C0-AOD-655

THE
UNIVERSITY OF WINNIPEG
PORTAGE & BALMORAL
WINNIPEG 2, MAN. CANADA
DISCARDED

A Concordance to the Poems of

EMILY DICKINSON

THE CORNELL CONCORDANCES

Supervisory Committee

M. H. Abrams
Ephim G. Fogel
William R. Keast
James A. Painter, *Computer Programmer*
S. M. Parrish, *General Editor*

POEMS OF MATTHEW ARNOLD
Edited by S. M. Parrish

POEMS OF W. B. YEATS
Edited by S. M. Parrish

POEMS OF EMILY DICKINSON
Edited by S. P. Rosenbaum

PS
1541
.Z49R6

A Concordance to the Poems of

EMILY DICKINSON

Edited by

Stanford Patrick
S. P. ROSENBAUM

Cornell University Press

ITHACA, NEW YORK

Copyright © 1964 by Cornell University

All rights reserved

CORNELL UNIVERSITY PRESS

First published 1964
Second printing 1967

The texts of Emily Dickinson's poems are quoted herein by permission of the Publishers and the Trustees of Amherst College from Thomas H. Johnson, editor, *The Poems of Emily Dickinson,* Cambridge, Mass., The Belknap Press of Harvard University Press, copyright 1951, 1955 by The President and Fellows of Harvard College.

Library of Congress Catalog Card Number: 64–25335

PRINTED IN THE UNITED STATES OF AMERICA

In Memory of

Stephen E. Whicher

PREFACE

DESCRIBING the difficulties of her own art in metaphors of another, Emily Dickinson once wrote,

> I found the words to every thought
> I ever had—but One—
> And that—defies me—
> As a Hand did try to chalk the Sun
>
> To Races—nurtured in the Dark—
> How would your own—begin?
> Can Blaze be shown in Cochineal—
> Or Noon—in Mazarin?

Readers who have sought the words Emily Dickinson so successfully found for her poetry have not always been as fortunate. For some time it was not even possible to find the poems as she wrote them, but with the publication in 1955 of Thomas H. Johnson's definitive three-volume variorum edition, *The Poems of Emily Dickinson,* they became fully available. The purpose of this concordance is to make "the words to every thought" in the poems of that edition equally available. For some this purpose will best be served by the use of the concordance to locate poems or parts of poems that have been forgotten. The publishing history of her work being what it is, this service is more important than it might be for other poets; lines and stanzas that appear in the early editions of Emily Dickinson's poetry as separate works can, through this concordance, be restored to the poems from which they were originally taken. Yet such a service hardly justifies the human and inhuman labor involved in making a computer concordance. Of far greater value is the index that the concordance provides to the words, and consequently to the images and ideas, of Emily Dickinson's art. And by indexing the words that present those images and ideas along with their contexts in the line—contexts which include the poet's alternative choices for these words—the concordance becomes much more useful than a listing that merely locates the isolated, inert words of her vocabulary. With its inclusion of variants and with its presentation of the entries in approximate chronological order under a given index word, this concordance is potentially helpful for studies of Emily Dickinson's poetic development. The concordance could also be indispensable for biographical and canonical studies, and the preservation at Cornell University of the tape from which the concordance was made allows for further possible studies of Emily Dickinson's metrics and methods of composition.

How electronic means were invoked to attain these humanistic ends is fully explained in James A. Painter's "Programmer's Preface" to *A Concordance to the Poems of W. B. Yeats* (Ithaca, N.Y., 1963). There is also a brief résumé of the computer techniques specifically used for the concordance of Emily Dickinson's poetry in my "Emily Dickinson and the Machine" (*Studies in Bibliography,* XVIII[1965]). The effective use of this concordance depends, however, not so much on understanding the technicalities of how the concordance was made as on being aware of the particular features of its format. These are described below under appropriate subheadings. The nature of the text of Emily Dickinson's poetry on which this concordance is based and the various modifications made in that text for the concordance are explained after the description of the format. The last section of the preface discusses what is probably the most difficult task in editing Emily Dickinson's poems, the treatment of her numerous and important variants.

FORMAT OF THE CONCORDANCE

Index Word

The alphabetically arranged index words consist of all the words in Emily Dickinson's poetry except the so-called "nonsignificant" omitted words listed below. Bracketed variant words and phrases are indexed along with the words from the main texts. When the entries under an index word are continued on the next page of the concordance, the index word is repeated and CONTINUED is printed in parentheses alongside the word. In its alphabetizing, the computer was instructed to treat the apostrophe as a letter; consequently such a form as the singular possessive of a noun follows the nominative singular but precedes the nominative plural.

The few hyphenated compounds in Emily Dickinson's poetry were automatically cross-referenced by the computer, which indexed the second half of the compound and then printed alongside it a SEE followed by the first part of the compound. Unhyphenated compounds were cross-referenced by the editor in the same way only when they were so unusual that a user in search of all occurrences of a word could not be expected to anticipate them. ASHINE, for instance, is cross-referenced from SHINE, but there is no reference from STIR to ASTIR. (Unusual compounds not hyphenated by Emily Dickinson, or groups of letters that belonged together as index "words," were also kept together to make possible such index entries as A—B—C, AUTO DA FE, and I. E.) Emily Dickinson's numerous misspellings, eccentric contractions, and uncommon variant spellings were cross-referenced *only when they are not either alphabetically adjacent to their familiar spellings or separated merely by different forms of the same word.* Thus WO was not cross-referenced to WOE, which follows it, but VAIL and VEIL, separated by forty-six entries, were cross-referenced. Much of the cross-referencing in the concordance is one way only—from the expected to the unexpected. EYE is cross-referenced to E'E but not vice versa. In instances where more than one spelling occurs in the text (CONCEIVE and CONCIEVE), cross-referencing was done both ways, lest the user suppose Emily Dickinson a consistent misspeller. But again, different spellings were not cross-referenced when adjacent to each other or separated only by forms of the same word. There could be, of course, no end to cross-referencing; the reader who wants to be certain he has all the forms of a particular word should consult the appendix, which contains a complete record of the poet's indexed vocabulary, arranged according to the frequency of the words.

Certain words in Emily Dickinson's poetic vocabulary were omitted from the indexing because the cost of including them would have been disproportionate to their value for users of the concordance. To index every occurrence of "the" and "a" would have entailed the addition of 6,138 and 2,681 lines, respectively—an increase in the bulk of the concordance of approximately 10 per cent. The number of these omitted words is quite small compared to the number customarily dropped from manual concordances. The sheer labor involved in a manual concordance makes it desirable to omit as many words as possible; but in a computer concordance the main considerations are space and consistency in the omission of low-frequency forms of high-frequency words. Examples of the kinds of words usually deleted from concordances but retained here are LIKE and AS (for lists of Emily Dickinson's similes), BE (for Emily Dickinson's unusual and extensive use of the subjunctive form of this verb), and the pronouns I, WE, YOU, HE, and SHE, along with their related forms (for their relevance to biographical and "persona" studies). Because the concordance provides the context of each word, it was not felt necessary to distinguish homographs among the indexed words. Among the unindexed words seven potentially important homographs appeared: the nouns ART, MAY, MIGHT, WILL, and WONT, the main verb WILT, and the adjective WONT. These were separated from “nonsignificant” verbs with the same spelling and then indexed. (No homographs were found among Emily Dickinson’s apostropheless contractions CANT and TWILL.)

The following is a complete list, together with their frequencies, of the words in Emily Dickinson’s vocabulary that were omitted from the indexing.

A	2681	’EM	2	OTHER	143	THOUGH	89
ALTHO’	1	FOR	845	OTHERS	23	THRO	2
ALTHOUGH	11	FROM	381	OTHER’S	9	THRO’	20
AM	79	HAD	298	SHALL	104	THROUGH	77
&	1	HAD’NT	1	SHALT	8	THUS	2
AN	371	HADST	1	SHANT	2	TIS	4
AND	2349	HAD’ST	3	SH’D	8	T’IS	5
ANOTHER	44	HAS	174	SHOULD	120	’TIS	161
ANOTHER’S	2	HAS’NT	2	SHOULD’NT	3	’TIS’NT	2
A’NT	1	HAST	16	SO	637	TO	2384
ARE	334	HATH	29	SO’S	1	TOO	236
ART (vb.)	221	HAVE	289	’T	1	TWAS	2
AT	421	HAV’NT	3	THAN	221	T’WAS	1
BOTH	25	HERE	84	THAT	1298	’TWAS	113
BUT	808	HERE’S	3	THAT’S	18	’TWAS’NT	6
BY	454	HOW	308	THE	6138	TWERE	2
CAN	179	HOWEVER	12	THEIR	215	T’WERE	1
CANNOT	117	IF	447	THEIRS	1	’TWERE	19
CAN’ST	3	IN	1223	THEIR’S	6	TWILL (vb.)	2
CANT (vb.)	9	INTO	34	THEM	138	’TWILL	10
C’D	3	IS	1201	THEMSELF	9	TWOULD	2
COULD	275	ISN’T	1	THEMSELVES	20	’TWOULD	15
COULD’NT	6	IS’NT	2	THEN	354	’TWOULD’NT	1
COULD’ST	4	IT	1256	THERE	220	UPON	302
DID	150	ITS	22	THEREFORE	15	WAS	506
DID’NT	8	IT’S	312	THERE’LL	1	WAS’NT	3
DIDST	1	ITSELF	104	THERE’S	29	WAS’T	2
DID’ST	4	MAY (vb.)	141	THESE	87	W’D	9
DINNA	2	MIGHT (vb.)	64	THEY	314	WERE	269
DO	170	MUST	127	THEY’D	5	WERT	8
DOES	45	NEITHER	22	THEY’LL	5	WH’	1
DOES’NT	11	NO	395	THEY’RE	9	WHAT	278
DONT	24	NOR	163	THIS	430	WHATSOE’ER	3
DON’T	1	NOT	828	THO	3	WHEN	486
DOST	7	NOW	131	THO’	27	WHERE	146
DOTH	38	OF	1996	’THO’	1	WHEREVER	4
EACH	74	ON	391	THOSE	89	WHETHER	20
EITHER	11	OR	460	THOSOEVER	1	WHICH	116

WHO . . .	223	WHOM . .	46	WILL (vb.)	208	WOULD . .	254
WHO'D . . .	1	WHOSE . .	105	WILT (aux.)	6	WOULDN'T .	1
WHOEVER .	3	WHO'VE . .	2	WITH . . .	603	WOULD'NT .	3
WHO'LL . .	2	WHY . . .	40	WONT (vb.)	15	WOULD'ST .	4

Several recent studies have shown that some of these omitted words could be very important in analyses of style. But for those who need them, all is not lost. It is possible for a computer to retrieve them from the complete magnetic tape of the concordance.

Text Line

Indented below each indexed word appear the lines of poetry containing that word. Many of the lines include bracketed insertions of variant words or phrases to be found in Emily Dickinson's manuscripts. (For the provenance of these variants and the methods used to include them in the text lines of the concordance, see the discussion of the text and variants, below.) The bracketed insertions *follow* the words for which they are variants. When more than one variant word or phrase is listed for the reading in a particular main text of Johnson's edition, the alternative variants are separated from one another within the brackets by slash marks. Thus Emily Dickinson's famous description of despair in poem number 640, together with the two variants written in the manuscript for the last word in the line, appears as follows in the concordance:

AND THAT WHITE SUSTENANCE—[EXERCISE/PRIVILEGE]

Here as elsewhere in the concordance the word or phrase that the variants replace can usually be determined simply by noting the number of syllables in the variant and in the words preceding the bracketed insertion.

The text lines under each index word are arranged in order, according to their poem and line numbers. A line is repeated if the index word occurs in it more than once. Widely spaced dots separate the text lines from the shortened first lines used as titles for the poems. These dots are omitted in lines longer than forty-six spaces, which are continued, indented, on the line below. Lines longer than sixty-nine spaces—all that an eighty-space IBM card could contain in addition to poem and line numbers—had to be divided and the parts preceded or followed by ellipses, indicated by three closely spaced dots, which should not be confused with the widely spaced ones that follow the text lines. Because of the shortness of Emily Dickinson's lines, even when extended with inserted variants, using part of a line instead of the whole was seldom necessary. An extreme illustration of how a line distended with bracketed variants had to be divided can be seen in the sixth line of number 1420. The line with all its variants reads as follows:

> BEFORE THE QUICK [RIPE/PEAL/DRUM/DRUMS/BELLS/BOMB/BURST /FLAGS/STEP/TICK/SHOUTS/PINK/RED/BLADE] OF DAY

The line had to be divided in two places in the concordance: the first section ends with an ellipsis after BOMB, the second begins with an ellipsis before BURST and ends with an ellipsis after RED, and the last section begins with an ellipsis before BLADE.

First Line

Under the heading FIRST LINE are given the shortened first lines of the poems from which the text lines are taken. These first lines serve, in effect, as titles for the poems, and they contain as many complete words of the first line as could be fitted into the twenty-four spaces available for them in the format of the concordance. In a dozen or so instances, the necessary shortening of the lines resulted in nearly identical titles (number 1244, THE BUTTERFLY'S, and number 1387, THE BUTTERFLY'S NUMIDIAN, for example), yet this method of identifying the poems seemed preferable to any other. To have identified the lines of a poem only by its number, for instance, would have assumed that readers of Emily Dickinson were more familiar with her poem numbers than readers of Shakespeare's sonnets appear to be with those numbers. Furthermore, using only Johnson's numbering of the poems would have rendered the concordance almost useless for anyone working from an edition or anthology that does not adopt Johnson's poem numbers. Another possible alternative—making up titles for the 1,749 poems Emily Dickinson left untitled—was unattractive if only because this had been tried, with some horrible results, by the poet's first editors. The use of shortened first lines as identifying titles in the concordance also obviated the need for a separate list of abbreviated titles like those in the Cornell concordances of Arnold and Yeats. The twenty-six titles that Emily Dickinson did use are treated as lines of poetry and indexed accordingly; they are distinguished by a "T" in the line-number column.

Poem Number

Poem numbers rather than page numbers of *The Poems of Emily Dickinson* are used to identify the source of the indexed lines because they have been adopted by other editors following Johnson. (If only page numbers had been employed, the concordance would be limited to use with Johnson's edition.) A more valuable result of giving the poem numbers—and one of the most significant features of the format of the concordance—is the roughly chronological order of these numbers. By arranging the lines under a particular index word according to the numbers of the poems in which they appear, the concordance presents in approximate chronological order the poet's uses of any indexed word. The following table of poem numbers and dates of composition is constructed from the approximate dates in *The Poems of Emily Dickinson*; with it the user of the concordance should be able to determine the approximate dates at which any indexed word was used by Emily Dickinson. In the right-hand columns of the table are the exceptions to the chronological sequence of poem numbers that Johnson discovered after the text of his edition went to press and noted in his introduction. (The date of number 1775 was established later.)

Poem number	*Approximate date*	*Exceptions*
1	1850	
2	1851	
3	1852	
4	1853	
5	1854	
6–57	1858	
58–151	1859	
152–216	1860	
217–298	1861	330–331, 687
299–664*	1862	688, 1072
665–807*	1863	
808–981	1864	
982–1066	1865	
1067–1103*	1866	1775
1104–1113	1867	
1114–1135	1868	
1136–1152	1869	
1153–1176*	1870	1222, 1770, 1774
1177–1204	1871	
1205–1242*	1872	
1243–1292	1873	
1293–1331	1874	1153
1332–1351	1875	
1352–1389*	1876	1575

* Poem numbers in this sequence that are exceptions to the assigned date can be found in the right-hand section of the table beside the dates to which they belong.

Poem number	Approximate date	Exceptions
1390–1431	1877	
1432–1452	1878	1218, 1237, 1314
1453–1482	1879	1385
1483–1508	1880	
1509–1536	1881	1771–1772
1537–1559	1882	1760
1560–1593*	1883	1768, 1773
1594–1636	1884	
1637–1646	1885	
1647–1648	1886	
1649–1775*	Undated	

* See note, page xiii.

Line Number

The number of the text line, as given in the main texts of Johnson's edition, appears in the last column on the concordance page. A "T" in this column instead of a number indicates that this line is one of the few titles supplied by Emily Dickinson. When a line number is preceded by a "V,"an *alternative* variant line is indicated; when a "V" is followed by no line number, an *additional* variant line is indicated. To explain more fully the origins of these variant lines, it is necessary to discuss the text on which this concordance is based and the methods needed to handle the variorum readings contained in that text.

BASIC TEXT OF THE CONCORDANCE

Unless the maker of a concordance attempts to re-edit a text in and through the concordance, his work will be only as good as the editions on which it is based. The chaotic early editions of Emily Dickinson's poetry provide a case in point. A partial concordance for these editions was done by Louise Kline Kelly as a doctoral dissertation at Pennsylvania State College in 1951. Confined to nouns, verbs, adjectives, and adverbs, Mrs. Kelly's "A Concordance of Emily Dickinson's Poems" gives the line-contexts of words occurring less than ten times in Emily Dickinson's poetry; words occurring more frequently are accompanied only by the page and line numbers of the editions where they may be found. Mrs. Kelly's dissertation was used by Johnson in preparing *The Poems of Emily Dickinson.* With its addition of forty-one new poems, its arrangement of the poems, and its inclusion of the numerous authorial variants for the poems, Johnson's edition rendered Mrs. Kelly's work obsolete. Yet as the acknowledgments in various works on Emily Dickinson testify, Mrs. Kelly's work has been a valuable aid to scholars and critics—and she has put the users of both Johnson's edition and this new concordance based on it considerably in her debt.

In his introduction to *The Poems of Emily Dickinson* Johnson wrote that the purpose of his edition was "to establish an accurate text of the poems and to give them as far as possible a chronology." Once a chronology—based on Mrs. Theodora Van Wagenen Ward's analysis of Emily Dickinson's changing handwriting—was established, the manuscripts were grouped together and the poems assigned numbers according to their place in the chronology. But before this could be done, Johnson had to select, from among the poems found in more than one manuscript, the texts that were to be given what he called "principal representation" in large type under the poem numbers. Holograph manuscripts survive for all but 119 of the 1,775 poems in the edition, and according to Johnson's classification these exist in one or more of three stages of composition: there are fair copies, which Emily Dickinson appears to have finished; there are semifinal drafts, which also appear to be finished except for alternative words or phrases written between the lines or at the sides or bottoms of the manuscripts; and finally there are work-sheet drafts, which range from rough jottings to elaborately reworked poems. Many of Emily Dickinson's poems are to be found in more than one manuscript state, and a number of them exist in two or more variant fair copies. In order to maintain the chronological order of the poems, Johnson chose, whenever possible, the earliest fair copy of each poem; other versions are given in smaller type below the main text. This decision has resulted in some misunderstanding and misuse of *The Poems of Emily Dickinson* because the text selected for principal representation is not always the best version of the poem. A later fair copy of an earlier semifinal draft may contain readings that are better poetry than those in the earliest fair copy; or the alternative words written at the bottom of a semifinal draft may be preferable to those in the body of the poem. Subsequent editors using Johnson's edition have too often selected a text of inferior poetry just because it was given principal representation in this edition. In order to base a concordance on *The Poems of Emily Dickinson* it was necessary to follow the main texts given by Johnson; yet it was also essential to present the numerous and important variants to the earliest fair copies or, in the absence of these, to whatever text was given principal representation under a poem number. A concordance to Johnson's variorum edition had, in other words, to be a variorum concordance. Before considering how these variants were included in the concordance, however, it is important to note certain modifications in Johnson's text that have been adopted in the concordance.

Changes in Wording Adopted for the Concordance

The basic text for this concordance is the 1958 second printing of the three-volume variorum *The Poems of Emily Dickinson,* published by Harvard University Press. (This edition should not be confused with the one-volume *The Complete Poems of Emily Dickinson,* also edited by Johnson and published in 1960, which is not a variorum text.) The second printing of *The Poems of Emily Dickinson* differs from the first mainly in its inclusion, on the verso of the title page to the edition's appendix, of a list entitled "Corrections." The substantive changes in the poetry of the edition to be found in this list and in the text of the concordance are the corrections of "teases" to "teazes" (poem 319, l. 6), "has" to "had" (1254, l. 1 of the work-sheet draft), "revelry" to "revery" (1526, l. 12 of the Todd transcript), and "the" to "a" (87, l. 2). Two dashes were added at the ends of lines (290, l. 4, and 299, l. 4 of the copy sent to Susan Dickinson). Also corrected in the text of the concordance were the errors noted by Charles R. Anderson in his *Emily Dickinson's Poetry* (New York, 1960), pages 312, 321, 324–325; these include the change of "the" to "this" (1068, l. 11 of the copy sent to Niles), the addition of a dash at the end of a line (1271, l. 7), and the addition of "swift" to the list of variants for the phrase "sudden legacy" (1333, l. 5 of the work-sheet draft). Corrections of obvious misprints that I have found while preparing Johnson's text for the concordance involved changing "unknow" to "unknown" (78, l. 8 of the penciled copy), "Feet" to "Fete" (794, variant note to l. 16), "world" to "would" (1133, variant note to l. 8), "he" to "her" (1496, variant note to l. 11), and "departure" to "departing" (1773, variant note to l. 3). Also corrected were the minor mistakes in the line- number listings of variants to poems 532, 577, 1479, 1508, and 1646. I have also added two titles to the twenty-six titles of Emily Dickinson's poems noted by Johnson in Appendix 8 of his edition: "Valentine Week," which Johnson gives as the first line to poem 1, and "Diagnosis of the Bible, by a Boy—" the title of a semifinal draft of poem 1545.

Changes in Spelling and Punctuation Adopted for the Concordance

The limitations of our IBM printing equipment necessitated five kinds of changes in the punctuation, spelling, and capitalization of *The Poems of Emily Dickinson.* Although the special print wheels made for the Cornell Concordances enabled this concordance to employ all the punctuation marks that Emily Dickinson used, it was not possible to reproduce lower-case letters. The brackets that Johnson occasionally used to indicate his insertion of a letter or his reconstruction of a torn manuscript were silently dropped because brackets were needed to include variants in the concordance. (The following poem and line numbers indicate all the places where brackets were used in Johnson's edition: number 43, l. 4; 58, l. 7; 233, l. 4; 264, l. 4; 371, l. 11; 373, l. 4; 419, l. 13; 588, l. 21; 608, l. 5; 976, l. 4; 1133, l. 2; and 1685, l. 6.) Twice in her poetry (62, l. 9, and 142, l. 11) Emily Dickinson used numbers in her text; these were spelled out in the concordance because her punctuation had to be coded by numbers to prepare it for the computer. The single quotation marks to be found in four of Emily Dickinson's poems (82, l. 4; 103, ll. 11, 16; 127, ll. 1, 2, 5; and 175, l. 1)—none of which followed double quotation marks—had to be changed to the double quotation marks usually found in her poetry because the computer's processes of alphabetization treated single quotation marks as if they were apostrophes. Finally, it was impractical to program a computer and a printer to print lines under or through words. As a result, the cancels and underlinings in Emily Dickinson's manuscripts are not reproduced in the concordance. Because less than 1 per cent of the more than 100,000 words in her manuscripts are canceled, this limitation is not very significant. There are even fewer instances of underlinings—almost all of them occur with variants in semifinal drafts—yet these have greater importance, because Emily Dickinson appears to have indicated to herself the alternative choices she preferred by underlining them. Nevertheless, Johnson notes instances where later fair copies of poems do not adopt the underlined variants of earlier drafts, and he concludes that "the mood of the moment played its part." One of the small sacrifices involved in applying a computer, with its peripheral equipment, to Emily Dickinson's poetry is the machine's inability to convey the results of these moods.

Changes in Emily Dickinson's Canon Not Adopted in the Concordance

In his review of Johnson's edition in the *New England Quarterly* (XXIX [1956], 242–243), Jay Leyda noted that the number of poems in Emily Dickinson's canon was less than the 1,775 given by Johnson because in three instances (331 and 342, 937 and 992, 1525 and 1616), poems numbered separately are actually variant versions of other poems in the canon. And after writing his review Leyda discovered that the last poem in *The Poems of Emily Dickinson* is actually a stanza from a lost variant version of poem 1068, which he located and which is given in Anderson's *Emily Dickinson's Poetry* (pp. 324–325); this version also includes one new variant ("candles" for "candle" in l. 18 of the Norcross transcript of poem 1068), which was adopted in the concordance. Except for the addition of this variant, these important modifications of Emily Dickinson's canon have *not* been adopted in the text of the concordance, however, because of the confusions that would result if all the poem numbers after number 331 were changed. In several instances, then, identical lines with different poem numbers will appear together in the concordance; the reader should not forget that these lines belong to versions or parts of the same poem.

VARIANTS

Only seven of Emily Dickinson's poems were published in her lifetime, none of them with her clear consent. Many of her poems are "unfinished" in the sense that she never made final choices among the variants in drafts and copies. If she "found the words to every thought" but one, she often failed to indicate finally what the words were; even in this line she wrote a variant, and the line appears in the concordance as I FOUND THE WORDS [PHRASE] TO EVERY THOUGHT. The principal problem in editing Emily Dickinson's poetry for the concordance was how to present in individual lines of poetry the variants that in Johnson's edition are given either in separate versions or as notes at the end of the poems. One solution would have been to expand all variants into variant lines, but, in addition to increasing the automatic word-frequency counts given in the appendix to the concordance, such a method would not show a crucial feature of the variant's context—the word or words for which the variants were introduced. A single method of handling all the variants was abandoned, therefore, and the kinds of variants were treated in different ways, according to whether they were words, phrases, lines, or complete versions of poems.

Variant Phrases

Although variant words could be enclosed within brackets and inserted into the lines after the words for which they were variants, variant phrases could not be handled in quite the same way. Frequently the phrases could not be matched, word for word, with the phrases in the main text, and breaking up the variant phrases would have ignored the unity—hence often the meaning—of the phrases. Sometimes it was impossible to do otherwise, but in many instances the words of a variant phrase could be kept together and inserted within brackets after the phrase in the main text; and as with variant words, it is usually possible for the reader to see how far back in the line the variant phrase refers by counting the syllables of the variant and of the words preceding it. When the variants differ in the number of syllables from the preceding phrases, the sense of the inserted phrase usually makes clear what words the variants replace; when it does not, the user of the concordance must have recourse to Johnson's edition.

Sometimes the editing of variants into the lines of the principal texts involved adding words from the texts to the phrases. In poem 1343, for instance, Emily Dickinson wrote as variants for the phrase "Was all that saved" first "alone sustained—" and simply "upheld—" after that. To make the position of the variants clearer, Johnson uses a bracketed "Alone" with "upheld." Here as elsewhere Johnson's clarification of variants was followed, and the line appears in the concordance as follows:

WAS ALL THAT SAVED [ALONE SUSTAINED—/ALONE UPHELD—] A BEE

In addition to the interpolations given by Johnson other words from the text were occasionally used to clarify the location of a variant. It should be stressed, however, that the editing procedure for variant phrases does not involve adding or removing words from Emily Dickinson's poetry, but simply filling out elliptical phrases with words from the main text or removing repetitions that the poet used to indicate the place of a variant phrase in a line. Even with these procedures it was not always possible to avoid repetition, as the example above shows. Nor was it always possible to keep the different words of a variant phrase together. Where keeping the words of a variant phrase together would have meant repeating nearly an entire line, it seemed better to separate the words than to swell the bulk of the concordance and the word frequencies. Sometimes the various combinations requiring insertion were too complex to be fitted together as one or more variant phrases; in these instances the phrases were treated word by word or were combined into separate variant lines. The texts involved in this kind of editing were almost always work-sheet drafts, the definitive reconstruction of which is impossible.

Variant Lines

Lines both numbered and marked with a "V" are those clearly variant to a particular line in the main text of Johnson's edition; the number of the variant line is the same as that of the line for which it is a variant. Unnumbered variant lines are taken from lines and stanzas of drafts that were not included in the versions given principal representation in *The Poems of Emily Dickinson.* Also treated as variant lines are phrases that lack only a word or two of being completely different variant lines; the missing words are supplied from the original lines. Complicated series of variants that could not be bracketed into lines of the main texts are also handled as variant lines. In the most involved cases—again work-sheet drafts in which Emily Dickinson's final decision cannot be definitively reconstructed—variant words and phrases are bracketed into lines that are themselves additional, unnumbered variant lines.

Variant Poems

For ten poems in Johnson's edition (148, 216, 433, 494, 824, 1213, 1282, 1357, 1358, and 1627) the texts given principal representation consist of two versions of one poem. Because these double versions constitute, in effect, two poems under one number, and because it was not possible in the format of the concordance to identify poems beyond their numbers and shortened first lines, it was necessary to combine each double version. Where there are only minor differences between versions (as in numbers 494, 1213, and 1282), certain words of one version are included as variants to the other. For double versions that contain more substantial variants, numbered and unnumbered variant lines are used. How these were employed can be illustrated by the best-known double-version poem, "Safe in their Alabaster Chambers—" (number 216). The earliest fair copy of the poem is the 1859 version, which was taken as the main text in the concordance; the lines of both the 1861 fair copy and its work-sheet draft are treated as variants to the 1859 version. The additional lines and stanzas of the 1861 manuscripts are not clearly variant to specific lines of the 1859 manuscript; hence they had to be listed as unnumbered, additional variant lines. And just as the arrangement in Johnson's edition does not imply any evaluation of the quality or authority of the two versions, so in the concordance the unnumbered variant lines are no less significant or valuable than the numbered ones.

Punctuation of Variants

When the punctuation with variant words differs from that of the main text in Johnson's edition, the difference usually consists in the addition of a dash following the variant. These differences are not reproduced in the concordance, because Emily Dickinson seems to have used the dash with variants mainly to separate alternative choices. The punctuation of variant phrases is followed exactly, however. When the final punctuation of a variant phrase is *identical* with that in the principal text, it is given *after* the bracketed variant phrase, indicating that the punctuation is the same for both the main-text reading and the variant. When the terminal punctuation of variant phrases *differs* from that in the main text, the variant punctuation follows the variant phrase *within* the brackets, and the final punctuation of the main-text phrase *precedes* the bracketed variants.

Omitted Variants

The Poems of Emily Dickinson includes certain types of variants that are irrelevant to the uses of the concordance. Variants in syntax alone, unaccompanied by variants in wording, were omitted from the concordance, as were changes in spelling and punctuation; variants in spelling that suggested different words ("straight" and "strait," for example) were retained in the concordance, however. Variants in line or stanza order were not included because there was no way of presenting them in the single lines of the concordance. Variants in published versions of poems were also excluded when versions of these poems were extant in manuscripts or authoritative transcripts; Johnson's inclusion of all published variants makes a fascinating record of editorial corruption, but there is no point in perpetuating these corruptions in a concordance. Three exceptions were made to this policy: the variants in published versions of poems 59 and 160 were included because they appear to derive from manuscripts now lost, and the published second stanza of poem 57 was retained because it poetically complements the stanza of a poem to be found in a manuscript, part of which has been torn off. Poems in Emily Dickinson's canon that have survived only in their published forms were, of course, included in the concordance.

Finally, it was not possible within the format of a computer concordance to indicate the numerous sources of the variants that had to be edited into the lines of the earliest finished text or included as numbered and unnumbered variant lines in preparing the text of Emily Dickinson's poems for the computer. Yet because it does not indicate whether variants derive from fair copies, semifinal drafts, work sheets, or transcripts, the concordance should not be taken as making new composite poems out of differing versions that a private poet left unfinished. By simply ignoring the bracketed insertions and the lines marked with "V" the user can determine all the poems chosen by Johnson as the principal texts of his edition. If the reader wants to find the source of a given variant in the concordance, he must return to the variorum edition. And it is worth stressing again that the concordance can be most effectively used in conjunction with *The Poems of Emily Dickinson.*

ACKNOWLEDGMENTS

Without the help of a number of individuals and institutions this concordance could not have been made. Professor S. M. Parrish, the general editor of the Cornell Concordances, anticipated and solved many of the problems that beset the making of a computer concordance, and the finished work owes much to his energy and enthusiasm. To the interest and ingenuity of James A. Painter, the computer programmer, are due special features of the concordance that might not have been possible without his help. The *sine qua non* of this concordance is, of course, Thomas H. Johnson's superb *The Poems of Emily Dickinson,* which was used by the kind permission of the Harvard University Press and the Trustees of Amherst College.

A grant from the Grant-in-Aid Fund of the Department of English, Cornell University, covered the clerical costs of preparing Emily Dickinson's poetry for the computer, and a research grant from the Graduate School of Indiana University made it possible for me to spend a summer preparing the text of the poems. The Cornell Aeronautical Laboratory, Buffalo, New York, generously made its computer and other facilities available. The Indiana University Computing Center gave free use of its peripheral equipment; I am grateful to Dale J. Hall, the executive director of the center, for helpful advice about the equipment's possibilities. The computer centers at Cornell and Brown universities also made their facilities available at crucial stages in the preparation of the concordance. Marta Petoe and James Free punched and verified the text of the poems with impressive accuracy and speed, and Sophia Boyatzes Blaydes helped greatly with the proofreading of the punched text.

To Professors M. H. Abrams, Ephim G. Fogel, William R. Keast, and especially the late Stephen E. Whicher—members of the Cornell Concordance Supervisory Committee—I am grateful for much helpful advice and criticism. My wife's multifarious aid and cheerful endurance are beyond gratitude.

S. P. Rosenbaum

Barrington, Rhode Island
April 1964

A Concordance to the Poems of

EMILY DICKINSON

	FIRST LINE	POEM		LINE
ABANDONED				
THAT FIRST ABANDONED [ABSCONDED] YEAR. . .	THE DISTANCE THAT THE	1742	V	4
ABASED				
DISPELLED [ABASED / WITHHELD / DEPRIVED] FROM THERE--	I HAVE NO LIFE BUT THIS	1398		4
ABASH				
THAT COULD ABASH THE LITTLE BIRD	"HOPE" IS THE THING WITH	254		7
ABASHETH				
AS MUCH ABASHETH ME!	AFRAID! OF WHOM AM I	608		4
ABASHING				
OUTSTARING [DEFYING / APPALLING / ABASHING] MASONRY--	TOO COLD IS THIS	1135		5
ABASHLESS				
AND BEES ABASHLESS PLAY, ...	WHERE EVERY BIRD IS BOLD	1758		2
ABATED				
ABATED--DISTANCE IS	DISTANCE--IS NOT THE	1155		3
ABATES				
DISSOLVES [ABATES / EXHALES]--THE SAME-- .	IN MANY AND REPORTLESS	1382		6
ABBEY				
AN ABBEY--A COCOON--	HE PARTS HIMSELF--LIKE	517		20
FAR SAFER, THROUGH AN ABBEY GALLOP, . . .	ONE NEED NOT BE A	670		9
ABBEYS				
WHICH FROM IT'S SOLEMN ABBEYS	THE FEET OF PEOPLE	7		23
ABBREVIATE				
ABBREVIATE ME THIS	THROUGH WHAT TRANSPORTS	1153		8
A--B--C				
AND LEAVE ME--JUST MY A--B--C	NOT IN THIS WORLD TO SEE	418		11
ABDICATE				
DELIGHT OF NATURE--ABDICATE--	TILL DEATH--IS NARROW	907		11
ABDICATED				
WHO ABDICATED AMBUSH	WHO ABDICATED AMBUSH	1616		1
ABDICATION				
EXCEPT BY ABDICATION--	ME FROM MYSELF--TO	642		11
THE ABDICATION OF BELIEF	THOSE--DYING THEN,	1551		6
ABDUCTED				
WHETHER BY DAY ABDUCTED	A DEW SUFFICED ITSELF--	1437		9
ABETS				
AND SO ABETS THE SHINING FLEET	LOVE CAN DO ALL BUT	1731		7
ABHOR				
AND ONE--THE FLOWERS ABHOR--	THERE IS AN ARID	782		6
EQUALLY TO ABHOR DELIGHT--	SUMMER IS SHORTER THAN	1506		7
ABHORRED				
POSSESSED [ABHORRED / WE OWNED] BEFORE-- .	DREAMS ARE THE SUBTLE	1376		6
TO THAT ABHORRED ABODE, ...	DROWNING IS NOT SO	1718		6
ABHORRENCE				
THEY FOUND TO OUR OBJECTION [ABHORRENCE]-- .	THOSE CATTLE SMALLER	1388		7
ABHORRENT				
ABHORRENT IS THE REST	WATER MAKES MANY BEDS	1428		5
ABHORS				
CONSTANCY ABHORS--	"FAITHFUL TO THE END"	1357		4
ABIDE				
WHERE DAFFODILS--ABIDE--	SHE DWELLETH IN THE	671		2
HIMSELF--ABIDE WITH THEE--	NO PRISONER BE--	720		3
THE FATHOMS THEY ABIDE--	SHE ROSE TO HIS	732		12
HIMSELF ABIDE, ...	SPRING IS THE PERIOD	844		4
DID [IF] IT ABIDE OR NO--	THESE HELD THEIR WICK	1390		8
AND STILL ABIDE--	THE THINGS THAT NEVER	1515		4
NO MATTER WHERE THE SAINTS ABIDE, ...	NO MATTER WHERE THE	1541		1
AND YET ABIDE [REMAIN] THE WORLD!	THERE CAME A WIND LIKE A	1593		17
WITH WINTER TO ABIDE	'TWAS HERE MY SUMMER	1756		6
ABIDES				
CHASE IT NOT, AND IT ABIDES--	BEAUTY--BE NOT CAUSED--	516		3
WE PASS, AND SHE ABIDES.	THE VEINS OF OTHER	811		5
A CRESCENT STILL ABIDES, ...	EACH THAT WE LOSE TAKES	1605		2
ABILITIES				
BENUMBED ABILITIES--	SUCH IS THE FORCE OF	787	V	8
ABILITY				
TO PROVE ABILITY. [SHOW SUPREMACY] . . .	IT ALWAYS FELT TO ME--A	597		16
WAS LAUGHTER AND ABILITY AND SIGHING . . .	THIS QUIET DUST WAS	813		3
OF THE ABILITY.	WHO SAW NO SUNRISE	1018		4
BECAUSE HE HAS ABILITY--	THE DEVIL--HAD HE	1479		3
ABJECT				
YOUR LIFE TOO ABJECT FOR ITSELF	TILL DEATH--IS NARROW	907		7
ABJECT IS HIS KNEE--	WHEN A LOVER IS A BEGGAR	1314		2
IN ABJECT [BOUNDLESS] POVERTY--	TAKE ALL AWAY FROM ME,	1640		5
ABJURED				
INCREASED TILL I ABJURED IT	ART THOU THE THING I	1282		7
ABLATIVE				
IS IMPUDENT [RENEGADE / INFIDEL / ABLATIVE] TO NATURE	THE JAY HIS CASTANET HAS	1635		4
AN ABLATIVE ESTATE [DELIGHT]--	THAT IT WILL NEVER COME	1741		6
BUT ABLATIVE TO SHOW.	THE JOY THAT HAS NO STEM	1744		4
ABLE				
'TIS ABLE AS A GOD--	TO BE ALIVE--IS POWER--	677		6
A ROBIN'S FAMINE [PALATE / HUNGER] ABLE-- .	DEPRIVED OF OTHER	773		9
YET ABLE TO CONTAIN	A COFFIN--IS A SMALL	943		2
ABLE AS THE DUST TO EQUIP IT'S FEATURE . .	SOME WE SEE NO MORE,	1221		8
ABLENESS				
OF OTHERS IN IT'S ABLENESS	NOT TO DISCOVER WEAKNESS	1054	V	5

	FIRST LINE	POEM	LINE
A'BLOSSOM			
A'BLOSSOM JUST WHEN I WENT IN	MY FIRST WELL DAY--SINCE	574	5
A-BLOW			
DAFFODILS A-BLOW	ABSENT PLACE--AN APRIL	927	2
ABODE			
TO WANDER--NOW--IS MY REPOSE [ABODE]--	I MEANT TO FIND HER WHEN	718	9
SO I--THE UNDIVINE ABODE	MY WORTHINESS IS ALL MY	751	13
REVISITING MY LATE ABODE	ALONE AND IN A	1167	9
ENOUGH--THE FIRST ABODE	UNTIL THE DESERT KNOWS	1291	10
BUT THAT THEY HAVE ABODE	THAN HEAVEN MORE REMOTE,	1436	14
ABODE IN AS SUPREME	THE WAY HOPE BUILDS HIS	1481	5
OF WHAT ASTUTE ABODE--	THE BAT IS DUN, WITH	1575	10
IGNITED THIS ABODE	THOUGH THE GREAT WATERS	1599	5
WITHOUT SUSPECTING OUR ABODE	EDEN IS THAT	1657	3
DIVIDES ABODE WITH ME	THE BLUNDER IS IN	1684	6
UNTUMBLED THIS ABODE	TO THEIR APARTMENT DEEP	1701	3
TO THAT ABHORRED ABODE,	DROWNING IS NOT SO	1718	6
NOT DEEMING OF HIS DREAD ABODE	NO MAN SAW AWE, NOR TO	1733	5
ABODES			
THE OCCUPANTS OF THESE ABODES--	HAVE ANY LIKE MYSELF	736	11
ABOLISH			
LOOK DOWN UPON [ABOLISH HIS] CAPTIVITY--	THEY SHUT ME UP IN PROSE	613	11
DID WE ABOLISH FROST	DID WE ABOLISH FROST	1014	1
ABOLISHED			
THIS INSTANT BE SUSPENDED [ABOLISHED]	BECAUSE THAT YOU ARE	1260	7
ABOLITION			
THIS MORTAL ABOLITION	THE SOUL'S SUPERIOR	306	9
ABOUT			
I DO NOT CARE ABOUT IT--	I HAD A GUINEA GOLDEN--	23	23
NOT FOR ME--TO PRATE ABOUT IT!	I CANT·TELL YOU--BUT YOU	65	13
WHAT IF THE POLES SH'D FRISK ABOUT	"ARCTURUS" IS HIS OTHER	70	22
AN ALTERED LOOK ABOUT THE HILLS--	AN ALTERED LOOK ABOUT	140	1
YOU CANNOT FIND OUT ALL ABOUT	DUST IS THE ONLY SECRET	153	3
AND GO ABOUT IT'S CARE--	IN EBON BOX, WHEN YEARS	169	18
THEN PRATE ABOUT "PREFERMENT"--	WAIT TILL THE MAJESTY OF	171	7
AND OLD SUNSHINE--ABOUT--	IT'S THOUGHTS--AND JUST	495	2
AND HEAVEN--ABOUT--	IT'S THOUGHTS--AND JUST	495	24
BUT SOMETHING AWKWARD IN [ODD ABOUT] THE FIT--	I COULD NOT PROVE THE	563	11
SHE DROPPED BRIGHT SCRAPS OF TINT, ABOUT--	MY FIRST WELL DAY--SINCE	574	19
THE SHAPES WE BURIED, DWELL ABOUT,	OF NEARNESS TO HER	607	5
DID PLACE ABOUT THE WEST--TONIGHT--	WHOLE GULFS--OF RED, AND	658	3
ABOUT THE PRICE--'TIS SMALL--	THE JUDGE IS LIKE THE	699	9
THAT ARISE AND SET ABOUT US--	DRAMA'S VITALLEST	741	2
THAT DARKNESS--IS ABOUT TO PASS--	PRESENTIMENT--IS THAT	764	4
AND SO I BEAR IT BIG ABOUT	THIS CHASM, SWEET, UPON	858	17
THE STARS ABOUT MY HEAD I FELT	I STEPPED FROM PLANK TO	875	3
ABOUT MY FEET THE SEA.	I STEPPED FROM PLANK TO	875	4
I NOTWITHSTANDING WENT [STOLE] ABOUT	A LOSS OF SOMETHING EVER	959	6
AND WAS [JUST / WHEN] ABOUT TO RING	SHALL I TAKE THEE, THE	1126	6
HER SYSTEMS RANGED [STOLE] ABOUT	THE WIND TOOK UP THE	1134	12
WAGGONS LIKE MESSENGERS HURRY ABOUT	AFTER THE SUN COMES OUT	1148	3
HE PREACHED UPON [ABOUT] "BREADTH" TILL IT ARGUED HIM [WE . . .	HE PREACHED UPON	1207	1
A WINGED SPARK DOTH SOAR ABOUT--	A WINGED SPARK DOTH SOAR	1468	1
WE TALKED WITH EACH OTHER ABOUT EACH OTHER	WE TALKED WITH EACH	1473	1
AND DOES'NT CARE ABOUT CAREERS	HOW HAPPY IS THE LITTLE	1510	3
WHO CARES ABOUT A BLUE BIRD'S TUNE--	A PANG IS MORE	1530	6
BUT PUTS HER CRAFT ABOUT	QUITE EMPTY, QUITE AT	1606	4
ABOVE			
FIERCE FROM THE CRAG ABOVE US	THROUGH LANE IT LAY--	9	11
PAPA ABOVE!	PAPA ABOVE!	61	1
I PAUSE ABOVE THAT VANISHED HEAD	WHERE I HAVE LOST, I	104	3
FINAL FAST--ABOVE--	BY A FLOWER--BY A LETTER	109	4
COCOON ABOVE! COCOON BELOW!	COCOON ABOVE! COCOON	129	1
THEN GAY ABOVE RECEDING GRASS	COCOON ABOVE! COCOON	129	8
SHE "NOTICES," ABOVE.	MAMA NEVER FORGETS HER	164	8
IN HER CASTLE ABOVE THEM--	SAFE IN THEIR ALABASTER	216	8
GRAND GO THE YEARS--IN THE CRESCENT--ABOVE THEM--	SAFE IN THEIR ALABASTER	216	V
THAT SHONE ABOVE THE FAGOT--	READ--SWEET--HOW OTHERS	260	9
GO ABOVE YOUR NERVE--	IF YOUR NERVE, DENY YOU	292	2
FROM TANKS--ABOVE MY HEAD--	DO PEOPLE MOULDER	432	8
ABOVE THE RIPEST ROSE--	WITHIN MY GARDEN, RIDES	500	6
STILL--STILL--MY HANDS ABOVE	ME PROVE IT NOW--WHOEVER	537	10
GOD GROWS ABOVE--SO THOSE WHO PRAY	MY PERIOD HAD COME FOR	564	5
OR SIMPLER PROVED--ABOVE--	IT TROUBLED ME AS ONCE I	600	12
UPON THE ROPES--ABOVE OUR HEAD--	THE LIGHTNING PLAYETH--	630	9
THE HEAVEN BELOW THE HEAVEN ABOVE--	ONE BLESSING HAD I THAN	756	13
OR COMMONWEALTH ABOVE	HE TOLD A HOMELY TALE	763	14
REDIGNIFIED [RE-ROYALIZED], ABOVE?	PERHAPS YOU THINK ME	833	8
HOW THE WATERS CLOSED ABOVE HIM	HOW THE WATERS CLOSED	923	1
BOLD ABOVE THE BOY	HOW THE WATERS CLOSED	923	6
ABOVE HIM IS TOO LOW A HIGHT	'TIS MY FIRST NIGHT	1122	3
OF HEAVEN ABOVE THE FIRMEST PROOF	IMMORTAL IS AN AMPLE	1205	5
ABOVE HIS SYNTHESIS	THE LILAC IS AN ANCIENT	1241	14
ABOVE MORTALITY--	BECAUSE THAT YOU ARE	1260	8
TWIXT FIRMAMENT ABOVE	A SINGLE CLOVER PLANK	1343	5
THESE HELD THEIR WICK ABOVE THE WEST--	THESE HELD THEIR WICK	1390	1
ABOVE OSTENSIBLE VICISSITUDE.	AFTER ALL BIRDS HAVE	1395	4
ABOVE THE HAUNTS OF MEN--	A WINGED SPARK DOTH SOAR	1468	6

	FIRST LINE	POEM		LINE
ABOVE (CONTINUED)				
ABOVE OBLIVION'S TIDE THERE IS A PIER	ABOVE OBLIVION'S TIDE	1531		1
WILL FAIL OF IT ABOVE--	WHO HAS NOT FOUND THE	1544		2
HE BOWED TO HEAVEN INSTEAD OF EARTH [EVERY HEAVEN ABOVE / . . .	THE BOBOLINK IS GONE--	1591		6
ABOVE HIM IS THE SKY--[BENEATH]	THE DITCH IS DEAR TO THE	1645		6
ABRAHAM				
ABRAHAM TO KILL HIM	ABRAHAM TO KILL HIM	1317		1
ABRAHAM WAS OLD--	ABRAHAM TO KILL HIM	1317		4
ABRAHAM COMPLIED--	ABRAHAM TO KILL HIM	1317		6
ABREAST				
A WILD BLUE SKY ABREAST OF WINDS	A WILD BLUE SKY ABREAST	1415		1
ABRIDGE				
ABRIDGE [IMPAIR / DEBAR / DEPRIVE] SOCIETY	WE MISS HER, NOT BECAUSE	993		4
ABRIDGES				
AND ABRIDGES THE RAIN.	THE PARASOL IS THE	1747		4
ABROAD				
BECAUSE--WHEN NEXT IT BURNS ABROAD	THE DOOMED--REGARD THE	294		3
THE SUNRISE SHOOK ABROAD	THE DAY CAME SLOW--TILL	304		6
OF ALL THE SOUNDS DESPATCHED ABROAD,	OF ALL THE SOUNDS	321		1
THE SUN, AS COMMON, WENT ABROAD,	THERE CAME A DAY AT	322		5
WOULD PUT ITSELF ABROAD	I CANNOT DANCE UPON MY	326		6
THAT HURRIED ALL AROUND [ABROAD]--	A BIRD CAME DOWN THE	328		10
EXCEPT TO STRAY ABROAD	FROM COCOON FORTH A	354		6
WOULD LEAP ABROAD LIKE ANTELOPE--	ALTHOUGH I PUT AWAY HIS	366		15
THAT PUTS THE HEART--ABROAD--	GOOD MORNING--MIDNIGHT--	425		12
I PUT MY PLEASURE ALL ABROAD--	IT WOULD NEVER BE COMMON	430		17
THAT JUST ABROAD HIS WINDOW	I ENVY SEAS, WHEREON HE	498		13
TO TELL HIM IT IS NOON, ABROAD--	I ENVY SEAS, WHEREON HE	498		19
SHE DANCES LIKE A BOMB, ABROAD,	THE SOUL HAS BANDAGED	512		13
I ASKED TO GO ABROAD,	MY FIRST WELL DAY--SINCE	574		2
NO SQUIRREL WENT ABROAD--	THE NIGHT WAS WIDE, AND	589		9
NO NEWS OF IT IS HAD ABROAD--	THE BATTLE FOUGHT	594		5
PERPETUAL BREAK [BE / GO] ABROAD	WHEN I WAS SMALL, A	596		18
IT MAKES NO DIFFERENCE ABROAD--	IT MAKES NO DIFFERENCE	620		1
AND FAR ABROAD ON SUMMER DAYS--	THE LOVE A LIFE CAN SHOW	673		8
DOTH SELDOM GO ABROAD--	THE SOUL THAT HATH A	674		2
AND THEN ABROAD THE WORLD HE GO	MY FAITH IS LARGER THAN	766		7
BEREAVED OF ALL, I WENT ABROAD--	BEREAVED OF ALL, I WENT	784		1
A COLOR STANDS ABROAD	A LIGHT EXISTS IN SPRING	812		5
AND STARTED ALL ABROAD--	THE WIND BEGUN TO KNEAD	824		6
NONE STIR ABROAD	SPRING IS THE PERIOD	844		6
HE HOISTS ABROAD AGAIN--	THESE ARE THE NIGHTS	1128		8
THE DAY ABROAD WAS HEARD--[RESUMED ABROAD]	THE WIND TOOK UP THE	1134		14
THE DAY ABROAD WAS HEARD--[RESUMED ABROAD]	THE WIND TOOK UP THE	1134		14
AND LET THE FLOODS ABROAD--	LIKE RAIN IT SOUNDED	1235		12
RIDE ABROAD IN OSTENTATION	BEES ARE BLACK, WITH	1405		3
WHOSE ALLIES GO NO MORE ASTRAY [ABROAD]	A CHILLY PEACE INFESTS	1443		5
AND HEAVEN BESIDE, AND HEAVEN ABROAD;	A PIT--BUT HEAVEN OVER	1712		2
ABROGATE				
AND ABROGATE--MY BEE--	I ENVY SEAS, WHEREON HE	498		22
ABRUPT				
ABRUPT--MECHANICALLY--	THERE'S BEEN A DEATH, IN	389		8
ABSCONDED				
ABSCONDED--SUDDENLY--	BEREAVEMENT IN THEIR	645		12
ABSCONDED DAINTILY [FLUENTLY]	A SPARROW TOOK A SLICE	1211	V	8
THAT FIRST ABANDONED [ABSCONDED] YEAR.	THE DISTANCE THAT THE	1742	V	4
ABSCONDING				
BY A DEPARTING [RETREATING / ABSCONDING] LIGHT	BY A DEPARTING LIGHT	1714		1
ABSCONDS				
AND THEN ABSCONDS FROM SIGHT.	PAIN HAS BUT ONE	1049		8
ABSENCE				
BE FAITHFUL--IN HIS ABSENCE--	HE FOUND MY BEING--SET	603		5
ABSENCE DISEMBODIES--SO DOES DEATH	ABSENCE DISEMBODIES--SO	860		1
IN HIS LONG ABSENCE WORN	EACH SCAR I'LL KEEP FOR	877		3
THE ABSENCE [JOURNEY] OF AN EYE--	WE MISS HER, NOT BECAUSE	993		2
CERTIFICATE OF ABSENCE--	WE'LL PASS WITHOUT THE	996		3
THE [DIM / FAR] ABSENCE OF THE WITCH DOES NOT [CANNOT]	LONG YEARS APART--CAN	1383		3
WHO SAYS THE ABSENCE OF A WITCH	LONG YEARS APART--CAN	1383	V	4
ABSENT				
THE ABSENT--MYSTIC--CREATURE--	TO DIE--TAKES JUST A	255		9
BUT SUFFERED AN [ABSENT THROUGH] EXCHANGE OF TERRITORY--	IT KNEW NO LAPSE, NOR	560		7
HIS ABSENT CHARACTER.	JUST AS HE SPOKE IT FROM	848		8
ABSENT PLACE--AN APRIL DAY--	ABSENT PLACE--AN APRIL	927		1
LED ABSENT, WERE PROCURED [OBTAINED] OF HEAVEN	TWO TRAVELLERS PERISHING	933		15
AS ABSENT AS A HUNDRED YEARS,	THE FACE WE CHOOSE TO	1141		3
ABSENTEE				
BRIGHT ABSENTEE!	I TEND MY FLOWERS FOR	339		2
ABSENTLY				
CARESSED A TRIGGER ABSENTLY	HE SCANNED IT--STAGGERED	1062		8
ABSOLUTE				
AND ANGUISH--ABSOLUTE--	I REASON, EARTH IS SHORT	301		2
BUT SEEMED ENGROSSED TO ABSOLUTE--	I WATCHED THE MOON	629		27
EACH--IT'S DIFFICULT [ABSOLUTE] IDEAL	GROWTH OF MAN--LIKE	750		5
THE ABSOLUTE--REMOVED [WITHDREW]	YOU CONSTITUTED TIME--	765		5
THE OBJECT ABSOLUTE--IS NOUGHT--	PERCEPTION OF AN OBJECT	1071		5
AND I, HOWEVER ABSOLUTE [ACCURATE]	BECAUSE THAT YOU ARE	1260		3
BUT INTIMATE [COMPETENT / ABSOLUTE /	THE MOST TRIUMPHANT BIRD	1265		6

	FIRST LINE	POEM	LINE
ABSOLUTE (CONTINUED)			
IMPUDENT] DELIGHT.			
IT'S ABSOLUTE EXTENT	TWO LENGTHS HAS EVERY	1295	2
SO ABSOLUTE.	THE MIND LIVES ON THE	1355	8
SO ABSOLUTE--MONOTONY	HIS MANSION IN THE POOL	1379 V	
IS ABSOLUTE AS GOD,	THAN HEAVEN MORE REMOTE,	1436	15
FULFILLING ABSOLUTE [SOME EXPRESS] DECREE	HOW HAPPY IS THE LITTLE	1510	9
ABSOLVED			
NEITHER--WOULD BE ABSOLVED--	LIKE EYES THAT LOOKED ON	458	13
ABSORB			
THE ONE THE OTHER WILL ABSORB--	THE BRAIN--IS WIDER THAN	632	7
BUT [AND] THAT THE OTHER DID ABSORB	I THOUGHT THAT NATURE	1286	3
ABSORBED			
AUGUST--ABSORBED--NUMB--[RESISTLESS--DUMB]	NO CROWD THAT HAS	515	16
FOR IT'S ABSORBED ATTENTION'S	THIS DUST, AND IT'S	936	11
ABSTEMIOUS			
MAKE AN ABSTEMIOUS ECSTASY	RATHER ARID DELIGHT	1679	3
ABSTEMIOUSLY			
ABSTEMIOUSLY.	PARTAKE AS DOTH THE BEE,	994	2
ABSTEMIOUSNESS			
THE BANQUET OF ABSTEMIOUSNESS	WHO NEVER WANTED--	1430	3
ABSTINENCE			
IT HALF ENDEARS THE ABSTINENCE--	UNTO MY BOOKS--SO GOOD	604	3
THAT ABSTINENCE OF MINE [ME] PRODUCE	I FIT FOR THEM--	1109	6
WHAT ABSTINENCE IS THERE--	HOPE IS A SUBTLE GLUTTON	1547	4
ABSURD			
MY PRACTISE HOW ABSURD	CONFERRING WITH MYSELF	1655	6
ABSURDITY			
WHAT A POMPOSITY [AN ABSURDITY / A PERVERSITY]	THAT THIS SHOULD FEEL	1112 V	7
ABUNDANCE			
NOW [SINCE] I [THAT] ABUNDANCE SEE--	OH SUMPTUOUS MOMENT	1125	5
ABUNDANT			
FROM AN ABUNDANT SKY.	SUPERFLUOUS WERE THE SUN	999	12
IMPREGNABLE AS [AS OPULENT IT / EXTRAVAGANT AS / ABUNDANT AS	YOU CANNOT TAKE ITSELF	1351	5
ABUNDANT [A FERVENT / A LOYAL / A GRACIOUS / AN AMPLE] END--	THE GENTIAN HAS A	1424	13
ABUTS			
WHILE HER FATHER ABUTS THE TEMPEST	THE PARASOL IS THE	1747	3
ABYSS			
JUST A DOME OF ABYSS IS BOWING [NODDING]	HOW THE OLD MOUNTAINS	291	19
IS BLISS THEN, SUCH ABYSS,	IS BLISS THEN, SUCH	340	1
YOU CANNOT SOLDER AN ABYSS [PLUG A SEPULCHRE]	TO FILL A GAP	546	5
THEN COVERS THE ABYSS WITH TRANCE--	THERE IS A PAIN--SO	599	3
BESIDE US LIKE A BLAND ABYSS	POWER IS A FAMILIAR	1238	3
FLOSS WONT SAVE YOU FROM AN ABYSS	FLOSS WONT SAVE YOU FROM	1322	1
THAT TILLING IT'S ABYSS,	I NEVER HEAR THAT ONE IS	1323	6
ABYSS'S			
IN AN ABYSS'S FACE!	WHAT MYSTERY PERVADES A	1400	8
ACCEDED			
THE WHICH ACCEDED TO--	A LITTLE EAST OF JORDAN,	59	12
ACCENT			
FROM ACCENT HARSH, OR RUTHLESS WORD--	WHERE I HAVE LOST, I	104	6
NOR MYSELF TO HIM--BY ACCENT--	CONSCIOUS AM I IN MY	679	11
AS ACCENT FADES [WANES] TO INTERVAL	THE MURMURING OF BEES,	1115	11
THE TREASON OF AN ACCENT	THE TREASON OF AN ACCENT	1358	1
THE ACCENT OF A COMING FOOT--	ELYSIUM IS AS FAR AS TO	1760	7
ACCENTED			
JUST HIS SIGH--ACCENTED--	TO KNOW JUST HOW HE	622	14
ACCENTS			
TAKE OTHER ACCENTS, AS SUCH I HEARD	I'M SAYING EVERY DAY	373	21
THIS--ADDRESSED DEPARTING ACCENTS--	THESE--SAW VISIONS--	758	5
THROUGH ACCENTS TERRIBLE AS DEATH	WHO WERE "THE FATHER AND	1258 V	5
WARM IN HER HAND THESE ACCENTS LIE	WARM IN HER HAND THESE	1313	1
ACCEPT			
ACCEPT THIS "BONNIE DOON,"	"SIC TRANSIT GLORIA	3	62
ACCEPT IT'S MOST [BEST]--	THE TEST OF LOVE--IS	573	9
"HAVE ALTERED--ACCEPT THE PILLAGE	I SAW THAT THE FLAKE WAS	1267	7
THAT NOT A BEGGAR WOULD ACCEPT	THAT SHORT--POTENTIAL	1307	7
ACCEPTED			
FOR THIS--ACCEPTED BREATH--	FOR THIS--ACCEPTED	195	1
THAT SUCH A DAY, PERMITTED [PERSUADED / ACCEPTED] SO,	HE TOUCHED ME, SO I LIVE	506	2
HEART THAT PROPOSED AS HEART THAT ACCEPTED	UP LIFE'S HILL WITH MY	1010	7
ACCEPTS			
ACCEPTS A BETTER LATITUDE--	'TIS NOT THAT DYING	335	7
ACCESSIBLE			
ACCESSIBLE TO THILL OF BEE--	A LITTLE ROAD--NOT MADE	647	3
ACCIDENT			
REMOVED FROM ACCIDENT OF LOSS	REMOVED FROM ACCIDENT OF	424	1
BY ACCIDENT OF GAIN	REMOVED FROM ACCIDENT OF	424	2
MAINTAIN--BY ACCIDENT THAT THEY PROCLAIM--	LIFE, AND DEATH, AND	706	6
OR ACCIDENT OF NOISE--	WHEN I HAVE SEEN THE SUN	888	6
BECAUSE BY ACCIDENT	HOW MANY SCHEMES MAY DIE	1150	6
FAR AFTER ACT OR ACCIDENT	WE LIKE A HAIRBREADTH	1175	3
TO WHAT DELICIOUS ACCIDENT	THE MOST TRIUMPHANT BIRD	1265	8
MEETING BY ACCIDENT,	MEETING BY ACCIDENT,	1548	1
ACCIDENTAL			
THERE STRAYED AN ACCIDENTAL RED	IT WAS A QUIET SEEMING	1419	4
IN ACCIDENTAL POWER--	APPARENTLY WITH NO	1624	4

	FIRST LINE	POEM	LINE
ACCLIMATED			
TILL ACCLIMATED--TO--	THE PROVINCE OF THE	539	12
THAN THINE ACCLIMATED CREATURE	SNOW BENEATH WHOSE	942	7
BUT ACCLIMATED--PINES NO MORE [GROPES NO MORE / LOSES SIGHT / . . .	THE INUNDATION OF THE	1425	7
ACCOMMODATE			
THOUGH THE FAITH ACCOMMODATE BUT TWO--	THE SWEETEST HERESY	387	4
ACCOMPANIED			
ACCOMPANIED WITH TEAR--	I HAD A GUINEA GOLDEN--	23	30
ACCOMPANIES			
ACCOMPANIES A STAR.	NO MATTER WHERE THE	1541	4
ACCOMPANY			
WHEN KATIE WALKS, THIS SIMPLE PAIR ACCOMPANY HER SIDE,	WHEN KATIE WALKS, THIS	222	1
ACCOMPANY THEIR FEET--	OF BEING IS A BIRD	653	10
EXCEPT IT'S MIND ACCOMPANY	WE MISS HER, NOT BECAUSE	993	3
TO ACCOMPANY--	NOT ANY MORE TO BE	1344	12
ACCOMPANYING			
ACCOMPANYING THE SUN--	THE TREES LIKE TASSELS--	606	4
A SPECTRE--INFINITE--ACCOMPANYING--	ONE NEED NOT BE A	670 V	19
NEW ACCOMPANYING--	ALL FORGOT FOR	966	4
ACCOMPLISH			
THAT SORT ACCOMPLISH WELL--	'TWAS FIGHTING FOR HIS	1188	2
ACCOMPLISHED			
THE MOST ACCOMPLISHED SHOT!	THERE IS A WORD	8	16
TO SEARCH [SEEK] FOR THE ACCOMPLISHED GUEST,	THE SOUL SHOULD ALWAYS	1055	7
COME UNTO ME ENACTED [ACCOMPLISHED] HOW . .	CONTAINED IN THIS SHORT	1165 V	
. . . ACCOMPLISHED / DISCERNING / ACCOUTRED / ESTABLISHED / . . .	HE PREACHED UPON	1207	8
ACCOMPLISHED IN SURPRISE--	HOW FITS HIS UMBER COAT	1371	10
WHO HAVE ACCOMPLISHED DEATH	THE OVERTAKELESSNESS OF	1691	2
ACCORDING			
'TIS DUKE, OR DWARF, ACCORDING	THE OUTER--FROM THE	451	3
ACCORDING AS HIS SKILL PREFER	JUST AS HE SPOKE IT FROM	848	5
ACCORDING TO OUR DEED.	THE SUN IS GAY OR STARK	878	2
ACCORDING TO THE LAW	ALONE AND IN A	1167	20
ACCORDINGLY			
TO BE HALLOWED--ACCORDINGLY--	BY MY WINDOW HAVE I FOR	797	25
ACCOST			
WHEN THRONES ACCOST MY HANDS--	MY REWARD FOR BEING, WAS	343	6
ONE ACCOST ME--	I'M SAYING EVERY DAY	373	25
ACCOST A THEME--SO--FAIR--	THE SOUL HAS BANDAGED	512	10
AND WE APPROACH [ACCOST] HIM--STERN--	THE LIGHTNING PLAYETH--	630	4
SO THE EYES ACCOST--AND SUNDER	SO THE EYES ACCOST--AND	752	1
LATER THAN LIGHT THY CONSCIOUSNESS ACCOST ME	AIR HAS NO RESIDENCE, NO	1060	7
A SPIRIT--HOW DOTH IT ACCOST--	'TIS WHITER THAN AN	1482	7
AND WE ACCOST NO MORE--[WE KNOW]	WE NEVER KNOW WE GO WHEN	1523	4
ACCOSTAL			
THESE RECEDED TO ACCOSTAL	KNOCK WITH TREMOR--	1325 V	6
ACCOSTED			
ACCOSTED BY A TIMID BIRD	A FIELD OF STUBBLE,	1407	5
ACCOSTS			
ACCOSTS MY OPEN EYE--	THE ANGLE OF A LANDSCAPE	375	6
NOT WHEN WE KNOW, THE POWER ACCOSTS--	LET ME NOT MAR THAT	1335	5
EXPERIMENT ESCORTS [ACCOSTS] US LAST--	EXPERIMENT ESCORTS US	1770	1
ACCOUNT			
WHO SINCE THEY WENT TO THEIR ACCOUNT	HOW DARE THE ROBINS SING	1724	3
ACCOUNTED			
AND THO' I'M SCARCE ACCOUNTED,	WHEN DIAMONDS ARE A	397	5
ARE SCARCE ACCOUNTED [COMPUTED]--HARMS--	ONE ANGUISH--IN A CROWD	565	12
LESS ACCOUNTED THAN	ALL FORGOT FOR	966	6
ACCOUTRED			
. . . ACCOMPLISHED / DISCERNING / ACCOUTRED / ESTABLISHED / . . .	HE PREACHED UPON	1207	8
ACCREDITED			
ACCREDITED--TODAY--	THIS DUST, AND IT'S	936	2
ACCRUE			
IF CONTENTMENT ACCRUE	RATHER ARID DELIGHT	1679	2
ACCURATE			
SO ACCURATE THE ONE	NO MAN CAN COMPASS A	477	8
AND I, HOWEVER ABSOLUTE [ACCURATE]	BECAUSE THAT YOU ARE	1260	3
ACCUSE			
SAY IF I ERRED? ACCUSE MY FARTHINGS--	SWEET--YOU FORGOT--BUT I	523	5
ACCUSED			
MY SOUL--ACCUSED ME--AND I QUAILED--	MY SOUL--ACCUSED ME--AND	753	1
ALL ELSE [THE WORLD] ACCUSED ME--AND I SMILED--	MY SOUL--ACCUSED ME--AND	753	3
ACCUSED--WERT THOU--AND MYSELF--TRIBUNAL--	WERT THOU BUT ILL--THAT	961	9
ACCUSTOMED			
FROM AN ACCUSTOMED [A FAMILIAR] FLOWER.	SHE WENT AS QUIET AS THE	149	2
AT THE ACCUSTOMED HOUR!	SHE WENT AS QUIET AS THE	149	4
THE FLOWERS, ACCUSTOMED, BLEW,	THERE CAME A DAY AT	322	6
I'M SOME ACCUSTOMED TO HIM GROWN,	I DREADED THAT FIRST	348	3
I'M SO ACCUSTOMED TO MY FATE--	IT MIGHT BE LONELIER	405	3
WE GROW ACCUSTOMED TO THE DARK--	WE GROW ACCUSTOMED TO	419	1
TILL I GET ACCUSTOMED--BUT THEN THE TOMB	IT DONT SOUND SO	426	11
FROM HIS ACCUSTOMED ROUTE--	HOW MANY SCHEMES MAY DIE	1150	8
AS AN ACCUSTOMED STIRRUP--	A SPARROW TOOK A SLICE	1211 V	7
A'CHASE			
THE STONES A'CHASE--	ONE NEED NOT BE A	670	10

	FIRST LINE	POEM	LINE
ACHE			
IT IS SIMPLE, TO ACHE IN THE BONE, OR THE RIND--	IT IS EASY TO WORK WHEN	244	5
HOW MANY TIMES IT ACHE FOR ME--TODAY--CONFESS--	YOU SEE I CANNOT SEE--	253	3
AND IT WILL ACHE--CONTENTED--ON--	BOUND--A TROUBLE--	269	8
TO ACHE IS HUMAN--NOT POLITE--	SHE DEALT HER PRETTY	479	9
TO ACHE--AND LIKE A SKATER'S BROOK--	'TWAS WARM--AT FIRST--	519	7
ACHES			
WINCES [ACHES] WITH DELIGHT	INCONCEIVABLY SOLEMN!	582	14
ACHIEVE			
MUST ACHIEVE--ITSELF--	GROWTH OF MAN--LIKE	750	6
ONCE TO ACHIEVE, ANNULS THE POWER	THOSE WHO HAVE BEEN IN	922	7
NO SERVICE HAST THOU, I WOULD NOT ACHIEVE [ATTEMPT] IT--	WERT THOU BUT ILL--THAT	961	17
WE ACHIEVE THE JOY--	SATISFACTION--IS THE	1036	6
TO UNDERTAKE IS TO ACHIEVE	TO UNDERTAKE IS TO	1070	1
HE FIRST ACHIEVE [ESPOUSE] THY FACE	MY HEART RAN SO TO THEE	1237	6
WE BLUSH, THAT HEAVEN IF WE ACHIEVE [BEHOLD]--	WHO WERE "THE FATHER AND	1258	21
THAT IS BEST WHICH IS NOT--ACHIEVE IT--	WHICH IS THE BEST--THE	1315	3
ACHIEVED			
HE--MUST HAVE ACHIEVED IN PERSON	HER SWEET TURN TO LEAVE	649	27
BUT HE WHO HAS ACHIEVED THE TOP [CREST]--	THE HALLOWING OF PAIN	772	7
DESPAIR'S ADVANTAGE IS ACHIEVED	DESPAIR'S ADVANTAGE IS	799	1
AS NEVER WAS ACHIEVED [BEHELD]--	THAT THIS SHOULD FEEL	1112	4
WHAT CONSTANCY MUST BE ACHIEVED	LONGING IS LIKE THE SEED	1255	7
ACHIEVEMENT			
AT DISTANCE, AND ACHIEVEMENT, STRAINS,	AS PLAN FOR NOON AND	960	5
ACHIEVEMENT CONTEMPLATING THEE [THIS / HERE]--	THAT ODD OLD MAN IS DEAD	1130	11
ACHIEVES			
THE SOUL ACHIEVES--HERSELF--	EXHILIRATION--IS WITHIN	383	5
THE CHANNEL OF THE DUST WHO ONCE ACHIEVES	OURSELVES WE DO INTER	1144	2
ACHIEVING			
FOR JOURNEY--OR CRUSADE'S ACHIEVING--	ONE CRUCIFIXION IS	553	11
AS BIRDS BEFORE ACHIEVING	THESE TESTED OUR HORIZON	886	3
ACHING			
OR WOULD THEY GO ON ACHING STILL	I MEASURE EVERY GRIEF I	561	21
IF I CAN EASE ONE LIFE THE ACHING	IF I CAN STOP ONE HEART	919	3
A'CHIRRUP			
WHAT SHALL I DO WHEN THE SKIES A'CHIRRUP	WHAT SHALL I DO WHEN THE	956	5
ACKNOWLEDGED			
ACKNOWLEDGED--OF THE BRAVE--	THERE IS A SHAME OF	551	6
ACKNOWLEDGED HIM A MAN.	FATE SLEW HIM, BUT HE	1031	8
ACKNOWLEDGEMENT			
LIFT, IN BEREAVED ACKNOWLEDGEMENT	I DREADED THAT FIRST	348	27
ACORN			
THAT THE ACORN THERE	TO VENERATE THE SIMPLE	57	9
NO ACORN--THEN--	ONE YEAR AGO--JOTS WHAT?	296	24
ACORN'S			
MINE--WAS AN ACORN'S BREAST--	ONE YEAR AGO--JOTS WHAT?	296	18
A COURTING			
ALL THINGS DO GO A COURTING, IN EARTH, OR SEA, OR AIR,	AWAKE YE MUSES NINE,	1	5
ACQUAINTANCE			
ACQUAINTANCE--JUST A FEW--	IF ANYBODY'S FRIEND BE	509	18
AND BROAD--SUNBURNED ACQUAINTANCE	I'M SORRY FOR THE DEAD--	529	5
CHRIST'S ACQUAINTANCE WITH HIM	LIFE--IS WHAT WE MAKE IT	698	3
WHO HIS OWN ACQUAINTANCE	NEVER FOR SOCIETY	746	3
NEW ACQUAINTANCE--THIS BABY MADE--	TRUDGING TO EDEN,	1020	8
PAIN HAS BUT ONE ACQUAINTANCE	PAIN HAS BUT ONE	1049	1
ACQUAINTANCES			
ETERNITY'S ACQUAINTANCES	WHO OCCUPIES THIS HOUSE?	892	31
MY BEST ACQUAINTANCES ARE THOSE	MY BEST ACQUAINTANCES	932	1
AS WERE THEY OLD ACQUAINTANCES--	A FACE DEVOID OF LOVE OR	1711	5
ACQUAINTED			
BUT SHE, AND DEATH, ACQUAINTED--	I READ MY SENTENCE--	412	11
ACQUAINTED MORE WITH THAT	OH GIVE IT MOTION--DECK	1527	6
ACQUIESCENCE			
ACQUIESCENCE--OR DEMURRAL--	HER SWEET TURN TO LEAVE	649	23
ACQUIRE			
ACQUIRE THE QUICK OF SKILL--	'TIS ONE BY ONE--THE	545	6
WE--DIFFICULT--ACQUIRE	AWAY FROM HOME ARE SOME	821	6
ACQUIRED			
ACQUIRED BY REVERSE--	NONE CAN EXPERIENCE	771	6
ACQUISITION			
IN THE ACQUISITION	KNOWS HOW TO FORGET!	433	V
ACQUITTED			
ACQUITTED--FROM THAT NAKED BAR--	TRIUMPH--MAY BE OF	455	15
ACRE			
HE CLAIMS THE PRETTY ACRE,	I HAD SOME THINGS THAT I	116	7
THAT ON THE ACRE LIES.	EXCEPT TO HEAVEN, SHE IS	154	8
DROPPED INTO THE ETHER ACRE--	DROPPED INTO THE ETHER	665	1
LATE--MY GARDEN [ACRE] OF A ROCK--	SOIL OF FLINT, IF STEADY	681	V
FOUR TREES--UPON A SOLITARY ACRE--	FOUR TREES--UPON A	742	1
THE ACRE GIVES THEM--PLACE--	FOUR TREES--UPON A	742	9
NOT AN ACRE OR A CAPTION	ONE DAY IS THERE OF THE	814	11
A CONSCIOUSNESS IT'S ACRE, AND	IT WAS A GRAVE, YET BORE	876	3
IN ACRES--IT'S [ACRE--OR] LOCATION	A NEARNESS TO	963	7
HE LIKES A BOGGY ACRE	A NARROW FELLOW IN THE	986	9
"GIVE OF THINE AN ACRE UNTO ME."	SAID DEATH TO PASSION	1033	2

	FIRST LINE	POEM	LINE
ACRE (CONTINUED)			
ELATE THE ACRE AT HIS FEET--	MY GOD--HE SEES THEE--	1178	6
AN ACRE FOR A BIRD TO CHOOSE	ON MY VOLCANO GROWS THE	1677	3
ACRES			
ACRES OF MASTS ARE STANDING	HOW THE OLD MOUNTAINS	291	V 19
ACRES OF JOINTS [SEAMS], WHERE HARVESTS WERE,	IT SIFTS FROM LEADEN	311	15
SKIRTS THE ACRES OF PERHAPS--	THEIR HIGHT IN HEAVEN	696	7
IN ACRES--IT'S [ACRE--OR] LOCATION	A NEARNESS TO	963	7
AND FETCH THE ACRES IN.	THE PRODUCTS OF MY FARM	1025	8
AS ACRES [COUNTIES] FROM THE FEET	IT WAS A QUIET WAY--	1053	10
IT LOOSENED ACRES, LIFTED SEAS	LIKE RAIN IT SOUNDED	1235	13
ACRID			
ALONE--TOO ACRID--BUT COMBINED	SURPRISE IS LIKE A	1306	3
ACRID WHATEVER FATE.	FRIGID AND SWEET HER	1318	4
ACROSS			
AND CREAK ACROSS MY SOUL [BRAIN]	I FELT A FUNERAL, IN MY	280	10
I GOT SO I COULD WALK ACROSS	I GOT SO I COULD HEAR	293	5
WHEN SUDDENLY ACROSS THE JUNE	THEY DROPPED LIKE FLAKES	409	4
THE ROPE THE NIGHTS WERE PUT ACROSS--	I SHOWED HER HIGHTS SHE	446	6
ACROSS MY MOUTH--IT BLURS IT--	I AM ALIVE--I GUESS--	470	7
JUST MAKING SIGNS--ACROSS--[IT SEEMED] TO THEE--	IF I MAY HAVE IT, WHEN	577	20
AROUND--ACROSS--UPON IT--	THERE IS A PAIN--SO	599	5
LONG STEPS ACROSS THE FEATURES TOOK	TWO TRAVELLERS PERISHING	933	9
ACROSS A BARN OR THROUGH A RUT	THE SKY IS LOW--THE	1075	3
A JAR ACROSS THE FLOWERS GOES	LIKE TRAINS OF CARS ON	1224	3
WHICH THOU HAST LEAPED ACROSS!	PASS TO THY RENDEZVOUS	1564	4
A CAP OF LEAD ACROSS THE SKY	A CAP OF LEAD ACROSS THE	1649	1
ACT			
PRESENTS IT--IN THE ACT--	THE FUTURE--NEVER SPOKE	672	6
WE THIRST AT FIRST--'TIS NATURE'S ACT--	WE THIRST AT FIRST--'TIS	726	1
WHEN ACT AND WILL ARE DONE	NOT WHAT WE DID, SHALL	823	2
FINDING IS THE FIRST ACT	FINDING IS THE FIRST ACT	870	1
OF JUNIOR OF FOURSCORE--'TWAS ACT	NOT ALL DIE EARLY, DYING	990	7
CRUMBLING IS NOT AN INSTANT'S ACT	CRUMBLING IS NOT AN	997	1
GOD MADE NO ACT WITHOUT A CAUSE,	GOD MADE NO ACT WITHOUT	1163	1
FAR AFTER ACT OR ACCIDENT	WE LIKE A HAIRBREADTH	1175	3
IT THEN GOES OUT AN ACT	A DEED KNOCKS FIRST AT	1216	5
THE ACT OF EVENING FELL	THE MOUNTAINS STOOD IN	1278	10
AND DURING IT'S ELECTRIC GALE [SPELL / STAY / MIGHT / ACT / SPAN]--	WITH PINIONS OF DISDAIN	1431	7
HOW LITTLE WORK [WHAT LITTLE ACT] IT BE--	WITH PINIONS OF DISDAIN	1431	10
I KNOW THEE BETTER FOR THE ACT	I SEE THEE CLEARER FOR	1666	5
THE GLEAM OF AN HEROIC ACT	THE GLEAM OF AN HEROIC	1687	1
ACTION			
I'LL INSTITUTE AN "ACTION"--	I HAD SOME THINGS THAT I	116	13
OF ACTION--SICKER FAR--	I TIE MY HAT--I CREASE	443	18
OR ORDER, OR APPARENT ACTION [SIGNAL / NOTICE]--	FOUR TREES--UPON A	742	3
THE LIGHT HIS ACTION, AND THE DARK	ALL CIRCUMSTANCES ARE	820	5
IN UNREMITTING ACTION	HOPE IS A STRANGE	1392	3
NOR ACTION [WISDOMS] NEW--	I HAVE NO LIFE BUT THIS	1398	6
REKINDLED BY SOME ACTION QUAINT	A WINGED SPARK DOTH SOAR	1468	9
THE DREAMS CONSOLIDATE IN ACTION--	THE LASSITUDES OF	1592	5
HIS ACTION LAID AWAY	JUDGEMENT IS JUSTEST	1671	3
ACTS			
A PRESENCE OF DEPARTED ACTS--	REMORSE--IS MEMORY--	744	3
HIS ORDINARY ACTS ARE FEATS	BEST WITCHCRAFT IS	1158	3
ACTUAL			
AN ACTUAL SUFFERING STRENGTHENS	THEY SAY THAT "TIME	686	3
NO NEARER--LEST THE ACTUAL--[REALITY-- / ITS PENURY-- / THE . . .	WHO NEVER WANTED--	1430	7
ACTUALIZE			
AND HAUNTING ACTUALIZE--TO LAST	JOY TO HAVE MERITED THE	788	23
ACTUALLY			
WE ACTUALLY HEAR	THE SPIRIT IS THE	733	2
ACUTE			
OMNIPOTENT--ACUTE--	REHEARSAL TO OURSELVES	379	4
ACUTE DEGREE--CONFERRED ON ME--	TITLE DIVINE--IS MINE!	1072	3
ACUTER			
WOULD BE ACUTER, WOULD IT NOT	TO ONE DENIED TO DRINK	490	3
WE SEE ACUTER [DISTINCTER / SINCERER], QUITE,	BY A DEPARTING LIGHT	1714	2
ADAM			
ADAM, AND EVE, HIS CONSORT, THE MOON, AND THEN THE SUN;	AWAKE YE MUSES NINE,	1	8
PUT DOWN THE APPLE, ADAM,	"SIC TRANSIT GLORIA	3	17
DOUBTLESS--"ADAM"--SCOWLED AT EDEN--	TAKING UP THE FAIR IDEAL	428	7
ADAM AND REPEAL.	PARADISE IS OF THE	1069	4
ADAM TAUGHT HER THRIFT	PARADISE IS THAT OLD	1119	6
PATENTED BY ADAM.	WHAT WE SEE WE KNOW	1195	8
ADAMANT			
INTO THE LAP OF ADAMANT--	I KNOW A PLACE WHERE	337	9
A COBWEB--WOVE IN ADAMANT--	I HAD NOT MINDED--WALLS	398	11
AND THEIR OPAQUEST ADAMANT--	THEY PUT US FAR APART--	474	11
BUT DROPPED LIKE ADAMANT.	'TWAS WARM--AT FIRST--	519	16
BLISTERS THE ADAMANT!	I'LL SEND THE FEATHER	687	6
THE SPIRIT SHOOK THE ADAMANT--	'TWAS CRISIS--ALL THE	948	11
COULD ADAMANT REFUSE	JUST ONCE! OH LEAST	1076	2
THE ONLY ADAMANT ESTATE	HOW FIRM ETERNITY MUST	1499	3
IS SHOD WITH ADAMANT--	YOU CANNOT MAKE	1508	8

	FIRST LINE	POEM	LINE
ADAMANT (CONTINUED)			
INSTINCT PURSUES THE ADAMANT,	THE SPIRIT LASTS--BUT IN	1576	17
ADAMANTINE			
HANDLE THE ADAMANTINE FINGERS	HOW MANY TIMES THESE LOW	187	7
ADD			
AND ADD "HOW COLD--IT GREW"--	I AM ALIVE--I GUESS--	470	14
AND WHO CAN ADD A CROWN	WHO COURT OBTAIN WITHIN	803	7
ADD AN AMBER CRUMB	HE IS ALIVE, THIS	1160	6
UNTO THE WHOLE--HOW ADD?	UNTO THE WHOLE--HOW ADD?	1341	1
ADDED			
AN ADDED STRUT IN CHANTICLEER--	AN ALTERED LOOK ABOUT	140	9
THERE ADDED THE DIVINE	I THOUGHT THAT NATURE	1286	6
HAS HE NO ADDED REALM	HOW SOFT THIS PRISON IS	1334	6
BUT TIME HAD ADDED NOT OBTAINED	A LITTLE SNOW WAS HERE	1444	5
ADDER			
KNOWS THE ADDER [ADDERS] TONGUE HIS COMING	WE LIKE MARCH.	1213	6
ADDERS			
KNOWS THE ADDER [ADDERS] TONGUE HIS COMING	WE LIKE MARCH.	1213	6
ADDETH			
ADDETH TO MY DEGREE--	THE MURMUR OF A BEE	155	12
ADDICTED			
LET ALL ADDICTED TO	A RAT SURRENDERED HERE	1340	5
ADDINGS			
BUT GROWN BY SLENDER ADDINGS	DEPRIVED OF OTHER	773	5
ADDRESS			
FROM OUR FAMILIAR LIFETIME [ADDRESS / GAZING / FINGERS / NOTICE]--	THOSE FAIR--FICTITIOUS	499	3
SHOULD ENDOW [ADDRESS / REWARD] THE DAY--	BLOOM UPON THE MOUNTAIN	667	6
AN EMIGRANT'S ADDRESS.	A SOUTH WIND--HAS A	719	4
ADDRESSED			
AN AGED BEE ADDRESSED US--	THE GENTIAN WEAVES HER	18	11
I NEVER SPOKE--UNLESS ADDRESSED--	I WAS THE SLIGHTEST IN	486	10
THIS--ADDRESSED DEPARTING ACCENTS--	THESE--SAW VISIONS--	758	5
CONTINUAL ADDRESSED--	REPORTLESS SUBJECTS, TO	1048	2
ADDRESSING			
ENTERTAIN--WITHOUT ADDRESSING	SO THE EYES ACCOST--AND	752	5
ADDS			
ADDS [GIVES] POIGNANCY TO WINTER--	CONJECTURING A CLIMATE	562	3
ADEQUATE			
SO ADEQUATE--IT FORMS--	OF BRONZE--AND BLAZE--	290	3
TO HIM OF ADEQUATE DESIRE	HEAVEN IS SO FAR OF THE	370	7
A TEMPERATURE JUST ADEQUATE	MORE LIFE--WENT OUT--	422	7
BUT THIS TIME--ADEQUATE--ERECT,	I'M CEDED--I'VE STOPPED	508	17
WHOSE ADEQUATE SUPPLY	WE THIRST AT FIRST--'TIS	726	6
THE ADEQUATE [COMPLEMENT] OF HELL--	REMORSE--IS MEMORY--	744	12
HOW ADEQUATE UNTO ITSELF	THIS CONSCIOUSNESS THAT	822	9
AND ADEQUATE, [CONSCIOUS AND] ERECT,	THE PROPS ASSIST THE	1142	4
ADEQUATE AS DRUMS	SOME WE SEE NO MORE,	1221	9
. . . A MIGHT / SO DELICATE A MIGHT / SO ADEQUATE A MIGHT / . . .	THE MOST TRIUMPHANT BIRD	1265	4
HOW ADEQUATE THE HUMAN HEART	WHAT MYSTERY PERVADES A	1400	V
AN ADEQUATE REPAST	WITH SWEETNESS UNABATED	1709	10
ADEQUATELY			
THAT I BE ADEQUATELY DRESSED,	I CANNOT SEE MY SOUL BUT	1262	6
ADHERE			
LAST TO ADHERE [AT THE SCENE] WHEN SUMMER CLEAVES [SUMMER . . .	AFTER ALL BIRDS HAVE	1395	7
ADHERES			
TO WHICH THE GRAVE ADHERES--	MORE THAN THE GRAVE IS	1503	3
ADHESION'S			
DIVISION IS ADHESION'S FORFEIT--ON HIGH	NOT SO THE INFINITE	1040	2
ADIEU			
DAY--DROPS YOU HER [HIS] RED ADIEU!	AH, TENERIFFE!	666	5
BROTHER OF OPHIR, BRIGHT ADIEU,	BROTHER OF INGOTS--AH	1366 V	1
BY AN ADIEU--	FACTS BY OUR SIDE ARE	1497	8
ADIEU FOR WHENCE [TILL WHEN]	FACTS BY OUR SIDE ARE	1497	9
IMAGE [FELLOW] OF LIGHT, ADIEU--	IMAGE OF LIGHT, ADIEU--	1556	1
ADJACENT			
NOR THAT ADJACENT, THAT BESIDE,	COUNT NOT THAT FAR THAT	1074	3
ADJACENT SUMS	UNTIL THE DESERT KNOWS	1291	9
WHICH WHILE YOU TASTE SO NATIVE [ADJACENT] SEEMS	YOUR THOUGHTS DONT HAVE	1452	5
ADJECTIVE			
AFFLICTIVE IS THE ADJECTIVE	BIRTHDAY OF BUT A SINGLE	1488	3
ADJOINING			
IN AN ADJOINING ROOM--	I DIED FOR BEAUTY--BUT	449	4
REVERTED TO ADJOINING LIVES--	IF HE WERE LIVING--DARE	734	9
TO AN ADJOINING ZONE--	THE SPRY ARMS OF THE	1103	4
ALIEN, THOUGH ADJOINING	NOW I KNEW I LOST HER--	1219	5
ADJOURN			
TRUTH ADJOURN YOUR BOON	LOVE IS DONE WHEN LOVE'S	1485	4
OTHER FRIENDS ADJOURN	GUEST AM I TO HAVE	1661	4
ADJOURNING			
BUT AN ADJOURNING HEART--	NOT SICKNESS STAINS THE	1613	4
ADJOURNS			
ADJOURNS HER SIGH--	WE WEAR OUR SOBER	1572	3
ADJUNCT			
OF THIS [WHOSE] ELECTRIC ADJUNCT	HOPE IS A STRANGE	1392	5
ADJURE			
BESEECH [ADJURE] EACH LITTLE BOY--	A LITTLE DOG THAT WAGS	1185	16

	FIRST LINE	POEM	LINE
ADJUST			
OR PRIESTS--ADJUST THE SYMBOLS--	IT WILL BE SUMMER--	342	19
THE DUST--CONNECT [ADJUST]--AND LIVE--	NO CROWD THAT HAS	515	8
HERSELF ADJUST HER TIDES--UNTO--	I COULD SUFFICE FOR HIM,	643	15
THESE--ADJUST--THAT RAN TO MEET US--	THESE--SAW VISIONS--	758	12
THAT I UNTO HIMSELF ADJUST	YOU CONSTITUTED TIME--	765	7
ADJUST THE HEAT--ELUDE THE WIND--	BLOOM--IS RESULT--TO	1058	11
BUT SO ADJUST MY DAILY NIGHT	LET ME NOT MAR THAT	1335	3
ADJUSTED			
ADJUSTED IN THE TOMB	I DIED FOR BEAUTY--BUT	449	2
ADJUSTED IT TO PLACE--	HE FOUND MY BEING--SET	603	2
ADJUSTED BY A STEM--	YOU'LL KNOW HER--BY HER	634	6
ALL BUT DEATH, CAN BE ADJUSTED--	ALL BUT DEATH, CAN BE	749	1
AND WHEN ADJUSTED LIKE A SEED	NO NOTICE GAVE SHE, BUT	804	13
AND THEN ADJUSTED HIS LITTLE NOTES,	A TRAIN WENT THROUGH A	1761	5
ADJUSTS			
ADJUSTS ITSELF TO MIDNIGHT--	WE GROW ACCUSTOMED TO	419	19
THAT ADJUSTS THE HAIR	CRISIS IS A HAIR	889	14
TRUST ADJUSTS HER "PERADVENTURE"--	TRUST ADJUSTS HER	1161	1
ADJUSTS IT'S TUMBLED HEAD--	A ROUTE OF EVANESCENCE	1463	6
ADMINISTER			
ADMINISTER HER ECSTASY,	THOSE FINAL CREATURES,--	1766	3
ADMIRABLER			
OR ADMIRABLER SHOW--	THE ONLY NEWS I KNOW	827	11
ADMIRALTY			
AN ADMIRALTY, LESS--	MY REWARD FOR BEING, WAS	343	3
ADMIRATIONS			
THE ADMIRATIONS--AND CONTEMPTS--OF TIME--	THE ADMIRATIONS--AND	906	1
ADMIRED			
BY BUTTERFLIES ADMIRED [ADORED / DESIRED]	THIS BAUBLE WAS	805	2
ADMIRING			
TO AN ADMIRING BOG!	I'M NOBODY! WHO ARE YOU?	288	8
TO AN ADMIRING SKY--	THE FACE I CARRY WITH ME	336	14
ADMISSION			
OBTAIN "ADMISSION" AS A CHILD	DEW--IS THE FRESHET IN	1097	11
ADMIT			
TICKETS ADMIT	UNIT, LIKE DEATH, FOR	408	6
IS SHUNNED, WE MUST ADMIT IT,	DROWNING IS NOT SO	1718	11
ADMITS			
ADMITS OF NO DEBATE--	THE PUNGENT ATOM IN THE	1191	2
IF "GOD IS LOVE" AS HE ADMITS	BECAUSE THAT YOU ARE	1260	33
ADMITTED			
THEMSELF--ADMITTED HOME--	THOSE FAIR--FICTITIOUS	499	22
EMBODIED [ADMITTED] SCARCELY TO ITSELF--IT MAY BE--	EACH LIFE CONVERGES TO	680	5
THAT IS ADMITTED--HERE--	THE SPIRIT IS THE	733	4
A SOUL ADMITTED TO ITSELF--	THERE IS A SOLITUDE OF	1695	7
ADMITTED HE A MAN	NO MAN SAW AWE, NOR TO	1733	2
ADMITTING			
A NOT ADMITTING OF THE WOUND	A GREAT HOPE FELL	1123	10
ADMONISH			
I ADMONISH THEE	SNOW BENEATH WHOSE	942	4
ADMONISHED			
ADMONISHED BY HER BUCKLED LIPS	THE RETICENT VOLCANO	1748	9
ADMONITION			
HER ADMONITION MILD--	NATURE--THE GENTLEST	790	4
INSPECT THE ADMONITION	HOW KNOW IT FROM A	1364	7
ADORATION			
OUR ADORATION STAIN [MAR / FLAW]	WE SHUN BECAUSE WE PRIZE	1429	3
ADORE			
AND FURTHEST--TO ADORE--	THE HEAVEN VESTS FOR	694	16
THE OTHER TO PREFER [ADORE]?	THERE IS A JUNE WHEN	930	16
FALL SOFTLY, AND ADORE--	THE LADY FEEDS HER	941	8
BUT NEARER [CLOSER / FURTHER / SIMPLY / MERELY] TO ADORE	BECAUSE HE LOVES HER	1229	10
DEPUTED [CONTENTED / CREATED] TO ADORE--	SUMMER--WE ALL HAVE SEEN	1386	9
ADORED			
WE ADORED--FOR WHOLE--	TAKING UP THE FAIR IDEAL	428	14
ADORED [BEHELD] WITH CAUTION--AS A BRITTLE HEAVEN--	EACH LIFE CONVERGES TO	680	9
BY BUTTERFLIES ADMIRED [ADORED / DESIRED]	THIS BAUBLE WAS	805	2
ITSELF, ADORED BEFORE	A FULL FED ROSE ON MEALS	1154	6
THE DOOM [LOT] TO BE ADORED	SUMMER--WE ALL HAVE SEEN	1386	V 9
ADORES			
MY FAITH THAT DARK ADORES--	THE FEET OF PEOPLE	7	22
ADORING			
GUSHED TOO FREE [FULL] FOR THE ADORING--	HER--"LAST POEMS"--	312	9
LIFTED ADORING--THEN--	THE BEGGAR LAD--DIES	717	14
ADORN			
ME TO ADORN--HOW--TELL--	I AM ASHAMED--I HIDE--	473	7
WE HASTEN TO ADORN--	TO DISAPPEAR ENHANCES--	1209	12
LEST MEN SPECIFICAL ADORN	I CANNOT SEE MY SOUL BUT	1262	8
ADORNED			
WERE EQUALLY--ADORNED--	THE DAY THAT I WAS	356	12
ADORNED, FOR A SUPERIOR GRACE--	"HEAVEN" HAS DIFFERENT	575	19
THE HOMELIEST--ADORNED	I THINK I WAS ENCHANTED	593	18
DAINTY ADORNED WITH VEINS AND TISSUES	AS THE STARVED MAELSTROM	872	7
ADORNING			
ADORNING ALL THE RULE--	'TIS ONE BY ONE--THE	545	8

	FIRST LINE	POEM	LINE
ADOWN			
ADOWN THE EMPTY STREET--	THE NIGHT WAS WIDE, AND	589	12
A QUEEN ADOWN A SATIN AISLE,	A CURIOUS CLOUD	1710	8
A-DREAMING			
SHOULD BE A-DREAMING LAID.	I CAUTIOUS, SCANNED MY	178	4
ADRIFT			
ADRIFT! A LITTLE BOAT ADRIFT!	ADRIFT! A LITTLE BOAT	30	1
ADRIFT! A LITTLE BOAT ADRIFT!	ADRIFT! A LITTLE BOAT	30	1
ADROIT			
TO HIS ADROIT CREATOR	THE BAT IS DUN, WITH	1575	13
ADROITER			
WHILE GOD'S ADROITER WILL	IT ALWAYS FELT TO ME--A	597	12
ADROITLY			
ADROITLY TURNING OUT	IF HE WERE LIVING--DARE	734	10
ADROITLY TURNING ROUND	THE SUN IN REINING TO	1636	4
ADULT			
ADULT AND URGENT GROWN--	THE WAY TO KNOW THE	1279	18
WHETHER ADULT DELIGHT IS [BE] PAIN	WONDER--IS NOT PRECISELY	1331	6
ADVANCE			
PUT THE THOUGHT IN ADVANCE--A YEAR--	IT DONT SOUND SO	426	15
ADVANCE UNMOVED--TO HER SUPREME--	TRIUMPH--MAY BE OF	455	7
TO STOP--OR PERISH--OR ADVANCE--	FROM BLANK TO BLANK--	761	4
ENFEEBLES--THE ADVANCE--	HAD I NOT THIS, OR THIS,	904	16
SHE STUNG HIM--SAPPED HIS FIRM ADVANCE--	FATE SLEW HIM, BUT HE	1031	5
THE STOCK'S ADVANCE AND RETROGRADE	MYSELF CAN READ THE	1089	3
DO ONE ADVANCE [OBTAIN] SO NEAR	THE MERCHANT OF THE	1131	10
ADVANCE IS LIFE'S CONDITION	ADVANCE IS LIFE'S	1652	1
ADVANCED			
OUR JOURNEY HAD ADVANCED--	OUR JOURNEY HAD ADVANCED	615	1
ADVANCED AND BREAKFASTED.	OUR LITTLE KINSMEN--	885	8
THERE CAME [ADVANCED] UNSUMMONED IN--	SHALL I TAKE THEE, THE	1126	8
ADVANCING			
ADVANCING ON CELESTIAL LISTS--	HAD I PRESUMED TO HOPE--	522	11
ADVANCING ON THE TRANSPORT	HOW NEWS MUST FEEL WHEN	1319	V 3
ADVANCING [DEPUTED] TO THY DEN--	OH FUTURE! THOU SECRETED	1631	8
AND GLEE'S ADVANCING SOUND	IN SNOW THOU COMEST	1669	4
ADVANTAGE			
OR IT'S ADVANTAGE--BLUE--	I WATCHED THE MOON	629	36
DESPAIR'S ADVANTAGE IS ACHIEVED	DESPAIR'S ADVANTAGE IS	799	1
ADVENTURE			
ADVENTURE MOST UNTO ITSELF	THIS CONSCIOUSNESS THAT	822	13
TENERIFFE'S ADVENTURE	THE JAY HIS CASTANET HAS	1635	V
ADVENTURES			
THE DAY'S ADVENTURES TELL	THE HILLS IN PURPLE	1016	2
ADVENTUROUS			
BAGS OF DOUBLOONS--ADVENTUROUS BEES	WHAT WOULD I GIVE TO SEE	247	18
ADVERSITY			
AS SOON--ADVERSITY	REVERSE CANNOT BEFALL	395	4
WOULD BE AN EASY ADVERSITY	HOW HAPPY I WAS IF I	898	3
TO THE [A / OUR] TEMERITY [EXTREMITY / ADVERSITY]--	SUMMER--WE ALL HAVE SEEN	1386	8
ADVERSITY IF IT MAY BE, OR	THE SPIRIT LASTS--BUT IN	1576	19
ADVERSITY IF IT MAY BE	THIS ME--THAT WALKS AND	1588	3
IS LIKE THE CHILD'S ADVERSITY	THE GOING FROM A WORLD	1603	3
LIKE AN ADVERSITY.	DROWNING IS NOT SO	1718	12
ADVERTISE			
DONT TELL! THEY'D BANISH US [ADVERTISE]--YOU KNOW!	I'M NOBODY! WHO ARE YOU?	288	4
WHEN WE ADVERTISE EXISTENCE	LAIN IN NATURE--SO	1288	3
ADVISE			
COULD A SHREWD ADVISE ME	I NEVER TOLD THE BURIED	11	18
ADVOCATE			
ADVOCATE THE AZURE	LIFT IT--WITH THE	1348	5
HIS ADVOCATE--HIS EDIFICE--	THE DITCH IS DEAR TO THE	1645	3
ADZ			
PLATED THE RESIDUE OF ADZ	NOT ANY MORE TO BE	1344	15
ADZE			
WERE CLOVEN WITH AN ADZE--	WE MET AS SPARKS--	958	4
AERIAL			
AND TAKES HER FAIR AERIAL GAIT	THE OVERTAKELESSNESS OF	1691	7
AESTHETICS			
HAVE A SYSTEM OF AESTHETICS--	FLOWERS--WELL--IF	137	13
AFAR			
WHEN LOVERS BE AFAR--	'TIS CUSTOMARY AS WE	440	4
AFAR [REMOTE / ASTRAY] UPON THE WIND	IT IS A LONESOME GLEE--	774	4
AND CRUMBLESS AND AFAR	THE LADY FEEDS HER	941	6
WHILE FAITHFUL AND AFAR	WARM IN HER HAND THESE	1313	2
AFFABLE			
. . . INTIMATE / AFFABLE / AFFLUENT / GRACIOUS] SO TO BE	YOUR THOUGHTS DONT HAVE	1452	6
AFFAIR			
WERE NONE OF OUR AFFAIR!.	IN EBON BOX, WHEN YEARS	169	20
'TWAS AN EVERYDAY AFFAIR--	HE FORGOT--AND I--	203	2
FOR SO MINUTE AFFAIR	I GOT SO I COULD HEAR	293	25
THAT--IS NOT STEEL'S AFFAIR--	SHE DEALT HER PRETTY	479	6
OF OUR'S, NONE AFFAIR--	WE TALKED AS GIRLS DO--	586	4
OR MERCURY'S AFFAIR--	NATURE AND GOD--I	835	8
THESE--ARE TIME'S AFFAIR--	COLOR--CASTE--	970	2
ASSISTING IN THE BRIGHT AFFAIR	BLOOM--IS RESULT--TO	1058	5
THE DEMAND [THE AFFAIR / AN AFFAIR] OF AWE?	SUMMER LAID HER SIMPLE	1363	8

	FIRST LINE	POEM	LINE
AFFAIR (CONTINUED)			
THE DEMAND [THE AFFAIR / AN AFFAIR] OF AWE?	SUMMER LAID HER SIMPLE	1363	8
AFFAIRS			
AND THE AFFAIRS OF JUNE	LIKE SOME OLD FASHIONED	302	4
AFFECT			
AFFECT US, AND RETURN--	THERE IS A JUNE WHEN	930	8
AFFECTING			
AFFECTING OUR CONTENT	A LIGHT EXISTS IN SPRING	812	18
AFFECTINGLY			
AFFECTINGLY AGAIN--	SUMMER HAS TWO	1422	4
AFFECTION			
AFFECTION DOES'NT KNOW	AMBITION CANNOT FIND HIM	68	2
WITH INFINITE AFFECTION--	NATURE--THE GENTLEST	790	21
SPEECH IS ONE SYMPTOM OF AFFECTION	SPEECH IS ONE SYMPTOM OF	1681	1
REARRANGE A "WIFE'S" AFFECTION!	REARRANGE A "WIFE'S"	1737	1
AFFECTS			
NATURE AFFECTS [WAS KNOWN] TO BE SEDATE	NATURE AFFECTS TO BE	1170	1
AFFIANCE			
AFFIANCE IT AGAIN	OH GIVE IT MOTION--DECK	1527	4
AFFIDAVIT			
GOOD AFFIDAVIT--	MINE--BY THE RIGHT OF	528	V 8
BUT AFFIDAVIT STANDS	"REMEMBER ME" IMPLORED	1180	10
TO AFFIDAVIT GIVEN.	SO MUCH OF HEAVEN HAS	1228	4
IF NOT AN AFFIDAVIT	THE FACT THAT EARTH IS	1408	3
AFFIRM			
OF IT'S VOICE--TO AFFIRM--WHEN THE WIND IS WITHIN--	BY MY WINDOW HAVE I FOR	797	13
AFFIRMED			
IS NOT AFFIRMED OF MATHEMATICS--	ONE CRUCIFIXION IS	553	3
AFFIRMING			
AFFIRMING [PRONOUNCING] IT A SOUL.	THE PROPS ASSIST THE	1142	12
AFFIXED			
UNLESS CONCEALED IN [INTRENCHED IN / AFFIXED TO / INLAID IN] THEE	HOW FIRM ETERNITY MUST	1499	8
AFFLICT			
'TWOULD'NT AFFLICT A ROBIN--	WHAT SHALL I DO WHEN THE	956	13
AFFLICTED			
THE SAME--AFFLICTED THOMAS--	TRUST IN THE UNEXPECTED	555	13
AFFLICTED FOR THE DAY.	WHO SAW NO SUNRISE	1018	6
AFFLICTION			
AN IMPERIAL AFFLICTION	THERE'S A CERTAIN SLANT	258	11
AFFLICTION WOULD NOT BE APPEASED--	SEVERER SERVICE OF	786	17
AFFLICTION FEELS IMPALPABLE	DESPAIR'S ADVANTAGE IS	799	11
AFFLICTION IS INFERRED	AS FROST IS BEST	951	3
AFFLICTION RANGES BOUNDLESSNESS--	A NEARNESS TO	963	3
AFFLICTION CANNOT STAY	A NEARNESS TO	963	6
AFFLICTION BUT A SPECULATION--AND WO	NOT SO THE INFINITE	1040	3
IS BEAUTY AN AFFLICTION--THEN?	SO GAY A FLOWER	1456	4
TO KNOW HER NOT--AFFLICTION--	TO SEE HER IS A PICTURE	1568	5
AFFLICTIVE			
AFFLICTIVE IS THE ADJECTIVE	BIRTHDAY OF BUT A SINGLE	1488	3
WHEN OPENING THE SABBATH IN THEIR AFFLICTIVE WAY	THE BOBOLINK IS GONE--	1591	5
AFFLICTS			
AFFLICTS ME WITH A DOUBLE LOSS--	EXCEPT THE HEAVEN HAD	472	7
'TIS THIS ENAMORS [AFFLICTS US] IN THE EAST--	THE LOVE A LIFE CAN SHOW	673	10
AFFLICTS ME--AS A SETTING SUN--	I LEARNED--AT LEAST--	944	30
AFFLUENCE			
WHAT NECKLACES [AFFLUENCE / LEGACY] COULD BE [FOR ME]--	A DROP FELL ON THE APPLE	794	8
OUR AFFLUENCE A WHIM	THE DAYS THAT WE CAN	1184	V 6
THE AFFLUENCE EVOLVED [CONFERRED / BESTOWED / INVOLVED]--	SUMMER--WE ALL HAVE SEEN	1386	10
AFFLUENT			
. . . INTIMATE / AFFABLE / AFFLUENT / GRACIOUS] SO TO BE	YOUR THOUGHTS DONT HAVE	1452	6
BUT AFFLUENT THE DOOM--	BIRTHDAY OF BUT A SINGLE	1488	4
AFFORD			
COULD YOU AFFORD TO SELL--	I CAME TO BUY A SMILE--	223	8
THEY CAN AFFORD A SUN	I RECKON--WHEN I COUNT	569	10
THE POOREST--COULD AFFORD--	OF BRUSSELS--IT WAS NOT	602	6
AS CREW OF MOUNTAINS--COULD AFFORD--	THEY CALLED ME TO THE	628	11
COULD SCARCE AFFORD ETERNITY	IT'S EASY TO INVENT A	724	7
WHY BLISS SO SCANTILY [CAUTIOUSLY] DISBURSE [EXPRESS / AFFORD]--	ONE BLESSING HAD I THAN	756	17
NO SINEW CAN AFFORD--	SUCH IS THE FORCE OF	787	5
AFFORDED			
IT HAD CREATED [AFFORDED] HER.	THIS BAUBLE WAS	805	8
HINT OF GLORY--IT AFFORDED--	ROBBED BY DEATH--BUT	971	7
AFFORDED DAY BY DAY.	THE STIMULUS, BEYOND THE	1001	4
AFFORDS			
AFFORDS THE SLY PRESUMPTION	TO HANG OUR HEAD--	105	5
AFFORDS A BLISS LIKE MURDER--	REHEARSAL TO OURSELVES	379	3
A PIERCING COMFORT IT AFFORDS	I MEASURE EVERY GRIEF I	561	35
YELLOW SHE AFFORDS	NATURE RARER USES YELLOW	1045	6
AFFRIGHT			
WHERE BELLS NO MORE AFFRIGHT THE MORN--	WHERE BELLS NO MORE	112	1
AFFRONT			
NO BALD DEATH--AFFRONT THEIR PARLORS--	SWEET--SAFE--HOUSES--	457	10
WOULD MORE AFFRONT THE SAND--	YOU'LL KNOW HER--BY HER	634	4

	FIRST LINE	POEM		LINE
AFFRONT (CONTINUED)				
AFFRONT TO HIM	SO LARGE MY WILL	1024		5
AFFRONT TO ME	SO LARGE MY WILL	1024		7
SUPPLY THE [INVITE SOME / ENDOW SOME / AFFRONT A / AFFRONT . . .	ART THOU THE THING I	1282		3
SUPPLY THE [INVITE SOME / ENDOW SOME / AFFRONT A / AFFRONT . . .	ART THOU THE THING I	1282		3
AND ALMOST COUNT IT AN AFFRONT	AS SUMMER INTO AUTUMN	1346		5
NOTHING AFFRONT THY SECRECY.	TO THE STANCH DUST	1402	V	7
BUT THAT IT WOULD AFFRONT US	THE FACT THAT EARTH IS	1408		7
AFFRONTED				
WHEN TRUTH--AFFRONTED LONG--	TRIUMPH--MAY BE OF	455		6
INDIGNANT [AFFRONTED]--THAT THE JOY WAS COME--	I THINK THE LONGEST HOUR	635		5
AND I AFFRONTED [DISCOURAGED] GREW	MY HEART RAN SO TO THEE	1237		3
AFFRONTED BY THE SNOW--	SWEET SKEPTICISM OF THE	1413		4
AFFRONTS				
A BOG--AFFRONTS MY SHOE--	A BURDOCK--CLAWED MY	229		6
TOO MUCH OF PROOF AFFRONTS BELIEF	SO MUCH OF HEAVEN HAS	1228		9
AFLOAT				
AN EASY BREEZE DO PUT AFLOAT	OF BEING IS A BIRD	653		3
A-FOG				
A-FOG FOR--SAY--WHOSE SAKE?	YOU KNOW THAT PORTRAIT	504		4
AFORETIME				
AFORETIME IN MY HAT--	"ARCTURUS" IS HIS OTHER	70		14
AFRAID				
EMBARRASSED--NOT AFRAID--	BAFFLED FOR JUST A DAY	17		2
THE BEE IS NOT AFRAID OF ME.	THE BEE IS NOT AFRAID OF	111		1
AND HE WAS BAREFOOT, I'M AFRAID!	I MET A KING THIS	166		4
THE PERFECT, NOWHERE BE AFRAID--	WHEN WE STAND ON THE	242		9
TILL WE--ARE LESS AFRAID--	READ--SWEET--HOW OTHERS	260		4
BETTER OF IT--CONTINUAL BE AFRAID--	A SECRET TOLD--	381		5
AFRAID! OF WHOM AM I AFRAID?	AFRAID! OF WHOM AM I	608		1
AFRAID! OF WHOM AM I AFRAID?	AFRAID! OF WHOM AM I	608		1
AFRAID TO TRUST THE MORN	AFRAID! OF WHOM AM I	608		10
WAS HE AFRAID--OR TRANQUIL--	TO KNOW JUST HOW HE	622		22
I'M NOT AFRAID TO KNOW--	THE SUN KEPT SETTING--	692		16
OF MEETING THEM--AFRAID--	IF HE WERE LIVING--DARE	734		4
DYING! TO BE AFRAID OF THEE	DYING! TO BE AFRAID OF	831		1
BE OF ME--AFRAID.	STRUCK, WAS I, NOR YET	925		16
AND THAT HE DID'NT LOOK AFRAID?	TRUDGING TO EDEN,	1020		6
WHERE I AM NOT AFRAID TO GO	HERE, WHERE THE DAISIES	1037		5
I AM AFRAID TO OWN A BODY--	I AM AFRAID TO OWN A	1090		1
I AM AFRAID TO OWN A SOUL--	I AM AFRAID TO OWN A	1090		2
NAPLES IS MORE AFRAID	WHEN ETNA BASKS AND	1146		2
THE GRASS DOES NOT APPEAR AFRAID,	WHAT MYSTERY PERVADES A	1400		9
AFRAID OF JOY,	WE SHUN IT ERE IT COMES,	1580		2
"AFRAID HE HISSED	IN WINTER IN MY ROOM	1670		24
AFRESH				
AFRESH ANNIHILATING ME	I NEVER HEAR THAT ONE IS	1323		3
IT'S IRON BUDS WILL SPROUT ANEW [AFRESH]	YOU CANNOT MAKE	1508		11
AFRICAN				
BUT AFRICAN EXUBERANCE	NO AUTUMN'S INTERCEPTING	1516		3
AFTER				
AFTER [UNTO] THE DAY!	LIKE HER THE SAINTS	60		6
RANK AFTER RANK, WITH EVEN FEET--	TO FIGHT ALOUD, IS VERY	126		11
ROBIN AFTER ROBIN	DUST IS THE ONLY SECRET	153		15
AFTER DINNER LIGHT--FOR FLOWERS--	MORNING--IS THE PLACE	197		3
AFTER PLAYING CROWN!	GOD PERMITS INDUSTRIOUS	231		8
AND AFTER THAT--THERE'S HEAVEN--	YOU'RE RIGHT--"THE WAY	234		9
FLUNG COLORED, AFTER RAIN,	DELIGHT IS AS THE FLIGHT	257		6
NIGHT AFTER NIGHT	THIS--IS THE LAND--THE	266		5
THE SOUL STARES AFTER IT, SECURE--	'TIS SO APPALLING--IT	281		3
THAT AFTER HORROR--THAT 'TWAS US--	THAT AFTER HORROR--THAT	286		1
INTO [BACK OF / AT THE / AFTER / UNTO / NEXT TO] SOLITUDE--	HOW THE OLD MOUNTAINS	291		20
AFTER GREAT PAIN, A FORMAL FEELING COMES--	AFTER GREAT PAIN, A	341		1
THE MORNING AFTER WO--	THE MORNING AFTER WO--	364		1
AND AFTER THAT--IS NONE--	THE RED--BLAZE--IS THE	469		4
TO MAKE ONE'S TOILETTE--AFTER DEATH	TO MAKE ONE'S TOILETTE--	485		1
AFTER A LIFE--A DEATH--WE'LL SAY--	IF I MAY HAVE IT, WHEN	577		11
HAPPENING IN AFTER AGES	SHELLS FROM THE COAST	693		3
AFTER SUN HAS [WHEN THE SUN IS] SET--	WHEN I HOPED, I	768		20
BULB AFTER BULB, IN SILVER ROLLED--	SPLIT THE LARK--AND	861		2
GUSH AFTER GUSH, RESERVED FOR YOU--	SPLIT THE LARK--AND	861		6
OUR LITTLE KINSMEN--AFTER RAIN	OUR LITTLE KINSMEN--	885		1
AFTER ETERNITY.	WHAT DID THEY DO SINCE I	900		12
WHAT DIFFERENCE, AFTER ALL, THOU MAK'ST	THE SUNSET STOPPED ON	950		7
FAR AFTER SUFFERING	AS ONE DOES SICKNESS	957		10
BUT FAR AFTER FROST--	EXCEPT THE SMALLER SIZE	1067	V	
THE MORNING AFTER DEATH	THE BUSTLE IN A HOUSE	1078		2
RETURNS US NOT, BUT AFTER TIME	EXHILIRATION IS THE	1118		5
AFTER A HUNDRED YEARS	AFTER A HUNDRED YEARS	1147		1
AFTER THE SUN COMES OUT	AFTER THE SUN COMES OUT	1148		1
FAR AFTER ACT OR ACCIDENT	WE LIKE A HAIRBREADTH	1175		3
PAID AFTER THEY HAVE CEASED TO WORK	ALL MEN FOR HONOR	1193		3
AFTER ALL BIRDS HAVE BEEN INVESTIGATED AND LAID ASIDE--	AFTER ALL BIRDS HAVE	1395		1
CREATION AFTER THIS?	HOW HUMAN NATURE DOTES	1417		13
RECURRENT TO THE AFTER MIND [THOUGHT]	THEIR BARRICADE AGAINST	1471		9
WILL EVER AFTER RUN	THE LIFE THAT TIED TOO	1535		2

	FIRST LINE	POEM	LINE
AFTER (CONTINUED)			
AND AFTER THAT A SHALL.	THERE ARE TWO MAYS	1618	3
WHAT RIPENESS AFTER THEN	'TWAS HERE MY SUMMER	1756	2
AFTERNOON			
SINCE THE MIGHTY AUTUMN AFTERNOON	GOING TO HEAVEN!	79	26
TILL SOME ODD AFTERNOON	OUR LIVES ARE SWISS--	80	3
ONE MITRED AFTERNOON--	ONE DIGNITY DELAYS FOR	98	2
OH WHAT AN AFTERNOON FOR HEAVEN, ...	ALL OVERGROWN BY CUNNING	148	V
ON TIME'S FIRST AFTERNOON!	MUSICIANS WRESTLE	157	12
I MET A KING THIS AFTERNOON!	I MET A KING THIS	166	1
EMERGED--A SUMMER AFTERNOON--	FROM COCOON FORTH A	354	3
AND AFTERNOON--AND BUTTERFLY--	FROM COCOON FORTH A	354	24
A MIGHTY AFTERNOON--	DEPARTED--TO THE	524	2
THE HILL--THE AFTERNOON--	"NATURE" IS WHAT WE SEE	668	2
NO HUE OF AFTERNOON--	THE SUN KEPT SETTING--	692	2
A SUMMER AFTERNOON--	NATURE--THE GENTLEST	790	10
SOME--NEWLY RAISED THIS AFTERNOON, ...	WHO OCCUPIES THIS HOUSE?	892	11
SOME WEDNESDAY AFTERNOON.	DEW--IS THE FRESHET IN	1097	12
OCCURS EACH AFTERNOON--	THE LARGEST FIRE EVER	1114	2
THE AFTERNOON IN EVENING DEEP	THE DAY GREW SMALL,	1140	3
IN ONE SHORT AFTERNOON	HOW MANY SCHEMES MAY DIE	1150	2
THIS AFTERNOON PUT ON--	THE BUTTERFLY'S	1244	3
A SUMMER'S AFTERNOON--	NOT ANY HIGHER STANDS	1256	8
BELOVED ONLY AFTERNOON	FROM ALL THE JAILS THE	1532	3
SEQUESTERED AFTERNOON--	AS IMPERCEPTIBLY AS	1540	8
A FURTHER AFTERNOON TO FAIL	I WATCHED HER FACE TO	1667	7
AFTERNOONS			
AFTERNOONS--TO PLAY--	GOD PERMITS INDUSTRIOUS	231	2
HER TEAZING PURPLES--AFTERNOONS--	"HEAVEN"--IS WHAT I	239	9
WINTER AFTERNOONS--	THERE'S A CERTAIN SLANT	258	2
BRIGHT WEDNESDAY AFTERNOONS--	I NEVER FELT AT HOME--	413	8
THE AFTERNOONS--TOGETHER SPENT--	I LEARNED--AT LEAST--	944	18
AFTERWARD			
AFTERWARD--IN THE MEADOW--	THROUGH THE DARK SOD--AS	392	5
AND SICKENED--EVER AFTERWARD	IT KNEW NO MEDICINE--	559	15
AND AFTERWARD--OR NAY--	I WATCHED THE MOON	629	26
'TIS KINGDOMS--AFTERWARD--THEY SAY--	BEHIND ME--DIPS ETERNITY	721	7
NOT AFTERWARD--BY MEN--	HAVE ANY LIKE MYSELF	736	24
AFTERWARD I LEARNED	MOST SHE TOUCHED ME BY	760	18
AND AN AFTERWARD OF RUM--	THE POPULAR HEART IS A	1226	4
A TRIFLE AFTERWARD	IN WINTER IN MY ROOM	1670	10
AFTERWARDS			
AFTERWARDS--DAY!	OUR SHARE OF NIGHT TO	113	8
AGAIN			
AND IS MUTE AGAIN--	THERE IS A WORD	8	5
TOSS THEIR DICE AGAIN!	WE LOSE--BECAUSE WE WIN	21	3
THEN SLEEPS IN STATE AGAIN--	ALL THESE MY BANNERS BE.	22	5
TO LOSE--IF ONE CAN FIND AGAIN--	ALL THESE MY BANNERS BE.	22	8
I PLIGHT AGAIN, ...	I KEEP MY PLEDGE.	46	5
WILL SURELY COME AGAIN.	I KEEP MY PLEDGE.	46	11
ONLY TO FAIL AGAIN!	I NEVER HEAR THE WORD	77	8
BACK TO THE LAWN AGAIN.	WE SHOULD NOT MIND SO	81	4
TOMORROW, NIGHT WILL COME AGAIN--	HEART, NOT SO HEAVY AS	83	17
WILL PEEP, AND PRANCE AGAIN.	AS CHILDREN BID THE	133	8
SOUL, WILT THOU TOSS AGAIN?	SOUL, WILT THOU TOSS	139	1
A SPIDER AT HIS TRADE AGAIN--	AN ALTERED LOOK ABOUT	140	8
I WILL INQUIRE AGAIN--	WHOSE ARE THE LITTLE	142	6
YOU STING--AGAIN!	YOU LOVE ME--YOU ARE	156	19
AND "FEW THERE BE"--CORRECT AGAIN-- . . .	YOU'RE RIGHT--"THE WAY	234	3
SAY IT AGAIN, SAXON [ENGLISH LANGUAGE]! . .	MANY A PHRASE HAS THE	276	15
WITH THOSE SAME BOOTS OF LEAD, AGAIN, . .	I FELT A FUNERAL, IN MY	280	11
UNTO THE EAST AGAIN--	IT SIFTS FROM LEADEN	311	8
COULD NOT AGAIN BE PROVED--	HEAVEN IS SO FAR OF THE	370	4
AND OPEN HOUSE--AGAIN--	THE WINTERS ARE SO SHORT	403	8
TO HAVE THE JOY OF FEELING IT--AGAIN-- . .	I'LL CLUTCH--AND CLUTCH	427	14
AGAIN, HE TAPPED--'TWAS FLURRIEDLY-- . . .	THE WIND--TAPPED LIKE A	436	19
THE HORROR WELCOMES HER, AGAIN, ...	THE SOUL HAS BANDAGED	512	23
AND WHEN AGAIN, AT DAWN, ...	"HEAVEN" HAS DIFFERENT	575	4
SHE'S "SORRY I AM DEAD"--AGAIN--	I CRIED AT PITY--NOT AT	588	21
SHOULD I AGAIN EXPERIENCE--	I THINK I WAS ENCHANTED	593	27
AND HE WOULD COME AGAIN--	HE FOUND MY BEING--SET	603	6
AND NOT BEGIN--AGAIN--	IT WOULD HAVE STARVED A	612	16
AND WHEN I LOOKED AGAIN--	THEY CALLED ME TO THE	628	14
AND MEN TOO STRAIGHT TO STOOP [BEND] AGAIN,	MY PORTION IS DEFEAT--	639	8
AGAIN--HIS VOICE IS AT THE DOOR--	AGAIN--HIS VOICE IS AT	663	1
I'D GIVE--TO LIVE THAT HOUR--AGAIN--	AGAIN--HIS VOICE IS AT	663	26
AGAIN.	EACH LIFE CONVERGES TO	680	20
DEBATED--ROSE AGAIN--	SHE STAKED HER FEATHERS	798	2
UNTO HIS NEST AGAIN	IF I CAN STOP ONE HEART	919	6
IT CANNOT BE AGAIN--	THIS MERIT HATH THE	979	2
WE QUESTIONED TO, AGAIN.	'TIS ANGUISH GRANDER	984	4
TOO LATE TO CHOOSE AGAIN.	WHICH IS BEST? HEAVEN--	1012	9
THAT LETS HIM OUT AGAIN.	WHO IS THE EAST?	1032	8
WE SHALL NOT WANT TO USE AGAIN	THE BUSTLE IN A HOUSE	1078	7
IF BLOSSOMS CAN BE BORN AGAIN	WHEN THEY COME BACK--IF	1080	3
HE MIGHT NOT LOOK AGAIN?	WHEN THEY COME BACK--IF	1080	12
CAN NEVER BE FITTED [MATCHED] AGAIN?	OF THE HEART THAT GOES	1098	4
WE WENT AND PLAYED AND CAME AGAIN	THIS SLOW DAY MOVED	1120	7
HE HOISTS ABROAD AGAIN--	THESE ARE THE NIGHTS	1128	8
AGAIN THE SMOKE FROM DWELLINGS ROSE [CURLED]	THE WIND TOOK UP THE	1134	13

	FIRST LINE	POEM	LINE
AGAIN (CONTINUED)			
SO MANY YEARS AGAIN--	I SHOULD NOT DARE TO BE	1197	2
WE TAMPER WITH "AGAIN"	TO DISAPPEAR ENHANCES--	1209	8
CONFRONTING US AGAIN!	THE BONE THAT HAS NO	1274	12
NOR AGAIN--	LEFT IN IMMORTAL YOUTH	1289	4
THAT IT WILL COME AGAIN.	LET ME NOT MAR THAT	1335	4
CONTRIVES THAT NONE GO OUT AGAIN--	NO PASSENGER WAS KNOWN	1406	4
AFFECTINGLY AGAIN--	SUMMER HAS TWO	1422	4
AND [BUT] NOT AGAIN THAT DEW BE SEEN	A DEW SUFFICED ITSELF--	1437	7
WHO DOUBT TO LIVE AGAIN--	THOSE NOT LIVE YET	1454	2
"AGAIN" IS OF A TWICE	THOSE NOT LIVE YET	1454	3
AFFIANCE IT AGAIN	OH GIVE IT MOTION--DECK	1527	4
I SHALL NOT LOOK AGAIN.	CONSULTING SUMMER'S	1715	4
THAT IT WILL NEVER COME AGAIN	THAT IT WILL NEVER COME	1741	1
"DISCIPLE, CALL AGAIN."	THERE COMES AN HOUR WHEN	1751	6
AND BOWED AND SANG AGAIN.	A TRAIN WENT THROUGH A	1761	6
AGAINST			
LEANING AGAINST THE--SUN--	I TASTE A LIQUOR NEVER	214	V 16
HE CAN LEAN AGAINST THE GRAVE,	IF YOUR NERVE, DENY YOU	292	3
SO I LOOP MY APRON, AGAINST THE MAJESTY	I'M SAYING EVERY DAY	373	12
AGAINST THE WIND--BE SEEN--	THERE IS A FLOWER THAT	380	16
BECAUSE SHE BREATHED AGAINST	FORGET! THE LADY WITH	438	3
AGAINST THE MAN--PERSUADED--	MYSELF WAS FORMED--A	488	11
AND THEN HE RUNS AGAINST	HE PARTS HIMSELF--LIKE	517	5
AND WENT AGAINST THE WORLD--	I TOOK MY POWER IN MY	540	2
AND BROKE [SMOTE] AGAINST MY EAR--	I YEARS HAD BEEN FROM	609	12
SECURE AGAINST IT'S OWN--	THE SOUL UNTO ITSELF	683	5
AGAINST ITSELF--	RENUNCIATION--IS A	745	11
CONSPIRE AGAINST [REPUDIATE] HIS OWN	WHO COURT OBTAIN WITHIN	803	9
PREFERRED AGAINST THE MIND	EXPERIENCE IS THE ANGLED	910	2
'SCAPING ONE--AGAINST THE OTHER	PATIENCE--HAS A QUIET	926	5
IS CAPITAL AGAINST DESPAIR--	SOMEWHAT, TO HOPE FOR,	1041	3
IS PROOF AGAINST THE SUN	THE BUTTERFLY'S NUMIDIAN	1387	3
THEIR BARRICADE AGAINST THE SKY	THEIR BARRICADE AGAINST	1471	1
PAUSING IN FRONT OF [AGAINST] OUR PALSIED [SENTENCED /	WE TALKED WITH EACH	1473	5
AND NOW AGAINST HIS SUBTLE NAME	HE LIVED THE LIFE OF	1525	3
AND NOW AGAINST HIS SUBTLE NAME	WHO ABDICATED AMBUSH	1616	3
AGAINST YOUR TROPIC BRIDE	'TWAS HERE MY SUMMER	1756	8
AGATE			
TO JOINT THIS AGATE WERE A WORK [FEAT]--	TOO COLD IS THIS	1135	4
AGE			
WITH JUST AN AGE--AND NAME--	WE DREAM--IT IS GOOD WE	531	14
AS SINEWS DO, WITH AGE--	THEY SAY THAT "TIME	686	4
EACH AGE A LENS	THE POETS LIGHT BUT	883	6
'TIS WELL THE NAME AND AGE	WHO OCCUPIES THIS HOUSE?	892	4
THE AGE OF THAT	AS OLD AS WOE--	1168	V 5
AGED			
AN AGED BEE ADDRESSED US--	THE GENTIAN WEAVES HER	18	11
EARLY AGED, AND OFTEN COLD,	SOME, TOO FRAGILE FOR	141	10
THE CHESTNUT AGED GROWS	HOW FITS HIS UMBER COAT	1371	7
AND AID AN AGED YEAR	THE GENTIAN HAS A	1424	12
AGENT			
SATISFACTION--IS THE AGENT	SATISFACTION--IS THE	1036	1
AGES			
AGES BENEATH THE MOULD--	I BRING AN UNACCUSTOMED	132	13
WHILE THE AGES STEAL--	JUST LOST, WHEN I WAS	160	17
WHOSE EMERALD NEST THE AGES SPIN	A FEATHER FROM THE	161	5
STAPLES OF AGES--HAVE BUCKLED THERE--	SAFE IN THEIR ALABASTER	216	V
TELL [STATE] IT THE AGES--TO A CYPHER--	BOUND--A TROUBLE--	269	7
THE QUIET AGES PICKED IT UP--	I MEANT TO HAVE BUT	476	19
MINE--LONG AS [WHILE] AGES STEAL!	MINE--BY THE RIGHT OF	528	9
PURPLES OF AGES--PAUSE [HALT] FOR YOU--	AH, TENERIFFE!	666	3
HAPPENING IN AFTER AGES	SHELLS FROM THE COAST	693	3
AGES COIL [LURK] WITHIN	PAIN--EXPANDS THE TIME--	967	2
IN AGES, OR A NIGHT--	NOT ALL DIE EARLY, DYING	990	4
AGGRANDIZED			
DELIGHT HAD AGGRANDIZED THE GATE	IT CAME AT LAST BUT	1230	7
AGGRANDIZEMENT			
OR UNFORESEEN AGGRANDIZEMENT	THE WAY TO KNOW THE	1279	19
BEHOLD HIS LOST AGGRANDIZEMENT [EMOLUMENT]	ONE OF THE ONES THAT	1466	27
AGGRAVATE			
ONLY TO AGGRAVATE [JUST TO INTENSIFY] THE DARK	FAIRER THROUGH FADING--	938	7
AGGREGATE			
LOVE IS ONE, NOT AGGREGATE--	SAFE DESPAIR IT IS THAT	1243	7
THE AGGREGATE OF	TO EARN IT BY DISDAINING	1427	6
AGILE			
HOW WENT THE AGILE KERNEL OUT	TOO COLD IS THIS	1135	6
AGLOW			
AGLOW--ALL RUDDY--WITH THE LIGHT	I SEE THEE BETTER--IN	611	11
AND ALL MY HOUSE AGLOW	TO MY SMALL HEARTH HIS	638	2
AGO			
THAT PASSED, AN HOUR AGO!	WITHIN MY REACH!	90	9
WENT HOME A CENTURY AGO	WHERE I HAVE LOST, I	104	15
LONG AGO AS CHRIST AND PETER--	HE FORGOT--AND I--	203	3
AS LAUGHTER--WAS--AN HOUR AGO--	WHAT IF I SAY I SHALL	277	10
WHEN I, AM LONG AGO,	OF BRONZE--AND BLAZE--	290	17
ONE YEAR AGO--JOTS WHAT?	ONE YEAR AGO--JOTS WHAT?	296	1
SO--TWELVE MONTHS AGO--	ONE YEAR AGO--JOTS WHAT?	296	25
I WORE--AN HOUR AGO--	I GAINED IT SO--	359	15

	FIRST LINE	POEM		LINE
AGO (CONTINUED)				
CENTURIES AGO--	SMILING BACK FROM	385		8
AND THO' 'TIS YEARS AGO--THAT DAY--	THE FIRST DAY'S NIGHT	410		15
A NIGHT OR TWO AGO--	THE MOON WAS BUT A CHIN	737		2
THIS THAT WOULD GREET--AN HOUR AGO--	THIS THAT WOULD GREET--	778		1
CENTURIES AGO--	KNOCK WITH TREMOR--	1325		7
AGONIZED				
BURST AGONIZED AND CLEAR!	SUCCESS IS COUNTED	67		12
SO AGONIZED URGED?	JUST ONCE! OH LEAST	1076	V	5
AGONIZING				
OR THE MOST AGONIZING SPY--	THE SOUL UNTO ITSELF	683		3
SUCH AGONIZING TERMS?	JUST ONCE! OH LEAST	1076		5
AGONY				
I--FROM AGONY--	MORNS LIKE THESE--WE	27		8
BREWED FROM DECADES OF AGONY!	THO' I GET HOME HOW LATE	207		8
I LIKE A LOOK OF AGONY,	I LIKE A LOOK OF AGONY,	241		1
THAT AT THE LAST, IT SHOULD NOT BE A NOVEL AGONY--	I READ MY SENTENCE--	412		10
UNTIL THE AGONY	'TWAS LIKE A MAELSTROM,	414		4
REQUIRES ENERGY--POSSIBLY AGONY--	TO PUT THIS WORLD DOWN,	527		3
AN AGONY PROCURES--	A NEARNESS TO	963		2
AGONY THAT ENACTED THERE	AFTER A HUNDRED YEARS	1147		3
AGONY IS FRUGAL.	SAFE DESPAIR IT IS THAT	1243		2
AGROUND				
AGROUND--UPON THE SANDS--	I STARTED EARLY--TOOK MY	520		8
AGROUND--IS HE?	THOSE NOT LIVE YET	1454		6
AH				
AH--BUT REMEMBERING ME--	GARLANDS FOR QUEENS, MAY	34		4
AH--BUT REMEMBERING THEE--	GARLANDS FOR QUEENS, MAY	34		5
AH LITTLE ROSE--HOW EASY	NOBODY KNOWS THIS LITTLE	35		11
AH! INDEED!	"SOWN IN DISHONOR"!	62		2
AH [OH] BUGLE! BY MY [THE] WINDOW	HEART, NOT SO HEAVY AS	83		19
AH, CURIOUS FRIEND!	MY FRIEND MUST BE A BIRD	92		6
AH ARISTOCRACY!	FOR EVERY BIRD A NEST--	143		8
AH, WHAT LEAGUES THERE WERE	AT LAST, TO BE	174		6
AH, NECROMANCY SWEET!	AH, NECROMANCY SWEET!	177		1
AH, WIZARD ERUDITE!	AH, NECROMANCY SWEET!	177		2
AH, WHAT A ROYAL SAKE	FOR THIS--ACCEPTED	195		5
AH, WHAT SAGACITY PERISHED HERE!	SAFE IN THEIR ALABASTER	216		11
AH! KATIE! SMILE AT FORTUNE, WITH TWO SO KNIT TO THEE!	WHEN KATIE WALKS, THIS	222		4
AH, PITY--THEN!	A BURDOCK--CLAWED MY	229		10
AH, MOON--AND STAR!	AH, MOON--AND STAR!	240		1
AH, THE SEA!	WILD NIGHTS--WILD NIGHTS	249		10
AH, FRIEND, YOU LITTLE KNEW	GOOD NIGHT! WHICH PUT	259		3
AH, THE BEWILDERING THREAD!	A SHADY FRIEND--FOR	278		10
AH, SIR, NONE!	ONE YEAR AGO--JOTS WHAT?	296		37
AH, THE BEE FLIES NOT	THE NEAREST DREAM	319		12
AH, SAID JULY--	ANSWER JULY--	386		5
AH, TO ATTAIN IT--	KNOWS HOW TO FORGET!	433		12
AH, TO BE ERUDITE	KNOWS HOW TO FORGET!	433	V	
UNTIL TOMORROW [THE EVENING]--HAPPY LETTER! [AH! BE BASHFUL]	GOING TO HIM! HAPPY	494		24
AH, PUSSY, OF THE SAND,	SHE SIGHTS A BIRD--SHE	507		8
AH, TENERIFFE!	AH, TENERIFFE!	666		1
AH, TENERIFFE!	AH, TENERIFFE!	666		9
AH, BRIG--GOOD NIGHT	IT TOSSED--AND TOSSED--	723		9
BROTHER OF INGOTS--[SISTER OF OPHIR--] AH PERU--	BROTHER OF INGOTS--AH	1366		1
AH! PIT! WITH HEAVEN OVER IT!	A PIT--BUT HEAVEN OVER	1712		9
AH, TOO, IT HAS A WING.	FAME IS A BEE.	1763		4
AID				
TO GO WITHOUT THE SPECTRE'S AID [HELP]	I LIVED ON DREAD--	770		8
AID IT IN THE COMING	I SUPPOSE THE TIME WILL	1381		2
AND AID AN AGED YEAR	THE GENTIAN HAS A	1424		12
AIDED				
I MIGHT HAVE AIDED--THEE--	'TIS SUNRISE--LITTLE	908		14
OR HOW THE AMBER AIDED IT--	THESE HELD THEIR WICK	1390		3
AILED				
WHAT AILED SO SMART A LITTLE MAID--	THE ROSE DID CAPER ON	208		7
AIM				
THE TRANSPORT OF THE AIM--	I FIT FOR THEM--	1109		9
NOR HEART WITHOUT AN AIM,	GOD MADE NO ACT WITHOUT	1163		2
AIMED				
I AIMED MY PEBBLE--BUT MYSELF	I TOOK MY POWER IN MY	540		5
AIMLESS				
AIMLESS CREPT [STOLE] THE GLOWS	ON THE WORLD YOU COLORED	1171		4
AIMS				
I SMILE UPON THE AIMS	I COULD NOT PROVE THE	563		6
IT AIMS ONCE--KILLS ONCE--CONQUERS ONCE--	'TWAS FIGHTING FOR HIS	1188		5
IF AIMS IMPEL THESE ASTRAL ONES	THE MOON UPON HER FLUENT	1528		5
AIR				
ALL THINGS DO GO A COURTING, IN EARTH, OR SEA, OR AIR,	AWAKE YE MUSES NINE,	1		5
TO INVEST EXISTENCE WITH A STATELY AIR,	TO VENERATE THE SIMPLE	57		7
FOR THE UPPER AIR!	TO VENERATE THE SIMPLE	57		11
ANECDOTES OF AIR IN DUNGEONS	TALK WITH PRUDENCE TO A	119		7
SIP OLD FRANKFORT AIR	MANY CROSS THE RHINE	123		3
AND SOFTLY [SWIFTLY] THRO' THE ALTERED AIR	THESE ARE THE DAYS WHEN	130		11
ALL DAY--AMONG THE CROWDED AIR	MUSICIANS WRESTLE	157		2

	FIRST LINE	POEM	LINE
AIR (CONTINUED)			
AND BLUE--BELOVED AIR!	TO LEARN THE TRANSPORT	167	8
AN AWFUL TEMPEST MASHED THE AIR--	AN AWFUL TEMPEST MASHED	198	1
AND WHISTLED IN THE AIR--	AN AWFUL TEMPEST MASHED	198	6
INEBRIATE OF AIR--AM I--	I TASTE A LIQUOR NEVER	214	5
SENT US OF THE AIR--	THERE'S A CERTAIN SLANT	258	12
AND NOW, REMOVED FROM AIR--	I BREATHED ENOUGH TO	272	2
O'ERTAKELESS, AS THE AIR--	HOW NOTELESS MEN, AND	282	8
THEN DROPPED [LOST] THE AIR--	ONE YEAR AGO--JOTS WHAT?	296	27
AND COULD NOT VALUE--AIR?	ONE YEAR AGO--JOTS WHAT?	296	31
TO AUTOCRATIC AIR--	THE SOUL'S SUPERIOR	306	12
ONE CLAW UPON THE AIR,	I CANNOT DANCE UPON MY	326	12
IN [ON] FAR [STILL] OCTOBER AIR.	THERE ARE TWO RIPENINGS	332	8
OF GROUND, OR AIR, OR OUGHT--	AFTER GREAT PAIN, A	341	6
AND THE SURPRISED AIR	I'M SAYING EVERY DAY	373	30
HE CARED AS MUCH AS ON THE AIR	OF COURSE--I PRAYED--	376	3
A SOFA TO THE AIR--	THE WIND--TAPPED LIKE A	436	8
WAS LIKE THE STILLNESS IN THE AIR--	I HEARD A FLY BUZZ--WHEN	465	3
WITH A SUSPICIOUS AIR--	I MEANT TO HAVE BUT	476	26
WHILE IT AND I LAP ONE AIR	WHILE IT IS ALIVE	491	3
OH JESUS--IN THE AIR--	AT LEAST--TO PRAY--IS	502	2
AS IF I BREATHED SUPERIOR AIR--	HE TOUCHED ME, SO I LIVE	506	8
AS JUST APPRENTICED TO THE AIR--	SHE'S HAPPY, WITH A NEW	535	4
WITH AIR.	TO FILL A GAP	546	6
IN SIGHT OF NATIVE AIR--	I MEASURE EVERY GRIEF I	561	32
VAST [WIDE] PRAIRIES OF AIR	MY PERIOD HAD COME FOR	564	12
UPHELD IN ROLLING AIR	I WATCHED THE MOON	629	18
THE TRUMPETS TELL IT TO THE AIR--	MY PORTION IS DEFEAT--	639	15
UPON A RAFT OF AIR	COULD I BUT RIDE	661	14
FAINTING! FLASKS OF AIR!	WOULD YOU LIKE SUMMER?	691	7
THEY SPURN THE AIR, AS 'TWERE TOO MEAN	YOU'VE SEEN BALLOONS SET	700	7
ROUND THE STEEP AIR--	OUT OF SIGHT? WHAT OF	703	4
THE ROYAL AIR--	PUBLICATION--IS THE	709	12
ROUGHEST AIR--WAS GOOD--	WHEN I HOPED, I	768	4
WADES--SO--THRO' POLAR AIR!	THROUGH THE STRAIT PASS	792	12
BANISH AIR FROM AIR--	BANISH AIR FROM AIR--	854	1
BANISH AIR FROM AIR--	BANISH AIR FROM AIR--	854	1
MOST SHUN THE PUBLIC AIR	BEST THINGS DWELL OUT OF	998	3
AIR HAS NO RESIDENCE, NO NEIGHBOR,	AIR HAS NO RESIDENCE, NO	1060	1
OH, HAPPY AIR!	AIR HAS NO RESIDENCE, NO	1060	4
AN INCOME IN THE AIR,	BECAUSE 'TWAS RICHES I	1093	6
I'M FEELING FOR THE AIR--	MY COCOON TIGHTENS--	1099	2
THE INMATES [PEASANTS] OF THE AIR	ALONE AND IN A	1167	14
THE PUNGENT ATOM IN THE AIR	THE PUNGENT ATOM IN THE	1191	1
A SEA OF SUMMER AIR	A SOFT SEA WASHED AROUND	1198	2
OF SECRETS IS [TRAVELLERS] THE AIR--	THE FROST WAS NEVER SEEN	1202	16
SEDUCTIVE IN THE AIR--	RISK IS THE HAIR THAT	1239	2
IT SOUNDED AS IF THE STREETS [AIR] WERE RUNNING	IT SOUNDED AS IF THE	1397	1
AND THEN--THE STREETS [AIR] STOOD STILL--	IT SOUNDED AS IF THE	1397	2
MIXING FRESHER AIR.	IT SOUNDED AS IF THE	1397	8
'TIS THREADED IN THE AIR--	TO MEND EACH TATTERED	1442	4
THAT MASSACRE OF AIR--	THEIR BARRICADE AGAINST	1471	10
WHAT FUNCTION [CUSTOMS] HATH THE AIR?	'TIS WHITER THAN AN	1482	8
FILLED WAS THE AIR WITH MERRY VENTURE	GLASS WAS THE STREET--IN	1498	3
AND FILLING ALL THE EARTH AND AIR [SKY]	HIS ORIENTAL HERESIES	1526	3
THEY STORM THE EARTH AND STUN THE AIR,	FROM ALL THE JAILS THE	1532	5
DESCRIBING IN THE AIR	THE BAT IS DUN, WITH	1575	6
AIRS			
WHO AIRS OF EXPECTATION BREATHES	'TIS MY FIRST NIGHT	1122	5
AIRS NO OCEANS KEEP--	I THINK THAT THE ROOT OF	1302	4
AISLE			
IN A CATHEDRAL AISLE,	I'VE HEARD AN ORGAN TALK	183	2
IN THAT OLD CHAPEL AISLE.	I'VE HEARD AN ORGAN TALK	183	8
A QUEEN ADOWN A SATIN AISLE,	A CURIOUS CLOUD	1710	8
AISLES			
HAS FURROWED OUT THE AISLES--	THE COLOR OF THE GRAVE	411	13
WHEN THE LAST SAINT--GOES UP THE AISLES--	BETTER--THAN MUSIC! FOR	503	18
HER VOICE AMONG THE AISLES	NATURE--THE GENTLEST	790	13
AJAR			
A PAIR OF SPECTACLES AJAR JUST STIR--	I KNOW SOME LONELY	289	19
FANCY THE SUNRISE--LEFT THE DOOR AJAR!	I KNOW SOME LONELY	289	40
HER DANCING EYES--AJAR--	SHE LAY AS IF AT PLAY	369	9
IF MOMENTLY [HER SWEET DOOR--] AJAR--	IT KNEW NO MEDICINE--	559	13
AJAR--SECURE--INVITING--	THE BODY GROWS WITHOUT--	578	5
WITH JUST THE DOOR AJAR	I CANNOT LIVE WITH YOU--	640	47
TILL ALL THE WORLD IS AJAR--	NOON--IS THE HINGE OF	931	4
THE SOUL SHOULD ALWAYS STAND AJAR	THE SOUL SHOULD ALWAYS	1055	1
A JAR			
A JAR ACROSS THE FLOWERS GOES	LIKE TRAINS OF CARS ON	1224	3
ALABASTER			
SAFE IN THEIR ALABASTER CHAMBERS--	SAFE IN THEIR ALABASTER	216	1
IT FILLS WITH ALABASTER WOOL	IT SIFTS FROM LEADEN	311	3
INVEST THIS ALABASTER ZEST	PRAISE IT--'TIS DEAD--	1384	6
ALACRITY			
WITH SWEET ALACRITY	THEY PUT US FAR APART--	474	14
ALARM			
BUT WHEN WINDS ALARM THE FOREST FOLK,	A FUZZY FELLOW, WITHOUT	173	10
AS LEGIONS OF ALARM	ONE ANGUISH--IN A CROWD	565	6
NO NUMB ALARM--LEST DIFFERENCE COME--	I THINK TO LIVE--MAY BE	646	13

	FIRST LINE	POEM	LINE
ALARM (CONTINUED)			
THE LONELINESS WHOSE WORST ALARM	THE LONELINESS ONE DARE	777	5
GOOD, WITHOUT ALARM	EXPECTATION--IS	807	6
WITHOUT DISCREET ALARM--	THESE ARE THE NIGHTS	1128	14
GHOST--MAY NOT ALARM--	WHEN I HOPED I FEARED--	1181	V 5
A SYMPTOM OF ALARM	THE FROST WAS NEVER SEEN	1202	6
HIS PLUSH ALARM	UPON A LILAC SEA	1337	3
ALARM IT'S WALLS AWAY--	GO NOT TOO NEAR A HOUSE	1434	4
ALARMED			
IN WHICH THE SOUL AT FIRST ESTRANGED [ALARMED / SUBMERGED]--	THE INUNDATION OF THE	1425	5
ALARMING			
WITH INFERENCE APPALLING [ALARMING]	WHO WERE "THE FATHER AND	1258	5
ALARMS			
SO DISTANT--TO ALARMS--	OF BRONZE--AND BLAZE--	290	5
ALARMS US--THO' HIS YELLOW FEET	THE LIGHTNING PLAYETH--	630	7
ALAS			
THE LIPS I W'D HAVE COOLED, ALAS--	I BRING AN UNACCUSTOMED	132	9
ALAS, HOW HEEDLESS WERE THE EYES--	ON THIS LONG STORM THE	194	7
ALAS, THAT WISDOM IS SO LARGE--	WE LEARNED THE WHOLE OF	568	11
ALAS--AND ART THOU SLEEPING YET?	'TIS SUNRISE--LITTLE	908	6
MY LITTLE MAID--'TIS NIGHT--ALAS	'TIS SUNRISE--LITTLE	908	9
BECOME, ALAS, MORE FAIR--	TO MAKE ROUTINE A	1196	8
A WANDERING "ALAS"--	A SINGLE CLOVER PLANK	1343	16
AN INFINITE ALAS--	THE DANDELION'S PALLID	1519	4
ALAS--THAT FROWNS [DUSK] SHOULD LIE IN WAIT	FROM ALL THE JAILS THE	1532	7
ALBAN			
WHO BUILT THIS LITTLE ALBAN HOUSE	BRING ME THE SUNSET IN A	128	19
ALBUMS			
SO MARTYRS ALBUMS SHOW!	BY SUCH AND SUCH AN	38	4
ALCOHOL			
YIELD SUCH AN ALCOHOL!	I TASTE A LIQUOR NEVER	214	4
ALDEN			
"MILES", AND "JOHN ALDEN" WERE SYNONYME--	GOD IS A DISTANT--	357	8
ALE			
LIFE HAS IT'S ALE--	WE--BEE AND I--LIVE BY	230	3
ALGEBRA			
AS WITH ALGEBRA!	BOUND--A TROUBLE--	269	6
TILL [WHERE] ALGEBRA IS EASIER--	IT TROUBLED ME AS ONCE I	600	11
ALIBI			
BY NATURE'S ALIBI--	THE SNOW THAT NEVER	1133	12
THE GERM [JOY] OF ALIBI--	THE MUSHROOM IS THE ELF	1298	10
OF ALIBI ART THOU	"TOMORROW"--WHOSE	1367	7
ALIEN			
ALIEN, THOUGH ADJOINING	NOW I KNEW I LOST HER--	1219	5
AND YET IT'S WHOLE CAREER [ALIEN PLACE / COVERT PLACE]	THE MUSHROOM IS THE ELF	1298	6
ALIEN AND VAIN WHATEVER CLIME	FRIGID AND SWEET HER	1318	3
ALIGHT			
THAT NEVER DID ALIGHT.	PEACE IS A FICTION OF	912	4
ALIGHT IN EVERY LAND	COSMOPOLITES WITHOUT A	1589	2
ALIGHTING			
PARTAKES WITHOUT ALIGHTING	WITHIN MY GARDEN, RIDES	500	7
ALIGHTING AT THE DWELLING	HOW NEWS MUST FEEL WHEN	1319	3
COMBINEDLY ALIGHTING--	A BEE HIS BURNISHED	1339	3
FOR AN ALIGHTING MINE--	ONE OF THE ONES THAT	1466	8
ALIKE			
WE TWO--LOOKED SO ALIKE--	'TWAS LOVE--NOT ME--	394	10
ALIKE TO HIM--ONE--	THE MALAY--TOOK THE	452	17
REGARDS LEAST CYPHERER ALIKE	'TIS ONE BY ONE--THE	545	13
HEEDLESS [PASSIVE]--ALIKE--OF [TO] POMP--OR [AND] PARTING	AH, TENERIFFE!	666	8
ALIKE INDIFFERENT--	FROM BLANK TO BLANK--	761	5
OF BEING, ARE ALIKE	THE OPENING AND THE	1047	2
AN ARC ALIKE INSCRUTABLE	THE BAT IS DUN, WITH	1575	7
ALIMENT			
WERE ALIMENT--	DELIGHT IS AS THE FLIGHT	257	9
THE ALIMENT OF IT	THE MIND LIVES ON THE	1355	7
ALIVE			
CAN KEEP THE SOUL ALIVE--	A LITTLE BREAD--A CRUST	159	3
IF I SHOULD'NT BE ALIVE	IF I SHOULD'NT BE ALIVE	182	1
TO LOOK UPON HER LIKE--ALIVE--	I WENT TO THANK HER--	363	9
IT FEELS A SHAME TO BE ALIVE--	IT FEELS A SHAME TO BE	444	1
I STAND ALIVE--TODAY--	I LIVE WITH HIM--I SEE	463	10
I AM ALIVE--I GUESS--	I AM ALIVE--I GUESS--	470	1
I AM ALIVE--BECAUSE	I AM ALIVE--I GUESS--	470	9
I AM ALIVE--BECAUSE	I AM ALIVE--I GUESS--	470	17
HOW GOOD--TO BE ALIVE!	I AM ALIVE--I GUESS--	470	25
ALIVE--TWO-FOLD--THE BIRTH I HAD--	I AM ALIVE--I GUESS--	470	27
WHILE IT IS ALIVE	WHILE IT IS ALIVE	491	1
THE THINKING HOW THEY WALKED ALIVE--	IF ANYBODY'S FRIEND BE	509	3
TO BE ALIVE--IS POWER--	TO BE ALIVE--IS POWER--	677	1
TO BE ALIVE--AND WILL!	TO BE ALIVE--IS POWER--	677	5
THE THOUGHT TO BE ALIVE--	I SOMETIMES DROP IT, FOR	708	2
BUT HE--WAS LEFT [REMAINED] ALIVE BECAUSE	HE FOUGHT LIKE THOSE	759	11
I'VE RANSOMED IT [FOUND IT--'TIS]--ALIVE--	HE TOLD A HOMELY TALE	763	16
WHO TILL THEY DIED, DID NOT ALIVE BECOME--	A DEATH BLOW IS A LIFE	816	2
AND ROOMS WHERE THOSE TO BE ALIVE	THE LAST NIGHT THAT SHE	1100	11
HE IS ALIVE, THIS MORNING--	HE IS ALIVE, THIS	1160	1
HE IS ALIVE--AND AWAKE--	HE IS ALIVE, THIS	1160	2

	FIRST LINE	POEM	LINE
ALIVE (CONTINUED)			
THE BOON OF ALL ALIVE--	BEHOLD THIS LITTLE BANE	1438	2
WHAT SURGEONS CALL ALIVE--	STILL OWN THEE--STILL	1633	2
ALL			
ALL THINGS DO GO A COURTING, IN EARTH, OR SEA, OR AIR,	AWAKE YE MUSES NINE,	1	5
HAST NEVER SILENT HOURS, AND MINUTES ALL TOO LONG,	AWAKE YE MUSES NINE,	1	29
YET HAVE ALL ROADS	MY WHEEL IS IN THE DARK!	10	7
WHICH SHORTENED ALL THE MILES--	ONE SISTER HAVE I IN OUR	14	16
AND BEAR TO ALL MY FRIENDS,	I WOULD DISTIL A CUP,	16	2
SHE NODS, AND ALL BEGIN--	BAFFLED FOR JUST A DAY	17	6
ALL THESE MY BANNERS BE.	ALL THESE MY BANNERS BE.	22	1
MY CHANCEL--ALL THE PLAIN	ALL THESE MY BANNERS BE.	22	6
AND ALL THE NIGHT ASHINE--	I HAD A GUINEA GOLDEN--	23	22
AND ALL DAY LONG, WITH DANCE AND GAME,	THERE IS A MORN BY MEN	24	4
IT'S ALL I HAVE TO BRING TODAY--	IT'S ALL I HAVE TO BRING	26	1
THIS, AND MY HEART, AND ALL THE FIELDS--	IT'S ALL I HAVE TO BRING	26	3
AND ALL THE MEADOWS WIDE--	IT'S ALL I HAVE TO BRING	26	4
THIS, AND MY HEART, AND ALL THE BEES	IT'S ALL I HAVE TO BRING	26	7
ALL THE ROOMS ARE FULL--	TAKEN FROM MEN--THIS	53	8
TO NIBBLE ALL THE DAY,	PAPA ABOVE!	61	7
NOT ONE OF ALL THE PURPLE HOST	SUCCESS IS COUNTED	67	5
THO' ALL THE REST ARE HERE--	AS BY THE DEAD WE LOVE	88	4
IS ALL THE REST I KNEW!	WENT UP A YEAR THIS	93	24
ONE DIGNITY DELAYS FOR ALL--	ONE DIGNITY DELAYS FOR	98	1
AND SHOUTS FILL ALL MY CHILDISH SKY,	I HAVE A KING, WHO DOES	103	10
WHAT ALL THE WORLD SUSPECT?	COCOON ABOVE! COCOON	129	3
I WILL GIVE HIM ALL THE DAISIES	FLOWERS--WELL--IF	137	7
BUT TENS HAVE WON AN ALL--	SOUL, WILT THOU TOSS	139	4
ALL THIS AND MORE I CANNOT TELL--	AN ALTERED LOOK ABOUT	140	13
THIS COVERT HAVE ALL THE CHILDREN	SOME, TOO FRAGILE FOR	141	9
YET WHO OF ALL THE THRONG	FOR EVERY BIRD A NEST--	143	16
OF ALL THE MARTIAL BLEST!	BLESS GOD, HE WENT AS	147	4
ALL OVERGROWN BY CUNNING MOSS,	ALL OVERGROWN BY CUNNING	148	1
ALL INTERSPERSED WITH WEED,	ALL OVERGROWN BY CUNNING	148	2
YET NOT IN ALL THE NESTS I MEET--	ALL OVERGROWN BY CUNNING	148	11
YOU CANNOT FIND OUT ALL ABOUT	DUST IS THE ONLY SECRET	153	3
THAT'S ALL.	THE MURMUR OF A BEE	155	10
ALL DAY--AMONG THE CROWDED AIR	MUSICIANS WRESTLE	157	2
A LITTLE PALMLEAF HAT WAS ALL,	I MET A KING THIS	166	3
BUT NOT AT ALL DISPOSED TO RUN!	I MET A KING THIS	166	16
HAVE VENTURED ALL UPON A THROW!	'TIS SO MUCH JOY! 'TIS	172	4
ALL THIS IN SUMMER.	A FUZZY FELLOW, WITHOUT	173	9
NOR HERB OF ALL THE PLAIN	AH, NECROMANCY SWEET!	177	6
UNWEARIED, ALL THE SUMMER LONG,	IF I COULD BRIBE THEM BY	179	10
ALL DAY AND NIGHT WITH BARK AND START--	WHAT SHALL I DO--IT	186	3
THAT WAS ALL I CARED TO KNOW.	HE WAS WEAK, AND I WAS	190	8
NOT ALL THE FRANKFORT BERRIES [VATS UPON THE RHINE]	I TASTE A LIQUOR NEVER	214	3
AND NOW YOU'VE LITTERED ALL THE EAST	SHE SWEEPS WITH	219	7
'TIS'NT ALL HOCK--WITH US--	WE--BEE AND I--LIVE BY	230	2
ALL--FOR HIM--STRAIGHTWAY--	GOD PERMITS INDUSTRIOUS	231	4
AND LIFE WOULD ALL BE SPRING!	THE SUN--JUST TOUCHED	232	4
THE SMOKE ALL CLEARED AWAY FROM IT--	WHEN WE STAND ON THE	242	3
IS ALL I OWN--	I HELD A JEWEL IN MY	245	8
ALL LIFE--TO KNOW EACH OTHER--	FOREVER AT HIS SIDE TO	246	10
THAT WAS ALL!	I CAN WADE GRIEF--	252	9
AND NEVER STOPS--AT ALL--	"HOPE" IS THE THING WITH	254	4
IS ALL THAT PINS THE SOUL	A SINGLE SCREW OF FLESH	263	2
THAT NOT FOR ALL THEIR HEAVEN CAN BOAST	A SINGLE SCREW OF FLESH	263	19
OF ALL THIS COMPOUND FRAME--	A WEIGHT WITH NEEDLES ON	264	6
IT BURNS--DISTINCT FROM ALL THE ROW--	ONE LIFE OF SO MUCH	270	11
I CEDED ALL OF DUST I KNEW--	DOUBT ME! MY DIM	275	11
AND WHEN THEY ALL WERE SEATED,	I FELT A FUNERAL, IN MY	280	5
AS ALL THE HEAVENS WERE A BELL,	I FELT A FUNERAL, IN MY	280	13
YET SMALL--SHE SIGHS--IF ALL--IS ALL--	THE DROP, THAT WRESTLES	284	5
YET SMALL--SHE SIGHS--IF ALL--IS ALL--	THE DROP, THAT WRESTLES	284	5
TOUCHING ALL THE GRASS	HOW THE OLD MOUNTAINS	291	10
AND ALL OUR SINEW TORE--	I GOT SO I COULD HEAR	293	8
AND I ESTEEMED ALL POVERTY	YOUR RICHES--TAUGHT ME--	299	7
I'M SURE 'TIS INDIA--ALL DAY--	YOUR RICHES--TAUGHT ME--	299	17
IT POWDERS ALL THE WOOD [FIELD].	IT SIFTS FROM LEADEN	311	2
WERE CLIMBING ALL THE WHILE--	I'LL TELL YOU HOW THE	318	12
OF ALL THE SOUNDS DESPATCHED ABROAD,	OF ALL THE SOUNDS	321	1
THAT [WHICH] MAKETH ALL THINGS NEW--	THERE CAME A DAY AT	322	8
AND SO WHEN ALL THE TIME HAD LEAKED [FAILED]--	THERE CAME A DAY AT	322	21
I'M GOING, ALL ALONG.	SOME KEEP THE SABBATH	324	12
ALL THESE--DID CONQUER--	OF TRIBULATION--THESE	325	5
AND ALL WE SAID--WAS	OF TRIBULATION--THESE	325	16
ALL FORESTS--STINTLESS STARS--	BEFORE I GOT MY EYE PUT	327	11
THAT HURRIED ALL AROUND [ABROAD]--	A BIRD CAME DOWN THE	328	10
AND STIR ALL DAY TO PRETTY TUNES	THE GRASS SO LITTLE HAS	333	5
AND THREAD THE DEWS, ALL NIGHT, LIKE PEARLS [PEARL]--	THE GRASS SO LITTLE HAS	333	9
ALL THE LETTERS I CAN [COULD] WRITE	ALL THE LETTERS I CAN	334	1
NOT ALL PIANOS IN THE WOODS	I DREADED THAT FIRST	348	7
I ROSE, AND ALL WAS PLAIN--	THE DAY THAT I WAS	356	9
THIS--WAS ALL--	I GAINED IT SO--	359	9
SURPASSES ALL THAT ROSE BEFORE--	THE MORNING AFTER WO--	364	3

ALL (CONTINUED)

	FIRST LINE	POEM	LINE
OR ALL DAY, CHASE THE BEE--	ALTHOUGH I PUT AWAY HIS	366	21
AND TELL YOU ALL YOUR DREAMS--WERE TRUE--	A PRECIOUS--MOULDERING	371	23
PUT FROM MY SIMPLE SPEECH ALL PLAIN WORD--	I'M SAYING EVERY DAY	373	20
NOT IN ALL THE MEADOW--	I'M SAYING EVERY DAY	373	24
THESE--NEVER STIR AT ALL--	THE ANGLE OF A LANDSCAPE	375	20
AND HE OWNED ALL THE MOURNERS--NOW--	THERE'S BEEN A DEATH, IN	389	15
CHOOSES IT'S LATCH, FROM ALL THE OTHER FASTENINGS--	IT'S COMING--THE	390	3
THE MOLD-LIFE--ALL FORGOTTEN--NOW--	THROUGH THE DARK SOD--AS	392	7
HAS SUFFERED ALL IT CAN--	THERE IS A LANGUOR OF	396	4
IN SENDING ALL THE BIRDS AWAY--	THE WINTERS ARE SO SHORT	403	3
AND ALL THE CATTLE--STARVED--	THE WINTERS ARE SO SHORT	403	12
NOT ALL THE SNOWS C'D MAKE IT WHITE--	THE COLOR OF THE GRAVE	411	19
NOT ALL THE SUMMERS--GREEN--	THE COLOR OF THE GRAVE	411	20
BECAUSE IT'S SUNDAY--ALL THE TIME--	I NEVER FELT AT HOME--	413	5
FROM HIM--AND HOLY GHOST--AND ALL--	I NEVER FELT AT HOME--	413	15
ALL THIS--AND MORE--IF I SHOULD TELL--	A MURMUR IN THE TREES--	416	11
STAINS--ALL WASHED--	TAKING UP THE FAIR IDEAL	428	15
SUCH BLISS--HAD I--FOR ALL THE YEARS--	IT WOULD NEVER BE COMMON	430	7
I PUT MY PLEASURE ALL ABROAD--	IT WOULD NEVER BE COMMON	430	17
AND DOWERED--ALL THE WORLD--	IT WOULD NEVER BE COMMON	430	20
'TIS THE ART, MOST OF ALL,	KNOWS HOW TO FORGET!	433	3
ALL OTHER LORE--	KNOWS HOW TO FORGET!	433	14
IN THIS, AS ALL, PREVAIL--	MUCH MADNESS IS DIVINEST	435	5
AND FAILED--AND ALL THE SUMMER LAUGHED--	GOD MADE A LITTLE	442	3
THAT RAVISHED ALL THE HILL--	GOD MADE A LITTLE	442	6
EACH OTHER'S FACE--WAS ALL THE DISC	THEY PUT US FAR APART--	474	23
I LEFT THE PLACE, WITH ALL MY MIGHT--	I MEANT TO HAVE BUT	476	17
ALL SWINDLERS--BE--INFER--	I MEANT TO HAVE BUT	476	28
THAT THIS WAS ALL--	I WAS THE SLIGHTEST IN	486	9
TO CLASP HER SOUL--FOR ALL--	THE WORLD--STANDS--	493	8
HOW EASY ALL CAN SEE	I ENVY SEAS, WHEREON HE	498	6
OF ALL TUNES I KNEW--AND MORE--	BETTER--THAN MUSIC! FOR	503	4
AND ALL THE DEAD, LIE DOWN--	IT WAS NOT DEATH, FOR I	510	2
IT WAS NOT NIGHT, FOR ALL THE BELLS	IT WAS NOT DEATH, FOR I	510	3
AND YET, IT TASTED, LIKE THEM ALL,	IT WAS NOT DEATH, FOR I	510	9
AND SPACE STARES ALL AROUND--	IT WAS NOT DEATH, FOR I	510	18
WHEN BURSTING ALL THE DOORS--	THE SOUL HAS BANDAGED	512	12
ALL MULTITUDES THAT WERE	NO CROWD THAT HAS	515	10
AND THEN HE LEANS WITH ALL HIS MIGHT	HE PARTS HIMSELF--LIKE	517	V 3
GAVE--EVEN AS TO ALL--	HER SWEET WEIGHT ON MY	518	10
TILL ALL THE SCENE--BE GONE.	'TWAS WARM--AT FIRST--	519	4
IT STRAIGHTENED--THAT WAS ALL--	'TWAS WARM--AT FIRST--	519	9
AS PRIDE WERE ALL IT COULD--	'TWAS WARM--AT FIRST--	519	12
FROM ALL THE NOISE [SOUND] OF FIELDS--	I'M SORRY FOR THE DEAD--	529	10
AND ALL THE NEIGHBOR'S LIVES--	I'M SORRY FOR THE DEAD--	529	16
TO ALL SURVIVING BUTTERFLIES	TWO BUTTERFLIES WENT OUT	533	V
SHE'S TEARFUL--IF SHE WEEP AT ALL--	SHE'S HAPPY, WITH A NEW	535	5
FOR BLISSFUL CAUSES--MOST OF ALL	SHE'S HAPPY, WITH A NEW	535	6
WAS ALL THE ONE THAT FELL--	I TOOK MY POWER IN MY	540	6
'TWAS SUNSET [SUNDOWN]--ALL THE DAY--	I HAD NO CAUSE TO BE	542	16
ADORNING ALL THE RULE--	'TIS ONE BY ONE--THE	545	8
WERE ALL THAT I COULD SEE--	MY PERIOD HAD COME FOR	564	14
I HUNTED [WORRIED] ALL THE SAND--	A DYING TIGER--MOANED	566	2
I RECKON--WHEN I COUNT AT ALL--	I RECKON--WHEN I COUNT	569	1
SO I WRITE--POETS--ALL--	I RECKON--WHEN I COUNT	569	8
ALL THESE--REMIND US OF THE PLACE	"HEAVEN" HAS DIFFERENT	575	15
IT TAKES ME ALL THE WHILE TO POISE--	I PRAYED, AT FIRST, A	576	20
I'LL TELL THEE ALL--HOW BALD [BLANK] IT GREW--	IF I MAY HAVE IT, WHEN	577	14
HOW ALL THE CLOCKS STOPPED IN THE WORLD--	IF I MAY HAVE IT, WHEN	577	16
ALL WADED--WE LOOK BACK FOR PLAY,	IF I MAY HAVE IT, WHEN	577	24
I HAD BEEN HUNGRY, ALL THE YEARS--	I HAD BEEN HUNGRY, ALL	579	1
I GAVE MYSELF TO HIM [HIM ALL MYSELF]--	I GAVE MYSELF TO HIM--	580	1
COMPLAINING ALL THE WHILE	I LIKE TO SEE IT LAP	585	11
OF ALL THE BIRDS THAT BE--	WHAT CARE THE DEAD, FOR	592	14
OF ALL THE BATTLES PREVALENT--	THE BATTLE FOUGHT	594	3
HIS FACE ALL VICTORY	WHEN I WAS SMALL, A	596	4
AGLOW--ALL RUDDY--WITH THE LIGHT	I SEE THEE BETTER--IN	611	11
THE BROOKS SLAM [BRAG]--ALL THE DAY--	IT MAKES NO DIFFERENCE	620	6
THE LIGHTNING PLAYETH--ALL THE WHILE--	THE LIGHTNING PLAYETH--	630	1
I THINK THE LONGEST HOUR OF ALL	I THINK THE LONGEST HOUR	635	1
BELIEVES ALL SHAM	THE CHILD'S FAITH IS NEW	637	7
YET SWAYING ALL--	THE CHILD'S FAITH IS NEW	637	16
AND ALL MY HOUSE AGLOW	TO MY SMALL HEARTH HIS	638	2
REPUDIATES IT, ALL THE MORE--	SIZE CIRCUMSCRIBES--IT	641	5
UNTO ALL [TO FOREIGN] HEART--	ME FROM MYSELF--TO	642	4
HAD ALL MY LIFE BUT BEEN [BEEN ONE / BEEN BLEAK] MISTAKE	I THINK TO LIVE--MAY BE	646	27
MINE TO STAY--WHEN ALL HAVE WANDERED--	PROMISE THIS--WHEN YOU	648	9
OF ALL HER GLORIES--	PROMISE THIS--WHEN YOU	648	V 32
ALL OTHER RICHES BE	WITHOUT THIS--THERE IS	655	2
OF ALL CONCEIVED JOY--	'TIS GOOD--THE LOOKING	660	4
TILL ALL THE GRIEF WITH SUMMER--WAVED [BLEW]	'TIS GOOD--THE LOOKING	660	7
AND FLIRT ALL DAY WITH BUTTERCUPS	COULD I BUT RIDE	661	5
AND ROW IN NOWHERE ALL DAY LONG	COULD I BUT RIDE	661	15
I LOOK ON ALL THIS WORLD CONTAINS--	AGAIN--HIS VOICE IS AT	663	11
OF ALL THE SOULS THAT STAND CREATE--	OF ALL THE SOULS THAT	664	1
TO ALL THE LISTS OF CLAY!	OF ALL THE SOULS THAT	664	12
I CHERISHED THEM FOR ALL--	SHELLS FROM THE COAST	693	2

ALL (CONTINUED)

	FIRST LINE	POEM	LINE
ALL THE OTHER DISTANCE	LIFE--IS WHAT WE MAKE IT	698	9
IT JUST REMINDED ME--'TWAS ALL--	A THOUGHT WENT UP MY	701	11
HEAVEN IS SHY OF EARTH--THAT'S ALL--	OUT OF SIGHT? WHAT OF	703	11
THAT DID IT TEAR ALL DAY,	I SOMETIMES DROP IT, FOR	708	6
ALL OTHER PLAUDIT BE	FAME OF MYSELF, TO	713	2
"I WANT"--IT PLEADED--ALL IT'S LIFE--	"I WANT"--IT PLEADED--	731	1
ALL SEASONS OF THE YEAR,	HAVE ANY LIKE MYSELF	736	20
OR SMALL--OR ANY SIZE AT ALL--	YOU SAID THAT I "WAS	738	3
HER PARTIES ALL [COMPANIES] ASTIR--	REMORSE--IS MEMORY--	744	2
ALL BUT DEATH, CAN BE ADJUSTED--	ALL BUT DEATH, CAN BE	749	1
MY WORTHINESS IS ALL MY DOUBT--	MY WORTHINESS IS ALL MY	751	1
HIS MERIT--ALL MY FEAR--	MY WORTHINESS IS ALL MY	751	2
ALL ELSE [THE WORLD] ACCUSED ME--AND I SMILED--	MY SOUL--ACCUSED ME--AND	753	3
BEST [ALL] HORIZON--GONE [KNOWN]--	NO BOBOLINK--REVERSE HIS	755	7
ALL CRUMPLED WAS THE CHEEK	HE TOLD A HOMELY TALE	763	5
ALL--IS THE PRICE OF ALL--	THE HALLOWING OF PAIN	772	8
ALL--IS THE PRICE OF ALL--	THE HALLOWING OF PAIN	772	8
AND YET [YET ALL] THE BAND WAS GONE--	THE BIRDS BEGUN AT FOUR	783	20
BEREAVED OF ALL, I WENT ABROAD--	BEREAVED OF ALL, I WENT	784	1
AS ALL MY STRATEGEM HAD BEEN	SEVERER SERVICE OF	786	19
WHEN ALL THE CHILDREN SLEEP--	NATURE--THE GENTLEST	790	17
IT MIGHT BE FAMINE--ALL AROUND--	GOD GAVE A LOAF TO EVERY	791	9
AM SOVREIGN OF THEM ALL--	GOD GAVE A LOAF TO EVERY	791	16
WHEN DEATH LIT ALL THE SHORTNESS UP [LIMIT--UP / BREVITY]	HER FINAL SUMMER WAS IT	795	7
THOUGH ALL THE VILLAGE LOOKED--	NO NOTICE GAVE SHE, BUT	804	10
HER GRACE IS ALL SHE HAS--	HER GRACE IS ALL SHE HAS	810	1
ALL I MAY, IF SMALL,	ALL I MAY, IF SMALL,	819	1
ALL CIRCUMSTANCES ARE THE FRAME	ALL CIRCUMSTANCES ARE	820	1
ALL LATITUDES EXIST FOR HIS	ALL CIRCUMSTANCES ARE	820	3
AND STARTED ALL ABROAD--	THE WIND BEGUN TO KNEAD	824	6
ITSELF IS ALL THE LIKE IT HAS--	LOVE RECKONS BY ITSELF--	826	4
IS BULLETINS ALL DAY	THE ONLY NEWS I KNOW	827	2
AND I AM ALL ALONE--	I CANNOT BUY IT--'TIS	840	6
THOUGH IT TOOK ALL MY STORE	I CANNOT BUY IT--'TIS	840	9
ALL DAYS, I DID NOT EARN THE SAME	I MADE SLOW RICHES BUT	843	5
AND GRANT US ALL THEIR COUNTENANCE	THEY ASK BUT OUR DELIGHT	868	3
ALL PRIZES TO OBTAIN--	HOW FORTUNATE THE GRAVE	897	2
MY NEED--WAS ALL I HAD--I SAID--	HAD I NOT THIS, OR THIS,	904	9
AND THIS OF ALL MY HOPES	AND THIS OF ALL MY HOPES	913	1
MADONNA DIM, TO WHOM ALL FEET MAY COME,	ONLY A SHRINE, BUT MINE	918	3
ALL MY MANSION TORN--	STRUCK, WAS I, NOR YET	925	10
TILL ALL THE WORLD IS AJAR--	NOON--IS THE HINGE OF	931	4
THROUGH ALL THEIR [IT'S] FORMER PLACES, WE	DEATH LEAVES US HOMESICK	935	5
IS ALL THAT'S LEFT THEM, NOW--	DEATH LEAVES US HOMESICK	935	8
FOR FREQUENT [OFTEN], ALL MY SENSE OBSCURED	WHAT I SEE NOT, I BETTER	939	5
AND ALL THE SEAS HE POPULATES	A COFFIN--IS A SMALL	943	7
THAT BELLS SHOULD RING TILL ALL SHOULD KNOW [HEAR]	OF TOLLING BELL I ASK	947	5
'TWAS CRISIS--ALL THE LENGTH HAD PASSED--	'TWAS CRISIS--ALL THE	948	1
WHAT DIFFERENCE, AFTER ALL, THOU MAK'ST	THE SUNSET STOPPED ON	950	7
BIOGRAPHY TO ALL WHO PASSED	THE HOLLOWS ROUND HIS	955	5
WHEN THE BEE HANGS ALL NOON IN THE BUTTERCUP	WHAT SHALL I DO WHEN THE	956	7
ALL HIS GOODS HAVE WINGS--	WHAT SHALL I DO WHEN THE	956	14
AND ALL THE EARTH STROVE COMMON ROUND--	DENIAL--IS THE ONLY FACT	965	5
ALL FORGOT FOR [THROUGH] RECOLLECTING	ALL FORGOT FOR	966	1
ALL FORSOOK, FOR JUST A STRANGER'S	ALL FORGOT FOR	966	3
OVERLOOKED I ALL--	ALL FORGOT FOR	966	12
AS IN SLEEP--ALL HUE FORGOTTEN--	COLOR--CASTE--	970	5
THE MISSING ALL, PREVENTED ME	THE MISSING ALL,	985	1
NOT ALL DIE EARLY, DYING YOUNG--	NOT ALL DIE EARLY, DYING	990	1
WHO KNOW HIS MEED OF ALL.	SO LARGE MY WILL	1024	8
WITH US, 'TIS HARVEST ALL THE YEAR	THE PRODUCTS OF MY FARM	1025	5
A GLASS OF WATER'S ALL,	THE DYING NEED BUT	1026	2
HE NEUTRALIZED THEM ALL--	FATE SLEW HIM, BUT HE	1031	4
ALL HIS EAST	SAID DEATH TO PASSION	1033	6
CAME ALL THE WAY FROM LIFE TO ME	I HEARD, AS IF I HAD NO	1039	3
SAVES SHE ALL OF THAT FOR SUNSETS	NATURE RARER USES YELLOW	1045	3
AND CHISELLED ALL MY TUNE	I'VE DROPPED MY BRAIN--	1046	14
TILL OF ALL OUR NATURE'S HOUSE	AS WILLING LID O'ER	1050	3
ROYAL--ALL BUT THE CROWN!	TITLE DIVINE--IS MINE!	1072	5
A NARROW WIND COMPLAINS ALL DAY	THE SKY IS LOW--THE	1075	5
I TAKE BACK ALL I SAY--	WHEN THEY COME BACK--IF	1080	16
ALL IT'S PURPLE FLED	REVOLUTION IS THE POD	1082	10
THAN ALL THE GOLDEN PRESENCE	WE LEARN IN THE	1083	7
SUPPLANTED ALL THE REST.	AT HALF PAST THREE, A	1084	8
THEMSELF ARE ALL I HAVE--	THEMSELF ARE ALL I HAVE	1094	1
THE FENCES ALL BUT RAN,	THE BIRD DID PRANCE--THE	1107	6
THAT ALL MY LIFE HAD ENTERED IT	A GREAT HOPE FELL	1123	12
TELL ALL THE TRUTH BUT TELL IT SLANT--	TELL ALL THE TRUTH BUT	1129	1
REPAIRED OF ALL BUT LONELINESS	THE SNOW THAT NEVER	1133	11
TILL ALL HER HELPLESS BEAUTY BENT	THE FROST OF DEATH WAS	1136	14
ALL MEN MEET [PASS / HASTE] AS IF	AFTER THE SUN COMES OUT	1148	5
BUT WHEN ALL SPACE HAS BEEN BEHELD	THE LIFE WE HAVE IS VERY	1162	5
AND ALL DOMINION SHOWN	THE LIFE WE HAVE IS VERY	1162	6
LEST THEY SHOULD COME--IS ALL MY FEAR	LEST THEY SHOULD COME--	1169	1
OF ALL WE ARE ALLOWED TO HOPE	"REMEMBER ME" IMPLORED	1180	9
WE LET GO ALL OF TIME WITHOUT	THE DAYS THAT WE CAN	1184	7

ALL (CONTINUED)

	FIRST LINE	POEM		LINE
WHO GAMBOLS ALL THE LIVING DAY	A LITTLE DOG THAT WAGS	1185		5
ALL THAT IS NAMED OF SUMMER DAYS	THE PUNGENT ATOM IN THE	1191		3
ALL MEN FOR HONOR HARDEST WORK	ALL MEN FOR HONOR	1193		1
IN ALL THE DEEPEST SKY	A SPARROW TOOK A SLICE	1211		6
NEWS IS HE OF ALL THE OTHERS--	WE LIKE MARCH.	1213		10
SILENCE IS ALL WE DREAD.	SILENCE IS ALL WE DREAD.	1251		1
WAS ALL THE ONE THAT PLAYED.	LIKE BROOMS OF STEEL	1252		11
TO ALL BUT FEALTY--	BECAUSE THAT YOU ARE	1260	V	8
IF "ALL IS POSSIBLE WITH" HIM	BECAUSE THAT YOU ARE	1260		37
CONFIRMING ALL WHO ANALYZE	CONFIRMING ALL WHO	1268		1
IT MADE US ALL ASHAMED [DEMEANED]	SO PROUD SHE WAS TO DIE	1272		2
AND NOT IN ALL THE UNIVERSE	HOW NEWS MUST FEEL WHEN	1319		11
ALL THOSE HILLS YOU LEFT FOR ME TO HUE-- .	DEAR MARCH--COME IN--	1320		15
YOU TOOK IT ALL WITH YOU--	DEAR MARCH--COME IN--	1320		17
THAT OWNED IT ALL--	THE VASTEST EARTHLY DAY	1328	V	4
UNKNOWN--FOR ALL THE TIMES WE MET--	WITHOUT A SMILE--WITHOUT	1330		4
OF FATE IF THIS IS ALL	HOW SOFT THIS PRISON IS	1334		5
WAS ALL OUR TIMID MOTHER WORE	LET ME NOT MAR THAT	1335		7
LET ALL ADDICTED TO	A RAT SURRENDERED HERE	1340		5
HAS "ALL" A FURTHER REALM--	UNTO THE WHOLE--HOW ADD?	1341		2
"WAS NOT" WAS ALL THE STATEMENT.	"WAS NOT" WAS ALL THE	1342		1
WAS ALL THAT SAVED [ALONE SUSTAINED-- / ALONE UPHELD--] A BEE	A SINGLE CLOVER PLANK	1343		2
THAT EVERY MAN [ALL THE WORLD] BEHOLD . .	YOU CANNOT TAKE ITSELF	1351		6
TAKE ALL AWAY--	TAKE ALL AWAY--	1365		1
IS ALL THAT LOVE CAN SPEAK--	LOVE'S STRICKEN "WHY"	1368		2
AND ESTIMATES THEM ALL--	THE SUN IS ONE--AND ON	1372		4
DO ALL BUT [ALMOST] INUNDATE--	HOW MUCH THE PRESENT	1380		8
SUMMER--WE ALL HAVE SEEN--	SUMMER--WE ALL HAVE SEEN	1386		1
EMBELLISH ALL WE OWN--	HOPE IS A STRANGE	1392		8
AFTER ALL BIRDS HAVE BEEN INVESTIGATED AND LAID ASIDE--	AFTER ALL BIRDS HAVE	1395		1
ECLIPSE--WAS ALL WE COULD SEE AT THE WINDOW	IT SOUNDED AS IF THE	1397		3
AND AWE--WAS ALL WE COULD FEEL.	IT SOUNDED AS IF THE	1397		4
ALL WE KNOW	OF PARADISE' EXISTENCE	1411		2
ESPOUSING EACH AND SPURNING ALL	HOW LONESOME THE WIND	1418		11
THE BOON OF ALL ALIVE--	BEHOLD THIS LITTLE BANE	1438		2
AND SHADE IS ALL THAT DEVASTATES THE STILLNESS	THESE FEVERED DAYS--TO	1441		3
SEEMS IT SOMETIMES THIS WOULD BE ALL-- . .	THESE FEVERED DAYS--TO	1441		4
BUT [THOUGH] ALL MANKIND DELIVER [CRUISE SOFTLY / ROW SOFTLY / . . .	A CHILLY PEACE INFESTS	1443		7
WAS ALL THE PRICE [TERMS] THERE WAS-- . .	HIS MIND LIKE FABRICS OF	1446		8
THE CONSCIENCE OF US ALL	BELSHAZZAR HAD A LETTER	1459		6
WHO FAILED TO TOUCH US ALL	ONE OF THE ONES THAT	1466		2
ARE ALL THAT CROSS HIS THRESHOLD--	THE ROBIN IS A GABRIEL	1483		12
ALL THAT I DO	ALL THAT I DO	1496		1
IN ALL IDENTITY--	HOW FIRM ETERNITY MUST	1499		4
THE [A] CRASH OF NOTHING, YET [AND] OF ALL--	MORE THAN THE GRAVE IS	1503		5
ALL THINGS SWEPT SOLE AWAY	ALL THINGS SWEPT SOLE	1512		1
BUT THINK ENLARGED OF ALL THAT THEY WILL TELL US	THE THINGS THAT NEVER	1515		7
AND FILLING ALL THE EARTH AND AIR [SKY] . .	HIS ORIENTAL HERESIES	1526		3
ENOUGH WILL NOT BE FOUND WHEN ALL HAVE DIED.	ABOVE OBLIVION'S TIDE	1531		7
FROM ALL THE JAILS THE BOYS AND GIRLS . .	FROM ALL THE JAILS THE	1532		1
IS ALL THE SOUL CAN DO.	ON THAT SPECIFIC PILLOW	1533		8
IF HE IS CAUGHT AT ALL--	THE LIFE THAT TIED TOO	1535		8
THAT WOULD EXPAND [BETRAY] US ALL--	THE LIFE THAT TIED TOO	1535	V	8
ALL THE BOYS WOULD COME--	THE BIBLE IS AN ANTIQUE	1545		14
ALL THE REST, HAVE DIED--	MY WARS ARE LAID AWAY IN	1549		8
THAN NO ILLUME AT ALL--	THOSE--DYING THEN,	1551		9
ALL OTHER BOUNTY SUDDEN CHAFF [NIGGARDLY] .	I GROPED FOR HIM BEFORE	1555		3
TWAS ALL [ALL WAS] DISTINCT TO ME--	LIVES HE IN ANY OTHER	1557		4
TWAS ALL [ALL WAS] DISTINCT TO ME--	LIVES HE IN ANY OTHER	1557		4
WHEN HEAVEN LOOKED UPON US ALL	NO BRIGADIER THROUGHOUT	1561		11
BUT THIS SLEW ALL BUT HIM--	SOME ARROWS SLAY BUT	1565		2
MORNING IS DUE TO ALL--	MORNING IS DUE TO ALL--	1577		1
FOR ALL THE REST OF LIFE--	THE FARTHEST THUNDER	1581		8
FIND ALL THE WITCHCRAFT THAT WE NEED . . .	WITCHCRAFT WAS HUNG, IN	1583		3
WE ALL HAVE FOLLOWED THEE--	EXPANSE CANNOT BE LOST--	1584		12
. . . ALL THE SAINTS HE KNEW / EVERY GOD HE KNEW]	THE BOBOLINK IS GONE--	1591		6
"ALL" ROGUES "SHALL HAVE THEIR PART IN" WHAT--	WHO IS IT SEEKS MY	1598		7
A MIRACLE FOR ALL!	NO LIFE CAN POMPLESS	1626		8
THERE IS A WORLD [TOMB / CHAIR / SEAT] FOR ALL	NO LIFE CAN POMPLESS	1626	V	8
NO CIRCUIT SAGE OF ALL THE COURSE [LINES] .	OH FUTURE! THOU SECRETED	1631		5
IT'S SIZE IS ALL THAT HELL CAN GUESS-- . .	SO GIVE ME BACK TO DEATH	1632		7
AND ALL THAT HEAVEN WAS [SURMISE]-- . . .	SO GIVE ME BACK TO DEATH	1632		8
TAKE ALL AWAY FROM ME, BUT LEAVE ME ECSTASY,	TAKE ALL AWAY FROM ME,	1640		1
AND I AM RICHER THEN THAN ALL MY FELLOW MEN--	TAKE ALL AWAY FROM ME,	1640		2
THAT ALL ALONG THE LINE	"RED SEA," INDEED! TALK	1642		6
THAT ALL MAY THEM--IT--EXAMINE [WITNESS IT AND MORE]	SOME ONE PREPARED THIS	1644		5
THAN NOT EXIST AT ALL--	ADVANCE IS LIFE'S	1652		8
ALL OF EVENING SOFTLY LIT	LIGHTLY STEPPED A YELLOW	1672		5
FEW--LOVE AT ALL	SOMETIMES WITH THE HEART	1680		4
CONCLUSION IS THE COURSE OF ALL	SUMMER BEGINS TO HAVE	1682		13
FAITHFUL WAS ALL THAT I COULD BOAST	THAT SHE FORGOT ME WAS	1683		5
YET MAN HAS NOT OF ALL THE THRONG	THE HILLS ERECT THEIR	1688		3
LET CHANGE TRANSFUSE ALL OTHER TRAITS . .	THE LOOK OF THEE, WHAT	1689		9

	FIRST LINE	POEM	LINE
ALL (CONTINUED)			
ENACT ALL OTHER BLAME	THE LOOK OF THEE, WHAT	1689	10
THE DEPTH IS ALL MY THOUGHT--	A PIT--BUT HEAVEN OVER	1712	10
PAID ALL THAT LIFE HAD EARNED	HOW DARE THE ROBINS SING	1724	5
IF ALL THE GRIEFS I AM TO HAVE	IF ALL THE GRIEFS I AM	1726	1
IF ALL THE JOYS I AM TO HAVE	IF ALL THE GRIEFS I AM	1726	5
THE SOUL THERE--ALL THE TIME.	IF EVER THE LID GETS OFF	1727	8
LOVE CAN DO ALL BUT RAISE THE DEAD	LOVE CAN DO ALL BUT	1731	1
PARTING IS ALL WE KNOW OF HEAVEN,	MY LIFE CLOSED TWICE	1732	7
AND ALL WE NEED OF HELL.	MY LIFE CLOSED TWICE	1732	8
ALL OTHER HEARTS [THINGS] I KNEW.	TO LOSE THEE--SWEETER	1754	2
"'TWAS ALL I HAD," SHE STRICKEN GASPED--	UPON THE GALLOWS HUNG A	1757	7
TILL ALL THE CHURCHYARD RANG;	A TRAIN WENT THROUGH A	1761	4
IT MAKES US THINK OF ALL THE DEAD	THE SADDEST NOISE, THE	1764	9
THAT LOVE IS ALL THERE IS,	THAT LOVE IS ALL THERE	1765	1
IS ALL WE KNOW OF LOVE;	THAT LOVE IS ALL THERE	1765	2
ALL THE REST IS PERJURY--	LAD OF ATHENS, FAITHFUL	1768	4
ALLEYS			
GREAT GLOBULES--IN THE ALLEYS--	THE NAME--OF IT--IS	656	5
ALLIED			
THAN TO HIMSELF, ALLIED,	TO THIS WORLD SHE	830	7
ALLIES			
WHOSE ALLIES GO NO MORE ASTRAY [ABROAD]	A CHILLY PEACE INFESTS	1443	5
ALLOTTED			
ALLOTTED TWO--	MY HEART RAN SO TO THEE	1237	8
ALLOW			
ALLOW ME, SIR, AT PARTING,	"SIC TRANSIT GLORIA	3	59
THE SUN DOES NOT ALLOW	TO INTERRUPT HIS YELLOW	591	2
PERMIT [ALLOW / BESTOW] ME THIS REPRIEVE	TRIED ALWAYS AND	1559	2
WILL NOT ALLOW AN AXIOM	EXPERIMENT ESCORTS US	1770	3
ALLOWED			
TO THOSE WHO DARE [ALLOWED] TO TRY--	I THINK TO LIVE--MAY BE	646	2
OF ALL WE ARE ALLOWED TO HOPE	"REMEMBER ME" IMPLORED	1180	9
THE ONES ALLOWED TO KNOW	THE MOON UPON HER FLUENT	1528	6
ALLOYS			
ALLOYS OUR FIRMER MOMENTS	THROUGH THOSE OLD	1753	13
ALL'S			
TO MAKE SURE ALL'S ASLEEP--	I KNOW SOME LONELY	289	10
A TREMOR JUST, THAT ALL'S NOT SURE.	UNIT, LIKE DEATH, FOR	408	16
ALLUDED			
ALLUDED TO NO TIME	WENT UP A YEAR THIS	93	10
ALLURE			
WHOSE POMPS ALLURE AND SPURN	OF THIS IS DAY COMPOSED	1675	5
ALLURED			
'TWAS THIS--ALLURED COLUMBUS--	TRUST IN THE UNEXPECTED	555	9
UNTIL ALLURED AWAY	THE WAY TO KNOW THE	1279	16
ALLURES			
ALLURES [ENSNARES] HIS JADED EYE	HIS ORIENTAL HERESIES	1526	6
ALMANAC'S			
AN ALMANAC'S AWARE--	I KNOW SOME LONELY	289	20
ALMANACS			
NO ALMANACS--NOR CLIMES--	ALONE, I CANNOT BE--	298	6
ALMIGHTY			
MERCY [POWER] OF THE ALMIGHTY BEGGING [ASKING]--	TELL AS A MARKSMAN--WERE	1152	22
OH THOU ALMIGHTY GOD!	REMEMBRANCE HAS A	1182	V 8
ALMOST			
ALMOST THY PLAUSIBILITY	THESE ARE THE DAYS WHEN	130	8
ALMOST A POWDERED FOOTMAN	WAIT TILL THE MAJESTY OF	171	3
ALMOST AS IF THEY CARED--	IF I'M LOST--NOW--	256	9
ELATE US--TILL WE ALMOST WEEP--	LIKE SOME OLD FASHIONED	302	11
WHEN NIGHT IS ALMOST DONE--	WHEN NIGHT IS ALMOST	347	1
OR BREAKING--ALMOST--WITH UNSPOKEN PAIN--	HOW SICK--TO WAIT--IN	368	4
ALMOST--CONTENTED--	I WENT TO HEAVEN--	374	13
AND LIFE STEPS ALMOST STRAIGHT.	WE GROW ACCUSTOMED TO	419	20
YOU ALMOST PITIED IT--YOU--IT WORKED SO--	GOING TO HIM! HAPPY	494	14
AND IMMORTALITY--CAN BE ALMOST--	IT'S THOUGHTS--AND JUST	495	27
YOU ALMOST BATHED YOUR TONGUE--	SHE SIGHTS A BIRD--SHE	507	10
YOU ALMOST FEEL THE DATE--	IF ANYBODY'S FRIEND BE	509	10
I ALMOST STROVE TO CLASP HIS HAND,	I TRIED TO THINK A	532	16
IT'S BETTER--ALMOST PEACE--	IT CEASED TO HURT ME,	584	15
HAVE SOBBED OURSELVES ALMOST TO SLEEP,	I CRIED AT PITY--NOT AT	588	23
OUR FEET WERE ALMOST COME	OUR JOURNEY HAD ADVANCED	615	2
WE ALMOST CEASE TO FEAR--	THE HEAVEN VESTS FOR	694	14
AND ALMOST TO SUFFICE	DEPRIVED OF OTHER	773	8
IT ALMOST SPEAKS TO YOU.	A LIGHT EXISTS IN SPRING	812	12
TILL I WHO WAS ALMOST BOLD	HOW HAPPY I WAS IF I	898	6
ALMOST A LONELINESS.	I HIDE MYSELF WITHIN MY	903	4
SOMETIMES, ALMOST MORE.	THIS WAS IN THE WHITE OF	995	8
ALMOST TO JEALOUSY--	SO PROUD SHE WAS TO DIE	1272	8
HAD ALMOST MADE IT FAIR--	WHILE WE WERE FEARING IT	1277	4
ALMOST BELIEVES IT TOO	THE MOST PATHETIC THING	1290	4
'TIS ALMOST CONSEQUENCE--	THAT SHORT--POTENTIAL	1307	4
IS ALMOST REVELRY [ECSTASY]--	THE SYMPTOM OF THE GALE	1327	4
AND ALMOST COUNT IT AN AFFRONT	AS SUMMER INTO AUTUMN	1346	5
DO ALL BUT [ALMOST] INUNDATE--	HOW MUCH THE PRESENT	1380	8
ALMOST WE WISH THE END	I DID NOT REACH THEE	1664	24
I ALMOST TOUCHED HER	TO-DAY OR THIS NOON	1702	3
IT ALMOST TOUCHED THE LAWNS.	A CURIOUS CLOUD	1710	5
ALMOST TOO HEAVENLY NEAR.	THE SADDEST NOISE, THE	1764	8

	FIRST LINE	POEM	LINE
ALMOST (CONTINUED)			
WE ALMOST WISH THOSE SIREN THROATS . . .	THE SADDEST NOISE, THE	1764	15
ALMS			
SMILING, AS THEY REQUEST AN ALMS-- . . .	IN RAGS MYSTERIOUS AS	117	5
AS IF I ASKED A COMMON ALMS, ...	AS IF I ASKED A COMMON	323	1
IRRESOLUTE OF [REVISITING FOR] ALMS-- . .	A FIELD OF STUBBLE,	1407	6
IS DIFFERENT FROM ANOTHER ALMS	IT CAME HIS TURN TO BEG	1500	3
ALOFT			
BUT HELD HER GRAVITY ALOFT--	NO NOTICE GAVE SHE, BUT	804	11
ALONE			
ALONE, I CANNOT BE--	ALONE, I CANNOT BE--	298	1
OCCUR TO HER--ALONE--	THE SOUL'S SUPERIOR	306	2
THAT [WHICH] TEETH OF FROSTS ALONE DISCLOSE	THERE ARE TWO RIPENINGS	332	7
THINKING--PERHAPS--THAT I LOOKED TIRED--OR ALONE--	HOW SICK--TO WAIT--IN	368	3
AND BACK IT SLID--AND I ALONE--	I SAW NO WAY--THE	378	5
AND I BECAME ALONE--	THE WIND--TAPPED LIKE A	436	20
HUMMING--FOR PROMISE--WHEN ALONE-- . . .	BETTER--THAN MUSIC! FOR	503	22
AND LEAVE THE SOUL--ALONE--	DEPARTED--TO THE	524	8
AND DEEM TO BE ALONE	DID YOU EVER STAND IN A	590	4
AND--THEN--WE ARE ALONE--	AGAIN--HIS VOICE IS AT	663	21
ALONE--IF ANGELS ARE "ALONE"--	AGAIN--HIS VOICE IS AT	663	22
ALONE--IF ANGELS ARE "ALONE"--	AGAIN--HIS VOICE IS AT	663	22
ALONE--IF THOSE "VAILED FACES"--BE-- . . .	AGAIN--HIS VOICE IS AT	663	24
BE [IS] NOT EXPRESSED BY SUNS--ALONE-- . .	ESSENTIAL OILS--ARE	675	3
FAITH--ALONE--	A FIRST MUTE COMING--	702	8
BUT IT STIR--ALONE--	GROWTH OF MAN--LIKE	750	4
TO LIVES THAT STAND ALONE--	TO OFFER BRAVE	767	2
ONLY ME--[STILL MYSELF-- / ME ALONE] WAS STILL--	WHEN I HOPED, I	768	16
AND THAT ITSELF ALONE	THIS CONSCIOUSNESS THAT	822	4
LOVE RECKONS BY ITSELF--ALONE--	LOVE RECKONS BY ITSELF--	826	1
AND I AM ALL ALONE--	I CANNOT BUY IT--'TIS	840	6
THE LORD ALONE IS BURNED--	THE SUN AND MOON MUST	871	4
ATTENDED, OR ALONE	A NARROW FELLOW IN THE	986	22
TO DISCOURSE ALONE--	THREE WEEKS PASSED SINCE	1061	6
THE EARTH AND I, ALONE, ...	THE SUN WENT DOWN--NO	1079	2
ALONE AND IN [OF] A CIRCUMSTANCE	ALONE AND IN A	1167	1
EVERYWHERE ALONE	WHEN I HOPED I FEARED--	1181	3
LEAVE ME NOT EVER THERE ALONE	REMEMBRANCE HAS A	1182	V 7
HAD LEFT THE DEAD ALONE	MY TRIUMPH LASTED TILL	1227	2
ALONE--TOO ACRID--BUT COMBINED	SURPRISE IS LIKE A	1306	3
WAS ALL THAT SAVED [ALONE SUSTAINED-- / ALONE UPHELD--] A BEE	A SINGLE CLOVER PLANK	1343	2
WAS ALL THAT SAVED [ALONE SUSTAINED-- / ALONE UPHELD--] A BEE	A SINGLE CLOVER PLANK	1343	2
NOT ALONE WE FLY--	LIFT IT--WITH THE	1348	2
THAT RAMBLES IN THE ROAD ALONE, ...	HOW HAPPY IS THE LITTLE	1510	2
ASSOCIATES OR GLOWS [BASKS] ALONE, ...	HOW HAPPY IS THE LITTLE	1510	8
CAN FIT BUT HIM ALONE	THE PATTERN OF THE SUN	1550	2
DOES NOT EMERGE ALONE	THE SPIRIT LASTS--BUT IN	1576	6
ALONE--IS NOT A TUNE--	THE SPIRIT LASTS--BUT IN	1576	8
BUT NOT ALONE, ...	EXPANSE CANNOT BE LOST--	1584	11
WITH LOVE ALONE HAD [WERE] BENT, ...	'TIS NOT THE SWAYING	1597	4
FOR CLIMBING IT ALONE?	THE GOING FROM A WORLD	1603	8
THE SAUNTERING ALONE	THROUGH THOSE OLD	1753	2
THE REVERY ALONE WILL DO, ...	TO MAKE A PRAIRIE IT	1755	4
ALONG			
GLID STEALTHILY ALONG--	THROUGH LANE IT LAY--	9	8
PARCHED THE FLOWERS THEY BEAR ALONG. . . .	ANGELS, IN THE EARLY	94	8
AS WE RIDE GRAND ALONG!	ONE DIGNITY DELAYS FOR	98	8
GUIDES STILL THE SUN ALONG THE CRAG . . .	A SOMETHING IN A	122	17
TRAILED--SLOW--ALONG THE ORCHARDS-- . . .	THE SUN--JUST TOUCHED	232	9
I'M GOING, ALL ALONG.	SOME KEEP THE SABBATH	324	12
THE BREEZES FETCH ALONG--	THE GRASS SO LITTLE HAS	333	6
ALONG APPOINTED SANDS--	THE MOON IS DISTANT FROM	429	4
ALONG MY GOLDEN LINES--	IT WOULD NEVER BE COMMON	430	29
THAT PILOT HIM ALONG--	NO MAN CAN COMPASS A	477	12
THAT GAZE UPON [GROW ALONG] HIS JOURNEY-- .	I ENVY SEAS, WHEREON HE	498	5
WHEN, FELON LED ALONG, ...	THE SOUL HAS BANDAGED	512	20
THE DIMPLES RAN ALONG--	HER SMILE WAS SHAPED	514	2
A VEIN--ALONG THE ROAD--	THE NAME--OF IT--IS	656	4
THIS SLOW DAY MOVED ALONG--	THIS SLOW DAY MOVED	1120	1
HE FORKED HIS WAY ALONG	THE FROST OF DEATH WAS	1136	13
AND CHASTENED STOLE ALONG	MY TRIUMPH LASTED TILL	1227	4
WHEN FRESHETS COME ALONG.	A STAGNANT PLEASURE LIKE	1281	8
AND EVERY BREEZE THAT RUN ALONG	A SAUCER HOLDS A CUP	1374	7
IT STOLE ALONG SO STEALTHY	IT STOLE ALONG SO	1457	1
HE DANCED ALONG THE DINGY DAYS	HE ATE AND DRANK THE	1587	5
THAT ALL ALONG THE LINE	"RED SEA," INDEED! TALK	1642	6
AND WENT ALONG.	IN WINTER IN MY ROOM	1670	9
ALOOF			
IT ONLY HELD ITSELF ALOOF	IT WAS NOT SAINT--IT WAS	1092	3
ALOUD			
TO FIGHT ALOUD, IS VERY BRAVE--	TO FIGHT ALOUD, IS VERY	126	1
I COULD NOT BEAR TO LIVE--ALOUD--	I WAS THE SLIGHTEST IN	486	12
ALOUD	EMBARRASSMENT OF ONE	662	4
ALPHABET			
IN TENDER--SOLEMN ALPHABET, ...	A SINGLE SCREW OF FLESH	263	9
THE ALPHABET--THE WORDS--	WE LEARNED THE WHOLE OF	568	2

	FIRST LINE	POEM	LINE
ALPINE			
INVOLVES ALPINE	I CANNOT BE ASHAMED	914	8
ALPS			
THE ALPS NEGLECT THEIR CURTAINS	OUR LIVES ARE SWISS--	80	4
THE SOLEMN ALPS--	OUR LIVES ARE SWISS--	80	8
THE SIREN ALPS	OUR LIVES ARE SWISS--	80	9
IMMORTAL ALPS LOOK DOWN--	IN LANDS I NEVER SAW--	124	2
ALSO			
BELLS, ALSO, IN THE VILLAGE	ONE DIGNITY DELAYS FOR	98	7
ALSO, WHO LAID THE RAINBOW'S PIERS, . . .	BRING ME THE SUNSET IN A	128	13
ALSO, WHO LEADS THE DOCILE SPHERES . . .	BRING ME THE SUNSET IN A	128	14
WHEN OURSELVES WERE ALSO DUSTY--	SMILING BACK FROM	385	7
OF EXPECTATION--ALSO--	THOSE FAIR--FICTITIOUS	499	17
THIS--ALSO--I HAVE LEARNT--	YOU TAUGHT ME WAITING	740	4
ALSO WITH BIRD AND ASTEROID	THE DUTIES OF THE WIND	1137	11
IT HAS A GARRET ALSO	REMEMBRANCE HAS A	1182	3
WHEN IT HAS ALSO BEEN--	MY TRIUMPH LASTED TILL	1227	10
OF HEAVEN AND HELL I ALSO YIELD	BECAUSE THAT YOU ARE	1260	29
REPORTLESS, ALSO, BUT SINCERE AS NATURE . .	IN MANY AND REPORTLESS	1382	3
BY PARTIES ALSO THAT I KNEW	THE FAIREST HOME I EVER	1423	3
ALTER			
ME, CHANGE! ME, ALTER!	ME, CHANGE! ME, ALTER!	268	1
SMILE--AND ALTER--AND PRATTLE--AND DIE-- .	LOVE--THOU ART HIGH--	453	15
ALTER! WHEN THE HILLS DO--	ALTER! WHEN THE HILLS DO	729	1
ALTERED			
AND SOFTLY [SWIFTLY] THRO' THE ALTERED AIR .	THESE ARE THE DAYS WHEN	130	11
AN ALTERED LOOK ABOUT THE HILLS--	AN ALTERED LOOK ABOUT	140	1
SHE'S BUSY--WITH AN ALTERED CARE--	SHE'S HAPPY, WITH A NEW	535	3
NOR WHEN IT ALTERED, I COULD SAY, ...	IT CEASED TO HURT ME,	584	5
NATURE--ALTERED SMALL--	ALL FORGOT FOR	966	10
WHEN ALTERED FREQUENTLY--	WHO WERE "THE FATHER AND	1258	20
"HAVE ALTERED--ACCEPT THE PILLAGE	I SAW THAT THE FLAKE WAS	1267	7
ALTERNATING			
BY ALTERNATING ZONE--	'TWAS AWKWARD, BUT IT	973	8
ALTERNATIVE			
ALTERNATIVE TO DIE	SEVERER SERVICE OF	786	22
ALTERS			
A VOICE THAT ALTERS--LOW	A MIEN TO MOVE A QUEEN--	283	16
EITHER THE DARKNESS ALTERS--	WE GROW ACCUSTOMED TO	419	17
HOW IT ALTERS THE WORLD--	AFTER THE SUN COMES OUT	1148	2
ALTITUDE			
THE ALTITUDE OF ME--	'TWAS JUST THIS TIME,	445	20
AN ALTITUDE OF DEATH, THAT COULD	YOU TAUGHT ME WAITING	740	5
A LULL			
WHEN THE TIDE'S A' LULL--	MANY A PHRASE HAS THE	276	6
ALWAY			
HOW MODESTLY--ALWAY--	I TEND MY FLOWERS FOR	339	25
SUCH HOUSES HAVE--ALWAY--	THERE'S BEEN A DEATH, IN	389	4
THAT I SHALL LOVE ALWAY--	THAT I DID ALWAYS LOVE	549	5
IT'S TEMPLE [CLOSET] STANDS, ALWAY, . . .	THE BODY GROWS WITHOUT--	578	4
ALWAY A FLOWER WOULD BE.	BECAUSE THE BEE MAY	869	6
ALWAYS			
AND SO I ALWAYS BEAR THE CUP	I BRING AN UNACCUSTOMED	132	17
THEY SAID THAT JESUS--ALWAYS CAME-- . . .	DYING! DYING IN THE	158	6
A CHEEK IS ALWAYS REDDER	A WOUNDED DEER--LEAPS	165	7
ALWAYS LOST THE WAY!	WE DONT CRY--TIM AND I,	196	20
IS IT ALWAYS PLEASANT--THERE--	WHAT IS--"PARADISE"--	215	8
THAT I DID ALWAYS LOVE	THAT I DID ALWAYS LOVE	549	1
IT ALWAYS FELT TO ME--A WRONG	IT ALWAYS FELT TO ME--A	597	1
DOES'NT--ALWAYS--MOVE--	"SPEECH"--IS A PRANK OF	688	4
ALWAYS MINE!	ALWAYS MINE!	839	1
THEY WONT FROWN ALWAYS--SOME SWEET DAY . .	THEY WONT FROWN ALWAYS--	874	1
THAT ALWAYS GUAGES A DEGREE	LEST THIS BE HEAVEN	1043	3
THE SOUL SHOULD ALWAYS STAND AJAR	THE SOUL SHOULD ALWAYS	1055	1
I ALWAYS FEEL A DOUBT	WHEN THEY COME BACK--IF	1080	2
I ALWAYS HAD A FEAR	WHEN THEY COME BACK--IF	1080	6
IS ALWAYS AT THE WINDOW	I KNOW SUSPENSE--IT	1285	5
IS ALWAYS AS THE CONTENTS	I THOUGHT THAT NATURE	1286	9
AS IF IT TARRIED ALWAYS	THE MUSHROOM IS THE ELF	1298	5
TRIED ALWAYS AND CONDEMNED BY THEE	TRIED ALWAYS AND	1559	1
HOW ALWAYS WRONG IS LOVE--	HOW FLEET--HOW	1771	2
A MARCHING			
A MARCHING TO THE SKIES!	"SIC TRANSIT GLORIA	3	52
AMAZED			
AND STOOD AMAZED BEFORE THE CHANGE [BOON / MORNS]	THE THRILL CAME SLOWLY	1495	7
AMAZES			
AMAZES THE HUMILITY	ENDANGER IT, AND THE	1658	3
AMAZING			
DISTILLS AMAZING SENSE	THIS WAS A POET--IT IS	448	2
FROM HIS AMAZING HOUSE--	WHEN I HAVE SEEN THE SUN	888	2
AMBER			
STILL REARS THE EAST HER AMBER FLAG-- . . .	A SOMETHING IN A	122	16
YOU DROPPED AN AMBER THREAD--	SHE SWEEPS WITH	219	6
WHO STRAYED BEYOND THE AMBER LINE	THE LONESOME FOR THEY	262	3
THE MORNING'S AMBER [LIGHTNING'S JOINTED] ROAD--	BEFORE I GOT MY EYE PUT	327	15
UPON HER AMBER SHOE--	I KNOW A PLACE WHERE	337	12
AND YET, WITH AMBER HANDS--	THE MOON IS DISTANT FROM	429	2
OH, SIGNOR, THINE, THE AMBER HAND--	THE MOON IS DISTANT FROM	429	9

	FIRST LINE	POEM	LINE
AMBER (CONTINUED)			
OF AMBER--FIT--	THE MALAY--TOOK THE	452	13
IT'S AMBER REVELATION	AN IGNORANCE A SUNSET	552	5
IN AMBER--LIES--	DELIGHT--BECOMES	572	6
APPROACHED [POSSESSED]--THE AMBER FLITS [MOVES]--A LITTLE--	DELIGHT--BECOMES	572	7
WITH EQUIPAGE OF AMBER--	HE FOUND MY BEING--SET	603	7
I ONLY SAW A SAPPHIRE [AN AMBER--] FARM--	THEY CALLED ME TO THE	628	3
DID INDEPENDENT, AMBER--	I WATCHED THE MOON	629	15
THE AMBER QUANTITY--	LEAST BEE THAT BREW--	676	5
SO HERE'S AN AMBER SILL--	THE JUDGE IS LIKE THE	699	4
AMBER--AMBER--DEW--DEW--	OUT OF SIGHT? WHAT OF	703	9
AMBER--AMBER--DEW--DEW--	OUT OF SIGHT? WHAT OF	703	9
HER LIPS OF AMBER NEVER PART--	THE MOON WAS BUT A CHIN	737	9
AT SETTING--THIS AND AMBER--	THE COLOR OF A QUEEN, IS	776	3
ADD AN AMBER CRUMB	HE IS ALIVE, THIS	1160	6
OR HOW THE AMBER AIDED IT--	THESE HELD THEIR WICK	1390	3
A SLOOP OF AMBER SLIPS AWAY	A SLOOP OF AMBER SLIPS	1622	1
AMBITION			
AMBITION CANNOT FIND HIM.	AMBITION CANNOT FIND HIM	68	1
AMBLING			
IS PUSHING [ROAMING / PLODDING / STARING / AMBLING] CLOSE BEHIND	ALL THAT I DO	1496	6
AMBUSCADE			
NEVER SUCH AN AMBUSCADE	PIGMY SERAPHS--GONE	138	9
AMBUSH			
'TIS A FOND AMBUSH--	I KNOW THAT HE EXISTS.	338	6
HE LIVED THE LIFE OF AMBUSH	HE LIVED THE LIFE OF	1525	1
WHO ABDICATED AMBUSH	WHO ABDICATED AMBUSH	1616	1
AMEN			
AND OF THE BREEZE--AMEN!	THE GENTIAN WEAVES HER	18	19
AMENABLE			
AMENABLE TO LAW--	THE WAY TO KNOW THE	1279	10
AMEND			
TEAZING [TAUNTING] WITH GLITTERING AMEND--	FAIRER THROUGH FADING--	938	6
AMENDED			
"FAITHFUL TO THE END" AMENDED	"FAITHFUL TO THE END"	1357	1
THE DEVIL--WITHOUT QUESTION [SO AMENDED--]	THE DEVIL--HAD HE	1479	7
AMENITY			
AS OF FRUGALITY [VELOCITY / AMENITY / PROPRIETY]--	A SPARROW TOOK A SLICE	1211	V 8
AMERICA			
IN NORTH AMERICA--	I'VE KNOWN A HEAVEN,	243	8
BAPTIZED [TO WIT] AMERICA--	TRUST IN THE UNEXPECTED	555	12
AND SOUTH AMERICA	VOLCANOES BE IN SICILY	1705	2
AMETHYST			
THE PEACE--THE FLIGHT--THE AMETHYST--	THE DAISY FOLLOWS SOFT	106	11
OPENS THE LID OF AMETHYST	AS WATCHERS HANG UPON	121	8
AND NOW, AN AMETHYST REMEMBRANCE	I HELD A JEWEL IN MY	245	7
THE STEEPLES SWAM IN AMETHYST--	I'LL TELL YOU HOW THE	318	3
BY MENACES OF AMETHYST	SUNSET THAT SCREENS,	1609	3
THAT [HIS] WHIFFLETREE OF AMETHYST	THE SUN IN REINING TO	1636	5
AMHERST			
FROM AMHERST TO CASHMERE!	IF I COULD BRIBE THEM BY	179	3
DO THEY KNOW THAT THIS IS "AMHERST"--	WHAT IS--"PARADISE"--	215	5
AMID			
A LADY RED--AMID THE HILL	A LADY RED--AMID THE	74	1
AMID NO BELLS NOR BRAVOES	WENT UP A YEAR THIS	93	3
LOW AMID THAT GLAD BELLES LETTRES	IF THE FOOLISH, CALL	168	17
STARS, AMID PROFOUND GALAXIES--	IF THE FOOLISH, CALL	168	19
AMISS			
I MUST NOT PUT MY FOOT AMISS	IS BLISS THEN, SUCH	340	2
DETERMINE THEE AMISS--	GO SLOW, MY SOUL, TO	1297	6
AMITIES			
DISTURBED THESE AMITIES.	I HAD SOME THINGS THAT I	116	4
AMMUNITION			
HER FADED [RUSTY] AMMUNITION	THE PAST IS SUCH A	1203	7
AMONG SEE 'MONG			
BUILDED OUR HEARTS AMONG.	ONE SISTER HAVE I IN OUR	14	8
THE YEARS AMONG,	ONE SISTER HAVE I IN OUR	14	18
SUCH TRUST HAD ONE AMONG US,	COULD LIVE--DID LIVE--	43	10
AMONG US NOT TODAY--	COULD LIVE--DID LIVE--	43	11
"PENIEL" HILLS BEYOND [AMONG],	A LITTLE EAST OF JORDAN,	59	14
MODEST, LET US WALK AMONG IT	I CANT TELL YOU--BUT YOU	65	9
BRED AS WE, AMONG THE MOUNTAINS,	EXULTATION IS THE GOING	76	5
MAY BE SEEN THE DEWS AMONG,	ANGELS, IN THE EARLY	94	2
MAY BE SEEN THE SANDS AMONG,	ANGELS, IN THE EARLY	94	6
AMONG ASTONISHED BOUGHS--	BRING ME THE SUNSET IN A	128	9
ALL DAY--AMONG THE CROWDED AIR	MUSICIANS WRESTLE	157	2
AMONG IT'S STORES TO FIND--	IN EBON BOX, WHEN YEARS	169	10
AMONG THE APRIL WOODS!	IF I COULD BRIBE THEM BY	179	9
BUT GIMBLETS--AMONG THE NERVE--	IT IS EASY TO WORK WHEN	244	6
AMONG THE CUNNING CELLS--	I BREATHED ENOUGH TO	272	6
AMONG THE PENSIVE [SMILING] TREES--	THE ONLY GHOST I EVER	274	12
BUT OFTENTIMES, AMONG MY MIND,	I CANNOT DANCE UPON MY	326	3
AND THEN 'TWAS PUT AMONG THE DUST	DEATH SETS A THING	360	11
LIKE BEADS--AMONG THE BOG--	HER SMILE WAS SHAPED	514	8
THAT DAY--THE DAYS AMONG--	THAT FIRST DAY, WHEN YOU	659	4
AMONG REDEEMED CHILDREN	THE BEGGAR LAD--DIES	717	9
THESE--WE HELD AMONG [FONDLED IN] OUR OWN--	THESE--SAW VISIONS--	758	9

	FIRST LINE	POEM	LINE
AMONG (CONTINUED)			
HER VOICE AMONG THE AISLES	NATURE--THE GENTLEST	790	13
AND NOW, AMONG CIRCUMFERENCE--	SHE STAKED HER FEATHERS	798	5
AT HOME [EASE]--AMONG THE BILLOWS--AS . .	SHE STAKED HER FEATHERS	798	7
AMONG THE OTHER SEASONS	SPRING IS THE PERIOD	844	3
IT SHOULD NOT BE AMONG	WHO OCCUPIES THIS HOUSE?	892	13
OR A GLEE AMONG THE GARRET	THAT IS SOLEMN WE HAVE	934	3
A MOURNER WALKED [LURKED] AMONG THE CHILDREN	A LOSS OF SOMETHING EVER	959	5
WAS RECENTLY AMONG US--	WE LEARN IN THE	1083	3
OR STROLL THE TOWN AMONG.	THE SPRY ARMS OF THE	1103	8
AMONG THE CERTAINTIES--	WE DO NOT KNOW THE TIME	1106	4
TO DWELL EXTENT AMONG, ...	THE DUTIES OF THE WIND	1137	6
"MADE FLESH AND DWELT AMONG US	A WORD MADE FLESH IS	1651	13
AMOUNT			
THE SAME AMOUNT REMAIN--	HOPE IS A SUBTLE GLUTTON	1547	8
AMPHITRITE			
BUT SHE, FORGETTING AMPHITRITE--	THE DROP, THAT WRESTLES	284	8
AMPLE			
I'VE KNOWN HER--FROM AN AMPLE NATION-- . .	THE SOUL SELECTS HER OWN	303	9
IT WILL BE AMPLE TIME FOR--ME--	JUST SO--JESUS--RAPS--	317	9
ETERNITY IS AMPLE, ...	THEY LEAVE US WITH THE	350	11
UPON AN AMPLE CRACK--	THE ANGLE OF A LANDSCAPE	375	4
WHO HATH THE AMPLE RHINE	EXHILIRATION--IS WITHIN	383	10
WHO OWN THE AMPLE SEA--	'TIS LITTLE I--COULD	466	2
AMPLE I	I HAD NO TIME TO HATE--	478	5
AN AMPLE LETTER--HOW YOU MISS--	YOU LOVE THE LORD--YOU	487	5
'TWAS SUCH AN AMPLE PEACE--	I HAD NO CAUSE TO BE	542	13
THAT FELT SO AMPLE--YESTERDAY--	I COULD NOT PROVE THE	563	7
I DID NOT KNOW THE AMPLE BREAD--	I HAD BEEN HUNGRY, ALL	579	9
AMPLE AS THE EYE--	'TWOULD EASE--A	682	13
TO LEND AN AMPLE SINEW	TO OFFER BRAVE	767	5
HOW AMPLE TO RELY	ON A COLUMNAR SELF--	789	2
AMPLE MAKE THIS BED--	AMPLE MAKE THIS BED--	829	1
AS TO BEHOLD HIS AMPLE [GENTLE] FLIGHT-- .	THE MERCHANT OF THE	1131	11
IS NOT SO AMPLE AS THE BREAST [HEART] . .	STEP LIGHTLY ON THIS	1183	3
IMMORTAL IS AN AMPLE WORD	IMMORTAL IS AN AMPLE	1205	1
HIS AMPLE--PLODDING STEED	LIKE BROOMS OF STEEL	1252	9
AND THANKED THE AMPLE FRIEND--	I WORKED FOR CHAFF AND	1269	6
. . . MIGHTY / GALLANT / SYLVAN / AMPLE / PERFECT] WAY	SUMMER--WE ALL HAVE SEEN	1386	6
ABUNDANT [A FERVENT / A LOYAL / A GRACIOUS / AN AMPLE] END--	THE GENTIAN HAS A	1424	13
SO EASY [KINDRED / FULLY / FREE / AMPLE SEEMS / BOUNTEOUS / . . .	YOUR THOUGHTS DONT HAVE	1452	6
AMPLER			
HIS OWN WAS [IS] AMPLER--BUT AS I	I SEND TWO SUNSETS--	308	5
FOR SOME--AN AMPLER ZERO--	MORE LIFE--WENT OUT--	422	9
FOR AMPLER COVETING--	GOD GAVE A LOAF TO EVERY	791	8
YET AMPLER THAN THE SUN--	A COFFIN--IS A SMALL	943	6
AMPLER [BOLDER] TO FLY AWAY	ARE FRIENDS DELIGHT OR	1199	5
AMPLEST			
MOST ENOUGH [AMPLEST]--DENIED?	PROMISE THIS--WHEN YOU	648	33
HER FOREHEAD IS OF AMPLEST BLONDE--	THE MOON WAS BUT A CHIN	737	5
AMPLITUDE			
OF AMPLITUDE, OR AWE--	SHE ROSE TO HIS	732	6
WHOSE AMPLITUDE NO END [CLOCK] INVADES-- .	WATER MAKES MANY BEDS	1428	7
AMPLY			
WHOSE PEAT LIFE--AMPLY VIVID--	MORE LIFE--WENT OUT--	422	17
IT WILL BE AMPLY EARLY	WHEN THE ASTRONOMER	851	7
AMPUTATE			
AMPUTATE MY FRECKLED BOSOM!	REARRANGE A "WIFE'S"	1737	3
AMPUTATED			
THAT HAND IS AMPUTATED NOW	THOSE--DYING THEN,	1551	4
AMULET			
FORGET! THE LADY WITH THE AMULET	FORGET! THE LADY WITH	438	1
THE LADY WITH THE AMULET--WILL FADE-- . .	FORGET! THE LADY WITH	438	9
AMULETS			
OR SPIKENARDS, PERISHING [AMULETS OF PINE]--	THE GRASS SO LITTLE HAS	333	16
ANALYSIS			
OMNIPOTENCE' INSPECTION [ANALYSIS]	AN IGNORANCE A SUNSET	552	7
OF HEAVEN, EASING ANALYSIS, ...	THE DEFINITION OF BEAUTY	988	3
TO TIME'S ANALYSIS--	THE LILAC IS AN ANCIENT	1241	16
ANALYSIS AS [LIKE] CAPSULE SEEMED	HE WAS MY HOST--HE WAS	1721	7
ANALYTIC			
WITH NARROW, PROBING, [ANALYTIC] EYES-- . .	I MEASURE EVERY GRIEF I	561	2
ANALYZE			
TO ANALYZE PERHAPS	THE FROST WAS NEVER SEEN	1202	17
CONFIRMING ALL WHO ANALYZE	CONFIRMING ALL WHO	1268	1
ANANIAS			
ANANIAS WAS'NT--	SO I PULL MY STOCKINGS	1201	8
ANATOMY			
"COMPARATIVE ANATOMY"--	A SCIENCE--SO THE SAVANS	100	2
ANCESTOR			
NEITHER PATRIARCH NOR PUSSY [ANCESTOR NOR URCHIN]	ONE DAY IS THERE OF THE	814	5
OF DAWN, THE ANCESTOR--	THE MOUNTAIN SAT UPON	975	8
GENESIS--BETHLEHEM'S ANCESTOR--	THE BIBLE IS AN ANTIQUE	1545	V 5
ANCESTORS			
PRESUMPTION WAS--HIS ANCESTORS	AS IMPERCEPTIBLY AS	1540	V

	FIRST LINE	POEM	LINE
ANCHOR			
AND ANCHOR "OFF THE BAR"	COULD I BUT RIDE	661	16
. . . SAIL SOFTLY / DO ANCHOR] HERE	A CHILLY PEACE INFESTS	1443	7
ANCHORED			
THAT ANCHORED THERE--I WEIGH	I TIE MY HAT--I CREASE	443	8
ANCHORS			
THE ANCHORS FAST--	ON THIS WONDROUS SEA	4	9
ANCIENT			
A WATCH--SOME ANCIENT [ANTIQUE] BROOCH	I KNOW SOME LONELY	289	28
AN ANCIENT FASHIONED HEART--	'TWAS AWKWARD, BUT IT	973	2
THE LILAC IS AN ANCIENT SHRUB	THE LILAC IS AN ANCIENT	1241	1
EDEN--THE ANCIENT HOMESTEAD--	THE BIBLE IS AN ANTIQUE	1545	5
ANCIENTER			
BUT ANCIENTER THAN THAT	THE LILAC IS AN ANCIENT	1241	2
ANCLE			
OUR PANTING ANCLE BARELY PASSED [GAINED],	OF TRIBULATION--THESE	325	13
UPON MY ANCLE--THEN MY SHOES	I STARTED EARLY--TOOK MY	520	19
ANCLES SEE ANKLES			
ANDES			
BUT ANDES IN THE BOSOMS WHERE	SHE SPED AS PETALS OF A	991	7
ANDRE'S			
'TWAS MAJOR ANDRE'S WAY--	THE MANNER OF IT'S DEATH	468	4
ANECDOTES			
ANECDOTES OF AIR IN DUNGEONS	TALK WITH PRUDENCE TO A	119	7
ANEMONE			
ANEMONE--	SUMMER FOR THEE, GRANT I	31	8
ANEMONE, AND BELL--	WHOSE ARE THE LITTLE	142	14
ANEMONES			
CAN THE ANEMONES	IF PAIN FOR PEACE	63	5
ANEW			
AND GIRT HIS LOINS ANEW	A LITTLE EAST OF JORDAN,	59	V 10
BUT PERISHES--TO LIVE ANEW--	SUSPENSE--IS HOSTILER	705	5
BUT JUST ANEW TO DIE--	SUSPENSE--IS HOSTILER	705	6
'TIS WELL TO HOARD ANEW--	OUR OWN POSSESSIONS--	1208	2
IT'S IRON BUDS WILL SPROUT ANEW [AFRESH]	YOU CANNOT MAKE	1508	11
THAT MEN ANEW EMBARK TO LIVE	IN SNOW THOU COMEST	1669	7
ANGEL			
A GYMNAST AND AN ANGEL [A WRESTLER]	A LITTLE EAST OF JORDAN,	59	3
THE ANGEL BEGGED PERMISSION	A LITTLE EAST OF JORDAN,	59	7
I'LL HAND IT TO THE ANGEL--	THE FACE I CARRY WITH ME	336	5
HIS IGNORANCE--THE ANGEL	NO MAN CAN COMPASS A	477	11
A PRAYER, THAT IT MORE ANGEL--PROVE--	THE WORLD--STANDS--	493	9
NEVER TO PASS THE ANGEL	A CLOUD WITHDREW FROM	895	9
ANGELS			
WHOSE PEASANTS ARE THE ANGELS--	THE FEET OF PEOPLE	7	19
IS WHERE THE ANGELS ARE--	THE GENTIAN WEAVES HER	18	8
SO ANGELS SAY--ON YESTERDAY--	ADRIFT! A LITTLE BOAT	30	9
ANGELS--TWICE DESCENDING	I NEVER LOST AS MUCH BUT	49	5
ANGELS! WRITE [MARK] "PROMOTED"	WHO NEVER LOST, ARE	73	15
THE ANGELS--HAPPENING THAT WAY	A POOR--TORN HEART-- A	78	9
ANGELS, IN THE EARLY MORNING	ANGELS, IN THE EARLY	94	1
ANGELS, WHEN THE SUN IS HOTTEST	ANGELS, IN THE EARLY	94	5
FOR SUCH, THE ANGELS GO--	TO FIGHT ALOUD, IS VERY	126	10
"BERNARDINE" ANGELS, UP THE HIGHT	SHE DIED--THIS WAS THE	150	V 5
THE ANGELS MUST HAVE SPIED,	SHE DIED--THIS WAS THE	150	6
EXCEPT FOR ANGELS--LONE.	EXCEPT TO HEAVEN, SHE IS	154	2
NOT PURSUED BY LEARNED ANGELS	IF THE FOOLISH, CALL	168	15
OBSEQUIOUS ANGELS WAIT!	WAIT TILL THE MAJESTY OF	171	10
GOD PERMITS INDUSTRIOUS ANGELS--	GOD PERMITS INDUSTRIOUS	231	1
GOD CALLS HOME--THE ANGELS--PROMPTLY--	GOD PERMITS INDUSTRIOUS	231	5
WOULD'NT THE ANGELS TRY ME--	WHY--DO THEY SHUT ME OUT	248	5
THE ANGELS--SOFTLY PEERED--	IF I'M LOST--NOW--	256	7
THE ANGELS--LABORED DILIGENT--	GOOD NIGHT! WHICH PUT	259	5
TO TEACH THE ANGELS, AVARICE,	ALTHOUGH I PUT AWAY HIS	366	32
THE ANGELS BUSTLE IN THE HALL--	A WIFE--AT DAYBREAK I	461	8
ALONE--IF ANGELS ARE "ALONE"--	AGAIN--HIS VOICE IS AT	663	22
AND ANGELS KNOW THE REST!	I HIDE MYSELF WITHIN MY	903	V 4
ON ANGELS--SQUANDERING FOR YOU	HIS BILL IS CLASPED--HIS	1102	11
FOR ANGELS RENT THE HOUSE NEXT OUR'S,	WHO HAS NOT FOUND THE	1544	3
BUT ANGELS HAVE THAT MODEST WAY	FOREVER HONORED BE THE	1570	7
ANGELS'			
ANGELS' BREATHLESS BALLOT	SOUL, WILT THOU TOSS	139	5
ANGER			
ANGER AS SOON AS FED IS DEAD--	MINE ENEMY IS GROWING	1509	7
ANGLE			
THAT ANGLE IN THE FLOOR,	I GOT SO I COULD HEAR	293	6
THE ANGLE OF A LANDSCAPE--	THE ANGLE OF A LANDSCAPE	375	1
WE COULD NOT GRASP IT'S SEGMENT [ANGLE]	WE SEE--COMPARATIVELY--	534	3
TILL BULLETS CLIPT AN ANGLE	WHEN I WAS SMALL, A	596	7
HE [FIRST]--MUST PASS THE CRYSTAL ANGLE [LIMIT]	HER SWEET TURN TO LEAVE	649	25
AND LEFT THE LITTLE ANGLE WORM	OUR LITTLE KINSMEN--	885	11
ANGLED			
EXPERIENCE IS THE ANGLED ROAD	EXPERIENCE IS THE ANGLED	910	1
ANGLEWORM			
HE BIT [SHOOK] AN ANGLEWORM IN HALVES	A BIRD CAME DOWN THE	328	3
ANGLO-FLORENTINE			
FROM THE ANGLO-FLORENTINE--	HER--"LAST POEMS"--	312	10
ANGUISH			
AN ANGUISH AT THE MENTION	A THROE UPON THE	71	5

	FIRST LINE	POEM	LINE
ANGUISH (CONTINUED)			
WE MUST AN ANGUISH PAY	FOR EACH EXTATIC INSTANT	125	2
THRO' WHAT TRANSPORTING ANGUISH	ALL OVERGROWN BY CUNNING	148	V
MIRTH IS THE MAIL OF ANGUISH--	A WOUNDED DEER--LEAPS	165	9
THIS IS THE SOVREIGN ANGUISH!	TO LEARN THE TRANSPORT	167	9
IF AT LENGTH, THE SMOULDERING ANGUISH	I HAVE NEVER SEEN	175	13
CHRIST WILL EXPLAIN EACH SEPARATE ANGUISH	I SHALL KNOW WHY--WHEN	193	3
I SHALL FORGET THE DROP OF ANGUISH	I SHALL KNOW WHY--WHEN	193	7
I MIND ME THAT OF ANGUISH--SENT--	I THINK JUST HOW MY	237	9
BY HOMELY ANGUISH STRUNG.	I LIKE A LOOK OF AGONY,	241	8
AS MANIFOLD FOR ANGUISH--	A WEIGHT WITH NEEDLES ON	264	7
AND ANGUISH--ABSOLUTE--	I REASON, EARTH IS SHORT	301	2
GIVE LITTLE ANGUISH--	GIVE LITTLE ANGUISH--	310	1
"DEFEAT", AN OUTGROWN ANGUISH,	OF TRIBULATION--THESE	325	11
WHICH ANGUISH WAS THE UTTEREST--THEN--	'TWAS LIKE A MAELSTROM,	414	24
ANGUISH--AND THE TOMB--	SWEET--SAFE--HOUSES--	457	13
WRUNG ME--WITH ANGUISH--	HE STRAINED MY FAITH--	497	9
EVE--AND THE ANGUISH--GRANDAME'S STORY--	BETTER--THAN MUSIC! FOR	503	15
THE ANGUISH--AND THE LOSS--	WE SEE--COMPARATIVELY--	534	10
ONE ANGUISH--IN A CROWD--	ONE ANGUISH--IN A CROWD	565	1
I COULD NOT SEE [FEEL] THE TROUBLE [ANGUISH] GO--	IT CEASED TO HURT ME,	584	2
OH, REWARD [RECOMPENSE] OF ANGUISH,	IN FALLING TIMBERS	614	11
IN AN EXTREMER ANGUISH	A DOUBT IF IT BE US	859	3
HOW HE STRETCHED HIS ANGUISH [SPIRIT] TO US	HOW THE WATERS CLOSED	923	3
'TIS ANGUISH GRANDER THAN DELIGHT	'TIS ANGUISH GRANDER	984	1
IMMEDIATELY--THAT ANGUISH STOOPED	SO PROUD SHE WAS TO DIE	1272	7
ONE JOY [SOUND] OF SO MUCH ANGUISH	ONE JOY OF SO MUCH	1420	1
THE ANGUISH [PATHOS] OF THE AVARICE	ONE THING OF IT WE	1464	7
WAS THE STRONG CUP OF ANGUISH BREWED FOR THE NAZARENE	PROUD OF MY BROKEN HEART	1736	6
ANGUISH--BARE OF ANODYNE!	REARRANGE A "WIFE'S"	1737	12
ANGUISH CAN TRAVEL TO ITS STAKE,	THE LONGEST DAY THAT GOD	1769	3
'TIS ANGUISH NOT A FEATHER HATH	TOO HAPPY TIME DISSOLVES	1774	3
ANIMALS			
LIKE ANIMALS IN PAIN	THE WIND DREW OFF	1694	9
ANKLES			
AS ANKLES OF A QUEEN--	IT SIFTS FROM LEADEN	311	18
ANNEALED			
OR LOVE ANNEALED OF LOVE	PERHAPS YOU THINK ME	833	6
ANNIHILATE			
ANNIHILATE A SINGLE CLAUSE--	TO LOSE ONE'S FAITH--	377	7
COULD NOW ANNIHILATE	BECAUSE THAT YOU ARE	1260	12
ANNIHILATING			
AFRESH ANNIHILATING ME	I NEVER HEAR THAT ONE IS	1323	3
ANNIHILATION			
ANNIHILATION--PLATED FRESH	SUSPENSE--IS HOSTILER	705	7
ALTHOUGH ANNIHILATION PILE	A PLATED LIFE--	806	7
ANNIVERSARY			
SUCH ANNIVERSARY SHALL BE--	ONE YEAR AGO--JOTS WHAT?	296	6
ANNO			
FROM ANNO DOMINIES--	FOREVER--IS COMPOSED OF	624	12
ANNOUNCED			
IT WAS ANNOUNCED TO ME	"SIC TRANSIT GLORIA	3	30
ANNOUNCING			
ANNOUNCING ME IN OTHER DELLS--	THERE IS A MORN BY MEN	24	23
ANNUAL			
HER ANNUAL SECRET KEEPS!	A LADY RED--AMID THE	74	2
RECEIVES IT'S ANNUAL REPLY!	AN ALTERED LOOK ABOUT	140	16
ANNUL			
LEST INTERVIEW--ANNUL A WANT	A CHARM INVESTS A FACE	421	7
AS SUNS--DISSOLVE [ANNUL] A STAR--	NO CROWD THAT HAS	515	12
FILMS CANNOT ANNUL	BANISH AIR FROM AIR--	854	7
ANNULLED			
ANNULLED--	IT KNEW NO LAPSE, NOR	560	6
ANNULS			
DYING--ANNULS THE POWER TO KILL.	IF ANY SINK, ASSURE THAT	358	8
ONCE TO ACHIEVE, ANNULS THE POWER	THOSE WHO HAVE BEEN IN	922	7
ANODYNE			
AN ANODYNE SO SWEET--	HEART, NOT SO HEAVY AS	83	8
ONLY ANODYNE--	NO BOBOLINK--REVERSE HIS	755	9
ANGUISH--BARE OF ANODYNE!	REARRANGE A "WIFE'S"	1737	12
ANODYNES			
AND THEN--THOSE LITTLE ANODYNES	THE HEART ASKS PLEASURE	536	3
ANOMALY			
WERE ANOMALY.	SATISFACTION--IS THE	1036	8
ANONYMOUS			
ANONYMOUS DELIGHT TO KNOW--	I SOMETIMES DROP IT, FOR	708	3
AS STARS THAT DROP ANONYMOUS	SUPERFLUOUS WERE THE SUN	999	11
ANSWER			
ANSWER ME TO WEAR?	BEFORE THE ICE IS IN THE	37	16
ANSWER JULY--	ANSWER JULY--	386	1
ANSWER THEE--ME--	ANSWER JULY--	386	9
AND ANSWER WHAT I DO--	A TONGUE--TO TELL HIM I	400	9
TO ANSWER--WHEREFORE WHEN HE PASS	"WHY DO I LOVE" YOU, SIR	480	4
THE ANSWER OF THE SEA UNTO	I COULD SUFFICE FOR HIM,	643	13
THAT ANSWER TO OUR FEET--	A PRISON GETS TO BE A	652	10
SINCE A RACK COULD'NT COAX A SYLLABLE [AN ANSWER]--NOW	GRIEF IS A MOUSE--	793	17
THAT I THE ANSWER MAY PURSUE	I'VE NONE TO TELL ME TO	881	11

	FIRST LINE	POEM	LINE
ANSWER (CONTINUED)			
WHEN THE SEA RETURN NO ANSWER	GRATITUDE--IS NOT THE	989	5
I MADE NO ANSWER OF THE TONGUE	IT WAS A QUIET WAY--	1053	3
BUT ANSWER OF THE EYES--	IT WAS A QUIET WAY--	1053	4
WOULD DOUBTLESS SPECIFY--[ANSWER ME]	WHO WERE "THE FATHER AND	1258	12
AND SHE WOULD TELL YOU [ANSWER] SIGHING--	CRISIS IS SWEET AND YET	1416	7
WHAT ANSWER [TIDINGS] WREST FROM THEE	STILL OWN THEE--STILL	1633	6
ANSWERED			
I BOLDLY ANSWERED--ENTERED THEN	THE WIND--TAPPED LIKE A	436	3
ANSWERED WOLFE [HE] "TO DIE"	WOLFE DEMANDED DURING	678	4
NOT TILL THE LAST WAS ANSWERED	WHAT DID THEY DO SINCE I	900	7
I'M ANSWERED IN A LONESOME TONE--	OF TOLLING BELL I ASK	947	3
ANSWERING			
TO THINK OF ANSWERING YOU!	GOING TO HEAVEN!	79	5
ANTEDATE			
DOTH LIKE A BUBBLE ANTEDATE	THE MUSHROOM IS THE ELF	1298	11
ANTEDATES			
THAT COMPREHENSION FLUCTUATES [ANTEDATES]	PERHAPS THEY DO NOT GO	1399	7
ANTELOPE			
AND A STIRRUP OF AN ANTELOPE--	AH, MOON--AND STAR!	240	11
WOULD LEAP ABROAD LIKE ANTELOPE--	ALTHOUGH I PUT AWAY HIS	366	15
ANTERIOR			
LOVE--IS ANTERIOR TO LIFE--	LOVE--IS ANTERIOR TO	917	1
OF IT'S ANTERIOR SUN.	DELIGHT'S DESPAIR AT	1299	8
ANTHRACITE			
SO ANTHRACITE, TO LIVE--	MORE LIFE--WENT OUT--	422	8
ANTI			
BUT JUST THE ANTI FAIR--AVERRING--FAIREST-- TRUEST TRUTH	EXTOL THEE--COULD I--	1643	3
ANTICIPATE			
STILL TO ANTICIPATE [CONJECTURE]--WERE NO LIMIT--	BOUND--A TROUBLE--	269	V
MEN--TO ANTICIPATE [PROPITIATE]	THE CHILD'S FAITH IS NEW	637	23
TIME [TIME'S] TO ANTICIPATE HIS GAZE--	FITTER TO SEE HIM, I MAY	968	9
ANTICIPATING			
ANTICIPATING US	THOSE FAIR--FICTITIOUS	499	18
ANTICIPATION			
BUT OUR ANTICIPATION	THESE TESTED OUR HORIZON	886	7
ANTICS			
FOR FRENZY OF [FRENZIES OF / ANTICS IN / ANTICS WITH] THE SUN--	TWO BUTTERFLIES WENT OUT	533	V
FOR FRENZY OF [FRENZIES OF / ANTICS IN / ANTICS WITH] THE SUN--	TWO BUTTERFLIES WENT OUT	533	V
ANTIDOTE			
'TIS ANTIDOTE TO TURN--	I THINK I WAS ENCHANTED	593	28
ANTIQUARY			
IF SOME LOVING ANTIQUARY,	I HAVE NEVER SEEN	175	17
ANTIQUATED			
BIRDS ARE ANTIQUATED FELLOWS!	I'M THE LITTLE "HEART'S	176	11
WHO MISS HIS ANTIQUATED WICK [LIGHT]--	THAT ODD OLD MAN IS DEAD	1130	5
AN [ITS] ANTIQUATED GRACE	AN ANTIQUATED GRACE	1345	1
WHOSE ANTIQUATED BLOSSOM	TRUSTY AS THE STARS	1369	6
AN ANTIQUATED TREE	AN ANTIQUATED TREE	1514	1
ANTIQUE			
PERHAPS, AN ANTIQUE TRINKET--	IN EBON BOX, WHEN YEARS	169	15
A WATCH--SOME ANCIENT [ANTIQUE] BROOCH	I KNOW SOME LONELY	289	28
TO MEET AN ANTIQUE BOOK--	A PRECIOUS--MOULDERING	371	2
TILL IT AN ANTIQUE FASHION SHOWS--	WE OUTGROW LOVE, LIKE	887	3
'TWAS WITH TEXT AND VILLAGE [ANTIQUE] SINGING	THREE WEEKS PASSED SINCE	1061	3
THE BIBLE IS AN ANTIQUE [UNTOLD] VOLUME--	THE BIBLE IS AN ANTIQUE	1545	1
ANTIQUER			
ANTIQUEST [ANTIQUER] FELT AT NOON	FURTHER IN SUMMER THAN	1068	9
ANTIQUEST			
ANTIQUEST [ANTIQUER] FELT AT NOON	FURTHER IN SUMMER THAN	1068	9
ANTIQUITY			
ANTIQUITY--	PINK--SMALL--AND	1332	12
ANTLERS			
THE ANTLERS GRAY--	A CURIOUS CLOUD	1710	4
ANVIL			
NEVER MIND MY BREATHLESS ANVIL!	BY A FLOWER--BY A LETTER	109	5
ANVIL'S			
WHOSE ANVIL'S EVEN RING	DARE YOU SEE A SOUL AT	365	10
ANXIOUS			
WHAT SKILFUL [ANXIOUS] POINTERS MOVE--	NOT TO DISCOVER WEAKNESS	1054	8
ANY			
OR ANY CHEEK AT NIGHTFALL	BEFORE THE ICE IS IN THE	37	3
ANY FORGOT BY VICTORY	DELAYED TILL SHE HAD	58	14
COULD SCARE US ANY MORE!	WHERE BELLS NO MORE	112	12
CAUTIOUS, HINT TO ANY CAPTIVE	TALK WITH PRUDENCE TO A	119	5
IF, HAPLY, ANY SAY TO ME	I BRING AN UNACCUSTOMED	132	20
THAT ANY BROOK IS THERE,	HAVE YOU GOT A BROOK IN	136	6
NOR ANY SCHOOLBOY ROB THE NEST	THIS HEART THAT BROKE SO	145	7
HAD'NT ANY PLAYMATES,	DUST IS THE ONLY SECRET	153	7
IF ANY ASK ME WHY--	THE MURMUR OF A BEE	155	3
IF ANY ASK ME HOW--	THE MURMUR OF A BEE	155	13
TO PEOPLE--ANY MORE!	THE FLOWER MUST NOT	206	6
NONE MAY TEACH IT--ANY--	THERE'S A CERTAIN SLANT	258	9
SING--AT IT'S PAIN--AS ANY WORKMAN--	BOUND--A TROUBLE--	269	9
THEY CANNOT TAKE ME [US]--ANY MORE!	WHAT IF I SAY I SHALL	277	7
IF ANY ARE NOT SURE--	'TIS SO APPALLING--IT	281	11

ANY (CONTINUED)

	FIRST LINE	POEM	LINE
NEVER ANY [ONE] BEND	IF YOUR NERVE, DENY YOU	292	6
IF ANY POWER BEHIND IT, BE,	I GOT SO I COULD HEAR	293	22
NOR ANY KNOW [KNEW] I KNOW THE ART	I CANNOT DANCE UPON MY	326	17
NOR ANY PLACARD BOAST ME--	I CANNOT DANCE UPON MY	326	19
AT ANY STORE--	IS BLISS THEN, SUCH	340	8
NONE BUY IT ANY MORE--	IS BLISS THEN, SUCH	340	11
IF ANY SINK, ASSURE THAT THIS, NOW STANDING--	IF ANY SINK, ASSURE THAT	358	1
HOW SICK--TO WAIT--IN ANY PLACE--BUT THINE--	HOW SICK--TO WAIT--IN	368	1
TOO TENDERLY, THAT ANY DOUBT	THE MONTHS HAVE ENDS--	423	7
'TWAS NEEDLESS--ANY SPEAK--	IT WOULD NEVER BE COMMON	430	12
FOR ANY SANTA CLAUS TO REACH	'TWAS JUST THIS TIME,	445	19
ANY--FOR THE PRESS OF SMILING--	SWEET--SAFE--HOUSES--	457	16
AND ANY ONE I KNEW	I WAS THE SLIGHTEST IN	486	15
BLUSHES, IF ANY SEE--	THIS WORLD IS NOT	501	14
OF ANY [UPON A] BUTTERCUP--	HE PARTS HIMSELF--LIKE	517	4
THAN ANY I HAD SEEN--	I TRIED TO THINK A	532	2
THOUGH NEVER YET, IN ANY PORT--	TWO BUTTERFLIES WENT OUT	533	7
NOR ANY NEED OF SURGERY--	IT KNEW NO MEDICINE--	559	3
COULD GIVE THEM ANY BALM--	I MEASURE EVERY GRIEF I	561	20
THAT ANY GAIN--	DELIGHT--BECOMES	572	4
YET ANY PASSING BY	TO INTERRUPT HIS YELLOW	591	12
TO KNOW IF ANY HUMAN EYES WERE NEAR	TO KNOW JUST HOW HE	622	2
AND WISHES--HAD HE ANY--	TO KNOW JUST HOW HE	622	13
NOR HELD UPON--OF [HAS IT ANY] BRIM--	YOU'LL KNOW HER--BY HER	634	20
TOO WIDE FOR ANY NIGHT BUT HEAVEN--	A PRISON GETS TO BE A	652	31
HAVE ANY LIKE MYSELF	HAVE ANY LIKE MYSELF	736	1
HAVE ANY LIKE MYSELF	HAVE ANY LIKE MYSELF	736	9
HAVE ANY LIKE MYSELF	HAVE ANY LIKE MYSELF	736	17
OR SMALL--OR ANY SIZE AT ALL--	YOU SAID THAT I "WAS	738	3
OR ANY [BEFORE THE] HARBOR BE--	I MANY TIMES THOUGHT	739	8
AT ANY OTHER PERIOD--	A LIGHT EXISTS IN SPRING	812	3
WRINKLED ANY SEA,	ONE DAY IS THERE OF THE	814	14
YET WAS NOT THE FOE--OF ANY--	STRUCK, WAS I, NOR YET	925	13
FORBID THAT ANY KNOW--	HOW FAR IS IT TO HEAVEN?	929 V	8
TOO YOUNG THAT ANY SHOULD SUSPECT	A LOSS OF SOMETHING EVER	959	4
I DWELT TOO LOW THAT ANY SEEK--	I WAS A PHEBE--NOTHING	1009	5
TOO SHY, THAT ANY BLAME--	I WAS A PHEBE--NOTHING	1009	6
GRACIOUS NOW TO ME AS ANY--	THREE WEEKS PASSED SINCE	1061	7
BORNE WITHOUT DISSENT OF EITHER [ANY]	THREE WEEKS PASSED SINCE	1061	9
'TIS NOT CONFERRED OF ANY	SUPERIORITY TO FATE	1081	3
THAT ANY OTHER BUY.	A DIAMOND ON THE HAND	1108	8
ARE ANY HOAR [BLEAK] FOR HIM?	THAT ODD OLD MAN IS DEAD	1130	6
WAITS ANY INDURATED MATE	THAT ODD OLD MAN IS DEAD	1130	7
LEST ANY DOUBT THAT WE ARE GLAD THAT THEY WERE BORN TODAY	LEST ANY DOUBT THAT WE	1156	1
IF ANY STRIKE ME ON THE STREET	ALONE AND IN A	1167	17
IF ANY TAKE [SEIZE] MY PROPERTY	ALONE AND IN A	1167	19
UNARMED IF ANY MEET HER	THE PAST IS SUCH A	1203	5
IT WALKED AS WET AS ANY WAVE	LIKE RAIN IT SOUNDED	1235	3
NOT ANY HIGHER STANDS THE GRAVE	NOT ANY HIGHER STANDS	1256	1
NOT ANY NEARER FOR THE CHILD	NOT ANY HIGHER STANDS	1256	3
IN ANY FOREST STIRRED	A WIND THAT ROSE	1259	3
NOR ANY COURSERS LIKE A PAGE	THERE IS NO FRIGATE LIKE	1263	3
NO ASSAULT, NOR ANY MENACE	DEATH'S WAYLAYING NOT	1296	5
HAD NATURE ANY SUPPLE [PLATED / OUTCAST] FACE	THE MUSHROOM IS THE ELF	1298	17
NOT ANY HOUSE THE FLOWERS KEEP--	THE NOTICE THAT IS	1310	5
IF NEWS HAVE ANY HEART	HOW NEWS MUST FEEL WHEN	1319	2
IF NEWS HAVE ANY THOUGHT	HOW NEWS MUST FEEL WHEN	1319	6
IN ANY TONE COMMENSURATE	I NEVER HEAR THAT ONE IS	1323	11
NOT ANY CAN RECALL--	THE SYMPTOM OF THE GALE	1327	10
NOT ANY MORE TO BE LACKED--	NOT ANY MORE TO BE	1344	1
NOT ANY MORE TO BE KNOWN--	NOT ANY MORE TO BE	1344	2
FROM ANY HUMAN [LIVING] SOUL--	YOU CANNOT TAKE ITSELF	1351	2
LIKE ANY PARASITE--	THE MIND LIVES ON THE	1355	2
NOR ANY DEATH--BUT LEST	I HAVE NO LIFE BUT THIS	1398	3
THAN ANY FEATHER SPECIFIED [RATIFIED / CERTIFIED]	WITH PINIONS OF DISDAIN	1431	3
NOT ANY TRANCE OF INDUSTRY	A CHILLY PEACE INFESTS	1443	3
AT ANY GATE BUT WOE'S--	TIME'S WILY CHARGERS	1458	2
FOR ANY GOLDEN FLEECE	ONE OF THE ONES THAT	1466	22
THAT ANY, HEARING, HAD INFERRED	A LITTLE OVERFLOWING	1467	2
NOT ANY VOICE IMPLY [DENOTE] IT HERE	'TIS WHITER THAN AN	1482	5
NOT ANY PORT	ALL THAT I DO	1496	7
NOR ANY FLIGHT [PAUSE]	ALL THAT I DO	1496	8
TO WHOM NOT ANY FACE COHERE [PRESENT / PROPOUND]--	HOW FIRM ETERNITY MUST	1499	7
SUMMER IS SHORTER THAN ANY ONE--	SUMMER IS SHORTER THAN	1506	1
IF ANY WOULD AVENGE	MINE ENEMY IS GROWING	1509	4
AND HAS'NT ANY TAX TO PAY	THE BUTTERFLY UPON THE	1521	3
AND HAS'NT ANY HOME	THE BUTTERFLY UPON THE	1521	4
LIVES HE IN ANY OTHER WORLD	LIVES HE IN ANY OTHER	1557	1
FOR ANY SWEET "COME IN"	THE HEART HAS MANY DOORS	1567	3
NOR ANY LEADER'S GRIM BATON	NO LADDER NEEDS THE BIRD	1574	3
TO TWO--NOT ANY MORE--	THE AUCTIONEER OF	1612	8
NOR ANY DART,	NOT SICKNESS STAINS THE	1613	2
TO ANY HAPPY FLOWER	APPARENTLY WITH NO	1624	2
A CLOVER, ANY TIME, TO HIM,	THE PEDIGREE OF HONEY	1627 V	3
NOT ANY COLOR WILL ENDURE	JUDGEMENT IS JUSTEST	1671	8
NOT ANY SUNNY TONE	NOT ANY SUNNY TONE	1674	1

	FIRST LINE	POEM	LINE
ANY (CONTINUED)			
FROM ANY FERVENT ZONE	NOT ANY SUNNY TONE	1674	2
BY ANY MAN BUT GOD--	TO THEIR APARTMENT DEEP	1701	4
A LAVA STEP AT ANY TIME	VOLCANOES BE IN SICILY	1705	5
ONE CROWN THAT NO ONE SEEKS [NOT ANY SEEK]	ONE CROWN THAT NO ONE	1735	1
NOT ANY HELL.	THE MOST IMPORTANT	1746	4
TO OTHER [ANY] SCENE OR OTHER SOUL	'TWAS HERE MY SUMMER	1756	3
ANYBODY			
LEST ANYBODY FIND--	SO BASHFUL WHEN I SPIED	91	4
FLOWERS--WELL--IF ANYBODY	FLOWERS--WELL--IF	137	1
ANYBODY FIND THE FOUNTAIN	FLOWERS--WELL--IF	137	5
WOULD ANYBODY CARE	ON SUCH A NIGHT, OR SUCH	146	2
WOULD ANYBODY SIGH	ON SUCH A NIGHT, OR SUCH	146	10
IF ANYBODY SNEER--	THE MURMUR OF A BEE	155	8
LEST ANYBODY SPY THE BLOOD	A WOUNDED DEER--LEAPS	165	11
HAS ANYBODY FOUND?	I LOST A WORLD--THE	181	2
CAN ANYBODY TELL?	THOSE FAIR--FICTITIOUS	499	8
ANYBODY'S			
IF ANYBODY'S FRIEND BE DEAD	IF ANYBODY'S FRIEND BE	509	1
ANYONE			
OR FROST, OR DEATH, OR ANYONE--	IF I COULD BRIBE THEM BY	179	5
TO ANYONE BUT GOD--	DEATH IS POTENTIAL TO	548	4
ANYTHING			
NOT ANYTHING IS STALE SO LONG	THE RIDDLE WE CAN GUESS	1222	3
NOT ANYTHING IS KNOWN	HOPE IS A STRANGE	1392	6
ANYWHERE			
IF I COULD FIND IT ANYWHERE	I CANNOT BUY IT--'TIS	840	7
FOR AN OFFENSE NOR HERE NOR THERE [ANYWHERE]	ALONE AND IN A	1167	23
GO WE ANYWHERE	HOW HUMAN NATURE DOTES	1417	12
SUSTAINS HIM [HER] ANYWHERE--	TO HER DERIDED HOME	1586 V	
APART			
THEY PUT US FAR APART--	THEY PUT US FAR APART--	474	1
SO WE MUST MEET APART--	I CANNOT LIVE WITH YOU--	640	45
APART--INTRINSIC--STAND--	OF ALL THE SOULS THAT	664	6
LONG YEARS APART--CAN MAKE NO	LONG YEARS APART--CAN	1383	1
APART, IT NEVER TALKS--	THE SPIRIT LASTS--BUT IN	1576	4
APARTMENT			
ASSASSIN HID IN OUR APARTMENT	ONE NEED NOT BE A	670	15
BUT NO APARTMENT FIND	TOO FEW THE MORNINGS BE,	1186	6
IN CHRYSOPRASE APARTMENTS [APARTMENT] HUNG	THE BUTTERFLY'S	1244	2
TO THEIR APARTMENT DEEP	TO THEIR APARTMENT DEEP	1701	1
APARTMENTS			
IN LOW APARTMENTS IN THE SOD--	SHE HIDETH HER THE LAST	557	7
IN CHRYSOPRASE APARTMENTS [APARTMENT] HUNG	THE BUTTERFLY'S	1244	2
APE			
NOT SATISFIED TO APE THE GREAT IN HIS SIMPLICITY	THAT THIS SHOULD FEEL	1112	5
APOCALYPSE			
BRIDES--AN APOCALYPSE--	"MORNING"--MEANS	300	7
. . . QUICK / SWIFT / WILD] EXPERIMENT [LEGACY / APOCALYPSE / . . .	A LITTLE MADNESS IN THE	1333	5
APOCALYPTIC			
AND THIS--THIS UNSURMISED [APOCALYPTIC] THING--	'TIS WHITER THAN AN	1482 V	9
APOLOGIZE			
WHO'LL APOLOGIZE FOR ME?	I'M THE LITTLE "HEART'S	176	8
TO THE SKIES--APOLOGIZE--	TAKE YOUR HEAVEN FURTHER	388	8
WE APOLOGIZE TO THEE	"HEAVENLY FATHER"--TAKE	1461	7
APOLOGY			
APOLOGY FOR HER	APOLOGY FOR HER	852	1
APOLOGY FOR ME.	APOLOGY FOR HER	852	4
I FELT APOLOGY WERE DUE	NO BRIGADIER THROUGHOUT	1561	13
APOSTACY			
OR PUCK'S APOSTACY.	THE WAY TO KNOW THE	1279	12
APOSTASY			
WITH GAY APOSTASY	HIS ORIENTAL HERESIES	1526	4
APOSTATE			
HAD NATURE AN APOSTATE--[ONE "ISCARIOT" / AN ISCARIOT,]	THE MUSHROOM IS THE ELF	1298	19
APOSTLE			
APOSTLE IS ASKEW!	"SOWN IN DISHONOR"!	62	8
BEHOLD SAID THE APOSTLE	SPEECH IS ONE SYMPTOM OF	1681	7
APPAL			
THAT--CAN APPAL BUT ONE--	A SECRET TOLD--	381	4
APPALLED			
WHEN TOO APPALLED TO STIR--	THE SOUL HAS BANDAGED	512	2
APPALLING			
BEAR WITHIN--APPALLING ORDNANCE,	I HAVE NEVER SEEN	175	5
AND APPALLING MEN--	I HAVE NEVER SEEN	175	8
SINCE THAT APPALLING DAY!	THE ONLY GHOST I EVER	274	16
'TIS SO APPALLING--IT EXHILIRATES--	'TIS SO APPALLING--IT	281	1
OF THE APPALLING TRADE--	THERE'S BEEN A DEATH, IN	389	18
OUTSTARING [DEFYING / APPALLING / ABASHING] MASONRY--	TOO COLD IS THIS	1135	5
WITH INFERENCE APPALLING [ALARMING]	WHO WERE "THE FATHER AND	1258	5
WHAT AN APPALLING BOON!	UPON THE GALLOWS HUNG A	1757 V	8
APPALLS			
'TIS THIS--INVITES--APPALLS--ENDOWS--	THE LOVE A LIFE CAN SHOW	673	13
APPALLS THIS [THAT] TROPIC BREAST--	NO AUTUMN'S INTERCEPTING	1516	2

	FIRST LINE	POEM	LINE
APPALS			
APPALS THAT TRIPOLI	HIS ORIENTAL HERESIES	1526 V	4
APPARATUS			
THIS SUMS THE APPARATUS	PRAYER IS THE LITTLE	437	7
MINOR--APPARATUS--HOPPER OF THE MILL--	LIFE, AND DEATH, AND	706	3
THE APPARATUS OF THE DARK	THE LIGHTNING IS A	1173	7
APPARELED			
APPARELED AS THE NEW	'TWAS A LONG PARTING--	625	10
WHO SO APPARELED HIS ESCAPE--	SOME ARROWS SLAY BUT	1565	3
APPARENT			
OR ORDER, OR APPARENT ACTION [SIGNAL / NOTICE]--	FOUR TREES--UPON A	742	3
WITHOUT APPARENT BURDEN	HIGH FROM THE EARTH I	1723	13
APPARENTLY			
APPARENTLY WITH NO SURPRISE	APPARENTLY WITH NO	1624	1
APPARITION			
AS APPARITION--SUBJECT	THE SOUL'S SUPERIOR	306	11
BEFORE AN APPARITION	TRUST IN THE UNEXPECTED	555	11
BUT, PROUD IN APPARITION--	WHEN I WAS SMALL, A	596	13
AN ORIENT'S APPARITION--	JOY TO HAVE MERITED THE	788	15
APPARITIONS			
BRIGHT KNOTS OF APPARITIONS	OF NEARNESS TO HER	607	15
APPARRELED			
SHOW THEM THIS MEEK APPARRELED THING	DELAYED TILL SHE HAD	58	16
APPEALED			
THE FLOWERS--APPEALED--A TIMID THRONG--	THE BIRDS REPORTED FROM	743	5
APPEALING			
APPEALING TO MYSELF,	HAD I NOT THIS, OR THIS,	904	2
APPEAR			
MAY LESS APPEAR	TO LOVE THEE YEAR BY	434	2
APPEAR--UNTO THE SEA--	I THINK TO LIVE--MAY BE	646	8
MAKE THAT APPEAR--	RENUNCIATION--IS A	745	15
DO LOWLIER--APPEAR--	MY WORTHINESS IS ALL MY	751	4
COMPARISON--APPEAR--	THIS DUST, AND IT'S	936	8
THE GRASS DOES NOT APPEAR AFRAID,	WHAT MYSTERY PERVADES A	1400	9
DOES NOT AT FIRST APPEAR;	THE DISTANCE THAT THE	1742	2
APPEARANCE			
A FIRM APPEARANCE STILL INFLATES	WE DO NOT KNOW THE TIME	1106	5
THOUGH NO APPEARANCE INDICATE--	TO MEND EACH TATTERED	1442	3
APPEARS			
AND AS THE ROSE APPEARS,	I HAVE A BIRD IN SPRING	5	5
SO PLAUSIBLE [TANGIBLE / POSITIVE] BECOMES [APPEARS]	I THINK TO LIVE--MAY BE	646	22
AS ELOQUENT APPEARS--	A LITTLE OVERFLOWING	1467	6
HOW SIMILAR APPEARS--	MORE THAN THE GRAVE IS	1503	6
HOW SLEEK THE WOE APPEARS	SOFTENED BY TIME'S	1738	2
APPEASE			
I PLAY AT RICHES--TO APPEASE	I PLAY AT RICHES--TO	801	1
APPEASED			
THE FRACTION--THAT APPEASED THE HEART	PRECIOUS TO ME--SHE	727	10
AFFLICTION WOULD NOT BE APPEASED--	SEVERER SERVICE OF	786	17
'TWERE NOT APPEASED OF MEN [MAN]	IT WAS A GRAVE, YET BORE	876	8
APPENINE			
OR MISTS--THE APPENINE--	THE THOUGHT BENEATH SO	210	4
DAWN--TO THE TENERIFFE [APPENINE]--	"MORNING"--MEANS	300	2
OUR APPENINE--A KNOLL--	WE SEE--COMPARATIVELY--	534	8
APPETITE			
THIS INSTIGATES AN APPETITE	THAT IT WILL NEVER COME	1741	7
APPLAUD			
'TWAS UNIVERSE--THAT DID APPLAUD [ATTEND]--	LIKE MIGHTY FOOT LIGHTS	595	5
AND YET THE CROWD APPLAUD, BELOW--	YOU'VE SEEN BALLOONS SET	700	11
APPLAUD HIM TO DISCOVER	HIS MANSION IN THE POOL	1379	13
APPLAUSE			
ASSISTANCE--OR APPLAUSE--	THE MOUNTAINS--GROW	757	4
NOR WAS IT FOR APPLAUSE [PARADE / RESULT]--	THE BIRDS BEGUN AT FOUR	783	13
SECURES APPLAUSE	T'IS EASIER TO PITY	1698	5
APPLE			
PUT DOWN THE APPLE, ADAM,	"SIC TRANSIT GLORIA	3	17
FELL FROM AN APPLE TREE!	"SIC TRANSIT GLORIA	3	32
THE APPLE ON THE TREE--	"HEAVEN"--IS WHAT I	239	2
A DROP FELL ON THE APPLE TREE--	A DROP FELL ON THE APPLE	794	1
RUDDY AS THAT COEVAL APPLE	TELL AS A MARKSMAN--WERE	1152	3
THE APPLE IN THE CELLAR SNUG	LIKE BROOMS OF STEEL	1252	10
AND IN CHINTZ [RED / PINK] THE APPLE	I SUPPOSE THE TIME WILL	1381	8
UPON THE APPLE TREE--	ONE OF THE ONES THAT	1466	28
WHOSE APPLE WINTERWORN	FOREVER HONORED BE THE	1570	2
APPLES			
IS JUST A BOUGH OF APPLES--	THE ANGLE OF A LANDSCAPE	375	7
I THOUGHT JUST HOW RED--APPLES WEDGED	'TWAS JUST THIS TIME,	445	9
APPLICATION			
NOW TO THE APPLICATION, TO THE READING OF THE ROLL,	AWAKE YE MUSES NINE,	1	25
APPLIED			
THE WORD APPLIED TO FILL	SHALL I TAKE THEE, THE	1126	10
APPOINTED			
ALONG APPOINTED SANDS--	THE MOON IS DISTANT FROM	429	4
FOR THE APPOINTED BEAM	A PRISON GETS TO BE A	652	6
AND THEY--APPOINTED CREATURES--	WHOLE GULFS--OF RED, AND	658	5
APPOINTED UNTO MEN--	THIS CONSCIOUSNESS THAT	822	8
LIKE TIME'S INSIDIOUS [INVADING	LIKE TIME'S INSIDIOUS	1236	1

	FIRST LINE	POEM	LINE
APPOINTED (CONTINUED)			
/ PRESUMING / APPOINTED / . . .			
APPOINTMENT			
APPOINTMENT STRICTLY KEPT--	YOU TAUGHT ME WAITING	740	2
APPOINTS			
THE LONGEST DAY THAT GOD APPOINTS	THE LONGEST DAY THAT GOD	1769	1
APPRECIATION			
UNCERTAIN GRASP, APPRECIATION	UNCERTAIN LEASE--	857	3
BUT IT'S STILL APPRECIATION	GRATITUDE--IS NOT THE	989	3
APPREHEND			
THE LUXURY TO APPREHEND	THE LUXURY TO APPREHEND	815	1
APPREHENSION			
THE CHIEFEST APPREHENSION	MY WORTHINESS IS ALL MY	751	7
NO APPREHENSION OF ANOTHER	AIR HAS NO RESIDENCE, NO	1060	3
APPREHENSION'S			
NO START [CLICK] IN APPREHENSION'S EAR, . .	I THINK TO LIVE--MAY BE	646	15
APPREHENSIONS			
APPREHENSIONS--ARE GOD'S INTRODUCTIONS-- .	BY MY WINDOW HAVE I FOR	797	24
APPRENTICED			
AS JUST APPRENTICED TO THE AIR--	SHE'S HAPPY, WITH A NEW	535	4
APPROACH			
APPROACH THAT TREE WITH CAUTION, THEN UP IT BOLDLY CLIMB,	AWAKE YE MUSES NINE,	1	35
AND WE APPROACH [ACCOST] HIM--STERN-- . .	THE LIGHTNING PLAYETH--	630	4
APPROACH ENCOURAGES.	WHO OCCUPIES THIS HOUSE?	892	8
UPON HIS RARE APPROACH--	GO SLOW, MY SOUL, TO	1297	2
AND DIM APPROACH	DEATH IS THE SUPPLE	1445	6
WHEN YOU APPROACH THE PLACE--	'TIS WHITER THAN AN	1482	4
APPROACHED			
NO PEDDLER'S CART--APPROACHED--	A HOUSE UPON THE HIGHT--	399	4
APPROACHED [POSSESSED]--THE AMBER FLITS [MOVES]--A LITTLE--	DELIGHT--BECOMES	572	7
APPROACHED--AND SPURNED THE NARROW GRASS-- .	I THINK I WAS ENCHANTED	593	11
APPROACHING			
TILL HIS BEST STEP APPROACHING	I SING TO USE THE	850	5
APPROPRIATE			
APPROPRIATE CREATURES TO HER CHANGE . . .	THE MURMURING OF BEES,	1115	9
APPROVING			
FOR AN APPROVING GOD.	APPARENTLY WITH NO	1624	8
APRICOT			
MIGHT IT AN APRICOT!	MY HEART UPON A LITTLE	1027	4
APRIL			
SOLVE OUR APRIL DAY!	I CANT TELL YOU--BUT YOU	65	4
"CHARMING APRIL DAY"!	I CANT TELL YOU--BUT YOU	65	16
WHEN APRIL WOODS ARE RED.	WHOSE ARE THE LITTLE	142	28
AMONG THE APRIL WOODS!	IF I COULD BRIBE THEM BY	179	9
TO APRIL--HURRIES ON--	YOU'LL KNOW HER--BY HER	634	24
AN APRIL BUT BEGUN--	THE ROBIN IS THE ONE	828	8
BUT DURING MARCH AND APRIL	SPRING IS THE PERIOD	844	5
ABSENT PLACE--AN APRIL DAY--	ABSENT PLACE--AN APRIL	927	1
WHO KNOCKS? THAT APRIL.	DEAR MARCH--COME IN--	1320	18
COVERT--IN APRIL--	PINK--SMALL--AND	1332	3
THE ORATOR OF APRIL	HIS MANSION IN THE POOL	1379	7
BONNET [JACKET] DUE IN APRIL--	NOT AT HOME TO CALLERS	1590	3
BETWEEN THE MARCH AND APRIL LINE--	THE SADDEST NOISE, THE	1764	5
APRILS			
I SIGHT THE APRILS--	SPRING COMES ON THE	1042	2
APRON			
THO' SHE WEAR A SILVER APRON--	THO' MY DESTINY BE	163	3
BUT--IF I STAINED MY APRON--	OVER THE FENCE--	251	6
BUT SAY MY APRON BRING THE STICKS	ALTHOUGH I PUT AWAY HIS	366	28
SO I LOOP MY APRON, AGAINST THE MAJESTY . .	I'M SAYING EVERY DAY	373	12
AND PAST MY APRON--AND MY BELT	I STARTED EARLY--TOOK MY	520	11
NATURE WAS IN AN OPAL [HER BERYL / HER BLUEST] APRON,	IT SOUNDED AS IF THE	1397	7
APRONS			
AND STILL THE APRONS FLY, [SCENE PREVAILS] .	SHE SWEEPS WITH	219	10
APTITUDE			
AN APTITUDE FOR BIRD--	I'VE DROPPED MY BRAIN--	1046	12
THE APTITUDE TO FLY	MY COCOON TIGHTENS--	1099	6
AQUATIC			
LAUNCH IT--THE AQUATIC	LIFT IT--WITH THE	1348	3
ARABLE			
IS AS ARABLE AS SPRING	WINTER UNDER CULTIVATION	1707	2
ARAGON SEE ARRAGON			
ARARAT'S			
BUT ARARAT'S A LEGEND--NOW--	THE WINTERS ARE SO SHORT	403	15
ARARATS			
ARARATS--WE TOOK--	WE TALKED WITH EACH	1473	8
ARBITRATE			
WHAT RIGHT HAD FIELDS TO ARBITRATE . . .	I WORKED FOR CHAFF AND	1269	3
ARC			
UPON A BASELESS ARC--	IT SIFTS FROM LEADEN	311	V
EXISTENCE'S WHOLE ARC, [WHOLE EYE / WHOLE RIM / SURMISE] FILLED UP,	I'M CEDED--I'VE STOPPED	508	12
SHE STAKED HER FEATHERS--GAINED AN ARC-- .	SHE STAKED HER FEATHERS	798	1
OVER THE ARC OF THE BIRD--	UNDER THE LIGHT, YET	949	10
UPON AN ARC OF WHITE.	A SPIDER SEWED AT NIGHT	1138	3
BUT THE ARC OF A LOVER'S CONJECTURE . . .	WE SHALL FIND THE CUBE	1484	3
AN ARC ALIKE INSCRUTABLE	THE BAT IS DUN, WITH	1575	7

	FIRST LINE	POEM	LINE
ARCH			
THROUGH THIS LOW ARCH OF FLESH--	I ROSE--BECAUSE HE SANK	616	13
ARCHANGEL'S			
THE SLOW--ARCHANGEL'S SYLLABLES	ON THIS LONG STORM THE	194	11
ARCHANGELS			
AS THEY SAY POLITE ARCHANGELS	I CANT TELL YOU--BUT YOU	65	11
ARCHER'S			
SPED BY AN ARCHER'S BOW.	I'VE GOT AN ARROW HERE.	1729	7
ARCHITECT			
THE SITE--OF IT--BY ARCHITECT	HEAVEN IS SO FAR OF THE	370	3
EDIFICE [ARCHITECT] OF OCEAN	FORTITUDE INCARNATE	1217	9
ARCHLY			
HOW ARCHLY SPARED THE HEAVEN "TO COME"-- .	THE MOON UPON HER FLUENT	1528	V
ARCHNESS			
VOUCHES, WITH HYPERBOLIC ARCHNESS-- . . .	GOD IS A DISTANT--	357	7
ARCS			
WORLDS SCOOP THEIR ARCS--	SAFE IN THEIR ALABASTER	216	V
ARCTIC			
AS IF SOME LITTLE ARCTIC FLOWER	AS IF SOME LITTLE ARCTIC	180	1
OR ARCTIC CREATURES, DIMLY STIRRED--	LIKE FLOWERS, THAT HEARD	513	7
FORSAKES THE ARCTIC RACE	WHEN THE ASTRONOMER	851	4
RESTORED IN ARCTIC CONFIDENCE	A WIND THAT ROSE	1259	8
ARCTURUS			
"ARCTURUS" IS HIS OTHER NAME--	"ARCTURUS" IS HIS OTHER	70	1
ARDENT			
. . . BONNIE / SPACIOUS / TROPIC / ARDENT / FRIENDLY / MAGIC / . . .	THE BIBLE IS AN ANTIQUE	1545	13
FOR MANY AN ARDENT [A FRUITLESS] YEAR. . .	THE DISTANCE THAT THE	1742	4
ARDOR			
FOR ARDOR OR FOR TEARS, ...	A LITTLE OVERFLOWING	1467	3
ARDUOUS			
MORE ARDUOUS [DIFFICULT] THAN BALLS-- . .	MY PORTION IS DEFEAT--	639	6
MORE ARDUOUS THERE IS--	HIS MIND LIKE FABRICS OF	1446	6
AREA			
IT'S INSUFFICIENT AREA	THE HEART HAS NARROW	928	7
A TOO MINUTE AREA	THIS DUST, AND IT'S	936	6
AND AREA SUPERIOR	TWO LENGTHS HAS EVERY	1295	3
ARGENT			
THE TERRITORY ARGENT--THAT	THE RED--BLAZE--IS THE	469	7
ARGUE			
I NEED NO FURTHER ARGUE--	DO PEOPLE MOULDER	432	13
I ARGUE [OFFER] THEE	THAT I DID ALWAYS LOVE	549	6
ARGUED			
HE PREACHED UPON [ABOUT] "BREADTH" TILL IT ARGUED HIM [WE . . .	HE PREACHED UPON	1207	1
ARGUES			
ARGUES THE ASTER STILL--	LIKE HER THE SAINTS	60	10
DEATH DOUBTS IT--ARGUES [REASONS] FROM THE GROUND--	DEATH IS A DIALOGUE	976	5
ARGUMENT			
THE STAR'S ETRUSCAN ARGUMENT	THE MOON UPON HER FLUENT	1528	3
ARGUMENTS			
SUCH THRENODIES [EXTACIES / REVENUES / ARGUMENTS] OF PEARL--	YOU'LL KNOW HER--BY HER	634	26
ARID			
THERE IS AN ARID PLEASURE--	THERE IS AN ARID	782	1
HOARY [EVIL / RIGID / WRINKLED / ARID / SHRUNKEN] THE FRUITION	FORTITUDE INCARNATE	1217	7
RATHER ARID DELIGHT	RATHER ARID DELIGHT	1679	1
ARISE			
DO NOT ARISE AND PLAY	OF ALL THE SOUNDS	321	18
AND OUR'S--A KINSMANSHIP EXPRESS [EXIST / SUBSIST / ARISE]--	A PRISON GETS TO BE A	652	3
THAT ARISE AND SET ABOUT US--	DRAMA'S VITALLEST	741	2
THE BIRD [DAY] WOULD NOT ARISE--	MY FAITH IS LARGER THAN	766	10
AND I ARISE--AND IN MY DREAM--	WHAT I SEE NOT, I BETTER	939	9
ARISE THIS SPECTRAL CANTICLE	FURTHER IN SUMMER THAN	1068	11
ARISE AND EVANESCE	WHAT TENEMENTS OF CLOVER	1338	6
ARISTOCRACY			
AH ARISTOCRACY!	FOR EVERY BIRD A NEST--	143	8
IS ARISTOCRACY--	THE PEDIGREE OF HONEY	1627	V 4
ARISTOCRAT			
A FRAIL [FLEET / BRIEF] ARISTOCRAT OF TIME .	SHE SPED AS PETALS OF A	991	3
ARITHMETIC			
ARITHMETIC OF HIM--	THE DAYS THAT WE CAN	1184	8
ARKS			
ARKS OF REPRIEVE HE OFFERED [OPENED] TO US--	WE TALKED WITH EACH	1473	7
ARM			
UNTO THE SHEPHERD'S ARM!	GOING TO HEAVEN!	79	10
IN WHICH IT CAUTIOUS ARM, ...	A WOUNDED DEER--LEAPS	165	10
AND WHOM HE FOUNDETH, WITH HIS ARM . . .	THEY LEAVE US WITH THE	350	5
THOSE--DANGLE EASY--ON MY ARM, ...	PERHAPS I ASKED TOO	352	6
HAST THOU NO ARM FOR ME?	AT LEAST--TO PRAY--IS	502	8
FURTHER THAN ARM COULD STRETCH	UNDER THE LIGHT, YET	949	5
BY ARM OF CHIVALRY.	THE FLAKE THE WIND	1361	4
BUT ARM IN ARM WITH TOUCH, YET TOUCH . . .	THE SPIRIT LASTS--BUT IN	1576	7
BUT ARM IN ARM WITH TOUCH, YET TOUCH . . .	THE SPIRIT LASTS--BUT IN	1576	7
NOR PUT HIS SPACIOUS ARM AROUND THEE . . .	BACK FROM THE CORDIAL	1625	3
ARMED			
CAN PIERCE AN ARMED MAN--	THERE IS A WORD	8	3

	FIRST LINE	POEM	LINE
ARMED (CONTINUED)			
WILL EMERGE [DECAMP] BUT ONCE--AND DUMB [ARMED]--	"SECRETS" IS A DAILY	1385	11
ARMIES			
WAS CROWDED DENSE WITH ARMIES--	THE SUN KEPT STOOPING--	152	9
TWO ARMIES, LOVE AND CERTAINTY	DYING! TO BE AFRAID OF	831	11
THEIR ARMIES ARE NO MORE.	THEIR BARRICADE AGAINST	1471	4
ARMS			
THAN ARMS, OR PEDIGREE.	I HAD SOME THINGS THAT I	116	12
HELD OF THOSE BRASS ARMS--	IF YOUR NERVE, DENY YOU	292	7
HER MERRY ARMS, HALF DROPT--	SHE LAY AS IF AT PLAY	369	5
THE MIDNIGHT'S DUSKY ARMS	THE SUNRISE RUNS FOR	710	13
WITH ARMS OF STEEL AT EITHER SIDE--	FAITH--IS THE PIERLESS	915	7
"ARMS OF MINE--SUFFICIENT PHAETON--	"UNTO ME?" I DO NOT KNOW	964	7
THE SPRY [LONG] ARMS OF THE WIND	THE SPRY ARMS OF THE	1103	1
NAY--LIFT THEMSELVES--FAME HAS NO ARMS--	ABOVE OBLIVION'S TIDE	1531	3
AROMA			
SORROW [AROMA]--NOW--IS POLITE [COURTEOUS]--AND STAYS--	SUMMER IS SHORTER THAN	1506	5
AROMATIC			
AROMATIC--LOW--	PINK--SMALL--AND	1332	2
AROSE			
THE MORNING LIT--THE BIRDS AROSE--	AN AWFUL TEMPEST MASHED	198	10
HOW WEAKNESS PASSED--OR FORCE--AROSE--	IF ANY SINK, ASSURE THAT	358	4
AND WISHFULNESS IN ME AROSE--	I HAD NO CAUSE TO BE	542	11
A JEALOUSY FOR HER AROSE	THE LAST NIGHT THAT SHE	1100	15
AROUND			
THE BOBOLINKS AROUND THE THRONE	WE SHOULD NOT MIND SO	81	11
DANCING AROUND THE SUN	FOR EVERY BIRD A NEST--	143	17
AROUND THIS QUIET COURTIER	WAIT TILL THE MAJESTY OF	171	9
AROUND IT'S FOREHEAD BOUND.	I LOST A WORLD--THE	181	4
HE PUT THE BELT AROUND MY LIFE--	HE PUT THE BELT AROUND	273	1
ARRANGED THEMSELVES AROUND THEIR PRINCE	THE DAY CAME SLOW--TILL	304	11
THAT HURRIED ALL AROUND [ABROAD]--	A BIRD CAME DOWN THE	328	10
THE EYES AROUND--HAD WRUNG THEM DRY--	I HEARD A FLY BUZZ--WHEN	465	5
DROP INTO TUNE--AROUND THE THRONE--	BETTER--THAN MUSIC! FOR	503	24
AND SPACE STARES ALL AROUND--	IT WAS NOT DEATH, FOR I	510	18
AROUND YOUR FIRESIDE--	ENDOW THE LIVING--WITH	521	4
IF I BELIEVED [SUPPOSED] GOD LOOKED AROUND,	I PRAYED, AT FIRST, A	576	5
AROUND A PILE OF MOUNTAINS--	I LIKE TO SEE IT LAP	585	5
AROUND--ACROSS--UPON IT--	THERE IS A PAIN--SO	599	5
I WATCHED THE MOON AROUND THE HOUSE	I WATCHED THE MOON	629	1
AND SO AROUND THE WORDS I WENT--	IF HE WERE LIVING--DARE	734	3
IT MIGHT BE FAMINE--ALL AROUND--	GOD GAVE A LOAF TO EVERY	791	9
THE STARS EXPRESS AROUND	THE SUN AND MOON MUST	871	2
THE SEASONS PLAYED AROUND HIS KNEES	THE MOUNTAIN SAT UPON	975	5
TILL WHEN AROUND A HIGHT	I HAD A DAILY BLISS	1057	5
A SOFT SEA WASHED AROUND THE HOUSE	A SOFT SEA WASHED AROUND	1198	1
AND NATURE LOOKS AROUND--	THE SYMPTOM OF THE GALE	1327	14
WHERE WATERS COOL AROUND THE MOSSES CRAWL--	THESE FEVERED DAYS--TO	1441	2
UNTIL THEY LOOK AROUND	FACTS BY OUR SIDE ARE	1497	2
THE TIGHTENING THE SOIL AROUND	YOU CANNOT MAKE	1508	3
AROUND US, EVERY DAY--	WITCHCRAFT WAS HUNG, IN	1583	4
NOR PUT HIS SPACIOUS ARM AROUND THEE	BACK FROM THE CORDIAL	1625	3
ARRAGON			
MEET ME IN ARRAGON--	I'M SAYING EVERY DAY	373	28
ARRAIGN			
ARRAIGN THE SUNNY BREVITY	THIS DOCILE ONE INTER	1752	3
ARRAIGNS			
ARRAIGNS IT AS IT SINGS.	NO LADDER NEEDS THE BIRD	1574	4
ARRANGE			
PATTIE, ARRANGE THE STARS;	"SIC TRANSIT GLORIA	3	14
HOW SHALL WE ARRANGE IT--	WE DONT CRY--TIM AND I,	196	25
DRILL SILENTLY [ARRANGE THE HEART] FOR HEAVEN--	TO HELP OUR BLEAKER	1064	4
ARRANGED			
ARRANGED THEMSELVES AROUND THEIR PRINCE	THE DAY CAME SLOW--TILL	304	11
HIS PALLID FURNITURE ARRANGED	IT CAME AT LAST BUT	1230	3
ARRAY			
ONE IN THE RED ARRAY--	SLEEP IS SUPPOSED TO BE	13	14
NOR SO SERENE ARRAY--	THERE IS A MORN BY MEN	24	15
WIND AND SUN--WILT THEE ARRAY!	POOR LITTLE HEART!	192	12
IN MEEK ARRAY--DISPLAY YOU--	I'LL CLUTCH--AND CLUTCH	427	21
CIRCUMFERENCE--DECAY [ARRAY]--	AN IGNORANCE A SUNSET	552	4
THE FINE--IMPALPABLE ARRAY--	THE TINT I CANNOT TAKE--	627	5
A BUTTERCUP'S ARRAY--	PRECIOUS TO ME--SHE	727	8
REMOTE--HER BEST ARRAY--	THE BIRDS REPORTED FROM	743	10
THE LOVE, THO, WILL ARRAY [INSTRUCT] ME RIGHT	FITTER TO SEE HIM, I MAY	968	21
WILL SO DISPLAY [ARRAY]	HOW DESTITUTE IS HE	1477	6
ARRAYED			
IN HOMELY INDUSTRY ARRAYED [ATTIRED]--	THE BIRDS BEGUN AT FOUR	783	11
ARRAYS			
IN AUTHORIZED ARRAYS--	WHOLE GULFS--OF RED, AND	658	6
ARREST			
TOO DISTANT TO ARREST THE FEET	THIS IS THE PLACE THEY	1264	5
IT'S SOUNDLESS TRAVELS JUST ARREST	HOW SOFT A CATERPILLAR	1448	5
ARRESTED			
ARRESTED IT--BEFORE--	THIS WAS A POET--IT IS	448	8
TILL ARRESTED [DISCOVERED] HERE	HAD WE KNOWN THE TON SHE	1124 V	4

	FIRST LINE	POEM	LINE
ARRESTLESS			
ARRESTLESS AS INVISIBLE--	IT IS A LONESOME GLEE--	774	7
ARRIVE			
WILL ARRIVE TO ME!	BEFORE THE ICE IS IN THE	37	8
ARRIVED			
WITHELD TO THE ARRIVED [DEBARRED / DENIED]--	CRISIS IS SWEET AND YET	1416 V	4
ARROGANCE			
DECADES OF ARROGANCE BETWEEN	A CLOCK STOPPED--	287	16
FOR ARROGANCE OF THEM--	OF BRONZE--AND BLAZE--	290	13
WAS EVER IDLENESS [ARROGANCE] LIKE THIS?	A LONG--LONG SLEEP--A	654	5
ARROGANT			
NOT SO ARROGANT--THIS NOON--	THESE--SAW VISIONS--	758	11
THEIR [THIS] ARROGANT CAMPAIGN--	A WILD BLUE SKY ABREAST	1415	8
ARROGANTLY			
SHUTS ARROGANTLY--IN THE GRAVE--	THE TINT I CANNOT TAKE--	627	23
ARROW			
UPON THINE ARROW HANG!	A DAY! HELP! HELP!	42	8
COULD [CAN] HOLD AN ARROW--TOO--	FOR LARGEST WOMAN'S	309	4
THAN THINE OLD ARROW IS A SHOT	DYING! TO BE AFRAID OF	831	4
TELL HIS ARROW SENT--	TELL AS A MARKSMAN--WERE	1152	23
OF RETROSPECT THE ARROW	TO MAKE ROUTINE A	1196	5
I'VE GOT AN ARROW HERE.	I'VE GOT AN ARROW HERE.	1729	1
BY BUT A SIMPLE ARROW	I'VE GOT AN ARROW HERE.	1729	6
ARROWS			
SOME ARROWS SLAY BUT WHOM THEY STRIKE--	SOME ARROWS SLAY BUT	1565	1
ARROWS ENAMORED OF HIS HEART [BREAST]--	ARROWS ENAMORED OF HIS	1629	1
ART			
THE ONLY TRADE [ART] THEY KNOW--	A BURDOCK--CLAWED MY	229	8
BEYOND THE ART TO EARN--	OF ALL THE SOUNDS	321	10
NOR ANY KNOW [KNEW] I KNOW THE ART	I CANNOT DANCE UPON MY	326	17
MY ART, A SUMMER DAY--HAD PATRONS--	WHEN DIAMONDS ARE A	397	6
'TIS THE ART, MOST OF ALL,	KNOWS HOW TO FORGET!	433	3
HAD WE THE ART OF BOARDS	MYSELF WAS FORMED--A	488	6
HAD I THE ART TO STUN MYSELF	I WOULD NOT PAINT--A	505	23
SHOULD BE THE ART [EXCLUSIVELY]--TO SAVE--	THE PROVINCE OF THE	539	2
SOME [MEN] SEEK IN ART--THE ART OF PEACE--	THE MARTYR POETS--DID	544	8
SOME [MEN] SEEK IN ART--THE ART OF PEACE--	THE MARTYR POETS--DID	544	8
NO OTHER ART--WOULD DO--	MY PERIOD HAD COME FOR	564	2
NOR LIKE HIMSELF--THE ART	IT WOULD HAVE STARVED A	612	13
HAD I ART--	ME FROM MYSELF--TO	642	2
ART OF SNOW--OR TRICK OF LILY	HER SWEET TURN TO LEAVE	649	15
YET [BUT] HAVE NO ART TO SAY--	"NATURE" IS WHAT WE SEE	668	10
HAVE I THE ART TO SAY--	A THOUGHT WENT UP MY	701	8
FOR I HAVE BUT THE POWER [ART] TO KILL,	MY LIFE HAD STOOD--A	754	23
WANT--IS A MEAGRE ART	NONE CAN EXPERIENCE	771	5
ONE ART TO RECOGNIZE, MUST BE,	HER GRACE IS ALL SHE HAS	810	3
ANOTHER ART, TO PRAISE.	HER GRACE IS ALL SHE HAS	810	4
TO OWN THE ART WITHIN THE SOUL	TO OWN THE ART WITHIN	855	1
WHEN ONCE THE ART IS OUT--	WHEN THEY COME BACK--IF	1080	4
WITH HIM THE SKILL [RIGHT / ART] REMAIN	ELIJAH'S WAGON KNEW NO	1254 V	6
A UNIVERSE'S UTTER ART	UPON HIS SADDLE SPRUNG A	1600 V	7
ARTERIAL			
ON FINE--ARTERIAL CANVAS--	THE OUTER--FROM THE	451	13
ARTERY			
THE BUNG OUT--OF [A LEAKAGE IN] AN ARTERY--	ONE ANGUISH--IN A CROWD	565	11
IT'S SINGLE [GIANT] ARTERY--	EMPTY MY HEART, OF THEE	587	2
AN ARTERY--UPON THE HILL--	THE NAME--OF IT--IS	656	3
WITH ARTERY AND VEIN--	OH GIVE IT MOTION--DECK	1527	2
ARTICLE			
LIKE FALLOW ARTICLE--	THE BAT IS DUN, WITH	1575	2
ARTICLES			
WITH ARTICLES OF CLAIM	ALONE AND IN A	1167	10
LIKE PARAGRAPHS [ARTICLES] OF WIND	WE LIKE A HAIRBREADTH	1175	4
ARTIFICE			
TOWARD ARTIFICE OF TIME--OR MEN--	MY SOUL--ACCUSED ME--AND	753	6
THE ARTIFICE [MYSTERY] OF STRENGTH--	NOT TO DISCOVER WEAKNESS	1054	2
ARTIFICIAL			
IN CUPS OF ARTIFICIAL DROWSE	BEREAVED OF ALL, I WENT	784	13
ARTILLERY			
ONE MUST TO THINE ARTILLERY	DYING! TO BE AFRAID OF	831	2
ARTISAN			
AND ARTISAN LIES [SMALL ESTATE STANDS--] STILL--	DEW--IS THE FRESHET IN	1097	4
ARTISANS			
THEN STILLS IT'S ARTISANS [MYRMIDONS]--LIKE GHOSTS [SWANS]--	IT SIFTS FROM LEADEN	311	19
ARTIST			
ARTIST--WHO DREW ME SO--	THE MURMUR OF A BEE	155	14
THE SPIDER AS AN ARTIST	THE SPIDER AS AN ARTIST	1275	1
ARTISTS			
ARTISTS WRESTLED HERE!	ARTISTS WRESTLED HERE!	110	1
ARTLESS			
THEIR ARTLESS CURRENCY--	THE MERCHANT OF THE	1131	8
ARTS			
EASIEST OF ARTS, THEY SAY	KNOWS HOW TO FORGET!	433 V	
AS			
AND AS THE SUMMER NEARS--	I HAVE A BIRD IN SPRING	5	4
AND AS THE ROSE APPEARS,	I HAVE A BIRD IN SPRING	5	5
AND AS OFT A CRANNY	FREQUENTLY THE WOODS ARE	6	7
PEDESTRIAN ONCE--AS WE--	THE FEET OF PEOPLE	7	12

AS (CONTINUED)

	FIRST LINE	POEM	LINE
HE STOOD AS NEAR	I NEVER TOLD THE BURIED	11	5
AS STOOD YOU HERE--	I NEVER TOLD THE BURIED	11	6
WHETHER AS [WHILE] I PONDER	I NEVER TOLD THE BURIED	11	16
THE OTHER, AS A BIRD HER NEST,	ONE SISTER HAVE I IN OUR	14	7
SHE DID NOT SING AS WE DID--	ONE SISTER HAVE I IN OUR	14	9
AS BUMBLE BEE OF JUNE.	ONE SISTER HAVE I IN OUR	14	12
AS IF THE STARS SOME SUMMER NIGHT	THERE IS A MORN BY MEN	24	16
JUST AS THE DUSK WAS BROWN	ADRIFT! A LITTLE BOAT	30	6
JUST AS THE DAWN WAS RED	ADRIFT! A LITTLE BOAT	30	10
FOR SUCH AS THEE TO DIE!	NOBODY KNOWS THIS LITTLE	35	12
TO BE RECEIVED AS HIGH--	WHEN I COUNT THE SEEDS	40	6
FROM SUCH A COMMON BALL AS THIS	A DAY! HELP! HELP!	42	3
FROM MARSHALLINGS AS SIMPLE	A DAY! HELP! HELP!	42	5
I NEVER LOST AS MUCH BUT TWICE,	I NEVER LOST AS MUCH BUT	49	1
FAR--AS THE EAST FROM EVEN--	TAKEN FROM MEN--THIS	53	9
DIM--AS THE BORDER STAR--	TAKEN FROM MEN--THIS	53	10
AS IT HAS USUAL DONE--	IF I SHOULD DIE,	54	6
IF BIRDS SHOULD BUILD AS EARLY	IF I SHOULD DIE,	54	7
AND BEES AS BUSTLING GO--	IF I SHOULD DIE,	54	8
AND TRADES AS BRISKLY FLY--	IF I SHOULD DIE,	54	14
BY CHIVALRIES AS TINY,	BY CHIVALRIES AS TINY,	55	1
EVANGELISTS [AS GENESIS] RECORD	A LITTLE EAST OF JORDAN,	59	2
MARTIAL AS SHE!	LIKE HER THE SAINTS	60	3
THE ROBINS STAND AS THICK TODAY	SOME RAINBOW--COMING	64	13
AS FLAKES OF SNOW STOOD [DID] YESTERDAY--	SOME RAINBOW--COMING	64	14
AS THEY SAY POLITE ARCHANGELS	I CANT TELL YOU--BUT YOU	65	11
AS HE DEFEATED--DYING--	SUCCESS IS COUNTED	67	9
BETTER AS THE DAISY	GLOWING IS HER BONNET,	72	5
AS IF THE "RESURRECTION"	A LADY RED--AMID THE	74	15
THEN SANK AS GAILY AS A TURK	SHE DIED AT PLAY,	75	4
THEN SANK AS GAILY AS A TURK	SHE DIED AT PLAY,	75	4
HER VESTMENTS AS THE SILVER FLEECE--	SHE DIED AT PLAY,	75	8
HER COUNTENANCE AS SPRAY.	SHE DIED AT PLAY,	75	9
BRED AS WE, AMONG THE MOUNTAINS,	EXULTATION IS THE GOING	76	5
AS SURE AS FLOCKS GO HOME AT NIGHT	GOING TO HEAVEN!	79	9
AS SURE AS FLOCKS GO HOME AT NIGHT	GOING TO HEAVEN!	79	9
HEART, NOT SO HEAVY AS MINE	HEART, NOT SO HEAVY AS	83	1
AS IT PASSED MY WINDOW	HEART, NOT SO HEAVY AS	83	3
IT WAS AS IF A BOBOLINK	HEART, NOT SO HEAVY AS	83	9
IT WAS AS IF A CHIRPING BROOK	HEART, NOT SO HEAVY AS	83	13
AS BY THE DEAD WE LOVE TO SIT,	AS BY THE DEAD WE LOVE	88	1
AS FOR THE LOST WE GRAPPLE	AS BY THE DEAD WE LOVE	88	3
SAUNTERED AS SOFT AWAY!	WITHIN MY REACH!	90	5
CHEERFUL--AS TO THE VILLAGE--	WENT UP A YEAR THIS	93	5
TRANQUIL--AS TO REPOSE--	WENT UP A YEAR THIS	93	6
CHASTENED--AS TO THE CHAPEL	WENT UP A YEAR THIS	93	7
AS WE RIDE GRAND ALONG!	ONE DIGNITY DELAYS FOR	98	8
IS THERE SUCH A THING AS "DAY"?	WILL THERE REALLY BE A	101	2
IF I WERE AS TALL AS THEY?	WILL THERE REALLY BE A	101	4
IF I WERE AS TALL AS THEY?	WILL THERE REALLY BE A	101	4
IT IS AS IF A HUNDRED DRUMS	I HAVE A KING, WHO DOES	103	8
FEELING AS IF THEIR PILLOW HEARD,	WHERE I HAVE LOST, I	104	7
FORGIVE US, IF AS DAYS DECLINE--	THE DAISY FOLLOWS SOFT	106	8
IN RAGS MYSTERIOUS AS THESE	IN RAGS MYSTERIOUS AS	117	1
SMILING, AS THEY REQUEST AN ALMS--	IN RAGS MYSTERIOUS AS	117	5
AS WATCHERS HANG UPON THE EAST,	AS WATCHERS HANG UPON	121	1
AS BEGGARS REVEL AT A FEAST	AS WATCHERS HANG UPON	121	2
AS BROOKS IN DESERTS BABBLE SWEET	AS WATCHERS HANG UPON	121	4
AS THAT SAME WATCHER, WHEN THE EAST	AS WATCHERS HANG UPON	121	7
AS SLOW HER FLAMBEAUX BURN AWAY	A SOMETHING IN A	122	2
I W'D AS SOON ATTEMPT TO WARM	I BRING AN UNACCUSTOMED	132	11
AS CHILDREN BID THE GUEST "GOOD NIGHT"	AS CHILDREN BID THE	133	1
AS CHILDREN CAPER WHEN THEY WAKE	AS CHILDREN BID THE	133	5
AS OF BRIAR AND LEAF DISPLAYED	PIGMY SERAPHS--GONE	138	10
A FURTIVE LOOK YOU KNOW AS WELL--	AN ALTERED LOOK ABOUT	140	14
BLESS GOD, HE WENT AS SOLDIERS,	BLESS GOD, HE WENT AS	147	1
SHE WENT AS QUIET AS THE DEW	SHE WENT AS QUIET AS THE	149	1
SHE WENT AS QUIET AS THE DEW	SHE WENT AS QUIET AS THE	149	1
SHE DROPT AS SOFTLY AS A STAR	SHE WENT AS QUIET AS THE	149	5
SHE DROPT AS SOFTLY AS A STAR	SHE WENT AS QUIET AS THE	149	5
BOLD AS [BOLDER THAN] A BRIGAND!	DUST IS THE ONLY SECRET	153	11
UNNOTICED AS A SINGLE DEW	EXCEPT TO HEAVEN, SHE IS	154	7
CONSCIOUS--AS OLD NAPOLEON,	A LITTLE BREAD--A CRUST	159	5
THEREFORE, AS ONE RETURNED, I FEEL,	JUST LOST, WHEN I WAS	160	7
SHE LOOKS DOWN JUST AS OFTEN	MAMA NEVER FORGETS HER	164	3
AND JUST AS TENDERLY	MAMA NEVER FORGETS HER	164	4
AS WHEN HER LITTLE MORTAL NEST	MAMA NEVER FORGETS HER	164	5
AS THEN TRANSPORTED ME!	I MET A KING THIS	166	20
AS BLIND MEN LEARN THE SUN!	TO LEARN THE TRANSPORT	167	2
IT IS JUST AS WELL!	IF THE FOOLISH, CALL	168	4
AS IF THE LITTLE EBON BOX	IN EBON BOX, WHEN YEARS	169	19
AS AN EVENING WEST,	PORTRAITS ARE TO DAILY	170	2
AND YET, AS POOR AS I,	'TIS SO MUCH JOY! 'TIS	172	3
AND YET, AS POOR AS I,	'TIS SO MUCH JOY! 'TIS	172	3
AS IF SOME LITTLE ARCTIC FLOWER	AS IF SOME LITTLE ARCTIC	180	1
I SAY, AS IF THIS LITTLE FLOWER	AS IF SOME LITTLE ARCTIC	180	9
A BLACK--AS OF A SPECTRE'S CLOAK	AN AWFUL TEMPEST MASHED	198	3
LONG AGO AS CHRIST AND PETER--	HE FORGOT--AND I--	203	3
WERE USELESS AS NEXT MORNING'S SUN--	I SHOULD NOT DARE TO	205	15

		FIRST LINE	POEM	LINE
AS	(CONTINUED)			
	AS LACES JUST REVEAL THE SURGE--	THE THOUGHT BENEATH SO	210	3
	AS THE FAINTING BEE--	COME SLOWLY--EDEN!	211	4
	MUCH AS FORMERLY?	DID THE HAREBELL LOOSE	213	4
	AS "A FATHER"--IN THE SKY--	WHAT IS--"PARADISE"--	215	12
	AS NEW ENGLAND USED TO BE!	WHAT IS--"PARADISE"--	215	18
	SOUNDLESS AS DOTS--ON A DISC OF SNOW--	SAFE IN THEIR ALABASTER	216	V
	WILL SUIT ME JUST AS WELL--	I CAME TO BUY A SMILE--	223	4
	JUST AS THE NIGHT KEEPS FETCHING STARS	I'VE NOTHING ELSE--TO	224	3
	AS SHOULD SOUND--TO ME--	TEACH HIM--WHEN HE MAKES	227	4
	WERE MY EAR--AS NEAR HIS NEST--	TEACH HIM--WHEN HE MAKES	227	5
	AS MY THOUGHT--TODAY--	TEACH HIM--WHEN HE MAKES	227	6
	AS SHOULD SOUND--	TEACH HIM--WHEN HE MAKES	227	7
	STOOPING AS LOW AS [BENDING LOW AT] THE OTTER'S [KITCHEN / . . .	BLAZING IN GOLD AND	228	5
	STOOPING AS LOW AS [BENDING LOW AT] THE OTTER'S [KITCHEN / . . .	BLAZING IN GOLD AND	228	5
	DAINTY--AS THE TRESS--ON HER DEFT HEAD--	WE--BEE AND I--LIVE BY	230	11
	AS THAT THE SLAVE--IS GONE.	THE LAMP BURNS SURE--	233	8
	AS SMALL--THEY SAY--AS I--	THE COURT IS FAR AWAY--	235	10
	AS SMALL--THEY SAY--AS I--	THE COURT IS FAR AWAY--	235	10
	AS IF AN AXLE, [A MUSCLE--] HELD--	WHEN WE STAND ON THE	242	16
	DISSOLVED AS UTTERLY--	I'VE KNOWN A HEAVEN,	243	13
	AS BIRD'S FAR NAVIGATION	I'VE KNOWN A HEAVEN,	243	14
	DOMINIONS--BROAD AS DEW--	WHAT WOULD I GIVE TO SEE	247	17
	TIMID AS A BIRD!	WHY--DO THEY SHUT ME OUT	248	4
	ALMOST AS IF THEY CARED--	IF I'M LOST--NOW--	256	9
	DELIGHT IS AS THE FLIGHT--	DELIGHT IS AS THE FLIGHT	257	1
	AS THE SCHOOLS WOULD SAY--	DELIGHT IS AS THE FLIGHT	257	3
	WOULD SUIT AS BRIGHT,	DELIGHT IS AS THE FLIGHT	257	7
	TOOK RAINBOWS, AS THE COMMON WAY,	DELIGHT IS AS THE FLIGHT	257	16
	AS IF A KINGDOM--CARED!	READ--SWEET--HOW OTHERS	260	7
	PASSIVE--AS GRANITE--LAPS MY MUSIC--	PUT UP MY LUTE!	261	4
	SOBBING--WILL SUIT--AS WELL AS PSALM!	PUT UP MY LUTE!	261	5
	SOBBING--WILL SUIT--AS WELL AS PSALM!	PUT UP MY LUTE!	261	5
	AS BIRDS--THAT TUMBLE FROM THE CLOUDS	THE LONESOME FOR THEY	262	7
	AS FAR FROM MINE, AS IF NO PLIGHT	A SINGLE SCREW OF FLESH	263	7
	AS FAR FROM MINE, AS IF NO PLIGHT	A SINGLE SCREW OF FLESH	263	7
	AS MANIFOLD FOR ANGUISH--	A WEIGHT WITH NEEDLES ON	264	7
	AS SPECIES--BE--FOR NAME--	A WEIGHT WITH NEEDLES ON	264	8
	AS WITH ALGEBRA!	BOUND--A TROUBLE--	269	6
	SING--AT IT'S PAIN--AS ANY WORKMAN--	BOUND--A TROUBLE--	269	9
	AND WOULD IT FEEL AS BIG--	A SOLEMN THING--IT WAS--	271	10
	AS HOVERING [GLIMMERING]--SEEN--THROUGH FOG--	A SOLEMN THING--IT WAS--	271	12
	DELIBERATE, AS A DUKE WOULD DO	HE PUT THE BELT AROUND	273	5
	TO LIVES THAT [AS] STOOP TO NOTICE MINE--	HE PUT THE BELT AROUND	273	13
	LOW AS THE LAUGHTER OF THE CRICKET,	MANY A PHRASE HAS THE	276	3
	LOUD, AS THE THUNDER'S TONGUE--	MANY A PHRASE HAS THE	276	4
	AS LAUGHTER--WAS--AN HOUR AGO--	WHAT IF I SAY I SHALL	277	10
	AS ALL THE HEAVENS WERE A BELL,	I FELT A FUNERAL, IN MY	280	13
	O'ERTAKELESS, AS THE AIR--	HOW NOTELESS MEN, AND	282	8
	AS TONE OF REALM	A MIEN TO MOVE A QUEEN--	283	20
	AS I--TOWARD [IN] THEE--	THE DROP, THAT WRESTLES	284	3
	JUST AS THE GRANITE CRUMB LET GO--	THAT AFTER HORROR--THAT	286	3
	THE SUN HAS GOT AS FAR	I KNOW SOME LONELY	289	33
	AS THE THIRD SYCAMORE--	I KNOW SOME LONELY	289	34
	AS A DUCHESS PASSED--	HOW THE OLD MOUNTAINS	291	12
	AS STAPLES--DRIVEN THROUGH--	I GOT SO I COULD HEAR	293	12
	AS MISERY--	I GOT SO I COULD HEAR	293	26
	AS TRUMPETS--ROLLED--	UNTO LIKE STORY--TROUBLE	295	16
	FEET, SMALL AS MINE--HAVE MARCHED IN REVOLUTION	UNTO LIKE STORY--TROUBLE	295	17
	AS OLD AS THEE--HOW SOON?	ONE YEAR AGO--JOTS WHAT?	296	34
	AS OLD AS THEE--HOW SOON?	ONE YEAR AGO--JOTS WHAT?	296	34
	IN LITTLE WEALTHS, AS GIRLS COULD [CAN] BOAST	YOUR RICHES--TAUGHT ME--	299	3
	TILL BROAD AS BUENOS AYRE--	YOUR RICHES--TAUGHT ME--	299	4
	AS INFINITE [BAGATELLES] TRADITION	LIKE SOME OLD FASHIONED	302	5
	AS CINDERELLA'S BAYS--	LIKE SOME OLD FASHIONED	302	6
	CONTENTED AS THE EYE	THE DIFFERENCE BETWEEN	305	6
	IS SELDOM--BUT AS FAIR	THE SOUL'S SUPERIOR	306	10
	AS APPARITION--SUBJECT	THE SOUL'S SUPERIOR	306	11
	HIS OWN WAS [IS] AMPLER--BUT AS I	I SEND TWO SUNSETS--	308	5
	AS ANKLES OF A QUEEN--	IT SIFTS FROM LEADEN	311	18
	DISPERSES, WHILE [AS] IT STAYS	IT SIFTS FROM LEADEN	311	V
	AS PLAYERS AT THE KEYS	HE FUMBLES AT YOUR SOUL	315	2
	AS IF SOME CARAVAN OF SOUND	OF ALL THE SOUNDS	321	29
	THE SUN, AS COMMON, WENT ABROAD,	THERE CAME A DAY AT	322	5
	AS IF NO SOUL THE [WHILE OUR TWO SOULS THAT] SOLSTICE PASSED	THERE CAME A DAY AT	322	7
	WAS NEEDLESS, AS AT SACRAMENT,	THERE CAME A DAY AT	322	11
	THE HOURS SLID FAST--AS HOURS WILL,	THERE CAME A DAY AT	322	17
	AS IF I ASKED A COMMON ALMS,	AS IF I ASKED A COMMON	323	1
	AS IF I ASKED THE ORIENT	AS IF I ASKED A COMMON	323	5
	REMEMBERED--AS THE MILE	OF TRIBULATION--THESE	325	12
	IT'S FULL AS OPERA--	I CANNOT DANCE UPON MY	326	20
	I LIKED AS WELL TO SEE--	BEFORE I GOT MY EYE PUT	327	2
	AS OTHER CREATURES, THAT HAVE EYES	BEFORE I GOT MY EYE PUT	327	3
	AS MUCH OF NOON AS I COULD TAKE	BEFORE I GOT MY EYE PUT	327	12
	AS MUCH OF NOON AS I COULD TAKE	BEFORE I GOT MY EYE PUT	327	12
	LEAP, PLASHLESS AS THEY SWIM.	A BIRD CAME DOWN THE	328	20

THE UNIVERSITY OF WINNIPEG
PORTAGE & BALMORAL
WINNIPEG 2, MAN. CANADA
DISCARDED

AS (CONTINUED)

	FIRST LINE	POEM	LINE
LIKE [AS] LOWLY SPICES, LAIN TO SLEEP [GONE TO SLEEP / LAID . . .	THE GRASS SO LITTLE HAS	333	15
ARE [WERE] NOT FAIR AS THIS--	ALL THE LETTERS I CAN	334	2
AS GABRIEL--NEVER CAPERED AT--	THE FACE I CARRY WITH ME	336	11
AS ONE THAT BORE HER MASTER'S NAME--	THE FACE I CARRY WITH ME	336	15
I HAD AS LIEF THEY BORE	I TEND MY FLOWERS FOR	339	19
AS FREEZING PERSONS, RECOLLECT THE SNOW--	AFTER GREAT PAIN, A	341	12
AS 'TWERE A BRIGHT BOQUET--	IT WILL BE SUMMER--	342	6
AS WOMEN--DO--THEIR GOWN--	IT WILL BE SUMMER--	342	18
SLOW--SLOW--AS FEET DID WEARY--GROW--	'TWAS THE OLD--ROAD--	344	10
BUT THEN--I'M NOT SO STAID--AS HE--	FUNNY--TO BE A CENTURY--	345	4
AND FAR FROM HEAVEN AS THE REST--	NOT PROBABLE--THE BAREST	346	3
CONFUSED BY SWEETS--AS MORTALS--ARE--	NOT PROBABLE--THE BAREST	346	6
EACH ONE SALUTES ME, AS HE GOES,	I DREADED THAT FIRST	348	25
AS HIMMALEH, SHALL STAND--	THEY LEAVE US WITH THE	350	6
AS WELL AS OUR OLD HOME!"	I FELT MY LIFE WITH BOTH	351	16
AS WELL AS OUR OLD HOME!"	I FELT MY LIFE WITH BOTH	351	16
FOR EARTHS, GROW THICK AS	PERHAPS I ASKED TOO	352	3
AS LADY FROM HER DOOR	FROM COCOON FORTH A	354	2
WHERE PARTIES--PHANTOM AS HERSELF--	FROM COCOON FORTH A	354	14
AS 'TWERE A TROPIC SHOW--	FROM COCOON FORTH A	354	17
AS CARBON IN THE COAL	THE DAY THAT I WAS	356	5
WOOS, AS HE STATES US--BY HIS SON--	GOD IS A DISTANT--	357	2
AS WELL THE SKY	I GAINED IT SO--	359	6
THOUGH IT BE LITTLE AS A DAFFODIL--	WHAT I CAN DO--I WILL--	361	2
THE LIGHTNING WAS AS NEW	IT STRUCK ME--EVERY DAY	362	2
AS IF THE CLOUD THAT INSTANT SLIT	IT STRUCK ME--EVERY DAY	362	3
AS NATURE DID NOT CARE--	THE MORNING AFTER WO--	364	5
FOR FOREHEAD LOW AS MINE, TO WEAR,	ALTHOUGH I PUT AWAY HIS	366	3
SHE LAY AS IF AT PLAY	SHE LAY AS IF AT PLAY	369	1
AS IF FOR LULL OF SPORT--	SHE LAY AS IF AT PLAY	369	6
AS IF THEIR OWNER WERE	SHE LAY AS IF AT PLAY	369	10
'TIS VAST--AS OUR CAPACITY--	HEAVEN IS SO FAR OF THE	370	5
AS FAIR--AS OUR IDEA--	HEAVEN IS SO FAR OF THE	370	6
AS FAIR--AS OUR IDEA--	HEAVEN IS SO FAR OF THE	370	6
AS ONE SHOULD COME TO TOWN--	A PRECIOUS--MOULDERING	371	22
TAKE OTHER ACCENTS, AS SUCH I HEARD	I'M SAYING EVERY DAY	373	21
BEAUTIFUL--AS PICTURES--	I WENT TO HEAVEN--	374	7
HE CARED AS MUCH AS ON THE AIR	OF COURSE--I PRAYED--	376	3
HE CARED AS MUCH AS ON THE AIR	OF COURSE--I PRAYED--	376	3
AS THAT DIVINER BRAND	EXHILIRATION--IS WITHIN	383	4
AS LATELY AS TODAY--	THERE'S BEEN A DEATH, IN	389	2
AS LATELY AS TODAY--	THERE'S BEEN A DEATH, IN	389	2
AS IF THE HOUSE WERE HIS--	THERE'S BEEN A DEATH, IN	389	14
IT'S EASY AS A SIGN--	THERE'S BEEN A DEATH, IN	389	22
TILL THEY ARE ORDERLY AS BUSTS--	A VISITOR IN MARL--	391	3
AND ELEGANT--AS GLASS--	A VISITOR IN MARL--	391	4
IS AS IT HAD NOT BEEN--	A VISITOR IN MARL--	391	12
THROUGH THE DARK SOD--AS EDUCATION--	THROUGH THE DARK SOD--AS	392	1
EXCEPT AS STIMULANTS--IN	DID OUR BEST MOMENT LAST	393	5
THAT CERTAIN AS IT COMES--	DID OUR BEST MOMENT LAST	393	10
'TWAS BASE AS JESUS--MOST!	'TWAS LOVE--NOT ME--	394	8
AS SOON--ADVERSITY	REVERSE CANNOT BEFALL	395	4
AS MISTS--OBLITERATE A CRAG.	THERE IS A LANGUOR OF	396	8
ONE WOULD AS SOON ASSAULT A PLUSH--	WHAT SOFT--CHERUBIC	401	3
IS NEAR AS I CAN GUESS--	I PAY--IN SATIN CASH--	402	4
AND THEN--A DAY AS HUGE	THE FIRST DAY'S NIGHT	410	9
AS YESTERDAYS IN PAIRS,	THE FIRST DAY'S NIGHT	410	10
MEET TRANQUILLY, AS FRIENDS--	I READ MY SENTENCE--	412	12
AS IF A GOBLIN WITH A GUAGE--	'TWAS LIKE A MAELSTROM,	414	10
AS IF YOUR SENTENCE STOOD--PRONOUNCED--	'TWAS LIKE A MAELSTROM,	414	18
A HUBBUB--AS OF FEET--	A MURMUR IN THE TREES--	416	6
NOT AUDIBLE--AS OUR'S--TO US--	A MURMUR IN THE TREES--	416	7
THEMSELF--AS DUMB--	IT IS DEAD--FIND IT--	417	10
AS WHEN THE NEIGHBOR HOLDS THE LAMP	WE GROW ACCUSTOMED TO	419	3
BUT AS THEY LEARN TO SEE--	WE GROW ACCUSTOMED TO	419	16
YOU'LL KNOW IT--AS YOU KNOW 'TIS NOON--	YOU'LL KNOW IT--AS YOU	420	1
AS YOU DO THE SUN--	YOU'LL KNOW IT--AS YOU	420	3
AS YOU WILL IN HEAVEN--	YOU'LL KNOW IT--AS YOU	420	5
OF RICHES--AS UNCONSCIOUS	REMOVED FROM ACCIDENT OF	424	5
AS IS THE BROWN MALAY	REMOVED FROM ACCIDENT OF	424	6
IT DONT SOUND SO TERRIBLE--QUITE--AS IT DID--	IT DONT SOUND SO	426	1
JUST AS HIGH--AS I--	I'LL CLUTCH--AND CLUTCH	427	19
JUST AS HIGH--AS I--	I'LL CLUTCH--AND CLUTCH	427	19
SHE LEADS HIM--DOCILE AS A BOY--	THE MOON IS DISTANT FROM	429	3
OR--IF IT SOMETIME--SHOWED--AS 'TWILL--	IT WOULD NEVER BE COMMON	430	5
I WALKED--AS WINGS--MY BODY BORE--	IT WOULD NEVER BE COMMON	430	13
AS BOOTS--WOULD BE--TO BIRDS--	IT WOULD NEVER BE COMMON	430	16
AS POSITIVELY LIVE	DO PEOPLE MOULDER	432	4
AS I, WHO TESTIFY IT	DO PEOPLE MOULDER	432	5
IN THIS, AS ALL, PREVAIL--	MUCH MADNESS IS DIVINEST	435	5
WERE AS IMPOSSIBLE AS HAND	THE WIND--TAPPED LIKE A	436	7
WERE AS IMPOSSIBLE AS HAND	THE WIND--TAPPED LIKE A	436	7
HIS FINGERS, AS HE PASSED	THE WIND--TAPPED LIKE A	436	14
LET GO A MUSIC--AS OF TUNES	THE WIND--TAPPED LIKE A	436	15
'TIS CUSTOMARY AS WE PART	'TIS CUSTOMARY AS WE	440	1
'TIS VARIOUS--AS THE VARIOUS TASTE--	'TIS CUSTOMARY AS WE	440	5
AS THE VERY LEAST	I TIE MY HAT--I CREASE	443	3
AS A COMPLETED MAN	I TIE MY HAT--I CREASE	443	14

		FIRST LINE	POEM	LINE
AS	(CONTINUED)			
	AS LIFE--DISSOLVED BE--FOR US--	IT FEELS A SHAME TO BE	444	15
	THE LARGER, AS HER [MY] FACE WITHDREW--	I SHOWED HER HIGHTS SHE	446	11
	AND SO, AS KINSMEN, MET A NIGHT--	I DIED FOR BEAUTY--BUT	449	9
	AS IS THE CENTRAL MOOD--	THE OUTER--FROM THE	451	4
	AS IS THE INNER BRAND--	THE OUTER--FROM THE	451	12
	I HEARD SUCH WORDS AS "RICH"--	IT WAS GIVEN TO ME BY	454	9
	AS WELL AS JESUS?	SO WELL THAT I CAN LIVE	456	3
	AS WELL AS JESUS?	SO WELL THAT I CAN LIVE	456	3
	AS I--LOVE THEE--	SO WELL THAT I CAN LIVE	456	6
	AS THE LAUGHTER--AND THE WHISPER--	SWEET--SAFE--HOUSES--	457	8
	AS FAR AS IT COULD SEE--	LIKE EYES THAT LOOKED ON	458	6
	AS FAR AS IT COULD SEE--	LIKE EYES THAT LOOKED ON	458	6
	AS HOPELESS--AS DIVINE--	LIKE EYES THAT LOOKED ON	458	12
	AS HOPELESS--AS DIVINE--	LIKE EYES THAT LOOKED ON	458	12
	AND SO WE MOVE AS FAR	WE DO NOT PLAY ON GRAVES	467	9
	AS ENEMIES--AWAY--	WE DO NOT PLAY ON GRAVES	467	10
	AS GRAINS UPON A SHORE--	A NIGHT--THERE LAY THE	471	6
	OVAL--AS FEUDAL LADIES WORE--	I AM ASHAMED--I HIDE--	473	14
	AS SEPARATE AS SEA	THEY PUT US FAR APART--	474	2
	AS SEPARATE AS SEA	THEY PUT US FAR APART--	474	2
	OUR SOULS SAW--JUST AS WELL--	THEY PUT US FAR APART--	474	12
	SUCH AS CONTENT--AND HEAVEN--	I MEANT TO HAVE BUT	476	2
	A HEAVEN NOT SO LARGE AS YOUR'S,	I MEANT TO HAVE BUT	476	11
	AS CHILDREN--SWINDLED FOR THE FIRST	I MEANT TO HAVE BUT	476	27
	AS ROUND A GOALLESS ROAD	NO MAN CAN COMPASS A	477	2
	REMEMBER--AS THOU GO--	WE COVER THEE--SWEET	482	4
	SUCH AS THESE--THE PEARLS	MY GARDEN--LIKE THE	484	4
	SHE FETCHES--SUCH AS ME	MY GARDEN--LIKE THE	484	5
	AS IF IT HELD BUT THE MIGHT OF A CHILD--	GOING TO HIM! HAPPY	494	13
	CROWDED--AS SACRAMENT--	IT'S THOUGHTS--AND JUST	495	6
	THOUGH WINTER FIRE--SING CLEAR AS PLOVER--	IT'S THOUGHTS--AND JUST	495	15
	AS FAR FROM PITY, AS COMPLAINT--	AS FAR FROM PITY, AS	496	1
	AS FAR FROM PITY, AS COMPLAINT--	AS FAR FROM PITY, AS	496	1
	AS COOL TO SPEECH--AS STONE--	AS FAR FROM PITY, AS	496	2
	AS COOL TO SPEECH--AS STONE--	AS FAR FROM PITY, AS	496	2
	AS NUMB TO REVELATION	AS FAR FROM PITY, AS	496	3
	AS IF MY TRADE WERE BONE--	AS FAR FROM PITY, AS	496	4
	AS FAR FROM TIME--AS HISTORY--	AS FAR FROM PITY, AS	496	5
	AS FAR FROM TIME--AS HISTORY--	AS FAR FROM PITY, AS	496	5
	AS NEAR YOURSELF--TODAY--	AS FAR FROM PITY, AS	496	6
	AS CHILDREN, TO THE RAINBOW'S SCARF--	AS FAR FROM PITY, AS	496	7
	AS HEAVEN [EDEN]--UNTO ME!	I ENVY SEAS, WHEREON HE	498	8
	ESTEEMING US--AS EXILE--	THOSE FAIR--FICTITIOUS	499	21
	AS 'TWERE A TRAVELLING MILL--	WITHIN MY GARDEN, RIDES	500	4
	AND PRAISES AS HE GOES,	WITHIN MY GARDEN, RIDES	500	8
	INVISIBLE, AS MUSIC--	THIS WORLD IS NOT	501	3
	BUT POSITIVE, AS SOUND--	THIS WORLD IS NOT	501	4
	AND SILENCED, AS THE AWFUL SEA	HE TOUCHED ME, SO I LIVE	506	5
	AS IF I BREATHED SUPERIOR AIR--	HE TOUCHED ME, SO I LIVE	506	8
	AS IF MY LIFE WERE SHAVEN,	IT WAS NOT DEATH, FOR I	510	13
	AS HOUSEWIVES DO, A FLY.	IF YOU WERE COMING IN	511	4
	AS DO THE BEE--DELIRIOUS BORNE--	THE SOUL HAS BANDAGED	512	15
	LIKE [AS] FLOWERS, THAT HEARD THE NEWS OF DEWS,	LIKE FLOWERS, THAT HEARD	513	1
	AND STILL IT HURT YOU, AS SOME BIRD	HER SMILE WAS SHAPED	514	3
	AS SUNS--DISSOLVE [ANNUL] A STAR--	NO CROWD THAT HAS	515	12
	GAVE--EVEN AS TO ALL--	HER SWEET WEIGHT ON MY	518	10
	BY SO MUCH--AS 'TWAS REAL--	HER SWEET WEIGHT ON MY	518	12
	AS PRIDE WERE ALL IT COULD--	'TWAS WARM--AT FIRST--	519	12
	AND MADE AS HE WOULD EAT ME UP--	I STARTED EARLY--TOOK MY	520	13
	AS WHOLLY AS A DEW	I STARTED EARLY--TOOK MY	520	14
	AS WHOLLY AS A DEW	I STARTED EARLY--TOOK MY	520	14
	AS GIANTS--GONE [CLAIMED] AWAY--	HAD I PRESUMED TO HOPE--	522	4
	AS UNTO CROWD--	TO HEAR AN ORIOLE SING	526	6
	MINE--LONG AS [WHILE] AGES STEAL!	MINE--BY THE RIGHT OF	528	9
	AS ONE SHOULD PRY THE WALLS--	I TRIED TO THINK A	532	13
	THAT AS MYSELF--COULD PITY HIM--	I TRIED TO THINK A	532	18
	AS JUST APPRENTICED TO THE AIR--	SHE'S HAPPY, WITH A NEW	535	4
	THAT HEAVEN PERMIT SO MEEK [FAINT] AS HER--	SHE'S HAPPY, WITH A NEW	535	7
	AS YET--MY HEART BE DRY--	ME PROVE IT NOW--WHOEVER	537	6
	FORGIVE THEM--EVEN AS MYSELF--	'TIS TRUE--THEY SHUT ME	538	11
	'TWAS NOT SO MUCH AS DAVID--HAD--	I TOOK MY POWER IN MY	540	3
	BUT I--WAS TWICE AS BOLD--	I TOOK MY POWER IN MY	540	4
	AS THE STARS--YOU KNEW LAST NIGHT--	SOME SUCH BUTTERFLY BE	541	7
	IN SEARCH OF SOMETHING [SOMEWHAT]--AS IT SEEMED--	I'VE SEEN A DYING EYE	547	3
	AS ASIATIC RAINS--	I CROSS TILL I AM WEARY	550	9
	BUT AS AN ENEMY'S SALUTE	I CROSS TILL I AM WEARY	550	12
	WE START--AS IF DETECTED	AN IGNORANCE A SUNSET	552	11
	AS MANY BE	ONE CRUCIFIXION IS	553	6
	AS PERSONS--OR PENINSULAS--	ONE CRUCIFIXION IS	553	7
	AS ONE HAD TESTIFIED--	TRUST IN THE UNEXPECTED	555	4
	AS WORTHILY [PRIVATELY] AS WE.	SHE HIDETH HER THE LAST	557	8
	AS WORTHILY [PRIVATELY] AS WE.	SHE HIDETH HER THE LAST	557	8
	AS IMPOTENT [POSSIBLE] WOULD BE	SHE HIDETH HER THE LAST	557	10
	AS MAKE OF [BREW FROM / MIX] OUR IMPERFECT [UNCOMELY / OBTUSER]	SHE HIDETH HER THE LAST	557	11
	TIS TERROR AS CONSUMMATE	ONE ANGUISH--IN A CROWD	565	5
	AS LEGIONS OF ALARM	ONE ANGUISH--IN A CROWD	565	6

AS (CONTINUED)

	FIRST LINE	POEM	LINE
AND QUICKENING [RIPENING]--AS WE SOWED--	HE GAVE AWAY HIS LIFE--	567	13
BE BEAUTIFUL AS THEY PREPARE [DISCLOSE]	I RECKON--WHEN I COUNT	569	13
AS DIFFICULT [CLARIFIED]	MUST BE A WO--	571	7
AS STALACTITE [VIOLET]--	MUST BE A WO--	571	8
EVEN AS THE GRACE--	MUST BE A WO--	571	12
AS IF BEFORE A CHILD	MY FIRST WELL DAY--SINCE	574	14
TO HAVE A GOD SO STRONG AS THAT	I PRAYED, AT FIRST, A	576	16
IF JUST AS SOON AS BREATH IS OUT	IF I MAY HAVE IT, WHEN	577	3
IF JUST AS SOON AS BREATH IS OUT	IF I MAY HAVE IT, WHEN	577	3
AS IF MY SOUL WERE DEAF AND DUMB--	IF I MAY HAVE IT, WHEN	577	19
AS BERRY--OF A MOUNTAIN BUSH--	I HAD BEEN HUNGRY, ALL	579	15
AS A HAND DID TRY TO CHALK THE SUN	I FOUND THE WORDS TO	581	4
THE GNAT'S SUPREMACY IS LARGE AS THINE--	A TOAD, CAN DIE OF LIGHT	583	7
AS CONSTANT AS THE CHILDISH FROCK [GOWN]--	IT CEASED TO HURT ME,	584	7
AS CONSTANT AS THE CHILDISH FROCK [GOWN]--	IT CEASED TO HURT ME,	584	7
AS NEEDLES--LADIES SOFTLY PRESS	IT CEASED TO HURT ME,	584	10
THEN--PROMPTER THAN [PUNCTUAL AS] A STAR	I LIKE TO SEE IT LAP	585	15
WE TALKED AS GIRLS DO--	WE TALKED AS GIRLS DO--	586	1
WE HANDLED DESTINIES, AS COOL--	WE TALKED AS GIRLS DO--	586	5
AS WE--DISPOSERS--BE--	WE TALKED AS GIRLS DO--	586	6
AS WE EVENTUAL--BE--	WE TALKED AS GIRLS DO--	586	10
THAT OFTEN AS A CLOUD IT MET--	THE NIGHT WAS WIDE, AND	589	3
AND FLY, AS 'TWERE PURSUING YOU?	DID YOU EVER STAND IN A	590	7
AS COOL [DISTINCT] AS SATYR'S DRUMS--	DID YOU EVER STAND IN A	590	14
AS COOL [DISTINCT] AS SATYR'S DRUMS--	DID YOU EVER STAND IN A	590	14
DOES NOT SO MUCH AS TURN HIS HEAD	TO INTERRUPT HIS YELLOW	591	7
AS THE MINUTEST BEE	TO INTERRUPT HIS YELLOW	591	14
POUR AS BLANK ON THEM	WHAT CARE THE DEAD, FOR	592	5
AS ON THE TIER [ROW] OF WALL	WHAT CARE THE DEAD, FOR	592	6
AND EQUALLY AS COOL--	WHAT CARE THE DEAD, FOR	592	8
THEMSELVES AS EASY FREEZE--	WHAT CARE THE DEAD, FOR	592	18
JUNE NOON--AS JANUARY NIGHT--	WHAT CARE THE DEAD, FOR	592	19
AS SOON THE SOUTH--HER BREEZE	WHAT CARE THE DEAD, FOR	592	20
THE BEES--BECAME AS BUTTERFLIES--	I THINK I WAS ENCHANTED	593	9
THE BUTTERFLIES--AS SWANS [MOONS]--	I THINK I WAS ENCHANTED	593	10
AS IF UNTO A JUBILEE [SACRAMENT]	I THINK I WAS ENCHANTED	593	19
AS LEGIONS OF A NIGHT	THE BATTLE FOUGHT	594	10
AS EVEN IN THE SKY--	WHEN I WAS SMALL, A	596	16
FOR BRAVERIES, REMOTE AS THIS [HIS]	WHEN I WAS SMALL, A	596	19
AS BOY--SHOULD DEAL WITH LESSER BOY--	IT ALWAYS FELT TO ME--A	597	15
OLD MAN ON NEBO! LATE AS THIS--	IT ALWAYS FELT TO ME--A	597	23
AS ONE WITHIN A SWOON--	THERE IS A PAIN--SO	599	6
IT TROUBLED ME AS ONCE I WAS--	IT TROUBLED ME AS ONCE I	600	1
AS FLAVORS--CHEER RETARDED GUESTS	UNTO MY BOOKS--SO GOOD	604	5
AND DANCING SOFTLY TO HIMSELF [AS HE KNITS]	THE SPIDER HOLDS A	605	3
AS IF HIMSELF WERE OPTIONAL	THE TREES LIKE TASSELS--	606	11
AS WE--IT WERE--THAT PERISHED--	OF NEARNESS TO HER	607	17
AS MUCH ABASHETH ME!	AFRAID! OF WHOM AM I	608	4
JUST AS THE CASE MAY BE--	AFRAID! OF WHOM AM I	608	8
AS DEITY DECREE--	AFRAID! OF WHOM AM I	608	V 8
AS SOON IMPEACH MY CROWN!	AFRAID! OF WHOM AM I	608	12
AS CAUTIOUSLY AS GLASS	I YEARS HAD BEEN FROM	609	22
AS CAUTIOUSLY AS GLASS	I YEARS HAD BEEN FROM	609	22
FOR RECOLLECTING SUCH AS WENT--	YOU'LL FIND--IT WHEN YOU	610	3
AS DID THEIR MARBLE NAMES	YOU'LL FIND--IT WHEN YOU	610	6
AS DYING--SAY IT DOES--	YOU'LL FIND--IT WHEN YOU	610	10
TO LIVE [DINE] SO SMALL AS I--	IT WOULD HAVE STARVED A	612	2
AS WHEN A LITTLE GIRL	THEY SHUT ME UP IN PROSE	613	2
THEY MIGHT AS WISE HAVE LODGED A BIRD	THEY SHUT ME UP IN PROSE	613	7
AND EASY AS A STAR	THEY SHUT ME UP IN PROSE	613	10
WAS DYING AS HE THOUGHT--OR DIFFERENT--	TO KNOW JUST HOW HE	622	6
NO DIFFERENT [AS INFINITE] OUR YEARS WOULD BE	FOREVER--IS COMPOSED OF	624	11
APPARELED AS THE NEW	'TWAS A LONG PARTING--	625	10
JUST AS [EQUAL] SURE--	ONLY GOD--DETECT THE	626	8
AS IF THEY JUST REPRESSED	THE TINT I CANNOT TAKE--	627	14
AS EVEN WHILE I LOOKED--DISSOLVED--	THEY CALLED ME TO THE	628	7
AS CREW OF MOUNTAINS--COULD AFFORD--	THEY CALLED ME TO THE	628	11
I GAZED [TURNED]--AS AT A STRANGER--	I WATCHED THE MOON	629	5
AS HARASS US--LIKE LIFE--AND DEATH--	I WATCHED THE MOON	629	25
NOR WE SO MUCH AS CHECK OUR SPEECH--	THE LIGHTNING PLAYETH--	630	11
AS SPONGES--BUCKETS--DO--	THE BRAIN--IS WIDER THAN	632	8
AS SYLLABLE FROM SOUND--	THE BRAIN--IS WIDER THAN	632	12
BUT AS SHE CLOSER STANDS--	YOU'LL KNOW HER--BY HER	634	16
A SWEET ENDEAVOR--BUT AS MARCH	YOU'LL KNOW HER--BY HER	634	23
IT SEEMS AS THOUGH THE TIME	I THINK THE LONGEST HOUR	635	4
SORROWFUL--AS CERTAIN--	THE CHILD'S FAITH IS NEW	637	22
AS PARADISE	I CANNOT LIVE WITH YOU--	640	36
CAPACIOUS AS THE SEA--	YOU LEFT ME--SIRE--TWO	644	6
IN DYING--'TIS AS IF OUR SOULS [WORLD / SELVES / SUN]	BEREAVEMENT IN THEIR	645	11
HE SHALL SEEK AS HIGH	HER SWEET TURN TO LEAVE	649	18
AS THE PALM--THAT SERVE THE DESERT--	HER SWEET TURN TO LEAVE	649	19
IT DEAL US [FURNISH]--STATED AS OUR FOOD--	A PRISON GETS TO BE A	652	7
AS PLASHING IN THE POOLS--	A PRISON GETS TO BE A	652	13
AS THIS PHANTASM [COMPANION] STEEL--	A PRISON GETS TO BE A	652	21
ARE PRESENT TO US--AS OUR OWN--	A PRISON GETS TO BE A	652	23
AND AS ESCAPELESS--QUITE--	A PRISON GETS TO BE A	652	24
AVOIDED--LIKE [AS] A DREAM--	A PRISON GETS TO BE A	652	30
AS DID [SHOULD] THE DOWN EMIT A TUNE--	OF BEING IS A BIRD	653	11

		FIRST LINE	POEM	LINE
AS	(CONTINUED)			
	AS IS THE TWITTER OF A BIRD--	WITHOUT THIS--THERE IS	655	3
	AS SEAMS--INCLUDE THE BALL?	WITHOUT THIS--THERE IS	655	8
	OF CHAMBERS AS THE CEDARS--	I DWELL IN POSSIBILITY--	657	5
	AS 'TWERE SPECIFIC [A SIGNAL] GROUND--	WHOLE GULFS--OF RED, AND	658	4
	DUE--PROMPTLY--AS A DRAMA--	WHOLE GULFS--OF RED, AND	658	7
	BE LARGER--AS THE SEA	'TIS GOOD--THE LOOKING	660	10
	AS DOTH THE MEADOW BEE	COULD I BUT RIDE	661	2
	FOR SUCH AN ONE--AS ME--	AGAIN--HIS VOICE IS AT	663	4
	I TAKE A FLOWER--AS I GO--	AGAIN--HIS VOICE IS AT	663	5
	FAR AS NORTH--AND EAST,	BLOOM UPON THE MOUNTAIN	667	14
	FAR AS SOUTH AND WEST--EXPANDING [DISCLOSING]--	BLOOM UPON THE MOUNTAIN	667	15
	AS THE PERUSAL OF	NO ROMANCE SOLD UNTO	669	3
	THE DOWER--AS THE DOOM--	THE FUTURE--NEVER SPOKE	672	10
	'TIS ABLE AS A GOD--	TO BE ALIVE--IS POWER--	677	6
	ADORED [BEHELD] WITH CAUTION--AS A BRITTLE HEAVEN--	EACH LIFE CONVERGES TO	680	9
	WERE HOPELESS, AS THE [A] RAINBOW'S RAIMENT	EACH LIFE CONVERGES TO	680	11
	AMPLE AS THE EYE--	'TWOULD EASE--A	682	13
	AS SINEWS DO, WITH AGE--	THEY SAY THAT "TIME	686	4
	AS TRINKET--WORN BY FADED CHILD--	I'LL SEND THE FEATHER	687	4
	AS ONE SHOULD SUE A STAR--	THE HEAVEN VESTS FOR	694	10
	AS IF THE SEA SHOULD PART	AS IF THE SEA SHOULD	695	1
	'TWAS BEST IMPERFECT--AS IT WAS--	THEIR HIGHT IN HEAVEN	696	3
	FAR AS PARADISE--	LIFE--IS WHAT WE MAKE IT	698	12
	IT IS AS SWANS--DISCARDED YOU,	YOU'VE SEEN BALLOONS SET	700	3
	THEY SPURN THE AIR, AS 'TWERE TOO MEAN	YOU'VE SEEN BALLOONS SET	700	7
	SUCH AS THESE--ARE STILL--	LIFE, AND DEATH, AND	706	2
	AS BORE IT SEALED WINE--	STRONG DRAUGHTS OF THEIR	711	4
	TO GO ELASTIC--OR AS ONE	STRONG DRAUGHTS OF THEIR	711	5
	HER DIMITIES--AS OLD	THE DAY UNDRESSED--	716	4
	EXACTLY [PRECISELY]--AS THE WORLD--	THE DAY UNDRESSED--	716	5
	BE WRINKLED--MUCH AS HER--	THE DAY UNDRESSED--	716	8
	AS ONE DETECT ON LANDINGS	A SOUTH WIND--HAS A	719	3
	AS ONE THAT DRUNKEN--STEPT--	IT TOSSED--AND TOSSED--	723	6
	BONDAGE AS PLAY--BE SWEET--	WHERE THOU ART--THAT--IS	725	7
	REMEMBERED--AS THE MILLINER'S FLOWER	PRECIOUS TO ME--SHE	727	12
	AS OF THE FREE--	LET US PLAY YESTERDAY--	728	34
	EVEN AS HERSELF--SIR--	ALTER! WHEN THE HILLS DO	729	7
	THE LIPS HAD PLACED AS WITH A "PLEASE"	"I WANT"--IT PLEADED--	731	7
	IT LAY UNMENTIONED--AS THE SEA	SHE ROSE TO HIS	732	9
	FOR OTHER SERVICES [PURPOSES]--AS SOUND--	THE SPIRIT IS THE	733	5
	AS LATELY AS THE SNOW--	HAVE ANY LIKE MYSELF	736	6
	AS LATELY AS THE SNOW--	HAVE ANY LIKE MYSELF	736	6
	AS WRECKED MEN--DEEM THEY SIGHT THE LAND--	I MANY TIMES THOUGHT	739	3
	AS HOPELESSLY AS I--	I MANY TIMES THOUGHT	739	6
	AS HOPELESSLY AS I--	I MANY TIMES THOUGHT	739	6
	CONFORM MY SOUL--AS TWERE A CHURCH,	MY WORTHINESS IS ALL MY	751	15
	GONE--AS SOON AS KNOWN--	SO THE EYES ACCOST--AND	752	8
	GONE--AS SOON AS KNOWN--	SO THE EYES ACCOST--AND	752	8
	AS TONGUES [THRONGS / EYES] OF DIAMOND HAD REVILED	MY SOUL--ACCUSED ME--AND	753	2
	IT IS AS A VESUVIAN FACE	MY LIFE HAD STOOD--A	754	11
	CONTENTED AS DESPAIR--	ONE BLESSING HAD I THAN	756	8
	AS ONE WHO FOR A FURTHER LIFE	HE FOUGHT LIKE THOSE	759	3
	AS OTHER MEN, WERE COY [SHY] OF DEATH--	HE FOUGHT LIKE THOSE	759	7
	'TWAS AS SPACE SAT SINGING	MOST SHE TOUCHED ME BY	760	15
	I SHUT MY EYES--AND GROPED AS WELL	FROM BLANK TO BLANK--	761	9
	AS 'TWERE A SPUR--UPON THE SOUL--	I LIVED ON DREAD--	770	6
	ARRESTLESS AS INVISIBLE--	IT IS A LONESOME GLEE--	774	7
	AND WOULD AS SOON SURMISE	THE LONELINESS ONE DARE	777	2
	AS IN IT'S GRAVE GO PLUMBING [MEASURING]	THE LONELINESS ONE DARE	777	3
	AS DIFFERENT FROM JOY--	THERE IS AN ARID	782	2
	AS FROST IS DIFFERENT FROM DEW--	THERE IS AN ARID	782	3
	A MUSIC NUMEROUS AS SPACE [MEASURELESS AS NOON]--	THE BIRDS BEGUN AT FOUR	783	3
	A MUSIC NUMEROUS AS SPACE [MEASURELESS AS NOON]--	THE BIRDS BEGUN AT FOUR	783	3
	BUT NEIGHBORING AS NOON--	THE BIRDS BEGUN AT FOUR	783	4
	AS BROOK BY BROOK BESTOWS ITSELF	THE BIRDS BEGUN AT FOUR	783	7
	FORGOTTEN, AS FULFILLED.	THE BIRDS BEGUN AT FOUR	783	24
	THE DARKNESS [TROUBLE] BRACED AS FIRM	SEVERER SERVICE OF	786	18
	AS ALL MY STRATEGEM HAD BEEN	SEVERER SERVICE OF	786	19
	AS FLOODS--ON WHITES OF WHEELS--	JOY TO HAVE MERITED THE	788	20
	SHE TURNS AS LONG AWAY	NATURE--THE GENTLEST	790	18
	AS WILL SUFFICE TO LIGHT HER LAMPS--	NATURE--THE GENTLEST	790	19
	HARMLESS--AS STREAKS OF METEOR--	THROUGH THE STRAIT PASS	792	7
	AT HOME [EASE]--AMONG THE BILLOWS--AS	SHE STAKED HER FEATHERS	798	7
	AS CAN NO OTHER MOUTH	DESPAIR'S ADVANTAGE IS	799	8
	AS DID OURSELVES PARTAKE--	DESPAIR'S ADVANTAGE IS	799	10
	BUT OFTEN AS MY LOT DISPLAYS	I PLAY AT RICHES--TO	801	9
	AS WE--WHO NEVER CAN--	I PLAY AT RICHES--TO	801	16
	AS SOME [US] SHE NEVER KNEW--	NO NOTICE GAVE SHE, BUT	804	20
	AS "BRANCH," [TRUNK] AND "JUGULAR."	THE VEINS OF OTHER	811	4
	THEN AS HORIZONS STEP	A LIGHT EXISTS IN SPRING	812	13
	AS TRADE HAD SUDDENLY ENCROACHED	A LIGHT EXISTS IN SPRING	812	19
	AS CERTAINTY CAN SEE	THE LUXURY TO APPREHEND	815	14
	AS CHILDREN, WHO REMAIN IN FACE	AWAY FROM HOME ARE SOME	821	7
	AS WOMEN DO A DOUGH--	THE WIND BEGUN TO KNEAD	824	2

AS (CONTINUED)

	FIRST LINE	POEM	LINE
AND THEN, AS IF THE HANDS	THE WIND BEGUN TO KNEAD	824	16
"AS LARGE AS I"--RELATE THE SUN	LOVE RECKONS BY ITSELF--	826	2
"AS LARGE AS I"--RELATE THE SUN	LOVE RECKONS BY ITSELF--	826	2
AS A SOD	TO THIS WORLD SHE	830	4
UNTIL IT BEND AS LOW AS DEATH	PERHAPS YOU THINK ME	833	7
UNTIL IT BEND AS LOW AS DEATH	PERHAPS YOU THINK ME	833	7
MY SECRET AS SECURE	NATURE AND GOD--I	835	6
AS HERSCHEL'S PRIVATE INTEREST	NATURE AND GOD--I	835	7
TRUTH--IS AS OLD AS GOD--	TRUTH--IS AS OLD AS GOD	836	1
TRUTH--IS AS OLD AS GOD--	TRUTH--IS AS OLD AS GOD	836	1
AND WILL ENDURE AS LONG AS HE	TRUTH--IS AS OLD AS GOD	836	3
AND WILL ENDURE AS LONG AS HE	TRUTH--IS AS OLD AS GOD	836	3
AS CERTAINLY AS DOOM--	IMPOSSIBILITY, LIKE WINE	838	8
AS CERTAINLY AS DOOM--	IMPOSSIBILITY, LIKE WINE	838	8
FAILLESS AS THE FAIR ROTATION	ALWAYS MINE!	839	4
OF TRINKETS, AS A GIRL.	A MOTH THE HUE OF THIS	841	6
WAS STEADY AS THE SUN	I MADE SLOW RICHES BUT	843	2
JUST AS HE SPOKE IT FROM HIS HANDS	JUST AS HE SPOKE IT FROM	848	1
ACCORDING AS HIS SKILL PREFER	JUST AS HE SPOKE IT FROM	848	5
FEELS EASY, AS WHEN DAY LETS GO	WHEN ONE HAS GIVEN UP	853	3
AS SCARCELY AS THE IODINE	WHEN ONE HAS GIVEN UP	853	7
AS SCARCELY AS THE IODINE	WHEN ONE HAS GIVEN UP	853	7
WITH SILENCE AS A COMPANY	TO OWN THE ART WITHIN	855	3
AS AN ESTATE PERPETUAL	TO OWN THE ART WITHIN	855	7
DISCLOSE AS 'TWERE A TOMB	THIS CHASM, SWEET, UPON	858	6
SUPERSTITION HELPS, AS WELL AS LOVE--	ABSENCE DISEMBODIES--SO	860	3
SUPERSTITION HELPS, AS WELL AS LOVE--	ABSENCE DISEMBODIES--SO	860	3
TENDERNESS DECREASES AS WE PROVE--	ABSENCE DISEMBODIES--SO	860	4
IT HOLDS AS LARGE A GLOW	LIGHT IS SUFFICIENT TO	862	6
PRECISELY, AS TO YOU [ME].	LIGHT IS SUFFICIENT TO	862	8
THAT DISAPPEARS AS COMES--	FAME IS THE TINT THAT	866	4
AS THE STARVED MAELSTROM LAPS THE NAVIES	AS THE STARVED MAELSTROM	872	1
AS THE VULTURE TEAZED	AS THE STARVED MAELSTROM	872	2
AS THE TIGER EASED	AS THE STARVED MAELSTROM	872	4
THEN, AS FLUNG ASIDE	RIBBONS OF THE YEAR--	873	4
AS A FADED BEAD	RIBBONS OF THE YEAR--	873	5
AS WHEN ON NOON	A SHADE UPON THE MIND	882	2
INHERE AS DO THE SUNS--	THE POETS LIGHT BUT	883	5
AS TO A HOSPITALITY	OUR LITTLE KINSMEN--	885	7
AS I OF HE, SO GOD OF ME	OUR LITTLE KINSMEN--	885	9
AS BIRDS BEFORE ACHIEVING	THESE TESTED OUR HORIZON	886	3
WHERE NOT SO MUCH AS HONEST DOG	WHO OCCUPIES THIS HOUSE?	892	7
UNTIL A PIONEER, AS	WHO OCCUPIES THIS HOUSE?	892	21
AS EASY THE SECRETING HER	OF CONSCIOUSNESS, HER	894	3
PROTRACTED AS THE BREEZE	OF SILKEN SPEECH AND	896	7
I RECOLLECT IT--AS WELL--	THE FIRST DAY THAT I WAS	902	4
AS MINISTRY.	BETWEEN MY COUNTRY--AND	905	4
THE DYING--AS IT WERE A HIGHT	THE ADMIRATIONS--AND	906	3
OR QUARTER--AS I SIGNIFY--	I MAKE HIS CRESCENT FILL	909	3
IT BEARS THE SOUL AS BOLD	FAITH--IS THE PIERLESS	915	5
AS IT WERE ROCKED IN STEEL	FAITH--IS THE PIERLESS	915	6
STILL--JUST AS EASY, IF IT BE THY WILL	ONLY A SHRINE, BUT MINE	918	10
AS OFT AS HE GO DOWN	WE CAN BUT FOLLOW TO THE	920	2
AS OFT AS HE GO DOWN	WE CAN BUT FOLLOW TO THE	920	2
MOST AS BIG AS I WAS,	IF IT HAD NO PENCIL	921	7
MOST AS BIG AS I WAS,	IF IT HAD NO PENCIL	921	7
OFTEN AS I DIE	STRUCK, WAS I, NOR YET	925	18
BEST--AT SETTING--AS IS NATURE'S--	STRUCK, WAS I, NOR YET	925	21
AND AS ITSELF DISCERNS	THE HEART HAS NARROW	928	6
AS FAR AS DEATH THIS WAY--	HOW FAR IS IT TO HEAVEN?	929	2
AS FAR AS DEATH THIS WAY--	HOW FAR IS IT TO HEAVEN?	929	2
AS FAR AS DEATH THIS WAY--	HOW FAR IS IT TO HEAVEN?	929	6
AS FAR AS DEATH THIS WAY--	HOW FAR IS IT TO HEAVEN?	929	6
AS SHOULD A FACE SUPPOSED THE GRAVE'S	THERE IS A JUNE WHEN	930	5
THE FORESTS AS THEY FROZE	TWO TRAVELLERS PERISHING	933	2
AS THOSE FIRST FURNISHED, SAID--	TWO TRAVELLERS PERISHING	933	16
AS IF IT WERE NOT BORN.	DEATH LEAVES US HOMESICK	935	4
AS IF MY BRAIN HAD SPLIT--	I FELT A CLEAVING IN MY	937	2
FAIRER THROUGH FADING--AS THE DAY	FAIRER THROUGH FADING--	938	1
AS SOMEONE HELD A LIGHT UNTO [UPON]	WHAT I SEE NOT, I BETTER	939	7
YET PRECIOUS AS THE HOUSE	ON THAT DEAR FRAME THE	940	2
AS HANDS THE GRAVE HAD GRIMED	ON THAT DEAR FRAME THE	940	6
AFFLICTS ME--AS A SETTING SUN--	I LEARNED--AT LEAST--	944	30
SHY AS THE WIND OF HIS CHAMBERS [LODGINGS]	THIS IS A BLOSSOM OF THE	945	5
SWIFT AS A FRESHET'S TONGUE	THIS IS A BLOSSOM OF THE	945	6
AS ONE MET SUDDEN [ENCOUNTERED] GENTLEFOLK	IT IS AN HONORABLE	946	3
THE MUSCLES GRAPPLED [STRUGGLED] AS WITH LEADS	'TWAS CRISIS--ALL THE	948	9
AS FROST IS BEST CONCEIVED	AS FROST IS BEST	951	1
IF WHEN [AS] THE SUN REVEAL,	AS FROST IS BEST	951	5
IF AS THE DAYS RESUME [INCREASE]	AS FROST IS BEST	951	7
THE DOOR AS INSTANT [SUDDEN] SHUT--AND I--	A DOOR JUST OPENED ON A	953	5
AS ONE DOES SICKNESS OVER	AS ONE DOES SICKNESS	957	1
AS ONE REWALKS A PRECIPICE	AS ONE DOES SICKNESS	957	5
WE MET AS SPARKS--DIVERGING FLINTS	WE MET AS SPARKS--	958	1
WE PARTED AS THE CENTRAL FLINT	WE MET AS SPARKS--	958	3
AS ONE BEMOANING A DOMINION	A LOSS OF SOMETHING EVER	959	7
AND FAINTER, TOO, AS WISENESS IS--	A LOSS OF SOMETHING EVER	959	10
AS PLAN FOR NOON AND PLAN FOR NIGHT	AS PLAN FOR NOON AND	960	1
ARE [FLIT / SHOW] AS THEY WERE NOT--	PAIN--EXPANDS THE TIME--	967	8

		FIRST LINE	POEM	LINE
AS	(CONTINUED)			
	AS IN SLEEP--ALL HUE FORGOTTEN--	COLOR--CASTE--	970	5
	AS TO ESTIMATE	ROBBED BY DEATH--BUT	971	V 16
	IT ONLY MOVED [SWERVED] AS DO THE SUNS--	'TWAS AWKWARD, BUT IT	973	5
	AS LIGHTNING ON A LANDSCAPE	THE SOUL'S DISTINCT	974	5
	AS SLEIGH BELLS SEEM [SOUND] IN SUMMER	AS SLEIGH BELLS SEEM IN	981	1
	'TIS TRANSPORT WILD AS THRILLS THE GRAVES	'TIS ANGUISH GRANDER	984	5
	THE GRASS DIVIDES AS WITH A COMB--	A NARROW FELLOW IN THE	986	5
	SHE SPED AS PETALS OF [FROM] A ROSE	SHE SPED AS PETALS OF A	991	1
	AS CRICKET OR AS BEE--	SHE SPED AS PETALS OF A	991	6
	AS CRICKET OR AS BEE--	SHE SPED AS PETALS OF A	991	6
	AS SLIGHTLY [SCARCELY] AS THE ROUTES [FLIGHTS] OF STARS--	WE MISS HER, NOT BECAUSE	993	5
	AS SLIGHTLY [SCARCELY] AS THE ROUTES [FLIGHTS] OF STARS--	WE MISS HER, NOT BECAUSE	993	5
	INCLUDE US [SCAN BETTER / CONVEY US]--AS THEY GO--	WE MISS HER, NOT BECAUSE	993	8
	PARTAKE AS DOTH THE BEE,	PARTAKE AS DOTH THE BEE,	994	1
	DRIFTS WERE AS DIFFICULT THEN TO THINK	THIS WAS IN THE WHITE OF	995	3
	AS DAISIES NOW TO BE SEEN--	THIS WAS IN THE WHITE OF	995	4
	EXHIBIT HERE, AS DOTH A BURR--	BEST THINGS DWELL OUT OF	998	7
	AS STARS THAT DROP ANONYMOUS	SUPERFLUOUS WERE THE SUN	999	11
	AS THAT ENDURED	THERE IS NO SILENCE IN	1004	2
	HEART THAT PROPOSED AS HEART THAT ACCEPTED	UP LIFE'S HILL WITH MY	1010	7
	SHE ROSE AS HIGH AS HIS OCCASION	SHE ROSE AS HIGH AS HIS	1011	1
	SHE ROSE AS HIGH AS HIS OCCASION	SHE ROSE AS HIGH AS HIS	1011	1
	HE--SOVREIGN AS THE SUN	SAID DEATH TO PASSION	1033	7
	AS BLEMISHLESS, AS HER.	HER LITTLE PARASOL TO	1038	8
	AS BLEMISHLESS, AS HER.	HER LITTLE PARASOL TO	1038	8
	I HEARD, AS IF I HAD NO EAR	I HEARD, AS IF I HAD NO	1039	1
	I SAW, AS IF MY EYE WERE ON	I HEARD, AS IF I HAD NO	1039	5
	I DWELT, AS IF MYSELF WERE OUT,	I HEARD, AS IF I HAD NO	1039	9
	AS, TILL THE BEE	SPRING COMES ON THE	1042	4
	A CHIEF INDIFFERENCE, AS FOREIGN	A SICKNESS OF THIS WORLD	1044	5
	AS BLOOM UPON A STALK.	THE OPENING AND THE	1047	4
	BUT FOREIGN AS THE DIALECT	REPORTLESS SUBJECTS, TO	1048	3
	AS WILLING LID O'ER WEARY EYE	AS WILLING LID O'ER	1050	1
	AND AS [WHEN] SHE VANISHES, REMORSE	I CANNOT MEET THE SPRING	1051	7
	AS IF THE CHECKS WERE GIVEN--	I NEVER SAW A MOOR--	1052	8
	WITH SWIFTNESS, AS OF CHARIOTS	IT WAS A QUIET WAY--	1053	7
	AND DISTANCE, AS OF WHEELS.	IT WAS A QUIET WAY--	1053	8
	AS ACRES [COUNTIES] FROM THE FEET	IT WAS A QUIET WAY--	1053	10
	AS MUCH THROUGH CONSCIOUSNESS [CONSCIOUS FAITH]	NOT TO DISCOVER WEAKNESS	1054	4
	AS PYRAMIDAL [ELEMENTAL / PLUPOTENTIAL] NERVE	NOT TO DISCOVER WEAKNESS	1054	6
	IT GREW AS I PURSUED	I HAD A DAILY BLISS	1057	4
	THEN OFFERED AS A BUTTERFLY	BLOOM--IS RESULT--TO	1058	7
	GRACIOUS NOW TO ME AS ANY--	THREE WEEKS PASSED SINCE	1061	7
	CAUGHT HELPLESS AT A SENSE AS IF	HE SCANNED IT--STAGGERED	1062	4
	AS WEST-INDIAN--	EXCEPT THE SMALLER SIZE	1067	V
	REMIT AS YET NO GRACE	FURTHER IN SUMMER THAN	1068	13
	BUT SIMULTANEOUS AS SOUND	FURTHER IN SUMMER THAN	1068	V
	AS DOWN HIS HEAVEN DROPT REMOTE [ECHOED FAINT]	JUST ONCE! OH LEAST	1076	8
	AS THE FRINGE	WHAT TWIGS WE HELD BY--	1086	6
	'TIS NEWS AS NULL AS NOTHING,	MYSELF CAN READ THE	1089	7
	'TIS NEWS AS NULL AS NOTHING,	MYSELF CAN READ THE	1089	7
	OBTAIN "ADMISSION" AS A CHILD	DEW--IS THE FRESHET IN	1097	11
	ITALICIZED--AS 'TWERE.	THE LAST NIGHT THAT SHE	1100	8
	AS WE WENT OUT AND IN	THE LAST NIGHT THAT SHE	1100	9
	THEN LIGHTLY [SOFTLY] AS A REED	THE LAST NIGHT THAT SHE	1100	22
	THE DIFFERENCE IS AS BIG	BETWEEN THE FORM OF LIFE	1101	2
	AS LIQUOR AT THE LIP BETWEEN	BETWEEN THE FORM OF LIFE	1101	3
	THE TWILIGHT STOOD [LEANED], AS STRANGERS DO	THE CRICKETS SANG	1104	6
	TO STAY AS IF, OR GO.	THE CRICKETS SANG	1104	8
	A VASTNESS, AS A NEIGHBOR, CAME,	THE CRICKETS SANG	1104	9
	A PEACE, AS HEMISPHERES AT HOME	THE CRICKETS SANG	1104	11
	AND DISTANT AS AN ORDER DONE	THE CRICKETS SANG	1104	V
	AND DOUBTFUL AS REPORT UPON	THE CRICKETS SANG	1104	V
	MINUTER LANDSCAPE AS OURSELVES	LIKE MEN AND WOMEN	1105	7
	AS EMIGRANTS WE COME	THE BIRD DID PRANCE--THE	1107	V 10
	'TIS AS HID AS DEATH	NONE WHO SAW IT EVER	1110	2
	'TIS AS HID AS DEATH	NONE WHO SAW IT EVER	1110	2
	GENERAL AS THE DANDELION	NONE WHO SAW IT EVER	1110	7
	THE SAME AS THOSE THAT LIVED	THAT THIS SHOULD FEEL	1112	2
	AS NEVER WAS ACHIEVED [BEHELD]--	THAT THIS SHOULD FEEL	1112	4
	AS MAKES ONE HIDE [HANG] IT'S HEAD	THAT THIS SHOULD FEEL	1112	V 4
	THE SMALL MUST [DO] DIE, THE SAME [AS WELL] AS HE--	THAT THIS SHOULD FEEL	1112	6
	THE SMALL MUST [DO] DIE, THE SAME [AS WELL] AS HE--	THAT THIS SHOULD FEEL	1112	6
	AS ACCENT FADES [WANES] TO INTERVAL	THE MURMURING OF BEES,	1115	11
	AS IF THEY COULD NOT HOIST THEMSELVES	THIS SLOW DAY MOVED	1120	3
	SOFT AS THE MASSACRE [MASSACRES] OF SUNS	SOFT AS THE MASSACRE OF	1127	1
	AS LIGHTNING TO THE CHILDREN EASED	TELL ALL THE TRUTH BUT	1129	5
	PRECISELY AS THE CALLS--	THE MERCHANT OF THE	1131	4
	AS TO BEHOLD HIS AMPLE [GENTLE] FLIGHT--	THE MERCHANT OF THE	1131	11
	LIKE WINTER AS A FACE	THE SNOW THAT NEVER	1133	9
	AS NEAR AS MEMORY--	THE SNOW THAT NEVER	1133	16
	AS NEAR AS MEMORY--	THE SNOW THAT NEVER	1133	16
	DID MAKE [PRESUMED] AS TO DEVOUR	THE WIND TOOK UP THE	1134	6

AS (CONTINUED)	FIRST LINE	POEM		LINE
YET [BUT] EASY AS THE [A] NARROW SNAKE	THE FROST OF DEATH WAS	1136		12
NATURE KNOWS AS WELL	HER SOVREIGN PEOPLE	1139		2
AND IS AS FOND OF SIGNIFYING	HER SOVREIGN PEOPLE	1139		3
AS IF FALLIBLE--	HER SOVREIGN PEOPLE	1139		4
AS ABSENT AS A HUNDRED YEARS,	THE FACE WE CHOOSE TO	1141		3
AS ABSENT AS A HUNDRED YEARS,	THE FACE WE CHOOSE TO	1141		3
THAT DOUBTS AS FERVENTLY AS IT BELIEVES.	OURSELVES WE DO INTER	1144		4
THAT DOUBTS AS FERVENTLY AS IT BELIEVES.	OURSELVES WE DO INTER	1144		4
MOTIONLESS AS PEACE	AFTER A HUNDRED YEARS	1147		4
ALL MEN MEET [PASS / HASTE] AS IF	AFTER THE SUN COMES OUT	1148		5
MEN EXPRESS AS IF	AFTER THE SUN COMES OUT	1148	V	5
FRESH AS A CARGO FROM BATIZE	AFTER THE SUN COMES OUT	1148		7
TELL AS A MARKSMAN--WERE FORGOTTEN	TELL AS A MARKSMAN--WERE	1152		1
RUDDY AS THAT COEVAL APPLE	TELL AS A MARKSMAN--WERE	1152		3
FRESH [NEW] AS MANKIND THAT HUMBLE STORY	TELL AS A MARKSMAN--WERE	1152		5
I WON AS NEAR AS THIS	THROUGH WHAT TRANSPORTS	1153		6
I WON AS NEAR AS THIS	THROUGH WHAT TRANSPORTS	1153		6
AS CHILDREN STRICTEST [STRICTLY] KEPT	CONTAINED IN THIS SHORT	1165		5
UNMANIFEST TO [UNWITNESSED OF THE / AS DOTH THE TIRED] SENSE	CONTAINED IN THIS SHORT	1165	V	
AS [FOR] A GYMNASIUM	ALONE AND IN A	1167		12
AS EACH WERE SPECIAL [LAWFUL / ONLY] HEIR--	ALONE AND IN A	1167		16
AS OLD AS WOE--	AS OLD AS WOE--	1168		1
AS OLD AS WOE--	AS OLD AS WOE--	1168		1
AS OLD AS BLISS [JOY]	AS OLD AS WOE--	1168		4
AS OLD AS BLISS [JOY]	AS OLD AS WOE--	1168		4
BOLD AS A BAILIFF'S HYMN--	A PROMPT--EXECUTIVE BIRD	1177		2
GOOD AS A NORSEMAN'S HYMN--	A PROMPT--EXECUTIVE BIRD	1177	V	2
AS A MAGISTRATE [BENEFIT]--	A PROMPT--EXECUTIVE BIRD	1177		8
AS A CHURCH REMAIN--	WHEN I HOPED I FEARED--	1181		4
IS NOT SO AMPLE AS THE BREAST [HEART]	STEP LIGHTLY ON THIS	1183		3
AS FAR AS CANNON DWELL	STEP LIGHTLY ON THIS	1183		6
AS FAR AS CANNON DWELL	STEP LIGHTLY ON THIS	1183		6
AS POSITIVE ARE WE	THE PUNGENT ATOM IN THE	1191		6
AS LIMIT OF DOMINION	THE PUNGENT ATOM IN THE	1191		7
AS ONE COMMUTED LED--	SOMEHOW MYSELF SURVIVED	1194		6
AS GOLD THE [A] PYRITES WOULD SHUN--	HE PREACHED UPON	1207		6
BUT "NEVER" FAR AS HONOR	TO DISAPPEAR ENHANCES--	1209		9
THAT JUST AS WE DISCERN	TO DISAPPEAR ENHANCES--	1209		14
AS SPECULATIONS FLEE	A SPARROW TOOK A SLICE	1211	V	6
AS AN ACCUSTOMED STIRRUP--	A SPARROW TOOK A SLICE	1211	V	7
AS A FAMILIAR STIRRUP [SADDLE]	A SPARROW TOOK A SLICE	1211	V	7
AS OF FRUGALITY [VELOCITY / AMENITY / PROPRIETY]--	A SPARROW TOOK A SLICE	1211	V	8
AS A FOREIGN RACE--	NOW I KNEW I LOST HER--	1219		6
GRAPPLES WITH A THEME STUBBORN AS SUBLIME	SOME WE SEE NO MORE,	1221		7
ABLE AS THE DUST TO EQUIP IT'S FEATURE	SOME WE SEE NO MORE,	1221		8
ADEQUATE AS DRUMS	SOME WE SEE NO MORE,	1221		9
AS YESTERDAY'S SURPRISE--	THE RIDDLE WE CAN GUESS	1222		4
AS FORESTS [BRANCHES] TOUCH THE WIND	BECAUSE HE LOVES HER	1229		8
HAD LOVE AS PUNCTUAL BEEN	IT CAME AT LAST BUT	1230		6
IT WALKED AS WET AS ANY WAVE	LIKE RAIN IT SOUNDED	1235		3
IT WALKED AS WET AS ANY WAVE	LIKE RAIN IT SOUNDED	1235		3
BUT SWEPT AS DRY AS SAND--	LIKE RAIN IT SOUNDED	1235		4
BUT SWEPT AS DRY AS SAND--	LIKE RAIN IT SOUNDED	1235		4
A COMING AS OF HOSTS WAS HEARD	LIKE RAIN IT SOUNDED	1235		7
PERSUASIVE AS PERDITION,	RISK IS THE HAIR THAT	1239		11
SO CHASTENED AS THE FLY--	THE BUTTERFLY IN HONORED	1246		4
WHITE AS AN INDIAN PIPE	WHITE AS AN INDIAN PIPE	1250		1
RED AS A CARDINAL FLOWER	WHITE AS AN INDIAN PIPE	1250		2
FABULOUS AS A MOON AT NOON	WHITE AS AN INDIAN PIPE	1250		3
ELIJAH'S HORSES AS UNIQUE	ELIJAH'S WAGON KNEW NO	1254		3
AS WAS HIS VEHICLE--	ELIJAH'S WAGON KNEW NO	1254		4
POSSESSION JUST AS LONG--	DOMINION LASTS UNTIL	1257		2
BUT THESE--ENDOWING AS THEY FLIT	DOMINION LASTS UNTIL	1257		3
THROUGH ACCENTS TERRIBLE AS DEATH	WHO WERE "THE FATHER AND	1258	V	5
AS PARADISE FICTITIOUS	BECAUSE THAT YOU ARE	1260		19
IF "GOD IS LOVE" AS HE ADMITS	BECAUSE THAT YOU ARE	1260		33
AS HE BESIDES CONCEDES	BECAUSE THAT YOU ARE	1260		38
BUT A CONFIDING GUEST CONSULT AS WELL,	I CANNOT SEE MY SOUL BUT	1262		4
THE SPIDER AS AN ARTIST	THE SPIDER AS AN ARTIST	1275		1
AND WENT OR WAITED AS THEY LIKED	THE MOUNTAINS STOOD IN	1278		3
PRECISELY AS THE JOY OF HIM--	THE WAY TO KNOW THE	1279		3
AS HERESIES OF TRANSPORT	THE WAY TO KNOW THE	1279		11
AS PARALLAX [FIRMAMENT] A FLAME--	I THOUGHT THAT NATURE	1286		4
IS ALWAYS AS THE CONTENTS	I THOUGHT THAT NATURE	1286		9
PRECISELY AS THE CANDIDATE [CHARACTER]	TWO LENGTHS HAS EVERY	1295	V	7
REMAIN THOU AS THOU ART.	TWO LENGTHS HAS EVERY	1295		12
AS IF IT TARRIED ALWAYS	THE MUSHROOM IS THE ELF	1298		5
I FEEL [FELT] AS IF THE GRASS WAS PLEASED	THE MUSHROOM IS THE ELF	1298		13
MAGNANIMOUS AS BIRD	NOT WITH A CLUB, THE	1304		9
IN SUCH AN EARTH AS OUR'S--	NOT WITH A CLUB, THE	1304		14
REQUIRED A BLOW AS VAST--	TO BREAK SO VAST A HEART	1312		2
GENERIC AS A QUARRY	WINTER IS GOOD--HIS HOAR	1316		5
AND HEARTY--AS A ROSE--	WINTER IS GOOD--HIS HOAR	1316		6
SHALL COMPREHEND [SCRUTINIZE] AS ONE	HOW NEWS MUST FEEL WHEN	1319		10
AS SOON AS [THE INSTANT THAT] YOU HAVE COME	DEAR MARCH--COME IN--	1320		24
AS SOON AS [THE INSTANT THAT] YOU HAVE COME	DEAR MARCH--COME IN--	1320		24
THAT BLAME IS JUST AS DEAR AS PRAISE	DEAR MARCH--COME IN--	1320		25

AS (CONTINUED)

	FIRST LINE	POEM	LINE
THAT BLAME IS JUST AS DEAR AS PRAISE	DEAR MARCH--COME IN--	1320	25
AND PRAISE AS MERE AS BLAME--	DEAR MARCH--COME IN--	1320	26
AND PRAISE AS MERE AS BLAME--	DEAR MARCH--COME IN--	1320	26
DOES NOT LOOK AS WELL--	FLOSS WONT SAVE YOU FROM	1322	V 4
FLEE AS IF YOU TROD UNTHINKING	KNOCK WITH TREMOR--	1325	4
AND MIGHT WE NOT AS WELL--	OUR LITTLE SECRETS SLINK	1326	4
AS IF IT WERE HIS OWN!	A LITTLE MADNESS IN THE	1333	6
DID NOT SO MUCH AS WRING FROM HIM	A SINGLE CLOVER PLANK	1343	15
AS WELL AS [BETTER THAN] PRIME	AN ANTIQUATED GRACE	1345	3
AS WELL AS [BETTER THAN] PRIME	AN ANTIQUATED GRACE	1345	3
AS SUMMER INTO AUTUMN SLIPS	AS SUMMER INTO AUTUMN	1346	1
IMPREGNABLE AS [AS OPULENT IT / EXTRAVAGANT AS / ABUNDANT AS . . .	YOU CANNOT TAKE ITSELF	1351	5
IMPREGNABLE AS [AS OPULENT IT / EXTRAVAGANT AS / ABUNDANT AS . . .	YOU CANNOT TAKE ITSELF	1351	5
IMPREGNABLE AS [AS OPULENT IT / EXTRAVAGANT AS / ABUNDANT AS . . .	YOU CANNOT TAKE ITSELF	1351	5
IMPREGNABLE AS [AS OPULENT IT / EXTRAVAGANT AS / ABUNDANT AS . . .	YOU CANNOT TAKE ITSELF	1351	5
. . . THE / LUXURIOUS AS THE] LIGHT	YOU CANNOT TAKE ITSELF	1351	5
BUT TAKE AWAY AS DIFFICULT [IMPOTENT / EASILY]	YOU CANNOT TAKE ITSELF	1351	7
AS UNDISCOVERED GOLD--	YOU CANNOT TAKE ITSELF	1351	8
TO MEET IT--NAMELESS AS IT IS--	THE LAST OF SUMMER IS	1353	5
AUDACIOUS AS WITHOUT A KNOCK	THE LAST OF SUMMER IS	1353	7
LAWFUL AS EQUILIBRIUM.	THE RAT IS THE CONCISEST	1356	10
WHERESOE'ER, OR WAS SHE--[SHE IS / OR AS WAS SHE]	SUMMER LAID HER SIMPLE	1363	7
IT'S FERVORS ARE AS FIRM--	HOW KNOW IT FROM A	1364	2
AND SUNDER AS THEY CAME--	HOW KNOW IT FROM A	1364	8
TRUSTY AS THE STARS	TRUSTY AS THE STARS	1369	1
PROMPT AS WHEN I LIT THEM	TRUSTY AS THE STARS	1369	3
DURABLE AS DAWN	TRUSTY AS THE STARS	1369	5
HE DOTH AS PUNCTUAL CALL	THE SUN IS ONE--AND ON	1372	2
AS ON THE CONSCIENTIOUS FLOWER	THE SUN IS ONE--AND ON	1372	3
AS FAME SHOULD BE--	HIS MANSION IN THE POOL	1379	12
REPORTLESS, ALSO, BUT SINCERE AS NATURE	IN MANY AND REPORTLESS	1382	3
AS ELIGIBLE [UNPERVERTED / UNDIVERTED / UNAVAILING] AS THE MOON	SUMMER--WE ALL HAVE SEEN	1386	7
AS ELIGIBLE [UNPERVERTED / UNDIVERTED / UNAVAILING] AS THE MOON	SUMMER--WE ALL HAVE SEEN	1386	7
UNKNOWN AS TO AN ECSTASY	SUMMER--WE ALL HAVE SEEN	1386	11
AS IF IT [HE] WERE [AS FREQUENTLY] UNDONE--	THE BUTTERFLY'S NUMIDIAN	1387	6
AS IF IT [HE] WERE [AS FREQUENTLY] UNDONE--	THE BUTTERFLY'S NUMIDIAN	1387	6
A SMILE SO SMALL AS MINE MIGHT BE	THEY MIGHT NOT NEED ME--	1391	3
PORTENTOUS AS OUR OWN, WHO KNOWS?	WHOSE PINK CAREER MAY	1394	2
IT SOUNDED AS IF THE STREETS [AIR] WERE RUNNING	IT SOUNDED AS IF THE	1397	1
AS WE [YOU] WHO STAY, SUPPOSE--	PERHAPS THEY DO NOT GO	1399	2
BETRAYS [REPORTS] US, AS HIS FIRST BETROTHAL	MARCH IS THE MONTH OF	1404	7
AS THOSE THAT DISSOLUTION SAW	IT WAS A QUIET SEEMING	1419	11
I SHUN IT AS I DO DESPAIR	ONE JOY OF SO MUCH	1420	3
AS FINER IS A GOING	SUMMER HAS TWO	1422	7
AS CASUAL [ODORLESS / INNOCENT] AS RAIN	THE GENTIAN HAS A	1424	6
AS CASUAL [ODORLESS / INNOCENT] AS RAIN	THE GENTIAN HAS A	1424	6
AND AS BENIGN--	THE GENTIAN HAS A	1424	7
IT IS AS OLD AS GOD--	HOW BRITTLE ARE THE	1433	5
IT IS AS OLD AS GOD--	HOW BRITTLE ARE THE	1433	5
IS ABSOLUTE AS GOD,	THAN HEAVEN MORE REMOTE,	1436	15
AS COMMON AS IT IS UNKNOWN	BEHOLD THIS LITTLE BANE	1438	3
AS COMMON AS IT IS UNKNOWN	BEHOLD THIS LITTLE BANE	1438	3
AS IF IT NEVER TORE	TO MEND EACH TATTERED	1442	6
AND SPACIOUS AS BEFORE--	TO MEND EACH TATTERED	1442	8
AND KINSMEN AS DIVULGELESS	DEATH IS THE SUPPLE	1445	11
AND KINDRED AS RESPONSIVE--	DEATH IS THE SUPPLE	1445	V 11
AND PAGEANTS AS IMPASSIVE	DEATH IS THE SUPPLE	1445	V 11
AS THRONGS [CLANS] OF DOWN--	DEATH IS THE SUPPLE	1445	12
AS PORCELAIN	DEATH IS THE SUPPLE	1445	V 12
AS GUILELESS AS A BIRD	WHOEVER DISENCHANTS	1451	5
AS GUILELESS AS A BIRD	WHOEVER DISENCHANTS	1451	5
AS GRAPHIC AS A STAR	WHOEVER DISENCHANTS	1451	6
AS GRAPHIC AS A STAR	WHOEVER DISENCHANTS	1451	6
AS IF IT WERE A WOE--	SO GAY A FLOWER	1456	3
WAS DIM AS TO THE WEALTHY	IT STOLE ALONG SO	1457	3
AS LONG AS HE CAN BLUSH	HIS CHEEK IS HIS	1460	2
AS LONG AS HE CAN BLUSH	HIS CHEEK IS HIS	1460	2
AS LIGHTLY AS AN OPTION GOWN	WE KNEW NOT THAT WE WERE	1462	5
AS LIGHTLY AS AN OPTION GOWN	WE KNEW NOT THAT WE WERE	1462	5
EXCEPT AS A SURMISE	BEFORE YOU THOUGHT OF	1465	2
AS IF FOR YOU TO CHOOSE--	BEFORE YOU THOUGHT OF	1465	10
HE CHEATS AS HE ENCHANTS	ONE OF THE ONES THAT	1466	14
AS ELOQUENT APPEARS--	A LITTLE OVERFLOWING	1467	6
AS IS A DISRESPECT	HOW DESTITUTE IS HE	1477	7
AS HE HAD NO ESTEEM	HOW DESTITUTE IS HE	1477	V 7
ABODE IN AS SUPREME	THE WAY HOPE BUILDS HIS	1481	5
AS IF IT WERE OF LEDGES SMIT	THE WAY HOPE BUILDS HIS	1481	7
AS COVERT AS A FUGITIVE,	THE ROBIN IS A GABRIEL	1483	13
AS COVERT AS A FUGITIVE,	THE ROBIN IS A GABRIEL	1483	13
AS CAPSULES ARE FOR FLOWER'S--	THE FACE IN EVANESCENCE	1490	4
AS IGNORANT OF THEIR RESUMPTION	FACTS BY OUR SIDE ARE	1497	12

AS (CONTINUED)

	FIRST LINE	POEM		LINE
AS YOU OR I [COWARDS DO]--	FACTS BY OUR SIDE ARE	1497		13
AS INTIMATE [MAGICAL]--AS FUGITIVE	OF WHOM SO DEAR	1504		4
AS INTIMATE [MAGICAL]--AS FUGITIVE	OF WHOM SO DEAR	1504		4
AS SUNSET ON THE SNOW--	OF WHOM SO DEAR	1504		5
SEVENTY YEARS IS SPENT AS QUICK	SUMMER IS SHORTER THAN	1506		3
AS AN ONLY DOLLAR--	SUMMER IS SHORTER THAN	1506		4
AS WHEN YOU CAME BEFORE	THE PILE OF YEARS IS NOT	1507		2
AND CATCH ME ERE [WHEN / AS] I DROP	THE PILE OF YEARS IS NOT	1507		8
ANGER AS SOON AS FED IS DEAD--	MINE ENEMY IS GROWING	1509		7
ANGER AS SOON AS FED IS DEAD--	MINE ENEMY IS GROWING	1509		7
AND [WHO] INDEPENDENT AS THE SUN	HOW HAPPY IS THE LITTLE	1510		7
HER TRIPLE SUIT AS SWEET	MY COUNTRY NEED NOT	1511		2
AS WHEN 'TWAS CUT AT LEXINGTON,	MY COUNTRY NEED NOT	1511		3
IS JUST AS HIGH AS YOU AND I,	THE BUTTERFLY UPON THE	1521		5
IS JUST AS HIGH AS YOU AND I,	THE BUTTERFLY UPON THE	1521		5
AS CONFIDENT OF HIM AS WE--	HE LIVED THE LIFE OF	1525		5
AS CONFIDENT OF HIM AS WE--	HE LIVED THE LIFE OF	1525		5
KNOW THAT WHICH MAKES THEM AS FORGOT	THE MOON UPON HER FLUENT	1528		7
AS DAWN FORGETS THEM--NOW--	THE MOON UPON HER FLUENT	1528		8
AS IF A DRUM [THE DRUMS] WENT ON AND ON	A PANG IS MORE	1530	V	
FOR SUCH A FOE [SWEET / GLEE / DAWN / SCENE / DEW / JOY] AS THIS--	FROM ALL THE JAILS THE	1532		8
HE IS JUST AS [STILL MORE] HIGH--	FOLLOW WISE ORION	1538		4
AS IMPERCEPTIBLY AS GRIEF	AS IMPERCEPTIBLY AS	1540		1
AS IMPERCEPTIBLY AS GRIEF	AS IMPERCEPTIBLY AS	1540		1
AS TWILIGHT LONG BEGUN,	AS IMPERCEPTIBLY AS	1540		6
AS [OF] GUEST, THAT [WHO] WOULD BE GONE--	AS IMPERCEPTIBLY AS	1540		12
AS SUDDENLY BE WORN	AS IMPERCEPTIBLY AS	1540	V	
AS OFTEN AS A CENTURY	MEETING BY ACCIDENT,	1548		3
AS OFTEN AS A CENTURY	MEETING BY ACCIDENT,	1548		3
AS MIDAS IS OF GOLD--	MEETING BY ACCIDENT,	1548		8
SO CIVIC AS THE JAY--	NO BRIGADIER THROUGHOUT	1561		2
AS GALLANTLY AS IF THE EAST	HER LOSSES MAKE OUR	1562		3
AS GALLANTLY AS IF THE EAST	HER LOSSES MAKE OUR	1562		3
AS EVERY PORTER KNOWS--	HER LOSSES MAKE OUR	1562		6
AS INNOCENT [DANGEROUS] AS JUNE--	TO SEE HER IS A PICTURE	1568		4
AS INNOCENT [DANGEROUS] AS JUNE--	TO SEE HER IS A PICTURE	1568		4
OF [TO] EVERY OTHER [AS GRACIOUS AS A] BOON--	TO SEE HER IS A PICTURE	1568	V	4
OF [TO] EVERY OTHER [AS GRACIOUS AS A] BOON--	TO SEE HER IS A PICTURE	1568	V	4
A WARMTH AS NEAR [SURE / FINE] AS IF THE SUN	TO SEE HER IS A PICTURE	1568		7
A WARMTH AS NEAR [SURE / FINE] AS IF THE SUN	TO SEE HER IS A PICTURE	1568		7
A GLEE AS SWEET AS IF THE STARS	TO SEE HER IS A PICTURE	1568	V	7
A GLEE AS SWEET AS IF THE STARS	TO SEE HER IS A PICTURE	1568	V	7
A PEACE AS PURE AS IF THE SKY	TO SEE HER IS A PICTURE	1568	V	7
A PEACE AS PURE AS IF THE SKY	TO SEE HER IS A PICTURE	1568	V	7
AS ROBINS [ROBIN]--SIRE AND SON--	FOREVER HONORED BE THE	1570		6
BUT SUMMER, FRILLED AS FOR A HOLIDAY	WE WEAR OUR SOBER	1572		2
ARRAIGNS IT AS IT SINGS.	NO LADDER NEEDS THE BIRD	1574		4
AS JESUS SAYS OF HIM,	NO LADDER NEEDS THE BIRD	1574		6
BUT AS THE SPIRIT FURNISHES--	THE SPIRIT LASTS--BUT IN	1576		3
THE THOUGHT IS [SCENE WAS] QUIET AS A FLAKE--	THE FARTHEST THUNDER	1581		17
THEN SWEPT AS LIGHTLY FROM DISDAIN	TO HER DERIDED HOME	1586		7
AS LADY FROM HER BOWER--	TO HER DERIDED HOME	1586		8
AS JESUS CITES [SAYS] OF HIM--	TO HER DERIDED HOME	1586		10
IS VALID AS A STAR--	TO HER DERIDED HOME	1586	V	
AS FROM AN EMERALD GHOST--	THERE CAME A WIND LIKE A	1593		6
AS MADE REALITY A DREAM	WITHIN THAT LITTLE HIVE	1607		3
AS CONFIDENT OF HIM AS WE--	WHO ABDICATED AMBUSH	1616		5
AS CONFIDENT OF HIM AS WE--	WHO ABDICATED AMBUSH	1616		5
AS THAT EXALTED [THOSE RESPLENDENT] HERE--	NO LIFE CAN POMPLESS	1626		4
AS FROM THE EARTH THE LIGHT [FAIR] BALLOON	AS FROM THE EARTH THE	1630		1
AS A BIRD	AS FROM THE EARTH THE	1630		8
MAKES NOT AS MUCH OF SOUND	THE SUN IN REINING TO	1636		2
AS CART OF MAN IN ROAD BELOW	THE SUN IN REINING TO	1636		3
ARE EVEN AS THYSELF--	GO THY GREAT WAY!	1638		3
A CHILL CAME UP AS FROM A SHAFT	A CAP OF LEAD ACROSS THE	1649		5
COHESIVE AS THE SPIRIT	A WORD MADE FLESH IS	1651		11
AS WE PASS HOUSES MUSING SLOW	AS WE PASS HOUSES MUSING	1653		1
WILL FEEL AS COOL AS LAND	I DID NOT REACH THEE	1664		11
WILL FEEL AS COOL AS LAND	I DID NOT REACH THEE	1664		11
AS FLOWER AT FALL OF FROST--	I WATCHED HER FACE TO	1667		8
BUT AS HE WAS A WORM	IN WINTER IN MY ROOM	1670		4
IN FEATURE AS THE WORM BEFORE	IN WINTER IN MY ROOM	1670		16
AS PATTERNS SWIM	IN WINTER IN MY ROOM	1670		30
AS AN ASTRAL HALL	LIGHTLY STEPPED A YELLOW	1672		6
PERIL AS A POSSESSION	PERIL AS A POSSESSION	1678		1
AS CLEAN AS FIRE	PERIL AS A POSSESSION	1678		7
AS CLEAN AS FIRE	PERIL AS A POSSESSION	1678		7
NOT SO GOOD AS JOY--	RATHER ARID DELIGHT	1679		4
WE SAY AS OF A STATION	THE BLUNDER IS IN	1684		3
AS THIS ETERNITY	THE BLUNDER IS IN	1684		8
PRECISELY AS IN MARCH IS HEARD	THE ONES THAT	1690		3
A WOMAN'S SHAWL AS BIG	THE SUN RETIRED TO A	1693		2
THEY TALK AS SLOW AS LEGENDS GROW	THEY TALK AS SLOW AS	1697		1
THEY TALK AS SLOW AS LEGENDS GROW	THEY TALK AS SLOW AS	1697		1
THEY LAUGH AS WISE AS PLOTS OF WIT	THEY TALK AS SLOW AS	1697		5
THEY LAUGH AS WISE AS PLOTS OF WIT	THEY TALK AS SLOW AS	1697		5
A RAPTURE AS OF LEGACIES--	TO TELL THE BEAUTY WOULD	1700		7
IS AS ARABLE AS SPRING	WINTER UNDER CULTIVATION	1707		2

	FIRST LINE	POEM		LINE
AS (CONTINUED)				
IS AS ARABLE AS SPRING	WINTER UNDER CULTIVATION	1707		2
T'IS EARLY AS OUR BREATH	WITCHCRAFT HAS NOT A	1708		2
AS COMPETITION DONE	WITH SWEETNESS UNABATED	1709		6
WOULD FEEL AS THOROUGHLY AT EASE	A FACE DEVOID OF LOVE OR	1711		4
AS WERE THEY OLD ACQUAINTANCES--	A FACE DEVOID OF LOVE OR	1711		5
AS SUBTLE AS TOMORROW	AS SUBTLE AS TOMORROW	1713		1
AS SUBTLE AS TOMORROW	AS SUBTLE AS TOMORROW	1713		1
AS THE ATTEMPT TO RISE.	DROWNING IS NOT SO	1718		2
ANALYSIS AS [LIKE] CAPSULE SEEMED	HE WAS MY HOST--HE WAS	1721		7
AS HE ESTEEMED THEM TRIFLES,	HIGH FROM THE EARTH I	1723		3
THEY COULD NOT BE SO BIG AS THIS	IF ALL THE GRIEFS I AM	1726		7
AS THE EYE BEHOLDS	"LETHE" IN MY FLOWER,	1730		6
AS THESE THAT TWICE BEFEL.	MY LIFE CLOSED TWICE	1732		6
IS AUTHORIZED AS PEACE	THE MOB WITHIN THE HEART	1745		4
THE WATERS CHASED HIM AS HE FLED,	THE WATERS CHASED HIM AS	1749		1
AS DAUNTLESS IN THE HOUSE OF DEATH	THIS DOCILE ONE INTER	1752		7
AS PLAYFUL IN THE DOOR OF DEATH	THIS DOCILE ONE INTER	1752	V	7
AS CONTENTED [FEARLESS] IN THE PORCH OF DEATH	THIS DOCILE ONE INTER	1752	V	7
AS HAPPY IN HER CRIB [BED] OF DUST	THIS DOCILE ONE INTER	1752	V	7
AS IF IT WERE HER OWN--	THIS DOCILE ONE INTER	1752		8
PERNICIOUS AS THE SUNSET	THROUGH THOSE OLD	1753		9
AS NATURE'S CURTAIN FELL	UPON THE GALLOWS HUNG A	1757		4
'TIS TWICE AS HEAVY AS IT WAS	WHICH MISSES MOST,	1759		4
'TIS TWICE AS HEAVY AS IT WAS	WHICH MISSES MOST,	1759		4
ELYSIUM IS AS FAR AS TO	ELYSIUM IS AS FAR AS TO	1760		1
ELYSIUM IS AS FAR AS TO	ELYSIUM IS AS FAR AS TO	1760		1
AS QUICKLY AS A SPEAR,	THE SADDEST NOISE, THE	1764		18
AS QUICKLY AS A SPEAR,	THE SADDEST NOISE, THE	1764		18
A SAILING				
A SAILING O'ER THE TIDE,	"SIC TRANSIT GLORIA	3		38
ASCEND				
ASCEND IN CEASELESS [BREAKS IN VICTORIOUS] CAROL--	TO LEARN THE TRANSPORT	167		13
HORIZONS--MUST ASCEND--	MY PERIOD HAD COME FOR	564		6
SO STATELY THEY ASCEND--	YOU'VE SEEN BALLOONS SET	700		2
HER ZEALOUS NOTE DELIGHTS IT TO ASCEND.	AFTER ALL BIRDS HAVE	1395	V	6
ASCEND WITH ME THE EMINENCE [TABLE LAND]	SUCH ARE THE INLETS OF	1421		3
ASCEND INCESSANTLY--	FAME IS THE ONE THAT	1475		4
ASCENDED				
ASCENDED FROM OUR VISION	WENT UP A YEAR THIS	93		21
OR SHE--HERSELF--ASCENDED	THE SOUL'S SUPERIOR	306		5
ASCENDING				
ASCENDING, THOUGH TERRENE--	THE ROAD WAS LIT WITH	1450		6
ASCENSION				
ASCENSION THAT FOR WHICH IT WAS,	AS FROM THE EARTH THE	1630		3
ASCERTAIN				
PLEASE GOD--SHALL ASCERTAIN!	MUSICIANS WRESTLE	157		18
HIS THOUGHT TO ASCERTAIN	A PRECIOUS--MOULDERING	371		10
TO ASCERTAIN [REGISTER] THE SIZE--	THE LONELINESS ONE DARE	777		4
THAT I COULD ASCERTAIN--	THE BIRDS BEGUN AT FOUR	783		14
TO ASCERTAIN THE HOUSE	THE SPRY ARMS OF THE	1103		9
I ASCERTAIN IT WITH A SHOCK--	CONSULTING SUMMER'S	1715		3
ASCERTAINED				
IS ASCERTAINED BY TASTING [TESTING]--	DESPAIR'S ADVANTAGE IS	799		7
ASCETIC				
A FEW ASCETIC EVES--	BESIDES THE AUTUMN POETS	131		6
ASCRIBE				
ASCRIBE NO LESS THE PRAISE--	THE BAT IS DUN, WITH	1575		14
A'SELF				
THAN UNARMED [MOONLESS], ONE'S A'SELF ENCOUNTER--	ONE NEED NOT BE A	670		11
ASHAMED				
SO PRETTY--SO ASHAMED!	SO BASHFUL WHEN I SPIED	91		2
THE LARK IS NOT ASHAMED	FOR EVERY BIRD A NEST--	143		13
OF DEITY--ASHAMED--	WHAT SOFT--CHERUBIC	401		8
BE SO--ASHAMED OF THEE--	WHAT SOFT--CHERUBIC	401		12
I AM ASHAMED--I HIDE--	I AM ASHAMED--I HIDE--	473		1
NO MORE ASHAMED--	I AM ASHAMED--I HIDE--	473		24
THAT YOU BE NOT ASHAMED	YOU TAUGHT ME WAITING	740		10
I'M NOT ASHAMED OF THAT	PERHAPS YOU THINK ME	833		2
I CANNOT BE ASHAMED	I CANNOT BE ASHAMED	914		1
WE SHALL HAVE SHUNNED UNTIL ASHAMED	WHO WERE "THE FATHER AND	1258		23
IT MADE US ALL ASHAMED [DEMEANED]	SO PROUD SHE WAS TO DIE	1272		2
HER [HIS] LOSSES MAKE OUR GAINS ASHAMED--	HER LOSSES MAKE OUR	1562		1
ASHES				
THE MEMORY OF MY ASHES	"SIC TRANSIT GLORIA	3		65
HIS ASHES [EMBERS]--WILL	GRIEF IS A MOUSE--	793		15
ASHES DENOTE THAT FIRE WAS--	ASHES DENOTE THAT FIRE	1063		1
ASHINE				
AND ALL THE NIGHT ASHINE--	I HAD A GUINEA GOLDEN--	23		22
ASHORE				
ASHORE AT LAST!	ON THIS WONDROUS SEA	4		12
ASIA				
PITY--THE PARD--THAT LEFT HER ASIA--	CIVILIZATION--SPURNS--	492		10
ASIATIC				
AS ASIATIC RAINS--	I CROSS TILL I AM WEARY	550		9
AND ASIATIC REST.	NO AUTUMN'S INTERCEPTING	1516		4
ASIDE				
HE'LL TAKE IT--SCAN IT--STEP ASIDE--	THE FACE I CARRY WITH ME	336		9

	FIRST LINE	POEM	LINE
ASIDE (CONTINUED)			
THEN, AS FLUNG ASIDE	RIBBONS OF THE YEAR--	873	4
AFTER ALL BIRDS HAVE BEEN INVESTIGATED AND LAID ASIDE--	AFTER ALL BIRDS HAVE	1395	1
ASK			
WE ASK THAT WE MAY BE.	THE GENTIAN WEAVES HER	18	14
I ASK, EACH NEW MAY MORN.	THERE IS A MORN BY MEN	24	21
PRAY DO NOT ASK ME HOW!	GOING TO HEAVEN!	79	3
MANY, WILL DOUBTLESS ASK ME,	SO BASHFUL WHEN I SPIED	91	11
IF ANY ASK ME WHY--	THE MURMUR OF A BEE	155	3
IF ANY ASK ME HOW--	THE MURMUR OF A BEE	155	13
ASK THE JOLLY CLOVERS!	WE--BEE AND I--LIVE BY	230	7
AND KINDLY ASK IT IN--	HE PUT THE BELT AROUND	273	14
TO ASK THE OWNER'S NAME--	I FELT MY LIFE WITH BOTH	351	7
"CONSCIOUS"? WONT YOU ASK THAT--	IT IS DEAD--FIND IT--	417	5
THAT "WHATSOEVER YE SHALL ASK--	I MEANT TO HAVE BUT	476	23
BUT--IF HE [SHE] ASK WHERE YOU ARE HID	GOING TO HIM! HAPPY	494	23
FOR [TO] THOSE WHO WORSHIP [TRUST IN / ASK OF] THEM--	I RECKON--WHEN I COUNT	569	14
AND ASK MY BUSINESS THERE--	I YEARS HAD BEEN FROM	609	6
TILL THE CHILDREN URGE [ASK]--	GLEE--THE GREAT STORM IS	619	11
OF HER FATHER--WHOSO ASK [CLAIM] HER--	HER SWEET TURN TO LEAVE	649	17
I HEAR HIM ASK THE SERVANT	AGAIN--HIS VOICE IS AT	663	3
I ONLY ASK A TUNE	THE JUDGE IS LIKE THE	699	10
IF HE WERE LIVING--DARE I ASK--	IF HE WERE LIVING--DARE	734	1
TO ASK WHAT TREASON MEANS.	WHEN THE ASTRONOMER	851	8
THEY ASK BUT OUR DELIGHT--	THEY ASK BUT OUR DELIGHT	868	1
OF TOLLING BELL I ASK THE CAUSE?	OF TOLLING BELL I ASK	947	1
PROVE [ASK]--ME--SWEET--IF I REGRET IT--	ALL FORGOT FOR	966	15
THAT HE'LL [HE] MISTAKE--AND ASK FOR ME	FITTER TO SEE HIM, I MAY	968	16
ASK [TO] HIM UNTO THE GALLOWS LED [CALLED]--	OH SUMPTUOUS MOMENT	1125	8
AND OF WHOEVER ASK THEIR WAY	COSMOPOLITES WITHOUT A	1589 V	3
"DID YOU" OR "DID YOU NOT," TO ASK--	WHO IS IT SEEKS MY	1598	3
OF GOD WE ASK ONE FAVOR,	OF GOD WE ASK ONE FAVOR,	1601	1
SHE DOES NOT ASK FOR NOON--	QUITE EMPTY, QUITE AT	1606	6
SHE DOES NOT ASK FOR BOON,	QUITE EMPTY, QUITE AT	1606	7
AND ASK IT OF THE TEARS,	TO TRY TO SPEAK, AND	1617	2
I DARE NOT ASK MY FEET--	A PIT--BUT HEAVEN OVER	1712	11
ASKED			
WHOSE ARE THE LITTLE BEDS, I ASKED	WHOSE ARE THE LITTLE	142	1
IT ASKED A CRUMB--OF ME.	"HOPE" IS THE THING WITH	254	12
I ASKED THE EAST,	DELIGHT IS AS THE FLIGHT	257	11
AS IF I ASKED A COMMON ALMS,	AS IF I ASKED A COMMON	323	1
AS IF I ASKED THE ORIENT	AS IF I ASKED A COMMON	323	5
PERHAPS I ASKED TOO LARGE--	PERHAPS I ASKED TOO	352	1
THE LIGHTNING--NEVER ASKED AN EYE	"WHY DO I LOVE" YOU, SIR	480	11
YOU ASKED THE COMPANY TO TEA--	IF ANYBODY'S FRIEND BE	509	17
I ASKED TO GO ABROAD,	MY FIRST WELL DAY--SINCE	574	2
THE SOUL THAT ASKED IT'S SHELTER	THE BODY GROWS WITHOUT--	578	7
I ASKED NO OTHER THING--	I ASKED NO OTHER THING--	621	1
ASKED HIM HIS NAME--HE LISPED ME "TROTWOOD"--	TRUDGING TO EDEN,	1020	3
HE ASKED IF I WAS HIS--	IT WAS A QUIET WAY--	1053	2
PROTECTION ASKED OF ME--	THESE STRANGERS, IN A	1096	2
TILL WE ARE ASKED [CALLED] TO RISE	WE NEVER KNOW HOW HIGH	1176	2
TILL ASKED TO TAKE IT OFF--	WE KNEW NOT THAT WE WERE	1462	6
I ASKED HUMILITY	I SAW THE WIND WITHIN	1502	4
ASKETH			
AND GIVE HER WHAT SHE ASKETH, JEWEL, OR BIRD, OR FLOWER--	AWAKE YE MUSES NINE,	1	38
A SOLDIER'S--BALLS! WHO ASKETH MORE,	A LITTLE BREAD--A CRUST	159	11
ASKEW			
APOSTLE IS ASKEW!	"SOWN IN DISHONOR"!	62	8
ASKING			
MERCY [POWER] OF THE ALMIGHTY BEGGING [ASKING]--	TELL AS A MARKSMAN--WERE	1152	22
ASKS			
AND ASKS A VANE, THE WAY--	THIS WORLD IS NOT	501	16
THE HEART ASKS PLEASURE [BLESSING]--FIRST--	THE HEART ASKS PLEASURE	536	1
ASKS NOTHING BUT RELEASE--[IT'S FLIGHT]	AS FROM THE EARTH THE	1630	2
ASLANT			
BUT--ONCE ASLANT	MUST BE A WO--	571	5
ASLEEP			
TOO SOUND ASLEEP DID LIE	ON SUCH A NIGHT, OR SUCH	146	12
BEING FAST ASLEEP,	IF I SHOULD'NT BE ALIVE	182	6
TO MAKE SURE ALL'S ASLEEP--	I KNOW SOME LONELY	289	10
. . . ASLEEP / LAID TO SLEEP]--	THE GRASS SO LITTLE HAS	333	15
TOO INFINITE ASLEEP	THE COLOR OF THE GRAVE	411	6
MAGICIANS BE ASLEEP--	I THINK I WAS ENCHANTED	593	30
OURSELVES--ASLEEP BELOW--	WE MISS HER, NOT BECAUSE	993	6
"MY FACES ARE ASLEEP--	THE FINGERS OF THE LIGHT	1000	6
WHERE TAX ASLEEP AND TITLE OFF	ALONE AND IN A	1167	13
ASPECTS			
THE PERSONS [TRANSPORTS / TREASURES / ASPECTS] OF PROGNOSTICATION	MARCH IS THE MONTH OF	1404	3
ASPERITY			
INVITED WITH ASPERITY	WINTER IS GOOD--HIS HOAR	1316	7
ASPHODEL			
SHE REACHED THE ASPHODEL!	ALL OVERGROWN BY CUNNING	148 V	
ASPIRE			
THE HUMMING BIRD--ASPIRE--	THERE IS A FLOWER THAT	380	4

	FIRST LINE	POEM	LINE
ASPIRE (CONTINUED)			
TO ENTER, IT WOULD NOT ASPIRE--	IT WOULD NOT KNOW IF IT	1579	5
ASPIRES			
HER PRIDE ASPIRES--	FOR EVERY BIRD A NEST--	143	12
ASPIRING			
A FEW--THE MORE ASPIRING	SUMMER--WE ALL HAVE SEEN	1386	3
ASSASSIN			
ASSASSIN HID IN OUR APARTMENT	ONE NEED NOT BE A	670	15
ASSASSIN OF A BIRD	HIS BILL IS CLASPED--HIS	1102	8
FELLED BY BUT ONE ASSASSIN--	COULD HOPE INSPECT HER	1283	7
THE BLONDE ASSASSIN PASSES ON--	APPARENTLY WITH NO	1624	5
ASSAULT			
ONE WOULD AS SOON ASSAULT A PLUSH--	WHAT SOFT--CHERUBIC	401	3
BUT SINCE MYSELF--ASSAULT ME--	ME FROM MYSELF--TO	642	5
WITHSTANDS UNTIL THE SWEET ASSAULT	LIKE TRAINS OF CARS ON	1224	5
NO ASSAULT, NOR ANY MENACE	DEATH'S WAYLAYING NOT	1296	5
MORE PRUDENT TO ASSAULT THE DAWN	HER SPIRIT ROSE TO SUCH	1486	4
ASSAULTED			
OFFENDED [INSULTED / ASSAULTED] BY THE WIND--	SHE SPED AS PETALS OF A	991	2
TO OUR ASSAULTED MINDS--	OF PAUL AND SILAS IT IS	1166	6
ASSAULTING			
OR AN ASSAULTING GUESS.	WHAT TENEMENTS OF CLOVER	1338	8
ASSEMBLE			
BUT WHERE THE BIRDS ASSEMBLE	WHO OCCUPIES THIS HOUSE?	892	15
ASSEMBLED			
WAS WAITING [ASSEMBLED] TO BE POURED	HIS BILL IS CLASPED--HIS	1102	6
ASSEMBLIES			
A [DO / OUR] SUMMER'S [NATURE'S] SOFT ASSEMBLIES GO	WITHOUT A SMILE--WITHOUT	1330	2
ASSEMBLING			
NEVER BRIDE HAD SUCH ASSEMBLING--	HER SWEET TURN TO LEAVE	649	9
ASSEMBLY			
AND THAT ASSEMBLY [COMPANION]--NOT FAR OFF	ON A COLUMNAR SELF--	789	11
HER HOUSEHOLD--HER ASSEMBLY--	NATURE--THE GENTLEST	790	11
UNTO SUCH, WERE SUCH ASSEMBLY	ONE DAY IS THERE OF THE	814	15
A MARROWLESS ASSEMBLY	THE BONE THAT HAS NO	1274	7
ASSENT			
ASSENT--AND YOU ARE SANE--	MUCH MADNESS IS DIVINEST	435	6
ASSERT			
ASSERT THEMSELVES--AND NOT BY TERMS--	YOU'LL KNOW IT--AS YOU	420	8
ASSERT HER VITAL PRIVILEGE--[HIS PRIMOGENITURE]	NO CROWD THAT HAS	515	7
ASSERTING			
ASSERTING FROM HIS PRISM	LIKE TIME'S INSIDIOUS	1236	7
ASSIDUOUSLY			
ASSIDUOUSLY [DELIBERATELY / DETERMINATELY / IMPERTINENTLY] CRAWLED	ALONE AND IN A	1167	4
ASSIGNABLE			
ASSIGNABLE--AND THEN IT WAS	I HEARD A FLY BUZZ--WHEN	465	11
ASSIGNS			
NATURE ASSIGNS THE SUN--	NATURE ASSIGNS THE SUN--	1336	1
ASSIST			
THE PROPS ASSIST THE HOUSE	THE PROPS ASSIST THE	1142	1
ASSISTANCE			
ASSISTANCE--OR APPLAUSE--	THE MOUNTAINS--GROW	757	4
TO OFFER BRAVE ASSISTANCE	TO OFFER BRAVE	767	1
TIS [IT] STILL IS AN ASSISTANCE	I SAW THE WIND WITHIN	1502	V
ASSISTED			
BUT TRANSACTION--IS ASSISTED	GROWTH OF MAN--LIKE	750	15
ASSISTED BY IT'S STIMULUS--	SUCH IS THE FORCE OF	787	3
TO BE ASSISTED OF REVERSE	DESPAIR'S ADVANTAGE IS	799	3
ASSISTED FAINT [SLOW] OF LOVE.	AS PLAN FOR NOON AND	960	8
ASSISTING			
ASSISTING IN THE BRIGHT AFFAIR	BLOOM--IS RESULT--TO	1058	5
ASSISTS			
ASSISTS THE STAGGERING MIND	A DOUBT IF IT BE US	859	2
DEATH TENDERLY ASSISTS HIM	PAIN HAS BUT ONE	1049	7
THE FORMER ASSISTS A SIREN	THE PARASOL IS THE	1747	5
ASSOCIATES			
ASSOCIATES OR GLOWS [BASKS] ALONE,	HOW HAPPY IS THE LITTLE	1510	8
AND ASSOCIATES WITH A FAN	THE PARASOL IS THE	1747	2
ASSOCIATION			
WITH FAIR ASSOCIATION--	IT IS A LONESOME GLEE--	774	3
ASSUAGE			
SURGEONS ASSUAGE IN VAIN,	AH, NECROMANCY SWEET!	177	5
TIME NEVER DID ASSUAGE--	THEY SAY THAT "TIME	686	2
ASSUAGES			
THEY SAY THAT "TIME ASSUAGES"--	THEY SAY THAT "TIME	686	1
ASSUMED			
I FOUND IT QUIETLY ASSUMED	ALONE AND IN A	1167	11
HAS BEEN ASSUMED TO BE--	THE INFINITE A SUDDEN	1309	2
A SUDDEN FREIGHT OF WIND ASSUMED [TOOK ON--]	A SINGLE CLOVER PLANK	1343	11
ASSUMES			
AND ASSUMES [INFERS]--FROM HOME--	HE WHO IN HIMSELF	969	4
ASSUMING			
THAT HINTS WITHOUT ASSUMING--	SEPTEMBER'S	1271	5
ASSUMPTION			
THE BUTTERFLY'S ASSUMPTION GOWN	THE BUTTERFLY'S	1244	1
ASSURE			
IF ANY SINK, ASSURE THAT THIS, NOW STANDING--	IF ANY SINK, ASSURE THAT	358	1

	FIRST LINE	POEM	LINE
ASSURE (CONTINUED)			
NOR THE LEAST SIGNAL, ME [MINE] ASSURE--	WERT THOU BUT ILL--THAT	961	4
TO WHERE THE STRONG ASSURE ME	BECAUSE MY BROOK IS	1200	7
ASSURED			
SO--CHILDREN--TOLD HOW [ASSURED THAT] BROOKS IN EDEN--	BETTER--THAN MUSIC! FOR	503	9
WHEN DEITY ASSURED [PRONOUNCED]	TRUST IN THE UNEXPECTED	555	14
NATURE IMPARTS THE LITTLE BLUE-BIRD--ASSURED	AFTER ALL BIRDS HAVE	1395	2
ASSUREDLY			
ASSUREDLY WILL LIE	THE BUTTERFLY IN HONORED	1246	2
GUEST OF MINE ASSUREDLY--	RECOLLECT THE FACE OF ME	1305	4
ASTER			
ARGUES THE ASTER STILL--	LIKE HER THE SAINTS	60	10
'TIS IRIS, SIR, AND ASTER--	WHOSE ARE THE LITTLE	142	13
THE ASTER--ON THE HILL	IT WILL BE SUMMER--	342	14
ASTERISK			
BUT JUST AN ASTERISK.	TOO COLD IS THIS	1135	9
THERE STANDS AN ASTERISK	HE LIVED THE LIFE OF	1525	4
THERE STANDS AN ASTERISK	WHO ABDICATED AMBUSH	1616	4
THE ASTERISK IS FOR THE DEAD,	OF GLORY NOT A BEAM IS	1647	3
ASTERISKS			
FOR WHAT ARE STARS BUT ASTERISKS	GO THY GREAT WAY!	1638	4
ASTEROID			
ALSO WITH BIRD AND ASTEROID	THE DUTIES OF THE WIND	1137	11
ASTERS			
WHILE ASTERS--	WHILE ASTERS--	331	1
ASTIR			
DRINKING TO HER NO MORE ASTIR,	I WOULD DISTIL A CUP,	16	3
WHILE THE OLD COUPLE, JUST ASTIR,	I KNOW SOME LONELY	289	39
HER PARTIES ALL [COMPANIES] ASTIR--	REMORSE--IS MEMORY--	744	2
ASTONISHED			
AND THE BEWILDERED GYMNAST [ASTONISHED WRESTLER]	A LITTLE EAST OF JORDAN,	59	15
INDEED I'M TOO ASTONISHED	GOING TO HEAVEN!	79	4
AMONG ASTONISHED BOUGHS--	BRING ME THE SUNSET IN A	128	9
ASTONISHES			
ASTONISHES THE GRASS,	THE DANDELION'S PALLID	1519	2
ASTONISHMENT			
. . . EXPERIENCE / ASTONISHMENT / PERIPHERY] OF GREEN--	A LITTLE MADNESS IN THE	1333	5
ASTRAL			
IF AIMS IMPEL THESE ASTRAL ONES	THE MOON UPON HER FLUENT	1528	5
AS AN ASTRAL HALL	LIGHTLY STEPPED A YELLOW	1672	6
ASTRAY			
PIGMY SERAPHS--GONE ASTRAY--	PIGMY SERAPHS--GONE	138	1
AFAR [REMOTE / ASTRAY] UPON THE WIND	IT IS A LONESOME GLEE--	774	4
WHOSE ALLIES GO NO MORE ASTRAY [ABROAD]	A CHILLY PEACE INFESTS	1443	5
ASTROLOGY			
THAT--IS ASTROLOGY.	NATURE ASSIGNS THE SUN--	1336	4
ASTRONOMER			
WHEN THE ASTRONOMER STOPS SEEKING	WHEN THE ASTRONOMER	851	1
ASTRONOMY			
AND BIND ASTRONOMY, IN PLACE, [FROM BLAME]	TO INTERRUPT HIS YELLOW	591	11
THAT--IS ASTRONOMY--	NATURE ASSIGNS THE SUN--	1336	2
ASTUTE			
REMOTE [ASTUTE / OBSCURE] TO UNDERSTAND	NATURE AFFECTS TO BE	1170	6
PERHAPS IS MORE ASTUTE	COME SHOW THY DURHAM	1542	8
OF WHAT ASTUTE ABODE--	THE BAT IS DUN, WITH	1575	10
ATE			
AND ATE THE FELLOW, RAW,	A BIRD CAME DOWN THE	328	4
HE ATE AND DRANK THE PRECIOUS WORDS--	HE ATE AND DRANK THE	1587	1
ATHEIST			
THE FOP--THE CARP--[THE DOG--THE TRAMP--]THE ATHEIST--	HOW MUCH THE PRESENT	1380	3
ATHENS			
LAD OF ATHENS, FAITHFUL BE	LAD OF ATHENS, FAITHFUL	1768	1
ATMOSPHERE			
CAPRICES OF THE ATMOSPHERE--	TO INTERRUPT HIS YELLOW	591	3
ATMOSPHERE, AND SUN ENDORSE [CONFIRM] IT--	GROWTH OF MAN--LIKE	750	3
IN THE ATMOSPHERE--	I THINK THAT THE ROOT OF	1302	8
ATMOSPHERES			
REELS IN REMOTER ATMOSPHERES--	WITHIN MY GARDEN, RIDES	500	11
ATOM			
CONCLUDING [DECIDING] HOW AN ATOM--FELL--	IT TROUBLED ME AS ONCE I	600	3
BEHOLD THE ATOM--I PREFERRED--	OF ALL THE SOULS THAT	664	11
OR AN ATOM PRESS	CRISIS IS A HAIR	889	10
UPON HIS ATOM SWIM--	MY GOD--HE SEES THEE--	1178	7
THE PUNGENT ATOM IN THE AIR	THE PUNGENT ATOM IN THE	1191	1
WOULD PAY [PAWN] EACH ATOM THAT I AM	SOMEWHERE UPON THE	1231	7
ATOM'S			
TO LEAVE ME IN THE ATOM'S TOMB--	OF COURSE--I PRAYED--	376	9
ATOMS			
HER BOW--TO ATOMS BLOWN--	THE FIRST DAY'S NIGHT	410	6
ON ATOMS--FEATURES PLACE--	NO CROWD THAT HAS	515	9
THE FACES OF THE ATOMS	THE CHEMICAL CONVICTION	954	5
AND MOUNTS TO BE TO ATOMS HURLED	RISK IS THE HAIR THAT	1239 V	7
ATONE			
THE HAPPINESS ATONE--	I THOUGHT THE TRAIN	1449	12
ATROPOS			
ATROPOS DECIDE!	I NEVER TOLD THE BURIED	11	21

	FIRST LINE	POEM	LINE
ATTACHES			
UNDUE SIGNIFICANCE A STARVING MAN ATTACHES	UNDUE SIGNIFICANCE A	439	1
ATTACKS			
MY FRIEND ATTACKS MY FRIEND!	MY FRIEND ATTACKS MY	118	1
ATTAIN			
AH, TO ATTAIN IT--	KNOWS HOW TO FORGET!	433	12
SHUDDER TO ATTAIN.	WHICH IS THE BEST--THE	1315	6
HE HUNGERS TO ATTAIN.	HIS ORIENTAL HERESIES	1526	V
ATTAINED			
THE CAMEL'S TRAIT--ATTAINED--	STRONG DRAUGHTS OF THEIR	711	6
MAY BE EASIER REACHED [BETTER ATTAINED / EASIER GAINED]--THIS WAY--	BY MY WINDOW HAVE I FOR	797	8
ATTAINMENTS			
TO MEASURE OUR ATTAINMENTS--	MYSELF WAS FORMED--A	488	5
ATTAR			
AND ATTAR SO IMMENSE	THIS WAS A POET--IT IS	448	4
THE ATTAR FROM THE ROSE	ESSENTIAL OILS--ARE	675	2
OF AN ENTIRE ATTAR	ONE OF THE ONES THAT	1466	15
ATTAR'S			
SOME ATTAR'S PERFIDY?	SWEET PIRATE OF THE	1546	5
ATTARS			
AND ATTARS THAT HAVE FAILED,	HIS ORIENTAL HERESIES	1526	V
ATTEMPT			
I W'D AS SOON ATTEMPT TO WARM	I BRING AN UNACCUSTOMED	132	11
ATTEMPT BY STRATEGY--	I GAINED IT SO--	359	7
O'ER THE CURLS ATTEMPT TO CAPER	HER SWEET TURN TO LEAVE	649	7
WITHOUT ATTEMPT--EXHAUSTION--	THE MOUNTAINS--GROW	757	3
INVITED DEATH--WITH BOLD ATTEMPT--	HE FOUGHT LIKE THOSE	759	5
FOOT OF THE BOLD DID LEAST ATTEMPT IT--	THOSE WHO HAVE BEEN IN	922	5
NO SERVICE HAST THOU, I WOULD NOT ACHIEVE [ATTEMPT] IT--	WERT THOU BUT ILL--THAT	961	17
WHEN DAY'S ATTEMPT IS DONE	FURTHER IN SUMMER THAN	1068	V
ATTEMPT IT, AND THE UNIVERSE	THE RIGHT TO PERISH	1692	3
AS THE ATTEMPT TO RISE.	DROWNING IS NOT SO	1718	2
ATTEMPTED			
ATTEMPTED OF THE HOUNDS	ONE ANGUISH--IN A CROWD	565	4
ATTEMPTED TO [DID TIMIDLY] EXPOUND	WE LEARNED THE WHOLE OF	568	9
ATTEMPTING			
ON ONE ATTEMPTING SHY	AS SUMMER INTO AUTUMN	1346	10
ATTEND			
'TWAS UNIVERSE--THAT DID APPLAUD [ATTEND]--	LIKE MIGHTY FOOT LIGHTS	595	5
ATTENDANCE			
THAT GENERAL ATTENDANCE	NO CROWD THAT HAS	515	3
THE HOUSEWIFE IN THY LOW ATTENDANCE	WERT THOU BUT ILL--THAT	961	15
ATTENDANTS			
WHAT DIGNIFIED ATTENDANTS!	ONE DIGNITY DELAYS FOR	98	9
ATTENDED			
ATTENDED BY A SINGLE HOUND	THIS CONSCIOUSNESS THAT	822	15
ATTENDED, OR ALONE	A NARROW FELLOW IN THE	986	22
ATTENDETH			
WHERE THIS ATTENDETH ME [THEE]--	FOR THIS--ACCEPTED	195	8
ATTENTION			
DEATH, BUT OUR RAPT ATTENTION	THE FEET OF PEOPLE	7	15
THEN--CLOSE THE VALVES [LIDS] OF HER ATTENTION--	THE SOUL SELECTS HER OWN	303	11
HER LEAST ATTENTION RAISE ON ME--	'TWOULD EASE--A	682	14
THEY--HIM--ATTENTION OF PASSER BY--	FOUR TREES--UPON A	742	10
THOUGH THINE ATTENTION STOP NOT ON ME	WERT THOU BUT ILL--THAT	961	3
EXTRINSIC TO ATTENTION	THE WAY TO KNOW THE	1279	13
ATTENTION'S			
FOR IT'S ABSORBED ATTENTION'S	THIS DUST, AND IT'S	936	11
ATTEST			
HE DOTH NOT ATTEST BY POSTURE--	CONSCIOUS AM I IN MY	679	3
ATTEST [REMIT] ME THIS AND THIS--	THROUGH WHAT TRANSPORTS	1153	4
ATTESTED			
ATTESTED TO THIS DAY	A DEW SUFFICED ITSELF--	1437	13
ATTESTS			
ATTESTS THE BIRD THAT'S GONE	I SEE THEE CLEARER FOR	1666	8
ATTIRED			
IN HOMELY INDUSTRY ARRAYED [ATTIRED]--	THE BIRDS BEGUN AT FOUR	783	11
ATTIRED TO DEFY,	THE WAY TO KNOW THE	1279	6
ATTIRETH			
ATTIRETH THAT IT HEAR	TO HEAR AN ORIOLE SING	526	8
ATTITUDE			
A FLYING ATTITUDE!	I NEVER HEAR THE WORD	77	4
LEAVING AN ATTITUDE [A MAGNITUDE] ON TIME	SHE SPED AS PETALS OF A	991	V 5
THERE'S SOMETHING IN THEIR ATTITUDE	MY COUNTRY NEED NOT	1511	7
ATTITUDES			
YOU--TOO--TAKE COBWEB ATTITUDES	TO HANG OUR HEAD--	105	7
TILL I TAKE VASTER ATTITUDES [MANNERS]--	OF BRONZE--AND BLAZE--	290	10
ATTRACTED			
ATTRACTED MORE UNTO--	WHO OCCUPIES THIS HOUSE?	892	24
ATTRACTS			
THE DEER ATTRACTS NO FURTHER [INVITES NO LONGER--]	THIS MERIT HATH THE	979	7
AUBURN			
WILL IDLE LIE--IN AUBURN--	WHEN ROSES CEASE TO	32	7
WHO SPUN THE AUBURN CLOTH?	HOW FITS HIS UMBER COAT	1371	5
AUCTION			
PUBLICATION--IS THE AUCTION	PUBLICATION--IS THE	709	1

	FIRST LINE	POEM	LINE
AUCTIONEER			
THE AUCTIONEER OF PARTING	THE AUCTIONEER OF	1612	1
AUDACIOUS			
AUDACIOUS AS WITHOUT A KNOCK	THE LAST OF SUMMER IS	1353	7
AUDACITY			
OH THE AUDACITY [POMPOSITY]--	THAT THIS SHOULD FEEL	1112	7
AUDIBLE			
NOT AUDIBLE--AS OUR'S--TO US--	A MURMUR IN THE TREES--	416	7
WHEN WE INSPECT--THAT'S AUDIBLE--	THE SPIRIT IS THE	733	3
IT'S DOOM IS AUDIBLE--	A DEED KNOCKS FIRST AT	1216	8
AUDIBLER			
AND THEN--BE AUDIBLER	I COULD SUFFICE FOR HIM,	643	12
'TIS AUDIBLER AT DUSK	FURTHER IN SUMMER THAN	1068	V
AUDIENCE			
THIS AUDIENCE OF IDLENESS	FROM COCOON FORTH A	354	20
OF ME--IN CHRIST'S BRIGHT AUDIENCE [LATITUDE]	YOU TAUGHT ME WAITING	740	11
WHEN THE AUDIENCE IS SCATTERED	DRAMA'S VITALLEST	741	6
OF IT'S AUDIENCE--	GROWTH OF MAN--LIKE	750	14
IN AN AUDIENCE--	SO THE EYES ACCOST--AND	752	2
AUDIENCES			
NOR HOPPED FOR [TO] AUDIENCES--LIKE BIRDS,	I CANNOT DANCE UPON MY	326	11
TWO [THE] WORLDS--LIKE AUDIENCES--DISPERSE [DISSOLVE / WITHDRAW / RETIRE]	DEPARTED--TO THE	524	7
AUDITORS			
HIS AUDITORS TWO WORLDS	HIS MANSION IN THE POOL	1379	5
AUGHT			
COULD I DO AUGHT ELSE--TO THEE?	HE FORGOT--AND I--	203	8
OF AUGHT PENINSULAR--	THE INUNDATION OF THE	1425	V 8
AUGMENTED			
AUGMENTED--SWEET--A HUNDRED FOLD--	WE COVER THEE--SWEET	482	11
AUGUR			
HIS BILL AN AUGUR IS	HIS BILL AN AUGUR IS	1034	1
THE AUGUR [SCAFFOLD] AND THE CARPENTER--	THE PROPS ASSIST THE	1142	7
AUGUST			
UPON AN AUGUST DAY?	IN LANDS I NEVER SAW--	124	8
AND LATER, IN AUGUST IT MAY BE--	HAVE YOU GOT A BROOK IN	136	13
AUGUST--ABSORBED--NUMB--[RESISTLESS--DUMB]	NO CROWD THAT HAS	515	16
AND CENTURIES OF AUGUST CEASE [FUSE / LAPSE / BLEND]	THERE IS A ZONE WHOSE	1056	7
WHEN AUGUST BURNING LOW	FURTHER IN SUMMER THAN	1068	10
AUGUST THE DUST OF THAT DOMAIN--	THAT SACRED CLOSET WHEN	1273	9
IN RECUSANCE AUGUST.	PRAISE IT--'TIS DEAD--	1384	9
AUGUSTAN			
LO, WHAT [THE] "AUGUSTAN" YEARS	IF PAIN FOR PEACE	63	2
AURORA			
THAT SHALL AURORA BE--	SLEEP IS SUPPOSED TO BE	13	11
FINGERS OF THE SLIM AURORA--	THESE--SAW VISIONS--	758	10
TILL THE INFINITE AURORA	STRUCK, WAS I, NOR YET	925	23
AURORA IS THE EFFORT	AURORA IS THE EFFORT	1002	1
AURORAL			
BY AN AURORAL STAIN	LET ME NOT MAR THAT	1335	2
THE AURORAL LIGHT.	MORNING IS DUE TO ALL--	1577	4
AURORAN			
AND WHEN AT NIGHT--AURORAN WIDTHS	THE COLOR OF A QUEEN, IS	776	5
AUSPICIOUSLY			
AUSPICIOUSLY WITHHELD--	THE BAT IS DUN, WITH	1575	12
AUSTERE			
SHE DREW AWAY AUSTERE--	THE BIRDS REPORTED FROM	743	14
OF AN AUSTERE TRAIT IN PLEASURE--	EXPECTATION--IS	807	5
WILT THOU, AUSTERE [RUSSIAN] SNOW?	SNOW BENEATH WHOSE	942	8
AUSTERER			
WITH THE [AN / THIS] AUSTERER SWEET--	I FIT FOR THEM--	1109	5
AUSTERITY			
IT SUITS HIS OWN AUSTERITY--	I THINK THE HEMLOCK	525	3
AUSTIN			
NEVER MIND FADED FORESTS, AUSTIN,	THERE IS ANOTHER SKY,	2	5
AUSTRIAN			
BEWARE AN AUSTRIAN	THE WIND DREW OFF	1694	11
AUTHENTIC			
FOR THE AUTHENTIC ORBIT	DELIGHT'S DESPAIR AT	1299	7
AUTHOR			
THE WRINKLED MAKER [AUTHOR] LIE	A WORD DROPPED CARELESS	1261	4
AUTHORITY			
THE PRIVILEGE [THE LIBERTY / AUTHORITY] TO SAY	HE PARTS HIMSELF--LIKE	517	14
TO OUR AUTHORITY--	WE TALKED AS GIRLS DO--	586	8
OF HIS AUTHORITY--	IT'S EASY TO INVENT A	724	4
AUTHORIZED			
IN AUTHORIZED ARRAYS--	WHOLE GULFS--OF RED, AND	658	6
WHO JUSTIFIED [AUTHORIZED] ELIJAH [THE FORMER]	ELIJAH'S WAGON KNEW NO	1254	7
IS AUTHORIZED AS PEACE	THE MOB WITHIN THE HEART	1745	4
AUTOCRATIC			
TO AUTOCRATIC AIR--	THE SOUL'S SUPERIOR	306	12
AUTO DA FE			
AUTO DA FE--AND JUDGMENT--	IT MAKES NO DIFFERENCE	620	9
AUTUMN			
SINCE THE MIGHTY AUTUMN AFTERNOON	GOING TO HEAVEN!	79	26
BESIDES THE AUTUMN POETS SING	BESIDES THE AUTUMN POETS	131	1
WHERE NO AUTUMN LIFTS HER PENCIL--	THO' MY DESTINY BE	163	15
OR GRISLY FROSTS--FIRST AUTUMN MORNS,	IT WAS NOT DEATH, FOR I	510	19
THE NAME--OF IT--IS "AUTUMN"--	THE NAME--OF IT--IS	656	1

	FIRST LINE	POEM	LINE
AUTUMN (CONTINUED)			
AUTUMN--OVERLOOKED MY KNITTING--	AUTUMN--OVERLOOKED MY	748	1
AS SUMMER INTO AUTUMN SLIPS	AS SUMMER INTO AUTUMN	1346	1
"THE SUMMER" THAN "THE AUTUMN," LEST	AS SUMMER INTO AUTUMN	1346	3
AUTUMN BEGINS TO BE INFERRED	SUMMER BEGINS TO HAVE	1682	5
BE THIS AN AUTUMN OR A SPRING	THE ONES THAT	1690	5
THE AUTUMN STARTED HOME--	WITH SWEETNESS UNABATED	1709	4
AUTUMN'S			
NO AUTUMN'S INTERCEPTING CHILL	NO AUTUMN'S INTERCEPTING	1516	1
NO AUTUMN'S INTERCEPTIVE CHILL,	HIS ORIENTAL HERESIES	1526 V	3
AUTUMNS			
TWO FULL AUTUMNS FOR THE SQUIRREL	TWICE HAD SUMMER HER	846	5
AUXILIARIES			
BUT THAT CLOUD AND IT'S AUXILIARIES	A CLOUD WITHDREW FROM	895	3
AUXILIARY			
BELLS FOR AN AUXILIARY	THE POPULAR HEART IS A	1226	3
AVAIL			
MAY NOT AT LAST AVAIL?	IF I COULD BRIBE THEM BY	179	16
AVAILED			
IT HAD AVAILED ME NOW.	A CLOUD WITHDREW FROM	895	8
AVALANCHES			
GIVE AVALANCHES--	GIVE LITTLE ANGUISH--	310	3
AVARICE			
TO TEACH THE ANGELS, AVARICE,	ALTHOUGH I PUT AWAY HIS	366	32
THE ANGUISH [PATHOS] OF THE AVARICE	ONE THING OF IT WE	1464	7
THE EYE BEGINS IT'S AVARICE	SUMMER BEGINS TO HAVE	1682	9
AVENGE			
IF ANY WOULD AVENGE	MINE ENEMY IS GROWING	1509	4
AVENGING			
THE SPRING AVENGING FLING	UPON A LILAC SEA	1337	5
AVERRING			
BUT JUST THE ANTI FAIR--AVERRING--FAIREST-- TRUEST TRUTH	EXTOL THEE--COULD I--	1643	3
AVERSE			
FOR THOSE AVERSE TO SLEEP--	WATER MAKES MANY BEDS	1428	2
WHY TO CORDIALITY SO AVERSE TO COME	GUEST AM I TO HAVE	1661	3
AVOCATION			
NOR AVOCATION--NOR CONCERN	I WATCHED THE MOON	629	23
AVOID			
AND AVOID IT'S BEE,	WHEN I COUNT THE SEEDS	40	10
NONE CAN AVOID THIS PURPLE--	ONE DIGNITY DELAYS FOR	98	3
WHY AVOID SO NARROWLY	GUEST AM I TO HAVE	1661	6
AVOIDED			
AVOIDED--LIKE [AS] A DREAM--	A PRISON GETS TO BE A	652	30
AVOWING			
DO THE [THY] AVOWING--	COME SHOW THY DURHAM	1542	6
AWAIT			
OUR FEET AWAIT!	IF PAIN FOR PEACE	63	3
IF IN THAT ROOM A FRIEND AWAIT	ELYSIUM IS AS FAR AS TO	1760	3
AWAITED			
AWAITED EVEN--HIM--	REMOVED FROM ACCIDENT OF	424	12
AWAITED THEIR--LOW BROWS--	LIKE FLOWERS, THAT HEARD	513	3
AWAITING			
AWAITING HER THAT DAY--	BLOOM--IS RESULT--TO	1058	14
AWAKE			
AWAKE YE MUSES NINE, SING ME A STRAIN DIVINE,	AWAKE YE MUSES NINE,	1	1
WHEN I AT LAST AWAKE.	I BRING AN UNACCUSTOMED	132	22
A LITTLE NOTE--WHEN YOU AWAKE--	YOU LOVE THE LORD--YOU	487	3
IT [THEY] WOULD HURT US--WERE WE AWAKE--	WE DREAM--IT IS GOOD WE	531	2
I HAD NO CAUSE TO BE AWAKE--	I HAD NO CAUSE TO BE	542	1
MY FINGERS WERE AWAKE--	THE SUN KEPT SETTING--	692	10
REMORSE--IS MEMORY--AWAKE--	REMORSE--IS MEMORY--	744	1
I WAKED, TO FIND IT FIRST AWAKE--	BEREAVED OF ALL, I WENT	784	9
HE IS ALIVE--AND AWAKE--	HE IS ALIVE, THIS	1160	2
AWAKEN			
MUST AWAKEN HER!	ON THIS LONG STORM THE	194	12
MAYBE--THAT--WOULD AWAKEN--THEM!	PUT UP MY LUTE!	261	10
AWAKENED			
AWAKENED MAID AND MAN	THE FINGERS OF THE LIGHT	1000	12
AWARD			
'TIS LIFE'S AWARD--TO DIE--	THE WHOLE OF IT CAME NOT	762	9
AWARDED			
CONSTANCY THRO' FIRE--AWARDED--	REARRANGE A "WIFE'S"	1737	11
AWARDS			
IN THE DELIGHTS [AWARDS] OF DUST--	PRAISE IT--'TIS DEAD--	1384	7
AWARE			
AN ALMANAC'S AWARE--	I KNOW SOME LONELY	289	20
NOR EVEN OF DEFEAT--AWARE--	THERE IS A FLOWER THAT	380	31
OF PARADISE--AWARE--	THEY PUT US FAR APART--	474	22
THIS CONSCIOUSNESS THAT IS AWARE	THIS CONSCIOUSNESS THAT	822	1
WILL BE THE ONE AWARE OF DEATH	THIS CONSCIOUSNESS THAT	822	3
OF HUMAN NATURE JUST AWARE	I THOUGHT THAT NATURE	1286	5
AWAY			
AND COME AWAY WITH ME,	"SIC TRANSIT GLORIA	3	18
GAVE HIS BREATH AWAY.	THERE IS A WORD	8	10
AND ONE, A HEDGE AWAY.	ONE SISTER HAVE I IN OUR	14	2
AND JUST TO TURN AWAY,	DISTRUSTFUL OF THE	20	2
HE, TOO, DID FLY AWAY--	I HAD A GUINEA GOLDEN--	23	12
TO PARADISE AWAY--	SO HAS A DAISY VANISHED	28	4
JUST A BRIDGE AWAY--	BEFORE THE ICE IS IN THE	37	12

AWAY (CONTINUED)

	FIRST LINE	POEM	LINE
I [HE] GRASPED--I [HE] BORE AWAY--	I ROBBED THE WOODS--	41	7
WHO MARSHALLED HER AWAY--	TAKEN FROM MEN--THIS	53	4
I HAVE BEEN CALLED AWAY--	IF I SHOULD CEASE TO	56	4
I.E. GATHERED AWAY,	LIKE HER THE SAINTS	60	8
WHEEL SOLEMNLY [POMPOUSLY] AWAY!	PAPA ABOVE!	61	9
FRITTERS ITSELF AWAY!	SOME RAINBOW--COMING	64	6
HIDDEN AWAY, CUNNINGLY,	SO FROM THE MOULD	66	4
MY FIGURES FILE [CIPHERS STEAL] AWAY.	LOW AT MY PROBLEM	69	6
GAMBOLLED AWAY	SHE DIED AT PLAY,	75	2
AND BORE HER SAFE AWAY.	WHOSE CHEEK IS THIS?	82	5
THEN BUBBLED SLOW AWAY!	HEART, NOT SO HEAVY AS	83	12
SAUNTERED AS SOFT AWAY!	WITHIN MY REACH!	90	5
I TRUDGE THE DAY AWAY--	I HAVE A KING, WHO DOES	103	3
THAT BECKONED IT AWAY!	'TWAS SUCH A LITTLE--	107	4
AS SLOW HER FLAMBEAUX BURN AWAY	A SOMETHING IN A	122	2
WITH IMPLEMENTS TO FLY AWAY,	BRING ME THE SUNSET IN A	128	23
I TURN MY BRIMMING EYES AWAY,	I BRING AN UNACCUSTOMED	132	6
TAKETH AWAY MY WILL--	THE MURMUR OF A BEE	155	7
WIPING AWAY THE VELVET DUST	IN EBON BOX, WHEN YEARS	169	3
PLUCKED FAR AWAY, SOME MORNING--	IN EBON BOX, WHEN YEARS	169	11
CAN I, THEREFORE, STAY AWAY?	I'M THE LITTLE "HEART'S	176	4
THE FORMER, BLEW AWAY.	I CAUTIOUS, SCANNED MY	178	6
AND RISEN UP--AND GONE AWAY,	I'VE HEARD AN ORGAN TALK	183	5
PUT MY PRETENSE--AWAY--	MAKE ME A PICTURE OF THE	188	8
AND THEN I COME AWAY--	SHE SWEEPS WITH	219	12
THE COURT IS FAR AWAY--	THE COURT IS FAR AWAY--	235	1
SOME DRIFTS WERE MOVED AWAY--	I THINK JUST HOW MY	237	10
THE SMOKE ALL CLEARED AWAY FROM IT--	WHEN WE STAND ON THE	242	3
NO LIGHTNING, SCARES [DRIVES] AWAY--	WHEN WE STAND ON THE	242	8
IF JOY--TO PUT MY PIECE AWAY	FOREVER AT HIS SIDE TO	246	8
TURNS SO--AWAY FROM YOU--	IF I'M LOST--NOW--	256	13
IT'S NAME IS PUT AWAY	A SINGLE SCREW OF FLESH	263	6
AND TURNED AWAY, IMPERIAL,	HE PUT THE BELT AROUND	273	3
THAT DIES AWAY IN DIMPLES	THE ONLY GHOST I EVER	274	11
DROP, LIKE A TAPESTRY, AWAY,	DOUBT ME! MY DIM	275	20
SCARES MUSLIN SOULS--AWAY--	A SHADY FRIEND--FOR	278	6
AND ECHOES--TRAINS AWAY,	I KNOW SOME LONELY	289	37
WHETTING AWAY THE HOURS	THE WIND DID'NT COME	316	14
AND LED THE FLOCK AWAY--	I'LL TELL YOU HOW THE	318	16
BEYOND THE TRAIT TO TAKE AWAY	OF ALL THE SOUNDS	321	11
AND DREAM THE DAYS AWAY,	THE GRASS SO LITTLE HAS	333	18
HER LORD--AWAY!	I TEND MY FLOWERS FOR	339	22
I WISHED THEY'D STAY AWAY	I DREADED THAT FIRST	348	18
NO BLOSSOM STAYED AWAY	I DREADED THAT FIRST	348	22
ALTHOUGH I PUT AWAY HIS LIFE--	ALTHOUGH I PUT AWAY HIS	366	1
HER LIFE HAD LEAPED AWAY--	SHE LAY AS IF AT PLAY	369	2
A HONEY BEAR AWAY	THERE IS A FLOWER THAT	380	6
THIS--PUT AWAY	FOR DEATH--OR RATHER	382	3
TO DRINK--OR SET AWAY	EXHILIRATION--IS WITHIN	383	6
THE DOCTOR--DRIVES AWAY--	THERE'S BEEN A DEATH, IN	389	6
IN SENDING ALL THE BIRDS AWAY--	THE WINTERS ARE SO SHORT	403	3
AND SWEPT THE WORLD AWAY--	THE WINTERS ARE SO SHORT	403	14
MYSELF WOULD RUN AWAY	I NEVER FELT AT HOME--	413	14
WHEN LIGHT IS PUT AWAY--	WE GROW ACCUSTOMED TO	419	2
THEY CANNOT PUT AWAY--	THE MONTHS HAVE ENDS--	423	12
HE TURNED AWAY!	GOOD MORNING--MIDNIGHT--	425	16
JUST SO FAR--GOES AWAY--	THE MOON IS DISTANT FROM	429	8
OR OPPORTUNITY--HER LORD AWAY?	FORGET! THE LADY WITH	438	8
AND THROW THE OLD--AWAY--	I TIE MY HAT--I CREASE	443	6
WE CANNOT PUT OURSELF AWAY	I TIE MY HAT--I CREASE	443	13
THIS SPARTAN PUT AWAY	IT FEELS A SHAME TO BE	444	6
WHERE MOSSES GO NO MORE AWAY--	I KNOW WHERE WELLS GROW	460	3
I GO NO MORE AWAY	I LIVE WITH HIM--I SEE	463	2
I WILLED MY KEEPSAKES--SIGNED AWAY	I HEARD A FLY BUZZ--WHEN	465	9
AS ENEMIES--AWAY--	WE DO NOT PLAY ON GRAVES	467	10
SLOW--NIGHT--THAT MUST BE WATCHED AWAY--	A NIGHT--THERE LAY THE	471	5
THEY TOOK AWAY OUR EYES--	THEY PUT US FAR APART--	474	5
AND THEN THE LADDER'S THROWN AWAY,	DOOM IS THE HOUSE	475	3
I THREW MY PRAYER AWAY--	I MEANT TO HAVE BUT	476	18
AND THEN--RELUCTANT--TURN AWAY	WE COVER THEE--SWEET	482	7
BY DECALOGUES--AWAY--	TO MAKE ONE'S TOILETTE--	485	8
THE WOMEN--PLUCKED [SLIPPED] AWAY	THOSE FAIR--FICTITIOUS	499	2
CUT THEE AWAY FROM ME--	YOU KNOW THAT PORTRAIT	504	14
THEN AWAY UPON A JIB--HE GOES--	HE PARTS HIMSELF--LIKE	517	8
MY BRIDE HAD SLIPPED AWAY--	HER SWEET WEIGHT ON MY	518	4
AS GIANTS--GONE [CLAIMED] AWAY--	HAD I PRESUMED TO HOPE--	522	4
AND WALK STEADY, AWAY,	TO PUT THIS WORLD DOWN,	527	2
IT SEEMS SO STRAIGHT TO LIE AWAY	I'M SORRY FOR THE DEAD--	529	9
AND THEN--TOGETHER BORE AWAY	TWO BUTTERFLIES WENT OUT	533	5
AND TRODDEN OUT [BLOTTED OUT-- / SHOVED AWAY--] THE MILLS--	THE BRAIN, WITHIN IT'S	556	8
AND PUTTETH HER AWAY	SHE HIDETH HER THE LAST	557	6
IT MOVED AWAY THE CHEEKS--	IT KNEW NO MEDICINE--	559	5
HE GAVE AWAY HIS LIFE--	HE GAVE AWAY HIS LIFE--	567	1
SHE PUT SOME FLOWERS AWAY--	MY FIRST WELL DAY--SINCE	574	10
THE ENTERING--TAKES AWAY--	I HAD BEEN HUNGRY, ALL	579	20
IS LEFT--TO PUT AWAY--	EMPTY MY HEART, OF THEE	587	9
AND DROVE AWAY THE LEAVES	THE NIGHT WAS WIDE, AND	589	6
AND PUSHED AWAY A SAIL	THREE TIMES--WE PARTED--	598	8

AWAY (CONTINUED)

	FIRST LINE	POEM		LINE
WHY HEAVEN DID NOT BREAK AWAY--	IT TROUBLED ME AS ONCE I	600		15
AND CITIES--OOZE [SLIP / SLIDE / MELT] AWAY--	A STILL--VOLCANO--LIFE--	601		12
THAN I COULD COAX A LEECH AWAY--[MODIFY A LEECH]	IT WOULD HAVE STARVED A	612		7
THIS--TOO--THE SHOWMAN RUBBED AWAY--	THEY CALLED ME TO THE	628		13
SLID CARELESSLY AWAY--	I WATCHED THE MOON	629		14
SUCH PRESENCE BEAR AWAY	BEREAVEMENT IN THEIR	645		10
IT HAD CAST AWAY--	HER SWEET TURN TO LEAVE	649		8
TO BASK THE CENTURIES AWAY--	A LONG--LONG SLEEP--A	654		7
THEN--EDDIES LIKE A ROSE--AWAY--	THE NAME--OF IT--IS	656		11
OR BETTER, RUN AWAY	COULD I BUT RIDE	661		8
TO GET AWAY FROM ME--	COULD I BUT RIDE	661		12
WHEN SENSE FROM SPIRIT--FILES AWAY--	OF ALL THE SOULS THAT	664		3
AND MISTS--ARE CARVED AWAY,	OF ALL THE SOULS THAT	664		10
SHOW [SHIFT] ITSELF AWAY--	BLOOM UPON THE MOUNTAIN	667		8
WICKS WIDE AWAY--	THE SUNRISE RUNS FOR	710		9
AND I HAD PUT AWAY	BECAUSE I COULD NOT STOP	712		6
DISSOLVING INTO DAWN AWAY,	BEHIND ME--DIPS ETERNITY	721		5
FADES FROM THE FIRMAMENT AWAY--	SWEET MOUNTAINS--YE TELL	722		11
AWAY FROM ME--	LET US PLAY YESTERDAY--	728		36
IN USING, WEAR AWAY,	SHE ROSE TO HIS	732		8
WHEN PEACE WAS FAR AWAY--	I MANY TIMES THOUGHT	739		2
BUT YOU MUST GO AWAY	THE BIRDS REPORTED FROM	743	V	4
SHE DREW AWAY AUSTERE--	THE BIRDS REPORTED FROM	743		14
AND CARRIED ME AWAY--	MY LIFE HAD STOOD--A	754		4
THE RELATIVE AWAY--	YOU CONSTITUTED TIME--	765		6
TO STEEP IT'S SHAPE AWAY--	BEREAVED OF ALL, I WENT	784		14
WHEN SHE HAD PUT AWAY HER WORK	SEVERER SERVICE OF	786		7
WHO PUT A HEAD AWAY	SEVERER SERVICE OF	786		14
HIS LAST DECADE [SLOW DECADES] AWAY,	JOY TO HAVE MERITED THE	788		22
SHE TURNS AS LONG AWAY	NATURE--THE GENTLEST	790		18
THE SUNSHINE THREW HIS HAT AWAY--	A DROP FELL ON THE APPLE	794		11
AND SIGNED THE FETE [SHOW / VAN] AWAY--	A DROP FELL ON THE APPLE	794		16
WHEN THE LATTER--IS PUT AWAY	BY MY WINDOW HAVE I FOR	797		19
OR NOONS REPORT AWAY	A LIGHT EXISTS IN SPRING	812		14
AWAY FROM HOME ARE SOME [THEY] AND I--	AWAY FROM HOME ARE SOME	821		1
AND THROW [THREW] AWAY THE ROAD--	THE WIND BEGUN TO KNEAD	824		8
HIMSELF [THAT HE] IS BORNE AWAY	TRUTH--IS AS OLD AS GOD	836		6
THEN, TURN MY FACE AWAY.	I CANNOT BUY IT--'TIS	840		12
TO KEEP THE DARK AWAY.	I SING TO USE THE	850		8
LIKE GLOW WORMS, FLEE AWAY--	THE SUN AND MOON MUST	871		8
OR TAKE AWAY [PALLIATE] A BRIAR.	IT WAS A GRAVE, YET BORE	876		12
WHY GIVE IF THOU MUST TAKE AWAY	A SHADE UPON THE MIND	882		7
LIGHTNING--LETS AWAY	STRUCK, WAS I, NOR YET	925		2
INTO THE DARKNESS [TWILIGHT / EVENING] DIPS AWAY--	FAIRER THROUGH FADING--	938		2
AND THEN AWAY TO YOU TO PASS--	I LEARNED--AT LEAST--	944		23
FLIT RUSSETLY AWAY	IT IS AN HONORABLE	946		8
RUB AWAY THE BRAND--	COLOR--CASTE--	970		8
IF HE PUT AWAY	COLOR--CASTE--	970		10
THE SPIRIT TURNS AWAY	DEATH IS A DIALOGUE	976		6
THIS [THE] WORLD DID DROP AWAY	IT WAS A QUIET WAY--	1053		9
AND PUTTING LOVE AWAY	THE BUSTLE IN A HOUSE	1078		6
THE SUN RAN MILES AWAY	THE BIRD DID PRANCE--THE	1107		2
WHEN IT HAS RODE AWAY.	THE FACE WE CHOOSE TO	1141		4
GREAT STREETS OF SILENCE LED AWAY	GREAT STREETS OF SILENCE	1159		1
WHOSE NAMELESS FATHOMS SLINK AWAY	CONTAINED IN THIS SHORT	1165		7
SHORED [PUSHED] THE SUN AWAY	ON THE WORLD YOU COLORED	1171		10
PUT THEIR WORK AWAY	THERE'S THE BATTLE OF	1174		4
AND RIDE AWAY.	TOO FEW THE MORNINGS BE,	1186		7
AND DROVE THE FOG AWAY--	THE SUN AND FOG	1190		4
AMPLER [BOLDER] TO FLY AWAY	ARE FRIENDS DELIGHT OR	1199		5
WORDS ARE HANDED [LANGUAGE IS DRIVEN] AWAY--	WHATEVER IT IS--SHE HAS	1204		8
THE WORDS ARE WITHERED [SPEECH IS STOLEN] AWAY	WHATEVER IT IS--SHE HAS	1204	V	8
THE MAN THAT [WHO] RUNS AWAY	TO DISAPPEAR ENHANCES--	1209		2
WAS FORFEITED AWAY--	A SPARROW TOOK A SLICE	1211		8
AND BOLDLY RODE AWAY--	A SPARROW TOOK A SLICE	1211	V	8
HERE IS LAID AWAY	FORTITUDE INCARNATE	1217		2
WHILE HE, VICTORIOUS TILTS AWAY	LIKE TRAINS OF CARS ON	1224		7
AND HE HAS HAULED AWAY.	SO MUCH OF HEAVEN HAS	1228		12
WHEN IT HAD PUSHED ITSELF AWAY	LIKE RAIN IT SOUNDED	1235		5
THEN LIKE ELIJAH RODE AWAY	LIKE RAIN IT SOUNDED	1235		15
AND DREW AWAY	MY HEART RAN SO TO THEE	1237		4
PUTS ITSELF SEVERE AWAY	SAFE DESPAIR IT IS THAT	1243		3
THEN CRUMBLE GRAND AWAY	TO PILE LIKE THUNDER TO	1247		2
TO TAKE US [ONE] LANDS AWAY	THERE IS NO FRIGATE LIKE	1263		2
UNTIL ALLURED AWAY	THE WAY TO KNOW THE	1279		16
AND TURNS SO WEAK AWAY--	I KNOW SUSPENSE--IT	1285		2
'TIS SO FAR AWAY--	YESTERDAY IS HISTORY,	1292		2
FLUTTER BOTH AWAY	YESTERDAY IS HISTORY,	1292		8
WHICH NEVER WENT AWAY?	THE INFINITE A SUDDEN	1309		4
IS BUT A MONTH FROM HERE [AWAY]--	THE NOTICE THAT IS	1310		2
HE STAYED AWAY A YEAR TO CALL	DEAR MARCH--COME IN--	1320		21
OUR LITTLE SECRETS SLINK AWAY--	OUR LITTLE SECRETS SLINK	1326		1
WERE SWEEPING HIM AWAY--	A SINGLE CLOVER PLANK	1343		8
WE TURN THE SUN [SPELL] AWAY,	AS SUMMER INTO AUTUMN	1346		4
BUT TAKE AWAY AS DIFFICULT [IMPOTENT / EASILY]	YOU CANNOT TAKE ITSELF	1351		7
TAKE ALL AWAY--	TAKE ALL AWAY--	1365		1
GOES NOR COMES AWAY	"SECRETS" IS A DAILY	1385		8

	FIRST LINE	POEM	LINE
AWAY (CONTINUED)			
. . . SWERVES / SUMMERS SWERVE] AWAY--	AFTER ALL BIRDS HAVE	1395	7
IT SWEEPS THE TENEMENT [TENEMENTS] AWAY	THE INUNDATION OF THE	1425	3
ALARM IT'S WALLS AWAY--	GO NOT TOO NEAR A HOUSE	1434	4
IT BEARS AWAY IN TRIUMPH	DEATH IS THE SUPPLE	1445	9
IT'S TREATISE FLEW AWAY	I THOUGHT THE TRAIN	1449	8
THOUGH GENERATIONS PASS AWAY,	A LITTLE OVERFLOWING	1467	4
TILL WHEN IT [AND THEN DOTH] SLIP AWAY	IT'S LITTLE ETHER HOOD	1501	5
ALL THINGS SWEPT SOLE AWAY	ALL THINGS SWEPT SOLE	1512	1
ENTIRELY AWAY.	HOW MUCH OF SOURCE	1517	4
AND QUAKE--AND TURN AWAY,	NOT SEEING, STILL WE	1518	5
SO SOAR AWAY AND NEVER SIGH	THE BUTTERFLY UPON THE	1521	7
OUR PROJECTS FLIT AWAY--	ON THAT SPECIFIC PILLOW	1533	2
AND SUMMER IS [SUMMER PASSED / SUMMERS ARE] AWAY--	THERE COMES A WARNING	1536	4
THE SUMMER LAPSED AWAY--	AS IMPERCEPTIBLY AS	1540	2
FOR SO TO SOAR AWAY	COME SHOW THY DURHAM	1542	10
MY WARS ARE LAID AWAY IN BOOKS--	MY WARS ARE LAID AWAY IN	1549	1
BY CHUMS THAT PASSED AWAY--	MY WARS ARE LAID AWAY IN	1549	10
WAS NEVER BLOWN AWAY--	NO BRIGADIER THROUGHOUT	1561	8
HE [SHE] RAN AWAY FROM EARTH--	CLIMBING TO REACH THE	1566	4
BLOSSOMS WILL RUN AWAY,	BLOSSOMS WILL RUN AWAY,	1578	1
AND FENCES FLED AWAY	THERE CAME A WIND LIKE A	1593	10
A SLOOP OF AMBER SLIPS AWAY	A SLOOP OF AMBER SLIPS	1622	1
NO LIFE CAN POMPLESS PASS AWAY--	NO LIFE CAN POMPLESS	1626	1
THAT LEADS AWAY FROM THEE--	OH FUTURE! THOU SECRETED	1631	4
BEFORE THOU DOST EXUDE [DISSOLVE] AWAY	STILL OWN THEE--STILL	1633	7
TAKE ALL AWAY FROM ME, BUT LEAVE ME ECSTASY,	TAKE ALL AWAY FROM ME,	1640	1
AND HONOR LEAGUES AWAY	THE DITCH IS DEAR TO THE	1645	8
UNTIL WE DRIVE AWAY	EDEN IS THAT	1657	4
HIS ACTION LAID AWAY	JUDGEMENT IS JUSTEST	1671	3
AND TRAILED LIKE ROBES AWAY;	A CURIOUS CLOUD	1710	7
THEY'D LAUGH AND RUN AWAY.	IF ALL THE GRIEFS I AM	1726	4
AND LETS THE BRAIN AWAY	IF EVER THE LID GETS OFF	1727	2
IT WILL NEVER GET AWAY	REARRANGE A "WIFE'S"	1737	18
MUST THRUST THE TEARS AWAY.	WHERE EVERY BIRD IS BOLD	1758	4
AWE			
AN AWE CAME ON THE TRINKET!	A CLOCK STOPPED--	287	6
AND SATISFIES AN AWE	I THINK THE HEMLOCK	525	4
AN AWE IF IT SHOULD BE LIKE THAT	"HEAVEN" HAS DIFFERENT	575	7
I LEANED UPON THE AWE--	I YEARS HAD BEEN FROM	609	9
OUR PACE TOOK SUDDEN AWE--	OUR JOURNEY HAD ADVANCED	615	5
THE SOUL SHOULD STAND [BE] IN AWE--	THE SOUL UNTO ITSELF	683	8
OF AMPLITUDE, OR AWE--	SHE ROSE TO HIS	732	6
A RANK--FOR [THE RANK OF / AN AWE OF--] IODINE--	THE COLOR OF A QUEEN, IS	776	8
MAKE THIS BED WITH AWE--	AMPLE MAKE THIS BED--	829	2
THE DEMAND [THE AFFAIR / AN AFFAIR] OF AWE?	SUMMER LAID HER SIMPLE	1363	8
THAT HATH NO OMEN HERE--BUT AWE--	GATHERED INTO THE EARTH,	1370	5
IN AWE AND INNOCENCE, WERE MEET.	WHOSE PINK CAREER MAY	1394	4
AND AWE--WAS ALL WE COULD FEEL.	IT SOUNDED AS IF THE	1397	4
AT WHAT IS AWE [DREAD] TO ME.	WHAT MYSTERY PERVADES A	1400	12
WE COMPREHENDED [POSTULATED / RECOLLECTED] BY THE AWE	IT WAS A QUIET SEEMING	1419	10
LIKE ONE THAT FED ON AWE.	HER SPIRIT ROSE TO SUCH	1486	3
CIRCUMFERENCE THOU BRIDE OF AWE	CIRCUMFERENCE THOU BRIDE	1620	1
WOULD POPULATE WITH AWE MY SOLITUDE	ON MY VOLCANO GROWS THE	1677	8
BEGETS AN AWE	PERIL AS A POSSESSION	1678	5
NO MAN SAW AWE, NOR TO HIS HOUSE	NO MAN SAW AWE, NOR TO	1733	1
AND GUILE [AWE] IS WHERE IT GOES.	SWEET IS THE SWAMP WITH	1740	8
AWED			
BUT AWED BEYOND MY ERRAND--	MY PERIOD HAD COME FOR	564	19
AWES			
AND AWES	WE INTRODUCE OURSELVES	1214	6
AWFUL			
SOME PALE REPORTER, FROM THE AWFUL DOORS	JUST LOST, WHEN I WAS	160	10
TRY--CAN YOU STIR THE AWFUL RIVET--	HOW MANY TIMES THESE LOW	187	3
AN AWFUL TEMPEST MASHED THE AIR--	AN AWFUL TEMPEST MASHED	198	1
A PRIVILEGE [LUXURY] SO AWFUL	I WOULD NOT PAINT--A	505	21
AND SILENCED, AS THE AWFUL SEA	HE TOUCHED ME, SO I LIVE	506	5
LEST BACK THE AWFUL DOOR SHOULD SPRING	I YEARS HAD BEEN FROM	609	19
TO FILL THE AWFUL VACUUM [LONGITUDE]	SEVERER SERVICE OF	786	3
OF CONSCIOUSNESS, HER AWFUL MATE	OF CONSCIOUSNESS, HER	894	1
AND THEN AN AWFUL LEISURE WAS	THE LAST NIGHT THAT SHE	1100	27
THE AWFUL MOMENT IS	WE DO NOT KNOW THE TIME	1106	2
BEHIND THE AWFUL POWER--	THE WIND TOOK UP THE	1134	8
MIDNIGHT'S AWFUL PATTERN	ON THE WORLD YOU COLORED	1171	11
THE AWFUL [SOLEMN] CUTLERY	THE LIGHTNING IS A	1173	4
AWFUL FATHER [FOUNDER] OF LOVE--	WHATEVER IT IS--SHE HAS	1204	2
OF THE AWFUL [SWINGING] SEA--	FORTITUDE INCARNATE	1217	4
THAT AWFUL STRANGER CONSCIOUSNESS	I NEVER HEAR THAT ONE IS	1323	15
WHEN DOWN SOME AWFUL BATTLEMENT	ESCAPE IS SUCH A	1347	7
IT'S AWFUL CHAMBER OPEN STANDS--	WATER MAKES MANY BEDS	1428	3
THAT AWFUL TRAGEDY	A DEW SUFFICED ITSELF--	1437	14
SHE TOOK THE AWFUL NEWS	I WATCHED HER FACE TO	1667	2
THOUGH BY HIS AWFUL RESIDENCE	NO MAN SAW AWE, NOR TO	1733	3
AWHILE			
THAT HOVERED THERE AWHILE--	ASHES DENOTE THAT FIRE	1063	4
AWKWARD			
THAT IN MY AWKWARD--GAZING--FACE--	IF I'M LOST--NOW--	256	6

	FIRST LINE	POEM	LINE
AWKWARD (CONTINUED)			
LEST WE TOO AWKWARD SHOW	THERE CAME A DAY AT	322	15
FLOWERS--TO KEEP THE EYES--FROM GOING AWKWARD--	IT'S THOUGHTS--AND JUST	495	12
BUT SOMETHING AWKWARD IN [ODD ABOUT] THE FIT--	I COULD NOT PROVE THE	563	11
HOW AWKWARD AT THE HYMN [PLAN]	I LEARNED--AT LEAST--	944	4
'TWAS AWKWARD, BUT IT FITTED ME--	'TWAS AWKWARD, BUT IT	973	1
AWKWARD--FALTERING--	SANG FROM THE HEART,	1059	10
PRESENT THE AWKWARD RIND--	EXCEPT THE SMALLER SIZE	1067	V
THE GRACE SO AWKWARD FOR HER SAKE	WARM IN HER HAND THESE	1313	3
BUT POMPOUS [SILLY / AWKWARD] JOY	MARCH IS THE MONTH OF	1404	6
AXE			
AN AXE SHRILL SINGING IN THE WOODS--	AN ALTERED LOOK ABOUT	140	11
BECAUSE IT'S MUSIC STIRS THE AXE	THE DOOMED--REGARD THE	294	7
AXIOM			
IF SUMMER WERE AN AXIOM--	THE SKIES CANT KEEP	191	11
WILL NOT ALLOW AN AXIOM	EXPERIMENT ESCORTS US	1770	3
AXIS			
THE EARTH UPON AN AXIS	"SIC TRANSIT GLORIA	3	33
ON IT'S AXIS TURNED!	FREQUENTLY THE WOODS ARE	6	10
THE FINE--UNVARYING AXIS	THE OUTER--FROM THE	451	5
A BORER IN THE AXIS	CRUMBLING IS NOT AN	997	7
WHOSE AXIS [OWNER] NEVER COMES.	WATER MAKES MANY BEDS	1428	8
AXLE			
AS IF AN AXLE, [A MUSCLE--] HELD--	WHEN WE STAND ON THE	242	16
BUT WHEN THE VITAL AXLE TURNS	IDEALS ARE THE FAIRY OIL	983	3
AXLES			
I HEARD IT'S AXLES GO	THIS SLOW DAY MOVED	1120	2
AYRE			
TILL BROAD AS BUENOS AYRE--	YOUR RICHES--TAUGHT ME--	299	4
AZOF			
AZOF--THE EQUINOX,	THE DUTIES OF THE WIND	1137	10
AZURE			
A DEPTH--AN AZURE--A PERFUME--	A SOMETHING IN A	122	5
TRACED AZURE ON HER HAND--	SHE BORE IT TILL THE	144	2
WHAT EDIFICES AZURE	WHAT TENEMENTS OF CLOVER	1338	3
ADVOCATE THE AZURE	LIFT IT--WITH THE	1348	5
LIKE AZURE DRIED	THE GENTIAN HAS A	1424	2
BABBLE			
AS BROOKS IN DESERTS BABBLE SWEET	AS WATCHERS HANG UPON	121	4
WITH BABBLE OF THE STYLES--	THE MANNER OF IT'S DEATH	468	10
BABBLE [CAROL] OF THE HAPPY	FORTITUDE INCARNATE	1217	5
BABBLER			
SO BABBLER, AND BOHEA--STAY THERE--	UNIT, LIKE DEATH, FOR	408	14
OR BABBLER--ENTERTAIN--	I FEAR A MAN OF FRUGAL	543	4
LET EVERY BABBLER [PRATER] BE	THE RETICENT VOLCANO	1748	10
BABBLERS			
THE JEHOVAHS--ARE NO BABBLERS--	ONLY GOD--DETECT THE	626	3
BABBLES			
BABBLES THE BEE IN A STOLID EAR,	SAFE IN THEIR ALABASTER	216	9
BABBLING			
ON HIS BABBLING--BERRY--LIPS--	TEACH HIM--WHEN HE MAKES	227	3
BABY			
BABY--	TEACH HIM--WHEN HE MAKES	227	T
NEW ACQUAINTANCE--THIS BABY MADE--	TRUDGING TO EDEN,	1020	8
BACCALAUREATE			
SEPTEMBER'S BACCALAUREATE	SEPTEMBER'S	1271	1
BACK			
FLINGING THE PROBLEM BACK	MY WHEEL IS IN THE DARK!	10	14
BACK TO HER NATIVE WOOD!	THERE'S SOMETHING	45	12
BACK TO THE LAWN AGAIN.	WE SHOULD NOT MIND SO	81	4
THESE ARE THE DAYS WHEN BIRDS COME BACK--	THESE ARE THE DAYS WHEN	130	1
WHEN BREATH BLEW [DREW] BACK,	JUST LOST, WHEN I WAS	160	4
AND THEN TO LAY THEM QUIET BACK--	IN EBON BOX, WHEN YEARS	169	17
COME BACK, AND DUST THE POND!	SHE SWEEPS WITH	219	4
TOO PLUMMETLESS--THAT IT COME BACK [RETURN]--	A SOLEMN THING--IT WAS--	271	7
INTO [BACK OF / AT THE / AFTER / UNTO / NEXT TO] SOLITUDE--	HOW THE OLD MOUNTAINS	291	20
SO FACES ON TWO DECKS, LOOK BACK,	THERE CAME A DAY AT	322	19
SHE--EACH YEAR--LEADS HER DAISIES BACK--	I KNOW A PLACE WHERE	337	3
THE LEAF--AT LOVE--TURNED BACK--	'TWAS THE OLD--ROAD--	344	13
IF THEY--TWINKLED BACK--	I FELT MY LIFE WITH BOTH	351	11
BUT TURNING BACK--'TWAS SLOW--	I WENT TO THANK HER--	363	10
A PASSAGE BACK--OR TWO--TO MAKE--	A PRECIOUS--MOULDERING	371	7
AND BACK IT SLID--AND I ALONE--	I SAW NO WAY--THE	378	5
SMILING BACK FROM CORONATION	SMILING BACK FROM	385	1
THE EARTH LAYS BACK THESE TIRED LIVES	THE MONTHS HAVE ENDS--	423	5
I FELT THE WILDERNESS ROLL BACK	IT WOULD NEVER BE COMMON	430	28
AND YET--EXISTENCE--SOME WAY BACK--	I TIE MY HAT--I CREASE	443	11
BE SLOWLY HANDED BACK--	TRIUMPH--MAY BE OF	455	10
THEN NUMERALS ARE DOWERED BACK--	'TIS ONE BY ONE--THE	545	7
TO PUT A CURRENT [THE WATERS] BACK--	THE BRAIN, WITHIN IT'S	556	5
BUT, LOOKING BACK--THE FIRST SO SEEMS	I RECKON--WHEN I COUNT	569	5
ALL WADED--WE LOOK BACK FOR PLAY,	IF I MAY HAVE IT, WHEN	577	24
BUT ONLY KNEW BY LOOKING BACK--	IT CEASED TO HURT ME,	584	3
PASS BACK AND FORTH, BEFORE MY BRAIN	WHEN I WAS SMALL, A	596	15
THE GRAVE YIELDS BACK HER ROBBERIES--	OF NEARNESS TO HER	607	13
LEST BACK THE AWFUL DOOR SHOULD SPRING	I YEARS HAD BEEN FROM	609	19
AND WHEN THIS WORLD--SETS FURTHER BACK--	YOU'LL FIND--IT WHEN YOU	610	9
DID THEY--COME BACK NO MORE?	GLEE--THE GREAT STORM IS	619	13

	FIRST LINE	POEM	LINE
BACK (CONTINUED)			
'TIS GOOD [WELL]--THE LOOKING BACK ON GRIEF--	'TIS GOOD--THE LOOKING	660	1
BUT DID NOT FINISH--SOME WAY BACK--	A THOUGHT WENT UP MY	701	3
THAT SWEPT HIS BEING--BACK--	GRIEF IS A MOUSE--	793	8
BACK--TOWARD TIME--	THE ADMIRATIONS--AND	906	14
TILL SUNRISE TAKE [CALL] US BACK TO SCENE--	I LEARNED--AT LEAST--	944	25
LOOKING BACK IS BEST THAT IS LEFT	THIS WAS IN THE WHITE OF	995	5
BIRDS, MOSTLY BACK--	BEE! I'M EXPECTING YOU!	1035	7
WHEN THEY COME BACK--IF BLOSSOMS DO--	WHEN THEY COME BACK--IF	1080	1
I TAKE BACK ALL I SAY--	WHEN THEY COME BACK--IF	1080	16
WE PRIED HIM BACK	THE FROST OF DEATH WAS	1136	9
AND NEVER COMING BACK	BECAUSE THAT YOU ARE	1260	2
LOOK BACK ON TIME, WITH KINDLY EYES--	LOOK BACK ON TIME, WITH	1478	1
THE THINGS THAT NEVER CAN COME BACK, ARE SEVERAL--	THE THINGS THAT NEVER	1515	1
WERE SWINGING AT HER [HIS] BACK.	HER LOSSES MAKE OUR	1562	4
BACK FROM THE CORDIAL GRAVE I DRAG THEE	BACK FROM THE CORDIAL	1625	1
SO GIVE ME BACK TO DEATH--	SO GIVE ME BACK TO DEATH	1632	1
HOW FAIR ON LOOKING BACK THE DAY	EDEN IS THAT	1657	5
THE ONES THAT DISAPPEARED ARE BACK	THE ONES THAT	1690	1
THEIR COMING BACK SEEMS POSSIBLE	THE DISTANCE THAT THE	1742	3
BACKS			
WE TURNED OUR BACKS UPON THE SUN	THEY PUT US FAR APART--	474	19
THE CLOUDS THEIR BACKS TOGETHER LAID	THE CLOUDS THEIR BACKS	1172	1
BACKWARD			
TO TAKE A BACKWARD [FINAL / PARTING] LOOK.	THESE ARE THE DAYS WHEN	130	3
ESCAPING BACKWARD TO PERCEIVE	ESCAPING BACKWARD TO	867	1
TRUDGING TO EDEN, LOOKING BACKWARD,	TRUDGING TO EDEN,	1020	1
GROPED BACKWARD AT HIMSELF	HE SCANNED IT--STAGGERED	1062	7
A GAIN UPON THE BACKWARD LEAVES	SUMMER BEGINS TO HAVE	1682	4
BAD			
AND BAD MEN--"GO TO JAIL"--	YOU'RE RIGHT--"THE WAY	234	11
BADE			
AND [THEN] BADE IT TO THE EAST	HE FOUND MY BEING--SET	603	4
BADINAGE			
WITH BADINAGE DIVINE--	ONE OF THE ONES THAT	1466	6
AND BADINAGE PARTOOK.	HIGH FROM THE EARTH I	1723	12
BAFFLE			
WHO BAFFLE KEY--	ALONE, I CANNOT BE--	298	4
SO I MUST BAFFLE AT THE HINT	MY COCOON TIGHTENS--	1099	9
BAFFLE, IF IT COST YOU	DEATH IS LIKE THE INSECT	1716	7
BAFFLED			
BAFFLED FOR JUST A DAY OR TWO--	BAFFLED FOR JUST A DAY	17	1
WHEREFORE, MY BAFFLED FINGERS	LOW AT MY PROBLEM	69	7
THESE ARE THE VISIONS FLITTED [FASHIONS--BAFFLED--] GUIDO--	HOW THE OLD MOUNTAINS	291	21
NOR PERSIAN, BAFFLED AT HER SHRINE	HE TOUCHED ME, SO I LIVE	506	16
THAT BAFFLED ME--	I PRAYED, AT FIRST, A	576	11
BAFFLES			
IT BECKONS, AND IT BAFFLES--	THIS WORLD IS NOT	501	5
AND BAFFLES QUEST--	GRIEF IS A MOUSE--	793	4
BAFFLING			
'TIS A BAFFLING EARTH--	IN FALLING TIMBERS	614	14
BAGATELLES			
AS INFINITE [BAGATELLES] TRADITION	LIKE SOME OLD FASHIONED	302	5
BAGGAGE			
BAGGAGE A [OF] STRAPPED PEARL--	DROPPED INTO THE ETHER	665	6
BAGS			
BAGS OF DOUBLOONS--ADVENTUROUS BEES	WHAT WOULD I GIVE TO SEE	247	18
BAHAMAS			
BERRIES OF THE BAHAMAS--HAVE I--	I COULD BRING YOU JEWELS	697	5
BAILIFF			
AND SENDS A BAILIFF THERE.	I HAD SOME THINGS THAT I	116	8
BAILIFF'S			
BOLD AS A BAILIFF'S HYMN--	A PROMPT--EXECUTIVE BIRD	1177	2
BAIT			
BAIT IT WITH THE BALSAM,	DEATH IS LIKE THE INSECT	1716	5
BAIZE			
THE VIOLIN IN BAIZE REPLACED--	LIKE SOME OLD FASHIONED	302	15
BAKES			
IN OVENS GREEN OUR MOTHER BAKES,	THE WORK OF HER THAT	1143	3
BALANCE			
TILL I COULD TAKE THE [CATCH MY] BALANCE	I PRAYED, AT FIRST, A	576	18
OF OPPOSITE--TO BALANCE ODD [EQUAL OUGHT]--	THE ZEROES--TAUGHT US--	689	5
BALANCED			
THEY BALANCED FILM WITH FILM,	I TOOK ONE DRAUGHT OF	1725	6
BALANCING			
NICELY BALANCING.	CRISIS IS A HAIR	889	8
BALCONY			
REMAINS BUT BALCONY	AS WILLING LID O'ER	1050	4
BALD			
THE TRUTH, IS BALD, AND COLD--	'TIS SO APPALLING--IT	281	9
NO BALD DEATH--AFFRONT THEIR PARLORS--	SWEET--SAFE--HOUSES--	457	10
AN INSTINCT [HUNGER] FOR THE HOAR [DREAR], THE BALD--	I THINK THE HEMLOCK	525	7
I'LL TELL THEE ALL--HOW BALD [BLANK] IT GREW--	IF I MAY HAVE IT, WHEN	577	14
BALES			
STREWS THE LANDING WITH OPAL BALES--	THIS--IS THE LAND--THE	266	7
BALK			
TO BALK THEE OF THY SACRED PREY--[THE	OH FUTURE! THOU SECRETED	1631	7

	FIRST LINE	POEM	LINE
BALK (CONTINUED)			
INNOCENCE / THE MYRIADS]			
BALKED			
BALKED IN THE VASTEST INSTANCE	COULD HOPE INSPECT HER	1283	5
BALKING			
BALKING OUR WIT	THE RAT IS THE CONCISEST	1356	5
BALL			
NONE CANNOT FIND WHO SEEKETH, ON THIS TERRESTIAL BALL!	AWAKE YE MUSES NINE,	1	12
FROM SUCH A COMMON BALL AS THIS	A DAY! HELP! HELP!	42	3
TILL THE BALL IS FULL--	HOW THE OLD MOUNTAINS	291	6
DREAD, BUT THE WHIZZING, BEFORE THE BALL--	IF ANY SINK, ASSURE THAT	358	6
WHEN THE BALL ENTERS, ENTERS SILENCE--	IF ANY SINK, ASSURE THAT	358	7
A SPECK UPON A BALL--	I SAW NO WAY--THE	378	6
THEN RECOLLECT A BALL, SHE GOT--	HER SMILE WAS SHAPED	514	5
THEN CAUGHT ME--LIKE A BALL--	THREE TIMES--WE PARTED--	598	6
THE SPIDER HOLDS A SILVER BALL	THE SPIDER HOLDS A	605	1
AS SEAMS--INCLUDE THE BALL?	WITHOUT THIS--THERE IS	655	8
ON BALL OF MAST IN BOSPORUS [FOREIGN PORT]--	THE DAY UNDRESSED--	716	15
IS FRUGAL OF IT'S BALL.	'TWAS FIGHTING FOR HIS	1188	4
BALLAD			
A CARELESS SNATCH--A BALLAD--	HEART, NOT SO HEAVY AS	83	5
THAN COULD BORDER BALLAD--	NEVER FOR SOCIETY	746	9
BEAR WITH THE BALLAD--	SANG FROM THE HEART,	1059	9
BALLAD'S			
REMANDED TO A BALLAD'S BARN	A FADED BOY--IN SALLOW	1524	7
BALLADS			
THEIR BALLADS WERE THE SAME--	I HAD A GUINEA GOLDEN--	23	14
OF BALLADS AND OF BARDS--	ONE OF THE ONES THAT	1466	20
BALLET			
THAT HAD I BALLET KNOWLEDGE--	I CANNOT DANCE UPON MY	326	5
BALLOON			
MYSELF ENDUED [UPHELD / UPBORNE / SUSTAINED] BALLOON	I WOULD NOT PAINT--A	505	14
OBSERVE--"'TWAS ONLY A BALLOON"--	YOU'VE SEEN BALLOONS SET	700	20
OF ONE [HIM] THAT LEANETH FROM [IN] BALLOON	IT WAS A QUIET WAY--	1053	11
AND SCUTTLE MY BALLOON--	I BET WITH EVERY WIND	1215	4
AS FROM THE EARTH THE LIGHT [FAIR] BALLOON	AS FROM THE EARTH THE	1630	1
BALLOONS			
YOU'VE SEEN BALLOONS SET--HAV'NT YOU?	YOU'VE SEEN BALLOONS SET	700	1
BALLOT			
ANGELS' BREATHLESS BALLOT	SOUL, WILT THOU TOSS	139	5
BALLOTS			
THE BALLOTS OF ETERNITY, WILL SHOW JUST THAT.	MY REWARD FOR BEING, WAS	343	11
BALLS			
A SOLDIER'S--BALLS! WHO ASKETH MORE,	A LITTLE BREAD--A CRUST	159	11
NOR TOSSED MY SHAPE IN EIDER BALLS,	I CANNOT DANCE UPON MY	326	13
HER EYES INCREASE TO BALLS--	SHE SIGHTS A BIRD--SHE	507	4
I'D WIND THE MONTHS IN BALLS--	IF YOU WERE COMING IN	511	6
HIS MIGHTY BALLS--IN DEATH WERE THICK--	A DYING TIGER--MOANED	566	5
HEAVES BALLS OF SPECKS, LIKE VICIOUS BOY	TO INTERRUPT HIS YELLOW	591	5
MORE ARDUOUS [DIFFICULT] THAN BALLS--	MY PORTION IS DEFEAT--	639	6
BESTOWED [HE GAVE] HIMSELF TO BALLS	HE FOUGHT LIKE THOSE	759	2
LIKE BALLS--UPON A FLOOR.	I FELT A CLEAVING IN MY	937	8
LIKE BALLS UPON A FLOOR--	THE DUST BEHIND I STROVE	992	4
FLING UP THY BALLS OF GOLD	MY GOD--HE SEES THEE--	1178	3
BALM			
THAN WHEN--A LITTLE DULL BALM GROWN--	YOU LOVE ME--YOU ARE	156	17
KILL YOUR BALM--AND IT'S ODORS BLESS YOU--	KILL YOUR BALM--AND IT'S	238	1
GIVE BALM--TO GIANTS--	I CAN WADE GRIEF--	252	13
NOR SUPPRESSED--WITH BALM--	CIVILIZATION--SPURNS--	492	13
COULD GIVE THEM ANY BALM--	I MEASURE EVERY GRIEF I	561	20
BALM TO [FOR] BALM--	I ROSE--BECAUSE HE SANK	616	11
BALM TO [FOR] BALM--	I ROSE--BECAUSE HE SANK	616	11
INVALIDATES THE BALM OF THAT RELIGION	OURSELVES WE DO INTER	1144	3
THAT WALK THIS PLANK OF BALM--	THIS IS THE PLACE THEY	1264	6
HE SUPPLANTS THE BALM.	DEATH'S WAYLAYING NOT	1296	8
TO DOOMS OF BALM--	UPON A LILAC SEA	1337	6
OH, SUBSIDY OF BALM!	UNTO THE WHOLE--HOW ADD?	1341	4
AND TOSSES LIKE A FLEET OF BALM--	SWEET SKEPTICISM OF THE	1413	3
HEAVEN THE BALM OF A SURLY TECHNICALITY!	HOW HAPPY IS THE LITTLE	1510 V	
BETTER A GRAVE OF BALM	NOT ANY SUNNY TONE	1674	4
BALMS			
ENTERS--AND IS LOST IN BALMS.	COME SLOWLY--EDEN!	211	8
AND HYBLA BALMS--	THE WORLD--FEELS DUSTY	715	12
AND BUT ONE SMILE--THAT MEAGRES [HUMBLES] BALMS--	ABOVE OBLIVION'S TIDE	1531	4
AND A CHILL [BLEAK] SMILE INLAID WITH BALMS--	ABOVE OBLIVION'S TIDE	1531 V	4
AND [THE] VENOMS HE MISTOOK FOR BALMS	ARROWS ENAMORED OF HIS	1629	3
BALSAM			
BAIT IT WITH THE BALSAM,	DEATH IS LIKE THE INSECT	1716	5
BALTIC			
ONE BALTIC--THEY--	EMPTY MY HEART, OF THEE	587	6
WHO'S BALTIC--	NOR MOUNTAIN HINDER ME	1029	3
BAN			
CONTINUAL BAN PROPOUNDETH HE	OF SILKEN SPEECH AND	896	8
BAND			
NOR "BAND"--IN BRASS AND SCARLET--DREST--	MUSICIANS WRESTLE	157	8
OF THE MYSTERIOUS BARD [BAND]!	TO LEARN THE TRANSPORT	167	16
WITH LEADER OF THE BAND--	'TIS ONE BY ONE--THE	545	14

	FIRST LINE	POEM	LINE
BAND (CONTINUED)			
NOR IS IT CLASPED UNTO OF BAND--	YOU'LL KNOW HER--BY HER	634	19
AND YET [YET ALL] THE BAND WAS GONE--	THE BIRDS BEGUN AT FOUR	783	20
BANDAGED			
THE SOUL HAS BANDAGED MOMENTS--	THE SOUL HAS BANDAGED	512	1
BELIEFS ARE BANDAGED, LIKE THE TONGUE	I NEVER HEAR THAT ONE IS	1323	9
BIG MY SECRET BUT IT'S BANDAGED--	REARRANGE A "WIFE'S"	1737	17
BANDIT			
ROBBED--WAS I--INTACT TO [YET MET NO] BANDIT--	STRUCK, WAS I, NOR YET	925	9
BANDITTI			
BANDITTI OFTEN PASSED US	THROUGH LANE IT LAY--	9	3
BANDS			
WHEN WINDS GO ROUND AND ROUND IN BANDS--	OF ALL THE SOUNDS	321	21
THO' BANDS OF SPICES--ROW--	WHERE THOU ART--THAT--IS	725	12
THE RIVET IN THE BANDS	MY FAITH IS LARGER THAN	766	16
THE MEETING BANDS OF SMITTEN FACE	'TIS ANGUISH GRANDER	984	3
BANE			
BEHOLD THIS LITTLE BANE--	BEHOLD THIS LITTLE BANE	1438	1
IS IMMORTALITY A BANE	IS IMMORTALITY A BANE	1728	1
BANISH			
DONT TELL! THEY'D BANISH US [ADVERTISE]--YOU KNOW!	I'M NOBODY! WHO ARE YOU?	288	4
AND BANISH ME--	I'LL CLUTCH--AND CLUTCH	427	24
ELSE--SAVIOR--BANISH ME--	'TIS TRUE--THEY SHUT ME	538	V 12
ME FROM MYSELF--TO BANISH--	ME FROM MYSELF--TO	642	1
BANISH AIR FROM AIR--	BANISH AIR FROM AIR--	854	1
BANISH--MY MANDOLIN	BIND ME--I STILL CAN	1005	2
BANISHED			
I'M BANISHED--NOW--YOU KNOW IT--	IF I'M LOST--NOW--	256	10
BANISHMENT			
THERE'S BANISHMENT FROM NATIVE EYES--	I MEASURE EVERY GRIEF I	561	31
BANJO			
NO BLACK BIRD BATES HIS BANJO--	IT MAKES NO DIFFERENCE	620	7
BANK			
A BANK OF DAY--	A SLASH OF BLUE--	204	8
THE OTHER, LIKE THE LITTLE BANK	I THINK TO LIVE--MAY BE	646	7
UPON A BANK [WITHIN A HUT] OF STONE	A LONG--LONG SLEEP--A	654	6
BANKER			
BURGLAR! BANKER--FATHER!	I NEVER LOST AS MUCH BUT	49	7
BANKRUPT			
BANKRUPT ONCE THROUGH HIS EXCESSES--	PARADISE IS THAT OLD	1119	7
BANKRUPTCY			
NO BANKRUPTCY [SEPULCHRE / WILDERNESS]--NO DOOM--	I THINK TO LIVE--MAY BE	646	16
BANKS			
THEN I HAVE "SHARES" IN PRIMROSE "BANKS"--	WHAT WOULD I GIVE TO SEE	247	15
THESE--ARE THE BANKS OF THE YELLOW SEA--	THIS--IS THE LAND--THE	266	2
OR BUTTERFLIES, OFF BANKS OF NOON	A BIRD CAME DOWN THE	328	19
BROOKS OF PLUSH--IN BANKS OF SATIN	SWEET--SAFE--HOUSES--	457	6
THE HEART HAS NARROW BANKS	THE HEART HAS NARROW	928	1
BANNED			
MYSELF--HAD BANNED THE TRIBES--	IT ALWAYS FELT TO ME--A	597	18
BANNER			
ONE WITH THE BANNER GAY--	SLEEP IS SUPPOSED TO BE	13	13
BANNERS			
ALL THESE MY BANNERS BE.	ALL THESE MY BANNERS BE.	22	1
MET BY THE GODS WITH BANNERS--	TAKEN FROM MEN--THIS	53	3
BANQUET			
DEPRIVED OF OTHER BANQUET,	DEPRIVED OF OTHER	773	1
TO BANQUET ON THY COUNTENANCE	THE LUXURY TO APPREHEND	815	11
OR FIND THE BANQUET MEAN--	WHO GOES TO DINE MUST	1223	2
THE BANQUET OF ABSTEMIOUSNESS	WHO NEVER WANTED--	1430	3
LET HIM BE QUICK--THE VIAND FLITS [BANQUET COOLS]--	MINE ENEMY IS GROWING	1509	5
BANQUET'S			
THEIR BANQUET'S REAL [TRUE]--	ONE YEAR AGO--JOTS WHAT?	296	11
BANQUETS			
'TIS BEGGARS--BANQUETS BEST [CAN] DEFINE--	I SHOULD HAVE BEEN TOO	313	22
BANQUETTINGS			
WITH BANQUETTINGS TO BE--	UNTO MY BOOKS--SO GOOD	604	6
BAPTIZED			
SNATCHES, FROM BAPTIZED GENERATIONS--	OVER AND OVER, LIKE A	367	5
BAPTIZED--THIS DAY--A BRIDE--	I AM ASHAMED--I HIDE--	473	27
BAPTIZED, BEFORE, WITHOUT THE CHOICE,	I'M CEDED--I'VE STOPPED	508	8
BAPTIZED [TO WIT] AMERICA--	TRUST IN THE UNEXPECTED	555	12
BAPTIZES			
NOT SUCH A STRAIN--THE CHURCH--BAPTIZES--	BETTER--THAN MUSIC! FOR	503	17
BAR			
ACQUITTED--FROM THAT NAKED BAR--	TRIUMPH--MAY BE OF	455	15
AND ANCHOR "OFF THE BAR"	COULD I BUT RIDE	661	16
LATCH [BAR / BIND] THEM SOFTLY--	THESE--SAW VISIONS--	758	2
HOW DIMMER THAN A SATURN'S BAR	WHAT TWIGS WE HELD BY--	1086	16
WITH THE INTERNAL BAR.	THROUGH THOSE OLD	1753	8
BARABBAS'			
STRONG CLUSTERS, FROM BARABBAS' TOMB--	TO PUT THIS WORLD DOWN,	527	11
BARBED			
IT HURLS IT'S BARBED SYLLABLES	THERE IS A WORD	8	4
BARBS			
BARBS HAS IT, LIKE A BEE!	MY FRIEND MUST BE A BIRD	92	5

	FIRST LINE	POEM	LINE
BARD			
OF THE MYSTERIOUS BARD [BAND]!	TO LEARN THE TRANSPORT	167	16
BECAUSE [THAT WERT] A BARD TOO SOON--	TOUCH LIGHTLY NATURE'S	1389	4
THE BARD TO SILENCE BORN--	TOUCH LIGHTLY NATURE'S	1389 V	4
BARDS			
OF BALLADS AND OF BARDS--	ONE OF THE ONES THAT	1466	20
BARE			
BARE YOUR JESSAMINE--TO THE STORM--	KILL YOUR BALM--AND IT'S	238	2
LOCKING BARE FEET OUT--	SWEET--SAFE--HOUSES--	457	5
BARE RHINE--	A TOAD, CAN DIE OF LIGHT	583	11
TELL WOULD NOT BARE HIS HEAD	TELL AS A MARKSMAN--WERE	1152	13
ANGUISH--BARE OF ANODYNE!	REARRANGE A "WIFE'S"	1737	12
BAREFOOT			
THERE--SANDALS FOR THE BAREFOOT--	A POOR--TORN HEART-- A	78	13
SMILING WHEN WE WALK BAREFOOT	IN RAGS MYSTERIOUS AS	117	7
AND HE WAS BAREFOOT, I'M AFRAID!	I MET A KING THIS	166	4
OF THIS BAREFOOT ESTATE!	I MET A KING THIS	166	28
I SHANT WALK THE "JASPER"--BAREFOOT--	WHAT IS--"PARADISE"--	215	15
SIFT HER, FROM BROW TO BAREFOOT!	DOUBT ME! MY DIM	275	18
JUST TO BE POOR--FOR BAREFOOT VISION [PLEASURE]	SWEET--YOU FORGOT--BUT I	523	11
THE BAREFOOT TIME FORGOTTEN--SO--	THE BEGGAR LAD--DIES	717	11
HAVE MISSED [LOST] A BAREFOOT CITIZEN--	HE TOLD A HOMELY TALE	763	15
YET [BUT] WHEN A BOY, AND BAREFOOT--	A NARROW FELLOW IN THE	986	11
BAREHEAD			
SHE'D PASS FOR BAREHEAD--SHORT WAY OFF--	YOU'LL KNOW HER--BY HER	634	15
BARELY			
OUR PANTING ANCLE BARELY PASSED [GAINED],	OF TRIBULATION--THESE	325	13
BAREST			
NOT PROBABLE--THE BAREST CHANCE--	NOT PROBABLE--THE BAREST	346	1
BARGAIN			
'TWOULD BE "A BARGAIN" FOR A JEW!	I CAME TO BUY A SMILE--	223	13
BARGEMEN			
TILL BYE AND BYE THESE BARGEMEN	THE FEET OF PEOPLE	7	7
BARK			
WHETHER MY BARK WENT DOWN AT SEA--	WHETHER MY BARK WENT	52	1
ALL DAY AND NIGHT WITH BARK AND START--	WHAT SHALL I DO--IT	186	3
AND MICE WONT BARK--	I KNOW SOME LONELY	289	16
IF MY BARK SINK	IF MY BARK SINK	1234	1
BARN			
I PUT THE LATTER IN A BARN--	I CAUTIOUS, SCANNED MY	178	5
ART THOU WITHIN THE LITTLE BARN	I CAUTIOUS, SCANNED MY	178	19
TOUCHING THE ROOF [FLOODING THE STEEPLE] AND TINTING THE BARN	BLAZING IN GOLD AND	228	6
WHEN GOING TO THE BARN--	THE JUDGE IS LIKE THE	699	6
THE REDBREAST OF THE BARN--	HE TOLD A HOMELY TALE	763	8
ACROSS A BARN OR THROUGH A RUT	THE SKY IS LOW--THE	1075	3
REMANDED TO A BALLAD'S BARN	A FADED BOY--IN SALLOW	1524	7
BARNS			
AND THEN, IN SOVREIGN BARNS TO DWELL--	THE GRASS SO LITTLE HAS	333	17
THE CATTLE FLUNG [FLED] TO BARNS--	THE WIND BEGUN TO KNEAD	824	14
OF BARNS FOR WINTER--BLAMELESS [IGNORANT]--	THOSE CATTLE SMALLER	1388	5
HAS VIEWS OF BRIDLES AND OF BARNS	THE LIFE THAT TIED TOO	1535 V	7
BAROMETER			
FOR HIS BAROMETER	'TIS MY FIRST NIGHT	1122	4
BARONIAL			
BARONIAL BEES--MARCH--ONE BY ONE--	SOME RAINBOW--COMING	64	11
BARRED			
WOODEN BARRED,	I KNOW SOME LONELY	289	3
WE BARRED THE WINDOWS AND THE DOORS	THERE CAME A WIND LIKE A	1593	5
BARRICADE			
THEIR BARRICADE AGAINST THE SKY	THEIR BARRICADE AGAINST	1471	1
BARS			
BUT I TUG CHILDISH AT MY BARS	I NEVER HEAR THE WORD	77	7
PUT GENTLY UP THE EVENING BARS--	I'LL TELL YOU HOW THE	318	15
AND GOLD TO OWN--IN SOLID BARS--	IT WAS GIVEN TO ME BY	454	15
BARS [BOLTS]--CANNOT CONCEAL!	MINE--BY THE RIGHT OF	528	4
THE BIRDS PUT UP THE BARS TO NESTS--	THE WIND BEGUN TO KNEAD	824	13
LET DOWN THE BARS, OH DEATH--	LET DOWN THE BARS, OH	1065	1
HOW SWEET THESE [THOSE] SULLEN BARS	HOW SOFT THIS PRISON IS	1334	2
NOR CLIMB THE BARS OF ECSTASY,	GO NOT TOO NEAR A HOUSE	1434	6
BARTSIA			
BARTSIA, IN THE BLANKET RED--	WHOSE ARE THE LITTLE	142	15
BASE			
'TWAS BASE AS JESUS--MOST!	'TWAS LOVE--NOT ME--	394	8
BASE MUST BE THE COWARD	LIFE--IS WHAT WE MAKE IT	698	15
ITSELF CAN REST [LIFT / BASE] UPON--	MY WORTHINESS IS ALL MY	751	12
CONVICTION--THAT GRANITIC BASE--	ON A COLUMNAR SELF--	789	7
SPREADS THE POND HER BASE OF LILIES	HOW THE WATERS CLOSED	923	5
BUT EXCEPT IT'S RUSSET BASE	REVOLUTION IS THE POD	1082	5
"I WILL GIVE" THE BASE PROVISO--	"FAITHFUL TO THE END"	1357 V	
BASELESS			
UPON A BASELESS ARC--	IT SIFTS FROM LEADEN	311 V	
BASELESS EMPEROR--	THE CHILD'S FAITH IS NEW	637	14
BASEMENT			
THE MERMAIDS IN THE BASEMENT	I STARTED EARLY--TOOK MY	520	3
BASES			
AT BASES OF THE TREES--	LIKE MIGHTY FOOT LIGHTS	595	2
BASHFUL			
SO BASHFUL WHEN I SPIED HER!	SO BASHFUL WHEN I SPIED	91	1

	FIRST LINE	POEM	LINE
BASHFUL (CONTINUED)			
WHERE BASHFUL FLOWERS BLOW,	HAVE YOU GOT A BROOK IN	136	2
BASHFUL--SIP THY JESSAMINES--	COME SLOWLY--EDEN!	211	3
THIS BASHFUL GLOBE OF OUR'S WOULD BE--	FUNNY--TO BE A CENTURY--	345	7
OUR BASHFUL FEET--	ME--COME! MY DAZZLED	431	6
UNTIL TOMORROW [THE EVENING]--HAPPY LETTER! [AH! BE BASHFUL]	GOING TO HIM! HAPPY	494	24
SOME BASHFUL SUMMER'S DAY--	THE HEAVEN VESTS FOR	694	4
BASHFUL HEAVEN--THY LOVERS SMALL--	OUT OF SIGHT? WHAT OF	703	12
BASIN			
WHEN WINDS--UPSET THE BASIN--	THE NAME--OF IT--IS	656	7
BASIS			
BUT EPOCH HAD NO BASIS HERE	GREAT STREETS OF SILENCE	1159	7
COULD HOPE INSPECT HER [IT'S] BASIS	COULD HOPE INSPECT HER	1283	1
THERE'S BASIS THERE--	PERIL AS A POSSESSION	1678	4
BASK			
TO BASK THE CENTURIES AWAY--	A LONG--LONG SLEEP--A	654	7
BASKET			
MY BASKET HOLDS--JUST--FIRMAMENTS--	PERHAPS I ASKED TOO	352	5
AND JUST MY BASKET--	I WAS THE SLIGHTEST IN	486	7
ESCAPE--IT IS THE BASKET [CITADEL]	ESCAPE IS SUCH A	1347	5
BASKING			
BASKING [WINNING] IN BETHLEEM	MY HEART RAN SO TO THEE	1237	15
BASKS			
WHEN ETNA BASKS AND PURRS	WHEN ETNA BASKS AND	1146	1
ASSOCIATES OR GLOWS [BASKS] ALONE,	HOW HAPPY IS THE LITTLE	1510	8
BASS			
WHOSE SHORT--SEPULCHRAL BASS	THE LIGHTNING PLAYETH--	630	6
IN MIGHTY--UNREMITTING BASS	THE HEART HAS NARROW	928	3
BASTINADOED			
BOYS THAT "BELIEVE" ARE VERY LONESOME [BASTINADOED]--	THE BIBLE IS AN ANTIQUE	1545	11
BAT			
THE BAT IS DUN, WITH WRINKLED WINGS--	THE BAT IS DUN, WITH	1575	1
BATES			
NO BLACK BIRD BATES HIS BANJO--	IT MAKES NO DIFFERENCE	620	7
BATHED			
YOU ALMOST BATHED YOUR TONGUE--	SHE SIGHTS A BIRD--SHE	507	10
AND BATHED THEM IN THE GLEE [SEA]--	A DROP FELL ON THE APPLE	794	14
BATIZE			
FRESH AS A CARGO FROM BATIZE	AFTER THE SUN COMES OUT	1148	7
BATON			
NOR ANY LEADER'S GRIM BATON	NO LADDER NEEDS THE BIRD	1574	3
BATTERED			
BY SOLDIERS BATTERED DOWN,	I NEVER HEAR THE WORD	77	6
BATTERIES			
THY BATTERIES DIVORCE.	DYING! TO BE AFRAID OF	831	9
BATTLE			
OH BATTLE PICTURESQUE!	MY FRIEND ATTACKS MY	118	2
HEROES--A BATTLE--	"MORNING"--MEANS	300 V	7
THE BATTLE FOUGHT BETWEEN THE SOUL	THE BATTLE FOUGHT	594	1
THERE'S [THAT'S] THE BATTLE OF BURGOYNE--	THERE'S THE BATTLE OF	1174	1
I HAVE ONE BATTLE MORE--	MY WARS ARE LAID AWAY IN	1549	2
BATTLEMENT			
A BATTLEMENT--OF STRAW--	I HAD NOT MINDED--WALLS	398	12
WHEN DOWN SOME AWFUL BATTLEMENT	ESCAPE IS SUCH A	1347	7
BATTLEMENTS			
DRUMS OFF THE PHANTOM BATTLEMENTS	OVER AND OVER, LIKE A	367	3
BATTLE'S			
IN BATTLE'S--HORRID BOWL?	IT FEELS A SHAME TO BE	444	16
BATTLES			
PEACE--BY IT'S BATTLES TOLD--	WATER, IS TAUGHT BY	135	4
OF ALL THE BATTLES PREVALENT--	THE BATTLE FOUGHT	594	3
BAUBLE			
THIS BAUBLE WAS PREFERRED OF BEES--	THIS BAUBLE WAS	805	1
BAY			
NEVER SAILED THE BAY!	COULD LIVE--DID LIVE--	43	13
OUT UPON THE BAY.	WHETHER MY BARK WENT	52	8
THAT TODDLED DOWN THE BAY!	'TWAS SUCH A LITTLE--	107	2
IF WRECKED UPON THE SHOAL [WHARF / CAPE / DOCK / BAY] OF THOUGHT	IF WRECKED UPON THE	1469	1
BAYONET			
THAT TAUNTS HER BAYONET.	MY COUNTRY NEED NOT	1511	8
BAYONET'S			
A BAYONET'S CONTRITION	MY TRIUMPH LASTED TILL	1227	15
BAYS			
AS CINDERELLA'S BAYS--	LIKE SOME OLD FASHIONED	302	6
BAZAAR			
THAT I COULD SHOW IT IN BAZAAR--	THE TINT I CANNOT TAKE--	627	3
BE			
THE LIFE DOTH PROVE THE PRECEPT, WHO OBEY SHALL HAPPY BE,	AWAKE YE MUSES NINE,	1	9
WHO WILL NOT SERVE THE SOVREIGN, BE HANGED ON FATAL TREE.	AWAKE YE MUSES NINE,	1	10
THOUGH IT BE DARKNESS THERE;	THERE IS ANOTHER SKY,	2	4
WILL CONSOLATION BE!	"SIC TRANSIT GLORIA	3	66
WHERE IT USED TO BE--	FREQUENTLY THE WOODS ARE	6	8
LEST I SH'D BE OLD FASHIONED	THE MORNS ARE MEEKER	12	7
SLEEP IS SUPPOSED TO BE	SLEEP IS SUPPOSED TO BE	13	1
MORN IS SUPPOSED TO BE	SLEEP IS SUPPOSED TO BE	13	7

		FIRST LINE	POEM	LINE
BE	(CONTINUED)			
	THAT SHALL AURORA BE--	SLEEP IS SUPPOSED TO BE	13	11
	WE ASK THAT WE MAY BE.	THE GENTIAN WEAVES HER	18	14
	ALL THESE MY BANNERS BE.	ALL THESE MY BANNERS BE.	22	1
	BE SURE YOU COUNT--SH'D I FORGET	IT'S ALL I HAVE TO BRING	26	5
	SUMMER FOR THEE, GRANT I MAY BE	SUMMER FOR THEE, GRANT I	31	1
	GARLANDS FOR QUEENS, MAY BE--	GARLANDS FOR QUEENS, MAY	34	1
	IT MIGHT A PILGRIM BE	NOBODY KNOWS THIS LITTLE	35	2
	WHAT AND IF IT BE	IT DID NOT SURPRISE ME--	39	10
	TO BE RECEIVED AS HIGH--	WHEN I COUNT THE SEEDS	40	6
	THERE MAY YET BE LAND!	ONCE MORE, MY NOW	48	8
	THERE MUST BE GUESTS IN EDEN--	TAKEN FROM MEN--THIS	53	7
	TWILL BE BECAUSE BEYOND THE ROSE	IF I SHOULD CEASE TO	56	3
	TWILL BE BECAUSE DEATH'S FINGER	IF I SHOULD CEASE TO	56	7
	COULD SHE HAVE GUESSED THAT IT WOULD BE--	DELAYED TILL SHE HAD	58	7
	OH IF THERE MAY DEPARTING [REMAINING] BE	DELAYED TILL SHE HAD	58	13
	THAT COULD NOT STOP TO BE A KING--	DELAYED TILL SHE HAD	58	17
	DOUBTFUL IF IT BE CROWNED!	DELAYED TILL SHE HAD	58	18
	MAY THIS "DISHONOR" BE?	"SOWN IN DISHONOR"!	62	3
	BE RECKONED UP?	IF PAIN FOR PEACE	63	6
	WONT BE "NEW FASHIONED" WHEN I COME--	"ARCTURUS" IS HIS OTHER	70	28
	WHO MAY EXPECTED BE?	A LADY RED--AMID THE	74	8
	AND YET IT WILL BE DONE	GOING TO HEAVEN!	79	8
	SOME THINGS THAT FLY THERE BE--	SOME THINGS THAT FLY	89	1
	SOME THINGS THAT STAY THERE BE--	SOME THINGS THAT FLY	89	4
	MY FRIEND MUST BE A BIRD--	MY FRIEND MUST BE A BIRD	92	1
	MORTAL, MY FRIEND MUST BE,	MY FRIEND MUST BE A BIRD	92	3
	MAY BE SEEN THE DEWS AMONG,	ANGELS, IN THE EARLY	94	2
	MAY BE SEEN THE SANDS AMONG,	ANGELS, IN THE EARLY	94	6
	WILL THERE REALLY BE A "MORNING"?	WILL THERE REALLY BE A	101	1
	"FATHER, THY WILL BE DONE" TODAY	I HAVE A KING, WHO DOES	103	16
	SURGEONS MUST BE VERY CAREFUL	SURGEONS MUST BE VERY	108	1
	"MANSIONS"! MANSIONS MUST BE WARM!	"HOUSES"--SO THE WISE	127	2
	WRITE ME HOW MANY NOTES THERE BE	BRING ME THE SUNSET IN A	128	7
	SOME OTHER THIRSTY THERE MAY BE	I BRING AN UNACCUSTOMED	132	14
	IF, HAPLY, MINE MAY BE THE DROP	I BRING AN UNACCUSTOMED	132	18
	AND LATER, IN AUGUST IT MAY BE--	HAVE YOU GOT A BROOK IN	136	13
	THAN BE "DUKE OF EXETER"--	PIGMY SERAPHS--GONE	138	15
	PILGRIM BE FOUND?	FOR EVERY BIRD A NEST--	143	6
	CAN NIGHTINGALE BE SEEN--	ALL OVERGROWN BY CUNNING	148	12
	THAT NIGHT WILL NEVER BE--	YOU LOVE ME--YOU ARE	156	9
	BE SURE YOU'RE SURE--YOU KNOW--	YOU LOVE ME--YOU ARE	156	14
	THO' MY DESTINY BE FUSTIAN--	THO' MY DESTINY BE	163	1
	HER'S BE DAMASK FINE--	THO' MY DESTINY BE	163	2
	OH BELLS, THAT IN THE STEEPLES BE!	'TIS SO MUCH JOY! 'TIS	172	14
	AT LAST, TO BE IDENTIFIED!	AT LAST, TO BE	174	1
	IN THE DUST, BE THROWN?	I HAVE NEVER SEEN	175	16
	I, MUST RESOLUTER BE!	I'M THE LITTLE "HEART'S	176	7
	EVER BE INDUCED TO DO!	I'M THE LITTLE "HEART'S	176	14
	SHOULD BE A-DREAMING LAID.	I CAUTIOUS, SCANNED MY	178	4
	IF I SHOULD'NT BE ALIVE	IF I SHOULD'NT BE ALIVE	182	1
	MAY YET, A TRANSPORT BE--	A TRANSPORT ONE CANNOT	184	2
	BE DEBONNAIRE! BE DEBONNAIRE!	POOR LITTLE HEART!	192	6
	BE DEBONNAIRE! BE DEBONNAIRE!	POOR LITTLE HEART!	192	6
	NO WILDERNESS--CAN BE	FOR THIS--ACCEPTED	195	7
	BETTER WILL BE THE EXTASY	THO' I GET HOME HOW LATE	207	3
	TRANSPORTING MUST THE MOMENT BE--	THO' I GET HOME HOW LATE	207	7
	WOULD THE EDEN BE AN EDEN,	DID THE HAREBELL LOOSE	213	7
	AS NEW ENGLAND USED TO BE!	WHAT IS--"PARADISE"--	215	18
	REJECTED--BE--OF HER?	COULD I--THEN--SHUT THE	220	3
	IT CANT BE "SUMMER"!	IT CANT BE "SUMMER"!	221	1
	IT CANT BE "DYING"!	IT CANT BE "SUMMER"!	221	6
	'TWOULD BE "A BARGAIN" FOR A JEW!	I CAME TO BUY A SMILE--	223	13
	AND LIFE WOULD ALL BE SPRING!	THE SUN--JUST TOUCHED	232	4
	AND "FEW THERE BE"--CORRECT AGAIN--	YOU'RE RIGHT--"THE WAY	234	3
	OR IT BE TOO LATE!	IF HE DISSOLVE--THEN--	236	9
	WHEN I SHALL BE "FORGIVEN"--	I THINK JUST HOW MY	237	2
	AND BE WITH [LEAP TO] YOU--TONIGHT!	AH, MOON--AND STAR!	240	12
	THE PERFECT, NOWHERE BE AFRAID--	WHEN WE STAND ON THE	242	9
	WILD NIGHTS SHOULD BE	WILD NIGHTS--WILD NIGHTS	249	3
	AND SORE MUST BE THE STORM--	"HOPE" IS THE THING WITH	254	6
	SHALL STILL MY TRANSPORT BE--	IF I'M LOST--NOW--	256	3
	HOW FOREIGN THAT CAN BE--	IF I'M LOST--NOW--	256	11
	THE EASTERN EXILES--BE--	THE LONESOME FOR THEY	262	2
	THAT NOT A PORE BE OVERLOOKED	A WEIGHT WITH NEEDLES ON	264	5
	AS SPECIES--BE--FOR NAME--	A WEIGHT WITH NEEDLES ON	264	8
	A WOMAN--WHITE--TO BE--	A SOLEMN THING--IT WAS--	271	2
	THAT ONE, TO BE QUITE SURE--	I BREATHED ENOUGH TO	272	4
	WHY, GOD, WOULD BE CONTENT	DOUBT ME! MY DIM	275	2
	IT CANNOT BE MY SPIRIT--	DOUBT ME! MY DIM	275	9
	HOW LARGER--BE?	THE DROP, THAT WRESTLES	284	6
	HOW DREARY--TO BE--SOMEBODY!	I'M NOBODY! WHO ARE YOU?	288	5
	IF ANY POWER BEHIND IT, BE,	I GOT SO I COULD HEAR	293	22
	SUCH ANNIVERSARY SHALL BE--	ONE YEAR AGO--JOTS WHAT?	296	6
	IN DOUBTFUL MEAL, IF IT BE POSSIBLE	ONE YEAR AGO--JOTS WHAT?	296	10
	IF TO BE "ELDER"--MEAN MOST PAIN--	ONE YEAR AGO--JOTS WHAT?	296	32
	ALONE, I CANNOT BE--	ALONE, I CANNOT BE--	298	1
	THEIR COMING, MAY BE KNOWN	ALONE, I CANNOT BE--	298	9
	BUT THIS, MUST BE A DIFFERENT WEALTH--	YOUR RICHES--TAUGHT ME--	299	15
	MIGHT I--BUT BE THE JEW--	YOUR RICHES--TAUGHT ME--	299	20

		FIRST LINE	POEM	LINE
BE	(CONTINUED)			
	SOMEHOW, IT WILL BE EVEN--	I REASON, EARTH IS SHORT	301	10
	WHEN [THO'] ORCHESTRA IS [BE] DUMB--	LIKE SOME OLD FASHIONED	302	14
	UNMOVED--AN EMPEROR BE KNEELING	THE SOUL SELECTS HER OWN	303	7
	HOW MIGHTY 'TWAS--TO BE	THE DAY CAME SLOW--TILL	304	14
	MINUTEST OF MANKIND SHOULD [MIGHT / COULD] BE--	THE ONE WHO COULD REPEAT	307	3
	BE IT'S GRAVE--SUFFICIENT SIGN--	HER--"LAST POEMS"--	312	15
	WHO'D BE THE FOOL TO STAY?	THE WIND DID'NT COME	316	21
	WOULD YOU BE THE FOOL TO STAY?	THE WIND DID'NT COME	316	23
	IT WILL BE AMPLE TIME FOR--ME--	JUST SO--JESUS--RAPS--	317	9
	IF SUCH AN OUTCAST BE--	OF ALL THE SOUNDS	321	26
	WHERE RESURRECTIONS [REVELATIONS]--BE--	THERE CAME A DAY AT	322	4
	FOR WHERE THE HOLIDAY SHOULD BE	SO GLAD WE ARE--A	329	3
	NOR HOW OURSELVES BE JUSTIFIED--	SO GLAD WE ARE--A	329	5
	THAT FACE--WILL JUST BE THINE--	THE FACE I CARRY WITH ME	336	4
	THY FLOWER--BE GAY--	I TEND MY FLOWERS FOR	339	21
	IT WILL BE SUMMER--EVENTUALLY.	IT WILL BE SUMMER--	342	1
	FUNNY--TO BE A CENTURY--	FUNNY--TO BE A CENTURY--	345	1
	THIS BASHFUL GLOBE OF OUR'S WOULD BE--	FUNNY--TO BE A CENTURY--	345	7
	HE'D BE TOO TALL, THE TALLEST ONE	I DREADED THAT FIRST	348	15
	HER PRETTY PARASOL BE SEEN	FROM COCOON FORTH A	354	9
	THE BLIND--ESTEEM IT BE	'TIS OPPOSITES--ENTICE--	355	5
	BE ONLY	'TIS OPPOSITES--ENTICE--	355	11
	THOUGH IT BE LITTLE AS A DAFFODIL--	WHAT I CAN DO--I WILL--	361	2
	THAT I CANNOT--MUST BE	WHAT I CAN DO--I WILL--	361	3
	OUR'S BE THE TOSSING--WILD THOUGH THE SEA--	HOW SICK--TO WAIT--IN	368	8
	OUR'S BE THE CARGO--UNLADEN--HERE--	HOW SICK--TO WAIT--IN	368	10
	COULD NOT AGAIN BE PROVED--	HEAVEN IS SO FAR OF THE	370	4
	WOULD BE ETERNITY--	I KNOW LIVES, I COULD	372	4
	"IF I SHOULD BE A QUEEN, TOMORROW"--	I'M SAYING EVERY DAY	373	2
	IF IT BE, I WAKE A BOURBON,	I'M SAYING EVERY DAY	373	5
	BUT THIS, MIGHT BE MY BRIEF TERM	I'M SAYING EVERY DAY	373	18
	BETTER TO BE READY--	I'M SAYING EVERY DAY	373	26
	I--COULD BE--	I WENT TO HEAVEN--	374	14
	BECAUSE ESTATES CAN BE	TO LOSE ONE'S FAITH--	377	3
	BELIEF--BUT ONCE--CAN BE--	TO LOSE ONE'S FAITH--	377	6
	HER FACE BE ROUNDER THAN THE MOON	THERE IS A FLOWER THAT	380	9
	BEFORE THE WORLD BE GREEN--	THERE IS A FLOWER THAT	380	14
	AGAINST THE WIND--BE SEEN--	THERE IS A FLOWER THAT	380	16
	AND WHEN THE HILLS BE FULL--	THERE IS A FLOWER THAT	380	21
	HER PUBLIC--BE THE NOON--	THERE IS A FLOWER THAT	380	25
	CEASES TO BE A SECRET--THEN--	A SECRET TOLD--	381	2
	BETTER OF IT--CONTINUAL BE AFRAID--	A SECRET TOLD--	381	5
	TWO BODIES--THEREFORE BE--	NO RACK CAN TORTURE ME--	384	7
	EXCEPT THYSELF MAY BE	NO RACK CAN TORTURE ME--	384	13
	MAY BE LUXURY--	SMILING BACK FROM	385	2
	OF HOW MANY BE--	SMILING BACK FROM	385	10
	WHERE BE THE MAIZE--	ANSWER JULY--	386	15
	WHERE BE THE HAZE--	ANSWER JULY--	386	16
	WHERE BE THE BUR?	ANSWER JULY--	386	17
	THERE'LL BE THAT DARK PARADE--	THERE'S BEEN A DEATH, IN	389	20
	IT'S FEE--TO BE OF GOLD--	A TONGUE--TO TELL HIM I	400	2
	THY PAY--IN DIAMONDS--BE--	A TONGUE--TO TELL HIM I	400	18
	MY MESSAGE--MUST BE TOLD--	A TONGUE--TO TELL HIM I	400	21
	THEN--LOOK FOR ME. BE SURE YOU SAY--	A TONGUE--TO TELL HIM I	400	28
	BE SO--ASHAMED OF THEE--	WHAT SOFT--CHERUBIC	401	12
	IT MIGHT BE LONELIER	IT MIGHT BE LONELIER	405	1
	IT MIGHT BE EASIER	IT MIGHT BE LONELIER	405	13
	CRITERION--BE SMALL--	IF WHAT WE COULD--WERE	407	2
	COULD IT BE MADNESS--THIS?	THE FIRST DAY'S NIGHT	410	20
	THAT AT THE LAST, IT SHOULD NOT BE A NOVEL AGONY--	I READ MY SENTENCE--	412	10
	AND EDEN'LL BE SO LONESOME	I NEVER FELT AT HOME--	413	7
	ECLIPSES BE--PREDICTED--	SUNSET AT NIGHT--IS	415	5
	WOULD NEVER BE BELIEVED--	A MURMUR IN THE TREES--	416	12
	WHERE THIS--IS SAID TO BE	NOT IN THIS WORLD TO SEE	418	3
	THAN THAT--BE SWEETER WISE--	NOT IN THIS WORLD TO SEE	418	9
	MIGHT SOME ONE ELSE--SO LEARNED--BE--	NOT IN THIS WORLD TO SEE	418	10
	FOR FEAR IT BE DISPELLED--	A CHARM INVESTS A FACE	421	4
	NEXT--ONE--MIGHT BE THE GOLDEN TOUCH--	I'LL CLUTCH--AND CLUTCH	427	2
	IT WOULD NEVER BE COMMON--MORE--I SAID--	IT WOULD NEVER BE COMMON	430	1
	AS BOOTS--WOULD BE--TO BIRDS--	IT WOULD NEVER BE COMMON	430	16
	MY HOLIDAY, SHALL BE	ME--COME! MY DAZZLED	431	7
	THAT THERE BE STANDING HERE--	DO PEOPLE MOULDER	432	10
	AH, TO BE ERUDITE	KNOWS HOW TO FORGET!	433	V
	IF IT BE INVENTION	KNOWS HOW TO FORGET!	433	V
	FOREVER MIGHT BE SHORT, I THOUGHT TO SHOW--	TO LOVE THEE YEAR BY	434	5
	WHEN LOVERS BE AFAR--	'TIS CUSTOMARY AS WE	440	4
	IT TRIED--TO BE A ROSE--	GOD MADE A LITTLE	442	2
	THE TIME 'TWILL BE TILL SIX O'CLOCK	I TIE MY HAT--I CREASE	443	9
	THERE MAY BE--MILES ON MILES OF NOUGHT--	I TIE MY HAT--I CREASE	443	17
	THOUGH LIFE'S REWARD--BE DONE--	I TIE MY HAT--I CREASE	443	31
	IT FEELS A SHAME TO BE ALIVE--	IT FEELS A SHAME TO BE	444	1
	THAT LIVES--LIKE DOLLARS--MUST BE PILED	IT FEELS A SHAME TO BE	444	11
	AS LIFE--DISSOLVED BE--FOR US--	IT FEELS A SHAME TO BE	444	15
	IT MAY BE--A RENOWN TO LIVE--	IT FEELS A SHAME TO BE	444	17
	PRAYING THAT I MIGHT BE	THE MALAY--TOOK THE	452	5
	TO GAIN, OR BE UNDONE--	THE MALAY--TOOK THE	452	16
	FOR FEAR IT WOULD BE GONE--	IT WAS GIVEN TO ME BY	454	8

		FIRST LINE	POEM	LINE
BE	(CONTINUED)			
	TRIUMPH--MAY BE OF SEVERAL KINDS--	TRIUMPH--MAY BE OF	455	1
	BY FAITH--BE OVERCOME--	TRIUMPH--MAY BE OF	455	4
	BE SLOWLY HANDED BACK--	TRIUMPH--MAY BE OF	455	10
	NEITHER--WOULD BE ABSOLVED--	LIKE EYES THAT LOOKED ON	458	13
	NEITHER WOULD BE A QUEEN	LIKE EYES THAT LOOKED ON	458	14
	THEN WHEREFORE BE THE TOOTH?	A TOOTH UPON OUR PEACE	459	3
	A WIFE--AT DAYBREAK I SHALL BE--	A WIFE--AT DAYBREAK I	461	1
	SO SOON TO BE A CHILD NO MORE--	A WIFE--AT DAYBREAK I	461	11
	BE JUDGMENT--WHAT IT MAY--	I LIVE WITH HIM--I SEE	463	16
	THE POWER TO BE TRUE TO YOU,	THE POWER TO BE TRUE TO	464	1
	BE WITNESSED--IN THE ROOM--	I HEARD A FLY BUZZ--WHEN	465	8
	WHAT PORTION OF ME BE	I HEARD A FLY BUZZ--WHEN	465	10
	HOW GOOD--TO BE ALIVE!	I AM ALIVE--I GUESS--	470	25
	HOW INFINITE--TO BE	I AM ALIVE--I GUESS--	470	26
	SLOW--NIGHT--THAT MUST BE WATCHED AWAY--	A NIGHT--THERE LAY THE	471	5
	TILL IT BE NIGHT--NO MORE--	A NIGHT--THERE LAY THE	471	8
	WHAT RIGHT HAVE I--TO BE A BRIDE--	I AM ASHAMED--I HIDE--	473	2
	MEEK--LET IT BE--TOO PROUD--FOR PRIDE--	I AM ASHAMED--I HIDE--	473	26
	THAT ONE SO HONEST--BE EXTANT--	I MEANT TO HAVE BUT	476	21
	ITSELF BE GIVEN YOU"--	I MEANT TO HAVE BUT	476	24
	ALL SWINDLERS--BE--INFER--	I MEANT TO HAVE BUT	476	28
	BE SETTING ON HIS PROGRESS--	NO MAN CAN COMPASS A	477	7
	SOME INDUSTRY MUST BE--	I HAD NO TIME TO HATE--	478	9
	BE LARGE ENOUGH FOR ME--	I HAD NO TIME TO HATE--	478	12
	THE WISDOM IT BE SO--	"WHY DO I LOVE" YOU, SIR	480	10
	THERE BE--PREFERRED BY DAINTIER FOLK--	"WHY DO I LOVE" YOU, SIR	480	16
	DENOTES THERE BE--A SEA--	MY GARDEN--LIKE THE	484	2
	WOULD BE ACUTER, WOULD IT NOT	TO ONE DENIED TO DRINK	490	3
	CANNOT BE STIFLED--WITH NARCOTIC--	CIVILIZATION--SPURNS--	492	12
	A DOUBT--IF IT BE FAIR--INDEED--	THE WORLD--STANDS--	493	5
	A GRATITUDE--THAT SUCH BE TRUE--	THE WORLD--STANDS--	493	13
	AND YOU--GOT SLEEPY--AND BEGGED TO BE ENDED--	GOING TO HIM! HAPPY	494	20
	UNTIL TOMORROW [THE EVENING]--HAPPY LETTER! [AH! BE BASHFUL]	GOING TO HIM! HAPPY	494	24
	AND IMMORTALITY--CAN BE ALMOST--	IT'S THOUGHTS--AND JUST	495	27
	MUST BE--I DESERVED--IT--	HE STRAINED MY FAITH--	497	V 10
	MYSELF--BE NOON TO HIM--	I ENVY SEAS, WHEREON HE	498	20
	WITH TRANSPORT, THAT WOULD BE A PAIN	THOSE FAIR--FICTITIOUS	499	19
	I'D RATHER BE THE ONE	I WOULD NOT PAINT--A	505	2
	I'D RATHER BE THE ONE	I WOULD NOT PAINT--A	505	10
	NOR WOULD I BE A POET--	I WOULD NOT PAINT--A	505	17
	WHAT WOULD THE DOWER BE,	I WOULD NOT PAINT--A	505	22
	IF ANYBODY'S FRIEND BE DEAD	IF ANYBODY'S FRIEND BE	509	1
	THAT YOUR'S AND MINE, SHOULD BE--	IF YOU WERE COMING IN	511	14
	CIRCUMFERENCE BE FULL--	NO CROWD THAT HAS	515	5
	WHAT PARALLEL [SCENERY] CAN BE--	NO CROWD THAT HAS	515	18
	BEAUTY--BE [IS] NOT CAUSED--IT IS--	BEAUTY--BE NOT CAUSED--	516	1
	BE LIMITED BY IGNORANCE--	HE PARTS HIMSELF--LIKE	517	15
	IN CABINETS--BE SHOWN--	HE PARTS HIMSELF--LIKE	517	18
	TILL ALL THE SCENE--BE GONE.	'TWAS WARM--AT FIRST--	519	4
	PRESUMING ME TO BE A MOUSE--	I STARTED EARLY--TOOK MY	520	7
	TILL HE BE JUSTIFIED BY DEATH--	HAD I PRESUMED TO HOPE--	522	15
	SO THAT THE SUM [LOVE] BE NEVER HINDERED	SWEET--YOU FORGOT--BUT I	523	3
	HAPPY IT BE FOR YOU--A BEGGAR'S--	SWEET--YOU FORGOT--BUT I	523	7
	JUST TO BE RICH--TO WASTE MY GUINEAS [GUINEA]	SWEET--YOU FORGOT--BUT I	523	9
	JUST TO BE POOR--FOR BAREFOOT VISION [PLEASURE]	SWEET--YOU FORGOT--BUT I	523	11
	MAY BE A COMMON THING--	TO HEAR AN ORIOLE SING	526	2
	SO WHETHER IT BE RUNE,	TO HEAR AN ORIOLE SING	526	10
	OR WHETHER IT BE NONE [DIN]	TO HEAR AN ORIOLE SING	526	11
	THEIR COMING, MENTIONED--BE--	TWO BUTTERFLIES WENT OUT	533	8
	BE THIS FATUITY [BIOGRAPHY]	TWO BUTTERFLIES WENT OUT	533	V
	AND THEN--IF IT SHOULD BE	THE HEART ASKS PLEASURE	536	6
	MAKE HASTE--[COME NEAR] THE SCRUPLE! DEATH BE SCANT	ME PROVE IT NOW--WHOEVER	537	3
	AS YET--MY HEART BE DRY--	ME PROVE IT NOW--WHOEVER	537	6
	NO PARADISE COULD BE--CONFERRED	'TIS TRUE--THEY SHUT ME	538	7
	SHOULD BE THE ART [EXCLUSIVELY]--TO SAVE--	THE PROVINCE OF THE	539	2
	THAT MAN--BE QUALIFIED	THE PROVINCE OF THE	539	8
	SOME SUCH BUTTERFLY BE SEEN	SOME SUCH BUTTERFLY BE	541	1
	I HAD NO CAUSE TO BE AWAKE--	I HAD NO CAUSE TO BE	542	1
	THAT WHEN THEIR MORTAL NAME [FAME] BE NUMB--	THE MARTYR POETS--DID	544	3
	AND THEN--BE SOLDERED DOWN	I'VE SEEN A DYING EYE	547	6
	WITHOUT DISCLOSING WHAT IT BE	I'VE SEEN A DYING EYE	547	7
	THAT LOVE IS [BE] LIFE--	THAT I DID ALWAYS LOVE	549	7
	ONE MORE--"YE BLESSED"--TO BE TOLD--	THERE IS A SHAME OF	551	7
	HOW MANY BE	ONE CRUCIFIXION IS	553	2
	AS MANY BE	ONE CRUCIFIXION IS	553	6
	AS IMPOTENT [POSSIBLE] WOULD BE	SHE HIDETH HER THE LAST	557	10
	IT WOULD NOT BE--TO DIE--	I MEASURE EVERY GRIEF I	561	12
	BE BEAUTIFUL AS THEY PREPARE [DISCLOSE]	I RECKON--WHEN I COUNT	569	13
	MUST BE A WO--	MUST BE A WO--	571	1
	IF SMALLER PATIENCE--BE--	THE TEST OF LOVE--IS	573	5
	AN AWE IF IT SHOULD BE LIKE THAT	"HEAVEN" HAS DIFFERENT	575	7
	ITSELF BE FAIRER--WE SUPPOSE--	"HEAVEN" HAS DIFFERENT	575	17
	BUT HOW OURSELF, SHALL BE	"HEAVEN" HAS DIFFERENT	575	18
	I COUNT THE FORCE 'TWOULD BE	I PRAYED, AT FIRST, A	576	15
	I'LL BE CONTENTED--SO [NOW]--	IF I MAY HAVE IT, WHEN	577	2
	PERMITTED--FACE TO FACE TO BE--	IF I MAY HAVE IT, WHEN	577	10

		FIRST LINE	POEM	LINE
BE	(CONTINUED)			
	CAN BLAZE BE SHOWN [DONE] IN COCHINEAL--	I FOUND THE WORDS TO	581	7
	AS WE--DISPOSERS--BE--	WE TALKED AS GIRLS DO--	586	6
	AS WE EVENTUAL--BE--	WE TALKED AS GIRLS DO--	586	10
	LIKE INTERMITTENT PLUSH, BE HEARD	THE NIGHT WAS WIDE, AND	589	11
	TO FEEL IF BLINDS BE FAST--	THE NIGHT WAS WIDE, AND	589	13
	AND DEEM TO BE ALONE	DID YOU EVER STAND IN A	590	4
	HOW GOBLIN IT WOULD BE--	DID YOU EVER STAND IN A	590	6
	OF ALL THE BIRDS THAT BE--	WHAT CARE THE DEAD, FOR	592	14
	HENCEFORWARD CHERISHED BE--	WHAT CARE THE DEAD, FOR	592	16
	THE DANGER [SORROW] TO BE SANE	I THINK I WAS ENCHANTED	593	26
	MAGICIANS BE ASLEEP--	I THINK I WAS ENCHANTED	593	30
	IF PRIDE SHALL BE IN PARADISE--	WHEN I WAS SMALL, A	596	9
	PERPETUAL BREAK [BE / GO] ABROAD	WHEN I WAS SMALL, A	596	18
	NO MOSES THERE CAN BE	IT ALWAYS FELT TO ME--A	597	6
	WHERE HUMAN FACES--BE--	THREE TIMES--WE PARTED--	598	12
	THEN--TOO--BE COMPREHENDED--	IT TROUBLED ME AS ONCE I	600	13
	BE FAITHFUL--IN HIS ABSENCE--	HE FOUND MY BEING--SET	603	5
	WITH BANQUETTINGS TO BE--	UNTO MY BOOKS--SO GOOD	604	6
	IT MAY BE WILDERNESS--WITHOUT--	UNTO MY BOOKS--SO GOOD	604	9
	JUST AS THE CASE MAY BE--	AFRAID! OF WHOM AM I	608	8
	THE LOVE OF THEE--A PRISM BE--	I SEE THEE BETTER--IN	611	3
	THE MINER'S LAMP--SUFFICIENT BE--	I SEE THEE BETTER--IN	611	7
	IT'S LITTLE PANELS BE	I SEE THEE BETTER--IN	611	10
	IT DEEM IT BE--CONTINUALLY--	I SEE THEE BETTER--IN	611	15
	NEITHER--COULD BE HEARD--	IN FALLING TIMBERS	614	8
	I THOUGHT IT WOULD BE OPPOSITE--	I ROSE--BECAUSE HE SANK	616	2
	TO KNOW JUST HOW HE SUFFERED--WOULD BE DEAR--	TO KNOW JUST HOW HE	622	1
	TILL LOVE THAT WAS--AND LOVE TOO BEST TO BE--	TO KNOW JUST HOW HE	622	25
	MEET--AND THE JUNCTION BE [MEAN] ETERNITY	TO KNOW JUST HOW HE	622	26
	WHEN EARTH--CANNOT BE HAD--	IT WAS TOO LATE FOR MAN	623	6
	NO DIFFERENT [AS INFINITE] OUR YEARS WOULD BE	FOREVER--IS COMPOSED OF	624	11
	WHILE OCEANS--AND THE NORTH MUST BE-- [DID PLAY]	OURSELVES WERE WED ONE	631	11
	WITH FINGERS--WHERE THE TOES SHOULD BE--	YOU'LL KNOW HER--BY HER	634	3
	FOR TRANSPORT IT BE SURE--	THE WAY I READ A	636	4
	IT WOULD BE LIFE--	I CANNOT LIVE WITH YOU--	640	2
	AND WERE YOU LOST, I WOULD BE--	I CANNOT LIVE WITH YOU--	640	37
	AND I--CONDEMNED TO BE	I CANNOT LIVE WITH YOU--	640	42
	HOW THIS BE	ME FROM MYSELF--TO	642	10
	"WOULD I BE WHOLE" HE SUDDEN BROACHED--	I COULD SUFFICE FOR HIM,	643	5
	AND THEN--BE AUDIBLER	I COULD SUFFICE FOR HIM,	643	12
	THERE BE IMMORTAL FRIENDS	BEREAVEMENT IN THEIR	645	6
	I THINK TO LIVE--MAY BE A BLISS [LIFE]	I THINK TO LIVE--MAY BE	646	1
	AND MAJESTY--BE EASIER--	I THINK TO LIVE--MAY BE	646	11
	WHAT PLENTY--IT WOULD BE--	I THINK TO LIVE--MAY BE	646	26
	PROMISE THIS--WHEN YOU BE DYING--	PROMISE THIS--WHEN YOU	648	1
	NOT WITH COINS--THOUGH THEY BE MINTED	PROMISE THIS--WHEN YOU	648	5
	BE MY LIPS--THE ONLY BUCKLE	PROMISE THIS--WHEN YOU	648	7
	IF THE LIFE BE TOO SURRENDERED--	PROMISE THIS--WHEN YOU	648	11
	IF MADONNA BE	PROMISE THIS--WHEN YOU	648	26
	CARRIAGES--BE SURE--AND GUESTS--TRUE [TOO]--	HER SWEET TURN TO LEAVE	649	3
	GARLAND BE INDEED--	HER SWEET TURN TO LEAVE	649	12
	DISTANCE--BE HER ONLY MOTION [SIGNAL]--	HER SWEET TURN TO LEAVE	649	21
	A PRISON GETS TO BE A FRIEND--	A PRISON GETS TO BE A	652	1
	ALL OTHER RICHES BE	WITHOUT THIS--THERE IS	655	2
	I WISHED A WAY [SORT] MIGHT BE	WITHOUT THIS--THERE IS	655	9
	AND COULD BE MIGHTY, IF I LIKED--	THAT FIRST DAY, WHEN YOU	659	3
	BE LARGER--AS THE SEA	'TIS GOOD--THE LOOKING	660	10
	I SAID "BUT JUST TO BE A BEE"	COULD I BUT RIDE	661	13
	ALONE--IF THOSE "VAILED FACES"--BE--	AGAIN--HIS VOICE IS AT	663	24
	WHOSE BE HER [THIS] RENOWN, OR FADING,	BLOOM UPON THE MOUNTAIN	667	11
	SO IMPOTENT OUR WISDOM IS [BE]	"NATURE" IS WHAT WE SEE	668	11
	ONE NEED NOT BE A CHAMBER--TO BE HAUNTED--	ONE NEED NOT BE A	670	1
	ONE NEED NOT BE A CHAMBER--TO BE HAUNTED--	ONE NEED NOT BE A	670	1
	ONE NEED NOT BE A HOUSE--	ONE NEED NOT BE A	670	2
	BE HORROR'S LEAST.	ONE NEED NOT BE A	670	16
	AND FETCH HER THEE--BE MINE--	SHE DWELLETH IN THE	671	8
	BUT WHEN THE NEWS BE RIPE--	THE FUTURE--NEVER SPOKE	672	5
	UPON HIMSELF BE VISITING	THE SOUL THAT HATH A	674	7
	BE [IS] NOT EXPRESSED BY SUNS--ALONE--	ESSENTIAL OILS--ARE	675	3
	TO BE ALIVE--IS POWER--	TO BE ALIVE--IS POWER--	677	1
	TO BE ALIVE--AND WILL!	TO BE ALIVE--IS POWER--	677	5
	THE MAKER [FURTHER]--OF OURSELVES--BE WHAT--	TO BE ALIVE--IS POWER--	677	7
	EMBODIED [ADMITTED] SCARCELY TO ITSELF--IT MAY BE--	EACH LIFE CONVERGES TO	680	5
	UNGAINED--IT MAY BE--BY [IN] A LIFE'S LOW VENTURE--	EACH LIFE CONVERGES TO	680	17
	I WOULD RATHER BE	'TWOULD EASE--A	682	6
	THE SOUL SHOULD STAND [BE] IN AWE--	THE SOUL UNTO ITSELF	683	8
	IF WHITE--A RED--MUST BE!	THE ZEROES--TAUGHT US--	689	6
	MY NEED OF THEE--BE DONE--	SHELLS FROM THE COAST	693	6
	BUT A PRESUMPTION BE--	AS IF THE SEA SHOULD	695	4
	THEMSELVES THE VERGE OF SEAS TO BE--	AS IF THE SEA SHOULD	695	7
	BASE MUST BE THE COWARD	LIFE--IS WHAT WE MAKE IT	698	15
	THE THOUGHT TO BE ALIVE--	I SOMETIMES DROP IT, FOR	708	2
	POVERTY--BE JUSTIFYING	PUBLICATION--IS THE	709	3
	IN THE PARCEL--BE THE MERCHANT	PUBLICATION--IS THE	709	13
	ALL OTHER PLAUDIT BE	FAME OF MYSELF, TO	713	2
	MY NAME BE ELSE SUPREME--	FAME OF MYSELF, TO	713	6

		FIRST LINE	POEM	LINE
BE	(CONTINUED)			
	MINE BE THE MINISTRY	THE WORLD--FEELS DUSTY	715	9
	BE WRINKLED--MUCH AS HER--	THE DAY UNDRESSED--	716	8
	THE FLICKERING BE SEEN	THE DAY UNDRESSED--	716	14
	TO REST [PAUSE]--TO REST [PAUSE / STAY / DWELL] WOULD BE	I MEANT TO FIND HER WHEN	718	10
	NO PRISONER BE--	NO PRISONER BE--	720	1
	BONDAGE AS PLAY--BE SWEET--	WHERE THOU ART--THAT--IS	725	7
	PRECIOUS TO ME--SHE STILL SHALL BE--	PRECIOUS TO ME--SHE	727	1
	SOMEWHAT DIFFERENT--MUST BE--	LET US PLAY YESTERDAY--	728	9
	MANACLES BE DIM--THEY SAY--	LET US PLAY YESTERDAY--	728	17
	BE THE PERFECT ONE--	ALTER! WHEN THE HILLS DO	729	4
	BUT ONLY TO HIMSELF--BE KNOWN	SHE ROSE TO HIS	732	11
	AND HOW IF HE BE DEAD--	IF HE WERE LIVING--DARE	734	2
	THOUGH HOW MAY THIS BE SO?	HAVE ANY LIKE MYSELF	736	8
	CONJECTURED WHO MAY BE	HAVE ANY LIKE MYSELF	736	10
	TWOULD SEEM THAT GOD SHOULD BE	HAVE ANY LIKE MYSELF	736	13
	MY [THE] VILLAGES BE SEEN--	HAVE ANY LIKE MYSELF	736	22
	BUT WHAT MUST BE THE SMILE	THE MOON WAS BUT A CHIN	737	10
	AND WHAT A PRIVILEGE TO BE	THE MOON WAS BUT A CHIN	737	13
	THEN "GREAT" IT BE--IF THAT PLEASE THEE--	YOU SAID THAT I "WAS	738	2
	AND I MUST BE RHINOCEROS	YOU SAID THAT I "WAS	738	10
	SO SAY--IF QUEEN IT BE--	YOU SAID THAT I "WAS	738	13
	OR OTHER THING--IF OTHER THING THERE BE--	YOU SAID THAT I "WAS	738	16
	OR ANY [BEFORE THE] HARBOR BE--	I MANY TIMES THOUGHT	739	8
	THAT YOU BE NOT ASHAMED	YOU TAUGHT ME WAITING	740	10
	ALL BUT DEATH, CAN BE ADJUSTED--	ALL BUT DEATH, CAN BE	749	1
	LEST I SHOULD INSUFFICIENT PROVE [BE]	MY WORTHINESS IS ALL MY	751	5
	BY THE FARMER BE--	NO BOBOLINK--REVERSE HIS	755	4
	WHOSE MUSIC BE HIS	NO BOBOLINK--REVERSE HIS	755	8
	WHY FLOODS BE SERVED TO US--IN BOWLS--	ONE BLESSING HAD I THAN	756	19
	'TWAS LIGHTER [FIRMER]--TO BE BLIND--	FROM BLANK TO BLANK--	761	10
	NATURE WILL--THAT IT BE NIGHT	WHEN I HOPED, I	768	19
	TWO--BE FINISHED USING--	ONE AND ONE--ARE ONE--	769	2
	MORE [TWO]--WOULD BE TOO VAST	ONE AND ONE--ARE ONE--	769	7
	THE [NOR] FACT OF FAMINE--COULD NOT BE [EXIST]	NONE CAN EXPERIENCE	771	3
	CANNOT BE [ENABLES] INDIGENCE	NONE CAN EXPERIENCE	771	8
	IF BLAME BE MY SIDE--FORFEIT ME--	IF BLAME BE MY SIDE--	775	1
	THE HORROR [CHASM] NOT TO BE SURVEYED--	THE LONELINESS ONE DARE	777	9
	OTHER FORCE--MAY BE PRESUMED TO MOVE--	THE TRUTH--IS STIRLESS--	780	2
	IF LOVE BE JUST BEYOND--	TO WAIT AN HOUR--IS LONG	781	2
	IF LOVE REWARD [BE AT] THE END--	TO WAIT AN HOUR--IS LONG	781	4
	AFFLICTION WOULD NOT BE APPEASED--	SEVERER SERVICE OF	786	17
	NO DRUG FOR CONSCIOUSNESS--CAN BE--	SEVERER SERVICE OF	786	21
	BETTER THAN NEW--COULD BE--FOR THAT--	JOY TO HAVE MERITED THE	788	7
	THOUGH NONE BE ON OUR SIDE--	ON A COLUMNAR SELF--	789	8
	BY TRAVELLER--BE HEARD--	NATURE--THE GENTLEST	790	6
	IT MIGHT BE FAMINE--ALL AROUND--	GOD GAVE A LOAF TO EVERY	791	9
	WHAT NECKLACES [AFFLUENCE / LEGACY] COULD BE [FOR ME]--	A DROP FELL ON THE APPLE	794	8
	A SMALLER, COULD NOT BE PERTURBED--	WHO GIANTS KNOW, WITH	796	5
	MAY BE EASIER REACHED [BETTER ATTAINED / EASIER GAINED]--THIS WAY--	BY MY WINDOW HAVE I FOR	797	8
	TO BE HALLOWED--ACCORDINGLY--	BY MY WINDOW HAVE I FOR	797	25
	HER STEADY BOAT BE SEEN--	SHE STAKED HER FEATHERS	798	6
	TO BE ASSISTED OF REVERSE	DESPAIR'S ADVANTAGE IS	799	3
	TOO HUNGRY TO BE BORNE	I PLAY AT RICHES--TO	801	10
	I DEEM MYSELF WHAT I WOULD BE--	I PLAY AT RICHES--TO	801	11
	HOW ['TIS] FITTER THEY WILL [I SHALL] BE--FOR [BY] WANT--	I PLAY AT RICHES--TO	801	21
	BE WHOLLY [CHIEFEST / UTMOST] BEAUTIFUL--	I PLAY AT RICHES--TO	801	24
	WHAT DAY BE DARK TO ME	SO SET IT'S SUN IN THEE	808	2
	ONE ART TO RECOGNIZE, MUST BE,	HER GRACE IS ALL SHE HAS	810	3
	THE LUXURY 'TWOULD BE	THE LUXURY TO APPREHEND	815	2
	AN EMIGRANT TO BE	AWAY FROM HOME ARE SOME	821	2
	WILL BE THE ONE AWARE OF DEATH	THIS CONSCIOUSNESS THAT	822	3
	IT'S PROPERTIES SHALL BE	THIS CONSCIOUSNESS THAT	822	10
	THE SOUL CONDEMNED TO BE--	THIS CONSCIOUSNESS THAT	822	14
	NOT WHAT WE DID, SHALL BE THE TEST	NOT WHAT WE DID, SHALL	823	1
	WITH THEM WOULD HARBOR BE--	AN HOUR IS A SEA	825	3
	IF OTHER NEWS THERE BE--	THE ONLY NEWS I KNOW	827	10
	BE IT'S MATTRESS STRAIGHT--	AMPLE MAKE THIS BED--	829	5
	BE IT'S PILLOW ROUND--	AMPLE MAKE THIS BED--	829	6
	DYING! TO BE AFRAID OF THEE	DYING! TO BE AFRAID OF	831	1
	BUT, ENEMY, BELOVED BE	DYING! TO BE AFRAID OF	831	8
	BETTER, TO BE FOUND,	GOOD TO HIDE, AND HEAR	842	2
	BE MINE THE DOOM--	BE MINE THE DOOM--	845	1
	IT WILL BE AMPLY EARLY	WHEN THE ASTRONOMER	851	7
	BE RENDERED BY THE BEE--	APOLOGY FOR HER	852	2
	TO HIM, IT WOULD BE DEATH--	THIS CHASM, SWEET, UPON	858	16
	A DOUBT IF IT BE US	A DOUBT IF IT BE US	859	1
	SAVED FOR YOUR EAR WHEN LUTES BE OLD.	SPLIT THE LARK--AND	861	4
	IT CAN BE HAD ON WINDOW PANES	LIGHT IS SUFFICIENT TO	862	3
	ALWAY A FLOWER WOULD BE.	BECAUSE THE BEE MAY	869	6
	WOULD BE MY FINAL INCH--	I STEPPED FROM PLANK TO	875	6
	THAT SOME THERE BE TOO NUMB TO NOTICE	A SHADE UPON THE MIND	882	5
	IN PLENTY MAY BE SEEN,	OUR LITTLE KINSMEN--	885	2
	WE IGNORANT MUST BE--	FROM US SHE WANDERED NOW	890	6
	IT SHOULD NOT BE AMONG	WHO OCCUPIES THIS HOUSE?	892	13
	A STRANGER HE MUST BE--	WHO OCCUPIES THIS HOUSE?	892	30

	FIRST LINE	POEM	LINE
BE (CONTINUED)			
THE SOUL CANNOT BE RID--	OF CONSCIOUSNESS, HER	894	2
SUPERIOR GLORY BE	A CLOUD WITHDREW FROM	895	2
WOULD BE AN EASY ADVERSITY	HOW HAPPY I WAS IF I	898	3
FOR NEWS THAT THEY BE SAVED--	SWEET, TO HAVE HAD THEM	901	2
OF FINITENESS--BE SPENT--	TILL DEATH--IS NARROW	907	4
THE LILY--WAITING TO BE WED--	'TIS SUNRISE--LITTLE	908	7
THAT NIGHT SHOULD BE TO THEE	'TIS SUNRISE--LITTLE	908	10
I CANNOT BE ASHAMED	I CANNOT BE ASHAMED	914	1
AND I CANNOT BE PROUD	I CANNOT BE ASHAMED	914	6
THE BRIDGE WOULD CEASE TO BE	FAITH--IS THE PIERLESS	915	10
STILL--JUST AS EASY, IF IT BE THY WILL	ONLY A SHRINE, BUT MINE	918	10
BE OF ME--AFRAID.	STRUCK, WAS I, NOR YET	925	16
BE IT BUT A PLAY	THAT IS SOLEMN WE HAVE	934	2
STILL [YET] TO BE EXPLAINED.	THAT IS SOLEMN WE HAVE	934	8
I LEARNED--AT LEAST--WHAT HOME COULD BE--	I LEARNED--AT LEAST--	944	1
WHEN PLAY BE DONE--	I LEARNED--AT LEAST--	944	14
BUT WHAT THAT PLACE COULD BE--	I LEARNED--AT LEAST--	944	29
WHERE DAWN--KNOWS HOW TO BE--	I LEARNED--AT LEAST--	944	31
WHEN IT IS LOST, THAT DAY SHALL BE	THIS IS A BLOSSOM OF THE	945	13
A GOOD NEWS SHOULD BE GIVEN.	OF TOLLING BELL I ASK	947	8
WHERE SUNSET HENCE MUST BE	THE SUNSET STOPPED ON	950	2
THAT NOUGHT BE LOST	THE CHEMICAL CONVICTION	954	2
PERMIT TO BE	WERT THOU BUT ILL--THAT	961	14
FOR LIFE--BE [IS / MEANS] LOVE--	WERT THOU BUT ILL--THAT	961	20
WHERE MAY BE YOUR HOUSE?	"UNTO ME?" I DO NOT KNOW	964	2
FITTER TO SEE HIM, I MAY BE	FITTER TO SEE HIM, I MAY	968	1
FOR EVIDENCE IT BE THE GRACE--	FITTER TO SEE HIM, I MAY	968	12
HE SEEK CONVICTION, THAT--BE THIS--	FITTER TO SEE HIM, I MAY	968	14
I SHALL BE PERFECT--IN HIS SIGHT--	FITTER TO SEE HIM, I MAY	968	22
A NATURE [SECTION] BE	BESIDES THIS MAY	977	8
IT CANNOT BE AGAIN--	THIS MERIT HATH THE	979	2
TO BE AN EMPEROR.	PURPLE--IS FASHIONABLE	980	4
LIKE THE REMEMBERING IT BE NOUGHT	NO OTHER CAN REDUCE	982	3
OR SUN'S EXTINCTION, BE OBSERVED	THE MISSING ALL,	985	5
AS DAISIES NOW TO BE SEEN--	THIS WAS IN THE WHITE OF	995	4
OR IF IT BE--BEFORE--	THIS WAS IN THE WHITE OF	995	6
GERM'S GERM BE WHERE?	BEST THINGS DWELL OUT OF	998	8
WHEN EXCELLENCE BE DEAD	SUPERFLUOUS WERE THE SUN	999	2
FOR EVERY DAY BE SAID	SUPERFLUOUS WERE THE SUN	999	4
SPOTLESS BE FROM BLAME	UP LIFE'S HILL WITH MY	1010	6
THE RESPITE TO BE DEAD.	TOO SCANTY 'TWAS TO DIE	1013	8
THE COUNTENANCE 'TWOULD BE.	WHO SAW NO SUNRISE	1018	2
A BERRY OR A BUN, WOULD BE,	MY HEART UPON A LITTLE	1027	3
LET IT BE	'TWAS MY ONE GLORY--	1028	2
WHO MAY BE PURPLE IF HE CAN	WHO IS THE EAST?	1032	3
WHO MAY BE YELLOW IF HE CAN	WHO IS THE EAST?	1032	7
OR BETTER, BE WITH ME--	BEE! I'M EXPECTING YOU!	1035	11
WILL GENTLE BE, TO HER.	HERE, WHERE THE DAISIES	1037	8
TO IMITATE BE MINE.	HER LITTLE PARASOL TO	1038	4
BE IT NE'ER SO FAR	SOMEWHAT, TO HOPE FOR,	1041	2
BE IT NE'ER SO KEEN--	SOMEWHAT, TO HOPE FOR,	1041	5
IF TERMINABLE, MAY BE BORNE.	SOMEWHAT, TO HOPE FOR,	1041	6
LEST THIS BE HEAVEN INDEED	LEST THIS BE HEAVEN	1043	1
A WORLD MUST BE	A SICKNESS OF THIS WORLD	1044	6
A WARRANT TO BE FAIR--	I CANNOT MEET THE SPRING	1051	4
AND WHAT A BILLOW BE.	I NEVER SAW A MOOR--	1052	4
HE WILL NOT BE OBLIGED TO WAIT	THE SOUL SHOULD ALWAYS	1055	3
TO BE A FLOWER, IS PROFOUND	BLOOM--IS RESULT--TO	1058	15
WHICH BE OUT OF SIGHT?	THREE WEEKS PASSED SINCE	1061	12
TOO TENDER, TO BE TOLD.	LET DOWN THE BARS, OH	1065	8
TOO WILLING, TO BE CALLED	LET DOWN THE BARS, OH	1065	V 8
NO ORDINANCE BE SEEN	FURTHER IN SUMMER THAN	1068	5
BE UNDERTAKING BLENT	TO UNDERTAKE IS TO	1070	2
COUNT NOT THAT FAR THAT CAN BE HAD,	COUNT NOT THAT FAR THAT	1074	1
BE CONSCIOUS OF A SIGH	JUST ONCE! OH LEAST	1076	7
IF BLOSSOMS CAN BE BORN AGAIN	WHEN THEY COME BACK--IF	1080	3
WHAT PARTY--ONE MAY BE	WHEN THEY COME BACK--IF	1080	14
EVERY SUMMER BE	REVOLUTION IS THE POD	1082	6
TEST IF IT BE DEAD.	REVOLUTION IS THE POD	1082	12
NOR IMPLEMENT, BE SEEN--	AT HALF PAST THREE, A	1084	10
MYSELF A FRECKLED--BE--	THEMSELF ARE ALL I HAVE	1094	2
WHAT MUST THE MIDNIGHTS--BE!	TO WHOM THE MORNINGS	1095	2
BE FOUND A REFUGEE--	THESE STRANGERS, IN A	1096	4
CAN NEVER BE FITTED [MATCHED] AGAIN?	OF THE HEART THAT GOES	1098	4
A POWER OF BUTTERFLY MUST BE--	MY COCOON TIGHTENS--	1099	5
AND ROOMS WHERE THOSE TO BE ALIVE	THE LAST NIGHT THAT SHE	1100	11
WAS WAITING [ASSEMBLED] TO BE POURED	HIS BILL IS CLASPED--HIS	1102	6
GORED THROUGH AND THROUGH WITH DEATH, TO BE	HIS BILL IS CLASPED--HIS	1102	7
SURFACES MAY [CAN] BE INVESTED [RELATED]	NONE WHO SAW IT EVER	1110	5
THERE IS A [GOOD] STRENGTH IN PROVING [KNOWING] THAT IT CAN BE	THERE IS A STRENGTH IN	1113	1
THE SHIP MIGHT BE OF SATIN HAD IT NOT TO FIGHT--	THERE IS A STRENGTH IN	1113	5
IS RICHER THAN COULD BE REVEALED	THERE IS ANOTHER	1116	7
BUT MUST IT BE CONFERRED,	A MINE THERE IS NO MAN	1117	2
POTOSI NEVER TO BE SPENT	A MINE THERE IS NO MAN	1117	5
SO BE HER'S THE ERROR--	HAD WE KNOWN THE TON SHE	1124	4
'TWILL NEVER BE THE SAME TO STARVE	OH SUMPTUOUS MOMENT	1125	4
BE STATIONED WITH THE CANDIDATES	SHALL I TAKE THEE, THE	1126	3

		FIRST LINE	POEM		LINE
BE	(CONTINUED)				
	OR EVERY MAN BE BLIND--	TELL ALL THE TRUTH BUT	1129		8
	IT MUST AT FIRST BE TRUE--	THE SMOULDERING EMBERS	1132	V	8
	THE VALUE COULD NOT BE--	THE SNOW THAT NEVER	1133		14
	TOO STIFF TO BENDED BE,	TOO COLD IS THIS	1135		3
	BE IT BUT FOR A DAY	THE FACE WE CHOOSE TO	1141		2
	NO MOMENT WILL THERE BE	IN THY LONG PARADISE OF	1145		2
	[SOME] IT MUST BE COMPETITIONS	HOW MANY SCHEMES MAY DIE	1150		11
	WITH DEATH TO BE	SOUL, TAKE THY RISK,	1151		2
	WERE BETTER THAN BE NOT	SOUL, TAKE THY RISK,	1151		3
	TO BE ESTEEMED NO MORE	A FULL FED ROSE ON MEALS	1154		8
	WERE IT TO BE THE LAST	WERE IT TO BE THE LAST	1164		1
	HOW INFINITE WOULD BE	WERE IT TO BE THE LAST	1164		2
	TOO DISTANT [SUBTLE] TO BE SEEN	CONTAINED IN THIS SHORT	1165	V	
	THE STAPLE MUST BE OPTIONAL	OF PAUL AND SILAS IT IS	1166		7
	RELUCTANT TO BE TOLD	ALONE AND IN A	1167		2
	BUT WHAT REDRESS CAN BE	ALONE AND IN A	1167		22
	NATURE AFFECTS [WAS KNOWN] TO BE SEDATE	NATURE AFFECTS TO BE	1170		1
	HOW GOOD [SAFE / FIRM / CALM] TO BE IN TOMBS	THE CLOUDS THEIR BACKS	1172		6
	WOULD BE A NORMAL [DAILY] THING	WE NEVER KNOW HOW HIGH	1176		6
	FOR FEAR TO BE A KING--	WE NEVER KNOW HOW HIGH	1176		8
	BE [ARE] UNEXPECTED FRIENDS.	"REMEMBER ME" IMPLORED	1180		12
	OURSELVES BE NOT PURSUED--	REMEMBRANCE HAS A	1182		8
	STEP LOFTY, FOR THIS NAME BE TOLD	STEP LIGHTLY ON THIS	1183		5
	TOO FEW THE MORNINGS BE,	TOO FEW THE MORNINGS BE,	1186		1
	NO LODGING CAN BE HAD	TOO FEW THE MORNINGS BE,	1186		3
	BY OTHER FINANCIERS BE DEEMED	THE VOICE THAT STANDS	1189		7
	THAT IT BE SAVED THE SAVED SUFFICE	SOMEHOW MYSELF SURVIVED	1194		3
	BE IT BUT A LITTLE--	WHAT WE SEE WE KNOW	1195		2
	I SHOULD NOT DARE TO BE SO SAD	I SHOULD NOT DARE TO BE	1197		1
	THAT NEVER COULD BE TRACED.	THE FROST WAS NEVER SEEN	1202		12
	WHATEVER IT IS [BE]--SHE HAS TRIED IT--	WHATEVER IT IS--SHE HAS	1204		1
	ONLY LEST SHE BE LONELY	WHATEVER IT IS--SHE HAS	1204		9
	MY NEIGHBOR BE--	THE SHOW IS NOT THE SHOW	1206		4
	THE SEA SAID "THEN YOU WILL BE A SEA--	THE SEA SAID "COME" TO	1210		3
	LET MY FIRST KNOWING BE OF THEE	LET MY FIRST KNOWING BE	1218		1
	IS LICENSED TO BE STILL.	IT'S HOUR WITH ITSELF	1225		8
	WHAT IS TO BE IS BEST DESCRIED	MY TRIUMPH LASTED TILL	1227		9
	THAT THERE MUST BE A HEAVEN	SO MUCH OF HEAVEN HAS	1228		2
	WHERE I FOR RIGHT TO BE [GO]--	SOMEWHERE UPON THE	1231		6
	ERE I BE THERE--	MY HEART RAN SO TO THEE	1237		16
	NOT DISTANT [FOREIGN]--NOT TO BE--	POWER IS A FAMILIAR	1238		2
	AND SEATS ITSELF TO BE LET GO	RISK IS THE HAIR THAT	1239		7
	AND MOUNTS TO BE TO ATOMS HURLED	RISK IS THE HAIR THAT	1239	V	7
	DISCLOSED [DISPLAYED] TO BE DENIED	THE BEGGAR AT THE DOOR	1240		4
	BE CURRENT WITH THE BLIND	THE LILAC IS AN ANCIENT	1241		18
	BY THESES BE DETAINED [PROFANED]--	THE LILAC IS AN ANCIENT	1241		20
	GARRISONED NO SOUL CAN BE	SAFE DESPAIR IT IS THAT	1243		5
	AND BE OF BUTTERCUPS THE FRIEND	THE BUTTERFLY'S	1244		5
	THIS--WOULD BE POETRY--	TO PILE LIKE THUNDER TO	1247		4
	OR COULD IT CEASE TO BE	HAD THIS ONE DAY NOT	1253		2
	IT SHALL AT LENGTH BE FOUND.	LONGING IS LIKE THE SEED	1255		4
	WHAT CONSTANCY MUST BE ACHIEVED	LONGING IS LIKE THE SEED	1255		7
	THAN TIME ENSUE TO BE--	WHO WERE "THE FATHER AND	1258		16
	HOWEVER FIRST [TRUE / DUE / JUST] IT BE	BECAUSE THAT YOU ARE	1260		6
	THIS INSTANT BE SUSPENDED [ABOLISHED]	BECAUSE THAT YOU ARE	1260		7
	THE "LIFE THAT IS TO BE," TO ME,	BECAUSE THAT YOU ARE	1260		21
	WE THINK THAT HE MUST BE	BECAUSE THAT YOU ARE	1260		34
	THAT I BE ADEQUATELY DRESSED,	I CANNOT SEE MY SOUL BUT	1262		6
	WHERE NONE OF US SHOULD [WOULD] BE	SO PROUD SHE WAS TO DIE	1272		6
	'TWILL BE A LABOR OF SURPRISE--	THAT SACRED CLOSET WHEN	1273		5
	OBLIGED TO BE INFERRED.	THE WAY TO KNOW THE	1279		4
	ETERNITY WILL BE	TWO LENGTHS HAS EVERY	1295		5
	OTHER COURTESY MAY BE--	RECOLLECT THE FACE OF ME	1305		6
	HAS BEEN ASSUMED TO BE--	THE INFINITE A SUDDEN	1309		2
	I WILL NOT BE PURSUED--	DEAR MARCH--COME IN--	1320		20
	NOTWITHSTANDING [TO BE SURE] A ROPE FOR A SOUVENIR	FLOSS WONT SAVE YOU FROM	1322		3
	IF SENTIMENT FOR ME [IT BE]	I SEND YOU A DECREPIT	1324		6
	SHOULD THEY BE AT HOME	KNOCK WITH TREMOR--	1325		3
	THE HEAVENS [TREES / SKY / FIELD] CANNOT BE FOUND--	THE SYMPTOM OF THE GALE	1327		6
	WHETHER ADULT DELIGHT IS [BE] PAIN	WONDER--IS NOT PRECISELY	1331		6
	BUT GOD BE WITH THE CLOWN--	A LITTLE MADNESS IN THE	1333		3
	NOT ANY MORE TO BE LACKED--	NOT ANY MORE TO BE	1344		1
	NOT ANY MORE TO BE KNOWN--	NOT ANY MORE TO BE	1344		2
	IT IS TO BE THE SAVED--	ESCAPE IS SUCH A	1347		10
	IF THAT IS [BE] FULL OF MEAT	THE MIND LIVES ON THE	1355		3
	BUT IF THE HEART OMIT [BE LEAN / BE THIN / DECLINE]	THE MIND LIVES ON THE	1355		5
	BUT IF THE HEART OMIT [BE LEAN / BE THIN / DECLINE]	THE MIND LIVES ON THE	1355		5
	OF SANCTITY TO BE--	THE TREASON OF AN ACCENT	1358	V	
	THAT SUCH A REALM COULD BE--	I SUED THE NEWS--YET	1360		2
	CONVICTED--COULD WE BE	A SAUCER HOLDS A CUP	1374		13
	DEATH WARRANTS ARE SUPPOSED [BELIEVED] TO BE	DEATH WARRANTS ARE	1375		1
	CAN BE NO BODE OF DAWN	HIS HEART WAS DARKER	1378		4
	AS FAME SHOULD BE--	HIS MANSION IN THE POOL	1379		12
	AND THE BEE BE BOOMING.	I SUPPOSE THE TIME WILL	1381		4
	I BELIEVE THE DAY WILL BE	I SUPPOSE THE TIME WILL	1381		9

BE (CONTINUED)

	FIRST LINE	POEM	LINE
THE DOOM [LOT] TO BE ADORED	SUMMER--WE ALL HAVE SEEN	1386	V 9
DEFIED TO BE DEFINED--	THESE HELD THEIR WICK	1390	4
I'LL LET MY HEART BE JUST IN SIGHT--	THEY MIGHT NOT NEED ME--	1391	2
A SMILE SO SMALL AS MINE MIGHT BE	THEY MIGHT NOT NEED ME--	1391	3
SUCH A VICTOR COULD NOT [CANNOT] BE--	LAY THIS LAUREL ON THE	1393	V
IT MAY BE KNOW SO CERTAINLY	PERHAPS THEY DO NOT GO	1399	5
RELATED SOMEHOW THEY MAY BE,	WHAT MYSTERY PERVADES A	1400	13
MY MAKER--LET ME BE	MY MAKER--LET ME BE	1403	1
LEST CERTAINTY BE SERE	SWEET SKEPTICISM OF THE	1413	6
BE HONOR AND NOT SHAME--	TO EARN IT BY DISDAINING	1427	8
HOW LITTLE WORK [WHAT LITTLE ACT] IT BE--	WITH PINIONS OF DISDAIN	1431	10
AND [BUT] NOT AGAIN THAT DEW BE SEEN	A DEW SUFFICED ITSELF--	1437	7
IT'S TANTAMOUNT BE FOUND--	BEHOLD THIS LITTLE BANE	1438	8
SEEMS IT SOMETIMES THIS WOULD BE ALL--	THESE FEVERED DAYS--TO	1441	4
WHO [THAT] MUST BE UP TO CALL THE WORLD	HOW GOOD HIS LAVA BED,	1447	3
TO WISER BE [GROW] TOO SOON--	I THOUGHT THE TRAIN	1449	10
. . . INTIMATE / AFFABLE / AFFLUENT / GRACIOUS] SO TO BE	YOUR THOUGHTS DONT HAVE	1452	6
I WOULD NOT BE--	A COUNTERFEIT--A PLATED	1453	2
OF THE DISK TO BE--	THOSE NOT LIVE YET	1454	9
THE SWEETS OF PILLAGE, CAN BE KNOWN	THE SWEETS OF PILLAGE,	1470	1
ESTRANGED FROM BEAUTY--NONE CAN BE--	ESTRANGED FROM BEAUTY--	1474	1
AND POWER TO BE FINITE CEASED	ESTRANGED FROM BEAUTY--	1474	3
OR BE THAT MOST INSOLVENT THING	FAME IS THE ONE THAT	1475	5
HOW OLD THE NEWS OF LOVE MUST [SHOULD] BE	HIS VOICE DECREPIT WAS	1476	3
WOULD BE THE BEST FRIEND--	THE DEVIL--HAD HE	1479	2
EACH ONE OF US SHALL BE--	'TIS WHITER THAN AN	1482	10
IT BE NOT TRAGEDY--	'TIS WHITER THAN AN	1482	12
WAS LEVELED, BUT FOR THAT TWOULD BE	THE SAVIOR MUST HAVE	1487	7
DISSENTING [DEFYING] TO BE WON	THE FACE IN EVANESCENCE	1490	6
BE ONCE DISCLOSED TO US	COULD THAT SWEET	1493	2
FOR HER [ONE] TO BE A [AN IMPENDING] BRIDE	ALL THAT I DO	1496	11
LET HIM BE QUICK--THE VIAND FLITS [BANQUET COOLS]--	MINE ENEMY IS GROWING	1509	5
HER TRAVELS DAILY BE	"GO TRAVELING WITH US!"	1513	2
HOW CHIEF THY SESSIONS BE--	HOW MUCH OF SOURCE	1517	2
AND HONEYS, IF HIS LIFE BE SPARED,	HIS ORIENTAL HERESIES	1526	V
IF SUCH PROSPECTIVE BE--	THE MOON UPON HER FLUENT	1528	V
AND CENTURIES 'TWILL BE AND MORE	'TIS SEASONS SINCE THE	1529	4
ENOUGH WILL NOT BE FOUND WHEN ALL HAVE DIED.	ABOVE OBLIVION'S TIDE	1531	7
WILL BE RETAKEN WITH A SHOT	THE LIFE THAT TIED TOO	1535	7
AS [OF] GUEST, THAT [WHO] WOULD BE GONE--	AS IMPERCEPTIBLY AS	1540	12
AS SUDDENLY BE WORN	AS IMPERCEPTIBLY AS	1540	V
AND IF IT BE NOT ME	COME SHOW THY DURHAM	1542	4
TO BE A SUN--	THE PATTERN OF THE SUN	1550	4
AND GOD CANNOT BE FOUND--	THOSE--DYING THEN,	1551	5
THAT CONSECRATED IT COULD BE	I GROPED FOR HIM BEFORE	1555	7
TO BE FORGOT BY THEE	TO BE FORGOT BY THEE	1560	1
TO BE REMEMBERED WHAT--	TO BE FORGOT BY THEE	1560	10
WORTHY TO BE FORGOT	TO BE FORGOT BY THEE	1560	11
BY WHICH TO BE UNDONE	TO SEE HER IS A PICTURE	1568	V
FOREVER HONORED [CHERISHED] BE THE TREE	FOREVER HONORED BE THE	1570	1
HOW LATE THEIR FEATHERS BE!	HOW SLOW THE WIND--	1571	3
WHAT WOULD THE EITHER BE?	THE SPIRIT LASTS--BUT IN	1576	12
ADVERSITY IF IT MAY BE, OR	THE SPIRIT LASTS--BUT IN	1576	19
HOW THEREFORE SAFE TO BE A FLOWER	IT WOULD NOT KNOW IF IT	1579	3
MAY NOT THIS BE	WE SHUN IT ERE IT COMES,	1580	6
EXPANSE CANNOT BE LOST--	EXPANSE CANNOT BE LOST--	1584	1
BUT WORK MIGHT BE ELECTRIC REST	THE BIRD HER PUNCTUAL	1585	7
ADVERSITY IF IT MAY BE	THIS ME--THAT WALKS AND	1588	3
KNOCK AND IT SHALL BE OPENED	COSMOPOLITES WITHOUT A	1589	7
LET EVERY BONDAGE BE,	IMMURED IN HEAVEN!	1594	3
THAT WE MAY BE FORGIVEN--	OF GOD WE ASK ONE FAVOR,	1601	2
YOUR REQUISITION BE.	PURSUING YOU IN YOUR	1602	4
POSSESSING THOU SHALT BE	CIRCUMFERENCE THOU BRIDE	1620	2
BETROTHED TO RIGHTEOUSNESS MIGHT BE	BETROTHED TO	1641	1
THAT EARTH SH'D BE SO BIG--	"RED SEA," INDEED! TALK	1642	10
WHOSE SOFT INHABITANTS TO BE	A LANE OF YELLOW LED THE	1650	3
COULD CONDESCENSION BE	A WORD MADE FLESH IS	1651	14
SUPPOSED TO BE A TERMINUS	ADVANCE IS LIFE'S	1652	3
IF THEY BE OCCUPIED	AS WE PASS HOUSES MUSING	1653	2
IF THEY BE OCCUPIED	AS WE PASS HOUSES MUSING	1653	4
LET IT BE IN SIGHT OF THEE--	BEAUTY CROWDS ME TILL I	1654	4
THE LAST SHALL BE THE LIGHTEST LOAD	I DID NOT REACH THEE	1664	18
WHO WOULD BE VERY GLAD	I KNOW OF PEOPLE IN THE	1665	2
I SHOULD NOT BE SO GLAD--	IF I COULD TELL HOW GLAD	1668	2
THAT NEW DILEMMA BE	IF I COULD TELL HOW GLAD	1668	6
IF OTHER SUMMERS BE	NATURE CAN DO NO MORE	1673	6
WHOSE SEAM COULD NOT BE SHEWN--	OF YELLOW WAS THE OUTER	1676	4
WOULD BE THE GENERAL THOUGHT--	ON MY VOLCANO GROWS THE	1677	4
MUST NOT BE INCURRED	RATHER ARID DELIGHT	1679	6
AUTUMN BEGINS TO BE INFERRED	SUMMER BEGINS TO HAVE	1682	5
AT MOST TO BE PERENNIAL	SUMMER BEGINS TO HAVE	1682	14
THAT THOU SHALT BE THE SAME--	THE LOOK OF THEE, WHAT	1689	12
BE THIS AN AUTUMN OR A SPRING	THE ONES THAT	1690	5
THE RIGHT TO PERISH MIGHT BE THO'T	THE RIGHT TO PERISH	1692	1
SOCIETY SHALL BE	THERE IS A SOLITUDE OF	1695	4
NOTWITHSTANDING IT NEVER BE KNOWN	TO DO A MAGNANIMOUS	1699	6
VOLCANOES BE IN SICILY	VOLCANOES BE IN SICILY	1705	1

	FIRST LINE	POEM	LINE
BE (CONTINUED)			
HER HOME TO BE WITH NATURE	WITH SWEETNESS UNABATED	1709	5
HER RESIDUE BE PAST--	WITH SWEETNESS UNABATED	1709	12
TO STIR WOULD BE TO SLIP--	A PIT--BUT HEAVEN OVER	1712	5
TO LOOK WOULD BE TO DROP--	A PIT--BUT HEAVEN OVER	1712	6
BUT DECOYED MAY BE.	DEATH IS LIKE THE INSECT	1716	4
WHO HEARS MAY BE INCREDULOUS,	HER FACE WAS IN A BED OF	1722	7
EXTINCT BE EVERY HUM	HOW DARE THE ROBINS SING	1724	13
THEY COULD NOT BE SO BIG AS THIS	IF ALL THE GRIEFS I AM	1726	7
AND THE WORLD--IF THE WORLD BE LOOKING ON--	IF EVER THE LID GETS OFF	1727	5
TO BE ENACTED NOW.	NO MAN SAW AWE, NOR TO	1733	12
DESERVING BE.	OH, HONEY OF AN HOUR,	1734	6
THAT IF IT BE, IT BE AT BEST	THAT IT WILL NEVER COME	1741	5
THAT IF IT BE, IT BE AT BEST	THAT IT WILL NEVER COME	1741	5
A CYCLE, IT MAY BE,	THE GRAVE MY LITTLE	1743	6
LET EVERY BABBLER [PRATER] BE	THE RETICENT VOLCANO	1748	10
NO CASPIAN COULD BE.	TO LOSE THEE--SWEETER	1754	8
BUT NATURE WILL BE READY	WERE NATURE MORTAL LADY	1762	7
IT IS ENOUGH, THE FREIGHT SHOULD BE	THAT LOVE IS ALL THERE	1765	3
LAD OF ATHENS, FAITHFUL BE	LAD OF ATHENS, FAITHFUL	1768	1
BEACH			
MY GARDEN--LIKE THE BEACH--	MY GARDEN--LIKE THE	484	1
BEAD			
AS A FADED BEAD	RIBBONS OF THE YEAR--	873	5
BEADS			
THE BEADS UPON THE FOREHEAD	I LIKE A LOOK OF AGONY,	241	7
THEY LOOKED LIKE FRIGHTENED BEADS, I THOUGHT--	A BIRD CAME DOWN THE	328	11
LIKE BEADS--AMONG THE BOG--	HER SMILE WAS SHAPED	514	8
BEAK			
THE LIGHTNING SHOWED A YELLOW HEAD [BEAK]--	THE WIND BEGUN TO KNEAD	824	11
DIPPED MY BEAK IN IT,	SANG FROM THE HEART,	1059	2
BEAM			
AND MORN SH'D BEAM--	IF I SHOULD DIE,	54	4
WAS NOT UPON THE "BEAM"--	I CAUTIOUS, SCANNED MY	178	10
AND RESTED, ON A BEAM--	TWO BUTTERFLIES WENT OUT	533	4
FOR THE APPOINTED BEAM	A PRISON GETS TO BE A	652	6
NOR BEAM WOULD IT NOR WARM--	THIS THAT WOULD GREET--	778	6
WITHOUT DELIGHT, OR BEAM--	DENIAL--IS THE ONLY FACT	965	6
BEFORE MY BEAM WAS SOWN,	EXPANSE CANNOT BE LOST--	1584	6
BEFORE MY MIND [SOUL / BEAM] WAS BORN	THIS ME--THAT WALKS AND	1588	6
OF GLORY NOT A BEAM IS LEFT	OF GLORY NOT A BEAM IS	1647	1
BEAR			
THEN BEAR HER TO THE GREENWOOD, AND BUILD FOR HER A BOWER,	AWAKE YE MUSES NINE,	1	37
AND BEAR TO ALL MY FRIENDS,	I WOULD DISTIL A CUP,	16	2
PARCHED THE FLOWERS THEY BEAR ALONG.	ANGELS, IN THE EARLY	94	8
THEY BEAR NO OTHER ERRAND,	MY NOSEGAYS ARE FOR	95	7
OUR SHARE OF NIGHT TO BEAR--	OUR SHARE OF NIGHT TO	113	1
TILL RANKS OF SEEDS THEIR WITNESS BEAR--	THESE ARE THE DAYS WHEN	130	10
THY WINDY WILL TO BEAR!	BESIDES THE AUTUMN POETS	131	16
AND SO I ALWAYS BEAR THE CUP	I BRING AN UNACCUSTOMED	132	17
AND THEN SHE CEASED TO BEAR IT--	SHE BORE IT TILL THE	144	7
I'LL BEAR IT BETTER NOW--	YOU LOVE ME--YOU ARE	156	15
BEAR WITHIN--APPALLING ORDNANCE,	I HAVE NEVER SEEN	175	5
AND COULD NOT BEAR TO SHUT UNTIL	I SHOULD NOT DARE TO	205	7
THEY BEAR THEIR DAUNTLESS [FEARLESS / TRANQUIL] HEADS,	WHEN WE STAND ON THE	242	10
AND LIVES CAN [WILL] BEAR IT!	BOUND--A TROUBLE--	269	2
TO BEAR THEM ORCHESTRA.	OF ALL THE SOUNDS	321	24
I COULD NOT BEAR THE BEES SHOULD COME,	I DREADED THAT FIRST	348	17
THE FOOT TO BEAR HIS ERRAND--	ALTHOUGH I PUT AWAY HIS	366	13
A HONEY BEAR AWAY	THERE IS A FLOWER THAT	380	6
IT BEAR TO OTHER EYES--	HOW MANY FLOWERS FAIL IN	404	8
BEAR YOU--FOR ORNAMENT	I'LL CLUTCH--AND CLUTCH	427	16
TO BEAR ON US UNSHADED--	I TIE MY HAT--I CREASE	443	23
HOW ILL THE CREATURES BEAR--	SHE DEALT HER PRETTY	479	8
I COULD NOT BEAR TO LIVE--ALOUD--	I WAS THE SLIGHTEST IN	486	12
I ENVY SEAS, WHEREON HE RIDES--[THAT BEAR HIM]	I ENVY SEAS, WHEREON HE	498	1
SUCH PRESENCE BEAR AWAY	BEREAVEMENT IN THEIR	645	10
BEAR [HOLD] ME--	A LITTLE ROAD--NOT MADE	647	8
THEN--TO HIM WHO BEAR	PUBLICATION--IS THE	709	10
THOUGH SHE FORGET THE NAME I BEAR--	PRECIOUS TO ME--SHE	727	2
WHAT DEED IS THEIR'S [THEY BEAR] UNTO THE GENERAL NATURE--	FOUR TREES--UPON A	742	13
BUT HER DISDAIN--'TWERE LIGHTER [COOLER] BEAR	MY SOUL--ACCUSED ME--AND	753	7
AND SO I BEAR IT BIG ABOUT	THIS CHASM, SWEET, UPON	858	17
HOW CAN I BEAR THEIR JOCUND FACES	WHAT SHALL I DO WHEN THE	956	11
FRAUD OF DEATH--TO BEAR--	ROBBED BY DEATH--BUT	971	10
ANOTHER BEAR IT'S DUPLICATE	I KNEW THAT I HAD GAINED	1022	7
BEAR WITH THE BALLAD--	SANG FROM THE HEART,	1059	9
EXCEPT TO BEAR	THERE IS A STRENGTH IN	1113	4
TRADITION BEAR WITH [SUFFER] ME	ONE OF THE ONES THAT	1466	26
T'IS GOOD TO BEAR	PERIL AS A POSSESSION	1678	2
HE CANNOT BEAR TO SEE	GOD IS INDEED A JEALOUS	1719	2
BEARD			
MY CACTUS--SPLITS HER BEARD	I TEND MY FLOWERS FOR	339	7
BEARDED			
MAKE ME BEARDED LIKE A MAN!	REARRANGE A "WIFE'S"	1737	4
BEARD'S			
OR BLUE BEARD'S GALLERIES--	LIKE SOME OLD FASHIONED	302	8

	FIRST LINE	POEM	LINE
BEARER			
JUST TWO--THE BEARER--	UNIT, LIKE DEATH, FOR	408	7
THE BEARER FROM AN EMERALD COURT	THE STEM OF A DEPARTED	1520	3
BEAREST			
HOW MANY BULLETS BEAREST?	WHO NEVER LOST, ARE	73	13
BEARING			
BEARING THE NEIGHBOR OUT OF SOUND	PEACE IS A FICTION OF	912	3
BEARS			
WHICH BEARS A SWORD	THERE IS A WORD	8	2
THAT BEARS ANOTHER'S--NAME--	THE WORLD--STANDS--	493	4
IT BEARS THE SOUL AS BOLD	FAITH--IS THE PIERLESS	915	5
THE TRADITION [HEROISM] BEARS--	TELL AS A MARKSMAN--WERE	1152	4
GRATITUDE BEARS	AN HONEST TEAR	1192	7
THAT BEARS THE HUMAN SOUL.	THERE IS NO FRIGATE LIKE	1263	8
IT BEARS AWAY IN TRIUMPH	DEATH IS THE SUPPLE	1445	9
BEAST			
DOUBTLESS AN ESTIMABLE BEAST,	I MET A KING THIS	166	15
BY THE TIME THAT MAN AND BEAST	THERE'S THE BATTLE OF	1174	3
BEAT			
AND BRING THE FIFE, AND TRUMPET, AND BEAT UPON THE DRUM--	AWAKE YE MUSES NINE,	1	39
DO WE "BEAT" OUR "WIFE"?	WE--BEE AND I--LIVE BY	230	8
THAT HAD IT BEAT A THOUSAND YEARS,	'TIS NOT THE SWAYING	1597	3
BEATIFIED			
BEATIFIED--	THE GENTIAN HAS A	1424	4
BEATING			
KEPT BEATING--BEATING--TILL I THOUGHT	I FELT A FUNERAL, IN MY	280	7
KEPT BEATING--BEATING--TILL I THOUGHT	I FELT A FUNERAL, IN MY	280	7
REPEAL THE BEATING GROUND--	IT WAS NOT DEATH, FOR I	510	20
BEATRICE			
AND BEATRICE WORE	A PRECIOUS--MOULDERING	371	18
BEAUTIFUL			
BEAUTIFUL--AS PICTURES--	I WENT TO HEAVEN--	374	7
THAT THEY ARE BEAUTIFUL--	HOW MANY FLOWERS FAIL IN	404	4
TRINKET--TO MAKE ME BEAUTIFUL--	I AM ASHAMED--I HIDE--	473	8
TOO BEAUTIFUL--FOR SHAPE TO PROVE--	THE WORLD--STANDS--	493	15
BE BEAUTIFUL AS THEY PREPARE [DISCLOSE]	I RECKON--WHEN I COUNT	569	13
THE DARK--FELT BEAUTIFUL--	I THINK I WAS ENCHANTED	593	4
BE WHOLLY [CHIEFEST / UTMOST] BEAUTIFUL--	I PLAY AT RICHES--TO	801	24
LEST IN A FACE SO BEAUTIFUL	WHEN THEY COME BACK--IF	1080	11
IN THY BEAUTIFUL HOUSE	WHATEVER IT IS--SHE HAS	1204	10
IS NOT BEAUTIFUL--	FLOSS WONT SAVE YOU FROM	1322	4
A BEAUTIFUL BUT BLEAK CONDITION	WONDER--IS NOT PRECISELY	1331	3
THOUGH ONE IS BEAUTIFUL FORGETTING [SECESSION]--	I'D RATHER RECOLLECT A	1349	3
INTO [UNTO] THE BEAUTIFUL.	AS IMPERCEPTIBLY AS	1540	16
ARE BEAUTIFUL--	THE WORDS THE HAPPY SAY	1750	4
BEAUTY			
I DIED FOR BEAUTY--BUT WAS SCARCE	I DIED FOR BEAUTY--BUT	449	1
"FOR BEAUTY", I REPLIED--	I DIED FOR BEAUTY--BUT	449	6
BEAUTY--BE [IS] NOT CAUSED--IT IS--	BEAUTY--BE NOT CAUSED--	516	1
HER BEAUTY--IS THE LOVE SHE DOTH--	BUT LITTLE CARMINE HATH	558	3
THE BEAUTY THAT REWARD HIM MOST [BEST]--	FITTER TO SEE HIM, I MAY	968	27
THE BEAUTY OF DEMAND [BELIEF]--AT REST--	FITTER TO SEE HIM, I MAY	968	28
THE DEFINITION OF BEAUTY IS	THE DEFINITION OF BEAUTY	988	1
TILL ALL HER HELPLESS BEAUTY BENT	THE FROST OF DEATH WAS	1136	14
BOLD LITTLE BEAUTY	PINK--SMALL--AND	1332	9
IS BEAUTY AN AFFLICTION--THEN?	SO GAY A FLOWER	1456	4
ESTRANGED FROM BEAUTY--NONE CAN BE--	ESTRANGED FROM BEAUTY--	1474	1
FOR BEAUTY IS INFINITY--	ESTRANGED FROM BEAUTY--	1474	2
DID BEAUTY EVER TAKE--	THE BIRD HER PUNCTUAL	1585	6
BEAUTY CROWDS ME TILL I DIE	BEAUTY CROWDS ME TILL I	1654	1
BEAUTY MERCY HAVE ON ME	BEAUTY CROWDS ME TILL I	1654	2
TO TELL THE BEAUTY WOULD DECREASE	TO TELL THE BEAUTY WOULD	1700	1
BEAUTY IS NATURE'S FACT.	THE EARTH HAS MANY KEYS.	1775	4
BEAUTY'S			
BEST BEAUTY'S WAY--	MUST BE A WO--	571	4
BECAME			
WHEN FROSTS TOO SHARP BECAME	ALL OVERGROWN BY CUNNING	148	6
A CYNIC, I BECAME.	I CAUTIOUS, SCANNED MY	178	12
AND I BECAME ALONE--	THE WIND--TAPPED LIKE A	436	20
THE BEES--BECAME AS BUTTERFLIES--	I THINK I WAS ENCHANTED	593	9
AND SO THE NIGHT BECAME.	THE CRICKETS SANG	1104	12
IN PROCESS OF THE NOON BECAME--	A FULL FED ROSE ON MEALS	1154	3
OUR NOON BECAME A WELL	A CAP OF LEAD ACROSS THE	1649	6
BUT CONSTANCY BECAME	THAT SHE FORGOT ME WAS	1683	6
BECAUSE			
WE LOSE--BECAUSE WE WIN--	WE LOSE--BECAUSE WE WIN	21	1
TWILL BE BECAUSE BEYOND THE ROSE	IF I SHOULD CEASE TO	56	3
TWILL BE BECAUSE DEATH'S FINGER	IF I SHOULD CEASE TO	56	7
BECAUSE IT FLIES!	MY FRIEND MUST BE A BIRD	92	2
BECAUSE IT DIES!	MY FRIEND MUST BE A BIRD	92	4
BECAUSE, SIR, LOVE IS SWEET!	THE DAISY FOLLOWS SOFT	106	6
GOOD NIGHT, BECAUSE WE MUST,	GOOD NIGHT, BECAUSE WE	114	1
BECAUSE--THEE--	I STOLE THEM FROM A BEE	200	2
BECAUSE--BECAUSE IF HE SHOULD DIE	I SHOULD NOT DARE TO	205	2
BECAUSE--BECAUSE IF HE SHOULD DIE	I SHOULD NOT DARE TO	205	2
BECAUSE I KNOW IT'S TRUE--	I LIKE A LOOK OF AGONY,	241	2
BECAUSE I GROW--WHERE ROBINS DO--	THE ROBIN'S MY CRITERION	285	2
BECAUSE, WE'RE ORCHARD SPRUNG--	THE ROBIN'S MY CRITERION	285	7

	FIRST LINE	POEM	LINE
BECAUSE (CONTINUED)			
BECAUSE, THROUGH DROPPING IT,	THE ROBIN'S MY CRITERION	285	11
BECAUSE I SEE--NEW ENGLANDLY--	THE ROBIN'S MY CRITERION	285	15
BECAUSE--WHEN NEXT IT BURNS ABROAD	THE DOOMED--REGARD THE	294	3
BECAUSE IT'S MUSIC STIRS THE AXE	THE DOOMED--REGARD THE	294	7
BECAUSE IT WAS A CHILD, YOU KNOW--	ONE YEAR AGO--JOTS WHAT?	296	30
BECAUSE ESTATES CAN BE	TO LOSE ONE'S FAITH--	377	3
BECAUSE WE LOVE THE WOUND	REHEARSAL TO OURSELVES	379	6
BECAUSE HE--NEVER TOLD--	A HOUSE UPON THE HIGHT--	399	12
BECAUSE THERE WAS A WINTER--ONCE--	THE WINTERS ARE SO SHORT	403	11
BECAUSE IT'S SUNDAY--ALL THE TIME--	I NEVER FELT AT HOME--	413	5
BECAUSE SHE BREATHED AGAINST	FORGET! THE LADY WITH	438	3
BECAUSE THE CAUSE WAS MINE--	LIKE EYES THAT LOOKED ON	458	10
BECAUSE THERE IS'NT ROOM--	WE DO NOT PLAY ON GRAVES	467	2
I AM ALIVE--BECAUSE	I AM ALIVE--I GUESS--	470	9
I AM ALIVE--BECAUSE	I AM ALIVE--I GUESS--	470	17
BECAUSE ESCAPE--IS DONE--	DOOM IS THE HOUSE	475	4
BECAUSE	I HAD NO TIME TO HATE--	478	2
BECAUSE--	"WHY DO I LOVE" YOU, SIR	480	2
BECAUSE HE KNOWS--AND	"WHY DO I LOVE" YOU, SIR	480	6
BECAUSE HE KNOWS IT CANNOT SPEAK--	"WHY DO I LOVE" YOU, SIR	480	13
BECAUSE HE'S SUNRISE--AND I SEE--	"WHY DO I LOVE" YOU, SIR	480	18
BECAUSE THE WINDS WOULD FIND IT OUT--	YOU CANNOT PUT A FIRE	530	7
MORE FAIR--BECAUSE IMPOSSIBLE	DELIGHT--BECOMES	572	3
BECAUSE THEY TOLD ME TO--	I PRAYED, AT FIRST, A	576	2
BECAUSE THEY LIKED ME "STILL"--	THEY SHUT ME UP IN PROSE	613	4
I ROSE--BECAUSE HE SANK--	I ROSE--BECAUSE HE SANK	616	1
BECAUSE YOUR FACE	I CANNOT LIVE WITH YOU--	640	22
BECAUSE YOU SATURATED SIGHT--	I CANNOT LIVE WITH YOU--	640	33
FOR EASE OF [FOR SIMPLE / BECAUSE OF] GIANTURE--	SIZE CIRCUMSCRIBES--IT	641	4
BECAUSE INTRINSIC SIZE	SIZE CIRCUMSCRIBES--IT	641	6
BECAUSE I COULD NOT STOP FOR DEATH--	BECAUSE I COULD NOT STOP	712	1
BUT HE--WAS LEFT [REMAINED] ALIVE BECAUSE	HE FOUGHT LIKE THOSE	759	11
BECAUSE 'TIS UNSUSTAINED	THE SERVICE WITHOUT HOPE	779	3
BECAUSE THEY LOOKED ON THEE BEFORE--	JOY TO HAVE MERITED THE	788	9
BECAUSE	UNCERTAIN LEASE--	857	6
BECAUSE THE BEE MAY BLAMELESS HUM	BECAUSE THE BEE MAY	869	1
BECAUSE THE FLOWERS UNAFRAID	BECAUSE THE BEE MAY	869	4
BECAUSE THE FOOD--EXTERMINATE--	HAD I NOT THIS, OR THIS,	904	11
BECAUSE I CANNOT SEE	I CANNOT BE ASHAMED	914	2
BECAUSE A HIGHT SO HIGH	I CANNOT BE ASHAMED	914	7
WE MISS HER, NOT BECAUSE WE SEE--	WE MISS HER, NOT BECAUSE	993	1
BECAUSE I FOUND HER KINSMANLESS,	MY SEASON'S FURTHEST	1019	3
AND NOW I KNOW 'TWAS LIGHT, BECAUSE	I HEARD, AS IF I HAD NO	1039	7
BECAUSE 'TWAS RICHES I COULD OWN,	BECAUSE 'TWAS RICHES I	1093	1
BUT DID BECAUSE [VASTER THAT] THEY DIED	I NOTICED PEOPLE	1149	7
BECAUSE BY ACCIDENT	HOW MANY SCHEMES MAY DIE	1150	6
BECAUSE HE WAS DETAINED	HOW MANY SCHEMES MAY DIE	1150	V 6
BECAUSE BESIDE [BEFORE] THE DOOR	HOW MANY SCHEMES MAY DIE	1150	10
SURPASSES IT, WE KNOW, BECAUSE	THE LIFE WE HAVE IS VERY	1162	3
BECAUSE HE IS A LITTLE BOY	A LITTLE DOG THAT WAGS	1185	7
BECAUSE MY BROOK IS FLUENT	BECAUSE MY BROOK IS	1200	1
BECAUSE MY BROOK IS SILENT	BECAUSE MY BROOK IS	1200	3
I THINK, BECAUSE HIS EMPTY PLATE	A SPARROW TOOK A SLICE	1211	3
BECAUSE HE LOVES HER	BECAUSE HE LOVES HER	1229	1
BECAUSE THAT YOU ARE GOING	BECAUSE THAT YOU ARE	1260	1
BECAUSE THAT DEATH IS FINAL [TREASON / DIFFERENT],	BECAUSE THAT YOU ARE	1260	5
BECAUSE HE IS A "JEALOUS GOD"	BECAUSE THAT YOU ARE	1260	35
BECAUSE THAT FEARING IT SO LONG	WHILE WE WERE FEARING IT	1277	3
BECAUSE "GOD TOOK HIM" MENTION--[TELL US]	"WAS NOT" WAS ALL THE	1342	7
BECAUSE IN GOING IS A DRAMA	I'D RATHER RECOLLECT A	1349	5
BECAUSE [THAT WERT] A BARD TOO SOON--	TOUCH LIGHTLY NATURE'S	1389	4
WE SHUN BECAUSE WE PRIZE HER FACE	WE SHUN BECAUSE WE PRIZE	1429	1
BECAUSE HE HAS ABILITY--	THE DEVIL--HAD HE	1479	3
BECAUSE THAT JUNIOR FOLIAGE IS DISRESPECTFUL NOW	AN ANTIQUATED TREE	1514	3
BECAUSE HE TRAVELS FREELY	THE BUTTERFLY OBTAINS	1685	5
BECAUSE THE HAND IS GONE?	WHICH MISSES MOST,	1759	5
BECK			
BY BECK, OR BURN, OR MOOR!	I WOULD DISTIL A CUP,	16	4
BECKONED			
THE SATYRS FINGERS BECKONED--	THROUGH LANE IT LAY--	9	13
THAT BECKONED IT AWAY!	'TWAS SUCH A LITTLE--	107	4
BECKONING			
BECKONING--ETRUSCAN INVITATION--	UNTO LIKE STORY--TROUBLE	295	23
BECKONS			
SHE BECKONS, AND THE WOODS START--	BAFFLED FOR JUST A DAY	17	5
IT BECKONS, AND IT BAFFLES--	THIS WORLD IS NOT	501	5
A "THIS WAY" BECKONS SPACIOUSLY--	NO LIFE CAN POMPLESS	1626	7
BECLOUDED			
WITH BECLOUDED EYES!	IF THE FOOLISH, CALL	168	8
BECOME			
BECOME SO WONDROUS DEAR--	AS BY THE DEAD WE LOVE	88	2
AND OCCIDENT--BECOME UNKNOWN--	THE ONE WHO COULD REPEAT	307	8
THEN CLOUDIER BECOME--	I'VE SEEN A DYING EYE	547	4
PHANTASMS [FICTITIOUS] BOTH BECOME	ONE BLESSING HAD I THAN	756	10
TO WIN, BECOME THEIR [MY] TURN--	I PLAY AT RICHES--TO	801	20
WHO TILL THEY DIED, DID NOT ALIVE BECOME--	A DEATH BLOW IS A LIFE	816	2

	FIRST LINE	POEM	LINE
BECOME (CONTINUED)			
FOR THEE A BEE DO I BECOME	BECAUSE THE BEE MAY	869	2
SUPERFLUOUS BECOME--	THE BIRD MUST SING TO	880	8
IF OTHER FLOWER BECOME.	THIS IS A BLOSSOM OF THE	945	12
WHAT WILL BECOME OF ME?	WHAT SHALL I DO WHEN THE	956	8
BY DISTANCES BECOME--	HERE, WHERE THE DAISIES	1037	10
MORE INTIMATE WITH US BECOME	THE MURMURING OF BEES,	1115	15
BECOME, ALAS, MORE FAIR--	TO MAKE ROUTINE A	1196	8
SO INTIMATE HAVE WE BECOME	THE DISTANCE THAT THE	1742	7
BECOMES			
DELIGHT--BECOMES PICTORIAL--	DELIGHT--BECOMES	572	1
SO PLAUSIBLE [TANGIBLE / POSITIVE] BECOMES [APPEARS]	I THINK TO LIVE--MAY BE	646	22
A [GENTLE] PENSIVE CUSTOM IT BECOMES	FURTHER IN SUMMER THAN	1068	7
BECOMES THAT CHERISHED [MAGIC] FACE	AN ANTIQUATED GRACE	1345	2
AND WINTER INSTANTLY BECOMES	THE DANDELION'S PALLID	1519	3
BECOMETH			
IT ILL BECOMETH ME--	I TEND MY FLOWERS FOR	339	23
ILL IT BECOMETH [IS IT BECOMING] ME TO DWELL SO WEALTHILY	TAKE ALL AWAY FROM ME,	1640	3
BECOMING			
WISDOM IS MORE BECOMING VIEWED	I WORKED FOR CHAFF AND	1269	7
WE TRY TO SHOW BECOMING FIRMNESS [CALMNESS]--	MARCH IS THE MONTH OF	1404	5
ILL IT BECOMETH [IS IT BECOMING] ME TO DWELL SO WEALTHILY	TAKE ALL AWAY FROM ME,	1640	3
BED			
PRAY LEAD ME TO HIS BED!	SEXTON! MY MASTER'S	96	2
I SOW SWEET FLOWER FROM GARDEN BED--	WHERE I HAVE LOST, I	104	2
STILL CHAFES IT'S NARROW BED--	A SOMETHING IN A	122	15
ANOTHER BED--A SHORT ONE--	'TWAS THE OLD--ROAD--	344	17
HER BED--A FUNNELED STONE--	I WENT TO THANK HER--	363	3
OF ROBINS IN THE TRUNDLE BED	A MURMUR IN THE TREES--	416	13
SO BRAVE--UPON IT'S LITTLE BED	WHY MAKE IT DOUBT--IT	462	4
AND WHEN I SOUGHT MY BED--	BEREAVED OF ALL, I WENT	784	6
AMPLE MAKE THIS BED--	AMPLE MAKE THIS BED--	829	1
MAKE THIS BED WITH AWE--	AMPLE MAKE THIS BED--	829	2
A REMOTER BED?	GRATITUDE--IS NOT THE	989	8
HOW GOOD HIS LAVA BED,	HOW GOOD HIS LAVA BED,	1447	1
FOR IS IT NOT HIS BED--	THE DITCH IS DEAR TO THE	1645	2
HER FACE WAS IN A BED OF HAIR,	HER FACE WAS IN A BED OF	1722	1
AS HAPPY IN HER CRIB [BED] OF DUST	THIS DOCILE ONE INTER	1752 V	7
BEDECKED			
BEDECKED WITH THEE	PINK--SMALL--AND	1332	10
BEDS			
WHOSE ARE THE LITTLE BEDS, I ASKED	WHOSE ARE THE LITTLE	142	1
WHOSE ARE THE BEDS--THE TINY BEDS	WHOSE ARE THE LITTLE	142	7
WHOSE ARE THE BEDS--THE TINY BEDS	WHOSE ARE THE LITTLE	142	7
WATER MAKES MANY BEDS	WATER MAKES MANY BEDS	1428	1
BEDTIME			
THEIR BEDTIME 'TIS, SHE SAID--	WHOSE ARE THE LITTLE	142	26
BEE SEE BUMBLE/BEE			
THE BEE DOTH COURT THE FLOWER, THE FLOWER HIS SUIT RECEIVES,	AWAKE YE MUSES NINE,	1	13
I HEAR THE BRIGHT BEE HUM;	THERE IS ANOTHER SKY,	2	12
"HOW DOTH THE BUSY BEE,"	"SIC TRANSIT GLORIA	3	2
AS BUMBLE BEE OF JUNE.	ONE SISTER HAVE I IN OUR	14	12
AN AGED BEE ADDRESSED US--	THE GENTIAN WEAVES HER	18	11
IN THE NAME OF THE BEE--	THE GENTIAN WEAVES HER	18	17
A FLASK OF DEW--A BEE OR TWO--	A SEPAL, PETAL, AND A	19	3
BEFORE THE BREATHLESS BEE--	DISTRUSTFUL OF THE	20	10
ONLY A BEE WILL MISS IT--	NOBODY KNOWS THIS LITTLE	35	5
AND AVOID IT'S BEE,	WHEN I COUNT THE SEEDS	40	10
BY EVERY SAINTED BEE--	I KEEP MY PLEDGE.	46	6
TO BREAK IT TO THE BEE--	I HAV'NT TOLD MY GARDEN	50	4
BARBS HAS IT, LIKE A BEE!	MY FRIEND MUST BE A BIRD	92	5
THE BEE IS NOT AFRAID OF ME.	THE BEE IS NOT AFRAID OF	111	1
HOW MANY CUPS THE BEE PARTAKES,	BRING ME THE SUNSET IN A	128	11
OH FRAUD THAT CANNOT CHEAT THE BEE--	THESE ARE THE DAYS WHEN	130	7
EXCEPT TO SOME WIDE-WANDERING BEE	EXCEPT TO HEAVEN, SHE IS	154	3
THE MURMUR [BUMBLE] OF A BEE	THE MURMUR OF A BEE	155	1
IF THE COWARD BUMBLE BEE	I'M THE LITTLE "HEART'S	176	5
I STOLE THEM FROM A BEE--	I STOLE THEM FROM A BEE	200	1
THE FLOWER MUST NOT BLAME THE BEE--	THE FLOWER MUST NOT	206	1
AS THE FAINTING BEE--	COME SLOWLY--EDEN!	211	4
TO THE LOVER BEE	DID THE HAREBELL LOOSE	213	2
WOULD THE BEE THE HAREBELL HALLOW	DID THE HAREBELL LOOSE	213	3
WHEN "LANDLORDS" TURN THE DRUNKEN BEE	I TASTE A LIQUOR NEVER	214	9
BABBLES THE BEE IN A STOLID EAR,	SAFE IN THEIR ALABASTER	216	9
WE--BEE AND I--LIVE BY THE QUAFFING--	WE--BEE AND I--LIVE BY	230	1
BEE--PLEDGES HIS--IN MINUTE FLAGONS--	WE--BEE AND I--LIVE BY	230	10
IT'S LIKE THE BEE--	IT'S LIKE THE LIGHT--	297	3
LIKE THE JUNE BEE--BEFORE THE SCHOOL BOY,	THE NEAREST DREAM	319	3
AH, THE BEE FLIES NOT	THE NEAREST DREAM	319	12
AND NOTWITHSTANDING BEE--THAT WORKED--	FROM COCOON FORTH A	354	18
OR ALL DAY, CHASE THE BEE--	ALTHOUGH I PUT AWAY HIS	366	21
AND BUT FOR THE BEE--	I'M SAYING EVERY DAY	373	23
HER PROGRESS--BY THE BEE--PROCLAIMED--	THERE IS A FLOWER THAT	380	27
WHERE IS THE BEE--	ANSWER JULY--	386	2
DENY! DID ROSE HER BEE--	FORGET! THE LADY WITH	438	5
THE BEE--IN MAUSOLEUM LAID--	FORGET! THE LADY WITH	438	10

	FIRST LINE	POEM	LINE
BEE (CONTINUED)			
WERT THOU A BUMBLE BEE--	COULD--I DO MORE--FOR	447	2
AND ABROGATE--MY BEE--	I ENVY SEAS, WHEREON HE	498	22
IT GOADS ME, LIKE THE GOBLIN BEE--	IF YOU WERE COMING IN	511	19
AS DO THE BEE--DELIRIOUS BORNE--	THE SOUL HAS BANDAGED	512	15
THE JULEP--OF THE BEE--	SHE HIDETH HER THE LAST	557	12
AS THE MINUTEST BEE	TO INTERRUPT HIS YELLOW	591	14
ARE NOTHING TO THE BEE--	IT MAKES NO DIFFERENCE	620	10
ACCESSIBLE TO THILL OF BEE--	A LITTLE ROAD--NOT MADE	647	3
AS DOTH THE MEADOW BEE	COULD I BUT RIDE	661	2
I SAID "BUT JUST TO BE A BEE"	COULD I BUT RIDE	661	13
SQUIRREL--ECLIPSE--THE BUMBLE BEE--	"NATURE" IS WHAT WE SEE	668	3
LEAST BEE THAT BREW--	LEAST BEE THAT BREW--	676	1
ELATE--A BEE--	'TWOULD EASE--A	682	2
CONFRONTS THE DAZZLED BEE.	PRECIOUS TO ME--SHE	727	14
IS WORTHLESS--TO THE BEE--	THERE IS AN ARID	782	8
REPELS THE HEALTHY BEE--	THERE IS AN ARID	782	V 8
BE RENDERED BY THE BEE--	APOLOGY FOR HER	852	2
BECAUSE THE BEE MAY BLAMELESS HUM	BECAUSE THE BEE MAY	869	1
FOR THEE A BEE DO I BECOME	BECAUSE THE BEE MAY	869	2
THAT BEE TO RIDE, OR FLOWER OF FURZE	BECAUSE THE BEE MAY	869	11
A TRAITOR IS THE BEE	OF SILKEN SPEECH AND	896	2
CROSS IT, AND OVERCOME THE BEE--	HEREIN A BLOSSOM LIES--	899	3
THE BEE--HAST THOU FORGOT?	'TIS SUNRISE--LITTLE	908	8
WHEN THE BEE HANGS ALL NOON IN THE BUTTERCUP	WHAT SHALL I DO WHEN THE	956	7
AS CRICKET OR AS BEE--	SHE SPED AS PETALS OF A	991	6
PARTAKE AS DOTH THE BEE,	PARTAKE AS DOTH THE BEE,	994	1
BEE! I'M EXPECTING YOU!	BEE! I'M EXPECTING YOU!	1035	1
AS, TILL THE BEE	SPRING COMES ON THE	1042	4
ESCAPE THE PROWLING BEE	BLOOM--IS RESULT--TO	1058	12
TO BEGGAR AND TO BEE	THESE ARE THE SIGNS TO	1077	8
THE BEE HAD PERISHED FROM THE SCENE	THE CRICKETS SANG	1104	V
THE BIRD DID PRANCE--THE BEE [BIRD] DID PLAY--	THE BIRD DID PRANCE--THE	1107	1
A DINNER FOR A BEE	A FULL FED ROSE ON MEALS	1154	2
FOR HELMSMAN [STEERSMAN] WAS THE BEE	A SOFT SEA WASHED AROUND	1198	6
I HEAR THE LEVEL BEE--	LIKE TRAINS OF CARS ON	1224	2
ARE FITTING FOR THE BEE,	WHAT TENEMENTS OF CLOVER	1338	2
A BEE HIS BURNISHED CARRIAGE	A BEE HIS BURNISHED	1339	1
WAS ALL THAT SAVED [ALONE SUSTAINED-- / ALONE UPHELD--] A BEE	A SINGLE CLOVER PLANK	1343	2
A BEE I PERSONALLY KNEW	A SINGLE CLOVER PLANK	1343	3
AND BUMBLE BEE WAS NOT--	A SINGLE CLOVER PLANK	1343	12
AND THE BEE BE BOOMING.	I SUPPOSE THE TIME WILL	1381	4
THOSE CATTLE SMALLER THAN A BEE	THOSE CATTLE SMALLER	1388	1
EXHILIRATE THE BEE,	HIS ORIENTAL HERESIES	1526	2
DOES NOT CONCERN THE BEE,	THE PEDIGREE OF HONEY	1627	2
CONSULTS THE BUMBLE BEE--	A DRUNKARD CANNOT MEET A	1628	12
TO MAKE A PRAIRIE IT TAKES A CLOVER AND ONE BEE,	TO MAKE A PRAIRIE IT	1755	1
ONE CLOVER, AND A BEE,	TO MAKE A PRAIRIE IT	1755	2
FAME IS A BEE.	FAME IS A BEE.	1763	1
BEEN			
WHERE NOT A FROST HAS BEEN;	THERE IS ANOTHER SKY,	2	10
A PACE HAD BEEN BETWEEN--	I NEVER TOLD THE BURIED	11	7
MY LIFE HAD FORFEIT BEEN.	I NEVER TOLD THE BURIED	11	9
IF SHE HAD BEEN THE MISTLETOE	IF SHE HAD BEEN THE	44	1
AND I HAD BEEN THE ROSE--	IF SHE HAD BEEN THE	44	2
I HAVE BEEN CALLED AWAY--	IF I SHOULD CEASE TO	56	4
IT MIGHT--HAVE BEEN THE LIGHT HOUSE SPARK--	GOOD NIGHT! WHICH PUT	259	7
IT MIGHT--HAVE BEEN THE WANING LAMP	GOOD NIGHT! WHICH PUT	259	10
A GIANT--EYE TO EYE WITH YOU, HAD BEEN--	ONE YEAR AGO--JOTS WHAT?	296	23
AND WHEN THE WRECK HAS BEEN--	THE DIFFERENCE BETWEEN	305	4
WHEN ORIENT HAVE BEEN OUTGROWN--	THE ONE WHO COULD REPEAT	307	7
DENYING THEY HAVE BEEN--	IT SIFTS FROM LEADEN	311	20
I SHOULD HAVE BEEN TOO GLAD, I SEE--	I SHOULD HAVE BEEN TOO	313	1
I SHOULD HAVE BEEN TOO SAVED--I SEE--	I SHOULD HAVE BEEN TOO	313	7
EARTH WOULD HAVE BEEN TOO MUCH--I SEE--	I SHOULD HAVE BEEN TOO	313	13
THEN HE HAS BEEN WITH THE MOWERS--	THE WIND DID'NT COME	316	13
"THAT MUST HAVE BEEN THE SUN"!	I'LL TELL YOU HOW THE	318	8
THIS MIGHT HAVE BEEN THE HAND	ALTHOUGH I PUT AWAY HIS	366	4
THERE'S BEEN A DEATH, IN THE OPPOSITE HOUSE,	THERE'S BEEN A DEATH, IN	389	1
IS AS IT HAD NOT BEEN--	A VISITOR IN MARL--	391	12
SO TERRIBLE--HAD BEEN ENDURED--	THE FIRST DAY'S NIGHT	410	3
MANY A BITTERNESS--HAD BEEN--	IT WOULD NEVER BE COMMON	430	3
AND IF IT HAD NOT BEEN SO FAR--	I WAS THE SLIGHTEST IN	486	14
THE LOSS HAD BEEN TO ME	HAD I PRESUMED TO HOPE--	522	2
I HAD BEEN HUNGRY, ALL THE YEARS--	I HAD BEEN HUNGRY, ALL	579	1
AND SO AND SO--HAD BEEN TO US [ME],	I CRIED AT PITY--NOT AT	588	15
I YEARS HAD BEEN FROM HOME	I YEARS HAD BEEN FROM	609	1
HAD BEEN LEGIBLE--TO ME--	TO KNOW JUST HOW HE	622	15
WHO TO HAVE HAD IT, WOULD HAVE BEEN	MY PORTION IS DEFEAT--	639	18
HAD ALL MY LIFE BUT BEEN [BEEN ONE / BEEN BLEAK] MISTAKE	I THINK TO LIVE--MAY BE	646	27
HAD ALL MY LIFE BUT BEEN [BEEN ONE / BEEN BLEAK] MISTAKE	I THINK TO LIVE--MAY BE	646	27
HAD ALL MY LIFE BUT BEEN [BEEN ONE / BEEN BLEAK] MISTAKE	I THINK TO LIVE--MAY BE	646	27
HAD I NOT BEEN	PROMISE THIS--WHEN YOU	648	32
THE OTHER'S ONE [FOOT]--HAD BEEN--	AGAIN--HIS VOICE IS AT	663	17
WHAT HATH MINGLED--BEEN--	A FIRST MUTE COMING--	702	6

	FIRST LINE	POEM	LINE
BEEN (CONTINUED)			
NO TUMULT THERE HAD BEEN	THE BIRDS BEGUN AT FOUR	783	18
AS ALL MY STRATEGEM HAD BEEN	SEVERER SERVICE OF	786	19
AND BEEN MYSELF THAT EASY [DISTANT] THING	I PLAY AT RICHES--TO	801	7
HAD THERE BEEN NO SHARP SUBTRACTION	ONE DAY IS THERE OF THE	814	9
HAD WE DIVINER BEEN--	NOT WHAT WE DID, SHALL	823	4
WHOM NOT TO KNOW HAS BEEN	HOW WELL I KNEW HER NOT	837	2
ON THE RIVERS BEEN--	TWICE HAD SUMMER HER	846	4
THOSE WHO HAVE BEEN IN THE GRAVE THE LONGEST--	THOSE WHO HAVE BEEN IN	922	1
HOW IGNORANT I HAD BEEN	I LEARNED--AT LEAST--	944	2
FOR EVIDENCE 'T HAS BEEN--	AS ONE DOES SICKNESS	957	12
THE SECOND HAD NOT BEEN.	THE FIRST WE KNEW OF HIM	1006	4
HAD IT BEEN MINE, TO PRINT!	ENDED, ERE IT BEGUN--	1088	5
HAD IT BEEN YOUR'S, TO READ!	ENDED, ERE IT BEGUN--	1088	6
TILL WHAT WE SPECULATE, HAS BEEN	THE MURMURING OF BEES,	1115	13
. . . [NAME HAS BEEN]	THE MURMURING OF BEES,	1115	V 13
BUT WHEN ALL SPACE HAS BEEN BEHELD	THE LIFE WE HAVE IS VERY	1162	5
THAT SUCH A BLISS HAS BEEN.	OF SO DIVINE A LOSS	1179	4
IT HAD BEEN HEAVEN BELOW.	IMMORTAL IS AN AMPLE	1205	8
WHEN IT HAS ALSO BEEN--	MY TRIUMPH LASTED TILL	1227	10
HAD LOVE AS PUNCTUAL BEEN	IT CAME AT LAST BUT	1230	6
HAD THIS ONE DAY NOT BEEN,	HAD THIS ONE DAY NOT	1253	1
THAN THEY HAVE BEEN DESCRIBED.	WHO WERE "THE FATHER AND	1258	8
WE BETTER FRIENDS HAD BEEN, PERHAPS,	WHO WERE "THE FATHER AND	1258	15
THE "LIFE THAT IS" WILL THEN HAVE BEEN	BECAUSE THAT YOU ARE	1260	17
HAS NEVER BEEN EMPLOYED--	THE SPIDER AS AN ARTIST	1275	2
HAVE NEVER BEEN BEGUN--	THE THINGS WE THOUGHT	1293	4
MISTAKEN OFT HAS BEEN	DELIGHT'S DESPAIR AT	1299	6
OTHER COURTESIES HAVE BEEN--	RECOLLECT THE FACE OF ME	1305	5
HAS BEEN ASSUMED TO BE--	THE INFINITE A SUDDEN	1309	2
AFTER ALL BIRDS HAVE BEEN INVESTIGATED AND LAID ASIDE--	AFTER ALL BIRDS HAVE	1395	1
THE SAVIOR MUST HAVE BEEN	THE SAVIOR MUST HAVE	1487	1
IT MIGHT HAVE BEEN TO LIVE	TO SEE HER IS A PICTURE	1568	V
HAS HUMAN NATURE BEEN.	NO MAN SAW AWE, NOR TO	1733	4
BEE'S			
THE MOUNTAIN GORSE--THE BEE'S!	THE JUGGLER'S HAT HER	330	2
THAN A BEE'S ETERNITY--	'TWOULD EASE--A	682	8
OH, FOR A BEE'S EXPERIENCE	HIS FEET ARE SHOD WITH	916	7
ENTITLED TO A BUMBLE BEE'S	OF NATURE I SHALL HAVE	1220	3
THE BUMBLE BEE'S RELIGION	HIS LITTLE HEARSE LIKE	1522	T
BEES SEE BUMBLE-BEES			
THIS, AND MY HEART, AND ALL THE BEES	IT'S ALL I HAVE TO BRING	26	7
AND BEES AS BUSTLING GO--	IF I SHOULD DIE,	54	8
BARONIAL BEES--MARCH--ONE BY ONE--	SOME RAINBOW--COMING	64	11
SO DRUNKEN, REEL HER BEES--	WE SHOULD NOT MIND SO	81	6
UNTIL THE BEES, FROM CLOVER ROWS	PERHAPS YOU'D LIKE TO	134	7
BEES EXCLUSIVE COTERIE--	PIGMY SERAPHS--GONE	138	4
THE BUMBLE BEES WILL WAKE THEM	WHOSE ARE THE LITTLE	142	27
BEES--BY THE FURLONG--	WHAT WOULD I GIVE TO SEE	247	11
BAGS OF DOUBLOONS--ADVENTUROUS BEES	WHAT WOULD I GIVE TO SEE	247	18
HER BEES HAVE A FICTITIOUS [AN ILLUSIVE] HUM--	LIKE SOME OLD FASHIONED	302	9
AND BEES TO ENTERTAIN--	THE GRASS SO LITTLE HAS	333	4
AND BEES--PICK UP--	I TEND MY FLOWERS FOR	339	10
THE BEES--WILL NOT DESPISE THE TUNE--	IT WILL BE SUMMER--	342	11
I COULD NOT BEAR THE BEES SHOULD COME,	I DREADED THAT FIRST	348	17
THERE IS A FLOWER THAT BEES PREFER--	THERE IS A FLOWER THAT	380	1
OR BEES--THAT THOUGHT THE SUMMER'S NAME	LIKE FLOWERS, THAT HEARD	513	4
THE BEES--BECAME AS BUTTERFLIES--	I THINK I WAS ENCHANTED	593	9
GO BLOSSOM TO THE BEES--I SAID--	THE BIRDS REPORTED FROM	743	7
THIS BAUBLE WAS PREFERRED OF BEES--	THIS BAUBLE WAS	805	1
WHERE BLOOM AND BEES	THIS QUIET DUST WAS	813	6
WHAT BEES--FOR US--TO HUM--	I LEARNED--AT LEAST--	944	10
OR BEES, AT CHRISTMAS SHOW--	AS SLEIGH BELLS SEEM IN	981	2
THE MURMURING OF BEES, HAS CEASED	THE MURMURING OF BEES,	1115	1
BEES--TO THEIR LOAVES OF HONEY	HE IS ALIVE, THIS	1160	5
BEES ARE BLACK, WITH GILT SURCINGLES--	BEES ARE BLACK, WITH	1405	1
HOME FLEW THE LOADED BEES	THE SUN RETIRED TO A	1693	6
IF BEES ARE FEW.	TO MAKE A PRAIRIE IT	1755	5
AND BEES ABASHLESS PLAY,	WHERE EVERY BIRD IS BOLD	1758	2
BEETLE			
TO LET A BEETLE PASS--	A BIRD CAME DOWN THE	328	8
BEETLE AT THE CANDLE--	LIFE, AND DEATH, AND	706	4
BEETLE'S			
UNDER THE BEETLE'S CELLAR	UNDER THE LIGHT, YET	949	3
BEETLES			
WHOM NONE BUT DAISIES [BEETLES], KNOW.	OF BRONZE--AND BLAZE--	290	19
THESE ARE THE NIGHTS THAT BEETLES LOVE--	THESE ARE THE NIGHTS	1128	1
BEFALL			
NO DREARIER, CAN BEFALL!	'TIS SO MUCH JOY! 'TIS	172	12
REVERSE CANNOT BEFALL	REVERSE CANNOT BEFALL	395	1
AND WHOSO IT BEFALL	THERE IS ANOTHER	1116	6
BEFALLEN			
THAT HAS BEFALLEN HIM.	FROM HIS SLIM PALACE IN	1300	4
BEFALLING			
BEFALLING NOT MY SIMPLE DAYS--	REMOVED FROM ACCIDENT OF	424	3
BEFEL			
AS THESE THAT TWICE BEFEL.	MY LIFE CLOSED TWICE	1732	6
BEFITS			
A MODESTY BEFITS THE SOUL	THE WORLD--STANDS--	493	3

BEFORE	FIRST LINE	POEM	LINE
I NE'ER BEHELD BEFORE!	"SIC TRANSIT GLORIA	3	24
BEFORE THE BREATHLESS BEE--	DISTRUSTFUL OF THE	20	10
BEFORE THE ICE IS IN THE POOLS--	BEFORE THE ICE IS IN THE	37	1
BEFORE THE SKATERS GO,	BEFORE THE ICE IS IN THE	37	2
BEFORE THE FIELDS HAVE FINISHED,	BEFORE THE ICE IS IN THE	37	5
BEFORE THE CHRISTMAS TREE,	BEFORE THE ICE IS IN THE	37	6
BEFORE THE DOOR OF GOD!	I NEVER LOST AS MUCH BUT	49	4
BEFORE THEIR FEET ARE COLD.	SOME, TOO FRAGILE FOR	141	4
AND--WAKING--LONG BEFORE THE MORN--	MUSICIANS WRESTLE	157	4
THE NIGHT BEFORE THE CROWN!	A LITTLE BREAD--A CRUST	159	6
BEFORE THE SEAL!	JUST LOST, WHEN I WAS	160	11
MY HEART WOULD WISH IT BROKE BEFORE--	I SHOULD NOT DARE TO	205	13
BEFORE THE BLACKBIRDS SING!	IT CANT BE "SUMMER"!	221	5
IT WAS DARK--BEFORE--	IF HE DISSOLVE--THEN--	236	3
BEFORE MY SIMPLE BOSOM--BROKE--	I THINK JUST HOW MY	237	11
THEY SLINK BEFORE THE CLAY,	A SINGLE SCREW OF FLESH	263	18
FOR THAT WAS THINE, BEFORE--	DOUBT ME! MY DIM	275	10
BEFORE THE FIRE'S EYES--	DOUBT ME! MY DIM	275	21
THEN SPRANG BEFORE THE HILLS	THE DAY CAME SLOW--TILL	304	2
BEFORE THEY DROP FULL MUSIC ON--	HE FUMBLES AT YOUR SOUL	315	3
LIKE THE JUNE BEE--BEFORE THE SCHOOL BOY,	THE NEAREST DREAM	319	3
BEFORE I GOT MY EYE PUT OUT	BEFORE I GOT MY EYE PUT	327	1
AND YESTERDAY, OR CENTURIES BEFORE?	AFTER GREAT PAIN, A	341	4
DREAD, BUT THE WHIZZING, BEFORE THE BALL--	IF ANY SINK, ASSURE THAT	358	6
SURPASSES ALL THAT ROSE BEFORE--	THE MORNING AFTER WO--	364	3
FACTS CENTURIES BEFORE	A PRECIOUS--MOULDERING	371	20
BEFORE THE WORLD BE GREEN--	THERE IS A FLOWER THAT	380	14
AND JUST BEFORE THE SUN--	A VISITOR IN MARL--	391	6
HAS MINISTERED BEFORE HIM--	THERE IS A LANGUOR OF	396	15
WHEN THAT YOU MET IT WITH BEFORE--	THE COLOR OF THE GRAVE	411	23
BUT JUST BEFORE THE SNOWS	GOD MADE A LITTLE	442	4
BEFORE WE MAY OBTAIN?	IT FEELS A SHAME TO BE	444	12
ARRESTED IT--BEFORE--	THIS WAS A POET--IT IS	448	8
AND EVERY SIGN BEFORE THE PLACE	A TOOTH UPON OUR PEACE	459	7
SAVIOR [MASTER]--I'VE SEEN THE FACE--BEFORE!	A WIFE--AT DAYBREAK I	461	13
THE DAY THAT WAS BEFORE--	A NIGHT--THERE LAY THE	471	2
I HAD NOT HOPED--BEFORE--	EXCEPT THE HEAVEN HAD	472	4
BEFORE A BUILDER CAME--	MYSELF WAS FORMED--A	488	4
TELL HIM [HER]--NIGHT [DAY] FINISHED--BEFORE WE FINISHED--	GOING TO HIM! HAPPY	494	18
I WAS USED--TO THE BIRDS--BEFORE--	BETTER--THAN MUSIC! FOR	503	2
AND NOW, I'M DIFFERENT FROM BEFORE,	HE TOUCHED ME, SO I LIVE	506	7
BAPTIZED, BEFORE, WITHOUT THE CHOICE,	I'M CEDED--I'VE STOPPED	508	8
CONTENTED, KNOWN, BEFORE--	LIKE FLOWERS, THAT HEARD	513	12
SACRAMENT, SAINTS PARTOOK [INDORSED] BEFORE US--	TO PUT THIS WORLD DOWN,	527	12
BEFORE AN APPARITION	TRUST IN THE UNEXPECTED	555	11
AS IF BEFORE A CHILD	MY FIRST WELL DAY--SINCE	574	14
BEFORE ANOTHER NIGHT.	WE TALKED AS GIRLS DO--	586	16
COULD WASTE [MELT] THE SNOW BEFORE THEIR GATE--	WHAT CARE THE DEAD, FOR	592	11
PASS BACK AND FORTH, BEFORE MY BRAIN	WHEN I WAS SMALL, A	596	15
AND NOW BEFORE THE DOOR	I YEARS HAD BEEN FROM	609	2
I NEVER SAW BEFORE	I YEARS HAD BEEN FROM	609	4
I LINGERED WITH BEFORE--	I YEARS HAD BEEN FROM	609	10
AND [BUT] NEVER WINCED [SHOOK / QUAKED] BEFORE.	I YEARS HAD BEEN FROM	609	16
BEFORE--WERE CITIES--BUT BETWEEN--	OUR JOURNEY HAD ADVANCED	615	7
ETERNITY'S WHITE [COOL] FLAG--BEFORE [IN FRONT]--	OUR JOURNEY HAD ADVANCED	615	11
THE WIDTH OF LIFE--BEFORE IT SPREADS [RUNS]	AT LEISURE IS THE SOUL	618	3
BEFORE THE JUDGMENT SEAT OF GOD--	'TWAS A LONG PARTING--	625	3
NOT EXORCISED BEFORE--	THE WAY I READ A	636	12
BEFORE DECISION--STOOPED TO SPEECH--	I COULD SUFFICE FOR HIM,	643	11
FITTER FEET--OF HER [FOR THE FEET] BEFORE US--	HER SWEET TURN TO LEAVE	649	13
HOW WELL I KNEW THE LIGHT BEFORE--	THE SUN KEPT SETTING--	692	13
THAT I HAVE HAD BEFORE--	A THOUGHT WENT UP MY	701	2
I'VE MET THE THING BEFORE--	A THOUGHT WENT UP MY	701	10
WE PAUSED BEFORE A HOUSE THAT SEEMED	BECAUSE I COULD NOT STOP	712	17
BEFORE ME--IMMORTALITY--	BEHIND ME--DIPS ETERNITY	721	2
BEFORE THE WEST BEGIN--	BEHIND ME--DIPS ETERNITY	721	6
'TIS MIRACLE BEFORE ME--THEN--	BEHIND ME--DIPS ETERNITY	721	13
OR ANY [BEFORE THE] HARBOR BE--	I MANY TIMES THOUGHT	739	8
THAN LIFE--HAD DONE--BEFORE IT--	YOU TAUGHT ME WAITING	740	7
IT'S PAST--SET DOWN BEFORE THE SOUL	REMORSE--IS MEMORY--	744	5
NATURE HESITATE--BEFORE	WHEN I HOPED, I	768	23
AND PERISH FROM BEFORE ITSELF	THE LONELINESS ONE DARE	777	7
BECAUSE THEY LOOKED ON THEE BEFORE--	JOY TO HAVE MERITED THE	788	9
BEST GRIEF IS TONGUELESS--BEFORE HE'LL TELL--	GRIEF IS A MOUSE--	793	13
BEFORE HE COMES WE WEIGH THE TIME!	BEFORE HE COMES WE WEIGH	834	1
MY BURIAL--BEFORE	THIS CHASM, SWEET, UPON	858	18
BEFORE THE PERISHING!	EACH SECOND IS THE LAST	879	8
AS BIRDS BEFORE ACHIEVING	THESE TESTED OUR HORIZON	886	3
BEFORE MYSELF WAS BORN	WHO OCCUPIES THIS HOUSE?	892	17
WHAT WE SAW BEFORE--	THE ADMIRATIONS--AND	906	8
UNTO THE THOUGHT BEFORE--	I FELT A CLEAVING IN MY	937	6
BEFORE IT EXISTS [EXPRESS] IN FIRE.	A MAN MAY MAKE A REMARK	952	8
BEFORE WE FELT THE DARK--	WE MET AS SPARKS--	958	6
BEFORE THE COMING FLAIL--	MIDSUMMER, WAS IT, WHEN	962	6

	FIRST LINE	POEM		LINE
BEFORE (CONTINUED)				
UNTO THE DISK BEFORE--	THE DUST BEHIND I STROVE	992		2
OR IF IT BE--BEFORE--	THIS WAS IN THE WHITE OF	995		6
BEFORE THIS MORTAL NOISE	IT WAS A QUIET WAY--	1053		6
ETERNITY IT WAS BEFORE	IT WAS A QUIET WAY--	1053		15
DEPART, BEFORE THE HOST HAVE SLID	THE SOUL SHOULD ALWAYS	1055		5
IT WAS--BEFORE--	WE LEARN IN THE	1083		8
WE PAUSE BEFORE A FURTHER PLUNGE	WHAT TWIGS WE HELD BY--	1086		4
THINGS OVERLOOKED BEFORE	THE LAST NIGHT THAT SHE	1100		6
MANY OWNED BEFORE--	PARADISE IS THAT OLD	1119		2
LIKE WORMS BENEATH [BEFORE] THE POWER--	THE WIND TOOK UP THE	1134	V	8
BECAUSE BESIDE [BEFORE] THE DOOR	HOW MANY SCHEMES MAY DIE	1150		10
ITSELF, ADORED BEFORE	A FULL FED ROSE ON MEALS	1154		6
I THE DAY BEFORE	ON THE WORLD YOU COLORED	1171		6
IT CHERISHES BEFORE.	HAD THIS ONE DAY NOT	1253		8
BEFORE IT SEE THE SUN!	LONGING IS LIKE THE SEED	1255		8
THIS IS THE PLACE THEY HOPED BEFORE,	THIS IS THE PLACE THEY	1264		1
BEFORE THEM LIES ESCAPELESS SEA--	THIS IS THE PLACE THEY	1264		7
I HOPED [LOOKED] FOR YOU BEFORE--	DEAR MARCH--COME IN--	1320		3
POSSESSED [ABHORRED / WE OWNED] BEFORE--	DREAMS ARE THE SUBTLE	1376		6
BEFORE IT'S EMBLEM FLEW--	SHE LAID HER DOCILE	1396		8
BEFORE THE QUICK [RIPE / PEAL / DRUM / DRUMS / BELLS / BOMB / . . .	ONE JOY OF SO MUCH	1420		6
AND SPACIOUS AS BEFORE--	TO MEND EACH TATTERED	1442		8
BEFORE YOU THOUGHT OF SPRING	BEFORE YOU THOUGHT OF	1465		1
BEFORE IDENTITY WAS CREASED [LEASED].	ESTRANGED FROM BEAUTY--	1474		4
AND STOOD AMAZED BEFORE THE CHANGE [BOON / MORNS]	THE THRILL CAME SLOWLY	1495		7
AND STOOD BEFORE THE SUDDENNESS	THE THRILL CAME SLOWLY	1495	V	7
AS WHEN YOU CAME BEFORE	THE PILE OF YEARS IS NOT	1507		2
ANOTHER MASSACRE BEFORE	'TIS SEASONS SINCE THE	1529		5
AND IF THOU LIVE BEFORE THOU WAKE--	NOW I LAY THEE DOWN TO	1539		3
I GROPED FOR HIM BEFORE I KNEW	I GROPED FOR HIM BEFORE	1555		1
BEFORE IT WAS IMPERATIVE	LIVES HE IN ANY OTHER	1557		3
BEFORE IT CAN FORGET	TO BE FORGOT BY THEE	1560	V	11
BEFORE MY MIND WAS SOWN,	THE SPIRIT LASTS--BUT IN	1576		22
BEFORE MY BEAM WAS SOWN,	EXPANSE CANNOT BE LOST--	1584		6
BEFORE MY MIND [SOUL / BEAM] WAS BORN	THIS ME--THAT WALKS AND	1588		6
BEFORE A FENCE WITHOUT A FARE	UPON HIS SADDLE SPRUNG A	1600		3
BEFORE THOU DOST EXUDE [DISSOLVE] AWAY	STILL OWN THEE--STILL	1633		7
DISPLAYED [PASS SLOW] BEFORE THE SIMPLEST [HUMBLEST] DOOR	SOME ONE PREPARED THIS	1644		4
BEFORE HE MAKES THE BEND	I DID NOT REACH THEE	1664		22
WHETHER SHE DIED BEFORE SHE HEARD	I WATCHED HER FACE TO	1667		3
IN FEATURE AS THE WORM BEFORE	IN WINTER IN MY ROOM	1670		16
MY LIFE CLOSED TWICE BEFORE ITS CLOSE;	MY LIFE CLOSED TWICE	1732		1
THE FOREIGNER BEFORE HE KNOCKS	WHERE EVERY BIRD IS BOLD	1758		3
THAT WAS TOO FAIR BEFORE--	WERE NATURE MORTAL LADY	1762		10
BEFRIEND				
BEFRIEND THEM, LEST YOURSELF IN HEAVEN	THESE STRANGERS, IN A	1096		3
BEG				
AND BEG ME PUT IT ON--	THE FACE I CARRY WITH ME	336		12
YOU BEG HIM NOT TO GO--	A PRECIOUS--MOULDERING	371		26
YOU BEG THE ROBIN IN YOUR BRAIN	YOU'LL KNOW HER--BY HER	634		27
IT CAME HIS TURN TO BEG--	IT CAME HIS TURN TO BEG	1500		1
NOR BEG, WITH DOMAINS IN MY POCKET--	LET ME NOT THIRST WITH	1772		2
BEGAN				
THEN SPACE--BEGAN TO TOLL,	I FELT A FUNERAL, IN MY	280		12
SUCH A PRAISE BEGAN	MOST SHE TOUCHED ME BY	760		14
TO CRAWL THE FROST BEGUN [BEGAN]--	THE FROST OF DEATH WAS	1136		8
AND THEN OUR WRATH BEGUN [BEGAN]--	THE FROST OF DEATH WAS	1136		15
BUT WHEN THE EARTH BEGAN TO JAR	IT WAS A QUIET SEEMING	1419		7
BEGET				
BEGET A FORCE	THE LASSITUDES OF	1592		2
BEGETS				
AND PRESENTS [BEGETS] HER SPOT--	WE LIKE MARCH.	1213		7
BEGETS AN AWE	PERIL AS A POSSESSION	1678		5
BEGGAR				
TWICE HAVE I STOOD A BEGGAR	I NEVER LOST AS MUCH BUT	49		3
TALK WITH PRUDENCE TO A BEGGAR	TALK WITH PRUDENCE TO A	119		1
THAT BEGGAR, WHEN AN HONORED GUEST,	AS WATCHERS HANG UPON	121		10
A BEGGAR--HERE AND THERE--	SOME--WORK FOR	406		9
OF BEGGAR--OR OF BIRD--	OF BRUSSELS--IT WAS NOT	602		8
THE BEGGAR LAD--DIES EARLY--	THE BEGGAR LAD--DIES	717		1
SANK THIS [THE] BEGGAR FROM THE SKY--	MOST SHE TOUCHED ME BY	760		10
'TWAS THE WINGED BEGGAR--	MOST SHE TOUCHED ME BY	760		17
TO BEGGAR AND TO BEE	THESE ARE THE SIGNS TO	1077		8
THE BEGGAR AT THE DOOR FOR FAME	THE BEGGAR AT THE DOOR	1240		1
THE BEGGAR AND HIS QUEEN	NOT ANY HIGHER STANDS	1256		6
FOR BEGGAR OR FOR CAT.	THE BONE THAT HAS NO	1274		4
THAT NOT A BEGGAR WOULD ACCEPT	THAT SHORT--POTENTIAL	1307		7
WHEN A LOVER IS A BEGGAR	WHEN A LOVER IS A BEGGAR	1314		1
WHAT HE BEGGED IS THEN THE BEGGAR--	WHEN A LOVER IS A BEGGAR	1314		5
I WATCHED THE PRECIOUS [SUBTLE] BEGGAR	I SAW THE WIND WITHIN	1502	V	
FROM SUCH A GIANT [BEGGAR] WERE WITHHELD	LOVE CAN DO ALL BUT	1731		3
BEGGARED				
MYSELF--WAS BEGGARED--TOO--	IT WOULD NEVER BE COMMON	430		24
BEGGAR'S				
THAT, WEARY OF THIS BEGGAR'S FACE--	IF I COULD BRIBE THEM BY	179		17
FOR THE CONTENTED--BEGGAR'S FACE	I GAINED IT SO--	359		14

	FIRST LINE	POEM	LINE
BEGGAR'S (CONTINUED)			
HAPPY IT BE FOR YOU--A BEGGAR'S--	SWEET--YOU FORGOT--BUT I	523	7
BEGGARS			
AS BEGGARS REVEL AT A FEAST	AS WATCHERS HANG UPON	121	2
TO MISS IT--BEGGARS SO--	YOUR RICHES--TAUGHT ME--	299	16
'TIS BEGGARS--BANQUETS BEST [CAN] DEFINE--	I SHOULD HAVE BEEN TOO	313	22
FOR DEEMING--BEGGARS--PLAY--	'TIS OPPOSITES--ENTICE--	355	8
BEGGARY			
AND BEING'S--BEGGARY--	TO LOSE ONE'S FAITH--	377	8
BEGGED			
THE ANGEL BEGGED PERMISSION	A LITTLE EAST OF JORDAN,	59	7
BEGGED IN THE MARKET PLACE--	I'M SAYING EVERY DAY	373	8
AND YOU--GOT SLEEPY--AND BEGGED TO BE ENDED--	GOING TO HIM! HAPPY	494	20
WHAT HE BEGGED IS THEN THE BEGGAR--	WHEN A LOVER IS A BEGGAR	1314	5
BEGGING			
WITH EYES IN DEATH--STILL BEGGING RAISED--	TWO SWIMMERS WRESTLED ON	201	8
MERCY [POWER] OF THE ALMIGHTY BEGGING [ASKING]--	TELL AS A MARKSMAN--WERE	1152	22
THE BEGGING FOR THE LIFE	IT CAME HIS TURN TO BEG	1500	2
THERE COMES AN HOUR WHEN BEGGING STOPS,	THERE COMES AN HOUR WHEN	1751	1
BEGIN			
SHE NODS, AND ALL BEGIN--	BAFFLED FOR JUST A DAY	17	6
THAT I MAY STRAIGHT BEGIN!	HEART! WE WILL FORGET	47	6
SO I BEGIN TO RANSACK!	I CAUTIOUS, SCANNED MY	178	17
WHO WERE SUFFICIENT TO [COULD BEGIN ON--] MISERY?	BOUND--A TROUBLE--	269	V
OR DID IT JUST BEGIN--	I MEASURE EVERY GRIEF I	561	6
HOW WOULD YOUR OWN--BEGIN?	I FOUND THE WORDS TO	581	6
BEGIN, AND LEAVE THEE OUT--	EMPTY MY HEART, OF THEE	587	3
AND NOT BEGIN--AGAIN--	IT WOULD HAVE STARVED A	612	16
I'LL BEGIN TO SOW	DONT PUT UP MY THREAD &	617	2
WHEN THE BIRDS BEGIN TO WHISTLE--	DONT PUT UP MY THREAD &	617	3
MY PERIOD BEGIN	SHELLS FROM THE COAST	693	8
BEFORE THE WEST BEGIN--	BEHIND ME--DIPS ETERNITY	721	6
THOSE WHO BEGIN TODAY--	THOSE WHO HAVE BEEN IN	922	2
FOR WHEN THE FROSTS BEGIN	THE PRODUCTS OF MY FARM	1025	6
WHEN THEY BEGIN, IF ROBINS MAY,	WHEN THEY COME BACK--IF	1080	5
BEGIN TO PERISH NOW.	I SHOULD NOT DARE TO BE	1197	8
AT DAY BREAK TO BEGIN HIS RACE	HE WENT BY SLEEP THAT	1662	3
BEGINNING			
BEGINNING WITH THE DAY	A TONGUE--TO TELL HIM I	400	10
BEGINNING ONCE IN JUNE--	SUMMER HAS TWO	1422	2
BEGINNING IN OCTOBER	SUMMER HAS TWO	1422	3
BEGINNING NOT TO OWN--	IT STOLE ALONG SO	1457	4
BEGINNINGS			
SUMMER HAS TWO BEGINNINGS--	SUMMER HAS TWO	1422	1
BEGINS			
WHEN BELLS STOP RINGING--CHURCH--BEGINS--	WHEN BELLS STOP RINGING	633	1
THE PENDULUM BEGINS TO COUNT--	I THINK THE LONGEST HOUR	635	9
THE HEART BEGINS TO CROWD--	I THINK THE LONGEST HOUR	635	12
BEGINS TO LIVE	A WORD IS DEAD	1212	5
SUMMER BEGINS TO HAVE THE LOOK	SUMMER BEGINS TO HAVE	1682	1
AUTUMN BEGINS TO BE INFERRED	SUMMER BEGINS TO HAVE	1682	5
THE EYE BEGINS IT'S AVARICE	SUMMER BEGINS TO HAVE	1682	9
BEGONE			
BEGONE--MY TOOTH HAS GROWN--	ART THOU THE THING I	1282	2
BEGS			
IT BEGS YOU GIVE IT WORK--	AT LEISURE IS THE SOUL	618	5
OF MINOR FABRICS [SYSTEMS] BEGS	A WORLD MADE PENNINILESS	1623	2
BEGUILE			
LIBERTY'S BEGUILE [FORESTALL]"	WOLFE DEMANDED DURING	678	8
BEGUILE IT MORE AND MORE--	WE SHUN IT ERE IT COMES,	1580	5
BEGUILED			
BEGUILED OF IMMORTALITY	HOW DARE THE ROBINS SING	1724	11
BEGUILES			
HEAVEN BEGUILES THE TIRED.	AS WATCHERS HANG UPON	121	6
BEGUILES THE CENTURIES OF WAY!	THO' I GET HOME HOW LATE	207	13
BEGUILING			
BEGUILING THUS THE WONDER	WENT UP A YEAR THIS	93	17
BEGUN			
THE BOBOLINKS--BEGUN--	I'LL TELL YOU HOW THE	318	6
THAT NIGHT--BEGUN--	A TONGUE--TO TELL HIM I	400	11
MY BOND--HAVE JUST BEGUN--	A TONGUE--TO TELL HIM I	400	25
THE PHEBES HAVE BEGUN--	THE WINTERS ARE SO SHORT	403	6
MY BRAIN--BEGUN TO LAUGH--	THE FIRST DAY'S NIGHT	410	13
DIFFERENCE--HAD BEGUN--	IT WOULD NEVER BE COMMON	430	2
WHOSE OWN--HAS JUST BEGUN--	NO MAN CAN COMPASS A	477	10
THE BODILESS--BEGUN--	DEPARTED--TO THE	524	6
WHEN ONCE IT HAS BEGUN--	ONE ANGUISH--IN A CROWD	565	16
WHEN IT BEGUN--OR IF THERE WERE	PAIN--HAS AN ELEMENT OF	650	3
THE BIRDS BEGUN AT FOUR O'CLOCK--	THE BIRDS BEGUN AT FOUR	783	1
MY OWN HAD JUST BEGUN.	SEVERER SERVICE OF	786	8
THEY DIED, VITALITY BEGUN.	A DEATH BLOW IS A LIFE	816	4
THE WIND BEGUN TO KNEAD [ROCK] THE GRASS--	THE WIND BEGUN TO KNEAD	824	1
AN APRIL BUT BEGUN--	THE ROBIN IS THE ONE	828	8
TERM OF LIGHT THIS DAY BEGUN!	ALWAYS MINE!	839	3
THE WALLS--BEGUN TO TELL--	TO MY QUICK EAR THE	891	6
ANOTHER HAD BEGUN--	'TWAS CRISIS--ALL THE	948	14
WHERE MORNING [SUNRISE] JUST BEGUN--	THE SUNSET STOPPED ON	950	6
SHE HAD BEGUN TO LIE--	SHE SPED AS PETALS OF A	991	8

	FIRST LINE	POEM	LINE
BEGUN (CONTINUED)			
ENDED, ERE IT BEGUN--	ENDED, ERE IT BEGUN--	1088	1
IN COUNTIES HAVE BEGUN.	MYSELF CAN READ THE	1089	6
OH LIFE, BEGUN IN FLUENT BLOOD	THAT ODD OLD MAN IS DEAD	1130	9
TO CRAWL THE FROST BEGUN [BEGAN]--	THE FROST OF DEATH WAS	1136	8
AND THEN OUR WRATH BEGUN [BEGAN]--	THE FROST OF DEATH WAS	1136	15
THE NORTH BEGUN TO PUSH	THE CLOUDS THEIR BACKS	1172	2
HIS RESEARCH HAS BUT JUST BEGUN--	THE LILAC IS AN ANCIENT	1241	13
HAVE NEVER BEEN BEGUN--	THE THINGS WE THOUGHT	1293	4
CONCLUDED AND BEGUN	BELSHAZZAR HAD A LETTER	1459	4
LOVE IS DONE WHEN LOVE'S BEGUN,	LOVE IS DONE WHEN LOVE'S	1485	1
AS TWILIGHT LONG BEGUN,	AS IMPERCEPTIBLY AS	1540	6
THAT THIS WHICH IS BEGUN	WHY SHOULD WE HURRY--WHY	1646	6
MY SENTENCE HAD BEGUN.	'TWAS HERE MY SUMMER	1756	4
BEHAVIOR			
MAKES THE BEHAVIOR SMALL--	THOSE--DYING THEN,	1551	7
BEHEADS			
THE FROST BEHEADS IT AT IT'S PLAY--	APPARENTLY WITH NO	1624	3
BEHELD			
I NE'ER BEHELD BEFORE!	"SIC TRANSIT GLORIA	3	24
IMPERFECTLY BEHELD--	A CHARM INVESTS A FACE	421	2
AN IGNORANCE BEHELD--	WE LEARNED THE WHOLE OF	568	6
UNBORN--EXCEPT THEY HAD BEHELD--	'TWAS A LONG PARTING--	625	11
ADORED [BEHELD] WITH CAUTION--AS A BRITTLE HEAVEN--	EACH LIFE CONVERGES TO	680	9
THE BLINDNESS THAT BEHELD AND BLEST--	WHO SAW NO SUNRISE	1018	7
I BEHELD HER NEXT	THREE WEEKS PASSED SINCE	1061	4
AS NEVER WAS ACHIEVED [BEHELD]--	THAT THIS SHOULD FEEL	1112	4
BUT WHEN ALL SPACE HAS BEEN BEHELD	THE LIFE WE HAVE IS VERY	1162	5
BEHIND			
BEHIND MY NATIVE TOWN.	FREQUENTLY THE WOODS ARE	6	4
AN HOUR BEHIND THE FLEETING BREATH--	DELAYED TILL SHE HAD	58	4
BEHIND THIS SOFT ECLIPSE--	I'M "WIFE"--I'VE	199	6
AND LEAVES THE SHREDS BEHIND--	SHE SWEEPS WITH	219	2
BEHIND THE HILL--THE HOUSE BEHIND--	"HEAVEN"--IS WHAT I	239	7
BEHIND THE HILL--THE HOUSE BEHIND--	"HEAVEN"--IS WHAT I	239	7
AND GOD FORBID I LOOK BEHIND--	THE ONLY GHOST I EVER	274	15
IF ANY POWER BEHIND IT, BE,	I GOT SO I COULD HEAR	293	22
THE HOMELIER TIME BEHIND.	I SHOULD HAVE BEEN TOO	313	6
A KIND BEHIND THE DOOR--	'TIS NOT THAT DYING	335	4
BEHIND THIS MORTAL BONE	NO RACK CAN TORTURE ME--	384	3
AND DAY THAT WAS BEHIND--WERE ONE--	A NIGHT--THERE LAY THE	471	3
YOU COULD HEAR THE BODDICE TUG, BEHIND YOU--	GOING TO HIM! HAPPY	494	12
AND HE--HE FOLLOWED--CLOSE BEHIND--	I STARTED EARLY--TOOK MY	520	17
BUT THAT'S--BEHIND [THIS--INVOLVES] THE GRAVE--	THERE IS A SHAME OF	551	8
TO STAY BEHIND--WITH JUST THE TOYS	YOU'LL FIND--IT WHEN YOU	610	15
BEHIND--A SEALED ROUTE--	OUR JOURNEY HAD ADVANCED	615	10
BEHIND THE SHELF	I CANNOT LIVE WITH YOU--	640	4
HER POLAR TIME--BEHIND--	I THINK TO LIVE--MAY BE	646	20
NE'ER SO FAR BEHIND--	PROMISE THIS--WHEN YOU	648	30
THE MINOR ONE--THAT GLEAMED [SHONE] BEHIND--	THAT FIRST DAY, WHEN YOU	659	7
WE WALK--I LEAVE MY DOG--AT HOME [BEHIND]--	AGAIN--HIS VOICE IS AT	663	18
OURSELF BEHIND OURSELF, CONCEALED--	ONE NEED NOT BE A	670	13
BEHIND ME--DIPS ETERNITY--	BEHIND ME--DIPS ETERNITY	721	1
'TIS MIRACLE BEHIND--BETWEEN--	BEHIND ME--DIPS ETERNITY	721	14
YOUR LIFE HAD LEFT BEHIND--	SEVERER SERVICE OF	786	4
THE LEAVING LOVE BEHIND.	DYING! TO BE AFRAID OF	831	6
BEHIND THE EYES OF GOD.	OF CONSCIOUSNESS, HER	894	4
BEHIND INFERIOR CLOUDS--OR ROUND	I MAKE HIS CRESCENT FILL	909	7
IT JOINS--BEHIND THE VAIL	FAITH--IS THE PIERLESS	915	8
HE LEAVE OURSELVES A SPHERE BEHIND--	WE CAN BUT FOLLOW TO THE	920	3
WHAT EITHER LEFT BEHIND	TWO TRAVELLERS PERISHING	933	6
AND THOSE THEY LEFT BEHIND	TWO TRAVELLERS PERISHING	933	14
DEATH LEAVES US HOMESICK, WHO BEHIND,	DEATH LEAVES US HOMESICK	935	1
THE THOUGHT BEHIND, I STROVE [TRIED] TO JOIN	I FELT A CLEAVING IN MY	937	5
HE LEFT BEHIND ONE DAY--SO LESS	FITTER TO SEE HIM, I MAY	968	13
TENETS--PUT BEHIND--	COLOR--CASTE--	970	6
THE DUST BEHIND I STROVE TO JOIN	THE DUST BEHIND I STROVE	992	1
THE GULF BEHIND WAS NOT,	IT WAS A QUIET WAY--	1053	13
BEHIND THE MOST UNCONSCIOUS [CONSUMMATE] CLOCK	NOT TO DISCOVER WEAKNESS	1054	7
BEHIND THE AWFUL POWER--	THE WIND TOOK UP THE	1134	8
THAT WE SO FAR BEHIND--	BECAUSE HE LOVES HER	1229	6
THE DAISY THAT HAS LOOKED BEHIND	THE CLOVER'S SIMPLE FAME	1232	7
BEHIND A PALL--	THE VASTEST EARTHLY DAY	1328	4
AND CROUCHED BEHIND HIS YELLOW DOOR	A WILD BLUE SKY ABREAST	1415	3
LOOK BEHIND--HE IS PURSUING THEE.	TO EARN IT BY DISDAINING	1427	4
IS PUSHING [ROAMING / PLODDING / STARING / AMBLING] CLOSE BEHIND	ALL THAT I DO	1496	6
FATE--FOLLOWING--BEHIND US BOLTS IT--	WE NEVER KNOW WE GO WHEN	1523	3
WITH A PRUDENTIAL LOOK BEHIND	THE LIFE THAT TIED TOO	1535	3
BEHIND THE HILL IS SORCERY	THE GOING FROM A WORLD	1603	5
THE EVENT WAS DIRECTLY BEHIND HIM	THE EVENT WAS DIRECTLY	1686	1
NATURE HAD LEFT BEHIND.	HIGH FROM THE EARTH I	1723	8
NOT DARING LOOK BEHIND;	THE WATERS CHASED HIM AS	1749	2
BEHOLD			
BEHOLD THE KEENEST MARKSMAN!	THERE IS A WORD	8	15
BEHOLD! WHOSE MULTITUDES ARE THESE?	SOME RAINBOW--COMING	64	22
BY FAITH MAY CLEAR BEHOLD	WE SHOULD NOT MIND SO	81	10
BEHOLD, WHAT CURIOUS ROOMS!	WHAT INN IS THIS	115	6

	FIRST LINE	POEM	LINE
BEHOLD (CONTINUED)			
PLEASE GOD, MIGHT I BEHOLD HIM	BLESS GOD, HE WENT AS	147	5
IT'S DISTANCE--TO BEHOLD--	YOUR RICHES--TAUGHT ME--	299	28
WE BEHOLD HER--GLORIFIED--	TAKING UP THE FAIR IDEAL	428	11
A FEW--BEHOLD THEE--	LOVE--THOU ART HIGH--	453	14
HOW PLEASANT TO BEHOLD A THING	THREE TIMES--WE PARTED--	598	11
COULD BEHOLD [REGARD] SO FAR [SMALL / DIM / SCARCE] A CREATURE--	PROMISE THIS--WHEN YOU	648	27
BEHOLD THE ATOM--I PREFERRED--	OF ALL THE SOULS THAT	664	11
AND WE BEHOLD--NO MORE	WE CAN BUT FOLLOW TO THE	920	8
I EQUALLY BEHOLD	WHAT I SEE NOT, I BETTER	939	6
AS TO BEHOLD HIS AMPLE [GENTLE] FLIGHT--	THE MERCHANT OF THE	1131	11
BEHOLD OUR [MY / THIS] SPACIOUS CITIZEN	NATURE AFFECTS TO BE	1170	7
WE BLUSH, THAT HEAVEN IF WE ACHIEVE [BEHOLD]--	WHO WERE "THE FATHER AND	1258	21
I FAMISH [PERISH] TO BEHOLD SO EMINENT A SIGHT [ANOTHER SUCH . . .	THE MOST TRIUMPHANT BIRD	1265	4
THAT EVERY MAN [ALL THE WORLD] BEHOLD	YOU CANNOT TAKE ITSELF	1351	6
BEHOLD THIS LITTLE BANE--	BEHOLD THIS LITTLE BANE	1438	1
BEHOLD HIS LOST AGGRANDIZEMENT [EMOLUMENT]	ONE OF THE ONES THAT	1466	27
BEHOLD HOW GREAT A FIRMAMENT	NO MATTER WHERE THE	1541	3
BEHOLD SAID THE APOSTLE	SPEECH IS ONE SYMPTOM OF	1681	7
BEHOLDING			
RECEIVING [BEHOLDING]--WHERE WE--PRAY--	THOSE FAIR--FICTITIOUS	499	16
BEHOLDS			
PERENNIAL BEHOLDS US--	I NEVER FELT AT HOME--	413	13
AS THE EYE BEHOLDS	"LETHE" IN MY FLOWER,	1730	6
BEHOOVETH			
NOR THIS BEHOOVETH ME.	SOME THINGS THAT FLY	89	6
BEING			
THOU ART A HUMAN SOLO, A BEING COLD, AND LONE,	AWAKE YE MUSES NINE,	1	27
OUR FATHERS BEING WEARY,	"SIC TRANSIT GLORIA	3	45
STILL, MY LITTLE GIPSEY BEING	THO' MY DESTINY BE	163	5
BEING FAST ASLEEP,	IF I SHOULD'NT BE ALIVE	182	6
THIS BEING COMFORT--THEN	I'M "WIFE"--I'VE	199	9
TWO LIVES--ONE BEING--NOW--	FOREVER AT HIS SIDE TO	246	5
AND BEING, BUT AN EAR,	I FELT A FUNERAL, IN MY	280	14
MY REWARD FOR BEING, WAS THIS.	MY REWARD FOR BEING, WAS	343	1
I TURNED MY BEING ROUND AND ROUND	I FELT MY LIFE WITH BOTH	351	5
YOU HEAR A BEING--DROP--	A SOLEMN THING WITHIN	483	6
I'M CEDED--I'VE STOPPED BEING THEIR'S--	I'M CEDED--I'VE STOPPED	508	1
A BEING--IMPOTENT TO END [STOP]--	ONE ANGUISH--IN A CROWD	565	15
IT SWALLOWS SUBSTANCE [BEING] UP--	THERE IS A PAIN--SO	599	2
HE FOUND MY BEING--SET IT UP--	HE FOUND MY BEING--SET	603	1
TO GAD MY LITTLE BEING OUT--	IT WOULD HAVE STARVED A	612	15
I OFFERED BEING--FOR IT--	I ASKED NO OTHER THING--	621	3
OF BEING IS A BIRD	OF BEING IS A BIRD	653	1
SUCH BEING FINITUDE!	TO BE ALIVE--IS POWER--	677	8
AND BEING UNDER LOCK--	THE LONELINESS ONE DARE	777	12
THAT SWEPT HIS BEING--BACK--	GRIEF IS A MOUSE--	793	8
WILL IN A SECOND FUTURE [BEING]--	THIS DUST, AND IT'S	936	3
TO BEING, SOMEWHERE--MOTION--BREATH--	I'VE DROPPED MY BRAIN--	1046	17
OF BEING, ARE ALIKE	THE OPENING AND THE	1047	2
A BEING HAS THE SAME--	THE BONE THAT HAS NO	1274	6
REDEMPTION [THY TOTAL / THY BEING]--FOR A KISS--	GO SLOW, MY SOUL, TO	1297	8
BEING'S			
AND BEING'S--BEGGARY--	TO LOSE ONE'S FAITH--	377	8
BEING'S PEASANTRY--	SMILING BACK FROM	385	4
IS BUT A PROVINCE--IN THE BEING'S [HUMAN] CENTRE--	ONE CRUCIFIXION IS	553	9
TO THAT ODD FORK IN BEING'S ROAD--	OUR JOURNEY HAD ADVANCED	615	3
FOR BEING'S MALADY--	SEVERER SERVICE OF	786	24
THEN HANDED ME MY BEING'S WORTH--	I TOOK ONE DRAUGHT OF	1725	7
BELATED			
A DOG'S BELATED FEET	THE NIGHT WAS WIDE, AND	589	10
BELIEF			
INDUCES MY BELIEF.	THESE ARE THE DAYS WHEN	130	9
BELIEF--BUT ONCE--CAN BE--	TO LOSE ONE'S FAITH--	377	6
HURLED MY BELIEF--	HE STRAINED MY FAITH--	497	5
FROM THE BELIEF THAT SOMEWHERE--	I TRIED TO THINK A	532	8
AND HELP BELIEF TO STRETCH [REACH]--	REMORSE--IS MEMORY--	744	8
AND INTACT [DIRECT / DISTINCT] BELIEF--	GROWTH OF MAN--LIKE	750	12
IS SENTENCE [EXILE] FROM BELIEF--AND HOME--	IF BLAME BE MY SIDE--	775	4
THE BEAUTY OF DEMAND [BELIEF]--AT REST--	FITTER TO SEE HIM, I MAY	968	28
PROPOUNDED TO BELIEF.	TO DIE--WITHOUT THE	1017	4
BELIEF [WITH NOUGHT / OUR FAITH] TO REGULATE--	THE LAST NIGHT THAT SHE	1100	28
THAT OBLIQUE BELIEF WHICH WE CALL CONJECTURE	SOME WE SEE NO MORE,	1221	6
TOO MUCH OF PROOF AFFRONTS BELIEF	SO MUCH OF HEAVEN HAS	1228	9
BELIEF, IT DOES NOT FIT SO WELL	WHO WERE "THE FATHER AND	1258	19
THAT MIGHTIEST BELIEF,	I NEVER HEAR THAT ONE IS	1323	4
THE ABDICATION OF BELIEF	THOSE--DYING THEN,	1551	6
BELIEF'S			
WHEN, STIRRING, FOR BELIEF'S DELIGHT,	HER SWEET WEIGHT ON MY	518	3
BELIEFS			
BELIEFS ARE BANDAGED, LIKE THE TONGUE	I NEVER HEAR THAT ONE IS	1323	9
BELIEVE			
WHEN I BELIEVE THE GARDEN	WHEN I COUNT THE SEEDS	40	7
I'M GLAD I DONT BELIEVE IT	GOING TO HEAVEN!	79	20
I AM GLAD THEY DID BELIEVE IT	GOING TO HEAVEN!	79	24
IT'S SORER TO BELIEVE!	SHE WENT AS QUIET AS THE	149	8

	FIRST LINE	POEM	LINE
BELIEVE (CONTINUED)			
AND MAKE BELIEVE I'M GETTING WARM	MAKE ME A PICTURE OF THE	188	3
I DO BELIEVE A SPECIES	DO PEOPLE MOULDER	432	3
THEY DONT BELIEVE IT NOW--	TIME DOES GO ON--	1121	5
WE START--TO LEARN THAT WE BELIEVE	WHO WERE "THE FATHER AND	1258	17
I MAKE BELIEVE UNTIL MY HEART	THE MOST PATHETIC THING	1290	3
I BELIEVE THE DAY WILL BE	I SUPPOSE THE TIME WILL	1381	9
I DONT BELIEVE A PEEVISH BIRD	I THOUGHT THE TRAIN	1449	3
AND HIGHER, I BELIEVE,	THE BUTTERFLY UPON THE	1521	6
BOYS THAT "BELIEVE" ARE VERY LONESOME [BASTINADOED]--	THE BIBLE IS AN ANTIQUE	1545	11
BENEFICENT, BELIEVE ME,	THE BAT IS DUN, WITH	1575	15
I'D NOT BELIEVE IT IF I HEARD	IN WINTER IN MY ROOM	1670	12
I AM SO HAPPY I BELIEVE	IF ALL THE GRIEFS I AM	1726	3
BELIEVING WHAT WE DON'T BELIEVE	THAT IT WILL NEVER COME	1741	3
BELIEVED			
WOULD NEVER BE BELIEVED--	A MURMUR IN THE TREES--	416	12
PROVIDED IT BELIEVED--	TRUST IN THE UNEXPECTED	555	16
IF I BELIEVED [SUPPOSED] GOD LOOKED AROUND,	I PRAYED, AT FIRST, A	576	5
DEATH WARRANTS ARE SUPPOSED [BELIEVED] TO BE	DEATH WARRANTS ARE	1375	1
A FEW OF US--BELIEVED--	SUMMER--WE ALL HAVE SEEN	1386	2
BELIEVES			
BELIEVES ALL SHAM	THE CHILD'S FAITH IS NEW	637	7
HE WHO IN HIMSELF BELIEVES--	HE WHO IN HIMSELF	969	1
THAT DOUBTS AS FERVENTLY AS IT BELIEVES.	OURSELVES WE DO INTER	1144	4
ALMOST BELIEVES IT TOO	THE MOST PATHETIC THING	1290	4
WHO WITNESSES, BELIEVES.	HER FACE WAS IN A BED OF	1722	8
BELIEVING			
BELIEVING IF IT INTERCEDE	LONGING IS LIKE THE SEED	1255	3
BELIEVING WHAT WE DON'T BELIEVE	THAT IT WILL NEVER COME	1741	3
BELL			
ANEMONE, AND BELL--	WHOSE ARE THE LITTLE	142	14
THE LITTLE CAGE OF "CURRER BELL"	ALL OVERGROWN BY CUNNING	148	3
AS ALL THE HEAVENS WERE A BELL,	I FELT A FUNERAL, IN MY	280	13
WITHOUT A MOMENT'S BELL--	THAT AFTER HORROR--THAT	286	10
AND FIRST [THEN]--AT THE BELL.	JUST SO--JESUS--RAPS--	317	4
AND INSTEAD OF TOLLING THE BELL, FOR CHURCH,	SOME KEEP THE SABBATH	324	7
BEYOND THE DIP OF BELL--	I SAW NO WAY--THE	378	8
SWINGING HER BERYL BELL--	THROUGH THE DARK SOD--AS	392	6
OF TOLLING BELL I ASK THE CAUSE?	OF TOLLING BELL I ASK	947	1
THE BELL WITHIN THE STEEPLE WILD	THERE CAME A WIND LIKE A	1593	13
BELLES			
BELLES FROM SOME LOST SUMMER DAY--	PIGMY SERAPHS--GONE	138	3
LOW AMID THAT GLAD BELLES LETTRES	IF THE FOOLISH, CALL	168	17
THE BELLES [GUESTS] OF PARADISE ARE FEW--	THE ROAD TO PARADISE IS	1491	7
BELLOWS			
HOW NUMB [COOL], THE BELLOWS FEELS!	I BREATHED ENOUGH TO	272	8
BELLS			
I WAIT THY FAR, FANTASTIC BELLS--	THERE IS A MORN BY MEN	24	22
THE BELLS OF GHENT W'D RING--	IF THOSE I LOVED WERE	29	4
THE CLOVER BELLS FORGOT.	"ARCTURUS" IS HIS OTHER	70	16
AMID NO BELLS NOR BRAVOES	WENT UP A YEAR THIS	93	3
BELLS, ALSO, IN THE VILLAGE	ONE DIGNITY DELAYS FOR	98	7
AND BELLS KEEP SAYING "VICTORY"	I HAVE A KING, WHO DOES	103	11
WHERE BELLS NO MORE AFFRIGHT THE MORN--	WHERE BELLS NO MORE	112	1
NOT FATHER'S BELLS--NOR FACTORIES,	WHERE BELLS NO MORE	112	11
OH BELLS, THAT IN THE STEEPLES BE!	'TIS SO MUCH JOY! 'TIS	172	14
SHOW ME THE BELLS--	ANSWER JULY--	386	12
AND BELLS--THAT BOLDLY RING [COME]	I ENVY SEAS, WHEREON HE	498	18
WHEN THE REDEMPTION STRIKES [SHAKES] HER BELLS--	BETTER--THAN MUSIC! FOR	503	20
IT WAS NOT NIGHT, FOR ALL THE BELLS	IT WAS NOT DEATH, FOR I	510	3
'TWAS SABBATH--WITH THE BELLS DIVORCED [REVERSED]--	I HAD NO CAUSE TO BE	542	15
AND IT IS BELLS--WITHIN--	UNTO MY BOOKS--SO GOOD	604	12
WHEN BELLS STOP RINGING--CHURCH--BEGINS--	WHEN BELLS STOP RINGING	633	1
THE POSITIVE [TRANSITIVE]--OF BELLS--	WHEN BELLS STOP RINGING	633	2
LESS PAEANS--FEWER BELLS--	MY PORTION IS DEFEAT--	639	3
WHEN THE BELLS REJOICE--	A FIRST MUTE COMING--	702	4
THE MIXING BELLS AND PALLS--	UPON CONCLUDED LIVES	735	4
NO BELLS HAVE PARADISE--	MY FAITH IS LARGER THAN	766	12
THE BUSHES--THEY WERE BELLS--	TO MY QUICK EAR THE	891	2
THE BELLS A WINTER NIGHT	PEACE IS A FICTION OF	912	2
THAT BELLS SHOULD RING TILL ALL SHOULD KNOW [HEAR]	OF TOLLING BELL I ASK	947	5
AS SLEIGH BELLS SEEM [SOUND] IN SUMMER	AS SLEIGH BELLS SEEM IN	981	1
HOW STILL THE BELLS IN STEEPLES STAND	HOW STILL THE BELLS IN	1008	1
THE BELLS AT DISTANCE CALLED--	GREAT STREETS OF SILENCE	1159	6
BELLS FOR AN AUXILIARY	THE POPULAR HEART IS A	1226	3
BEFORE THE QUICK [RIPE / PEAL / DRUM / DRUMS / BELLS / BOMB / . . .	ONE JOY OF SO MUCH	1420	6
PUT ON YOUR MUFF [BELLS] FOR WINTER	THE JAY HIS CASTANET HAS	1635	2
BELONG			
BUT BOTH BELONG TO ME.	ONE SISTER HAVE I IN OUR	14	4
DO THE BUDS TO THEM BELONG?	ANGELS, IN THE EARLY	94	4
IT SHALL BELONG TO ME--	IF I MAY HAVE IT, WHEN	577	4
MINE BELONG YOUR LATEST SIGHING--	PROMISE THIS--WHEN YOU	648	3
THOUGHT BELONG TO HIM WHO GAVE IT--	PUBLICATION--IS THE	709	9
LADY, DID HE BELONG TO THEE?	TRUDGING TO EDEN,	1020	4
ETERNALLY BELONG.	DOMINION LASTS UNTIL	1257	4

	FIRST LINE	POEM	LINE
BELONG (CONTINUED)			
TO STEALTHILY BELONG?	FEW, YET ENOUGH,	1596	5
BELONGED			
THE THING BELONGED TO US--	WE SEE--COMPARATIVELY--	534	12
THE FELLOW WILL GO WHERE HE BELONGED--	IF EVER THE LID GETS OFF	1727	3
BELOVED			
FOR EACH BELOVED HOUR	FOR EACH EXTATIC INSTANT	125	5
AND BLUE--BELOVED AIR!	TO LEARN THE TRANSPORT	167	8
FOR THAT BELOVED HEART--	FOREVER AT HIS SIDE TO	246	9
JUST REVELATION--TO THE BELOVED--	"MORNING"--MEANS	300	5
THROUGH THEIR BELOVED BLAME--	'TIS TRUE--THEY SHUT ME	538	8
THIS ONE--BELOVED OF MANKIND	WHAT CARE THE DEAD, FOR	592	15
FOR HIS BELOVED NEED--	MY WORTHINESS IS ALL MY	751	6
BUT, ENEMY, BELOVED BE	DYING! TO BE AFRAID OF	831	8
LEST THIS BELOVED CHARGE	LOVE--IS THAT LATER	924	10
IT'S [THAT] BELOVED RECOGNITION	STRUCK, WAS I, NOR YET	925	19
THE FEATURES SO BELOVED--	WHAT I SEE NOT, I BETTER	939	8
FOR THE BRAVE [BOLD] BELOVED--	ROBBED BY DEATH--BUT	971	8
UNTIL THYSELF, BELOVED.	DISTANCE--IS NOT THE	1155	4
ON A BELOVED FACE	LIKE TIME'S INSIDIOUS	1236	2
BELOVED ONLY AFTERNOON	FROM ALL THE JAILS THE	1532	3
BELOW			
AND ONE BELOW, THIS MORNING	THE GENTIAN WEAVES HER	18	7
TO A HAND BELOW.	DISTRUSTFUL OF THE	20	16
FROM ENTERPRISE BELOW!	IF I SHOULD DIE,	54	10
NEW WEARY SLEEP BELOW--	NEW FEET WITHIN MY	99	6
WHO ARE THESE BELOW?	WHAT INN IS THIS	115	10
COCOON ABOVE! COCOON BELOW!	COCOON ABOVE! COCOON	129	1
OR STIRRING HOUSE BELOW--	ON SUCH A NIGHT, OR SUCH	146	14
WHOSE VOICES--TRAINED--[STANZA, HUSHED,] BELOW--	TO LEARN THE TRANSPORT	167	12
TO SAY WHAT TRANCE BELOW	FOR THIS--ACCEPTED	195	15
I NEVER FELT AT HOME--BELOW--	I NEVER FELT AT HOME--	413	1
AND IN THE ORCHARD FAR BELOW--	A SOLEMN THING WITHIN	483	5
UNCERTAIN [INDIFFERENT]--TO RETURN BELOW--	HE PARTS HIMSELF--LIKE	517	11
MYSELF TOO FAR BELOW	I WATCHED THE MOON	629	34
IT SPRINKLES BONNETS--FAR BELOW--	THE NAME--OF IT--IS	656	9
THE LOVE A LIFE [CHILD] CAN SHOW BELOW	THE LOVE A LIFE CAN SHOW	673	1
AND YET THE CROWD APPLAUD, BELOW--	YOU'VE SEEN BALLOONS SET	700	11
UPON THE WORLD BELOW--	THE MOON WAS BUT A CHIN	737	4
THE HEAVEN BELOW THE HEAVEN ABOVE--	ONE BLESSING HAD I THAN	756	13
IF COMMONWEALTH BELOW,	HE TOLD A HOMELY TALE	763	13
OURSELVES--ASLEEP BELOW--	WE MISS HER, NOT BECAUSE	993	6
NOT SO THE INFINITE RELATIONS--BELOW	NOT SO THE INFINITE	1040	1
AT NIGHT BENEATH [BELOW] THE STAR	THE SNOW THAT NEVER	1133	6
IT HAD BEEN HEAVEN BELOW.	IMMORTAL IS AN AMPLE	1205	8
THE VALLEYS STOPPED BELOW	THE MOUNTAINS STOOD IN	1278	2
AND FIRMAMENT BELOW	A SINGLE CLOVER PLANK	1343	6
THE ONES I LOVED BELOW	I SHALL NOT MURMUR IF AT	1410	2
NO BRIDGE BELOW DOTH TOTTER SO--	HOW BRITTLE ARE THE	1433	3
WHO HAS NOT FOUND THE HEAVEN--BELOW--	WHO HAS NOT FOUND THE	1544	1
BELOW, THE BODY SPEAKS,	THE SPIRIT LASTS--BUT IN	1576	2
AS CART OF MAN IN ROAD BELOW	THE SUN IN REINING TO	1636	3
HOW RED THE FIRE ROCKS BELOW	ON MY VOLCANO GROWS THE	1677	5
BELSHAZZAR			
BELSHAZZAR HAD A LETTER--	BELSHAZZAR HAD A LETTER	1459	1
BELSHAZZAR'S			
BELSHAZZAR'S CORRESPONDENT	BELSHAZZAR HAD A LETTER	1459	3
BELT			
HE PUT THE BELT AROUND MY LIFE--	HE PUT THE BELT AROUND	273	1
IT'S MADE OF FATHOMS--AND A BELT--	I KNOW WHERE WELLS GROW	460	5
A BELT OF JAGGED STONE--	I KNOW WHERE WELLS GROW	460	6
AND PAST MY APRON--AND MY BELT	I STARTED EARLY--TOOK MY	520	11
MINE--TO BELT YOUR EYE--	PROMISE THIS--WHEN YOU	648	4
ON MY BELT--TOO--	NO MATTER--NOW--SWEET--	704	12
THE STARS--THE TRINKETS AT HER BELT--	THE MOON WAS BUT A CHIN	737	19
WHOSE ESOTERIC BELT	DID LIFE'S PENURIOUS	1717	7
BELTED			
BELTED DOWN WITH EMERALD--	PIGMY SERAPHS--GONE	138	6
BEMOANING			
AS ONE BEMOANING A DOMINION	A LOSS OF SOMETHING EVER	959	7
BEMUMBED			
THAT SOMETHING--HAD OBSCURED [BEMUMBED] THE TRACK--	IT CEASED TO HURT ME,	584	4
BENCH			
THE BENCH, WHERE WE HAD TOILED--	MYSELF WAS FORMED--A	488	10
BEND			
NEVER ANY [ONE] BEND	IF YOUR NERVE, DENY YOU	292	6
NONE ON ME, BEND SUPERCILIOUS--	I'M SAYING EVERY DAY	373	6
TO BEND THE EYE	MUST BE A WO--	571	3
AND MEN TOO STRAIGHT TO STOOP [BEND] AGAIN,	MY PORTION IS DEFEAT--	639	8
UNTIL IT BEND AS LOW AS DEATH	PERHAPS YOU THINK ME	833	7
BEFORE HE MAKES THE BEND	I DID NOT REACH THEE	1664	22
BENDED			
TOO STIFF TO BENDED BE,	TOO COLD IS THIS	1135	3
BENDING			
LOW AT MY PROBLEM BENDING,	LOW AT MY PROBLEM	69	1
STOOPING AS LOW AS [BENDING LOW AT] THE OTTER'S [KITCHEN / . . .	BLAZING IN GOLD AND	228	5
THE LILACS--BENDING MANY A YEAR--	IT WILL BE SUMMER--	342	9

	FIRST LINE	POEM		LINE
BENDING (CONTINUED)				
THEN BENDING [STOOPING] FROM THE SKY--	NATURE--THE GENTLEST	790		20
OBLIVION BENDING OVER [ENFOLDING] HIM	THE DITCH IS DEAR TO THE	1645		7
BENDS				
THAT BENDS A KNEE TO THEE	CIRCUMFERENCE THOU BRIDE	1620	V	4
BENEATH				
BENEATH THE SUN MAY FIND.	I HAD A GUINEA GOLDEN--	23		36
SHE SLEPT BENEATH A TREE--	SHE SLEPT BENEATH A TREE	25		1
THAT ARE SOWN BENEATH,	WHEN I COUNT THE SEEDS	40		2
AGES BENEATH THE MOULD--	I BRING AN UNACCUSTOMED	132		13
BENEATH THE VILLAGE DOOR,	PERHAPS YOU'D LIKE TO	134		6
BENEATH HIS FADED JACKET'S BLUE--	I MET A KING THIS	166		6
THE THOUGHT BENEATH SO SLIGHT A FILM--	THE THOUGHT BENEATH SO	210		1
BENEATH HIS TABERNACLES, PLAY,	I THINK THE HEMLOCK	525		15
THE WAYWARD NUN--BENEATH THE HILL--	SWEET MOUNTAINS--YE TELL	722		8
SNOW BENEATH WHOSE CHILLY SOFTNESS	SNOW BENEATH WHOSE	942		1
TURNS UNPERCEIVED BENEATH OUR FEET	DEW--IS THE FRESHET IN	1097		3
'TIS MY FIRST NIGHT BENEATH THE SUN	'TIS MY FIRST NIGHT	1122		1
AT NIGHT BENEATH [BELOW] THE STAR	THE SNOW THAT NEVER	1133		6
LIKE WORMS BENEATH [BEFORE] THE POWER--	THE WIND TOOK UP THE	1134	V	8
IS THERE NO SWEET BENEATH THE SUN	OUR LITTLE SECRETS SLINK	1326		7
BENEATH THE SECOND SUN--	A FIELD OF STUBBLE,	1407		2
THE SHIP BENEATH THE DRAW	THOSE NOT LIVE YET	1454		5
ABOVE HIM IS THE SKY--[BENEATH]	THE DITCH IS DEAR TO THE	1645		6
BENEDICTION				
WHOSE HOMELY BENEDICTION	TO OFFER BRAVE	767		7
WHICH BOTH OF BENEDICTION	HIGH FROM THE EARTH I	1723		11
BENEFACTOR				
TO HER BENEFACTOR	MOST SHE TOUCHED ME BY	760		19
BENEFICENT				
BENEFICENT, BELIEVE ME,	THE BAT IS DUN, WITH	1575		15
BENEFIT				
AND HERE AND THERE A BENEFIT	THE PRODUCTS OF MY FARM	1025		3
AS A MAGISTRATE [BENEFIT]--	A PROMPT--EXECUTIVE BIRD	1177		8
BENIGN				
AND AS BENIGN--	THE GENTIAN HAS A	1424		7
BENT				
SHE BENT HER DOCILE SAILS--	WHETHER MY BARK WENT	52		4
WHEN THAT BENT STRIPE	DELIGHT IS AS THE FLIGHT	257		12
BENT TO THE SCAFFOLD, OR IN DUNGEONS--CHANTED [WAITED]--	UNTO LIKE STORY--TROUBLE	295		5
BUT WHEN HIS POWER DROPPED [BENT]--	I ROSE--BECAUSE HE SANK	616		3
MY SOUL GREW [FELT / BENT / STOOD] STRAIGHT.	I ROSE--BECAUSE HE SANK	616		4
THESE WERE BENT--MY SIGHT GOT CROOKED--	DONT PUT UP MY THREAD &	617		5
BENT TO THE WATER, STRUGGLED [SHIVERED] SCARCE--	THE LAST NIGHT THAT SHE	1100		23
THEN GAVE [BENT / BOWED] THE EAST UNTO THE WEST	THE WIND TOOK UP THE	1134		3
TILL ALL HER HELPLESS BEAUTY BENT	THE FROST OF DEATH WAS	1136		14
WITH LOVE ALONE HAD [WERE] BENT,	'TIS NOT THE SWAYING	1597		4
BENUMBED SEE BEMUMBED				
BENUMBED ABILITIES--	SUCH IS THE FORCE OF	787	V	8
BENUMBING				
THAT DULL--BENUMBING TIME	'TWAS CRISIS--ALL THE	948		2
BEQUEATHES				
BEQUEATHES THIS FINAL PLANT	THE LILAC IS AN ANCIENT	1241		6
BEQUEATHING				
BEQUEATHING--RATHER--TO THEIR WORK--	THE MARTYR POETS--DID	544		6
BEQUEATHS				
BEQUEATHS HIM TO THE NIGHT.	HOW DARE THE ROBINS SING	1724		12
BEQUEST				
AND THIS BEQUEST OF WINGS	HE ATE AND DRANK THE	1587		6
BEREAVED				
LIFT, IN BEREAVED ACKNOWLEDGEMENT	I DREADED THAT FIRST	348		27
BEREAVED OF ALL, I WENT ABROAD--	BEREAVED OF ALL, I WENT	784		1
NO LESS BEREAVED WAS I	BEREAVED OF ALL, I WENT	784		2
BEREAVEMENT				
BEREAVEMENT IN THEIR DEATH TO FEEL	BEREAVEMENT IN THEIR	645		1
BEREAVES				
BEREAVES THE MIND	SO GAY A FLOWER	1456		2
BEREFT				
BEREFT I WAS--OF WHAT I KNEW NOT	A LOSS OF SOMETHING EVER	959		3
BERNARDINE				
"BERNARDINE" ANGELS, UP THE HIGHT	SHE DIED--THIS WAS THE	150	V	5
A MORE BERNARDINE GIRL--	I'VE HEARD AN ORGAN TALK	183		6
BERRIES				
NOT ALL THE FRANKFORT BERRIES [VATS UPON THE RHINE]	I TASTE A LIQUOR NEVER	214		3
BERRIES ARE NICE!	OVER THE FENCE--	251		5
BERRIES, IN MY NATIVE TOWN--	PERHAPS I ASKED TOO	352		4
WHERE SQUIRRELS PLAY--AND BERRIES DIE--	DOOM IS THE HOUSE	475		7
ILL! WE HAVE BERRIES, FOR THE PARCHING!	WOULD YOU LIKE SUMMER?	691		3
BERRIES OF THE BAHAMAS--HAVE I--	I COULD BRING YOU JEWELS	697		5
AND THE BERRIES STARE	WHAT SHALL I DO WHEN THE	956		10
BERRY				
ON HIS BABBLING--BERRY--LIPS--	TEACH HIM--WHEN HE MAKES	227		3
THE BLACK BERRY--WEARS A THORN IN HIS SIDE--	THE BLACK BERRY--WEARS A	554		1
HE OFFERS [SPICES / FLAVORS] HIS BERRY, JUST THE SAME	THE BLACK BERRY--WEARS A	554		3
BRAVE BLACK BERRY--	THE BLACK BERRY--WEARS A	554		12

	FIRST LINE	POEM	LINE
BERRY (CONTINUED)			
AS BERRY--OF A MOUNTAIN BUSH--	I HAD BEEN HUNGRY, ALL	579	15
A BERRY FROM OUR TABLE	DEPRIVED OF OTHER	773	11
NATURE, HAD'ST THOU NOT A BERRY	TWICE HAD SUMMER HER	846	7
FOR BUT A BERRY OF DOMINGO	AS THE STARVED MAELSTROM	872	15
A BERRY OR A BUN, WOULD BE, ...	MY HEART UPON A LITTLE	1027	3
THOUGH FIRST UPON A BERRY FAT	CONFERRING WITH MYSELF	1655	3
BERRY'S			
THE BERRY'S CHEEK IS PLUMPER--	THE MORNS ARE MEEKER	12	3
BERYL			
WHOSE BERYL EGG, WHAT SCHOOL BOYS HUNT . .	A FEATHER FROM THE	161	7
SWINGING HER BERYL BELL--	THROUGH THE DARK SOD--AS	392	6
HER CHEEK--A BERYL HEWN--	THE MOON WAS BUT A CHIN	737	6
BERYL--AND THIS, AT NOON--	THE COLOR OF A QUEEN, IS	776	4
NATURE WAS IN AN OPAL [HER BERYL / HER BLUEST] APRON,	IT SOUNDED AS IF THE	1397	7
BESEECH			
BESEECH [ADJURE] EACH LITTLE BOY-- . . .	A LITTLE DOG THAT WAGS	1185	16
BESEECHING			
AND HANDS--BESEECHING--THROWN!	TWO SWIMMERS WRESTLED ON	201	9
LEST MY BESEECHING FACE--AT LAST-- . . .	COULD I--THEN--SHUT THE	220	2
BESEEMETH			
AND EARTH IS QUITE COQUETTISH, AND BESEEMETH IN VAIN TO SUE.	AWAKE YE MUSES NINE,	1	24
BESETS			
BESETS THE SIGHT	WHY SHOULD WE HURRY--WHY	1646	9
BESIDE			
THIS, AND MY HEART BESIDE--	IT'S ALL I HAVE TO BRING	26	2
DOMINIONS DOWERLESS--BESIDE THIS GRACE-- .	MY REWARD FOR BEING, WAS	343	9
AND WHOM YOU TOLD IT TO--BESIDE--	A SECRET TOLD--	381	7
WITH EASE--AND YOU--BESIDE--	THE BRAIN--IS WIDER THAN	632	4
BESIDE YOUR PALACE [TWINKLING / GLIMMERING] DOOR--	THE MOON WAS BUT A CHIN	737	16
NOR THAT ADJACENT, THAT BESIDE, ...	COUNT NOT THAT FAR THAT	1074	3
A UNIVERSE BESIDE--	A MINE THERE IS NO MAN	1117	4
AND THERE WERE [WAS] TROUGHS [SPACE / ROOM] BESIDE	A GREAT HOPE FELL	1123	13
BECAUSE BESIDE [BEFORE] THE DOOR	HOW MANY SCHEMES MAY DIE	1150	10
BESIDE [TO THINE] INFINITY	CONTAINED IN THIS SHORT	1165	8
BESIDE US LIKE A BLAND ABYSS	POWER IS A FAMILIAR	1238	3
THAN LEAST [BESIDE] VITALITY.	THE HARM OF YEARS IS ON	1280	8
BESIDE GOD'S SHALL [WILL] NOT TELL-- . . .	OUR LITTLE SECRETS SLINK	1326	2
BESIDE THIS TRAVELLING BIRD	CONFERRING WITH MYSELF	1655	8
AND HEAVEN BESIDE, AND HEAVEN ABROAD; . .	A PIT--BUT HEAVEN OVER	1712	2
BESIDES			
BESIDES THE AUTUMN POETS SING	BESIDES THE AUTUMN POETS	131	1
TO PUSH, AND PIERCE, BESIDES--	A WEIGHT WITH NEEDLES ON	264	2
AND LITTLE BOYS--BESIDES--	THERE'S BEEN A DEATH, IN	389	16
BESIDES--IT IS'NT EVEN--IT SLANTS	WE DO NOT PLAY ON GRAVES	467	3
AND THIS--BESIDES, IN--THEE!	I AM ALIVE--I GUESS--	470	28
IF TOWN IT HAVE--BEYOND [BESIDES] ITSELF-- .	A LITTLE ROAD--NOT MADE	647	5
BESIDES THIS MAY	BESIDES THIS MAY	977	1
BESIDES THE DEEPEST CELLAR	REMEMBRANCE HAS A	1182	5
AS HE BESIDES CONCEDES	BECAUSE THAT YOU ARE	1260	38
BESIDES IDENTITY	THAT SACRED CLOSET WHEN	1273	6
BESIDES--SUSPENSE IS NEIGHBORLY	I KNOW SUSPENSE--IT	1285	3
BEST			
LOVE THE DULL LAD--BEST--	DID WE DISOBEY HIM?	267	7
BEST GIANT MADE--	IF YOUR NERVE, DENY YOU	292	8
WHICH BORE IT BEST?	ONE YEAR AGO--JOTS WHAT?	296	28
BEST--WHEN IT'S DONE--	IT'S LIKE THE LIGHT--	297	10
THE BEST VITALITY	I REASON, EARTH IS SHORT	301	6
'TIS BEGGARS--BANQUETS BEST [CAN] DEFINE-- .	I SHOULD HAVE BEEN TOO	313	22
WITHIN HIS CLOSET--BEST YOU CAN	EXHILIRATION--IS WITHIN	383	11
DID OUR BEST MOMENT LAST--	DID OUR BEST MOMENT LAST	393	1
BRING ME MY BEST PRIDE--	I AM ASHAMED--I HIDE--	473	23
BUT HE, THE BEST LOGICIAN, ...	WITHIN MY GARDEN, RIDES	500	17
ON SO BEST [BROAD] A HEART--	SWEET--YOU FORGOT--BUT I	523	10
HIS BEST [GOOD] NORWEGIAN WINES--	I THINK THE HEMLOCK	525	12
MY BEST--WAS GONE TO SLEEP--	I HAD NO CAUSE TO BE	542	2
A BEST DISGRACE--A BRAVE MAN FEELS-- . . .	THERE IS A SHAME OF	551	5
BEST BEAUTY'S WAY--	MUST BE A WO--	571	4
ACCEPT IT'S MOST [BEST]--	THE TEST OF LOVE--IS	573	9
AND IN THE GRAVE--I SEE THEE BEST-- . . .	I SEE THEE BETTER--IN	611	9
I TOLD HIM BEST--MUST PASS	I ROSE--BECAUSE HE SANK	616	12
AND IF HE SPOKE--WHAT NAME WAS BEST-- . .	TO KNOW JUST HOW HE	622	18
TILL LOVE THAT WAS--AND LOVE TOO BEST TO BE--	TO KNOW JUST HOW HE	622	25
THE TINT I CANNOT TAKE--IS BEST--	THE TINT I CANNOT TAKE--	627	1
POURED LIKE THIS--MY WHOLE [BEST] LIBATION--	PROMISE THIS--WHEN YOU	648	13
BEST GAINS--MUST HAVE THE LOSSES' TEST-- .	BEST GAINS--MUST HAVE	684	1
'TWAS BEST IMPERFECT--AS IT WAS--	THEIR HIGHT IN HEAVEN	696	3
THIS--THE BEST ENACT [MORE EXERT]	DRAMA'S VITALLEST	741	5
REMOTE--HER BEST ARRAY--	THE BIRDS REPORTED FROM	743	10
HER FAVOR--IS THE BEST DISDAIN	MY SOUL--ACCUSED ME--AND	753	5
BEST [ALL] HORIZON--GONE [KNOWN]-- . . .	NO BOBOLINK--REVERSE HIS	755	7
THIS--THEN--IS BEST FOR CONFIDENCE-- . . .	THE TRUTH--IS STIRLESS--	780	3
BEST GRIEF IS TONGUELESS--BEFORE HE'LL TELL--	GRIEF IS A MOUSE--	793	13
AND SANCTITY, ARE BEST	THE ROBIN IS THE ONE	828	12
BEST, TO KNOW AND TELL, ...	GOOD TO HIDE, AND HEAR	842	6
TILL HIS BEST STEP APPROACHING	I SING TO USE THE	850	5

	FIRST LINE	POEM	LINE
BEST (CONTINUED)			
BEST--AT SETTING--AS IS NATURE'S--	STRUCK, WAS I, NOR YET	925	21
MY BEST ACQUAINTANCES ARE THOSE	MY BEST ACQUAINTANCES	932	1
AS FROST IS BEST CONCEIVED	AS FROST IS BEST	951	1
THE BEAUTY THAT REWARD HIM MOST [BEST]--	FITTER TO SEE HIM, I MAY	968	27
IS BEST DISCLOSED BY DANGER	THE SOUL'S DISTINCT	974	3
LOOKING BACK IS BEST THAT IS LEFT	THIS WAS IN THE WHITE OF	995	5
BEST THINGS DWELL OUT OF SIGHT	BEST THINGS DWELL OUT OF	998	1
WHICH IS BEST? HEAVEN--	WHICH IS BEST? HEAVEN--	1012	1
EARTH AT THE BEST	SO LARGE MY WILL	1024	9
WHEN BEST MEN DIE.	A SICKNESS OF THIS WORLD	1044	2
THE GEM WERE BEST UNKNOWN--	A DIAMOND ON THE HAND	1108	4
BEST WITCHCRAFT IS GEOMETRY	BEST WITCHCRAFT IS	1158	1
SHINE THY BEST--	MY GOD--HE SEES THEE--	1178	2
WHAT IS TO BE IS BEST DESCRIED	MY TRIUMPH LASTED TILL	1227	9
INVESTMENT'S BEST EXPOSITOR	THE INCIDENTS OF LOVE	1248	3
WHICH IS THE BEST--THE MOON OR THE CRESCENT?	WHICH IS THE BEST--THE	1315	1
THAT IS BEST WHICH IS NOT--ACHIEVE IT--	WHICH IS THE BEST--THE	1315	3
AND TRUE [BEST / REAL / BLAND / FINE / FAIR] THE OTHER . . .	I'D RATHER RECOLLECT A	1349	4
NATURE WAS IN THE BEST OF HUMORS	IT SOUNDED AS IF THE	1397	V 7
HE DOUBTLESS DID HIS BEST--	LOOK BACK ON TIME, WITH	1478	2
WOULD BE THE BEST FRIEND--	THE DEVIL--HAD HE	1479	2
TO HER WHO LOVES THEE BEST,	COME SHOW THY DURHAM	1542	2
BUT CHOSE THE BEST--NEGLECTING ME--TILL	MY WARS ARE LAID AWAY IN	1549	7
THAT IF IT BE, IT BE AT BEST	THAT IT WILL NEVER COME	1741	5
BESTIR			
THE DREAMY BUTTERFLIES BESTIR!	SOME RAINBOW--COMING	64	7
NO DAYBREAK--CAN BESTIR--	ON THIS LONG STORM THE	194	10
BESTIRS			
BESTIRS HER PUZZLED WINGS	ONCE MORE, MY NOW	48	2
BESTIRS ITSELF--PUTS ON IT'S COAT,	THE SUMMER THAT WE DID	1773	5
BESTOW			
THE HEAVEN GOD BESTOW--	THE WAY I READ A	636	16
POSSIBLY BESTOW	HER SWEET TURN TO LEAVE	649	16
UPON HER FRIEND SHE COULD CONFER [BESTOW]	THE MOON WAS BUT A CHIN	737	11
TO BESTOW A WORLD	ALL I MAY, IF SMALL,	819	5
SO WINGS BESTOW ON ME	BECAUSE THE BEE MAY	869	9
WE SO NEW BESTOW	SNOW BENEATH WHOSE	942	6
SOME PASSING YEAR--A TRAIT [CHARM] BESTOW	FITTER TO SEE HIM, I MAY	968	4
PERMIT [ALLOW / BESTOW] ME THIS REPRIEVE	TRIED ALWAYS AND	1559	2
BESTOWAL			
BREAD OF HEAVEN RESENTS BESTOWAL	WHEN A LOVER IS A BEGGAR	1314	7
BESTOWED			
BESTOWED [HE GAVE] HIMSELF TO BALLS	HE FOUGHT LIKE THOSE	759	2
FOR PATTERN IS THE MIND BESTOWED	WHO GOES TO DINE MUST	1223	5
THE AFFLUENCE EVOLVED [CONFERRED / BESTOWED / INVOLVED]--	SUMMER--WE ALL HAVE SEEN	1386	10
BESTOWED A SUMMER LONG	TO HER DERIDED HOME	1586	5
BESTOWING			
WOULD A SMILE'S MINUTE BESTOWING	SO MUCH SUMMER	651	4
BESTOWS			
AS BROOK BY BROOK BESTOWS ITSELF	THE BIRDS BEGUN AT FOUR	783	7
A SUMPTUOUSNESS BESTOWS [SUPPLIES]	THE LUXURY TO APPREHEND	815	12
BESTOWS [CONFERRED] A SINGLE FRIEND--	A COFFIN--IS A SMALL	943	10
BET			
I BET WITH EVERY WIND THAT BLEW	I BET WITH EVERY WIND	1215	1
BETAKES			
BETAKES HIMSELF TO DIE.	HIS ORIENTAL HERESIES	1526	V 8
BETHLEEM			
UTTERED IN BETHLEEM!	"THEY HAVE NOT CHOSEN ME	85	4
BASKING [WINNING] IN BETHLEEM	MY HEART RAN SO TO THEE	1237	15
BETHLEHEM			
FAINT STAR OF BETHLEHEM--	IF HE DISSOLVE--THEN--	236	6
THE ROAD TO BETHLEHEM	THE SAVIOR MUST HAVE	1487	5
HE PASSED THROUGH BETHLEHEM--	"AND WITH WHAT BODY DO	1492	8
SUBJECTS--BETHLEHEM--	THE BIBLE IS AN ANTIQUE	1545	4
BETHLEHEM'S			
GENESIS--BETHLEHEM'S ANCESTOR--	THE BIBLE IS AN ANTIQUE	1545	V 5
BETHOUGHT			
TYRANNY BETHOUGHT	TELL AS A MARKSMAN--WERE	1152	17
BETIDES			
WHATEVER PRANK BETIDES!	"ARCTURUS" IS HIS OTHER	70	25
BETIMES			
BETIMES AN ORATORIO--	ONE OF THE ONES THAT	1466	11
BETOKEN			
DOTH BETOKEN HIM.	DEATH'S WAYLAYING NOT	1296	6
BETRAY			
SHOULD A SHREWD BETRAY ME--	I NEVER TOLD THE BURIED	11	20
IT NEVER DID BETRAY	THE BODY GROWS WITHOUT--	578	6
OTHER--COULD BETRAY--	LIFE--IS WHAT WE MAKE IT	698	6
AND DOES NO TIMIDITY BETRAY	WHAT MYSTERY PERVADES A	1400	16
THAT WOULD EXPAND [BETRAY] US ALL--	THE LIFE THAT TIED TOO	1535	V 8
BETRAYED			
FOR WHOM BETRAYED THE DELL--	SO BASHFUL WHEN I SPIED	91	10
WAS HAUGHTY AND BETRAYED.	I WORKED FOR CHAFF AND	1269	2
BETRAYS			
BETRAYS THE SOLITUDE.	NEW FEET WITHIN MY	99	4
BETRAYS [REPORTS] US, AS HIS FIRST BETROTHAL	MARCH IS THE MONTH OF	1404	7
BETRAYS A BOY.	MARCH IS THE MONTH OF	1404	8

	FIRST LINE	POEM	LINE
BETROTHAL			
BETRAYS [REPORTS] US, AS HIS FIRST BETROTHAL	MARCH IS THE MONTH OF	1404	7
BETROTHED			
BETROTHED--WITHOUT THE SWOON	TITLE DIVINE--IS MINE!	1072	6
BETROTHED TO RIGHTEOUSNESS MIGHT BE	BETROTHED TO	1641	1
BETTER			
BETTER AS THE DAISY	GLOWING IS HER BONNET,	72	5
I'LL BEAR IT BETTER NOW--	YOU LOVE ME--YOU ARE	156	15
BETTER WILL BE THE EXTASY	THO' I GET HOME HOW LATE	207	3
BUBBLE! "FORGIVE"--"SOME BETTER"--BUBBLE!	KILL YOUR BALM--AND IT'S	238	7
HOW BETTER, THAN A GEM!	YOUR RICHES--TAUGHT ME--	299	24
ACCEPTS A BETTER LATITUDE--	'TIS NOT THAT DYING	335	7
BETTER TO BE READY--	I'M SAYING EVERY DAY	373	26
'TWERE BETTER CHARITY	OF COURSE--I PRAYED--	376	8
BETTER OF IT--CONTINUAL BE AFRAID--	A SECRET TOLD--	381	5
DREAMS--ARE WELL--BUT WAKING'S BETTER,	DREAMS--ARE WELL--BUT	450	1
IF ONE WAKE AT MIDNIGHT--BETTER--	DREAMS--ARE WELL--BUT	450	3
BETTER--THAN MUSIC! FOR I--WHO HEARD IT--	BETTER--THAN MUSIC! FOR	503	1
BUBBLED A BETTER--MELODY--	BETTER--THAN MUSIC! FOR	503	10
'TWAS BETTER--THE PERCEIVING NOT--	TRUST IN THE UNEXPECTED	555	15
IT'S BETTER--ALMOST PEACE--	IT CEASED TO HURT ME,	584	15
I SEE THEE BETTER--IN THE DARK--	I SEE THEE BETTER--IN	611	1
I SEE THEE BETTER FOR THE YEARS	I SEE THEE BETTER--IN	611	5
BETTER STITCHES--SO--	DONT PUT UP MY THREAD &	617	4
OR BETTER, RUN AWAY	COULD I BUT RIDE	661	8
BETTER THAN LARGER VALUES--	THEIR HIGHT IN HEAVEN	696	13
BETTER--COULD I BRING?	I COULD BRING YOU JEWELS	697	12
BETTER 'TIS TO FAIL--THERE--	OUT OF SIGHT? WHAT OF	703	6
BETTER [BRAVER] ENTERTAIN	NEVER FOR SOCIETY	746	8
'TIS BETTER THAN THE EIDER-DUCK'S	MY LIFE HAD STOOD--A	754	15
BETTER THAN NEW--COULD BE--FOR THAT--	JOY TO HAVE MERITED THE	788	7
MAY BE EASIER REACHED [BETTER ATTAINED / EASIER GAINED]--THIS WAY--	BY MY WINDOW HAVE I FOR	797	8
BETTER, TO BE FOUND,	GOOD TO HIDE, AND HEAR	842	2
WE HAVE UNDERSTOOD FOR BETTER	THAT IS SOLEMN WE HAVE	934	7
WHAT [WHEN] I SEE NOT, I BETTER SEE--	WHAT I SEE NOT, I BETTER	939	1
INCLUDE US [SCAN BETTER / CONVEY US]--AS THEY GO--	WE MISS HER, NOT BECAUSE	993	8
OR BETTER, BE WITH ME--	BEE! I'M EXPECTING YOU!	1035	11
IT SUITS HIM BETTER THAN A CHECK	THE MERCHANT OF THE	1131	7
WERE BETTER THAN BE NOT	SOUL, TAKE THY RISK,	1151	3
BETTER [RATHER] THAN THE TOMBS	FORTITUDE INCARNATE	1217	12
IS BETTER [SWEETER] THAN ENAMELED REALMS	THE CLOVER'S SIMPLE FAME	1232	3
BETTER THAN ON A DREAM INTRUDE	THE SUBURBS OF A SECRET	1245	3
WE BETTER FRIENDS HAD BEEN, PERHAPS,	WHO WERE "THE FATHER AND	1258	15
AS WELL AS [BETTER THAN] PRIME	AN ANTIQUATED GRACE	1345	3
BETTER AN IGNIS FATUUS	THOSE--DYING THEN,	1551	8
A BETTER COAT IF HE POSSESSED	TO TRY TO SPEAK, AND	1617	5
IS BETTER WE CONSIDER	ADVANCE IS LIFE'S	1652	7
I KNOW THEE BETTER FOR THE ACT	I SEE THEE CLEARER FOR	1666	5
BETTER A GRAVE OF BALM	NOT ANY SUNNY TONE	1674	4
BETWEEN			
A PACE HAD BEEN BETWEEN--	I NEVER TOLD THE BURIED	11	7
LIE BETWEEN THEM NOW.	AMBITION CANNOT FIND HIM	68	4
WHILE LIKE A GUARD BETWEEN--	OUR LIVES ARE SWISS--	80	7
BETWEEN OUR FEET, AND DAY!	AT LAST, TO BE	174	7
A LITTLE PURPLE--SLIPPED BETWEEN--	A SLASH OF BLUE--	204	5
DECADES OF ARROGANCE BETWEEN	A CLOCK STOPPED--	287	16
THE DIFFERENCE BETWEEN DESPAIR	THE DIFFERENCE BETWEEN	305	1
BETWEEN THE INSTANT OF A WRECK--	THE DIFFERENCE BETWEEN	305	3
BETWEEN MY FINITE EYES--	BEFORE I GOT MY EYE PUT	327	13
COULD NOT DECIDE [DISCERN / CONCLUDE] BETWEEN--	SO GLAD WE ARE--A	329	8
AND PERISH--BUT A BOUGH BETWEEN--	NOT PROBABLE--THE BAREST	346	8
BETWEEN THE BLISS--AND ME--	I GAINED IT SO--	359	4
BETWEEN MY CURTAIN AND THE WALL	THE ANGLE OF A LANDSCAPE	375	3
THE STUBBLE'S JOINTS BETWEEN--	'TWAS JUST THIS TIME,	445	10
WE TALKED BETWEEN THE ROOMS--	I DIED FOR BEAUTY--BUT	449	10
BETWEEN THE HEAVES OF STORM--	I HEARD A FLY BUZZ--WHEN	465	4
BETWEEN THE LIGHT--AND ME--	I HEARD A FLY BUZZ--WHEN	465	14
A NIGHT--THERE LAY THE DAYS BETWEEN--	A NIGHT--THERE LAY THE	471	1
OF THIS, THAT IS BETWEEN,	IF YOU WERE COMING IN	511	18
DISCOURSE BETWEEN THE TOIL--	I'M SORRY FOR THE DEAD--	529	6
BETWEEN HIMSELF--AND HORROR'S TWIN--	I TRIED TO THINK A	532	14
AND THEN A TRACT BETWEEN	'TIS ONE BY ONE--THE	545	2
AND WHETHER--COULD THEY CHOOSE BETWEEN--	I MEASURE EVERY GRIEF I	561	11
AND CRAWL BETWEEN	I LIKE TO SEE IT LAP	585	10
BETWEEN WHOSE YELLOW EYE--	DID YOU EVER STAND IN A	590	10
THE BATTLE FOUGHT BETWEEN THE SOUL	THE BATTLE FOUGHT	594	1
THAT HUNCH [PILE] THEMSELVES BETWEEN--	I SEE THEE BETTER--IN	611	6
BEFORE--WERE CITIES--BUT BETWEEN--	OUR JOURNEY HAD ADVANCED	615	7
BETWEEN ETERNITY AND TIME--	YOU LEFT ME--SIRE--TWO	644	7
OUR SOUL AND THEIR'S--BETWEEN--	BEREAVEMENT IN THEIR	645	4
BETWEEN IT'S PONDEROUS FACE	A PRISON GETS TO BE A	652	2
BETWEEN DIVERGING GOLDS--	THAT FIRST DAY, WHEN YOU	659	6
MYSELF--THE TERM BETWEEN--	BEHIND ME--DIPS ETERNITY	721	3
'TIS MIRACLE BEHIND--BETWEEN--	BEHIND ME--DIPS ETERNITY	721	14
THAT PLY BETWEEN IT AND THE SKY	BY MY WINDOW HAVE I FOR	797	V 6
EXPERIENCE BETWEEN	THIS CONSCIOUSNESS THAT	822	6
BETWEEN A FEW, AND ME--	AN HOUR IS A SEA	825	2

	FIRST LINE	POEM	LINE
BETWEEN (CONTINUED)			
THAT DISTANCE WAS BETWEEN US	THAT DISTANCE WAS	863	1
THE SEA AND SPAR BETWEEN.	EACH SECOND IS THE LAST	879	4
A SEPULCHRE, BETWEEN--	HEREIN A BLOSSOM LIES--	899	2
BETWEEN MY COUNTRY--AND THE OTHERS--	BETWEEN MY COUNTRY--AND	905	1
BUT FLOWERS--NEGOTIATE BETWEEN US--	BETWEEN MY COUNTRY--AND	905	3
TOO NARROW IS THE RIGHT BETWEEN--	TOO LITTLE WAY THE HOUSE	911	5
INFINITES--BETWEEN--	PATIENCE--HAS A QUIET	926	4
THE GULF BETWEEN THE HAND AND HER	THE LADY FEEDS HER	941	5
BETWEEN OURSELVES AND THE DEAD!	UNDER THE LIGHT, YET	949	16
WE KNEW BY CHANGE BETWEEN ITSELF	WE MET AS SPARKS--	958	7
DEATH IS A DIALOGUE BETWEEN	DEATH IS A DIALOGUE	976	1
BETWEEN OURSELF AND HEAVEN.	LEST THIS BE HEAVEN	1043	4
THOUGH SUNSET LIE BETWEEN--	COUNT NOT THAT FAR THAT	1074	2
CIRCUMFERENCE BETWEEN.	AT HALF PAST THREE, A	1084	12
BETWEEN HER FINAL ROOM	THE LAST NIGHT THAT SHE	1100	10
BETWEEN THE FORM OF LIFE AND LIFE	BETWEEN THE FORM OF LIFE	1101	1
AS LIQUOR AT THE LIP BETWEEN	BETWEEN THE FORM OF LIFE	1101	3
IF I COULD CRAWL BETWEEN	THE SPRY ARMS OF THE	1103	2
BETWEEN HIS [THE] HOLIDAY	THE BIRD DID PRANCE--THE	1107	4
HIMSELF AND HER BETWEEN,	THE FROST OF DEATH WAS	1136	11
WITH FIRMAMENTS [CENTURIES] BETWEEN	CONTAINED IN THIS SHORT	1165 V	
BETWEEN IT'S RUMOR AND IT'S FACE--	THE SYMPTOM OF THE GALE	1327	3
WITHIN [BETWEEN] HIS RUSSET LIPS--	A SAUCER HOLDS A CUP	1374	10
THE FLASH [FLARE / GLARE / BLARE] BETWEEN THE CREVICES OF CRASH--	IT WAS A QUIET SEEMING	1419 V	
AND HESITATED ME BETWEEN	MY WARS ARE LAID AWAY IN	1549	5
THAT TOOK THY FACE BETWEEN	I SEE THEE CLEARER FOR	1666	2
BETWEEN THE MARCH AND APRIL LINE--	THE SADDEST NOISE, THE	1764	5
BEWARE			
BEWARE, LEST THIS LITTLE BROOK OF LIFE,	HAVE YOU GOT A BROOK IN	136	15
BEWARE.	A RAT SURRENDERED HERE	1340	6
BEWARE AN AUSTRIAN	THE WIND DREW OFF	1694	11
'TIS EASY TO BEWARE	THROUGH THOSE OLD	1753	6
BEWILDERED			
PHILIP--WHEN BEWILDERED [QUESTIONED EAGER]	IF THOSE I LOVED WERE	29	7
ONCE MORE, MY NOW BEWILDERED DOVE	ONCE MORE, MY NOW	48	1
AND THE BEWILDERED GYMNAST [ASTONISHED WRESTLER]	A LITTLE EAST OF JORDAN,	59	15
STARING--BEWILDERED [DEFRAUDED]--AT THE MOCKING SKY--	THE NEAREST DREAM	319	10
AND I, BEWILDERED, STAND--	AS IF I ASKED A COMMON	323	4
BEWILDERING			
AH, THE BEWILDERING THREAD!	A SHADY FRIEND--FOR	278	10
BEYOND			
HATH PASSED BEYOND THE MOON,	"SIC TRANSIT GLORIA	3	64
LEARNETH BEYOND THE SEA	I HAVE A BIRD IN SPRING	5	10
HAVE PASSED BEYOND THE SUN--	WHEN ROSES CEASE TO	32	4
TWILL BE BECAUSE BEYOND THE ROSE	IF I SHOULD CEASE TO	56	3
"PENIEL" HILLS BEYOND [AMONG],	A LITTLE EAST OF JORDAN,	59	14
HER SIMPLE HAUNTS BEYOND!	SO BASHFUL WHEN I SPIED	91	8
WHO STRAYED BEYOND THE AMBER LINE	THE LONESOME FOR THEY	262	3
BEYOND MY POWER TO DEEM [DREAM]--	YOUR RICHES--TAUGHT ME--	299	22
ENDEAR THE SHORE [COAST] BEYOND--	I SHOULD HAVE BEEN TOO	313	21
BEYOND THE ART TO EARN--	OF ALL THE SOUNDS	321	10
BEYOND THE TRAIT TO TAKE AWAY	OF ALL THE SOUNDS	321	11
BEYOND THE DIP OF BELL--	I SAW NO WAY--THE	378	8
NOW--TO RING A DOOR BEYOND	TAKE YOUR HEAVEN FURTHER	388	6
DOOM IT BEYOND THE REST--	'TWAS LOVE--NOT ME--	394	6
BEYOND THE BROKER'S INSIGHT--	SOME--WORK FOR	406	11
BUT PEERS BEYOND HER MESH--	A CHARM INVESTS A FACE	421	5
BEYOND OUR FAINT [SMALL] CONJECTURE--	THOSE FAIR--FICTITIOUS	499	11
A SPECIES [SEQUEL] STANDS BEYOND--	THIS WORLD IS NOT	501	2
BEYOND THAT--UNCONSPICUOUS	DEATH IS POTENTIAL TO	548	3
BUT AWED BEYOND MY ERRAND--	MY PERIOD HAD COME FOR	564	19
BEYOND MY LIMIT TO CONCEIVE--	I THINK TO LIVE--MAY BE	646	3
IF TOWN IT HAVE--BEYOND [BESIDES] ITSELF--	A LITTLE ROAD--NOT MADE	647	5
THEIR RIBBONS JUST BEYOND THE EYE--	YOU'VE SEEN BALLOONS SET	700	9
BEYOND NESCESSITY--	FAME OF MYSELF, TO	713	4
IT ENDS BEYOND	FROM BLANK TO BLANK--	761	7
IF LOVE BE JUST BEYOND--	TO WAIT AN HOUR--IS LONG	781	2
THIS TIME--BEYOND THE ESTIMATE [INFERENCE]	SHE STAKED HER FEATHERS	798	3
BEYOND MY BOUNDARY--	I'VE NONE TO TELL ME TO	881	6
OF RIVER OR OF RIDGE [OF FATHOM OR OF LEAGUE] BEYOND	HOW FAR IS IT TO HEAVEN?	929	3
THE STIMULUS, BEYOND THE GRAVE	THE STIMULUS, BEYOND THE	1001	1
THOUGH CENTURIES BEYOND,	I'VE DROPPED MY BRAIN--	1046	18
INCREASED [ENLARGED] BEYOND MY UTMOST SCOPE	I HAD A DAILY BLISS	1057	7
BEYOND MACHINERY	TOO COLD IS THIS	1135 V	5
BEYOND THE REALM OF BIRD--	A WIND THAT ROSE	1259	5
BEYOND IT'S DULL [SLOW]--CONTROL	WITH PINIONS OF DISDAIN	1431	6
BEYOND EARTH'S TRAFFICKING FRONTIER,	NOT THAT HE GOES--WE	1435	3
FROM JUST A PURPLE FLOWER BEYOND	OF DEATH I TRY TO THINK	1558	13
MAJESTIC IS TO ME BEYOND	THE OVERTAKELESSNESS OF	1691	3
BEYOND THE HOPE OF TOUCH	THE OVERTAKELESSNESS OF	1691	8
BEYOND WHICH SUMMER HESITATES,	THE SADDEST NOISE, THE	1764	7
BIBLE			
DIAGNOSIS OF THE BIBLE, BY A BOY--	THE BIBLE IS AN ANTIQUE	1545	T
THE BIBLE IS AN ANTIQUE [UNTOLD] VOLUME--	THE BIBLE IS AN ANTIQUE	1545	1

	FIRST LINE	POEM	LINE
BID			
AND BID THE WORLD GOODMORROW, AND GO TO GLORY HOME!	AWAKE YE MUSES NINE,	1	40
AS CHILDREN BID THE GUEST "GOOD NIGHT"	AS CHILDREN BID THE	133	1
BIDS			
MY COUNTRY BIDS ME GO;	"SIC TRANSIT GLORIA	3	26
BIER			
IS NOTHING BUT A BIER.	THE NOTICE THAT IS	1310	8
BIG			
AND WOULD IT FEEL AS BIG--	A SOLEMN THING--IT WAS--	271	10
AND SO I BEAR IT BIG ABOUT	THIS CHASM, SWEET, UPON	858	17
MOST AS BIG AS I WAS,	IF IT HAD NO PENCIL	921	7
THE DIFFERENCE IS AS BIG	BETWEEN THE FORM OF LIFE	1101	2
THAT EARTH SH'D BE SO BIG--	"RED SEA," INDEED! TALK	1642	10
A WOMAN'S SHAWL AS BIG	THE SUN RETIRED TO A	1693	2
THEY COULD NOT BE SO BIG AS THIS	IF ALL THE GRIEFS I AM	1726	7
BIG MY SECRET BUT IT'S BANDAGED--	REARRANGE A "WIFE'S"	1737	17
BIGGEST			
I'D GIVE MY BIGGEST BOBOLINK!	WHAT WOULD I GIVE TO SEE	247	5
BILL			
HIS BILL AN AUGUR IS	HIS BILL AN AUGUR IS	1034	1
HIS BILL IS CLASPED [LOCKED]--HIS EYE FORSOOK [ESTRANGED]--	HIS BILL IS CLASPED--HIS	1102	1
IN ONE CONSUMMATE BILL,	HOW DARE THE ROBINS SING	1724	6
BILLION			
A RUGGED BILLION MILES--	THE SAVIOR MUST HAVE	1487	8
BILLOW			
HIS COUNTENANCE--A BILLOW--	THE WIND--TAPPED LIKE A	436	13
MUCH BILLOW HATH THE SEA--	EMPTY MY HEART, OF THEE	587	5
AND WHAT A BILLOW BE.	I NEVER SAW A MOOR--	1052	4
A BILLOW WHISPERED IN HIS EAR,	THE WATERS CHASED HIM AS	1749	3
BILLOW'S			
RETREATING UP, A BILLOW'S HIGHT	ESCAPING BACKWARD TO	867	5
BILLOWS			
THEN, HOW THE FIRE EBBS LIKE BILLOWS--	HOW THE OLD MOUNTAINS	291	9
THREE TIMES--THE BILLOWS THREW [TOSSED] ME UP--	THREE TIMES--WE PARTED--	598	5
AT HOME [EASE]--AMONG THE BILLOWS--AS	SHE STAKED HER FEATHERS	798	7
THE BILLOWS OF CIRCUMFERENCE	A SINGLE CLOVER PLANK	1343	7
OR BILLOWS, LIKE A SHORE--	NOT KNOWING WHEN THE	1619	4
BIN			
UNTO A NEIGHBOR'S BIN.	THE PRODUCTS OF MY FARM	1025	4
IT'S TRIUMPHS [PUMPKINS]--TO THE BIN--	A FIELD OF STUBBLE,	1407	4
BIND			
BIND ONE--THE OTHER FLY--	NO RACK CAN TORTURE ME--	384	8
NO BONE HAD HE TO BIND HIM--	THE WIND--TAPPED LIKE A	436	9
AND BIND ASTRONOMY, IN PLACE, [FROM BLAME]	TO INTERRUPT HIS YELLOW	591	11
THAN BIND PHILOSOPHER--	I WATCHED THE MOON	629	20
LATCH [BAR / BIND] THEM SOFTLY--	THESE--SAW VISIONS--	758	2
BIND ME--I STILL CAN SING--	BIND ME--I STILL CAN	1005	1
CATCH [TRAP / BIND] A DROP OF DEW	FOLLOW WISE ORION	1538	V
BINDLESS			
BUT WE DEMAND [BINDLESS IS] THE FLAME	FAME IS THE ONE THAT	1475	8
BINDS			
THE ORCHIS BINDS HER FEATHER ON	SOME RAINBOW--COMING	64	16
THE MAN--UPON THE WOMAN--BINDS--	THE WORLD--STANDS--	493	7
THAT AN IMMORTAL BINDS.	OF PAUL AND SILAS IT IS	1166	8
BIOGRAPHER			
HIS CHEEK IS HIS BIOGRAPHER--	HIS CHEEK IS HIS	1460	1
BIOGRAPHY			
BE THIS FATUITY [BIOGRAPHY]	TWO BUTTERFLIES WENT OUT	533	V
BIOGRAPHY TO ALL WHO PASSED	THE HOLLOWS ROUND HIS	955	5
BIRD SEE BLUE-BIRD,HUMMING-BIRD			
AND GIVE HER WHAT SHE ASKETH, JEWEL, OR BIRD, OR FLOWER--	AWAKE YE MUSES NINE,	1	38
I HAVE A BIRD IN SPRING	I HAVE A BIRD IN SPRING	5	1
KNOWING THAT BIRD OF MINE	I HAVE A BIRD IN SPRING	5	8
KNOWING THAT BIRD OF MINE	I HAVE A BIRD IN SPRING	5	26
THE OTHER, AS A BIRD HER NEST,	ONE SISTER HAVE I IN OUR	14	7
ONLY A BIRD WILL WONDER--	NOBODY KNOWS THIS LITTLE	35	9
THE PATRIARCH'S BIRD RETURNED,	ONCE MORE, MY NOW	48	6
ORCHARD, AND BUTTERCUP, AND BIRD--	A LADY RED--AMID THE	74	11
MY FRIEND MUST BE A BIRD--	MY FRIEND MUST BE A BIRD	92	1
HAS IT FEATHERS LIKE A BIRD?	WILL THERE REALLY BE A	101	6
AND IF I DONT--THE LITTLE BIRD	I HAVE A KING, WHO DOES	103	13
A VERY FEW--A BIRD OR TWO--	THESE ARE THE DAYS WHEN	130	2
FOR EVERY BIRD A NEST--	FOR EVERY BIRD A NEST--	143	1
OR GIDDY BIRD IN ORCHARD--	ON SUCH A NIGHT, OR SUCH	146	15
THIS BIRD--OBSERVING OTHERS	ALL OVERGROWN BY CUNNING	148	5
BUILDS, LIKE A BIRD, TOO!	DUST IS THE ONLY SECRET	153	13
IT IS NOT BIRD--IT HAS NO NEST--	MUSICIANS WRESTLE	157	7
IF THEY W'D LINGER FOR A BIRD	IF I COULD BRIBE THEM BY	179	7
A BIRD--BY CHANCE--THAT GOES THAT WAY--	THE SKIES CANT KEEP	191	5
IF I SHOULD BRIBE THE LITTLE BIRD--	THE SKIES CANT KEEP	191	7
STAB THE BIRD--THAT BUILT IN YOUR BOSOM--	KILL YOUR BALM--AND IT'S	238	5
TIMID AS A BIRD!	WHY--DO THEY SHUT ME OUT	248	4
THAT COULD ABASH THE LITTLE BIRD	"HOPE" IS THE THING WITH	254	7
HIS MIEN [GAIT], WAS SOUNDLESS, LIKE THE [A] BIRD--	THE ONLY GHOST I EVER	274	5
HARKS FOR [DETECTS] THE MEADOW BIRD--	THE DOOMED--REGARD THE	294	6

	FIRST LINE	POEM	LINE
BIRD (CONTINUED)			
JOYFUL--FOR WHOM THE MEADOW BIRD	THE DOOMED--REGARD THE	294	11
A BIRD CAME DOWN THE WALK--	A BIRD CAME DOWN THE	328	1
PLAY IT WERE A HUMMING BIRD--	ALL THE LETTERS I CAN	334	7
THE SOUTHERN CUSTOM--OF THE BIRD--	'TIS NOT THAT DYING	335	5
WHAT IF THE BIRD FROM JOUNEY FAR--	NOT PROBABLE--THE BAREST	346	5
A BIRD--HAD STAMPED HER FOOT--	OF COURSE--I PRAYED--	376	4
THE HUMMING BIRD--ASPIRE--	THERE IS A FLOWER THAT	380	4
A BIRD--IF THEY--PREFER--	IT'S THOUGHTS--AND JUST	495	14
WITHIN MY GARDEN, RIDES A BIRD	WITHIN MY GARDEN, RIDES	500	1
SHE SIGHTS A BIRD--SHE CHUCKLES--	SHE SIGHTS A BIRD--SHE	507	1
BY TROPIC HINT--SOME TRAVELLED BIRD	LIKE FLOWERS, THAT HEARD	513	8
AND STILL IT HURT YOU, AS SOME BIRD	HER SMILE WAS SHAPED	514	3
IT IS NOT OF THE BIRD	TO HEAR AN ORIOLE SING	526	4
IF SPOKEN BY THE DISTANT BIRD--	TWO BUTTERFLIES WENT OUT	533	9
AND KNEW ONE BIRD A TUNE--	WHAT CARE THE DEAD, FOR	592	12
OF BEGGAR--OR OF BIRD--	OF BRUSSELS--IT WAS NOT	602	8
A BIRD SAT CARELESS ON THE FENCE--	THE TREES LIKE TASSELS--	606	17
THEY MIGHT AS WISE HAVE LODGED A BIRD	THEY SHUT ME UP IN PROSE	613	7
NO BLACK BIRD BATES HIS BANJO--	IT MAKES NO DIFFERENCE	620	7
OF BEING IS A BIRD	OF BEING IS A BIRD	653	1
AS IS THE TWITTER OF A BIRD--	WITHOUT THIS--THERE IS	655	3
SEE THE BIRD--REACH IT!	OUT OF SIGHT? WHAT OF	703	2
AND THE BIRD FELL--	LET US PLAY YESTERDAY--	728	16
THE BIRD [DAY] WOULD NOT ARISE--	MY FAITH IS LARGER THAN	766	10
BIRD WENT PRAISING EVERYWHERE--	WHEN I HOPED, I	768	15
A BIRD TO OVERHEAR	IT IS A LONESOME GLEE--	774	5
OR TOO IMPETUOUS BIRD--	NATURE--THE GENTLEST	790	8
GOD GAVE A LOAF TO EVERY BIRD--	GOD GAVE A LOAF TO EVERY	791	1
IF [GRANT] THE BIRD AND THE FARMER--DEEM IT A "PINE"--	BY MY WINDOW HAVE I FOR	797	3
WAS JUSTIFIED OF BIRD--	THIS BAUBLE WAS	805	4
FOR THY WANDERING BIRD?	TWICE HAD SUMMER HER	846	8
NOW, DO YOU DOUBT THAT YOUR BIRD WAS TRUE?	SPLIT THE LARK--AND	861	8
THE BIRD MUST SING TO EARN THE CRUMB	THE BIRD MUST SING TO	880	1
UNTIL A LITTLE BIRD	OUR LITTLE KINSMEN--	885	6
NOT THE SMALLEST BIRD	STRUCK, WAS I, NOR YET	925	14
THE LADY FEEDS HER LITTLE BIRD	THE LADY FEEDS HER	941	1
THE LITTLE BIRD WOULD NOT DISSENT [DEMUR]	THE LADY FEEDS HER	941	3
OVER THE ARC OF THE BIRD--	UNDER THE LIGHT, YET	949	10
THE "BIRD WITHIN THE HAND"	WHICH IS BEST? HEAVEN--	1012	5
AN APTITUDE FOR BIRD--	I'VE DROPPED MY BRAIN--	1046	12
OF THE POOREST BIRD.	SANG FROM THE HEART,	1059	8
A NAMELESS BIRD--A STRANGER	THE SUN WENT DOWN--NO	1079	7
AT HALF PAST THREE, A SINGLE BIRD	AT HALF PAST THREE, A	1084	1
ASSASSIN OF A BIRD	HIS BILL IS CLASPED--HIS	1102	8
THE BIRD DID PRANCE--THE BEE [BIRD] DID PLAY--	THE BIRD DID PRANCE--THE	1107	1
THE BIRD DID PRANCE--THE BEE [BIRD] DID PLAY--	THE BIRD DID PRANCE--THE	1107	1
THE TRANSPORT [RAPTURE / TRIUMPH / RIOT] OF THE BIRD--	THE WIND TOOK UP THE	1134	16
ALSO WITH BIRD AND ASTEROID	THE DUTIES OF THE WIND	1137	11
NOR BY RELAY OF BIRD	DISTANCE--IS NOT THE	1155	2
A PROMPT--EXECUTIVE [BOLD, INSPIRITING] BIRD IS THE JAY--	A PROMPT--EXECUTIVE BIRD	1177	1
WHERE RODE THE BIRD	LIKE BROOMS OF STEEL	1252	7
BEYOND THE REALM OF BIRD--	A WIND THAT ROSE	1259	5
THE MOST TRIUMPHANT BIRD I EVER KNEW OR MET	THE MOST TRIUMPHANT BIRD	1265	1
FROM EVERY OTHER BIRD	THE WAY TO KNOW THE	1279	2
THE BIRD OF BIRDS IS GONE--	THE WAY TO KNOW THE	1279	22
MAGNANIMOUS AS BIRD	NOT WITH A CLUB, THE	1304	9
WHEN THE BIRD WILL CROWD THE TREE	I SUPPOSE THE TIME WILL	1381	3
OR EVERY BIRD WILL POINT AT THEE	TOUCH LIGHTLY NATURE'S	1389	3
A BLUE BIRD	AFTER ALL BIRDS HAVE	1395	T
ACCOSTED BY A TIMID BIRD	A FIELD OF STUBBLE,	1407	5
WITH USUALLY [GENERALLY] A SOBER BIRD--	A FIELD OF STUBBLE,	1407 V	5
I DONT BELIEVE A PEEVISH BIRD	I THOUGHT THE TRAIN	1449	3
AS GUILELESS AS A BIRD	WHOEVER DISENCHANTS	1451	5
BLUE BIRD	BEFORE YOU THOUGHT OF	1465	T
DEPARTED WAS THE BIRD--	AS IMPERCEPTIBLY AS	1540 V	
NO LADDER NEEDS THE BIRD BUT SKIES	NO LADDER NEEDS THE BIRD	1574	1
THE BIRD HER PUNCTUAL MUSIC BRINGS	THE BIRD HER PUNCTUAL	1585	1
UPON HIS SADDLE SPRUNG A [SPRANG THE] BIRD	UPON HIS SADDLE SPRUNG A	1600	1
OR HAS IT [SHE] FEATHERS, LIKE A BIRD,	NOT KNOWING WHEN THE	1619	3
AS A BIRD	AS FROM THE EARTH THE	1630	8
IF BIRD THE SILENCE CONTRADICT	A LANE OF YELLOW LED THE	1650	5
BESIDE THIS TRAVELLING BIRD	CONFERRING WITH MYSELF	1655	8
ATTESTS THE BIRD THAT'S GONE	I SEE THEE CLEARER FOR	1666	8
AN ACRE FOR A BIRD TO CHOOSE	ON MY VOLCANO GROWS THE	1677	3
HIGH FROM THE EARTH I HEARD A BIRD;	HIGH FROM THE EARTH I	1723	1
WHERE EVERY BIRD IS BOLD TO GO	WHERE EVERY BIRD IS BOLD	1758	1
A BIRD BROKE FORTH AND SANG,	A TRAIN WENT THROUGH A	1761	2
BIRDLING			
THIS WAS BUT A BIRDLING--	IT DID NOT SURPRISE ME--	39	9
BIRD'S			
I CAME TO BUILD THE BIRD'S NEST,	SEXTON! MY MASTER'S	96	3
AS BIRD'S FAR NAVIGATION	I'VE KNOWN A HEAVEN,	243	14
WHO CARES ABOUT A BLUE BIRD'S TUNE--	A PANG IS MORE	1530	6
BIRDS			
HERE ARE THE BIRDS THAT SOUGHT THE SUN	THERE IS A MORN BY MEN	24	10
REMARK THAT BIRDS HAVE FLED!	THERE'S SOMETHING	45	16

	FIRST LINE	POEM	LINE
BIRDS (CONTINUED)			
AND BIRDS CAN FLUTTER DOWN--	I OFTEN PASSED THE	51	12
IF BIRDS SHOULD BUILD AS EARLY	IF I SHOULD DIE,	54	7
BIRDS--HOURS--THE BUMBLEBEE--	SOME THINGS THAT FLY	89	2
EXCEPT THE BIRDS WERE HERE!	THE RAINBOW NEVER TELLS	97	8
THESE ARE THE DAYS WHEN BIRDS COME BACK--	THESE ARE THE DAYS WHEN	130	1
BIRDS, BY THE SNOW.	WATER, IS TAUGHT BY	135	6
AND BLUSHING BIRDS GO DOWN TO DRINK,	HAVE YOU GOT A BROOK IN	136	3
MAMA NEVER FORGETS HER BIRDS,	MAMA NEVER FORGETS HER	164	1
BIRDS ARE ANTIQUATED FELLOWS!	I'M THE LITTLE "HEART'S	176	11
AND BIRDS, OF FOREIGN TONGUE!	AS IF SOME LITTLE ARCTIC	180	8
THE BIRDS ROSE SMILING, IN THEIR NESTS--	ON THIS LONG STORM THE	194	5
THE MORNING LIT--THE BIRDS AROSE--	AN AWFUL TEMPEST MASHED	198	10
PIPE THE SWEET BIRDS IN IGNORANT CADENCE--	SAFE IN THEIR ALABASTER	216	10
BIRDS WILL PASS ME	I SHALL KEEP SINGING!	250	2
AS BIRDS--THAT TUMBLE FROM THE CLOUDS	THE LONESOME FOR THEY	262	7
THE BIRDS--IN DOCILE ROWS	THE DAY CAME SLOW--TILL	304	10
IT SCATTERS LIKE THE BIRDS	IT SIFTS FROM LEADEN	311	V
AND BIRDS TAKE PLACES, OVERHEAD,	OF ALL THE SOUNDS	321	23
NOR HOPPED FOR [TO] AUDIENCES--LIKE BIRDS,	I CANNOT DANCE UPON MY	326	11
THE MOTIONS OF THE DIPPING BIRDS--	BEFORE I GOT MY EYE PUT	327	14
WE--ARE THE BIRDS--THAT STAY.	'TIS NOT THAT DYING	335	8
THE BIRDS DECLAIM THEIR TUNES--	THE MORNING AFTER WO--	364	9
IN SENDING ALL THE BIRDS AWAY--	THE WINTERS ARE SO SHORT	403	3
AS BOOTS--WOULD BE--TO BIRDS--	IT WOULD NEVER BE COMMON	430	16
OF NUMEROUS HUMMING BIRDS AT ONCE	THE WIND--TAPPED LIKE A	436	11
I WAS USED--TO THE BIRDS--BEFORE--	BETTER--THAN MUSIC! FOR	503	2
THE TRIUMPH OF THE BIRDS	"HEAVEN" HAS DIFFERENT	575	10
THE BIRDS AND I, HAD OFTEN SHARED	I HAD BEEN HUNGRY, ALL	579	11
OF ALL THE BIRDS THAT BE--	WHAT CARE THE DEAD, FOR	592	14
WHEN THE BIRDS BEGIN TO WHISTLE--	DONT PUT UP MY THREAD &	617	3
NO DIFFERENT THE BIRDS--	OF BEING IS A BIRD	653	8
THE BIRDS REPORTED FROM THE SOUTH--	THE BIRDS REPORTED FROM	743	1
THE BIRDS BEGUN AT FOUR O'CLOCK--	THE BIRDS BEGUN AT FOUR	783	1
THE BIRDS JOCOSER [REDOUBLED] SUNG--	A DROP FELL ON THE APPLE	794	10
THE BIRDS PUT UP THE BARS TO NESTS--	THE WIND BEGUN TO KNEAD	824	13
AS BIRDS BEFORE ACHIEVING	THESE TESTED OUR HORIZON	886	3
BUT WHERE THE BIRDS ASSEMBLE	WHO OCCUPIES THIS HOUSE?	892	15
WITH ONLY BIRDS [BLOOM] TO INTERRUPT	I LEARNED--AT LEAST--	944	11
OR BIRDS--CONFIRMED PERPETUAL	'TWAS AWKWARD, BUT IT	973	7
BIRDS, MOSTLY BACK--	BEE! I'M EXPECTING YOU!	1035	7
FURTHER IN SUMMER THAN THE BIRDS	FURTHER IN SUMMER THAN	1068	1
BIRDS ARE RESUMING FOR HIM--	HE IS ALIVE, THIS	1160	3
WITH THE BLUE BIRDS EXERCISING [BUCCANEERING]	WE LIKE MARCH.	1213	12
BIRDS WITH DISMAY [SURPRISE]	TO FLEE FROM MEMORY	1242	5
THE BIRD OF BIRDS IS GONE--	THE WAY TO KNOW THE	1279	22
THE BIRDS ENAMOR CARE--	THE NOTICE THAT IS	1310	6
I GOT YOUR LETTER, AND THE BIRDS--	DEAR MARCH--COME IN--	1320	11
YET BIRDS EXAMINE IT AND FLEE--	HOW KNOW IT FROM A	1364	5
AFTER ALL BIRDS HAVE BEEN INVESTIGATED AND LAID ASIDE--	AFTER ALL BIRDS HAVE	1395	1
WHY BIRDS, A SUMMER MORNING	ONE JOY OF SO MUCH	1420	5
THE METEOR OF BIRDS,	ONE OF THE ONES THAT	1466	18
TO VENERABLE BIRDS	AN ANTIQUATED TREE	1514	4
NOT BIRDS ENTIRELY--BUT MINDS--	A PANG IS MORE	1530	3
THE PRESBYTERIAN BIRDS CAN NOW RESUME THE MEETING	THE BOBOLINK IS GONE--	1591	3
THE BIRDS SHE LOST--	QUITE EMPTY, QUITE AT	1606	9
A TABERNACLE IS FOR BIRDS	TALK NOT TO ME OF SUMMER	1634	3
THE BIRDS, THEY MAKE IT IN THE SPRING,	THE SADDEST NOISE, THE	1764	3
BIRMINGHAM			
DO BIRMINGHAM [MANCHESTER] ECLIPSE--	A SAUCER HOLDS A CUP	1374	12
BIRTH			
ALIVE--TWO-FOLD--THE BIRTH I HAD--	I AM ALIVE--I GUESS--	470	27
BIRTHDAY			
ONE--BIRTHDAY MORE--OR TEN?	ONE YEAR AGO--JOTS WHAT?	296	35
CHRIST'S BIRTHDAY	THE SAVIOR MUST HAVE	1487	T
BIRTHDAY OF BUT A SINGLE PANG	BIRTHDAY OF BUT A SINGLE	1488	1
BISCAYAN			
OR BISCAYAN HYMN--	NEVER FOR SOCIETY	746	10
BISECT			
DID BUT A SNAKE BISECT THE BRAKE	I NEVER TOLD THE BURIED	11	8
TILL HURRICANE BISECT	THE HEART HAS NARROW	928	5
BISECTED			
AND A BISECTED COACH	DEATH IS THE SUPPLE	1445	8
BISECTED NOW, BY BLEAKER GRIEFS,	SOFTENED BY TIME'S	1738	5
BISECTING			
BY IT'S BISECTING	OF PARADISE' EXISTENCE	1411	5
BIT			
AND JUST A BIT OF "CROWN"--	GOING TO HEAVEN!	79	17
HE BIT [SHOOK] AN ANGLEWORM IN HALVES	A BIRD CAME DOWN THE	328	3
BUT NOT TO MAKE A "BIT OF NOISE"	A LITTLE DOG THAT WAGS	1185	15
BITE			
NOT A SLEET COULD BITE ME--	WHEN I HOPED, I	768	5
BITTER			
BITTER CONTESTED FARTHINGS--	FOR EACH EXTATIC INSTANT	125	7
THE SLEET--THE BITTER WIND--	THE BEGGAR LAD--DIES	717	12
BITTERER			
NO BITTERER DEBAR	YOU TAUGHT ME WAITING	740	6

	FIRST LINE	POEM	LINE
BITTEREST			
A TROUBLE LOOKS BITTEREST--	IT DONT SOUND SO	426	6
BITTERNESS			
MANY A BITTERNESS--HAD BEEN--	IT WOULD NEVER BE COMMON	430	3
BLACK			
A BONNET BLACK--A DUSK SURPLICE--	WHERE I HAVE LOST, I	104	10
A BLACK--AS OF A SPECTRE'S CLOAK	AN AWFUL TEMPEST MASHED	198	3
THE BLACK BERRY--WEARS A THORN IN HIS SIDE--	THE BLACK BERRY--WEARS A	554	1
BRAVE BLACK BERRY--	THE BLACK BERRY--WEARS A	554	12
NO BLACK BIRD BATES HIS BANJO--	IT MAKES NO DIFFERENCE	620	7
MY WITNESS--WAS THE CRAPE [BLACK] I BORE--	THE BIRDS REPORTED FROM	743	19
BUT IN THIS BLACK RECEPTACLE	HIS HEART WAS DARKER	1378	3
BEES ARE BLACK, WITH GILT SURCINGLES--	BEES ARE BLACK, WITH	1405	1
BLACKBIRDS			
BEFORE THE BLACKBIRDS SING!	IT CANT BE "SUMMER"!	221	5
BLACKENED			
THE WILTED [BLACKENED] COUNTENANCE	AS FROST IS BEST	951	8
BLACKSMITH			
LEAST VILLAGE HAS [BOASTS] IT'S BLACKSMITH	DARE YOU SEE A SOUL AT	365	9
BLADE			
. . . BLADE] OF DAY	ONE JOY OF SO MUCH	1420	6
BLADES			
SHE DEALT HER PRETTY WORDS LIKE BLADES--	SHE DEALT HER PRETTY	479	1
BLAME			
THE FLOWER MUST NOT BLAME THE BEE--	THE FLOWER MUST NOT	206	1
NOT BURDOCK'S--BLAME--	A BURDOCK--CLAWED MY	229	2
WHO IS TO BLAME? THE WEAVER?	A SHADY FRIEND--FOR	278	9
WITHOUT A STINT--WITHOUT A BLAME,	YOUR RICHES--TAUGHT ME--	299	19
AND BLAME THE SCANTY LOVE	WE COVER THEE--SWEET	482	9
BLAME THE LITTLE [EMPTY / CHILDISH] HAND	SWEET--YOU FORGOT--BUT I	523	6
THROUGH THEIR BELOVED BLAME--	'TIS TRUE--THEY SHUT ME	538	8
WAS PARADISE--TO BLAME--	IT KNEW NO MEDICINE--	559	12
'TWAS NOT MY BLAME--WHO SPED TOO SLOW--	A DYING TIGER--MOANED	566	9
'TWAS NOT HIS BLAME--WHO DIED	A DYING TIGER--MOANED	566	10
AND BIND ASTRONOMY, IN PLACE, [FROM BLAME]	TO INTERRUPT HIS YELLOW	591	11
IF BLAME BE MY SIDE--FORFEIT ME--	IF BLAME BE MY SIDE--	775	1
THE BLAME THAT I WAS CHOSEN [COMMON]--THEN--	FITTER TO SEE HIM, I MAY	968	8
WAS MY RETRIEVELESS BLAME--	IT BLOOMED AND DROPT, A	978	12
TOO SHY, THAT ANY BLAME--	I WAS A PHEBE--NOTHING	1009	6
SPOTLESS BE FROM BLAME	UP LIFE'S HILL WITH MY	1010	6
'TWAS'NT MY BLAME--	SANG FROM THE HEART,	1059	12
IS SHE SO MUCH TO BLAME?	IF NATURE SMILES--THE	1085	4
TOMORROW WERE, A BLAME	THE LAST NIGHT THAT SHE	1100	12
OUR PREMISES TO BLAME.	GOD MADE NO ACT WITHOUT	1163	4
THAT BLAME IS JUST AS DEAR AS PRAISE	DEAR MARCH--COME IN--	1320	25
AND PRAISE AS MERE AS BLAME--	DEAR MARCH--COME IN--	1320	26
ENACT ALL OTHER BLAME	THE LOOK OF THEE, WHAT	1689	10
BLISS WAS MOST TO BLAME.	HAD I KNOWN THAT THE	1720	8
BLAMED			
THIS NEW CIRCUMFERENCE--HAVE BLAMED--	I SHOULD HAVE BEEN TOO	313	5
YET BLAMED THE FATE THAT FRACTURED--[FLUNG IT] LESS	IT DROPPED SO LOW--IN MY	747	5
BLAMELESS			
HER BLAMELESS MYSTERY--	A SOLEMN THING--IT WAS--	271	4
BLAMELESS OF A NAME--	BLOOM UPON THE MOUNTAIN	667	2
BECAUSE THE BEE MAY BLAMELESS HUM	BECAUSE THE BEE MAY	869	1
OF BARNS FOR WINTER--BLAMELESS [IGNORANT]--	THOSE CATTLE SMALLER	1388	5
BLANCH			
IN PIROUETTE TO BLANCH A TROUPE--	I CANNOT DANCE UPON MY	326	7
THE SURGEON--DOES NOT BLANCH--AT PAIN--	THERE IS A LANGUOR OF	396	9
BLAND			
BESIDE US LIKE A BLAND ABYSS	POWER IS A FAMILIAR	1238	3
AND TRUE [BEST / REAL / BLAND / FINE / FAIR] THE OTHER . . .	I'D RATHER RECOLLECT A	1349	4
A DEVOTEE HAS OFT [COOL / BLAND] CONSIGNED	DEATH WARRANTS ARE	1375	5
A BLAND UNCERTAINTY	WHY SHOULD WE HURRY--WHY	1646	8
THE POINT WITH BLAND PREVISION	THEY TALK AS SLOW AS	1697	7
BLANDLY			
IT'S CURTAINS BLANDLY SWEEP--	WATER MAKES MANY BEDS	1428	4
BLANK			
OUR BLANK IN BLISS TO FILL	OUR SHARE OF NIGHT TO	113	3
OUR BLANK IN SCORNING--	OUR SHARE OF NIGHT TO	113	4
BUT BLANK--AND STEADY WILDERNESS--	LIKE EYES THAT LOOKED ON	458	3
I'LL TELL THEE ALL--HOW BALD [BLANK] IT GREW--	IF I MAY HAVE IT, WHEN	577	14
POUR AS BLANK ON THEM	WHAT CARE THE DEAD, FOR	592	5
AND CHIPS OF BLANK--IN BOYISH EYES--	MY PORTION IS DEFEAT--	639	10
PAIN--HAS AN ELEMENT OF BLANK--	PAIN--HAS AN ELEMENT OF	650	1
FROM BLANK TO BLANK--	FROM BLANK TO BLANK--	761	1
FROM BLANK TO BLANK--	FROM BLANK TO BLANK--	761	1
WHOSE WILL--A NUMB SIGNIFICANCE--[BLANK INTELLIGENCE]	DENIAL--IS THE ONLY FACT	965	3
TO BREATHE MY BLANK WITHOUT THEE	THROUGH WHAT TRANSPORTS	1153	3
BLANKET			
BARTSIA, IN THE BLANKET RED--	WHOSE ARE THE LITTLE	142	15
BLANKET WEALTHIER THE NEIGHBOR	SNOW BENEATH WHOSE	942	5
BLANKETLESS			
BRIGHT FIRES--THE BLANKETLESS--	'TIS OPPOSITES--ENTICE--	355	3
BLARE			
THE FLASH [FLARE / GLARE / BLARE] BETWEEN THE CREVICES OF CRASH--	IT WAS A QUIET SEEMING	1419	V

	FIRST LINE	POEM	LINE
BLASPHEME			
IT'S SWEET PARADE--BLASPHEME THE PLACE-- .	IT MIGHT BE LONELIER	405	11
BLAST			
A LITTLE BRIG I KNEW--O'ERTOOK BY BLAST-- .	IT TOSSED--AND TOSSED--	723	2
'TWAS UNDESERVED BLAST--	TO BREAK SO VAST A HEART	1312	4
BLAZE			
NOONS BLAZE!	IF PAIN FOR PEACE	63	12
OF BRONZE--AND BLAZE--	OF BRONZE--AND BLAZE--	290	1
OF UNANNOINTED BLAZE.	DARE YOU SEE A SOUL AT	365	8
WITH HAMMER, AND WITH BLAZE	DARE YOU SEE A SOUL AT	365	14
THE RED--BLAZE--IS THE MORNING--	THE RED--BLAZE--IS THE	469	1
AND BLAZE--THE BUTTERFLIES!	AS FAR FROM PITY, AS	496	12
CAN BLAZE BE SHOWN [DONE] IN COCHINEAL-- .	I FOUND THE WORDS TO	581	7
BUT THIS LITTLE BLAZE	I COULD BRING YOU JEWELS	697	6
TO ONE WHO NEVER FELT IT BLAZE--	LOVE RECKONS BY ITSELF--	826	3
BLAZED			
BLAZED OPEN--SUDDENLY--	IF I'M LOST--NOW--	256	5
BLAZING			
BLAZING IN GOLD AND QUENCHING IN PURPLE . .	BLAZING IN GOLD AND	228	1
THE NORTH--HER BLAZING SIGN	THE SUNRISE RUNS FOR	710	10
GO TIMID, LEST [SHOULD] HIS FINAL [TESTING / BLAZING / LOFTY] EYE	GO SLOW, MY SOUL, TO	1297	5
BLEAK			
AND SO OF WO, BLEAK DREADED--COME, . . .	'TIS SO APPALLING--IT	281	21
HAD ALL MY LIFE BUT BEEN [BEEN ONE / BEEN BLEAK] MISTAKE	I THINK TO LIVE--MAY BE	646	27
ARE ANY HOAR [BLEAK] FOR HIM?	THAT ODD OLD MAN IS DEAD	1130	6
BY THAT BLEAK EXULTATION	THROUGH WHAT TRANSPORTS	1153	5
A BEAUTIFUL BUT BLEAK CONDITION	WONDER--IS NOT PRECISELY	1331	3
AND A CHILL [BLEAK] SMILE INLAID WITH BALMS--	ABOVE OBLIVION'S TIDE	1531	V 4
BLEAKER			
TO HELP OUR BLEAKER PARTS	TO HELP OUR BLEAKER	1064	1
BISECTED NOW, BY BLEAKER GRIEFS, ...	SOFTENED BY TIME'S	1738	5
BLEAKNESS			
ON THE BLEAKNESS OF MY LOT	SOIL OF FLINT, IF STEADY	681	V
BLEATING			
WHOSE BLEATING CEASES TO REPEAT	LET DOWN THE BARS, OH	1065	3
BLEATS			
FAITH BLEATS [FAINTS] TO UNDERSTAND-- . .	I SHOULD HAVE BEEN TOO	313	24
BLEEDING			
SET BLEEDING FEET TO MINUETS	HEART, NOT SO HEAVY AS	83	15
LIMIT--HOW DEEP A BLEEDING GO!	BOUND--A TROUBLE--	269	3
BLEEDS			
MY [ONE] JUSTICE BLEEDS--FOR THEE! . . .	IT ALWAYS FELT TO ME--A	597	24
BLEMISHLESS			
AS BLEMISHLESS, AS HER.	HER LITTLE PARASOL TO	1038	8
BLEND			
AND CENTURIES OF AUGUST CEASE [FUSE / LAPSE / BLEND]	THERE IS A ZONE WHOSE	1056	7
BLENT			
BE UNDERTAKING BLENT	TO UNDERTAKE IS TO	1070	2
BLESS			
EXCEPT [UNTIL] THOU BLESSME"--STRANGER [SIGNOR]!	A LITTLE EAST OF JORDAN,	59	11
BLESS GOD, HE WENT AS SOLDIERS, ...	BLESS GOD, HE WENT AS	147	1
KILL YOUR BALM--AND IT'S ODORS BLESS YOU-- .	KILL YOUR BALM--AND IT'S	238	1
YOU SEE--GOD BLESS HIS SUDDENNESS-- . . .	BEFORE YOU THOUGHT OF	1465	3
BLESSED			
THE BLESSED ETHER--TAUGHT THEM--	THE LONESOME FOR THEY	262	9
'TWERE BLESSED TO HAVE SEEN--	I'VE SEEN A DYING EYE	547	8
ONE MORE--"YE BLESSED"--TO BE TOLD-- . . .	THERE IS A SHAME OF	551	7
BY BLESSED HEALTH OBSCURED--	AS ONE DOES SICKNESS	957	4
BLESSEDER			
YET BLESSEDER--THAN WE--	THOSE FAIR--FICTITIOUS	499	14
'TWAS BLESSEDER--THE SEEING NOT--	TRUST IN THE UNEXPECTED	555	V 15
BLESSES			
WHICH BLESSES MOST, ...	WHICH MISSES MOST,	1759	6
BLESSING			
THE HEART ASKS PLEASURE [BLESSING]--FIRST--	THE HEART ASKS PLEASURE	536	1
ONE BLESSING HAD I THAN THE REST	ONE BLESSING HAD I THAN	756	1
BLEST			
OF ALL THE MARTIAL BLEST!	BLESS GOD, HE WENT AS	147	4
THE BLINDNESS THAT BEHELD AND BLEST-- . .	WHO SAW NO SUNRISE	1018	7
BLEW			
WHEN BREATH BLEW [DREW] BACK, ...	JUST LOST, WHEN I WAS	160	4
THE FORMER, BLEW AWAY.	I CAUTIOUS, SCANNED MY	178	6
THE FLOWERS, ACCUSTOMED, BLEW, ...	THERE CAME A DAY AT	322	6
AND FLOWER--THAT ZEALOUS BLEW--	FROM COCOON FORTH A	354	19
BLEW OUT ITSELF--FOR FEAR--	THE NIGHT WAS WIDE, AND	589	4
TILL ALL THE GRIEF WITH SUMMER--WAVED [BLEW]	'TIS GOOD--THE LOOKING	660	7
I BET WITH EVERY WIND THAT BLEW	I BET WITH EVERY WIND	1215	1
I KNEW IT BLEW FOR ME--	I SAW THE WIND WITHIN	1502	2
BLIND			
AS BLIND MEN LEARN THE SUN!	TO LEARN THE TRANSPORT	167	2
THE BLIND--ESTEEM IT BE	'TIS OPPOSITES--ENTICE--	355	5
MAKE THE BLIND--LEAP--	LET US PLAY YESTERDAY--	728	12
'TWAS LIGHTER [FIRMER]--TO BE BLIND-- . .	FROM BLANK TO BLANK--	761	10
HIS MIND WERE GOING BLIND--	HE SCANNED IT--STAGGERED	1062	5
THE DILIGENCE WERE NOT MORE BLIND	WHAT TWIGS WE HELD BY--	1086	13
SO BLIND WITH [FULL OF] JOY HE COULD	THE BIRD DID PRANCE--THE	1107	3

	FIRST LINE	POEM	LINE
BLIND (CONTINUED)			
NOT CHOOSE OR EVERY MAN BE BLIND--	TELL ALL THE TRUTH BUT	1129	8
BE CURRENT WITH THE BLIND	THE LILAC IS AN ANCIENT	1241	18
HOW WELL THAT [PRUDENT] WE ARE BLIND-- . .	HAD WE OUR SENSES	1284	6
BLINDED			
THINE EYES ARE SADLY BLINDED, BUT YET THOU MAYEST SEE	AWAKE YE MUSES NINE,	1	33
RETREATING BLINDED DOWN	ESCAPING BACKWARD TO	867.	6
BLINDING			
WITH STEADY--DRIFTING--[SUDDEN--BLINDING] GRAINS	I CROSS TILL I AM WEARY	550	7
BLINDNESS			
BLINDNESS--ON THE DAWN--	IF HE DISSOLVE--THEN--	236	5
WE WONDERED AT OUR BLINDNESS	HER FINAL SUMMER WAS IT	795	9
THE BLINDNESS THAT BEHELD AND BLEST-- . .	WHO SAW NO SUNRISE	1018	7
BLINDS			
TO FEEL IF BLINDS BE FAST--	THE NIGHT WAS WIDE, AND	589	13
BLISS			
HAD NOT THE BLISS SO SLOW A PACE	DELAYED TILL SHE HAD	58	10
NEXT BLISS!	WHERE I HAVE LOST, I	104	16
THIS PLACE IS BLISS--THIS TOWN IS HEAVEN-- .	WHERE BELLS NO MORE	112	7
OUR BLANK IN BLISS TO FILL	OUR SHARE OF NIGHT TO	113	3
BLISS IS BUT BLISS, AND BREATH BUT BREATH! .	'TIS SO MUCH JOY! 'TIS	172	8
BLISS IS BUT BLISS, AND BREATH BUT BREATH! .	'TIS SO MUCH JOY! 'TIS	172	8
MY KINGDOM'S WORTH OF BLISS!	WHAT WOULD I GIVE TO SEE	247	29
I PONDERED HOW THE BLISS WOULD LOOK-- . .	A SOLEMN THING--IT WAS--	271	9
JUST TO MAKE BLISS	I KNOW THAT HE EXISTS.	338	7
IS BLISS THEN, SUCH ABYSS, ...	IS BLISS THEN, SUCH	340	1
BUT BLISS, IS SOLD JUST ONCE.	IS BLISS THEN, SUCH	340	9
MY PREMIUM--MY BLISS--	MY REWARD FOR BEING, WAS	343	2
BETWEEN THE BLISS--AND ME--	I GAINED IT SO--	359	4
AFFORDS A BLISS LIKE MURDER--	REHEARSAL TO OURSELVES	379	3
SUCH BLISS--HAD I--FOR ALL THE YEARS-- . .	IT WOULD NEVER BE COMMON	430	7
BLISS--WERE AN ODDITY--WITHOUT THEE-- . .	LOVE--THOU ART HIGH--	453	16
WHEN BLISS DISCLOSED A HUNDRED TOES [WINGS]--	SHE SIGHTS A BIRD--SHE	507	11
A COMMON BLISS	MUST BE A WO--	571	9
'TIS BLISS [WEALTH / RIGHT] I CANNOT WEIGH--	IF I MAY HAVE IT, WHEN	577	6
I THINK TO LIVE--MAY BE A BLISS [LIFE] . .	I THINK TO LIVE--MAY BE	646	1
BLISS OF DEATH--LIFE'S BLISS EXTOL THRO [SURPASS IN / EXCEL IN]	PROMISE THIS--WHEN YOU	648	15
BLISS OF DEATH--LIFE'S BLISS EXTOL THRO [SURPASS IN / EXCEL IN]	PROMISE THIS--WHEN YOU	648	15
A PERFECT--PARALYZING BLISS--	ONE BLESSING HAD I THAN	756	7
WHY BLISS SO SCANTILY [CAUTIOUSLY] DISBURSE [EXPRESS / AFFORD]--	ONE BLESSING HAD I THAN	756	17
THE BLISS TO CAUTERIZE--	THE WHOLE OF IT CAME NOT	762	4
I HAD A DAILY BLISS	I HAD A DAILY BLISS	1057	1
BLISS IS FRUGAL OF HER LEASES	PARADISE IS THAT OLD	1119	5
I REACHED THE STOLID BLISS	THROUGH WHAT TRANSPORTS	1153	2
AS OLD AS BLISS [JOY]	AS OLD AS WOE--	1168	4
THAT SUCH A BLISS HAS BEEN.	OF SO DIVINE A LOSS	1179	4
IS OF ITSELF A BLISS--	TO OWN A SUSAN OF MY OWN	1401	2
A MOB OF SOLID BLISS--	FROM ALL THE JAILS THE	1532	6
AND ECONOMICAL OF BLISS	MEETING BY ACCIDENT,	1548	7
BLISS IS THE PLAYTHING [TRINKET] OF THE CHILD--	BLISS IS THE PLAYTHING	1553	1
THE IMPLEMENTS OF BLISS ARE FEW--	NO LADDER NEEDS THE BIRD	1574	5
OF BLISS THE CODES [THE IMPLEMENTS OF BLISS] ARE FEW--	TO HER DERIDED HOME	1586	9
OF BLISS THE CODES [THE IMPLEMENTS OF BLISS] ARE FEW--	TO HER DERIDED HOME	1586	9
WERE A RECEIPTED BLISS	THE ECSTASY TO GUESS	1608	2
ARE OBSOLETE TO BLISS--	THEIR DAPPLED	1611	4
BLISS WAS MOST TO BLAME.	HAD I KNOWN THAT THE	1720	8
TO THIS REVOLTING BLISS	THE WATERS CHASED HIM AS	1749	8
BLISS'			
BLISS' EARLY SHAPE	I HAD THE GLORY--THAT	349	5
BLISSFUL			
FOR BLISSFUL CAUSES--MOST OF ALL	SHE'S HAPPY, WITH A NEW	535	6
BUT LEAVES A SUMPTUOUS [BLISSFUL] DESTITUTION--	IN MANY AND REPORTLESS	1382	7
THE REELING [BLISSFUL] ORIOLE--	ONE OF THE ONES THAT	1466	4
IN BLISSFUL [LUSCIOUS / SUMPTUOUS] REVERY .	HIS ORIENTAL HERESIES	1526	V
BLISTER			
THIS THIRST WOULD BLISTER--EASIER--NOW-- .	ONE YEAR AGO--JOTS WHAT?	296	16
BLISTERED			
IT BLISTERED TO MY DREAM--	IT STRUCK ME--EVERY DAY	362	6
BLISTERS			
BLISTERS THE ADAMANT!	I'LL SEND THE FEATHER	687	6
BLITHE			
HOW VERY BLITHE THE FINGERS [MAIDEN] . . .	IF RECOLLECTING WERE	33	7
BLOCK			
IT GAINS THE BLOCK--AND NOW--IT GAINS THE DOOR--	IT'S COMING--THE	390	2
THE OTHER SIDE THE BLOCK--	I HAD NOT MINDED--WALLS	398	4
BLOCK IT UP	TO FILL A GAP	546	3
AND LOOK--AND SHUDDER, AND BLOCK YOUR BREATH--	DID YOU EVER STAND IN A	590	3
DID BLOCK THE GILDED HANDS--	I THINK THE LONGEST HOUR	635	6
DRIFT MAY BLOCK WITHIN IT	ABSENT PLACE--AN APRIL	927	5

	FIRST LINE	POEM	LINE
BLOCK (CONTINUED)			
TO WHICH MY FAITH PINNED BLOCK BY BLOCK . .	FALSEHOOD OF THEE COULD	1007	3
TO WHICH MY FAITH PINNED BLOCK BY BLOCK . .	FALSEHOOD OF THEE COULD	1007	3
TO CRUCIFIX OR BLOCK [STAKE]	DEATH WARRANTS ARE	1375	6
BLOCKED			
UNTIL IT BLOCKED MY EYES--	THE FIRST DAY'S NIGHT	410	12
AND BLOCKED THE COMING IN.	IT CAME AT LAST BUT	1230	8
BLOCKS			
AND MY HORIZON BLOCKS	I CROSS TILL I AM WEARY	550	6
BLONDE			
THAT COVERS MYSTERY WITH BLONDE--	THE TINT I CANNOT TAKE--	627	V 19
HORSES OF BLONDE--AND COACH OF SILVER-- . .	DROPPED INTO THE ETHER	665	5
UPON A SEA OF BLONDE--	YOU'VE SEEN BALLOONS SET	700	6
HER FOREHEAD IS OF AMPLEST BLONDE--	THE MOON WAS BUT A CHIN	737	5
AND WITH A BLONDE PUSH	BANISH AIR FROM AIR--	854	10
CHRYSALIS OF BLONDE--OR UMBER--	COLOR--CASTE--	970	11
THE BLONDE ASSASSIN PASSES ON--	APPARENTLY WITH NO	1624	5
BLOOD			
WITHOUT A QUICKER BLOOD, ...	I NEVER HEAR THE WORD	77	2
LEST ANYBODY SPY THE BLOOD	A WOUNDED DEER--LEAPS	165	11
I'VE RUBIES--LIKE THE EVENING BLOOD-- . .	I CAME TO BUY A SMILE--	223	11
BLOOD OF HIS BLOOD--	FOREVER AT HIS SIDE TO	246	4
BLOOD OF HIS BLOOD--	FOREVER AT HIS SIDE TO	246	4
DWELL IN ONE BLOOD	WHILE IT IS ALIVE	491	4
IT IS A TRUTH [FACT]--OF BLOOD--	WE DREAM--IT IS GOOD WE	531	6
THE HUE--OF IT--IS BLOOD--	THE NAME--OF IT--IS	656	2
AND CREWS--OF SOLID BLOOD--	WHOLE GULFS--OF RED, AND	658	2
BY BUT A CRUMB OF BLOOD, FASTS SCARLET . .	AS THE STARVED MAELSTROM	872	5
OH LIFE, BEGUN IN FLUENT BLOOD	THAT ODD OLD MAN IS DEAD	1130	9
BUT STATE WITH CREEPING BLOOD	IN WINTER IN MY ROOM	1670	13
BLOOM			
FOR THEE TO BLOOM, I'LL SKIP THE TOMB . .	SUMMER FOR THEE, GRANT I	31	5
WHEN ROSES CEASE TO BLOOM, SIR, ...	WHEN ROSES CEASE TO	32	1
TO BLOOM SO, BYE AND BYE--	WHEN I COUNT THE SEEDS	40	3
BLOOM ETERNALLY!	THO' MY DESTINY BE	163	12
OR BUTTERFLIES--THAT "BLOOM"?	MAKE ME A PICTURE OF THE	188	11
HAUNT THE PERENNIAL BLOOM--	FOR THIS--ACCEPTED	195	11
THE BUTTERCUP'S, MY WHIM FOR BLOOM-- . . .	THE ROBIN'S MY CRITERION	285	6
CREATOR--SHALL I--BLOOM?	GOD MADE A LITTLE	442	12
FILAMENTS OF BLOOM, PONTIUS PILATE SOWED-- .	TO PUT THIS WORLD DOWN,	527	10
AND IN THE PLACE [STEAD] OF BLOOM	IT KNEW NO MEDICINE--	559	8
'TIS TRUE, YOUR GARDEN LED THE BLOOM, . .	OURSELVES WERE WED ONE	631	13
NO GOBLIN--ON THE BLOOM--	I THINK TO LIVE--MAY BE	646	14
BLOOM UPON THE MOUNTAIN--STATED--	BLOOM UPON THE MOUNTAIN	667	1
BLOOM I STROVE TO RAISE--	SOIL OF FLINT, IF STEADY	681	V
WHERE BLOOM AND BEES	THIS QUIET DUST WAS	813	6
THE ROSE CONTENT MAY BLOOM	THE BIRD MUST SING TO	880	4
BUT THE RECOLLECTING OF BLOOM	HOW HAPPY I WAS IF I	898	4
WITH ONLY BIRDS [BLOOM] TO INTERRUPT . . .	I LEARNED--AT LEAST--	944	11
IN CONSUMMATED BLOOM--	MIDSUMMER, WAS IT, WHEN	962	4
A SINGLE BLOOM WE CONSTITUTE	HERE, WHERE THE DAISIES	1037	11
AS BLOOM UPON A STALK.	THE OPENING AND THE	1047	4
BLOOM--IS RESULT--TO MEET A FLOWER . . .	BLOOM--IS RESULT--TO	1058	1
EXCELLENT IS BLOOM	REVOLUTION IS THE POD	1082	4
BLOOMED			
IT BLOOMED AND DROPT, A SINGLE NOON-- . .	IT BLOOMED AND DROPT, A	978	1
BLOOMING			
BLOOMING--TRIPPING--FLOWING--	SO HAS A DAISY VANISHED	28	7
BLOOMS			
TO VANQUISH OTHER BLOOMS.	LIKE TRAINS OF CARS ON	1224	8
BLOSSOM SEE A'BLOSSOM			
PICK BY FAITH IT'S BLOSSOM	WHEN I COUNT THE SEEDS	40	9
BLOSSOM AND I--	I KEEP MY PLEDGE.	46	9
A BLOSSOM, OR A BOOK, ...	BY CHIVALRIES AS TINY,	55	2
WHICH BLOSSOM IN THE DARK.	BY CHIVALRIES AS TINY,	55	4
NO BLOSSOM STAYED AWAY	I DREADED THAT FIRST	348	22
YET INTERDICT--MY BLOSSOM--	I ENVY SEAS, WHEREON HE	498	21
THE MORNINGS BLOSSOM INTO NOONS--	IT MAKES NO DIFFERENCE	620	3
BUT, BLOSSOM, WERE I, ...	'TWOULD EASE--A	682	5
GO BLOSSOM TO THE BEES--I SAID--	THE BIRDS REPORTED FROM	743	7
HEREIN A BLOSSOM LIES--	HEREIN A BLOSSOM LIES--	899	1
THIS IS A BLOSSOM OF THE BRAIN--	THIS IS A BLOSSOM OF THE	945	1
WHOSE ANTIQUATED BLOSSOM	TRUSTY AS THE STARS	1369	6
AND EVERY BLOSSOM ON THE BUSH	A ROUTE OF EVANESCENCE	1463	5
UNOBTRUSIVE BLOSSOM	FOLLOW WISE ORION	1538	V
BLOSSOMS			
MY DEPARTING BLOSSOMS	THE GENTIAN WEAVES HER	18	3
AND ROW MY BLOSSOMS O'ER!	SUMMER FOR THEE, GRANT I	31	6
HER BLOSSOMS, LIKE A DREAM--	LIKE SOME OLD FASHIONED	302	10
AND PILED HER BLOSSOMS ON--	THE MORNING AFTER WO--	364	6
I PUT NEW BLOSSOMS IN THE GLASS--	I TIE MY HAT--I CREASE	443	5
TO JUST VIBRATING BLOSSOMS!	WITHIN MY GARDEN, RIDES	500	19
BY BLOSSOMS GRADUAL [COMMON] PROCESS-- . .	HE GAVE AWAY HIS LIFE--	567	11
BLOSSOMS STAND NEGATIVE, ...	SPRING COMES ON THE	1042	5
WHEN THEY COME BACK--IF BLOSSOMS DO-- . .	WHEN THEY COME BACK--IF	1080	1
IF BLOSSOMS CAN BE BORN AGAIN	WHEN THEY COME BACK--IF	1080	3
BLOSSOMS--DRESS FOR HIS SAKE.	HE IS ALIVE, THIS	1160	4
BLOSSOMS WILL RUN AWAY, ...	BLOSSOMS WILL RUN AWAY,	1578	1
BLOT			
TILL THE HOUSES BLOT	HOW THE OLD MOUNTAINS	291	14

	FIRST LINE	POEM	LINE
BLOTTED			
AND TRODDEN OUT [BLOTTED OUT-- / SHOVED AWAY--] THE MILLS--	THE BRAIN, WITHIN IT'S	556	8
BLOW SEE A-BLOW			
IN CASE THE WIND SHOULD BLOW!	"SIC TRANSIT GLORIA	3	28
WHERE BASHFUL FLOWERS BLOW,	HAVE YOU GOT A BROOK IN	136	2
WHICH UPON THE HILLSIDE BLOW.	FLOWERS--WELL--IF	137	8
FOR THE ETHERIAL BLOW	HE FUMBLES AT YOUR SOUL	315	6
AND NEWER FASHIONS BLOW--	THERE IS A FLOWER THAT	380	22
THAT GETS A STAGGERING BLOW--	AT LEISURE IS THE SOUL	618	2
A DEATH BLOW IS A LIFE BLOW TO SOME	A DEATH BLOW IS A LIFE	816	1
A DEATH BLOW IS A LIFE BLOW TO SOME	A DEATH BLOW IS A LIFE	816	1
I CAN RETURN THE BLOW--	ALONE AND IN A	1167	18
REQUIRED A BLOW AS VAST--	TO BREAK SO VAST A HEART	1312	2
BLOWN			
A FLOWER SUPERFLUOUS BLOWN.	EXCEPT TO HEAVEN, SHE IS	154	4
HER BOW--TO ATOMS BLOWN--	THE FIRST DAY'S NIGHT	410	6
BLOWN TREMULOUS IN GLASS--	THE WIND--TAPPED LIKE A	436	16
WAS NEVER BLOWN AWAY--	NO BRIGADIER THROUGHOUT	1561	8
BLOWS			
THEY WILL NOT STIR FOR BLOWS--	TIME'S WILY CHARGERS	1458	4
BLUE			
DO THE BLUE HAVENS BY THE HAND	A POOR--TORN HEART-- A	78	15
WHO SPUN THE BREADTHS OF BLUE!	BRING ME THE SUNSET IN A	128	6
BY WITHES OF SUPPLE BLUE?	BRING ME THE SUNSET IN A	128	15
A BLUE AND GOLD MISTAKE.	THESE ARE THE DAYS WHEN	130	6
BLUE SEA! WILT WELCOME ME?	MY RIVER RUNS TO THEE--	162	2
BENEATH HIS FADED JACKET'S BLUE--	I MET A KING THIS	166	6
AND BLUE--BELOVED AIR!	TO LEARN THE TRANSPORT	167	8
HEAVEN DOES NOT CHANGE HER BLUE.	I'M THE LITTLE "HEART'S	176	12
A SLASH OF BLUE--	A SLASH OF BLUE--	204	1
FROM INNS OF MOLTEN BLUE--	I TASTE A LIQUOR NEVER	214	8
STRAITS OF BLUE	WHAT WOULD I GIVE TO SEE	247	12
OR BLUE BEARD'S GALLERIES--	LIKE SOME OLD FASHIONED	302	8
THAN GAIN--MY BLUE PENINSULA--	IT MIGHT BE LONELIER	405	15
WITH BLUE--UNCERTAIN STUMBLING BUZZ--	I HEARD A FLY BUZZ--WHEN	465	13
THEN MADE BLUE FACES IN MY FACE--	THREE TIMES--WE PARTED--	598	7
YET BLUE--AND SOLID [EASY]--STOOD--	IT TROUBLED ME AS ONCE I	600	6
AND TUMBLE--BLUE--ON ME--	IT TROUBLED ME AS ONCE I	600	16
OR IT'S ADVANTAGE--BLUE--	I WATCHED THE MOON	629	36
FOR--HOLD THEM--BLUE TO BLUE--	THE BRAIN--IS WIDER THAN	632	6
FOR--HOLD THEM--BLUE TO BLUE--	THE BRAIN--IS WIDER THAN	632	6
BLUE IS BLUE--THE WORLD THROUGH--	OUT OF SIGHT? WHAT OF	703	8
BLUE IS BLUE--THE WORLD THROUGH--	OUT OF SIGHT? WHAT OF	703	8
THE NOON UNWINDS HER BLUE	THE SUNRISE RUNS FOR	710	4
THE OCEAN'S HEART TOO SMOOTH--TOO BLUE--	IT TOSSED--AND TOSSED--	723	11
HER DIMITIES--OF BLUE--	THE MOON WAS BUT A CHIN	737	20
OBSCURED WITH RUDDIER [NEARER / COMELIER] BLUE--	ONE BLESSING HAD I THAN	756	14
PRICKLED BLUE [RAW] AND COOL--	WHEN I HOPED, I	768	14
AND BLUE MONOTONY	THE HEART HAS NARROW	928	4
PRODIGAL OF BLUE	NATURE RARER USES YELLOW	1045	4
WITH THE BLUE BIRDS EXERCISING [BUCCANEERING]	WE LIKE MARCH.	1213	12
A BLUE BIRD	AFTER ALL BIRDS HAVE	1395	T
A WILD BLUE SKY ABREAST OF WINDS	A WILD BLUE SKY ABREAST	1415	1
BLUE BIRD	BEFORE YOU THOUGHT OF	1465	T
WHO CARES ABOUT A BLUE BIRD'S TUNE--	A PANG IS MORE	1530	6
THE SHEET WAS BLUE--	A CURIOUS CLOUD	1710	3
BLUE-BIRD			
NATURE IMPARTS THE LITTLE BLUE-BIRD--ASSURED	AFTER ALL BIRDS HAVE	1395	2
BLUEST			
NATURE WAS IN AN OPAL [HER BERYL / HER BLUEST] APRON,	IT SOUNDED AS IF THE	1397	7
BLUNDER			
AND MAKE MUCH BLUNDER, IF AT LAST	MY COCOON TIGHTENS--	1099	11
THE BLUNDER IS IN ESTIMATE	THE BLUNDER IS IN	1684	1
BLUNDERED			
HAD YOU EARLIER BLUNDERED IN	TAKE YOUR HEAVEN FURTHER	388	3
BLUR			
THAT--DOES NOT BLUR MY GEM!	ONE LIFE OF SO MUCH	270	10
AND WOULD IT BLUR THE CHRISTMAS GLEE	'TWAS JUST THIS TIME,	445	17
BLURS			
ACROSS MY MOUTH--IT BLURS IT--	I AM ALIVE--I GUESS--	470	7
BLUSH			
HAS LOST A BLUSH TODAY?	WHOSE CHEEK IS THIS?	82	3
WHERE IS THE BLUSH--	ANSWER JULY--	386	3
WOULD NOT BLUSH TO OWN--	DONT PUT UP MY THREAD &	617	8
THE SMOULDERING EMBERS BLUSH--	THE SMOULDERING EMBERS	1132	1
WE BLUSH, THAT HEAVEN IF WE ACHIEVE [BEHOLD]--	WHO WERE "THE FATHER AND	1258	21
IT CANNOT GLOW [THRILL / BLUSH]--	PRAISE IT--'TIS DEAD--	1384	2
AS LONG AS HE CAN BLUSH	HIS CHEEK IS HIS	1460	2
BLUSH, MY SPIRIT, IN THY FASTNESS--	REARRANGE A "WIFE'S"	1737	5
BLUSH, MY UNACKNOWLEDGED CLAY--	REARRANGE A "WIFE'S"	1737	6
BLUSHES			
BLUSHES, IF ANY SEE--	THIS WORLD IS NOT	501	14
BLUSHING			
AND BORE HER STRUGGLING, BLUSHING,	SO BASHFUL WHEN I SPIED	91	7
AND BLUSHING BIRDS GO DOWN TO DRINK,	HAVE YOU GOT A BROOK IN	136	3
BOANERGES			
AND [THEN] NEIGH LIKE BOANERGES--	I LIKE TO SEE IT LAP	585	14

	FIRST LINE	POEM	LINE
BOARD			
SUCH PLENTY SMILES UPON MY BOARD--	GOD GAVE A LOAF TO EVERY	791	11
BOARDS			
WITHOUT THE SOUND OF BOARDS	I'VE KNOWN A HEAVEN,	243	4
HAD WE THE ART OF BOARDS	MYSELF WAS FORMED--A	488	6
BOAST			
THAT NOT FOR ALL THEIR HEAVEN CAN BOAST	A SINGLE SCREW OF FLESH	263	19
IN LITTLE WEALTHS, AS GIRLS COULD [CAN] BOAST	YOUR RICHES--TAUGHT ME--	299	3
NOR ANY PLACARD BOAST ME--	I CANNOT DANCE UPON MY	326	19
FAITHFUL WAS ALL THAT I COULD BOAST	THAT SHE FORGOT ME WAS	1683	5
THOU CAN'ST NOT BOAST, LIKE JESUS, DRUNKEN WITHOUT COMPANION	PROUD OF MY BROKEN HEART	1736	5
BOASTING			
BOASTING [WOOING] MY PREMIUM--	MY HEART RAN SO TO THEE	1237	14
BOASTS			
LEAST VILLAGE HAS [BOASTS] IT'S BLACKSMITH	DARE YOU SEE A SOUL AT	365	9
BOAT			
ADRIFT! A LITTLE BOAT-ADRIFT!	ADRIFT! A LITTLE BOAT	30	1
WILL NO ONE GUIDE A LITTLE BOAT	ADRIFT! A LITTLE BOAT	30	3
ONE LITTLE BOAT GAVE UP IT'S STRIFE	ADRIFT! A LITTLE BOAT	30	7
ONE LITTLE BOAT--O'ERSPENT WITH GALES--	ADRIFT! A LITTLE BOAT	30	11
'TWAS SUCH A LITTLE--LITTLE BOAT	'TWAS SUCH A LITTLE--	107	1
HER STEADY BOAT BE SEEN--	SHE STAKED HER FEATHERS	798	6
BOBADILO			
DOWER ITSELF--FOR BOBADILO--	I COULD BRING YOU JEWELS	697	11
BOBOLINK			
THE BOBOLINK WAS THERE--	THE GENTIAN WEAVES HER	18	10
BY BOBOLINK FROM LANE.	I KEEP MY PLEDGE.	46	8
IT WAS AS IF A BOBOLINK	HEART, NOT SO HEAVY AS	83	9
I'D GIVE MY BIGGEST BOBOLINK!	WHAT WOULD I GIVE TO SEE	247	5
WITH A BOBOLINK FOR A CHORISTER--	SOME KEEP THE SABBATH	324	3
THE BOBOLINK--THE SEA--	"NATURE" IS WHAT WE SEE	668	6
NO BOBOLINK--REVERSE HIS SINGING	NO BOBOLINK--REVERSE HIS	755	1
BRAVE BOBOLINK--	NO BOBOLINK--REVERSE HIS	755	10
THE WAY TO KNOW THE BOBOLINK	THE WAY TO KNOW THE	1279	1
THE BOBOLINK IS GONE--THE ROWDY OF THE MEADOW--	THE BOBOLINK IS GONE--	1591	1
HEAR THE BOBOLINK!	"LETHE" IN MY FLOWER,	1730	4
BOBOLINKS			
THE BOBOLINKS AROUND THE THRONE	WE SHOULD NOT MIND SO	81	11
THE BOBOLINKS--BEGUN--	I'LL TELL YOU HOW THE	318	6
BODDICE			
HER BODDICE ROSE AND FELL--	THE ROSE DID CAPER ON	208	2
A VEST THAT LIKE HER BODDICE, DANCED--	THE ROSE DID CAPER ON	208	13
AND MAKE THE BODDICE GAY--	TO MAKE ONE'S TOILETTE--	485	6
YOU COULD HEAR THE BODDICE TUG, BEHIND YOU--	GOING TO HIM! HAPPY	494	12
AND PAST MY BODDICE [BOSOM / BUCKLE]--TOO--	I STARTED EARLY--TOOK MY	520	12
BODE			
CAN BE NO BODE OF DAWN	HIS HEART WAS DARKER	1378	4
BODIES			
TWO BODIES--THEREFORE BE--	NO RACK CAN TORTURE ME--	384	7
BODILESS			
THE BODILESS--BEGUN--	DEPARTED--TO THE	524	6
IT'S BODILESS CAMPAIGN	THE BATTLE FOUGHT	594	6
BODY			
I WALKED--AS WINGS--MY BODY BORE--	IT WOULD NEVER BE COMMON	430	13
THE BODY GROWS WITHOUT [OUTSIDE]--	THE BODY GROWS WITHOUT--	578	1
THE BODY--BORROWS [THE PRUDENT--CARRIES] A [THE] REVOLVER--	ONE NEED NOT BE A	670	17
HOW EXCELLENT A BODY [GIANT], THAT	THE TRUTH--IS STIRLESS--	780	7
MY BODY BUT WITHIN	I HEARD, AS IF I HAD NO	1039	10
I AM AFRAID TO OWN A BODY--	I AM AFRAID TO OWN A	1090	1
THE BODY IS A SOUL--	WITH PINIONS OF DISDAIN	1431	8
"AND WITH WHAT BODY DO THEY COME?"--	"AND WITH WHAT BODY DO	1492	1
"BODY!" THEN REAL--A FACE AND EYES--	"AND WITH WHAT BODY DO	1492	5
BELOW, THE BODY SPEAKS,	THE SPIRIT LASTS--BUT IN	1576	2
BOG			
REVISITING THE BOG!	SOME RAINBOW--COMING	64	18
A BOG--AFFRONTS MY SHOE--	A BURDOCK--CLAWED MY	229	6
TO AN ADMIRING BOG!	I'M NOBODY! WHO ARE YOU?	288	8
THE WILD ROSE--REDDEN IN THE BOG--	IT WILL BE SUMMER--	342	13
LIKE BEADS--AMONG THE BOG--	HER SMILE WAS SHAPED	514	8
BOGGY			
HE LIKES A BOGGY ACRE	A NARROW FELLOW IN THE	986	9
BOGS			
WHAT ELSE HAVE BOGS--TO DO--	A BURDOCK--CLAWED MY	229	7
BOHEA			
SO BABBLER, AND BOHEA--STAY THERE--	UNIT, LIKE DEATH, FOR	408	14
BOILING			
KEPT NARROWING IT'S BOILING WHEEL	'TWAS LIKE A MAELSTROM,	414	3
INTO THE BOILING SAND--	GLEE--THE GREAT STORM IS	619	4
BOLD			
AND SPORTSMAN IS NOT BOLD.	SOME, TOO FRAGILE FOR	141	8
BOLD AS [BOLDER THAN] A BRIGAND!	DUST IS THE ONLY SECRET	153	11
THAT I--GROWN BOLD--	UNTO LIKE STORY--TROUBLE	295	14
BOLD--WERE IT ENEMY--BRIEF--WERE IT FRIEND--	IT'S COMING--THE	390	6
THE DIFFERENCE--MADE ME BOLD--	IT WAS GIVEN TO ME BY	454	16
NO BOLD SICKNESS COME	SWEET--SAFE--HOUSES--	457	11
WAS THE LEOPARD--BOLD?	CIVILIZATION--SPURNS--	492	2
AND WHEN--SOME NIGHT--BOLD--SLASHING CLOUDS	YOU KNOW THAT PORTRAIT	504	13

	FIRST LINE	POEM	LINE
BOLD (CONTINUED)			
BUT I--WAS TWICE AS BOLD--	I TOOK MY POWER IN MY	540	4
MORNING'S BOLD FACE--STARES IN THE WINDOW--	I COULD DIE--TO KNOW--	570	5
INVITED DEATH--WITH BOLD ATTEMPT--	HE FOUGHT LIKE THOSE	759	5
BY DEATH'S BOLD EXHIBITION	THERE IS A FINISHED	856	5
TILL I WHO WAS ALMOST BOLD	HOW HAPPY I WAS IF I	898	6
TO THAT BOLD PERSON, GOD--	WHAT DID THEY DO SINCE I	900	16
IT BEARS THE SOUL AS BOLD	FAITH--IS THE PIERLESS	915	5
FOOT OF THE BOLD DID LEAST ATTEMPT IT--	THOSE WHO HAVE BEEN IN	922	5
BOLD ABOVE THE BOY	HOW THE WATERS CLOSED	923	6
FOR THE BRAVE [BOLD] BELOVED--	ROBBED BY DEATH--BUT	971	8
TOO BRIGHT [BOLD] FOR OUR INFIRM DELIGHT	TELL ALL THE TRUTH BUT	1129	3
A PROMPT--EXECUTIVE [BOLD, INSPIRITING] BIRD IS THE JAY--	A PROMPT--EXECUTIVE BIRD	1177	1
BOLD AS A BAILIFF'S HYMN--	A PROMPT--EXECUTIVE BIRD	1177	2
BOLD IT WERE TO DIE	WE LIKE MARCH.	1213	11
CAVIL OF THE BOLD	FORTITUDE INCARNATE	1217	6
I DO NOT KNOW THE MAN SO BOLD	I NEVER HEAR THAT ONE IS	1323	13
BOLD LITTLE BEAUTY	PINK--SMALL--AND	1332	9
CAN STAND SO CLOSE AND LOOK SO BOLD	WHAT MYSTERY PERVADES A	1400	11
WHERE EVERY BIRD IS BOLD TO GO	WHERE EVERY BIRD IS BOLD	1758	1
BOLDER			
BOLD AS [BOLDER THAN] A BRIGAND!	DUST IS THE ONLY SECRET	153	11
THERE KNITS A BOLDER ONE--	NO RACK CAN TORTURE ME--	384	4
AND YET SO BOLDER EVERY DAY	THIS CHASM, SWEET, UPON	858	11
IN THY BOLDER SEA--	ALL FORGOT FOR	966	14
AMPLER [BOLDER] TO FLY AWAY	ARE FRIENDS DELIGHT OR	1199	5
WITH BOLDER PLAYMATES STRAYING	OF DEATH I TRY TO THINK	1558	10
BOLDEST			
GRIEF IS A JUGGLER--BOLDEST AT THE PLAY--	GRIEF IS A MOUSE--	793	9
THE BOLDEST MIND WILL PINE	THE MIND LIVES ON THE	1355 V	6
BY AND BY--THE BOLDEST STOLE OUT OF HIS COVERT	IT SOUNDED AS IF THE	1397	5
THE BOLDEST [BRAVEST] LEAPED, AND CLUTCHED IT--	OF DEATH I TRY TO THINK	1558	16
BOLDLY			
APPROACH THAT TREE WITH CAUTION, THEN UP IT BOLDLY CLIMB,	AWAKE YE MUSES NINE,	1	35
I BOLDLY ANSWERED--ENTERED THEN	THE WIND--TAPPED LIKE A	436	3
AND BELLS--THAT BOLDLY RING [COME]	I ENVY SEAS, WHEREON HE	498	18
THAT TRUSTS HER--BOLDLY UP--	THE TRUTH--IS STIRLESS--	780	12
AND BOLDLY RODE AWAY--	A SPARROW TOOK A SLICE	1211 V	8
GO [BUT] BOLDLY--FOR THOU PAID'ST HIS PRICE	GO SLOW, MY SOUL, TO	1297	7
DROVE BOLDLY TO A ROSE--	A BEE HIS BURNISHED	1339	2
HE GAILY [BOLDLY] INTERRUPTED THAT OVERFLOWING DAY	THE BOBOLINK IS GONE--	1591	4
WALK BOLDLY UP AND KNOCK	T'WAS COMFORT IN HER	1703	4
BOLIVIAN			
IN FAR--BOLIVIAN GROUND--	REVERSE CANNOT BEFALL	395	6
BOLT			
BUT WE BOLT THE DOOR TIGHT	WE DONT CRY--TIM AND I,	196	3
WITHOUT A BOLT--THAT I COULD PROVE--	IT TROUBLED ME AS ONCE I	600	7
AND CLICK [BOLT]--AND SUDDENNESS.	THE SOUL'S DISTINCT	974	8
THE BOLT UNTO [UPON] THE DOOR--	THE SOUL SHOULD ALWAYS	1055	6
BUT [AND] I WOULD NOT EXCHANGE THE BOLT [FLASH]	THE FARTHEST THUNDER	1581	7
BOLTS			
WITH BOLTS OF MELODY!	I WOULD NOT PAINT--A	505	24
BARS [BOLTS]--CANNOT CONCEAL!	MINE--BY THE RIGHT OF	528	4
HE BOLTS THE DOOR--	ONE NEED NOT BE A	670	18
FATE--FOLLOWING--BEHIND US BOLTS IT--	WE NEVER KNOW WE GO WHEN	1523	3
BOMB			
BUT SINCE WE GOT A BOMB--	I TIE MY HAT--I CREASE	443	27
SHE DANCES LIKE A BOMB, ABROAD,	THE SOUL HAS BANDAGED	512	13
A BOMB--TO JUSTIFY--	TO INTERRUPT HIS YELLOW	591	16
A BOMB UPON THE CEILING	THESE ARE THE NIGHTS	1128	9
BEFORE THE QUICK [RIPE / PEAL / DRUM / DRUMS / BELLS / BOMB / . . .	ONE JOY OF SO MUCH	1420	6
BOND			
SIGN ME THE BOND!	WHAT WOULD I GIVE TO SEE	247	23
WE GAVE NO OTHER BOND--	THERE CAME A DAY AT	322	24
MY BOND--HAVE JUST BEGUN--	A TONGUE--TO TELL HIM I	400	25
UPON A PLANET'S BOND--	THROUGH THE STRAIT PASS	792	8
IT'S BOND IT'S FRIEND--	THE GENTIAN HAS A	1424	10
BONDAGE			
BONDAGE AS PLAY--BE SWEET--	WHERE THOU ART--THAT--IS	725	7
LET EVERY BONDAGE BE,	IMMURED IN HEAVEN!	1594	3
BONDS			
WOULD'NT BONDS HURT MORE	LET US PLAY YESTERDAY--	728	27
OTHER BONDS DECAY	GUEST AM I TO HAVE	1661	5
BONE			
BY WHICH A SINGLE BONE--	A SCIENCE--SO THE SAVANS	100	3
IT IS SIMPLE, TO ACHE IN THE BONE, OR THE RIND--	IT IS EASY TO WORK WHEN	244	5
AND INNER THAN THE BONE--	OF ALL THE SOUNDS	321	14
BEHIND THIS MORTAL BONE	NO RACK CAN TORTURE ME--	384	3
NO BONE HAD HE TO BIND HIM--	THE WIND--TAPPED LIKE A	436	9
OR WANTONED WITH A BONE--	SHE DEALT HER PRETTY	479	4
AS IF MY TRADE WERE BONE--	AS FAR FROM PITY, AS	496	4
SOME POLAR EXPIATION--AN OMEN IN THE BONE	I TRIED TO THINK A	532	3
WOULD DROP [SPILL] HIM--BONE BY BONE.	THERE IS A PAIN--SO	599	8

	FIRST LINE	POEM		LINE
BONE (CONTINUED)				
WOULD DROP [SPILL] HIM--BONE BY BONE.	THERE IS A PAIN--SO	599		8
TIS POPULOUS WITH BONE AND STAIN--	MY PORTION IS DEFEAT--	639		7
STANDS WITHOUT A BONE--	THE TRUTH--IS STIRLESS--	780		8
I STROVE TO WEARY BRAIN AND BONE--	SEVERER SERVICE OF	786		9
AND ZERO AT THE BONE--	A NARROW FELLOW IN THE	986		24
THE BONE THAT HAS NO MARROW,	THE BONE THAT HAS NO	1274		1
A BONE HAS OBLIGATIONS--	THE BONE THAT HAS NO	1274		5
LIKE DOG A BONE	THE MIND LIVES ON THE	1355	V	8
DEFEATED OF A BONE	THE WIND DREW OFF	1694		3
BONNET				
GLOWING IS HER BONNET,	GLOWING IS HER BONNET,	72		1
A BONNET BLACK--A DUSK SURPLICE--	WHERE I HAVE LOST, I	104		10
UNTIES HER YELLOW BONNET	PERHAPS YOU'D LIKE TO	134		5
NO MORE HER TIMID BONNET	SHE BORE IT TILL THE	144		11
KISSING HER [IT'S] BONNET TO THE MEADOW	BLAZING IN GOLD AND	228		7
I COULD BORROW A BONNET	AH, MOON--AND STAR!	240		8
A BONNET LIKE A DUKE--	A MIEN TO MOVE A QUEEN--	283		9
UPON A BONNET BOUND--	THE COLOR OF THE GRAVE	411		22
THEN STANDS UPON THE BONNET	HE PARTS HIMSELF--LIKE	517		3
BONNET OF EVERLASTING LACES--	DROPPED INTO THE ETHER	665		3
HER BONNET IS THE FIRMAMENT--	THE MOON WAS BUT A CHIN	737		17
MY BONNET BUT TO TIE	I SING TO USE THE	850		2
BONNET [JACKET] DUE IN APRIL--	NOT AT HOME TO CALLERS	1590		3
BONNETS				
WHOSE BONNETS TOUCH THE FIRMAMENT--	IN LANDS I NEVER SAW--	124		3
THE HILLS UNTIED THEIR BONNETS--	I'LL TELL YOU HOW THE	318		5
IT SPRINKLES BONNETS--FAR BELOW--	THE NAME--OF IT--IS	656		9
BONNIE				
ACCEPT THIS "BONNIE DOON,"	"SIC TRANSIT GLORIA	3		62
TOLL--FOR THE BONNIE SOULS--	GLEE--THE GREAT STORM IS	619		6
. . . BONNIE / SPACIOUS / TROPIC / ARDENT / FRIENDLY / MAGIC / . . .	THE BIBLE IS AN ANTIQUE	1545		13
BOOK				
A BLOSSOM, OR A BOOK,	BY CHIVALRIES AS TINY,	55		2
WAIT! LOOK! HER LITTLE BOOK--	'TWAS THE OLD--ROAD--	344		12
A BOOK I HAVE--A FRIEND GAVE--	DEATH SETS A THING	360		13
TO MEET AN ANTIQUE BOOK--	A PRECIOUS--MOULDERING	371		2
I WOULD NOT CHOOSE--A BOOK TO KNOW	NOT IN THIS WORLD TO SEE	418		8
ODDEST OF SCIENCES--BOOK EVER BORE--	KNOWS HOW TO FORGET!	433		10
IS IT IN A BOOK?	KNOWS HOW TO FORGET!	433	V	
RABBI OF THE WISE BOOK	KNOWS HOW TO FORGET!	433	V	
I READ IN AN OLD FASHIONED BOOK	I KNOW WHERE WELLS GROW	460		13
AT NIGHT, MY LITTLE LAMP, AND BOOK--	I WAS THE SLIGHTEST IN	486		3
A CHAPTER--THEN THE MIGHTY BOOK--	WE LEARNED THE WHOLE OF	568		3
THE REVELATIONS OF THE BOOK	THE MURMURING OF BEES,	1115		7
THERE IS NO [WAS NEVER] FRIGATE LIKE A BOOK	THERE IS NO FRIGATE LIKE	1263		1
IS POETRY, THOUGH NEVER IN A BOOK IT LIE--	TO SEE THE SUMMER SKY	1472		2
THEY REGISTERED IN NATURE'S BOOK	FOREVER HONORED BE THE	1570		5
WAS BUT A BOOK--WHAT LIBERTY	HE ATE AND DRANK THE	1587		7
PERUSER OF ENCHANTING BOOK	SUMMER BEGINS TO HAVE	1682		2
BOOKS				
BOOKS--WHEN THE UNIT--	IT'S THOUGHTS--AND JUST	495		7
UNTO MY BOOKS--SO GOOD TO TURN--	UNTO MY BOOKS--SO GOOD	604		1
MY WARS ARE LAID AWAY IN BOOKS--	MY WARS ARE LAID AWAY IN	1549		1
BOOMING				
AND THE BEE BE BOOMING.	I SUPPOSE THE TIME WILL	1381		4
BOON				
HURRAH FOR DANIEL BOON!	"SIC TRANSIT GLORIA	3		10
THE BOON OF ALL ALIVE--	BEHOLD THIS LITTLE BANE	1438		2
TRUTH ADJOURN YOUR BOON	LOVE IS DONE WHEN LOVE'S	1485		4
THE THRILL CAME SLOWLY LIKE A BOON [LIGHT] FOR	THE THRILL CAME SLOWLY	1495		1
AND STOOD AMAZED BEFORE THE CHANGE [BOON / MORNS]	THE THRILL CAME SLOWLY	1495		7
OF [TO] EVERY OTHER [AS GRACIOUS AS A] BOON--	TO SEE HER IS A PICTURE	1568	V	4
SHE DOES NOT ASK FOR BOON,	QUITE EMPTY, QUITE AT	1606		7
OH, WHAT A LIVID BOON!	UPON THE GALLOWS HUNG A	1757		8
WHAT AN APPALLING BOON!	UPON THE GALLOWS HUNG A	1757	V	8
BOOT				
AND A CHAMOIS' SILVER BOOT--	AH, MOON--AND STAR!	240		10
THAN SAVE MY BOOT--	IS BLISS THEN, SUCH	340		5
VERDICT FOR BOOT!	IS BLISS THEN, SUCH	340		14
A LITTLE BOOT I KNOW--	ALTHOUGH I PUT AWAY HIS	366		14
THAN THIS QUAINT CREATURE'S BOOT--	YOU'LL KNOW HER--BY HER	634		5
HER'S IS THE SMALLEST BOOT--	A FLOWER WILL NOT	1621		3
BOOTS				
WITH THOSE SAME BOOTS OF LEAD, AGAIN,	I FELT A FUNERAL, IN MY	280		11
AS BOOTS--WOULD BE--TO BIRDS--	IT WOULD NEVER BE COMMON	430		16
BOOTY				
THAT WAS A WONDROUS BOOTY--	I NEVER TOLD THE BURIED	11		10
WOULD I RESTORE MY BOOTY	WHAT DID THEY DO SINCE I	900		15
THE BOOTY AND THE SORROW	ONE THING OF IT WE	1464		3
BOQUET SEE BOUQUET				
IN LIFE'S DIVERSE BOQUET--	WENT UP A YEAR THIS	93		14
AS 'TWERE A BRIGHT BOQUET--	IT WILL BE SUMMER--	342		6
NOUGHT BUT BOQUET?	COULD--I DO MORE--FOR	447		4
BORDER				
DIM--AS THE BORDER STAR--	TAKEN FROM MEN--THIS	53		10
THAN COULD BORDER BALLAD--	NEVER FOR SOCIETY	746		9
AND THE LITTLE BORDER--DUSKER--	AUTUMN--OVERLOOKED MY	748		7

	FIRST LINE	POEM	LINE
BORE			
LONG YEARS OF PRACTISE BORE	THE FEET OF PEOPLE	7	6
BORE HIS RIDDLE IN!	IF THOSE I LOVED WERE	29	8
I [HE] GRASPED--I [HE] BORE AWAY--	I ROBBED THE WOODS--	41	7
AND BORE HER SAFE AWAY.	WHOSE CHEEK IS THIS?	82	5
AND BORE HER STRUGGLING, BLUSHING,	SO BASHFUL WHEN I SPIED	91	7
SHE BORE IT TILL THE SIMPLE VEINS	SHE BORE IT TILL THE	144	1
AND SURE I AM, THE CREST HE BORE	I MET A KING THIS	166	7
THAT BORE ANOTHER ROSE--	THE ROSE DID CAPER ON	208	10
HOW MANY TIMES THEY--BORE THE FAITHFUL WITNESS--	READ--SWEET--HOW OTHERS	260	5
WHICH BORE IT BEST?	ONE YEAR AGO--JOTS WHAT?	296	28
AS ONE THAT BORE HER MASTER'S NAME--	THE FACE I CARRY WITH ME	336	15
I HAD AS LIEF THEY BORE	I TEND MY FLOWERS FOR	339	19
THE STIFF HEART QUESTIONS WAS IT HE, THAT BORE,	AFTER GREAT PAIN, A	341	3
I WALKED--AS WINGS--MY BODY BORE--	IT WOULD NEVER BE COMMON	430	13
ODDEST OF SCIENCES--BOOK EVER BORE--	KNOWS HOW TO FORGET!	433	10
AND BORE MY JEWEL--HOME--	THE MALAY--TOOK THE	452	8
OR BORE THE GARDEN IN THE BRAIN	WITHIN MY GARDEN, RIDES	500	15
AND THEN--TOGETHER BORE AWAY	TWO BUTTERFLIES WENT OUT	533	5
MYSELF--WHO BORE IT--DO--	'TIS TRUE--THEY SHUT ME	538	10
OUR LORD--INDEED--MADE [BORE] COMPOUND WITNESS--	ONE CRUCIFIXION IS	553	13
I WONDER IF THEY BORE IT LONG--	I MEASURE EVERY GRIEF I	561	5
AND BORE IT IN MY HAND--	A DYING TIGER--MOANED	566	4
AS BORE IT SEALED WINE--	STRONG DRAUGHTS OF THEIR	711	4
MY WITNESS--WAS THE CRAPE [BLACK] I BORE--	THE BIRDS REPORTED FROM	743	19
ONE MUST REVERSE HAVE [ITSELF HAVE / HAVE PREVIOUS] BORE--	DESPAIR'S ADVANTAGE IS	799	4
IT WAS A GRAVE, YET BORE NO STONE	IT WAS A GRAVE, YET BORE	876	1
BUT EVERY TEAR I BORE	EACH SCAR I'LL KEEP FOR	877	5
SUBSISTING ON THE LIGHT WE BORE	WE MET AS SPARKS--	958	5
BORE DEATH FROM PASSION	SAID DEATH TO PASSION	1033	5
AND THEN HE BORE ME ON [HIGH]	IT WAS A QUIET WAY--	1053	5
HAD WE KNOWN THE TON [WEIGHT / LOAD] SHE BORE	HAD WE KNOWN THE TON SHE	1124	1
THAT BORE HIM FROM THE TOMB--	OBTAINING BUT OUR OWN	1543	4
SHE [HE] BORE LIFE'S EMPTY PACK	HER LOSSES MAKE OUR	1562	2
THAT BORE IT THROUGH THE TOMB,	'TIS NOT THE SWAYING	1597	6
THE ONE WHO BORE HIM TOTTERED IN,--	UPON THE GALLOWS HUNG A	1757	5
BORED			
BORED AT SO BRAVE A ROOT	AND THIS OF ALL MY HOPES	913	8
BORER			
A BORER IN THE AXIS	CRUMBLING IS NOT AN	997	7
BORN			
BUT, WERE I CUCKOO BORN--	THE ROBIN'S MY CRITERION	285	3
BUT, WERE I BRITAIN BORN,	THE ROBIN'S MY CRITERION	285	8
HE LIVED--WHERE DREAMS WERE BORN--	A PRECIOUS--MOULDERING	371	24
BORN INFINITER [EVERLASTING]--NOW--	'TWAS A LONG PARTING--	625	12
SHE WORE WHEN SHE WAS BORN--	YOU'LL KNOW HER--BY HER	634	12
THE BOUGH WHERE SHE WAS BORN--	SHE STAKED HER FEATHERS	798	8
IF HOME OR FOREIGN BORN--	IT WAS A GRAVE, YET BORE	876	6
BEFORE MYSELF WAS BORN	WHO OCCUPIES THIS HOUSE?	892	17
AS IF IT WERE NOT BORN.	DEATH LEAVES US HOMESICK	935	4
AND ARE TOO SELDOM BORN--	FAME'S BOYS AND GIRLS,	1066	2
BORN--BRIDALLED--SHROUDED--	TITLE DIVINE--IS MINE!	1072	10
IF BLOSSOMS CAN BE BORN AGAIN	WHEN THEY COME BACK--IF	1080	3
LEST ANY DOUBT THAT WE ARE GLAD THAT THEY WERE BORN TODAY	LEST ANY DOUBT THAT WE	1156	1
HE IS PRISM BORN.	WHICH IS THE BEST--THE	1315	8
THE BARD TO SILENCE BORN--	TOUCH LIGHTLY NATURE'S	1389 V	4
BEFORE MY MIND [SOUL / BEAM] WAS BORN	THIS ME--THAT WALKS AND	1588	6
BORNE SEE BOURNE			
UPON THE WATERS BORNE--	TWO SWIMMERS WRESTLED ON	201	7
UNTIL--DELIRIOUS--BORNE--	I THINK JUST HOW MY	237	14
AND THE BORNE--	UNIT, LIKE DEATH, FOR	408	8
BORNE ON A DUSKY BREAST--	THE MALAY--TOOK THE	452	11
TO GAIN IT, MEN HAVE BORNE	THIS WORLD IS NOT	501	10
AS DO THE BEE--DELIRIOUS BORNE--	THE SOUL HAS BANDAGED	512	15
OF SPICE--I INFER FROM THE ODORS BORNE--	BY MY WINDOW HAVE I FOR	797	12
TOO HUNGRY TO BE BORNE	I PLAY AT RICHES--TO	801	10
HIMSELF [THAT HE] IS BORNE AWAY	TRUTH--IS AS OLD AS GOD	836	6
IF TERMINABLE, MAY BE BORNE.	SOMEWHAT, TO HOPE FOR,	1041	6
BORNE WITHOUT DISSENT OF EITHER [ANY]	THREE WEEKS PASSED SINCE	1061	9
IS STERILE BORNE TO SOME--	THE VOICE THAT STANDS	1189	2
I COULD HAVE BORNE THE SHADE	HAD I NOT SEEN THE SUN	1233	2
FOR THOU HAST BORNE A UNIVERSE	HOW MUCH OF SOURCE	1517	3
BURDEN--BORNE SO FAR TRIUMPHANT--	REARRANGE A "WIFE'S"	1737	13
BUT HER FATHER IS BORNE AND HONORED,	THE PARASOL IS THE	1747	7
OR HEART SO GENTLY BORNE,	WHICH MISSES MOST,	1759	3
BOROUGHS			
AND BOROUGHS [LIMITS] WHERE WE LIVE--	LIKE MEN AND WOMEN	1105	8
BORROW			
IF YOU WOULD LIKE TO BORROW,	PERHAPS YOU'D LIKE TO	134	3
I COULD BORROW A BONNET	AH, MOON--AND STAR!	240	8
MY DUPLICATE--TO BORROW--	I TRIED TO THINK A	532	6
ONE THING OF IT WE [THEE I] BORROW	ONE THING OF IT WE	1464	1
BORROWED			
WE BORROWED AT HER GRAVE--	THE IMMORTALITY SHE GAVE	1648	2
AND BORROWED TO THIS DAY.	THE PARASOL IS THE	1747	8

	FIRST LINE	POEM	LINE
BORROWS			
THE BODY--BORROWS [THE PRUDENT--CARRIES] A [THE] REVOLVER--	ONE NEED NOT BE A	670	17
BOSOM			
ONE WITHIN MY BOSOM	IT DID NOT SURPRISE ME--	39	11
HER LOVING BOSOM LAY--	DELAYED TILL SHE HAD	58	3
WHO CHARGE WITHIN THE BOSOM	TO FIGHT ALOUD, IS VERY	126	3
STILL, MY LITTLE SUNBURNT BOSOM	THO' MY DESTINY BE	163	7
BEFORE MY SIMPLE BOSOM--BROKE--	I THINK JUST HOW MY	237	11
STAB THE BIRD--THAT BUILT IN YOUR BOSOM--	KILL YOUR BALM--AND IT'S	238	5
AND HELD IT IN OUR BOSOM--	I TIE MY HAT--I CREASE	443	28
AND PAST MY BODDICE [BOSOM / BUCKLE]--TOO--	I STARTED EARLY--TOOK MY	520	12
UPON HER BOSOM--ONE--	THE SUNRISE RUNS FOR	710	16
UPON HER BOSOM [PETALS / SOFTNESS] PILED--	NO NOTICE GAVE SHE, BUT	804	8
AMPUTATE MY FRECKLED BOSOM!	REARRANGE A "WIFE'S"	1737	3
BOSOMS			
THE BOSOMS WHERE THE FROST HAS LAIN	I BRING AN UNACCUSTOMED	132	12
BUT ANDES IN THE BOSOMS WHERE	SHE SPED AS PETALS OF A	991	7
BOSPORUS			
ON BALL OF MAST IN BOSPORUS [FOREIGN PORT]--	THE DAY UNDRESSED--	716	15
BOTTOM			
AT BOTTOM OF MY MIND--	IT DROPPED SO LOW--IN MY	747	4
AT MIDDLE [BOTTOM / CENTRE] OF THE HILL--	THE HALLOWING OF PAIN	772	6
BOUGH			
PINE BOUGH	A FEATHER FROM THE	161	T
SOMETIME, UPON A BOUGH,	A FUZZY FELLOW, WITHOUT	173	6
AND PERISH--BUT A BOUGH BETWEEN--	NOT PROBABLE--THE BAREST	346	8
IS JUST A BOUGH OF APPLES--	THE ANGLE OF A LANDSCAPE	375	7
UPON MY EMERALD BOUGH,	THE ANGLE OF A LANDSCAPE	375	14
THE BOUGH WHERE SHE WAS BORN--	SHE STAKED HER FEATHERS	798	8
SITTING [RIDING] A BOUGH LIKE A BRIGADIER	A PROMPT--EXECUTIVE BIRD	1177	5
AND BOUGH AND STEEPLE	TO-DAY OR THIS NOON	1702	6
BOUGHS			
BUILD IN GAYER BOUGHS,	IT DID NOT SURPRISE ME--	39	6
AMONG ASTONISHED BOUGHS--	BRING ME THE SUNSET IN A	128	9
WHEREFORE WHEN BOUGHS ARE FREE--	FOR EVERY BIRD A NEST--	143	4
WHEN WINTER SHOOK THE BOUGHS!	IF I COULD BRIBE THEM BY	179	12
LIKE THAT OLD MEASURE IN THE BOUGHS--	OF ALL THE SOUNDS	321	3
I CRAVE HIM GRACE OF SUMMER BOUGHS,	OF ALL THE SOUNDS	321	25
BOUGHT			
NOW--HAVE I BOUGHT IT--	WHAT WOULD I GIVE TO SEE	247	21
WE BOUGHT--TO EASE THEIR PLACE--	YOU'LL FIND--IT WHEN YOU	610	16
THOUGH BOUGHT IN PARADISE--	JOY TO HAVE MERITED THE	788	8
BOUGHT, CARRIED HOME	SO LARGE MY WILL	1024	11
I WATCHED [BOUGHT] THE FLUTTERING [VANQUISHED] SPIRIT	I SAW THE WIND WITHIN	1502	V
BOUND			
AND SUMMER'S BROWS WERE BOUND.	THERE IS A MORN BY MEN	24	12
AROUND IT'S FOREHEAD BOUND.	I LOST A WORLD--THE	181	4
BOUND--A TROUBLE--	BOUND--A TROUBLE--	269	1
BOUND TO OPPOSING LANDS--	THERE CAME A DAY AT	322	20
EACH BOUND THE OTHER'S CRUCIFIX--	THERE CAME A DAY AT	322	23
UPON A BONNET BOUND--	THE COLOR OF THE GRAVE	411	22
BOUNDARIES			
HIS BOUNDARIES [SOPHISTRIES]--FORGOT--	THE SPIDER HOLDS A	605	12
YOU LEFT ME BOUNDARIES OF PAIN--	YOU LEFT ME--SIRE--TWO	644	5
BOUNDARY			
BEYOND MY BOUNDARY--	I'VE NONE TO TELL ME TO	881	6
BOUNDLESS			
IT WAS A BOUNDLESS PLACE TO ME	HE TOUCHED ME, SO I LIVE	506	4
ON IT'S BOUNDLESS [MIGHTY / SUBTLE] SHELF--	SUMMER LAID HER SIMPLE	1363	2
IN ABJECT [BOUNDLESS] POVERTY--	TAKE ALL AWAY FROM ME,	1640	5
BOUNDLESSNESS			
AFFLICTION RANGES BOUNDLESSNESS--	A NEARNESS TO	963	3
BOUNTEOUS			
BOUNTEOUS PREPARED--	TWICE HAD SUMMER HER	846	6
SO EASY [KINDRED / FULLY / FREE / AMPLE SEEMS / BOUNTEOUS / . . .	YOUR THOUGHTS DONT HAVE	1452	6
BOUNTIFUL			
HOW BOUNTIFUL THE DREAM--	I THINK TO LIVE--MAY BE	646	25
BOUNTIFUL COLORED, MY MORNING ROSE	AND THIS OF ALL MY HOPES	913	3
BOUNTY			
WHO BOUNTY--HAVE NOT KNOWN--	NONE CAN EXPERIENCE	771	2
A BOUNTY IN PROSPECTIVE, NOW	HOW WELL I KNEW HER NOT	837	3
THOU PAUSED AT, FOR A PASSING [DOUBTFUL] BOUNTY--	WERT THOU BUT ILL--THAT	961	7
IT IS BOUNTY--TO SUSPENSE'S	ROBBED BY DEATH--BUT	971	11
COULD BOUNTY BUT REMAIN	ARE FRIENDS DELIGHT OR	1199	2
ALL OTHER BOUNTY SUDDEN CHAFF [NIGGARDLY]	I GROPED FOR HIM BEFORE	1555	3
BOUQUET SEE BOQUET			
LIFE'S BOUQUET	TO EARN IT BY DISDAINING	1427	7
BOURBON			
IF IT BE, I WAKE A BOURBON,	I'M SAYING EVERY DAY	373	5
BOURNE			
. . . BOURNE	THERE IS A STRENGTH IN	1113	[illegible]
BOUT			
AND CAUGHT A RIDE [TOOK A BOUT] WITH HIM	TWO BUTTERFLIES WENT OUT	533	V [illegible]
HE OUTSTRIPPED TIME WITH BUT A BOUT,	HE OUTSTRIPPED TIME WITH	865	[illegible]
BOW			
AND BOW TO EVERYTHING--	THE GRASS SO LITTLE HAS	333	[illegible]

	FIRST LINE	POEM	LINE
BOW (CONTINUED)			
HER BOW--TO ATOMS BLOWN--	THE FIRST DAY'S NIGHT	410	6
AND HEMLOCKS--BOW--TO GOD--	DOOM IS THE HOUSE	475	8
NOR GLOW, WOULD IT, NOR BOW--	THIS THAT WOULD GREET--	778	4
WITH A GLANCE AND A BOW	A CLOUD WITHDREW FROM	895	10
WITH HERE AND THERE A MIGHTY BOW	LIKE MEN AND WOMEN	1105	3
SPED BY AN ARCHER'S BOW. . . . . -	I'VE GOT AN ARROW HERE.	1729	7
BOWED			
THEN GAVE [BENT / BOWED] THE EAST UNTO THE WEST	THE WIND TOOK UP THE	1134	3
HE BOWED TO HEAVEN INSTEAD OF EARTH [EVERY HEAVEN ABOVE / . . .	THE BOBOLINK IS GONE--	1591	6
AND BOWED AND SANG AGAIN.	A TRAIN WENT THROUGH A	1761	6
BOWER			
THEN BEAR HER TO THE GREENWOOD, AND BUILD FOR HER A BOWER,	AWAKE YE MUSES NINE,	1	37
AS LADY FROM HER BOWER--	TO HER DERIDED HOME	1586	8
BOWING			
CANT PUT THE PUPPET BOWING--	A CLOCK STOPPED--	287	4
JUST A DOME OF ABYSS IS BOWING [NODDING] .	HOW THE OLD MOUNTAINS	291	19
AND BOWING--WITH A MIGHTY LOOK--	I STARTED EARLY--TOOK MY	520	23
THE CRUEL--SMILING--BOWING WORLD-- . . .	THE BEGGAR LAD--DIES	717	5
A BOWING INTERCOURSE.	THE DUTIES OF THE WIND	1137	12
BOWL			
IN BATTLE'S--HORRID BOWL?	IT FEELS A SHAME TO BE	444	16
BOWLS			
WHY FLOODS BE SERVED TO US--IN BOWLS-- . .	ONE BLESSING HAD I THAN	756	19
BOWS			
AND SCIENCE BOWS THEM IN--	SUNSET AT NIGHT--IS	415	6
PAST BOWS, AND INVITATIONS--	IF ANYBODY'S FRIEND BE	509	21
THAT BOWS--AND DISAPPEARS--	WHOLE GULFS--OF RED, AND	658	8
BOX			
IN EBON BOX, WHEN YEARS HAVE FLOWN . . .	IN EBON BOX, WHEN YEARS	169	1
AS IF THE LITTLE EBON BOX	IN EBON BOX, WHEN YEARS	169	19
AND THEN I HEARD THEM LIFT A BOX	I FELT A FUNERAL, IN MY	280	9
I GOT SO I COULD STIR THE BOX--	I GOT SO I COULD HEAR	293	9
BOXES			
AND THE BOXES SHUT--	DRAMA'S VITALLEST	741	7
BOY			
NEVER WAS A BOY--	DUST IS THE ONLY SECRET	153	6
OH, DEAR,--I GUESS IF HE WERE A BOY-- . .	OVER THE FENCE--	251	8
LIKE THE JUNE BEE--BEFORE THE SCHOOL BOY, .	THE NEAREST DREAM	319	3
HEEDLESS OF THE BOY--	THE NEAREST DREAM	319	9
I USED TO--WHEN A BOY--	THERE'S BEEN A DEATH, IN	389	12
IF ONCE MORE--PARDON--BOY--	A TONGUE--TO TELL HIM I	400	14
SHE LEADS HIM--DOCILE AS A BOY--	THE MOON IS DISTANT FROM	429	3
TO PARTRIDGE--AND TO BOY--	THE BLACK BERRY--WEARS A	554	4
HEAVES BALLS OF SPECKS, LIKE VICIOUS BOY .	TO INTERRUPT HIS YELLOW	591	5
TODAY--HER ONLY BOY	WHEN I WAS SMALL, A	596	2
THAT WOMAN AND HER BOY	WHEN I WAS SMALL, A	596	14
AS BOY--SHOULD DEAL WITH LESSER BOY-- . .	IT ALWAYS FELT TO ME--A	597	15
AS BOY--SHOULD DEAL WITH LESSER BOY-- . .	IT ALWAYS FELT TO ME--A	597	15
WHEN MEMORY WAS A BOY--	A PRISON GETS TO BE A	652	14
BY PLAYING GLACIERS--WHEN A BOY--	THE ZEROES--TAUGHT US--	689	3
OR BOY--	FOUR TREES--UPON A	742	12
BOLD ABOVE THE BOY	HOW THE WATERS CLOSED	923	6
STONE OF STOLID BOY--	STRUCK, WAS I, NOR YET	925	6
YET [BUT] WHEN A BOY, AND BAREFOOT-- . . .	A NARROW FELLOW IN THE	986	11
A HOARY BOY, I'VE KNOWN TO DROP	NOT ALL DIE EARLY, DYING	990	5
I MET SOMEBODY'S LITTLE BOY	TRUDGING TO EDEN,	1020	2
MAKE OF HIS ONLY BOY A TARGET	TELL AS A MARKSMAN--WERE	1152	18
REMINDED BY A BOY	A LITTLE DOG THAT WAGS	1185	4
BECAUSE HE IS A LITTLE BOY	A LITTLE DOG THAT WAGS	1185	7
BESEECH [ADJURE] EACH LITTLE BOY--	A LITTLE DOG THAT WAGS	1185	16
BOY THAT LIVED FOR "OUGHT TO [OR'TER]" . .	SO I PULL MY STOCKINGS	1201	4
BY BOY DESCRIED--	NOT WITH A CLUB, THE	1304	10
BETRAYS A BOY.	MARCH IS THE MONTH OF	1404	8
TO THIS LABORIOUS BOY--	HOW GOOD HIS LAVA BED,	1447	2
A FADED BOY--IN SALLOW CLOTHES	A FADED BOY--IN SALLOW	1524	1
DIAGNOSIS OF THE BIBLE, BY A BOY--	THE BIBLE IS AN ANTIQUE	1545	T
THE SACRED STEALTH [HAPPY GUILT] OF BOY AND GIRL	BLISS IS THE PLAYTHING	1553	3
BOYISH			
AND CHIPS OF BLANK--IN BOYISH EYES--	MY PORTION IS DEFEAT--	639	10
BOYS SEE NEWS-BOYS			
WHOSE BERYL EGG, WHAT SCHOOL BOYS HUNT . .	A FEATHER FROM THE	161	7
LITTLE BOYS HATS--AND STUBBLE--	THE WIND DIDN'T COME	316	18
THAT [WHICH] LITTLE YELLOW BOYS AND GIRLS .	I'LL TELL YOU HOW THE	318	11
AND LITTLE BOYS--BESIDES--	THERE'S BEEN A DEATH, IN	389	16
THOSE BOYS AND GIRLS, IN CANVAS--	THOSE FAIR--FICTITIOUS	499	5
WHEN MEN--AND BOYS--AND CARTS [LARKS]--AND JUNE,	I'M SORRY FOR THE DEAD--	529	19
PURSUED OF LITTLE BOYS	WHEN I HAVE SEEN THE SUN	888	8
AND BOYS WERE POSSIBLE.	WHO OCCUPIES THIS HOUSE?	892	16
FAME'S BOYS AND GIRLS, WHO NEVER DIE . . .	FAME'S BOYS AND GIRLS,	1066	1
SINCE HE AND I WERE BOYS	THE SAVIOR MUST HAVE	1487	6
HEARTY WITH BOYS THE ROAD--	GLASS WAS THE STREET--IN	1498	4
THE BOYS THAT WHISTLED ARE EXTINCT-- . . .	A FADED BOY--IN SALLOW	1524	5
FROM ALL THE JAILS THE BOYS AND GIRLS . .	FROM ALL THE JAILS THE	1532	1
BOYS THAT "BELIEVE" ARE VERY LONESOME	THE BIBLE IS AN ANTIQUE	1545	11

	FIRST LINE	POEM	LINE
BOYS (CONTINUED)			
[BASTINADOED]--			
OTHER BOYS ARE "LOST"--	THE BIBLE IS AN ANTIQUE	1545	12
ALL THE BOYS WOULD COME--	THE BIBLE IS AN ANTIQUE	1545	14
WHY BOYS ARE FRIENDLY--	THE BIBLE IS AN ANTIQUE	1545	V
BRACED			
THE DARKNESS [TROUBLE] BRACED AS FIRM	SEVERER SERVICE OF	786	18
BRAG			
THE BROOKS SLAM [BRAG]--ALL THE DAY--	IT MAKES NO DIFFERENCE	620	6
BRAID			
THAT'S EASIER--THAN BRAID THE HAIR--	TO MAKE ONE'S TOILETTE--	485	5
BRAIN			
BRAIN OF HIS BRAIN--	FOREVER AT HIS SIDE TO	246	3
BRAIN OF HIS BRAIN--	FOREVER AT HIS SIDE TO	246	3
I FELT A FUNERAL, IN MY BRAIN,	I FELT A FUNERAL, IN MY	280	1
AND CREAK ACROSS MY SOUL [BRAIN]	I FELT A FUNERAL, IN MY	280	10
YOUR BRAIN--TO BUBBLE COOL--	HE FUMBLES AT YOUR SOUL	315	10
MY BRAIN--BEGUN TO LAUGH--	THE FIRST DAY'S NIGHT	410	13
MY BRAIN KEEPS GIGGLING--STILL.	THE FIRST DAY'S NIGHT	410	16
THOSE EVENINGS OF THE BRAIN--	WE GROW ACCUSTOMED TO	419	10
I RUN IT OVER--"DEAD", BRAIN, "DEAD."	IT DONT SOUND SO	426	2
OR BORE THE GARDEN IN THE BRAIN	WITHIN MY GARDEN, RIDES	500	15
THE BRAIN, WITHIN IT'S GROOVE	THE BRAIN, WITHIN IT'S	556	1
PASS BACK AND FORTH, BEFORE MY BRAIN	WHEN I WAS SMALL, A	596	15
AND SEEN MY BRAIN--GO ROUND--	THEY SHUT ME UP IN PROSE	613	6
THE BRAIN--IS WIDER THAN THE SKY--	THE BRAIN--IS WIDER THAN	632	1
THE BRAIN IS DEEPER THAN THE SEA--	THE BRAIN--IS WIDER THAN	632	5
THE BRAIN IS JUST THE WEIGHT OF GOD--	THE BRAIN--IS WIDER THAN	632	9
YOU BEG THE ROBIN IN YOUR BRAIN	YOU'LL KNOW HER--BY HER	634	27
THE BRAIN HAS CORRIDORS--SURPASSING	ONE NEED NOT BE A	670	3
I STROVE TO WEARY BRAIN AND BONE--	SEVERER SERVICE OF	786	9
AS IF MY BRAIN HAD SPLIT--	I FELT A CLEAVING IN MY	937	2
YOUR PROBLEM [LABOR]--OF THE BRAIN--	I LEARNED--AT LEAST--	944	15
THIS IS A BLOSSOM OF THE BRAIN--	THIS IS A BLOSSOM OF THE	945	1
OF A SINGLE BRAIN--	PAIN--EXPANDS THE TIME--	967	4
I'VE DROPPED MY BRAIN--MY SOUL IS NUMB--	I'VE DROPPED MY BRAIN--	1046	1
AND LETS THE BRAIN AWAY	IF EVER THE LID GETS OFF	1727	2
WHEN THEY DISLOCATE MY BRAIN!	REARRANGE A "WIFE'S"	1737	2
BRAKE			
DID BUT A SNAKE BISECT THE BRAKE	I NEVER TOLD THE BURIED	11	8
AND THEN THE BRAKE IS STILL!	A WOUNDED DEER--LEAPS	165	4
HOW THE DUN BRAKE IS DRAPED IN CINDER [TIPPED IN TINSEL]	HOW THE OLD MOUNTAINS	291	3
AND THEN, I [HE] BRAKE MY [HIS] LIFE--AND LO,	I SHOWED HER HIGHTS SHE	446	9
BRAMBLE			
THROUGH LANE IT LAY--THRO' BRAMBLE--	THROUGH LANE IT LAY--	9	1
BRANCH			
AS "BRANCH," [TRUNK] AND "JUGULAR."	THE VEINS OF OTHER	811	4
BRANCHES			
THE WIND DOTH WOO THE BRANCHES, THE BRANCHES THEY ARE WON,	AWAKE YE MUSES NINE,	1	15
THE WIND DOTH WOO THE BRANCHES, THE BRANCHES THEY ARE WON,	AWAKE YE MUSES NINE,	1	15
THE BRANCHES ON MY HAND	I AM ALIVE--I GUESS--	470	2
AS FORESTS [BRANCHES] TOUCH THE WIND	BECAUSE HE LOVES HER	1229	8
BRAND			
AS THAT DIVINER BRAND	EXHILIRATION--IS WITHIN	383	4
AS IS THE INNER BRAND--	THE OUTER--FROM THE	451	12
WITH THE BRAND [STAMP] OF THE GENTILE DRINKER	TO PUT THIS WORLD DOWN,	527	14
RUB AWAY THE BRAND--	COLOR--CASTE--	970	8
BRASS			
NOR "BAND"--IN BRASS AND SCARLET--DREST--	MUSICIANS WRESTLE	157	8
HELD OF THOSE BRASS ARMS--	IF YOUR NERVE, DENY YOU	292	7
BRAVE			
IT WAS THE BRAVE COLUMBUS,	"SIC TRANSIT GLORIA	3	37
COURAGE! MY BRAVE COLUMBA!	ONCE MORE, MY NOW	48	7
BRAVE--BROKEN HEARTED STATEMENT--	"THEY HAVE NOT CHOSEN ME	85	3
TO FIGHT ALOUD, IS VERY BRAVE--	TO FIGHT ALOUD, IS VERY	126	1
BRAVE--SHINES THE SUN THROUGH THE FRECKLED PANE--	HOW MANY TIMES THESE LOW	187	10
THEN WE HIDE OUR BRAVE FACE	WE DONT CRY--TIM AND I,	196	5
THE BRAVE EYES FILM--	YOU SEE I CANNOT SEE--	253	5
BRAVE NAMES OF MEN--	READ--SWEET--HOW OTHERS	260	12
WHEN MEN SO BRAVE--ARE DEAD--	IT FEELS A SHAME TO BE	444	2
SO BRAVE--UPON IT'S LITTLE BED	WHY MAKE IT DOUBT--IT	462	4
A BEST DISGRACE--A BRAVE MAN FEELS--	THERE IS A SHAME OF	551	5
ACKNOWLEDGED--OF THE BRAVE--	THERE IS A SHAME OF	551	6
BRAVE BLACK BERRY--	THE BLACK BERRY--WEARS A	554	12
FLAGS, ARE A BRAVE SIGHT--	INCONCEIVABLY SOLEMN!	582	8
NO CASQUE SO BRAVE	I ROSE--BECAUSE HE SANK	616	14
A LONG--LONG [VAST--VAST / BRAVE--BRAVE] SLEEP--A FAMOUS--SLEEP--	A LONG--LONG SLEEP--A	654	[illegible]
A LONG--LONG [VAST--VAST / BRAVE--BRAVE] SLEEP--A FAMOUS--SLEEP--	A LONG--LONG SLEEP--A	654	[illegible]
BRAVE BOBOLINK--	NO BOBOLINK--REVERSE HIS	755	1[illegible]
TO OFFER BRAVE ASSISTANCE	TO OFFER BRAVE	767	
BORED AT SO BRAVE A ROOT	AND THIS OF ALL MY HOPES	913	
FOR THE BRAVE [BOLD] BELOVED--	ROBBED BY DEATH--BUT	971	
SMILED TOO BRAVE FOR THE DETECTING [OUR DETECTION]	HAD WE KNOWN THE TON SHE	1124	V

	FIRST LINE	POEM	LINE
BRAVE (CONTINUED)			
BUT BRAVE AT LAST WITH BUGLES	DEATH IS THE SUPPLE	1445	7
NOT SICKNESS STAINS THE BRAVE,	NOT SICKNESS STAINS THE	1613	1
BRAVER			
BETTER [BRAVER] ENTERTAIN	NEVER FOR SOCIETY	746	8
BRAVERIES			
FOR BRAVERIES, REMOTE AS THIS [HIS]	WHEN I WAS SMALL, A	596	19
FOR BRAVERIES JUST SEALED [PROVED] IN THIS	WHEN I WAS SMALL, A	596	V 19
BRAVEST			
GRANT GOD, HE CHARGE THE BRAVEST	BLESS GOD, HE WENT AS	147	3
THE BRAVEST--OF THE HOST--	THERE IS A FLOWER THAT	380	29
THE BRAVEST--GROPE A LITTLE--	WE GROW ACCUSTOMED TO	419	13
THE BRAVEST DIE	FACTS BY OUR SIDE ARE	1497	11
THE BOLDEST [BRAVEST] LEAPED, AND CLUTCHED IT--	OF DEATH I TRY TO THINK	1558	16
BRAVO			
IF BRAVO, SOMETIMES SWERVE--	THE TEST OF LOVE--IS	573	7
BRAVOES			
AMID NO BELLS NOR BRAVOES	WENT UP A YEAR THIS	93	3
I'M CONFIDENT THAT BRAVOES	WHEN I WAS SMALL, A	596	17
BRAWLING			
WHOSE WATERS ARE THE BRAWLING [NAMELESS] BROOK	CONTAINED IN THIS SHORT	1165	V 7
BRAYED			
THESE, ARE NOT BRAYED OF TONGUE--	THE SOUL HAS BANDAGED	512	24
BRAZIL			
BRAZIL? HE TWIRLED A BUTTON--	I ASKED NO OTHER THING--	621	5
HAUNTS CANDLES IN BRAZIL.	A MOTH THE HUE OF THIS	841	2
BRAZILIAN			
ON BRAZILIAN PAMPAS--	SOME SUCH BUTTERFLY BE	541	2
AND LEFT BRAZILIAN THREADS	MY FIRST WELL DAY--SINCE	574	20
BREACH			
BREACH A SECOND CANNOT FILL--	LONG YEARS APART--CAN	1383	2
BREAD			
THY CONSECRATED BREAD TO TAKE	THESE ARE THE DAYS WHEN	130	17
A LITTLE BREAD--A CRUST--A CRUMB--	A LITTLE BREAD--A CRUST	159	1
I DID NOT KNOW THE AMPLE BREAD--	I HAD BEEN HUNGRY, ALL	579	9
NOR HEARD THE TIMID CRY FOR "BREAD"--	THE BEGGAR LAD--DIES	717	7
TO TASTE HER MYSTIC BREAD--	THESE ARE THE SIGNS TO	1077	4
BUT BREAD IS THAT DIVINER [MAJESTIC] THING	THE BEGGAR AT THE DOOR	1240	3
BREAD OF HEAVEN RESENTS BESTOWAL	WHEN A LOVER IS A BEGGAR	1314	7
BREADTH			
TILL ONE BREADTH COVER TWO--	THE SUNRISE RUNS FOR	710	5
A GRAVE--IS A RESTRICTED [AN INFERIOR] BREADTH--	A COFFIN--IS A SMALL	943	5
HE PREACHED UPON [ABOUT] "BREADTH" TILL IT ARGUED HIM [WE . . .	HE PREACHED UPON	1207	1
BREADTHS			
WHO SPUN THE BREADTHS OF BLUE!	BRING ME THE SUNSET IN A	128	6
LIKE BREADTHS OF TOPAZ--PACKED A NIGHT--	THE DAY CAME SLOW--TILL	304	7
OF SMALL AND SPICY YARDS [BREADTHS]--	OF BRUSSELS--IT WAS NOT	602	9
BREAK			
THAT IS THE BREAK OF DAY!	SLEEP IS SUPPOSED TO BE	13	15
TO BREAK IT TO THE BEE--	I HAV'NT TOLD MY GARDEN	50	4
ONLY TO BREAK IN WILDER SONG	IF I COULD BRIBE THEM BY	179	11
I WOULD NOT BREAK THEE--	POOR LITTLE HEART!	192	8
GLOBE ROSES--BREAK THEIR SATIN FLAKE--	I TEND MY FLOWERS FOR	339	16
HOW COULD I BREAK MY WORD?	A MURMUR IN THE TREES--	416	18
WHILE COLOR'S REVELATIONS BREAK--	AS FAR FROM PITY, AS	496	11
PERPETUAL BREAK [BE / GO] ABROAD	WHEN I WAS SMALL, A	596	18
WHY HEAVEN DID NOT BREAK AWAY--	IT TROUBLED ME AS ONCE I	600	15
TO BREAK FOR YOU--	IT TOSSED--AND TOSSED--	723	12
IN IT WAIT TILL JUDGMENT BREAK	AMPLE MAKE THIS BED--	829	3
BUT WHEN I BREAK IT WITH THE NEWS	THE MOST PATHETIC THING	1290	5
TO BREAK SO VAST A HEART	TO BREAK SO VAST A HEART	1312	1
THE HUGEST HEARTS THAT BREAK.	LOVE'S STRICKEN "WHY"	1368	4
AT DAY BREAK TO BEGIN HIS RACE	HE WENT BY SLEEP THAT	1662	3
PROUD OF MY BROKEN HEART, SINCE THOU DIDST BREAK IT,	PROUD OF MY BROKEN HEART	1736	1
AN EAR CAN BREAK A HUMAN HEART	THE SADDEST NOISE, THE	1764	17
BREAKERS			
WHERE NO BREAKERS ROAR--	ON THIS WONDROUS SEA	4	5
BREAKFAST			
TO BREAKFAST--TO [AND] RETURN--	A LITTLE EAST OF JORDAN,	59	8
TAKING VILLAGES FOR BREAKFAST,	I HAVE NEVER SEEN	175	7
EPICURES--DATE A BREAKFAST--BY IT--	"MORNING"--MEANS	300	6
THE EAGLE'S GOLDEN BREAKFAST STRANGLES [DAZZLES]--THEM--	VICTORY COMES LATE--	690	12
NO BREAKFAST IF IT GUARANTY	THE BIRD MUST SING TO	880	3
ENTICED TO BREAKFAST FROM THE SKY	FOREVER HONORED BE THE	1570	3
BREAKFASTED			
ADVANCED AND BREAKFASTED.	OUR LITTLE KINSMEN--	885	8
BREAKING			
THE BREAKING OF THE DAY.	SLEEP IS SUPPOSED TO BE	13	9
THE BREAKING OF THE DAY	THE MURMUR OF A BEE	155	11
SINCE BREAKING THEN--SINCE BREAKING THEN--	I SHOULD NOT DARE TO	205	14
SINCE BREAKING THEN--SINCE BREAKING THEN--	I SHOULD NOT DARE TO	205	14
BREAKING IN BRIGHT ORTHOGRAPHY	MANY A PHRASE HAS THE	276	9
THAT SENSE WAS BREAKING THROUGH--	I FELT A FUNERAL, IN MY	280	4
OR BREAKING--ALMOST--WITH UNSPOKEN PAIN--	HOW SICK--TO WAIT--IN	368	4
IF I CAN STOP ONE HEART FROM BREAKING	IF I CAN STOP ONE HEART	919	1

	FIRST LINE	POEM	LINE
BREAKS			
SUCH TRANSPORT BREAKS UPON THE TOWN	MUSICIANS WRESTLE	157	5
ASCEND IN CEASELESS [BREAKS IN VICTORIOUS] CAROL--	TO LEARN THE TRANSPORT	167	13
BREAKS UP MY FEET--	I CAN WADE GRIEF--	252	5
A HAPPY LIP--BREAKS SUDDEN--	A HAPPY LIP--BREAKS	353	1
BREAST			
ON IT'S BREAST TO LIE--	NOBODY KNOWS THIS LITTLE	35	8
IT WEARS A SPRIG UPON IT'S BREAST--	THERE'S SOMETHING	45	3
HER BREAST IS FIT FOR PEARLS,	HER BREAST IS FIT FOR	84	1
THE PURPLE BROOK WITHIN THE BREAST	A SOMETHING IN A	122	14
FOR A SIMPLE BREAST LIKE MINE--	FLOWERS--WELL--IF	137	10
HIS MUSKET ON HIS BREAST--	BLESS GOD, HE WENT AS	147	2
SWELLED--LIKE HORIZONS--IN MY BREAST [VEST]--	A SOLEMN THING--IT WAS--	271	15
MINE--WAS AN ACORN'S BREAST--	ONE YEAR AGO--JOTS WHAT?	296	18
BORNE ON A DUSKY BREAST--	THE MALAY--TOOK THE	452	11
I GROPED [PERISHED / DWELT] UPON HIS BREAST--	HE TOUCHED ME, SO I LIVE	506	3
CROWNED--CROWING [WHIMPERING / DANGLING]--ON MY FATHER'S BREAST--	I'M CEDED--I'VE STOPPED	508	15
THE RIVER REACHES TO MY BREAST--	ME PROVE IT NOW--WHOEVER	537	9
LIKE COLUMNS--IN THE BREAST--	THE TINT I CANNOT TAKE--	627	V 16
AND CHOOSES WAINSCOT IN THE BREAST	GRIEF IS A MOUSE--	793	2
THAT WEARING ON YOUR BREAST--	I HIDE MYSELF WITHIN MY	903	V 2
HIS BREAST, A SINGLE ONYX	HIS FEET ARE SHOD WITH	916	3
UPON HIS BREAST, A CLOSING SOUL	THIS IS A BLOSSOM OF THE	945	15
OCCUPY MY HOUSE [BREAST]"--	"UNTO ME?" I DO NOT KNOW	964	12
IS NOT SO AMPLE AS THE BREAST [HEART]	STEP LIGHTLY ON THIS	1183	3
DUNGEONED IN THE HUMAN BREAST	"SECRETS" IS A DAILY	1385	5
UNWORTHY OF HER BREAST	UNWORTHY OF HER BREAST	1414	1
APPALLS THIS [THAT] TROPIC BREAST--	NO AUTUMN'S INTERCEPTING	1516	2
THAT LOWLY BREAST [HOMESTEAD SWEET] WHERE BUTTERFLIES	HIS ORIENTAL HERESIES	1526	7
COME SHOW THY DURHAM BREAST	COME SHOW THY DURHAM	1542	1
ARROWS ENAMORED OF HIS HEART [BREAST]--	ARROWS ENAMORED OF HIS	1629	1
BREASTS			
IF BROADCLOTH HEARTS [BREASTS] ARE FIRMER--	A SHADY FRIEND--FOR	278	7
BREATH			
GAVE HIS BREATH AWAY.	THERE IS A WORD	8	10
AN HOUR BEHIND THE FLEETING BREATH--	DELAYED TILL SHE HAD	58	4
COMPUTES THE STAMENS IN A BREATH--	"ARCTURUS" IS HIS OTHER	70	11
A HURRY IN THE BREATH--	A THROE UPON THE	71	2
FOR IT W'D STOP MY BREATH--	GOING TO HEAVEN!	79	21
AND WHEN HER BREATH WAS DONE	SHE DIED--THIS WAS THE	150	2
WHEN BREATH BLEW [DREW] BACK,	JUST LOST, WHEN I WAS	160	4
BLISS IS BUT BLISS, AND BREATH BUT BREATH!	'TIS SO MUCH JOY! 'TIS	172	8
BLISS IS BUT BLISS, AND BREATH BUT BREATH!	'TIS SO MUCH JOY! 'TIS	172	8
YET HELD MY BREATH, THE WHILE--	I'VE HEARD AN ORGAN TALK	183	4
FOR THIS--ACCEPTED BREATH--	FOR THIS--ACCEPTED	195	1
'TIS JUST THE PRICE OF BREATH--	YOU'RE RIGHT--"THE WAY	234	6
SHADOWS--HOLD THEIR BREATH--	THERE'S A CERTAIN SLANT	258	14
I SIMULATE THE BREATH, SO WELL--	I BREATHED ENOUGH TO	272	3
JUST LET GO THE BREATH--	'TIS SO APPALLING--IT	281	16
WITHOUT THAT FORCING, IN MY BREATH--	I GOT SO I COULD HEAR	293	11
STRAIGHTEN--LOOK CAUTIOUS FOR THEIR BREATH--	GIVE LITTLE ANGUISH--	310	5
YOUR BREATH HAS TIME [CHANCE] TO STRAIGHTEN--	HE FUMBLES AT YOUR SOUL	315	9
THAN ORDINARY BREATH--	MORE LIFE--WENT OUT--	422	2
PHYSICIAN'S--PROOF OF BREATH--	I AM ALIVE--I GUESS--	470	8
IF JUST AS SOON AS BREATH IS OUT	IF I MAY HAVE IT, WHEN	577	3
AND LOOK--AND SHUDDER, AND BLOCK YOUR BREATH--	DID YOU EVER STAND IN A	590	3
THREE TIMES--WE PARTED--BREATH--AND I--	THREE TIMES--WE PARTED--	598	1
. . . WEARIED--] BREATH--DID NOT--	THREE TIMES--WE PARTED--	598	13
THEY STRUGGLE--SOME--FOR BREATH--	YOU'VE SEEN BALLOONS SET	700	10
WITH A REMAINING BREATH	THIS CHASM, SWEET, UPON	858	14
TO SUSPEND THE BREATH	CRISIS IS A HAIR	889	5
TO BEING, SOMEWHERE--MOTION--BREATH--	I'VE DROPPED MY BRAIN--	1046	17
A DEPARTING BREATH--	NONE WHO SAW IT EVER	1110	4
HOW OUT OF BREATH YOU ARE--	DEAR MARCH--COME IN--	1320	6
A SHORTER BREATH OF DAY	THERE COMES A WARNING	1536	2
T'IS EARLY AS OUR BREATH	WITCHCRAFT HAS NOT A	1708	2
BREATHE			
BREATHE IN EAR MORE MODERN	IT DID NOT SURPRISE ME--	39	7
WHERE WOMEN BREATHE--	I'LL CLUTCH--AND CLUTCH	427	17
AND COULD NOT BREATHE WITHOUT A KEY,	IT WAS NOT DEATH, FOR I	510	15
THE MAIMED MAY PAUSE, AND BREATHE,	THIS MERIT HATH THE	979	5
TO BREATHE MY BLANK WITHOUT THEE	THROUGH WHAT TRANSPORTS	1153	3
TO BREATHE--CORRODE THE RAPTURE	THE TREASON OF AN ACCENT	1358	V
IN MY OWN GRAVE I BREATHE	SO GIVE ME BACK TO DEATH	1632	5
BREATHED			
I BREATHED ENOUGH TO TAKE THE TRICK--	I BREATHED ENOUGH TO	272	1
WE BREATHED--	ONE YEAR AGO--JOTS WHAT?	296	26
BECAUSE SHE BREATHED AGAINST	FORGET! THE LADY WITH	438	3
AS IF I BREATHED SUPERIOR AIR--	HE TOUCHED ME, SO I LIVE	506	8
THERE BREATHED A MAN--	IN FALLING TIMBERS	614	2
COULD THEY--KNOW--HE BREATHED [LIVED]--	IN FALLING TIMBERS	614	6
THAT HAVING BREATHED	OH WHAT A GRACE IS THIS,	1615	3
BREATHES			
LEOPARD BREATHES--AT LAST!	WITH THEE, IN THE DESERT	209	4
WHO AIRS OF EXPECTATION BREATHES	'TIS MY FIRST NIGHT	1122	5
A WORD THAT BREATHES DISTINCTLY	A WORD MADE FLESH IS	1651	9

	FIRST LINE	POEM	LINE
BREATHING			
NOT PORTLY, MIND! BUT BREATHING--WARM--	A LITTLE BREAD--A CRUST	159	4
WITHOUT A TIGHTER BREATHING	A NARROW FELLOW IN THE	986	23
A BREATHING WOMAN	I'VE DROPPED MY BRAIN--	1046	7
FOR BREATHING IS THE ONLY WORK	NO MAN SAW AWE, NOR TO	1733	11
BREATHLESS			
WHEREVER RUNS THE BREATHLESS SUN--	THERE IS A WORD	8	11
BEFORE THE BREATHLESS BEE--	DISTRUSTFUL OF THE	20	10
SO BREATHLESS TILL I PASSED HER--	SO BASHFUL WHEN I SPIED	91	5
NEVER MIND MY BREATHLESS ANVIL!	BY A FLOWER--BY A LETTER	109	5
ANGELS' BREATHLESS BALLOT	SOUL, WILT THOU TOSS	139	5
WOULD SCAN THE MIGHTY [EAGER / BREATHLESS / HURRYING / . . .	TO FLEE FROM MEMORY	1242	6
BREATHS			
AND BREATHS WERE GATHERING FIRM	I HEARD A FLY BUZZ--WHEN	465	6
SAID PASSION, THROUGH CONTRACTING BREATHS	SAID DEATH TO PASSION	1033	3
BRED			
BRED AS WE, AMONG THE MOUNTAINS,	EXULTATION IS THE GOING	76	5
BREEDS			
INFECTION IN THE SENTENCE BREEDS	A WORD DROPPED CARELESS	1261	5
BREEZE			
AND OF THE BREEZE--AMEN!	THE GENTIAN WEAVES HER	18	19
A BREEZE--A CAPER IN THE TREES--	A SEPAL, PETAL, AND A	19	4
ONLY A BREEZE WILL SIGH--	NOBODY KNOWS THIS LITTLE	35	10
LIGHT LAUGHS THE BREEZE	SAFE IN THEIR ALABASTER	216	7
HIS LAUGHTER, LIKE THE BREEZE	THE ONLY GHOST I EVER	274	10
PRIVATE--LIKE THE BREEZE--	IT'S LIKE THE LIGHT--	297	6
UPON THE NEAREST BREEZE--	HOW MANY FLOWERS FAIL IN	404	6
AS SOON THE SOUTH--HER BREEZE	WHAT CARE THE DEAD, FOR	592	20
AN EASY BREEZE DO PUT AFLOAT	OF BEING IS A BIRD	653	3
PROTRACTED AS THE BREEZE	OF SILKEN SPEECH AND	896	7
EXHILIRATION IS THE BREEZE	EXHILIRATION IS THE	1118	1
THE GALE [BREEZE] WERE NOT SO FINE	WE LIKE A HAIRBREADTH	1175	6
AND A DISSEMBLING BREEZE	SEPTEMBER'S	1271	4
AND EVERY BREEZE THAT RUN ALONG	A SAUCER HOLDS A CUP	1374	7
THE DEPREDATION OF A BREEZE	GO NOT TOO NEAR A HOUSE	1434	2
AND THEN HE SPIED A BREEZE,	HIGH FROM THE EARTH I	1723	4
BREEZES			
THE TIDY BREEZES, WITH THEIR BROOMS--	A LADY RED--AMID THE	74	5
THE BREEZES MADDER PLAY;	THE BEE IS NOT AFRAID OF	111	6
THE BREEZES FETCH ALONG--	THE GRASS SO LITTLE HAS	333	6
THE BREEZES BROUGHT DEJECTED LUTES--	A DROP FELL ON THE APPLE	794	13
BREEZES CARESS	TO THE STANCH DUST	1402 V	5
BRETHEREN			
WE BRETHEREN, ARE", HE SAID--	I DIED FOR BEAUTY--BUT	449	8
OR BRETHEREN, HAD HE--	HE TOLD A HOMELY TALE	763	12
BREVITY			
WHEN DEATH LIT ALL THE SHORTNESS UP [LIMIT--UP / BREVITY]	HER FINAL SUMMER WAS IT	795	7
ARRAIGN THE SUNNY BREVITY	THIS DOCILE ONE INTER	1752	3
BREW			
AS MAKE OF [BREW FROM / MIX] OUR IMPERFECT [UNCOMELY / OBTUSER] . . .	SHE HIDETH HER THE LAST	557	11
LEAST BEE THAT BREW--	LEAST BEE THAT BREW--	676	1
BREWED			
BREWED FROM DECADES OF AGONY!	THO' I GET HOME HOW LATE	207	8
I TASTE A LIQUOR NEVER BREWED--	I TASTE A LIQUOR NEVER	214	1
WAS THE STRONG CUP OF ANGUISH BREWED FOR THE NAZARENE	PROUD OF MY BROKEN HEART	1736	6
BREWS			
THAT BREWS THAT RARE VARIETY!	THE NEAREST DREAM	319	13
BRIAR			
AS OF BRIAR AND LEAF DISPLAYED	PIGMY SERAPHS--GONE	138	10
OR TAKE AWAY [PALLIATE] A BRIAR.	IT WAS A GRAVE, YET BORE	876	12
OFTENER THROUGH REALM OF BRIAR	FAR FROM LOVE THE	1021	3
BRIBE			
IF I COULD BRIBE THEM BY A ROSE	IF I COULD BRIBE THEM BY	179	1
IF I SHOULD BRIBE THE LITTLE BIRD--	THE SKIES CANT KEEP	191	7
A TRIUMPH--WHEN TEMPTATION'S BRIBE	TRIUMPH--MAY BE OF	455	9
BRICK			
WITH THEIR BRICK SHOULDERS--	I COULD DIE--TO KNOW--	570	8
BRIDAL			
WAS BRIDAL--E'ER LIKE THIS?	'TWAS A LONG PARTING--	625	13
BRIDALLED			
BORN--BRIDALLED--SHROUDED--	TITLE DIVINE--IS MINE!	1072	10
BRIDE			
THE BRIDE, AND THEN THE BRIDEGROOM, THE TWO, AND THEN THE ONE,	AWAKE YE MUSES NINE,	1	7
THE WORM DOTH WOO THE MORTAL, DEATH CLAIMS A LIVING BRIDE,	AWAKE YE MUSES NINE,	1	21
DISCARD HIS BRIDE--	FORGET! THE LADY WITH	438	11
HOW SHORT IT TAKES TO MAKE IT BRIDE--	A WIFE--AT DAYBREAK I	461	4
WHAT RIGHT HAVE I--TO BE A BRIDE--	I AM ASHAMED--I HIDE--	473	2
BAPTIZED--THIS DAY--A BRIDE--	I AM ASHAMED--I HIDE--	473	27
MY BRIDE HAD SLIPPED AWAY--	HER SWEET WEIGHT ON MY	518	4
NEVER BRIDE HAD SUCH ASSEMBLING--	HER SWEET TURN TO LEAVE	649	9
BRIDE OF THE FATHER AND THE SON	GIVEN IN MARRIAGE UNTO	817	3
BRIDE OF THE HOLY GHOST.	GIVEN IN MARRIAGE UNTO	817	4
AND HALF OF DAY, THE BRIDE.	TO THIS WORLD SHE	830	9
FOR HER [ONE] TO BE A [AN IMPENDING] BRIDE	ALL THAT I DO	1496	11

	FIRST LINE	POEM	LINE
BRIDE (CONTINUED)			
CIRCUMFERENCE THOU BRIDE OF AWE	CIRCUMFERENCE THOU BRIDE	1620	1
AGAINST YOUR TROPIC BRIDE	'TWAS HERE MY SUMMER	1756	8
BRIDEGROOM			
THE BRIDE, AND THEN THE BRIDEGROOM, THE TWO, AND THEN THE ONE,	AWAKE YE MUSES NINE,	1	7
WHAT, AND IF, OURSELF A BRIDEGROOM--	HER--"LAST POEMS"--	312	18
NEIGHBOR--AND FRIEND--AND BRIDEGROOM--	GLEE--THE GREAT STORM IS	619	7
BRIDES			
BRIDES--AN APOCALYPSE--	"MORNING"--MEANS	300	7
THESE ARE THE BRIDES OF PERMANENCE	DOMINION LASTS UNTIL	1257	7
BRIDGE			
JUST A BRIDGE AWAY--	BEFORE THE ICE IS IN THE	37	12
FAITH--IS THE PIERLESS BRIDGE	FAITH--IS THE PIERLESS	915	1
THE BRIDGE WOULD CEASE TO BE	FAITH--IS THE PIERLESS	915	10
NO BRIDGE BELOW DOTH TOTTER SO--	HOW BRITTLE ARE THE	1433	3
BRIDGES			
AND THE BRIDGES OFTEN GO--	HAVE YOU GOT A BROOK IN	136	12
BUT NEVER I MIND THE STEEPEST [BRIDGES]--	TIE THE STRINGS TO MY	279	9
BRIDGET			
BY EVERY BROOM AND BRIDGET	THE SPIDER AS AN ARTIST	1275	5
BRIDLES			
HAS VIEWS OF BRIDLES AND OF BARNS	THE LIFE THAT TIED TOO	1535	V 7
BRIEF			
A BRIEF, BUT PATIENT ILLNESS--	THE GENTIAN WEAVES HER	18	5
WHEN TIME'S BRIEF MASQUERADE WAS DONE	"ARCTURUS" IS HIS OTHER	70	20
A BRIEF CAMPAIGN OF STING AND SWEET	A LITTLE BREAD--A CRUST	159	8
I THOUGHT THAT STORM--WAS BRIEF--	IT STRUCK ME--EVERY DAY	362	9
BUT THIS, MIGHT BE MY BRIEF TERM	I'M SAYING EVERY DAY	373	18
BOLD--WERE IT ENEMY--BRIEF--WERE IT FRIEND--	IT'S COMING--THE	390	6
AND THEN, 'TWAS BRIEF AND LOW--	I WAS THE SLIGHTEST IN	486	11
THE HARM THEY DID--WAS SHORT [BRIEF]--AND SINCE	'TIS TRUE--THEY SHUT ME	538	9
IMPANELLED FROM NO SUMMER BRIEF--	TO MY SMALL HEARTH HIS	638	5
AND THIS BRIEF TRAGEDY OF [DRAMA IN THE] FLESH--	OF ALL THE SOULS THAT	664	7
A FRAIL [FLEET / BRIEF] ARISTOCRAT OF TIME	SHE SPED AS PETALS OF A	991	3
FOR HER BRIEF CREST--	SHE ROSE AS HIGH AS HIS	1011	4
BRITTLE AND BRIEF IN QUALITY--	A PROMPT--EXECUTIVE BIRD	1177	3
BRIEF STRUGGLE FOR CAPACITY	I THOUGHT THAT NATURE	1286	7
A BRIEF CAREER OF CHEER	A RAT SURRENDERED HERE	1340	2
BRIEFER			
A SUMMER BRIEFER THAN THE FIRST	THERE IS A JUNE WHEN	930	3
BRIEFLY			
RECORDING BRIEFLY--"LOST"--	I KNOW A PLACE WHERE	337	4
FOR TWO DIVIDED, BRIEFLY,	THE GRAVE MY LITTLE	1743	5
BRIG			
ONE PORT--SUFFICES--FOR A BRIG--LIKE MINE--	HOW SICK--TO WAIT--IN	368	7
A LITTLE BRIG I KNEW--O'ERTOOK BY BLAST--	IT TOSSED--AND TOSSED--	723	2
AH, BRIG--GOOD NIGHT	IT TOSSED--AND TOSSED--	723	9
BRIGADIER			
SO GAY, SO BRIGADIER--	THE SUN KEPT STOOPING--	152	10
AND MEN--TOO BRIGADIER--	A MIEN TO MOVE A QUEEN--	283	V 24
SITTING [RIDING] A BOUGH LIKE A BRIGADIER	A PROMPT--EXECUTIVE BIRD	1177	5
SATAN--THE BRIGADIER--	THE BIBLE IS AN ANTIQUE	1545	6
NO BRIGADIER THROUGHOUT THE YEAR	NO BRIGADIER THROUGHOUT	1561	1
BRIGAND			
BOLD AS [BOLDER THAN] A BRIGAND!	DUST IS THE ONLY SECRET	153	11
BRIGHT			
I HEAR THE BRIGHT BEE HUM;	THERE IS ANOTHER SKY,	2	12
IN A SERENER BRIGHT,	I HAVE A BIRD IN SPRING	5	19
BRIGHT MELODY FOR ME	I HAVE A BIRD IN SPRING	5	29
IN BRIGHT DETACHMENT [DETACHMENTS] STAND!	SOME RAINBOW--COMING	64	21
A SOMETHING SO TRANSPORTING BRIGHT	A SOMETHING IN A	122	8
SOME SAY--THAT BRIGHT MAJORITY	MUSICIANS WRESTLE	157	14
TO STRANGE, BRIGHT CROWDS OF FLOWERS--	AS IF SOME LITTLE ARCTIC	180	7
BY MY LONG BRIGHT--AND LONGER--TRUST--	I THINK JUST HOW MY	237	15
WOULD SUIT AS BRIGHT,	DELIGHT IS AS THE FLIGHT	257	7
BREAKING IN BRIGHT ORTHOGRAPHY	MANY A PHRASE HAS THE	276	9
DRILLED BRIGHT--	UNTO LIKE STORY--TROUBLE	295	22
BRIGHT ABSENTEE!	I TEND MY FLOWERS FOR	339	2
AS 'TWERE A BRIGHT BOQUET--	IT WILL BE SUMMER--	342	6
IN CHAMBERS BRIGHT--	'TWAS THE OLD--ROAD--	344	19
BRIGHT FIRES--THE BLANKETLESS--	'TIS OPPOSITES--ENTICE--	355	3
WITH BRIGHT PINS OF BUTTERCUP--	I'M SAYING EVERY DAY	373	13
BRIGHT WEDNESDAY AFTERNOONS--	I NEVER FELT AT HOME--	413	8
IT'S BRIGHT [FAIR] IMPOSSIBILITY	I WOULD NOT PAINT--A	505	3
OR WIND'S BRIGHT SIGNAL TO THE EAR--	LIKE FLOWERS, THAT HEARD	513	10
SHE DROPPED BRIGHT SCRAPS OF TINT, ABOUT--	MY FIRST WELL DAY--SINCE	574	19
BRIGHT FLOWERS SLIT A CALYX	THE TREES LIKE TASSELS--	606	21
BRIGHT KNOTS OF APPARITIONS	OF NEARNESS TO HER	607	15
OF ME--IN CHRIST'S BRIGHT AUDIENCE [LATITUDE]	YOU TAUGHT ME WAITING	740	11
HE HELPED TO MAKE TOO BRIGHT	THE SUN IS GAY OR STARK	878	6
ASSISTING IN THE BRIGHT AFFAIR	BLOOM--IS RESULT--TO	1058	5
TOO BRIGHT [BOLD] FOR OUR INFIRM DELIGHT	TELL ALL THE TRUTH BUT	1129	3
'TWAS SUCH AN EVENING BRIGHT AND STIFF	THAT ODD OLD MAN IS DEAD	1130	3
EACH BRIGHT MORTALITY	A FULL FED ROSE ON MEALS	1154	4
IMPEDING [IMPEDE THE] NAVIGATION BRIGHT [FAIR]	A STAGNANT PLEASURE LIKE	1281	5
THIS WHOLE [SUDDEN / FAIR / GAY / BRIGHT / FLEET / SWEET / . . .	A LITTLE MADNESS IN THE	1333	5

	FIRST LINE	POEM		LINE
BRIGHT (CONTINUED)				
BROTHER OF OPHIR, BRIGHT ADIEU, ...	BROTHER OF INGOTS--AH	1366	V	1
THE TREES WERE BRIGHT AND STILL--	THE ROAD WAS LIT WITH	1450		2
TO THE BRIGHT EAST SHE FLIES, ...	TO THE BRIGHT EAST SHE	1573		1
AND EVERY CLAMOR BRIGHT	THE FARTHEST THUNDER	1581		14
GLORY IS THAT BRIGHT TRAGIC THING	GLORY IS THAT BRIGHT	1660		1
BRIGHTER				
HERE IS A BRIGHTER GARDEN, ...	THERE IS ANOTHER SKY,	2		9
BRIGHTEST				
THAT THOU ART TRITEST--BRIGHTEST [SWEETEST] TRUTH--	EXTOL THEE--COULD I--	1643	V	4
BRIM				
NOR HELD UPON--OF [HAS IT ANY] BRIM-- . .	YOU'LL KNOW HER--BY HER	634		20
BRIMMING				
NO BRIMMING TANKARDS FLOW--	WHAT INN IS THIS	115		8
I TURN MY BRIMMING EYES AWAY, ...	I BRING AN UNACCUSTOMED	132		6
BRIMS				
AND DECKS [BRIMS / FILLS / SWELLS] THE RAYS	BY A DEPARTING LIGHT	1714		6
BRINDLED				
IT'S TOILS [CORN] TO BRINDLED PEOPLE [NATIONS] THRUST [CAST]--	A FIELD OF STUBBLE,	1407		3
BRING				
AND BRING THE FIFE, AND TRUMPET, AND BEAT UPON THE DRUM--	AWAKE YE MUSES NINE,	1		39
IT'S ALL I HAVE TO BRING TODAY--	IT'S ALL I HAVE TO BRING	26		1
I, MY RIDDLE BRING	IF THOSE I LOVED WERE	29	V	8
I BRING MY ROSE.	I KEEP MY PLEDGE.	46		4
IF I SHOULD CEASE TO BRING A ROSE	IF I SHOULD CEASE TO	56		1
EXCEPT IT QUIET BRING	WE SHOULD NOT MIND SO	81		2
BRING ME THE SUNSET IN A CUP, ...	BRING ME THE SUNSET IN A	128		1
I BRING AN UNACCUSTOMED WINE	I BRING AN UNACCUSTOMED	132		1
WONT SOMEBODY BRING THE LIGHT	DYING! DYING IN THE	158		2
I'LL FETCH [BRING] THEE BROOKS	MY RIVER RUNS TO THEE--	162		5
I'D BRING THEM EVERY FLOWER THAT GROWS . .	IF I COULD BRIBE THEM BY	179		2
FATHER--I BRING THEE--NOT MYSELF--	SAVIOR! I'VE NO ONE ELSE	217	V	5
I BROUGHT [BRING] THEE THE IMPERIAL [DEPARTED] HEART	SAVIOR! I'VE NO ONE ELSE	217		7
I'VE NOTHING ELSE--TO BRING, YOU KNOW-- . .	I'VE NOTHING ELSE--TO	224		1
BUT--I SHALL BRING A FULLER TUNE--	I SHALL KEEP SINGING!	250		8
IF HE BRING ODORS OF CLOVERS--	THE WIND DID'NT COME	316		11
BUT SAY MY APRON BRING THE STICKS	ALTHOUGH I PUT AWAY HIS	366		28
BRING ME MY BEST PRIDE--	I AM ASHAMED--I HIDE--	473		23
I BRING THEE PROOF	THAT I DID ALWAYS LOVE	549		2
CAPTIVE! WE BRING REPRIEVE OF ROSES! . . .	WOULD YOU LIKE SUMMER?	691		6
I COULD BRING YOU JEWELS--HAD I A MIND TO--	I COULD BRING YOU JEWELS	697		1
I COULD BRING YOU ODORS FROM ST DOMINGO-- .	I COULD BRING YOU JEWELS	697		3
BETTER--COULD I BRING?	I COULD BRING YOU JEWELS	697		12
BRINGING				
TO BRINGING THEE TO JUSTICE, AND MARSHALLING THY SOUL:	AWAKE YE MUSES NINE,	1		26
SO I KEEP BRINGING THESE--	I'VE NOTHING ELSE--TO	224		2
BRINGING STILL MY "PLEA FOR CULTURE." . .	THE LUXURY TO APPREHEND	815	V	
BRINGS				
THE BIRD HER PUNCTUAL MUSIC BRINGS	THE BIRD HER PUNCTUAL	1585		1
A [THE] LOOSENED SPIRIT BRINGS--	HE ATE AND DRANK THE	1587		8
AND BRINGS HIS HAMMER DOWN--	THE AUCTIONEER OF	1612		4
BRISKLY				
AND TRADES AS BRISKLY FLY--	IF I SHOULD DIE,	54		14
BRITAIN				
BUT, WERE I BRITAIN BORN, ...	THE ROBIN'S MY CRITERION	285		8
GREAT BRITAIN DISAPPROVES, "THE STARS"; . .	MY COUNTRY NEED NOT	1511		5
BRITISH				
"GENERAL, THE BRITISH"--"EASY"	WOLFE DEMANDED DURING	678		3
WHEN THE LONE BRITISH LADY	WHEN THE ASTRONOMER	851		3
ON HIS BRITISH SKY.	WE LIKE MARCH.	1213		13
BRITTLE				
PREPARES YOUR BRITTLE NATURE [SUBSTANCE] .	HE FUMBLES AT YOUR SOUL	315		5
REDEMPTION--BRITTLE LADY--	WHAT SOFT--CHERUBIC	401		11
ADORED [BEHELD] WITH CAUTION--AS A BRITTLE HEAVEN--	EACH LIFE CONVERGES TO	680		9
EATS OFF THE BRITTLE LINE--	I SOMETIMES DROP IT, FOR	708		14
BRITTLE AND BRIEF IN QUALITY--	A PROMPT--EXECUTIVE BIRD	1177		3
HOW BRITTLE ARE THE PIERS	HOW BRITTLE ARE THE	1433		1
UPON WHAT BRITTLE [FICKLE / TRIFLING] PIERS	HOW BRITTLE ARE THE	1433	V	1
BROACHED				
"WOULD I BE WHOLE" HE SUDDEN BROACHED-- . .	I COULD SUFFICE FOR HIM,	643		5
INSTEAD OF MORNING--HAD'ST THOU BROACHED .	'TIS SUNRISE--LITTLE	908		11
BROAD				
I NEVER HEAR OF PRISONS BROAD	I NEVER HEAR THE WORD	77		5
DOMINIONS--BROAD AS DEW--	WHAT WOULD I GIVE TO SEE	247		17
TILL BROAD AS BUENOS AYRE--	YOUR RICHES--TAUGHT ME--	299		4
ON SO BEST [BROAD] A HEART--	SWEET--YOU FORGOT--BUT I	523		10
AND BROAD--SUNBURNED ACQUAINTANCE	I'M SORRY FOR THE DEAD--	529		5
UPON THE BROAD POSSESSION [LAWFUL MANOR--] .	IT ALWAYS FELT TO ME--A	597		21
UNTIL IT SETTLED BROAD [FULL / FIRM]--ON PARADISE--	TO KNOW JUST HOW HE	622		4
DEATH--THOSOEVER BROAD, ...	SUSPENSE--IS HOSTILER	705		2
THE SUN--WITH JUST [BROAD] DELIGHT	THE MOUNTAINS--GROW	757		6
HER INVITATION BROAD	THESE ARE THE SIGNS TO	1077		2
THE PLEASURES OF THE WIND ARE BROAD, . . .	THE DUTIES OF THE WIND	1137		5

	FIRST LINE	POEM	LINE
BROAD (CONTINUED)			
THE BROAD ARE TOO BROAD TO DEFINE	HE PREACHED UPON	1207	2
THE BROAD ARE TOO BROAD TO DEFINE	HE PREACHED UPON	1207	2
BROADCLOTH			
IF BROADCLOTH HEARTS [BREASTS] ARE FIRMER--	A SHADY FRIEND--FOR	278	7
BROADER			
TRAVERSE BROADER FORESTS--	IT DID NOT SURPRISE ME--	39	5
BROADEST			
BROADEST OF SOVREIGNTIES--	THE CHILD'S FAITH IS NEW	637	11
THE BROADEST LAND THAT GROWS	STEP LIGHTLY ON THIS	1183	2
BROCADE			
BUT WHERE MY MOMENT OF BROCADE--	IT WOULD NEVER BE COMMON	430	32
MULTITUDE BROCADE--	RIBBONS OF THE YEAR--	873	2
BROKE SEE BRAKE			
THIS HEART THAT BROKE SO LONG--	THIS HEART THAT BROKE SO	145	1
MY HEART WOULD WISH IT BROKE BEFORE--	I SHOULD NOT DARE TO	205	13
BEFORE MY SIMPLE BOSOM--BROKE--	I THINK JUST HOW MY	237	11
AND THEN A PLANK IN REASON, BROKE,	I FELT A FUNERAL, IN MY	280	17
WHEN SOMETHING BROKE--	'TWAS LIKE A MAELSTROM,	414	8
CONVULSIVE, WHILE THE MUSIC CRASHED [BROKE]--	HER SMILE WAS SHAPED	514	7
BROKE--PERFECT--FROM THE POD--	HE GAVE AWAY HIS LIFE--	567	16
AND BROKE [SMOTE] AGAINST MY EAR--	I YEARS HAD BEEN FROM	609	12
WHAT ONE BROKE OFF WITH	TO KNOW JUST HOW HE	622	20
QUAINT--OR BROKE--	I CANNOT LIVE WITH YOU--	640	10
THOUGH THE RING IS UNWHOLE, AND THE COMPANY BROKE	OF THE HEART THAT GOES	1098	3
GOD BROKE HIS CONTRACT TO HIS LAMB	HOW RUTHLESS ARE THE	1439	3
HE [AND] BROKE THEM, FEARING PUNISHMENT	CLIMBING TO REACH THE	1566	3
A BIRD BROKE FORTH AND SANG,	A TRAIN WENT THROUGH A	1761	2
BROKEN			
BRAVE--BROKEN HEARTED STATEMENT--	"THEY HAVE NOT CHOSEN ME	85	3
IN BROKEN MATHEMATICS	AS BY THE DEAD WE LOVE	88	5
I CAN MURMUR BROKEN,	MUTE THY CORONATION--	151	7
HAD PARTED [BROKEN] RANK,	OF ALL THE SOUNDS	321	31
TILL THE BROKEN CREATURES--	TAKING UP THE FAIR IDEAL	428	13
I WISH I HAD NOT BROKEN IT--	THE MOST PATHETIC THING	1290	7
NOT WITH A CLUB, THE HEART IS BROKEN	NOT WITH A CLUB, THE	1304	1
UNTO A BROKEN HEART	UNTO A BROKEN HEART	1704	1
PROUD OF MY BROKEN HEART, SINCE THOU DIDST BREAK IT,	PROUD OF MY BROKEN HEART	1736	1
BROKER			
THE BROKER CANNOT CHEAT.	ALL THESE MY BANNERS BE.	22	11
BROKER'S			
BEYOND THE BROKER'S INSIGHT--	SOME--WORK FOR	406	11
BROKERS			
TERMED BY THE BROKERS--"DEATH"!	YOU'RE RIGHT--"THE WAY	234	8
BRONTE			
WHEN "BRONTE" ENTERED THERE!	ALL OVERGROWN BY CUNNING	148	V
BRONZE			
OF BRONZE--AND BLAZE--	OF BRONZE--AND BLAZE--	290	1
IS DURABLER THAN BRONZE--	AN HONEST TEAR	1192	2
BROOCH			
A WATCH--SOME ANCIENT [ANTIQUE] BROOCH	I KNOW SOME LONELY	289	28
I BROOCH AND EARRINGS FOR MYSELF,	WHEN DIAMONDS ARE A	397	3
BROOCH--FROZEN ON--	DROPPED INTO THE ETHER	665	4
BROOCHES			
OR BROOCHES--WHEN THE EMPEROR--	'TIS LITTLE I--COULD	466	3
BROOD			
WITH ONLY BUTTERFLIES TO BROOD	THE GRASS SO LITTLE HAS	333	3
OF A DEPENDENT BROOD.	HIGH FROM THE EARTH I	1723	16
BROODS			
FORCES THE BROODS IN LONELY VALLEYS	AS THE STARVED MAELSTROM	872	3
BROOK			
IT WAS AS IF A CHIRPING BROOK	HEART, NOT SO HEAVY AS	83	13
THE PURPLE BROOK WITHIN THE BREAST	A SOMETHING IN A	122	14
STILL, IS THE BUSTLE IN THE BROOK--	BESIDES THE AUTUMN POETS	131	9
HAVE YOU GOT A BROOK IN YOUR LITTLE HEART,	HAVE YOU GOT A BROOK IN	136	1
THAT ANY BROOK IS THERE,	HAVE YOU GOT A BROOK IN	136	6
WHY, LOOK OUT FOR THE LITTLE BROOK IN MARCH,	HAVE YOU GOT A BROOK IN	136	9
BEWARE, LEST THIS LITTLE BROOK OF LIFE,	HAVE YOU GOT A BROOK IN	136	15
TO ACHE--AND LIKE A SKATER'S BROOK--	'TWAS WARM--AT FIRST--	519	7
AS BROOK BY BROOK BESTOWS ITSELF	THE BIRDS BEGUN AT FOUR	783	7
AS BROOK BY BROOK BESTOWS ITSELF	THE BIRDS BEGUN AT FOUR	783	7
A FEW WENT OUT TO HELP THE BROOK	A DROP FELL ON THE APPLE	794	5
THE WELL UPON THE BROOK	THE WELL UPON THE BROOK	1091	1
WHOSE WATERS ARE THE BRAWLING [NAMELESS] BROOK	CONTAINED IN THIS SHORT	1165	V 7
BECAUSE MY BROOK IS FLUENT	BECAUSE MY BROOK IS	1200	1
BECAUSE MY BROOK IS SILENT	BECAUSE MY BROOK IS	1200	3
THE SEA SAID "COME" TO THE BROOK--	THE SEA SAID "COME" TO	1210	1
THE BROOK SAID "LET ME GROW"--	THE SEA SAID "COME" TO	1210	2
I WANT A BROOK--COME NOW"!	THE SEA SAID "COME" TO	1210	4
IS BUT THE LIKENESS OF THE BROOK	OF DEATH I TRY TO THINK	1558	3
TO WHERE A BROOK THAT SEEMED A SEA	OF DEATH I TRY TO THINK	1558	11
BROOKS			
SO BUBBLE BROOKS IN DESERTS	DISTRUSTFUL OF THE	20	11
THE BROOKS LAUGH LOUDER WHEN I COME--	THE BEE IS NOT AFRAID OF	111	5
AS BROOKS IN DESERTS BABBLE SWEET	AS WATCHERS HANG UPON	121	4
I'LL FETCH [BRING] THEE BROOKS	MY RIVER RUNS TO THEE--	162	5
THAT BROOKS IN MEADOWS RUN!	TO LEARN THE TRANSPORT	167	4
BROOKS OF PLUSH--IN BANKS OF SATIN	SWEET--SAFE--HOUSES--	457	6

	FIRST LINE	POEM	LINE
BROOKS (CONTINUED)			
SO--CHILDREN--TOLD HOW [ASSURED THAT] BROOKS IN EDEN--	BETTER--THAN MUSIC! FOR	503	9
THE BROOKS SLAM [BRAG]--ALL THE DAY-- . .	IT MAKES NO DIFFERENCE	620	6
LET BROOKS--RENEW OF BROOKS--	THE WELL UPON THE BROOK	1091	3
LET BROOKS--RENEW OF BROOKS--	THE WELL UPON THE BROOK	1091	3
BROOM			
THEN DANGLE FROM [PERISH BY] THE HOUSEWIFE'S BROOM--	THE SPIDER HOLDS A	605	11
SELECT A REVERENTIAL BROOM--	THAT SACRED CLOSET WHEN	1273	3
BY EVERY BROOM AND BRIDGET	THE SPIDER AS AN ARTIST	1275	5
BROOMS			
THE TIDY BREEZES, WITH THEIR BROOMS-- . .	A LADY RED--AMID THE	74	5
SHE SWEEPS WITH MANY-COLORED BROOMS-- . .	SHE SWEEPS WITH	219	1
AND STILL, SHE PLIES HER SPOTTED BROOMS, [THRIFT]	SHE SWEEPS WITH	219	9
TILL BROOMS FADE SOFTLY INTO STARS-- . . .	SHE SWEEPS WITH	219	11
LIKE BROOMS OF STEEL	LIKE BROOMS OF STEEL	1252	1
BROTHER			
PRITHEE, MY BROTHER, ...	THERE IS ANOTHER SKY,	2	13
AND CALL YOUR BROTHER MARS!	"SIC TRANSIT GLORIA	3	16
SOME EPAULETTED BROTHER	THERE IS A WORD	8	9
BROTHER OF INGOTS--[SISTER OF OPHIR--] AH PERU--	BROTHER OF INGOTS--AH	1366	1
BROTHER OF OPHIR, BRIGHT ADIEU, ...	BROTHER OF INGOTS--AH	1366	V 1
THE BROTHER OF THE UNIVERSE	NO BRIGADIER THROUGHOUT	1561	7
BROTHERS			
BROTHERS AND SISTERS--WHO PREFERRED THE GLORY--	UNTO LIKE STORY--TROUBLE	295	3
BROTHERS OF PARADISE	TO THE BRIGHT EAST SHE	1573	2
BROUGHT			
TIME BROUGHT ME OTHER ROBINS--	I HAD A GUINEA GOLDEN--	23	13
BROUGHT OUT THEIR BURS AND MOSSES	I ROBBED THE WOODS--	41	4
IS IT BROUGHT FROM FAMOUS COUNTRIES . . .	WILL THERE REALLY BE A	101	7
I BROUGHT [BRING] THEE THE IMPERIAL [DEPARTED] HEART	SAVIOR! I'VE NO ONE ELSE	217	7
BROUGHT ME--FROM FIRMAMENTAL SEAS-- . . .	WHAT WOULD I GIVE TO SEE	247	19
THE BREEZES BROUGHT DEJECTED LUTES-- . . .	A DROP FELL ON THE APPLE	794	13
BROW			
ON THIS SOLDIER'S BROW!	WHO NEVER LOST, ARE	73	16
HER BROW IS FIT FOR THRONES	HER BREAST IS FIT FOR	84	3
INVESTS SO MEAN A BROW!	WAIT TILL THE MAJESTY OF	171	2
SIFT HER, FROM BROW TO BAREFOOT!	DOUBT ME! MY DIM	275	18
A CHEEK--PERCHANCE A BROW--	THE OUTER--FROM THE	451	14
SKILL--TO HOLD MY BROW LIKE AN EARL-- . .	I AM ASHAMED--I HIDE--	473	16
THE VERY BROW--THE STOOPING EYES-- . . .	YOU KNOW THAT PORTRAIT	504	3
THAN WHATEVER BROW	HER SWEET TURN TO LEAVE	649	14
BROWN			
FREQUENTLY ARE BROWN.	FREQUENTLY THE WOODS ARE	6	2
THE NUTS ARE GETTING BROWN--	THE MORNS ARE MEEKER	12	2
JUST AS THE DUSK WAS BROWN	ADRIFT! A LITTLE BOAT	30	6
FROM MY BROWN CIGAR.	MANY CROSS THE RHINE	123	4
WE JUST SHUT OUR BROWN EYE	WE DONT CRY--TIM AND I,	196	11
AS IS THE BROWN MALAY	REMOVED FROM ACCIDENT OF	424	6
TIGHT FITTING--ORANGE--BROWN--	YOU'LL KNOW HER--BY HER	634	10
OF INDIGO AND BROWN--	BEFORE YOU THOUGHT OF	1465	8
WHOSE COAT OF ELEMENTAL BROWN	HOW HAPPY IS THE LITTLE	1510	5
BROWS			
AND SUMMER'S BROWS WERE BOUND.	THERE IS A MORN BY MEN	24	12
AWAITED THEIR--LOW BROWS--	LIKE FLOWERS, THAT HEARD	513	3
TO LIFT HER BROWS ON YOU--	SWEET MOUNTAINS--YE TELL	722	12
BRUISE			
OR IN PROTRACTED BRUISE	I WATCHED HER FACE TO	1667	4
BRUISES			
POUNCE ON HIS BRUISES--ONE--SAY--OR THREE--	GRIEF IS A MOUSE--	793	11
BRUSH			
WHOSE FINGERS COMB [BRUSH] THE SKY-- . . .	OF ALL THE SOUNDS	321	6
THE BRUSH WITHOUT THE HAND--	THE OUTER--FROM THE	451	10
I'D BRUSH THE SUMMER BY	IF YOU WERE COMING IN	511	2
BRUSHED			
OR BRUSHED A ROYAL GOWN--	HE TOUCHED ME, SO I LIVE	506	9
BRUSSELS			
OF BRUSSELS--IT WAS NOT--	OF BRUSSELS--IT WAS NOT	602	1
BRYANT'S			
GONE--MR BRYANT'S "GOLDEN ROD"--	BESIDES THE AUTUMN POETS	131	7
BUBBLE			
SO BUBBLE BROOKS IN DESERTS	DISTRUSTFUL OF THE	20	11
BUBBLE! "FORGIVE"--"SOME BETTER"--BUBBLE! .	KILL YOUR BALM--AND IT'S	238	7
BUBBLE! "FORGIVE"--"SOME BETTER"--BUBBLE! .	KILL YOUR BALM--AND IT'S	238	7
YOUR BRAIN--TO BUBBLE COOL--	HE FUMBLES AT YOUR SOUL	315	10
BUBBLE! BUBBLE!	DYING AT MY MUSIC!	1003	2
BUBBLE! BUBBLE!	DYING AT MY MUSIC!	1003	2
DOTH LIKE A BUBBLE ANTEDATE	THE MUSHROOM IS THE ELF	1298	11
AND LIKE A BUBBLE, HIE--	THE MUSHROOM IS THE ELF	1298	12
HIS ELOQUENCE A BUBBLE	HIS MANSION IN THE POOL	1379	11
BUBBLED			
THEN BUBBLED SLOW AWAY!	HEART, NOT SO HEAVY AS	83	12
NOT ON RECORD--BUBBLED OTHER, ...	HER--"LAST POEMS"--	312	4
BUBBLED A BETTER--MELODY--	BETTER--THAN MUSIC! FOR	503	10
AND SHOUTED [BUBBLED / GURGLED] LET US PRAY--	THE BOBOLINK IS GONE--	1591	7

	FIRST LINE	POEM	LINE
BUBBLED (CONTINUED)			
IT QUIVERED THROUGH [BUBBLED IN] THE GRASS	THERE CAME A WIND LIKE A	1593	2
BUBBLES			
OOZED SO IN CRIMSON BUBBLES	SO HAS A DAISY VANISHED	28	5
BUCANEERS			
BUCANEERS OF BUZZ.	BEES ARE BLACK, WITH	1405	2
BUCCANEER			
WHAT BUCCANEER WOULD RIDE	DOWN TIME'S QUAINT	1656	8
BUCCANEERING			
WITH THE BLUE BIRDS EXERCISING [BUCCANEERING]	WE LIKE MARCH.	1213	12
BUCKET			
IT HAS NO BUCKET--WERE I RICH	I KNOW WHERE WELLS GROW	460	9
A BUCKET I WOULD BUY--	I KNOW WHERE WELLS GROW	460	10
BUCKETS			
THE WELLS HAVE BUCKETS TO THEM THERE--	I KNOW WHERE WELLS GROW	460	15
AS SPONGES--BUCKETS--DO--	THE BRAIN--IS WIDER THAN	632	-8
BUCKLE			
I HEARD THE BUCKLE SNAP--	HE PUT THE BELT AROUND	273	2
AND PAST MY BODDICE [BOSOM / BUCKLE]--TOO--	I STARTED EARLY--TOOK MY	520	12
BE MY LIPS--THE ONLY BUCKLE	PROMISE THIS--WHEN YOU	648	7
BUCKLED			
STAPLES OF AGES--HAVE BUCKLED THERE--	SAFE IN THEIR ALABASTER	216 V	
ADMONISHED BY HER BUCKLED LIPS	THE RETICENT VOLCANO	1748	9
BUCKLES			
EAGLES ON MY BUCKLES--	NO MATTER--NOW--SWEET--	704	11
BUD			
WHERE IS THE BUD--	ANSWER JULY--	386	7
JUST OBVIATED BUD--	HE GAVE AWAY HIS LIFE--	567	14
NEVER BUD FROM A STEM	AND THIS OF ALL MY HOPES	913	5
UNTO AN EQUAL BUD	THE OPENING AND THE	1047	6
TO PACK THE BUD--OPPOSE THE WORM--	BLOOM--IS RESULT--TO	1058	9
. . . RECEIPTED / EXPENDED] BUD	CRISIS IS SWEET AND YET	1416	8
THE HOUR [SESSION] OF HER BUD--	CRISIS IS SWEET AND YET	1416 V	8
THE TRANSPORT [RAPTURE] OF THE BUD	CRISIS IS SWEET AND YET	1416 V	8
THE TUBE UPLIFTS A SIGNAL BUD	THE DANDELION'S PALLID	1519	5
BUDS			
MY BUDS COMMEMORATE--	IF I SHOULD CEASE TO	56	6
DO THE BUDS TO THEM BELONG?	ANGELS, IN THE EARLY	94	4
IT'S IRON BUDS WILL SPROUT ANEW [AFRESH]	YOU CANNOT MAKE	1508	11
BUENOS			
TILL BROAD AS BUENOS AYRE--	YOUR RICHES--TAUGHT ME--	299	4
BUGLE			
AH [OH] BUGLE! BY MY [THE] WINDOW	HEART, NOT SO HEAVY AS	83	19
THERE CAME A WIND LIKE A BUGLE--	THERE CAME A WIND LIKE A	1593	1
BUGLES			
BUT BRAVE AT LAST WITH BUGLES	DEATH IS THE SUPPLE	1445	7
WHOSE BUGLES CALL THE LEAST OF US	TALK NOT TO ME OF SUMMER	1634	7
BUILD			
THEN BEAR HER TO THE GREENWOOD, AND BUILD FOR HER A BOWER,	AWAKE YE MUSES NINE,	1	37
SO BUILD THE HILLOCKS GAILY	ALL THESE MY BANNERS BE.	22	12
BUILD IN GAYER BOUGHS,	IT DID NOT SURPRISE ME--	39	6
IF BIRDS SHOULD BUILD AS EARLY	IF I SHOULD DIE,	54	7
I--A SPARROW--BUILD THERE	HER BREAST IS FIT FOR	84	6
I CAME TO BUILD THE BIRD'S NEST,	SEXTON! MY MASTER'S	96	3
TO BUILD UPON THE GROUND	FOR EVERY BIRD A NEST--	143	14
WE--TEMPLES BUILD--I SAID--	MYSELF WAS FORMED--A	488	12
AND OWLS DO BUILD IN OAKS--	THE JUDGE IS LIKE THE	699	3
WERE I COMPELLED TO BUILD	WHO OCCUPIES THIS HOUSE?	892	12
BUILDED			
BUILDED OUR HEARTS AMONG.	ONE SISTER HAVE I IN OUR	14	8
TENDERNESS BUILDED THERE.	THIS HEART THAT BROKE SO	145	8
THE MASON BUILDED, YESTERDAY,	WHAT CARE THE DEAD, FOR	592	7
BUILDER			
BEFORE A BUILDER CAME--	MYSELF WAS FORMED--A	488	4
BUILDING			
BUILDING WHERE SCHOOLBOY DARE NOT LOOK,	SOME, TOO FRAGILE FOR	141	7
BUILDS			
BUILDS, LIKE A BIRD, TOO!	DUST IS THE ONLY SECRET	153	13
THE WAY HOPE BUILDS HIS HOUSE	THE WAY HOPE BUILDS HIS	1481	1
BUILT			
I DONT KNOW HIM; SNUGLY BUILT!	"HOUSES"--SO THE WISE	127	6
WHO BUILT THIS LITTLE ALBAN HOUSE	BRING ME THE SUNSET IN A	128	19
STAB THE BIRD--THAT BUILT IN YOUR BOSOM--	KILL YOUR BALM--AND IT'S	238	5
THE MIND WAS BUILT FOR MIGHTY FREIGHT	A GREAT HOPE FELL	1123	6
UNTIL THE HOUSE IS BUILT	THE PROPS ASSIST THE	1142	2
BUILT OF BUT JUST A SYLLABLE	LOVE'S STRICKEN "WHY"	1368	3
INDEED--'TWAS BUILT BY HIM--	HOW BRITTLE ARE THE	1433	6
BULB			
MANY A BULB WILL RISE--	SO FROM THE MOULD	66	3
BULB AFTER BULB, IN SILVER ROLLED--	SPLIT THE LARK--AND	861	2
BULB AFTER BULB, IN SILVER ROLLED--	SPLIT THE LARK--AND	861	2
BULK			
UNCONSCIOUS THAT HIS SINGLE FLEET [BULK / SAIL]	WHO GIANTS KNOW, WITH	796	7
BULLETINS			
IS BULLETINS ALL DAY	THE ONLY NEWS I KNOW	827	2
BULLETS			
HOW MANY BULLETS BEAREST?	WHO NEVER LOST, ARE	73	13
TILL BULLETS CLIPT AN ANGLE	WHEN I WAS SMALL, A	596	7

	FIRST LINE	POEM	LINE
BULLION			
THE BULLION OF TODAY--	SOME--WORK FOR	406	6
BULWARK			
IT IS A TIMID BULWARK	I SAW THE WIND WITHIN	1502	V
BUMBLE			
AS BUMBLE BEE OF JUNE.	ONE SISTER HAVE I IN OUR	14	12
THE BUMBLE BEES WILL WAKE THEM	WHOSE ARE THE LITTLE	142	27
THE MURMUR [BUMBLE] OF A BEE	THE MURMUR OF A BEE	155	1
IF THE COWARD BUMBLE BEE	I'M THE LITTLE "HEART'S	176	5
WERT THOU A BUMBLE BEE	COULD--I DO MORE--FOR	447	2
SQUIRREL--ECLIPSE--THE BUMBLE BEE-- . . .	"NATURE" IS WHAT WE SEE	668	3
ENTITLED TO A BUMBLE BEE'S	OF NATURE I SHALL HAVE	1220	3
AND BUMBLE BEE WAS NOT--	A SINGLE CLOVER PLANK	1343	12
THE BUMBLE BEE'S RELIGION	HIS LITTLE HEARSE LIKE	1522	T
CONSULTS THE BUMBLE BEE--	A DRUNKARD CANNOT MEET A	1628	12
BUMBLEBEE			
BIRDS--HOURS--THE BUMBLEBEE--	SOME THINGS THAT FLY	89	2
TO SUBDUE THE BUMBLEBEE.	PIGMY SERAPHS--GONE	138	17
BUMBLEBEES			
WHEN BUMBLEBEES IN SOLEMN FLIGHT	WHEN ROSES CEASE TO	32	3
BUMBLEBEES COME--	SOUTH WINDS JOSTLE THEM	86	2
BUMBLE-BEES			
OF BUMBLE-BEES AND OTHER NATIONS	THE MOST IMPORTANT	1746	7
BUN			
A BERRY OR A BUN, WOULD BE, ...	MY HEART UPON A LITTLE	1027	3
I WON IT WITH A BUN--	THIS DIRTY--LITTLE--	1311	3
BUNDLE			
TO PUT THIS WORLD DOWN, LIKE A BUNDLE-- . .	TO PUT THIS WORLD DOWN,	527	1
UP LIFE'S HILL WITH MY LITTLE BUNDLE . . .	UP LIFE'S HILL WITH MY	1010	1
BUNDLES			
BUT SMALLER BUNDLES--CRAM.	PERHAPS I ASKED TOO	352	7
BUNG			
THE BUNG OUT--OF [A LEAKAGE IN] AN ARTERY--	ONE ANGUISH--IN A CROWD	565	11
BUNKER			
LAID DOWN ON BUNKER HILL!	"SIC TRANSIT GLORIA	3	46
BUOYANT			
'TIS NATURE'S BUOYANT JUICES	THE GENTIAN HAS A	1424	3
BUR SEE BURR			
IF [WHEN] HE LEAVE A BUR AT THE DOOR . . .	THE WIND DID'NT COME	316	7
A PROCESS IN THE BUR--	THERE ARE TWO RIPENINGS	332	6
WHERE BE THE BUR?	ANSWER JULY--	386	17
BURDEN			
EFFACE THE BURDEN [MONSTER / STATURE / SPECTRE / TROUBLE / . . .	THE PILE OF YEARS IS NOT	1507	7
WITHOUT APPARENT BURDEN	HIGH FROM THE EARTH I	1723	13
BURDEN--BORNE SO FAR TRIUMPHANT--	REARRANGE A "WIFE'S"	1737	13
BURDOCK			
A BURDOCK--CLAWED [TWITCHED] MY GOWN-- . .	A BURDOCK--CLAWED MY	229	1
BURDOCK'S			
NOT BURDOCK'S--BLAME--	A BURDOCK--CLAWED MY	229	2
THE BURDOCK'S DEN--	A BURDOCK--CLAWED MY	229	5
BURGLAR			
THE BURGLAR CANNOT ROB--THEN--	ALL THESE MY BANNERS BE.	22	10
BURGLAR! BANKER--FATHER!	I NEVER LOST AS MUCH BUT	49	7
BURGOYNE			
THERE'S [THAT'S] THE BATTLE OF BURGOYNE-- .	THERE'S THE BATTLE OF	1174	1
BURGUND			
BUT IT'S DIM CHAT OF THINGS BURGUND, WE KNOW--	WE--BEE AND I--LIVE BY	230	V 4
BURGUNDY			
BUT IT'S MANY A LAY OF THE DIM BURGUNDY-- .	WE--BEE AND I--LIVE BY	230	4
BURIAL			
SET ORDERLY, FOR BURIAL, ...	IT WAS NOT DEATH, FOR I	510	11
COUNTRY BURIAL	AMPLE MAKE THIS BED--	829	T
MY BURIAL--BEFORE	THIS CHASM, SWEET, UPON	858	18
THROUGH HAZE OF BURIAL--	MIDSUMMER, WAS IT, WHEN	962	8
IN STRESS OF BURIAL--	AS IMPERCEPTIBLY AS	1540	V
A TRAIN WENT THROUGH A BURIAL GATE, . . .	A TRAIN WENT THROUGH A	1761	1
BURIED			
I NEVER TOLD THE BURIED GOLD	I NEVER TOLD THE BURIED	11	1
PERSUADED OF THE BURIED GOLD--	TRUST IN THE UNEXPECTED	555	3
THE SHAPES WE BURIED, DWELL ABOUT, ...	OF NEARNESS TO HER	607	5
IN FALLING [CRASHING] TIMBERS BURIED-- . .	IN FALLING TIMBERS	614	1
"WAS BURIED"--"BURIED"! "HE!"	IF HE WERE LIVING--DARE	734	15
"WAS BURIED"--"BURIED"! "HE!"	IF HE WERE LIVING--DARE	734	15
BURMAH			
THE SPLENDOR OF A BURMAH	ONE OF THE ONES THAT	1466	17
BURN			
BY BECK, OR BURN, OR MOOR!	I WOULD DISTIL A CUP,	16	4
BURN SO THE EVENING SPIRES	DISTRUSTFUL OF THE	20	13
AND NOON SHOULD BURN--	IF I SHOULD DIE,	54	5
NOR CONSTELLATION BURN--	A POOR--TORN HEART-- A	78	6
AS SLOW HER FLAMBEAUX BURN AWAY	A SOMETHING IN A	122	2
TO THINK JUST HOW THE FIRE WILL BURN-- . .	THO' I GET HOME HOW LATE	207	9
HOW THE HEMLOCKS BURN--	HOW THE OLD MOUNTAINS	291	2
BURN HIM IN THE PUBLIC SQUARE--	GRIEF IS A MOUSE--	793	14
WHAT TRIPLE LENSES BURN UPON	OF CONSCIOUSNESS, HER	894	7
THAT SCRUTINY CAN BURN--	JUDGEMENT IS JUSTEST	1671	9
BURNED			
IT BURNED ME--IN THE NIGHT--	IT STRUCK ME--EVERY DAY	362	5
REVEAL THE WIDTH THAT BURNED--	THE RED--BLAZE--IS THE	469	6

	FIRST LINE	POEM	LINE
BURNED (CONTINUED)			
BURNED [GLOWED] ON--UNTIL THROUGH DISSOLUTION--	IT KNEW NO LAPSE, NOR	560	3
LIKE MIGHTY FOOT LIGHTS--BURNED THE RED . .	LIKE MIGHTY FOOT LIGHTS	595	1
THE LORD ALONE IS BURNED--	THE SUN AND MOON MUST	871	4
BURNING			
SOME BURNING NOON GO DRY!	HAVE YOU GOT A BROOK IN	136	16
WHEN AUGUST BURNING LOW	FURTHER IN SUMMER THAN	1068	10
BURNISH			
WITH SPOTS OF BURNISH ROASTED ON	THE BUTTERFLY'S NUMIDIAN	1387	2
BURNISHED			
THE CAPSULES BURNISHED SEEDS THE STARS-- .	THE LILAC IS AN ANCIENT	1241	11
A BEE HIS BURNISHED CARRIAGE	A BEE HIS BURNISHED	1339	1
BURNS			
THE LAMP BURNS SURE--WITHIN--	THE LAMP BURNS SURE--	233	1
THE LAMP--BURNS GOLDEN--ON--	THE LAMP BURNS SURE--	233	6
IT BURNS--DISTINCT FROM ALL THE ROW-- . .	ONE LIFE OF SO MUCH	270	11
BECAUSE--WHEN NEXT IT BURNS ABROAD . . .	THE DOOMED--REGARD THE	294	3
BURR SEE BUR			
EXHIBIT HERE, AS DOTH A BURR--	BEST THINGS DWELL OUT OF	998	7
BURROWED			
THEN, IF IT HAVE BURROWED	DEATH IS LIKE THE INSECT	1716	9
BURS			
BROUGHT OUT THEIR BURS AND MOSSES	I ROBBED THE WOODS--	41	4
BURST			
BURST AGONIZED AND CLEAR!	SUCCESS IS COUNTED	67	12
WHAT IF I BURST THE FLESHLY GATE--	WHAT IF I SAY I SHALL	277	2
UNTIL IT BURST THE HEARTS	HE GAVE AWAY HIS LIFE--	567	5
QUICK! BURST THE WINDOWS!	DYING AT MY MUSIC!	1003	4
. . . BURST / FLAGS / STEP / TICK / SHOUTS / PINK / RED / . . .	ONE JOY OF SO MUCH	1420	6
WOULD BURST THE LONELINESS--	COULD THAT SWEET	1493	4
BURSTING			
WHEN BURSTING ALL THE DOORS--	THE SOUL HAS BANDAGED	512	12
BURY			
BURY ME, IN SUCH A SHROUD OF RED!	IF THIS IS "FADING"	120	4
THEY BURY, IN THE GRAVE?	DO PEOPLE MOULDER	432	2
BUSH			
FROM A SUPERIOR BUSH--	THE WIND--TAPPED LIKE A	436	12
AS BERRY--OF A MOUNTAIN BUSH--	I HAD BEEN HUNGRY, ALL	579	15
THE WIND PURSUED THE LITTLE BUSH--	THE NIGHT WAS WIDE, AND	589	5
SHE STAKED HER WINGS--AND GAINED A BUSH-- .	SHE STAKED HER FEATHERS	798 V	1
THE "BUSH" MAY YIELD ME	WHICH IS BEST? HEAVEN--	1012	7
AND EVERY BLOSSOM ON THE BUSH	A ROUTE OF EVANESCENCE	1463	5
BUSHES			
THE BUSHES [ORCHARDS / MEADOWS]--SPANGLES FLUNG--	A DROP FELL ON THE APPLE	794	12
THE BUSHES--THEY WERE BELLS--	TO MY QUICK EAR THE	891	2
BUSIER			
WOULD DEEM OURSELVES--THE BUSIER	TO INTERRUPT HIS YELLOW	591	13
BUSINESS			
A SAILOR'S BUSINESS IS THE SHORE!	A LITTLE BREAD--A CRUST	159	10
MY BUSINESS IS, TO FIND!	I CAUTIOUS, SCANNED MY	178	16
MY BUSINESS WERE SO DEAR!	IF I COULD BRIBE THEM BY	179	6
MY BUSINESS, WITH THE CLOUD, ...	I GOT SO I COULD HEAR	293	21
AND THAT IS HIS BUSINESS--NOT OUR'S-- . .	THE WIND DID'NT COME	316	12
AND ASK MY BUSINESS THERE--	I YEARS HAD BEEN FROM	609	6
"MY BUSINESS BUT [JUST] A LIFE I LEFT . .	I YEARS HAD BEEN FROM	609	7
WARRANT [BUSINESS] IN EVERY LINE-- . . .	A PROMPT--EXECUTIVE BIRD	1177	4
BUST			
UPON THE FOREHEAD OF A BUST--	THE DIFFERENCE BETWEEN	305	7
BUSTLE			
STILL, IS THE BUSTLE IN THE BROOK--	BESIDES THE AUTUMN POETS	131	9
THE ANGELS BUSTLE IN THE HALL--	A WIFE--AT DAYBREAK I	461	8
THE BUSTLE IN A HOUSE	THE BUSTLE IN A HOUSE	1078	1
THAT BUSTLE SO ILLUSTRIOUS	THAT SHORT--POTENTIAL	1307	3
BUSTLED			
HANDS BUSTLED AT THE MOORINGS--	WENT UP A YEAR THIS	93	19
BUSTLES			
THERE PUBLISHES [BUSTLES BUT] A TEAR-- . .	SO GLAD WE ARE--A	329	4
BUSTLING			
AND BEES AS BUSTLING GO--	IF I SHOULD DIE,	54	8
BUSTS			
TILL THEY ARE ORDERLY AS BUSTS--	A VISITOR IN MARL--	391	3
BUSY			
"HOW DOTH THE BUSY BEE,"	"SIC TRANSIT GLORIA	3	2
SOME IN THE BUSY TOMB	MY WHEEL IS IN THE DARK!	10	10
I CHECK MY BUSY PENCIL, ...	LOW AT MY PROBLEM	69	5
HER BUSY FOOT SHE PLIED--	WHOSE ARE THE LITTLE	142	18
BUSY NEEDLES, AND SPOOLS OF THREAD-- . . .	ON SUCH A NIGHT, OR SUCH	146	19
IT MATTERS NOT THE BUSY WICK--	THE LAMP BURNS SURE--	233	3
THE BUSY EYES--CONGEALED--	'TWAS WARM--AT FIRST--	519	8
THE BUSY CARTS--THE FRAGRANT COCKS-- . . .	I'M SORRY FOR THE DEAD--	529	11
SHE'S BUSY--WITH AN ALTERED CARE--	SHE'S HAPPY, WITH A NEW	535	3
BUSY WITH MAJESTY--	TO INTERRUPT HIS YELLOW	591	8
TO RECOLLECT HOW BUSY GRASS	'TIS GOOD--THE LOOKING	660	5
THE BUSY DARLING LAY--	HER FINAL SUMMER WAS IT	795	14
SO BUSY WAS SHE--FINISHING--	HER FINAL SUMMER WAS IT	795	15
BUTTERCUP			
ORCHARD, AND BUTTERCUP, AND BIRD--	A LADY RED--AMID THE	74	11

	FIRST LINE	POEM	LINE
BUTTERCUP (CONTINUED)			
WITH BRIGHT PINS OF BUTTERCUP--	I'M SAYING EVERY DAY	373	13
OF ANY [UPON A] BUTTERCUP--	HE PARTS HIMSELF--LIKE	517	4
WHEN THE BEE HANGS ALL NOON IN THE BUTTERCUP	WHAT SHALL I DO WHEN THE	956	7
BUTTERCUP'S			
THE BUTTERCUP'S, MY WHIM FOR BLOOM-- . . .	THE ROBIN'S MY CRITERION	285	6
A BUTTERCUP'S ARRAY--	PRECIOUS TO ME--SHE	727	8
THE BUTTERCUP'S [LEONTODON'S] ESCUTSCHEON--	TO HER DERIDED HOME	1586 V	
BUTTERCUPS			
WHETHER IT'S BUTTERCUPS--THAT "SKIM"-- . .	MAKE ME A PICTURE OF THE	188	10
AND FLIRT ALL DAY WITH BUTTERCUPS	COULD I BUT RIDE	661	5
AND BE OF BUTTERCUPS THE FRIEND	THE BUTTERFLY'S	1244	5
BUTTERFLIES			
THE DREAMY BUTTERFLIES BESTIR!	SOME RAINBOW--COMING	64	7
BUTTERFLIES PAUSE	SOUTH WINDS JOSTLE THEM	86	5
BUTTERFLIES FROM ST DOMINGO	FLOWERS--WELL--IF	137	11
EXCEPT BY [FOR] BUTTERFLIES	EXCEPT TO HEAVEN, SHE IS	154	6
OR BUTTERFLIES--THAT "BLOOM"?	MAKE ME A PICTURE OF THE	188	11
WHEN BUTTERFLIES--RENOUNCE THEIR "DRAMS"-- .	I TASTE A LIQUOR NEVER	214	11
NAVIES OF BUTTERFLIES--SAILED THRO'-- . .	WHAT WOULD I GIVE TO SEE	247	13
AND SO WITH BUTTERFLIES--	DELIGHT IS AS THE FLIGHT	257	20
OR BUTTERFLIES, OFF BANKS OF NOON	A BIRD CAME DOWN THE	328	19
WITH ONLY BUTTERFLIES TO BROOD	THE GRASS SO LITTLE HAS	333	3
AND BUTTERFLIES--DESIRE--	THERE IS A FLOWER THAT	380	2
AND BLAZE--THE BUTTERFLIES!	AS FAR FROM PITY, AS	496	12
TWO BUTTERFLIES WENT OUT AT NOON-- . . .	TWO BUTTERFLIES WENT OUT	533	1
TO ALL SURVIVING BUTTERFLIES	TWO BUTTERFLIES WENT OUT	533 V	
THE BEES--BECAME AS BUTTERFLIES--	I THINK I WAS ENCHANTED	593	9
THE BUTTERFLIES--AS SWANS [MOONS]-- . . .	I THINK I WAS ENCHANTED	593	10
BY BUTTERFLIES ADMIRED [ADORED / DESIRED] .	THIS BAUBLE WAS	805	2
FOR BUTTERFLIES AND ME--	WHAT TENEMENTS OF CLOVER	1338	4
THAT LOWLY BREAST [HOMESTEAD SWEET] WHERE BUTTERFLIES	HIS ORIENTAL HERESIES	1526	7
BUTTERFLY			
DECEIVES THE BUTTERFLY;	ONE SISTER HAVE I IN OUR	14	19
AND OF THE BUTTERFLY--	THE GENTIAN WEAVES HER	18	18
ONLY A BUTTERFLY, ...	NOBODY KNOWS THIS LITTLE	35	6
WHEREAS I TOOK THE BUTTERFLY	"ARCTURUS" IS HIS OTHER	70	13
AND COUNTLESS BUTTERFLY!	A SCIENCE--SO THE SAVANS	100	12
I KNOW THE BUTTERFLY.	THE BEE IS NOT AFRAID OF	111	2
A BUTTERFLY TO GO!	COCOON ABOVE! COCOON	129	9
OF THE BUTTERFLY!	A FUZZY FELLOW, WITHOUT	173	20
IF THE BUTTERFLY DELAY	I'M THE LITTLE "HEART'S	176	3
FROM COCOON FORTH A BUTTERFLY	FROM COCOON FORTH A	354	1
AND AFTERNOON--AND BUTTERFLY--	FROM COCOON FORTH A	354	24
AND ONCE--A BUTTERFLY--	WHEN DIAMONDS ARE A	397	8
OR WILE OF BUTTERFLY	FORGET! THE LADY WITH	438	7
SOME SUCH BUTTERFLY BE SEEN	SOME SUCH BUTTERFLY BE	541	1
OR CART OF BUTTERFLY--	A LITTLE ROAD--NOT MADE	647	4
'TWOULD EASE--A BUTTERFLY--	'TWOULD EASE--A	682	1
DEFRAUDED I A BUTTERFLY--	DEFRAUDED I A BUTTERFLY	730	1
EQUAL BUTTERFLY--	COLOR--CASTE--	970	12
THEN OFFERED AS A BUTTERFLY	BLOOM--IS RESULT--TO	1058	7
A POWER OF BUTTERFLY MUST BE--	MY COCOON TIGHTENS--	1099	5
FOR CAPTAIN WAS THE BUTTERFLY	A SOFT SEA WASHED AROUND	1198	5
THE BUTTERFLY IN HONORED DUST	THE BUTTERFLY IN HONORED	1246	1
NOR TRY TO TIE THE BUTTERFLY, ...	GO NOT TOO NEAR A HOUSE	1434	5
THE BUTTERFLY UPON THE SKY, ...	THE BUTTERFLY UPON THE	1521	1
SWEET HOMESTEAD WHERE THE BUTTERFLY . . .	HIS ORIENTAL HERESIES	1526 V	7
DELAY THE BUTTERFLY	THE PEDIGREE OF HONEY	1627	4
THE BUTTERFLY OBTAINS	THE BUTTERFLY OBTAINS	1685	1
BUTTERFLY'S			
THE BUTTERFLY'S ASSUMPTION GOWN	THE BUTTERFLY'S	1244	1
THE BUTTERFLY'S NUMIDIAN GOWN	THE BUTTERFLY'S NUMIDIAN	1387	1
BUTTON			
BRAZIL? HE TWIRLED A BUTTON--	I ASKED NO OTHER THING--	621	5
WITHOUT A BUTTON--I C'D VOUCH--	YOU'LL KNOW HER--BY HER	634	7
BUTTONED			
LONG BUTTONED IN THE MOLD	OF NEARNESS TO HER	607	10
BUTTONHOLE			
I'LL DECK TRADITION'S BUTTONHOLE-- . . .	IF SHE HAD BEEN THE	44	7
BUY			
PERHAPS YOU'D LIKE TO BUY A FLOWER, . . .	PERHAPS YOU'D LIKE TO	134	1
I CAME TO BUY A SMILE--TODAY--	I CAME TO BUY A SMILE--	223	1
FOR YET TO BUY ANOTHER PAIR	IS BLISS THEN, SUCH	340	6
NONE BUY IT ANY MORE--	IS BLISS THEN, SUCH	340	11
FOR THE THINGS 'TWOULD BUY--	FOR DEATH--OR RATHER	382	2
THE THINGS THAT DEATH WILL BUY	FOR DEATH--OR RATHER	382	5
SO, I COULD BUY IT--	KNOWS HOW TO FORGET!	433 V	
A BUCKET I WOULD BUY--	I KNOW WHERE WELLS GROW	460	10
BUT TILL THE MERCHANT BUY--	I GAVE MYSELF TO HIM--	580	10
TO SOMETIMES HEAR "RICH PEOPLE" BUY . . .	I CRIED AT PITY--NOT AT	588	9
THE WINDS DID BUY IT OF THE WOODS-- . . .	OF BRUSSELS--IT WAS NOT	602	3
SPICES? BUY HERE!	WOULD YOU LIKE SUMMER?	691	2
I CANNOT BUY IT--'TIS NOT SOLD--	I CANNOT BUY IT--'TIS	840	1
THAT ANY OTHER BUY.	A DIAMOND ON THE HAND	1108	8
LEST SOME ONE ELSE SHOULD [RICHER PEOPLE] BUY	A DIAMOND ON THE HAND	1108 V	8
WE BUY WITH CONTRAST--PANG IS GOOD . . .	THE SNOW THAT NEVER	1133	15
BUT SHE MUST BUY MY SHELTER	I SAW THE WIND WITHIN	1502	3

	FIRST LINE	POEM	LINE
BUZZ			
BUZZ THE DULL FLIES--ON THE CHAMBER WINDOW--	HOW MANY TIMES THESE LOW	187	9
I HEARD A FLY BUZZ--WHEN I DIED--	I HEARD A FLY BUZZ--WHEN	465	1
WITH BLUE--UNCERTAIN STUMBLING BUZZ--	I HEARD A FLY BUZZ--WHEN	465	13
OR PETALS, OR A DOWER OF BUZZ	BECAUSE THE BEE MAY	869	10
BUCANEERS OF BUZZ.	BEES ARE BLACK, WITH	1405	2
BYE SEE GOOD-BYE			
GOOD BYE, SIR, I AM GOING;	"SIC TRANSIT GLORIA	3	57
TILL BYE AND BYE THESE BARGEMEN	THE FEET OF PEOPLE	7	7
TILL BYE AND BYE THESE BARGEMEN	THE FEET OF PEOPLE	7	7
TO BLOOM SO, BYE AND BYE--	WHEN I COUNT THE SEEDS	40	3
TO BLOOM SO, BYE AND BYE--	WHEN I COUNT THE SEEDS	40	3
AND BYE AND BYE--A CHANGE--	FOREVER AT HIS SIDE TO	246	12
AND BYE AND BYE--A CHANGE--	FOREVER AT HIS SIDE TO	246	12
GROWN BYE AND BYE	THE CHILD'S FAITH IS NEW	637	17
GROWN BYE AND BYE	THE CHILD'S FAITH IS NEW	637	17
BYSTANDERS			
THE BYSTANDERS WILL TELL!	WENT UP A YEAR THIS	93	4
BY-THYME			
IN A BY-THYME!	WE--BEE AND I--LIVE BY	230	18
CABINETS			
HE SITS ERECT IN "CABINETS"--	"ARCTURUS" IS HIS OTHER	70	15
IN CABINETS--BE SHOWN--	HE PARTS HIMSELF--LIKE	517	18
CACTUS			
MY CACTUS--SPLITS HER BEARD	I TEND MY FLOWERS FOR	339	7
CADENCE			
PIPE THE SWEET BIRDS IN IGNORANT CADENCE--	SAFE IN THEIR ALABASTER	216	10
LET ME NOT SPILL [LOSE / WASTE]--IT'S SMALLEST CADENCE--	BETTER--THAN MUSIC! FOR	503	21
OF CADENCE OR OF PAUSE	FURTHER IN SUMMER THAN	1068	V
CADENCES			
CADENCES TOO GRAND	OVER AND OVER, LIKE A	367	6
CAESAR			
GREAT CAESAR! CONDESCEND	GREAT CAESAR! CONDESCEND	102	1
AND CAESAR--MEAN--	THE CHILD'S FAITH IS NEW	637	12
CAESARS			
THESE ARE CAESARS--	KNOCK WITH TREMOR--	1325	2
CAGE			
THE LITTLE CAGE OF "CURRER BELL"	ALL OVERGROWN BY CUNNING	148	3
CAGES			
WITH HOLY GHOSTS IN CAGES!	A TRANSPORT ONE CANNOT	184	7
CAJOLES			
CAJOLES A MOMENT WITH THE SPIRES	IT RISES--PASSES--ON OUR	1023	3
CAJOLING			
CAJOLING CONSTERNATION	THE ROBIN IS A GABRIEL	1483	14
CAKES			
CAKES REIGN BUT A DAY,	BLOSSOMS WILL RUN AWAY,	1578	2
CALAMITY			
VAGUE CALAMITY--	ROBBED BY DEATH--BUT	971	12
OR QUICK CALAMITY--	THE SOUL'S DISTINCT	974	4
CALCULATIONS			
THAN LIFE'S SWEET [NEW] CALCULATIONS--	UPON CONCLUDED LIVES	735	3
CALL			
AND CALL YOUR BROTHER MARS!	"SIC TRANSIT GLORIA	3	16
IN WHICH MY CALL WOULD COME--	I OFTEN PASSED THE	51	6
I'D RATHER CALL HIM "STAR."	"ARCTURUS" IS HIS OTHER	70	2
IF THE FOOLISH, CALL THEM "FLOWERS"--	IF THE FOOLISH, CALL	168	1
WHEN OTHERS CALL IT "DAY"!	MAKE ME A PICTURE OF THE	188	4
THE SAGES--CALL IT SMALL--	A SOLEMN THING--IT WAS--	271	14
YET NOT TOO FAR [NEAR ENOUGH--] TO COME AT CALL--	HE PUT THE BELT AROUND	273	9
DUNGEONS CAN [MAY] CALL--AND GUNS IMPLORE--	WHAT IF I SAY I SHALL	277	8
I THINK, THEY CALL IT "GOD"--	I GOT SO I COULD HEAR	293	14
AND FAR I HEARD HIS SILVER CALL	I HAD NOT MINDED--WALLS	398	3
MIDNIGHT--GOOD NIGHT! I HEAR THEM CALL,	A WIFE--AT DAYBREAK I	461	7
A SORT THEY CALL "DESPAIR"--	I MEASURE EVERY GRIEF I	561	30
THAT MEN CALL "PARADISE"--	"HEAVEN" HAS DIFFERENT	575	16
TO CALL THE LITTLE GIRL	THEY WONT FROWN ALWAYS--	874	6
SOME CALL EXPERIENCE.	I STEPPED FROM PLANK TO	875	8
ALTHOUGH TO THEIR CELESTIAL CALL	MY BEST ACQUAINTANCES	932	5
TILL SUNRISE TAKE [CALL] US BACK TO SCENE--	I LEARNED--AT LEAST--	944	25
THAT OBLIQUE BELIEF WHICH WE CALL CONJECTURE	SOME WE SEE NO MORE,	1221	6
HE STAYED AWAY A YEAR TO CALL	DEAR MARCH--COME IN--	1320	21
HE DOTH AS PUNCTUAL CALL	THE SUN IS ONE--AND ON	1372	2
THEY CANNOT CALL, THEY'RE DUMB,	THAN HEAVEN MORE REMOTE,	1436	12
WHO [THAT] MUST BE UP TO CALL THE WORLD	HOW GOOD HIS LAVA BED,	1447	3
TO THAT PINK STRANGER WE CALL DUST--	OH GIVE IT MOTION--DECK	1527	5
WHAT SURGEONS CALL ALIVE--	STILL OWN THEE--STILL	1633	2
WHOSE BUGLES CALL THE LEAST OF US	TALK NOT TO ME OF SUMMER	1634	7
"DISCIPLE, CALL AGAIN."	THERE COMES AN HOUR WHEN	1751	6
CALLED			
I WAS NOT CALLED--	I KEEP MY PLEDGE.	46	2
BY DAISY CALLED FROM HILLSIDE--	I KEEP MY PLEDGE.	46	7
I HAVE BEEN CALLED AWAY--	IF I SHOULD CEASE TO	56	4
WHERE THE PLACE CALLED "MORNING" LIES!	WILL THERE REALLY BE A	101	12
I HAD SOME THINGS THAT I CALLED MINE--	I HAD SOME THINGS THAT I	116	1
AND GOD, THAT HE CALLED HIS,	I HAD SOME THINGS THAT I	116	2
CALLED HEAVEN--	FOREVER AT HIS SIDE TO	246	13
CALLED TO MY FULL--THE CRESCENT DROPPED--	I'M CEDED--I'VE STOPPED	508	11
BUT CALLED THE OTHERS--CLEAR--	I HAD NO CAUSE TO BE	542	5

	FIRST LINE	POEM		LINE
CALLED (CONTINUED)				
THEY CALLED ME TO THE WINDOW, FOR	THEY CALLED ME TO THE	628		1
THE TRACK CALLED LAND.	AN EVERYWHERE OF SILVER	884		4
TOO WILLING, TO BE CALLED	LET DOWN THE BARS, OH	1065	V	8
ASK [TO] HIM UNTO THE GALLOWS LED [CALLED]--	OH SUMPTUOUS MOMENT	1125		8
THE BELLS AT DISTANCE CALLED--	GREAT STREETS OF SILENCE	1159		6
TILL WE ARE ASKED [CALLED] TO RISE	WE NEVER KNOW HOW HIGH	1176		2
THE NOTICE THAT IS CALLED THE SPRING	THE NOTICE THAT IS	1310		1
THE MAPLES NEVER KNEW THAT YOU WERE COMING--TILL I CALLED	DEAR MARCH--COME IN--	1320		12
WHOSE TITLE IS [DISCREETLY CALLED] "THE SOUL."	TO TRY TO SPEAK, AND	1617		8
CALLERS				
NOT AT HOME TO CALLERS	NOT AT HOME TO CALLERS	1590		1
CALLETH				
MY COUNTRY CALLETH ME;	"SIC TRANSIT GLORIA	3		58
CALLING				
OF THEIR PECULIAR CALLING	THOSE CATTLE SMALLER	1388		13
CALLS				
OR DO WHAT THE NURSE CALLS "DIE"--	WHAT IS--"PARADISE"--	215		14
GOD CALLS HOME--THE ANGELS--PROMPTLY--	GOD PERMITS INDUSTRIOUS	231		5
PRECISELY AS THE CALLS--	THE MERCHANT OF THE	1131		4
CALM				
THE [AN] ELEPHANT'S--CALM EYES	A BURDOCK--CLAWED MY	229		12
NAY--HOLD IT--IT IS CALM--	I TIE MY HAT--I CREASE	443		29
MATCH ME THE SOLID CALM--	THIS THAT WOULD GREET--	778		8
THAT CALM IS BUT A WALL	THE HEART HAS NARROW	928		9
HOW GOOD [SAFE / FIRM / CALM] TO BE IN TOMBS	THE CLOUDS THEIR BACKS	1172		6
CALMNESS				
WE TRY TO SHOW BECOMING FIRMNESS [CALMNESS]--	MARCH IS THE MONTH OF	1404		5
CALUMNIES				
OF CALUMNIES [JEALOUSIES]--OR FLIES.	SIZE CIRCUMSCRIBES--IT	641		8
CALVARIES				
JUSTIFIED--THROUGH [BY] CALVARIES OF LOVE--	THERE CAME A DAY AT	322		28
CALVARY				
THE PALM--WITHOUT THE CALVARY--	I SHOULD HAVE BEEN TOO	313		17
THE QUEEN OF CALVARY--	I DREADED THAT FIRST	348		24
SOME KEY OF CALVARY--	THE MORNING AFTER WO--	364		16
BUT CALVARY--	THAT I DID ALWAYS LOVE	549		12
ONE CALVARY--EXHIBITED TO STRANGER--	ONE CRUCIFIXION IS	553		5
IN PASSING CALVARY--	I MEASURE EVERY GRIEF I	561		36
AT THOSE OLD TIMES--IN CALVARY.	IF I MAY HAVE IT, WHEN	577		25
FOR PASSING CALVARY--	IT MAKES NO DIFFERENCE	620		8
CASHMERE--OR CALVARY--THE SAME--	WHERE THOU ART--THAT--IS	725		2
EMPRESS OF CALVARY!	TITLE DIVINE--IS MINE!	1072		4
RASHNESS OF CALVARY--	SPURN THE TEMERITY--	1432		2
CALYX				
I'LL DWELL IN CALYX--GRAY--	I TEND MY FLOWERS FOR	339		24
BRIGHT FLOWERS SLIT A CALYX	THE TREES LIKE TASSELS--	606		21
THE CALYX IS THE EARTH--	THE LILAC IS AN ANCIENT	1241		10
CAMBRIC				
THAT TOOK IT'S CAMBRIC WAY--	THE BEGGAR LAD--DIES	717		6
CAME				
THE WOLF CAME PEERING CURIOUS--	THROUGH LANE IT LAY--	9		5
ONE CAME THE ROAD THAT I CAME--	ONE SISTER HAVE I IN OUR	14		5
ONE CAME THE ROAD THAT I CAME--	ONE SISTER HAVE I IN OUR	14		5
I CAME TO BUILD THE BIRD'S NEST,	SEXTON! MY MASTER'S	96		3
THEY SAID THAT JESUS--ALWAYS CAME--	DYING! DYING IN THE	158		6
UNTIL IT PUZZLED CAME	AS IF SOME LITTLE ARCTIC	180		4
NOR, FOR MYSELF, I CAME SO FAR--	SAVIOR! I'VE NO ONE ELSE	217		5
I CAME TO BUY A SMILE--TODAY--	I CAME TO BUY A SMILE--	223		1
AN AWE CAME ON THE TRINKET!	A CLOCK STOPPED--	287		6
CAME ONCE A WORLD--DID YOU?	ONE YEAR AGO--JOTS WHAT?	296		14
THE DAY CAME SLOW--TILL FIVE O'CLOCK--	THE DAY CAME SLOW--TILL	304		1
THERE CAME A DAY AT SUMMER'S FULL,	THERE CAME A DAY AT	322		1
A BIRD CAME DOWN THE WALK--	A BIRD CAME DOWN THE	328		1
UNTIL THE CORONATION CAME--	THE DAY THAT I WAS	356		3
WITH EVERY MORN THAT CAME--	IT STRUCK ME--EVERY DAY	362		8
WE CAME TO FLESH--UPON--	I TIE MY HAT--I CREASE	443		16
AND WHEN THANKSGIVING, CAME,	'TWAS JUST THIS TIME,	445		14
BEFORE A BUILDER CAME--	MYSELF WAS FORMED--A	488		4
CAME OUT TO LOOK AT ME--	I STARTED EARLY--TOOK MY	520		4
TO MY SMALL HEARTH HIS FIRE CAME--	TO MY SMALL HEARTH HIS	638		1
CAME THE DARKER WAY--	HER SWEET TURN TO LEAVE	649		2
NOR WHERE IT WENT--NOR WHY IT CAME	A THOUGHT WENT UP MY	701		5
AND CAME MY WAY NO MORE--	A THOUGHT WENT UP MY	701		12
I MEANT TO FIND HER WHEN I CAME--	I MEANT TO FIND HER WHEN	718		1
THE WHOLE OF IT CAME NOT AT ONCE--	THE WHOLE OF IT CAME NOT	762		1
THEN CAME ONE DROP OF GIANT RAIN--	THE WIND BEGUN TO KNEAD	824		15
BUT CAME ANOTHER DAY	IT BLOOMED AND DROPT, A	978		6
CAME ALL THE WAY FROM LIFE TO ME	I HEARD, AS IF I HAD NO	1039		3
IT FITTED THEM, CAME IN.	I HEARD, AS IF I HAD NO	1039		8
AT LENGTH THE NOTICE CAME.	THE LAST NIGHT THAT SHE	1100		20
A VASTNESS, AS A NEIGHBOR, CAME,	THE CRICKETS SANG	1104		9
WE WENT AND PLAYED AND CAME AGAIN	THIS SLOW DAY MOVED	1120		7
THERE CAME [ADVANCED] UNSUMMONED IN--	SHALL I TAKE THEE, THE	1126		8
THE DAY THAT A COMPANION CAME	SOME DAYS RETIRED FROM	1157		3
THE SOUL CAME HOME FROM TRIPS [FROM TOWNS / FROM SCENES / TO SLEEP]	CONTAINED IN THIS SHORT	1165	V	
IT CAME AT LAST BUT PROMPTER DEATH	IT CAME AT LAST BUT	1230		1
THE WAY IS CLOSED THEY CAME.	THIS IS THE PLACE THEY	1264		8

	FIRST LINE	POEM	LINE
CAME (CONTINUED)			
THAN WHEN THE CRICKET CAME--	'TWAS LATER WHEN THE	1276	2
THAN WHEN THE WINTER CAME	'TWAS LATER WHEN THE	1276	6
WHILE WE WERE [I WAS] FEARING IT, IT CAME--	WHILE WE WERE FEARING IT	1277	1
BUT CAME WITH LESS OF FEAR	WHILE WE WERE FEARING IT	1277	2
TILL HUMAN NATURE CAME	I THOUGHT THAT NATURE	1286	2
AND SUNDER AS THEY CAME--	HOW KNOW IT FROM A	1364	8
FROM SUCH A VELVET WORLD IT COMES [CAME]	HOW SOFT A CATERPILLAR	1448	3
PROVOKING LOVER, WHEN YOU CAME	I THOUGHT THE TRAIN	1449	7
THE THRILL CAME SLOWLY LIKE A BOON [LIGHT] FOR	THE THRILL CAME SLOWLY	1495	1
IT CAME HIS TURN TO BEG--	IT CAME HIS TURN TO BEG	1500	1
AS WHEN YOU CAME BEFORE	THE PILE OF YEARS IS NOT	1507	2
THERE COMES [CAME] A WARNING LIKE A SPY	THERE COMES A WARNING	1536	1
THE WINDS CAME CLOSER UP--	AS IMPERCEPTIBLY AS	1540	V
A WEED OF SUMMER CAME--	TO HER DERIDED HOME	1586	2
THERE CAME A WIND LIKE A BUGLE--	THERE CAME A WIND LIKE A	1593	1
A CHILL CAME UP AS FROM A SHAFT	A CAP OF LEAD ACROSS THE	1649	5
I CAME UPON A WORM	IN WINTER IN MY ROOM	1670	2
THAT NEVER CAME,	AS SUBTLE AS TOMORROW	1713	2
CAMEL'S			
THE CAMEL'S TRAIT--ATTAINED--	STRONG DRAUGHTS OF THEIR	711	6
CAMEST			
THOU ONLY CAMEST TO MANKIND	WITHIN THY GRAVE!	1552	3
CAMP			
THAT LIT THE DRUMMER FROM THE CAMP	GOOD NIGHT! WHICH PUT	259	11
CAMPAIGN			
A BRIEF CAMPAIGN OF STING AND SWEET	A LITTLE BREAD--A CRUST	159	8
IT'S BODILESS CAMPAIGN	THE BATTLE FOUGHT	594	6
IN THAT CAMPAIGN INSCRUTABLE	'TWAS FIGHTING FOR HIS	1188	7
THEIR [THIS] ARROGANT CAMPAIGN--	A WILD BLUE SKY ABREAST	1415	8
CANAAN			
"CANAAN" DENIED--	IF THE FOOLISH, CALL	168	10
TO LET HIM SEE--THE CANAAN--	IT ALWAYS FELT TO ME--A	597	3
CANCELED			
CANCELED LIKE DAWN	LEFT IN IMMORTAL YOUTH	1289	7
CANCELLED			
WHEN CANCELLED BY THE FROST--	THERE IS A FLOWER THAT	380	32
THE FLESH--SURRENDERED--CANCELLED [SHIFTED]--	DEPARTED--TO THE	524	5
CANDID			
CANDID--IN MAY--	PINK--SMALL--AND	1332	4
FASHIONED BY THY CANDID HAND	"HEAVENLY FATHER"--TAKE	1461	3
CANDIDATE			
FOR THE SUSPENDED CANDIDATE	SHALL I TAKE THEE, THE	1126	7
GO MAKE THEE FAIR MY CANDIDATE	OH SHADOW ON THE GRASS,	1187	3
A CANDIDATE FOR MORNING CHANCE	SOMEHOW MYSELF SURVIVED	1194	7
PRECISELY AS THE CANDIDATE [CHARACTER]	TWO LENGTHS HAS EVERY	1295	V 7
CANDIDATES			
BE STATIONED WITH THE CANDIDATES	SHALL I TAKE THEE, THE	1126	3
CANDLE			
GOOD NIGHT! WHICH PUT THE CANDLE OUT?	GOOD NIGHT! WHICH PUT	259	1
BEETLE AT THE CANDLE--	LIFE, AND DEATH, AND	706	4
HER CANDLE SO EXPIRE	THE DAY UNDRESSED--	716	13
THE LORD A CANDLE ENTERTAINS	THE SUN AND MOON MUST	871	12
AT CANDLE [CANDLES] IT IS HERE;	FURTHER IN SUMMER THAN	1068	V
CANDLES			
HAUNTS CANDLES IN BRAZIL.	A MOTH THE HUE OF THIS	841	2
AT CANDLE [CANDLES] IT IS HERE;	FURTHER IN SUMMER THAN	1068	V
CANDOR			
"UNCHANGED" I URGED WITH A CANDOR	I SAW THAT THE FLAKE WAS	1267	3
CANDOR--MY TEPID FRIEND--	CANDOR--MY TEPID FRIEND	1537	1
CANES			
SAUNTERING GENTLEMEN--WITH CANES--	IT WILL BE SUMMER--	342	3
CANNON			
AS FAR AS CANNON DWELL	STEP LIGHTLY ON THIS	1183	6
THE POPULAR HEART IS A CANNON FIRST--	THE POPULAR HEART IS A	1226	1
CANNON'S			
DID YOU EVER LOOK IN A CANNON'S FACE--	DID YOU EVER STAND IN A	590	9
CANTICLE			
ARISE THIS SPECTRAL CANTICLE	FURTHER IN SUMMER THAN	1068	11
CANTONS			
WHOSE CANTONS DOT THE SKIES--	THE FEET OF PEOPLE	7	20
CANVAS			
NIGHT IS THE MORNING'S CANVAS	THE FEET OF PEOPLE	7	13
ON FINE--ARTERIAL CANVAS--	THE OUTER--FROM THE	451	13
THOSE BOYS AND GIRLS, IN CANVAS--	THOSE FAIR--FICTITIOUS	499	5
CAP			
HER CAP IS SMALL--AND SNUG--	YOU'LL KNOW HER--BY HER	634	13
HIS HEAD, A CAP AND FRILL	HIS BILL AN AUGUR IS	1034	2
A CAP OF LEAD ACROSS THE SKY	A CAP OF LEAD ACROSS THE	1649	1
CAPABILITIES			
SLOW CAPABILITIES.	SUCH IS THE FORCE OF	787	8
CAPACIOUS			
CAPACIOUS AS THE SEA--	YOU LEFT ME--SIRE--TWO	644	6
CAPACITY			
'TIS VAST--AS OUR CAPACITY--	HEAVEN IS SO FAR OF THE	370	5
AND HER--CAPACITY--	THERE IS A FLOWER THAT	380	8
NEITHER--THY CAPACITY--	'TWOULD EASE--A	682	4
A DIM CAPACITY FOR WINGS	MY COCOON TIGHTENS--	1099	3
CAPACITY TO TERMINATE	TO MAKE ROUTINE A	1196	3
BRIEF STRUGGLE FOR CAPACITY	I THOUGHT THAT NATURE	1286	7

	FIRST LINE	POEM	LINE
CARE (CONTINUED)			
WHAT CARE THE DEAD, FOR CHANTICLEER--	WHAT CARE THE DEAD, FOR	592	1
WHAT CARE THE DEAD FOR DAY?	WHAT CARE THE DEAD, FOR	592	2
WHAT CARE THE DEAD FOR SUMMER?	WHAT CARE THE DEAD, FOR	592	9
WHAT [NOR] CARE THE DEAD FOR WINTER?	WHAT CARE THE DEAD, FOR	592	17
MY HAND, WITH TREMBLING CARE	I YEARS HAD BEEN FROM	609	18
I COULD NOT CARE--TO GAIN	WITHOUT THIS--THERE IS	655	5
RETIRED [LAID DOWN] WITHOUT A CARE--	THE DAY UNDRESSED--	716	12
AND INFINITER CARE--	NATURE--THE GENTLEST	790	22
IF ONE CARE TO, THAT IS,	GOOD TO HIDE, AND HEAR	842	3
A NEW--DIVINER--CARE--	I LEARNED--AT LEAST--	944	24
LET US DISCOURSE [DISCLOSE]--WITH CARE--	A MAN MAY MAKE A REMARK	952	6
I SHOULD NOT CARE TO STOP	THE SPRY ARMS OF THE	1103	5
THAT SAILED WITHOUT A CARE--	A SOFT SEA WASHED AROUND	1198	4
THE BIRDS ENAMOR CARE--	THE NOTICE THAT IS	1310	6
BUT SUMMER DOES NOT CARE--	SUMMER--WE ALL HAVE SEEN	1386	5
AND DOES'NT CARE ABOUT CAREERS	HOW HAPPY IS THE LITTLE	1510	3
WHEN WE HAVE CEASED TO CARE	WHEN WE HAVE CEASED TO	1706	1
HIS REMEDY FOR CARE,--	HIGH FROM THE EARTH I	1723	18
CARED			
THAT WAS ALL I CARED TO KNOW.	HE WAS WEAK, AND I WAS	190	8
ALMOST AS IF THEY CARED--	IF I'M LOST--NOW--	256	9
AS IF A KINGDOM--CARED!	READ--SWEET--HOW OTHERS	260	7
SINCE THE SOLE EAR I CARED TO CHARM--	PUT UP MY LUTE!	261	3
HE CARED AS MUCH AS ON THE AIR	OF COURSE--I PRAYED--	376	3
OF ONLY TASTE WE CARED TO PLEASE	TO MAKE ONE'S TOILETTE--	485	3
NO OTHER--STOPPED [CARED] TO EARN--	TO OFFER BRAVE	767	8
I EVER CARED TO EARN--	THE STARS ARE OLD, THAT	1249	4
CAREER			
AND YET IT'S WHOLE CAREER [ALIEN PLACE / COVERT PLACE]	THE MUSHROOM IS THE ELF	1298	6
A BRIEF CAREER OF CHEER	A RAT SURRENDERED HERE	1340	2
WHOSE PINK CAREER MAY HAVE A CLOSE	WHOSE PINK CAREER MAY	1394	1
TO FILL IT'S FRINGED CAREER [SPHERE]	THE GENTIAN HAS A	1424	11
INTENT UPON IT'S OWN CAREER [MISSION QUAINT / CIRCUIT QUAINT]	HOW SOFT A CATERPILLAR	1448	7
THE LOWLIEST CAREER	NO LIFE CAN POMPLESS	1626	2
SUPERFLUOUS MY WHOLE CAREER	CONFERRING WITH MYSELF	1655	7
CAREERS			
AND DOES'NT CARE ABOUT CAREERS	HOW HAPPY IS THE LITTLE	1510	3
CAREFUL			
SURGEONS MUST BE VERY CAREFUL	SURGEONS MUST BE VERY	108	1
IN CAREFUL FITTED GROUND	NO NOTICE GAVE SHE, BUT	804	14
CAREFULLY			
BY SHUNNING CAREFULLY THE PLACE [SPOT / SITE]	HAVE ANY LIKE MYSELF	736	19
CAREFULLY CHERISHING THE SPOT	THIS IS A BLOSSOM OF THE	945	11
CARELESS			
A CARELESS SNATCH--A BALLAD--	HEART, NOT SO HEAVY AS	83	5
I TASTED--CARELESS--THEN--	ONE YEAR AGO--JOTS WHAT?	296	12
A BIRD SAT CARELESS ON THE FENCE--	THE TREES LIKE TASSELS--	606	17
WE TALK IN CARELESS [VENTURE]--AND IN TOSS--	AGAIN--HIS VOICE IS AT	663	13
IF CIRCASSIAN--HE IS CARELESS--	COLOR--CASTE--	970	9
A WORD DROPPED CARELESS ON A PAGE	A WORD DROPPED CARELESS	1261	1
CARELESSLY			
SLID CARELESSLY AWAY--	I WATCHED THE MOON	629	14
CARES			
WHO CARES ABOUT A BLUE BIRD'S TUNE--	A PANG IS MORE	1530	6
HOW PALTRY LOOKED MY CARES	CONFERRING WITH MYSELF	1655	5
CARESS			
CARESS HER FREEZING HAIR--	THE SOUL HAS BANDAGED	512	6
BREEZES CARESS	TO THE STANCH DUST	1402	V 5
AND HALF CARESS--	NOT SEEING, STILL WE	1518	4
CARESSED			
CARESSED A TRIGGER ABSENTLY	HE SCANNED IT--STAGGERED	1062	8
CARESSES			
CARESSES--AND IS GONE--	A VISITOR IN MARL--	391	8
CARGO			
HER CARGO--IS OF DEW--	MY EYE IS FULLER THAN MY	202	2
OUR'S BE THE CARGO--UNLADEN--HERE--	HOW SICK--TO WAIT--IN	368	10
THE CARGO OF THEMSELVES--	SUCH IS THE FORCE OF	787	6
FRESH AS A CARGO FROM BATIZE	AFTER THE SUN COMES OUT	1148	7
CARGOES			
THE SUBTLE CARGOES--LIE--	I GAVE MYSELF TO HIM--	580	12
CARLO			
TELL CARLO--	WHAT SHALL I DO--IT	186	14
CARMINE			
PUT ON HER CARMINE SUIT	SHE SLEPT BENEATH A TREE	25	5
THE CARMINE--TINGLES WARM--	I AM ALIVE--I GUESS--	470	5
BUT LITTLE CARMINE HATH HER FACE--	BUT LITTLE CARMINE HATH	558	1
CARNATIONS			
SO SPICY HER CARNATIONS NOD--	WE SHOULD NOT MIND SO	81	5
CARNATIONS--TIP THEIR SPICE--	I TEND MY FLOWERS FOR	339	9
CARNIVAL			
FIND CONSTERNATION'S CARNIVAL	ENDANGER IT, AND THE	1658	7
CARNIVALS			
SOME CARNIVALS OF CLOUDS--	"HEAVEN" HAS DIFFERENT	575	12
CAROL			
ASCEND IN CEASELESS [BREAKS IN VICTORIOUS] CAROL--	TO LEARN THE TRANSPORT	167	13
"CAROL FOR HIM--WHEN I AM GONE"!	KILL YOUR BALM--AND IT'S	238	8

	FIRST LINE	POEM	LINE
CAROL (CONTINUED)			
BABBLE [CAROL] OF THE HAPPY	FORTITUDE INCARNATE	1217	5
CAROLLED			
CAROLLED, AND PAUSED [MUSED], AND CAROLLED--	HEART, NOT SO HEAVY AS	83	11
CAROLLED, AND PAUSED [MUSED], AND CAROLLED--	HEART, NOT SO HEAVY AS	83	11
CARP			
THE FOP--THE CARP--[THE DOG--THE TRAMP--]THE ATHEIST--	HOW MUCH THE PRESENT	1380	3
CARPENTER			
OR RIP OF NAIL--OR CARPENTER--	I'VE KNOWN A HEAVEN,	243	5
MYSELF WAS FORMED--A CARPENTER--	MYSELF WAS FORMED--A	488	1
UNTIL THE TENDER CARPENTER [SOVREIGN CARPENTER / UNSUSPECTING . . .	A GREAT HOPE FELL	1123	16
UNTIL THE TENDER CARPENTER [SOVREIGN CARPENTER / UNSUSPECTING . . .	A GREAT HOPE FELL	1123	16
THE AUGUR [SCAFFOLD] AND THE CARPENTER-- .	THE PROPS ASSIST THE	1142	7
CARPENTERS			
. . . CARPENTERS]	A GREAT HOPE FELL	1123	16
CARRARA			
BUT HER CARRARA GUIDE POST--	HER FINAL SUMMER WAS IT	795	11
WHO WROUGHT CARRARA IN ME	I'VE DROPPED MY BRAIN--	1046	13
CARRIAGE			
THE CARRIAGE HELD BUT JUST OURSELVES-- . .	BECAUSE I COULD NOT STOP	712	3
A BEE HIS BURNISHED CARRIAGE	A BEE HIS BURNISHED	1339	1
HIMSELF--HIS CARRIAGE WAS--[CARRIAGE IS-- / EQUIPAGE.]	A BEE HIS BURNISHED	1339	4
HIMSELF--HIS CARRIAGE WAS--[CARRIAGE IS-- / EQUIPAGE.]	A BEE HIS BURNISHED	1339	4
CARRIAGES			
CARRIAGES--BE SURE--AND GUESTS--TRUE [TOO]--	HER SWEET TURN TO LEAVE	649	3
CARRIED			
CARRIED BY MEN TODAY--	TAKEN FROM MEN--THIS	53	2
AND CARRIED IT TO GOD--	A POOR--TORN HEART-- A	78	12
THE HEART I CARRIED [CHERISHED] IN MY OWN--	SAVIOR! I'VE NO ONE ELSE	217	9
NO DEAD, WERE EVER CARRIED DOWN--	A HOUSE UPON THE HIGHT--	399	3
WHEN I WAS CARRIED BY THE FARMS--	'TWAS JUST THIS TIME,	445	3
AND CARRIED, WE SUPPOSE--[I SUPPOSED] TO HEAVEN,	I CRIED AT PITY--NOT AT	588	11
AND CARRIED ME AWAY--	MY LIFE HAD STOOD--A	754	4
BOUGHT, CARRIED HOME	SO LARGE MY WILL	1024	11
CARRIES			
AND CARRIES ONE--OUT OF IT--TO GOD-- . . .	IT'S COMING--THE	390	8
THE BODY--BORROWS [THE PRUDENT--CARRIES] A [THE] REVOLVER--	ONE NEED NOT BE A	670	17
THAT CARRIES IN THE SUN.	WHO IS THE EAST?	1032	4
HE CARRIES A CIRCUMFERENCE	HIS MIND OF MAN, A	1663	3
CARRY			
THEY'LL CARRY--HIM!	I CAN WADE GRIEF--	252	16
AND THE ODD FLAMBEAU, NO MEN CARRY . . .	HOW THE OLD MOUNTAINS	291	15
TO CARRY IN THE HAND--	I SEND TWO SUNSETS--	308	8
THE FACE I CARRY WITH ME--LAST--	THE FACE I CARRY WITH ME	336	1
CARRYING			
BY SOME ONE CARRYING A LIGHT--	OURSELVES WERE WED ONE	631	7
CARS			
IS WHEN THE CARS HAVE COME--	I THINK THE LONGEST HOUR	635	2
LIKE TRAINS OF CARS ON TRACKS OF PLUSH . .	LIKE TRAINS OF CARS ON	1224	1
CART			
NO PEDDLER'S CART--APPROACHED--	A HOUSE UPON THE HIGHT--	399	4
OR CART OF BUTTERFLY--	A LITTLE ROAD--NOT MADE	647	4
AS CART OF MAN IN ROAD BELOW	THE SUN IN REINING TO	1636	3
CARTS			
AND CARTS WENT STOOPING ROUND THE FIELDS .	'TWAS JUST THIS TIME,	445	11
THE BUSY CARTS--THE FRAGRANT COCKS-- . . .	I'M SORRY FOR THE DEAD--	529	11
WHEN MEN--AND BOYS--AND CARTS [LARKS]--AND JUNE,	I'M SORRY FOR THE DEAD--	529	19
CARTS--JOGGLE BY--	I COULD DIE--TO KNOW--	570	4
CARVED			
THEN CARVED [HE WROTE] HIS NAME--UPON IT-- .	HE FOUND MY BEING--SET	603	3
AND MISTS--ARE CARVED AWAY, ...	OF ALL THE SOULS THAT	664	10
VITALITY IS CARVED AND COOL.	I'VE DROPPED MY BRAIN--	1046	5
CASE			
IN CASE THE WIND SHOULD BLOW!	"SIC TRANSIT GLORIA	3	28
JUST AS THE CASE MAY BE--	AFRAID! OF WHOM AM I	608	8
WITH WHICH WE CITE THIS MIGHTIEST CASE . .	"REMEMBER ME" IMPLORED	1180	7
CASEMENT			
THRICE TO THE FLOATING CASEMENT	ONCE MORE, MY NOW	48	5
CASES			
CASES OF DESPAIR--	DID OUR BEST MOMENT LAST	393	6
THE PARTIES IN BOTH CASES	THE LEAVES LIKE WOMEN,	987	5
CASH			
I PAY--IN SATIN CASH--	I PAY--IN SATIN CASH--	402	1
CASHMERE			
SOME VISION OF THE WORLD CASHMERE--	SOME RAINBOW--COMING	64	2
ON THEIR PASSAGE CASHMERE--	SOUTH WINDS JOSTLE THEM	86	6
LO, A TINT CASHMERE!	ARTISTS WRESTLED HERE!	110	2
FROM AMHERST TO CASHMERE!	IF I COULD BRIBE THEM BY	179	3
FABRICS OF CASHMERE--	I AM ASHAMED--I HIDE--	473	9
CASHMERE--OR CALVARY--THE SAME--	WHERE THOU ART--THAT--IS	725	2
CASK			
NAKED OF FLASK--NAKED OF CASK--	A TOAD, CAN DIE OF LIGHT	583	10

	FIRST LINE	POEM	LINE
CASKETS			
FROM POLAR CASKETS--FETCHED ME--	THE ANGLE OF A LANDSCAPE	375	17
CASPIAN			
MY CASPIAN--THEE.	LEAST RIVERS--DOCILE TO	212	2
MURMURING, LIKE OLD CASPIAN CHOIRS,	MANY A PHRASE HAS THE	276	5
A CASPIAN WERE CROWDED--	THE BIRD DID PRANCE--THE	1107	11
THAT CASPIAN FACT	UNTIL THE DESERT KNOWS	1291	5
THE CASPIAN HAS ITS REALMS OF SAND,	TO LOSE THEE--SWEETER	1754	5
NO CASPIAN COULD BE.	TO LOSE THEE--SWEETER	1754	8
CASQUE			
NO CASQUE SO BRAVE	I ROSE--BECAUSE HE SANK	616	14
CAST			
HOW MANY CAST A NAMELESS POD	HOW MANY FLOWERS FAIL IN	404	5
JUST TO CAST HER DOWN	TAKING UP THE FAIR IDEAL	428	2
IT HAD CAST AWAY--	HER SWEET TURN TO LEAVE	649	8
ITSELF THE ONLY PRINCE CAST OUT--	A LOSS OF SOMETHING EVER	959	8
THE GARMENT CAST,	WHAT TWIGS WE HELD BY--	1086	8
TO CAST THE SHIPS, AT SEA,	THE DUTIES OF THE WIND	1137	2
THROW [GIVE / CAST] NOT TO THE DIVINE	THE MIND LIVES ON THE	1355	V 7
IT'S TOILS [CORN] TO BRINDLED PEOPLE [NATIONS] THRUST [CAST]--	A FIELD OF STUBBLE,	1407	3
CASTANET			
THE JAY HIS CASTANET HAS STRUCK	THE JAY HIS CASTANET HAS	1635	1
CASTE			
COLOR--CASTE--DENOMINATION--	COLOR--CASTE--	970	1
CASTLE			
IN HER CASTLE ABOVE THEM--	SAFE IN THEIR ALABASTER	216	8
OUTSIDE THE CASTLE [CENTRE / CITY]--THAT CONTAIN [PRESENT]--	THE SPIRIT IS THE	733	7
THIS LATEST LEISURE EQUAL LULLS [CASTLE EQUAL HOLDS]	NOT ANY HIGHER STANDS	1256	5
CAST'S			
YOU'VE SEEN IT ON A CAST'S FACE [CHEEK]--	IT KNEW NO MEDICINE--	559	11
CASUAL			
AS CASUAL [ODORLESS / INNOCENT] AS RAIN	THE GENTIAN HAS A	1424	6
IN CASUAL [COMPETENT] SIMPLICITY--	HOW HAPPY IS THE LITTLE	1510	10
CASUALLY			
AND CASUALLY GLANCE	BLOOM--IS RESULT--TO	1058	2
CAT			
O'ERPOWERED BY THE CAT!	PAPA ABOVE!	61	3
THE CAT REPRIEVES THE MOUSE	THE WHOLE OF IT CAME NOT	762	5
THE CAT THAT IN THE CORNER DWELLS [SITS]	A LITTLE DOG THAT WAGS	1185	9
FOR BEGGAR OR FOR CAT.	THE BONE THAT HAS NO	1274	4
CATACOMB			
OR SOME ELF'S CATACOMB?	DRAB HABITATION OF WHOM?	893	5
BUT NONE WILL PASS THE [MAN'S] CATACOMB	THE BUTTERFLY IN HONORED	1246	3
CATARACT			
UPON THE CATARACT.	WHEN ONE HAS GIVEN UP	853	8
CATCH			
OH, COULD YOU CATCH HER LAST REFRAIN--	KILL YOUR BALM--AND IT'S	238	6
SO STATIONED I COULD CATCH THE MINT	I WAS THE SLIGHTEST IN	486	5
TILL I COULD TAKE THE [CATCH MY] BALANCE	I PRAYED, AT FIRST, A	576	18
AND CATCH ME ERE [WHEN / AS] I DROP	THE PILE OF YEARS IS NOT	1507	8
CATCH [TRAP / BIND] A DROP OF DEW	FOLLOW WISE ORION	1538	V
CATCHING			
BY CATCHING AT THE TWIGS THAT GROW	I GAINED IT SO--	359	3
CATERPILLAR			
BY MEN, YCLEPT CATERPILLAR!	A FUZZY FELLOW, WITHOUT	173	17
HOW SOFT A CATERPILLAR STEPS--	HOW SOFT A CATERPILLAR	1448	1
CATHEDRAL			
IN A CATHEDRAL AISLE,	I'VE HEARD AN ORGAN TALK	183	2
OF CATHEDRAL TUNES--	THERE'S A CERTAIN SLANT	258	4
CATO			
WHAT CATO COULD'NT PROVE ME	THE RAINBOW NEVER TELLS	97	7
CATO'S			
GATHERED BY CATO'S DAUGHTER,	GREAT CAESAR! CONDESCEND	102	3
CATTLE			
AND ALL THE CATTLE--STARVED--	THE WINTERS ARE SO SHORT	403	12
OF OPAL CATTLE--FEEDING FAR	THEY CALLED ME TO THE	628	5
NOR CATTLE WERE--NOR SOIL--	THEY CALLED ME TO THE	628	8
THE CATTLE FLUNG [FLED] TO BARNS--	THE WIND BEGUN TO KNEAD	824	14
THOSE CATTLE SMALLER THAN A BEE	THOSE CATTLE SMALLER	1388	1
THOSE CATTLE ARE THE FLY--	THOSE CATTLE SMALLER	1388	4
CAUCUS			
IMPS IN EAGER CAUCUS	SOUL, WILT THOU TOSS	139	7
CAUGHT			
CAUGHT SUNRISE FIRST--AND SUNSET--LAST--	A HOUSE UPON THE HIGHT--	399	7
AND CAUGHT A RIDE [TOOK A BOUT] WITH HIM	TWO BUTTERFLIES WENT OUT	533	V 4
. . . [LOST / CAUGHT] THEMSELVES	TWO BUTTERFLIES WENT OUT	533	V
I CAUGHT THE DRIPPING OF A ROCK	A DYING TIGER--MOANED	566	3
THEN CAUGHT ME--LIKE A BALL--	THREE TIMES--WE PARTED--	598	6
CAUGHT HELPLESS AT A SENSE AS IF	HE SCANNED IT--STAGGERED	1062	4
NATURE, LIKE US IS SOMETIMES CAUGHT	THE SKY IS LOW--THE	1075	7
AND WHEN THE NOISE IS CAUGHT	THE SYMPTOM OF THE GALE	1327	13
IN WHICH THE HEART IS CAUGHT	ESCAPE IS SUCH A	1347	6
IF HE IS CAUGHT AT ALL--	THE LIFE THAT TIED TOO	1535	8
CAUSE			
BECAUSE THE CAUSE WAS MINE--	LIKE EYES THAT LOOKED ON	458	10
I HAD NO CAUSE TO BE AWAKE--	I HAD NO CAUSE TO BE	542	1
THERE IS THE VARIOUS CAUSE--	I MEASURE EVERY GRIEF I	561	26

	FIRST LINE	POEM	LINE
CAUSE (CONTINUED)			
DELIGHT WITHOUT A CAUSE--	IT IS A LONESOME GLEE--	774	6
MOST--I LOVE THE CAUSE THAT SLEW ME.	STRUCK, WAS I, NOR YET	925	17
OF TOLLING BELL I ASK THE CAUSE?	OF TOLLING BELL I ASK	947	1
WOULD CAUSE ONE SCARCELY TO SUSPECT	BLOOM--IS RESULT--TO	1058	3
GOD MADE NO ACT WITHOUT A CAUSE,	GOD MADE NO ACT WITHOUT	1163	1
WITHOUT AN EARTHLY CAUSE	A LITTLE DOG THAT WAGS	1185	6
THEY INDICATE OR CAUSE	THEIR BARRICADE AGAINST	1471	6
ARE SO FOR THAT MOST FATAL [MIGHTY] CAUSE	DECLAIMING WATERS NONE	1595	3
CAUSED			
BEAUTY--BE [IS] NOT CAUSED--IT IS--	BEAUTY--BE NOT CAUSED--	516	1
INSERT THE THING THAT CAUSED IT--	TO FILL A GAP	546	2
CAUSES			
FOR BLISSFUL CAUSES--MOST OF ALL	SHE'S HAPPY, WITH A NEW	535	6
CAUTERIZE			
THE BLISS TO CAUTERIZE--	THE WHOLE OF IT CAME NOT	762	4
CAUTION			
APPROACH THAT TREE WITH CAUTION, THEN UP IT BOLDLY CLIMB,	AWAKE YE MUSES NINE,	1	35
IS REVELATION'S LIMIT [CAUTION],	EMBARRASSMENT OF ONE	662	3
ADORED [BEHELD] WITH CAUTION--AS A BRITTLE HEAVEN--	EACH LIFE CONVERGES TO	680	9
I TOUCHED WITH CAUTION--LEST THEY CRACK [SLIT]--	IF HE WERE LIVING--DARE	734	7
CAUTIOUS			
CAUTIOUS, HINT TO ANY CAPTIVE	TALK WITH PRUDENCE TO A	119	5
THE CAUTIOUS GRAVE EXPOSES,	SOME, TOO FRAGILE FOR	141	6
IN WHICH IT CAUTIOUS ARM,	A WOUNDED DEER--LEAPS	165	10
I CAUTIOUS, SCANNED MY LITTLE LIFE--	I CAUTIOUS, SCANNED MY	178	1
STRAIGHTEN--LOOK CAUTIOUS FOR THEIR BREATH--	GIVE LITTLE ANGUISH--	310	5
LIKE ONE IN DANGER, CAUTIOUS,	A BIRD CAME DOWN THE	328	13
TELL HIM [HER]--JUST HOW SHE SEALED YOU--CAUTIOUS!	GOING TO HIM! HAPPY	494	22
CAUTIOUS--WE JAR EACH OTHER--	WE DREAM--IT IS GOOD WE	531	9
A SLOW AND CAUTIOUS WAY	I STEPPED FROM PLANK TO	875	2
OF CAUTIOUS MELODY.	AT HALF PAST THREE, A	1084	4
CAUTIOUSLY			
AS CAUTIOUSLY AS GLASS	I YEARS HAD BEEN FROM	609	22
WHY BLISS SO SCANTILY [CAUTIOUSLY] DISBURSE [EXPRESS / AFFORD]--	ONE BLESSING HAD I THAN	756	17
CAVALIER			
THAT IT IS NOT A CAVALIER,	IT WOULD NOT KNOW IF IT	1579	7
CAVALRY			
THE CAVALRY OF WO--	TO FIGHT ALOUD, IS VERY	126	4
CAVE			
IN CAVE IF I PRESUMED TO HIDE	TO MY QUICK EAR THE	891	5
CAVERN'S			
DID YOU EVER STAND IN A CAVERN'S MOUTH--	DID YOU EVER STAND IN A	590	1
CAVERNS			
ICICLES--CRAWL FROM POLAR CAVERNS--	SAFE IN THEIR ALABASTER	216	V
IT'S CAVERNS AND IT'S CORRIDORS	THE LONELINESS ONE DARE	777	15
CAVIL			
CAVIL OF THE BOLD	FORTITUDE INCARNATE	1217	6
CAVILER			
OH, CAVILER, FOR YOU!	DOUBT ME! MY DIM	275	25
TILL CAVILER [PERJURY] INSINUATES	WHOEVER DISENCHANTS	1451	V 7
CAW			
AND WITH IRONIC CAW	FAME IS A FICKLE FOOD	1659	7
CEASE			
WHEN ROSES CEASE TO BLOOM, SIR,	WHEN ROSES CEASE TO	32	1
IF I SHOULD CEASE TO BRING A ROSE	IF I SHOULD CEASE TO	56	1
IF I SHOULD CEASE TO TAKE THE NAMES	IF I SHOULD CEASE TO	56	5
THAN SACRIFICE, AND CEASE--	TO LOVE THEE YEAR BY	434	3
THAT WHEN THEIR CONSCIOUS FINGERS CEASE--	THE MARTYR POETS--DID	544	7
WE ALMOST CEASE TO FEAR--	THE HEAVEN VESTS FOR	694	14
THEN CEASE [CEASED], LIKE THESE--	THIS QUIET DUST WAS	813	8
THE HUNGER--DOES NOT CEASE--	HAD I NOT THIS, OR THIS,	904	12
THE BRIDGE WOULD CEASE TO BE	FAITH--IS THE PIERLESS	915	10
CEASE TO IDENTIFY--	THIS DUST, AND IT'S	936	4
THE SUMMER WOULD NOT CEASE--	DID WE ABOLISH FROST	1014	2
AND CENTURIES OF AUGUST CEASE [FUSE / LAPSE / BLEND]	THERE IS A ZONE WHOSE	1056	7
NOR KNOW I WHEN IT CEASE,	FURTHER IN SUMMER THAN	1068	V
AND CEASE TO RECOLLECT	THE PROPS ASSIST THE	1142	6
REMEMBER IT CAN CEASE--	TO MAKE ROUTINE A	1196	2
OR COULD IT CEASE TO BE	HAD THIS ONE DAY NOT	1253	2
FOR WHICH I CEASE TO LIVE--	TRIED ALWAYS AND	1559	4
DOES THAT KNOW--NOW--OR DOES IT CEASE--	THE SPIRIT LASTS--BUT IN	1576	13
CEASED			
DELAYED TILL SHE HAD CEASED TO KNOW--	DELAYED TILL SHE HAD	58	1
AND THEN SHE CEASED TO BEAR IT--	SHE BORE IT TILL THE	144	7
AND I HAVE CEASED TO WONDER WHY--	I SHALL KNOW WHY--WHEN	193	2
BUT TELL HIM THAT IT CEASED TO FEEL--	THERE IS A LANGUOR OF	396	11
THAT NEVER CEASED TO FALL--	I WAS THE SLIGHTEST IN	486	6
IT CEASED TO HURT ME, THOUGH SO SLOW	IT CEASED TO HURT ME,	584	1
AT NEWS THAT HE CEASED HUMAN NATURE	TO KNOW JUST HOW HE	622	11
WHEN HER'S HAD CEASED TO RUN--	SEVERER SERVICE OF	786	6
THEN CEASE [CEASED], LIKE THESE--	THIS QUIET DUST WAS	813	8
THE MURMURING OF BEES, HAS CEASED	THE MURMURING OF BEES,	1115	1
PAID AFTER THEY HAVE CEASED TO WORK	ALL MEN FOR HONOR	1193	3

	FIRST LINE	POEM	LINE
CEASED (CONTINUED)			
MURMURED--IT HAS CEASED--	"SECRETS" IS A DAILY	1385	4
AND POWER TO BE FINITE CEASED	ESTRANGED FROM BEAUTY--	1474	3
NOR EVER CEASED TO RUN	IN WINTER IN MY ROOM	1670	35
WHEN WE HAVE CEASED TO CARE	WHEN WE HAVE CEASED TO	1706	1
CEASELESS			
ASCEND IN CEASELESS [BREAKS IN VICTORIOUS] CAROL--	TO LEARN THE TRANSPORT	167	13
IN CEASELESS--SALARY--	ONE LIFE OF SO MUCH	270	4
TO CEASELESS POVERTY--	THIS WAS A POET--IT IS	448	12
IN CEASELESS ROSEMARY--	ESSENTIAL OILS--ARE	675	8
CEASES			
CEASES TO BE A SECRET--THEN--	A SECRET TOLD--	381	2
CHASE IT, AND IT CEASES--	BEAUTY--BE NOT CAUSED--	516	2
WHOSE BLEATING CEASES TO REPEAT	LET DOWN THE BARS, OH	1065	3
CEDAR			
AND TELL YOUR CEDAR FLOOR--	YOU CANNOT PUT A FIRE	530	8
HER CEDAR CITADEL.	FALSEHOOD OF THEE COULD	1007	4
TO WALK ON SEAS [TIDES] REQUIRES CEDAR FEET	THERE IS A STRENGTH IN	1113	6
NO ZEPHYR FELLED THIS CEDAR STRAIGHT--	TO BREAK SO VAST A HEART	1312	3
REAL MEMORY, LIKE CEDAR FEET	YOU CANNOT MAKE	1508	7
CEDARS			
OF CHAMBERS AS THE CEDARS--	I DWELL IN POSSIBILITY--	657	5
WHEN OLDEST CEDARS SWERVE--	THE TRUTH--IS STIRLESS--	780	4
CEDED			
I CEDED ALL OF DUST I KNEW--	DOUBT ME! MY DIM	275	11
I'M CEDED--I'VE STOPPED BEING THEIR'S--	I'M CEDED--I'VE STOPPED	508	1
BY SPECULATION CEDED	THE THINGS WE THOUGHT	1293	7
CEILING			
FEARLESS--THE COBWEB SWINGS FROM THE CEILING--	HOW MANY TIMES THESE LOW	187	11
A BOMB UPON THE CEILING	THESE ARE THE NIGHTS	1128	9
CEILINGS			
RAISED SOFTLY TO THE CEILINGS [HORIZONS]--	I WOULD NOT PAINT--A	505	11
CELEBRATE			
AND SPICIEST AT FADING--INDICATE [CELEBRATE]--	THEY HAVE A LITTLE ODOR	785	3
OR TERROR--THAT DO DECORATE [CELEBRATE / GENERATE]	HIS VOICE DECREPIT WAS	1476	7
CELEBRATED			
OR CELEBRATED DAYS--	FOREVER--IS COMPOSED OF	624	10
CELEBRATED PART AT TABLE	ONE DAY IS THERE OF THE	814	3
CELEBRATES			
A MINOR NATION CELEBRATES	FURTHER IN SUMMER THAN	1068	3
CELERITY			
AND DOOM'S CELERITY.	A DEW SUFFICED ITSELF--	1437	16
CELESTIAL			
WHERE WE--WITH LATE--CELESTIAL FACE--	MUSICIANS WRESTLE	157	17
HOW LONG AT THAT CELESTIAL WICK	GOOD NIGHT! WHICH PUT	259	4
AND CELESTIAL WOMEN--	READ--SWEET--HOW OTHERS	260	13
IT DEALS CELESTIAL [FLINGS A CRYSTAL] VAIL	IT SIFTS FROM LEADEN	311	12
WHOSE RARE--CELESTIAL--STIR--	I WOULD NOT PAINT--A	505	6
ADVANCING ON CELESTIAL LISTS--	HAD I PRESUMED TO HOPE--	522	11
OH THOU CELESTIAL HOST--	GIVEN IN MARRIAGE UNTO	817	2
ALTHOUGH TO THEIR CELESTIAL CALL	MY BEST ACQUAINTANCES	932	5
OF A CELESTIAL SEA--	I LEARNED--AT LEAST--	944	8
OF THE CELESTIAL FACE	AURORA IS THE EFFORT	1002	2
WITHOUT CELESTIAL MAIL--	THE LAST OF SUMMER IS	1353	6
LOVE CELESTIAL TOO--	IS IT TOO LATE TO TOUCH	1637	4
CELL			
WHAT A CELL!	IMMURED IN HEAVEN!	1594	2
CELLAR			
UNDER THE BEETLE'S CELLAR	UNDER THE LIGHT, YET	949	3
BESIDES THE DEEPEST CELLAR	REMEMBRANCE HAS A	1182	5
THE APPLE IN THE CELLAR SNUG	LIKE BROOMS OF STEEL	1252	10
CELLARS			
THE CELLARS OF THE SOUL--	IT'S HOUR WITH ITSELF	1225	6
CELLS			
AMONG THE CUNNING CELLS--	I BREATHED ENOUGH TO	272	6
WITHIN OPPOSING CELLS--	I TRIED TO THINK A	532	15
CENOTAPH			
THIS CENOTAPH	AN HONEST TEAR	1192	3
CENSURE			
PURSUING [SUBDUING] WINDS THAT CENSURE [SUNDER] US	NO BRIGADIER THROUGHOUT	1561	5
CENTIPEDE			
MURMURED "RESURGAM"--"CENTIPEDE"!	"ARCTURUS" IS HIS OTHER	70	7
CENTRAL			
AS IS THE CENTRAL MOOD--	THE OUTER--FROM THE	451	4
GLOWS CENTRAL--LIKE A JEWEL	THAT FIRST DAY, WHEN YOU	659	5
WE PARTED AS THE CENTRAL FLINT	WE MET AS SPARKS--	958	3
THAT FEEDS THE SACRED [CENTRAL] LIGHT.	HER FACE WAS IN A BED OF	1722	4
CENTRE			
IS BUT A PROVINCE--IN THE BEING'S [HUMAN] CENTRE--	ONE CRUCIFIXION IS	553	9
EACH LIFE CONVERGES TO SOME CENTRE--	EACH LIFE CONVERGES TO	680	1
OUTSIDE THE CASTLE [CENTRE / CITY]--THAT CONTAIN [PRESENT]--	THE SPIRIT IS THE	733	7
AT CENTRE OF THE SEA--	I MANY TIMES THOUGHT	739	4
AT MIDDLE [BOTTOM / CENTRE] OF THE HILL--	THE HALLOWING OF PAIN	772	6
CENTRES			
THE STOLID RAFTERS [CENTRES / HOURS /	THE SMOULDERING EMBERS	1132	6

	FIRST LINE	POEM	LINE
CENTRES (CONTINUED)			
INSTANTS / SECONDS] GLOW THE SITES OF CENTRES STIRRED	LIKE RAIN IT SOUNDED	1235	14
CENTS			
IS THE MINUTE PER CENTS--	THE INCIDENTS OF LOVE	1248	4
CENTURIES			
THRO' CENTURIES OF NOON	WHERE BELLS NO MORE	112	6
SLOW TRAMP THE CENTURIES,	JUST LOST, WHEN I WAS	160	18
BEGUILES THE CENTURIES OF WAY!	THO' I GET HOME HOW LATE	207	13
WILL ENTERTAIN THE CENTURIES	OF BRONZE--AND BLAZE--	290	16
AND YESTERDAY, OR CENTURIES BEFORE?	AFTER GREAT PAIN, A	341	4
FACTS CENTURIES BEFORE	A PRECIOUS--MOULDERING	371	20
CENTURIES AGO--	SMILING BACK FROM	385	8
AND NOW--THEY'RE CENTURIES FROM THAT--	IF ANYBODY'S FRIEND BE	509	12
IF ONLY CENTURIES, DELAYED,	IF YOU WERE COMING IN	511	9
THROUGH CENTURIES OF NERVE--	I MEASURE EVERY GRIEF I	561	22
TO BASK THE CENTURIES AWAY--	A LONG--LONG SLEEP--A	654	7
SINCE THEN--'TIS CENTURIES--AND YET	BECAUSE I COULD NOT STOP	712	21
CENTURIES REMOVED	ALL BUT DEATH, CAN BE	749 V	4
THOUGH CENTURIES BEYOND,	I'VE DROPPED MY BRAIN--	1046	18
THE CENTURIES OF JUNE	THERE IS A ZONE WHOSE	1056	6
AND CENTURIES OF AUGUST CEASE [FUSE / LAPSE / BLEND]	THERE IS A ZONE WHOSE	1056	7
WITH FIRMAMENTS [CENTURIES] BETWEEN	CONTAINED IN THIS SHORT	1165 V	
AT DISTANCES OF CENTURIES	A WORD DROPPED CARELESS	1261	7
CENTURIES AGO--	KNOCK WITH TREMOR--	1325	7
CENTURIES DELAYED	THE THRILL CAME SLOWLY	1495	2
AND CENTURIES 'TWILL BE AND MORE	'TIS SEASONS SINCE THE	1529	4
CENTURIES FROM HIS SOUL	THE EVENT WAS DIRECTLY	1686	8
CENTURY			
WENT HOME A CENTURY AGO	WHERE I HAVE LOST, I	104	15
FUNNY--TO BE A CENTURY--	FUNNY--TO BE A CENTURY--	345	1
IN JUST THE DRESS HIS CENTURY WORE--	A PRECIOUS--MOULDERING	371	3
BUT ONCE A CENTURY, THE ROSE	THE BIRD MUST SING TO	880	7
AS OFTEN AS A CENTURY	MEETING BY ACCIDENT,	1548	3
CEREMENTS			
WHEN CEREMENTS LET GO	'TIS ANGUISH GRANDER	984	6
CEREMONIOUS			
THE NERVES SIT CEREMONIOUS, LIKE TOMBS--	AFTER GREAT PAIN, A	341	2
CERTAIN			
BUT CERTAIN JUNE!	FOR THIS--ACCEPTED	195	12
THERE'S A CERTAIN SLANT OF LIGHT,	THERE'S A CERTAIN SLANT	258	1
I'M OLD ENOUGH, TODAY, I'M CERTAIN--THEN--	ONE YEAR AGO--JOTS WHAT?	296	33
SIMPLE SALUTE--AND CERTAIN RECOGNITION--	IT'S COMING--THE	390	5
THAT CERTAIN AS IT COMES--	DID OUR BEST MOMENT LAST	393	10
WHEN CERTAIN IT MUST DIE--	THE MANNER OF IT'S DEATH	468	2
IF CERTAIN, WHEN THIS LIFE WAS OUT--	IF YOU WERE COMING IN	511	13
SORROWFUL--AS CERTAIN--	THE CHILD'S FAITH IS NEW	637	22
THE CERTAIN PREY TO TEAZE--	THE WHOLE OF IT CAME NOT	762 V	4
SUCCESSFUL CERTAIN, IF AT LAST,	HOW FORTUNATE THE GRAVE	897	3
YET CERTAIN AM I OF THE SPOT	I NEVER SAW A MOOR--	1052	7
THE CIRCUMSPECT ARE CERTAIN	THE BUTTERFLY OBTAINS	1685	7
CERTAINLY			
GOD WOULD CERTAINLY SCOLD!	OVER THE FENCE--	251	7
AS CERTAINLY AS DOOM--	IMPOSSIBILITY, LIKE WINE	838	8
HE TELLS US CERTAINLY	BECAUSE THAT YOU ARE	1260	36
IT MAY BE KNOW SO CERTAINLY	PERHAPS THEY DO NOT GO	1399	5
CERTAINTIES			
BUT CERTAINTIES OF SUN [NOON]--	I THINK TO LIVE--MAY BE	646	17
AMONG THE CERTAINTIES--	WE DO NOT KNOW THE TIME	1106	4
CERTAINTY			
WHEN PLATO--WAS A CERTAINTY--	A PRECIOUS--MOULDERING	371	15
TO WITNESS TO THE CERTAINTY	I LIVE WITH HIM--I SEE	463	11
FOR CERTAINTY SHE TAKE HER WAY	THE MOON WAS BUT A CHIN	737	15
HOW GOOD THE CERTAINTY	ON A COLUMNAR SELF--	789	4
AS CERTAINTY CAN SEE	THE LUXURY TO APPREHEND	815	14
SUBMIT THAT HOME--AND CERTAINTY	THE ROBIN IS THE ONE	828	11
TWO ARMIES, LOVE AND CERTAINTY	DYING! TO BE AFRAID OF	831	11
AND CERTAINTY THAT ONE	THE DYING NEED BUT	1026	6
IS THE UNCERTAIN CERTAINTY--	OF PARADISE' EXISTENCE	1411	3
LEST CERTAINTY BE SERE	SWEET SKEPTICISM OF THE	1413	6
CERTIFICATE			
WITHOUT DEBATE [CERTIFICATE]--OR PAUSE--	FOREVER--IS COMPOSED OF	624	9
CERTIFICATE	THE GOOD WILL OF A	849	4
CERTIFICATE OF ABSENCE--	WE'LL PASS WITHOUT THE	996	3
CERTIFICATE FOR IMMORTALITY.	THAT SUCH HAVE DIED	1030	4
BUT DEIGN THIS LEAST CERTIFICATE	THE LOOK OF THEE, WHAT	1689	11
CERTIFIED			
IS FREELY CERTIFIED	THE SPIDER AS AN ARTIST	1275	4
THAN ANY FEATHER SPECIFIED [RATIFIED / CERTIFIED]	WITH PINIONS OF DISDAIN	1431	3
UNCERTIFIED [NOT CERTIFIED] OF SCENE	THE MOB WITHIN THE HEART	1745	5
CERTIFYING			
BY CONTRAST CERTIFYING	THE WAY TO KNOW THE	1279	21
T'WERE FITTER CERTIFYING	THE BUTTERFLY OBTAINS	1685	11
CHAFE			
SOME CHAFE IT'S IDLE HAND--	THERE'S SOMETHING	45	6
CHAFES			
STILL CHAFES IT'S NARROW BED--	A SOMETHING IN A	122	15

	FIRST LINE	POEM	LINE
CHAFF			
I WORKED FOR CHAFF AND EARNING WHEAT . . .	I WORKED FOR CHAFF AND	1269	1
I TASTED WHEAT AND HATED CHAFF	I WORKED FOR CHAFF AND	1269	5
ALL OTHER BOUNTY SUDDEN CHAFF [NIGGARDLY] .	I GROPED FOR HIM BEFORE	1555	3
CHAFING			
CHAFING THE SHELL--	LET US PLAY YESTERDAY--	728	14
CHAGRIN			
SOME MORNING OF CHAGRIN--	WE SEE--COMPARATIVELY--	534	14
TILL NATURE IN CHAGRIN	I BET WITH EVERY WIND	1215	2
TO YOUR CHAGRIN	HIS MANSION IN THE POOL	1379	14
CHAIN			
AND HANDLED WITH A CHAIN--	MUCH MADNESS IS DIVINEST	435	8
CHAIR			
SLIPPED QUIET FROM IT'S CHAIR--	ON SUCH A NIGHT, OR SUCH	146	4
BY YOUR CHAIR--OR, ON THE MAT--	WHAT SHALL I DO--IT	186	9
TO OFFER WHOM A CHAIR	THE WIND--TAPPED LIKE A	436	6
HER LITTLE ROCKING CHAIR TO DRAW-- . . .	THE NIGHT WAS WIDE, AND	589	15
IN HIS TREMENDOUS [ETERNAL / ENORMOUS] CHAIR--	THE MOUNTAIN SAT UPON	975	2
ESPIES THAT FICKLE CHAIR	RISK IS THE HAIR THAT	1239	6
AND TAKE A ROSY CHAIR.	THE NOTICE THAT IS	1310	4
THERE IS A WORLD [TOMB / CHAIR / SEAT] FOR ALL	NO LIFE CAN POMPLESS	1626	V 8
CHALK			
AS A HAND DID TRY TO CHALK THE SUN . . .	I FOUND THE WORDS TO	581	4
CHALLENGED			
AND THEN, UNJADED, CHALLENGED GOD	HE OUTSTRIPPED TIME WITH	865	3
CHALLENGING			
WERE CHALLENGING DESPAIR.	I LIVED ON DREAD--	770	9
CHAMBER			
FROM OFF HIS CHAMBER DOOR--	SEXTON! MY MASTER'S	96	6
CHAMBER, AND STATE, AND THRONG--	ONE DIGNITY DELAYS FOR	98	6
BUZZ THE DULL FLIES--ON THE CHAMBER WINDOW--	HOW MANY TIMES THESE LOW	187	9
ROUND HER CHAMBER HUMS--	COME SLOWLY--EDEN!	211	6
I KNOW NOT WHICH THY CHAMBER IS [PALACES]--	AT LEAST--TO PRAY--IS	502	3
ONE NEED NOT BE A CHAMBER--TO BE HAUNTED-- .	ONE NEED NOT BE A	670	1
CONSCIOUS AM I IN MY CHAMBER, ...	CONSCIOUS AM I IN MY	679	1
AT A WINDOW [IN A CHAMBER] FACING WEST-- .	WHEN I HOPED, I	768	3
IT'S AWFUL CHAMBER OPEN STANDS--	WATER MAKES MANY BEDS	1428	3
SURVEYED MY CHAMBER FLOOR	IN WINTER IN MY ROOM	1670	15
CHAMBERS			
SAFE IN THEIR ALABASTER CHAMBERS-- . . .	SAFE IN THEIR ALABASTER	216	1
IN CHAMBERS BRIGHT--	'TWAS THE OLD--ROAD--	344	19
OF CHAMBERS AS THE CEDARS--	I DWELL IN POSSIBILITY--	657	5
SHY AS THE WIND OF HIS CHAMBERS [LODGINGS] .	THIS IS A BLOSSOM OF THE	945	5
THE WIND--UNTO HIS [IT'S] CHAMBERS WENT . .	THE WIND TOOK UP THE	1134	9
CHAMOIS'			
AND A CHAMOIS' SILVER BOOT--	AH, MOON--AND STAR!	240	10
CHANCE			
A BIRD--BY CHANCE--THAT GOES THAT WAY-- . .	THE SKIES CANT KEEP	191	5
MORNING MEANS JUST RISK [CHANCE]--TO THE LOVER--	"MORNING"--MEANS	300	4
YOUR BREATH HAS TIME [CHANCE] TO STRAIGHTEN--	HE FUMBLES AT YOUR SOUL	315	9
NOT PROBABLE--THE BAREST CHANCE--	NOT PROBABLE--THE BAREST	346	1
YOUR CHANCE IN HARVEST MOVES	A SOLEMN THING WITHIN	483	14
WITHOUT A CHANCE, OR SPAR--	IT WAS NOT DEATH, FOR I	510	22
TO TAKE MY CHANCE [RISK] WITH PAIN-- . . .	MY FIRST WELL DAY--SINCE	574	6
A THRUST--AND THEN FOR LIFE A CHANCE-- . .	THE WHOLE OF IT CAME NOT	762	3
TOO HAPPY--FOR [IN] MY SPARROW'S CHANCE-- .	GOD GAVE A LOAF TO EVERY	791	7
CHANCE SOVREIGN ON A MINE--	I PLAY AT RICHES--TO	801	18
TO FAIL WITHIN A CHANCE--	EACH SECOND IS THE LAST	879	5
HIS SUIT A CHANCE	OF SILKEN SPEECH AND	896	5
PROPORTIONED TO THE CHANCE--	HAD I NOT THIS, OR THIS,	904	14
TOO IMMINENT THE CHANCE--	TOO LITTLE WAY THE HOUSE	911	6
AND NOW THE CHANCE HAD COME--	'TWAS CRISIS--ALL THE	948	4
I'VE STILL A CHANCE TO STRAIN	I'VE DROPPED MY BRAIN--	1046	16
THE CARD--THE CHANCE--THE FRIEND--	WE DO NOT KNOW THE TIME	1106	6
SOUL, TAKE THY RISK [RISKS / CHANCE], . .	SOUL, TAKE THY RISK,	1151	1
A CANDIDATE FOR MORNING CHANCE	SOMEHOW MYSELF SURVIVED	1194	7
ESCAPE IT--THERE IS BUT A CHANCE--	POWER IS A FAMILIAR	1238	5
WITHOUT THE CHANCE OF LIFE	I NEVER HEAR THAT ONE IS	1323	2
LUCK IS NOT CHANCE--	LUCK IS NOT CHANCE--	1350	1
IF THEY THE CHANCE HAD HAD	I KNOW OF PEOPLE IN THE	1665	4
CHANCED			
I MIGHT HAVE CHANCED THAT WAY!	WITHIN MY REACH!	90	3
CHANCEL			
MY CHANCEL--ALL THE PLAIN	ALL THESE MY BANNERS BE.	22	6
COULD KEEP A CHANCEL, COOL--	IT WAS NOT DEATH, FOR I	510	8
CHANCE'S			
A CHANCE'S FAINTEST TINCTURE	IMPOSSIBILITY, LIKE WINE	838	5
THAN PERISH FROM THE CHANCE'S LIST	EACH SECOND IS THE LAST	879	7
CHANCES			
HIS SCRUTINY OF CHANCES	AS ONE DOES SICKNESS	957	3
HIS CHANCES [DOCTRINES / DOGMAS] A REDOUBT--	NO BRIGADIER THROUGHOUT	1561	V 22
THAT HOLDS MY CHANCES UP.	A PIT--BUT HEAVEN OVER	1712	8
CHANGE			
HEAVEN DOES NOT CHANGE HER BLUE.	I'M THE LITTLE "HEART'S	176	12
AND BYE AND BYE--A CHANGE--	FOREVER AT HIS SIDE TO	246	12
ME, CHANGE! ME, ALTER!	ME, CHANGE! ME, ALTER!	268	1
I COULD NOT HAVE DEFINED THE CHANGE-- . .	I THINK I WAS ENCHANTED	593	21
IS EXEMPT FROM CHANGE--	ALL BUT DEATH, CAN BE	749	8
NO NOTICE GAVE SHE, BUT A CHANGE--	NO NOTICE GAVE SHE, BUT	804	1

	FIRST LINE	POEM	LINE
CHANGE (CONTINUED)			
WE KNEW BY CHANGE BETWEEN ITSELF	WE MET AS SPARKS--	958	7
I ONLY MUST NOT CHANGE SO FAIR	FITTER TO SEE HIM, I MAY	968	19
IN CHANGE--UNERUDITE--	'TWAS AWKWARD, BUT IT	973	4
APPROPRIATE CREATURES TO HER CHANGE . . .	THE MURMURING OF BEES,	1115	9
AND STOOD AMAZED BEFORE THE CHANGE [BOON / MORNS]	THE THRILL CAME SLOWLY	1495	7
MY COUNTRY NEED NOT CHANGE HER GOWN, . . .	MY COUNTRY NEED NOT	1511	1
WITHOUT A CHANGE OF WINGS, ...	TO THE BRIGHT EAST SHE	1573	4
LET CHANGE TRANSFUSE ALL OTHER TRAITS . .	THE LOOK OF THEE, WHAT	1689	9
CHANGED			
PERHAPS THE "KINGDOM OF HEAVEN'S" CHANGED--	"ARCTURUS" IS HIS OTHER	70	26
WHILE RAPTURE CHANGED IT'S DRESS	THE THRILL CAME SLOWLY	1495	6
CHANGES			
I HINTED CHANGES--LAPSE OF TIME--	IF HE WERE LIVING--DARE	734	5
CHANNEL			
THE CHANNEL OF THE DUST WHO ONCE ACHIEVES .	OURSELVES WE DO INTER	1144	2
CHANT			
LET US CHANT IT SOFTLY--	ALL THESE MY BANNERS BE.	22	18
WE CHANT--FOR CHEER--WHEN THE WINES--FAIL--	WE--BEE AND I--LIVE BY	230	5
WHO [HE] NEVER HEARD THAT FLESHLESS CHANT--	OF ALL THE SOUNDS	321	27
THAT MURMUR SO--CHANT SO--FAR--	AGAIN--HIS VOICE IS AT	663	V 25
HIS LABOR IS A CHANT--	HIS FEET ARE SHOD WITH	916	5
CHANTED			
BENT TO THE SCAFFOLD, OR IN DUNGEONS--CHANTED [WAITED]--	UNTO LIKE STORY--TROUBLE	295	5
CHANTICLEER			
AN ADDED STRUT IN CHANTICLEER--	AN ALTERED LOOK ABOUT	140	9
FOR CHANTICLEER TO WAKE IT--	ON SUCH A NIGHT, OR SUCH	146	13
SCREAMS CHANTICLEER	I KNOW SOME LONELY	289	35
WHAT CARE THE DEAD, FOR CHANTICLEER-- . .	WHAT CARE THE DEAD, FOR	592	1
CHANTING			
SCOOPING UP THE DUST AND CHANTING "LIVE"! .	WHILE IT IS ALIVE	491	10
CHANTING TO PARADISE--	BIND ME--I STILL CAN	1005	5
CHANTS			
I SANG FIRM--EVEN--[STRAIGHT--STEADY] CHANTS--	I ROSE--BECAUSE HE SANK	616	6
CHAOS			
BUT, MOST, LIKE CHAOS--STOPLESS--COOL-- . .	IT WAS NOT DEATH, FOR I	510	21
CHAOSES			
WHOLE CHAOSES [OBLIVIONS] ON HIM--	A PLATED LIFE--	806	8
CHAPEAU			
IN THEIR CHAPEAUX [A CHAPEAU] OF FIRE, . .	LIKE HER THE SAINTS	60	2
CHAPEAUX			
IN THEIR CHAPEAUX [A CHAPEAU] OF FIRE, . .	LIKE HER THE SAINTS	60	2
CHAPEL			
CHASTENED--AS TO THE CHAPEL	WENT UP A YEAR THIS	93	7
IN THAT OLD CHAPEL AISLE.	I'VE HEARD AN ORGAN TALK	183	8
CHAPTER			
A CHAPTER--THEN THE MIGHTY BOOK--	WE LEARNED THE WHOLE OF	568	3
CHARACTER			
THEN, FOR CHARACTER--	I AM ASHAMED--I HIDE--	473	19
HIS ABSENT CHARACTER.	JUST AS HE SPOKE IT FROM	848	8
PRECISELY AS THE CANDIDATE [CHARACTER] . .	TWO LENGTHS HAS EVERY	1295	V 7
HIS CHARACTER--A TONIC--	NO BRIGADIER THROUGHOUT	1561	21
RENOUNCHED THEIR CHARACTER	ARROWS ENAMORED OF HIS	1629	V 4
CHARCOAL			
POWDER EXISTS IN CHARCOAL [ELEMENTS / SULPHURETS]--	A MAN MAY MAKE A REMARK	952	7
CHARGE			
WHO CHARGE WITHIN THE BOSOM	TO FIGHT ALOUD, IS VERY	126	3
GRANT GOD, HE CHARGE THE BRAVEST	BLESS GOD, HE WENT AS	147	3
THERE'S NOT A CHARGE TO ME	OF ALL THE SOUNDS	321	2
AND TELL HIM--CHARGE THEE SPEAK IT PLAIN-- .	A TONGUE--TO TELL HIM I	400	7
A SPICY CHARGE, MY LITTLE POSTS [FRIENDS]--	THE BIRDS REPORTED FROM	743	3
WHO SHALL CHARGE THE VANITY	RIBBONS OF THE YEAR--	873	7
LEST THIS BELOVED CHARGE	LOVE--IS THAT LATER	924	10
I CHARGE HIM FLY [FLEE]	THE PAST IS SUCH A	1203	6
SO WE EVADE THE CHARGE OF YEARS	AS SUMMER INTO AUTUMN	1346	9
CHARGED			
STRANGE THAT THE FEET SO PRECIOUS CHARGED .	ON SUCH A NIGHT, OR SUCH	146	23
CHARGED, FROM MY CHIMNEY CORNER--	THE SUN KEPT STOOPING--	152	13
CHARGED US TO FORGET HIM--	DID WE DISOBEY HIM?	267	3
CHARGERS			
TIME'S WILY CHARGERS WILL NOT WAIT	TIME'S WILY CHARGERS	1458	1
CHARIOT			
HOW FRUGAL IS THE CHARIOT	THERE IS NO FRIGATE LIKE	1263	7
CHARIOTS			
THE CHARIOTS WAIT--	IF HE DISSOLVE--THEN--	236	11
UNMOVED--SHE NOTES THE CHARIOTS--PAUSING-- .	THE SOUL SELECTS HER OWN	303	5
OF CHARIOTS, THAT HIM CONVEY--	I ENVY SEAS, WHEREON HE	498	3
LIKE CHARIOTS--IN THE VEST--	THE TINT I CANNOT TAKE--	627	16
WITH SWIFTNESS, AS OF CHARIOTS	IT WAS A QUIET WAY--	1053	7
CHARITY			
NATURE IN CHARITY--	GARLANDS FOR QUEENS, MAY	34	7
'TWERE BETTER CHARITY	OF COURSE--I PRAYED--	376	8
"SWEET LADY--CHARITY"--	THE BEGGAR LAD--DIES	717	8
PLEA ITSELF--FOR CHARITY--	MOST SHE TOUCHED ME BY	760	4
RESERVE--FOR CHARITY--	DEPRIVED OF OTHER	773	12
CHARM			
HAPLY--YOUR SUMMER NIGHT TO CHARM-- . . .	KILL YOUR BALM--AND IT'S	238	4

	FIRST LINE	POEM	LINE
CHARM (CONTINUED)			
SINCE THE SOLE EAR I CARED TO CHARM--	PUT UP MY LUTE!	261	3
A CHARM INVESTS A FACE	A CHARM INVESTS A FACE	421	1
PRESERVED THE CHARM [VISION SURE / VISION CLEAR] SECURE	HAVE ANY LIKE MYSELF	736	18
SOME PASSING YEAR--A TRAIT [CHARM] BESTOW	FITTER TO SEE HIM, I MAY	968	4
WITH IT'S [A] REMAINING CHARM	THESE ARE THE NIGHTS	1128	16
SERPENT CANNOT [MAY NOT] CHARM--	WHEN I HOPED I FEARED--	1181	6
CHARMED			
ON SILVER MATTERS CHARMED A SNAKE	THE TREES LIKE TASSELS--	606	19
CHARMING			
"CHARMING APRIL DAY"!	I CANT TELL YOU--BUT YOU	65	16
CHARMS			
A THUNDER STORM COMBINES THE CHARMS	A CAP OF LEAD ACROSS THE	1649	7
CHART			
DONE WITH THE CHART!	WILD NIGHTS--WILD NIGHTS	249	8
ON DOOM'S CONSUMMATE CHART	TWO LENGTHS HAS EVERY	1295	10
CHARTED			
IS MAPPED AND CHARTED TOO.	"ARCTURUS" IS HIS OTHER	70	21
CHARTER			
DELIRIOUS CHARTER!	MINE--BY THE RIGHT OF	528	8
WERE BUT MINE--THE CHARTER OF THE LEAST FLY--	I COULD DIE--TO KNOW--	570	6
HAS A FICTITIOUS CHARTER	COULD HOPE INSPECT HER	1283	3
HER CHARTER IS FICTITIOUS	COULD HOPE INSPECT HER	1283	V 3
CHASE SEE A'CHASE			
THE HEAVEN WE CHASE,	THE NEAREST DREAM	319	2
OR ALL DAY, CHASE THE BEE--	ALTHOUGH I PUT AWAY HIS	366	21
CHASE IT, AND IT CEASES--	BEAUTY--BE NOT CAUSED--	516	2
CHASE IT NOT, AND IT ABIDES--	BEAUTY--BE NOT CAUSED--	516	3
THEN CHASE ITSELF DOWN HILL--	I LIKE TO SEE IT LAP	585	13
OR CHASE HIM IF HE DO	COULD I BUT RIDE	661	10
CHASED			
THEN LOST [STAKED / CHASED] THEMSELVES AND FOUND . . .	TWO BUTTERFLIES WENT OUT	533	V
TILL GRAVITATION CHASED [HUMBLED / EJECTED / FOUNDERED / . . .	TWO BUTTERFLIES WENT OUT	533	V
UNTIL A ZEPHYR PUSHED [CHASED / FLUNG / SPURNED / SCOURGED] THEM	TWO BUTTERFLIES WENT OUT	533	V
WE CHASED HIM TO HIS DEN--	THE FROST OF DEATH WAS	1136	17
THE WATERS CHASED HIM AS HE FLED,	THE WATERS CHASED HIM AS	1749	1
CHASM			
THE HORROR [CHASM] NOT TO BE SURVEYED--	THE LONELINESS ONE DARE	777	9
THIS CHASM, SWEET, UPON MY LIFE	THIS CHASM, SWEET, UPON	858	1
CHASTEN			
HIM YOU CHASTEN, [THOU CHASTENEST-- / YOU CHASTENED] THAT IS [WAS] HE!	LAY THIS LAUREL ON THE	1393	4
CHASTENED			
CHASTENED--AS TO THE CHAPEL	WENT UP A YEAR THIS	93	7
YOU WOULD CHASTENED STARE--	THERE'S THE BATTLE OF	1174	8
AND CHASTENED STOLE ALONG	MY TRIUMPH LASTED TILL	1227	4
SO CHASTENED AS THE FLY--	THE BUTTERFLY IN HONORED	1246	4
IS SHRUNKEN [SHRIVELLED / DWINDLED / CHASTENED] SMALL	THE VASTEST EARTHLY DAY	1328	2
DETERRED BY [FOR CHASTENED / SUBDUED TO] RETROSPECT.	THE LAST OF SUMMER IS	1353	2
HIM YOU CHASTEN, [THOU CHASTENEST-- / YOU CHASTENED] THAT IS [WAS] HE!	LAY THIS LAUREL ON THE	1393	4
CHASTENEST			
HIM YOU CHASTEN, [THOU CHASTENEST-- / YOU CHASTENED] THAT IS [WAS] HE!	LAY THIS LAUREL ON THE	1393	4
CHASTENS			
A MEDITATION CHASTENS SPEECH	SUMMER BEGINS TO HAVE	1682	10
CHASTISE			
DO NOT CHASTISE THE DOVE--	WHATEVER IT IS--SHE HAS	1204	4
CHASTISING			
IS NOT OUR'S THE CHASTISING--	WHATEVER IT IS--SHE HAS	1204	3
CHAT			
CHAT OF THE "EARLY DEAD"--	THERE'S SOMETHING	45	14
BUT IT'S DIM CHAT OF THINGS BURGUND, WE KNOW--	WE--BEE AND I--LIVE BY	230	V 4
CHATTED			
AND CHATTED CLOSE WITH THIS GRAND THING	IF ANYBODY'S FRIEND BE	509	19
CHATTER			
NO CHATTER--HERE--NO TEA--	UNIT, LIKE DEATH, FOR	408	13
CHEAT			
THE BROKER CANNOT CHEAT.	ALL THESE MY BANNERS BE.	22	11
OH FRAUD THAT CANNOT CHEAT THE BEE--	THESE ARE THE DAYS WHEN	130	7
THAT THEY WILL CHEAT THE SIGHT--	DELIGHT IS AS THE FLIGHT	257	22
TO CHEAT HERSELF, IT SEEMED SHE TRIED--	MY FIRST WELL DAY--SINCE	574	13
CHEATED SEE LONG-CHEATED			
I SHALL NOT CHEATED WAKE--	YOU LOVE ME--YOU ARE	156	3
UNTIL THE CHEATED EYE	THE TINT I CANNOT TAKE--	627	22
CHEATS			
HE CHEATS AS HE ENCHANTS	ONE OF THE ONES THAT	1466	14
CHECK			
I CHECK MY BUSY PENCIL,	LOW AT MY PROBLEM	69	5
NOR WE SO MUCH AS CHECK OUR SPEECH--	THE LIGHTNING PLAYETH--	630	11
IT SUITS HIM BETTER THAN A CHECK	THE MERCHANT OF THE	1131	7
CHECKS			
THE FORMER--CHECKS--ON FAME--	SOME--WORK FOR	406	4
AS IF THE CHECKS WERE GIVEN--	I NEVER SAW A MOOR--	1052	8

	FIRST LINE	POEM	LINE
CHEEK			
THE BERRY'S CHEEK IS PLUMPER--	THE MORNS ARE MEEKER	12	3
OR ANY CHEEK AT NIGHTFALL	BEFORE THE ICE IS IN THE	37	3
GLOWING IS HER CHEEK,	GLOWING IS HER BONNET,	72	2
WHOSE CHEEK IS THIS?	WHOSE CHEEK IS THIS?	82	1
BUT WHICH THE CHEEK--	WHOSE CHEEK IS THIS?	82	8
VENICE COULD NOT SHOW A CHEEK	PIGMY SERAPHS--GONE	138	7
RHODORA'S CHEEK IS CRIMSON,	WHOSE ARE THE LITTLE	142	23
A CHEEK IS ALWAYS REDDER	A WOUNDED DEER--LEAPS	165	7
PERHAPS A FLOWER'S SHRIVELLED CHEEK	IN EBON BOX, WHEN YEARS	169	9
THE ROSE DID CAPER ON HER CHEEK--	THE ROSE DID CAPER ON	208	1
TILL OPPOSITE--I SPIED A CHEEK	THE ROSE DID CAPER ON	208	9
THE SMALLEST ONE UPON YOUR FACE [CHEEK]	I CAME TO BUY A SMILE--	223	3
AND NOT THE PILLOW AT YOUR CHEEK	'TIS SO APPALLING--IT	281	17
UPON MY SIMPLE CHEEK--	IT WOULD NEVER BE COMMON	430	10
A CHEEK--PERCHANCE A BROW--	THE OUTER--FROM THE	451	14
STILL TOILING AT THE CHEEK	A SOLEMN THING WITHIN	483	8
THE VERY PATTERN OF THE CHEEK--	YOU KNOW THAT PORTRAIT	504	5
YOU'VE SEEN IT ON A CAST'S FACE [CHEEK]--	IT KNEW NO MEDICINE--	559	11
THE CHEEK OF LIBERTY--	A PRISON GETS TO BE A	652	20
HER CHEEK--A BERYL HEWN--	THE MOON WAS BUT A CHIN	737	6
ALL CRUMPLED WAS THE CHEEK	HE TOLD A HOMELY TALE	763	5
I THOUGHT YOU'D CHOOSE A VELVET CHEEK	THEMSELF ARE ALL I HAVE	1094	3
OH CHEEK [HEART] WITHIN THE COAL	THE SMOULDERING EMBERS	1132	2
HIS CHEEK IS HIS BIOGRAPHER--	HIS CHEEK IS HIS	1460	1
CHEEKED			
AND REDDER CHEEKED ONES--IN THEIR STEAD [PLACE]--	MY FIRST WELL DAY--SINCE	574	11
CHEEKS			
IT MOVED AWAY THE CHEEKS--	IT KNEW NO MEDICINE--	559	5
TO CUSHIONS CHEEKS--	IT CEASED TO HURT ME,	584	11
CHEER			
WE CHANT--FOR CHEER--WHEN THE WINES--FAIL--	WE--BEE AND I--LIVE BY	230	5
TO KEEP HERSELF IN CHEER--	I THINK I WAS ENCHANTED	593	14
AS FLAVORS--CHEER RETARDED GUESTS	UNTO MY BOOKS--SO GOOD	604	5
AND THEN THE CHEER TOO SOLEMN GREW	TWO TRAVELLERS PERISHING	933	7
HER UNDECAYING CHEER	THESE ARE THE SIGNS TO	1077	10
A BRIEF CAREER OF CHEER	A RAT SURRENDERED HERE	1340	2
CHEERED			
I CHEERED MY FAINTING PRINCE--	I ROSE--BECAUSE HE SANK	616	5
CHEERFUL			
CHEERFUL--AS TO THE VILLAGE--	WENT UP A YEAR THIS	93	5
CHEERS			
THREE CHEERS, SIR, FOR THE GENTLEMAN	"SIC TRANSIT GLORIA	3	11
CHEMICAL			
THE CHEMICAL CONVICTION	THE CHEMICAL CONVICTION	954	1
CHEMIST			
ONLY THE CHEMIST CAN DISCLOSE	ASHES DENOTE THAT FIRE	1063	7
THE HAPPY [THE CHEMIST / THE RANSOMED / A LOVER] MAY [CAN] REPAY,	THE FARTHEST THUNDER	1581	10
CHEMISTRY			
THEY PROVE ONE CHEMISTRY--	'TIS GOOD--THE LOOKING	660	V 12
CHERISH			
TO CHERISH, AND [RECOLLECT] TO WRITE	WE TALKED AS GIRLS DO--	586	14
MY STRONG MADONNAS--CHERISH STILL--	SWEET MOUNTAINS--YE TELL	722	7
LICENSE TO THINK OF [CHERISH] US--	WHATEVER IT IS--SHE HAS	1204	12
AND IMPOTENT TO CHERISH	TO DISAPPEAR ENHANCES--	1209	11
CHERISHED			
THE HEART I CARRIED [CHERISHED] IN MY OWN--	SAVIOR! I'VE NO ONE ELSE	217	9
HENCEFORWARD CHERISHED BE--	WHAT CARE THE DEAD, FOR	592	16
I CHERISHED THEM FOR ALL--	SHELLS FROM THE COAST	693	2
YOU CHERISHED"--"LEARNED WATERS--	THE SEA SAID "COME" TO	1210	7
THAT WHAT WE CHERISHED, SO UNKNOWN [VALUED SO DEVOID / HOARDED . . .	SO PROUD SHE WAS TO DIE	1272	3
BECOMES THAT CHERISHED [MAGIC] FACE	AN ANTIQUATED GRACE	1345	2
IS CHERISHED OF [BY] THE CROW	AN ANTIQUATED TREE	1514	2
FOREVER HONORED [CHERISHED] BE THE TREE	FOREVER HONORED BE THE	1570	1
CHERISHES			
IT CHERISHES BEFORE.	HAD THIS ONE DAY NOT	1253	8
CHERISHING			
CHERISHING--OUR POOR IDEAL--	TAKING UP THE FAIR IDEAL	428	9
DENIED THE CHERISHING	ENDOW THE LIVING--WITH	521	6
TILL THEY--THE CHERISHING DENY--	ENDOW THE LIVING--WITH	521	7
CAREFULLY CHERISHING THE SPOT	THIS IS A BLOSSOM OF THE	945	11
CHERRIES			
CHERRIES--SUIT ROBINS--	VICTORY COMES LATE--	690	11
CHERUBIC			
WHAT SOFT--CHERUBIC CREATURES--	WHAT SOFT--CHERUBIC	401	1
WITH HER CHERUBIC QUANTITY--	THE ROBIN IS THE ONE	828	7
CHERUBIM			
THE CHERUBIM--WITHDREW--	I MEANT TO HAVE BUT	476	14
AND CHERUBIM--AND SERAPHIM--	'TWAS A LONG PARTING--	625	15
THE CHERUBIM REVEAL--	SHALL I TAKE THEE, THE	1126	12
THAT WAFTS THE CHERUBIM.	NO LADDER NEEDS THE BIRD	1574	8
CHESTNUT			
THE CHESTNUT AGED GROWS	HOW FITS HIS UMBER COAT	1371	7
HIS LOTUS IS A CHESTNUT	THE JAY HIS CASTANET HAS	1635	6
CHID			
CHID MY PERFIDY--	DISTRUSTFUL OF THE	20	4
I WOKE--AND CHID MY HONEST FINGERS,	I HELD A JEWEL IN MY	245	5

	FIRST LINE	POEM	LINE
CHIEF			
IS NOTHING THAT IS CHIEF,	EMBARRASSMENT OF ONE	662	5
I WANT--WAS CHIEF IT SAID	"I WANT"--IT PLEADED--	731	2
A CHIEF INDIFFERENCE, AS FOREIGN	A SICKNESS OF THIS WORLD	1044	5
A LETTER CHIEF TO ME	MYSELF CAN READ THE	1089	2
AN ECSTASY IN CHIEF--	ONE OF THE ONES THAT	1466	12
'TIS PENURY IN CHIEF--	IT CAME HIS TURN TO BEG	1500	4
HOW CHIEF THY SESSIONS BE--	HOW MUCH OF SOURCE	1517	2
CHIEFER			
THE CHIEFER PART, FOR TIME--	SOME--WORK FOR	406	2
THAT CHIEFER TO THE SKIES	TO THIS WORLD SHE	830	6
CHIEFEST			
WHILE CHIEFEST--OF [IN] THE CROWD--	LIKE MIGHTY FOOT LIGHTS	595	6
THE CHIEFEST APPREHENSION	MY WORTHINESS IS ALL MY	751	7
BE WHOLLY [CHIEFEST / UTMOST] BEAUTIFUL--	I PLAY AT RICHES--TO	801	24
THE SHORTER FATE--IS OFTENER THE CHIEFEST	UNCERTAIN LEASE--	857	5
IS ESTEEMED IN HEAVEN THE CHIEFEST--	"UNTO ME?" I DO NOT KNOW	964	11
TOGETHER CHIEFEST [CHIEFLY] THEY ARE FOUND	AS OLD AS WOE--	1168	7
CHIEFLY			
WE CHIEFLY WONDER THEN	SO LARGE MY WILL	1024	14
TOGETHER CHIEFEST [CHIEFLY] THEY ARE FOUND	AS OLD AS WOE--	1168	7
WE CHIEFLY HAVE!	UNWORTHY OF HER BREAST	1414	6
CHILD			
PERMIT A CHILD TO JOIN.	THESE ARE THE DAYS WHEN	130	15
THAT EVER ROCKED A CHILD.	WHOSE ARE THE LITTLE	142	20
THOU SHALT--THYSELF--ONE DAY--A CHILD--	THE COURT IS FAR AWAY--	235	7
HALF CHILD--HALF HEROINE--	A MIEN TO MOVE A QUEEN--	283	2
BECAUSE IT WAS A CHILD, YOU KNOW--	ONE YEAR AGO--JOTS WHAT?	296	30
A SINGLE RAGGED CHILD--	A TONGUE--TO TELL HIM I	400	4
SO SOON TO BE A CHILD NO MORE--	A WIFE--AT DAYBREAK I	461	11
AS IF IT HELD BUT THE MIGHT OF A CHILD--	GOING TO HIM! HAPPY	494	13
AND EACH TO EACH, A CHILD--	WE LEARNED THE WHOLE OF	568	8
AS IF BEFORE A CHILD	MY FIRST WELL DAY--SINCE	574	14
"POOR CHILD"--AND SOMETHING IN HER VOICE	I CRIED AT PITY--NOT AT	588	3
FOR I WAS ONCE A CHILD--	IT TROUBLED ME AS ONCE I	600	2
AND YET I WAS A LIVING CHILD--	IT WOULD HAVE STARVED A	612	3
THE LOVE A LIFE [CHILD] CAN SHOW BELOW	THE LOVE A LIFE CAN SHOW	673	1
AS TRINKET--WORN BY FADED CHILD--	I'LL SEND THE FEATHER	687	4
IMPATIENT OF NO CHILD--	NATURE--THE GENTLEST	790	2
LOSE MY WAY LIKE A LITTLE CHILD	HOW HAPPY I WAS IF I	898	7
LEADS THE CHOSEN CHILD,	FAR FROM LOVE THE	1021	2
OBTAIN "ADMISSION" AS A CHILD	DEW--IS THE FRESHET IN	1097	11
WHEN BUT A LITTLE CHILD--	I NOTICED PEOPLE	1149	2
A FACT WITHELD THE LITTLE CHILD--	I NOTICED PEOPLE	1149	8
NOT ANY NEARER FOR THE CHILD	NOT ANY HIGHER STANDS	1256	3
WE [I] PONDERED WHEN A CHILD,	WHO WERE "THE FATHER AND	1258	2
BLISS IS THE PLAYTHING [TRINKET] OF THE CHILD--	BLISS IS THE PLAYTHING	1553	1
I DO REMEMBER WHEN A CHILD	OF DEATH I TRY TO THINK	1558	9
CHILDHOOD			
TODAY IS FAR FROM CHILDHOOD--	ONE SISTER HAVE I IN OUR	14	13
IN EVERLASTING KEEPSAKE [CHILDHOOD]--	THOSE FAIR--FICTITIOUS	499	7
MY CHILDHOOD, AND THE STRING OF SPOOLS,	I'M CEDED--I'VE STOPPED	508	6
BY CHILDHOOD [DISTANCE] FORTIFIED	WHO WERE "THE FATHER AND	1258	6
CHILDHOOD--SOME FORMS OF HOPE--THE DEAD--	THE THINGS THAT NEVER	1515	2
THAT ONLY CHILDHOOD KNOWS.	SWEET IS THE SWAMP WITH	1740	6
CHILDHOOD'S			
I FUMBLE AT MY CHILDHOOD'S PRAYER	A WIFE--AT DAYBREAK I	461	10
DIVINER THAN THE CHILDHOOD'S--	WE LEARNED THE WHOLE OF	568	7
'TIS "CONSCIENCE"--CHILDHOOD'S NURSE--	WHO IS IT SEEKS MY	1598	4
THAT THREATENED CHILDHOOD'S CITADEL	SOFTENED BY TIME'S	1738	3
THAT DEVASTATED CHILDHOOD'S REALM,	SOFTENED BY TIME'S	1738	7
CHILDISH			
BUT I TUG CHILDISH AT MY BARS	I NEVER HEAR THE WORD	77	7
AND SHOUTS FILL ALL MY CHILDISH SKY,	I HAVE A KING, WHO DOES	103	10
STRUCK UP MY CHILDISH	DELIGHT IS AS THE FLIGHT	257	13
AND I, MY CHILDISH PLUMES,	I DREADED THAT FIRST	348	26
BLAME THE LITTLE [EMPTY / CHILDISH] HAND	SWEET--YOU FORGOT--BUT I	523	6
EACH TIME MY CHILDISH EYE	I PRAYED, AT FIRST, A	576	6
IN CHILDISH [SOLEMN] HONESTY--	I PRAYED, AT FIRST, A	576	8
AS CONSTANT AS THE CHILDISH FROCK [GOWN]--	IT CEASED TO HURT ME,	584	7
THE CHILDISH HANDS THAT TEAZED FOR PENCE	THE BEGGAR LAD--DIES	717	13
CHILDREN			
THESE CHILDREN FLUTTERED HOME.	THROUGH LANE IT LAY--	9	17
THE CHILDREN OF WHOSE TURBANED SEAS--	SOME RAINBOW--COMING	64	23
BY WHICH CHILDREN SLOW	I CANT TELL YOU--BUT YOU	65	18
I HOPE THE "CHILDREN" THERE	"ARCTURUS" IS HIS OTHER	70	27
NEW CHILDREN PLAY UPON THE GREEN--	NEW FEET WITHIN MY	99	5
WHERE TIRED CHILDREN PLACID SLEEP	WHERE BELLS NO MORE	112	5
COULD THE CHILDREN FIND THE WAY THERE--	"HOUSES"--SO THE WISE	127	7
AS CHILDREN BID THE GUEST "GOOD NIGHT"	AS CHILDREN BID THE	133	1
AS CHILDREN CAPER WHEN THEY WAKE	AS CHILDREN BID THE	133	5
THIS COVERT HAVE ALL THE CHILDREN	SOME, TOO FRAGILE FOR	141	9
THE CHILDREN HURRY BY--	THERE'S BEEN A DEATH, IN	389	10
THE MANNER OF THE CHILDREN--	THE MONTHS HAVE ENDS--	423	9
AS CHILDREN--SWINDLED FOR THE FIRST	I MEANT TO HAVE BUT	476	27
AS CHILDREN, TO THE RAINBOW'S SCARF--	AS FAR FROM PITY, AS	496	7
SO--CHILDREN--TOLD HOW [ASSURED THAT] BROOKS IN EDEN--	BETTER--THAN MUSIC! FOR	503	9
CHILDREN--MATURED [GROWN UP]--ARE	BETTER--THAN MUSIC! FOR	503	13

	FIRST LINE	POEM		LINE
CHILDREN (CONTINUED)				
WISER--MOSTLY-- BUT CHILDREN ON THE DON,	I THINK THE HEMLOCK	525		14
FOR CHILDREN, MADE OF GOLD--	I CRIED AT PITY--NOT AT	588		12
THE WINDS--LIKE CHILDREN--LULLED--	THREE TIMES--WE PARTED--	598		14
SINCE WE--OLD MORNINGS, CHILDREN--PLAYED--	OF NEARNESS TO HER	607		11
OR HUMBLEST PATCHWORK--CHILDREN DO [MAY]--	AT LEISURE IS THE SOUL	618		7
TILL THE CHILDREN URGE [ASK]--	GLEE--THE GREAT STORM IS	619		11
AND THE CHILDREN--NO FURTHER QUESTION--	GLEE--THE GREAT STORM IS	619		16
WE PASSED THE SCHOOL, WHERE CHILDREN STROVE	BECAUSE I COULD NOT STOP	712		9
AMONG REDEEMED CHILDREN	THE BEGGAR LAD--DIES	717		9
WHEN ALL THE CHILDREN SLEEP--	NATURE--THE GENTLEST	790		17
AS CHILDREN, WHO REMAIN IN FACE	AWAY FROM HOME ARE SOME	821		7
A MOURNER WALKED [LURKED] AMONG THE CHILDREN	A LOSS OF SOMETHING EVER	959		5
LIKE CHILDREN ROUND A SIRE--	THE MOUNTAIN SAT UPON	975		6
THE TERROR [TRANSPORT] OF THE CHILDREN	THESE ARE THE NIGHTS	1128		5
AS LIGHTNING TO THE CHILDREN EASED	TELL ALL THE TRUTH BUT	1129		5
TO CHILDREN HE IS SMALL [LEAST] IN PRICE	THE MERCHANT OF THE	1131		5
AS CHILDREN STRICTEST [STRICTLY] KEPT	CONTAINED IN THIS SHORT	1165		5
BY SEASONS OR HIS CHILDREN--	THE WAY TO KNOW THE	1279		17
ISAAC--TO HIS CHILDREN	ABRAHAM TO KILL HIM	1317		9
TO HEAR THE CHILDREN PLAY	T'WAS COMFORT IN HER	1703		6
CHILDREN'S				
DISTRACTS THE CHILDREN'S FINGERS--	'TIS ONE BY ONE--THE	545		11
CHILD'S				
THE CHILD'S FAITH IS NEW--	THE CHILD'S FAITH IS NEW	637		1
IS LIKE THE CHILD'S ADVERSITY	THE GOING FROM A WORLD	1603		3
CHILL				
FIRST--CHILL--THEN STUPOR--THEN THE LETTING GO--	AFTER GREAT PAIN, A	341		13
A CHILL--LIKE FROST UPON A GLASS--	'TWAS WARM--AT FIRST--	519		3
THE DEWS DREW QUIVERING AND CHILL--	BECAUSE I COULD NOT STOP	712		14
THE FASCINATING CHILL THAT MUSIC LEAVES [OF MUSIC]	THE FASCINATING CHILL	1480		1
NO AUTUMN'S INTERCEPTING CHILL	NO AUTUMN'S INTERCEPTING	1516		1
NO AUTUMN'S INTERCEPTIVE CHILL,	HIS ORIENTAL HERESIES	1526	V	3
AND A CHILL [BLEAK] SMILE INLAID WITH BALMS--	ABOVE OBLIVION'S TIDE	1531	V	4
AND A GREEN CHILL UPON THE HEAT	THERE CAME A WIND LIKE A	1593		3
A CHILL CAME UP AS FROM A SHAFT	A CAP OF LEAD ACROSS THE	1649		5
CHILLED				
CHILLED--OR WEARY--	JUST SO--JESUS--RAPS--	317		8
CHILLEST				
I'VE HEARD IT IN THE CHILLEST LAND--	"HOPE" IS THE THING WITH	254		9
CHILLY				
SNOW BENEATH WHOSE CHILLY SOFTNESS	SNOW BENEATH WHOSE	942		1
A CHILLY [LONESOME / WARNING] PEACE INFESTS THE GRASS	A CHILLY PEACE INFESTS	1443		1
CHIMBORAZO				
TAKING TURNS--AT THE CHIMBORAZO--	LOVE--THOU ART HIGH--	453		5
CHIME				
CHIME [STRIKE]--NOON!	IT'S LIKE THE LIGHT--	297		12
CHIMNEY				
CHARGED, FROM MY CHIMNEY CORNER--	THE SUN KEPT STOOPING--	152		13
IN HIS CHIMNEY CORNER STAY,	I'M THE LITTLE "HEART'S	176		6
THE PATTERN OF A CHIMNEY--	THE ANGLE OF A LANDSCAPE	375		9
THE CHIMNEY--AND THE HILL--	THE ANGLE OF A LANDSCAPE	375		18
WHOSE CHIMNEY NEVER SMOKED--	A HOUSE UPON THE HIGHT--	399		5
BY CHIMNEY--NOR BY DOOR	MY PERIOD HAD COME FOR	564		10
OVER THE COMET'S CHIMNEY--	UNDER THE LIGHT, YET	949		11
CHIN				
IT VARIES--IN THE CHIN--	YOU KNOW THAT PORTRAIT	504		6
THE MOON WAS BUT A CHIN OF GOLD	THE MOON WAS BUT A CHIN	737		1
CHINK				
POSSESSION--HAS A SWEETER CHINK	BECAUSE 'TWAS RICHES I	1093		7
CHINTZ				
IN PLACID [CHINTZ AND] LILY SLEEPS!	A LADY RED--AMID THE	74		4
AND IN CHINTZ [RED / PINK] THE APPLE	I SUPPOSE THE TIME WILL	1381		8
CHIPS				
AND CHIPS OF BLANK--IN BOYISH EYES--	MY PORTION IS DEFEAT--	639		10
CHIRPING				
IT WAS AS IF A CHIRPING BROOK	HEART, NOT SO HEAVY AS	83		13
CHIRRUPT SEE A'CHIRRUPT				
CHISELLED				
AND CHISELLED ALL MY TUNE	I'VE DROPPED MY BRAIN--	1046		14
CHIVALRIES				
BY CHIVALRIES AS TINY,	BY CHIVALRIES AS TINY,	55		1
CHIVALRY				
NATURE IN CHIVALRY--	GARLANDS FOR QUEENS, MAY	34		6
THEIR CHIVALRY CONSUMES--	LIKE TRAINS OF CARS ON	1224		6
WHEN DISCIPLINE [CHIVALRY / TYRANNY] WAS DONE	THE THINGS WE THOUGHT	1293		10
PARAGON OF CHIVALRY.	RECOLLECT THE FACE OF ME	1305		8
BY ARM OF CHIVALRY.	THE FLAKE THE WIND	1361		4
CHOICE				
BY MY OWN CHOICE, AND THEE--	TIE THE STRINGS TO MY	279		12
WHEN CHOICE OF LIFE--IS PAST--	THE MANNER OF IT'S DEATH	468		5
BAPTIZED, BEFORE, WITHOUT THE CHOICE,	I'M CEDED--I'VE STOPPED	508		8
CHOIRS				
MURMURING, LIKE OLD CASPIAN CHOIRS,	MANY A PHRASE HAS THE	276		5
CHOOSE				
JOVE! CHOOSE YOUR COUNSEL--	I HAD SOME THINGS THAT I	116		15

	FIRST LINE	POEM	LINE
CHOOSE (CONTINUED)			
LET ME--CHOOSE!	ONE YEAR AGO--JOTS WHAT?	296	36
CHOOSE ONE--	THE SOUL SELECTS HER OWN	303	10
CHOOSE THE ENVOY--AND SPURN THE GROOM--	GOD IS A DISTANT--	357	6
I WOULD NOT CHOOSE--A BOOK TO KNOW	NOT IN THIS WORLD TO SEE	418	8
OR ETNA'S SCARLETS, CHOOSE--	MORE LIFE--WENT OUT--	422	20
'TIS DEEMED A PRIVILEGE TO CHOOSE--	THE MANNER OF IT'S DEATH	468	3
SO SEEMED TO CHOOSE MY DOOR--	EXCEPT THE HEAVEN HAD	472	2
WITH WILL [POWER] TO CHOOSE, OR TO REJECT,	I'M CEDED--I'VE STOPPED	508	18
AND I CHOOSE, JUST A CROWN [THRONE]--	I'M CEDED--I'VE STOPPED	508	19
AND WHETHER--COULD THEY CHOOSE BETWEEN--	I MEASURE EVERY GRIEF I	561	11
"WHICH CHOOSE I"?	THE FIRST DAY THAT I WAS	902	13
"WHICH CHOOSE THEY"?	THE FIRST DAY THAT I WAS	902	15
COMPELLING HIM TO CHOOSE HIMSELF	EXPERIENCE IS THE ANGLED	910	7
TOO LATE TO CHOOSE AGAIN.	WHICH IS BEST? HEAVEN--	1012	9
I THOUGHT YOU'D CHOOSE A VELVET CHEEK	THEMSELF ARE ALL I HAVE	1094	3
SO BLIND WITH [FULL OF] JOY HE COULD NOT CHOOSE	THE BIRD DID PRANCE--THE	1107	3
TILL WHAT WE COULD NOT SEE [FACE / CHOOSE / PROVE] HAS COME . . .	THE MURMURING OF BEES,	1115	V 13
THE FACE WE CHOOSE TO MISS--	THE FACE WE CHOOSE TO	1141	1
AS IF FOR YOU TO CHOOSE--	BEFORE YOU THOUGHT OF	1465	10
AN ACRE FOR A BIRD TO CHOOSE	ON MY VOLCANO GROWS THE	1677	3
CHOOSES			
CHOOSES IT'S LATCH, FROM ALL THE OTHER FASTENINGS--	IT'S COMING--THE	390	3
AND CHOOSES WAINSCOT IN THE BREAST	GRIEF IS A MOUSE--	793	2
CHOOSING			
SO CHOOSING BUT A GOWN--	I HAD NO CAUSE TO BE	542	17
RENUNCIATION--IS THE CHOOSING	RENUNCIATION--IS A	745	10
BUT FOR MINOR [INNER] CHOOSING--	ONE AND ONE--ARE ONE--	769	4
CHORALS			
WAIT YOUR CHORALS--	SANG FROM THE HEART,	1059	14
CHORISTER			
WITH A BOBOLINK FOR A CHORISTER--	SOME KEEP THE SABBATH	324	3
CHOSE			
I CHOSE THIS SINGLE STAR	ONE SISTER HAVE I IN OUR	14	25
THE GRACE THAT I--WAS CHOSE--	THE DAY THAT I WAS	356	13
I CHOSE--DAY--	GOOD MORNING--MIDNIGHT--	425	14
TO THAT MUNIFICENCE, THAT CHOSE--	THE WORLD--STANDS--	493	11
HE CHOSE--MATURITY--	HE GAVE AWAY HIS LIFE--	567	12
YOU CHOSE THE NEWER NAMES [TIMES]--	YOU'LL FIND--IT WHEN YOU	610	8
COCHINEAL--I CHOSE--FOR DEEMING	AUTUMN--OVERLOOKED MY	748	5
. . . CHOSE [SIGNED]--	NO NOTICE GAVE SHE, BUT	804	17
BUT CHOSE THE BEST--NEGLECTING ME--TILL	MY WARS ARE LAID AWAY IN	1549	7
CHOSEN			
"THEY HAVE NOT CHOSEN ME," HE SAID,	"THEY HAVE NOT CHOSEN ME	85	1
"BUT I HAVE CHOSEN THEM!"	"THEY HAVE NOT CHOSEN ME	85	2
OR PLAYED HIS CHOSEN TUNE--	ALTHOUGH I PUT AWAY HIS	366	8
THE BLAME THAT I WAS CHOSEN [COMMON]--THEN--	FITTER TO SEE HIM, I MAY	968	8
LEADS THE CHOSEN CHILD,	FAR FROM LOVE THE	1021	2
CHRIST			
CHRIST ROBS THE NEST--	DUST IS THE ONLY SECRET	153	14
CHRIST WILL EXPLAIN EACH SEPARATE ANGUISH	I SHALL KNOW WHY--WHEN	193	3
LONG AGO AS CHRIST AND PETER--	HE FORGOT--AND I--	203	3
JUST SO--JESUS [CHRIST]--RAPS--	JUST SO--JESUS--RAPS--	317	1
SAY, JESUS CHRIST OF NAZARETH--	AT LEAST--TO PRAY--IS	502	7
FORGET IT--LORD [CHRIST]--OF THEM--	'TIS TRUE--THEY SHUT ME	538	4
CHRIST--OMITTED--ME--	PROMISE THIS--WHEN YOU	648	28
CHRIST--STOOPED UNTIL HE TOUCHED THE GRAVE--	PERHAPS YOU THINK ME	833	3
CHRISTIAN			
THROUGHOUT A CHRISTIAN LAND--	THE SPIDER AS AN ARTIST	1275	6
CHRISTMAS			
BEFORE THE CHRISTMAS TREE,	BEFORE THE ICE IS IN THE	37	6
AND WOULD IT BLUR THE CHRISTMAS GLEE	'TWAS JUST THIS TIME,	445	17
OR BEES, AT CHRISTMAS SHOW--	AS SLEIGH BELLS SEEM IN	981	2
CHRIST'S			
CHRIST'S ACQUAINTANCE WITH HIM	LIFE--IS WHAT WE MAKE IT	698	3
OF ME--IN CHRIST'S BRIGHT AUDIENCE [LATITUDE]	YOU TAUGHT ME WAITING	740	11
CHRIST'S BIRTHDAY	THE SAVIOR MUST HAVE	1487	T
'TWAS CHRIST'S OWN PERSONAL EXPANSE	OBTAINING BUT OUR OWN	1543	3
CHRONICLE			
IN SILVER CHRONICLE.	THE ROBIN FOR THE CRUMB	864	4
CHRYSALIS			
AN HOUR IN CHRYSALIS TO PASS,	COCOON ABOVE! COCOON	129	7
THEN SUNRISE KISSED MY CHRYSALIS--	THREE TIMES--WE PARTED--	598	15
CHRYSALIS OF BLONDE--OR UMBER--	COLOR--CASTE--	970	11
CHRYSOLITE			
SHOULD SWING THEIR CUPS OF CHRYSOLITE--	THERE IS A MORN BY MEN	24	17
WITH CUFFS OF CHRYSOLITE!	IT CANT BE "SUMMER"!	221	10
CHRYSOPHRAS			
WITH CHRYSOPHRAS, INLAID.	HIS FEET ARE SHOD WITH	916	4
CHRYSOPRASE			
IN CHRYSOPRASE APARTMENTS [APARTMENT] HUNG	THE BUTTERFLY'S	1244	2
CHUBBY			
AND CHUBBY DAFFODIL.	WHOSE ARE THE LITTLE	142	16
CHUCKLED			
THE CREATURES CHUCKLED ON THE ROOFS--	AN AWFUL TEMPEST MASHED	198	5
CHUCKLES			
SHE SIGHTS A BIRD--SHE CHUCKLES--	SHE SIGHTS A BIRD--SHE	507	1

	FIRST LINE	POEM	LINE
CHUMS			
BY CHUMS THAT PASSED AWAY--	MY WARS ARE LAID AWAY IN	1549	10
CHURCH			
EACH WAS TO EACH THE SEALED CHURCH,	THERE CAME A DAY AT	322	13
SOME KEEP THE SABBATH GOING TO CHURCH--	SOME KEEP THE SABBATH	324	1
AND INSTEAD OF TOLLING THE BELL, FOR CHURCH,	SOME KEEP THE SABBATH	324	7
NOT SUCH A STRAIN--THE CHURCH--BAPTIZES--	BETTER--THAN MUSIC! FOR	503	17
WITH WATER, IN THE COUNTRY CHURCH	I'M CEDED--I'VE STOPPED	508	3
WHEN BELLS STOP RINGING--CHURCH--BEGINS--	WHEN BELLS STOP RINGING	633	1
AND DOME [SPIRE / CHURCH]--AND WINDOW PANE--	THE DAY UNDRESSED--	716	16
AND POSSIBLY A CHURCH--	HAVE ANY LIKE MYSELF	736	4
CONFORM MY SOUL--AS TWERE A CHURCH,	MY WORTHINESS IS ALL MY	751	15
AS A CHURCH REMAIN--	WHEN I HOPED I FEARED--	1181	4
CHURCHES			
THE CHURCHES ARE SO FREQUENT--	THE SWEETEST HERESY	387	5
CHURCHYARD			
TILL ALL THE CHURCHYARD RANG;	A TRAIN WENT THROUGH A	1761	4
CICATRICE			
THE CICATRICE OF YEARS--	HE TOLD A HOMELY TALE	763	4
CIGAR			
FROM MY BROWN CIGAR.	MANY CROSS THE RHINE	123	4
CIMITAR			
NOR PIERCE WITH CIMITAR--	NO RACK CAN TORTURE ME--	384	6
CINDER			
HOW THE DUN BRAKE IS DRAPED IN CINDER [TIPPED IN TINSEL]	HOW THE OLD MOUNTAINS	291	3
CINDERELLA'S			
AS CINDERELLA'S BAYS--	LIKE SOME OLD FASHIONED	302	6
CINNAMON			
OF SYCAMORE--OR CINNAMON--	WHAT CARE THE DEAD, FOR	592	21
CIPHER SEE CYPHER			
AND CIPHER AT THE SIGN	MY COCOON TIGHTENS--	1099	10
CIPHERS			
MY FIGURES FILE [CIPHERS STEAL] AWAY.	LOW AT MY PROBLEM	69	6
CIRCASSIAN			
OR WHAT CIRCASSIAN LAND?	SOME RAINBOW--COMING	64	24
IF CIRCASSIAN--HE IS CARELESS--	COLOR--CASTE--	970	9
CIRCLE			
OR A CIRCLE HESITATE	CRISIS IS A HAIR	889	11
CIRCUIT			
THAT MAKE THE CIRCUIT OF THE REST--	HE PUT THE BELT AROUND	273	11
MY LITTLE CIRCUIT WOULD HAVE SHAMED	I SHOULD HAVE BEEN TOO	313	4
BUT A DEMURER CIRCUIT [MEASURE]--	A PRISON GETS TO BE A	652	15
EXIST AN [FULFILLED THEIR] ORIENTAL CIRCUIT	THIS QUIET DUST WAS	813	7
SUCCESS IN CIRCUIT LIES	TELL ALL THE TRUTH BUT	1129	2
INTENT UPON IT'S OWN CAREER [MISSION QUAINT / CIRCUIT QUAINT]	HOW SOFT A CATERPILLAR	1448	7
THEY MAKE THEIR CIRCUIT FAIR	NO MATTER WHERE THE	1541	2
NO CIRCUIT SAGE OF ALL THE COURSE [LINES]	OH FUTURE! THOU SECRETED	1631	5
ITS CIRCUIT JUST THE SAME	A PIT--BUT HEAVEN OVER	1712	15
CIRCUMFERENCE			
THIS NEW CIRCUMFERENCE--HAVE BLAMED--	I SHOULD HAVE BEEN TOO	313	5
IN PURPOSELESS CIRCUMFERENCE--	FROM COCOON FORTH A	354	16
WENT OUT UPON CIRCUMFERENCE--	I SAW NO WAY--THE	378	7
CIRCUMFERENCE BE FULL--	NO CROWD THAT HAS	515	5
AND THEN ESPIED [THEN OVERTOOK--] CIRCUMFERENCE	TWO BUTTERFLIES WENT OUT	533 V	3
CIRCUMFERENCE--DECAY [ARRAY]--	AN IGNORANCE A SUNSET	552	4
WHEN COGS--STOP--THAT'S CIRCUMFERENCE--	WHEN BELLS STOP RINGING	633	3
AND NOW, AMONG CIRCUMFERENCE--	SHE STAKED HER FEATHERS	798	5
I FEAR ME THIS CIRCUMFERENCE	TIME FEELS SO VAST THAT	802	3
CIRCUMFERENCE--	THE POETS LIGHT BUT	883	8
IN CIRCUMFERENCE	CRISIS IS A HAIR	889	12
CIRCUMFERENCE WITHOUT RELIEF--	A COFFIN--IS A SMALL	943	11
THE MINUTE CIRCUMFERENCE	PAIN--EXPANDS THE TIME--	967	3
CIRCUMFERENCE BETWEEN.	AT HALF PAST THREE, A	1084	12
THE BILLOWS OF CIRCUMFERENCE	A SINGLE CLOVER PLANK	1343	7
CIRCUMFERENCE THOU BRIDE OF AWE	CIRCUMFERENCE THOU BRIDE	1620	1
HE CARRIES A CIRCUMFERENCE	HIS MIND OF MAN, A	1663	3
CIRCUMSCRIBES			
SIZE CIRCUMSCRIBES--IT HAS NO ROOM	SIZE CIRCUMSCRIBES--IT	641	1
CIRCUMSCRIPTION			
CIRCUMSCRIPTION--ENABLES WO--	BOUND--A TROUBLE--	269 V	
CIRCUMSPECT			
OF SUMMER'S CIRCUMSPECT.	THE MUSHROOM IS THE ELF	1298	16
THE CIRCUMSPECT ARE CERTAIN	THE BUTTERFLY OBTAINS	1685	7
CIRCUMSTANCE			
A CIRCUMSTANCE OR TWO!	"SOWN IN DISHONOR"!	62	10
FOR CIRCUMSTANCE THE SAME--	I HAD NO CAUSE TO BE	542	12
REPORT BY SIGN A CIRCUMSTANCE	THE FUTURE--NEVER SPOKE	672 V	3
IS AN UNFURNISHED CIRCUMSTANCE	TO OWN THE ART WITHIN	855	5
SINCE NO ONE KNOWS HIS CIRCUMSTANCE--	WHO OCCUPIES THIS HOUSE?	892	3
THE MINOR CIRCUMSTANCE	BLOOM--IS RESULT--TO	1058	4
OR CIRCUMSTANCE OF LOT	THERE IS ANOTHER	1116	4
ALONE AND IN [OF] A CIRCUMSTANCE	ALONE AND IN A	1167	1
EACH CIRCUMSTANCE UNKNOWN,	LONGING IS LIKE THE SEED	1255	6
OR CIRCUMSTANCE PRUDENTIAL	I SEND YOU A DECREPIT	1324	7
CIRCUMSTANCES			
ESCAPE FROM CIRCUMSTANCES--	FOR DEATH--OR RATHER	382	7
ALL CIRCUMSTANCES ARE THE FRAME	ALL CIRCUMSTANCES ARE	820	1

	FIRST LINE	POEM	LINE
CIRCUMSTANCES (CONTINUED)			
IN HUMBLE CIRCUMSTANCES--	THE ROBIN IS A GABRIEL	1483	2
CIRCUMVENT			
TO SOUND OR CIRCUMVENT--	THE RAT IS THE CONCISEST	1356	6
CIRCUMVENTION			
THE CIRCUMVENTION OF THE SHAFT [THOUGHT / SITE / FACT]	AS SUMMER INTO AUTUMN	1346	11
CITADEL			
BUT EVERY MESH--A CITADEL--	I HAD NOT MINDED--WALLS	398	15
HER CEDAR CITADEL.	FALSEHOOD OF THEE COULD	1007	4
ESCAPE--IT IS THE BASKET [CITADEL]	ESCAPE IS SUCH A	1347	5
OR FAME ERECT HER SITELESS CITADEL	SOCIETY FOR ME MY MISERY	1534	V
THAT THREATENED CHILDHOOD'S CITADEL	SOFTENED BY TIME'S	1738	3
CITADELS			
CITADELS--DISSOLVED--	ALL BUT DEATH, CAN BE	749	4
CITE			
WITH WHICH WE CITE THIS MIGHTIEST CASE	"REMEMBER ME" IMPLORED	1180	7
THE ONES THAT [WHO] CITE HER MOST	WHAT MYSTERY PERVADES A	1400	18
CITES			
AS JESUS CITES [SAYS] OF HIM--	TO HER DERIDED HOME	1586	10
CITIES			
AND CITIES--OOZE [SLIP / SLIDE / MELT] AWAY--	A STILL--VOLCANO--LIFE--	601	12
BEFORE--WERE CITIES--BUT BETWEEN--	OUR JOURNEY HAD ADVANCED	615	7
CITIZEN			
A TRACT OF CITIZEN--	MORE LIFE--WENT OUT--	422	16
HAVE MISSED [LOST] A BAREFOOT CITIZEN--	HE TOLD A HOMELY TALE	763	15
OF EVERY CITIZEN.	WHO OCCUPIES THIS HOUSE?	892	28
A CITIZEN [RUDIMENT] OF PARADISE	A COFFIN--IS A SMALL	943	3
WHERE EACH IS CITIZEN--	THE BIRD DID PRANCE--THE	1107	8
BEHOLD OUR [MY / THIS] SPACIOUS CITIZEN	NATURE AFFECTS TO BE	1170	7
THE SMALLEST CITIZEN THAT FLIES	A SAUCER HOLDS A CUP	1374	15
CITY			
OUTSIDE THE CASTLE [CENTRE / CITY]--THAT CONTAIN [PRESENT]--	THE SPIRIT IS THE	733	7
CIVIC			
SO CIVIC AS THE JAY--	NO BRIGADIER THROUGHOUT	1561	2
CIVILITY			
FOR HIS CIVILITY--	BECAUSE I COULD NOT STOP	712	8
CIVILIZATION			
CIVILIZATION--SPURNS--THE LEOPARD!	CIVILIZATION--SPURNS--	492	1
CLAD			
STILL--CLAD IN YOUR MAIL OF ICES--	AH, TENERIFFE!	666	6
AND CREATURES CLAD IN MIRACLE [VICTORY]	'TIS ANGUISH GRANDER	984	7
CLAIM			
AND CLAIM THE RANK TO DIE!	ONE DIGNITY DELAYS FOR	98	16
TILL, RECENTLY A RIVAL CLAIM	I HAD SOME THINGS THAT I	116	3
PRESENTS A CLAIM INVISIBLE--	I LIVE WITH HIM--I SEE	463	7
OF HER FATHER--WHOSO ASK [CLAIM] HER--	HER SWEET TURN TO LEAVE	649	17
WITH ARTICLES OF CLAIM	ALONE AND IN A	1167	10
CLAIMED			
AS GIANTS--GONE [CLAIMED] AWAY--	HAD I PRESUMED TO HOPE--	522	4
CLAIMS			
THE WORM DOTH WOO THE MORTAL, DEATH CLAIMS A LIVING BRIDE,	AWAKE YE MUSES NINE,	1	21
HE CLAIMS THE PRETTY ACRE,	I HAD SOME THINGS THAT I	116	7
TODAY'S--HAVE VASTER CLAIMS [FORM]--	I COULD NOT PROVE THE	563	8
CLAMBERED			
NOVEMBER LEFT--THEN CLAMBERED UP	THE NIGHT WAS WIDE, AND	589	7
CLAMOR			
THE CLAMOR FOR THEIR LOVELINESS	COULD THAT SWEET	1493	3
AND EVERY CLAMOR BRIGHT	THE FARTHEST THUNDER	1581	14
CLAMORING			
THE CLAMORING FOR GOLD--	I PLAY AT RICHES--TO	801	2
CLAMORS			
THAT CLAMORS FOR HIS HEAD--	THE DOOMED--REGARD THE	294	8
CLANS			
AS THRONGS [CLANS] OF DOWN--	DEATH IS THE SUPPLE	1445	12
CLAP			
I CLAP MY HANDS TO SEE--	A SOMETHING IN A	122	9
CLAPS			
CLAPS MY MURMURING LIP!	IF I SHOULD CEASE TO	56	8
CLARIFIED			
AS DIFFICULT [CLARIFIED]	MUST BE A WO--	571	7
WHEN CONSTANCY IS CLARIFIED	HOW HUMAN NATURE DOTES	1417	7
CLARIFIES			
THAT CLARIFIES THE SIGHT	BY A DEPARTING LIGHT	1714	5
CLARIFY			
TO CLARIFY THE SIGHT	OF THEIR PECULIAR LIGHT	1362	3
CLARIFYING			
AND CLARIFYING SCENERY	HOW LONESOME THE WIND	1418	8
CLASP			
WHEN KATIE KNEELS, THEIR LOVING HANDS STILL CLASP HER PIOUS KNEE--	WHEN KATIE WALKS, THIS	222	3
TO CLASP HER SOUL--FOR ALL--	THE WORLD--STANDS--	493	8
I ALMOST STROVE TO CLASP HIS HAND,	I TRIED TO THINK A	532	16
CLASP HEMISPHERES, AND HOMES	THE SUNRISE RUNS FOR	710	14
CLASPED			
CLASPED YET--TO HIM--AND ME--	NOT IN THIS WORLD TO SEE	418	6
NOR IS IT CLASPED UNTO OF BAND--	YOU'LL KNOW HER--BY HER	634	19
HIS BILL IS CLASPED [LOCKED]--HIS EYE	HIS BILL IS CLASPED--HIS	1102	1

	FIRST LINE	POEM	LINE
CLASPED (CONTINUED)			
FORSOOK [ESTRANGED]--			
CLASPS			
OR CLASPS A ROCK, WITH BOTH HIS HANDS--	THE BLACK BERRY--WEARS A	554	7
CLASS			
AND HAS HER IN A "CLASS"!	"ARCTURUS" IS HIS OTHER	70	12
ANOTHER CLASS REMIND ME [REMINDS ME OF]	A LITTLE DOG THAT WAGS	1185	13
CLASSES			
OF TRANSPORT'S WORKING CLASSES--	THE ROBIN IS A GABRIEL	1483	4
CLASSICS			
MY CLASSICS VAIL THEIR FACES--	THE FEET OF PEOPLE	7	21
CLASSIFY			
IF THE SAVANS "CLASSIFY" THEM	IF THE FOOLISH, CALL	168	3
CLASSIFYING			
DEATH'S DIVINER CLASSIFYING	COLOR--CASTE--	970	3
CLAUS			
FOR ANY SANTA CLAUS TO REACH	'TWAS JUST THIS TIME,	445	19
CLAUSE			
ANNIHILATE A SINGLE CLAUSE--	TO LOSE ONE'S FAITH--	377	7
IN IT'S EXTREMEST CLAUSE--	I READ MY SENTENCE--	412	4
FROM [OF / IN] THE HEAVENLY CLAUSE--	"FAITHFUL TO THE END"	1357	2
CLAW			
ONE CLAW UPON THE AIR,	I CANNOT DANCE UPON MY	326	12
UPON ME--LIKE A CLAW--	IT WOULD HAVE STARVED A	612	5
AND THEN A LIVID TOE [CLAW]--	THE WIND BEGUN TO KNEAD	824	12
THE INSTANT HOLDING IN IT'S CLAW	'TWAS CRISIS--ALL THE	948	5
OFTENER BY THE CLAW OF DRAGON	FAR FROM LOVE THE	1021	5
PROPITIATION'S CLAW--	IN WINTER IN MY ROOM	1670	23
CLAWED			
A BURDOCK--CLAWED [TWITCHED] MY GOWN--	A BURDOCK--CLAWED MY	229	1
CLAWS			
THE CLAWS THAT CLUNG, LIKE LIFELESS GLOVES	HIS BILL IS CLASPED--HIS	1102	3
CLAY			
TO SUCH A MODEST CLAY,	WAIT TILL THE MAJESTY OF	171	14
THEY SLINK BEFORE THE CLAY,	A SINGLE SCREW OF FLESH	263	18
TO ALL THE LISTS OF CLAY!	OF ALL THE SOULS THAT	664	12
AN OVERCOAT OF CLAY.	DEATH IS A DIALOGUE	976	8
WHEN CONSCIOUSNESS AND CLAY	POWER IS A FAMILIAR	1238	6
BLUSH, MY UNACKNOWLEDGED CLAY--	REARRANGE A "WIFE'S"	1737	6
CLEAN			
AS CLEAN AS FIRE	PERIL AS A POSSESSION	1678	7
CLEAR			
SO CLEAR OF VICTORY	SUCCESS IS COUNTED	67	8
BURST AGONIZED AND CLEAR!	SUCCESS IS COUNTED	67	12
BY FAITH MAY CLEAR BEHOLD	WE SHOULD NOT MIND SO	81	10
CLEAR STRAINS OF HYMN	READ--SWEET--HOW OTHERS	260	10
THOUGH WINTER FIRE--SING CLEAR AS PLOVER--	IT'S THOUGHTS--AND JUST	495	15
BUT CALLED THE OTHERS--CLEAR--	I HAD NO CAUSE TO BE	542	5
PRESERVED THE CHARM [VISION SURE / VISION CLEAR] SECURE	HAVE ANY LIKE MYSELF	736	18
WE DISTINGUISH CLEAR--	THE ADMIRATIONS--AND	906	6
THE CRICKET SPOKE SO CLEAR	AS IMPERCEPTIBLY AS	1540	V
CLEARED			
THE SMOKE ALL CLEARED AWAY FROM IT--	WHEN WE STAND ON THE	242	3
CLEARER			
I SEE THEE CLEARER FOR THE GRAVE	I SEE THEE CLEARER FOR	1666	1
CLEARING			
THROUGH CLEARING AND THRO' WOOD--	THROUGH LANE IT LAY--	9	2
A CLEARING AT THE END--	MY WHEEL IS IN THE DARK!	10	8
CLEAVE			
AND SLOWNESS--THEN THE SCAFFOLDS DROP [SCAFFOLDS CLEAVE / . . .	THE PROPS ASSIST THE	1142	11
CLEAVES			
LAST TO ADHERE [AT THE SCENE] WHEN SUMMER CLEAVES [SUMMER . . .	AFTER ALL BIRDS HAVE	1395	7
CLEAVING			
I FELT A CLEAVING IN MY MIND--	I FELT A CLEAVING IN MY	937	1
CLEF			
TO FIT SOME CRUCIFIXAL CLEF--	THE MORNING AFTER WO--	364	15
CLEMATIS			
CLEMATIS--JOURNEYING FAR--	'TIS CUSTOMARY AS WE	440	6
CLEMENCY			
A CLEMENCY SO COMMON--	THE HEAVEN VESTS FOR	694	13
THE CLEMENCY OF DEITY	ELIZABETH TOLD ESSEX	1321	3
CLEOPATRA'S			
LIKE CLEOPATRA'S COMPANY--	THE TINT I CANNOT TAKE--	627	7
CLERGYMAN			
GOD PREACHES, A NOTED CLERGYMAN--	SOME KEEP THE SABBATH	324	9
CLERGYMEN			
CLERGYMEN SAY--	WE DONT CRY--TIM AND I,	196	22
CLERKS			
AND CLERKS IN COUNTING ROOMS	YOU'VE SEEN BALLOONS SET	700	19
CLICK			
NO START [CLICK] IN APPREHENSION'S EAR,	I THINK TO LIVE--MAY BE	646	15
AND CLICK [BOLT]--AND SUDDENNESS.	THE SOUL'S DISTINCT	974	8
CLIMATE			
THE CLIMATE OF THE GRAVE	MORE LIFE--WENT OUT--	422	6
CONJECTURING A CLIMATE	CONJECTURING A CLIMATE	562	1
CLIMB			
APPROACH THAT TREE WITH CAUTION, THEN	AWAKE YE MUSES NINE,	1	35

	FIRST LINE	POEM	LINE
CLIMB (CONTINUED)			
UP IT BOLDLY CLIMB,			
I CLIMB THE "HILL OF SCIENCE,"	"SIC TRANSIT GLORIA	3	21
"OH COULD WE CLIMB WHERE MOSES STOOD,	WHERE BELLS NO MORE	112	9
OR IF IT DARE--TO CLIMB YOUR DIZZY KNEE--	WHAT SHALL I DO--IT	186	10
I COULD CLIMB--IF I TRIED, I KNOW--	OVER THE FENCE--	251	4
HE'D--CLIMB--IF HE COULD!	OVER THE FENCE--	251	9
THEY STRIVE TO CLIMB--IN VAIN--	THE LONESOME FOR THEY	262	6
"WOULD'ST CLIMB," I [HE] SAID?	I SHOWED HER HIGHTS SHE	446	2
I CANNOT CLIMB THEE--	LOVE--THOU ART HIGH--	453	2
NOR CLIMB THE BARS OF ECSTASY,	GO NOT TOO NEAR A HOUSE	1434	6
SOFTLY CLIMB	THE PILE OF YEARS IS NOT	1507	V
AM I INCLINED TO CLIMB	VOLCANOES BE IN SICILY	1705	6
CLIMBED			
HAVE CLIMBED THE DISTANT HILL--	DELAYED TILL SHE HAD	58	9
WHO NEVER CLIMBED THE WEARY LEAGUE--	WHO NEVER LOST, ARE	73	5
WE KNOW [SAY] HE HAS CLIMBED A FIR--	THE WIND DID'NT COME	316	8
CLIMBING			
WERE CLIMBING ALL THE WHILE--	I'LL TELL YOU HOW THE	318	12
BY CLIMBING SLOW--	I GAINED IT SO--	359	2
CLIMBING TO REACH [WHO "MEDDLED" WITH] THE COSTLY HEARTS	CLIMBING TO REACH THE	1566	1
FOR CLIMBING IT ALONE?	THE GOING FROM A WORLD	1603	8
CLIMBS			
SOFTLY MY FUTURE CLIMBS THE STAIR,	A WIFE--AT DAYBREAK I	461	9
CLIME			
THE HOUR, AND THE CLIME [ZONE]--	LONGING IS LIKE THE SEED	1255	5
ALIEN AND VAIN WHATEVER CLIME	FRIGID AND SWEET HER	1318	3
THE GREAT EXCHANGE OF CLIME--	WERE NATURE MORTAL LADY	1762	4
CLIMES			
ON THEIR WAY TO YELLOWER CLIMES--	I SHALL KEEP SINGING!	250	3
NO ALMANACS--NOR CLIMES--	ALONE, I CANNOT BE--	298	6
FROM HEAVY LADEN LANDS [CLIMES] TO THEE	THE BIRD DID PRANCE--THE	1107	9
CLING			
I CLING TO NOWHERE TILL I FALL--	MORE THAN THE GRAVE IS	1503	4
CLIPT			
TILL BULLETS CLIPT AN ANGLE	WHEN I WAS SMALL, A	596	7
CLOAK			
A BLACK--AS OF A SPECTRE'S CLOAK	AN AWFUL TEMPEST MASHED	198	3
CLOCK			
A CLOCK STOPPED--	A CLOCK STOPPED--	287	1
WITH JUST A CLOCK--	I KNOW SOME LONELY	289	14
AND THE OLD CLOCK KEPT NEIGHING "DAY"!	GOING TO HIM! HAPPY	494	19
BEHIND THE MOST UNCONSCIOUS [CONSUMMATE] CLOCK	NOT TO DISCOVER WEAKNESS	1054	7
AND YET WE KNEW THAT GENTLE CLOCK	'TWAS LATER WHEN THE	1276	3
WHOSE AMPLITUDE NO END [CLOCK] INVADES--	WATER MAKES MANY BEDS	1428	7
AND THE HOOFS OF THE CLOCK--	WE TALKED WITH EACH	1473	4
THE CLOCK STRIKES ONE THAT JUST STRUCK TWO--	THE CLOCK STRIKES ONE	1569	1
TO HEAR THE LIVING CLOCK	T'WAS COMFORT IN HER	1703	2
CONSULTING SUMMER'S CLOCK,	CONSULTING SUMMER'S	1715	1
CLOCKS			
TILL THOSE TWO TROUBLED--LITTLE CLOCKS	THE ROSE DID CAPER ON	208	15
AND THE EVERLASTING CLOCKS--	IT'S LIKE THE LIGHT--	297	11
HOW ALL THE CLOCKS STOPPED IN THE WORLD--	IF I MAY HAVE IT, WHEN	577	16
BY CLOCKS, 'TWAS MORNING, AND FOR NIGHT	GREAT STREETS OF SILENCE	1159	5
CLOG			
VITALITY TO CLOG	SEVERER SERVICE OF	786	12
THAT IT WOULD CLOG THE COGS	DID LIFE'S PENURIOUS	1717	5
CLOSE			
MY VELVET LIFE TO CLOSE--	IF SHE HAD BEEN THE	44	4
CLOSE TO THE TWO I LOST--	GOING TO HEAVEN!	79	15
AND SHUT THE WINDOWS DOWN SO CLOSE	BRING ME THE SUNSET IN A	128	20
AT DAY'S SUPERIOR CLOSE!	ME, CHANGE! ME, ALTER!	268	6
THEN--CLOSE THE VALVES [LIDS] OF HER ATTENTION--	THE SOUL SELECTS HER OWN	303	11
THE LITTLE TRACKS--CLOSE PREST--	'TWAS THE OLD--ROAD--	344	8
THE SOUL SO CLOSE ON PARADISE--	NOT PROBABLE--THE BAREST	346	4
I FELT THE COLUMNS CLOSE--	I SAW NO WAY--THE	378	2
AND CHATTED CLOSE WITH THIS GRAND THING	IF ANYBODY'S FRIEND BE	509	19
AND HE--HE FOLLOWED--CLOSE BEHIND--	I STARTED EARLY--TOOK MY	520	17
BUT NOT THE GRIEF--THAT NESTLED CLOSE	IT CEASED TO HURT ME,	584	9
TO OUR ENDEAVOR--NOT SO REAL [TRUE / CLOSE / NEAR]	A PRISON GETS TO BE A	652	19
SO CLOSE ON PARADISE--	I SOMETIMES DROP IT, FOR	708	12
THEN, DARLING, IT WILL CLOSE	THIS CHASM, SWEET, UPON	858	10
THE OPENING AND THE CLOSE	THE OPENING AND THE	1047	1
TOO NEAR [CLOSE] THOU ART FOR FAME--	THE BIRD DID PRANCE--THE	1107	12
STANDS THE SUN SO CLOSE AND MIGHTY	WE LIKE MARCH.	1213	8
TO PILE LIKE THUNDER TO IT'S CLOSE	TO PILE LIKE THUNDER TO	1247	1
THE LAST [CLOSE] OF SUMMER IS DELIGHT--[A TIME / RESULT--SURVEY]	THE LAST OF SUMMER IS	1353	1
WHOSE PINK CAREER MAY HAVE A CLOSE	WHOSE PINK CAREER MAY	1394	1
CAN STAND SO CLOSE AND LOOK SO BOLD	WHAT MYSTERY PERVADES A	1400	11
IS PUSHING [ROAMING / PLODDING / STARING / AMBLING] CLOSE BEHIND	ALL THAT I DO	1496	6
OF SWARTHY DAYS HE IS THE CLOSE [KNELL]	THE JAY HIS CASTANET HAS	1635	5
SHE DWELT SO CLOSE	TO-DAY OR THIS NOON	1702	2
MY LIFE CLOSED TWICE BEFORE ITS CLOSE;	MY LIFE CLOSED TWICE	1732	1
AT NIGHT'S DELICIOUS CLOSE.	THE SADDEST NOISE, THE	1764	4
THAT, FAITHFUL TO THE CLOSE,	THOSE FINAL CREATURES,--	1766	2

	FIRST LINE	POEM	LINE
CLOSED			
THEN--REVELATION CLOSED--	WE LEARNED THE WHOLE OF	568	4
HOW THE WATERS CLOSED ABOVE HIM	HOW THE WATERS CLOSED	923	1
THE SUMMER CLOSED UPON ITSELF	MIDSUMMER, WAS IT, WHEN	962	3
WAS IGNORANT THAT NATURE CLOSED	IT BLOOMED AND DROPT, A	978	V 19
THE WAY IS CLOSED THEY CAME.	THIS IS THE PLACE THEY	1264	8
MORE THAN THE GRAVE IS CLOSED TO ME--	MORE THAN THE GRAVE IS	1503	1
MY LIFE CLOSED TWICE BEFORE ITS CLOSE;	MY LIFE CLOSED TWICE	1732	1
CLOSELY			
AND YET--INSPECTED CLOSELY	HOPE IS A SUBTLE GLUTTON	1547	3
CLOSER			
AND CLOSER TO THE FIRE--	THE NIGHT WAS WIDE, AND	589	14
CLOSER--SO I--AT MY SLEEPING [SIGHING]--	DONT PUT UP MY THREAD &	617	19
BUT AS SHE CLOSER STANDS--	YOU'LL KNOW HER--BY HER	634	16
SHONE CLOSER BY--	I CANNOT LIVE WITH YOU--	640	28
BUT NEARER [CLOSER / FURTHER / SIMPLY / MERELY] TO ADORE	BECAUSE HE LOVES HER	1229	10
PERHAPS COME [COMES] CLOSER, FOR THE LAPSE [FLIGHT]	PERHAPS THEY DO NOT GO	1399	3
THE WINDS CAME CLOSER UP--	AS IMPERCEPTIBLY AS	1540	V
CLOSES			
AND THEN--HE CLOSES UP--	HE PARTS HIMSELF--LIKE	517	2
THEN--THE LICENSE [VISION / PAGEANT] CLOSES--	SOME SUCH BUTTERFLY BE	541	4
AND THEN IT CLOSES AT YOUR FEET	A NARROW FELLOW IN THE	986	7
OF THE HEART THAT GOES IN, AND CLOSES THE DOOR	OF THE HEART THAT GOES	1098	1
CLOSES THE [HIS] SHUTTER AND GOES IN--	HOW LONESOME THE WIND	1418	4
CLOSET			
UPON THE CLOSET SHELVES--	DEATH SETS A THING	360	12
WITHIN HIS CLOSET--BEST YOU CAN	EXHILIRATION--IS WITHIN	383	11
IT'S TEMPLE [CLOSET] STANDS, ALWAY,	THE BODY GROWS WITHOUT--	578	4
THEY PUT ME IN THE CLOSET--	THEY SHUT ME UP IN PROSE	613	3
THAT SACRED CLOSET WHEN YOU SWEEP--	THAT SACRED CLOSET WHEN	1273	1
CLOSING			
TO EYES THAT CLOSING GO--	DISTRUSTFUL OF THE	20	14
THE CLOSING OF HER EYES--	SHE HIDETH HER THE LAST	557	4
UPON HIS BREAST, A CLOSING SOUL	THIS IS A BLOSSOM OF THE	945	15
A CLOSING OF THE SIMPLE LID [GATE]	A GREAT HOPE FELL	1123	14
INQUIRE OF THE PROUDEST [FULLEST / CLOSING] ROSE	CRISIS IS SWEET AND YET	1416	5
TILL WITH THE SETTING [CLOSING] SUN	IT WAS A QUIET SEEMING	1419	3
CLOTH			
WHO SPUN THE AUBURN CLOTH?	HOW FITS HIS UMBER COAT	1371	5
CLOTHES			
IN THOSE PRIMEVAL CLOTHES--	HOW FITS HIS UMBER COAT	1371	8
OF THEIR [HER] CORPOREAL CLOTHES--	PERHAPS THEY DO NOT GO	1399	4
A FADED BOY--IN SALLOW CLOTHES	A FADED BOY--IN SALLOW	1524	1
CLOUD			
THE COLOR, ON THE CRUISING CLOUD--	"HEAVEN"--IS WHAT I	239	5
A MEMBER OF THE CLOUD.	HE PUT THE BELT AROUND	273	8
MY BUSINESS, WITH THE CLOUD,	I GOT SO I COULD HEAR	293	21
WITH AN OPPOSING CLOUD--	FROM COCOON FORTH A	354	13
AS IF THE CLOUD THAT INSTANT SLIT	IT STRUCK ME--EVERY DAY	362	3
THAT OFTEN AS A CLOUD IT MET--	THE NIGHT WAS WIDE, AND	589	3
AND HAD [OWNED] ESTATES OF CLOUD	THE TREES LIKE TASSELS--	606	12
AND NEXT--I MET HER ON A CLOUD--	I WATCHED THE MOON	629	33
A CLOUD THE MIGHTY SUN ENCLOSES	A SHADE UPON THE MIND	882	3
A CLOUD WITHDREW FROM THE SKY	A CLOUD WITHDREW FROM	895	1
BUT THAT CLOUD AND IT'S AUXILIARIES	A CLOUD WITHDREW FROM	895	3
UPON A WHEEL OF CLOUD.	LIKE RAIN IT SOUNDED	1235	16
THE POPPY [WARRANT] IN THE CLOUD	IT WAS A QUIET SEEMING	1419	12
BY MILLINERY OF THE CLOUD	SUMMER BEGINS TO HAVE	1682	6
THE SUN RETIRED TO A CLOUD	THE SUN RETIRED TO A	1693	1
VOLCANIC CLOUD	THE WIND DREW OFF	1694	5
A CURIOUS CLOUD SURPRISED THE SKY,	A CURIOUS CLOUD	1710	1
CLOUDIER			
THEN CLOUDIER BECOME--	I'VE SEEN A DYING EYE	547	4
CLOUDING			
TO THE FAILING [DYING / CLOUDING] EYE	ROBBED BY DEATH--BUT	971	2
CLOUDS			
THE CLOUDS--LIKE LISTLESS ELEPHANTS--	ON THIS LONG STORM THE	194	3
THE CLOUDS WERE GAUNT, AND FEW--	AN AWFUL TEMPEST MASHED	198	2
AS BIRDS--THAT TUMBLE FROM THE CLOUDS	THE LONESOME FOR THEY	262	7
THEN--TO THE ROYAL CLOUDS	THE NEAREST DREAM	319	7
AND WHEN--SOME NIGHT--BOLD--SLASHING CLOUDS	YOU KNOW THAT PORTRAIT	504	13
GREAT CLOUDS--LIKE USHERS--LEANING [PLACING]--	DEPARTED--TO THE	524	3
SOME CARNIVALS OF CLOUDS--	"HEAVEN" HAS DIFFERENT	575	12
AND MEASURES WITH THE CLOUDS	OF BEING IS A BIRD	653	6
BEHIND INFERIOR CLOUDS--OR ROUND	I MAKE HIS CRESCENT FILL	909	7
THE SKY IS LOW--THE CLOUDS ARE MEAN.	THE SKY IS LOW--THE	1075	1
THE CLOUDS THEIR BACKS TOGETHER LAID	THE CLOUDS THEIR BACKS	1172	1
CLOVE			
CLOVE TO THE ROOT [CORE]--	NO BOBOLINK--REVERSE HIS	755	5
CLOVEN			
WERE CLOVEN WITH AN ADZE--	WE MET AS SPARKS--	958	4
CLOVER			
WHICH IN THE CLOVER DWELL.	IT'S ALL I HAVE TO BRING	26	8
THE CLOVER BELLS FORGOT.	"ARCTURUS" IS HIS OTHER	70	16
UNTIL THE BEES, FROM CLOVER ROWS	PERHAPS YOU'D LIKE TO	134	7
STOOPS--TO AN EASY CLOVER--	THE NEAREST DREAM	319	5
THE CLOVER WARM AND THICK--	BEE! I'M EXPECTING YOU!	1035	8

	FIRST LINE	POEM		LINE
CLOVER (CONTINUED)				
WHAT TENEMENTS OF CLOVER	WHAT TENEMENTS OF CLOVER	1338		1
A SINGLE CLOVER PLANK [SPAR]	A SINGLE CLOVER PLANK	1343		1
AND [HE] PANTING [HEAVY / LANGUID] ON A CLOVER LEAN	THE BUTTERFLY'S NUMIDIAN	1387		5
FATIGUED AT LAST, A CLOVER PLAIN [LOW]	HIS ORIENTAL HERESIES	1526		5
A CLOVER, ANY TIME, TO HIM,	THE PEDIGREE OF HONEY	1627	V	3
TO MAKE A PRAIRIE IT TAKES A CLOVER AND ONE BEE,	TO MAKE A PRAIRIE IT	1755		1
ONE CLOVER, AND A BEE,	TO MAKE A PRAIRIE IT	1755		2
CLOVER'S				
UNDER THE CLOVER'S ROOT [FOOT],	UNDER THE LIGHT, YET	949		4
THE [A] CLOVER'S SIMPLE FAME	THE CLOVER'S SIMPLE FAME	1232		1
OR CLOVER'S RETROSPECT--	A FADED BOY--IN SALLOW	1524		8
CLOVERS				
ASK THE JOLLY CLOVERS!	WE--BEE AND I--LIVE BY	230		7
I'D DAISIES SPURN [CLOVERS--SCORN]--	THE ROBIN'S MY CRITERION	285		9
IF HE BRING ODORS OF CLOVERS--	THE WIND DID'NT COME	316		11
THE CLOVERS--UNDERSTOOD--	FROM COCOON FORTH A	354		8
OF CLOVERS, AND OF NOON!	HIS FEET ARE SHOD WITH	916		8
CLOWN				
BUT GOD BE WITH THE CLOWN--	A LITTLE MADNESS IN THE	1333		3
CLOY				
AND [OR] IN THE DESERT--CLOY--	I THINK THE HEMLOCK	525		6
CLUB				
NOT WITH A CLUB, THE HEART IS BROKEN	NOT WITH A CLUB, THE	1304		1
CLUE				
I TAKE THE CLUE DIVINE--	MY COCOON TIGHTENS--	1099		12
CLUMSY				
REFERS MY CLUMSY [DULLER] EYE--	WITHIN MY GARDEN, RIDES	500		18
CLUNG				
THE CLAWS THAT CLUNG, LIKE LIFELESS GLOVES	HIS BILL IS CLASPED--HIS	1102		3
CLUSTER				
GREENER LEAN--OR FONDER CLUSTER [LATER LINGER]	PROMISE THIS--WHEN YOU	648		23
NO CLUSTER--YE [YOU] SHALL FIND--	EXCEPT THE SMALLER SIZE	1067	V	
BUT FROM LIFE'S CONSUMMATE CLUSTER--	DEATH'S WAYLAYING NOT	1296		7
CLUSTERS				
STRONG CLUSTERS, FROM BARABBAS' TOMB--	TO PUT THIS WORLD DOWN,	527		11
CLUTCH				
LOOK, HOW I CLUTCH IT	I GAINED IT SO--	359		10
I'LL CLUTCH--AND CLUTCH--	I'LL CLUTCH--AND CLUTCH	427		1
I'LL CLUTCH--AND CLUTCH--	I'LL CLUTCH--AND CLUTCH	427		1
WITHIN THE CLUTCH OF THOUGHT--	I TRIED TO THINK A	532		9
WE CLUTCH THE GRACE THE TIGHTER	LIKE TIME'S INSIDIOUS	1236		3
UNTIL CONSTRAINED TO CLUTCH IT	OF DEATH I TRY TO THINK	1558		14
WHICH QUESTION SHALL I CLUTCH--	STILL OWN THEE--STILL	1633		5
CLUTCHED				
CLUTCHED TIGHT, BY GREEDY HANDS--	THERE CAME A DAY AT	322		18
I CLUTCHED AT SOUNDS--	IT WOULD NEVER BE COMMON	430		25
THE BOLDEST [BRAVEST] LEAPED, AND CLUTCHED IT--	OF DEATH I TRY TO THINK	1558		16
COACH				
COACH, IT INSURES, AND FOOTMEN--	ONE DIGNITY DELAYS FOR	98		5
I QUESTION IF THE ROYAL COACH	I MET A KING THIS	166		25
AND WE ARE WAITING FOR THE COACH--	I THINK THE LONGEST HOUR	635		3
HORSES OF BLONDE--AND COACH OF SILVER--	DROPPED INTO THE ETHER	665		5
PREVAIL UPON THE COACH--	GO SLOW, MY SOUL, TO	1297		4
AND A BISECTED COACH	DEATH IS THE SUPPLE	1445		8
COACHES				
OF TASSELS--AND OF COACHES--SOON--	THERE'S BEEN A DEATH, IN	389		21
HUM BY--IN MUFFLED COACHES--	SWEET--SAFE--HOUSES--	457		14
COAL				
AS CARBON IN THE COAL	THE DAY THAT I WAS	356		5
OH CHEEK [HEART] WITHIN THE COAL	THE SMOULDERING EMBERS	1132		2
COALS				
COALS--FROM A ROLLING [PASSING] LOAD--RATTLE--HOW--NEAR--	I COULD DIE--TO KNOW--	570		9
COAST				
THAT LICKED IT FROM THE COAST--	'TWAS SUCH A LITTLE--	107		6
TURNED SLOWLY TO HIS NATIVE COAST--	AN AWFUL TEMPEST MASHED	198		12
ENDEAR THE SHORE [COAST] BEYOND--	I SHOULD HAVE BEEN TOO	313		21
SHELLS FROM THE COAST MISTAKING--	SHELLS FROM THE COAST	693		1
COAT				
TO HIM WHOM NEVER RAGGED--COAT	THE BEGGAR LAD--DIES	717		15
HOW FITS HIS UMBER COAT	HOW FITS HIS UMBER COAT	1371		1
WHOSE COAT OF ELEMENTAL BROWN	HOW HAPPY IS THE LITTLE	1510		5
WHOSE CORPORATION [UNSUSPECTING / WELL INTENTIONED] COAT	AN ANTIQUATED TREE	1514		5
A BETTER COAT IF HE POSSESSED	TO TRY TO SPEAK, AND	1617		5
AND WEARS A PROPER COAT	THE BUTTERFLY OBTAINS	1685		6
BESTIRS ITSELF--PUTS ON IT'S COAT,	THE SUMMER THAT WE DID	1773		5
COAX				
THAN I COULD COAX A LEECH AWAY--[MODIFY A LEECH]	IT WOULD HAVE STARVED A	612		7
SINCE A RACK COULD'NT COAX A SYLLABLE [AN ANSWER]--NOW	GRIEF IS A MOUSE--	793		17
COBWEB				
YOU--TOO--TAKE COBWEB ATTITUDES	TO HANG OUR HEAD--	105		7
FEARLESS--THE COBWEB SWINGS FROM THE CEILING--	HOW MANY TIMES THESE LOW	187		11
A COBWEB--WOVE IN ADAMANT--	I HAD NOT MINDED--WALLS	398		11

	FIRST LINE	POEM	LINE
COBWEB (CONTINUED)			
'TIS FIRST A COBWEB ON THE SOUL	CRUMBLING IS NOT AN	997	5
COCHINEAL			
PURPLE AND COCHINEAL	LIKE HER THE SAINTS	60	5
CAN BLAZE BE SHOWN [DONE] IN COCHINEAL--	I FOUND THE WORDS TO	581	7
COCHINEAL--I CHOSE--FOR DEEMING	AUTUMN--OVERLOOKED MY	748	5
PARDON THE COCHINEAL--	SANG FROM THE HEART,	1059	5
A RUSH OF COCHINEAL--	A ROUTE OF EVANESCENCE	1463	4
COCKADE			
WHO ONCE THE COCKADE WORE--	THE SUN KEPT STOOPING--	152	12
COCKS			
THE BUSY CARTS--THE FRAGRANT COCKS--	I'M SORRY FOR THE DEAD--	529	11
COCOA			
TILL HE ESTEEM HIS DATES AND COCOA	AS THE STARVED MAELSTROM	872	11
COCOON			
SO FROM COCOON	SO FROM THE MOULD	66	6
COCOON ABOVE! COCOON BELOW!	COCOON ABOVE! COCOON	129	1
COCOON ABOVE! COCOON BELOW!	COCOON ABOVE! COCOON	129	1
STEALTHY COCOON, WHY HIDE YOU SO	COCOON ABOVE! COCOON	129	2
FROM COCOON FORTH A BUTTERFLY	FROM COCOON FORTH A	354	1
AN ABBEY--A COCOON--	HE PARTS HIMSELF--LIKE	517	20
MY COCOON TIGHTENS--COLORS TEAZE--	MY COCOON TIGHTENS--	1099	1
CODES			
OF BLISS THE CODES [THE IMPLEMENTS OF BLISS] ARE FEW--	TO HER DERIDED HOME	1586	9
CODICIL			
WITH THAT OLD CODICIL OF DOUBT?	WHICH IS BEST? HEAVEN--	1012	3
CO-ETERNITY			
A CO-ETERNITY--	TRUTH--IS AS OLD AS GOD	836	4
COEVAL			
RUDDY AS THAT COEVAL APPLE	TELL AS A MARKSMAN--WERE	1152	3
OR LOVE--THE TWO COEVAL COME--	TO PILE LIKE THUNDER TO	1247	5
COEVAL CARDINAL--	IMAGE OF LIGHT, ADIEU--	1556	5
COFFEE			
IN A COFFEE CUP,	IS IT TRUE, DEAR SUE?	218	6
COFFERS			
AND COFFERS HEAPED WITH TEARS!	FOR EACH EXTATIC INSTANT	125	8
COFFIN			
THERE WERE JUST SUCH COFFIN	IT DID NOT SURPRISE ME--	39	15
A COFFIN--IS A SMALL DOMAIN,	A COFFIN--IS A SMALL	943	1
COGS			
WHEN COGS--STOP--THAT'S CIRCUMFERENCE--	WHEN BELLS STOP RINGING	633	3
THAT IT WOULD CLOG THE COGS	DID LIFE'S PENURIOUS	1717	5
COHERE			
TO WHOM NOT ANY FACE COHERE [PRESENT / PROPOUND]--	HOW FIRM ETERNITY MUST	1499	7
COHESIVE			
COHESIVE AS THE SPIRIT	A WORD MADE FLESH IS	1651	11
COIL			
HIS YARN [COIL] OF PEARL--UNWINDS [EXPENDS]--	THE SPIDER HOLDS A	605	4
AGES COIL [LURK] WITHIN	PAIN--EXPANDS THE TIME--	967	2
COIN			
IS THAT OLD-FASHIONED COIN	LUCK IS NOT CHANCE--	1350	6
COINS			
NOT WITH COINS--THOUGH THEY BE MINTED	PROMISE THIS--WHEN YOU	648	5
COLD			
THOU ART A HUMAN SOLO, A BEING COLD, AND LONE,	AWAKE YE MUSES NINE,	1	27
OR PERPLEXED--OR COLD--	I OFTEN PASSED THE	51	14
ARE SO SUPERFLUOUS COLD--	I BRING AN UNACCUSTOMED	132	10
BEFORE THEIR FEET ARE COLD.	SOME, TOO FRAGILE FOR	141	4
EARLY AGED, AND OFTEN COLD,	SOME, TOO FRAGILE FOR	141	10
THE TRUTH, IS BALD, AND COLD--	'TIS SO APPALLING--IT	281	9
THE COLD WILL FORCE YOUR TIGHTEST DOOR	ALTHOUGH I PUT AWAY HIS	366	26
A POWER OF RENOWNED COLD,	MORE LIFE--WENT OUT--	422	5
AND ADD "HOW COLD--IT GREW"--	I AM ALIVE--I GUESS--	470	14
THE FINGERS GREW TOO COLD	'TWAS WARM--AT FIRST--	519	6
IT CROWDED COLD TO COLD--	'TWAS WARM--AT FIRST--	519	10
IT CROWDED COLD TO COLD--	'TWAS WARM--AT FIRST--	519	10
THE HEMLOCK'S NATURE THRIVES--ON COLD--	I THINK THE HEMLOCK	525	9
'TIS TRUE--THEY SHUT ME IN THE COLD--	'TIS TRUE--THEY SHUT ME	538	1
THERE'S GRIEF OF WANT--AND GRIEF OF COLD--	I MEASURE EVERY GRIEF I	561	29
TO PALLIATE A COLD--	CONJECTURING A CLIMATE	562	6
AND SUNSHINE PINCHED ME--'TWAS SO COLD--	IF I MAY HAVE IT, WHEN	577	17
IT'S SOMEWHAT IN THE COLD--	THE BEGGAR LAD--DIES	717	2
I KNEW NO MORE OF WANT--OR COLD--	ONE BLESSING HAD I THAN	756	9
NOR SCRUPULOUS OF COLD	NO NOTICE GAVE SHE, BUT	804	6
THEY'LL RECOLLECT HOW COLD I LOOKED	THEY WONT FROWN ALWAYS--	874	3
AND PERISH OF THE COLD.	HOW HAPPY I WAS IF I	898	8
TOO COLD IS THIS	TOO COLD IS THIS	1135	1
BUT WITH ITSELF DID COLD ENGAGE [COMMUNE]	A WIND THAT ROSE	1259	4
TO COME SO FAR SO COLD A DAY	THE SAVIOR MUST HAVE	1487	3
TWO DESERTS BUT THE YEAR IS COLD	I DID NOT REACH THEE	1664	7
COLONNADE			
A MIST'S SLOW COLONNADE--	I MAKE HIS CRESCENT FILL	909	8
COLOR			
THE COLOR, ON THE CRUISING CLOUD--	"HEAVEN"--IS WHAT I	239	5
WITHOUT A COLOR, BUT THE LIGHT	DARE YOU SEE A SOUL AT	365	7
THE COLOR OF THE GRAVE IS GREEN--	THE COLOR OF THE GRAVE	411	1
THE COLOR OF THE GRAVE IS WHITE--	THE COLOR OF THE GRAVE	411	9
THE COLOR OF THE GRAVE WITHIN--	THE COLOR OF THE GRAVE	411	17

	FIRST LINE	POEM	LINE
COLOR (CONTINUED)			
YOU'VE SEEN THE COLOR--MAYBE--	THE COLOR OF THE GRAVE	411	21
OF TERRITORY--COLOR--	AN IGNORANCE A SUNSET	552	3
THE COLOR TOO REMOTE	THE TINT I CANNOT TAKE--	627	2
THE VERY COLOR OF MY HAIR--	PRECIOUS TO ME--SHE	727	4
THE COLOR OF A QUEEN, IS THIS--	THE COLOR OF A QUEEN, IS	776	1
THE COLOR OF A SUN	THE COLOR OF A QUEEN, IS	776	2
AND FORGET THE COLOR [FIGURE] OF THE DAY--	SEVERER SERVICE OF	786	16
A COLOR STANDS ABROAD	A LIGHT EXISTS IN SPRING	812	5
COLOR--CASTE--DENOMINATION--	COLOR--CASTE--	970	1
NO COLOR IN THE RAINBOW	THE DYING NEED BUT	1026	7
NOT ANY COLOR WILL ENDURE	JUDGEMENT IS JUSTEST	1671	8
OR DEEPER COLOR IN THE SHAWL	SUMMER BEGINS TO HAVE	1682	7
COLORED SEE MANY-COLORED			
FLUNG COLORED, AFTER RAIN,	DELIGHT IS AS THE FLIGHT	257	6
THEN NATURE RAISED A COLORED HAND	A DROP FELL ON THE APPLE	794	V 15
BOUNTIFUL COLORED, MY MORNING ROSE	AND THIS OF ALL MY HOPES	913	3
ON THE WORLD YOU COLORED	ON THE WORLD YOU COLORED	1171	1
COLOR'S			
WHILE COLOR'S REVELATIONS BREAK--	AS FAR FROM PITY, AS	496	11
COLORS			
HOW MANY COLORS TAKEN	WHO NEVER LOST, ARE	73	11
THE COLORS OF THE COMMONEST--	YOUR RICHES--TAUGHT ME--	299	11
COLORS--FROM VERA CRUZ--	I COULD BRING YOU JEWELS	697	4
WASTES OF LIVES--RESOWN WITH COLORS	ALL BUT DEATH, CAN BE	749	5
MY COCOON TIGHTENS--COLORS TEAZE--	MY COCOON TIGHTENS--	1099	1
COLOSSAL			
OF THE COLOSSAL SUBSTANCE	THE SOUL'S SUPERIOR	306	15
COLUMBA			
COURAGE! MY BRAVE COLUMBA!	ONCE MORE, MY NOW	48	7
COLUMBINE			
AND FOR COLUMBINE--	ALL THESE MY BANNERS BE.	22	15
COLUMBUS			
IT WAS THE BRAVE COLUMBUS,	"SIC TRANSIT GLORIA	3	37
'TWAS THIS--ALLURED COLUMBUS--	TRUST IN THE UNEXPECTED	555	9
COLUMNAR			
ON A COLUMNAR SELF--	ON A COLUMNAR SELF--	789	1
COLUMNS			
I FELT THE COLUMNS CLOSE--	I SAW NO WAY--THE	378	2
LIKE COLUMNS--IN THE BREAST--	THE TINT I CANNOT TAKE--	627	V 16
WOULD PIERCE HIS COLUMNS THRO'--	"RED SEA," INDEED! TALK	1642	4
COMB			
WHOSE FINGERS COMB [BRUSH] THE SKY--	OF ALL THE SOUNDS	321	6
THE GRASS DIVIDES AS WITH A COMB--	A NARROW FELLOW IN THE	986	5
COMBINATION			
A COMBINATION IS	SEPTEMBER'S	1271	2
COMBINE			
IS FLAVORLESS--COMBINE	IMPOSSIBILITY, LIKE WINE	838	4
COMBINED			
CONTAINED [COMBINED / COMPRISED] IN THIS SHORT [PLAIN] LIFE	CONTAINED IN THIS SHORT	1165	1
ALONE--TOO ACRID--BUT COMBINED	SURPRISE IS LIKE A	1306	3
COMBINED WITHOUT A SEAM	HOW FITS HIS UMBER COAT	1371	3
COMBINEDLY			
COMBINEDLY ALIGHTING--	A BEE HIS BURNISHED	1339	3
COMBINES			
A THUNDER STORM COMBINES THE CHARMS	A CAP OF LEAD ACROSS THE	1649	7
COME			
INTO MY GARDEN COME!	THERE IS ANOTHER SKY,	2	14
AND COME AWAY WITH ME,	"SIC TRANSIT GLORIA	3	18
THE VALLEY MURMURED "COME"--	THROUGH LANE IT LAY--	9	14
WILL SURELY COME AGAIN.	I KEEP MY PLEDGE.	46	11
IN WHICH MY CALL WOULD COME--	I OFTEN PASSED THE	51	6
THE DAISIES DARE TO COME HERE--	I OFTEN PASSED THE	51	11
WONT BE "NEW FASHIONED" WHEN I COME--	"ARCTURUS" IS HIS OTHER	70	28
TOMORROW, NIGHT WILL COME AGAIN--	HEART, NOT SO HEAVY AS	83	17
BUMBLEBEES COME--	SOUTH WINDS JOSTLE THEM	86	2
THE BROOKS LAUGH LOUDER WHEN I COME--	THE BEE IS NOT AFRAID OF	111	5
THESE ARE THE DAYS WHEN BIRDS COME BACK--	THESE ARE THE DAYS WHEN	130	1
AND COME NEXT HOUR TO LOOK.	I BRING AN UNACCUSTOMED	132	7
AND THE SNOWS COME HURRYING FROM THE HILLS,	HAVE YOU GOT A BROOK IN	136	11
TILL DAFFODILS HAD COME AND GONE	SHE BORE IT TILL THE	144	5
WHEN THE ROBINS COME,	IF I SHOULD'NT BE ALIVE	182	2
SHALL [MAY] IT COME?	WHAT SHALL I DO--IT	186	13
LET'S PLAY THOSE--NEVER COME!	MAKE ME A PICTURE OF THE	188	14
NO FEAR OF FROST TO COME	FOR THIS--ACCEPTED	195	10
SO SURE I'D COME--SO SURE I'D COME--	I SHOULD NOT DARE TO	205	10
SO SURE I'D COME--SO SURE I'D COME--	I SHOULD NOT DARE TO	205	10
COME SLOWLY--EDEN!	COME SLOWLY--EDEN!	211	1
FROM MANZANILLA COME!	I TASTE A LIQUOR NEVER	214	16
I SHOULD'NT LIKE TO COME	IS IT TRUE, DEAR SUE?	218	3
HIST! WHIST! I'D COME!	IS IT TRUE, DEAR SUE?	218	11
COME BACK, AND DUST THE POND!	SHE SWEEPS WITH	219	4
AND THEN I COME AWAY--	SHE SWEEPS WITH	219	12
UNLESS THEY DID'NT COME--	I'VE NOTHING ELSE--TO	224	6
SUPPOSED THAT HE HAD COME TO DWELL--	THE SUN--JUST TOUCHED	232	3
TOO PLUMMETLESS--THAT IT COME BACK [RETURN]--	A SOLEMN THING--IT WAS--	271	7
YET NOT TOO FAR [NEAR ENOUGH--] TO COME AT CALL--	HE PUT THE BELT AROUND	273	9
AND SO OF WO, BLEAK DREADED--COME,	'TIS SO APPALLING--IT	281	21

	FIRST LINE	POEM	LINE
COME (CONTINUED)			
THE WIND DID'NT COME FROM THE ORCHARD--TODAY--	THE WIND DID'NT COME	316	1
I COULD NOT BEAR THE BEES SHOULD COME,	I DREADED THAT FIRST	348	17
THE SURGEON, WILL NOT COME--	ALTHOUGH I PUT AWAY HIS	366	23
AS ONE SHOULD COME TO TOWN--	A PRECIOUS--MOULDERING	371	22
THAT WHEN THE HILLS--COME DOWN--	A TONGUE--TO TELL HIM I	400	23
THE FIRST DAY'S NIGHT HAD COME--	THE FIRST DAY'S NIGHT	410	1
OR STAR--COME OUT--WITHIN--	WE GROW ACCUSTOMED TO	419	12
ME--COME! MY DAZZLED FACE	ME--COME! MY DAZZLED	431	1
AND LIKE A HOST--"COME IN"	THE WIND--TAPPED LIKE A	436	2
THE TYRIAN WOULD NOT COME	GOD MADE A LITTLE	442	10
THEMSELF, SHOULD COME TO ME--	'TWAS JUST THIS TIME,	445	24
NO BOLD SICKNESS COME	SWEET--SAFE--HOUSES--	457	11
AND PEOPLE COME--	WE DO NOT PLAY ON GRAVES	467	4
SO VISITORS MAY COME--	I AM ALIVE--I GUESS--	470	12
EXCEPT THE HEAVEN HAD COME SO NEAR--	EXCEPT THE HEAVEN HAD	472	1
AND BELLS--THAT BOLDLY RING [COME]	I ENVY SEAS, WHEREON HE	498	18
THE WAY OURSELF, MUST COME--	THOSE FAIR--FICTITIOUS	499	24
INTO THIS PORT, IF I MIGHT COME,	HE TOUCHED ME, SO I LIVE	506	13
SHE FEELS SOME GHASTLY FRIGHT COME UP	THE SOUL HAS BANDAGED	512	3
THE HEAVEN--UNEXPECTED COME,	LIKE FLOWERS, THAT HEARD	513	13
WHAT COME OF HIM--AT NIGHT--	HE PARTS HIMSELF--LIKE	517	13
WHAT COME OF HIM--THAT DAY--	HE PARTS HIMSELF--LIKE	517	16
MAKE HASTE--[COME NEAR] THE SCRUPLE! DEATH BE SCANT	ME PROVE IT NOW--WHOEVER	537	3
MY PERIOD HAD COME FOR PRAYER--	MY PERIOD HAD COME FOR	564	1
FORGIVE ME, IF THE GRAVE COME [SEEM] SLOW--	IF I MAY HAVE IT, WHEN	577	26
MY NOON HAD COME--TO DINE--	I HAD BEEN HUNGRY, ALL	579	2
AND HE WOULD COME AGAIN--	HE FOUND MY BEING--SET	603	6
OUR FEET WERE ALMOST COME	OUR JOURNEY HAD ADVANCED	615	2
DID THEY--COME BACK NO MORE?	GLEE--THE GREAT STORM IS	619	13
FOR INTERVIEW--HAD COME--	'TWAS A LONG PARTING--	625	2
IS WHEN THE CARS HAVE COME--	I THINK THE LONGEST HOUR	635	2
INDIGNANT [AFFRONTED]--THAT THE JOY WAS COME--	I THINK THE LONGEST HOUR	635	5
NO NUMB ALARM--LEST DIFFERENCE COME--	I THINK TO LIVE--MAY BE	646	13
WE COME TO LOOK WITH GRATITUDE [FONDNESS / PLEASURE]	A PRISON GETS TO BE A	652	5
COME, AND DISAPPEAR--	BLOOM UPON THE MOUNTAIN	667	10
OF HIS PROFOUND [OPAQUE] TO COME--	THE FUTURE--NEVER SPOKE	672	4
SO I MAY COME--	WHERE THOU ART--THAT--IS	725	5
I MANY TIMES THOUGHT PEACE HAD COME	I MANY TIMES THOUGHT	739	1
BUT IF THE LADY COME	THE BIRD MUST SING TO	880	6
IF IT COME IN SLEEP	CRISIS IS A HAIR	889	4
MADONNA DIM, TO WHOM ALL FEET MAY COME,	ONLY A SHRINE, BUT MINE	918	3
THE STARS THAT STATED COME TO TOWN	MY BEST ACQUAINTANCES	932	3
AND NOW THE CHANCE HAD COME--	'TWAS CRISIS--ALL THE	948	4
OR ONLY HEAVEN TO COME	WHICH IS BEST? HEAVEN--	1012	2
HUELESS TO ME UNTIL THOU COME	SPRING COMES ON THE	1042	3
THE TIRED FLOCKS COME IN	LET DOWN THE BARS, OH	1065	2
WHEN THEY COME BACK--IF BLOSSOMS DO--	WHEN THEY COME BACK--IF	1080	1
WERE SEAS TO CROSS TO COME	THE BIRD DID PRANCE--THE	1107	10
AS EMIGRANTS WE COME	THE BIRD DID PRANCE--THE	1107	V 10
HAS SIMULTANEOUS COME.	THE MURMURING OF BEES,	1115	4
TILL WHAT WE COULD NOT SEE [FACE / CHOOSE / PROVE] HAS COME	THE MURMURING OF BEES,	1115	V 13
I TOLD MY SOUL TO COME--	THIS SLOW DAY MOVED	1120	5
COME UNTO ME ENACTED [ACCOMPLISHED] HOW	CONTAINED IN THIS SHORT	1165	V
LEST THEY SHOULD COME--IS ALL MY FEAR	LEST THEY SHOULD COME--	1169	1
THAT COME TO EARTH TO STAY,	TOO FEW THE MORNINGS BE,	1186	5
THE SEA SAID "COME" TO THE BROOK--	THE SEA SAID "COME" TO	1210	1
I WANT A BROOK--COME NOW"!	THE SEA SAID "COME" TO	1210	4
SOMEHOW THIS HAD COME--	NOW I KNEW I LOST HER--	1219	12
OR LOVE--THE TWO COEVAL COME--	TO PILE LIKE THUNDER TO	1247	5
WHEN FRESHETS COME ALONG.	A STAGNANT PLEASURE LIKE	1281	8
BUT HOW CAN THAT STUPENDOUS COME	THE INFINITE A SUDDEN	1309	3
DEAR MARCH--COME IN--	DEAR MARCH--COME IN--	1320	1
OH MARCH, COME RIGHT UP STAIRS WITH ME--	DEAR MARCH--COME IN--	1320	9
AS SOON AS [THE INSTANT THAT] YOU HAVE COME	DEAR MARCH--COME IN--	1320	24
THAT IT WILL COME AGAIN.	LET ME NOT MAR THAT	1335	4
I SUPPOSE THE TIME WILL COME	I SUPPOSE THE TIME WILL	1381	1
I SUPPOSE THE TIME WILL COME	I SUPPOSE THE TIME WILL	1381	5
NOR TIE TO EARTHS TO COME--	I HAVE NO LIFE BUT THIS	1398	5
NOR PLEA FOR WORLD [WORLDS] TO COME	I HAVE NO LIFE BUT THIS	1398	V 5
PERHAPS COME [COMES] CLOSER, FOR THE LAPSE [FLIGHT]	PERHAPS THEY DO NOT GO	1399	3
MY SOUL, TO FIND THEM, COME,	THAN HEAVEN MORE REMOTE,	1436	11
I THOUGHT THE TRAIN WOULD NEVER COME--	I THOUGHT THE TRAIN	1449	1
THEY COME A SINGLE TIME	YOUR THOUGHTS DONT HAVE	1452	2
TO COME SO FAR SO COLD A DAY	THE SAVIOR MUST HAVE	1487	3
THAT THERE ARE LESS TO COME--	BIRTHDAY OF BUT A SINGLE	1488	2
"AND WITH WHAT BODY DO THEY COME?"--	"AND WITH WHAT BODY DO	1492	1
THEN THEY DO COME--REJOICE!	"AND WITH WHAT BODY DO	1492	2
THE THINGS THAT NEVER CAN COME BACK, ARE SEVERAL--	THE THINGS THAT NEVER	1515	1
HOW ARCHLY SPARED THE HEAVEN "TO COME"--	THE MOON UPON HER FLUENT	1528	V
COME NOT TO PLAY WITH ME--	CANDOR--MY TEPID FRIEND	1537	2
COME SHOW THY DURHAM BREAST	COME SHOW THY DURHAM	1542	1
ALL THE BOYS WOULD COME--	THE BIBLE IS AN ANTIQUE	1545	14
FOR ANY SWEET "COME IN"	THE HEART HAS MANY DOORS	1567	3
ENTICED TO COME.	TO THE BRIGHT EAST SHE	1573	6

	FIRST LINE	POEM	LINE
COME (CONTINUED)			
"COME UNTO ME" THE MOIETY	NO LADDER NEEDS THE BIRD	1574	7
"COME UNTO ME" THE MOIETY	TO HER DERIDED HOME	1586	11
HOW MUCH CAN COME	THERE CAME A WIND LIKE A	1593	15
NOR DOUBT OF SCENE TO COME,	NOT SICKNESS STAINS THE	1613	3
NOT KNOWING WHEN THE DAWN WILL [HERSELF MAY] COME,	NOT KNOWING WHEN THE	1619	1
WHY TO CORDIALITY SO AVERSE TO COME	GUEST AM I TO HAVE	1661	3
WHATEVER FLOWER FAIL TO COME	NATURE CAN DO NO MORE	1673	3
INFORMED THE HOUR HAD COME	WITH SWEETNESS UNABATED	1709	2
WOULD ONLY COME TODAY,	IF ALL THE GRIEFS I AM	1726	2
WOULD ONLY COME TODAY,	IF ALL THE GRIEFS I AM	1726	6
THAT IT WILL NEVER COME AGAIN	THAT IT WILL NEVER COME	1741	1
"COME HOME WITH ME, MY FRIEND;	THE WATERS CHASED HIM AS	1749	4
COMELIER			
OBSCURED WITH RUDDIER [NEARER / COMELIER] BLUE--	ONE BLESSING HAD I THAN	756	14
COMELY			
SIX TRUE, AND COMELY MAIDENS SITTING UPON THE TREE;	AWAKE YE MUSES NINE,	1	34
THE FROST HIMSELF [ITSELF] SO COMELY	LIKE TIME'S INSIDIOUS	1236	5
COMES			
HE REACHES [COMES TO] TOWN AT NIGHTFALL--	THE GUEST IS GOLD AND	15	5
ANOTHER PROBLEM COMES--	LOW AT MY PROBLEM	69	2
AND IF I DO--WHEN MORNING COMES--	I HAVE A KING, WHO DOES	103	7
WHERE SCRABBLE NEVER COMES--	WHERE BELLS NO MORE	112	2
PECULIAR TRAVELLER COMES?	WHAT INN IS THIS	115	3
DEATH COMES	I LIKE A LOOK OF AGONY,	241	V
AND THEN THE PRETTY SUNSHINE COMES--	TO DIE--TAKES JUST A	255	7
WHEN IT COMES, THE LANDSCAPE LISTENS--	THERE'S A CERTAIN SLANT	258	13
AFTER GREAT PAIN, A FORMAL FEELING COMES--	AFTER GREAT PAIN, A	341	1
THAT CERTAIN AS IT COMES--	DID OUR BEST MOMENT LAST	393	10
AND RECESS--NEVER COMES--	I NEVER FELT AT HOME--	413	6
SAY "WHEN TOMORROW COMES THIS WAY--	IT DONT SOUND SO	426	8
HE COMES JUST SO FAR--TOWARD THE TOWN--	THE MOON IS DISTANT FROM	429	7
DEATH--IS BUT ONE--AND COMES BUT ONCE--	I MEASURE EVERY GRIEF I	561	27
SO WHEN SHE COMES THIS WAY,	I CRIED AT PITY--NOT AT	588	18
THE [OUR] MOULDERING PLAYMATE COMES--	OF NEARNESS TO HER	607	8
VICTORY COMES LATE--	VICTORY COMES LATE--	690	1
WHEN THY THIRST COMES--	THE WORLD--FEELS DUSTY	715	10
BEFORE HE COMES WE WEIGH THE TIME!	BEFORE HE COMES WE WEIGH	834	1
THAT DISAPPEARS AS COMES--	FAME IS THE TINT THAT	866	4
SPRING COMES ON THE WORLD--	SPRING COMES ON THE	1042	1
THAT COMES A SINGLE TIME A YEAR	THE SNOW THAT NEVER	1133	3
AFTER THE SUN COMES OUT	AFTER THE SUN COMES OUT	1148	1
NOR MISSILE [VENGEANCE] EVER COMES	THE CLOUDS THEIR BACKS	1172	8
IT COMES, WITHOUT A CONSTERNATION--	IN MANY AND REPORTLESS	1382	5
GOES NOR COMES AWAY	"SECRETS" IS A DAILY	1385	8
PERHAPS COME [COMES] CLOSER, FOR THE LAPSE [FLIGHT]	PERHAPS THEY DO NOT GO	1399	3
WHEN MOST IS PAST--IT COMES--	THE GENTIAN HAS A	1424	8
WHOSE AXIS [OWNER] NEVER COMES.	WATER MAKES MANY BEDS	1428	8
FROM SUCH A VELVET WORLD IT COMES [CAME]	HOW SOFT A CATERPILLAR	1448	3
THERE COMES [CAME] A WARNING LIKE A SPY	THERE COMES A WARNING	1536	1
WE SHUN IT ERE IT COMES,	WE SHUN IT ERE IT COMES,	1580	1
MORNING THAT COMES BUT ONCE,	MORNING THAT COMES BUT	1610	1
THE SEA COMES LAST--STEP MERRY FEET	I DID NOT REACH THEE	1664	14
COMES UP TO FACE THE SKIES,	DROWNING IS NOT SO	1718	4
THERE COMES AN HOUR WHEN BEGGING STOPS,	THERE COMES AN HOUR WHEN	1751	1
COMEST			
IN SNOW THOU COMEST	IN SNOW THOU COMEST	1669	1
IN FEAR THOU COMEST	IN SNOW THOU COMEST	1669	5
COMET'S			
OVER THE COMET'S CHIMNEY--	UNDER THE LIGHT, YET	949	11
COMFORT			
THIS BEING COMFORT--THEN	I'M "WIFE"--I'VE	199	9
A HAGGARD COMFORT SPRINGS	I TRIED TO THINK A	532	7
A PIERCING COMFORT IT AFFORDS	I MEASURE EVERY GRIEF I	561	35
I RECOLLECTED [ROSE TO COMFORT--] HER--	THE BIRDS REPORTED FROM	743	16
TO SOME DULL COMFORT THOSE OBTAIN	SEVERER SERVICE OF	786	13
WHAT COMFORT WAS IT WISDOM--WAS--	DENIAL--IS THE ONLY FACT	965	7
WOULD IT COMFORT--TO KNOW I MET HIM--	TRUDGING TO EDEN,	1020	5
T'WAS COMFORT IN HER DYING ROOM	T'WAS COMFORT IN HER	1703	1
COMFORTABLE			
'TIS VERY COMFORTABLE INDEED	TO MEND EACH TATTERED	1442	7
COMFORTED			
CONFRONTING EYES LONG--COMFORTED--	I'LL SEND THE FEATHER	687	5
COMFORTING			
AND NOVEL [SO MUCH] COMFORTING	I PLAY AT RICHES--TO	801	12
COMFORTS			
COMFORTS--SEARCH--LIKE THIS--	TAKING UP THE FAIR IDEAL	428	12
THEIR HIGHT IN HEAVEN COMFORTS NOT--	THEIR HIGHT IN HEAVEN	696	1
COMING			
AND NIGHT IS COMING DOWN!	ADRIFT! A LITTLE BOAT	30	2
SOME RAINBOW--COMING FROM THE FAIR!	SOME RAINBOW--COMING	64	1
AND I MEET, COMING THRO' THE DEWS	A SOMETHING IN A	122	21
AND SEE IF DOLLIE'S COMING! WAIT!	DYING! DYING IN THE	158	10
AND THAT I--AM COMING--TOO--	WHAT IS--"PARADISE"--	215	6
THEIR COMING, MAY BE KNOWN	ALONE, I CANNOT BE--	298	9
IT'S COMING--THE POSTPONELESS CREATURE--	IT'S COMING--THE	390	1

	FIRST LINE	POEM	LINE
COMING (CONTINUED)			
I'M COMING HOME--	GOOD MORNING--MIDNIGHT--	425	2
ETERNITY, I'M COMING--SIR, ...	A WIFE--AT DAYBREAK I	461	12
IF YOU WERE COMING IN THE FALL, ...	IF YOU WERE COMING IN	511	1
THEIR COMING, MENTIONED--BE--	TWO BUTTERFLIES WENT OUT	533	8
A FIRST MUTE COMING--	A FIRST MUTE COMING--	702	1
BEFORE THE COMING FLAIL--	MIDSUMMER, WAS IT, WHEN	962	6
HIS WRINKLED COMING HOME?	THAT ODD OLD MAN IS DEAD	1130	8
KNOWS THE ADDER [ADDERS] TONGUE HIS COMING .	WE LIKE MARCH.	1213	6
AND BLOCKED THE COMING IN.	IT CAME AT LAST BUT	1230	8
A COMING AS OF HOSTS WAS HEARD	LIKE RAIN IT SOUNDED	1235	7
AND NEVER COMING BACK	BECAUSE THAT YOU ARE	1260	2
THE MAPLES NEVER KNEW THAT YOU WERE COMING--TILL I CALLED	DEAR MARCH--COME IN--	1320	12
AID IT IN THE COMING	I SUPPOSE THE TIME WILL	1381	2
ARE COMING NOW--	MARCH IS THE MONTH OF	1404	4
CONSIDERS COMING TWICE--	MORNING THAT COMES BUT	1610	2
THEIR COMING BACK SEEMS POSSIBLE	THE DISTANCE THAT THE	1742	3
THE ACCENT OF A COMING FOOT--	ELYSIUM IS AS FAR AS TO	1760	7
COMISSARY			
WANT--A QUIET COMISSARY	SATISFACTION--IS THE	1036	3
COMMAND			
OBEDIENT TO THE LEAST COMMAND	THE MOON IS DISTANT FROM	429	11
OR GROPES, AT MY COMMAND	I MAKE HIS CRESCENT FILL	909	6
SUCH PLUSHES AT COMMAND	HOW SOFT A CATERPILLAR	1448	4
COMMANDER			
WITHOUT COMMANDER! COUNTLESS! STILL! . . .	SOME RAINBOW--COMING	64	19
COMMANDMENT			
HIS WEARIEST COMMANDMENT--	ALTHOUGH I PUT AWAY HIS	366	17
COMMEMORATE			
MY BUDS COMMEMORATE--	IF I SHOULD CEASE TO	56	6
THE DIRK COMMEMORATE--ITSELF	REHEARSAL TO OURSELVES	379	7
COMMEMORATE DISHONOR	PERHAPS YOU THINK ME	833	5
COMMENCES			
AND ESTIMATES [ENFORCES / COMMENCES / REPLEVYS / CONFISCATES] . . .	PERHAPS THEY DO NOT GO	1399	8
COMMEND			
I TENDERER COMMEND	MY SEASON'S FURTHEST	1019	2
WE COMMEND OURSELVES TO THEE	RECOLLECT THE FACE OF ME	1305	7
COMMENSURATE			
IN ANY TONE COMMENSURATE	I NEVER HEAR THAT ONE IS	1323	11
COMMENTATORS			
COULD COMMENTATORS ON THE SIGN	DEW--IS THE FRESHET IN	1097	9
COMMERCE			
THAT COMMERCE WILL CONTINUE--	IF I SHOULD DIE,	54	13
AND IT'S COMMERCE--IF COMMERCE IT HAVE-- .	BY MY WINDOW HAVE I FOR	797	11
AND IT'S COMMERCE--IF COMMERCE IT HAVE-- .	BY MY WINDOW HAVE I FOR	797	11
COMMIT			
WE SAFE [SOFT] COMMIT THEE--	TO THE STANCH DUST	1402	2
COMMITTED			
HER MESSAGE IS COMMITTED	THIS IS MY LETTER TO THE	441	5
COMMON			
UPON A COMMON SUMMER'S MORN--	A SEPAL, PETAL, AND A	19	2
FROM SUCH A COMMON BALL AS THIS	A DAY! HELP! HELP!	42	3
TOOK RAINBOWS, AS THE COMMON WAY, ...	DELIGHT IS AS THE FLIGHT	257	16
WHEN HEAVEN--WAS TOO COMMON--TO MISS-- . .	THE LONESOME FOR THEY	262	11
WHEN FARTHER [SHARPER] PARTED, THAN THE COMMON WO--	ONE YEAR AGO--JOTS WHAT?	296	8
THE SUN, AS COMMON, WENT ABROAD, ...	THERE CAME A DAY AT	322	5
AS IF I ASKED A COMMON ALMS, ...	AS IF I ASKED A COMMON	323	1
A DUCHESS WERE TOO COMMON	THE GRASS SO LITTLE HAS	333	11
RED--IS THE FIRE'S COMMON TINT--	DARE YOU SEE A SOUL AT	365	3
IT'S SUCH A COMMON--GLORY--	WHAT SOFT--CHERUBIC	401	9
IT WOULD NEVER BE COMMON--MORE--I SAID-- .	IT WOULD NEVER BE COMMON	430	1
IS COMMON, THOUGH, NOW--	KNOWS HOW TO FORGET!	433	V
MAY BE A COMMON THING--	TO HEAR AN ORIOLE SING	526	2
BY BLOSSOMS GRADUAL [COMMON] PROCESS-- . .	HE GAVE AWAY HIS LIFE--	567	11
A COMMON BLISS	MUST BE A WO--	571	9
DEATH IS THE COMMON [MUTUAL / EQUAL] RIGHT .	A TOAD, CAN DIE OF LIGHT	583	2
IT SEEMED THE COMMON WAY, ...	I CRIED AT PITY--NOT AT	588	6
AND JUST THE MEANEST [COMMON / FAINTEST] TUNES	I THINK I WAS ENCHANTED	593	12
A CLEMENCY SO COMMON--	THE HEAVEN VESTS FOR	694	13
DRAMA'S VITALLEST EXPRESSION IS THE COMMON DAY	DRAMA'S VITALLEST	741	1
IS EASY [COMMON], POSSIBLY--	AWAY FROM HOME ARE SOME	821	4
AND ALL THE EARTH STROVE COMMON ROUND-- . .	DENIAL--IS THE ONLY FACT	965	5
THE BLAME THAT I WAS CHOSEN [COMMON]--THEN--	FITTER TO SEE HIM, I MAY	968	8
IT WAS A COMMON NIGHT	THE LAST NIGHT THAT SHE	1100	2
TO CUSTOM COMMON GROWN	A DIAMOND ON THE HAND	1108	2
AS COMMON AS IT IS UNKNOWN	BEHOLD THIS LITTLE BANE	1438	3
COMMONER			
WEAR NOTHING COMMONER THAN SNOW--	OF TRIBULATION--THESE	325	7
LIBERTY--COMMONER--	LET US PLAY YESTERDAY--	728	19
COMMONEST			
THE COLORS OF THE COMMONEST--	YOUR RICHES--TAUGHT ME--	299	11
COMMONLY			
THE PARLOR--COMMONLY--IT IS--	I AM ALIVE--I GUESS--	470	11
COMMONWEALTH			
IF COMMONWEALTH BELOW, ...	HE TOLD A HOMELY TALE	763	13
OR COMMONWEALTH ABOVE	HE TOLD A HOMELY TALE	763	14

	FIRST LINE	POEM	LINE
COMMUNE			
PERMITTED TO COMMUNE THIS--TIME--	THERE CAME A DAY AT	322	14
BUT WITH ITSELF DID COLD ENGAGE [COMMUNE] .	A WIND THAT ROSE	1259	4
COMMUNICATE			
ONCE TO COMMUNICATE--	THOSE WHO HAVE BEEN IN	922	8
COMMUNICATION			
THE PERFECTEST COMMUNICATION	SPEECH IS ONE SYMPTOM OF	1681	3
COMMUNION			
OH LAST COMMUNION IN THE HAZE--	THESE ARE THE DAYS WHEN	130	14
OF THE COMMUNION [SACRAMENTAL] WINE . . .	YOUR THOUGHTS DONT HAVE	1452	4
COMMUTE			
TO WHOSO WOULD COMMUTE THIS FACE	BECAUSE THAT YOU ARE	1260	31
COMMUTED			
AS ONE COMMUTED LED--	SOMEHOW MYSELF SURVIVED	1194	6
WHILE THEIR COMMUTED FEET	HOW MUCH THE PRESENT	1380	6
COMPACT			
THE MISERY A COMPACT	LIKE EYES THAT LOOKED ON	458	11
NOR I--HERSELF--OUR COMPACT--	THE BIRDS REPORTED FROM	743	V 23
INVIOLABLE COMPACT	THE LEAVES LIKE WOMEN,	987	7
COMPANIES			
HER PARTIES ALL [COMPANIES] ASTIR--	REMORSE--IS MEMORY--	744	2
COMPANION			
WILT HAVE NO KIND COMPANION, THOU REAP'ST WHAT THOU HAST SOWN.	AWAKE YE MUSES NINE,	1	28
DOUBT ME! MY DIM [FAINT] COMPANION! . . .	DOUBT ME! MY DIM	275	1
AS THIS PHANTASM [COMPANION] STEEL--	A PRISON GETS TO BE A	652	21
AND THAT ASSEMBLY [COMPANION]--NOT FAR OFF .	ON A COLUMNAR SELF--	789	11
THE DAY THAT A COMPANION CAME	SOME DAYS RETIRED FROM	1157	3
THOU CAN'ST NOT BOAST, LIKE JESUS, DRUNKEN WITHOUT COMPANION	PROUD OF MY BROKEN HEART	1736	5
COMPANY			
FOR HUMBLER COMPANY	A MIEN TO MOVE A QUEEN--	283	5
RECORDLESS COMPANY--	ALONE, I CANNOT BE--	298	3
IN SEAMLESS COMPANY--	OF ALL THE SOUNDS	321	33
AND TWO OR THREE--FOR COMPANY--	IT'S THOUGHTS--AND JUST	495	4
YOU ASKED THE COMPANY TO TEA--	IF ANYBODY'S FRIEND BE	509	17
LIKE CLEOPATRA'S COMPANY--	THE TINT I CANNOT TAKE--	627	7
OF HIS COMPANY--	CONSCIOUS AM I IN MY	679	8
FOR SHOW, OR COMPANY--	HAVE ANY LIKE MYSELF	736	16
A STATELY--SHRIVEN--COMPANY--	THROUGH THE STRAIT PASS	792	5
IN MINOR COMPANY--	WHO GIANTS KNOW, WITH	796	4
WITH SILENCE AS A COMPANY	TO OWN THE ART WITHIN	855	3
AND WEALTH--AND COMPANY.	A DOOR JUST OPENED ON A	953	4
AND A COMPANY--OUR PLEASURE	THREE WEEKS PASSED SINCE	1061	5
THOUGH THE RING IS UNWHOLE, AND THE COMPANY BROKE	OF THE HEART THAT GOES	1098	3
AND MORTAL COMPANY--	IN THY LONG PARADISE OF	1145	4
IN EVERY COMPANY--	POWER IS A FAMILIAR	1238	4
WHERE HOPE AND HE PART COMPANY--	DROWNING IS NOT SO	1718	7
HIS PUNGENT COMPANY	EXPERIMENT ESCORTS US	1770	2
COMPARATIVE			
"COMPARATIVE ANATOMY"--	A SCIENCE--SO THE SAVANS	100	2
THROUGH THEIR COMPARATIVE.	TWO--WERE IMMORTAL TWICE	800	8
COMPARATIVELY			
WE SEE--COMPARATIVELY--	WE SEE--COMPARATIVELY--	534	1
COMPARE			
BUT WHY COMPARE?	I'M "WIFE"--I'VE	199	11
HOW DEATH'S GIFTS MAY COMPARE--	FOR DEATH--OR RATHER	382	10
SO INFINITE COMPARE	THERE IS A JUNE WHEN	930	14
WITH THIS THAT MAY COMPARE--	OUR LITTLE SECRETS SLINK	1326	8
AND YET IF YOU COMPARE THE LASTS, ...	A FLOWER WILL NOT	1621	2
COMPARED			
COMPARED WITH THE DELICIOUS THROE	SWEET SKEPTICISM OF THE	1413	7
COMPARED WITH THAT PROFOUNDER SITE	THERE IS A SOLITUDE OF	1695	5
COMPARISON			
EFFACE IN THE COMPARISON--	NO CROWD THAT HAS	515	11
IN THE COMPARISON--	THE CHILD'S FAITH IS NEW	637	13
COMPARISON--APPEAR--	THIS DUST, AND IT'S	936	8
COMPASS			
DONE WITH THE COMPASS--	WILD NIGHTS--WILD NIGHTS	249	7
NO MAN CAN COMPASS A DESPAIR--	NO MAN CAN COMPASS A	477	1
TO CREDIT [COMPASS]--'TIS'NT TRUE!	NO ROMANCE SOLD UNTO	669	7
TO COMPASS PARADISE--	JOY TO HAVE MERITED THE	788	4
COMPASSED			
WHO CONSTERNATION COMPASSED	I YEARS HAD BEEN FROM	609	15
COMPASSION			
TRANSPORTED WITH COMPASSION	THE HIMMALEH WAS KNOWN	481	3
COMPASSION FOR INTEGRITY	THE SWEETS OF PILLAGE,	1470	3
TIME COMPASSION TOOK--	WE TALKED WITH EACH	1473	6
COMPELLED			
WERE I COMPELLED TO BUILD	WHO OCCUPIES THIS HOUSE?	892	12
COMPELLETH			
THE SUNRISE--SIR--COMPELLETH ME--	"WHY DO I LOVE" YOU, SIR	480	17
COMPELLING			
COMPELLING HIM TO CHOOSE HIMSELF	EXPERIENCE IS THE ANGLED	910	7
MORNING--THE EAST COMPELLING THE SILL . .	NOON--IS THE HINGE OF	931	3
COMPENSATE			
SO I GET HOME--'TWILL COMPENSATE--	THO' I GET HOME HOW LATE	207	2
BUT WILL THE SECRET COMPENSATE	THE GOING FROM A WORLD	1603	7

	FIRST LINE	POEM	LINE
COMPENSATED			
OF COMPENSATED TRUST.	"REMEMBER ME" IMPLORED	1180	8
COMPENSATES			
HE--COMPENSATES--IMMEDIATELY--	SOME--WORK FOR	406	3
COMPENSATION			
BUT NOT FOR COMPENSATION--	LIGHT IS SUFFICIENT TO	862	5
A COMPENSATION FAIR [GAY]	COSMOPOLITES WITHOUT A	1589	6
COMPETE			
THROUGH IT--COMPETE WITH DEATH--	FOR THIS--ACCEPTED	195	2
COMPETELESS			
BUT THEIR COMPETELESS SHOW	OF BRONZE--AND BLAZE--	290	15
COMPETENCE			
A COMPETENCE SO GAY	COSMOPOLITES WITHOUT A	1589	V 6
COMPETENT			
WAS COMPETENT TO ME--	I COULD NOT PROVE THE	563	10
. . . SO COMPETENT A SIGHT]	THE MOST TRIUMPHANT BIRD	1265	4
BUT INTIMATE [COMPETENT / ABSOLUTE / IMPUDENT] DELIGHT.	THE MOST TRIUMPHANT BIRD	1265	6
TOO OBDURATE [COMPETENT / SUMPTUOUS] FOR SNOWS--	A LITTLE SNOW WAS HERE	1444	8
IN CASUAL [COMPETENT] SIMPLICITY--	HOW HAPPY IS THE LITTLE	1510	10
COMPETENT TO KILL IT,	DEATH IS LIKE THE INSECT	1716	3
COMPETES			
THAT TOO COMPETES WITH HEAVEN.	OF GOD WE ASK ONE FAVOR,	1601	8
COMPETING			
GO RAPID, LEST COMPETING DEATH	GO SLOW, MY SOUL, TO	1297	3
FIRST AT THE MARCH--COMPETING WITH THE WIND--	AFTER ALL BIRDS HAVE	1395	5
IN OUR COMPETING DAYS	I SAW THE WIND WITHIN	1502	V
COMPETITION			
DAY AND I--IN COMPETITION RAN--	I SEND TWO SUNSETS--	308	2
OUR SINGLE [ONLY] COMPETITION	NO OTHER CAN REDUCE	982	7
A COMPETITION IN MY SENSE	I CANNOT MEET THE SPRING	1051	5
AS COMPETITION DONE	WITH SWEETNESS UNABATED	1709	6
COMPETITIONS			
WHAT COMPETITIONS RAN--	A PRECIOUS--MOULDERING	371	14
[SOME] IT MUST BE COMPETITIONS	HOW MANY SCHEMES MAY DIE	1150	11
THE COMPETITIONS OF THE SKY	THE COMPETITIONS OF THE	1494	1
COMPETITOR			
FAINT DOUBT--AND FAR COMPETITOR--	I CROSS TILL I AM WEARY	550	16
COMPLACENCE			
PERPETUAL PRESUMPTION [COMPLACENCE] TOOK	ALONE AND IN A	1167	15
COMPLAIN			
OF PARISHES, COMPLAIN.	WE MISS A KINSMAN MORE	1087	8
SHALL THE PLAYFELLOW HEART COMPLAIN	OF THE HEART THAT GOES	1098	2
COMPLAINED			
HIMSELF HAD NOT COMPLAINED. [HITHERTO CONCEALED--]	THE HOLLOWS ROUND HIS	955	4
COMPLAINING			
COMPLAINING ALL THE WHILE	I LIKE TO SEE IT LAP	585	11
COMPLAINS			
A NARROW WIND COMPLAINS ALL DAY	THE SKY IS LOW--THE	1075	5
COMPLAINT			
AS FAR FROM PITY, AS COMPLAINT--	AS FAR FROM PITY, AS	496	1
COMPLEMENT			
THE ADEQUATE [COMPLEMENT] OF HELL--	REMORSE--IS MEMORY--	744	12
COMPLETED			
AS A COMPLETED MAN	I TIE MY HAT--I CREASE	443	14
COMPLEXION			
AND HIS COMPLEXION, DUN!	A FUZZY FELLOW, WITHOUT	173	4
HALF HER COMPLEXION OF THE SUN--	FAIRER THROUGH FADING--	938	3
COMPLICATE			
QUITE OPPOSITE--HOW COMPLICATE	EXPERIENCE IS THE ANGLED	910	5
COMPLIED			
THE EASY GUEST COMPLIED	THE FINGERS OF THE LIGHT	1000	9
ABRAHAM COMPLIED--	ABRAHAM TO KILL HIM	1317	6
COMPLIMENTS			
HE COMPLIMENTS EXISTENCE	THE WAY TO KNOW THE	1279	15
THE COMPLIMENTS OF PARADISE	COSMOPOLITES WITHOUT A	1589	3
COMPOSE			
COMPOSE AN EVENING SKY--	A SLASH OF BLUE--	204	4
COMPOSED			
OF SUNSHINE--AND OF SERE--COMPOSED--	OF BRUSSELS--IT WAS NOT	602	11
FOREVER--IS COMPOSED OF NOWS--	FOREVER--IS COMPOSED OF	624	1
FOR GREATNESS, THAT IS ILL AT EASE [COMPOSED]	WHO GIANTS KNOW, WITH	796	3
OF THIS IS DAY COMPOSED	OF THIS IS DAY COMPOSED	1675	1
COMPOSER			
BUT THE COMPOSER--PERFECT MOZART--	BETTER--THAN MUSIC! FOR	503	7
COMPOUND			
OF ALL THIS COMPOUND FRAME--	A WEIGHT WITH NEEDLES ON	264	6
OUR LORD--INDEED--MADE [BORE] COMPOUND WITNESS--	ONE CRUCIFIXION IS	553	13
A COMPOUND MANNER,	TO THIS WORLD SHE	830	3
'TIS COMPOUND VISION--	THE ADMIRATIONS--AND	906	9
COMPREHEND			
TO COMPREHEND A NECTAR	SUCCESS IS COUNTED	67	3
TO COMPREHEND THE WHOLE--	I RECKON--WHEN I COUNT	569	6
COULD YOU COMPREHEND IT	THERE'S THE BATTLE OF	1174	7
SHALL COMPREHEND [SCRUTINIZE] AS ONE	HOW NEWS MUST FEEL WHEN	1319	10
THAT ONE SHOULD COMPREHEND THE WORTH	HIS MIND LIKE FABRICS OF	1446	7
YOU CANNOT COMPREHEND ITS PRICE [WORTH]	YOUR THOUGHTS DONT HAVE	1452	7

	FIRST LINE	POEM	LINE
COMPREHENDED			
THEN--TOO--BE COMPREHENDED--	IT TROUBLED ME AS ONCE I	600	13
WE COMPREHENDED [POSTULATED / RECOLLECTED] BY THE AWE	IT WAS A QUIET SEEMING	1419	10
COMPREHENDETH			
THAT COMPREHENDETH ME	AFRAID! OF WHOM AM I	608	6
COMPREHENSION			
MOULD MY SLOW MIND TO THIS COMPREHENSION--	KNOWS HOW TO FORGET!	433	9
PERHAPS--THE COMPREHENSION--	"WAS NOT" WAS ALL THE	1342	3
THAT COMPREHENSION FLUCTUATES [ANTEDATES]	PERHAPS THEY DO NOT GO	1399	7
TO SITUATIONS [EXHIBITION / COMPREHENSION] NEW	ON THAT SPECIFIC PILLOW	1533	6
A GRASP ON COMPREHENSION LAID	NO MAN SAW AWE, NOR TO	1733	7
COMPREHENSIVE			
IN COMPREHENSIVE DAY--	LEFT IN IMMORTAL YOUTH	1289	8
COMPRISE			
DO NOT COMPRISE THE SKIES--	WHO GIANTS KNOW, WITH	796	8
THE EFFORT TO COMPRISE IT [OF COMPRISING]	ON THAT SPECIFIC PILLOW	1533	7
COMPRISED			
COMPRISED IN PRAYER--	PRAYER IS THE LITTLE	437	8
CONTAINED [COMBINED / COMPRISED] IN THIS SHORT [PLAIN] LIFE	CONTAINED IN THIS SHORT	1165	1
COMPRISING			
FOR THE SOUL'S COMPRISING--	ONE AND ONE--ARE ONE--	769	8
THE EFFORT TO COMPRISE IT [OF COMPRISING]	ON THAT SPECIFIC PILLOW	1533	7
COMPROMISE			
AND SO MEN COMPROMISE--	A MIEN TO MOVE A QUEEN--	283	24
HOW INFINITE THE COMPROMISE	THERE ARE TWO MAYS	1618	4
COMPROMISED			
HAS COMPROMISED IT'S POWER--	THE CLOVER'S SIMPLE FAME	1232	8
NOR SIMPLIFIED [COMPROMISED] HER GHOST.	WHAT MYSTERY PERVADES A	1400	20
COMPUTED			
ARE SCARCE ACCOUNTED [COMPUTED]--HARMS--	ONE ANGUISH--IN A CROWD	565	12
MYSELF CONJECTURED [COMPUTED] WERE THEY PEARLS--	A DROP FELL ON THE APPLE	794	7
COMPUTED HOW THE GIRTH?	HOW FITS HIS UMBER COAT	1371	6
COMPUTES			
COMPUTES THE STAMENS IN A BREATH--	"ARCTURUS" IS HIS OTHER	70	11
COMRADE			
SO TRUST HIM, COMRADE--	THEY LEAVE US WITH THE	350	9
COMRADES			
HIS COMRADES, SHIFTED LIKE THE FLAKES	HE FOUGHT LIKE THOSE	759	9
CON			
WHEN I CON THE PEOPLE	WHEN I COUNT THE SEEDS	40	4
TO CON THE FADED SYLLABLES	IN EBON BOX, WHEN YEARS	169	7
AND SO I CON THAT THING--"FORGIVEN"--	I THINK JUST HOW MY	237	13
TO CON THEE OER AND OER--	WE COVER THEE--SWEET	482	8
CONCAVE			
CONVEX--AND CONCAVE WITNESS--	THE ADMIRATIONS--AND	906	13
CONCEAL			
BARS [BOLTS]--CANNOT CONCEAL!	MINE--BY THE RIGHT OF	528	4
WOULD HELP HIM TO CONCEAL,	TO TRY TO SPEAK, AND	1617	6
CONCEALED			
OURSELF BEHIND OURSELF, CONCEALED--	ONE NEED NOT BE A	670	13
HIMSELF HAD NOT COMPLAINED. [HITHERTO CONCEALED--]	THE HOLLOWS ROUND HIS	955	4
AND NEVER QUITE CONCEALED	THE LIGHTNING IS A	1173	6
UNLESS CONCEALED IN [INTRENCHED IN / AFFIXED TO / INLAID IN] THEE	HOW FIRM ETERNITY MUST	1499	8
CONCEDE			
THE PRESENCE TO CONCEDE	AS SUMMER INTO AUTUMN	1346	6
CONCEDES			
MEADOWS OF MAJESTY CONCEDES [IMPLIES]	MY COCOON TIGHTENS--	1099	7
AS HE BESIDES CONCEDES	BECAUSE THAT YOU ARE	1260	38
CONCEIT			
THE OCEAN--SMILES--AT HER CONCEIT--	THE DROP, THAT WRESTLES	284	7
AT OUR CONCEIT	SO LARGE MY WILL	1024	15
CONCEIVE SEE CONCIEVE			
BEYOND MY LIMIT TO CONCEIVE--	I THINK TO LIVE--MAY BE	646	3
THE QUALITY CONCEIVE [PERCEIVE]	TWO--WERE IMMORTAL TWICE	800	6
SO HUGE, SO HOPELESS TO CONCEIVE	MY LIFE CLOSED TWICE	1732	5
CONCEIVED			
OF ALL CONCEIVED JOY--	'TIS GOOD--THE LOOKING	660	4
AS FROST IS BEST CONCEIVED	AS FROST IS BEST	951	1
CONCEIVELESS			
PRECIOUS! IT WAS CONCEIVELESS FAIR	ON THAT DEAR FRAME THE	940	5
CONCENTRATE			
DO CONCENTRATE HIS COUNTENANCE	THE SUN AND MOON MUST	871	7
WILL CONCENTRATE IT'S OFFICERS--	THE RIGHT TO PERISH	1692	5
CONCEPTION			
WOULD STIR HIS SLOW CONCEPTION--	REMOVED FROM ACCIDENT OF	424	9
CONCERN			
ON THEMES CONCERN OUR MUTUAL MIND--	A PRECIOUS--MOULDERING	371	11
NOR AVOCATION--NOR CONCERN	I WATCHED THE MOON	629	23
ARE IGNORANT OF IT'S CONCERN	DEATH LEAVES US HOMESICK	935	3
PROCEEDS WITHOUT CONCERN--	THE LARGEST FIRE EVER	1114	4
TO THOSE THEY MOST CONCERN--	HOW MANY SCHEMES MAY DIE	1150	4
DOES NOT CONCERN THE BEE,	THE PEDIGREE OF HONEY	1627	2
CONCERNING			
CONCERNING THE STUPENDOUSNESS	HOW NEWS MUST FEEL WHEN	1319	7

	FIRST LINE	POEM	LINE
CONCERNLESS			
WHILE COOL--CONCERNLESS NO--	A CLOCK STOPPED--	287	13
CONCIEVE SEE CONCEIVE			
AND MADDER--TO CONCIEVE--	I SOMETIMES DROP IT, FOR	708	4
CONCISEST			
THE RAT IS THE CONCISEST TENANT.	THE RAT IS THE CONCISEST	1356	1
CONCLUDE			
CONCLUDE THE WONDER GAY--	A SOMETHING IN A	122	20
COULD NOT DECIDE [DISCERN / CONCLUDE] BETWEEN--	SO GLAD WE ARE--A	329	8
AND DEITY CONCLUDE--	A TONGUE--TO TELL HIM I	400	27
SUSPENSE--DOES NOT CONCLUDE--	SUSPENSE--IS HOSTILER	705	4
CONCLUDED			
THE RAPTURE OF A FINISHED [CONCLUDED] DAY--	"HEAVEN" HAS DIFFERENT	575	13
UPON CONCLUDED LIVES	UPON CONCLUDED LIVES	735	1
A TOO CONCLUDED SHOW	THIS DUST, AND IT'S	936	10
CONCLUDED AND BEGUN	BELSHAZZAR HAD A LETTER	1459	4
CONCLUDES			
CONCLUDES HIS GLISTENING INTERVIEW--	A VISITOR IN MARL--	391	7
CONCLUDING			
CONCLUDING [DECIDING] HOW AN ATOM--FELL--	IT TROUBLED ME AS ONCE I	600	3
CONCLUSION			
THIS WORLD IS NOT CONCLUSION.	THIS WORLD IS NOT	501	1
MAKES EFFORT AT CONCLUSION	AS PLAN FOR NOON AND	960	7
BY NO CONCLUSION [DERISION] HINDERED	A SPARROW TOOK A SLICE	1211	V 7
CONCLUSION TURNED ON ME	MY TRIUMPH LASTED TILL	1227	6
CONCLUSION IS THE COURSE OF ALL	SUMMER BEGINS TO HAVE	1682	13
CONCLUSIVE			
. . . CONCLUSIVE] A MAN!	HE PREACHED UPON	1207	8
CONCOMITANT			
IS BUT THE GLEAM CONCOMITANT	THE FARTHEST THUNDER	1581	15
CONDEMN			
IT DID NOT CONDEMN--	THE BIBLE IS AN ANTIQUE	1545	16
CONDEMNED			
CONDEMNED--BUT JUST--TO SEE--	THEY PUT US FAR APART--	474	16
OF HIS CONDEMNED LIP?	TO ONE DENIED TO DRINK	490	8
AND I--CONDEMNED TO BE	I CANNOT LIVE WITH YOU--	640	42
THE SOUL CONDEMNED TO BE--	THIS CONSCIOUSNESS THAT	822	14
TRIED ALWAYS AND CONDEMNED BY THEE	TRIED ALWAYS AND	1559	1
CONDENSED			
OF IT'S CONDENSED DESPATCH	REMORSE--IS MEMORY--	744	V 8
CONDENSES			
CONDENSES LIKE A FLOCK	IT SIFTS FROM LEADEN	311	V
CONDESCEND			
GREAT CAESAR! CONDESCEND	GREAT CAESAR! CONDESCEND	102	1
DO WE CONDESCEND--	WE DONT CRY--TIM AND I,	196	10
CONDESCENDED			
THE SILENCE CONDESCENDED--	MY PERIOD HAD COME FOR	564	17
CONDESCENDING			
HOW CONDESCENDING TO DESCEND	THE BUTTERFLY'S	1244	4
CONDESCENSION			
COULD CONDESCENSION BE	A WORD MADE FLESH IS	1651	14
CONDITION			
THE FROSTS WERE HER CONDITION--	GOD MADE A LITTLE	442	9
EFFORT--IS THE SOLE CONDITION--	GROWTH OF MAN--LIKE	750	9
HALF THE CONDITION [DISTINCTION], THY REVERSE--TO FOLLOW--	WERT THOU BUT ILL--THAT	961	11
A WISHFULNESS THEIR FAR CONDITION	A SICKNESS OF THIS WORLD	1044	3
A BEAUTIFUL BUT BLEAK CONDITION	WONDER--IS NOT PRECISELY	1331	3
ADVANCE IS LIFE'S CONDITION	ADVANCE IS LIFE'S	1652	1
CONDITIONS			
HAS VANQUISHED [SATED] FLAME'S CONDITIONS,	DARE YOU SEE A SOUL AT	365	5
TOUCHED TO CONDITIONS	SPRING COMES ON THE	1042	6
CONDUCT			
CONDUCT THE PLEASING SCENE!	IF I SHOULD DIE,	54	18
OF THEIR IMPERIAL CONDUCT--	WHEN I WAS SMALL, A	596	11
CONDUCTED			
CONDUCTED FIRST	DEATH IS THE SUPPLE	1445	4
CONFEDERATE			
BUT HER CONFEDERATE.	TO HIS SIMPLICITY	1352	4
CONFEDERATES			
LATER, HIS FAINT CONFEDERATES	TO PUT THIS WORLD DOWN,	527	7
CONFER			
A TRINKET--TO CONFER--	'TIS CUSTOMARY AS WE	440	2
CONFER UPON THE EYE--	AN IGNORANCE A SUNSET	552	2
CONFER UPON MY FLOWER--	THE GRACE--MYSELF--MIGHT	707	2
UPON HER FRIEND SHE COULD CONFER [BESTOW]	THE MOON WAS BUT A CHIN	737	11
HE MAY EXCHANGE [CONFER] WITH ME	BECAUSE THAT YOU ARE	1260	26
STAYING CANNOT [COULD NOT] CONFER	I'D RATHER RECOLLECT A	1349	6
CONFERRED			
NO PARADISE COULD BE--CONFERRED	'TIS TRUE--THEY SHUT ME	538	7
TO MY QUICK EAR THE LEAVES--CONFERRED--	TO MY QUICK EAR THE	891	1
BESTOWS [CONFERRED] A SINGLE FRIEND--	A COFFIN--IS A SMALL	943	10
ACUTE DEGREE--CONFERRED ON ME--	TITLE DIVINE--IS MINE!	1072	3
'TIS NOT CONFERRED OF ANY	SUPERIORITY TO FATE	1081	3
BUT MUST IT BE CONFERRED,	A MINE THERE IS NO MAN	1117	2
THE AFFLUENCE EVOLVED [CONFERRED / BESTOWED / INVOLVED]--	SUMMER--WE ALL HAVE SEEN	1386	10
CONFERRING			
'TIS DULL--CONFERRING	HER--"LAST POEMS"--	312	12

	FIRST LINE	POEM	LINE
CONFERRING (CONTINUED)			
CONFERRING WITH MYSELF	CONFERRING WITH MYSELF	1655	1
CONFESS			
HOW MANY TIMES IT ACHE FOR ME--TODAY--CONFESS--	YOU SEE I CANNOT SEE--	253	3
CONFIDE			
GOD THE SON--CONFIDE [DISCLOSE] IT--	ONLY GOD--DETECT THE	626	5
I MAY CONFIDE MY FLOWER--	HERE, WHERE THE DAISIES	1037	6
CONFIDE IN ME.	SWEET PIRATE OF THE	1546	6
CONFIDED			
CONFIDED ARE HIS PROJECTS PINK	THE RETICENT VOLCANO	1748	3
CONFIDENCE			
THIS--THEN--IS BEST FOR CONFIDENCE--	THE TRUTH--IS STIRLESS--	780	3
SAGACIOUS [EXCLUSIVE] CONFIDENCE--	THE LEAVES LIKE WOMEN,	987	2
RESTORED IN ARCTIC CONFIDENCE	A WIND THAT ROSE	1259	8
CONFIDENT			
BUT CONFIDENT [DILIGENT / RESOLUTE] DESPAIR--	HAD I PRESUMED TO HOPE--	522	10
YET CONFIDENT THEY RUN	I COULD NOT PROVE THE	563	2
I'M CONFIDENT THAT BRAVOES	WHEN I WAS SMALL, A	596	17
AND WAS HE CONFIDENT UNTIL	TO KNOW JUST HOW HE	622	16
NEVER A WORM SO CONFIDENT	AND THIS OF ALL MY HOPES	913	7
CONFIDENT AND STRAIGHT--	A PROMPT--EXECUTIVE BIRD	1177	6
AS CONFIDENT OF HIM AS WE--	HE LIVED THE LIFE OF	1525	5
AS CONFIDENT OF HIM AS WE--	WHO ABDICATED AMBUSH	1616	5
CONFIDENTIAL			
WITH CONFIDENTIAL MOAN--	THE HEALED HEART SHOWS	1440	2
CONFIDENTLY			
I CONFIDENTLY SEE!	SOME RAINBOW--COMING	64	3
CONFIDES			
BUT DISTANCE HIS DELIGHTS CONFIDES	'TIS MY FIRST NIGHT	1122	7
CONFIDING			
BUT A CONFIDING GUEST CONSULT AS WELL,	I CANNOT SEE MY SOUL BUT	1262	4
AND THIS CONFIDING [MECHANIC / SUBJUNCTIVE] STONE	SHE LAID HER DOCILE	1396	2
WAS THAT CONFIDING PRODIGAL [MINUTE DOMINGO]	ONE OF THE ONES THAT	1466	3
OR IS IT THE CONFIDING SHEEN	THE FACE IN EVANESCENCE	1490	5
CONFIRM			
THE HEAVEN TO CONFIRM--	HER SWEET WEIGHT ON MY	518	6
THE FAILURE BUT CONFIRM THE GRACE	HAD I PRESUMED TO HOPE--	522	7
CONFIRM [WITHDRAW]--IN VICTORY--	AN IGNORANCE A SUNSET	552	10
NOR CONFIRM--BY WORD--	CONSCIOUS AM I IN MY	679	4
ATMOSPHERE, AND SUN ENDORSE [CONFIRM] IT--	GROWTH OF MAN--LIKE	750	3
THE MIDNIGHT TO CONFIRM--	SEVERER SERVICE OF	786	20
NOT ONLY MUST CONFIRM US	THE FACT THAT EARTH IS	1408	5
CONFIRMED			
TITLED--CONFIRMED--	MINE--BY THE RIGHT OF	528	7
'TWERE SUDDENLY CONFIRMED [ORDAINED]--	I THINK I WAS ENCHANTED	593	20
OR BIRDS--CONFIRMED PERPETUAL	'TWAS AWKWARD, BUT IT	973	7
CONFIRMING			
CONFIRMING ALL WHO ANALYZE	CONFIRMING ALL WHO	1268	1
CONFIRMS			
CONFIRMS IT AT IT'S ENTRANCE--AND	LOVE--IS THAT LATER	924	3
CONFISCATED			
OUR CONFISCATED GODS--	BECAUSE THAT YOU ARE	1260	40
CONFISCATES			
AND ESTIMATES [ENFORCES / COMMENCES / REPLEVYS / CONFISCATES]	PERHAPS THEY DO NOT GO	1399	8
CONFLICT			
SOME CONFLICT WITH THOSE UPPER FRIENDS	A WILD BLUE SKY ABREAST	1415	5
CONFORM			
CONFORM MY SOUL--AS TWERE A CHURCH,	MY WORTHINESS IS ALL MY	751	15
CONFRONT			
ESCAPING FORWARD, TO CONFRONT	ESCAPING BACKWARD TO	867	3
CONFRONTING			
THAN A SOLID DAWN--CONFRONTING--	DREAMS--ARE WELL--BUT	450	7
CONFRONTING SUDDEN PELF--	THERE IS A SHAME OF	551	2
THAN IT'S [AN] INTERIOR CONFRONTING--	ONE NEED NOT BE A	670	7
CONFRONTING EYES LONG--COMFORTED--	I'LL SEND THE FEATHER	687	5
SALUTING [CONFRONTING / CONTRASTING]--IN THE ROAD--	UPON CONCLUDED LIVES	735	8
CONFRONTING US AGAIN!	THE BONE THAT HAS NO	1274	12
CONFRONTS			
CONFRONTS THE DAZZLED BEE.	PRECIOUS TO ME--SHE	727	14
CONFUSED			
CONFUSED BY SWEETS--AS MORTALS--ARE--	NOT PROBABLE--THE BAREST	346	6
CONFUSION			
WHAT CONFUSION WOULD COVER THE INNOCENT JESUS	HE PREACHED UPON	1207	7
CONGEALED			
THE BUSY EYES--CONGEALED--	'TWAS WARM--AT FIRST--	519	8
CONGENIAL			
IT'S SUCH CONGENIAL TIMES [WAY]	I'M SORRY FOR THE DEAD--	529	2
IN A CONGENIAL GROUND.	THE MOB WITHIN THE HEART	1745	8
CONJECTURE			
STILL TO ANTICIPATE [CONJECTURE]--WERE NO LIMIT--	BOUND--A TROUBLE--	269	V
WHOSE FATE--CONJECTURE KNEW--	A HOUSE UPON THE HIGHT--	399	9
BEYOND OUR FAINT [SMALL] CONJECTURE--	THOSE FAIR--FICTITIOUS	499	11
CONJECTURE FLOURISHING--	THESE ARE THE NIGHTS	1128	12
THAT OBLIQUE BELIEF WHICH WE CALL CONJECTURE	SOME WE SEE NO MORE,	1221	6
MISERIES OF CONJECTURE	WHETHER THEY HAVE	1329	5

	FIRST LINE	POEM	LINE
CONJECTURE (CONTINUED)			
BUT THE ARC OF A LOVER'S CONJECTURE	WE SHALL FIND THE CUBE	1484	3
THE SAGE [WISE] CANNOT CONJECTURE	FACTS BY OUR SIDE ARE	1497	10
CONJECTURED			
CONJECTURED, AND WAKED SUDDEN IN--	'TIS SO MUCH JOY! 'TIS	172	17
CONJECTURED WHO MAY BE	HAVE ANY LIKE MYSELF	736	10
MYSELF CONJECTURED [COMPUTED] WERE THEY PEARLS--	A DROP FELL ON THE APPLE	794	7
CONJECTURE'S			
INTO CONJECTURE'S PRESENCE--	THAT AFTER HORROR--THAT	286	11
CONJECTURING			
CONJECTURING A CLIMATE	CONJECTURING A CLIMATE	562	1
CONJUGATE			
WE CONJUGATE HER SKILL	THE VEINS OF OTHER	811	6
CONJUROR			
ENAMORED--OF THE CONJUROR--	"HEAVEN"--IS WHAT I	239	11
CONNECT			
THE DUST--CONNECT [ADJUST]--AND LIVE--	NO CROWD THAT HAS	515	8
CONNECTION			
THE SOUL'S DISTINCT CONNECTION	THE SOUL'S DISTINCT	974	1
CONNOISSEUR			
YOUR CONNOISSEUR IN LIQUORS	A DRUNKARD CANNOT MEET A	1628	11
CONQUER			
LEST THAT SHOULD CONQUER ME.	I HAV'NT TOLD MY GARDEN	50	2
ALL THESE--DID CONQUER--	OF TRIBULATION--THESE	325	5
CONQUER MORTALITY--	GIVEN IN MARRIAGE UNTO	817	8
CONQUERED			
CONQUERED WITH THE ROBIN--	ON THE WORLD YOU COLORED	1171	7
CONQUEROR			
IN WHICH WE EACH WERE CONQUEROR	'TIS SEASONS SINCE THE	1529	2
CONQUERS			
BUT GRAPPLING, CONQUERS IT--	'TIS SO APPALLING--IT	281	6
IT AIMS ONCE--KILLS ONCE--CONQUERS ONCE--	'TWAS FIGHTING FOR HIS	1188	5
CONSCIENCE			
THE CONSCIENCE OF US ALL	BELSHAZZAR HAD A LETTER	1459	6
'TIS "CONSCIENCE"--CHILDHOOD'S NURSE--	WHO IS IT SEEKS MY	1598	4
CONSCIENTIOUS			
AS ON THE CONSCIENTIOUS FLOWER	THE SUN IS ONE--AND ON	1372	3
HER CONSCIENTIOUS VOICE WILL SOAR UNMOVED	AFTER ALL BIRDS HAVE	1395	3
CONSCIOUS			
CONSCIOUS--AS OLD NAPOLEON,	A LITTLE BREAD--A CRUST	159	5
FAILED LIKE THEMSELVES--AND CONSCIOUS THAT IT ROSE--	IF ANY SINK, ASSURE THAT	358	2
"CONSCIOUS"? WONT YOU ASK THAT--	IT IS DEAD--FIND IT--	417	5
AND "WAS IT CONSCIOUS--WHEN IT STEPPED	I AM ALIVE--I GUESS--	470	15
SHE WAS CONSCIOUS--	CIVILIZATION--SPURNS--	492	6
THAT WHEN THEIR CONSCIOUS FINGERS CEASE--	THE MARTYR POETS--DID	544	7
HOW CONSCIOUS CONSCIOUSNESS--COULD GROW--	TO KNOW JUST HOW HE	622	24
OURSELVES ARE CONSCIOUS HE EXIST--	THE LIGHTNING PLAYETH--	630	3
CONSCIOUS AM I IN MY CHAMBER,	CONSCIOUS AM I IN MY	679	1
THE SPIRIT IS THE CONSCIOUS EAR.	THE SPIRIT IS THE	733	1
OF SAVORS--MAKE US CONSCIOUS--	DESPAIR'S ADVANTAGE IS	799	9
AS MUCH THROUGH CONSCIOUSNESS [CONSCIOUS FAITH]	NOT TO DISCOVER WEAKNESS	1054	4
BE CONSCIOUS OF A SIGH	JUST ONCE! OH LEAST	1076	7
AND ADEQUATE, [CONSCIOUS AND] ERECT,	THE PROPS ASSIST THE	1142	4
CONSCIOUSER			
FOR CONSCIOUSER [TOTALLER] ECLIPSE--	THE WHOLE OF IT CAME NOT	762	12
CONSCIOUSLY			
BUT THIS TIME, CONSCIOUSLY, OF GRACE--	I'M CEDED--I'VE STOPPED	508	9
CONSCIOUSNESS			
CAPTIVITY IS CONSCIOUSNESS--	NO RACK CAN TORTURE ME--	384	15
ENVELOPES CONSCIOUSNESS--	THERE IS A LANGUOR OF	396	7
POSSESS EACH SEPARATE CONSCIOUSNESS--	NO CROWD THAT HAS	515	15
HOW CONSCIOUS CONSCIOUSNESS--COULD GROW--	TO KNOW JUST HOW HE	622	24
CONSCIOUSNESS?	ME FROM MYSELF--TO	642	8
YOUR CONSCIOUSNESS--AND ME--	YOU LEFT ME--SIRE--TWO	644	8
WITH CONSCIOUSNESS SUSPENDED--	THE LONELINESS ONE DARE	777	11
NO DRUG FOR CONSCIOUSNESS--CAN BE--	SEVERER SERVICE OF	786	21
THE CONSCIOUSNESS OF THEE.	THE LUXURY TO APPREHEND	815	16
THIS CONSCIOUSNESS THAT IS AWARE	THIS CONSCIOUSNESS THAT	822	1
A CONSCIOUSNESS IT'S ACRE, AND	IT WAS A GRAVE, YET BORE	876	3
OF CONSCIOUSNESS, HER AWFUL MATE	OF CONSCIOUSNESS, HER	894	1
EACH CONSCIOUSNESS MUST EMIGRATE	TOO LITTLE WAY THE HOUSE	911	7
HIS--SHORTEST CONSCIOUSNESS--	NO OTHER CAN REDUCE	982 V	
AS MUCH THROUGH CONSCIOUSNESS [CONSCIOUS FAITH]	NOT TO DISCOVER WEAKNESS	1054	4
AND CONSCIOUSNESS--IS NOON.	THERE IS A ZONE WHOSE	1056	8
LATER THAN LIGHT THY CONSCIOUSNESS ACCOST ME	AIR HAS NO RESIDENCE, NO	1060	7
WHEN THE PREFACE PERISHED FROM CONSCIOUSNESS	ENDED, ERE IT BEGUN--	1088	3
WITHOUT THE DATE, LIKE CONSCIOUSNESS OR IMMORTALITY--	LEST ANY DOUBT THAT WE	1156	3
WHEN CONSCIOUSNESS AND CLAY	POWER IS A FAMILIAR	1238	6
THE YAWNING CONSCIOUSNESS,	I NEVER HEAR THAT ONE IS	1323	8
THE CONSCIOUSNESS OF THIS.	I NEVER HEAR THAT ONE IS	1323 V	8
THAT AWFUL STRANGER CONSCIOUSNESS	I NEVER HEAR THAT ONE IS	1323	15
COSTUMELESS CONSCIOUSNESS--	THOSE NOT LIVE YET	1454	10
CONSCIOUSNESS'			
TOO INFINITE FOR CONSCIOUSNESS'	SUCH IS THE FORCE OF	787	7

	FIRST LINE	POEM	LINE
CONSECRATE			
SOME OTHER THOU WILT [DID'ST] CONSECRATE-- .	OH SHADOW ON THE GRASS,	1187	7
MAY STIMULATE [CONSECRATE] AN EYE	A WORD DROPPED CARELESS	1261	2
CONSECRATED			
THY CONSECRATED BREAD TO TAKE	THESE ARE THE DAYS WHEN	130	17
THAT CONSECRATED ME--	SOMEWHERE UPON THE	1231	4
THAT CONSECRATED IT COULD BE	I GROPED FOR HIM BEFORE	1555	7
CONSECUTIVE			
CONSECUTIVE AND SLOW--	CRUMBLING IS NOT AN	997	10
CONSENT			
LIKE THIS CONSENT OF LANGUAGE	A WORD MADE FLESH IS	1651	15
CONSENTED			
CONSENTED, AND WAS DEAD--	THE LAST NIGHT THAT SHE	1100	24
CONSENTING			
DESCENDING [CONSENTING / ESTABLISHED / IMPARTED] TO ENAMOR US	THE FACE IN EVANESCENCE	1490	7
CONSEQUENCE			
ONE LIFE OF SO MUCH CONSEQUENCE!	ONE LIFE OF SO MUCH	270	1
FOR SORDID EXCELLENCE [CONSEQUENCE]	I CANNOT LIVE WITH YOU--	640	35
OUR MORTAL CONSEQUENCE	NO OTHER CAN REDUCE	982	2
MORTAL CONSEQUENCE	NO OTHER CAN REDUCE	982	V
'TIS ALMOST CONSEQUENCE--	THAT SHORT--POTENTIAL	1307	4
AND GRAPHIC CONSEQUENCE	AS IMPERCEPTIBLY AS	1540	V
CONSIDER			
THAT YOU--SO LATE--"CONSIDER" ME--	I THINK JUST HOW MY	237	7
CONSIDER IT UNTO MYSELF	ESCAPE IS SUCH A	1347	3
IS BETTER WE CONSIDER	ADVANCE IS LIFE'S	1652	7
CONSIDERED			
AND OUR'S SURRENDERED [CONSIDERED] FOR IT'S SAKE	THE FACE IN EVANESCENCE	1490	3
I WAS REGARDED [CONSIDERED] THEN	TO BE FORGOT BY THEE	1560	7
CONSIDERS			
CONSIDERS COMING TWICE--	MORNING THAT COMES BUT	1610	2
CONSIGNED			
A DEVOTEE HAS OFT [COOL / BLAND] CONSIGNED .	DEATH WARRANTS ARE	1375	5
CONSOLATION			
WILL CONSOLATION BE;	"SIC TRANSIT GLORIA	3	66
AND HE NO CONSOLATION	I HAD A GUINEA GOLDEN--	23	35
CONSOLED			
NOR WHAT CONSOLED IT, I COULD TRACE-- . .	IT CEASED TO HURT ME,	584	13
CONSOLELESSLY			
CONSOLELESSLY PRESUME--	'TIS NOT THE SWAYING	1597	8
CONSOLES			
CONSOLES A WO SO MONSTROUS	I SOMETIMES DROP IT, FOR	708	5
CONSOLIDATE			
THE DREAMS CONSOLIDATE IN ACTION-- . . .	THE LASSITUDES OF	1592	5
CONSOLIDATES			
AND THEN CONSOLIDATES	ASHES DENOTE THAT FIRE	1063	6
CONSORT			
ADAM, AND EVE, HIS CONSORT, THE MOON, AND THEN THE SUN;	AWAKE YE MUSES NINE,	1	8
CONSPICUOUS			
THOUGH SPOKES--SPIN--MORE CONSPICUOUS . .	THE OUTER--FROM THE	451	7
A PANG IS MORE CONSPICUOUS IN SPRING . . .	A PANG IS MORE	1530	1
CONSPIRE			
CONSPIRE AGAINST [REPUDIATE] HIS OWN . . .	WHO COURT OBTAIN WITHIN	803	9
CONSTANCY			
OUR CONSTANCY FORGOT--	IN EBON BOX, WHEN YEARS	169	14
WHAT CONSTANCY MUST BE ACHIEVED	LONGING IS LIKE THE SEED	1255	7
CONSTANCY WITH A PROVISO	"FAITHFUL TO THE END"	1357	3
CONSTANCY ABHORS--	"FAITHFUL TO THE END"	1357	4
IT SHAMES THE CONSTANCY THAT FLED	SHE LAID HER DOCILE	1396	7
WHEN CONSTANCY IS CLARIFIED	HOW HUMAN NATURE DOTES	1417	7
BUT CONSTANCY BECAME	THAT SHE FORGOT ME WAS	1683	6
CONSTANCY THRO' FIRE--AWARDED--	REARRANGE A "WIFE'S"	1737	11
CONSTANCY'S			
FAITH IS CONSTANCY'S RESULT--	HE WHO IN HIMSELF	969	3
CONSTANT			
AS CONSTANT AS THE CHILDISH FROCK [GOWN]-- .	IT CEASED TO HURT ME,	584	7
MY CONSTANT--REVERENTIAL FACE	MY BEST ACQUAINTANCES	932	7
SO CONSTANT TO IT'S STOLID TRUST, ...	SHE LAID HER DOCILE	1396	5
CONSTELLATION			
NOR CONSTELLATION BURN--	A POOR--TORN HEART-- A	78	6
CONSTERNATION			
WHO CONSTERNATION COMPASSED	I YEARS HAD BEEN FROM	609	15
IT COMES, WITHOUT A CONSTERNATION--	IN MANY AND REPORTLESS	1382	5
CAJOLING CONSTERNATION	THE ROBIN IS A GABRIEL	1483	14
CONSTERNATION'S			
FIND CONSTERNATION'S CARNIVAL	ENDANGER IT, AND THE	1658	7
CONSTITUTE			
TO CONSTITUTE THEM--GAINS--	BEST GAINS--MUST HAVE	684	2
A SINGLE BLOOM WE CONSTITUTE	HERE, WHERE THE DAISIES	1037	11
CONSTITUTED			
YOU CONSTITUTED TIME--	YOU CONSTITUTED TIME--	765	1
CONSTRAINED			
UNTIL CONSTRAINED TO CLUTCH IT	OF DEATH I TRY TO THINK	1558	14
CONSTRUCTED			
CONSTRUCTED FOR THE WINDS--	YOU'LL KNOW HER--BY HER	634	14
CONSTRUCTS			
WHOSE SUN CONSTRUCTS PERPETUAL NOON . . .	THERE IS A ZONE WHOSE	1056	3

	FIRST LINE	POEM	LINE
CONSULATE			
. . . MOST POMPOUS] CONSULATE.	AN ANTIQUATED TREE	1514	7
CONSULT			
CONSULT YOUR EYE!	YOU'LL KNOW IT--AS YOU	420	15
BUT A CONFIDING GUEST CONSULT AS WELL, . .	I CANNOT SEE MY SOUL BUT	1262	4
CONSULTING			
CONSULTING SUMMER'S CLOCK, ...	CONSULTING SUMMER'S	1715	1
CONSULTS			
CONSULTS THE BUMBLE BEE--	A DRUNKARD CANNOT MEET A	1628	12
CONSUME			
EXPERIENCE EITHER AND CONSUME--	TO PILE LIKE THUNDER TO	1247	7
CONSUMED			
NEVER YET--CONSUMED--	THE RED--BLAZE--IS THE	469	8
AND WHATSOEVER IS CONSUMED	HOPE IS A SUBTLE GLUTTON	1547	7
"AM NOT CONSUMED," OLD MOSES WROTE, . . .	NO MAN SAW AWE, NOR TO	1733	13
CONSUMES			
CONSUMES AND NO [WITHOUT] REPORT TO MEN . .	THE LARGEST FIRE EVER	1114	5
THEIR CHIVALRY CONSUMES--	LIKE TRAINS OF CARS ON	1224	6
CONSUMMATE			
TIS TERROR AS CONSUMMATE	ONE ANGUISH--IN A CROWD	565	5
BEHIND THE MOST UNCONSCIOUS [CONSUMMATE] CLOCK	NOT TO DISCOVER WEAKNESS	1054	7
IN THAT UNCOMMON [CONSUMMATE] SCENE-- . .	ELIJAH'S WAGON KNEW NO	1254	V 8
ON DOOM'S CONSUMMATE CHART	TWO LENGTHS HAS EVERY	1295	10
BUT FROM LIFE'S CONSUMMATE CLUSTER--	DEATH'S WAYLAYING NOT	1296	7
IS FAME'S CONSUMMATE FEE--	TO EARN IT BY DISDAINING	1427	2
IN ONE CONSUMMATE BILL, ...	HOW DARE THE ROBINS SING	1724	6
SOFTENED BY TIME'S CONSUMMATE PLUSH, ...	SOFTENED BY TIME'S	1738	1
CONSUMMATED			
JUST CONSUMMATED--NOW--	A HAPPY LIP--BREAKS	353	4
IN CONSUMMATED BLOOM--	MIDSUMMER, WAS IT, WHEN	962	4
IS CONSUMMATED EQUALLY	NOT ALL DIE EARLY, DYING	990	3
AND CONSUMMATED DULL!	THAT ODD OLD MAN IS DEAD	1130	10
THEIR MOMENT CONSUMMATED--	A BEE HIS BURNISHED	1339	9
CONTAIN			
A TRANSPORT ONE CANNOT CONTAIN	A TRANSPORT ONE CANNOT	184	1
TOO SCANT--BY CUBITS--TO CONTAIN	IT MIGHT BE LONELIER	405	7
THE ONE THE OTHER WILL CONTAIN [INCLUDE] .	THE BRAIN--IS WIDER THAN	632	3
IT'S INFINITE CONTAIN	PAIN--HAS AN ELEMENT OF	650	6
OUTSIDE THE CASTLE [CENTRE / CITY]--THAT CONTAIN [PRESENT]--	THE SPIRIT IS THE	733	7
THAT HEAVEN IF HEAVEN--MUST CONTAIN . . .	TWO TRAVELLERS PERISHING	933	5
YET ABLE TO CONTAIN	A COFFIN--IS A SMALL	943	2
IF IT CONTAIN A KERNEL?	EXPERIMENT TO ME	1073	3
THE POWER TO CONTAIN	I THOUGHT THAT NATURE	1286	8
CONTAINED			
AND REASONS NOT CONTAINED--	"WHY DO I LOVE" YOU, SIR	480	14
'TWAS'NT CONTAINED--LIKE OTHER STANZA-- . .	BETTER--THAN MUSIC! FOR	503	5
WHEN IT HAS JUST CONTAINED A LIFE	THIS CHASM, SWEET, UPON	858	9
CONTAINED [COMBINED / COMPRISED] IN THIS SHORT [PLAIN] LIFE	CONTAINED IN THIS SHORT	1165	1
CONTAINS			
I LOOK ON ALL THIS WORLD CONTAINS--	AGAIN--HIS VOICE IS AT	663	11
WHAT FORTITUDE THE SOUL CONTAINS, ...	ELYSIUM IS AS FAR AS TO	1760	5
CONTEMN			
OR COULD SHE ONE CONTEMN--	THE MUSHROOM IS THE ELF	1298	18
COULD SHE A SON CONTEMN	THE MUSHROOM IS THE ELF	1298	V 18
CONTEMPLATE			
COULD CONTEMPLATE THE JOURNEY	COULD LIVE--DID LIVE--	43	8
UNLESS [UNTIL] IT CONTEMPLATE	TO BE FORGOT BY THEE	1560	5
A CRATER I MAY CONTEMPLATE	VOLCANOES BE IN SICILY	1705	7
CONTEMPLATED			
IT CONTEMPLATED--SMILING--	A HAPPY LIP--BREAKS	353	3
CONTEMPLATING			
ACHIEVEMENT CONTEMPLATING THEE [THIS / HERE]--	THAT ODD OLD MAN IS DEAD	1130	11
CONTEMPLATION			
OR CONTEMPLATION FAILS.	SHE SWEEPS WITH	219	V 12
BUT CONTEMPLATION FOR	NO OTHER CAN REDUCE	982	5
TO CONTEMPLATION--[TO SPECTACLE, BUT] NOT TO TOUCH--	THE LILAC IS AN ANCIENT	1241	7
THE LASSITUDES OF CONTEMPLATION	THE LASSITUDES OF	1592	1
CONTEMPT			
CONTEMPT OF GENERATIONS	THIS WORLD IS NOT	501	11
CONTEMPTS			
THE ADMIRATIONS--AND CONTEMPTS--OF TIME-- .	THE ADMIRATIONS--AND	906	1
CONTENDED			
IS A TOO ESTABLISHED FORTUNE [SECURE POSSESSION / CONTENDED . . .	EXPECTATION--IS	807	7
CONTENDING			
CONTENDING WITH THE GRASS--	THERE IS A FLOWER THAT	380	17
CONTENT			
WHY, GOD, WOULD BE CONTENT	DOUBT ME! MY DIM	275	2
SUCH AS CONTENT--AND HEAVEN--	I MEANT TO HAVE BUT	476	2
WE WERE CONTENT TO SHOW--	WE COVER THEE--SWEET	482	10
MAKE FRUGAL--ONES--CONTENT--	IT'S THOUGHTS--AND JUST	495	3
NOT QUITE--CONTENT--	IT'S THOUGHTS--AND JUST	495	28
ENAMORED--IMPOTENT--CONTENT--	I WOULD NOT PAINT--A	505	19
SHE'S HAPPY, WITH A NEW CONTENT--	SHE'S HAPPY, WITH A NEW	535	1
TO KNOW IF HE WAS PATIENT--PART CONTENT-- .	TO KNOW JUST HOW HE	622	5
A HEAVENLY FATHER WOULD SUFFICE [CONTENT] .	YOU LEFT ME--SIRE--TWO	644	3
FOR SOMETHING PASSIVER--CONTENT	A PRISON GETS TO BE A	652	27

	FIRST LINE	POEM	LINE
CONTRADICT			
IF BIRD THE SILENCE CONTRADICT	A LANE OF YELLOW LED THE	1650	5
CONTRAST			
STIMULATED--BY THE CONTRAST--	SMILING BACK FROM	385	11
ENTITLES US--BY CONTRAST--	THIS WAS A POET--IT IS	448	11
IN CONTRAST WITH THE LOVE--	I MEASURE EVERY GRIEF I	561	24
LOST DOUBLY--BUT BY CONTRAST--MOST--	A DOOR JUST OPENED ON A	953	7
WE BUY WITH CONTRAST--PANG IS GOOD	THE SNOW THAT NEVER	1133	15
BY CONTRAST CERTIFYING	THE WAY TO KNOW THE	1279	21
IN CONTRAST WITH THE [THOSE] THINGS THAT SING	A PANG IS MORE	1530	2
A CONTRAST TO OUR RESPITES.	HIGH FROM THE EARTH I	1723	19
CONTRASTED			
CONTRASTED WITH THE CURRENCY	SOME--WORK FOR	406	7
CONTRASTING			
SALUTING [CONFRONTING / CONTRASTING]--IN THE ROAD--	UPON CONCLUDED LIVES	735	8
CONTRASTING WHICH, MY QUALITY	MY WORTHINESS IS ALL MY	751	3
CONTRITION			
A BAYONET'S CONTRITION	MY TRIUMPH LASTED TILL	1227	15
CONTRIVES			
CONTRIVES THAT NONE GO OUT AGAIN--	NO PASSENGER WAS KNOWN	1406	4
CONTROL			
"WHICH OBTAIN [CONTROLLED / CONTROL] THE DAY"?	WOLFE DEMANDED DURING	678	2
HIS TIDES--DO I CONTROL--	I MAKE HIS CRESCENT FILL	909	4
BEYOND IT'S DULL [SLOW]--CONTROL	WITH PINIONS OF DISDAIN	1431	6
CONTROLLED			
"WHICH OBTAIN [CONTROLLED / CONTROL] THE DAY"?	WOLFE DEMANDED DURING	678	2
THE DAY CONTROLLED [RESUMED] THE WORLD--	THE BIRDS BEGUN AT FOUR	783	22
CONTROVERTIBLE			
IS NOT A CONTROVERTIBLE--	DO PEOPLE MOULDER	432	15
CONTUSION			
CONTUSION OF THE HUSK	TOO COLD IS THIS	1135	7
CONVALESCENT			
IN CONVALESCENT MIND,	AS ONE DOES SICKNESS	957	2
TO GO IT'S CONVALESCENT WAY	THE HEALED HEART SHOWS	1440	5
CONVENIENT			
MINE--IS THE MORE CONVENIENT	I SEND TWO SUNSETS--	308	7
FROM A CONVENIENT GRASS--	A BIRD CAME DOWN THE	328	6
THE MORE CONVENIENT WAY--	THE BODY GROWS WITHOUT--	578	2
AND HEAVEN--A CONVENIENT GRACE	HAVE ANY LIKE MYSELF	736	15
OR LOVE'S CONVENIENT THINGS,	TO THE BRIGHT EAST SHE	1573	5
CONVENIENT TO THE LONGING	THROUGH THOSE OLD	1753	15
CONVERGES			
EACH LIFE CONVERGES TO SOME CENTRE--	EACH LIFE CONVERGES TO	680	1
CONVERSATION			
HIS CONVERSATION--SELDOM--	THE ONLY GHOST I EVER	274	9
HIS CONVERSATION--WITH THE SEA--	YOU'LL KNOW IT--AS YOU	420	13
HOW FAIR HER CONVERSATION--	NATURE--THE GENTLEST	790	9
CONVERSION			
CONVERSION OF THE MIND	I THINK I WAS ENCHANTED	593	22
CONVERT			
EACH OTHER'S CONVERT--	THE SWEETEST HERESY	387	3
CONVEX			
CONVEX--AND CONCAVE WITNESS--	THE ADMIRATIONS--AND	906	13
CONVEY			
OF CHARIOTS, THAT HIM CONVEY--	I ENVY SEAS, WHEREON HE	498	3
THE WISE CONVEY IT HOME	THIS IS A BLOSSOM OF THE	945	10
WAGONS--HAVE YOU--TO CONVEY ME?	"UNTO ME?" I DO NOT KNOW	964	5
INCLUDE US [SCAN BETTER / CONVEY US]--AS THEY GO--	WE MISS HER, NOT BECAUSE	993	8
CONVEY MY DYING KISS--	"GO TELL IT"--WHAT A	1554	V 8
CONVEYING			
TILL IT DEPART, PERSUADING [CONVEYING] MINE--	AIR HAS NO RESIDENCE, NO	1060	8
CONVICTED			
CONVICTED OF ITSELF--	THERE IS A SHAME OF	551	4
CONVICTED ME--OF ME--	I CRIED AT PITY--NOT AT	588	V 4
CONVICTED--SENTENCED--ERMINE--NOT TO ME	WERT THOU BUT ILL--THAT	961	10
CONVICTED--COULD WE BE	A SAUCER HOLDS A CUP	1374	13
CONVICTION			
CONVICTION MIGHT, OF ME--	I FELT MY LIFE WITH BOTH	351	12
HAD THE TRIUMPH NO CONVICTION	SMILING BACK FROM	385	9
CONVICTION--EVERY DAY--	I LIVE WITH HIM--I SEE	463	14
FOR FIRM CONVICTION OF A MOUSE	THE WAY I READ A	636	11
CONVICTION--THAT GRANITIC BASE--	ON A COLUMNAR SELF--	789	7
I SHALL MEET WITH CONVICTION I SOMEWHERE MET	BY MY WINDOW HAVE I FOR	797	20
BUT SATIETY--CONVICTION	EXPECTATION--IS	807	3
THE CHEMICAL CONVICTION	THE CHEMICAL CONVICTION	954	1
HE SEEK CONVICTION, THAT--BE THIS--	FITTER TO SEE HIM, I MAY	968	14
THERE IS A MARITIME CONVICTION	I THINK THAT THE ROOT OF	1302	7
A WARRANT, A CONVICTION,	AS SUBTLE AS TOMORROW	1713	3
CONVICTIONS			
SUCH DIMITY CONVICTIONS--	WHAT SOFT--CHERUBIC	401	5
CONVICTS			
RETURNS--SUGGESTS--CONVICTS--ENCHANTS--	THE LOVE A LIFE CAN SHOW	673	15
CONVINCE			
OH LOVER--LIFE COULD NOT CONVINCE--	ME PROVE IT NOW--WHOEVER	537	7
CONVINCED			
CONVINCED MYSELF OF ME--	I CRIED AT PITY--NOT AT	588	4
I AM CONVINCED WAS THIS	NO MAN SAW AWE, NOR TO	1733	16

	FIRST LINE	POEM	LINE
CONVINCING			
YET IS SHE MORE CONVINCING	THE RAINBOW NEVER TELLS	97	3
CONVULSION			
MEN DO NOT SHAM CONVULSION,	I LIKE A LOOK OF AGONY,	241	3
CONVULSION--PLAYING ROUND--	THROUGH THE STRAIT PASS	792	6
CONVULSIVE			
CONVULSIVE, WHILE THE MUSIC CRASHED [BROKE]--	HER SMILE WAS SHAPED	514	7
THE HEART CONVULSIVE LEARNS	THE HEART HAS NARROW	928	8
COOL			
SO STILL--SO COOL--	OUR LIVES ARE SWISS--	80	2
STROKE THE COOL FOREHEAD--HOT SO OFTEN--	HOW MANY TIMES THESE LOW	187	5
HOW NUMB [COOL], THE BELLOWS FEELS!	I BREATHED ENOUGH TO	272	8
WHILE COOL--CONCERNLESS NO--	A CLOCK STOPPED--	287	13
YOUR BRAIN--TO BUBBLE COOL--	HE FUMBLES AT YOUR SOUL	315	10
COOL OF EYE, AND CRITICAL OF WORK--	A SOLEMN THING WITHIN	483	10
HAS MADE THE TOILETTE COOL	TO MAKE ONE'S TOILETTE--	485	2
AS COOL TO SPEECH--AS STONE--	AS FAR FROM PITY, AS	496	2
COULD KEEP A CHANCEL, COOL--	IT WAS NOT DEATH, FOR I	510	8
BUT, MOST, LIKE CHAOS--STOPLESS--COOL--	IT WAS NOT DEATH, FOR I	510	21
COOL US TO SHAFTS OF GRANITE--	WE DREAM--IT IS GOOD WE	531	13
WE--TELL A HURT--TO COOL IT--	THE BLACK BERRY--WEARS A	554	9
WE HANDLED DESTINIES, AS COOL--	WE TALKED AS GIRLS DO--	586	5
AS COOL [DISTINCT] AS SATYR'S DRUMS--	DID YOU EVER STAND IN A	590	14
AND EQUALLY AS COOL--	WHAT CARE THE DEAD, FOR	592	8
ETERNITY'S WHITE [COOL] FLAG--BEFORE [IN FRONT]--	OUR JOURNEY HAD ADVANCED	615	11
NOT A FROST COULD [NO NOVEMBER] COOL--	WHEN I HOPED, I	768	6
PRICKLED BLUE [RAW] AND COOL--	WHEN I HOPED, I	768	14
OR COOL ONE PAIN	IF I CAN STOP ONE HEART	919	4
A FLOOR TOO COOL FOR CORN--	A NARROW FELLOW IN THE	986	10
VITALITY IS CARVED AND COOL.	I'VE DROPPED MY BRAIN--	1046	5
FEELS TRANSITIVE AND COOL.	THAT ODD OLD MAN IS DEAD	1130	12
A DEVOTEE HAS OFT [COOL / BLAND] CONSIGNED	DEATH WARRANTS ARE	1375	5
WHERE WATERS COOL AROUND THE MOSSES CRAWL--	THESE FEVERED DAYS--TO	1441	2
WILL FEEL AS COOL AS LAND	I DID NOT REACH THEE	1664	11
COOLED			
THE LIPS I W'D HAVE COOLED, ALAS--	I BRING AN UNACCUSTOMED	132	9
THAT COOLED THE FOREHEAD OF THE HILL--	FORGET! THE LADY WITH	438	13
COOLED BY THE MORSEL FOR A MOMENT	AS THE STARVED MAELSTROM	872	9
COOLER			
IT'S COOLER THAN THE DAWN--	I OFTEN PASSED THE	51	10
THAT COOLER [WHITER] HOST.	ONE NEED NOT BE A	670	8
THERE'S NOTHING COOLER FALLS--	UPON CONCLUDED LIVES	735	2
BUT HER DISDAIN--'TWERE LIGHTER [COOLER] BEAR	MY SOUL--ACCUSED ME--AND	753	7
THOUGH COOLER THAN THE WATER WAS	I COULD NOT DRINK IT,	818	3
COOLING			
FLAGONS, AND COOLING TAMARIND!	WHO NEVER LOST, ARE	73	4
COOLLY			
THE PUNCTURE--COOLLY TRIES--	A WEIGHT WITH NEEDLES ON	264	4
TOYED COOLLY WITH THE FINAL INCH	'TWAS LIKE A MAELSTROM,	414	5
THEN--SEESAWING--COOLLY--ON IT--	ROBBED BY DEATH--BUT	971	15
COOLS			
COOLS--LIKE THE RAIN--	THE WORLD--FEELS DUSTY	715	8
LET HIM BE QUICK--THE VIAND FLITS [BANQUET COOLS]--	MINE ENEMY IS GROWING	1509	5
COPIED			
THE FOREHEAD COPIED STONE--	'TWAS WARM--AT FIRST--	519	5
COPY			
IN THAT IMMORTAL COPY	BELSHAZZAR HAD A LETTER	1459	5
COQUETTE			
GESTURE COQUETTE--AND SHAKE YOUR HEAD!	GOING TO HIM! HAPPY	494	25
COQUETTISH			
AND EARTH IS QUITE COQUETTISH, AND BESEEMETH IN VAIN TO SUE.	AWAKE YE MUSES NINE,	1	24
CORAL			
MY FUSCHZIA'S CORAL SEAMS	I TEND MY FLOWERS FOR	339	3
CORALS			
WHOSE HISSING CORALS PART--AND SHUT--	A STILL--VOLCANO--LIFE--	601	11
CORDAGE			
WHAT ARE THE SINEWS OF SUCH CORDAGE FOR	THERE IS A STRENGTH IN	1113	3
CORDIAL			
AND DO I SMILE, SUCH CORDIAL LIGHT	MY LIFE HAD STOOD--A	754	9
WITHOUT A CORDIAL INTERVIEW	SPRING IS THE PERIOD	844	7
HER PANTING NOTE [JOYFUL CRY / CORDIAL NOTE] EXALTS US-- . . .	AFTER ALL BIRDS HAVE	1395	6
BACK FROM THE CORDIAL GRAVE I DRAG THEE	BACK FROM THE CORDIAL	1625	1
HOW CORDIAL IS THE MYSTERY!	NO LIFE CAN POMPLESS	1626	5
THE MAKER'S CORDIAL VISAGE,	DROWNING IS NOT SO	1718	9
CORDIALITY			
THE CORDIALITY OF DEATH--	THAT AFTER HORROR--THAT	286	15
OF CORDIALITY--	A NARROW FELLOW IN THE	986	20
WHY TO CORDIALITY SO AVERSE TO COME	GUEST AM I TO HAVE	1661	3
"NO CORDIALITY"--	IN WINTER IN MY ROOM	1670	26
CORDIALLY			
RECEIVE ME CORDIALLY--	THE BEE IS NOT AFRAID OF	111	4
CORDILLERA			
FLICKERS UPON CORDILLERA--	ME, CHANGE! ME, ALTER!	268	5
A FURROW--OUR CORDILLERA--	WE SEE--COMPARATIVELY--	534	7
WHO'S CORDILLERA?	NOR MOUNTAIN HINDER ME	1029	4

	FIRST LINE	POEM	LINE
COST (CONTINUED)			
THAT COST ME MY HONEST HEART--	I SAW THAT THE FLAKE WAS	1267	4
NOTWITHSTANDING IT COST US EXISTENCE ONCE .	TO DO A MAGNANIMOUS	1699	7
BAFFLE, IF IT COST YOU	DEATH IS LIKE THE INSECT	1716	7
COSTLIER			
A COSTLIER ONE	EACH SCAR I'LL KEEP FOR	877	4
THE LIVING, SWEET, IS COSTLIER--	TOO SCANTY 'TWAS TO DIE	1013	3
COSTLY			
'TIS COSTLY--SO ARE PURPLES!	YOU'RE RIGHT--"THE WAY	234	5
TOO COSTLY FOR REPAIRS.	DEATH SETS A THING	360	20
CLIMBING TO REACH [WHO "MEDDLED" WITH] THE COSTLY HEARTS	CLIMBING TO REACH THE	1566	1
COSTS			
PERCEPTION OF AN OBJECT COSTS	PERCEPTION OF AN OBJECT	1071	1
COSTUME			
THEIR COSTUME, OF A SUNDAY, ...	IF ANYBODY'S FRIEND BE	509	5
COSTUMELESS			
COSTUMELESS CONSCIOUSNESS--	THOSE NOT LIVE YET	1454	10
COSTUMES			
LIKE COSTUMES GRANDSIRES WORE.	WE OUTGROW LOVE, LIKE	887	4
COTEMPORANEOUS			
COTEMPORANEOUS NOUGHT	NO OTHER CAN REDUCE	982	6
COTERIE			
BEES EXCLUSIVE COTERIE--	PIGMY SERAPHS--GONE	138	4
COTTAGE			
TO MAKE YOUR COTTAGE GAY--	ALTHOUGH I PUT AWAY HIS	366	29
YOUR COTTAGE--FACED THE SUN--	OURSELVES WERE WED ONE	631	10
THE TENANT OF THE NARROW COTTAGE, WERT THOU--	WERT THOU BUT ILL--THAT	961	13
THE GRAVE MY LITTLE COTTAGE IS, ...	THE GRAVE MY LITTLE	1743	1
COTTAGES			
TIM--SEE COTTAGES--	WE DONT CRY--TIM AND I,	196	13
THE SUNSET STOPPED [DROPPED] ON COTTAGES .	THE SUNSET STOPPED ON	950	1
THE SUNSET STOPPED ON COTTAGES	THE SUNSET STOPPED ON	950	5
COUCH			
UPON A COUCH OF FLOWERS.	SHE DIED AT PLAY,	75	5
COUNSEL			
JOVE! CHOOSE YOUR COUNSEL--	I HAD SOME THINGS THAT I	116	15
COUNT			
BE SURE YOU COUNT--SH'D I FORGET	IT'S ALL I HAVE TO BRING	26	5
WHEN I COUNT THE SEEDS	WHEN I COUNT THE SEEDS	40	1
AND WEAR--IF GOD SHOULD COUNT ME FIT-- . .	A SOLEMN THING--IT WAS--	271	3
COUNT--HOARD--THEN LOSE--	I'LL CLUTCH--AND CLUTCH	427	12
I'D COUNT THEM ON MY HAND, ...	IF YOU WERE COMING IN	511	10
I RECKON--WHEN I COUNT AT ALL--	I RECKON--WHEN I COUNT	569	1
I COUNT THE FORCE 'TWOULD BE	I PRAYED, AT FIRST, A	576	15
THE PENDULUM BEGINS TO COUNT--	I THINK THE LONGEST HOUR	635	9
WE CANNOT COUNT--ON HIGH!	AGAIN--HIS VOICE IS AT	663	25
BUT HE MUST [SHOULD] COUNT THE DROPS--HIMSELF--	AGAIN--HIS VOICE IS AT	663	28
I COULD NOT COUNT THEIR FORCE--	THE BIRDS BEGUN AT FOUR	783	5
WERE HE TO COUNT THEM O'ER	EACH SCAR I'LL KEEP FOR	877	6
COUNT NOT THAT FAR THAT CAN BE HAD, ...	COUNT NOT THAT FAR THAT	1074	1
AND ALMOST COUNT IT AN AFFRONT	AS SUMMER INTO AUTUMN	1346	5
I SHALL NOT COUNT THE JOURNEY ONE	I DID NOT REACH THEE	1664	5
COUNTED			
I COUNTED TILL THEY DANCED SO	I COUNTED TILL THEY	36	1
SUCCESS IS COUNTED SWEETEST	SUCCESS IS COUNTED	67	1
THEN I HAD COUNTED IT UNTIL	THEIR HIGHT IN HEAVEN	696	11
COUNTENANCE			
HER COUNTENANCE AS SPRAY.	SHE DIED AT PLAY,	75	9
OF VELVET, IS HIS COUNTENANCE, ...	A FUZZY FELLOW, WITHOUT	173	3
HER STURDY LITTLE COUNTENANCE	THERE IS A FLOWER THAT	380	15
HIS COUNTENANCE--A BILLOW--	THE WIND--TAPPED LIKE A	436	13
JEHOVAH'S COUNTENANCE--	TRIUMPH--MAY BE OF	455	16
FIT [STRAIN] HIS COUNTENANCE--	BLOOM UPON THE MOUNTAIN	667	18
REFRACTED BUT A COUNTENANCE--	THE GRACE--MYSELF--MIGHT	707	3
BY NO COUNTENANCE--	GROWTH OF MAN--LIKE	750	16
SO MAY [CAN] COUNTENANCE	SO THE EYES ACCOST--AND	752	4
COUNTENANCE OF ONE	SO THE EYES ACCOST--AND	752	6
TO BANQUET ON THY COUNTENANCE	THE LUXURY TO APPREHEND	815	11
AND GRANT US ALL THEIR COUNTENANCE	THEY ASK BUT OUR DELIGHT	868	3
DO CONCENTRATE HIS COUNTENANCE	THE SUN AND MOON MUST	871	7
THE WILTED [BLACKENED] COUNTENANCE	AS FROST IS BEST	951	8
THE TRANSPORT OF HIS COUNTENANCE	THE FINGERS OF THE LIGHT	1000	11
HIS COUNTENANCE TO SEE	THE STIMULUS, BEYOND THE	1001	2
THE COUNTENANCE 'TWOULD BE.	WHO SAW NO SUNRISE	1018	2
COULD COUNTENANCE DISCLOSE	IT'S HOUR WITH ITSELF	1225	4
AND NOTHING IN THE COUNTENANCE	HOW KNOW IT FROM A	1364	3
HER COUNTENANCE IT DID INFLATE	HER SPIRIT ROSE TO SUCH	1486	2
COUNTENANCES			
TO COUNTENANCES NEW!	WENT UP A YEAR THIS	93	22
THEIR COUNTENANCES KID	UNTO MY BOOKS--SO GOOD	604	14
COUNTER			
I'M PLEADING AT THE "COUNTER"--SIR--	I CAME TO BUY A SMILE--	223	7
A COUNTER HAS AND SALES	THE MERCHANT OF THE	1131	2
COUNTERACT			
TO COUNTERACT A KNOCK--	THE WAY I READ A	636	6
OR COUNTERACT THE STAIN--	AS FROST IS BEST	951	10
COUNTERFEIT			
AT LEAST--A COUNTERFEIT--	IT'S THOUGHTS--AND JUST	495	25

	FIRST LINE	POEM	LINE
COUNTERFEIT (CONTINUED)			
SIMPLICITY FLED FROM HIS COUNTERFEIT PRESENCE	HE PREACHED UPON	1207	5
HOW COUNTERFEIT THE WHITE	UNWORTHY OF HER BREAST	1414	5
A COUNTERFEIT--A PLATED PERSON--	A COUNTERFEIT--A PLATED	1453	1
COUNTERFEITS			
OF COUNTERFEITS HE IS SO SHY	THE MERCHANT OF THE	1131	9
COUNTERPASS			
MAY PASS--AND COUNTERPASS--	THE LIGHTNING PLAYETH--	630	8
COUNTESS			
LOOP UP A COUNTESS--WITH YOU--	I'LL CLUTCH--AND CLUTCH	427	10
COUNTIES			
AS ACRES [COUNTIES] FROM THE FEET	IT WAS A QUIET WAY--	1053	10
IN COUNTIES HAVE BEGUN.	MYSELF CAN READ THE	1089	6
COUNTING			
AND CLERKS IN COUNTING ROOMS	YOU'VE SEEN BALLOONS SET	700	19
COUNTLESS			
WITHOUT COMMANDER! COUNTLESS! STILL!	SOME RAINBOW--COMING	64	19
AND COUNTLESS BUTTERFLY!	A SCIENCE--SO THE SAVANS	100	12
COUNTRIES			
IS IT BROUGHT FROM FAMOUS COUNTRIES	WILL THERE REALLY BE A	101	7
IN THOSE DIM COUNTRIES WHERE THEY GO,	I DREADED THAT FIRST	348	19
COUNTRY			
MY COUNTRY BIDS ME GO!	"SIC TRANSIT GLORIA	3	26
MY COUNTRY CALLETH ME!	"SIC TRANSIT GLORIA	3	58
SURELY, SUCH A COUNTRY	BAFFLED FOR JUST A DAY	17	7
IN COUNTRY FAR FROM HERE--	I HAD A GUINEA GOLDEN--	23	32
WHOSE DYING EYES, NO COUNTRY	TO FIGHT ALOUD, IS VERY	126	7
BY HEADS REJECTED--IN THE LOWER COUNTRY--	UNTO LIKE STORY--TROUBLE	295	11
THE JUGGLER'S HAT HER COUNTRY IS--	THE JUGGLER'S HAT HER	330	1
IN JUST A COUNTRY TOWN--	THERE'S BEEN A DEATH, IN	389	24
WITH WATER, IN THE COUNTRY CHURCH	I'M CEDED--I'VE STOPPED	508	3
TO A FICTITIOUS COUNTRY [SUMMER / SEASON]	CONJECTURING A CLIMATE	562	5
COUNTRY BURIAL	AMPLE MAKE THIS BED--	829	T
BETWEEN MY COUNTRY--AND THE OTHERS--	BETWEEN MY COUNTRY--AND	905	1
WERT THOU BUT STRANGER IN UNGRACIOUS COUNTRY--	WERT THOU BUT ILL--THAT	961	5
MY COUNTRY NEED NOT CHANGE HER GOWN,	MY COUNTRY NEED NOT	1511	1
COUNTRYMAN			
YET BY THIS COUNTRYMAN--	HOW FITS HIS UMBER COAT	1371	11
COUNTRYMEN			
FOR LOVE OF HER--SWEET--COUNTRYMEN--	THIS IS MY LETTER TO THE	441	7
COUNTRY'S			
MY COUNTRY'S WARDROBE	MY COUNTRY NEED NOT	1511	T
COUNTS			
WHO COUNTS THE WAMPUM OF THE NIGHT	BRING ME THE SUNSET IN A	128	17
COUNTS HIS NECTARS--	COME SLOWLY--EDEN!	211	7
'TIS ONE BY ONE--THE FATHER COUNTS--	'TIS ONE BY ONE--THE	545	1
COUPLE			
WHILE THE OLD COUPLE, JUST ASTIR,	I KNOW SOME LONELY	289	39
COURAGE			
COURAGE! MY BRAVE COLUMBA!	ONCE MORE, MY NOW	48	7
I TOLD MYSELF, "TAKE COURAGE, FRIEND--	I FELT MY LIFE WITH BOTH	351	13
COURIERS			
BY COURIERS WITHIN--	ALONE, I CANNOT BE--	298	10
COURSE			
I'D GIVE--I'D GIVE MY LIFE--OF COURSE--	WHAT WOULD I GIVE TO SEE	247	2
OF COURSE--I PRAYED--	OF COURSE--I PRAYED--	376	1
A THREADLESS WAY [COURSE]	FROM BLANK TO BLANK--	761	2
THE SUN SUBSIDING ON HIS COURSE	THE LILAC IS AN ANCIENT	1241	5
NO CIRCUIT SAGE OF ALL THE COURSE [LINES]	OH FUTURE! THOU SECRETED	1631	5
CONCLUSION IS THE COURSE OF ALL	SUMMER BEGINS TO HAVE	1682	13
COURSERS			
NOR ANY COURSERS LIKE A PAGE	THERE IS NO FRIGATE LIKE	1263	3
COURT			
THE BEE DOTH COURT THE FLOWER, THE FLOWER HIS SUIT RECEIVES,	AWAKE YE MUSES NINE,	1	13
THE COURT IS FAR AWAY--	THE COURT IS FAR AWAY--	235	1
COURT IS A STATELY PLACE--	I'M SAYING EVERY DAY	373	10
I'LL SHOW YOU AT THE COURT--	I'LL CLUTCH--AND CLUTCH	427	15
WHO COURT OBTAIN WITHIN HIMSELF	WHO COURT OBTAIN WITHIN	803	1
THE BEARER FROM AN EMERALD COURT	THE STEM OF A DEPARTED	1520	3
COURTEOUS			
SORROW [AROMA]--NOW--IS POLITE [COURTEOUS]--AND STAYS--	SUMMER IS SHORTER THAN	1506	5
A [THE] COURTEOUS, YET [BUT] HARROWING GRACE,	AS IMPERCEPTIBLY AS	1540	11
COURTESIES			
NEARER TO YOUR COURTESIES	TAKE YOUR HEAVEN FURTHER	388	9
OTHER COURTESIES HAVE BEEN--	RECOLLECT THE FACE OF ME	1305	5
COURTESY			
AND COURTESY FORBID [FORBIDS]	THE SOUL THAT HATH A	674	5
FITTER COURTESY	CONSCIOUS AM I IN MY	679	6
SUFFICIENT COURTESY.	MY BEST ACQUAINTANCES	932	8
OR TRAILING [SWEEPING] COURTESY	LIKE MEN AND WOMEN	1105	4
AND LARGE [MOST] IN COURTESY--	THE MERCHANT OF THE	1131	6
THAT COURTESY WILL FAIR REMAIN	"REMEMBER ME" IMPLORED	1180	5
THE EPICURE OF FIRMAMENTS [VEHICLES / COURTESY / PURPOSES]	A SPARROW TOOK A SLICE	1211 V	7
OTHER COURTESY MAY BE--	RECOLLECT THE FACE OF ME	1305	6
COURTIER			
FOLD A TINY COURTIER	MUTE THY CORONATION--	151	3
AROUND THIS QUIET COURTIER	WAIT TILL THE MAJESTY OF	171	9

	FIRST LINE	POEM	LINE
CRAPE			
A CRAPE UPON THE HAT--	TO DIE--TAKES JUST A	255	6
DRESSES EACH HOUSE IN CRAPE, AND ICICLE-- .	IT'S COMING--THE	390	7
MY WITNESS--WAS THE CRAPE [BLACK] I BORE-- .	THE BIRDS REPORTED FROM	743	19
CRASH			
AND HIT A WORLD, AT EVERY PLUNGE [CRASH], .	I FELT A FUNERAL, IN MY	280	19
YOU HEARD NO NOISE [CRASH]	A GREAT HOPE FELL	1123	2
THE FLASH [FLARE / GLARE / BLARE] BETWEEN THE CREVICES OF CRASH--	IT WAS A QUIET SEEMING	1419	V
THE [A] CRASH OF NOTHING, YET [AND] OF ALL--	MORE THAN THE GRAVE IS	1503	5
A CRASH WITHOUT A SOUND, ...	THE FARTHEST THUNDER	1581	18
CRASHED			
CONVULSIVE, WHILE THE MUSIC CRASHED [BROKE]--	HER SMILE WAS SHAPED	514	7
CRASHE'S			
SLIPPING--IS CRASHE'S LAW.	CRUMBLING IS NOT AN	997	12
CRASHING			
IN FALLING [CRASHING] TIMBERS BURIED-- . .	IN FALLING TIMBERS	614	1
CRATER			
A CRATER I MAY CONTEMPLATE	VOLCANOES BE IN SICILY	1705	7
CRAVAT			
GIVE THE ONE IN RED CRAVAT, ...	IF I SHOULD'NT BE ALIVE	182	3
CRAVE			
I CRAVE HIM GRACE OF SUMMER BOUGHS, . . .	OF ALL THE SOUNDS	321	25
CRAVED			
IT CRAVED THE GRACE TO WORSHIP	THE HEAVEN VESTS FOR	694	3
CRAWL			
ICICLES--CRAWL FROM POLAR CAVERNS-- . . .	SAFE IN THEIR ALABASTER	216	V
I FELT SIROCCOS--CRAWL--	IT WAS NOT DEATH, FOR I	510	6
AND CRAWL BETWEEN	I LIKE TO SEE IT LAP	585	10
IF I COULD CRAWL BETWEEN	THE SPRY ARMS OF THE	1103	2
TO CRAWL THE FROST BEGUN [BEGAN]-- . . .	THE FROST OF DEATH WAS	1136	8
WHERE WATERS COOL AROUND THE MOSSES CRAWL--	THESE FEVERED DAYS--TO	1441	2
CRAWLED			
HAVE CRAWLED TOO FAR!	I KNOW THAT HE EXISTS.	338	16
THAT CRAWLED LEAGUES OFF--I LIKED TO SEE-- .	THREE TIMES--WE PARTED--	598	9
A REEF--CRAWLED EASY FROM THE SEA	I SOMETIMES DROP IT, FOR	708	13
ASSIDUOUSLY [DELIBERATELY / DETERMINATELY / IMPERTINENTLY] CRAWLED	ALONE AND IN A	1167	4
CRAWLS			
HOW A SMALL DUSK CRAWLS ON THE VILLAGE . .	HOW THE OLD MOUNTAINS	291	13
SHE FLATTENS--THEN SHE CRAWLS--	SHE SIGHTS A BIRD--SHE	507	2
CRAYON			
IN CRAYON, OR IN WOOL, ...	DEATH SETS A THING	360	6
CRAYONS			
THE PURPLE CRAYONS STAND.	SHE BORE IT TILL THE	144	4
CREAK			
AND CREAK ACROSS MY SOUL [BRAIN]	I FELT A FUNERAL, IN MY	280	10
CREASE			
AND DRAGONS--IN THE CREASE--	I HAD NOT MINDED--WALLS	398	16
I TIE MY HAT--I CREASE MY SHAWL--	I TIE MY HAT--I CREASE	443	1
CANNOT CORRECT [EFFACE] THE CREASE . . .	AS FROST IS BEST	951	9
PRESENT ME FROM SEPULCHRAL CREASE	HER LITTLE PARASOL TO	1038	7
THOUGH [WHILE / BUT] WE RESENT THE CREASE .	LIKE TIME'S INSIDIOUS	1236	4
CAN [COULD] MAKE A [NO] DENT [CREASE / SEAM] THEREON [UPON]--	THIS ME--THAT WALKS AND	1588	8
CREASED			
BEFORE IDENTITY WAS CREASED [LEASED]. . .	ESTRANGED FROM BEAUTY--	1474	4
CREASES			
OVERTAKE THE CREASES	BEAUTY--BE NOT CAUSED--	516	4
THAT SEARCHES HUMAN NATURE'S CREASES . . .	PERIL AS A POSSESSION	1678	6
CREATE			
OF ALL THE SOULS THAT STAND CREATE-- . . .	OF ALL THE SOULS THAT	664	1
CREATED			
IT HAD CREATED [AFFORDED] HER.	THIS BAUBLE WAS	805	8
WHILE EVERYTHING CREATED HID	TO PILE LIKE THUNDER TO	1247	3
MADDEST HEART THAT GOD CREATED	LAIN IN NATURE--SO	1288	5
DEPUTED [CONTENTED / CREATED] TO ADORE-- .	SUMMER--WE ALL HAVE SEEN	1386	9
CREATES			
WHILE SHE CREATES AND FEDERATES	THE VEINS OF OTHER	811	7
CREATION			
CREATION--POWERLESS--	MY REWARD FOR BEING, WAS	343	V
CREATION--LOOKING ON--	DEPARTED--TO THE	524	4
CREATION STOPPED [THE HEAVENS PAUSED]--FOR ME--	MY PERIOD HAD COME FOR	564	18
CREATION--IMPOTENT TO HELP--	IT WAS TOO LATE FOR MAN	623	3
CREATION--BUT THE GAMBOL	IT'S EASY TO INVENT A	724	3
CREATION SEEMED A MIGHTY CRACK--	TO MY QUICK EAR THE	891	7
INITIAL OF CREATION, AND	LOVE--IS ANTERIOR TO	917	3
SAHARA [CONTENTMENT / CREATION / HIS STATUS] DIES	UNTIL THE DESERT KNOWS	1291	6
CREATION AFTER THIS?	HOW HUMAN NATURE DOTES	1417	13
CREATION O'ER--	THE GENTIAN HAS A	1424	17
CREATOR			
CREATOR--SHALL I--BLOOM?	GOD MADE A LITTLE	442	12
CREATOR--WAS IT YOU?	MY PERIOD HAD COME FOR	564	4
WHITE--UNTO THE WHITE CREATOR--	PUBLICATION--IS THE	709	7
BUT NOT TO OUR CREATOR--	THE FASCINATING CHILL	1480	8
TO HIS ADROIT CREATOR	THE BAT IS DUN, WITH	1575	13
CREATOR'S			
TO THE CREATOR'S HOUSE--	NO OTHER CAN REDUCE	982	V

	FIRST LINE	POEM	LINE
CREATURE			
THE ABSENT--MYSTIC--CREATURE--	TO DIE--TAKES JUST A	255	9
THEY'RE HERE, THOUGH! NOT A CREATURE FAILED--	I DREADED THAT FIRST	348	21
EXCEPT A PERISHED CREATURE	DEATH SETS A THING	360	3
ON HERE AND THERE--A CREATURE--	THE MORNING AFTER WO--	364	13
IT'S COMING--THE POSTPONELESS CREATURE--	IT'S COMING--THE	390	1
THE CREATURE LYING THERE--	THERE IS A LANGUOR OF	396	12
A CREATURE GASPED "REPREIVE"!	'TWAS LIKE A MAELSTROM,	414	23
TO EVERY CREATURE--THAT I MET--	IT WOULD NEVER BE COMMON	430	19
THERE ROSE A PURPLE CREATURE--	GOD MADE A LITTLE	442	5
THERE DWELLS ONE OTHER CREATURE	I TRIED TO THINK A	532	10
COULD BEHOLD [REGARD] SO FAR [SMALL / DIM / SCARCE] A CREATURE--	PROMISE THIS--WHEN YOU	648	27
THE GILDED CREATURE STRAINS--AND SPINS--	YOU'VE SEEN BALLOONS SET	700	13
MANY'S THE GALLANT--OVERWHELMED CREATURE	FINITE--TO FAIL, BUT	847	3
THAN THINE ACCLIMATED CREATURE	SNOW BENEATH WHOSE	942	7
SOME WRETCHED CREATURE, SAVIOR TAKE	SOME WRETCHED CREATURE,	1111	1
THE FORFEIT IS OF CREATURE FAIR	A FULL FED ROSE ON MEALS	1154	5
THE PAST IS SUCH A CURIOUS CREATURE	THE PAST IS SUCH A	1203	1
TO LASH THE MAGIC CREATURE	NOT WITH A CLUB, THE	1304	5
A FINE--ESTRANGING CREATURE--	THE FASCINATING CHILL	1480	6
CREATURE'S			
THAN THIS QUAINT CREATURE'S BOOT--	YOU'LL KNOW HER--BY HER	634	5
FOR THE DEPARTED CREATURE'S SAKE	ASHES DENOTE THAT FIRE	1063	3
CREATURES			
THE CREATURES CHUCKLED ON THE ROOFS--	AN AWFUL TEMPEST MASHED	198	5
AS OTHER CREATURES, THAT HAVE EYES	BEFORE I GOT MY EYE PUT	327	3
WHERE OTHER CREATURES PUT THEIR EYES--	BEFORE I GOT MY EYE PUT	327	20
WHAT SOFT--CHERUBIC CREATURES--	WHAT SOFT--CHERUBIC	401	1
TILL THE BROKEN CREATURES--	TAKING UP THE FAIR IDEAL	428	13
HOW ILL THE CREATURES BEAR--	SHE DEALT HER PRETTY	479	8
OR ARCTIC CREATURES, DIMLY STIRRED--	LIKE FLOWERS, THAT HEARD	513	7
INSTEAD OF PASSIVE CREATURES,	ENDOW THE LIVING--WITH	521	5
OF PERSONS [CREATURES] OUTSIDE WINDOWS--	I HAD BEEN HUNGRY, ALL	579	19
FROM MINIATURE CREATURES	THE TREES LIKE TASSELS--	606	3
AND THEY--APPOINTED CREATURES--	WHOLE GULFS--OF RED, AND	658	5
FOR CREATURES SO RENOWNED--	YOU'VE SEEN BALLOONS SET	700	8
HOW MORE THE FINISHED CREATURES	THE CHEMICAL CONVICTION	954	7
AND CREATURES CLAD IN MIRACLE [VICTORY]	'TIS ANGUISH GRANDER	984	7
APPROPRIATE CREATURES TO HER CHANGE	THE MURMURING OF BEES,	1115	9
BUT HOW SHALL FINISHED CREATURES	THE BONE THAT HAS NO	1274	9
THOSE FINAL CREATURES,--WHO THEY ARE--	THOSE FINAL CREATURES,--	1766	1
CREDIBILITY			
'TIS FICTION'S--TO DILUTE [CONTRACT] TO PLAUSIBILITY [CREDIBILITY]	NO ROMANCE SOLD UNTO	669	5
OF CREDIBILITY--	ENDANGER IT, AND THE	1658	4
CREDIBILITY'S			
FOR CREDIBILITY'S PRESUMPTION [TEMERITY]	EACH LIFE CONVERGES TO	680	7
CREDIT			
COULD'ST CREDIT ME? COULD'ST CREDIT ME?	POOR LITTLE HEART!	192	9
COULD'ST CREDIT ME? COULD'ST CREDIT ME?	POOR LITTLE HEART!	192	9
TO CREDIT [COMPASS]--'TIS'NT TRUE!	NO ROMANCE SOLD UNTO	669	7
CREDITS			
AND NO ONE CREDITS NOAH--	THE WINTERS ARE SO SHORT	403	16
CREDITS THE WORLD--	THE CHILD'S FAITH IS NEW	637	9
CREDULOUS			
THE CREDULOUS--DECOY--	"HEAVEN"--IS WHAT I	239	10
CREEP			
WHERE TWO COULD CREEP--	I KNOW SOME LONELY	289	7
TOWARD WHICH FORCES CREEP	CRISIS IS A HAIR	889	2
NO RIBALDRY MAY CREEP	TO THEIR APARTMENT DEEP	1701	2
CREEPING			
BUT STATE WITH CREEPING BLOOD	IN WINTER IN MY ROOM	1670	13
CREEPS			
THAT WHEN THE SNOW CREEPS SLOWLY	SEXTON! MY MASTER'S	96	5
CREPT			
TILL SUNDOWN CREPT--A STEADY TIDE--	FROM COCOON FORTH A	354	22
UNTIL THERE CREPT UPON	'TWAS WARM--AT FIRST--	519	2
AIMLESS CREPT [STOLE] THE GLOWS	ON THE WORLD YOU COLORED	1171	4
CRESCENT			
GRAND GO THE YEARS--IN THE CRESCENT--ABOVE THEM--	SAFE IN THEIR ALABASTER	216	V
WHEN CRESCENT--THOU ART WORN--I NOTE [MIND]--	YOU KNOW THAT PORTRAIT	504	11
CALLED TO MY FULL--THE CRESCENT DROPPED--	I'M CEDED--I'VE STOPPED	508	11
A CRESCENT IN THE SEA--	BEHIND ME--DIPS ETERNITY	721	15
I MAKE HIS CRESCENT FILL OR LACK--	I MAKE HIS CRESCENT FILL	909	1
AND EVERY CRESCENT HOLD--	MY GOD--HE SEES THEE--	1178	5
WHICH IS THE BEST--THE MOON OR THE CRESCENT?	WHICH IS THE BEST--THE	1315	1
WITHOLDING NOT A CRESCENT	A BEE HIS BURNISHED	1339	7
SHE [HE] LAID HER [HIS] DOCILE CRESCENT DOWN	SHE LAID HER DOCILE	1396	1
A CRESCENT STILL ABIDES,	EACH THAT WE LOSE TAKES	1605	2
HER CRESCENT REIMBURSE	NATURE CAN DO NO MORE	1673	5
CREST			
BUT I HAVE [HAD] NOT A CREST.	HER BREAST IS FIT FOR	84	4
AND SURE I AM, THE CREST HE BORE	I MET A KING THIS	166	7
BUT HE WHO HAS ACHIEVED THE TOP [CREST]--	THE HALLOWING OF PAIN	772	7
FOR HER BRIEF CREST--	SHE ROSE AS HIGH AS HIS	1011	4
CRESTED			
OFT A HEAD IS CRESTED	FREQUENTLY THE WOODS ARE	6	5

	FIRST LINE	POEM	LINE
CRESTS			
UNTO GUESSED CRESTS, MY MOANING FANCY, LEADS [LURES] ME,	UNTO LIKE STORY--TROUBLE	295	9
CRESTS--WILL DO--	NO MATTER--NOW--SWEET--	704	10
CREVICES			
THE FLASH [FLARE / GLARE / BLARE] BETWEEN THE CREVICES OF CRASH--	IT WAS A QUIET SEEMING	1419	V
CREW			
AS CREW OF MOUNTAINS--COULD AFFORD--	THEY CALLED ME TO THE	628	11
TO CREW AND YOU--	IT TOSSED--AND TOSSED--	723	10
FIFTH, NO CREW--	FINDING IS THE FIRST ACT	870	6
FOR THE DELIGHTED CREW.	A SOFT SEA WASHED AROUND	1198	8
CREWS			
AND CREWS--OF SOLID BLOOD--	WHOLE GULFS--OF RED, AND	658	2
CRIB			
AS HAPPY IN HER CRIB [BED] OF DUST	THIS DOCILE ONE INTER	1752	V 7
CRIBS			
MY FLOWERS FROM A HUNDRED CRIBS	AS CHILDREN BID THE	133	7
CRICKET			
LOW AS THE LAUGHTER OF THE CRICKET,	MANY A PHRASE HAS THE	276	3
THOUGH BUT FOR THE CRICKET--JUST,	I'M SAYING EVERY DAY	373	22
THUNDER--THE CRICKET--	"NATURE" IS WHAT WE SEE	668	7
OF THE MINUTEST CRICKET--	NATURE--THE GENTLEST	790	15
AS CRICKET OR AS BEE--	SHE SPED AS PETALS OF A	991	6
MY CRICKET	FURTHER IN SUMMER THAN	1068	T
THAN WHEN THE CRICKET CAME--	'TWAS LATER WHEN THE	1276	2
'TWAS SOONER WHEN THE CRICKET WENT	'TWAS LATER WHEN THE	1276	5
THE CRICKET SPOKE SO CLEAR	AS IMPERCEPTIBLY AS	1540	V
THE CRICKET DROPS A SABLE LINE	THE JAY HIS CASTANET HAS	1635	7
THE CRICKET IS HER UTMOST	THE EARTH HAS MANY KEYS.	1775	7
CRICKETS			
THE CRICKETS SANG	THE CRICKETS SANG	1104	1
OF CRICKETS--CROWS--AND RETROSPECTS	SEPTEMBER'S	1271	3
CRIED			
AND CRIED "GIVE ME"--	OF COURSE--I PRAYED--	376	5
I CRIED AT PITY--NOT AT PAIN--	I CRIED AT PITY--NOT AT	588	1
CRIER			
COULD BUT A CRIER OF THE JOY	DELAYED TILL SHE HAD	58	8
CRIER'S			
THE CRIER'S VOICE W'D [WOULD] TELL ME--	IF THOSE I LOVED WERE	29	2
CRIME			
THE CRIME, FROM US, IS HIDDEN--	OF GOD WE ASK ONE FAVOR,	1601	4
CRIMSON			
THE GUEST IS GOLD AND CRIMSON--	THE GUEST IS GOLD AND	15	1
I HAD A CRIMSON ROBIN--	I HAD A GUINEA GOLDEN--	23	9
OOZED SO IN CRIMSON BUBBLES	SO HAS A DAISY VANISHED	28	5
RHODORA'S CHEEK IS CRIMSON,	WHOSE ARE THE LITTLE	142	23
NO CRIMSON--MORE--	I TEND MY FLOWERS FOR	339	20
AND SO I SEND MY CRIMSON SCOUTS	WHERE ROSES WOULD NOT	1582	3
CRISIS			
CRISIS IS A HAIR	CRISIS IS A HAIR	889	1
'TWAS CRISIS--ALL THE LENGTH HAD PASSED--	'TWAS CRISIS--ALL THE	948	1
FROM SINKING [IN CRISIS / IN HAZARD] IN THE SKY--	A SINGLE CLOVER PLANK	1343	4
CRISIS IS SWEET AND YET THE HEART	CRISIS IS SWEET AND YET	1416	1
CRITERION			
THE ROBIN'S MY CRITERION FOR TUNE--	THE ROBIN'S MY CRITERION	285	1
CRITERION--BE SMALL--	IF WHAT WE COULD--WERE	407	2
CRITERION SOURCES [NATURES] HERE	TO UNDERTAKE IS TO	1070	8
CRITICAL			
COOL OF EYE, AND CRITICAL OF WORK--	A SOLEMN THING WITHIN	483	10
CRITICIZE			
MUST NOT CRITICIZE	IF THE FOOLISH, CALL	168	6
CRITICS			
THE "FOOLISH TUN" THE CRITICS SAY--	RISK IS THE HAIR THAT	1239	9
CROCUS			
THE CROCUS--TILL SHE RISES	THE FEET OF PEOPLE	7	3
OF THE CROCUS KNOW--	ALL THESE MY BANNERS BE.	22	17
THE CROCUS STIRS HER LIDS--	WHOSE ARE THE LITTLE	142	22
CROOKED			
I ENVY CROOKED [SPEECHLESS] HILLS	I ENVY SEAS, WHEREON HE	498	4
THESE WERE BENT--MY SIGHT GOT CROOKED--	DONT PUT UP MY THREAD &	617	5
THE SUN GOES CROOKED--	I DID NOT REACH THEE	1664	20
CROONED			
EDEN--A LEGEND--DIMLY TOLD [LEARNED / CROONED]--	BETTER--THAN MUSIC! FOR	503	14
CROSS			
MANY CROSS THE RHINE	MANY CROSS THE RHINE	123	1
OR TELL GOD--HOW CROSS WE ARE--	WHAT IS--"PARADISE"--	215	10
THERE'S THAT LONG [THEN THERE'S THAT] TOWN OF WHITE--TO CROSS--	IT CANT BE "SUMMER"!	221	4
THE LADY CROSS, OR NOT?	IS BLISS THEN, SUCH	340	13
'TWAS SHORT--TO CROSS THE SEA--	I WENT TO THANK HER--	363	8
I CANNOT CROSS THEE--	LOVE--THOU ART HIGH--	453	8
I CROSS TILL I AM WEARY	I CROSS TILL I AM WEARY	550	1
TO NOTE THE FASHIONS--OF THE CROSS--	I MEASURE EVERY GRIEF I	561	37
TO PAY--A CROSS--	MUST BE A WO--	571	15
NOR STOP TO CROSS OURSELVES--	THE LIGHTNING PLAYETH--	630	12
I CROSS THE HALL WITH MINGLED STEPS--	AGAIN--HIS VOICE IS AT	663	9
CROSS IT, AND OVERCOME THE BEE--	HEREIN A BLOSSOM LIES--	899	3

	FIRST LINE	POEM	LINE
CROSS (CONTINUED)			
WERE SEAS TO CROSS TO COME	THE BIRD DID PRANCE--THE	1107	10
ARE ALL THAT CROSS HIS THRESHOLD--	THE ROBIN IS A GABRIEL	1483	12
THREE RIVERS AND A HILL TO CROSS	I DID NOT REACH THEE	1664	3
CROSS'			
THE CROSS'--REQUEST--	THE TEST OF LOVE--IS	573	12
CROSSED			
AND CROSSED A THOUSAND TREES	UPON HIS SADDLE SPRUNG A	1600	2
ONE DESERT CROSSED--	I DID NOT REACH THEE	1664	9
CROUCH			
CROUCH LOW TO GUARD HIS PRIZE.	I NEVER TOLD THE BURIED	11	4
THEN CROUCH WITHIN THE DOOR--	DARE YOU SEE A SOUL AT	365	2
SHAME NEED NOT CROUCH	HOW MANY SCHEMES MAY DIE	1150	V
SHAME NEED NOT CROUCH	NOT WITH A CLUB, THE	1304	13
CROUCHED			
AND CROUCHED BEHIND HIS YELLOW DOOR	A WILD BLUE SKY ABREAST	1415	3
CROW			
IS CHERISHED OF [BY] THE CROW	AN ANTIQUATED TREE	1514	2
THE SWEET DERISION OF THE CROW	IN SNOW THOU COMEST	1669	3
THE PHEBE AND THE CROW	THE ONES THAT	1690	2
CROWD			
THE CROWD RESPECTFUL GREW--	WENT UP A YEAR THIS	93	20
YET--NOT SO DENSE A CROWD--	ONE LIFE OF SO MUCH	270	14
AND CROWD THE LITTLE ROOM--	IT MIGHT BE LONELIER	405	6
NO CROWD THAT HAS OCCURRED	NO CROWD THAT HAS	515	1
AS UNTO CROWD--	TO HEAR AN ORIOLE SING	526	6
ONE ANGUISH--IN A CROWD--	ONE ANGUISH--IN A CROWD	565	1
WHILE CHIEFEST--OF [IN] THE CROWD--	LIKE MIGHTY FOOT LIGHTS	595	6
THE HEART BEGINS TO CROWD--	I THINK THE LONGEST HOUR	635	12
DIVINER CROWD AT HOME [WITHIN]--	THE SOUL THAT HATH A	674	3
AND YET THE CROWD APPLAUD, BELOW--	YOU'VE SEEN BALLOONS SET	700	11
THE CROWD--RETIRE WITH AN OATH--	YOU'VE SEEN BALLOONS SET	700	17
I TRIED TO DROP [SHIFT] IT IN THE CROWD--	BEREAVED OF ALL, I WENT	784	11
SUFFICE US--FOR A CROWD--	ON A COLUMNAR SELF--	789	9
AND SCANT TO HIM THE CROWD--	OF CONSCIOUSNESS, HER	894	6
WHEN THE BIRD WILL CROWD THE TREE	I SUPPOSE THE TIME WILL	1381	3
YET [AND] NONE HATH SUCH A CROWD.	HOW BRITTLE ARE THE	1433	4
CROWDED			
AND THO' THE SKIES ARE CROWDED--	I HAD A GUINEA GOLDEN--	23	21
WAS CROWDED DENSE WITH ARMIES--	THE SUN KEPT STOOPING--	152	9
ALL DAY--AMONG THE CROWDED AIR	MUSICIANS WRESTLE	157	2
CROWDED--AS SACRAMENT--	IT'S THOUGHTS--AND JUST	495	6
IT CROWDED COLD TO COLD--	'TWAS WARM--AT FIRST--	519	10
UPON MY THRONGING [CROWDED / HAPPY] MIND--	MY WORTHINESS IS ALL MY	751	8
A CASPIAN WERE CROWDED--	THE BIRD DID PRANCE--THE	1107	11
CROWDS			
TO STRANGE, BRIGHT CROWDS OF FLOWERS--	AS IF SOME LITTLE ARCTIC	180	7
BEAUTY CROWDS ME TILL I DIE	BEAUTY CROWDS ME TILL I	1654	1
CROWING			
CROWNED--CROWING [WHIMPERING / DANGLING]--ON MY FATHER'S BREAST--	I'M CEDED--I'VE STOPPED	508	15
CROWN			
AND JUST A BIT OF "CROWN"--	GOING TO HEAVEN!	79	17
NONE EVADE THIS CROWN!	ONE DIGNITY DELAYS FOR	98	4
THE NIGHT BEFORE THE CROWN!	A LITTLE BREAD--A CRUST	159	6
HE HAD NOT ON A CROWN INDEED,	I MET A KING THIS	166	2
THE FELLOW CANNOT TOUCH THIS CROWN--	FOR THIS--ACCEPTED	195	3
FITTEST THE CROWN!	FOR THIS--ACCEPTED	195	17
AFTER PLAYING CROWN!	GOD PERMITS INDUSTRIOUS	231	8
FELT FEEBLY--FOR HER CROWN--	THE SUN--JUST TOUCHED	232	14
ON THE [A] HEAD TOO HIGH TO CROWN--	HER--"LAST POEMS"--	312	13
RETURN--WITH SUCH A CROWN	THE FACE I CARRY WITH ME	336	10
TO ME--SURPASSED THE CROWN	THE DAY THAT I WAS	356	14
OR A SPLINTERED CROWN--	TAKING UP THE FAIR IDEAL	428	4
AND I CHOOSE, JUST A CROWN [THRONE]--	I'M CEDED--I'VE STOPPED	508	19
AS SOON IMPEACH MY CROWN!	AFRAID! OF WHOM AM I	608	12
AND WHO CAN ADD A CROWN	WHO COURT OBTAIN WITHIN	803	7
ROYAL--ALL BUT THE CROWN!	TITLE DIVINE--IS MINE!	1072	5
WERE WITNESS FOR THE CROWN--	THE SUN WENT DOWN--NO	1079	8
SPARE YOUR "CROWN OF LIFE"--	"FAITHFUL TO THE END"	1357	V
WAS FERVOR'S SUDDEN CROWN--	THE PRETTY RAIN FROM	1426	8
ONE CROWN THAT NO ONE SEEKS [NOT ANY SEEK]	ONE CROWN THAT NO ONE	1735	1
NONE SUSPECT ME OF THE CROWN,	REARRANGE A "WIFE'S"	1737	14
CROWNED			
DOUBTFUL IF IT BE CROWNED!	DELAYED TILL SHE HAD	58	18
THE DAY THAT I WAS CROWNED	THE DAY THAT I WAS	356	1
CROWNED--CROWING [WHIMPERING / DANGLING]--ON MY FATHER'S BREAST--	I'M CEDED--I'VE STOPPED	508	15
BUT YOU--WERE CROWNED [YOUR'S WAS FIRST--] IN JUNE--	OURSELVES WERE WED ONE	631	16
CROWNS			
BUT CROWNS INSTEAD, AND COURTIERS--	SHE BORE IT TILL THE	144	13
"CROWNS OF LIFE" ARE SERVILE PRIZES	"FAITHFUL TO THE END"	1357	5
CROWS			
OF CRICKETS--CROWS--AND RETROSPECTS	SEPTEMBER'S	1271	3
WHOSE CRUMBS THE CROWS INSPECT	FAME IS A FICKLE FOOD	1659	6
CRUCIFIX			
JESUS! THY CRUCIFIX	JESUS! THY CRUCIFIX	225	1
EACH BOUND THE OTHER'S CRUCIFIX--	THERE CAME A DAY AT	322	23
TO CRUCIFIX OR BLOCK [STAKE]	DEATH WARRANTS ARE	1375	6

	FIRST LINE	POEM	LINE
CRUCIFIX (CONTINUED)			
SHOUTS EVEN FROM THE CRUCIFIX, ...	THE AUCTIONEER OF	1612	3
SEE! I USURPED THY CRUCIFIX TO HONOR MINE! .	PROUD OF MY BROKEN HEART	1736	8
CRUCIFIXAL			
TO FIT SOME CRUCIFIXAL CLEF--	THE MORNING AFTER WO--	364	15
LIFT SUCH A CRUCIFIXAL SIGN	HE TOUCHED ME, SO I LIVE	506	17
CRUCIFIXION			
STEP MARTIAL--AT MY CRUCIFIXION--	UNTO LIKE STORY--TROUBLE	295	15
AND CRUCIFIXION, SHOWN--	THIS WORLD IS NOT	501	12
FLAVORS OF THAT OLD CRUCIFIXION--	TO PUT THIS WORLD DOWN,	527	9
ONE CRUCIFIXION IS RECORDED--ONLY--	ONE CRUCIFIXION IS	553	1
THERE'S NEWER--NEARER CRUCIFIXION	ONE CRUCIFIXION IS	553	15
CRUCIFY			
SO SAVIOR--CRUCIFY--	I SHOULD HAVE BEEN TOO	313	18
CRUEL			
THE CRUEL--SMILING--BOWING WORLD--	THE BEGGAR LAD--DIES	717	5
HOW CRUEL ARE THE KIND--	HOW RUTHLESS ARE THE	1439	2
CRUELLY			
MADE CRUELLY MORE DEAR.	THE SADDEST NOISE, THE	1764	12
CRUISE			
BUT [THOUGH] ALL MANKIND DELIVER [CRUISE SOFTLY / ROW SOFTLY / . . .	A CHILLY PEACE INFESTS	1443	7
CRUISING			
CRUISING ROUND THE PURPLE LINE--	FLOWERS--WELL--IF	137	12
THE COLOR, ON THE CRUISING CLOUD--	"HEAVEN"--IS WHAT I	239	5
CRUMB			
A LITTLE BREAD--A CRUST--A CRUMB--	A LITTLE BREAD--A CRUST	159	1
A MEMORIAL CRUMB.	IF I SHOULD'NT BE ALIVE	182	4
IT ASKED A CRUMB--OF ME.	"HOPE" IS THE THING WITH	254	12
JUST AS THE GRANITE CRUMB LET GO--	THAT AFTER HORROR--THAT	286	3
I OFFERED HIM A CRUMB	A BIRD CAME DOWN THE	328	14
FOR WHOSE RELUCTANT CRUMB--	'TIS NOT THAT DYING	335	10
'TWAS SO UNLIKE THE CRUMB	I HAD BEEN HUNGRY, ALL	579	10
CRUMB OF MINE	SO MUCH SUMMER	651	9
WERE A CRUMB MY WHOLE POSSESSION--	MOST SHE TOUCHED ME BY	760	5
BUT THE CRUMB PARTOOK--DEPARTED--	MOST SHE TOUCHED ME BY	760	11
BUT JUST A CRUMB--TO ME--	GOD GAVE A LOAF TO EVERY	791	2
I DEEM THAT I--WITH BUT A CRUMB--	GOD GAVE A LOAF TO EVERY	791	15
IS LADEN WITH A SINGLE CRUMB	THE LUXURY TO APPREHEND	815	15
THE ROBIN FOR THE CRUMB	THE ROBIN FOR THE CRUMB	864	1
BY BUT A CRUMB OF BLOOD, FASTS SCARLET . .	AS THE STARVED MAELSTROM	872	5
THE BIRD MUST SING TO EARN THE CRUMB . . .	THE BIRD MUST SING TO	880	1
ADD AN AMBER CRUMB	HE IS ALIVE, THIS	1160	6
WHOSE TILLAGE [PASTURE] IS THE PASSING [WANDERING] CRUMB--	THOSE CATTLE SMALLER	1388	3
CRUMBLE			
THEN CRUMBLE GRAND AWAY	TO PILE LIKE THUNDER TO	1247	2
'TWOULD CRUMBLE WITH THE WEIGHT.	COULD MORTAL LIP DIVINE	1409	4
CRUMBLED			
THE THUNDER CRUMBLED LIKE A STUFF	THE CLOUDS THEIR BACKS	1172	5
CRUMBLESS			
AND CRUMBLESS AND AFAR	THE LADY FEEDS HER	941	6
CRUMBLESS AND HOMELESS, OF BUT ONE REQUEST--	QUITE EMPTY, QUITE AT	1606	8
CRUMBLING			
I LAUGHED A CRUMBLING [WOODEN] LAUGH . . .	I YEARS HAD BEEN FROM	609	13
CRUMBLING IS NOT AN INSTANT'S ACT	CRUMBLING IS NOT AN	997	1
TO CRUMBLING MEN LIKE ME [THEE]	HOW FIRM ETERNITY MUST	1499	2
CRUMBS			
CRUMBS--FIT SUCH LITTLE MOUTHS--	VICTORY COMES LATE--	690	10
WHOSE CRUMBS THE CROWS INSPECT	FAME IS A FICKLE FOOD	1659	6
CRUMPLED			
ALL CRUMPLED WAS THE CHEEK	HE TOLD A HOMELY TALE	763	5
CRUNCHES			
THEN MASHES IT TO DEATH [CRUNCHES]--	THE WHOLE OF IT CAME NOT	762	8
CRUSADE'S			
FOR JOURNEY--OR CRUSADE'S ACHIEVING-- . .	ONE CRUCIFIXION IS	553	11
CRUSH			
AND CRUSH OUR PRETTY PLAY--	WE DO NOT PLAY ON GRAVES	467	8
CRUST			
A LITTLE BREAD--A CRUST--A CRUMB--	A LITTLE BREAD--A CRUST	159	1
CRUZ			
COLORS--FROM VERA CRUZ--	I COULD BRING YOU JEWELS	697	4
CRY			
CRY "IT'S I", "TAKE DOLLIE", ...	I OFTEN PASSED THE	51	17
WILL NOT CRY WITH JOY "POMPEII"!	I HAVE NEVER SEEN	175	19
WE DONT CRY--TIM AND I, ...	WE DONT CRY--TIM AND I,	196	1
NOT TO CRY--TIM AND I--	WE DONT CRY--TIM AND I,	196	7
AND LEST I--CRY--	WE DONT CRY--TIM AND I,	196	16
BUT NO MAN HEARD HIM CRY--	THE BLACK BERRY--WEARS A	554	2
NOR HEARD THE TIMID CRY FOR "BREAD"-- . .	THE BEGGAR LAD--DIES	717	7
WHEN THE CRY IS MEANT	TELL AS A MARKSMAN--WERE	1152	25
HER PANTING NOTE [JOYFUL CRY / CORDIAL NOTE] EXALTS US-- . . .	AFTER ALL BIRDS HAVE	1395	6
CRYPTS			
WHEN THOU UPON THEIR CRYPTS INTRUDE . . .	BECAUSE THE BEE MAY	869	8
CRYSTAL			
IT DEALS CELESTIAL [FLINGS A CRYSTAL] VAIL .	IT SIFTS FROM LEADEN	311	12
HE [FIRST]--MUST PASS THE CRYSTAL ANGLE [LIMIT]	HER SWEET TURN TO LEAVE	649	25
MATCH ME THE SILVER [CRYSTAL] RETICENCE-- .	THIS THAT WOULD GREET--	778	7

	FIRST LINE	POEM	LINE
CUBE			
WE SHALL FIND THE CUBE OF THE RAINBOW. . .	WE SHALL FIND THE CUBE	1484	1
CUBES			
WHILE CUBES IN A DROP	BANISH AIR FROM AIR--	854	4
CUBIT			
OR A CUBIT--OR SO?	AH, MOON--AND STAR!	240	7
TILL EVERY CUBIT PLAY WITH THEE	MY GOD--HE SEES THEE--	1178	4
CUBIT'S			
OVER THE CUBIT'S HEAD, ...	UNDER THE LIGHT, YET	949	12
CUBITS			
TOO SCANT--BY CUBITS--TO CONTAIN	IT MIGHT BE LONELIER	405	7
DID NOT OURSELVES THE CUBITS WARP	WE NEVER KNOW HOW HIGH	1176	7
CUCKOO			
BUT, WERE I CUCKOO BORN--	THE ROBIN'S MY CRITERION	285	3
CUFFS			
WITH CUFFS OF CHRYSOLITE!	IT CANT BE "SUMMER"!	221	10
CUIRASS			
OUR IGNORANCE--OUR CUIRASS IS--	WE KNEW NOT THAT WE WERE	1462	3
CULMINATE			
CULMINATE--IN REST--	BLOOM UPON THE MOUNTAIN	667	16
CULPABLER			
IS CULPABLER THAN SHAME.	THE BONE THAT HAS NO	1274	8
CULPRIT			
STIRS THE CULPRIT--LIFE!	SURGEONS MUST BE VERY	108	4
CULTIVATE			
CULTIVATE--OF MEN	NEVER FOR SOCIETY	746	4
CULTIVATION			
WINTER UNDER CULTIVATION	WINTER UNDER CULTIVATION	1707	1
CULTURE			
BRINGING STILL MY "PLEA FOR CULTURE." . .	THE LUXURY TO APPREHEND	815	V
CUNNING			
NOT SO, SAID CUNNING [QUOTH WILY] JACOB! .	A LITTLE EAST OF JORDAN,	59	9
ALL OVERGROWN BY CUNNING MOSS, ...	ALL OVERGROWN BY CUNNING	148	1
WITH CUNNING CARE SHE WOVE--	MAMA NEVER FORGETS HER	164	6
AMONG THE CUNNING CELLS--	I BREATHED ENOUGH TO	272	6
CUNNING REDS OF MORNING	LET US PLAY YESTERDAY--	728	11
OH CUNNING WRECK THAT TOLD NO TALE . . .	A GREAT HOPE FELL	1123	4
DESCRIED BY CUNNING MEN	OH FUTURE! THOU SECRETED	1631	6
CUNNINGLY			
HIDDEN AWAY, CUNNINGLY, ...	SO FROM THE MOULD	66	4
CUP			
I WOULD DISTIL A CUP, ...	I WOULD DISTIL A CUP,	16	1
IN THIS CUP OF MINE.	MANY CROSS THE RHINE	123	2
BRING ME THE SUNSET IN A CUP, ...	BRING ME THE SUNSET IN A	128	1
AND SO I ALWAYS BEAR THE CUP	I BRING AN UNACCUSTOMED	132	17
IN A COFFEE CUP, ...	IS IT TRUE, DEAR SUE?	218	6
NOON--OUR LAST CUP--	WE--BEE AND I--LIVE BY	230	15
WHO INDORSED [ENFORCED] THE CUP--	TO PUT THIS WORLD DOWN,	527	15
LIKE A CUP--	I CANNOT LIVE WITH YOU--	640	8
HELD UP HIS CUP FOR LIGHT.	THE FINGERS OF THE LIGHT	1000	16
A SAUCER HOLDS A CUP	A SAUCER HOLDS A CUP	1374	1
CUP, IT WAS YOUR FAULT, ...	HAD I KNOWN THAT THE	1720	5
WAS THE STRONG CUP OF ANGUISH BREWED FOR THE NAZARENE	PROUD OF MY BROKEN HEART	1736	6
CUPBOARDS			
SNUG IN SERAPHIC CUPBOARDS	PAPA ABOVE!	61	6
CUPIDITY			
TO HIS CUPIDITY--	A BEE HIS BURNISHED	1339	8
CUPID'S			
CUPID'S SERMON	MINE ENEMY IS GROWING	1509	T
CUPS			
SHOULD SWING THEIR CUPS OF CHRYSOLITE-- . .	THERE IS A MORN BY MEN	24	17
HOW MANY CUPS THE BEE PARTAKES, ...	BRING ME THE SUNSET IN A	128	11
IN CUPS OF ARTIFICIAL DROWSE	BEREAVED OF ALL, I WENT	784	13
CURDLED			
THE FINEST HONEY--CURDLED--	THERE IS AN ARID	782	7
CURELESS			
REMORSE IS CURELESS--THE DISEASE	REMORSE--IS MEMORY--	744	9
CURIOSITY			
THIS CURIOSITY--	WITHIN MY GARDEN, RIDES	500	16
THE CURIOSITY	I WATCHED THE MOON	629	10
HAD I THE CURIOSITY	IT WAS A GRAVE, YET BORE	876	7
HOMESICK CURIOSITY	ABSENT PLACE--AN APRIL	927	3
FOR CURIOSITY.	THE MISSING ALL,	985	8
OF CURIOSITY--	HOW HUMAN NATURE DOTES	1417	8
A CURIOSITY	THE HILLS ERECT THEIR	1688	4
CURIOUS			
THE WOLF CAME PEERING CURIOUS--	THROUGH LANE IT LAY--	9	5
I [HE] SCANNED THEIR TRINKETS CURIOUS-- . .	I ROBBED THE WOODS--	41	6
AT SUCH A CURIOUS EARTH!	GOING TO HEAVEN!	79	23
AH, CURIOUS FRIEND!	MY FRIEND MUST BE A BIRD	92	6
BEHOLD, WHAT CURIOUS ROOMS!	WHAT INN IS THIS	115	6
THROUGH GENTLE [CURIOUS / EASY] MIRACLE OF DEATH--	THOSE FAIR--FICTITIOUS	499	23
TO SEE [REACH / TOUCH] THIS CURIOUS FRIEND--	MY PERIOD HAD COME FOR	564	8
AND TOUCHED THE CURIOUS WINE--	I HAD BEEN HUNGRY, ALL	579	4
AND HEALTH, AND LAUGHTER, CURIOUS THINGS-- .	I CRIED AT PITY--NOT AT	588	7
IT SEEMS A CURIOUS TOWN--	WHO OCCUPIES THIS HOUSE?	892	9
THE PAST IS SUCH A CURIOUS CREATURE . . .	THE PAST IS SUCH A	1203	1
A CURIOUS CLOUD SURPRISED THE SKY, ...	A CURIOUS CLOUD	1710	1

	FIRST LINE	POEM	LINE
CURL			
A CURL, PERHAPS, FROM FOREHEADS	IN EBON BOX, WHEN YEARS	169	13
PRESENTS ME WITH A SINGLE CURL	'TIS CUSTOMARY AS WE	440	7
AND DRESS [CURL] THE SLEEPY DAY--	HOW GOOD HIS LAVA BED,	1447	4
CURLED			
AGAIN THE SMOKE FROM DWELLINGS ROSE [CURLED]	THE WIND TOOK UP THE	1134	13
CURLING			
AND HARRIET, AND SUSAN, AND SHE WITH CURLING HAIR!	AWAKE YE MUSES NINE,	1	32
CURLS			
THEN CURLS ITSELF IN CAPRICORN	IT SIFTS FROM LEADEN	311	V
O'ER THE CURLS ATTEMPT TO CAPER	HER SWEET TURN TO LEAVE	649	7
AND FROCKS AND CURLS.	THIS QUIET DUST WAS	813	4
CURRENCY			
CONTRASTED WITH THE CURRENCY	SOME--WORK FOR	406	7
THEIR ARTLESS CURRENCY--	THE MERCHANT OF THE	1131	8
CURRENT			
TO PUT A CURRENT [THE WATERS] BACK--	THE BRAIN, WITHIN IT'S	556	5
BE CURRENT WITH THE BLIND	THE LILAC IS AN ANCIENT	1241	18
CURRENT'S			
TO A CURRENT'S EAR--	I THINK THAT THE ROOT OF	1302	6
CURRER			
THE LITTLE CAGE OF "CURRER BELL"	ALL OVERGROWN BY CUNNING	148	3
CURRICLE			
I ONLY KNOW [SIGH]--NO CURRICLE [VEHICLE] THAT RUMBLE THERE	A LITTLE ROAD--NOT MADE	647	7
CURTAIL			
CURTAIL [CONTRACT] ETERNITY!	SOMEWHERE UPON THE	1231	12
CURTAIL SO	IT CAME HIS TURN TO BEG	1500	V
CURTAILED			
CURTAILED BY YOUR OBSCURING [REMOVING] FACE	BECAUSE THAT YOU ARE	1260	27
CURTAIN			
BETWEEN MY CURTAIN AND THE WALL	THE ANGLE OF A LANDSCAPE	375	3
AS NATURE'S CURTAIN FELL	UPON THE GALLOWS HUNG A	1757	4
CURTAINS			
ONE THE CURTAINS DREW--	MORNS LIKE THESE--WE	27	10
THE ALPS NEGLECT THEIR CURTAINS	OUR LIVES ARE SWISS--	80	4
AND PASSED THEIR CURTAINS BY--	I HAD NO CAUSE TO BE	542	6
IT'S CURTAINS BLANDLY SWEEP--	WATER MAKES MANY BEDS	1428	4
CURTNESS			
THE CURTNESS OF THE JAY--	THE ONES THAT	1690	4
CURVE			
CURVE BY CURVE--SWEEP BY SWEEP--	OUT OF SIGHT? WHAT OF	703	3
CURVE BY CURVE--SWEEP BY SWEEP--	OUT OF SIGHT? WHAT OF	703	3
CURVED			
LIKE RAIN IT SOUNDED TILL IT CURVED [SWELLED]	LIKE RAIN IT SOUNDED	1235	1
CUSHIONS			
TO CUSHIONS CHEEKS--	IT CEASED TO HURT ME,	584	11
THAT CUSHIONS MYSTERY WITH TULLE, ...	THE TINT I CANNOT TAKE--	627	19
CUSTOM			
THE SOUTHERN CUSTOM--OF THE BIRD--	'TIS NOT THAT DYING	335	5
MORTALITY'S OLD CUSTOM--	SHE DEALT HER PRETTY	479	11
A CUSTOM [HABIT] OF THE SOUL	AS ONE DOES SICKNESS	957	9
A [GENTLE] PENSIVE CUSTOM IT BECOMES	FURTHER IN SUMMER THAN	1068	7
TO CUSTOM COMMON GROWN	A DIAMOND ON THE HAND	1108	2
CUSTOMARY			
'TIS CUSTOMARY AS WE PART	'TIS CUSTOMARY AS WE	440	1
CUSTOMS			
AND CUSTOMS AT "ST. JAMES"!	THE MANNER OF IT'S DEATH	468	12
TAWNY--HER CUSTOMS--	CIVILIZATION--SPURNS--	492	5
WHAT FUNCTION [CUSTOMS] HATH THE AIR? . . .	'TIS WHITER THAN AN	1482	8
CUT			
CUT THEE AWAY FROM ME--	YOU KNOW THAT PORTRAIT	504	14
THERE IS A JUNE WHEN CORN IS CUT	THERE IS A JUNE WHEN	930	1
NOR CAN YOU CUT REMEMBRANCE DOWN	YOU CANNOT MAKE	1508	9
AS WHEN 'TWAS CUT AT LEXINGTON, ...	MY COUNTRY NEED NOT	1511	3
CUTICLE			
A CUTICLE OF DUST	CRUMBLING IS NOT AN	997	6
CUTLERY			
THE AWFUL [SOLEMN] CUTLERY	THE LIGHTNING IS A	1173	4
HIS CUTLERY--HE KEEPS	A SAUCER HOLDS A CUP	1374	9
CYCLE			
A CYCLE, IT MAY BE, ...	THE GRAVE MY LITTLE	1743	6
CYCLES			
WHILE UNSUSPECTING CYCLES	PAPA ABOVE!	61	8
AND THE CYCLES WHEEL!	JUST LOST, WHEN I WAS	160	19
CYNIC			
A CYNIC, I BECAME.	I CAUTIOUS, SCANNED MY	178	12
CYPHER SEE CIPHER			
TELL [STATE] IT THE AGES--TO A CYPHER-- . .	BOUND--A TROUBLE--	269	7
CYPHERER			
REGARDS LEAST CYPHERER ALIKE	'TIS ONE BY ONE--THE	545	13
CYPHERLESS			
SET CYPHERLESS--TO TEACH THE EYE	'TIS ONE BY ONE--THE	545	3
CZAR			
'TWAS POSSIBLY A CZAR PETITE--	I MET A KING THIS	166	11
I'M CZAR--I'M "WOMAN" NOW--	I'M "WIFE"--I'VE	199	3
CZARS			
THAT EMPIRE--IS OF CZARS--	THE COURT IS FAR AWAY--	235	9

	FIRST LINE	POEM	LINE
DAFFODIL			
REASONS THE DAFFODIL	LIKE HER THE SAINTS	60	11
UNTIL THE DAFFODIL	PERHAPS YOU'D LIKE TO	134	4
AND CHUBBY DAFFODIL.	WHOSE ARE THE LITTLE	142	16
DAFFODIL DOWRIES--SPICY "STOCKS"-- . . .	WHAT WOULD I GIVE TO SEE	247	16
ON SEAS OF DAFFODIL--	WHERE SHIPS OF PURPLE--	265	2
THOUGH IT BE LITTLE AS A DAFFODIL-- . . .	WHAT I CAN DO--I WILL--	361	2
SURFEIT! WHEN THE DAFFODIL	ALTER! WHEN THE HILLS DO	729	5
DAFFODIL DELIGHT BUT	ABSENT PLACE--AN APRIL	927	7
DAFFODILS			
TILL DAFFODILS HAD COME AND GONE	SHE BORE IT TILL THE	144	5
AND THEY--THE DAFFODILS!	THE SKIES CANT KEEP	191	4
I DARED NOT MEET THE DAFFODILS--	I DREADED THAT FIRST	348	9
WHERE DAFFODILS--ABIDE--	SHE DWELLETH IN THE	671	2
DAFFODILS A-BLOW	ABSENT PLACE--AN APRIL	927	2
DAILY			
IS DAILY DRUNKEN THERE--	HAVE YOU GOT A BROOK IN	136	8
PORTRAITS [PICTURES] ARE TO DAILY FACES . .	PORTRAITS ARE TO DAILY	170	1
THE DAILY OWN--OF LOVE	I GAVE MYSELF TO HIM--	580	8
UPON A DAILY STREET	IT IS AN HONORABLE	946	4
I HAD A DAILY BLISS	I HAD A DAILY BLISS	1057	1
WOULD BE A NORMAL [DAILY] THING	WE NEVER KNOW HOW HIGH	1176	6
TOO MIGHTY FOR THE DAILY MIND	I NEVER HEAR THAT ONE IS	1323	5
BUT SO ADJUST MY DAILY NIGHT	LET ME NOT MAR THAT	1335	3
"SECRETS" IS A DAILY WORD	"SECRETS" IS A DAILY	1385	1
OUR FAITH DOTH DAILY TREAD--	HOW BRITTLE ARE THE	1433 V	2
HER TRAVELS DAILY BE	"GO TRAVELING WITH US!"	1513	2
THE MEN THAT DAILY LIVE	DID LIFE'S PENURIOUS	1717	3
DAINTIER			
MANGLE DAINTIER--TERRIBLER--	IT IS EASY TO WORK WHEN	244	7
THERE BE--PREFERRED BY DAINTIER FOLK-- . .	"WHY DO I LOVE" YOU, SIR	480	16
DAINTILY			
ABSCONDED DAINTILY [FLUENTLY]	A SPARROW TOOK A SLICE	1211 V	8
DAINTY			
DAINTY--AS THE TRESS--ON HER DEFT HEAD-- .	WE--BEE AND I--LIVE BY	230	11
SO DAINTY OF PUBLICITY--	FUNNY--TO BE A CENTURY--	345	8
TUCKS--OF DAINTY INTERSPERSION--	DONT PUT UP MY THREAD &	617	11
DAINTY ADORNED WITH VEINS AND TISSUES . .	AS THE STARVED MAELSTROM	872	7
A PENCIL IN AN IDOL'S [DAINTY] HAND . . .	DEATH WARRANTS ARE	1375	4
DAISIES			
THE DAISIES DARE TO COME HERE--	I OFTEN PASSED THE	51	11
WHEN WE WITH DAISIES LIE--	IF I SHOULD DIE,	54	12
DAISIES POINT THE WAY THERE--	SEXTON! MY MASTER'S	96	7
I WILL GIVE HIM ALL THE DAISIES	FLOWERS--WELL--IF	137	7
INDOLENT HOUSEWIFE--IN DAISIES--LAIN! . .	HOW MANY TIMES THESE LOW	187	12
I'D DAISIES SPURN [CLOVERS--SCORN]-- . . .	THE ROBIN'S MY CRITERION	285	9
WHOM NONE BUT DAISIES [BEETLES], KNOW. . .	OF BRONZE--AND BLAZE--	290	19
SHE--EACH YEAR--LEADS HER DAISIES BACK-- .	I KNOW A PLACE WHERE	337	3
LOW DAISIES--DOT--	I TEND MY FLOWERS FOR	339	6
AS DAISIES NOW TO BE SEEN--	THIS WAS IN THE WHITE OF	995	4
HERE, WHERE THE DAISIES FIT MY HEAD . . .	HERE, WHERE THE DAISIES	1037	1
DAISY			
LEAVING NOOKS FOR DAISY	ALL THESE MY BANNERS BE.	22	14
SO HAS A DAISY VANISHED	SO HAS A DAISY VANISHED	28	1
THE DAISY WOULD IMPEL ME.	IF THOSE I LOVED WERE	29	6
BY DAISY CALLED FROM HILLSIDE--	I KEEP MY PLEDGE.	46	7
BETTER AS THE DAISY	GLOWING IS HER BONNET,	72	5
SOVREIGN! KNOW A DAISY	"THEY HAVE NOT CHOSEN ME	85	7
A DIFFERENCE--A DAISY--	WENT UP A YEAR THIS	93	23
THE DAISY, TO RECEIVE, ...	GREAT CAESAR! CONDESCEND	102	2
THE DAISY FOLLOWS SOFT THE SUN--	THE DAISY FOLLOWS SOFT	106	1
A MYRIAD DAISY PLAY--	IN LANDS I NEVER SAW--	124	6
'TIS DAISY, IN THE SHORTEST--	WHOSE ARE THE LITTLE	142	9
THY DAISY--	I TEND MY FLOWERS FOR	339	26
BUT JUST A DAISY--DEEP--	THE COLOR OF THE GRAVE	411	8
UNTO THE DAISY LOW--	THE HIMMALEH WAS KNOWN	481	2
WOULD IT MAKE THE DAISY, ...	IF IT HAD NO PENCIL	921	6
THE DAISY THAT HAS LOOKED BEHIND	THE CLOVER'S SIMPLE FAME	1232	7
DAM			
THE SAGEST [ONLY] TIME TO DAM THE SEA IS WHEN THE SEA IS GONE--	WE SEND THE WAVE TO FIND	1604	7
DAMAGE			
THE RUIN [HAVOC / DAMAGE] WAS WITHIN . . .	A GREAT HOPE FELL	1123	3
DAMASK			
FOR MY LITTLE DAMASK MAID--	PIGMY SERAPHS--GONE	138	11
HER'S BE DAMASK FINE--	THO' MY DESTINY BE	163	2
HE TAKETH DAMASK RESIDENCE--	A FUZZY FELLOW, WITHOUT	173	11
DAME			
IF RUFF IT WAS OF DAME	A SPIDER SEWED AT NIGHT	1138	4
DAMES			
OF VANISHED DAMES--AND MEN!	MUSICIANS WRESTLE	157	15
DAMS			
THAT HELD THE DAMS--HAD PARTED HOLD-- . .	THE WIND BEGUN TO KNEAD	824	17
OR DAMS--OF EXTASY--	THE PUNGENT ATOM IN THE	1191	8
DAMSEL			
OH THE EARTH WAS MADE FOR LOVERS, FOR DAMSEL, AND HOPELESS SWAIN,	AWAKE YE MUSES NINE,	1	3
EARTH IS A MERRY DAMSEL, AND HEAVEN A KNIGHT SO TRUE,	AWAKE YE MUSES NINE,	1	23
"THOU WERT WITH HIM"--QUOTH "THE DAMSEL"? .	HE FORGOT--AND I--	203	5

	FIRST LINE	POEM	LINE
DAMSONS			
THAT LAWFUL ORCHARDS [DAMSONS] MOCKS--	FORBIDDEN FRUIT A FLAVOR	1377	2
DANCE			
AND ALL DAY LONG, WITH DANCE AND GAME,	THERE IS A MORN BY MEN	24	4
LIKE THEE TO DANCE--LIKE THEE TO SING--	THERE IS A MORN BY MEN	24	19
I CANNOT DANCE UPON MY TOES--	I CANNOT DANCE UPON MY	326	1
INSTINCTS FOR DANCE--A CAPER PART--	I'VE DROPPED MY BRAIN--	1046	11
DANCED			
I COUNTED TILL THEY DANCED SO	I COUNTED TILL THEY	36	1
A VEST THAT LIKE HER BODDICE, DANCED--	THE ROSE DID CAPER ON	208	13
HE DANCED ALONG THE DINGY DAYS	HE ATE AND DRANK THE	1587	5
DANCER			
HOW DUMB [STILL] THE DANCER LIES--	AS FAR FROM PITY, AS	496	10
DANCES			
SHE DANCES LIKE A BOMB, ABROAD,	THE SOUL HAS BANDAGED	512	13
DANCING			
DANCING AROUND THE SUN	FOR EVERY BIRD A NEST--	143	17
HER DANCING EYES--AJAR--	SHE LAY AS IF AT PLAY	369	9
AND DANCING SOFTLY TO HIMSELF [AS HE KNITS]	THE SPIDER HOLDS A	605	3
DANDELION			
GENERAL AS THE DANDELION	NONE WHO SAW IT EVER	1110	7
DANDELION'S			
UPON A DANDELION'S SLEEVE--	I STARTED EARLY--TOOK MY	520	15
AND DANDELION'S DRAMA	IT'S LITTLE ETHER HOOD	1501	7
THE DANDELION'S PALLID TUBE	THE DANDELION'S PALLID	1519	1
THE DANDELION'S SHIELD	TO HER DERIDED HOME	1586	V
DANDELIONS			
AND DANDELIONS GOLD.	WE SHOULD NOT MIND SO	81	12
DANES			
OF DANES, UNTO THE REST.	REPORTLESS SUBJECTS, TO	1048	4
DANGER			
LIKE ONE IN DANGER, CAUTIOUS,	A BIRD CAME DOWN THE	328	13
AND OFTEN SINCE, IN DANGER,	I PRAYED, AT FIRST, A	576	14
THE DANGER [SORROW] TO BE SANE	I THINK I WAS ENCHANTED	593	26
WHO DANGER--AND THE DEAD--HAD FACED--	I YEARS HAD BEEN FROM	609	V 15
DANGER! WHAT IS THAT TO HER?	OUT OF SIGHT? WHAT OF	703	5
IN DANGER--OTHER IMPETUS	I LIVED ON DREAD--	770	4
DANGER--DEEPENS SUM--	EXPECTATION--IS	807	8
FRAUD OF DISTANCE--FRAUD OF DANGER,	ROBBED BY DEATH--BUT	971	9
IS BEST DISCLOSED BY DANGER	THE SOUL'S DISTINCT	974	3
DANGER DISINTEGRATES SATIETY	PERIL AS A POSSESSION	1678	3
DANGEROUS			
DEMUR--YOU'RE STRAIGHTWAY DANGEROUS--	MUCH MADNESS IS DIVINEST	435	7
FOR THAT DEAR--DISTANT--DANGEROUS--SAKE--	WHY MAKE IT DOUBT--IT	462	7
AS INNOCENT [DANGEROUS] AS JUNE--	TO SEE HER IS A PICTURE	1568	4
DANGEROUSLY			
SO DANGEROUSLY NEAR.	THE SADDEST NOISE, THE	1764	20
DANGLE			
THOSE--DANGLE EASY--ON MY ARM,	PERHAPS I ASKED TOO	352	6
THEN DANGLE FROM [PERISH BY] THE HOUSEWIFE'S BROOM--	THE SPIDER HOLDS A	605	11
DANGLED			
THAT JUST NOW DANGLED STILL--	A CLOCK STOPPED--	287	5
DANGLES			
AND DANGLES LIKE A MOTE	HE PARTS HIMSELF--LIKE	517	9
DANGLING			
CROWNED--CROWING [WHIMPERING / DANGLING]--ON MY FATHER'S BREAST--	I'M CEDED--I'VE STOPPED	508	15
DANIEL			
HURRAH FOR DANIEL BOON!	"SIC TRANSIT GLORIA	3	10
DANTE			
THE GOWN THAT DANTE--DEIFIED--	A PRECIOUS--MOULDERING	371	19
DAPPERER			
BUT DAPPERER--MORE SWEET--	A MURMUR IN THE TREES--	416	8
DAPPLED			
FROM SPOTTED [DAPPLED] NOOKS--	MY RIVER RUNS TO THEE--	162	6
AND DAPPLED COWSLIP DELLS--	WHAT WOULD I GIVE TO SEE	247	14
THOUGH SHUTTING LIKE A DAPPLED FAN	THE BUTTERFLY'S NUMIDIAN	1387	V 4
A DIMPLED [FLORID / DAPPLED] ROAD	THE ROAD TO PARADISE IS	1491	5
THEIR DAPPLED JOURNEY TO THEMSELVES	COSMOPOLITES WITHOUT A	1589	5
THEIR DAPPLED IMPORTUNITY	THEIR DAPPLED	1611	1
DARE			
THE DAISIES DARE TO COME HERE--	I OFTEN PASSED THE	51	11
BUILDING WHERE SCHOOLBOY DARE NOT LOOK,	SOME, TOO FRAGILE FOR	141	7
DARE I PRESUME TO SEE	I MET A KING THIS	166	18
MIGHT DARE TO TOUCH IT NOW!	WAIT TILL THE MAJESTY OF	171	4
A LORD, MIGHT DARE TO LIFT THE HAT	WAIT TILL THE MAJESTY OF	171	13
OR IF IT DARE--TO CLIMB YOUR DIZZY KNEE--	WHAT SHALL I DO--IT	186	10
I SHOULD NOT DARE TO LEAVE MY FRIEND,	I SHOULD NOT DARE TO	205	1
WHERE OTHERS, DARE NOT GO [WALK] AT NOON,	WHEN WE STAND ON THE	242	11
THE STARS DARE SHINE OCCASIONALLY	WHEN WE STAND ON THE	242	13
THAT I DARE TO TELL?	HOW THE OLD MOUNTAINS	291	8
DARE YOU SEE A SOUL AT THE WHITE HEAT?	DARE YOU SEE A SOUL AT	365	1
THE LADY DARE NOT LIFT HER VAIL	A CHARM INVESTS A FACE	421	3
I DID NOT DARE TO EAT--OR SLEEP--	IT WAS GIVEN TO ME BY	454	7
THAT SOMETHING--IT DID DO--OR DARE--	WHY MAKE IT DOUBT--IT	462	9
TO THOSE WHO DARE [ALLOWED] TO TRY--	I THINK TO LIVE--MAY BE	646	2
TO MAR [DARE]--	EACH LIFE CONVERGES TO	680	8
DARE NOT VENTURE--NOW--	LIFE--IS WHAT WE MAKE IT	698	16
IF HE WERE LIVING--DARE I ASK--	IF HE WERE LIVING--DARE	734	1

	FIRST LINE	POEM	LINE
DARE (CONTINUED)			
HOW DARE I, THEREFORE, STINT A FAITH . . .	MY FAITH IS LARGER THAN	766	13
THE LONELINESS ONE DARE NOT SOUND-- . . .	THE LONELINESS ONE DARE	777	1
I DARE NOT EAT IT--THO' I STARVE-- . . .	GOD GAVE A LOAF TO EVERY	791	3
DIVIDE LIGHT IF YOU DARE--	BANISH AIR FROM AIR--	854	2
I SHOULD NOT DARE TO BE SO SAD	I SHOULD NOT DARE TO BE	1197	1
HE DARE IN LONELY [LONESOME / SECRET] PLACE	I NEVER HEAR THAT ONE IS	1323	14
"IF YOU DARE"?	NOT SEEING, STILL WE	1518	8
I DARE NOT WRITE UNTIL I HEAR--	A PANG IS MORE	1530	V
TO DARE AND PERISH THERE?	IT WOULD NOT KNOW IF IT	1579	8
WHERE ROSES WOULD NOT DARE TO GO, ...	WHERE ROSES WOULD NOT	1582	1
I DARE NOT ASK MY FEET--	A PIT--BUT HEAVEN OVER	1712	11
THE TRUTH I DO NOT DARE TO KNOW	CONSULTING SUMMER'S	1715	7
HOW DARE THE ROBINS SING, ...	HOW DARE THE ROBINS SING	1724	1
WHILE WE WHO DARE TO LIVE	THIS DOCILE ONE INTER	1752	2
DARED			
BUT SINCE JESUS DARED--	"THEY HAVE NOT CHOSEN ME	85	6
I DARED NOT MEET THE DAFFODILS--	I DREADED THAT FIRST	348	9
I DARED NOT ENTER [OPEN], LEST A FACE . .	I YEARS HAD BEEN FROM	609	3
I DARED TO SHOW A TRESS OF THEIR'S . . .	PRECIOUS TO ME--SHE	727	6
SINCE I HOPED I DARED	WHEN I HOPED I FEARED--	1181	2
DARES			
THAT DARES [FEARS] TO COVET THEE	CIRCUMFERENCE THOU BRIDE	1620	4
DARING			
THE PILLOW OF THIS DARING HEAD	NO BRIGADIER THROUGHOUT	1561	17
NOT DARING LOOK BEHIND;	THE WATERS CHASED HIM AS	1749	2
DARK			
MY FAITH THAT DARK ADORES--	THE FEET OF PEOPLE	7	22
MY WHEEL IS IN THE DARK!	MY WHEEL IS IN THE DARK!	10	1
WHICH BLOSSOM IN THE DARK.	BY CHIVALRIES AS TINY,	55	4
TO FIND THE WINDOWS DARK--	YOU LOVE ME--YOU ARE	156	11
'TWAS'NT DARK--FOR HE WENT--TOO--	HE WAS WEAK, AND I WAS	190	6
WHEN NIGHT--DESCENDING--DUMB--AND DARK-- .	THO' I GET HOME HOW LATE	207	5
IT WAS DARK--BEFORE--	IF HE DISSOLVE--THEN--	236	3
SOME SAILOR--ROWING IN THE DARK--	GOOD NIGHT! WHICH PUT	259	8
THERE'LL BE THAT DARK PARADE--	THERE'S BEEN A DEATH, IN	389	20
THROUGH THE DARK SOD--AS EDUCATION-- . . .	THROUGH THE DARK SOD--AS	392	1
WOULD INTERRUPT THE DARK--	IT MIGHT BE LONELIER	405	5
WE GROW ACCUSTOMED TO THE DARK--	WE GROW ACCUSTOMED TO	419	1
THEN--FIT OUR VISION TO THE DARK--	WE GROW ACCUSTOMED TO	419	7
TO RACES--NURTURED IN THE DARK--	I FOUND THE WORDS TO	581	5
THE DARK--FELT BEAUTIFUL--	I THINK I WAS ENCHANTED	593	4
WHEN IT WAS DARK ENOUGH TO DO [SHOW] . . .	A STILL--VOLCANO--LIFE--	601	3
I SEE THEE BETTER--IN THE DARK--	I SEE THEE BETTER--IN	611	1
TO THOSE WHOSE DARK--HATH SO--SURPASSING SUN--	I SEE THEE BETTER--IN	611	14
AND OVERTAKEN IN THE DARK--	OURSELVES WERE WED ONE	631	5
DARK SHALL OVERTAKE THE HILL--	WHEN I HOPED, I	768	V 21
BUT SKIRTED IN THE DARK--	THE LONELINESS ONE DARE	777	10
OF THAT VAST DARK--	GRIEF IS A MOUSE--	793	7
WHAT DAY BE DARK TO ME	SO SET IT'S SUN IN THEE	808	2
THE LIGHT HIS ACTION, AND THE DARK	ALL CIRCUMSTANCES ARE	820	5
TO KEEP THE DARK AWAY.	I SING TO USE THE	850	8
ONLY TO AGGRAVATE [JUST TO INTENSIFY] THE DARK	FAIRER THROUGH FADING--	938	7
BEFORE WE FELT THE DARK--	WE MET AS SPARKS--	958	6
I SEEK THE DARK	I FIT FOR THEM--	1109	2
THE APPARATUS OF THE DARK	THE LIGHTNING IS A	1173	7
DARKER			
A DARKER RIBBON--FOR A DAY--	TO DIE--TAKES JUST A	255	5
CAME THE DARKER WAY--	HER SWEET TURN TO LEAVE	649	2
HIS HEART WAS DARKER THAN THE STARLESS NIGHT	HIS HEART WAS DARKER	1378	1
DARKNESS			
THOUGH IT BE DARKNESS THERE!	THERE IS ANOTHER SKY,	2	4
EITHER THE DARKNESS ALTERS--	WE GROW ACCUSTOMED TO	419	17
AND DARKNESS ON THE SCHOOL	'TIS ONE BY ONE--THE	545	10
THAT DARKNESS--IS ABOUT TO PASS--	PRESENTIMENT--IS THAT	764	4
DARKNESS INTERSECT HER FACE--	WHEN I HOPED, I	768	21
THE DARKNESS [TROUBLE] BRACED AS FIRM . .	SEVERER SERVICE OF	786	18
INTO THE DARKNESS [TWILIGHT / EVENING] DIPS AWAY--	FAIRER THROUGH FADING--	938	2
COULD THAT SWEET DARKNESS WHERE THEY DWELL .	COULD THAT SWEET	1493	[illegible]
DARKNESSES			
AND SO OF LARGER--DARKNESSES--	WE GROW ACCUSTOMED TO	419	[illegible]
DARLING			
THE BUSY DARLING LAY--	HER FINAL SUMMER WAS IT	795	1[illegible]
THEN, DARLING, IT WILL CLOSE	THIS CHASM, SWEET, UPON	858	1[illegible]
DARLINGS			
THE DARLINGS OF THE SOIL	THEY ASK BUT OUR DELIGHT	868	[illegible]
DART			
'TWILL ENTER LIKE A DART!	HOW NEWS MUST FEEL WHEN	1319	
NOR ANY DART, ...	NOT SICKNESS STAINS THE	1613	
I THE DART REVERE.	I'VE GOT AN ARROW HERE.	1729	
DARTING			
A DARTING FEAR--A POMP--A TEAR--	A DARTING FEAR--A POMP--	87	
DATE			
MIGHT DATE A VICTORY!	A DAY! HELP! HELP!	42	
EPICURES--DATE A BREAKFAST--BY IT--	"MORNING"--MEANS	300	
BUT NATURE LOST THE DATE OF THIS--	IT STRUCK ME--EVERY DAY	362	1
THE DATE, AND MANNER, OF THE SHAME-- . . .	I READ MY SENTENCE--	412	
YOU ALMOST FEEL THE DATE--	IF ANYBODY'S FRIEND BE	509	1
I COULD NOT TELL THE DATE OF MINE--	I MEASURE EVERY GRIEF I	561	

	FIRST LINE	POEM	LINE
DATE (CONTINUED)			
SIMPLY EXTINCTION'S DATE--	EMPTY MY HEART, OF THEE	587	4
WITHOUT THE DATE, LIKE CONSCIOUSNESS OR IMMORTALITY--	LEST ANY DOUBT THAT WE	1156	3
OH FAITHFUL FROST [SLEET] THAT KEPT THE DATE	IT CAME AT LAST BUT	1230	5
ANOTHER DATE OF THEE--	SOMEWHERE UPON THE	1231	10
RESUMING AT A MUTUAL DATE	THE SPIRIT LASTS--BUT IN	1576	15
DATED			
BUT DATED WITH THE DEAD.	SOMEHOW MYSELF SURVIVED	1194	8
DATELESS			
A DATELESS--MELODY--	IT'S LIKE THE LIGHT--	297	4
HIMSELF--HIS DATELESS DYNASTY--	BEHIND ME--DIPS ETERNITY	721	10
UPON HIS DATELESS FAME	SUPERFLUOUS WERE THE SUN	999	9
DATES			
REMOVE THE DATES--TO THESE--	FOREVER--IS COMPOSED OF	624	6
TILL HE ESTEEM HIS DATES AND COCOA	AS THE STARVED MAELSTROM	872	11
STILL STATES TO DATES THAT HAVE FORGOT	SHE LAID HER DOCILE	1396	3
DATING			
BY DATING IT A SUDDEN FEAST.	I CANNOT SEE MY SOUL BUT	1262	10
DAUGHTER			
GATHERED BY CATO'S DAUGHTER,	GREAT CAESAR! CONDESCEND	102	3
THE PARASOL IS THE UMBRELLA'S DAUGHTER,	THE PARASOL IS THE	1747	1
DAUNTLESS			
THEY BEAR THEIR DAUNTLESS [FEARLESS / TRANQUIL] HEADS,	WHEN WE STAND ON THE	242	10
AS DAUNTLESS IN THE HOUSE OF DEATH	THIS DOCILE ONE INTER	1752	7
DAVID			
'TWAS NOT SO MUCH AS DAVID--HAD--	I TOOK MY POWER IN MY	540	3
DAVID--THE TROUBADOUR--	THE BIBLE IS AN ANTIQUE	1545	8
DAWN			
UNTO THE DIFFERENT DAWN!	THERE IS A MORN BY MEN	24	24
JUST AS THE DAWN WAS RED	ADRIFT! A LITTLE BOAT	30	10
IT'S COOLER THAN THE DAWN--	I OFTEN PASSED THE	51	10
INHALES THE DIFFERENT DAWN.	A DARTING FEAR--A POMP--	87	4
ON SUCH A DAWN, OR SUCH A DAWN--	ON SUCH A NIGHT, OR SUCH	146	9
ON SUCH A DAWN, OR SUCH A DAWN--	ON SUCH A NIGHT, OR SUCH	146	9
BLINDNESS--ON THE DAWN--	IF HE DISSOLVE--THEN--	236	5
DAWN--TO THE TENERIFFE [APPENINE]--	"MORNING"--MEANS	300	2
AND SHATTER [FLOOD] ME WITH DAWN!	AS IF I ASKED A COMMON	323	8
BUT SUNSET ON THE DAWN	SUNSET AT NIGHT--IS	415	2
DREAMING--OF THE DAWN--	DREAMS--ARE WELL--BUT	450	4
THAN A SOLID DAWN--CONFRONTING--	DREAMS--ARE WELL--BUT	450	7
AND WHEN AGAIN, AT DAWN,	"HEAVEN" HAS DIFFERENT	575	4
DISSOLVING INTO DAWN AWAY,	BEHIND ME--DIPS ETERNITY	721	5
THEIR PERIOD FOR DAWN--	THE BIRDS BEGUN AT FOUR	783	2
EVERY DAWN, IS FIRST.	ALWAYS MINE!	839	9
WHERE DAWN--KNOWS HOW TO BE--	I LEARNED--AT LEAST--	944	31
OF DAWN, THE ANCESTOR--	THE MOUNTAIN SAT UPON	975	8
THAN DAWN IN [ON] TIMBUCTOO.	AS SLEIGH BELLS SEEM IN	981	8
AND FASTENED IT IN DAWN.	IT WAS A QUIET WAY--	1053	20
THE SOUL RETURNING SOFT AT NIGHT [STILL BY DAWN / LOTH BY DAWN]	CONTAINED IN THIS SHORT	1165	3
THE SOUL RETURNING SOFT AT NIGHT [STILL BY DAWN / LOTH BY DAWN]	CONTAINED IN THIS SHORT	1165	3
CANCELED LIKE DAWN	LEFT IN IMMORTAL YOUTH	1289	7
DURABLE AS DAWN	TRUSTY AS THE STARS	1369	5
CAN BE NO BODE OF DAWN	HIS HEART WAS DARKER	1378	4
MORE PRUDENT TO ASSAULT THE DAWN	HER SPIRIT ROSE TO SUCH	1486	4
AS DAWN FORGETS THEM--NOW--	THE MOON UPON HER FLUENT	1528	8
FOR SUCH A FOE [SWEET / GLEE / DAWN / SCENE / DEW / JOY] AS THIS--	FROM ALL THE JAILS THE	1532	8
NOT KNOWING WHEN THE DAWN WILL [HERSELF MAY] COME,	NOT KNOWING WHEN THE	1619	1
AND PRESENCE, SIMPLY DAWN--	SOME SAY GOODNIGHT--AT	1739	6
DAWNS			
ENCAMPING ON A THOUSAND DAWNS	HOW LONESOME THE WIND	1418	10
TWO DAWNS UPON A SINGLE MORN,	MORNING THAT COMES BUT	1610	3
DAY SEE TO-DAY			
NIGHT UNTO DAY IS MARRIED, MORN UNTO EVENTIDE;	AWAKE YE MUSES NINE,	1	22
ON PATRIOTIC DAY,	THERE IS A WORD	8	8
WHEREVER ROAMS THE DAY--	THERE IS A WORD	8	12
THE BREAKING OF THE DAY.	SLEEP IS SUPPOSED TO BE	13	9
THAT IS THE BREAK OF DAY!	SLEEP IS SUPPOSED TO BE	13	15
BAFFLED FOR JUST A DAY OR TWO--	BAFFLED FOR JUST A DAY	17	1
WHO SANG FULL MANY A DAY	I HAD A GUINEA GOLDEN--	23	10
AND ALL DAY LONG, WITH DANCE AND GAME,	THERE IS A MORN BY MEN	24	4
AND REVEL TILL THE DAY--	THERE IS A MORN BY MEN	24	18
UPON THIS SUMMER'S DAY	WHEN ROSES CEASE TO	32	6
ON A SUMMER'S DAY--	BEFORE THE ICE IS IN THE	37	10
A DAY! HELP! HELP! ANOTHER DAY!	A DAY! HELP! HELP!	42	1
A DAY! HELP! HELP! ANOTHER DAY!	A DAY! HELP! HELP!	42	1
THE DAY THAT I SHALL GO--	I HAV'NT TOLD MY GARDEN	50	12
UPON A FESTAL DAY,	IF I SHOULD CEASE TO	56	2
AFTER [UNTO] THE DAY!	LIKE HER THE SAINTS	60	6
TO NIBBLE ALL THE DAY,	PAPA ABOVE!	61	7
SOLVE OUR APRIL DAY!	I CANT TELL YOU--BUT YOU	65	4
"CHARMING APRIL DAY"!	I CANT TELL YOU--BUT YOU	65	16
I SLEW A WORM THE OTHER DAY--	"ARCTURUS" IS HIS OTHER	70	5
ON REVOLUTION DAY?	WHO NEVER LOST, ARE	73	12
NOR NOTICED THAT THE EBBING DAY	A POOR--TORN HEART-- A	78	3

	FIRST LINE	POEM	LINE
DAY (CONTINUED)			
TO PICK ANOTHER DAY;	WENT UP A YEAR THIS	93	16
UPON A WINTER'S DAY,	A SCIENCE--SO THE SAVANS	100	9
IS THERE SUCH A THING AS "DAY"?	WILL THERE REALLY BE A	101	2
I TRUDGE THE DAY AWAY--	I HAVE A KING, WHO DOES	103	3
IN PARLORS, SHUT BY DAY.	I HAVE A KING, WHO DOES	103	6
WHEREFORE, OH SUMMER'S DAY?	THE BEE IS NOT AFRAID OF	111	8
AFTERWARDS--DAY!	OUR SHARE OF NIGHT TO	113	8
A SOMETHING IN A SUMMER'S DAY	A SOMETHING IN A	122	1
ANOTHER SUMMER'S DAY!	A SOMETHING IN A	122	22
UPON AN AUGUST DAY?	IN LANDS I NEVER SAW--	124	8
WHO'LL LET ME OUT SOME GALA DAY	BRING ME THE SUNSET IN A	128	22
BELLES FROM SOME LOST SUMMER DAY--	PIGMY SERAPHS--GONE	138	3
THE BREAKING OF THE DAY	THE MURMUR OF A BEE	155	11
ALL DAY--AMONG THE CROWDED AIR	MUSICIANS WRESTLE	157	2
BETWEEN OUR FEET, AND DAY!	AT LAST, TO BE	174	7
I LOST A WORLD--THE OTHER DAY!	I LOST A WORLD--THE	181	1
ALL DAY AND NIGHT WITH BARK AND START--	WHAT SHALL I DO--IT	186	3
WHEN OTHERS CALL IT "DAY"!	MAKE ME A PICTURE OF THE	188	4
DAY KNOCKED--AND WE MUST PART--	HE WAS WEAK, AND I WAS	190	9
A BANK OF DAY--	A SLASH OF BLUE--	204	8
AND THE JUGGLER OF DAY IS GONE	BLAZING IN GOLD AND	228	8
THOU SHALT--THYSELF--ONE DAY--A CHILD--	THE COURT IS FAR AWAY--	235	7
GRANT ME--THAT DAY--THE ROYALTY--	THE COURT IS FAR AWAY--	235	11
THE DAY WAS WARM, AND WINDS WERE PROSY--	I HELD A JEWEL IN MY	245	3
ROSES A DAY FROM ZENZIBAR--	WHAT WOULD I GIVE TO SEE	247	9
A DARKER RIBBON--FOR A DAY--	TO DIE--TAKES JUST A	255	5
SINCE THAT APPALLING DAY!	THE ONLY GHOST I EVER	274	16
DAY--RATTLES--TOO	I KNOW SOME LONELY	289	31
PRECEDES ENAMORED--DAY--	THE DOOMED--REGARD THE	294	10
I'M SURE 'TIS INDIA--ALL DAY--	YOUR RICHES--TAUGHT ME--	299	17
TO HAVE A SMILE FOR MINE--EACH DAY,	YOUR RICHES--TAUGHT ME--	299	23
THE DAY CAME SLOW--TILL FIVE O'CLOCK--	THE DAY CAME SLOW--TILL	304	1
THE PARLOR--OF THE DAY--	THE DAY CAME SLOW--TILL	304	16
THE ONE WHO [THAT] COULD REPEAT THE SUMMER DAY--	THE ONE WHO COULD REPEAT	307	1
DAY AND I--IN COMPETITION RAN--	I SEND TWO SUNSETS--	308	2
HIS WAY--OF A JUNE DAY--	THE WIND DID'NT COME	316	16
OF A JUNE DAY	THE WIND DID'NT COME	316	V 16
THERE CAME A DAY AT SUMMER'S FULL,	THERE CAME A DAY AT	322	1
AND STIR ALL DAY TO PRETTY TUNES	THE GRASS SO LITTLE HAS	333	5
THE DAY THAT I WAS CROWNED	THE DAY THAT I WAS	356	1
BUT WHEN THE DAY DECLINED	THE DAY THAT I WAS	356	10
IT STRUCK ME--EVERY DAY--	IT STRUCK ME--EVERY DAY	362	1
OR ALL DAY, CHASE THE BEE--	ALTHOUGH I PUT AWAY HIS	366	21
SOME FEBUARY DAY,	ALTHOUGH I PUT AWAY HIS	366	27
I'M SAYING EVERY DAY	I'M SAYING EVERY DAY	373	1
MY ART, A SUMMER DAY--HAD PATRONS--	WHEN DIAMONDS ARE A	397	6
BEGINNING WITH THE DAY	A TONGUE--TO TELL HIM I	400	10
AND THEN--A DAY AS HUGE	THE FIRST DAY'S NIGHT	410	9
AND THO' 'TIS YEARS AGO--THAT DAY--	THE FIRST DAY'S NIGHT	410	15
BUT THERE'S THE "JUDGMENT DAY"!	I NEVER FELT AT HOME--	413	16
THAT NEARER, EVERY DAY,	'TWAS LIKE A MAELSTROM,	414	2
WHO WEARY OF THE DAY--	THE MONTHS HAVE ENDS--	423	10
DAY--GOT TIRED OF ME--	GOOD MORNING--MIDNIGHT--	425	3
SO--GOODNIGHT--DAY!	GOOD MORNING--MIDNIGHT--	425	8
I CHOSE--DAY--	GOOD MORNING--MIDNIGHT--	425	14
I SHALL HAVE WADED DOWN ONE DAY".	IT DONT SOUND SO	426	9
LEADING TO NO DAY--	DREAMS--ARE WELL--BUT	450	8
CONVICTION--EVERY DAY--	I LIVE WITH HIM--I SEE	463	14
THE YELLOW--DAY--IS FALLING--	THE RED--BLAZE--IS THE	469	3
THE DAY THAT WAS BEFORE--	A NIGHT--THERE LAY THE	471	2
AND DAY THAT WAS BEHIND--WERE ONE--	A NIGHT--THERE LAY THE	471	3
BAPTIZED--THIS DAY--A BRIDE--	I AM ASHAMED--I HIDE--	473	27
YOU WRITE HIM--EVERY DAY--	YOU LOVE THE LORD--YOU	487	2
AND FURTHER IN THE DAY.	YOU LOVE THE LORD--YOU	487	4
TELL HIM [HER]--NIGHT [DAY] FINISHED--BEFORE WE FINISHED--	GOING TO HIM! HAPPY	494	18
AND THE OLD CLOCK KEPT NEIGHING "DAY"!	GOING TO HIM! HAPPY	494	19
THAT SUCH A DAY, PERMITTED [PERSUADED / ACCEPTED] SO,	HE TOUCHED ME, SO I LIVE	506	2
HOW WARM, THEY WERE, ON SUCH A DAY,	IF ANYBODY'S FRIEND BE	509	9
WHAT COME OF HIM--THAT DAY--	HE PARTS HIMSELF--LIKE	517	16
'TWAS SUNSET [SUNDOWN]--ALL THE DAY--	I HAD NO CAUSE TO BE	542	16
MY FIRST WELL DAY--SINCE MANY ILL--	MY FIRST WELL DAY--SINCE	574	1
THE RAPTURE OF A FINISHED [CONCLUDED] DAY--	"HEAVEN" HAS DIFFERENT	575	13
FOR I HAD WORN IT, EVERY DAY,	IT CEASED TO HURT ME,	584	6
WHAT CARE THE DEAD FOR DAY?	WHAT CARE THE DEAD, FOR	592	2
THE FAR THEATRICALS OF DAY	LIKE MIGHTY FOOT LIGHTS	595	3
OF NATURE'S--SUMMER DAY!	THE TREES LIKE TASSELS--	606	28
WHAT NEED OF DAY--	I SEE THEE BETTER--IN	611	13
THE BROOKS SLAM [BRAG]--ALL THE DAY--	IT MAKES NO DIFFERENCE	620	6
WAS IT A PLEASANT DAY TO DIE--	TO KNOW JUST HOW HE	622	7
SUCH A DAY--	TO KNOW JUST HOW HE	622	12
NAY, NATURE, ['TWAS FURTHER--] IT WAS DAY--	TO MY SMALL HEARTH HIS	638	8
A TIME [DAY] WHEN IT WAS NOT--	PAIN--HAS AN ELEMENT OF	650	4
THAT INTERRUPT THE DAY	A PRISON GETS TO BE A	652	18
WHOSE FEATURES--DAY AND NIGHT--	A PRISON GETS TO BE A	652	22
THAT FIRST DAY, WHEN YOU PRAISED ME, SWEET,	THAT FIRST DAY, WHEN YOU	659	1
THAT DAY--THE DAYS AMONG--	THAT FIRST DAY, WHEN YOU	659	4

DAY (CONTINUED)

	FIRST LINE	POEM		LINE
TO RE-ENDURE A DAY--	'TIS GOOD--THE LOOKING	660		2
AND FLIRT ALL DAY WITH BUTTERCUPS	COULD I BUT RIDE	661		5
AND ROW IN NOWHERE ALL DAY LONG	COULD I BUT RIDE	661		15
DAY--DROPS YOU HER [HIS] RED ADIEU!	AH, TENERIFFE!	666		5
SHOULD ENDOW [ADDRESS / REWARD] THE DAY-- .	BLOOM UPON THE MOUNTAIN	667		6
"WHICH OBTAIN [CONTROLLED / CONTROL] THE DAY"?	WOLFE DEMANDED DURING	678		2
SOME BASHFUL SUMMER'S DAY--	THE HEAVEN VESTS FOR	694		4
THAT DID IT TEAR ALL DAY, ...	I SOMETIMES DROP IT, FOR	708		6
FEELS SHORTER THAN THE DAY	BECAUSE I COULD NOT STOP	712		22
THE DAY UNDRESSED--HERSELF--	THE DAY UNDRESSED--	716		1
HER LATEST WORSHIP--WHEN THE DAY	SWEET MOUNTAINS--YE TELL	722		10
GOD DOES IT--EVERY DAY--	IT'S EASY TO INVENT A	724		2
IF OUGHT SHE MISSED IN HER NEW DAY, . . .	SHE ROSE TO HIS	732		5
YOU SAID THAT I "WAS GREAT"--ONE DAY-- . .	YOU SAID THAT I "WAS	738		1
DRAMA'S VITALLEST EXPRESSION IS THE COMMON DAY	DRAMA'S VITALLEST	741		1
LEST DAY--	RENUNCIATION--IS A	745		7
IN CORNERS--TILL A DAY	MY LIFE HAD STOOD--A	754		2
AND WHEN AT NIGHT--OUR GOOD DAY DONE-- . .	MY LIFE HAD STOOD--A	754		13
THE BIRD [DAY] WOULD NOT ARISE--	MY FAITH IS LARGER THAN	766		10
JUST THE DAY IT WAS--	WHEN I HOPED, I	768		10
AND THE DAY THAT I DESPAIRED--	WHEN I HOPED, I	768		17
THE DAY CONTROLLED [RESUMED] THE WORLD-- .	THE BIRDS BEGUN AT FOUR	783		22
AND FORGET THE COLOR [FIGURE] OF THE DAY-- .	SEVERER SERVICE OF	786		16
WHAT DAY BE DARK TO ME	SO SET IT'S SUN IN THEE	808		2
ONE DAY IS THERE OF THE SERIES	ONE DAY IS THERE OF THE	814		1
TERMED THANKSGIVING DAY.	ONE DAY IS THERE OF THE	814		2
TWERE THANKSGIVING DAY.	ONE DAY IS THERE OF THE	814		16
IS BULLETINS ALL DAY	THE ONLY NEWS I KNOW	827		2
AND HALF OF DAY, THE BRIDE.	TO THIS WORLD SHE	830		9
AND PERISH ON THE DAY	TRUTH--IS AS OLD AS GOD	836		5
TERM OF LIGHT THIS DAY BEGUN!	ALWAYS MINE!	839		3
WE JOURNEY TO THE DAY	I SING TO USE THE	850		6
FEELS EASY, AS WHEN DAY LETS GO	WHEN ONE HAS GIVEN UP	853		3
THE DAY MUST FOLLOW TOO.	THIS CHASM, SWEET, UPON	858		4
AND YET SO BOLDER EVERY DAY	THIS CHASM, SWEET, UPON	858		11
SOME HOURS IN [OF] THE DAY.	LIGHT IS SUFFICIENT TO	862		4
THAT HUNTED FOR THE DAY--	THE SUN AND MOON MUST	871		11
THEY WONT FROWN ALWAYS--SOME SWEET DAY . .	THEY WONT FROWN ALWAYS--	874		1
OR AN EXPENDED DAY	THE SUN IS GAY OR STARK	878		5
AND LEAVE A DAY AT EVERY DOOR	WHEN I HAVE SEEN THE SUN	888		3
THE FIRST DAY THAT I WAS A LIFE	THE FIRST DAY THAT I WAS	902		1
THE LAST DAY THAT I WAS A LIFE	THE FIRST DAY THAT I WAS	902		3
NO STATION IN THE DAY?	'TIS SUNRISE--LITTLE	908		2
AND FRONT A MUTUAL DAY--	I MAKE HIS CRESCENT FILL	909		10
ABSENT PLACE--AN APRIL DAY--	ABSENT PLACE--AN APRIL	927		1
NOON--IS THE HINGE OF DAY--	NOON--IS THE HINGE OF	931		1
FAIRER THROUGH FADING--AS THE DAY	FAIRER THROUGH FADING--	938		1
WHEN IT IS LOST, THAT DAY SHALL BE	THIS IS A BLOSSOM OF THE	945		13
WERE THE DAY YEAR LONG, ...	UNDER THE LIGHT, YET	949		8
A FLINT UNTO THIS DAY--PERHAPS--	WE MET AS SPARKS--	958	V	7
HOW LONG A DAY I COULD ENDURE	WERT THOU BUT ILL--THAT	961		2
THE DAY THE HEAVEN DIED--	DENIAL--IS THE ONLY FACT	965		4
HE LEFT BEHIND ONE DAY--SO LESS	FITTER TO SEE HIM, I MAY	968		13
BUT CAME ANOTHER DAY	IT BLOOMED AND DROPT, A	978		6
HE WERE SUPERFLUOUS EVERY DAY	SUPERFLUOUS WERE THE SUN	999		3
FOR EVERY DAY BE SAID	SUPERFLUOUS WERE THE SUN	999		4
AFFORDED DAY BY DAY.	THE STIMULUS, BEYOND THE	1001		4
AFFORDED DAY BY DAY.	THE STIMULUS, BEYOND THE	1001		4
AFFLICTED FOR THE DAY.	WHO SAW NO SUNRISE	1018		6
THE EVENING ON THE DAY LEANS	AS WILLING LID O'ER	1050		2
AWAITING HER THAT DAY--	BLOOM--IS RESULT--TO	1058		14
IN A DAY--	TITLE DIVINE--IS MINE!	1072		11
A NARROW WIND COMPLAINS ALL DAY	THE SKY IS LOW--THE	1075		5
THEIR SEAM [SEAMS] THE DAY UPON.	THE CRICKETS SANG	1104		4
THIS SLOW DAY MOVED ALONG--	THIS SLOW DAY MOVED	1120		1
THE DIFFERENCE OF DAY	OH SUMPTUOUS MOMENT	1125		7
THE DAY ABROAD WAS HEARD--[RESUMED ABROAD] .	THE WIND TOOK UP THE	1134		14
THE DAY GREW SMALL, SURROUNDED TIGHT . . .	THE DAY GREW SMALL,	1140		1
BE IT BUT FOR A DAY	THE FACE WE CHOOSE TO	1141		2
TELL--THIS DAY [TILL NOW] ENDURES	TELL AS A MARKSMAN--WERE	1152		2
THE DAY THAT A COMPANION CAME	SOME DAYS RETIRED FROM	1157		3
THE MARROW OF THE DAY	ALONE AND IN A	1167		26
I THE DAY BEFORE	ON THE WORLD YOU COLORED	1171		6
IN THE GOODS OF DAY--	ON THE WORLD YOU COLORED	1171		12
OVER, EVERY DAY, ...	THERE'S THE BATTLE OF	1174		2
WHO GAMBOLS ALL THE LIVING DAY	A LITTLE DOG THAT WAGS	1185		5
HER MARTIAL DAY [TIME] FORGOT	A LITTLE DOG THAT WAGS	1185		10
THE GOVERNMENT OF DAY--	THE SUN AND FOG	1190		2
AND ENTERED WITH THE DAY--	SOMEHOW MYSELF SURVIVED	1194		2
THAT DAY.	A WORD IS DEAD	1212		6
NATURE TOOK THE DAY	NOW I KNEW I LOST HER--	1219		14
HAD THIS ONE DAY NOT BEEN, ...	HAD THIS ONE DAY NOT	1253		1
WERE EVERY OTHER DAY!	HAD THIS ONE DAY NOT	1253		4
IN COMPREHENSIVE DAY--	LEFT IN IMMORTAL YOUTH	1289		8
TWO LENGTHS HAS EVERY DAY--	TWO LENGTHS HAS EVERY	1295		1
THE DAY SHE GOES	THE DAY SHE GOES	1308		1
OR DAY SHE STAYS	THE DAY SHE GOES	1308		2
OUR SALARY THE LONGEST DAY	THE NOTICE THAT IS	1310		7
THE VASTEST EARTHLY DAY	THE VASTEST EARTHLY DAY	1328		1

	FIRST LINE	POEM	LINE
DAY (CONTINUED)			
UPON A SUMMER'S DAY	THE LONG SIGH OF THE	1359	2
HOW KNOW IT FROM A SUMMER'S DAY?	HOW KNOW IT FROM A	1364	1
I BELIEVE THE DAY WILL BE	I SUPPOSE THE TIME WILL	1381	9
IT WAS A QUIET SEEMING DAY--	IT WAS A QUIET SEEMING	1419	1
. . . BLADE] OF DAY	ONE JOY OF SO MUCH	1420	6
SO LET US GATHER--EVERY DAY--	TO EARN IT BY DISDAINING	1427	5
THE DAY WENT OUT TO PLAY	A DEW SUFFICED ITSELF--	1437	6
WHETHER BY DAY ABDUCTED	A DEW SUFFICED ITSELF--	1437	9
ATTESTED TO THIS DAY	A DEW SUFFICED ITSELF--	1437	13
AND DRESS [CURL] THE SLEEPY DAY--	HOW GOOD HIS LAVA BED,	1447	4
YOUR THOUGHTS DONT HAVE WORDS EVERY DAY	YOUR THOUGHTS DONT HAVE	1452	1
WITHOUT DAY.	LOVE IS DONE WHEN LOVE'S	1485	5
TO COME SO FAR SO COLD A DAY	THE SAVIOR MUST HAVE	1487	3
BUT IT IS RISING [HIGHER / FURTHER] EVERY DAY	THE PILE OF YEARS IS NOT	1507	3
A SHORTER BREATH OF DAY	THERE COMES A WARNING	1536	2
THE DAY ENSUING--	COME SHOW THY DURHAM	1542	12
A FEBUARY [JANUARY] DAY,	NO BRIGADIER THROUGHOUT	1561	6
CAKES REIGN BUT A DAY,	BLOSSOMS WILL RUN AWAY,	1578	2
AROUND US, EVERY DAY--	WITCHCRAFT WAS HUNG, IN	1583	4
SOME FAIR OR STORMY DAY,	THIS ME--THAT WALKS AND	1588	2
WISHING YOU GOOD DAY--	NOT AT HOME TO CALLERS	1590	4
HE GAILY [BOLDLY] INTERRUPTED THAT OVERFLOWING DAY	THE BOBOLINK IS GONE--	1591	4
THOSE LOOKED THAT LIVED--[THE LIVING LOOKED] THAT DAY--	THERE CAME A WIND LIKE A	1593	12
TO MEASURE OFF ANOTHER DAY	APPARENTLY WITH NO	1624	7
THIS JANUARY DAY	A DRUNKARD CANNOT MEET A	1628	4
WE DWELL IN EVERY DAY	EDEN IS THAT	1657	2
HOW FAIR ON LOOKING BACK THE DAY	EDEN IS THAT	1657	5
AT DAY BREAK TO BEGIN HIS RACE	HE WENT BY SLEEP THAT	1662	3
BUT MY FEET SLIP NEARER EVERY DAY	I DID NOT REACH THEE	1664	2
OF THIS IS DAY COMPOSED	OF THIS IS DAY COMPOSED	1675	1
I NEVER TO THIS DAY	HE WAS MY HOST--HE WAS	1721	2
TILL THE DAY ITS WEARY KEEPER	REARRANGE A "WIFE'S"	1737	19
I SAY GOODNIGHT BY DAY--	SOME SAY GOODNIGHT--AT	1739	2
AND BORROWED TO THIS DAY.	THE PARASOL IS THE	1747	8
THE LONGEST DAY THAT GOD APPOINTS	THE LONGEST DAY THAT GOD	1769	1
DAYBREAK			
NO DAYBREAK--CAN BESTIR--	ON THIS LONG STORM THE	194	10
A WIFE--AT DAYBREAK I SHALL BE--	A WIFE--AT DAYBREAK I	461	1
AT DAYBREAK OVERCOME!	HOW DARE THE ROBINS SING	1724	16
DAYLIGHT			
TILL JEALOUS DAYLIGHT INTERRUPT--	WHAT I SEE NOT, I BETTER	939	11
DAY'S			
DAY'S DEPARTING TIDE--	SO HAS A DAISY VANISHED	28	6
AT DAY'S SUPERIOR CLOSE!	ME, CHANGE! ME, ALTER!	268	6
THE LOST--DAY'S FACE--	'TIS OPPOSITES--ENTICE--	355	4
THE FIRST DAY'S NIGHT HAD COME--	THE FIRST DAY'S NIGHT	410	1
DAY'S GREAT PROGENITOR--	RENUNCIATION--IS A	745	8
THE DAY'S ADVENTURES TELL	THE HILLS IN PURPLE	1016	2
WHEN DAY'S ATTEMPT IS DONE	FURTHER IN SUMMER THAN	1068	V
DAYS			
WHEN SUMMER DAYS ARE FLOWN!	SUMMER FOR THEE, GRANT I	31	2
TO VENERATE THE SIMPLE DAYS	TO VENERATE THE SIMPLE	57	1
FORGIVE US, IF AS DAYS DECLINE--	THE DAISY FOLLOWS SOFT	106	8
THESE ARE THE DAYS WHEN BIRDS COME BACK--	THESE ARE THE DAYS WHEN	130	1
THESE ARE THE DAYS WHEN SKIES RESUME	THESE ARE THE DAYS WHEN	130	4
OH SACRAMENT OF SUMMER DAYS,	THESE ARE THE DAYS WHEN	130	13
A FEW PROSAIC DAYS	BESIDES THE AUTUMN POETS	131	2
REELING--THRO ENDLESS SUMMER DAYS--	I TASTE A LIQUOR NEVER	214	7
A SHADY FRIEND--FOR TORRID DAYS--	A SHADY FRIEND--FOR	278	1
HID GOLDEN, FOR THE WHOLE OF DAYS,	OF ALL THE SOUNDS	321	15
AND DREAM THE DAYS AWAY,	THE GRASS SO LITTLE HAS	333	18
WAS LIKE THE OTHER DAYS--	THE DAY THAT I WAS	356	2
BEFALLING NOT MY SIMPLE DAYS--	REMOVED FROM ACCIDENT OF	424	3
DEEP DUG--FOR SUMMER DAYS--	I KNOW WHERE WELLS GROW	460	2
A NIGHT--THERE LAY THE DAYS BETWEEN--	A NIGHT--THERE LAY THE	471	1
THE DAYS--TO MIGHTY METRES STEPT--	I THINK I WAS ENCHANTED	593	17
FAR ENDS OF TIRED [HOMELY] DAYS--	UNTO MY BOOKS--SO GOOD	604	2
OR CELEBRATED DAYS--	FOREVER--IS COMPOSED OF	624	10
I THINK THE DAYS--COULD EVERY ONE	I THINK TO LIVE--MAY BE	646	9
THAT DAY--THE DAYS AMONG--	THAT FIRST DAY, WHEN YOU	659	4
AND FAR ABROAD ON SUMMER DAYS--	THE LOVE A LIFE CAN SHOW	673	8
ON [TO] PLAINER DAYS, WHOSE TABLE FAR	THE LUXURY TO APPREHEND	815	13
ALL DAYS, I DID NOT EARN THE SAME	I MADE SLOW RICHES BUT	843	5
THE TALELESS DAYS WENT ON	TWO TRAVELLERS PERISHING	933	12
IF AS THE DAYS RESUME [INCREASE]	AS FROST IS BEST	951	7
GRANDFATHER OF THE DAYS IS HE	THE MOUNTAIN SAT UPON	975	7
SOME DAYS RETIRED FROM THE REST	SOME DAYS RETIRED FROM	1157	1
THE DAYS THAT WE CAN SPARE	THE DAYS THAT WE CAN	1184	1
ALL THAT IS NAMED OF SUMMER DAYS	THE PUNGENT ATOM IN THE	1191	3
SIMPLER ARE THE DAYS THAN THE SUPPOSITION	SOME WE SEE NO MORE,	1221	3
OF FUTURE DAYS	THAN HEAVEN MORE REMOTE,	1436	9
THESE FEVERED DAYS--TO TAKE THEM TO THE FOREST	THESE FEVERED DAYS--TO	1441	1
IN OUR COMPETING DAYS	I SAW THE WIND WITHIN	1502	V
HE SPENDS THE EVENING OF HIS DAYS [NOONS]	HIS ORIENTAL HERESIES	1526	V
AND THAT DISSOLVES THE DAYS	TO THE BRIGHT EAST SHE	1573	10
IT FOUNDS THE HOMES AND DECKS THE DAYS	THE FARTHEST THUNDER	1581	13
HE DANCED ALONG THE DINGY DAYS	HE ATE AND DRANK THE	1587	5

	FIRST LINE	POEM	LINE
DAYS (CONTINUED)			
OF SWARTHY DAYS HE IS THE CLOSE [KNELL]	THE JAY HIS CASTANET HAS	1635	5
THE NATIONS AND THE DAYS--	SOME ONE PREPARED THIS	1644	3
THE POMP OF SUMMER [ETHIOPIAN] DAYS	SOME ONE PREPARED THIS	1644	6
OF OTHER SUMMER DAYS	NATURE CAN DO NO MORE	1673	4
THESE ARE THE DAYS THAT REINDEER LOVE	THESE ARE THE DAYS THAT	1696	1
DAZZINGLY			
DAZZINGLY DECAMPING	FOLLOW WISE ORION	1538	3
DAZZLE			
THE TRUTH MUST DAZZLE GRADUALLY [MODERATELY]	TELL ALL THE TRUTH BUT	1129	7
DAZZLED			
THAT DAZZLED, YESTERDAY,	I'VE KNOWN A HEAVEN,	243	10
WITHDRAWS--AND LEAVES THE DAZZLED SOUL	DID OUR BEST MOMENT LAST	393	11
ME--COME! MY DAZZLED FACE	ME--COME! MY DAZZLED	431	1
NOWHERE TO HIDE MY DAZZLED FACE--	I AM ASHAMED--I HIDE--	473	4
CONFRONTS THE DAZZLED BEE.	PRECIOUS TO ME--SHE	727	14
THAT WOULD TO [UN TO] SENSE HAVE DAZZLED	CONTAINED IN THIS SHORT	1165	V
DAZZLES			
THE EAGLE'S GOLDEN BREAKFAST STRANGLES [DAZZLES]--THEM--	VICTORY COMES LATE--	690	12
DAZZLING			
IN EASY--EVEN--DAZZLING PACE--	OF BEING IS A BIRD	653	7
UNKNOWN HIS SHIMMERING [GIDDY / DAZZLING] ULTIMATE--	THE ROAD WAS LIT WITH	1450	7
SO DAZZLING WE MISTAKE HIM	ONE OF THE ONES THAT	1466	7
IN RAVISHED [DAZZLING / SIMPLE] HOLINESS--	THE THRILL CAME SLOWLY	1495	8
DEAD			
CHAT OF THE "EARLY DEAD"--	THERE'S SOMETHING	45	14
AS BY THE DEAD WE LOVE TO SIT,	AS BY THE DEAD WE LOVE	88	1
GIVE GENTLY TO THE DEAD--	THIS HEART THAT BROKE SO	145	4
THE DEAD SHALL GO IN WHITE--	IT CANT BE "SUMMER"!	221	8
"FOUND DEAD"--"OF NECTAR"--	WE--BEE AND I--LIVE BY	230	16
THE NEWS WOULD STRIKE ME DEAD--	BEFORE I GOT MY EYE PUT	327	17
NO DEAD, WERE EVER CARRIED DOWN--	A HOUSE UPON THE HIGHT--	399	3
THE COY DEAD--NONE--	UNIT, LIKE DEATH, FOR	408	12
TO GIBBETS, AND THE DEAD--	'TWAS LIKE A MAELSTROM,	414	21
IT IS DEAD--FIND IT--	IT IS DEAD--FIND IT--	417	1
I RUN IT OVER--"DEAD", BRAIN, "DEAD."	IT DONT SOUND SO	426	2
I RUN IT OVER--"DEAD", BRAIN, "DEAD."	IT DONT SOUND SO	426	2
DENY THAT I--AM DEAD--	DO PEOPLE MOULDER	432	6
HE TOLD ME, DEATH WAS DEAD--	DO PEOPLE MOULDER	432	16
WHEN MEN SO BRAVE--ARE DEAD--	IT FEELS A SHAME TO BE	444	2
UNTO THE DEAD	WE PRAY--TO HEAVEN--	489	8
IF ANYBODY'S FRIEND BE DEAD	IF ANYBODY'S FRIEND BE	509	1
AND ALL THE DEAD, LIE DOWN--	IT WAS NOT DEATH, FOR I	510	2
YOU SQUANDER ON [SPEND UPON] THE DEAD,	ENDOW THE LIVING--WITH	521	2
I'M SORRY FOR THE DEAD--TODAY--	I'M SORRY FOR THE DEAD--	529	1
AND DRAMA--IS NEVER [SELDOM] DEAD--	WE DREAM--IT IS GOOD WE	531	8
BUT 'TWAS--THE FACT THAT HE WAS DEAD--	A DYING TIGER--MOANED	566	12
IF I MAY HAVE IT, WHEN IT'S DEAD,	IF I MAY HAVE IT, WHEN	577	1
SHE'S "SORRY I AM DEAD"--AGAIN--	I CRIED AT PITY--NOT AT	588	21
WHAT CARE THE DEAD, FOR CHANTICLEER--	WHAT CARE THE DEAD, FOR	592	1
WHAT CARE THE DEAD FOR DAY?	WHAT CARE THE DEAD, FOR	592	2
WHAT CARE THE DEAD FOR SUMMER?	WHAT CARE THE DEAD, FOR	592	9
WHAT [NOR] CARE THE DEAD FOR WINTER?	WHAT CARE THE DEAD, FOR	592	17
WHO DANGER--AND THE DEAD--HAD FACED--	I YEARS HAD BEEN FROM	609	V 15
THE FOREST OF THE DEAD--	OUR JOURNEY HAD ADVANCED	615	8
AND WHEN SO NEWLY DEAD--	"I WANT"--IT PLEADED--	731	4
AND HOW IF HE BE DEAD--	IF HE WERE LIVING--DARE	734	2
HER--WITNESS--WAS HER DEAD--	THE BIRDS REPORTED FROM	743	20
IF EAGER FOR THE DEAD	THE SUN IS GAY OR STARK	878	4
MOST PRECIOUS ARE THE DEAD--	SWEET, TO HAVE HAD THEM	901	6
BETWEEN OURSELVES AND THE DEAD!	UNDER THE LIGHT, YET	949	16
WHEN EXCELLENCE BE DEAD	SUPERFLUOUS WERE THE SUN	999	2
THE RESPITE TO BE DEAD.	TOO SCANTY 'TWAS TO DIE	1013	8
TEST IF IT BE DEAD.	REVOLUTION IS THE POD	1082	12
CONSENTED, AND WAS DEAD--	THE LAST NIGHT THAT SHE	1100	24
THAT ODD OLD MAN IS DEAD A YEAR--	THAT ODD OLD MAN IS DEAD	1130	1
OF THE ELDER DEAD	AFTER A HUNDRED YEARS	1147	8
BUT DATED WITH THE DEAD.	SOMEHOW MYSELF SURVIVED	1194	8
A WORD IS DEAD	A WORD IS DEAD	1212	1
HAD LEFT THE DEAD ALONE	MY TRIUMPH LASTED TILL	1227	2
IS NOTHING TO THE DEAD.	MY TRIUMPH LASTED TILL	1227	16
ON THE LONGED FOR [SOLDERED] DEAD	LAIN IN NATURE--SO	1288	8
I NEVER HEAR THAT ONE IS DEAD [HAS DIED]	I NEVER HEAR THAT ONE IS	1323	1
WOULD STRIKE US INSTANT DEAD	I NEVER HEAR THAT ONE IS	1323	12
PRAISE IT--'TIS DEAD--	PRAISE IT--'TIS DEAD--	1384	1
ANGER AS SOON AS FED IS DEAD--	MINE ENEMY IS GROWING	1509	7
CHILDHOOD--SOME FORMS OF HOPE--THE DEAD--	THE THINGS THAT NEVER	1515	2
THE ASTERISK IS FOR THE DEAD,	OF GLORY NOT A BEAM IS	1647	3
HOW DEAD WE ARE--	NOT ANY SUNNY TONE	1674	9
T'IS EASIER TO PITY THOSE WHEN DEAD	T'IS EASIER TO PITY	1698	1
LOVE CAN DO ALL BUT RAISE THE DEAD	LOVE CAN DO ALL BUT	1731	1
THE DISTANCE THAT THE DEAD HAVE GONE	THE DISTANCE THAT THE	1742	1
IT MAKES US THINK OF ALL THE DEAD	THE SADDEST NOISE, THE	1764	9
DEADEN			
THAT DEADEN SUFFERING--	THE HEART ASKS PLEASURE	536	4
DEADLY			
HAVE SOMETIMES PROVED DEADLY SWEET!	TALK WITH PRUDENCE TO A	119	8
TO FOE OF HIS--I'M DEADLY FOE--	MY LIFE HAD STOOD--A	754	17

	FIRST LINE	POEM	LINE
DEAF			
AS IF MY SOUL WERE DEAF AND DUMB--	IF I MAY HAVE IT, WHEN	577	19
BUT I AM DEAF--TODAY--	THE BIRDS REPORTED FROM	743	4
DEAL			
AND A DEAL OF SAD REFLECTION, AND WAILING INSTEAD OF SONG?	AWAKE YE MUSES NINE,	1	30
DEAL WITH THE SOUL	BOUND--A TROUBLE--	269	5
AND DEAL OCCASIONAL SMILES	HE PUT THE BELT AROUND	273	12
AS BOY--SHOULD DEAL WITH LESSER BOY--	IT ALWAYS FELT TO ME--A	597	15
IT DEAL US [FURNISH]--STATED AS OUR FOOD--	A PRISON GETS TO BE A	652	7
DEALS			
IT DEALS CELESTIAL [FLINGS A CRYSTAL] VAIL	IT SIFTS FROM LEADEN	311	12
DEALS--ONE--IMPERIAL--THUNDERBOLT--	HE FUMBLES AT YOUR SOUL	315	11
DEALT			
I DEALT A WORD OF GOLD	IT WOULD NEVER BE COMMON	430	18
SHE DEALT HER PRETTY WORDS LIKE BLADES--	SHE DEALT HER PRETTY	479	1
SHE DEALT A [THE] FASHION TO THE NUT--	MY FIRST WELL DAY--SINCE	574	17
SCANTILY DEALT TO THE SUMMER MORNING	SPLIT THE LARK--AND	861	3
DEAR			
BECOME SO WONDROUS DEAR--	AS BY THE DEAD WE LOVE	88	2
DEAR, OLD FASHIONED, LITTLE FLOWER!	I'M THE LITTLE "HEART'S	176	9
MY BUSINESS WERE SO DEAR!	IF I COULD BRIBE THEM BY	179	6
IS IT TRUE, DEAR SUE?	IS IT TRUE, DEAR SUE?	218	1
OH, DEAR,--I GUESS IF HE WERE A BOY--	OVER THE FENCE--	251	8
HOWEVER, DEAR,	TO LOVE THEE YEAR BY	434	4
FOR THAT DEAR--DISTANT--DANGEROUS--SAKE--	WHY MAKE IT DOUBT--IT	462	7
TO KNOW JUST HOW HE SUFFERED--WOULD BE DEAR--	TO KNOW JUST HOW HE	622	1
OURSELVES WERE WED ONE SUMMER--DEAR--	OURSELVES WERE WED ONE	631	1
JUST [STILL] TO FOLLOW YOUR DEAR FEATURE--	PROMISE THIS--WHEN YOU	648	29
ON THAT DEAR FRAME THE YEARS HAD WORN	ON THAT DEAR FRAME THE	940	1
THE DYING NEED BUT LITTLE, DEAR,	THE DYING NEED BUT	1026	1
TOO DEAR THE [WERE] SUMMER EVENING	THESE ARE THE NIGHTS	1128	13
DEAR MARCH--COME IN--	DEAR MARCH--COME IN--	1320	1
DEAR MARCH, HOW ARE YOU, AND THE REST--	DEAR MARCH--COME IN--	1320	7
THAT BLAME IS JUST AS DEAR AS PRAISE	DEAR MARCH--COME IN--	1320	25
DEAR TO THE MOSS--	PINK--SMALL--AND	1332	5
OR DEAR INIQUITY--	ONE JOY OF SO MUCH	1420	4
OF WHOM SO DEAR	OF WHOM SO DEAR	1504	1
IS IT TOO LATE TO TOUCH YOU, DEAR?	IS IT TOO LATE TO TOUCH	1637	1
THE DITCH IS DEAR TO THE DRUNKEN MAN	THE DITCH IS DEAR TO THE	1645	1
WITH THEIR DEAR RETROSPECT.	THE DISTANCE THAT THE	1742	8
MADE CRUELLY MORE DEAR.	THE SADDEST NOISE, THE	1764	12
DEARER			
DEARER TO UNDERSTAND--	I KNOW WHERE WELLS GROW	460	20
IS DEARER THAN REDEMPTION--	TO SEE HER IS A PICTURE	1568	V
DEARTH			
PROPORTIONED TO HIS SEVERAL DEARTH	THERE IS A FLOWER THAT	380	7
DEATH			
THE WORM DOTH WOO THE MORTAL, DEATH CLAIMS A LIVING BRIDE,	AWAKE YE MUSES NINE,	1	21
DEATH, BUT OUR RAPT ATTENTION	THE FEET OF PEOPLE	7	15
DEATH DID NOT NOTICE ME.	I KEEP MY PLEDGE.	46	3
LATER BY JUST AN HOUR THAN DEATH--	DELAYED TILL SHE HAD	58	5
DENOMINATED "DEATH"--	A THROE UPON THE	71	4
DEATH, THE ONLY ONE	DUST IS THE ONLY SECRET	153	2
DEATH WONT HURT--NOW DOLLIE'S HERE!	DYING! DYING IN THE	158	12
'TIS BUT THE EXTASY OF DEATH--	A WOUNDED DEER--LEAPS	165	3
WAIT TILL THE MAJESTY OF DEATH	WAIT TILL THE MAJESTY OF	171	1
LIFE IS BUT LIFE! AND DEATH, BUT DEATH!	'TIS SO MUCH JOY! 'TIS	172	7
LIFE IS BUT LIFE! AND DEATH, BUT DEATH!	'TIS SO MUCH JOY! 'TIS	172	7
OR FROST, OR DEATH, OR ANYONE--	IF I COULD BRIBE THEM BY	179	5
THE QUIET NONCHALANCE OF DEATH--	ON THIS LONG STORM THE	194	9
THROUGH IT--COMPETE WITH DEATH--	FOR THIS--ACCEPTED	195	2
WITH EYES IN DEATH--STILL BEGGING RAISED--	TWO SWIMMERS WRESTLED ON	201	8
TERMED BY THE BROKERS--"DEATH"!	YOU'RE RIGHT--"THE WAY	234	8
THE EYES GLAZE ONCE--AND THAT IS DEATH--	I LIKE A LOOK OF AGONY,	241	5
DEATH COMES	I LIKE A LOOK OF AGONY,	241	V
ON THE LOOK OF DEATH--	THERE'S A CERTAIN SLANT	258	16
LOOKING AT DEATH, IS DYING--	'TIS SO APPALLING--IT	281	15
THE CORDIALITY OF DEATH--	THAT AFTER HORROR--THAT	286	15
BUT MAKE NO SYLLABLE--LIKE DEATH--	GIVE LITTLE ANGUISH--	310	6
DEATH SETS A THING SIGNIFICANT	DEATH SETS A THING	360	1
FOR DEATH--OR RATHER	FOR DEATH--OR RATHER	382	1
THE THINGS THAT DEATH WILL BUY	FOR DEATH--OR RATHER	382	5
THERE'S BEEN A DEATH, IN THE OPPOSITE HOUSE,	THERE'S BEEN A DEATH, IN	389	1
UNIT, LIKE DEATH, FOR WHOM?	UNIT, LIKE DEATH, FOR	408	1
BUT SHE, AND DEATH, ACQUAINTED--	I READ MY SENTENCE--	412	11
A SORT, THAT SHALL NOT TASTE OF DEATH--	DO PEOPLE MOULDER	432	11
HE TOLD ME, DEATH WAS DEAD--	DO PEOPLE MOULDER	432	16
WHEN THAT OLD IMPERATOR--DEATH--	TRIUMPH--MAY BE OF	455	3
NO BALD DEATH--AFFRONT THEIR PARLORS--	SWEET--SAFE--HOUSES--	457	10
THE MANNER OF IT'S DEATH	THE MANNER OF IT'S DEATH	468	1
NOT EITHER--NOTICED DEATH--	THEY PUT US FAR APART--	474	21
TO MAKE ONE'S TOILETTE--AFTER DEATH	TO MAKE ONE'S TOILETTE--	485	1
UNTIL DEATH TOUCHES IT	WHILE IT IS ALIVE	491	2
LOVE [FAITH] IS LIKE DEATH, DURING THE GRAVE	WHILE IT IS ALIVE	491	8
THROUGH GENTLE [CURIOUS / EASY] MIRACLE OF DEATH--	THOSE FAIR--FICTITIOUS	499	23
IT WAS NOT DEATH, FOR I STOOD UP,	IT WAS NOT DEATH, FOR I	510	1
TILL HE BE JUSTIFIED BY DEATH--	HAD I PRESUMED TO HOPE--	522	15

DEATH (CONTINUED)

	FIRST LINE	POEM	LINE
MAKE HASTE--[COME NEAR] THE SCRUPLE! DEATH BE SCANT	ME PROVE IT NOW--WHOEVER	537	3
MIGHT DEATH--ENABLE THEE--	ME PROVE IT NOW--WHOEVER	537	8
MISTAKE DEFEAT FOR DEATH--EACH TIME--	THE PROVINCE OF THE	539	11
DEATH IS POTENTIAL TO THAT MAN	DEATH IS POTENTIAL TO	548	1
DEATH--IS BUT ONE--AND COMES BUT ONCE--	I MEASURE EVERY GRIEF I	561	27
HIS MIGHTY BALLS--IN DEATH WERE THICK--	A DYING TIGER--MOANED	566	5
THE TEST OF LOVE--IS DEATH--	THE TEST OF LOVE--IS	573	1
AFTER A LIFE--A DEATH--WE'LL SAY--	IF I MAY HAVE IT, WHEN	577	11
FOR DEATH WAS THAT--	IF I MAY HAVE IT, WHEN	577	12
DEATH IS THE COMMON [MUTUAL / EQUAL] RIGHT	A TOAD, CAN DIE OF LIGHT	583	2
FOR THESE--WERE ONLY PUT TO DEATH--	IT ALWAYS FELT TO ME--A	597	11
NOT DEATH--FOR WHO IS HE?	AFRAID! OF WHOM AM I	608	2
LIKE THE GRACE--OF DEATH--	IN FALLING TIMBERS	614	16
AS HARASS US--LIKE LIFE--AND DEATH--	I WATCHED THE MOON	629	25
BEREAVEMENT IN THEIR DEATH TO FEEL	BEREAVEMENT IN THEIR	645	1
WHOM DEATH SEE FIRST--'TIS NEWS OF THIS	BEREAVEMENT IN THEIR	645	7
BLISS OF DEATH--LIFE'S BLISS EXTOL THRO [SURPASS IN / EXCEL IN]	PROMISE THIS--WHEN YOU	648	15
EVEN FOR DEATH, A FAIRY MEDICINE.	WOULD YOU LIKE SUMMER?	691	8
DEATH--WE DO NOT KNOW--	LIFE--IS WHAT WE MAKE IT	698	2
THEY WOULD NOT ENCORE--DEATH--	YOU'VE SEEN BALLOONS SET	700	12
SUSPENSE--IS HOSTILER THAN DEATH--	SUSPENSE--IS HOSTILER	705	1
DEATH--THOSOEVER BROAD,	SUSPENSE--IS HOSTILER	705	2
IS JUST DEATH, AND CANNOT INCREASE--	SUSPENSE--IS HOSTILER	705	3
LIFE, AND DEATH, AND GIANTS--	LIFE, AND DEATH, AND	706	1
BECAUSE I COULD NOT STOP FOR DEATH--	BECAUSE I COULD NOT STOP	712	1
DEATH--HAD THE SAME DESIGN--	I MEANT TO FIND HER WHEN	718	2
BUT DEATH HAD TOLD HER SO THE [SPECIFIC TOLD HER / ENAMORED ...	I MEANT TO FIND HER WHEN	718	7
DEATH BUT THE DRIFT OF EASTERN GRAY,	BEHIND ME--DIPS ETERNITY	721	4
AN ALTITUDE OF DEATH, THAT COULD	YOU TAUGHT ME WAITING	740	5
ALL BUT DEATH, CAN BE ADJUSTED--	ALL BUT DEATH, CAN BE	749	1
DEATH--UNTO ITSELF--EXCEPTION--	ALL BUT DEATH, CAN BE	749	7
INVITED DEATH--WITH BOLD ATTEMPT--	HE FOUGHT LIKE THOSE	759	5
BUT DEATH WAS COY OF HIM	HE FOUGHT LIKE THOSE	759	6
AS OTHER MEN, WERE COY [SHY] OF DEATH--	HE FOUGHT LIKE THOSE	759	7
THEN MASHES IT TO DEATH [CRUNCHES]--	THE WHOLE OF IT CAME NOT	762	8
LIFE--JUST--OR DEATH--	ONE AND ONE--ARE ONE--	769	5
WHEN DEATH LIT ALL THE SHORTNESS UP [LIMIT--UP / BREVITY]	HER FINAL SUMMER WAS IT	795	7
THE WORTHINESS OF DEATH	DESPAIR'S ADVANTAGE IS	799	6
A DEATH BLOW IS A LIFE BLOW TO SOME	A DEATH BLOW IS A LIFE	816	1
WILL BE THE ONE AWARE OF DEATH	THIS CONSCIOUSNESS THAT	822	3
UNTIL IT BEND AS LOW AS DEATH	PERHAPS YOU THINK ME	833	7
TO HIM, IT WOULD BE DEATH--	THIS CHASM, SWEET, UPON	858	16
ABSENCE DISEMBODIES--SO DOES DEATH	ABSENCE DISEMBODIES--SO	860	1
IGNORANT IS IT LIFE OR DEATH	CRISIS IS A HAIR	889	7
TILL DEATH--IS NARROW LOVING--	TILL DEATH--IS NARROW	907	1
POSTERIOR--TO DEATH--	LOVE--IS ANTERIOR TO	917	2
DEATH IS THE OTHER [FURTHER] WAY--	THOSE WHO HAVE BEEN IN	922	4
LOVE--IS THAT LATER THING THAN DEATH--	LOVE--IS THAT LATER	924	1
TASTES DEATH--THE FIRST--TO HAND [PASS / PROVE] THE STING	LOVE--IS THAT LATER	924	5
AS FAR AS DEATH THIS WAY--	HOW FAR IS IT TO HEAVEN?	929	2
AS FAR AS DEATH THIS WAY--	HOW FAR IS IT TO HEAVEN?	929	6
DEATH LEAVES US HOMESICK, WHO BEHIND,	DEATH LEAVES US HOMESICK	935	1
SO DIFFER LIFE AND DEATH	AS PLAN FOR NOON AND	960	2
WHAT DEATH--KNOWS SO WELL--	COLOR--CASTE--	970	14
ROBBED BY DEATH--BUT THAT WAS EASY--	ROBBED BY DEATH--BUT	971	1
FRAUD OF DEATH--TO BEAR--	ROBBED BY DEATH--BUT	971	10
FOR TECHNICALITY OF DEATH--	'TWAS AWKWARD, BUT IT	973	11
DEATH IS A DIALOGUE BETWEEN	DEATH IS A DIALOGUE	976	1
"DISSOLVE" SAYS DEATH--THE SPIRIT "SIR	DEATH IS A DIALOGUE	976	3
DEATH DOUBTS IT--ARGUES [REASONS] FROM THE GROUND--	DEATH IS A DIALOGUE	976	5
THE FIRST WE KNEW OF HIM WAS DEATH--	THE FIRST WE KNEW OF HIM	1006	1
SAID DEATH TO PASSION	SAID DEATH TO PASSION	1033	1
BORE DEATH FROM PASSION	SAID DEATH TO PASSION	1033	5
WERE IT A WITCHCRAFT--WERE IT DEATH--	I'VE DROPPED MY BRAIN--	1046	15
AND THAT IS DEATH--	PAIN HAS BUT ONE	1049	2
DEATH TENDERLY ASSISTS HIM	PAIN HAS BUT ONE	1049	7
DEATH IS THE WEALTH	SANG FROM THE HEART,	1059	7
DEATH TWISTS THE STRINGS--	SANG FROM THE HEART,	1059	11
LET DOWN THE BARS, OH DEATH--	LET DOWN THE BARS, OH	1065	1
THE MORNING AFTER DEATH	THE BUSTLE IN A HOUSE	1078	2
GORED THROUGH AND THROUGH WITH DEATH, TO BE	HIS BILL IS CLASPED--HIS	1102	7
'TIS AS HID AS DEATH	NONE WHO SAW IT EVER	1110	2
THAT THIS SHOULD FEEL THE NEED OF DEATH	THAT THIS SHOULD FEEL	1112	1
THE FROST OF DEATH WAS ON THE PANE--	THE FROST OF DEATH WAS	1136	1
WE HATED DEATH AND HATED LIFE	THE FROST OF DEATH WAS	1136	18
WITH DEATH TO BE	SOUL, TAKE THY RISK,	1151	2
THREATENED FOR THAT WITH DEATH--BY GESSLER--	TELL AS A MARKSMAN--WERE	1152	16
THAT SURPASSES DEATH--	TELL AS A MARKSMAN--WERE	1152	19
WENT TO HEAVEN PERHAPS AT DEATH	SO I PULL MY STOCKINGS	1201	5
OF DEATH THE STERNEST [SHARPEST] FUNCTION [FEATURE]	TO DISAPPEAR ENHANCES--	1209	13
IT CAME AT LAST BUT PROMPTER DEATH	IT CAME AT LAST BUT	1230	1
THROUGH ACCENTS TERRIBLE AS DEATH	WHO WERE "THE FATHER AND	1258	V 5

	FIRST LINE	POEM	LINE
DEATH (CONTINUED)			
BECAUSE THAT DEATH IS FINAL [TREASON / DIFFERENT],	BECAUSE THAT YOU ARE	1260	5
GO RAPID, LEST COMPETING DEATH	GO SLOW, MY SOUL, TO	1297	3
IS THE ECLAT OF DEATH--	THAT SHORT--POTENTIAL	1307	5
DEATH WARRANTS ARE SUPPOSED [BELIEVED] TO BE	DEATH WARRANTS ARE	1375	1
NOR ANY DEATH--BUT LEST	I HAVE NO LIFE BUT THIS	1398	3
DEATH IS THE SUPPLE SUITOR	DEATH IS THE SUPPLE	1445	1
DEATH--SO--THE HYPHEN OF THE SEA--	THOSE NOT LIVE YET	1454	7
OF DEATH I TRY TO THINK LIKE THIS--	OF DEATH I TRY TO THINK	1558	1
SO GIVE ME BACK TO DEATH--	SO GIVE ME BACK TO DEATH	1632	1
THE DEATH I NEVER FEARED	SO GIVE ME BACK TO DEATH	1632	2
NOW DEATH USURPS MY PREMIUM	I DID NOT REACH THEE	1664	33
WHO HAVE ACCOMPLISHED DEATH	THE OVERTAKELESSNESS OF	1691	2
A SOLITUDE OF DEATH, BUT THESE	THERE IS A SOLITUDE OF	1695	3
THE MOMENT OF OUR DEATH--	WITCHCRAFT HAS NOT A	1708	4
DEATH IS LIKE THE INSECT	DEATH IS LIKE THE INSECT	1716	1
AND NOW, WHAT LIFE OR DEATH CAN DO	HOW DARE THE ROBINS SING	1724	7
AS DAUNTLESS IN THE HOUSE OF DEATH	THIS DOCILE ONE INTER	1752	7
AS PLAYFUL IN THE DOOR OF DEATH	THIS DOCILE ONE INTER	1752	V 7
AS CONTENTED [FEARLESS] IN THE PORCH OF DEATH	THIS DOCILE ONE INTER	1752	V 7
DEATHLESS			
HER DEATHLESS SYLLABLE.	STEP LIGHTLY ON THIS	1183	8
LAUREL--VAIL YOUR [THY] DEATHLESS TREE--	LAY THIS LAUREL ON THE	1393	3
DEATHLESSNESS			
DUKE IN A MOMENT OF DEATHLESSNESS	I AM AFRAID TO OWN A	1090	7
DEATH'S			
TWILL BE BECAUSE DEATH'S FINGER	IF I SHOULD CEASE TO	56	7
IN DEATH'S--STIFF--STARE--	I KNOW THAT HE EXISTS.	338	12
HOW DEATH'S GIFTS MAY COMPARE--	FOR DEATH--OR RATHER	382	10
DEATH'S SINGLE PRIVACY	I LIVE WITH HIM--I SEE	463	4
WITH DEATH'S ETHERIAL SCORN--	ENDOW THE LIVING--WITH	521	8
OF DEATH'S TREMENDOUS NEARNESS--	I TRIED TO THINK A	532	4
OR IS THIS DEATH'S EXPERIMENT--	I CROSS TILL I AM WEARY	550	24
AND DEATH'S SURPRISE,	MY PORTION IS DEFEAT--	639	12
DEATH'S PRIVILEGE?	I CANNOT LIVE WITH YOU--	640	20
BY DEATH'S BOLD EXHIBITION	THERE IS A FINISHED	856	5
DEATH'S DIVINER CLASSIFYING	COLOR--CASTE--	970	3
DEATH'S LARGE--DEMOCRATIC FINGERS	COLOR--CASTE--	970	7
DEATH'S WAYLAYING NOT THE SHARPEST	DEATH'S WAYLAYING NOT	1296	1
IN DEATH'S IMMEDIATELY--	ONE JOY OF SO MUCH	1420	12
DEBAR			
NO BITTERER DEBAR	YOU TAUGHT ME WAITING	740	6
ABRIDGE [IMPAIR / DEBAR / DEPRIVE] SOCIETY	WE MISS HER, NOT BECAUSE	993	4
DEBARRED			
WITHELD TO THE ARRIVED [DEBARRED / DENIED]--	CRISIS IS SWEET AND YET	1416	V 4
DEBASE			
EXHILIRATE--DEBASE--	AN IGNORANCE A SUNSET	552	6
DEBASES			
DEFACES [DEBASES / SURPASSES] THAT OF WINE--	WHO NEVER WANTED--	1430	4
DEBATE			
WITHOUT DEBATE [CERTIFICATE]--OR PAUSE--	FOREVER--IS COMPOSED OF	624	9
THAN DEBATE--HERE--	OUT OF SIGHT? WHAT OF	703	7
AND THE DEBATE WAS DONE.	SAID DEATH TO PASSION	1033	9
ADMITS OF NO DEBATE--	THE PUNGENT ATOM IN THE	1191	2
DEBATED			
DEBATED--ROSE AGAIN--	SHE STAKED HER FEATHERS	798	2
THE SECOND POISED--DEBATED--SHOT--	'TWAS CRISIS--ALL THE	948	13
THE VERY FOOD DEBATED	A WORD MADE FLESH IS	1651	7
DEBATES			
DEBATES IF IT WILL GO--	THE SKY IS LOW--THE	1075	4
DEBAUCHEE			
THE DEBAUCHEE OF DEWS!	BRING ME THE SUNSET IN A	128	12
AND DEBAUCHEE OF DEW--	I TASTE A LIQUOR NEVER	214	6
DEBONNAIRE			
BE DEBONNAIRE! BE DEBONNAIRE!	POOR LITTLE HEART!	192	6
BE DEBONNAIRE! BE DEBONNAIRE!	POOR LITTLE HEART!	192	6
DEBT			
SWEET DEBT OF LIFE--EACH NIGHT TO OWE--	I GAVE MYSELF TO HIM--	580	15
DECADE			
HIS LAST DECADE [SLOW DECADES] AWAY,	JOY TO HAVE MERITED THE	788	22
AND EVERY LIMIT A DECADE--	I'VE DROPPED MY BRAIN--	1046	19
DECADE HAD HASTENED [HURRIED / GATHERED] TO DECADE--	A LITTLE SNOW WAS HERE	1444	4
DECADE HAD HASTENED [HURRIED / GATHERED] TO DECADE--	A LITTLE SNOW WAS HERE	1444	4
DECADES			
BREWED FROM DECADES OF AGONY!	THO' I GET HOME HOW LATE	207	8
DECADES OF ARROGANCE BETWEEN	A CLOCK STOPPED--	287	16
HIS LAST DECADE [SLOW DECADES] AWAY,	JOY TO HAVE MERITED THE	788	22
DECALOGUE			
HE RECOGNIZED HIS MAKER--OVERTURNED THE DECALOGUE--	THE BOBOLINK IS GONE--	1591	8
HE SWUNG UPON THE DECALOGUE	THE BOBOLINK IS GONE--	1591	9
DECALOGUES			
BY DECALOGUES--AWAY--	TO MAKE ONE'S TOILETTE--	485	8
DECAMP			
WILL EMERGE [DECAMP] BUT ONCE--AND DUMB [ARMED]--	"SECRETS" IS A DAILY	1385	11

	FIRST LINE	POEM	LINE
DECAMPING			
FOR HIS DECAMPING WANTS--	ONE OF THE ONES THAT	1466	16
DAZZINGLY DECAMPING	FOLLOW WISE ORION	1538	3
DECAY			
CANNOT [COULD NOT] EXCEL DECAY,	I REASON, EARTH IS SHORT	301	7
THROUGH DECAY [FATIGUE / THE LAPSE] OF YOU--	SWEET--YOU FORGOT--BUT I	523	4
CIRCUMFERENCE--DECAY [ARRAY]--	AN IGNORANCE A SUNSET	552	4
AND WONDER--AND DECAY	HE GAVE AWAY HIS LIFE--	567	10
WITH LIMIT [LICENSE] OF DECAY--	TO MY SMALL HEARTH HIS	638	6
THE GENERAL ROSE--DECAY--	ESSENTIAL OILS--ARE	675	5
SO WHEN THE HILLS DECAY--	MY FAITH IS LARGER THAN	766	2
WEDLOCK OF WILL, DECAY--	GIVEN IN MARRIAGE UNTO	817	6
THOUGH PYRAMIDS DECAY	IT IS AN HONORABLE	946	6
THE GLORY OF DECAY	THE HARM OF YEARS IS ON	1280	6
SEQUESTERED FROM DECAY	LEFT IN IMMORTAL YOUTH	1289	6
TRADITIONS RIPEN AND DECAY,	A LITTLE OVERFLOWING	1467	5
OTHER BONDS DECAY	GUEST AM I TO HAVE	1661	5
DECAYED			
IN THAT THEY HAVE DECAYED.	THE OPENING AND THE	1047	8
DECAYS			
ARE ORGANIZED DECAYS.	CRUMBLING IS NOT AN	997	4
WHEN OBELISK DECAYS	AN HONEST TEAR	1192	8
DECEIVES			
DECEIVES THE BUTTERFLY!	ONE SISTER HAVE I IN OUR	14	19
MY SCRUTINY DECEIVES.	WHOSE CHEEK IS THIS?	82	10
THE WISE DECEIVES	"TOMORROW"--WHOSE	1367	2
DECEIVES PERHAPS THE UNIVERSE	YOU CANNOT MAKE	1508	5
DECIDE			
ATROPOS DECIDE!	I NEVER TOLD THE BURIED	11	21
COULD NOT DECIDE [DISCERN / CONCLUDE] BETWEEN--	SO GLAD WE ARE--A	329	8
SAY, FOOT, DECIDE THE POINT--	IS BLISS THEN, SUCH	340	12
OURSELF CANNOT DECIDE--	WHEN I WAS SMALL, A	596	10
THAT WOULD [WILL] NOT LET THE EYE DECIDE	THESE HELD THEIR WICK	1390	7
DECIDING			
CONCLUDING [DECIDING] HOW AN ATOM--FELL--	IT TROUBLED ME AS ONCE I	600	3
DECIDUOUS			
FOREVER IS DECIDUOUS [RECURRENT]--	SUMMER HAS TWO	1422	11
DECIMALS			
THEN QUIVERED OUT OF DECIMALS--	A CLOCK STOPPED--	287	8
DECISION			
BEFORE DECISION--STOOPED TO SPEECH--	I COULD SUFFICE FOR HIM,	643	11
TIME'S DECISION SHOOK--	WE TALKED WITH EACH	1473 V	6
WE MAKE THE WISE DISTINCTION [SAGE DECISION] STILL,	WE SEND THE WAVE TO FIND	1604	5
DECK			
I'LL DECK TRADITION'S BUTTONHOLE--	IF SHE HAD BEEN THE	44	7
AND SO I DECK, A LITTLE,	I'M SAYING EVERY DAY	373	4
OH GIVE IT MOTION--DECK IT SWEET	OH GIVE IT MOTION--DECK	1527	1
DECKS			
SO FACES ON TWO DECKS, LOOK BACK,	THERE CAME A DAY AT	322	19
AND DECKS--TO SEAT THE SKIES--	THEY CALLED ME TO THE	628	12
IT FOUNDS THE HOMES AND DECKS THE DAYS	THE FARTHEST THUNDER	1581	13
AND DECKS [BRIMS / FILLS / SWELLS] THE RAYS	BY A DEPARTING LIGHT	1714	6
DECLAIM			
THE BIRDS DECLAIM THEIR TUNES--	THE MORNING AFTER WO--	364	9
DECLAIMING			
DECLAIMING WATERS NONE MAY DREAD--	DECLAIMING WATERS NONE	1595	1
DECLARE			
YET ELOQUENT DECLARE	THE RAINBOW NEVER TELLS	97	6
BUT THE FIR IS WHERE--DECLARE--	THE WIND DID'NT COME	316	9
I DECLARE--HOW RED THEIR FACES GREW--	DEAR MARCH--COME IN--	1320	13
THIS TRUTH ENDEAR [DECLARE]--	THE GENTIAN HAS A	1424	15
DECLINE			
FORGIVE US, IF AS DAYS DECLINE--	THE DAISY FOLLOWS SOFT	106	8
FOR WHOM I MUST DECLINE?	HE PUT THE BELT AROUND	273	16
BUT IF THE HEART OMIT [BE LEAN / BE THIN / DECLINE]	THE MIND LIVES ON THE	1355	5
DECLINED			
BUT WHEN THE DAY DECLINED	THE DAY THAT I WAS	356	10
TILL WHEN THE RED DECLINED--	THESE HELD THEIR WICK	1390	2
BUT SO DECLINED IN WORTH	WHEN WE HAVE CEASED TO	1706	5
DECLINES			
WHAT IT DECLINES	TO BE FORGOT BY THEE	1560	6
AND THEN DECLINES FOREVER	DROWNING IS NOT SO	1718	5
DECLIVITY			
OF LIFE'S DECLIVITY.	AS SUMMER INTO AUTUMN	1346	12
DECOMPOSITION			
TRANSPORT'S DECOMPOSITION FOLLOWS--	WHICH IS THE BEST--THE	1315	7
DECORATE			
OR TERROR--THAT DO DECORATE [CELEBRATE / GENERATE]	HIS VOICE DECREPIT WAS	1476	7
WOULD DECORATE OBLIVION'S	AN ANTIQUATED TREE	1514	6
DECOY			
THE CREDULOUS--DECOY--	"HEAVEN"--IS WHAT I	239	10
DECOYED			
BUT DECOYED MAY BE.	DEATH IS LIKE THE INSECT	1716	4
DECOYING			
DECOYING BUT TO GREET US--	OF DEATH I TRY TO THINK	1558	8

	FIRST LINE	POEM		LINE
DECOYS				
THE SPRING DECOYS.	I HAVE A BIRD IN SPRING	5		3
DECOYS IT'S TRAVELLER [PASSENGER]	RISK IS THE HAIR THAT	1239		12
DECREASE				
TO TELL THE BEAUTY WOULD DECREASE	TO TELL THE BEAUTY WOULD	1700		1
DECREASES				
TENDERNESS DECREASES AS WE PROVE--	ABSENCE DISEMBODIES--SO	860		4
DECREE				
AS DEITY DECREE--	AFRAID! OF WHOM AM I	608	V	8
NEITHER [OR] DECREE PROHIBIT HIM--	THE RAT IS THE CONCISEST	1356		9
FULFILLING ABSOLUTE [SOME EXPRESS] DECREE	HOW HAPPY IS THE LITTLE	1510		9
NOT JOY, BUT A DECREE	EXPANSE CANNOT BE LOST--	1584		2
DECREPIT				
I SEND YOU A DECREPIT FLOWER	I SEND YOU A DECREPIT	1324		1
HIS VOICE DECREPIT WAS WITH JOY--	HIS VOICE DECREPIT WAS	1476		1
DEDICATED				
HENCEFORTH, A DEDICATED SORT--	HE PUT THE BELT AROUND	273		7
DEDUCTING				
DEDUCTING ME--	HIS MANSION IN THE POOL	1379		6
DEED				
A KINGDOM'S TITLE DEED--	HE PUT THE BELT AROUND	273		6
WHAT DEED IS THEIR'S [THEY BEAR] UNTO THE GENERAL NATURE--	FOUR TREES--UPON A	742		13
ACCORDING TO OUR DEED.	THE SUN IS GAY OR STARK	878		2
A DEED, IN EVERY PLACE--	WHEN I HAVE SEEN THE SUN	888		4
A DEED KNOCKS FIRST AT THOUGHT	A DEED KNOCKS FIRST AT	1216		1
YOU'D THINK [SWEAR] HE TOOK A DEED	HOW DESTITUTE IS HE	1477	V	7
AND SWELLS THE SCANTEST DEED	I KNOW OF PEOPLE IN THE	1665		6
DEEDS				
PROTECTED BY THEIR DEEDS--	WHEN WE STAND ON THE	242		12
DEEM				
DOUBTLESS, WE SHOULD DEEM SUPERFLUOUS	IF THE FOOLISH, CALL	168		13
BEYOND MY POWER TO DEEM [DREAM]--	YOUR RICHES--TAUGHT ME--	299		22
AND DEEM OURSELF A FOOL--	WE PLAY AT PASTE--	320		4
SO GLAD WE ARE--A STRANGER'D DEEM	SO GLAD WE ARE--A	329		1
I COULD [DID] NOT DEEM THESE [THAT] PLANETARY FORCES	IT KNEW NO LAPSE, NOR	560		5
THE EAST--WOULD DEEM EXTRAVAGANT--	I RECKON--WHEN I COUNT	569		11
AND DEEM TO BE ALONE	DID YOU EVER STAND IN A	590		4
WOULD DEEM OURSELVES--THE BUSIER	TO INTERRUPT HIS YELLOW	591		13
IT DEEM IT BE--CONTINUALLY--	I SEE THEE BETTER--IN	611		15
WHAT LIBERTY! SO CAPTIVES DEEM	COULD I BUT RIDE	661		17
I COULD NOT DEEM IT LATE--TO HEAR	"I WANT"--IT PLEADED--	731		5
AS WRECKED MEN--DEEM THEY SIGHT THE LAND--	I MANY TIMES THOUGHT	739		3
I DEEM THAT I--WITH BUT A CRUMB--	GOD GAVE A LOAF TO EVERY	791		15
IF [GRANT] THE BIRD AND THE FARMER--DEEM IT A "PINE"--	BY MY WINDOW HAVE I FOR	797		3
I DEEM MYSELF WHAT I WOULD BE--	I PLAY AT RICHES--TO	801		11
DEEM MY SUPPER DRY	AS THE STARVED MAELSTROM	872		14
DEEM UNPLAUSIBLE [INCREDIBLE]	COLOR--CASTE--	970		16
WE DEEM WE DREAM--	TO THE BRIGHT EAST SHE	1573		9
OR EVEN IF I DEEM I DO	HIS MIND OF MAN, A	1663		5
DEEMED				
I HAD NOT DEEMED A VEST	THE MALAY--TOOK THE	452		12
'TIS DEEMED A PRIVILEGE TO CHOOSE--	THE MANNER OF IT'S DEATH	468		3
SHE NEVER DEEMED--SHE HURT--	SHE DEALT HER PRETTY	479		5
BUT NEVER DEEMED THE DRIPPING PRIZE	LIKE FLOWERS, THAT HEARD	513		2
I DEEMED ETERNITY	YOU CONSTITUTED TIME--	765		2
BY OTHER FINANCIERS BE DEEMED	THE VOICE THAT STANDS	1189		7
DEEMING				
FOR DEEMING--BEGGARS--PLAY--	'TIS OPPOSITES--ENTICE--	355		8
TILL THEN--DREAMING [DEEMING] I AM SOWING	DONT PUT UP MY THREAD &	617		17
COCHINEAL--I CHOSE--FOR DEEMING	AUTUMN--OVERLOOKED MY	748		5
DEEMING WHERE	WE'LL PASS WITHOUT THE	996		4
NOT DEEMING OF HIS DREAD ABODE	NO MAN SAW AWE, NOR TO	1733		5
DEEMS				
DEEMS HIS DOMINION	THE CHILD'S FAITH IS NEW	637		10
DEEP				
ONCE MORE HER MISTRESS, ON THE DEEP	ONCE MORE, MY NOW	48		3
INTO DEEP ETERNITY--	EXULTATION IS THE GOING	76		4
DEEP IN OUR HAND--	WE DONT CRY--TIM AND I,	196		6
LIMIT--HOW DEEP A BLEEDING GO!	BOUND--A TROUBLE--	269		3
A SECOND MORE, HAD DROPPED TOO DEEP	THAT AFTER HORROR--THAT	286		5
THO' DRIFTED DEEP, IN PARIAN--	IT WILL BE SUMMER--	342		7
SO LIGHT--SO DEEP--	SHE LAY AS IF AT PLAY	369		16
BUT JUST A DAISY--DEEP--	THE COLOR OF THE GRAVE	411		8
LOVE--THOU ART DEEP--	LOVE--THOU ART HIGH--	453		7
DEEP DUG--FOR SUMMER DAYS--	I KNOW WHERE WELLS GROW	460		2
A SMILE, TO SHOW YOU, WHEN THIS DEEP	IF I MAY HAVE IT, WHEN	577		23
JUST--HOW--DEEP--	AGAIN--HIS VOICE IS AT	663		16
DEEP [LOW] PILLOW--TO HAVE SHARED--	MY LIFE HAD STOOD--A	754		16
THE AFTERNOON IN EVENING DEEP	THE DAY GREW SMALL,	1140		3
BUT THE SEA [DEEP] IS OLD	FORTITUDE INCARNATE	1217		8
IT WOULD NOT SOUND SO DEEP	I THINK THAT THE ROOT OF	1302		2
DEEP IS THE SCHEDULE	THOSE NOT LIVE YET	1454		8
THAT THEY ARE STILL THE DEEP,	THOUGH THE GREAT WATERS	1599		2
TO THEIR APARTMENT DEEP	TO THEIR APARTMENT DEEP	1701		1
WOULD STAND SO DEEP IN JOY	DID LIFE'S PENURIOUS	1717		4
DEEPENED				
THE SUMMER DEEPENED, WHILE WE STROVE--	MY FIRST WELL DAY--SINCE	574		9

	FIRST LINE	POEM	LINE
DEEPENS			
DANGER--DEEPENS SUM--	EXPECTATION--IS	807	8
DEEPER			
A DEEPER TWILIGHT ON THE LAWN--	AN ALTERED LOOK ABOUT	140	4
DEEPER AND DEEPER GREW THE STAIN	THE SUN KEPT STOOPING--	152	5
DEEPER AND DEEPER GREW THE STAIN	THE SUN KEPT STOOPING--	152	5
THE BRAIN IS DEEPER THAN THE SEA--	THE BRAIN--IS WIDER THAN	632	5
DEEPER THAN WITHOUT--	ABSENT PLACE--AN APRIL	927	6
OR DEEPER COLOR IN THE SHAWL	SUMMER BEGINS TO HAVE	1682	7
DEEPEST			
THE DEEPEST HID IS SIGHTED FIRST	OF CONSCIOUSNESS, HER	894	5
BESIDES THE DEEPEST CELLAR	REMEMBRANCE HAS A	1182	5
IN ALL THE DEEPEST SKY	A SPARROW TOOK A SLICE	1211	6
DEER			
A WOUNDED DEER--LEAPS HIGHEST--	A WOUNDED DEER--LEAPS	165	1
THE DEER ATTRACTS NO FURTHER [INVITES NO LONGER--]	THIS MERIT HATH THE	979	7
DEFACE			
TO DEFACE THEIR STATELY TREASURES--	SWEET--SAFE--HOUSES--	457	12
THE PEACE CANNOT DEFACE--	A TOOTH UPON OUR PEACE	459	2
DEFACED			
BUT [WHEN / IF] DEFACED VICARIOUSLY-- . .	HE WHO IN HIMSELF	969	7
DEFACES			
DEFACES [DEBASES / SURPASSES] THAT OF WINE--	WHO NEVER WANTED--	1430	4
DEFAULT			
LEAVING ON NATURE--A DEFAULT	SHE SPED AS PETALS OF A	991	5
DEFAULTER			
JUDAS--THE GREAT [FIRST] DEFAULTER--	THE BIBLE IS AN ANTIQUE	1545	7
DEFAULTING			
BY ONE DEFAULTING [HEROIC] FACE	THE VASTEST EARTHLY DAY	1328	3
DEFEAT			
DEFEAT MEANS NOTHING BUT DEFEAT, ...	'TIS SO MUCH JOY! 'TIS	172	11
DEFEAT MEANS NOTHING BUT DEFEAT, ...	'TIS SO MUCH JOY! 'TIS	172	11
DEFEAT WHETS VICTORY--THEY SAY--	I SHOULD HAVE BEEN TOO	313	19
"DEFEAT", AN OUTGROWN ANGUISH, ...	OF TRIBULATION--THESE	325	11
NOR EVEN OF DEFEAT--AWARE--	THERE IS A FLOWER THAT	380	31
MISTAKE DEFEAT FOR DEATH--EACH TIME-- . .	THE PROVINCE OF THE	539	11
NOR THIS--DEFEAT MY PACE--	I CROSS TILL I AM WEARY	550	10
MY PORTION IS DEFEAT--TODAY--	MY PORTION IS DEFEAT--	639	1
DEFEAT--A SOMEWHAT SLOWER--[SOMETHING DUMBER] MEANS--	MY PORTION IS DEFEAT--	639	5
BUT VANQUISHED HER [HIM] WITH MY DEFEAT . .	THE STARS ARE OLD, THAT	1249	7
DEFEATED			
AS HE DEFEATED--DYING--	SUCCESS IS COUNTED	67	9
THAT VANQUISHED HER--DEFEATED FEAT--	THE PRETTY RAIN FROM	1426	7
DEFEATED OF A BONE	THE WIND DREW OFF	1694	3
DEFENCES			
FOR HER JUGULAR DEFENCES--	ROBBED BY DEATH--BUT	971	5
DEFENDING			
THE STONE--THAT TELLS DEFENDING WHOM . . .	IT FEELS A SHAME TO BE	444	5
DEFER			
WHY PARADISE DEFER [DEMUR]--	ONE BLESSING HAD I THAN	756	18
DEFERENCE			
IN GENTLE DEFERENCE TO ME--	I DREADED THAT FIRST	348	23
IN DEFERENCE TO HIM	HOW DARE THE ROBINS SING	1724	14
DEFERRED			
SURVEYED [DELAYED / DEFERRED] INFINITY-- .	I COULD SUFFICE FOR HIM,	643	4
DEFIANT			
WAS [SAT] THE DEFIANT SUN--	A WILD BLUE SKY ABREAST	1415	4
DEFIANT OF A ROAD --	THE MOON UPON HER FLUENT	1528	2
DEFIED			
DEFIED TO BE DEFINED--	THESE HELD THEIR WICK	1390	4
DEFIES			
DEFIES IMPRISONMENT!	COCOON ABOVE! COCOON	129	6
AND THAT--DEFIES ME--	I FOUND THE WORDS TO	581	3
DEFIES TOPOGRAPHY.	HOW FAR IS IT TO HEAVEN?	929	8
THE EXCELLENCE [QUALITY] DEFIES US--	TO DISAPPEAR ENHANCES--	1209	15
DEFILES			
AND THAT PROFANES [POLLUTES / DEFILES] THE POWER	THE CLOVER'S SIMPLE FAME	1232	V 6
DEFINE			
CAN THE EXTASY DEFINE--	FLOWERS--WELL--IF	137	2
'TIS BEGGARS--BANQUETS BEST [CAN] DEFINE-- .	I SHOULD HAVE BEEN TOO	313	22
CAN THE DUMB--DEFINE [DIVULGE] THE DIVINE? .	BY MY WINDOW HAVE I FOR	797	14
THE BROAD ARE TOO BROAD TO DEFINE	HE PREACHED UPON	1207	2
DEFINED			
I COULD NOT HAVE DEFINED THE CHANGE-- . .	I THINK I WAS ENCHANTED	593	21
DEFIED TO BE DEFINED--	THESE HELD THEIR WICK	1390	4
DEFINITELY			
NOR DEFINITELY, WHAT IT WAS--	A THOUGHT WENT UP MY	701	7
DEFINITION			
CAN TELL THE DEFINITION	SUCCESS IS COUNTED	67	7
THE DEFINITION OF MELODY--IS--	BY MY WINDOW HAVE I FOR	797	15
THAT DEFINITION IS NONE--	BY MY WINDOW HAVE I FOR	797	16
THE DEFINITION OF BEAUTY IS	THE DEFINITION OF BEAUTY	988	1
THAT DEFINITION IS NONE--	THE DEFINITION OF BEAUTY	988	2
DEFORMED			
DEFORMED MEN--PONDER GRACE--	'TIS OPPOSITES--ENTICE--	355	2
DEFORMING			
DEFORMING--DWINDLING--GULPHING UP-- . . .	I HAD THE GLORY--THAT	349	6

	FIRST LINE	POEM	LINE
DEFRAUDED			
STARING--BEWILDERED [DEFRAUDED]--AT THE MOCKING SKY--	THE NEAREST DREAM	319	10
DEFRAUDED I A BUTTERFLY--	DEFRAUDED I A BUTTERFLY	730	1
NOT ONE BY HEAVEN DEFRAUDED STAY--	NOT ONE BY HEAVEN	1303	1
DEFRAUDED OF IT'S SONG.	AS FROM THE EARTH THE	1630	9
DEFRAYS			
DEFRAYS THE DROSS OF IT--	ONE THING OF IT WE	1464	8
DEFT			
DAINTY--AS THE TRESS--ON HER DEFT HEAD--	WE--BEE AND I--LIVE BY	230	11
DEFY			
ATTIRED TO DEFY,	THE WAY TO KNOW THE	1279	6
DEFYING			
OUTSTARING [DEFYING / APPALLING / ABASHING] MASONRY--	TOO COLD IS THIS	1135	5
DISSENTING [DEFYING] TO BE WON	THE FACE IN EVANESCENCE	1490	6
DEGRADES			
DEMEANS [DEGRADES] THE DRESS I WEAR--	MY COCOON TIGHTENS--	1099	4
AND THAT DEGRADES [PROFANES] THE FLOWER--	THE CLOVER'S SIMPLE FAME	1232	6
DEGREE			
BY PEOPLE OF DEGREE	SLEEP IS SUPPOSED TO BE	13	8
LAURELS--FOR RARE DEGREE	GARLANDS FOR QUEENS, MAY	34	2
ADDETH TO MY DEGREE--	THE MURMUR OF A BEE	155	12
WHOSE FARTHEST OF DEGREE,	DOUBT ME! MY DIM	275	14
TOO LIFTED--FOR THE SCANT DEGREE	I SHOULD HAVE BEEN TOO	313	2
THAT--SIR--WAS MY DEGREE--	THE FACE I CARRY WITH ME	336	6
A FISHERMAN'S--DEGREE--	WHAT SOFT--CHERUBIC	401	10
HE NEVER MISSES A DEGREE--	THE MOON IS DISTANT FROM	429	5
NOT OBVIATED OF DEGREE--	CONJECTURING A CLIMATE	562	7
WE--OCCUPY--DEGREE [TOO--PARTAKE]--	WE TALKED AS GIRLS DO--	586	12
I FEEL THE OLD DEGREE--	AGAIN--HIS VOICE IS AT	663	2
DEGREE--OR SHAME--	WHERE THOU ART--THAT--IS	725	3
THE NEEDLE--TO THE NORTH DEGREE--	THROUGH THE STRAIT PASS	792	11
THAT ALWAYS GUAGES A DEGREE	LEST THIS BE HEAVEN	1043	3
ACUTE DEGREE--CONFERRED ON ME--	TITLE DIVINE--IS MINE!	1072	3
DEGREELESS			
INTO DEGREELESS NOON--	A CLOCK STOPPED--	287	9
DEGREES			
IT'S ONLY FAINTER--BY DEGREES--	TO DIE--TAKES JUST A	255	3
HE STUNS YOU BY DEGREES--	HE FUMBLES AT YOUR SOUL	315	4
'TWAS MURDER BY DEGREES--	THE WHOLE OF IT CAME NOT	762	2
DEIFIED			
THE GOWN THAT DANTE--DEIFIED--	A PRECIOUS--MOULDERING	371	19
ITS STIGMA [FORFEIT] DEIFIED	ONE CROWN THAT NO ONE	1735	4
DEIGN			
WITHOUT A [BUT DEIGN NO] SYLLABLE--	HOW NOTELESS MEN, AND	282	12
BUT DEIGN THIS LEAST CERTIFICATE	THE LOOK OF THEE, WHAT	1689	11
DEIGNED			
HAD SCARCELY DEIGNED TO LIE--	HER SWEET WEIGHT ON MY	518	2
DEITY			
THAT STANDS FOR DEITY, TO MINE,	A SINGLE SCREW OF FLESH	263	3
AND DEITY CONCLUDE--	A TONGUE--TO TELL HIM I	400	27
OF DEITY--ASHAMED--	WHAT SOFT--CHERUBIC	401	8
DEITY WILL SEE TO IT	BEAUTY--BE NOT CAUSED--	516	7
WHEN DEITY ASSURED [PRONOUNCED]	TRUST IN THE UNEXPECTED	555	14
LIKE DEITY--TO KEEP--	I THINK I WAS ENCHANTED	593	32
AS DEITY DECREE--	AFRAID! OF WHOM AM I	608	V 8
IN THAT SMALL DEITY	THE HEAVEN VESTS FOR	694	2
THE THRIFTY DEITY	IT'S EASY TO INVENT A	724	6
'TIS TRUE--THAT DEITY TO STOOP	MY WORTHINESS IS ALL MY	751	9
'TWAS THEREFORE DEITY	YOU CONSTITUTED TIME--	765	4
LEST FIRMAMENT [UNIVERSE / DEITY] SHOULD FAIL FOR ME--	MY FAITH IS LARGER THAN	766	15
OF DEITY [UNIVERSE] AND MEN--	THE BIRDS BEGUN AT FOUR	783	16
NAY, IT IS DEITY--	UNABLE ARE THE LOVED TO	809	3
NAY--IT IS DEITY--	UNABLE ARE THE LOVED TO	809	V 6
A LIFELESS DEITY.	TRUTH--IS AS OLD AS GOD	836	8
FOR DEITY	A SICKNESS OF THIS WORLD	1044	8
"JUST ONCE" SWEET DEITY?	JUST ONCE! OH LEAST	1076	9
THE CLEMENCY OF DEITY	ELIZABETH TOLD ESSEX	1321	3
OR DEITY--	IN MANY AND REPORTLESS	1382	4
IS DEITY--	EXPANSE CANNOT BE LOST--	1584	3
THE JOYFUL LITTLE DEITY	HOW FLEET--HOW	1771	3
DEITY'S			
WHETHER DEITY'S GUILTLESS--	I CAUTIOUS, SCANNED MY	178	15
DEJECTED			
THE BREEZES BROUGHT DEJECTED LUTES--	A DROP FELL ON THE APPLE	794	13
AND THAT DEJECTED FLEET	ENDANGER IT, AND THE	1658	6
DELAPIDATION'S			
DELAPIDATION'S PROCESSES	CRUMBLING IS NOT AN	997	3
DELAY			
IF THE BUTTERFLY DELAY	I'M THE LITTLE "HEART'S	176	3
THEY STRIVE--AND YET DELAY--	I CROSS TILL I AM WEARY	550	22
WHILE I DELAY [DELAYED] TO GUESS [DRESS]	OH SHADOW ON THE GRASS,	1187	6
IS [WAS] SHORTER THAN A [THE] SNAKE'S DELAY [EVENT / REPLY]	THE MUSHROOM IS THE ELF	1298	7
THEN SUE IT TO DELAY	WE SHUN IT ERE IT COMES,	1580	3
DELAY THE BUTTERFLY	THE PEDIGREE OF HONEY	1627	4
DELAYED			
DELAYED TILL SHE HAD CEASED TO KNOW--	DELAYED TILL SHE HAD	58	1

	FIRST LINE	POEM	LINE
DELAYED (CONTINUED)			
DELAYED TILL IN IT'S VEST OF SNOW	DELAYED TILL SHE HAD	58	2
IF ONLY CENTURIES, DELAYED,	IF YOU WERE COMING IN	511	9
SURVEYED [DELAYED / DEFERRED] INFINITY--	I COULD SUFFICE FOR HIM,	643	4
WHILE I DELAY [DELAYED] TO GUESS [DRESS]	OH SHADOW ON THE GRASS,	1187	6
CENTURIES DELAYED	THE THRILL CAME SLOWLY	1495	2
DELAYING			
THAT WILL RECEIVE [DELAYING ITS] REPLY	ONE JOY OF SO MUCH	1420	10
DELAYS			
ONE DIGNITY DELAYS FOR ALL--	ONE DIGNITY DELAYS FOR	98	1
WITH GAY DELAYS HE GOES	BEFORE YOU THOUGHT OF	1465	12
DELIBERATE			
DELIBERATE, AS A DUKE WOULD DO	HE PUT THE BELT AROUND	273	5
DELIBERATELY			
ASSIDUOUSLY [DELIBERATELY / DETERMINATELY / IMPERTINENTLY] CRAWLED	ALONE AND IN A	1167	4
DELIBERATELY [LOOK SQUARELY IN THE] FACE--	I NEVER HEAR THAT ONE IS	1323	16
DELICATE			
. . . A MIGHT / SO DELICATE A MIGHT / SO ADEQUATE A MIGHT / . . .	THE MOST TRIUMPHANT BIRD	1265	4
DELICIOUS			
TO DWELL--DELICIOUS--ON--	I WOULD NOT PAINT--A	505	4
TO WHAT DELICIOUS ACCIDENT	THE MOST TRIUMPHANT BIRD	1265	8
COMPARED WITH THE DELICIOUS THROE	SWEET SKEPTICISM OF THE	1413	7
DELICIOUS ROBIN--	COME SHOW THY DURHAM	1542	3
AT NIGHT'S DELICIOUS CLOSE.	THE SADDEST NOISE, THE	1764	4
DELIGHT			
ON EAR TOO FAR FOR THE DELIGHT,	AS WATCHERS HANG UPON	121	5
DELIGHT IS AS THE FLIGHT--	DELIGHT IS AS THE FLIGHT	257	1
WITH LAST [LEAST] DELIGHT I OWN!	DOUBT ME! MY DIM	275	8
WITH DIFFERENT DELIGHT--	THE DOOMED--REGARD THE	294	2
A FASHIONLESS DELIGHT--	IT'S LIKE THE LIGHT--	297	2
OF A WITHDRAWN DELIGHT--	REHEARSAL TO OURSELVES	379	2
TO PERISH--OF DELIGHT--	IT MIGHT BE LONELIER	405	16
AND WOULD DELIGHT TO SEE--	YOU LOVE THE LORD--YOU	487	6
INHERITING DELIGHT	THOSE FAIR--FICTITIOUS	499	10
WHEN, STIRRING, FOR BELIEF'S DELIGHT,	HER SWEET WEIGHT ON MY	518	3
IT NOTES [GAINS] DELIGHT	MUST BE A WO--	571	6
DELIGHT--BECOMES PICTORIAL--	DELIGHT--BECOMES	572	1
WINCES [ACHES] WITH DELIGHT	INCONCEIVABLY SOLEMN!	582	14
ANONYMOUS DELIGHT TO KNOW--	I SOMETIMES DROP IT, FOR	708	3
WHAT THOU DOST--IS DELIGHT--	WHERE THOU ART--THAT--IS	725	6
THE SUN--WITH JUST [BROAD] DELIGHT	THE MOUNTAINS--GROW	757	6
DELIGHT WITHOUT A CAUSE--	IT IS A LONESOME GLEE--	774	6
THEY ASK BUT OUR DELIGHT--	THEY ASK BUT OUR DELIGHT	868	1
A FIXED DELIGHT,	THESE TESTED OUR HORIZON	886	6
DELIGHT OF NATURE--ABDICATE--	TILL DEATH--IS NARROW	907	11
DAFFODIL DELIGHT BUT	ABSENT PLACE--AN APRIL	927	7
WITHOUT DELIGHT, OR BEAM--	DENIAL--IS THE ONLY FACT	965	6
IT'S [THE] FIRST--DELIGHT--AND THEN--SURPRISE--	FITTER TO SEE HIM, I MAY	968	10
'TIS ANGUISH GRANDER THAN DELIGHT	'TIS ANGUISH GRANDER	984	1
HER PALATE TO DELIGHT	MY HEART UPON A LITTLE	1027	2
REPUBLIC OF DELIGHT, I THOUGHT	THE BIRD DID PRANCE--THE	1107	7
TOO BRIGHT [BOLD] FOR OUR INFIRM DELIGHT	TELL ALL THE TRUTH BUT	1129	3
WHEN THE DELIGHT IS DUST	"REMEMBER ME" IMPLORED	1180	6
FOR WHAT DEPARTMENT OF DELIGHT	THE PUNGENT ATOM IN THE	1191	5
ARE FRIENDS DELIGHT OR PAIN?	ARE FRIENDS DELIGHT OR	1199	1
OF UNOBTAINED DELIGHT----	TO DISAPPEAR ENHANCES--	1209	20
DELIGHT HAD AGGRANDIZED THE GATE	IT CAME AT LAST BUT	1230	7
A WIND THAT WOKE A LONE DELIGHT	A WIND THAT ROSE	1259	6
BUT INTIMATE [COMPETENT / ABSOLUTE / IMPUDENT] DELIGHT.	THE MOST TRIUMPHANT BIRD	1265	6
IS THAT DELIGHT IS LESS	DELIGHT'S DESPAIR AT	1299	2
AN EDIBLE DELIGHT.	SURPRISE IS LIKE A	1306	4
BUT FOR THE NIGGARDLY DELIGHT	OUR LITTLE SECRETS SLINK	1326	5
WHETHER ADULT DELIGHT IS [BE] PAIN	WONDER--IS NOT PRECISELY	1331	6
THE LAST [CLOSE] OF SUMMER IS DELIGHT--[A TIME / RESULT--SURVEY]	THE LAST OF SUMMER IS	1353	1
AND THEN--ENFORCES THEIR DELIGHT	THE WORTHLESSNESS OF	1373	3
IS IT DELIGHT OR WOE--	HIS VOICE DECREPIT WAS	1476	6
EQUALLY TO ABHOR DELIGHT--	SUMMER IS SHORTER THAN	1506	7
THE MODERATE DRINKER OF DELIGHT	A DRUNKARD CANNOT MEET A	1628	7
REFORMED TO NOTHING BUT DELIGHT WHICH	ARROWS ENAMORED OF HIS	1629 V	
RATHER ARID DELIGHT	RATHER ARID DELIGHT	1679	1
HAST THOU DELIGHT OR FEAR	THE LOOK OF THEE, WHAT	1689	6
AN ABLATIVE ESTATE [DELIGHT]--	THAT IT WILL NEVER COME	1741	6
DELIGHTED			
THAT WHATSOE'ER DELIGHTED IT,	ALTHOUGH I PUT AWAY HIS	366	11
FOR THE DELIGHTED CREW.	A SOFT SEA WASHED AROUND	1198	8
DELIGHT'S			
DELIGHT'S DESPAIR AT SETTING	DELIGHT'S DESPAIR AT	1299	1
DELIGHTS			
BUT DISTANCE HIS DELIGHTS CONFIDES	'TIS MY FIRST NIGHT	1122	7
FOR THE DELIGHTS	TOO FEW THE MORNINGS BE,	1186	4
WINTER IS GOOD--HIS HOAR DELIGHTS	WINTER IS GOOD--HIS HOAR	1316	1
IN THE DELIGHTS [AWARDS] OF DUST--	PRAISE IT--'TIS DEAD--	1384	7
HER ZEALOUS NOTE DELIGHTS IT TO ASCEND.	AFTER ALL BIRDS HAVE	1395 V	6
DELINEATION			
VANDYKES DELINEATION	THE TREES LIKE TASSELS--	606	27

	FIRST LINE	POEM	LINE
DELINQUENT			
FOR MY DELINQUENT PALACES--	A LOSS OF SOMETHING EVER	959	12
DELIRIOUS			
UNTIL--DELIRIOUS--BORNE--	I THINK JUST HOW MY	237	14
OF YOUR DELIRIOUS HEM--	'TWAS LIKE A MAELSTROM,	414	6
AS DO THE BEE--DELIRIOUS BORNE--	THE SOUL HAS BANDAGED	512	15
DELIRIOUS CHARTER!	MINE--BY THE RIGHT OF	528	8
AND GROPED DELIRIOUS, FOR MORN--	IT TOSSED--AND TOSSED--	723	4
DELIRIUM			
SOME RUMOR OF DELIRIUM,	LIKE FLOWERS, THAT HEARD	513	5
DELIRIUM--DIVERTS THE WRETCH	I SOMETIMES DROP IT, FOR	708	9
DELIVER			
BUT [THOUGH] ALL MANKIND DELIVER [CRUISE SOFTLY / ROW SOFTLY / . . .	A CHILLY PEACE INFESTS	1443	7
DELIVERED			
DELIVERED STRAIGHTER TO THE HEART	DYING! TO BE AFRAID OF	831	5
OF A [ITS] DELIVERED SYLLABLE	COULD MORTAL LIP DIVINE	1409	3
DELL			
FOR WHOM BETRAYED THE DELL--	SO BASHFUL WHEN I SPIED	91	10
IN EXTASY--AND DELL--	THROUGH THE DARK SOD--AS	392	8
DELLS			
ANNOUNCING ME IN OTHER DELLS--	THERE IS A MORN BY MEN	24	23
AND DAPPLED COWSLIP DELLS--	WHAT WOULD I GIVE TO SEE	247	14
DELUGE			
AND SO THERE WAS A DELUGE--	THE WINTERS ARE SO SHORT	403	13
DELUSIVE			
WHILE THAT DELUSIVE [OBLIGING / ENCHANTING] HAIR	RISK IS THE HAIR THAT	1239	10
WITH A REVOLVING [DELUSIVE / DISSEMBLING / DISSOLVING / . . .	A ROUTE OF EVANESCENCE	1463	2
TO A DELUSIVE LILAC	HIS LITTLE HEARSE LIKE	1522	3
DEMAND			
YOUR LOW [MEEK] EYES--DEMAND--	PROMISE THIS--WHEN YOU	648	8
TO DEMAND, IN YOUR LOW FAVOR	PROMISE THIS--WHEN YOU	648	21
I--HASTENED TO DEMAND	SEVERER SERVICE OF	786	2
THE BEAUTY OF DEMAND [BELIEF]--AT REST--	FITTER TO SEE HIM, I MAY	968	28
DID WE [I] DEMAND TODAY	WHO WERE "THE FATHER AND	1258	10
THE DEMAND [THE AFFAIR / AN AFFAIR] OF AWE?	SUMMER LAID HER SIMPLE	1363	8
BUT WE DEMAND [BINDLESS IS] THE FLAME	FAME IS THE ONE THAT	1475	8
ENDANGER IT, AND THE DEMAND	ENDANGER IT, AND THE	1658	1
DEMANDED			
WOLFE DEMANDED DURING DYING	WOLFE DEMANDED DURING	678	1
DEMANDETH			
AND THE FATHER FOND DEMANDETH THE MAIDEN FOR HIS SON.	AWAKE YE MUSES NINE,	1	16
DEMANDS			
DEMANDS THE [MY] LITTLE KING	A SAUCER HOLDS A CUP	1374	6
DEMEAN			
TO STATE THE SPELL DEMEAN	TO TELL THE BEAUTY WOULD	1700	2
DEMEANED			
IT MADE US ALL ASHAMED [DEMEANED]	SO PROUD SHE WAS TO DIE	1272	2
DEMEANING			
DEMEANING BY EXCLUSIVE WEALTH	A MINE THERE IS NO MAN	1117	3
DEMEANS			
DEMEANS [DEGRADES] THE DRESS I WEAR--	MY COCOON TIGHTENS--	1099	4
DEMIJOHN			
A LITTLE TRUST--A DEMIJOHN--	A LITTLE BREAD--A CRUST	159	2
DEMOCRAT			
THIS DEMOCRAT IS DRESSED,	WAIT TILL THE MAJESTY OF	171	6
TO GAIN THE PURPLE DEMOCRAT	THERE IS A FLOWER THAT	380	3
PROPITIATE THIS DEMOCRAT	NOT ANY HIGHER STANDS	1256	7
DEMOCRATIC			
DEATH'S LARGE--DEMOCRATIC FINGERS	COLOR--CASTE--	970	7
DEMOLISHES			
AN INSTANT'S PUSH DEMOLISHES	THE HEART HAS NARROW	928	11
DEMOSTHENES			
DEMOSTHENES HAS VANISHED	HIS MANSION IN THE POOL	1379	15
DEMUR			
DEMUR--YOU'RE STRAIGHTWAY DANGEROUS--	MUCH MADNESS IS DIVINEST	435	7
WHY PARADISE DEFER [DEMUR]--	ONE BLESSING HAD I THAN	756	18
IF WE DEMUR, IT'S GAPING SIDES	THIS CHASM, SWEET, UPON	858	5
THE LITTLE BIRD WOULD NOT DISSENT [DEMUR]	THE LADY FEEDS HER	941	3
DEMURER			
BUT A DEMURER CIRCUIT [MEASURE]--	A PRISON GETS TO BE A	652	15
DEMURRAL			
ACQUIESCENCE--OR DEMURRAL--	HER SWEET TURN TO LEAVE	649	23
DEMURRED			
IT MADE NO SIGNAL, NOR DEMURRED,	'TWAS WARM--AT FIRST--	519	15
TYRANNY DEMURRED--	ABRAHAM TO KILL HIM	1317	8
DEN			
THE BURDOCK'S DEN--	A BURDOCK--CLAWED MY	229	5
WE CHASED HIM TO HIS DEN--	THE FROST OF DEATH WAS	1136	17
ADVANCING [DEPUTED] TO THY DEN--	OH FUTURE! THOU SECRETED	1631	8
DENIAL			
DENIAL--IS THE ONLY FACT	DENIAL--IS THE ONLY FACT	965	1
DENIED			
FINGERS DENIED THE PLUCKING,	MY NOSEGAYS ARE FOR	95	3
"CANAAN" DENIED--	IF THE FOOLISH, CALL	168	10
WHERE PRESENCE--IS DENIED THEM.	PRAYER IS THE LITTLE	437	3
TO ONE DENIED TO DRINK	TO ONE DENIED TO DRINK	490	1

	FIRST LINE	POEM	LINE
DENIED (CONTINUED)			
WHAT IS FORBIDDEN [DENIED] UTTERLY	I ENVY SEAS, WHEREON HE	498	7
DENIED THE CHERISHING	ENDOW THE LIVING--WITH	521	6
NO OTHER--WAS DENIED--	I ASKED NO OTHER THING--	621	2
MOST ENOUGH [AMPLEST]--DENIED?	PROMISE THIS--WHEN YOU	648	33
DENIED THE SMALL DESIRE	IT WAS A GRAVE, YET BORE	876	10
PERCEIVED BY THE DENIED--	DENIAL--IS THE ONLY FACT	965	2
DISCLOSED [DISPLAYED] TO BE DENIED	THE BEGGAR AT THE DOOR	1240	4
TO DENIZEN DENIED	CRISIS IS SWEET AND YET	1416	4
WITHELD TO THE ARRIVED [DEBARRED / DENIED]--	CRISIS IS SWEET AND YET	1416	V 4
OURSELVES, DENIED THE PRIVILEGE,	'TIS NOT THE SWAYING	1597	7
IT IS DENIED THE GODS--	A LETTER IS A JOY OF	1639	2
DENIES			
AND WISHES--AND DENIES--	A CHARM INVESTS A FACE	421	6
STANDARD DENIES	UNTIL THE DESERT KNOWS	1291	V 6
DENIZEN			
DENIZEN OF SIGNIFICANCE	NOT ANY MORE TO BE	1344	3
TO DENIZEN DENIED	CRISIS IS SWEET AND YET	1416	4
DENOMINATED			
DENOMINATED "DEATH"--	A THROE UPON THE	71	4
DENOMINATED MORN.	SOME SAY GOODNIGHT--AT	1739	8
DENOMINATION			
COLOR--CASTE--DENOMINATION--	COLOR--CASTE--	970	1
DENOTE			
ASHES DENOTE THAT FIRE WAS--	ASHES DENOTE THAT FIRE	1063	1
SILENCE--DENOTE--	TO THE STANCH DUST	1402	5
NOT ANY VOICE IMPLY [DENOTE] IT HERE	'TIS WHITER THAN AN	1482	5
DENOTED			
DENOTED BY THE WHITE.	OF TRIBULATION--THESE	325	2
DENOTES			
DENOTES THERE BE--A SEA--	MY GARDEN--LIKE THE	484	2
HIS DRESS DENOTES HIM SOCIALLY,	THE ROBIN IS A GABRIEL	1483	3
DENOUNCED			
THAN I REVILED [DENOUNCED] MYSELF,	IT DROPPED SO LOW--IN MY	747	6
DENSE			
THAT IN SO DENSE A FUZZ--	TO HANG OUR HEAD--	105	6
WAS CROWDED DENSE WITH ARMIES--	THE SUN KEPT STOOPING--	152	9
YET--NOT SO DENSE A CROWD--	ONE LIFE OF SO MUCH	270	14
DENT			
COULD MAKE A DENT THEREON--	THE SPIRIT LASTS--BUT IN	1576	24
COULD MAKE A DENT THEREON--	EXPANSE CANNOT BE LOST--	1584	8
CAN [COULD] MAKE A [NO] DENT [CREASE / SEAM] THEREON [UPON]--	THIS ME--THAT WALKS AND	1588	8
DENUDED			
IS A MINUTER [DENUDED] PAGEANT	THE HARM OF YEARS IS ON	1280	7
DENY			
IF YOUR NERVE, DENY YOU--	IF YOUR NERVE, DENY YOU	292	1
DENY THAT I--AM DEAD--	DO PEOPLE MOULDER	432	6
DENY! DID ROSE HER BEE--	FORGET! THE LADY WITH	438	5
TILL THEY--THE CHERISHING DENY--	ENDOW THE LIVING--WITH	521	7
DENY SHE IS A ROBIN--NOW--	YOU'LL KNOW HER--BY HER	634	V 27
NEVER DENY ME--NEVER FLY--	SWEET MOUNTAINS--YE TELL	722	2
DENYING			
DENYING THEY HAVE BEEN--	IT SIFTS FROM LEADEN	311	20
DENYING THAT IT WAS--	IT SIFTS FROM LEADEN	311	V
DENYING [DISPUTING] THAT THEY DIED.	ON THAT DEAR FRAME THE	940	8
A SELF DENYING HOUSEHOLD,	THE ROBIN IS A GABRIEL	1483	10
DEPART			
AND THOUGH THEY NOW DEPART,	I HAVE A BIRD IN SPRING	5	16
ONE MIGHT DEPART AT OPTION	IF I SHOULD DIE,	54	9
BUT JUST TO HEAR THE GRACE DEPART--	EXCEPT THE HEAVEN HAD	472	5
WHEN HE DEPART [DEPARTS], AN EMPTINESS	BEFORE HE COMES WE WEIGH	834	3
A LIFE QUITE READY TO DEPART	THIS CHASM, SWEET, UPON	858	19
DEPART, BEFORE THE HOST HAVE SLID	THE SOUL SHOULD ALWAYS	1055	5
TILL IT DEPART, PERSUADING [CONVEYING] MINE--	AIR HAS NO RESIDENCE, NO	1060	8
IMPART--DEPART--	IMAGE OF LIGHT, ADIEU--	1556	6
DEPARTED			
HAD DEPARTED ME?	IT DID NOT SURPRISE ME--	39	12
OUR DEPARTED ARE.	TAKEN FROM MEN--THIS	53	12
"DEPARTED"--BOTH--THEY SAY!	LIKE HER THE SAINTS	60	7
I BROUGHT [BRING] THEE THE IMPERIAL [DEPARTED] HEART	SAVIOR! I'VE NO ONE ELSE	217	7
DEPARTED--TO THE JUDGMENT--	DEPARTED--TO THE	524	1
A PRESENCE OF DEPARTED ACTS--	REMORSE--IS MEMORY--	744	3
BUT THE CRUMB PARTOOK--DEPARTED--	MOST SHE TOUCHED ME BY	760	11
THE NEARER THEY DEPARTED US	SWEET, TO HAVE HAD THEM	901	3
DEPARTED [ENTRUSTED] ME!	THE CHEMICAL CONVICTION	954	8
DEPARTED, OR AT HOME--	HERE, WHERE THE DAISIES	1037	12
FOR THE DEPARTED CREATURE'S SAKE	ASHES DENOTE THAT FIRE	1063	3
DEPARTED STANDARDS AND THE FEW	TO UNDERTAKE IS TO	1070	7
DEPARTED WITH THE TORMENT	TO MAKE ROUTINE A	1196	7
DEPARTED, OR AT HOME--	THE DAY SHE GOES	1308	5
TO HER RESCINDED [SURRENDERED / RECEDING / DEPARTED / . . .	CRISIS IS SWEET AND YET	1416	8
THE STEM OF A DEPARTED FLOWER	THE STEM OF A DEPARTED	1520	1
DEPARTED WAS THE BIRD--	AS IMPERCEPTIBLY AS	1540	V
DEPARTING			
MY DEPARTING BLOSSOMS	THE GENTIAN WEAVES HER	18	3
DAY'S DEPARTING TIDE--	SO HAS A DAISY VANISHED	28	6
OH IF THERE MAY DEPARTING [REMAINING] BE	DELAYED TILL SHE HAD	58	13

	FIRST LINE	POEM	LINE
DEPARTING (CONTINUED)			
WITH A DEPARTING--SAPPHIRE--FEATURE--	HOW THE OLD MOUNTAINS	291	11
THIS--ADDRESSED DEPARTING ACCENTS--	THESE--SAW VISIONS--	758	5
A DEPARTING BREATH--	NONE WHO SAW IT EVER	1110	4
DEPARTING THEN [NEXT]--FOREVER--	SUMMER HAS TWO	1422	9
DEPARTING LIKE A PAGEANT	ONE OF THE ONES THAT	1466	19
BY A DEPARTING [RETREATING / ABSCONDING] LIGHT	BY A DEPARTING LIGHT	1714	1
ON [OF] HER DEPARTING SPAN	THIS DOCILE ONE INTER	1752	5
INSTRUCTS US BY DEPARTING [DERISION] NOW [MORE]	THE SUMMER THAT WE DID	1773	3
DEPARTMENT			
LOOKING ON--IS THE DEPARTMENT	GROWTH OF MAN--LIKE	750	13
FOR WHAT DEPARTMENT OF DELIGHT	THE PUNGENT ATOM IN THE	1191	5
DEPARTS			
WHEN HE DEPART [DEPARTS], AN EMPTINESS	BEFORE HE COMES WE WEIGH	834	3
THE PALATE OF THE HATE DEPARTS--	MINE ENEMY IS GROWING	1509	3
DEPARTURE			
A [THE] HOST'S DEPARTURE WHEN	THE SOUL THAT HATH A	674	6
OF DRESSING, OR DEPARTURE--	THE BIRDS BEGUN AT FOUR	783	19
DEPARTURE FROM A HINGE	THE MISSING ALL,	985	4
ENDEAR IN THE DEPARTURE	WE LEARN IN THE	1083	5
A WORLD MADE PENNINILESS BY THAT [HIS] DEPARTURE	A WORLD MADE PENNINILESS	1623	1
AND OUR DEPARTURE TAKE	SWEET IS THE SWAMP WITH	1740	4
AND BY DEPARTURE MORE.	WERE NATURE MORTAL LADY	1762	12
DEPEND			
WERE FOOLISH TO DEPEND--	THE WELL UPON THE BROOK	1091	2
DEPENDENT			
OF A DEPENDENT BROOD.	HIGH FROM THE EARTH I	1723	16
DEPENDS			
ON WHICH SO VAST DEPENDS--	MY FAITH IS LARGER THAN	766	14
DEPLORE			
THAT WE DEPLORE PECULIARLY	A WILD BLUE SKY ABREAST	1415	7
AND WHAT WE NOW DEPLORE.	THE SADDEST NOISE, THE	1764	14
DEPLOYS			
DIPS--EVADES--TEAZES--DEPLOYS--	THE NEAREST DREAM	319	6
DEPORT			
LET US DIVIDE [DEPORT]--WITH SKILL--	A MAN MAY MAKE A REMARK	952	5
DEPORTMENTS			
LET ME NOT SHAME THEIR SUBLIME DEPORTMENTS--	UNTO LIKE STORY--TROUBLE	295	21
DEPOSE			
NO MAN [FATE] DEPOSE	WHO COURT OBTAIN WITHIN	803	5
DEPOSE HIM LIKE A FASHION	THE HARM OF YEARS IS ON	1280	3
DEPOSED			
DEPOSED--AT LENGTH [LAST], THE GRAVE--	THERE CAME A DAY AT	322	26
DEPOSES			
HE DEPOSES DOOM	WHEN I HOPED I FEARED--	1181	7
DEPOSIT			
DEPOSIT IN A STONE	WHAT CARE THE DEAD, FOR	592	22
DEPOSITING			
DEPOSITING HIS THUNDER	THESE ARE THE NIGHTS	1128	7
DEPOSITS			
DEPOSITS HIM WITH GOD--	LOVE--IS THAT LATER	924	8
DEPRECIATE			
DEPRECIATE THE VISION--	I GAVE MYSELF TO HIM--	580	9
DEPREDATION			
THE DEPREDATION OF A BREEZE	GO NOT TOO NEAR A HOUSE	1434	2
DEPRIVE			
OF THIS--COULD MAN DEPRIVE ME--	THE POWER TO BE TRUE TO	464	5
ABRIDGE [IMPAIR / DEBAR / DEPRIVE] SOCIETY	WE MISS HER, NOT BECAUSE	993	4
AND DOWER AND DEPRIVE	OF THIS IS DAY COMPOSED	1675	6
DEPRIVED			
DEPRIVED OF OTHER BANQUET,	DEPRIVED OF OTHER	773	1
DISPELLED [ABASED / WITHHELD / DEPRIVED] FROM THERE--	I HAVE NO LIFE BUT THIS	1398	4
EXCEPT THAT IT DEPRIVED OF THEE--	SO GIVE ME BACK TO DEATH	1632	3
AND NOW, BY LIFE DEPRIVED,	SO GIVE ME BACK TO DEATH	1632	4
DEPTH			
A DEPTH--AN AZURE--A PERFUME--	A SOMETHING IN A	122	5
THE DEPTH UPON MY SOUL WAS NOTCHED--	JOY TO HAVE MERITED THE	788	19
UPON THE DEPTH OF THEE--	IN SNOW THOU COMEST	1669	8
THE DEPTH IS ALL MY THOUGHT--	A PIT--BUT HEAVEN OVER	1712	10
DEPTHS			
DEPTHS OF RUBY, UNDRAINED,	ALL THE LETTERS I CAN	334	5
DEPUTED			
DEPUTED [CONTENTED / CREATED] TO ADORE--	SUMMER--WE ALL HAVE SEEN	1386	9
THE WHOLE OF IMMORTALITY INTRENCHED [SECRETED / DEPUTED]	HE LIVED THE LIFE OF	1525	7
DEPUTED FROM WHAT FIRMAMENT--	THE BAT IS DUN, WITH	1575	9
ADVANCING [DEPUTED] TO THY DEN--	OH FUTURE! THOU SECRETED	1631	8
DEPUTIES			
FAINT DEPUTIES OF HEAT--	LIKE BROOMS OF STEEL	1252	6
DEPUTY			
NO DEPUTY SUFFICE--	AN HONEST TEAR	1192	6
DERIDED			
TO HER DERIDED HOME	TO HER DERIDED HOME	1586	1
DERIDING			
AND RODE IMMENSITY [DERIDING BY--]	A SPARROW TOOK A SLICE	1211	V 8
DERISION			
OURSELVES WE DO INTER WITH SWEET DERISION.	OURSELVES WE DO INTER	1144	1

	FIRST LINE	POEM	LINE
DERISION (CONTINUED)			
BY NO CONCLUSION [DERISION] HINDERED	A SPARROW TOOK A SLICE	1211	V 7
THE SWEET DERISION OF THE CROW	IN SNOW THOU COMEST	1669	3
INSTRUCTS US BY DEPARTING [DERISION] NOW [MORE]	THE SUMMER THAT WE DID	1773	3
DERIVE			
MY POVERTY AND I DERIVE--	I PLAY AT RICHES--TO	801	13
DERIVES			
DERIVES IT'S MAGNITUDE--	THE OUTER--FROM THE	451	2
DESCEND			
NOR NOTICED NIGHT DID SOFT DESCEND--	A POOR--TORN HEART-- A	78	5
FROM WHICH HE DOTH DESCEND IN PLUSH	A FUZZY FELLOW, WITHOUT	173	7
THE LUNGS ARE STIRLESS--MUST DESCEND	I BREATHED ENOUGH TO	272	5
WE SOBERLY DESCEND	EXHILIRATION IS THE	1118	6
HOW CONDESCENDING TO DESCEND	THE BUTTERFLY'S	1244	4
TO SUDDENLY DESCEND	THOSE CATTLE SMALLER	1388	10
DESCENDING			
ANGELS--TWICE DESCENDING	I NEVER LOST AS MUCH BUT	49	5
WHEN NIGHT--DESCENDING--DUMB--AND DARK--	THO' I GET HOME HOW LATE	207	5
DESCENDING [CONSENTING / ESTABLISHED / IMPARTED] TO ENAMOR US	THE FACE IN EVANESCENCE	1490	7
DESCRIBED			
THAN THEY HAVE BEEN DESCRIBED.	WHO WERE "THE FATHER AND	1258	8
DESCRIBING			
DESCRIBING IN THE AIR	THE BAT IS DUN, WITH	1575	6
DESCRIED			
NEW HOUSES ON THE HILL DESCRIED--	HAVE ANY LIKE MYSELF	736	3
WHAT IS TO BE IS BEST DESCRIED	MY TRIUMPH LASTED TILL	1227	9
BY BOY DESCRIED--	NOT WITH A CLUB, THE	1304	10
DESCRIED I--BY [IN] THE DISTANT [GAINING] LIGHT	THE ROAD WAS LIT WITH	1450	3
DESCRIED BY CUNNING MEN	OH FUTURE! THOU SECRETED	1631	6
DESCRY			
THOUGH LATELY I DESCRY	I KNOW SUSPENSE--IT	1285	6
DESERT			
NO DESERT NOON--	FOR THIS--ACCEPTED	195	9
WITH THEE, IN THE DESERT--	WITH THEE, IN THE DESERT	209	1
WOULD BUT THE "MEMNON" OF THE DESERT--	PUT UP MY LUTE!	261	6
AND [OR] IN THE DESERT--CLOY--	I THINK THE HEMLOCK	525	6
A DESERT--FIND--	I CROSS TILL I AM WEARY	550	5
AS THE PALM--THAT SERVE THE DESERT--	HER SWEET TURN TO LEAVE	649	19
THROUGH DESERT OR THE WILDERNESS	STRONG DRAUGHTS OF THEIR	711	3
UNTIL THE DESERT KNOWS	UNTIL THE DESERT KNOWS	1291	1
ONE DESERT AND A SEA	I DID NOT REACH THEE	1664	4
ONE DESERT CROSSED--	I DID NOT REACH THEE	1664	9
DESERTS			
SO BUBBLE BROOKS IN DESERTS	DISTRUSTFUL OF THE	20	11
AS BROOKS IN DESERTS BABBLE SWEET	AS WATCHERS HANG UPON	121	4
OFF [ON] DESERTS, IN THE SKY,	OF ALL THE SOUNDS	321	30
DESERTS--NEVER REBUKED HER SATIN--	CIVILIZATION--SPURNS--	492	3
TWO DESERTS BUT THE YEAR IS COLD	I DID NOT REACH THEE	1664	7
TWO DESERTS AND THE SEA!	I DID NOT REACH THEE	1664	32
DESERVE			
DO WE DESERVE--A THING--	IT FEELS A SHAME TO BE	444	10
DOES NOT DESERVE THE [HAS NEVER TASTED] SPRING--	A DRUNKARD CANNOT MEET A	1628	8
DESERVED			
MUST BE--I DESERVED--IT--	HE STRAINED MY FAITH--	497	V 10
DESERVING			
DESERVING BE.	OH, HONEY OF AN HOUR,	1734	6
DESIGN			
WITHOUT DESIGN--THAT I COULD TRACE	FROM COCOON FORTH A	354	5
DEATH--HAD THE SAME DESIGN--	I MEANT TO FIND HER WHEN	718	2
WITHOUT DESIGN	FOUR TREES--UPON A	742	2
DISHONOR HIS DESIGN--	JUST AS HE SPOKE IT FROM	848	4
LODGED BY DESIGN OR HAPPENING	THIS IS A BLOSSOM OF THE	945	3
WE HOVERED BY DESIGN--	MEETING BY ACCIDENT,	1548	2
DESIGNATE			
OF VICTORS, DESIGNATE--	OF TRIBULATION--THESE	325	4
OR INTIMATE [DESIGNATE] IT THERE	'TIS WHITER THAN AN	1482	6
DESIGNATED			
UNTIL THE DESIGNATED LIGHT	DARE YOU SEE A SOUL AT	365	15
DESIGNED			
AND I DESIGNED TO STAY--	I SEND YOU A DECREPIT	1324	4
DESIRE			
TO HIM OF ADEQUATE DESIRE	HEAVEN IS SO FAR OF THE	370	7
AND BUTTERFLIES--DESIRE--	THERE IS A FLOWER THAT	380	2
I KNOW NOT WHICH, DESIRE, OR GRANT [RIGHT / SIGHT]--	I PLAY AT RICHES--TO	801	23
DENIED THE SMALL DESIRE	IT WAS A GRAVE, YET BORE	876	10
I FEEL THE OLD DESIRE--	I CANNOT MEET THE SPRING	1051	2
TO HER DESIRE SEEMED--	SO PROUD SHE WAS TO DIE	1272	4
THAT WE DESIRE WITH OURSELVES	GOD IS INDEED A JEALOUS	1719	V 3
DESIRED			
BY BUTTERFLIES ADMIRED [ADORED / DESIRED]	THIS BAUBLE WAS	805	2
WHEN WE [I] DESIRED TO KNOW,	WHO WERE "THE FATHER AND	1258	14
DESIRELESS			
OF HER DESIRELESS LOT	A LITTLE DOG THAT WAGS	1185	12
DESIRE'S			
DESIRE'S PERFECT GOAL--	WHO NEVER WANTED--	1430	6

	FIRST LINE	POEM	LINE
DESIRES			
THE LITTLE WREN DESIRES--	FOR EVERY BIRD A NEST--	143	9
DESIST			
BUT I MUST DESIST--	THE BIBLE IS AN ANTIQUE	1545	V 10
DESOLATION			
THE DESOLATION ONLY MISSED	THE THRILL CAME SLOWLY	1495	5
DESPAIR			
'TIS THE SEAL DESPAIR--	THERE'S A CERTAIN SLANT	258	10
NOT SUBJECT TO [SUPREMER THAN / SUPERIOR TO] DESPAIR--	I GOT SO I COULD HEAR	293	23
THE DIFFERENCE BETWEEN DESPAIR	THE DIFFERENCE BETWEEN	305	1
CASES OF DESPAIR--	DID OUR BEST MOMENT LAST	393	6
NO MAN CAN COMPASS A DESPAIR--	NO MAN CAN COMPASS A	477	1
SUCH SUMPTUOUS--DESPAIR--	I WOULD NOT PAINT--A	505	8
TO JUSTIFY--DESPAIR.	IT WAS NOT DEATH, FOR I	510	24
BUT CONFIDENT [DILIGENT / RESOLUTE] DESPAIR--	HAD I PRESUMED TO HOPE--	522	10
TO QUALIFY DESPAIR	THE PROVINCE OF THE	539	9
A SORT THEY CALL "DESPAIR"--	I MEASURE EVERY GRIEF I	561	30
DESPAIR--	I CANNOT LIVE WITH YOU--	640	50
AND ENTERTAIN DESPAIR--	THE HEAVEN VESTS FOR	694	12
WHAT THOU DOST NOT--DESPAIR--	WHERE THOU ART--THAT--IS	725	13
CONTENTED AS DESPAIR--	ONE BLESSING HAD I THAN	756	8
WERE CHALLENGING DESPAIR.	I LIVED ON DREAD--	770	9
BY SUFFERING--DESPAIR--	DESPAIR'S ADVANTAGE IS	799	2
JUST SAVES IT FROM DESPAIR	SUPERFLUOUS WERE THE SUN	999	6
IS CAPITAL AGAINST DESPAIR--	SOMEWHAT, TO HOPE FOR,	1041	3
[THAT] SURVEYING HIS DESPAIR	HOW MANY SCHEMES MAY DIE	1150	13
SAFE DESPAIR IT IS THAT RAVES--	SAFE DESPAIR IT IS THAT	1243	1
WE MAY [AND WE] INHALE DESPAIR	A WORD DROPPED CARELESS	1261	6
A FITTING--A DESPAIR--	WHILE WE WERE FEARING IT	1277	6
DELIGHT'S DESPAIR AT SETTING	DELIGHT'S DESPAIR AT	1299	1
NOTWITHSTANDING [TO RETAIN] DESPAIR--	NOT ANY MORE TO BE	1344	8
I SHUN IT AS I DO DESPAIR	ONE JOY OF SO MUCH	1420	3
DISPLAYED [UNROLLED] TO THE DESPAIR	HIS MIND LIKE FABRICS OF	1446	2
BUT MAY IT NOT DESPAIR	IT WOULD NOT KNOW IF IT	1579	6
THE PRICES OF DESPAIR	THE AUCTIONEER OF	1612	6
WE ENVY THE DESPAIR	SOFTENED BY TIME'S	1738	6
DESPAIRED			
AND THE DAY THAT I DESPAIRED--	WHEN I HOPED, I	768	17
DESPAIR'S			
DESPAIR'S ADVANTAGE IS ACHIEVED	DESPAIR'S ADVANTAGE IS	799	1
DESPATCH			
OF IT'S CONDENSED DESPATCH	REMORSE--IS MEMORY--	744	V 8
OF A DESPATCH OF PINK.	THE STEM OF A DEPARTED	1520	4
DESPATCHED			
OF ALL THE SOUNDS DESPATCHED ABROAD,	OF ALL THE SOUNDS	321	1
DESPISE			
'TIS MINNOWS CAN [SHOULD] DESPISE!	A BURDOCK--CLAWED MY	229	11
THE BEES--WILL NOT DESPISE THE TUNE--	IT WILL BE SUMMER--	342	11
IF HAPLY--SHE MIGHT NOT DESPISE	PRECIOUS TO ME--SHE	727	7
WE SPEEDILY DESPISE--	THE RIDDLE WE CAN GUESS	1222	2
DESPOILED			
MY SUMMER--IS DESPOILED--	THE WINTERS ARE SO SHORT	403	10
DESPOT			
WHICH IS THE DESPOT, NEITHER KNOWS--	I MAKE HIS CRESCENT FILL	909	11
NO DESPOT BUT THE KING OF DOWN	HOW SOFT THIS PRISON IS	1334	3
DESTINIES			
WE HANDLED DESTINIES, AS COOL--	WE TALKED AS GIRLS DO--	586	5
DESTINY			
THO' MY DESTINY BE FUSTIAN--	THO' MY DESTINY BE	163	1
WORTHY--THE DESTINY--	THE MALAY--TOOK THE	452	6
AND FELT [THOUGHT] "HOW VAST A DESTINY"--	A DEW SUFFICED ITSELF--	1437	3
BY SUPERSEDING DESTINY	THE MOON UPON HER FLUENT	1528	V
IS RATIFIED BY DESTINY,	MEETING BY ACCIDENT,	1548	5
BUT DESTINY IS OLD	MEETING BY ACCIDENT,	1548	6
DESTITUTE			
HOW DESTITUTE IS HE	HOW DESTITUTE IS HE	1477	1
'TIS TRUE THE DROUGHT IS DESTITUTE,	TO LOSE THEE--SWEETER	1754	3
DESTITUTION			
SUCH DESTITUTION THAT	TILL DEATH--IS NARROW	907	6
BUT LEAVES A SUMPTUOUS [BLISSFUL] DESTITUTION--	IN MANY AND REPORTLESS	1382	7
DESTROY			
MIGHT YET [STILL] REPLY [DESTROY].	THE PAST IS SUCH A	1203	8
DETACHMENT			
IN BRIGHT DETACHMENT [DETACHMENTS] STAND!	SOME RAINBOW--COMING	64	21
DETACHMENTS			
IN BRIGHT DETACHMENT [DETACHMENTS] STAND!	SOME RAINBOW--COMING	64	21
DETAIN			
WHY DID'NT WE DETAIN [RETAIN] THEM [IT]?	HOW NOTELESS MEN, AND	282	9
DETAINED			
BECAUSE HE WAS DETAINED	HOW MANY SCHEMES MAY DIE	1150	V 6
BY THESES BE DETAINED [PROFANED]--	THE LILAC IS AN ANCIENT	1241	20
DETAINED VITALITY.	NO MAN SAW AWE, NOR TO	1733	8
DETECT			
THE NORTH CANNOT DETECT	A STILL--VOLCANO--LIFE--	601	8
ONLY GOD--DETECT THE SORROW [POSSESS THE SECRET]--	ONLY GOD--DETECT THE	626	1
AS ONE DETECT ON LANDINGS	A SOUTH WIND--HAS A	719	3
THE OTHER TO DETECT	BECAUSE THAT YOU ARE	1260	10

	FIRST LINE	POEM	LINE
DETECT (CONTINUED)			
ON WHAT IT CANT DETECT.	HOW HUMAN NATURE DOTES	1417	2
DETECTED			
WE START--AS IF DETECTED	AN IGNORANCE A SUNSET	552	11
UNTIL A MIGHT DETECTED ME	I HEARD, AS IF I HAD NO	1039	11
DETECTING			
SMILED TOO BRAVE FOR THE DETECTING [OUR DETECTION]	HAD WE KNOWN THE TON SHE	1124	V 3
DETECTION			
SMILED TOO BRAVE FOR THE DETECTING [OUR DETECTION]	HAD WE KNOWN THE TON SHE	1124	V 3
DETECTS			
HARKS FOR [DETECTS] THE MEADOW BIRD--	THE DOOMED--REGARD THE	294	6
DETENTION			
NOT OF DETENTION IS FRUITION--	WHICH IS THE BEST--THE	1315	5
DETERMINATELY			
ASSIDUOUSLY [DELIBERATELY / DETERMINATELY / IMPERTINENTLY] CRAWLED	ALONE AND IN A	1167	4
DETERMINE			
DETERMINE THEE AMISS--	GO SLOW, MY SOUL, TO	1297	6
DETERRED			
DETERRED BY [FOR CHASTENED / SUBDUED TO] RETROSPECT.	THE LAST OF SUMMER IS	1353	2
DETRIMENT			
OF DETRIMENT DIVINE?	THE FACE IN EVANESCENCE	1490	8
DEVASTATED			
THAT DEVASTATED CHILDHOOD'S REALM,	SOFTENED BY TIME'S	1738	7
DEVASTATES			
AND SHADE IS ALL THAT DEVASTATES THE STILLNESS	THESE FEVERED DAYS--TO	1441	3
DEVELOPE			
DEVELOPE PEARL, AND WEED,	SHE ROSE TO HIS	732	10
DEVELOPED			
ON OUR DEVELOPED EYES	IF PAIN FOR PEACE	63	11
SUFFICIENTLY DEVELOPED--HE'D HIRE US	MYSELF WAS FORMED--A	488	7
DEVELOPED FROM WITHIN--	HER FINAL SUMMER WAS IT	795	6
DEVELOPES			
UNCERTAIN LEASE--DEVELOPES LUSTRE	UNCERTAIN LEASE--	857	1
EXHIBITS [DEVELOPES] SHEETS OF PLACE--	THE SOUL'S DISTINCT	974	6
DEVIL			
THE DEVIL--HAD HE FIDELITY	THE DEVIL--HAD HE	1479	1
THE DEVIL--WITHOUT QUESTION [SO AMENDED--]	THE DEVIL--HAD HE	1479	7
DEVILS			
RUIN IS FORMAL--DEVILS WORK	CRUMBLING IS NOT AN	997	9
BUT DEVILS CANNOT MEND--	THE DEVIL--HAD HE	1479	4
DEVISE			
TO DEVISE ONCE MORE	PROMISE THIS--WHEN YOU	648	10
DEVISED			
WITH DUNGEONS--THEY DEVISED--	THEY PUT US FAR APART--	474	9
DEVISING			
DEVISING, I AM SURE--	SHE LAY AS IF AT PLAY	369	14
DEVOID			
THAT WHAT WE CHERISHED, SO UNKNOWN [VALUED SO DEVOID / HOARDED . . .	SO PROUD SHE WAS TO DIE	1272	3
A FACE DEVOID OF LOVE OR GRACE,	A FACE DEVOID OF LOVE OR	1711	1
DEVOTEE			
A DEVOTEE HAS OFT [COOL / BLAND] CONSIGNED	DEATH WARRANTS ARE	1375	5
DEVOUR			
DID MAKE [PRESUMED] AS TO DEVOUR	THE WIND TOOK UP THE	1134	6
DEVOURED			
WHEN NIGHT DEVOURED THE ROAD--	OF TRIBULATION--THESE	325	14
DEW			
I SPILT THE DEW--	ONE SISTER HAVE I IN OUR	14	23
A FLASK OF DEW--A BEE OR TWO--	A SEPAL, PETAL, AND A	19	3
AND SHE IS OF THE DEW--	IF SHE HAD BEEN THE	44	6
AND SAY HOW MANY DEW,	BRING ME THE SUNSET IN A	128	3
SHE WENT AS QUIET AS THE DEW	SHE WENT AS QUIET AS THE	149	1
NOT LIKE THE DEW, DID SHE RETURN	SHE WENT AS QUIET AS THE	149	3
UNNOTICED AS A SINGLE DEW	EXCEPT TO HEAVEN, SHE IS	154	7
MORNING--IS THE PLACE FOR DEW--	MORNING--IS THE PLACE	197	1
HER CARGO--IS OF DEW--	MY EYE IS FULLER THAN MY	202	2
AND DEBAUCHEE OF DEW--	I TASTE A LIQUOR NEVER	214	6
DOMINIONS--BROAD AS DEW--	WHAT WOULD I GIVE TO SEE	247	17
AND THEN HE DRANK A DEW	A BIRD CAME DOWN THE	328	5
AND SPICES--AND THE DEW--	I KNOW A PLACE WHERE	337	10
AT THE FULL DEW--	I WENT TO HEAVEN--	374	6
A GOBLIN--DRANK MY DEW--	IT WOULD NEVER BE COMMON	430	22
AS WHOLLY AS A DEW	I STARTED EARLY--TOOK MY	520	14
NO DEW UPON THE GRASS--	THE SUN KEPT SETTING--	692	6
AMBER--AMBER--DEW--DEW--	OUT OF SIGHT? WHAT OF	703	9
AMBER--AMBER--DEW--DEW--	OUT OF SIGHT? WHAT OF	703	9
WE WANT THE DEW--THEN--	THE WORLD--FEELS DUSTY	715	3
DOTH OF THE DEW--	ALTER! WHEN THE HILLS DO	729	6
HER EYE UNTO THE SUMMER DEW	THE MOON WAS BUT A CHIN	737	7
AS FROST IS DIFFERENT FROM DEW--	THERE IS AN ARID	782	3
OBTAIN IT'S RIGHT OF DEW--	BLOOM--IS RESULT--TO	1058	10
DEW--IS THE FRESHET IN THE GRASS--	DEW--IS THE FRESHET IN	1097	1
THE LOW GRASS LOADED WITH THE DEW	THE CRICKETS SANG	1104	5
KNOWN ONLY TO THE DEW--	DOMINION LASTS UNTIL	1257	6
OR INUNDATION OF A DEW	GO NOT TOO NEAR A HOUSE	1434	3
A DEW SUFFICED ITSELF--	A DEW SUFFICED ITSELF--	1437	1

	FIRST LINE	POEM	LINE
DEW (CONTINUED)			
AND [BUT] NOT AGAIN THAT DEW BE SEEN	A DEW SUFFICED ITSELF--	1437	7
FOR SUCH A FOE [SWEET / GLEE / DAWN / SCENE / DEW / JOY] AS THIS--	FROM ALL THE JAILS THE	1532	8
CATCH [TRAP / BIND] A DROP OF DEW	FOLLOW WISE ORION	1538	V
WHOSE GARDEN WRESTLES WITH THE DEW,	HOW DARE THE ROBINS SING	1724	15
BUT THEN, I HAD THE DEW!	TO LOSE THEE--SWEETER	1754	4
DEWS			
MAY BE SEEN THE DEWS AMONG,	ANGELS, IN THE EARLY	94	2
AND I MEET, COMING THRO' THE DEWS	A SOMETHING IN A	122	21
THE DEBAUCHEE OF DEWS!	BRING ME THE SUNSET IN A	128	12
AND THREAD THE DEWS, ALL NIGHT, LIKE PEARLS [PEARL]--	THE GRASS SO LITTLE HAS	333	9
LIKE [AS] FLOWERS, THAT HEARD THE NEWS OF DEWS,	LIKE FLOWERS, THAT HEARD	513	1
AND WHEN THE DEWS DREW OFF	I ROSE--BECAUSE HE SANK	616	8
LARGEST [NEWEST / FRESHEST] DEWS OF MORN	PROMISE THIS--WHEN YOU	648	20
THE DEWS DREW QUIVERING AND CHILL--	BECAUSE I COULD NOT STOP	712	14
DEWS OF THESSALY, TO FETCH--	THE WORLD--FEELS DUSTY	715	11
DIADEM			
INTACT--IN DIADEM!	ONE LIFE OF SO MUCH	270	12
ON SUBJECTS DIADEM--	A MIEN TO MOVE A QUEEN--	283	21
DIADEM--OR DUCAL SHOWING [SYMBOL / TOKEN]--	HER--"LAST POEMS"--	312	14
WERE DULL FOR DIADEM--	THE DAY THAT I WAS	356	8
MAKE--A DIADEM--AND MEND MY OLD ONE--	I'LL CLUTCH--AND CLUTCH	427	11
A DIADEM TO FIT A DOME--	'TIS LITTLE I--COULD	466	7
WITH ONE SMALL [JUST ONE] DIADEM.	I'M CEDED--I'VE STOPPED	508	13
A FUTILE DIADEM--	FAME OF MYSELF, TO	713	8
WITHOUT HER DIADEM.	THE SKY IS LOW--THE	1075	8
THEN--MY DIADEM PUT ON.	REARRANGE A "WIFE'S"	1737	16
DIADEMS			
DIADEMS--DROP--AND DOGES--SURRENDER--	SAFE IN THEIR ALABASTER	216	V
THE WANT OF DIADEMS!	THE SUN--JUST TOUCHED	232	12
AND SCARCE OF DIADEMS--	YOUR RICHES--TAUGHT ME--	299	12
AND DIADEMS--A TALE--	WHEN DIAMONDS ARE A	397	2
DIAGNOSIS			
DIAGNOSIS OF THE BIBLE, BY A BOY--	THE BIBLE IS AN ANTIQUE	1545	T
DIAGRAM			
A DIAGRAM--OF RAPTURE!	A TRANSPORT ONE CANNOT	184	5
DIAL			
EARLIER, BY THE DIAL,	I OFTEN PASSED THE	51	7
THE DIAL LIFE--	A CLOCK STOPPED--	287	17
DIALECT			
BUT FOREIGN AS THE DIALECT	REPORTLESS SUBJECTS, TO	1048	3
DIALOGUE			
DEATH IS A DIALOGUE BETWEEN	DEATH IS A DIALOGUE	976	1
DIAMETERS			
OF HIS DIAMETERS--	TIME FEELS SO VAST THAT	802	8
DIAMOND			
A DIAMOND--OVERTAKE	REVERSE CANNOT BEFALL	395	5
JOURNEY OF DOWN--AND WHIP OF DIAMOND--	DROPPED INTO THE ETHER	665	7
FOR DUTIES DIAMOND--	YOU'VE SEEN BALLOONS SET	700	4
AS TONGUES [THRONGS / EYES] OF DIAMOND HAD REVILED	MY SOUL--ACCUSED ME--AND	753	2
A DIAMOND ON THE HAND	A DIAMOND ON THE HAND	1108	1
DID THE DIAMOND GROW	NONE WHO SAW IT EVER	1110	6
DIAMONDS			
I'VE DIAMONDS--ON MY FINGERS--	I CAME TO BUY A SMILE--	223	9
YOU KNOW WHAT DIAMONDS ARE?	I CAME TO BUY A SMILE--	223	10
THEN--DIAMONDS--WHICH THE SNOW	THE ANGLE OF A LANDSCAPE	375	16
WHEN DIAMONDS ARE A LEGEND,	WHEN DIAMONDS ARE A	397	1
THY PAY--IN DIAMONDS--BE--	A TONGUE--TO TELL HIM I	400	18
DIAMONDS--WAIT--	I'LL CLUTCH--AND CLUTCH	427	4
AND DIAMONDS--JUMBLED ON--	I KNOW WHERE WELLS GROW	460	8
OR DIAMONDS--WHEN HAVE I	'TIS LITTLE I--COULD	466	6
DICE			
TOSS THEIR DICE AGAIN!	WE LOSE--BECAUSE WE WIN	21	3
DICE--TO THE MAID--	"MORNING"--MEANS	300	3
A DICE--A DOUBT--	THESE TESTED OUR HORIZON	886	8
DIE			
FOR SUCH AS THEE TO DIE!	NOBODY KNOWS THIS LITTLE	35	12
COULD DIE--DID DIE--	COULD LIVE--DID LIVE--	43	2
COULD DIE--DID DIE--	COULD LIVE--DID LIVE--	43	2
SHOULD HAVE THE FACE TO DIE.	I HAV'NT TOLD MY GARDEN	50	8
IF I SHOULD DIE,	IF I SHOULD DIE,	54	1
AND CLAIM THE RANK TO DIE!	ONE DIGNITY DELAYS FOR	98	16
PEACOCK PRESUMES TO DIE!	IF THIS IS "FADING"	120	9
'TWERE EASIER TO DIE--	THE MURMUR OF A BEE	155	4
TO DIE OF THIRST--SUSPECTING	TO LEARN THE TRANSPORT	167	3
WE MEN AND WOMEN DIE!	IT'S SUCH A LITTLE THING	189	4
WE MUST DIE--BY AND BY--	WE DONT CRY--TIM AND I,	196	21
BECAUSE--BECAUSE IF HE SHOULD DIE	I SHOULD NOT DARE TO	205	2
OR DO WHAT THE NURSE CALLS "DIE"--	WHAT IS--"PARADISE"--	215	14
NEXT SUN--TO DIE--	SHOULD YOU BUT FAIL AT--	226	4
LAYING HER [IT'S] SPOTTED FACE TO DIE	BLAZING IN GOLD AND	228	4
TO GAIN HIS GRACE--I'D DIE!	THE COURT IS FAR AWAY--	235	4
TO DIE--TAKES JUST A LITTLE WHILE--	TO DIE--TAKES JUST A	255	1
THE MAN--TO DIE--TOMORROW--	THE DOOMED--REGARD THE	294	5
I REASON, WE COULD [SHOULD] DIE--	I REASON, EARTH IS SHORT	301	5
WHEN THEY DO NOT DIE--	NATURE--SOMETIMES SEARS	314	4

		FIRST LINE	POEM	LINE
DIE	(CONTINUED)			
	DIE OFTENER--NOT SO VITALLY--	NATURE--SOMETIMES SEARS	314	8
	AND EVEN WHEN IT DIES [DIE]--TO PASS	THE GRASS SO LITTLE HAS	333	13
	I--SHOULD DIE OF THE ODDITY--	FUNNY--TO BE A CENTURY--	345	3
	AND--WHEN I DIE--	I'LL CLUTCH--AND CLUTCH	427	20
	I THINK THE MEN WHO DIE--	IT FEELS A SHAME TO BE	444	18
	SMILE--AND ALTER--AND PRATTLE--AND DIE--	LOVE--THOU ART HIGH--	453	15
	INTERRUPT--TO DIE--	SWEET--SAFE--HOUSES--	457	17
	WHEN CERTAIN IT MUST DIE--	THE MANNER OF IT'S DEATH	468	2
	THEY SUMMONED US TO DIE--	THEY PUT US FAR APART--	474	13
	WHERE SQUIRRELS PLAY--AND BERRIES DIE--	DOOM IS THE HOUSE	475	7
	JUST LOCKING UP--TO DIE.	SHE DEALT HER PRETTY	479	12
	HOW NOTELESS--I COULD DIE--	I WAS THE SLIGHTEST IN	486	17
	RELATE--WHEN NEIGHBORS DIE--	WE PRAY--TO HEAVEN--	489	3
	'TIS HONOR--THOUGH I DIE--	HAD I PRESUMED TO HOPE--	522	13
	WHAT HARM? MEN DIE--EXTERNALLY--	WE DREAM--IT IS GOOD WE	531	5
	THE PRIVILEGE [LIBERTY / LUXURY] TO DIE--	THE HEART ASKS PLEASURE	536	8
	THEY PERISH [STAGGER]--DO WE DIE--	I CROSS TILL I AM WEARY	550	23
	IT WOULD NOT BE--TO DIE--	I MEASURE EVERY GRIEF I	561	12
	I COULD [WOULD] DIE--TO KNOW--	I COULD DIE--TO KNOW--	570	1
	TO FADE [DIE]--TOMORROW--RAINBOWS HELD [THRUST]	MY FIRST WELL DAY--SINCE	574	15
	A TOAD, CAN DIE OF LIGHT--	A TOAD, CAN DIE OF LIGHT	583	1
	THE QUESTION OF "TO DIE"--	DID YOU EVER STAND IN A	590	12
	FOR THINKING--WHILE I DIE--	THREE TIMES--WE PARTED--	598	10
	YOU'LL FIND--IT WHEN YOU TRY TO DIE--	YOU'LL FIND--IT WHEN YOU	610	1
	WAS IT A PLEASANT DAY TO DIE--	TO KNOW JUST HOW HE	622	7
	CONTENTEDER--TO DIE--	MY PORTION IS DEFEAT--	639	19
	I COULD NOT DIE--WITH YOU--	I CANNOT LIVE WITH YOU--	640	13
	ANSWERED WOLFE [HE] "TO DIE"	WOLFE DEMANDED DURING	678	4
	BUT JUST ANEW TO DIE--	SUSPENSE--IS HOSTILER	705	6
	'TWOULD LOOK TOO FAR--TO DIE--	I SOMETIMES DROP IT, FOR	708	8
	WHEN WE STOP TO DIE--	THE WORLD--FEELS DUSTY	715	2
	AND LATER--WHEN WE DIE--	WE THIRST AT FIRST--'TIS	726	2
	WITHOUT--THE POWER TO DIE--	MY LIFE HAD STOOD--A	754	24
	OF GREEDINESS [URGENCY / VEHEMENCE] TO DIE--	HE FOUGHT LIKE THOSE	759	12
	'TIS LIFE'S AWARD--TO DIE--	THE WHOLE OF IT CAME NOT	762	9
	ALTERNATIVE TO DIE	SEVERER SERVICE OF	786	22
	UNABLE ARE THE LOVED TO DIE	UNABLE ARE THE LOVED TO	809	1
	UNABLE THEY THAT LOVE [ARE THE LOVED]--TO DIE	UNABLE ARE THE LOVED TO	809	4
	THY LITTLE PLAN TO DIE--	'TIS SUNRISE--LITTLE	908	12
	OFTEN AS I DIE	STRUCK, WAS I, NOR YET	925	18
	TO DIE--OR LIVE--	WERT THOU BUT ILL--THAT	961	18
	NOT ALL DIE EARLY, DYING YOUNG--	NOT ALL DIE EARLY, DYING	990	1
	TOO SCANTY 'TWAS TO DIE FOR YOU,	TOO SCANTY 'TWAS TO DIE	1013	1
	TO DIE--WITHOUT THE DYING	TO DIE--WITHOUT THE	1017	1
	THE TRANQUILLER TO DIE--	THAT SUCH HAVE DIED	1030	2
	WHEN BEST MEN DIE.	A SICKNESS OF THIS WORLD	1044	2
	FAME'S BOYS AND GIRLS, WHO NEVER DIE	FAME'S BOYS AND GIRLS,	1066	1
	WHO WOULD EXULT TO DIE	SOME WRETCHED CREATURE,	1111	2
	THE SMALL MUST [DO] DIE, THE SAME [AS WELL] AS HE--	THAT THIS SHOULD FEEL	1112	6
	THAT MANY DIE WITHOUT--	THERE IS ANOTHER	1116	2
	DO HE EXIST, OR DIE,	THE DUTIES OF THE WIND	1137	14
	HOW MANY SCHEMES MAY DIE	HOW MANY SCHEMES MAY DIE	1150	1
	OR WAS OBLIGED TO DIE	SOME DAYS RETIRED FROM	1157	4
	ARE THOSE A FUNCTION DIE	THE DAYS THAT WE CAN	1184	2
	BOLD IT WERE TO DIE	WE LIKE MARCH.	1213	11
	SO PROUD [PLEASED / FAIN] SHE WAS TO DIE	SO PROUD SHE WAS TO DIE	1272	1
	TO DIE IS NOT TO GO--	TWO LENGTHS HAS EVERY	1295	9
	IN INANITION DIE	"WAS NOT" WAS ALL THE	1342	6
	TO DIE DIVINELY ONCE A TWILIGHT--[AN EVENING / A LIMIT]	I'D RATHER RECOLLECT A	1349	7
	TO DIE--WAS LITTLE FATE--	TO HIS SIMPLICITY	1352	2
	EXCEPT TO THOSE WHO DIE--	SUMMER HAS TWO	1422	12
	AND VOCAL--WHEN WE DIE--	A COUNTERFEIT--A PLATED	1453	7
	NOR WHEN--WE ARE TO DIE--	WE KNEW NOT THAT WE WERE	1462	2
	IT'S OCCUPANT MUST DIE	FAME IS THE ONE THAT	1475	2
	THE BRAVEST DIE	FACTS BY OUR SIDE ARE	1497	11
	HAVE FELT [THOUGHT] IT MEET TO DIE--	HIS ORIENTAL HERESIES	1526	8
	BETAKES HIMSELF TO DIE.	HIS ORIENTAL HERESIES	1526 V	8
	WE WEAR OUR SOBER DRESSES WHEN WE DIE,	WE WEAR OUR SOBER	1572	1
	THIS ME--THAT WALKS AND WORKS--MUST DIE,	THIS ME--THAT WALKS AND	1588	1
	HAS NOT THE POWER TO DIE	A WORD MADE FLESH IS	1651	10
	BEAUTY CROWDS ME TILL I DIE	BEAUTY CROWDS ME TILL I	1654	1
	MEN EAT OF IT AND DIE	FAME IS A FICKLE FOOD	1659	10
	YOU CANNOT EVEN DIE	THE RIGHT TO PERISH	1692	6
	AND THIS OF OURS MUST DIE	T'WAS COMFORT IN HER	1703	9
DIED				
	SHE DIED AT PLAY,	SHE DIED AT PLAY,	75	1
	SHE DIED--THIS WAS THE WAY SHE DIED.	SHE DIED--THIS WAS THE	150	1
	SHE DIED--THIS WAS THE WAY SHE DIED.	SHE DIED--THIS WAS THE	150	1
	OR WHO DIED--YESTERDAY!	WHAT IF I SAY I SHALL	277	12
	REMIND US THAT WE DIED.	REHEARSAL TO OURSELVES	379	8
	THEY WONDER IF IT DIED--ON THAT--	THERE'S BEEN A DEATH, IN	389	11
	THE REAL ONE DIED FOR THEE--	'TWAS LOVE--NOT ME--	394	3
	DULL HEARTS HAVE DIED	KNOWS HOW TO FORGET!	433 V	
	'TWAS JUST THIS TIME, LAST YEAR, I DIED.	'TWAS JUST THIS TIME,	445	1
	I DIED FOR BEAUTY--BUT WAS SCARCE	I DIED FOR BEAUTY--BUT	449	1
	WHEN ONE WHO DIED FOR TRUTH, WAS LAIN	I DIED FOR BEAUTY--BUT	449	3

	FIRST LINE	POEM		LINE
DIED (CONTINUED)				
I HEARD A FLY BUZZ--WHEN I DIED--	I HEARD A FLY BUZZ--WHEN	465		1
'TWAS NOT HIS BLAME--WHO DIED	A DYING TIGER--MOANED	566		10
WHEN I WAS SMALL, A WOMAN DIED--	WHEN I WAS SMALL, A	596		1
WHO TILL THEY DIED, DID NOT ALIVE BECOME--	A DEATH BLOW IS A LIFE	816		2
WHO HAD THEY LIVED, HAD DIED BUT WHEN	A DEATH BLOW IS A LIFE	816		3
THEY DIED, VITALITY BEGUN.	A DEATH BLOW IS A LIFE	816		4
DENYING [DISPUTING] THAT THEY DIED.	ON THAT DEAR FRAME THE	940		8
MIDSUMMER, WAS IT, WHEN THEY DIED--	MIDSUMMER, WAS IT, WHEN	962		1
THE DAY THE HEAVEN DIED--	DENIAL--IS THE ONLY FACT	965		4
NOT PERIOD--THAT DIED.	NOT ALL DIE EARLY, DYING	990		8
THOSE THAT DIED.	WE'LL PASS WITHOUT THE	996		8
THAT SUCH HAVE DIED ENABLE US	THAT SUCH HAVE DIED	1030		1
BUT DID BECAUSE [VASTER THAT] THEY DIED	I NOTICED PEOPLE	1149		7
TO ONE THAT NEVER DIED--	WHO WERE "THE FATHER AND	1258	V	6
OF WHICH IT DIED--	NOT WITH A CLUB, THE	1304		12
I NEVER HEAR THAT ONE IS DEAD [HAS DIED]	I NEVER HEAR THAT ONE IS	1323		1
ENOUGH WILL NOT BE FOUND WHEN ALL HAVE DIED.	ABOVE OBLIVION'S TIDE	1531		7
ALL THE REST, HAVE DIED--	MY WARS ARE LAID AWAY IN	1549		8
WHETHER SHE DIED BEFORE SHE HEARD	I WATCHED HER FACE TO	1667		3
DIEMAN'S				
INTO VAN DIEMAN'S LAND.	IF YOU WERE COMING IN	511		12
DIES				
BECAUSE IT DIES!	MY FRIEND MUST BE A BIRD	92		4
THAT DIES AWAY IN DIMPLES	THE ONLY GHOST I EVER	274		11
AND EVEN WHEN IT DIES [DIE]--TO PASS	THE GRASS SO LITTLE HAS	333		13
WHO DIES--AND TO HIS FRIEND--	DEATH IS POTENTIAL TO	548		2
THE BEGGAR LAD--DIES EARLY--	THE BEGGAR LAD--DIES	717		1
MAY EACH THAT DIES--	AN HONEST TEAR	1192		4
SAHARA [CONTENTMENT / CREATION / HIS STATUS] DIES	UNTIL THE DESERT KNOWS	1291		6
DIFFER				
AND THEY WILL DIFFER--IF THEY DO--	THE BRAIN--IS WIDER THAN	632		11
SO DIFFER LIFE AND DEATH	AS PLAN FOR NOON AND	960		2
OR DIFFER, IF THEY DO,	THE OPENING AND THE	1047		3
DIFFERED				
BUT DIFFERED IN RETURNING--	ALL OVERGROWN BY CUNNING	148		9
DIFFERENCE				
A DIFFERENCE--A DAISY--	WENT UP A YEAR THIS	93		23
BUT INTERNAL DIFFERENCE,	THERE'S A CERTAIN SLANT	258		7
THE DIFFERENCE BETWEEN DESPAIR	THE DIFFERENCE BETWEEN	305		1
DIFFERENCE--HAD BEGUN--	IT WOULD NEVER BE COMMON	430		2
THE DIFFERENCE--MADE ME BOLD--	IT WAS GIVEN TO ME BY	454		16
IT MAKES NO DIFFERENCE ABROAD--	IT MAKES NO DIFFERENCE	620		1
NO NUMB ALARM--LEST DIFFERENCE COME--	I THINK TO LIVE--MAY BE	646		13
WHAT DIFFERENCE, AFTER ALL, THOU MAK'ST	THE SUNSET STOPPED ON	950		7
YET [BUT] A DRUIDIC DIFFERENCE	FURTHER IN SUMMER THAN	1068		15
NOR DIFFERENCE IT KNOWS	FURTHER IN SUMMER THAN	1068	V	
THE DIFFERENCE IS AS BIG	BETWEEN THE FORM OF LIFE	1101		2
THE DIFFERENCE OF DAY	OH SUMPTUOUS MOMENT	1125		7
WHAT DIFFERENCE IN SUBSTANCE LIES	THE VOICE THAT STANDS	1189		5
WHAT DIFFERENCE IS ON HER FACE	BECAUSE HE LOVES HER	1229		3
DIFFERENT				
IT WAS A DIFFERENT TUNE--	ONE SISTER HAVE I IN OUR	14		10
UNTO THE DIFFERENT DAWN!	THERE IS A MORN BY MEN	24		24
INHALES THE DIFFERENT DAWN.	A DARTING FEAR--A POMP--	87		4
FOR HEAVEN IS A DIFFERENT THING,	'TIS SO MUCH JOY! 'TIS	172		16
WITH DIFFERENT DELIGHT--	THE DOOMED--REGARD THE	294		2
A DIFFERENT PERU--	YOUR RICHES--TAUGHT ME--	299		6
BUT THIS, MUST BE A DIFFERENT WEALTH--	YOUR RICHES--TAUGHT ME--	299		15
BUT DYING--IS A DIFFERENT WAY--	'TIS NOT THAT DYING	335		3
THIS--WAS DIFFERENT--'TWAS TRANSLATION--	BETTER--THAN MUSIC! FOR	503		3
AND NOW, I'M DIFFERENT FROM BEFORE,	HE TOUCHED ME, SO I LIVE	506		7
"HEAVEN" HAS DIFFERENT SIGNS--TO ME--	"HEAVEN" HAS DIFFERENT	575		1
LIFE--IS A DIFFERENT [ANOTHER] THING--	A TOAD, CAN DIE OF LIGHT	583		8
WAS DYING AS HE THOUGHT--OR DIFFERENT--	TO KNOW JUST HOW HE	622		6
'TIS NOT A DIFFERENT TIME--	FOREVER--IS COMPOSED OF	624		2
NO DIFFERENT [AS INFINITE] OUR YEARS WOULD BE	FOREVER--IS COMPOSED OF	624		11
'TIS TRUE--OUR FUTURES DIFFERENT LAY--	OURSELVES WERE WED ONE	631		9
HOW DIFFERENT VICTORY	MY PORTION IS DEFEAT--	639		16
NO DIFFERENT THE BIRDS--	OF BEING IS A BIRD	653		8
AND VASTER [THIS ONE / DIFFERENT]--OF THE WORLD'S.	THAT FIRST DAY, WHEN YOU	659		8
SOMEWHAT DIFFERENT--MUST BE--	LET US PLAY YESTERDAY--	728		9
AS DIFFERENT FROM JOY--	THERE IS AN ARID	782		2
AS FROST IS DIFFERENT FROM DEW--	THERE IS AN ARID	782		3
MADE NATURE DIFFERENT	THE LAST NIGHT THAT SHE	1100		4
BECAUSE THAT DEATH IS FINAL [TREASON / DIFFERENT],	BECAUSE THAT YOU ARE	1260		5
DIFFERENT IS HE--	WHEN A LOVER IS A BEGGAR	1314		4
IS DIFFERENT FROM ANOTHER ALMS	IT CAME HIS TURN TO BEG	1500		3
HOW DIFFERENT WE ARE!	HIGH FROM THE EARTH I	1723		20
RETURNING IS A DIFFERENT ROUTE	NO MAN SAW AWE, NOR TO	1733		9
DIFFERENTLY				
HAD GOD WILLED DIFFERENTLY.	I CRIED AT PITY--NOT AT	588		16
DIFFICULT				
AND "DIFFICULT THE GATE"--	YOU'RE RIGHT--"THE WAY	234		2
MAKES WORK DIFFICULT--THEN--	IT IS EASY TO WORK WHEN	244		4
IS DIFFICULT, AND STILL--	TO MAKE ONE'S TOILETTE--	485		4
IT IS TOO DIFFICULT A GRACE--	I RECKON--WHEN I COUNT	569		15

	FIRST LINE	POEM	LINE
DIFFICULT (CONTINUED)			
AS DIFFICULT [CLARIFIED]	MUST BE A WO--	571	7
MORE ARDUOUS [DIFFICULT] THAN BALLS--	MY PORTION IS DEFEAT--	639	6
EACH--IT'S DIFFICULT [ABSOLUTE] IDEAL	GROWTH OF MAN--LIKE	750	5
WE--DIFFICULT--ACQUIRE	AWAY FROM HOME ARE SOME	821	6
KEEPS MAKING NOVEMBER DIFFICULT	HOW HAPPY I WAS IF I	898	5
DRIFTS WERE AS DIFFICULT THEN TO THINK	THIS WAS IN THE WHITE OF	995	3
IS DIFFICULT TO GAIN	SUPERIORITY TO FATE	1081	2
BUT TAKE AWAY AS DIFFICULT [IMPOTENT / EASILY]	YOU CANNOT TAKE ITSELF	1351	7
DIFFIDENT			
BY INNOCENT [ELOQUENT / HALLOWED / HEAVENLY / DIFFIDENT] SURPRISE--	THE PRETTY RAIN FROM	1426	4
DIFFUSES			
A DROWSINESS--DIFFUSES--	THERE IS A LANGUOR OF	396	5
DIGGERS			
NEVER SLACKED THE DIGGERS--	IN FALLING TIMBERS	614	9
DIGNIFIED			
WHAT DIGNIFIED ATTENDANTS!	ONE DIGNITY DELAYS FOR	98	9
DIGNITY			
ONE DIGNITY DELAYS FOR ALL--	ONE DIGNITY DELAYS FOR	98	1
DIKES			
AND IT SHOULD LIFT IT'S PURPLE DIKES,	AS IF I ASKED A COMMON	323	7
DILAPIDATIONS SEE DELAPIDATIONS			
DILEMMA			
THAT NEW DILEMMA BE	IF I COULD TELL HOW GLAD	1668	6
DILIGENCE			
TILL DUSK OBSTRUCTS THE DILIGENCE--	SHE SWEEPS WITH	219	V 11
UNTO THE SAINTS' SLOW DILIGENCE [INDUSTRY]--	EACH LIFE CONVERGES TO	680	15
THERE IS NO DILIGENCE LIKE THAT	THE SERVICE WITHOUT HOPE	779	7
BUT DILIGENCE--IS SHARPER--	HAD I NOT THIS, OR THIS,	904	13
THE DILIGENCE WERE NOT MORE BLIND	WHAT TWIGS WE HELD BY--	1086	13
DILIGENT			
THE ANGELS--LABORED DILIGENT--	GOOD NIGHT! WHICH PUT	259	5
BUT CONFIDENT [DILIGENT / RESOLUTE] DESPAIR--	HAD I PRESUMED TO HOPE--	522	10
DILUTE			
'TIS FICTION'S--TO DILUTE [CONTRACT] TO PLAUSIBILITY [CREDIBILITY]	NO ROMANCE SOLD UNTO	669	5
DIM			
DIM--AS THE BORDER STAR--	TAKEN FROM MEN--THIS	53	10
HOW DIM IT SOUNDS!	GOING TO HEAVEN!	79	7
DIM--LONG EXPECTANT EYES,	MY NOSEGAYS ARE FOR	95	2
BUT IT'S MANY A LAY OF THE DIM BURGUNDY--	WE--BEE AND I--LIVE BY	230	4
BUT IT'S DIM CHAT OF THINGS BURGUND, WE KNOW--	WE--BEE AND I--LIVE BY	230	V 4
MINE--GET SO DIM!	YOU SEE I CANNOT SEE--	253	7
DOUBT ME! MY DIM [FAINT] COMPANION!	DOUBT ME! MY DIM	275	1
TOO RESCUED--FEAR TOO DIM TO ME	I SHOULD HAVE BEEN TOO	313	8
IN THOSE DIM COUNTRIES WHERE THEY GO,	I DREADED THAT FIRST	348	19
COULD BEHOLD [REGARD] SO FAR [SMALL / DIM / SCARCE] A CREATURE--	PROMISE THIS--WHEN YOU	648	27
MANACLES BE DIM--THEY SAY--	LET US PLAY YESTERDAY--	728	17
MADONNA DIM, TO WHOM ALL FEET MAY COME,	ONLY A SHRINE, BUT MINE	918	3
A DIM CAPACITY FOR WINGS	MY COCOON TIGHTENS--	1099	3
THE [DIM / FAR] ABSENCE OF THE WITCH DOES NOT [CANNOT]	LONG YEARS APART--CAN	1383	3
AND DIM APPROACH	DEATH IS THE SUPPLE	1445	6
WAS DIM AS TO THE WEALTHY	IT STOLE ALONG SO	1457	3
DIMENSIONS			
REMEMBERING THE DIMENSIONS	OUR OWN POSSESSIONS--	1208	3
DIMINISHED			
IN IT'S DIMINISHED PLANE.	A COFFIN--IS A SMALL	943	4
DIMINUET			
WITHOUT DIMINUET PROCEED!	OH WHAT A GRACE IS THIS,	1615	5
DIMINUTION			
IT KNEW NO LAPSE, NOR DIMINUTION--	IT KNEW NO LAPSE, NOR	560	1
BY DIMINUTION IT WAS NOT	I KNEW THAT I HAD GAINED	1022	3
DIMITIES			
HER DIMITIES--AS OLD	THE DAY UNDRESSED--	716	4
HER DIMITIES--OF BLUE--	THE MOON WAS BUT A CHIN	737	20
DIMITY			
SUCH DIMITY CONVICTIONS--	WHAT SOFT--CHERUBIC	401	5
DIMLY			
COULD DIMLY RECOLLECT A GRACE [FORCE]--	I GOT SO I COULD HEAR	293	13
EDEN--A LEGEND--DIMLY TOLD [LEARNED / CROONED]--	BETTER--THAN MUSIC! FOR	503	14
OR ARCTIC CREATURES, DIMLY STIRRED--	LIKE FLOWERS, THAT HEARD	513	7
DIMMER			
HOW DIMMER THAN A SATURN'S BAR	WHAT TWIGS WE HELD BY--	1086	16
'TIS DIMMER THAN A LACE--	'TIS WHITER THAN AN	1482	2
DIMNESS			
A DIMNESS LIKE A FOG	THERE IS A LANGUOR OF	396	6
WHEN DIMNESS--LOOKS THE ODDITY--	OF NEARNESS TO HER	607	3
DIMPLE			
A DIMPLE AT A TIME--	IT KNEW NO MEDICINE--	559	6
A DIMPLE IN THE TOMB	A DIMPLE IN THE TOMB	1489	1
DIMPLED			
A DIMPLED [FLORID / DAPPLED] ROAD	THE ROAD TO PARADISE IS	1491	5
'TIS SEASONS SINCE THE DIMPLED WAR	'TIS SEASONS SINCE THE	1529	1
DIMPLES			
THAT DIES AWAY IN DIMPLES	THE ONLY GHOST I EVER	274	11
AND GET THE DIMPLES READY--	WHEN NIGHT IS ALMOST	347	5

	FIRST LINE	POEM	LINE
DIMPLES (CONTINUED)			
I PUSHED MY DIMPLES BY, AND WAITED--	I FELT MY LIFE WITH BOTH	351	10
AND SHOWED THEIR DIMPLES--TOO--	I MEANT TO HAVE BUT	476	16
THE DIMPLES RAN ALONG--	HER SMILE WAS SHAPED	514	2
THESE--HELD DIMPLES--	THESE--SAW VISIONS--	758	3
DIN			
OR WHETHER IT BE NONE [DIN]	TO HEAR AN ORIOLE SING	526	11
DINE			
MY NOON HAD COME--TO DINE--	I HAD BEEN HUNGRY, ALL	579	2
TO LIVE [DINE] SO SMALL AS I--	IT WOULD HAVE STARVED A	612	2
UNLESS [EXCEPT] WE DINE ON TIPTOE--	VICTORY COMES LATE--	690	9
WHO GOES TO DINE MUST TAKE HIS FEAST	WHO GOES TO DINE MUST	1223	1
AND DINE [GROW] WITHOUT LIKE GOD--	ART THOU THE THING I	1282	8
DINES			
TO SEE IT FLASHING WHEN HE DINES	A SAUCER HOLDS A CUP	1374	11
DINGLE			
FOR WHOM I ROBBED THE DINGLE--	SO BASHFUL WHEN I SPIED	91	9
DINGY			
HE DANCED ALONG THE DINGY DAYS	HE ATE AND DRANK THE	1587	5
DINING			
IN NATURE'S--DINING ROOM--	I HAD BEEN HUNGRY, ALL	579	12
HIS DINING ROOM DO [DOTH] SWING,	A SAUCER HOLDS A CUP	1374	8
DINNER			
AFTER DINNER LIGHT--FOR FLOWERS--	MORNING--IS THE PLACE	197	3
AND SEEK [GAIN] A DINNER FOR MYSELF--	IT WOULD HAVE STARVED A	612	11
A DINNER FOR A BEE	A FULL FED ROSE ON MEALS	1154	2
DIP			
DIP--AND VANISH LIKE ORIOLES!	THIS--IS THE LAND--THE	266	9
BEYOND THE DIP OF BELL--	I SAW NO WAY--THE	378	8
AND DIP [MIX] YOUR FINGERS IN THE FROST--	IF ANYBODY'S FRIEND BE	509	15
WHOSE MEMORY DROWNS ME, LIKE THE DIP	I LEARNED--AT LEAST--	944	7
DIPPED			
DIPPED MY BEAK IN IT,	SANG FROM THE HEART,	1059	2
DIPPING			
THE MOTIONS OF THE DIPPING BIRDS--	BEFORE I GOT MY EYE PUT	327	14
DIPS			
DIPS--EVADES--TEAZES--DEPLOYS--	THE NEAREST DREAM	319	6
BEHIND ME--DIPS ETERNITY--	BEHIND ME--DIPS ETERNITY	721	1
INTO THE DARKNESS [TWILIGHT / EVENING] DIPS AWAY--	FAIRER THROUGH FADING--	938	2
DIRECT			
AND INTACT [DIRECT / DISTINCT] BELIEF--	GROWTH OF MAN--LIKE	750	12
AND MET THE GAZE--DIRECT--	NO NOTICE GAVE SHE, BUT	804	12
DIRECTION			
BY THE DIRECTION OF HALLOWED SPECTRES--	THE BIBLE IS AN ANTIQUE	1545	V 3
DIRECTLY			
DIRECTLY IN THE FOREHEAD--	WE GROW ACCUSTOMED TO	419	15
DIRECTLY IN HIS EYE--	TO INTERRUPT HIS YELLOW	591	6
WAS DISTINCTLY [DIRECTLY] TOLD--	ABRAHAM TO KILL HIM	1317	2
THE EVENT WAS DIRECTLY BEHIND HIM	THE EVENT WAS DIRECTLY	1686	1
DIRGE			
UNTO ITSELF A DIRGE	HIS LITTLE HEARSE LIKE	1522	2
DIRK			
WE WILL NOT DROP THE DIRK--	REHEARSAL TO OURSELVES	379	5
THE DIRK COMMEMORATE--ITSELF	REHEARSAL TO OURSELVES	379	7
DIRKS			
WITH DIRKS OF MELODY	ONE JOY OF SO MUCH	1420	8
DIRT			
UNDER THE GRASS AND THE DIRT,	UNDER THE LIGHT, YET	949	2
DIRTY			
THIS DIRTY--LITTLE--HEART	THIS DIRTY--LITTLE--	1311	1
DISAPPEAR			
PLUCK UP IT'S STAKES, AND DISAPPEAR--	I'VE KNOWN A HEAVEN,	243	3
COME, AND DISAPPEAR--	BLOOM UPON THE MOUNTAIN	667	10
TO DISAPPEAR ENHANCES--	TO DISAPPEAR ENHANCES--	1209	1
DISAPPEARED			
THEN DISAPPEARED	THESE TESTED OUR HORIZON	886	2
TO FIND THE SPECIES DISAPPEARED--	IT BLOOMED AND DROPT, A	978	7
I NOTICED PEOPLE DISAPPEARED	I NOTICED PEOPLE	1149	1
MY STRANGER DISAPPEARED	CONFERRING WITH MYSELF	1655	2
THE ONES THAT DISAPPEARED ARE BACK	THE ONES THAT	1690	1
DISAPPEARS			
THAT BOWS--AND DISAPPEARS--	WHOLE GULFS--OF RED, AND	658	8
THAT DISAPPEARS AS COMES--	FAME IS THE TINT THAT	866	4
DISAPPOINT			
IF I SHOULD DISAPPOINT THE EYES	I SHOULD NOT DARE TO	205	5
THE WEALTH MIGHT DISAPPOINT--	I GAVE MYSELF TO HIM--	580	5
GREAT NATURE NOT TO DISAPPOINT	BLOOM--IS RESULT--TO	1058	13
DISAPPOINTED			
I HEARD RECEDE THE DISAPPOINTED TIDE!	JUST LOST, WHEN I WAS	160	6
SWEEP BY OUR DISAPPOINTED HEADS	HOW NOTELESS MEN, AND	282	11
DISAPPOINTING			
THAN FROM A DISAPPOINTING GOD	THERE COMES AN HOUR WHEN	1751	5
DISAPPOINTMENT			
THE SEED OF DISAPPOINTMENT GREW	THIS IS THE PLACE THEY	1264	3
DISAPPROVES			
GREAT BRITAIN DISAPPROVES, "THE STARS";	MY COUNTRY NEED NOT	1511	5
DISARMS			
DISARMS THE LITTLE INTERVAL--	LOVE--IS THAT LATER	924	7

	FIRST LINE	POEM	LINE
DISASTER			
ENABLE IN DISASTER	THE CHEMICAL CONVICTION	954	3
DISAVOWS			
SO DRUNK HE DISAVOWS IT	ONE OF THE ONES THAT	1466	5
DISBAND			
AND WHEN THE HEAVENS--DISBAND--	A TONGUE--TO TELL HIM I	400	26
DISBURSE			
WHY BLISS SO SCANTILY [CAUTIOUSLY] DISBURSE [EXPRESS / AFFORD]--	ONE BLESSING HAD I THAN	756	17
DISC			
SOUNDLESS AS DOTS--ON A DISC OF SNOW--	SAFE IN THEIR ALABASTER	216	V
WHO ONLY SHOWS HIS MARBLE DISC [GRANITE FACE]--	GIVE LITTLE ANGUISH--	310	7
EACH OTHER'S FACE--WAS ALL THE DISC	THEY PUT US FAR APART--	474	23
BUT SINCE WE HOLD A MUTUAL DISC--	I MAKE HIS CRESCENT FILL	909	9
OH FOR A DISC TO THE DISTANCE	UNDER THE LIGHT, YET	949	15
DISCARD			
DISCARD HIS BRIDE--	FORGET! THE LADY WITH	438	11
DISCARDED			
DISCARDED OF THE HOUSEWIFE--	I CANNOT LIVE WITH YOU--	640	9
IT IS AS SWANS--DISCARDED YOU,	YOU'VE SEEN BALLOONS SET	700	3
DISCERN			
COULD NOT DECIDE [DISCERN / CONCLUDE] BETWEEN--	SO GLAD WE ARE--A	329	8
IS GIFTED TO DISCERN	SOME--WORK FOR	406	10
THAT JUST AS WE DISCERN	TO DISAPPEAR ENHANCES--	1209	14
DISCERNED			
DISCERNED--STILL WITHOLDEN	TRUST IN THE UNEXPECTED	555	7
DISCERNIBLE			
DISCERNIBLE TO NOT A FRIEND	CONTAINED IN THIS SHORT	1165	V
DISCERNING			
TO A DISCERNING EYE--	MUCH MADNESS IS DIVINEST	435	2
. . . ACCOMPLISHED / DISCERNING / ACCOUTRED / ESTABLISHED / . . .	HE PREACHED UPON	1207	8
DISCERNS			
THE QUEEN, DISCERNS LIKE ME--	THE ROBIN'S MY CRITERION	285	16
AND AS ITSELF DISCERNS	THE HEART HAS NARROW	928	6
DISCIPLE			
"DISCIPLE, CALL AGAIN."	THERE COMES AN HOUR WHEN	1751	6
DISCIPLINE			
STRANDED, THRO' DISCIPLINE,	I CAN WADE GRIEF--	252	11
THE DISCIPLINE OF MAN--	EXPERIENCE IS THE ANGLED	910	6
WHEN DISCIPLINE [CHIVALRY / TYRANNY] WAS DONE	THE THINGS WE THOUGHT	1293	10
DISCLOSE			
THAT [WHICH] TEETH OF FROSTS ALONE DISCLOSE	THERE ARE TWO RIPENINGS	332	7
WHEN NOT A MOON DISCLOSE A SIGN--	WE GROW ACCUSTOMED TO	419	11
BE BEAUTIFUL AS THEY PREPARE [DISCLOSE]	I RECKON--WHEN I COUNT	569	13
GOD THE SON--CONFIDE [DISCLOSE] IT--	ONLY GOD--DETECT THE	626	5
DISCLOSE AS 'TWERE A TOMB	THIS CHASM, SWEET, UPON	858	6
LET US DISCOURSE [DISCLOSE]--WITH CARE--	A MAN MAY MAKE A REMARK	952	6
ONLY THE CHEMIST CAN DISCLOSE	ASHES DENOTE THAT FIRE	1063	7
OUR PROPS DISCLOSE	WHAT TWIGS WE HELD BY--	1086	9
COULD COUNTENANCE DISCLOSE	IT'S HOUR WITH ITSELF	1225	4
DID I DISCLOSE	ON MY VOLCANO GROWS THE	1677	7
IF IMMORTALITY UNVEIL [DISCLOSE]	MY LIFE CLOSED TWICE	1732	3
DISCLOSED			
WHEN BLISS DISCLOSED A HUNDRED TOES [WINGS]--	SHE SIGHTS A BIRD--SHE	507	11
INDEFINITE DISCLOSED--	FROM BLANK TO BLANK--	761	8
AN INSTANT'S WIDTH OF WARMTH DISCLOSED--	A DOOR JUST OPENED ON A	953	3
IS BEST DISCLOSED BY DANGER	THE SOUL'S DISTINCT	974	3
OF MANSIONS NEVER QUITE DISCLOSED	THE LIGHTNING IS A	1173	5
DISCLOSED [DISPLAYED] TO BE DENIED	THE BEGGAR AT THE DOOR	1240	4
BE ONCE DISCLOSED TO US	COULD THAT SWEET	1493	2
DISCLOSER			
OF PICTURES, THE DISCLOSER--	THIS WAS A POET--IT IS	448	9
DISCLOSES			
DISCLOSES JUST A HUE--	I'VE KNOWN A HEAVEN,	243	15
DISCLOSING			
WITHOUT DISCLOSING WHAT IT BE	I'VE SEEN A DYING EYE	547	7
FAR AS SOUTH AND WEST--EXPANDING [DISCLOSING]--	BLOOM UPON THE MOUNTAIN	667	15
DISCLOSURE			
ETERNITY'S DISCLOSURE	THE SOUL'S SUPERIOR	306	13
DISCOMFIT			
AND THE SURRENDER [DISCOMFIT]--MINE--	I MEANT TO FIND HER WHEN	718	4
DISCONTENT			
AND LEAVE IT WITH A DISCONTENT	THE TINT I CANNOT TAKE--	627	11
DISCORD			
EACH LITTLE DISCORD HERE	I HAVE A BIRD IN SPRING	5	23
DISCOUNT			
WITH BUT THE "DISCOUNT" OF THE GRAVE--	YOU'RE RIGHT--"THE WAY	234	7
DISCOURAGE			
WHICH UTTERED, WOULD DISCOURAGE NATURE	THERE IS NO SILENCE IN	1004	3
DISCOURAGED			
AND I AFFRONTED [DISCOURAGED] GREW	MY HEART RAN SO TO THEE	1237	3
DISCOURAGEMENT			
IF A DISCOURAGEMENT WITHOLD ME--	UP LIFE'S HILL WITH MY	1010	3
DISCOURSE			
DISCOURSE BETWEEN THE TOIL--	I'M SORRY FOR THE DEAD--	529	6
LET US DISCOURSE [DISCLOSE]--WITH CARE--	A MAN MAY MAKE A REMARK	952	6

	FIRST LINE	POEM	LINE
DISCOURSE (CONTINUED)			
TO DISCOURSE ALONE--	THREE WEEKS PASSED SINCE	1061	6
DISCOVER			
WHEN A FRACTURE--WE DISCOVER--	TAKING UP THE FAIR IDEAL	428	3
NOT TO DISCOVER WEAKNESS IS	NOT TO DISCOVER WEAKNESS	1054	1
APPLAUD HIM TO DISCOVER	HIS MANSION IN THE POOL	1379	13
BUT DISCOVER IT NO MORE	EDEN IS THAT	1657	8
DISCOVERED			
DISCOVERED IS WITHOUT SURPRISE	THE LARGEST FIRE EVER	1114	3
TILL ARRESTED [DISCOVERED] HERE	HAD WE KNOWN THE TON SHE	1124	V 4
DISCOVERY			
SHALL MAKE DISCOVERY.	THIS CONSCIOUSNESS THAT	822	12
FOURTH, NO DISCOVERY--	FINDING IS THE FIRST ACT	870	5
WAS NO DISCOVERY.	HOW FAR IS IT TO HEAVEN?	929	4
DISCOVERY NOT GOD HIMSELF	BECAUSE THAT YOU ARE	1260	11
DISCPLINE			
BUT DISCPLINE UNTO	I KNEW THAT I HAD GAINED	1022	4
DISCREET			
WITHOUT DISCREET ALARM--	THESE ARE THE NIGHTS	1128	14
DISPARAGEMENT DISCREET,--	MY COUNTRY NEED NOT	1511	6
AN ECSTASY DISCREET	BETROTHED TO	1641	2
DISCREETLY			
WHOSE TITLE IS [DISCREETLY CALLED] "THE SOUL."	TO TRY TO SPEAK, AND	1617	8
DISCRETION			
DISCRETION IN THE INTERVAL	BEFORE YOU THOUGHT OF	1465	11
DISCS			
THE DISCS THAT SATISFIED OUR SIGHT--	WHAT TWIGS WE HELD BY--	1086	15
DISDAIN			
HER FAVOR--IS THE BEST DISDAIN	MY SOUL--ACCUSED ME--AND	753	5
BUT HER DISDAIN--'TWERE LIGHTER [COOLER] BEAR	MY SOUL--ACCUSED ME--AND	753	7
HER [HIS] INFINITE DISDAIN	THE STARS ARE OLD, THAT	1249	6
WITH PINIONS OF DISDAIN	WITH PINIONS OF DISDAIN	1431	1
THEN SWEPT AS LIGHTLY FROM DISDAIN	TO HER DERIDED HOME	1586	7
DISDAINED			
DISDAINED THEM, FROM THE SKY--	FROM COCOON FORTH A	354	21
DISDAINED [REFUSED] TO RANKLE THERE--	ARROWS ENAMORED OF HIS	1629	4
DISDAINFUL			
UNCONSCIOUS [DISDAINFUL] OF HIS SMARTNESS.	THE SUMMER THAT WE DID	1773	8
DISDAINING			
DISDAINING MEN, AND OXYGEN,	OF BRONZE--AND BLAZE--	290	12
TO EARN IT BY DISDAINING IT	TO EARN IT BY DISDAINING	1427	1
DISEASE			
REMORSE IS CURELESS--THE DISEASE	REMORSE--IS MEMORY--	744	9
SOME DISEASE HAD VEXT	THREE WEEKS PASSED SINCE	1061	2
DISEMBODIES			
ABSENCE DISEMBODIES--SO DOES DEATH	ABSENCE DISEMBODIES--SO	860	1
DISENCHANTS			
WHOEVER DISENCHANTS	WHOEVER DISENCHANTS	1451	1
DISENTHRALL			
SHOULD DISENTHRALL THY SOUL--	WHO NEVER WANTED--	1430	8
DISGRACE			
A BEST DISGRACE--A BRAVE MAN FEELS--	THERE IS A SHAME OF	551	5
TO DISGRACE OF PRICE--	PUBLICATION--IS THE	709	16
OR A DISGRACE--	THE PAST IS SUCH A	1203	4
LEST SIGHT'S [PROOF'S] INEFFABLE DISGRACE	WE SHUN BECAUSE WE PRIZE	1429	2
DISHEVELED			
IN HER DISHEVELED SANCTITY--	THE DITCH IS DEAR TO THE	1645	5
DISHEVELS			
DISHEVELS EVERY PRIME	LIKE TIME'S INSIDIOUS	1236	6
DISHONOR			
"SOWN IN DISHONOR"!	"SOWN IN DISHONOR"!	62	1
MAY THIS "DISHONOR" BE?	"SOWN IN DISHONOR"!	62	3
THY DISHONOR SHARED!	"THEY HAVE NOT CHOSEN ME	85	8
COULD DISPARAGE [DISHONOR] A FLAMINGO--	AUTUMN--OVERLOOKED MY	748	3
COMMEMORATE DISHONOR	PERHAPS YOU THINK ME	833	5
DISHONOR HIS DESIGN--	JUST AS HE SPOKE IT FROM	848	4
DISHONORED			
AN [SOME] ISLAND IN DISHONORED GRASS--	OF BRONZE--AND BLAZE--	290	18
DISINTEGRATES			
DANGER DISINTEGRATES SATIETY	PERIL AS A POSSESSION	1678	3
DISK			
UNTO THE DISK BEFORE--	THE DUST BEHIND I STROVE	992	2
OF THE DISK TO BE--	THOSE NOT LIVE YET	1454	9
FOR SHEEN MUST HAVE A DISK	THE PATTERN OF THE SUN	1550	3
DIVESTED IS OF EVERY DISK	JUDGEMENT IS JUSTEST	1671	4
DISLOCATE			
WHEN THEY DISLOCATE MY BRAIN!	REARRANGE A "WIFE'S"	1737	2
DISMAY			
BIRDS WITH DISMAY [SURPRISE]	TO FLEE FROM MEMORY	1242	5
THERE IS A FITTING--A [TOTAL IN] DISMAY--	WHILE WE WERE FEARING IT	1277	5
THE SECOND OF DISMAY--	THE SYMPTOM OF THE GALE	1327	2
BUT TO INVITE BY THAT DISMAY	OF DEATH I TRY TO THINK	1558	5
LIKE OUR DISMAY AT THEE?	WE SHUN IT ERE IT COMES,	1580	8
DISMISS			
DISPARAGE OR DISMISS--	THEIR DAPPLED	1611	2
DISOBEDIENCE'			
FOR THE DISOBEDIENCE' SAKE	SO I PULL MY STOCKINGS	1201	3
DISOBEY			
DID WE DISOBEY HIM?	DID WE DISOBEY HIM?	267	1

	FIRST LINE	POEM	LINE
DISOWNED			
WE SPURNED [DISOWNED]--	LUCK IS NOT CHANCE--	1350	7
DISPARAGE			
COULD DISPARAGE [DISHONOR] A FLAMINGO-- . .	AUTUMN--OVERLOOKED MY	748	3
DISPARAGE OR DISMISS--	THEIR DAPPLED	1611	2
DISPARAGEMENT			
THEN WANED [TO WANE] WITHOUT DISPARAGEMENT .	THESE HELD THEIR WICK	1390	5
DISPARAGEMENT DISCREET,--	MY COUNTRY NEED NOT	1511	6
TO KNOW HER AN INTEMPERANCE [A DISPARAGEMENT / AN EMBARRASSMENT]	TO SEE HER IS A PICTURE	1568	3
DISPARITY			
OH DISPARITY--	WHEN A LOVER IS A BEGGAR	1314	6
DISPEL			
DISPROVE [DISPEL] THAT AND YOU MAY--	POWER IS A FAMILIAR	1238	8
DISPELLED			
FOR FEAR IT BE DISPELLED--	A CHARM INVESTS A FACE	421	4
DISPELLED [ABASED / WITHHELD / DEPRIVED] FROM THERE--	I HAVE NO LIFE BUT THIS	1398	4
DISPELS			
BUT MINE--DISPELS--IN TEARS.	I SHALL NOT MURMUR IF AT	1410	8
DISPERSE			
TWO [THE] WORLDS--LIKE AUDIENCES--DISPERSE [DISSOLVE / WITHDRAW / RETIRE]	DEPARTED--TO THE	524	7
DISPERSE IT--SLAY IT--	YOU CANNOT MAKE	1508	V
DISPERSES			
DISPERSES, WHILE [AS] IT STAYS	IT SIFTS FROM LEADEN	311	V
DISPLAY			
IN MEEK ARRAY--DISPLAY YOU--	I'LL CLUTCH--AND CLUTCH	427	21
DO IT NOT DISPLAY	ALL I MAY, IF SMALL,	819	2
WILL SO DISPLAY [ARRAY]	HOW DESTITUTE IS HE	1477	6
IN HER SERENE DISPLAY;	THE PARASOL IS THE	1747	6
DISPLAYED			
AS OF BRIAR AND LEAF DISPLAYED	PIGMY SERAPHS--GONE	138	10
BUT IN THEIR ROOM [STEAD]--A SEA--DISPLAYED--	THEY CALLED ME TO THE	628	9
DISCLOSED [DISPLAYED] TO BE DENIED . . .	THE BEGGAR AT THE DOOR	1240	4
DISPLAYED [UNROLLED] TO THE DESPAIR . . .	HIS MIND LIKE FABRICS OF	1446	2
DISPLAYED [PASS SLOW] BEFORE THE SIMPLEST [HUMBLEST] DOOR	SOME ONE PREPARED THIS	1644	4
DISPLAYS			
THE SUMMER GNAT DISPLAYS--	WHO GIANTS KNOW, WITH	796	6
BUT OFTEN AS MY LOT DISPLAYS	I PLAY AT RICHES--TO	801	9
AND THAT, SO LEAST DISPLAYS--	HER GRACE IS ALL SHE HAS	810	2
DISPOSED			
BUT NOT AT ALL DISPOSED TO RUN!	I MET A KING THIS	166	16
DISPOSERS			
AS WE--DISPOSERS--BE--	WE TALKED AS GIRLS DO--	586	6
DISPROVE			
DISPROVE [DISPEL] THAT AND YOU MAY--	POWER IS A FAMILIAR	1238	8
DISPUTE			
BUT PLOTTED WITH TIME TO DISPUTE--	I SAW THAT THE FLAKE WAS	1267	2
HIS FUTURE--A DISPUTE--	NO BRIGADIER THROUGHOUT	1561	22
DISPUTING			
DENYING [DISPUTING] THAT THEY DIED.	ON THAT DEAR FRAME THE	940	8
DISRESPECT			
AS IS A DISRESPECT	HOW DESTITUTE IS HE	1477	7
DISRESPECTFUL			
BECAUSE THAT JUNIOR FOLIAGE IS DISRESPECTFUL NOW	AN ANTIQUATED TREE	1514	3
DISSECT			
I DISSECT [REVIEW] THE PLAY	ONE DAY IS THERE OF THE	814	6
DISSEMBLER			
A PLEADER--A DISSEMBLER--	ONE OF THE ONES THAT	1466	9
DISSEMBLING			
AND A DISSEMBLING BREEZE	SEPTEMBER'S	1271	4
WHAT A DISSEMBLING FRIEND--	WITHOUT A SMILE--WITHOUT	1330	6
IN A DISSEMBLING HUE	THESE HELD THEIR WICK	1390	6
WITH A REVOLVING [DELUSIVE / DISSEMBLING / DISSOLVING / . . .	A ROUTE OF EVANESCENCE	1463	2
DISSEMINATED			
DISSEMINATED IN HER HAIR--	A LITTLE SNOW WAS HERE	1444	2
DISSEMINATING			
DISSEMINATING THEIR	THE POETS LIGHT BUT	883	7
DISSENT			
THE LITTLE BIRD WOULD NOT DISSENT [DEMUR] .	THE LADY FEEDS HER	941	3
BORNE WITHOUT DISSENT OF EITHER [ANY] . .	THREE WEEKS PASSED SINCE	1061	9
HERE WAS NO NOTICE--NO DISSENT	GREAT STREETS OF SILENCE	1159	3
DISSENTING			
DISSENTING [DEFYING] TO BE WON	THE FACE IN EVANESCENCE	1490	6
DISSIPATE			
ENACT--AND TERMINATE [DISSIPATE]--	THE BATTLE FOUGHT	594	12
DISSOLUTE			
THAT HE IS DISSOLUTE	THE BUTTERFLY OBTAINS	1685	8
DISSOLUTION			
THE DISSOLUTION--IN HIMSELF--	THE PROVINCE OF THE	539	7
BURNED [GLOWED] ON--UNTIL THROUGH DISSOLUTION--	IT KNEW NO LAPSE, NOR	560	3
AS THOSE THAT DISSOLUTION SAW	IT WAS A QUIET SEEMING	1419	11
DISSOLVE			
IF HE DISSOLVE--THEN--THERE IS NOTHING--MORE--	IF HE DISSOLVE--THEN--	236	1
AS SUNS--DISSOLVE [ANNUL] A STAR--	NO CROWD THAT HAS	515	12

	FIRST LINE	POEM	LINE
DISTILS			
DISTILS UNCERTAIN PAIN--	THE LOVE A LIFE CAN SHOW	673	9
DISTINCT			
IT BURNS--DISTINCT FROM ALL THE ROW--	ONE LIFE OF SO MUCH	270	11
AS COOL [DISTINCT] AS SATYR'S DRUMS--	DID YOU EVER STAND IN A	590	14
AND INTACT [DIRECT / DISTINCT] BELIEF--	GROWTH OF MAN--LIKE	750	12
THE SOUL'S DISTINCT CONNECTION	THE SOUL'S DISTINCT	974	1
THE FLOWER--DISTINCT AND RED--	IT BLOOMED AND DROPT, A	978	2
IS MORE DISTINCT THAN OUR'S--	THE FACE IN EVANESCENCE	1490	2
TWAS ALL [ALL WAS] DISTINCT TO ME--	LIVES HE IN ANY OTHER	1557	4
MADE NO DISTINCT REPLY.	THE WATERS CHASED HIM AS	1749	10
DISTINCTER			
THE FORMER LOVE--DISTINCTER GROWS--	YOU'LL FIND--IT WHEN YOU	610	11
WE SEE ACUTER [DISTINCTER / SINCERER], QUITE,	BY A DEPARTING LIGHT	1714	2
DISTINCTION			
HALF THE CONDITION [DISTINCTION], THY REVERSE--TO FOLLOW--	WERT THOU BUT ILL--THAT	961	11
IN SOFT DISTINCTION LIE	SOME DAYS RETIRED FROM	1157	2
WE MAKE THE WISE DISTINCTION [SAGE DECISION] STILL,	WE SEND THE WAVE TO FIND	1604	5
DISTINCTLY			
IS MORE DISTINCTLY SEEN--	THE THOUGHT BENEATH SO	210	2
WAS DISTINCTLY [DIRECTLY] TOLD--	ABRAHAM TO KILL HIM	1317	2
A WORD THAT BREATHES DISTINCTLY	A WORD MADE FLESH IS	1651	9
DISTINCTNESS			
DISTINCTNESS--EASY--SEEMS--	OF NEARNESS TO HER	607	4
DISTINGUISH			
WE DISTINGUISH CLEAR--	THE ADMIRATIONS--AND	906	6
DISTINGUISHED			
THAN AN EARL'S DISTINGUISHED FACE--	PIGMY SERAPHS--GONE	138	13
ONE ENVIES THE DISTINGUISHED DUST--	IT FEELS A SHAME TO BE	444	3
MYSELF DISTINGUISHED GOD--	LIKE MIGHTY FOOT LIGHTS	595	8
DISTINGUISHED FOR THE GRAVITY	WHO OCCUPIES THIS HOUSE?	892	27
DO THEE DISTINGUISHED GRACE--	WHAT I SEE NOT, I BETTER	939	10
SIN--A DISTINGUISHED PRECIPICE	THE BIBLE IS AN ANTIQUE	1545	9
DISTRACTS			
DISTRACTS THE CHILDREN'S FINGERS--	'TIS ONE BY ONE--THE	545	11
DISTRUSTFUL			
DISTRUSTFUL OF THE GENTIAN--	DISTRUSTFUL OF THE	20	1
DISTURBED			
DISTURBED THESE AMITIES.	I HAD SOME THINGS THAT I	116	4
DITCH			
AND GO TO PIECES ON THE STONES [IN THE DITCH]	IT DROPPED SO LOW--IN MY	747	3
THE DITCH IS DEAR TO THE DRUNKEN MAN	THE DITCH IS DEAR TO THE	1645	1
DITCHES			
DITCHES FOR REALMS AND A TRIP TO JAIL	THE POPULAR HEART IS A	1226	7
DITTIES			
BY DITTIES TO THE ENEMY	THE ROBIN IS A GABRIEL	1483	15
DITTY			
AND WHEN THIS MOURNFUL DITTY	I HAD A GUINEA GOLDEN--	23	29
A DITTY OF THE STREET--	HEART, NOT SO HEAVY AS	83	6
THE DITTY [SERMON] IS THAT NATURE SINGS--	THE WORTHLESSNESS OF	1373	2
DIVE			
THAT I WOULD INSTANT DIVE--	ONE LIFE OF SO MUCH	270	6
DIVER			
BUT I WAS NOT A "DIVER"--	HER BREAST IS FIT FOR	84	2
DIVERGING			
BETWEEN DIVERGING GOLDS--	THAT FIRST DAY, WHEN YOU	659	6
WE MET AS SPARKS--DIVERGING FLINTS	WE MET AS SPARKS--	958	1
DIVER'S			
PEARLS ARE THE DIVER'S FARTHINGS	THE FEET OF PEOPLE	7	9
DIVERSE			
IN LIFE'S DIVERSE BOQUET--	WENT UP A YEAR THIS	93	14
DIVERSIFIED			
DIVERSIFIED BY NIGHT--	LIKE EYES THAT LOOKED ON	458	4
A PLATED LIFE--DIVERSIFIED	A PLATED LIFE--	806	1
AND THIS OF OUR'S, DIVERSIFIED	THERE IS A JUNE WHEN	930	11
DIVERSIFY			
HIMSELF--HIMSELF DIVERSIFY--	BEHIND ME--DIPS ETERNITY	721	11
DIVERSION			
DIVERSION FROM THE DYING THEME	T'WAS COMFORT IN HER	1703	5
DIVERTS			
DELIRIUM--DIVERTS THE WRETCH	I SOMETIMES DROP IT, FOR	708	9
DIVEST			
NO EASIER DIVEST--	NO RACK CAN TORTURE ME--	384	10
DIVESTED			
DIVESTED OF IT'S MEAT	ENDANGER IT, AND THE	1658	8
DIVESTED IS OF EVERY DISK	JUDGEMENT IS JUSTEST	1671	4
DIVIDE			
WE MIGHT E'EN DIVIDE--	I NEVER TOLD THE BURIED	11	19
THAN OARS DIVIDE THE OCEAN,	A BIRD CAME DOWN THE	328	17
THAT OBSCURE [DIVIDE] HER FACE--	HER SWEET TURN TO LEAVE	649	26
AND WEDGE CANNOT DIVIDE	ON A COLUMNAR SELF--	789	6
DIVIDE LIGHT IF YOU DARE--	BANISH AIR FROM AIR--	854	2
LET US DIVIDE [DEPORT]--WITH SKILL--	A MAN MAY MAKE A REMARK	952	5
DIVIDED			
DIVIDED--BY A WORLD--	OF NEARNESS TO HER	607	12
THAN FLAKE OF SNOW, DIVIDED WITH [IMPRINTED SWIFT]	HE TOLD A HOMELY TALE	763	7
FOR TWO DIVIDED, BRIEFLY,	THE GRAVE MY LITTLE	1743	5

	FIRST LINE	POEM	LINE
DIVIDEND			
THE GOOD MAN'S--"DIVIDEND"--	YOU'RE RIGHT--"THE WAY	234	10
TRANSPORT'S DOUBTFUL DIVIDEND	WHAT WE SEE WE KNOW	1195	7
DIVIDES			
THE GRASS DIVIDES AS WITH A COMB--	A NARROW FELLOW IN THE	986	5
DIVIDES ABODE WITH ME	THE BLUNDER IS IN	1684	6
DIVINE			
AWAKE YE MUSES NINE, SING ME A STRAIN DIVINE,	AWAKE YE MUSES NINE,	1	1
THE DIVINE INTOXICATION	EXULTATION IS THE GOING	76	7
I, A LESS DIVINE--	THO' MY DESTINY BE	163	4
TO [ON] HER DIVINE MAJORITY--	THE SOUL SELECTS HER OWN	303	3
SO DIVINE--	HER--"LAST POEMS"--	312	6
IN ODORS SO DIVINE--	THE GRASS SO LITTLE HAS	333	14
THIS--TO HEAVEN DIVINE HAS GONE--	TAKE YOUR HEAVEN FURTHER	388	2
A GRANT OF THE DIVINE--	DID OUR BEST MOMENT LAST	393	9
AS HOPELESS--AS DIVINE--	LIKE EYES THAT LOOKED ON	458	12
OR ONLY A DIVINE.	TO HEAR AN ORIOLE SING	526	3
'TWAS A DIVINE INSANITY--	I THINK I WAS ENCHANTED	593	25
IN DUPLICATE DIVINE--	BEHIND ME--DIPS ETERNITY	721	12
IS HUMAN--BUT DIVINE	TO OFFER BRAVE	767	4
CAN THE DUMB--DEFINE [DIVULGE] THE DIVINE?	BY MY WINDOW HAVE I FOR	797	14
INSTRUCTS TO THE DIVINE.	ESCAPING BACKWARD TO	867	8
STAKING OUR ENTIRE [DIVINE] POSSESSION	ROBBED BY DEATH--BUT	971	13
TITLE DIVINE--IS MINE!	TITLE DIVINE--IS MINE!	1072	1
I TAKE THE CLUE DIVINE--	MY COCOON TIGHTENS--	1099	12
IT'S TENTACLES [RESONANCE] DIVINE.	WE LIKE A HAIRBREADTH	1175	8
OF SO DIVINE A LOSS	OF SO DIVINE A LOSS	1179	1
THERE ADDED THE DIVINE	I THOUGHT THAT NATURE	1286	6
'TIS ECSTASY'S REVEALED [DIVINE / SUBLIME / REVERED] REVIEW--	THE LAST OF SUMMER IS	1353	3
THROW [GIVE / CAST] NOT TO THE DIVINE	THE MIND LIVES ON THE	1355 V	7
COULD MORTAL LIP DIVINE	COULD MORTAL LIP DIVINE	1409	1
SHAME IS THE TINT DIVINE.	SHAME IS THE SHAWL OF	1412	8
WITH BADINAGE DIVINE--	ONE OF THE ONES THAT	1466	6
WERE THOROUGHLY [DURABLY] DIVINE	THE DEVIL--HAD HE	1479	8
OF DETRIMENT DIVINE?	THE FACE IN EVANESCENCE	1490	8
FOR THE DIVINE PERDITION	HIS LITTLE HEARSE LIKE	1522	7
AN ERROR SO DIVINE	MEETING BY ACCIDENT,	1548	4
AN ERRAND SO DIVINE,	WE SEND THE WAVE TO FIND	1604	2
IS IT, OR NOT, DIVINE--	"RED SEA," INDEED! TALK	1642	8
IS A DIVINE INTEMPERANCE	THROUGH THOSE OLD	1753	3
DIVINELY			
TO DIE DIVINELY ONCE A TWILIGHT--[AN EVENING / A LIMIT]	I'D RATHER RECOLLECT A	1349	7
DIVINER			
AS THAT DIVINER BRAND	EXHILIRATION--IS WITHIN	383	4
DIVINER THAN THE CHILDHOOD'S--	WE LEARNED THE WHOLE OF	568	7
OF THAT DIVINER THING	THE LOVE A LIFE CAN SHOW	673	3
DIVINER CROWD AT HOME [WITHIN]--	THE SOUL THAT HATH A	674	3
HAD WE DIVINER BEEN--	NOT WHAT WE DID, SHALL	823	4
A NEW--DIVINER--CARE--	I LEARNED--AT LEAST--	944	24
DEATH'S DIVINER CLASSIFYING	COLOR--CASTE--	970	3
WERE TENDERER--DIVINER	MY TRIUMPH LASTED TILL	1227	13
BUT BREAD IS THAT DIVINER [MAJESTIC] THING	THE BEGGAR AT THE DOOR	1240	3
DIVINEST			
THEN--ON DIVINEST TIPTOE--STANDING--	JUST SO--JESUS--RAPS--	317	5
MUCH MADNESS IS DIVINEST SENSE--	MUCH MADNESS IS DIVINEST	435	1
IS HIS DIVINEST GRIEF--	THE SWEETS OF PILLAGE,	1470	4
DIVING			
I'M DIVING--JUST A LITTLE LATE--	I'LL CLUTCH--AND CLUTCH	427	5
DIVINITY			
THO' THE DIVINITY--	'TIS OPPOSITES--ENTICE--	355	10
PRESENT DIVINITY--	IT FEELS A SHAME TO BE	444	20
OF HIS DIVINITY--	I PRAYED, AT FIRST, A	576	13
DIVINITY DWELLS UNDER SEAL.	EMBARRASSMENT OF ONE	662	7
FADE I UNTO DIVINITY--	'TWOULD EASE--A	682	11
REVERSED DIVINITY--	TWO--WERE IMMORTAL TWICE	800	4
INTO DIVINITY.	UNABLE ARE THE LOVED TO	809	6
FROM HER DIVINITY	SUMMER--WE ALL HAVE SEEN	1386 V	8
THE STINT NOR THE DIVINITY	YOUR THOUGHTS DONT HAVE	1452 V	8
DIVISION			
SHOW ME DIVISION [COULD] CAN SPLIT OR PARE--	WHILE IT IS ALIVE	491	6
DIVISION IS ADHESION'S FORFEIT--ON HIGH	NOT SO THE INFINITE	1040	2
DIVISIONS			
THE FOUR DIVISIONS OF THE EARTH	THE WIND TOOK UP THE	1134	5
DIVORCE			
THY BATTERIES DIVORCE.	DYING! TO BE AFRAID OF	831	9
CONTINUAL DIVORCE.	OF SILKEN SPEECH AND	896	9
DIVORCED			
'TWAS SABBATH--WITH THE BELLS DIVORCED [REVERSED]--	I HAD NO CAUSE TO BE	542	15
DIVULGE			
CAN THE DUMB--DEFINE [DIVULGE] THE DIVINE?	BY MY WINDOW HAVE I FOR	797	14
THE VANITY DIVULGE	HIS LITTLE HEARSE LIKE	1522	4
DIVULGELESS			
AND KINSMEN AS DIVULGELESS	DEATH IS THE SUPPLE	1445	11
DIVULGING			
DIVULGING IT WOULD REST MY HEART	I SHALL NOT MURMUR IF AT	1410	5
DIZZY			
OR IF IT DARE--TO CLIMB YOUR DIZZY KNEE--	WHAT SHALL I DO--IT	186	10

	FIRST LINE	POEM	LINE
DIZZY (CONTINUED)			
OUR DIZZY [SCANTY] ESTIMATE--	THOSE FAIR--FICTITIOUS	499	12
WHOSE SPOKES A DIZZY MUSIC MAKE	WITHIN MY GARDEN, RIDES	500	3
DNIEPER			
AND DNIEPER WRESTLERS, RUN.	I THINK THE HEMLOCK	525	16
DOCILE			
SHE BENT HER DOCILE SAILS--	WHETHER MY BARK WENT	52	4
ALSO, WHO LEADS THE DOCILE SPHERES . . .	BRING ME THE SUNSET IN A	128	14
LEAST RIVERS--DOCILE TO SOME SEA.	LEAST RIVERS--DOCILE TO	212	1
THE BIRDS--IN DOCILE ROWS	THE DAY CAME SLOW--TILL	304	10
SHE LEADS HIM--DOCILE AS A BOY--	THE MOON IS DISTANT FROM	429	3
STOP--DOCILE AND OMNIPOTENT	I LIKE TO SEE IT LAP	585	16
SHE [HE] LAID HER [HIS] DOCILE CRESCENT DOWN	SHE LAID HER DOCILE	1396	1
A DOCILE GENTLEMAN--	THE SAVIOR MUST HAVE	1487	2
THIS DOCILE ONE INTER	THIS DOCILE ONE INTER	1752	1
DOCK			
IF WRECKED UPON THE SHOAL [WHARF / CAPE / DOCK / BAY] OF THOUGHT	IF WRECKED UPON THE	1469	1
DOCTOR SEE DR			
THE DOCTOR--DRIVES AWAY--	THERE'S BEEN A DEATH, IN	389	6
DOCTOR'S			
IT WILL NOT STIR FOR DOCTOR'S--	A CLOCK STOPPED--	287	10
DOCTRINES			
HIS CHANCES [DOCTRINES / DOGMAS] A REDOUBT--	NO BRIGADIER THROUGHOUT	1561	V 22
DOE			
AND YET, UNTO THE SINGLE DOE	ONE ANGUISH--IN A CROWD	565	3
AND NOW WE HUNT THE DOE--	MY LIFE HAD STOOD--A	754	6
DOG			
AND I REJOIN MY DOG, ...	WITHIN MY GARDEN, RIDES	500	12
I STARTED EARLY--TOOK MY DOG--	I STARTED EARLY--TOOK MY	520	1
WE WALK--I LEAVE MY DOG--AT HOME [BEHIND]--	AGAIN--HIS VOICE IS AT	663	18
WHERE NOT SO MUCH AS HONEST DOG	WHO OCCUPIES THIS HOUSE?	892	7
A LITTLE DOG THAT WAGS HIS TAIL	A LITTLE DOG THAT WAGS	1185	1
OF SUCH A LITTLE DOG AM I	A LITTLE DOG THAT WAGS	1185	3
MAKES HE MUD FOR DOG AND PEDDLER, ...	WE LIKE MARCH.	1213	4
LIKE DOG A BONE	THE MIND LIVES ON THE	1355	V 8
THE FOP--THE CARP--[THE DOG--THE TRAMP--]THE ATHEIST--	HOW MUCH THE PRESENT	1380	3
DOGES			
DIADEMS--DROP--AND DOGES--SURRENDER-- . .	SAFE IN THEIR ALABASTER	216	V
DOGMAS			
HIS CHANCES [DOCTRINES / DOGMAS] A REDOUBT--	NO BRIGADIER THROUGHOUT	1561	V 22
DOG'S			
A DOG'S BELATED FEET	THE NIGHT WAS WIDE, AND	589	10
DOGS			
LIKE HUNGRY DOGS	THE WIND DREW OFF	1694	2
DOING			
'TIS DYING--I AM DOING--BUT	THE SUN KEPT SETTING--	692	15
DOLL			
THAT SUCH A DOLL SHOULD GROW	THE HIMMALEH WAS KNOWN	481	4
DOLLAR			
AS AN ONLY DOLLAR--	SUMMER IS SHORTER THAN	1506	4
DOLLARS			
THAT LIVES--LIKE DOLLARS--MUST BE PILED . .	IT FEELS A SHAME TO BE	444	11
I KNEW THE DOLLARS BY THEIR NAMES-- . . .	BECAUSE 'TWAS RICHES I	1093	3
DOLLIE			
CRY "IT'S I", "TAKE DOLLIE", ...	I OFTEN PASSED THE	51	17
AND DOLLIE--GONE!	YOU LOVE ME--YOU ARE	156	7
AND NO MORE DOLLIE--MARK--	YOU LOVE ME--YOU ARE	156	12
DOLLIE'S			
AND SEE IF DOLLIE'S COMING! WAIT!	DYING! DYING IN THE	158	10
DEATH WONT HURT--NOW DOLLIE'S HERE! . . .	DYING! DYING IN THE	158	12
DOLLS			
AND LITTLE GIRLS--WITH DOLLS--	IT WILL BE SUMMER--	342	4
AND THEY CAN PUT IT WITH MY DOLLS, . . .	I'M CEDED--I'VE STOPPED	508	5
DOMAIN			
A COFFIN--IS A SMALL DOMAIN, ...	A COFFIN--IS A SMALL	943	1
AUGUST THE DUST OF THAT DOMAIN--	THAT SACRED CLOSET WHEN	1273	9
DOMAINS			
NOR BEG, WITH DOMAINS IN MY POCKET-- . . .	LET ME NOT THIRST WITH	1772	2
DOME			
JUST A DOME OF ABYSS IS BOWING [NODDING] .	HOW THE OLD MOUNTAINS	291	19
AND AN ORCHARD, FOR A DOME--	SOME KEEP THE SABBATH	324	4
A DIADEM TO FIT A DOME--	'TIS LITTLE I--COULD	466	7
AND DOME [SPIRE / CHURCH]--AND WINDOW PANE--	THE DAY UNDRESSED--	716	16
OR DOME OF WORM--	DRAB HABITATION OF WHOM?	893	3
DOMENICHINO			
DOMENICHINO DROPPED HIS PENCIL--	HOW THE OLD MOUNTAINS	291	23
DOMINGO			
BUTTERFLIES FROM ST DOMINGO	FLOWERS--WELL--IF	137	11
I COULD BRING YOU ODORS FROM ST DOMINGO-- .	I COULD BRING YOU JEWELS	697	3
FOR BUT A BERRY OF DOMINGO	AS THE STARVED MAELSTROM	872	15
WAS THAT CONFIDING PRODIGAL [MINUTE DOMINGO]	ONE OF THE ONES THAT	1466	3
DOMINIE			
A DOMINIE IN GRAY--	I'LL TELL YOU HOW THE	318	14
DOMINIES			
FROM ANNO DOMINIES--	FOREVER--IS COMPOSED OF	624	12
DOMINION			
THE MOMENTS OF DOMINION	THE TINT I CANNOT TAKE--	627	9
DEEMS HIS DOMINION	THE CHILD'S FAITH IS NEW	637	10

	FIRST LINE	POEM	LINE
DOMINION (CONTINUED)			
AS ONE BEMOANING A DOMINION	A LOSS OF SOMETHING EVER	959	7
AND ALL DOMINION SHOWN	THE LIFE WE HAVE IS VERY	1162	6
AS LIMIT OF DOMINION	THE PUNGENT ATOM IN THE	1191	7
DOMINION LASTS UNTIL OBTAINED--	DOMINION LASTS UNTIL	1257	1
AND TILL DOMINION SET	THE MOST TRIUMPHANT BIRD	1265	3
AND GIVE DOMINION ROOM.	THE HARM OF YEARS IS ON	1280	4
MEANS DOMINION	GLORY IS THAT BRIGHT	1660	3
DOMINIONS			
DOMINIONS--BROAD AS DEW--	WHAT WOULD I GIVE TO SEE	247	17
YOU DRIFTED YOUR DOMINIONS--	YOUR RICHES--TAUGHT ME--	299	5
DOMINIONS DOWERLESS--BESIDE THIS GRACE-- .	MY REWARD FOR BEING, WAS	343	9
DON			
FOR HER OLD LOVER--DON THE SUN!	SOME RAINBOW--COMING	64	17
BUT CHILDREN ON THE DON, ...	I THINK THE HEMLOCK	525	14
DONE			
UNTIL THE FIGHT IS DONE;	"SIC TRANSIT GLORIA	3	54
I SAW THE SUN--HIS PLUNDER DONE	I NEVER TOLD THE BURIED	11	3
AND ORIOLE--ARE DONE!	SUMMER FOR THEE, GRANT I	31	4
AND VIOLETS ARE DONE--	WHEN ROSES CEASE TO	32	2
WHEN YOU HAVE DONE, PRAY TELL ME	HEART! WE WILL FORGET	47	5
AS IT HAS USUAL DONE--	IF I SHOULD DIE,	54	6
WHEN TIME'S BRIEF MASQUERADE WAS DONE . .	"ARCTURUS" IS HIS OTHER	70	20
AND YET IT WILL BE DONE	GOING TO HEAVEN!	79	8
"FATHER, THY WILL BE DONE" TODAY	I HAVE A KING, WHO DOES	103	16
AND WHEN HIS GOLDEN WALK IS DONE--	THE DAISY FOLLOWS SOFT	106	2
AND WHEN HER BREATH WAS DONE	SHE DIED--THIS WAS THE	150	2
YET--KNOW NOT WHAT WAS DONE TO ME	I'VE HEARD AN ORGAN TALK	183	7
THE GALES--INDEED--WERE DONE--	ON THIS LONG STORM THE	194	6
THAT THEY HAVE DONE EXPECTING ME--	THO' I GET HOME HOW LATE	207	4
DONE WITH THE COMPASS--	WILD NIGHTS--WILD NIGHTS	249	7
DONE WITH THE CHART!	WILD NIGHTS--WILD NIGHTS	249	8
DONE--	DELIGHT IS AS THE FLIGHT	257	26
NOT FOR THE SORROW, DONE ME--	MANY A PHRASE HAS THE	276	13
YOUR'S, IS DONE--	'TIS SO APPALLING--IT	281	20
BEST--WHEN IT'S DONE--	IT'S LIKE THE LIGHT--	297	10
WHEN SUMMERTIME IS DONE--	LIKE SOME OLD FASHIONED	302	2
SINCE GRIEF AND JOY ARE DONE	SO GLAD WE ARE--A	329	6
WHEN SACRAMENT--IS DONE--	IT WILL BE SUMMER--	342	20
WHEN NIGHT IS ALMOST DONE--	WHEN NIGHT IS ALMOST	347	1
BUT THAT OLD SORT--WAS DONE--	IT WOULD NEVER BE COMMON	430	4
OR WOMAN--WHEN THE ERRAND'S DONE	I TIE MY HAT--I CREASE	443	15
THOUGH LIFE'S REWARD--BE DONE--	I TIE MY HAT--I CREASE	443	31
BECAUSE ESCAPE--IS DONE--	DOOM IS THE HOUSE	475	4
PERHAPS 'TIS KINDLY--DONE US--	WE SEE--COMPARATIVELY--	534	9
AND SERIES THAT ARE DONE--	I COULD NOT PROVE THE	563	4
AND THEN--THE LIST IS DONE--	I RECKON--WHEN I COUNT	569	4
CAN BLAZE BE SHOWN [DONE] IN COCHINEAL-- .	I FOUND THE WORDS TO	581	7
TO THAT OLD MOSES--DONE--	IT ALWAYS FELT TO ME--A	597	2
BUT WHEN SPADES HAD DONE--	IN FALLING TIMBERS	614	10
THEN I--MY TIMID SERVICE DONE--	I THINK THE LONGEST HOUR	635	13
AND SUBTERFUGE--IS DONE--	OF ALL THE SOULS THAT	664	4
MY NEED OF THEE--BE DONE--	SHELLS FROM THE COAST	693	6
THAN LIFE--HAD DONE--BEFORE IT--	YOU TAUGHT ME WAITING	740	7
AND WHEN AT NIGHT--OUR GOOD DAY DONE-- . .	MY LIFE HAD STOOD--A	754	13
BY SIX, THE FLOOD [GUSH] HAD DONE-- . . .	THE BIRDS BEGUN AT FOUR	783	17
I COULD [MIGHT] HAVE DONE A SIN	I PLAY AT RICHES--TO	801	6
WHEN ACT AND WILL ARE DONE	NOT WHAT WE DID, SHALL	823	2
FURTHEST SHINING--DONE--	STRUCK, WAS I, NOR YET	925	12
WHEN PLAY BE DONE--	I LEARNED--AT LEAST--	944	14
BUT WHEN HER WORST WAS DONE	FATE SLEW HIM, BUT HE	1031	6
AND THE DEBATE WAS DONE.	SAID DEATH TO PASSION	1033	9
DONE PERFECTER ON STONE.	I'VE DROPPED MY BRAIN--	1046	4
SO INTRICATELY DONE	BLOOM--IS RESULT--TO	1058	6
WHOSE WANDERING IS DONE--	LET DOWN THE BARS, OH	1065	4
WHEN DAY'S ATTEMPT IS DONE	FURTHER IN SUMMER THAN	1068	V
AND DISTANT AS AN ORDER DONE	THE CRICKETS SANG	1104	V
WHEN NATURE'S LAUGH IS DONE	THE MURMURING OF BEES,	1115	6
THE TOIL OF FELLOWS DONE--	THE WORK OF HER THAT	1143	2
HER CRAFT WERE DONE--	COULD HOPE INSPECT HER	1283	2
WE OTHER THINGS HAVE DONE	THE THINGS WE THOUGHT	1293	2
WHEN DISCIPLINE [CHIVALRY / TYRANNY] WAS DONE	THE THINGS WE THOUGHT	1293	10
SUSPICION IT WAS DONE	IT STOLE ALONG SO	1457	2
LOVE IS DONE WHEN LOVE'S BEGUN, ...	LOVE IS DONE WHEN LOVE'S	1485	1
THAT WHICH TO THIS IS DONE, ...	THE SPIRIT LASTS--BUT IN	1576	14
AS COMPETITION DONE	WITH SWEETNESS UNABATED	1709	6
DOOM			
DOOM IT BEYOND THE REST--	'TWAS LOVE--NOT ME--	394	6
DOOM IS THE HOUSE WITHOUT THE DOOR--	DOOM IS THE HOUSE	475	1
IT'S INDIVIDUAL DOOM	NO CROWD THAT HAS	515	14
NO BANKRUPTCY [SEPULCHRE / WILDERNESS]--NO DOOM--	I THINK TO LIVE--MAY BE	646	16
THE DOWER--AS THE DOOM--	THE FUTURE--NEVER SPOKE	672	10
TO HIM--TO LIVE--WAS DOOM--	HE FOUGHT LIKE THOSE	759	8
BUT DOOM ME NOT TO FORFEIT THEE--	IF BLAME BE MY SIDE--	775	2
AS CERTAINLY AS DOOM--	IMPOSSIBILITY, LIKE WINE	838	8
BE MINE THE DOOM--	BE MINE THE DOOM--	845	1
THE FAVORITE OF DOOM.	THIS CHASM, SWEET, UPON	858	8
HE DEPOSES DOOM	WHEN I HOPED I FEARED--	1181	7
IT'S DOOM IS AUDIBLE--	A DEED KNOCKS FIRST AT	1216	8

	FIRST LINE	POEM	LINE
DOOM (CONTINUED)			
ON THE FOOT OF DOOM--	KNOCK WITH TREMOR--	1325	5
THE DOOM [LOT] TO BE ADORED	SUMMER--WE ALL HAVE SEEN	1386	V 9
BUT AFFLUENT THE DOOM--	BIRTHDAY OF BUT A SINGLE	1488	4
IF DOOM ITSELF WERE THE RESULT,	OF DEATH I TRY TO THINK	1558	15
WERE DOOM ITSELF THE PENALTY--	OF DEATH I TRY TO THINK	1558	V 15
AND DOOM A FALLACY--	THE DITCH IS DEAR TO THE	1645	V 8
WHOSE DOOM TO WHOM [THEM]	A PIT--BUT HEAVEN OVER	1712	17
FELICITY OR DOOM--	ELYSIUM IS AS FAR AS TO	1760	4
DOOMED			
OR DOOMED LIE--	SHOULD YOU BUT FAIL AT--	226	3
THE DOOMED--REGARD THE SUNRISE	THE DOOMED--REGARD THE	294	1
THEN--DOOMED NEW--	LET US PLAY YESTERDAY--	728	32
DOOM'S			
ON DOOM'S CONSUMMATE CHART	TWO LENGTHS HAS EVERY	1295	10
AND DOOM'S CELERITY.	A DEW SUFFICED ITSELF--	1437	16
THE DOOM'S ELECTRIC MOCCASIN	THERE CAME A WIND LIKE A	1593	7
DOOMS			
TO DOOMS OF BALM--	UPON A LILAC SEA	1337	6
DOON			
ACCEPT THIS "BONNIE DOON,"	"SIC TRANSIT GLORIA	3	62
DOOR			
HE STOPS AT EVERY DOOR--	THE GUEST IS GOLD AND	15	6
BEFORE THE DOOR OF GOD!	I NEVER LOST AS MUCH BUT	49	4
FROM OFF HIS CHAMBER DOOR--	SEXTON! MY MASTER'S	96	6
AT SOME IMPOSING DOOR!	IN RAGS MYSTERIOUS AS	117	6
BENEATH THE VILLAGE DOOR,	PERHAPS YOU'D LIKE TO	134	6
NEAREST THE DOOR--TO WAKE THE FIRST--	WHOSE ARE THE LITTLE	142	11
'TWAS'NT FAR--THE DOOR WAS NEAR--	HE WAS WEAK, AND I WAS	190	5
BUT WE BOLT THE DOOR TIGHT	WE DONT CRY--TIM AND I,	196	3
TOO OFTEN AT HER DOOR--	THE FLOWER MUST NOT	206	3
OUT OF THE FOXGLOVE'S DOOR--	I TASTE A LIQUOR NEVER	214	10
HOAR--IS THE WINDOW--AND NUMB--THE DOOR--	SAFE IN THEIR ALABASTER	216	V
COULD I--THEN--SHUT THE DOOR--	COULD I--THEN--SHUT THE	220	1
BUT DONT--SHUT THE DOOR!	WHY--DO THEY SHUT ME OUT	248	8
FANCY THE SUNRISE--LEFT THE DOOR AJAR!	I KNOW SOME LONELY	289	40
LIFT THE FLESH DOOR--	IF YOUR NERVE, DENY YOU	292	10
THEN--SHUTS THE DOOR--	THE SOUL SELECTS HER OWN	303	2
IF [WHEN] HE LEAVE A BUR AT THE DOOR	THE WIND DID'NT COME	316	7
AND THRUM UPON THE DOOR,	OF ALL THE SOUNDS	321	22
A KIND BEHIND THE DOOR--	'TIS NOT THAT DYING	335	4
AS LADY FROM HER DOOR	FROM COCOON FORTH A	354	2
THEN CROUCH WITHIN THE DOOR--	DARE YOU SEE A SOUL AT	365	2
THE COLD WILL FORCE YOUR TIGHTEST DOOR	ALTHOUGH I PUT AWAY HIS	366	26
HER MORNING AT THE DOOR--	SHE LAY AS IF AT PLAY	369	13
NOW--TO RING A DOOR BEYOND	TAKE YOUR HEAVEN FURTHER	388	6
IT GAINS THE BLOCK--AND NOW--IT GAINS THE DOOR--	IT'S COMING--THE	390	2
THAT PERISHED BY THE DOOR--	THIS WAS A POET--IT IS	448	6
THE VISION FLUTTERS IN THE DOOR,	A WIFE--AT DAYBREAK I	461	V 12
WHICH DOOR IS MINE--AND NOT MISTAKE--	I AM ALIVE--I GUESS--	470	23
SO SEEMED TO CHOOSE MY DOOR--	EXCEPT THE HEAVEN HAD	472	2
DOOM IS THE HOUSE WITHOUT THE DOOR--	DOOM IS THE HOUSE	475	1
IF MOMENTLY [HER SWEET DOOR--] AJAR--	IT KNEW NO MEDICINE--	559	13
BY CHIMNEY--NOR BY DOOR	MY PERIOD HAD COME FOR	564	10
NEWS-BOYS SALUTE THE DOOR--	I COULD DIE--TO KNOW--	570	3
AT IT'S OWN STABLE DOOR--	I LIKE TO SEE IT LAP	585	17
AND NOW BEFORE THE DOOR	I YEARS HAD BEEN FROM	609	2
THAT I COULD FEAR A DOOR	I YEARS HAD BEEN FROM	609	14
LEST BACK THE AWFUL DOOR SHOULD SPRING	I YEARS HAD BEEN FROM	609	19
WHEN WINTER SHAKE THE DOOR--	GLEE--THE GREAT STORM IS	619	10
'TIS FIRST--I LOCK THE DOOR--	THE WAY I READ A	636	2
AND NARROW AT THE FLOOR [DOOR]	THE WAY I READ A	636	10
WITH JUST THE DOOR AJAR	I CANNOT LIVE WITH YOU--	640	47
AGAIN--HIS VOICE IS AT THE DOOR--	AGAIN--HIS VOICE IS AT	663	1
I--SILENT [SPEECHLESS]--PASS THE DOOR--	AGAIN--HIS VOICE IS AT	663	10
HE BOLTS THE DOOR--	ONE NEED NOT BE A	670	18
BESIDE YOUR PALACE [TWINKLING / GLIMMERING] DOOR--	THE MOON WAS BUT A CHIN	737	16
I REINFORCED [ONLY SEALED] THE DOOR--	THE BIRDS REPORTED FROM	743	6
AT WINDOW--AND AT DOOR--	REMORSE--IS MEMORY--	744	4
NEXT DOOR TO MINE THE PAIN.	HOW WELL I KNEW HER NOT	837	4
TO SHUT THE DOOR AND IT WENT OUT	I CANNOT BUY IT--'TIS	840	5
AND SHUT THE DOOR UNTO MY HOUSE	I SING TO USE THE	850	3
THEN THEY WILL HASTEN TO THE DOOR	THEY WONT FROWN ALWAYS--	874	5
AND LEAVE A DAY AT EVERY DOOR	WHEN I HAVE SEEN THE SUN	888	3
ARE WRIT UPON THE DOOR	WHO OCCUPIES THIS HOUSE?	892	5
THAN TO THE EARTHEN DOOR--	WE CAN BUT FOLLOW TO THE	920	6
EVENING--THE TISSUE [FOLDING] DOOR--	NOON--IS THE HINGE OF	931	2
A DOOR JUST [THERE] OPENED ON A STREET [TO A HOUSE]--	A DOOR JUST OPENED ON A	953	1
THE DOOR AS INSTANT [SUDDEN] SHUT--AND I--	A DOOR JUST OPENED ON A	953	5
AND MINE--THE DOOR	WERT THOU BUT ILL--THAT	961	6
OF ME--WHEN FIRST UNTO THE DOOR	FITTER TO SEE HIM, I MAY	968	17
THE BOLT UNTO [UPON] THE DOOR--	THE SOUL SHOULD ALWAYS	1055	6
NO EAR, NO DOOR,	AIR HAS NO RESIDENCE, NO	1060	2
OF THE HEART THAT GOES IN, AND CLOSES THE DOOR	OF THE HEART THAT GOES	1098	1
THEN REVERSED THE DOOR--	PARADISE IS THAT OLD	1119	4
BECAUSE BESIDE [BEFORE] THE DOOR	HOW MANY SCHEMES MAY DIE	1150	10
THE BEGGAR AT THE DOOR FOR FAME	THE BEGGAR AT THE DOOR	1240	1

	FIRST LINE	POEM	LINE
DOOR (CONTINUED)			
LOCK THE DOOR--	DEAR MARCH--COME IN--	1320	19
OUT OF THE PURPLE DOOR	DREAMS ARE THE SUBTLE	1376	4
AND CROUCHED BEHIND HIS YELLOW DOOR	A WILD BLUE SKY ABREAST	1415	3
WHAT DOOR--WHAT HOUR--RUN--RUN--MY SOUL!	"AND WITH WHAT BODY DO	1492	3
WE JEST AND SHUT THE DOOR--	WE NEVER KNOW WE GO WHEN	1523	2
I OPEN EVERY DOOR,	NOT KNOWING WHEN THE	1619	2
WHEN AT MY VERY DOOR ARE THOSE POSSESSING MORE,	TAKE ALL AWAY FROM ME,	1640	4
DISPLAYED [PASS SLOW] BEFORE THE SIMPLEST [HUMBLEST] DOOR	SOME ONE PREPARED THIS	1644	4
WE SAUNTERED FROM THE DOOR	EDEN IS THAT	1657	6
AS PLAYFUL IN THE DOOR OF DEATH	THIS DOCILE ONE INTER	1752	V 7
THE OPENING OF A DOOR--	ELYSIUM IS AS FAR AS TO	1760	8
DOORS			
SOME PALE REPORTER, FROM THE AWFUL DOORS	JUST LOST, WHEN I WAS	160	10
THE SHIVERERS ROUND FARMER'S DOORS--	'TIS NOT THAT DYING	335	9
WHEN BURSTING ALL THE DOORS--	THE SOUL HAS BANDAGED	512	12
SUPERIOR--FOR DOORS--	I DWELL IN POSSIBILITY--	657	4
THE HEART HAS MANY DOORS--	THE HEART HAS MANY DOORS	1567	1
WE BARRED THE WINDOWS AND THE DOORS	THERE CAME A WIND LIKE A	1593	5
DORMANT			
IN DORMANT NATURE--LAIN--	A MAN MAY MAKE A REMARK	952	4
DOT			
WHOSE CANTONS DOT THE SKIES--	THE FEET OF PEOPLE	7	20
LOW DAISIES--DOT--	I TEND MY FLOWERS FOR	339	6
THAT DOT HIS DISTANT EAVES--	I ENVY SEAS, WHEREON HE	498	10
LIKE A DOTTED DOT--	DONT PUT UP MY THREAD &	617	12
DOTE			
TOO SURE--TO DOTE UPON!	THE LONESOME FOR THEY	262	12
DOTES			
HOW HUMAN NATURE DOTES	HOW HUMAN NATURE DOTES	1417	1
DOTS			
SOUNDLESS AS DOTS--ON A DISC OF SNOW--	SAFE IN THEIR ALABASTER	216	V
DOTTED			
LIKE A DOTTED DOT--	DONT PUT UP MY THREAD &	617	12
DOUBLE			
AFFLICTS ME WITH A DOUBLE LOSS--	EXCEPT THE HEAVEN HAD	472	7
DOUBLE ESTATE--ENTAILED AT PLEASURE	I AM AFRAID TO OWN A	1090	5
NOR IS DYING DOUBLE--	SAFE DESPAIR IT IS THAT	1243	8
DOUBLET			
OF ERMINE IS HIS DOUBLET--	THE GUEST IS GOLD AND	15	3
DOUBLOONS			
BAGS OF DOUBLOONS--ADVENTUROUS BEES	WHAT WOULD I GIVE TO SEE	247	18
DOUBLY			
LOST DOUBLY--BUT BY CONTRAST--MOST--	A DOOR JUST OPENED ON A	953	7
HOW DOUBLY MORE	WE LEARN IN THE	1083	6
DOUBT			
EACH LITTLE DOUBT AND FEAR,	I HAVE A BIRD IN SPRING	5	22
A JEALOUS ZEPHYR--NOT A DOUBT--	GOOD NIGHT! WHICH PUT	259	2
DOUBT ME! MY DIM [FAINT] COMPANION!	DOUBT ME! MY DIM	275	1
THEY DOUBT TO WITNESS IT--	THE DOOMED--REGARD THE	294	4
FOR DOUBT, THAT I SHOULD KNOW THE SOUND--	I FELT MY LIFE WITH BOTH	351	8
FROM DUNGEON'S LUXURY OF DOUBT	'TWAS LIKE A MAELSTROM,	414	20
TOO TENDERLY, THAT ANY DOUBT	THE MONTHS HAVE ENDS--	423	7
AND DOUBT THAT YOU ARE MINE--	I'LL CLUTCH--AND CLUTCH	427	13
WHY MAKE IT DOUBT--IT HURTS IT SO--	WHY MAKE IT DOUBT--IT	462	1
A DOUBT--IF IT BE FAIR--INDEED--	THE WORLD--STANDS--	493	5
ME PROVE IT NOW--WHOEVER [WHATEVER] DOUBT	ME PROVE IT NOW--WHOEVER	537	1
THIS--DOST THOU DOUBT--SWEET--	THAT I DID ALWAYS LOVE	549	9
FAINT DOUBT--AND FAR COMPETITOR--	I CROSS TILL I AM WEARY	550	16
I DO NOT DOUBT THE SELF I WAS	I COULD NOT PROVE THE	563	9
NEVER HAD A DOUBT--	THE CHILD'S FAITH IS NEW	637	5
MY WORTHINESS IS ALL MY DOUBT--	MY WORTHINESS IS ALL MY	751	1
A DOUBT IF IT BE US	A DOUBT IF IT BE US	859	1
NOW, DO YOU DOUBT THAT YOUR BIRD WAS TRUE?	SPLIT THE LARK--AND	861	8
A DICE--A DOUBT--	THESE TESTED OUR HORIZON	886	8
WITH THAT OLD CODICIL OF DOUBT?	WHICH IS BEST? HEAVEN--	1012	3
I ALWAYS FEEL A DOUBT	WHEN THEY COME BACK--IF	1080	2
LEST ANY DOUBT THAT WE ARE GLAD THAT THEY WERE BORN TODAY	LEST ANY DOUBT THAT WE	1156	1
WHO DOUBT TO LIVE AGAIN--	THOSE NOT LIVE YET	1454	2
OF THAT, THERE IS NO DOUBT.	WE SHALL FIND THE CUBE	1484	2
WE CANNOT DOUBT--	THOUGH THE GREAT WATERS	1599	3
NOR DOUBT OF SCENE TO COME,	NOT SICKNESS STAINS THE	1613	3
I DOUBT IF EVEN THAT	LOVE CAN DO ALL BUT	1731	2
DOUBTED			
BUT I NEVER DOUBTED HIM--	HE STRAINED MY FAITH--	497	10
DOUBTFUL			
DOUBTFUL IF IT BE CROWNED!	DELAYED TILL SHE HAD	58	18
IN DOUBTFUL MEAL, IF IT BE POSSIBLE	ONE YEAR AGO--JOTS WHAT?	296	10
AT FIRST--A DOUBTFUL TONE--	YOU'LL KNOW HER--BY HER	634	22
THOU PAUSED AT, FOR A PASSING [DOUBTFUL] BOUNTY--	WERT THOU BUT ILL--THAT	961	7
AND DOUBTFUL AS REPORT UPON	THE CRICKETS SANG	1104	V
TRANSPORT'S DOUBTFUL DIVIDEND	WHAT WE SEE WE KNOW	1195	7
DOUBTING			
TELL I MY DOUBTING HEART	I HAVE A BIRD IN SPRING	5	17
THE SAILOR DOUBTING TURNS--	WHEN THE ASTRONOMER	851	6

	FIRST LINE	POEM		LINE
DOUBTLESS				
MANY, WILL DOUBTLESS ASK ME,	SO BASHFUL WHEN I SPIED	91		11
DOUBTLESS AN ESTIMABLE BEAST,	I MET A KING THIS	166		15
DOUBTLESS THE FIRST EXCURSION	I MET A KING THIS	166		23
DOUBTLESS, WE SHOULD DEEM SUPERFLUOUS	IF THE FOOLISH, CALL	168		13
DOUBTLESS--"ADAM"--SCOWLED AT EDEN--	TAKING UP THE FAIR IDEAL	428		7
THE FAULT--WAS DOUBTLESS ISRAEL'S--	IT ALWAYS FELT TO ME--A	597		17
TO NEIGHBORS DOUBTLESS OF THEIR OWN	LIKE MEN AND WOMEN	1105		5
LOCATION DOUBTLESS HE WOULD PLEAD [URGE]	SO MUCH OF HEAVEN HAS	1228		7
INDIFFERENT SEASONS DOUBTLESS PLAY	SOMEWHERE UPON THE	1231		5
WOULD DOUBTLESS SPECIFY--[ANSWER ME]	WHO WERE "THE FATHER AND	1258		12
DOUBTLESS SECRETS LIE--	"SECRETS" IS A DAILY	1385		6
HE DOUBTLESS DID HIS BEST--	LOOK BACK ON TIME, WITH	1478		2
DOUBTLESS, HE THOUGHT IT MEET OF HIM	A TRAIN WENT THROUGH A	1761		7
DOUBTS				
DEATH DOUBTS IT--ARGUES [REASONS] FROM THE GROUND--	DEATH IS A DIALOGUE	976		5
THAT DOUBTS AS FERVENTLY AS IT BELIEVES.	OURSELVES WE DO INTER	1144		4
OF IMMORTALITY WHO DOUBTS	BECAUSE THAT YOU ARE	1260		25
DOUGH				
AS WOMEN DO A DOUGH--	THE WIND BEGUN TO KNEAD	824		2
DOVE				
ONCE MORE, MY NOW BEWILDERED DOVE	ONCE MORE, MY NOW	48		1
DO NOT CHASTISE THE DOVE--	WHATEVER IT IS--SHE HAS	1204		4
DOWER				
AND DOWER LATITUDES FAR ON--	DELIGHT IS AS THE FLIGHT	257		23
SAY QUICK, THAT I MAY [SO I CAN] DOWER THEE	DOUBT ME! MY DIM	275		7
TO DOWER--SO GREAT--	MY REWARD FOR BEING, WAS	343	V	
WHAT WOULD THE DOWER BE,	I WOULD NOT PAINT--A	505		22
THE DOWER--AS THE DOOM--	THE FUTURE--NEVER SPOKE	672		10
DOWER ITSELF--FOR BOBADILO--	I COULD BRING YOU JEWELS	697		11
WHEN SUMMER'S EVERLASTING DOWER--	PRECIOUS TO ME--SHE	727		13
OR PETALS, OR A DOWER OF BUZZ	BECAUSE THE BEE MAY	869		10
HAS FORFEITED THE DOWER	THE CLOVER'S SIMPLE FAME	1232	V	8
DREAMS ARE THE SUBTLE DOWER	DREAMS ARE THE SUBTLE	1376		1
AND DOWER AND DEPRIVE	OF THIS IS DAY COMPOSED	1675		6
TILL MY MINUTEST DOWER,	OH, HONEY OF AN HOUR,	1734		4
DOWERED				
AND DOWERED--ALL THE WORLD--	IT WOULD NEVER BE COMMON	430		20
THEN NUMERALS ARE DOWERED BACK--	'TIS ONE BY ONE--THE	545		7
DOWERLESS				
DOMINIONS DOWERLESS--BESIDE THIS GRACE--	MY REWARD FOR BEING, WAS	343		9
SO LATE A DOWERLESS GIRL--	I AM ASHAMED--I HIDE--	473		3
DOWER'S				
THAT BUT THE DOWER'S FRACTION--	REMOVED FROM ACCIDENT OF	424		11
DOWERS				
HAS DOWERS OF PROSPECTIVE	CRISIS IS SWEET AND YET	1416		3
DOWN SEE ADOWN				
PUT DOWN THE APPLE, ADAM,	"SIC TRANSIT GLORIA	3		17
LAID DOWN ON BUNKER HILL;	"SIC TRANSIT GLORIA	3		46
THE OWL LOOKED PUZZLED DOWN--	THROUGH LANE IT LAY--	9		6
DOWN WH', ON EITHER HAND	SLEEP IS SUPPOSED TO BE	13		5
BUT UP AND DOWN THE HILLS	ONE SISTER HAVE I IN OUR	14		14
I SAT ME DOWN TO SIGH.	I HAD A GUINEA GOLDEN--	23		8
AND NIGHT IS COMING DOWN!	ADRIFT! A LITTLE BOAT	30		2
AND GURGLED DOWN AND DOWN.	ADRIFT! A LITTLE BOAT	30		8
AND GURGLED DOWN AND DOWN.	ADRIFT! A LITTLE BOAT	30		8
TO NOTE THE REBELS DOWN.	I COUNTED TILL THEY	36		4
AND BIRDS CAN FLUTTER DOWN--	I OFTEN PASSED THE	51		12
WHETHER MY BARK WENT DOWN AT SEA--	WHETHER MY BARK WENT	52		1
BY SOLDIERS BATTERED DOWN,	I NEVER HEAR THE WORD	77		6
THAT SAT IT DOWN TO REST--	A POOR--TORN HEART-- A	78		2
THAT TODDLED DOWN THE BAY!	'TWAS SUCH A LITTLE--	107		2
IMMORTAL ALPS LOOK DOWN--	IN LANDS I NEVER SAW--	124		2
AND SHUT THE WINDOWS DOWN SO CLOSE	BRING ME THE SUNSET IN A	128		20
AND BLUSHING BIRDS GO DOWN TO DRINK,	HAVE YOU GOT A BROOK IN	136		3
BELTED DOWN WITH EMERALD--	PIGMY SERAPHS--GONE	138		6
AND WITH THE SAINTS SAT DOWN.	SHE BORE IT TILL THE	144		8
SHE LOOKS DOWN JUST AS OFTEN	MAMA NEVER FORGETS HER	164		3
WENT WANDERING DOWN THE LATITUDES	AS IF SOME LITTLE ARCTIC	180		3
HORIZONS--STRAGGLED DOWN--	ON THIS LONG STORM THE	194		4
TO MY NESCESSITY--STOOPED DOWN!	FOR THIS--ACCEPTED	195		6
SO SUNSET SHUTS MY QUESTION DOWN	IT CANT BE "SUMMER"!	221		9
GONE DOWN!	IF HE DISSOLVE--THEN--	236		7
AND LIKE THE TREES, LOOK DOWN--	WHEN WE STAND ON THE	242		2
FAR DOWN THE DUSTIEST ROAD!	ONE LIFE OF SO MUCH	270		16
AND IT'S PARTLY [MANY A MILE], DOWN HILL--	TIE THE STRINGS TO MY	279		8
AND I DROPPED DOWN, AND DOWN--	I FELT A FUNERAL, IN MY	280		18
AND I DROPPED DOWN, AND DOWN--	I FELT A FUNERAL, IN MY	280		18
THE MOON--SLIDES DOWN THE STAIR,	I KNOW SOME LONELY	289		23
AT PERIOD OF GOING DOWN--	THE ONE WHO COULD REPEAT	307		5
PUT HER DOWN--IN ITALY?	HER--"LAST POEMS"--	312		19
THEN QUIVER DOWN--WITH TUFTS OF TUNE--	OF ALL THE SOUNDS	321		7
A BIRD CAME DOWN THE WALK--	A BIRD CAME DOWN THE	328		1
LATHED--WITH DOWN--	I WENT TO HEAVEN--	374		4
NO DEAD, WERE EVER CARRIED DOWN--	A HOUSE UPON THE HIGHT--	399		3
THAT WHEN THE HILLS--COME DOWN--	A TONGUE--TO TELL HIM I	400		23
I SHALL HAVE WADED DOWN ONE DAY".	IT DONT SOUND SO	426		9
JUST TO CAST HER DOWN	TAKING UP THE FAIR IDEAL	428		2
I NEVER PUT IT DOWN--	IT WAS GIVEN TO ME BY	454		6

	FIRST LINE	POEM	LINE
DOWN (CONTINUED)			
INLAID WITH EMERALD--HALF WAY DOWN--	I KNOW WHERE WELLS GROW	460	7
LEST NOON IN [DOWN] EVERLASTING NIGHT--	I ENVY SEAS, WHEREON HE	498	23
AND ALL THE DEAD, LIE DOWN--	IT WAS NOT DEATH, FOR I	510	2
TO PUT THIS WORLD DOWN, LIKE A BUNDLE--	TO PUT THIS WORLD DOWN,	527	1
GO DOWN THE FIELDS TO "HAY"--	I'M SORRY FOR THE DEAD--	529	20
AND THEN--BE SOLDERED DOWN	I'VE SEEN A DYING EYE	547	6
THEN CHASE ITSELF DOWN HILL--	I LIKE TO SEE IT LAP	585	13
LOOK DOWN UPON [ABOLISH HIS] CAPTIVITY--	THEY SHUT ME UP IN PROSE	613	11
WHERE I PUT IT DOWN--	DONT PUT UP MY THREAD &	617	14
FORTY--GONE DOWN TOGETHER--	GLEE--THE GREAT STORM IS	619	3
WHERE YOU HAD PUT ME DOWN--	OURSELVES WERE WED ONE	631	6
TO SHUT THE OTHER'S GAZE DOWN--	I CANNOT LIVE WITH YOU--	640	15
THE LIKEST TO THE DOWN	OF BEING IS A BIRD	653	2
AS DID [SHOULD] THE DOWN EMIT A TUNE--	OF BEING IS A BIRD	653	11
JOURNEY OF DOWN--AND WHIP OF DIAMOND--	DROPPED INTO THE ETHER	665	7
WEARY! FURLOUGHS OF DOWN!	WOULD YOU LIKE SUMMER?	691	4
THE DUST IN STREETS--GO DOWN--	YOU'VE SEEN BALLOONS SET	700	18
RETIRED [LAID DOWN] WITHOUT A CARE--	THE DAY UNDRESSED--	716	12
IT'S PAST--SET DOWN BEFORE THE SOUL	REMORSE--IS MEMORY--	744	5
INDICATIVE THAT SUNS GO DOWN--	PRESENTIMENT--IS THAT	764	2
AND WHEN THE SUN GO DOWN--	NATURE--THE GENTLEST	790	12
RETREATING BLINDED DOWN	ESCAPING BACKWARD TO	867	6
AS OFT AS HE GO DOWN	WE CAN BUT FOLLOW TO THE	920	2
AND ONCE TO LET IT DOWN	HER LITTLE PARASOL TO	1038	2
LET DOWN THE BARS, OH DEATH--	LET DOWN THE BARS, OH	1065	1
AS DOWN HIS HEAVEN DROPT REMOTE [ECHOED FAINT]	JUST ONCE! OH LEAST	1076	8
THE SUN WENT DOWN--NO MAN LOOKED ON--	THE SUN WENT DOWN--NO	1079	1
PERPETUAL NAIL IT DOWN--	A GREAT HOPE FELL	1123	17
THE SUN TOOK DOWN HIS YELLOW WHIP	THE SUN AND FOG	1190	3
WHEN WE HAVE PUT IT DOWN--	I SHOULD NOT DARE TO BE	1197	4
OF SHADOWS [RIPPLES] GOING DOWN	A STAGNANT PLEASURE LIKE	1281	6
PUT DOWN YOUR HAT--	DEAR MARCH--COME IN--	1320	4
NO DESPOT BUT THE KING OF DOWN	HOW SOFT THIS PRISON IS	1334	3
WHEN DOWN SOME AWFUL BATTLEMENT	ESCAPE IS SUCH A	1347	7
THAN IF ESCORTED TO IT'S DOWN	THE FLAKE THE WIND	1361	3
SHE [HE] LAID HER [HIS] DOCILE CRESCENT DOWN	SHE LAID HER DOCILE	1396	1
TO HOLD THE FEELING DOWN	THE PRETTY RAIN FROM	1426	6
AS THRONGS [CLANS] OF DOWN--	DEATH IS THE SUPPLE	1445	12
NOR CAN YOU CUT REMEMBRANCE DOWN	YOU CANNOT MAKE	1508	9
NOW I LAY THEE DOWN TO SLEEP--	NOW I LAY THEE DOWN TO	1539	1
AND BRINGS HIS HAMMER DOWN--	THE AUCTIONEER OF	1612	4
DOWN TIME'S QUAINT STREAM	DOWN TIME'S QUAINT	1656	1
I SET ME DOWN	IN WINTER IN MY ROOM	1670	38
DOWNIEST			
UPON THE DOWNIEST--MORN--	IT WOULD NEVER BE COMMON	430	6
DOWRIES			
DAFFODIL DOWRIES--SPICY "STOCKS"--	WHAT WOULD I GIVE TO SEE	247	16
DOZEN			
A HALF A DOZEN KISSED THE EAVES--	A DROP FELL ON THE APPLE	794	3
DR			
YOU AND I, AND DR HOLLAND,	THO' MY DESTINY BE	163	11
DRAB			
DRAB HABITATION OF WHOM?	DRAB HABITATION OF WHOM?	893	1
DRAG			
BACK FROM THE CORDIAL GRAVE I DRAG THEE	BACK FROM THE CORDIAL	1625	1
DRAGON			
OR MAKE A DRAGON--MOVE--	IT WOULD HAVE STARVED A	612	8
OFTENER BY THE CLAW OF DRAGON	FAR FROM LOVE THE	1021	5
DRAGONS			
AND DRAGONS--IN THE CREASE--	I HAD NOT MINDED--WALLS	398	16
DRAM			
AND IN THE FORMER DRAM	IMPOSSIBILITY, LIKE WINE	838	6
A SINGLE DRAM OF HEAVEN!	I TOOK ONE DRAUGHT OF	1725	8
DRAMA			
BUT WE--ARE DYING IN DRAMA--	WE DREAM--IT IS GOOD WE	531	7
AND DRAMA--IS NEVER [SELDOM] DEAD--	WE DREAM--IT IS GOOD WE	531	8
DUE--PROMPTLY--AS A DRAMA--	WHOLE GULFS--OF RED, AND	658	7
AND THIS BRIEF TRAGEDY OF [DRAMA IN THE] FLESH--	OF ALL THE SOULS THAT	664	7
BECAUSE IN GOING IS A DRAMA	I'D RATHER RECOLLECT A	1349	5
'TIS DRAMA--IF HYPOTHESIS	'TIS WHITER THAN AN	1482	11
AND DANDELION'S DRAMA	IT'S LITTLE ETHER HOOD	1501	7
A SNAKE IS SUMMER'S [NATURE'S] TREASON [DRAMA],	SWEET IS THE SWAMP WITH	1740	7
DRAMA'S			
DRAMA'S VITALLEST EXPRESSION IS THE COMMON DAY	DRAMA'S VITALLEST	741	1
DRAMS			
WHEN BUTTERFLIES--RENOUNCE THEIR "DRAMS"--	I TASTE A LIQUOR NEVER	214	11
SUPPORTS ME LIKE IMPERIAL DRAMS	THE STIMULUS, BEYOND THE	1001	3
DRANK			
AND THEN HE DRANK A DEW	A BIRD CAME DOWN THE	328	5
A GOBLIN--DRANK MY DEW--	IT WOULD NEVER BE COMMON	430	22
HE ATE AND DRANK THE PRECIOUK WORDS--	HE ATE AND DRANK THE	1587	1
DRAPED			
HOW THE DUN BRAKE IS DRAPED IN CINDER [TIPPED IN TINSEL]	HOW THE OLD MOUNTAINS	291	3
DRAPED FOR THEE!	I TEND MY FLOWERS FOR	339	27
DRAUGHT			
AND YET YOUR LITTLE DRAUGHT OF LIFE	HAVE YOU GOT A BROOK IN	136	7

	FIRST LINE	POEM	LINE
DRAUGHT (CONTINUED)			
I TOOK ONE DRAUGHT OF LIFE--	I TOOK ONE DRAUGHT OF	1725	1
DRAUGHTS			
STRONG DRAUGHTS OF THEIR REFRESHING MINDS	STRONG DRAUGHTS OF THEIR	711	1
DRAW			
THEIR HOCK, AND SHERRY, DRAW,	PERHAPS YOU'D LIKE TO	134	8
DRAW ME A ROBIN--ON A STEM--	MAKE ME A PICTURE OF THE	188	5
HER LITTLE ROCKING CHAIR TO DRAW--	THE NIGHT WAS WIDE, AND	589	15
THEN DRAW MY LITTLE LETTER FORTH	THE WAY I READ A	636	7
FROM LIFE TO DRAW--	OF LIFE TO OWN--	1294	2
THE SHIP BENEATH THE DRAW	THOSE NOT LIVE YET	1454	5
THAT WE HAVE HAD TO DRAW	I DID NOT REACH THEE	1664	19
DRAWER			
AND PUT IT IN A DRAWER--	YOU CANNOT PUT A FIRE	530	6
BUT [WHILE] THIS--IN LADY'S DRAWER	ESSENTIAL OILS--ARE	675	6
TO GAIN RENOWN OF LADY'S DRAWER	THE BIRD MUST SING TO	880	5
AND PUT IT IN THE DRAWER--	WE OUTGROW LOVE, LIKE	887	2
CONTENT IF NATURE'S DRAWER	HER LITTLE PARASOL TO	1038	6
IN IT'S SYLVAN DRAWER--	SUMMER LAID HER SIMPLE	1363	6
DRAWERS			
IN HER MYSTERIOUS DRAWERS--	THE MONTHS HAVE ENDS--	423	6
AND PUT THEM EACH IN SEPARATE DRAWERS,	IF YOU WERE COMING IN	511	7
DRAWN			
WAS TIGHT AND SURLY DRAWN	A CAP OF LEAD ACROSS THE	1649	2
DREAD			
TO KNOW THE WORST, LEAVES NO DREAD MORE--	'TIS SO APPALLING--IT	281	4
DREAD, BUT THE WHIZZING, BEFORE THE BALL--	IF ANY SINK, ASSURE THAT	358	6
I LIVED ON DREAD--	I LIVED ON DREAD--	770	1
FOR DREAD OCCASION PLANNED	A GREAT HOPE FELL	1123	7
SILENCE IS ALL WE DREAD.	SILENCE IS ALL WE DREAD.	1251	1
AT WHAT IS AWE [DREAD] TO ME.	WHAT MYSTERY PERVADES A	1400	12
DECLAIMING WATERS NONE MAY DREAD--	DECLAIMING WATERS NONE	1595	1
NOT DEEMING OF HIS DREAD ABODE	NO MAN SAW AWE, NOR TO	1733	5
DREADED			
AND SO OF WO, BLEAK DREADED--COME,	'TIS SO APPALLING--IT	281	21
I DREADED THAT FIRST ROBIN, SO,	I DREADED THAT FIRST	348	1
DREAM			
ROUND A LEDGE OF DREAM!	I CANT TELL YOU--BUT YOU	65	8
IF, HAPLY, THRO' A DREAM, TO PEEP	I HAVE A KING, WHO DOES	103	5
SO I AM HEARING HIM, I'LL DREAM,	MAKE ME A PICTURE OF THE	188	6
NOR TO DREAM--HE AND ME--	WE DONT CRY--TIM AND I,	196	9
BEYOND MY POWER TO DEEM [DREAM]--	YOUR RICHES--TAUGHT ME--	299	22
HER BLOSSOMS, LIKE A DREAM--	LIKE SOME OLD FASHIONED	302	10
THE NEAREST [MADDEST] DREAM RECEDES--UNREALIZED--	THE NEAREST DREAM	319	1
AND DREAM THE DAYS AWAY,	THE GRASS SO LITTLE HAS	333	18
IT BLISTERED TO MY DREAM--	IT STRUCK ME--EVERY DAY	362	6
AND LET YOU FROM A DREAM--	'TWAS LIKE A MAELSTROM,	414	9
HAD HE THE POWER TO DREAM	REMOVED FROM ACCIDENT OF	424	10
'TIS VARIED BY THE DREAM	DOOM IS THE HOUSE	475	5
IT HAD ESTEEMED THE DREAM--	THE WORLD--STANDS--	493	14
IF 'TWAS A DREAM--MADE SOLID--JUST	HER SWEET WEIGHT ON MY	518	5
WE DREAM [ARE DREAMING / SHOULD DREAM]--IT IS GOOD WE ARE DREAMING--	WE DREAM--IT IS GOOD WE	531	1
WE DREAM [ARE DREAMING / SHOULD DREAM]--IT IS GOOD WE ARE DREAMING--	WE DREAM--IT IS GOOD WE	531	1
IT'S PRUDENTER--TO DREAM--	WE DREAM--IT IS GOOD WE	531	16
TO JUSTIFY THE DREAM--	I RECKON--WHEN I COUNT	569	16
WHILE I--DREAM [WAIT]--HERE--	I COULD DIE--TO KNOW--	570	12
HOW BOUNTIFUL THE DREAM--	I THINK TO LIVE--MAY BE	646	25
AVOIDED--LIKE [AS] A DREAM--	A PRISON GETS TO BE A	652	30
IT WAS THE LIMIT OF MY DREAM--	ONE BLESSING HAD I THAN	756	5
AND I ARISE--AND IN MY DREAM--	WHAT I SEE NOT, I BETTER	939	9
BETTER THAN ON A DREAM INTRUDE	THE SUBURBS OF A SECRET	1245	3
LET ME NOT MAR THAT PERFECT DREAM	LET ME NOT MAR THAT	1335	1
LIKE RAIMENT OF A DREAM--	HOW FITS HIS UMBER COAT	1371	4
WE DEEM WE DREAM--	TO THE BRIGHT EAST SHE	1573	9
AS MADE REALITY A DREAM	WITHIN THAT LITTLE HIVE	1607	3
THIS WAS A DREAM--	IN WINTER IN MY ROOM	1670	39
TO DREAM--TO SAP THE PROP	A PIT--BUT HEAVEN OVER	1712	7
DREAMED			
OR IF MYSELF WERE DREAMED OF HER--	HER SWEET WEIGHT ON MY	518	7
"WE DREAMED IT"? SHE INTERROGATES--	THE SYMPTOM OF THE GALE	1327	15
DREAMING SEE A-DREAMING			
SHE'S DREAMING OF THE WOODS!	WHOSE ARE THE LITTLE	142	24
DREAMING--OF THE DAWN--	DREAMS--ARE WELL--BUT	450	4
WE DREAM [ARE DREAMING / SHOULD DREAM]--IT IS GOOD WE ARE DREAMING--	WE DREAM--IT IS GOOD WE	531	1
WE DREAM [ARE DREAMING / SHOULD DREAM]--IT IS GOOD WE ARE DREAMING--	WE DREAM--IT IS GOOD WE	531	1
TILL THEN--DREAMING [DEEMING] I AM SOWING	DONT PUT UP MY THREAD &	617	17
DREAMS			
IN DREAMS I SEE THEM RISE,	"SIC TRANSIT GLORIA	3	50
RIP--WHILE THE SOWER--DREAMS--	I TEND MY FLOWERS FOR	339	4
AND TELL YOU ALL YOUR DREAMS--WERE TRUE--	A PRECIOUS--MOULDERING	371	23
HE LIVED--WHERE DREAMS WERE BORN--	A PRECIOUS--MOULDERING	371	24
DREAMS--ARE WELL--BUT WAKING'S BETTER,	DREAMS--ARE WELL--BUT	450	1
DREAMS TINT THE SLEEP--	LET US PLAY YESTERDAY--	728	10
GALLOPED IN DREAMS--	UNTIL THE DESERT KNOWS	1291	12
DREAMS ARE THE SUBTLE DOWER	DREAMS ARE THE SUBTLE	1376	1

	FIRST LINE	POEM	LINE
DREAMS (CONTINUED)			
THE DREAMS CONSOLIDATF IN ACTION-- . . .	THE LASSITUDES OF	1592	5
AND DREAMS, REALITY--	WITHIN THAT LITTLE HIVE	1607	4
DREAMY			
THE DREAMY BUTTERFLIES BESTIR!	SOME RAINBOW--COMING	64	7
DREAR			
AN INSTINCT [HUNGER] FOR THE HOAR [DREAR], THE BALD--	I THINK THE HEMLOCK	525	7
DREARIER			
NO DREARIER, CAN BEFALL!	'TIS SO MUCH JOY! 'TIS	172	12
DREARY			
I MISSED MINE--HOW DREARY--MARBLES-- . . .	GOD PERMITS INDUSTRIOUS	231	7
HOW DREARY--TO BE--SOMEBODY!	I'M NOBODY! WHO ARE YOU?	288	5
DREGS			
THE GODS [STARS / HEAVENS / SKIES / SUNS] BUT DREGS	A WORLD MADE PENNINILESS	1623	4
DRESS			
FOR YOU KNOW WE DO NOT MIND OUR DRESS . .	GOING TO HEAVEN!	79	18
IN JUST THE DRESS HIS CENTURY WORE-- . . .	A PRECIOUS--MOULDERING	371	3
TILL IN PURER DRESS--	TAKING UP THE FAIR IDEAL	428	10
ENABLED BY HIS ROYAL DRESS--	LIKE MIGHTY FOOT LIGHTS	595	7
DEMEANS [DEGRADES] THE DRESS I WEAR-- . .	MY COCOON TIGHTENS--	1099	4
BLOSSOMS--DRESS FOR HIS SAKE.	HE IS ALIVE, THIS	1160	4
WHILE I DELAY [DELAYED] TO GUESS [DRESS] .	OH SHADOW ON THE GRASS,	1187	6
WHEN THE CORN IN SILK [GILT] WILL DRESS . .	I SUPPOSE THE TIME WILL	1381	7
AND DRESS [CURL] THE SLEEPY DAY--	HOW GOOD HIS LAVA BED,	1447	4
HIS DRESS DENOTES HIM SOCIALLY, ...	THE ROBIN IS A GABRIEL	1483	3
WHILE RAPTURE CHANGED IT'S DRESS	THE THRILL CAME SLOWLY	1495	6
DRESSED			
WHO DRESSED IN FROCKS OF PUREST SNOW . . .	WHERE I HAVE LOST, I	104	14
THIS DEMOCRAT IS DRESSED, ...	WAIT TILL THE MAJESTY OF	171	6
WAS DRESSED IN MECHLIN--SO--	THE ONLY GHOST I EVER	274	2
DRESSED TO MEET YOU--	TAKE YOUR HEAVEN FURTHER	388	11
THAT I BE ADEQUATELY DRESSED, ...	I CANNOT SEE MY SOUL BUT	1262	6
DRESSES			
DRESSES EACH HOUSE IN CRAPE, AND ICICLE-- .	IT'S COMING--THE	390	7
WE WEAR OUR SOBER DRESSES WHEN WE DIE, . .	WE WEAR OUR SOBER	1572	1
DRESSING			
OF DRESSING, OR DEPARTURE--	THE BIRDS BEGUN AT FOUR	783	19
DREST			
NOR "BAND"--IN BRASS AND SCARLET--DREST-- .	MUSICIANS WRESTLE	157	8
PROCURING HIM PERPETUAL DREST	I CANNOT SEE MY SOUL BUT	1262	9
DREW			
ONE THE CURTAINS DREW--	MORNS LIKE THESE--WE	27	10
THE WONDROUS NEARER DREW--	WENT UP A YEAR THIS	93	18
ARTIST--WHO DREW ME SO--	THE MURMUR OF A BEE	155	14
WHEN BREATH BLEW [DREW] BACK	JUST LOST, WHEN I WAS	160	4
NO MAN DREW.	I WENT TO HEAVEN--	374	8
TEMERITY--DREW NEAR--	IT KNEW NO MEDICINE--	559	14
I TREMBLING DREW THE TABLE NEAR--	I HAD BEEN HUNGRY, ALL	579	3
AND WHEN THE DEWS DREW OFF	I ROSE--BECAUSE HE SANK	616	8
THE DEWS DREW QUIVERING AND CHILL-- . . .	BECAUSE I COULD NOT STOP	712	14
SHE DREW AWAY AUSTERE--	THE BIRDS REPORTED FROM	743	14
AND WE--IMPLORING DREW--	NO NOTICE GAVE SHE, BUT	804	18
TILL MYSTERY IMPATIENT DREW	TWO TRAVELLERS PERISHING	933	13
AND DREW THE HEAD ERECT--	THE LAST NIGHT THAT SHE	1100	26
AND DREW AWAY	MY HEART RAN SO TO THEE	1237	4
THE DUSK DREW EARLIER IN--	AS IMPERCEPTIBLY AS	1540	9
THE WIND DREW OFF	THE WIND DREW OFF	1694	1
SO LOW IT LEANED--THEN STATELIER DREW-- . .	A CURIOUS CLOUD	1710	6
DRIED			
LIKE AZURE DRIED	THE GENTIAN HAS A	1424	2
DRIFT			
DEATH BUT THE DRIFT OF EASTERN GRAY, . . .	BEHIND ME--DIPS ETERNITY	721	4
DRIFT MAY BLOCK WITHIN IT	ABSENT PLACE--AN APRIL	927	5
DRIFTED			
YOU DRIFTED YOUR DOMINIONS--	YOUR RICHES--TAUGHT ME--	299	5
THO' DRIFTED DEEP, IN PARIAN--	IT WILL BE SUMMER--	342	7
DRIFTING			
WITH STEADY--DRIFTING--[SUDDEN--BLINDING] GRAINS	I CROSS TILL I AM WEARY	550	7
DRIFTS			
SOME DRIFTS WERE MOVED AWAY--	I THINK JUST HOW MY	237	10
YOU WOULD NOT KNOW IT FROM THE DRIFTS-- . .	THE COLOR OF THE GRAVE	411	11
DRIFTS WERE AS DIFFICULT THEN TO THINK . .	THIS WAS IN THE WHITE OF	995	3
THE SNOW THAT NEVER DRIFTS--	THE SNOW THAT NEVER	1133	1
DRILL			
DRILL SILENTLY [ARRANGE THE HEART] FOR HEAVEN--	TO HELP OUR BLEAKER	1064	4
MOTIONED ITSELF TO DRILL	THE EVENT WAS DIRECTLY	1686	5
DRILLED			
DRILLED BRIGHT--	UNTO LIKE STORY--TROUBLE	295	22
DRILLS			
WHO DRILLS [NAILS] HIS WELCOME IN-- . . .	THAT AFTER HORROR--THAT	286	16
DRINK			
DRINK, AND ARE GONE--	SOUTH WINDS JOSTLE THEM	86	4
AND SUMMON THEM TO DRINK;	I BRING AN UNACCUSTOMED	132	4
AND BLUSHING BIRDS GO DOWN TO DRINK, . . .	HAVE YOU GOT A BROOK IN	136	3
I SHALL BUT DRINK THE MORE!	I TASTE A LIQUOR NEVER	214	12
TO DRINK--OR SET AWAY	EXHILIRATION--IS WITHIN	383	6

	FIRST LINE	POEM	LINE
DRINK (CONTINUED)			
TO ONE DENIED TO DRINK	TO ONE DENIED TO DRINK	490	1
A DYING TIGER--MOANED FOR DRINK--	A DYING TIGER--MOANED	566	1
TO DRINK--ENABLES MINE	STRONG DRAUGHTS OF THEIR	711	2
LOGARITHM--HAD I--FOR DRINK--	LET US PLAY YESTERDAY--	728	7
I COULD NOT DRINK IT, SWEET [SUE],	I COULD NOT DRINK IT,	818	1
OF WHICH THEY WHO DRINK	"LETHE" IN MY FLOWER,	1730	2
DRINKER			
WITH THE BRAND [STAMP] OF THE GENTILE DRINKER	TO PUT THIS WORLD DOWN,	527	14
THE MODERATE DRINKER OF DELIGHT	A DRUNKARD CANNOT MEET A	1628	7
DRINKING			
DRINKING TO HER NO MORE ASTIR,	I WOULD DISTIL A CUP,	16	3
DRIP			
HOW THE OLD MOUNTAINS DRIP WITH SUNSET	HOW THE OLD MOUNTAINS	291	1
AND LET HIM HEAR IT DRIP	TO ONE DENIED TO DRINK	490	6
IF THE TUNE DRIP TOO MUCH	SANG FROM THE HEART,	1059	3
DRIPPING			
YET KNOW IT'S DRIPPING FEET	MY WHEEL IS IN THE DARK!	10	3
BUT NEVER DEEMED THE DRIPPING PRIZE	LIKE FLOWERS, THAT HEARD	513	2
I CAUGHT THE DRIPPING OF A ROCK	A DYING TIGER--MOANED	566	3
DRIVE			
TO DRIVE HER FROM THE HALL?	IF I COULD BRIBE THEM BY	179	19
UNTIL WE DRIVE AWAY	EDEN IS THAT	1657	4
DRIVEN			
AS STAPLES--DRIVEN THROUGH--	I GOT SO I COULD HEAR	293	12
WORDS ARE HANDED [LANGUAGE IS DRIVEN] AWAY--	WHATEVER IT IS--SHE HAS	1204	8
DRIVES			
NO LIGHTNING, SCARES [DRIVES] AWAY--	WHEN WE STAND ON THE	242	8
THE DOCTOR--DRIVES AWAY--	THERE'S BEEN A DEATH, IN	389	6
DRIVES PONDEROUS PERPENDICULAR	THESE ARE THE NIGHTS	1128	3
DRIVING			
IS SOFTLY DRIVING NOW--	THE SNOW THAT NEVER	1133	4
DROP			
IF, HAPLY, MINE MAY BE THE DROP	I BRING AN UNACCUSTOMED	132	18
I SHALL FORGET THE DROP OF ANGUISH	I SHALL KNOW WHY--WHEN	193	7
DIADEMS--DROP--AND DOGES--SURRENDER--	SAFE IN THEIR ALABASTER	216	V
I DROP MY HEART--UNSHRIVEN!	I THINK JUST HOW MY	237	16
A TIMID [HALLOWED] THING--TO DROP A LIFE	A SOLEMN THING--IT WAS--	271	5
DROP, LIKE A TAPESTRY, AWAY,	DOUBT ME! MY DIM	275	20
THE DROP, THAT WRESTLES IN THE SEA--	THE DROP, THAT WRESTLES	284	1
BEFORE THEY DROP FULL MUSIC ON--	HE FUMBLES AT YOUR SOUL	315	3
THEN, DROP THE PASTE--	WE PLAY AT PASTE--	320	3
DROP SPICY TO THE GROUND--	THERE ARE TWO RIPENINGS	332	4
WE WILL NOT DROP THE DIRK--	REHEARSAL TO OURSELVES	379	5
MY--DROP--OF INDIA?	IT WOULD NEVER BE COMMON	430	33
WE'RE FEARING THAT THEIR HEARTS WILL DROP--	WE DO NOT PLAY ON GRAVES	467	7
YOU HEAR A BEING--DROP--	A SOLEMN THING WITHIN	483	6
DROP GABRIEL--AND ME--	I ENVY SEAS, WHEREON HE	498	24
DROP INTO TUNE--AROUND THE THRONE--	BETTER--THAN MUSIC! FOR	503	24
PATENT, EVERY DROP,	TO PUT THIS WORLD DOWN,	527	13
WOULD DROP [SPILL] HIM--BONE BY BONE.	THERE IS A PAIN--SO	599	8
EXCEEDS IT'S UNREMEMBERED [UNDEVELOPED] DROP--	'TIS GOOD--THE LOOKING	660	11
JUST A DROP--	VICTORY COMES LATE--	690	6
TILL THESE FAINT TABERNACLES DROP	THE HEAVEN VESTS FOR	694	7
I SOMETIMES DROP IT, FOR A QUICK--	I SOMETIMES DROP IT, FOR	708	1
I TRIED TO DROP [SHIFT] IT IN THE CROWD--	BEREAVED OF ALL, I WENT	784	11
A DROP FELL ON THE APPLE TREE--	A DROP FELL ON THE APPLE	794	1
THEN CAME ONE DROP OF GIANT RAIN--	THE WIND BEGUN TO KNEAD	824	15
WHILE CUBES IN A DROP	BANISH AIR FROM AIR--	854	4
WHEN SUNRISE THROUGH A FISSURE DROP	THIS CHASM, SWEET, UPON	858	3
A MAN MAY MAKE [DROP] A REMARK--	A MAN MAY MAKE A REMARK	952	1
DROP A TUNE ON ME--	WHAT SHALL I DO WHEN THE	956	6
A HOARY BOY, I'VE KNOWN TO DROP	NOT ALL DIE EARLY, DYING	990	5
AS STARS THAT DROP ANONYMOUS	SUPERFLUOUS WERE THE SUN	999	11
FATE SLEW HIM, BUT HE DID NOT DROP--	FATE SLEW HIM, BUT HE	1031	1
THIS [THE] WORLD DID DROP AWAY	IT WAS A QUIET WAY--	1053	9
AND SLOWNESS--THEN THE SCAFFOLDS DROP	THE PROPS ASSIST THE	1142	11
[SCAFFOLDS CLEAVE / . . .			
. . . STAGINGS DROP]	THE PROPS ASSIST THE	1142	11
AND CATCH ME ERE [WHEN / AS] I DROP	THE PILE OF YEARS IS NOT	1507	8
CATCH [TRAP / BIND] A DROP OF DEW	FOLLOW WISE ORION	1538	V
TO LOOK WOULD BE TO DROP--	A PIT--BUT HEAVEN OVER	1712	6
DROPPED			
YOU DROPPED A PURPLE RAVELLING IN--	SHE SWEEPS WITH	219	5
YOU DROPPED AN AMBER THREAD--	SHE SWEEPS WITH	219	6
AND I DROPPED DOWN, AND DOWN--	I FELT A FUNERAL, IN MY	280	18
A SECOND MORE, HAD DROPPED TOO DEEP	THAT AFTER HORROR--THAT	286	5
DOMENICHINO DROPPED HIS PENCIL--	HOW THE OLD MOUNTAINS	291	23
THEN DROPPED [LOST] THE AIR--	ONE YEAR AGO--JOTS WHAT?	296	27
THEY DROPPED LIKE FLAKES--	THEY DROPPED LIKE FLAKES	409	1
THEY DROPPED LIKE STARS--	THEY DROPPED LIKE FLAKES	409	2
MY PALACES--DROPPED TENANTLESS--	IT WOULD NEVER BE COMMON	430	23
THE NAME THEY DROPPED UPON MY FACE	I'M CEDED--I'VE STOPPED	508	2
CALLED TO MY FULL--THE CRESCENT DROPPED--	I'M CEDED--I'VE STOPPED	508	11
SUBTRACTING, TILL MY FINGERS DROPPED	IF YOU WERE COMING IN	511	11
BUT DROPPED LIKE ADAMANT.	'TWAS WARM--AT FIRST--	519	16
SHE DROPPED BRIGHT SCRAPS OF TINT, ABOUT--	MY FIRST WELL DAY--SINCE	574	19
BUT WHEN HIS POWER DROPPED [BENT]--	I ROSE--BECAUSE HE SANK	616	3
DROPPED INTO THE ETHER ACRE--	DROPPED INTO THE ETHER	665	1
THEN DROPPED FROM SIGHT--	IT TOSSED--AND TOSSED--	723	8

	FIRST LINE	POEM	LINE
DROPPED (CONTINUED)			
IT DROPPED SO LOW--IN MY REGARD--	IT DROPPED SO LOW--IN MY	747	1
TO HAUNT--TILL TIME HAVE DROPPED	JOY TO HAVE MERITED THE	788	21
THE SUNSET STOPPED [DROPPED] ON COTTAGES .	THE SUNSET STOPPED ON	950	1
DROPPED--MY FATE--A TIMID PEBBLE-- . . .	ALL FORGOT FOR	966	13
I'VE DROPPED MY BRAIN--MY SOUL IS NUMB-- .	I'VE DROPPED MY BRAIN--	1046	1
DROPPED THE LOOP	HE SCANNED IT--STAGGERED	1062	2
DROPPED BY MEMORY--	AFTER A HUNDRED YEARS	1147	12
AND THEN I DROPPED MY VICTORY	MY TRIUMPH LASTED TILL	1227	3
A WORD DROPPED CARELESS ON A PAGE	A WORD DROPPED CARELESS	1261	1
DROPPING			
BECAUSE, THROUGH DROPPING IT, ...	THE ROBIN'S MY CRITERION	285	11
THE DUSK KEPT DROPPING--DROPPING--STILL . .	THE SUN KEPT SETTING--	692	5
THE DUSK KEPT DROPPING--DROPPING--STILL . .	THE SUN KEPT SETTING--	692	5
DROPS			
SO--MANY--DROPS--OF VITAL SCARLET-- . . .	BOUND--A TROUBLE--	269	4
BUT HE MUST [SHOULD] COUNT THE DROPS--HIMSELF--	AGAIN--HIS VOICE IS AT	663	28
DAY--DROPS YOU HER [HIS] RED ADIEU! . . .	AH, TENERIFFE!	666	5
WHICH HELPLESS NATURE DROPS	SHAME IS THE SHAWL OF	1412	5
THE CRICKET DROPS A SABLE LINE	THE JAY HIS CASTANET HAS	1635	7
THE DROPS ON NATURE'S FOREHEAD STOOD . . .	THE SUN RETIRED TO A	1693	5
DROPT			
SHE DROPT AS SOFTLY AS A STAR	SHE WENT AS QUIET AS THE	149	5
HER MERRY ARMS, HALF DROPT--	SHE LAY AS IF AT PLAY	369	5
AND YOU DROPT, LOST, ...	'TWAS LIKE A MAELSTROM,	414	7
SHE ROSE TO HIS REQUIREMENT--DROPT . . .	SHE ROSE TO HIS	732	1
WHO SOMETHING LOST [DROPT], THE SEEKING [LOOKING] FOR	DEATH LEAVES US HOMESICK	935	7
IT BLOOMED AND DROPT, A SINGLE NOON-- . .	IT BLOOMED AND DROPT, A	978	1
THE LITTLE NOTE THAT OTHERS DROPT	I WAS A PHEBE--NOTHING	1009	3
AS DOWN HIS HEAVEN DROPT REMOTE [ECHOED FAINT]	JUST ONCE! OH LEAST	1076	8
IT'S YELLOW SHORTNESS DROPT--	THE DAY GREW SMALL,	1140	4
BY INADVERTENT FINGERS DROPT	THE LIGHTNING IS A	1173	3
THE REST OF LIFE IS DROPT--	ESCAPE IS SUCH A	1347	8
DROSS			
AND REALMS--JUST DROSS--	MY REWARD FOR BEING, WAS	343	5
DEFRAYS THE DROSS OF IT--	ONE THING OF IT WE	1464	8
DROUGHT			
'TIS TRUE THE DROUGHT IS DESTITUTE, . . .	TO LOSE THEE--SWEETER	1754	3
DROUGHTLESS			
I KNOW WHERE WELLS GROW--DROUGHTLESS WELLS--	I KNOW WHERE WELLS GROW	460	1
DROVE			
AND DROVE AWAY THE LEAVES	THE NIGHT WAS WIDE, AND	589	6
WE SLOWLY DROVE--HE KNEW NO HASTE	BECAUSE I COULD NOT STOP	712	5
AND DROVE THE FOG AWAY--	THE SUN AND FOG	1190	4
DROVE BOLDLY TO A ROSE--	A BEE HIS BURNISHED	1339	2
WHO DROVE A LONESOME COW	A FADED BOY--IN SALLOW	1524	2
DROWN			
THE RIVER COULD NOT DROWN--	READ--SWEET--HOW OTHERS	260	11
DROWNED			
AND BOTH WERE WRECKED [DROWNED / QUENCHED / WHELMED] IN NOON--	TWO BUTTERFLIES WENT OUT	533	V
DROWNING			
DROWNING IS NOT SO PITIFUL	DROWNING IS NOT SO	1718	1
DROWNS			
WHOSE MEMORY DROWNS ME, LIKE THE DIP . . .	I LEARNED--AT LEAST--	944	7
DROWSE			
IN CUPS OF ARTIFICIAL DROWSE	BEREAVED OF ALL, I WENT	784	13
DROWSIEST			
AT THE DROWSIEST--	TO KNOW JUST HOW HE	622	21
DROWSINESS			
A DROWSINESS--DIFFUSES--	THERE IS A LANGUOR OF	396	5
DROWSING			
MY FEET KEPT DROWSING--DROWSING--STILL . .	THE SUN KEPT SETTING--	692	9
MY FEET KEPT DROWSING--DROWSING--STILL . .	THE SUN KEPT SETTING--	692	9
DROWSY			
HE WENT BY SLEEP THAT DROWSY ROUTE . . .	HE WENT BY SLEEP THAT	1662	1
DRUG			
NO DRUG FOR CONSCIOUSNESS--CAN BE-- . . .	SEVERER SERVICE OF	786	21
DRUID			
SINCE I AM OF THE DRUID, ...	IF SHE HAD BEEN THE	44	5
DRUIDIC			
YET [BUT] A DRUIDIC DIFFERENCE	FURTHER IN SUMMER THAN	1068	15
DRUM			
AND BRING THE FIFE, AND TRUMPET, AND BEAT UPON THE DRUM--	AWAKE YE MUSES NINE,	1	39
A SERVICE, LIKE A DRUM--	I FELT A FUNERAL, IN MY	280	6
FIRM TO THE DRUM--	UNTO LIKE STORY--TROUBLE	295	18
THE EARTH HAS SEEMED TO ME A DRUM, . . .	WHEN I HAVE SEEN THE SUN	888	7
SUBSEQUENT A DRUM--	THE POPULAR HEART IS A	1226	2
BEFORE THE QUICK [RIPE / PEAL / DRUM / DRUMS / BELLS / BOMB / . . .	ONE JOY OF SO MUCH	1420	6
AS IF A DRUM [THE DRUMS] WENT ON AND ON . .	A PANG IS MORE	1530	V
DRUMMER			
THAT LIT THE DRUMMER FROM THE CAMP . . .	GOOD NIGHT! WHICH PUT	259	11
DRUMS			
IT IS AS IF A HUNDRED DRUMS	I HAVE A KING, WHO DOES	103	8
OF THEIR UNTHINKING DRUMS--	I DREADED THAT FIRST	348	28
DRUMS OFF THE PHANTOM BATTLEMENTS	OVER AND OVER, LIKE A	367	3

	FIRST LINE	POEM	LINE
DRUMS (CONTINUED)			
ARE DRUMS TOO NEAR--	INCONCEIVABLY SOLEMN!	582	15
THE DRUMS TO HEAR--	INCONCEIVABLY SOLEMN!	582	V 15
AS COOL [DISTINCT] AS SATYR'S DRUMS--	DID YOU EVER STAND IN A	590	14
THE DRUMS DONT FOLLOW ME--WITH TUNES--	MY PORTION IS DEFEAT--	639	4
ADEQUATE AS DRUMS	SOME WE SEE NO MORE,	1221	9
MY TRIUMPH LASTED TILL THE DRUMS	MY TRIUMPH LASTED TILL	1227	1
BEFORE THE QUICK [RIPE / PEAL / DRUM / DRUMS / BELLS / BOMB / . . .	ONE JOY OF SO MUCH	1420	6
AS IF A DRUM [THE DRUMS] WENT ON AND ON	A PANG IS MORE	1530	V
DRUNK			
DO WE "GET DRUNK"?	WE--BEE AND I--LIVE BY	230	6
SO DRUNK HE DISAVOWS IT	ONE OF THE ONES THAT	1466	5
I SHOULD HAVE DRUNK [MIXED] IT STRONGER.	HAD I KNOWN THAT THE	1720	4
DRUNKARD			
THAT LIKE THE DRUNKARD GOES--	THE ROSE DID CAPER ON	208	12
A DRUNKARD CANNOT MEET A CORK	A DRUNKARD CANNOT MEET A	1628	1
DRUNKEN			
SO DRUNKEN, REEL HER BEES--	WE SHOULD NOT MIND SO	81	6
IS DAILY DRUNKEN THERE--	HAVE YOU GOT A BROOK IN	136	8
HER PRETTY SPEECH--LIKE DRUNKEN MEN--	THE ROSE DID CAPER ON	208	3
WHEN "LANDLORDS" TURN THE DRUNKEN BEE	I TASTE A LIQUOR NEVER	214	9
AND I TIP--DRUNKEN--	I CAN WADE GRIEF--	252	6
AS ONE THAT DRUNKEN--STEPT--	IT TOSSED--AND TOSSED--	723	6
THE DITCH IS DEAR TO THE DRUNKEN MAN	THE DITCH IS DEAR TO THE	1645	1
THOU CAN'ST NOT BOAST, LIKE JESUS, DRUNKEN WITHOUT COMPANION	PROUD OF MY BROKEN HEART	1736	5
DRY			
SOME BURNING NOON GO DRY!	HAVE YOU GOT A BROOK IN	136	16
THE EYES AROUND--HAD WRUNG THEM DRY--	I HEARD A FLY BUZZ--WHEN	465	5
AS YET--MY HEART BE DRY--	ME PROVE IT NOW--WHOEVER	537	6
HONORS--TASTE DRY--	THE WORLD--FEELS DUSTY	715	4
'TWAS A DRY WINE--	LET US PLAY YESTERDAY--	728	8
DEEM MY SUPPER DRY	AS THE STARVED MAELSTROM	872	14
I KNOW 'TIS DRY--	BECAUSE MY BROOK IS	1200	2
MAKES HE FORESTS [FOREST] DRY.	WE LIKE MARCH.	1213	5
BUT SWEPT AS DRY AS SAND--	LIKE RAIN IT SOUNDED	1235	4
DUCAL			
DIADEM--OR DUCAL SHOWING [SYMBOL / TOKEN]--	HER--"LAST POEMS"--	312	14
AND I TURNED--DUCAL--	HOW SICK--TO WAIT--IN	368	5
DUCAL--AT LAST--STAND UP BY THEE--	LOVE--THOU ART HIGH--	453	6
OF THE DUCAL HAT--	TELL AS A MARKSMAN--WERE	1152	15
DUCATS			
OF MORE ESTEEM THAN DUCATS--	I LOST A WORLD--THE	181	7
DUCHESS			
AS A DUCHESS PASSED--	HOW THE OLD MOUNTAINS	291	12
A DUCHESS WERE TOO COMMON	THE GRASS SO LITTLE HAS	333	11
DUCK'S SEE EIDER-DUCK'S			
DUDS			
WITH DUDS OF EMERALD!	SHE SWEEPS WITH	219	8
DUE			
TO SEE THAT NONE IS DUE?	BRING ME THE SUNSET IN A	128	18
THAT ERE THE FROSTS ARE DUE--	'TIS NOT THAT DYING	335	6
SO MIDNIGHT'S--DUE--AT NOON.	SUNSET AT NIGHT--IS	415	4
DUE--PROMPTLY--AS A DRAMA--	WHOLE GULFS--OF RED, AND	658	7
THAT YOU WERE DUE--	BEE! I'M EXPECTING YOU!	1035	4
ETERNITY WAS DUE.	IT WAS A QUIET WAY--	1053	16
THAT THIS WAS DUE WHERE MOST [SOME] WE FEAR	"REMEMBER ME" IMPLORED	1180	11
HOWEVER FIRST [TRUE / DUE / JUST] IT BE	BECAUSE THAT YOU ARE	1260	6
'TIS HARDER KNOWING IT IS DUE	WHILE WE WERE FEARING IT	1277	7
DUE IN PARADISE TODAY	RECOLLECT THE FACE OF ME	1305	3
OF IGNOMINY'S DUE	A RAT SURRENDERED HERE	1340	4
I FELT APOLOGY WERE DUE	NO BRIGADIER THROUGHOUT	1561	13
MORNING IS DUE TO ALL--	MORNING IS DUE TO ALL--	1577	1
BONNET [JACKET] DUE IN APRIL--	NOT AT HOME TO CALLERS	1590	3
DUG			
DEEP DUG--FOR SUMMER DAYS--	I KNOW WHERE WELLS GROW	460	2
DUKE			
THAN BE "DUKE OF EXETER"--	PIGMY SERAPHS--GONE	138	15
DELIBERATE, AS A DUKE WOULD DO	HE PUT THE BELT AROUND	273	5
A BONNET LIKE A DUKE--	A MIEN TO MOVE A QUEEN--	283	9
'TIS DUKE, OR DWARF, ACCORDING	THE OUTER--FROM THE	451	3
DUKE IN A MOMENT OF DEATHLESSNESS	I AM AFRAID TO OWN A	1090	7
FOR EITHER DUKE OR ROBIN	SHE COULD NOT LIVE UPON	1505	6
DUKES			
DUKES--FOR SETTING SUN!	MORNING--IS THE PLACE	197	4
DULL			
THAN WHEN--A LITTLE DULL BALM GROWN--	YOU LOVE ME--YOU ARE	156	17
BUZZ THE DULL FLIES--ON THE CHAMBER WINDOW--	HOW MANY TIMES THESE LOW	187	9
LOVE THE DULL LAD--BEST--	DID WE DISOBEY HIM?	267	7
'TIS DULL--CONFERRING	HER--"LAST POEMS"--	312	12
WERE DULL FOR DIADEM--	THE DAY THAT I WAS	356	8
DULL HEARTS HAVE DIED	KNOWS HOW TO FORGET!	433	V
TO THAT DULL GIRL?	NO MATTER--NOW--SWEET--	704	4
TELL WHICH--IT'S DULL TO GUESS--	YOU SAID THAT I "WAS	738	9
TO SOME DULL COMFORT THOSE OBTAIN	SEVERER SERVICE OF	786	13
NOT TOO DULL--	GOOD TO HIDE, AND HEAR	842	8
WORN--NOW--AND DULL--SWEET,	IF IT HAD NO PENCIL	921	3
THAT DULL--BENUMBING TIME	'TWAS CRISIS--ALL THE	948	2
AND CONSUMMATED DULL!	THAT ODD OLD MAN IS DEAD	1130	10

	FIRST LINE	POEM	LINE
DULL (CONTINUED)			
BEYOND IT'S DULL [SLOW]--CONTROL	WITH PINIONS OF DISDAIN	1431	6
DULLER			
TO US--THE DULLER SCHOLARS [CORNETS]	TO LEARN THE TRANSPORT	167	15
REFERS MY CLUMSY [DULLER] EYE--	WITHIN MY GARDEN, RIDES	500	18
INSIDE A JACKET DULLER--	YOU'LL KNOW HER--BY HER	634	11
WHEN DULLER THAN OUR DULLNESS	HER FINAL SUMMER WAS IT	795	13
DULLEST			
THE FEEBLEST [DULLEST]--OR THE WAYWARDEST--	NATURE--THE GENTLEST	790	3
DULLNESS			
WHEN DULLER THAN OUR DULLNESS	HER FINAL SUMMER WAS IT	795	13
DUM			
"DUM VIVIMUS VIVAMUS,"	"SIC TRANSIT GLORIA	3	3
DUMB			
WHEN NIGHT--DESCENDING--DUMB--AND DARK--	THO' I GET HOME HOW LATE	207	5
SO OVER HORROR, IT HALF CAPTIVATES [DUMB FASCINATES]--	'TIS SO APPALLING--IT	281	2
AND SHAME [SCORN] WENT STILL [DUMB]--	UNTO LIKE STORY--TROUBLE	295	8
WHEN [THO'] ORCHESTRA IS [BE] DUMB--	LIKE SOME OLD FASHIONED	302	14
THEMSELF--AS DUMB--	IT IS DEAD--FIND IT--	417	10
HOW DUMB [STILL] THE DANCER LIES--	AS FAR FROM PITY, AS	496	10
AUGUST--ABSORBED--NUMB--[RESISTLESS--DUMB]	NO CROWD THAT HAS	515	16
AS IF MY SOUL WERE DEAF AND DUMB--	IF I MAY HAVE IT, WHEN	577	19
NOR WILL HE--LIKE THE DUMB--	THE FUTURE--NEVER SPOKE	672	2
PARALYSIS--OUR PRIMER--DUMB [NUMB]--	THE ZEROES--TAUGHT US--	689	7
CAN THE DUMB--DEFINE [DIVULGE] THE DIVINE?	BY MY WINDOW HAVE I FOR	797	14
NOT DUMB--I HAD A SORT THAT MOVED--	I'VE DROPPED MY BRAIN--	1046	9
MOTION, AND AM DUMB.	HE IS ALIVE, THIS	1160	8
WILL EMERGE [DECAMP] BUT ONCE--AND DUMB [ARMED]--	"SECRETS" IS A DAILY	1385	11
THEY CANNOT CALL, THEY'RE DUMB,	THAN HEAVEN MORE REMOTE,	1436	12
DUMBER			
DEFEAT--A SOMEWHAT SLOWER--[SOMETHING DUMBER] MEANS--	MY PORTION IS DEFEAT--	639	5
DUMBLY			
DUMBLY TESTIFY--	NATURE--SOMETIMES SEARS	314	6
DUN			
AND HIS COMPLEXION, DUN!	A FUZZY FELLOW, WITHOUT	173	4
HOW THE DUN BRAKE IS DRAPED IN CINDER [TIPPED IN TINSEL]	HOW THE OLD MOUNTAINS	291	3
NEVER A GOWN OF DUN--MORE--	I AM ASHAMED--I HIDE--	473	10
SPOTTED--HER DUN GOWN--	CIVILIZATION--SPURNS--	492	7
IN DUN, OR FAIR--	TO HEAR AN ORIOLE SING	526	9
IN HUE--A MELLOW DUN--	OF BRUSSELS--IT WAS NOT	602	10
THE BAT IS DUN, WITH WRINKLED WINGS--	THE BAT IS DUN, WITH	1575	1
DUNCE			
WERE HIMSELF--SUCH A DUNCE--	DID WE DISOBEY HIM?	267	5
RISE--STILL THE DUNCE--	KNOWS HOW TO FORGET!	433	7
DUNGEON			
A DUNGEON BUT A KINSMAN IS	HOW SOFT THIS PRISON IS	1334	7
DUNGEONED			
LONG DUNGEONED FROM HIS ROSE--	THE SOUL HAS BANDAGED	512	16
DUNGEONED IN THE HUMAN BREAST	"SECRETS" IS A DAILY	1385	5
DUNGEON'S			
FROM DUNGEON'S LUXURY OF DOUBT	'TWAS LIKE A MAELSTROM,	414	20
DUNGEONS			
ANECDOTES OF AIR IN DUNGEONS	TALK WITH PRUDENCE TO A	119	7
DUNGEONS CAN [MAY] CALL--AND GUNS IMPLORE--	WHAT IF I SAY I SHALL	277	8
BENT TO THE SCAFFOLD, OR IN DUNGEONS--CHANTED [WAITED]--	UNTO LIKE STORY--TROUBLE	295	5
WITH DUNGEONS--THEY DEVISED--	THEY PUT US FAR APART--	474	9
WHO TIGHT IN DUNGEONS ARE.	COULD I BUT RIDE	661	18
WOULD'NT DUNGEONS SORER GRATE	LET US PLAY YESTERDAY--	728	29
DUPLICATE			
THE DUPLICATE--I MEAN--	THE COLOR OF THE GRAVE	411	18
WHAT DUPLICATE--EXIST--	NO CROWD THAT HAS	515	17
MY DUPLICATE--TO BORROW--	I TRIED TO THINK A	532	6
IN DUPLICATE DIVINE--	BEHIND ME--DIPS ETERNITY	721	12
HIM [WHOM] IT DUPLICATE--	ABSENT PLACE--AN APRIL	927	8
ANOTHER BEAR IT'S DUPLICATE	I KNEW THAT I HAD GAINED	1022	7
DUPLICITY			
FOR THINE OWN DUPLICITY--	"HEAVENLY FATHER"--TAKE	1461	8
DURABLE			
DURABLE AS DAWN	TRUSTY AS THE STARS	1369	5
DURABLER			
IS DURABLER THAN BRONZE--	AN HONEST TEAR	1192	2
DURABLY			
WERE THOROUGHLY [DURABLY] DIVINE	THE DEVIL--HAD HE	1479	8
DURHAM			
COME SHOW THY DURHAM BREAST	COME SHOW THY DURHAM	1542	1
DURING			
DURING MY EDUCATION,	"SIC TRANSIT GLORIA	3	29
LOVE [FAITH] IS LIKE DEATH, DURING THE GRAVE	WHILE IT IS ALIVE	491	8
WOLFE DEMANDED DURING DYING	WOLFE DEMANDED DURING	678	1
BUT DURING MARCH AND APRIL	SPRING IS THE PERIOD	844	5
AND DURING IT'S ELECTRIC GALE [SPELL / STAY / MIGHT / ACT / SPAN]--	WITH PINIONS OF DISDAIN	1431	7
DUSK			
JUST AS THE DUSK WAS BROWN	ADRIFT! A LITTLE BOAT	30	6
A BONNET BLACK--A DUSK SURPLICE--	WHERE I HAVE LOST, I	104	10

	FIRST LINE	POEM	LINE
DUSK (CONTINUED)			
TILL DUSK OBSTRUCTS THE DILIGENCE-- . . .	SHE SWEEPS WITH	219	V 11
HOW A SMALL DUSK CRAWLS ON THE VILLAGE . .	HOW THE OLD MOUNTAINS	291	13
THE DUSK KEPT DROPPING--DROPPING--STILL . .	THE SUN KEPT SETTING--	692	5
'TIS AUDIBLER AT DUSK	FURTHER IN SUMMER THAN	1068	V
AND WENT THE WAY OF DUSK	HE LIVED THE LIFE OF	1525	2
ALAS--THAT FROWNS [DUSK] SHOULD LIE IN WAIT	FROM ALL THE JAILS THE	1532	7
THE DUSK DREW EARLIER IN--	AS IMPERCEPTIBLY AS	1540	9
AND WENT THE WAY OF DUSK, ...	WHO ABDICATED AMBUSH	1616	2
DUSKER			
AND THE LITTLE BORDER--DUSKER--	AUTUMN--OVERLOOKED MY	748	7
DUSKY			
BORNE ON A DUSKY BREAST--	THE MALAY--TOOK THE	452	11
THE MIDNIGHT'S DUSKY ARMS	THE SUNRISE RUNS FOR	710	13
REMOTEST [FANTASTIC / MOST GRACIOUS / MOST DUSKY / . . .	AN ANTIQUATED TREE	1514	7
DUST			
HOW INTRICATE THE DUST!	GOOD NIGHT, BECAUSE WE	114	2
DUST IS THE ONLY SECRET--	DUST IS THE ONLY SECRET	153	1
WIPING AWAY THE VELVET DUST	IN EBON BOX, WHEN YEARS	169	3
IN THE DUST, BE THROWN?	I HAVE NEVER SEEN	175	16
COME BACK, AND DUST THE POND!	SHE SWEEPS WITH	219	4
I CEDED ALL OF DUST I KNEW--	DOUBT ME! MY DIM	275	11
IF HE FLING SAND [DUST], AND PEBBLE-- . .	THE WIND DID'NT COME	316	17
I CANNOT VOUCH THE MERRY DUST	OF ALL THE SOUNDS	321	17
TOO LITTLE--DUST--	MY REWARD FOR BEING, WAS	343	V
AND THEN 'TWAS PUT AMONG THE DUST	DEATH SETS A THING	360	11
THE DUST, WILL VEX YOUR FAME--	ALTHOUGH I PUT AWAY HIS	366	25
ONE ENVIES THE DISTINGUISHED DUST-- . . .	IT FEELS A SHAME TO BE	444	3
AND FLING A DUST--THE WHILE.	THE OUTER--FROM THE	451	8
SCOOPING UP THE DUST AND CHANTING "LIVE"! .	WHILE IT IS ALIVE	491	10
THE DUST--CONNECT [ADJUST]--AND LIVE-- . .	NO CROWD THAT HAS	515	8
AND OVERLOOK--THE DUST--	THE TEST OF LOVE--IS	573	10
THE DUST IN STREETS--GO DOWN--	YOU'VE SEEN BALLOONS SET	700	18
THE DUST REPLACED, IN HOISTED ROADS-- . .	A DROP FELL ON THE APPLE	794	9
THIS QUIET DUST WAS GENTLEMEN AND LADIES .	THIS QUIET DUST WAS	813	1
THE DUST DID SCOOP ITSELF LIKE HANDS-- . .	THE WIND BEGUN TO KNEAD	824	7
DWELT HESITATING, HALF OF DUST, ...	TO THIS WORLD SHE	830	8
NOT FOR ITSELF, THE DUST IS SHY, ...	DYING! TO BE AFRAID OF	831	7
WE GO NO FURTHER WITH THE DUST	WE CAN BUT FOLLOW TO THE	920	5
THIS DUST, AND IT'S FEATURE--	THIS DUST, AND IT'S	936	1
THE SPIRIT AND THE DUST.	DEATH IS A DIALOGUE	976	2
THE DUST BEHIND I STROVE TO JOIN	THE DUST BEHIND I STROVE	992	1
A CUTICLE OF DUST	CRUMBLING IS NOT AN	997	6
THEN SOUGHT THE DUST--	SHE ROSE AS HIGH AS HIS	1011	2
AND SPIRIT TURNED [THE SPIRIT SAID] UNTO THE DUST	I HEARD, AS IF I HAD NO	1039	13
THE CHANNEL OF THE DUST WHO ONCE ACHIEVES .	OURSELVES WE DO INTER	1144	2
WHEN THE DELIGHT IS DUST	"REMEMBER ME" IMPLORED	1180	6
ABLE AS THE DUST TO EQUIP IT'S FEATURE . .	SOME WE SEE NO MORE,	1221	8
THE BUTTERFLY IN HONORED DUST	THE BUTTERFLY IN HONORED	1246	1
AUGUST THE DUST OF THAT DOMAIN--	THAT SACRED CLOSET WHEN	1273	9
FROM HIS SLIM PALACE IN THE DUST	FROM HIS SLIM PALACE IN	1300	1
IN THE DELIGHTS [AWARDS] OF DUST-- . . .	PRAISE IT--'TIS DEAD--	1384	7
TO THE STANCH [UNWILLING] DUST	TO THE STANCH DUST	1402	1
MORE RESPECTFUL--"WE ARE DUST"--	"HEAVENLY FATHER"--TAKE	1461	6
TO THAT PINK STRANGER WE CALL DUST-- . . .	OH GIVE IT MOTION--DECK	1527	5
I PRAY THE LORD THY DUST TO KEEP-- . . .	NOW I LAY THEE DOWN TO	1539	2
NOR THAT HIS FRAME WAS DUST--	HE ATE AND DRANK THE	1587	4
. . . AT] THE DUST	AS FROM THE EARTH THE	1630	5
THEY WEIGHED ME, DUST BY DUST--	I TOOK ONE DRAUGHT OF	1725	5
THEY WEIGHED ME, DUST BY DUST--	I TOOK ONE DRAUGHT OF	1725	5
WERE FLESH [DUST] EQUIVALENT	LOVE CAN DO ALL BUT	1731	4
AS HAPPY IN HER CRIB [BED] OF DUST . . .	THIS DOCILE ONE INTER	1752	V 7
DUSTIEST			
FAR DOWN THE DUSTIEST ROAD!	ONE LIFE OF SO MUCH	270	16
DUSTY			
THIS DUSTY HEART ESPIED--	A POOR--TORN HEART-- A	78	10
UPON A [THE] DUSTY [TOILSOME] WAY--	HEART, NOT SO HEAVY AS	83	14
WHEN OURSELVES WERE ALSO DUSTY--	SMILING BACK FROM	385	7
THE WORLD--FEELS DUSTY	THE WORLD--FEELS DUSTY	715	1
DUTIES			
DUTIES--OF GOSSAMER--	I WENT TO HEAVEN--	374	11
LIFE'S LITTLE DUTIES DO--PRECISELY-- . . .	I TIE MY HAT--I CREASE	443	2
FOR DUTIES DIAMOND--	YOU'VE SEEN BALLOONS SET	700	4
THE DUTIES OF THE WIND ARE FEW, ...	THE DUTIES OF THE WIND	1137	1
DUTY			
IF DUTY LIVE--CONTENTED	TO HIS SIMPLICITY	1352	3
THE PEA THAT DUTY LOCKS--	FORBIDDEN FRUIT A FLAVOR	1377	4
DWARF			
'TIS DUKE, OR DWARF, ACCORDING	THE OUTER--FROM THE	451	3
DWELL			
WHICH IN THE CLOVER DWELL.	IT'S ALL I HAVE TO BRING	26	8
I HAD RATHER DWELL LIKE HER	PIGMY SERAPHS--GONE	138	14
SUPPOSED THAT HE HAD COME TO DWELL-- . . .	THE SUN--JUST TOUCHED	232	3
DWELL TIMIDLY, WITH THEE!	DOUBT ME! MY DIM	275	17
AND THEN, IN SOVREIGN BARNS TO DWELL-- . .	THE GRASS SO LITTLE HAS	333	17
I'LL DWELL IN CALYX--GRAY--	I TEND MY FLOWERS FOR	339	24
DWELL IN ONE BLOOD	WHILE IT IS ALIVE	491	4
WHO STAY [DWELL] UPON THE WALL	THOSE FAIR--FICTITIOUS	499	6

	FIRST LINE	POEM	LINE
DWELL (CONTINUED)			
TO DWELL--DELICIOUS--ON--	I WOULD NOT PAINT--A	505	4
THE SHAPES WE BURIED, DWELL ABOUT,	OF NEARNESS TO HER	607	5
I DWELL IN POSSIBILITY--	I DWELL IN POSSIBILITY--	657	1
AND DWELL A LITTLE EVERYWHERE [GENERALLY]	COULD I BUT RIDE	661	7
DO HE DWELL--OR NAY--KNOW I--	CONSCIOUS AM I IN MY	679	18
TO REST [PAUSE]--TO REST [PAUSE / STAY / DWELL] WOULD BE	I MEANT TO FIND HER WHEN	718	10
BEST THINGS DWELL OUT OF SIGHT	BEST THINGS DWELL OUT OF	998	1
OWN [DWELL] IN EDEN NOTWITHSTANDING	PARADISE IS OF THE	1069	3
TO DWELL EXTENT AMONG,	THE DUTIES OF THE WIND	1137	6
AS FAR AS CANNON DWELL	STEP LIGHTLY ON THIS	1183	6
WHO HAS INVITED ME WITH HIM TO DWELL;	I CANNOT SEE MY SOUL BUT	1262	3
ENABLE HIM [EACH] TO DWELL--	YOU CANNOT TAKE ITSELF	1351	4
TO DWELL IN SUCH A PLACE--	THE FACT THAT EARTH IS	1408	8
COULD THAT SWEET DARKNESS WHERE THEY DWELL	COULD THAT SWEET	1493	1
ILL IT BECOMETH [IS IT BECOMING] ME TO DWELL SO WEALTHILY	TAKE ALL AWAY FROM ME,	1640	3
WE DWELL IN EVERY DAY	EDEN IS THAT	1657	2
UNNOTICED DWELL,	THE MOST IMPORTANT	1746	2
DWELLETH			
SOMETIME, HE DWELLETH IN THE GRASS!	A FUZZY FELLOW, WITHOUT	173	5
SHE DWELLETH IN THE GROUND--	SHE DWELLETH IN THE	671	1
DWELLING			
THE LITTLE DWELLING HOUSES RISE	THE COLOR OF THE GRAVE	411	15
WAS SUCH REMAINING [STILL DWELLING] THERE?"	I YEARS HAD BEEN FROM	609	8
IN THE NEAREST ORCHARD DWELLING [WAITING]	STRUCK, WAS I, NOR YET	925	15
ALIGHTING AT THE DWELLING	HOW NEWS MUST FEEL WHEN	1319	3
AND DWELLING THERE TODAY--	THE MOON UPON HER FLUENT	1528	V
DWELLINGS			
AGAIN THE SMOKE FROM DWELLINGS ROSE [CURLED]	THE WIND TOOK UP THE	1134	13
DWELLS			
THERE DWELLS ONE OTHER CREATURE	I TRIED TO THINK A	532	10
DIVINITY DWELLS UNDER SEAL.	EMBARRASSMENT OF ONE	662	7
THE CAT THAT IN THE CORNER DWELLS [SITS]	A LITTLE DOG THAT WAGS	1185	9
DWELT			
I GROPED [PERISHED / DWELT] UPON HIS BREAST--	HE TOUCHED ME, SO I LIVE	506	3
BUT FONDEST, DWELT UPON OURSELF	WE TALKED AS GIRLS DO--	586	9
THENCEFORWARD--WE--TOGETHER DWELT [WALKED]--	THE BIRDS REPORTED FROM	743	21
DWELT HESITATING, HALF OF DUST,	TO THIS WORLD SHE	830	8
I DWELT TOO LOW THAT ANY SEEK--	I WAS A PHEBE--NOTHING	1009	5
I DWELT, AS IF MYSELF WERE OUT,	I HEARD, AS IF I HAD NO	1039	9
"MADE FLESH AND DWELT AMONG US	A WORD MADE FLESH IS	1651	13
SHE DWELT SO CLOSE	TO-DAY OR THIS NOON	1702	2
DWINDLED			
HOME EFFACED--HER FACES DWINDLED--	ALL FORGOT FOR	966	9
IS SHRUNKEN [SHRIVELLED / DWINDLED / CHASTENED] SMALL	THE VASTEST EARTHLY DAY	1328	2
DWINDLING			
DEFORMING--DWINDLING--GULPHING UP--	I HAD THE GLORY--THAT	349	6
DYER			
SOME DYER OF A DISTANT TREE	SUMMER BEGINS TO HAVE	1682	11
DYES			
DYES--SAID HE--HAVE I--	AUTUMN--OVERLOOKED MY	748	2
SHE HAS FULFILLED HER DYES	NATURE CAN DO NO MORE	1673	2
DYING			
ON EARS THAT DYING LIE--	DISTRUSTFUL OF THE	20	12
AS HE DEFEATED--DYING--	SUCCESS IS COUNTED	67	9
IF THIS IS "DYING"	IF THIS IS "FADING"	120	3
WHOSE DYING EYES, NO COUNTRY	TO FIGHT ALOUD, IS VERY	126	7
DYING! DYING IN THE NIGHT!	DYING! DYING IN THE	158	1
DYING! DYING IN THE NIGHT!	DYING! DYING IN THE	158	1
IT CANT BE "DYING"!	IT CANT BE "SUMMER"!	221	6
LOOKING AT DEATH, IS DYING--	'TIS SO APPALLING--IT	281	15
'TIS NOT THAT DYING HURTS US SO--	'TIS NOT THAT DYING	335	1
BUT DYING--IS A DIFFERENT WAY--	'TIS NOT THAT DYING	335	3
DYING--ANNULS THE POWER TO KILL.	IF ANY SINK, ASSURE THAT	358	8
THE DYING--BUT A SYLLABLE--	UNIT, LIKE DEATH, FOR	408	11
HOW "THEY ARE DYING MOSTLY--NOW"--	THE MANNER OF IT'S DEATH	468	11
BUT WE--ARE DYING IN DRAMA--	WE DREAM--IT IS GOOD WE	531	7
I'VE SEEN A DYING EYE	I'VE SEEN A DYING EYE	547	1
A DYING TIGER--MOANED FOR DRINK--	A DYING TIGER--MOANED	566	1
AS DYING--SAY IT DOES--	YOU'LL FIND--IT WHEN YOU	610	10
IT WAS DYING--THEN--	IN FALLING TIMBERS	614	12
WAS DYING AS HE THOUGHT--OR DIFFERENT--	TO KNOW JUST HOW HE	622	6
IN DYING--'TIS AS IF OUR SOULS [WORLD / SELVES / SUN]	BEREAVEMENT IN THEIR	645	11
PROMISE THIS--WHEN YOU BE DYING--	PROMISE THIS--WHEN YOU	648	1
WOLFE DEMANDED DURING DYING	WOLFE DEMANDED DURING	678	1
AND DYING--LIFETIME--	'TWOULD EASE--A	682	12
'TIS DYING--I AM DOING--BUT	THE SUN KEPT SETTING--	692	15
FLAGS--VEX A DYING FACE--	THE WORLD--FEELS DUSTY	715	5
TO EARS THE DYING SIDE--	UPON CONCLUDED LIVES	735	6
THAN DYING HALF [PART]--THEN RALLYING	THE WHOLE OF IT CAME NOT	762	11
DYING! TO BE AFRAID OF THEE	DYING! TO BE AFRAID OF	831	1
FIGHT STERNLY IN A DYING EYE	DYING! TO BE AFRAID OF	831	10
THE DYING--AS IT WERE A HIGHT	THE ADMIRATIONS--AND	906	3
RALLIES HER GLOW [THE WEST], LIKE A DYING FRIEND--	FAIRER THROUGH FADING--	938	5
TO THE FAILING [DYING / CLOUDING] EYE	ROBBED BY DEATH--BUT	971	2

	FIRST LINE	POEM	LINE
DYING (CONTINUED)			
NOT ALL DIE EARLY, DYING YOUNG--	NOT ALL DIE EARLY, DYING	990	1
DYING AT MY MUSIC!	DYING AT MY MUSIC!	1003	1
THE DYING, IS A TRIFLE, PAST,	TOO SCANTY 'TWAS TO DIE	1013	5
THE DYING MULTIFOLD--WITHOUT	TOO SCANTY 'TWAS TO DIE	1013	7
HOW MANY THINGS THE DYING PLAY	WERE IT BUT ME THAT	1015	3
TO DIE--WITHOUT THE DYING	TO DIE--WITHOUT THE	1017	1
THE DYING NEED BUT LITTLE, DEAR,	THE DYING NEED BUT	1026	1
EXCEPT THE DYING--THIS TO US	THE LAST NIGHT THAT SHE	1100	3
THY PRIVILEGE OF DYING	THROUGH WHAT TRANSPORTS	1153	7
NOR IS DYING DOUBLE--	SAFE DESPAIR IT IS THAT	1243	8
THOSE--DYING THEN,	THOSE--DYING THEN,	1551	1
I GIVE [SEND] MY DYING KISS--	"GO TELL IT"--WHAT A	1554	8
CONVEY MY DYING KISS--	"GO TELL IT"--WHAT A	1554 V	8
THAT DYING I MAY EARN THE LOOK [GAZE]	TRIED ALWAYS AND	1559	3
T'WAS COMFORT IN HER DYING ROOM	T'WAS COMFORT IN HER	1703	1
DIVERSION FROM THE DYING THEME	T'WAS COMFORT IN HER	1703	5
DYNASTIES			
DYNASTIES REPAIRED--	ALL BUT DEATH, CAN BE	749	2
DYNASTY			
SUFFICIENT DYNASTY--	MY REWARD FOR BEING, WAS	343 V	
HIMSELF--HIS DATELESS DYNASTY--	BEHIND ME--DIPS ETERNITY	721	10
EAGER			
PHILIP--WHEN BEWILDERED [QUESTIONED EAGER]	IF THOSE I LOVED WERE	29	7
IMPS IN EAGER CAUCUS	SOUL, WILT THOU TOSS	139	7
THE EAGER LOOK--ON LANDSCAPES--	THE TINT I CANNOT TAKE--	627	13
IF EAGER FOR THE DEAD	THE SUN IS GAY OR STARK	878	4
THE HOLLOWS ROUND HIS EAGER EYES	THE HOLLOWS ROUND HIS	955	1
WOULD SCAN THE MIGHTY [EAGER / BREATHLESS / HURRYING / ...	TO FLEE FROM MEMORY	1242	6
EAGERNESS			
FOR COVETING [EAGERNESS] TO LOOK AT THEE--	IF I MAY HAVE IT, WHEN	577	27
HAVE I THE EAGERNESS	WHAT DID THEY DO SINCE I	900	4
EAGLE			
THE EAGLE OF HIS NEST	NO RACK CAN TORTURE ME--	384	9
EAGLE'S			
THE EAGLE'S GOLDEN BREAKFAST STRANGLES [DAZZLES]--THEM--	VICTORY COMES LATE--	690	12
EAGLES			
EAGLES ON MY BUCKLES--	NO MATTER--NOW--SWEET--	704	11
EAR			
BREATHE IN EAR MORE MODERN	IT DID NOT SURPRISE ME--	39	7
ON WHOSE FORBIDDEN EAR	SUCCESS IS COUNTED	67	10
YET TO MY IRRITATED EAR	HEART, NOT SO HEAVY AS	83	7
ON EAR TOO FAR FOR THE DELIGHT,	AS WATCHERS HANG UPON	121	5
UPON HER PUZZLED EAR--	ALL OVERGROWN BY CUNNING	148 V	
BY EAR UNHEARD,	JUST LOST, WHEN I WAS	160	14
BABBLES THE BEE IN A STOLID EAR,	SAFE IN THEIR ALABASTER	216	9
WERE MY EAR--AS NEAR HIS NEST--	TEACH HIM--WHEN HE MAKES	227	5
SINCE THE SOLE EAR I CARED TO CHARM--	PUT UP MY LUTE!	261	3
AND BEING, BUT AN EAR,	I FELT A FUNERAL, IN MY	280	14
AND ON THE EAR CAN [DOTH] GO	A MIEN TO MOVE A QUEEN--	283	17
AND EAR--AND HEAVEN--NUMB--	LIKE SOME OLD FASHIONED	302	16
BUT JUST HIS EAR COULD KNOW	ALTHOUGH I PUT AWAY HIS	366	10
ME--HEAR! MY FOREIGN EAR	ME--COME! MY DAZZLED	431	3
BY MEANS OF IT--IN GOD'S EAR--	PRAYER IS THE LITTLE	437	5
TO OUR--EAR--	IT'S THOUGHTS--AND JUST	495	16
THE EAR RINGS OF PIZARRO	I ENVY SEAS, WHEREON HE	498	15
IT'S FINER--OWN THE EAR--	I WOULD NOT PAINT--A	505	13
OR WIND'S BRIGHT SIGNAL TO THE EAR--	LIKE FLOWERS, THAT HEARD	513	10
THE FASHION OF THE EAR	TO HEAR AN ORIOLE SING	526	7
BUT THE [A] FINE EAR	INCONCEIVABLY SOLEMN!	582	13
EXTEMPORIZING IN YOUR EAR	DID YOU EVER STAND IN A	590	13
COULD THRILL [PENETRATE] THEIR MORTISED EAR	WHAT CARE THE DEAD, FOR	592	13
ENAMORING THE EAR	THE TREES LIKE TASSELS--	606	6
AND BROKE [SMOTE] AGAINST MY EAR--	I YEARS HAD BEEN FROM	609	12
SHE SQUANDERS ON YOUR HEAD [EAR]	YOU'LL KNOW HER--BY HER	634	25
NO START [CLICK] IN APPREHENSION'S EAR,	I THINK TO LIVE--MAY BE	646	15
THIGH [EYE] OF GRANITE--AND THEW [EAR]--OF STEEL--	AH, TENERIFFE!	666	7
THE SPIRIT IS THE CONSCIOUS EAR.	THE SPIRIT IS THE	733	1
THERE HANGS A SMALLER [MINOR] EAR	THE SPIRIT IS THE	733	6
WISER MEN [ONE / EAR] MAY WEARY--	NEVER FOR SOCIETY	746	5
I COULD NOT MISS AN EAR--	GOD GAVE A LOAF TO EVERY	791	10
PRICKS HIS EAR--REPORT TO HEAR	GRIEF IS A MOUSE--	793	6
CAN ONE FIND THE RARE EAR	GOOD TO HIDE, AND HEAR	842	7
SAVED FOR YOUR EAR WHEN LUTES BE OLD.	SPLIT THE LARK--AND	861	4
TO MY QUICK EAR THE LEAVES--CONFERRED--	TO MY QUICK EAR THE	891	1
I HEARD, AS IF I HAD NO EAR	I HEARD, AS IF I HAD NO	1039	1
REPORTLESS MEASURES, TO THE EAR	REPORTLESS SUBJECTS, TO	1048	5
NO EAR, NO DOOR,	AIR HAS NO RESIDENCE, NO	1060	2
UNTO A MISER'S EAR--	BECAUSE 'TWAS RICHES I	1093	8
THAT ONLY TO THE EAR OF GOD	A DEED KNOCKS FIRST AT	1216	7
TO A CURRENT'S EAR--	I THINK THAT THE ROOT OF	1302	6
THAT MAKES THE EAR INORDINATE	THE LONG SIGH OF THE	1359	7
WARM THIS INCLEMENT EAR	PRAISE IT--'TIS DEAD--	1384	3
NOTHING WITH A TONGUE OR EAR--[AN EAR OR TONGUE--]	"SECRETS" IS A DAILY	1385	9
NOTHING WITH A TONGUE OR EAR--[AN EAR OR TONGUE--]	"SECRETS" IS A DAILY	1385	9

	FIRST LINE	POEM	LINE
EAR (CONTINUED)			
A BILLOW WHISPERED IN HIS EAR,	THE WATERS CHASED HIM AS	1749	3
AN EAR CAN BREAK A HUMAN HEART	THE SADDEST NOISE, THE	1764	17
WE WISH THE EAR HAD NOT A HEART	THE SADDEST NOISE, THE	1764	19
EARL			
FOR 'TWAS TOO STATELY FOR AN EARL--	I MET A KING THIS	166	9
OR THE EARL--AN EARL?	DID THE HAREBELL LOOSE	213	8
OR THE EARL--AN EARL?	DID THE HAREBELL LOOSE	213	8
NOT--I--THE EARL--	THE MALAY--TOOK THE	452	2
SKILL--TO HOLD MY BROW LIKE AN EARL--	I AM ASHAMED--I HIDE--	473	16
OF EARL AND MIDGE	A TOAD, CAN DIE OF LIGHT	583	4
RIDING TO MEET THE EARL--	DROPPED INTO THE ETHER	665	8
BUT WHEN I'M EARL--	NO MATTER--NOW--SWEET--	704	2
WHEN I'M EARL?	NO MATTER--NOW--SWEET--	704	8
AN INDIAMAN--AN EARL--	GOD GAVE A LOAF TO EVERY	791	14
EACH OCCUPANT AN EARL	NO LIFE CAN POMPLESS	1626	V 8
EARLDOM			
AN EARLDOM OUT OF SIGHT TO HOLD,	BECAUSE 'TWAS RICHES I	1093	5
EARLIER			
EARLIER, BY THE DIAL,	I OFTEN PASSED THE	51	7
HAD YOU EARLIER BLUNDERED IN	TAKE YOUR HEAVEN FURTHER	388	3
THE DUSK DREW EARLIER IN--	AS IMPERCEPTIBLY AS	1540	9
EARL'S			
THAN AN EARL'S DISTINGUISHED FACE--	PIGMY SERAPHS--GONE	138	13
EARLY			
CHAT OF THE "EARLY DEAD"--	THERE'S SOMETHING	45	14
IF BIRDS SHOULD BUILD AS EARLY	IF I SHOULD DIE,	54	7
ANGELS, IN THE EARLY MORNING	ANGELS, IN THE EARLY	94	1
AND SOW THE EARLY SEED--	SEXTON! MY MASTER'S	96	4
EARLY AGED, AND OFTEN COLD,	SOME, TOO FRAGILE FOR	141	10
OR EARLY TASK TO DO?	ON SUCH A NIGHT, OR SUCH	146	16
OR [NOR] "EARLY HISTORY"--	DUST IS THE ONLY SECRET	153	8
IT'S EARLY--YET--FOR "SPRING"!	IT CANT BE "SUMMER"!	221	3
BLISS' EARLY SHAPE	I HAD THE GLORY--THAT	349	5
I STARTED EARLY--TOOK MY DOG--	I STARTED EARLY--TOOK MY	520	1
THAT HURT THEM EARLY--SUCH A LAPSE	I MEASURE EVERY GRIEF I	561	19
BUT EARLY, YET, FOR GOD--	IT WAS TOO LATE FOR MAN	623	2
THE BEGGAR LAD--DIES EARLY--	THE BEGGAR LAD--DIES	717	1
FROM THE EARLY SUM--	ONE DAY IS THERE OF THE	814	10
IT WILL BE AMPLY EARLY	WHEN THE ASTRONOMER	851	7
EARLY AND SERE, IT'S END	AND THIS OF ALL MY HOPES	913	4
NOT ALL DIE EARLY, DYING YOUNG--	NOT ALL DIE EARLY, DYING	990	1
BY EARLY, STOOPING NIGHT--	THE DAY GREW SMALL,	1140	2
T'IS EARLY AS OUR BREATH	WITCHCRAFT HAS NOT A	1708	2
EARN			
BEYOND THE ART TO EARN--	OF ALL THE SOUNDS	321	10
EARN HER OWN SURPRISE!	I KNOW THAT HE EXISTS.	338	8
TO EARN A MINE--WOULD RUN	A TONGUE--TO TELL HIM I	400	5
MYSELF HAD JUST TO EARN--	REMOVED FROM ACCIDENT OF	424	4
I COULD NOT HOPE--FOR MINE--[TO EARN]	I HAD BEEN HUNGRY, ALL	579	8
NO OTHER--STOPPED [CARED] TO EARN--	TO OFFER BRAVE	767	8
ALL DAYS, I DID NOT EARN THE SAME	I MADE SLOW RICHES BUT	843	5
THE BIRD MUST SING TO EARN THE CRUMB	THE BIRD MUST SING TO	880	1
BUT POSSIBLE TO EARN	SUPERIORITY TO FATE	1081	4
BUT ARE NOT KNOWN TO EARN--	ALL MEN FOR HONOR	1193	2
I EVER CARED TO EARN--	THE STARS ARE OLD, THAT	1249	4
TO EARN IT BY DISDAINING IT	TO EARN IT BY DISDAINING	1427	1
THAT DYING I MAY EARN THE LOOK [GAZE]	TRIED ALWAYS AND	1559	3
EARNED			
MYSELF HAD EARNED IT--ME,	BECAUSE 'TWAS RICHES I	1093	2
IS EARNED--	LUCK IS NOT CHANCE--	1350	4
WITH THE ENCOMIUM IT EARNED	PRAISE IT--'TIS DEAD--	1384	4
PAID ALL THAT LIFE HAD EARNED	HOW DARE THE ROBINS SING	1724	5
EARNEST			
PROVE PIERCING EARNEST--	I KNOW THAT HE EXISTS.	338	10
EARNING			
I WORKED FOR CHAFF AND EARNING WHEAT	I WORKED FOR CHAFF AND	1269	1
EARNS			
ONE EARNS [GETS] BY MEASURING THE GRAVE--	MY FIRST WELL DAY--SINCE	574	27
EARRING			
EARRING--OR STONE--	I KNOW SOME LONELY	289	27
EARRINGS			
I BROOCH AND EARRINGS FOR MYSELF,	WHEN DIAMONDS ARE A	397	3
EARS			
ON EARS THAT DYING LIE--	DISTRUSTFUL OF THE	20	12
TO HOLD MY LIFE, AND HOLD MY EARS	I CRIED AT PITY--NOT AT	588	19
AND HELD MY EARS, AND LIKE A THIEF	I YEARS HAD BEEN FROM	609	23
TO EARS THE DYING SIDE--	UPON CONCLUDED LIVES	735	6
EARTH			
OH THE EARTH WAS MADE FOR LOVERS, FOR DAMSEL, AND HOPELESS SWAIN,	AWAKE YE MUSES NINE,	1	3
ALL THINGS DO GO A COURTING, IN EARTH, OR SEA, OR AIR,	AWAKE YE MUSES NINE,	1	5
EARTH IS A MERRY DAMSEL, AND HEAVEN A KNIGHT SO TRUE,	AWAKE YE MUSES NINE,	1	23
AND EARTH IS QUITE COQUETTISH, AND BESEEMETH IN VAIN TO SUE.	AWAKE YE MUSES NINE,	1	24
THE EARTH UPON AN AXIS	"SIC TRANSIT GLORIA	3	33
AND THE EARTH [WORLD]--THEY TELL ME--	FREQUENTLY THE WOODS ARE	6	9
AT SUCH A CURIOUS EARTH!	GOING TO HEAVEN!	79	23

	FIRST LINE	POEM	LINE
EARTH (CONTINUED)			
HID HEAVEN AND EARTH FROM VIEW.	AN AWFUL TEMPEST MASHED	198	4
I THINK THAT EARTH FEELS SO	I'M "WIFE"--I'VE	199	7
I REASON, EARTH IS SHORT--	I REASON, EARTH IS SHORT	301	1
EARTH WOULD HAVE BEEN TOO MUCH--I SEE--	I SHOULD HAVE BEEN TOO	313	13
THE EARTH REVERSED HER HEMISPHERES--	I SAW NO WAY--THE	378	3
THE EARTH LAYS BACK THESE TIRED LIVES	THE MONTHS HAVE ENDS--	423	5
'TIS HIS TO STIMULATE THE EARTH--	TO INTERRUPT HIS YELLOW	591	9
'TIS A BAFFLING EARTH--	IN FALLING TIMBERS	614	14
WHEN EARTH--CANNOT BE HAD--	IT WAS TOO LATE FOR MAN	623	6
HEAVEN IS SHY OF EARTH--THAT'S ALL--	OUT OF SIGHT? WHAT OF	703	11
FOR INLANDS--THE EARTH IS THE UNDER SIDE--	BY MY WINDOW HAVE I FOR	797	9
HE THREW A MENACE AT THE EARTH--	THE WIND BEGUN TO KNEAD	824	V 3
HIDING INDIVIDUALS FROM THE EARTH	ABSENCE DISEMBODIES--SO	860	2
THE EARTH HAS SEEMED TO ME A DRUM,	WHEN I HAVE SEEN THE SUN	888	7
THE EXPONENT OF EARTH--	LOVE--IS ANTERIOR TO	917	4
THE FOOT UPON THE EARTH	AS PLAN FOR NOON AND	960	4
AND ALL THE EARTH STROVE COMMON ROUND--	DENIAL--IS THE ONLY FACT	965	5
TO MAKE ME FAIREST OF THE EARTH--	FITTER TO SEE HIM, I MAY	968	5
THE SINGLE FLOWER OF THE EARTH	IT BLOOMED AND DROPT, A	978	17
THERE IS NO SILENCE IN THE EARTH--SO SILENT	THERE IS NO SILENCE IN	1004	1
EARTH AT THE BEST	SO LARGE MY WILL	1024	9
WHICH IF THEY DO NOT FIT FOR EARTH	TO HELP OUR BLEAKER	1064	3
ENACTED UPON EARTH--	THE BUSTLE IN A HOUSE	1078	4
THE EARTH AND I, ALONE,	THE SUN WENT DOWN--NO	1079	2
THE EARTH AND I AND ONE	THE SUN WENT DOWN--NO	1079	6
THE FOUR DIVISIONS OF THE EARTH	THE WIND TOOK UP THE	1134	5
THAT COME TO EARTH TO STAY,	TOO FEW THE MORNINGS BE,	1186	5
OF STRANGERS IS THE EARTH THE INN	THE FROST WAS NEVER SEEN	1202	15
SO MUCH OF HEAVEN HAS GONE FROM EARTH	SO MUCH OF HEAVEN HAS	1228	1
SOMEWHERE UPON THE GENERAL EARTH	SOMEWHERE UPON THE	1231	1
THE CALYX IS THE EARTH--	THE LILAC IS AN ANCIENT	1241	10
WE COULD NOT LOOK UPON THE EARTH [WORLD]--	HAD WE OUR SENSES	1284	7
IN SUCH AN EARTH AS OUR'S--	NOT WITH A CLUB, THE	1304	14
GATHERED INTO THE EARTH,	GATHERED INTO THE EARTH,	1370	1
AT HIS NEW WHITE HOUSE THE EARTH	I SUPPOSE THE TIME WILL	1381	11
THE FACT THAT EARTH IS HEAVEN--	THE FACT THAT EARTH IS	1408	1
THERE WAS NO HARM IN EARTH OR SKY--	IT WAS A QUIET SEEMING	1419	2
BUT WHEN THE EARTH BEGAN TO JAR	IT WAS A QUIET SEEMING	1419	7
AND FILLING ALL THE EARTH AND AIR [SKY]	HIS ORIENTAL HERESIES	1526	3
THEY STORM THE EARTH AND STUN THE AIR,	FROM ALL THE JAILS THE	1532	5
HE [SHE] RAN AWAY FROM EARTH--	CLIMBING TO REACH THE	1566	4
HE BOWED TO HEAVEN INSTEAD OF EARTH [EVERY HEAVEN ABOVE / . . .	THE BOBOLINK IS GONE--	1591	6
AS FROM THE EARTH THE LIGHT [FAIR] BALLOON	AS FROM THE EARTH THE	1630	1
A LETTER IS A JOY OF EARTH--	A LETTER IS A JOY OF	1639	1
THAT EARTH SH'D BE SO BIG--	"RED SEA," INDEED! TALK	1642	10
MY RIGHT TO WALK UPON THE EARTH	I KNOW OF PEOPLE IN THE	1665	7
THE MAJESTIES OF EARTH	THE OVERTAKELESSNESS OF	1691	4
FOR WHICH WE GAVE THE EARTH	WHEN WE HAVE CEASED TO	1706	3
HIGH FROM THE EARTH I HEARD A BIRD;	HIGH FROM THE EARTH I	1723	1
THE EARTH HAS MANY KEYS.	THE EARTH HAS MANY KEYS.	1775	1
EARTHEN			
THAN TO THE EARTHEN DOOR--	WE CAN BUT FOLLOW TO THE	920	6
EARTHLY			
SUPREMEST EARTHLY SUM--	ONE BLESSING HAD I THAN	756	12
MY EARTHLY HOUR [HUMAN LIFE] TO ME	SOME WRETCHED CREATURE,	1111	V 4
ONE [THIS] REQUISITE HAS FIRE THAT LASTS [EARTHLY FIRE / MORTAL FIRE]	THE SMOULDERING EMBERS	1132	7
WHEN I SHALL LONG FOR EARTHLY PLAY	IN THY LONG PARADISE OF	1145	3
WITHOUT AN EARTHLY CAUSE	A LITTLE DOG THAT WAGS	1185	6
THE VASTEST EARTHLY DAY	THE VASTEST EARTHLY DAY	1328	1
THE WORTHLESSNESS [EMPTINESS] OF EARTHLY THINGS	THE WORTHLESSNESS OF	1373	1
EARTHQUAKE			
THOU SETTEST [STIRREST] EARTHQUAKE IN THE SOUTH--	AT LEAST--TO PRAY--IS	502	5
A QUIET--EARTHQUAKE STYLE--	A STILL--VOLCANO--LIFE--	601	5
EARTH'S			
WHEN FRIEND--AND EARTH'S OCCASION	THE SOUL'S SUPERIOR	306	3
BEYOND EARTH'S TRAFFICKING FRONTIER,	NOT THAT HE GOES--WE	1435	3
IS EARTH'S CORROBORATION	THE FASCINATING CHILL	1480	2
EARTHS			
FOR EARTHS, GROW THICK AS	PERHAPS I ASKED TOO	352	3
NOR TIE TO EARTHS TO COME--	I HAVE NO LIFE BUT THIS	1398	5
EASE			
I'M THE LITTLE "HEART'S EASE"!	I'M THE LITTLE "HEART'S	176	1
NOR WILL I, THE LITTLE HEART'S EASE--	I'M THE LITTLE "HEART'S	176	13
RENOWNED TO EASE [STIR] EXTREMITY--	I GOT SO I COULD HEAR	293	15
WE BOUGHT--TO EASE THEIR PLACE--	YOU'LL FIND--IT WHEN YOU	610	16
WITH EASE--AND YOU--BESIDE--	THE BRAIN--IS WIDER THAN	632	4
FOR EASE OF [FOR SIMPLE / BECAUSE OF] GIANTURE--	SIZE CIRCUMSCRIBES--IT	641	4
'TWOULD EASE--A BUTTERFLY--	'TWOULD EASE--A	682	1
FOR GREATNESS, THAT IS ILL AT EASE [COMPOSED]	WHO GIANTS KNOW, WITH	796	3
AT HOME [EASE]--AMONG THE BILLOWS--AS	SHE STAKED HER FEATHERS	798	7
IF I CAN EASE ONE LIFE THE ACHING	IF I CAN STOP ONE HEART	919	3
WOULD FEEL AS THOROUGHLY AT EASE	A FACE DEVOID OF LOVE OR	1711	4
EASED			
NOR EASED--OF LATITUDE--	CONJECTURING A CLIMATE	562	8

	FIRST LINE	POEM	LINE
EASED (CONTINUED)			
AS THE TIGER EASED	AS THE STARVED MAELSTROM	872	4
AS LIGHTNING TO THE CHILDREN EASED	TELL ALL THE TRUTH BUT	1129	5
EASEL			
FOR THE EASEL HERE	ARTISTS WRESTLED HERE!	110	5
EASES			
SHE EASES FROM HER TEETH	THE WHOLE OF IT CAME NOT	762	6
EASIER			
'TWERE EASIER TO DIE--	THE MURMUR OF A BEE	155	4
IS EASIER TO FIND--	A SHADY FRIEND--FOR	278	2
THIS THIRST WOULD BLISTER--EASIER--NOW--	ONE YEAR AGO--JOTS WHAT?	296	16
NO EASIER DIVEST--	NO RACK CAN TORTURE ME--	384	10
IT MIGHT BE EASIER	IT MIGHT BE LONELIER	405	13
OTHERS--EXTINGUISH EASIER--	MORE LIFE--WENT OUT--	422	13
'TWOULD GIVE AN EASIER--PAIN--	IT WOULD NEVER BE COMMON	430	8
THAT'S EASIER--THAN BRAID THE HAIR--	TO MAKE ONE'S TOILETTE--	485	5
THAT'S EASIER--THAN THE OTHER FILM	YOU KNOW THAT PORTRAIT	504	15
'TWERE EASIER FOR YOU--	THE BRAIN, WITHIN IT'S	556	4
OR HAS AN EASIER SIZE.	I MEASURE EVERY GRIEF I	561	4
TILL [WHERE] ALGEBRA IS EASIER--	IT TROUBLED ME AS ONCE I	600	11
THE EASIER TO LET GO--	YOU'LL FIND--IT WHEN YOU	610	2
AND MAJESTY--BE EASIER--	I THINK TO LIVE--MAY BE	646	11
EASIER--FOR THE SKY--	LET US PLAY YESTERDAY--	728	26
MAY BE EASIER REACHED [BETTER ATTAINED / EASIER GAINED]--THIS WAY--	BY MY WINDOW HAVE I FOR	797	8
MAY BE EASIER REACHED [BETTER ATTAINED / EASIER GAINED]--THIS WAY--	BY MY WINDOW HAVE I FOR	797	8
THAN WANE [LIVE] IS EASIER--	I'D RATHER RECOLLECT A	1349	8
T'IS EASIER TO PITY THOSE WHEN DEAD	T'IS EASIER TO PITY	1698	1
EASIEST			
EASIEST OF ARTS, THEY SAY	KNOWS HOW TO FORGET!	433	V
'TIS EASIEST TO LIE	HERE, WHERE THE DAISIES	1037	2
EASILY			
COULD EASILY OUTGROW--	I KNOW LIVES, I COULD	372	8
WERE EASILY SUPPLIED	THE BEGGAR AT THE DOOR	1240	2
BUT TAKE AWAY AS DIFFICULT [IMPOTENT / EASILY]	YOU CANNOT TAKE ITSELF	1351	7
EASING			
EASING MY FAMINE	LET US PLAY YESTERDAY--	728	5
OF HEAVEN, EASING ANALYSIS,	THE DEFINITION OF BEAUTY	988	3
EAST			
EAST OF ETERNITY--	SLEEP IS SUPPOSED TO BE	13	12
FAR--AS THE EAST FROM EVEN--	TAKEN FROM MEN--THIS	53	9
A LITTLE EAST OF [OVER] JORDAN,	A LITTLE EAST OF JORDAN,	59	1
AS WATCHERS HANG UPON THE EAST,	AS WATCHERS HANG UPON	121	1
AS THAT SAME WATCHER, WHEN THE EAST	AS WATCHERS HANG UPON	121	7
STILL REARS THE EAST HER AMBER FLAG--	A SOMETHING IN A	122	16
EAST INDIA--FOR YOU!	MY EYE IS FULLER THAN MY	202	4
AND NOW YOU'VE LITTERED ALL THE EAST	SHE SWEEPS WITH	219	7
I ASKED THE EAST,	DELIGHT IS AS THE FLIGHT	257	11
THE VANE A LITTLE TO THE EAST--	A SHADY FRIEND--FOR	278	5
THE PURPLE COULD NOT KEEP THE EAST--	THE DAY CAME SLOW--TILL	304	5
UNBROKEN FOREHEAD FROM THE EAST	IT SIFTS FROM LEADEN	311	7
UNTO THE EAST AGAIN--	IT SIFTS FROM LEADEN	311	8
WHEN THE EAST IS RED?	GOOD MORNING--MIDNIGHT--	425	10
UNTO [OVER] THE EAST, AND VICTORY--	A WIFE--AT DAYBREAK I	461	6
THE EAST--WOULD DEEM EXTRAVAGANT--	I RECKON--WHEN I COUNT	569	11
AND [THEN] BADE IT TO THE EAST	HE FOUND MY BEING--SET	603	4
OF RESURRECTION? IS THE EAST	AFRAID! OF WHOM AM I	608	9
FAR AS NORTH--AND EAST,	BLOOM UPON THE MOUNTAIN	667	14
'TIS THIS ENAMORS [AFFLICTS US] IN THE EAST--	THE LOVE A LIFE CAN SHOW	673	10
THE EAST--HER PURPLE TROTH	THE SUNRISE RUNS FOR	710	2
THE SUN ENGROSSED THE EAST--	THE BIRDS BEGUN AT FOUR	783	21
THEN ORIENT SHOWED [THE EAST PUT OUT / NATURE PUT OUT] A SINGLE FLAG,	A DROP FELL ON THE APPLE	794	15
OLD, INDEED, THE EAST,	ALWAYS MINE!	839	7
HIS EYE, IT IS THE EAST AND WEST--	THE SUN AND MOON MUST	871	5
MORNING--THE EAST COMPELLING THE SILL	NOON--IS THE HINGE OF	931	3
WHO IS THE EAST?	WHO IS THE EAST?	1032	1
ALL HIS EAST	SAID DEATH TO PASSION	1033	6
THE PURPLE IN THE EAST IS SET	THESE ARE THE SIGNS TO	1077	11
THEN GAVE [BENT / BOWED] THE EAST UNTO THE WEST	THE WIND TOOK UP THE	1134	3
HIS MIND LIKE FABRICS OF THE EAST	HIS MIND LIKE FABRICS OF	1446	1
AS GALLANTLY AS IF THE EAST	HER LOSSES MAKE OUR	1562	3
TO THE BRIGHT EAST SHE FLIES,	TO THE BRIGHT EAST SHE	1573	1
EASTER			
SUNSET--AT EASTER--	IF HE DISSOLVE--THEN--	236	4
EASTERN			
THE EASTERN EXILES--BE--	THE LONESOME FOR THEY	262	2
OF PEARLS IN EASTERN WATERS,	REMOVED FROM ACCIDENT OF	424	7
DEATH BUT THE DRIFT OF EASTERN GRAY,	BEHIND ME--DIPS ETERNITY	721	4
EASY			
AH LITTLE ROSE--HOW EASY	NOBODY KNOWS THIS LITTLE	35	11
IT IS EASY TO WORK WHEN THE SOUL IS AT PLAY--	IT IS EASY TO WORK WHEN	244	1
HOW EASY, TORMENT, NOW--	'TIS SO APPALLING--IT	281	7
NOT EASY TO SURPRISE!	I KNOW SOME LONELY	289	12
SUFFOCATE--WITH EASY WO--	HER--"LAST POEMS"--	312	17
STOOPS--TO AN EASY CLOVER--	THE NEAREST DREAM	319	5
I MENTION--EASY--HERE--	I CANNOT DANCE UPON MY	326	18
THOSE--DANGLE EASY--ON MY ARM,	PERHAPS I ASKED TOO	352	6

	FIRST LINE	POEM		LINE
EASY (CONTINUED)				
TELL THAT THE WORST, IS EASY IN A MOMENT--	IF ANY SINK, ASSURE THAT	358		5
IT'S EASY AS A SIGN--	THERE'S BEEN A DEATH, IN	389		22
HOW EASY ALL CAN SEE	I ENVY SEAS, WHEREON HE	498		6
THROUGH GENTLE [CURIOUS / EASY] MIRACLE OF DEATH--	THOSE FAIR--FICTITIOUS	499		23
AND OUT [BY], AND EASY ON--	I WOULD NOT PAINT--A	505		12
THAT TIPS SO FREQUENT, [SLIPS SO EASY] NOW,	I PRAYED, AT FIRST, A	576		19
THEMSELVES AS EASY FREEZE--	WHAT CARE THE DEAD, FOR	592		18
YET BLUE--AND SOLID [EASY]--STOOD--	IT TROUBLED ME AS ONCE I	600		6
DISTINCTNESS--EASY--SEEMS--	OF NEARNESS TO HER	607		4
AND EASY AS A STAR	THEY SHUT ME UP IN PROSE	613		10
AN EASY BREEZE DO PUT AFLOAT	OF BEING IS A BIRD	653		3
IN EASY--EVEN--DAZZLING PACE--	OF BEING IS A BIRD	653		7
"GENERAL, THE BRITISH"--"EASY"	WOLFE DEMANDED DURING	678		3
A REEF--CRAWLED EASY FROM THE SEA	I SOMETIMES DROP IT, FOR	708		13
IT'S EASY TO INVENT A LIFE--	IT'S EASY TO INVENT A	724		1
IT'S EASY TO EFFACE IT--	IT'S EASY TO INVENT A	724		5
SO EASY TO THE SKY--	HAVE ANY LIKE MYSELF	736		12
AND BEEN MYSELF THAT EASY [DISTANT] THING	I PLAY AT RICHES--TO	801		7
IS EASY [COMMON], POSSIBLY--	AWAY FROM HOME ARE SOME	821		4
FEELS EASY, AS WHEN DAY LETS GO	WHEN ONE HAS GIVEN UP	853		3
AS EASY THE SECRETING HER	OF CONSCIOUSNESS, HER	894		3
WOULD BE AN EASY ADVERSITY	HOW HAPPY I WAS IF I	898		3
STILL--JUST AS EASY, IF IT BE THY WILL	ONLY A SHRINE, BUT MINE	918		10
ROBBED BY DEATH--BUT THAT WAS EASY--	ROBBED BY DEATH--BUT	971		1
THE EASY GUEST COMPLIED	THE FINGERS OF THE LIGHT	1000		9
AND EASY SWEEPS OF SKY--	MY COCOON TIGHTENS--	1099		8
YET [BUT] EASY AS THE [A] NARROW SNAKE	THE FROST OF DEATH WAS	1136		12
SPRANG LIGHTLY TO [ROSE SOFTLY IN / TURNED EASY IN] THE SKY	A SPARROW TOOK A SLICE	1211	V	6
TO HIM WHO EASY OWNS--	I CANNOT WANT IT MORE--	1301		6
SO EASY [KINDRED / FULLY / FREE / AMPLE SEEMS / BOUNTEOUS / . . .	YOUR THOUGHTS DONT HAVE	1452		6
AN EASY MORNING'S RIDE--	A ROUTE OF EVANESCENCE	1463		8
SO EASY [SUPPLE / PLIANT] TO REPAIR.	SOFTENED BY TIME'S	1738		8
'TIS EASY TO BEWARE	THROUGH THOSE OLD	1753		6
HER TREASURES WERE SO EASY	THE SUMMER THAT WE DID	1773		2
EAT				
I DID NOT DARE TO EAT--OR SLEEP--	IT WAS GIVEN TO ME BY	454		7
AND MADE AS HE WOULD EAT ME UP--	I STARTED EARLY--TOOK MY	520		13
I DARE NOT EAT IT--THO' I STARVE--	GOD GAVE A LOAF TO EVERY	791		3
WHICH SHE WAS TAUGHT TO EAT--	BETROTHED TO	1641		4
MEN EAT OF IT AND DIE	FAME IS A FICKLE FOOD	1659		10
EATS				
EATS OFF THE BRITTLE LINE--	I SOMETIMES DROP IT, FOR	708		14
EAVES				
THAT DOT HIS DISTANT EAVES--	I ENVY SEAS, WHEREON HE	498		10
AND FRETTED IN THE EAVES--	THE NIGHT WAS WIDE, AND	589		8
A HALF A DOZEN KISSED THE EAVES--	A DROP FELL ON THE APPLE	794		3
THE PRETTY RAIN FROM THOSE SWEET EAVES	THE PRETTY RAIN FROM	1426		1
EBBED				
AND ME IT WERE--THAT EBBED FROM THEE	I'VE NONE TO TELL ME TO	881		8
EBBING				
NOR NOTICED THAT THE EBBING DAY	A POOR--TORN HEART-- A	78		3
EBBS				
THEN, HOW THE FIRE EBBS LIKE BILLOWS--	HOW THE OLD MOUNTAINS	291		9
EBON				
IN EBON BOX, WHEN YEARS HAVE FLOWN	IN EBON BOX, WHEN YEARS	169		1
AS IF THE LITTLE EBON BOX	IN EBON BOX, WHEN YEARS	169		19
ECCENTRIC				
OF HER ECCENTRIC FAMILY--	IF NATURE SMILES--THE	1085		3
IN HIS ECCENTRIC [PECULIAR] STYLE	ELIJAH'S WAGON KNEW NO	1254	V	8
ECCENTRICITIES				
HIS ECCENTRICITIES--	THE BAT IS DUN, WITH	1575		16
ECCENTRICITY				
THE ECCENTRICITY--	DELIGHT IS AS THE FLIGHT	257		18
ECHO				
ECHO HAS NO MAGISTRATE--	FOLLOW WISE ORION	1538	V	
ECHOED				
AS DOWN HIS HEAVEN DROPT REMOTE [ECHOED FAINT]	JUST ONCE! OH LEAST	1076		8
ECHOES				
BUT--THE ECHOES--STIFFEN [SILENCE--STIFFENS]--	SAFE IN THEIR ALABASTER	216	V	
AND ECHOES--TRAINS AWAY,	I KNOW SOME LONELY	289		37
ECLAT				
IS THE ECLAT OF DEATH--	THAT SHORT--POTENTIAL	1307		5
ECLIPSE				
BEHIND THIS SOFT ECLIPSE--	I'M "WIFE"--I'VE	199		6
TRIBES OF ECLIPSE--IN TENTS OF MARBLE--	SAFE IN THEIR ALABASTER	216	V	
ECLIPSE--AT MIDNIGHT--	IF HE DISSOLVE--THEN--	236		2
SQUIRREL--ECLIPSE--THE BUMBLE BEE--	"NATURE" IS WHAT WE SEE	668		3
FOR CONSCIOUSER [TOTALLER] ECLIPSE--	THE WHOLE OF IT CAME NOT	762		12
DO BIRMINGHAM [MANCHESTER] ECLIPSE--	A SAUCER HOLDS A CUP	1374		12
ECLIPSE--WAS ALL WE COULD SEE AT THE WINDOW	IT SOUNDED AS IF THE	1397		3
ECLIPSES				
ECLIPSES BE--PREDICTED--	SUNSET AT NIGHT--IS	415		5
ECLIPSES--SUNS--IMPLY--	THE ZEROES--TAUGHT US--	689	V	6
ECONOMICAL				
WAS GOD SO ECONOMICAL?	VICTORY COMES LATE--	690		7
AND ECONOMICAL OF BLISS	MEETING BY ACCIDENT,	1548		7

	FIRST LINE	POEM	LINE
ECONOMY			
'TIS ECONOMY	ALL I MAY, IF SMALL,	819	4
THE SOUL WITH STRICT ECONOMY	SUPERIORITY TO FATE	1081	7
IN OUR ECONOMY	THE DAYS THAT WE CAN	1184	4
ECSTASIES SEE EXTACIES			
WITH ECSTASIES OF STEALTH	A WORD MADE FLESH IS	1651	6
ECSTASY SEE EXTASY			
IS ALMOST REVELRY [ECSTASY]--	THE SYMPTOM OF THE GALE	1327	4
MIGHT ECSTASY TRANSFER--	THE TREASON OF AN ACCENT	1358	2
UNKNOWN AS TO AN ECSTASY	SUMMER--WE ALL HAVE SEEN	1386	11
NOR CLIMB THE BARS OF ECSTASY,	GO NOT TOO NEAR A HOUSE	1434	6
AN ECSTASY IN CHIEF--	ONE OF THE ONES THAT	1466	12
BY ROUTES OF ECSTASY	"GO TRAVELING WITH US!"	1513	3
THE ECSTASY TO GUESS	THE ECSTASY TO GUESS	1608	1
THE SON [A WOE] OF ECSTASY--	A SLOOP OF AMBER SLIPS	1622	4
NOR LINEAGE OF ECSTASY	THE PEDIGREE OF HONEY	1627	3
TAKE ALL AWAY FROM ME, BUT LEAVE ME ECSTASY,	TAKE ALL AWAY FROM ME,	1640	1
AN ECSTASY DISCREET	BETROTHED TO	1641	2
MAKE AN ABSTEMIOUS ECSTASY	RATHER ARID DELIGHT	1679	3
ADMINISTER HER ECSTASY,	THOSE FINAL CREATURES,--	1766	3
ECSTASY'S			
'TIS ECSTASY'S REVEALED [DIVINE / SUBLIME / REVERED] REVIEW--	THE LAST OF SUMMER IS	1353	3
OF ECSTASY'S IMPEDIMENT--	THE FASCINATING CHILL	1480	3
ECSTATIC			
THIS ECSTATIC NATION	THE HEART IS THE CAPITAL	1354	7
ECSTATICALLY			
ECSTATICALLY LEAP--	FROM ALL THE JAILS THE	1532	2
EDDIED			
UNTO THE LIPS IT EDDIED THROUGH--	I'VE NONE TO TELL ME TO	881	12
EDDIES			
IN EDDIES OF [FATHOMS IN / RAPIDS OF / GAMBOLS WITH / ...	TWO BUTTERFLIES WENT OUT	533	V
THEN--EDDIES LIKE A ROSE--AWAY--	THE NAME--OF IT--IS	656	11
EDEN			
THERE MUST BE GUESTS IN EDEN--	TAKEN FROM MEN--THIS	53	7
SOFT FALL THE SOUNDS OF EDEN	ALL OVERGROWN BY CUNNING	148	V
EDEN IS OLD FASHIONED, TOO!	I'M THE LITTLE "HEART'S	176	10
TO EDEN, WANDERED IN--	AS IF SOME LITTLE ARCTIC	180	10
COME SLOWLY--EDEN!	COME SLOWLY--EDEN!	211	1
WOULD THE EDEN BE AN EDEN,	DID THE HAREBELL LOOSE	213	7
WOULD THE EDEN BE AN EDEN,	DID THE HAREBELL LOOSE	213	7
DO THEY WEAR "NEW SHOES"--IN "EDEN"--	WHAT IS--"PARADISE"--	215	7
MAYBE--"EDEN" A'NT SO LONESOME	WHAT IS--"PARADISE"--	215	17
ROWING IN EDEN--	WILD NIGHTS--WILD NIGHTS	249	9
DOUBTLESS--"ADAM"--SCOWLED AT EDEN--	TAKING UP THE FAIR IDEAL	428	7
AS HEAVEN [EDEN]--UNTO ME!	I ENVY SEAS, WHEREON HE	498	8
SO--CHILDREN--TOLD HOW [ASSURED THAT] BROOKS IN EDEN--	BETTER--THAN MUSIC! FOR	503	9
EDEN--A LEGEND--DIMLY TOLD [LEARNED / CROONED]--	BETTER--THAN MUSIC! FOR	503	14
TRUDGING TO EDEN, LOOKING BACKWARD,	TRUDGING TO EDEN,	1020	1
OWN [DWELL] IN EDEN NOTWITHSTANDING	PARADISE IS OF THE	1069	3
EDEN--THE ANCIENT HOMESTEAD--	THE BIBLE IS AN ANTIQUE	1545	5
EDEN IS THAT OLD-FASHIONED HOUSE	EDEN IS THAT	1657	1
EDEN'LL			
AND EDEN'LL BE SO LONESOME	I NEVER FELT AT HOME--	413	7
EDEN'S			
IS EDEN'S INNUENDO	NOT SEEING, STILL WE	1518	7
EDIBLE			
AN EDIBLE DELIGHT.	SURPRISE IS LIKE A	1306	4
IS EDIBLE TO LONGING,	THE JOY THAT HAS NO STEM	1744	3
EDIFICE			
THIS EDIFICE REMAIN--	JUST AS HE SPOKE IT FROM	848	2
EDIFICE [ARCHITECT] OF OCEAN	FORTITUDE INCARNATE	1217	9
NOR RAFTER--HAS [MARS / KNOWS] THAT EDIFICE	THE WAY HOPE BUILDS HIS	1481	3
HIS ADVOCATE--HIS EDIFICE--	THE DITCH IS DEAR TO THE	1645	3
EDIFICES			
WHAT EDIFICES AZURE	WHAT TENEMENTS OF CLOVER	1338	3
EDITION			
THOSE WHO READ THE SAME EDITION--	IF THE FOOLISH, CALL	168	7
EDUCATION			
DURING MY EDUCATION,	"SIC TRANSIT GLORIA	3	29
THROUGH THE DARK SOD--AS EDUCATION--	THROUGH THE DARK SOD--AS	392	1
E'E			
TO WIPE MY WEEPING E'E.	"SIC TRANSIT GLORIA	3	60
E'EN			
WE MIGHT E'EN DIVIDE--	I NEVER TOLD THE BURIED	11	19
OF TWINE E'EN SUPERFINE,	FOR EVERY BIRD A NEST--	143	11
POSSIBLY, E'EN YOU HAD SEEN	TAKE YOUR HEAVEN FURTHER	388	4
ETHERIAL GUEST AT E'EN AN OUTCAST'S PILLOW--	AIR HAS NO RESIDENCE, NO	1060	5
E'ER			
WAS BRIDAL--E'ER LIKE THIS?	'TWAS A LONG PARTING--	625	13
WHERE E'ER I PLY	ALL THAT I DO	1496	5
EFFACE			
EFFACE IN THE COMPARISON--	NO CROWD THAT HAS	515	11
IT'S EASY TO EFFACE IT--	IT'S EASY TO INVENT A	724	5
CANNOT CORRECT [EFFACE] THE CREASE	AS FROST IS BEST	951	9
YOU EFFACE THE SHEEN.	WHICH IS THE BEST--THE	1315	4
EFFACE THE BURDEN [MONSTER / STATURE	THE PILE OF YEARS IS NOT	1507	7

	FIRST LINE	POEM	LINE
EFFACE (CONTINUED)			
/ SPECTRE / TROUBLE / . . .			
EFFACED			
HOME EFFACED--HER FACES DWINDLED--	ALL FORGOT FOR	966	9
EFFACELESS			
AND AN [THE] EFFACELESS "FEW" ARE LIFTED THERE--	ABOVE OBLIVION'S TIDE	1531	2
EFFACES			
BUT SEARCH EFFACES HIM	THE FROST WAS NEVER SEEN	1202	8
EFFACES THE SURMISE--	THEIR BARRICADE AGAINST	1471	8
EFFACING			
TO KEEP IT FROM EFFACING	AN EVERYWHERE OF SILVER	884	3
OF HER EFFACING FATHOM	THE TREASON OF AN ACCENT	1358	3
EFFECT			
AND MINE--SOME FOOLISHER EFFECT--	I LEARNED--AT LEAST--	944	16
BY SUBSEQUENT EFFECT--	AS FROST IS BEST	951	4
EFFERVESCE			
THAT EFFERVESCED [EFFERVESCE] FROM HER.	HER SPIRIT ROSE TO SUCH	1486	6
EFFERVESCED			
THAT EFFERVESCED [EFFERVESCE] FROM HER.	HER SPIRIT ROSE TO SUCH	1486	6
EFFLORESCENCE			
EFFLORESCENCE OF A SUNSET--	BLOOM UPON THE MOUNTAIN	667	3
EFFORT			
TO EFFORT UNDIVINE--	TRUST IN THE UNEXPECTED	555	8
EFFORT--IS THE SOLE CONDITION--	GROWTH OF MAN--LIKE	750	9
MAKES EFFORT AT CONCLUSION	AS PLAN FOR NOON AND	960	7
AURORA IS THE EFFORT	AURORA IS THE EFFORT	1002	1
THE EFFORT TO COMPRISE IT [OF COMPRISING]	ON THAT SPECIFIC PILLOW	1533	7
EFFULGENCIES			
MINUTE EFFULGENCIES AND WINDS--	A PANG IS MORE	1530	4
EGG			
IS THE EGG OF FORESTS	TO VENERATE THE SIMPLE	57	10
WHOSE BERYL EGG, WHAT SCHOOL BOYS HUNT	A FEATHER FROM THE	161	7
EGG-LIFE			
STILL AT THE EGG-LIFE--	LET US PLAY YESTERDAY--	728	13
EGGS			
WHAT WHEN THE EGGS FLY OFF IN MUSIC	WHAT SHALL I DO WHEN THE	956	3
EGYPTIAN			
AND PERHAPS A PHRASE IN EGYPTIAN [LATIN INSCRIPTION]--	WE DREAM--IT IS GOOD WE	531	15
EIDER			
NOR TOSSED MY SHAPE IN EIDER BALLS,	I CANNOT DANCE UPON MY	326	13
AND EIDER--NAMES--	I WENT TO HEAVEN--	374	12
EIDER-DUCK'S			
'TIS BETTER THAN THE EIDER-DUCK'S	MY LIFE HAD STOOD--A	754	15
EIGHTEEN			
SOME EIGHTEEN THOUSAND YEARS--	AS OLD AS WOE--	1168	3
EJECTED			
TILL GRAVITATION CHASED [HUMBLED / EJECTED / FOUNDERED / . . .	TWO BUTTERFLIES WENT OUT	533	V
ELASTIC			
TO GO ELASTIC--OR AS ONE	STRONG DRAUGHTS OF THEIR	711	5
ELATE			
THEY WOULD ELATE A SPRITE	A MIEN TO MOVE A QUEEN--	283	14
ELATE US--TILL WE ALMOST WEEP--	LIKE SOME OLD FASHIONED	302	11
ELATE--A BEE--	'TWOULD EASE--A	682	2
UPON HIS HIP ELATE	THE FINGERS OF THE LIGHT	1000	14
ELATE THE ACRE AT HIS FEET--	MY GOD--HE SEES THEE--	1178	6
SEDULOUS [TOO ELATE] OF HER MULTITUDES	NOT ANY MORE TO BE	1344	7
ELATE PHILOSOPHER.	THE BAT IS DUN, WITH	1575	8
ELDER			
IF TO BE "ELDER"--MEAN MOST PAIN--	ONE YEAR AGO--JOTS WHAT?	296	32
ELDER, TODAY, A SESSION WISER	A LOSS OF SOMETHING EVER	959	9
OF THE ELDER DEAD	AFTER A HUNDRED YEARS	1147	8
ELDERLY			
TO MAKE LIPS ELDERLY	HIS VOICE DECREPIT WAS	1476	4
ELECT			
OF HIS ELECT CONTENT--	MY WORTHINESS IS ALL MY	751	14
ELECTED			
I HAVE ELECTED--ONE--	OF ALL THE SOULS THAT	664	2
ELECTION			
ELECTION--VOTE--	MY REWARD FOR BEING, WAS	343	10
MINE--BY THE RIGHT OF THE WHITE ELECTION!	MINE--BY THE RIGHT OF	528	1
ELECTRIC			
OF HER ELECTRIC HAIR--	'TIS CUSTOMARY AS WE	440	8
OF THIS [WHOSE] ELECTRIC ADJUNCT	HOPE IS A STRANGE	1392	5
AND DURING IT'S ELECTRIC GALE [SPELL / STAY / MIGHT / ACT / SPAN]--	WITH PINIONS OF DISDAIN	1431	7
BUT WORK MIGHT BE ELECTRIC REST	THE BIRD HER PUNCTUAL	1585	7
THE DOOM'S ELECTRIC MOCCASIN	THERE CAME A WIND LIKE A	1593	7
IT'S FERVOR THE ELECTRIC OAR,	'TIS NOT THE SWAYING	1597	5
ELECTRICAL			
ELECTRICAL THE EMBRYO	FAME IS THE ONE THAT	1475	7
ELECTRICITY			
TO ELECTRICITY--	THE FARTHEST THUNDER	1581	12
ELEGANT			
AND ELEGANT--AS GLASS--	A VISITOR IN MARL--	391	4
ELEGY			
OF THESE NO ELEGY.	SOME THINGS THAT FLY	89	3
HAS OUGHT BUT ELEGY!	THE DOOMED--REGARD THE	294	12

	FIRST LINE	POEM	LINE
ELEGY (CONTINUED)			
ELEGY OF INTEGRITY.	AFTER ALL BIRDS HAVE	1395	8
OF ELEGY TO ME.	THE EARTH HAS MANY KEYS.	1775	8
ELEMENT			
BUT MAGIC--HATH AN ELEMENT	I THINK I WAS ENCHANTED	593	31
PAIN--HAS AN ELEMENT OF BLANK--	PAIN--HAS AN ELEMENT OF	650	1
LIKE ELEMENT--ARE THEY--	THERE IS AN ARID	782	4
AT HALF PAST SEVEN, ELEMENT	AT HALF PAST THREE, A	1084	9
HER DISTANCES [ELEMENT] PROPITIATE	BECAUSE HE LOVES HER	1229	7
ELEMENTAL			
AN ELEMENTAL RUST--	CRUMBLING IS NOT AN	997	8
AS PYRAMIDAL [ELEMENTAL / PLUPOTENTIAL] NERVE	NOT TO DISCOVER WEAKNESS	1054	6
THE UNDEVELOPED [ELEMENTAL] FREIGHT	COULD MORTAL LIP DIVINE	1409	2
THE ELEMENTAL VEIL	SHAME IS THE SHAWL OF	1412	4
WHOSE COAT OF ELEMENTAL BROWN	HOW HAPPY IS THE LITTLE	1510	5
ELEMENTS			
POWDER EXISTS IN CHARCOAL [ELEMENTS / SULPHURETS]--	A MAN MAY MAKE A REMARK	952	7
ELEMENTS UNALTERED--	NOW I KNEW I LOST HER--	1219	9
ELEPHANT'S			
THE [AN] ELEPHANT'S--CALM EYES	A BURDOCK--CLAWED MY	229	12
ELEPHANTS			
THE CLOUDS--LIKE LISTLESS ELEPHANTS--	ON THIS LONG STORM THE	194	3
ELF			
THE MUSHROOM IS THE ELF OF PLANTS--	THE MUSHROOM IS THE ELF	1298	1
ELF'S			
OR SOME ELF'S CATACOMB?	DRAB HABITATION OF WHOM?	893	5
ELICIT			
I FAILED TO MAKE [ELICIT NO] REPLY--	MY BEST ACQUAINTANCES	932	6
ELIGIBLE			
AS ELIGIBLE [UNPERVERTED / UNDIVERTED / UNAVAILING] AS THE MOON	SUMMER--WE ALL HAVE SEEN	1386	7
ON ELIGIBLE WALLS--	THOSE CATTLE SMALLER	1388	8
ELIGIBLY			
BUT ELIGIBLY FAIR	THIS DIRTY--LITTLE--	1311	5
ELIJAH			
THEN LIKE ELIJAH RODE AWAY	LIKE RAIN IT SOUNDED	1235	15
WHO JUSTIFIED [AUTHORIZED] ELIJAH [THE FORMER]	ELIJAH'S WAGON KNEW NO	1254	7
ELIJAH'S			
ELIJAH'S WAGON KNEW [HAD] NO THILL	ELIJAH'S WAGON KNEW NO	1254	1
ELIJAH'S HORSES AS UNIQUE	ELIJAH'S WAGON KNEW NO	1254	3
ELIJAH'S JOURNEY TO PORTRAY	ELIJAH'S WAGON KNEW NO	1254	5
ELIZA			
THERE'S SARAH, AND ELIZA, AND EMELINE SO FAIR,	AWAKE YE MUSES NINE,	1	31
ELIZABETH			
ELIZABETH TOLD ESSEX	ELIZABETH TOLD ESSEX	1321	1
ELLIPSE			
WHEN YOU TROUBLED THE ELLIPSE--	LET US PLAY YESTERDAY--	728	15
ELM			
A TROUBADOUR UPON THE ELM	NEW FEET WITHIN MY	99	3
ELOQUENCE			
THAT ELOQUENCE IS WHEN THE HEART	CONFIRMING ALL WHO	1268	3
HIS ELOQUENCE A BUBBLE	HIS MANSION IN THE POOL	1379	11
ELOQUENT			
YET ELOQUENT DECLARE	THE RAINBOW NEVER TELLS	97	6
BY INNOCENT [ELOQUENT / HALLOWED / HEAVENLY / DIFFIDENT] SURPRISE--	THE PRETTY RAIN FROM	1426	4
AS ELOQUENT APPEARS--	A LITTLE OVERFLOWING	1467	6
ELOQUENTLY			
MORE ELOQUENTLY LIE	THE FLAKE THE WIND	1361	2
ELSE			
OR ELSE A PEACOCK'S PURPLE TRAIN	SOME RAINBOW--COMING	64	4
ELSE PERISHED IN THE STONE--	A SCIENCE--SO THE SAVANS	100	6
COULD I DO AUGHT ELSE--TO THEE?	HE FORGOT--AND I--	203	8
SAVIOR! I'VE NO ONE ELSE TO TELL--	SAVIOR! I'VE NO ONE ELSE	217	1
THE ONE THAT NO ONE ELSE WOULD MISS	I CAME TO BUY A SMILE--	223	5
I'VE NOTHING ELSE--TO BRING, YOU KNOW--	I'VE NOTHING ELSE--TO	224	1
WHAT ELSE HAVE BOGS--TO DO--	A BURDOCK--CLAWED MY	229	7
MIGHT SOME ONE ELSE--SO LEARNED--BE--	NOT IN THIS WORLD TO SEE	418	10
AND FITTING NO ONE ELSE--	I AM ALIVE--I GUESS--	470	20
OR ELSE--FORGIVE NOT ME--	'TIS TRUE--THEY SHUT ME	538	12
ELSE--SAVIOR--BANISH ME--	'TIS TRUE--THEY SHUT ME	538	V 12
"BUT--MADAM--IS THERE NOTHING ELSE--	I ASKED NO OTHER THING--	621	7
COULD I--DO ELSE--WITH MINE?	I COULD SUFFICE FOR HIM,	643	16
MY NAME BE ELSE SUPREME--	FAME OF MYSELF, TO	713	6
ALL ELSE [THE WORLD] ACCUSED ME--AND I SMILED--	MY SOUL--ACCUSED ME--AND	753	3
LEST SOME ONE ELSE SHOULD [RICHER PEOPLE] BUY	A DIAMOND ON THE HAND	1108	V 8
ELSEWHERE			
I GO--TO ELSEWHERE GO NO MORE--	FITTER TO SEE HIM, I MAY	968	18
NOT ELSEWHERE--IF IN PARADISE	BEHOLD THIS LITTLE BANE	1438	7
ELUDE			
TO ELUDE ME SO!	GOOD NIGHT, BECAUSE WE	114	6
FRESH GILDED--TO ELUDE THE EYES	A HAPPY LIP--BREAKS	353	7
ADJUST THE HEAT--ELUDE THE WIND--	BLOOM--IS RESULT--TO	1058	11
AND THEN ELUDE STABILITY	SUMMER BEGINS TO HAVE	1682	15
ELUDES			
THAN IT RESISTS [EVADES / ELUDES]--THE HOUND--	THIS MERIT HATH THE	979	8
ELUDES THE FINDING OUT.	WE SHALL FIND THE CUBE	1484	4

	FIRST LINE	POEM	LINE
ELVES			
THE EYES OF MANY ELVES--	BESIDES THE AUTUMN POETS	131	12
ELYSIUM			
ELYSIUM IS AS FAR AS TO	ELYSIUM IS AS FAR AS TO	1760	1
EMACIATE			
EMACIATE THE WIT--	THE MIND LIVES ON THE	1355	6
EMBARK			
THAT MEN ANEW EMBARK TO LIVE	IN SNOW THOU COMEST	1669	7
EMBARKED			
EMBARKED UPON A TWIG TODAY	THE MOST TRIUMPHANT BIRD	1265	2
EMBARRASSED			
EMBARRASSED--NOT AFRAID--	BAFFLED FOR JUST A DAY	17	2
EMBARRASSES			
EMBARRASSES	SO LARGE MY WILL	1024	3
EMBARRASSMENT			
EMBARRASSMENT OF ONE ANOTHER	EMBARRASSMENT OF ONE	662	1
TO KNOW HER AN INTEMPERANCE [A DISPARAGEMENT / AN EMBARRASSMENT]	TO SEE HER IS A PICTURE	1568	3
EMBARRASSMENTS			
EMBARRASSMENTS	WE INTRODUCE OURSELVES	1214	5
EMBELLISH			
DID NOON--ENAMEL [ENABLE / EMBELLISH]--IN HERSELF	THIS BAUBLE WAS	805	5
NEW HORIZONS--THEY EMBELLISH [REPLENISH]--	UNFULFILLED TO	972	7
EMBELLISH ALL WE OWN--	HOPE IS A STRANGE	1392	8
EMBERS			
HIS ASHES [EMBERS]--WILL	GRIEF IS A MOUSE--	793	15
THE SMOULDERING EMBERS BLUSH--	THE SMOULDERING EMBERS	1132	1
THE SMOULDERING EMBERS SMILE--	THE SMOULDERING EMBERS	1132	4
THE EMBERS OF A THOUSAND YEARS	LONG YEARS APART--CAN	1383	5
EMBLEM			
BEFORE IT'S EMBLEM FLEW--	SHE LAID HER DOCILE	1396	8
EMBLEMS			
THY SACRED EMBLEMS TO PARTAKE--	THESE ARE THE DAYS WHEN	130	16
EMBODIED			
EMBODIED [ADMITTED] SCARCELY TO ITSELF--IT MAY BE--	EACH LIFE CONVERGES TO	680	5
EMBOLDEN			
ITSELF--EXHIBIT [ENABLE / EMBOLDEN]--MINE--	BUT LITTLE CARMINE HATH	558	4
EMBRACE			
THE WAKING IN A GNAT'S--EMBRACE--	WE SEE--COMPARATIVELY--	534	15
HIS GLITTERING EMBRACE--	ESCAPING BACKWARD TO	867	4
EMBRYO			
THE EMBRYO ENDOWED--	SUMMER--WE ALL HAVE SEEN	1386	12
ELECTRICAL THE EMBRYO	FAME IS THE ONE THAT	1475	7
A STATESMAN'S EMBRYO--	A FADED BOY--IN SALLOW	1524	4
EMELINE			
THERE'S SARAH, AND ELIZA, AND EMELINE SO FAIR,	AWAKE YE MUSES NINE,	1	31
EMERALD			
BELTED DOWN WITH EMERALD--	PIGMY SERAPHS--GONE	138	6
WHOSE EMERALD NEST THE AGES SPIN	A FEATHER FROM THE	161	5
WITH DUDS OF EMERALD!	SHE SWEEPS WITH	219	8
UPON MY EMERALD BOUGH,	THE ANGLE OF A LANDSCAPE	375	14
INLAID WITH EMERALD--HALF WAY DOWN--	I KNOW WHERE WELLS GROW	460	7
OF EMERALD SCANT--HER GOWN--	BUT LITTLE CARMINE HATH	558	2
AND HIS EMERALD SWING--	I COULD BRING YOU JEWELS	697	10
THESE EMERALD SEAMS ENCLOSE.	STEP LIGHTLY ON THIS	1183	4
A RESONANCE OF EMERALD--	A ROUTE OF EVANESCENCE	1463	3
THE BEARER FROM AN EMERALD COURT	THE STEM OF A DEPARTED	1520	3
AS FROM AN EMERALD GHOST--	THERE CAME A WIND LIKE A	1593	6
EMERALDS			
I WAKE--TO FIND NO--EMERALDS--	THE ANGLE OF A LANDSCAPE	375	15
EMERGE			
WHEN I HAVE SEEN THE SUN EMERGE	WHEN I HAVE SEEN THE SUN	888	1
EMERGE A SINGLE NOON	THERE IS A JUNE WHEN	930	6
THEY EMERGE FROM HIS OBSCURING--	COLOR--CASTE--	970	13
WILL EMERGE [DECAMP] BUT ONCE--AND DUMB [ARMED]--	"SECRETS" IS A DAILY	1385	11
DOES NOT EMERGE ALONE	THE SPIRIT LASTS--BUT IN	1576	6
EMERGED			
EMERGED--A SUMMER AFTERNOON--	FROM COCOON FORTH A	354	3
EMERGENCY			
IN AN EMERGENCY.	"FAITH" IS A FINE	185	4
TO IT'S EMERGENCY--	WHAT MYSTERY PERVADES A	1400	V
EMERGES			
EMERGES IN THE SPRING!	A FUZZY FELLOW, WITHOUT	173	14
EMIGRANT			
AN EMIGRANT TO BE	AWAY FROM HOME ARE SOME	821	2
THE EMIGRANT OF LIGHT, IT IS	WHO SAW NO SUNRISE	1018	5
EMIGRANT'S			
AN EMIGRANT'S ADDRESS.	A SOUTH WIND--HAS A	719	4
EMIGRANTS			
AS EMIGRANTS WE COME	THE BIRD DID PRANCE--THE	1107	V 10
EMIGRATE			
EACH CONSCIOUSNESS MUST EMIGRATE	TOO LITTLE WAY THE HOUSE	911	7
EMILY			
SOME LIKE "EMILY."	TEACH HIM--WHEN HE MAKES	227	9
EMINENCE			
FROM EMINENCE REMOTE	THESE ARE THE NIGHTS	1128	2
ASCEND WITH ME THE EMINENCE [TABLE LAND]	SUCH ARE THE INLETS OF	1421	3

	FIRST LINE	POEM	LINE
EMINENT			
EMINENT TODAY	AMBITION CANNOT FIND HIM	68	6
I FAMISH [PERISH] TO BEHOLD SO EMINENT A SIGHT [ANOTHER SUCH . . .	THE MOST TRIUMPHANT BIRD	1265	4
EMINENTLY			
SO SCANT, SO EMINENTLY SMALL	WHAT TWIGS WE HELD BY--	1086	10
EMIT			
AS DID [SHOULD] THE DOWN EMIT A TUNE--	OF BEING IS A BIRD	653	11
EMITS			
THAT RIDES--EMITS [SUPPORTS] A THUNDER--	TO INTERRUPT HIS YELLOW	591	15
EMOLUMENT			
NO EMOLUMENT.	"FAITHFUL TO THE END"	1357	8
BEHOLD HIS LOST AGGRANDIZEMENT [EMOLUMENT] .	ONE OF THE ONES THAT	1466	27
EMPEROR			
THE EMPEROR WILL SAY?	WHO NEVER LOST, ARE	73	10
UNMOVED--AN EMPEROR BE KNEELING	THE SOUL SELECTS HER OWN	303	7
OR BROOCHES--WHEN THE EMPEROR--	'TIS LITTLE I--COULD	466	3
BASELESS EMPEROR--	THE CHILD'S FAITH IS NEW	637	14
THE EMPEROR [MIGHTIEST] OF MEN--	THE SOUL THAT HATH A	674	8
TO BE AN EMPEROR.	PURPLE--IS FASHIONABLE	980	4
EMPEROR'S			
FROM AN EMPEROR'S HAND--	PROMISE THIS--WHEN YOU	648	6
EMPERORS			
WHERE EMPERORS [MONARCHS] GREW--	I ROSE--BECAUSE HE SANK	616	17
EMPERY			
TILL NUMBER'S EMPERY--	PRECIOUS TO ME--SHE	727	11
EMPHASIZE			
THE SERVICE EMPHASIZE;	FURTHER IN SUMMER THAN	1068	V
EMPHASIZED			
EMPHASIZED AND GONE	GLASS WAS THE STREET--IN	1498	6
EMPHATIC			
OR AN EMPHATIC THUMB--	MY LIFE HAD STOOD--A	754	20
EMPIRE			
THAT EMPIRE--IS OF CZARS--	THE COURT IS FAR AWAY--	235	9
EMPIRE--STATE--	MY REWARD FOR BEING, WAS	343	V
EMPLOY			
FIND QUAINT EMPLOY--	MY WHEEL IS IN THE DARK!	10	11
EMPLOY THEIR HOLIDAY.	THERE IS A MORN BY MEN	24	6
EMPLOYED			
EMPLOYED A FACT TO VISIT ME	I BET WITH EVERY WIND	1215	3
HAS NEVER BEEN EMPLOYED--	THE SPIDER AS AN ARTIST	1275	2
EMPOWERED			
EMPOWERED WITH WHAT MALIGNITY	THE BAT IS DUN, WITH	1575	11
EMPRESS			
EMPRESS OF CALVARY!	TITLE DIVINE--IS MINE!	1072	4
EMPTIED			
OR EMPTIED BY THE SUN	A DEW SUFFICED ITSELF--	1437	10
EMPTINESS			
WHEN HE DEPART [DEPARTS], AN EMPTINESS	BEFORE HE COMES WE WEIGH	834	3
THE WORTHLESSNESS [EMPTINESS] OF EARTHLY THINGS	THE WORTHLESSNESS OF	1373	1
EMPTY			
AND EMPTY SKIES	DELIGHT IS AS THE FLIGHT	257	17
A SUMMER'S [THE SUMMERS] EMPTY ROOM--	IT SIFTS FROM LEADEN	311	14
THEN--HELD AN EMPTY PANE--	A HOUSE UPON THE HIGHT--	399	8
BLAME THE LITTLE [EMPTY / CHILDISH] HAND	SWEET--YOU FORGOT--BUT I	523	6
EMPTY MY HEART, OF THEE--	EMPTY MY HEART, OF THEE	587	1
ADOWN THE EMPTY STREET--	THE NIGHT WAS WIDE, AND	589	12
'TWAS EMPTY--BUT THE FIRST	THE FIRST DAY THAT I WAS	902	7
I THINK, BECAUSE HIS EMPTY PLATE	A SPARROW TOOK A SLICE	1211	3
EMPTY THE HEARTS THAT PURCHASED YOU--	BROTHER OF INGOTS--AH	1366	2
SHE [HE] BORE LIFE'S EMPTY PACK	HER LOSSES MAKE OUR	1562	2
LIFE'S EMPTY PACK IS HEAVIEST,	HER LOSSES MAKE OUR	1562	5
QUITE EMPTY, QUITE AT REST,	QUITE EMPTY, QUITE AT	1606	1
THE STATURE OF THE EMPTY NEST	I SEE THEE CLEARER FOR	1666	7
ENABLE			
ENABLE THEE TO GUESS	JESUS! THY CRUCIFIX	225	2
MIGHT DEATH--ENABLE THEE--	ME PROVE IT NOW--WHOEVER	537	8
ITSELF--EXHIBIT [ENABLE / EMBOLDEN]--MINE--	BUT LITTLE CARMINE HATH	558	4
ETERNITY ENABLE THE ENDEAVORING	EACH LIFE CONVERGES TO	680	19
DID NOON--ENAMEL [ENABLE / EMBELLISH]--IN HERSELF	THIS BAUBLE WAS	805	5
ENABLE IN DISASTER	THE CHEMICAL CONVICTION	954	3
THAT SUCH HAVE DIED ENABLE US	THAT SUCH HAVE DIED	1030	1
ENABLE HIM [EACH] TO DWELL--	YOU CANNOT TAKE ITSELF	1351	4
ENABLED			
ENABLED BY HIS ROYAL DRESS--	LIKE MIGHTY FOOT LIGHTS	595	7
ENABLED OF THE EYE--	A LITTLE ROAD--NOT MADE	647	2
ENABLED TO INFER.	THERE IS A FINISHED	856	8
TO MEET [AT MEETING] SO ENABLED [LEARNED / RELIGIOUS / . . .	HE PREACHED UPON	1207	8
ENABLES			
CIRCUMSCRIPTION--ENABLES WO--	BOUND--A TROUBLE--	269	V
TO DRINK--ENABLES MINE	STRONG DRAUGHTS OF THEIR	711	2
CANNOT BE [ENABLES] INDIGENCE	NONE CAN EXPERIENCE	771	8
ENABLING			
ENABLING THE MINUTEST--	THE HEAVEN VESTS FOR	694	15
LIGHT--ENABLING LIGHT--	THE ADMIRATIONS--AND	906	10
INFORMING [ENLIGHTENING / ENABLING]--MISERY--	A DOOR JUST OPENED ON A	953	8

	FIRST LINE	POEM	LINE
ENACT			
ENACT--AND TERMINATE [DISSIPATE]--	THE BATTLE FOUGHT	594	12
THIS--THE BEST ENACT [MORE EXERT]	DRAMA'S VITALLEST	741	5
NATURE CANNOT ENACT A FRIEND--	NATURE ASSIGNS THE SUN--	1336	3
ENACT ALL OTHER BLAME	THE LOOK OF THEE, WHAT	1689	10
ENACTED			
IT WERE INFINITE [TENDERER] ENACTED	DRAMA'S VITALLEST	741	12
ENACTED UPON EARTH--	THE BUSTLE IN A HOUSE	1078	4
AGONY THAT ENACTED THERE	AFTER A HUNDRED YEARS	1147	3
COME UNTO ME ENACTED [ACCOMPLISHED] HOW	CONTAINED IN THIS SHORT	1165	V
A TRAGEDY ENACTED	T'IS EASIER TO PITY	1698	4
TO BE ENACTED NOW.	NO MAN SAW AWE, NOR TO	1733	12
ENACTING			
THAT TRAGEDY ENACTING	T'IS EASIER TO PITY	1698	6
ENACTS			
ENACTS INTOXICATION	THE LONG SIGH OF THE	1359	3
ENAMEL			
DID NOON--ENAMEL [ENABLE / EMBELLISH]--IN HERSELF	THIS BAUBLE WAS	805	5
ENAMELED			
IS BETTER [SWEETER] THAN ENAMELED REALMS	THE CLOVER'S SIMPLE FAME	1232	3
ENAMELLED			
A FINGER OF ENAMELLED FIRE--	MY SOUL--ACCUSED ME--AND	753	8
ENAMOR			
TO LACK--ENAMOR THEE--	'TIS OPPOSITES--ENTICE--	355	9
ENAMOR--IN PROSPECTIVE--	UNTO MY BOOKS--SO GOOD	604	15
THE BIRDS ENAMOR CARE--	THE NOTICE THAT IS	1310	6
DESCENDING [CONSENTING / ESTABLISHED / IMPARTED] TO ENAMOR US	THE FACE IN EVANESCENCE	1490	7
ENAMORED			
ENAMORED OF THE PARTING WEST--	THE DAISY FOLLOWS SOFT	106	10
ENAMORED--OF THE CONJUROR--	"HEAVEN"--IS WHAT I	239	11
PRECEDES ENAMORED--DAY--	THE DOOMED--REGARD THE	294	10
ENAMORED--IMPOTENT--CONTENT--	I WOULD NOT PAINT--A	505	19
BUT DEATH HAD TOLD HER SO THE [SPECIFIC TOLD HER / ENAMORED . . .	I MEANT TO FIND HER WHEN	718	7
ENAMORED MOST OF THEE--	MY MAKER--LET ME BE	1403	2
TO HIS ENAMORED MIND	ALL THAT I DO	1496	3
THE MESSENGER ENAMORED TOO,	WE SEND THE WAVE TO FIND	1604	3
ARROWS ENAMORED OF HIS HEART [BREAST]--	ARROWS ENAMORED OF HIS	1629	1
ENAMORING			
ENAMORING THE EAR	THE TREES LIKE TASSELS--	606	6
ENAMORS			
'TIS THIS ENAMORS [AFFLICTS US] IN THE EAST--	THE LOVE A LIFE CAN SHOW	673	10
ENCAMPING			
ENCAMPING ON A THOUSAND DAWNS	HOW LONESOME THE WIND	1418	10
ENCHANT			
HER MEMORIES [MEMORY] LIKE STRAINS--REVIEW [ENCHANT]--	LIKE SOME OLD FASHIONED	302	13
ENCHANTED			
WHETHER TO ISLES ENCHANTED	WHETHER MY BARK WENT	52	3
I THINK I WAS ENCHANTED	I THINK I WAS ENCHANTED	593	1
FOR THIS ENCHANTED SIZE--	ONE BLESSING HAD I THAN	756	4
UPON ENCHANTED GROUND--	EXHILIRATION IS THE	1118	8
ENCHANTING			
WHILE THAT DELUSIVE [OBLIGING / ENCHANTING] HAIR	RISK IS THE HAIR THAT	1239	10
PERUSER OF ENCHANTING BOOK	SUMMER BEGINS TO HAVE	1682	2
ENCHANTING BY REMAINING,	WERE NATURE MORTAL LADY	1762	11
ENCHANTLESS			
THE ENCHANTLESS POD	LAIN IN NATURE--SO	1288	2
ENCHANTMENT			
HIS PRESENCE IS ENCHANTMENT--	A PRECIOUS--MOULDERING	371	25
ENCHANTMENT MAKES INGREDIENT	IMPOSSIBILITY, LIKE WINE	838	7
ENCHANTMENT'S			
ENCHANTMENT'S PERIHELION	DELIGHT'S DESPAIR AT	1299	5
ENCHANTMENT'S SYNDICATE [POSTULATE / TESTAMENT].	THE LAST OF SUMMER IS	1353	4
ENCHANTS			
RETURNS--SUGGESTS--CONVICTS--ENCHANTS--	THE LOVE A LIFE CAN SHOW	673	15
HE CHEATS AS HE ENCHANTS	ONE OF THE ONES THAT	1466	14
ENCLOSE			
THESE EMERALD SEAMS ENCLOSE.	STEP LIGHTLY ON THIS	1183	4
IF ONLY TO ENCLOSE THE SAINTS	SO MUCH OF HEAVEN HAS	1228	3
ENCLOSED			
ENCLOSED 'TWAS NOT OF RAIL	IT WAS A GRAVE, YET BORE	876	2
ENCLOSES			
THE THOUGHTFUL GRAVE ENCLOSES--	SOME, TOO FRAGILE FOR	141	2
A CLOUD THE MIGHTY SUN ENCLOSES	A SHADE UPON THE MIND	882	3
ENCOMIUM			
WITH THE ENCOMIUM IT EARNED	PRAISE IT--'TIS DEAD--	1384	4
ENCORE			
THE HOUSE ENCORE ME SO--	I CANNOT DANCE UPON MY	326	16
THEY WOULD NOT ENCORE--DEATH--	YOU'VE SEEN BALLOONS SET	700	12
ENCORES			
RECEIPTED WITH ENCORES	TALK NOT TO ME OF SUMMER	1634	V
ENCOUNTER			
ENCOUNTER IN MY GARDEN	BAFFLED FOR JUST A DAY	17	3
THAN UNARMED [MOONLESS], ONE'S A'SELF ENCOUNTER--	ONE NEED NOT BE A	670	11

	FIRST LINE	POEM	LINE
ENCOUNTERED			
AS ONE MET SUDDEN [ENCOUNTERED] GENTLEFOLK	IT IS AN HONORABLE	946	3
ENCOUNTERING			
AND SO ENCOUNTERING A FLY	A DRUNKARD CANNOT MEET A	1628	3
ENCOURAGE			
THEIR MORTAL FATE--ENCOURAGE SOME--	THE MARTYR POETS--DID	544	4
ENCOURAGEMENT			
AND TOWARD ENCOURAGEMENT	TO UNDERTAKE IS TO	1070	4
ENCOURAGES			
APPROACH ENCOURAGES.	WHO OCCUPIES THIS HOUSE?	892	8
ENCROACHED			
AS TRADE HAD SUDDENLY ENCROACHED	A LIGHT EXISTS IN SPRING	812	19
END			
A CLEARING AT THE END--	MY WHEEL IS IN THE DARK!	10	8
TO SEE TO THE END--	WE DONT CRY--TIM AND I,	196	12
AND AT MY FINGER'S END--	I AM ALIVE--I GUESS--	470	4
A BEING--IMPOTENT TO END [STOP]--	ONE ANGUISH--IN A CROWD	565	15
IF END I GAINED [REACHED]	FROM BLANK TO BLANK--	761	6
BY STINT [END]--REWARDED WORK--	THE SERVICE WITHOUT HOPE	779	4
IF LOVE REWARD [BE AT] THE END--	TO WAIT AN HOUR--IS LONG	781	4
THIS, IS THE SILENT END	AND THIS OF ALL MY HOPES	913	2
EARLY AND SERE, IT'S END	AND THIS OF ALL MY HOPES	913	4
OR ESTIMATE--OR END--	A COFFIN--IS A SMALL	943	12
AND SHOW AND END--	EXCEPT THE SMALLER SIZE	1067	4
TO THEIR ENTRANCING END	WITHOUT A SMILE--WITHOUT	1330	3
"FAITHFUL TO THE END" AMENDED	"FAITHFUL TO THE END"	1357	1
ABUNDANT [A FERVENT / A LOYAL / A GRACIOUS / AN AMPLE] END--	THE GENTIAN HAS A	1424	13
WHOSE AMPLITUDE NO END [CLOCK] INVADES--	WATER MAKES MANY BEDS	1428	7
ALMOST WE WISH THE END	I DID NOT REACH THEE	1664	24
ENDANGER			
ENDANGER IT, AND THE DEMAND	ENDANGER IT, AND THE	1658	1
ENDANGERING			
WITHOUT ERASING [ENDANGERING] SIGHT--	A STILL--VOLCANO--LIFE--	601	4
ENDEAR			
TOO DISTANT--TO ENDEAR--	A MIEN TO MOVE A QUEEN--	283	23
ENDEAR THE SHORE [COAST] BEYOND--	I SHOULD HAVE BEEN TOO	313	21
ENDEAR IN THE DEPARTURE	WE LEARN IN THE	1083	5
THIS TRUTH ENDEAR [DECLARE]--	THE GENTIAN HAS A	1424	15
ENDEARMENT			
NOT MURMUR--NOT ENDEARMENT--	"GO TELL IT"--WHAT A	1554	3
ENDEARS			
IT HALF ENDEARS THE ABSTINENCE--	UNTO MY BOOKS--SO GOOD	604	3
ENDEAVOR			
I'LL DO SEAMS--A QUEEN'S ENDEAVOR	DONT PUT UP MY THREAD &	617	7
A SWEET ENDEAVOR--BUT AS MARCH	YOU'LL KNOW HER--BY HER	634	23
'TWAS MORE PITIFUL ENDEAVOR	HER SWEET TURN TO LEAVE	649	5
TO OUR ENDEAVOR--NOT SO REAL [TRUE / CLOSE / NEAR]	A PRISON GETS TO BE A	652	19
ENDEAVORING			
ETERNITY ENABLE THE ENDEAVORING	EACH LIFE CONVERGES TO	680	19
WITH "IF I COULD" ENDEAVORING	WHICH MISSES MOST,	1759	9
ENDEAVORS			
MY WILL ENDEAVORS FOR IT'S WORD	TO TELL THE BEAUTY WOULD	1700	5
ENDED			
POETS--ENDED--	HER--"LAST POEMS"--	312	2
AND YOU--GOT SLEEPY--AND BEGGED TO BE ENDED--	GOING TO HIM! HAPPY	494	20
THAT IS SOLEMN [TENDER / SACRED] WE HAVE ENDED	THAT IS SOLEMN WE HAVE	934	1
ENDED, ERE IT BEGUN--	ENDED, ERE IT BEGUN--	1088	1
WHEN A [THE] SUBJECT IS FINISHED [ENDED / TAKEN]--	WHATEVER IT IS--SHE HAS	1204	7
PRECISELY HOW IT ENDED [IS IT KNOWN]	I SAW THE WIND WITHIN	1502	V
ENDLESS			
REELING--THRO ENDLESS SUMMER DAYS--	I TASTE A LIQUOR NEVER	214	7
ENDORSE			
ATMOSPHERE, AND SUN ENDORSE [CONFIRM] IT--	GROWTH OF MAN--LIKE	750	3
ENDORSEMENT			
JUST HIS OWN ENDORSEMENT--	LIFE--IS WHAT WE MAKE IT	698	7
ENDOW			
ENDOW THE LIVING--WITH THE TEARS--	ENDOW THE LIVING--WITH	521	1
EVER COULD ENDOW--	HER SWEET TURN TO LEAVE	649	V 16
SHOULD ENDOW [ADDRESS / REWARD] THE DAY--	BLOOM UPON THE MOUNTAIN	667	6
SUPPLY THE [INVITE SOME / ENDOW SOME / AFFRONT A / AFFRONT ...	ART THOU THE THING I	1282	3
ENDOWAL			
BUT STATE--ENDOWAL--FOCUS--	WE PRAY--TO HEAVEN--	489	10
ENDOWED			
YESTERDAY--ENDOWED WITH PARADISE.	I'VE DROPPED MY BRAIN--	1046	8
THE EMBRYO ENDOWED--	SUMMER--WE ALL HAVE SEEN	1386	12
ENDOWING			
BUT THESE--ENDOWING AS THEY FLIT	DOMINION LASTS UNTIL	1257	3
ENDOWS			
'TIS THIS--INVITES--APPALLS--ENDOWS--	THE LOVE A LIFE CAN SHOW	673	13
HER GALLANT NOTE ENDOWS US LIKE A FRIEND	AFTER ALL BIRDS HAVE	1395	V 6
ENDS			
AND THERE, THE MATTER ENDS--	I READ MY SENTENCE--	412	14
THE MONTHS HAVE ENDS--THE YEARS--A KNOT--	THE MONTHS HAVE ENDS--	423	1
FAR ENDS OF TIRED [HOMELY] DAYS--	UNTO MY BOOKS--SO GOOD	604	2
BUT SLOWEST INSTANT--ENDS--	I THINK THE LONGEST HOUR	635	8
IT ENDS BEYOND	FROM BLANK TO BLANK--	761	7

	FIRST LINE	POEM	LINE
ENDUED			
MYSELF ENDUED [UPHELD / UPBORNE / SUSTAINED] BALLOON	I WOULD NOT PAINT--A	505	14
ENDURE SEE RE-ENDURE			
THE SUNRISE SCATTERS--THESE ENDURE--	THE BATTLE FOUGHT	594	11
AND WILL ENDURE AS LONG AS HE	TRUTH--IS AS OLD AS GOD	836	3
IT PERISH, OR ENDURE--	JUST AS HE SPOKE IT FROM	848	6
HOW LONG A DAY I COULD ENDURE	WERT THOU BUT ILL--THAT	961	2
NOT ANY COLOR WILL ENDURE	JUDGEMENT IS JUSTEST	1671	8
THAT IT CAN SO ENDURE	ELYSIUM IS AS FAR AS TO	1760	6
ENDURED			
SO TERRIBLE--HAD BEEN ENDURED--	THE FIRST DAY'S NIGHT	410	3
BUT HE THAT HATH ENDURED	THE PROVINCE OF THE	539	6
ENDURED, UNHELPED [RESIGNED]--UNKNOWN.	THE HOLLOWS ROUND HIS	955	8
THIS, TOO, I ENDURED--	ROBBED BY DEATH--BUT	971	6
AS THAT ENDURED	THERE IS NO SILENCE IN	1004	2
ENDURES			
TELL--THIS DAY [TILL NOW] ENDURES	TELL AS A MARKSMAN--WERE	1152	2
ENEMIES			
AS ENEMIES--AWAY--	WE DO NOT PLAY ON GRAVES	467	10
ENEMY			
I STAY MINE ENEMY!	"SIC TRANSIT GLORIA	3	4
THINE ENEMY--	NO RACK CAN TORTURE ME--	384	14
BOLD--WERE IT ENEMY--BRIEF--WERE IT FRIEND--	IT'S COMING--THE	390	6
AN ENEMY--COULD SEND--	THE SOUL UNTO ITSELF	683	4
BUT, ENEMY, BELOVED BE	DYING! TO BE AFRAID OF	831	8
WHO MINE ENEMY?	STRUCK, WAS I, NOR YET	925	8
WHO WAS NOT ENEMY OF ME	HERE, WHERE THE DAISIES	1037	7
AND STEM [STEMS] AN ENEMY	WHAT MYSTERY PERVADES A	1400	V
BY DITTIES TO THE ENEMY	THE ROBIN IS A GABRIEL	1483	15
MINE ENEMY [MY FOE] IS GROWING OLD--	MINE ENEMY IS GROWING	1509	1
TO SOUND [TEST] THE ENEMY--	WHERE ROSES WOULD NOT	1582	4
ENEMY'S			
BUT AS AN ENEMY'S SALUTE	I CROSS TILL I AM WEARY	550	12
ENERGY			
REQUIRES ENERGY--POSSIBLY AGONY--	TO PUT THIS WORLD DOWN,	527	3
ENFEEBLES			
ENFEEBLES--THE ADVANCE--	HAD I NOT THIS, OR THIS,	904	16
ENFOLD			
AND I WILL ENFOLD!	I OFTEN PASSED THE	51	18
SUFFICIENT TO ENFOLD HIM	THE TREES LIKE TASSELS--	606	13
ENFOLDING			
OBLIVION BENDING OVER [ENFOLDING] HIM	THE DITCH IS DEAR TO THE	1645	7
ENFOLDS			
MY TIMIDNESS ENFOLDS--	YOU SEE I CANNOT SEE--	253	11
ENFORCE			
AND SANCTITY--ENFORCE THEE--	TO THE STANCH DUST	1402	6
ENFORCED			
WHO INDORSED [ENFORCED] THE CUP--	TO PUT THIS WORLD DOWN,	527	15
WAS INNOCENT [IGNORANT / NOT ENFORCED / UNENFORCED] OF WHEEL	ELIJAH'S WAGON KNEW NO	1254	2
WE ARE ENFORCED TO SAIL	DOWN TIME'S QUAINT	1656	3
ENFORCES			
AND THEN--ENFORCES THEIR DELIGHT	THE WORTHLESSNESS OF	1373	3
AND ESTIMATES [ENFORCES / COMMENCES / REPLEVYS / CONFISCATES] . . .	PERHAPS THEY DO NOT GO	1399	8
ENFRANCHIZED			
YOU HAVE PASSED ENFRANCHIZED FEET!	TALK WITH PRUDENCE TO A	119	6
ENGAGE			
BUT WITH ITSELF DID COLD ENGAGE [COMMUNE]	A WIND THAT ROSE	1259	4
ENGINERY			
AN ENGINERY OF EQUITY	DEATH WARRANTS ARE	1375	2
ENGLAND			
AS NEW ENGLAND USED TO BE!	WHAT IS--"PARADISE"--	215	18
IN A NEW ENGLAND TOWN--	THE BUTTERFLY'S	1244	6
ON OUR NEW ENGLAND FARMS--	A FIELD OF STUBBLE,	1407	8
OF THE NEW ENGLAND FARMER--	THE ROBIN IS A GABRIEL	1483	6
ENGLANDLY			
BECAUSE I SEE--NEW ENGLANDLY--	THE ROBIN'S MY CRITERION	285	15
ENGLISH			
MANY A PHRASE HAS THE ENGLISH LANGUAGE--	MANY A PHRASE HAS THE	276	1
SAY IT AGAIN, SAXON [ENGLISH LANGUAGE]!	MANY A PHRASE HAS THE	276	15
ENGROSS			
ENGROSS MY FINITY--	TIME FEELS SO VAST THAT	802	4
ENGROSSED			
BUT SEEMED ENGROSSED TO ABSOLUTE--	I WATCHED THE MOON	629	27
THE SUN ENGROSSED THE EAST--	THE BIRDS BEGUN AT FOUR	783	21
OBTAINED [ENGROSSED] MY LODGINGS, ERE MYSELF--	BEREAVED OF ALL, I WENT	784	5
WE WERE LISTENING TO [TOO ENGROSSED WITH] THE SECONDS . . .	WE TALKED WITH EACH	1473	3
ENGULPH			
ENGULPH THEE IN THE NIGHT--	LET MY FIRST KNOWING BE	1218	4
ENHANCES			
ENHANCES NATURE NOW	FURTHER IN SUMMER THAN	1068	16
TO DISAPPEAR ENHANCES--	TO DISAPPEAR ENHANCES--	1209	1
ENHANCING			
ENHANCING WHAT WE SEE	SUNSET THAT SCREENS,	1609	2
ENJOINING			
ENJOINING SECRECY--	THE LEAVES LIKE WOMEN,	987	6
ENJOINING US TO PART	AN ANTIQUATED GRACE	1345	4

	FIRST LINE	POEM	LINE
ENLARGE			
ENLARGE MY MESSAGE--IF TOO VAST	A TONGUE--TO TELL HIM I	400	16
ENLARGED			
WITH MODESTIES ENLARGED.	OUR LITTLE KINSMEN--	885	12
FOR IT'S ENLARGED INSPECTION'S	THIS DUST, AND IT'S	936	7
INCREASED [ENLARGED] BEYOND MY UTMOST SCOPE	I HAD A DAILY BLISS	1057	7
BUT THINK ENLARGED OF ALL THAT THEY WILL TELL US	THE THINGS THAT NEVER	1515	7
ENLARGES			
ENLARGES [SUBMERGES] EVERY SOUL--	THE INUNDATION OF THE	1425	2
ENLARGING			
ENLARGING LONELINESS.	FURTHER IN SUMMER THAN	1068	8
ENLIGHTENED			
ENLIGHTENED TO A LARGER PAIN--	I MEASURE EVERY GRIEF I	561	23
IT'S PAST--ENLIGHTENED TO PERCEIVE	PAIN--HAS AN ELEMENT OF	650	7
ENLIGHTENING			
ENLIGHTENING SO WELL--	I PLAY AT RICHES--TO	801	22
INFORMING [ENLIGHTENING / ENABLING]--MISERY--	A DOOR JUST OPENED ON A	953	8
ENLIST			
TO ENLIST THE TOMB.	SOME WE SEE NO MORE,	1221	10
ENMITY			
COULD FINISH--ENMITY--	I HAD NO TIME TO HATE--	478	6
ENO'			
SPARE THE TENANT--LONG ENO'--	IT'S THOUGHTS--AND JUST	495	8
ENORMOUS			
THAT SUCH ENORMOUS PEARL	IT FEELS A SHAME TO BE	444	14
IN HIS TREMENDOUS [ETERNAL / ENORMOUS] CHAIR--	THE MOUNTAIN SAT UPON	975	2
ENOUGH			
ROYALTY ENOUGH FOR ME	PIGMY SERAPHS--GONE	138	16
IS PLENTY! IS ENOUGH!	A LITTLE BREAD--A CRUST	159	9
BUT THAT IS NOT ENOUGH!	WHAT WOULD I GIVE TO SEE	247	3
I BREATHED ENOUGH TO TAKE THE TRICK--	I BREATHED ENOUGH TO	272	1
YET NOT TOO FAR [NEAR ENOUGH--] TO COME AT CALL--	HE PUT THE BELT AROUND	273	9
SEE WHERE IT HURT ME--THAT'S ENOUGH--	WHAT IF I SAY I SHALL	277	5
I'M OLD ENOUGH, TODAY, I'M CERTAIN--THEN--	ONE YEAR AGO--JOTS WHAT?	296	33
AND HEAVEN--NOT ENOUGH FOR ME--	I SHOULD HAVE BEEN TOO	313	14
AND QUICK ENOUGH, IF TRUE.	THEY LEAVE US WITH THE	350	12
ENOUGH ESTATE--TO SEE--	'TIS OPPOSITES--ENTICE--	355	6
NOT LOUD ENOUGH--FOR WIND--	A MURMUR IN THE TREES--	416	2
A STAR--NOT FAR ENOUGH TO SEEK--	A MURMUR IN THE TREES--	416	3
NOR NEAR ENOUGH--TO FIND--	A MURMUR IN THE TREES--	416	4
ENOUGH TO KNOW!	KNOWS HOW TO FORGET!	433	V
BUT LARGE ENOUGH--FOR ME--	I MEANT TO HAVE BUT	476	12
BE LARGE ENOUGH FOR ME--	I HAD NO TIME TO HATE--	478	12
ENOUGH FOR US	"WHY DO I LOVE" YOU, SIR	480	9
I NEVER LIVED [DID NOT LIVE]--ENOUGH--	THAT I DID ALWAYS LOVE	549	4
AND NOT ENOUGH OF ME	EMPTY MY HEART, OF THEE	587	8
WHEN IT WAS DARK ENOUGH TO DO [SHOW]	A STILL--VOLCANO--LIFE--	601	3
MOST ENOUGH [AMPLEST]--DENIED?	PROMISE THIS--WHEN YOU	648	33
OUR NOVEL [ROMANCE]--WHEN 'TIS SMALL ENOUGH	NO ROMANCE SOLD UNTO	669	6
OMNIPOTENCE--ENOUGH--	TO BE ALIVE--IS POWER--	677	4
IS ENOUGH FOR ME--	'TWOULD EASE--A	682	10
BUT YOU HAVE ENOUGH--OF THOSE--	I COULD BRING YOU JEWELS	697	2
JUST LONG ENOUGH TO TASTE--	LET US PLAY YESTERDAY--	728	31
JUST LONG ENOUGH FOR HOPE TO TEAZE [STIR]--	THE WHOLE OF IT CAME NOT	762	7
WELL ENOUGH FOR SCHOOLS--	ONE AND ONE--ARE ONE--	769	3
'TIS SUMPTUOUS ENOUGH FOR ME--	DEPRIVED OF OTHER	773	7
SOCIETY ENOUGH.	PAIN HAS BUT ONE	1049	4
OF NATURE I SHALL HAVE ENOUGH	OF NATURE I SHALL HAVE	1220	1
I THOUGHT THAT NATURE WAS ENOUGH	I THOUGHT THAT NATURE	1286	1
ENOUGH--THE FIRST ABODE	UNTIL THE DESERT KNOWS	1291	10
WHEN LARGE ENOUGH TO RUN	THE THINGS WE THOUGHT	1293	6
NUMEROUS ENOUGH--	THE HEART IS THE CAPITAL	1354	6
ENOUGH WILL NOT BE FOUND WHEN ALL HAVE DIED.	ABOVE OBLIVION'S TIDE	1531	7
FEW, YET ENOUGH,	FEW, YET ENOUGH,	1596	1
ENOUGH IS ONE--	FEW, YET ENOUGH,	1596	2
IT IS ENOUGH, THE FREIGHT SHOULD BE	THAT LOVE IS ALL THERE	1765	3
ENROLLED			
ENROLLED UPON THE HEMISPHERE [FIRMAMENT]	THE DAY UNDRESSED--	716	7
ENSNARES			
ALLURES [ENSNARES] HIS JADED EYE	HIS ORIENTAL HERESIES	1526	6
ENSUE			
THAN TIME ENSUE TO BE--	WHO WERE "THE FATHER AND	1258	16
ENSUING			
THE DAY ENSUING--	COME SHOW THY DURHAM	1542	12
THE FINE--ENSUING RIGHT	OH WHAT A GRACE IS THIS,	1615	4
ENTAILED			
DOUBLE ESTATE--ENTAILED AT PLEASURE	I AM AFRAID TO OWN A	1090	5
ENTER			
THAT "ENTER IN--THEREAT"--	YOU'RE RIGHT--"THE WAY	234	4
I DARED NOT ENTER [OPEN], LEST A FACE	I YEARS HAD BEEN FROM	609	3
WE ENTER BUT THE GAIN,	OF SO DIVINE A LOSS	1179	2
'TWILL ENTER LIKE A DART!	HOW NEWS MUST FEEL WHEN	1319	4
TO ENTER, IT WOULD NOT ASPIRE--	IT WOULD NOT KNOW IF IT	1579	5
FORGOT TO RANKLE [ENTER] THERE	ARROWS ENAMORED OF HIS	1629	2
ENTERED			
WHEN "BRONTE" ENTERED THERE!	ALL OVERGROWN BY CUNNING	148	V
I BOLDLY ANSWERED--ENTERED THEN	THE WIND--TAPPED LIKE A	436	3
'TIS ENTERED FROM THE SUN--	DOOM IS THE HOUSE	475	2

	FIRST LINE	POEM	LINE
ENTERED (CONTINUED)			
THAT ALL MY LIFE HAD ENTERED IT	A GREAT HOPE FELL	1123	12
PHANTOMS ENTERED "AND NOT YOU."	TRUST ADJUSTS HER	1161	2
AND ENTERED WITH THE DAY--	SOMEHOW MYSELF SURVIVED	1194	2
WHEN I HAVE ENTERED THESE	OF NATURE I SHALL HAVE	1220	2
ENTERING			
THE ENTERING--TAKES AWAY--	I HAD BEEN HUNGRY, ALL	579	20
WITHOUT THE ENTERING--	IT ALWAYS FELT TO ME--A	597	4
ENTERPRISE			
FROM ENTERPRISE BELOW!	IF I SHOULD DIE,	54	10
ON MISCELLANEOUS ENTERPRISE	FROM COCOON FORTH A	354	7
ENTERS			
ENTERS--AND IS LOST IN BALMS.	COME SLOWLY--EDEN!	211	8
WHEN THE BALL ENTERS, ENTERS SILENCE-- . .	IF ANY SINK, ASSURE THAT	358	7
WHEN THE BALL ENTERS, ENTERS SILENCE-- . .	IF ANY SINK, ASSURE THAT	358	7
ENTERS--WITH A "YOU KNOW ME--SIR"? . . .	IT'S COMING--THE	390	4
ENTERTAIN			
WILL ENTERTAIN THE CENTURIES	OF BRONZE--AND BLAZE--	290	16
AND BEES TO ENTERTAIN--	THE GRASS SO LITTLE HAS	333	4
OR BABBLER--ENTERTAIN--	I FEAR A MAN OF FRUGAL	543	4
TO ENTERTAIN A PEARL--	SHELLS FROM THE COAST	693	4
AND ENTERTAIN DESPAIR--	THE HEAVEN VESTS FOR	694	12
BETTER [BRAVER] ENTERTAIN	NEVER FOR SOCIETY	746	8
ENTERTAIN--WITHOUT ADDRESSING	SO THE EYES ACCOST--AND	752	5
THE SOUL TO ENTERTAIN	TO OWN THE ART WITHIN	855	2
SPECULATE, OR FORESTS ENTERTAIN.	THE DUTIES OF THE WIND	1137	8
ENTERTAINED			
I ENTERTAINED MYSELF--	DEPRIVED OF OTHER	773	2
ENTERTAINING			
FOR ENTERTAINING PLATED WARES	IT DROPPED SO LOW--IN MY	747	7
ENTERTAINS			
THE GIANT TOLERATES [ENTERTAINS] NO GNAT .	SIZE CIRCUMSCRIBES--IT	641	3
THE LORD A CANDLE ENTERTAINS	THE SUN AND MOON MUST	871	12
AND FAILS, BUT ENTERTAINS	TO TELL THE BEAUTY WOULD	1700	6
ENTHRALL			
COULD SO ENTHRALL A MAN	NO ROMANCE SOLD UNTO	669	2
WHAT TERROR WOULD ENTHRALL THE STREET . .	IT'S HOUR WITH ITSELF	1225	3
ENTHRALLING			
AT THAT ENTHRALLING GALLOP	SWEET IS THE SWAMP WITH	1740	5
ENTICE			
'TIS OPPOSITES--ENTICE--	'TIS OPPOSITES--ENTICE--	355	1
TO SEDUCE [ENTICE / PERSUADE] THE SUN . .	PROMISE THIS--WHEN YOU	648	18
ENTICED			
UNTO LIKE STORY--TROUBLE HAS ENTICED ME-- .	UNTO LIKE STORY--TROUBLE	295	1
ENTICED TO BREAKFAST FROM THE SKY	FOREVER HONORED BE THE	1570	3
ENTICED TO COME.	TO THE BRIGHT EAST SHE	1573	6
ENTIRE			
MY SOUL'S ENTIRE INCOME--	ONE LIFE OF SO MUCH	270	3
STAKING OUR ENTIRE [DIVINE] POSSESSION . .	ROBBED BY DEATH--BUT	971	13
AND AN ENTIRE UNIVERSE	A SOFT SEA WASHED AROUND	1198	7
STAKE AN ENTIRE STORE	HOW MUCH THE PRESENT	1380	4
OF AN ENTIRE ATTAR	ONE OF THE ONES THAT	1466	15
ENTIRELY			
ENTIRELY FOR ME--	THERE CAME A DAY AT	322	2
ENTIRELY THE WEST	WHEN ONE HAS GIVEN UP	853	4
ENTIRELY FOR THEE--	THE SUN AND MOON MUST	871	13
ENTIRELY UNKNOWN	HOW MANY SCHEMES MAY DIE	1150	3
BUT ONCE--ENTIRELY--	WHO WERE "THE FATHER AND	1258	18
ENTIRELY AWAY.	HOW MUCH OF SOURCE	1517	4
NOT BIRDS ENTIRELY--BUT MINDS--	A PANG IS MORE	1530	3
ENTITLED			
ENTITLED TO MYSELF--PRECISE--	I AM ALIVE--I GUESS--	470	19
ENTITLED TO A BUMBLE BEE'S	OF NATURE I SHALL HAVE	1220	3
ENTITLED "MEMORY"--	THAT SACRED CLOSET WHEN	1273	2
TO WHICH THE LAW ENTITLED HIM.	UPON THE GALLOWS HUNG A	1757	3
ENTITLES			
ENTITLES US--BY CONTRAST--	THIS WAS A POET--IT IS	448	11
ENTOMBED			
ENTOMBED BY WHOM, FOR WHAT OFFENCE	IT WAS A GRAVE, YET BORE	876	5
OR IS ENTOMBED SO STILL	A DEED KNOCKS FIRST AT	1216	6
ENTOMBER			
THE ENTOMBER OF ITSELF, ...	REVOLUTION IS THE POD	1082	7
ENTOMOLOGY			
TO ENTOMOLOGY--	TWO BUTTERFLIES WENT OUT	533	V
SUPPLIED BY ENTOMOLOGY	THESE ARE THE NIGHTS	1128	15
IN ENTOMOLOGY--	THE BUTTERFLY OBTAINS	1685	4
ENTRANCE			
CONFIRMS IT AT IT'S ENTRANCE--AND	LOVE--IS THAT LATER	924	3
FIND ENTRANCE THERE	NOT ANY SUNNY TONE	1674	3
ENTRANCING			
TO THEIR ENTRANCING END	WITHOUT A SMILE--WITHOUT	1330	3
ENTREAT			
ENTREAT US TENDERLY	DEATH SETS A THING	360	4
ENTREATED			
WHEN SKILL ENTREATED IT--THE LAST--	"I WANT"--IT PLEADED--	731	3
ENTREATY			
STOLID TO LOVE'S SUPREME [SUBLIME] ENTREATY	TELL AS A MARKSMAN--WERE	1152	20
ENTRENCHED			
TRUST ENTRENCHED IN NARROW PAIN--	REARRANGE A "WIFE'S"	1737	10

	FIRST LINE	POEM	LINE
ENTRUST			
TO WHOM HE COULD ENTRUST HIS WAVERING GAZE--	TO KNOW JUST HOW HE	622	3
ENTRUSTED			
DEPARTED [ENTRUSTED] ME!	THE CHEMICAL CONVICTION	954	8
ENVELOPES			
ENVELOPES CONSCIOUSNESS--	THERE IS A LANGUOR OF	396	7
ENVIES			
ONE ENVIES THE DISTINGUISHED DUST--	IT FEELS A SHAME TO BE	444	3
ENVOY			
CHOOSE THE ENVOY--AND SPURN THE GROOM--	GOD IS A DISTANT--	357	6
ENVY			
I ENVY SEAS, WHEREON HE RIDES--[THAT BEAR HIM]	I ENVY SEAS, WHEREON HE	498	1
I ENVY SPOKES OF WHEELS	I ENVY SEAS, WHEREON HE	498	2
I ENVY CROOKED [SPEECHLESS] HILLS	I ENVY SEAS, WHEREON HE	498	4
I ENVY NESTS OF SPARROWS--	I ENVY SEAS, WHEREON HE	498	9
I ENVY LIGHT--THAT WAKES HIM--	I ENVY SEAS, WHEREON HE	498	17
OF ENVY, OR OF MEN--	SHE STAKED HER FEATHERS	798	4
WE ENVY THE DESPAIR	SOFTENED BY TIME'S	1738	6
EPAULETTED			
SOME EPAULETTED BROTHER	THERE IS A WORD	8	9
IN EPAULETTED WHITE--	BLESS GOD, HE WENT AS	147	6
EPICURE			
AN EPICURE OF ME	THE LUXURY TO APPREHEND	815	4
THE EPICURE OF FIRMAMENTS [VEHICLES / COURTESY / PURPOSES]	A SPARROW TOOK A SLICE	1211	V 7
AN EPICURE--A THIEF--	ONE OF THE ONES THAT	1466	10
EPICURES			
EPICURES--DATE A BREAKFAST--BY IT--	"MORNING"--MEANS	300	6
EPIGEA			
HUSH! EPIGEA WAKENS!	WHOSE ARE THE LITTLE	142	21
EPITAPH			
EPITAPH	SHE LAID HER DOCILE	1396	T
EPOCH			
BUT EPOCH HAD NO BASIS HERE	GREAT STREETS OF SILENCE	1159	7
EQUAL			
DEATH IS THE COMMON [MUTUAL / EQUAL] RIGHT	A TOAD, CAN DIE OF LIGHT	583	2
JUST AS [EQUAL] SURE--	ONLY GOD--DETECT THE	626	8
EQUAL PARADISE--	HER SWEET TURN TO LEAVE	649	28
OF OPPOSITE--TO BALANCE ODD [EQUAL OUGHT]--	THE ZEROES--TAUGHT US--	689	5
EQUAL BUTTERFLY--	COLOR--CASTE--	970	12
WILL EQUAL GLOW, AND THOUGHT NO MORE	IT BLOOMED AND DROPT, A	978	5
THAT FROM AN EQUAL SEED	THE OPENING AND THE	1047	5
UNTO AN EQUAL BUD	THE OPENING AND THE	1047	6
THAT OPENS WITH AN EQUAL WIDTH	THESE ARE THE SIGNS TO	1077	7
THEY ARE OF EQUAL YEARS	AS OLD AS WOE--	1168	6
THIS LATEST LEISURE EQUAL LULLS [CASTLE EQUAL HOLDS]	NOT ANY HIGHER STANDS	1256	5
THIS LATEST LEISURE EQUAL LULLS [CASTLE EQUAL HOLDS]	NOT ANY HIGHER STANDS	1256	5
EQUALLY			
WERE EQUALLY--ADORNED--	THE DAY THAT I WAS	356	12
DO PEOPLE MOULDER EQUALLY,	DO PEOPLE MOULDER	432	1
AND EQUALLY AS COOL--	WHAT CARE THE DEAD, FOR	592	8
THEY'RE WATER--EQUALLY--	'TIS GOOD--THE LOOKING	660	12
EQUALLY PERISH FROM OUR PRACTISE--	THOSE WHO HAVE BEEN IN	922	3
I EQUALLY BEHOLD	WHAT I SEE NOT, I BETTER	939	6
IS CONSUMMATED EQUALLY	NOT ALL DIE EARLY, DYING	990	3
EQUALLY PLAUSIBLY	EXPERIMENT TO ME	1073	6
ARE EQUALLY SUPREME--	THE DAY SHE GOES	1308	3
EQUALLY TO ABHOR DELIGHT--	SUMMER IS SHORTER THAN	1506	7
EQUALLY RETAIN HIM--	SUMMER IS SHORTER THAN	1506	8
WE ARE MOLESTED EQUALLY	WHY SHOULD WE HURRY--WHY	1646	3
EQUATION			
SOME NEW EQUATION, GIVEN--	I REASON, EARTH IS SHORT	301	11
EQUATOR			
EQUATOR--NEVER CAN--	THAT DISTANCE WAS	863	4
EQUILIBRIUM			
LAWFUL AS EQUILIBRIUM.	THE RAT IS THE CONCISEST	1356	10
EQUINOX			
AZOF--THE EQUINOX,	THE DUTIES OF THE WIND	1137	10
EQUIP			
ABLE AS THE DUST TO EQUIP IT'S FEATURE	SOME WE SEE NO MORE,	1221	8
EQUIPAGE			
WITH EQUIPAGE OF AMBER--	HE FOUND MY BEING--SET	603	7
HIMSELF--HIS CARRIAGE WAS--[CARRIAGE IS-- / EQUIPAGE.]	A BEE HIS BURNISHED	1339	4
EQUITY			
NATURE IN EQUITY--	GARLANDS FOR QUEENS, MAY	34	8
SO NOT IN EQUITY--	ALONE AND IN A	1167	24
AN ENGINERY OF EQUITY	DEATH WARRANTS ARE	1375	2
EQUIVALENT			
WERE FLESH [DUST] EQUIVALENT	LOVE CAN DO ALL BUT	1731	4
ERASE			
ERASE THE ROOT--NO TREE--	EMPTY MY HEART, OF THEE	587	11
ERASING			
WITHOUT ERASING [ENDANGERING] SIGHT--	A STILL--VOLCANO--LIFE--	601	4
ERE			
THAT ERE THE FROSTS ARE DUE--	'TIS NOT THAT DYING	335	6
OBTAINED [ENGROSSED] MY LODGINGS, ERE MYSELF--	BEREAVED OF ALL, I WENT	784	5
THE FIRST--SWEET, PROVED I, [THAT WAS]	WERT THOU BUT ILL--THAT	961	19

	FIRST LINE	POEM	LINE
ERE (CONTINUED)			
ERE I SAW THEE--			
ENDED, ERE IT BEGUN--	ENDED, ERE IT BEGUN--	1088	1
ERE I BE THERE--	MY HEART RAN SO TO THEE	1237	16
AND CATCH ME ERE [WHEN / AS] I DROP	THE PILE OF YEARS IS NOT	1507	8
WE SHUN IT ERE IT COMES,	WE SHUN IT ERE IT COMES,	1580	1
ERECT			
HE SITS ERECT IN "CABINETS"--	"ARCTURUS" IS HIS OTHER	70	15
AND MEET THE ROAD--ERECT--	WE GROW ACCUSTOMED TO	419	8
BUT THIS TIME--ADEQUATE--ERECT,	I'M CEDED--I'VE STOPPED	508	17
AND DREW THE HEAD ERECT--	THE LAST NIGHT THAT SHE	1100	26
AND ADEQUATE, [CONSCIOUS AND] ERECT,	THE PROPS ASSIST THE	1142	4
SHAME--STAND ERECT--	NOT WITH A CLUB, THE	1304	15
OR FAME ERECT HER SITELESS CITADEL	SOCIETY FOR ME MY MISERY	1534	V
THE HILLS ERECT THEIR PURPLE HEADS	THE HILLS ERECT THEIR	1688	1
ERECTS			
ERECTS IN IODINE--	THE SUNRISE RUNS FOR	710	11
ERMINE			
OF ERMINE IS HIS DOUBLET--	THE GUEST IS GOLD AND	15	3
HOW POMP SURPASSING ERMINE	ONE DIGNITY DELAYS FOR	98	13
VAILING THE ERMINE SO.	IN RAGS MYSTERIOUS AS	117	4
IN THINE ERMINE, SIR,	MUTE THY CORONATION--	151	4
BUT SURE I AM HE ERMINE WORE	I MET A KING THIS	166	5
ERMINE--MY FAMILIAR GOWN--	NO MATTER--NOW--SWEET--	704	13
CONVICTED--SENTENCED--ERMINE--NOT TO ME	WERT THOU BUT ILL--THAT	961	10
ERRAND			
THIS IS THE ERRAND OF THE EYE	WHETHER MY BARK WENT	52	7
THEY BEAR NO OTHER ERRAND,	MY NOSEGAYS ARE FOR	95	7
THE FOOT TO BEAR HIS ERRAND--	ALTHOUGH I PUT AWAY HIS	366	13
BUT AWED BEYOND MY ERRAND--	MY PERIOD HAD COME FOR	564	19
I HAVE AN ERRAND IMMINENT	THE SPRY ARMS OF THE	1103	3
AN ERRAND SO DIVINE,	WE SEND THE WAVE TO FIND	1604	2
ERRAND'S			
OR WOMAN--WHEN THE ERRAND'S DONE	I TIE MY HAT--I CREASE	443	15
ERRED			
SAY IF I ERRED? ACCUSE MY FARTHINGS--	SWEET--YOU FORGOT--BUT I	523	5
ERROR			
SO BE HER'S THE ERROR--	HAD WE KNOWN THE TON SHE	1124	4
AN ERROR SO DIVINE	MEETING BY ACCIDENT,	1548	4
ERRORS			
CORRECTING ERRORS OF THE SKY	HOW LONESOME THE WIND	1418	7
ERUDITE			
AH, WIZARD ERUDITE!	AH, NECROMANCY SWEET!	177	2
AH, TO BE ERUDITE	KNOWS HOW TO FORGET!	433	V
ESCAPADE			
THE ESCAPADE FROM GOD--	OF CONSCIOUSNESS, HER	894	8
ESCAPE SEE 'SCAPE			
I NEVER HEAR THE WORD "ESCAPE"	I NEVER HEAR THE WORD	77	1
ESCAPE FROM CIRCUMSTANCES--	FOR DEATH--OR RATHER	382	7
BECAUSE ESCAPE--IS DONE--	DOOM IS THE HOUSE	475	4
THE SOUL HAS MOMENTS OF ESCAPE--	THE SOUL HAS BANDAGED	512	11
ESCAPE--OR SUBSTITUTE--	THE FUTURE--NEVER SPOKE	672	8
ESCAPE THE PROWLING BEE	BLOOM--IS RESULT--TO	1058	12
ESCAPE IT--THERE IS BUT A CHANCE--	POWER IS A FAMILIAR	1238	5
ESCAPE IS SUCH A THANKFUL WORD	ESCAPE IS SUCH A	1347	1
ESCAPE--IT IS THE BASKET [CITADEL]	ESCAPE IS SUCH A	1347	5
OUR SUMMER MADE HER LIGHT ESCAPE	AS IMPERCEPTIBLY AS	1540	15
WHO SO APPARELED HIS ESCAPE--	SOME ARROWS SLAY BUT	1565	3
ESCAPE MORE SLOWLY	EXPANSE CANNOT BE LOST--	1584	13
ESCAPED			
AND PASS ESCAPED--TO THEE!	WHAT IF I SAY I SHALL	277	3
ESCAPED THE HOUSE UNSEEN--	'TWAS CRISIS--ALL THE	948	16
ESCAPELESS			
AND AS ESCAPELESS--QUITE--	A PRISON GETS TO BE A	652	24
BEFORE THEM LIES ESCAPELESS SEA--	THIS IS THE PLACE THEY	1264	7
ESCAPES			
HOW MUCH OF SOURCE ESCAPES WITH THEE--	HOW MUCH OF SOURCE	1517	1
THE LIFE THAT TIED TOO TIGHT ESCAPES	THE LIFE THAT TIED TOO	1535	1
ESCAPING SEE 'SCAPING			
ESCAPING BACKWARD TO PERCEIVE	ESCAPING BACKWARD TO	867	1
ESCAPING FORWARD, TO CONFRONT	ESCAPING BACKWARD TO	867	3
OF MEN ESCAPING	TO FLEE FROM MEMORY	1242	7
ESCORT			
ESTABLISH MARCH, THE FLOODS ESCORT,	THE DUTIES OF THE WIND	1137	3
ESCORTED			
THAN IF ESCORTED TO IT'S DOWN	THE FLAKE THE WIND	1361	3
ESCORTS			
EXPERIMENT ESCORTS [ACCOSTS] US LAST--	EXPERIMENT ESCORTS US	1770	1
ESCUTSCHEON SEE SCUTCHEON			
PRESENT OUR MEEK ESCUTSCHEON	ONE DIGNITY DELAYS FOR	98	15
THE BUTTERCUP'S [LEONTODON'S] ESCUTSCHEON--	TO HER DERIDED HOME	1586	V
ESOTERIC			
KEEPS ESOTERIC TIME	'TWAS LATER WHEN THE	1276	8
LIKE SIGNAL ESOTERIC SIPS	YOUR THOUGHTS DONT HAVE	1452	3
WHOSE ESOTERIC BELT	DID LIFE'S PENURIOUS	1717	7
ESPIED			
THIS DUSTY HEART ESPIED--	A POOR--TORN HEART-- A	78	10
HER TRUDGING FEET ESPIED--	SHE DIED--THIS WAS THE	150	V 6
AND THEN ESPIED [THEN OVERTOOK--] CIRCUMFERENCE	TWO BUTTERFLIES WENT OUT	533	V 3

	FIRST LINE	POEM	LINE
ESPIES			
ESPIES THAT FICKLE CHAIR	RISK IS THE HAIR THAT	1239	6
ESPOUSE			
HE FIRST ACHIEVE [ESPOUSE] THY FACE . . .	MY HEART RAN SO TO THEE	1237	6
ESPOUSED			
ESPOUSED A VIOLET, ...	TO THIS WORLD SHE	830	5
ESPOUSING			
ESPOUSING EACH AND SPURNING ALL	HOW LONESOME THE WIND	1418	11
ESPY			
HOW MANY I ESPY	A MURMUR IN THE TREES--	416	14
ESSAY			
CRACKLING WITH FEVER, THEY ESSAY, ...	I BRING AN UNACCUSTOMED	132	5
ESSENTIAL			
ESSENTIAL OILS--ARE WRUNG--	ESSENTIAL OILS--ARE	675	1
ESSENTIAL HOST, IN LIFE'S FAINT, WAILING INN,	AIR HAS NO RESIDENCE, NO	1060	6
A MORE ESSENTIAL THING.	THE PEDIGREE OF HONEY	1627	8
ESSEX			
ELIZABETH TOLD ESSEX	ELIZABETH TOLD ESSEX	1321	1
WHEN SUING--LIKE HER ESSEX	ELIZABETH TOLD ESSEX	1321	7
ESTABLISH			
ESTABLISH MARCH, THE FLOODS ESCORT, . . .	THE DUTIES OF THE WIND	1137	3
ESTABLISHED			
IS A TOO ESTABLISHED FORTUNE [SECURE POSSESSION / CONTENDED . . .	EXPECTATION--IS	807	7
IN IT'S ESTABLISHED PLACE--	'TWAS AWKWARD, BUT IT	973	10
. . . ACCOMPLISHED / DISCERNING / ACCOUTRED / ESTABLISHED / . . .	HE PREACHED UPON	1207	8
DESCENDING [CONSENTING / ESTABLISHED / IMPARTED] TO ENAMOR US	THE FACE IN EVANESCENCE	1490	7
ESTABLISHES			
ESTABLISHES, AND TERMINATES--	THE BATTLE FOUGHT	594	7
ESTATE			
OF THIS BAREFOOT ESTATE!	I MET A KING THIS	166	28
FOR LIFE'S ESTATE WITH YOU--	YOUR RICHES--TAUGHT ME--	299	8
ENOUGH ESTATE--TO SEE--	'TIS OPPOSITES--ENTICE--	355	6
THE LOSS OF AN ESTATE--	TO LOSE ONE'S FAITH--	377	2
AS AN ESTATE PERPETUAL	TO OWN THE ART WITHIN	855	7
THE [A] ROSE IS AN ESTATE--	PARTAKE AS DOTH THE BEE,	994	3
FOR SURETIES OF HER STAUNCH ESTATE . . .	THESE ARE THE SIGNS TO	1077	9
DOUBLE ESTATE--ENTAILED AT PLEASURE . . .	I AM AFRAID TO OWN A	1090	5
AND ARTISAN LIES [SMALL ESTATE STANDS--] STILL--	DEW--IS THE FRESHET IN	1097	4
RELINQUISHED OUR ESTATE--	THE PUNGENT ATOM IN THE	1191	4
RETIRED, AND RESUMED HIS TRANSITIVE ESTATE--	THE MOST TRIUMPHANT BIRD	1265	7
THAT INDESTRUCTIBLE ESTATE	YOU CANNOT TAKE ITSELF	1351	3
THE ONLY ADAMANT ESTATE	HOW FIRM ETERNITY MUST	1499	3
AN ABLATIVE ESTATE [DELIGHT]--	THAT IT WILL NEVER COME	1741	6
ESTATES			
BECAUSE ESTATES CAN BE	TO LOSE ONE'S FAITH--	377	3
AND HAD [OWNED] ESTATES OF CLOUD	THE TREES LIKE TASSELS--	606	12
PERPLEXED! ESTATES OF VIOLET TROUBLE NE'ER LOOKED ON!	WOULD YOU LIKE SUMMER?	691	5
ESTEEM			
OF MORE ESTEEM THAN DUCATS--	I LOST A WORLD--THE	181	7
THE BLIND--ESTEEM IT BE	'TIS OPPOSITES--ENTICE--	355	5
IN HEAVENLY ESTEEM--	'TIS TRUE--THEY SHUT ME	538	6
A TRIFLE--IN HIS OWN ESTEEM [ESTIMATE]-- .	HE GAVE AWAY HIS LIFE--	567	3
THAT I ESTEEM THE FICTION--REAL [TRUE]-- .	I THINK TO LIVE--MAY BE	646	23
BUT [JUST] INSTINCT ESTEEM [REPORT] HIM . .	CONSCIOUS AM I IN MY	679	19
I SCARCE ESTEEM LOCATION'S NAME--	WHERE THOU ART--THAT--IS	725	4
WHO OWN--ESTEEM THE OPULENCE--	I PLAY AT RICHES--TO	801	15
TILL HE ESTEEM HIS DATES AND COCOA . . .	AS THE STARVED MAELSTROM	872	11
AN UNKNOWN ESTEEM [CONTENT] POSSESSING-- .	ALL FORGOT FOR	966	7
I CANNOT HELP ESTEEM	WHICH IS BEST? HEAVEN--	1012	4
AS HE HAD NO ESTEEM	HOW DESTITUTE IS HE	1477	V 7
ESTEEMED			
AND I ESTEEMED ALL POVERTY	YOUR RICHES--TAUGHT ME--	299	7
IT HAD ESTEEMED THE DREAM--	THE WORLD--STANDS--	493	14
TO SO ESTEEMED A SIZE	DEPRIVED OF OTHER	773	6
ESTEEMED ME NEVER RUDE	MY BEST ACQUAINTANCES	932	4
IS ESTEEMED IN HEAVEN THE CHIEFEST-- . . .	"UNTO ME?" I DO NOT KNOW	964	11
THE THINGS ESTEEMED, FOR THINGS THAT ARE! .	WHAT TWIGS WE HELD BY--	1086	17
TO BE ESTEEMED NO MORE	A FULL FED ROSE ON MEALS	1154	8
AS HE ESTEEMED THEM TRIFLES, ...	HIGH FROM THE EARTH I	1723	3
ESTEEMING			
ESTEEMING US--AS EXILE--	THOSE FAIR--FICTITIOUS	499	21
ESTIMABLE			
DOUBTLESS AN ESTIMABLE BEAST, ...	I MET A KING THIS	166	15
ESTIMATE			
WE ESTIMATE OUR PRIZE	AS BY THE DEAD WE LOVE	88	6
AND ESTIMATE THE PEARL--	YOUR RICHES--TAUGHT ME--	299	30
OUR DIZZY [SCANTY] ESTIMATE--	THOSE FAIR--FICTITIOUS	499	12
PAST WHAT OURSELF CAN ESTIMATE [UNDERSTAND]--	IF ANYBODY'S FRIEND BE	509	23
A TRIFLE--IN HIS OWN ESTEEM [ESTIMATE]-- .	HE GAVE AWAY HIS LIFE--	567	3
THIS TIME--BEYOND THE ESTIMATE [INFERENCE] .	SHE STAKED HER FEATHERS	798	3
REORGANIZES ESTIMATE	THE ADMIRATIONS--AND	906	4
OR ESTIMATE--OR END--	A COFFIN--IS A SMALL	943	12
ESTIMATE--WHO CAN--	ALL FORGOT FOR	966	8
AS TO ESTIMATE	ROBBED BY DEATH--BUT	971	V 16
JEHOVAH'S ESTIMATE.	NO OTHER CAN REDUCE	982	8

	FIRST LINE	POEM	LINE
ESTIMATE (CONTINUED)			
I LEARNED TO ESTIMATE.	I HAD A DAILY BLISS	1057	8
BUT IN A SQUIRREL'S ESTIMATE	A SAUCER HOLDS A CUP	1374	3
OR OUT OF SIGHT OF ESTIMATE	FAME IS THE ONE THAT	1475	3
AND ESTIMATE IT'S SIZE--	SO GIVE ME BACK TO DEATH	1632	6
THE BLUNDER IS IN ESTIMATE	THE BLUNDER IS IN	1684	1
ESTIMATES			
HIS PRETTY ESTIMATES	THE CHILD'S FAITH IS NEW	637	19
OUR ESTIMATES A SCHEME [FORSOOK]--	THE DAYS THAT WE CAN	1184	5
AND ESTIMATES THEM ALL--	THE SUN IS ONE--AND ON	1372	4
AND ESTIMATES [ENFORCES / COMMENCES / REPLEVYS / CONFISCATES] ...	PERHAPS THEY DO NOT GO	1399	8
ESTIMATING			
AT ESTIMATING PAIN--	NO MAN CAN COMPASS A	477	9
ESTRANGED			
HIS BILL IS CLASPED [LOCKED]--HIS EYE FORSOOK [ESTRANGED]--	HIS BILL IS CLASPED--HIS	1102	1
ESTRANGED, HOWEVER INTIMATE--	WITHOUT A SMILE--WITHOUT	1330	5
IN WHICH THE SOUL AT FIRST ESTRANGED [ALARMED / SUBMERGED]--	THE INUNDATION OF THE	1425	5
ESTRANGED FROM BEAUTY--NONE CAN BE--	ESTRANGED FROM BEAUTY--	1474	1
THAT MAKE THE WATER LIVE, ESTRANGED	THE SPIRIT LASTS--BUT IN	1576	11
ESTRANGING			
A FINE--ESTRANGING CREATURE--	THE FASCINATING CHILL	1480	6
ETCHINGS			
OBLITERATE THE ETCHINGS	DEATH SETS A THING	360	19
ETERNAL			
STILL THE ETERNAL RULE	'TIS ONE BY ONE--THE	545	12
IN THEIR ETERNAL FACES	THE MOUNTAINS--GROW	757	5
AND THE ETERNAL FUNCTION	THERE IS A FINISHED	856	7
IN HIS TREMENDOUS [ETERNAL / ENORMOUS] CHAIR--	THE MOUNTAIN SAT UPON	975	2
BUT HER ETERNAL HOUSE--	OF GLORY NOT A BEAM IS	1647	2
ETERNALLY			
BLOOM ETERNALLY!	THO' MY DESTINY BE	163	12
ETERNALLY FROM VIEW--	THE TREES LIKE TASSELS--	606	14
ETERNALLY BELONG.	DOMINION LASTS UNTIL	1257	4
ETERNALLY UNKNOWN	A DEW SUFFICED ITSELF--	1437	12
IS PINK ETERNALLY.	BLOSSOMS WILL RUN AWAY,	1578	4
ETERNITIES			
GAMMUTS [TRIPLETS] OF ETERNITIES	PAIN--EXPANDS THE TIME--	967	7
ETERNITY SEE CO-ETERNITY			
LAND HO! ETERNITY!	ON THIS WONDROUS SEA	4	11
EAST OF ETERNITY--	SLEEP IS SUPPOSED TO BE	13	12
INTO DEEP ETERNITY--	EXULTATION IS THE GOING	76	4
GRIEF--HILLS--ETERNITY--	SOME THINGS THAT FLY	89	5
JUST GIRT ME FOR THE ONSET WITH ETERNITY,	JUST LOST, WHEN I WAS	160	3
INTO ETERNITY--	A SINGLE SCREW OF FLESH	263	12
ETERNITY--UNTIL--	A SOLEMN THING--IT WAS--	271	8
SOMETIMES--NOT OFTEN--IN ETERNITY--	ONE YEAR AGO--JOTS WHAT?	296	7
THE BALLOTS OF ETERNITY, WILL SHOW JUST THAT.	MY REWARD FOR BEING, WAS	343	11
ETERNITY IS AMPLE,	THEY LEAVE US WITH THE	350	11
WOULD BE ETERNITY--	I KNOW LIVES, I COULD	372	4
AN ETERNITY--PUT ON--	TAKE YOUR HEAVEN FURTHER	388	5
ETERNITY--	LOVE--THOU ART HIGH--	453	18
ETERNITY, I'M COMING--SIR,	A WIFE--AT DAYBREAK I	461	12
AND TAKE [TASTE] ETERNITY--	IF YOU WERE COMING IN	511	16
ETERNITY--BY TERM--	OUR JOURNEY HAD ADVANCED	615	4
MEET--AND THE JUNCTION BE [MEAN] ETERNITY	TO KNOW JUST HOW HE	622	26
BETWEEN ETERNITY AND TIME--	YOU LEFT ME--SIRE--TWO	644	7
ETERNITY ENABLE THE ENDEAVORING	EACH LIFE CONVERGES TO	680	19
THAN A BEE'S ETERNITY--	'TWOULD EASE--A	682	8
IN FULL ETERNITY--	THE HEAVEN VESTS FOR	694	8
ETERNITY--IS THOSE--	AS IF THE SEA SHOULD	695	8
WERE TOWARD ETERNITY--	BECAUSE I COULD NOT STOP	712	24
BEHIND ME--DIPS ETERNITY--	BEHIND ME--DIPS ETERNITY	721	1
COULD SCARCE AFFORD ETERNITY	IT'S EASY TO INVENT A	724	7
YOU--AND ETERNITY--THE	LET US PLAY YESTERDAY--	728	3
TOWARD ETERNITY--	"I WANT"--IT PLEADED--	731	8
I DEEMED ETERNITY	YOU CONSTITUTED TIME--	765	2
TO WAIT ETERNITY--IS SHORT--	TO WAIT AN HOUR--IS LONG	781	3
AT LEAST--ETERNITY--	JOY TO HAVE MERITED THE	788	24
ETERNITY--OBTAINED--IN TIME--	TWO--WERE IMMORTAL TWICE	800	3
FOR AN ETERNITY--	TIME FEELS SO VAST THAT	802	2
PERCHANCE [THREE--WITH / AND SOME] ETERNITY--	THE ONLY NEWS I KNOW	827	6
THAT SECURES ETERNITY	CRISIS IS A HAIR	889	15
AFTER ETERNITY.	WHAT DID THEY DO SINCE I	900	12
NEED [MISS]--ONCE IN AN ETERNITY--	LOVE--IS THAT LATER	924	11
TO TARRY AN ETERNITY--	NO OTHER CAN REDUCE	982	V
AND MET [UNTO] ETERNITY	I HEARD, AS IF I HAD NO	1039	16
ETERNITY IT WAS BEFORE	IT WAS A QUIET WAY--	1053	15
ETERNITY WAS DUE.	IT WAS A QUIET WAY--	1053	16
UNTIL ETERNITY.	THE BUSTLE IN A HOUSE	1078	8
CURTAIL [CONTRACT] ETERNITY!	SOMEWHERE UPON THE	1231	12
ETERNITY, PRESUMPTION	BECAUSE THAT YOU ARE	1260	13
ETERNITY WILL BE	TWO LENGTHS HAS EVERY	1295	5
THE TORRENTS [WATERS] OF ETERNITY	HOW MUCH THE PRESENT	1380	7
HOW FIRM ETERNITY MUST LOOK	HOW FIRM ETERNITY MUST	1499	1
THE GRAVE AND THAT ETERNITY	MORE THAN THE GRAVE IS	1503	2
THAN FROM ETERNITY	IF I COULD TELL HOW GLAD	1668	8
ETERNITY IS THERE	THE BLUNDER IS IN	1684	2

	FIRST LINE	POEM	LINE
ETERNITY (CONTINUED)			
AS THIS ETERNITY	THE BLUNDER IS IN	1684	8
ETERNITY'S			
ETERNITY'S DISCLOSURE	THE SOUL'S SUPERIOR	306	13
ETERNITY'S VAST [WIDE] POCKET, PICKED--	EMPTY MY HEART, OF THEE	587	14
ETERNITY'S WHITE [COOL] FLAG--BEFORE [IN FRONT]--	OUR JOURNEY HAD ADVANCED	615	11
ETERNITY'S ACQUAINTANCES	WHO OCCUPIES THIS HOUSE?	892	31
ETHER			
THE BLESSED ETHER--TAUGHT THEM--	THE LONESOME FOR THEY	262	9
THROUGH VILLAGES OF ETHER--	I WOULD NOT PAINT--A	505	13
IF MET IN ETHER SEA	TWO BUTTERFLIES WENT OUT	533	10
DROPPED INTO THE ETHER ACRE--	DROPPED INTO THE ETHER	665	1
UPON AN ETHER STREET.	IT WAS A QUIET WAY--	1053	12
IT'S LITTLE ETHER HOOD	IT'S LITTLE ETHER HOOD	1501	1
UPON AN ETHER SEA,	A SLOOP OF AMBER SLIPS	1622	2
ETHEREAL			
THAN MERIT THE ETHEREAL SCORN	HER SPIRIT ROSE TO SUCH	1486	5
ETHERIAL			
A RAISED--ETHERIAL THING!	THE SUN--JUST TOUCHED	232	6
FOR THE ETHERIAL BLOW	HE FUMBLES AT YOUR SOUL	315	6
WITH DEATH'S ETHERIAL SCORN--	ENDOW THE LIVING--WITH	521	8
OR THAT ETHERIAL [SERAPHIC] GAIN	MY FIRST WELL DAY--SINCE	574	26
OR THAT ETHERIAL ZONE	FROM US SHE WANDERED NOW	890	4
AND THAT ETHERIAL SPARK.	WE MET AS SPARKS--	958	8
ETHERIAL GUEST AT E'EN AN OUTCAST'S PILLOW--	AIR HAS NO RESIDENCE, NO	1060	5
TO THAT ETHERIAL THRONG	FEW, YET ENOUGH,	1596	3
TO THEIR [WHOSE] ETHERIAL HOMES	TALK NOT TO ME OF SUMMER	1634	6
ETHICS			
OF INDUSTRY AND MORALS [ETHICS]	HIS LITTLE HEARSE LIKE	1522	5
ETHIOP			
THE ETHIOP WITHIN.	MORE LIFE--WENT OUT--	422	12
ETHIOP--HER GOLD--	CIVILIZATION--SPURNS--	492	4
ETHIOPIAN			
THE POMP OF SUMMER [ETHIOPIAN] DAYS	SOME ONE PREPARED THIS	1644	6
ETIQUETTE			
THE OBLOQUIES OF ETIQUETTE	THEIR DAPPLED	1611	3
ETIQUETTES			
HAVE ETIQUETTES	WE INTRODUCE OURSELVES	1214	4
ETNA			
WHEN ETNA BASKS AND PURRS	WHEN ETNA BASKS AND	1146	1
ETNA'S			
OR ETNA'S SCARLETS, CHOOSE--	MORE LIFE--WENT OUT--	422	20
ETRUSCAN			
BECKONING--ETRUSCAN INVITATION--	UNTO LIKE STORY--TROUBLE	295	23
THE STAR'S ETRUSCAN ARGUMENT	THE MOON UPON HER FLUENT	1528	3
EULOGY			
THAT THOU ART THAT TRITEST EULOGY	EXTOL THEE--COULD I--	1643	V 4
EVADE			
NONE EVADE THIS CROWN!	ONE DIGNITY DELAYS FOR	98	4
SO WE EVADE THE CHARGE OF YEARS	AS SUMMER INTO AUTUMN	1346	9
EVADES			
DIPS--EVADES--TEAZES--DEPLOYS--	THE NEAREST DREAM	319	6
THAN IT RESISTS [EVADES / ELUDES]--THE HOUND--	THIS MERIT HATH THE	979	8
EVANESCE			
ARISE AND EVANESCE	WHAT TENEMENTS OF CLOVER	1338	6
EVANESCENCE			
A ROUTE OF EVANESCENCE	A ROUTE OF EVANESCENCE	1463	1
THE FACE IN EVANESCENCE LAIN	THE FACE IN EVANESCENCE	1490	1
EVANGELISTS			
EVANGELISTS [AS GENESIS] RECORD,	A LITTLE EAST OF JORDAN,	59	2
EVE			
ADAM, AND EVE, HIS CONSORT, THE MOON, AND THEN THE SUN;	AWAKE YE MUSES NINE,	1	8
FROM OUT MY SUMMER'S EVE--	SHE WENT AS QUIET AS THE	149	6
EVE--AND THE ANGUISH--GRANDAME'S STORY--	BETTER--THAN MUSIC! FOR	503	15
EVEN			
FAR--AS THE EAST FROM EVEN--	TAKEN FROM MEN--THIS	53	9
RANK AFTER RANK, WITH EVEN FEET--	TO FIGHT ALOUD, IS VERY	126	11
SOME, WOULD EVEN TRUDGE TONIGHT!	"HOUSES"--SO THE WISE	127	8
I SENT IT--EVEN NOW?	WHAT SHALL I DO--IT	186	7
NOTCHING THE FALL OF THE EVEN SUN!	BOUND--A TROUBLE--	269	10
EVEN A TEAR--	A MIEN TO MOVE A QUEEN--	283	7
SOMEHOW, IT WILL BE EVEN--	I REASON, EARTH IS SHORT	301	10
IT MAKES AN EVEN FACE	IT SIFTS FROM LEADEN	311	5
AND EVEN IN THE URN,	OF ALL THE SOUNDS	321	16
AND EVEN WHEN IT DIES [DIE]--TO PASS	THE GRASS SO LITTLE HAS	333	13
'TWAS EVEN THAT 'TWAS MINE--	THE DAY THAT I WAS	356	16
WHOSE ANVIL'S EVEN RING	DARE YOU SEE A SOUL AT	365	10
NOR EVEN OF DEFEAT--AWARE--	THERE IS A FLOWER THAT	380	31
EVEN THROUGH THEM--THIS	IT IS DEAD--FIND IT--	417	8
AWAITED EVEN--HIM--	REMOVED FROM ACCIDENT OF	424	12
TO MAKE AN EVEN SUM--	'TWAS JUST THIS TIME,	445	16
BESIDES--IT IS'NT EVEN--IT SLANTS	WE DO NOT PLAY ON GRAVES	467	3
AND LIFE AND I--KEEP EVEN--	I MEANT TO HAVE BUT	476	4
OR EVEN A REPORT OF LAND--	IT WAS NOT DEATH, FOR I	510	23
GAVE--EVEN AS TO ALL--	HER SWEET WEIGHT ON MY	518	10
AND EVEN WHEN WITH CORDS--	'TWAS WARM--AT FIRST--	519	13
FORGIVE THEM--EVEN AS MYSELF--	'TIS TRUE--THEY SHUT ME	538	11
EVEN AS THE GRACE--	MUST BE A WO--	571	12

	FIRST LINE	POEM	LINE
EVEN (CONTINUED)			
AND EVEN WHEN THE SNOW	TO INTERRUPT HIS YELLOW	591	4
AS EVEN IN THE SKY--	WHEN I WAS SMALL, A	596	16
I SANG FIRM--EVEN--[STRAIGHT--STEADY] CHANTS--	I ROSE--BECAUSE HE SANK	616	6
AS EVEN WHILE I LOOKED--DISSOLVED--	THEY CALLED ME TO THE	628	7
NOR EVEN NOW--SO SWEET--	A PRISON GETS TO BE A	652	12
IF THAT--INDEED [EVEN THAT]--REDEEM--	A PRISON GETS TO BE A	652	32
IN EASY--EVEN--DAZZLING PACE--	OF BEING IS A BIRD	653	7
EVEN FOR DEATH, A FAIRY MEDICINE.	WOULD YOU LIKE SUMMER?	691	8
EVEN AS HERSELF--SIR--	ALTER! WHEN THE HILLS DO	729	7
NOT EVEN GOD--CAN HEAL--	REMORSE--IS MEMORY--	744	10
'TWAS EVEN WITH THE HILLS--	JOY TO HAVE MERITED THE	788	18
THE MARTYRS--EVEN [STEADY]--TROD.	THROUGH THE STRAIT PASS	792	2
LIST EVEN UNTO ME.	BECAUSE THE BEE MAY	869	3
I OFFER EVEN THAT--	TOO SCANTY 'TWAS TO DIE	1013	4
THERE IS A ZONE WHOSE EVEN YEARS	THERE IS A ZONE WHOSE	1056	1
YET [BUT] EVEN ON HIS SCARLET SHELF	THE FROST OF DEATH WAS	1136	7
YET EVEN THIS SHALL ROUSE [STIR] ITSELF	A STAGNANT PLEASURE LIKE	1281	7
IS WHOLESOME EVEN FOR THE KING,	A LITTLE MADNESS IN THE	1333	2
EVEN NATURE HERSELF	NOT ANY MORE TO BE	1344	5
NOT EVEN A PROGNOSTIC'S PUSH	THE SPIRIT LASTS--BUT IN	1576	23
NOT EVEN A PROGNOSTIC'S PUSH	EXPANSE CANNOT BE LOST--	1584	7
NOT [THAT] EVEN A PROGNOSTIC'S PUSH [FOOT]	THIS ME--THAT WALKS AND	1588	7
SHOUTS EVEN FROM THE CRUCIFIX,	THE AUCTIONEER OF	1612	3
ARE EVEN AS THYSELF--	GO THY GREAT WAY!	1638	3
OR EVEN IF I DEEM I DO	HIS MIND OF MAN, A	1663	5
YOU CANNOT EVEN DIE	THE RIGHT TO PERISH	1692	6
I DOUBT IF EVEN THAT	LOVE CAN DO ALL BUT	1731	2
EVENING			
BURN SO THE EVENING SPIRES	DISTRUSTFUL OF THE	20	13
TILL--THE EVENING NEARING	MORNS LIKE THESE--WE	27	9
WENT UP A YEAR THIS EVENING!	WENT UP A YEAR THIS	93	1
GOOD EVENING, GENTLE FELLOW MEN!	IF THIS IS "FADING"	120	8
AS AN EVENING WEST,	PORTRAITS ARE TO DAILY	170	2
COMPOSE AN EVENING SKY--	A SLASH OF BLUE--	204	4
OH HOUSEWIFE IN THE EVENING WEST--	SHE SWEEPS WITH	219	3
I'VE RUBIES--LIKE THE EVENING BLOOD--	I CAME TO BUY A SMILE--	223	11
PUT GENTLY UP THE EVENING BARS--	I'LL TELL YOU HOW THE	318	15
BUT MILES OF SPARKS--AT EVENING--	THE RED--BLAZE--IS THE	469	5
UNTIL TOMORROW [THE EVENING]--HAPPY LETTER! [AH! BE BASHFUL]	GOING TO HIM! HAPPY	494	24
AND THE MOUNTAIN TO THE EVENING	BLOOM UPON THE MOUNTAIN	667	17
EVENING--THE TISSUE [FOLDING] DOOR--	NOON--IS THE HINGE OF	931	2
INTO THE DARKNESS [TWILIGHT / EVENING] DIPS AWAY--	FAIRER THROUGH FADING--	938	2
THE EVENING ON THE DAY LEANS	AS WILLING LID O'ER	1050	2
TOO DEAR THE [WERE] SUMMER EVENING	THESE ARE THE NIGHTS	1128	13
'TWAS SUCH AN EVENING BRIGHT AND STIFF	THAT ODD OLD MAN IS DEAD	1130	3
THE AFTERNOON IN EVENING DEEP	THE DAY GREW SMALL,	1140	3
PRESUMPTUOUS EVENING SAID--	WHEN MEMORY IS FULL	1266	4
THE ACT OF EVENING FELL	THE MOUNTAINS STOOD IN	1278	10
AT EVENING, IT IS NOT--	THE MUSHROOM IS THE ELF	1298	2
TO DIE DIVINELY ONCE A TWILIGHT--[AN EVENING / A LIMIT]	I'D RATHER RECOLLECT A	1349	7
HE SPENDS THE EVENING OF HIS DAYS [NOONS]	HIS ORIENTAL HERESIES	1526	V
ALL OF EVENING SOFTLY LIT	LIGHTLY STEPPED A YELLOW	1672	5
EVENING'S			
BY EVENING'S SABRES [SABRE] SLAIN	SOFT AS THE MASSACRE OF	1127	2
TO EVENING'S SEA--	"GO TRAVELING WITH US!"	1513	4
EVENINGS			
LIKE HER THE EVENINGS STEAL	LIKE HER THE SAINTS	60	4
THOSE EVENINGS OF THE BRAIN--	WE GROW ACCUSTOMED TO	419	10
EVENLY			
RUNS EVENLY--AND TRUE--	THE BRAIN, WITHIN IT'S	556	2
EVENT			
THERE IS IN FEVER OR EVENT--	'TWAS CRISIS--ALL THE	948	3
EVENT INEFFABLE--	WHO WERE "THE FATHER AND	1258	22
IS [WAS] SHORTER THAN A [THE] SNAKE'S DELAY [EVENT / REPLY]	THE MUSHROOM IS THE ELF	1298	7
THIS HARROWING EVENT	A SINGLE CLOVER PLANK	1343	13
T'IS THIS EXPANDS THE LEAST EVENT	I KNOW OF PEOPLE IN THE	1665	5
THE EVENT WAS DIRECTLY BEHIND HIM	THE EVENT WAS DIRECTLY	1686	1
A THIRD EVENT TO ME,	MY LIFE CLOSED TWICE	1732	4
EVENTIDE			
NIGHT UNTO DAY IS MARRIED, MORN UNTO EVENTIDE!	AWAKE YE MUSES NINE,	1	22
EVENTS			
ARE MORE THAN IT'S EVENTS--	THE INCIDENTS OF LOVE	1248	2
EVENTUAL			
AS WE EVENTUAL--BE--	WE TALKED AS GIRLS DO--	586	10
EVENTUALLY			
IT WILL BE SUMMER--EVENTUALLY.	IT WILL BE SUMMER--	342	1
EVER			
EVER SERENE AND FAIR,	THERE IS ANOTHER SKY,	2	2
WHOSE LEAF IS EVER GREEN;	THERE IS ANOTHER SKY,	2	8
THAT EVER KISSED THE SPADE!	I NEVER TOLD THE BURIED	11	13
NOR EVER GUESSED THE STATELY SAILS	'TWAS SUCH A LITTLE--	107	7
THAT EVER ROCKED A CHILD.	WHOSE ARE THE LITTLE	142	20
THESE SOVREIGNS EVER TOOK!	I MET A KING THIS	166	24
EVER BE INDUCED TO DO!	I'M THE LITTLE "HEART'S	176	14
SO IF I GET LOST--THERE--EVER--	WHAT IS--"PARADISE"--	215	13

	FIRST LINE	POEM	LINE
EVER (CONTINUED)			
AND EVER SINCE--THE PURPLE MOAT	THE LONESOME FOR THEY	262	5
THE ONLY GHOST I EVER SAW	THE ONLY GHOST I EVER	274	1
WERE YOU EVER THERE?	THE WIND DID'NT COME	316	10
NO DEAD, WERE EVER CARRIED DOWN--	A HOUSE UPON THE HIGHT--	399	3
OR EVER TOOK A NAP--	I NEVER FELT AT HOME--	413	10
ODDEST OF SCIENCES--BOOK EVER BORE--	KNOWS HOW TO FORGET!	433	10
NOR EVER TURN TO TELL ME WHY--	WHY MAKE IT DOUBT--IT	462	12
AND SICKENED--EVER AFTERWARD	IT KNEW NO MEDICINE--	559	15
I EVER HAD--BUT ONE--	I FOUND THE WORDS TO	581	2
EVER WENT BY ONE--	INCONCEIVABLY SOLEMN!	582	10
DID YOU EVER STAND IN A CAVERN'S MOUTH--	DID YOU EVER STAND IN A	590	1
DID YOU EVER LOOK IN A CANNON'S FACE--	DID YOU EVER STAND IN A	590	9
EVER COULD ENDOW--	HER SWEET TURN TO LEAVE	649	V 16
WAS EVER IDLENESS [ARROGANCE] LIKE THIS?	A LONG--LONG SLEEP--A	654	5
EVER HE MINDED OCCUPYING	NO BOBOLINK--REVERSE HIS	755	3
SHOULD EVER THESE EXPLORING HANDS	I PLAY AT RICHES--TO	801	17
A LOSS OF SOMETHING EVER FELT I--	A LOSS OF SOMETHING EVER	959	1
NONE [THEY] WHO SAW IT EVER TOLD IT	NONE WHO SAW IT EVER	1110	1
THE LARGEST FIRE EVER KNOWN	THE LARGEST FIRE EVER	1114	1
NOR MISSILE [VENGEANCE] EVER COMES	THE CLOUDS THEIR BACKS	1172	8
THAT EVER MASON LAID--	REMEMBRANCE HAS A	1182	6
LEAVE ME NOT EVER THERE ALONE	REMEMBRANCE HAS A	1182	V 7
I EVER CARED TO EARN--	THE STARS ARE OLD, THAT	1249	4
NOR EVER SAW HIS HOUSE NOR FURNITURE,	I CANNOT SEE MY SOUL BUT	1262	2
THE MOST TRIUMPHANT BIRD I EVER KNEW OR MET	THE MOST TRIUMPHANT BIRD	1265	1
WHOSE LIMIT NONE HAVE EVER SEEN,	WHAT MYSTERY PERVADES A	1400	5
THE FAIREST HOME I EVER KNEW	THE FAIREST HOME I EVER	1423	1
WILL EVER AFTER RUN	THE LIFE THAT TIED TOO	1535	2
DID BEAUTY EVER TAKE--	THE BIRD HER PUNCTUAL	1585	6
OR EVER TO REMAIN--	HE WENT BY SLEEP THAT	1662	4
NOR EVER CEASED TO RUN	IN WINTER IN MY ROOM	1670	35
IF EVER THE LID GETS OFF MY HEAD	IF EVER THE LID GETS OFF	1727	1
MORE THAN WIFEHOOD EVER MAY!	REARRANGE A "WIFE'S"	1737	8
EVERGREENS			
IS PUNGENT EVERGREENS--	NO BRIGADIER THROUGHOUT	1561	18
EVERLASTING			
MEEK AT WHOSE EVERLASTING FEET	IN LANDS I NEVER SAW--	124	5
INTO THE EVERLASTING SNOW?	DYING! DYING IN THE	158	4
THAT EVERLASTING--SINGS!	A FEATHER FROM THE	161	2
WAIT TILL IN EVERLASTING ROBES	WAIT TILL THE MAJESTY OF	171	5
THEN I WILL, WHEN ON THE EVERLASTING HILL	ME, CHANGE! ME, ALTER!	268	2
INTACT, IN EVERLASTING FLAKE--	DOUBT ME! MY DIM	275	24
HELD FAST IN EVERLASTING RACE--	TIE THE STRINGS TO MY	279	11
AND THE EVERLASTING CLOCKS--	IT'S LIKE THE LIGHT--	297	11
THEIR EVERLASTING FASHIONS--SET--	WHILE ASTERS--	331	3
HER EVERLASTING FASHION--SET--	IT WILL BE SUMMER--	342	15
GIBRALTAR'S EVERLASTING SHOE	THEY LEAVE US WITH THE	350	7
SLOW GOLD--BUT EVERLASTING--	SOME--WORK FOR	406	5
LEST NOON IN [DOWN] EVERLASTING NIGHT--	I ENVY SEAS, WHEREON HE	498	23
IN EVERLASTING KEEPSAKE [CHILDHOOD]--	THOSE FAIR--FICTITIOUS	499	7
ILL FLUTTERED OUT--IN EVERLASTING WELL--	TO KNOW JUST HOW HE	622	17
BORN INFINITER [EVERLASTING]--NOW--	'TWAS A LONG PARTING--	625	12
AND FOR AN EVERLASTING ROOF	I DWELL IN POSSIBILITY--	657	7
BONNET OF EVERLASTING LACES--	DROPPED INTO THE ETHER	665	3
WHEN SUMMER'S EVERLASTING DOWER--	PRECIOUS TO ME--SHE	727	13
OR THE EVERLASTING--	ONE AND ONE--ARE ONE--	769	6
THEIR FAITH--THE EVERLASTING TROTH--	THROUGH THE STRAIT PASS	792	9
UNTO THE EVERLASTING SPRING	NO NOTICE GAVE SHE, BUT	804	15
HOW SCANT, BY EVERLASTING LIGHT	WHAT TWIGS WE HELD BY--	1086	14
HOW EVERLASTING ARE THE LIPS	DOMINION LASTS UNTIL	1257	5
THAT WRAPS THE EVERLASTING HILL	SUMMER BEGINS TO HAVE	1682	8
TILL EVERLASTING LIFE [RITE] UNITE	THE GRAVE MY LITTLE	1743	7
EVERY			
HE STOPS AT EVERY DOOR--	THE GUEST IS GOLD AND	15	6
BY EVERY SAINTED BEE--	I KEEP MY PLEDGE.	46	6
AN HOUR, AND GAY ON EVERY TREE	COCOON ABOVE! COCOON	129	4
FOR EVERY BIRD A NEST--	FOR EVERY BIRD A NEST--	143	1
HOUSEHOLDS IN EVERY TREE--	FOR EVERY BIRD A NEST--	143	5
FOR EVERY LITTLE KNOLL--	ON SUCH A NIGHT, OR SUCH	146	18
I'D BRING THEM EVERY FLOWER THAT GROWS	IF I COULD BRIBE THEM BY	179	2
AND HIT A WORLD, AT EVERY PLUNGE [CRASH],	I FELT A FUNERAL, IN MY	280	19
AND PAUSED AT EVERY POUND	I FELT MY LIFE WITH BOTH	351	6
IT STRUCK ME--EVERY DAY--	IT STRUCK ME--EVERY DAY	362	1
WITH EVERY MORN THAT CAME--	IT STRUCK ME--EVERY DAY	362	8
PRONOUNCING EVERY WORD	THE MORNING AFTER WO--	364	10
I'M SAYING EVERY DAY	I'M SAYING EVERY DAY	373	1
THAT EVERY TIME I WAKE--	THE ANGLE OF A LANDSCAPE	375	2
BUT EVERY MESH--A CITADEL--	I HAD NOT MINDED--WALLS	398	15
BUT GOD CAN SUMMON EVERY FACE	THEY DROPPED LIKE FLAKES	409	8
THAT NEARER, EVERY DAY,	'TWAS LIKE A MAELSTROM,	414	2
THAT EVERY SIGH--MAY LIFT YOU	I'LL CLUTCH--AND CLUTCH	427	18
TO EVERY CREATURE--THAT I MET--	IT WOULD NEVER BE COMMON	430	19
AND EVERY SIGN BEFORE THE PLACE	A TOOTH UPON OUR PEACE	459	7
CONVICTION--EVERY DAY--	I LIVE WITH HIM--I SEE	463	14
AND EVERY ONE UNBARED A NERVE	SHE DEALT HER PRETTY	479	3
A LITTLE NEARER--EVERY SUN	A SOLEMN THING WITHIN	483	15
YOU WRITE HIM--EVERY DAY--	YOU LOVE THE LORD--YOU	487	2
TILL EVERY SPICE IS TASTED--	WITHIN MY GARDEN, RIDES	500	9
AND FLED WITH EVERY ONE--	SHE SIGHTS A BIRD--SHE	507	12

	FIRST LINE	POEM	LINE
EVERY (CONTINUED)			
EVERY TIME--FOR TWO--	SWEET--YOU FORGOT--BUT I	523	2
PATENT, EVERY DROP,	TO PUT THIS WORLD DOWN,	527	13
AND EVERY SEPARATE URCHIN'S SUM--	'TIS ONE BY ONE--THE	545	15
I MEASURE EVERY GRIEF I MEET	I MEASURE EVERY GRIEF I	561	1
ON EVERY SHOULDER THAT SHE MET [SHE COULD REACH]--	MY FIRST WELL DAY--SINCE	574	21
INSOLVENT--EVERY NOON--	I GAVE MYSELF TO HIM--	580	16
I FOUND THE WORDS [PHRASE] TO EVERY THOUGHT	I FOUND THE WORDS TO	581	1
FOR I HAD WORN IT, EVERY DAY,	IT CEASED TO HURT ME,	584	6
WE SPECULATED FAIR, ON EVERY SUBJECT, BUT THE GRAVE--	WE TALKED AS GIRLS DO--	586	3
AND GOD--AT EVERY GATE--	OUR JOURNEY HAD ADVANCED	615	12
ON EVERY SIDE OF MINE	OURSELVES WERE WED ONE	631	12
I THINK THE DAYS--COULD EVERY ONE	I THINK TO LIVE--MAY BE	646	9
MY PRICE FOR EVERY STAIN!	AGAIN--HIS VOICE IS AT	663	29
EXISTS IN EVERY HUMAN NATURE	EACH LIFE CONVERGES TO	680	3
GOD DOES IT--EVERY DAY--	IT'S EASY TO INVENT A	724	2
AND EVERY TIME I SPEAK FOR HIM--	MY LIFE HAD STOOD--A	754	7
TRUTH STAYS HERSELF--AND EVERY MAN	THE TRUTH--IS STIRLESS--	780	11
JOY TO HAVE PERISHED EVERY STEP--	JOY TO HAVE MERITED THE	788	3
GOD GAVE A LOAF TO EVERY BIRD--	GOD GAVE A LOAF TO EVERY	791	1
SEES EVERY MAN A KING--	WHO COURT OBTAIN WITHIN	803	2
EVERY DAWN, IS FIRST.	ALWAYS MINE!	839	9
AND EVERY NIGHT, IT NUMBERED MORE	I MADE SLOW RICHES BUT	843	3
AND YET SO BOLDER EVERY DAY	THIS CHASM, SWEET, UPON	858	11
BUT EVERY TEAR I BORE	EACH SCAR I'LL KEEP FOR	877	5
AND LEAVE A DAY AT EVERY DOOR	WHEN I HAVE SEEN THE SUN	888	3
A DEED, IN EVERY PLACE--	WHEN I HAVE SEEN THE SUN	888	4
OF EVERY CITIZEN.	WHO OCCUPIES THIS HOUSE?	892	28
FROM EVERY HUMAN HEART	TOO LITTLE WAY THE HOUSE	911	2
THOU KNOWEST EVERY WO--	ONLY A SHRINE, BUT MINE	918	5
EVERY SECOND TIME--	HE WHO IN HIMSELF	969	6
HE WERE SUPERFLUOUS EVERY DAY	SUPERFLUOUS WERE THE SUN	999	3
FOR EVERY DAY BE SAID	SUPERFLUOUS WERE THE SUN	999	4
HE LABORETH AT EVERY TREE	HIS BILL AN AUGUR IS	1034	3
AND EVERY GRASS THAT PLAYS OUTSIDE	HERE, WHERE THE DAISIES	1037	3
AND EVERY LIMIT A DECADE--	I'VE DROPPED MY BRAIN--	1046	19
IS EVERY ONE I MEET	EXPERIMENT TO ME	1073	2
EVERY SUMMER BE	REVOLUTION IS THE POD	1082	6
OR EVERY MAN BE BLIND--	TELL ALL THE TRUTH BUT	1129	8
WERE EVERY STORM [GALE / SNOW] SO SPICE [FAIR / SWEET]	THE SNOW THAT NEVER	1133	13
OVER, EVERY DAY,	THERE'S THE BATTLE OF	1174	2
WARRANT [BUSINESS] IN EVERY LINE--	A PROMPT--EXECUTIVE BIRD	1177	4
TILL EVERY CUBIT PLAY WITH THEE	MY GOD--HE SEES THEE--	1178	4
AND EVERY CRESCENT HOLD--	MY GOD--HE SEES THEE--	1178	5
I BET WITH EVERY WIND THAT BLEW	I BET WITH EVERY WIND	1215	1
DISHEVELS EVERY PRIME	LIKE TIME'S INSIDIOUS	1236	6
IN EVERY COMPANY--	POWER IS A FAMILIAR	1238	4
WERE EVERY OTHER DAY!	HAD THIS ONE DAY NOT	1253	4
BY EVERY BROOM AND BRIDGET	THE SPIDER AS AN ARTIST	1275	5
FROM EVERY OTHER BIRD	THE WAY TO KNOW THE	1279	2
TWO LENGTHS HAS EVERY DAY--	TWO LENGTHS HAS EVERY	1295	1
WHAT NEWS WILL DO WHEN EVERY MAN	HOW NEWS MUST FEEL WHEN	1319	9
BUT I TELL YOU EVERY STEP IS A TROUGH [SLUICE]--	FLOSS WONT SAVE YOU FROM	1322	5
AND EVERY STOP A WELL--	FLOSS WONT SAVE YOU FROM	1322	6
IN EVERY HUMAN SOUL--	PINK--SMALL--AND	1332	8
THAT EVERY MAN [ALL THE WORLD] BEHOLD	YOU CANNOT TAKE ITSELF	1351	6
OF EVERY TARE--	"TOMORROW"--WHOSE	1367	6
AND EVERY BREEZE THAT RUN ALONG	A SAUCER HOLDS A CUP	1374	7
OR EVERY BIRD WILL POINT AT THEE	TOUCH LIGHTLY NATURE'S	1389	3
LIKE LOOKING EVERY TIME YOU PLEASE	WHAT MYSTERY PERVADES A	1400	7
ENLARGES [SUBMERGES] EVERY SOUL--	THE INUNDATION OF THE	1425	2
SO LET US GATHER--EVERY DAY--	TO EARN IT BY DISDAINING	1427	5
YOUR THOUGHTS DONT HAVE WORDS EVERY DAY	YOUR THOUGHTS DONT HAVE	1452	1
AND EVERY BLOSSOM ON THE BUSH	A ROUTE OF EVANESCENCE	1463	5
AND WITH A FLAG AT EVERY TURN	THEIR BARRICADE AGAINST	1471	3
WHO FINDS IT EVERY TIME	HOW DESTITUTE IS HE	1477	3
BUT IT IS RISING [HIGHER / FURTHER] EVERY DAY	THE PILE OF YEARS IS NOT	1507	3
AND EVERY RIGHTEOUS [FOUNDED] THING	HIS LITTLE HEARSE LIKE	1522	6
AS EVERY PORTER KNOWS--	HER LOSSES MAKE OUR	1562	6
OF [TO] EVERY OTHER [AS GRACIOUS AS A] BOON--	TO SEE HER IS A PICTURE	1568	V 4
WITH EVERY FUTURE ONE?	THE SPIRIT LASTS--BUT IN	1576	16
AND EVERY CLAMOR BRIGHT	THE FARTHEST THUNDER	1581	14
AROUND US, EVERY DAY--	WITCHCRAFT WAS HUNG, IN	1583	4
ALIGHT IN EVERY LAND	COSMOPOLITES WITHOUT A	1589	2
HE BOWED TO HEAVEN INSTEAD OF EARTH [EVERY HEAVEN ABOVE / . . .	THE BOBOLINK IS GONE--	1591	6
. . . ALL THE SAINTS HE KNEW / EVERY GOD HE KNEW]	THE BOBOLINK IS GONE--	1591	6
LET EVERY BONDAGE BE,	IMMURED IN HEAVEN!	1594	3
I OPEN EVERY DOOR,	NOT KNOWING WHEN THE	1619	2
POSSESSED BY EVERY HALLOWED KNIGHT	CIRCUMFERENCE THOU BRIDE	1620	3
WHEN EVERY WAY WE FLY	WHY SHOULD WE HURRY--WHY	1646	2
WE DWELL IN EVERY DAY	EDEN IS THAT	1657	2
BUT MY FEET SLIP NEARER EVERY DAY	I DID NOT REACH THEE	1664	2
DIVESTED IS OF EVERY DISK	JUDGEMENT IS JUSTEST	1671	4
EXTINCT BE EVERY HUM	HOW DARE THE ROBINS SING	1724	13

	FIRST LINE	POEM	LINE
EVERY (CONTINUED)			
LET EVERY BABBLER [PRATER] BE	THE RETICENT VOLCANO	1748	10
FOR EVERY PALATE IN THE YEAR,"--	THE WATERS CHASED HIM AS	1749	7
WHERE EVERY BIRD IS BOLD TO GO	WHERE EVERY BIRD IS BOLD	1758	1
EVERYDAY			
'TWAS AN EVERYDAY AFFAIR--	HE FORGOT--AND I--	203	2
EVERYONE			
OF EVERYONE BUT HERE AND THERE	HIS MIND LIKE FABRICS OF	1446	3
EVERYTHING			
OLD FASHIONED--NAUGHTY--EVERYTHING--	"ARCTURUS" IS HIS OTHER	70	32
AND BOW TO EVERYTHING--	THE GRASS SO LITTLE HAS	333	8
WHEN EVERYTHING THAT TICKED--HAS STOPPED--	IT WAS NOT DEATH, FOR I	510	17
WHILE EVERYTHING TO CORNERS SLUNK	THE WIND TOOK UP THE	1134	7
WHILE EVERYTHING CREATED HID	TO PILE LIKE THUNDER TO	1247	3
OF EVERYTHING BUT HE--	BECAUSE THAT YOU ARE	1260	28
AND EVERYTHING THAT HAS AN INN	HOW LONESOME THE WIND	1418	3
AND EVERYTHING UNKNOWN,	THE GOING FROM A WORLD	1603	6
EVERYTHING YOU ARE.	DEATH IS LIKE THE INSECT	1716	8
EVERYWHERE			
A FLOWER EXPECTED EVERYWHERE--	AN ALTERED LOOK ABOUT	140	10
MUSICIANS WRESTLE [WRESTLING] EVERYWHERE--	MUSICIANS WRESTLE	157	1
REPAIRING EVERYWHERE--	FROM COCOON FORTH A	354	4
I'M KNOCKING--EVERYWHERE--	AT LEAST--TO PRAY--IS	502	4
AND DWELL A LITTLE EVERYWHERE [GENERALLY]	COULD I BUT RIDE	661	7
BIRD WENT PRAISING EVERYWHERE--	WHEN I HOPED, I	768	15
WILLS SILENCE--EVERYWHERE--	NATURE--THE GENTLEST	790	24
AN EVERYWHERE OF SILVER	AN EVERYWHERE OF SILVER	884	1
HIS INQUEST, EVERYWHERE--	THE MOUNTAIN SAT UPON	975	4
EVERYWHERE ALONE	WHEN I HOPED I FEARED--	1181	3
EVE'S			
QUAINTLY INFER--EVE'S GREAT SURRENDER--	BETTER--THAN MUSIC! FOR	503	11
EVES			
A FEW ASCETIC EVES--	BESIDES THE AUTUMN POETS	131	6
EVIDENCE			
PLUCKS AT A TWIG OF EVIDENCE--	THIS WORLD IS NOT	501	15
THIS TIMID LIFE OF EVIDENCE	THEIR HIGHT IN HEAVEN	696	15
FOR EVIDENCE 'T HAS BEEN--	AS ONE DOES SICKNESS	957	12
FOR EVIDENCE IT BE THE GRACE--	FITTER TO SEE HIM, I MAY	968	12
JUST LAYING OFF FOR EVIDENCE	DEATH IS A DIALOGUE	976	7
AND OF FEAR NO EVIDENCE GIVES HE	WHAT MYSTERY PERVADES A	1400	V 16
PERCEIVING THEE IS EVIDENCE	EXTOL THEE--COULD I--	1643	5
EVIL			
HOARY [EVIL / RIGID / WRINKLED / ARID / SHRUNKEN] THE FRUITION	FORTITUDE INCARNATE	1217	7
EVOKES			
EVOKES [PROVOKES] SO SWEET A TORMENT--	I WOULD NOT PAINT--A	505	7
EVOLVED			
THE AFFLUENCE EVOLVED [CONFERRED / BESTOWED / INVOLVED]--	SUMMER--WE ALL HAVE SEEN	1386	10
EXACTING			
BY HER EXACTING LIGHT	UNWORTHY OF HER BREAST	1414	4
EXACTING THIS REPLY--	THE SPIRIT LASTS--BUT IN	1576	18
EXACTLY			
EXACTLY [PRECISELY]--AS THE WORLD--	THE DAY UNDRESSED--	716	5
EXACTNESS			
WITH SCRUPULOUS EXACTNESS--	I TIE MY HAT--I CREASE	443	32
EXALT			
NO OTHER CAN EXALT OUR	NO OTHER CAN REDUCE	982	V
EXALTED			
AS THAT EXALTED [THOSE RESPLENDENT] HERE--	NO LIFE CAN POMPLESS	1626	4
EXALTS			
HER PANTING NOTE [JOYFUL CRY / CORDIAL NOTE] EXALTS US--	AFTER ALL BIRDS HAVE	1395	6
EXAMINE			
YET BIRDS EXAMINE IT AND FLEE--	HOW KNOW IT FROM A	1364	5
THAT ALL MAY THEM--IT--EXAMINE [WITNESS IT AND MORE]	SOME ONE PREPARED THIS	1644	5
EXAMPLE			
EXAMPLE--AND MONITION	TWO BUTTERFLIES WENT OUT	533	V
EXASPERATE			
THE FLAKE THE WIND EXASPERATE	THE FLAKE THE WIND	1361	1
EXCEEDING			
YET DOTH EXCEEDING RUN!	A FUZZY FELLOW, WITHOUT	173	2
EXCEEDS			
EXCEEDS IT'S UNREMEMBERED [UNDEVELOPED] DROP--	'TIS GOOD--THE LOOKING	660	11
EXCEL			
CANNOT [COULD NOT] EXCEL DECAY,	I REASON, EARTH IS SHORT	301	7
HIMSELF--THE HEAVEN EXCEL--	THE POWER TO BE TRUE TO	464	6
BLISS OF DEATH--LIFE'S BLISS EXTOL THRO [SURPASS IN / EXCEL IN]	PROMISE THIS--WHEN YOU	648	15
EXCELLENCE			
FOR SORDID EXCELLENCE [CONSEQUENCE]	I CANNOT LIVE WITH YOU--	640	35
THE WORTHINESS [EXCELLENCE / QUALITY] OF SUFFERING LIKE	DESPAIR'S ADVANTAGE IS	799	5
WHEN EXCELLENCE BE DEAD	SUPERFLUOUS WERE THE SUN	999	2
THE EXCELLENCE [QUALITY] DEFIES US--	TO DISAPPEAR ENHANCES--	1209	15
EXCELLENT			
HOW EXCELLENT THE HEAVEN--	IT WAS TOO LATE FOR MAN	623	5
HOW EXCELLENT A BODY [GIANT], THAT	THE TRUTH--IS STIRLESS--	780	7
EXCELLENT AND FAIR.	AMPLE MAKE THIS BED--	829	4

	FIRST LINE	POEM	LINE
EXCUSE			
AND THEN--EXCUSE FROM PAIN--	THE HEART ASKS PLEASURE	536	2
THE LEAVES OBTAINED EXCUSE--	THE DAY GREW SMALL,	1140	6
BUT WHAT EXCUSE HAVE I?	SO MUCH OF HEAVEN HAS	1228	8
EXECUTE			
HIS OFFICE--BUT TO EXECUTE	THE FUTURE--NEVER SPOKE	672	11
EXECUTIVE			
A PROMPT--EXECUTIVE [BOLD, INSPIRITING] BIRD IS THE JAY--	A PROMPT--EXECUTIVE BIRD	1177	1
EXECUTORS			
THEY STARTLED, LIKE EXECUTORS	NATURE AND GOD--I	835	3
EXEGESIS			
IN TRANSPORT'S EXEGESIS	A DEW SUFFICED ITSELF--	1437	V 15
EXEMPT			
IS EXEMPT FROM CHANGE--	ALL BUT DEATH, CAN BE	749	8
EXERCISE			
AND THAT WHITE SUSTENANCE--[EXERCISE / PRIVILEGE]	I CANNOT LIVE WITH YOU--	640	49
EXERCISING			
WITH THE BLUE BIRDS EXERCISING [BUCCANEERING]	WE LIKE MARCH.	1213	12
EXERT			
THIS--THE BEST ENACT [MORE EXERT]	DRAMA'S VITALLEST	741	5
EXERTION			
PATIENCE--IS THE SMILE'S [MOUTH'S / LOVE'S] EXERTION	PATIENCE--HAS A QUIET	926	7
EXETER			
THAN BE "DUKE OF EXETER"--	PIGMY SERAPHS--GONE	138	15
TO EXETER--	I'M SAYING EVERY DAY	373	33
EXHALE			
EXHALE IN OFFERING.	EXHILIRATION--IS WITHIN	383	12
AND YEARS--EXHALE IN YEARS--	FOREVER--IS COMPOSED OF	624	8
EXHALED			
FOR PERIOD EXHALED.	GREAT STREETS OF SILENCE	1159	8
EXHALES			
DISSOLVES [ABATES / EXHALES]--THE SAME--	IN MANY AND REPORTLESS	1382	6
EXHAUSTION			
WITHOUT ATTEMPT--EXHAUSTION--	THE MOUNTAINS--GROW	757	3
EXHIBIT			
EXHIBIT--I SUPPOSE	NO CROWD THAT HAS	515	2
ITSELF--EXHIBIT [ENABLE / EMBOLDEN]--MINE--	BUT LITTLE CARMINE HATH	558	4
EXHIBIT LOVE--SOMEWHAT--	TILL DEATH--IS NARROW	907	12
EXHIBIT HERE, AS DOTH A BURR--	BEST THINGS DWELL OUT OF	998	7
EXHIBIT WORTHIER.	WHO GOES TO DINE MUST	1223	8
EXHIBITED			
ONE CALVARY--EXHIBITED TO STRANGER--	ONE CRUCIFIXION IS	553	5
FOR LOT--EXHIBITED TO	A FIRST MUTE COMING--	702	7
EXHIBITING			
EXHIBITING--TO THESE--	LIKE MIGHTY FOOT LIGHTS	595	4
EXHIBITION			
BY DEATH'S BOLD EXHIBITION	THERE IS A FINISHED	856	5
TO SITUATIONS [EXHIBITION / COMPREHENSION] NEW	ON THAT SPECIFIC PILLOW	1533	6
EXHIBITS			
EXHIBITS [DEVELOPES] SHEETS OF PLACE--	THE SOUL'S DISTINCT	974	6
EXHILARATE			
DOES NOT EXHILARATE.	THAT IT WILL NEVER COME	1741	4
EXHILIRATE			
EXHILIRATE--DEBASE--	AN IGNORANCE A SUNSET	552	6
EXHILIRATE THE BEE,	HIS ORIENTAL HERESIES	1526	2
EXHILIRATES			
'TIS SO APPALLING--IT EXHILIRATES--	'TIS SO APPALLING--IT	281	1
EXHILIRATES THE MAN	IMPOSSIBILITY, LIKE WINE	838	2
EXHILIRATION			
EXHILIRATION--IS WITHIN--	EXHILIRATION--IS WITHIN	383	1
EXHILIRATION IS THE BREEZE	EXHILIRATION IS THE	1118	1
EXIGENCIES			
AND EXIGENCIES NEVER FEARS--	HOW HAPPY IS THE LITTLE	1510	4
WHAT EXIGENCIES WERE--	WERE NATURE MORTAL LADY	1762	6
EXILE			
ESTEEMING US--AS EXILE--	THOSE FAIR--FICTITIOUS	499	21
IS SENTENCE [EXILE] FROM BELIEF--AND HOME--	IF BLAME BE MY SIDE--	775	4
HOW MEAGRE, WHAT AN EXILE--IS A LIE,	A COUNTERFEIT--A PLATED	1453	6
EXILES			
THE EASTERN EXILES--BE--	THE LONESOME FOR THEY	262	2
EXIST			
WHAT DUPLICATE--EXIST--	NO CROWD THAT HAS	515	17
OURSELVES ARE CONSCIOUS HE EXIST--	THE LIGHTNING PLAYETH--	630	3
AND OUR'S--A KINSMANSHIP EXPRESS [EXIST / SUBSIST / ARISE]--	A PRISON GETS TO BE A	652	3
AND ARE TODAY--IF WE EXIST--	HAVE ANY LIKE MYSELF	736	7
THE [NOR] FACT OF FAMINE--COULD NOT BE [EXIST]	NONE CAN EXPERIENCE	771	3
A VALUE [NATURE] STRUGGLE--IT EXIST--	A PLATED LIFE--	806	5
EXIST AN [FULFILLED THEIR] ORIENTAL CIRCUIT	THIS QUIET DUST WAS	813	7
ALL LATITUDES EXIST FOR HIS	ALL CIRCUMSTANCES ARE	820	3
TWO SEASONS, IT IS SAID, EXIST--	THERE IS A JUNE WHEN	930	9
LIKE THE REMEMBERING IT EXIST--	NO OTHER CAN REDUCE	982	V
THAT OTHERS COULD EXIST	THE LAST NIGHT THAT SHE	1100	13
DO HE EXIST, OR DIE,	THE DUTIES OF THE WIND	1137	14
ITSELF EXIST TODAY--	SOMEWHERE UPON THE	1231	2
YET DOES NOT EXIST--	"SECRETS" IS A DAILY	1385	2
THAN NOT EXIST AT ALL--	ADVANCE IS LIFE'S	1652	8

	FIRST LINE	POEM	LINE
EXISTENCE			
TO INVEST EXISTENCE WITH A STATELY AIR, . .	TO VENERATE THE SIMPLE	57	7
THAT MADE EXISTENCE--HOME!	EXCEPT TO HEAVEN, SHE IS	154	12
AND YET--EXISTENCE--SOME WAY BACK--	I TIE MY HAT--I CREASE	443	11
EXISTENCE--IN ITSELF--	TO BE ALIVE--IS POWER--	677	2
IN HIM EXISTENCE SERVE OR SET	ALL CIRCUMSTANCES ARE	820	7
EXISTENCE--THIS TRAVERSED	THE ONLY NEWS I KNOW	827	9
THAT YOU, WHO WERE EXISTENCE	BECAUSE THAT YOU ARE	1260	15
A WHOLE EXISTENCE THROUGH.	WHILE WE WERE FEARING IT	1277	12
HE COMPLIMENTS EXISTENCE	THE WAY TO KNOW THE	1279	15
WHEN WE ADVERTISE EXISTENCE	LAIN IN NATURE--SO	1288	3
EXISTENCE HAS A STATED WIDTH	THE DAY SHE GOES	1308	4
OF PARADISE' EXISTENCE	OF PARADISE' EXISTENCE	1411	1
THROUGH WHICH EXISTENCE STRAYS	TO THE BRIGHT EAST SHE	1573	11
EXISTENCE WITH A WALL	ADVANCE IS LIFE'S	1652	6
NOTWITHSTANDING IT COST US EXISTENCE ONCE .	TO DO A MAGNANIMOUS	1699	7
PRECISELY AN EXISTENCE--	I TOOK ONE DRAUGHT OF	1725	3
EXISTENCE'S			
EXISTENCE'S WHOLE ARC, [WHOLE EYE / WHOLE RIM / SURMISE] FILLED UP,	I'M CEDED--I'VE STOPPED	508	12
EXISTENCES			
IN ONE OR TWO [MORE] EXISTENCES--	AFRAID! OF WHOM AM I	608	7
EXISTING			
EXISTING, WHILE WE STARE, ...	HOW NOTELESS MEN, AND	282	6
EXISTS			
THAT THERE EXISTS--A GOLD--	YOUR RICHES--TAUGHT ME--	299	26
I KNOW THAT HE EXISTS.	I KNOW THAT HE EXISTS.	338	1
THAT POPOCATAPEL EXISTS--	MORE LIFE--WENT OUT--	422	19
EXISTS IN EVERY HUMAN NATURE	EACH LIFE CONVERGES TO	680	3
A LIGHT EXISTS IN SPRING	A LIGHT EXISTS IN SPRING	812	1
POWDER EXISTS IN CHARCOAL [ELEMENTS / SULPHURETS]--	A MAN MAY MAKE A REMARK	952	7
BEFORE IT EXISTS [EXPRESS] IN FIRE.	A MAN MAY MAKE A REMARK	952	8
FIRE EXISTS THE FIRST IN LIGHT	ASHES DENOTE THAT FIRE	1063	5
THAT SOMEWHERE, THERE EXISTS, ...	THE HEART HAS MANY DOORS	1567	7
EXISTS AND IT'S INDORSEMENT	SPEECH IS ONE SYMPTOM OF	1681	5
EXODY			
MORE LOYAL FOR THE EXODY	FROM HIS SLIM PALACE IN	1300	3
EXORBITANT			
TOO EXORBITANT [EXTRAVAGANT / IMPORTUNATE] .	SO MUCH SUMMER	651	5
EXORCISED			
NOT EXORCISED BEFORE--	THE WAY I READ A	636	12
EXPAND			
THAT WOULD EXPAND [BETRAY] US ALL--	THE LIFE THAT TIED TOO	1535	V 8
EXPANDING			
FAR AS SOUTH AND WEST--EXPANDING [DISCLOSING]--	BLOOM UPON THE MOUNTAIN	667	15
EXPANDS			
PAIN--EXPANDS THE TIME--	PAIN--EXPANDS THE TIME--	967	1
T'IS THIS EXPANDS THE LEAST EVENT	I KNOW OF PEOPLE IN THE	1665	5
EXPANSE			
EXCEPT THROUGH THIS EXTENT [EXPANSE]-- . . .	I HAVE NO LIFE BUT THIS	1398	7
'TWAS CHRIST'S OWN PERSONAL EXPANSE	OBTAINING BUT OUR OWN	1543	3
EXPANSE CANNOT BE LOST--	EXPANSE CANNOT BE LOST--	1584	1
EXPECTANT			
DIM--LONG EXPECTANT EYES, ...	MY NOSEGAYS ARE FOR	95	2
EXPECTATION			
A SUDDEN EXPECTATION, ...	I NEVER HEAR THE WORD	77	3
EACH--WITH A ROBIN'S EXPECTATION--	I SHALL KEEP SINGING!	250	4
BUT GRAVITY--AND EXPECTATION--AND FEAR-- .	UNIT, LIKE DEATH, FOR	408	15
OF EXPECTATION--ALSO--	THOSE FAIR--FICTITIOUS	499	17
A PRESENCE--FOR AN EXPECTATION--	RENUNCIATION--IS A	745	3
THEIR EXPECTATION--FAIR [SURE]--	THROUGH THE STRAIT PASS	792	10
EXPECTATION--IS CONTENTMENT--	EXPECTATION--IS	807	1
WHO AIRS OF EXPECTATION BREATHES	'TIS MY FIRST NIGHT	1122	5
MARCH IS THE MONTH OF EXPECTATION.	MARCH IS THE MONTH OF	1404	1
EXPECTED			
WHO MAY EXPECTED BE?	A LADY RED--AMID THE	74	8
A FLOWER EXPECTED EVERYWHERE--	AN ALTERED LOOK ABOUT	140	10
EXPECTING			
THAT THEY HAVE DONE EXPECTING ME--	THO' I GET HOME HOW LATE	207	4
BEE! I'M EXPECTING YOU!	BEE! I'M EXPECTING YOU!	1035	1
EXPEDITION			
THIRD, EXPEDITION FOR	FINDING IS THE FIRST ACT	870	3
EXPEND			
EXPEND THEIR FURTHEST [INMOST] POUND-- . . .	I FEAR A MAN OF FRUGAL	543	6
THEIR VOICES [NUMBERS] DID EXPEND	THE BIRDS BEGUN AT FOUR	783	6
EXPENDED			
OR AN EXPENDED DAY	THE SUN IS GAY OR STARK	878	5
. . . RECEIPTED / EXPENDED] BUD	CRISIS IS SWEET AND YET	1416	8
EXPENDS			
HIS YARN [COIL] OF PEARL--UNWINDS [EXPENDS]--	THE SPIDER HOLDS A	605	4
EXPENDS ITSELF ON THIS.	I CANNOT WANT IT MORE--	1301	4
EXPENSE			
BUT RAPTURE'S EXPENSE	RATHER ARID DELIGHT	1679	5
EXPENSIVE			
LOOK TOO EXPENSIVE!	I KNOW THAT HE EXISTS.	338	14
FORTUNE'S EXPENSIVE SMILE	LUCK IS NOT CHANCE--	1350	3
EXPERIENCE			
SHOULD I AGAIN EXPERIENCE--	I THINK I WAS ENCHANTED	593	27

	FIRST LINE	POEM	LINE
EXPRESSION			
DRAMA'S VITALLEST EXPRESSION IS THE COMMON DAY	DRAMA'S VITALLEST	741	1
EXQUISITE			
SO PLAUSIBLE [EXQUISITE]--THEY SEEM--	LIKE SOME OLD FASHIONED	302	12
AN EXQUISITE REPLY!	WITHIN MY GARDEN, RIDES	500	20
TOO EXQUISITE--TO TELL--	THE TINT I CANNOT TAKE--	627	12
. . . ARE TENDEREST--/ WERE EXQUISITE] EXTENTS	CONTAINED IN THIS SHORT	1165	2
EXTACIES SEE ECSTASIES			
SUCH THRENODIES [EXTACIES / REVENUES / ARGUMENTS] OF PEARL--	YOU'LL KNOW HER--BY HER	634	26
EXTANT			
THAT ONE SO HONEST--BE EXTANT--	I MEANT TO HAVE BUT	476	21
THE SCANTEST HEART EXTANT	TILL DEATH--IS NARROW	907	2
THE MAGIC PASSIVE BUT EXTANT	SOMEWHERE UPON THE	1231	3
EXTASY SEE ECSTASY			
AN EXTASY OF PARTING	A THROE UPON THE	71	3
TRANSCENDING EXTASY.	A SOMETHING IN A	122	6
TO THE EXTASY.	FOR EACH EXTATIC INSTANT	125	4
IN THE NEW ROBIN'S EXTASY	BRING ME THE SUNSET IN A	128	8
YOUR SECRET, PERCHED IN EXTASY	COCOON ABOVE! COCOON	129	5
CAN THE EXTASY DEFINE--	FLOWERS--WELL--IF	137	2
'TIS BUT THE EXTASY OF DEATH--	A WOUNDED DEER--LEAPS	165	3
UNTO IT'S EXTASY!	A TRANSPORT ONE CANNOT	184	4
BETTER WILL BE THE EXTASY	THO' I GET HOME HOW LATE	207	3
IN EXTASY--AND DELL--	THROUGH THE DARK SOD--AS	392	8
A FINER SHAME OF EXTASY--	THERE IS A SHAME OF	551	3
FOR EXTASY--OF IT	OF BEING IS A BIRD	653	12
BUT INDEPENDANT EXTASY	THE BIRDS BEGUN AT FOUR	783	15
OR DAMS--OF EXTASY--	THE PUNGENT ATOM IN THE	1191	8
EXTATIC			
FOR EACH EXTATIC INSTANT	FOR EACH EXTATIC INSTANT	125	1
EXTATIC CONTRACT!	WHAT WOULD I GIVE TO SEE	247	27
BUT FOR EXTATIC NEED	BETWEEN THE FORM OF LIFE	1101	6
WITH THE EXTATIC LIMIT	TO DISAPPEAR ENHANCES--	1209	19
EXTEMPORANEOUS			
EXTEMPORANEOUS STALLS	THOSE CATTLE SMALLER	1388	6
EXTEMPORIZING			
EXTEMPORIZING IN YOUR EAR	DID YOU EVER STAND IN A	590	13
EXTEND			
HER PRACTICES [QUALITIES] EXTEND	NATURE AFFECTS TO BE	1170	4
EXTENDED			
EXTENDED HEMPEN HANDS--	I STARTED EARLY--TOOK MY	520	6
EXTENDED INSCRUTABLY--	BY MY WINDOW HAVE I FOR	797	V 25
EXTENT			
TO DWELL EXTENT AMONG,	THE DUTIES OF THE WIND	1137	6
THE SMALLEST HUMAN HEART'S EXTENT	THE LIFE WE HAVE IS VERY	1162	7
IT'S ABSOLUTE EXTENT	TWO LENGTHS HAS EVERY	1295	2
EXCEPT THROUGH THIS EXTENT [EXPANSE]--	I HAVE NO LIFE BUT THIS	1398	7
OBTAINING BUT OUR [HIS] OWN EXTENT	OBTAINING BUT OUR OWN	1543	1
EXTENTS			
. . . ARE TENDEREST--/ WERE EXQUISITE] EXTENTS	CONTAINED IN THIS SHORT	1165	2
EXTERIOR			
EXTERIOR--TO TIME--	THIS WAS A POET--IT IS	448	16
EXTERMINATE			
BECAUSE THE FOOD--EXTERMINATE--	HAD I NOT THIS, OR THIS,	904	11
EXTERNAL			
WITHOUT EXTERNAL SOUND	THERE CAME A DAY AT	322	22
EXTERNAL GHOST	ONE NEED NOT BE A	670	6
EXTERNALLY			
WHAT HARM? MEN DIE--EXTERNALLY--	WE DREAM--IT IS GOOD WE	531	5
EXTINCT			
IT'S MEANING [IMPORT] IS EXTINCT--	HOW HUMAN NATURE DOTES	1417	4
PROSPECTIVE IS EXTINCT.	HOW HUMAN NATURE DOTES	1417	V 4
THE BOYS THAT WHISTLED ARE EXTINCT--	A FADED BOY--IN SALLOW	1524	5
EXTINCT BE EVERY HUM	HOW DARE THE ROBINS SING	1724	13
EXTINCTION			
OR SUN'S EXTINCTION, BE OBSERVED	THE MISSING ALL,	985	5
EXTINCTION'S			
SIMPLY EXTINCTION'S DATE--	EMPTY MY HEART, OF THEE	587	4
EXTINGUISH			
AND MIGHT EXTINGUISH ME!	'TIS SO MUCH JOY! 'TIS	172	18
OTHERS--EXTINGUISH EASIER--	MORE LIFE--WENT OUT--	422	13
UNTO US--THE SUNS EXTINGUISH--	UNFULFILLED TO	972	5
EXTINGUISHED			
EXTINGUISHED--NOW--FOR YOU!	GOOD NIGHT! WHICH PUT	259	6
EXTINGUISHED--IN THE SEA--	FROM COCOON FORTH A	354	25
EXTOL			
BLISS OF DEATH--LIFE'S BLISS EXTOL THRO [SURPASS IN / EXCEL IN]	PROMISE THIS--WHEN YOU	648	15
EXTOL THEE--COULD I--THEN I WILL	EXTOL THEE--COULD I--	1643	1
EXTORTED			
EXTORTED FROM THE SEA--	THE FEET OF PEOPLE	7	10
EXTRAVAGANCE			
EXTRAVAGANCE	MUST BE A WO--	571	14
EXTRAVAGANT			
THE EAST--WOULD DEEM EXTRAVAGANT--	I RECKON--WHEN I COUNT	569	11
TOO EXORBITANT [EXTRAVAGANT / IMPORTUNATE] .	SO MUCH SUMMER	651	5
IMPREGNABLE AS [AS OPULENT IT / EXTRAVAGANT AS / ABUNDANT AS . . .	YOU CANNOT TAKE ITSELF	1351	5

	FIRST LINE	POEM	LINE
EXTREMELY			
WERE HE TO TELL--EXTREMELY SORRY	FUNNY--TO BE A CENTURY--	345	6
EXTREMER			
IN AN EXTREMER ANGUISH	A DOUBT IF IT BE US	859	3
EXTREMEST			
IN IT'S EXTREMEST CLAUSE--	I READ MY SENTENCE--	412	4
EXTREMITY			
THINE [THY] EXTREMITY	LOW AT MY PROBLEM	69	V 8
YET, NEVER, IN EXTREMITY,	"HOPE" IS THE THING WITH	254	11
RENOWNED TO EASE [STIR] EXTREMITY--	I GOT SO I COULD HEAR	293	15
I MADE MY SOUL FAMILIAR--WITH HER EXTREMITY--	I READ MY SENTENCE--	412	9
IN TUMULT--OR EXTREMITY--	ON A COLUMNAR SELF--	789	3
TO THE [A / OUR] TEMERITY [EXTREMITY / ADVERSITY]--	SUMMER--WE ALL HAVE SEEN	1386	8
EXTRINSIC			
EXTRINSIC TO ATTENTION	THE WAY TO KNOW THE	1279	13
EXUBERANCE			
BUT AFRICAN EXUBERANCE	NO AUTUMN'S INTERCEPTING	1516	3
EXUDE			
BEFORE THOU DOST EXUDE [DISSOLVE] AWAY	STILL OWN THEE--STILL	1633	7
EXULT			
WHO WOULD EXULT TO DIE	SOME WRETCHED CREATURE,	1111	2
EXULTANT			
AND SHOT--EXULTANT ON!	ADRIFT! A LITTLE BOAT	30	13
EXULTATION			
EXULTATION IS THE GOING	EXULTATION IS THE GOING	76	1
BY THAT BLEAK EXULTATION	THROUGH WHAT TRANSPORTS	1153	5
WHAT EXULTATION IN THE WOE--	"RED SEA," INDEED! TALK	1642	11
EYE SEE E'E			
THE WAVE WITH EYE SO PENSIVE, LOOKETH TO SEE THE MOON,	AWAKE YE MUSES NINE,	1	18
THE SHUTTING OF THE EYE.	SLEEP IS SUPPOSED TO BE	13	3
STILL IN HER EYE	ONE SISTER HAVE I IN OUR	14	20
UNTO MY FRUGAL EYE--	I HAD A GUINEA GOLDEN--	23	6
SHALL MEET THE EYE OF TRAITOR	I HAD A GUINEA GOLDEN--	23	31
THIS IS THE ERRAND OF THE EYE	WHETHER MY BARK WENT	52	7
SO TO THE EYE PROSPECTIVE LED,	A SCIENCE--SO THE SAVANS	100	7
WHEREFORE MINE EYE THY SILVER MISTS,	THE BEE IS NOT AFRAID OF	111	7
HOW PROUD TO SHUT THE EYE!	IF THIS IS "FADING"	120	7
UNSCRUTINIZED BY EYE--	JUST LOST, WHEN I WAS	160	15
YET--TO MY FRUGAL EYE,	I LOST A WORLD--THE	181	6
WE JUST SHUT OUR BROWN EYE	WE DONT CRY--TIM AND I,	196	11
MY EYE IS FULLER THAN MY VASE--	MY EYE IS FULLER THAN MY	202	1
AND STILL--MY HEART--MY EYE OUTWEIGHS--	MY EYE IS FULLER THAN MY	202	3
FOREVER FROM THE EYE--	HOW NOTELESS MEN, AND	282	4
AN ORLEANS IN THE EYE	A MIEN TO MOVE A QUEEN--	283	3
A GIANT--EYE TO EYE WITH YOU, HAD BEEN--	ONE YEAR AGO--JOTS WHAT?	296	23
A GIANT--EYE TO EYE WITH YOU, HAD BEEN--	ONE YEAR AGO--JOTS WHAT?	296	23
CONTENTED AS THE EYE	THE DIFFERENCE BETWEEN	305	6
TO A REVERING--EYE	THE SOUL'S SUPERIOR	306	V 14
BEFORE I GOT MY EYE PUT OUT	BEFORE I GOT MY EYE PUT	327	1
THE EYE HAD HURRIED BY	DEATH SETS A THING	360	2
ACCOSTS MY OPEN EYE--	THE ANGLE OF A LANDSCAPE	375	6
NO EYE COULD FIND THE PLACE--	THEY DROPPED LIKE FLAKES	409	7
CONSULT YOUR EYE!	YOU'LL KNOW IT--AS YOU	420	15
OBEDIENT TO HER EYE	THE MOON IS DISTANT FROM	429	6
THINE EYE IMPOSE ON ME--	THE MOON IS DISTANT FROM	429	12
I FELT IT PUBLISH--IN MY EYE--	IT WOULD NEVER BE COMMON	430	11
TO A DISCERNING EYE--	MUCH MADNESS IS DIVINEST	435	2
ONE EYE UPON THE HEAVEN RENOUNCED--	TRIUMPH--MAY BE OF	455	11
THE FILM UPON THE EYE	SHE DEALT HER PRETTY	479	10
THE LIGHTNING--NEVER ASKED AN EYE	"WHY DO I LOVE" YOU, SIR	480	11
COOL OF EYE, AND CRITICAL OF WORK--	A SOLEMN THING WITHIN	483	10
TO SUFFOCATE THE EYE--	IT'S THOUGHTS--AND JUST	495	18
REFERS MY CLUMSY [DULLER] EYE--	WITHIN MY GARDEN, RIDES	500	18
EXISTENCE'S WHOLE ARC, [WHOLE EYE / WHOLE RIM / SURMISE] FILLED UP,	I'M CEDED--I'VE STOPPED	508	12
SET CYPHERLESS--TO TEACH THE EYE	'TIS ONE BY ONE--THE	545	3
I'VE SEEN A DYING EYE	I'VE SEEN A DYING EYE	547	1
CONFER UPON THE EYE--	AN IGNORANCE A SUNSET	552	2
TO BEND THE EYE	MUST BE A WO--	571	3
EACH TIME MY CHILDISH EYE	I PRAYED, AT FIRST, A	576	6
THEIR FAR PARADES--ORDER [HALT] ON THE EYE	INCONCEIVABLY SOLEMN!	582	5
BUT NO TRUE EYE	INCONCEIVABLY SOLEMN!	582	9
BETWEEN WHOSE YELLOW EYE--	DID YOU EVER STAND IN A	590	10
DIRECTLY IN HIS EYE--	TO INTERRUPT HIS YELLOW	591	6
GOES SAFELY [STEADY]--WHERE AN OPEN EYE--	THERE IS A PAIN--SO	599	7
AND A SILENCE--THE TELLER'S EYE--	GLEE--THE GREAT STORM IS	619	15
THAT SWAGGERS ON THE EYE	THE TINT I CANNOT TAKE--	627	6
UNTIL THE CHEATED EYE	THE TINT I CANNOT TAKE--	627	22
ON MY HOMESICK EYE--	I CANNOT LIVE WITH YOU--	640	26
ENABLED OF THE EYE--	A LITTLE ROAD--NOT MADE	647	2
MINE--TO BELT YOUR EYE--	PROMISE THIS--WHEN YOU	648	4
IMPREGNABLE OF EYE--	I DWELL IN POSSIBILITY--	657	6
I MIGHT SURPRISE [NOT PLEASE] HIS EYE!	AGAIN--HIS VOICE IS AT	663	8
THIGH [EYE] OF GRANITE--AND THEW [EAR]--OF STEEL--	AH, TENERIFFE!	666	7
AMPLE AS THE EYE--	'TWOULD EASE--A	682	13
THEIR RIBBONS JUST BEYOND THE EYE--	YOU'VE SEEN BALLOONS SET	700	9
HER EYE UNTO THE SUMMER DEW	THE MOON WAS BUT A CHIN	737	7

	FIRST LINE	POEM	LINE
EYE (CONTINUED)			
THE HEART--TO STIMULATE THE EYE	THE BIRDS REPORTED FROM	743	11
ON WHOM I LAY A YELLOW EYE--	MY LIFE HAD STOOD--A	754	19
AND PUT OUT HER EYE--	WHEN I HOPED, I	768	22
LEST IF HE FLINCH--THE EYE THAT WAY	GRIEF IS A MOUSE--	793	10
FIGHT STERNLY IN A DYING EYE	DYING! TO BE AFRAID OF	831	10
BUT JUST TO LOOK IT IN THE EYE--	I CANNOT BUY IT--'TIS	840	10
HIS EYE, IT IS THE EAST AND WEST--	THE SUN AND MOON MUST	871	5
OH HINDERED EYE	THE SUN AND MOON MUST	871	10
AND A TORRID EYE.	AS THE STARVED MAELSTROM	872	16
NO EYE HATH SEEN AND LIVED	FROM US SHE WANDERED NOW	890	5
TOO SLENDER FOR THE EYE	FAITH--IS THE PIERLESS	915	4
THROUGH FAITH--MY HAZEL EYE	WHAT I SEE NOT, I BETTER	939	2
TO THE FAILING [DYING / CLOUDING] EYE	ROBBED BY DEATH--BUT	971	2
INCOMPLETE--TO EYE--	UNFULFILLED TO	972	2
THE EYE REJECTS THE OIL.	IDEALS ARE THE FAIRY OIL	983	4
THE ABSENCE [JOURNEY] OF AN EYE--	WE MISS HER, NOT BECAUSE	993	2
AND COULD NOT FIND IT'S EYE.	WHO SAW NO SUNRISE	1018	8
I SAW, AS IF MY EYE WERE ON	I HEARD, AS IF I HAD NO	1039	5
AS WILLING LID O'ER WEARY EYE	AS WILLING LID O'ER	1050	1
HIS BILL IS CLASPED [LOCKED]--HIS EYE FORSOOK [ESTRANGED]--	HIS BILL IS CLASPED--HIS	1102	1
TO A MAGICIAN'S EYE--	BEST WITCHCRAFT IS	1158	V 2
"EYE HATH NOT SEEN" MAY POSSIBLY	THE LILAC IS AN ANCIENT	1241	17
MAY STIMULATE [CONSECRATE] AN EYE	A WORD DROPPED CARELESS	1261	2
GO TIMID, LEST [SHOULD] HIS FINAL [TESTING / BLAZING / LOFTY] EYE	GO SLOW, MY SOUL, TO	1297	5
THAT HERD UPON THE EYE--	THOSE CATTLE SMALLER	1388	2
THAT WOULD [WILL] NOT LET THE EYE DECIDE	THESE HELD THEIR WICK	1390	7
MY SLOW--TERRESTRIAL EYE	HOW SOFT A CATERPILLAR	1448	6
I KNOW HIS EYE	ALL THAT I DO	1496	4
ALLURES [ENSNARES] HIS JADED EYE	HIS ORIENTAL HERESIES	1526	6
TILL YOU WASTE [FURL / LAME] YOUR EYE--	FOLLOW WISE ORION	1538	2
THE EYE INQUIRES WITH A SIGH	"RED SEA," INDEED! TALK	1642	9
A LANE OF YELLOW LED THE EYE	A LANE OF YELLOW LED THE	1650	1
THE EYE BEGINS IT'S AVARICE	SUMMER BEGINS TO HAVE	1682	9
AS THE EYE BEHOLDS	"LETHE" IN MY FLOWER,	1730	6
EYELIDS			
TO EYELIDS IN THE SEPULCHRE--	AS FAR FROM PITY, AS	496	9
EYES			
THINE EYES ARE SADLY BLINDED, BUT YET THOU MAYEST SEE	AWAKE YE MUSES NINE,	1	33
TO EYES THAT CLOSING GO--	DISTRUSTFUL OF THE	20	14
ON OUR DEVELOPED EYES	IF PAIN FOR PEACE	63	11
FROM SAGACIOUS EYES.	SO FROM THE MOULD	66	5
TO OUR PENURIOUS EYES!	AS BY THE DEAD WE LOVE	88	8
DIM--LONG EXPECTANT EYES,	MY NOSEGAYS ARE FOR	95	2
WHOSE DYING EYES, NO COUNTRY	TO FIGHT ALOUD, IS VERY	126	7
THE EYES OF MANY ELVES--	BESIDES THE AUTUMN POETS	131	12
I TURN MY BRIMMING EYES AWAY,	I BRING AN UNACCUSTOMED	132	6
TILL PLEADING, ROUND HER QUIET EYES	SHE BORE IT TILL THE	144	3
WITH BECLOUDED EYES!	IF THE FOOLISH, CALL	168	8
ALAS, HOW HEEDLESS WERE THE EYES--	ON THIS LONG STORM THE	194	7
THE MONSTER'S FADED EYES	AN AWFUL TEMPEST MASHED	198	11
WITH EYES IN DEATH--STILL BEGGING RAISED--	TWO SWIMMERS WRESTLED ON	201	8
IF I SHOULD DISAPPOINT THE EYES	I SHOULD NOT DARE TO	205	5
JUST HOW LONG-CHEATED EYES WILL TURN--	THO' I GET HOME HOW LATE	207	10
TO OUR FAMILIAR EYES--	I'VE NOTHING ELSE--TO	224	4
THE [AN] ELEPHANT'S--CALM EYES	A BURDOCK--CLAWED MY	229	12
TILL HAIR--AND EYES--AND TIMID HEAD--	I THINK JUST HOW MY	237	3
THE EYES GLAZE ONCE--AND THAT IS DEATH--	I LIKE A LOOK OF AGONY,	241	5
THE BRAVE EYES FILM--	YOU SEE I CANNOT SEE--	253	5
MY EYES JUST TURNED TO SEE,	A SINGLE SCREW OF FLESH	263	10
BEFORE THE FIRE'S EYES--	DOUBT ME! MY DIM	275	21
OLD FASHIONED EYES--	I KNOW SOME LONELY	289	11
FAINT-GOING LIVES [EYES]--THEIR LAPSE FROM SIGHING--	"MORNING"--MEANS	300	9
AS OTHER CREATURES, THAT HAVE EYES	BEFORE I GOT MY EYE PUT	327	3
BETWEEN MY FINITE EYES--	BEFORE I GOT MY EYE PUT	327	13
WHERE OTHER CREATURES PUT THEIR EYES--	BEFORE I GOT MY EYE PUT	327	20
HE GLANCED WITH RAPID EYES	A BIRD CAME DOWN THE	328	9
FROM OUR GROSS EYES.	I KNOW THAT HE EXISTS.	338	4
FRESH GILDED--TO ELUDE THE EYES	A HAPPY LIP--BREAKS	353	7
HER DANCING EYES--AJAR--	SHE LAY AS IF AT PLAY	369	9
THE LOOKING IN HIS EYES--	I HAD NOT MINDED--WALLS	398	8
IT BEAR TO OTHER EYES--	HOW MANY FLOWERS FAIL IN	404	8
UNTIL IT BLOCKED MY EYES--	THE FIRST DAY'S NIGHT	410	12
REVIEWED IT WITH MY EYES,	I READ MY SENTENCE--	412	2
AND WHEN THE FILM HAD STITCHED YOUR EYES	'TWAS LIKE A MAELSTROM,	414	22
TOO TELESCOPIC EYES	I TIE MY HAT--I CREASE	443	22
EYES WERE NOT MEANT TO KNOW.	THE OUTER--FROM THE	451	16
LIKE EYES THAT LOOKED ON WASTES--	LIKE EYES THAT LOOKED ON	458	1
THE EYES AROUND--HAD WRUNG THEM DRY--	I HEARD A FLY BUZZ--WHEN	465	5
THEY TOOK AWAY OUR EYES--	THEY PUT US FAR APART--	474	5
WHEN EYES THAT FONDLED IT ARE WRENCHED	TO MAKE ONE'S TOILETTE--	485	7
AND THEN YOU WISHED YOU HAD EYES IN YOUR PAGES--	GOING TO HIM! HAPPY	494	8
FLOWERS--TO KEEP THE EYES--FROM GOING AWKWARD--	IT'S THOUGHTS--AND JUST	495	12
THE VERY BROW--THE STOOPING EYES--	YOU KNOW THAT PORTRAIT	504	3

	FIRST LINE	POEM	LINE
EYES (CONTINUED)			
HER EYES INCREASE TO BALLS--	SHE SIGHTS A BIRD--SHE	507	4
THE BUSY EYES--CONGEALED--	'TWAS WARM--AT FIRST--	519	8
AND EITHER--OPEN THE [IT'S] EYES--	WE DREAM--IT IS GOOD WE	531	10
SWEPT BY MY SEARCHING EYES--THE LAST--	ME PROVE IT NOW--WHOEVER	537	15
THE CLOSING OF HER EYES--	SHE HIDETH HER THE LAST	557	4
WITH NARROW, PROBING, [ANALYTIC] EYES--	I MEASURE EVERY GRIEF I	561	2
AND ONLY NAILS THE EYES--	I MEASURE EVERY GRIEF I	561	28
THERE'S BANISHMENT FROM NATIVE EYES--	I MEASURE EVERY GRIEF I	561	31
BUT IN EACH OTHER'S EYES	WE LEARNED THE WHOLE OF	568	5
FROM OUR UNFITTED [UNFURNISHED] EYES.	MY FIRST WELL DAY--SINCE	574	24
NOT YET, OUR EYES CAN SEE--	"HEAVEN" HAS DIFFERENT	575	20
TO KNOW IF ANY HUMAN EYES WERE NEAR	TO KNOW JUST HOW HE	622	2
OF ONE ANOTHER'S EYES--	'TWAS A LONG PARTING--	625	8
WAS SCARCE UPON MY EYES	I WATCHED THE MOON	629	30
ON FRESH EYES--	THE CHILD'S FAITH IS NEW	637	4
AND CHIPS OF BLANK--IN BOYISH EYES--	MY PORTION IS DEFEAT--	639	10
AND I HAD NO MORE EYES	I CANNOT LIVE WITH YOU--	640	34
YOUR LOW [MEEK] EYES--DEMAND--	PROMISE THIS--WHEN YOU	648	8
AND IN IT'S NARROW EYES--	A PRISON GETS TO BE A	652	4
BUT OUR UNFURNISHED EYES--	NOT "REVELATION"--'TIS--	685	2
CONFRONTING EYES LONG--COMFORTED--	I'LL SEND THE FEATHER	687	5
IT PLEASED MY NARROW EYES--	THEIR HIGHT IN HEAVEN	696	12
THOSE SAME UNVARYING EYES	SWEET MOUNTAINS--YE TELL	722	3
THE PUTTING OUT OF EYES--	RENUNCIATION--IS A	745	5
SO THE EYES ACCOST--AND SUNDER	SO THE EYES ACCOST--AND	752	1
AS TONGUES [THRONGS / EYES] OF DIAMOND HAD REVILED	MY SOUL--ACCUSED ME--AND	753	2
SO LARGER TO MY EYES	ONE BLESSING HAD I THAN	756	2
I SHUT MY EYES--AND GROPED AS WELL	FROM BLANK TO BLANK--	761	9
WITH THESE OLD FASHIONED EYES--	JOY TO HAVE MERITED THE	788	6
THAT OUR IGNOBLE EYES	TWO--WERE IMMORTAL TWICE	800	5
BEHIND THE EYES OF GOD.	OF CONSCIOUSNESS, HER	894	4
IN THE OTHER'S EYES.	STRUCK, WAS I, NOR YET	925	24
THE HOLLOWS ROUND HIS EAGER EYES	THE HOLLOWS ROUND HIS	955	1
WE KNOW THAT THEIR SUPERIOR EYES	WE MISS HER, NOT BECAUSE	993	7
BUT ANSWER OF THE EYES--	IT WAS A QUIET WAY--	1053	4
HAD WE THE EYES WITHIN OUR HEAD [HEADS]--	HAD WE OUR SENSES	1284	5
TO THE LOWER EYES--	LIFT IT--WITH THE	1348	6
TO KEEP IT FROM INFESTING EYES--	SHAME IS THE SHAWL OF	1412	3
HER UNINTENDING EYES--	THE PRETTY RAIN FROM	1426	2
LOOK BACK ON TIME, WITH KINDLY EYES--	LOOK BACK ON TIME, WITH	1478	1
"BODY!" THEN REAL--A FACE AND EYES--	"AND WITH WHAT BODY DO	1492	5
BOTH EYES HIS WAY	IN WINTER IN MY ROOM	1670	33
FABLE			
STILL [HOW / SO] FABLE--IN THE ISLES OF SPICE--	I GAVE MYSELF TO HIM--	580	11
FABLES			
OUTVISIONS [OUT FABLES] PARADISE!	IF I MAY HAVE IT, WHEN	577	29
FABRICS			
FABRICS OF CASHMERE--	I AM ASHAMED--I HIDE--	473	9
ARE FABRICS TRULY TORN--	THE HEALED HEART SHOWS	1440	4
HIS MIND LIKE FABRICS OF THE EAST	HIS MIND LIKE FABRICS OF	1446	1
OF MINOR FABRICS [SYSTEMS] BEGS	A WORLD MADE PENNINILESS	1623	2
FABULOUS			
TO OTHERS, FABULOUS--	REPORTLESS SUBJECTS, TO	1048	8
FABULOUS AS A MOON AT NOON	WHITE AS AN INDIAN PIPE	1250	3
FACE			
SHOULD HAVE THE FACE TO DIE.	I HAV'NT TOLD MY GARDEN	50	8
WHO KNOWS BUT THIS SURRENDERED FACE	DELAYED TILL SHE HAD	58	11
LOOKING FOR HER FACE.	GLOWING IS HER BONNET,	72	10
WHAT ROSY FACE	WHOSE CHEEK IS THIS?	82	2
THEN VAIL MY TOO INSPECTING FACE	A SOMETHING IN A	122	10
THAN AN EARL'S DISTINGUISHED FACE--	PIGMY SERAPHS--GONE	138	13
WHOSE BUT HER SHY--IMMORTAL FACE	SHE BORE IT TILL THE	144	15
AND SOMEBODY HAS LOST THE FACE	EXCEPT TO HEAVEN, SHE IS	154	11
WHERE WE--WITH LATE--CELESTIAL FACE--	MUSICIANS WRESTLE	157	17
IN THE HUMAN FACE	I HAVE NEVER SEEN	175	10
THAT, WEARY OF THIS BEGGAR'S FACE--	IF I COULD BRIBE THEM BY	179	17
THEN WE HIDE OUR BRAVE FACE	WE DONT CRY--TIM AND I,	196	5
SPIED A FACE--	TWO SWIMMERS WRESTLED ON	201	6
LEST MY BESEECHING FACE--AT LAST--	COULD I--THEN--SHUT THE	220	2
THE SMALLEST ONE UPON YOUR FACE [CHEEK]	I CAME TO BUY A SMILE--	223	3
JESUS! THY SECOND FACE	JESUS! THY CRUCIFIX	225	4
LAYING HER [IT'S] SPOTTED FACE TO DIE	BLAZING IN GOLD AND	228	4
WHAT WOULD I GIVE TO SEE HIS FACE?	WHAT WOULD I GIVE TO SEE	247	1
ONE HOUR--OF HER SOVREIGN'S FACE"!	WHAT WOULD I GIVE TO SEE	247	26
TOO VAGUE--THE FACE--	YOU SEE I CANNOT SEE--	253	8
THAT IN MY AWKWARD--GAZING--FACE--	IF I'M LOST--NOW--	256	6
YOU'LL KNOW--SIR--WHEN THE SAVIOR'S FACE	IF I'M LOST--NOW--	256	12
IS LIKE A FACE OF STEEL--	THAT AFTER HORROR--THAT	286	12
WHO ONLY SHOWS HIS MARBLE DISC [GRANITE FACE]--	GIVE LITTLE ANGUISH--	310	7
IT MAKES AN EVEN FACE	IT SIFTS FROM LEADEN	311	5
THE FACE I CARRY WITH ME--LAST--	THE FACE I CARRY WITH ME	336	1
THAT FACE--WILL JUST BE THINE--	THE FACE I CARRY WITH ME	336	4
THE LOST--DAY'S FACE--	'TIS OPPOSITES--ENTICE--	355	4
FOR THE CONTENTED--BEGGAR'S FACE	I GAINED IT SO--	359	14
HER FACE BE ROUNDER THAN THE MOON	THERE IS A FLOWER THAT	380	9
THEN MY FACE TAKE HER RECOMPENSE--	I HAD NOT MINDED--WALLS	398	7

FACE (CONTINUED)

	FIRST LINE	POEM	LINE
UNTO THE LADY'S FACE--	I HAD NOT MINDED--WALLS	398	14
BUT GOD CAN SUMMON EVERY FACE	THEY DROPPED LIKE FLAKES	409	8
UNROLLED IT'S HORROR IN MY FACE--	THE FIRST DAY'S NIGHT	410	11
BUT DO ONE FACE US SUDDENLY--	SUNSET AT NIGHT--IS	415	7
NOT IN THIS WORLD TO SEE HIS FACE--	NOT IN THIS WORLD TO SEE	418	1
A CHARM INVESTS A FACE	A CHARM INVESTS A FACE	421	1
TURN IT, A LITTLE--FULL IN THE FACE	IT DONT SOUND SO	426	5
ME--COME! MY DAZZLED FACE	ME--COME! MY DAZZLED	431	1
THE LARGER, AS HER [MY] FACE WITHDREW--	I SHOWED HER HIGHTS SHE	446	11
SO LOOKED THE FACE I LOOKED UPON--	LIKE EYES THAT LOOKED ON	458	7
SAVIOR [MASTER]--I'VE SEEN THE FACE--BEFORE!	A WIFE--AT DAYBREAK I	461	13
I LIVE WITH HIM--I SEE HIS FACE--	I LIVE WITH HIM--I SEE	463	1
UNTIL UPON MY FACE	THE POWER TO BE TRUE TO	464	2
NOWHERE TO HIDE MY DAZZLED FACE--	I AM ASHAMED--I HIDE--	473	4
EACH OTHER'S FACE--WAS ALL THE DISC	THEY PUT US FAR APART--	474	23
A SMILE SUFFUSED JEHOVAH'S FACE--	I MEANT TO HAVE BUT	476	13
WE COVER THEE--SWEET FACE--	WE COVER THEE--SWEET	482	1
MY GIPSY FACE--TRANSFIGURED NOW--	HE TOUCHED ME, SO I LIVE	506	11
THE NAME THEY DROPPED UPON MY FACE	I'M CEDED--I'VE STOPPED	508	2
OF OUR INFERIOR FACE--	AN IGNORANCE A SUNSET	552	8
BUT LITTLE CARMINE HATH HER FACE--	BUT LITTLE CARMINE HATH	558	1
YOU'VE SEEN IT ON A CAST'S FACE [CHEEK]--	IT KNEW NO MEDICINE--	559	11
INFINITUDE--HAD'ST THOU NO FACE	MY PERIOD HAD COME FOR	564	15
MORNING'S BOLD FACE--STARES IN THE WINDOW--	I COULD DIE--TO KNOW--	570	5
PERMITTED--FACE TO FACE TO BE--	IF I MAY HAVE IT, WHEN	577	10
PERMITTED--FACE TO FACE TO BE--	IF I MAY HAVE IT, WHEN	577	10
DID YOU EVER LOOK IN A CANNON'S FACE--	DID YOU EVER STAND IN A	590	9
'TIS LATE YOUR SUNRISE VEX THEIR FACE--	WHAT CARE THE DEAD, FOR	592	3
HIS FACE ALL VICTORY	WHEN I WAS SMALL, A	596	4
THEN MADE BLUE FACES IN MY FACE--	THREE TIMES--WE PARTED--	598	7
I DARED NOT ENTER [OPEN], LEST A FACE	I YEARS HAD BEEN FROM	609	3
AND DID THE SUNSHINE FACE HIS WAY--	TO KNOW JUST HOW HE	622	8
HOW HOSPITABLE--THEN--THE FACE	IT WAS TOO LATE FOR MAN	623	7
BECAUSE YOUR FACE	I CANNOT LIVE WITH YOU--	640	22
'TWAS FACE TO FACE WITH NATURE--FORCED--	I COULD SUFFICE FOR HIM,	643	7
'TWAS FACE TO FACE WITH NATURE--FORCED--	I COULD SUFFICE FOR HIM,	643	7
'TWAS FACE TO FACE WITH GOD--	I COULD SUFFICE FOR HIM,	643	8
'TWAS FACE TO FACE WITH GOD--	I COULD SUFFICE FOR HIM,	643	8
ROUND SOME OTHER FACE--	PROMISE THIS--WHEN YOU	648	24
THAT OBSCURE [DIVIDE] HER FACE--	HER SWEET TURN TO LEAVE	649	26
BETWEEN IT'S PONDEROUS FACE	A PRISON GETS TO BE A	652	2
MY FACE TO JUSTIFY--	AGAIN--HIS VOICE IS AT	663	6
JUST HIS FACE--NOTHING MORE!	AGAIN--HIS VOICE IS AT	663	12
THAT FAINTS UPON THE FACE OF NOON--	THE LOVE A LIFE CAN SHOW	673	4
AND WANDERED IN MY FACE--	THE SUN KEPT SETTING--	692	8
FLAGS--VEX A DYING FACE--	THE WORLD--FEELS DUSTY	715	5
IN FACE OF THE SUSPENSE--	IF HE WERE LIVING--DARE	734	14
AND NOW SHE TURNS HER PERFECT FACE	THE MOON WAS BUT A CHIN	737	3
IT IS AS A VESUVIAN FACE	MY LIFE HAD STOOD--A	754	11
COULD I SUCH A PLEA [FACE] WITHSTAND--	MOST SHE TOUCHED ME BY	760	8
UPON HIS INFANT FACE WAS SET	HE TOLD A HOMELY TALE	763	3
DARKNESS INTERSECT HER FACE--	WHEN I HOPED, I	768	21
PARDON--TO LOOK UPON THY FACE--	JOY TO HAVE MERITED THE	788	5
IN WHICH HIS FACE IS SET--	ALL CIRCUMSTANCES ARE	820	2
AS CHILDREN, WHO REMAIN IN FACE	AWAY FROM HOME ARE SOME	821	7
THEN, TURN MY FACE AWAY.	I CANNOT BUY IT--'TIS	840	12
FOR HIS PLEIAD'S FACE--	WHEN THE ASTRONOMER	851	2
SINCE SOMEWHERE THY SWEET FACE HAS SPILLED	I'VE NONE TO TELL ME TO	881	5
AS SHOULD A FACE SUPPOSED THE GRAVE'S	THERE IS A JUNE WHEN	930	5
MY CONSTANT--REVERENTIAL FACE	MY BEST ACQUAINTANCES	932	7
EXCEPT FOR THE ITALIC FACE	THE HOLLOWS ROUND HIS	955	7
THE TURNING O'ER AND O'ER MY FACE	FITTER TO SEE HIM, I MAY	968	11
UNCONSCIOUS WAS--GREAT NATURE'S FACE	IT BLOOMED AND DROPT, A	978	19
THE MEETING BANDS OF SMITTEN FACE	'TIS ANGUISH GRANDER	984	3
OF THE CELESTIAL FACE	AURORA IS THE EFFORT	1002	2
A FLOWER'S UNOBTRUSIVE FACE	THE DYING NEED BUT	1026	3
LEST IN A FACE SO BEAUTIFUL	WHEN THEY COME BACK--IF	1080	11
A WISDOM, WITHOUT FACE, OR NAME,	THE CRICKETS SANG	1104	10
TILL WHAT WE COULD NOT SEE [FACE / CHOOSE / PROVE] HAS COME	THE MURMURING OF BEES,	1115	V 13
THAT IT WAS FEBUARY'S FOOT [FACE / SELF]	THE SNOW THAT NEVER	1133	7
LIKE WINTER AS A FACE	THE SNOW THAT NEVER	1133	9
THE FACE WE CHOOSE TO MISS--	THE FACE WE CHOOSE TO	1141	1
OH UNELECTED FACE--	OH SHADOW ON THE GRASS,	1187	8
THE FACE THAT MAKES THE MORNING MEAN	THE VOICE THAT STANDS	1189	3
TO LOOK HER IN THE FACE	THE PAST IS SUCH A	1203	2
ON HER FACE AND TONGUE.	NOW I KNEW I LOST HER--	1219	4
WHAT DIFFERENCE IS ON HER FACE	BECAUSE HE LOVES HER	1229	3
ON A BELOVED FACE	LIKE TIME'S INSIDIOUS	1236	2
HE FIRST ACHIEVE [ESPOUSE] THY FACE	MY HEART RAN SO TO THEE	1237	6
HIMSELF HAVE NOT A FACE.	SILENCE IS ALL WE DREAD.	1251	4
UNLESS IN MY REDEEMER'S FACE	BECAUSE THAT YOU ARE	1260	23
CURTAILED BY YOUR OBSCURING [REMOVING] FACE	BECAUSE THAT YOU ARE	1260	27
TO WHOSO WOULD COMMUTE THIS FACE	BECAUSE THAT YOU ARE	1260	31
HAD NATURE ANY SUPPLE [PLATED / OUTCAST] FACE	THE MUSHROOM IS THE ELF	1298	17
RECOLLECT THE FACE OF ME	RECOLLECT THE FACE OF ME	1305	1
FRIGID AND SWEET HER PARTING FACE--	FRIGID AND SWEET HER	1318	1
DELIBERATELY [LOOK SQUARELY IN THE] FACE--	I NEVER HEAR THAT ONE IS	1323	16
BETWEEN IT'S RUMOR AND IT'S FACE--	THE SYMPTOM OF THE GALE	1327	3

	FIRST LINE	POEM	LINE
FACE (CONTINUED)			
BY ONE DEFAULTING [HEROIC] FACE	THE VASTEST EARTHLY DAY	1328	3
BECOMES THAT CHERISHED [MAGIC] FACE	AN ANTIQUATED GRACE	1345	2
IN AN ABYSS'S FACE!	WHAT MYSTERY PERVADES A	1400	8
THAN A REMAINING FACE--	SUMMER HAS TWO	1422	8
WE SHUN BECAUSE WE PRIZE HER FACE	WE SHUN BECAUSE WE PRIZE	1429	1
THE FACE IN EVANESCENCE LAIN	THE FACE IN EVANESCENCE	1490	1
"BODY!" THEN REAL--A FACE AND EYES--	"AND WITH WHAT BODY DO	1492	5
TO WHOM NOT ANY FACE COHERE [PRESENT / PROPOUND]--	HOW FIRM ETERNITY MUST	1499	7
. . . MOUNTAIN] WITH YOUR FACE	THE PILE OF YEARS IS NOT	1507	7
A FLOWER TO HELP HIS STRAIGHTENED FACE	AS IMPERCEPTIBLY AS	1540	V
WITH PLAIN INSPECTING FACE--	WHO IS IT SEEKS MY	1598	2
WE COULD NOT FIND THE MIGHTY FACE	A CAP OF LEAD ACROSS THE	1649	3
THAT TOOK THY FACE BETWEEN	I SEE THEE CLEARER FOR	1666	2
I WATCHED HER FACE TO SEE WHICH WAY	I WATCHED HER FACE TO	1667	1
FROM HER LUSTRAL FACE	LIGHTLY STEPPED A YELLOW	1672	4
A FACE DEVOID OF LOVE OR GRACE,	A FACE DEVOID OF LOVE OR	1711	1
A HATEFUL, HARD, SUCCESSFUL FACE,	A FACE DEVOID OF LOVE OR	1711	2
A FACE WITH WHICH A STONE	A FACE DEVOID OF LOVE OR	1711	3
COMES UP TO FACE THE SKIES,	DROWNING IS NOT SO	1718	4
HER FACE WAS IN A BED OF HAIR,	HER FACE WAS IN A BED OF	1722	1
"YET SAW HIM FACE TO FACE"--	NO MAN SAW AWE, NOR TO	1733	14
"YET SAW HIM FACE TO FACE"--	NO MAN SAW AWE, NOR TO	1733	14
FACED			
WHO DANGER--AND THE DEAD--HAD FACED--	I YEARS HAD BEEN FROM	609	V 15
YOUR COTTAGE--FACED THE SUN--	OURSELVES WERE WED ONE	631	10
FACES			
MY CLASSICS VAIL THEIR FACES--	THE FEET OF PEOPLE	7	21
WITH OUR FACES VAILED--	I CANT TELL YOU--BUT YOU	65	10
NEVER MIND THE SOOTY FACES	BY A FLOWER--BY A LETTER	109	7
TOO MUCH PATHOS IN THEIR FACES	FLOWERS--WELL--IF	137	9
PORTRAITS [PICTURES] ARE TO DAILY FACES	PORTRAITS ARE TO DAILY	170	1
LIKE HER TRANSLATED FACES--	YOU SEE I CANNOT SEE--	253	13
LOOK--FEED UPON EACH OTHER'S FACES--SO--	ONE YEAR AGO--JOTS WHAT?	296	9
SO FACES ON TWO DECKS, LOOK BACK,	THERE CAME A DAY AT	322	19
AND HANG THEIR FACES SO--	WE DO NOT PLAY ON GRAVES	467	6
MY TOOLS TOOK HUMAN--FACES--	MYSELF WAS FORMED--A	488	9
THEN MADE BLUE FACES IN MY FACE--	THREE TIMES--WE PARTED--	598	7
WHERE HUMAN FACES--BE--	THREE TIMES--WE PARTED--	598	12
ALONE--IF THOSE "VAILED FACES"--BE--	AGAIN--HIS VOICE IS AT	663	24
IN THEIR ETERNAL FACES	THE MOUNTAINS--GROW	757	5
THEIR FACES [FOREHEADS]--UPON GOD--	THROUGH THE STRAIT PASS	792	4
THAT COULD I SNATCH THEIR FACES	WHAT DID THEY DO SINCE I	900	5
THE FACES OF THE ATOMS	THE CHEMICAL CONVICTION	954	5
HOW CAN I BEAR THEIR JOCUND FACES	WHAT SHALL I DO WHEN THE	956	11
HOME EFFACED--HER FACES DWINDLED--	ALL FORGOT FOR	966	9
"MY FACES ARE ASLEEP--	THE FINGERS OF THE LIGHT	1000	6
TO WHERE THE FINISHED FACES	MY TRIUMPH LASTED TILL	1227	5
I DECLARE--HOW RED THEIR FACES GREW--	DEAR MARCH--COME IN--	1320	13
. . . FOUNDERING] FACES	WE TALKED WITH EACH	1473	5
FACILITATE			
PERUSAL--TO FACILITATE--	REMORSE--IS MEMORY--	744	7
FACING			
AT A WINDOW [IN A CHAMBER] FACING WEST--	WHEN I HOPED, I	768	3
FACT			
REVEALS THE FACT THAT ONE IS RAPT	HOW NOTELESS MEN, AND	282	3
GREW BY THE FACT, AND NOT THE UNDERSTANDING	IF ANY SINK, ASSURE THAT	358	3
IT IS A TRUTH [FACT]--OF BLOOD--	WE DREAM--IT IS GOOD WE	531	6
BUT 'TWAS--THE FACT THAT HE WAS DEAD--	A DYING TIGER--MOANED	566	12
THE [NOR] FACT OF FAMINE--COULD NOT BE [EXIST]	NONE CAN EXPERIENCE	771	3
EXCEPT FOR FACT OF CORN--	NONE CAN EXPERIENCE	771	4
DENIAL--IS THE ONLY FACT	DENIAL--IS THE ONLY FACT	965	1
A FACT WITHELD THE LITTLE CHILD--	I NOTICED PEOPLE	1149	8
EMPLOYED A FACT TO VISIT ME	I BET WITH EVERY WIND	1215	3
THE NEED [FACT / LIFE] IS NOT OF [FOR] ME--	I KNOW SUSPENSE--IT	1285	8
THAT CASPIAN FACT	UNTIL THE DESERT KNOWS	1291	5
THAN A FACT [NEWS] OF IRON	WHETHER THEY HAVE	1329	7
THE CIRCUMVENTION OF THE SHAFT [THOUGHT / SITE / FACT]	AS SUMMER INTO AUTUMN	1346	11
THE FACT THAT EARTH IS HEAVEN--	THE FACT THAT EARTH IS	1408	1
BEAUTY IS NATURE'S FACT.	THE EARTH HAS MANY KEYS.	1775	4
FACTORIES			
NOT FATHER'S BELLS--NOR FACTORIES,	WHERE BELLS NO MORE	112	11
FACTS			
FACTS CENTURIES BEFORE	A PRECIOUS--MOULDERING	371	20
FACTS BY OUR SIDE ARE NEVER SUDDEN	FACTS BY OUR SIDE ARE	1497	1
FADE			
OH LET ME IMMEDIATELY "FADE"!	IF THIS IS "FADING"	120	2
I WINNOWED WHAT WOULD FADE	I CAUTIOUS, SCANNED MY	178	2
TILL BROOMS FADE SOFTLY INTO STARS--	SHE SWEEPS WITH	219	11
THE LADY WITH THE AMULET--WILL FADE--	FORGET! THE LADY WITH	438	9
TO FADE [DIE]--TOMORROW--RAINBOWS HELD [THRUST]	MY FIRST WELL DAY--SINCE	574	15
FADE I UNTO DIVINITY--	'TWOULD EASE--A	682	11
FADED			
NEVER MIND FADED FORESTS, AUSTIN,	THERE IS ANOTHER SKY,	2	5
BENEATH HIS FADED JACKET'S BLUE--	I MET A KING THIS	166	6
TO CON THE FADED SYLLABLES	IN EBON BOX, WHEN YEARS	169	7
THE MONSTER'S FADED EYES	AN AWFUL TEMPEST MASHED	198	11

	FIRST LINE	POEM	LINE
FADED (CONTINUED)			
FOR THAT OLD--FADED MIDNIGHT--	WHEN NIGHT IS ALMOST	347	7
AS TRINKET--WORN BY FADED CHILD--	I'LL SEND THE FEATHER	687	4
AS A FADED BEAD	RIBBONS OF THE YEAR--	873	5
HIS FADED LAMP WENT OUT.	THAT ODD OLD MAN IS DEAD	1130	4
HER FADED [RUSTY] AMMUNITION	THE PAST IS SUCH A	1203	7
IT IS A FADED [PHANTOM] MEAT--	MINE ENEMY IS GROWING	1509	6
A FADED BOY--IN SALLOW CLOTHES	A FADED BOY--IN SALLOW	1524	1
WRITTEN BY FADED [UNKNOWN] MEN	THE BIBLE IS AN ANTIQUE	1545	2
FADELESS			
IN THE FADELESS ORCHARDS	"LETHE" IN MY FLOWER,	1730	3
FADES			
FADES FROM THE FIRMAMENT AWAY--	SWEET MOUNTAINS--YE TELL	722	11
AS ACCENT FADES [WANES] TO INTERVAL . . .	THE MURMURING OF BEES,	1115	11
FADING			
VAST--IN IT'S FADING RATIO	AS BY THE DEAD WE LOVE	88	7
IF THIS IS "FADING"	IF THIS IS "FADING"	120	1
WHOSE BE HER [THIS] RENOWN, OR FADING, . .	BLOOM UPON THE MOUNTAIN	667	11
CONTENT OF FADING	'TWOULD EASE--A	682	9
AND SPICIEST AT FADING--INDICATE [CELEBRATE]--	THEY HAVE A LITTLE ODOR	785	3
THAT FADING FROM YOUR VASE, ...	I HIDE MYSELF WITHIN MY	903	2
FAIRER THROUGH FADING--AS THE DAY	FAIRER THROUGH FADING--	938	1
FAGOT			
THAT SHONE ABOVE THE FAGOT--	READ--SWEET--HOW OTHERS	260	9
FAIL			
MY FIGURES FAIL TO TELL ME	THE FEET OF PEOPLE	7	17
ONLY TO FAIL AGAIN!	I NEVER HEAR THE WORD	77	8
IF I SHOULD FAIL, WHAT POVERTY!	'TIS SO MUCH JOY! 'TIS	172	2
AND IF INDEED I FAIL, ...	'TIS SO MUCH JOY! 'TIS	172	9
SHOULD YOU BUT FAIL AT--SEA--	SHOULD YOU BUT FAIL AT--	226	1
WE CHANT--FOR CHEER--WHEN THE WINES--FAIL--	WE--BEE AND I--LIVE BY	230	5
TO FAIL--IS INFIDEL--	THE SWEETEST HERESY	387	8
HOW MANY FLOWERS FAIL IN WOOD--	HOW MANY FLOWERS FAIL IN	404	1
TO FAIL--WITH LAND IN SIGHT--	IT MIGHT BE LONELIER	405	14
BETTER 'TIS TO FAIL--THERE--	OUT OF SIGHT? WHAT OF	703	6
TURN ON ME--WHEN I FAIL--OR FEIGN, . . .	SWEET MOUNTAINS--YE TELL	722	4
LEST FIRMAMENT [UNIVERSE / DEITY] SHOULD FAIL FOR ME--	MY FAITH IS LARGER THAN	766	15
FINITE--TO FAIL, BUT INFINITE TO VENTURE-- .	FINITE--TO FAIL, BUT	847	1
TO FAIL WITHIN A CHANCE--	EACH SECOND IS THE LAST	879	5
CANNOT PERISH, THOUGH IT FAIL	HE WHO IN HIMSELF	969	5
FAIL IN AN INSTANT, NO MAN DID	CRUMBLING IS NOT AN	997	11
WILL FAIL OF IT ABOVE--	WHO HAS NOT FOUND THE	1544	2
A FURTHER AFTERNOON TO FAIL	I WATCHED HER FACE TO	1667	7
WHATEVER FLOWER FAIL TO COME	NATURE CAN DO NO MORE	1673	3
FAILED			
WHEN FORMULA [FILAMENT], HAD FAILED-- . .	I GOT SO I COULD HEAR	293	16
AND SO WHEN ALL THE TIME HAD LEAKED [FAILED]--	THERE CAME A DAY AT	322	21
THEY'RE HERE, THOUGH; NOT A CREATURE FAILED--	I DREADED THAT FIRST	348	21
FAILED LIKE THEMSELVES--AND CONSCIOUS THAT IT ROSE--	IF ANY SINK, ASSURE THAT	358	2
AND FAILED--AND ALL THE SUMMER LAUGHED-- .	GOD MADE A LITTLE	442	3
HE QUESTIONED SOFTLY "WHY I FAILED"? . . .	I DIED FOR BEAUTY--BUT	449	5
AND THEN THE WINDOWS FAILED--AND THEN . .	I HEARD A FLY BUZZ--WHEN	465	15
NOT A NERVE FAILED!	HE STRAINED MY FAITH--	497	8
AND FAILED TO WAKE THEM UP--	I HAD NO CAUSE TO BE	542	4
IT FAILED FROM MEN--	IT KNEW NO LAPSE, NOR	560	4
AND WHEN YOUR LITTLE LIFETIME FAILED, . .	OURSELVES WERE WED ONE	631	3
WHEN ONE [YOU] HAS FAILED TO STOP THEM-- .	TO OFFER BRAVE	767	3
I FAILED TO MAKE [ELICIT NO] REPLY-- . . .	MY BEST ACQUAINTANCES	932	6
WERE IT BUT THEY, THAT FAILED!	WERE IT BUT ME THAT	1015	2
WHO FAILED TO TOUCH US ALL	ONE OF THE ONES THAT	1466	2
AND ATTARS THAT HAVE FAILED, ...	HIS ORIENTAL HERESIES	1526	V
FAILEST			
SO WHEN THOU FAILEST, NOBODY.	I'VE NONE TO TELL ME TO	881	2
FAILING			
TO THOSE WHO FAILING NEW--	THE PROVINCE OF THE	539	10
FAR FEET OF FAILING MEN--	UNTO MY BOOKS--SO GOOD	604	10
TO THE FAILING [DYING / CLOUDING] EYE . .	ROBBED BY DEATH--BUT	971	2
FAILLESS			
FAILLESS AS THE FAIR ROTATION	ALWAYS MINE!	839	4
BUT WELLS--OF FAILLESS GROUND!	THE WELL UPON THE BROOK	1091	4
FAILS			
OR CONTEMPLATION FAILS.	SHE SWEEPS WITH	219	V 12
HE FAILS TO FEAR--	ONE NEED NOT BE A	670	V 20
AND FAILS, BUT ENTERTAINS	TO TELL THE BEAUTY WOULD	1700	6
FAILURE			
THE FAILURE BUT CONFIRM THE GRACE	HAD I PRESUMED TO HOPE--	522	7
'TIS FAILURE--NOT OF HOPE--	HAD I PRESUMED TO HOPE--	522	9
BY FAILURE OF IRREVERENCE	WHOEVER DISENCHANTS	1451	3
FAIN			
SO PROUD [PLEASED / FAIN] SHE WAS TO DIE .	SO PROUD SHE WAS TO DIE	1272	1
FAINT			
FAINT STAR OF BETHLEHEM--	IF HE DISSOLVE--THEN--	236	6
DOUBT ME! MY DIM [FAINT] COMPANION! . . .	DOUBT ME! MY DIM	275	1
TO SCAN A GHOST, IS FAINT--	'TIS SO APPALLING--IT	281	5
BEYOND OUR FAINT [SMALL] CONJECTURE-- . .	THOSE FAIR--FICTITIOUS	499	11
HUMMING--UNTIL MY FAINT REHEARSAL-- . . .	BETTER--THAN MUSIC! FOR	503	23
WITH FAINT--TERRESTRIAL POWER--	HAD I PRESUMED TO HOPE--	522	12
LATER, HIS FAINT CONFEDERATES	TO PUT THIS WORLD DOWN,	527	7

	FIRST LINE	POEM	LINE
FAINT (CONTINUED)			
THAT HEAVEN PERMIT SO MEEK [FAINT] AS HER--	SHE'S HAPPY, WITH A NEW	535	7
FAINT DOUBT--AND FAR COMPETITOR--	I CROSS TILL I AM WEARY	550	16
TILL THESE FAINT TABERNACLES DROP	THE HEAVEN VESTS FOR	694	7
ASSISTED FAINT [SLOW] OF LOVE.	AS PLAN FOR NOON AND	960	8
ESSENTIAL HOST, IN LIFE'S FAINT, WAILING INN,	AIR HAS NO RESIDENCE, NO	1060	6
AS DOWN HIS HEAVEN DROPT REMOTE [ECHOED FAINT]	JUST ONCE! OH LEAST	1076	8
FAINT DEPUTIES OF HEAT--	LIKE BROOMS OF STEEL	1252	6
FAINTED			
SO LONG I FAINTED, TO MYSELF	I CRIED AT PITY--NOT AT	588	5
FAINTER			
IT'S ONLY FAINTER--BY DEGREES--	TO DIE--TAKES JUST A	255	3
FAINTER LEAVES--TO FURTHER SEASONS--	NATURE--SOMETIMES SEARS	314	5
BY FAINTER HAMMERS--FURTHER HEARD--	HE FUMBLES AT YOUR SOUL	315	7
THROUGH FAINTER NERVE--	THE TEST OF LOVE--IS	573	8
AND FAINTER, TOO, AS WISENESS IS--	A LOSS OF SOMETHING EVER	959	10
FAINTEST			
AND JUST THE MEANEST [COMMON / FAINTEST] TUNES	I THINK I WAS ENCHANTED	593	12
A CHANCE'S FAINTEST TINCTURE	IMPOSSIBILITY, LIKE WINE	838	5
FAINT-GOING			
FAINT-GOING LIVES [EYES]--THEIR LAPSE FROM SIGHING--	"MORNING"--MEANS	300	9
FAINTING			
AS THE FAINTING BEE--	COME SLOWLY--EDEN!	211	4
I CHEERED MY FAINTING PRINCE--	I ROSE--BECAUSE HE SANK	616	5
FAINTING! FLASKS OF AIR!	WOULD YOU LIKE SUMMER?	691	7
OR HELP ONE FAINTING ROBIN	IF I CAN STOP ONE HEART	919	5
AND FAINTING, ON HER YELLOW KNEE	THE LADY FEEDS HER	941	7
FAINTLY			
SEEKS FAINTLY [SOFTLY / FURTIVE] FOR IT'S SHORE	THE INUNDATION OF THE	1425	6
FAINTS			
FAITH BLEATS [FAINTS] TO UNDERSTAND--	I SHOULD HAVE BEEN TOO	313	24
THAT FAINTS UPON THE FACE OF NOON--	THE LOVE A LIFE CAN SHOW	673	4
FAIR			
GOD HATH MADE NOTHING SINGLE BUT THEE IN HIS WORLD SO FAIR!	AWAKE YE MUSES NINE,	1	6
THERE'S SARAH, AND ELIZA, AND EMELINE SO FAIR,	AWAKE YE MUSES NINE,	1	31
EVER SERENE AND FAIR,	THERE IS ANOTHER SKY,	2	2
TO HER FAIR REPOSE.	MORNS LIKE THESE--WE	27	4
SOME RAINBOW--COMING FROM THE FAIR!	SOME RAINBOW--COMING	64	1
AND IN THE MIDST SO FAIR,	SHE BORE IT TILL THE	144	14
IN THE FAIR SCHOOLROOM OF THE SKY--	I SHALL KNOW WHY--WHEN	193	4
WORN FAIR	UNTO LIKE STORY--TROUBLE	295	10
IS SELDOM--BUT AS FAIR	THE SOUL'S SUPERIOR	306	10
ARE [WERE] NOT FAIR AS THIS--	ALL THE LETTERS I CAN	334	2
BUT, LEST THE SOUL--LIKE FAIR "PRISCILLA"	GOD IS A DISTANT--	357	5
AS FAIR--AS OUR IDEA--	HEAVEN IS SO FAR OF THE	370	6
YOU--ARE NOT SO FAIR--MIDNIGHT--	GOOD MORNING--MIDNIGHT--	425	13
TAKING UP THE FAIR IDEAL,	TAKING UP THE FAIR IDEAL	428	1
FAR FASHIONS--FAIR--	I AM ASHAMED--I HIDE--	473	15
A DOUBT--IF IT BE FAIR--INDEED--	THE WORLD--STANDS--	493	5
THOSE FAIR [NEW]--FICTITIOUS PEOPLE--	THOSE FAIR--FICTITIOUS	499	1
IT'S BRIGHT [FAIR] IMPOSSIBILITY	I WOULD NOT PAINT--A	505	3
ACCOST A THEME--SO--FAIR--	THE SOUL HAS BANDAGED	512	10
IN DUN, OR FAIR--	TO HEAR AN ORIOLE SING	526	9
MORE FAIR--BECAUSE IMPOSSIBLE	DELIGHT--BECOMES	572	3
WE SPECULATED FAIR, ON EVERY SUBJECT, BUT THE GRAVE--	WE TALKED AS GIRLS DO--	586	3
REMOTEST--WHEN MOST FAIR [NEAR]	THE TREES LIKE TASSELS--	606	8
AND THOUGHT OF THEM--SO FAIR INVITES--	YOU'LL FIND--IT WHEN YOU	610	13
TO SALUTE SO FAIR A FOREHEAD--	HER SWEET TURN TO LEAVE	649	11
TOO FAIR	EACH LIFE CONVERGES TO	680	6
A FIRST FAIR GOING--	A FIRST MUTE COMING--	702	3
WITH FAIR ASSOCIATION--	IT IS A LONESOME GLEE--	774	3
HOW FAIR HER CONVERSATION--	NATURE--THE GENTLEST	790	9
MY GARNER SHOWS SO FAIR--	GOD GAVE A LOAF TO EVERY	791	12
THEIR EXPECTATION--FAIR [SURE]--	THROUGH THE STRAIT PASS	792	10
EXCELLENT AND FAIR.	AMPLE MAKE THIS BED--	829	4
FAILLESS AS THE FAIR ROTATION	ALWAYS MINE!	839	4
TWICE HAD SUMMER HER FAIR VERDURE	TWICE HAD SUMMER HER	846	1
PRECIOUS! IT WAS CONCEIVELESS FAIR	ON THAT DEAR FRAME THE	940	5
I ONLY MUST NOT CHANGE SO FAIR	FITTER TO SEE HIM, I MAY	968	19
HOW FAIR	BESIDES THIS MAY	977	4
A WARRANT TO BE FAIR--	I CANNOT MEET THE SPRING	1051	4
PERCEPTION SETS IT FAIR	PERCEPTION OF AN OBJECT	1071	6
WERE EVERY STORM [GALE / SNOW] SO SPICE [FAIR / SWEET]	THE SNOW THAT NEVER	1133	13
THE FORFEIT IS OF CREATURE FAIR	A FULL FED ROSE ON MEALS	1154	5
MISERY, HOW FAIR	ON THE WORLD YOU COLORED	1171	8
THAT COURTESY WILL FAIR REMAIN	"REMEMBER ME" IMPLORED	1180	5
GO MAKE THEE FAIR MY CANDIDATE	OH SHADOW ON THE GRASS,	1187	3
BECOME, ALAS, MORE FAIR--	TO MAKE ROUTINE A	1196	8
FAIR PLAY--	THE SHOW IS NOT THE SHOW	1206	5
WE WILL PRY AND SEE IF SHE IS FAIR	BECAUSE HE LOVES HER	1229	2
IN THE OPINION FAIR	CONFIRMING ALL WHO	1268	2
HAD ALMOST MADE IT FAIR--	WHILE WE WERE FEARING IT	1277	4
IMPEDING [IMPEDE THE] NAVIGATION BRIGHT [FAIR]	A STAGNANT PLEASURE LIKE	1281	5
BUT ELIGIBLY FAIR	THIS DIRTY--LITTLE--	1311	5
THIS WHOLE [SUDDEN / FAIR / GAY / BRIGHT	A LITTLE MADNESS IN THE	1333	5

	FIRST LINE	POEM	LINE
FAIR (CONTINUED)			
/ FLEET / SWEET / . . .			
AND TRUE [BEST / REAL / BLAND / FINE / FAIR] THE OTHER . . .	I'D RATHER RECOLLECT A	1349	4
THOSE IT FITS, TOO FAIR TO WEAR IT--	"FAITHFUL TO THE END"	1357	V
THERE IS A NEEDLE FAIR	TO MEND EACH TATTERED	1442	2
THEIR ROUTES ARE FAIR--	THE THINGS THAT NEVER	1515	6
THEY MAKE THEIR CIRCUIT FAIR	NO MATTER WHERE THE	1541	2
HE FEEDS UPON THE FAIR--	HOPE IS A SUBTLE GLUTTON	1547	2
SOME FAIR OR STORMY DAY,	THIS ME--THAT WALKS AND	1588	2
A COMPENSATION FAIR [GAY]	COSMOPOLITES WITHOUT A	1589	6
WHAT METTLE FAIR	THE LASSITUDES OF	1592	6
AS FROM THE EARTH THE LIGHT [FAIR] BALLOON	AS FROM THE EARTH THE	1630	1
BUT JUST THE ANTI FAIR--AVERRING--FAIREST-- TRUEST TRUTH	EXTOL THEE--COULD I--	1643	3
HOW FAIR ON LOOKING BACK THE DAY	EDEN IS THAT	1657	5
I SHRANK--"HOW FAIR YOU ARE"!	IN WINTER IN MY ROOM	1670	22
AND TAKES HER FAIR AERIAL GAIT	THE OVERTAKELESSNESS OF	1691	7
THAT WAS TOO FAIR BEFORE--	WERE NATURE MORTAL LADY	1762	10
FAIRER			
ITSELF BE FAIRER--WE SUPPOSE--	"HEAVEN" HAS DIFFERENT	575	17
A FAIRER HOUSE THAN PROSE--	I DWELL IN POSSIBILITY--	657	2
THE FAIRER--FOR THE FARNESS--	A SOUTH WIND--HAS A	719	7
FAIRER THROUGH FADING--AS THE DAY	FAIRER THROUGH FADING--	938	1
TO MAKE SOME TRIFLE FAIRER	WERE NATURE MORTAL LADY	1762	9
FAIREST			
THOSE WERE THE FAIREST INGOTS	I NEVER TOLD THE BURIED	11	12
OF VISITERS--THE FAIREST--	I DWELL IN POSSIBILITY--	657	9
TO MAKE ME FAIREST OF THE EARTH--	FITTER TO SEE HIM, I MAY	968	5
THE FAIREST HOME I EVER KNEW	THE FAIREST HOME I EVER	1423	1
BUT JUST THE ANTI FAIR--AVERRING--FAIREST-- TRUEST TRUTH	EXTOL THEE--COULD I--	1643	3
FAIRLY			
MOSES WAS'NT FAIRLY USED--	SO I PULL MY STOCKINGS	1201	7
FAIRNESS			
AND FAIRNESS--AND RENOWN--	SHE DWELLETH IN THE	671	6
FAIRY			
MIGHT SCARE THE QUIET FAIRY	THERE'S SOMETHING	45	11
AND THEN HIS FAIRY [MICROSCOPIC] GIG	WITHIN MY GARDEN, RIDES	500	10
EVEN FOR DEATH, A FAIRY MEDICINE.	WOULD YOU LIKE SUMMER?	691	8
SO FAIRY [FOREIGN]--SO FICTITIOUS	AS SLEIGH BELLS SEEM IN	981	3
IDEALS ARE THE FAIRY OIL	IDEALS ARE THE FAIRY OIL	983	1
FAITH			
MY FAITH THAT DARK ADORES--	THE FEET OF PEOPLE	7	22
PICK BY FAITH IT'S BLOSSOM	WHEN I COUNT THE SEEDS	40	9
THROUGH FAITH IN ONE HE MET NOT,	COULD LIVE--DID LIVE--	43	4
BY FAITH MAY CLEAR BEHOLD	WE SHOULD NOT MIND SO	81	10
THIS FAITH THAT WATCHED FOR STAR IN VAIN,	THIS HEART THAT BROKE SO	145	3
"FAITH" IS A FINE INVENTION	"FAITH" IS A FINE	185	1
IF I SHOULD STAB THE PATIENT FAITH	I SHOULD NOT DARE TO	205	9
READ THEN--OF FAITH--	READ--SWEET--HOW OTHERS	260	8
FAITH--THE EXPERIMENT OF OUR LORD--	"MORNING"--MEANS	300	10
FAITH BLEATS [FAINTS] TO UNDERSTAND--	I SHOULD HAVE BEEN TOO	313	24
TO LOSE ONE'S FAITH--SURPASS	TO LOSE ONE'S FAITH--	377	1
REPLENISHED--FAITH CANNOT--	TO LOSE ONE'S FAITH--	377	4
THOUGH THE FAITH ACCOMMODATE BUT TWO--	THE SWEETEST HERESY	387	4
HER FAITH--NO FEAR--	THROUGH THE DARK SOD--AS	392	4
IT HELPS TO STIMULATE THE FAITH	'TIS CUSTOMARY AS WE	440	3
BY FAITH--BE OVERCOME--	TRIUMPH--MAY BE OF	455	4
LOVE [FAITH] IS LIKE LIFE--MERELY [ONLY THE] LONGER	WHILE IT IS ALIVE	491	7
LOVE [FAITH] IS LIKE DEATH, DURING THE GRAVE	WHILE IT IS ALIVE	491	8
LOVE [FAITH] IS THE FELLOW OF THE RESURRECTION	WHILE IT IS ALIVE	491	9
HE STRAINED MY FAITH--	HE STRAINED MY FAITH--	497	1
FAITH SLIPS--AND LAUGHS, AND RALLIES--	THIS WORLD IS NOT	501	13
A FICTION SUPERSEDING FAITH--	HER SWEET WEIGHT ON MY	518	11
THE CHILD'S FAITH IS NEW--	THE CHILD'S FAITH IS NEW	637	1
FAITH--ALONE--	A FIRST MUTE COMING--	702	8
MY FAITH IS LARGER THAN THE HILLS--	MY FAITH IS LARGER THAN	766	1
MY FAITH MUST TAKE THE PURPLE WHEEL	MY FAITH IS LARGER THAN	766	3
HOW DARE I, THEREFORE, STINT A FAITH	MY FAITH IS LARGER THAN	766	13
THEIR FAITH--THE EVERLASTING TROTH--	THROUGH THE STRAIT PASS	792	9
IT--SUGGESTS TO OUR FAITH--	BY MY WINDOW HAVE I FOR	797	17
PEACE IS A FICTION OF OUR FAITH--	PEACE IS A FICTION OF	912	1
FAITH--IS THE PIERLESS BRIDGE	FAITH--IS THE PIERLESS	915	1
THROUGH FAITH--MY HAZEL EYE	WHAT I SEE NOT, I BETTER	939	2
FAITH IS CONSTANCY'S RESULT--	HE WHO IN HIMSELF	969	3
BUT TO FAITH--A REVOLUTION	UNFULFILLED TO	972	3
THAT SYLLABLE WHOSE FAITH	SUPERFLUOUS WERE THE SUN	999	5
TO WHICH MY FAITH PINNED BLOCK BY BLOCK	FALSEHOOD OF THEE COULD	1007	3
AS MUCH THROUGH CONSCIOUSNESS [CONSCIOUS FAITH]	NOT TO DISCOVER WEAKNESS	1054	4
OF FAITH OF OTHERS IN ITSELF	NOT TO DISCOVER WEAKNESS	1054	5
BELIEF [WITH NOUGHT / OUR FAITH] TO REGULATE--	THE LAST NIGHT THAT SHE	1100	28
NOT FORSOOK [FORGOT] OF FAITH--	TELL AS A MARKSMAN--WERE	1152	21
THE SCIENTIST OF FAITH	THE LILAC IS AN ANCIENT	1241	12
ON WHICH OUR FAITH DOTH TREAD--	HOW BRITTLE ARE THE	1433	2
OUR FAITH DOTH DAILY TREAD--	HOW BRITTLE ARE THE	1433	V 2
TO MEND EACH TATTERED FAITH	TO MEND EACH TATTERED	1442	1
MY FAITH CANNOT REPLY	LIVES HE IN ANY OTHER	1557	2

	FIRST LINE	POEM		LINE
FAITHFUL				
HOW MANY TIMES THEY--BORE THE FAITHFUL WITNESS--	READ--SWEET--HOW OTHERS	260		5
BE FAITHFUL--IN HIS ABSENCE--	HE FOUND MY BEING--SET	603		5
FROM FURTHEST SPIRIT [FAITHFUL / GOOD MAN]--GOD--	ON A COLUMNAR SELF--	789		12
OH FAITHFUL FROST [SLEET] THAT KEPT THE DATE	IT CAME AT LAST BUT	1230		5
WHILE FAITHFUL AND AFAR	WARM IN HER HAND THESE	1313		2
"FAITHFUL TO THE END" AMENDED	"FAITHFUL TO THE END"	1357		1
FAITHFUL WAS ALL THAT I COULD BOAST	THAT SHE FORGOT ME WAS	1683		5
HE WAS THE FAITHFUL FATHER	HIGH FROM THE EARTH I	1723		15
THAT, FAITHFUL TO THE CLOSE,	THOSE FINAL CREATURES,--	1766		2
LAD OF ATHENS, FAITHFUL BE	LAD OF ATHENS, FAITHFUL	1768		1
FALL				
WHO FALL--AND NONE OBSERVE--	TO FIGHT ALOUD, IS VERY	126		6
SOFT FALL THE SOUNDS OF EDEN	ALL OVERGROWN BY CUNNING	148	V	
IF EITHER OF HER "SPARROWS FALL",	MAMA NEVER FORGETS HER	164		7
NOTCHING THE FALL OF THE EVEN SUN!	BOUND--A TROUBLE--	269		10
SO I SHALL NEVER FALL--	TIE THE STRINGS TO MY	279		6
AND ODORS FALL	I TEND MY FLOWERS FOR	339		13
LEST IT FALL--	I GAINED IT SO--	359		11
NOT SO SOFTLY FALL	SWEET--SAFE--HOUSES--	457		7
THAT NEVER CEASED TO FALL--	I WAS THE SLIGHTEST IN	486		6
IF YOU WERE COMING IN THE FALL,	IF YOU WERE COMING IN	511		1
HIS OWN WOULD FALL SO MORE	EACH SCAR I'LL KEEP FOR	877		7
FALL SOFTLY, AND ADORE--	THE LADY FEEDS HER	941		8
SHE FELLED--HE DID NOT FALL--	FATE SLEW HIM, BUT HE	1031		2
I CLING TO NOWHERE TILL I FALL--	MORE THAN THE GRAVE IS	1503		4
AS FLOWER AT FALL OF FROST--	I WATCHED HER FACE TO	1667		8
FALLACY				
A FALLACY, A FIGMENT, WE KNEW--	NOT SO THE INFINITE	1040		4
AND DOOM A FALLACY--	THE DITCH IS DEAR TO THE	1645	V	8
FALLEN				
HOW SAFE HIS FALLEN HEAD	THE DITCH IS DEAR TO THE	1645		4
FALLIBLE				
AS IF FALLIBLE--	HER SOVREIGN PEOPLE	1139		4
FALLING				
THE SYMBOL [FALLING / FIGURE] OF A WORD	THERE CAME A DAY AT	322		10
THE YELLOW--DAY--IS FALLING--	THE RED--BLAZE--IS THE	469		3
IN FALLING [CRASHING] TIMBERS BURIED--	IN FALLING TIMBERS	614		1
FALLOW				
LIKE FALLOW ARTICLE--	THE BAT IS DUN, WITH	1575		2
FALLS				
THERE'S NOTHING COOLER FALLS--	UPON CONCLUDED LIVES	735		2
WHEN NATURE FALLS UPON HERSELF	THE WIND DREW OFF	1694		10
FALSEHOOD				
FALSEHOOD OF THEE COULD I SUPPOSE	FALSEHOOD OF THEE COULD	1007		1
FALTER				
FALTER! WHEN THE SUN	ALTER! WHEN THE HILLS DO	729		2
FALTERING				
AWKWARD--FALTERING--	SANG FROM THE HEART,	1059		10
FAME				
A MODEST LOT--A FAME PETITE--	A LITTLE BREAD--A CRUST	159		7
THE DUST, WILL VEX YOUR FAME--	ALTHOUGH I PUT AWAY HIS	366		25
THE FORMER--CHECKS--ON FAME--	SOME--WORK FOR	406		4
MY PARADISE--THE FAME	ME--COME! MY DAZZLED	431		9
THAT WHEN THEIR MORTAL NAME [FAME] BE NUMB--	THE MARTYR POETS--DID	544		3
BUT MAGNIFIED--BY FAME--	HE GAVE AWAY HIS LIFE--	567		4
ON THE HEAVENLY FAME--	I CANNOT LIVE WITH YOU--	640		40
OR A FIFE'S FAME--	LIFE, AND DEATH, AND	706		5
FAME OF MYSELF, TO JUSTIFY,	FAME OF MYSELF, TO	713		1
FAME OF MYSELF TO LACK--ALTHOUGH	FAME OF MYSELF, TO	713		5
SUFFICIENT FAME--	BE MINE THE DOOM--	845		2
FAME IS THE TINT THAT SCHOLARS LEAVE	FAME IS THE TINT THAT	866		1
WITHOUT THE INCIDENT OF FAME	WHEN I HAVE SEEN THE SUN	888		5
UPON HIS DATELESS FAME	SUPERFLUOUS WERE THE SUN	999		9
UPON THE FLOORS OF FAME--	I WAS A PHEBE--NOTHING	1009		8
TOO NEAR [CLOSE] THOU ART FOR FAME--	THE BIRD DID PRANCE--THE	1107		12
OR FLAG SUBSIST OR FAME EXPORT	STEP LIGHTLY ON THIS	1183		7
THE [A] CLOVER'S SIMPLE FAME	THE CLOVER'S SIMPLE FAME	1232		1
THE BEGGAR AT THE DOOR FOR FAME	THE BEGGAR AT THE DOOR	1240		1
GATHERED TO THAT STRANGE FAME--	GATHERED INTO THE EARTH,	1370		3
AS FAME SHOULD BE--	HIS MANSION IN THE POOL	1379		12
FAME IS THE ONE THAT DOES NOT STAY--	FAME IS THE ONE THAT	1475		1
NAY--LIFT THEMSELVES--FAME HAS NO ARMS--	ABOVE OBLIVION'S TIDE	1531		3
OR FAME ERECT HER SITELESS CITADEL	SOCIETY FOR ME MY MISERY	1534	V	
FAME IS A FICKLE FOOD	FAME IS A FICKLE FOOD	1659		1
FAME IS A BEE.	FAME IS A BEE.	1763		1
FAMELESS				
UPON A FAMELESS FLOWER--	TO HER DERIDED HOME	1586		6
FAME'S				
FAME'S BOYS AND GIRLS, WHO NEVER DIE	FAME'S BOYS AND GIRLS,	1066		1
IS FAME'S CONSUMMATE FEE--	TO EARN IT BY DISDAINING	1427		2
FAMES				
WHEN LESSER FAMES INVITE--	I HAD THE GLORY--THAT	349		3
FAMILIAR				
COULD GO FROM SCENE FAMILIAR	COULD LIVE--DID LIVE--	43		6
FROM AN ACCUSTOMED [A FAMILIAR] FLOWER.	SHE WENT AS QUIET AS THE	149		2
TO OUR FAMILIAR EYES--	I'VE NOTHING ELSE--TO	224		4
THE ODE FAMILIAR--RULES THE NOON--	THE ROBIN'S MY CRITERION	285		5

	FIRST LINE	POEM	LINE
FAMILIAR (CONTINUED)			
HE TRAVERSES--FAMILIAR--	A PRECIOUS--MOULDERING	371	21
I MADE MY SOUL FAMILIAR--WITH HER EXTREMITY--	I READ MY SENTENCE--	412	9
FROM THE FAMILIAR SPECIES	THIS WAS A POET--IT IS	448	5
FROM OUR FAMILIAR LIFETIME [ADDRESS / GAZING / FINGERS / NOTICE]--	THOSE FAIR--FICTITIOUS	499	3
FAMILIAR, IN THE ROOMS--	OF NEARNESS TO HER	607	6
THE UNOBTRUSIVE [MOST FAMILIAR] GUEST-- . .	'TWAS A LONG PARTING--	625	16
ERMINE--MY FAMILIAR GOWN--	NO MATTER--NOW--SWEET--	704	13
AS A FAMILIAR STIRRUP [SADDLE]	A SPARROW TOOK A SLICE	1211	V 7
POWER IS A FAMILIAR GROWTH--	POWER IS A FAMILIAR	1238	1
ON THE FAMILIAR ROAD	UNTIL THE DESERT KNOWS	1291	11
FAMILIARITIES			
FAMILIARITIES.	OF NATURE I SHALL HAVE	1220	4
FAMILY			
I KNOW THE FAMILY	PARTAKE AS DOTH THE BEE,	994	V 3
OF HER ECCENTRIC FAMILY--	IF NATURE SMILES--THE	1085	3
OR FOR FAMILY	NOW I KNEW I LOST HER--	1219	18
FAMINE			
EASING MY FAMINE	LET US PLAY YESTERDAY--	728	5
WERE THERE FAMINE IN THE LAND--	MOST SHE TOUCHED ME BY	760	6
THE [NOR] FACT OF FAMINE--COULD NOT BE [EXIST]	NONE CAN EXPERIENCE	771	3
A ROBIN'S FAMINE [PALATE / HUNGER] ABLE-- .	DEPRIVED OF OTHER	773	9
IT MIGHT BE FAMINE--ALL AROUND--	GOD GAVE A LOAF TO EVERY	791	9
I, OF A FINER FAMINE	AS THE STARVED MAELSTROM	872	13
FAMISH			
WHICH WAS TO FAMISH, THEN OR NOW--	OH SUMPTUOUS MOMENT	1125	6
I FAMISH [PERISH] TO BEHOLD SO EMINENT A SIGHT [ANOTHER SUCH . . .	THE MOST TRIUMPHANT BIRD	1265	4
FAMISHED			
I TELL THE WHILE I WAITED [FAMISHED]-- . .	ART THOU THE THING I	1282	5
FAMISHING			
TO WHOSOEVER FAMISHING	THESE ARE THE SIGNS TO	1077	3
FOR JUST ONE PLAUDIT FAMISHING, ...	THE IMMORTALITY SHE GAVE	1648	3
FAMOUS			
IS IT BROUGHT FROM FAMOUS COUNTRIES . . .	WILL THERE REALLY BE A	101	7
A LONG--LONG [VAST--VAST / BRAVE--BRAVE] SLEEP--A FAMOUS--SLEEP--	A LONG--LONG SLEEP--A	654	1
FAN			
A GNAT'S MINUTEST FAN	MORE LIFE--WENT OUT--	422	14
CAN GO, ITSELF, WITHOUT A FAN--	YOU CANNOT PUT A FIRE	530	3
BUT STROVE TO STIR THE LIFELESS [FLICKERING] FAN	THREE TIMES--WE PARTED--	598	3
DID FAN AND ROCK, WITH SUDDEN LIGHT-- . .	TO MY SMALL HEARTH HIS	638	3
BUT THE LEAST FAN	THE WORLD--FEELS DUSTY	715	6
A FAN, PERHAPS, A FRIEND'S REGRET	THE DYING NEED BUT	1026	5
BUT [YET] PRONE TO SHUT IT'S [HIS] SPOTTED [SUBTLE] FAN	THE BUTTERFLY'S NUMIDIAN	1387	4
THOUGH SHUTTING LIKE A DAPPLED FAN	THE BUTTERFLY'S NUMIDIAN	1387	V 4
THE SOUTH UNROLLED A PURPLE FAN	THE SUN RETIRED TO A	1693	7
AND ASSOCIATES WITH A FAN	THE PARASOL IS THE	1747	2
FANCIED			
THAT FANCIED THEY COULD HOLD--	HE GAVE AWAY HIS LIFE--	567	6
FANCY			
BY SAVORY FANCY SPREAD--	AS WATCHERS HANG UPON	121	3
FANCY THE SUNRISE--LEFT THE DOOR AJAR! . .	I KNOW SOME LONELY	289	40
UNTO GUESSED CRESTS, MY MOANING FANCY, LEADS [LURES] ME,	UNTO LIKE STORY--TROUBLE	295	9
THE SHIVERING [FREEZING] FANCY TURNS . . .	CONJECTURING A CLIMATE	562	4
FANTASTIC			
I WAIT THY FAR, FANTASTIC BELLS--	THERE IS A MORN BY MEN	24	22
FANTASTIC SAILORS--MINGLE--	WHERE SHIPS OF PURPLE--	265	3
REMOTEST [FANTASTIC / MOST GRACIOUS / MOST DUSKY / . . .	AN ANTIQUATED TREE	1514	7
FANTASY			
MY [HIS] FANTASY TO PLEASE.	I ROBBED THE WOODS--	41	5
HIS FANTASY DID PLEASE	UPON HIS SADDLE SPRUNG A	1600	4
FAR			
WHEN I AM FAR FROM THEE!	"SIC TRANSIT GLORIA	3	8
HOW FAR THE VILLAGE LIES--	THE FEET OF PEOPLE	7	18
TODAY IS FAR FROM CHILDHOOD--	ONE SISTER HAVE I IN OUR	14	13
IN COUNTRY FAR FROM HERE--	I HAD A GUINEA GOLDEN--	23	32
I WAIT THY FAR, FANTASTIC BELLS--	THERE IS A MORN BY MEN	24	22
HASTENING FROM FAR JOURNEY--	NOBODY KNOWS THIS LITTLE	35	7
FAR--AS THE EAST FROM EVEN--	TAKEN FROM MEN--THIS	53	9
ON EAR TOO FAR FOR THE DELIGHT, ...	AS WATCHERS HANG UPON	121	5
FLUTTER TOO FAR FOR ME--	A SOMETHING IN A	122	12
TELL ME HOW FAR THE MORNING LEAPS--	BRING ME THE SUNSET IN A	128	4
FAR SUPERIOR TO MINE.	FLOWERS--WELL--IF	137	14
I WOULD FAR PREFER, ...	THO' MY DESTINY BE	163	6
PLUCKED FAR AWAY, SOME MORNING--	IN EBON BOX, WHEN YEARS	169	11
'TWAS'NT FAR--THE DOOR WAS NEAR--	HE WAS WEAK, AND I WAS	190	5
WE ARE FAR TOO GRAND--	WE DONT CRY--TIM AND I,	196	2
WE ARE FAR TOO GRAND--	WE DONT CRY--TIM AND I,	196	8
NOR, FOR MYSELF, I CAME SO FAR--	SAVIOR! I'VE NO ONE ELSE	217	5
THE COURT IS FAR AWAY--	THE COURT IS FAR AWAY--	235	1
YOU ARE VERY FAR--	AH, MOON--AND STAR!	240	2
THOUGH YOU'RE VERY FAR--	AH, MOON--AND STAR!	240	14
AS BIRD'S FAR NAVIGATION	I'VE KNOWN A HEAVEN,	243	14
HOW MANY TIMES FOR MY FAR SAKE	YOU SEE I CANNOT SEE--	253	4

	FIRST LINE	POEM	LINE
FAR (CONTINUED)			
TOO FAR--THE STRENGTH--	YOU SEE I CANNOT SEE--	253	10
AND DOWER LATITUDES FAR ON--	DELIGHT IS AS THE FLIGHT	257	23
AS FAR FROM MINE, AS IF NO PLIGHT	A SINGLE SCREW OF FLESH	263	7
FAR DOWN THE DUSTIEST ROAD!	ONE LIFE OF SO MUCH	270	16
YET NOT TOO FAR [NEAR ENOUGH--] TO COME AT CALL--	HE PUT THE BELT AROUND	273	9
THE SUN HAS GOT AS FAR	I KNOW SOME LONELY	289	33
IT'S FAR--FAR TREASURE TO SURMISE--	YOUR RICHES--TAUGHT ME--	299	29
IT'S FAR--FAR TREASURE TO SURMISE--	YOUR RICHES--TAUGHT ME--	299	29
IN [ON] FAR [STILL] OCTOBER AIR,	THERE ARE TWO RIPENINGS	332	8
HAVE CRAWLED TOO FAR!	I KNOW THAT HE EXISTS.	338	16
AND FAR FROM HEAVEN AS THE REST--	NOT PROBABLE--THE BAREST	346	3
WHAT IF THE BIRD FROM JOUNEY FAR--	NOT PROBABLE--THE BAREST	346	5
HEAVEN IS SO FAR OF THE MIND	HEAVEN IS SO FAR OF THE	370	1
IN FAR--BOLIVIAN GROUND--	REVERSE CANNOT BEFALL	395	6
AND FAR I HEARD HIS SILVER CALL	I HAD NOT MINDED--WALLS	398	3
THAT SO FAR--TRUTH IS TRUE?	A TONGUE--TO TELL HIM I	400	8
A STAR--NOT FAR ENOUGH TO SEEK--	A MURMUR IN THE TREES--	416	3
HE COMES JUST SO FAR--TOWARD THE TOWN--	THE MOON IS DISTANT FROM	429	7
JUST SO FAR--GOES AWAY--	THE MOON IS DISTANT FROM	429	8
FAR OFF--HE SIGHS--AND THEREFORE--HOPELESS--	UNDUE SIGNIFICANCE A	439	3
CLEMATIS--JOURNEYING FAR--	'TIS CUSTOMARY AS WE	440	6
OF ACTION--SICKER FAR--	I TIE MY HAT--I CREASE	443	18
AS FAR AS IT COULD SEE--	LIKE EYES THAT LOOKED ON	458	6
AND SO WE MOVE AS FAR	WE DO NOT PLAY ON GRAVES	467	9
JUST LOOKING ROUND TO SEE HOW FAR	WE DO NOT PLAY ON GRAVES	467	11
FAR FASHIONS--FAIR--	I AM ASHAMED--I HIDE--	473	15
THEY PUT US FAR APART--	THEY PUT US FAR APART--	474	1
AND IN THE ORCHARD FAR BELOW--	A SOLEMN THING WITHIN	483	5
AND IF IT HAD NOT BEEN SO FAR--	I WAS THE SLIGHTEST IN	486	14
AS FAR FROM PITY, AS COMPLAINT--	AS FAR FROM PITY, AS	496	1
AS FAR FROM TIME--AS HISTORY--	AS FAR FROM PITY, AS	496	5
FAINT DOUBT--AND FAR COMPETITOR--	I CROSS TILL I AM WEARY	550	16
AND PARTS OF HIS FAR PLAN	I PRAYED, AT FIRST, A	576	10
THEIR FAR PARADES--ORDER [HALT] ON THE EYE	INCONCEIVABLY SOLEMN!	582	5
BY FAR THE GREATER ONE--	THE BATTLE FOUGHT	594	4
THE FAR THEATRICALS OF DAY	LIKE MIGHTY FOOT LIGHTS	595	3
THE HEAVENS WEIGHED THE MOST--BY FAR [WERE THE WEIGHTIEST--FAR]--	IT TROUBLED ME AS ONCE I	600	5
THE HEAVENS WEIGHED THE MOST--BY FAR [WERE THE WEIGHTIEST--FAR]--	IT TROUBLED ME AS ONCE I	600	5
FAR ENDS OF TIRED [HOMELY] DAYS--	UNTO MY BOOKS--SO GOOD	604	2
FAR FEET OF FAILING MEN--	UNTO MY BOOKS--SO GOOD	604	10
FAR PSALTERIES OF SUMMER--	THE TREES LIKE TASSELS--	606	5
OF OPAL CATTLE--FEEDING FAR	THEY CALLED ME TO THE	628	5
MYSELF TOO FAR BELOW	I WATCHED THE MOON	629	34
COULD BEHOLD [REGARD] SO FAR [SMALL / DIM / SCARCE] A CREATURE--	PROMISE THIS--WHEN YOU	648	27
NE'ER SO FAR BEHIND--	PROMISE THIS--WHEN YOU	648	30
IT SPRINKLES BONNETS--FAR BELOW--	THE NAME--OF IT--IS	656	9
THAT MURMUR SO--CHANT SO--FAR--	AGAIN--HIS VOICE IS AT	663	V 25
FAR AS NORTH--AND EAST,	BLOOM UPON THE MOUNTAIN	667	14
FAR AS SOUTH AND WEST--EXPANDING [DISCLOSING]--	BLOOM UPON THE MOUNTAIN	667	15
FAR SAFER, OF A MIDNIGHT MEETING	ONE NEED NOT BE A	670	5
FAR SAFER, THROUGH AN ABBEY GALLOP,	ONE NEED NOT BE A	670	9
AND FAR ABROAD ON SUMMER DAYS--	THE LOVE A LIFE CAN SHOW	673	8
FAR AS PARADISE--	LIFE--IS WHAT WE MAKE IT	698	12
'TWOULD LOOK TOO FAR--TO DIE--	I SOMETIMES DROP IT, FOR	708	8
THEIR FAR--SLOW--VIOLET GAZE--	SWEET MOUNTAINS--YE TELL	722	6
WHEN PEACE WAS FAR AWAY--	I MANY TIMES THOUGHT	739	2
AND THAT ASSEMBLY [COMPANION]--NOT FAR OFF	ON A COLUMNAR SELF--	789	11
WHAT DISTANCE FAR	SO SET IT'S SUN IN THEE	808	3
ON [TO] PLAINER DAYS, WHOSE TABLE FAR	THE LUXURY TO APPREHEND	815	13
OH POOR AND FAR--	THE SUN AND MOON MUST	871	9
TO OUR FAR, VASCILLATING FEET	FAITH--IS THE PIERLESS	915	11
HOW FAR IS IT TO HEAVEN?	HOW FAR IS IT TO HEAVEN?	929	1
AS FAR AS DEATH THIS WAY--	HOW FAR IS IT TO HEAVEN?	929	2
HOW FAR IS IT TO HELL?	HOW FAR IS IT TO HEAVEN?	929	5
AS FAR AS DEATH THIS WAY--	HOW FAR IS IT TO HEAVEN?	929	6
HOW FAR LEFT HAND THE SEPULCHRE	HOW FAR IS IT TO HEAVEN?	929	7
THOU FROM HERE, SO FAR?	WHAT SHALL I DO WHEN THE	956	12
FAR AFTER SUFFERING	AS ONE DOES SICKNESS	957	10
THIS IS FAR FROM THENCE--	"UNTO ME?" I DO NOT KNOW	964	6
FAR FROM LOVE THE HEAVENLY FATHER	FAR FROM LOVE THE	1021	1
BE IT NE'ER SO FAR	SOMEWHAT, TO HOPE FOR,	1041	2
A WISHFULNESS THEIR FAR CONDITION	A SICKNESS OF THIS WORLD	1044	3
BUT FAR AFTER FROST--	EXCEPT THE SMALLER SIZE	1067	V
THAT SITUATES SO FAR--	PERCEPTION OF AN OBJECT	1071	8
THAT 'TIS SO HEAVENLY FAR--	PERCEPTION OF AN OBJECT	1071	V 8
COUNT NOT THAT FAR THAT CAN BE HAD,	COUNT NOT THAT FAR THAT	1074	1
FAR AFTER ACT OR ACCIDENT	WE LIKE A HAIRBREADTH	1175	3
AS FAR AS CANNON DWELL	STEP LIGHTLY ON THIS	1183	6
BUT "NEVER" FAR AS HONOR	TO DISAPPEAR ENHANCES--	1209	9
THAT WE SO FAR BEHIND--	BECAUSE HE LOVES HER	1229	6
NOT HOPING FOR HIS NOTICE VAST [FAR / FINE]	BECAUSE HE LOVES HER	1229	9
'TIS GLORY'S FAR SUFFICIENCY [OVERTAKELESSNESS]	BECAUSE HE LOVES HER	1229	11
'TIS SO FAR AWAY--	YESTERDAY IS HISTORY,	1292	2

	FIRST LINE	POEM	LINE
FAR (CONTINUED)			
THE [DIM / FAR] ABSENCE OF THE WITCH DOES NOT [CANNOT]	LONG YEARS APART--CAN	1383	3
PERHAPS THEY DO [SHE DOES] NOT GO SO FAR	PERHAPS THEY DO NOT GO	1399	1
THE WATER LIVES SO FAR--	WHAT MYSTERY PERVADES A	1400	2
TO COME SO FAR SO COLD A DAY	THE SAVIOR MUST HAVE	1487	3
WILL SEE HOW FAR FROM HOME	IF EVER THE LID GETS OFF	1727	6
BURDEN--BORNE SO FAR TRIUMPHANT--	REARRANGE A "WIFE'S"	1737	13
ELYSIUM IS AS FAR AS TO	ELYSIUM IS AS FAR AS TO	1760	1
FARE			
BEFORE A FENCE WITHOUT A FARE	UPON HIS SADDLE SPRUNG A	1600	3
FARED			
MIRACULOUSLY FARED	CONFERRING WITH MYSELF	1655	4
FAREWELL			
THEN, FAREWELL, TUSCARORA,	"SIC TRANSIT GLORIA	3	67
AND FAREWELL, SIR, TO THEE!	"SIC TRANSIT GLORIA	3	68
FARM			
AND WALTZED UPON A FARM--	TWO BUTTERFLIES WENT OUT	533	2
I ONLY SAW A SAPPHIRE [AN AMBER--] FARM--	THEY CALLED ME TO THE	628	3
NOR FARM--NOR OPAL HERD--WAS THERE--	THEY CALLED ME TO THE	628	15
THE PRODUCTS OF MY FARM ARE THESE	THE PRODUCTS OF MY FARM	1025	1
FARMER			
AND FROM A THRIVING FARMER--	I CAUTIOUS, SCANNED MY	178	11
"MORNING"--MEANS "MILKING"--TO THE FARMER--	"MORNING"--MEANS	300	1
BY THE FARMER BE--	NO BOBOLINK--REVERSE HIS	755	4
IF [GRANT] THE BIRD AND THE FARMER--DEEM IT A "PINE"--	BY MY WINDOW HAVE I FOR	797	3
OF THE NEW ENGLAND FARMER--	THE ROBIN IS A GABRIEL	1483	6
FARMER'S			
THE SHIVERERS ROUND FARMER'S DOORS--	'TIS NOT THAT DYING	335	9
FARMERS			
ARE THEY "FARMERS"--	WHAT IS--"PARADISE"--	215	3
THOSE FARMERS--AND THEIR WIVES--	I'M SORRY FOR THE DEAD--	529	14
FARMERS CORN	FAME IS A FICKLE FOOD	1659	9
FARMING			
SET SEPARATE [PUT QUIET--] FROM THE FARMING--	I'M SORRY FOR THE DEAD--	529	15
FARMS			
WHEN I WAS CARRIED BY THE FARMS--	'TWAS JUST THIS TIME,	445	3
ON OUR NEW ENGLAND FARMS--	A FIELD OF STUBBLE,	1407	8
FARNESS			
THE FAIRER--FOR THE FARNESS--	A SOUTH WIND--HAS A	719	7
FARTHER			
AND WE LOOK FARTHER ON!	OUR LIVES ARE SWISS--	80	5
FARTHER THAN YOU--	AH, MOON--AND STAR!	240	4
THERE IS ONE--FARTHER THAN YOU--	AH, MOON--AND STAR!	240	15
WHEN FARTHER [SHARPER] PARTED, THAN THE COMMON WO--	ONE YEAR AGO--JOTS WHAT?	296	8
FURTHER [FARTHER] THAN THAT--	THE WIND DID'NT COME	316	2
AND GOLDEN HANG--WHILE FARTHER UP--	A SOLEMN THING WITHIN	483	3
THE SOUL CAN FARTHER FLY	WITH PINIONS OF DISDAIN	1431	2
FARTHEST			
WHOSE FARTHEST OF DEGREE,	DOUBT ME! MY DIM	275	14
GENEVA'S FARTHEST SKILL	A CLOCK STOPPED--	287	3
THE FARTHEST THUNDER THAT I HEARD	THE FARTHEST THUNDER	1581	1
FARTHINGS			
PEARLS ARE THE DIVER'S FARTHINGS	THE FEET OF PEOPLE	7	9
BITTER CONTESTED FARTHINGS--	FOR EACH EXTATIC INSTANT	125	7
SAY IF I ERRED? ACCUSE MY FARTHINGS--	SWEET--YOU FORGOT--BUT I	523	5
FASCINATED			
STILL FASCINATED TO PRESUME	I MEASURE EVERY GRIEF I	561	39
FASCINATES			
SO OVER HORROR, IT HALF CAPTIVATES [DUMB FASCINATES]--	'TIS SO APPALLING--IT	281	2
FASCINATING			
THE FASCINATING CHILL THAT MUSIC LEAVES [OF MUSIC]	THE FASCINATING CHILL	1480	1
FASHION			
OUR PORTION--IN THE FASHION--	DELIGHT IS AS THE FLIGHT	257	25
IN SOME ODD FASHION [PATTERN] OF IT'S OWN,	OF ALL THE SOUNDS	321	19
HER EVERLASTING FASHION--SET--	IT WILL BE SUMMER--	342	15
WOULD PIERCE ME WITH A FASHION	I DREADED THAT FIRST	348	11
FASHION MY SPIRIT QUAINT--WHITE--	I AM ASHAMED--I HIDE--	473	20
THE FASHION OF THE EAR	TO HEAR AN ORIOLE SING	526	7
SHE DEALT A [THE] FASHION TO THE NUT--	MY FIRST WELL DAY--SINCE	574	17
THE FASHION OF THE GOWN I WEAR--	PRECIOUS TO ME--SHE	727	3
TILL IT AN ANTIQUE FASHION SHOWS--	WE OUTGROW LOVE, LIKE	887	3
DEPOSE HIM LIKE A FASHION	THE HARM OF YEARS IS ON	1280	3
FASHIONABLE			
TO SOME FASHIONABLE LADY	I CANT TELL YOU--BUT YOU	65	15
PURPLE--IS FASHIONABLE TWICE--	PURPLE--IS FASHIONABLE	980	1
FASHIONED SEE OLD-FASHIONED,NEW-FASHIONED			
LEST I SH'D BE OLD FASHIONED	THE MORNS ARE MEEKER	12	7
GOD'S OLD FASHIONED VOWS--	IT DID NOT SURPRISE ME--	39	8
WONT BE "NEW FASHIONED" WHEN I COME--	"ARCTURUS" IS HIS OTHER	70	28
OLD FASHIONED--NAUGHTY--EVERYTHING--	"ARCTURUS" IS HIS OTHER	70	32
DEAR, OLD FASHIONED, LITTLE FLOWER!	I'M THE LITTLE "HEART'S	176	9
EDEN IS OLD FASHIONED, TOO!	I'M THE LITTLE "HEART'S	176	10
OLD FASHIONED EYES--	I KNOW SOME LONELY	289	11
LIKE SOME OLD FASHIONED MIRACLE	LIKE SOME OLD FASHIONED	302	1
I READ IN AN OLD FASHIONED BOOK	I KNOW WHERE WELLS GROW	460	13

	FIRST LINE	POEM	LINE
FASHIONED (CONTINUED)			
IS FASHIONED FOR [FITTED TO] HIS HAND--	'TIS ONE BY ONE--THE	545	16
WITH THESE OLD FASHIONED EYES--	JOY TO HAVE MERITED THE	788	6
AN ANCIENT FASHIONED HEART--	'TWAS AWKWARD, BUT IT	973	2
FASHIONED BY THY CANDID HAND	"HEAVENLY FATHER"--TAKE	1461	3
FASHIONING			
FASHIONING WHAT SHE IS,	TO THE BRIGHT EAST SHE	1573	7
FASHIONLESS			
A FASHIONLESS DELIGHT--	IT'S LIKE THE LIGHT--	297	2
FASHIONS			
IN VANISHED FASHIONS SET!	IN EBON BOX, WHEN YEARS	169	16
HIS FASHIONS, QUAINT, MOSAIC--	THE ONLY GHOST I EVER	274	7
THESE ARE THE VISIONS FLITTED [FASHIONS--BAFFLED--] GUIDO--	HOW THE OLD MOUNTAINS	291	21
THEIR EVERLASTING FASHIONS--SET--	WHILE ASTERS--	331	3
AND NEWER FASHIONS BLOW--	THERE IS A FLOWER THAT	380	22
FAR FASHIONS--FAIR--	I AM ASHAMED--I HIDE--	473	15
AND FASHIONS--INTERVENE--	YOU KNOW THAT PORTRAIT	504	8
TO NOTE THE FASHIONS--OF THE CROSS--	I MEASURE EVERY GRIEF I	561	37
THIS WORLD, AND IT'S SPECIES [NATIONS / FASHIONS / SYMBOLS / . . .	THIS DUST, AND IT'S	936	9
FAST			
THE ANCHORS FAST--	ON THIS WONDROUS SEA	4	9
FAST IN A SAFER HAND	I HAVE A BIRD IN SPRING	5	13
NOT SO FAST!	"SOWN IN DISHONOR"!	62	7
FINAL FAST--ABOVE--	BY A FLOWER--BY A LETTER	109	4
BEING FAST ASLEEP,	IF I SHOULD'NT BE ALIVE	182	6
OR MAKE HIM FAST	IS'IT TRUE, DEAR SUE?	218	9
HELD FAST IN EVERLASTING RACE--	TIE THE STRINGS TO MY	279	11
THE HOURS SLID FAST--AS HOURS WILL,	THERE CAME A DAY AT	322	17
THEN--STEPPED MORE FAST--	'TWAS THE OLD--ROAD--	344	7
TO FEEL IF BLINDS BE FAST--	THE NIGHT WAS WIDE, AND	589	13
THE WIND--UNROLLED IT FAST--	OF BRUSSELS--IT WAS NOT	602	13
FASTEN			
ON MOSES--SEEMED TO FASTEN	IT ALWAYS FELT TO ME--A	597	13
. . . IT / SANCTION IT / FASTEN IT] YOURSELF.	SUMMER LAID HER SIMPLE	1363	4
FASTENED			
AND FASTENED IT IN DAWN.	IT WAS A QUIET WAY--	1053	20
HARDENED [FASTENED] WITH I KNOW--	WHETHER THEY HAVE	1329	8
UPON IT'S FASTENED LIPS LAY WORDS--	OH GIVE IT MOTION--DECK	1527	3
THAT FASTENED IT SO LONG	AS FROM THE EARTH THE	1630	6
FASTENINGS			
CHOOSES IT'S LATCH, FROM ALL THE OTHER FASTENINGS--	IT'S COMING--THE	390	3
FASTER			
IF I WELD THE RIVET FASTER--	BY A FLOWER--BY A LETTER	109	3
NO FASTER THAN A MILE AT ONCE	NO MAN CAN COMPASS A	477	3
FASTIDIOUS			
WITH HER FASTIDIOUS FOREHEAD?	AFRAID! OF WHOM AM I	608	11
FASTNESS			
BLUSH, MY SPIRIT, IN THY FASTNESS--	REARRANGE A "WIFE'S"	1737	5
FASTS			
BY BUT A CRUMB OF BLOOD, FASTS SCARLET	AS THE STARVED MAELSTROM	872	5
FAT			
THE MIND IS FAT.	THE MIND LIVES ON THE	1355	4
'TIS STARVING MAKES IT FAT--	MINE ENEMY IS GROWING	1509	8
THOUGH FIRST UPON A BERRY FAT	CONFERRING WITH MYSELF	1655	3
FATAL			
WHO WILL NOT SERVE THE SOVREIGN, BE HANGED ON FATAL TREE.	AWAKE YE MUSES NINE,	1	10
MORTALITY IS FATAL--	"SIC TRANSIT GLORIA	3	41
ARE SO FOR THAT MOST FATAL [MIGHTY] CAUSE	DECLAIMING WATERS NONE	1595	3
AND SCANS WITH [WITH WHAT A] FATAL PROMPTNESS	THE SUMMER THAT WE DID	1773	6
FATALLER			
OR ODIOUSER [FATALLER / OTHERWISE] OFFEND--	THOSE CATTLE SMALLER	1388	12
FATE			
FOREVER OF HIS FATE TO TASTE--	FOREVER AT HIS SIDE TO	246	6
WHOSE FATE--CONJECTURE KNEW--	A HOUSE UPON THE HIGHT--	399	9
I'M SO ACCUSTOMED TO MY FATE--	IT MIGHT BE LONELIER	405	3
IT'S LITTLE FATE TO STIPULATE--	THE MANNER OF IT'S DEATH	468	7
TO SUCH A FATE--TO MINISTER.	SHE'S HAPPY, WITH A NEW	535	8
THEIR MORTAL FATE--ENCOURAGE SOME--	THE MARTYR POETS--DID	544	4
YOU TAUGHT ME FORTITUDE OF FATE--	YOU TAUGHT ME WAITING	740	3
YET BLAMED THE FATE THAT FRACTURED--[FLUNG IT] LESS	IT DROPPED SO LOW--IN MY	747	5
NO MAN [FATE] DEPOSE	WHO COURT OBTAIN WITHIN	803	5
WHOM FATE [TRAIT] ORDAIN--	WHO COURT OBTAIN WITHIN	803	6
THE SHORTER FATE--IS OFTENER THE CHIEFEST	UNCERTAIN LEASE--	857	5
DROPPED--MY FATE--A TIMID PEBBLE--	ALL FORGOT FOR	966	13
WHEN FATE HATH TAUNTED LAST	THIS MERIT HATH THE	979	3
MATURITY OF FATE	NOT ALL DIE EARLY, DYING	990	2
FATE SLEW HIM, BUT HE DID NOT DROP--	FATE SLEW HIM, BUT HE	1031	1
SUPERIORITY TO FATE	SUPERIORITY TO FATE	1081	1
ACRID WHATEVER FATE.	FRIGID AND SWEET HER	1318	4
FATE HAS BOTH TO SELL--	FLOSS WONT SAVE YOU FROM	1322	V 8
OF FATE IF THIS IS ALL	HOW SOFT THIS PRISON IS	1334	5
TO DIE--WAS LITTLE FATE--	TO HIS SIMPLICITY	1352	2
WHEN FATE INCORPORATED US--	ESTRANGED FROM BEAUTY--	1474	V 4
FATE--FOLLOWING--BEHIND US BOLTS IT--	WE NEVER KNOW WE GO WHEN	1523	3

	FIRST LINE	POEM	LINE
FATE'S			
FATE'S--TELEGRAM--TO HIM--	THE FUTURE--NEVER SPOKE	672	12
FATHER			
AND THE FATHER FOND DEMANDETH THE MAIDEN FOR HIS SON.	AWAKE YE MUSES NINE,	1	16
BURGLAR! BANKER--FATHER!	I NEVER LOST AS MUCH BUT	49	7
I HOPE THE FATHER IN THE SKIES	"ARCTURUS" IS HIS OTHER	70	30
"FATHER, THY WILL BE DONE" TODAY	I HAVE A KING, WHO DOES	103	16
FATHER! THEY WONT TELL ME,	GOOD NIGHT, BECAUSE WE	114	7
"MANY MANSIONS", BY "HIS FATHER",	"HOUSES"--SO THE WISE	127	5
SPARROWS, UNNOTICED BY THE FATHER--	SOME, TOO FRAGILE FOR	141	11
NOBODY KNEW "HIS FATHER"--	DUST IS THE ONLY SECRET	153	5
SO KEEP YOUR SECRET--FATHER!	THE SKIES CANT KEEP	191	13
AS "A FATHER"--IN THE SKY--	WHAT IS--"PARADISE"--	215	12
FATHER--I BRING THEE--NOT MYSELF--	SAVIOR! I'VE NO ONE ELSE	217 V	5
KNOW GOD THE FATHER--AND THE SON.	YOU'LL KNOW IT--AS YOU	420	6
'TIS ONE BY ONE--THE FATHER COUNTS--	'TIS ONE BY ONE--THE	545	1
A HEAVENLY FATHER WOULD SUFFICE [CONTENT]	YOU LEFT ME--SIRE--TWO	644	3
OF HER FATHER--WHOSO ASK [CLAIM] HER--	HER SWEET TURN TO LEAVE	649	17
I'VE HEARD MY FATHER TELL--	THE JUDGE IS LIKE THE	699	2
OR FATHER--ON THE SEA--	HE TOLD A HOMELY TALE	763	10
OR FATHER IN THE FIRMAMENT--	HE TOLD A HOMELY TALE	763	11
BRIDE OF THE FATHER AND THE SON	GIVEN IN MARRIAGE UNTO	817	3
FAR FROM LOVE THE HEAVENLY FATHER	FAR FROM LOVE THE	1021	1
AWFUL FATHER [FOUNDER] OF LOVE--	WHATEVER IT IS--SHE HAS	1204	2
WHO WERE "THE FATHER AND THE SON"	WHO WERE "THE FATHER AND	1258	1
WHO ARE "THE FATHER AND THE SON"	WHO WERE "THE FATHER AND	1258	9
"THE FATHER AND THE SON" HIMSELF	WHO WERE "THE FATHER AND	1258	11
THE FATHER OF THE MINE	LUCK IS NOT CHANCE--	1350	5
"HEAVENLY FATHER"--TAKE TO THEE	"HEAVENLY FATHER"--TAKE	1461	1
FATHER I OBSERVED TO HEAVEN	LIGHTLY STEPPED A YELLOW	1672	7
HE WAS THE FAITHFUL FATHER	HIGH FROM THE EARTH I	1723	15
JUPITER! MY FATHER!	"LETHE" IN MY FLOWER,	1730	7
WHILE HER FATHER ABUTS THE TEMPEST	THE PARASOL IS THE	1747	3
BUT HER FATHER IS BORNE AND HONORED,	THE PARASOL IS THE	1747	7
FATHER'D			
IF FATHER'D MULTIPLY THE PLATES--	'TWAS JUST THIS TIME,	445	15
FATHER'S			
FROM OFF MY FATHER'S TREE!	"SIC TRANSIT GLORIA	3	20
NOT FATHER'S BELLS--NOR FACTORIES,	WHERE BELLS NO MORE	112	11
CROWNED--CROWING [WHIMPERING / DANGLING]--ON MY FATHER'S BREAST--	I'M CEDED--I'VE STOPPED	508	15
THE PORTER OF MY FATHER'S LODGE	AFRAID! OF WHOM AM I	608	3
BUT OVERLOOKED MY FATHER'S HOUSE--	THE WIND BEGUN TO KNEAD	824	19
FATHERS			
OUR FATHERS BEING WEARY,	"SIC TRANSIT GLORIA	3	45
FATHOM			
OF RIVER OR OF RIDGE [OF FATHOM OR OF LEAGUE] BEYOND	HOW FAR IS IT TO HEAVEN?	929	3
OF HER EFFACING FATHOM	THE TREASON OF AN ACCENT	1358	3
HIMSELF--AT WHATSOEVER FATHOM	THE THINGS THAT NEVER	1515	12
FATHOMED			
HE FATHOMED ME--	IN WINTER IN MY ROOM	1670	27
FATHOMING			
FATHOMING WHAT SHE WAS,	TO THE BRIGHT EAST SHE	1573	8
FATHOMS			
IT'S MADE OF FATHOMS--AND A BELT--	I KNOW WHERE WELLS GROW	460	5
IN EDDIES OF [FATHOMS IN / RAPIDS OF / GAMBOLS WITH / . . .	TWO BUTTERFLIES WENT OUT	533 V	
THE FATHOMS THEY ABIDE--	SHE ROSE TO HIS	732	12
WHOSE NAMELESS FATHOMS SLINK AWAY	CONTAINED IN THIS SHORT	1165	7
LOOK TO IT BY IT'S FATHOMS [CONTENTS]	REMEMBRANCE HAS A	1182	7
HE FATHOMS WHO OBTAINS.	I CANNOT WANT IT MORE--	1301	8
IT WAS A PIT--WITH FATHOMS UNDER IT	A PIT--BUT HEAVEN OVER	1712	14
FATIGUE			
BUT THAT THYSELF FATIGUE OF US--	WE COVER THEE--SWEET	482	3
THROUGH DECAY [FATIGUE / THE LAPSE] OF YOU--	SWEET--YOU FORGOT--BUT I	523	4
TO HARASS TO FATIGUE	SEVERER SERVICE OF	786	10
WHAT WINE IN THE FATIGUE!	"RED SEA," INDEED! TALK	1642	12
FATIGUED			
FATIGUED AT LAST, A CLOVER PLAIN [LOW]	HIS ORIENTAL HERESIES	1526	5
FATUITY			
BE THIS FATUITY [BIOGRAPHY]	TWO BUTTERFLIES WENT OUT	533 V	
FATUUS			
BETTER AN IGNIS FATUUS	THOSE--DYING THEN,	1551	8
FAULT			
THE FAULT--WAS DOUBTLESS ISRAEL'S--	IT ALWAYS FELT TO ME--A	597	17
CUP, IT WAS YOUR FAULT,	HAD I KNOWN THAT THE	1720	5
FAVOR			
A FAVOR SO REMOTE--	HAD I PRESUMED TO HOPE--	522	6
TO DEMAND, IN YOUR LOW FAVOR	PROMISE THIS--WHEN YOU	648	21
HER FAVOR--IS THE BEST DISDAIN	MY SOUL--ACCUSED ME--AND	753	5
OF GOD WE ASK ONE FAVOR,	OF GOD WE ASK ONE FAVOR,	1601	1
FAVORABLY			
THOUGH FAVORABLY MENTIONED	THE BUTTERFLY OBTAINS	1685	3
FAVORITE			
HIS FAVORITE REFRAIN.	THE JUDGE IS LIKE THE	699	12
THE FAVORITE OF DOOM.	THIS CHASM, SWEET, UPON	858	8
FAVORITES			
TO FAVORITES--A FEW--	THE SOUL'S SUPERIOR	306	14

	FIRST LINE	POEM	LINE
FEALTY			
TO ALL BUT FEALTY--	BECAUSE THAT YOU ARE	1260	V 8
FEAR			
EACH LITTLE DOUBT AND FEAR,	I HAVE A BIRD IN SPRING	5	22
I SHALL NOT FEAR THE SNOW.	DISTRUSTFUL OF THE	20	8
A DARTING FEAR--A POMP--A TEAR--	A DARTING FEAR--A POMP--	87	1
I SHOULD NOT FEAR THE FOE THEN--	BLESS GOD, HE WENT AS	147	7
I SHOULD NOT FEAR THE FIGHT!	BLESS GOD, HE WENT AS	147	8
I SHALL NOT FEAR MISTAKE--	YOU LOVE ME--YOU ARE	156	2
NO FEAR OF FROST TO COME	FOR THIS--ACCEPTED	195	10
FOR FEAR OF JOGGLING HIM!	IS IT TRUE, DEAR SUE?	218	4
TOO SMALL--TO FEAR--	A MIEN TO MOVE A QUEEN--	283	22
IF HE FEAR TO SWERVE--	IF YOUR NERVE, DENY YOU	292	4
AND FEAR--IS LIKE THE ONE	THE DIFFERENCE BETWEEN	305	2
TOO RESCUED--FEAR TOO DIM TO ME	I SHOULD HAVE BEEN TOO	313	8
WITHOUT THE FEAR--TO JUSTIFY--	I SHOULD HAVE BEEN TOO	313	16
FOR FEAR I SPOIL MY SHOE?	IS BLISS THEN, SUCH	340	3
FOR FEAR THEIR YELLOW GOWN	I DREADED THAT FIRST	348	10
HER FAITH--NO FEAR--	THROUGH THE DARK SOD--AS	392	4
BUT GRAVITY--AND EXPECTATION--AND FEAR--	UNIT, LIKE DEATH, FOR	408	15
NO FEAR YOU'LL MISS THE ROAD.	A MURMUR IN THE TREES--	416	20
FOR FEAR IT BE DISPELLED--	A CHARM INVESTS A FACE	421	4
FOR FEAR IT WOULD BE GONE--	IT WAS GIVEN TO ME BY	454	8
BUT--THE INSTEAD--THE PINCHING FEAR	WHY MAKE IT DOUBT--IT	462	8
FOR FEAR THE NUMBERS FUSE--	IF YOU WERE COMING IN	511	8
I FEAR A MAN OF FRUGAL [SCANTY] SPEECH--	I FEAR A MAN OF FRUGAL	543	1
I FEAR A SILENT MAN--	I FEAR A MAN OF FRUGAL	543	2
I FEAR THAT HE IS GRAND--	I FEAR A MAN OF FRUGAL	543	8
FOR FEAR I HEAR HER SAY	I CRIED AT PITY--NOT AT	588	20
BLEW OUT ITSELF--FOR FEAR--	THE NIGHT WAS WIDE, AND	589	4
OF LIFE? 'TWERE ODD I FEAR A THING	AFRAID! OF WHOM AM I	608	5
THAT I COULD FEAR A DOOR	I YEARS HAD BEEN FROM	609	14
FOR FEAR THE SQUIRRELS--KNOW.	THE TINT I CANNOT TAKE--	627	20
HE FAILS TO FEAR--	ONE NEED NOT BE A	670	V 20
NO TREASON IT CAN FEAR--	THE SOUL UNTO ITSELF	683	6
WE ALMOST CEASE TO FEAR--	THE HEAVEN VESTS FOR	694	14
TOO NEAR TO HEAVEN--TO FEAR--	THE DAY UNDRESSED--	716	10
HIS MERIT--ALL MY FEAR--	MY WORTHINESS IS ALL MY	751	2
A FEAR WILL URGE IT WHERE	I LIVED ON DREAD--	770	7
I FEAR ME THIS--IS LONELINESS--	THE LONELINESS ONE DARE	777	13
I FEAR ME THIS CIRCUMFERENCE	TIME FEELS SO VAST THAT	802	3
OR I SHOULD FEAR TO PAUSE	WHO OCCUPIES THIS HOUSE?	892	6
I ALWAYS HAD A FEAR	WHEN THEY COME BACK--IF	1080	6
AND CANNOT, BUT ARE MAD WITH [FOR] FEAR	A DIAMOND ON THE HAND	1108	7
LEST THEY SHOULD COME--IS ALL MY FEAR	LEST THEY SHOULD COME--	1169	1
FOR FEAR TO BE A KING--	WE NEVER KNOW HOW HIGH	1176	8
THAT THIS WAS DUE WHERE MOST [SOME] WE FEAR	"REMEMBER ME" IMPLORED	1180	11
UNKNOWN THE WORST WE FEAR--	THE FROST WAS NEVER SEEN	1202	14
BUT CAME WITH LESS OF FEAR	WHILE WE WERE FEARING IT	1277	2
AND FRAUD AND FEAR.	A RAT SURRENDERED HERE	1340	3
HOW SHORT WE HAVE TO FEAR	PERHAPS THEY DO NOT GO	1399	6
AND OF FEAR NO EVIDENCE GIVES HE	WHAT MYSTERY PERVADES A	1400	V 16
OF TRANSPORT THRILLED WITH FEAR--	SWEET SKEPTICISM OF THE	1413	8
SERAPHIC FEAR--	NOT SEEING, STILL WE	1518	6
IN FEAR THOU COMEST	IN SNOW THOU COMEST	1669	5
HAST THOU DELIGHT OR FEAR	THE LOOK OF THEE, WHAT	1689	6
FEARED			
I--FEARED THE SEA--TOO MUCH	THE MALAY--TOOK THE	452	3
WHEN I FEARED--I RECOLLECT	WHEN I HOPED, I	768	9
WHEN I HOPED I FEARED--	WHEN I HOPED I FEARED--	1181	1
I SUED THE NEWS--YET FEARED--THE NEWS	I SUED THE NEWS--YET	1360	1
THE DEATH I NEVER FEARED	SO GIVE ME BACK TO DEATH	1632	2
FEARING			
WE'RE FEARING THAT THEIR HEARTS WILL DROP--	WE DO NOT PLAY ON GRAVES	467	7
AND MY FIRST FEARING, LEST UNKNOWNS	LET MY FIRST KNOWING BE	1218	3
WHILE WE WERE [I WAS] FEARING IT, IT CAME--	WHILE WE WERE FEARING IT	1277	1
BECAUSE THAT FEARING IT SO LONG	WHILE WE WERE FEARING IT	1277	3
HE [AND] BROKE THEM, FEARING PUNISHMENT	CLIMBING TO REACH THE	1566	3
FEARLESS			
FEARLESS--THE COBWEB SWINGS FROM THE CEILING--	HOW MANY TIMES THESE LOW	187	11
THEY BEAR THEIR DAUNTLESS [FEARLESS / TRANQUIL] HEADS,	WHEN WE STAND ON THE	242	10
AS CONTENTED [FEARLESS] IN THE PORCH OF DEATH	THIS DOCILE ONE INTER	1752	V 7
FEARS			
A SEPULCHRE, FEARS FROST, NO MORE--	'TIS SO APPALLING--IT	281	V 4
AND SHOW ME TO MY FEARS--	IF HE WERE LIVING--DARE	734	8
AND EXIGENCIES NEVER FEARS--	HOW HAPPY IS THE LITTLE	1510	4
THAT DARES [FEARS] TO COVET THEE	CIRCUMFERENCE THOU BRIDE	1620	4
FEAST			
AS BEGGARS REVEL AT A FEAST	AS WATCHERS HANG UPON	121	2
WHO GOES TO DINE MUST TAKE HIS FEAST	WHO GOES TO DINE MUST	1223	1
BY DATING IT A SUDDEN FEAST.	I CANNOT SEE MY SOUL BUT	1262	10
FEAT			
PROVE THE FEAT--THAT MADE THE PELLET MINE--	GOD GAVE A LOAF TO EVERY	791	6
IS SUCH A FEAT [STROKE / HIGHT / PASS] OF IRONY	THAT THIS SHOULD FEEL	1112	3
TO JOINT THIS AGATE WERE A WORK [FEAT]--	TOO COLD IS THIS	1135	4
THAT VANQUISHED HER--DEFEATED FEAT--	THE PRETTY RAIN FROM	1426	7
FEATHER			
FEATHER BY FEATHER--ON THE PLAIN	SOME RAINBOW--COMING	64	5

	FIRST LINE	POEM	LINE
FEATHER (CONTINUED)			
FEATHER BY FEATHER--ON THE PLAIN	SOME RAINBOW--COMING	64	5
THE ORCHIS BINDS HER FEATHER ON	SOME RAINBOW--COMING	64	16
A FEATHER FROM THE WHIPPOWIL	A FEATHER FROM THE	161	1
A FEATHER ON EACH SHOULDER!	A FUZZY FELLOW, WITHOUT	173	15
I'LL SEND THE FEATHER FROM MY HAT!	I'LL SEND THE FEATHER	687	1
THAN ANY FEATHER SPECIFIED [RATIFIED / CERTIFIED]	WITH PINIONS OF DISDAIN	1431	3
'TIS ANGUISH NOT A FEATHER HATH	TOO HAPPY TIME DISSOLVES	1774	3
FEATHERS			
HAS IT FEATHERS LIKE A BIRD?	WILL THERE REALLY BE A	101	6
"HOPE" IS THE THING WITH FEATHERS--	"HOPE" IS THE THING WITH	254	1
AND HE UNROLLED HIS FEATHERS	A BIRD CAME DOWN THE	328	15
PERSUADE OUR FEATHERS HOME	'TIS NOT THAT DYING	335	12
SHE STAKED HER FEATHERS--GAINED AN ARC--	SHE STAKED HER FEATHERS	798	1
HIS FEATHERS WILTED LOW--	HIS BILL IS CLASPED--HIS	1102	2
LIFT IT--WITH THE FEATHERS	LIFT IT--WITH THE	1348	1
HOW LATE THEIR FEATHERS BE!	HOW SLOW THE WIND--	1571	3
OR HAS IT [SHE] FEATHERS, LIKE A BIRD,	NOT KNOWING WHEN THE	1619	3
FEATS			
MEN, AND FEATS--	I'VE KNOWN A HEAVEN,	243	12
HIS ORDINARY ACTS ARE FEATS	BEST WITCHCRAFT IS	1158	3
IN FEATS INSCRUTABLE--	ELIJAH'S WAGON KNEW NO	1254	8
FEATURE			
WITH A DEPARTING--SAPPHIRE--FEATURE--	HOW THE OLD MOUNTAINS	291	11
JUST [STILL] TO FOLLOW YOUR DEAR FEATURE--	PROMISE THIS--WHEN YOU	648	29
INDICATING, BY NO MUSCLE [FEATURE]--	BLOOM UPON THE MOUNTAIN	667	19
THIS DUST, AND IT'S FEATURE--	THIS DUST, AND IT'S	936	1
OF DEATH THE STERNEST [SHARPEST] FUNCTION [FEATURE]	TO DISAPPEAR ENHANCES--	1209	13
ABLE AS THE DUST TO EQUIP IT'S FEATURE	SOME WE SEE NO MORE,	1221	8
IN FEATURE AS THE WORM BEFORE	IN WINTER IN MY ROOM	1670	16
FEATURES			
A THROE UPON THE FEATURES--	A THROE UPON THE	71	1
FEATURES KEEP THEIR PLACE--	I HAVE NEVER SEEN	175	12
I JUDGED MY FEATURES--JARRED MY HAIR--	I FELT MY LIFE WITH BOTH	351	9
ON ATOMS--FEATURES PLACE--	NO CROWD THAT HAS	515	9
AND WHEN THE SOLEMN FEATURES	AN IGNORANCE A SUNSET	552	9
WHOSE FEATURES--DAY AND NIGHT--	A PRISON GETS TO BE A	652	22
THE FEATURES ARE THE SAME--	JOY TO HAVE MERITED THE	788	12
LONG STEPS ACROSS THE FEATURES TOOK	TWO TRAVELLERS PERISHING	933	9
THE FEATURES SO BELOVED--	WHAT I SEE NOT, I BETTER	939	8
FROM FEATURES OTHERS WEAR.	BECAUSE HE LOVES HER	1229	4
FEBUARY			
SOME FEBUARY DAY,	ALTHOUGH I PUT AWAY HIS	366	27
FEBUARY HOUR--	WHITE AS AN INDIAN PIPE	1250	4
A FEBUARY [JANUARY] DAY,	NO BRIGADIER THROUGHOUT	1561	6
FEBUARY'S			
THAT IT WAS FEBUARY'S FOOT [FACE / SELF]	THE SNOW THAT NEVER	1133	7
FED			
A FULL FED ROSE ON MEALS OF TINT	A FULL FED ROSE ON MEALS	1154	1
LIKE ONE THAT FED ON AWE.	HER SPIRIT ROSE TO SUCH	1486	3
ANGER AS SOON AS FED IS DEAD--	MINE ENEMY IS GROWING	1509	7
THE COWS THAT FED AND THANKED	A FADED BOY--IN SALLOW	1524	6
FEDERATES			
WHILE SHE CREATES AND FEDERATES	THE VEINS OF OTHER	811	7
FEE			
IT'S FEE--TO BE OF GOLD--	A TONGUE--TO TELL HIM I	400	2
IS FAME'S CONSUMMATE FEE--	TO EARN IT BY DISDAINING	1427	2
FEEBLE			
AND MOUNTAINS--FEEBLE--LEAN--	THE TRUTH--IS STIRLESS--	780	6
FEEBLEST			
THE FEEBLEST [DULLEST]--OR THE WAYWARDEST--	NATURE--THE GENTLEST	790	3
FEEBLY			
FELT FEEBLY--FOR HER CROWN--	THE SUN--JUST TOUCHED	232	14
FEED			
LOOK--FEED UPON EACH OTHER'S FACES--SO--	ONE YEAR AGO--JOTS WHAT?	296	9
AND STOP TO FEED ITSELF AT TANKS--	I LIKE TO SEE IT LAP	585	3
TO FEED UPON THE RETROGRADE--	HAD I NOT THIS, OR THIS,	904	15
GO SLOW, MY SOUL, TO FEED THYSELF	GO SLOW, MY SOUL, TO	1297	1
FEEDING			
OF OPAL CATTLE--FEEDING FAR	THEY CALLED ME TO THE	628	5
FEEDS			
THE LADY FEEDS HER LITTLE BIRD	THE LADY FEEDS HER	941	1
HE FEEDS UPON THE FAIR--	HOPE IS A SUBTLE GLUTTON	1547	2
THAT FEEDS THE SACRED [CENTRAL] LIGHT.	HER FACE WAS IN A BED OF	1722	4
FEEL			
I SHALL NOT FEEL THE SLEET--THEN--	DISTRUSTFUL OF THE	20	7
I CANT TELL YOU--BUT YOU FEEL IT--	I CANT TELL YOU--BUT YOU	65	1
THEREFORE, AS ONE RETURNED, I FEEL,	JUST LOST, WHEN I WAS	160	7
AND WOULD IT FEEL AS BIG--	A SOLEMN THING--IT WAS--	271	10
BUT TELL HIM THAT IT CEASED TO FEEL--	THERE IS A LANGUOR OF	396	11
AND THIS ONE--DO NOT FEEL THE SAME--	THE FIRST DAY'S NIGHT	410	19
I SHALL NOT FEEL AT HOME--I KNOW--	I NEVER FELT AT HOME--	413	3
TO FEEL ITSELF GET RIPE--	A SOLEMN THING WITHIN	483	2
A WONDERFUL--TO FEEL THE SUN	A SOLEMN THING WITHIN	483	7
AND WONDER HOW THE FINGERS FEEL	I WOULD NOT PAINT--A	505	5
YOU ALMOST FEEL THE DATE--	IF ANYBODY'S FRIEND BE	509	10
DONT FEEL A LONESOME WAY--	I'M SORRY FOR THE DEAD--	529	18
HOW PRAYER WOULD FEEL [SOUND]--TO ME--	I PRAYED, AT FIRST, A	576	4

	FIRST LINE	POEM	LINE
FEEL (CONTINUED)			
I COULD NOT SEE [FEEL] THE TROUBLE [ANGUISH] GO--	IT CEASED TO HURT ME,	584	2
TO FEEL IF BLINDS BE FAST--	THE NIGHT WAS WIDE, AND	589	13
YOU CANNOT FEEL THE SEAM--	YOU'LL KNOW HER--BY HER	634	18
BEREAVEMENT IN THEIR DEATH TO FEEL	BEREAVEMENT IN THEIR	645	1
I FEEL THE OLD DEGREE--	AGAIN--HIS VOICE IS AT	663	2
I WONDER HOW THE RICH--MAY FEEL--	GOD GAVE A LOAF TO EVERY	791	13
YOU, UNSUSPECTING, FEEL FOR ME [WEAR ME TOO]--	I HIDE MYSELF WITHIN MY	903	3
BUT COULD NOT MAKE IT FEEL [TELL].	'TWAS CRISIS--ALL THE	948	12
I FEEL FOR THEM A TRANSPORT	A NARROW FELLOW IN THE	986	19
OLDER FEEL THAN THE HOPE THAT PROMPTED--	UP LIFE'S HILL WITH MY	1010	5
I FEEL THE OLD DESIRE--	I CANNOT MEET THE SPRING	1051	2
I ALWAYS FEEL A DOUBT	WHEN THEY COME BACK--IF	1080	2
THAT THIS SHOULD FEEL THE NEED OF DEATH	THAT THIS SHOULD FEEL	1112	1
I FEEL [FELT] AS IF THE GRASS WAS PLEASED	THE MUSHROOM IS THE ELF	1298	13
HOW NEWS MUST FEEL WHEN TRAVELLING	HOW NEWS MUST FEEL WHEN	1319	1
WE FEEL A JOY--	IN MANY AND REPORTLESS	1382	2
AND AWE--WAS ALL WE COULD FEEL.	IT SOUNDED AS IF THE	1397	4
WE FEEL IT BY THE FLUCTUATION	MARCH IS THE MONTH OF	1404 V	3
HOW LONESOME THE WIND MUST FEEL NIGHTS--	HOW LONESOME THE WIND	1418	1
HOW POMPOUS THE WIND MUST FEEL NOONS	HOW LONESOME THE WIND	1418	5
HOW MIGHTY THE WIND MUST FEEL MORNS	HOW LONESOME THE WIND	1418	9
TO SEEM [FEEL] LIKE PERFIDY--	AS IMPERCEPTIBLY AS	1540	4
WILL FEEL AS COOL AS LAND	I DID NOT REACH THEE	1664	11
WOULD FEEL AS THOROUGHLY AT EASE	A FACE DEVOID OF LOVE OR	1711	4
PROUD OF THE PAIN I DID NOT FEEL TILL THEE,	PROUD OF MY BROKEN HEART	1736	2
BUT THOSE THE SILENT FEEL	THE WORDS THE HAPPY SAY	1750	3
FEELING			
FEELING AS IF THEIR PILLOW HEARD,	WHERE I HAVE LOST, I	104	7
AFTER GREAT PAIN, A FORMAL FEELING COMES--	AFTER GREAT PAIN, A	341	1
TO HAVE THE JOY OF FEELING IT--AGAIN--	I'LL CLUTCH--AND CLUTCH	427	14
AND COULD [DID] NOT KNOW THE FEELING 'TWAS--	'TIS TRUE--THEY SHUT ME	538	3
THERE IS A FINISHED FEELING	THERE IS A FINISHED	856	1
I'M FEELING FOR THE AIR--	MY COCOON TIGHTENS--	1099	2
TO HOLD THE FEELING DOWN	THE PRETTY RAIN FROM	1426	6
BY FEELING IT IS GONE--	A WINGED SPARK DOTH SOAR	1468	8
FEELS			
I THINK THAT EARTH FEELS SO	I'M "WIFE"--I'VE	199	7
HOW NUMB [COOL], THE BELLOWS FEELS!	I BREATHED ENOUGH TO	272	8
FEELS HER WHITE FOOT--NO TREPIDATION--	THROUGH THE DARK SOD--AS	392	3
IT FEELS A SHAME TO BE ALIVE--	IT FEELS A SHAME TO BE	444	1
SHE FEELS SOME GHASTLY FRIGHT COME UP	THE SOUL HAS BANDAGED	512	3
THAT FEELS TO HER--LIKE SACRAMENT--	SHE'S HAPPY, WITH A NEW	535	2
A BEST DISGRACE--A BRAVE MAN FEELS--	THERE IS A SHAME OF	551	5
IT FEELS SO OLD A PAIN--	I MEASURE EVERY GRIEF I	561	8
FEELS SHORTER THAN THE DAY	BECAUSE I COULD NOT STOP	712	22
THE WORLD--FEELS DUSTY	THE WORLD--FEELS DUSTY	715	1
AFFLICTION FEELS IMPALPABLE	DESPAIR'S ADVANTAGE IS	799	11
TIME FEELS SO VAST THAT WERE IT NOT	TIME FEELS SO VAST THAT	802	1
BUT HUMAN NATURE FEELS.	A LIGHT EXISTS IN SPRING	812	8
FEELS EASY, AS WHEN DAY LETS GO	WHEN ONE HAS GIVEN UP	853	3
IT FEELS LIKE POVERTY	BECAUSE 'TWAS RICHES I	1093	4
FEELS TRANSITIVE AND COOL.	THAT ODD OLD MAN IS DEAD	1130	12
FEET			
THE FEET OF PEOPLE WALKING HOME	THE FEET OF PEOPLE	7	1
YET KNOW IT'S DRIPPING FEET	MY WHEEL IS IN THE DARK!	10	3
SOME WITH NEW--STATELY FEET--	MY WHEEL IS IN THE DARK!	10	12
HERE TO LIGHT MEASURE, MOVE THE FEET	THERE IS A MORN BY MEN	24	7
OUR FEET AWAIT!	IF PAIN FOR PEACE	63	3
SAVE BY FEET UNNUMBERED	GLOWING IS HER BONNET,	72	11
SET BLEEDING FEET TO MINUETS	HEART, NOT SO HEAVY AS	83	15
NEW FEET WITHIN MY GARDEN GO--	NEW FEET WITHIN MY	99	1
HAS IT FEET LIKE WATER LILIES?	WILL THERE REALLY BE A	101	5
SITS SHILY AT HIS FEET--	THE DAISY FOLLOWS SOFT	106	3
YOU HAVE PASSED ENFRANCHIZED FEET!	TALK WITH PRUDENCE TO A	119	6
MEEK AT WHOSE EVERLASTING FEET	IN LANDS I NEVER SAW--	124	5
RANK AFTER RANK, WITH EVEN FEET--	TO FIGHT ALOUD, IS VERY	126	11
BEFORE THEIR FEET ARE COLD.	SOME, TOO FRAGILE FOR	141	4
THESE FEET THAT NEVER FLAGGED--	THIS HEART THAT BROKE SO	145	2
AND TRUDGING FEET FROM SCHOOL--	ON SUCH A NIGHT, OR SUCH	146	20
STRANGE THAT THE FEET SO PRECIOUS CHARGED	ON SUCH A NIGHT, OR SUCH	146	23
HER TRUDGING FEET ESPIED--	SHE DIED--THIS WAS THE	150 V	6
THICKER AND THICKER STOOD THE FEET	THE SUN KEPT STOOPING--	152	7
I HEAR HER FEET UPON THE STAIR!	DYING! DYING IN THE	158	11
TO STAY THE HOMESICK--HOMESICK FEET	TO LEARN THE TRANSPORT	167	5
A FUZZY FELLOW, WITHOUT FEET,	A FUZZY FELLOW, WITHOUT	173	1
BETWEEN OUR FEET, AND DAY!	AT LAST, TO BE	174	7
HOW MANY TIMES THESE LOW FEET STAGGERED--	HOW MANY TIMES THESE LOW	187	1
THEN AT THE FEET OF THE OLD HORIZON	BLAZING IN GOLD AND	228	3
I'LL SEEK HIS ROYAL FEET--	THE COURT IS FAR AWAY--	235	5
BREAKS UP MY FEET--	I CAN WADE GRIEF--	252	5
FEET, SMALL AS MINE--HAVE MARCHED IN REVOLUTION	UNTO LIKE STORY--TROUBLE	295	17
THE FEET, MECHANICAL, GO ROUND--	AFTER GREAT PAIN, A	341	5
SLOW--SLOW--AS FEET DID WEARY--GROW--	'TWAS THE OLD--ROAD--	344	10
OH, GROPING FEET--	NOT PROBABLE--THE BAREST	346	9
AND WHERE HIS FEET HAVE RUN--	A VISITOR IN MARL--	391	10
A HUBBUB--AS OF FEET--	A MURMUR IN THE TREES--	416	6
THE FEET--I FORMER USED--	IT WOULD NEVER BE COMMON	430	14

	FIRST LINE	POEM	LINE
FEET (CONTINUED)			
OUR BASHFUL FEET--	ME--COME! MY DAZZLED	431	6
LOCKING BARE FEET OUT--	SWEET--SAFE--HOUSES--	457	5
WE STOOD UPON OUR STAPLED FEET--	THEY PUT US FAR APART--	474	15
URGING THE FEET--THAT WOULD--NOT--FLY--	BETTER--THAN MUSIC! FOR	503	12
MY FEET, TOO, THAT HAD WANDERED SO--	HE TOUCHED ME, SO I LIVE	506	10
SHE RUNS WITHOUT THE LOOK OF FEET--	SHE SIGHTS A BIRD--SHE	507	3
NOR FIRE--FOR JUST MY [TWO] MARBLE FEET	IT WAS NOT DEATH, FOR I	510	7
WITH SHACKLES [IRONS] ON THE PLUMED FEET,	THE SOUL HAS BANDAGED	512	21
THE RIVER REACHES TO MY FEET--	ME PROVE IT NOW--WHOEVER	537	5
I SHOUT UNTO MY FEET--	I CROSS TILL I AM WEARY	550	19
I COULD NOT PROVE THE YEARS HAD FEET--	I COULD NOT PROVE THE	563	1
I FIND MY FEET HAVE FURTHER GOALS--	I COULD NOT PROVE THE	563	5
A DOG'S BELATED FEET	THE NIGHT WAS WIDE, AND	589	10
FAR FEET OF FAILING MEN--	UNTO MY BOOKS--SO GOOD	604	10
OUR FEET WERE ALMOST COME	OUR JOURNEY HAD ADVANCED	615	2
OUR FEET--RELUCTANT--LED--	OUR JOURNEY HAD ADVANCED	615	6
ALARMS US--THO' HIS YELLOW FEET	THE LIGHTNING PLAYETH--	630	7
FITTER FEET--OF HER [FOR THE FEET] BEFORE US--	HER SWEET TURN TO LEAVE	649	13
FITTER FEET--OF HER [FOR THE FEET] BEFORE US--	HER SWEET TURN TO LEAVE	649	13
THAT ANSWER TO OUR FEET--	A PRISON GETS TO BE A	652	10
ACCOMPANY THEIR FEET--	OF BEING IS A BIRD	653	10
MY FEET KEPT DROWSING--DROWSING--STILL	THE SUN KEPT SETTING--	692	9
THEIR LIQUID FEET GO SOFTLY OUT	YOU'VE SEEN BALLOONS SET	700	5
AND SOMEWHAT IN THE TRUDGING FEET--	THE BEGGAR LAD--DIES	717	3
IF TRUDGING FEET MAY STAND--	THE BEGGAR LAD--DIES	717	10
I PUSHED MECHANIC FEET--	FROM BLANK TO BLANK--	761	3
AND IF HIS YELLOW FEET SHOULD MISS--	MY FAITH IS LARGER THAN	766	9
THEIR FEET--UPON TEMPTATION--	THROUGH THE STRAIT PASS	792	3
THE MORE THEIR FEET RETIRE.	AWAY FROM HOME ARE SOME	821	8
OUR UNDERMINING FEET TO MEET	ESCAPING BACKWARD TO	867	7
ABOUT MY FEET THE SEA.	I STEPPED FROM PLANK TO	875	4
IF WILDERNESS PREVENT HER FEET	FROM US SHE WANDERED NOW	890	3
TO OUR FAR, VASCILLATING FEET	FAITH--IS THE PIERLESS	915	11
HIS FEET ARE SHOD WITH GAUZE--	HIS FEET ARE SHOD WITH	916	1
MADONNA DIM, TO WHOM ALL FEET MAY COME,	ONLY A SHRINE, BUT MINE	918	3
AND THEN IT CLOSES AT YOUR FEET	A NARROW FELLOW IN THE	986	7
THEY LEAP UPON THEIR SILVER FEET	HOW STILL THE BELLS IN	1008	3
AS ACRES [COUNTIES] FROM THE FEET	IT WAS A QUIET WAY--	1053	10
TURNS UNPERCEIVED BENEATH OUR FEET	DEW--IS THE FRESHET IN	1097	3
TO WALK ON SEAS [TIDES] REQUIRES CEDAR FEET	THERE IS A STRENGTH IN	1113	6
ELATE THE ACRE AT HIS FEET--	MY GOD--HE SEES THEE--	1178	6
TOO DISTANT TO ARREST THE FEET	THIS IS THE PLACE THEY	1264	5
FRIGID AND FLEET MY FEET--	FRIGID AND SWEET HER	1318	2
HIS MITTENS AT HIS FEET	HIS MANSION IN THE POOL	1379	9
WHILE THEIR COMMUTED FEET	HOW MUCH THE PRESENT	1380	6
REAL MEMORY, LIKE CEDAR FEET	YOU CANNOT MAKE	1508	7
BUT MY FEET SLIP NEARER EVERY DAY	I DID NOT REACH THEE	1664	2
THE SEA COMES LAST--STEP MERRY FEET	I DID NOT REACH THEE	1664	14
I DARE NOT ASK MY FEET--	A PIT--BUT HEAVEN OVER	1712	11
FEIGN			
IMPOSSIBLE TO FEIGN	I LIKE A LOOK OF AGONY,	241	6
TURN ON ME--WHEN I FAIL--OR FEIGN,	SWEET MOUNTAINS--YE TELL	722	4
FELICITY			
THAT SEEKETH HIS FELICITY	THE FLOWER MUST NOT	206	2
BUT HAD THEY THE FELICITY [HAD THE READINESS]	WHO WERE "THE FATHER AND	1258	13
WHEN IN THY FELICITY,	RECOLLECT THE FACE OF ME	1305	2
WITH SHRILL FELICITY	NO BRIGADIER THROUGHOUT	1561	4
FELICITY OR DOOM--	ELYSIUM IS AS FAR AS TO	1760	4
FELL			
FELL FROM AN APPLE TREE!	"SIC TRANSIT GLORIA	3	32
BUT WHERE IT FELL	THERE IS A WORD	8	6
HER BODDICE ROSE AND FELL--	THE ROSE DID CAPER ON	208	2
HOW KINSMEN FELL--	UNTO LIKE STORY--TROUBLE	295	2
LIKE HAMMERS--DID THEY KNOW THEY FELL	THE MORNING AFTER WO--	364	11
WAS ALL THE ONE THAT FELL--	I TOOK MY POWER IN MY	540	6
CONCLUDING [DECIDING] HOW AN ATOM--FELL--	IT TROUBLED ME AS ONCE I	600	3
AND THE BIRD FELL--	LET US PLAY YESTERDAY--	728	16
A DROP FELL ON THE APPLE TREE--	A DROP FELL ON THE APPLE	794	1
A GREAT HOPE FELL	A GREAT HOPE FELL	1123	1
THE FORESTS GALLOPED TILL THEY FELL	THE CLOUDS THEIR BACKS	1172	3
AND ROSE AND FELL THE MAGIC PLANKS	A SOFT SEA WASHED AROUND	1198	3
THE ACT OF EVENING FELL	THE MOUNTAINS STOOD IN	1278	10
TILL IT FELL,	NOT WITH A CLUB, THE	1304	6
LAUREL--FELL YOUR [THY] FUTILE TREE--	LAY THIS LAUREL ON THE	1393	V
FELL, THEY WILL SAY, IN "SKIRMISH"!	I'VE GOT AN ARROW HERE.	1729	4
AS NATURE'S CURTAIN FELL	UPON THE GALLOWS HUNG A	1757	4
FELLED			
SHE FELLED--HE DID NOT FALL--	FATE SLEW HIM, BUT HE	1031	2
FELLED BY BUT ONE ASSASSIN--	COULD HOPE INSPECT HER	1283	7
NO ZEPHYR FELLED THIS CEDAR STRAIGHT--	TO BREAK SO VAST A HEART	1312	3
FELLOW SEE PLAYFELLOW			
GOOD EVENING, GENTLE FELLOW MEN!	IF THIS IS "FADING"	120	8
A FUZZY FELLOW, WITHOUT FEET,	A FUZZY FELLOW, WITHOUT	173	1
THE FELLOW CANNOT TOUCH THIS CROWN--	FOR THIS--ACCEPTED	195	3
HE'S A TRANSITIVE FELLOW--VERY--	THE WIND DID'NT COME	316	5
AND ATE THE FELLOW, RAW,	A BIRD CAME DOWN THE	328	4
THE SWARTHY FELLOW SWAM--	THE MALAY--TOOK THE	452	7
LOVE [FAITH] IS THE FELLOW OF THE RESURRECTION	WHILE IT IS ALIVE	491	9
NEVER A FELLOW MATCHED THIS TOPAZ--	I COULD BRING YOU JEWELS	697	9

	FIRST LINE	POEM	LINE
FELLOW (CONTINUED)			
WAS THE PINE AT MY WINDOW A "FELLOW	BY MY WINDOW HAVE I FOR	797	22
A NARROW FELLOW IN THE GRASS	A NARROW FELLOW IN THE	986	1
BUT NEVER MET THIS FELLOW	A NARROW FELLOW IN THE	986	21
A FELLOW IN THE SKIES	BEFORE YOU THOUGHT OF	1465	4
IMAGE [FELLOW] OF LIGHT, ADIEU--	IMAGE OF LIGHT, ADIEU--	1556	1
AND I AM RICHER THEN THAN ALL MY FELLOW MEN--	TAKE ALL AWAY FROM ME,	1640	2
A JOYOUS GOING FELLOW	HIGH FROM THE EARTH I	1723	9
THE FELLOW WILL GO WHERE HE BELONGED--	IF EVER THE LID GETS OFF	1727	3
FELLOWMEN			
FOR LITTLE FELLOWMEN--	THE SAVIOR MUST HAVE	1487	4
FELLOWS			
BIRDS ARE ANTIQUATED FELLOWS!	I'M THE LITTLE "HEART'S	176	11
KNOW WHAT THE SAPPHIRE FELLOWS, DO,	THE SKIES CANT KEEP	191	15
THE TOIL OF FELLOWS DONE--	THE WORK OF HER THAT	1143	2
BUT FIRMAMENTS WERE NOT HIS FELLOWS--	A WORLD MADE PENNINILESS	1623	V 3
THY FELLOWS ARE THEY REALMS OR THEMES	THE LOOK OF THEE, WHAT	1689	5
FELLOWSHIP			
FOR FELLOWSHIP [SYMPATHY]--AT NIGHT--	THE MOUNTAINS--GROW	757	8
FELON			
WHEN, FELON LED ALONG,	THE SOUL HAS BANDAGED	512	20
FELT			
THAT I FELT MARTIAL STIRRINGS	THE SUN KEPT STOOPING--	152	11
JUST FELT [HEARD] THE WORLD GO BY!	JUST LOST, WHEN I WAS	160	2
SHE FELT HERSELF SUPREMER--	THE SUN--JUST TOUCHED	232	5
FELT FEEBLY--FOR HER CROWN--	THE SUN--JUST TOUCHED	232	14
I FELT A FUNERAL, IN MY BRAIN,	I FELT A FUNERAL, IN MY	280	1
I FELT MY LIFE WITH BOTH MY HANDS	I FELT MY LIFE WITH BOTH	351	1
I FELT THE COLUMNS CLOSE--	I SAW NO WAY--THE	378	2
I NEVER FELT AT HOME--BELOW--	I NEVER FELT AT HOME--	413	1
UNTIL YOU FELT YOUR SECOND	'TWAS LIKE A MAELSTROM,	414	12
I FELT IT PUBLISH--IN MY EYE--	IT WOULD NEVER BE COMMON	430	11
I FELT THE WILDERNESS ROLL BACK	IT WOULD NEVER BE COMMON	430	28
I FELT SIROCCOS--CRAWL--	IT WAS NOT DEATH, FOR I	510	6
I FELT HIS SILVER HEEL	I STARTED EARLY--TOOK MY	520	18
THAT FELT SO AMPLE--YESTERDAY--	I COULD NOT PROVE THE	563	7
HOW MIDNIGHT FELT, AT FIRST--TO ME--	IF I MAY HAVE IT, WHEN	577	15
MYSELF FELT ILL--AND ODD--	I HAD BEEN HUNGRY, ALL	579	14
THE DARK--FELT BEAUTIFUL--	I THINK I WAS ENCHANTED	593	4
IT ALWAYS FELT TO ME--A WRONG	IT ALWAYS FELT TO ME--A	597	1
MY SOUL GREW [FELT / BENT / STOOD] STRAIGHT.	I ROSE--BECAUSE HE SANK	616	4
TO ONE WHO NEVER FELT IT BLAZE--	LOVE RECKONS BY ITSELF--	826	3
THE STARS ABOUT MY HEAD I FELT	I STEPPED FROM PLANK TO	875	3
I FELT A CLEAVING IN MY MIND--	I FELT A CLEAVING IN MY	937	1
BEFORE WE FELT THE DARK--	WE MET AS SPARKS--	958	6
A LOSS OF SOMETHING EVER FELT I--	A LOSS OF SOMETHING EVER	959	1
ANTIQUEST [ANTIQUER] FELT AT NOON	FURTHER IN SUMMER THAN	1068	9
I FELT MYSELF A [THE] VISITOR	ALONE AND IN A	1167	7
WE FELT HOW NEIGHBORLY A THING	THE MOUNTAINS STOOD IN	1278	11
I FEEL [FELT] AS IF THE GRASS WAS PLEASED	THE MUSHROOM IS THE ELF	1298	13
HE HAS NOT LIVED WHO HAS NOT FELT--	WONDER--IS NOT PRECISELY	1331	4
IS OFTEN SEEN--BUT SELDOM FELT,	A FIELD OF STUBBLE,	1407	7
AND FELT [THOUGHT] "HOW VAST A DESTINY"--	A DEW SUFFICED ITSELF--	1437	3
HAVE FELT [THOUGHT] IT MEET TO DIE--	HIS ORIENTAL HERESIES	1526	8
I FELT APOLOGY WERE DUE	NO BRIGADIER THROUGHOUT	1561	13
THAT NEVER FELT THE SUN	GLORY IS THAT BRIGHT	1660	5
I FELT IT SECOND PAIN	THAT SHE FORGOT ME WAS	1683	2
FENCE			
ON FENCE--AND ROOF--AND TWIG!	SOME RAINBOW--COMING	64	15
OVER THE FENCE--	OVER THE FENCE--	251	1
OVER THE FENCE--	OVER THE FENCE--	251	3
IT REACHES TO THE FENCE--	IT SIFTS FROM LEADEN	311	9
HE SOMETIMES HOLDS UPON THE FENCE--	THE BLACK BERRY--WEARS A	554	5
A BIRD SAT CARELESS ON THE FENCE--	THE TREES LIKE TASSELS--	606	17
A FENCE [WORLD] OR TWO FROM THEE--	MY MAKER--LET ME BE	1403	V 2
BEFORE A FENCE WITHOUT A FARE	UPON HIS SADDLE SPRUNG A	1600	3
FENCES			
OLD NEIGHBORS HAVE AT FENCES--	I'M SORRY FOR THE DEAD--	529	3
THAT MAKES THE FENCES SMILE--	I'M SORRY FOR THE DEAD--	529	8
THE FENCES ALL BUT RAN,	THE BIRD DID PRANCE--THE	1107	6
AND FENCES FLED AWAY	THERE CAME A WIND LIKE A	1593	10
FERN			
FERN ODORS ON UNTRAVELLED ROADS--	AN ALTERED LOOK ABOUT	140	12
FEROCIOUS			
MAKES THAT FEROCIOUS ROOM	A DIMPLE IN THE TOMB	1489	2
FERRET			
THE FERRET--CANNOT FIND--	THE COLOR OF THE GRAVE	411	24
FERVENT			
ABUNDANT [A FERVENT / A LOYAL / A GRACIOUS / AN AMPLE] END--	THE GENTIAN HAS A	1424	13
FROM ANY FERVENT ZONE	NOT ANY SUNNY TONE	1674	2
FERVENTLY			
THAT DOUBTS AS FERVENTLY AS IT BELIEVES.	OURSELVES WE DO INTER	1144	4
FERVOR			
IT'S FERVOR THE ELECTRIC OAR,	'TIS NOT THE SWAYING	1597	5
FERVOR'S			
WAS FERVOR'S SUDDEN CROWN--	THE PRETTY RAIN FROM	1426	8
FERVORS			
IT'S FERVORS ARE AS FIRM--	HOW KNOW IT FROM A	1364	2

	FIRST LINE	POEM	LINE
FESTAL			
UPON A FESTAL DAY,	IF I SHOULD CEASE TO	56	2
FESTIVAL			
AND FESTIVAL MAINTAIN	TO OWN THE ART WITHIN	855	4
FETCH			
I'LL FETCH [BRING] THEE BROOKS	MY RIVER RUNS TO THEE--	162	5
THE BREEZES FETCH ALONG--	THE GRASS SO LITTLE HAS	333	6
FETCH THE SEAM I MISSED--	DONT PUT UP MY THREAD &	617	18
TO FETCH HER GRACE--AND HUE--	SHE DWELLETH IN THE	671	5
AND FETCH HER THEE--BE MINE--	SHE DWELLETH IN THE	671	8
DEWS OF THESSALY, TO FETCH--	THE WORLD--FEELS DUSTY	715	11
AND FETCH THE ACRES IN.	THE PRODUCTS OF MY FARM	1025	8
FETCHED			
FROM POLAR CASKETS--FETCHED ME--	THE ANGLE OF A LANDSCAPE	375	17
FETCHES			
SHE FETCHES--SUCH AS ME	MY GARDEN--LIKE THE	484	5
FETCHING			
JUST AS THE NIGHT KEEPS FETCHING STARS	I'VE NOTHING ELSE--TO	224	3
FETE			
AND SIGNED THE FETE [SHOW / VAN] AWAY--	A DROP FELL ON THE APPLE	794	16
FEUDAL			
OVAL--AS FEUDAL LADIES WORE--	I AM ASHAMED--I HIDE--	473	14
FEVER			
CRACKLING WITH FEVER, THEY ESSAY,	I BRING AN UNACCUSTOMED	132	5
THERE IS IN FEVER OR EVENT--	'TWAS CRISIS--ALL THE	948	3
FEVERED			
THESE FEVERED DAYS--TO TAKE THEM TO THE FOREST	THESE FEVERED DAYS--TO	1441	1
FEW			
A VERY FEW--A BIRD OR TWO--	THESE ARE THE DAYS WHEN	130	2
A FEW PROSAIC DAYS	BESIDES THE AUTUMN POETS	131	2
A FEW INCISIVE MORNINGS--	BESIDES THE AUTUMN POETS	131	5
A FEW ASCETIC EVES--	BESIDES THE AUTUMN POETS	131	6
THE CLOUDS WERE GAUNT, AND FEW--	AN AWFUL TEMPEST MASHED	198	2
AND "FEW THERE BE"--CORRECT AGAIN--	YOU'RE RIGHT--"THE WAY	234	3
TO FAVORITES--A FEW--	THE SOUL'S SUPERIOR	306	14
A SMILE TOO FEW--A WORD TOO MUCH	NOT PROBABLE--THE BAREST	346	2
A FEW--AND THEY BY RISK--PROCURE--	DID OUR BEST MOMENT LAST	393	3
A FEW--BEHOLD THEE--	LOVE--THOU ART HIGH--	453	14
ACQUAINTANCE--JUST A FEW--	IF ANYBODY'S FRIEND BE	509	18
A FEW WENT OUT TO HELP THE BROOK	A DROP FELL ON THE APPLE	794	5
THE PRIVILEGE OF FEW--	TWO--WERE IMMORTAL TWICE	800	2
BETWEEN A FEW, AND ME--	AN HOUR IS A SEA	825	2
WITH HURRIED--FEW--EXPRESS REPORTS	THE ROBIN IS THE ONE	828	3
WHEN IT IS FOUND, A FEW REJOICE	THIS IS A BLOSSOM OF THE	945	9
DEPARTED STANDARDS AND THE FEW	TO UNDERTAKE IS TO	1070	7
THE DUTIES OF THE WIND ARE FEW,	THE DUTIES OF THE WIND	1137	1
TOO FEW THE MORNINGS BE,	TOO FEW THE MORNINGS BE,	1186	1
A FEW OF US--BELIEVED--	SUMMER--WE ALL HAVE SEEN	1386	2
A FEW--THE MORE ASPIRING	SUMMER--WE ALL HAVE SEEN	1386	3
THE BELLES [GUESTS] OF PARADISE ARE FEW--	THE ROAD TO PARADISE IS	1491	7
AND AN [THE] EFFACELESS "FEW" ARE LIFTED THERE--	ABOVE OBLIVION'S TIDE	1531	2
THE IMPLEMENTS OF BLISS ARE FEW--	NO LADDER NEEDS THE BIRD	1574	5
TO AN IMPERIAL FEW--	MORNING IS DUE TO ALL--	1577	3
OF BLISS THE CODES [THE IMPLEMENTS OF BLISS] ARE FEW--	TO HER DERIDED HOME	1586	9
FEW, YET ENOUGH,	FEW, YET ENOUGH,	1596	1
REMAINED A FEW SLOW YEARS WITH US	I WATCHED HER FACE TO	1667	5
FEW--LOVE AT ALL	SOMETIMES WITH THE HEART	1680	4
IF BEES ARE FEW.	TO MAKE A PRAIRIE IT	1755	5
FEWER			
LESS PAEANS--FEWER BELLS--	MY PORTION IS DEFEAT--	639	3
FICKLE			
THOUGH IT SHOWS SO FICKLE	WHAT WE SEE WE KNOW	1195	4
ESPIES THAT FICKLE CHAIR	RISK IS THE HAIR THAT	1239	6
UPON A MOMENT'S SHALLOW [FICKLE] RIM	HOW MUCH THE PRESENT	1380	5
UPON WHAT BRITTLE [FICKLE / TRIFLING] PIERS	HOW BRITTLE ARE THE	1433 V	1
FAME IS A FICKLE FOOD	FAME IS A FICKLE FOOD	1659	1
FICTION			
A FICTION SUPERSEDING FAITH--	HER SWEET WEIGHT ON MY	518	11
THAT I ESTEEM THE FICTION--REAL [TRUE]--	I THINK TO LIVE--MAY BE	646	23
PEACE IS A FICTION OF OUR FAITH--	PEACE IS A FICTION OF	912	1
FICTION'S			
'TIS FICTION'S--TO DILUTE [CONTRACT] TO PLAUSIBILITY [CREDIBILITY]	NO ROMANCE SOLD UNTO	669	5
FICTITIOUS			
HER BEES HAVE A FICTITIOUS [AN ILLUSIVE] HUM--	LIKE SOME OLD FASHIONED	302	9
THOSE FAIR [NEW]--FICTITIOUS PEOPLE--	THOSE FAIR--FICTITIOUS	499	1
TO A FICTITIOUS COUNTRY [SUMMER / SEASON]	CONJECTURING A CLIMATE	562	5
THE REAL [TRUTH]--FICTITIOUS SEEMS--	I THINK TO LIVE--MAY BE	646	24
HOW MANY THE FICTITIOUS SHORES--	I MANY TIMES THOUGHT	739	7
PHANTASMS [FICTITIOUS] BOTH BECOME	ONE BLESSING HAD I THAN	756	10
SO FAIRY [FOREIGN]--SO FICTITIOUS	AS SLEIGH BELLS SEEM IN	981	3
AS PARADISE FICTITIOUS	BECAUSE THAT YOU ARE	1260	19
HAS A FICTITIOUS CHARTER	COULD HOPE INSPECT HER	1283	3
HER CHARTER IS FICTITIOUS	COULD HOPE INSPECT HER	1283 V	3
FIDELITY			
FIDELITY IS GAIN	THE GENTIAN HAS A	1424	16
THAN SUCH FIDELITY.	THE HEALED HEART SHOWS	1440	8
THE DEVIL--HAD HE FIDELITY	THE DEVIL--HAD HE	1479	1

	FIRST LINE	POEM	LINE
FIDELITY (CONTINUED)			
MY FIDELITY--	GUEST AM I TO HAVE	1661	7
FIELD			
THE FIELD A SCARLET GOWN--	THE MORNS ARE MEEKER	12	6
A LADY WHITE, WITHIN THE FIELD	A LADY RED--AMID THE	74	3
IT POWDERS ALL THE WOOD [FIELD].	IT SIFTS FROM LEADEN	311	2
CONTRACTING IN A FIELD	FROM COCOON FORTH A	354	10
YOU WOULD NOT KNOW IT FROM THE FIELD--	THE COLOR OF THE GRAVE	411	3
THE HEAVENS [TREES / SKY / FIELD] CANNOT BE FOUND--	THE SYMPTOM OF THE GALE	1327	6
A FIELD OF STUBBLE, LYING SERE	A FIELD OF STUBBLE,	1407	1
FIELDS			
NEVER MIND SILENT FIELDS--	THERE IS ANOTHER SKY,	2	6
THIS, AND MY HEART, AND ALL THE FIELDS--	IT'S ALL I HAVE TO BRING	26	3
FROM THE FIELDS TODAY--	SO HAS A DAISY VANISHED	28	2
BEFORE THE FIELDS HAVE FINISHED,	BEFORE THE ICE IS IN THE	37	5
STILLER--THAN THE FIELDS	I WENT TO HEAVEN--	374	5
AND CARTS WENT STOOPING ROUND THE FIELDS	'TWAS JUST THIS TIME,	445	11
FROM ALL THE NOISE [SOUND] OF FIELDS--	I'M SORRY FOR THE DEAD--	529	10
GO DOWN THE FIELDS TO "HAY"--	I'M SORRY FOR THE DEAD--	529	20
WE PASSED THE FIELDS OF GAZING GRAIN--	BECAUSE I COULD NOT STOP	712	11
ON SOLITARY FIELDS	A LIGHT EXISTS IN SPRING	812	6
WINDS OF SUMMER FIELDS	AFTER A HUNDRED YEARS	1147	9
WHAT RIGHT HAD FIELDS TO ARBITRATE	I WORKED FOR CHAFF AND	1269	3
FIEND			
WHEN GOD--REMEMBERED--AND THE FIEND	'TWAS LIKE A MAELSTROM,	414	16
FIERCE			
FIERCE FROM THE CRAG ABOVE US	THROUGH LANE IT LAY--	9	11
FIERCER			
GROWS A FIERCER THING	AS THE STARVED MAELSTROM	872	10
FIERCEST			
IMPALED HIM ON HER FIERCEST STAKES--	FATE SLEW HIM, BUT HE	1031	3
FIFE			
AND BRING THE FIFE, AND TRUMPET, AND BEAT UPON THE DRUM--	AWAKE YE MUSES NINE,	1	39
FIFE'S			
OR A FIFE'S FAME--	LIFE, AND DEATH, AND	706	5
FIFTEEN			
CORINTHIANS ONE. FIFTEEN. NARRATES	"SOWN IN DISHONOR"!	62	9
FIFTH			
FIFTH, NO CREW--	FINDING IS THE FIRST ACT	870	6
FIGHT			
UNTIL THE FIGHT IS DONE;	"SIC TRANSIT GLORIA	3	54
TO FIGHT ALOUD, IS VERY BRAVE--	TO FIGHT ALOUD, IS VERY	126	1
I SHOULD NOT FEAR THE FIGHT!	BLESS GOD, HE WENT AS	147	8
FIGHT STERNLY IN A DYING EYE	DYING! TO BE AFRAID OF	831	10
THE SHIP MIGHT BE OF SATIN HAD IT NOT TO FIGHT--	THERE IS A STRENGTH IN	1113	5
FIGHTING			
LIKE SAILORS FIGHTING WITH A LEAK	THE FROST OF DEATH WAS	1136	3
'TWAS FIGHTING FOR HIS LIFE HE WAS--	'TWAS FIGHTING FOR HIS	1188	1
FIGMENT			
NO TRACE--NO FIGMENT OF THE THING	I'VE KNOWN A HEAVEN,	243	9
A FALLACY, A FIGMENT, WE KNEW--	NOT SO THE INFINITE	1040	4
FIGURE			
THE SERPENT'S SATIN FIGURE	THROUGH LANE IT LAY--	9	7
NO MORE HER PATIENT FIGURE	SHE BORE IT TILL THE	144	9
IF SUCH A LITTLE FIGURE	ON SUCH A NIGHT, OR SUCH	146	3
BUT THAT THE LITTLE FIGURE	ON SUCH A NIGHT, OR SUCH	146	7
THAT SUCH A LITTLE FIGURE	ON SUCH A NIGHT, OR SUCH	146	11
THERE WAS A LITTLE FIGURE PLUMP	ON SUCH A NIGHT, OR SUCH	146	17
HER LITTLE FIGURE AT THE GATE	SHE DIED--THIS WAS THE	150	5
THE SYMBOL [FALLING / FIGURE] OF A WORD	THERE CAME A DAY AT	322	10
LEAST FIGURE--ON THE ROAD--	A TONGUE--TO TELL HIM I	400	29
SHE PRESENTED HER SMALL FIGURE--	MOST SHE TOUCHED ME BY	760	3
AND FORGET THE COLOR [FIGURE] OF THE DAY--	SEVERER SERVICE OF	786	16
THE FIGURE OF A NUT	EXPERIMENT TO ME	1073	4
HIS [THIS] FIGURE INTIMATE	THESE ARE THE NIGHTS	1128	4
UNTIL HIS LITTLE FIGURE	A SPARROW TOOK A SLICE	1211	7
HIS LITTLE HEARSE LIKE FIGURE	HIS LITTLE HEARSE LIKE	1522	1
THE FIGURE WAS WITHDRAWN--	A CAP OF LEAD ACROSS THE	1649	4
FIGURES			
MY FIGURES FAIL TO TELL ME	THE FEET OF PEOPLE	7	17
MY FIGURES FILE [CIPHERS STEAL] AWAY.	LOW AT MY PROBLEM	69	6
THE FIGURES HUNCHED, WITH PAIN--	A CLOCK STOPPED--	287	7
LIKE JUGGLER'S FLOWERS [FIGURES] SITUATES	IT SIFTS FROM LEADEN	311	V
THE FIGURES I HAVE SEEN	IT WAS NOT DEATH, FOR I	510	10
WHEN FIGURES SHOW THEIR ROYAL FRONT--	OF ALL THE SOULS THAT	664	9
THEIR PURPLE FIGURES RISE	THE MOUNTAINS--GROW	757	2
FILAMENT			
WHEN FORMULA [FILAMENT], HAD FAILED--	I GOT SO I COULD HEAR	293	16
A FILAMENT--A LAW--	I HAD NOT MINDED--WALLS	398	10
IS BUT A FILAMENT, I KNOW,	THE LOVE A LIFE CAN SHOW	673	2
FILAMENTS			
FILAMENTS OF BLOOM, PONTIUS PILATE SOWED--	TO PUT THIS WORLD DOWN,	527	10
TO PUT OFF FILAMENTS LIKE THIS	WITH PINIONS OF DISDAIN	1431	11
FILE			
MY FIGURES FILE [CIPHERS STEAL] AWAY.	LOW AT MY PROBLEM	69	6
WHAT IF I FILE THIS MORTAL--OFF--	WHAT IF I SAY I SHALL	277	4

	FIRST LINE	POEM	LINE
FILES			
WHEN SENSE FROM SPIRIT--FILES AWAY--	OF ALL THE SOULS THAT	664	3
FILL			
AND SHOUTS FILL ALL MY CHILDISH SKY,	I HAVE A KING, WHO DOES	103	10
OUR BLANK IN BLISS TO FILL	OUR SHARE OF NIGHT TO	113	3
THE SLAVE--FORGETS--TO FILL--	THE LAMP BURNS SURE--	233	5
'TWOULD SCARCELY FILL A TWO--	I KNOW LIVES, I COULD	372	6
AND FILL MY LUNGS, FOR WITNESS--	DO PEOPLE MOULDER	432	7
WHILE OTHER--WENT THE SEA TO FILL--	FORGET! THE LADY WITH	438	14
TO FILL A GAP	TO FILL A GAP	546	1
TO FILL THE AWFUL VACUUM [LONGITUDE]	SEVERER SERVICE OF	786	3
I MAKE HIS CRESCENT FILL OR LACK--	I MAKE HIS CRESCENT FILL	909	1
THE WORD APPLIED TO FILL	SHALL I TAKE THEE, THE	1126	10
BREACH A SECOND CANNOT FILL--	LONG YEARS APART--CAN	1383	2
TO FILL IT'S FRINGED CAREER [SPHERE]	THE GENTIAN HAS A	1424	11
FILLED			
EXISTENCE'S WHOLE ARC, [WHOLE EYE / WHOLE RIM / SURMISE] FILLED UP,	I'M CEDED--I'VE STOPPED	508	12
AND THOUGH THEIR PLACES SOMEWHAT FILLED--	YOU'LL FIND--IT WHEN YOU	610	5
THAT FILLED THE LISPING FULL.	THEY WONT FROWN ALWAYS--	874	8
THE CORN, HER FURTHEST KERNEL FILLED	MIDSUMMER, WAS IT, WHEN	962	5
IT FILLED THE WELLS, IT PLEASED THE POOLS	LIKE RAIN IT SOUNDED	1235	9
FILLED WAS THE AIR WITH MERRY VENTURE	GLASS WAS THE STREET--IN	1498	3
FILLING			
AND FILLING ALL THE EARTH AND AIR [SKY]	HIS ORIENTAL HERESIES	1526	3
FILLS			
A TYRIAN LIGHT THE VILLAGE FILLS--	AN ALTERED LOOK ABOUT	140	2
IT FILLS WITH ALABASTER WOOL	IT SIFTS FROM LEADEN	311	3
OH, WHEN THE SQUIRREL FILLS HIS POCKETS	WHAT SHALL I DO WHEN THE	956	9
AND DECKS [BRIMS / FILLS / SWELLS] THE RAYS	BY A DEPARTING LIGHT	1714	6
FILM			
THE THOUGHT BENEATH SO SLIGHT A FILM--	THE THOUGHT BENEATH SO	210	1
THE BRAVE EYES FILM--	YOU SEE I CANNOT SEE--	253	5
AND WHEN THE FILM HAD STITCHED YOUR EYES	'TWAS LIKE A MAELSTROM,	414	22
THE FILM UPON THE EYE	SHE DEALT HER PRETTY	479	10
THAT'S EASIER--THAN THE OTHER FILM	YOU KNOW THAT PORTRAIT	504	15
I HELPED [STAYED] HIS FILM--WITH HYMN--	I ROSE--BECAUSE HE SANK	616	7
THEY BALANCED FILM WITH FILM,	I TOOK ONE DRAUGHT OF	1725	6
THEY BALANCED FILM WITH FILM,	I TOOK ONE DRAUGHT OF	1725	6
FILMS			
I TOUCHED THE TOPS OF FILMS--	IT WOULD NEVER BE COMMON	430	27
FILMS CANNOT ANNUL	BANISH AIR FROM AIR--	854	7
FINAL			
FINAL FAST--ABOVE--	BY A FLOWER--BY A LETTER	109	4
TO TAKE A BACKWARD [FINAL / PARTING] LOOK.	THESE ARE THE DAYS WHEN	130	3
TOYED COOLLY WITH THE FINAL INCH	'TWAS LIKE A MAELSTROM,	414	5
AND IF THE FURTHER [OTHER / FINAL] HEAVEN--	I RECKON--WHEN I COUNT	569	12
HER FINAL SUMMER WAS IT--	HER FINAL SUMMER WAS IT	795	1
WOULD BE MY FINAL INCH--	I STEPPED FROM PLANK TO	875	6
BETWEEN HER FINAL ROOM	THE LAST NIGHT THAT SHE	1100	10
OUR FINAL INTERVIEW.	WERE IT TO BE THE LAST	1164	4
LEAN FORWARD FOR A FINAL GLANCE--	POWER IS A FAMILIAR	1238	7
BEQUEATHES THIS FINAL PLANT	THE LILAC IS AN ANCIENT	1241	6
BECAUSE THAT DEATH IS FINAL [TREASON / DIFFERENT],	BECAUSE THAT YOU ARE	1260	5
GO TIMID, LEST [SHOULD] HIS FINAL [TESTING / BLAZING / LOFTY] EYE	GO SLOW, MY SOUL, TO	1297	5
THOSE FINAL CREATURES,--WHO THEY ARE--	THOSE FINAL CREATURES,--	1766	1
FINALLEST			
THIS--WAS MY FINALLEST OCCASION--	THE FIRST DAY THAT I WAS	902	9
FINALLY			
THEY MAY NOT FINALLY SAY, YES--	IF I COULD BRIBE THEM BY	179	18
FINALLY, NO GOLDEN FLEECE--	FINDING IS THE FIRST ACT	870	7
HE WILL REFUND US FINALLY	BECAUSE THAT YOU ARE	1260	39
FINANCIERS			
BY OTHER FINANCIERS BE DEEMED	THE VOICE THAT STANDS	1189	7
FIND			
NONE CANNOT FIND WHO SEEKETH, ON THIS TERRESTIAL BALL!	AWAKE YE MUSES NINE,	1	12
FIND QUAINT EMPLOY--	MY WHEEL IS IN THE DARK!	10	11
TO LOSE--IF ONE CAN FIND AGAIN--	ALL THESE MY BANNERS BE.	22	8
THAT WHEN I COULD NOT FIND IT--	I HAD A GUINEA GOLDEN--	23	7
BENEATH THE SUN MAY FIND.	I HAD A GUINEA GOLDEN--	23	36
AMBITION CANNOT FIND HIM.	AMBITION CANNOT FIND HIM	68	1
A CORONET TO FIND!	WHO NEVER LOST, ARE	73	2
TO FIND THAT WHAT ONE WAKED FOR,	A DARTING FEAR--A POMP--	87	3
LEST ANYBODY FIND--	SO BASHFUL WHEN I SPIED	91	4
AND SUBSEQUENT, TO FIND	TO HANG OUR HEAD--	105	2
COULD THE CHILDREN FIND THE WAY THERE--	"HOUSES"--SO THE WISE	127	7
ANYBODY FIND THE FOUNTAIN	FLOWERS--WELL--IF	137	5
SINCE I COULD NEVER FIND HER	SHE DIED--THIS WAS THE	150	7
YOU CANNOT FIND OUT ALL ABOUT	DUST IS THE ONLY SECRET	153	3
TO FIND THE SUNRISE LEFT--	YOU LOVE ME--YOU ARE	156	5
TO FIND THE WINDOWS DARK--	YOU LOVE ME--YOU ARE	156	11
AMONG IT'S STORES TO FIND--	IN EBON BOX, WHEN YEARS	169	10
MY BUSINESS IS, TO FIND!	I CAUTIOUS, SCANNED MY	178	16
OH FIND IT--SIR--FOR ME!	I LOST A WORLD--THE	181	8
TO FIND OUR WAY HOME--	I'VE NOTHING ELSE--TO	224	8
WE CAN FIND NO SCAR,	THERE'S A CERTAIN SLANT	258	6
IS EASIER TO FIND--	A SHADY FRIEND--FOR	278	2

	FIRST LINE	POEM	LINE
FIND (CONTINUED)			
I WAKE--TO FIND NO--EMERALDS--	THE ANGLE OF A LANDSCAPE	375	15
NO EYE COULD FIND THE PLACE--	THEY DROPPED LIKE FLAKES	409	7
TO HELP THE FOND--TO FIND IT--	THE COLOR OF THE GRAVE	411	5
THE FERRET--CANNOT FIND--	THE COLOR OF THE GRAVE	411	24
NOR NEAR ENOUGH--TO FIND--	A MURMUR IN THE TREES--	416	4
IT IS DEAD--FIND IT--	IT IS DEAD--FIND IT--	417	1
SHE [I] COULD NOT FIND HER [MY] YES-- . .	I SHOWED HER HIGHTS SHE	446	8
DID HE FIND IT SUPPLE?	HE STRAINED MY FAITH--	497	2
BECAUSE THE WINDS WOULD FIND IT OUT-- . .	YOU CANNOT PUT A FIRE	530	7
A DESERT--FIND--	I CROSS TILL I AM WEARY	550	5
I FIND MY FEET HAVE FURTHER GOALS-- . . .	I COULD NOT PROVE THE	563	5
YOU'LL FIND--IT WHEN YOU TRY TO DIE-- . .	YOU'LL FIND--IT WHEN YOU	610	1
I MEANT TO FIND HER WHEN I CAME--	I MEANT TO FIND HER WHEN	718	1
I WAKED, TO FIND IT FIRST AWAKE--	BEREAVED OF ALL, I WENT	784	9
THEREIN THYSELF SHALT FIND	SOTO! EXPLORE THYSELF!	832	2
IF I COULD FIND IT ANYWHERE	I CANNOT BUY IT--'TIS	840	7
CAN ONE FIND THE RARE EAR	GOOD TO HIDE, AND HEAR	842	7
UNTIL IT FOOTING FIND.	A DOUBT IF IT BE US	859	4
SPLIT THE LARK--AND YOU'LL FIND THE MUSIC--	SPLIT THE LARK--AND	861	1
LOOSE THE FLOOD--YOU SHALL FIND IT PATENT--	SPLIT THE LARK--AND	861	5
I COULD NOT FIND A PRIVACY	TO MY QUICK EAR THE	891	3
I FIND MYSELF STILL SOFTLY SEARCHING	A LOSS OF SOMETHING EVER	959	11
TO FIND THE SPECIES DISAPPEARED--	IT BLOOMED AND DROPT, A	978	7
INDEMNITY TO FIND--	SHE SPED AS PETALS OF A	991	4
I LEFT HER I COULD FIND HER	WE'LL PASS WITHOUT THE	996	5
AND COULD NOT FIND IT'S EYE.	WHO SAW NO SUNRISE	1018	8
NO CLUSTER--YE [YOU] SHALL FIND--	EXCEPT THE SMALLER SIZE	1067	V
BUT NO APARTMENT FIND	TOO FEW THE MORNINGS BE,	1186	6
I FIND IT TO INFER.	THE FROST WAS NEVER SEEN	1202	20
OR FIND THE BANQUET MEAN--	WHO GOES TO DINE MUST	1223	2
MY SOUL, TO FIND THEM, COME, ...	THAN HEAVEN MORE REMOTE,	1436	11
I FIND ONE ON MY HAND	HOW SOFT A CATERPILLAR	1448	2
WE SHALL FIND THE CUBE OF THE RAINBOW. . .	WE SHALL FIND THE CUBE	1484	1
WHAT HEART WOULD RISK [COULD FIND] THE WAY--	WHERE ROSES WOULD NOT	1582	2
FIND ALL THE WITCHCRAFT THAT WE NEED . . .	WITCHCRAFT WAS HUNG, IN	1583	3
WE SEND THE WAVE TO FIND THE WAVE--	WE SEND THE WAVE TO FIND	1604	1
WE COULD NOT FIND THE MIGHTY FACE	A CAP OF LEAD ACROSS THE	1649	3
FIND CONSTERNATION'S CARNIVAL	ENDANGER IT, AND THE	1658	7
FIND ENTRANCE THERE	NOT ANY SUNNY TONE	1674	3
FINDING			
JUST FINDING OUT--WHAT PUZZLED US--	FOREVER AT HIS SIDE TO	246	15
FINDING IS THE FIRST ACT	FINDING IS THE FIRST ACT	870	1
ELUDES THE FINDING OUT.	WE SHALL FIND THE CUBE	1484	4
FINDS			
HE--WAKING--FINDS THE FLOWER THERE--	THE DAISY FOLLOWS SOFT	106	4
WHO FINDS IT EVERY TIME	HOW DESTITUTE IS HE	1477	3
FINE			
GENTILITY IS FINE, ...	"SIC TRANSIT GLORIA	3	42
IF I WERE HALF SO FINE MYSELF	"SOWN IN DISHONOR"!	62	4
UNDERNEATH THEIR FINE INCISIONS	SURGEONS MUST BE VERY	108	3
PERHAPS OF TWIG SO FINE--	FOR EVERY BIRD A NEST--	143	10
HER'S BE DAMASK FINE--	THO' MY DESTINY BE	163	2
TO A FINE, PEDANTIC SUNSHINE--	PORTRAITS ARE TO DAILY	170	3
"FAITH" IS A FINE INVENTION	"FAITH" IS A FINE	185	1
AND MAKE ITSELF SO FINE	THE GRASS SO LITTLE HAS	333	10
THAT FINE PROSPERITY	REVERSE CANNOT BEFALL	395	2
I'LL STRING YOU--IN FINE NECKLACE--	I'LL CLUTCH--AND CLUTCH	427	7
THE FINE--UNVARYING AXIS	THE OUTER--FROM THE	451	5
ON FINE--ARTERIAL CANVAS--	THE OUTER--FROM THE	451	13
BUT THE [A] FINE EAR	INCONCEIVABLY SOLEMN!	582	13
HEMS--TOO FINE FOR LADY'S TRACING	DONT PUT UP MY THREAD &	617	9
THE FINE--IMPALPABLE ARRAY--	THE TINT I CANNOT TAKE--	627	5
THAT FINE SUSPICION, NATURES MUST	TO UNDERTAKE IS TO	1070	5
THE GALE [BREEZE] WERE NOT SO FINE	WE LIKE A HAIRBREADTH	1175	6
NOT HOPING FOR HIS NOTICE VAST [FAR / FINE]	BECAUSE HE LOVES HER	1229	9
AND TRUE [BEST / REAL / BLAND / FINE / FAIR] THE OTHER . . .	I'D RATHER RECOLLECT A	1349	4
A FINE--ESTRANGING CREATURE--	THE FASCINATING CHILL	1480	6
FOLLOW WISE [FINE] ORION	FOLLOW WISE ORION	1538	1
A WARMTH AS NEAR [SURE / FINE] AS IF THE SUN	TO SEE HER IS A PICTURE	1568	7
THE FINE--ENSUING RIGHT	OH WHAT A GRACE IS THIS,	1615	4
GUILELESS, YET OF SUCH GLORY FINE	"RED SEA," INDEED! TALK	1642	5
FINER			
THEN, FINER THAN A LADY, ...	A FUZZY FELLOW, WITHOUT	173	13
IT'S FINER--NOT TO KNOW--	THE SKIES CANT KEEP	191	10
STANDS SYMBOL FOR THE FINER FORGE	DARE YOU SEE A SOUL AT	365	11
LIT WITH A FINER PHOSPHOR--	MORE LIFE--WENT OUT--	422	3
THERE'S TRIUMPH OF THE FINER MIND	TRIUMPH--MAY BE OF	455	5
IT'S FINER--OWN THE EAR--	I WOULD NOT PAINT--A	505	18
THIS MORNING'S FINER VERDICT--	WE SEE--COMPARATIVELY--	534	5
A FINER SHAME OF EXTASY--	THERE IS A SHAME OF	551	3
BY FINER GRAVITATIONS--	I WATCHED THE MOON	629	19
SO FINER 'TIS THAN WOOL--	YOU'LL KNOW HER--BY HER	634	17
IT INTIMATES THE FINER WANT--	WE THIRST AT FIRST--'TIS	726	5
I, OF A FINER FAMINE	AS THE STARVED MAELSTROM	872	13
TILL I HAVE FINER [VAINER / FURTHER] TRIED--	SHALL I TAKE THEE, THE	1126	4
AS FINER IS A GOING	SUMMER HAS TWO	1422	7
FINEST			
WINNOW HER FINEST FONDNESS--	DOUBT ME! MY DIM	275	22

	FIRST LINE	POEM	LINE
FINEST (CONTINUED)			
THE SMALLEST [FINEST] GAMBOGE HAND	YOU'LL KNOW HER--BY HER	634	2
THE FINEST HONEY--CURDLED--	THERE IS AN ARID	782	7
DOES FINEST GLORY FIT!	THE MOST TRIUMPHANT BIRD	1265	9
THIS MORNING'S FINEST SYLLABLE	WHEN MEMORY IS FULL	1266	3
IS PRECISELY THE FINEST OF JOYS--	TO DO A MAGNANIMOUS	1699	4
FINGER			
TWILL BE BECAUSE DEATH'S FINGER	IF I SHOULD CEASE TO	56	7
A PURPLE FINGER ON THE SLOPE--	AN ALTERED LOOK ABOUT	140	6
AND JUST THE STEEPLE'S FINGER--	THE ANGLE OF A LANDSCAPE	375	19
A FINGER OF ENAMELLED FIRE--	MY SOUL--ACCUSED ME--AND	753	8
HER GOLDEN FINGER ON HER LIP--	NATURE--THE GENTLEST	790	23
AND A SUSPICION, LIKE A FINGER	A LOSS OF SOMETHING EVER	959	13
TILL YOUR WRINKLED FINGER	ON THE WORLD YOU COLORED	1171	9
FINGER'S			
AND AT MY FINGER'S END--	I AM ALIVE--I GUESS--	470	4
FINGERS			
THE SATYRS FINGERS BECKONED--	THROUGH LANE IT LAY--	9	13
HOW VERY BLITHE THE FINGERS [MAIDEN]	IF RECOLLECTING WERE	33	7
WHEREFORE, MY BAFFLED FINGERS	LOW AT MY PROBLEM	69	7
TOO LATE FOR STRIVING FINGERS	WITHIN MY REACH!	90	8
FINGERS DENIED THE PLUCKING,	MY NOSEGAYS ARE FOR	95	3
NEW FINGERS STIR THE SOD--	NEW FEET WITHIN MY	99	2
THE WIZARD FINGERS NEVER REST--	A SOMETHING IN A	122	13
WHOSE FINGERS STRING THE STALACTITE--	BRING ME THE SUNSET IN A	128	16
MESMERIC FINGERS SOFTLY TOUCH	BESIDES THE AUTUMN POETS	131	11
FOR, WHEN FROSTS, THEIR PUNCTUAL FINGERS	THO' MY DESTINY BE	163	9
HANDLE THE ADAMANTINE FINGERS	HOW MANY TIMES THESE LOW	187	7
HER FINGERS FUMBLED AT HER WORK--	THE ROSE DID CAPER ON	208	5
I'VE DIAMONDS--ON MY FINGERS--	I CAME TO BUY A SMILE--	223	9
I HELD A JEWEL IN MY FINGERS--	I HELD A JEWEL IN MY	245	1
I WOKE--AND CHID MY HONEST FINGERS,	I HELD A JEWEL IN MY	245	5
THAT SLIPPED MY SIMPLE FINGERS THROUGH--	YOUR RICHES--TAUGHT ME--	299	31
WHOSE FINGERS COMB [BRUSH] THE SKY--	OF ALL THE SOUNDS	321	6
IS GOTTEN NOT OF [WITH] FINGERS--	OF ALL THE SOUNDS	321	13
HIS FINGERS ARE THE SIZE OF FISTS--	THEY LEAVE US WITH THE	350	3
WITH "THIS WAS LAST HER FINGERS DID"--	DEATH SETS A THING	360	7
AT REST--HIS FINGERS ARE--	DEATH SETS A THING	360	16
BUT WHOM HIS FINGERS TOUCHED--	A VISITOR IN MARL--	391	9
A WIND WITH FINGERS--GOES--	THEY DROPPED LIKE FLAKES	409	5
HIS FINGERS, AS HE PASSED	THE WIND--TAPPED LIKE A	436	14
FINGERS--TO FRAME MY ROUND HAIR	I AM ASHAMED--I HIDE--	473	13
TELL HIM [HER] JUST HOW THE FINGERS HURRIED--	GOING TO HIM! HAPPY	494	6
FROM OUR FAMILIAR LIFETIME [ADDRESS / GAZING / FINGERS / NOTICE]--	THOSE FAIR--FICTITIOUS	499	3
AND WONDER HOW THE FINGERS FEEL	I WOULD NOT PAINT--A	505	5
AND DIP [MIX] YOUR FINGERS IN THE FROST--	IF ANYBODY'S FRIEND BE	509	15
SUBTRACTING, TILL MY FINGERS DROPPED	IF YOU WERE COMING IN	511	11
SALUTE HER--WITH LONG FINGERS--	THE SOUL HAS BANDAGED	512	5
RUNS [PUTS] HIS FINGERS THRO' IT--	BEAUTY--BE NOT CAUSED--	516	6
THE FINGERS GREW TOO COLD	'TWAS WARM--AT FIRST--	519	6
THAT WHEN THEIR CONSCIOUS FINGERS CEASE--	THE MARTYR POETS--DID	544	7
DISTRACTS THE CHILDREN'S FINGERS--	'TIS ONE BY ONE--THE	545	11
THEN [I] MOVED MY FINGERS OFF	I YEARS HAD BEEN FROM	609	21
WITH FINGERS--WHERE THE TOES SHOULD BE--	YOU'LL KNOW HER--BY HER	634	3
AND PUSH IT WITH MY FINGERS--NEXT--	THE WAY I READ A	636	3
MY FINGERS WERE AWAKE--	THE SUN KEPT SETTING--	692	10
OF FINGERS GOING BY--	WE THIRST AT FIRST--'TIS	726	4
FINGERS OF THE SLIM AURORA--	THESE--SAW VISIONS--	758	10
DEATH'S LARGE--DEMOCRATIC FINGERS	COLOR--CASTE--	970	7
THE FINGERS OF THE LIGHT	THE FINGERS OF THE LIGHT	1000	1
BY INADVERTENT FINGERS DROPT	THE LIGHTNING IS A	1173	3
FINISH			
COULD FINISH--ENMITY--	I HAD NO TIME TO HATE--	478	6
BUT DID NOT FINISH--SOME WAY BACK--	A THOUGHT WENT UP MY	701	3
WHILE SHE MUST FINISH QUITE	THE LAST NIGHT THAT SHE	1100	14
WILL FINISH WITH THE SUN.	THE LONGEST DAY THAT GOD	1769	2
FINISHED			
BEFORE THE FIELDS HAVE FINISHED,	BEFORE THE ICE IS IN THE	37	5
I'M "WIFE"--I'VE FINISHED THAT--	I'M "WIFE"--I'VE	199	1
AND FINISHED [GOT THROUGH--] KNOWING--THEN--	I FELT A FUNERAL, IN MY	280	20
I FINISHED TWO--AND SEVERAL STARS--	I SEND TWO SUNSETS--	308	3
YOU THOUGHT WAS FINISHED--	A SOLEMN THING WITHIN	483	9
TELL HIM [HER]--NIGHT [DAY] FINISHED--BEFORE WE FINISHED--	GOING TO HIM! HAPPY	494	18
TELL HIM [HER]--NIGHT [DAY] FINISHED--BEFORE WE FINISHED--	GOING TO HIM! HAPPY	494	18
IS FINISHED USING, NOW,	I'M CEDED--I'VE STOPPED	508	4
I'VE FINISHED THREADING--TOO--	I'M CEDED--I'VE STOPPED	508	7
THE RAPTURE OF A FINISHED [CONCLUDED] DAY--	"HEAVEN" HAS DIFFERENT	575	13
TWO--BE FINISHED USING--	ONE AND ONE--ARE ONE--	769	2
THE GRAVE--WAS FINISHED--BUT THE SPADE	BEREAVED OF ALL, I WENT	784	15
THERE IS A FINISHED FEELING	THERE IS A FINISHED	856	1
HOW MORE THE FINISHED CREATURES	THE CHEMICAL CONVICTION	954	7
AND WORKMEN FINISHED ONE BY ONE	THE CRICKETS SANG	1104	3
WHEN A [THE] SUBJECT IS FINISHED [ENDED / TAKEN]--	WHATEVER IT IS--SHE HAS	1204	7
TO WHERE THE FINISHED FACES	MY TRIUMPH LASTED TILL	1227	5
BUT HOW SHALL FINISHED CREATURES	THE BONE THAT HAS NO	1274	9

	FIRST LINE	POEM	LINE
FINISHING			
SO BUSY WAS SHE--FINISHING--	HER FINAL SUMMER WAS IT	795	15
FINITE			
BETWEEN MY FINITE EYES--	BEFORE I GOT MY EYE PUT	327	13
I'M FINITE--I CANT SEE--	THEIR HIGHT IN HEAVEN	696	4
FINITE--TO FAIL, BUT INFINITE TO VENTURE--	FINITE--TO FAIL, BUT	847	1
THE FINITE--FURNISHED	THE ADMIRATIONS--AND	906	11
AND POWER TO BE FINITE CEASED	ESTRANGED FROM BEAUTY--	1474	3
FINITE INFINITY.	THERE IS A SOLITUDE OF	1695	8
FINITENESS			
OF FINITENESS--BE SPENT--	TILL DEATH--IS NARROW	907	4
FINITUDE			
SUCH BEING FINITUDE!	TO BE ALIVE--IS POWER--	677	8
FINITY			
ENGROSS MY FINITY--	TIME FEELS SO VAST THAT	802	4
FINLAND			
AND FINLAND OF THE YEAR	THESE ARE THE DAYS THAT	1696	4
FIR			
WHAT WILL THE OAK [FIR] TREE SAY?	I ROBBED THE WOODS--	41	9
WE KNOW [SAY] HE HAS CLIMBED A FIR--	THE WIND DID'NT COME	316	8
BUT THE FIR IS WHERE--DECLARE--	THE WIND DID'NT COME	316	9
FIRE			
IN THEIR CHAPEAUX [A CHAPEAU] OF FIRE,	LIKE HER THE SAINTS	60	2
FIRE, AND SMOKE, AND GUN,	I HAVE NEVER SEEN	175	6
"WARMED THEM" AT THE "TEMPLE FIRE".	HE FORGOT--AND I--	203	4
TO THINK JUST HOW THE FIRE WILL BURN--	THO' I GET HOME HOW LATE	207	9
THEN, HOW THE FIRE EBBS LIKE BILLOWS--	HOW THE OLD MOUNTAINS	291	9
AND LET THE FIRE THROUGH--	IT STRUCK ME--EVERY DAY	362	4
THOUGH WINTER FIRE--SING CLEAR AS PLOVER--	IT'S THOUGHTS--AND JUST	495	15
NOR FIRE--FOR JUST MY [TWO] MARBLE FEET	IT WAS NOT DEATH, FOR I	510	7
YOU CANNOT [NO MAN--] PUT A FIRE OUT--	YOU CANNOT PUT A FIRE	530	1
AND CLOSER TO THE FIRE--	THE NIGHT WAS WIDE, AND	589	14
TO MY SMALL HEARTH HIS FIRE CAME--	TO MY SMALL HEARTH HIS	638	1
WE LEARNED TO LIKE THE FIRE	THE ZEROES--TAUGHT US--	689	2
A FINGER OF ENAMELLED FIRE--	MY SOUL--ACCUSED ME--AND	753	8
BEFORE IT EXISTS [EXPRESS] IN FIRE.	A MAN MAY MAKE A REMARK	952	8
ASHES DENOTE THAT FIRE WAS--	ASHES DENOTE THAT FIRE	1063	1
FIRE EXISTS THE FIRST IN LIGHT	ASHES DENOTE THAT FIRE	1063	5
THE LARGEST FIRE EVER KNOWN	THE LARGEST FIRE EVER	1114	1
ONE [THIS] REQUISITE HAS FIRE THAT LASTS [EARTHLY FIRE / MORTAL FIRE]	THE SMOULDERING EMBERS	1132	7
ONE [THIS] REQUISITE HAS FIRE THAT LASTS [EARTHLY FIRE / MORTAL FIRE]	THE SMOULDERING EMBERS	1132	7
ONE [THIS] REQUISITE HAS FIRE THAT LASTS [EARTHLY FIRE / MORTAL FIRE]	THE SMOULDERING EMBERS	1132	7
HIS INTERESTS OF FIRE	THE MOUNTAINS STOOD IN	1278	6
THAT FONDLED THEM WHEN THEY WERE FIRE	LONG YEARS APART--CAN	1383	7
HOW RED THE FIRE ROCKS BELOW	ON MY VOLCANO GROWS THE	1677	5
AS CLEAN AS FIRE	PERIL AS A POSSESSION	1678	7
CONSTANCY THRO' FIRE--AWARDED--	REARRANGE A "WIFE'S"	1737	11
FIRE'S			
BEFORE THE FIRE'S EYES--	DOUBT ME! MY DIM	275	21
RED--IS THE FIRE'S COMMON TINT--	DARE YOU SEE A SOUL AT	365	3
FIRES			
NO RUDDY FIRES ON THE HEARTH--	WHAT INN IS THIS	115	7
BRIGHT FIRES--THE BLANKETLESS--	'TIS OPPOSITES--ENTICE--	355	3
BY FIRES OF THE SUN.	THE WORK OF HER THAT	1143	4
FIRESIDE			
AROUND YOUR FIRESIDE--	ENDOW THE LIVING--WITH	521	4
ROUND OUR NEW FIRESIDE--BUT FOR THIS--	I LEARNED--AT LEAST--	944	5
FIRING			
THE FIRING IN HEAVEN,	HIS BILL IS CLASPED--HIS	1102	10
FIRM			
FIRM TO THE DRUM--	UNTO LIKE STORY--TROUBLE	295	18
AND BREATHS WERE GATHERING FIRM	I HEARD A FLY BUZZ--WHEN	465	6
I SANG FIRM--EVEN--[STRAIGHT--STEADY] CHANTS--	I ROSE--BECAUSE HE SANK	616	6
UNTIL IT SETTLED BROAD [FULL / FIRM]--ON PARADISE--	TO KNOW JUST HOW HE	622	4
FOR FIRM CONVICTION OF A MOUSE	THE WAY I READ A	636	11
THE DARKNESS [TROUBLE] BRACED AS FIRM	SEVERER SERVICE OF	786	18
TILL I AM FIRM IN HEAVEN	A CLOUD WITHDREW FROM	895	11
SHE STUNG HIM--SAPPED HIS FIRM ADVANCE--	FATE SLEW HIM, BUT HE	1031	5
A FIRM APPEARANCE STILL INFLATES	WE DO NOT KNOW THE TIME	1106	5
HOW GOOD [SAFE / FIRM / CALM] TO BE IN TOMBS	THE CLOUDS THEIR BACKS	1172	6
IT'S FERVORS ARE AS FIRM--	HOW KNOW IT FROM A	1364	2
AND HE PRONOUNCED IT FIRM.	HOW BRITTLE ARE THE	1433	8
WHOSE GOLD IS FIRM	HOW DESTITUTE IS HE	1477	2
NOT THAT IT IS NOT FIRM [HAS NOT ROOM]	THE ROAD TO PARADISE IS	1491	3
HOW FIRM ETERNITY MUST LOOK	HOW FIRM ETERNITY MUST	1499	1
FIRMAMENT			
WHOSE BONNETS TOUCH THE FIRMAMENT--	IN LANDS I NEVER SAW--	124	3
FOR A FIRMAMENT--	AH, MOON--AND STAR!	240	6
HE--IS MORE THAN A FIRMAMENT--FROM ME--	AH, MOON--AND STAR!	240	16
FIRMAMENT--	DELIGHT IS AS THE FLIGHT	257	14
UNDER ONE SACRAMENT [FIRMAMENT]	WHILE IT IS ALIVE	491	5
THEN STEPPED STRAIGHT THROUGH THE FIRMAMENT	TWO BUTTERFLIES WENT OUT	533	3
THE WRENCHING--FOR HIS FIRMAMENT	WE SEE--COMPARATIVELY--	534	11
ENROLLED UPON THE HEMISPHERE [FIRMAMENT]	THE DAY UNDRESSED--	716	7
FADES FROM THE FIRMAMENT AWAY--	SWEET MOUNTAINS--YE TELL	722	11
HER BONNET IS THE FIRMAMENT--	THE MOON WAS BUT A CHIN	737	17

	FIRST LINE	POEM		LINE
FIRMAMENT (CONTINUED)				
OR FATHER IN THE FIRMAMENT--	HE TOLD A HOMELY TALE	763		11
LEST FIRMAMENT [UNIVERSE / DEITY] SHOULD FAIL FOR ME--	MY FAITH IS LARGER THAN	766		15
AS PARALLAX [FIRMAMENT] A FLAME--	I THOUGHT THAT NATURE	1286		4
TWIXT FIRMAMENT ABOVE	A SINGLE CLOVER PLANK	1343		5
AND FIRMAMENT BELOW	A SINGLE CLOVER PLANK	1343		6
AND FIRMAMÊNT SALUTE THEE,	TO THE STANCH DUST	1402	V	6
BEHOLD HOW GREAT A FIRMAMENT	NO MATTER WHERE THE	1541		3
DEPUTED FROM WHAT FIRMAMENT--	THE BAT IS DUN, WITH	1575		9
FIRMAMENTAL				
BROUGHT ME--FROM FIRMAMENTAL SEAS--	WHAT WOULD I GIVE TO SEE	247		19
THE FIRMAMENTAL LILAC	THE LILAC IS AN ANCIENT	1241		3
WERE IT A FIRMAMENTAL PRODUCT--	I THINK THAT THE ROOT OF	1302		3
FIRMAMENT'S				
THE FIRMAMENT'S--TO PLUCK HER--	SHE DWELLETH IN THE	671		7
FIRMAMENTS				
TO FIRMAMENTS OF SUN--	AS IF SOME LITTLE ARCTIC	180		6
AND FIRMAMENTS--ROW--	SAFE IN THEIR ALABASTER	216	V	
THE UNIVERSE--IS [FIRMAMENTS--ARE] STILL--	HE FUMBLES AT YOUR SOUL	315		14
MY BASKET HOLDS--JUST--FIRMAMENTS--	PERHAPS I ASKED TOO	352		5
WITH FIRMAMENTS [CENTURIES] BETWEEN	CONTAINED IN THIS SHORT	1165	V	
THE EPICURE OF FIRMAMENTS [VEHICLES / COURTESY / PURPOSES]	A SPARROW TOOK A SLICE	1211	V	7
BUT FIRMAMENTS WERE NOT HIS FELLOWS--	A WORLD MADE PENNINILESS	1623	V	3
FIRMER				
FLUTTERING FIRST--THEN FIRMER	MORNS LIKE THESE--WE	27		3
IF BROADCLOTH HEARTS [BREASTS] ARE FIRMER--	A SHADY FRIEND--FOR	278		7
'TWAS LIGHTER [FIRMER]--TO BE BLIND--	FROM BLANK TO BLANK--	761		10
THE HOUSES FIRMER ROOT--	THE SYMPTOM OF THE GALE	1327		5
ALLOYS OUR FIRMER MOMENTS	THROUGH THOSE OLD	1753		13
FIRMEST				
PUT ME IN ON THE FIRMEST [TIGHTEST / HIGHEST] SIDE--	TIE THE STRINGS TO MY	279		5
OF HEAVEN ABOVE THE FIRMEST PROOF	IMMORTAL IS AN AMPLE	1205		5
FIRMNESS				
WE TRY TO SHOW BECOMING FIRMNESS [CALMNESS]--	MARCH IS THE MONTH OF	1404		5
FIRST				
WHO FIRST OBSERVED THE MOON!	"SIC TRANSIT GLORIA	3		12
FLUTTERING FIRST--THEN FIRMER	MORNS LIKE THESE--WE	27		3
IF NIGHT STANDS FIRST--THEN NOON	IF PAIN FOR PEACE	63		7
OF THE FIRST LEAGUE OUT FROM LAND?	EXULTATION IS THE GOING	76		8
IF YOU SH'D GET THERE FIRST	GOING TO HEAVEN!	79		13
NEAREST THE DOOR--TO WAKE THE FIRST--	WHOSE ARE THE LITTLE	142		11
ON TIME'S FIRST AFTERNOON!	MUSICIANS WRESTLE	157		12
DOUBTLESS THE FIRST EXCURSION	I MET A KING THIS	166		23
AT FIRST, REPEAT IT SLOW!	'TIS SO MUCH JOY! 'TIS	172		15
FIRST--AT THE VAT--AND LATEST AT THE VINE--	WE--BEE AND I--LIVE BY	230		14
LAST [FIRST]--AT THE KNOCKER--	JUST SO--JESUS--RAPS--	317		3
AND FIRST [THEN]--AT THE BELL.	JUST SO--JESUS--RAPS--	317		4
FIRST--CHILL--THEN STUPOR--THEN THE LETTING GO--	AFTER GREAT PAIN, A	341		13
I DREADED THAT FIRST ROBIN, SO,	I DREADED THAT FIRST	348		1
TILL THAT FIRST SHOUT GOT BY--	I DREADED THAT FIRST	348		6
YOU, SIR, TAUGHT FIRST--TO ME.	ALTHOUGH I PUT AWAY HIS	366		33
THE FIRST--A GNAT'S HORIZON	I KNOW LIVES, I COULD	372		7
CAUGHT SUNRISE FIRST--AND SUNSET--LAST--	A HOUSE UPON THE HIGHT--	399		7
THE FIRST DAY'S NIGHT HAD COME--	THE FIRST DAY'S NIGHT	410		1
AS CHILDREN--SWINDLED FOR THE FIRST	I MEANT TO HAVE BUT	476		27
SHE LEAPS, BUT ROBIN LEAPED THE FIRST--	SHE SIGHTS A BIRD--SHE	507		7
MY SECOND RANK--TOO SMALL THE FIRST--	I'M CEDED--I'VE STOPPED	508		14
OR GRISLY FROSTS--FIRST AUTUMN MORNS,	IT WAS NOT DEATH, FOR I	510		19
'TWAS WARM--AT FIRST--LIKE US--	'TWAS WARM--AT FIRST--	519		1
THE HEART ASKS PLEASURE [BLESSING]--FIRST--	THE HEART ASKS PLEASURE	536		1
AND IS THE FIRST, TO RISE--	SHE HIDETH HER THE LAST	557		2
FIRST--POETS--THEN THE SUN--	I RECKON--WHEN I COUNT	569		2
BUT, LOOKING BACK--THE FIRST SO SEEMS	I RECKON--WHEN I COUNT	569		5
MY FIRST WELL DAY--SINCE MANY ILL--	MY FIRST WELL DAY--SINCE	574		1
I PRAYED, AT FIRST, A LITTLE GIRL,	I PRAYED, AT FIRST, A	576		1
HOW MIDNIGHT FELT, AT FIRST--TO ME--	IF I MAY HAVE IT, WHEN	577		15
WHEN FIRST A SOMBRE [LITTLE] GIRL--	I THINK I WAS ENCHANTED	593		2
WHAT LAST [FIRST]	TO KNOW JUST HOW HE	622		19
BUT YOU--WERE CROWNED [YOUR'S WAS FIRST--] IN JUNE--	OURSELVES WERE WED ONE	631		16
AT FIRST--A DOUBTFUL TONE--	YOU'LL KNOW HER--BY HER	634		22
'TIS FIRST--I LOCK THE DOOR--	THE WAY I READ A	636		2
WHOM DEATH SEE FIRST--'TIS NEWS OF THIS	BEREAVEMENT IN THEIR	645		7
HE [FIRST]--MUST PASS THE CRYSTAL ANGLE [LIMIT]	HER SWEET TURN TO LEAVE	649		25
SO MISERABLE A SOUND--AT FIRST--	A PRISON GETS TO BE A	652		11
THAT FIRST DAY, WHEN YOU PRAISED ME, SWEET,	THAT FIRST DAY, WHEN YOU	659		1
FIRST TIME THEY TRY THE SKY!	AGAIN--HIS VOICE IS AT	663		23
HE HATH TRAVERSED FIRST--	LIFE--IS WHAT WE MAKE IT	698		10
A FIRST MUTE COMING--	A FIRST MUTE COMING--	702		1
A FIRST FAIR GOING--	A FIRST MUTE COMING--	702		3
A FIRST EXCHANGE--OF	A FIRST MUTE COMING--	702		5
I FIRST SURMISED THE HORSES HEADS	BECAUSE I COULD NOT STOP	712		23
. . . TOLD HER] FIRST--	I MEANT TO FIND HER WHEN	718		7
WE THIRST AT FIRST--'TIS NATURE'S ACT--	WE THIRST AT FIRST--'TIS	726		1
'TWAS THE FIRST MIRACLE	LET US PLAY YESTERDAY--	728		23

	FIRST LINE	POEM	LINE
FIRST (CONTINUED)			
OR FIRST PROSPECTIVE--OR THE GOLD	SHE ROSE TO HIS	732	7
'TIS FIRST [YOU SEE] HE STEPS UPON THE VANE--	MY FAITH IS LARGER THAN	766	5
AT FIRST--A SCANT NUTRITION--[PLAIN REGALING]	DEPRIVED OF OTHER	773	3
I WAKED, TO FIND IT FIRST AWAKE--	BEREAVED OF ALL, I WENT	784	9
SO FIRST AM I SUPPLIED--	THE LUXURY TO APPREHEND	815	8
TILL YOU HAD TASTED FIRST,	I COULD NOT DRINK IT,	818	2
EVERY DAWN, IS FIRST.	ALWAYS MINE!	839	9
MUST FIRST PRESENT	THE GOOD WILL OF A	849	3
FINDING IS THE FIRST ACT	FINDING IS THE FIRST ACT	870	1
THE DEEPEST HID IS SIGHTED FIRST	OF CONSCIOUSNESS, HER	894	5
FIRST SUITOR NOT IN VAIN.	HOW FORTUNATE THE GRAVE	897	4
THE FIRST DAY THAT I WAS A LIFE	THE FIRST DAY THAT I WAS	902	1
'TWAS STILLER--THOUGH THE FIRST	THE FIRST DAY THAT I WAS	902	5
'TWAS EMPTY--BUT THE FIRST	THE FIRST DAY THAT I WAS	902	7
A FIRST NESCESSITY.	FAITH--IS THE PIERLESS	915	12
TASTES DEATH--THE FIRST--TO HAND [PASS / PROVE] THE STING	LOVE--IS THAT LATER	924	5
A SUMMER BRIEFER THAN THE FIRST	THERE IS A JUNE WHEN	930	3
MAY NOT OUR SECOND WITH IT'S FIRST	THERE IS A JUNE WHEN	930	13
AS THOSE FIRST FURNISHED, SAID--	TWO TRAVELLERS PERISHING	933	16
IN WHICH WE FIRST EXPERIENCED LIGHT	ON THAT DEAR FRAME THE	940	3
MAKE THEIR FIRST REPOSE THIS WINTER	SNOW BENEATH WHOSE	942	3
THE FIRST THAT I COULD RECOLLECT	A LOSS OF SOMETHING EVER	959	2
THE FIRST--SWEET, PROVED I, [THAT WAS] ERE I SAW THEE--	WERT THOU BUT ILL--THAT	961	19
IT'S [THE] FIRST--DELIGHT--AND THEN--SURPRISE--	FITTER TO SEE HIM, I MAY	968	10
OF ME--WHEN FIRST UNTO THE DOOR	FITTER TO SEE HIM, I MAY	968	17
'TIS FIRST A COBWEB ON THE SOUL	CRUMBLING IS NOT AN	997	5
THE FIRST WE KNEW OF HIM WAS DEATH--	THE FIRST WE KNEW OF HIM	1006	1
EXCEPT THE FIRST HAD JUSTIFIED	THE FIRST WE KNEW OF HIM	1006	3
FIRE EXISTS THE FIRST IN LIGHT	ASHES DENOTE THAT FIRE	1063	5
'TIS MY FIRST NIGHT BENEATH THE SUN	'TIS MY FIRST NIGHT	1122	1
IT MUST AT FIRST BE TRUE--	THE SMOULDERING EMBERS	1132	V 8
A LOAD IS FIRST IMPOSSIBLE	I SHOULD NOT DARE TO BE	1197	3
THE FLOWERS NOTICE FIRST	THE FROST WAS NEVER SEEN	1202	4
A DEED KNOCKS FIRST AT THOUGHT	A DEED KNOCKS FIRST AT	1216	1
LET MY FIRST KNOWING BE OF THEE	LET MY FIRST KNOWING BE	1218	1
AND MY FIRST FEARING, LEST UNKNOWNS	LET MY FIRST KNOWING BE	1218	3
THE POPULAR HEART IS A CANNON FIRST--	THE POPULAR HEART IS A	1226	1
HE FIRST ACHIEVE [ESPOUSE] THY FACE	MY HEART RAN SO TO THEE	1237	6
HOWEVER FIRST [TRUE / DUE / JUST] IT BE	BECAUSE THAT YOU ARE	1260	6
ENOUGH--THE FIRST ABODE	UNTIL THE DESERT KNOWS	1291	10
FIRST AT THE MARCH--COMPETING WITH THE WIND--	AFTER ALL BIRDS HAVE	1395	5
BETRAYS [REPORTS] US, AS HIS FIRST BETROTHAL	MARCH IS THE MONTH OF	1404	7
IN WHICH THE SOUL AT FIRST ESTRANGED [ALARMED / SUBMERGED]--	THE INUNDATION OF THE	1425	5
CONDUCTED FIRST	DEATH IS THE SUPPLE	1445	4
A SPECK OF RAPTURE--FIRST PERCEIVED	A WINGED SPARK DOTH SOAR	1468	7
WHERE HE DOES NOT [FIRST] PRESIDE	ALL THAT I DO	1496	V 9
AND FIRST PRONOUNCED "A FIT."	MY COUNTRY NEED NOT	1511	4
JUDAS--THE GREAT [FIRST] DEFAULTER--	THE BIBLE IS AN ANTIQUE	1545	7
THOUGH FIRST UPON A BERRY FAT	CONFERRING WITH MYSELF	1655	3
THAT MADE THEE FIRST UNKNOWN	I SEE THEE CLEARER FOR	1666	6
FIRST TIME TOGETHER THROWN.	A FACE DEVOID OF LOVE OR	1711	6
IS SHORTER THAN THE FIRST.	CONSULTING SUMMER'S	1715	6
HAD I KNOWN THAT THE FIRST WAS THE LAST	HAD I KNOWN THAT THE	1720	1
HAD I KNOWN THAT THE LAST WAS THE FIRST	HAD I KNOWN THAT THE	1720	3
DOES NOT AT FIRST APPEAR;	THE DISTANCE THAT THE	1742	2
THAT FIRST ABANDONED [ABSCONDED] YEAR.	THE DISTANCE THAT THE	1742	V 4
THE RIOT GIVEN AT THE FIRST	THE MOB WITHIN THE HEART	1745	3
FISH			
MY PANTRY HAS A FISH	THE WATERS CHASED HIM AS	1749	6
FISHERMAN			
FOR FISHERMAN TO PLUMB--	THAT AFTER HORROR--THAT	286	6
FISHERMAN'S			
A FISHERMAN'S--DEGREE--	WHAT SOFT--CHERUBIC	401	10
FISSURE			
WHEN SUNRISE THROUGH A FISSURE DROP	THIS CHASM, SWEET, UPON	858	3
FISSURES			
THROUGH FISSURES IN	THE WIND DREW OFF	1694	4
FIST			
TO "TOBY'S" FIST--	IS IT TRUE, DEAR SUE?	218	10
FISTS			
AND SHOOK THEIR FISTS--	AN AWFUL TEMPEST MASHED	198	7
HIS FINGERS ARE THE SIZE OF FISTS--	THEY LEAVE US WITH THE	350	3
HIS FISTS, THE SIZE OF MEN--	THEY LEAVE US WITH THE	350	4
AND OAKS UNTWIST [UNKNOT / UNKNIT / UNCLINCH] THEIR FISTS--	THE TRUTH--IS STIRLESS--	780	5
FIT			
THE SMALLEST "ROBE" WILL FIT ME	GOING TO HEAVEN!	79	16
HER BREAST IS FIT FOR PEARLS,	HER BREAST IS FIT FOR	84	1
HER BROW IS FIT FOR THRONES	HER BREAST IS FIT FOR	84	3
HER HEART IS FIT FOR HOME [REST]--	HER BREAST IS FIT FOR	84	5
AND WEAR--IF GOD SHOULD COUNT ME FIT--	A SOLEMN THING--IT WAS--	271	3
NONE BUT THE NUT--OCTOBER FIT--	THE ROBIN'S MY CRITERION	285	10
TO FIT SOME CRUCIFIXAL CLEF--	THE MORNING AFTER WO--	364	15
THEN--FIT OUR VISION TO THE DARK--	WE GROW ACCUSTOMED TO	419	7
HOW LIKE "A FIT"--THEN--	IT DONT SOUND SO	426	16

	FIRST LINE	POEM	LINE
FIT (CONTINUED)			
OF AMBER--FIT--	THE MALAY--TOOK THE	452	13
A DIADEM TO FIT A DOME--	'TIS LITTLE I--COULD	466	7
BUT SOMETHING AWKWARD IN [ODD ABOUT] THE FIT--	I COULD NOT PROVE THE	563	11
TO FIT IT'S SIDES [RIBS]	I LIKE TO SEE IT LAP	585	9
THE SEASONS--FIT--THE SAME--	IT MAKES NO DIFFERENCE	620	2
FIT [STRAIN] HIS COUNTENANCE--	BLOOM UPON THE MOUNTAIN	667	18
CRUMBS--FIT SUCH LITTLE MOUTHS--	VICTORY COMES LATE--	690	10
FIT FOR HER RECEPTION--NOW--	THESE--SAW VISIONS--	758	15
FIT.	BANISH AIR FROM AIR--	854	6
BUT COULD NOT MAKE THEM FIT.	I FELT A CLEAVING IN MY	937	4
HERE, WHERE THE DAISIES FIT MY HEAD	HERE, WHERE THE DAISIES	1037	1
WHICH IF THEY DO NOT FIT FOR EARTH	TO HELP OUR BLEAKER	1064	3
I FIT FOR THEM--	I FIT FOR THEM--	1109	1
TILL I AM THOROUGH FIT.	I FIT FOR THEM--	1109	3
BELIEF, IT DOES NOT FIT SO WELL	WHO WERE "THE FATHER AND	1258	19
DOES FINEST GLORY FIT!	THE MOST TRIUMPHANT BIRD	1265	9
IT IS NOT FIT FOR TABLE	THE BONE THAT HAS NO	1274	3
AND FIRST PRONOUNCED "A FIT."	MY COUNTRY NEED NOT	1511	4
CAN FIT BUT HIM ALONE	THE PATTERN OF THE SUN	1550	2
FITNESS			
IT'S FITNESS GROWING LIKE THE FLOOD	THE THRILL CAME SLOWLY	1495	3
FITS			
AND THIS WORN SHOE JUST FITS THE TRACK--	'TWAS THE OLD--ROAD--	344	15
THE FOX FITS THE HOUND--	GOOD TO HIDE, AND HEAR	842	4
THOSE IT FITS, TOO FAIR TO WEAR IT--	"FAITHFUL TO THE END"	1357	V
HOW FITS HIS UMBER COAT	HOW FITS HIS UMBER COAT	1371	1
FITTED			
AND FITTED TO A FRAME,	IT WAS NOT DEATH, FOR I	510	14
IS FASHIONED FOR [FITTED TO] HIS HAND--	'TIS ONE BY ONE--THE	545	16
I FITTED TO THE LATCH	I YEARS HAD BEEN FROM	609	17
IN CAREFUL FITTED GROUND	NO NOTICE GAVE SHE, BUT	804	14
'TWAS AWKWARD, BUT IT FITTED ME--	'TWAS AWKWARD, BUT IT	973	1
I FITTED INTO PLACE--	I WAS A PHEBE--NOTHING	1009	4
IT FITTED THEM, CAME IN.	I HEARD, AS IF I HAD NO	1039	8
CAN NEVER BE FITTED [MATCHED] AGAIN?	OF THE HEART THAT GOES	1098	4
FITTED ITSELF TO HIMSELF LIKE A ROBE	THE EVENT WAS DIRECTLY	1686	3
FITTER			
FITTER FEET--OF HER [FOR THE FEET] BEFORE US--	HER SWEET TURN TO LEAVE	649	13
FITTER COURTESY	CONSCIOUS AM I IN MY	679	6
HOW ['TIS] FITTER THEY WILL [I SHALL] BE--FOR [BY] WANT--	I PLAY AT RICHES--TO	801	21
FITTER TO SEE HIM, I MAY BE	FITTER TO SEE HIM, I MAY	968	1
T'WERE FITTER CERTIFYING	THE BUTTERFLY OBTAINS	1685	11
FITTEST			
FITTEST THE CROWN!	FOR THIS--ACCEPTED	195	17
FITTING			
AND FITTING NO ONE ELSE--	I AM ALIVE--I GUESS--	470	20
TIGHT FITTING--ORANGE--BROWN--	YOU'LL KNOW HER--BY HER	634	10
THERE IS A FITTING--A [TOTAL IN] DISMAY--	WHILE WE WERE FEARING IT	1277	5
A FITTING--A DESPAIR--	WHILE WE WERE FEARING IT	1277	6
ARE FITTING FOR THE BEE,	WHAT TENEMENTS OF CLOVER	1338	2
FIVE			
THE DAY CAME SLOW--TILL FIVE O'CLOCK--	THE DAY CAME SLOW--TILL	304	1
FIX			
I COULD NOT FIX THE YEAR--	A THOUGHT WENT UP MY	701	4
FIXED			
FIXED FULL, AND STEADY, ON HIS OWN	I PRAYED, AT FIRST, A	576	7
A FIXED DELIGHT,	THESE TESTED OUR HORIZON	886	6
FLAG			
WHO TOOK THE FLAG TODAY	SUCCESS IS COUNTED	67	6
STILL REARS THE EAST HER AMBER FLAG--	A SOMETHING IN A	122	16
SUNRISE--HAST THOU A FLAG FOR ME?	A WIFE--AT DAYBREAK I	461	2
ETERNITY'S WHITE [COOL] FLAG--BEFORE [IN FRONT]--	OUR JOURNEY HAD ADVANCED	615	11
THEN ORIENT SHOWED [THE EAST PUT OUT / NATURE PUT OUT] A SINGLE FLAG,	A DROP FELL ON THE APPLE	794	15
OR FLAG SUBSIST OR FAME EXPORT	STEP LIGHTLY ON THIS	1183	7
AND WITH A FLAG AT EVERY TURN	THEIR BARRICADE AGAINST	1471	3
FLAGGED			
THESE FEET THAT NEVER FLAGGED--	THIS HEART THAT BROKE SO	145	2
FLAGON'S			
RECKON THE MORNING'S FLAGON'S UP	BRING ME THE SUNSET IN A	128	2
FLAGONS			
FLAGONS, AND COOLING TAMARIND!	WHO NEVER LOST, ARE	73	4
THOSE THIRSTY LIPS TO FLAGONS PRESSED,	AS WATCHERS HANG UPON	121	11
BEE--PLEDGES HIS--IN MINUTE FLAGONS--	WE--BEE AND I--LIVE BY	230	10
FLAGS			
THE FLAGS OF NATIONS SWANG.	A DAY! HELP! HELP!	42	6
HUNG OUT IT'S FLAGS OF SNOW--	THE HIMMALEH WAS KNOWN	481	6
FLAGS, ARE A BRAVE SIGHT--	INCONCEIVABLY SOLEMN!	582	8
LIKE HINDERED FLAGS--SWEET HOISTED--	THE TREES LIKE TASSELS--	606	23
FLAGS--VEX A DYING FACE--	THE WORLD--FEELS DUSTY	715	5
. . . BURST / FLAGS / STEP / TICK / SHOUTS / PINK / RED / . . .	ONE JOY OF SO MUCH	1420	6
FLAIL			
BEFORE THE COMING FLAIL--	MIDSUMMER, WAS IT, WHEN	962	6
FLAKE			
INTACT, IN EVERLASTING FLAKE--	DOUBT ME! MY DIM	275	24
GLOBE ROSES--BREAK THEIR SATIN FLAKE--	I TEND MY FLOWERS FOR	339	16

	FIRST LINE	POEM	LINE
FLAKE (CONTINUED)			
THAN FLAKE OF SNOW, DIVIDED WITH [IMPRINTED SWIFT]	HE TOLD A HOMELY TALE	763	7
A TRAVELLING FLAKE OF SNOW	THE SKY IS LOW--THE	1075	2
I SAW THAT THE FLAKE WAS ON IT	I SAW THAT THE FLAKE WAS	1267	1
THE FLAKE THE WIND EXASPERATE	THE FLAKE THE WIND	1361	1
THE THOUGHT IS [SCENE WAS] QUIET AS A FLAKE--	THE FARTHEST THUNDER	1581	17
MERELY FLAKE OR PETAL	"LETHE" IN MY FLOWER,	1730	5
FLAKES			
SNOW FLAKES	I COUNTED TILL THEY	36	T
AS FLAKES OF SNOW STOOD [DID] YESTERDAY--	SOME RAINBOW--COMING	64	14
AND STEPPED LIKE FLAKES OF SNOW--	THE ONLY GHOST I EVER	274	4
THEY DROPPED LIKE FLAKES--	THEY DROPPED LIKE FLAKES	409	1
HIS COMRADES, SHIFTED LIKE THE FLAKES	HE FOUGHT LIKE THOSE	759	9
SOFT STIRS THE NEWS [STIR THE FLAKES] OF LIGHT	THE SMOULDERING EMBERS	1132	5
FLAMBEAU			
AND THE ODD FLAMBEAU, NO MEN CARRY	HOW THE OLD MOUNTAINS	291	15
FLAMBEAUX			
AS SLOW HER FLAMBEAUX BURN AWAY	A SOMETHING IN A	122	2
FLAME			
AND SPLIT THEIR PODS OF FLAME--	IT MAKES NO DIFFERENCE	620	4
FORCE FLAME	BANISH AIR FROM AIR--	854	9
AS PARALLAX [FIRMAMENT] A FLAME--	I THOUGHT THAT NATURE	1286	4
BUT WE DEMAND [BINDLESS IS] THE FLAME	FAME IS THE ONE THAT	1475	8
FLAME'S			
HAS VANQUISHED [SATED] FLAME'S CONDITIONS,	DARE YOU SEE A SOUL AT	365	5
FLAMINGO			
HAVE I THE LIP OF THE FLAMINGO	HOW THE OLD MOUNTAINS	291	7
COULD DISPARAGE [DISHONOR] A FLAMINGO--	AUTUMN--OVERLOOKED MY	748	3
FLANKED			
DID LEAP, FULL FLANKED, UPON THE HOST--	ONE ANGUISH--IN A CROWD	565	7
FORTITUDE--FLANKED [STANCHED] WITH MELODY.	AFTER ALL BIRDS HAVE	1395	V 8
FLAP			
FLAP PAST IT TO THE	FAME IS A FICKLE FOOD	1659	8
FLARE			
THE FLASH [FLARE / GLARE / BLARE] BETWEEN THE CREVICES OF CRASH--	IT WAS A QUIET SEEMING	1419	V
FLASH			
NOT YET SUSPECTED--[STILL UNSUSPECTED] BUT FOR FLASH [FORK]--	THE SOUL'S DISTINCT	974	7
THE FLASH [FLARE / GLARE / BLARE] BETWEEN THE CREVICES OF CRASH--	IT WAS A QUIET SEEMING	1419	V
BUT [AND] I WOULD NOT EXCHANGE THE BOLT [FLASH]	THE FARTHEST THUNDER	1581	7
FLASHING			
TO SEE IT FLASHING WHEN HE DINES	A SAUCER HOLDS A CUP	1374	11
FLASK			
A FLASK OF DEW--A BEE OR TWO--	A SEPAL, PETAL, AND A	19	3
NAKED OF FLASK--NAKED OF CASK--	A TOAD, CAN DIE OF LIGHT	583	10
FLASKS			
FROM FLASKS--SO SMALL--	I TEND MY FLOWERS FOR	339	14
FAINTING! FLASKS OF AIR!	WOULD YOU LIKE SUMMER?	691	7
FLATTENS			
SHE FLATTENS--THEN SHE CRAWLS--	SHE SIGHTS A BIRD--SHE	507	2
FLATTERED			
FLATTERED BY OBEISANCE	ABRAHAM TO KILL HIM	1317	7
FLAUNTED			
THE TRUTH NEVER FLAUNTED [HOISTED] A SIGN--	HE PREACHED UPON	1207	4
FLAVOR			
ITALIC FLAVOR YIELD--	WINTER IS GOOD--HIS HOAR	1316	2
FORBIDDEN FRUIT A FLAVOR HAS	FORBIDDEN FRUIT A FLAVOR	1377	1
FLAVORLESS			
IS FLAVORLESS--COMBINE	IMPOSSIBILITY, LIKE WINE	838	4
FLAVORS			
FLAVORS OF THAT OLD CRUCIFIXION--	TO PUT THIS WORLD DOWN,	527	9
HE OFFERS [SPICES / FLAVORS] HIS BERRY, JUST THE SAME	THE BLACK BERRY--WEARS A	554	3
AS FLAVORS--CHEER RETARDED GUESTS	UNTO MY BOOKS--SO GOOD	604	5
FLAW			
EXCEPT IT HAVE THE FLAW--	WHEN WE STAND ON THE	242	6
OUR ADORATION STAIN [MAR / FLAW]	WE SHUN BECAUSE WE PRIZE	1429	3
FLED			
REMARK THAT BIRDS HAVE FLED!	THERE'S SOMETHING	45	16
HERSELF--THOUGH--FLED!	'TWAS THE OLD--ROAD--	344	16
AT WHAT O'CLOCK TO HEAVEN--THEY FLED--	WE PRAY--TO HEAVEN--	489	4
AND FLED WITH EVERY ONE--	SHE SIGHTS A BIRD--SHE	507	12
FLED [STOLE] GASPING FROM THE HOUSE--	I YEARS HAD BEEN FROM	609	24
AND SHE HAD PAST, WITH [FLED WITH / TRUSTED / HEARKENED] HIM--	I MEANT TO FIND HER WHEN	718	8
THE CATTLE FLUNG [FLED] TO BARNS--	THE WIND BEGUN TO KNEAD	824	14
ALL IT'S PURPLE FLED	REVOLUTION IS THE POD	1082	10
SIMPLICITY FLED FROM HIS COUNTERFEIT PRESENCE	HE PREACHED UPON	1207	5
IT SHAMES THE CONSTANCY THAT FLED	SHE LAID HER DOCILE	1396	7
AND HUMAN NATURE HID [POPULATION FLED]	IT WAS A QUIET SEEMING	1419	9
AND FENCES FLED AWAY	THERE CAME A WIND LIKE A	1593	10
THE WATERS CHASED HIM AS HE FLED,	THE WATERS CHASED HIM AS	1749	1
FLEE			
OFFEND THE VISION--AND IT FLEE--	WHY MAKE IT DOUBT--IT	462	10
LIKE GLOW WORMS, FLEE AWAY--	THE SUN AND MOON MUST	871	8
I TRY TO FLEE	BECAUSE MY BROOK IS	1200	6

	FIRST LINE	POEM	LINE
FLIGHT			
WHEN BUMBLEBEES IN SOLEMN FLIGHT	WHEN ROSES CEASE TO	32	3
THE PEACE--THE FLIGHT--THE AMETHYST--	THE DAISY FOLLOWS SOFT	106	11
DELIGHT IS AS THE FLIGHT--	DELIGHT IS AS THE FLIGHT	257	1
EXCEPT THAT FLIGHT	DELIGHT IS AS THE FLIGHT	257	8
AS TO BEHOLD HIS AMPLE [GENTLE] FLIGHT--	THE MERCHANT OF THE	1131	11
PERHAPS COME [COMES] CLOSER, FOR THE LAPSE [FLIGHT]	PERHAPS THEY DO NOT GO	1399	3
NOR ANY FLIGHT [PAUSE]	ALL THAT I DO	1496	8
OH NO, BUT ON SOME OTHER FLIGHT--	WITHIN THY GRAVE!	1552	2
ASKS NOTHING BUT RELEASE--[IT'S FLIGHT]	AS FROM THE EARTH THE	1630	2
THERE'S SOMETHING IN THE FLIGHT	BY A DEPARTING LIGHT	1714	4
FLIGHTS			
AS SLIGHTLY [SCARCELY] AS THE ROUTES [FLIGHTS] OF STARS--	WE MISS HER, NOT BECAUSE	993	5
FLINCH			
LEST IF HE FLINCH--THE EYE THAT WAY	GRIEF IS A MOUSE--	793	10
FLING			
AND SHE WILL FLING HER MADDEST PERFUME--	KILL YOUR BALM--AND IT'S	238	3
IF HE FLING SAND [DUST], AND PEBBLE--	THE WIND DID'NT COME	316	17
THEY FLING THEIR SPEECH	PRAYER IS THE LITTLE	437	4
AND FLING A DUST--THE WHILE.	THE OUTER--FROM THE	451	8
FLING SUDDENLY ON MEN--	THE COLOR OF A QUEEN, IS	776	6
FRUITLESSER TO FLING--	PATIENCE--HAS A QUIET	926	6
FLING UP THY BALLS OF GOLD	MY GOD--HE SEES THEE--	1178	3
THE SPRING AVENGING FLING	UPON A LILAC SEA	1337	5
THEN FLING US POOR	DREAMS ARE THE SUBTLE	1376	3
FLINGING			
FLINGING THE PROBLEM BACK	MY WHEEL IS IN THE DARK!	10	14
FLINGS			
HER TROUBLED QUESTION FLINGS--	ONCE MORE, MY NOW	48	4
IT DEALS CELESTIAL [FLINGS A CRYSTAL] VAIL	IT SIFTS FROM LEADEN	311	12
SOMEBODY FLINGS A MATTRASS OUT--	THERE'S BEEN A DEATH, IN	389	9
THEN--FLINGS IN PARADISE--	THE LOVE A LIFE CAN SHOW	673	16
FLINT			
SOIL OF FLINT, IF STEADY [STEADFAST] TILLED--	SOIL OF FLINT, IF STEADY	681	1
WE PARTED AS THE CENTRAL FLINT	WE MET AS SPARKS--	958	3
A FLINT UNTO THIS DAY--PERHAPS--	WE MET AS SPARKS--	958	V 7
WOULD NOT A GOD OF FLINT	JUST ONCE! OH LEAST	1076	6
FLINTS			
WE MET AS SPARKS--DIVERGING FLINTS	WE MET AS SPARKS--	958	1
FLIPPANT			
A FLIPPANT FLY UPON THE PANE--	AN ALTERED LOOK ABOUT	140	7
FLIRT			
AND FLIRT ALL DAY WITH BUTTERCUPS	COULD I BUT RIDE	661	5
FLIT			
THE SEASONS FLIT--I'M TAUGHT--	THE ROBIN'S MY CRITERION	285	12
FLIT RUSSETLY AWAY	IT IS AN HONORABLE	946	8
ARE [FLIT / SHOW] AS THEY WERE NOT--	PAIN--EXPANDS THE TIME--	967	8
BUT THESE--ENDOWING AS THEY FLIT	DOMINION LASTS UNTIL	1257	3
OUR PROJECTS FLIT AWAY--	ON THAT SPECIFIC PILLOW	1533	2
FLITS			
APPROACHED [POSSESSED]--THE AMBER FLITS [MOVES]--A LITTLE--	DELIGHT--BECOMES	572	7
FLITS--GLIMMERS--PROVES--DISSOLVES--	THE LOVE A LIFE CAN SHOW	673	14
FLITS STEAM.	BANISH AIR FROM AIR--	854	12
LET HIM BE QUICK--THE VIAND FLITS [BANQUET COOLS]--	MINE ENEMY IS GROWING	1509	5
FLITTED			
THESE ARE THE VISIONS FLITTED [FASHIONS--BAFFLED--] GUIDO--	HOW THE OLD MOUNTAINS	291	21
REMITTED--SINCE IT FLITTED IT	PRAISE IT--'TIS DEAD--	1384	8
BUT THESE THE FLITTED SEED,	THAN HEAVEN MORE REMOTE,	1436	3
FLITTING			
HE VISITED--STILL FLITTING--	THE WIND--TAPPED LIKE A	436	17
OPINION IS A FLITTING THING,	OPINION IS A FLITTING	1455	1
FLOATING			
THRICE TO THE FLOATING CASEMENT	ONCE MORE, MY NOW	48	5
THE OBJECT FLOATING AT HIS SIDE	THE WATERS CHASED HIM AS	1749	9
FLOCK			
CONDENSES LIKE A FLOCK	IT SIFTS FROM LEADEN	311	V
AND LED THE FLOCK AWAY--	I'LL TELL YOU HOW THE	318	16
FLOCKS			
AS SURE AS FLOCKS GO HOME AT NIGHT	GOING TO HEAVEN!	79	9
THE TIRED FLOCKS COME IN	LET DOWN THE BARS, OH	1065	2
FLOOD			
WORLDS [THE MILLER]--A FLOOD--	"MORNING"--MEANS	300	8
AND SHATTER [FLOOD] ME WITH DAWN!	AS IF I ASKED A COMMON	323	8
YOU CANNOT FOLD A FLOOD--	YOU CANNOT PUT A FIRE	530	5
BY SIX, THE FLOOD [GUSH] HAD DONE--	THE BIRDS BEGUN AT FOUR	783	17
LOOSE THE FLOOD--YOU SHALL FIND IT PATENT--	SPLIT THE LARK--AND	861	5
IT'S FITNESS GROWING LIKE THE FLOOD	THE THRILL CAME SLOWLY	1495	3
FLOODED			
SMALLER--THAT COVERED [FLOODED / SATED] VISION--HERE--	RENUNCIATION--IS A	745	16
FLOODING			
TOUCHING THE ROOF [FLOODING THE STEEPLE] AND TINTING THE BARN	BLAZING IN GOLD AND	228	6
FLOODS			
FROM WHICH FLOODS SO CONTRA FLOW--	FLOWERS--WELL--IF	137	6

	FIRST LINE	POEM	LINE
FLOODS (CONTINUED)			
WHEN FLOODS HAVE SLIT THE HILLS--	THE BRAIN, WITHIN IT'S	556	6
WHY FLOODS BE SERVED TO US--IN BOWLS--	ONE BLESSING HAD I THAN	756	19
AS FLOODS--ON WHITES OF WHEELS--	JOY TO HAVE MERITED THE	788	20
ESTABLISH MARCH, THE FLOODS ESCORT,	THE DUTIES OF THE WIND	1137	3
THE VOICE THAT STANDS FOR FLOODS TO ME	THE VOICE THAT STANDS	1189	1
AND LET THE FLOODS ABROAD--	LIKE RAIN IT SOUNDED	1235	12
FLOOR			
UPON THEIR GOLDEN FLOOR!	IN RAGS MYSTERIOUS AS	117	8
THAT ANGLE IN THE FLOOR,	I GOT SO I COULD HEAR	293	6
UPON MY GARDEN FLOOR--	I TEND MY FLOWERS FOR	339	17
AND FRIGATES--IN THE UPPER FLOOR	I STARTED EARLY--TOOK MY	520	5
AND TELL YOUR CEDAR FLOOR--	YOU CANNOT PUT A FIRE	530	8
AND LEAVE ME IN THE FLOOR--	I YEARS HAD BEEN FROM	609	20
AND NARROW AT THE FLOOR [DOOR]	THE WAY I READ A	636	10
LIKE BALLS--UPON A FLOOR.	I FELT A CLEAVING IN MY	937	8
A FLOOR TOO COOL FOR CORN--	A NARROW FELLOW IN THE	986	10
LIKE BALLS UPON A FLOOR--	THE DUST BEHIND I STROVE	992	4
MORTALITY'S GROUND FLOOR	IF MY BARK SINK	1234	3
FROM RECOLLECTION'S FLOOR	THE PILE OF YEARS IS NOT	1507	4
INHERITED THE FLOOR--	AS IMPERCEPTIBLY AS	1540	V
SURVEYED MY CHAMBER FLOOR	IN WINTER IN MY ROOM	1670	15
FLOORLESS			
WHERE HE IS FLOORLESS	WHAT MYSTERY PERVADES A	1400	15
FLOORS			
UPON THE FLOORS OF FAME--	I WAS A PHEBE--NOTHING	1009	8
FLORA			
THE FLORA UNIMPEACHABLE	THE LILAC IS AN ANCIENT	1241	15
FLORENTINE SEE ANGLO-FLORENTINE			
FLORID			
A DIMPLED [FLORID / DAPPLED] ROAD	THE ROAD TO PARADISE IS	1491	5
FLOSS			
A SEPULCHRE OF QUAINTEST FLOSS--	HE PARTS HIMSELF--LIKE	517	19
FLOSS WONT SAVE YOU FROM AN ABYSS	FLOSS WONT SAVE YOU FROM	1322	1
NOW WILL YOU HAVE THE ROPE OR THE FLOSS?	FLOSS WONT SAVE YOU FROM	1322	7
A MANSE OF MECHLIN AND OF FLOSS [GLOSS / SUN]--	THE FAIREST HOME I EVER	1423	5
FLOURISHING			
CONJECTURE FLOURISHING--	THESE ARE THE NIGHTS	1128	12
FLOW			
NO BRIMMING TANKARDS FLOW--	WHAT INN IS THIS	115	8
FROM WHICH FLOODS SO CONTRA FLOW--	FLOWERS--WELL--IF	137	6
FLOWED			
FLOWED SILVER TO THE WEST--	A POOR--TORN HEART-- A	78	4
FLOWER			
THE BEE DOTH COURT THE FLOWER, THE FLOWER HIS SUIT RECEIVES,	AWAKE YE MUSES NINE,	1	13
THE BEE DOTH COURT THE FLOWER, THE FLOWER HIS SUIT RECEIVES,	AWAKE YE MUSES NINE,	1	13
AND GIVE HER WHAT SHE ASKETH, JEWEL, OR BIRD, OR FLOWER--	AWAKE YE MUSES NINE,	1	38
THY FLOWER--FOREVERMORE!	SUMMER FOR THEE, GRANT I	31	9
I PULL A FLOWER FROM THE WOODS--	"ARCTURUS" IS HIS OTHER	70	9
WE SHOULD NOT MIND SO SMALL A FLOWER--	WE SHOULD NOT MIND SO	81	1
THAT WHOSO SEES THIS LITTLE FLOWER	WE SHOULD NOT MIND SO	81	9
THIS MEEKEST FLOWER OF THE MEAD	A SCIENCE--SO THE SAVANS	100	8
I SOW SWEET FLOWER FROM GARDEN BED--	WHERE I HAVE LOST, I	104	2
HE--WAKING--FINDS THE FLOWER THERE--	THE DAISY FOLLOWS SOFT	106	4
WE ARE THE FLOWER--THOU THE SUN!	THE DAISY FOLLOWS SOFT	106	7
BY A FLOWER--BY A LETTER--	BY A FLOWER--BY A LETTER	109	1
PERHAPS YOU'D LIKE TO BUY A FLOWER,	PERHAPS YOU'D LIKE TO	134	1
A FLOWER EXPECTED EVERYWHERE--	AN ALTERED LOOK ABOUT	140	10
FROM AN ACCUSTOMED [A FAMILIAR] FLOWER.	SHE WENT AS QUIET AS THE	149	2
A FLOWER SUPERFLUOUS BLOWN.	EXCEPT TO HEAVEN, SHE IS	154	4
DEAR, OLD FASHIONED, LITTLE FLOWER!	I'M THE LITTLE "HEART'S	176	9
I'D BRING THEM EVERY FLOWER THAT GROWS	IF I COULD BRIBE THEM BY	179	2
AS IF SOME LITTLE ARCTIC FLOWER	AS IF SOME LITTLE ARCTIC	180	1
I SAY, AS IF THIS LITTLE FLOWER	AS IF SOME LITTLE ARCTIC	180	9
THE FLOWER MUST NOT BLAME THE BEE--	THE FLOWER MUST NOT	206	1
REACHING LATE HIS FLOWER,	COME SLOWLY--EDEN!	211	5
THY FLOWER--BE GAY--	I TEND MY FLOWERS FOR	339	21
AND FLOWER--THAT ZEALOUS BLEW--	FROM COCOON FORTH A	354	19
THAT SOWED THE FLOWER, HE PREFERRED--	ALTHOUGH I PUT AWAY HIS	366	5
THERE IS A FLOWER THAT BEES PREFER--	THERE IS A FLOWER THAT	380	1
AND SO I PIECED IT, WITH A FLOWER, NOW.	TO LOVE THEE YEAR BY	434	6
AND PUT A FLOWER ON IT--	WE DO NOT PLAY ON GRAVES	467	5
OR LIKE A STEMLESS FLOWER--	I WATCHED THE MOON	629	17
I TAKE A FLOWER--AS I GO--	AGAIN--HIS VOICE IS AT	663	5
FLOWER OF A SINGLE SUNSET--	BLOOM UPON THE MOUNTAIN	667	V 3
CONFER UPON MY FLOWER--	THE GRACE--MYSELF--MIGHT	707	2
REMEMBERED--AS THE MILLINER'S FLOWER	PRECIOUS TO ME--SHE	727	12
THE MOST UNWORTHY FLOWER--	NATURE--THE GENTLEST	790	16
THE GOOD WILL OF A FLOWER	THE GOOD WILL OF A	849	1
ALWAY A FLOWER WOULD BE.	BECAUSE THE BEE MAY	869	6
THAT BEE TO RIDE, OR FLOWER OF FURZE	BECAUSE THE BEE MAY	869	11
OR SACRIFICIAL FLOWER--	IT WAS A GRAVE, YET BORE	876	V 12
I HIDE MYSELF WITHIN MY FLOWER,	I HIDE MYSELF WITHIN MY	903	1
SO OF THE FLOWER OF THE SOUL	THIS IS A BLOSSOM OF THE	945	7
IF OTHER FLOWER BECOME.	THIS IS A BLOSSOM OF THE	945	12
THE FLOWER OF OUR LORD.	THIS IS A BLOSSOM OF THE	945	16

	FIRST LINE	POEM	LINE
FLOWER (CONTINUED)			
THE FLOWER--DISTINCT AND RED--	IT BLOOMED AND DROPT, A	978	2
THE SINGLE FLOWER OF THE EARTH	IT BLOOMED AND DROPT, A	978	17
MY SEASON'S FURTHEST FLOWER--	MY SEASON'S FURTHEST	1019	1
I MAY CONFIDE MY FLOWER--	HERE, WHERE THE DAISIES	1037	6
BLOOM--IS RESULT--TO MEET A FLOWER	BLOOM--IS RESULT--TO	1058	1
TO BE A FLOWER, IS PROFOUND	BLOOM--IS RESULT--TO	1058	15
"SECURE [PROTECT] YOUR FLOWER" SAID HE.	THE FROST OF DEATH WAS	1136	2
OUR PASSIVE FLOWER WE HELD TO SEA--	THE FROST OF DEATH WAS	1136	5
AND THAT DEGRADES [PROFANES] THE FLOWER--	THE CLOVER'S SIMPLE FAME	1232	6
THE FLOWER OF OCCIDENT.	THE LILAC IS AN ANCIENT	1241	8
RED AS A CARDINAL FLOWER	WHITE AS AN INDIAN PIPE	1250	2
I SEND YOU A DECREPIT FLOWER	I SEND YOU A DECREPIT	1324	1
AS ON THE CONSCIENTIOUS FLOWER	THE SUN IS ONE--AND ON	1372	3
A SPIDER AND A FLOWER--	THE FAIREST HOME I EVER	1423	4
SO GAY A FLOWER	SO GAY A FLOWER	1456	1
AND THEN A SHOUTING FLOWER,--	THE DANDELION'S PALLID	1519	6
THE STEM OF A DEPARTED FLOWER	THE STEM OF A DEPARTED	1520	1
A FLOWER TO HELP HIS STRAIGHTENED FACE	AS IMPERCEPTIBLY AS	1540	V
TO THE SAME FLOWER HESPERIAN,	OF DEATH I TRY TO THINK	1558	7
FROM JUST A PURPLE FLOWER BEYOND	OF DEATH I TRY TO THINK	1558	13
THIS GALLANT LITTLE FLOWER--	IT WOULD NOT KNOW IF IT	1579	2
HOW THEREFORE SAFE TO BE A FLOWER	IT WOULD NOT KNOW IF IT	1579	3
UPON A FAMELESS FLOWER--	TO HER DERIDED HOME	1586	6
A FLOWER WILL NOT TROUBLE HER, IT HAS SO SMALL A FOOT,	A FLOWER WILL NOT	1621	1
TO ANY HAPPY FLOWER	APPARENTLY WITH NO	1624	2
OR FLOWER PRESUME TO SHOW	A LANE OF YELLOW LED THE	1650	6
AS FLOWER AT FALL OF FROST--	I WATCHED HER FACE TO	1667	8
WHATEVER FLOWER FAIL TO COME	NATURE CAN DO NO MORE	1673	3
"LETHE" IN MY FLOWER,	"LETHE" IN MY FLOWER,	1730	1
MY UNFREQUENTED FLOWER	OH, HONEY OF AN HOUR,	1734	5
FLOWER'S			
PERHAPS A FLOWER'S SHRIVELLED CHEEK	IN EBON BOX, WHEN YEARS	169	9
A FLOWER'S UNOBTRUSIVE FACE	THE DYING NEED BUT	1026	3
AS CAPSULES ARE FOR FLOWER'S--	THE FACE IN EVANESCENCE	1490	4
FLOWERS			
IN ITS UNFADING FLOWERS	THERE IS ANOTHER SKY,	2	11
THEN TAKE MY FLOWERS--PRAY!	WHEN ROSES CEASE TO	32	8
UPON A COUCH OF FLOWERS.	SHE DIED AT PLAY,	75	5
PARCHED THE FLOWERS THEY BEAR ALONG.	ANGELS, IN THE EARLY	94	8
MY FLOWERS TURN FROM FORUMS--	THE RAINBOW NEVER TELLS	97	5
MY FLOWERS RAISE THEIR PRETTY LIPS--	AS CHILDREN BID THE	133	3
MY FLOWERS FROM A HUNDRED CRIBS	AS CHILDREN BID THE	133	7
WHERE BASHFUL FLOWERS BLOW,	HAVE YOU GOT A BROOK IN	136	2
FLOWERS--WELL--IF ANYBODY	FLOWERS--WELL--IF	137	1
WITH WHICH FLOWERS HUMBLE MEN!	FLOWERS--WELL--IF	137	4
IF THE FOOLISH, CALL THEM "FLOWERS"--	IF THE FOOLISH, CALL	168	1
TO STRANGE, BRIGHT CROWDS OF FLOWERS--	AS IF SOME LITTLE ARCTIC	180	7
AFTER DINNER LIGHT--FOR FLOWERS--	MORNING--IS THE PLACE	197	3
LIKE JUGGLER'S FLOWERS [FIGURES] SITUATES	IT SIFTS FROM LEADEN	311	V
THE FLOWERS, ACCUSTOMED, BLEW,	THERE CAME A DAY AT	322	6
I TEND MY FLOWERS FOR THEE--	I TEND MY FLOWERS FOR	339	1
WHO INFLUENCES FLOWERS--	A VISITOR IN MARL--	391	2
HOW MANY FLOWERS FAIL IN WOOD--	HOW MANY FLOWERS FAIL IN	404	1
FLOWERS--TO KEEP THE EYES--FROM GOING AWKWARD--	IT'S THOUGHTS--AND JUST	495	12
LIKE [AS] FLOWERS, THAT HEARD THE NEWS OF DEWS,	LIKE FLOWERS, THAT HEARD	513	1
SHE PUT SOME FLOWERS AWAY--	MY FIRST WELL DAY--SINCE	574	10
BRIGHT FLOWERS SLIT A CALYX	THE TREES LIKE TASSELS--	606	21
WILD FLOWERS--KINDLE IN THE WOODS--	IT MAKES NO DIFFERENCE	620	5
THE FLOWERS--APPEALED--A TIMID THRONG--	THE BIRDS REPORTED FROM	743	5
THE FLOWERS WOULD SLUMBER ON [SLEEP UPON--] THEIR STEMS--	MY FAITH IS LARGER THAN	766	11
YET ONE--REJOICES FLOWERS--	THERE IS AN ARID	782	5
AND ONE--THE FLOWERS ABHOR--	THERE IS AN ARID	782	6
THE VEINS OF OTHER FLOWERS	THE VEINS OF OTHER	811	1
THE SCARLET FLOWERS ARE	THE VEINS OF OTHER	811	2
BECAUSE THE FLOWERS UNAFRAID	BECAUSE THE BEE MAY	869	4
BUT FLOWERS--NEGOTIATE BETWEEN US--	BETWEEN MY COUNTRY--AND	905	3
MUCH FLOWERS OF THIS AND FURTHER ZONES	IT BLOOMED AND DROPT, A	978	13
THE FLOWERS NOTICE FIRST	THE FROST WAS NEVER SEEN	1202	4
TO PLANETS AND TO FLOWERS	WE INTRODUCE OURSELVES	1214	2
A JAR ACROSS THE FLOWERS GOES	LIKE TRAINS OF CARS ON	1224	3
NOT ANY HOUSE THE FLOWERS KEEP--	THE NOTICE THAT IS	1310	5
LIKE FLOWERS IN A PLOT--	HER FACE WAS IN A BED OF	1722	2
FLOWING			
BLOOMING--TRIPPING--FLOWING--	SO HAS A DAISY VANISHED	28	7
FLOWN			
THOUGH FLOWN--	I HAVE A BIRD IN SPRING	5	9
THOUGH FLOWN	I HAVE A BIRD IN SPRING	5	27
WHEN SUMMER DAYS ARE FLOWN!	SUMMER FOR THEE, GRANT I	31	2
IN EBON BOX, WHEN YEARS HAVE FLOWN	IN EBON BOX, WHEN YEARS	169	1
MORE FLOWN INDEED	THAN HEAVEN MORE REMOTE,	1436	4
FLOWS			
AND NOBODY KNOWS, SO STILL IT FLOWS,	HAVE YOU GOT A BROOK IN	136	5
FLUCTUATES			
THAT COMPREHENSION FLUCTUATES [ANTEDATES]	PERHAPS THEY DO NOT GO	1399	7

	FIRST LINE	POEM	LINE
FLUCTUATION			
WE FEEL IT BY THE FLUCTUATION	MARCH IS THE MONTH OF	1404	V 3
FLUENT			
RECITED FLUENT--HERE--	I SHOULD HAVE BEEN TOO	313	12
OH LIFE, BEGUN IN FLUENT BLOOD	THAT ODD OLD MAN IS DEAD	1130	9
BECAUSE MY BROOK IS FLUENT	BECAUSE MY BROOK IS	1200	1
THE MOON UPON HER FLUENT ROUTE	THE MOON UPON HER FLUENT	1528	1
FLUENTLY			
ABSCONDED DAINTILY [FLUENTLY]	A SPARROW TOOK A SLICE	1211	V 8
FLUNG			
FLUNG COLORED, AFTER RAIN, ...	DELIGHT IS AS THE FLIGHT	257	6
UNTIL A ZEPHYR PUSHED [CHASED / FLUNG / SPURNED / SCOURGED] THEM	TWO BUTTERFLIES WENT OUT	533	V
YET BLAMED THE FATE THAT FRACTURED--[FLUNG IT] LESS	IT DROPPED SO LOW--IN MY	747	5
THE BUSHES [ORCHARDS / MEADOWS]--SPANGLES FLUNG--	A DROP FELL ON THE APPLE	794	12
HE FLUNG A HAND FULL AT THE PLAIN--	THE WIND BEGUN TO KNEAD	824	3
THE CATTLE FLUNG [FLED] TO BARNS--	THE WIND BEGUN TO KNEAD	824	14
THEN, AS FLUNG ASIDE	RIBBONS OF THE YEAR--	873	4
FLURRIEDLY			
AGAIN, HE TAPPED--'TWAS FLURRIEDLY--	THE WIND--TAPPED LIKE A	436	19
FLUTE			
FLUTE--OR WOMAN--	HER--"LAST POEMS"--	312	5
FLUTES			
SO SILVER STEAL A HUNDRED FLUTES	WE SHOULD NOT MIND SO	81	7
OR SKIP TO FLUTES--	ALTHOUGH I PUT AWAY HIS	366	20
FLUTTER			
AND BIRDS CAN FLUTTER DOWN--	I OFTEN PASSED THE	51	12
FLUTTER TOO FAR FOR ME--	A SOMETHING IN A	122	12
FLUTTER BOTH AWAY	YESTERDAY IS HISTORY,	1292	8
FLUTTERED			
THESE CHILDREN FLUTTERED HOME.	THROUGH LANE IT LAY--	9	17
THAT FLUTTERED PANTING, HERE--	THIS HEART THAT BROKE SO	145	6
THE MORNING--FLUTTERED--STAGGERED--	THE SUN--JUST TOUCHED	232	13
ILL FLUTTERED OUT--IN EVERLASTING WELL-- .	TO KNOW JUST HOW HE	622	17
FLUTTERING			
THE FLUTTERING OF HER FRINGES	DISTRUSTFUL OF THE	20	3
FLUTTERING FIRST--THEN FIRMER	MORNS LIKE THESE--WE	27	3
. . . THRILLING / FLUTTERING / COWERING] VAN	TO FLEE FROM MEMORY	1242	6
I WATCHED [BOUGHT] THE FLUTTERING [VANQUISHED] SPIRIT	I SAW THE WIND WITHIN	1502	V
FLUTTERS			
THE VISION FLUTTERS IN THE DOOR, ...	A WIFE--AT DAYBREAK I	461	V 12
FLY			
HE, TOO, DID FLY AWAY--	I HAD A GUINEA GOLDEN--	23	12
AND TRADES AS BRISKLY FLY--	IF I SHOULD DIE,	54	14
SOME THINGS THAT FLY THERE BE--	SOME THINGS THAT FLY	89	1
WITH IMPLEMENTS TO FLY AWAY, ...	BRING ME THE SUNSET IN A	128	23
A FLIPPANT FLY UPON THE PANE--	AN ALTERED LOOK ABOUT	140	7
AND STILL THE APRONS FLY, [SCENE PREVAILS] .	SHE SWEEPS WITH	219	10
BIND ONE--THE OTHER FLY--	NO RACK CAN TORTURE ME--	384	8
THAT SPICES FLY	UNDUE SIGNIFICANCE A	439	7
I HEARD A FLY BUZZ--WHEN I DIED--	I HEARD A FLY BUZZ--WHEN	465	1
THERE INTERPOSED A FLY--	I HEARD A FLY BUZZ--WHEN	465	12
WHO SAW THEM--WHEREFORE FLY?	WE PRAY--TO HEAVEN--	489	5
WHERE--OMNIPRESENCE--FLY?	WE PRAY--TO HEAVEN--	489	11
THE WEALTHY [HAPPY] FLY, UPON HIS PANE-- .	I ENVY SEAS, WHEREON HE	498	11
URGING THE FEET--THAT WOULD--NOT--FLY-- . .	BETTER--THAN MUSIC! FOR	503	12
AS HOUSEWIVES DO, A FLY.	IF YOU WERE COMING IN	511	4
WERE BUT MINE--THE CHARTER OF THE LEAST FLY--	I COULD DIE--TO KNOW--	570	6
AND FLY, AS 'TWERE PURSUING YOU?	DID YOU EVER STAND IN A	590	7
THE PRIVILEGE TO FLY	IT WOULD HAVE STARVED A	612	10
NEVER DENY ME--NEVER FLY--	SWEET MOUNTAINS--YE TELL	722	2
WHAT WHEN THE EGGS FLY OFF IN MUSIC . . .	WHAT SHALL I DO WHEN THE	956	3
I--DO NOT FLY, SO WHEREFORE	WHAT SHALL I DO WHEN THE	956	15
OF MONAD OR OF FLY	SHE SPED AS PETALS OF A	991	V 6
YOURS, FLY.	BEE! I'M EXPECTING YOU!	1035	12
THE APTITUDE TO FLY	MY COCOON TIGHTENS--	1099	6
AMPLER [BOLDER] TO FLY AWAY	ARE FRIENDS DELIGHT OR	1199	5
I CHARGE HIM FLY [FLEE]	THE PAST IS SUCH A	1203	6
MANY WOULD FLY [SOAR]	TO FLEE FROM MEMORY	1242	3
SO CHASTENED AS THE FLY--	THE BUTTERFLY IN HONORED	1246	4
NOT ALONE WE FLY--	LIFT IT--WITH THE	1348	2
THOSE CATTLE ARE THE FLY--	THOSE CATTLE SMALLER	1388	4
THE SOUL CAN FARTHER FLY	WITH PINIONS OF DISDAIN	1431	2
AND LEST IT FLY, ...	WE SHUN IT ERE IT COMES,	1580	4
AND SO ENCOUNTERING A FLY	A DRUNKARD CANNOT MEET A	1628	3
WHEN EVERY WAY WE FLY	WHY SHOULD WE HURRY--WHY	1646	2
OR TOO MUCH WEIGHT TO FLY--	TOO HAPPY TIME DISSOLVES	1774	4
FLYING			
A FLYING ATTITUDE!	I NEVER HEAR THE WORD	77	4
STOOPING--PLUCKING--SMILING--FLYING-- . .	ANGELS, IN THE EARLY	94	3
STOOPING--PLUCKING--SIGHING--FLYING-- . .	ANGELS, IN THE EARLY	94	7
THE FLYING TIDINGS TOLD--	THERE CAME A WIND LIKE A	1593	14
FOCUS			
BUT STATE--ENDOWAL--FOCUS--	WE PRAY--TO HEAVEN--	489	10
THE FOCUS OF MY PRAYER--	ONE BLESSING HAD I THAN	756	6
FOE			
I SHOULD NOT FEAR THE FOE THEN--	BLESS GOD, HE WENT AS	147	7

	FIRST LINE	POEM	LINE
FOE (CONTINUED)			
TO FOE OF HIS--I'M DEADLY FOE--	MY LIFE HAD STOOD--A	754	17
TO FOE OF HIS--I'M DEADLY FOE--	MY LIFE HAD STOOD--A	754	17
YET WAS NOT THE FOE--OF ANY--	STRUCK, WAS I, NOR YET	925	13
A FOE SO RETICENT--	THE RAT IS THE CONCISEST	1356	8
MINE ENEMY [MY FOE] IS GROWING OLD--	MINE ENEMY IS GROWING	1509	1
FOR SUCH A FOE [SWEET / GLEE / DAWN / SCENE / DEW / JOY] AS THIS--	FROM ALL THE JAILS THE	1532	8
A FOE WHOM I HAVE NEVER SEEN	MY WARS ARE LAID AWAY IN	1549	3
FOG SEE A-FOG			
AS HOVERING [GLIMMERING]--SEEN--THROUGH FOG--	A SOLEMN THING--IT WAS--	271	12
A DIMNESS LIKE A FOG	THERE IS A LANGUOR OF	396	6
AND THEN--OBSCURE WITH FOG--	I'VE SEEN A DYING EYE	547	5
THE SUN AND FOG CONTESTED	THE SUN AND FOG	1190	1
AND DROVE THE FOG AWAY--	THE SUN AND FOG	1190	4
NO STATURE HAS IT, LIKE A FOG	'TIS WHITER THAN AN	1482	3
FOLD SEE TWO-FOLD			
PARIS COULD NOT LAY THE FOLD	PIGMY SERAPHS--GONE	138	5
LAMBS FOR WHOM TIME HAD NOT A FOLD.	SOME, TOO FRAGILE FOR	141	12
FOLD A TINY COURTIER	MUTE THY CORONATION--	151	3
AUGMENTED--SWEET--A HUNDRED FOLD--	WE COVER THEE--SWEET	482	11
YOU CANNOT FOLD A FLOOD--	YOU CANNOT PUT A FIRE	530	5
THINE THE SECUREST [PATERNAL] FOLD	LET DOWN THE BARS, OH	1065	6
FOLDED			
WHEN FOLDED IN PERPETUAL SEAM	A WORD DROPPED CARELESS	1261	3
FOLDING			
MY LIFETIME FOLDING UP--	HE PUT THE BELT AROUND	273	4
EVENING--THE TISSUE [FOLDING] DOOR--	NOON--IS THE HINGE OF	931	2
FOLDS			
TILL SUMMER FOLDS HER MIRACLE--	IT WILL BE SUMMER--	342	17
FOLIAGE			
BECAUSE THAT JUNIOR FOLIAGE IS DISRESPECTFUL NOW	AN ANTIQUATED TREE	1514	3
THE FOLIAGE OF THE MIND	TALK NOT TO ME OF SUMMER	1634	2
BUT FOLIAGE OF STERILITY	THEY TALK AS SLOW AS	1697	3
FOLK			
BUT WHEN WINDS ALARM THE FOREST FOLK,	A FUZZY FELLOW, WITHOUT	173	10
THERE BE--PREFERRED BY DAINTIER FOLK--	"WHY DO I LOVE" YOU, SIR	480	16
FOLKS			
TO FOLKS IN HEAVEN--NOW--	I'M "WIFE"--I'VE	199	8
RANSOMED FOLKS--WONT LAUGH AT ME--	WHAT IS--"PARADISE"--	215	16
FOLLOW			
WHEN KATIE RUNS UNWEARIED THEY FOLLOW ON THE ROAD,	WHEN KATIE WALKS, THIS	222	2
WE FOLLOW THEE UNTIL	WE COVER THEE--SWEET	482	5
TO FOLLOW HER SUPERIOR ROAD [PACE]--	I WATCHED THE MOON	629	35
THE DRUMS DONT FOLLOW ME--WITH TUNES--	MY PORTION IS DEFEAT--	639	4
JUST [STILL] TO FOLLOW YOUR DEAR FEATURE--	PROMISE THIS--WHEN YOU	648	29
WITH NO POLICE TO FOLLOW	COULD I BUT RIDE	661	9
THE DAY MUST FOLLOW TOO.	THIS CHASM, SWEET, UPON	858	4
WE CAN BUT FOLLOW TO THE SUN--	WE CAN BUT FOLLOW TO THE	920	1
HALF THE CONDITION [DISTINCTION], THY REVERSE--TO FOLLOW--	WERT THOU BUT ILL--THAT	961	11
FOLLOW WISE [FINE] ORION	FOLLOW WISE ORION	1538	1
FOLLOWED			
AND HE--HE FOLLOWED--CLOSE BEHIND--	I STARTED EARLY--TOOK MY	520	17
I ROSE--IT FOLLOWED ME--	BEREAVED OF ALL, I WENT	784	10
WE ALL HAVE FOLLOWED THEE--	EXPANSE CANNOT BE LOST--	1584	12
AND THEN, THAT WE HAVE FOLLOWED THEM,	THE DISTANCE THAT THE	1742	5
FOLLOWING			
'TIS MOSTLY--FOLLOWING--	WE CAN BUT FOLLOW TO THE	920	4
FATE--FOLLOWING--BEHIND US BOLTS IT--	WE NEVER KNOW WE GO WHEN	1523	3
FOLLOWS			
THE DAISY FOLLOWS SOFT THE SUN--	THE DAISY FOLLOWS SOFT	106	1
TRANSPORT'S DECOMPOSITION FOLLOWS--	WHICH IS THE BEST--THE	1315	7
FOND			
AND THE FATHER FOND DEMANDETH THE MAIDEN FOR HIS SON.	AWAKE YE MUSES NINE,	1	16
'TIS A FOND AMBUSH--	I KNOW THAT HE EXISTS.	338	6
TO HELP THE FOND--TO FIND IT--	THE COLOR OF THE GRAVE	411	5
A FOND--ILLUSIVE WAY--	MY FIRST WELL DAY--SINCE	574	12
FOND, AND LATE--	WE TALKED AS GIRLS DO--	586	2
NATURE IS FOND, I SOMETIMES THINK,	A MOTH THE HUE OF THIS	841	5
TO SINK, IF WE HAD LABORED, FOND	WHAT TWIGS WE HELD BY--	1086	12
AND IS AS FOND OF SIGNIFYING	HER SOVREIGN PEOPLE	1139	3
IT'S FOND SUBJECTION WEAR--	WARM IN HER HAND THESE	1313	4
FONDER			
GREENER LEAN--OR FONDER CLUSTER [LATER LINGER]	PROMISE THIS--WHEN YOU	648	23
FONDEST			
BUT FONDEST, DWELT UPON OURSELF	WE TALKED AS GIRLS DO--	586	9
FONDLED			
WHEN EYES THAT FONDLED IT ARE WRENCHED	TO MAKE ONE'S TOILETTE--	485	7
THESE--WE HELD AMONG [FONDLED IN] OUR OWN--	THESE--SAW VISIONS--	758	9
THAT FONDLED THEM WHEN THEY WERE FIRE	LONG YEARS APART--CAN	1383	7
FONDLY			
AND SHE WILL POINT UNDOUBTEDLY [YOU FONDLY-- / YOU LONGINGLY]	CRISIS IS SWEET AND YET	1416	V 7
FONDNESS			
WINNOW HER FINEST FONDNESS--	DOUBT ME! MY DIM	275	22
AND COULD NOT KNOW HOW FONDNESS GREW	ONE YEAR AGO--JOTS WHAT?	296	19

	FIRST LINE	POEM	LINE
FONDNESS (CONTINUED)			
TO THAT NEW MARRIAGE [FONDNESS],	THERE CAME A DAY AT	322	27
WE COME TO LOOK WITH GRATITUDE [FONDNESS / PLEASURE]	A PRISON GETS TO BE A	652	5
FOOD			
TO FOOD--	UNDUE SIGNIFICANCE A	439	2
IT DEAL US [FURNISH]--STATED AS OUR FOOD--	A PRISON GETS TO BE A	652	7
TILL FOR A FURTHER FOOD	THE LUXURY TO APPREHEND	815	6
BECAUSE THE FOOD--EXTERMINATE--	HAD I NOT THIS, OR THIS,	904	11
A PURER FOOD FOR THEM, IF I SUCCEED,	I FIT FOR THEM--	1109	7
THE MYSTERY OF FOOD	ART THOU THE THING I	1282	6
FOR THIS FORESHADOWED [UNSULLIED] FOOD	I GROPED FOR HIM BEFORE	1555	4
THE ONLY FOOD THAT GROWS	I GROPED FOR HIM BEFORE	1555	8
THE VERY FOOD DEBATED	A WORD MADE FLESH IS	1651	7
FAME IS A FICKLE FOOD	FAME IS A FICKLE FOOD	1659	1
FOOD'S			
WITH FOOD'S NESCESSITY	IT WOULD HAVE STARVED A	612	4
FOOL			
WHO'D BE THE FOOL TO STAY?	THE WIND DID'NT COME	316	21
WOULD YOU BE THE FOOL TO STAY?	THE WIND DID'NT COME	316	23
AND DEEM OURSELF A FOOL--	WE PLAY AT PASTE--	320	4
I MUMBLED--LIKE A FOOL--	THE FIRST DAY'S NIGHT	410	14
FOOLISH			
IF THE FOOLISH, CALL THEM "FLOWERS"--	IF THE FOOLISH, CALL	168	1
WERE FOOLISH TO DEPEND--	THE WELL UPON THE BROOK	1091	2
THE "FOOLISH TUN" THE CRITICS SAY--	RISK IS THE HAIR THAT	1239	9
FOOLISHER			
AND MINE--SOME FOOLISHER EFFECT--	I LEARNED--AT LEAST--	944	16
FOOT			
MY FOOT IS ON THE TIDE!	MY WHEEL IS IN THE DARK!	10	5
SHE RECOGNIZED THE FOOT--	SHE SLEPT BENEATH A TREE	25	4
CAN SUCH A FOOT EXPLORE	WHO NEVER LOST, ARE	73	6
A PRINT OF A VERMILLION FOOT--	AN ALTERED LOOK ABOUT	140	5
HER BUSY FOOT SHE PLIED--	WHOSE ARE THE LITTLE	142	18
HE HAD [WORE] NO SANDAL ON HIS FOOT--	THE ONLY GHOST I EVER	274	3
I MUST NOT PUT MY FOOT AMISS	IS BLISS THEN, SUCH	340	2
I'D RATHER SUIT MY FOOT	IS BLISS THEN, SUCH	340	4
SAY, FOOT, DECIDE THE POINT--	IS BLISS THEN, SUCH	340	12
WITH NOSEGAYS AT THE HEAD AND FOOT--	I WENT TO THANK HER--	363	4
THE FOOT TO BEAR HIS ERRAND--	ALTHOUGH I PUT AWAY HIS	366	13
A BIRD--HAD STAMPED HER FOOT--	OF COURSE--I PRAYED--	376	4
FEELS HER WHITE FOOT--NO TREPIDATION--	THROUGH THE DARK SOD--AS	392	3
TO THE VERY SQUARE--HIS FOOT IS PASSING--	I COULD DIE--TO KNOW--	570	10
LIKE MIGHTY FOOT LIGHTS--BURNED THE RED	LIKE MIGHTY FOOT LIGHTS	595	1
LIKE MINE--FOR NOT A FOOT--NOR HAND--	I WATCHED THE MOON	629	11
YOU'LL KNOW HER--BY HER FOOT--	YOU'LL KNOW HER--BY HER	634	1
THE OTHER'S ONE [FOOT]--HAD BEEN--	AGAIN--HIS VOICE IS AT	663	17
HIS SURE FOOT PRECEDING--	LIFE--IS WHAT WE MAKE IT	698	13
IT'S WHITE FOOT TRIPPED--	IT TOSSED--AND TOSSED--	723	7
STEPPED WITH SO GAY A FOOT	AND THIS OF ALL MY HOPES	913	6
FOOT OF THE BOLD DID LEAST ATTEMPT IT--	THOSE WHO HAVE BEEN IN	922	5
UNDER THE CLOVER'S ROOT [FOOT],	UNDER THE LIGHT, YET	949	4
THE FOOT UPON THE EARTH	AS PLAN FOR NOON AND	960	4
THE FOOT UPON THE GRAVE	AS PLAN FOR NOON AND	960	6
THAT IT WAS FEBUARY'S FOOT [FACE / SELF]	THE SNOW THAT NEVER	1133	7
ON THE FOOT OF DOOM--	KNOCK WITH TREMOR--	1325	5
NOT [THAT] EVEN A PROGNOSTIC'S PUSH [FOOT]	THIS ME--THAT WALKS AND	1588	7
A FLOWER WILL NOT TROUBLE HER, IT HAS SO SMALL A FOOT,	A FLOWER WILL NOT	1621	1
HAST THOU A HAND OR FOOT	THE LOOK OF THEE, WHAT	1689	2
THE ACCENT OF A COMING FOOT--	ELYSIUM IS AS FAR AS TO	1760	7
FOOTING			
TILL RAPTURE MISSED THEM [HER FOOTING-- / PENINSULA]	TWO BUTTERFLIES WENT OUT	533	V
UNTIL IT FOOTING FIND.	A DOUBT IF IT BE US	859	4
FOOTLESS			
A RAPID--FOOTLESS GUEST--	THE WIND--TAPPED LIKE A	436	5
FOOTMAN			
ALMOST A POWDERED FOOTMAN	WAIT TILL THE MAJESTY OF	171	3
BUT TEACH THE FOOTMAN FROM VEVAY--	THE FLOWER MUST NOT	206	4
FOOTMEN			
COACH, IT INSURES, AND FOOTMEN--	ONE DIGNITY DELAYS FOR	98	5
ROUND WHICH THE FOOTMEN WAIT	I MET A KING THIS	166	26
FOP			
THE FOP--THE CARP--[THE DOG--THE TRAMP--]THE ATHEIST--	HOW MUCH THE PRESENT	1380	3
FORBID			
THOUGH GOD FORBID IT LIFT THE LID--	A TRANSPORT ONE CANNOT	184	3
"FORBID US NOT"--	TEACH HIM--WHEN HE MAKES	227	8
COULD--I--FORBID?	WHY--DO THEY SHUT ME OUT	248	12
AND GOD FORBID I LOOK BEHIND--	THE ONLY GHOST I EVER	274	15
AND COURTESY FORBID [FORBIDS]	THE SOUL THAT HATH A	674	5
FORBID THAT ANY KNOW--	HOW FAR IS IT TO HEAVEN?	929	V 8
BY SPIDER, OR FORBID IT LORD	ALONE AND IN A	1167	27
FORBIDDEN			
ON WHOSE FORBIDDEN EAR	SUCCESS IS COUNTED	67	10
WHAT IS FORBIDDEN [DENIED] UTTERLY	I ENVY SEAS, WHEREON HE	498	7
FORBIDDEN FRUIT A FLAVOR HAS	FORBIDDEN FRUIT A FLAVOR	1377	1
FORBIDS			
FORBIDS PUBLICITY,	I HAD SOME THINGS THAT I	116	10

	FIRST LINE	POEM	LINE
FORBIDS (CONTINUED)			
AND COURTESY FORBID [FORBIDS]	THE SOUL THAT HATH A	674	5
FORCE			
COULD DIMLY RECOLLECT A GRACE [FORCE]--	I GOT SO I COULD HEAR	293	13
HOW WEAKNESS PASSED--OR FORCE--AROSE--	IF ANY SINK, ASSURE THAT	358	4
THE COLD WILL FORCE YOUR TIGHTEST DOOR	ALTHOUGH I PUT AWAY HIS	366	26
TO FORCE HER SLEEP--	SHE LAY AS IF AT PLAY	369	15
I COUNT THE FORCE 'TWOULD BE	I PRAYED, AT FIRST, A	576	15
AND HE--I PUSHED--WITH SUDDEN FORCE--	IF HE WERE LIVING--DARE	734	13
OTHER FORCE--MAY BE PRESUMED TO MOVE--	THE TRUTH--IS STIRLESS--	780	2
HOW VIGOROUS A FORCE	THE TRUTH--IS STIRLESS--	780	9
I COULD NOT COUNT THEIR FORCE--	THE BIRDS BEGUN AT FOUR	783	5
SUCH IS THE FORCE [STRENGTH] OF HAPPINESS--	SUCH IS THE FORCE OF	787	1
A FURTHER FORCE [FUND] OF LIFE	HER FINAL SUMMER WAS IT	795	5
A FORCE ILLEGIBLE.	ALL CIRCUMSTANCES ARE	820	8
FORCE FLAME	BANISH AIR FROM AIR--	854	9
BY FORCE OF [SCANNING] IT'S RESULT--	AS FROST IS BEST	951	2
MY HUMAN NATURE'S FULLEST FORCE	I CANNOT WANT IT MORE--	1301	3
"NOTHING" IS THE FORCE	BY HOMELY GIFT AND	1563	4
BEGET A FORCE	THE LASSITUDES OF	1592	2
BUT WHEN I CANNOT MAKE THE FORCE	IF I COULD TELL HOW GLAD	1668	3
FORCED			
ARE FORCED TO KEEP THEIR ROOMS--	WHERE BELLS NO MORE	112	4
'TWAS FACE TO FACE WITH NATURE--FORCED--	I COULD SUFFICE FOR HIM,	643	7
FORCES			
WHOSE FORCES SPHERIC WIND [ROUND]	THERE ARE TWO RIPENINGS	332	2
I COULD [DID] NOT DEEM THESE [THAT] PLANETARY FORCES	IT KNEW NO LAPSE, NOR	560	5
PATIENCE OF OPPOSING FORCES--	GROWTH OF MAN--LIKE	750	11
FORCES THE BROODS IN LONELY VALLEYS	AS THE STARVED MAELSTROM	872	3
TOWARD WHICH FORCES CREEP	CRISIS IS A HAIR	889	2
PAST WHICH FORCES RETROGRADE	CRISIS IS A HAIR	889	3
IS AN INSECT'S FUTILE FORCES	PATIENCE--HAS A QUIET	926	3
MEAN OF FORCES--STAND BY HER WING,	PATIENCE--HAS A QUIET	926	V
FORGET HIS MORNING FORCES--	THE HARM OF YEARS IS ON	1280	5
FORCING			
WITHOUT THAT FORCING, IN MY BREATH--	I GOT SO I COULD HEAR	293	11
FORD			
WHO SLOWLY FORD THE MYSTERY	PASS TO THY RENDEZVOUS	1564	3
FOREBORE			
OF SHRINKING WAYS--SHE DID NOT [FOREBORE HER] FRIGHT	NO NOTICE GAVE SHE, BUT	804	9
FORECLOSED			
EACH FORECLOSED A NEWS--	AFTER THE SUN COMES OUT	1148	6
FORECLOSING			
. . . FORECLOSING / REPEALING] WRINKLE	LIKE TIME'S INSIDIOUS	1236	1
FOREFATHERS			
THEIR FOREFATHERS--HAVE HUMMED--	IT WILL BE SUMMER--	342	12
FOREFINGER			
SOMETIMES--A VANE'S FOREFINGER--	THE ANGLE OF A LANDSCAPE	375	11
FOREHEAD			
ON HER FOREHEAD LAY,	THO' MY DESTINY BE	163	10
AROUND IT'S FOREHEAD BOUND.	I LOST A WORLD--THE	181	4
STROKE THE COOL FOREHEAD--HOT SO OFTEN--	HOW MANY TIMES THESE LOW	187	5
HER UNANNOINTED FOREHEAD--	THE SUN--JUST TOUCHED	232	15
THE BEADS UPON THE FOREHEAD	I LIKE A LOOK OF AGONY,	241	7
UPON THE FOREHEAD OF A BUST--	THE DIFFERENCE BETWEEN	305	7
UNBROKEN FOREHEAD FROM THE EAST	IT SIFTS FROM LEADEN	311	7
FOR FOREHEAD LOW AS MINE, TO WEAR,	ALTHOUGH I PUT AWAY HIS	366	3
THE FOREHEAD OF A HILL--	THE ANGLE OF A LANDSCAPE	375	10
DIRECTLY IN THE FOREHEAD--	WE GROW ACCUSTOMED TO	419	15
THAT COOLED THE FOREHEAD OF THE HILL--	FORGET! THE LADY WITH	438	13
AND SUMMER HID HER FOREHEAD--	GOD MADE A LITTLE	442	7
THE FOREHEAD COPIED STONE--	'TWAS WARM--AT FIRST--	519	5
WITH HER FASTIDIOUS FOREHEAD?	AFRAID! OF WHOM AM I	608	11
THAT HELD HIS FOREHEAD STIFF--	I ROSE--BECAUSE HE SANK	616	9
TO SALUTE SO FAIR A FOREHEAD--	HER SWEET TURN TO LEAVE	649	11
BUT ONLY ON MY FOREHEAD STOPPED--	THE SUN KEPT SETTING--	692	7
HER FOREHEAD IS OF AMPLEST BLONDE--	THE MOON WAS BUT A CHIN	737	5
TOUCHES MY FOREHEAD NOW AND THEN	A LOSS OF SOMETHING EVER	959	14
COULD LIFT MY FOREHEAD FROM MY WORK	THE MISSING ALL,	985	7
THE DROPS ON NATURE'S FOREHEAD STOOD	THE SUN RETIRED TO A	1693	5
FOREHEADS			
A CURL, PERHAPS, FROM FOREHEADS	IN EBON BOX, WHEN YEARS	169	13
THEIR FACES [FOREHEADS]--UPON GOD--	THROUGH THE STRAIT PASS	792	4
FOREIGN			
SOME SAILOR, SKIRTING FOREIGN [NOVEL] SHORES--	JUST LOST, WHEN I WAS	160	9
UPON A FOREIGN SHORE--	TO LEARN THE TRANSPORT	167	6
AND BIRDS, OF FOREIGN TONGUE!	AS IF SOME LITTLE ARCTIC	180	8
HOW FOREIGN THAT CAN BE--	IF I'M LOST--NOW--	256	11
SO FOREIGN TO MY OWN--	I DREADED THAT FIRST	348	12
ME--HEAR! MY FOREIGN EAR	ME--COME! MY DAZZLED	431	3
I READ THAT FOREIGN LADY--	I THINK I WAS ENCHANTED	593	3
GLOW PLAIN--AND FOREIGN	I CANNOT LIVE WITH YOU--	640	25
UNTO ALL [TO FOREIGN] HEART--	ME FROM MYSELF--TO	642	4
ON BALL OF MAST IN BOSPORUS [FOREIGN PORT]--	THE DAY UNDRESSED--	716	15
THE HABIT OF A FOREIGN SKY	AWAY FROM HOME ARE SOME	821	5
IF HOME OR FOREIGN BORN--	IT WAS A GRAVE, YET BORE	876	6
SO FAIRY [FOREIGN]--SO FICTITIOUS	AS SLEIGH BELLS SEEM IN	981	3
A CHIEF INDIFFERENCE, AS FOREIGN	A SICKNESS OF THIS WORLD	1044	5

	FIRST LINE	POEM	LINE
FOREIGN (CONTINUED)			
BUT FOREIGN AS THE DIALECT	REPORTLESS SUBJECTS, TO	1048	3
THESE STRANGERS, IN A FOREIGN WORLD,	THESE STRANGERS, IN A	1096	1
AS A FOREIGN RACE--	NOW I KNEW I LOST HER--	1219	6
NOT DISTANT [FOREIGN]--NOT TO BE--	POWER IS A FAMILIAR	1238	2
THE MORNING FOREIGN SHONE--	AS IMPERCEPTIBLY AS	1540	10
FOREIGNER			
OUR SPECULATIONS OF THE FOREIGNER!	BESIDES THIS MAY	977	5
A HEART SOMETIMES A FOREIGNER,	PARTING WITH THEE	1614	3
THE FOREIGNER BEFORE HE KNOCKS	WHERE EVERY BIRD IS BOLD	1758	3
FOREIGNERS			
FOREIGNERS [KNOW NOT YOU]--THIS MORNING--	SOME SUCH BUTTERFLY BE	541	8
FOREIGNHOOD			
AND FOR THE FOREIGNHOOD.	A SOUTH WIND--HAS A	719	8
FORESHADOWED			
FOR THIS FORESHADOWED [UNSULLIED] FOOD	I GROPED FOR HIM BEFORE	1555	4
FOREST			
HERE IS A LITTLE FOREST,	THERE IS ANOTHER SKY,	2	7
BUT WHEN WINDS ALARM THE FOREST FOLK,	A FUZZY FELLOW, WITHOUT	173	10
THE FOREST OF THE DEAD--	OUR JOURNEY HAD ADVANCED	615	8
IN FOREST--AND THE HILL--	NATURE--THE GENTLEST	790	5
MAKES HE FORESTS [FOREST] DRY.	WE LIKE MARCH.	1213	5
IN ANY FOREST STIRRED	A WIND THAT ROSE	1259	3
THESE FEVERED DAYS--TO TAKE THEM TO THE FOREST	THESE FEVERED DAYS--TO	1441	1
FORESTALL			
LIBERTY'S BEGUILE [FORESTALL]"	WOLFE DEMANDED DURING	678	8
FORESTALLING			
THE ONLY ONE--FORESTALLING MINE--	I LIVE WITH HIM--I SEE	463	5
FORESTALLING PREPARATION--	THE FUTURE--NEVER SPOKE	672	7
FORESTS			
NEVER MIND FADED FORESTS, AUSTIN,	THERE IS ANOTHER SKY,	2	5
TRAVERSE BROADER FORESTS--	IT DID NOT SURPRISE ME--	39	5
NOR TELL THE LOVING FORESTS	I HAV'NT TOLD MY GARDEN	50	11
IS THE EGG OF FORESTS	TO VENERATE THE SIMPLE	57	10
WHEN WINDS TAKE [HOLD] FORESTS IN THEIR PAWS--	HE FUMBLES AT YOUR SOUL	315	13
ALL FORESTS--STINTLESS STARS--	BEFORE I GOT MY EYE PUT	327	11
THE FORESTS AS THEY FROZE	TWO TRAVELLERS PERISHING	933	2
WE SPY THE FORESTS AND THE HILLS	DEW--IS THE FRESHET IN	1097	5
SPECULATE, OR FORESTS ENTERTAIN,	THE DUTIES OF THE WIND	1137	8
THE FORESTS GALLOPED TILL THEY FELL	THE CLOUDS THEIR BACKS	1172	3
MAKES HE FORESTS [FOREST] DRY.	WE LIKE MARCH.	1213	5
AS FORESTS [BRANCHES] TOUCH THE WIND	BECAUSE HE LOVES HER	1229	8
FORETOLD			
FORETOLD LOCATIONS--	THE THINGS THAT NEVER	1515	10
FOREVER			
FOREVER INTERVENE!	OUR LIVES ARE SWISS--	80	10
FOREVER AT HIS SIDE TO WALK--	FOREVER AT HIS SIDE TO	246	1
FOREVER OF HIS FATE TO TASTE--	FOREVER AT HIS SIDE TO	246	6
THE WHOLE OF ME--FOREVER--	DOUBT ME! MY DIM	275	5
FOREVER FROM THE EYE--	HOW NOTELESS MEN, AND	282	4
FOREVER MIGHT BE SHORT, I THOUGHT TO SHOW--	TO LOVE THEE YEAR BY	434	5
FOREVER--IS COMPOSED OF NOWS--	FOREVER--IS COMPOSED OF	624	1
STAMPED--OCCASIONALLY--[IN INSTANCES] FOREVER--	SO THE EYES ACCOST--AND	752	3
ARE FOREVER LOST TO ME	A CLOUD WITHDREW FROM	895	4
DEPARTING THEN [NEXT]--FOREVER--	SUMMER HAS TWO	1422	9
FOREVER--UNTIL MAY--	SUMMER HAS TWO	1422	10
FOREVER IS DECIDUOUS [RECURRENT]--	SUMMER HAS TWO	1422	11
FOREVER HONORED [CHERISHED] BE THE TREE	FOREVER HONORED BE THE	1570	1
AND THEN DECLINES FOREVER	DROWNING IS NOT SO	1718	5
FOREVERMORE			
SUE--FOREVERMORE!	ONE SISTER HAVE I IN OUR	14	27
THY FLOWER--FOREVERMORE!	SUMMER FOR THEE, GRANT I	31	9
FORFEIT			
MY LIFE HAD FORFEIT BEEN.	I NEVER TOLD THE BURIED	11	9
FORFEIT PROBITY--	CONSCIOUS AM I IN MY	679	12
IF BLAME BE MY SIDE--FORFEIT ME--	IF BLAME BE MY SIDE--	775	1
BUT DOOM ME NOT TO FORFEIT THEE--	IF BLAME BE MY SIDE--	775	2
TO FORFEIT THEE? THE VERY NAME	IF BLAME BE MY SIDE--	775	3
DIVISION IS ADHESION'S FORFEIT--ON HIGH	NOT SO THE INFINITE	1040	2
THE FORFEIT IS OF CREATURE FAIR	A FULL FED ROSE ON MEALS	1154	5
WHATEVER REALM I FORFEIT, LORD,	TO OWN A SUSAN OF MY OWN	1401	3
ITS STIGMA [FORFEIT] DEIFIED	ONE CROWN THAT NO ONE	1735	4
FORFEITED			
WAS FORFEITED AWAY--	A SPARROW TOOK A SLICE	1211	8
HAS FORFEITED THE DOWER	THE CLOVER'S SIMPLE FAME	1232	V 8
FORGE			
TUGGING AT THE FORGE!	BY A FLOWER--BY A LETTER	109	8
IT [SHE] QUIVERS FROM THE FORGE	DARE YOU SEE A SOUL AT	365	6
STANDS SYMBOL FOR THE FINER FORGE	DARE YOU SEE A SOUL AT	365	11
REPUDIATE THE FORGE--	DARE YOU SEE A SOUL AT	365	16
FORGET			
BE SURE YOU COUNT--SH'D I FORGET	IT'S ALL I HAVE TO BRING	26	5
HEART! WE WILL FORGET HIM!	HEART! WE WILL FORGET	47	1
YOU MAY FORGET THE WARMTH HE GAVE--	HEART! WE WILL FORGET	47	3
I WILL FORGET THE LIGHT!	HEART! WE WILL FORGET	47	4
DID THEY FORGET THEE?	POOR LITTLE HEART!	192	2
I SHALL FORGET THE DROP OF ANGUISH	I SHALL KNOW WHY--WHEN	193	7
AND HELPS US TO FORGET--	TO DIE--TAKES JUST A	255	8
CHARGED US TO FORGET HIM--	DID WE DISOBEY HIM?	267	3

	FIRST LINE	POEM	LINE
FORGET (CONTINUED)			
FORGET THE SECRET OF HIS WING	NOT PROBABLE--THE BAREST	346	7
THE SAINTS FORGET	ME--COME! MY DAZZLED	431	5
KNOWS HOW TO FORGET!	KNOWS HOW TO FORGET!	433	1
HOW TO FORGET!	KNOWS HOW TO FORGET!	433	11
FORGET! THE LADY WITH THE AMULET	FORGET! THE LADY WITH	438	1
PERMISSION TO FORGET--	THEY PUT US FAR APART--	474	18
FORGET IT--LORD [CHRIST]--OF THEM--	'TIS TRUE--THEY SHUT ME	538	4
NOR DOES THE NIGHT FORGET	THE SUNRISE RUNS FOR	710	7
THOUGH SHE FORGET THE NAME I BEAR--	PRECIOUS TO ME--SHE	727	2
THIS--IF I FORGET	WHEN I HOPED, I	768	18
AND FORGET THE COLOR [FIGURE] OF THE DAY--	SEVERER SERVICE OF	786	16
WHEN I FORGET TO TEAZE--	THEY WONT FROWN ALWAYS--	874	2
HOW HAPPY I WAS IF I COULD FORGET	HOW HAPPY I WAS IF I	898	1
FORGET HIS MORNING FORCES--	THE HARM OF YEARS IS ON	1280	5
THE POWER TO FORGET--	ONE THING OF IT WE	1464	6
BUT THEIR'S FORGET IN PRAISE	I SAW THE WIND WITHIN	1502	V
THE HEART CANNOT FORGET	TO BE FORGOT BY THEE	1560	4
BEFORE IT CAN FORGET	TO BE FORGOT BY THEE	1560	V 11
THAT I WAS WORTHY TO FORGET	THAT SHE FORGOT ME WAS	1683	3
FORGETS			
MAMA NEVER FORGETS HER BIRDS,	MAMA NEVER FORGETS HER	164	1
THE SLAVE--FORGETS--TO FILL--	THE LAMP BURNS SURE--	233	5
FORGETS HER OWN LOCALITY--	THE DROP, THAT WRESTLES	284	2
AND PAIN--IS MISSED--IN [FORGETS--FOR--] PRAISE--	UNTO MY BOOKS--SO GOOD	604	4
AS DAWN FORGETS THEM--NOW--	THE MOON UPON HER FLUENT	1528	8
FORGETTING			
IF RECOLLECTING [OH IF REMEMBERING] WERE FORGETTING,	IF RECOLLECTING WERE	33	1
AND IF FORGETTING, RECOLLECTING,	IF RECOLLECTING WERE	33	3
BUT SHE, FORGETTING AMPHITRITE--	THE DROP, THAT WRESTLES	284	8
OR ARE FORGETTING NOW	WHETHER THEY HAVE	1329	2
THOUGH ONE IS BEAUTIFUL FORGETTING [SECESSION]--	I'D RATHER RECOLLECT A	1349	3
FORGETTING TO RETURN,	WE SEND THE WAVE TO FIND	1604	4
FORGIVE			
FORGIVE US, IF AS DAYS DECLINE--	THE DAISY FOLLOWS SOFT	106	8
BUBBLE! "FORGIVE"--"SOME BETTER"--BUBBLE!	KILL YOUR BALM--AND IT'S	238	7
FORGIVE IT--LAST--	'TWAS LOVE--NOT ME--	394	7
FORGIVE THEM--EVEN AS MYSELF--	'TIS TRUE--THEY SHUT ME	538	11
OR ELSE--FORGIVE NOT ME--	'TIS TRUE--THEY SHUT ME	538	12
FORGIVE ME, IF THE GRAVE COME [SEEM] SLOW--	IF I MAY HAVE IT, WHEN	577	26
FORGIVE ME, IF TO STROKE [TOUCH / GREET] THY FROST	IF I MAY HAVE IT, WHEN	577	28
BUT MARCH, FORGIVE ME--AND	DEAR MARCH--COME IN--	1320	14
THAT SHE [HERSELF] COULD NOT FORGIVE	ELIZABETH TOLD ESSEX	1321	2
FORGIVEN			
WHEN I SHALL BE "FORGIVEN"--	I THINK JUST HOW MY	237	2
AND SO I CON THAT THING--"FORGIVEN"--	I THINK JUST HOW MY	237	13
THAT WE MAY BE FORGIVEN--	OF GOD WE ASK ONE FAVOR,	1601	2
FORGIVENESS			
HIS SWEET FORGIVENESS--	HE STRAINED MY FAITH--	497	14
FORGOT			
IS A SOUL "FORGOT!"	THERE IS A WORD	8	18
HOW NEAR I HAD FORGOT.	IF RECOLLECTING WERE	33	4
AND THE NEST FORGOT,	IT DID NOT SURPRISE ME--	39	4
ANY FORGOT BY VICTORY	DELAYED TILL SHE HAD	58	14
THE CLOVER BELLS FORGOT.	"ARCTURUS" IS HIS OTHER	70	16
OUR CONSTANCY FORGOT--	IN EBON BOX, WHEN YEARS	169	14
HE FORGOT--AND I--REMEMBERED--	HE FORGOT--AND I--	203	1
I AM THE ONE FORGOT THEE SO--	SAVIOR! I'VE NO ONE ELSE	217	3
I MET ONE--FORGOT MY SCHOOLMATES--	GOD PERMITS INDUSTRIOUS	231	3
AN INSTANT HAD FORGOT	SHE LAY AS IF AT PLAY	369	7
FORGOT SHE WORE IT AT HER HEART	FORGET! THE LADY WITH	438	2
SWEET--YOU FORGOT--BUT I REMEMBERED	SWEET--YOU FORGOT--BUT I	523	1
OF HEAVENLY LOVE--FORGOT--	I TRIED TO THINK A	532	11
HIS BOUNDARIES [SOPHISTRIES]--FORGOT--	THE SPIDER HOLDS A	605	12
I WAS SO HAPPY I FORGOT	I CANNOT BUY IT--'TIS	840	4
THE BEE--HAST THOU FORGOT?	'TIS SUNRISE--LITTLE	908	8
ALL FORGOT FOR [THROUGH] RECOLLECTING	ALL FORGOT FOR	966	1
SHE MENTIONED, AND FORGOT--	THE LAST NIGHT THAT SHE	1100	21
NOT FORSOOK [FORGOT] OF FAITH--	TELL AS A MARKSMAN--WERE	1152	21
HER MARTIAL DAY [TIME] FORGOT	A LITTLE DOG THAT WAGS	1185	10
YOURSELF FORGOT TO LIVE--	BECAUSE THAT YOU ARE	1260	16
HAS FORGOT IT IS THERE--	NOT ANY MORE TO BE	1344	6
STILL STATES TO DATES THAT HAVE FORGOT	SHE LAID HER DOCILE	1396	3
IT'S LOT--WERE IT FORGOT--	THE GENTIAN HAS A	1424	14
KNOW THAT WHICH MAKES THEM AS FORGOT	THE MOON UPON HER FLUENT	1528	7
HOW SWEET IF I AM NOT FORGOT	MY WARS ARE LAID AWAY IN	1549	9
TO BE FORGOT BY THEE	TO BE FORGOT BY THEE	1560	1
WORTHY TO BE FORGOT	TO BE FORGOT BY THEE	1560	11
REMEMBERS IT FORGOT--	PARTING WITH THEE	1614	4
FORGOT TO RANKLE [ENTER] THERE	ARROWS ENAMORED OF HIS	1629	2
THAT SHE FORGOT ME WAS THE LEAST	THAT SHE FORGOT ME WAS	1683	1
FORGOTTEN			
THE MOLD-LIFE--ALL FORGOTTEN--NOW--	THROUGH THE DARK SOD--AS	392	7
THE BAREFOOT TIME FORGOTTEN--SO--	THE BEGGAR LAD--DIES	717	11
FORGOTTEN, AS FULFILLED.	THE BIRDS BEGUN AT FOUR	783	24
AS IN SLEEP--ALL HUE FORGOTTEN--	COLOR--CASTE--	970	5

	FIRST LINE	POEM	LINE
FORGOTTEN (CONTINUED)			
TELL AS A MARKSMAN--WERE FORGOTTEN	TELL AS A MARKSMAN--WERE	1152	1
WHETHER THEY HAVE [IT HAS] FORGOTTEN	WHETHER THEY HAVE	1329	1
FORK			
TO THAT ODD FORK IN BEING'S ROAD--	OUR JOURNEY HAD ADVANCED	615	3
NOT YET SUSPECTED--[STILL UNSUSPECTED] BUT FOR FLASH [FORK]--	THE SOUL'S DISTINCT	974	7
THE LIGHTNING IS A YELLOW FORK	THE LIGHTNING IS A	1173	1
FORKED			
HE FORKED HIS WAY ALONG	THE FROST OF DEATH WAS	1136	13
FORM			
AND THEN THE PIOUS FORM	I READ MY SENTENCE--	412	6
TODAY'S--HAVE VASTER CLAIMS [FORM]--	I COULD NOT PROVE THE	563	8
BETWEEN THE FORM OF LIFE AND LIFE	BETWEEN THE FORM OF LIFE	1101	1
SECRETED IN HIS FORM	IN WINTER IN MY ROOM	1670	29
FORMAL			
AFTER GREAT PAIN, A FORMAL FEELING COMES--	AFTER GREAT PAIN, A	341	1
RUIN IS FORMAL--DEVILS WORK	CRUMBLING IS NOT AN	997	9
FORMED			
MYSELF WAS FORMED--A CARPENTER--	MYSELF WAS FORMED--A	488	1
FORMER			
THE FORMER, BLEW AWAY.	I CAUTIOUS, SCANNED MY	178	6
THAT--WAS A FORMER TIME--	I FELT MY LIFE WITH BOTH	351	14
ARE ONE--AND YET THE FORMER	THE DAY THAT I WAS	356	7
ONES WE FORMER KNEW--	SMILING BACK FROM	385	6
THE FORMER--CHECKS--ON FAME--	SOME--WORK FOR	406	4
THE FEET--I FORMER USED--	IT WOULD NEVER BE COMMON	430	14
THE FORMER LOVE--DISTINCTER GROWS--	YOU'LL FIND--IT WHEN YOU	610	11
I THINK THE HEART I FORMER WORE	I THINK TO LIVE--MAY BE	646	5
AND IN THE FORMER DRAM	IMPOSSIBILITY, LIKE WINE	838	6
THROUGH ALL THEIR [IT'S] FORMER PLACES, WE	DEATH LEAVES US HOMESICK	935	5
UPON A FORMER GARMENT SHOWS	WHAT TWIGS WE HELD BY--	1086	7
WE STERN AND FORMER KNEW	THE SNOW THAT NEVER	1133	10
WHO JUSTIFIED [AUTHORIZED] ELIJAH [THE FORMER]	ELIJAH'S WAGON KNEW NO	1254	7
THE FORMER ASSISTS A SIREN	THE PARASOL IS THE	1747	5
FORMERLY			
MUCH AS FORMERLY?	DID THE HAREBELL LOOSE	213	4
AND SQUIRRELS, FORMERLY.	WHO OCCUPIES THIS HOUSE?	892	20
FORMS			
SO ADEQUATE--IT FORMS--	OF BRONZE--AND BLAZE--	290	3
CHILDHOOD--SOME FORMS OF HOPE--THE DEAD--	THE THINGS THAT NEVER	1515	2
FORMULA			
WHEN FORMULA [FILAMENT], HAD FAILED--	I GOT SO I COULD HEAR	293	16
NOR FORMULA--HAD SHE--	I WATCHED THE MOON	629	12
WITHOUT THE FORMULA OF SOUND	A LIGHT EXISTS IN SPRING	812	15
WITHOUT THE FORMULA.	SOMEHOW MYSELF SURVIVED	1194	4
WITHOUT A FORMULA WE FOUGHT	'TIS SEASONS SINCE THE	1529	7
FORSAKE			
DID THEY FORSAKE THEE?	POOR LITTLE HEART!	192	5
THEMSELVES FORSAKE--CONTENTED,	A SICKNESS OF THIS WORLD	1044	7
FORSAKES			
FORSAKES THE ARCTIC RACE	WHEN THE ASTRONOMER	851	4
THE FROG FORSAKES--	HIS MANSION IN THE POOL	1379	2
FORSOOK			
ALL FORSOOK, FOR JUST A STRANGER'S	ALL FORGOT FOR	966	3
HIS BILL IS CLASPED [LOCKED]--HIS EYE FORSOOK [ESTRANGED]--	HIS BILL IS CLASPED--HIS	1102	1
NOT FORSOOK [FORGOT] OF FAITH--	TELL AS A MARKSMAN--WERE	1152	21
OUR ESTIMATES A SCHEME [FORSOOK]--	THE DAYS THAT WE CAN	1184	5
FORSWEARS			
NATURE FORSWEARS	PINK--SMALL--AND	1332	11
FORTH			
FROM COCOON FORTH A BUTTERFLY	FROM COCOON FORTH A	354	1
PASS BACK AND FORTH, BEFORE MY BRAIN	WHEN I WAS SMALL, A	596	15
THEN DRAW MY LITTLE LETTER FORTH	THE WAY I READ A	636	7
A BIRD BROKE FORTH AND SANG,	A TRAIN WENT THROUGH A	1761	2
FORTHWITH			
THE STOUTEST [FORTHWITH THE] MIND IS WAN	THE MIND LIVES ON THE	1355 V	6
FORTIFIED			
BY CHILDHOOD [DISTANCE] FORTIFIED	WHO WERE "THE FATHER AND	1258	6
FORTITUDE			
YOU TAUGHT ME FORTITUDE OF FATE--	YOU TAUGHT ME WAITING	740	3
WITH FORTITUDE OF OBSTACLE	TO UNDERTAKE IS TO	1070	3
FORTITUDE INCARNATE	FORTITUDE INCARNATE	1217	1
FORTITUDE--FLANKED [STANCHED] WITH MELODY.	AFTER ALL BIRDS HAVE	1395 V	8
WHAT FORTITUDE THE SOUL CONTAINS,	ELYSIUM IS AS FAR AS TO	1760	5
FORTRESS			
FROM SOME OLD FORTRESS ON THE SUN	SOME RAINBOW--COMING	64	10
INVINCIBLE [IMPREGNABLE] MY FORTRESS	ME FROM MYSELF--TO	642	3
FORTUNATE			
HOW FORTUNATE THE GRAVE--	HOW FORTUNATE THE GRAVE	897	1
FORTUNE			
AH! KATIE! SMILE AT FORTUNE, WITH TWO SO KNIT TO THEE!	WHEN KATIE WALKS, THIS	222	4
HIMSELF--TO HIM--A FORTUNE--	THIS WAS A POET--IT IS	448	15
FOR THIS NEW VALUE [FORTUNE / PORTION] IN THE SOUL--	ONE BLESSING HAD I THAN	756	11
IS A TOO ESTABLISHED FORTUNE [SECURE POSSESSION / CONTENDED . . .	EXPECTATION--IS	807	7
GRACE OF RANK--AND GRACE OF FORTUNE	ALL FORGOT FOR	966 V	5

	FIRST LINE	POEM	LINE
FORTUNE'S			
FORTUNE'S EXPENSIVE SMILE	LUCK IS NOT CHANCE--	1350	3
FORTY			
FORTY--GONE DOWN TOGETHER--	GLEE--THE GREAT STORM IS	619	3
BUT THE FORTY--	GLEE--THE GREAT STORM IS	619	12
FORUMS			
MY FLOWERS TURN FROM FORUMS--	THE RAINBOW NEVER TELLS	97	5
IN WATERS [FORUMS] GREEN--	HIS MANSION IN THE POOL	1379	16
FORWARD			
ESCAPING FORWARD, TO CONFRONT	ESCAPING BACKWARD TO	867	3
AND FORWARD--	THE ADMIRATIONS--AND	906	15
LEAN FORWARD FOR A FINAL GLANCE--	POWER IS A FAMILIAR	1238	7
FOUGHT			
THE BATTLE FOUGHT BETWEEN THE SOUL . . .	THE BATTLE FOUGHT	594	1
HE FOUGHT LIKE THOSE WHO'VE NOUGHT TO LOSE--	HE FOUGHT LIKE THOSE	759	1
WE FOUGHT MORTALITY.	THE FROST OF DEATH WAS	1136	4
WITHOUT A FORMULA WE FOUGHT	'TIS SEASONS SINCE THE	1529	7
FOUL			
FOR SO FOUL A THING	PUBLICATION--IS THE	709	4
FOUND			
NOR BY THE WOOD ARE FOUND--	THERE IS A MORN BY MEN	24	9
IF THOSE I LOVED WERE FOUND	IF THOSE I LOVED WERE	29	3
FOUND HE HAD WORSTED GOD!	A LITTLE EAST OF JORDAN,	59	16
NOT FOUND, ...	LIKE HER THE SAINTS	60	9
WHOM I HAVE NEVER FOUND	GOING TO HEAVEN!	79	25
I FOUND HER--"PLEIAD"--IN THE WOODS . . .	WHOSE CHEEK IS THIS?	82	4
PILGRIM BE FOUND?	FOR EVERY BIRD A NEST--	143	6
HAS ANYBODY FOUND?	I LOST A WORLD--THE	181	2
"FOUND DEAD"--"OF NECTAR"--	WE--BEE AND I--LIVE BY	230	16
THERE--PARADISE--IS FOUND!	"HEAVEN"--IS WHAT I	239	8
THAT I WAS FOUND--	IF I'M LOST--NOW--	256	2
COULD MAR IT--IF IT FOUND--	REVERSE CANNOT BEFALL	395	8
THEN LOST [STAKED / CHASED] THEMSELVES AND FOUND . . .	TWO BUTTERFLIES WENT OUT	533	V
NOR WAS I HUNGRY--SO I FOUND	I HAD BEEN HUNGRY, ALL	579	17
SOME--FOUND IT--MUTUAL GAIN--	I GAVE MYSELF TO HIM--	580	14
I FOUND THE WORDS [PHRASE] TO EVERY THOUGHT	I FOUND THE WORDS TO	581	1
HE FOUND MY BEING--SET IT UP--	HE FOUND MY BEING--SET	603	1
I'VE RANSOMED IT [FOUND IT--'TIS]--ALIVE-- .	HE TOLD A HOMELY TALE	763	16
BETTER, TO BE FOUND, ...	GOOD TO HIDE, AND HEAR	842	2
WHEN IT IS FOUND, A FEW REJOICE	THIS IS A BLOSSOM OF THE	945	9
BECAUSE I FOUND HER KINSMANLESS, ...	MY SEASON'S FURTHEST	1019	3
BE FOUND A REFUGEE--	THESE STRANGERS, IN A	1096	4
WHOSE STATEMENT IS NOT FOUND--	EXHILIRATION IS THE	1118	4
I FOUND IT QUIETLY ASSUMED	ALONE AND IN A	1167	11
TOGETHER CHIEFEST [CHIEFLY] THEY ARE FOUND .	AS OLD AS WOE--	1168	7
IT SHALL AT LENGTH BE FOUND.	LONGING IS LIKE THE SEED	1255	4
THE HEAVENS [TREES / SKY / FIELD] CANNOT BE FOUND--	THE SYMPTOM OF THE GALE	1327	6
THEY FOUND TO OUR OBJECTION [ABHORRENCE]-- .	THOSE CATTLE SMALLER	1388	7
IT'S TANTAMOUNT BE FOUND--	BEHOLD THIS LITTLE BANE	1438	8
ENOUGH WILL NOT BE FOUND WHEN ALL HAVE DIED.	ABOVE OBLIVION'S TIDE	1531	7
WHO HAS NOT FOUND THE HEAVEN--BELOW-- . .	WHO HAS NOT FOUND THE	1544	1
AND GOD CANNOT BE FOUND--	THOSE--DYING THEN,	1551	5
IT'S EXPLANATION FOUND--	THE FARTHEST THUNDER	1581	20
FOUNDED			
WAS FOUNDED IN AN HOUR	THE FAIREST HOME I EVER	1423	2
AND EVERY RIGHTEOUS [FOUNDED] THING . . .	HIS LITTLE HEARSE LIKE	1522	6
FOUNDER			
AWFUL FATHER [FOUNDER] OF LOVE--	WHATEVER IT IS--SHE HAS	1204	2
FOUNDERED			
TILL GRAVITATION CHASED [HUMBLED / EJECTED / FOUNDERED / . . .	TWO BUTTERFLIES WENT OUT	533	V
FOUNDERING			
HOW OFTEN FOUNDERING AT SEA	A GREAT HOPE FELL	1123	8
. . . FOUNDERING] FACES	WE TALKED WITH EACH	1473	5
FOUNDETH			
AND WHOM HE FOUNDETH, WITH HIS ARM . . .	THEY LEAVE US WITH THE	350	5
FOUNDS			
IT FOUNDS THE HOMES AND DECKS THE DAYS . .	THE FARTHEST THUNDER	1581	13
FOUNTAIN			
ANYBODY FIND THE FOUNTAIN	FLOWERS--WELL--IF	137	5
FOUR			
FOUR--HAVE RECOVERED THE LAND--	GLEE--THE GREAT STORM IS	619	2
FOUR TREES--UPON A SOLITARY ACRE--	FOUR TREES--UPON A	742	1
THE BIRDS BEGUN AT FOUR O'CLOCK--	THE BIRDS BEGUN AT FOUR	783	1
AT HALF PAST FOUR, EXPERIMENT	AT HALF PAST THREE, A	1084	5
THE FOUR DIVISIONS OF THE EARTH	THE WIND TOOK UP THE	1134	5
FOURSCORE			
OF JUNIOR OF FOURSCORE--'TWAS ACT	NOT ALL DIE EARLY, DYING	990	7
FOURTH			
FOURTH, NO DISCOVERY--	FINDING IS THE FIRST ACT	870	5
FOX			
THE FOX FITS THE HOUND--	GOOD TO HIDE, AND HEAR	842	4
DISTANCE--IS NOT THE REALM OF FOX	DISTANCE--IS NOT THE	1155	1
FOXGLOVE'S			
OUT OF THE FOXGLOVE'S DOOR--	I TASTE A LIQUOR NEVER	214	10
FRACTION			
WITH BUT A FRACTION OF THE LIFE [LOVE]-- .	DOUBT ME! MY DIM	275	3
THAT BUT THE DOWER'S FRACTION--	REMOVED FROM ACCIDENT OF	424	11

	FIRST LINE	POEM	LINE
FRACTION (CONTINUED)			
CONTENT HER SMALLEST FRACTION HELP	LEAST BEE THAT BREW--	676	4
THE FRACTION--THAT APPEASED THE HEART	PRECIOUS TO ME--SHE	727	10
FRACTIONS			
YET HESITATING FRACTIONS--BOTH	I COULD SUFFICE FOR HIM,	643	3
FRACTURE			
WHEN A FRACTURE--WE DISCOVER--	TAKING UP THE FAIR IDEAL	428	3
TWICE A WINTER'S SILVER FRACTURE	TWICE HAD SUMMER HER	846	3
JUGS--A UNIVERSE'S FRACTURE [RUPTURE]	BEES ARE BLACK, WITH	1405	7
FRACTURED			
YET BLAMED THE FATE THAT FRACTURED--[FLUNG IT] LESS	IT DROPPED SO LOW--IN MY	747	5
MY FRACTURED TRUST--	THE CHEMICAL CONVICTION	954	4
FRAGILE			
SOME, TOO FRAGILE FOR WINTER WINDS	SOME, TOO FRAGILE FOR	141	1
FRAGRANT			
THE BUSY CARTS--THE FRAGRANT COCKS--	I'M SORRY FOR THE DEAD--	529	11
THE TRANSIENT, FRAGRANT SNOW	THE SNOW THAT NEVER	1133	2
FRAIL			
"OH LORD--HOW FRAIL ARE WE"!	"ARCTURUS" IS HIS OTHER	70	8
FRAIL LITTLE HEART!	POOR LITTLE HEART!	192	7
A FRAIL [FLEET / BRIEF] ARISTOCRAT OF TIME	SHE SPED AS PETALS OF A	991	3
FRAME			
OF ALL THIS COMPOUND FRAME--	A WEIGHT WITH NEEDLES ON	264	6
FINGERS--TO FRAME MY ROUND HAIR	I AM ASHAMED--I HIDE--	473	13
AND FITTED TO A FRAME,	IT WAS NOT DEATH, FOR I	510	14
ALL CIRCUMSTANCES ARE THE FRAME	ALL CIRCUMSTANCES ARE	820	1
ON THAT DEAR FRAME THE YEARS HAD WORN	ON THAT DEAR FRAME THE	940	1
OUR MUTUAL FRAME--THAT HAPLY	NO OTHER CAN REDUCE	982	V 7
NOR THAT HIS FRAME WAS DUST--	HE ATE AND DRANK THE	1587	4
'TIS NOT THE SWAYING FRAME WE MISS,	'TIS NOT THE SWAYING	1597	1
FRAMES			
OF MECHLIN--FRAMES--	I WENT TO HEAVEN--	374	10
FRANK			
WITH FRANK TRANQUILITY	A BEE HIS BURNISHED	1339	6
FRANKFORT			
SIP OLD FRANKFORT AIR	MANY CROSS THE RHINE	123	3
NOT ALL THE FRANKFORT BERRIES [VATS UPON THE RHINE]	I TASTE A LIQUOR NEVER	214	3
FRANTIC			
TRIPS FRANTIC IN A TREE--	YOU'VE SEEN BALLOONS SET	700	14
IN FRANTIC MELODY!	HOW STILL THE BELLS IN	1008	4
FRAUD			
OH FRAUD THAT CANNOT CHEAT THE BEE--	THESE ARE THE DAYS WHEN	130	7
FRAUD [LIE] CANNOT PRESUME--	HE WHO IN HIMSELF	969	2
FRAUD OF DISTANCE--FRAUD OF DANGER,	ROBBED BY DEATH--BUT	971	9
FRAUD OF DISTANCE--FRAUD OF DANGER,	ROBBED BY DEATH--BUT	971	9
FRAUD OF DEATH--TO BEAR--	ROBBED BY DEATH--BUT	971	10
THE SUN IN PLACE--NO OTHER FRAUD	IT BLOOMED AND DROPT, A	978	9
AND FRAUD AND FEAR.	A RAT SURRENDERED HERE	1340	3
FRECKLED			
MY FRECKLED MONARCH HELD THE REIN--	I MET A KING THIS	166	14
BRAVE--SHINES THE SUN THROUGH THE FRECKLED PANE--	HOW MANY TIMES THESE LOW	187	10
HAD I--A FRECKLED MAIDEN,	DOUBT ME! MY DIM	275	13
OF FRECKLED HUMAN NATURE--	WHAT SOFT--CHERUBIC	401	7
MYSELF A FRECKLED--BE--	THEMSELF ARE ALL I HAVE	1094	2
A FRECKLED SHRINE--	THIS DIRTY--LITTLE--	1311	4
AMPUTATE MY FRECKLED BOSOM!	REARRANGE A "WIFE'S"	1737	3
FREE			
WHEREFORE WHEN BOUGHS ARE FREE--	FOR EVERY BIRD A NEST--	143	4
AND TERROR'S FREE--	'TIS SO APPALLING--IT	281	23
GUSHED TOO FREE [FULL] FOR THE ADORING--	HER--"LAST POEMS"--	312	9
TO THE NEW FREE--	LET US PLAY YESTERDAY--	728	18
ON THE MAN--FREE--	LET US PLAY YESTERDAY--	728	30
AS OF THE FREE--	LET US PLAY YESTERDAY--	728	34
SO EASY [KINDRED / FULLY / FREE / AMPLE SEEMS / BOUNTEOUS / . . .	YOUR THOUGHTS DONT HAVE	1452	6
AND THE SUN WILL FREE IT [LOOSE HIM]	FOLLOW WISE ORION	1538	V
FREEDOM			
NOT WHO TOILS FOR FREEDOM	NOW I KNEW I LOST HER--	1219	17
FREELY			
IS FREELY CERTIFIED	THE SPIDER AS AN ARTIST	1275	4
IS FREELY MINE.	THIS DIRTY--LITTLE--	1311	2
BECAUSE HE TRAVELS FREELY	THE BUTTERFLY OBTAINS	1685	5
FREEZE			
THEMSELVES AS EASY FREEZE--	WHAT CARE THE DEAD, FOR	592	18
AND SEE YOU--FREEZE--	I CANNOT LIVE WITH YOU--	640	18
FREEZING			
AS FREEZING PERSONS, RECOLLECT THE SNOW--	AFTER GREAT PAIN, A	341	12
CARESS HER FREEZING HAIR--	THE SOUL HAS BANDAGED	512	6
THE SHIVERING [FREEZING] FANCY TURNS	CONJECTURING A CLIMATE	562	4
AND IS HELD LOW TO FREEZING LIPS--	VICTORY COMES LATE--	690	2
FREIGHT			
UNCONSCIOUS OF THE SCARLET FREIGHT--	HOW MANY FLOWERS FAIL IN	404	7
'TWAS LOWERED, LIKE A WEIGHT [FREIGHT]--	'TWAS WARM--AT FIRST--	519	14
BUT THE HEART WITH THE HEAVIEST FREIGHT ON--	"SPEECH"--IS A PRANK OF	688	3
IS THE PREVAILING [SUPERIOR] FREIGHT.	BEFORE HE COMES WE WEIGH	834	4
IT MAGNIFIES OUR FREIGHT	THE SUN IS GAY OR STARK	878	8
THE MIND WAS BUILT FOR MIGHTY FREIGHT	A GREAT HOPE FELL	1123	6

	FIRST LINE	POEM	LINE
FREIGHT (CONTINUED)			
BUT SHE STRAIGHTER WALKED FOR FREIGHT	HAD WE KNOWN THE TON SHE	1124	3
THE SUBTERRANEAN FREIGHT	IT'S HOUR WITH ITSELF	1225	5
OF IT'S PERCEIVELESS FREIGHT!	HOW NEWS MUST FEEL WHEN	1319	8
A SUDDEN FREIGHT OF WIND ASSUMED [TOOK ON--]	A SINGLE CLOVER PLANK	1343	11
THE UNDEVELOPED [ELEMENTAL] FREIGHT	COULD MORTAL LIP DIVINE	1409	2
IT IS ENOUGH, THE FREIGHT SHOULD BE	THAT LOVE IS ALL THERE	1765	3
FRENZIED			
AND SWUNG THEIR FRENZIED HAIR.	AN AWFUL TEMPEST MASHED	198	9
FRENZIES			
FOR FRENZY OF [FRENZIES OF / ANTICS IN / ANTICS WITH] THE SUN--	TWO BUTTERFLIES WENT OUT	533	V
FRENZY			
FOR FRENZY OF [FRENZIES OF / ANTICS IN / ANTICS WITH] THE SUN--	TWO BUTTERFLIES WENT OUT	533	V
FREQUENT			
IT'S FREQUENT VISITOR--	A MIEN TO MOVE A QUEEN--	283	8
THE CHURCHES ARE SO FREQUENT--	THE SWEETEST HERESY	387	5
THAT TIPS SO FREQUENT, [SLIPS SO EASY] NOW,	I PRAYED, AT FIRST, A	576	19
FOR FREQUENT [OFTEN], ALL MY SENSE OBSCURED	WHAT I SEE NOT, I BETTER	939	5
FREQUENTLY			
FREQUENTLY THE WOODS ARE PINK--	FREQUENTLY THE WOODS ARE	6	1
FREQUENTLY ARE BROWN.	FREQUENTLY THE WOODS ARE	6	2
FREQUENTLY THE HILLS UNDRESS	FREQUENTLY THE WOODS ARE	6	3
'TIS FREQUENTLY THE WAY--	THE MORNING AFTER WO--	364	2
WHEN ALTERED FREQUENTLY--	WHO WERE "THE FATHER AND	1258	20
AS IF IT [HE] WERE [AS FREQUENTLY] UNDONE--	THE BUTTERFLY'S NUMIDIAN	1387	6
FRESH			
FRESH GILDED--TO ELUDE THE EYES	A HAPPY LIP--BREAKS	353	7
IT SICKENED FRESH UPON MY SIGHT--	IT STRUCK ME--EVERY DAY	362	7
AND SUPERSEDES THE FRESH--	YOU'LL FIND--IT WHEN YOU	610	12
ON FRESH EYES--	THE CHILD'S FAITH IS NEW	637	4
ANNIHILATION--PLATED FRESH	SUSPENSE--IS HOSTILER	705	7
FRESH AS A CARGO FROM BATIZE	AFTER THE SUN COMES OUT	1148	7
FRESH [NEW] AS MANKIND THAT HUMBLE STORY	TELL AS A MARKSMAN--WERE	1152	5
A FUNCTION FRESH OBTAIN?	THE BONE THAT HAS NO	1274	10
THAT HIM REFRESH [MAKE HIM FRESH]--	THE LASSITUDES OF	1592	4
FRESHER			
MIXING FRESHER AIR.	IT SOUNDED AS IF THE	1397	8
FRESHEST			
LARGEST [NEWEST / FRESHEST] DEWS OF MORN	PROMISE THIS--WHEN YOU	648	20
FRESHET			
DEW--IS THE FRESHET IN THE GRASS--	DEW--IS THE FRESHET IN	1097	1
FRESHET'S			
SWIFT AS A FRESHET'S TONGUE	THIS IS A BLOSSOM OF THE	945	6
FRESHETS			
WHEN FRESHETS COME ALONG.	A STAGNANT PLEASURE LIKE	1281	8
FRET			
LIVES WILL FRET--	GIVE LITTLE ANGUISH--	310	2
FRETTED			
AND FRETTED IN THE EAVES--	THE NIGHT WAS WIDE, AND	589	8
FRIEND			
I HAVE A MISSING FRIEND--	I HAD A GUINEA GOLDEN--	23	26
MY FRIEND MUST BE A BIRD--	MY FRIEND MUST BE A BIRD	92	1
MORTAL, MY FRIEND MUST BE,	MY FRIEND MUST BE A BIRD	92	3
AH, CURIOUS FRIEND!	MY FRIEND MUST BE A BIRD	92	6
MY FRIEND ATTACKS MY FRIEND!	MY FRIEND ATTACKS MY	118	1
MY FRIEND ATTACKS MY FRIEND!	MY FRIEND ATTACKS MY	118	1
TO PREVENT A FRIEND--	WE DONT CRY--TIM AND I,	196	4
I SHOULD NOT DARE TO LEAVE MY FRIEND,	I SHOULD NOT DARE TO	205	1
AH, FRIEND, YOU LITTLE KNEW	GOOD NIGHT! WHICH PUT	259	3
A SHADY FRIEND--FOR TORRID DAYS--	A SHADY FRIEND--FOR	278	1
WHEN FRIEND--AND EARTH'S OCCASION	THE SOUL'S SUPERIOR	306	3
WAS SAYING TO A FRIEND--	I SEND TWO SUNSETS--	308	6
I TOLD MYSELF, "TAKE COURAGE, FRIEND--	I FELT MY LIFE WITH BOTH	351	13
A BOOK I HAVE--A FRIEND GAVE--	DEATH SETS A THING	360	13
BOLD--WERE IT ENEMY--BRIEF--WERE IT FRIEND--	IT'S COMING--THE	390	6
WHERE EACH--HAS LEFT A FRIEND--	THE COLOR OF THE GRAVE	411	16
IF ANYBODY'S FRIEND BE DEAD	IF ANYBODY'S FRIEND BE	509	1
WHO DIES--AND TO HIS FRIEND--	DEATH IS POTENTIAL TO	548	2
THE LONGEST--FOR THE FRIEND--	DEATH IS POTENTIAL TO	548	6
TO SEE [REACH / TOUCH] THIS CURIOUS FRIEND--	MY PERIOD HAD COME FOR	564	8
NEIGHBOR--AND FRIEND--AND BRIDEGROOM--	GLEE--THE GREAT STORM IS	619	7
A PRISON GETS TO BE A FRIEND--	A PRISON GETS TO BE A	652	1
OF A SHAPELESS FRIEND--	CONSCIOUS AM I IN MY	679	2
IS AN IMPERIAL FRIEND--	THE SOUL UNTO ITSELF	683	2
SEEK--FRIEND--AND SEE--	OUT OF SIGHT? WHAT OF	703	10
UPON HER FRIEND SHE COULD CONFER [BESTOW]	THE MOON WAS BUT A CHIN	737	11
MY SOUL--THAT MORNING--WAS MY FRIEND--	MY SOUL--ACCUSED ME--AND	753	4
HAVE LEFT EXPOSED A FRIEND--	DYING! TO BE AFRAID OF	831	3
THE SECOND--TO IT'S FRIEND--	LOVE--IS THAT LATER	924	6
RALLIES HER GLOW [THE WEST], LIKE A DYING FRIEND--	FAIRER THROUGH FADING--	938	5
BESTOWS [CONFERRED] A SINGLE FRIEND--	A COFFIN--IS A SMALL	943	10
A GRACE WITHOUT A FRIEND.	MY SEASON'S FURTHEST	1019	4
THAN THE HAND OF FRIEND	FAR FROM LOVE THE	1021	6
"OLD FRIEND, THOU KNOWEST [KNEWEST] ME,"	I HEARD, AS IF I HAD NO	1039	14
THE CARD--THE CHANCE--THE FRIEND--	WE DO NOT KNOW THE TIME	1106	6
NOT WANT OF FRIEND OCCASIONS IT	THERE IS ANOTHER	1116	3
DISCERNIBLE TO NOT A FRIEND	CONTAINED IN THIS SHORT	1165	V

	FIRST LINE	POEM	LINE
FRIEND (CONTINUED)			
A FRIEND TOO STRAIGHT TO STOOP	CONTAINED IN THIS SHORT	1165	V
THE STATUTE IS MY LEARNED FRIEND	ALONE AND IN A	1167	21
OR FRIEND OR NATURE--STRANDED THEN	THE DAYS THAT WE CAN	1184	3
AND BE OF BUTTERCUPS THE FRIEND	THE BUTTERFLY'S	1244	5
FOR HIS LESS PRICELESS FRIEND.	BECAUSE THAT YOU ARE	1260	32
AND THANKED THE AMPLE FRIEND--	I WORKED FOR CHAFF AND	1269	6
WHAT A DISSEMBLING FRIEND--	WITHOUT A SMILE--WITHOUT	1330	6
NATURE CANNOT ENACT A FRIEND--	NATURE ASSIGNS THE SUN--	1336	3
TEMPTATION IS THE FRIEND	A RAT SURRENDERED HERE	1340	10
. . . LIKE A FRIEND--	AFTER ALL BIRDS HAVE	1395	6
HER GALLANT NOTE ENDOWS US LIKE A FRIEND	AFTER ALL BIRDS HAVE	1395	V 6
WORD TO A FRIEND	I HAVE NO LIFE BUT THIS	1398	T
INTRENCHMENTS STIMULATE [INTRENCHMENT STIMULATE] A FRIEND	WHAT MYSTERY PERVADES A	1400	V
PROSPECTIVE IS THE FRIEND	HOW HUMAN NATURE DOTES	1417	5
IT'S BOND IT'S FRIEND--	THE GENTIAN HAS A	1424	10
WOULD BE THE BEST FRIEND--	THE DEVIL--HAD HE	1479	2
CANDOR--MY TEPID FRIEND--	CANDOR--MY TEPID FRIEND	1537	1
TO OWN HER FOR A FRIEND	TO SEE HER IS A PICTURE	1568	6
NO FRIEND HAVE I THAT SO PERSISTS	THE BLUNDER IS IN	1684	7
"COME HOME WITH ME, MY FRIEND!	THE WATERS CHASED HIM AS	1749	4
IF IN THAT ROOM A FRIEND AWAIT	ELYSIUM IS AS FAR AS TO	1760	3
FRIENDLY			
. . . BONNIE / SPACIOUS / TROPIC / ARDENT / FRIENDLY / MAGIC / . . .	THE BIBLE IS AN ANTIQUE	1545	13
WHY BOYS ARE FRIENDLY--	THE BIBLE IS AN ANTIQUE	1545	V
FRIEND'S			
STIRRED BY A FRIEND'S HAND--	THE WORLD--FEELS DUSTY	715	7
A FAN, PERHAPS, A FRIEND'S REGRET	THE DYING NEED BUT	1026	5
FRIENDS			
AND BEAR TO ALL MY FRIENDS,	I WOULD DISTIL A CUP,	16	2
MEET TRANQUILLY, AS FRIENDS--	I READ MY SENTENCE--	412	12
THERE BE IMMORTAL FRIENDS	BEREAVEMENT IN THEIR	645	6
A SPICY CHARGE, MY LITTLE POSTS [FRIENDS]--	THE BIRDS REPORTED FROM	743	3
WITH SEPARATING FRIENDS	THE MURMURING OF BEES,	1115	12
BE [ARE] UNEXPECTED FRIENDS.	"REMEMBER ME" IMPLORED	1180	12
ARE FRIENDS DELIGHT OR PAIN?	ARE FRIENDS DELIGHT OR	1199	1
WE BETTER FRIENDS HAD BEEN, PERHAPS,	WHO WERE "THE FATHER AND	1258	15
GOOD FRIENDS WITH TIME	AN ANTIQUATED GRACE	1345	6
SOME CONFLICT WITH THOSE UPPER FRIENDS	A WILD BLUE SKY ABREAST	1415	5
OTHER FRIENDS ADJOURN	GUEST AM I TO HAVE	1661	4
FRIENDSHIP			
IN TOKEN OF OUR FRIENDSHIP	"SIC TRANSIT GLORIA	3	61
FRIGATE			
BY FRIGATE, OR BY MERCHANTMAN--	TWO BUTTERFLIES WENT OUT	533	11
THERE IS NO [WAS NEVER] FRIGATE LIKE A BOOK	THERE IS NO FRIGATE LIKE	1263	1
FRIGATES			
AND FRIGATES--IN THE UPPER FLOOR	I STARTED EARLY--TOOK MY	520	5
FRIGHT			
SEEN MAGIC--THROUGH THE FRIGHT	DELIGHT IS AS THE FLIGHT	257	21
IT SETS THE FRIGHT AT LIBERTY--	'TIS SO APPALLING--IT	281	22
SHE FEELS SOME GHASTLY FRIGHT COME UP	THE SOUL HAS BANDAGED	512	3
OF SHRINKING WAYS--SHE DID NOT [FOREBORE HER] FRIGHT	NO NOTICE GAVE SHE, BUT	804	9
FRIGHTENED			
WHEN FRIGHTENED--HOME TO THEE I RUN--	YOU LOVE ME--YOU ARE	156	10
THEY LOOKED LIKE FRIGHTENED BEADS, I THOUGHT--	A BIRD CAME DOWN THE	328	11
THAT FRIGHTENED--BUT AN HOUR--	WHEN NIGHT IS ALMOST	347	8
FRIGID			
FOR FRIGID--HOUR OF MIND--	A SHADY FRIEND--FOR	278	4
FRIGID AND SWEET HER PARTING FACE--	FRIGID AND SWEET HER	1318	1
FRIGID AND FLEET MY FEET--	FRIGID AND SWEET HER	1318	2
FRILL			
AND COVENANT GENTIANS--FRILL!	WHILE ASTERS--	331	4
AND COVENANT GENTIANS--FRILL--	IT WILL BE SUMMER--	342	16
HIS HEAD, A CAP AND FRILL	HIS BILL AN AUGUR IS	1034	2
FRILLED			
BUT SUMMER, FRILLED AS FOR A HOLIDAY	WE WEAR OUR SOBER	1572	2
FRINGE			
AS THE FRINGE	WHAT TWIGS WE HELD BY--	1086	6
FRINGED			
TO FILL IT'S FRINGED CAREER [SPHERE]	THE GENTIAN HAS A	1424	11
FRINGES			
THE GENTIAN WEAVES HER FRINGES--	THE GENTIAN WEAVES HER	18	1
THE FLUTTERING OF HER FRINGES	DISTRUSTFUL OF THE	20	3
FRISK			
WHAT IF THE POLES SH'D FRISK ABOUT	"ARCTURUS" IS HIS OTHER	70	22
FRITTERS			
FRITTERS ITSELF AWAY!	SOME RAINBOW--COMING	64	6
FRO			
ROCKED SOFTER--TO AND FRO--	ON SUCH A NIGHT, OR SUCH	146	8
AND MOURNERS TO AND FRO	I FELT A FUNERAL, IN MY	280	2
FROCK			
WILL THE FROCK I WEPT IN	BEFORE THE ICE IS IN THE	37	15
THE FROCK I USED TO WEAR--	IT WOULD NEVER BE COMMON	430	31
AS CONSTANT AS THE CHILDISH FROCK [GOWN]--	IT CEASED TO HURT ME,	584	7
FROCKS			
WHO DRESSED IN FROCKS OF PUREST SNOW	WHERE I HAVE LOST, I	104	14
AND FROCKS AND CURLS.	THIS QUIET DUST WAS	813	4

	FIRST LINE	POEM		LINE
FROG				
HOW PUBLIC--LIKE A FROG--	I'M NOBODY! WHO ARE YOU?	288		6
THE LONG SIGH OF THE FROG	THE LONG SIGH OF THE	1359		1
THE FROG FORSAKES--	HIS MANSION IN THE POOL	1379		2
FROGS				
THE FROGS GOT HOME LAST WEEK--	BEE! I'M EXPECTING YOU!	1035		5
FROLIC				
SWEETER THAN A VANISHED FROLIC	I CANT TELL YOU--BUT YOU	65		5
FRONT				
ETERNITY'S WHITE [COOL] FLAG--BEFORE [IN FRONT]--	OUR JOURNEY HAD ADVANCED	615		11
WHEN FIGURES SHOW THEIR ROYAL FRONT--	OF ALL THE SOULS THAT	664		9
AND FRONT A MUTUAL DAY--	I MAKE HIS CRESCENT FILL	909		10
REMEMBRANCE HAS A REAR AND FRONT--	REMEMBRANCE HAS A	1182		1
IN THE FRONT OF TROUBLE--	SAFE DESPAIR IT IS THAT	1243		6
PAUSING IN FRONT OF [AGAINST] OUR PALSIED [SENTENCED / . . .	WE TALKED WITH EACH	1473		5
FRONTIER				
THE GLIMMERING FRONTIER THAT	THEIR HIGHT IN HEAVEN	696		6
AND GOD, FOR A FRONTIER.	I AM AFRAID TO OWN A	1090		8
BEYOND EARTH'S TRAFFICKING FRONTIER,	NOT THAT HE GOES--WE	1435		3
THAT MAGICAL FRONTIER	THE SADDEST NOISE, THE	1764		6
FRONTING				
FRONTING US--WITH [TURNING US--THEIR] NIGHT.	UNFULFILLED TO	972		8
FROST				
WHERE NOT A FROST HAS BEEN;	THERE IS ANOTHER SKY,	2		10
THE BOSOMS WHERE THE FROST HAS LAIN	I BRING AN UNACCUSTOMED	132		12
TENDERLY TUCKING THEM IN FROM FROST	SOME, TOO FRAGILE FOR	141		3
OR FROST, OR DEATH, OR ANYONE--	IF I COULD BRIBE THEM BY	179		5
THEN--SKIP--THE FROST--UPON THE LEA--	MAKE ME A PICTURE OF THE	188		12
NO FEAR OF FROST TO COME	FOR THIS--ACCEPTED	195		10
A SEPULCHRE, FEARS FROST, NO MORE--	'TIS SO APPALLING--IT	281	V	4
WITH SUCH A PRACTISED FROST--	I KNOW A PLACE WHERE	337		2
WHEN CANCELLED BY THE FROST--	THERE IS A FLOWER THAT	380		32
A FROST MORE NEEDLE KEEN	MORE LIFE--WENT OUT--	422		10
AND DIP [MIX] YOUR FINGERS IN THE FROST--	IF ANYBODY'S FRIEND BE	509		15
IT WAS NOT FROST, FOR ON MY FLESH [KNEES]	IT WAS NOT DEATH, FOR I	510		5
THE FROST--POSSESS [OBTAIN] THE WORLD--	HE PARTS HIMSELF--LIKE	517		17
A CHILL--LIKE FROST UPON A GLASS--	'TWAS WARM--AT FIRST--	519		3
FORGIVE ME, IF TO STROKE [TOUCH / GREET] THY FROST	IF I MAY HAVE IT, WHEN	577		28
WITHOUT MY RIGHT OF FROST--	I CANNOT LIVE WITH YOU--	640		19
TOO RAPT WITH FROST	VICTORY COMES LATE--	690		3
NOT A FROST COULD [NO NOVEMBER] COOL--	WHEN I HOPED, I	768		6
AS FROST IS DIFFERENT FROM DEW--	THERE IS AN ARID	782		3
THOUGH RIME BY RIME, THE STEADY FROST	NO NOTICE GAVE SHE, BUT	804		7
WITH PROSPECT, AND WITH FROST--	THERE IS A JUNE WHEN	930		12
AS FROST IS BEST CONCEIVED	AS FROST IS BEST	951		1
DID WE ABOLISH FROST	DID WE ABOLISH FROST	1014		1
BUT FAR AFTER FROST--	EXCEPT THE SMALLER SIZE	1067	V	
THE FROST OF DEATH WAS ON THE PANE--	THE FROST OF DEATH WAS	1136		1
TO CRAWL THE FROST BEGUN [BEGAN]--	THE FROST OF DEATH WAS	1136		8
THE FROST WAS NEVER SEEN--	THE FROST WAS NEVER SEEN	1202		1
OH FAITHFUL FROST [SLEET] THAT KEPT THE DATE	IT CAME AT LAST BUT	1230		5
THE FROST HIMSELF [ITSELF] SO COMELY	LIKE TIME'S INSIDIOUS	1236		5
THE FROST BEHEADS IT AT IT'S PLAY--	APPARENTLY WITH NO	1624		3
AS FLOWER AT FALL OF FROST--	I WATCHED HER FACE TO	1667		8
FROSTS				
WHEN FROSTS TOO SHARP BECAME	ALL OVERGROWN BY CUNNING	148		6
FOR, WHEN FROSTS, THEIR PUNCTUAL FINGERS	THO' MY DESTINY BE	163		9
WHERE MIDNIGHT FROSTS--HAD LAIN!	I SHOULD NOT DARE TO	205		16
FROSTS UNHOOK--IN THE NORTHERN ZONES--	SAFE IN THEIR ALABASTER	216	V	
THAT [WHICH] TEETH OF FROSTS ALONE DISCLOSE	THERE ARE TWO RIPENINGS	332		7
THAT ERE THE FROSTS ARE DUE--	'TIS NOT THAT DYING	335		6
THE FROSTS WERE HER CONDITION--	GOD MADE A LITTLE	442		9
OR GRISLY FROSTS--FIRST AUTUMN MORNS,	IT WAS NOT DEATH, FOR I	510		19
FOR MINE--IN FROSTS--WAS SOWN--	OURSELVES WERE WED ONE	631		14
HER FROSTS TO PONDER--THEN IT WAS	THE BIRDS REPORTED FROM	743		15
FOR WHEN THE FROSTS BEGIN	THE PRODUCTS OF MY FARM	1025		6
FROWN				
NEED--A KEEPER--FROWN?	CIVILIZATION--SPURNS--	492		9
THEY WONT FROWN ALWAYS--SOME SWEET DAY	THEY WONT FROWN ALWAYS--	874		1
WHOSE POMPOUS FROWN WAS NUTRIMENT	NO BRIGADIER THROUGHOUT	1561		15
FROWNS				
ALAS--THAT FROWNS [DUSK] SHOULD LIE IN WAIT	FROM ALL THE JAILS THE	1532		7
FROZE				
YET HOW NATURE FROZE--	WHEN I HOPED, I	768		12
THE FORESTS AS THEY FROZE	TWO TRAVELLERS PERISHING	933		2
FROZEN				
AND YOU WERE FROZEN LED	'TWAS LIKE A MAELSTROM,	414		19
BROOCH--FROZEN ON--	DROPPED INTO THE ETHER	665		4
FRUCTIFIED				
FRUCTIFIED IN SAND--	SOIL OF FLINT, IF STEADY	681		4
THE SPIRIT FRUCTIFIED--	THIS IS A BLOSSOM OF THE	945		4
FRUGAL				
UNTO MY FRUGAL EYE--	I HAD A GUINEA GOLDEN--	23		6
YET--TO MY FRUGAL EYE,	I LOST A WORLD--THE	181		6
MAKE FRUGAL--ONES--CONTENT--	IT'S THOUGHTS--AND JUST	495		3
I FEAR A MAN OF FRUGAL [SCANTY] SPEECH--	I FEAR A MAN OF FRUGAL	543		1
IT WAS WITHIN THE FRUGAL PURSE	OF BRUSSELS--IT WAS NOT	602		7

	FIRST LINE	POEM		LINE
FRUGAL (CONTINUED)				
BLISS IS FRUGAL OF HER LEASES	PARADISE IS THAT OLD	1119		5
IS FRUGAL OF IT'S BALL.	'TWAS FIGHTING FOR HIS	1188		4
AGONY IS FRUGAL.	SAFE DESPAIR IT IS THAT	1243		2
HOW FRUGAL IS THE CHARIOT	THERE IS NO FRIGATE LIKE	1263		7
FRUGALITY				
AS OF FRUGALITY [VELOCITY / AMENITY / PROPRIETY]--	A SPARROW TOOK A SLICE	1211	V	8
FRUIT				
THE FRUIT PERVERSE TO PLUCKING, ...	TO DISAPPEAR ENHANCES--	1209		17
FORBIDDEN FRUIT A FLAVOR HAS	FORBIDDEN FRUIT A FLAVOR	1377		1
FRUITION				
HOARY [EVIL / RIGID / WRINKLED / ARID / SHRUNKEN] THE FRUITION	FORTITUDE INCARNATE	1217		7
NOT OF DETENTION IS FRUITION--	WHICH IS THE BEST--THE	1315		5
FRUITLESS				
MANY THINGS--ARE FRUITLESS--	IN FALLING TIMBERS	614		13
FOR MANY AN ARDENT [A FRUITLESS] YEAR. . .	THE DISTANCE THAT THE	1742		4
FRUITLESSER				
FRUITLESSER TO FLING--	PATIENCE--HAS A QUIET	926		6
FUCHSIA'S SEE FUSCHZIA'S				
FUGITIVE				
AS COVERT AS A FUGITIVE, ...	THE ROBIN IS A GABRIEL	1483		13
A FUGITIVE REKNOWN--	THE ROBIN IS A GABRIEL	1483	V	
AS INTIMATE [MAGICAL]--AS FUGITIVE . . .	OF WHOM SO DEAR	1504		4
FULFILLED				
FORGOTTEN, AS FULFILLED.	THE BIRDS BEGUN AT FOUR	783		24
EXIST AN [FULFILLED THEIR] ORIENTAL CIRCUIT	THIS QUIET DUST WAS	813		7
SHE HAS FULFILLED HER DYES	NATURE CAN DO NO MORE	1673		2
FULFILLING				
FULFILLING ABSOLUTE [SOME EXPRESS] DECREE .	HOW HAPPY IS THE LITTLE	1510		9
FULL				
AND THO' FULL MANY A MORNING, ...	"SIC TRANSIT GLORIA	3		47
WHO SANG FULL MANY A DAY	I HAD A GUINEA GOLDEN--	23		10
ALL THE ROOMS ARE FULL--	TAKEN FROM MEN--THIS	53		8
FULL ROYAL IS HIS RETINUE!	WAIT TILL THE MAJESTY OF	171		11
FULL PURPLE IS HIS STATE!	WAIT TILL THE MAJESTY OF	171		12
THE SEA IS FULL--I KNOW IT!	ONE LIFE OF SO MUCH	270		9
TILL THE BALL IS FULL--	HOW THE OLD MOUNTAINS	291		6
TILL GOD'S FULL TIME [WHOLE--WILL]-- . . .	UNTO LIKE STORY--TROUBLE	295		6
GUSHED TOO FREE [FULL] FOR THE ADORING-- .	HER--"LAST POEMS"--	312		9
BEFORE THEY DROP FULL MUSIC ON--	HE FUMBLES AT YOUR SOUL	315		3
THERE CAME A DAY AT SUMMER'S FULL, . . .	THERE CAME A DAY AT	322		1
IT'S FULL AS OPERA--	I CANNOT DANCE UPON MY	326		20
AT THE FULL DEW--	I WENT TO HEAVEN--	374		6
AND WHEN THE HILLS BE FULL--	THERE IS A FLOWER THAT	380		21
TURN IT, A LITTLE--FULL IN THE FACE . . .	IT DONT SOUND SO	426		5
ARE FULL OF MORNING GLORY--	I AM ALIVE--I GUESS--	470		3
WHEN MOON'S AT FULL--'TIS THOU--I SAY-- . .	YOU KNOW THAT PORTRAIT	504		9
CALLED TO MY FULL--THE CRESCENT DROPPED-- .	I'M CEDED--I'VE STOPPED	508		11
CIRCUMFERENCE BE FULL--	NO CROWD THAT HAS	515		5
DID LEAP, FULL FLANKED, UPON THE HOST-- . .	ONE ANGUISH--IN A CROWD	565		7
FIXED FULL, AND STEADY, ON HIS OWN . . .	I PRAYED, AT FIRST, A	576		7
WITH MOSS--THEY NEVER GREW SO FULL-- . . .	YOU'LL FIND--IT WHEN YOU	610		7
UNTIL IT SETTLED BROAD [FULL / FIRM]--ON PARADISE--	TO KNOW JUST HOW HE	622		4
IN FULL ETERNITY--	THE HEAVEN VESTS FOR	694		8
LIFE'S LATITUDES LEANT OVER--FULL-- . . .	ONE BLESSING HAD I THAN	756		15
HE FLUNG A HAND FULL AT THE PLAIN-- . . .	THE WIND BEGUN TO KNEAD	824		3
A HAND FULL AT THE SKY--	THE WIND BEGUN TO KNEAD	824		4
TWO FULL AUTUMNS FOR THE SQUIRREL	TWICE HAD SUMMER HER	846		5
THAT FILLED THE LISPING FULL.	THEY WONT FROWN ALWAYS--	874		8
WAS FULL--	THE FIRST DAY THAT I WAS	902		8
HIS NATURE IS AT FULL	I MAKE HIS CRESCENT FILL	909		2
A FULL, AND PERFECT TIME--	MIDSUMMER, WAS IT, WHEN	962		2
SO BLIND WITH [FULL OF] JOY HE COULD NOT CHOOSE	THE BIRD DID PRANCE--THE	1107		3
A FULL FED ROSE ON MEALS OF TINT	A FULL FED ROSE ON MEALS	1154		1
WHEN MEMORY IS FULL	WHEN MEMORY IS FULL	1266		1
IF THAT IS [BE] FULL OF MEAT	THE MIND LIVES ON THE	1355		3
IN NATURE--THEY ARE FULL--	DECLAIMING WATERS NONE	1595		4
THE GRASS IS FULL.	THE MOST IMPORTANT	1746		8
FULLER				
MY EYE IS FULLER THAN MY VASE--	MY EYE IS FULLER THAN MY	202		1
BUT--I SHALL BRING A FULLER TUNE--	I SHALL KEEP SINGING!	250		8
FULLEST				
MY HUMAN NATURE'S FULLEST FORCE	I CANNOT WANT IT MORE--	1301		3
INQUIRE OF THE PROUDEST [FULLEST / CLOSING] ROSE	CRISIS IS SWEET AND YET	1416		5
FULLY				
INVIGORATED, WADED [FULLY]	A SPARROW TOOK A SLICE	1211		5
SO EASY [KINDRED / FULLY / FREE / AMPLE SEEMS / BOUNTEOUS / . . .	YOUR THOUGHTS DONT HAVE	1452		6
FUMBLE				
DO FUMBLE AT THE STRAIN--	THE LONESOME FOR THEY	262		8
I FUMBLE AT MY CHILDHOOD'S PRAYER	A WIFE--AT DAYBREAK I	461		10
FUMBLED				
HER FINGERS FUMBLED AT HER WORK--	THE ROSE DID CAPER ON	208		5
I FUMBLED AT MY NERVE--	I YEARS HAD BEEN FROM	609	V	9

	FIRST LINE	POEM	LINE
FUMBLES			
HE FUMBLES AT YOUR SOUL	HE FUMBLES AT YOUR SOUL	315	1
FUN			
WOULD NOT THE FUN [JOKE]	I KNOW THAT HE EXISTS.	338	13
FOR FUN--AT YOU--	SHE LAY AS IF AT PLAY	369	12
THAT MAKES THE HEART PUT UP IT'S FUN--	SEPTEMBER'S	1271	7
FUNCTION			
WITHOUT A FURTHER FUNCTION--	TO BE ALIVE--IS POWER--	677	3
WHEN LARGER FUNCTION--	RENUNCIATION--IS A	745	14
AND THE ETERNAL FUNCTION	THERE IS A FINISHED	856	7
ARE THOSE A FUNCTION DIE	THE DAYS THAT WE CAN	1184	2
OF DEATH THE STERNEST [SHARPEST] FUNCTION [FEATURE]	TO DISAPPEAR ENHANCES--	1209	13
A FUNCTION FRESH OBTAIN?	THE BONE THAT HAS NO	1274	10
WHAT FUNCTION [CUSTOMS] HATH THE AIR?	'TIS WHITER THAN AN	1482	8
FUND			
A FURTHER FORCE [FUND] OF LIFE	HER FINAL SUMMER WAS IT	795	5
FUNDAMENTAL			
A FUNDAMENTAL PAUSE	CRUMBLING IS NOT AN	997	2
AND TAKES IT'S FUNDAMENTAL PLACE	WE DO NOT KNOW THE TIME	1106	3
WE FUNDAMENTAL KNOW	IMMORTAL IS AN AMPLE	1205	6
AT FUNDAMENTAL SIGNALS	TWO LENGTHS HAS EVERY	1295	7
FROM FUNDAMENTAL LAWS.	TWO LENGTHS HAS EVERY	1295	8
BY FUNDAMENTAL PALATES	THE JOY THAT HAS NO STEM	1744	5
FUNERAL			
I FELT A FUNERAL, IN MY BRAIN,	I FELT A FUNERAL, IN MY	280	1
WE THOUGHT THE MIGHTY [MONSTROUS] FUNERAL--	'TIS GOOD--THE LOOKING	660	3
'TIS CORONAL--AND FUNERAL--	UPON CONCLUDED LIVES	735	7
THE FUNERAL OF GOD,	THIS IS A BLOSSOM OF THE	945	14
FUNNELED			
HER BED--A FUNNELED STONE--	I WENT TO THANK HER--	363	3
FUNNY			
FUNNY--TO BE A CENTURY--	FUNNY--TO BE A CENTURY--	345	1
FURL			
TILL YOU WASTE [FURL / LAME] YOUR EYE--	FOLLOW WISE ORION	1538	2
FURLONG			
BEES--BY THE FURLONG--	WHAT WOULD I GIVE TO SEE	247	11
A FURLONG THAN A LEAGUE	WE MISS A KINSMAN MORE	1087	5
FURLOUGHS			
WEARY! FURLOUGHS OF DOWN!	WOULD YOU LIKE SUMMER?	691	4
FURNISH			
IT DEAL US [FURNISH]--STATED AS OUR FOOD--	A PRISON GETS TO BE A	652	7
THAT MAY FURNISH THE FUSE [IGNITION] UNTO A SPARK	A MAN MAY MAKE A REMARK	952	3
FURNISHED			
THE NIGHT WAS WIDE, AND FURNISHED SCANT	THE NIGHT WAS WIDE, AND	589	1
THE FINITE--FURNISHED	THE ADMIRATIONS--AND	906	11
AS THOSE FIRST FURNISHED, SAID--	TWO TRAVELLERS PERISHING	933	16
FURNISHES			
BUT AS THE SPIRIT FURNISHES--	THE SPIRIT LASTS--BUT IN	1576	3
FURNITURE			
FOR PETTY FURNITURE--	SIZE CIRCUMSCRIBES--IT	641	2
HIS PALLID FURNITURE ARRANGED	IT CAME AT LAST BUT	1230	3
NOR EVER SAW HIS HOUSE NOR FURNITURE,	I CANNOT SEE MY SOUL BUT	1262	2
AND GALLOP ON THE FURNITURE--	THOSE CATTLE SMALLER	1388	11
FURROW			
A FURROW--OUR CORDILLERA--	WE SEE--COMPARATIVELY--	534	7
LEAVE MY NEEDLE IN THE FURROW--	DONT PUT UP MY THREAD &	617	13
NO FURROW ON THE GLOW	FURTHER IN SUMMER THAN	1068	14
FURROWED			
HAS FURROWED OUT THE AISLES--	THE COLOR OF THE GRAVE	411	13
FURTHER			
A LITTLE FURTHER ON--	WHOSE ARE THE LITTLE	142	10
LOOK FURTHER ON!	A BURDOCK--CLAWED MY	229	13
FAINTER LEAVES--TO FURTHER SEASONS--	NATURE--SOMETIMES SEARS	314	5
BY FAINTER HAMMERS--FURTHER HEARD--	HE FUMBLES AT YOUR SOUL	315	7
FURTHER [FARTHER] THAN THAT--	THE WIND DID'NT COME	316	2
AND FURTHER TO PARADE A JOY	THE MORNING AFTER WO--	364	7
NO FURTHER 'TIS, THAN HERE--	HEAVEN IS SO FAR OF THE	370	8
TAKE YOUR HEAVEN FURTHER ON--	TAKE YOUR HEAVEN FURTHER	388	1
TO STRETCH A LITTLE FURTHER	THE MONTHS HAVE ENDS--	423	3
I NEED NO FURTHER ARGUE--	DO PEOPLE MOULDER	432	13
AND COULD SHE [I], FURTHER, "NO"?	I SHOWED HER HIGHTS SHE	446	12
AND FURTHER IN THE DAY.	YOU LOVE THE LORD--YOU	487	4
IN FURTHER INFINITE--	HAD I PRESUMED TO HOPE--	522	8
OUR GIANTS--FURTHER ON--	WE SEE--COMPARATIVELY--	534	16
A LITTLE FURTHER REACHES--INSTEAD--	THE BLACK BERRY--WEARS A	554	11
I FIND MY FEET HAVE FURTHER GOALS--	I COULD NOT PROVE THE	563	5
AND IF THE FURTHER [OTHER / FINAL] HEAVEN--	I RECKON--WHEN I COUNT	569	12
THE MINGLED [UNDER / FURTHER] SIDE	I PRAYED, AT FIRST, A	576	12
AND WHEN THIS WORLD--SETS FURTHER BACK--	YOU'LL FIND--IT WHEN YOU	610	9
AND THE CHILDREN--NO FURTHER QUESTION--	GLEE--THE GREAT STORM IS	619	16
LET MONTHS DISSOLVE IN FURTHER [OTHER] MONTHS--	FOREVER--IS COMPOSED OF	624	7
AND FURTHER NORTH--REMOVE.	I THINK THE LONGEST HOUR	635	16
NAY, NATURE, ['TWAS FURTHER--] IT WAS DAY--	TO MY SMALL HEARTH HIS	638	8
WITHOUT A FURTHER FUNCTION--	TO BE ALIVE--IS POWER--	677	3
THE MAKER [FURTHER]--OF OURSELVES--BE WHAT--	TO BE ALIVE--IS POWER--	677	7
AND SHOW A FURTHER SEA--	AS IF THE SEA SHOULD	695	2
AND THAT--A FURTHER--AND THE THREE	AS IF THE SEA SHOULD	695	3

	FIRST LINE	POEM	LINE
FURTHER (CONTINUED)			
UPON THE FURTHER HAND--	YOU TAUGHT ME WAITING	740	12
THEY SEVERALLY--RETARD--OR FURTHER [PROMOTE--OR HINDER]--	FOUR TREES--UPON A	742	15
AS ONE WHO FOR A FURTHER LIFE	HE FOUGHT LIKE THOSE	759	3
HAD NOT A FURTHER USE--	HE FOUGHT LIKE THOSE	759	4
A FURTHER FORCE [FUND] OF LIFE	HER FINAL SUMMER WAS IT	795	5
TILL FOR A FURTHER FOOD	THE LUXURY TO APPREHEND	815	6
HAD I BUT FURTHER SCANNED	A CLOUD WITHDREW FROM	895	5
WE GO NO FURTHER WITH THE DUST	WE CAN BUT FOLLOW TO THE	920	5
DEATH IS THE OTHER [FURTHER] WAY--	THOSE WHO HAVE BEEN IN	922	4
FURTHER THAN ARM COULD STRETCH	UNDER THE LIGHT, YET	949	5
FURTHER THAN SUNSHINE COULD	UNDER THE LIGHT, YET	949	7
FURTHER THAN GUESS CAN GALLOP	UNDER THE LIGHT, YET	949	13
FURTHER THAN RIDDLE RIDE--	UNDER THE LIGHT, YET	949	14
MUCH FLOWERS OF THIS AND FURTHER ZONES	IT BLOOMED AND DROPT, A	978	13
THE DEER ATTRACTS NO FURTHER [INVITES NO LONGER--]	THIS MERIT HATH THE	979	7
AND OPENS FURTHER ON--	A NARROW FELLOW IN THE	986	8
A SUMMER FURTHER I MUST WEAR,	HER LITTLE PARASOL TO	1038	5
FURTHER IN SUMMER THAN THE BIRDS	FURTHER IN SUMMER THAN	1068	1
IS FURTHER THAN THE SUN.	COUNT NOT THAT FAR THAT	1074	4
WE PAUSE BEFORE A FURTHER PLUNGE	WHAT TWIGS WE HELD BY--	1086	4
TILL I HAVE FINER [VAINER / FURTHER] TRIED--	SHALL I TAKE THEE, THE	1126	4
BUT NEARER [CLOSER / FURTHER / SIMPLY / MERELY] TO ADORE	BECAUSE HE LOVES HER	1229	10
HAS "ALL" A FURTHER REALM--	UNTO THE WHOLE--HOW ADD?	1341	2
BUT IT IS RISING [HIGHER / FURTHER] EVERY DAY	THE PILE OF YEARS IS NOT	1507	3
WERE FURTHER OFF	I DID NOT REACH THEE	1664	25
A FURTHER AFTERNOON TO FAIL	I WATCHED HER FACE TO	1667	7
FROM MATHEMATICS FURTHER OFF	IF I COULD TELL HOW GLAD	1668	7
FURTHEST			
EXPEND THEIR FURTHEST [INMOST] POUND--	I FEAR A MAN OF FRUGAL	543	6
WHAT WAS HIS FURTHEST MIND--OF HOME--OR GOD--	TO KNOW JUST HOW HE	622	9
AND THEN I GO THE FURTHEST OFF	THE WAY I READ A	636	5
WITHDREW THE FURTHEST STAR	I COULD SUFFICE FOR HIM,	643	10
PRESENCE--IS HIS FURTHEST LICENSE--	CONSCIOUS AM I IN MY	679	9
AND FURTHEST--TO ADORE--	THE HEAVEN VESTS FOR	694	16
FROM FURTHEST SPIRIT [FAITHFUL / GOOD MAN]--GOD--	ON A COLUMNAR SELF--	789	12
IT SHOWS THE FURTHEST TREE	A LIGHT EXISTS IN SPRING	812	10
UPON THE FURTHEST SLOPE YOU KNOW	A LIGHT EXISTS IN SPRING	812	11
FURTHEST SHINING--DONE--	STRUCK, WAS I, NOR YET	925	12
THE CORN, HER FURTHEST KERNEL FILLED	MIDSUMMER, WAS IT, WHEN	962	5
AND THROWN HER FURTHEST STONE--	THIS MERIT HATH THE	979	4
MY SEASON'S FURTHEST FLOWER--	MY SEASON'S FURTHEST	1019	1
FURTIVE			
A FURTIVE LOOK YOU KNOW AS WELL--	AN ALTERED LOOK ABOUT	140	14
SEEKS FAINTLY [SOFTLY / FURTIVE] FOR IT'S SHORE	THE INUNDATION OF THE	1425	6
FURZE			
THAT BEE TO RIDE, OR FLOWER OF FURZE	BECAUSE THE BEE MAY	869	11
FUSCHZIA'S			
MY FUSCHZIA'S CORAL SEAMS	I TEND MY FLOWERS FOR	339	3
FUSE			
FOR FEAR THE NUMBERS FUSE--	IF YOU WERE COMING IN	511	8
THAT MAY FURNISH THE FUSE [IGNITION] UNTO A SPARK	A MAN MAY MAKE A REMARK	952	3
AND CENTURIES OF AUGUST CEASE [FUSE / LAPSE / BLEND]	THERE IS A ZONE WHOSE	1056	7
THE POSSIBLE'S SLOW FUSE IS LIT	THE GLEAM OF AN HEROIC	1687	3
FUSTIAN			
THO' MY DESTINY BE FUSTIAN--	THO' MY DESTINY BE	163	1
FUTILE			
FUTILE--THE WINDS--	WILD NIGHTS--WILD NIGHTS	249	5
A FUTILE DIADEM--	FAME OF MYSELF, TO	713	8
IS AN INSECT'S FUTILE FORCES	PATIENCE--HAS A QUIET	926	3
LAUREL--FELL YOUR [THY] FUTILE TREE--	LAY THIS LAUREL ON THE	1393	V
FUTURE			
SOFTLY MY FUTURE CLIMBS THE STAIR,	A WIFE--AT DAYBREAK I	461	9
IT HAS NO FUTURE--BUT ITSELF--	PAIN--HAS AN ELEMENT OF	650	5
THE FUTURE--NEVER SPOKE--	THE FUTURE--NEVER SPOKE	672	1
HIS SPACIOUS FUTURE--	NO BOBOLINK--REVERSE HIS	755	6
A LEISURE OF THE FUTURE--	THERE IS A FINISHED	856	3
WILL IN A SECOND FUTURE [BEING]--	THIS DUST, AND IT'S	936	3
OF FUTURE DAYS	THAN HEAVEN MORE REMOTE,	1436	9
HIS FUTURE--A DISPUTE--	NO BRIGADIER THROUGHOUT	1561	22
WITH EVERY FUTURE ONE?	THE SPIRIT LASTS--BUT IN	1576	16
OH FUTURE! THOU SECRETED PEACE	OH FUTURE! THOU SECRETED	1631	1
FUTURES			
'TIS TRUE--OUR FUTURES DIFFERENT LAY--	OURSELVES WERE WED ONE	631	9
FUZZ			
THAT IN SO DENSE A FUZZ--	TO HANG OUR HEAD--	105	6
AND SUBSIST ON FUZZ.	BEES ARE BLACK, WITH	1405	4
FUZZ ORDAINED--NOT FUZZ CONTINGENT--	BEES ARE BLACK, WITH	1405	5
FUZZ ORDAINED--NOT FUZZ CONTINGENT--	BEES ARE BLACK, WITH	1405	5
FUZZY			
A FUZZY FELLOW, WITHOUT FEET,	A FUZZY FELLOW, WITHOUT	173	1
GABLES			
THE GAMBRELS [GABLES] OF THE SKY--	I DWELL IN POSSIBILITY--	657	8

	FIRST LINE	POEM	LINE
GABLES (CONTINUED)			
AND MADE THE GABLES LAUGH--	A DROP FELL ON THE APPLE	794	4
GABRIEL			
GET GABRIEL--TO TELL--THE ROYAL SYLLABLE--	FOR THIS--ACCEPTED	195	13
AS GABRIEL--NEVER CAPERED AT--	THE FACE I CARRY WITH ME	336	11
DROP GABRIEL--AND ME--	I ENVY SEAS, WHEREON HE	498	24
THO' GABRIEL--PRAISE ME--SIR--	WHERE THOU ART--THAT--IS	725	14
THE ROBIN IS A GABRIEL [TROUBADOUR]	THE ROBIN IS A GABRIEL	1483	1
GABRIEL'S			
AND HINDERS GABRIEL'S WING--	THE LOVE A LIFE CAN SHOW	673	6
GABRIELS			
TWO GABRIELS YESTERMORN.	FOREVER HONORED BE THE	1570	4
GAD			
TO GAD MY LITTLE BEING OUT--	IT WOULD HAVE STARVED A	612	15
GAG			
BUT THEY COULD GAG THE TICK--	I KNOW SOME LONELY	289	15
GAIETY			
A PLASH OF OARS, A GAIETY--	I'VE KNOWN A HEAVEN,	243	16
GAILY			
SO BUILD THE HILLOCKS GAILY	ALL THESE MY BANNERS BE.	22	12
THEN SANK AS GAILY AS A TURK	SHE DIED AT PLAY,	75	4
AND GAILY GALLOPED BY--	A SPARROW TOOK A SLICE	1211	V 8
HE GAILY [BOLDLY] INTERRUPTED THAT OVERFLOWING DAY	THE BOBOLINK IS GONE--	1591	4
GAIN			
AND IF I GAIN! OH GUN AT SEA!	'TIS SO MUCH JOY! 'TIS	172	13
TO GAIN HIS GRACE--I'D DIE!	THE COURT IS FAR AWAY--	235	4
WITHOUT--TREMENDOUS GAIN--	I GOT SO I COULD HEAR	293	2
BY ROBBER, SINCE THE GAIN	OF ALL THE SOUNDS	321	12
TO GAIN THE PURPLE DEMOCRAT	THERE IS A FLOWER THAT	380	3
AND GAIN THE SKY	NO RACK CAN TORTURE ME--	384	11
THAN GAIN--MY BLUE PENINSULA--	IT MIGHT BE LONELIER	405	15
BY ACCIDENT OF GAIN	REMOVED FROM ACCIDENT OF	424	2
TO GAIN, OR BE UNDONE--	THE MALAY--TOOK THE	452	16
TO GAIN IT, MEN HAVE BORNE	THIS WORLD IS NOT	501	10
HAD I PRESUMED TO GAIN	HAD I PRESUMED TO HOPE--	522	5
THIS--IS THE SECOND GAIN--	HAD I PRESUMED TO HOPE--	522	16
TO JEOPARDIZE THE GAIN?	I CROSS TILL I AM WEARY	550	17
THAT ANY GAIN--	DELIGHT--BECOMES	572	4
OR THAT ETHERIAL [SERAPHIC] GAIN	MY FIRST WELL DAY--SINCE	574	26
SOME--FOUND IT--MUTUAL GAIN--	I GAVE MYSELF TO HIM--	580	14
AND SEEK [GAIN] A DINNER FOR MYSELF--	IT WOULD HAVE STARVED A	612	11
I COULD NOT CARE--TO GAIN	WITHOUT THIS--THERE IS	655	5
HAS IMPETUS OF GAIN--	THE SERVICE WITHOUT HOPE	779	5
GAIN--SATIETY--	EXPECTATION--IS	807	2
I MADE SLOW RICHES BUT MY GAIN	I MADE SLOW RICHES BUT	843	1
BUT MY PERCEIVELESS GAIN	I MADE SLOW RICHES BUT	843	6
TO GAIN RENOWN OF LADY'S DRAWER	THE BIRD MUST SING TO	880	5
BUT GAIN--THRO' LOSS--THROUGH GRIEF [PAIN]--OBTAIN--	FITTER TO SEE HIM, I MAY	968	26
PERCEPTION IN ITSELF A GAIN	PERCEPTION OF AN OBJECT	1071	3
IS DIFFICULT TO GAIN	SUPERIORITY TO FATE	1081	2
WE ENTER BUT THE GAIN,	OF SO DIVINE A LOSS	1179	2
FIDELITY IS GAIN	THE GENTIAN HAS A	1424	16
A GAIN UPON THE BACKWARD LEAVES	SUMMER BEGINS TO HAVE	1682	4
TO LOSE THEE--SWEETER THAN TO GAIN	TO LOSE THEE--SWEETER	1754	1
GAINED			
I HOPE TWAS HONEST GAINED.	I NEVER TOLD THE BURIED	11	11
HAVE GAINED! YES! HESITATED SO--	'TIS SO MUCH JOY! 'TIS	172	5
OUR PANTING ANCLE BARELY PASSED [GAINED],	OF TRIBULATION--THESE	325	13
I GAINED IT SO--	I GAINED IT SO--	359	1
I SAID I GAINED IT--	I GAINED IT SO--	359	8
WORTHIEST--TO HAVE GAINED--	PROMISE THIS--WHEN YOU	648	V 33
IF END I GAINED [REACHED]	FROM BLANK TO BLANK--	761	6
MAY BE EASIER REACHED [BETTER ATTAINED / EASIER GAINED]--THIS WAY--	BY MY WINDOW HAVE I FOR	797	8
SHE STAKED HER FEATHERS--GAINED AN ARC--	SHE STAKED HER FEATHERS	798	1
SHE STAKED HER WINGS--AND GAINED A BUSH--	SHE STAKED HER FEATHERS	798	V 1
WERE IT BUT ME THAT GAINED THE HIGHT--	WERE IT BUT ME THAT	1015	1
I KNEW THAT I HAD GAINED	I KNEW THAT I HAD GAINED	1022	1
GAINING			
DESCRIED I--BY [IN] THE DISTANT [GAINING] LIGHT	THE ROAD WAS LIT WITH	1450	3
GAINS			
IT GAINS THE BLOCK--AND NOW--IT GAINS THE DOOR--	IT'S COMING--THE	390	2
IT GAINS THE BLOCK--AND NOW--IT GAINS THE DOOR--	IT'S COMING--THE	390	2
IT NOTES [GAINS] DELIGHT	MUST BE A WO--	571	6
HE GAINS THE SKILL	THE CHILD'S FAITH IS NEW	637	21
BEST GAINS--MUST HAVE THE LOSSES' TEST--	BEST GAINS--MUST HAVE	684	1
TO CONSTITUTE THEM--GAINS--	BEST GAINS--MUST HAVE	684	2
SEEN POOREST--THRO' OUR GAINS--	I LEARNED--AT LEAST--	944	21
HER [HIS] LOSSES MAKE OUR GAINS ASHAMED--	HER LOSSES MAKE OUR	1562	1
GAIT			
HIS MIEN [GAIT], WAS SOUNDLESS, LIKE THE [A] BIRD--	THE ONLY GHOST I EVER	274	5
THIS GAVE ME THAT PRECARIOUS GAIT	I STEPPED FROM PLANK TO	875	7
THOU SHALT GO AT SUCH A GAIT OF JOY	IN SNOW THOU COMEST	1669	6
AND TAKES HER FAIR AERIAL GAIT	THE OVERTAKELESSNESS OF	1691	7

	FIRST LINE	POEM		LINE
GALA				
WHO'LL LET ME OUT SOME GALA DAY	BRING ME THE SUNSET IN A	128		22
GALAXIES				
STARS, AMID PROFOUND GALAXIES--	IF THE FOOLISH, CALL	168		19
GALE				
AND SWEETEST--IN THE GALE--IS HEARD-- . .	"HOPE" IS THE THING WITH	254		5
WERE EVERY STORM [GALE / SNOW] SO SPICE [FAIR / SWEET]	THE SNOW THAT NEVER	1133		13
THE GALE [BREEZE] WERE NOT SO FINE . . .	WE LIKE A HAIRBREADTH	1175		6
THE SYMPTOM OF THE GALE--	THE SYMPTOM OF THE GALE	1327		1
A GALE	IT SOUNDED AS IF THE	1397		T
AND DURING IT'S ELECTRIC GALE [SPELL / STAY / MIGHT / ACT / SPAN]--	WITH PINIONS OF DISDAIN	1431		7
OUR PERCHANCE A GALE	DOWN TIME'S QUAINT	1656		5
GALES				
ONE LITTLE BOAT--O'ERSPENT WITH GALES-- . .	ADRIFT! A LITTLE BOAT	30		11
WHETHER SHE MET WITH GALES--	WHETHER MY BARK WENT	52		2
THERE--GATHERED FROM THE GALES--	A POOR--TORN HEART-- A	78		14
WHEN, WERE THE GALES PROPITIOUS--	WENT UP A YEAR THIS	93		11
THE GALES--INDEED--WERE DONE--	ON THIS LONG STORM THE	194		6
GALLANT				
'TWAS SUCH A GALLANT--GALLANT SEA	'TWAS SUCH A LITTLE--	107		3
'TWAS SUCH A GALLANT--GALLANT SEA	'TWAS SUCH A LITTLE--	107		3
BY GALLANT--MOULDERING HAND!	IN EBON BOX, WHEN YEARS	169		12
MANY'S THE GALLANT--OVERWHELMED CREATURE .	FINITE--TO FAIL, BUT	847		3
. . . MIGHTY / GALLANT / SYLVAN / AMPLE / PERFECT] WAY	SUMMER--WE ALL HAVE SEEN	1386		6
HER GALLANT NOTE ENDOWS US LIKE A FRIEND .	AFTER ALL BIRDS HAVE	1395	V	6
THIS GALLANT LITTLE FLOWER--	IT WOULD NOT KNOW IF IT	1579		2
GALLANTER				
BUT GALLANTER, I KNOW	TO FIGHT ALOUD, IS VERY	126		2
GALLANTLY				
AS GALLANTLY AS IF THE EAST	HER LOSSES MAKE OUR	1562		3
GALLERIES				
WHOSE GALLERIES--ARE SUNRISE--	A FEATHER FROM THE	161		3
OR BLUE BEARD'S GALLERIES--	LIKE SOME OLD FASHIONED	302		8
GALLERY				
ITSELF--A GALLERY [VATICAN] TOO RARE-- . .	IT'S THOUGHTS--AND JUST	495		10
GALLOP				
FAR SAFER, THROUGH AN ABBEY GALLOP, . . .	ONE NEED NOT BE A	670		9
FURTHER THAN GUESS CAN GALLOP	UNDER THE LIGHT, YET	949		13
AND GALLOP ON THE FURNITURE--	THOSE CATTLE SMALLER	1388		11
AT THAT ENTHRALLING GALLOP	SWEET IS THE SWAMP WITH	1740		5
GALLOPED				
THE FORESTS GALLOPED TILL THEY FELL . . .	THE CLOUDS THEIR BACKS	1172		3
AND GAILY GALLOPED BY--	A SPARROW TOOK A SLICE	1211	V	8
GALLOPED IN DREAMS--	UNTIL THE DESERT KNOWS	1291		12
GALLOWS				
ASK [TO] HIM UNTO THE GALLOWS LED [CALLED]--	OH SUMPTUOUS MOMENT	1125		8
UPON THE GALLOWS HUNG A WRETCH, ...	UPON THE GALLOWS HUNG A	1757		1
GAMBLERS				
GAMBLERS--RECOLLECTING WHICH	WE LOSE--BECAUSE WE WIN	21		2
GAMBOGE				
THE SMALLEST [FINEST] GAMBOGE HAND . . .	YOU'LL KNOW HER--BY HER	634		2
GAMBOL				
AND GAMBOL I MAY NEVER NAME--	THERE IS A MORN BY MEN	24		5
CREATION--BUT THE GAMBOL	IT'S EASY TO INVENT A	724		3
GAMBOLLED				
GAMBOLLED AWAY	SHE DIED AT PLAY,	75		2
GAMBOLS				
IN EDDIES OF [FATHOMS IN / RAPIDS OF / GAMBOLS WITH / . . .	TWO BUTTERFLIES WENT OUT	533	V	
. . . GAMBOLS OF] THE SUN--	TWO BUTTERFLIES WENT OUT	533	V	
WHO GAMBOLS ALL THE LIVING DAY	A LITTLE DOG THAT WAGS	1185		5
GAMBRELS				
THE GAMBRELS [GABLES] OF THE SKY-- . . .	I DWELL IN POSSIBILITY--	657		8
GAME				
AND ALL DAY LONG, WITH DANCE AND GAME, . .	THERE IS A MORN BY MEN	24		4
GAMMUTS				
GAMMUTS [TRIPLETS] OF ETERNITIES	PAIN--EXPANDS THE TIME--	967		7
GAP				
TO FILL A GAP	TO FILL A GAP	546		1
GAPING				
IF WE DEMUR, IT'S GAPING SIDES	THIS CHASM, SWEET, UPON	858		5
GARDEN				
HERE IS A BRIGHTER GARDEN, ...	THERE IS ANOTHER SKY,	2		9
INTO MY GARDEN COME!	THERE IS ANOTHER SKY,	2		14
ENCOUNTER IN MY GARDEN	BAFFLED FOR JUST A DAY	17		3
WHEN I BELIEVE THE GARDEN	WHEN I COUNT THE SEEDS	40		7
I HAV'NT TOLD MY GARDEN YET--	I HAV'NT TOLD MY GARDEN	50		1
OUR LITTLE GARDEN THAT WE LOST	WE SHOULD NOT MIND SO	81		3
NEW FEET WITHIN MY GARDEN GO--	NEW FEET WITHIN MY	99		1
I SOW SWEET FLOWER FROM GARDEN BED-- . . .	WHERE I HAVE LOST, I	104		2
THE PROPERTY, MY GARDEN, ...	I HAD SOME THINGS THAT I	116		5
UPON MY GARDEN FLOOR--	I TEND MY FLOWERS FOR	339		17
MY GARDEN--LIKE THE BEACH--	MY GARDEN--LIKE THE	484		1
WITHIN MY GARDEN, RIDES A BIRD	WITHIN MY GARDEN, RIDES	500		1
OR BORE THE GARDEN IN THE BRAIN	WITHIN MY GARDEN, RIDES	500		15
'TIS TRUE, YOUR GARDEN LED THE BLOOM, . .	OURSELVES WERE WED ONE	631		13
LATE--MY GARDEN [ACRE] OF A ROCK-- . . .	SOIL OF FLINT, IF STEADY	681	V	

	FIRST LINE	POEM	LINE
GARDEN (CONTINUED)			
WHAT MORNINGS IN OUR GARDEN--GUESSED--	I LEARNED--AT LEAST--	944	9
THE GARDEN [LANDSCAPE] KEEP [SHOW / OWN / HOLD] THE GASH--	AS FROST IS BEST	951	6
THE GARDEN GETS THE ONLY SHOT	THE FROST WAS NEVER SEEN	1202	11
WHOSE GARDEN WRESTLES WITH THE DEW,	HOW DARE THE ROBINS SING	1724	15
GARLAND			
GARLAND BE INDEED--	HER SWEET TURN TO LEAVE	649	12
GARLANDS			
GARLANDS FOR QUEENS, MAY BE--	GARLANDS FOR QUEENS, MAY	34	1
GARMENT			
UPON A FORMER GARMENT SHOWS	WHAT TWIGS WE HELD BY--	1086	7
THE GARMENT CAST,	WHAT TWIGS WE HELD BY--	1086	8
THE GARMENT OF SURPRISE	LET ME NOT MAR THAT	1335	6
GARMENTS			
THE TEMPESTS TOUCHED OUR GARMENTS--	THROUGH LANE IT LAY--	9	9
GARNER			
MY GARNER SHOWS SO FAIR--	GOD GAVE A LOAF TO EVERY	791	12
GARNET			
WHEN YOU--HOLD--GARNET TO GARNET--	TITLE DIVINE--IS MINE!	1072	8
WHEN YOU--HOLD--GARNET TO GARNET--	TITLE DIVINE--IS MINE!	1072	8
THAN WHEN SHE SHOWS HER GARNET TOOTH--	WHEN ETNA BASKS AND	1146	3
GARRET			
FROM OUR GARRET GO	PUBLICATION--IS THE	709	6
OR A GLEE AMONG THE GARRET	THAT IS SOLEMN WE HAVE	934	3
IT HAS A GARRET ALSO	REMEMBRANCE HAS A	1182	3
GARRISONED			
GARRISONED NO SOUL CAN BE	SAFE DESPAIR IT IS THAT	1243	5
GARTER			
HER GARTER--WAS OF GOLD--	THE DAY UNDRESSED--	716	2
GASH			
THE GARDEN [LANDSCAPE] KEEP [SHOW / OWN / HOLD] THE GASH--	AS FROST IS BEST	951	6
GASPED			
A CREATURE GASPED "REPREIVE"!	'TWAS LIKE A MAELSTROM,	414	23
"'TWAS ALL I HAD," SHE STRICKEN GASPED--	UPON THE GALLOWS HUNG A	1757	7
GASPING			
FLED [STOLE] GASPING FROM THE HOUSE--	I YEARS HAD BEEN FROM	609	24
GATE			
PASS ROYAL THRO' THE GATE--	MY WHEEL IS IN THE DARK!	10	13
HER LITTLE FIGURE AT THE GATE	SHE DIED--THIS WAS THE	150	5
SOMEBODY RUN TO THE GREAT GATE	DYING! DYING IN THE	158	9
AND "DIFFICULT THE GATE"--	YOU'RE RIGHT--"THE WAY	234	2
WHAT IF I BURST THE FLESHLY GATE--	WHAT IF I SAY I SHALL	277	2
AT HER LOW GATE--	THE SOUL SELECTS HER OWN	303	6
COULD WASTE [MELT] THE SNOW BEFORE THEIR GATE--	WHAT CARE THE DEAD, FOR	592	11
AND GOD--AT EVERY GATE--	OUR JOURNEY HAD ADVANCED	615	12
THE WIND COULD WAIT WITHOUT THE GATE	THE SPRY ARMS OF THE	1103	7
A CLOSING OF THE SIMPLE LID [GATE]	A GREAT HOPE FELL	1123	14
DELIGHT HAD AGGRANDIZED THE GATE	IT CAME AT LAST BUT	1230	7
AT ANY GATE BUT WOE'S--	TIME'S WILY CHARGERS	1458	2
THE RUMOR'S GATE WAS SHUT SO TIGHT	THE SPIRIT LASTS--BUT IN	1576	21
WHOSE RUMOR'S GATE WAS SHUT SO TIGHT	EXPANSE CANNOT BE LOST--	1584	5
THE RUMOR'S GATE WAS SHUT SO TIGHT	THIS ME--THAT WALKS AND	1588	5
A TRAIN WENT THROUGH A BURIAL GATE,	A TRAIN WENT THROUGH A	1761	1
GATES			
THAT ONCE--ON ME--THOSE JASPER GATES	IF I'M LOST--NOW--	256	4
GATHER			
PRAY GATHER ME--	SUMMER FOR THEE, GRANT I	31	7
THE HAND THAT PAUSED TO GATHER	WHEN ROSES CEASE TO	32	5
TO GATHER PARADISE--	I DWELL IN POSSIBILITY--	657	12
SO LET US GATHER--EVERY DAY--	TO EARN IT BY DISDAINING	1427	5
BUT IMPOTENT TO GATHER,	THROUGH THOSE OLD	1753	11
GATHERED			
THAT [WHO] GATHERED THIS [THESE], TODAY!	IF RECOLLECTING WERE	33	8
I.E. GATHERED AWAY,	LIKE HER THE SAINTS	60	8
THERE--GATHERED FROM THE GALES--	A POOR--TORN HEART-- A	78	14
GATHERED BY CATO'S DAUGHTER,	GREAT CAESAR! CONDESCEND	102	3
GATHERED FROM MANY WANDERINGS--	ALL OVERGROWN BY CUNNING	148	V
INDIFFERENT HANGING [GATHERED] NOW--	HIS BILL IS CLASPED--HIS	1102	4
SECUREST GATHERED THEN	TO DISAPPEAR ENHANCES--	1209	16
GATHERED INTO THE EARTH,	GATHERED INTO THE EARTH,	1370	1
GATHERED TO THAT STRANGE FAME--	GATHERED INTO THE EARTH,	1370	3
SINCE IT WAS GATHERED [TETHERED] HERE--	PRAISE IT--'TIS DEAD--	1384	5
DECADE HAD HASTENED [HURRIED / GATHERED] TO DECADE--	A LITTLE SNOW WAS HERE	1444	4
I GATHERED FROM HIS TALK	HIGH FROM THE EARTH I	1723	10
GATHERING			
AND BREATHS WERE GATHERING FIRM	I HEARD A FLY BUZZ--WHEN	465	6
GATHERS			
IT GATHERS RUDDY [STANDS IN--RUDDY / MAKES VERMILLION--] POOLS--	THE NAME--OF IT--IS	656	10
GAUDY			
WE AND OUR PLOTTING HEART [GAUDY HEART / SCHEMING TINSEL / . . .	AN ANTIQUATED GRACE	1345	5
THOUGH GAUDY INFLUENCE	AS IMPERCEPTIBLY AS	1540	V
RESUMES HIS GAUDY INDUSTRY	SUMMER BEGINS TO HAVE	1682	12
GAUGE SEE GUAGE			

	FIRST LINE	POEM	LINE
GAUNT			
THE CLOUDS WERE GAUNT, AND FEW--	AN AWFUL TEMPEST MASHED	198	2
GAUZE			
UPON A PLANE OF GAUZE!	TO HANG OUR HEAD--	105	8
ONCE WITNESSED OF THE GAUZE--	A SINGLE SCREW OF FLESH	263	5
AND THOUGH I HAD NO GOWN OF GAUZE--	I CANNOT DANCE UPON MY	326	9
HIS FEET ARE SHOD WITH GAUZE--	HIS FEET ARE SHOD WITH	916	1
OF UNATTEMPTED GAUZE	THE HEART HAS NARROW	928	10
GAVE			
GAVE HIS BREATH AWAY.	THERE IS A WORD	8	10
ONE LITTLE BOAT GAVE UP IT'S STRIFE	ADRIFT! A LITTLE BOAT	30	7
YOU MAY FORGET THE WARMTH HE GAVE--	HEART! WE WILL FORGET	47	3
WE GAVE NO OTHER BOND--	THERE CAME A DAY AT	322	24
A BOOK I HAVE--A FRIEND GAVE--	DEATH SETS A THING	360	13
AND SO TO MEND HER--GAVE ME WORK	THE FIRST DAY'S NIGHT	410	7
GAVE--EVEN AS TO ALL--	HER SWEET WEIGHT ON MY	518	10
HE GAVE AWAY HIS LIFE--	HE GAVE AWAY HIS LIFE--	567	1
I GAVE MYSELF TO HIM [HIM ALL MYSELF]--	I GAVE MYSELF TO HIM--	580	1
I MET [GAVE] HIM--	I ROSE--BECAUSE HE SANK	616	10
THOUGHT BELONG TO HIM WHO GAVE IT--	PUBLICATION--IS THE	709	9
BESTOWED [HE GAVE] HIMSELF TO BALLS	HE FOUGHT LIKE THOSE	759	2
GOD GAVE A LOAF TO EVERY BIRD--	GOD GAVE A LOAF TO EVERY	791	1
NO NOTICE GAVE SHE, BUT A CHANGE--	NO NOTICE GAVE SHE, BUT	804	1
THIS GAVE ME THAT PRECARIOUS GAIT	I STEPPED FROM PLANK TO	875	7
THEN GAVE [BENT / BOWED] THE EAST UNTO THE WEST	THE WIND TOOK UP THE	1134	3
I GAVE HIM LEAVE TO LIVE	IT CAME HIS TURN TO BEG	1500	6
TO WHICH HE [SHE] GAVE THE WORTH,	CLIMBING TO REACH THE	1566	2
THE IMMORTALITY SHE GAVE	THE IMMORTALITY SHE GAVE	1648	1
FOR WHICH WE GAVE THE EARTH	WHEN WE HAVE CEASED TO	1706	3
GAY			
ONE WITH THE BANNER GAY--	SLEEP IS SUPPOSED TO BE	13	13
HIS CAPUCHIN GAY--	THE GUEST IS GOLD AND	15	4
AND TO MOURN, WERE GAY,	IF RECOLLECTING WERE	33	6
HOW GAY UPON YOUR TABLE	IF SHE HAD BEEN THE	44	3
LEAP SO HIGHLAND GAY,	SO FROM THE MOULD	66	8
CONCLUDE THE WONDER GAY--	A SOMETHING IN A	122	20
AN HOUR, AND GAY ON EVERY TREE	COCOON ABOVE! COCOON	129	4
THEN GAY ABOVE RECEDING GRASS	COCOON ABOVE! COCOON	129	8
SO GAY, SO BRIGADIER--	THE SUN KEPT STOOPING--	152	10
GAY LITTLE HEART--	POOR LITTLE HEART!	192	10
GAY, GHASTLY, HOLIDAY!	'TIS SO APPALLING--IT	281	24
THY FLOWER--BE GAY--	I TEND MY FLOWERS FOR	339	21
TO MAKE YOUR COTTAGE GAY--	ALTHOUGH I PUT AWAY HIS	366	29
MERRY, AND NOUGHT, AND GAY, AND NUMB--	OF COURSE--I PRAYED--	376	10
GLAD--GAY--HOUSES--	SWEET--SAFE--HOUSES--	457	2
GAY--LIKE LIGHT--	I AM ASHAMED--I HIDE--	473	22
AND MAKE THE BODDICE GAY--	TO MAKE ONE'S TOILETTE--	485	6
THINGS SO [TOO] GAY	INCONCEIVABLY SOLEMN!	582	2
THE SUN IS GAY OR STARK	THE SUN IS GAY OR STARK	878	1
STEPPED WITH SO GAY A FOOT	AND THIS OF ALL MY HOPES	913	6
I TELL IT GAY TO THOSE WHO SUFFER NOW--	TIME DOES GO ON--	1121	2
WITHIN A CAPSULE GAY,	THIS IS THE PLACE THEY	1264	4
THIS WHOLE [SUDDEN / FAIR / GAY / BRIGHT / FLEET / SWEET / ...	A LITTLE MADNESS IN THE	1333	5
GAY WERE GETHSEMANE	SPURN THE TEMERITY--	1432	3
SO GAY A FLOWER	SO GAY A FLOWER	1456	1
WITH GAY DELAYS HE GOES	BEFORE YOU THOUGHT OF	1465	12
WITH GAY APOSTASY	HIS ORIENTAL HERESIES	1526	4
A COMPENSATION FAIR [GAY]	COSMOPOLITES WITHOUT A	1589	6
A COMPETENCE SO GAY	COSMOPOLITES WITHOUT A	1589	V 6
GAY FROM AN UNANNOINTED [SWEET FROM A SURREPTITIOUS] TWIG	THE BOBOLINK IS GONE--	1591	12
AND THEN A GAY UNKNOWN	OF THIS IS DAY COMPOSED	1675	4
GAYER			
WITH GAYER SANDALS GO--	THE FEET OF PEOPLE	7	2
THE MAPLE WEARS A GAYER SCARF--	THE MORNS ARE MEEKER	12	5
BUILD IN GAYER BOUGHS,	IT DID NOT SURPRISE ME--	39	6
GAZE			
WHAT GAZE!	IF PAIN FOR PEACE	63	9
GAZE PERPLEXEDLY!	SO FROM THE MOULD	66	11
THAT GAZE UPON [GROW ALONG] HIS JOURNEY--	I ENVY SEAS, WHEREON HE	498	5
TO WHOM HE COULD ENTRUST HIS WAVERING GAZE--	TO KNOW JUST HOW HE	622	3
A HEAVEN IN A GAZE--	'TWAS A LONG PARTING--	625	6
SHE VAULTED OUT OF GAZE--	I WATCHED THE MOON	629	32
TO SHUT THE OTHER'S GAZE DOWN--	I CANNOT LIVE WITH YOU--	640	15
THEIR FAR--SLOW--VIOLET GAZE--	SWEET MOUNTAINS--YE TELL	722	6
AND MET THE GAZE--DIRECT--	NO NOTICE GAVE SHE, BUT	804	12
TIME [TIME'S] TO ANTICIPATE HIS GAZE--	FITTER TO SEE HIM, I MAY	968	9
THAT DYING I MAY EARN THE LOOK [GAZE]	TRIED ALWAYS AND	1559	3
TILL IT IS OUT OF GAZE.	LOVE CAN DO ALL BUT	1731	8
GAZED			
I GAZED [TURNED]--AS AT A STRANGER--	I WATCHED THE MOON	629	5
GAZES			
THE [IT'S] SPIRIT LOOKS UPON [TURNS UPON / GAZES AT / GLANCES ...	AS FROM THE EARTH THE	1630	5
GAZING			
THAT IN MY AWKWARD--GAZING--FACE--	IF I'M LOST--NOW--	256	6
FROM OUR FAMILIAR LIFETIME [ADDRESS / GAZING / FINGERS / NOTICE]--	THOSE FAIR--FICTITIOUS	499	3

	FIRST LINE	POEM	LINE
GAZING (CONTINUED)			
WE PASSED THE FIELDS OF GAZING GRAIN--	BECAUSE I COULD NOT STOP	712	11
GEM			
THE GEM WAS GONE--	I HELD A JEWEL IN MY	245	6
THAT--DOES NOT BLUR MY GEM!	ONE LIFE OF SO MUCH	270	10
HOW BETTER, THAN A GEM!	YOUR RICHES--TAUGHT ME--	299	24
AND CARBON IN THE GEM	THE DAY THAT I WAS	356	6
INSTEAD I'LL SAY OF GEM	EACH SCAR I'LL KEEP FOR	877	2
THE GEM WERE BEST UNKNOWN--	A DIAMOND ON THE HAND	1108	4
GEMS			
BUT JUST THE NAMES, OF GEMS--	YOUR RICHES--TAUGHT ME--	299	10
GEM-TACTICS			
LEARNED GEM-TACTICS--	WE PLAY AT PASTE--	320	7
GENERAL			
BUT GENERAL HOMES	ALONE, I CANNOT BE--	298	7
THAT GENERAL ATTENDANCE	NO CROWD THAT HAS	515	3
THE GENERAL HEAVENS--UPON--	OF BEING IS A BIRD	653	4
THE GENERAL ROSE--DECAY--	ESSENTIAL OILS--ARE	675	5
"GENERAL, THE BRITISH"--"EASY"	WOLFE DEMANDED DURING	678	3
WHAT DEED IS THEIR'S [THEY BEAR] UNTO THE GENERAL NATURE--	FOUR TREES--UPON A	742	13
ON NATURE'S PERFECT [GENERAL] SUM--	IT BLOOMED AND DROPT, A	978	10
GENERAL AS THE DANDELION	NONE WHO SAW IT EVER	1110	7
SOMEWHERE UPON THE GENERAL EARTH	SOMEWHERE UPON THE	1231	1
HOW GENERAL A GRACE	MY HEART RAN SO TO THEE	1237	7
WOULD BE THE GENERAL THOUGHT--	ON MY VOLCANO GROWS THE	1677	4
GENERALLY			
AND DWELL A LITTLE EVERYWHERE [GENERALLY]	COULD I BUT RIDE	661	7
WITH USUALLY [GENERALLY] A SOBER BIRD--	A FIELD OF STUBBLE,	1407	V 5
GENERATE			
OR TERROR--THAT DO DECORATE [CELEBRATE / GENERATE]	HIS VOICE DECREPIT WAS	1476	7
GENERATIONS			
SNATCHES, FROM BAPTIZED GENERATIONS--	OVER AND OVER, LIKE A	367	5
CONTEMPT OF GENERATIONS	THIS WORLD IS NOT	501	11
THOUGH GENERATIONS PASS AWAY,	A LITTLE OVERFLOWING	1467	4
GENERIC			
GENERIC AS A QUARRY	WINTER IS GOOD--HIS HOAR	1316	5
GENESIS			
EVANGELISTS [AS GENESIS] RECORD	A LITTLE EAST OF JORDAN,	59	2
WHOSE GENESIS WAS JUNE.	THE MURMURING OF BEES,	1115	8
GENESIS--BETHLEHEM'S ANCESTOR--	THE BIBLE IS AN ANTIQUE	1545	V 5
A VAGABOND [SORCERER] FROM GENESIS	THE CLOCK STRIKES ONE	1569	3
GENESIS'			
IN GENESIS' NEW HOUSE,	TRUSTY AS THE STARS	1369	4
GENEVA'S			
GENEVA'S FARTHEST SKILL	A CLOCK STOPPED--	287	3
GENIAL			
SO GENIAL IN THE MAIN	A WILD BLUE SKY ABREAST	1415	6
GENIUS			
NEGLECTED SON OF GENIUS	THE SPIDER AS AN ARTIST	1275	7
GENOA			
WHEN [TILL] GENOA--WITHDREW	TRUST IN THE UNEXPECTED	555	10
GENTIAN			
THE GENTIAN WEAVES HER FRINGES--	THE GENTIAN WEAVES HER	18	1
DISTRUSTFUL OF THE GENTIAN--	DISTRUSTFUL OF THE	20	1
GOD MADE A LITTLE GENTIAN--	GOD MADE A LITTLE	442	1
THE GENTIAN HAS A PARCHED COROLLA--	THE GENTIAN HAS A	1424	1
GENTIANS			
AND COVENANT GENTIANS--FRILL!	WHILE ASTERS--	331	4
AND COVENANT GENTIANS--FRILL--	IT WILL BE SUMMER--	342	16
GENTILE			
WITH THE BRAND [STAMP] OF THE GENTILE DRINKER	TO PUT THIS WORLD DOWN,	527	14
GENTILITY			
GENTILITY IS FINE,	"SIC TRANSIT GLORIA	3	42
GENTLE			
FOR SIGHING, AND GENTLE WHISPERING, AND UNITY MADE OF TWAIN.	AWAKE YE MUSES NINE,	1	4
GOOD EVENING, GENTLE FELLOW MEN!	IF THIS IS "FADING"	120	8
IN GENTLE DEFERENCE TO ME--	I DREADED THAT FIRST	348	23
THROUGH GENTLE [CURIOUS / EASY] MIRACLE OF DEATH--	THOSE FAIR--FICTITIOUS	499	23
THE HOUSEWIFE'S GENTLE TASK--	THE NIGHT WAS WIDE, AND	589	17
IT WAS A GENTLE PRICE--	OF BRUSSELS--IT WAS NOT	602	5
LIKE GENTLE INFAMY--	SO LARGE MY WILL	1024	4
WILL GENTLE BE, TO HER.	HERE, WHERE THE DAISIES	1037	8
A [GENTLE] PENSIVE CUSTOM IT BECOMES	FURTHER IN SUMMER THAN	1068	7
AS TO BEHOLD HIS AMPLE [GENTLE] FLIGHT--	THE MERCHANT OF THE	1131	11
AND YET WE KNEW THAT GENTLE CLOCK	'TWAS LATER WHEN THE	1276	3
HOW RUTHLESS ARE THE GENTLE--	HOW RUTHLESS ARE THE	1439	1
GENTLEFOLK			
AS ONE MET SUDDEN [ENCOUNTERED] GENTLEFOLK	IT IS AN HONORABLE	946	3
GENTLEMAN			
THREE CHEERS, SIR, FOR THE GENTLEMAN	"SIC TRANSIT GLORIA	3	11
OH, IF I--WERE THE GENTLEMAN	WHY--DO THEY SHUT ME OUT	248	9
A DOCILE GENTLEMAN--	THE SAVIOR MUST HAVE	1487	2
GENTLEMEN			
THAT GENTLEMEN SO SPRIGHTLY	IF I SHOULD DIE,	54	17
WHERE VERY NIMBLE GENTLEMEN	WHERE BELLS NO MORE	112	3
WHEN GENTLEMEN CAN [FOR GENTLEMEN WHO] SEE--	"FAITH" IS A FINE	185	2

	FIRST LINE	POEM	LINE
GENTLEMEN (CONTINUED)			
SAUNTERING GENTLEMEN--WITH CANES--	IT WILL BE SUMMER--	342	3
THIS QUIET DUST WAS GENTLEMEN AND LADIES	THIS QUIET DUST WAS	813	1
GENTLEST			
NATURE--THE GENTLEST MOTHER IS,	NATURE--THE GENTLEST	790	1
GENTLEWOMEN			
THESE GENTLEWOMEN ARE--	WHAT SOFT--CHERUBIC	401	2
GENTLY			
GIVE GENTLY TO THE DEAD--	THIS HEART THAT BROKE SO	145	4
WHERE SHIPS OF PURPLE--GENTLY TOSS--	WHERE SHIPS OF PURPLE--	265	1
PUT GENTLY UP THE EVENING BARS--	I'LL TELL YOU HOW THE	318	15
AND NATURE GENTLY [SOFTLY] OWNED HER	SHE COULD NOT LIVE UPON	1505	4
GENTLY REPLACING	GLORY IS THAT BRIGHT	1660	6
OR HEART SO GENTLY BORNE,	WHICH MISSES MOST,	1759	3
GENUINE			
MORE GENUINE WERE PERFIDY	THE HEALED HEART SHOWS	1440	7
GEOGRAPHY			
THERE'S NO GEOGRAPHY--	WE PRAY--TO HEAVEN--	489	9
I JUDGE FROM MY GEOGRAPHY	VOLCANOES BE IN SICILY	1705	3
GEOMETRIC			
A GEOMETRIC JOY--	A PRISON GETS TO BE A	652	16
GEOMETRY			
BEST WITCHCRAFT IS GEOMETRY	BEST WITCHCRAFT IS	1158	1
GERANIUM			
AND ONE GERANIUM--	I WAS THE SLIGHTEST IN	486	4
GERANIUMS			
GERANIUMS--TINT--AND SPOT--	I TEND MY FLOWERS FOR	339	5
GERM			
GERM'S GERM BE WHERE?	BEST THINGS DWELL OUT OF	998	8
THE GERM [JOY] OF ALIBI--	THE MUSHROOM IS THE ELF	1298	10
A LIGHTNING IN THE GERM--	FAME IS THE ONE THAT	1475	6
GERMINATION			
'TIS RAPTURE'S GERMINATION	THE FASCINATING CHILL	1480	4
GERM'S			
GERM'S GERM BE WHERE?	BEST THINGS DWELL OUT OF	998	8
GESSLER			
THREATENED FOR THAT WITH DEATH--BY GESSLER--	TELL AS A MARKSMAN--WERE	1152	16
GESTURE			
GESTURE COQUETTE--AND SHAKE YOUR HEAD!	GOING TO HIM! HAPPY	494	25
MUCH GESTURE, FROM THE PULPIT--	THIS WORLD IS NOT	501	17
GET			
IF YOU SH'D GET THERE FIRST	GOING TO HEAVEN!	79	13
GET GABRIEL--TO TELL--THE ROYAL SYLLABLE--	FOR THIS--ACCEPTED	195	13
GET SAINTS--WITH NEW--UNSTEADY TONGUE--	FOR THIS--ACCEPTED	195	14
THO' I GET HOME HOW LATE--HOW LATE--	THO' I GET HOME HOW LATE	207	1
SO I GET HOME--'TWILL COMPENSATE--	THO' I GET HOME HOW LATE	207	2
SO IF I GET LOST--THERE--EVER--	WHAT IS--"PARADISE"--	215	13
DO WE "GET DRUNK"?	WE--BEE AND I--LIVE BY	230	6
MINE--GET SO DIM!	YOU SEE I CANNOT SEE--	253	7
AND A HOARSE "GET OUT OF THE WAY, I SAY,"	THE WIND DID'NT COME	316	20
AND GET THE DIMPLES READY--	WHEN NIGHT IS ALMOST	347	5
TILL I GET ACCUSTOMED--BUT THEN THE TOMB	IT DONT SOUND SO	426	11
AND THEN, I WANTED TO GET OUT,	'TWAS JUST THIS TIME,	445	7
TO FEEL ITSELF GET RIPE--	A SOLEMN THING WITHIN	483	2
TO GET AWAY FROM ME--	COULD I BUT RIDE	661	12
YOU'LL GET MY LETTER BY	BEE! I'M EXPECTING YOU!	1035	9
THE NEARER HER THEY GET.	WHAT MYSTERY PERVADES A	1400	24
IT WILL NEVER GET AWAY	REARRANGE A "WIFE'S"	1737	18
GETHSEMANE			
GETHSEMANE CAN TELL	ALL OVERGROWN BY CUNNING	148 V	
THE REEFS IN OLD GETHSEMANE	I SHOULD HAVE BEEN TOO	313	20
GETHSEMANE--	ONE CRUCIFIXION IS	553	8
GAY WERE GETHSEMANE	SPURN THE TEMERITY--	1432	3
GETS			
ONE EARNS [GETS] BY MEASURING THE GRAVE--	MY FIRST WELL DAY--SINCE	574	27
THAT GETS A STAGGERING BLOW--	AT LEISURE IS THE SOUL	618	2
A PRISON GETS TO BE A FRIEND--	A PRISON GETS TO BE A	652	1
THE GARDEN GETS THE ONLY SHOT	THE FROST WAS NEVER SEEN	1202	11
AND GETS THE LOOK AT THEE--	I DID NOT REACH THEE	1664	34
IF EVER THE LID GETS OFF MY HEAD	IF EVER THE LID GETS OFF	1727	1
GETTING			
THE NUTS ARE GETTING BROWN--	THE MORNS ARE MEEKER	12	2
AND MAKE BELIEVE I'M GETTING WARM	MAKE ME A PICTURE OF THE	188	3
SO INSTEAD OF GETTING TO HEAVEN, AT LAST--	SOME KEEP THE SABBATH	324	11
GHASTLY			
GAY, GHASTLY, HOLIDAY!	'TIS SO APPALLING--IT	281	24
SHE FEELS SOME GHASTLY FRIGHT COME UP	THE SOUL HAS BANDAGED	512	3
GHENT			
THE BELLS OF GHENT W'D RING--	IF THOSE I LOVED WERE	29	4
GHOST			
HER GHOST STROLLED SOFTLY O'ER THE HILL	SHE DIED AT PLAY,	75	6
THE ONLY GHOST I EVER SAW	THE ONLY GHOST I EVER	274	1
TO SCAN A GHOST, IS FAINT--	'TIS SO APPALLING--IT	281	5
FROM HIM--AND HOLY GHOST--AND ALL--	I NEVER FELT AT HOME--	413	15
EXTERNAL GHOST	ONE NEED NOT BE A	670	6
BRIDE OF THE HOLY GHOST.	GIVEN IN MARRIAGE UNTO	817	4
GHOST--MAY NOT ALARM--	WHEN I HOPED I FEARED--	1181 V	5
NOR SIMPLIFIED [COMPROMISED] HER GHOST.	WHAT MYSTERY PERVADES A	1400	20
AS FROM AN EMERALD GHOST--	THERE CAME A WIND LIKE A	1593	6

	FIRST LINE	POEM	LINE
GHOSTS			
WITH HOLY GHOSTS IN CAGES!	A TRANSPORT ONE CANNOT	184	7
THEN STILLS IT'S ARTISANS [MYRMIDONS]--LIKE GHOSTS [SWANS]--	IT SIFTS FROM LEADEN	311	19
A TERRITORY FOR THE GHOSTS--	WHO OCCUPIES THIS HOUSE?	892	19
GIANT			
SOME STRIDING--GIANT--LOVE--	A SINGLE SCREW OF FLESH	263	16
BEST GIANT MADE--	IF YOUR NERVE, DENY YOU	292	8
A GIANT--EYE TO EYE WITH YOU, HAD BEEN--	ONE YEAR AGO--JOTS WHAT?	296	23
IT'S SINGLE [GIANT] ARTERY--	EMPTY MY HEART, OF THEE	587	2
THE GIANT TOLERATES [ENTERTAINS] NO GNAT	SIZE CIRCUMSCRIBES--IT	641	3
HOW EXCELLENT A BODY [GIANT], THAT	THE TRUTH--IS STIRLESS--	780	7
THEN CAME ONE DROP OF GIANT RAIN--	THE WIND BEGUN TO KNEAD	824	15
WERE IT GIANT LONG,	UNDER THE LIGHT, YET	949	6
THE GIANT AT THE OTHER SIDE	I SHOULD NOT DARE TO BE	1197	7
BUT GIVE A GIANT ROOM	I THOUGHT THAT NATURE	1286	10
AND YOU WILL [SHALL] LODGE A GIANT	I THOUGHT THAT NATURE	1286	11
A GIANT IS YOUR TENANT	I THOUGHT THAT NATURE	1286	V 11
FROM SUCH A GIANT [BEGGAR] WERE WITHHELD	LOVE CAN DO ALL BUT	1731	3
GIANTS			
GIVE BALM--TO GIANTS--	I CAN WADE GRIEF--	252	13
AS GIANTS--GONE [CLAIMED] AWAY--	HAD I PRESUMED TO HOPE--	522	4
OUR GIANTS--FURTHER ON--	WE SEE--COMPARATIVELY--	534	16
I TOOK FOR GIANTS--PRACTISING	I THINK I WAS ENCHANTED	593	15
WOULD [DID / MIGHT] GIANTS--UNDERSTAND?	IT TROUBLED ME AS ONCE I	600	8
LIFE, AND DEATH, AND GIANTS--	LIFE, AND DEATH, AND	706	1
WHO GIANTS KNOW, WITH LESSER MEN	WHO GIANTS KNOW, WITH	796	1
GIANTURE			
FOR EASE OF [FOR SIMPLE / BECAUSE OF] GIANTURE--	SIZE CIRCUMSCRIBES--IT	641	4
GIBBETS			
TO GIBBETS, AND THE DEAD--	'TWAS LIKE A MAELSTROM,	414	21
GIBRALTAR			
GIBRALTAR COULD SURRENDER	I SAW THE WIND WITHIN	1502	V
GIBRALTAR'S			
GIBRALTAR'S EVERLASTING SHOE	THEY LEAVE US WITH THE	350	7
GIDDY			
OR GIDDY BIRD IN ORCHARD--	ON SUCH A NIGHT, OR SUCH	146	15
OR A SQUIRREL, WHOSE GIDDY PENINSULA	BY MY WINDOW HAVE I FOR	797	7
UNKNOWN HIS SHIMMERING [GIDDY / DAZZLING] ULTIMATE--	THE ROAD WAS LIT WITH	1450	7
GIFT			
A WHITER GIFT--WITHIN--	THE WORLD--STANDS--	493	10
IT IS THE GIFT OF SCREWS--	ESSENTIAL OILS--ARE	675	4
SINCE GIFT OF THEE--	SOCIETY FOR ME MY MISERY	1534	2
BY HOMELY GIFT AND HINDERED WORDS	BY HOMELY GIFT AND	1563	1
THE GIFT IS GIVEN	WHEN WE HAVE CEASED TO	1706	2
GIFTED			
IS GIFTED TO DISCERN	SOME--WORK FOR	406	10
GIFTS			
WITH GIFTS OF LIFE	FOR DEATH--OR RATHER	382	9
HOW DEATH'S GIFTS MAY COMPARE--	FOR DEATH--OR RATHER	382	10
GIG			
AND THEN HIS FAIRY [MICROSCOPIC] GIG	WITHIN MY GARDEN, RIDES	500	10
GIGANTIC			
TO US--GIGANTIC SUM--	HE GAVE AWAY HIS LIFE--	567	2
GIGGLE			
WHEN THE JAY WILL GIGGLE	I SUPPOSE THE TIME WILL	1381	10
GIGGLING			
MY BRAIN KEEPS GIGGLING--STILL.	THE FIRST DAY'S NIGHT	410	16
GILDED			
NODS [STARES] FROM THE GILDED POINTERS--	A CLOCK STOPPED--	287	14
FRESH GILDED--TO ELUDE THE EYES	A HAPPY LIP--BREAKS	353	7
DID BLOCK THE GILDED HANDS--	I THINK THE LONGEST HOUR	635	6
THE GILDED CREATURE STRAINS--AND SPINS--	YOU'VE SEEN BALLOONS SET	700	13
IS TINCTURED [GILDED] FOR AN INSTANT	TO DISAPPEAR ENHANCES--	1209	3
GILT			
IS GILT WITH SACRIFICE--	A TOOTH UPON OUR PEACE	459	8
WHEN THE CORN IN SILK [GILT] WILL DRESS	I SUPPOSE THE TIME WILL	1381	7
BEES ARE BLACK, WITH GILT SURCINGLES--	BEES ARE BLACK, WITH	1405	1
GIMBLETS			
BUT GIMBLETS--AMONG THE NERVE--	IT IS EASY TO WORK WHEN	244	6
GIPSEY			
STILL, MY LITTLE GIPSEY BEING	THO' MY DESTINY BE	163	5
GIPSY			
MY GIPSY FACE--TRANSFIGURED NOW--	HE TOUCHED ME, SO I LIVE	506	11
GIRD			
TO GIRD US FOR THE SUN,	IF PAIN FOR PEACE	63	8
GIRDLE			
DID THE HAREBELL LOOSE HER GIRDLE	DID THE HAREBELL LOOSE	213	1
GIRL			
WILL LIFT HIS LITTLE GIRL--	"ARCTURUS" IS HIS OTHER	70	31
A MORE BERNARDINE GIRL--	I'VE HEARD AN ORGAN TALK	183	6
WHILE JUST [YET] A GIRL AT SCHOOL.	YOUR RICHES--TAUGHT ME--	299	32
WHEN SAPPHO--WAS A LIVING GIRL--	A PRECIOUS--MOULDERING	371	17
BUT--PLEASE TAKE A LITTLE GIRL--	GOOD MORNING--MIDNIGHT--	425	15
WHEN I WAS A LITTLE GIRL--	IT WAS GIVEN TO ME BY	454	2
SO LATE A DOWERLESS GIRL--	I AM ASHAMED--I HIDE--	473	3
I PRAYED, AT FIRST, A LITTLE GIRL,	I PRAYED, AT FIRST, A	576	1
WHEN FIRST A SOMBRE [LITTLE] GIRL--	I THINK I WAS ENCHANTED	593	2

	FIRST LINE	POEM	LINE
GIRL (CONTINUED)			
AS WHEN A LITTLE GIRL	THEY SHUT ME UP IN PROSE	613	2
TO THAT DULL GIRL?	NO MATTER--NOW--SWEET--	704	4
I--THE GIRL AT SCHOOL--	LET US PLAY YESTERDAY--	728	2
OF TRINKETS, AS A GIRL.	A MOTH THE HUE OF THIS	841	6
OF THE MAKER'S GIRL?	RIBBONS OF THE YEAR--	873	8
TO CALL THE LITTLE GIRL	THEY WONT FROWN ALWAYS--	874	6
THE SACRED STEALTH [HAPPY GUILT] OF BOY AND GIRL	BLISS IS THE PLAYTHING	1553	3
GIRLHOOD'S			
AND MARKED MY GIRLHOOD'S NAME--	I AM ALIVE--I GUESS--	470	21
GIRL'S			
HOW ODD THE GIRL'S LIFE LOOKS	I'M "WIFE"--I'VE	199	5
GIRLS			
IN LITTLE WEALTHS, AS GIRLS COULD [CAN] BOAST	YOUR RICHES--TAUGHT ME--	299	3
THAT [WHICH] LITTLE YELLOW BOYS AND GIRLS	I'LL TELL YOU HOW THE	318	11
AND LITTLE GIRLS--WITH DOLLS--	IT WILL BE SUMMER--	342	4
THOSE BOYS AND GIRLS, IN CANVAS--	THOSE FAIR--FICTITIOUS	499	5
WE TALKED AS GIRLS DO--	WE TALKED AS GIRLS DO--	586	1
WHEN GIRLS TO WOMEN, SOFTLY RAISED	WE TALKED AS GIRLS DO--	586	11
AND LADS AND GIRLS--	THIS QUIET DUST WAS	813	2
FAME'S BOYS AND GIRLS, WHO NEVER DIE	FAME'S BOYS AND GIRLS,	1066	1
FROM ALL THE JAILS THE BOYS AND GIRLS	FROM ALL THE JAILS THE	1532	1
GIRT			
AND GIRT HIS LOINS ANEW	A LITTLE EAST OF JORDAN,	59	V 10
JUST GIRT ME FOR THE ONSET WITH ETERNITY,	JUST LOST, WHEN I WAS	160	3
GIRTH			
COMPUTED HOW THE GIRTH?	HOW FITS HIS UMBER COAT	1371	6
GIVE			
AND GIVE HER WHAT SHE ASKETH, JEWEL, OR BIRD, OR FLOWER--	AWAKE YE MUSES NINE,	1	38
I WILL GIVE HIM ALL THE DAISIES	FLOWERS--WELL--IF	137	7
GIVE GENTLY TO THE DEAD--	THIS HEART THAT BROKE SO	145	4
GIVE THE ONE IN RED CRAVAT,	IF I SHOULD'NT BE ALIVE	182	3
WHAT WOULD I GIVE TO SEE HIS FACE?	WHAT WOULD I GIVE TO SEE	247	1
I'D GIVE--I'D GIVE MY LIFE--OF COURSE--	WHAT WOULD I GIVE TO SEE	247	2
I'D GIVE--I'D GIVE MY LIFE--OF COURSE--	WHAT WOULD I GIVE TO SEE	247	2
I'D GIVE MY BIGGEST BOBOLINK!	WHAT WOULD I GIVE TO SEE	247	5
I'D GIVE HER--	WHAT WOULD I GIVE TO SEE	247	8
GIVE BALM--TO GIANTS--	I CAN WADE GRIEF--	252	13
GIVE HIMMALEH--	I CAN WADE GRIEF--	252	15
GIVE LITTLE ANGUISH--	GIVE LITTLE ANGUISH--	310	1
GIVE AVALANCHES--	GIVE LITTLE ANGUISH--	310	3
AND CRIED "GIVE ME"--	OF COURSE--I PRAYED--	376	5
'TWOULD GIVE AN EASIER--PAIN--	IT WOULD NEVER BE COMMON	430	8
I WOULD GIVE YOU--	KNOWS HOW TO FORGET!	433	13
THEY GIVE US PRESENTS MOST--YOU KNOW--	IT WAS GIVEN TO ME BY	454	3
GREAT SPIRIT--GIVE TO ME	I MEANT TO HAVE BUT	476	10
TO GIVE YOUR CORE--A LOOK--	A SOLEMN THING WITHIN	483	12
COULD GIVE THEM ANY BALM--	I MEASURE EVERY GRIEF I	561	20
GIVE SPICES--UNTO MEN--	WHAT CARE THE DEAD, FOR	592	24
IT BEGS YOU GIVE IT WORK--	AT LEISURE IS THE SOUL	618	5
I'D GIVE--TO LIVE THAT HOUR--AGAIN--	AGAIN--HIS VOICE IS AT	663	26
SHOW ME THEM [GIVE THEM ME--]--SAID I--	AUTUMN--OVERLOOKED MY	748	4
WHY GIVE IF THOU MUST TAKE AWAY	A SHADE UPON THE MIND	882	7
"GIVE OF THINE AN ACRE UNTO ME."	SAID DEATH TO PASSION	1033	2
GIVE ME THE CORKLESS	BETWEEN THE FORM OF LIFE	1101	V
I GIVE THEE GUARANTY.	"REMEMBER ME" IMPLORED	1180	4
GIVE HER FOR HER TRANSGRESSION	WHATEVER IT IS--SHE HAS	1204	11
AND GIVE DOMINION ROOM.	THE HARM OF YEARS IS ON	1280	4
BUT GIVE A GIANT ROOM	I THOUGHT THAT NATURE	1286	10
THROW [GIVE / CAST] NOT TO THE DIVINE	THE MIND LIVES ON THE	1355	V 7
"I WILL GIVE" THE BASE PROVISO--	"FAITHFUL TO THE END"	1357	V
OH GIVE IT MOTION--DECK IT SWEET	OH GIVE IT MOTION--DECK	1527	1
I GIVE [SEND] MY DYING KISS--	"GO TELL IT"--WHAT A	1554	8
SO GIVE ME BACK TO DEATH--	SO GIVE ME BACK TO DEATH	1632	1
GIVEN			
I'VE KNOWN PERMISSION GIVEN	A THROE UPON THE	71	7
SOME NEW EQUATION, GIVEN--	I REASON, EARTH IS SHORT	301	11
SO THIS SORT--ARE NOT GIVEN--	DID OUR BEST MOMENT LAST	393	4
IT WAS GIVEN TO ME BY THE GODS--	IT WAS GIVEN TO ME BY	454	1
ITSELF BE GIVEN YOU"--	I MEANT TO HAVE BUT	476	24
THE MOUNTAIN--AT A GIVEN DISTANCE--	DELIGHT--BECOMES	572	5
THE SUMMIT IS NOT GIVEN	THE HALLOWING OF PAIN	772	4
GIVEN IN MARRIAGE UNTO THEE	GIVEN IN MARRIAGE UNTO	817	1
WHEN ONE HAS GIVEN UP ONE'S LIFE	WHEN ONE HAS GIVEN UP	853	1
A GOOD NEWS SHOULD BE GIVEN.	OF TOLLING BELL I ASK	947	8
AN OBSTACLE IS GIVEN	LEST THIS BE HEAVEN	1043	2
AS IF THE CHECKS WERE GIVEN--	I NEVER SAW A MOOR--	1052	8
SALUBRIOUS HOURS ARE GIVEN	TO HELP OUR BLEAKER	1064	2
TO AFFIDAVIT GIVEN.	SO MUCH OF HEAVEN HAS	1228	4
GIVEN TO ME WITHOUT THE SUIT	FRIGID AND SWEET HER	1318	5
GIVEN FOR THE GIVING, SOLELY, [THE MAJESTY]	"FAITHFUL TO THE END"	1357	7
THE GIFT IS GIVEN	WHEN WE HAVE CEASED TO	1706	2
THE RIOT GIVEN AT THE FIRST	THE MOB WITHIN THE HEART	1745	3
GIVES			
HEAVENLY HURT, IT GIVES US--	THERE'S A CERTAIN SLANT	258	5
ADDS [GIVES] POIGNANCY TO WINTER--	CONJECTURING A CLIMATE	562	3
THE ACRE GIVES THEM--PLACE--	FOUR TREES--UPON A	742	9
GOD SENDS [GIVES] US WOMEN--	TITLE DIVINE--IS MINE!	1072	7

	FIRST LINE	POEM	LINE
GIVES (CONTINUED)			
AND OF FEAR NO EVIDENCE GIVES HE	WHAT MYSTERY PERVADES A	1400	V 16
GIVING			
GIVEN FOR THE GIVING, SOLELY, [THE MAJESTY]	"FAITHFUL TO THE END"	1357	7
GLACIERS			
BY PLAYING GLACIERS--WHEN A BOY--	THE ZEROES--TAUGHT US--	689	3
GLAD			
I'M GLAD I DONT BELIEVE IT	GOING TO HEAVEN!	79	20
I AM GLAD THEY DID BELIEVE IT	GOING TO HEAVEN!	79	24
HALF GLAD WHEN IT IS NIGHT, AND SLEEP,	I HAVE A KING, WHO DOES	103	4
LOW AMID THAT GLAD BELLES LETTRES	IF THE FOOLISH, CALL	168	17
I SHOULD HAVE BEEN TOO GLAD, I SEE--	I SHOULD HAVE BEEN TOO	313	1
SO GLAD WE ARE--A STRANGER'D DEEM	SO GLAD WE ARE--A	329	1
GLAD--GAY--HOUSES--	SWEET--SAFE--HOUSES--	457	2
LEST ANY DOUBT THAT WE ARE GLAD THAT THEY WERE BORN TODAY	LEST ANY DOUBT THAT WE	1156	1
HOW GLAD I AM--	DEAR MARCH--COME IN--	1320	2
WHO WOULD BE VERY GLAD	I KNOW OF PEOPLE IN THE	1665	2
IF I COULD TELL HOW GLAD I WAS	IF I COULD TELL HOW GLAD	1668	1
I SHOULD NOT BE SO GLAD--	IF I COULD TELL HOW GLAD	1668	2
GLADDENED			
NEVER GLADDENED TREE--	DREAMS--ARE WELL--BUT	450	6
GLANCE			
WITHOUT A GLANCE MY WAY--	I ASKED NO OTHER THING--	621	6
WITH A GLANCE AND A BOW	A CLOUD WITHDREW FROM	895	10
AND GLANCE SECURELY ROUND--	THIS MERIT HATH THE	979	6
AND CASUALLY GLANCE	BLOOM--IS RESULT--TO	1058	2
LEAN FORWARD FOR A FINAL GLANCE--	POWER IS A FAMILIAR	1238	7
GLANCED			
HE GLANCED WITH RAPID EYES	A BIRD CAME DOWN THE	328	9
GLANCES			
THE [IT'S] SPIRIT LOOKS UPON [TURNS UPON / GAZES AT / GLANCES	AS FROM THE EARTH THE	1630	5
GLANCING			
THEN--GLANCING NARROW, AT THE WALL--	THE WAY I READ A	636	9
GLARE			
THE FLASH [FLARE / GLARE / BLARE] BETWEEN THE CREVICES OF CRASH--	IT WAS A QUIET SEEMING	1419	V
GLASS			
A MONSTER WITH A GLASS	"ARCTURUS" IS HIS OTHER	70	10
THE HANDS STILL HUG THE TARDY GLASS--	I BRING AN UNACCUSTOMED	132	8
I HELD MY SPIRIT TO THE GLASS,	I FELT MY LIFE WITH BOTH	351	3
AND ELEGANT--AS GLASS--	A VISITOR IN MARL--	391	4
BLOWN TREMULOUS IN GLASS--	THE WIND--TAPPED LIKE A	436	16
I PUT NEW BLOSSOMS IN THE GLASS--	I TIE MY HAT--I CREASE	443	5
AND IF I HOLD A GLASS	I AM ALIVE--I GUESS--	470	6
A CHILL--LIKE FROST UPON A GLASS--	'TWAS WARM--AT FIRST--	519	3
AS CAUTIOUSLY AS GLASS	I YEARS HAD BEEN FROM	609	22
TO LIFT HER GLASS--UPON--	I WATCHED THE MOON	629	8
A GLASS OF WATER'S ALL,	THE DYING NEED BUT	1026	2
BUT JUST HIS LID [LIP] OF GLASS--	WHAT MYSTERY PERVADES A	1400	6
GLASS WAS THE STREET--IN TINSEL PERIL	GLASS WAS THE STREET--IN	1498	1
MY PARLOR IS OF SHRIVEN GLASS,	THE WATERS CHASED HIM AS	1749	5
GLASSES			
CAN READ WITHOUT IT'S GLASSES	BELSHAZZAR HAD A LETTER	1459	7
GLAZE			
THE EYES GLAZE ONCE--AND THAT IS DEATH--	I LIKE A LOOK OF AGONY,	241	5
SHOULD THE GLEE--GLAZE--	I KNOW THAT HE EXISTS.	338	11
GLAZES			
THAT GLAZES HOLIDAY--	YOU KNOW THAT PORTRAIT	504	16
GLEAM			
WILL GLEAM [STIR] AND UNDERSTAND	LONG YEARS APART--CAN	1383	8
IS BUT THE GLEAM CONCOMITANT	THE FARTHEST THUNDER	1581	15
THE GLEAM OF AN HEROIC ACT	THE GLEAM OF AN HEROIC	1687	1
GLEAMED			
THE LIGHTNING'S POINARDS GLEAMED--	THROUGH LANE IT LAY--	9	10
THE MINOR ONE--THAT GLEAMED [SHONE] BEHIND--	THAT FIRST DAY, WHEN YOU	659	7
GLEE			
AND I, FOR GLEE,	DELIGHT IS AS THE FLIGHT	257	15
A GLEE POSSESSETH ME,	I CANNOT DANCE UPON MY	326	4
SHOULD THE GLEE--GLAZE--	I KNOW THAT HE EXISTS.	338	11
THEY'D MODIFY THE GLEE	THE MORNING AFTER WO--	364	14
AND WOULD IT BLUR THE CHRISTMAS GLEE	'TWAS JUST THIS TIME,	445	17
GLEE--THE GREAT STORM IS OVER--	GLEE--THE GREAT STORM IS	619	1
IT IS A LONESOME GLEE--	IT IS A LONESOME GLEE--	774	1
AND BATHED THEM IN THE GLEE [SEA]--	A DROP FELL ON THE APPLE	794	14
OR A GLEE AMONG THE GARRET	THAT IS SOLEMN WE HAVE	934	3
FOR SERVICE [HONOR / WELCOME] OR FOR GLEE--	A CHILLY PEACE INFESTS	1443	6
THAT PURLED A MOMENT SINCE WITH GLEE--	HIS VOICE DECREPIT WAS	1476	5
FOR SUCH A FOE [SWEET / GLEE / DAWN / SCENE / DEW / JOY] AS THIS--	FROM ALL THE JAILS THE	1532	8
A GLEE AS SWEET AS IF THE STARS	TO SEE HER IS A PICTURE	1568	V 7
GLEE'S			
AND GLEE'S ADVANCING SOUND	IN SNOW THOU COMEST	1669	4
GLID			
GLID STEALTHILY ALONG--	THROUGH LANE IT LAY--	9	8
GLIMMER			
GLIMMER ON THE STREET--	HOW THE OLD MOUNTAINS	291	16
GLIMMERING			
AS HOVERING [GLIMMERING]--SEEN--THROUGH FOG--	A SOLEMN THING--IT WAS--	271	12

	FIRST LINE	POEM	LINE
GLIMMERING (CONTINUED)			
THE GLIMMERING FRONTIER THAT	THEIR HIGHT IN HEAVEN	696	6
BESIDE YOUR PALACE [TWINKLING / GLIMMERING] DOOR--	THE MOON WAS BUT A CHIN	737	16
GLIMMERS			
FLITS--GLIMMERS--PROVES--DISSOLVES--	THE LOVE A LIFE CAN SHOW	673	14
GLISTENING			
CONCLUDES HIS GLISTENING INTERVIEW--	A VISITOR IN MARL--	391	7
GLITTERING			
HOW GLITTERING THEY SHONE--	SHE DEALT HER PRETTY	479	2
THE GLITTERING RETINUE OF NERVES--	SEVERER SERVICE OF	786	11
HIS GLITTERING EMBRACE--	ESCAPING BACKWARD TO	867	4
TEAZING [TAUNTING] WITH GLITTERING AMEND--	FAIRER THROUGH FADING--	938	6
GLOAT			
THAT [TILL] I MAY [CAN] GLOAT ON THEE--	OH SUMPTUOUS MOMENT	1125	3
BUT THERE--SO GLOAT TO HESITATE	TIME'S WILY CHARGERS	1458	3
GLOBE			
GLOBE ROSES--BREAK THEIR SATIN FLAKE--	I TEND MY FLOWERS FOR	339	16
THIS BASHFUL GLOBE OF OUR'S WOULD BE--	FUNNY--TO BE A CENTURY--	345	7
GLOBE DID NOT TEACH IT	KNOWS HOW TO FORGET!	433	V
GLOBULES			
GREAT GLOBULES--IN THE ALLEYS--	THE NAME--OF IT--IS	656	5
GLOOM			
PROCLAIMING TO THE GLOOM	NOT ANY SUNNY TONE	1674	8
GLORIA			
"SIC TRANSIT GLORIA MUNDI,"	"SIC TRANSIT GLORIA	3	1
GLORIES			
OF ALL HER GLORIES--	PROMISE THIS--WHEN YOU	648	V 32
GLORIFIED			
WE BEHOLD HER--GLORIFIED--	TAKING UP THE FAIR IDEAL	428	11
GLORY			
AND BID THE WORLD GOODMORROW, AND GO TO GLORY HOME!	AWAKE YE MUSES NINE,	1	40
AND THEN TO GLORY RUN!	MY FRIEND ATTACKS MY	118	8
LIKE MORNING GLORY!	POOR LITTLE HEART!	192	11
MOST LIKE THEIR GLORY SHOW--	FOR THIS--ACCEPTED	195	16
BROTHERS AND SISTERS--WHO PREFERRED THE GLORY--	UNTO LIKE STORY--TROUBLE	295	3
WAS'T GLORY? THAT--WILL DO ['TWAS JUST YOU]--	ONE YEAR AGO--JOTS WHAT?	296	4
SPELL SLOWER--GLORY--	ONE YEAR AGO--JOTS WHAT?	296	5
HER GLORY I SHOULD KNOW--	YOUR RICHES--TAUGHT ME--	299	14
I HAD THE GLORY--THAT WILL DO--	I HAD THE GLORY--THAT	349	1
IT'S SUCH A COMMON--GLORY--	WHAT SOFT--CHERUBIC	401	9
BY GLORY--	YOU'LL KNOW IT--AS YOU	420	2
BY GLORY--	YOU'LL KNOW IT--AS YOU	420	4
ARE FULL OF MORNING GLORY--	I AM ALIVE--I GUESS--	470	3
HALF SHRINKING FROM THE GLORY	THE HEAVEN VESTS FOR	694	5
THEIR GLORY--NOUGHT TO ME--	THEIR HIGHT IN HEAVEN	696	2
QUESTION IF HIS GLORY	ALTER! WHEN THE HILLS DO	729	3
THE LARGER GLORY FOR THE LESS	HE OUTSTRIPPED TIME WITH	865	7
SUPERIOR GLORY BE	A CLOUD WITHDREW FROM	895	2
HINT OF GLORY--IT AFFORDED--	'ROBBED BY DEATH--BUT	971	7
'TWAS MY ONE GLORY--	'TWAS MY ONE GLORY--	1028	1
AND THEN I HATED GLORY	MY TRIUMPH LASTED TILL	1227	7
DOES FINEST GLORY FIT!	THE MOST TRIUMPHANT BIRD	1265	9
THE GLORY OF DECAY	THE HARM OF YEARS IS ON	1280	6
THAT LONESOME GLORY	GATHERED INTO THE EARTH,	1370	4
GUILELESS, YET OF SUCH GLORY FINE	"RED SEA," INDEED! TALK	1642	5
OF GLORY NOT A BEAM IS LEFT	OF GLORY NOT A BEAM IS	1647	1
GLORY IS THAT BRIGHT TRAGIC THING	GLORY IS THAT BRIGHT	1660	1
AND PENURY FOR GLORY	OF THIS IS DAY COMPOSED	1675	7
GLORY'S			
'TIS GLORY'S FAR SUFFICIENCY [OVERTAKELESSNESS]	BECAUSE HE LOVES HER	1229	11
GLOSS			
A MANSE OF MECHLIN AND OF FLOSS [GLOSS / SUN]--	THE FAIREST HOME I EVER	1423	5
GLOVE			
LIKE A PANTHER IN THE GLOVE--	IT IS EASY TO WORK WHEN	244	8
WITH INSULATORS--AND A GLOVE--	THE LIGHTNING PLAYETH--	630	5
SUMMER LAID HER SUPPLE GLOVE	SUMMER LAID HER SIMPLE	1363	5
GLOVES			
THE CLAWS THAT CLUNG, LIKE LIFELESS GLOVES	HIS BILL IS CLASPED--HIS	1102	3
GLOW			
AT SUNSET, OR A LESSER GLOW	ME, CHANGE! ME, ALTER!	268	4
A LIGHT, FOR HER [ME], DID SOLEMN GLOW,	I SHOWED HER HIGHTS SHE	446	10
GLOW PLAIN--AND FOREIGN	I CANNOT LIVE WITH YOU--	640	25
UPON THE VALLEY GLOW--	MY LIFE HAD STOOD--A	754	10
NOR GLOW, WOULD IT, NOR BOW--	THIS THAT WOULD GREET--	778	4
IT HOLDS AS LARGE A GLOW	LIGHT IS SUFFICIENT TO	862	6
LIKE GLOW WORMS, FLEE AWAY--	THE SUN AND MOON MUST	871	8
HAD I SECURED THE GLOW	A CLOUD WITHDREW FROM	895	6
RALLIES HER GLOW [THE WEST], LIKE A DYING FRIEND--	FAIRER THROUGH FADING--	938	5
WILL EQUAL GLOW, AND THOUGHT NO MORE	IT BLOOMED AND DROPT, A	978	5
NO FURROW ON THE GLOW	FURTHER IN SUMMER THAN	1068	14
THE STOLID RAFTERS [CENTRES / HOURS / INSTANTS / SECONDS] GLOW	THE SMOULDERING EMBERS	1132	6
IT CANNOT GLOW [THRILL / BLUSH]--	PRAISE IT--'TIS DEAD--	1384	2
ILLUMINES [SUFFUSES] WITH A GLOW	OF WHOM SO DEAR	1504	3

	FIRST LINE	POEM	LINE
GLOWED			
BURNED [GLOWED] ON--UNTIL THROUGH DISSOLUTION--	IT KNEW NO LAPSE, NOR	560	3
GLOWING			
GLOWING IS HER BONNET,	GLOWING IS HER BONNET,	72	1
GLOWING IS HER CHEEK,	GLOWING IS HER BONNET,	72	2
GLOWING IS HER KIRTLE,	GLOWING IS HER BONNET,	72	3
I COULD HOLD THE LATEST GLOWING--	ROBBED BY DEATH--BUT	971	3
GLOWS			
GLOWS CENTRAL--LIKE A JEWEL	THAT FIRST DAY, WHEN YOU	659	5
AIMLESS CREPT [STOLE] THE GLOWS	ON THE WORLD YOU COLORED	1171	4
GLOWS IMPOTENT ON THEM--	THE VOICE THAT STANDS	1189	4
YET NEWER GLOWS THE ONLY GOLD	THE STARS ARE OLD, THAT	1249	3
ASSOCIATES OR GLOWS [BASKS] ALONE,	HOW HAPPY IS THE LITTLE	1510	8
GLUTTON			
HOPE IS A SUBTLE GLUTTON--	HOPE IS A SUBTLE GLUTTON	1547	1
GNASH			
THE GNASH OF NORTHERN WINDS	I THINK THE HEMLOCK	525	10
GNASHED			
AND GNASHED THEIR TEETH--	AN AWFUL TEMPEST MASHED	198	8
GNAT			
IT WOULD HAVE STARVED A GNAT--	IT WOULD HAVE STARVED A	612	1
NOR LIKE THE GNAT--HAD I--	IT WOULD HAVE STARVED A	612	9
THE GIANT TOLERATES [ENTERTAINS] NO GNAT	SIZE CIRCUMSCRIBES--IT	641	3
THE SUMMER GNAT DISPLAYS--	WHO GIANTS KNOW, WITH	796	6
MADE LOUD OBEISANCE AND THE GNAT	THE FINGERS OF THE LIGHT	1000	15
THIS IS THE GNAT THAT MANGLES MEN--	WONDER--IS NOT PRECISELY	1331	8
GNAT'S			
THE FIRST--A GNAT'S HORIZON	I KNOW LIVES, I COULD	372	7
A GNAT'S MINUTEST FAN	MORE LIFE--WENT OUT--	422	14
THE WAKING IN A GNAT'S--EMBRACE--	WE SEE--COMPARATIVELY--	534	15
THE GNAT'S SUPREMACY IS LARGE AS THINE--	A TOAD, CAN DIE OF LIGHT	583	7
GNOME			
OR PORCH OF GNOME--	DRAB HABITATION OF WHOM?	893	4
OR SHROUD OF GNOME	A SPIDER SEWED AT NIGHT	1138	5
GNOMES			
LIKE GNOMES--	ALONE, I CANNOT BE--	298	8
GO			
ALL THINGS DO GO A COURTING, IN EARTH, OR SEA, OR AIR,	AWAKE YE MUSES NINE,	1	5
AND BID THE WORLD GOODMORROW, AND GO TO GLORY HOME!	AWAKE YE MUSES NINE,	1	40
MY COUNTRY BIDS ME GO;	"SIC TRANSIT GLORIA	3	26
WITH GAYER SANDALS GO--	THE FEET OF PEOPLE	7	2
GO ROUND AND ROUND.	MY WHEEL IS IN THE DARK!	10	4
LET US GO WITH THEE!	THE GENTIAN WEAVES HER	18	16
I WILL SINGING GO--	DISTRUSTFUL OF THE	20	6
TO EYES THAT CLOSING GO--	DISTRUSTFUL OF THE	20	14
BEFORE THE SKATERS GO,	BEFORE THE ICE IS IN THE	37	2
COULD GO FROM SCENE FAMILIAR	COULD LIVE--DID LIVE--	43	6
THE DAY THAT I SHALL GO--	I HAV'NT TOLD MY GARDEN	50	12
AND BEES AS BUSTLING GO--	IF I SHOULD DIE,	54	8
"I WILL NOT LET THEE GO	A LITTLE EAST OF JORDAN,	59	10
ARE PREPARED TO GO!	I CANT TELL YOU--BUT YOU	65	20
TO GO AND INTERFERE!	"ARCTURUS" IS HIS OTHER	70	4
WHERE I PROPOSED TO GO	"ARCTURUS" IS HIS OTHER	70	19
AS SURE AS FLOCKS GO HOME AT NIGHT	GOING TO HEAVEN!	79	9
WITHIN THE MEADOWS GO--	WITHIN MY REACH!	90	7
NEW FEET WITHIN MY GARDEN GO--	NEW FEET WITHIN MY	99	1
I WOULD GO, TO KNOW!	GOOD NIGHT, BECAUSE WE	114	3
THE SHINING COURTIERS GO--	IN RAGS MYSTERIOUS AS	117	2
AND LETS THE MORNING GO--	AS WATCHERS HANG UPON	121	9
FOR SUCH, THE ANGELS GO--	TO FIGHT ALOUD, IS VERY	126	10
A BUTTERFLY TO GO!	COCOON ABOVE! COCOON	129	9
AND BLUSHING BIRDS GO DOWN TO DRINK,	HAVE YOU GOT A BROOK IN	136	3
AND THE BRIDGES OFTEN GO--	HAVE YOU GOT A BROOK IN	136	12
SOME BURNING NOON GO DRY!	HAVE YOU GOT A BROOK IN	136	16
SO I CAN SEE WHICH WAY TO GO	DYING! DYING IN THE	158	3
JUST FELT [HEARD] THE WORLD GO BY!	JUST LOST, WHEN I WAS	160	2
A MARQUIS WOULD NOT GO SO GRAND!	I MET A KING THIS	166	10
AND GO ABOUT IT'S CARE--	IN EBON BOX, WHEN YEARS	169	18
THE UNIVERSE WOULD GO!	A TRANSPORT ONE CANNOT	184	8
AND YET, IT WILL NOT GO--	WHAT SHALL I DO--IT	186	4
HER NEEDLE WOULD NOT GO--	THE ROSE DID CAPER ON	208	6
GRAND GO THE YEARS--IN THE CRESCENT--ABOVE THEM--	SAFE IN THEIR ALABASTER	216	V
THE DEAD SHALL GO IN WHITE--	IT CANT BE "SUMMER"!	221	8
AND BAD MEN--"GO TO JAIL"--	YOU'RE RIGHT--"THE WAY	234	11
SO I CAN NEVER [AND I CANNOT] GO!	AH, MOON--AND STAR!	240	17
WHERE OTHERS, DARE NOT GO [WALK] AT NOON,	WHEN WE STAND ON THE	242	11
AND SUNS, GO SURER, FOR THEIR PROOF,	WHEN WE STAND ON THE	242	15
WILL LET IT'S KEEPSAKE--GO	A SINGLE SCREW OF FLESH	263	20
LIMIT--HOW DEEP A BLEEDING GO!	BOUND--A TROUBLE--	269	3
THEN, I AM READY TO GO!	TIE THE STRINGS TO MY	279	2
THEN [NOW]--I AM READY TO GO!	TIE THE STRINGS TO MY	279	16
JUST LET GO THE BREATH--	'TIS SO APPALLING--IT	281	16
AND ON THE EAR CAN [DOTH] GO	A MIEN TO MOVE A QUEEN--	283	17
JUST AS THE GRANITE CRUMB LET GO--	THAT AFTER HORROR--THAT	286	3
GO ABOVE YOUR NERVE--	IF YOUR NERVE, DENY YOU	292	2
WHERE HE TURNED SO, AND I TURNED--HOW	I GOT SO I COULD HEAR	293	7

	FIRST LINE	POEM	LINE
GO (CONTINUED)			
[LET GO]--			
WHEN THEY LET GO THE IGNOMINY--SMILING--	UNTO LIKE STORY--TROUBLE	295	7
WHEN WINDS GO ROUND AND ROUND IN BANDS--	OF ALL THE SOUNDS	321	21
WHEN I GO OUT OF TIME--	THE FACE I CARRY WITH ME	336	2
THE FEET, MECHANICAL, GO ROUND--	AFTER GREAT PAIN, A	341	5
FIRST--CHILL--THEN STUPOR--THEN THE LETTING GO--	AFTER GREAT PAIN, A	341	13
IN THOSE DIM COUNTRIES WHERE THEY GO,	I DREADED THAT FIRST	348	19
TO NOWHERE--SEEMED TO GO	FROM COCOON FORTH A	354	15
AND I A PAUPER GO--	I GAINED IT SO--	359	12
I NEVER WOULD LET GO--	ALTHOUGH I PUT AWAY HIS	366	12
YOU BEG HIM NOT TO GO--	A PRECIOUS--MOULDERING	371	26
LET GO, THEN, OVERCOME--	'TWAS LIKE A MAELSTROM,	414	17
SO GO YOUR WAY--AND I'LL GO MINE--	A MURMUR IN THE TREES--	416	19
SO GO YOUR WAY--AND I'LL GO MINE--	A MURMUR IN THE TREES--	416	19
BUT STARS--GO SLOW--FOR NIGHT--	I'LL CLUTCH--AND CLUTCH	427	6
STILL TO SHOW--HOW RICH I GO--	I'LL CLUTCH--AND CLUTCH	427	22
LET GO A MUSIC--AS OF TUNES	THE WIND--TAPPED LIKE A	436	15
WHERE MOSSES GO NO MORE AWAY--	I KNOW WHERE WELLS GROW	460	3
I GO NO MORE AWAY	I LIVE WITH HIM--I SEE	463	2
REMEMBER--AS THOU GO--	WE COVER THEE--SWEET	482	4
SAGACITY, MUST GO--	THIS WORLD IS NOT	501	8
GO DOWN THE FIELDS TO "HAY"--	I'M SORRY FOR THE DEAD--	529	20
CAN GO, ITSELF, WITHOUT A FAN--	YOU CANNOT PUT A FIRE	530	3
AND THEN--TO GO TO SLEEP--	THE HEART ASKS PLEASURE	536	5
OR WOULD THEY GO ON ACHING STILL	I MEASURE EVERY GRIEF I	561	21
I ASKED TO GO ABROAD,	MY FIRST WELL DAY--SINCE	574	2
I COULD NOT SEE [FEEL] THE TROUBLE [ANGUISH] GO--	IT CEASED TO HURT ME,	584	2
PERPETUAL BREAK [BE / GO] ABROAD	WHEN I WAS SMALL, A	596	18
THREE TIMES--HE WOULD NOT GO--	THREE TIMES--WE PARTED--	598	2
THE EASIER TO LET GO--	YOU'LL FIND--IT WHEN YOU	610	2
AND SEEN MY BRAIN--GO ROUND--	THEY SHUT ME UP IN PROSE	613	6
AND THEN I GO THE FURTHEST OFF	THE WAY I READ A	636	5
I TAKE A FLOWER--AS I GO--	AGAIN--HIS VOICE IS AT	663	5
DOTH SELDOM GO ABROAD--	THE SOUL THAT HATH A	674	2
THEIR LIQUID FEET GO SOFTLY OUT	YOU'VE SEEN BALLOONS SET	700	5
THE DUST IN STREETS--GO DOWN--	YOU'VE SEEN BALLOONS SET	700	18
FROM OUR GARRET GO	PUBLICATION--IS THE	709	6
TO GO ELASTIC--OR AS ONE	STRONG DRAUGHTS OF THEIR	711	5
AND THE SUN--GO ON--	RESTS AT NIGHT	714	6
BUT YOU MUST GO AWAY	THE BIRDS REPORTED FROM	743 V	4
GO BLOSSOM TO THE BEES--I SAID--	THE BIRDS REPORTED FROM	743	7
THE LETTING GO	RENUNCIATION--IS A	745	2
AND GO TO PIECES ON THE STONES [IN THE DITCH]	IT DROPPED SO LOW--IN MY	747	3
INDICATIVE THAT SUNS GO DOWN--	PRESENTIMENT--IS THAT	764	2
AND THEN ABROAD THE WORLD HE GO	MY FAITH IS LARGER THAN	766	7
TO GO WITHOUT THE SPECTRE'S AID [HELP]	I LIVED ON DREAD--	770	8
AS IN IT'S GRAVE GO PLUMBING [MEASURING]	THE LONELINESS ONE DARE	777	3
AND WHEN THE SUN GO DOWN--	NATURE--THE GENTLEST	790	12
FEELS EASY, AS WHEN DAY LETS GO	WHEN ONE HAS GIVEN UP	853	3
THEMSELVES--GO OUT--	THE POETS LIGHT BUT	883	2
THOSE THAT ROSE [TURNED] TO GO--	SWEET, TO HAVE HAD THEM	901	8
AS OFT AS HE GO DOWN	WE CAN BUT FOLLOW TO THE	920	2
WE GO NO FURTHER WITH THE DUST	WE CAN BUT FOLLOW TO THE	920	5
LIKE INDIVIDUALS GO	DEATH LEAVES US HOMESICK	935	6
I GO--TO ELSEWHERE GO NO MORE--	FITTER TO SEE HIM, I MAY	968	18
I GO--TO ELSEWHERE GO NO MORE--	FITTER TO SEE HIM, I MAY	968	18
WHEN CEREMENTS LET GO	'TIS ANGUISH GRANDER	984	6
GO UP BY TWO AND TWO.	'TIS ANGUISH GRANDER	984	8
INCLUDE US [SCAN BETTER / CONVEY US]--AS THEY GO--	WE MISS HER, NOT BECAUSE	993	8
WHERE I AM NOT AFRAID TO GO	HERE, WHERE THE DAISIES	1037	5
GO PARALLEL, PERFECTED	THE OPENING AND THE	1047	7
DEBATES IF IT WILL GO--	THE SKY IS LOW--THE	1075	4
TO STAY AS IF, OR GO.	THE CRICKETS SANG	1104	8
I HEARD IT'S AXLES GO	THIS SLOW DAY MOVED	1120	2
TIME DOES GO ON--	TIME DOES GO ON--	1121	1
SLOWER GO	OH SUMPTUOUS MOMENT	1125	2
AND NOWHERE WAS TO GO--	THE FROST OF DEATH WAS	1136	19
WE LET GO ALL OF TIME WITHOUT	THE DAYS THAT WE CAN	1184	7
GO MAKE THEE FAIR MY CANDIDATE	OH SHADOW ON THE GRASS,	1187	3
BUT THEY THAT GO--	THE SHOW IS NOT THE SHOW	1206	2
THE SEA SAID "GO" TO THE SEA--	THE SEA SAID "COME" TO	1210	5
WHERE I FOR RIGHT TO BE [GO]--	SOMEWHERE UPON THE	1231	6
AND SEATS ITSELF TO BE LET GO	RISK IS THE HAIR THAT	1239	7
SO SATISFIED TO GO	SO PROUD SHE WAS TO DIE	1272	5
TO DIE IS NOT TO GO--	TWO LENGTHS HAS EVERY	1295	9
GO SLOW, MY SOUL, TO FEED THYSELF	GO SLOW, MY SOUL, TO	1297	1
GO RAPID, LEST COMPETING DEATH	GO SLOW, MY SOUL, TO	1297	3
GO TIMID, LEST [SHOULD] HIS FINAL [TESTING / BLAZING / LOFTY] EYE	GO SLOW, MY SOUL, TO	1297	5
GO [BUT] BOLDLY--FOR THOU PAID'ST HIS PRICE	GO SLOW, MY SOUL, TO	1297	7
A [DO / OUR] SUMMER'S [NATURE'S] SOFT ASSEMBLIES GO	WITHOUT A SMILE--WITHOUT	1330	2
SUING IT NOT TO GO	NOT ANY MORE TO BE	1344	10
PERHAPS THEY DO [SHE DOES] NOT GO SO FAR	PERHAPS THEY DO NOT GO	1399	1
CONTRIVES THAT NONE GO OUT AGAIN--	NO PASSENGER WAS KNOWN	1406	4
WHERE GO WE--	HOW HUMAN NATURE DOTES	1417	11

	FIRST LINE	POEM	LINE
GO (CONTINUED)			
GO WE ANYWHERE	HOW HUMAN NATURE DOTES	1417	12
GO NOT TOO NEAR A HOUSE OF ROSE--	GO NOT TOO NEAR A HOUSE	1434	1
TO GO IT'S CONVALESCENT WAY	THE HEALED HEART SHOWS	1440	5
WHOSE ALLIES GO NO MORE ASTRAY [ABROAD] . .	A CHILLY PEACE INFESTS	1443	5
"GO TRAVELING WITH US!"	"GO TRAVELING WITH US!"	1513	1
WE NEVER KNOW WE GO WHEN WE ARE GOING-- . .	WE NEVER KNOW WE GO WHEN	1523	1
"GO TELL IT"--WHAT A MESSAGE--	"GO TELL IT"--WHAT A	1554	1
WHERE ROSES WOULD NOT DARE TO GO, ...	WHERE ROSES WOULD NOT	1582	1
AND MUCH CAN GO, ...	THERE CAME A WIND LIKE A	1593	16
AND WINDS DO GO THAT WAY AT NOON [TIMES] .	TALK NOT TO ME OF SUMMER	1634	5
GO THY GREAT WAY!	GO THY GREAT WAY!	1638	1
TO WHICH WITHOUT A TICKET GO	SOME ONE PREPARED THIS	1644	2
SO SHORT WE HAVE TO GO	I DID NOT REACH THEE	1664	15
THOU SHALT GO WITH THE RESUMING GROUND . .	IN SNOW THOU COMEST	1669	2
THOU SHALT GO AT SUCH A GAIT OF JOY . . .	IN SNOW THOU COMEST	1669	6
NO OTHER ONE MAY GO	UNTO A BROKEN HEART	1704	2
THE FELLOW WILL GO WHERE HE BELONGED-- . .	IF EVER THE LID GETS OFF	1727	3
GO MANACLE YOUR ICICLE	'TWAS HERE MY SUMMER	1756	7
WHERE EVERY BIRD IS BOLD TO GO	WHERE EVERY BIRD IS BOLD	1758	1
WOULD GO AND SING NO MORE.	THE SADDEST NOISE, THE	1764	16
GOAD			
THOU DID'ST [COULD'ST] NOT GOAD SO LONG-- .	ART THOU THE THING I	1282	V 4
GOADS			
IT GOADS ME, LIKE THE GOBLIN BEE-- . . .	IF YOU WERE COMING IN	511	19
GOAL			
SHOULD REACH SO SMALL A GOAL!	ON SUCH A NIGHT, OR SUCH	146	24
WHAT MERIT HAD THE GOAL--	I CROSS TILL I AM WEARY	550	14
A GOAL--	EACH LIFE CONVERGES TO	680	4
AND IMPETUS OF GOAL--	THE SERVICE WITHOUT HOPE	779	6
A WORM, HIS UTMOST GOAL.	HIS BILL AN AUGUR IS	1034	4
DESIRE'S PERFECT GOAL--	WHO NEVER WANTED--	1430	6
GOALLESS			
AS ROUND A GOALLESS ROAD	NO MAN CAN COMPASS A	477	2
GOALS			
I FIND MY FEET HAVE FURTHER GOALS-- . . .	I COULD NOT PROVE THE	563	5
GOBLIN			
AS IF A GOBLIN WITH A GUAGE--	'TWAS LIKE A MAELSTROM,	414	10
A GOBLIN--DRANK MY DEW--	IT WOULD NEVER BE COMMON	430	22
IT GOADS ME, LIKF THE GOBLIN BEE--	IF YOU WERE COMING IN	511	19
SIP, GOBLIN, FROM THE VERY LIPS	THE SOUL HAS BANDAGED	512	7
HOW GOBLIN IT WOULD BE--	DID YOU EVER STAND IN A	590	6
NO GOBLIN--ON THE BLOOM--	I THINK TO LIVE--MAY BE	646	14
GOD			
GOD HATH MADE NOTHING SINGLE BUT THEE IN HIS WORLD SO FAIR!	AWAKE YE MUSES NINE,	1	6
ARE YE THEN WITH GOD?	SO HAS A DAISY VANISHED	28	8
BEFORE THE DOOR OF GOD!	I NEVER LOST AS MUCH BUT	49	4
FOUND HE HAD WORSTED GOD!	A LITTLE EAST OF JORDAN,	59	16
DO IN MEETING GOD!	I CANT TELL YOU--BUT YOU	65	12
AND CARRIED IT TO GOD--	A POOR--TORN HEART-- A	78	12
AND GOD, THAT HE CALLED HIS, ...	I HAD SOME THINGS THAT I	116	2
BLESS GOD, HE WENT AS SOLDIERS, ...	BLESS GOD, HE WENT AS	147	1
GRANT GOD, HE CHARGE THE BRAVEST	BLESS GOD, HE WENT AS	147	3
PLEASE GOD, MIGHT I BEHOLD HIM	BLESS GOD, HE WENT AS	147	5
TAKE CARE--FOR GOD IS HERE [NEAR]-- . . .	THE MURMUR OF A BEE	155	9
PLEASE GOD--SHALL ASCERTAIN!	MUSICIANS WRESTLE	157	18
THOUGH GOD FORBID IT LIFT THE LID-- . . .	A TRANSPORT ONE CANNOT	184	3
OH GOD! THE OTHER ONE!	TWO SWIMMERS WRESTLED ON	201	4
OR TELL GOD--HOW CROSS WE ARE--	WHAT IS--"PARADISE"--	215	10
I'D HARASS GOD	SHOULD YOU BUT FAIL AT--	226	6
GOD PERMITS INDUSTRIOUS ANGELS--	GOD PERMITS INDUSTRIOUS	231	1
GOD CALLS HOME--THE ANGELS--PROMPTLY-- . .	GOD PERMITS INDUSTRIOUS	231	5
WOULD BUT SOME GOD--INFORM HIM--	IF HE DISSOLVE--THEN--	236	8
GOD WOULD CERTAINLY SCOLD!	OVER THE FENCE--	251	7
AND WEAR--IF GOD SHOULD COUNT ME FIT-- . .	A SOLEMN THING--IT WAS--	271	3
AND GOD FORBID I LOOK BEHIND--	THE ONLY GHOST I EVER	274	15
WHY, GOD, WOULD BE CONTENT	DOUBT ME! MY DIM	275	2
I THINK, THEY CALL IT "GOD"--	I GOT SO I COULD HEAR	293	14
GOD--SPELL THE WORD! I--CANT--	ONE YEAR AGO--JOTS WHAT?	296	2
GOD PREACHES, A NOTED CLERGYMAN--	SOME KEEP THE SABBATH	324	9
GOD IS A DISTANT--STATELY LOVER--	GOD IS A DISTANT--	357	1
AND DID GOD CARE?	OF COURSE--I PRAYED--	376	2
AND CARRIES ONE--OUT OF IT--TO GOD-- . . .	IT'S COMING--THE	390	8
BUT GOD CAN SUMMON EVERY FACE	THEY DROPPED LIKE FLAKES	409	8
THAT "GOD HAVE MERCY" ON THE SOUL	I READ MY SENTENCE--	412	7
IF GOD COULD MAKE A VISIT--	I NEVER FELT AT HOME--	413	9
WHEN GOD--REMEMBERED--AND THE FIEND . . .	'TWAS LIKE A MAELSTROM,	414	16
KNOW GOD THE FATHER--AND THE SON.	YOU'LL KNOW IT--AS YOU	420	6
GOD MADE A LITTLE GENTIAN--	GOD MADE A LITTLE	442	1
NICKNAMED BY GOD--	LOVE--THOU ART HIGH--	453	17
HER GOD--HER ONLY THRONG--	TRIUMPH--MAY BE OF	455	8
AND HEMLOCKS--BOW--TO GOD--	DOOM IS THE HOUSE	475	8
BY THE SON OF GOD--	TO PUT THIS WORLD DOWN,	527	6
TO ANYONE BUT GOD--	DEATH IS POTENTIAL TO	548	4
OF THESE TWO--GOD REMEMBERS	DEATH IS POTENTIAL TO	548	5
ITSELF DISSOLVED--OF GOD--	DEATH IS POTENTIAL TO	548	8
GOD GROWS ABOVE--SO THOSE WHO PRAY . . .	MY PERIOD HAD COME FOR	564	5
THEN SUMMER--THEN THE HEAVEN OF GOD-- . .	I RECKON--WHEN I COUNT	569	3
IF I BELIEVED [SUPPOSED] GOD LOOKED AROUND,	I PRAYED, AT FIRST, A	576	5

GOD (CONTINUED)

	FIRST LINE	POEM	LINE
TO HAVE A GOD SO STRONG AS THAT	I PRAYED, AT FIRST, A	576	16
AND GOD, A QUIET PARTY	WE TALKED AS GIRLS DO--	586	7
HAD GOD WILLED DIFFERENTLY.	I CRIED AT PITY--NOT AT	588	16
MYSELF DISTINGUISHED GOD--	LIKE MIGHTY FOOT LIGHTS	595	8
AND GOD--AT EVERY GATE--	OUR JOURNEY HAD ADVANCED	615	12
WHAT WAS HIS FURTHEST MIND--OF HOME--OR GOD--	TO KNOW JUST HOW HE	622	9
BUT EARLY, YET, FOR GOD--	IT WAS TOO LATE FOR MAN	623	2
OF OUR OLD [NEW] NEIGHBOR--GOD--	IT WAS TOO LATE FOR MAN	623	8
BEFORE THE JUDGMENT SEAT OF GOD--	'TWAS A LONG PARTING--	625	3
ONLY GOD--DETECT THE SORROW [POSSESS THE SECRET]--	ONLY GOD--DETECT THE	626	1
ONLY GOD--	ONLY GOD--DETECT THE	626	2
UNTO GOD--	ONLY GOD--DETECT THE	626	4
GOD THE SON--CONFIDE [DISCLOSE] IT--	ONLY GOD--DETECT THE	626	5
GOD THE SPIRIT'S HONOR--	ONLY GOD--DETECT THE	626	7
THE BRAIN IS JUST THE WEIGHT OF GOD--	THE BRAIN--IS WIDER THAN	632	9
THE HEAVEN GOD BESTOW--	THE WAY I READ A	636	16
'TWAS FACE TO FACE WITH GOD--	I COULD SUFFICE FOR HIM,	643	8
AND GOD	EMBARRASSMENT OF ONE	662	2
'TIS ABLE AS A GOD--	TO BE ALIVE--IS POWER--	677	6
WAS GOD SO ECONOMICAL?	VICTORY COMES LATE--	690	7
GOD KEEP HIS OATH [VOW] TO SPARROWS--	VICTORY COMES LATE--	690	13
TOO NEAR TO GOD--TO PRAY--	THE DAY UNDRESSED--	716	9
GOD DOES IT--EVERY DAY--	IT'S EASY TO INVENT A	724	2
GOD OF THE MANACLE	LET US PLAY YESTERDAY--	728	33
TWOULD SEEM THAT GOD SHOULD BE	HAVE ANY LIKE MYSELF	736	13
BUT GOD--	FOUR TREES--UPON A	742	8
NOT EVEN GOD--CAN HEAL--	REMORSE--IS MEMORY--	744	10
FROM FURTHEST SPIRIT [FAITHFUL / GOOD MAN]--GOD--	ON A COLUMNAR SELF--	789	12
GOD GAVE A LOAF TO EVERY BIRD--	GOD GAVE A LOAF TO EVERY	791	1
THEIR FACES [FOREHEADS]--UPON GOD--	THROUGH THE STRAIT PASS	792	4
IS GOD--THE ONLY STREET--	THE ONLY NEWS I KNOW	827	8
NATURE AND GOD--I NEITHER KNEW	NATURE AND GOD--I	835	1
TRUTH--IS AS OLD AS GOD--	TRUTH--IS AS OLD AS GOD	836	1
EXPRESS FROM GOD.	SPRING IS THE PERIOD	844	2
WITH GOD.	SPRING IS THE PERIOD	844	8
AND THEN, UNJADED, CHALLENGED GOD	HE OUTSTRIPPED TIME WITH	865	3
OH GOD	A SHADE UPON THE MIND	882	6
AS I OF HE, SO GOD OF ME	OUR LITTLE KINSMEN--	885	9
BEHIND THE EYES OF GOD.	OF CONSCIOUSNESS, HER	894	4
THE ESCAPADE FROM GOD--	OF CONSCIOUSNESS, HER	894	8
TO THAT BOLD PERSON, GOD--	WHAT DID THEY DO SINCE I	900	16
TOWARD THE GOD OF HIM--	THE ADMIRATIONS--AND	906	16
DEPOSITS HIM WITH GOD--	LOVE--IS THAT LATER	924	8
THE FUNERAL OF GOD,	THIS IS A BLOSSOM OF THE	945	14
I NEVER SPOKE WITH GOD	I NEVER SAW A MOOR--	1052	5
GROPED UP, TO SEE IF GOD WERE [WAS] THERE--	HE SCANNED IT--STAGGERED	1062	6
GOD SENDS [GIVES] US WOMEN--	TITLE DIVINE--IS MINE!	1072	7
WOULD NOT A GOD OF FLINT	JUST ONCE! OH LEAST	1076	6
THE INTERDICT OF GOD--	ENDED, ERE IT BEGUN--	1088	8
AND GOD, FOR A FRONTIER.	I AM AFRAID TO OWN A	1090	8
GOD IT IS SAID REPLIES IN PERSON	TELL AS A MARKSMAN--WERE	1152	24
GOD MADE NO ACT WITHOUT A CAUSE,	GOD MADE NO ACT WITHOUT	1163	1
MY GOD--HE SEES THEE--	MY GOD--HE SEES THEE--	1178	1
OH THOU ALMIGHTY GOD!	REMEMBRANCE HAS A	1182	V 8
THAT ONLY TO THE EAR OF GOD	A DEED KNOCKS FIRST AT	1216	7
THANK GOD THE LOUDEST PLACE HE MADE	IT'S HOUR WITH ITSELF	1225	7
OH GOD OF WIDTH, DO NOT FOR US	SOMEWHERE UPON THE	1231	11
FOR NONE SEE GOD AND LIVE--	TO PILE LIKE THUNDER TO	1247	8
DISCOVERY NOT GOD HIMSELF	BECAUSE THAT YOU ARE	1260	11
IF "GOD IS LOVE" AS HE ADMITS	BECAUSE THAT YOU ARE	1260	33
BECAUSE HE IS A "JEALOUS GOD"	BECAUSE THAT YOU ARE	1260	35
AND DINE [GROW] WITHOUT LIKE GOD--	ART THOU THE THING I	1282	8
SUBSISTING NOW [SINCE] LIKE GOD--	ART THOU THE THING I	1282	V 8
MADDEST HEART THAT GOD CREATED	LAIN IN NATURE--SO	1288	5
BUT GOD BE WITH THE CLOWN--	A LITTLE MADNESS IN THE	1333	3
BECAUSE "GOD TOOK HIM" MENTION--[TELL US]	"WAS NOT" WAS ALL THE	1342	7
IT IS AS OLD AS GOD--	HOW BRITTLE ARE THE	1433	5
IS ABSOLUTE AS GOD,	THAN HEAVEN MORE REMOTE,	1436	15
GOD BROKE HIS CONTRACT TO HIS LAMB	HOW RUTHLESS ARE THE	1439	3
BY HIS INTRUSION, GOD IS KNOWN--	WE KNEW NOT THAT WE WERE	1462	7
YOU SEE--GOD BLESS HIS SUDDENNESS--	BEFORE YOU THOUGHT OF	1465	3
OF THE SAGACIOUS GOD--	IT'S LITTLE ETHER HOOD	1501	4
SUBSTANTIATE A GOD--	THE MOON UPON HER FLUENT	1528	4
AND GOD CANNOT BE FOUND--	THOSE--DYING THEN,	1551	5
. . . ALL THE SAINTS HE KNEW / EVERY GOD HE KNEW]	THE BOBOLINK IS GONE--	1591	6
THE PHOSPHORUS OF GOD--	WHO IS IT SEEKS MY	1598	8
NO VACILLATING GOD	THOUGH THE GREAT WATERS	1599	4
OF GOD WE ASK ONE FAVOR,	OF GOD WE ASK ONE FAVOR,	1601	1
FOR AN APPROVING GOD.	APPARENTLY WITH NO	1624	8
BY ANY MAN BUT GOD--	TO THEIR APARTMENT DEEP	1701	4
FOR HE IS GRASPED OF GOD.	DROWNING IS NOT SO	1718	8
GOD IS INDEED A JEALOUS GOD--	GOD IS INDEED A JEALOUS	1719	1
GOD IS INDEED A JEALOUS GOD--	GOD IS INDEED A JEALOUS	1719	1
THAN FROM A DISAPPOINTING GOD	THERE COMES AN HOUR WHEN	1751	5
THE LONGEST DAY THAT GOD APPOINTS	THE LONGEST DAY THAT GOD	1769	1

	FIRST LINE	POEM	LINE
GOD'S			
GOD'S OLD FASHIONED VOWS--	IT DID NOT SURPRISE ME--	39	8
TILL GOD'S FULL TIME [WHOLE--WILL]--	UNTO LIKE STORY--TROUBLE	295	6
BY MEANS OF IT--IN GOD'S EAR--	PRAYER IS THE LITTLE	437	5
WHILE GOD'S ADROITER WILL	IT ALWAYS FELT TO ME--A	597	12
APPREHENSIONS--ARE GOD'S INTRODUCTIONS--	BY MY WINDOW HAVE I FOR	797	24
BESIDE GOD'S SHALL [WILL] NOT TELL--	OUR LITTLE SECRETS SLINK	1326	2
THEY WENT TO GOD'S RIGHT HAND--	THOSE--DYING THEN,	1551	3
GODS			
MET BY THE GODS WITH BANNERS--	TAKEN FROM MEN--THIS	53	3
SO GREATER THAN THE GODS CAN SHOW,	A SINGLE SCREW OF FLESH	263	17
PERMITTED GODS [MEN], AND ME--	OF ALL THE SOUNDS	321	8
AND THE GODS--A LIE--	TAKING UP THE FAIR IDEAL	428	6
GODS USED TO KNOW--	KNOWS HOW TO FORGET!	433	8
IT WAS GIVEN TO ME BY THE GODS--	IT WAS GIVEN TO ME BY	454	1
OUR CONFISCATED GODS--	BECAUSE THAT YOU ARE	1260	40
THE GODS [STARS / HEAVENS / SKIES / SUNS] BUT DREGS	A WORLD MADE PENNINILESS	1623	4
IT IS DENIED THE GODS--	A LETTER IS A JOY OF	1639	2
GOER			
OF GOER BY--	A MIEN TO MOVE A QUEEN--	283	12
GOES			
FOR MY WILL GOES THE OTHER WAY,	I HAVE A KING, WHO DOES	103	17
SOME LITTLE WREN GOES SEEKING ROUND--	FOR EVERY BIRD A NEST--	143	3
A BIRD--BY CHANCE--THAT GOES THAT WAY--	THE SKIES CANT KEEP	191	5
THAT LIKE THE DRUNKARD GOES--	THE ROSE DID CAPER ON	208	12
WHEN IT GOES, 'TIS LIKE THE DISTANCE	THERE'S A CERTAIN SLANT	258	15
EACH ONE SALUTES ME, AS HE GOES,	I DREADED THAT FIRST	348	25
THE MINISTER--GOES STIFFLY IN--	THERE'S BEEN A DEATH, IN	389	13
A WIND WITH FINGERS--GOES--	THEY DROPPED LIKE FLAKES	409	5
JUST SO FAR--GOES AWAY--	THE MOON IS DISTANT FROM	429	8
AND PRAISES AS HE GOES,	WITHIN MY GARDEN, RIDES	500	8
WHEN THE LAST SAINT--GOES UP THE AISLES--	BETTER--THAN MUSIC! FOR	503	18
THEN AWAY UPON A JIB--HE GOES--	HE PARTS HIMSELF--LIKE	517	8
GOES SAFELY [STEADY]--WHERE AN OPEN EYE--	THERE IS A PAIN--SO	599	7
GOES WITH US--JUST A LITTLE WAY--	AGAIN--HIS VOICE IS AT	663	20
OF THE HEART THAT GOES IN, AND CLOSES THE DOOR	OF THE HEART THAT GOES	1098	1
IT THEN GOES OUT AN ACT	A DEED KNOCKS FIRST AT	1216	5
WHO GOES TO DINE MUST TAKE HIS FEAST	WHO GOES TO DINE MUST	1223	1
A JAR ACROSS THE FLOWERS GOES	LIKE TRAINS OF CARS ON	1224	3
THE DAY SHE GOES	THE DAY SHE GOES	1308	1
BUT WELCOME WHEN HE GOES.	WINTER IS GOOD--HIS HOAR	1316	8
GOES NOR COMES AWAY	"SECRETS" IS A DAILY	1385	8
SHE TAKES [GOES] HER GRACIOUS [SPACIOUS / SUBTLE / SIMPLE / . . .	SUMMER--WE ALL HAVE SEEN	1386	6
CLOSES THE [HIS] SHUTTER AND GOES IN--	HOW LONESOME THE WIND	1418	4
NOT THAT HE GOES--WE LOVE HIM MORE	NOT THAT HE GOES--WE	1435	1
WITH GAY DELAYS HE GOES	BEFORE YOU THOUGHT OF	1465	12
THE SUN GOES CROOKED--	I DID NOT REACH THEE	1664	20
AND GUILE [AWE] IS WHERE IT GOES.	SWEET IS THE SWAMP WITH	1740	8
GOING SEE FAINT-GOING			
GOOD BYE, SIR, I AM GOING;	"SIC TRANSIT GLORIA	3	57
WHEN GOING HOME FROM SCHOOL--	I OFTEN PASSED THE	51	2
EXULTATION IS THE GOING	EXULTATION IS THE GOING	76	1
GOING TO HEAVEN!	GOING TO HEAVEN!	79	1
GOING TO HEAVEN!	GOING TO HEAVEN!	79	6
PERHAPS YOU'RE GOING TOO!	GOING TO HEAVEN!	79	11
WHEN WE ARE GOING HOME--	GOING TO HEAVEN!	79	19
MY MIND WAS GOING NUMB--	I FELT A FUNERAL, IN MY	280	8
THEIR GOING--IS NOT--	ALONE, I CANNOT BE--	298	11
AT PERIOD OF GOING DOWN--	THE ONE WHO COULD REPEAT	307	5
SOME KEEP THE SABBATH GOING TO CHURCH--	SOME KEEP THE SABBATH	324	1
I'M GOING, ALL ALONG.	SOME KEEP THE SABBATH	324	12
AND SEE THE PEOPLE--GOING BY--	FUNNY--TO BE A CENTURY--	345	2
WERE GOING--I HAD OFTEN THOUGHT	I WAS THE SLIGHTEST IN	486	16
GOING TO HIM [HER]! HAPPY LETTER!	GOING TO HIM! HAPPY	494	1
FLOWERS--TO KEEP THE EYES--FROM GOING AWKWARD--	IT'S THOUGHTS--AND JUST	495	12
WHEN GOING TO THE BARN--	THE JUDGE IS LIKE THE	699	6
A FIRST FAIR GOING--	A FIRST MUTE COMING--	702	3
OF FINGERS GOING BY--	WE THIRST AT FIRST--'TIS	726	4
WHERE SAINTS, AND OUR PLAIN GOING NEIGHBOR	BESIDES THIS MAY	977	9
JUST GOING HOME FROM SCHOOL.	THE HILLS IN PURPLE	1016	4
HIS MIND WERE GOING BLIND--	HE SCANNED IT--STAGGERED	1062	5
BECAUSE THAT YOU ARE GOING	BECAUSE THAT YOU ARE	1260	1
MEANT NOUGHT BUT GOING HOME--	'TWAS LATER WHEN THE	1276	4
OF SHADOWS [RIPPLES] GOING DOWN	A STAGNANT PLEASURE LIKE	1281	6
AT PARTING--SHE WAS GOING SOUTH	I SEND YOU A DECREPIT	1324	3
BECAUSE IN GOING IS A DRAMA	I'D RATHER RECOLLECT A	1349	5
AS FINER IS A GOING	SUMMER HAS TWO	1422	7
WE NEVER KNOW WE GO WHEN WE ARE GOING--	WE NEVER KNOW WE GO WHEN	1523	1
THE GOING FROM A WORLD WE KNOW	THE GOING FROM A WORLD	1603	1
HIS "GOING, GOING, GONE"	THE AUCTIONEER OF	1612	2
HIS "GOING, GOING, GONE"	THE AUCTIONEER OF	1612	2
AND MOURNERS MEET IT GOING OUT	WITCHCRAFT HAS NOT A	1708	3
A JOYOUS GOING FELLOW	HIGH FROM THE EARTH I	1723	9
GOOD-BYE--THE GOING UTTER ME--	SOME SAY GOODNIGHT--AT	1739	3
GOLCONDA			
I'M SURE [I KNOW] IT IS GOLCONDA--	YOUR RICHES--TAUGHT ME--	299	21

	FIRST LINE	POEM	LINE
GOLD			
I NEVER TOLD THE BURIED GOLD	I NEVER TOLD THE BURIED	11	1
THE GUEST IS GOLD AND CRIMSON--	THE GUEST IS GOLD AND	15	1
SCARLET AND GOLD	SO FROM THE MOULD	66	2
AND DANDELIONS GOLD.	WE SHOULD NOT MIND SO	81	12
STANDS REPRESENTATIVE IN GOLD	A SCIENCE--SO THE SAVANS	100	10
A BLUE AND GOLD MISTAKE.	THESE ARE THE DAYS WHEN	130	6
A WAVE OF GOLD--	A SLASH OF BLUE--	204	7
BLAZING IN GOLD AND QUENCHING IN PURPLE	BLAZING IN GOLD AND	228	1
PARALYZED, WITH GOLD--	HOW THE OLD MOUNTAINS	291	24
THAT THERE EXISTS--A GOLD--	YOUR RICHES--TAUGHT ME--	299	26
IT'S FEE--TO BE OF GOLD--	A TONGUE--TO TELL HIM I	400	2
AND HIS--IN SOLID GOLD--	A TONGUE--TO TELL HIM I	400	19
SLOW GOLD--BUT EVERLASTING--	SOME--WORK FOR	406	5
I DEALT A WORD OF GOLD	IT WOULD NEVER BE COMMON	430	18
TO TAKE THE NAME OF GOLD--	IT WAS GIVEN TO ME BY	454	14
AND GOLD TO OWN--IN SOLID BARS--	IT WAS GIVEN TO ME BY	454	15
OR GOLD--WHO AM THE PRINCE OF MINES--	'TIS LITTLE I--COULD	466	5
ETHIOP--HER GOLD--	CIVILIZATION--SPURNS--	492	4
PERSUADED OF THE BURIED GOLD--	TRUST IN THE UNEXPECTED	555	3
FOR CHILDREN, MADE OF GOLD--	I CRIED AT PITY--NOT AT	588	12
AND NOT REDUCE--THE GOLD--	WITHOUT THIS--THERE IS	655	12
HER GARTER--WAS OF GOLD--	THE DAY UNDRESSED--	716	2
OR FIRST PROSPECTIVE--OR THE GOLD	SHE ROSE TO HIS	732	7
THE MOON WAS BUT A CHIN OF GOLD	THE MOON WAS BUT A CHIN	737	1
THE CLAMORING FOR GOLD--	I PLAY AT RICHES--TO	801	2
WITH GOLD AND SILVER PAIN	A PLATED LIFE--	806	2
HIS HELMET, IS OF GOLD,	HIS FEET ARE SHOD WITH	916	2
GOLD--TO GOLD--	TITLE DIVINE--IS MINE!	1072	9
GOLD--TO GOLD--	TITLE DIVINE--IS MINE!	1072	9
FLING UP THY BALLS OF GOLD	MY GOD--HE SEES THEE--	1178	3
AS GOLD THE [A] PYRITES WOULD SHUN--	HE PREACHED UPON	1207	6
YET NEWER GLOWS THE ONLY GOLD	THE STARS ARE OLD, THAT	1249	3
AS UNDISCOVERED GOLD--	YOU CANNOT TAKE ITSELF	1351	8
FOR THOUGH HIS [THE] PRICE WAS NOT OF GOLD--	HIS MIND LIKE FABRICS OF	1446	5
WHOSE GOLD IS FIRM	HOW DESTITUTE IS HE	1477	2
AS MIDAS IS OF GOLD--	MEETING BY ACCIDENT,	1548	8
WITH THAT SEVEREST GOLD	THROUGH THOSE OLD	1753	14
GOLDEN			
IN A MORE GOLDEN LIGHT	I HAVE A BIRD IN SPRING	5	20
I HAD A GUINEA GOLDEN--	I HAD A GUINEA GOLDEN--	23	1
AND WHEN HIS GOLDEN WALK IS DONE--	THE DAISY FOLLOWS SOFT	106	2
UPON THEIR GOLDEN FLOOR!	IN RAGS MYSTERIOUS AS	117	8
GONE--MR BRYANT'S "GOLDEN ROD"--	BESIDES THE AUTUMN POETS	131	7
THE LAMP--BURNS GOLDEN--ON--	THE LAMP BURNS SURE--	233	6
HID GOLDEN, FOR THE WHOLE OF DAYS,	OF ALL THE SOUNDS	321	15
NEXT--ONE--MIGHT BE THE GOLDEN TOUCH--	I'LL CLUTCH--AND CLUTCH	427	2
ALONG MY GOLDEN LINES--	IT WOULD NEVER BE COMMON	430	29
AND GOLDEN HANG--WHILE FARTHER UP--	A SOLEMN THING WITHIN	483	3
BUT--THERE--THE GOLDEN SAME--	YOU KNOW THAT PORTRAIT	504	12
THE EAGLE'S GOLDEN BREAKFAST STRANGLES [DAZZLES]--THEM--	VICTORY COMES LATE--	690	12
LOOKS LONG--AND LAST--AND GOLDEN--	THE MOUNTAINS--GROW	757	7
TO DO HIS GOLDEN WILL--	MY FAITH IS LARGER THAN	766	8
HER GOLDEN FINGER ON HER LIP--	NATURE--THE GENTLEST	790	23
THE "GOLDEN FLEECE"	FINDING IS THE FIRST ACT	870	4
FINALLY, NO GOLDEN FLEECE--	FINDING IS THE FIRST ACT	870	7
THAN ALL THE GOLDEN PRESENCE	WE LEARN IN THE	1083	7
FOR ANY GOLDEN FLEECE	ONE OF THE ONES THAT	1466	22
GOLDS			
BETWEEN DIVERGING GOLDS--	THAT FIRST DAY, WHEN YOU	659	6
GOLIAH			
WAS IT GOLIAH--WAS TOO LARGE--	I TOOK MY POWER IN MY	540	7
GOLIAH--SO WOULD YOU--	THE MOST PATHETIC THING	1290	8
GONE			
ROBIN IS GONE.	I HAVE A BIRD IN SPRING	5	6
THAN THE REST HAVE GONE.	I OFTEN PASSED THE	51	8
DRINK, AND ARE GONE--	SOUTH WINDS JOSTLE THEM	86	4
GONE--MR BRYANT'S "GOLDEN ROD"--	BESIDES THE AUTUMN POETS	131	7
PIGMY SERAPHS--GONE ASTRAY--	PIGMY SERAPHS--GONE	138	1
TILL DAFFODILS HAD COME AND GONE	SHE BORE IT TILL THE	144	5
AND DOLLIE--GONE!	YOU LOVE ME--YOU ARE	156	7
AND "JESUS"! WHERE IS JESUS GONE?	DYING! DYING IN THE	158	5
AND RISEN UP--AND GONE AWAY,	I'VE HEARD AN ORGAN TALK	183	5
WHILE I WAS GONE--AND I--TOO LATE--	I SHOULD NOT DARE TO	205	3
AND THE JUGGLER OF DAY IS GONE	BLAZING IN GOLD AND	228	8
AS THAT THE SLAVE--IS GONE.	THE LAMP BURNS SURE--	233	8
GONE DOWN!	IF HE DISSOLVE--THEN--	236	7
"CAROL FOR HIM--WHEN I AM GONE"!	KILL YOUR BALM--AND IT'S	238	8
THE GEM WAS GONE--	I HELD A JEWEL IN MY	245	6
HAD GONE TO SLEEP--THAT SOUNDEST TIME--	TO DIE--TAKES JUST A	255	11
FOR THEY'RE NEVER GONE--	ALONE, I CANNOT BE--	298	12
LIKE [AS] LOWLY SPICES, LAIN TO SLEEP [GONE TO SLEEP / LAID ...	THE GRASS SO LITTLE HAS	333	15
THIS--TO HEAVEN DIVINE HAS GONE--	TAKE YOUR HEAVEN FURTHER	388	2
CARESSES--AND IS GONE--	A VISITOR IN MARL--	391	8
FOR FEAR IT WOULD BE GONE--	IT WAS GIVEN TO ME BY	454	8
TILL ALL THE SCENE--BE GONE.	'TWAS WARM--AT FIRST--	519	4
AS GIANTS--GONE [CLAIMED] AWAY--	HAD I PRESUMED TO HOPE--	522	4
MY BEST--WAS GONE TO SLEEP--	I HAD NO CAUSE TO BE	542	2

	FIRST LINE	POEM	LINE
GONE (CONTINUED)			
I NOTE THAT SOME--GONE PATIENT LONG-- . .	I MEASURE EVERY GRIEF I	561	13
FORTY--GONE DOWN TOGETHER--	GLEE--THE GREAT STORM IS	619	3
GONE--AS SOON AS KNOWN--	SO THE EYES ACCOST--AND	752	8
BEST [ALL] HORIZON--GONE [KNOWN]-- . . .	NO BOBOLINK--REVERSE HIS	755	7
AND YET [YET ALL] THE BAND WAS GONE-- . .	THE BIRDS BEGUN AT FOUR	783	20
SO INFINITE--WHEN GONE--	JOY TO HAVE MERITED THE	788	14
EXCEPT THAT IT IS GONE	DEATH LEAVES US HOMESICK	935	2
"A SOUL HAS GONE TO HEAVEN"	OF TOLLING BELL I ASK	947	2
A SOUL HAD GONE TO HEAVEN	OF TOLLING BELL I ASK	947	6
GONE WESTERLY, TODAY--	THE SUNSET STOPPED ON	950	4
IT WRINKLED, AND WAS GONE--	A NARROW FELLOW IN THE	986	16
AND INFINITE IS GONE--	IT RISES--PASSES--ON OUR	1023	4
PERCEIVE, WHEN YOU ARE GONE.	THE DYING NEED BUT	1026	8
NOT THAT SHE WAS GONE--	NOW I KNEW I LOST HER--	1219	2
SO MUCH OF HEAVEN HAS GONE FROM EARTH . .	SO MUCH OF HEAVEN HAS	1228	1
THE BIRD OF BIRDS IS GONE--	THE WAY TO KNOW THE	1279	22
THE NEWS THAT SHE [HE] IS GONE--	SHE LAID HER DOCILE	1396	4
BY FEELING IT IS GONE--	A WINGED SPARK DOTH SOAR	1468	8
EMPHASIZED AND GONE	GLASS WAS THE STREET--IN	1498	6
AS [OF] GUEST, THAT [WHO] WOULD BE GONE-- .	AS IMPERCEPTIBLY AS	1540	12
BUT THE TROOPS ARE GONE!	EXPANSE CANNOT BE LOST--	1584	16
THE BOBOLINK IS GONE--THE ROWDY OF THE MEADOW--	THE BOBOLINK IS GONE--	1591	1
THE SAGEST [ONLY] TIME TO DAM THE SEA IS WHEN THE SEA IS GONE--	WE SEND THE WAVE TO FIND	1604	7
HIS "GOING, GOING, GONE"	THE AUCTIONEER OF	1612	2
ATTESTS THE BIRD THAT'S GONE	I SEE THEE CLEARER FOR	1666	8
THE DISTANCE THAT THE DEAD HAVE GONE . . .	THE DISTANCE THAT THE	1742	1
BECAUSE THE HAND IS GONE?	WHICH MISSES MOST,	1759	5
GOOD			
GOOD BYE, SIR, I AM GOING!	"SIC TRANSIT GLORIA	3	57
GOOD NIGHT, BECAUSE WE MUST, ...	GOOD NIGHT, BECAUSE WE	114	1
GOOD EVENING, GENTLE FELLOW MEN!	IF THIS IS "FADING"	120	8
AS CHILDREN BID THE GUEST "GOOD NIGHT" . .	AS CHILDREN BID THE	133	1
THE GOOD MAN'S--"DIVIDEND"--	YOU'RE RIGHT--"THE WAY	234	10
GOOD NIGHT! WHICH PUT THE CANDLE OUT? . .	GOOD NIGHT! WHICH PUT	259	1
FOR OUR HOARSE GOOD NIGHT--	'TWAS THE OLD--ROAD--	344	21
GOOD MORNING--MIDNIGHT--	GOOD MORNING--MIDNIGHT--	425	1
AND THEREFORE--GOOD--	UNDUE SIGNIFICANCE A	439	4
MIDNIGHT--GOOD NIGHT! I HEAR THEM CALL, . .	A WIFE--AT DAYBREAK I	461	7
HOW GOOD--TO BE ALIVE!	I AM ALIVE--I GUESS--	470	25
HIS BEST [GOOD] NORWEGIAN WINES--	I THINK THE HEMLOCK	525	12
GOOD AFFIDAVIT--	MINE--BY THE RIGHT OF	528 V	8
WE DREAM [ARE DREAMING / SHOULD DREAM]--IT IS GOOD WE ARE DREAMING--	WE DREAM--IT IS GOOD WE	531	1
UNTO MY BOOKS--SO GOOD TO TURN--	UNTO MY BOOKS--SO GOOD	604	1
'TIS GOOD [WELL]--THE LOOKING BACK ON GRIEF--	'TIS GOOD--THE LOOKING	660	1
AH, BRIG--GOOD NIGHT	IT TOSSED--AND TOSSED--	723	9
AND WHEN AT NIGHT--OUR GOOD DAY DONE-- . .	MY LIFE HAD STOOD--A	754	13
ROUGHEST AIR--WAS GOOD--	WHEN I HOPED, I	768	4
HOW GOOD THE CERTAINTY	ON A COLUMNAR SELF--	789	4
FROM FURTHEST SPIRIT [FAITHFUL / GOOD MAN]--GOD--	ON A COLUMNAR SELF--	789	12
HER WARM [STRAIGHT / GOOD / QUICK / SAFE] RETURN, IF SO SHE . . .	NO NOTICE GAVE SHE, BUT	804	17
GOOD, WITHOUT ALARM	EXPECTATION--IS	807	6
GOOD TO HIDE, AND HEAR 'EM HUNT!	GOOD TO HIDE, AND HEAR	842	1
GOOD TO KNOW, AND NOT TELL, ...	GOOD TO HIDE, AND HEAR	842	5
THE GOOD WILL OF A FLOWER	THE GOOD WILL OF A	849	1
SWEET [GOOD], TO HAVE HAD THEM LOST . . .	SWEET, TO HAVE HAD THEM	901	1
A GOOD NEWS SHOULD BE GIVEN.	OF TOLLING BELL I ASK	947	8
THERE IS A [GOOD] STRENGTH IN PROVING [KNOWING] THAT IT CAN BE . . .	THERE IS A STRENGTH IN	1113	1
WE BUY WITH CONTRAST--PANG IS GOOD . . .	THE SNOW THAT NEVER	1133	15
HOW GOOD [SAFE / FIRM / CALM] TO BE IN TOMBS	THE CLOUDS THEIR BACKS	1172	6
GOOD AS A NORSEMAN'S HYMN--	A PROMPT--EXECUTIVE BIRD	1177 V	2
MUCH IS THE MIEN [GOOD IS THE LOOK] OF HIM IN MARCH	A PROMPT--EXECUTIVE BIRD	1177	7
RICHES WERE GOOD--	ARE FRIENDS DELIGHT OR	1199	3
WINTER IS GOOD--HIS HOAR DELIGHTS	WINTER IS GOOD--HIS HOAR	1316	1
"GOOD MORNING"--WE PROPOUND?	THE SYMPTOM OF THE GALE	1327	16
GOOD FRIENDS WITH TIME	AN ANTIQUATED GRACE	1345	6
HOW GOOD HIS LAVA BED, ...	HOW GOOD HIS LAVA BED,	1447	1
TRUTH IS GOOD HEALTH--AND SAFETY, AND THE SKY.	A COUNTERFEIT--A PLATED	1453	5
TO REND IT WITH GOOD NIGHT--	WITHIN THY GRAVE!	1552	4
WISHING YOU GOOD DAY--	NOT AT HOME TO CALLERS	1590	4
T'IS GOOD TO BEAR	PERIL AS A POSSESSION	1678	2
NOT SO GOOD AS JOY--	RATHER ARID DELIGHT	1679	4
HOWEVER GOOD TO SEE, ...	DROWNING IS NOT SO	1718	10
GOOD-BY			
TO SAY GOOD-BY TO MEN.	A TRAIN WENT THROUGH A	1761	8
GOODBYE			
GOODBYE TO THE LIFE I USED TO LIVE-- . . .	TIE THE STRINGS TO MY	279	13
TO WITNESS HER GOODBYE--	WE GROW ACCUSTOMED TO	419	4
GOOD-BYE			
GOOD-BYE--THE GOING UTTER ME--	SOME SAY GOODNIGHT--AT	1739	3
GOODMORROW			
AND BID THE WORLD GOODMORROW, AND GO TO GLORY HOME!	AWAKE YE MUSES NINE,	1	40

	FIRST LINE	POEM	LINE
GOODNIGHT			
SO--GOODNIGHT--DAY!	GOOD MORNING--MIDNIGHT--	425	8
SOME SAY GOODNIGHT--AT NIGHT--	SOME SAY GOODNIGHT--AT	1739	1
I SAY GOODNIGHT BY DAY--	SOME SAY GOODNIGHT--AT	1739	2
GOODNIGHT, I STILL REPLY--	SOME SAY GOODNIGHT--AT	1739	4
GOODS			
ALL HIS GOODS HAVE WINGS--	WHAT SHALL I DO WHEN THE	956	14
IN THE GOODS OF DAY--	ON THE WORLD YOU COLORED	1171	12
GORED			
GORED THROUGH AND THROUGH WITH DEATH, TO BE	HIS BILL IS CLASPED--HIS	1102	7
GORSE			
THE MOUNTAIN GORSE--THE BEE'S!	THE JUGGLER'S HAT HER	330	2
GOSSAMER			
DUTIES--OF GOSSAMER--	I WENT TO HEAVEN--	374	11
FOR ONLY GOSSAMER, MY GOWN--	BECAUSE I COULD NOT STOP	712	15
GOSSIPED			
THE THUNDERS [THUNDER] GOSSIPED LOW--	THE WIND BEGUN TO KNEAD	824	10
GOSSIPPED			
ONE GOSSIPPED IN THE LANE	THE TREES LIKE TASSELS--	606	18
GOT			
HAVE YOU GOT A BROOK IN YOUR LITTLE HEART,	HAVE YOU GOT A BROOK IN	136	1
TILL I GOT IN--	IS IT TRUE, DEAR SUE?	218	8
THAT--GOT THROUGH!	IT CANT BE "SUMMER"!	221	2
AND FINISHED [GOT THROUGH--] KNOWING--THEN--	I FELT A FUNERAL, IN MY	280	20
THE SUN HAS GOT AS FAR	I KNOW SOME LONELY	289	33
I GOT SO I COULD HEAR [THINK / TAKE] HIS NAME--	I GOT SO I COULD HEAR	293	1
I GOT SO I COULD WALK ACROSS	I GOT SO I COULD HEAR	293	5
I GOT SO I COULD STIR THE BOX--	I GOT SO I COULD HEAR	293	9
BEFORE I GOT MY EYE PUT OUT	BEFORE I GOT MY EYE PUT	327	1
TILL THAT FIRST SHOUT GOT BY--	I DREADED THAT FIRST	348	6
DAY--GOT TIRED OF ME--	GOOD MORNING--MIDNIGHT--	425	3
BUT SINCE WE GOT A BOMB--	I TIE MY HAT--I CREASE	443	27
HAD I--THE JEWEL--GOT--	THE MALAY--TOOK THE	452	10
AND YOU--GOT SLEEPY--AND BEGGED TO BE ENDED--	GOING TO HIM! HAPPY	494	20
THEN RECOLLECT A BALL, SHE GOT--	HER SMILE WAS SHAPED	514	5
THEN HOW THE GRIEF GOT SLEEPY--SOME--	IF I MAY HAVE IT, WHEN	577	18
THESE WERE BENT--MY SIGHT GOT CROOKED--	DONT PUT UP MY THREAD &	617	5
THE FROGS GOT HOME LAST WEEK--	BEE! I'M EXPECTING YOU!	1035	5
I GOT YOUR LETTER, AND THE BIRDS--	DEAR MARCH--COME IN--	1320	11
I'VE GOT AN ARROW HERE.	I'VE GOT AN ARROW HERE.	1729	1
GOTTEN			
IS GOTTEN NOT OF [WITH] FINGERS--	OF ALL THE SOUNDS	321	13
GOURMAND			
GRIEF IS A GOURMAND--SPARE HIS LUXURY--	GRIEF IS A MOUSE--	793	12
GOVERNMENT			
THE GOVERNMENT OF DAY--	THE SUN AND FOG	1190	2
GOWN			
THE FIELD A SCARLET GOWN--	THE MORNS ARE MEEKER	12	6
AND WORE MY LAST YEAR'S GOWN--	ONE SISTER HAVE I IN OUR	14	6
A BURDOCK--CLAWED [TWITCHED] MY GOWN--	A BURDOCK--CLAWED MY	229	1
AND THOUGH I HAD NO GOWN OF GAUZE--	I CANNOT DANCE UPON MY	326	9
AS WOMEN--DO--THEIR GOWN--	IT WILL BE SUMMER--	342	18
FOR FEAR THEIR YELLOW GOWN	I DREADED THAT FIRST	348	10
THE GOWN THAT DANTE--DEIFIED--	A PRECIOUS--MOULDERING	371	19
MY OLD GOWN--ON--	I'M SAYING EVERY DAY	373	29
AND RUDDIER THAN THE GOWN	THERE IS A FLOWER THAT	380	10
I PUSH A PETAL FROM MY GOWN	I TIE MY HAT--I CREASE	443	7
NEVER A GOWN OF DUN--MORE--	I AM ASHAMED--I HIDE--	473	10
SPOTTED--HER DUN GOWN--	CIVILIZATION--SPURNS--	492	7
OR BRUSHED A ROYAL GOWN--	HE TOUCHED ME, SO I LIVE	506	9
SO CHOOSING BUT A GOWN--	I HAD NO CAUSE TO BE	542	17
OF EMERALD SCANT--HER GOWN--	BUT LITTLE CARMINE HATH	558	2
AS CONSTANT AS THE CHILDISH FROCK [GOWN]--	IT CEASED TO HURT ME,	584	7
WEARING THE SOD GOWN--	DROPPED INTO THE ETHER	665	2
ERMINE--MY FAMILIAR GOWN--	NO MATTER--NOW--SWEET--	704	13
FOR ONLY GOSSAMER, MY GOWN--	BECAUSE I COULD NOT STOP	712	15
THE FASHION OF THE GOWN I WEAR--	PRECIOUS TO ME--SHE	727	3
THE BUTTERFLY'S ASSUMPTION GOWN	THE BUTTERFLY'S	1244	1
THE BUTTERFLY'S NUMIDIAN GOWN	THE BUTTERFLY'S NUMIDIAN	1387	1
AS LIGHTLY AS AN OPTION GOWN	WE KNEW NOT THAT WE WERE	1462	5
MY COUNTRY NEED NOT CHANGE HER GOWN,	MY COUNTRY NEED NOT	1511	1
A HOMOGENEOUS GOWN.	AS IMPERCEPTIBLY AS	1540	V
GOWNS			
THE SPANGLED GOWNS, A LESSER RANK	OF TRIBULATION--THESE	325	3
GRACE			
LEST SUCH A SUBTLE--SHIMMERING GRACE	A SOMETHING IN A	122	11
I HAD RATHER WEAR HER GRACE	PIGMY SERAPHS--GONE	138	12
TO GAIN HIS GRACE--I'D DIE!	THE COURT IS FAR AWAY--	235	4
NIGGARD GRACE!	WHAT WOULD I GIVE TO SEE	247	28
COULD DIMLY RECOLLECT A GRACE [FORCE]--	I GOT SO I COULD HEAR	293	13
WAS'T GRACE? NOT THAT--	ONE YEAR AGO--JOTS WHAT?	296	3
I CRAVE HIM GRACE OF SUMMER BOUGHS,	OF ALL THE SOUNDS	321	25
DOMINIONS DOWERLESS--BESIDE THIS GRACE--	MY REWARD FOR BEING, WAS	343	9
TO PEER THIS GRACE--	MY REWARD FOR BEING, WAS	343	V
DEFORMED MEN--PONDER GRACE--	'TIS OPPOSITES--ENTICE--	355	2
THE GRACE THAT I--WAS CHOSE--	THE DAY THAT I WAS	356	13
THAT WAS THE WITNESS FOR THE GRACE--	THE DAY THAT I WAS	356	15
UNFITTED BY AN INSTANT'S GRACE	I GAINED IT SO--	359	13
THE GRACE SO UNAVOIDABLE--	THE SWEETEST HERESY	387	7

	FIRST LINE	POEM		LINE
GRACE (CONTINUED)				
TO VITALIZE THE GRACE--	A TOOTH UPON OUR PEACE	459		4
BUT JUST TO HEAR THE GRACE DEPART--	EXCEPT THE HEAVEN HAD	472		5
NO ONE TO TEACH ME THAT NEW GRACE--	I AM ASHAMED--I HIDE--	473		5
AND GRACE WOULD GRANT THE PAIR--	I MEANT TO HAVE BUT	476		8
BUT THIS TIME, CONSCIOUSLY, OF GRACE--	I'M CEDED--I'VE STOPPED	508		9
THE FAILURE BUT CONFIRM THE GRACE .	HAD I PRESUMED TO HOPE--	522		7
AT LAST--THE GRACE [THE GRACE IS JUST] IN SIGHT--	I CROSS TILL I AM WEARY	550		18
AT LAST--THE GRACE [THE GRACE IS JUST] IN SIGHT--	I CROSS TILL I AM WEARY	550		18
IT IS TOO DIFFICULT A GRACE--	I RECKON--WHEN I COUNT	569		15
EVEN AS THE GRACE--	MUST BE A WO--	571		12
PUT UP--TO HIDE [HOLD] HER PARTING GRACE	MY FIRST WELL DAY--SINCE	574		23
ADORNED, FOR A SUPERIOR GRACE--	"HEAVEN" HAS DIFFERENT	575		19
IT LOOKS TOO TAWDRY GRACE	YOU'LL FIND--IT WHEN YOU	610		14
LIKE THE GRACE--OF DEATH--	IN FALLING TIMBERS	614		16
THAT NEW GRACE	I CANNOT LIVE WITH YOU--	640		24
TO FETCH HER GRACE--AND HUE--	SHE DWELLETH IN THE	671		5
IT CRAVED THE GRACE TO WORSHIP	THE HEAVEN VESTS FOR	694		3
THE GRACE--MYSELF--MIGHT NOT OBTAIN--	THE GRACE--MYSELF--MIGHT	707		1
OF THE HEAVENLY GRACE--	PUBLICATION--IS THE	709		14
AND HEAVEN--A CONVENIENT GRACE	HAVE ANY LIKE MYSELF	736		15
THE SUMMER GRACE, FOR NOTICE STROVE--	THE BIRDS REPORTED FROM	743		9
HER GRACE IS ALL SHE HAS--	HER GRACE IS ALL SHE HAS	810		1
OLD THE GRACE, BUT NEW THE SUBJECTS--	ALWAYS MINE!	839		6
HIS SERVICE TO THE NEWEST GRACE	OF SILKEN SPEECH AND	896		3
THE GRACE NEXT TO IT--HEAL?	ONLY A SHRINE, BUT MINE	918		8
THOUGH THEIR REPEATED GRACE	MY BEST ACQUAINTANCES	932	V	5
DO THEE DISTINGUISHED GRACE--	WHAT I SEE NOT, I BETTER	939		10
GRACE OF WEALTH, AND GRACE OF STATION	ALL FORGOT FOR	966		5
GRACE OF WEALTH, AND GRACE OF STATION	ALL FORGOT FOR	966		5
GRACE OF RANK--AND GRACE OF FORTUNE	ALL FORGOT FOR	966	V	5
GRACE OF RANK--AND GRACE OF FORTUNE	ALL FORGOT FOR	966	V	5
FOR THE LONG HINDRANCE--GRACE--TO ME--	FITTER TO SEE HIM, I MAY	968		2
FOR EVIDENCE IT BE THE GRACE--	FITTER TO SEE HIM, I MAY	968		12
A GRACE WITHOUT A FRIEND.	MY SEASON'S FURTHEST	1019		4
SO GRADUAL THE GRACE	FURTHER IN SUMMER THAN	1068		6
REMIT AS YET NO GRACE	FURTHER IN SUMMER THAN	1068		13
SO SMALL A GRACE	JUST ONCE! OH LEAST	1076		3
IS A SPECIFIC GRACE--	TO MAKE ROUTINE A	1196		4
WE CLUTCH THE GRACE THE TIGHTER	LIKE TIME'S INSIDIOUS	1236		3
HOW GENERAL A GRACE	MY HEART RAN SO TO THEE	1237		7
THE GRACE SO AWKWARD FOR HER SAKE	WARM IN HER HAND THESE	1313		3
AN [ITS] ANTIQUATED GRACE	AN ANTIQUATED GRACE	1345		1
BUT GRAPHICER FOR GRACE--	SUMMER HAS TWO	1422		6
A [THE] COURTEOUS, YET [BUT] HARROWING GRACE,	AS IMPERCEPTIBLY AS	1540		11
AND IN THE HEAVENLY GRACE--	THE BIRD HER PUNCTUAL	1585		4
IF GRACE COULD TALK.	THE ECSTASY TO GUESS	1608		3
OH WHAT A GRACE IS THIS,	OH WHAT A GRACE IS THIS,	1615		1
IS THERE NO WANDERING ROUTE OF GRACE	OH FUTURE! THOU SECRETED	1631		3
A FACE DEVOID OF LOVE OR GRACE,	A FACE DEVOID OF LOVE OR	1711		1
GRACIOUS				
GRACIOUS NOW TO ME AS ANY--	THREE WEEKS PASSED SINCE	1061		7
GRACIOUS UNTO NONE--	THREE WEEKS PASSED SINCE	1061		8
HOW GRACIOUS	A SOFT SEA WASHED AROUND	1198	V	
SHE TAKES [GOES] HER GRACIOUS [SPACIOUS / SUBTLE / SIMPLE / . . .	SUMMER--WE ALL HAVE SEEN	1386		6
ABUNDANT [A FERVENT / A LOYAL / A GRACIOUS / AN AMPLE] END--	THE GENTIAN HAS A	1424		13
. . . INTIMATE / AFFABLE / AFFLUENT / GRACIOUS] SO TO BE	YOUR THOUGHTS DONT HAVE	1452		6
REMOTEST [FANTASTIC / MOST GRACIOUS / MOST DUSKY / . . .	AN ANTIQUATED TREE	1514		7
OF [TO] EVERY OTHER [AS GRACIOUS AS A] BOON--	TO SEE HER IS A PICTURE	1568	V	4
GRACIOUSLY				
OH SEA--LOOK GRACIOUSLY--	MY RIVER RUNS TO THEE--	162		4
GRADUAL				
BY BLOSSOMS GRADUAL [COMMON] PROCESS--	HE GAVE AWAY HIS LIFE--	567		11
SO GRADUAL THE GRACE	FURTHER IN SUMMER THAN	1068		6
GRADUALLY				
THE TRUTH MUST DAZZLE GRADUALLY [MODERATELY]	TELL ALL THE TRUTH BUT	1129		7
GRAIN				
WE PASSED THE FIELDS OF GAZING GRAIN--	BECAUSE I COULD NOT STOP	712		11
GRAINS				
AS GRAINS UPON A SHORE--	A NIGHT--THERE LAY THE	471		6
WITH STEADY--DRIFTING--[SUDDEN--BLINDING] GRAINS	I CROSS TILL I AM WEARY	550		7
GRAND				
SLEEP IS THE STATION GRAND	SLEEP IS SUPPOSED TO BE	13		4
AS WE RIDE GRAND ALONG!	ONE DIGNITY DELAYS FOR	98		8
A MARQUIS WOULD NOT GO SO GRAND!	I MET A KING THIS	166		10
AT THAT GRAND "RIGHT HAND"!	IF THE FOOLISH, CALL	168		20
WE ARE FAR TOO GRAND--	WE DONT CRY--TIM AND I,	196		2
WE ARE FAR TOO GRAND--	WE DONT CRY--TIM AND I,	196		8
GRAND GO THE YEARS--IN THE CRESCENT--ABOVE THEM--	SAFE IN THEIR ALABASTER	216	V	
AN ORNAMENT TOO GRAND	ALTHOUGH I PUT AWAY HIS	366		2
CADENCES TOO GRAND	OVER AND OVER, LIKE A	367		6
THOSE WATERS SOUND SO GRAND--	I KNOW WHERE WELLS GROW	460		18

	FIRST LINE	POEM	LINE
GRAND (CONTINUED)			
AND CHATTED CLOSE WITH THIS GRAND THING	IF ANYBODY'S FRIEND BE	509	19
I FEAR THAT HE IS GRAND--	I FEAR A MAN OF FRUGAL	543	8
AND USHERED GRAND OLD MOSES	IT ALWAYS FELT TO ME--A	597	19
UPON OCCASION, GRAND	NATURE AFFECTS TO BE	1170	2
THEN CRUMBLE GRAND AWAY	TO PILE LIKE THUNDER TO	1247	2
GRANDAME'S			
EVE--AND THE ANGUISH--GRANDAME'S STORY--	BETTER--THAN MUSIC! FOR	503	15
GRANDER			
'TIS ANGUISH GRANDER THAN DELIGHT	'TIS ANGUISH GRANDER	984	1
GRANDFATHER			
GRANDFATHER OF THE DAYS IS HE	THE MOUNTAIN SAT UPON	975	7
GRANDMAMA			
TO MATCH THE GRANDMAMA--	I KNOW SOME LONELY	289	29
GRANDSIRES			
LIKE COSTUMES GRANDSIRES WORE.	WE OUTGROW LOVE, LIKE	887	4
GRANITE			
WITH MY GRANITE LIP!	IF I SHOULD'NT BE ALIVE	182	8
PASSIVE--AS GRANITE--LAPS MY MUSIC--	PUT UP MY LUTE!	261	4
JUST AS THE GRANITE CRUMB LET GO--	THAT AFTER HORROR--THAT	286	3
WHO ONLY SHOWS HIS MARBLE DISC [GRANITE FACE]--	GIVE LITTLE ANGUISH--	310	7
COOL US TO SHAFTS OF GRANITE--	WE DREAM--IT IS GOOD WE	531	13
THIGH [EYE] OF GRANITE--AND THEW [EAR]--OF STEEL--	AH, TENERIFFE!	666	7
NOVEMBER HUNG HIS GRANITE HAT	THE DAY GREW SMALL,	1140	7
GRANITIC			
CONVICTION--THAT GRANITIC BASE--	ON A COLUMNAR SELF--	789	7
GRANT			
GRANT THAT REPENTANCE SOLEMN	I HAD A GUINEA GOLDEN--	23	33
SUMMER FOR THEE, GRANT I MAY BE	SUMMER FOR THEE, GRANT I	31	1
GRANT ME, OH LORD, A SUNNY MIND--	BESIDES THE AUTUMN POETS	131	15
GRANT GOD, HE CHARGE THE BRAVEST	BLESS GOD, HE WENT AS	147	3
GRANT THAT WE MAY STAND,	IF THE FOOLISH, CALL	168	18
GRANT ME--THAT DAY--THE ROYALTY--	THE COURT IS FAR AWAY--	235	11
WITH JUST THE GRANT TO DO--	ALTHOUGH I PUT AWAY HIS	366	16
A GRANT OF THE DIVINE--	DID OUR BEST MOMENT LAST	393	9
AND GRACE WOULD GRANT THE PAIR--	I MEANT TO HAVE BUT	476	8
IF [GRANT] THE BIRD AND THE FARMER--DEEM IT A "PINE"--	BY MY WINDOW HAVE I FOR	797	3
I KNOW NOT WHICH, DESIRE, OR GRANT [RIGHT / SIGHT]--	I PLAY AT RICHES--TO	801	23
AND GRANT US ALL THEIR COUNTENANCE	THEY ASK BUT OUR DELIGHT	868	3
TO THEE--GRANT ME--	ONLY A SHRINE, BUT MINE	918	11
I SCANNED HIS NARROW REALM [GRANT]	IT CAME HIS TURN TO BEG	1500	5
GRANTED			
JUST GRANTED, FOR THE PERIL'S SAKE--	A SINGLE SCREW OF FLESH	263	15
NO WEDLOCK--GRANTED ME--	I LIVE WITH HIM--I SEE	463	8
GRANTED I CAN PICK 'EM--	WHAT WE SEE WE KNOW	1195	6
GRAPE			
YIELDED GRAPE--AND MAISE--	SOIL OF FLINT, IF STEADY	681	V
GRAPHIC			
AS GRAPHIC AS A STAR	WHOEVER DISENCHANTS	1451	6
AND GRAPHIC CONSEQUENCE	AS IMPERCEPTIBLY AS	1540	V
GRAPHICER			
BUT GRAPHICER FOR GRACE--	SUMMER HAS TWO	1422	6
GRAPPLE			
AS FOR THE LOST WE GRAPPLE	AS BY THE DEAD WE LOVE	88	3
GRAPPLED			
THE MUSCLES GRAPPLED [STRUGGLED] AS WITH LEADS	'TWAS CRISIS--ALL THE	948	9
GRAPPLES			
GRAPPLES WITH A THEME STUBBORN AS SUBLIME	SOME WE SEE NO MORE,	1221	7
GRAPPLING			
BUT GRAPPLING, CONQUERS IT--	'TIS SO APPALLING--IT	281	6
GRASP			
WE COULD NOT GRASP IT'S SEGMENT [ANGLE]	WE SEE--COMPARATIVELY--	534	3
UNCERTAIN GRASP, APPRECIATION	UNCERTAIN LEASE--	857	3
A GRASP ON COMPREHENSION LAID	NO MAN SAW AWE, NOR TO	1733	7
GRASPED			
I [HE] GRASPED--I [HE] BORE AWAY--	I ROBBED THE WOODS--	41	7
FOR HE IS GRASPED OF GOD.	DROWNING IS NOT SO	1718	8
GRASPLESS			
THEIR GRASPLESS MANNERS--MOCK US--	THE TINT I CANNOT TAKE--	627	21
GRASS			
THEN GAY ABOVE RECEDING GRASS	COCOON ABOVE! COCOON	129	8
THE SMALLEST HOUSEWIFE IN THE GRASS,	EXCEPT TO HEAVEN, SHE IS	154	9
SOMETIME, HE DWELLETH IN THE GRASS!	A FUZZY FELLOW, WITHOUT	173	5
AN [SOME] ISLAND IN DISHONORED GRASS--	OF BRONZE--AND BLAZE--	290	18
TOUCHING ALL THE GRASS	HOW THE OLD MOUNTAINS	291	10
FROM A CONVENIENT GRASS--	A BIRD CAME DOWN THE	328	6
THE GRASS SO LITTLE HAS TO DO--	THE GRASS SO LITTLE HAS	333	1
THE GRASS SO LITTLE HAS TO DO	THE GRASS SO LITTLE HAS	333	19
I WISHED THE GRASS WOULD HURRY--	I DREADED THAT FIRST	348	13
CONTENDING WITH THE GRASS--	THERE IS A FLOWER THAT	380	17
THEY PERISHED IN THE SEAMLESS GRASS--	THEY DROPPED LIKE FLAKES	409	6
THE WIND DOES NOT REQUIRE THE GRASS	"WHY DO I LOVE" YOU, SIR	480	3
APPROACHED--AND SPURNED THE NARROW GRASS--	I THINK I WAS ENCHANTED	593	11
LIT UP THE LOW--INFERIOR GRASS--	I THINK I WAS ENCHANTED	593	V 11
LEST THE JEALOUS GRASS	PROMISE THIS--WHEN YOU	648	22
TO RECOLLECT HOW BUSY GRASS	'TIS GOOD--THE LOOKING	660	5

	FIRST LINE	POEM	LINE
GRASS (CONTINUED)			
NO DEW UPON THE GRASS--	THE SUN KEPT SETTING--	692	6
THE NOTICE [MONITION] TO THE STARTLED GRASS	PRESENTIMENT--IS THAT	764	3
THE WIND BEGUN TO KNEAD [ROCK] THE GRASS--	THE WIND BEGUN TO KNEAD	824	1
UNDER THE GRASS AND THE DIRT,	UNDER THE LIGHT, YET	949	2
A NARROW FELLOW IN THE GRASS	A NARROW FELLOW IN THE	986	1
THE GRASS DIVIDES AS WITH A COMB--	A NARROW FELLOW IN THE	986	5
AND EVERY GRASS THAT PLAYS OUTSIDE	HERE, WHERE THE DAISIES	1037	3
PATHETIC FROM THE GRASS	FURTHER IN SUMMER THAN	1068	2
DEW--IS THE FRESHET IN THE GRASS--	DEW--IS THE FRESHET IN	1097	1
THE LOW GRASS LOADED WITH THE DEW	THE CRICKETS SANG	1104	5
OH SHADOW ON THE GRASS,	OH SHADOW ON THE GRASS,	1187	1
OH SHADOW ON THE GRASS	OH SHADOW ON THE GRASS,	1187	5
I FEEL [FELT] AS IF THE GRASS WAS PLEASED	THE MUSHROOM IS THE ELF	1298	13
TRANSPIRING IN THE GRASS	A SINGLE CLOVER PLANK	1343	14
THE GRASS DOES NOT APPEAR AFRAID,	WHAT MYSTERY PERVADES A	1400	9
A CHILLY [LONESOME / WARNING] PEACE INFESTS THE GRASS	A CHILLY PEACE INFESTS	1443	1
ASTONISHES THE GRASS,	THE DANDELION'S PALLID	1519	2
THE HORSE THAT SCENTS THE LIVING GRASS	THE LIFE THAT TIED TOO	1535	5
IT QUIVERED THROUGH [BUBBLED IN] THE GRASS	THERE CAME A WIND LIKE A	1593	2
ON MY VOLCANO GROWS THE GRASS	ON MY VOLCANO GROWS THE	1677	1
THE GRASS IS FULL.	THE MOST IMPORTANT	1746	8
GRATE			
WOULD'NT DUNGEONS SORER GRATE	LET US PLAY YESTERDAY--	728	29
BUT THAT GRATE INVIOLATE--	"SECRETS" IS A DAILY	1385	7
GRATEFUL			
WAS GRATEFUL FOR THE ROSES	WENT UP A YEAR THIS	93	13
AND GRATEFUL THAT A THING	THE FIRST DAY'S NIGHT	410	2
GRATITUDE			
A GRATITUDE--THAT SUCH BE TRUE--	THE WORLD--STANDS--	493	13
BUT THERE IS NO GRATITUDE	IN FALLING TIMBERS	614	15
WE COME TO LOOK WITH GRATITUDE [FONDNESS / PLEASURE]	A PRISON GETS TO BE A	652	5
'TWOULD MAGNIFY--THE GRATITUDE--	WITHOUT THIS--THERE IS	655	11
'TWAS MY LAST GRATITUDE	LET US PLAY YESTERDAY--	728	21
MAKING [PAYING] GRATITUDE	MOST SHE TOUCHED ME BY	760	20
GRATITUDE--IS NOT THE MENTION	GRATITUDE--IS NOT THE	989	1
GRATITUDE BEARS	AN HONEST TEAR	1192	7
LEST GRATITUDE REVIVE THE SNAKE [MY THOUGHT]	IT CAME HIS TURN TO BEG	1500	7
GRATITUDE'S			
IS GRATITUDE'S SWEET POVERTY,	TO TRY TO SPEAK, AND	1617	3
GRAVE			
THE THOUGHTFUL GRAVE ENCLOSES--	SOME, TOO FRAGILE FOR	141	2
THE CAUTIOUS GRAVE EXPOSES,	SOME, TOO FRAGILE FOR	141	6
WITH BUT THE "DISCOUNT" OF THE GRAVE--	YOU'RE RIGHT--"THE WAY	234	7
HE CAN LEAN AGAINST THE GRAVE,	IF YOUR NERVE, DENY YOU	292	3
BE IT'S GRAVE--SUFFICIENT SIGN--	HER--"LAST POEMS"--	312	15
DEPOSED--AT LENGTH [LAST], THE GRAVE--	THERE CAME A DAY AT	322	26
THE GRAVE IS STRICT--	UNIT, LIKE DEATH, FOR	408	5
THE COLOR OF THE GRAVE IS GREEN--	THE COLOR OF THE GRAVE	411	1
THE OUTER GRAVE--I MEAN--	THE COLOR OF THE GRAVE	411	2
THE COLOR OF THE GRAVE IS WHITE--	THE COLOR OF THE GRAVE	411	9
THE OUTER GRAVE--I MEAN--	THE COLOR OF THE GRAVE	411	10
THE COLOR OF THE GRAVE WITHIN--	THE COLOR OF THE GRAVE	411	17
THE CLIMATE OF THE GRAVE	MORE LIFE--WENT OUT--	422	6
THEY BURY, IN THE GRAVE?	DO PEOPLE MOULDER	432	2
GRAVE SAINTS STOLE OUT TO LOOK AT ME--	I MEANT TO HAVE BUT	476	15
THE GRAVE WOULD HINDER ME--	I HAD NO TIME TO HATE--	478	3
LOVE [FAITH] IS LIKE DEATH, DURING THE GRAVE	WHILE IT IS ALIVE	491	8
THE LONG RESTRICTED [SUBJECTED] GRAVE	NO CROWD THAT HAS	515	6
THE SCIENCE OF THE GRAVE	THE PROVINCE OF THE	539	4
BUT THAT'S--BEHIND [THIS--INVOLVES] THE GRAVE--	THERE IS A SHAME OF	551	8
ONE EARNS [GETS] BY MEASURING THE GRAVE--	MY FIRST WELL DAY--SINCE	574	27
UNTIL THEY LOCK IT IN THE GRAVE,	IF I MAY HAVE IT, WHEN	577	5
FOR THO' THEY LOCK THEE IN THE GRAVE,	IF I MAY HAVE IT, WHEN	577	7
FORGIVE ME, IF THE GRAVE COME [SEEM] SLOW--	IF I MAY HAVE IT, WHEN	577	26
WE SPECULATED FAIR, ON EVERY SUBJECT, BUT THE GRAVE--	WE TALKED AS GIRLS DO--	586	3
JUST WHEN THE GRAVE AND I--	I CRIED AT PITY--NOT AT	588	22
THE GRAVE YIELDS BACK HER ROBBERIES--	OF NEARNESS TO HER	607	13
AND IN THE GRAVE--I SEE THEE BEST--	I SEE THEE BETTER--IN	611	9
IT SPURN THE GRAVE--	I ROSE--BECAUSE HE SANK	616	15
SHUTS ARROGANTLY--IN THE GRAVE--	THE TINT I CANNOT TAKE--	627	23
IF MOTHER--IN THE GRAVE--	HE TOLD A HOMELY TALE	763	9
AS IN IT'S GRAVE GO PLUMBING [MEASURING]	THE LONELINESS ONE DARE	777	3
THE GRAVE PRECEDED ME--	BEREAVED OF ALL, I WENT	784	4
THE GRAVE IT WAS REPOSED UPON	BEREAVED OF ALL, I WENT	784	7
THE GRAVE--WAS FINISHED--BUT THE SPADE	BEREAVED OF ALL, I WENT	784	15
CHRIST--STOOPED UNTIL HE TOUCHED THE GRAVE--	PERHAPS YOU THINK ME	833	3
IT WAS A GRAVE, YET BORE NO STONE	IT WAS A GRAVE, YET BORE	876	1
HOW FORTUNATE THE GRAVE--	HOW FORTUNATE THE GRAVE	897	1
THOSE WHO HAVE BEEN IN THE GRAVE THE LONGEST--	THOSE WHO HAVE BEEN IN	922	1
AS HANDS THE GRAVE HAD GRIMED	ON THAT DEAR FRAME THE	940	6
A GRAVE--IS A RESTRICTED [AN INFERIOR] BREADTH--	A COFFIN--IS A SMALL	943	5
THE OTHER SIDE THE GRAVE.	'TWAS CRISIS--ALL THE	948	8
THE FOOT UPON THE GRAVE	AS PLAN FOR NOON AND	960	6
THE STIMULUS, BEYOND THE GRAVE	THE STIMULUS, BEYOND THE	1001	1

	FIRST LINE	POEM	LINE
GRAVE (CONTINUED)			
NOT ANY HIGHER STANDS THE GRAVE	NOT ANY HIGHER STANDS	1256	1
MORE THAN THE GRAVE IS CLOSED TO ME--	MORE THAN THE GRAVE IS	1503	1
THE GRAVE AND THAT ETERNITY	MORE THAN THE GRAVE IS	1503	2
TO WHICH THE GRAVE ADHERES--	MORE THAN THE GRAVE IS	1503	3
WITHIN THY GRAVE!	WITHIN THY GRAVE!	1552	1
BACK FROM THE CORDIAL GRAVE I DRAG THEE	BACK FROM THE CORDIAL	1625	1
IN MY OWN GRAVE I BREATHE	SO GIVE ME BACK TO DEATH	1632	5
TO THY REPORTLESS GRAVE--	STILL OWN THEE--STILL	1633	4
WE BORROWED AT HER GRAVE--	THE IMMORTALITY SHE GAVE	1648	2
THE GRAVE BUT A RELAY	ADVANCE IS LIFE'S	1652	2
I KNOW OF PEOPLE IN THE GRAVE	I KNOW OF PEOPLE IN THE	1665	1
I SEE THEE CLEARER FOR THE GRAVE	I SEE THEE CLEARER FOR	1666	1
BETTER A GRAVE OF BALM	NOT ANY SUNNY TONE	1674	4
LEADS IT THROUGH THE GRAVE TO THEE.	REARRANGE A "WIFE'S"	1737	20
THE GRAVE MY LITTLE COTTAGE IS,	THE GRAVE MY LITTLE	1743	1
THAT SPARKLED TO [SPARKLES IN] THE GRAVE	THIS DOCILE ONE INTER	1752	4
GRAVE'S			
MINE--BY THE GRAVE'S REPEAL--	MINE--BY THE RIGHT OF	528	6
AS SHOULD A FACE SUPPOSED THE GRAVE'S	THERE IS A JUNE WHEN	930	5
GRAVES			
WE DO NOT PLAY ON GRAVES--	WE DO NOT PLAY ON GRAVES	467	1
WHEREVER I SUSPECTED GRAVES--	IF HE WERE LIVING--DARE	734	11
EXPERIENCED AT GRAVES--	THERE IS A FINISHED	856	2
'TIS TRANSPORT WILD AS THRILLS THE GRAVES	'TIS ANGUISH GRANDER	984	5
GRAVITATES			
GRAVITATES WITHIN--	GROWTH OF MAN--LIKE	750	2
GRAVITATION			
THAT GRAVITATION, STUMBLING,	"SIC TRANSIT GLORIA	3	31
TILL GRAVITATION CHASED [HUMBLED / EJECTED / FOUNDERED / . . .	TWO BUTTERFLIES WENT OUT	533	V
GRAVITATIONS			
BY FINER GRAVITATIONS--	I WATCHED THE MOON	629	19
GRAVITY			
IT HAS A SIMPLE GRAVITY	THERE'S SOMETHING	45	7
BUT GRAVITY--AND EXPECTATION--AND FEAR--	UNIT, LIKE DEATH, FOR	408	15
BUT HELD HER GRAVITY ALOFT--	NO NOTICE GAVE SHE, BUT	804	11
DISTINGUISHED FOR THE GRAVITY	WHO OCCUPIES THIS HOUSE?	892	27
GRAY			
AN OPAL GUEST AND GRAY--	THE GUEST IS GOLD AND	15	2
A SWEEP OF GRAY--	A SLASH OF BLUE--	204	2
A DOMINIE IN GRAY--	I'LL TELL YOU HOW THE	318	14
I'LL DWELL IN CALYX--GRAY--	I TEND MY FLOWERS FOR	339	24
DEATH BUT THE DRIFT OF EASTERN GRAY,	BEHIND ME--DIPS ETERNITY	721	4
THE ANTLERS GRAY--	A CURIOUS CLOUD	1710	4
GRAYEST			
REVERE [RESPECT] THE GRAYEST PILE	ASHES DENOTE THAT FIRE	1063	2
GRAZE			
AND HUNGRY AND MUST GRAZE	LOVE CAN DO ALL BUT	1731	6
GREAT			
THE HIGH DO SEEK THE LOWLY, THE GREAT DO SEEK THE SMALL,	AWAKE YE MUSES NINE,	1	11
GREAT CAESAR! CONDESCEND	GREAT CAESAR! CONDESCEND	102	1
SOMEBODY RUN TO THE GREAT GATE	DYING! DYING IN THE	158	9
ITSELF, TOO GREAT [VAST], FOR INTERRUPTING--MORE--	I GOT SO I COULD HEAR	293	27
AFTER GREAT PAIN, A FORMAL FEELING COMES--	AFTER GREAT PAIN, A	341	1
TO DOWER--SO GREAT--	MY REWARD FOR BEING, WAS	343	V
THE PRICE IS GREAT--SUBLIMELY PAID--	IT FEELS A SHAME TO BE	444	9
GREAT SPIRIT--GIVE TO ME	I MEANT TO HAVE BUT	476	10
A LANDSCAPE--NOT SO GREAT	IT'S THOUGHTS--AND JUST	495	17
QUAINTLY INFER--EVE'S GREAT SURRENDER--	BETTER--THAN MUSIC! FOR	503	11
GREAT CLOUDS--LIKE USHERS--LEANING [PLACING]--	DEPARTED--TO THE	524	3
THAN THIS GREAT PURCHASER SUSPECT,	I GAVE MYSELF TO HIM--	580	7
GLEE--THE GREAT STORM IS OVER--	GLEE--THE GREAT STORM IS	619	1
GREAT GLOBULES--IN THE ALLEYS--	THE NAME--OF IT--IS	656	5
IS THAT GREAT WATER IN THE WEST--	WE THIRST AT FIRST--'TIS	726	7
YOU SAID THAT I "WAS GREAT"--ONE DAY--	YOU SAID THAT I "WAS	738	1
THEN "GREAT" IT BE--IF THAT PLEASE THEE--	YOU SAID THAT I "WAS	738	2
DAY'S GREAT PROGENITOR--	RENUNCIATION--IS A	745	8
UNCONSCIOUS WAS--GREAT NATURE'S FACE	IT BLOOMED AND DROPT, A	978	19
WITH "I AM GREAT AND CANNOT WAIT	THE FINGERS OF THE LIGHT	1000	3
GREAT NATURE NOT TO DISAPPOINT	BLOOM--IS RESULT--TO	1058	13
BY THIS GREAT LIGHT UPON OUR MINDS	THE LAST NIGHT THAT SHE	1100	7
NOT SATISFIED TO APE THE GREAT IN HIS SIMPLICITY	THAT THIS SHOULD FEEL	1112	5
A GREAT HOPE FELL	A GREAT HOPE FELL	1123	1
GREAT STREETS OF SILENCE LED AWAY	GREAT STREETS OF SILENCE	1159	1
THE LIFE WE HAVE IS VERY GREAT.	THE LIFE WE HAVE IS VERY	1162	1
GREAT BRITAIN DISAPPROVES, "THE STARS";	MY COUNTRY NEED NOT	1511	5
BEHOLD HOW GREAT A FIRMAMENT	NO MATTER WHERE THE	1541	3
JUDAS--THE GREAT [FIRST] DEFAULTER--	THE BIBLE IS AN ANTIQUE	1545	7
THOUGH THE GREAT WATERS SLEEP,	THOUGH THE GREAT WATERS	1599	1
GO THY GREAT WAY!	GO THY GREAT WAY!	1638	1
TOO GREAT IT SEEMS	I DID NOT REACH THEE	1664	26
THE GREAT EXCHANGE OF CLIME--	WERE NATURE MORTAL LADY	1762	4
GREATER			
SO GREATER THAN THE GODS CAN SHOW,	A SINGLE SCREW OF FLESH	263	17
WERE GREATER THAN ITSELF--THOUGH HE	THE ONE WHO COULD REPEAT	307	2
BY FAR THE GREATER ONE--	THE BATTLE FOUGHT	594	4

	FIRST LINE	POEM	LINE
GREATNESS			
FOR GREATNESS, THAT IS ILL AT EASE [COMPOSED]	WHO GIANTS KNOW, WITH	796	3
GREATNESS'			
A VALUE--FOR THE GREATNESS' SAKE--	HAD I PRESUMED TO HOPE--	522	3
GREED			
BUT FOR THE GREED [VAUNT / LIKE] OF HIM--	MY HEART RAN SO TO THEE	1237	13
GREEDINESS			
OF GREEDINESS [URGENCY / VEHEMENCE] TO DIE--	HE FOUGHT LIKE THOSE	759	12
GREEDY			
'TWAS SUCH A GREEDY, GREEDY WAVE	'TWAS SUCH A LITTLE--	107	5
'TWAS SUCH A GREEDY, GREEDY WAVE	'TWAS SUCH A LITTLE--	107	5
CLUTCHED TIGHT, BY GREEDY HANDS--	THERE CAME A DAY AT	322	18
GREEK			
LONG, AT IT'S GREEK--	KNOWS HOW TO FORGET!	433	5
THE MEREST GREEK COULD THAT.	TOO SCANTY 'TWAS TO DIE	1013	2
GREEN			
WHOSE LEAF IS EVER GREEN;	THERE IS ANOTHER SKY,	2	8
WHOSE MAIDS UPON REMOTER GREEN	THERE IS A MORN BY MEN	24	2
NE'ER SUCH A RING ON SUCH A GREEN--	THERE IS A MORN BY MEN	24	14
PEOPLE UPON THAT MYSTIC GREEN--	THERE IS A MORN BY MEN	24	20
FROM A VANISHED GREEN!	I CANT TELL YOU--BUT YOU	65	6
NEW CHILDREN PLAY UPON THE GREEN--	NEW FEET WITHIN MY	99	5
SINCE YORKSHIRE HILLS ARE GREEN--	ALL OVERGROWN BY CUNNING	148	10
OR LITTLE JOHN--OF LINCOLN GREEN--	LIKE SOME OLD FASHIONED	302	7
HER GREEN PEOPLE RECOLLECT IT	NATURE--SOMETIMES SEARS	314	3
A SPHERE OF SIMPLE GREEN--	THE GRASS SO LITTLE HAS	333	2
BEFORE THE WORLD BE GREEN--	THERE IS A FLOWER THAT	380	14
THE COLOR OF THE GRAVE IS GREEN--	THE COLOR OF THE GRAVE	411	1
NOT ALL THE SUMMERS--GREEN--	THE COLOR OF THE GRAVE	411	20
THAT--WAS IN THE GREEN--	THIS WAS IN THE WHITE OF	995	2
IN OVENS GREEN OUR MOTHER BAKES,	THE WORK OF HER THAT	1143	3
. . . EXPERIENCE / ASTONISHMENT / PERIPHERY] OF GREEN--	A LITTLE MADNESS IN THE	1333	5
IN WATERS [FORUMS] GREEN--	HIS MANSION IN THE POOL	1379	16
AND A GREEN CHILL UPON THE HEAT	THERE CAME A WIND LIKE A	1593	3
GREENER			
GREENER LEAN--OR FONDER CLUSTER [LATER LINGER]	PROMISE THIS--WHEN YOU	648	23
GREENWOOD			
THEN BEAR HER TO THE GREENWOOD, AND BUILD FOR HER A BOWER,	AWAKE YE MUSES NINE,	1	37
GREET			
FORGIVE ME, IF TO STROKE [TOUCH / GREET] THY FROST	IF I MAY HAVE IT, WHEN	577	28
THIS THAT WOULD GREET--AN HOUR AGO--	THIS THAT WOULD GREET--	778	1
DECOYING BUT TO GREET US--	OF DEATH I TRY TO THINK	1558	8
GREW			
AND THEN THEY GREW SO JOLLY	I COUNTED TILL THEY	36	5
THE CROWD RESPECTFUL GREW--	WENT UP A YEAR THIS	93	20
DEEPER AND DEEPER GREW THE STAIN	THE SUN KEPT STOOPING--	152	5
TILL MINE TOO HEAVY GREW--	SAVIOR! I'VE NO ONE ELSE	217	10
IN WHICH HIS LETTERS GREW	I GOT SO I COULD HEAR	293	10
AND COULD NOT KNOW HOW FONDNESS GREW	ONE YEAR AGO--JOTS WHAT?	296	19
GREW BY THE FACT, AND NOT THE UNDERSTANDING	IF ANY SINK, ASSURE THAT	358	3
AND ADD "HOW COLD--IT GREW"--	I AM ALIVE--I GUESS--	470	14
THE FINGERS GREW TOO COLD	'TWAS WARM--AT FIRST--	519	6
SUCH LUXURY--IT GREW--	I TRIED TO THINK A	532	17
I'LL TELL THEE ALL--HOW BALD [BLANK] IT GREW--	IF I MAY HAVE IT, WHEN	577	14
THE WAVES GREW SLEEPY--[THE OCEAN--TIRED-- / THE OCEAN-- . . .	THREE TIMES--WE PARTED--	598	13
WITH MOSS--THEY NEVER GREW SO FULL--	YOU'LL FIND--IT WHEN YOU	610	7
MY SOUL GREW [FELT / BENT / STOOD] STRAIGHT.	I ROSE--BECAUSE HE SANK	616	4
WHERE EMPERORS [MONARCHS] GREW--	I ROSE--BECAUSE HE SANK	616	17
AND THEN THE CHEER TOO SOLEMN GREW	TWO TRAVELLERS PERISHING	933	7
IT GREW AS I PURSUED	I HAD A DAILY BLISS	1057	4
UNTIL IT GREW SO WIDE	A GREAT HOPE FELL	1123	11
THE DAY GREW SMALL, SURROUNDED TIGHT	THE DAY GREW SMALL,	1140	1
IMMEDIATELY GREW	ALONE AND IN A	1167	6
AND I AFFRONTED [DISCOURAGED] GREW	MY HEART RAN SO TO THEE	1237	3
THE SEED OF DISAPPOINTMENT GREW	THIS IS THE PLACE THEY	1264	3
I DECLARE--HOW RED THEIR FACES GREW--	DEAR MARCH--COME IN--	1320	13
HIS SPIRIT GREW ROBUST--	HE ATE AND DRANK THE	1587	2
GRIEF			
GRIEF--HILLS--ETERNITY--	SOME THINGS THAT FLY	89	5
IF GRIEF--THE LARGEST PART--	FOREVER AT HIS SIDE TO	246	7
I CAN WADE GRIEF--	I CAN WADE GRIEF--	252	1
SINCE GRIEF AND JOY ARE DONE	SO GLAD WE ARE--A	329	6
I MEASURE EVERY GRIEF I MEET	I MEASURE EVERY GRIEF I	561	1
THERE'S GRIEF OF WANT--AND GRIEF OF COLD--	I MEASURE EVERY GRIEF I	561	29
THERE'S GRIEF OF WANT--AND GRIEF OF COLD--	I MEASURE EVERY GRIEF I	561	29
THEN HOW THE GRIEF GOT SLEEPY--SOME--	IF I MAY HAVE IT, WHEN	577	18
BUT NOT THE GRIEF--THAT NESTLED CLOSE	IT CEASED TO HURT ME,	584	9
'TIS GOOD [WELL]--THE LOOKING BACK ON GRIEF--	'TIS GOOD--THE LOOKING	660	1
TILL ALL THE GRIEF WITH SUMMER--WAVED [BLEW]	'TIS GOOD--THE LOOKING	660	7
GRIEF IS A MOUSE--	GRIEF IS A MOUSE--	793	1
GRIEF IS A THIEF--QUICK STARTLED--	GRIEF IS A MOUSE--	793	5
GRIEF IS A JUGGLER--BOLDEST AT THE PLAY--	GRIEF IS A MOUSE--	793	9
GRIEF IS A GOURMAND--SPARE HIS LUXURY--	GRIEF IS A MOUSE--	793	12
BEST GRIEF IS TONGUELESS--BEFORE HE'LL TELL--	GRIEF IS A MOUSE--	793	13
BUT GAIN--THRO' LOSS--THROUGH GRIEF [PAIN]--OBTAIN--	FITTER TO SEE HIM, I MAY	968	26

	FIRST LINE	POEM	LINE
GRIEF (CONTINUED)			
IS HIS DIVINEST GRIEF--	THE SWEETS OF PILLAGE,	1470	4
AS IMPERCEPTIBLY AS GRIEF	AS IMPERCEPTIBLY AS	1540	1
GRIEFS			
IF ALL THE GRIEFS I AM TO HAVE	IF ALL THE GRIEFS I AM	1726	1
BISECTED NOW, BY BLEAKER GRIEFS,	SOFTENED BY TIME'S	1738	5
GRIEVE			
AND THAT'S THE WAY TO GRIEVE--	THE BUTTERFLY UPON THE	1521	8
GRIEVED			
BUT THIS SORT, GRIEVED MYSELF,	'TWAS JUST THIS TIME,	445	21
THE GRIEVED--ARE MANY--I AM TOLD--	I MEASURE EVERY GRIEF I	561	25
GRIM			
NOR ANY LEADER'S GRIM BATON	NO LADDER NEEDS THE BIRD	1574	3
GRIMACE			
A VULGAR GRIMACE IN THE FLESH--	SHE DEALT HER PRETTY	479	7
GRIMED			
AS HANDS THE GRAVE HAD GRIMED	ON THAT DEAR FRAME THE	940	6
GRIN			
WITH A METALLIC GRIN--	THAT AFTER HORROR--THAT	286	14
GRINNING			
SOME GRINNING MORN--	YOU LOVE ME--YOU ARE	156	4
GRISLY			
OR GRISLY FROSTS--FIRST AUTUMN MORNS,	IT WAS NOT DEATH, FOR I	510	19
GROOM			
CHOOSE THE ENVOY--AND SPURN THE GROOM--	GOD IS A DISTANT--	357	6
GROOVE			
I'D TUNNEL--TILL MY GROOVE	I HAD NOT MINDED--WALLS	398	5
THE BRAIN, WITHIN IT'S GROOVE	THE BRAIN, WITHIN IT'S	556	1
PROPORTIONED TO THE GROOVE.	THAT LOVE IS ALL THERE	1765	4
GROPE			
TILL I STIR [GROPE / START], AND WEEP--	MANY A PHRASE HAS THE	276	12
THE BRAVEST--GROPE A LITTLE--	WE GROW ACCUSTOMED TO	419	13
GROPED			
I GROPED AT SHAPES--	IT WOULD NEVER BE COMMON	430	26
I GROPED [PERISHED / DWELT] UPON HIS BREAST--	HE TOUCHED ME, SO I LIVE	506	3
AND GROPED DELIRIOUS, FOR MORN--	IT TOSSED--AND TOSSED--	723	4
I SHUT MY EYES--AND GROPED AS WELL	FROM BLANK TO BLANK--	761	9
GROPED UP, TO SEE IF GOD WERE [WAS] THERE--	HE SCANNED IT--STAGGERED	1062	6
GROPED BACKWARD AT HIMSELF	HE SCANNED IT--STAGGERED	1062	7
I GROPED FOR HIM BEFORE I KNEW	I GROPED FOR HIM BEFORE	1555	1
GROPES			
OR GROPES, AT MY COMMAND	I MAKE HIS CRESCENT FILL	909	6
BUT ACCLIMATED--PINES NO MORE [GROPES NO MORE / LOSES SIGHT / . . .	THE INUNDATION OF THE	1425	7
GROPING			
OH, GROPING FEET--	NOT PROBABLE--THE BAREST	346	9
GROSS			
FROM OUR GROSS EYES.	I KNOW THAT HE EXISTS.	338	4
GROUND			
I LEFT THEM IN THE GROUND.	GOING TO HEAVEN!	79	27
TO BUILD UPON THE GROUND	FOR EVERY BIRD A NEST--	143	14
DROP SPICY TO THE GROUND--	THERE ARE TWO RIPENINGS	332	4
OF GROUND, OR AIR, OR OUGHT--	AFTER GREAT PAIN, A	341	6
IN FAR--BOLIVIAN GROUND--	REVERSE CANNOT BEFALL	395	6
OF THE LOW GROUND?	IT IS DEAD--FIND IT--	417	6
REPEAL THE BEATING GROUND--	IT WAS NOT DEATH, FOR I	510	20
AND SPREAD IT ON THE GROUND--	OF BRUSSELS--IT WAS NOT	602	14
AS 'TWERE SPECIFIC [A SIGNAL] GROUND--	WHOLE GULFS--OF RED, AND	658	4
SHE DWELLETH IN THE GROUND--	SHE DWELLETH IN THE	671	1
A SWELLING OF THE GROUND--	BECAUSE I COULD NOT STOP	712	18
THE CORNICE--IN THE GROUND--	BECAUSE I COULD NOT STOP	712	20
I HEARD IT HIT THE GROUND--	IT DROPPED SO LOW--IN MY	747	2
IN CAREFUL FITTED GROUND	NO NOTICE GAVE SHE, BUT	804	14
INTERRUPT THIS GROUND--	AMPLE MAKE THIS BED--	829	8
THE TEPID GROUND UPON.	OUR LITTLE KINSMEN--	885	4
DEATH DOUBTS IT--ARGUES [REASONS] FROM THE GROUND--	DEATH IS A DIALOGUE	976	5
BUT WELLS--OF FAILLESS GROUND!	THE WELL UPON THE BROOK	1091	4
FOR INDIES IN THE GROUND!	A MINE THERE IS NO MAN	1117	8
THAT LIFTS US FROM THE GROUND	EXHILIRATION IS THE	1118	2
UPON ENCHANTED GROUND--	EXHILIRATION IS THE	1118	8
MORTALITY'S GROUND FLOOR	IF MY BARK SINK	1234	3
THAT WRESTLES IN THE GROUND,	LONGING IS LIKE THE SEED	1255	2
TAKE COVERT IN THE GROUND--	THE SYMPTOM OF THE GALE	1327	8
PROTRUDING FROM THE GROUND--	FACTS BY OUR SIDE ARE	1497	4
THOU SHALT GO WITH THE RESUMING GROUND	IN SNOW THOU COMEST	1669	2
IN A CONGENIAL GROUND.	THE MOB WITHIN THE HEART	1745	8
GROUNDS			
THROUGH THOSE OLD GROUNDS OF MEMORY,	THROUGH THOSE OLD	1753	1
GROUPS			
TO LITTLE GROUPS OF CONTINENTS	THE HILLS IN PURPLE	1016	3
YIELD GROUPS OF ONES--	EXCEPT THE SMALLER SIZE	1067	V
GROW			
STRAWBERRIES--GROW--	OVER THE FENCE--	251	2
BECAUSE I GROW--WHERE ROBINS DO--	THE ROBIN'S MY CRITERION	285	2
SLOW--SLOW--AS FEET DID WEARY--GROW--	'TWAS THE OLD--ROAD--	344	10
FOR EARTHS, GROW THICK AS	PERHAPS I ASKED TOO	352	3
BY CATCHING AT THE TWIGS THAT GROW	I GAINED IT SO--	359	3
WE GROW ACCUSTOMED TO THE DARK--	WE GROW ACCUSTOMED TO	419	1
I KNOW WHERE WELLS GROW--DROUGHTLESS WELLS--	I KNOW WHERE WELLS GROW	460	1

	FIRST LINE	POEM	LINE
GROW (CONTINUED)			
THAT SUCH A DOLL SHOULD GROW	THE HIMMALEH WAS KNOWN	481	4
THAT GAZE UPON [GROW ALONG] HIS JOURNEY--	I ENVY SEAS, WHEREON HE	498	5
TO LET THE ORCHARDS GROW--	THE TREES LIKE TASSELS--	606	16
HOW CONSCIOUS CONSCIOUSNESS--COULD GROW--	TO KNOW JUST HOW HE	622	24
THE STEPS GROW THICKER--IN THE HALL--	I THINK THE LONGEST HOUR	635	11
THE MOUNTAINS--GROW UNNOTICED--	THE MOUNTAINS--GROW	757	1
WITH SUMMERS, AND WITH WINTERS, GROW,	FITTER TO SEE HIM, I MAY	968	3
I ONLY MUST NOT GROW SO NEW	FITTER TO SEE HIM, I MAY	968	15
THE LARGER--SLOWER GROW	EXCEPT THE SMALLER SIZE	1067	5
DID THE DIAMOND GROW	NONE WHO SAW IT EVER	1110	6
THE BROOK SAID "LET ME GROW"--	THE SEA SAID "COME" TO	1210	2
THAT LETS IT'S RUSHES GROW	A STAGNANT PLEASURE LIKE	1281	2
AND DINE [GROW] WITHOUT LIKE GOD--	ART THOU THE THING I	1282	8
TO WISER BE [GROW] TOO SOON--	I THOUGHT THE TRAIN	1449	10
YOU CANNOT MAKE REMEMBRANCE GROW	YOU CANNOT MAKE	1508	1
THEY TALK AS SLOW AS LEGENDS GROW	THEY TALK AS SLOW AS	1697	1
GROWING			
INFERRED THE LESS BY GROWING THAN	I MADE SLOW RICHES BUT	843	7
IT'S FITNESS GROWING LIKE THE FLOOD	THE THRILL CAME SLOWLY	1495	3
MINE ENEMY [MY FOE] IS GROWING OLD--	MINE ENEMY IS GROWING	1509	1
BUT GROWING LIKE A HURRICANE	THE MOB WITHIN THE HEART	1745	7
GROWN			
WHICH WHEN TO PATIENCE GROWN,	A THROE UPON THE	71	6
THAN WHEN--A LITTLE DULL BALM GROWN--	YOU LOVE ME--YOU ARE	156	17
GROWN TAWNY NOW, WITH TIME--	IN EBON BOX, WHEN YEARS	169	6
THAT I--GROWN BOLD--	UNTO LIKE STORY--TROUBLE	295	14
REGARDLESS GROWN,	AFTER GREAT PAIN, A	341	8
I'M SOME ACCUSTOMED TO HIM GROWN,	I DREADED THAT FIRST	348	3
BUT I, GROWN SHREWDER--SCAN THE SKIES	I MEANT TO HAVE BUT	476	25
CHILDREN--MATURED [GROWN UP]--ARE WISER--MOSTLY--	BETTER--THAN MUSIC! FOR	503	13
GROWN BYE AND BYE	THE CHILD'S FAITH IS NEW	637	17
BUT GROWN BY SLENDER ADDINGS	DEPRIVED OF OTHER	773	5
THE SUM THAT IT HAD GROWN.	I MADE SLOW RICHES BUT	843	8
A CAPITOL HAS GROWN	WHO OCCUPIES THIS HOUSE?	892	26
TO CUSTOM COMMON GROWN	A DIAMOND ON THE HAND	1108	2
GROWN IN [BY] THE REPETITION HOARY	TELL AS A MARKSMAN--WERE	1152	7
ADULT AND URGENT GROWN--	THE WAY TO KNOW THE	1279	18
BEGONE--MY TOOTH HAS GROWN--	ART THOU THE THING I	1282	2
WHEN IT SHALL ONCE HAVE GROWN--	YOU CANNOT MAKE	1508	10
GROWS			
I'D BRING THEM EVERY FLOWER THAT GROWS	IF I COULD BRIBE THEM BY	179	2
A SMALLER PURPLE GROWS--	ME, CHANGE! ME, ALTER!	268	3
AND SUNRISE GROWS SO NEAR	WHEN NIGHT IS ALMOST	347	2
GOD GROWS ABOVE--SO THOSE WHO PRAY	MY PERIOD HAD COME FOR	564	5
THE BODY GROWS WITHOUT [OUTSIDE]--	THE BODY GROWS WITHOUT--	578	1
THE FORMER LOVE--DISTINCTER GROWS--	YOU'LL FIND--IT WHEN YOU	610	11
SO TURBULENT IT GROWS	THIS CHASM, SWEET, UPON	858	12
GROWS A FIERCER THING	AS THE STARVED MAELSTROM	872	10
THE BROADEST LAND THAT GROWS	STEP LIGHTLY ON THIS	1183	2
THAT WATER GROWS	UNTIL THE DESERT KNOWS	1291	2
THE CHESTNUT AGED GROWS	HOW FITS HIS UMBER COAT	1371	7
THE ONLY FOOD THAT GROWS	I GROPED FOR HIM BEFORE	1555	8
IT ONLY SWEETER GROWS.	HER LOSSES MAKE OUR	1562	8
ON MY VOLCANO GROWS THE GRASS	ON MY VOLCANO GROWS THE	1677	1
THE MADDEST NOISE THAT GROWS,--	THE SADDEST NOISE, THE	1764	2
GROWTH			
AND WHEN WE TURNED TO NOTE THE GROWTH--	HE GAVE AWAY HIS LIFE--	567	15
GROWTH OF MAN--LIKE GROWTH OF NATURE--	GROWTH OF MAN--LIKE	750	1
GROWTH OF MAN--LIKE GROWTH OF NATURE--	GROWTH OF MAN--LIKE	750	1
AND THEN IF WE ARE TRUE TO PLAN [GROWTH]	WE NEVER KNOW HOW HIGH	1176	3
POWER IS A FAMILIAR GROWTH--	POWER IS A FAMILIAR	1238	1
GRUMBLED			
. . . GRUMBLED] THEM	TWO BUTTERFLIES WENT OUT	533	V
GUAGE			
TO GUAGE THE SLEEP--	I KNOW SOME LONELY	289	V 10
AS IF A GOBLIN WITH A GUAGE--	'TWAS LIKE A MAELSTROM,	414	10
GUAGES			
THAT ALWAYS GUAGES A DEGREE	LEST THIS BE HEAVEN	1043	3
GUAGING			
THAT I STOPPED GUAGING--SATISFIED--	ONE BLESSING HAD I THAN	756	3
GUARANTY			
NO BREAKFAST IF IT GUARANTY	THE BIRD MUST SING TO	880	3
I GIVE THEE GUARANTY.	"REMEMBER ME" IMPLORED	1180	4
PARTAKING THEE A GUARANTY	EXTOL THEE--COULD I--	1643	7
GUARD			
CROUCH LOW TO GUARD HIS PRIZE.	I NEVER TOLD THE BURIED	11	4
WHILE LIKE A GUARD BETWEEN--	OUR LIVES ARE SWISS--	80	7
WHOM I HAVE LOST, I PIOUS GUARD	WHERE I HAVE LOST, I	104	5
MINE--TO GUARD YOUR NARROW PRECINCT--	PROMISE THIS--WHEN YOU	648	17
I GUARD MY MASTER'S HEAD--	MY LIFE HAD STOOD--A	754	14
THEN HOVERS--AN INFERIOR GUARD--	LOVE--IS THAT LATER	924	9
GUESS			
ENABLE THEE TO GUESS	JESUS! THY CRUCIFIX	225	2
I GUESS--	YOU'RE RIGHT--"THE WAY	234	12
OH, DEAR,--I GUESS IF HE WERE A BOY--	OVER THE FENCE--	251	8
I MUST GUESS--	YOU SEE I CANNOT SEE--	253	2
BUT I GUESS GUESSING HURTS--	YOU SEE I CANNOT SEE--	253	6
SO SAFER GUESS--WITH JUST MY SOUL	BEFORE I GOT MY EYE PUT	327	18

	FIRST LINE	POEM	LINE
GUINEA			
I HAD A GUINEA GOLDEN--	I HAD A GUINEA GOLDEN--	23	1
AND GUINEA IN THE SAND.	I HAD A GUINEA GOLDEN--	23	28
JUST TO BE RICH--TO WASTE MY GUINEAS [GUINEA]	SWEET--YOU FORGOT--BUT I	523	9
A GUINEA AT A SIGHT--	THE TINT I CANNOT TAKE--	627	4
WITH THE GUINEA [GUINEAS]	SO MUCH SUMMER	651	7
GUINEAS			
JUST TO BE RICH--TO WASTE MY GUINEAS [GUINEA]	SWEET--YOU FORGOT--BUT I	523	9
WITH THE GUINEA [GUINEAS]	SO MUCH SUMMER	651	7
GUITAR			
TOUCH LIGHTLY NATURE'S SWEET GUITAR	TOUCH LIGHTLY NATURE'S	1389	1
GULF			
THE GULF BETWEEN THE HAND AND HER	THE LADY FEEDS HER	941	5
THE GULF BEHIND WAS NOT,	IT WAS A QUIET WAY--	1053	13
GULFS			
WHOLE GULFS--OF RED, AND FLEETS--OF RED--	WHOLE GULFS--OF RED, AND	658	1
GULPHING			
DEFORMING--DWINDLING--GULPHING UP--	I HAD THE GLORY--THAT	349	6
GUN			
HAD I A MIGHTY GUN	MY FRIEND ATTACKS MY	118	6
AND IF I GAIN! OH GUN AT SEA!	'TIS SO MUCH JOY! 'TIS	172	13
FIRE, AND SMOKE, AND GUN,	I HAVE NEVER SEEN	175	6
MY LIFE HAD STOOD--A LOADED GUN--	MY LIFE HAD STOOD--A	754	1
GUNS			
DUNGEONS CAN [MAY] CALL--AND GUNS IMPLORE--	WHAT IF I SAY I SHALL	277	8
THEY THWARTED US WITH GUNS--	THEY PUT US FAR APART--	474	6
GURGLE			
AND TIME SH'D GURGLE ON--	IF I SHOULD DIE,	54	3
GURGLED			
AND GURGLED DOWN AND DOWN.	ADRIFT! A LITTLE BOAT	30	8
AND SHOUTED [BUBBLED / GURGLED] LET US PRAY--	THE BOBOLINK IS GONE--	1591	7
GUSH			
BY SIX, THE FLOOD [GUSH] HAD DONE--	THE BIRDS BEGUN AT FOUR	783	17
GUSH AFTER GUSH, RESERVED FOR YOU--	SPLIT THE LARK--AND	861	6
GUSH AFTER GUSH, RESERVED FOR YOU--	SPLIT THE LARK--AND	861	6
GUSHED			
GUSHED TOO FREE [FULL] FOR THE ADORING--	HER--"LAST POEMS"--	312	9
GUSHES			
THE SMITTEN ROCK THAT GUSHES!	A WOUNDED DEER--LEAPS	165	5
GUST			
THAT GUST AND STORM ARE BY,	THE RAINBOW NEVER TELLS	97	2
GUSTS			
WHEN GUSTS REVERSE THE SNOW--	HE FOUGHT LIKE THOSE	759	10
GYMNASIUM			
AS [FOR] A GYMNASIUM	ALONE AND IN A	1167	12
GYMNAST			
A GYMNAST AND AN ANGEL [A WRESTLER]	A LITTLE EAST OF JORDAN,	59	3
AND THE BEWILDERED GYMNAST [ASTONISHED WRESTLER]	A LITTLE EAST OF JORDAN,	59	15
GYMNASTIC			
BY WAY OF A GYMNASTIC	"SIC TRANSIT GLORIA	3	35
HABILIMENT			
OF IMPUDENT HABILIMENT	THE WAY TO KNOW THE	1279	5
HABILIMENTS			
INSPIRITING HABILIMENTS	BEFORE YOU THOUGHT OF	1465	7
HABIT			
HIS HABIT--IS SEVERE--	THERE IS A LANGUOR OF	396	10
AND SMALLER, BY HABIT--	IT DONT SOUND SO	426	13
A HABIT--OF A LAUREATE--	THEY HAVE A LITTLE ODOR	785	4
THE HABIT OF A FOREIGN SKY	AWAY FROM HOME ARE SOME	821	5
A CUSTOM [HABIT] OF THE SOUL	AS ONE DOES SICKNESS	957	9
IF ONESELF IS NOT IN THE HABIT OF HIM	TO DO A MAGNANIMOUS	1699	3
HABITATION			
DRAB HABITATION OF WHOM?	DRAB HABITATION OF WHOM?	893	1
HAGGARD			
A HAGGARD COMFORT SPRINGS	I TRIED TO THINK A	532	7
HAIR			
AND HARRIET, AND SUSAN, AND SHE WITH CURLING HAIR!	AWAKE YE MUSES NINE,	1	32
LIFT--IF YOU CARE--THE LISTLESS HAIR--	HOW MANY TIMES THESE LOW	187	6
AND SWUNG THEIR FRENZIED HAIR.	AN AWFUL TEMPEST MASHED	198	9
TILL HAIR--AND EYES--AND TIMID HEAD--	I THINK JUST HOW MY	237	3
OUR SAVIOR, BY A HAIR--	THAT AFTER HORROR--THAT	286	4
NO RINGLET, TO MY HAIR,	I CANNOT DANCE UPON MY	326	10
IT'S TIME TO SMOOTH THE HAIR--	WHEN NIGHT IS ALMOST	347	4
I JUDGED MY FEATURES--JARRED MY HAIR--	I FELT MY LIFE WITH BOTH	351	9
BUT 'TIS A SINGLE HAIR--	I HAD NOT MINDED--WALLS	398	9
OF HER ELECTRIC HAIR--	'TIS CUSTOMARY AS WE	440	8
FINGERS--TO FRAME MY ROUND HAIR	I AM ASHAMED--I HIDE--	473	13
THAT'S EASIER--THAN BRAID THE HAIR--	TO MAKE ONE'S TOILETTE--	485	5
SOME MANNER OF THE HAIR--	IF ANYBODY'S FRIEND BE	509	6
CARESS HER FREEZING HAIR--	THE SOUL HAS BANDAGED	512	6
THE VERY COLOR OF MY HAIR--	PRECIOUS TO ME--SHE	727	4
THEY KNEW THE HAIR TO--	SEVERER SERVICE OF	786	15
CRISIS IS A HAIR	CRISIS IS A HAIR	889	1
THAT ADJUSTS THE HAIR	CRISIS IS A HAIR	889	14
AND WE--WE PLACED THE HAIR--	THE LAST NIGHT THAT SHE	1100	25
THAT REACHES TO OUR UTMOST HAIR	WE LIKE A HAIRBREADTH	1175	7

	FIRST LINE	POEM	LINE
HAIR (CONTINUED)			
RISK IS THE HAIR THAT HOLDS THE TUN [ONE] .	RISK IS THE HAIR THAT	1239	1
BY THAT PERFIDIOUS HAIR--	RISK IS THE HAIR THAT	1239	8
WHILE THAT DELUSIVE [OBLIGING / ENCHANTING] HAIR	RISK IS THE HAIR THAT	1239	10
DISSEMINATED IN HER HAIR--	A LITTLE SNOW WAS HERE	1444	2
WITH MARTIAL HAND SHE STROKES THE HAIR . .	WHO IS IT SEEKS MY	1598	5
HER FACE WAS IN A BED OF HAIR, ...	HER FACE WAS IN A BED OF	1722	1
HAIRBREADTH			
WE [I] LIKE A HAIRBREADTH 'SCAPE	WE LIKE A HAIRBREADTH	1175	1
HAIR'S			
ON A HAIR'S RESULT--	ROBBED BY DEATH--BUT	971	14
HALCYON			
FOR MISERIES SO HALCYON	I THOUGHT THE TRAIN	1449	11
HIS IS THE HALCYON TABLE--	HOPE IS A SUBTLE GLUTTON	1547	5
HALF			
IF I WERE HALF SO FINE MYSELF	"SOWN IN DISHONOR"!	62	4
HALF GLAD WHEN IT IS NIGHT, AND SLEEP, . .	I HAVE A KING, WHO DOES	103	4
HALF A TRANSPORT--HALF A TROUBLE-- . . .	FLOWERS--WELL--IF	137	3
HALF A TRANSPORT--HALF A TROUBLE-- . . .	FLOWERS--WELL--IF	137	3
SO OVER HORROR, IT HALF CAPTIVATES [DUMB FASCINATES]--	'TIS SO APPALLING--IT	281	2
HALF CHILD--HALF HEROINE--	A MIEN TO MOVE A QUEEN--	283	2
HALF CHILD--HALF HEROINE--	A MIEN TO MOVE A QUEEN--	283	2
ROBIN--UTTERED [PUBLISHED / LAVISHED] HALF THE TUNE--	HER--"LAST POEMS"--	312	8
HER MERRY ARMS, HALF DROPT--	SHE LAY AS IF AT PLAY	369	5
INLAID WITH EMERALD--HALF WAY DOWN-- . . .	I KNOW WHERE WELLS GROW	460	7
A HALF [TOO] UNCONSCIOUS [AN INSUFFICIENT] QUEEN--	I'M CEDED--I'VE STOPPED	508	16
WITH HALF A SMILE, AND HALF A SPURN, . . .	IF YOU WERE COMING IN	511	3
WITH HALF A SMILE, AND HALF A SPURN, . . .	IF YOU WERE COMING IN	511	3
I OFFER THEM THE WHOLE [HALF] OF HEAVEN . .	I CROSS TILL I AM WEARY	550	20
IT HALF ENDEARS THE ABSTINENCE--	UNTO MY BOOKS--SO GOOD	604	3
IN HALF THE PERIOD--	THE SPIDER HOLDS A	605	8
THEN HALF--THEN UTTER HID--	THE TREES LIKE TASSELS--	606	10
HALF SHRINKING FROM THE GLORY	THE HEAVEN VESTS FOR	694	5
THAN DYING HALF [PART]--THEN RALLYING	THE WHOLE OF IT CAME NOT	762	11
A HALF A DOZEN KISSED THE EAVES--	A DROP FELL ON THE APPLE	794	3
DWELT HESITATING, HALF OF DUST, ...	TO THIS WORLD SHE	830	8
AND HALF OF DAY, THE BRIDE.	TO THIS WORLD SHE	830	9
I'M TEMPTED HALF TO STITCH IT UP	THIS CHASM, SWEET, UPON	858	13
HALF HER COMPLEXION OF THE SUN--	FAIRER THROUGH FADING--	938	3
HALF THE CONDITION [DISTINCTION], THY REVERSE--TO FOLLOW--	WERT THOU BUT ILL--THAT	961	11
I SHALL IMPUTE WITH HALF A PAIN	FITTER TO SEE HIM, I MAY	968	7
RETROSPECTION IS PROSPECT'S HALF, ...	THIS WAS IN THE WHITE OF	995	7
I HALF INDIFFERENT VIEWED	I HAD A DAILY BLISS	1057	2
AT HALF PAST THREE, A SINGLE BIRD	AT HALF PAST THREE, A	1084	1
AT HALF PAST FOUR, EXPERIMENT	AT HALF PAST THREE, A	1084	5
AT HALF PAST SEVEN, ELEMENT	AT HALF PAST THREE, A	1084	9
AND HALF CARESS--	NOT SEEING, STILL WE	1518	4
BUT HALF THE HOURS REMAIN.	CONSULTING SUMMER'S	1715	2
THE SECOND HALF OF JOY	CONSULTING SUMMER'S	1715	5
WE MORE THAN HALF SUSPECT, ...	THE DISTANCE THAT THE	1742	6
HALL			
TO DRIVE HER FROM THE HALL?	IF I COULD BRIBE THEM BY	179	19
THE ANGELS BUSTLE IN THE HALL--	A WIFE--AT DAYBREAK I	461	8
THE STEPS GROW THICKER--IN THE HALL-- . .	I THINK THE LONGEST HOUR	635	11
I CROSS THE HALL WITH MINGLED STEPS-- . .	AGAIN--HIS VOICE IS AT	663	9
AS AN ASTRAL HALL	LIGHTLY STEPPED A YELLOW	1672	6
HALLELUJAH			
THE LIPS AT HALLELUJAH	THE FEET OF PEOPLE	7	5
HALLELUJAHS			
STRONG [SURE] HALLELUJAHS ROLL--	THIS WORLD IS NOT	501	18
HALLOW			
WOULD THE BEE THE HAREBELL HALLOW	DID THE HAREBELL LOOSE	213	3
BUT HALLOW JUST THE SNOW	DOUBT ME! MY DIM	275	23
HALLOWED			
A TIMID [HALLOWED] THING--TO DROP A LIFE .	A SOLEMN THING--IT WAS--	271	5
TO BE HALLOWED--ACCORDINGLY--	BY MY WINDOW HAVE I FOR	797	25
HALLOWED NAME--	SANG FROM THE HEART,	1059	16
BY INNOCENT [ELOQUENT / HALLOWED / HEAVENLY / DIFFIDENT] SURPRISE--	THE PRETTY RAIN FROM	1426	4
BY THE DIRECTION OF HALLOWED SPECTRES-- . .	THE BIBLE IS AN ANTIQUE	1545 V	3
A SINGLE [ROYAL / SIGNAL / HALLOWED] TIME .	TO BE FORGOT BY THEE	1560	9
POSSESSED BY EVERY HALLOWED KNIGHT . . .	CIRCUMFERENCE THOU BRIDE	1620	3
HALLOWING			
THE HALLOWING OF PAIN	THE HALLOWING OF PAIN	772	1
LIKE HALLOWING OF HEAVEN, ...	THE HALLOWING OF PAIN	772	2
HALLUCINATION			
THOUGH IT'S HALLUCINATION	"TOMORROW"--WHOSE	1367	3
HALT			
THEIR FAR PARADES--ORDER [HALT] ON THE EYE .	INCONCEIVABLY SOLEMN!	582	5
PURPLES OF AGES--PAUSE [HALT] FOR YOU-- . .	AH, TENERIFFE!	666	3
BUT LET OUR OBSERVATION SHUT [HALT] . . .	NATURE AFFECTS TO BE	1170	3
THAT, TOO, HALT A LITTLE--	I SUPPOSE THE TIME WILL	1381	12
HALTS			
IT TRAVERSES--YET HALTS--	IT SIFTS FROM LEADEN	311 V	
WHAT RUSSET HALTS IN NATURE'S MARCH . . .	THEIR BARRICADE AGAINST	1471	5

	FIRST LINE	POEM	LINE
HALVED			
HIS SMALL UMBRELLA QUAINTLY HALVED	THE BAT IS DUN, WITH	1575	5
HALVES			
HE BIT [SHOOK] AN ANGLEWORM IN HALVES	A BIRD CAME DOWN THE	328	3
AT HALVES--	MYSELF WAS FORMED--A	488	8
HAME			
I KEPT THE "HOUSE AT HAME."	I HAD A GUINEA GOLDEN--	23	16
HAMLET			
"HAMLET" TO HIMSELF WERE HAMLET--	DRAMA'S VITALLEST	741	8
"HAMLET" TO HIMSELF WERE HAMLET--	DRAMA'S VITALLEST	741	8
HAMMER			
WITH HAMMER, AND WITH BLAZE	DARE YOU SEE A SOUL AT	365	14
AND BRINGS HIS HAMMER DOWN--	THE AUCTIONEER OF	1612	4
HAMMERS			
BY FAINTER HAMMERS--FURTHER HEARD--	HE FUMBLES AT YOUR SOUL	315	7
LIKE HAMMERS--DID THEY KNOW THEY FELL	THE MORNING AFTER WO--	364	11
HAMMOCK'S			
THE HAMMOCK'S MOTION LULLS THE HEADS	I SOMETIMES DROP IT, FOR	708	11
HAND			
AND WHEN THE HAND THAT PLUCKED IT	"SIC TRANSIT GLORIA	3	63
FAST IN A SAFER HAND	I HAVE A BIRD IN SPRING	5	13
DOWN WH', ON EITHER HAND	SLEEP IS SUPPOSED TO BE	13	5
I HELD HER HAND THE TIGHTER--	ONE SISTER HAVE I IN OUR	14	15
TO A HAND BELOW.	DISTRUSTFUL OF THE	20	16
THE HAND THAT PAUSED TO GATHER	WHEN ROSES CEASE TO	32	5
SOME CHAFE IT'S IDLE HAND--	THERE'S SOMETHING	45	6
DO THE BLUE HAVENS BY THE HAND	A POOR--TORN HEART-- A	78	15
TRACED AZURE ON HER HAND--	SHE BORE IT TILL THE	144	2
AT THAT GRAND "RIGHT HAND"!	IF THE FOOLISH, CALL	168	20
BY GALLANT--MOULDERING HAND!	IN EBON BOX, WHEN YEARS	169	12
DEEP IN OUR HAND--	WE DONT CRY--TIM AND I,	196	6
AND THEY--WERE THE LITTLE HAND--THAT KNOCKED--	WHY--DO THEY SHUT ME OUT	248	11
WHEN I COULD TAKE IT IN MY HAND--	A SOLEMN THING--IT WAS--	271	11
ONE--HAND THE TOOLS--	I KNOW SOME LONELY	289	8
HOW THE OLD STEEPLES HAND THE SCARLET	HOW THE OLD MOUNTAINS	291	5
TO CARRY IN THE HAND--	I SEND TWO SUNSETS--	308	8
THE WIND DOES--WORKING LIKE A HAND,	OF ALL THE SOUNDS	321	5
AND IN MY WONDERING HAND	AS IF I ASKED A COMMON	323	2
I'LL HAND IT TO THE ANGEL--	THE FACE I CARRY WITH ME	336	5
POISED LIGHTLY ON HIS HAND,	THEY LEAVE US WITH THE	350	8
THIS MIGHT HAVE BEEN THE HAND	ALTHOUGH I PUT AWAY HIS	366	4
AT THE LORD'S RIGHT HAND.	OVER AND OVER, LIKE A	367	8
HIS VENERABLE HAND TO TAKE--	A PRECIOUS--MOULDERING	371	5
IS THE UTMOST OF YOUR HAND--	TAKE YOUR HEAVEN FURTHER	388	7
OH, SIGNOR, THINE, THE AMBER HAND--	THE MOON IS DISTANT FROM	429	9
WERE AS IMPOSSIBLE AS HAND	THE WIND--TAPPED LIKE A	436	7
THE BRUSH WITHOUT THE HAND--	THE OUTER--FROM THE	451	10
I KEPT IT IN MY HAND--	IT WAS GIVEN TO ME BY	454	5
THE BRANCHES ON MY HAND	I AM ALIVE--I GUESS--	470	2
I'D COUNT THEM ON MY HAND,	IF YOU WERE COMING IN	511	10
BLAME THE LITTLE [EMPTY / CHILDISH] HAND	SWEET--YOU FORGOT--BUT I	523	6
I ALMOST STROVE TO CLASP HIS HAND,	I TRIED TO THINK A	532	16
I TOOK MY POWER IN MY HAND--	I TOOK MY POWER IN MY	540	1
IS FASHIONED FOR [FITTED TO] HIS HAND--	'TIS ONE BY ONE--THE	545	16
AND BORE IT IN MY HAND--	A DYING TIGER--MOANED	566	4
AS A HAND DID TRY TO CHALK THE SUN	I FOUND THE WORDS TO	581	4
MY HAND, WITH TREMBLING CARE	I YEARS HAD BEEN FROM	609	18
LIKE MINE--FOR NOT A FOOT--NOR HAND--	I WATCHED THE MOON	629	11
THE SMALLEST [FINEST] GAMBOGE HAND	YOU'LL KNOW HER--BY HER	634	2
FROM AN EMPEROR'S HAND--	PROMISE THIS--WHEN YOU	648	6
WILL REFUND [REWARD / REPAY] THE HAND--	SOIL OF FLINT, IF STEADY	681	2
STIRRED BY A FRIEND'S HAND--	THE WORLD--FEELS DUSTY	715	7
UPON THE FURTHER HAND--	YOU TAUGHT ME WAITING	740	12
THEN NATURE RAISED A COLORED HAND	A DROP FELL ON THE APPLE	794	V 15
HE FLUNG A HAND FULL AT THE PLAIN--	THE WIND BEGUN TO KNEAD	824	3
A HAND FULL AT THE SKY--	THE WIND BEGUN TO KNEAD	824	4
TO PERISH IN HER HAND!	BE MINE THE DOOM--	845	3
IT--MAY JOLT THE HAND	CRISIS IS A HAIR	889	13
SHALL STAND TO OUR RIGHT HAND--	SWEET, TO HAVE HAD THEM	901	5
TASTES DEATH--THE FIRST--TO HAND [PASS / PROVE] THE STING	LOVE--IS THAT LATER	924	5
HOW FAR LEFT HAND THE SEPULCHRE	HOW FAR IS IT TO HEAVEN?	929	7
THE GULF BETWEEN THE HAND AND HER	THE LADY FEEDS HER	941	5
THE "BIRD WITHIN THE HAND"	WHICH IS BEST? HEAVEN--	1012	5
THAN THE HAND OF FRIEND	FAR FROM LOVE THE	1021	6
WITH HAT IN HAND, POLITE AND NEW	THE CRICKETS SANG	1104	7
A DIAMOND ON THE HAND	A DIAMOND ON THE HAND	1108	1
EXCEPT FOR IT'S MARAUDING HAND	IMMORTAL IS AN AMPLE	1205	7
AT DISTANCE THAN AT HAND.	I WORKED FOR CHAFF AND	1269	8
I TAKE THEE BY THE HAND--	THE SPIDER AS AN ARTIST	1275	8
WARM IN HER HAND THESE ACCENTS LIE	WARM IN HER HAND THESE	1313	1
A PENCIL IN AN IDOL'S [DAINTY] HAND	DEATH WARRANTS ARE	1375	4
NO HAND HATH [HAS] HE--	HIS MANSION IN THE POOL	1379	10
UNCOVERED BY THE HAND	LONG YEARS APART--CAN	1383	6
I FIND ONE ON MY HAND	HOW SOFT A CATERPILLAR	1448	2
IT'S JOURNEY NEVER WAKES MY HAND	HOW SOFT A CATERPILLAR	1448	V
FASHIONED BY THY CANDID HAND	"HEAVENLY FATHER"--TAKE	1461	3
THEY WENT TO GOD'S RIGHT HAND--	THOSE--DYING THEN,	1551	3
THAT HAND IS AMPUTATED NOW	THOSE--DYING THEN,	1551	4
WERE SHINING IN YOUR [ONE'S] HAND.	TO SEE HER IS A PICTURE	1568	8

	FIRST LINE	POEM	LINE
HAND (CONTINUED)			
FROM THESE [THOSE] WITHIN MY HAND	COSMOPOLITES WITHOUT A	1589	4
WITH MARTIAL HAND SHE STROKES THE HAIR	WHO IS IT SEEKS MY	1598	5
HE SHALL NOT TAKE THY HAND	BACK FROM THE CORDIAL	1625	2
TO PAY FOR THY RIGHT HAND	I DID NOT REACH THEE	1664	13
HAST THOU A HAND OR FOOT	THE LOOK OF THEE, WHAT	1689	2
HER HAND WAS WHITER THAN THE SPERM	HER FACE WAS IN A BED OF	1722	3
LOVING THE HAND THAT SENT IT	I'VE GOT AN ARROW HERE.	1729	2
THE HAND THAT TENDS,	WHICH MISSES MOST,	1759	2
BECAUSE THE HAND IS GONE?	WHICH MISSES MOST,	1759	5
HANDED			
BE SLOWLY HANDED BACK--	TRIUMPH--MAY BE OF	455	10
WORDS ARE HANDED [LANGUAGE IS DRIVEN] AWAY--	WHATEVER IT IS--SHE HAS	1204	8
WAS HANDED NATURE TWICE--	A SPARROW TOOK A SLICE	1211	4
AND HANDED TO THE TREES	THE SUN RETIRED TO A	1693	8
THEN HANDED ME MY BEING'S WORTH--	I TOOK ONE DRAUGHT OF	1725	7
HANDLE			
HANDLE THE ADAMANTINE FINGERS	HOW MANY TIMES THESE LOW	187	7
IDENTITY TO QUESTION [HANDLE]	AS ONE DOES SICKNESS	957	11
HANDLED			
AND HANDLED WITH A CHAIN--	MUCH MADNESS IS DIVINEST	435	8
WE HANDLED DESTINIES, AS COOL--	WE TALKED AS GIRLS DO--	586	5
HANDS			
HANDS BUSTLED AT THE MOORINGS--	WENT UP A YEAR THIS	93	19
I CLAP MY HANDS TO SEE--	A SOMETHING IN A	122	9
THE HANDS STILL HUG THE TARDY GLASS--	I BRING AN UNACCUSTOMED	132	8
AND HANDS--BESEECHING--THROWN!	TWO SWIMMERS WRESTLED ON	201	9
WHEN KATIE KNEELS, THEIR LOVING HANDS STILL CLASP HER PIOUS KNEE--	WHEN KATIE WALKS, THIS	222	3
MORE HANDS--TO HOLD--THESE ARE BUT TWO--	A SINGLE SCREW OF FLESH	263	13
AND HANDS--SO SLIGHT--	A MIEN TO MOVE A QUEEN--	283	13
AND SHAPE MY HANDS--	I GOT SO I COULD HEAR	293	17
HANDS--NOT SO STOUT--HOISTED THEM--IN WITNESS--	UNTO LIKE STORY--TROUBLE	295	19
AND OUR NEW HANDS	WE PLAY AT PASTE--	320	6
CLUTCHED TIGHT, BY GREEDY HANDS--	THERE CAME A DAY AT	322	18
WHEN THRONES ACCOST MY HANDS--	MY REWARD FOR BEING, WAS	343	6
I FELT MY LIFE WITH BOTH MY HANDS	I FELT MY LIFE WITH BOTH	351	1
AND YET, WITH AMBER HANDS--	THE MOON IS DISTANT FROM	429	2
TO HANDS I CANNOT SEE--	THIS IS MY LETTER TO THE	441	6
EXTENDED HEMPEN HANDS--	I STARTED EARLY--TOOK MY	520	6
STILL--STILL--MY HANDS ABOVE	ME PROVE IT NOW--WHOEVER	537	10
OR CLASPS A ROCK, WITH BOTH HIS HANDS--	THE BLACK BERRY--WEARS A	554	7
AND TAKE THE SUNSHINE IN MY HANDS,	MY FIRST WELL DAY--SINCE	574	3
THEN BOTH HER HANDS OF HAZE	MY FIRST WELL DAY--SINCE	574	22
IN UNPERCEIVED HANDS--	THE SPIDER HOLDS A	605	2
TO STILL IT'S NOISY [HELP IT'S VACANT] HANDS--	AT LEISURE IS THE SOUL	618	8
DID BLOCK THE GILDED HANDS--	I THINK THE LONGEST HOUR	635	6
THE SPREADING WIDE MY NARROW HANDS	I DWELL IN POSSIBILITY--	657	11
THE CHILDISH HANDS THAT TEAZED FOR PENCE	THE BEGGAR LAD--DIES	717	13
SHOULD EVER THESE EXPLORING HANDS	I PLAY AT RICHES--TO	801	17
THE DUST DID SCOOP ITSELF LIKE HANDS--	THE WIND BEGUN TO KNEAD	824	7
AND THEN, AS IF THE HANDS	THE WIND BEGUN TO KNEAD	824	16
JUST AS HE SPOKE IT FROM HIS HANDS	JUST AS HE SPOKE IT FROM	848	1
AS HANDS THE GRAVE HAD GRIMED	ON THAT DEAR FRAME THE	940	6
HAVE PERISHED IN MY HANDS	IT BLOOMED AND DROPT, A	978	14
WHAT MISERS WRING THEIR HANDS TONIGHT	A MINE THERE IS NO MAN	1117	7
"THE HOUSE NOT MADE WITH HANDS" IT WAS--	I SUED THE NEWS--YET	1360	3
HANDSOME			
AND IN THE HANDSOME SKIES	I NEVER FELT AT HOME--	413	2
HANG			
UPON THINE ARROW HANG!	A DAY! HELP! HELP!	42	8
TO HANG OUR HEAD--OSTENSIBLY--	TO HANG OUR HEAD--	105	1
AS WATCHERS HANG UPON THE EAST,	AS WATCHERS HANG UPON	121	1
SO I CAN HANG IT IN MY ROOM--	MAKE ME A PICTURE OF THE	188	2
PROVIDED IT DO HOPELESS--HANG--	"HEAVEN"--IS WHAT I	239	3
TILL WEIGHTS--WILL HANG--	I CAN WADE GRIEF--	252	12
MY STOCKING HANG TOO HIGH	'TWAS JUST THIS TIME,	445	18
AND HANG THEIR FACES SO--	WE DO NOT PLAY ON GRAVES	467	6
AND GOLDEN HANG--WHILE FARTHER UP--	A SOLEMN THING WITHIN	483	3
AND LATER HANG--	EXCEPT THE SMALLER SIZE	1067	6
AS MAKES ONE HIDE [HANG] IT'S HEAD	THAT THIS SHOULD FEEL	1112 V	4
HANGED			
WHO WILL NOT SERVE THE SOVREIGN, BE HANGED ON FATAL TREE.	AWAKE YE MUSES NINE,	1	10
HANGING			
AND WINDOWS HANGING LOW,	I KNOW SOME LONELY	289	4
INDIFFERENT HANGING [GATHERED] NOW--	HIS BILL IS CLASPED--HIS	1102	4
HANGS			
HANGS SO DISTANT HEAVEN--	DISTRUSTFUL OF THE	20	15
THE SACKCLOTH--HANGS UPON THE NAIL--	IT WOULD NEVER BE COMMON	430	30
THERE HANGS A SMALLER [MINOR] EAR	THE SPIRIT IS THE	733	6
WHEN THE BEE HANGS ALL NOON IN THE BUTTERCUP	WHAT SHALL I DO WHEN THE	956	7
HAPLY			
IF, HAPLY, THRO' A DREAM, TO PEEP	I HAVE A KING, WHO DOES	103	5
IF, HAPLY, MINE MAY BE THE DROP	I BRING AN UNACCUSTOMED	132	18
IF, HAPLY, ANY SAY TO ME	I BRING AN UNACCUSTOMED	132	20
HAPLY--YOUR SUMMER NIGHT TO CHARM--	KILL YOUR BALM--AND IT'S	238	4
OR HAPLY, MISTLETOE--	THE ONLY GHOST I EVER	274	8
AND HAPLY, IN THE WORLD--	THE BEGGAR LAD--DIES	717	4

	FIRST LINE	POEM	LINE
HAPLY (CONTINUED)			
IF HAPLY--SHE MIGHT NOT DESPISE	PRECIOUS TO ME--SHE	727	7
OF SHADOW, OR OF SQUIRREL, HAPLY--	FOUR TREES--UPON A	742	11
OUR MUTUAL FRAME--THAT HAPLY	NO OTHER CAN REDUCE	982	V 7
HAPPEN			
THAT HAPPEN ON THE SOUL	THE TINT I CANNOT TAKE--	627	10
HAPPENED			
SINCE MIDNIGHT--HAPPENED--SAY--	A TONGUE--TO TELL HIM I	400	13
HAPPENING			
THE ANGELS--HAPPENING THAT WAY	A POOR--TORN HEART-- A	78	9
HAPPENING IN AFTER AGES	SHELLS FROM THE COAST	693	3
LODGED BY DESIGN OR HAPPENING	THIS IS A BLOSSOM OF THE	945	3
HAPPENS			
THAT HAPPENS TO ME NOW.	IF ALL THE GRIEFS I AM	1726	8
HAPPILY			
OR, HAPPILY [POSSIBLY], RENOWN--	THE WAY TO KNOW THE	1279	20
HAPPINESS			
SUCH IS THE FORCE [STRENGTH] OF HAPPINESS--	SUCH IS THE FORCE OF	787	1
THE HAPPINESS ATONE--	I THOUGHT THE TRAIN	1449	12
WE REPRIMAND THE HAPPINESS	OF GOD WE ASK ONE FAVOR,	1601	7
HAPPY			
THE LIFE DOTH PROVE THE PRECEPT, WHO OBEY SHALL HAPPY BE,	AWAKE YE MUSES NINE,	1	9
THE MORNING--HAPPY THING--	THE SUN--JUST TOUCHED	232	2
THE HAPPY WINDS--THEIR TIMBRELS TOOK--	THE DAY CAME SLOW--TILL	304	9
A HAPPY LIP--BREAKS SUDDEN--	A HAPPY LIP--BREAKS	353	1
"HAPPY"? WHICH IS WISER--	IT IS DEAD--FIND IT--	417	3
GOING TO HIM [HER]! HAPPY LETTER!	GOING TO HIM! HAPPY	494	1
UNTIL TOMORROW [THE EVENING]--HAPPY LETTER! [AH! BE BASHFUL]	GOING TO HIM! HAPPY	494	24
THE WEALTHY [HAPPY] FLY, UPON HIS PANE--	I ENVY SEAS, WHEREON HE	498	11
THE HAPPY--HAPPY LEAVES--	I ENVY SEAS, WHEREON HE	498	12
THE HAPPY--HAPPY LEAVES--	I ENVY SEAS, WHEREON HE	498	12
HAPPY IT BE FOR YOU--A BEGGAR'S--	SWEET--YOU FORGOT--BUT I	523	7
SHE'S HAPPY, WITH A NEW CONTENT--	SHE'S HAPPY, WITH A NEW	535	1
UPON MY THRONGING [CROWDED / HAPPY] MIND--	MY WORTHINESS IS ALL MY	751	8
TOO HAPPY--FOR [IN] MY SPARROW'S CHANCE--	GOD GAVE A LOAF TO EVERY	791	7
I WAS SO HAPPY I FORGOT	I CANNOT BUY IT--'TIS	840	4
HOW HAPPY I WAS IF I COULD FORGET	HOW HAPPY I WAS IF I	898	1
OH, HAPPY AIR!	AIR HAS NO RESIDENCE, NO	1060	4
THE JOY THAT IN HIS HAPPY THROAT	HIS BILL IS CLASPED--HIS	1102	5
BABBLE [CAROL] OF THE HAPPY	FORTITUDE INCARNATE	1217	5
HOW HAPPY IS [INVINCIBLE] THE LITTLE STONE	HOW HAPPY IS THE LITTLE	1510	1
THE SACRED STEALTH [HAPPY GUILT] OF BOY AND GIRL	BLISS IS THE PLAYTHING	1553	3
THE HAPPY [THE CHEMIST / THE RANSOMED / A LOVER] MAY [CAN] REPAY,	THE FARTHEST THUNDER	1581	10
TO ANY HAPPY FLOWER	APPARENTLY WITH NO	1624	2
I AM SO HAPPY I BELIEVE	IF ALL THE GRIEFS I AM	1726	3
THE WORDS THE HAPPY SAY	THE WORDS THE HAPPY SAY	1750	1
AS HAPPY IN HER CRIB [BED] OF DUST	THIS DOCILE ONE INTER	1752	V 7
TOO HAPPY TIME DISSOLVES ITSELF	TOO HAPPY TIME DISSOLVES	1774	1
HARANGUER			
HARANGUER--I CAN OVERTAKE--	I FEAR A MAN OF FRUGAL	543	3
HARASS			
I'D HARASS GOD	SHOULD YOU BUT FAIL AT--	226	6
AS HARASS US--LIKE LIFE--AND DEATH--	I WATCHED THE MOON	629	25
AND TROUBLE [HARASS] ME--NO MORE--	THE BIRDS REPORTED FROM	743	8
TO HARASS TO FATIGUE	SEVERER SERVICE OF	786	10
CAN HARASS ME NO MORE--	THIS CHASM, SWEET, UPON	858	20
HARBOR			
OR ANY [BEFORE THE] HARBOR BE--	I MANY TIMES THOUGHT	739	8
WITH THEM WOULD HARBOR BE--	AN HOUR IS A SEA	825	3
HARD			
DID WRESTLE LONG AND HARD--	A LITTLE EAST OF JORDAN,	59	4
THEN STRUGGLING HARD	FROM COCOON FORTH A	354	12
A HATEFUL, HARD, SUCCESSFUL FACE,	A FACE DEVOID OF LOVE OR	1711	2
HARDENED			
HARDENED [FASTENED] WITH I KNOW--	WHETHER THEY HAVE	1329	8
HARDER			
THAT LOOKS A HARDER SKILL TO US--	ONLY A SHRINE, BUT MINE	918	9
'TIS HARDER KNOWING IT IS DUE	WHILE WE WERE FEARING IT	1277	7
HARDEST			
THIS IS THE HARDEST MIRACLE	TO DIE--WITHOUT THE	1017	3
ALL MEN FOR HONOR HARDEST WORK	ALL MEN FOR HONOR	1193	1
HARDLY			
I'M HARDLY JUSTIFIED	THE WINTERS ARE SO SHORT	403	2
HER TEETH CAN HARDLY STAND--	SHE SIGHTS A BIRD--SHE	507	6
HER NIGHT DOTH HARDLY RECOMPENSE	SHE HIDETH HER THE LAST	557	3
HARE			
HOUND CANNOT OVERTAKE THE HARE	THIS HEART THAT BROKE SO	145	5
HAREBELL			
DID THE HAREBELL LOOSE HER GIRDLE	DID THE HAREBELL LOOSE	213	1
WOULD THE BEE THE HAREBELL HALLOW	DID THE HAREBELL LOOSE	213	3
HARK			
IMPELLED TO HARK--	THE HEART HAS MANY DOORS	1567	4
HARKS			
HARKS FOR [DETECTS] THE MEADOW BIRD--	THE DOOMED--REGARD THE	294	6
HARM			
THE ROBBING--COULD NOT HARM--	THIS WAS A POET--IT IS	448	14

	FIRST LINE	POEM	LINE
HARM (CONTINUED)			
WHAT HARM? MEN DIE--EXTERNALLY--	WE DREAM--IT IS GOOD WE	531	5
THE HARM THEY DID--WAS SHORT [BRIEF]--AND SINCE	'TIS TRUE--THEY SHUT ME	538	9
SOME THOUSANDS--ON THE HARM--	I MEASURE EVERY GRIEF I	561	18
NONE STIR [HARM] THE SECOND TIME--	MY LIFE HAD STOOD--A	754	18
SPECTRE CANNOT HARM--	WHEN I HOPED I FEARED--	1181	5
HE IS KING [PRINCE] OF HARM--	WHEN I HOPED I FEARED--	1181	V 7
IT WILL NOT HARM HER MAGIC PACE	BECAUSE HE LOVES HER	1229	5
THE HARM OF YEARS IS ON HIM--	THE HARM OF YEARS IS ON	1280	1
HATE CANNOT HARM	THE RAT IS THE CONCISEST	1356	7
THERE WAS NO HARM IN EARTH OR SKY-- . . .	IT WAS A QUIET SEEMING	1419	2
HARMLESS			
HARMLESS--AS STREAKS OF METEOR--	THROUGH THE STRAIT PASS	792	7
HARMONY			
NAY--NATURE IS HARMONY [MELODY]--	"NATURE" IS WHAT WE SEE	668	8
HARMS			
ARE SCARCE ACCOUNTED [COMPUTED]--HARMS-- .	ONE ANGUISH--IN A CROWD	565	12
HARRIET			
AND HARRIET, AND SUSAN, AND SHE WITH CURLING HAIR!	AWAKE YE MUSES NINE,	1	32
HARROWING			
WITH HARROWING IODINE--	THE LOVE A LIFE CAN SHOW	673	12
THIS HARROWING EVENT	A SINGLE CLOVER PLANK	1343	13
A [THE] COURTEOUS, YET [BUT] HARROWING GRACE,	AS IMPERCEPTIBLY AS	1540	11
HARSH			
FROM ACCENT HARSH, OR RUTHLESS WORD-- . .	WHERE I HAVE LOST, I	104	6
HARVEST			
YOUR CHANCE IN HARVEST MOVES	A SOLEMN THING WITHIN	483	14
WITH US, 'TIS HARVEST ALL THE YEAR	THE PRODUCTS OF MY FARM	1025	5
HARVESTS			
ACRES OF JOINTS [SEAMS], WHERE HARVESTS WERE,	IT SIFTS FROM LEADEN	311	15
HASPS			
TRY--CAN YOU LIFT THE HASPS OF STEEL! . .	HOW MANY TIMES THESE LOW	187	4
HASTE			
HASTE! LEST WHILE YOU'RE LAGGING	HEART! WE WILL FORGET	47	7
MAKE HASTE--[COME NEAR] THE SCRUPLE! DEATH BE SCANT	ME PROVE IT NOW--WHOEVER	537	3
WE SLOWLY DROVE--HE KNEW NO HASTE	BECAUSE I COULD NOT STOP	712	5
THE SUN AND MOON MUST MAKE THEIR HASTE-- .	THE SUN AND MOON MUST	871	1
ALL MEN MEET [PASS / HASTE] AS IF	AFTER THE SUN COMES OUT	1148	5
INERTIA OR HASTE--	HIS MANSION IN THE POOL	1379	V
HASTEN			
THEN THEY WILL HASTEN TO THE DOOR	THEY WONT FROWN ALWAYS--	874	5
WE HASTEN TO ADORN--	TO DISAPPEAR ENHANCES--	1209	12
HASTENED			
I--HASTENED TO DEMAND	SEVERER SERVICE OF	786	2
DECADE HAD HASTENED [HURRIED / GATHERED] TO DECADE--	A LITTLE SNOW WAS HERE	1444	4
HASTENING			
HASTENING FROM FAR JOURNEY--	NOBODY KNOWS THIS LITTLE	35	7
HASTILY			
AND HURRIEDLY [HASTILY] WITHDREW	ALONE AND IN A	1167	8
HAT			
WILL TAKE HIS HAT, AND RUN!	"SIC TRANSIT GLORIA	3	56
AFORETIME IN MY HAT--	"ARCTURUS" IS HIS OTHER	70	14
A LITTLE PALMLEAF HAT WAS ALL, ...	I MET A KING THIS	166	3
A LORD, MIGHT DARE TO LIFT THE HAT	WAIT TILL THE MAJESTY OF	171	13
A CRAPE UPON THE HAT--	TO DIE--TAKES JUST A	255	6
NOR THREATEN [JOGGLE / OGLE] A HAT--	THE WIND DID'NT COME	316	4
THE JUGGLER'S HAT HER COUNTRY IS--	THE JUGGLER'S HAT HER	330	1
HER VERY HAT--	'TWAS THE OLD--ROAD--	344	14
I TIE MY HAT--I CREASE MY SHAWL--	I TIE MY HAT--I CREASE	443	1
I'LL SEND THE FEATHER FROM MY HAT!	I'LL SEND THE FEATHER	687	1
THE SUNSHINE THREW HIS HAT AWAY--	A DROP FELL ON THE APPLE	794	11
WHOSE UNCLAIMED HAT AND JACKET	HOW THE WATERS CLOSED	923	7
AND MAKES ONE LIFT ONE'S HAT	IT IS AN HONORABLE	946	2
WITH HAT IN HAND, POLITE AND NEW	THE CRICKETS SANG	1104	7
WE MISS HIS STATED HAT.	THAT ODD OLD MAN IS DEAD	1130	2
NOVEMBER HUNG HIS GRANITE HAT	THE DAY GREW SMALL,	1140	7
OF THE DUCAL HAT--	TELL AS A MARKSMAN--WERE	1152	15
PUT DOWN YOUR HAT--	DEAR MARCH--COME IN--	1320	4
SUMMER LAID HER SIMPLE HAT	SUMMER LAID HER SIMPLE	1363	1
THAT WILL NOT LIFT IT'S HAT--	OH GIVE IT MOTION--DECK	1527	8
LOOSED THE MOON HER SILVER HAT	LIGHTLY STEPPED A YELLOW	1672	3
HATE			
I HAD NO TIME TO HATE--	I HAD NO TIME TO HATE--	478	1
HATE CANNOT HARM	THE RAT IS THE CONCISEST	1356	7
THE PALATE OF THE HATE DEPARTS--	MINE ENEMY IS GROWING	1509	3
HATED			
THEY HATED MOTION SO--	THIS SLOW DAY MOVED	1120	4
WE HATED DEATH AND HATED LIFE	THE FROST OF DEATH WAS	1136	18
WE HATED DEATH AND HATED LIFE	THE FROST OF DEATH WAS	1136	18
AND THEN I HATED GLORY	MY TRIUMPH LASTED TILL	1227	7
I TASTED WHEAT AND HATED CHAFF	I WORKED FOR CHAFF AND	1269	5
THAT MAKES IT HATED SO--	ADVANCE IS LIFE'S	1652	4
HATEFUL			
A HATEFUL, HARD, SUCCESSFUL FACE, ...	A FACE DEVOID OF LOVE OR	1711	2
HATS			
THEIR HUNDRED HATS THEY RAISE!	ONE DIGNITY DELAYS FOR	98	12

	FIRST LINE	POEM	LINE
HATS (CONTINUED)			
TILL SERAPHS SWING THEIR SNOWY HATS--	I TASTE A LIQUOR NEVER	214	13
LITTLE BOYS HATS--AND STUBBLE--	THE WIND DID'NT COME	316	18
HAUGHTY			
HIS HAUGHTY--SPANGLED HEMS--	THE SUN--JUST TOUCHED	232	10
WAS HAUGHTY AND BETRAYED.	I WORKED FOR CHAFF AND	1269	2
HAULED			
AND HE HAS HAULED AWAY.	SO MUCH OF HEAVEN HAS	1228	12
HAUNT			
HAUNT THE PERENNIAL BLOOM--	FOR THIS--ACCEPTED	195	11
THE DISTANCE WOULD NOT HAUNT ME SO--	EXCEPT THE HEAVEN HAD	472	3
TO HAUNT--TILL TIME HAVE DROPPED	JOY TO HAVE MERITED THE	788	21
AND HAUNT THE WORLD.	THERE IS NO SILENCE IN	1004	4
HAUNTED			
HAUNTED BY NATIVE LANDS, THE WHILE--	TO LEARN THE TRANSPORT	167	7
ONE NEED NOT BE A CHAMBER--TO BE HAUNTED--	ONE NEED NOT BE A	670	1
HAVE NEVER PASSED [SCALED] HER HAUNTED HOUSE,	WHAT MYSTERY PERVADES A	1400	19
HAUNTING			
HAUNTING THE HEART--	YOU SEE I CANNOT SEE--	253	12
AND HAUNTING ACTUALIZE--TO LAST	JOY TO HAVE MERITED THE	788	23
HINDERING--HAUNTING--PERISHING--	FAIRER THROUGH FADING--	938	4
HAUNTS			
HER SIMPLE HAUNTS BEYOND!	SO BASHFUL WHEN I SPIED	91	8
HAUNTS CANDLES IN BRAZIL.	A MOTH THE HUE OF THIS	841	2
ABOVE THE HAUNTS OF MEN--	A WINGED SPARK DOTH SOAR	1468	6
HAVENS			
DO THE BLUE HAVENS BY THE HAND	A POOR--TORN HEART-- A	78	15
HAVING			
WHICH HAVING SOWN WITH CARE,	I HAD SOME THINGS THAT I	116	6
WHOSE HAVING LIVED IS HELD BY US IN NOBLE HOLIDAY	LEST ANY DOUBT THAT WE	1156	2
NOR WE WHO HAVING ONCE INHALED [WAYLAID] IT--	IN MANY AND REPORTLESS	1382	11
THAT HAVING BREATHED	OH WHAT A GRACE IS THIS,	1615	3
HAVOC			
THE RUIN [HAVOC / DAMAGE] WAS WITHIN	A GREAT HOPE FELL	1123	3
HAWORTH			
IN QUIET "HAWORTH" LAID.	ALL OVERGROWN BY CUNNING	148	4
HAY			
AND LO--MY PRICELESS HAY	I CAUTIOUS, SCANNED MY	178	8
NOR STOP TO PLAY WITH THE HAY--	THE WIND DID'NT COME	316	3
TO SWEET PAUSES OF HAY--	THE WIND DID'NT COME	316	15
I WISH I WERE A HAY--	THE GRASS SO LITTLE HAS	333	20
WHERE MEN MADE HAY--	FROM COCOON FORTH A	354	11
AND MEN THAT MADE THE HAY--	FROM COCOON FORTH A	354	23
WHERE IS THE HAY?	ANSWER JULY--	386	4
IT'S TIME O' YEAR FOR HAY.	I'M SORRY FOR THE DEAD--	529	4
GO DOWN THE FIELDS TO "HAY"--	I'M SORRY FOR THE DEAD--	529	20
HAZARD			
BY JUST SUCH A HAZARD	SOUL, WILT THOU TOSS	139	2
FROM SINKING [IN CRISIS / IN HAZARD] IN THE SKY--	A SINGLE CLOVER PLANK	1343	4
HAZARDOUS			
A MERCIFUL [HAZARDOUS] MISTAKE	DEATH WARRANTS ARE	1375	3
HAZE			
OH LAST COMMUNION IN THE HAZE--	THESE ARE THE DAYS WHEN	130	14
AND THAT SIDE OF THE HAZE--	BESIDES THE AUTUMN POETS	131	4
WHERE BE THE HAZE--	ANSWER JULY--	386	16
THEN BOTH HER HANDS OF HAZE	MY FIRST WELL DAY--SINCE	574	22
THROUGH HAZE OF BURIAL--	MIDSUMMER, WAS IT, WHEN	962	8
THE MOUNTAINS STOOD IN HAZE--	THE MOUNTAINS STOOD IN	1278	1
HAZEL			
PROVE ME--MY HAZEL [SWIMMING] WITNESSES	JOY TO HAVE MERITED THE	788	11
THROUGH FAITH--MY HAZEL EYE	WHAT I SEE NOT, I BETTER	939	2
HE			
NO MORE HE SINGETH MOURNFUL, HER SADNESS SHE DOTH LOSE.	AWAKE YE MUSES NINE,	1	*20
HE STOOD AS NEAR	I NEVER TOLD THE BURIED	11	5
HE REACHES [COMES TO] TOWN AT NIGHTFALL--	THE GUEST IS GOLD AND	15	5
HE STOPS AT EVERY DOOR--	THE GUEST IS GOLD AND	15	6
HE, TOO, DID FLY AWAY--	I HAD A GUINEA GOLDEN--	23	12
AND HE NO CONSOLATION	I HAD A GUINEA GOLDEN--	23	35
I [HE] SCANNED THEIR TRINKETS CURIOUS--	I ROBBED THE WOODS--	41	6
I [HE] GRASPED--I [HE] BORE AWAY--	I ROBBED THE WOODS--	41	7
I [HE] GRASPED--I [HE] BORE AWAY--	I ROBBED THE WOODS--	41	7
THROUGH FAITH IN ONE HE MET NOT,	COULD LIVE--DID LIVE--	43	4
YOU MAY FORGET THE WARMTH HE GAVE--	HEART! WE WILL FORGET	47	3
FOUND HE HAD WORSTED GOD!	A LITTLE EAST OF JORDAN,	59	16
AS HE DEFEATED--DYING--	SUCCESS IS COUNTED	67	9
HE SITS ERECT IN "CABINETS"--	"ARCTURUS" IS HIS OTHER	70	15
"THEY HAVE NOT CHOSEN ME," HE SAID,	"THEY HAVE NOT CHOSEN ME	85	1
HE--WAKING--FINDS THE FLOWER THERE--	THE DAISY FOLLOWS SOFT	106	4
AND GOD, THAT HE CALLED HIS,	I HAD SOME THINGS THAT I	116	2
HE CLAIMS THE PRETTY ACRE,	I HAD SOME THINGS THAT I	116	7
AND HE TURNS SATIRIST!	MY FRIEND ATTACKS MY	118	4
BLESS GOD, HE WENT AS SOLDIERS,	BLESS GOD, HE WENT AS	147	1
GRANT GOD, HE CHARGE THE BRAVEST	BLESS GOD, HE WENT AS	147	3
PERHAPS HE DOES'NT KNOW THE HOUSE--	DYING! DYING IN THE	158	7
HE HAD NOT ON A CROWN INDEED,	I MET A KING THIS	166	2
AND HE WAS BAREFOOT, I'M AFRAID!	I MET A KING THIS	166	4
BUT SURE I AM HE ERMINE WORE	I MET A KING THIS	166	5

HE (CONTINUED)	FIRST LINE	POEM	LINE
AND SURE I AM, THE CREST HE BORE	I MET A KING THIS	166	7
SOMETIME, HE DWELLETH IN THE GRASS!	A FUZZY FELLOW, WITHOUT	173	5
FROM WHICH HE DOTH DESCEND IN PLUSH	A FUZZY FELLOW, WITHOUT	173	7
HE TAKETH DAMASK RESIDENCE--	A FUZZY FELLOW, WITHOUT	173	11
HE WAS WEAK, AND I WAS STRONG--THEN--	HE WAS WEAK, AND I WAS	190	1
SO HE LET ME LEAD HIM IN--	HE WAS WEAK, AND I WAS	190	2
I WAS WEAK, AND HE WAS STRONG THEN--	HE WAS WEAK, AND I WAS	190	3
'TWAS'NT DARK--FOR HE WENT--TOO--	HE WAS WEAK, AND I WAS	190	6
'TWAS'NT LOUD, FOR HE SAID NOUGHT--	HE WAS WEAK, AND I WAS	190	7
HE STROVE--AND I STROVE--TOO--	HE WAS WEAK, AND I WAS	190	11
HE WILL TELL ME WHAT "PETER" PROMISED--	I SHALL KNOW WHY--WHEN	193	5
NOR TO DREAM--HE AND ME--	WE DONT CRY--TIM AND I,	196	9
I--TOO--IF HE--	WE DONT CRY--TIM AND I,	196	24
HE PARDONED ME!	I STOLE THEM FROM A BEE	200	4
HE FORGOT--AND I--REMEMBERED--	HE FORGOT--AND I--	203	1
BECAUSE--BECAUSE IF HE SHOULD DIE	I SHOULD NOT DARE TO	205	2
UNTIL HE LET YOU IN!	SHOULD YOU BUT FAIL AT--	226	7
TEACH HIM--WHEN HE MAKES THE NAMES--	TEACH HIM--WHEN HE MAKES	227	1
HE AND I--REVEL--	WE--BEE AND I--LIVE BY	230	13
SUPPOSED THAT HE HAD COME TO DWELL--	THE SUN--JUST TOUCHED	232	3
IF HE DISSOLVE--THEN--THERE IS NOTHING--MORE--	IF HE DISSOLVE--THEN--	236	1
WILL HE HEED?	IF HE DISSOLVE--THEN--	236	15
HE--IS MORE THAN A FIRMAMENT--FROM ME--	AH, MOON--AND STAR!	240	16
OH, DEAR,--I GUESS IF HE WERE A BOY--	OVER THE FENCE--	251	8
HE'D--CLIMB--IF HE COULD!	OVER THE FENCE--	251	9
WHEN HE--SURRENDERED TO THE SUNRISE--	PUT UP MY LUTE!	261	9
HE PUT THE BELT AROUND MY LIFE--	HE PUT THE BELT AROUND	273	1
HE HAD [WORE] NO SANDAL ON HIS FOOT--	THE ONLY GHOST I EVER	274	3
HE CAN LEAN AGAINST THE GRAVE,	IF YOUR NERVE, DENY YOU	292	3
IF HE FEAR TO SWERVE--	IF YOUR NERVE, DENY YOU	292	4
WHERE HE TURNED SO, AND I TURNED--HOW [LET GO]--	I GOT SO I COULD HEAR	293	7
WERE GREATER THAN ITSELF--THOUGH HE	THE ONE WHO COULD REPEAT	307	2
AND HE--COULD REPRODUCE THE SUN--	THE ONE WHO COULD REPEAT	307	4
WHILE HE--WAS MAKING ONE--	I SEND TWO SUNSETS--	308	4
HE FUMBLES AT YOUR SOUL	HE FUMBLES AT YOUR SOUL	315	1
HE STUNS YOU BY DEGREES--	HE FUMBLES AT YOUR SOUL	315	4
IF [WHEN] HE LEAVE A BUR AT THE DOOR	THE WIND DID'NT COME	316	7
WE KNOW [SAY] HE HAS CLIMBED A FIR--	THE WIND DID'NT COME	316	8
IF HE BRING ODORS OF CLOVERS--	THE WIND DID'NT COME	316	11
THEN HE HAS BEEN WITH THE MOWERS--	THE WIND DID'NT COME	316	13
A WAY HE HAS	THE WIND DID'NT COME	316	V 16
IF HE FLING SAND [DUST], AND PEBBLE--	THE WIND DID'NT COME	316	17
HE--DOES'NT WEARY--	JUST SO--JESUS--RAPS--	317	2
MIGHT HE BUT SPY THE LADY'S [HIDING] SOUL--	JUST SO--JESUS--RAPS--	317	6
WHEN HE--RETIRES--	JUST SO--JESUS--RAPS--	317	7
BUT HOW HE SET--I KNOW NOT--	I'LL TELL YOU HOW THE	318	9
WHO [HE] NEVER HEARD THAT FLESHLESS CHANT--	OF ALL THE SOUNDS	321	27
HE DID NOT KNOW I SAW--	A BIRD CAME DOWN THE	328	2
HE BIT [SHOOK] AN ANGLEWORM IN HALVES	A BIRD CAME DOWN THE	328	3
AND THEN HE DRANK A DEW	A BIRD CAME DOWN THE	328	5
HE GLANCED WITH RAPID EYES	A BIRD CAME DOWN THE	328	9
HE STIRRED HIS VELVET HEAD	A BIRD CAME DOWN THE	328	12
AND HE UNROLLED HIS FEATHERS	A BIRD CAME DOWN THE	328	15
I KNOW THAT HE EXISTS.	I KNOW THAT HE EXISTS.	338	1
HE HAS HID HIS RARE LIFE	I KNOW THAT HE EXISTS.	338	3
THE STIFF HEART QUESTIONS WAS IT HE, THAT BORE,	AFTER GREAT PAIN, A	341	3
BUT THEN--I'M NOT SO STAID--AS HE--	FUNNY--TO BE A CENTURY--	345	4
HE KEEPS HIS SECRETS SAFELY--VERY--	FUNNY--TO BE A CENTURY--	345	5
WERE HE TO TELL--EXTREMELY SORRY	FUNNY--TO BE A CENTURY--	345	6
BUT HE IS MASTERED, NOW,	I DREADED THAT FIRST	348	2
HE HURTS A LITTLE, THOUGH--	I DREADED THAT FIRST	348	4
EACH ONE SALUTES ME, AS HE GOES,	I DREADED THAT FIRST	348	25
BUT HE--IS NOT A MAN--	THEY LEAVE US WITH THE	350	2
AND WHOM HE FOUNDETH, WITH HIS ARM	THEY LEAVE US WITH THE	350	5
WOOS, AS HE STATES US--BY HIS SON--	GOD IS A DISTANT--	357	2
THAT SOWED THE FLOWER, HE PREFERRED--	ALTHOUGH I PUT AWAY HIS	366	5
TO TIMES WHEN HE--WAS YOUNG--	A PRECIOUS--MOULDERING	371	8
HE TRAVERSES--FAMILIAR--	A PRECIOUS--MOULDERING	371	21
HE LIVED--WHERE DREAMS WERE BORN--	A PRECIOUS--MOULDERING	371	24
HE CARED AS MUCH AS ON THE AIR	OF COURSE--I PRAYED--	376	3
AND HE OWNED ALL THE MOURNERS--NOW--	THERE'S BEEN A DEATH, IN	389	15
AND WHATSOEVER MOUTH HE KISSED--	A VISITOR IN MARL--	391	11
AND HE WILL TELL YOU--SKILL IS LATE--	THERE IS A LANGUOR OF	396	13
A MIGHTIER THAN HE--	THERE IS A LANGUOR OF	396	14
BECAUSE HE--NEVER TOLD--	A HOUSE UPON THE HIGHT--	399	12
SAY RUBIES--IF HE HESITATE--	A TONGUE--TO TELL HIM I	400	20
HE--COMPENSATES--IMMEDIATELY--	SOME--WORK FOR	406	3
MORE LIFE--WENT OUT--WHEN HE WENT	MORE LIFE--WENT OUT--	422	1
HAD HE THE POWER TO DREAM	REMOVED FROM ACCIDENT OF	424	10
HE TURNED AWAY!	GOOD MORNING--MIDNIGHT--	425	16
HE NEVER MISSES A DEGREE--	THE MOON IS DISTANT FROM	429	5
HE COMES JUST SO FAR--TOWARD THE TOWN--	THE MOON IS DISTANT FROM	429	7
HE TOLD ME, DEATH WAS DEAD--	DO PEOPLE MOULDER	432	16
NO BONE HAD HE TO BIND HIM--	THE WIND--TAPPED LIKE A	436	9
HIS FINGERS, AS HE PASSED	THE WIND--TAPPED LIKE A	436	14
HE VISITED--STILL FLITTING--	THE WIND--TAPPED LIKE A	436	17
AGAIN, HE TAPPED--'TWAS FLURRIEDLY--	THE WIND--TAPPED LIKE A	436	19

		FIRST LINE	POEM	LINE
HE	(CONTINUED)			
	IF THEN HE HEAR--	PRAYER IS THE LITTLE	437	6
	FAR OFF--HE SIGHS--AND THEREFORE--HOPELESS--	UNDUE SIGNIFICANCE A	439	3
	I [HE] SHOWED HER [ME] HIGHTS SHE [I] NEVER SAW--	I SHOWED HER HIGHTS SHE	446	1
	"WOULD'ST CLIMB," I [HE] SAID?	I SHOWED HER HIGHTS SHE	446	2
	"WITH ME--" I [HE] SAID--WITH ME?	I SHOWED HER HIGHTS SHE	446	4
	I [HE] SHOWED HER [ME] SECRETS--MORNING'S NEST--	I SHOWED HER HIGHTS SHE	446	5
	AND THEN, I [HE] BRAKE MY [HIS] LIFE--AND LO,	I SHOWED HER HIGHTS SHE	446	9
	THE POET--IT IS HE--	THIS WAS A POET--IT IS	448	10
	HE QUESTIONED SOFTLY "WHY I FAILED"?	I DIED FOR BEAUTY--BUT	449	5
	WE BRETHEREN, ARE", HE SAID--	I DIED FOR BEAUTY--BUT	449	8
	THAT HE--LOVED MEN--	SO WELL THAT I CAN LIVE	456	5
	AND THAT--BY RIGHT THAT HE	I LIVE WITH HIM--I SEE	463	6
	TO ANSWER--WHEREFORE WHEN HE PASS	"WHY DO I LOVE" YOU, SIR	480	4
	BECAUSE HE KNOWS--AND	"WHY DO I LOVE" YOU, SIR	480	6
	WHEREFORE IT SHUT--WHEN HE WAS BY--	"WHY DO I LOVE" YOU, SIR	480	12
	BECAUSE HE KNOWS IT CANNOT SPEAK--	"WHY DO I LOVE" YOU, SIR	480	13
	HE SHIFTS THE STEM--A LITTLE--	A SOLEMN THING WITHIN	483	11
	BUT--IF HE [SHE] ASK WHERE YOU ARE HID	GOING TO HIM! HAPPY	494	23
	HE STRAINED MY FAITH--	HE STRAINED MY FAITH--	497	1
	DID HE FIND IT SUPPLE?	HE STRAINED MY FAITH--	497	2
	BUT--DID HE SHATTER--IT?	HE STRAINED MY FAITH--	497	6
	HE DID NEVER SAY--	HE STRAINED MY FAITH--	497	12
	I ENVY SEAS, WHEREON HE RIDES--[THAT BEAR HIM]	I ENVY SEAS, WHEREON HE	498	1
	HE NEVER STOPS, BUT SLACKENS	WITHIN MY GARDEN, RIDES	500	5
	AND PRAISES AS HE GOES,	WITHIN MY GARDEN, RIDES	500	8
	AND HE AND I, PERPLEX US	WITHIN MY GARDEN, RIDES	500	13
	BUT HE, THE BEST LOGICIAN,	WITHIN MY GARDEN, RIDES	500	17
	HE TOUCHED ME, SO I LIVE TO KNOW	HE TOUCHED ME, SO I LIVE	506	1
	HE PARTS HIMSELF--LIKE LEAVES--	HE PARTS HIMSELF--LIKE	517	1
	AND THEN--HE CLOSES UP--	HE PARTS HIMSELF--LIKE	517	2
	AND THEN HE LEANS WITH ALL HIS MIGHT	HE PARTS HIMSELF--LIKE	517	V 3
	AND THEN HE RUNS AGAINST	HE PARTS HIMSELF--LIKE	517	5
	THEN AWAY UPON A JIB--HE GOES--	HE PARTS HIMSELF--LIKE	517	8
	AND MADE AS HE WOULD EAT ME UP--	I STARTED EARLY--TOOK MY	520	13
	AND HE--HE FOLLOWED--CLOSE BEHIND--	I STARTED EARLY--TOOK MY	520	17
	AND HE--HE FOLLOWED--CLOSE BEHIND--	I STARTED EARLY--TOOK MY	520	17
	NO ONE [MAN] HE SEEMED TO KNOW--	I STARTED EARLY--TOOK MY	520	22
	TILL HE BE JUSTIFIED BY DEATH--	HAD I PRESUMED TO HOPE--	522	15
	TO SATIN RACES--HE IS NOUGHT--	I THINK THE HEMLOCK	525	13
	PERHAPS HE--PITIED ME--	I TRIED TO THINK A	532	19
	HE--TOO--COULD PITY ME--	I TRIED TO THINK A	532	V 19
	BUT HE THAT HATH ENDURED	THE PROVINCE OF THE	539	6
	BUT HE WHO WEIGHETH--WHILE THE REST--	I FEAR A MAN OF FRUGAL	543	5
	I FEAR THAT HE IS GRAND--	I FEAR A MAN OF FRUGAL	543	8
	HE OFFERS [SPICES / FLAVORS] HIS BERRY, JUST THE SAME	THE BLACK BERRY--WEARS A	554	3
	HE SOMETIMES HOLDS UPON THE FENCE--	THE BLACK BERRY--WEARS A	554	5
	HIS HOUSE WAS NOT--NO SIGN HAD HE--	MY PERIOD HAD COME FOR	564	9
	BUT 'TWAS--THE FACT THAT HE WAS DEAD--	A DYING TIGER--MOANED	566	12
	HE GAVE AWAY HIS LIFE--	HE GAVE AWAY HIS LIFE--	567	1
	HE CHOSE--MATURITY--	HE GAVE AWAY HIS LIFE--	567	12
	UNCERTAIN IF MYSELF, OR HE,	MY FIRST WELL DAY--SINCE	574	7
	AND HE PASSED [WENT] QUICKLY [SOFTLY] ROUND--	WHEN I WAS SMALL, A	596	8
	'TWAS LITTLE--HE SHOULD SEE--	IT ALWAYS FELT TO ME--A	597	22
	THREE TIMES--HE WOULD NOT GO--	THREE TIMES--WE PARTED--	598	2
	UPHOLSTERER OF THE PINES [SEA / LAND / HILLS]--IS HE--	OF BRUSSELS--IT WAS NOT	602	15
	HE FOUND MY BEING--SET IT UP--	HE FOUND MY BEING--SET	603	1
	THEN CARVED [HE WROTE] HIS NAME--UPON IT--	HE FOUND MY BEING--SET	603	3
	AND HE WOULD COME AGAIN--	HE FOUND MY BEING--SET	603	6
	AND DANCING SOFTLY TO HIMSELF [AS HE KNITS]	THE SPIDER HOLDS A	605	3
	HE PLIES FROM NOUGHT TO NOUGHT--	THE SPIDER HOLDS A	605	5
	IN JUST THE JACKET THAT HE WORE--	OF NEARNESS TO HER	607	9
	NOT DEATH--FOR WHO IS HE?	AFRAID! OF WHOM AM I	608	2
	HOW MIGHTIER HE--THAN I--	IT WOULD HAVE STARVED A	612	12
	COULD HE--KNOW--THEY SOUGHT HIM--	IN FALLING TIMBERS	614	5
	COULD THEY--KNOW--HE BREATHED [LIVED]--	IN FALLING TIMBERS	614	6
	I ROSE--BECAUSE HE SANK--	I ROSE--BECAUSE HE SANK	616	1
	BRAZIL? HE TWIRLED A BUTTON--	I ASKED NO OTHER THING--	621	5
	TO KNOW JUST HOW HE SUFFERED--WOULD BE DEAR--	TO KNOW JUST HOW HE	622	1
	TO WHOM HE COULD ENTRUST HIS WAVERING GAZE--	TO KNOW JUST HOW HE	622	3
	TO KNOW IF HE WAS PATIENT--PART CONTENT--	TO KNOW JUST HOW HE	622	5
	WAS DYING AS HE THOUGHT--OR DIFFERENT--	TO KNOW JUST HOW HE	622	6
	AT NEWS THAT HE CEASED HUMAN NATURE	TO KNOW JUST HOW HE	622	11
	AND WISHES--HAD HE ANY--	TO KNOW JUST HOW HE	622	13
	AND WAS HE CONFIDENT UNTIL	TO KNOW JUST HOW HE	622	16
	AND IF HE SPOKE--WHAT NAME WAS BEST--	TO KNOW JUST HOW HE	622	18
	WAS HE AFRAID--OR TRANQUIL--	TO KNOW JUST HOW HE	622	22
	MIGHT HE KNOW	TO KNOW JUST HOW HE	622	23
	BUT WHEN HE SINGETH--THEN--	THE LIGHTNING PLAYETH--	630	2
	OURSELVES ARE CONSCIOUS HE EXIST--	THE LIGHTNING PLAYETH--	630	3
	HE GAINS THE SKILL	THE CHILD'S FAITH IS NEW	637	21
	EXCEPT THAT YOU THAN HE	I CANNOT LIVE WITH YOU--	640	27
	HE--COULD SUFFICE FOR ME--	I COULD SUFFICE FOR HIM,	643	2
	"WOULD I BE WHOLE" HE SUDDEN BROACHED--	I COULD SUFFICE FOR HIM,	643	5
	HAD HE THE OFFER OF--	YOU LEFT ME--SIRE--TWO	644	4
	HE SHALL SEEK AS HIGH	HER SWEET TURN TO LEAVE	649	18

		FIRST LINE	POEM	LINE
HE	(CONTINUED)			
	HE [FIRST]--MUST PASS THE CRYSTAL ANGLE [LIMIT]	HER SWEET TURN TO LEAVE	649	25
	HE--MUST HAVE ACHIEVED IN PERSON	HER SWEET TURN TO LEAVE	649	27
	OR CHASE HIM IF HE DO	COULD I BUT RIDE	661	10
	TILL HE SHOULD JUMP PENINSULAS	COULD I BUT RIDE	661	11
	HE NEVER SAW ME--IN THIS LIFE--	AGAIN--HIS VOICE IS AT	663	7
	BUT HE MUST [SHOULD] COUNT THE DROPS--HIMSELF--	AGAIN--HIS VOICE IS AT	663	28
	HE BOLTS THE DOOR--	ONE NEED NOT BE A	670	18
	HE FAILS TO FEAR--	ONE NEED NOT BE A	670	V 20
	NOR WILL HE--LIKE THE DUMB--	THE FUTURE--NEVER SPOKE	672	2
	ANSWERED WOLFE [HE] "TO DIE"	WOLFE DEMANDED DURING	678	4
	"SWEET" SAID HE "MY OWN SURRENDER	WOLFE DEMANDED DURING	678	7
	HE DOTH NOT ATTEST BY POSTURE--	CONSCIOUS AM I IN MY	679	3
	NEITHER HE TO ME	CONSCIOUS AM I IN MY	679	10
	NEITHER IF HE VISIT OTHER--	CONSCIOUS AM I IN MY	679	17
	DO HE DWELL--OR NAY--KNOW I--	CONSCIOUS AM I IN MY	679	18
	HE--WOULD TRUST NO STRANGER--	LIFE--IS WHAT WE MAKE IT	698	5
	HE HATH TRAVERSED FIRST--	LIFE--IS WHAT WE MAKE IT	698	10
	HE KINDLY STOPPED FOR ME--	BECAUSE I COULD NOT STOP	712	2
	WE SLOWLY DROVE--HE KNEW NO HASTE	BECAUSE I COULD NOT STOP	712	5
	OR RATHER--HE PASSED US--	BECAUSE I COULD NOT STOP	712	13
	IF HE WERE LIVING--DARE I ASK--	IF HE WERE LIVING--DARE	734	1
	AND HOW IF HE BE DEAD--	IF HE WERE LIVING--DARE	734	2
	AND HE--I PUSHED--WITH SUDDEN FORCE--	IF HE WERE LIVING--DARE	734	13
	"WAS BURIED"--"BURIED"! "HE!"	IF HE WERE LIVING--DARE	734	15
	HE SHALL SEEK IN VAIN--	NEVER FOR SOCIETY	746	2
	DYES--SAID HE--HAVE I--	AUTUMN--OVERLOOKED MY	748	2
	THOUGH I THAN HE--MAY LONGER LIVE	MY LIFE HAD STOOD--A	754	21
	HE LONGER MUST--THAN I--	MY LIFE HAD STOOD--A	754	22
	EVER HE MINDED OCCUPYING	NO BOBOLINK--REVERSE HIS	755	3
	HE FOUGHT LIKE THOSE WHO'VE NOUGHT TO LOSE--	HE FOUGHT LIKE THOSE	759	1
	BESTOWED [HE GAVE] HIMSELF TO BALLS	HE FOUGHT LIKE THOSE	759	2
	BUT HE--WAS LEFT [REMAINED] ALIVE BECAUSE	HE FOUGHT LIKE THOSE	759	11
	HE TOLD A HOMELY TALE	HE TOLD A HOMELY TALE	763	1
	OR BRETHEREN, HAD HE--	HE TOLD A HOMELY TALE	763	12
	'TIS FIRST [YOU SEE] HE STEPS UPON THE VANE--	MY FAITH IS LARGER THAN	766	5
	AND THEN ABROAD THE WORLD HE GO	MY FAITH IS LARGER THAN	766	7
	BUT HE WHO HAS ACHIEVED THE TOP [CREST]--	THE HALLOWING OF PAIN	772	7
	RED PILGRIM, HE AND I--	DEPRIVED OF OTHER	773	10
	LEST IF HE FLINCH--THE EYE THAT WAY	GRIEF IS A MOUSE--	793	10
	HE FLUNG A HAND FULL AT THE PLAIN--	THE WIND BEGUN TO KNEAD	824	3
	HE THREW A MENACE AT THE EARTH--	THE WIND BEGUN TO KNEAD	824	V 3
	CHRIST--STOOPED UNTIL HE TOUCHED THE GRAVE--	PERHAPS YOU THINK ME	833	3
	BEFORE HE COMES WE WEIGH THE TIME!	BEFORE HE COMES WE WEIGH	834	1
	WHEN HE DEPART [DEPARTS], AN EMPTINESS	BEFORE HE COMES WE WEIGH	834	3
	AND WILL ENDURE AS LONG AS HE	TRUTH--IS AS OLD AS GOD	836	3
	HIMSELF [THAT HE] IS BORNE AWAY	TRUTH--IS AS OLD AS GOD	836	6
	JUST AS HE SPOKE IT FROM HIS HANDS	JUST AS HE SPOKE IT FROM	848	1
	HE OUTSTRIPPED TIME WITH BUT A BOUT,	HE OUTSTRIPPED TIME WITH	865	1
	HE OUTSTRIPPED STARS AND SUN	HE OUTSTRIPPED TIME WITH	865	2
	AND HE AND HE IN MIGHTY LIST	HE OUTSTRIPPED TIME WITH	865	5
	AND HE AND HE IN MIGHTY LIST	HE OUTSTRIPPED TIME WITH	865	5
	THE NORTH AND SOUTH WHEN HE	THE SUN AND MOON MUST	871	6
	TILL HE MEET A MAN	AS THE STARVED MAELSTROM	872	6
	TILL HE ESTEEM HIS DATES AND COCOA	AS THE STARVED MAELSTROM	872	11
	WERE HE TO COUNT THEM O'ER	EACH SCAR I'LL KEEP FOR	877	6
	IF MERRY, HE IS MERRIER--	THE SUN IS GAY OR STARK	878	3
	HE HELPED TO MAKE TOO BRIGHT	THE SUN IS GAY OR STARK	878	6
	AS I OF HE, SO GOD OF ME	OUR LITTLE KINSMEN--	885	9
	A STRANGER HE MUST BE--	WHO OCCUPIES THIS HOUSE?	892	30
	CONTINUAL BAN PROPOUNDETH HE	OF SILKEN SPEECH AND	896	8
	BUT HE WHOSE LOSS PROCURES YOU	TILL DEATH--IS NARROW	907	5
	HE HOLDS SUPERIOR IN THE SKY	I MAKE HIS CRESCENT FILL	909	5
	AS OFT AS HE GO DOWN	WE CAN BUT FOLLOW TO THE	920	2
	HE LEAVE OURSELVES A SPHERE BEHIND--	WE CAN BUT FOLLOW TO THE	920	3
	HOW HE STRETCHED HIS ANGUISH [SPIRIT] TO US	HOW THE WATERS CLOSED	923	3
	AND ALL THE SEAS HE POPULATES	A COFFIN--IS A SMALL	943	7
	AND LANDS HE LOOKS UPON	A COFFIN--IS A SMALL	943	8
	HE LEFT BEHIND ONE DAY--SO LESS	FITTER TO SEE HIM, I MAY	968	13
	HE SEEK CONVICTION, THAT--BE THIS--	FITTER TO SEE HIM, I MAY	968	14
	THAT HE'LL [HE] MISTAKE--AND ASK FOR ME	FITTER TO SEE HIM, I MAY	968	16
	IF HE PERCEIVE THE OTHER TRUTH--	FITTER TO SEE HIM, I MAY	968	23
	HE WHO IN HIMSELF BELIEVES--	HE WHO IN HIMSELF	969	1
	IF CIRCASSIAN--HE IS CARELESS--	COLOR--CASTE--	970	9
	IF HE PUT AWAY	COLOR--CASTE--	970	10
	GRANDFATHER OF THE DAYS IS HE	THE MOUNTAIN SAT UPON	975	7
	HE LIKES A BOGGY ACRE	A NARROW FELLOW IN THE	986	9
	SINCE HEAVEN AND HE ARE ONE.	THE DEFINITION OF BEAUTY	988	4
	HE WERE SUPERFLUOUS EVERY DAY	SUPERFLUOUS WERE THE SUN	999	3
	ASKED HIM HIS NAME--HE LISPED ME "TROTWOOD"--	TRUDGING TO EDEN,	1020	3
	LADY, DID HE BELONG TO THEE?	TRUDGING TO EDEN,	1020	4
	AND THAT HE DID'NT LOOK AFRAID?	TRUDGING TO EDEN,	1020	6
	FATE SLEW HIM, BUT HE DID NOT DROP--	FATE SLEW HIM, BUT HE	1031	1
	SHE FELLED--HE DID NOT FALL--	FATE SLEW HIM, BUT HE	1031	2
	HE NEUTRALIZED THEM ALL--	FATE SLEW HIM, BUT HE	1031	4
	AND HE--UNMOVED REGARDED HER--	FATE SLEW HIM, BUT HE	1031	7
	WHO MAY BE PURPLE IF HE CAN	WHO IS THE EAST?	1032	3
	WHO MAY BE YELLOW IF HE CAN	WHO IS THE EAST?	1032	7

		FIRST LINE	POEM		LINE
HE	(CONTINUED)				
	HE--SOVREIGN AS THE SUN	SAID DEATH TO PASSION	1033		7
	HE LABORETH AT EVERY TREE	HIS BILL AN AUGUR IS	1034		3
	HE ASKED IF I WAS HIS--	IT WAS A QUIET WAY--	1053		2
	AND THEN HE BORE ME ON [HIGH]	IT WAS A QUIET WAY--	1053		5
	HE WILL NOT BE OBLIGED TO WAIT	THE SOUL SHOULD ALWAYS	1055		3
	HE SCANNED IT--STAGGERED--	HE SCANNED IT--STAGGERED	1062		1
	HE TRIUMPHED, AND WENT ON--	THE SUN WENT DOWN--NO	1079		4
	HE MIGHT NOT LOOK AGAIN?	WHEN THEY COME BACK--IF	1080		12
	SO BLIND WITH [FULL OF] JOY HE COULD NOT CHOOSE	THE BIRD DID PRANCE--THE	1107		3
	THE SMALL MUST [DO] DIE, THE SAME [AS WELL] AS HE--	THAT THIS SHOULD FEEL	1112		6
	HE HOISTS ABROAD AGAIN--	THESE ARE THE NIGHTS	1128		8
	TO CHILDREN HE IS SMALL [LEAST] IN PRICE	THE MERCHANT OF THE	1131		5
	OF COUNTERFEITS HE IS SO SHY	THE MERCHANT OF THE	1131		9
	"SECURE [PROTECT] YOUR FLOWER" SAID HE.	THE FROST OF DEATH WAS	1136		2
	HE FORKED HIS WAY ALONG	THE FROST OF DEATH WAS	1136		13
	DO HE EXIST, OR DIE,	THE DUTIES OF THE WIND	1137		14
	TOO WISE HE SEEMS FOR WAKELESSNESS,	THE DUTIES OF THE WIND	1137		15
	BECAUSE HE WAS DETAINED	HOW MANY SCHEMES MAY DIE	1150	V	6
	HE VARIED BY A RIBBON'S WIDTH	HOW MANY SCHEMES MAY DIE	1150		7
	HE IS ALIVE, THIS MORNING--	HE IS ALIVE, THIS	1160		1
	HE IS ALIVE--AND AWAKE--	HE IS ALIVE, THIS	1160		2
	FROM NEITHER OF THEM THO' HE TRY	AS OLD AS WOE--	1168		9
	MY GOD--HE SEES THEE--	MY GOD--HE SEES THEE--	1178		1
	HE DEPOSES DOOM	WHEN I HOPED I FEARED--	1181		7
	HE IS KING [PRINCE] OF HARM--	WHEN I HOPED I FEARED--	1181	V	7
	BECAUSE HE IS A LITTLE BOY	A LITTLE DOG THAT WAGS	1185		7
	'TWAS FIGHTING FOR HIS LIFE HE WAS--	'TWAS FIGHTING FOR HIS	1188		1
	AND PERHAPS HE DID'NT	SO I PULL MY STOCKINGS	1201		6
	HE PREACHED UPON [ABOUT] "BREADTH" TILL IT ARGUED HIM [WE . . .	HE PREACHED UPON	1207		1
	. . . KNEW HE WAS] NARROW--	HE PREACHED UPON	1207		1
	THE SEA SAID "I AM HE	THE SEA SAID "COME" TO	1210		6
	HE IS NEW AND HIGH--	WE LIKE MARCH.	1213		3
	MAKES HE MUD FOR DOG AND PEDDLER,	WE LIKE MARCH.	1213		4
	MAKES HE FORESTS [FOREST] DRY.	WE LIKE MARCH.	1213		5
	NEWS IS HE OF ALL THE OTHERS--	WE LIKE MARCH.	1213		10
	WHILE HE, VICTORIOUS TILTS AWAY	LIKE TRAINS OF CARS ON	1224		7
	THANK GOD THE LOUDEST PLACE HE MADE	IT'S HOUR WITH ITSELF	1225		7
	LOCATION DOUBTLESS HE WOULD PLEAD [URGE]	SO MUCH OF HEAVEN HAS	1228		7
	AND HE HAS HAULED AWAY.	SO MUCH OF HEAVEN HAS	1228		12
	BECAUSE HE LOVES HER	BECAUSE HE LOVES HER	1229		1
	HE FIRST ACHIEVE [ESPOUSE] THY FACE	MY HEART RAN SO TO THEE	1237		6
	HAD HE OBLIQUITY	MY HEART RAN SO TO THEE	1237		11
	HE MAY EXCHANGE [CONFER] WITH ME	BECAUSE THAT YOU ARE	1260		26
	OF EVERYTHING BUT HE--	BECAUSE THAT YOU ARE	1260		28
	IF "GOD IS LOVE" AS HE ADMITS	BECAUSE THAT YOU ARE	1260		33
	WE THINK THAT HE MUST BE	BECAUSE THAT YOU ARE	1260		34
	BECAUSE HE IS A "JEALOUS GOD"	BECAUSE THAT YOU ARE	1260		35
	HE TELLS US CERTAINLY	BECAUSE THAT YOU ARE	1260		36
	AS HE BESIDES CONCEDES	BECAUSE THAT YOU ARE	1260		38
	HE WILL REFUND US FINALLY	BECAUSE THAT YOU ARE	1260		39
	FOR HE INSURES TO NONE	I CANNOT SEE MY SOUL BUT	1262		7
	THEY SAY THAT HE CAN HEAL--	IS HEAVEN A PHYSICIAN?	1270		2
	HE COMPLIMENTS EXISTENCE	THE WAY TO KNOW THE	1279		15
	HE SUPPLANTS THE BALM.	DEATH'S WAYLAYING NOT	1296		8
	HE RELEGATES THE REALM,	FROM HIS SLIM PALACE IN	1300		2
	HE FATHOMS WHO OBTAINS.	I CANNOT WANT IT MORE--	1301		8
	ALTHOUGH HE SEEM TO STEAL	NOT ONE BY HEAVEN	1303		2
	HE RESTITUTES IN SOME SWEET WAY	NOT ONE BY HEAVEN	1303		3
	HAD HE THE POWER TO SPURN--	THAT SHORT--POTENTIAL	1307		8
	DIFFERENT IS HE--	WHEN A LOVER IS A BEGGAR	1314		4
	WHAT HE BEGGED IS THEN THE BEGGAR--	WHEN A LOVER IS A BEGGAR	1314		5
	HE IS PRISM BORN.	WHICH IS THE BEST--THE	1315		8
	BUT WELCOME WHEN HE GOES.	WINTER IS GOOD--HIS HOAR	1316		8
	HE STAYED AWAY A YEAR TO CALL	DEAR MARCH--COME IN--	1320		21
	HE DARE IN LONELY [LONESOME / SECRET] PLACE	I NEVER HEAR THAT ONE IS	1323		14
	HE KEPT HIS WORD A TRILLION YEARS	OUR LITTLE SECRETS SLINK	1326		3
	HE HAS NOT LIVED WHO HAS NOT FELT--	WONDER--IS NOT PRECISELY	1331		4
	HAS HE NO ADDED REALM	HOW SOFT THIS PRISON IS	1334		6
	HE HAS OBLIGATION	LIFT IT--WITH THE	1348		7
	HE PAYS NO RENT.	THE RAT IS THE CONCISEST	1356		2
	HE DOTH AS PUNCTUAL CALL	THE SUN IS ONE--AND ON	1372		2
	HIS CUTLERY--HE KEEPS	A SAUCER HOLDS A CUP	1374		9
	TO SEE IT FLASHING WHEN HE DINES	A SAUCER HOLDS A CUP	1374		11
	HE RISES ON A LOG	HIS MANSION IN THE POOL	1379		3
	NO HAND HATH [HAS] HE--	HIS MANSION IN THE POOL	1379		10
	AND [HE] PANTING [HEAVY / LANGUID] ON A CLOVER LEAN	THE BUTTERFLY'S NUMIDIAN	1387		5
	AS IF IT [HE] WERE [AS FREQUENTLY] UNDONE--	THE BUTTERFLY'S NUMIDIAN	1387		6
	HIM YOU CHASTEN, [THOU CHASTENEST-- / YOU CHASTENED] THAT IS [WAS] HE!	LAY THIS LAUREL ON THE	1393		4
	SHE [HE] LAID HER [HIS] DOCILE CRESCENT DOWN	SHE LAID HER DOCILE	1396		1
	THE NEWS THAT SHE [HE] IS GONE--	SHE LAID HER DOCILE	1396		4
	I OFTEN WONDER HE	WHAT MYSTERY PERVADES A	1400		10
	WHERE HE IS FLOORLESS	WHAT MYSTERY PERVADES A	1400		15
	AND OF FEAR NO EVIDENCE GIVES HE	WHAT MYSTERY PERVADES A	1400	V	16
	HE LOVES [SEEKS] WHAT SPURNS [SHUNS] HIM--	TO EARN IT BY DISDAINING	1427		3

		FIRST LINE	POEM		LINE
HE	(CONTINUED)				
	LOOK BEHIND--HE IS PURSUING THEE.	TO EARN IT BY DISDAINING	1427		4
	HE SENT HIS SON TO TEST THE PLANK, . . .	HOW BRITTLE ARE THE	1433		7
	AND HE PRONOUNCED IT FIRM.	HOW BRITTLE ARE THE	1433		8
	NOT THAT HE GOES--WE LOVE HIM MORE . . .	NOT THAT HE GOES--WE	1435		1
	WHO LED US WHILE HE STAYED.	NOT THAT HE GOES--WE	1435		2
	FOR WHAT HE MOVED, HE MADE.	NOT THAT HE GOES--WE	1435		4
	FOR WHAT HE MOVED, HE MADE.	NOT THAT HE GOES--WE	1435		4
	BUT HE INDORSED THE SHEEN [SCENE]-- . . .	THE ROAD WAS LIT WITH	1450		8
	AGROUND--IS HE?	THOSE NOT LIVE YET	1454		6
	THAT IS HE--	THOSE NOT LIVE YET	1454		11
	HE NEVER HAD BUT ONE--	BELSHAZZAR HAD A LETTER	1459		2
	AS LONG AS HE CAN BLUSH	HIS CHEEK IS HIS	1460		2
	PAST THAT, HE SINS IN PEACE--	HIS CHEEK IS HIS	1460		4
	WITH GAY DELAYS HE GOES	BEFORE YOU THOUGHT OF	1465		12
	SO DRUNK HE DISAVOWS IT	ONE OF THE ONES THAT	1466		5
	HE CHEATS AS HE ENCHANTS	ONE OF THE ONES THAT	1466		14
	HE CHEATS AS HE ENCHANTS	ONE OF THE ONES THAT	1466		14
	ARKS OF REPRIEVE HE OFFERED [OPENED] TO US--	WE TALKED WITH EACH	1473		7
	HOW DESTITUTE IS HE	HOW DESTITUTE IS HE	1477		1
	AS HE HAD NO ESTEEM	HOW DESTITUTE IS HE	1477	V	7
	YOU'D THINK [SWEAR] HE TOOK A DEED . . .	HOW DESTITUTE IS HE	1477	V	7
	HE DOUBTLESS DID HIS BEST--	LOOK BACK ON TIME, WITH	1478		2
	THE DEVIL--HAD HE FIDELITY	THE DEVIL--HAD HE	1479		1
	BECAUSE HE HAS ABILITY--	THE DEVIL--HAD HE	1479		3
	THAT WOULD BUT HE RESIGN	THE DEVIL--HAD HE	1479		6
	HE HAS THE PUNCTUALITY	THE ROBIN IS A GABRIEL	1483		5
	SINCE HE AND I WERE BOYS	THE SAVIOR MUST HAVE	1487		6
	HE PASSED THROUGH BETHLEHEM--	"AND WITH WHAT BODY DO	1492		8
	BUT HE DOTH THERE PRESIDE	ALL THAT I DO	1496		9
	WHERE HE DOES NOT [FIRST] PRESIDE	ALL THAT I DO	1496	V	9
	HE LIVED THE LIFE OF AMBUSH	HE LIVED THE LIFE OF	1525		1
	HE SPENDS THE EVENING OF HIS DAYS [NOONS] .	HIS ORIENTAL HERESIES	1526	V	
	RECOUNTING NECTARS HE HAS KNOWN	HIS ORIENTAL HERESIES	1526	V	
	HE HUNGERS TO ATTAIN.	HIS ORIENTAL HERESIES	1526	V	
	IF HE IS CAUGHT AT ALL--	THE LIFE THAT TIED TOO	1535		8
	HE IS JUST AS [STILL MORE] HIGH--	FOLLOW WISE ORION	1538		4
	HE FEEDS UPON THE FAIR--	HOPE IS A SUBTLE GLUTTON	1547		2
	LIVES HE IN ANY OTHER WORLD	LIVES HE IN ANY OTHER	1557		1
	THE SNOW AND HE ARE INTIMATE--	NO BRIGADIER THROUGHOUT	1561		9
	SHE [HE] BORE LIFE'S EMPTY PACK	HER LOSSES MAKE OUR	1562		2
	TO WHICH HE [SHE] GAVE THE WORTH, ...	CLIMBING TO REACH THE	1566		2
	HE [AND] BROKE THEM, FEARING PUNISHMENT . .	CLIMBING TO REACH THE	1566		3
	HE [SHE] RAN AWAY FROM EARTH--	CLIMBING TO REACH THE	1566		4
	HE ATE AND DRANK THE PRECIOUS WORDS-- . .	HE ATE AND DRANK THE	1587		1
	HE KNEW NO MORE THAT HE WAS POOR, ...	HE ATE AND DRANK THE	1587		3
	HE KNEW NO MORE THAT HE WAS POOR, ...	HE ATE AND DRANK THE	1587		3
	HE DANCED ALONG THE DINGY DAYS	HE ATE AND DRANK THE	1587		5
	HE GAILY [BOLDLY] INTERRUPTED THAT OVERFLOWING DAY	THE BOBOLINK IS GONE--	1591		4
	HE BOWED TO HEAVEN INSTEAD OF EARTH [EVERY HEAVEN ABOVE / . . .	THE BOBOLINK IS GONE--	1591		6
	. . . ALL THE SAINTS HE KNEW / EVERY GOD HE KNEW]	THE BOBOLINK IS GONE--	1591		6
	. . . ALL THE SAINTS HE KNEW / EVERY GOD HE KNEW]	THE BOBOLINK IS GONE--	1591		6
	HE RECOGNIZED HIS MAKER--OVERTURNED THE DECALOGUE--	THE BOBOLINK IS GONE--	1591		8
	HE SWUNG UPON THE DECALOGUE	THE BOBOLINK IS GONE--	1591		9
	AND THEN HE LIFTED UP HIS THROAT	UPON HIS SADDLE SPRUNG A	1600		5
	FOR WHAT, HE IS PRESUMED TO KNOW--	OF GOD WE ASK ONE FAVOR,	1601		3
	HE ONLY SELLS THE WILDERNESS, ...	THE AUCTIONEER OF	1612		5
	THE TATTERS THAT HE WEARS--	TO TRY TO SPEAK, AND	1617		4
	A BETTER COAT IF HE POSSESSED	TO TRY TO SPEAK, AND	1617		5
	HE SHALL NOT TAKE THY HAND	BACK FROM THE CORDIAL	1625		2
	AND [THE] VENOMS HE MISTOOK FOR BALMS . .	ARROWS ENAMORED OF HIS	1629		3
	OF SWARTHY DAYS HE IS THE CLOSE [KNELL] . .	THE JAY HIS CASTANET HAS	1635		5
	IT MAY EXPIRE IF HE--	A WORD MADE FLESH IS	1651		12
	HE WENT BY SLEEP THAT DROWSY ROUTE . . .	HE WENT BY SLEEP THAT	1662		1
	HE CARRIES A CIRCUMFERENCE	HIS MIND OF MAN, A	1663		3
	HE OTHERWISE MAY KNOW	HIS MIND OF MAN, A	1663		6
	BEFORE HE MAKES THE BEND	I DID NOT REACH THEE	1664		22
	BUT AS HE WAS A WORM	IN WINTER IN MY ROOM	1670		4
	WHEN HE WAS MEAN AND NEW	IN WINTER IN MY ROOM	1670		20
	"AFRAID HE HISSED	IN WINTER IN MY ROOM	1670		24
	HE FATHOMED ME--	IN WINTER IN MY ROOM	1670		27
	LEST HE PURSUE	IN WINTER IN MY ROOM	1670		34
	MEANWHILE HE IS SO NEAR	THE BLUNDER IS IN	1684		4
	HE JOINS ME IN MY RAMBLE	THE BLUNDER IS IN	1684		5
	BECAUSE HE TRAVELS FREELY	THE BUTTERFLY OBTAINS	1685		5
	THAT HE IS DISSOLUTE	THE BUTTERFLY OBTAINS	1685		8
	HAD HE THE HOMELY SCUTCHEON	THE BUTTERFLY OBTAINS	1685		9
	YET HE DID NOT GUESS	THE EVENT WAS DIRECTLY	1686		2
	AND THEN HE SULKED IN MERCURY	THE SUN RETIRED TO A	1693		3
	WHERE HOPE AND HE PART COMPANY--	DROWNING IS NOT SO	1718		7
	FOR HE IS GRASPED OF GOD.	DROWNING IS NOT SO	1718		8
	HE CANNOT BEAR TO SEE	GOD IS INDEED A JEALOUS	1719		2
	HE WAS MY HOST--HE WAS MY GUEST, ...	HE WAS MY HOST--HE WAS	1721		1
	HE WAS MY HOST--HE WAS MY GUEST, ...	HE WAS MY HOST--HE WAS	1721		1
	OR HE INVITED ME.	HE WAS MY HOST--HE WAS	1721		4

	FIRST LINE	POEM	LINE
HE (CONTINUED)			
HE TROD UPON THE TREES	HIGH FROM THE EARTH I	1723	2
AS HE ESTEEMED THEM TRIFLES,	HIGH FROM THE EARTH I	1723	3
AND THEN HE SPIED A BREEZE,	HIGH FROM THE EARTH I	1723	4
HE WAS THE FAITHFUL FATHER	HIGH FROM THE EARTH I	1723	15
THE FELLOW WILL GO WHERE HE BELONGED--	IF EVER THE LID GETS OFF	1727	3
ADMITTED HE A MAN	NO MAN SAW AWE, NOR TO	1733	2
HE RECOLLECTS IT WELL.	ONE CROWN THAT NO ONE	1735	8
THE WATERS CHASED HIM AS HE FLED,	THE WATERS CHASED HIM AS	1749	1
THE FOREIGNER BEFORE HE KNOCKS	WHERE EVERY BIRD IS BOLD	1758	3
DOUBTLESS, HE THOUGHT IT MEET OF HIM	A TRAIN WENT THROUGH A	1761	7
HEAD			
OFT A HEAD IS CRESTED	FREQUENTLY THE WOODS ARE	6	5
I PAUSE ABOVE THAT VANISHED HEAD	WHERE I HAVE LOST, I	104	3
TO HANG OUR HEAD--OSTENSIBLY--	TO HANG OUR HEAD--	105	1
DAINTY--AS THE TRESS--ON HER DEFT HEAD--	WE--BEE AND I--LIVE BY	230	11
TILL HAIR--AND EYES--AND TIMID HEAD--	I THINK JUST HOW MY	237	3
THAT CLAMORS FOR HIS HEAD--	THE DOOMED--REGARD THE	294	8
ON THE [A] HEAD TOO HIGH TO CROWN--	HER--"LAST POEMS"--	312	13
HE STIRRED HIS VELVET HEAD	A BIRD CAME DOWN THE	328	12
PUTS OUT A RUFFLED HEAD--	I TEND MY FLOWERS FOR	339	12
TO TOUCH HER HEAD!	'TWAS THE OLD--ROAD--	344	22
WITH NOSEGAYS AT THE HEAD AND FOOT--	I WENT TO THANK HER--	363	4
FROM TANKS--ABOVE MY HEAD--	DO PEOPLE MOULDER	432	8
PERMITTED--SUCH A HEAD--	IT FEELS A SHAME TO BE	444	4
GESTURE COQUETTE--AND SHAKE YOUR HEAD!	GOING TO HIM! HAPPY	494	25
DOES NOT SO MUCH AS TURN HIS HEAD	TO INTERRUPT HIS YELLOW	591	7
BUT LIKE A HEAD--A GUILLOTINE	I WATCHED THE MOON	629	13
UPON THE ROPES--ABOVE OUR HEAD--	THE LIGHTNING PLAYETH--	630	9
SHE SQUANDERS ON YOUR HEAD [EAR]	YOU'LL KNOW HER--BY HER	634	25
I GUARD MY MASTER'S HEAD--	MY LIFE HAD STOOD--A	754	14
THE PILLOW FOR MY HEAD--	BEREAVED OF ALL, I WENT	784	8
WHO PUT A HEAD AWAY	SEVERER SERVICE OF	786	14
THE LIGHTNING SHOWED A YELLOW HEAD [BEAK]--	THE WIND BEGUN TO KNEAD	824	11
THE STARS ABOUT MY HEAD I FELT	I STEPPED FROM PLANK TO	875	3
OVER THE CUBIT'S HEAD,	UNDER THE LIGHT, YET	949	12
HIS HEAD, A CAP AND FRILL	HIS BILL AN AUGUR IS	1034	2
HERE, WHERE THE DAISIES FIT MY HEAD	HERE, WHERE THE DAISIES	1037	1
AND DREW THE HEAD ERECT--	THE LAST NIGHT THAT SHE	1100	26
AS MAKES ONE HIDE [HANG] IT'S HEAD	THAT THIS SHOULD FEEL	1112 V	4
TELL WOULD NOT BARE HIS HEAD	TELL AS A MARKSMAN--WERE	1152	13
HAD WE THE EYES WITHIN OUR HEAD [HEADS]--	HAD WE OUR SENSES	1284	5
AND THAT IS WHY I LAY MY HEAD	ESCAPE IS SUCH A	1347	11
ADJUSTS IT'S TUMBLED HEAD--	A ROUTE OF EVANESCENCE	1463	6
DOTH SIT UPON IT'S HEAD--	IT'S LITTLE ETHER HOOD	1501	2
THE PILLOW OF THIS DARING HEAD	NO BRIGADIER THROUGHOUT	1561	17
UPON MY WINCING HEAD--	WHO IS IT SEEKS MY	1598	6
HOW SAFE HIS FALLEN HEAD	THE DITCH IS DEAR TO THE	1645	4
IF EVER THE LID GETS OFF MY HEAD	IF EVER THE LID GETS OFF	1727	1
AND YET [ALTHOUGH] THE HIGHEST HEAD	ONE CROWN THAT NO ONE	1735	2
HEADLANDS			
PAST THE HOUSES--PAST THE HEADLANDS--	EXULTATION IS THE GOING	76	3
HEADS			
AND STAND UPON THEIR HEADS!	"ARCTURUS" IS HIS OTHER	70	23
SOME SHOOK THEIR HEADS, AND OTHERS SMILED--	WHOSE ARE THE LITTLE	142	3
FROM WHAT W'D LAST TILL HEADS LIKE MINE	I CAUTIOUS, SCANNED MY	178	3
THEY BEAR THEIR DAUNTLESS [FEARLESS / TRANQUIL] HEADS,	WHEN WE STAND ON THE	242	10
SWEEP BY OUR DISAPPOINTED HEADS	HOW NOTELESS MEN, AND	282	11
BY HEADS REJECTED--IN THE LOWER COUNTRY--	UNTO LIKE STORY--TROUBLE	295	11
OLD VOLUMES SHAKE THEIR VELLUM HEADS	A PRECIOUS--MOULDERING	371	27
ON THE HEADS THAT STARTED WITH US--	SMILING BACK FROM	385	3
THE HAMMOCK'S MOTION LULLS THE HEADS	I SOMETIMES DROP IT, FOR	708	11
I FIRST SURMISED THE HORSES HEADS	BECAUSE I COULD NOT STOP	712	23
HAD WE THE EYES WITHIN OUR HEAD [HEADS]--	HAD WE OUR SENSES	1284	5
THE HILLS ERECT THEIR PURPLE HEADS	THE HILLS ERECT THEIR	1688	1
HEAL			
CAN HEAL!	AH, NECROMANCY SWEET!	177	7
NOT EVEN GOD--CAN HEAL--	REMORSE--IS MEMORY--	744	10
THE GRACE NEXT TO IT--HEAL?	ONLY A SHRINE, BUT MINE	918	8
THEY SAY THAT HE CAN HEAL--	IS HEAVEN A PHYSICIAN?	1270	2
HEALED			
THE HEALED HEART SHOWS IT'S SHALLOW SCAR	THE HEALED HEART SHOWS	1440	1
HEALTH			
AND HEALTH, AND LAUGHTER, CURIOUS THINGS--	I CRIED AT PITY--NOT AT	588	7
BY BLESSED HEALTH OBSCURED--	AS ONE DOES SICKNESS	957	4
TRUTH IS GOOD HEALTH--AND SAFETY, AND THE SKY.	A COUNTERFEIT--A PLATED	1453	5
HEALTHY			
REPELS THE HEALTHY BEE--	THERE IS AN ARID	782 V	8
HEAPED			
AND COFFERS HEAPED WITH TEARS!	FOR EACH EXTATIC INSTANT	125	8
HEAR			
I HEAR THE BRIGHT BEE HUM;	THERE IS ANOTHER SKY,	2	12
I NEVER HEAR THE WORD "ESCAPE"	I NEVER HEAR THE WORD	77	1
I NEVER HEAR OF PRISONS BROAD	I NEVER HEAR THE WORD	77	5
PERHAPS THEY DID NOT HEAR, I SAID,	WHOSE ARE THE LITTLE	142	5
I HEAR THE SILVER STRIFE--	MUSICIANS WRESTLE	157	3
I HEAR HER FEET UPON THE STAIR!	DYING! DYING IN THE	158	11
WHAT IF THEY HEAR ME!	IF I COULD BRIBE THEM BY	179	13
THEY HEAR MY UNEXPECTED KNOCK--	THO' I GET HOME HOW LATE	207	6

	FIRST LINE	POEM	LINE
HEAR (CONTINUED)			
I GOT SO I COULD HEAR [THINK / TAKE] HIS NAME--	I GOT SO I COULD HEAR	293	1
ME--HEAR! MY FOREIGN EAR	ME--COME! MY DAZZLED	431	3
IF THEN HE HEAR--	PRAYER IS THE LITTLE	437	6
MIDNIGHT--GOOD NIGHT! I HEAR THEM CALL,	A WIFE--AT DAYBREAK I	461	7
I LIVE WITH HIM--I HEAR HIS VOICE--	I LIVE WITH HIM--I SEE	463	9
BUT JUST TO HEAR THE GRACE DEPART--	EXCEPT THE HEAVEN HAD	472	5
YOU HEAR A BEING--DROP--	A SOLEMN THING WITHIN	483	6
AND LET HIM HEAR IT DRIP	TO ONE DENIED TO DRINK	490	6
YOU COULD HEAR THE BODDICE TUG, BEHIND YOU--	GOING TO HIM! HAPPY	494	12
TO HEAR AN ORIOLE SING	TO HEAR AN ORIOLE SING	526	1
ATTIRETH THAT IT HEAR	TO HEAR AN ORIOLE SING	526	8
THE DRUMS TO HEAR--	INCONCEIVABLY SOLEMN!	582	V 15
I LIKE TO SEE [HEAR] IT LAP THE MILES--	I LIKE TO SEE IT LAP	585	1
TO SOMETIMES HEAR "RICH PEOPLE" BUY	I CRIED AT PITY--NOT AT	588	9
FOR FEAR I HEAR HER SAY	I CRIED AT PITY--NOT AT	588	20
I HEAR HIM ASK THE SERVANT	AGAIN--HIS VOICE IS AT	663	3
NATURE IS WHAT WE HEAR--	"NATURE" IS WHAT WE SEE	668	5
I COULD NOT DEEM IT LATE--TO HEAR	"I WANT"--IT PLEADED--	731	5
WE ACTUALLY HEAR	THE SPIRIT IS THE	733	2
THE OTHER--ONLY--HEAR--	THE SPIRIT IS THE	733	8
PRICKS HIS EAR--REPORT TO HEAR	GRIEF IS A MOUSE--	793	6
GOOD TO HIDE, AND HEAR 'EM HUNT!	GOOD TO HIDE, AND HEAR	842	1
THAT BELLS SHOULD RING TILL ALL SHOULD KNOW [HEAR]	OF TOLLING BELL I ASK	947	5
I HEAR THE LEVEL BEE--	LIKE TRAINS OF CARS ON	1224	2
IS PLAY I HEAR FROM YOU--	THE MOST PATHETIC THING	1290	2
I NEVER HEAR THAT ONE IS DEAD [HAS DIED]	I NEVER HEAR THAT ONE IS	1323	1
THE NAME TO HEAR	OF WHOM SO DEAR	1504	2
I DARE NOT WRITE UNTIL I HEAR--	A PANG IS MORE	1530	V
TO HEAR HER IS A TUNE--	TO SEE HER IS A PICTURE	1568	2
TO HEAR THE LIVING CLOCK	T'WAS COMFORT IN HER	1703	2
TO HEAR THE CHILDREN PLAY	T'WAS COMFORT IN HER	1703	6
WHEN MEN AND WOMEN HEAR	HOW DARE THE ROBINS SING	1724	2
HEAR THE BOBOLINK!	"LETHE" IN MY FLOWER,	1730	4
HEARD			
OF WHICH I HAVE NEVER HEARD?	WILL THERE REALLY BE A	101	8
WITHIN THE ORCHARD, IS NOT HEARD,	I HAVE A KING, WHO DOES	103	14
FEELING AS IF THEIR PILLOW HEARD,	WHERE I HAVE LOST, I	104	7
JUST FELT [HEARD] THE WORLD GO BY!	JUST LOST, WHEN I WAS	160	2
I HEARD RECEDE THE DISAPPOINTED TIDE!	JUST LOST, WHEN I WAS	160	6
I'VE HEARD THE HUNTER TELL--	A WOUNDED DEER--LEAPS	165	2
MY TAMBORIN WERE SOONEST HEARD	IF I COULD BRIBE THEM BY	179	8
I'VE HEARD AN ORGAN TALK, SOMETIMES--	I'VE HEARD AN ORGAN TALK	183	1
AND SWEETEST--IN THE GALE--IS HEARD--	"HOPE" IS THE THING WITH	254	5
I'VE HEARD IT IN THE CHILLEST LAND--	"HOPE" IS THE THING WITH	254	9
I HEARD THE BUCKLE SNAP--	HE PUT THE BELT AROUND	273	2
I HAVE HEARD BUT ONE--	MANY A PHRASE HAS THE	276	2
AND THEN I HEARD THEM LIFT A BOX	I FELT A FUNERAL, IN MY	280	9
BY FAINTER HAMMERS--FURTHER HEARD--	HE FUMBLES AT YOUR SOUL	315	7
WHO [HE] NEVER HEARD THAT FLESHLESS CHANT--	OF ALL THE SOUNDS	321	27
IN KINGDOMS--YOU HAVE HEARD THE RAISED--	THE FACE I CARRY WITH ME	336	7
I'VE HEARD MEN SAY--	I'M SAYING EVERY DAY	373	11
TAKE OTHER ACCENTS, AS SUCH I HEARD	I'M SAYING EVERY DAY	373	21
AND FAR I HEARD HIS SILVER CALL	I HAD NOT MINDED--WALLS	398	3
ALTHOUGH I HEARD THEM TRY--	A MURMUR IN THE TREES--	416	16
I KNOW I HEARD THE CORN,	'TWAS JUST THIS TIME,	445	2
I HEARD SUCH WORDS AS "RICH"--	IT WAS GIVEN TO ME BY	454	9
I HEARD A FLY BUZZ--WHEN I DIED--	I HEARD A FLY BUZZ--WHEN	465	1
BETTER--THAN MUSIC! FOR I--WHO HEARD IT--	BETTER--THAN MUSIC! FOR	503	1
BUT--I WAS TELLING A TUNE--I HEARD--	BETTER--THAN MUSIC! FOR	503	16
LIKE [AS] FLOWERS, THAT HEARD THE NEWS OF DEWS,	LIKE FLOWERS, THAT HEARD	513	1
BUT NO MAN HEARD HIM CRY--	THE BLACK BERRY--WEARS A	554	2
I HEARD A WOMAN SAY	I CRIED AT PITY--NOT AT	588	2
LIKE INTERMITTENT PLUSH, BE HEARD	THE NIGHT WAS WIDE, AND	589	11
NEITHER--COULD BE HEARD--	IN FALLING TIMBERS	614	8
HEARD [HELD] OPPOSITE THE SEA--	WITHOUT THIS--THERE IS	655	4
I'VE HEARD MY FATHER TELL--	THE JUDGE IS LIKE THE	699	2
NOR HEARD THE TIMID CRY FOR "BREAD"--	THE BEGGAR LAD--DIES	717	7
I HEARD IT HIT THE GROUND--	IT DROPPED SO LOW--IN MY	747	2
BY TRAVELLER--BE HEARD--	NATURE--THE GENTLEST	790	6
TOGETHER HEARD THEM STRENGTHENING	TWO TRAVELLERS PERISHING	933	3
I HEARD, AS IF I HAD NO EAR	I HEARD, AS IF I HAD NO	1039	1
AND THEN I KNEW I HEARD.	I HEARD, AS IF I HAD NO	1039	4
I HEARD IT'S AXLES GO	THIS SLOW DAY MOVED	1120	2
YOU HEARD NO NOISE [CRASH]	A GREAT HOPE FELL	1123	2
THE DAY ABROAD WAS HEARD--[RESUMED ABROAD]	THE WIND TOOK UP THE	1134	14
TELL HAD A SON--THE ONES THAT KNEW [HEARD] IT	TELL AS A MARKSMAN--WERE	1152	9
A COMING AS OF HOSTS WAS HEARD	LIKE RAIN IT SOUNDED	1235	7
THE FARTHEST THUNDER THAT I HEARD	THE FARTHEST THUNDER	1581	1
IT ONLY HEARD THEM PLAY--	PURSUING YOU IN YOUR	1602	6
WHETHER SHE DIED BEFORE SHE HEARD	I WATCHED HER FACE TO	1667	3
I'D NOT BELIEVE IT IF I HEARD	IN WINTER IN MY ROOM	1670	12
IS HEARD OF NONE	SPEECH IS ONE SYMPTOM OF	1681	4
PRECISELY AS IN MARCH IS HEARD	THE ONES THAT	1690	3
HIGH FROM THE EARTH I HEARD A BIRD;	HIGH FROM THE EARTH I	1723	1
HEARING			
SO I AM HEARING HIM, I'LL DREAM,	MAKE ME A PICTURE OF THE	188	6

	FIRST LINE	POEM	LINE
HEARING (CONTINUED)			
THE HEARING HIM PUT HIS PLAYTHINGS UP	IT IS EASY TO WORK WHEN	244	3
THAT ANY, HEARING, HAD INFERRED	A LITTLE OVERFLOWING	1467	2
HEARKENED			
AND SHE HAD PAST, WITH [FLED WITH / TRUSTED / HEARKENED] HIM--	I MEANT TO FIND HER WHEN	718	8
HEARS			
WHO HEARS MAY BE INCREDULOUS,	HER FACE WAS IN A BED OF	1722	7
HEARSE			
HIS LITTLE HEARSE LIKE FIGURE	HIS LITTLE HEARSE LIKE	1522	1
HEART			
TELL I MY DOUBTING HEART	I HAVE A BIRD IN SPRING	5	17
TO HIM WHO KEEPS AN ORCHIS' HEART--	ALL THESE MY BANNERS BE.	22	20
THIS, AND MY HEART BESIDE--	IT'S ALL I HAVE TO BRING	26	2
THIS, AND MY HEART, AND ALL THE FIELDS--	IT'S ALL I HAVE TO BRING	26	3
THIS, AND MY HEART, AND ALL THE BEES	IT'S ALL I HAVE TO BRING	26	7
IN THE HEART INSTEAD?	IT DID NOT SURPRISE ME--	39	16
WITH UNPUZZLED HEART--	COULD LIVE--DID LIVE--	43	9
HEART! WE WILL FORGET HIM!	HEART! WE WILL FORGET	47	1
A POOR--TORN HEART--A TATTERED HEART--	A POOR--TORN HEART-- A	78	1
A POOR--TORN HEART--A TATTERED HEART--	A POOR--TORN HEART-- A	78	1
THIS DUSTY HEART ESPIED--	A POOR--TORN HEART-- A	78	10
HEART, NOT SO HEAVY AS MINE	HEART, NOT SO HEAVY AS	83	1
HER HEART IS FIT FOR HOME [REST]--	HER BREAST IS FIT FOR	84	5
HAVE YOU GOT A BROOK IN YOUR LITTLE HEART,	HAVE YOU GOT A BROOK IN	136	1
THIS HEART THAT BROKE SO LONG--	THIS HEART THAT BROKE SO	145	1
THIS LITTLE HOUND WITHIN THE HEART	WHAT SHALL I DO--IT	186	2
POOR LITTLE HEART!	POOR LITTLE HEART!	192	1
PROUD LITTLE HEART!	POOR LITTLE HEART!	192	4
FRAIL LITTLE HEART!	POOR LITTLE HEART!	192	7
GAY LITTLE HEART--	POOR LITTLE HEART!	192	10
AND STILL--MY HEART--MY EYE OUTWEIGHS--	MY EYE IS FULLER THAN MY	202	3
SHOULD REACH THE HEART THAT WANTED ME--	I SHOULD NOT DARE TO	205	4
MY HEART WOULD WISH IT BROKE BEFORE--	I SHOULD NOT DARE TO	205	13
I BROUGHT [BRING] THEE THE IMPERIAL [DEPARTED] HEART	SAVIOR! I'VE NO ONE ELSE	217	7
THE HEART I CARRIED [CHERISHED] IN MY OWN--	SAVIOR! I'VE NO ONE ELSE	217	9
I DROP MY HEART--UNSHRIVEN!	I THINK JUST HOW MY	237	16
FOR THAT BELOVED HEART--	FOREVER AT HIS SIDE TO	246	9
TO A HEART IN PORT--	WILD NIGHTS--WILD NIGHTS	249	6
HAUNTING THE HEART--	YOU SEE I CANNOT SEE--	253	12
FOR LARGEST WOMAN'S HEART I KNEW--	FOR LARGEST WOMAN'S	309	1
AND YET THE LARGEST WOMAN'S HEART	FOR LARGEST WOMAN'S	309	3
HEART! I AM KNOCKING--LOW AT THEE.	JUST SO--JESUS--RAPS--	317	11
FOR MINE--I TELL YOU THAT MY HEART	BEFORE I GOT MY EYE PUT	327	7
HER HEART MISGIVES HER, FOR HER VOW--	I KNOW A PLACE WHERE	337	7
THE STIFF HEART QUESTIONS WAS IT HE, THAT BORE,	AFTER GREAT PAIN, A	341	3
THAT PUTS THE HEART--ABROAD--	GOOD MORNING--MIDNIGHT--	425	12
FORGOT SHE WORE IT AT HER HEART	FORGET! THE LADY WITH	438	2
FOR IT WOULD SPLIT HIS [HER] HEART, TO KNOW IT--	GOING TO HIM! HAPPY	494	16
IT'S THOUGHTS--AND JUST ONE HEART--	IT'S THOUGHTS--AND JUST	495	1
IT'S THOUGHTS--AND JUST TWO HEART--	IT'S THOUGHTS--AND JUST	495	23
HER SWEET WEIGHT ON MY HEART A NIGHT	HER SWEET WEIGHT ON MY	518	1
ON SO BEST [BROAD] A HEART--	SWEET--YOU FORGOT--BUT I	523	10
THE HEART ASKS PLEASURE [BLESSING]--FIRST--	THE HEART ASKS PLEASURE	536	1
AS YET--MY HEART BE DRY--	ME PROVE IT NOW--WHOEVER	537	6
EMPTY MY HEART, OF THEE--	EMPTY MY HEART, OF THEE	587	1
THE HEART BEGINS TO CROWD--	I THINK THE LONGEST HOUR	635	12
UNTO ALL [TO FOREIGN] HEART--	ME FROM MYSELF--TO	642	4
I THINK THE HEART I FORMER WORE	I THINK TO LIVE--MAY BE	646	5
MY HEART TO SUBDIVIDE--	WITHOUT THIS--THERE IS	655	10
BUT THE HEART WITH THE HEAVIEST FREIGHT ON--	"SPEECH"--IS A PRANK OF	688	3
THE OCEAN'S HEART TOO SMOOTH--TOO BLUE--	IT TOSSED--AND TOSSED--	723	11
THE FRACTION--THAT APPEASED THE HEART	PRECIOUS TO ME--SHE	727	10
IN THE HUMAN HEART--	DRAMA'S VITALLEST	741	13
THE HEART--TO STIMULATE THE EYE	THE BIRDS REPORTED FROM	743	11
DELIVERED STRAIGHTER TO THE HEART	DYING! TO BE AFRAID OF	831	5
THE SCANTEST HEART EXTANT	TILL DEATH--IS NARROW	907	2
FROM EVERY HUMAN HEART	TOO LITTLE WAY THE HOUSE	911	2
IF I CAN STOP ONE HEART FROM BREAKING	IF I CAN STOP ONE HEART	919	1
THE HEART HAS NARROW BANKS	THE HEART HAS NARROW	928	1
THE HEART CONVULSIVE LEARNS	THE HEART HAS NARROW	928	8
AN ANCIENT FASHIONED HEART--	'TWAS AWKWARD, BUT IT	973	2
HEART THAT PROPOSED AS HEART THAT ACCEPTED	UP LIFE'S HILL WITH MY	1010	7
HEART THAT PROPOSED AS HEART THAT ACCEPTED	UP LIFE'S HILL WITH MY	1010	7
MY HEART UPON A LITTLE PLATE	MY HEART UPON A LITTLE	1027	1
SANG FROM THE HEART, SIRE,	SANG FROM THE HEART,	1059	1
DRILL SILENTLY [ARRANGE THE HEART] FOR HEAVEN--	TO HELP OUR BLEAKER	1064	4
THE SWEEPING UP THE HEART	THE BUSTLE IN A HOUSE	1078	5
OF THE HEART THAT GOES IN, AND CLOSES THE DOOR	OF THE HEART THAT GOES	1098	1
SHALL THE PLAYFELLOW HEART COMPLAIN	OF THE HEART THAT GOES	1098	2
OH CHEEK [HEART] WITHIN THE COAL	THE SMOULDERING EMBERS	1132	2
NOR HEART WITHOUT AN AIM,	GOD MADE NO ACT WITHOUT	1163	2
IS NOT SO AMPLE AS THE BREAST [HEART]	STEP LIGHTLY ON THIS	1183	3
MY NOMINATED HEART--	OH SHADOW ON THE GRASS,	1187	4
THE POPULAR HEART IS A CANNON FIRST--	THE POPULAR HEART IS A	1226	1
MY HEART RAN SO TO THEE	MY HEART RAN SO TO THEE	1237	1

	FIRST LINE	POEM	LINE
HEART (CONTINUED)			
THAT COST ME MY HONEST HEART--	I SAW THAT THE FLAKE WAS	1267	4
THAT ELOQUENCE IS WHEN THE HEART	CONFIRMING ALL WHO	1268	3
THAT MAKES THE HEART PUT UP IT'S FUN--	SEPTEMBER'S	1271	7
MADDEST HEART THAT GOD CREATED	LAIN IN NATURE--SO	1288	5
I MAKE BELIEVE UNTIL MY HEART	THE MOST PATHETIC THING	1290	3
NOT WITH A CLUB, THE HEART IS BROKEN	NOT WITH A CLUB, THE	1304	1
PUT UP MY HEART THY HOARY WORK	THE NOTICE THAT IS	1310	3
THIS DIRTY--LITTLE--HEART	THIS DIRTY--LITTLE--	1311	1
TO BREAK SO VAST A HEART	TO BREAK SO VAST A HEART	1312	1
IF NEWS HAVE ANY HEART	HOW NEWS MUST FEEL WHEN	1319	2
WE AND OUR PLOTTING HEART [GAUDY HEART / SCHEMING TINSEL / . . .	AN ANTIQUATED GRACE	1345	5
WE AND OUR PLOTTING HEART [GAUDY HEART / SCHEMING TINSEL / . . .	AN ANTIQUATED GRACE	1345	5
. . . POUTING HEART]	AN ANTIQUATED GRACE	1345	5
IN WHICH THE HEART IS CAUGHT	ESCAPE IS SUCH A	1347	6
THE HEART IS THE CAPITAL OF THE MIND--	THE HEART IS THE CAPITAL	1354	1
THE HEART AND THE MIND TOGETHER MAKE	THE HEART IS THE CAPITAL	1354	3
THE MIND LIVES ON THE HEART	THE MIND LIVES ON THE	1355	1
BUT IF THE HEART OMIT [BE LEAN / BE THIN / DECLINE]	THE MIND LIVES ON THE	1355	5
TO THE STATELY HEART,	"FAITHFUL TO THE END"	1357	6
BUT THE HEART WITHDRAWS--	"FAITHFUL TO THE END"	1357	V
HIS HEART WAS DARKER THAN THE STARLESS NIGHT	HIS HEART WAS DARKER	1378	1
I'LL LET MY HEART BE JUST IN SIGHT--	THEY MIGHT NOT NEED ME--	1391	2
A PATENT OF THE HEART--	HOPE IS A STRANGE	1392	2
HOW ADEQUATE THE HUMAN HEART	WHAT MYSTERY PERVADES A	1400	V
DIVULGING IT WOULD REST MY HEART	I SHALL NOT MURMUR IF AT	1410	5
SWEET SKEPTICISM OF THE HEART--	SWEET SKEPTICISM OF THE	1413	1
CRISIS IS SWEET AND YET THE HEART	CRISIS IS SWEET AND YET	1416	1
TOOK HER OWN HEART, INCLUDING OUR'S,	THE PRETTY RAIN FROM	1426	3
THE HEALED HEART SHOWS IT'S SHALLOW SCAR	THE HEALED HEART SHOWS	1440	1
I TAUGHT MY HEART A HUNDRED TIMES	I THOUGHT THE TRAIN	1449	5
AND WHILE BY STEPPING [STANDING] ON MY HEART	THE PILE OF YEARS IS NOT	1507	5
SWEET PIRATE OF THE HEART,	SWEET PIRATE OF THE	1546	1
THE HEART CANNOT FORGET	TO BE FORGOT BY THEE	1560	4
THE HUMAN HEART IS TOLD	BY HOMELY GIFT AND	1563	2
THE HEART HAS MANY DOORS--	THE HEART HAS MANY DOORS	1567	1
WHAT HEART WOULD RISK [COULD FIND] THE WAY--	WHERE ROSES WOULD NOT	1582	2
IT'S PLACE IS IN THE HUMAN HEART	THE BIRD HER PUNCTUAL	1585	3
IT IS THE STEADFAST HEART,	'TIS NOT THE SWAYING	1597	2
RANGE FROM A SINGLE HUMAN HEART	THE AUCTIONEER OF	1612	7
BUT AN ADJOURNING HEART--	NOT SICKNESS STAINS THE	1613	4
A HEART SOMETIMES A FOREIGNER,	PARTING WITH THEE	1614	3
ARROWS ENAMORED OF HIS HEART [BREAST]--	ARROWS ENAMORED OF HIS	1629	1
SOMETIMES WITH THE HEART	SOMETIMES WITH THE HEART	1680	1
UNTO A BROKEN HEART	UNTO A BROKEN HEART	1704	1
PROUD OF MY BROKEN HEART, SINCE THOU DIDST BREAK IT,	PROUD OF MY BROKEN HEART	1736	1
THE MOB WITHIN THE HEART	THE MOB WITHIN THE HEART	1745	1
OR HEART SO GENTLY BORNE,	WHICH MISSES MOST,	1759	3
AN EAR CAN BREAK A HUMAN HEART	THE SADDEST NOISE, THE	1764	17
WE WISH THE EAR HAD NOT A HEART	THE SADDEST NOISE, THE	1764	19
HEARTED SEE SIMPLE-HEARTED			
BRAVE--BROKEN HEARTED STATEMENT--	"THEY HAVE NOT CHOSEN ME	85	3
HEARTH			
NO RUDDY FIRES ON THE HEARTH--	WHAT INN IS THIS	115	7
TO MY SMALL HEARTH HIS FIRE CAME--	TO MY SMALL HEARTH HIS	638	1
HEARTIER			
IS HEARTIER THAN WE--	A SAUCER HOLDS A CUP	1374	16
HEART'S			
I'M THE LITTLE "HEART'S EASE"!	I'M THE LITTLE "HEART'S	176	1
NOR WILL I, THE LITTLE HEART'S EASE--	I'M THE LITTLE "HEART'S	176	13
THE SMALLEST HUMAN HEART'S EXTENT	THE LIFE WE HAVE IS VERY	1162	7
HEARTS			
BUILDED OUR HEARTS AMONG.	ONE SISTER HAVE I IN OUR	14	8
HOW IS IT HEARTS, WITH THEE?	I CAUTIOUS, SCANNED MY	178	18
IF BROADCLOTH HEARTS [BREASTS] ARE FIRMER--	A SHADY FRIEND--FOR	278	7
DULL HEARTS HAVE DIED	KNOWS HOW TO FORGET!	433	V
WE'RE FEARING THAT THEIR HEARTS WILL DROP--	WE DO NOT PLAY ON GRAVES	467	7
UNTIL IT BURST THE HEARTS	HE GAVE AWAY HIS LIFE--	567	5
EMPTY THE HEARTS THAT PURCHASED YOU--	BROTHER OF INGOTS--AH	1366	2
THE HUGEST HEARTS THAT BREAK.	LOVE'S STRICKEN "WHY"	1368	4
CLIMBING TO REACH [WHO "MEDDLED" WITH] THE COSTLY HEARTS	CLIMBING TO REACH THE	1566	1
ALL OTHER HEARTS [THINGS] I KNEW.	TO LOSE THEE--SWEETER	1754	2
HEARTY			
AND HEARTY--AS A ROSE--	WINTER IS GOOD--HIS HOAR	1316	6
HEARTY WITH BOYS THE ROAD--	GLASS WAS THE STREET--IN	1498	4
HAD BUT THE TALE A WARBLING [THRILLING / TYPIC / HEARTY / . . .	THE BIBLE IS AN ANTIQUE	1545	13
HEAT			
DARE YOU SEE A SOUL AT THE WHITE HEAT?	DARE YOU SEE A SOUL AT	365	1
ADJUST THE HEAT--ELUDE THE WIND--	BLOOM--IS RESULT--TO	1058	11
FAINT DEPUTIES OF HEAT--	LIKE BROOMS OF STEEL	1252	6
AND A GREEN CHILL UPON THE HEAT	THERE CAME A WIND LIKE A	1593	3
HEATHER			
YET KNOW I HOW THE HEATHER LOOKS	I NEVER SAW A MOOR--	1052	3

	FIRST LINE	POEM	LINE
HEAVEN			
EARTH IS A MERRY DAMSEL, AND HEAVEN A KNIGHT SO TRUE,	AWAKE YE MUSES NINE,	1	23
HANGS SO DISTANT HEAVEN--	DISTRUSTFUL OF THE	20	15
I HAD A STAR IN HEAVEN--	I HAD A GUINEA GOLDEN--	23	17
WHAT ONCE WAS "HEAVEN"	"ARCTURUS" IS HIS OTHER	70	17
GOING TO HEAVEN!	GOING TO HEAVEN!	79	1
GOING TO HEAVEN!	GOING TO HEAVEN!	79	6
THIS PLACE IS BLISS--THIS TOWN IS HEAVEN--	WHERE BELLS NO MORE	112	7
HEAVEN BEGUILES THE TIRED.	AS WATCHERS HANG UPON	121	6
HEAVEN TO US, IF TRUE.	AS WATCHERS HANG UPON	121	12
OH WHAT AN AFTERNOON FOR HEAVEN,	ALL OVERGROWN BY CUNNING	148	V
EXCEPT TO HEAVEN, SHE IS NOUGHT.	EXCEPT TO HEAVEN, SHE IS	154	1
FOR HEAVEN IS A DIFFERENT THING,	'TIS SO MUCH JOY! 'TIS	172	16
HEAVEN DOES NOT CHANGE HER BLUE.	I'M THE LITTLE "HEART'S	176	12
HID HEAVEN AND EARTH FROM VIEW.	AN AWFUL TEMPEST MASHED	198	4
TO FOLKS IN HEAVEN--NOW--	I'M "WIFE"--I'VE	199	8
AND AFTER THAT--THERE'S HEAVEN--	YOU'RE RIGHT--"THE WAY	234	9
ARE OUT OF SIGHT--IN HEAVEN--	I THINK JUST HOW MY	237	4
"HEAVEN"--IS WHAT I CANNOT REACH!	"HEAVEN"--IS WHAT I	239	1
THAT--"HEAVEN" IS--TO ME!	"HEAVEN"--IS WHAT I	239	4
I'VE KNOWN A HEAVEN, LIKE A TENT--	I'VE KNOWN A HEAVEN,	243	1
CALLED HEAVEN--	FOREVER AT HIS SIDE TO	246	13
WHY--DO THEY SHUT ME OUT OF HEAVEN?	WHY--DO THEY SHUT ME OUT	248	1
WHEN HEAVEN--WAS TOO COMMON--TO MISS--	THE LONESOME FOR THEY	262	11
THAT NOT FOR ALL THEIR HEAVEN CAN BOAST	A SINGLE SCREW OF FLESH	263	19
SOME DISTANT HEAVEN,	DOUBT ME! MY DIM	275	16
I REASON, THAT IN HEAVEN--	I REASON, EARTH IS SHORT	301	9
AND EAR--AND HEAVEN--NUMB--	LIKE SOME OLD FASHIONED	302	16
AND HEAVEN--NOT ENOUGH FOR ME--	I SHOULD HAVE BEEN TOO	313	14
THE HEAVEN WE CHASE,	THE NEAREST DREAM	319	2
SO INSTEAD OF GETTING TO HEAVEN, AT LAST--	SOME KEEP THE SABBATH	324	11
THAT STOPS--AT HEAVEN--	'TWAS THE OLD--ROAD--	344	4
AND FAR FROM HEAVEN AS THE REST--	NOT PROBABLE--THE BAREST	346	3
BUT WE MIGHT LEARN TO LIKE THE HEAVEN,	I FELT MY LIFE WITH BOTH	351	15
HEAVEN IS SO FAR OF THE MIND	HEAVEN IS SO FAR OF THE	370	1
I WENT TO HEAVEN--	I WENT TO HEAVEN--	374	1
TAKE YOUR HEAVEN FURTHER ON--	TAKE YOUR HEAVEN FURTHER	388	1
THIS--TO HEAVEN DIVINE HAS GONE--	TAKE YOUR HEAVEN FURTHER	388	2
'TWOULD SUPERSEDE THE HEAVEN--	DID OUR BEST MOMENT LAST	393	2
AS YOU WILL IN HEAVEN--	YOU'LL KNOW IT--AS YOU	420	5
ONE EYE UPON THE HEAVEN RENOUNCED--	TRIUMPH--MAY BE OF	455	11
THE HEAVEN HATH A HELL--	A TOOTH UPON OUR PEACE	459	5
HIMSELF--THE HEAVEN EXCEL--	THE POWER TO BE TRUE TO	464	6
EXCEPT THE HEAVEN HAD COME SO NEAR--	EXCEPT THE HEAVEN HAD	472	1
SUCH AS CONTENT--AND HEAVEN--	I MEANT TO HAVE BUT	476	2
A HEAVEN NOT SO LARGE AS YOUR'S,	I MEANT TO HAVE BUT	476	11
AND MINE'S--IN HEAVEN--YOU SEE.	YOU LOVE THE LORD--YOU	487	8
WE PRAY--TO HEAVEN--	WE PRAY--TO HEAVEN--	489	1
WE PRATE--OF HEAVEN--	WE PRAY--TO HEAVEN--	489	2
AT WHAT O'CLOCK TO HEAVEN--THEY FLED--	WE PRAY--TO HEAVEN--	489	4
IS HEAVEN A PLACE--A SKY--A TREE?	WE PRAY--TO HEAVEN--	489	6
AND HEAVEN--ABOUT--	IT'S THOUGHTS--AND JUST	495	24
AS HEAVEN [EDEN]--UNTO ME!	I ENVY SEAS, WHEREON HE	498	8
THE HEAVEN--UNEXPECTED COME,	LIKE FLOWERS, THAT HEARD	513	13
THE HEAVEN TO CONFIRM--	HER SWEET WEIGHT ON MY	518	6
THAT HEAVEN PERMIT SO MEEK [FAINT] AS HER--	SHE'S HAPPY, WITH A NEW	535	7
I OFFER THEM THE WHOLE [HALF] OF HEAVEN	I CROSS TILL I AM WEARY	550	20
THEN SUMMER--THEN THE HEAVEN OF GOD--	I RECKON--WHEN I COUNT	569	3
AND IF THE FURTHER [OTHER / FINAL] HEAVEN--	I RECKON--WHEN I COUNT	569	12
"HEAVEN" HAS DIFFERENT SIGNS--TO ME--	"HEAVEN" HAS DIFFERENT	575	1
BUT HEAVEN MADE BOTH, IMPOSSIBLE	WE TALKED AS GIRLS DO--	586	15
AND CARRIED, WE SUPPOSE--[I SUPPOSED] TO HEAVEN,	I CRIED AT PITY--NOT AT	588	11
OR ONLY HEAVEN--AT NOON--	I THINK I WAS ENCHANTED	593	6
WHY HEAVEN DID NOT BREAK AWAY--	IT TROUBLED ME AS ONCE I	600	15
HOW EXCELLENT THE HEAVEN--	IT WAS TOO LATE FOR MAN	623	5
A HEAVEN IN A GAZE--	'TWAS A LONG PARTING--	625	6
A HEAVEN OF HEAVENS--THE PRIVILEGE	'TWAS A LONG PARTING--	625	7
AND SIGH FOR LACK OF HEAVEN--BUT NOT	THE WAY I READ A	636	15
THE HEAVEN GOD BESTOW--	THE WAY I READ A	636	16
FOR YOU--SERVED HEAVEN--YOU KNOW,	I CANNOT LIVE WITH YOU--	640	30
FOR MY HEAVEN--	PROMISE THIS--WHEN YOU	648	31
TOO WIDE FOR ANY NIGHT BUT HEAVEN--	A PRISON GETS TO BE A	652	31
NAY--NATURE IS HEAVEN--	"NATURE" IS WHAT WE SEE	668	4
ADORED [BEHELD] WITH CAUTION--AS A BRITTLE HEAVEN--	EACH LIFE CONVERGES TO	680	9
THE HEAVEN VESTS FOR EACH	THE HEAVEN VESTS FOR	694	1
THEIR HIGHT IN HEAVEN COMFORTS NOT--	THEIR HIGHT IN HEAVEN	696	1
HEAVEN IS SHY OF EARTH--THAT'S ALL--	OUT OF SIGHT? WHAT OF	703	11
BASHFUL HEAVEN--THY LOVERS SMALL--	OUT OF SIGHT? WHAT OF	703	12
TOO NEAR TO HEAVEN--TO FEAR--	THE DAY UNDRESSED--	716	10
AND HEAVEN--A CONVENIENT GRACE	HAVE ANY LIKE MYSELF	736	15
THE HEAVEN YOU KNOW--TO UNDERSTAND	YOU TAUGHT ME WAITING	740	9
THE HEAVEN BELOW THE HEAVEN ABOVE--	ONE BLESSING HAD I THAN	756	13
THE HEAVEN BELOW THE HEAVEN ABOVE--	ONE BLESSING HAD I THAN	756	13
LIKE HALLOWING OF HEAVEN,	THE HALLOWING OF PAIN	772	2
TILL I AM FIRM IN HEAVEN	A CLOUD WITHDREW FROM	895	11
HOW FAR IS IT TO HEAVEN?	HOW FAR IS IT TO HEAVEN?	929	1
THAT HEAVEN IF HEAVEN--MUST CONTAIN	TWO TRAVELLERS PERISHING	933	5

	FIRST LINE	POEM	LINE
HEAVEN (CONTINUED)			
THAT HEAVEN IF HEAVEN--MUST CONTAIN	TWO TRAVELLERS PERISHING	933	5
LED ABSENT, WERE PROCURED [OBTAINED] OF HEAVEN	TWO TRAVELLERS PERISHING	933	15
"A SOUL HAS GONE TO HEAVEN"	OF TOLLING BELL I ASK	947	2
IS HEAVEN THEN A PRISON?	OF TOLLING BELL I ASK	947	4
A SOUL HAD GONE TO HEAVEN	OF TOLLING BELL I ASK	947	6
FOR THE SITE OF THE KINGDOM OF HEAVEN--	A LOSS OF SOMETHING EVER	959	16
IS ESTEEMED IN HEAVEN THE CHIEFEST--	"UNTO ME?" I DO NOT KNOW	964	11
THE DAY THE HEAVEN DIED--	DENIAL--IS THE ONLY FACT	965	4
OF HEAVEN, EASING ANALYSIS,	THE DEFINITION OF BEAUTY	988	3
SINCE HEAVEN AND HE ARE ONE.	THE DEFINITION OF BEAUTY	988	4
WHICH IS BEST? HEAVEN--	WHICH IS BEST? HEAVEN--	1012	1
OR ONLY HEAVEN TO COME	WHICH IS BEST? HEAVEN--	1012	2
LEST THIS BE HEAVEN INDEED	LEST THIS BE HEAVEN	1043	1
BETWEEN OURSELF AND HEAVEN.	LEST THIS BE HEAVEN	1043	4
NOR VISITED IN HEAVEN--	I NEVER SAW A MOOR--	1052	6
THAT IF THE HEAVEN INQUIRE	THE SOUL SHOULD ALWAYS	1055	2
DRILL SILENTLY [ARRANGE THE HEART] FOR HEAVEN--	TO HELP OUR BLEAKER	1064	4
AS DOWN HIS HEAVEN DROPT REMOTE [ECHOED FAINT]	JUST ONCE! OH LEAST	1076	8
BEFRIEND THEM, LEST YOURSELF IN HEAVEN	THESE STRANGERS, IN A	1096	3
THE FIRING IN HEAVEN,	HIS BILL IS CLASPED--HIS	1102	10
WENT TO HEAVEN PERHAPS AT DEATH	SO I PULL MY STOCKINGS	1201	5
OF HEAVEN ABOVE THE FIRMEST PROOF	IMMORTAL IS AN AMPLE	1205	5
IT HAD BEEN HEAVEN BELOW.	IMMORTAL IS AN AMPLE	1205	8
SO MUCH OF HEAVEN HAS GONE FROM EARTH	SO MUCH OF HEAVEN HAS	1228	1
THAT THERE MUST BE A HEAVEN	SO MUCH OF HEAVEN HAS	1228	2
WE BLUSH, THAT HEAVEN IF WE ACHIEVE [BEHOLD]--	WHO WERE "THE FATHER AND	1258	21
OF HEAVEN AND HELL I ALSO YIELD	BECAUSE THAT YOU ARE	1260	29
IS HEAVEN A PHYSICIAN?	IS HEAVEN A PHYSICIAN?	1270	1
IS HEAVEN AN EXCHEQUER?	IS HEAVEN A PHYSICIAN?	1270	5
THE HEAVEN, IN WHICH WE HOPED TO PAUSE	THE THINGS WE THOUGHT	1293	9
NOT ONE BY HEAVEN DEFRAUDED STAY--	NOT ONE BY HEAVEN	1303	1
BREAD OF HEAVEN RESENTS BESTOWAL	WHEN A LOVER IS A BEGGAR	1314	7
THE FACT THAT EARTH IS HEAVEN--	THE FACT THAT EARTH IS	1408	1
WHETHER HEAVEN IS HEAVEN OR NOT	THE FACT THAT EARTH IS	1408	2
WHETHER HEAVEN IS HEAVEN OR NOT	THE FACT THAT EARTH IS	1408	2
THAN HEAVEN MORE REMOTE,	THAN HEAVEN MORE REMOTE,	1436	1
FOR HEAVEN IS THE ROOT,	THAN HEAVEN MORE REMOTE,	1436	2
HEAVEN THE BALM OF A SURLY TECHNICALITY!	HOW HAPPY IS THE LITTLE	1510	V
HOW ARCHLY SPARED THE HEAVEN "TO COME"--	THE MOON UPON HER FLUENT	1528	V
WHO HAS NOT FOUND THE HEAVEN--BELOW--	WHO HAS NOT FOUND THE	1544	1
WHEN HEAVEN LOOKED UPON US ALL	NO BRIGADIER THROUGHOUT	1561	11
OLD SUITOR HEAVEN,	WE SHUN IT ERE IT COMES,	1580	7
HE BOWED TO HEAVEN INSTEAD OF EARTH [EVERY HEAVEN ABOVE / . . .	THE BOBOLINK IS GONE--	1591	6
HE BOWED TO HEAVEN INSTEAD OF EARTH [EVERY HEAVEN ABOVE / . . .	THE BOBOLINK IS GONE--	1591	6
IMMURED IN HEAVEN!	IMMURED IN HEAVEN!	1594	1
THAT TOO COMPETES WITH HEAVEN.	OF GOD WE ASK ONE FAVOR,	1601	8
AND ALL THAT HEAVEN WAS [SURMISE]--	SO GIVE ME BACK TO DEATH	1632	8
FATHER I OBSERVED TO HEAVEN	LIGHTLY STEPPED A YELLOW	1672	7
AND MORTGAGED HEAVEN	WHEN WE HAVE CEASED TO	1706	4
A PIT--BUT HEAVEN OVER IT--	A PIT--BUT HEAVEN OVER	1712	1
AND HEAVEN BESIDE, AND HEAVEN ABROAD;	A PIT--BUT HEAVEN OVER	1712	2
AND HEAVEN BESIDE, AND HEAVEN ABROAD;	A PIT--BUT HEAVEN OVER	1712	2
WITH HEAVEN OVER IT.	A PIT--BUT HEAVEN OVER	1712	4
AH! PIT! WITH HEAVEN OVER IT!	A PIT--BUT HEAVEN OVER	1712	9
A SINGLE DRAM OF HEAVEN!	I TOOK ONE DRAUGHT OF	1725	8
PARTING IS ALL WE KNOW OF HEAVEN,	MY LIFE CLOSED TWICE	1732	7
THEY HAVE A HEAVEN EACH INSTANT [MINUTE]	THE MOST IMPORTANT	1746	3
HEAVENLY			
HEAVENLY HURT, IT GIVES US--	THERE'S A CERTAIN SLANT	258	5
THESE HEAVENLY MOMENTS ARE--	DID OUR BEST MOMENT LAST	393	8
OF HEAVENLY LOVE--FORGOT--	I TRIED TO THINK A	532	11
IN HEAVENLY ESTEEM--	'TIS TRUE--THEY SHUT ME	538	6
ON THE HEAVENLY FAME--	I CANNOT LIVE WITH YOU--	640	40
A HEAVENLY FATHER WOULD SUFFICE [CONTENT]	YOU LEFT ME--SIRE--TWO	644	3
OF THE HEAVENLY GRACE--	PUBLICATION--IS THE	709	14
AT HEAVENLY--HOPELESS DISTANCES--	THIS BAUBLE WAS	805	3
FAR FROM LOVE THE HEAVENLY FATHER	FAR FROM LOVE THE	1021	1
THAT 'TIS SO HEAVENLY FAR--	PERCEPTION OF AN OBJECT	1071	V 8
FROM [OF / IN] THE HEAVENLY CLAUSE--	"FAITHFUL TO THE END"	1357	2
BY INNOCENT [ELOQUENT / HALLOWED / HEAVENLY / DIFFIDENT] SURPRISE--	THE PRETTY RAIN FROM	1426	4
"HEAVENLY FATHER"--TAKE TO THEE	"HEAVENLY FATHER"--TAKE	1461	1
AND IN THE HEAVENLY GRACE--	THE BIRD HER PUNCTUAL	1585	4
THAT THOU ART HEAVENLY	EXTOL THEE--COULD I--	1643	4
IN HEAVENLY REVIEWING	WITH SWEETNESS UNABATED	1709	11
ALMOST TOO HEAVENLY NEAR.	THE SADDEST NOISE, THE	1764	8
HEAVEN'S			
RATHER--HEAVEN'S "PETER PARLEY"!	I CANT TELL YOU--BUT YOU	65	17
PERHAPS THE "KINGDOM OF HEAVEN'S" CHANGED--	"ARCTURUS" IS HIS OTHER	70	26
HEAVENS			
AS ALL THE HEAVENS WERE A BELL,	I FELT A FUNERAL, IN MY	280	13
THE HEAVENS WITH A SMILE,	HOW NOTELESS MEN, AND	282	10
I SAW NO WAY--THE HEAVENS WERE STITCHED--	I SAW NO WAY--THE	378	1
AND WHEN THE HEAVENS--DISBAND--	A TONGUE--TO TELL HIM I	400	26
MAKES THE HEAVENS PORTABLE--	TAKING UP THE FAIR IDEAL	428	5
CREATION STOPPED [THE HEAVENS	MY PERIOD HAD COME FOR	564	18

	FIRST LINE	POEM	LINE
HEAVENS (CONTINUED)			
PAUSED]--FOR ME--			
AND ON THE HEAVENS--UNROLLED--	HE GAVE AWAY HIS LIFE--	567	8
THE HEAVENS STRIPPED--	EMPTY MY HEART, OF THEE	587	13
AND YET THE HEAVENS--HELD--	IT TROUBLED ME AS ONCE I	600	4
THE HEAVENS WEIGHED THE MOST--BY FAR [WERE THE WEIGHTIEST--FAR]--	IT TROUBLED ME AS ONCE I	600	5
A HEAVEN OF HEAVENS--THE PRIVILEGE . . .	'TWAS A LONG PARTING--	625	7
THE GENERAL HEAVENS--UPON--	OF BEING IS A BIRD	653	4
THE HEAVENS [TREES / SKY / FIELD] CANNOT BE FOUND--	THE SYMPTOM OF THE GALE	1327	6
THE GODS [STARS / HEAVENS / SKIES / SUNS] BUT DREGS	A WORLD MADE PENNINILESS	1623	4
HEAVES			
BETWEEN THE HEAVES OF STORM--	I HEARD A FLY BUZZ--WHEN	465	4
HEAVES BALLS OF SPECKS, LIKE VICIOUS BOY .	TO INTERRUPT HIS YELLOW	591	5
HEAVIER			
YET--STRANGEST--HEAVIER SINCE IT WENT-- . .	SAVIOR! I'VE NO ONE ELSE	217	11
EACH HEAVIER THAN THE LAST	I WATCHED HER FACE TO	1667	6
HEAVIEST			
BUT THE HEART WITH THE HEAVIEST FREIGHT ON--	"SPEECH"--IS A PRANK OF	688	3
LIFE'S EMPTY PACK IS HEAVIEST, ...	HER LOSSES MAKE OUR	1562	5
HEAVY			
HEART, NOT SO HEAVY AS MINE	HEART, NOT SO HEAVY AS	83	1
TILL MINE TOO HEAVY GREW--	SAVIOR! I'VE NO ONE ELSE	217	10
THE THIMBLE WEIGHED TOO HEAVY--	DEATH SETS A THING	360	9
'TIS HEAVY AND 'TIS LIGHT.	BEFORE HE COMES WE WEIGH	834	2
FROM HEAVY LADEN LANDS [CLIMES] TO THEE . .	THE BIRD DID PRANCE--THE	1107	9
AND [HE] PANTING [HEAVY / LANGUID] ON A CLOVER LEAN	THE BUTTERFLY'S NUMIDIAN	1387	5
'TIS TWICE AS HEAVY AS IT WAS	WHICH MISSES MOST,	1759	4
HECTIC			
JUST WHERE THE HECTIC STINGS!	A WOUNDED DEER--LEAPS	165	8
HE'D			
HE'D--CLIMB--IF HE COULD!	OVER THE FENCE--	251	9
HE'D BE TOO TALL, THE TALLEST ONE	I DREADED THAT FIRST	348	15
SUFFICIENTLY DEVELOPED--HE'D HIRE US . . .	MYSELF WAS FORMED--A	488	7
HEDGE			
AND ONE, A HEDGE AWAY.	ONE SISTER HAVE I IN OUR	14	2
HOW NONCHALANT THE HEDGE!	A LADY RED--AMID THE	74	14
HEED			
WILL HE HEED?	IF HE DISSOLVE--THEN--	236	15
HEEDING			
AND WHEN I WAS NOT HEEDING, ...	I HAD A GUINEA GOLDEN--	23	19
HEEDLESS			
NOR HEEDLESS BY THE WAY	I HAV'NT TOLD MY GARDEN	50	14
ALAS, HOW HEEDLESS WERE THE EYES--	ON THIS LONG STORM THE	194	7
HEEDLESS OF THE BOY--	THE NEAREST DREAM	319	9
HEEDLESS [PASSIVE]--ALIKE--OF [TO] POMP--OR [AND] PARTING	AH, TENERIFFE!	666	8
UNTIL THEY HEEDLESS TUMBLE IN	A STAGNANT PLEASURE LIKE	1281	3
HEEL			
I FELT HIS SILVER HEEL	I STARTED EARLY--TOOK MY	520	18
HEFT			
THAT OPPRESSES, LIKE THE HEFT	THERE'S A CERTAIN SLANT	258	3
THAT IF THE FLESH RESIST THE HEFT--	A WEIGHT WITH NEEDLES ON	264	3
FOR--HEFT THEM--POUND FOR POUND--	THE BRAIN--IS WIDER THAN	632	10
HEIGHT SEE HIGHT			
HEIR			
THE LAWFUL HEIR--FOR THEE--	DEFRAUDED I A BUTTERFLY	730	2
UPON AN UNSUSPECTING HEIR--	I AM AFRAID TO OWN A	1090	6
AS EACH WERE SPECIAL [LAWFUL / ONLY] HEIR--	ALONE AND IN A	1167	16
HELD			
HELD IN A TRUER LAND	I HAVE A BIRD IN SPRING	5	14
I HELD HER HAND THE TIGHTER--	ONE SISTER HAVE I IN OUR	14	15
SHE IS HELD TODAY--	WHETHER MY BARK WENT	52	6
MY FRECKLED MONARCH HELD THE REIN-- . . .	I MET A KING THIS	166	14
YET HELD MY BREATH, THE WHILE--	I'VE HEARD AN ORGAN TALK	183	4
AS IF AN AXLE, [A MUSCLE--] HELD--	WHEN WE STAND ON THE	242	16
I HELD A JEWEL IN MY FINGERS--	I HELD A JEWEL IN MY	245	1
HELD FAST IN EVERLASTING RACE--	TIE THE STRINGS TO MY	279	11
HELD OF THOSE BRASS ARMS--	IF YOUR NERVE, DENY YOU	292	7
YOU MARVEL HOW THEY HELD--	I TEND MY FLOWERS FOR	339	15
I HELD MY SPIRIT TO THE GLASS, ...	I FELT MY LIFE WITH BOTH	351	3
HELD SLANTING, IN THE SKY--	THE ANGLE OF A LANDSCAPE	375	8
THEN--HELD AN EMPTY PANE--	A HOUSE UPON THE HIGHT--	399	8
AND HELD IT IN OUR BOSOM--	I TIE MY HAT--I CREASE	443	28
BUT SOMETHING HELD MY WILL.	'TWAS JUST THIS TIME,	445	8
AS IF IT HELD BUT THE MIGHT OF A CHILD-- .	GOING TO HIM! HAPPY	494	13
TO FADE [DIE]--TOMORROW--RAINBOWS HELD [THRUST]	MY FIRST WELL DAY--SINCE	574	15
AND YET THE HEAVENS--HELD--	IT TROUBLED ME AS ONCE I	600	4
AND HELD MY EARS, AND LIKE A THIEF . . .	I YEARS HAD BEEN FROM	609	23
I HELD SO HIGH, FOR THEE--	I SEE THEE BETTER--IN	611	12
THAT HELD HIS FOREHEAD STIFF--	I ROSE--BECAUSE HE SANK	616	9
NOR HELD UPON--OF [HAS IT ANY] BRIM-- . .	YOU'LL KNOW HER--BY HER	634	20
HEARD [HELD] OPPOSITE THE SEA--	WITHOUT THIS--THERE IS	655	4
AND IS HELD LOW TO FREEZING LIPS--	VICTORY COMES LATE--	690	2
THE CARRIAGE HELD BUT JUST OURSELVES-- . .	BECAUSE I COULD NOT STOP	712	3
THESE--HELD DIMPLES--	THESE--SAW VISIONS--	758	3

	FIRST LINE	POEM	LINE
HELD (CONTINUED)			
THESE--WE HELD AMONG [FONDLED IN] OUR OWN--	THESE--SAW VISIONS--	758	9
BUT HELD HER GRAVITY ALOFT--	NO NOTICE GAVE SHE, BUT	804	11
THAT HELD THE DAMS--HAD PARTED HOLD--	THE WIND BEGUN TO KNEAD	824	17
IT HELD A HUMAN SOUL.	IT WAS A GRAVE, YET BORE	876	4
IT JUST HELD TWO, NOR THOSE IT HELD	I'VE NONE TO TELL ME TO	881	4
IT JUST HELD TWO, NOR THOSE IT HELD	I'VE NONE TO TELL ME TO	881	4
AS SOMEONE HELD A LIGHT UNTO [UPON]	WHAT I SEE NOT, I BETTER	939	7
THAT HELD HIM FROM PERDITION	AS ONE DOES SICKNESS	957	7
HELD UP HIS CUP FOR LIGHT.	THE FINGERS OF THE LIGHT	1000	16
WHAT TWIGS WE HELD BY--	WHAT TWIGS WE HELD BY--	1086	1
IT ONLY HELD ITSELF ALOOF	IT WAS NOT SAINT--IT WAS	1092	3
OUR PASSIVE FLOWER WE HELD TO SEA--	THE FROST OF DEATH WAS	1136	5
WHOSE HAVING LIVED IS HELD BY US IN NOBLE HOLIDAY	LEST ANY DOUBT THAT WE	1156	2
THESE HELD THEIR WICK ABOVE THE WEST--	THESE HELD THEIR WICK	1390	1
THE PRISM NEVER HELD THE HUES,	PURSUING YOU IN YOUR	1602	5
THE TREES HELD UP	THE WIND DREW OFF	1694	7
HE'LL			
HE'LL TELL ME!	WHAT SHALL I DO--IT	186	15
HE'LL TAKE IT--SCAN IT--STEP ASIDE--	THE FACE I CARRY WITH ME	336	9
AND THEN--HE'LL TURN ME ROUND AND ROUND--	THE FACE I CARRY WITH ME	336	13
BEST GRIEF IS TONGUELESS--BEFORE HE'LL TELL--	GRIEF IS A MOUSE--	793	13
THAT HE'LL [HE] MISTAKE--AND ASK FOR ME	FITTER TO SEE HIM, I MAY	968	16
HE'LL SIGH--"THE OTHER--[REAL ONE] SHE--IS WHERE?"	FITTER TO SEE HIM, I MAY	968	20
HELL			
THE HEAVEN HATH A HELL--	A TOOTH UPON OUR PEACE	459	5
THAT SELF--WERE HELL TO ME--	I CANNOT LIVE WITH YOU--	640	44
THE ADEQUATE [COMPLEMENT] OF HELL--	REMORSE--IS MEMORY--	744	12
HOW FAR IS IT TO HELL?	HOW FAR IS IT TO HEAVEN?	929	5
OF HEAVEN AND HELL I ALSO YIELD	BECAUSE THAT YOU ARE	1260	29
IT'S SIZE IS ALL THAT HELL CAN GUESS--	SO GIVE ME BACK TO DEATH	1632	7
OF WINTER AND OF HELL	A CAP OF LEAD ACROSS THE	1649	8
AND ALL WE NEED OF HELL.	MY LIFE CLOSED TWICE	1732	8
IN WHATSOEVER HELL	ONE CROWN THAT NO ONE	1735	6
NOT ANY HELL.	THE MOST IMPORTANT	1746	4
TOO SULLIED FOR THE HELL	UPON THE GALLOWS HUNG A	1757	2
HELMET			
HIS HELMET, IS OF GOLD,	HIS FEET ARE SHOD WITH	916	2
HELMSMAN			
FOR HELMSMAN [STEERSMAN] WAS THE BEE	A SOFT SEA WASHED AROUND	1198	6
HELP			
A DAY! HELP! HELP! ANOTHER DAY!	A DAY! HELP! HELP!	42	1
A DAY! HELP! HELP! ANOTHER DAY!	A DAY! HELP! HELP!	42	1
ANOTHER LAD--HELP THEE--	A TONGUE--TO TELL HIM I	400	17
TO HELP THE FOND--TO FIND IT--	THE COLOR OF THE GRAVE	411	5
AND NOT A SINEW--STIRRED--COULD HELP,	'TWAS LIKE A MAELSTROM,	414	14
I OFFERED IT NO HELP--	LIKE EYES THAT LOOKED ON	458	9
TO STILL IT'S NOISY [HELP IT'S VACANT] HANDS--	AT LEISURE IS THE SOUL	618	8
CREATION--IMPOTENT TO HELP--	IT WAS TOO LATE FOR MAN	623	3
CONTENT HER SMALLEST FRACTION HELP	LEAST BEE THAT BREW--	676	4
AND HELP BELIEF TO STRETCH [REACH]--	REMORSE--IS MEMORY--	744	8
TO GO WITHOUT THE SPECTRE'S AID [HELP]	I LIVED ON DREAD--	770	8
A FEW WENT OUT TO HELP THE BROOK	A DROP FELL ON THE APPLE	794	5
THAT [WHO] WENT TO HELP THE SEA--	A DROP FELL ON THE APPLE	794	6
OR HELP ONE FAINTING ROBIN	IF I CAN STOP ONE HEART	919	5
WITH WHICH WE HELP THE WHEEL	IDEALS ARE THE FAIRY OIL	983	2
I CANNOT HELP ESTEEM	WHICH IS BEST? HEAVEN--	1012	4
TO HELP OUR BLEAKER PARTS	TO HELP OUR BLEAKER	1064	1
OF MIGHT TO HELP, SO PITIFUL	WHAT TWIGS WE HELD BY--	1086	11
A FLOWER TO HELP HIS STRAIGHTENED FACE	AS IMPERCEPTIBLY AS	1540	V
WOULD HELP HIM TO CONCEAL,	TO TRY TO SPEAK, AND	1617	6
SO THAT WILL HELP THE SAND	I DID NOT REACH THEE	1664	8
HELPED			
TILL WE--ARE HELPED--	READ--SWEET--HOW OTHERS	260	6
I HELPED [STAYED] HIS FILM--WITH HYMN--	I ROSE--BECAUSE HE SANK	616	7
HE HELPED TO MAKE TOO BRIGHT	THE SUN IS GAY OR STARK	878	6
WE HAD HELPED THE TERROR	HAD WE KNOWN THE TON SHE	1124	2
IS HELPED [SOOTHED] BY THE REGRET	WHAT MYSTERY PERVADES A	1400	22
HELPLESS			
SO HELPLESS WHEN I TURNED	SO BASHFUL WHEN I SPIED	91	6
WEIGH, HELPLESS, IN HIS PAWS--	'TWAS LIKE A MAELSTROM,	414	13
CAUGHT HELPLESS AT A SENSE AS IF	HE SCANNED IT--STAGGERED	1062	4
TILL ALL HER HELPLESS BEAUTY BENT	THE FROST OF DEATH WAS	1136	14
WHICH HELPLESS NATURE DROPS	SHAME IS THE SHAWL OF	1412	5
HELPS			
AND HELPS US TO FORGET--	TO DIE--TAKES JUST A	255	8
IT HELPS TO STIMULATE THE FAITH	'TIS CUSTOMARY AS WE	440	3
SUPERSTITION HELPS, AS WELL AS LOVE--	ABSENCE DISEMBODIES--SO	860	3
HEM			
UPON THE POLAR HEM--	AS IF SOME LITTLE ARCTIC	180	2
OF YOUR DELIRIOUS HEM--	'TWAS LIKE A MAELSTROM,	414	6
WEAR YOU ON HEM--	I'LL CLUTCH--AND CLUTCH	427	9
WITH SPICES--IN THE HEM--	THE TREES LIKE TASSELS--	606	24
AND ONE UPON HER HEM--	THE SUNRISE RUNS FOR	710	17
HEMISPHERE			
ENROLLED UPON THE HEMISPHERE [FIRMAMENT]	THE DAY UNDRESSED--	716	7
PENURY [HEMISPHERE] AND HOME?	FRIGID AND SWEET HER	1318	8

	FIRST LINE	POEM	LINE
HEMISPHERES			
THE EARTH REVERSED HER HEMISPHERES--	I SAW NO WAY--THE	378	3
CLASP HEMISPHERES, AND HOMES	THE SUNRISE RUNS FOR	710	14
A PEACE, AS HEMISPHERES AT HOME	THE CRICKETS SANG	1104	11
HEMLOCK			
WHAT WILL THE SOLEMN HEMLOCK--	I ROBBED THE WOODS--	41	8
I THINK THE HEMLOCK LIKES TO STAND	I THINK THE HEMLOCK	525	1
HEMLOCK'S			
THE HEMLOCK'S NATURE THRIVES--ON COLD--	I THINK THE HEMLOCK	525	9
HEMLOCKS			
HOW THE HEMLOCKS BURN--	HOW THE OLD MOUNTAINS	291	2
AND HEMLOCKS--BOW--TO GOD--	DOOM IS THE HOUSE	475	8
HEMPEN			
EXTENDED HEMPEN HANDS--	I STARTED EARLY--TOOK MY	520	6
HEMS			
WHAT WE TOUCH THE HEMS OF	BEFORE THE ICE IS IN THE	37	9
HIS HAUGHTY--SPANGLED HEMS--	THE SUN--JUST TOUCHED	232	10
HEMS--TOO FINE FOR LADY'S TRACING	DONT PUT UP MY THREAD &	617	9
HENCE			
WHERE SUNSET HENCE MUST BE	THE SUNSET STOPPED ON	950	2
A PERIOD FROM HENCE	NO OTHER CAN REDUCE	982	4
A PERIOD FROM HENCE--	NO OTHER CAN REDUCE	982	V
HENCEFORTH			
HENCEFORTH--FOR HER--WHAT HOLIDAY!	THE SUN--JUST TOUCHED	232	7
HENCEFORTH--HER ONLY ONE!	THE SUN--JUST TOUCHED	232	16
HENCEFORTH, A DEDICATED SORT--	HE PUT THE BELT AROUND	273	7
HENCEFORTH I TAKE MY LIVING PLACE	SOMEHOW MYSELF SURVIVED	1194	5
HENCEFORTH TO REMEMBER	NOW I KNEW I LOST HER--	1219	13
HENCEFORWARD			
HENCEFORWARD CHERISHED BE--	WHAT CARE THE DEAD, FOR	592	16
HER			
NO MORE HE SINGETH MOURNFUL, HER SADNESS SHE DOTH LOSE.	AWAKE YE MUSES NINE,	1	20
THEN BEAR HER TO THE GREENWOOD, AND BUILD FOR HER A BOWER,	AWAKE YE MUSES NINE,	1	37
THEN BEAR HER TO THE GREENWOOD, AND BUILD FOR HER A BOWER,	AWAKE YE MUSES NINE,	1	37
AND GIVE HER WHAT SHE ASKETH, JEWEL, OR BIRD, OR FLOWER--	AWAKE YE MUSES NINE,	1	38
THE OTHER, AS A BIRD HER NEST,	ONE SISTER HAVE I IN OUR	14	7
HERSELF TO HER A MUSIC	ONE SISTER HAVE I IN OUR	14	11
I HELD HER HAND THE TIGHTER--	ONE SISTER HAVE I IN OUR	14	15
AND STILL HER HUM	ONE SISTER HAVE I IN OUR	14	17
STILL IN HER EYE	ONE SISTER HAVE I IN OUR	14	20
DRINKING TO HER NO MORE ASTIR,	I WOULD DISTIL A CUP,	16	3
THE GENTIAN WEAVES HER FRINGES--	THE GENTIAN WEAVES HER	18	1
THE FLUTTERING OF HER FRINGES	DISTRUSTFUL OF THE	20	3
I TOUCHED HER CRADLE MUTE--	SHE SLEPT BENEATH A TREE	25	3
PUT ON HER CARMINE SUIT	SHE SLEPT BENEATH A TREE	25	5
TO HER FAIR REPOSE.	MORNS LIKE THESE--WE	27	4
SHE WILL STIR HER PINIONS	IT DID NOT SURPRISE ME--	39	3
BACK TO HER NATIVE WOOD!	THERE'S SOMETHING	45	12
HER OATH, AND MINE--	I KEEP MY PLEDGE.	46	10
BESTIRS HER PUZZLED WINGS	ONCE MORE, MY NOW	48	2
ONCE MORE HER MISTRESS, ON THE DEEP	ONCE MORE, MY NOW	48	3
HER TROUBLED QUESTION FLINGS--	ONCE MORE, MY NOW	48	4
SHE BENT HER DOCILE SAILS--	WHETHER MY BARK WENT	52	4
WHO MARSHALLED HER AWAY--	TAKEN FROM MEN--THIS	53	4
HER LOVING BOSOM LAY--	DELAYED TILL SHE HAD	58	3
IN HER IMPERIAL ROUND--	DELAYED TILL SHE HAD	58	15
LIKE HER THE SAINTS RETIRE,	LIKE HER THE SAINTS	60	1
LIKE HER THE EVENINGS STEAL	LIKE HER THE SAINTS	60	4
THE ORCHIS BINDS HER FEATHER ON	SOME RAINBOW--COMING	64	16
FOR HER OLD LOVER--DON THE SUN!	SOME RAINBOW--COMING	64	17
AND HAS HER IN A "CLASS"!	"ARCTURUS" IS HIS OTHER	70	12
GLOWING IS HER BONNET,	GLOWING IS HER BONNET,	72	1
GLOWING IS HER CHEEK,	GLOWING IS HER BONNET,	72	2
GLOWING IS HER KIRTLE,	GLOWING IS HER BONNET,	72	3
LOOKING FOR HER FACE.	GLOWING IS HER BONNET,	72	10
HER ANNUAL SECRET KEEPS!	A LADY RED--AMID THE	74	2
HER LEASE OF SPOTTED HOURS,	SHE DIED AT PLAY,	75	3
HER GHOST STROLLED SOFTLY O'ER THE HILL	SHE DIED AT PLAY,	75	6
HER VESTMENTS AS THE SILVER FLEECE--	SHE DIED AT PLAY,	75	8
HER COUNTENANCE AS SPRAY.	SHE DIED AT PLAY,	75	9
SO SPICY HER CARNATIONS NOD--	WE SHOULD NOT MIND SO	81	5
SO DRUNKEN, REEL HER BEES--	WE SHOULD NOT MIND SO	81	6
I FOUND HER--"PLEIAD"--IN THE WOODS	WHOSE CHEEK IS THIS?	82	4
AND BORE HER SAFE AWAY.	WHOSE CHEEK IS THIS?	82	5
HER BREAST IS FIT FOR PEARLS,	HER BREAST IS FIT FOR	84	1
HER BROW IS FIT FOR THRONES	HER BREAST IS FIT FOR	84	3
HER HEART IS FIT FOR HOME [REST]--	HER BREAST IS FIT FOR	84	5
SO BASHFUL WHEN I SPIED HER!	SO BASHFUL WHEN I SPIED	91	1
SO HIDDEN IN HER LEAFLETS	SO BASHFUL WHEN I SPIED	91	3
SO BREATHLESS TILL I PASSED HER--	SO BASHFUL WHEN I SPIED	91	5
AND BORE HER STRUGGLING, BLUSHING,	SO BASHFUL WHEN I SPIED	91	7
HER SIMPLE HAUNTS BEYOND!	SO BASHFUL WHEN I SPIED	91	8
AS SLOW HER FLAMBEAUX BURN AWAY	A SOMETHING IN A	122	2
STILL REARS THE EAST HER AMBER FLAG--	A SOMETHING IN A	122	16
UNTIES HER YELLOW BONNET	PERHAPS YOU'D LIKE TO	134	5
I HAD RATHER WEAR HER GRACE	PIGMY SERAPHS--GONE	138	12

HER (CONTINUED)

	FIRST LINE	POEM	LINE
I HAD RATHER DWELL LIKE HER	PIGMY SERAPHS--GONE	138	14
NEVER THE TREASURES IN HER NEST	SOME, TOO FRAGILE FOR	141	5
HER BUSY FOOT SHE PLIED--	WHOSE ARE THE LITTLE	142	18
THE CROCUS STIRS HER LIDS--	WHOSE ARE THE LITTLE	142	22
HER PRIDE ASPIRES--	FOR EVERY BIRD A NEST--	143	12
HER MODEST HOUSE--	FOR EVERY BIRD A NEST--	143	15
TRACED AZURE ON HER HAND--	SHE BORE IT TILL THE	144	2
TILL PLEADING, ROUND HER QUIET EYES	SHE BORE IT TILL THE	144	3
NO MORE HER PATIENT FIGURE	SHE BORE IT TILL THE	144	9
NO MORE HER TIMID BONNET	SHE BORE IT TILL THE	144	11
WHOSE BUT HER SHY--IMMORTAL FACE	SHE BORE IT TILL THE	144	15
UPON HER PUZZLED EAR--	ALL OVERGROWN BY CUNNING	148	V
AND WHEN HER BREATH WAS DONE	SHE DIED--THIS WAS THE	150	2
TOOK UP HER SIMPLE WARDROBE	SHE DIED--THIS WAS THE	150	3
HER LITTLE FIGURE AT THE GATE	SHE DIED--THIS WAS THE	150	5
HER TRUDGING FEET ESPIED--	SHE DIED--THIS WAS THE	150	V 6
SINCE I COULD NEVER FIND HER	SHE DIED--THIS WAS THE	150	7
YET TAKE HER FROM THE LAWN	EXCEPT TO HEAVEN, SHE IS	154	10
I HEAR HER FEET UPON THE STAIR!	DYING! DYING IN THE	158	11
TO HER ROSIER,	THO' MY DESTINY BE	163	8
ON HER FOREHEAD LAY,	THO' MY DESTINY BE	163	10
WHERE NO AUTUMN LIFTS HER PENCIL--	THO' MY DESTINY BE	163	15
MAMA NEVER FORGETS HER BIRDS,	MAMA NEVER FORGETS HER	164	1
AS WHEN HER LITTLE MORTAL NEST	MAMA NEVER FORGETS HER	164	5
IF EITHER OF HER "SPARROWS FALL",	MAMA NEVER FORGETS HER	164	7
HEAVEN DOES NOT CHANGE HER BLUE.	I'M THE LITTLE "HEART'S	176	12
TO DRIVE HER FROM THE HALL?	IF I COULD BRIBE THEM BY	179	19
MUST AWAKEN HER!	ON THIS LONG STORM THE	194	12
HER CARGO--IS OF DEW--	MY EYE IS FULLER THAN MY	202	2
TOO OFTEN AT HER DOOR--	THE FLOWER MUST NOT	206	3
THE ROSE DID CAPER ON HER CHEEK--	THE ROSE DID CAPER ON	208	1
HER BODDICE ROSE AND FELL--	THE ROSE DID CAPER ON	208	2
HER PRETTY SPEECH--LIKE DRUNKEN MEN--	THE ROSE DID CAPER ON	208	3
HER FINGERS FUMBLED AT HER WORK--	THE ROSE DID CAPER ON	208	5
HER FINGERS FUMBLED AT HER WORK--	THE ROSE DID CAPER ON	208	5
HER NEEDLE WOULD NOT GO--	THE ROSE DID CAPER ON	208	6
A VEST THAT LIKE HER BODDICE, DANCED--	THE ROSE DID CAPER ON	208	13
ROUND HER CHAMBER HUMS--	COME SLOWLY--EDEN!	211	6
DID THE HAREBELL LOOSE HER GIRDLE	DID THE HAREBELL LOOSE	213	1
YIELD HER MOAT OF PEARL--	DID THE HAREBELL LOOSE	213	6
IN HER CASTLE ABOVE THEM--	SAFE IN THEIR ALABASTER	216	8
AND STILL, SHE PLIES HER SPOTTED BROOMS, [THRIFT]	SHE SWEEPS WITH	219	9
REJECTED--BE--OF HER?	COULD I--THEN--SHUT THE	220	3
WHEN KATIE WALKS, THIS SIMPLE PAIR ACCOMPANY HER SIDE,	WHEN KATIE WALKS, THIS	222	1
WHEN KATIE KNEELS, THEIR LOVING HANDS STILL CLASP HER PIOUS KNEE--	WHEN KATIE WALKS, THIS	222	3
LAYING HER [IT'S] SPOTTED FACE TO DIE	BLAZING IN GOLD AND	228	4
KISSING HER [IT'S] BONNET TO THE MEADOW	BLAZING IN GOLD AND	228	7
DAINTY--AS THE TRESS--ON HER DEFT HEAD--	WE--BEE AND I--LIVE BY	230	11
HENCEFORTH--FOR HER--WHAT HOLIDAY!	THE SUN--JUST TOUCHED	232	7
MEANWHILE--HER WHEELING KING--	THE SUN--JUST TOUCHED	232	8
FELT FEEBLY--FOR HER CROWN--	THE SUN--JUST TOUCHED	232	14
HER UNANNOINTED FOREHEAD--	THE SUN--JUST TOUCHED	232	15
HENCEFORTH--HER ONLY ONE!	THE SUN--JUST TOUCHED	232	16
AT HER PHOSPHORIC TOIL!	THE LAMP BURNS SURE--	233	4
AND SHE WILL FLING HER MADDEST PERFUME--	KILL YOUR BALM--AND IT'S	238	3
OH, COULD YOU CATCH HER LAST REFRAIN--	KILL YOUR BALM--AND IT'S	238	6
HER TEAZING PURPLES--AFTERNOONS--	"HEAVEN"--IS WHAT I	239	9
I'D GIVE HER--	WHAT WOULD I GIVE TO SEE	247	8
TO HER--WHO PLEDGES THIS--	WHAT WOULD I GIVE TO SEE	247	25
ONE HOUR--OF HER SOVREIGN'S FACE"!	WHAT WOULD I GIVE TO SEE	247	26
LIKE HER TRANSLATED FACES--	YOU SEE I CANNOT SEE--	253	13
HER PURPLE TRAFFIC	THIS--IS THE LAND--THE	266	6
HER BLAMELESS MYSTERY--	A SOLEMN THING--IT WAS--	271	4
SIFT HER, FROM BROW TO BAREFOOT!	DOUBT ME! MY DIM	275	18
STRAIN TILL YOUR [HER] LAST SURMISE--	DOUBT ME! MY DIM	275	19
WINNOW HER FINEST FONDNESS--	DOUBT ME! MY DIM	275	22
FORGETS HER OWN LOCALITY--	THE DROP, THAT WRESTLES	284	2
THE OCEAN--SMILES--AT HER CONCEIT--	THE DROP, THAT WRESTLES	284	7
SUCH [SOME] SPIRIT MAKES [TELL] HER PERPETUAL MENTION,	UNTO LIKE STORY--TROUBLE	295	13
HER GLORY I SHOULD KNOW--	YOUR RICHES--TAUGHT ME--	299	14
HER BEES HAVE A FICTITIOUS [AN ILLUSIVE] HUM--	LIKE SOME OLD FASHIONED	302	9
HER BLOSSOMS, LIKE A DREAM--	LIKE SOME OLD FASHIONED	302	10
HER MEMORIES [MEMORY] LIKE STRAINS--REVIEW [ENCHANT]--	LIKE SOME OLD FASHIONED	302	13
THE SOUL SELECTS HER OWN SOCIETY--	THE SOUL SELECTS HER OWN	303	1
TO [ON] HER DIVINE MAJORITY--	THE SOUL SELECTS HER OWN	303	3
AT HER LOW GATE--	THE SOUL SELECTS HER OWN	303	6
UPON HER [ON HER RUSH] MAT--	THE SOUL SELECTS HER OWN	303	8
UPON HER [ON HER RUSH] MAT--	THE SOUL SELECTS HER OWN	303	8
I'VE KNOWN HER--FROM AN AMPLE NATION--	THE SOUL SELECTS HER OWN	303	9
THEN--CLOSE THE VALVES [LIDS] OF HER ATTENTION--	THE SOUL SELECTS HER OWN	303	11
OCCUR TO HER--ALONE--	THE SOUL'S SUPERIOR	306	2
THAN HER OMNIPOTENT--	THE SOUL'S SUPERIOR	306	8
HER--"LAST POEMS"--	HER--"LAST POEMS"--	312	1

HER (CONTINUED)

	FIRST LINE	POEM	LINE
SILVER--PERISHED--WITH HER TONGUE--	HER--"LAST POEMS"--	312	3
PUT HER DOWN--IN ITALY?	HER--"LAST POEMS"--	312	19
HER GREEN PEOPLE RECOLLECT IT	NATURE--SOMETIMES SEARS	314	3
THE JUGGLER'S HAT HER COUNTRY IS--	THE JUGGLER'S HAT HER	330	1
AS ONE THAT BORE HER MASTER'S NAME--	THE FACE I CARRY WITH ME	336	15
SHE--EACH YEAR--LEADS HER DAISIES BACK--	I KNOW A PLACE WHERE	337	3
HER HEART MISGIVES HER, FOR HER VOW--	I KNOW A PLACE WHERE	337	7
HER HEART MISGIVES HER, FOR HER VOW--	I KNOW A PLACE WHERE	337	7
HER HEART MISGIVES HER, FOR HER VOW--	I KNOW A PLACE WHERE	337	7
UPON HER AMBER SHOE--	I KNOW A PLACE WHERE	337	12
EARN HER OWN SURPRISE!	I KNOW THAT HE EXISTS	338	8
MY CACTUS--SPLITS HER BEARD	I TEND MY FLOWERS FOR	339	7
TO SHOW HER THROAT--	I TEND MY FLOWERS FOR	339	8
HER LORD--AWAY!	I TEND MY FLOWERS FOR	339	22
HER EVERLASTING FASHION--SET--	IT WILL BE SUMMER--	342	15
TILL SUMMER FOLDS HER MIRACLE--	IT WILL BE SUMMER--	342	17
WAIT! LOOK! HER LITTLE BOOK--	'TWAS THE OLD--ROAD--	344	12
HER VERY HAT--	'TWAS THE OLD--ROAD--	344	14
TO TOUCH HER HEAD!	'TWAS THE OLD--ROAD--	344	22
AN HONOR, THOUGHT CAN TURN HER TO	I HAD THE GLORY--THAT	349	2
AS LADY FROM HER DOOR	FROM COCOON FORTH A	354	2
HER PRETTY PARASOL BE SEEN	FROM COCOON FORTH A	354	9
WITH "THIS WAS LAST HER FINGERS DID"--	DEATH SETS A THING	360	7
I WENT TO THANK HER--	I WENT TO THANK HER--	363	1
HER BED--A FUNNELED STONE--	I WENT TO THANK HER--	363	3
WHO WENT TO THANK HER--	I WENT TO THANK HER--	363	6
TO LOOK UPON HER LIKE--ALIVE--	I WENT TO THANK HER--	363	9
AND PILED HER BLOSSOMS ON--	THE MORNING AFTER WO--	364	6
HER VICTIM STARED UPON--	THE MORNING AFTER WO--	364	8
HER LIFE HAD LEAPED AWAY--	SHE LAY AS IF AT PLAY	369	2
HER MERRY ARMS, HALF DROPT--	SHE LAY AS IF AT PLAY	369	5
HER DANCING EYES--AJAR--	SHE LAY AS IF AT PLAY	369	9
HER MORNING AT THE DOOR--	SHE LAY AS IF AT PLAY	369	13
TO FORCE HER SLEEP--	SHE LAY AS IF AT PLAY	369	15
A BIRD--HAD STAMPED HER FOOT--	OF COURSE--I PRAYED--	376	4
THE EARTH REVERSED HER HEMISPHERES--	I SAW NO WAY--THE	378	3
AND HER--CAPACITY--	THERE IS A FLOWER THAT	380	8
HER FACE BE ROUNDER THAN THE MOON	THERE IS A FLOWER THAT	380	9
HER STURDY LITTLE COUNTENANCE	THERE IS A FLOWER THAT	380	15
HER PUBLIC--BE THE NOON--	THERE IS A FLOWER THAT	380	25
HER PROVIDENCE--THE SUN--	THERE IS A FLOWER THAT	380	26
HER PROGRESS--BY THE BEE--PROCLAIMED--	THERE IS A FLOWER THAT	380	27
FEELS HER WHITE FOOT--NO TREPIDATION--	THROUGH THE DARK SOD--AS	392	3
HER FAITH--NO FEAR--	THROUGH THE DARK SOD--AS	392	4
SWINGING HER BERYL BELL--	THROUGH THE DARK SOD--AS	392	6
IN HER UNFURNISHED ROOMS--	DID OUR BEST MOMENT LAST	393	12
THEN MY FACE TAKE HER RECOMPENSE--	I HAD NOT MINDED--WALLS	398	7
HAD NATURE--IN HER MONSTROUS HOUSE	A TONGUE--TO TELL HIM I	400	3
SHE SAID HER STRINGS WERE SNAPT--	THE FIRST DAY'S NIGHT	410	5
HER BOW--TO ATOMS BLOWN--	THE FIRST DAY'S NIGHT	410	6
AND SO TO MEND HER--GAVE ME WORK	THE FIRST DAY'S NIGHT	410	7
I MADE MY SOUL FAMILIAR--WITH HER EXTREMITY--	I READ MY SENTENCE--	412	9
TO WITNESS HER GOODBYE--	WE GROW ACCUSTOMED TO	419	4
THE LADY DARE NOT LIFT HER VAIL	A CHARM INVESTS A FACE	421	3
BUT PEERS BEYOND HER MESH--	A CHARM INVESTS A FACE	421	5
IN HER MYSTERIOUS DRAWERS--	THE MONTHS HAVE ENDS--	423	6
JUST TO CAST HER DOWN	TAKING UP THE FAIR IDEAL	428	2
WE BEHOLD HER--GLORIFIED--	TAKING UP THE FAIR IDEAL	428	11
OBEDIENT TO HER EYE	THE MOON IS DISTANT FROM	429	6
FORGOT SHE WORE IT AT HER HEART	FORGET! THE LADY WITH	438	2
DENY! DID ROSE HER BEE--	FORGET! THE LADY WITH	438	5
OR OPPORTUNITY--HER LORD AWAY?	FORGET! THE LADY WITH	438	8
OF HER ELECTRIC HAIR--	'TIS CUSTOMARY AS WE	440	8
HER MESSAGE IS COMMITTED	THIS IS MY LETTER TO THE	441	5
FOR LOVE OF HER--SWEET--COUNTRYMEN--	THIS IS MY LETTER TO THE	441	7
AND SUMMER HID HER FOREHEAD--	GOD MADE A LITTLE	442	7
THE FROSTS WERE HER CONDITION--	GOD MADE A LITTLE	442	9
I [HE] SHOWED HER [ME] HIGHTS SHE [I] NEVER SAW--	I SHOWED HER HIGHTS SHE	446	1
I [HE] SHOWED HER [ME] SECRETS--MORNING'S NEST--	I SHOWED HER HIGHTS SHE	446	5
SHE [I] COULD NOT FIND HER [MY] YES--	I SHOWED HER HIGHTS SHE	446	8
A LIGHT, FOR HER [ME], DID SOLEMN GLOW,	I SHOWED HER HIGHTS SHE	446	10
THE LARGER, AS HER [MY] FACE WITHDREW--	I SHOWED HER HIGHTS SHE	446	11
ADVANCE UNMOVED--TO HER SUPREME--	TRIUMPH--MAY BE OF	455	7
HER GOD--HER ONLY THRONG--	TRIUMPH--MAY BE OF	455	8
HER GOD--HER ONLY THRONG--	TRIUMPH--MAY BE OF	455	8
AND HER UNSOWN PENINSULA--	THEY PUT US FAR APART--	474	3
SHE DEALT HER PRETTY WORDS LIKE BLADES--	SHE DEALT HER PRETTY	479	1
SHE CANNOT KEEP HER PLACE.	"WHY DO I LOVE" YOU, SIR	480	5
WHERE TENT BY TENT--HER UNIVERSE	THE HIMMALEH WAS KNOWN	481	5
DESERTS--NEVER REBUKED HER SATIN--	CIVILIZATION--SPURNS--	492	3
ETHIOP--HER GOLD--	CIVILIZATION--SPURNS--	492	4
TAWNY--HER CUSTOMS--	CIVILIZATION--SPURNS--	492	5
SPOTTED--HER DUN GOWN--	CIVILIZATION--SPURNS--	492	7
PITY--THE PARD--THAT LEFT HER ASIA--	CIVILIZATION--SPURNS--	492	10
TO CLASP HER SOUL--FOR ALL--	THE WORLD--STANDS--	493	8
GOING TO HIM [HER]! HAPPY LETTER!	GOING TO HIM! HAPPY	494	1
TELL HIM [HER]--	GOING TO HIM! HAPPY	494	2

HER (CONTINUED)

	FIRST LINE	POEM	LINE
TELL HIM [HER] THE PAGE I DID'NT WRITE--[NEVER WROTE!]	GOING TO HIM! HAPPY	494	3
TELL HIM [HER]--I ONLY SAID THE SYNTAX--	GOING TO HIM! HAPPY	494	4
TELL HIM [HER] JUST HOW THE FINGERS HURRIED--	GOING TO HIM! HAPPY	494	6
TELL HIM [HER]--IT WAS'NT A PRACTISED WRITER--	GOING TO HIM! HAPPY	494	10
TELL HIM [HER]--NO--YOU MAY QUIBBLE THERE--	GOING TO HIM! HAPPY	494	15
FOR IT WOULD SPLIT HIS [HER] HEART, TO KNOW IT--	GOING TO HIM! HAPPY	494	16
TELL HIM [HER]--NIGHT [DAY] FINISHED--BEFORE WE FINISHED--	GOING TO HIM! HAPPY	494	18
TELL HIM [HER]--JUST HOW SHE SEALED YOU--CAUTIOUS!	GOING TO HIM! HAPPY	494	22
WHEN THE REDEMPTION STRIKES [SHAKES] HER BELLS--	BETTER--THAN MUSIC! FOR	503	20
NOR PERSIAN, BAFFLED AT HER SHRINE	HE TOUCHED ME, SO I LIVE	506	16
TO HER IMPERIAL SUN.	HE TOUCHED ME, SO I LIVE	506	18
HER EYES INCREASE TO BALLS--	SHE SIGHTS A BIRD--SHE	507	4
HER JAWS STIR--TWITCHING [MOUTH STIRS--LONGING]--HUNGRY--	SHE SIGHTS A BIRD--SHE	507	5
HER TEETH CAN HARDLY STAND--	SHE SIGHTS A BIRD--SHE	507	6
AND STOP TO LOOK AT HER--	THE SOUL HAS BANDAGED	512	4
SALUTE HER--WITH LONG FINGERS--	THE SOUL HAS BANDAGED	512	5
CARESS HER FREEZING HAIR--	THE SOUL HAS BANDAGED	512	6
THE HORROR WELCOMES HER, AGAIN,	THE SOUL HAS BANDAGED	512	23
HER SMILE WAS SHAPED LIKE OTHER SMILES--	HER SMILE WAS SHAPED	514	1
ASSERT HER VITAL PRIVILEGE--[HIS PRIMOGENITURE]	NO CROWD THAT HAS	515	7
HER SWEET WEIGHT ON MY HEART A NIGHT	HER SWEET WEIGHT ON MY	518	1
OR IF MYSELF WERE DREAMED OF HER--	HER SWEET WEIGHT ON MY	518	7
TILL RAPTURE MISSED THEM [HER FOOTING-- / PENINSULA]	TWO BUTTERFLIES WENT OUT	533	V
THAT FEELS TO HER--LIKE SACRAMENT--	SHE'S HAPPY, WITH A NEW	535	2
THAT HEAVEN PERMIT SO MEEK [FAINT] AS HER--	SHE'S HAPPY, WITH A NEW	535	7
SHE HIDETH HER THE LAST--	SHE HIDETH HER THE LAST	557	1
HER NIGHT DOTH HARDLY RECOMPENSE	SHE HIDETH HER THE LAST	557	3
THE CLOSING OF HER EYES--	SHE HIDETH HER THE LAST	557	4
SHE DOTH HER PURPLE WORK--	SHE HIDETH HER THE LAST	557	5
AND PUTTETH HER AWAY	SHE HIDETH HER THE LAST	557	6
TO IMITATE HER LIFE	SHE HIDETH HER THE LAST	557	9
BUT LITTLE CARMINE HATH HER FACE--	BUT LITTLE CARMINE HATH	558	1
OF EMERALD SCANT--HER GOWN--	BUT LITTLE CARMINE HATH	558	2
HER BEAUTY--IS THE LOVE SHE DOTH--	BUT LITTLE CARMINE HATH	558	3
IF MOMENTLY [HER SWEET DOOR--] AJAR--	IT KNEW NO MEDICINE--	559	13
THEN BOTH HER HANDS OF HAZE	MY FIRST WELL DAY--SINCE	574	22
PUT UP--TO HIDE [HOLD] HER PARTING GRACE	MY FIRST WELL DAY--SINCE	574	23
"POOR CHILD"--AND SOMETHING IN HER VOICE	I CRIED AT PITY--NOT AT	588	3
FOR FEAR I HEAR HER SAY	I CRIED AT PITY--NOT AT	588	20
HER LITTLE ROCKING CHAIR TO DRAW--	THE NIGHT WAS WIDE, AND	589	15
AS SOON THE SOUTH--HER BREEZE	WHAT CARE THE DEAD, FOR	592	20
TODAY--HER ONLY BOY	WHEN I WAS SMALL, A	596	2
TO LOOK AT HER--HOW SLOWLY	WHEN I WAS SMALL, A	596	5
THAT WOMAN AND HER BOY	WHEN I WAS SMALL, A	596	14
OF NEARNESS TO HER SUNDERED THINGS	OF NEARNESS TO HER	607	1
THE GRAVE YIELDS BACK HER ROBBERIES--	OF NEARNESS TO HER	607	13
WITH HER FASTIDIOUS FOREHEAD?	AFRAID! OF WHOM AM I	608	11
TO LIFT HER GLASS--UPON--	I WATCHED THE MOON	629	8
SUSTAIN HER IN THE SKY--	I WATCHED THE MOON	629	16
HER TOILETTE--TO SUFFICE--	I WATCHED THE MOON	629	22
AND NEXT--I MET HER ON A CLOUD--	I WATCHED THE MOON	629	33
TO FOLLOW HER SUPERIOR ROAD [PACE]--	I WATCHED THE MOON	629	35
YOU'LL KNOW HER--BY HER FOOT--	YOU'LL KNOW HER--BY HER	634	1
YOU'LL KNOW HER--BY HER FOOT--	YOU'LL KNOW HER--BY HER	634	1
YOU'LL KNOW HER--BY HER VEST--	YOU'LL KNOW HER--BY HER	634	9
YOU'LL KNOW HER--BY HER VEST--	YOU'LL KNOW HER--BY HER	634	9
HER CAP IS SMALL--AND SNUG--	YOU'LL KNOW HER--BY HER	634	13
YOU'LL KNOW HER--BY HER VOICE--	YOU'LL KNOW HER--BY HER	634	21
YOU'LL KNOW HER--BY HER VOICE--	YOU'LL KNOW HER--BY HER	634	21
HERSELF ADJUST HER TIDES--UNTO--	I COULD SUFFICE FOR HIM,	643	15
HER POLAR TIME--BEHIND--	I THINK TO LIVE--MAY BE	646	20
OF ALL HER GLORIES--	PROMISE THIS--WHEN YOU	648	V 32
HER SWEET TURN TO LEAVE THE HOMESTEAD	HER SWEET TURN TO LEAVE	649	1
FITTER FEET--OF HER [FOR THE FEET] BEFORE US--	HER SWEET TURN TO LEAVE	649	13
OF HER FATHER--WHOSO ASK [CLAIM] HER--	HER SWEET TURN TO LEAVE	649	17
OF HER FATHER--WHOSO ASK [CLAIM] HER--	HER SWEET TURN TO LEAVE	649	17
DISTANCE--BE HER ONLY MOTION [SIGNAL]--	HER SWEET TURN TO LEAVE	649	21
THAT OBSCURE [DIVIDE] HER FACE--	HER SWEET TURN TO LEAVE	649	26
SUNSET--REVIEWS HER SAPPHIRE REGIMENT [REGIMENTS]--	AH, TENERIFFE!	666	4
DAY--DROPS YOU HER [HIS] RED ADIEU!	AH, TENERIFFE!	666	5
WHOSE BE HER [THIS] RENOWN, OR FADING,	BLOOM UPON THE MOUNTAIN	667	11
TO HER SIMPLICITY [SINCERITY]	"NATURE" IS WHAT WE SEE	668	12
HER MAKER--HER METROPOLIS--	SHE DWELLETH IN THE	671	3
HER MAKER--HER METROPOLIS--	SHE DWELLETH IN THE	671	3
THE UNIVERSE--HER MAID--	SHE DWELLETH IN THE	671	4
TO FETCH HER GRACE--AND HUE--	SHE DWELLETH IN THE	671	5
THE FIRMAMENT'S--TO PLUCK HER--	SHE DWELLETH IN THE	671	7
AND FETCH HER THEE--BE MINE--	SHE DWELLETH IN THE	671	8
CONTENT HER SMALLEST FRACTION HELP	LEAST BEE THAT BREW--	676	4
HER LEAST ATTENTION RAISE ON ME--	'TWOULD EASE--A	682	14

	FIRST LINE	POEM	LINE
HER (CONTINUED)			
TEARS OPEN HER IMPERIAL VEINS--	YOU'VE SEEN BALLOONS SET	700	15
DANGER! WHAT IS THAT TO HER?	OUT OF SIGHT? WHAT OF	703	5
FOR I--INHABIT HER--	THE GRACE--MYSELF--MIGHT	707	4
THE EAST--HER PURPLE TROTH	THE SUNRISE RUNS FOR	710	2
THE NOON UNWINDS HER BLUE	THE SUNRISE RUNS FOR	710	4
THE NORTH--HER BLAZING SIGN	THE SUNRISE RUNS FOR	710	10
UPON HER BOSOM--ONE--	THE SUNRISE RUNS FOR	710	16
AND ONE UPON HER HEM--	THE SUNRISE RUNS FOR	710	17
HER GARTER--WAS OF GOLD--	THE DAY UNDRESSED--	716	2
HER PETTICOAT--OF PURPLE PLAIN [JUST]--	THE DAY UNDRESSED--	716	3
HER DIMITIES--AS OLD	THE DAY UNDRESSED--	716	4
BE WRINKLED--MUCH AS HER--	THE DAY UNDRESSED--	716	8
HER CANDLE SO EXPIRE	THE DAY UNDRESSED--	716	13
I MEANT TO FIND HER WHEN I CAME--	I MEANT TO FIND HER WHEN	718	1
I MEANT TO TELL HER HOW I LONGED	I MEANT TO FIND HER WHEN	718	5
BUT DEATH HAD TOLD HER SO THE [SPECIFIC TOLD HER / ENAMORED . . .	I MEANT TO FIND HER WHEN	718	7
BUT DEATH HAD TOLD HER SO THE [SPECIFIC TOLD HER / ENAMORED . . .	I MEANT TO FIND HER WHEN	718	7
. . . TOLD HER] FIRST--	I MEANT TO FIND HER WHEN	718	7
WITH MIDNIGHT TO THE NORTH OF HER--	BEHIND ME--DIPS ETERNITY	721	16
AND MIDNIGHT TO THE SOUTH OF HER--	BEHIND ME--DIPS ETERNITY	721	17
HER LATEST WORSHIP--WHEN THE DAY	SWEET MOUNTAINS--YE TELL	722	10
TO LIFT HER BROWS ON YOU--	SWEET MOUNTAINS--YE TELL	722	12
THE PLAYTHINGS OF HER LIFE	SHE ROSE TO HIS	732	2
IF OUGHT SHE MISSED IN HER NEW DAY,	SHE ROSE TO HIS	732	5
AND NOW SHE TURNS HER PERFECT FACE	THE MOON WAS BUT A CHIN	737	3
HER FOREHEAD IS OF AMPLEST BLONDE--	THE MOON WAS BUT A CHIN	737	5
HER CHEEK--A BERYL HEWN--	THE MOON WAS BUT A CHIN	737	6
HER EYE UNTO THE SUMMER DEW	THE MOON WAS BUT A CHIN	737	7
HER LIPS OF AMBER NEVER PART--	THE MOON WAS BUT A CHIN	737	9
UPON HER FRIEND SHE COULD CONFER [BESTOW]	THE MOON WAS BUT A CHIN	737	11
WERE SUCH HER SILVER WILL--	THE MOON WAS BUT A CHIN	737	12
FOR CERTAINTY SHE TAKE HER WAY	THE MOON WAS BUT A CHIN	737	15
HER BONNET IS THE FIRMAMENT--	THE MOON WAS BUT A CHIN	737	17
THE UNIVERSE--[THE VALLEYS--ARE] HER SHOE--	THE MOON WAS BUT A CHIN	737	18
THE STARS--THE TRINKETS AT HER BELT--	THE MOON WAS BUT A CHIN	737	19
HER DIMITIES--OF BLUE--	THE MOON WAS BUT A CHIN	737	20
REMOTE--HER BEST ARRAY--	THE BIRDS REPORTED FROM	743	10
HER FROSTS TO PONDER--THEN IT WAS	THE BIRDS REPORTED FROM	743	15
I RECOLLECTED [ROSE TO COMFORT--] HER--	THE BIRDS REPORTED FROM	743	16
I OFFERED HER NO WORD--	THE BIRDS REPORTED FROM	743	18
HER--WITNESS--WAS HER DEAD--	THE BIRDS REPORTED FROM	743	20
HER--WITNESS--WAS HER DEAD--	THE BIRDS REPORTED FROM	743	20
I [SHE] NEVER QUESTIONED HER [ME]--	THE BIRDS REPORTED FROM	743	22
HER PARTIES ALL [COMPANIES] ASTIR--	REMORSE--IS MEMORY--	744	2
UNTO HER SACRAMENT--	MY WORTHINESS IS ALL MY	751	16
HER FAVOR--IS THE BEST DISDAIN	MY SOUL--ACCUSED ME--AND	753	5
BUT HER DISDAIN--'TWERE LIGHTER [COOLER] BEAR	MY SOUL--ACCUSED ME--AND	753	7
FIT FOR HER RECEPTION--NOW--	THESE--SAW VISIONS--	758	15
MOST SHE TOUCHED ME BY HER MUTENESS--	MOST SHE TOUCHED ME BY	760	1
SHE PRESENTED HER SMALL FIGURE--	MOST SHE TOUCHED ME BY	760	3
NOT UPON HER KNEE TO THANK ME	MOST SHE TOUCHED ME BY	760	9
TO HER BENEFACTOR	MOST SHE TOUCHED ME BY	760	19
SHE EASES FROM HER TEETH	THE WHOLE OF IT CAME NOT	762	6
DARKNESS INTERSECT HER FACE--	WHEN I HOPED, I	768	21
AND PUT OUT HER EYE--	WHEN I HOPED, I	768	22
THAT TRUSTS HER--BOLDLY UP--	THE TRUTH--IS STIRLESS--	780	12
WHEN SHE HAD PUT AWAY HER WORK	SEVERER SERVICE OF	786	7
HER ADMONITION MILD--	NATURE--THE GENTLEST	790	4
HOW FAIR HER CONVERSATION--	NATURE--THE GENTLEST	790	9
HER HOUSEHOLD--HER ASSEMBLY--	NATURE--THE GENTLEST	790	11
HER HOUSEHOLD--HER ASSEMBLY--	NATURE--THE GENTLEST	790	11
HER VOICE AMONG THE AISLES	NATURE--THE GENTLEST	790	13
AS WILL SUFFICE TO LIGHT HER LAMPS--	NATURE--THE GENTLEST	790	19
HER GOLDEN FINGER ON HER LIP--	NATURE--THE GENTLEST	790	23
HER GOLDEN FINGER ON HER LIP--	NATURE--THE GENTLEST	790	23
HER FINAL SUMMER WAS IT--	HER FINAL SUMMER WAS IT	795	1
PERVADED HER, WE THOUGHT	HER FINAL SUMMER WAS IT	795	4
BUT HER CARRARA GUIDE POST--	HER FINAL SUMMER WAS IT	795	11
SHE STAKED HER FEATHERS--GAINED AN ARC--	SHE STAKED HER FEATHERS	798	1
SHE STAKED HER WINGS--AND GAINED A BUSH--	SHE STAKED HER FEATHERS	798	V 1
HER STEADY BOAT BE SEEN--	SHE STAKED HER FEATHERS	798	6
UPON HER BOSOM [PETALS / SOFTNESS] PILED--	NO NOTICE GAVE SHE, BUT	804	8
OF SHRINKING WAYS--SHE DID NOT [FOREBORE HER] FRIGHT	NO NOTICE GAVE SHE, BUT	804	9
BUT HELD HER GRAVITY ALOFT--	NO NOTICE GAVE SHE, BUT	804	11
HER WARM [STRAIGHT / GOOD / QUICK / SAFE] RETURN, IF SO SHE . . .	NO NOTICE GAVE SHE, BUT	804	17
IT HAD CREATED [AFFORDED] HER.	THIS BAUBLE WAS	805	8
HER GRACE IS ALL SHE HAS--	HER GRACE IS ALL SHE HAS	810	1
WE CONJUGATE HER SKILL	THE VEINS OF OTHER	811	6
WITH HER CHERUBIC QUANTITY--	THE ROBIN IS THE ONE	828	7
THAT SPEECHLESS FROM HER NEST	THE ROBIN IS THE ONE	828	10
HOW WELL I KNEW HER NOT	HOW WELL I KNEW HER NOT	837	1
TO PERISH IN HER HAND!	BE MINE THE DOOM--	845	3
TWICE HAD SUMMER HER FAIR VERDURE	TWICE HAD SUMMER HER	846	1
APOLOGY FOR HER	APOLOGY FOR HER	852	1
REMAIN IN HER REGRET	WHEN ONE HAS GIVEN UP	853	6

HER (CONTINUED)

	FIRST LINE	POEM	LINE
HER TARRYING, UNKNOWN,	FROM US SHE WANDERED NOW	890	2
IF WILDERNESS PREVENT HER FEET	FROM US SHE WANDERED NOW	890	3
OF CONSCIOUSNESS, HER AWFUL MATE	OF CONSCIOUSNESS, HER	894	1
AS EASY THE SECRETING HER	OF CONSCIOUSNESS, HER	894	3
SPREADS THE POND HER BASE OF LILIES	HOW THE WATERS CLOSED	923	5
MEAN OF FORCES--STAND BY HER WING,	PATIENCE--HAS A QUIET	926	V
HALF HER COMPLEXION OF THE SUN--	FAIRER THROUGH FADING--	938	3
RALLIES HER GLOW [THE WEST], LIKE A DYING FRIEND--	FAIRER THROUGH FADING--	938	5
THE LADY FEEDS HER LITTLE BIRD	THE LADY FEEDS HER	941	1
THE GULF BETWEEN THE HAND AND HER	THE LADY FEEDS HER	941	5
AND FAINTING, ON HER YELLOW KNEE	THE LADY FEEDS HER	941	7
THE CORN, HER FURTHEST KERNEL FILLED	MIDSUMMER, WAS IT, WHEN	962	5
HOME EFFACED--HER FACES DWINDLED--	ALL FORGOT FOR	966	9
FOR HER JUGULAR DEFENCES--	ROBBED BY DEATH--BUT	971	5
AND THROWN HER FURTHEST STONE--	THIS MERIT HATH THE	979	4
WE MISS HER, NOT BECAUSE WE SEE--	WE MISS HER, NOT BECAUSE	993	1
I LEFT HER I COULD FIND HER	WE'LL PASS WITHOUT THE	996	5
I LEFT HER I COULD FIND HER	WE'LL PASS WITHOUT THE	996	5
HER CEDAR CITADEL.	FALSEHOOD OF THEE COULD	1007	4
FOR HER BRIEF CREST--	SHE ROSE AS HIGH AS HIS	1011	4
BECAUSE I FOUND HER KINSMANLESS,	MY SEASON'S FURTHEST	1019	3
HER PALATE TO DELIGHT	MY HEART UPON A LITTLE	1027	2
IMPALED HIM ON HER FIERCEST STAKES--	FATE SLEW HIM, BUT HE	1031	3
BUT WHEN HER WORST WAS DONE	FATE SLEW HIM, BUT HE	1031	6
AND HE--UNMOVED REGARDED HER--	FATE SLEW HIM, BUT HE	1031	7
WILL GENTLE BE, TO HER.	HERE, WHERE THE DAISIES	1037	8
HER LITTLE PARASOL TO LIFT	HER LITTLE PARASOL TO	1038	1
HER WHOLE RESPONSIBILITY--	HER LITTLE PARASOL TO	1038	3
AS BLEMISHLESS, AS HER.	HER LITTLE PARASOL TO	1038	8
WITH SOMETHING HID IN HER--	I CANNOT MEET THE SPRING	1051	6
I SAW NO MORE OF HER.	I CANNOT MEET THE SPRING	1051	8
OR SHY OF TROUBLING HER	THE SOUL SHOULD ALWAYS	1055	4
HER VISITOR, NO MORE--	THE SOUL SHOULD ALWAYS	1055	8
AWAITING HER THAT DAY--	BLOOM--IS RESULT--TO	1058	14
THREE WEEKS PASSED SINCE I HAD SEEN HER--	THREE WEEKS PASSED SINCE	1061	1
I BEHELD HER NEXT	THREE WEEKS PASSED SINCE	1061	4
WITHOUT HER DIADEM.	THE SKY IS LOW--THE	1075	8
HER INVITATION BROAD	THESE ARE THE SIGNS TO	1077	2
TO TASTE HER MYSTIC BREAD--	THESE ARE THE SIGNS TO	1077	4
FOR SURETIES OF HER STAUNCH ESTATE	THESE ARE THE SIGNS TO	1077	9
HER UNDECAYING CHEER	THESE ARE THE SIGNS TO	1077	10
UNTIL TO HER SURPRISE	SUPERIORITY TO FATE	1081	6
AND LO, HER SILVER PRINCIPLE	AT HALF PAST THREE, A	1084	7
OF HER ECCENTRIC FAMILY--	IF NATURE SMILES--THE	1085	3
BETWEEN HER FINAL ROOM	THE LAST NIGHT THAT SHE	1100	10
A JEALOUSY FOR HER AROSE	THE LAST NIGHT THAT SHE	1100	15
APPROPRIATE CREATURES TO HER CHANGE	THE MURMURING OF BEES,	1115	9
BLISS IS FRUGAL OF HER LEASES	PARADISE IS THAT OLD	1119	5
ADAM TAUGHT HER THRIFT	PARADISE IS THAT OLD	1119	6
HER SUBJECTS SCATTERED INTO PLACE	THE WIND TOOK UP THE	1134	11
HER SYSTEMS RANGED [STOLE] ABOUT	THE WIND TOOK UP THE	1134	12
HIMSELF AND HER BETWEEN,	THE FROST OF DEATH WAS	1136	11
TILL ALL HER HELPLESS BEAUTY BENT	THE FROST OF DEATH WAS	1136	14
HER SOVREIGN PEOPLE	HER SOVREIGN PEOPLE	1139	1
THE WORK OF HER THAT WENT,	THE WORK OF HER THAT	1143	1
THAN WHEN SHE SHOWS HER GARNET TOOTH--	WHEN ETNA BASKS AND	1146	3
TRUST ADJUSTS HER "PERADVENTURE"--	TRUST ADJUSTS HER	1161	1
HER PRACTICES [QUALITIES] EXTEND	NATURE AFFECTS TO BE	1170	4
HER DEATHLESS SYLLABLE.	STEP LIGHTLY ON THIS	1183	8
HER MARTIAL DAY [TIME] FORGOT	A LITTLE DOG THAT WAGS	1185	10
OF HER DESIRELESS LOT	A LITTLE DOG THAT WAGS	1185	12
TO LOOK HER IN THE FACE	THE PAST IS SUCH A	1203	2
UNARMED IF ANY MEET HER	THE PAST IS SUCH A	1203	5
HER FADED [RUSTY] AMMUNITION	THE PAST IS SUCH A	1203	7
GIVE HER FOR HER TRANSGRESSION	WHATEVER IT IS--SHE HAS	1204	11
GIVE HER FOR HER TRANSGRESSION	WHATEVER IT IS--SHE HAS	1204	11
AND PRESENTS [BEGETS] HER SPOT--	WE LIKE MARCH.	1213	7
NOW I KNEW I LOST HER--	NOW I KNEW I LOST HER--	1219	1
ON HER FACE AND TONGUE.	NOW I KNEW I LOST HER--	1219	4
THAT IMITATING HER	WHO GOES TO DINE MUST	1223	6
BECAUSE HE LOVES HER	BECAUSE HE LOVES HER	1229	1
WHAT DIFFERENCE IS ON HER FACE	BECAUSE HE LOVES HER	1229	3
IT WILL NOT HARM HER MAGIC PACE	BECAUSE HE LOVES HER	1229	5
HER DISTANCES [ELEMENT] PROPITIATE	BECAUSE HE LOVES HER	1229	7
HER [HIS] INFINITE DISDAIN	THE STARS ARE OLD, THAT	1249	6
BUT VANQUISHED HER [HIM] WITH MY DEFEAT	THE STARS ARE OLD, THAT	1249	7
TO HER DESIRE SEEMED--	SO PROUD SHE WAS TO DIE	1272	4
HER SORCERER WITHDRAWN!	THE WAY TO KNOW THE	1279	24
COULD HOPE INSPECT HER [IT'S] BASIS	COULD HOPE INSPECT HER	1283	1
HER CRAFT WERE DONE--	COULD HOPE INSPECT HER	1283	2
HER CHARTER IS FICTITIOUS	COULD HOPE INSPECT HER	1283	V 3
WARM IN HER HAND THESE ACCENTS LIE	WARM IN HER HAND THESE	1313	1
THE GRACE SO AWKWARD FOR HER SAKE	WARM IN HER HAND THESE	1313	3
FRIGID AND SWEET HER PARTING FACE--	FRIGID AND SWEET HER	1318	1
WHEN SUING--LIKE HER ESSEX	ELIZABETH TOLD ESSEX	1321	7
HER MOTIVE FOR [OBJECT IN] THE SOUVENIR	I SEND YOU A DECREPIT	1324	5
REMAINED FOR HER--OF RAPTURE	A BEE HIS BURNISHED	1339	11
SEDULOUS [TOO ELATE] OF HER MULTITUDES	NOT ANY MORE TO BE	1344	7

HER (CONTINUED)

	FIRST LINE	POEM		LINE
BUT HER CONFEDERATE.	TO HIS SIMPLICITY	1352		4
OF HER EFFACING FATHOM	THE TREASON OF AN ACCENT	1358		3
SUMMER LAID HER SIMPLE HAT	SUMMER LAID HER SIMPLE	1363		1
SUMMER LAID HER SUPPLE GLOVE	SUMMER LAID HER SIMPLE	1363		5
SHE TAKES [GOES] HER GRACIOUS [SPACIOUS / SUBTLE / SIMPLE / . . .	SUMMER--WE ALL HAVE SEEN	1386		6
FROM HER DIVINITY	SUMMER--WE ALL HAVE SEEN	1386	V	8
HER CONSCIENTIOUS VOICE WILL SOAR UNMOVED	AFTER ALL BIRDS HAVE	1395		3
HER PANTING NOTE [JOYFUL CRY / CORDIAL NOTE] EXALTS US-- . . .	AFTER ALL BIRDS HAVE	1395		6
HER ZEALOUS NOTE DELIGHTS IT TO ASCEND.	AFTER ALL BIRDS HAVE	1395	V	6
HER GALLANT NOTE ENDOWS US LIKE A FRIEND	AFTER ALL BIRDS HAVE	1395	V	6
SHE [HE] LAID HER [HIS] DOCILE CRESCENT DOWN	SHE LAID HER DOCILE	1396		1
NATURE WAS IN AN OPAL [HER BERYL / HER BLUEST] APRON,	IT SOUNDED AS IF THE	1397		7
NATURE WAS IN AN OPAL [HER BERYL / HER BLUEST] APRON,	IT SOUNDED AS IF THE	1397		7
OF THEIR [HER] CORPOREAL CLOTHES--	PERHAPS THEY DO NOT GO	1399		4
THE ONES THAT [WHO] CITE HER MOST	WHAT MYSTERY PERVADES A	1400		18
HAVE NEVER PASSED [SCALED] HER HAUNTED HOUSE,	WHAT MYSTERY PERVADES A	1400		19
NOR SIMPLIFIED [COMPROMISED] HER GHOST.	WHAT MYSTERY PERVADES A	1400		20
TO PITY THOSE THAT [WHO] KNOW HER NOT	WHAT MYSTERY PERVADES A	1400		21
THAT THOSE WHO KNOW HER, KNOW HER LESS	WHAT MYSTERY PERVADES A	1400		23
THAT THOSE WHO KNOW HER, KNOW HER LESS	WHAT MYSTERY PERVADES A	1400		23
THE NEARER HER THEY GET.	WHAT MYSTERY PERVADES A	1400		24
REPUGNANT TO HER PROBITY--	SHAME IS THE SHAWL OF	1412		7
UNWORTHY OF HER BREAST	UNWORTHY OF HER BREAST	1414		1
BY HER EXACTING LIGHT	UNWORTHY OF HER BREAST	1414		4
TO HER RESCINDED [SURRENDERED / RECEDING / DEPARTED / . . .	CRISIS IS SWEET AND YET	1416		8
THE HOUR [SESSION] OF HER BUD--	CRISIS IS SWEET AND YET	1416	V	8
HER UNINTENDING EYES--	THE PRETTY RAIN FROM	1426		2
TOOK HER OWN HEART, INCLUDING OUR'S,	THE PRETTY RAIN FROM	1426		3
THE WRESTLE IN HER SIMPLE THROAT	THE PRETTY RAIN FROM	1426		5
THAT VANQUISHED HER--DEFEATED FEAT--	THE PRETTY RAIN FROM	1426		7
WE SHUN BECAUSE WE PRIZE HER FACE	WE SHUN BECAUSE WE PRIZE	1429		1
DISSEMINATED IN HER HAIR--	A LITTLE SNOW WAS HERE	1444		2
HER WORDS DID TOTTER SO	HIS VOICE DECREPIT WAS	1476		2
HER SPIRIT ROSE TO SUCH A HIGHT	HER SPIRIT ROSE TO SUCH	1486		1
HER COUNTENANCE IT DID INFLATE	HER SPIRIT ROSE TO SUCH	1486		2
THAT EFFERVESCED [EFFERVESCE] FROM HER.	HER SPIRIT ROSE TO SUCH	1486		6
FOR HER [ONE] TO BE A [AN IMPENDING] BRIDE	ALL THAT I DO	1496		11
I SAW THE WIND WITHIN HER	I SAW THE WIND WITHIN	1502		1
THE PRESENT DID NOT KNOW HER	SHE COULD NOT LIVE UPON	1505		2
AND NATURE GENTLY [SOFTLY] OWNED HER	SHE COULD NOT LIVE UPON	1505		4
MY COUNTRY NEED NOT CHANGE HER GOWN,	MY COUNTRY NEED NOT	1511		1
HER TRIPLE SUIT AS SWEET	MY COUNTRY NEED NOT	1511		2
THAT TAUNTS HER BAYONET.	MY COUNTRY NEED NOT	1511		8
HER TRAVELS DAILY BE	"GO TRAVELING WITH US!"	1513		2
THE MOON UPON HER FLUENT ROUTE	THE MOON UPON HER FLUENT	1528		1
OR FAME ERECT HER SITELESS CITADEL	SOCIETY FOR ME MY MISERY	1534	V	
OUR SUMMER MADE HER LIGHT ESCAPE	AS IMPERCEPTIBLY AS	1540		15
TO HER WHO LOVES THEE BEST,	COME SHOW THY DURHAM	1542		2
HER [HIS] LOSSES MAKE OUR GAINS ASHAMED--	HER LOSSES MAKE OUR	1562		1
WERE SWINGING AT HER [HIS] BACK.	HER LOSSES MAKE OUR	1562		4
TO SEE HER IS A PICTURE--	TO SEE HER IS A PICTURE	1568		1
TO HEAR HER IS A TUNE--	TO SEE HER IS A PICTURE	1568		2
TO KNOW HER AN INTEMPERANCE [A DISPARAGEMENT / AN EMBARRASSMENT]	TO SEE HER IS A PICTURE	1568		3
TO KNOW HER NOT--AFFLICTION--	TO SEE HER IS A PICTURE	1568		5
TO OWN HER FOR A FRIEND	TO SEE HER IS A PICTURE	1568		6
ADJOURNS HER SIGH--	WE WEAR OUR SOBER	1572		3
REMIT HER HOME,	TO THE BRIGHT EAST SHE	1573		3
THE BIRD HER PUNCTUAL MUSIC BRINGS	THE BIRD HER PUNCTUAL	1585		1
WHAT RESPITE FROM HER THRILLING TOIL	THE BIRD HER PUNCTUAL	1585		5
TO HER DERIDED HOME	TO HER DERIDED HOME	1586		1
SHE DID NOT KNOW HER STATION LOW	TO HER DERIDED HOME	1586		3
AS LADY FROM HER BOWER--	TO HER DERIDED HOME	1586		8
SUSTAINS HIM [HER] ANYWHERE--	TO HER DERIDED HOME	1586	V	
THE ROBIN LOCKS HER NEST, AND TRIES HER WINGS.	QUITE EMPTY, QUITE AT	1606		2
THE ROBIN LOCKS HER NEST, AND TRIES HER WINGS.	QUITE EMPTY, QUITE AT	1606		2
BUT PUTS HER CRAFT ABOUT	QUITE EMPTY, QUITE AT	1606		4
A FLOWER WILL NOT TROUBLE HER, IT HAS SO SMALL A FOOT,	A FLOWER WILL NOT	1621		1
IN HER DISHEVELED SANCTITY--	THE DITCH IS DEAR TO THE	1645		5
BUT HER ETERNAL HOUSE--	OF GLORY NOT A BEAM IS	1647		2
WE BORROWED AT HER GRAVE--	THE IMMORTALITY SHE GAVE	1648		2
I WATCHED HER FACE TO SEE WHICH WAY	I WATCHED HER FACE TO	1667		1
LOOSED THE MOON HER SILVER HAT	LIGHTLY STEPPED A YELLOW	1672		3
FROM HER LUSTRAL FACE	LIGHTLY STEPPED A YELLOW	1672		4
SHE HAS FULFILLED HER DYES	NATURE CAN DO NO MORE	1673		2
HER CRESCENT REIMBURSE	NATURE CAN DO NO MORE	1673		5
TO HER, BY HER INNOMINATE	THAT SHE FORGOT ME WAS	1683		7
TO HER, BY HER INNOMINATE	THAT SHE FORGOT ME WAS	1683		7
THE SOUL HER "NOT AT HOME"	THE OVERTAKELESSNESS OF	1691		5
AND TAKES HER FAIR AERIAL GAIT	THE OVERTAKELESSNESS OF	1691		7
I ALMOST TOUCHED HER	TO-DAY OR THIS NOON	1702		3
T'WAS COMFORT IN HER DYING ROOM	T'WAS COMFORT IN HER	1703		1
HER HOME TO BE WITH NATURE	WITH SWEETNESS UNABATED	1709		5

	FIRST LINE	POEM	LINE
HER (CONTINUED)			
HER RESIDUE BE PAST--	WITH SWEETNESS UNABATED	1709	12
HER FACE WAS IN A BED OF HAIR,	HER FACE WAS IN A BED OF	1722	1
HER HAND WAS WHITER THAN THE SPERM	HER FACE WAS IN A BED OF	1722	3
HER TONGUE MORE TENDER [TIMID / MAGIC] THAN THE TUNE [TONE]	HER FACE WAS IN A BED OF	1722	5
WHILE HER FATHER ABUTS THE TEMPEST	THE PARASOL IS THE	1747	3
IN HER SERENE DISPLAY;	THE PARASOL IS THE	1747	6
BUT HER FATHER IS BORNE AND HONORED,	THE PARASOL IS THE	1747	7
BUT THE LATTER, HER SIRE, IS HONORED	THE PARASOL IS THE	1747	V 7
JEHOVAH TOLD TO HER	THE RETICENT VOLCANO	1748	6
ADMONISHED BY HER BUCKLED LIPS	THE RETICENT VOLCANO	1748	9
ON [OF] HER DEPARTING SPAN	THIS DOCILE ONE INTER	1752	5
AS HAPPY IN HER CRIB [BED] OF DUST	THIS DOCILE ONE INTER	1752	V 7
AS IF IT WERE HER OWN--	THIS DOCILE ONE INTER	1752	8
TO PACK HER TRUNK AND ORDER	WERE NATURE MORTAL LADY	1762	3
ADMINISTER HER ECSTASY,	THOSE FINAL CREATURES,--	1766	3
HER TREASURES WERE SO EASY	THE SUMMER THAT WE DID	1773	2
BUT WITNESS FOR HER LAND,	THE EARTH HAS MANY KEYS.	1775	5
AND WITNESS FOR HER SEA,	THE EARTH HAS MANY KEYS.	1775	6
THE CRICKET IS HER UTMOST	THE EARTH HAS MANY KEYS.	1775	7
HERB			
NOR HERB OF ALL THE PLAIN	AH, NECROMANCY SWEET!	177	6
HERD			
AND JUST A SINGLE HERD--	THEY CALLED ME TO THE	628	4
NOR FARM--NOR OPAL HERD--WAS THERE--	THEY CALLED ME TO THE	628	15
THAT HERD UPON THE EYE--	THOSE CATTLE SMALLER	1388	2
HEREIN			
HEREIN A BLOSSOM LIES--	HEREIN A BLOSSOM LIES--	899	1
HERES			
"HERE!" THERE ARE TYPIC "HERES"--	THE THINGS THAT NEVER	1515	9
HERESIES			
AS HERESIES OF TRANSPORT	THE WAY TO KNOW THE	1279	11
HIS ORIENTAL HERESIES	HIS ORIENTAL HERESIES	1526	1
HERESY			
THE SWEETEST HERESY RECIEVED	THE SWEETEST HERESY	387	1
HERMETIC			
OF AN HERMETIC MIND--	STRONG DRAUGHTS OF THEIR	711	8
IN AN HERMETIC MEMORY	A CLOUD WITHDREW FROM	895	7
HERO			
BUT AN IMMORTAL HERO	"SIC TRANSIT GLORIA	3	55
HEROES			
HEROES--A BATTLE--	"MORNING"--MEANS	300	V 7
FOR HEROES THAN FOR MEN--	NOT ANY HIGHER STANDS	1256	2
HEROIC			
RASCALITY, HEROIC,	"SIC TRANSIT GLORIA	3	43
BY ONE DEFAULTING [HEROIC] FACE	THE VASTEST EARTHLY DAY	1328	3
THE GLEAM OF AN HEROIC ACT	THE GLEAM OF AN HEROIC	1687	1
HEROINE			
HALF CHILD--HALF HEROINE--	A MIEN TO MOVE A QUEEN--	283	2
HEROISM			
THE TRADITION [HEROISM] BEARS--	TELL AS A MARKSMAN--WERE	1152	4
THE HEROISM WE RECITE	WE NEVER KNOW HOW HIGH	1176	5
HER'S			
HER'S BE DAMASK FINE--	THO' MY DESTINY BE	163	2
WHEN HER'S HAD CEASED TO RUN--	SEVERER SERVICE OF	786	6
SO BE HER'S THE ERROR--	HAD WE KNOWN THE TON SHE	1124	4
HER'S IS THE SMALLEST BOOT--	A FLOWER WILL NOT	1621	3
HERSCHEL'S			
AS HERSCHEL'S PRIVATE INTEREST	NATURE AND GOD--I	835	7
HERSELF			
HERSELF TO HER A MUSIC	ONE SISTER HAVE I IN OUR	14	11
SHE FELT HERSELF SUPREMER--	THE SUN--JUST TOUCHED	232	5
SHE KNOWS HERSELF AN INCENSE [OFFERING] SMALL--	THE DROP, THAT WRESTLES	284	4
OR SHE--HERSELF--ASCENDED	THE SOUL'S SUPERIOR	306	5
HERSELF--THOUGH--FLED!	'TWAS THE OLD--ROAD--	344	16
WHERE PARTIES--PHANTOM AS HERSELF--	FROM COCOON FORTH A	354	14
NEAR KINSMAN TO HERSELF--	THERE IS A FLOWER THAT	380	18
THE SOUL ACHIEVES--HERSELF--	EXHILIRATION--IS WITHIN	383	5
DID HOIST HERSELF, TO SING,	HER SMILE WAS SHAPED	514	4
TO CHEAT HERSELF, IT SEEMED SHE TRIED--	MY FIRST WELL DAY--SINCE	574	13
THAT NATURE MURMURED TO HERSELF	I THINK I WAS ENCHANTED	593	13
TO KEEP HERSELF IN CHEER--	I THINK I WAS ENCHANTED	593	14
HERSELF ADJUST HER TIDES--UNTO--	I COULD SUFFICE FOR HIM,	643	15
THE DAY UNDRESSED--HERSELF--	THE DAY UNDRESSED--	716	1
EVEN AS HERSELF--SIR--	ALTER! WHEN THE HILLS DO	729	7
NOR I--HERSELF--OUR COMPACT--	THE BIRDS REPORTED FROM	743	V 23
TO HERSELF--AND MEN [MAN]--	MOST SHE TOUCHED ME BY	760	16
TRUTH STAYS HERSELF--AND EVERY MAN	THE TRUTH--IS STIRLESS--	780	11
DID NOON--ENAMEL [ENABLE / EMBELLISH]--IN HERSELF	THIS BAUBLE WAS	805	5
HERSELF, WITHOUT A PARLIAMENT	APOLOGY FOR HER	852	3
NOR SEPARATE, HERSELF AND ME	HERE, WHERE THE DAISIES	1037	9
THAT SHE [HERSELF] COULD NOT FORGIVE	ELIZABETH TOLD ESSEX	1321	2
EVEN NATURE HERSELF	NOT ANY MORE TO BE	1344	5
OR NATURE SPENDING WITH HERSELF	AS IMPERCEPTIBLY AS	1540	7
NOT KNOWING WHEN THE DAWN WILL [HERSELF MAY] COME,	NOT KNOWING WHEN THE	1619	1
WHEN NATURE FALLS UPON HERSELF	THE WIND DREW OFF	1694	10

	FIRST LINE	POEM	LINE
HERSELF (CONTINUED)			
IS RAPTURE HERSELF SPURN--	TO DO A MAGNANIMOUS	1699	8
HE'S			
HE'S A TRANSITIVE FELLOW--VERY--	THE WIND DID'NT COME	316	5
BECAUSE HE'S SUNRISE--AND I SEE--	"WHY DO I LOVE" YOU, SIR	480	18
UNTIL HE'S PAST THE PAIN--	I SOMETIMES DROP IT, FOR	708	16
HE'S [THAT'S / 'TIS] LIABLE WITH THEM	HAD WE OUR SENSES	1284	4
HESITATE			
HOVER--HESITATE--	SOUTH WINDS JOSTLE THEM	86	3
SAY RUBIES--IF HE HESITATE--	A TONGUE--TO TELL HIM I	400	20
NATURE HESITATE--BEFORE	WHEN I HOPED, I	768	23
OR A CIRCLE HESITATE	CRISIS IS A HAIR	889	11
BUT THERE--SO GLOAT TO HESITATE	TIME'S WILY CHARGERS	1458	3
HESITATED			
HAVE GAINED! YES! HESITATED SO--	'TIS SO MUCH JOY! 'TIS	172	5
AND HESITATED ME BETWEEN	MY WARS ARE LAID AWAY IN	1549	5
HESITATES			
AND WHOSE "I'LL MEET YOU" HESITATES	SUPERFLUOUS WERE THE SUN	999	7
BEYOND WHICH SUMMER HESITATES,	THE SADDEST NOISE, THE	1764	7
HESITATING			
YET HESITATING FRACTIONS--BOTH	I COULD SUFFICE FOR HIM,	643	3
DWELT HESITATING, HALF OF DUST,	TO THIS WORLD SHE	830	8
HESITATION			
NOT A HESITATION--	ABRAHAM TO KILL HIM	1317	5
HESPERIAN			
TO THE SAME FLOWER HESPERIAN,	OF DEATH I TRY TO THINK	1558	7
HESPERIDES			
THE SUMMERS OF [IN] HESPERIDES	EXCEPT THE SMALLER SIZE	1067	7
HEWN			
HER CHEEK--A BERYL HEWN--	THE MOON WAS BUT A CHIN	737	6
IN YELLOWER YELLOW HEWN	OF YELLOW WAS THE OUTER	1676	2
HID			
HID HEAVEN AND EARTH FROM VIEW.	AN AWFUL TEMPEST MASHED	198	4
HID GOLDEN, FOR THE WHOLE OF DAYS,	OF ALL THE SOUNDS	321	15
HID, LIP, FOR THEE--	ALL THE LETTERS I CAN	334	6
HE HAS HID HIS RARE LIFE	I KNOW THAT HE EXISTS.	338	3
A HYACINTH--I HID--	I TEND MY FLOWERS FOR	339	11
AND SUMMER HID HER FOREHEAD--	GOD MADE A LITTLE	442	7
BUT--IF HE [SHE] ASK WHERE YOU ARE HID	GOING TO HIM! HAPPY	494	23
THEN HALF--THEN UTTER HID--	THE TREES LIKE TASSELS--	606	10
ASSASSIN HID IN OUR APARTMENT	ONE NEED NOT BE A	670	15
THE DEEPEST HID IS SIGHTED FIRST	OF CONSCIOUSNESS, HER	894	5
WITH SOMETHING HID IN HER--	I CANNOT MEET THE SPRING	1051	6
'TIS AS HID AS DEATH	NONE WHO SAW IT EVER	1110	2
WHILE EVERYTHING CREATED HID	TO PILE LIKE THUNDER TO	1247	3
AND HUMAN NATURE HID [POPULATION FLED]	IT WAS A QUIET SEEMING	1419	9
HIDDEN			
HIDDEN AWAY, CUNNINGLY,	SO FROM THE MOULD	66	4
SO HIDDEN IN HER LEAFLETS	SO BASHFUL WHEN I SPIED	91	3
THE CRIME, FROM US, IS HIDDEN--	OF GOD WE ASK ONE FAVOR,	1601	4
HIDE			
STEALTHY COCOON, WHY HIDE YOU SO	COCOON ABOVE! COCOON	129	2
THEN WE HIDE OUR BRAVE FACE	WE DONT CRY--TIM AND I,	196	5
THAN "HIDE AND SEEK"--	ALTHOUGH I PUT AWAY HIS	366	19
WHOSE NIGHTGOWNS COULD NOT HIDE THE WINGS--	A MURMUR IN THE TREES--	416	15
I AM ASHAMED--I HIDE--	I AM ASHAMED--I HIDE--	473	1
NOWHERE TO HIDE MY DAZZLED FACE--	I AM ASHAMED--I HIDE--	473	4
NO MORE TO HIDE--	I AM ASHAMED--I HIDE--	473	25
THE SEPULCHRE, COULD HIDE.	MY FIRST WELL DAY--SINCE	574	16
PUT UP--TO HIDE [HOLD] HER PARTING GRACE	MY FIRST WELL DAY--SINCE	574	23
THAT IF THE SPIRIT--LIKE TO HIDE	THE BODY GROWS WITHOUT--	578	3
HIDE--TOO--FROM THEE--	OUT OF SIGHT? WHAT OF	703	13
GOOD TO HIDE, AND HEAR 'EM HUNT!	GOOD TO HIDE, AND HEAR	842	1
NOR ROBINS, ROBINS NEED NOT HIDE	BECAUSE THE BEE MAY	869	7
IN CAVE IF I PRESUMED TO HIDE	TO MY QUICK EAR THE	891	5
I HIDE MYSELF WITHIN MY FLOWER,	I HIDE MYSELF WITHIN MY	903	1
AS MAKES ONE HIDE [HANG] IT'S HEAD	THAT THIS SHOULD FEEL	1112	V 4
CAN [MAY] HUMAN NATURE HIDE	AS OLD AS WOE--	1168	10
OR THOSE THAT HIDE, AND ARE.	THAN HEAVEN MORE REMOTE,	1436	6
TO HIDE MY STRATEGY TOO LATE	I THOUGHT THE TRAIN	1449	9
NOT GUESSING, SMILE AND HIDE	NOT SEEING, STILL WE	1518	3
HIDETH			
SHE HIDETH HER THE LAST--	SHE HIDETH HER THE LAST	557	1
HIDING			
MIGHT HE BUT SPY THE LADY'S [HIDING] SOUL--	JUST SO--JESUS--RAPS--	317	6
HIDING INDIVIDUALS FROM THE EARTH	ABSENCE DISEMBODIES--SO	860	2
HIE			
AND LIKE A BUBBLE, HIE--	THE MUSHROOM IS THE ELF	1298	12
HIGH			
THE HIGH DO SEEK THE LOWLY, THE GREAT DO SEEK THE SMALL,	AWAKE YE MUSES NINE,	1	11
TO BE RECEIVED AS HIGH--	WHEN I COUNT THE SEEDS	40	6
PERHAPS A HOME TOO HIGH--	FOR EVERY BIRD A NEST--	143	7
HAS THE SIGNIFICANCE, ON HIGH,	I MET A KING THIS	166	27
BUT, OH, SO HIGH!	WE DONT CRY--TIM AND I,	196	14
ON THE [A] HEAD TOO HIGH TO CROWN--	HER--"LAST POEMS"--	312	13
IT HUNG SO HIGH	I GAINED IT SO--	359	5
ON TWIGS OF SINGING--RATHER HIGH--	I'M SAYING EVERY DAY	373	17
JUST AS HIGH--AS I--	I'LL CLUTCH--AND CLUTCH	427	19
MY STOCKING HANG TOO HIGH	'TWAS JUST THIS TIME,	445	18

	FIRST LINE	POEM	LINE
HIGH (CONTINUED)			
LOVE--THOU ART HIGH--	LOVE--THOU ART HIGH--	453	1
ARE SO HIGH UP--YOU SEE--	I KNOW WHERE WELLS GROW	460	12
THE THING SO TOWERING HIGH	WE SEE--COMPARATIVELY--	534	2
I HELD SO HIGH, FOR THEE--	I SEE THEE BETTER--IN	611	12
HE SHALL SEEK AS HIGH	HER SWEET TURN TO LEAVE	649	18
WE CANNOT COUNT--ON HIGH!	AGAIN--HIS VOICE IS AT	663	25
HOW HIGH--	EACH LIFE CONVERGES TO	680	14
HIS TABLE'S SPREAD TOO HIGH FOR US--	VICTORY COMES LATE--	690	8
AND RETURNED ON HIGH--	MOST SHE TOUCHED ME BY	760	12
BECAUSE A HIGHT SO HIGH	I CANNOT BE ASHAMED	914	7
SHE ROSE AS HIGH AS HIS OCCASION	SHE ROSE AS HIGH AS HIS	1011	1
DIVISION IS ADHESION'S FORFEIT--ON HIGH	NOT SO THE INFINITE	1040	2
AND THEN HE BORE ME ON [HIGH]	IT WAS A QUIET WAY--	1053	5
WE NEVER KNOW HOW HIGH WE ARE	WE NEVER KNOW HOW HIGH	1176	1
HE IS NEW AND HIGH--	WE LIKE MARCH.	1213	3
THE PILE OF YEARS IS NOT SO HIGH	THE PILE OF YEARS IS NOT	1507	1
IS JUST AS HIGH AS YOU AND I,	THE BUTTERFLY UPON THE	1521	5
HE IS JUST AS [STILL MORE] HIGH--	FOLLOW WISE ORION	1538	4
WITHOUT THE HIGH PREROGATIVE	UNTO A BROKEN HEART	1704	3
HIGH FROM THE EARTH I HEARD A BIRD;	HIGH FROM THE EARTH I	1723	1
HIGHER			
THAN ONE OF HIGHER TEMPERATURE	A SHADY FRIEND--FOR	278	3
AND HOLD NO HIGHER THAN THE PLAIN--	A TONGUE--TO TELL HIM I	400	24
THEN--HIGHER THAN THE LAND	THE COLOR OF THE GRAVE	411	14
FOR NOTHING HIGHER THAN ITSELF	MY WORTHINESS IS ALL MY	751	11
NOT ANY HIGHER STANDS THE GRAVE	NOT ANY HIGHER STANDS	1256	1
BUT IT IS RISING [HIGHER / FURTHER] EVERY DAY	THE PILE OF YEARS IS NOT	1507	3
AND HIGHER, I BELIEVE,	THE BUTTERFLY UPON THE	1521	6
HIGHEST			
A WOUNDED DEER--LEAPS HIGHEST--	A WOUNDED DEER--LEAPS	165	1
PUT ME IN ON THE FIRMEST [TIGHTEST / HIGHEST] SIDE--	TIE THE STRINGS TO MY	279	5
AND YET [ALTHOUGH] THE HIGHEST HEAD	ONE CROWN THAT NO ONE	1735	2
HIGHLAND			
LEAP SO HIGHLAND GAY,	SO FROM THE MOULD	66	8
HIGHT			
"BERNARDINE" ANGELS, UP THE HIGHT	SHE DIED--THIS WAS THE	150	V 5
TO TOO REMOTE A HIGHT	THE SOUL'S SUPERIOR	306	6
A HOUSE UPON THE HIGHT--	A HOUSE UPON THE HIGHT--	399	1
THEIR HIGHT IN HEAVEN COMFORTS NOT--	THEIR HIGHT IN HEAVEN	696	1
THE HIGHT I RECOLLECT--	JOY TO HAVE MERITED THE	788	17
RETREATING UP, A BILLOW'S HIGHT	ESCAPING BACKWARD TO	867	5
THE DYING--AS IT WERE A HIGHT	THE ADMIRATIONS--AND	906	3
BECAUSE A HIGHT SO HIGH	I CANNOT BE ASHAMED	914	7
WERE IT BUT ME THAT GAINED THE HIGHT--	WERE IT BUT ME THAT	1015	1
TILL WHEN AROUND A HIGHT	I HAD A DAILY BLISS	1057	5
IS SUCH A FEAT [STROKE / HIGHT / PASS] OF IRONY	THAT THIS SHOULD FEEL	1112	3
ABOVE HIM IS TOO LOW A HIGHT	'TIS MY FIRST NIGHT	1122	3
HER SPIRIT ROSE TO SUCH A HIGHT	HER SPIRIT ROSE TO SUCH	1486	1
THE HIGHT OF OUR PORTENTOUS [UNKNOWING] NEIGHBOR	FACTS BY OUR SIDE ARE	1497	5
ITSELF, THE PURPLE ON THE HIGHT	SOME SAY GOODNIGHT--AT	1739	7
HIGHTS			
I [HE] SHOWED HER [ME] HIGHTS SHE [I] NEVER SAW--	I SHOWED HER HIGHTS SHE	446	1
OR OTHER HIGHTS OF OTHER ONES	YOU SAID THAT I "WAS	738	7
HILL			
I CLIMB THE "HILL OF SCIENCE,"	"SIC TRANSIT GLORIA	3	21
LAID DOWN ON BUNKER HILL;	"SIC TRANSIT GLORIA	3	46
UPON THE HILL--THAT LIES--	I NEVER TOLD THE BURIED	11	2
HAVE CLIMBED THE DISTANT HILL--	DELAYED TILL SHE HAD	58	9
THE REGIMENTS OF WOOD AND HILL	SOME RAINBOW--COMING	64	20
FROM THE SUMMER HILL	GLOWING IS HER BONNET,	72	6
A LADY RED--AMID THE HILL	A LADY RED--AMID THE	74	1
SWEEP VALE--AND HILL--AND TREE!	A LADY RED--AMID THE	74	6
HER GHOST STROLLED SOFTLY O'ER THE HILL	SHE DIED AT PLAY,	75	6
THE RED UPON THE HILL	THE MURMUR OF A BEE	155	6
BEHIND THE HILL--THE HOUSE BEHIND--	"HEAVEN"--IS WHAT I	239	7
THEN I WILL, WHEN ON THE EVERLASTING HILL	ME, CHANGE! ME, ALTER!	268	2
AND IT'S PARTLY [MANY A MILE], DOWN HILL--	TIE THE STRINGS TO MY	279	8
ON THE HILL--	WHILE ASTERS--	331	2
THE ASTER--ON THE HILL	IT WILL BE SUMMER--	342	14
THE FOREHEAD OF A HILL--	THE ANGLE OF A LANDSCAPE	375	10
THE CHIMNEY--AND THE HILL--	THE ANGLE OF A LANDSCAPE	375	18
OR PERISH FROM THE HILL--	HOW MANY FLOWERS FAIL IN	404	2
THAT COOLED THE FOREHEAD OF THE HILL--	FORGET! THE LADY WITH	438	13
THAT RAVISHED ALL THE HILL--	GOD MADE A LITTLE	442	6
A HILL--PERHAPS--	IT'S THOUGHTS--AND JUST	495	19
THEN CHASE ITSELF DOWN HILL--	I LIKE TO SEE IT LAP	585	13
UPON SO VAIN A HILL--	THEY CALLED ME TO THE	628	6
AN ARTERY--UPON THE HILL--	THE NAME--OF IT--IS	656	3
THE HILL--THE AFTERNOON--	"NATURE" IS WHAT WE SEE	668	2
KEEPS WITH THE HILL--	THE SUNRISE RUNS FOR	710	3
THE WAYWARD NUN--BENEATH THE HILL--	SWEET MOUNTAINS--YE TELL	722	8
NEW HOUSES ON THE HILL DESCRIED--	HAVE ANY LIKE MYSELF	736	3
AND THEN--UPON THE HILL--	MY FAITH IS LARGER THAN	766	6
DARK SHALL OVERTAKE THE HILL--	WHEN I HOPED, I	768	V 21
AT MIDDLE [BOTTOM / CENTRE] OF THE HILL--	THE HALLOWING OF PAIN	772	6

	FIRST LINE	POEM	LINE
HILL (CONTINUED)			
IN FOREST--AND THE HILL--	NATURE--THE GENTLEST	790	5
UP LIFE'S HILL WITH MY LITTLE BUNDLE	UP LIFE'S HILL WITH MY	1010	1
UPON THE HILL TONIGHT--	THE LILAC IS AN ANCIENT	1241	4
MARROWS OF THE HILL.	BEES ARE BLACK, WITH	1405	6
A TRAVELLER [HORSEMAN] ON A HILL--	THE ROAD WAS LIT WITH	1450	4
AND SCARCELY HAD THE HILL--	AS IMPERCEPTIBLY AS	1540	V
WHOSE VISTA IS A HILL,	THE GOING FROM A WORLD	1603	4
BEHIND THE HILL IS SORCERY	THE GOING FROM A WORLD	1603	5
THREE RIVERS AND A HILL TO CROSS	I DID NOT REACH THEE	1664	3
THREE RIVERS AND THE HILL ARE PASSED	I DID NOT REACH THEE	1664	31
THAT WRAPS THE EVERLASTING HILL	SUMMER BEGINS TO HAVE	1682	8
HILLOCKS			
SO BUILD THE HILLOCKS GAILY	ALL THESE MY BANNERS BE.	22	12
HILLS			
FREQUENTLY THE HILLS UNDRESS	FREQUENTLY THE WOODS ARE	6	3
BUT UP AND DOWN THE HILLS	ONE SISTER HAVE I IN OUR	14	14
"PENIEL" HILLS BEYOND [AMONG],	A LITTLE EAST OF JORDAN,	59	14
GRIEF--HILLS--ETERNITY--	SOME THINGS THAT FLY	89	5
AND THE SNOWS COME HURRYING FROM THE HILLS,	HAVE YOU GOT A BROOK IN	136	11
AN ALTERED LOOK ABOUT THE HILLS--	AN ALTERED LOOK ABOUT	140	1
SINCE YORKSHIRE HILLS ARE GREEN--	ALL OVERGROWN BY CUNNING	148	10
THE HILLS TO MEET HIM ROSE!	THE SUN KEPT STOOPING--	152	2
TO THE HILLS RETURN!	I HAVE NEVER SEEN	175	20
THEY TELL IT TO THE HILLS--	THE SKIES CANT KEEP	191	2
THE HILLS JUST TELL THE ORCHARDS--	THE SKIES CANT KEEP	191	3
THE SOUND ONES, LIKE THE HILLS--SHALL STAND [STAND UP]--	WHEN WE STAND ON THE	242	7
AND KISS THE HILLS, FOR ME, JUST ONCE--	TIE THE STRINGS TO MY	279	15
HERE'S A KEEPSAKE FOR THE HILLS	TIE THE STRINGS TO MY	279	V 15
THEN SPRANG BEFORE THE HILLS	THE DAY CAME SLOW--TILL	304	2
THE HILLS UNTIED THEIR BONNETS--	I'LL TELL YOU HOW THE	318	5
AND WHEN THE HILLS BE FULL--	THERE IS A FLOWER THAT	380	21
THAT WHEN THE HILLS--COME DOWN--	A TONGUE--TO TELL HIM I	400	23
THE HILLS--HAVE A WAY--THEN--	GOOD MORNING--MIDNIGHT--	425	11
I ENVY CROOKED [SPEECHLESS] HILLS	I ENVY SEAS, WHEREON HE	498	4
WHEN FLOODS HAVE SLIT THE HILLS--	THE BRAIN, WITHIN IT'S	556	6
AND SETTLES IN THE HILLS--	"HEAVEN" HAS DIFFERENT	575	6
UPHOLSTERER OF THE PINES [SEA / LAND / HILLS]--IS HE--	OF BRUSSELS--IT WAS NOT	602	15
AND LEAVES ME WITH THE HILLS.	THE NAME--OF IT--IS	656	V 12
ALTER! WHEN THE HILLS DO--	ALTER! WHEN THE HILLS DO	729	1
MY FAITH IS LARGER THAN THE HILLS--	MY FAITH IS LARGER THAN	766	1
SO WHEN THE HILLS DECAY--	MY FAITH IS LARGER THAN	766	2
'TWAS EVEN WITH THE HILLS--	JOY TO HAVE MERITED THE	788	18
THE HILLS IN PURPLE SYLLABLES	THE HILLS IN PURPLE	1016	1
WE SPY THE FORESTS AND THE HILLS	DEW--IS THE FRESHET IN	1097	5
UPON THE HILLS TODAY--	LIKE MEN AND WOMEN	1105	2
IT PULLED THE SPIGOT FROM THE HILLS	LIKE RAIN IT SOUNDED	1235	11
ALL THOSE HILLS YOU LEFT FOR ME TO HUE--	DEAR MARCH--COME IN--	1320	15
THE HILLS ERECT THEIR PURPLE HEADS	THE HILLS ERECT THEIR	1688	1
HILLSIDE			
BY DAISY CALLED FROM HILLSIDE--	I KEEP MY PLEDGE.	46	7
WHICH UPON THE HILLSIDE BLOW.	FLOWERS--WELL--IF	137	8
HILLSIDES			
THE HILLSIDES MUST NOT KNOW IT--	I HAV'NT TOLD MY GARDEN	50	9
HIM			
WHO LOOKS FOR HIM AT MORNING	THE GUEST IS GOLD AND	15	7
I PRAY HIM TOO--EXPLORE	THE GUEST IS GOLD AND	15	8
TO HIM WHO KEEPS AN ORCHIS' HEART--	ALL THESE MY BANNERS BE.	22	20
HEART! WE WILL FORGET HIM!	HEART! WE WILL FORGET	47	1
I REMEMBER HIM!	HEART! WE WILL FORGET	47	8
AMBITION CANNOT FIND HIM.	AMBITION CANNOT FIND HIM	68	1
I'D RATHER CALL HIM "STAR."	"ARCTURUS" IS HIS OTHER	70	2
WE MIGHT LOOK FOR HIM!	WENT UP A YEAR THIS	93	12
I DONT KNOW HIM; SNUGLY BUILT!	"HOUSES"--SO THE WISE	127	6
I WILL GIVE HIM ALL THE DAISIES	FLOWERS--WELL--IF	137	7
PLEASE GOD, MIGHT I BEHOLD HIM	BLESS GOD, HE WENT AS	147	5
THE HILLS TO MEET HIM ROSE!	THE SUN KEPT STOOPING--	152	2
THIS WAY, JESUS, LET HIM PASS!	DYING! DYING IN THE	158	8
SCAN LIKE HIM, THE STATELY LANDSCAPE	IF THE FOOLISH, CALL	168	11
YOU'D SCARCE RECOGNIZE HIM!	A FUZZY FELLOW, WITHOUT	173	16
SO I AM HEARING HIM, I'LL DREAM,	MAKE ME A PICTURE OF THE	188	6
SO HE LET ME LEAD HIM IN--	HE WAS WEAK, AND I WAS	190	2
SO I LET HIM LEAD ME--HOME.	HE WAS WEAK, AND I WAS	190	4
"THOU WERT WITH HIM"--QUOTH "THE DAMSEL"?	HE FORGOT--AND I--	203	5
FOR FEAR OF JOGGLING HIM!	IS IT TRUE, DEAR SUE?	218	4
IF I COULD SHUT HIM UP	IS IT TRUE, DEAR SUE?	218	5
OR TIE HIM TO A PIN	IS IT TRUE, DEAR SUE?	218	7
OR MAKE HIM FAST	IS IT TRUE, DEAR SUE?	218	9
TEACH HIM--WHEN HE MAKES THE NAMES--	TEACH HIM--WHEN HE MAKES	227	1
ALL--FOR HIM--STRAIGHTWAY--	GOD PERMITS INDUSTRIOUS	231	4
WOULD BUT SOME GOD--INFORM HIM--	IF HE DISSOLVE--THEN--	236	8
HIS LITTLE SPANIEL--TELL HIM!	IF HE DISSOLVE--THEN--	236	14
"CAROL FOR HIM--WHEN I AM GONE"!	KILL YOUR BALM--AND IT'S	238	8
THE HEARING HIM PUT HIS PLAYTHINGS UP	IT IS EASY TO WORK WHEN	244	3
THAT MAKES TWO--HIM--AND LIFE!	WHAT WOULD I GIVE TO SEE	247	6
THEY'LL CARRY--HIM!	I CAN WADE GRIEF--	252	16
THAT VANQUISHED HIM--	PUT UP MY LUTE!	261	8
DID WE DISOBEY HIM?	DID WE DISOBEY HIM?	267	1

HIM (CONTINUED)	FIRST LINE	POEM	LINE
CHARGED US TO FORGET HIM--	DID WE DISOBEY HIM?	267	3
I'D SWEAR BY HIM--	THE ROBIN'S MY CRITERION	285	4
AND HIM--	A CLOCK STOPPED--	287	18
I CRAVE HIM GRACE OF SUMMER BOUGHS,	OF ALL THE SOUNDS	321	25
I OFFERED HIM A CRUMB	A BIRD CAME DOWN THE	328	14
AND ROWED HIM SOFTER HOME--	A BIRD CAME DOWN THE	328	16
I'M SOME ACCUSTOMED TO HIM GROWN,	I DREADED THAT FIRST	348	3
SO TRUST HIM, COMRADE--	THEY LEAVE US WITH THE	350	9
HAD NOTCHED THE PLACE THAT PLEASED HIM--	DEATH SETS A THING	360	15
TO HIM OF ADEQUATE DESIRE	HEAVEN IS SO FAR OF THE	370	7
YOU BEG HIM NOT TO GO--	A PRECIOUS--MOULDERING	371	26
JUST HIM--NOT ME--	'TWAS LOVE--NOT ME--	394	4
BUT TELL HIM THAT IT CEASED TO FEEL--	THERE IS A LANGUOR OF	396	11
HAS MINISTERED BEFORE HIM--	THERE IS A LANGUOR OF	396	15
A TONGUE--TO TELL HIM I AM TRUE!	A TONGUE--TO TELL HIM I	400	1
AND TELL HIM--CHARGE THEE SPEAK IT PLAIN--	A TONGUE--TO TELL HIM I	400	7
THE SACRAMENT--OF HIM--	IT MIGHT BE LONELIER	405	8
TOLD TO HIM--	UNIT, LIKE DEATH, FOR	408	4
THE JURY VOTED HIM--	I READ MY SENTENCE--	412	8
FROM HIM--AND HOLY GHOST--AND ALL--	I NEVER FELT AT HOME--	413	15
CLASPED YET--TO HIM--AND ME--	NOT IN THIS WORLD TO SEE	418	6
AWAITED EVEN--HIM--	REMOVED FROM ACCIDENT OF	424	12
HOW COULD I--OF HIM?	GOOD MORNING--MIDNIGHT--	425	4
SHE LEADS HIM--DOCILE AS A BOY--	THE MOON IS DISTANT FROM	429	3
NO BONE HAD HE TO BIND HIM--	THE WIND--TAPPED LIKE A	436	9
WHAT LITTLE OF HIM WE--POSSESSED	IT FEELS A SHAME TO BE	444	7
HIMSELF--TO HIM--A FORTUNE--	THIS WAS A POET--IT IS	448	15
ALIKE TO HIM--ONE--	THE MALAY--TOOK THE	452	17
I LIVE WITH HIM--I SEE HIS FACE--	I LIVE WITH HIM--I SEE	463	1
I LIVE WITH HIM--I HEAR HIS VOICE--	I LIVE WITH HIM--I SEE	463	9
THAT PILOT HIM ALONG--	NO MAN CAN COMPASS A	477	12
YOU WRITE HIM--EVERY DAY--	YOU LOVE THE LORD--YOU	487	2
THAN LETTING HIM SURMISE?	TO ONE DENIED TO DRINK	490	4
TO LEAD HIM TO THE WELL	TO ONE DENIED TO DRINK	490	5
AND LET HIM HEAR IT DRIP	TO ONE DENIED TO DRINK	490	6
REMIND HIM, WOULD IT NOT, SOMEWHAT	TO ONE DENIED TO DRINK	490	7
SINCE I WAS WED--TO HIM--	THE WORLD--STANDS--	493	2
GOING TO HIM [HER]! HAPPY LETTER!	GOING TO HIM! HAPPY	494	1
TELL HIM [HER]--	GOING TO HIM! HAPPY	494	2
TELL HIM [HER] THE PAGE I DID'NT WRITE--[NEVER WROTE!]	GOING TO HIM! HAPPY	494	3
TELL HIM [HER]--I ONLY SAID THE SYNTAX--	GOING TO HIM! HAPPY	494	4
TELL HIM [HER] JUST HOW THE FINGERS HURRIED--	GOING TO HIM! HAPPY	494	6
TELL HIM [HER]--IT WAS'NT A PRACTISED WRITER--	GOING TO HIM! HAPPY	494	10
TELL HIM [HER]--NO--YOU MAY QUIBBLE THERE--	GOING TO HIM! HAPPY	494	15
TELL HIM [HER]--NIGHT [DAY] FINISHED--BEFORE WE FINISHED--	GOING TO HIM! HAPPY	494	18
TELL HIM [HER]--JUST HOW SHE SEALED YOU--CAUTIOUS!	GOING TO HIM! HAPPY	494	22
BUT I NEVER DOUBTED HIM--	HE STRAINED MY FAITH--	497	10
I ENVY SEAS, WHEREON HE RIDES--[THAT BEAR HIM]	I ENVY SEAS, WHEREON HE	498	1
OF CHARIOTS, THAT HIM CONVEY--	I ENVY SEAS, WHEREON HE	498	3
I ENVY LIGHT--THAT WAKES HIM--	I ENVY SEAS, WHEREON HE	498	17
TO TELL HIM IT IS NOON, ABROAD--	I ENVY SEAS, WHEREON HE	498	19
MYSELF--BE NOON TO HIM--	I ENVY SEAS, WHEREON HE	498	20
PERISH WITH HIM--THAT KEYLESS RHYME!	BETTER--THAN MUSIC! FOR	503	8
WHAT COME OF HIM--AT NIGHT--	HE PARTS HIMSELF--LIKE	517	13
WHAT COME OF HIM--THAT DAY--	HE PARTS HIMSELF--LIKE	517	16
WITH HIM REMAIN--WHO UNTO ME--	HER SWEET WEIGHT ON MY	518	9
IS SWEETEST NUTRIMENT--TO HIM--	I THINK THE HEMLOCK	525	11
THAT AS MYSELF--COULD PITY HIM--	I TRIED TO THINK A	532	18
AND CAUGHT A RIDE [TOOK A BOUT] WITH HIM	TWO BUTTERFLIES WENT OUT	533	V 4
BUT NO MAN HEARD HIM CRY--	THE BLACK BERRY--WEARS A	554	2
WHILE I WAS REACHING HIM--	A DYING TIGER--MOANED	566	11
AND TOLD HIM WHAT I'D LIKE, TODAY,	I PRAYED, AT FIRST, A	576	9
I GAVE MYSELF TO HIM [HIM ALL MYSELF]--	I GAVE MYSELF TO HIM--	580	1
I GAVE MYSELF TO HIM [HIM ALL MYSELF]--	I GAVE MYSELF TO HIM--	580	1
TO LET HIM SEE--THE CANAAN--	IT ALWAYS FELT TO ME--A	597	3
BUT TITLED HIM--TO SEE--	IT ALWAYS FELT TO ME--A	597	V 22
WOULD DROP [SPILL] HIM--BONE BY BONE.	THERE IS A PAIN--SO	599	8
SUFFICIENT TO ENFOLD HIM	THE TREES LIKE TASSELS--	606	13
COULD HE--KNOW--THEY SOUGHT HIM--	IN FALLING TIMBERS	614	5
I MET [GAVE] HIM--	I ROSE--BECAUSE HE SANK	616	10
I TOLD HIM BEST--MUST PASS	I ROSE--BECAUSE HE SANK	616	12
I TOLD HIM WORLDS [A WORLD] I KNEW	I ROSE--BECAUSE HE SANK	616	16
I LIFTED HIM--	I ROSE--BECAUSE HE SANK	616	23
TO HIM--SUMS MISERY--	IT MAKES NO DIFFERENCE	620	12
AND WE APPROACH [ACCOST] HIM--STERN--	THE LIGHTNING PLAYETH--	630	4
TO HIM WHO HAS IT--AND THE ONE	MY PORTION IS DEFEAT--	639	17
I COULD SUFFICE FOR HIM, I KNEW--	I COULD SUFFICE FOR HIM,	643	1
OR CHASE HIM IF HE DO	COULD I BUT RIDE	661	10
I HEAR HIM ASK THE SERVANT	AGAIN--HIS VOICE IS AT	663	3
INDIFFERENT TO HIM--	THE FUTURE--NEVER SPOKE	672	9
FATE'S--TELEGRAM--TO HIM--	THE FUTURE--NEVER SPOKE	672	12
NEITHER PLACE--NEED I PRESENT HIM--	CONSCIOUS AM I IN MY	679	5
NOR MYSELF TO HIM--BY ACCENT--	CONSCIOUS AM I IN MY	679	11
WEARINESS OF HIM, WERE QUAINTER	CONSCIOUS AM I IN MY	679	13
BUT [JUST] INSTINCT ESTEEM [REPORT] HIM	CONSCIOUS AM I IN MY	679	19
CHRIST'S ACQUAINTANCE WITH HIM	LIFE--IS WHAT WE MAKE IT	698	3

	FIRST LINE	POEM	LINE
HIM (CONTINUED)			
JUSTIFY HIM--THOUGH--	LIFE--IS WHAT WE MAKE IT	698	4
THOUGHT BELONG TO HIM WHO GAVE IT--	PUBLICATION--IS THE	709	9
THEN--TO HIM WHO BEAR	PUBLICATION--IS THE	709	10
TO HIM WHOM NEVER RAGGED--COAT	THE BEGGAR LAD--DIES	717	15
AND SHE HAD PAST, WITH [FLED WITH / TRUSTED / HEARKENED] HIM--	I MEANT TO FIND HER WHEN	718	8
THEY--HIM--ATTENTION OF PASSER BY--	FOUR TREES--UPON A	742	10
NEED YOU--UNTO HIM--	NEVER FOR SOCIETY	746	12
AND EVERY TIME I SPEAK FOR HIM--	MY LIFE HAD STOOD--A	754	7
BUT DEATH WAS COY OF HIM	HE FOUGHT LIKE THOSE	759	6
TO HIM--TO LIVE--WAS DOOM--	HE FOUGHT LIKE THOSE	759	8
TO HIM WHO STRIVES SEVERE	THE HALLOWING OF PAIN	772	5
BURN HIM IN THE PUBLIC SQUARE--	GRIEF IS A MOUSE--	793	14
TO HIM WHO DOTH CONTINUAL	WHO COURT OBTAIN WITHIN	803	8
WHOLE CHAOSES [OBLIVIONS] ON HIM--	A PLATED LIFE--	806	8
IN HIM EXISTENCE SERVE OR SET	ALL CIRCUMSTANCES ARE	820	7
TO HIM, IT WOULD BE DEATH--	THIS CHASM, SWEET, UPON	858	16
EACH SCAR I'LL KEEP FOR HIM	EACH SCAR I'LL KEEP FOR	877	1
AND SCANT TO HIM THE CROWD--	OF CONSCIOUSNESS, HER	894	6
TOWARD THE GOD OF HIM--	THE ADMIRATIONS--AND	906	16
COMPELLING HIM TO CHOOSE HIMSELF	EXPERIENCE IS THE ANGLED	910	7
HOW THE WATERS CLOSED ABOVE HIM	HOW THE WATERS CLOSED	923	1
DEPOSITS HIM WITH GOD--	LOVE--IS THAT LATER	924	8
HIM [WHOM] IT DUPLICATE--	ABSENT PLACE--AN APRIL	927	8
TO HIM WHO ON IT'S SMALL [LOW] REPOSE	A COFFIN--IS A SMALL	943	9
THAT HELD HIM FROM PERDITION	AS ONE DOES SICKNESS	957	7
FITTER TO SEE HIM, I MAY BE	FITTER TO SEE HIM, I MAY	968	1
THE BEAUTY THAT REWARD HIM MOST [BEST]--	FITTER TO SEE HIM, I MAY	968	27
SOME KNOW HIM [IT] WHOM WE KNEW--	BESIDES THIS MAY	977	6
YOU MAY HAVE MET HIM--DID YOU NOT	A NARROW FELLOW IN THE	986	3
THE FIRST WE KNEW OF HIM WAS DEATH--	THE FIRST WE KNEW OF HIM	1006	1
ASKED HIM HIS NAME--HE LISPED ME "TROTWOOD"--	TRUDGING TO EDEN,	1020	3
WOULD IT COMFORT--TO KNOW I MET HIM--	TRUDGING TO EDEN,	1020	5
AFFRONT TO HIM	SO LARGE MY WILL	1024	5
FATE SLEW HIM, BUT HE DID NOT DROP--	FATE SLEW HIM, BUT HE	1031	1
IMPALED HIM ON HER FIERCEST STAKES--	FATE SLEW HIM, BUT HE	1031	3
SHE STUNG HIM--SAPPED HIS FIRM ADVANCE--	FATE SLEW HIM, BUT HE	1031	5
ACKNOWLEDGED HIM A MAN.	FATE SLEW HIM, BUT HE	1031	8
THAT LETS HIM OUT AGAIN.	WHO IS THE EAST?	1032	8
DEATH TENDERLY ASSISTS HIM	PAIN HAS BUT ONE	1049	7
OF ONE [HIM] THAT LEANETH FROM [IN] BALLOON	IT WAS A QUIET WAY--	1053	11
HOW SOME ONE [PARTIES] TREATED HIM	THE SKY IS LOW--THE	1075	6
ABOVE HIM IS TOO LOW A HIGHT	'TIS MY FIRST NIGHT	1122	3
TO THOSE WHO VISIT HIM	'TIS MY FIRST NIGHT	1122	8
ASK [TO] HIM UNTO THE GALLOWS LED [CALLED]--	OH SUMPTUOUS MOMENT	1125	8
ARE ANY HOAR [BLEAK] FOR HIM?	THAT ODD OLD MAN IS DEAD	1130	6
IT SUITS HIM BETTER THAN A CHECK	THE MERCHANT OF THE	1131	7
WE PRIED HIM BACK	THE FROST OF DEATH WAS	1136	9
WE HUNTED HIM TO HIS RAVINE	THE FROST OF DEATH WAS	1136	16
WE CHASED HIM TO HIS DEN--	THE FROST OF DEATH WAS	1136	17
BIRDS ARE RESUMING FOR HIM--	HE IS ALIVE, THIS	1160	3
HIM--TO REGALE--ME--ONLY--	HE IS ALIVE, THIS	1160	7
MUCH IS THE MIEN [GOOD IS THE LOOK] OF HIM IN MARCH	A PROMPT--EXECUTIVE BIRD	1177	7
IN THY LONG RACE WITH HIM!	MY GOD--HE SEES THEE--	1178	9
WHO HATH SUFFERED HIM--	WHEN I HOPED I FEARED--	1181	8
ARITHMETIC OF HIM--	THE DAYS THAT WE CAN	1184	8
BUT SEARCH EFFACES HIM	THE FROST WAS NEVER SEEN	1202	8
I CHARGE HIM FLY [FLEE]	THE PAST IS SUCH A	1203	6
HE PREACHED UPON [ABOUT] "BREADTH" TILL IT ARGUED HIM [WE . . .	HE PREACHED UPON	1207	1
AND OF "TRUTH" UNTIL IT PROCLAIMED HIM A LIAR--	HE PREACHED UPON	1207	3
UNLESS YOU LEAVE HIM--THEN RETURN	SO MUCH OF HEAVEN HAS	1228	11
THAT NONE CAN PUNISH HIM	LIKE TIME'S INSIDIOUS	1236	8
BUT FOR THE GREED [VAUNT / LIKE] OF HIM--	MY HEART RAN SO TO THEE	1237	13
BUT VANQUISHED HER [HIM] WITH MY DEFEAT	THE STARS ARE OLD, THAT	1249	7
EXPIRE WITH HIM THE SKILL	ELIJAH'S WAGON KNEW NO	1254	6
WITH HIM THE SKILL [RIGHT / ART] REMAIN	ELIJAH'S WAGON KNEW NO	1254	V 6
IF "ALL IS POSSIBLE WITH" HIM	BECAUSE THAT YOU ARE	1260	37
WHO HAS INVITED ME WITH HIM TO DWELL;	I CANNOT SEE MY SOUL BUT	1262	3
WHAT RAIMENT HONOR HIM THE MOST,	I CANNOT SEE MY SOUL BUT	1262	5
PROCURING HIM PERPETUAL DREST	I CANNOT SEE MY SOUL BUT	1262	9
PRECISELY AS THE JOY OF HIM--	THE WAY TO KNOW THE	1279	3
THE HARM OF YEARS IS ON HIM--	THE HARM OF YEARS IS ON	1280	1
DEPOSE HIM LIKE A FASHION	THE HARM OF YEARS IS ON	1280	3
BUT LET HIM ONCE SUSPECT	UNTIL THE DESERT KNOWS	1291	4
DOTH BETOKEN HIM.	DEATH'S WAYLAYING NOT	1296	6
THAT MUSHROOM--IT IS HIM!	THE MUSHROOM IS THE ELF	1298	20
THAT HAS BEFALLEN HIM.	FROM HIS SLIM PALACE IN	1300	4
TO HIM WHO EASY OWNS--	I CANNOT WANT IT MORE--	1301	6
TO HIM WHO SEES	THIS DIRTY--LITTLE--	1311	6
ABRAHAM TO KILL HIM	ABRAHAM TO KILL HIM	1317	1
REMAINED FOR HIM--TO FLEE--	A BEE HIS BURNISHED	1339	10
BECAUSE "GOD TOOK HIM" MENTION--[TELL US]	"WAS NOT" WAS ALL THE	1342	7
WERE SWEEPING HIM AWAY--	A SINGLE CLOVER PLANK	1343	8
DID NOT SO MUCH AS WRING FROM HIM	A SINGLE CLOVER PLANK	1343	15
ENABLE HIM [EACH] TO DWELL--	YOU CANNOT TAKE ITSELF	1351	4
NEITHER [OR] DECREE PROHIBIT HIM--	THE RAT IS THE CONCISEST	1356	9

	FIRST LINE	POEM	LINE
HIM (CONTINUED)			
TO SEEK THEM [HIM] BY--	OF THEIR PECULIAR LIGHT	1362	4
APPLAUD HIM TO DISCOVER	HIS MANSION IN THE POOL	1379	13
HIM YOU CHASTEN, [THOU CHASTENEST-- / YOU CHASTENED] THAT IS [WAS] HE!	LAY THIS LAUREL ON THE	1393	4
HE LOVES [SEEKS] WHAT SPURNS [SHUNS] HIM--	TO EARN IT BY DISDAINING	1427	3
REMAINS TO HIM UNKNOWN--	WHO NEVER WANTED--	1430	2
INDEED--'TWAS BUILT BY HIM--	HOW BRITTLE ARE THE	1433	6
NOT THAT HE GOES--WE LOVE HIM MORE	NOT THAT HE GOES--WE	1435	1
SO DAZZLING WE MISTAKE HIM	ONE OF THE ONES THAT	1466	7
HIS DRESS DENOTES HIM SOCIALLY,	THE ROBIN IS A GABRIEL	1483	3
I GAVE HIM LEAVE TO LIVE	IT CAME HIS TURN TO BEG	1500	6
SEE HOW WELL WE SPURN HIM--	SUMMER IS SHORTER THAN	1506	6
EQUALLY RETAIN HIM--	SUMMER IS SHORTER THAN	1506	8
LET HIM BE QUICK--THE VIAND FLITS [BANQUET COOLS]--	MINE ENEMY IS GROWING	1509	5
AS CONFIDENT OF HIM AS WE--	HE LIVED THE LIFE OF	1525	5
AND THE SUN WILL FREE IT [LOOSE HIM]	FOLLOW WISE ORION	1538	V
THAT BORE HIM FROM THE TOMB--	OBTAINING BUT OUR OWN	1543	4
CAN FIT BUT HIM ALONE	THE PATTERN OF THE SUN	1550	2
I GROPED FOR HIM BEFORE I KNEW	I GROPED FOR HIM BEFORE	1555	1
BUT THIS SLEW ALL BUT HIM--	SOME ARROWS SLAY BUT	1565	2
AS JESUS SAYS OF HIM,	NO LADDER NEEDS THE BIRD	1574	6
AS JESUS CITES [SAYS] OF HIM--	TO HER DERIDED HOME	1586	10
SUSTAINS HIM [HER] ANYWHERE--	TO HER DERIDED HOME	1586	V
THAT HIM REFRESH [MAKE HIM FRESH]--	THE LASSITUDES OF	1592	4
THAT HIM REFRESH [MAKE HIM FRESH]--	THE LASSITUDES OF	1592	4
AS CONFIDENT OF HIM AS WE--	WHO ABDICATED AMBUSH	1616	5
WOULD HELP HIM TO CONCEAL,	TO TRY TO SPEAK, AND	1617	6
A CLOVER, ANY TIME, TO HIM,	THE PEDIGREE OF HONEY	1627	V 3
ABOVE HIM IS THE SKY--[BENEATH]	THE DITCH IS DEAR TO THE	1645	6
OBLIVION BENDING OVER [ENFOLDING] HIM	THE DITCH IS DEAR TO THE	1645	7
I MEET HIM WITH A START	HIS MIND OF MAN, A	1663	2
NOT QUITE WITH HIM AT HOME	IN WINTER IN MY ROOM	1670	6
SECURED HIM BY A STRING	IN WINTER IN MY ROOM	1670	7
I TIED HIM--TOO	IN WINTER IN MY ROOM	1670	19
PROJECTED HIM.	IN WINTER IN MY ROOM	1670	31
THE EVENT WAS DIRECTLY BEHIND HIM	THE EVENT WAS DIRECTLY	1686	1
IF ONESELF IS NOT IN THE HABIT OF HIM	TO DO A MAGNANIMOUS	1699	3
THAT WE HAD RATHER NOT WITH HIM	GOD IS INDEED A JEALOUS	1719	3
AND NOT WITH HIM TO PLAY.	GOD IS INDEED A JEALOUS	1719	V 4
IF I INVITED HIM COULD TELL,	HE WAS MY HOST--HE WAS	1721	3
TO HIM WHOSE MORTAL LIGHT	HOW DARE THE ROBINS SING	1724	10
BEQUEATHS HIM TO THE NIGHT.	HOW DARE THE ROBINS SING	1724	12
IN DEFERENCE TO HIM	HOW DARE THE ROBINS SING	1724	14
"YET SAW HIM FACE TO FACE"--	NO MAN SAW AWE, NOR TO	1733	14
THAT CORONATION PIERCES HIM	ONE CROWN THAT NO ONE	1735	7
THE WATERS CHASED HIM AS HE FLED,	THE WATERS CHASED HIM AS	1749	1
TO WHICH THE LAW ENTITLED HIM.	UPON THE GALLOWS HUNG A	1757	3
THE ONE WHO BORE HIM TOTTERED IN,--	UPON THE GALLOWS HUNG A	1757	5
DOUBTLESS, HE THOUGHT IT MEET OF HIM	A TRAIN WENT THROUGH A	1761	7
HIMMALEH			
GIVE HIMMALEH--	I CAN WADE GRIEF--	252	15
AS HIMMALEH, SHALL STAND--	THEY LEAVE US WITH THE	350	6
THE HIMMALEH WAS KNOWN TO STOOP	THE HIMMALEH WAS KNOWN	481	1
TO SQUIRREL IN THE HIMMALEH	LIGHT IS SUFFICIENT TO	862	7
HIMSELF			
WERE HIMSELF--SUCH A DUNCE--	DID WE DISOBEY HIM?	267	5
AND TOUCH THE PANTOMIME--HIMSELF,	I BREATHED ENOUGH TO	272	7
OF ME, HIMSELF WAS SHY--	THE ONLY GHOST I EVER	274	14
HIMSELF--A TELESCOPE	I NEVER FELT AT HOME--	413	12
HIMSELF--COULD HAVE THE SKIES--	NOT IN THIS WORLD TO SEE	418	12
HIMSELF--TO HIM--A FORTUNE--	THIS WAS A POET--IT IS	448	15
SEVERER TRIUMPH--BY HIMSELF	TRIUMPH--MAY BE OF	455	13
HIMSELF--THE HEAVEN EXCEL--	THE POWER TO BE TRUE TO	464	6
HE PARTS HIMSELF--LIKE LEAVES--	HE PARTS HIMSELF--LIKE	517	1
BETWEEN HIMSELF--AND HORROR'S TWIN--	I TRIED TO THINK A	532	14
THE DISSOLUTION--IN HIMSELF--	THE PROVINCE OF THE	539	7
AND TOOK HIMSELF, FOR PAY,	I GAVE MYSELF TO HIM--	580	2
AND DANCING SOFTLY TO HIMSELF [AS HE KNITS]	THE SPIDER HOLDS A	605	3
AS IF HIMSELF WERE OPTIONAL	THE TREES LIKE TASSELS--	606	11
NOR LIKE HIMSELF--THE ART	IT WOULD HAVE STARVED A	612	13
HIMSELF HAS BUT TO WILL	THEY SHUT ME UP IN PROSE	613	9
BUT HE MUST [SHOULD] COUNT THE DROPS--HIMSELF--	AGAIN--HIS VOICE IS AT	663	28
UPON HIMSELF BE VISITING	THE SOUL THAT HATH A	674	7
HIMSELF--ABIDE WITH THEE--	NO PRISONER BE--	720	3
HIMSELF--HIS DATELESS DYNASTY--	BEHIND ME--DIPS ETERNITY	721	10
HIMSELF--HIMSELF DIVERSIFY--	BEHIND ME--DIPS ETERNITY	721	11
HIMSELF--HIMSELF DIVERSIFY--	BEHIND ME--DIPS ETERNITY	721	11
BUT ONLY TO HIMSELF--BE KNOWN	SHE ROSE TO HIS	732	11
"HAMLET" TO HIMSELF WERE HAMLET--	DRAMA'S VITALLEST	741	8
BESTOWED [HE GAVE] HIMSELF TO BALLS	HE FOUGHT LIKE THOSE	759	2
THAT I UNTO HIMSELF ADJUST	YOU CONSTITUTED TIME--	765	7
WHO COURT OBTAIN WITHIN HIMSELF	WHO COURT OBTAIN WITHIN	803	1
THAN TO HIMSELF, ALLIED,	TO THIS WORLD SHE	830	7
HIMSELF [THAT HE] IS BORNE AWAY	TRUTH--IS AS OLD AS GOD	836	6
HIMSELF ABIDE,	SPRING IS THE PERIOD	844	4
COMPELLING HIM TO CHOOSE HIMSELF	EXPERIENCE IS THE ANGLED	910	7
HIMSELF HAD NOT COMPLAINED. [HITHERTO	THE HOLLOWS ROUND HIS	955	4

	FIRST LINE	POEM	LINE
HIMSELF (CONTINUED)			
CONCEALED--]			
HE WHO IN HIMSELF BELIEVES--	HE WHO IN HIMSELF	969	1
GROPED BACKWARD AT HIMSELF	HE SCANNED IT--STAGGERED	1062	7
HIMSELF AND HER BETWEEN,	THE FROST OF DEATH WAS	1136	11
HIMSELF HIMSELF INFORM.	A SPIDER SEWED AT NIGHT	1138	6
HIMSELF HIMSELF INFORM.	A SPIDER SEWED AT NIGHT	1138	6
THE FROST HIMSELF [ITSELF] SO COMELY	LIKE TIME'S INSIDIOUS	1236	5
HIMSELF HAVE NOT A FACE.	SILENCE IS ALL WE DREAD.	1251	4
"THE FATHER AND THE SON" HIMSELF	WHO WERE "THE FATHER AND	1258	11
DISCOVERY NOT GOD HIMSELF	BECAUSE THAT YOU ARE	1260	11
HIMSELF--HIS CARRIAGE WAS--[CARRIAGE IS-- / EQUIPAGE.]	A BEE HIS BURNISHED	1339	4
HIMSELF--AT WHATSOEVER FATHOM	THE THINGS THAT NEVER	1515	12
BETAKES HIMSELF TO DIE.	HIS ORIENTAL HERESIES	1526	V 8
FITTED ITSELF TO HIMSELF LIKE A ROBE	THE EVENT WAS DIRECTLY	1686	3
HINDER			
THE GRAVE WOULD HINDER ME--	I HAD NO TIME TO HATE--	478	3
WHAT COULD IT HINDER SO--TO SAY?	GOING TO HIM! HAPPY	494	21
LET NOT MY WITNESS HINDER THEM [THEM IMPAIR--]	'TIS TRUE--THEY SHUT ME	538	5
IT HINDER FROM THE WEST	I CROSS TILL I AM WEARY	550	11
THEY SEVERALLY--RETARD--OR FURTHER [PROMOTE--OR HINDER]--	FOUR TREES--UPON A	742	15
'TWAS NOT THY WONT, TO HINDER SO--	'TIS SUNRISE--LITTLE	908	3
NOR MOUNTAIN HINDER ME	NOR MOUNTAIN HINDER ME	1029	1
HINDER IT A LITTLE	I SUPPOSE THE TIME WILL	1381	6
HINDERED			
LIKE HINDERED RUBIES--OR THE LIGHT	THE DAY CAME SLOW--TILL	304	3
SO THAT THE SUM [LOVE] BE NEVER HINDERED	SWEET--YOU FORGOT--BUT I	523	3
LIKE HINDERED FLAGS--SWEET HOISTED--	THE TREES LIKE TASSELS--	606	23
AND HINDERED BUT A MOUND	NO NOTICE GAVE SHE, BUT	804	16
OH HINDERED EYE	THE SUN AND MOON MUST	871	10
WHAT HINDERED ME	THE BIRD DID PRANCE--THE	1107	V
BY NO CONCLUSION [DERISION] HINDERED	A SPARROW TOOK A SLICE	1211	V 7
BY HOMELY GIFT AND HINDERED WORDS	BY HOMELY GIFT AND	1563	1
HINDERING			
HINDERING--HAUNTING--PERISHING--	FAIRER THROUGH FADING--	938	4
HINDERS			
AND HINDERS GABRIEL'S WING--	THE LOVE A LIFE CAN SHOW	673	6
HINDRANCE			
FOR THE LONG HINDRANCE--GRACE--TO ME--	FITTER TO SEE HIM, I MAY	968	2
HINGE			
NOON--IS THE HINGE OF DAY--	NOON--IS THE HINGE OF	931	1
DEPARTURE FROM A HINGE	THE MISSING ALL,	985	4
HINT			
HINT THAT WITHIN THE RIDDLE	I HAV'NT TOLD MY GARDEN	50	15
CAUTIOUS, HINT TO ANY CAPTIVE	TALK WITH PRUDENCE TO A	119	5
SALUTE, AND PASS, WITHOUT A HINT--	I READ MY SENTENCE--	412	13
BY TROPIC HINT--SOME TRAVELLED BIRD	LIKE FLOWERS, THAT HEARD	513	8
A HINT OF PORTS AND PEOPLES--	A SOUTH WIND--HAS A	719	5
HINT OF GLORY--IT AFFORDED--	ROBBED BY DEATH--BUT	971	7
SO I MUST BAFFLE AT THE HINT	MY COCOON TIGHTENS--	1099	9
WITHOUT A HINT FROM ME,	IF EVER THE LID GETS OFF	1727	4
HINTED			
I HINTED CHANGES--LAPSE OF TIME--	IF HE WERE LIVING--DARE	734	5
HINTS			
'TIS THIS--IN MUSIC--HINTS AND SWAYS--	THE LOVE A LIFE CAN SHOW	673	7
THAT HINTS WITHOUT ASSUMING--	SEPTEMBER'S	1271	5
SUCH HINTS OF HONEY LAY	WITHIN THAT LITTLE HIVE	1607	2
HIP			
UPON HIS HIP ELATE	THE FINGERS OF THE LIGHT	1000	14
HIRE			
SUFFICIENTLY DEVELOPED--HE'D HIRE US	MYSELF WAS FORMED--A	488	7
HIS			
GOD HATH MADE NOTHING SINGLE BUT THEE IN HIS WORLD SO FAIR!	AWAKE YE MUSES NINE,	1	6
ADAM, AND EVE, HIS CONSORT, THE MOON, AND THEN THE SUN;	AWAKE YE MUSES NINE,	1	8
THE BEE DOTH COURT THE FLOWER, THE FLOWER HIS SUIT RECEIVES,	AWAKE YE MUSES NINE,	1	13
AND THE FATHER FOND DEMANDETH THE MAIDEN FOR HIS SON.	AWAKE YE MUSES NINE,	1	16
WILL TAKE HIS HAT, AND RUN!	"SIC TRANSIT GLORIA	3	56
GAVE HIS BREATH AWAY.	THERE IS A WORD	8	10
I SAW THE SUN--HIS PLUNDER DONE	I NEVER TOLD THE BURIED	11	3
CROUCH LOW TO GUARD HIS PRIZE.	I NEVER TOLD THE BURIED	11	4
OF ERMINE IS HIS DOUBLET--	THE GUEST IS GOLD AND	15	3
HIS CAPUCHIN GAY--	THE GUEST IS GOLD AND	15	4
MAY SEIZE UPON HIS MIND--	I HAD A GUINEA GOLDEN--	23	34
BORE HIS RIDDLE IN!	IF THOSE I LOVED WERE	29	8
MY [HIS] FANTASY TO PLEASE.	I ROBBED THE WOODS--	41	5
TO INTRODUCE HIS SOUL.	COULD LIVE--DID LIVE--	43	5
AND GIRT HIS LOINS ANEW	A LITTLE EAST OF JORDAN,	59	V 10
"ARCTURUS" IS HIS OTHER NAME--	"ARCTURUS" IS HIS OTHER	70	1
WILL LIFT HIS LITTLE GIRL--	"ARCTURUS" IS HIS OTHER	70	31
PRAY LEAD ME TO HIS BED!	SEXTON! MY MASTER'S	96	2
FROM OFF HIS CHAMBER DOOR--	SEXTON! MY MASTER'S	96	6
AND WHEN HIS GOLDEN WALK IS DONE--	THE DAISY FOLLOWS SOFT	106	2
SITS SHILY AT HIS FEET--	THE DAISY FOLLOWS SOFT	106	3
AND GOD, THAT HE CALLED HIS,	I HAD SOME THINGS THAT I	116	2

HIS (CONTINUED)	FIRST LINE	POEM	LINE
HIS CARAVAN OF RED--	A SOMETHING IN A	122	18
"MANY MANSIONS", BY "HIS FATHER",	"HOUSES"--SO THE WISE	127	5
A SPIDER AT HIS TRADE AGAIN--	AN ALTERED LOOK ABOUT	140	8
HIS MUSKET ON HIS BREAST--	BLESS GOD, HE WENT AS	147	2
HIS MUSKET ON HIS BREAST--	BLESS GOD, HE WENT AS	147	2
ON HIS SIDE [PART], WHAT TRANSACTION!	THE SUN KEPT STOOPING--	152	3
IN HIS "NATIVE TOWN."	DUST IS THE ONLY SECRET	153	4
NOBODY KNEW "HIS FATHER"--	DUST IS THE ONLY SECRET	153	5
BENEATH HIS FADED JACKET'S BLUE--	I MET A KING THIS	166	6
HIS ROYAL STATE PARTOOK!	I MET A KING THIS	166	22
FULL ROYAL IS HIS RETINUE!	WAIT TILL THE MAJESTY OF	171	11
FULL PURPLE IS HIS STATE!	WAIT TILL THE MAJESTY OF	171	12
OF VELVET, IS HIS COUNTENANCE,	A FUZZY FELLOW, WITHOUT	173	3
AND HIS COMPLEXION, DUN!	A FUZZY FELLOW, WITHOUT	173	4
IN HIS CHIMNEY CORNER STAY,	I'M THE LITTLE "HEART'S	176	6
AND I--FOR WONDER AT HIS WOE--	I SHALL KNOW WHY--WHEN	193	6
TURNED SLOWLY TO HIS NATIVE COAST--	AN AWFUL TEMPEST MASHED	198	12
THAT SEEKETH HIS FELICITY	THE FLOWER MUST NOT	206	2
REACHING LATE HIS FLOWER,	COME SLOWLY--EDEN!	211	5
COUNTS HIS NECTARS--	COME SLOWLY--EDEN!	211	7
ON HIS BABBLING--BERRY--LIPS--	TEACH HIM--WHEN HE MAKES	227	3
WERE MY EAR--AS NEAR HIS NEST--	TEACH HIM--WHEN HE MAKES	227	5
BEE--PLEDGES HIS--IN MINUTE FLAGONS--	WE--BEE AND I--LIVE BY	230	10
HIS HAUGHTY--SPANGLED HEMS--	THE SUN--JUST TOUCHED	232	10
TO GAIN HIS GRACE--I'D DIE!	THE COURT IS FAR AWAY--	235	4
I'LL SEEK HIS ROYAL FEET--	THE COURT IS FAR AWAY--	235	5
SAY--THAT A LITTLE LIFE--FOR HIS--	IF HE DISSOLVE--THEN--	236	12
HIS LITTLE SPANIEL--TELL HIM!	IF HE DISSOLVE--THEN--	236	14
THE HEARING HIM PUT HIS PLAYTHINGS UP	IT IS EASY TO WORK WHEN	244	3
FOREVER AT HIS SIDE TO WALK--	FOREVER AT HIS SIDE TO	246	1
BRAIN OF HIS BRAIN--	FOREVER AT HIS SIDE TO	246	3
BLOOD OF HIS BLOOD--	FOREVER AT HIS SIDE TO	246	4
FOREVER OF HIS FATE TO TASTE--	FOREVER AT HIS SIDE TO	246	6
WHAT WOULD I GIVE TO SEE HIS FACE?	WHAT WOULD I GIVE TO SEE	247	1
AND LEFT HIS PROCESS--SATISFIED--	HE PUT THE BELT AROUND	273	V 3
HE HAD [WORE] NO SANDAL ON HIS FOOT--	THE ONLY GHOST I EVER	274	3
HIS MIEN [GAIT], WAS SOUNDLESS, LIKE THE [A] BIRD--	THE ONLY GHOST I EVER	274	5
HIS FASHIONS, QUAINT, MOSAIC--	THE ONLY GHOST I EVER	274	7
HIS CONVERSATION--SELDOM--	THE ONLY GHOST I EVER	274	9
HIS LAUGHTER, LIKE THE BREEZE	THE ONLY GHOST I EVER	274	10
WHO DRILLS [NAILS] HIS WELCOME IN--	THAT AFTER HORROR--THAT	286	16
DOMENICHINO DROPPED HIS PENCIL--	HOW THE OLD MOUNTAINS	291	23
I GOT SO I COULD HEAR [THINK / TAKE] HIS NAME--	I GOT SO I COULD HEAR	293	1
IN WHICH HIS LETTERS GREW	I GOT SO I COULD HEAR	293	10
THAT CLAMORS FOR HIS HEAD--	THE DOOMED--REGARD THE	294	8
HIS NAME--REMAIN--	THE ONE WHO COULD REPEAT	307	9
HIS OWN WAS [IS] AMPLER--BUT AS I	I SEND TWO SUNSETS--	308	5
WHO ONLY SHOWS HIS MARBLE DISC [GRANITE FACE]--	GIVE LITTLE ANGUISH--	310	7
AND THAT IS HIS BUSINESS--NOT OUR'S--	THE WIND DID'NT COME	316	12
HIS WAY--OF A JUNE DAY--	THE WIND DID'NT COME	316	16
LIFTS [SPREADS] HIS LIGHT PINNACE--	THE NEAREST DREAM	319	8
HE STIRRED HIS VELVET HEAD	A BIRD CAME DOWN THE	328	12
AND HE UNROLLED HIS FEATHERS	A BIRD CAME DOWN THE	328	15
HE HAS HID HIS RARE LIFE	I KNOW THAT HE EXISTS.	338	3
HE KEEPS HIS SECRETS SAFELY--VERY--	FUNNY--TO BE A CENTURY--	345	5
FORGET THE SECRET OF HIS WING	NOT PROBABLE--THE BAREST	346	7
HIS FINGERS ARE THE SIZE OF FISTS--	THEY LEAVE US WITH THE	350	3
HIS FISTS, THE SIZE OF MEN--	THEY LEAVE US WITH THE	350	4
AND WHOM HE FOUNDETH, WITH HIS ARM	THEY LEAVE US WITH THE	350	5
POISED LIGHTLY ON HIS HAND,	THEY LEAVE US WITH THE	350	8
WOOS, AS HE STATES US--BY HIS SON--	GOD IS A DISTANT--	357	2
AT REST--HIS FINGERS ARE--	DEATH SETS A THING	360	16
ALTHOUGH I PUT AWAY HIS LIFE--	ALTHOUGH I PUT AWAY HIS	366	1
OR PUSHED THE PEBBLE FROM HIS PATH--	ALTHOUGH I PUT AWAY HIS	366	7
OR PLAYED HIS CHOSEN TUNE--	ALTHOUGH I PUT AWAY HIS	366	8
BUT JUST HIS EAR COULD KNOW	ALTHOUGH I PUT AWAY HIS	366	10
THE FOOT TO BEAR HIS ERRAND--	ALTHOUGH I PUT AWAY HIS	366	13
HIS WEARIEST COMMANDMENT--	ALTHOUGH I PUT AWAY HIS	366	17
IN JUST THE DRESS HIS CENTURY WORE--	A PRECIOUS--MOULDERING	371	3
HIS VENERABLE HAND TO TAKE--	A PRECIOUS--MOULDERING	371	5
HIS QUAINT OPINIONS--TO INSPECT--	A PRECIOUS--MOULDERING	371	9
HIS THOUGHT TO ASCERTAIN	A PRECIOUS--MOULDERING	371	10
HIS PRESENCE IS ENCHANTMENT--	A PRECIOUS--MOULDERING	371	25
PROPORTIONED TO HIS SEVERAL DEARTH	THERE IS A FLOWER THAT	380	7
WITHIN HIS CLOSET--BEST YOU CAN	EXHILIRATION--IS WITHIN	383	11
THE EAGLE OF HIS NEST	NO RACK CAN TORTURE ME--	384	9
AS IF THE HOUSE WERE HIS--	THERE'S BEEN A DEATH, IN	389	14
CONCLUDES HIS GLISTENING INTERVIEW--	A VISITOR IN MARL--	391	7
BUT WHOM HIS FINGERS TOUCHED--	A VISITOR IN MARL--	391	9
AND WHERE HIS FEET HAVE RUN--	A VISITOR IN MARL--	391	10
HIS HABIT--IS SEVERE--	THERE IS A LANGUOR OF	396	10
AND FAR I HEARD HIS SILVER CALL	I HAD NOT MINDED--WALLS	398	3
PUSHED SUDDEN THRO' TO HIS--	I HAD NOT MINDED--WALLS	398	6
THE LOOKING IN HIS EYES--	I HAD NOT MINDED--WALLS	398	8
AND HIS--IN SOLID GOLD--	A TONGUE--TO TELL HIM I	400	19
ON HIS REPEALLESS--LIST.	THEY DROPPED LIKE FLAKES	409	9

HIS (CONTINUED)

	FIRST LINE	POEM	LINE
WEIGH, HELPLESS, IN HIS PAWS--	'TWAS LIKE A MAELSTROM,	414	13
NOT IN THIS WORLD TO SEE HIS FACE--	NOT IN THIS WORLD TO SEE	418	1
HIS LISP--IS LIGHTNING--AND THE SUN--	YOU'LL KNOW IT--AS YOU	420	12
HIS CONVERSATION--WITH THE SEA--	YOU'LL KNOW IT--AS YOU	420	13
MARKED HIS--WHAT HOLIDAY	REMOVED FROM ACCIDENT OF	424	8
WOULD STIR HIS SLOW CONCEPTION--	REMOVED FROM ACCIDENT OF	424	9
FOR HIS PERJURY!	TAKING UP THE FAIR IDEAL	428	8
HIS SPEECH WAS LIKE THE PUSH	THE WIND--TAPPED LIKE A	436	10
HIS COUNTENANCE--A BILLOW--	THE WIND--TAPPED LIKE A	436	13
HIS FINGERS, AS HE PASSED	THE WIND--TAPPED LIKE A	436	14
DISCARD HIS BRIDE--	FORGET! THE LADY WITH	438	11
AND THEN, I [HE] BRAKE MY [HIS] LIFE--AND LO,	I SHOWED HER HIGHTS SHE	446	9
I LIVE WITH HIM--I SEE HIS FACE--	I LIVE WITH HIM--I SEE	463	1
I LIVE WITH HIM--I HEAR HIS VOICE--	I LIVE WITH HIM--I SEE	463	9
THE JUDGMENT PUSH HIS PICTURE--	THE POWER TO BE TRUE TO	464	3
BE SETTING ON HIS PROGRESS--	NO MAN CAN COMPASS A	477	7
HIS IGNORANCE--THE ANGEL	NO MAN CAN COMPASS A	477	11
BUT THEN HIS HOUSE--IS BUT A STEP--	YOU LOVE THE LORD--YOU	487	7
OF HIS CONDEMNED LIP?	TO ONE DENIED TO DRINK	490	8
FOR IT WOULD SPLIT HIS [HER] HEART, TO KNOW IT--	GOING TO HIM! HAPPY	494	16
HIS SWEET FORGIVENESS--	HE STRAINED MY FAITH--	497	14
THAT GAZE UPON [GROW ALONG] HIS JOURNEY--	I ENVY SEAS, WHEREON HE	498	5
THAT DOT HIS DISTANT EAVES--	I ENVY SEAS, WHEREON HE	498	10
THE WEALTHY [HAPPY] FLY, UPON HIS PANE--	I ENVY SEAS, WHEREON HE	498	11
THAT JUST ABROAD HIS WINDOW	I ENVY SEAS, WHEREON HE	498	13
AND THEN HIS FAIRY [MICROSCOPIC] GIG	WITHIN MY GARDEN, RIDES	500	10
I GROPED [PERISHED / DWELT] UPON HIS BREAST--	HE TOUCHED ME, SO I LIVE	506	3
LONG DUNGEONED FROM HIS ROSE--	THE SOUL HAS BANDAGED	512	16
ASSERT HER VITAL PRIVILEGE--[HIS PRIMOGENITURE]	NO CROWD THAT HAS	515	7
RUNS [PUTS] HIS FINGERS THRO' IT--	BEAUTY--BE NOT CAUSED--	516	6
AND THEN HE LEANS WITH ALL HIS MIGHT	HE PARTS HIMSELF--LIKE	517 V	3
I FELT HIS SILVER HEEL	I STARTED EARLY--TOOK MY	520	18
IT SUITS HIS OWN AUSTERITY--	I THINK THE HEMLOCK	525	3
HIS BEST [GOOD] NORWEGIAN WINES--	I THINK THE HEMLOCK	525	12
BENEATH HIS TABERNACLES, PLAY,	I THINK THE HEMLOCK	525	15
LATER, HIS FAINT CONFEDERATES	TO PUT THIS WORLD DOWN,	527	7
I ALMOST STROVE TO CLASP HIS HAND,	I TRIED TO THINK A	532	16
THE WRENCHING--FOR HIS FIRMAMENT	WE SEE--COMPARATIVELY--	534	11
IS FASHIONED FOR [FITTED TO] HIS HAND--	'TIS ONE BY ONE--THE	545	16
WHO DIES--AND TO HIS FRIEND--	DEATH IS POTENTIAL TO	548	2
THE BLACK BERRY--WEARS A THORN IN HIS SIDE--	THE BLACK BERRY--WEARS A	554	1
HE OFFERS [SPICES / FLAVORS] HIS BERRY, JUST THE SAME	THE BLACK BERRY--WEARS A	554	3
OR CLASPS A ROCK, WITH BOTH HIS HANDS--	THE BLACK BERRY--WEARS A	554	7
HIS TALISMANIC STONE	TRUST IN THE UNEXPECTED	555	6
HIS HOUSE WAS NOT--NO SIGN HAD HE--	MY PERIOD HAD COME FOR	564	9
COULD I INFER HIS RESIDENCE--	MY PERIOD HAD COME FOR	564	11
HIS MIGHTY BALLS--IN DEATH WERE THICK--	A DYING TIGER--MOANED	566	5
'TWAS NOT HIS BLAME--WHO DIED	A DYING TIGER--MOANED	566	10
HE GAVE AWAY HIS LIFE--	HE GAVE AWAY HIS LIFE--	567	1
A TRIFLE--IN HIS OWN ESTEEM [ESTIMATE]--	HE GAVE AWAY HIS LIFE--	567	3
TO THE VERY SQUARE--HIS FOOT IS PASSING--	I COULD DIE--TO KNOW--	570	10
FIXED FULL, AND STEADY, ON HIS OWN	I PRAYED, AT FIRST, A	576	7
AND PARTS OF HIS FAR PLAN	I PRAYED, AT FIRST, A	576	10
OF HIS DIVINITY--	I PRAYED, AT FIRST, A	576	13
TO INTERRUPT HIS YELLOW PLAN	TO INTERRUPT HIS YELLOW	591	1
DIRECTLY IN HIS EYE--	TO INTERRUPT HIS YELLOW	591	6
DOES NOT SO MUCH AS TURN HIS HEAD	TO INTERRUPT HIS YELLOW	591	7
'TIS HIS TO STIMULATE THE EARTH--	TO INTERRUPT HIS YELLOW	591	9
ENABLED BY HIS ROYAL DRESS--	LIKE MIGHTY FOOT LIGHTS	595	7
HIS FACE ALL VICTORY	WHEN I WAS SMALL, A	596	4
FOR BRAVERIES, REMOTE AS THIS [HIS]	WHEN I WAS SMALL, A	596	19
THEN CARVED [HE WROTE] HIS NAME--UPON IT--	HE FOUND MY BEING--SET	603	3
BE FAITHFUL--IN HIS ABSENCE--	HE FOUND MY BEING--SET	603	5
HIS YARN [COIL] OF PEARL--UNWINDS [EXPENDS]--	THE SPIDER HOLDS A	605	4
PURSUES HIS PEARLY STRANDS--	THE SPIDER HOLDS A	605 V	4
SUPPLANTS OUR TAPESTRIES WITH HIS--	THE SPIDER HOLDS A	605	7
HIS CONTINENTS [THEORIES] OF LIGHT--	THE SPIDER HOLDS A	605	10
HIS BOUNDARIES [SOPHISTRIES]--FORGOT--	THE SPIDER HOLDS A	605	12
EXCEPT IT WERE A WHIM OF HIS	THE TREES LIKE TASSELS--	606	15
LOOK DOWN UPON [ABOLISH HIS] CAPTIVITY--	THEY SHUT ME UP IN PROSE	613	11
BUT WHEN HIS POWER DROPPED [BENT]--	I ROSE--BECAUSE HE SANK	616	3
I HELPED [STAYED] HIS FILM--WITH HYMN--	I ROSE--BECAUSE HE SANK	616	7
THAT HELD HIS FOREHEAD STIFF--	I ROSE--BECAUSE HE SANK	616	9
NO BLACK BIRD BATES HIS BANJO--	IT MAKES NO DIFFERENCE	620	7
HIS SEPARATION FROM HIS ROSE--	IT MAKES NO DIFFERENCE	620	11
HIS SEPARATION FROM HIS ROSE--	IT MAKES NO DIFFERENCE	620	11
TO WHOM HE COULD ENTRUST HIS WAVERING GAZE--	TO KNOW JUST HOW HE	622	3
AND DID THE SUNSHINE FACE HIS WAY--	TO KNOW JUST HOW HE	622	8
WHAT WAS HIS FURTHEST MIND--OF HOME--OR GOD--	TO KNOW JUST HOW HE	622	9
JUST HIS SIGH--ACCENTED--	TO KNOW JUST HOW HE	622	14
ALARMS US--THO' HIS YELLOW FEET	THE LIGHTNING PLAYETH--	630	7
WHOLE--LIKE HIS PRINCIPLE--	THE CHILD'S FAITH IS NEW	637	2
DEEMS HIS DOMINION	THE CHILD'S FAITH IS NEW	637	10
HIS PRETTY ESTIMATES	THE CHILD'S FAITH IS NEW	637	19
TO MY SMALL HEARTH HIS FIRE CAME--	TO MY SMALL HEARTH HIS	638	1
OUR LIFE--HIS PORCELAIN--	I CANNOT LIVE WITH YOU--	640	7

HIS (CONTINUED)

	FIRST LINE	POEM	LINE
AGAIN--HIS VOICE IS AT THE DOOR--	AGAIN--HIS VOICE IS AT	663	1
I MIGHT SURPRISE [NOT PLEASE] HIS EYE!	AGAIN--HIS VOICE IS AT	663	8
JUST HIS FACE--NOTHING MORE!	AGAIN--HIS VOICE IS AT	663	12
DAY--DROPS YOU HER [HIS] RED ADIEU!	AH, TENERIFFE!	666	5
FIT [STRAIN] HIS COUNTENANCE--	BLOOM UPON THE MOUNTAIN	667	18
THE [HIS] EXPERIENCE--	BLOOM UPON THE MOUNTAIN	667	20
HIS INDIVIDUAL ONE--	NO ROMANCE SOLD UNTO	669	4
OF HIS PROFOUND [OPAQUE] TO COME--	THE FUTURE--NEVER SPOKE	672	4
HIS OFFICE--BUT TO EXECUTE	THE FUTURE--NEVER SPOKE	672	11
MONTCALM, HIS OPPOSING SPIRIT	WOLFE DEMANDED DURING	678	5
OF HIS COMPANY--	CONSCIOUS AM I IN MY	679	8
PRESENCE--IS HIS FURTHEST LICENSE--	CONSCIOUS AM I IN MY	679	9
HIS TABLE'S SPREAD TOO HIGH FOR US--	VICTORY COMES LATE--	690	8
GOD KEEP HIS OATH [VOW] TO SPARROWS--	VICTORY COMES LATE--	690	13
FOR HIS MEAN SAKE TO LEAVE THE ROW	THE HEAVEN VESTS FOR	694	11
AND HIS EMERALD SWING--	I COULD BRING YOU JEWELS	697	10
JUST HIS OWN ENDORSEMENT--	LIFE--IS WHAT WE MAKE IT	698	7
HIS SURE FOOT PRECEDING--	LIFE--IS WHAT WE MAKE IT	698	13
HIS FAVORITE REFRAIN.	THE JUDGE IS LIKE THE	699	12
FOR HIS CIVILITY--	BECAUSE I COULD NOT STOP	712	8
BUT THE SUCCESS--WAS HIS--IT SEEMS--	I MEANT TO FIND HER WHEN	718	3
HIMSELF--HIS DATELESS DYNASTY--	BEHIND ME--DIPS ETERNITY	721	10
OF HIS AUTHORITY--	IT'S EASY TO INVENT A	724	4
BUT HIS PERTURBLESS PLAN	IT'S EASY TO INVENT A	724	10
QUESTION IF HIS GLORY	ALTER! WHEN THE HILLS DO	729	3
SHE ROSE TO HIS REQUIREMENT--DROPT	SHE ROSE TO HIS	732	1
OF HIS JULIET,	DRAMA'S VITALLEST	741	11
FOR 'TIS HIS INSTITUTION--AND	REMORSE--IS MEMORY--	744	11
WHO HIS OWN ACQUAINTANCE	NEVER FOR SOCIETY	746	3
HIS MERIT--ALL MY FEAR--	MY WORTHINESS IS ALL MY	751	2
FOR HIS BELOVED NEED--	MY WORTHINESS IS ALL MY	751	6
OF HIS ELECT CONTENT--	MY WORTHINESS IS ALL MY	751	14
TO FOE OF HIS--I'M DEADLY FOE--	MY LIFE HAD STOOD--A	754	17
NO BOBOLINK--REVERSE HIS SINGING	NO BOBOLINK--REVERSE HIS	755	1
HIS SPACIOUS FUTURE--	NO BOBOLINK--REVERSE HIS	755	6
WHOSE MUSIC BE HIS	NO BOBOLINK--REVERSE HIS	755	8
HIS COMRADES, SHIFTED LIKE THE FLAKES	HE FOUGHT LIKE THOSE	759	9
UPON HIS INFANT FACE WAS SET	HE TOLD A HOMELY TALE	763	3
TO DO HIS GOLDEN WILL--	MY FAITH IS LARGER THAN	766	8
AND IF HIS YELLOW FEET SHOULD MISS--	MY FAITH IS LARGER THAN	766	9
HIS LAST DECADE [SLOW DECADES] AWAY,	JOY TO HAVE MERITED THE	788	22
FOR HIS SHY HOUSE--	GRIEF IS A MOUSE--	793	3
PRICKS HIS EAR--REPORT TO HEAR	GRIEF IS A MOUSE--	793	6
THAT SWEPT HIS BEING--BACK--	GRIEF IS A MOUSE--	793	8
POUNCE ON HIS BRUISES--ONE--SAY--OR THREE--	GRIEF IS A MOUSE--	793	11
GRIEF IS A GOURMAND--SPARE HIS LUXURY--	GRIEF IS A MOUSE--	793	12
HIS ASHES [EMBERS]--WILL	GRIEF IS A MOUSE--	793	15
THE SUNSHINE THREW HIS HAT AWAY--	A DROP FELL ON THE APPLE	794	11
UNCONSCIOUS THAT HIS SINGLE FLEET [BULK / SAIL]	WHO GIANTS KNOW, WITH	796	7
TO HIS EXCLUSION, WHO PREPARE	TIME FEELS SO VAST THAT	802	5
OF HIS DIAMETERS--	TIME FEELS SO VAST THAT	802	8
CONSPIRE AGAINST [REPUDIATE] HIS OWN	WHO COURT OBTAIN WITHIN	803	9
IN WHICH HIS FACE IS SET--	ALL CIRCUMSTANCES ARE	820	2
ALL LATITUDES EXIST FOR HIS	ALL CIRCUMSTANCES ARE	820	3
THE LIGHT HIS ACTION, AND THE DARK	ALL CIRCUMSTANCES ARE	820	5
THE LEISURE OF HIS WILL--	ALL CIRCUMSTANCES ARE	820	6
HIS TWIN IDENTITY	TRUTH--IS AS OLD AS GOD	836	2
YET UPON HIS PURPLE PROGRAMME	ALWAYS MINE!	839	8
JUST AS HE SPOKE IT FROM HIS HANDS	JUST AS HE SPOKE IT FROM	848	1
DISHONOR HIS DESIGN--	JUST AS HE SPOKE IT FROM	848	4
ACCORDING AS HIS SKILL PREFER	JUST AS HE SPOKE IT FROM	848	5
HIS ABSENT CHARACTER.	JUST AS HE SPOKE IT FROM	848	8
TILL HIS BEST STEP APPROACHING	I SING TO USE THE	850	5
FOR HIS PLEIAD'S FACE--	WHEN THE ASTRONOMER	851	2
WHEN TO HIS COVENANT NEEDLE	WHEN THE ASTRONOMER	851	5
HIS GLITTERING EMBRACE--	ESCAPING BACKWARD TO	867	4
HIS EYE, IT IS THE EAST AND WEST--	THE SUN AND MOON MUST	871	5
DO CONCENTRATE HIS COUNTENANCE	THE SUN AND MOON MUST	871	7
AND PARTAKES--HIS TONGUE	AS THE STARVED MAELSTROM	872	8
TILL HE ESTEEM HIS DATES AND COCOA	AS THE STARVED MAELSTROM	872	11
IN HIS LONG ABSENCE WORN	EACH SCAR I'LL KEEP FOR	877	3
HIS OWN WOULD FALL SO MORE	EACH SCAR I'LL KEEP FOR	877	7
HIS MIGHTY PLEASURE SUITS US NOT	THE SUN IS GAY OR STARK	878	7
FROM HIS AMAZING HOUSE--	WHEN I HAVE SEEN THE SUN	888	2
SINCE NO ONE KNOWS HIS CIRCUMSTANCE--	WHO OCCUPIES THIS HOUSE?	892	3
HIS SERVICE TO THE NEWEST GRACE	OF SILKEN SPEECH AND	896	3
HIS SUIT A CHANCE	OF SILKEN SPEECH AND	896	5
HIS TROTH A TERM	OF SILKEN SPEECH AND	896	6
YOURSELF, FOR HIS PURSUIT	TILL DEATH--IS NARROW	907	10
I MAKE HIS CRESCENT FILL OR LACK--	I MAKE HIS CRESCENT FILL	909	1
HIS NATURE IS AT FULL	I MAKE HIS CRESCENT FILL	909	2
HIS TIDES--DO I CONTROL--	I MAKE HIS CRESCENT FILL	909	4
HIS PREAPPOINTED PAIN--	EXPERIENCE IS THE ANGLED	910	8
HIS FEET ARE SHOD WITH GAUZE--	HIS FEET ARE SHOD WITH	916	1
HIS HELMET, IS OF GOLD,	HIS FEET ARE SHOD WITH	916	2
HIS BREAST, A SINGLE ONYX	HIS FEET ARE SHOD WITH	916	3
HIS LABOR IS A CHANT--	HIS FEET ARE SHOD WITH	916	5
HIS IDLENESS--A TUNE--	HIS FEET ARE SHOD WITH	916	6

		FIRST LINE	POEM	LINE
HIS	(CONTINUED)			
	UNTO HIS NEST AGAIN	IF I CAN STOP ONE HEART	919	6
	HOW HE STRETCHED HIS ANGUISH [SPIRIT] TO US	HOW THE WATERS CLOSED	923	3
	POWER TO PERCEIVE HIS PROCESS	STRUCK, WAS I, NOR YET	925	3
	SHY AS THE WIND OF HIS CHAMBERS [LODGINGS]	THIS IS A BLOSSOM OF THE	945	5
	UPON HIS BREAST, A CLOSING SOUL	THIS IS A BLOSSOM OF THE	945	15
	FOR TREASON NOT OF HIS, BUT LIFE'S,	THE SUNSET STOPPED ON	950	3
	THE HOLLOWS ROUND HIS EAGER EYES	THE HOLLOWS ROUND HIS	955	1
	OH, WHEN THE SQUIRREL FILLS HIS POCKETS	WHAT SHALL I DO WHEN THE	956	9
	ALL HIS GOODS HAVE WINGS--	WHAT SHALL I DO WHEN THE	956	14
	HIS SCRUTINY OF CHANCES	AS ONE DOES SICKNESS	957	3
	TIME [TIME'S] TO ANTICIPATE HIS GAZE--	FITTER TO SEE HIM, I MAY	968	9
	I SHALL BE PERFECT--IN HIS SIGHT--	FITTER TO SEE HIM, I MAY	968	22
	THEY EMERGE FROM HIS OBSCURING--	COLOR--CASTE--	970	13
	IN HIS TREMENDOUS [ETERNAL / ENORMOUS] CHAIR--	THE MOUNTAIN SAT UPON	975	2
	HIS OBSERVATION OMNIFOLD,	THE MOUNTAIN SAT UPON	975	3
	HIS INQUEST, EVERYWHERE--	THE MOUNTAIN SAT UPON	975	4
	THE SEASONS PLAYED AROUND HIS KNEES	THE MOUNTAIN SAT UPON	975	5
	HIS--SHORTEST CONSCIOUSNESS--	NO OTHER CAN REDUCE	982	V
	HIS NOTICE SUDDEN [INSTANT] IS--	A NARROW FELLOW IN THE	986	4
	UPON HIS DATELESS FAME	SUPERFLUOUS WERE THE SUN	999	9
	THE TRANSPORT OF HIS COUNTENANCE	THE FINGERS OF THE LIGHT	1000	11
	UPON HIS HIP ELATE	THE FINGERS OF THE LIGHT	1000	14
	HELD UP HIS CUP FOR LIGHT.	THE FINGERS OF THE LIGHT	1000	16
	HIS COUNTENANCE TO SEE	THE STIMULUS, BEYOND THE	1001	2
	SHE ROSE AS HIGH AS HIS OCCASION	SHE ROSE AS HIGH AS HIS	1011	1
	ASKED HIM HIS NAME--HE LISPED ME "TROTWOOD"--	TRUDGING TO EDEN,	1020	3
	WHO KNOW HIS MEED OF ALL.	SO LARGE MY WILL	1024	8
	SHE STUNG HIM--SAPPED HIS FIRM ADVANCE--	FATE SLEW HIM, BUT HE	1031	5
	ALL HIS EAST	SAID DEATH TO PASSION	1033	6
	HIS BILL AN AUGUR IS	HIS BILL AN AUGUR IS	1034	1
	HIS HEAD, A CAP AND FRILL	HIS BILL AN AUGUR IS	1034	2
	A WORM, HIS UTMOST GOAL.	HIS BILL AN AUGUR IS	1034	4
	HE ASKED IF I WAS HIS--	IT WAS A QUIET WAY--	1053	2
	HIS MIND WERE GOING BLIND--	HE SCANNED IT--STAGGERED	1062	5
	AS DOWN HIS HEAVEN DROPT REMOTE [ECHOED FAINT]	JUST ONCE! OH LEAST	1076	8
	HIS BILL IS CLASPED [LOCKED]--HIS EYE FORSOOK [ESTRANGED]--	HIS BILL IS CLASPED--HIS	1102	1
	HIS BILL IS CLASPED [LOCKED]--HIS EYE FORSOOK [ESTRANGED]--	HIS BILL IS CLASPED--HIS	1102	1
	HIS FEATHERS WILTED LOW--	HIS BILL IS CLASPED--HIS	1102	2
	THE JOY THAT IN HIS HAPPY THROAT	HIS BILL IS CLASPED--HIS	1102	5
	BETWEEN HIS [THE] HOLIDAY	THE BIRD DID PRANCE--THE	1107	4
	NOT SATISFIED TO APE THE GREAT IN HIS SIMPLICITY	THAT THIS SHOULD FEEL	1112	5
	BANKRUPT ONCE THROUGH HIS EXCESSES--	PARADISE IS THAT OLD	1119	7
	FOR HIS BAROMETER	'TIS MY FIRST NIGHT	1122	4
	BUT DISTANCE HIS DELIGHTS CONFIDES	'TIS MY FIRST NIGHT	1122	7
	HIS [THIS] FIGURE INTIMATE	THESE ARE THE NIGHTS	1128	4
	DEPOSITING HIS THUNDER	THESE ARE THE NIGHTS	1128	7
	WE MISS HIS STATED HAT.	THAT ODD OLD MAN IS DEAD	1130	2
	HIS FADED LAMP WENT OUT.	THAT ODD OLD MAN IS DEAD	1130	4
	WHO MISS HIS ANTIQUATED WICK [LIGHT]--	THAT ODD OLD MAN IS DEAD	1130	5
	HIS WRINKLED COMING HOME?	THAT ODD OLD MAN IS DEAD	1130	8
	AS TO BEHOLD HIS AMPLE [GENTLE] FLIGHT--	THE MERCHANT OF THE	1131	11
	AND OPENING HIS [IT'S] MOUTH	THE WIND TOOK UP THE	1134	4
	THE WIND--UNTO HIS [IT'S] CHAMBERS WENT	THE WIND TOOK UP THE	1134	9
	YET [BUT] EVEN ON HIS SCARLET SHELF	THE FROST OF DEATH WAS	1136	7
	HE FORKED HIS WAY ALONG	THE FROST OF DEATH WAS	1136	13
	WE HUNTED HIM TO HIS RAVINE	THE FROST OF DEATH WAS	1136	16
	WE CHASED HIM TO HIS DEN--	THE FROST OF DEATH WAS	1136	17
	HIS STRATEGY	A SPIDER SEWED AT NIGHT	1138	8
	NOVEMBER HUNG HIS GRANITE HAT	THE DAY GREW SMALL,	1140	7
	FROM HIS ACCUSTOMED ROUTE--	HOW MANY SCHEMES MAY DIE	1150	8
	[THAT] SURVEYING HIS DESPAIR	HOW MANY SCHEMES MAY DIE	1150	13
	TELL WOULD NOT BARE HIS HEAD	TELL AS A MARKSMAN--WERE	1152	13
	MAKE OF HIS ONLY BOY A TARGET	TELL AS A MARKSMAN--WERE	1152	18
	TELL HIS ARROW SENT--	TELL AS A MARKSMAN--WERE	1152	23
	HIS ORDINARY ACTS ARE FEATS	BEST WITCHCRAFT IS	1158	3
	BLOSSOMS--DRESS FOR HIS SAKE.	HE IS ALIVE, THIS	1160	4
	IDLE HIS VERMILLION	ON THE WORLD YOU COLORED	1171	3
	ELATE THE ACRE AT HIS FEET--	MY GOD--HE SEES THEE--	1178	6
	UPON HIS ATOM SWIM--	MY GOD--HE SEES THEE--	1178	7
	A LITTLE DOG THAT WAGS HIS TAIL	A LITTLE DOG THAT WAGS	1185	1
	'TWAS FIGHTING FOR HIS LIFE HE WAS--	'TWAS FIGHTING FOR HIS	1188	1
	THE SUN TOOK DOWN HIS YELLOW WHIP	THE SUN AND FOG	1190	3
	SIMPLICITY FLED FROM HIS COUNTERFEIT PRESENCE	HE PREACHED UPON	1207	5
	I THINK, BECAUSE HIS EMPTY PLATE	A SPARROW TOOK A SLICE	1211	3
	UNTIL HIS LITTLE FIGURE	A SPARROW TOOK A SLICE	1211	7
	HIS SHOES ARE PURPLE--	WE LIKE MARCH.	1213	2
	KNOWS THE ADDER [ADDERS] TONGUE HIS COMING	WE LIKE MARCH.	1213	6
	ON HIS BRITISH SKY.	WE LIKE MARCH.	1213	13
	HIS IS PENURY	NOW I KNEW I LOST HER--	1219	16
	WHO GOES TO DINE MUST TAKE HIS FEAST	WHO GOES TO DINE MUST	1223	1
	NOT HOPING FOR HIS NOTICE VAST [FAR / FINE]	BECAUSE HE LOVES HER	1229	9
	HIS PALLID FURNITURE ARRANGED	IT CAME AT LAST BUT	1230	3
	AND HIS METALLIC PEACE--	IT CAME AT LAST BUT	1230	4
	ASSERTING FROM HIS PRISM	LIKE TIME'S INSIDIOUS	1236	7
	THE SUN SUBSIDING ON HIS COURSE	THE LILAC IS AN ANCIENT	1241	5
	HIS RESEARCH HAS BUT JUST BEGUN--	THE LILAC IS AN ANCIENT	1241	13

HIS (CONTINUED)	FIRST LINE	POEM	LINE
ABOVE HIS SYNTHESIS	THE LILAC IS AN ANCIENT	1241	14
HER [HIS] INFINITE DISDAIN	THE STARS ARE OLD, THAT	1249	6
HIS AMPLE--PLODDING STEED	LIKE BROOMS OF STEEL	1252	9
AS WAS HIS VEHICLE--	ELIJAH'S WAGON KNEW NO	1254	4
IN HIS ECCENTRIC [PECULIAR] STYLE	ELIJAH'S WAGON KNEW NO	1254	V 8
THE BEGGAR AND HIS QUEEN	NOT ANY HIGHER STANDS	1256	6
FOR HIS LESS PRICELESS FRIEND.	BECAUSE THAT YOU ARE	1260	32
NOR EVER SAW HIS HOUSE NOR FURNITURE,	I CANNOT SEE MY SOUL BUT	1262	2
RETIRED, AND RESUMED HIS TRANSITIVE ESTATE--	THE MOST TRIUMPHANT BIRD	1265	7
THOUGH HIS SURPASSING MERIT	THE SPIDER AS AN ARTIST	1275	3
HIS INTERESTS OF FIRE	THE MOUNTAINS STOOD IN	1278	6
BY SEASONS OR HIS CHILDREN--	THE WAY TO KNOW THE	1279	17
FORGET HIS MORNING FORCES--	THE HARM OF YEARS IS ON	1280	5
HIS SANDS SUFFICE	UNTIL THE DESERT KNOWS	1291	3
SAHARA [CONTENTMENT / CREATION / HIS STATUS] DIES	UNTIL THE DESERT KNOWS	1291	6
SILENCE--IS HIS NAME--	DEATH'S WAYLAYING NOT	1296	4
UPON HIS RARE APPROACH--	GO SLOW, MY SOUL, TO	1297	2
GO TIMID, LEST [SHOULD] HIS FINAL [TESTING / BLAZING / LOFTY] EYE	GO SLOW, MY SOUL, TO	1297	5
GO [BUT] BOLDLY--FOR THOU PAID'ST HIS PRICE	GO SLOW, MY SOUL, TO	1297	7
FROM HIS SLIM PALACE IN THE DUST	FROM HIS SLIM PALACE IN	1300	1
SECRETED IN HIS WILL--	NOT ONE BY HEAVEN	1303	4
ABJECT IS HIS KNEE--	WHEN A LOVER IS A BEGGAR	1314	2
WINTER IS GOOD--HIS HOAR DELIGHTS	WINTER IS GOOD--HIS HOAR	1316	1
ISAAC--TO HIS CHILDREN	ABRAHAM TO KILL HIM	1317	9
HE KEPT HIS WORD A TRILLION YEARS	OUR LITTLE SECRETS SLINK	1326	3
SUSPENSE--IS HIS MATURER SISTER--	WONDER--IS NOT PRECISELY	1331	5
AS IF IT WERE HIS OWN!	A LITTLE MADNESS IN THE	1333	6
HOW SOFT THIS [HIS] PRISON IS	HOW SOFT THIS PRISON IS	1334	1
HIS PLUSH ALARM	UPON A LILAC SEA	1337	3
A BEE HIS BURNISHED CARRIAGE	A BEE HIS BURNISHED	1339	1
HIMSELF--HIS CARRIAGE WAS--[CARRIAGE IS-- EQUIPAGE.]	A BEE HIS BURNISHED	1339	4
THE ROSE RECEIVED HIS VISIT	A BEE HIS BURNISHED	1339	5
TO HIS CUPIDITY--	A BEE HIS BURNISHED	1339	8
TO HIS SIMPLICITY	TO HIS SIMPLICITY	1352	1
BUT HIS RECEDING SWELL	THE LONG SIGH OF THE	1359	5
OF THEIR [HIS] PECULIAR LIGHT	OF THEIR PECULIAR LIGHT	1362	1
HOW FITS HIS UMBER COAT	HOW FITS HIS UMBER COAT	1371	1
HIS DINING ROOM DO [DOTH] SWING,	A SAUCER HOLDS A CUP	1374	8
HIS CUTLERY--HE KEEPS	A SAUCER HOLDS A CUP	1374	9
WITHIN [BETWEEN] HIS RUSSET LIPS--	A SAUCER HOLDS A CUP	1374	10
HIS HEART WAS DARKER THAN THE STARLESS NIGHT	HIS HEART WAS DARKER	1378	1
HIS MANSION IN THE POOL	HIS MANSION IN THE POOL	1379	1
HIS AUDITORS TWO WORLDS	HIS MANSION IN THE POOL	1379	5
HIS MITTENS AT HIS FEET	HIS MANSION IN THE POOL	1379	9
HIS MITTENS AT HIS FEET	HIS MANSION IN THE POOL	1379	9
HIS ELOQUENCE A BUBBLE	HIS MANSION IN THE POOL	1379	11
AT HIS NEW WHITE HOUSE THE EARTH	I SUPPOSE THE TIME WILL	1381	11
INVALIDATE [INVALIDATES] THE [A / HIS] SPELL--	LONG YEARS APART--CAN	1383	4
BUT [YET] PRONE TO SHUT IT'S [HIS] SPOTTED [SUBTLE] FAN	THE BUTTERFLY'S NUMIDIAN	1387	4
SHE [HE] LAID HER [HIS] DOCILE CRESCENT DOWN	SHE LAID HER DOCILE	1396	1
BY AND BY--THE BOLDEST STOLE OUT OF HIS COVERT	IT SOUNDED AS IF THE	1397	5
BUT JUST HIS LID [LIP] OF GLASS--	WHAT MYSTERY PERVADES A	1400	6
BETRAYS [REPORTS] US, AS HIS FIRST BETROTHAL	MARCH IS THE MONTH OF	1404	7
AND CROUCHED BEHIND HIS YELLOW DOOR	A WILD BLUE SKY ABREAST	1415	3
CLOSES THE [HIS] SHUTTER AND GOES IN--	HOW LONESOME THE WIND	1418	4
THEN SOARING TO HIS TEMPLE [TURRET] TALL--	HOW LONESOME THE WIND	1418	12
HIS OUTLETS--WOULD YOU SEE [KNOW]	SUCH ARE THE INLETS OF	1421	2
HE SENT HIS SON TO TEST THE PLANK,	HOW BRITTLE ARE THE	1433	7
GOD BROKE HIS CONTRACT TO HIS LAMB	HOW RUTHLESS ARE THE	1439	3
GOD BROKE HIS CONTRACT TO HIS LAMB	HOW RUTHLESS ARE THE	1439	3
HIS MIND LIKE FABRICS OF THE EAST	HIS MIND LIKE FABRICS OF	1446	1
FOR THOUGH HIS [THE] PRICE WAS NOT OF GOLD--	HIS MIND LIKE FABRICS OF	1446	5
HOW GOOD HIS LAVA BED,	HOW GOOD HIS LAVA BED,	1447	1
UNKNOWN HIS SHIMMERING [GIDDY / DAZZLING] ULTIMATE--	THE ROAD WAS LIT WITH	1450	7
HIS CHEEK IS HIS BIOGRAPHER--	HIS CHEEK IS HIS	1460	1
HIS CHEEK IS HIS BIOGRAPHER--	HIS CHEEK IS HIS	1460	1
BY HIS INTRUSION, GOD IS KNOWN--	WE KNEW NOT THAT WE WERE	1462	7
YOU SEE--GOD BLESS HIS SUDDENNESS--	BEFORE YOU THOUGHT OF	1465	3
BUT HIS SERAPHIC SELF--	BEFORE YOU THOUGHT OF	1465	16
FOR HIS DECAMPING WANTS--	ONE OF THE ONES THAT	1466	16
BEHOLD HIS LOST AGGRANDIZEMENT [EMOLUMENT]	ONE OF THE ONES THAT	1466	27
IS HIS DIVINEST GRIEF--	THE SWEETS OF PILLAGE,	1470	4
HIS VOICE DECREPIT WAS WITH JOY--	HIS VOICE DECREPIT WAS	1476	1
HE DOUBTLESS DID HIS BEST--	LOOK BACK ON TIME, WITH	1478	2
HOW SOFTLY SINKS THAT [HIS] TREMBLING SUN	LOOK BACK ON TIME, WITH	1478	3
THE WAY HOPE BUILDS HIS HOUSE	THE WAY HOPE BUILDS HIS	1481	1
HIS DRESS DENOTES HIM SOCIALLY,	THE ROBIN IS A GABRIEL	1483	3
ARE ALL THAT CROSS HIS THRESHOLD--	THE ROBIN IS A GABRIEL	1483	12
TO HIS ENAMORED MIND	ALL THAT I DO	1496	3
I KNOW HIS EYE	ALL THAT I DO	1496	4
TILL SUMMONED TO HIS RECOGNITION	FACTS BY OUR SIDE ARE	1497	7
IT CAME HIS TURN TO BEG--	IT CAME HIS TURN TO BEG	1500	1
I SCANNED HIS NARROW REALM [GRANT]	IT CAME HIS TURN TO BEG	1500	5
THOUGH SMUGGLED HIS [MY] REPRIEVE	IT CAME HIS TURN TO BEG	1500	8

	FIRST LINE	POEM	LINE
HIS (CONTINUED)			
HIS NATIVE LAND--	THE THINGS THAT NEVER	1515	13
HIS LITTLE HEARSE LIKE FIGURE	HIS LITTLE HEARSE LIKE	1522	1
AND NOW AGAINST HIS SUBTLE NAME	HE LIVED THE LIFE OF	1525	3
HIS ORIENTAL HERESIES	HIS ORIENTAL HERESIES	1526	1
ALLURES [ENSNARES] HIS JADED EYE	HIS ORIENTAL HERESIES	1526	6
HE SPENDS THE EVENING OF HIS DAYS [NOONS]	HIS ORIENTAL HERESIES	1526	V
AND HONEYS, IF HIS LIFE BE SPARED,	HIS ORIENTAL HERESIES	1526	V
A FLOWER TO HELP HIS STRAIGHTENED FACE	AS IMPERCEPTIBLY AS	1540	V
PRESUMPTION WAS--HIS ANCESTORS	AS IMPERCEPTIBLY AS	1540	V
OBTAINING BUT OUR [HIS] OWN EXTENT	OBTAINING BUT OUR OWN	1543	1
HIS IS THE HALCYON TABLE--	HOPE IS A SUBTLE GLUTTON	1547	5
HIS LARDER--TERSE AND MILITANT--	NO BRIGADIER THROUGHOUT	1561	19
HIS CHARACTER--A TONIC--	NO BRIGADIER THROUGHOUT	1561	21
HIS FUTURE--A DISPUTE--	NO BRIGADIER THROUGHOUT	1561	22
HIS CHANCES [DOCTRINES / DOGMAS] A REDOUBT--	NO BRIGADIER THROUGHOUT	1561	V 22
HER [HIS] LOSSES MAKE OUR GAINS ASHAMED--	HER LOSSES MAKE OUR	1562	1
WERE SWINGING AT HER [HIS] BACK.	HER LOSSES MAKE OUR	1562	4
WHO SO APPARELED HIS ESCAPE--	SOME ARROWS SLAY BUT	1565	3
AND NOT A SONG PERVADE HIS LIPS--	THE BAT IS DUN, WITH	1575	3
HIS SMALL UMBRELLA QUAINTLY HALVED	THE BAT IS DUN, WITH	1575	5
TO HIS ADROIT CREATOR	THE BAT IS DUN, WITH	1575	13
HIS ECCENTRICITIES--	THE BAT IS DUN, WITH	1575	16
HIS SCENE, INFINITY--	EXPANSE CANNOT BE LOST--	1584	4
HIS SPIRIT GREW ROBUST--	HE ATE AND DRANK THE	1587	2
NOR THAT HIS FRAME WAS DUST--	HE ATE AND DRANK THE	1587	4
HE RECOGNIZED HIS MAKER--OVERTURNED THE DECALOGUE--	THE BOBOLINK IS GONE--	1591	8
UPON HIS SADDLE SPRUNG A [SPRANG THE] BIRD	UPON HIS SADDLE SPRUNG A	1600	1
HIS FANTASY DID PLEASE	UPON HIS SADDLE SPRUNG A	1600	4
AND THEN HE LIFTED UP HIS THROAT	UPON HIS SADDLE SPRUNG A	1600	5
HIS "GOING, GOING, GONE"	THE AUCTIONEER OF	1612	2
AND BRINGS HIS HAMMER DOWN--	THE AUCTIONEER OF	1612	4
AND NOW AGAINST HIS SUBTLE NAME	WHO ABDICATED AMBUSH	1616	3
A WORLD MADE PENNINILESS BY THAT [HIS] DEPARTURE	A WORLD MADE PENNINILESS	1623	1
BUT FIRMAMENTS WERE NOT HIS FELLOWS--	A WORLD MADE PENNINILESS	1623	V 3
NOR PUT HIS SPACIOUS ARM AROUND THEE	BACK FROM THE CORDIAL	1625	3
THE MOWER IS TUNING HIS SCYTHE	BACK FROM THE CORDIAL	1625	V
ARROWS ENAMORED OF HIS HEART [BREAST]--	ARROWS ENAMORED OF HIS	1629	1
THE JAY HIS CASTANET HAS STRUCK	THE JAY HIS CASTANET HAS	1635	1
THE TIPPET THAT IGNORES [RESISTS] HIS VOICE	THE JAY HIS CASTANET HAS	1635	3
HIS LOTUS IS A CHESTNUT	THE JAY HIS CASTANET HAS	1635	6
THAT [HIS] WHIFFLETREE OF AMETHYST	THE SUN IN REINING TO	1636	5
WOULD PIERCE HIS COLUMNS THRO'--	"RED SEA," INDEED! TALK	1642	4
FOR IS IT NOT HIS BED--	THE DITCH IS DEAR TO THE	1645	2
HIS ADVOCATE--HIS EDIFICE--	THE DITCH IS DEAR TO THE	1645	3
HIS ADVOCATE--HIS EDIFICE--	THE DITCH IS DEAR TO THE	1645	3
HOW SAFE HIS FALLEN HEAD	THE DITCH IS DEAR TO THE	1645	4
AT DAY BREAK TO BEGIN HIS RACE	HE WENT BY SLEEP THAT	1662	3
HIS MIND OF MAN, A SECRET MAKES	HIS MIND OF MAN, A	1663	1
SECRETED IN HIS FORM	IN WINTER IN MY ROOM	1670	29
BOTH EYES HIS WAY	IN WINTER IN MY ROOM	1670	33
HIS ACTION LAID AWAY	JUDGEMENT IS JUSTEST	1671	3
BUT HIS SINCERITY	JUDGEMENT IS JUSTEST	1671	5
RESUMES HIS GAUDY INDUSTRY	SUMMER BEGINS TO HAVE	1682	12
RELISHED HIS IGNORANCE	THE EVENT WAS DIRECTLY	1686	4
AND LET HIS FLESH	THE EVENT WAS DIRECTLY	1686	7
CENTURIES FROM HIS SOUL	THE EVENT WAS DIRECTLY	1686	8
I GATHERED FROM HIS TALK	HIGH FROM THE EARTH I	1723	10
HIS REMEDY FOR CARE,--	HIGH FROM THE EARTH I	1723	18
NO MAN SAW AWE, NOR TO HIS HOUSE	NO MAN SAW AWE, NOR TO	1733	1
THOUGH BY HIS AWFUL RESIDENCE	NO MAN SAW AWE, NOR TO	1733	3
NOT DEEMING OF HIS DREAD ABODE	NO MAN SAW AWE, NOR TO	1733	5
HIS NEVER SLUMBERING PLAN;	THE RETICENT VOLCANO	1748	2
CONFIDED ARE HIS PROJECTS PINK	THE RETICENT VOLCANO	1748	3
A BILLOW WHISPERED IN HIS EAR,	THE WATERS CHASED HIM AS	1749	3
THE OBJECT FLOATING AT HIS SIDE	THE WATERS CHASED HIM AS	1749	9
AND TRILLED, AND QUIVERED, AND SHOOK HIS THROAT	A TRAIN WENT THROUGH A	1761	3
AND THEN ADJUSTED HIS LITTLE NOTES,	A TRAIN WENT THROUGH A	1761	5
HIS PUNGENT COMPANY	EXPERIMENT ESCORTS US	1770	2
UNCONSCIOUS [DISDAINFUL] OF HIS SMARTNESS.	THE SUMMER THAT WE DID	1773	8
HISSED			
"AFRAID HE HISSED	IN WINTER IN MY ROOM	1670	24
HISSING			
WHOSE HISSING CORALS PART--AND SHUT--	A STILL--VOLCANO--LIFE--	601	11
HIST			
HIST! WHIST! I'D COME!	IS IT TRUE, DEAR SUE?	218	11
HISTORIES			
PATHETIC HISTORIES--ALTHOUGH	THE HOLLOWS ROUND HIS	955	3
HISTORY			
OR [NOR] "EARLY HISTORY"--	DUST IS THE ONLY SECRET	153	8
AS FAR FROM TIME--AS HISTORY--	AS FAR FROM PITY, AS	496	5
OR HISTORY--	ONE CRUCIFIXION IS	553	4
NOR HISTORY--RECORD IT--	THE BATTLE FOUGHT	594	9
SUM THE HISTORY--	HOW THE WATERS CLOSED	923	8
YESTERDAY IS HISTORY,	YESTERDAY IS HISTORY,	1292	1
WITCHCRAFT WAS HUNG, IN HISTORY,	WITCHCRAFT WAS HUNG, IN	1583	1
BUT HISTORY AND I	WITCHCRAFT WAS HUNG, IN	1583	2

	FIRST LINE	POEM	LINE
HIT			
AND HIT A WORLD, AT EVERY PLUNGE [CRASH],	I FELT A FUNERAL, IN MY	280	19
AND SOMETIMES HIT A TREE	WE GROW ACCUSTOMED TO	419	14
THE TREES LIKE TASSELS--HIT--AND SWUNG--	THE TREES LIKE TASSELS--	606	1
I HEARD IT HIT THE GROUND--	IT DROPPED SO LOW--IN MY	747	2
HITHER			
UPON THE HITHER SIDE	CRISIS IS SWEET AND YET	1416	2
HITHERTO			
HIMSELF HAD NOT COMPLAINED. [HITHERTO CONCEALED--]	THE HOLLOWS ROUND HIS	955	4
IS HITHERTO [PRUDENTLY] UNKNOWN	I SAW THE WIND WITHIN	1502	V
HIVE			
WITHIN THAT LITTLE HIVE	WITHIN THAT LITTLE HIVE	1607	1
HO			
HO! PILOT, HO!	ON THIS WONDROUS SEA	4	3
HO! PILOT, HO!	ON THIS WONDROUS SEA	4	3
LAND HO! ETERNITY!	ON THIS WONDROUS SEA	4	11
HOAR			
HOAR--IS THE WINDOW--AND NUMB--THE DOOR--	SAFE IN THEIR ALABASTER	216	V
AN INSTINCT [HUNGER] FOR THE HOAR [DREAR], THE BALD--	I THINK THE HEMLOCK	525	7
ARE ANY HOAR [BLEAK] FOR HIM?	THAT ODD OLD MAN IS DEAD	1130	6
WINTER IS GOOD--HIS HOAR DELIGHTS	WINTER IS GOOD--HIS HOAR	1316	1
HOARD			
COUNT--HOARD--THEN LOSE--	I'LL CLUTCH--AND CLUTCH	427	12
'TIS WELL TO HOARD ANEW--	OUR OWN POSSESSIONS--	1208	2
HOARDED			
BUT HOARDED IN THE MIND	A MINE THERE IS NO MAN	1117	6
THAT WHAT WE CHERISHED, SO UNKNOWN [VALUED SO DEVOID / HOARDED . . .	SO PROUD SHE WAS TO DIE	1272	3
HOARSE			
AND A HOARSE "GET OUT OF THE WAY, I SAY,"	THE WIND DID'NT COME	316	20
FOR OUR HOARSE GOOD NIGHT--	'TWAS THE OLD--ROAD--	344	21
IS HOARSE TODAY--	HIS MANSION IN THE POOL	1379	8
HOARY			
A HOARY BOY, I'VE KNOWN TO DROP	NOT ALL DIE EARLY, DYING	990	5
GROWN IN [BY] THE REPETITION HOARY	TELL AS A MARKSMAN--WERE	1152	7
HOARY [EVIL / RIGID / WRINKLED / ARID / SHRUNKEN] THE FRUITION	FORTITUDE INCARNATE	1217	7
PUT UP MY HEART THY HOARY WORK	THE NOTICE THAT IS	1310	3
HOCK			
THEIR HOCK, AND SHERRY, DRAW,	PERHAPS YOU'D LIKE TO	134	8
'TIS'NT ALL HOCK--WITH US--	WE--BEE AND I--LIVE BY	230	2
LET ME NOT THIRST WITH THIS HOCK AT MY LIP,	LET ME NOT THIRST WITH	1772	1
HOE			
DO THEY "HOE"--	WHAT IS--"PARADISE"--	215	4
HOIST			
DID HOIST HERSELF, TO SING,	HER SMILE WAS SHAPED	514	4
AS IF THEY COULD NOT HOIST THEMSELVES	THIS SLOW DAY MOVED	1120	3
HOISTED			
HANDS--NOT SO STOUT--HOISTED THEM--IN WITNESS--	UNTO LIKE STORY--TROUBLE	295	19
LIKE HINDERED FLAGS--SWEET HOISTED--	THE TREES LIKE TASSELS--	606	23
THE DUST REPLACED, IN HOISTED ROADS--	A DROP FELL ON THE APPLE	794	9
THE TRUTH NEVER FLAUNTED [HOISTED] A SIGN--	HE PREACHED UPON	1207	4
HOISTS			
HE HOISTS ABROAD AGAIN--	THESE ARE THE NIGHTS	1128	8
HOLD			
TO HOLD A LETTER TO THE LIGHT--	IN EBON BOX, WHEN YEARS	169	5
I HAD NOT STRENGTH [POWER] TO HOLD--	SAVIOR! I'VE NO ONE ELSE	217	8
SHADOWS--HOLD THEIR BREATH--	THERE'S A CERTAIN SLANT	258	14
MORE HANDS--TO HOLD--THESE ARE BUT TWO--	A SINGLE SCREW OF FLESH	263	13
BUT THAT WILL HOLD--	'TIS SO APPALLING--IT	281	10
COULD [CAN] HOLD AN ARROW--TOO--	FOR LARGEST WOMAN'S	309	4
WHEN WINDS TAKE [HOLD] FORESTS IN THEIR PAWS--	HE FUMBLES AT YOUR SOUL	315	13
AND HOLD THE SUNSHINE IN IT'S LAP	THE GRASS SO LITTLE HAS	333	7
AND HOLD NO HIGHER THAN THE PLAIN--	A TONGUE--TO TELL HIM I	400	24
NAY--HOLD IT--IT IS CALM--	I TIE MY HAT--I CREASE	443	29
TO HOLD OUR SENSES--ON--	I TIE MY HAT--I CREASE	443	33
AND IF I HOLD A GLASS	I AM ALIVE--I GUESS--	470	6
SKILL--TO HOLD MY BROW LIKE AN EARL--	I AM ASHAMED--I HIDE--	473	16
MY LIPS JUST HOLD THE NAME--	YOU KNOW THAT PORTRAIT	504	10
AND HOLD UPON THE TWIG,	HER SMILE WAS SHAPED	514	6
IT COULD NOT HOLD A SIGH--	I HAD NO CAUSE TO BE	542	14
THAT FANCIED THEY COULD HOLD--	HE GAVE AWAY HIS LIFE--	567	6
PUT UP--TO HIDE [HOLD] HER PARTING GRACE	MY FIRST WELL DAY--SINCE	574	23
TO HOLD MY LIFE [THE LIGHT] FOR ME	I PRAYED, AT FIRST, A	576	17
MYSELF--CAN OWN [HOLD] THE KEY--	IF I MAY HAVE IT, WHEN	577	8
TO HOLD MY LIFE, AND HOLD MY EARS	I CRIED AT PITY--NOT AT	588	19
TO HOLD MY LIFE, AND HOLD MY EARS	I CRIED AT PITY--NOT AT	588	19
FOR--HOLD THEM--BLUE TO BLUE--	THE BRAIN--IS WIDER THAN	632	6
TO HOLD MISTAKEN	THE CHILD'S FAITH IS NEW	637	18
BEAR [HOLD] ME--	A LITTLE ROAD--NOT MADE	647	8
THAT HELD THE DAMS--HAD PARTED HOLD--	THE WIND BEGUN TO KNEAD	824	17
WILL HOLD YOU TILL YOUR PRIVILEGE	TILL DEATH--IS NARROW	907	3
BUT SINCE WE HOLD A MUTUAL DISC--	I MAKE HIS CRESCENT FILL	909	9
THE GARDEN [LANDSCAPE] KEEP [SHOW / OWN / HOLD] THE GASH--	AS FROST IS BEST	951	6
I COULD HOLD THE LATEST GLOWING--	ROBBED BY DEATH--BUT	971	3
HOLD ME TILL THE OCTAVE'S RUN!	DYING AT MY MUSIC!	1003	3

	FIRST LINE	POEM	LINE
HOLD (CONTINUED)			
WHEN YOU--HOLD--GARNET TO GARNET--	TITLE DIVINE--IS MINE!	1072	8
AN EARLDOM OUT OF SIGHT TO HOLD,	BECAUSE !TWAS RICHES I	1093	5
AND HOLD THE WICK OF MINE TO IT	THE SPRY ARMS OF THE	1103	11
AND EVERY CRESCENT HOLD--	MY GOD--HE SEES THEE--	1178	5
TO HOLD THE FEELING DOWN	THE PRETTY RAIN FROM	1426	6
HOLDING			
THE INSTANT HOLDING IN IT'S CLAW	'TWAS CRISIS--ALL THE	948	5
HOLDS			
MY BASKET HOLDS--JUST--FIRMAMENTS--	PERHAPS I ASKED TOO	352	5
AS WHEN THE NEIGHBOR HOLDS THE LAMP	WE GROW ACCUSTOMED TO	419	3
HE SOMETIMES HOLDS UPON THE FENCE--	THE BLACK BERRY--WEARS A	554	5
THE SPIDER HOLDS A SILVER BALL	THE SPIDER HOLDS A	605	1
MY LIFE JUST HOLDS THE TRENCH--	IF HE WERE LIVING--DARE	734	16
THAT HOLDS WITHOUT A PROP--	THE TRUTH--IS STIRLESS--	780	10
IT HOLDS AS LARGE A GLOW	LIGHT IS SUFFICIENT TO	862	6
HE HOLDS SUPERIOR IN THE SKY	I MAKE HIS CRESCENT FILL	909	5
THAT HOLDS IN UNDISPUTED LEASE	TOO LITTLE WAY THE HOUSE	911	3
HOLDS A SUN ON ME--	STRUCK, WAS I, NOR YET	925	20
RISK IS THE HAIR THAT HOLDS THE TUN [ONE]	RISK IS THE HAIR THAT	1239	1
THIS LATEST LEISURE EQUAL LULLS [CASTLE EQUAL HOLDS]	NOT ANY HIGHER STANDS	1256	5
A SAUCER HOLDS A CUP	A SAUCER HOLDS A CUP	1374	1
A SAUCER HOLDS A LOAF.	A SAUCER HOLDS A CUP	1374	4
AND HOLDS SCARCE [JUST] ONE.	THE ROAD TO PARADISE IS	1491	2
THAT HOLDS MY CHANCES UP.	A PIT--BUT HEAVEN OVER	1712	8
HOLIDAY			
EMPLOY THEIR HOLIDAY.	THERE IS A MORN BY MEN	24	6
HENCEFORTH--FOR HER--WHAT HOLIDAY!	THE SUN--JUST TOUCHED	232	7
SOME MADDER HOLIDAY--	THE LONESOME FOR THEY	262	4
GAY, GHASTLY, HOLIDAY!	'TIS SO APPALLING--IT	281	24
SOME QUAINTER HOLIDAY,	OF ALL THE SOUNDS	321	20
FOR WHERE THE HOLIDAY SHOULD BE	SO GLAD WE ARE--A	329	3
'TIS NOT OF HOLIDAY	EXHILIRATION--IS WITHIN	383	8
MARKED HIS--WHAT HOLIDAY	REMOVED FROM ACCIDENT OF	424	8
MY HOLIDAY, SHALL BE	ME--COME! MY DAZZLED	431	7
UPON A HOLIDAY--	IT'S THOUGHTS--AND JUST	495	5
THAT GLAZES HOLIDAY--	YOU KNOW THAT PORTRAIT	504	16
BUT HOLIDAY--EXCLUDES THE NIGHT--	UNTO MY BOOKS--SO GOOD	604	11
BUT FOR HOLIDAY	HER SWEET TURN TO LEAVE	649	4
REFLEX HOLIDAY.	ONE DAY IS THERE OF THE	814	8
OR A HOLIDAY	THAT IS SOLEMN WE HAVE	934	4
BETWEEN HIS [THE] HOLIDAY	THE BIRD DID PRANCE--THE	1107	4
WHOSE HAVING LIVED IS HELD BY US IN NOBLE HOLIDAY	LEST ANY DOUBT THAT WE	1156	2
BUT SUMMER, FRILLED AS FOR A HOLIDAY	WE WEAR OUR SOBER	1572	2
HOLIDAYS			
PLAYMATES, AND HOLIDAYS, AND NUTS--	ON SUCH A NIGHT, OR SUCH	146	21
BUT HOLIDAYS OF WAR--	THEIR BARRICADE AGAINST	1471	12
HOLINESS			
EXCEPT FOR HOLINESS--	THOSE FAIR--FICTITIOUS	499	20
OF MINTED HOLINESS.	THE GOOD WILL OF A	849	5
IN RAVISHED [DAZZLING / SIMPLE] HOLINESS--	THE THRILL CAME SLOWLY	1495	8
HOLLAND			
YOU AND I, AND DR HOLLAND,	THO' MY DESTINY BE	163	11
HOLLOW			
THAT TUN IS HOLLOW--BUT THE TUN--	RISK IS THE HAIR THAT	1239	3
HOLLOWS			
THE HOLLOWS ROUND HIS EAGER EYES	THE HOLLOWS ROUND HIS	955	1
HOLY			
WITH HOLY GHOSTS IN CAGES!	A TRANSPORT ONE CANNOT	184	7
FROM HIM--AND HOLY GHOST--AND ALL--	I NEVER FELT AT HOME--	413	15
BRIDE OF THE HOLY GHOST.	GIVEN IN MARRIAGE UNTO	817	4
AT THE SUGGESTION OF HOLY SPECTRES--	THE BIBLE IS AN ANTIQUE	1545	3
HOME SEE HAME			
AND BID THE WORLD GOODMORROW, AND GO TO GLORY HOME!	AWAKE YE MUSES NINE,	1	40
THE FEET OF PEOPLE WALKING HOME	THE FEET OF PEOPLE	7	1
THESE CHILDREN FLUTTERED HOME.	THROUGH LANE IT LAY--	9	17
WHEN GOING HOME FROM SCHOOL--	I OFTEN PASSED THE	51	2
AS SURE AS FLOCKS GO HOME AT NIGHT	GOING TO HEAVEN!	79	9
WHEN WE ARE GOING HOME--	GOING TO HEAVEN!	79	19
WENDING LATE HOME--	HEART, NOT SO HEAVY AS	83	2
HER HEART IS FIT FOR HOME [REST]--	HER BREAST IS FIT FOR	84	5
WENT HOME A CENTURY AGO	WHERE I HAVE LOST, I	104	15
PERHAPS A HOME TOO HIGH--	FOR EVERY BIRD A NEST--	143	7
THAT MADE EXISTENCE--HOME!	EXCEPT TO HEAVEN, SHE IS	154	12
WHEN FRIGHTENED--HOME TO THEE I RUN--	YOU LOVE ME--YOU ARE	156	10
SO I LET HIM LEAD ME--HOME.	HE WAS WEAK, AND I WAS	190	4
MISTRESS IS "NOT AT HOME"--TO SAY--	THE FLOWER MUST NOT	206	5
THO' I GET HOME HOW LATE--HOW LATE--	THO' I GET HOME HOW LATE	207	1
SO I GET HOME--'TWILL COMPENSATE--	THO' I GET HOME HOW LATE	207	2
TO FIND OUR WAY HOME--	I'VE NOTHING ELSE--TO	224	8
GOD CALLS HOME--THE ANGELS--PROMPTLY--	GOD PERMITS INDUSTRIOUS	231	5
I KEEP IT, STAYING AT HOME--	SOME KEEP THE SABBATH	324	2
AND ROWED HIM SOFTER HOME--	A BIRD CAME DOWN THE	328	16
PERSUADE OUR FEATHERS HOME	'TIS NOT THAT DYING	335	12
AS WELL AS OUR OLD HOME!"	I FELT MY LIFE WITH BOTH	351	16
I NEVER FELT AT HOME--BELOW--	I NEVER FELT AT HOME--	413	1
I SHALL NOT FEEL AT HOME--I KNOW--	I NEVER FELT AT HOME--	413	3

	FIRST LINE	POEM	LINE
HOME (CONTINUED)			
A HURRYING HOME OF LITTLE MEN	A MURMUR IN THE TREES--	416	9
I'M COMING HOME--	GOOD MORNING--MIDNIGHT--	425	2
AND BORE MY JEWEL--HOME--	THE MALAY--TOOK THE	452	8
HOME TO THE HUT! WHAT LOT	THE MALAY--TOOK THE	452	9
THEMSELF--ADMITTED HOME--	THOSE FAIR--FICTITIOUS	499	22
WHEN TURNING, HUNGRY, HOME	I HAD BEEN HUNGRY, ALL	579	6
THAT TIME--TO TAKE IT HOME--	HE FOUND MY BEING--SET	603	8
I YEARS HAD BEEN FROM HOME	I YEARS HAD BEEN FROM	609	1
WHAT WAS HIS FURTHEST MIND--OF HOME--OR GOD--	TO KNOW JUST HOW HE	622	9
AND LATITUDE OF HOME--	FOREVER--IS COMPOSED OF	624	4
WE WALK--I LEAVE MY DOG--AT HOME [BEHIND]--	AGAIN--HIS VOICE IS AT	663	18
DIVINER CROWD AT HOME [WITHIN]--	THE SOUL THAT HATH A	674	3
WHERE THOU ART--THAT--IS HOME--	WHERE THOU ART--THAT--IS	725	1
IS SENTENCE [EXILE] FROM BELIEF--AND HOME--	IF BLAME BE MY SIDE--	775	4
AT HOME [EASE]--AMONG THE BILLOWS--AS	SHE STAKED HER FEATHERS	798	7
AWAY FROM HOME ARE SOME [THEY] AND I--	AWAY FROM HOME ARE SOME	821	1
SUBMIT THAT HOME--AND CERTAINTY	THE ROBIN IS THE ONE	828	11
IF HOME OR FOREIGN BORN--	IT WAS A GRAVE, YET BORE	876	6
OR A LEAVING HOME, OR LATER,	THAT IS SOLEMN WE HAVE	934	5
I LEARNED--AT LEAST--WHAT HOME COULD BE--	I LEARNED--AT LEAST--	944	1
AND THEN RETURN--AND NIGHT [TRUST]--AND HOME--	I LEARNED--AT LEAST--	944	22
THIS SEEMS A HOME--	I LEARNED--AT LEAST--	944	27
AND HOME IS NOT--	I LEARNED--AT LEAST--	944	28
THE WISE CONVEY IT HOME	THIS IS A BLOSSOM OF THE	945	10
THE SPOILER OF OUR HOME?	DENIAL--IS THE ONLY FACT	965	8
HOME EFFACED--HER FACES DWINDLED--	ALL FORGOT FOR	966	9
AND ASSUMES [INFERS]--FROM HOME--	HE WHO IN HIMSELF	969	4
HOMELESSNESS, FOR HOME--	UP LIFE'S HILL WITH MY	1010	8
JUST GOING HOME FROM SCHOOL.	THE HILLS IN PURPLE	1016	4
BOUGHT, CARRIED HOME	SO LARGE MY WILL	1024	11
THE FROGS GOT HOME LAST WEEK--	BEE! I'M EXPECTING YOU!	1035	5
DEPARTED, OR AT HOME--	HERE, WHERE THE DAISIES	1037	12
AND IS THE SOUL AT HOME	THE SPRY ARMS OF THE	1103	10
A PEACE, AS HEMISPHERES AT HOME	THE CRICKETS SANG	1104	11
HIS WRINKLED COMING HOME?	THAT ODD OLD MAN IS DEAD	1130	8
THE SOUL CAME HOME FROM TRIPS [FROM TOWNS / FROM SCENES / TO SLEEP]	CONTAINED IN THIS SHORT	1165	V
AND SO MUCH MORE AT HOME THAN I	ALONE AND IN A	1167	5
AND WILL AT HOME AND WELL	A DEED KNOCKS FIRST AT	1216	4
MEANT NOUGHT BUT GOING HOME--	'TWAS LATER WHEN THE	1276	4
BUT [THO'] PERHAPS 'TIS WELL THEY'RE NOT AT HOME	HAD WE OUR SENSES	1284	2
DEPARTED, OR AT HOME--	THE DAY SHE GOES	1308	5
PENURY [HEMISPHERE] AND HOME?	FRIGID AND SWEET HER	1318	8
SHOULD THEY BE AT HOME	KNOCK WITH TREMOR--	1325	3
INCARCERATION--HOME.	HOW SOFT THIS PRISON IS	1334	8
AT HOME--IN PARADISE.	LET ME NOT MAR THAT	1335	8
IT HAS NO HOME--	IN MANY AND REPORTLESS	1382	10
THE FAIREST HOME I EVER KNEW	THE FAIREST HOME I EVER	1423	1
A HOME--	A DIMPLE IN THE TOMB	1489	3
AND HAS'NT ANY HOME	THE BUTTERFLY UPON THE	1521	4
REMIT HER HOME,	TO THE BRIGHT EAST SHE	1573	3
HOMELESS AT HOME.	TO THE BRIGHT EAST SHE	1573	12
TO HER DERIDED HOME	TO HER DERIDED HOME	1586	1
NOT AT HOME TO CALLERS	NOT AT HOME TO CALLERS	1590	1
NOT QUITE WITH HIM AT HOME	IN WINTER IN MY ROOM	1670	6
TOWARD HUMAN NATURE'S HOME	NOT ANY SUNNY TONE	1674	5
THE SOUL HER "NOT AT HOME"	THE OVERTAKELESSNESS OF	1691	5
HOME FLEW THE LOADED BEES	THE SUN RETIRED TO A	1693	6
VESUVIUS AT HOME	VOLCANOES BE IN SICILY	1705	8
THE AUTUMN STARTED HOME--	WITH SWEETNESS UNABATED	1709	4
HER HOME TO BE WITH NATURE	WITH SWEETNESS UNABATED	1709	5
WILL SEE HOW FAR FROM HOME	IF EVER THE LID GETS OFF	1727	6
"COME HOME WITH ME, MY FRIEND;	THE WATERS CHASED HIM AS	1749	4
HOMELESS			
HOMELESS AT HOME.	TO THE BRIGHT EAST SHE	1573	12
CRUMBLESS AND HOMELESS, OF BUT ONE REQUEST--	QUITE EMPTY, QUITE AT	1606	8
HOMELESSNESS			
HOMELESSNESS, FOR HOME--	UP LIFE'S HILL WITH MY	1010	8
HOMELIER			
THE HOMELIER TIME BEHIND.	I SHOULD HAVE BEEN TOO	313	6
A HOMELIER MATURING--	THERE ARE TWO RIPENINGS	332	5
HOMELIEST			
THE HOMELIEST--ADORNED	I THINK I WAS ENCHANTED	593	18
HOMELY			
BY HOMELY ANGUISH STRUNG.	I LIKE A LOOK OF AGONY,	241	8
OR SMOOTHED A HOMELY PAIN,	ALTHOUGH I PUT AWAY HIS	366	6
MAKING THAT HOMELY, AND SEVERE,	LIKE FLOWERS, THAT HEARD	513	11
AND LAUGH, A HOMELY SPECIES	I'M SORRY FOR THE DEAD--	529	7
FAR ENDS OF TIRED [HOMELY] DAYS--	UNTO MY BOOKS--SO GOOD	604	2
HE TOLD A HOMELY TALE	HE TOLD A HOMELY TALE	763	1
WHOSE HOMELY BENEDICTION	TO OFFER BRAVE	767	7
IN HOMELY INDUSTRY ARRAYED [ATTIRED]--	THE BIRDS BEGUN AT FOUR	783	11
BY HOMELY GIFT AND HINDERED WORDS	BY HOMELY GIFT AND	1563	1
HAD HE THE HOMELY SCUTCHEON	THE BUTTERFLY OBTAINS	1685	9
HOMES			
BUT GENERAL HOMES	ALONE, I CANNOT BE--	298	7
CLASP HEMISPHERES, AND HOMES	THE SUNRISE RUNS FOR	710	14
IN A METROPOLIS OF HOMES	AWAY FROM HOME ARE SOME	821	3

	FIRST LINE	POEM	LINE
HOMES (CONTINUED)			
IT FOUNDS THE HOMES AND DECKS THE DAYS	THE FARTHEST THUNDER	1581	13
TO THEIR [WHOSE] ETHERIAL HOMES	TALK NOT TO ME OF SUMMER	1634	6
HOMESICK			
TO STAY THE HOMESICK--HOMESICK FEET	TO LEARN THE TRANSPORT	167	5
TO STAY THE HOMESICK--HOMESICK FEET	TO LEARN THE TRANSPORT	167	5
WONT THEY SCOLD US--WHEN WE'RE HUNGRY [HOMESICK]--	WHAT IS--"PARADISE"--	215	9
HOMESICK FOR STEADFAST HONEY--	THE NEAREST DREAM	319	11
"HOMESICK"? MANY MET IT--	IT IS DEAD--FIND IT--	417	7
A TROUBLE LEST THEY'RE HOMESICK--	I'M SORRY FOR THE DEAD--	529	13
ON MY HOMESICK EYE--	I CANNOT LIVE WITH YOU--	640	26
HOMESICK CURIOSITY	ABSENT PLACE--AN APRIL	927	3
DEATH LEAVES US HOMESICK, WHO BEHIND,	DEATH LEAVES US HOMESICK	935	1
HOMESICKNESS			
WERE TO THEM NOW, HOMESICKNESS	WHAT DID THEY DO SINCE I	900	11
HOMESTEAD			
HER SWEET TURN TO LEAVE THE HOMESTEAD	HER SWEET TURN TO LEAVE	649	1
THAT LOWLY BREAST [HOMESTEAD SWEET] WHERE BUTTERFLIES	HIS ORIENTAL HERESIES	1526	7
SWEET HOMESTEAD WHERE THE BUTTERFLY	HIS ORIENTAL HERESIES	1526 V	7
EDEN--THE ANCIENT HOMESTEAD--	THE BIBLE IS AN ANTIQUE	1545	5
HOMOGENEOUS			
A HOMOGENEOUS GOWN.	AS IMPERCEPTIBLY AS	1540 V	
HONEST			
I HOPE TWAS HONEST GAINED.	I NEVER TOLD THE BURIED	11	11
I WOKE--AND CHID MY HONEST FINGERS,	I HELD A JEWEL IN MY	245	5
THAT ONE SO HONEST--BE EXTANT--	I MEANT TO HAVE BUT	476	21
WHERE NOT SO MUCH AS HONEST DOG	WHO OCCUPIES THIS HOUSE?	892	7
AN HONEST TEAR	AN HONEST TEAR	1192	1
THAT COST ME MY HONEST HEART--	I SAW THAT THE FLAKE WAS	1267	4
HONESTLY			
I HONESTLY SUPPOSE--	A LITTLE DOG THAT WAGS	1185	8
HONESTY			
IN CHILDISH [SOLEMN] HONESTY--	I PRAYED, AT FIRST, A	576	8
IN SOLEMN [TIMID] HONESTY	THE BODY GROWS WITHOUT--	578	8
HONEY			
HOMESICK FOR STEADFAST HONEY--	THE NEAREST DREAM	319	11
A HONEY BEAR AWAY	THERE IS A FLOWER THAT	380	6
THE FINEST HONEY--CURDLED--	THERE IS AN ARID	782	7
BEES--TO THEIR LOAVES OF HONEY	HE IS ALIVE, THIS	1160	5
IN VAIN TO PUNISH HONEY--	HER LOSSES MAKE OUR	1562	7
SUCH HINTS OF HONEY LAY	WITHIN THAT LITTLE HIVE	1607	2
THE PEDIGREE OF HONEY	THE PEDIGREE OF HONEY	1627	1
OH, HONEY OF AN HOUR,	OH, HONEY OF AN HOUR,	1734	1
HONEY'S			
A HONEY'S WEIGHT [WORTH]	LEAST BEE THAT BREW--	676	2
HONEYS			
AND HONEYS, IF HIS LIFE BE SPARED,	HIS ORIENTAL HERESIES	1526 V	
HONOR			
IN HONOR OF THE SUN!	"SIC TRANSIT GLORIA	3	36
FOR OUR MUTUAL HONOR,	AMBITION CANNOT FIND HIM	68	7
AN HONOR, THOUGHT CAN TURN HER TO	I HAD THE GLORY--THAT	349	2
'TIS HONOR--THOUGH I DIE--	HAD I PRESUMED TO HOPE--	522	13
GOD THE SPIRIT'S HONOR--	ONLY GOD--DETECT THE	626	7
THIS WERE AN HONOR HONORLESS--	FAME OF MYSELF, TO	713	7
HONOR--IS IT'S OWN PAWN--	TITLE DIVINE--IS MINE!	1072 V	
ALL MEN FOR HONOR HARDEST WORK	ALL MEN FOR HONOR	1193	1
BUT "NEVER" FAR AS HONOR	TO DISAPPEAR ENHANCES--	1209	9
WHAT RAIMENT HONOR HIM THE MOST,	I CANNOT SEE MY SOUL BUT	1262	5
HONOR, THE SHORTEST ROUTE TO YOU.	BROTHER OF INGOTS--AH	1366 V	2
BE HONOR AND NOT SHAME--	TO EARN IT BY DISDAINING	1427	8
FOR SERVICE [HONOR / WELCOME] OR FOR GLEE--	A CHILLY PEACE INFESTS	1443	6
AND HONOR LEAGUES AWAY	THE DITCH IS DEAR TO THE	1645	8
HONOR IS THEN THE SAFEST HUE	JUDGEMENT IS JUSTEST	1671	6
SEE! I USURPED THY CRUCIFIX TO HONOR MINE!	PROUD OF MY BROKEN HEART	1736	8
HONORABLE			
TO TAKE THE HONORABLE WORK	SHE ROSE TO HIS	732	3
IT IS AN HONORABLE THOUGHT	IT IS AN HONORABLE	946	1
HONORED			
THAT BEGGAR, WHEN AN HONORED GUEST,	AS WATCHERS HANG UPON	121	10
THE BUTTERFLY IN HONORED DUST	THE BUTTERFLY IN HONORED	1246	1
FOREVER HONORED [CHERISHED] BE THE TREE	FOREVER HONORED BE THE	1570	1
BUT HER FATHER IS BORNE AND HONORED,	THE PARASOL IS THE	1747	7
BUT THE LATTER, HER SIRE, IS HONORED	THE PARASOL IS THE	1747 V	7
HONORLESS			
THIS WERE AN HONOR HONORLESS--	FAME OF MYSELF, TO	713	7
HONORS			
OF HONORS THERE--	UNTO LIKE STORY--TROUBLE	295	12
HONORS--TASTE DRY--	THE WORLD--FEELS DUSTY	715	4
HOOD			
IT'S LITTLE ETHER HOOD	IT'S LITTLE ETHER HOOD	1501	1
HOODED			
SEEMS IT TO MY HOODED THINKING	ONE DAY IS THERE OF THE	814	7
HOODS			
SHE TIED THE HOODS TO SEEDS--	MY FIRST WELL DAY--SINCE	574	18
HOOFS			
SWIFTER THAN THE HOOFS OF HORSEMEN	I CANT TELL YOU--BUT YOU	65	7
AND THE HOOFS OF THE CLOCK--	WE TALKED WITH EACH	1473	4

	FIRST LINE	POEM	LINE
HOOKED			
THE HOUSE WAS HOOKED	LIKE BROOMS OF STEEL	1252	4
HOOTING			
IN HORRID--HOOTING STANZA--	I LIKE TO SEE IT LAP	585	12
HOPE			
I HOPE TWAS HONEST GAINED.	I NEVER TOLD THE BURIED	11	11
I HOPE I'M READY FOR "THE WORST"--	"ARCTURUS" IS HIS OTHER	70	24
I HOPE THE "CHILDREN" THERE	"ARCTURUS" IS HIS OTHER	70	27
I HOPE THE FATHER IN THE SKIES	"ARCTURUS" IS HIS OTHER	70	30
"HOPE" IS THE THING WITH FEATHERS--	"HOPE" IS THE THING WITH	254	1
I AM NOT USED TO HOPE--	IT MIGHT BE LONELIER	405	9
THROUGH KNOWING--WHERE WE ONLY HOPE [GUESS]--	THOSE FAIR--FICTITIOUS	499	15
HAD I PRESUMED TO HOPE--	HAD I PRESUMED TO HOPE--	522	1
'TIS FAILURE--NOT OF HOPE--	HAD I PRESUMED TO HOPE--	522	9
I COULD NOT HOPE--FOR MINE--[TO EARN]	I HAD BEEN HUNGRY, ALL	579	8
RETREAT--WAS OUT OF HOPE--	OUR JOURNEY HAD ADVANCED	615	9
THE SLOW EXCHANGE OF HOPE--	A PRISON GETS TO BE A	652	26
JUST LONG ENOUGH FOR HOPE TO TEAZE [STIR]--	THE WHOLE OF IT CAME NOT	762	7
HOPE IT WAS THAT KEPT ME WARM--	WHEN I HOPED, I	768	7
THE SERVICE WITHOUT HOPE--	THE SERVICE WITHOUT HOPE	779	1
OLDER FEEL THAN THE HOPE THAT PROMPTED--	UP LIFE'S HILL WITH MY	1010	5
SOMEWHAT, TO HOPE FOR,	SOMEWHAT, TO HOPE FOR,	1041	1
A GREAT HOPE FELL	A GREAT HOPE FELL	1123	1
OF ALL WE ARE ALLOWED TO HOPE	"REMEMBER ME" IMPLORED	1180	9
COULD HOPE INSPECT HER [IT'S] BASIS	COULD HOPE INSPECT HER	1283	1
BY HOPE OR HORROR LENT--	TWO LENGTHS HAS EVERY	1295	4
HOPE IS A STRANGE INVENTION--	HOPE IS A STRANGE	1392	1
WITHIN IT'S REACH [HOPE], THOUGH YET [AND JUST] UNGRASPED	WHO NEVER WANTED--	1430	5
THE WAY HOPE BUILDS HIS HOUSE	THE WAY HOPE BUILDS HIS	1481	1
CHILDHOOD--SOME FORMS OF HOPE--THE DEAD--	THE THINGS THAT NEVER	1515	2
HOPE IS A SUBTLE GLUTTON--	HOPE IS A SUBTLE GLUTTON	1547	1
BEYOND THE HOPE OF TOUCH	THE OVERTAKELESSNESS OF	1691	8
WHERE HOPE AND HE PART COMPANY--	DROWNING IS NOT SO	1718	7
HOPED			
I HAD NOT HOPED--BEFORE--	EXCEPT THE HEAVEN HAD	472	4
WHEN I HOPED, I RECOLLECT	WHEN I HOPED, I	768	1
WHEN I HOPED I FEARED--	WHEN I HOPED I FEARED--	1181	1
SINCE I HOPED I DARED	WHEN I HOPED I FEARED--	1181	2
THIS IS THE PLACE THEY HOPED BEFORE,	THIS IS THE PLACE THEY	1264	1
THE HEAVEN, IN WHICH WE HOPED TO PAUSE	THE THINGS WE THOUGHT	1293	9
I HOPED [LOOKED] FOR YOU BEFORE--	DEAR MARCH--COME IN--	1320	3
HOPELESS			
OH THE EARTH WAS MADE FOR LOVERS, FOR DAMSEL, AND HOPELESS SWAIN,	AWAKE YE MUSES NINE,	1	3
PROVIDED IT DO HOPELESS--HANG--	"HEAVEN"--IS WHAT I	239	3
FAR OFF--HE SIGHS--AND THEREFORE--HOPELESS--	UNDUE SIGNIFICANCE A	439	3
AS HOPELESS--AS DIVINE--	LIKE EYES THAT LOOKED ON	458	12
WERE HOPELESS, AS THE [A] RAINBOW'S RAIMENT	EACH LIFE CONVERGES TO	680	11
AT HEAVENLY--HOPELESS DISTANCES--	THIS BAUBLE WAS	805	3
SO HUGE, SO HOPELESS TO CONCEIVE	MY LIFE CLOSED TWICE	1732	5
HOPELESSLY			
AS HOPELESSLY AS I--	I MANY TIMES THOUGHT	739	6
HOPE'S			
AND HOPE'S NECROLOGY	A DEW SUFFICED ITSELF--	1437	V 16
HOPES			
THE HOPES SO JUICY RIPENING--	SHE SIGHTS A BIRD--SHE	507	9
AND THIS OF ALL MY HOPES	AND THIS OF ALL MY HOPES	913	1
WITHIN ITS PRECINCTS HOPES HAVE PLAYED,--	SWEET HOURS HAVE	1767	3
HOPING			
STOP HOPING, NOW--	'TIS SO APPALLING--IT	281	14
NOT HOPING FOR HIS NOTICE VAST [FAR / FINE]	BECAUSE HE LOVES HER	1229	9
WHERE I AM HOPING NOW.	THIS IS THE PLACE THEY	1264	2
HOPPED			
NOR HOPPED FOR [TO] AUDIENCES--LIKE BIRDS,	I CANNOT DANCE UPON MY	326	11
AND THEN HOPPED SIDEWISE TO THE WALL	A BIRD CAME DOWN THE	328	7
HOPPER			
MINOR--APPARATUS--HOPPER OF THE MILL--	LIFE, AND DEATH, AND	706	3
HORIZON			
THEN AT THE FEET OF THE OLD HORIZON	BLAZING IN GOLD AND	228	3
THE FIRST--A GNAT'S HORIZON	I KNOW LIVES, I COULD	372	7
AND MY HORIZON BLOCKS	I CROSS TILL I AM WEARY	550	6
IN A NEIGHBORING HORIZON--	SO THE EYES ACCOST--AND	752	7
BEST [ALL] HORIZON--GONE [KNOWN]--	NO BOBOLINK--REVERSE HIS	755	7
THESE TESTED OUR HORIZON--	THESE TESTED OUR HORIZON	886	1
. . . INSURANCE-- / TO THE HORIZON--]	THE LARGEST FIRE EVER	1114	7
HORIZONS			
HORIZONS--STRAGGLED DOWN--	ON THIS LONG STORM THE	194	4
MERCHANTMEN--POISE UPON HORIZONS--	THIS--IS THE LAND--THE	266	8
SWELLED--LIKE HORIZONS--IN MY BREAST [VEST]--	A SOLEMN THING--IT WAS--	271	15
RAISED SOFTLY TO THE CEILINGS [HORIZONS]--	I WOULD NOT PAINT--A	505	11
HORIZONS--MUST ASCEND--	MY PERIOD HAD COME FOR	564	6
THEN AS HORIZONS STEP	A LIGHT EXISTS IN SPRING	812	13
NEW HORIZONS--THEY EMBELLISH [REPLENISH]--	UNFULFILLED TO	972	7
HORIZONTAL			
THAN WITH THIS HORIZONTAL ONE	OH GIVE IT MOTION--DECK	1527	7
HORNS			
'TWAS LIKE A SHEET WITH HORNS!	A CURIOUS CLOUD	1710	2
HORRID			
IN BATTLE'S--HORRID BOWL?	IT FEELS A SHAME TO BE	444	16

	FIRST LINE	POEM	LINE
HORRID (CONTINUED)			
IN HORRID--HOOTING STANZA--	I LIKE TO SEE IT LAP	585	12
STARE STOLID [VACANT / HORRID] INTO MINE	I YEARS HAD BEEN FROM	609	5
HORRID SAND PARTITION--	IN FALLING TIMBERS	614	7
HORROR			
SO OVER HORROR, IT HALF CAPTIVATES [DUMB FASCINATES]--	'TIS SO APPALLING--IT	281	2
THAT AFTER HORROR--THAT 'TWAS US--	THAT AFTER HORROR--THAT	286	1
A HORROR SO REFINED	WHAT SOFT--CHERUBIC	401	6
UNROLLED IT'S HORROR IN MY FACE--	THE FIRST DAY'S NIGHT	410	11
THE HORROR WELCOMES HER, AGAIN,	THE SOUL HAS BANDAGED	512	23
IN SUCH A PLACE, WHAT HORROR,	DID YOU EVER STAND IN A	590	5
THE HORROR [CHASM] NOT TO BE SURVEYED--	THE LONELINESS ONE DARE	777	9
BY HOPE OR HORROR LENT--	TWO LENGTHS HAS EVERY	1295	4
HORROR'S			
BETWEEN HIMSELF--AND HORROR'S TWIN--	I TRIED TO THINK A	532	14
BE HORROR'S LEAST.	ONE NEED NOT BE A	670	16
HORSE			
IF I MUST TELL YOU, OF A HORSE	I MET A KING THIS	166	13
SOME UNSUSPECTING HORSE WAS TIED	HOW MANY SCHEMES MAY DIE	1150	12
THE HORSE THAT SCENTS THE LIVING GRASS	THE LIFE THAT TIED TOO	1535	5
HORSEMAN			
A TRAVELLER [HORSEMAN] ON A HILL--	THE ROAD WAS LIT WITH	1450	4
HORSEMEN			
SWIFTER THAN THE HOOFS OF HORSEMEN	I CANT TELL YOU--BUT YOU	65	7
HORSES			
JUST A LOOK AT THE HORSES--	TIE THE STRINGS TO MY	279	3
HORSES OF BLONDE--AND COACH OF SILVER--	DROPPED INTO THE ETHER	665	5
I FIRST SURMISED THE HORSES HEADS	BECAUSE I COULD NOT STOP	712	23
ELIJAH'S HORSES AS UNIQUE	ELIJAH'S WAGON KNEW NO	1254	3
AND MENTION TO MY HORSES	I KNOW SUSPENSE--IT	1285	7
HOSPITABLE			
HOW HOSPITABLE--THEN--THE FACE	IT WAS TOO LATE FOR MAN	623	7
HOSPITABLE INTUITION	CONSCIOUS AM I IN MY	679	7
THE HOSPITABLE PALL	NO LIFE CAN POMPLESS	1626	6
HOSPITALITY			
AS TO A HOSPITALITY	OUR LITTLE KINSMEN--	885	7
THE HOSPITALITY	THESE ARE THE SIGNS TO	1077	6
OH HOSPITALITY [MAGNANIMITY]!	"REMEMBER ME" IMPLORED	1180	2
HOST			
NOT ONE OF ALL THE PURPLE HOST	SUCCESS IS COUNTED	67	5
THE BRAVEST--OF THE HOST--	THERE IS A FLOWER THAT	380	29
AND LIKE A HOST--"COME IN"	THE WIND--TAPPED LIKE A	436	2
DID LEAP, FULL FLANKED, UPON THE HOST--	ONE ANGUISH--IN A CROWD	565	7
A PARADISE--THE HOST--	'TWAS A LONG PARTING--	625	14
THAT COOLER [WHITER] HOST.	ONE NEED NOT BE A	670	8
OH THOU CELESTIAL HOST--	GIVEN IN MARRIAGE UNTO	817	2
DEPART, BEFORE THE HOST HAVE SLID	THE SOUL SHOULD ALWAYS	1055	5
ESSENTIAL HOST, IN LIFE'S FAINT, WAILING INN,	AIR HAS NO RESIDENCE, NO	1060	6
HE WAS MY HOST--HE WAS MY GUEST,	HE WAS MY HOST--HE WAS	1721	1
HOSTILER			
SUSPENSE--IS HOSTILER THAN DEATH--	SUSPENSE--IS HOSTILER	705	1
HOST'S			
A [THE] HOST'S DEPARTURE WHEN	THE SOUL THAT HATH A	674	6
HOSTS			
THE HOSTS OF WITNESS STAND!	SLEEP IS SUPPOSED TO BE	13	6
THE [FOR] HOSTS--DO VISIT ME--	ALONE, I CANNOT BE--	298	2
A COMING AS OF HOSTS WAS HEARD	LIKE RAIN IT SOUNDED	1235	7
HOT			
STROKE THE COOL FOREHEAD--HOT SO OFTEN--	HOW MANY TIMES THESE LOW	187	5
THAT OUR MINDS ARE HOT.	WE LIKE MARCH.	1213	9
WHEN NIGHTS ARE HOT AND SERE--	A WINGED SPARK DOTH SOAR	1468	4
HOTTEST			
ANGELS, WHEN THE SUN IS HOTTEST	ANGELS, IN THE EARLY	94	5
HOUND			
HOUND CANNOT OVERTAKE THE HARE	THIS HEART THAT BROKE SO	145	5
THIS LITTLE HOUND WITHIN THE HEART	WHAT SHALL I DO--IT	186	2
ATTENDED BY A SINGLE HOUND	THIS CONSCIOUSNESS THAT	822	15
THE FOX FITS THE HOUND--	GOOD TO HIDE, AND HEAR	842	4
THAN IT RESISTS [EVADES / ELUDES]--THE HOUND--	THIS MERIT HATH THE	979	8
HOUNDS			
ATTEMPTED OF THE HOUNDS	ONE ANGUISH--IN A CROWD	565	4
HOUR			
AN HOUR TO PREPARE,	THE GENTIAN WEAVES HER	18	6
AN HOUR BEHIND THE FLEETING BREATH--	DELAYED TILL SHE HAD	58	4
LATER BY JUST AN HOUR THAN DEATH--	DELAYED TILL SHE HAD	58	5
THAT PASSED, AN HOUR AGO!	WITHIN MY REACH!	90	9
FOR EACH BELOVED HOUR	FOR EACH EXTATIC INSTANT	125	5
AN HOUR, AND GAY ON EVERY TREE	COCOON ABOVE! COCOON	129	4
AN HOUR IN CHRYSALIS TO PASS,	COCOON ABOVE! COCOON	129	7
AND COME NEXT HOUR TO LOOK.	I BRING AN UNACCUSTOMED	132	7
BUT NOT AN HOUR MORE!	PERHAPS YOU'D LIKE TO	134	10
AT THE ACCUSTOMED HOUR!	SHE WENT AS QUIET AS THE	149	4
ONE HOUR--OF HER SOVREIGN'S FACE"!	WHAT WOULD I GIVE TO SEE	247	26
AS LAUGHTER--WAS--AN HOUR AGO--	WHAT IF I SAY I SHALL	277	10
FOR FRIGID--HOUR OF MIND--	A SHADY FRIEND--FOR	278	4
THIS IS THE HOUR OF LEAD--	AFTER GREAT PAIN, A	341	10
THAT FRIGHTENED--BUT AN HOUR--	WHEN NIGHT IS ALMOST	347	8
I WORE--AN HOUR AGO--	I GAINED IT SO--	359	15
AN HOUR TO REAR SUPREME	THE SPIDER HOLDS A	605	9

	FIRST LINE	POEM		LINE
HOUR (CONTINUED)				
I THINK THE LONGEST HOUR OF ALL	I THINK THE LONGEST HOUR	635		1
I'D GIVE--TO LIVE THAT HOUR--AGAIN--	AGAIN--HIS VOICE IS AT	663		26
THIS THAT WOULD GREET--AN HOUR AGO--	THIS THAT WOULD GREET--	778		1
TO WAIT AN HOUR--IS LONG--	TO WAIT AN HOUR--IS LONG	781		1
AN HOUR IS A SEA	AN HOUR IS A SEA	825		1
ANOTHER HOUR TO ME	SOME WRETCHED CREATURE,	1111		4
MY EARTHLY HOUR [HUMAN LIFE] TO ME	SOME WRETCHED CREATURE,	1111	V	4
IT'S HOUR WITH ITSELF	IT'S HOUR WITH ITSELF	1225		1
FEBUARY HOUR--	WHITE AS AN INDIAN PIPE	1250		4
THE HOUR, AND THE CLIME [ZONE]--	LONGING IS LIKE THE SEED	1255		5
THAT ONLY [MERELY] LASTS AN HOUR	IN THIS SHORT LIFE	1287		2
THAT MAKE US RICH AN HOUR--	DREAMS ARE THE SUBTLE	1376		2
WHICH RAPTURE [TRIUMPH / HOUR / MOMENT]-- SHE PREFERRED	CRISIS IS SWEET AND YET	1416		6
THE HOUR [SESSION] OF HER BUD--	CRISIS IS SWEET AND YET	1416	V	8
WAS FOUNDED IN AN HOUR	THE FAIREST HOME I EVER	1423		2
WHAT DOOR--WHAT HOUR--RUN--RUN--MY SOUL!	"AND WITH WHAT BODY DO	1492		3
INFORMED THE HOUR HAD COME	WITH SWEETNESS UNABATED	1709		2
OH, HONEY OF AN HOUR,	OH, HONEY OF AN HOUR,	1734		1
THERE COMES AN HOUR WHEN BEGGING STOPS,	THERE COMES AN HOUR WHEN	1751		1
AND HAVE AN HOUR TO SPARE.	WERE NATURE MORTAL LADY	1762		8
HOURS				
HAST NEVER SILENT HOURS, AND MINUTES ALL TOO LONG,	AWAKE YE MUSES NINE,	1		29
HER LEASE OF SPOTTED HOURS,	SHE DIED AT PLAY,	75		3
BIRDS--HOURS--THE BUMBLEBEE--	SOME THINGS THAT FLY	89		2
SO--WONDERING--THRO' THE HOURS MEEK	I HAVE A KING, WHO DOES	103		2
WHETTING AWAY THE HOURS	THE WIND DID'NT COME	316		14
THE HOURS SLID FAST--AS HOURS WILL,	THERE CAME A DAY AT	322		17
THE HOURS SLID FAST--AS HOURS WILL,	THERE CAME A DAY AT	322		17
KEPT MEASURING THE HOURS--	'TWAS LIKE A MAELSTROM,	414		11
AND SWINGS UPON THE HOURS,	THE SOUL HAS BANDAGED	512		14
SOME HOURS IN [OF] THE DAY.	LIGHT IS SUFFICIENT TO	862		4
SALUBRIOUS HOURS ARE GIVEN	TO HELP OUR BLEAKER	1064		2
THE STOLID RAFTERS [CENTRES / HOURS / INSTANTS / SECONDS] GLOW	THE SMOULDERING EMBERS	1132		6
BUT HALF THE HOURS REMAIN.	CONSULTING SUMMER'S	1715		2
SWEET HOURS HAVE PERISHED HERE;	SWEET HOURS HAVE	1767		1
HOUSE				
ONE SISTER HAVE I IN OUR HOUSE,	ONE SISTER HAVE I IN OUR	14		1
I KEPT THE "HOUSE AT HAME."	I HAD A GUINEA GOLDEN--	23		16
WHO BUILT THIS LITTLE ALBAN HOUSE	BRING ME THE SUNSET IN A	128		19
HER MODEST HOUSE--	FOR EVERY BIRD A NEST--	143		15
OR STIRRING HOUSE BELOW--	ON SUCH A NIGHT, OR SUCH	146		14
PERHAPS HE DOES'NT KNOW THE HOUSE--	DYING! DYING IN THE	158		7
BEHIND THE HILL--THE HOUSE BEHIND--	"HEAVEN"--IS WHAT I	239		7
IT MIGHT--HAVE BEEN THE LIGHT HOUSE SPARK--	GOOD NIGHT! WHICH PUT	259		7
BUT WE--STOOD--WHISPERING IN THE HOUSE--	OF TRIBULATION--THESE	325		15
THE HOUSE ENCORE ME SO--	I CANNOT DANCE UPON MY	326		16
THERE'S BEEN A DEATH, IN THE OPPOSITE HOUSE,	THERE'S BEEN A DEATH, IN	389		1
AS IF THE HOUSE WERE HIS--	THERE'S BEEN A DEATH, IN	389		14
TO TAKE THE MEASURE OF THE HOUSE--	THERE'S BEEN A DEATH, IN	389		19
DRESSES EACH HOUSE IN CRAPE, AND ICICLE--	IT'S COMING--THE	390		7
A HOUSE UPON THE HIGHT--	A HOUSE UPON THE HIGHT--	399		1
HAD NATURE--IN HER MONSTROUS HOUSE	A TONGUE--TO TELL HIM I	400		3
AND OPEN HOUSE--AGAIN--	THE WINTERS ARE SO SHORT	403		8
I DO NOT OWN A HOUSE--	I AM ALIVE--I GUESS--	470		18
DOOM IS THE HOUSE WITHOUT THE DOOR--	DOOM IS THE HOUSE	475		1
I WAS THE SLIGHTEST IN THE HOUSE--	I WAS THE SLIGHTEST IN	486		1
BUT THEN HIS HOUSE--IS BUT A STEP--	YOU LOVE THE LORD--YOU	487		7
HIS HOUSE WAS NOT--NO SIGN HAD HE--	MY PERIOD HAD COME FOR	564		9
HOUSES HUNCH THE HOUSE	I COULD DIE--TO KNOW--	570		7
FLED [STOLE] GASPING FROM THE HOUSE--	I YEARS HAD BEEN FROM	609		24
I WATCHED THE MOON AROUND THE HOUSE	I WATCHED THE MOON	629		1
AND ALL MY HOUSE AGLOW	TO MY SMALL HEARTH HIS	638		2
A FAIRER HOUSE THAN PROSE--	I DWELL IN POSSIBILITY--	657		2
ONE NEED NOT BE A HOUSE--	ONE NEED NOT BE A	670		2
FROM HOUSE TO HOUSE 'TWAS NOON--	THE SUN KEPT SETTING--	692		4
FROM HOUSE TO HOUSE 'TWAS NOON--	THE SUN KEPT SETTING--	692		4
THE HOUSE OF SUPPOSITION--	THEIR HIGHT IN HEAVEN	696		5
AND IF IT SERVE YOU FOR A HOUSE--	THE JUDGE IS LIKE THE	699		7
IN THE STRANGER'S HOUSE--	A FIRST MUTE COMING--	702		2
WE PAUSED BEFORE A HOUSE THAT SEEMED	BECAUSE I COULD NOT STOP	712		17
FOR HIS SHY HOUSE--	GRIEF IS A MOUSE--	793		3
BUT OVERLOOKED MY FATHER'S HOUSE--	THE WIND BEGUN TO KNEAD	824		19
AND SHUT THE DOOR UNTO MY HOUSE	I SING TO USE THE	850		3
FROM HIS AMAZING HOUSE--	WHEN I HAVE SEEN THE SUN	888		2
WHO OCCUPIES THIS HOUSE?	WHO OCCUPIES THIS HOUSE?	892		1
THE OWNER OF THIS HOUSE	WHO OCCUPIES THIS HOUSE?	892		29
TOO LITTLE WAY THE HOUSE MUST LIE	TOO LITTLE WAY THE HOUSE	911		1
YET PRECIOUS AS THE HOUSE	ON THAT DEAR FRAME THE	940		2
ESCAPED THE HOUSE UNSEEN--	'TWAS CRISIS--ALL THE	948		16
A DOOR JUST [THERE] OPENED ON A STREET [TO A HOUSE]--	A DOOR JUST OPENED ON A	953		1
WHERE MAY BE YOUR HOUSE?	"UNTO ME?" I DO NOT KNOW	964		2
OCCUPY MY HOUSE [BREAST]"--	"UNTO ME?" I DO NOT KNOW	964		12
TO THE CREATOR'S HOUSE--	NO OTHER CAN REDUCE	982	V	
TILL OF ALL OUR NATURE'S HOUSE	AS WILLING LID O'ER	1050		3
THESE ARE THE RITES OF NATURE'S HOUSE--	THESE ARE THE SIGNS TO	1077		5

	FIRST LINE	POEM	LINE
HOUSE (CONTINUED)			
THE BUSTLE IN A HOUSE	THE BUSTLE IN A HOUSE	1078	1
TO ASCERTAIN THE HOUSE	THE SPRY-ARMS OF THE	1103	9
THE PROPS ASSIST THE HOUSE	THE PROPS ASSIST THE	1142	1
UNTIL THE HOUSE IS BUILT	THE PROPS ASSIST THE	1142	2
THE HOUSE SUPPORT [SUSTAIN] ITSELF . . .	THE PROPS ASSIST THE	1142	5
'TIS SOMETHING LIKE A HOUSE--	REMEMBRANCE HAS A	1182	2
A SOFT SEA WASHED AROUND THE HOUSE . . .	A SOFT SEA WASHED AROUND	1198	1
IN THY BEAUTIFUL HOUSE	WHATEVER IT IS--SHE HAS	1204	10
HAD OCCUPIED THE HOUSE--	IT CAME AT LAST BUT	1230	2
THE HOUSE WAS HOOKED	LIKE BROOMS OF STEEL	1252	4
NOR EVER SAW HIS HOUSE NOR FURNITURE, . .	I CANNOT SEE MY SOUL BUT	1262	2
NOT ANY HOUSE THE FLOWERS KEEP--	THE NOTICE THAT IS	1310	5
"THE HOUSE NOT MADE WITH HANDS" IT WAS-- .	I SUED THE NEWS--YET	1360	3
IN GENESIS' NEW HOUSE, ...	TRUSTY AS THE STARS	1369	4
AT HIS NEW WHITE HOUSE THE EARTH	I SUPPOSE THE TIME WILL	1381	11
HAVE NEVER PASSED [SCALED] HER HAUNTED HOUSE,	WHAT MYSTERY PERVADES A	1400	19
GO NOT TOO NEAR A HOUSE OF ROSE--	GO NOT TOO NEAR A HOUSE	1434	1
THE WAY HOPE BUILDS HIS HOUSE	THE WAY HOPE BUILDS HIS	1481	1
ILLUMINATE THE HOUSE!	"AND WITH WHAT BODY DO	1492	4
FOR ANGELS RENT THE HOUSE NEXT OUR'S, . .	WHO HAS NOT FOUND THE	1544	3
BUT HER ETERNAL HOUSE--	OF GLORY NOT A BEAM IS	1647	2
EDEN IS THAT OLD-FASHIONED HOUSE	EDEN IS THAT	1657	1
NO MAN SAW AWE, NOR TO HIS HOUSE	NO MAN SAW AWE, NOR TO	1733	1
WHERE "KEEPING HOUSE" FOR THEE	THE GRAVE MY LITTLE	1743	2
AS DAUNTLESS IN THE HOUSE OF DEATH . . .	THIS DOCILE ONE INTER	1752	7
HOUSEHOLD			
HER HOUSEHOLD--HER ASSEMBLY--	NATURE--THE GENTLEST	790	11
A SELF DENYING HOUSEHOLD, ...	THE ROBIN IS A GABRIEL	1483	10
HOUSEHOLDS			
HOUSEHOLDS IN EVERY TREE--	FOR EVERY BIRD A NEST--	143	5
HOUSES			
PAST THE HOUSES--PAST THE HEADLANDS-- . .	EXULTATION IS THE GOING	76	3
"HOUSES"--SO THE WISE MEN TELL ME-- . . .	"HOUSES"--SO THE WISE	127	1
I KNOW SOME LONELY HOUSES OFF THE ROAD . .	I KNOW SOME LONELY	289	1
TILL THE HOUSES BLOT	HOW THE OLD MOUNTAINS	291	14
SUCH HOUSES HAVE--ALWAY--	THERE'S BEEN A DEATH, IN	389	4
THE LITTLE DWELLING HOUSES RISE	THE COLOR OF THE GRAVE	411	15
TO HOUSES UNPERCEIVED--	A MURMUR IN THE TREES--	416	10
SWEET--SAFE--HOUSES--	SWEET--SAFE--HOUSES--	457	1
GLAD--GAY--HOUSES--	SWEET--SAFE--HOUSES--	457	2
HOUSES HUNCH THE HOUSE	I COULD DIE--TO KNOW--	570	7
NEW HOUSES ON THE HILL DESCRIED--	HAVE ANY LIKE MYSELF	736	3
SOME HOUSES VERY OLD, ...	WHO OCCUPIES THIS HOUSE?	892	10
THE HOUSES FIRMER ROOT--	THE SYMPTOM OF THE GALE	1327	5
AND HOUSES VANISHED WITH A ROAR	IT WAS A QUIET SEEMING	1419	8
AND RIVERS WHERE THE HOUSES RAN	THERE CAME A WIND LIKE A	1593	11
AS WE PASS HOUSES MUSING SLOW	AS WE PASS HOUSES MUSING	1653	1
'TIS THEN WE SIGH FOR HOUSES, ...	SWEET IS THE SWAMP WITH	1740	3
HOUSEWIFE			
THE SMALLEST HOUSEWIFE IN THE GRASS, . . .	EXCEPT TO HEAVEN, SHE IS	154	9
INDOLENT HOUSEWIFE--IN DAISIES--LAIN! . .	HOW MANY TIMES THESE LOW	187	12
OH HOUSEWIFE IN THE EVENING WEST-- . . .	SHE SWEEPS WITH	219	3
DISCARDED OF THE HOUSEWIFE--	I CANNOT LIVE WITH YOU--	640	9
THE HOUSEWIFE IN THY LOW ATTENDANCE . . .	WERT THOU BUT ILL--THAT	961	15
HOUSEWIFE'S			
THE HOUSEWIFE'S GENTLE TASK--	THE NIGHT WAS WIDE, AND	589	17
THEN DANGLE FROM [PERISH BY] THE HOUSEWIFE'S BROOM--	THE SPIDER HOLDS A	605	11
HOUSEWIVES			
PRITHEE, MY PRETTY HOUSEWIVES!	A LADY RED--AMID THE	74	7
AS HOUSEWIVES DO, A FLY.	IF YOU WERE COMING IN	511	4
HOVER			
HOVER--HESITATE--	SOUTH WINDS JOSTLE THEM	86	3
HOVERED			
THE LOVER--HOVERED--O'ER--	THE SOUL HAS BANDAGED	512	8
THAT HOVERED THERE AWHILE--	ASHES DENOTE THAT FIRE	1063	4
WE HOVERED BY DESIGN--	MEETING BY ACCIDENT,	1548	2
HOVERING			
AS HOVERING [GLIMMERING]--SEEN--THROUGH FOG--	A SOLEMN THING--IT WAS--	271	12
A STRANGER HOVERING ROUND	THE FROST WAS NEVER SEEN	1202	5
HOVERS			
THEN HOVERS--AN INFERIOR GUARD--	LOVE--IS THAT LATER	924	9
HUBBUB			
A HUBBUB--AS OF FEET--	A MURMUR IN THE TREES--	416	6
HUE			
DISCLOSES JUST A HUE--	I'VE KNOWN A HEAVEN,	243	15
IN HUE--A MELLOW DUN--	OF BRUSSELS--IT WAS NOT	602	10
THE HUE--OF IT--IS BLOOD--	THE NAME--OF IT--IS	656	2
TO FETCH HER GRACE--AND HUE--	SHE DWELLETH IN THE	671	5
NO HUE OF AFTERNOON--	THE SUN KEPT SETTING--	692	2
A MOTH THE HUE OF THIS	A MOTH THE HUE OF THIS	841	1
AS IN SLEEP--ALL HUE FORGOTTEN--	COLOR--CASTE--	970	5
THAN ANOTHER HUE.	NATURE RARER USES YELLOW	1045	2
ALL THOSE HILLS YOU LEFT FOR ME TO HUE-- .	DEAR MARCH--COME IN--	1320	15
IN A DISSEMBLING HUE	THESE HELD THEIR WICK	1390	6
A STROLLING HUE, ONE WOULD HAVE SAID . . .	IT WAS A QUIET SEEMING	1419	5
HONOR IS THEN THE SAFEST HUE	JUDGEMENT IS JUSTEST	1671	6
HUELESS			
HUELESS TO ME UNTIL THOU COME	SPRING COMES ON THE	1042	3

	FIRST LINE	POEM	LINE
HUES			
OF INDEPENDENT HUES	BEFORE YOU THOUGHT OF	1465	5
THE PRISM NEVER HELD THE HUES,	PURSUING YOU IN YOUR	1602	5
HUG			
THE HANDS STILL HUG THE TARDY GLASS--	I BRING AN UNACCUSTOMED	132	8
HUGE			
AND THEN--A DAY AS HUGE	THE FIRST DAY'S NIGHT	410	9
HUGEST [THE HUGE] OF CORE	EXCEPT THE SMALLER SIZE	1067	V
SO HUGE, SO HOPELESS TO CONCEIVE	MY LIFE CLOSED TWICE	1732	5
HUGEST			
HUGEST [THE HUGE] OF CORE	EXCEPT THE SMALLER SIZE	1067	V
THE HUGEST HEARTS THAT BREAK.	LOVE'S STRICKEN "WHY"	1368	4
HUM			
I HEAR THE BRIGHT BEE HUM;	THERE IS ANOTHER SKY,	2	12
AND STILL HER HUM	ONE SISTER HAVE I IN OUR	14	17
HER BEES HAVE A FICTITIOUS [AN ILLUSIVE] HUM--	LIKE SOME OLD FASHIONED	302	9
HUM BY--IN MUFFLED COACHES--	SWEET--SAFE--HOUSES--	457	14
BECAUSE THE BEE MAY BLAMELESS HUM	BECAUSE THE BEE MAY	869	1
WHAT BEES--FOR US--TO HUM--	I LEARNED--AT LEAST--	944	10
BY A HUM.	SPRING COMES ON THE	1042	7
EXTINCT BE EVERY HUM	HOW DARE THE ROBINS SING	1724	13
HUMAN			
THOU ART A HUMAN SOLO, A BEING COLD, AND LONE,	AWAKE YE MUSES NINE,	1	27
I THINK I'D SHOOT THE HUMAN RACE	MY FRIEND ATTACKS MY	118	7
IN THE HUMAN FACE	I HAVE NEVER SEEN	175	10
OF FRECKLED HUMAN NATURE--	WHAT SOFT--CHERUBIC	401	7
TO ACHE IS HUMAN--NOT POLITE--	SHE DEALT HER PRETTY	479	9
MY TOOLS TOOK HUMAN--FACES--	MYSELF WAS FORMED--A	488	9
IS BUT A PROVINCE--IN THE BEING'S [HUMAN] CENTRE--	ONE CRUCIFIXION IS	553	9
WHERE HUMAN FACES--BE--	THREE TIMES--WE PARTED--	598	12
TO KNOW IF ANY HUMAN EYES WERE NEAR	TO KNOW JUST HOW HE	622	2
AT NEWS THAT HE CEASED HUMAN NATURE	TO KNOW JUST HOW HE	622	11
EXISTS IN EVERY HUMAN NATURE	EACH LIFE CONVERGES TO	680	3
BUT REDUCE NO HUMAN SPIRIT	PUBLICATION--IS THE	709	15
IN THE HUMAN HEART--	DRAMA'S VITALLEST	741	13
IS HUMAN--BUT DIVINE	TO OFFER BRAVE	767	4
BUT HUMAN NATURE FEELS.	A LIGHT EXISTS IN SPRING	812	8
IT HELD A HUMAN SOUL.	IT WAS A GRAVE, YET BORE	876	4
FROM EVERY HUMAN HEART	TOO LITTLE WAY THE HOUSE	911	2
MY EARTHLY HOUR [HUMAN LIFE] TO ME	SOME WRETCHED CREATURE,	1111	V 4
THOSE WHO DID [THAT DO] NOT TO HUMAN NATURE	TELL AS A MARKSMAN--WERE	1152	11
THE SMALLEST HUMAN HEART'S EXTENT	THE LIFE WE HAVE IS VERY	1162	7
CAN [MAY] HUMAN NATURE HIDE	AS OLD AS WOE--	1168	10
THAT BEARS THE HUMAN SOUL.	THERE IS NO FRIGATE LIKE	1263	8
TILL HUMAN NATURE CAME	I THOUGHT THAT NATURE	1286	2
OF HUMAN NATURE JUST AWARE	I THOUGHT THAT NATURE	1286	5
MY HUMAN NATURE'S FULLEST FORCE	I CANNOT WANT IT MORE--	1301	3
IN EVERY HUMAN SOUL--	PINK--SMALL--AND	1332	8
FROM ANY HUMAN [LIVING] SOUL--	YOU CANNOT TAKE ITSELF	1351	2
IN SORDID HUMAN LIFE	A SAUCER HOLDS A CUP	1374	2
DUNGEONED IN THE HUMAN BREAST	"SECRETS" IS A DAILY	1385	5
HOW ADEQUATE THE HUMAN HEART	WHAT MYSTERY PERVADES A	1400	V
HOW HUMAN NATURE DOTES	HOW HUMAN NATURE DOTES	1417	1
AND HUMAN NATURE HID [POPULATION FLED]	IT WAS A QUIET SEEMING	1419	9
A SINGLE HUMAN SOUL	WHOEVER DISENCHANTS	1451	2
IN HUMAN NATURE'S WEST--	LOOK BACK ON TIME, WITH	1478	4
THE HUMAN HEART IS TOLD	BY HOMELY GIFT AND	1563	2
IT'S PLACE IS IN THE HUMAN HEART	THE BIRD HER PUNCTUAL	1585	3
RANGE FROM A SINGLE HUMAN HEART	THE AUCTIONEER OF	1612	7
TO POINT A HUMAN LIFE?	GO THY GREAT WAY!	1638	5
THE MIGHT OF HUMAN LOVE--	THE IMMORTALITY SHE GAVE	1648	4
TOWARD HUMAN NATURE'S HOME	NOT ANY SUNNY TONE	1674	5
THAT SEARCHES HUMAN NATURE'S CREASES	PERIL AS A POSSESSION	1678	6
HAS HUMAN NATURE BEEN.	NO MAN SAW AWE, NOR TO	1733	4
CAN HUMAN NATURE NOT SURVIVE [PROCEED]	THE RETICENT VOLCANO	1748	7
AN EAR CAN BREAK A HUMAN HEART	THE SADDEST NOISE, THE	1764	17
HUMBLE			
THIS HUMBLE TOURIST ROSE!	WENT UP A YEAR THIS	93	8
WITH WHICH FLOWERS HUMBLE MEN:	FLOWERS--WELL--IF	137	4
FRESH [NEW] AS MANKIND THAT HUMBLE STORY	TELL AS A MARKSMAN--WERE	1152	5
AN HUMBLE PURCHASER--	HIS MIND LIKE FABRICS OF	1446	4
IN HUMBLE CIRCUMSTANCES--	THE ROBIN IS A GABRIEL	1483	2
HUMBLED			
TILL GRAVITATION CHASED [HUMBLED / EJECTED / FOUNDERED / . . .	TWO BUTTERFLIES WENT OUT	533	V
HUMBLER			
FOR HUMBLER COMPANY	A MIEN TO MOVE A QUEEN--	283	5
HUMBLES			
AND BUT ONE SMILE--THAT MEAGRES [HUMBLES] BALMS--	ABOVE OBLIVION'S TIDE	1531	4
HUMBLEST			
OR HUMBLEST PATCHWORK--CHILDREN DO [MAY]--	AT LEISURE IS THE SOUL	618	7
DISPLAYED [PASS SLOW] BEFORE THE SIMPLEST [HUMBLEST] DOOR	SOME ONE PREPARED THIS	1644	4
HUMILITY			
BUT THE HUMILITY.	A BEE HIS BURNISHED	1339	12
I ASKED HUMILITY	I SAW THE WIND WITHIN	1502	4
BUT SHE MUST [MY PRICE / HUMILITY] PAY FOR SUCCOR	I SAW THE WIND WITHIN	1502	V

	FIRST LINE	POEM	LINE
HUMILITY (CONTINUED)			
AMAZES THE HUMILITY	ENDANGER IT, AND THE	1658	3
NOT TO PARTAKE THY PASSION, MY HUMILITY.	PROUD OF MY BROKEN HEART	1736	4
HUMMED			
THEIR FOREFATHERS--HAVE HUMMED--	IT WILL BE SUMMER--	342	12
HUMMING			
THE STORM DOTH WALK THE SEASHORE HUMMING A MOURNFUL TUNE,	AWAKE YE MUSES NINE,	1	17
HUMMING THE QUAINTEST LULLABY	WHOSE ARE THE LITTLE	142	19
BY A HUMMING CORONER--	WE--BEE AND I--LIVE BY	230	17
PLAY IT WERE A HUMMING BIRD--	ALL THE LETTERS I CAN	334	7
THE HUMMING BIRD--ASPIRE--	THERE IS A FLOWER THAT	380	4
OF NUMEROUS HUMMING BIRDS AT ONCE	THE WIND--TAPPED LIKE A	436	11
HUMMING--FOR PROMISE--WHEN ALONE--	BETTER--THAN MUSIC! FOR	503	22
HUMMING--UNTIL MY FAINT REHEARSAL--	BETTER--THAN MUSIC! FOR	503	23
HUMMING-BIRD			
HUMMING-BIRD	A ROUTE OF EVANESCENCE	1463	T
HUMORS			
NATURE WAS IN THE BEST OF HUMORS	IT SOUNDED AS IF THE	1397 V	7
HUMS			
ROUND HER CHAMBER HUMS--	COME SLOWLY--EDEN!	211	6
WHOSE MORNING NEVER HUMS--	WATER MAKES MANY BEDS	1428 V	8
HUNCH			
HOUSES HUNCH THE HOUSE	I COULD DIE--TO KNOW--	570	7
THAT HUNCH [PILE] THEMSELVES BETWEEN--	I SEE THEE BETTER--IN	611	6
HUNCHED			
THE FIGURES HUNCHED, WITH PAIN--	A CLOCK STOPPED--	287	7
HUNDRED			
AND THEY MAKE MERRY WEDDING, WHOSE GUESTS ARE HUNDRED LEAVES;	AWAKE YE MUSES NINE,	1	14
SO SILVER STEAL A HUNDRED FLUTES	WE SHOULD NOT MIND SO	81	7
FROM OUT A HUNDRED TREES--	WE SHOULD NOT MIND SO	81	8
THEIR HUNDRED HATS THEY RAISE!	ONE DIGNITY DELAYS FOR	98	12
IT IS AS IF A HUNDRED DRUMS	I HAVE A KING, WHO DOES	103	8
MY FLOWERS FROM A HUNDRED CRIBS	AS CHILDREN BID THE	133	7
AUGMENTED--SWEET--A HUNDRED FOLD--	WE COVER THEE--SWEET	482	11
WHEN BLISS DISCLOSED A HUNDRED TOES [WINGS]--	SHE SIGHTS A BIRD--SHE	507	11
AS ABSENT AS A HUNDRED YEARS,	THE FACE WE CHOOSE TO	1141	3
AFTER A HUNDRED YEARS	AFTER A HUNDRED YEARS	1147	1
WITH HUNDRED WEIGHTS--TO SPARE--	RISK IS THE HAIR THAT	1239	4
I TAUGHT MY HEART A HUNDRED TIMES	I THOUGHT THE TRAIN	1449	5
HUNDREDS			
HUNDREDS HAVE LOST INDEED--	SOUL, WILT THOU TOSS	139	3
HUNG			
WHEN LAST YEAR'S DISTAFF IDLE HUNG	THERE IS A MORN BY MEN	24	11
IT HUNG SO HIGH	I GAINED IT SO--	359	5
HUNG OUT IT'S FLAGS OF SNOW--	THE HIMMALEH WAS KNOWN	481	6
I HUNG UPON THE PEG, AT NIGHT.	IT CEASED TO HURT ME,	584	8
NOVEMBER HUNG HIS GRANITE HAT	THE DAY GREW SMALL,	1140	7
IN CHRYSOPRASE APARTMENTS [APARTMENT] HUNG	THE BUTTERFLY'S	1244	2
WITCHCRAFT WAS HUNG, IN HISTORY,	WITCHCRAFT WAS HUNG, IN	1583	1
UPON THE GALLOWS HUNG A WRETCH,	UPON THE GALLOWS HUNG A	1757	1
HUNGER			
AN INSTINCT [HUNGER] FOR THE HOAR [DREAR], THE BALD--	I THINK THE HEMLOCK	525	7
THAT HUNGER--WAS A WAY	I HAD BEEN HUNGRY, ALL	579	18
NO HUNGER--HAD SHE--NOR AN INN--	I WATCHED THE MOON	629	21
A ROBIN'S FAMINE [PALATE / HUNGER] ABLE--	DEPRIVED OF OTHER	773	9
THE HUNGER--DOES NOT CEASE--	HAD I NOT THIS, OR THIS,	904	12
HUNGERED			
AND HUNGERED FOR--THE SAME--	A PRISON GETS TO BE A	652	8
HUNGERS			
HE HUNGERS TO ATTAIN.	HIS ORIENTAL HERESIES	1526 V	
HUNGRY			
THE HUNGRY VULTURE SCREAMED--	THROUGH LANE IT LAY--	9	12
REVERENTLY, TO THE HUNGRY	TALK WITH PRUDENCE TO A	119	3
WONT THEY SCOLD US--WHEN WE'RE HUNGRY [HOMESICK]--	WHAT IS--"PARADISE"--	215	9
HER JAWS STIR--TWITCHING [MOUTH STIRS--LONGING]--HUNGRY--	SHE SIGHTS A BIRD--SHE	507	5
I HAD BEEN HUNGRY, ALL THE YEARS--	I HAD BEEN HUNGRY, ALL	579	1
WHEN TURNING, HUNGRY, HOME	I HAD BEEN HUNGRY, ALL	579	6
NOR WAS I HUNGRY--SO I FOUND	I HAD BEEN HUNGRY, ALL	579	17
TOO HUNGRY TO BE BORNE	I PLAY AT RICHES--TO	801	10
LIKE HUNGRY DOGS	THE WIND DREW OFF	1694	2
AND HUNGRY AND MUST GRAZE	LOVE CAN DO ALL BUT	1731	6
HUNT			
WHOSE BERYL EGG, WHAT SCHOOL BOYS HUNT	A FEATHER FROM THE	161	7
AND NOW WE HUNT THE DOE--	MY LIFE HAD STOOD--A	754	6
GOOD TO HIDE, AND HEAR 'EM HUNT!	GOOD TO HIDE, AND HEAR	842	1
HUNTED			
THAT HUNTED--HUNTED SO--TO SEE--	I SHOULD NOT DARE TO	205	6
THAT HUNTED--HUNTED SO--TO SEE--	I SHOULD NOT DARE TO	205	6
I HUNTED [WORRIED] ALL THE SAND--	A DYING TIGER--MOANED	566	2
THAT HUNTED FOR THE DAY--	THE SUN AND MOON MUST	871	11
WE HUNTED HIM TO HIS RAVINE	THE FROST OF DEATH WAS	1136	16
HUNTER			
I'VE HEARD THE HUNTER TELL--	A WOUNDED DEER--LEAPS	165	2
HURLED			
HURLED MY BELIEF--	HE STRAINED MY FAITH--	497	5

	FIRST LINE	POEM	LINE
HURLED (CONTINUED)			
AND THEY WERE HURLED FROM NOON--	TWO BUTTERFLIES WENT OUT	533	V
AND MOUNTS TO BE TO ATOMS HURLED	RISK IS THE HAIR THAT	1239	V 7
HURLS			
IT HURLS IT'S BARBED SYLLABLES	THERE IS A WORD	8	4
HURRAH			
HURRAH FOR PETER PARLEY!	"SIC TRANSIT GLORIA	3	9
HURRAH FOR DANIEL BOON!	"SIC TRANSIT GLORIA	3	10
HURRICANE			
A PRIVILEGE OF HURRICANE [MISERY]	I MEANT TO FIND HER WHEN	718	11
TILL HURRICANE BISECT	THE HEART HAS NARROW	928	5
BUT GROWING LIKE A HURRICANE	THE MOB WITHIN THE HEART	1745	7
HURRIED			
SOME RUBY TROWSERS HURRIED ON--	A SLASH OF BLUE--	204	6
THAT HURRIED ALL AROUND [ABROAD]--	A BIRD CAME DOWN THE	328	10
THE EYE HAD HURRIED BY	DEATH SETS A THING	360	2
TELL HIM [HER] JUST HOW THE FINGERS HURRIED--	GOING TO HIM! HAPPY	494	6
THE THUNDER HURRIED SLOW--	THE WIND BEGUN TO KNEAD	824	V 10
WITH HURRIED--FEW--EXPRESS REPORTS	THE ROBIN IS THE ONE	828	3
DECADE HAD HASTENED [HURRIED / GATHERED] TO DECADE--	A LITTLE SNOW WAS HERE	1444	4
HURRIEDLY			
AND HURRIEDLY [HASTILY] WITHDREW	ALONE AND IN A	1167	8
HURRIES			
HURRIES A TIMID LEAF.	THESE ARE THE DAYS WHEN	130	12
TO APRIL--HURRIES ON--	YOU'LL KNOW HER--BY HER	634	24
HURRY			
A HURRY IN THE BREATH--	A THROE UPON THE	71	2
I WISHED THE GRASS WOULD HURRY--	I DREADED THAT FIRST	348	13
THE CHILDREN HURRY BY--	THERE'S BEEN A DEATH, IN	389	10
IT MADE THE HURRY PLAIN--	HER FINAL SUMMER WAS IT	795	8
A HURRY WITH A LINGERING, MIXED,	I CANNOT MEET THE SPRING	1051	3
THESE--HURRY TO A SPHERE	EXCEPT THE SMALLER SIZE	1067	3
WAGGONS LIKE MESSENGERS HURRY ABOUT	AFTER THE SUN COMES OUT	1148	3
WHY SHOULD WE [I] HURRY--WHY INDEED	WHY SHOULD WE HURRY--WHY	1646	1
HURRYING			
AND THE SNOWS COME HURRYING FROM THE HILLS,	HAVE YOU GOT A BROOK IN	136	11
A HURRYING HOME OF LITTLE MEN	A MURMUR IN THE TREES--	416	9
WHEN HURRYING TO SCHOOL--	IT WAS GIVEN TO ME BY	454	10
ONE HURRYING TO REST--	I CROSS TILL I AM WEARY	550	13
WHEN HURRYING TO THE TOWN	HE TOLD A HOMELY TALE	763	V 8
WOULD SCAN THE MIGHTY [EAGER / BREATHLESS / HURRYING / . . .	TO FLEE FROM MEMORY	1242	6
HURT			
DEATH WONT HURT--NOW DOLLIE'S HERE!	DYING! DYING IN THE	158	12
AND "YOU'RE HURT" EXCLAIM!	A WOUNDED DEER--LEAPS	165	12
THEY SAY IT DOES'NT HURT--	TO DIE--TAKES JUST A	255	2
HEAVENLY HURT, IT GIVES US--	THERE'S A CERTAIN SLANT	258	5
SEE WHERE IT HURT ME--THAT'S ENOUGH--	WHAT IF I SAY I SHALL	277	5
YOU SAID IT HURT YOU--MOST--	ONE YEAR AGO--JOTS WHAT?	296	17
AND MANY HURT,	I REASON, EARTH IS SHORT	301	3
SHE NEVER DEEMED--SHE HURT--	SHE DEALT HER PRETTY	479	5
AND STILL IT HURT YOU, AS SOME BIRD	HER SMILE WAS SHAPED	514	3
IT [THEY] WOULD HURT US--WERE WE AWAKE--	WE DREAM--IT IS GOOD WE	531	2
WE--TELL A HURT--TO COOL IT--	THE BLACK BERRY--WEARS A	554	9
THAT HURT THEM EARLY--SUCH A LAPSE	I MEASURE EVERY GRIEF I	561	19
THE PLENTY HURT ME--'TWAS SO NEW--	I HAD BEEN HUNGRY, ALL	579	13
IT CEASED TO HURT ME, THOUGH SO SLOW	IT CEASED TO HURT ME,	584	1
WOULD'NT BONDS HURT MORE	LET US PLAY YESTERDAY--	728	27
HURTS			
BUT I GUESS GUESSING HURTS--	YOU SEE I CANNOT SEE--	253	6
'TIS NOT THAT DYING HURTS US SO--	'TIS NOT THAT DYING	335	1
'TIS LIVING--HURTS US MORE--	'TIS NOT THAT DYING	335	2
HE HURTS A LITTLE, THOUGH--	I DREADED THAT FIRST	348	4
WHY MAKE IT DOUBT--IT HURTS IT SO--	WHY MAKE IT DOUBT--IT	462	1
I WONDER IF IT HURTS TO LIVE--	I MEASURE EVERY GRIEF I	561	9
HUSBAND			
"MY HUSBAND"--WOMEN SAY--	TITLE DIVINE--IS MINE!	1072	12
HUSH			
HUSH! EPIGEA WAKENS!	WHOSE ARE THE LITTLE	142	21
HUSH--ONLY TO ME!	MANY A PHRASE HAS THE	276	16
HUSHED			
WHOSE VOICES--TRAINED--[STANZA, HUSHED,] BELOW--	TO LEARN THE TRANSPORT	167	12
HUSK			
CONTUSION OF THE HUSK	TOO COLD IS THIS	1135	7
HUT			
HOME TO THE HUT! WHAT LOT	THE MALAY--TOOK THE	452	9
UPON A BANK [WITHIN A HUT] OF STONE	A LONG--LONG SLEEP--A	654	6
AT MORNING, IN A TRUFFLED HUT	THE MUSHROOM IS THE ELF	1298	3
HYACINTH			
A HYACINTH--I HID--	I TEND MY FLOWERS FOR	339	11
WITH REVERENTIAL HYACINTH--	TWO TRAVELLERS PERISHING	933	11
HYBLA			
AND HYBLA BALMS--	THE WORLD--FEELS DUSTY	715	12
HYMN			
IT IS NOT HYMN FROM PULPIT READ--	MUSICIANS WRESTLE	157	10
TIM--READS A LITTLE HYMN--	WE DONT CRY--TIM AND I,	196	17
CLEAR STRAINS OF HYMN	READ--SWEET--HOW OTHERS	260	10
I HELPED [STAYED] HIS FILM--WITH HYMN--	I ROSE--BECAUSE HE SANK	616	7

	FIRST LINE	POEM		LINE
HYMN (CONTINUED)				
AND SO WITH THEWS OF HYMN--	I ROSE--BECAUSE HE SANK	616		20
OR BISCAYAN HYMN--	NEVER FOR SOCIETY	746		10
HOW AWKWARD AT THE HYMN [PLAN]	I LEARNED--AT LEAST--	944		4
BOLD AS A BAILIFF'S HYMN--	A PROMPT--EXECUTIVE BIRD	1177		2
GOOD AS A NORSEMAN'S HYMN--	A PROMPT--EXECUTIVE BIRD	1177	V	2
HYPERBOLE				
THIS LIMITLESS HYPERBOLE	'TIS WHITER THAN AN	1482		9
HYPERBOLIC				
VOUCHES, WITH HYPERBOLIC ARCHNESS--	GOD IS A DISTANT--	357		7
HYPHEN				
DEATH--SO--THE HYPHEN OF THE SEA--	THOSE NOT LIVE YET	1454		7
HYPOTHESIS				
'TIS DRAMA--IF HYPOTHESIS	'TIS WHITER THAN AN	1482		11
I				
I HEAR THE BRIGHT BEE HUM;	THERE IS ANOTHER SKY,	2		12
I STAY MINE ENEMY!	"SIC TRANSIT GLORIA	3		4
WHEN I AM FAR FROM THEE!	"SIC TRANSIT GLORIA	3		8
I CLIMB THE "HILL OF SCIENCE,"	"SIC TRANSIT GLORIA	3		21
I "VIEW THE LANDSCAPE O'ER;"	"SIC TRANSIT GLORIA	3		22
I NE'ER BEHELD BEFORE!	"SIC TRANSIT GLORIA	3		24
OF WHERE I WOULD RESIDE!	"SIC TRANSIT GLORIA	3		40
IN DREAMS I SEE THEM RISE,	"SIC TRANSIT GLORIA	3		50
GOOD BYE, SIR, I AM GOING;	"SIC TRANSIT GLORIA	3		57
THITHER I PILOT THEE--	ON THIS WONDROUS SEA	4		10
I HAVE A BIRD IN SPRING	I HAVE A BIRD IN SPRING	5		1
YET DO I NOT REPINE	I HAVE A BIRD IN SPRING	5		7
TELL I MY DOUBTING HEART	I HAVE A BIRD IN SPRING	5		17
I SEE	I HAVE A BIRD IN SPRING	5		21
THEN WILL I NOT REPINE,	I HAVE A BIRD IN SPRING	5		25
I WAS WONT TO SEE--	FREQUENTLY THE WOODS ARE	6		6
I CANNOT SEE A SPOKE	MY WHEEL IS IN THE DARK!	10		2
AT YOU AND I!	MY WHEEL IS IN THE DARK!	10		15
I NEVER TOLD THE BURIED GOLD	I NEVER TOLD THE BURIED	11		1
I SAW THE SUN--HIS PLUNDER DONE	I NEVER TOLD THE BURIED	11		3
I HOPE TWAS HONEST GAINED.	I NEVER TOLD THE BURIED	11		11
WHETHER AS [WHILE] I PONDER	I NEVER TOLD THE BURIED	11		16
LEST I SH'D BE OLD FASHIONED	THE MORNS ARE MEEKER	12		7
ONE SISTER HAVE I IN OUR HOUSE,	ONE SISTER HAVE I IN OUR	14		1
ONE CAME THE ROAD THAT I CAME--	ONE SISTER HAVE I IN OUR	14		5
I HELD HER HAND THE TIGHTER--	ONE SISTER HAVE I IN OUR	14		15
I SPILT THE DEW--	ONE SISTER HAVE I IN OUR	14		23
I CHOSE THIS SINGLE STAR	ONE SISTER HAVE I IN OUR	14		25
I PRAY HIM TOO--EXPLORE	THE GUEST IS GOLD AND	15		8
I WOULD DISTIL A CUP,	I WOULD DISTIL A CUP,	16		1
I WAS NEVER IN!	BAFFLED FOR JUST A DAY	17		8
I WILL SINGING GO--	DISTRUSTFUL OF THE	20		6
I SHALL NOT FEEL THE SLEET--THEN--	DISTRUSTFUL OF THE	20		7
I SHALL NOT FEAR THE SNOW.	DISTRUSTFUL OF THE	20		8
I SOW MY PAGEANTRY	ALL THESE MY BANNERS BE.	22		2
YOU AND I THE SECRET	ALL THESE MY BANNERS BE.	22		16
I HAD A GUINEA GOLDEN--	I HAD A GUINEA GOLDEN--	23		1
I LOST IT IN THE SAND--	I HAD A GUINEA GOLDEN--	23		2
THAT WHEN I COULD NOT FIND IT--	I HAD A GUINEA GOLDEN--	23		7
I SAT ME DOWN TO SIGH.	I HAD A GUINEA GOLDEN--	23		8
I HAD A CRIMSON ROBIN--	I HAD A GUINEA GOLDEN--	23		9
I KEPT THE "HOUSE AT HAME."	I HAD A GUINEA GOLDEN--	23		16
I HAD A STAR IN HEAVEN--	I HAD A GUINEA GOLDEN--	23		17
AND WHEN I WAS NOT HEEDING,	I HAD A GUINEA GOLDEN--	23		19
I DO NOT CARE ABOUT IT--	I HAD A GUINEA GOLDEN--	23		23
I HAVE A MISSING FRIEND--	I HAD A GUINEA GOLDEN--	23		26
AND GAMBOL I MAY NEVER NAME--	THERE IS A MORN BY MEN	24		5
NE'ER SAW I SUCH A WONDROUS SCENE--	THERE IS A MORN BY MEN	24		13
I ASK, EACH NEW MAY MORN.	THERE IS A MORN BY MEN	24		21
I WAIT THY FAR, FANTASTIC BELLS--	THERE IS A MORN BY MEN	24		22
I TOUCHED HER CRADLE MUTE--	SHE SLEPT BENEATH A TREE	25		3
IT'S ALL I HAVE TO BRING TODAY--	IT'S ALL I HAVE TO BRING	26		1
BE SURE YOU COUNT--SH'D I FORGET	IT'S ALL I HAVE TO BRING	26		5
I--FROM AGONY--	MORNS LIKE THESE--WE	27		8
IF THOSE I LOVED WERE LOST	IF THOSE I LOVED WERE	29		1
IF THOSE I LOVED WERE FOUND	IF THOSE I LOVED WERE	29		3
DID THOSE I LOVED REPOSE	IF THOSE I LOVED WERE	29		5
I, MY RIDDLE BRING	IF THOSE I LOVED WERE	29	V	8
SUMMER FOR THEE, GRANT I MAY BE	SUMMER FOR THEE, GRANT I	31		1
THEN I REMEMBER NOT.	IF RECOLLECTING WERE	33		2
HOW NEAR I HAD FORGOT.	IF RECOLLECTING WERE	33		4
DID I NOT TAKE IT FROM THE WAYS	NOBODY KNOWS THIS LITTLE	35		3
I COUNTED TILL THEY DANCED SO	I COUNTED TILL THEY	36		1
AND THEN I TOOK A PENCIL	I COUNTED TILL THEY	36		3
I DID RESIGN THE PRIG,	I COUNTED TILL THEY	36		6
WILL THE FROCK I WEPT IN	BEFORE THE ICE IS IN THE	37		15
SO I SAID--OR THOUGHT--	IT DID NOT SURPRISE ME--	39		2
WHEN I COUNT THE SEEDS	WHEN I COUNT THE SEEDS	40		1
WHEN I CON THE PEOPLE	WHEN I COUNT THE SEEDS	40		4
WHEN I BELIEVE THE GARDEN	WHEN I COUNT THE SEEDS	40		7
I CAN SPARE THIS SUMMER, UNRELUCTANTLY.	WHEN I COUNT THE SEEDS	40		11
I [WHO] ROBBED THE WOODS--	I ROBBED THE WOODS--	41		1
I [HE] SCANNED THEIR TRINKETS CURIOUS--	I ROBBED THE WOODS--	41		6
I [HE] GRASPED--I [HE] BORE AWAY--	I ROBBED THE WOODS--	41		7
I [HE] GRASPED--I [HE] BORE AWAY--	I ROBBED THE WOODS--	41		7

I (CONTINUED)

	FIRST LINE	POEM	LINE
AND I HAD BEEN THE ROSE--	IF SHE HAD BEEN THE	44	2
SINCE I AM OF THE DRUID,	IF SHE HAD BEEN THE	44	5
I DO NOT UNDERSTAND!	THERE'S SOMETHING	45	8
I WOULD NOT WEEP IF I WERE THEY--	THERE'S SOMETHING	45	9
I WOULD NOT WEEP IF I WERE THEY--	THERE'S SOMETHING	45	9
I KEEP MY PLEDGE.	I KEEP MY PLEDGE.	46	1
I WAS NOT CALLED--	I KEEP MY PLEDGE.	46	2
I BRING MY ROSE.	I KEEP MY PLEDGE.	46	4
I PLIGHT AGAIN,	I KEEP MY PLEDGE.	46	5
BLOSSOM AND I--	I KEEP MY PLEDGE.	46	9
YOU AND I--TONIGHT!	HEART! WE WILL FORGET	47	2
I WILL FORGET THE LIGHT!	HEART! WE WILL FORGET	47	4
THAT I MAY STRAIGHT BEGIN!	HEART! WE WILL FORGET	47	6
I REMEMBER HIM!	HEART! WE WILL FORGET	47	8
I NEVER LOST AS MUCH BUT TWICE,	I NEVER LOST AS MUCH BUT	49	1
TWICE HAVE I STOOD A BEGGAR	I NEVER LOST AS MUCH BUT	49	3
I AM POOR ONCE MORE!	I NEVER LOST AS MUCH BUT	49	8
I HAV'NT TOLD MY GARDEN YET--	I HAV'NT TOLD MY GARDEN	50	1
I HAV'NT QUITE THE STRENGTH NOW	I HAV'NT TOLD MY GARDEN	50	3
I WILL NOT NAME IT IN THE STREET	I HAV'NT TOLD MY GARDEN	50	5
WHERE I HAVE RAMBLED SO--	I HAV'NT TOLD MY GARDEN	50	10
THE DAY THAT I SHALL GO--	I HAV'NT TOLD MY GARDEN	50	12
I OFTEN PASSED THE VILLAGE	I OFTEN PASSED THE	51	1
I DID NOT KNOW THE YEAR THEN--	I OFTEN PASSED THE	51	5
CRY "IT'S I", "TAKE DOLLIE",	I OFTEN PASSED THE	51	17
AND I WILL ENFOLD!	I OFTEN PASSED THE	51	18
IF I SHOULD DIE,	IF I SHOULD DIE,	54	1
IF I SHOULD CEASE TO BRING A ROSE	IF I SHOULD CEASE TO	56	1
I HAVE BEEN CALLED AWAY--	IF I SHOULD CEASE TO	56	4
IF I SHOULD CEASE TO TAKE THE NAMES	IF I SHOULD CEASE TO	56	5
THAT FROM YOU OR I,	TO VENERATE THE SIMPLE	57	4
"I WILL NOT LET THEE GO	A LITTLE EAST OF JORDAN,	59	10
IF I WERE HALF SO FINE MYSELF	"SOWN IN DISHONOR"!	62	4
I CONFIDENTLY SEE!	SOME RAINBOW--COMING	64	3
I CANT TELL YOU--BUT YOU FEEL IT--	I CANT TELL YOU--BUT YOU	65	1
I CHECK MY BUSY PENCIL,	LOW AT MY PROBLEM	69	5
I SLEW A WORM THE OTHER DAY--	"ARCTURUS" IS HIS OTHER	70	5
I PULL A FLOWER FROM THE WOODS--	"ARCTURUS" IS HIS OTHER	70	9
WHEREAS I TOOK THE BUTTERFLY	"ARCTURUS" IS HIS OTHER	70	13
WHERE I PROPOSED TO GO	"ARCTURUS" IS HIS OTHER	70	19
I HOPE I'M READY FOR "THE WORST"--	"ARCTURUS" IS HIS OTHER	70	24
I HOPE THE "CHILDREN" THERE	"ARCTURUS" IS HIS OTHER	70	27
WONT BE "NEW FASHIONED" WHEN I COME--	"ARCTURUS" IS HIS OTHER	70	28
I HOPE THE FATHER IN THE SKIES	"ARCTURUS" IS HIS OTHER	70	30
I NEVER HEAR THE WORD "ESCAPE"	I NEVER HEAR THE WORD	77	1
I NEVER HEAR OF PRISONS BROAD	I NEVER HEAR THE WORD	77	5
BUT I TUG CHILDISH AT MY BARS	I NEVER HEAR THE WORD	77	7
I DONT KNOW WHEN--	GOING TO HEAVEN!	79	2
CLOSE TO THE TWO I LOST--	GOING TO HEAVEN!	79	15
I'M GLAD I DONT BELIEVE IT	GOING TO HEAVEN!	79	20
I AM GLAD THEY DID BELIEVE IT	GOING TO HEAVEN!	79	24
WHOM I HAVE NEVER FOUND	GOING TO HEAVEN!	79	25
I LEFT THEM IN THE GROUND.	GOING TO HEAVEN!	79	27
I FOUND HER--"PLEIAD"--IN THE WOODS	WHOSE CHEEK IS THIS?	82	4
I PRAY YOU PASS [STROLL] ONCE MORE.	HEART, NOT SO HEAVY AS	83	20
BUT I WAS NOT A "DIVER"--	HER BREAST IS FIT FOR	84	2
BUT I HAVE [HAD] NOT A CREST.	HER BREAST IS FIT FOR	84	4
I--A SPARROW--BUILD THERE	HER BREAST IS FIT FOR	84	6
"BUT I HAVE CHOSEN THEM!"	"THEY HAVE NOT CHOSEN ME	85	2
I COULD NOT HAVE TOLD IT,	"THEY HAVE NOT CHOSEN ME	85	5
I--SOFTLY PLUCKING,	SOUTH WINDS JOSTLE THEM	86	7
CAN I EXPOUND THE SKIES?	SOME THINGS THAT FLY	89	8
I COULD HAVE TOUCHED!	WITHIN MY REACH!	90	2
I MIGHT HAVE CHANCED THAT WAY!	WITHIN MY REACH!	90	3
SO BASHFUL WHEN I SPIED HER!	SO BASHFUL WHEN I SPIED	91	1
SO BREATHLESS TILL I PASSED HER--	SO BASHFUL WHEN I SPIED	91	5
SO HELPLESS WHEN I TURNED	SO BASHFUL WHEN I SPIED	91	6
FOR WHOM I ROBBED THE DINGLE--	SO BASHFUL WHEN I SPIED	91	9
BUT I SHALL NEVER TELL!	SO BASHFUL WHEN I SPIED	91	12
I RECOLLECT IT WELL!	WENT UP A YEAR THIS	93	2
IS ALL THE REST I KNEW!	WENT UP A YEAR THIS	93	24
AND I, NO OTHER PRAYER.	MY NOSEGAYS ARE FOR	95	8
I CAME TO BUILD THE BIRD'S NEST,	SEXTON! MY MASTER'S	96	3
WHEN SIMPLE YOU, AND I,	ONE DIGNITY DELAYS FOR	98	14
COULD I SEE IT FROM THE MOUNTAINS	WILL THERE REALLY BE A	101	3
IF I WERE AS TALL AS THEY?	WILL THERE REALLY BE A	101	4
OF WHICH I HAVE NEVER HEARD?	WILL THERE REALLY BE A	101	8
I HAVE A KING, WHO DOES NOT SPEAK--	I HAVE A KING, WHO DOES	103	1
I TRUDGE THE DAY AWAY--	I HAVE A KING, WHO DOES	103	3
AND IF I DO--WHEN MORNING COMES--	I HAVE A KING, WHO DOES	103	7
AND IF I DONT--THE LITTLE BIRD	I HAVE A KING, WHO DOES	103	13
AND I OMIT TO PRAY	I HAVE A KING, WHO DOES	103	15
WHERE I HAVE LOST, I SOFTER TREAD--	WHERE I HAVE LOST, I	104	1
WHERE I HAVE LOST, I SOFTER TREAD--	WHERE I HAVE LOST, I	104	1
I SOW SWEET FLOWER FROM GARDEN BED--	WHERE I HAVE LOST, I	104	2
I PAUSE ABOVE THAT VANISHED HEAD	WHERE I HAVE LOST, I	104	3
WHOM I HAVE LOST, I PIOUS GUARD	WHERE I HAVE LOST, I	104	5
WHOM I HAVE LOST, I PIOUS GUARD	WHERE I HAVE LOST, I	104	5
WHEN I HAVE LOST, YOU'LL KNOW BY THIS--	WHERE I HAVE LOST, I	104	9

I (CONTINUED)

	FIRST LINE	POEM	LINE
WHY, I HAVE LOST, THE PEOPLE KNOW	WHERE I HAVE LOST, I	104	13
IF I WELD THE RIVET FASTER--	BY A FLOWER--BY A LETTER	109	3
I KNOW THE BUTTERFLY.	THE BEE IS NOT AFRAID OF	111	2
THE BROOKS LAUGH LOUDER WHEN I COME--	THE BEE IS NOT AFRAID OF	111	5
I WOULD GO, TO KNOW!	GOOD NIGHT, BECAUSE WE	114	3
I HAD SOME THINGS THAT I CALLED MINE--	I HAD SOME THINGS THAT I	116	1
I HAD SOME THINGS THAT I CALLED MINE--	I HAD SOME THINGS THAT I	116	1
I RETAIN "SHAW"!	I HAD SOME THINGS THAT I	116	16
THEN I TURN SOLDIER TOO,	MY FRIEND ATTACKS MY	118	3
HAD I A MIGHTY GUN	MY FRIEND ATTACKS MY	118	6
I THINK I'D SHOOT THE HUMAN RACE	MY FRIEND ATTACKS MY	118	7
I CLAP MY HANDS TO SEE--	A SOMETHING IN A	122	9
AND I MEET, COMING THRO' THE DEWS	A SOMETHING IN A	122	21
IN LANDS I NEVER SAW--THEY SAY	IN LANDS I NEVER SAW--	124	1
WHICH, SIR, ARE YOU AND WHICH AM I	IN LANDS I NEVER SAW--	124	7
BUT GALLANTER, I KNOW	TO FIGHT ALOUD, IS VERY	126	2
I DONT KNOW HIM; SNUGLY BUILT!	"HOUSES"--SO THE WISE	127	6
I BRING AN UNACCUSTOMED WINE	I BRING AN UNACCUSTOMED	132	1
I TURN MY BRIMMING EYES AWAY,	I BRING AN UNACCUSTOMED	132	6
THE LIPS I W'D HAVE COOLED, ALAS--	I BRING AN UNACCUSTOMED	132	9
I W'D AS SOON ATTEMPT TO WARM	I BRING AN UNACCUSTOMED	132	11
AND SO I ALWAYS BEAR THE CUP	I BRING AN UNACCUSTOMED	132	17
WHEN I AT LAST AWAKE.	I BRING AN UNACCUSTOMED	132	22
BUT I COULD NEVER SELL--	PERHAPS YOU'D LIKE TO	134	2
WHY, I WILL LEND UNTIL JUST THEN,	PERHAPS YOU'D LIKE TO	134	9
I WILL GIVE HIM ALL THE DAISIES	FLOWERS--WELL--IF	137	7
I HAD RATHER WEAR HER GRACE	PIGMY SERAPHS--GONE	138	12
I HAD RATHER DWELL LIKE HER	PIGMY SERAPHS--GONE	138	14
ALL THIS AND MORE I CANNOT TELL--	AN ALTERED LOOK ABOUT	140	13
WHOSE ARE THE LITTLE BEDS, I ASKED	WHOSE ARE THE LITTLE	142	1
PERHAPS THEY DID NOT HEAR, I SAID,	WHOSE ARE THE LITTLE	142	5
I WILL INQUIRE AGAIN--	WHOSE ARE THE LITTLE	142	6
I CANNOT TELL THE SUM,	SHE BORE IT TILL THE	144	6
PLEASE GOD, MIGHT I BEHOLD HIM	BLESS GOD, HE WENT AS	147	5
I SHOULD NOT FEAR THE FOE THEN--	BLESS GOD, HE WENT AS	147	7
I SHOULD NOT FEAR THE FIGHT!	BLESS GOD, HE WENT AS	147	8
YET NOT IN ALL THE NESTS I MEET--	ALL OVERGROWN BY CUNNING	148	11
SINCE I COULD NEVER FIND HER	SHE DIED--THIS WAS THE	150	7
I CAN MURMUR BROKEN,	MUTE THY CORONATION--	151	7
MASTER, IT WAS I--	MUTE THY CORONATION--	151	8
THAT I FELT MARTIAL STIRRINGS	THE SUN KEPT STOOPING--	152	11
I SHALL NOT FEAR MISTAKE--	YOU LOVE ME--YOU ARE	156	2
I SHALL NOT CHEATED WAKE--	YOU LOVE ME--YOU ARE	156	3
I NEED NOT START--YOU'RE SURE--	YOU LOVE ME--YOU ARE	156	8
WHEN FRIGHTENED--HOME TO THEE I RUN--	YOU LOVE ME--YOU ARE	156	10
I HEAR THE SILVER STRIFE--	MUSICIANS WRESTLE	157	3
I THINK IT THAT "NEW LIFE"!	MUSICIANS WRESTLE	157	6
SO I CAN SEE WHICH WAY TO GO	DYING! DYING IN THE	158	3
I HEAR HER FEET UPON THE STAIR!	DYING! DYING IN THE	158	11
JUST LOST, WHEN I WAS SAVED!	JUST LOST, WHEN I WAS	160	1
I HEARD RECEDE THE DISAPPOINTED TIDE!	JUST LOST, WHEN I WAS	160	6
THEREFORE, AS ONE RETURNED, I FEEL,	JUST LOST, WHEN I WAS	160	7
I, A LESS DIVINE--	THO' MY DESTINY BE	163	4
I WOULD FAR PREFER,	THO' MY DESTINY BE	163	6
YOU AND I, AND DR HOLLAND,	THO' MY DESTINY BE	163	11
I MET A KING THIS AFTERNOON!	I MET A KING THIS	166	1
BUT SURE I AM HE ERMINE WORE	I MET A KING THIS	166	5
AND SURE I AM, THE CREST HE BORE	I MET A KING THIS	166	7
IF I MUST TELL YOU, OF A HORSE	I MET A KING THIS	166	13
AND SUCH A WAGON! WHILE I LIVE	I MET A KING THIS	166	17
DARE I PRESUME TO SEE	I MET A KING THIS	166	18
I QUESTION IF THE ROYAL COACH	I MET A KING THIS	166	25
IF I SHOULD FAIL, WHAT POVERTY!	'TIS SO MUCH JOY! 'TIS	172	2
AND YET, AS POOR AS I,	'TIS SO MUCH JOY! 'TIS	172	3
AND IF INDEED I FAIL,	'TIS SO MUCH JOY! 'TIS	172	9
AND IF I GAIN! OH GUN AT SEA!	'TIS SO MUCH JOY! 'TIS	172	13
BY ME! BUT WHO AM I,	A FUZZY FELLOW, WITHOUT	173	18
I HAVE NEVER SEEN "VOLCANOES"--	I HAVE NEVER SEEN	175	1
I DONT CARE FOR POUTING SKIES!	I'M THE LITTLE "HEART'S	176	2
CAN I, THEREFORE, STAY AWAY?	I'M THE LITTLE "HEART'S	176	4
I, MUST RESOLUTER BE!	I'M THE LITTLE "HEART'S	176	7
NOR WILL I, THE LITTLE HEART'S EASE--	I'M THE LITTLE "HEART'S	176	13
THAT I INSTIL THE PAIN	AH, NECROMANCY SWEET!	177	4
I CAUTIOUS, SCANNED MY LITTLE LIFE--	I CAUTIOUS, SCANNED MY	178	1
I WINNOWED WHAT WOULD FADE	I CAUTIOUS, SCANNED MY	178	2
I PUT THE LATTER IN A BARN--	I CAUTIOUS, SCANNED MY	178	5
I WENT ONE WINTER MORNING	I CAUTIOUS, SCANNED MY	178	7
A CYNIC, I BECAME.	I CAUTIOUS, SCANNED MY	178	12
SO I BEGIN TO RANSACK!	I CAUTIOUS, SCANNED MY	178	17
IF I COULD BRIBE THEM BY A ROSE	IF I COULD BRIBE THEM BY	179	1
I WOULD NOT STOP FOR NIGHT, OR STORM--	IF I COULD BRIBE THEM BY	179	4
I SAY, AS IF THIS LITTLE FLOWER	AS IF SOME LITTLE ARCTIC	180	9
I LOST A WORLD--THE OTHER DAY!	I LOST A WORLD--THE	181	1
IF I SHOULD'NT BE ALIVE	IF I SHOULD'NT BE ALIVE	182	1
IF I COULD'NT THANK YOU,	IF I SHOULD'NT BE ALIVE	182	5
WHAT SHALL I DO--IT WHIMPERS SO--	WHAT SHALL I DO--IT	186	1
I SENT IT--EVEN NOW?	WHAT SHALL I DO--IT	186	7
SO I CAN HANG IT IN MY ROOM--	MAKE ME A PICTURE OF THE	188	2
SO I AM HEARING HIM, I'LL DREAM,	MAKE ME A PICTURE OF THE	188	6

I		FIRST LINE	POEM	LINE
	(CONTINUED)			
	HE WAS WEAK, AND I WAS STRONG--THEN--	HE WAS WEAK, AND I WAS	190	1
	I WAS WEAK, AND HE WAS STRONG THEN--	HE WAS WEAK, AND I WAS	190	3
	SO I LET HIM LEAD ME--HOME.	HE WAS WEAK, AND I WAS	190	4
	THAT WAS ALL I CARED TO KNOW.	HE WAS WEAK, AND I WAS	190	8
	HE STROVE--AND I STROVE--TOO--	HE WAS WEAK, AND I WAS	190	11
	IF I SHOULD BRIBE THE LITTLE BIRD--	THE SKIES CANT KEEP	191	7
	I THINK I WONT--HOWEVER--	THE SKIES CANT KEEP	191	9
	I THINK I WONT--HOWEVER--	THE SKIES CANT KEEP	191	9
	I WOULD NOT--IF I COULD,	THE SKIES CANT KEEP	191	14
	I WOULD NOT--IF I COULD,	THE SKIES CANT KEEP	191	14
	I WOULD NOT BREAK THEE--	POOR LITTLE HEART!	192	8
	I SHALL KNOW WHY--WHEN TIME IS OVER--	I SHALL KNOW WHY--WHEN	193	1
	AND I HAVE CEASED TO WONDER WHY--	I SHALL KNOW WHY--WHEN	193	2
	AND I--FOR WONDER AT HIS WOE--	I SHALL KNOW WHY--WHEN	193	6
	I SHALL FORGET THE DROP OF ANGUISH	I SHALL KNOW WHY--WHEN	193	7
	WE DONT CRY--TIM AND I,	WE DONT CRY--TIM AND I,	196	1
	NOT TO CRY--TIM AND I--	WE DONT CRY--TIM AND I,	196	7
	THEN--WE SHAKE--TIM AND I--	WE DONT CRY--TIM AND I,	196	15
	AND LEST I--CRY--	WE DONT CRY--TIM AND I,	196	16
	PLEASE, SIR, I AND TIM--	WE DONT CRY--TIM AND I,	196	19
	TIM--SHALL--IF I--DO--	WE DONT CRY--TIM AND I,	196	23
	I--TOO--IF HE--	WE DONT CRY--TIM AND I,	196	24
	I--"TIM"--AND--ME!	WE DONT CRY--TIM AND I,	196	28
	I THINK THAT EARTH FEELS SO	I'M "WIFE"--I'VE	199	7
	I STOLE THEM FROM A BEE--	I STOLE THEM FROM A BEE	200	1
	HE FORGOT--AND I--REMEMBERED--	HE FORGOT--AND I--	203	1
	COULD I DO AUGHT ELSE--TO THEE?	HE FORGOT--AND I--	203	8
	I SHOULD NOT DARE TO LEAVE MY FRIEND,	I SHOULD NOT DARE TO	205	1
	WHILE I WAS GONE--AND I--TOO LATE--	I SHOULD NOT DARE TO	205	3
	WHILE I WAS GONE--AND I--TOO LATE--	I SHOULD NOT DARE TO	205	3
	IF I SHOULD DISAPPOINT THE EYES	I SHOULD NOT DARE TO	205	5
	IF I SHOULD STAB THE PATIENT FAITH	I SHOULD NOT DARE TO	205	9
	THO' I GET HOME HOW LATE--HOW LATE--	THO' I GET HOME HOW LATE	207	1
	SO I GET HOME--'TWILL COMPENSATE--	THO' I GET HOME HOW LATE	207	2
	TILL OPPOSITE--I SPIED A CHEEK	THE ROSE DID CAPER ON	208	9
	I TASTE A LIQUOR NEVER BREWED--	I TASTE A LIQUOR NEVER	214	1
	INEBRIATE OF AIR--AM I--	I TASTE A LIQUOR NEVER	214	5
	I SHALL BUT DRINK THE MORE!	I TASTE A LIQUOR NEVER	214	12
	AND THAT I--AM COMING--TOO--	WHAT IS--"PARADISE"--	215	6
	SO IF I GET LOST--THERE--EVER--	WHAT IS--"PARADISE"--	215	13
	I SHANT WALK THE "JASPER"--BAREFOOT--	WHAT IS--"PARADISE"--	215	15
	AND SO I TROUBLE THEE.	SAVIOR! I'VE NO ONE ELSE	217	2
	I AM THE ONE FORGOT THEE SO--	SAVIOR! I'VE NO ONE ELSE	217	3
	NOR, FOR MYSELF, I CAME SO FAR--	SAVIOR! I'VE NO ONE ELSE	217	5
	FATHER--I BRING THEE--NOT MYSELF--	SAVIOR! I'VE NO ONE ELSE	217	V 5
	I BROUGHT [BRING] THEE THE IMPERIAL [DEPARTED] HEART	SAVIOR! I'VE NO ONE ELSE	217	7
	I HAD NOT STRENGTH [POWER] TO HOLD--	SAVIOR! I'VE NO ONE ELSE	217	8
	THE HEART I CARRIED [CHERISHED] IN MY OWN--	SAVIOR! I'VE NO ONE ELSE	217	9
	I SHOULD'NT LIKE TO COME	IS IT TRUE, DEAR SUE?	218	3
	IF I COULD SHUT HIM UP	IS IT TRUE, DEAR SUE?	218	5
	TILL I GOT IN--	IS IT TRUE, DEAR SUE?	218	8
	AND THEN I COME AWAY--	SHE SWEEPS WITH	219	12
	COULD I--THEN--SHUT THE DOOR--	COULD I--THEN--SHUT THE	220	1
	I CAME TO BUY A SMILE--TODAY--	I CAME TO BUY A SMILE--	223	1
	SAY--MAY I HAVE IT--SIR?	I CAME TO BUY A SMILE--	223	14
	SO I KEEP BRINGING THESE--	I'VE NOTHING ELSE--TO	224	2
	WE--BEE AND I--LIVE BY THE QUAFFING--	WE--BEE AND I--LIVE BY	230	1
	I--NEVER WED--	WE--BEE AND I--LIVE BY	230	9
	HE AND I--REVEL--	WE--BEE AND I--LIVE BY	230	13
	I MET ONE--FORGOT MY SCHOOLMATES--	GOD PERMITS INDUSTRIOUS	231	3
	I MISSED MINE--HOW DREARY--MARBLES--	GOD PERMITS INDUSTRIOUS	231	7
	I GUESS--	YOU'RE RIGHT--"THE WAY	234	12
	NO UMPIRE--HAVE I--	THE COURT IS FAR AWAY--	235	2
	AS SMALL--THEY SAY--AS I--	THE COURT IS FAR AWAY--	235	10
	I THINK JUST HOW MY SHAPE WILL RISE--	I THINK JUST HOW MY	237	1
	WHEN I SHALL BE "FORGIVEN"--	I THINK JUST HOW MY	237	2
	I THINK JUST HOW MY LIPS WILL WEIGH--	I THINK JUST HOW MY	237	5
	I MIND ME THAT OF ANGUISH--SENT--	I THINK JUST HOW MY	237	9
	AND SO I CON THAT THING--"FORGIVEN"--	I THINK JUST HOW MY	237	13
	I DROP MY HEART--UNSHRIVEN!	I THINK JUST HOW MY	237	16
	"CAROL FOR HIM--WHEN I AM GONE"!	KILL YOUR BALM--AND IT'S	238	8
	"HEAVEN"--IS WHAT I CANNOT REACH!	"HEAVEN"--IS WHAT I	239	1
	I COULD BORROW A BONNET	AH, MOON--AND STAR!	240	8
	SO I CAN NEVER [AND I CANNOT] GO!	AH, MOON--AND STAR!	240	17
	I LIKE A LOOK OF AGONY,	I LIKE A LOOK OF AGONY,	241	1
	BECAUSE I KNOW IT'S TRUE--	I LIKE A LOOK OF AGONY,	241	2
	I HELD A JEWEL IN MY FINGERS--	I HELD A JEWEL IN MY	245	1
	I SAID "'TWILL KEEP"--	I HELD A JEWEL IN MY	245	4
	I WOKE--AND CHID MY HONEST FINGERS,	I HELD A JEWEL IN MY	245	5
	IS ALL I OWN--	I HELD A JEWEL IN MY	245	8
	WHAT WOULD I GIVE TO SEE HIS FACE?	WHAT WOULD I GIVE TO SEE	247	1
	THEN I HAVE "SHARES" IN PRIMROSE "BANKS"--	WHAT WOULD I GIVE TO SEE	247	15
	NOW--HAVE I BOUGHT IT--	WHAT WOULD I GIVE TO SEE	247	21
	"I VOW TO PAY	WHAT WOULD I GIVE TO SEE	247	24
	DID I SING--TOO LOUD?	WHY--DO THEY SHUT ME OUT	248	2
	BUT--I CAN SAY A LITTLE "MINOR"	WHY--DO THEY SHUT ME OUT	248	3
	JUST--SEE--IF I TROUBLED THEM--	WHY--DO THEY SHUT ME OUT	248	7
	OH, IF I--WERE THE GENTLEMAN	WHY--DO THEY SHUT ME OUT	248	9

I (CONTINUED)	FIRST LINE	POEM	LINE
COULD--I--FORBID?	WHY--DO THEY SHUT ME OUT	248	12
WERE I WITH THEE	WILD NIGHTS--WILD NIGHTS	249	2
MIGHT I BUT MOOR--TONIGHT--	WILD NIGHTS--WILD NIGHTS	249	11
I SHALL KEEP SINGING!	I SHALL KEEP SINGING!	250	1
I--WITH MY REDBREAST--	I SHALL KEEP SINGING!	250	5
LATE--WHEN I TAKE MY PLACE IN SUMMER--	I SHALL KEEP SINGING!	250	7
BUT--I SHALL BRING A FULLER TUNE--	I SHALL KEEP SINGING!	250	8
I COULD CLIMB--IF I TRIED, I KNOW--	OVER THE FENCE--	251	4
I COULD CLIMB--IF I TRIED, I KNOW--	OVER THE FENCE--	251	4
I COULD CLIMB--IF I TRIED, I KNOW--	OVER THE FENCE--	251	4
BUT--IF I STAINED MY APRON--	OVER THE FENCE--	251	6
OH, DEAR,--I GUESS IF HE WERE A BOY--	OVER THE FENCE--	251	8
I CAN WADE GRIEF--	I CAN WADE GRIEF--	252	1
AND I TIP--DRUNKEN--	I CAN WADE GRIEF--	252	6
YOU SEE I CANNOT SEE--YOUR LIFETIME--	YOU SEE I CANNOT SEE--	253	1
I MUST GUESS--	YOU SEE I CANNOT SEE--	253	2
BUT I GUESS GUESSING HURTS--	YOU SEE I CANNOT SEE--	253	6
THAT I WAS FOUND--	IF I'M LOST--NOW--	256	2
I ASKED THE EAST,	DELIGHT IS AS THE FLIGHT	257	11
AND I, FOR GLEE,	DELIGHT IS AS THE FLIGHT	257	15
SINCE THE SOLE EAR I CARED TO CHARM--	PUT UP MY LUTE!	261	3
THEN I WILL, WHEN ON THE EVERLASTING HILL	ME, CHANGE! ME, ALTER!	268	2
YET I--FOR IT--WOULD PAY--	ONE LIFE OF SO MUCH	270	2
THAT I WOULD INSTANT DIVE--	ONE LIFE OF SO MUCH	270	6
ALTHOUGH--I KNEW--TO TAKE IT--	ONE LIFE OF SO MUCH	270	7
THE SEA IS FULL--I KNOW IT!	ONE LIFE OF SO MUCH	270	9
THE LIFE IS THICK--I KNOW IT!	ONE LIFE OF SO MUCH	270	13
A SOLEMN THING--IT WAS--I SAID--	A SOLEMN THING--IT WAS--	271	1
I PONDERED HOW THE BLISS WOULD LOOK--	A SOLEMN THING--IT WAS--	271	9
WHEN I COULD TAKE IT IN MY HAND--	A SOLEMN THING--IT WAS--	271	11
AND I SNEERED--SOFTLY--"SMALL"!	A SOLEMN THING--IT WAS--	271	16
I BREATHED ENOUGH TO TAKE THE TRICK--	I BREATHED ENOUGH TO	272	1
I SIMULATE THE BREATH, SO WELL--	I BREATHED ENOUGH TO	272	3
I HEARD THE BUCKLE SNAP--	HE PUT THE BELT AROUND	273	2
FOR WHOM I MUST DECLINE?	HE PUT THE BELT AROUND	273	16
THE ONLY GHOST I EVER SAW	THE ONLY GHOST I EVER	274	1
AND GOD FORBID I LOOK BEHIND--	THE ONLY GHOST I EVER	274	15
SAY QUICK, THAT I MAY [SO I CAN] DOWER THEE	DOUBT ME! MY DIM	275	7
SAY QUICK, THAT I MAY [SO I CAN] DOWER THEE	DOUBT ME! MY DIM	275	7
WITH LAST [LEAST] DELIGHT I OWN!	DOUBT ME! MY DIM	275	8
I CEDED ALL OF DUST I KNEW--	DOUBT ME! MY DIM	275	11
I CEDED ALL OF DUST I KNEW--	DOUBT ME! MY DIM	275	11
HAD I--A FRECKLED MAIDEN,	DOUBT ME! MY DIM	275	13
I HAVE HEARD BUT ONE--	MANY A PHRASE HAS THE	276	2
TILL I STIR [GROPE / START], AND WEEP--	MANY A PHRASE HAS THE	276	12
WHAT IF I SAY I SHALL NOT WAIT!	WHAT IF I SAY I SHALL	277	1
WHAT IF I SAY I SHALL NOT WAIT!	WHAT IF I SAY I SHALL	277	1
WHAT IF I BURST THE FLESHLY GATE--	WHAT IF I SAY I SHALL	277	2
WHAT IF I FILE THIS MORTAL--OFF--	WHAT IF I SAY I SHALL	277	4
THEN, I AM READY TO GO!	TIE THE STRINGS TO MY	279	2
SO I SHALL NEVER FALL--	TIE THE STRINGS TO MY	279	6
BUT NEVER I MIND THE STEEPEST [BRIDGES]--	TIE THE STRINGS TO MY	279	9
AND NEVER I MIND THE SEA--	TIE THE STRINGS TO MY	279	10
GOODBYE TO THE LIFE I USED TO LIVE--	TIE THE STRINGS TO MY	279	13
AND THE WORLD I USED TO KNOW--	TIE THE STRINGS TO MY	279	14
THEN [NOW]--I AM READY TO GO!	TIE THE STRINGS TO MY	279	16
I FELT A FUNERAL, IN MY BRAIN,	I FELT A FUNERAL, IN MY	280	1
KEPT BEATING--BEATING--TILL I THOUGHT	I FELT A FUNERAL, IN MY	280	7
AND THEN I HEARD THEM LIFT A BOX	I FELT A FUNERAL, IN MY	280	9
AND I, AND SILENCE, SOME STRANGE RACE	I FELT A FUNERAL, IN MY	280	15
AND I DROPPED DOWN, AND DOWN--	I FELT A FUNERAL, IN MY	280	18
AS I--TOWARD [IN] THEE--	THE DROP, THAT WRESTLES	284	3
BECAUSE I GROW--WHERE ROBINS DO--	THE ROBIN'S MY CRITERION	285	2
BUT, WERE I CUCKOO BORN--	THE ROBIN'S MY CRITERION	285	3
BUT, WERE I BRITAIN BORN,	THE ROBIN'S MY CRITERION	285	8
BECAUSE I SEE--NEW ENGLANDLY--	THE ROBIN'S MY CRITERION	285	15
I KNOW SOME LONELY HOUSES OFF THE ROAD	I KNOW SOME LONELY	289	1
TILL I TAKE VASTER ATTITUDES [MANNERS]--	OF BRONZE--AND BLAZE--	290	10
WHEN I, AM LONG AGO,	OF BRONZE--AND BLAZE--	290	17
HAVE I THE LIP OF THE FLAMINGO	HOW THE OLD MOUNTAINS	291	7
THAT I DARE TO TELL?	HOW THE OLD MOUNTAINS	291	8
I GOT SO I COULD HEAR [THINK / TAKE] HIS NAME--	I GOT SO I COULD HEAR	293	1
I GOT SO I COULD HEAR [THINK / TAKE] HIS NAME--	I GOT SO I COULD HEAR	293	1
I GOT SO I COULD WALK ACROSS	I GOT SO I COULD HEAR	293	5
I GOT SO I COULD WALK ACROSS	I GOT SO I COULD HEAR	293	5
WHERE HE TURNED SO, AND I TURNED--HOW [LET GO]--	I GOT SO I COULD HEAR	293	7
I GOT SO I COULD STIR THE BOX--	I GOT SO I COULD HEAR	293	9
I GOT SO I COULD STIR THE BOX--	I GOT SO I COULD HEAR	293	9
I THINK, THEY CALL IT "GOD"--	I GOT SO I COULD HEAR	293	14
THAT I--GROWN BOLD--	UNTO LIKE STORY--TROUBLE	295	14
GOD--SPELL THE WORD! I--CANT--	ONE YEAR AGO--JOTS WHAT?	296	2
I TASTED--CARELESS--THEN--	ONE YEAR AGO--JOTS WHAT?	296	12
I DID NOT KNOW THE WINE	ONE YEAR AGO--JOTS WHAT?	296	13
PERHAPS--I COULD'NT--	ONE YEAR AGO--JOTS WHAT?	296	21
ALONE, I CANNOT BE--	ALONE, I CANNOT BE--	298	1
AND I ESTEEMED ALL POVERTY	YOUR RICHES--TAUGHT ME--	299	7

	FIRST LINE	POEM	LINE
I (CONTINUED)			
OF MINES, I LITTLE KNOW--MYSELF--	YOUR RICHES--TAUGHT ME--	299	9
SO MUCH, THAT DID I MEET THE QUEEN--	YOUR RICHES--TAUGHT ME--	299	13
HER GLORY I SHOULD KNOW--	YOUR RICHES--TAUGHT ME--	299	14
MIGHT I--BUT BE THE JEW--	YOUR RICHES--TAUGHT ME--	299	20
I'M SURE [I KNOW] IT IS GOLCONDA--	YOUR RICHES--TAUGHT ME--	299	21
ALTHO' I PROVE IT, JUST IN TIME	YOUR RICHES--TAUGHT ME--	299	27
I REASON, EARTH IS SHORT--	I REASON, EARTH IS SHORT	301	1
I REASON, WE COULD [SHOULD] DIE--	I REASON, EARTH IS SHORT	301	5
I REASON, THAT IN HEAVEN--	I REASON, EARTH IS SHORT	301	9
THE LINGERING--AND THE STAIN--I MEAN--	THE ONE WHO COULD REPEAT	307	6
I SEND TWO SUNSETS--	I SEND TWO SUNSETS--	308	1
DAY AND I--IN COMPETITION RAN--	I SEND TWO SUNSETS--	308	2
I FINISHED TWO--AND SEVERAL STARS--	I SEND TWO SUNSETS--	308	3
HIS OWN WAS [IS] AMPLER--BUT AS I	I SEND TWO SUNSETS--	308	5
FOR LARGEST WOMAN'S HEART I KNEW--	FOR LARGEST WOMAN'S	309	1
'TIS LITTLE I CAN DO--	FOR LARGEST WOMAN'S	309	2
I TENDERER, TURN ME TO.	FOR LARGEST WOMAN'S	309	6
I SHOULD HAVE BEEN TOO GLAD, I SEE--	I SHOULD HAVE BEEN TOO	313	1
I SHOULD HAVE BEEN TOO GLAD, I SEE--	I SHOULD HAVE BEEN TOO	313	1
I SHOULD HAVE BEEN TOO SAVED--I SEE--	I SHOULD HAVE BEEN TOO	313	7
I SHOULD HAVE BEEN TOO SAVED--I SEE--	I SHOULD HAVE BEEN TOO	313	7
THAT I COULD SPELL THE PRAYER	I SHOULD HAVE BEEN TOO	313	9
I KNEW SO PERFECT--YESTERDAY--	I SHOULD HAVE BEEN TOO	313	10
EARTH WOULD HAVE BEEN TOO MUCH--I SEE--	I SHOULD HAVE BEEN TOO	313	13
I SHOULD HAVE HAD THE JOY	I SHOULD HAVE BEEN TOO	313	15
AND A HOARSE "GET OUT OF THE WAY, I SAY,"	THE WIND DID'NT COME	316	20
HEART! I AM KNOCKING--LOW AT THEE.	JUST SO--JESUS--RAPS--	317	11
THEN I SAID SOFTLY TO MYSELF--	I'LL TELL YOU HOW THE	318	7
BUT HOW HE SET--I KNOW NOT--	I'LL TELL YOU HOW THE	318	9
I CANNOT VOUCH THE MERRY DUST	OF ALL THE SOUNDS	321	17
I CRAVE HIM GRACE OF SUMMER BOUGHS,	OF ALL THE SOUNDS	321	25
I THOUGHT THAT SUCH WERE FOR THE SAINTS,	THERE CAME A DAY AT	322	3
AS IF I ASKED A COMMON ALMS,	AS IF I ASKED A COMMON	323	1
AND I, BEWILDERED, STAND--	AS IF I ASKED A COMMON	323	4
AS IF I ASKED THE ORIENT	AS IF I ASKED A COMMON	323	5
I KEEP IT, STAYING AT HOME--	SOME KEEP THE SABBATH	324	2
I JUST WEAR MY WINGS--	SOME KEEP THE SABBATH	324	6
I CANNOT DANCE UPON MY TOES--	I CANNOT DANCE UPON MY	326	1
THAT HAD I BALLET KNOWLEDGE--	I CANNOT DANCE UPON MY	326	5
AND THOUGH I HAD NO GOWN OF GAUZE--	I CANNOT DANCE UPON MY	326	9
TILL I WAS OUT OF SIGHT, IN SOUND,	I CANNOT DANCE UPON MY	326	15
NOR ANY KNOW [KNEW] I KNOW THE ART	I CANNOT DANCE UPON MY	326	17
I MENTION--EASY--HERE--	I CANNOT DANCE UPON MY	326	18
BEFORE I GOT MY EYE PUT OUT	BEFORE I GOT MY EYE PUT	327	1
I LIKED AS WELL TO SEE--	BEFORE I GOT MY EYE PUT	327	2
THAT I MIGHT HAVE THE SKY	BEFORE I GOT MY EYE PUT	327	6
FOR MINE--I TELL YOU THAT MY HEART	BEFORE I GOT MY EYE PUT	327	7
AS MUCH OF NOON AS I COULD TAKE	BEFORE I GOT MY EYE PUT	327	12
FOR MINE--TO LOOK AT WHEN I LIKED--	BEFORE I GOT MY EYE PUT	327	16
HE DID NOT KNOW I SAW--	A BIRD CAME DOWN THE	328	2
THEY LOOKED LIKE FRIGHTENED BEADS, I THOUGHT--	A BIRD CAME DOWN THE	328	11
I OFFERED HIM A CRUMB	A BIRD CAME DOWN THE	328	14
I WISH I WERE A HAY--	THE GRASS SO LITTLE HAS	333	20
I WISH I WERE A HAY--	THE GRASS SO LITTLE HAS	333	20
ALL THE LETTERS I CAN [COULD] WRITE	ALL THE LETTERS I CAN	334	1
THE FACE I CARRY WITH ME--LAST--	THE FACE I CARRY WITH ME	336	1
WHEN I GO OUT OF TIME--	THE FACE I CARRY WITH ME	336	2
I KNOW A PLACE WHERE SUMMER STRIVES	I KNOW A PLACE WHERE	337	1
I KNOW THAT HE EXISTS.	I KNOW THAT HE EXISTS.	338	1
I TEND MY FLOWERS FOR THEE--	I TEND MY FLOWERS FOR	339	1
A HYACINTH--I HID--	I TEND MY FLOWERS FOR	339	11
I HAD AS LIEF THEY BORE	I TEND MY FLOWERS FOR	339	19
I MUST NOT PUT MY FOOT AMISS	IS BLISS THEN, SUCH	340	2
FOR FEAR I SPOIL MY SHOE?	IS BLISS THEN, SUCH	340	3
I--SHOULD DIE OF THE ODDITY--	FUNNY--TO BE A CENTURY--	345	3
I DREADED THAT FIRST ROBIN, SO,	I DREADED THAT FIRST	348	1
I THOUGHT IF I COULD ONLY LIVE	I DREADED THAT FIRST	348	5
I THOUGHT IF I COULD ONLY LIVE	I DREADED THAT FIRST	348	5
I DARED NOT MEET THE DAFFODILS--	I DREADED THAT FIRST	348	9
I WISHED THE GRASS WOULD HURRY--	I DREADED THAT FIRST	348	13
I COULD NOT BEAR THE BEES SHOULD COME,	I DREADED THAT FIRST	348	17
I WISHED THEY'D STAY AWAY	I DREADED THAT FIRST	348	18
AND I, MY CHILDISH PLUMES,	I DREADED THAT FIRST	348	26
I HAD THE GLORY--THAT WILL DO--	I HAD THE GLORY--THAT	349	1
YOU FOR YOU, AND I, FOR YOU AND ME	THEY LEAVE US WITH THE	350	10
I FELT MY LIFE WITH BOTH MY HANDS	I FELT MY LIFE WITH BOTH	351	1
I HELD MY SPIRIT TO THE GLASS,	I FELT MY LIFE WITH BOTH	351	3
I TURNED MY BEING ROUND AND ROUND	I FELT MY LIFE WITH BOTH	351	5
FOR DOUBT, THAT I SHOULD KNOW THE SOUND--	I FELT MY LIFE WITH BOTH	351	8
I JUDGED MY FEATURES--JARRED MY HAIR--	I FELT MY LIFE WITH BOTH	351	9
I PUSHED MY DIMPLES BY, AND WAITED--	I FELT MY LIFE WITH BOTH	351	10
I TOLD MYSELF, "TAKE COURAGE, FRIEND--	I FELT MY LIFE WITH BOTH	351	13
PERHAPS I ASKED TOO LARGE--	PERHAPS I ASKED TOO	352	1
I TAKE--NO LESS THAN SKIES--	PERHAPS I ASKED TOO	352	2
WITHOUT DESIGN--THAT I COULD TRACE	FROM COCOON FORTH A	354	5
THE DAY THAT I WAS CROWNED	THE DAY THAT I WAS	356	1
I ROSE, AND ALL WAS PLAIN--	THE DAY THAT I WAS	356	9
THE GRACE THAT I--WAS CHOSE--	THE DAY THAT I WAS	356	13
I GAINED IT SO--	I GAINED IT SO--	359	1

I (CONTINUED)

	FIRST LINE	POEM	LINE
I SAID I GAINED IT--	I GAINED IT SO--	359	8
I SAID I GAINED IT--	I GAINED IT SO--	359	8
LOOK, HOW I CLUTCH IT	I GAINED IT SO--	359	10
AND I A PAUPER GO--	I GAINED IT SO--	359	12
I WORE--AN HOUR AGO--	I GAINED IT SO--	359	15
A BOOK I HAVE--A FRIEND GAVE--	DEATH SETS A THING	360	13
NOW--WHEN I READ--I READ NOT--	DEATH SETS A THING	360	17
NOW--WHEN I READ--I READ NOT--	DEATH SETS A THING	360	17
WHAT I CAN DO--I WILL--	WHAT I CAN DO--I WILL--	361	1
WHAT I CAN DO--I WILL--	WHAT I CAN DO--I WILL--	361	1
THAT I CANNOT--MUST BE	WHAT I CAN DO--I WILL--	361	3
I THOUGHT THAT STORM--WAS BRIEF--	IT STRUCK ME--EVERY DAY	362	9
I WENT TO THANK HER--	I WENT TO THANK HER--	363	1
ALTHOUGH I PUT AWAY HIS LIFE--	ALTHOUGH I PUT AWAY HIS	366	1
I NEVER WOULD LET GO--	ALTHOUGH I PUT AWAY HIS	366	12
A LITTLE BOOT I KNOW--	ALTHOUGH I PUT AWAY HIS	366	14
THAT I MAY TAKE THAT PROMISE	ALTHOUGH I PUT AWAY HIS	366	30
I KNEW LAST NIGHT--WHEN SOMEONE TRIED TO TWINE--	HOW SICK--TO WAIT--IN	368	2
THINKING--PERHAPS--THAT I LOOKED TIRED--OR ALONE--	HOW SICK--TO WAIT--IN	368	3
AND I TURNED--DUCAL--	HOW SICK--TO WAIT--IN	368	5
DEVISING, I AM SURE--	SHE LAY AS IF AT PLAY	369	14
A PRIVILEGE--I THINK--	A PRECIOUS--MOULDERING	371	4
I KNOW LIVES, I COULD MISS	I KNOW LIVES, I COULD	372	1
I KNOW LIVES, I COULD MISS	I KNOW LIVES, I COULD	372	1
"IF I SHOULD BE A QUEEN, TOMORROW"--	I'M SAYING EVERY DAY	373	2
AND SO I DECK, A LITTLE,	I'M SAYING EVERY DAY	373	4
IF IT BE, I WAKE A BOURBON,	I'M SAYING EVERY DAY	373	5
SO I LOOP MY APRON, AGAINST THE MAJESTY	I'M SAYING EVERY DAY	373	12
TAKE OTHER ACCENTS, AS SUCH I HEARD	I'M SAYING EVERY DAY	373	21
I WENT TO HEAVEN--	I WENT TO HEAVEN--	374	1
I--COULD BE--	I WENT TO HEAVEN--	374	14
THAT EVERY TIME I WAKE--	THE ANGLE OF A LANDSCAPE	375	2
I WAKE--TO FIND NO--EMERALDS--	THE ANGLE OF A LANDSCAPE	375	15
OF COURSE--I PRAYED--	OF COURSE--I PRAYED--	376	1
I HAD NOT HAD--BUT FOR YOURSELF--	OF COURSE--I PRAYED--	376	7
I SAW NO WAY--THE HEAVENS WERE STITCHED--	I SAW NO WAY--THE	378	1
I FELT THE COLUMNS CLOSE--	I SAW NO WAY--THE	378	2
I TOUCHED THE UNIVERSE--	I SAW NO WAY--THE	378	4
AND BACK IT SLID--AND I ALONE--	I SAW NO WAY--THE	378	5
I KNOW IT, BY THE NUMB LOOK	THERE'S BEEN A DEATH, IN	389	3
I USED TO--WHEN A BOY--	THERE'S BEEN A DEATH, IN	389	12
I BROOCH AND EARRINGS FOR MYSELF,	WHEN DIAMONDS ARE A	397	3
I HAD NOT MINDED--WALLS--	I HAD NOT MINDED--WALLS	398	1
AND FAR I HEARD HIS SILVER CALL	I HAD NOT MINDED--WALLS	398	3
A TONGUE--TO TELL HIM I AM TRUE!	A TONGUE--TO TELL HIM I	400	1
AND ANSWER WHAT I DO--	A TONGUE--TO TELL HIM I	400	9
SAY--LAST I SAID--WAS THIS--	A TONGUE--TO TELL HIM I	400	22
I PAY--IN SATIN CASH--	I PAY--IN SATIN CASH--	402	1
IS NEAR AS I CAN GUESS--	I PAY--IN SATIN CASH--	402	4
I AM NOT USED TO HOPE--	IT MIGHT BE LONELIER	405	9
I TOLD MY SOUL TO SING--	THE FIRST DAY'S NIGHT	410	4
I MUMBLED--LIKE A FOOL--	THE FIRST DAY'S NIGHT	410	14
THAT PERSON THAT I WAS--	THE FIRST DAY'S NIGHT	410	18
THE OUTER GRAVE--I MEAN--	THE COLOR OF THE GRAVE	411	2
THE OUTER GRAVE--I MEAN--	THE COLOR OF THE GRAVE	411	10
THE DUPLICATE--I MEAN--	THE COLOR OF THE GRAVE	411	18
I READ MY SENTENCE--STEADILY--	I READ MY SENTENCE--	412	1
TO SEE THAT I MADE NO MISTAKE	I READ MY SENTENCE--	412	3
I MADE MY SOUL FAMILIAR--WITH HER EXTREMITY--	I READ MY SENTENCE--	412	9
I NEVER FELT AT HOME--BELOW--	I NEVER FELT AT HOME--	413	1
I SHALL NOT FEEL AT HOME--I KNOW--	I NEVER FELT AT HOME--	413	3
I SHALL NOT FEEL AT HOME--I KNOW--	I NEVER FELT AT HOME--	413	3
I DONT LIKE PARADISE--	I NEVER FELT AT HOME--	413	4
ALL THIS--AND MORE--IF I SHOULD TELL--	A MURMUR IN THE TREES--	416	11
HOW MANY I ESPY	A MURMUR IN THE TREES--	416	14
ALTHOUGH I HEARD THEM TRY--	A MURMUR IN THE TREES--	416	16
BUT THEN I PROMISED NE'ER TO TELL--	A MURMUR IN THE TREES--	416	17
HOW COULD I BREAK MY WORD?	A MURMUR IN THE TREES--	416	18
SOUNDS LONG--UNTIL I READ THE PLACE	NOT IN THIS WORLD TO SEE	418	2
I WOULD NOT CHOOSE--A BOOK TO KNOW	NOT IN THIS WORLD TO SEE	418	8
HOW COULD I--OF HIM?	GOOD MORNING--MIDNIGHT--	425	4
I LIKED TO STAY--	GOOD MORNING--MIDNIGHT--	425	6
I CAN LOOK--CANT I--	GOOD MORNING--MIDNIGHT--	425	9
I CAN LOOK--CANT I--	GOOD MORNING--MIDNIGHT--	425	9
I CHOSE--DAY--	GOOD MORNING--MIDNIGHT--	425	14
I RUN IT OVER--"DEAD", BRAIN, "DEAD."	IT DONT SOUND SO	426	2
I SHALL HAVE WADED DOWN ONE DAY".	IT DONT SOUND SO	426	9
I SUPPOSE IT WILL INTERRUPT ME SOME	IT DONT SOUND SO	426	10
TILL I GET ACCUSTOMED--BUT THEN THE TOMB	IT DONT SOUND SO	426	11
JUST AS HIGH--AS I--	I'LL CLUTCH--AND CLUTCH	427	19
AND--WHEN I DIE--	I'LL CLUTCH--AND CLUTCH	427	20
STILL TO SHOW--HOW RICH I GO--	I'LL CLUTCH--AND CLUTCH	427	22
IT WOULD NEVER BE COMMON--MORE--I SAID--	IT WOULD NEVER BE COMMON	430	1
SUCH BLISS--HAD I--FOR ALL THE YEARS--	IT WOULD NEVER BE COMMON	430	7
I'D SO MUCH JOY--I TOLD IT--RED--	IT WOULD NEVER BE COMMON	430	9
I FELT IT PUBLISH--IN MY EYE--	IT WOULD NEVER BE COMMON	430	11
I WALKED--AS WINGS--MY BODY BORE--	IT WOULD NEVER BE COMMON	430	13

		FIRST LINE	POEM	LINE
I	(CONTINUED)			
	THE FEET--I FORMER USED--	IT WOULD NEVER BE COMMON	430	14
	I PUT MY PLEASURE ALL ABROAD--	IT WOULD NEVER BE COMMON	430	17
	I DEALT A WORD OF GOLD	IT WOULD NEVER BE COMMON	430	18
	TO EVERY CREATURE--THAT I MET--	IT WOULD NEVER BE COMMON	430	19
	I CLUTCHED AT SOUNDS--	IT WOULD NEVER BE COMMON	430	25
	I GROPED AT SHAPES--	IT WOULD NEVER BE COMMON	430	26
	I TOUCHED THE TOPS OF FILMS--	IT WOULD NEVER BE COMMON	430	27
	I FELT THE WILDERNESS ROLL BACK	IT WOULD NEVER BE COMMON	430	28
	THE FROCK I USED TO WEAR--	IT WOULD NEVER BE COMMON	430	31
	I DO BELIEVE A SPECIES	DO PEOPLE MOULDER	432	3
	AS I, WHO TESTIFY IT	DO PEOPLE MOULDER	432	5
	DENY THAT I--AM DEAD--	DO PEOPLE MOULDER	432	6
	I SAY TO YOU, SAID JESUS--	DO PEOPLE MOULDER	432	9
	I NEED NO FURTHER ARGUE--	DO PEOPLE MOULDER	432	13
	I SHOULD LIKE TO KNOW--	KNOWS HOW TO FORGET!	433	4
	I--WHO PORED--PATIENT--	KNOWS HOW TO FORGET!	433	6
	I WOULD GIVE YOU--	KNOWS HOW TO FORGET!	433	13
	I WENT TO SCHOOL	KNOWS HOW TO FORGET!	433	V
	SO, I COULD BUY IT--	KNOWS HOW TO FORGET!	433	V
	FOREVER MIGHT BE SHORT, I THOUGHT TO SHOW--	TO LOVE THEE YEAR BY	434	5
	AND SO I PIECED IT, WITH A FLOWER, NOW.	TO LOVE THEE YEAR BY	434	6
	I BOLDLY ANSWERED--ENTERED THEN	THE WIND--TAPPED LIKE A	436	3
	AND I BECAME ALONE--	THE WIND--TAPPED LIKE A	436	20
	TO HANDS I CANNOT SEE--	THIS IS MY LETTER TO THE	441	6
	CREATOR--SHALL I--BLOOM?	GOD MADE A LITTLE	442	12
	I TIE MY HAT--I CREASE MY SHAWL--	I TIE MY HAT--I CREASE	443	1
	I TIE MY HAT--I CREASE MY SHAWL--	I TIE MY HAT--I CREASE	443	1
	I PUT NEW BLOSSOMS IN THE GLASS--	I TIE MY HAT--I CREASE	443	5
	I PUSH A PETAL FROM MY GOWN	I TIE MY HAT--I CREASE	443	7
	THAT ANCHORED THERE--I WEIGH	I TIE MY HAT--I CREASE	443	8
	I HAVE SO MUCH TO DO--	I TIE MY HAT--I CREASE	443	10
	I THINK THE MEN WHO DIE--	IT FEELS A SHAME TO BE	444	18
	'TWAS JUST THIS TIME, LAST YEAR, I DIED.	'TWAS JUST THIS TIME,	445	1
	I KNOW I HEARD THE CORN,	'TWAS JUST THIS TIME,	445	2
	I KNOW I HEARD THE CORN,	'TWAS JUST THIS TIME,	445	2
	WHEN I WAS CARRIED BY THE FARMS--	'TWAS JUST THIS TIME,	445	3
	I THOUGHT HOW YELLOW IT WOULD LOOK--	'TWAS JUST THIS TIME,	445	5
	AND THEN, I WANTED TO GET OUT,	'TWAS JUST THIS TIME,	445	7
	I THOUGHT JUST HOW RED--APPLES WEDGED	'TWAS JUST THIS TIME,	445	9
	I WONDERED WHICH WOULD MISS ME, LEAST,	'TWAS JUST THIS TIME,	445	13
	AND SO, I THOUGHT THE OTHER WAY,	'TWAS JUST THIS TIME,	445	22
	I [HE] SHOWED HER [ME] HIGHTS SHE [I] NEVER SAW--	I SHOWED HER HIGHTS SHE	446	1
	I [HE] SHOWED HER [ME] HIGHTS SHE [I] NEVER SAW--	I SHOWED HER HIGHTS SHE	446	1
	"WOULD'ST CLIMB," I [HE] SAID?	I SHOWED HER HIGHTS SHE	446	2
	SHE [I] SAID--"NOT SO"--	I SHOWED HER HIGHTS SHE	446	3
	"WITH ME--" I [HE] SAID--WITH ME?	I SHOWED HER HIGHTS SHE	446	4
	I [HE] SHOWED HER [ME] SECRETS--MORNING'S NEST--	I SHOWED HER HIGHTS SHE	446	5
	SHE [I] COULD NOT FIND HER [MY] YES--	I SHOWED HER HIGHTS SHE	446	8
	AND THEN, I [HE] BRAKE MY [HIS] LIFE--AND LO,	I SHOWED HER HIGHTS SHE	446	9
	AND COULD SHE [I], FURTHER, "NO"?	I SHOWED HER HIGHTS SHE	446	12
	COULD--I DO MORE--FOR THEE--	COULD--I DO MORE--FOR	447	1
	SINCE FOR THE QUEEN, HAVE I--	COULD--I DO MORE--FOR	447	3
	I DIED FOR BEAUTY--BUT WAS SCARCE	I DIED FOR BEAUTY--BUT	449	1
	HE QUESTIONED SOFTLY "WHY I FAILED"?	I DIED FOR BEAUTY--BUT	449	5
	"FOR BEAUTY", I REPLIED--	I DIED FOR BEAUTY--BUT	449	6
	"AND I--FOR TRUTH--THEMSELF ARE ONE--	I DIED FOR BEAUTY--BUT	449	7
	NOT--I--THE EARL--	THE MALAY--TOOK THE	452	2
	I--FEARED THE SEA--TOO MUCH	THE MALAY--TOOK THE	452	3
	PRAYING THAT I MIGHT BE	THE MALAY--TOOK THE	452	5
	HAD I--THE JEWEL--GOT--	THE MALAY--TOOK THE	452	10
	I HAD NOT DEEMED A VEST	THE MALAY--TOOK THE	452	12
	I--WOOED IT--TOO--	THE MALAY--TOOK THE	452	15
	I CANNOT CLIMB THEE--	LOVE--THOU ART HIGH--	453	2
	I CANNOT CROSS THEE--	LOVE--THOU ART HIGH--	453	8
	WHEN I WAS A LITTLE GIRL--	IT WAS GIVEN TO ME BY	454	2
	I KEPT IT IN MY HAND--	IT WAS GIVEN TO ME BY	454	5
	I NEVER PUT IT DOWN--	IT WAS GIVEN TO ME BY	454	6
	I DID NOT DARE TO EAT--OR SLEEP--	IT WAS GIVEN TO ME BY	454	7
	I HEARD SUCH WORDS AS "RICH"--	IT WAS GIVEN TO ME BY	454	9
	SO WELL THAT I CAN LIVE WITHOUT--	SO WELL THAT I CAN LIVE	456	1
	I LOVE THEE--THEN HOW WELL IS THAT?	SO WELL THAT I CAN LIVE	456	2
	AS I--LOVE THEE--	SO WELL THAT I CAN LIVE	456	6
	SO LOOKED THE FACE I LOOKED UPON--	LIKE EYES THAT LOOKED ON	458	7
	I OFFERED IT NO HELP--	LIKE EYES THAT LOOKED ON	458	9
	I KNOW WHERE WELLS GROW--DROUGHTLESS WELLS--	I KNOW WHERE WELLS GROW	460	1
	IT HAS NO BUCKET--WERE I RICH	I KNOW WHERE WELLS GROW	460	9
	A BUCKET I WOULD BUY--	I KNOW WHERE WELLS GROW	460	10
	I READ IN AN OLD FASHIONED BOOK	I KNOW WHERE WELLS GROW	460	13
	I THINK A LITTLE WELL--LIKE MINE--	I KNOW WHERE WELLS GROW	460	19
	A WIFE--AT DAYBREAK I SHALL BE--	A WIFE--AT DAYBREAK I	461	1
	AT MIDNIGHT, I AM BUT [YET] A MAID,	A WIFE--AT DAYBREAK I	461	3
	THEN--MIDNIGHT, I HAVE PASSED FROM THEE	A WIFE--AT DAYBREAK I	461	5
	MIDNIGHT--GOOD NIGHT! I HEAR THEM CALL,	A WIFE--AT DAYBREAK I	461	7
	I FUMBLE AT MY CHILDHOOD'S PRAYER	A WIFE--AT DAYBREAK I	461	10
	I LIVE WITH HIM--I SEE HIS FACE--	I LIVE WITH HIM--I SEE	463	1
	I LIVE WITH HIM--I SEE HIS FACE--	I LIVE WITH HIM--I SEE	463	1

I (CONTINUED)	FIRST LINE	POEM	LINE
I GO NO MORE AWAY	I LIVE WITH HIM--I SEE	463	2
I LIVE WITH HIM--I HEAR HIS VOICE--	I LIVE WITH HIM--I SEE	463	9
I LIVE WITH HIM--I HEAR HIS VOICE--	I LIVE WITH HIM--I SEE	463	9
I STAND ALIVE--TODAY--	I LIVE WITH HIM--I SEE	463	10
I HEARD A FLY BUZZ--WHEN I DIED--	I HEARD A FLY BUZZ--WHEN	465	1
I HEARD A FLY BUZZ--WHEN I DIED--	I HEARD A FLY BUZZ--WHEN	465	1
I WILLED MY KEEPSAKES--SIGNED AWAY	I HEARD A FLY BUZZ--WHEN	465	9
I COULD NOT SEE TO SEE--	I HEARD A FLY BUZZ--WHEN	465	16
'TIS LITTLE I--COULD CARE FOR PEARLS--	'TIS LITTLE I--COULD	466	1
OR DIAMONDS--WHEN HAVE I	'TIS LITTLE I--COULD	466	6
I AM ALIVE--I GUESS--	I AM ALIVE--I GUESS--	470	1
I AM ALIVE--I GUESS--	I AM ALIVE--I GUESS--	470	1
AND IF I HOLD A GLASS	I AM ALIVE--I GUESS--	470	6
I AM ALIVE--BECAUSE	I AM ALIVE--I GUESS--	470	9
I AM NOT IN A ROOM--	I AM ALIVE--I GUESS--	470	10
I AM ALIVE--BECAUSE	I AM ALIVE--I GUESS--	470	17
I DO NOT OWN A HOUSE--	I AM ALIVE--I GUESS--	470	18
ALIVE--TWO-FOLD--THE BIRTH I HAD--	I AM ALIVE--I GUESS--	470	27
I HAD NOT HOPED--BEFORE--	EXCEPT THE HEAVEN HAD	472	4
I NEVER THOUGHT TO SEE--	EXCEPT THE HEAVEN HAD	472	6
I AM ASHAMED--I HIDE--	I AM ASHAMED--I HIDE--	473	1
I AM ASHAMED--I HIDE--	I AM ASHAMED--I HIDE--	473	1
WHAT RIGHT HAVE I--TO BE A BRIDE--	I AM ASHAMED--I HIDE--	473	2
"I SEE THEE" EACH RESPONDED STRAIGHT	THEY PUT US FAR APART--	474	7
I MEANT TO HAVE BUT MODEST NEEDS--	I MEANT TO HAVE BUT	476	1
AND LIFE AND I--KEEP EVEN--	I MEANT TO HAVE BUT	476	4
AND SO--UPON THIS WISE--I PRAYED--	I MEANT TO HAVE BUT	476	9
I LEFT THE PLACE, WITH ALL MY MIGHT--	I MEANT TO HAVE BUT	476	17
I THREW MY PRAYER AWAY--	I MEANT TO HAVE BUT	476	18
BUT I, GROWN SHREWDER--SCAN THE SKIES	I MEANT TO HAVE BUT	476	25
I HAD NO TIME TO HATE--	I HAD NO TIME TO HATE--	478	1
AMPLE I	I HAD NO TIME TO HATE--	478	5
NOR HAD I TIME TO LOVE--	I HAD NO TIME TO HATE--	478	7
I THOUGHT	I HAD NO TIME TO HATE--	478	11
"WHY DO I LOVE" YOU, SIR?	"WHY DO I LOVE" YOU, SIR	480	1
BECAUSE HE'S SUNRISE--AND I SEE--	"WHY DO I LOVE" YOU, SIR	480	18
I LOVE THEE--	"WHY DO I LOVE" YOU, SIR	480	20
I WAS THE SLIGHTEST IN THE HOUSE--	I WAS THE SLIGHTEST IN	486	1
I TOOK THE SMALLEST ROOM--	I WAS THE SLIGHTEST IN	486	2
SO STATIONED I COULD CATCH THE MINT	I WAS THE SLIGHTEST IN	486	5
I NEVER SPOKE--UNLESS ADDRESSED--	I WAS THE SLIGHTEST IN	486	10
I COULD NOT BEAR TO LIVE--ALOUD--	I WAS THE SLIGHTEST IN	486	12
AND ANY ONE I KNEW	I WAS THE SLIGHTEST IN	486	15
WERE GOING--I HAD OFTEN THOUGHT	I WAS THE SLIGHTEST IN	486	16
HOW NOTELESS--I COULD DIE--	I WAS THE SLIGHTEST IN	486	17
MY PLANE--AND I, TOGETHER WROUGHT	MYSELF WAS FORMED--A	488	3
WE--TEMPLES BUILD--I SAID--	MYSELF WAS FORMED--A	488	12
WHILE IT AND I LAP ONE AIR	WHILE IT IS ALIVE	491	3
SINCE I WAS WED--TO HIM--	THE WORLD--STANDS--	493	2
TELL HIM [HER] THE PAGE I DID'NT WRITE--[NEVER WROTE!]	GOING TO HIM! HAPPY	494	3
TELL HIM [HER]--I ONLY SAID THE SYNTAX--	GOING TO HIM! HAPPY	494	4
AND THEN YOU AND I, WERE SILENTER.	GOING TO HIM! HAPPY	494	17
BUT I NEVER DOUBTED HIM--	HE STRAINED MY FAITH--	497	10
MUST BE--I DESERVED--IT--	HE STRAINED MY FAITH--	497	V 10
STABBED--WHILE I SUED	HE STRAINED MY FAITH--	497	13
I ENVY SEAS, WHEREON HE RIDES--[THAT BEAR HIM]	I ENVY SEAS, WHEREON HE	498	1
I ENVY SPOKES OF WHEELS	I ENVY SEAS, WHEREON HE	498	2
I ENVY CROOKED [SPEECHLESS] HILLS	I ENVY SEAS, WHEREON HE	498	4
I ENVY NESTS OF SPARROWS--	I ENVY SEAS, WHEREON HE	498	9
I ENVY LIGHT--THAT WAKES HIM--	I ENVY SEAS, WHEREON HE	498	17
AND I REJOIN MY DOG,	WITHIN MY GARDEN, RIDES	500	12
AND HE AND I, PERPLEX US	WITHIN MY GARDEN, RIDES	500	13
I KNOW NOT WHICH THY CHAMBER IS [PALACES]--	AT LEAST--TO PRAY--IS	502	3
BETTER--THAN MUSIC! FOR I--WHO HEARD IT--	BETTER--THAN MUSIC! FOR	503	1
I WAS USED--TO THE BIRDS--BEFORE--	BETTER--THAN MUSIC! FOR	503	2
OF ALL TUNES I KNEW--AND MORE--	BETTER--THAN MUSIC! FOR	503	4
BUT--I WAS TELLING A TUNE--I HEARD--	BETTER--THAN MUSIC! FOR	503	16
BUT--I WAS TELLING A TUNE--I HEARD--	BETTER--THAN MUSIC! FOR	503	16
WHEN MOON'S AT FULL--'TIS THOU--I SAY--	YOU KNOW THAT PORTRAIT	504	9
WHEN CRESCENT--THOU ART WORN--I NOTE [MIND]--	YOU KNOW THAT PORTRAIT	504	11
I WOULD NOT PAINT--A PICTURE--	I WOULD NOT PAINT--A	505	1
I WOULD NOT TALK, LIKE CORNETS--	I WOULD NOT PAINT--A	505	9
NOR WOULD I BE A POET--	I WOULD NOT PAINT--A	505	17
HAD I THE ART TO STUN MYSELF	I WOULD NOT PAINT--A	505	23
HE TOUCHED ME, SO I LIVE TO KNOW	HE TOUCHED ME, SO I LIVE	506	1
I GROPED [PERISHED / DWELT] UPON HIS BREAST--	HE TOUCHED ME, SO I LIVE	506	3
AS IF I BREATHED SUPERIOR AIR--	HE TOUCHED ME, SO I LIVE	506	8
INTO THIS PORT, IF I MIGHT COME,	HE TOUCHED ME, SO I LIVE	506	13
AND I CHOOSE, JUST A CROWN [THRONE]--	I'M CEDED--I'VE STOPPED	508	19
IT WAS NOT DEATH, FOR I STOOD UP,	IT WAS NOT DEATH, FOR I	510	1
I FELT SIROCCOS--CRAWL--	IT WAS NOT DEATH, FOR I	510	6
THE FIGURES I HAVE SEEN	IT WAS NOT DEATH, FOR I	510	10
IF I COULD SEE YOU IN A YEAR,	IF YOU WERE COMING IN	511	5
EXHIBIT--I SUPPOSE	NO CROWD THAT HAS	515	2
I STARTED EARLY--TOOK MY DOG--	I STARTED EARLY--TOOK MY	520	1
AND THEN--I STARTED--TOO--	I STARTED EARLY--TOOK MY	520	16
I FELT HIS SILVER HEEL	I STARTED EARLY--TOOK MY	520	18
HAD I PRESUMED TO HOPE--	HAD I PRESUMED TO HOPE--	522	1

I (CONTINUED)

	FIRST LINE	POEM	LINE
HAD I PRESUMED TO GAIN	HAD I PRESUMED TO HOPE--	522	5
'TIS HONOR--THOUGH I DIE--	HAD I PRESUMED TO HOPE--	522	13
SWEET--YOU FORGOT--BUT I REMEMBERED	SWEET--YOU FORGOT--BUT I	523	1
SAY IF I ERRED? ACCUSE MY FARTHINGS--	SWEET--YOU FORGOT--BUT I	523	5
I THINK THE HEMLOCK LIKES TO STAND	I THINK THE HEMLOCK	525	1
I TRIED TO THINK A LONELIER THING	I TRIED TO THINK A	532	1
THAN ANY I HAD SEEN--	I TRIED TO THINK A	532	2
I PROBED RETRIEVELESS THINGS	I TRIED TO THINK A	532	5
I PLUCKED AT OUR PARTITION	I TRIED TO THINK A	532	12
I ALMOST STROVE TO CLASP HIS HAND,	I TRIED TO THINK A	532	16
I TOOK MY POWER IN MY HAND--	I TOOK MY POWER IN MY	540	1
BUT I--WAS TWICE AS BOLD--	I TOOK MY POWER IN MY	540	4
I AIMED MY PEBBLE--BUT MYSELF	I TOOK MY POWER IN MY	540	5
OR WAS MYSELF [JUST MYSELF / ONLY ME / I]--TOO SMALL?	I TOOK MY POWER IN MY	540	8
I HAD NO CAUSE TO BE AWAKE--	I HAD NO CAUSE TO BE	542	1
SWEET MORNING--WHEN I OVERSLEEP--	I HAD NO CAUSE TO BE	542	7
I LOOKED AT SUNRISE--ONCE--	I HAD NO CAUSE TO BE	542	9
AND THEN I LOOKED AT THEM--	I HAD NO CAUSE TO BE	542	10
THE ONLY RAIMENT I SHOULD NEED--	I HAD NO CAUSE TO BE	542	19
I STRUGGLED--AND WAS THERE--	I HAD NO CAUSE TO BE	542	20
I FEAR A MAN OF FRUGAL [SCANTY] SPEECH--	I FEAR A MAN OF FRUGAL	543	1
I FEAR A SILENT MAN--	I FEAR A MAN OF FRUGAL	543	2
HARANGUER--I CAN OVERTAKE--	I FEAR A MAN OF FRUGAL	543	3
OF THIS MAN--I AM WARY--	I FEAR A MAN OF FRUGAL	543	7
I FEAR THAT HE IS GRAND--	I FEAR A MAN OF FRUGAL	543	8
THAT I DID ALWAYS LOVE	THAT I DID ALWAYS LOVE	549	1
I BRING THEE PROOF	THAT I DID ALWAYS LOVE	549	2
THAT TILL I LOVED	THAT I DID ALWAYS LOVE	549	3
I NEVER LIVED [DID NOT LIVE]--ENOUGH--	THAT I DID ALWAYS LOVE	549	4
THAT I SHALL LOVE ALWAY--	THAT I DID ALWAYS LOVE	549	5
I ARGUE [OFFER] THEE	THAT I DID ALWAYS LOVE	549	6
THEN HAVE I	THAT I DID ALWAYS LOVE	549	10
I CROSS TILL I AM WEARY	I CROSS TILL I AM WEARY	550	1
I CROSS TILL I AM WEARY	I CROSS TILL I AM WEARY	550	1
I SHOUT UNTO MY FEET--	I CROSS TILL I AM WEARY	550	19
I OFFER THEM THE WHOLE [HALF] OF HEAVEN	I CROSS TILL I AM WEARY	550	20
I COULD [DID] NOT DEEM THESE [THAT] PLANETARY FORCES	IT KNEW NO LAPSE, NOR	560	5
I MEASURE EVERY GRIEF I MEET	I MEASURE EVERY GRIEF I	561	1
I MEASURE EVERY GRIEF I MEET	I MEASURE EVERY GRIEF I	561	1
I WONDER IF IT WEIGHS LIKE MINE--	I MEASURE EVERY GRIEF I	561	3
I WONDER IF THEY BORE IT LONG--	I MEASURE EVERY GRIEF I	561	5
I COULD NOT TELL THE DATE OF MINE--	I MEASURE EVERY GRIEF I	561	7
I WONDER IF IT HURTS TO LIVE--	I MEASURE EVERY GRIEF I	561	9
I NOTE THAT SOME--GONE PATIENT LONG--	I MEASURE EVERY GRIEF I	561	13
I WONDER IF WHEN YEARS HAVE PILED--	I MEASURE EVERY GRIEF I	561	17
THE GRIEVED--ARE MANY--I AM TOLD--	I MEASURE EVERY GRIEF I	561	25
AND THOUGH I MAY NOT GUESS THE KIND--	I MEASURE EVERY GRIEF I	561	33
I COULD NOT PROVE THE YEARS HAD FEET--	I COULD NOT PROVE THE	563	1
AM I, FROM SYMPTOMS THAT ARE PAST	I COULD NOT PROVE THE	563	3
I FIND MY FEET HAVE FURTHER GOALS--	I COULD NOT PROVE THE	563	5
I SMILE UPON THE AIMS	I COULD NOT PROVE THE	563	6
I DO NOT DOUBT THE SELF I WAS	I COULD NOT PROVE THE	563	9
I DO NOT DOUBT THE SELF I WAS	I COULD NOT PROVE THE	563	9
PROVES THAT--OUTGROWN--I SEE--	I COULD NOT PROVE THE	563	12
AND SO I STEPPED [STOOD] UPON THE NORTH	MY PERIOD HAD COME FOR	564	7
COULD I INFER HIS RESIDENCE--	MY PERIOD HAD COME FOR	564	11
WERE ALL THAT I COULD SEE--	MY PERIOD HAD COME FOR	564	14
THAT I MIGHT LOOK ON THEE?	MY PERIOD HAD COME FOR	564	16
I WORSHIPPED--DID NOT "PRAY"--	MY PERIOD HAD COME FOR	564	20
I HUNTED [WORRIED] ALL THE SAND--	A DYING TIGER--MOANED	566	2
I CAUGHT THE DRIPPING OF A ROCK	A DYING TIGER--MOANED	566	3
BUT SEARCHING--I COULD SEE	A DYING TIGER--MOANED	566	6
WHILE I WAS REACHING HIM--	A DYING TIGER--MOANED	566	11
I RECKON--WHEN I COUNT AT ALL--	I RECKON--WHEN I COUNT	569	1
I RECKON--WHEN I COUNT AT ALL--	I RECKON--WHEN I COUNT	569	1
SO I WRITE--POETS--ALL--	I RECKON--WHEN I COUNT	569	8
I COULD [WOULD] DIE--TO KNOW--	I COULD DIE--TO KNOW--	570	1
WHILE I--DREAM [WAIT]--HERE--	I COULD DIE--TO KNOW--	570	12
I ASKED TO GO ABROAD,	MY FIRST WELL DAY--SINCE	574	2
A'BLOSSOM JUST WHEN I WENT IN	MY FIRST WELL DAY--SINCE	574	5
SOMETIMES, I THINK THAT NOON	"HEAVEN" HAS DIFFERENT	575	2
I PRAYED, AT FIRST, A LITTLE GIRL,	I PRAYED, AT FIRST, A	576	1
IF I BELIEVED [SUPPOSED] GOD LOOKED AROUND,	I PRAYED, AT FIRST, A	576	5
I COUNT THE FORCE 'TWOULD BE	I PRAYED, AT FIRST, A	576	15
TILL I COULD TAKE THE [CATCH MY] BALANCE	I PRAYED, AT FIRST, A	576	18
IF I MAY HAVE IT, WHEN IT'S DEAD,	IF I MAY HAVE IT, WHEN	577	1
'TIS BLISS [WEALTH / RIGHT] I CANNOT WEIGH--	IF I MAY HAVE IT, WHEN	577	6
THINK OF IT LOVER! I AND THEE	IF I MAY HAVE IT, WHEN	577	9
I'LL TELL YOU HOW I TRIED TO KEEP	IF I MAY HAVE IT, WHEN	577	22
I HAD BEEN HUNGRY, ALL THE YEARS--	I HAD BEEN HUNGRY, ALL	579	1
I TREMBLING DREW THE TABLE NEAR--	I HAD BEEN HUNGRY, ALL	579	3
'TWAS THIS ON TABLES I HAD SEEN--	I HAD BEEN HUNGRY, ALL	579	5
I LOOKED IN WINDOWS, FOR THE WEALTH [THINGS]	I HAD BEEN HUNGRY, ALL	579	7
I COULD NOT HOPE--FOR MINE--[TO EARN]	I HAD BEEN HUNGRY, ALL	579	8
I DID NOT KNOW THE AMPLE BREAD--	I HAD BEEN HUNGRY, ALL	579	9
THE BIRDS AND I, HAD OFTEN SHARED	I HAD BEEN HUNGRY, ALL	579	11
NOR WAS I HUNGRY--SO I FOUND	I HAD BEEN HUNGRY, ALL	579	17

	FIRST LINE	POEM	LINE
I (CONTINUED)			
NOR WAS I HUNGRY--SO I FOUND	I HAD BEEN HUNGRY, ALL	579	17
I GAVE MYSELF TO HIM [HIM ALL MYSELF]--	I GAVE MYSELF TO HIM--	580	1
I FOUND THE WORDS [PHRASE] TO EVERY THOUGHT	I FOUND THE WORDS TO	581	1
I EVER HAD--BUT ONE--	I FOUND THE WORDS TO	581	2
I COULD NOT SEE [FEEL] THE TROUBLE [ANGUISH] GO--	IT CEASED TO HURT ME,	584	2
NOR WHEN IT ALTERED, I COULD SAY,	IT CEASED TO HURT ME,	584	5
FOR I HAD WORN IT, EVERY DAY,	IT CEASED TO HURT ME,	584	6
I HUNG UPON THE PEG, AT NIGHT.	IT CEASED TO HURT ME,	584	8
NOR WHAT CONSOLED IT, I COULD TRACE--	IT CEASED TO HURT ME,	584	13
I LIKE TO SEE [HEAR] IT LAP THE MILES--	I LIKE TO SEE IT LAP	585	1
I CRIED AT PITY--NOT AT PAIN--	I CRIED AT PITY--NOT AT	588	1
I HEARD A WOMAN SAY	I CRIED AT PITY--NOT AT	588	2
SO LONG I FAINTED, TO MYSELF	I CRIED AT PITY--NOT AT	588	5
AND CARRIED, WE SUPPOSE--[I SUPPOSED] TO HEAVEN,	I CRIED AT PITY--NOT AT	588	11
I WISH I KNEW THAT WOMAN'S NAME--	I CRIED AT PITY--NOT AT	588	17
I WISH I KNEW THAT WOMAN'S NAME--	I CRIED AT PITY--NOT AT	588	17
FOR FEAR I HEAR HER SAY	I CRIED AT PITY--NOT AT	588	20
SHE'S "SORRY I AM DEAD"--AGAIN--	I CRIED AT PITY--NOT AT	588	21
JUST WHEN THE GRAVE AND I--	I CRIED AT PITY--NOT AT	588	22
I THINK I WAS ENCHANTED	I THINK I WAS ENCHANTED	593	1
I THINK I WAS ENCHANTED	I THINK I WAS ENCHANTED	593	1
I READ THAT FOREIGN LADY--	I THINK I WAS ENCHANTED	593	3
I HAD NOT POWER TO TELL--	I THINK I WAS ENCHANTED	593	8
I TOOK FOR GIANTS--PRACTISING	I THINK I WAS ENCHANTED	593	15
I COULD NOT HAVE DEFINED THE CHANGE--	I THINK I WAS ENCHANTED	593	21
SHOULD I AGAIN EXPERIENCE--	I THINK I WAS ENCHANTED	593	27
WHEN I WAS SMALL, A WOMAN DIED--	WHEN I WAS SMALL, A	596	1
THREE TIMES--WE PARTED--BREATH--AND I--	THREE TIMES--WE PARTED--	598	1
THAT CRAWLED LEAGUES OFF--I LIKED TO SEE--	THREE TIMES--WE PARTED--	598	9
FOR THINKING--WHILE I DIE--	THREE TIMES--WE PARTED--	598	10
AND I STOOD UP--AND LIVED--	THREE TIMES--WE PARTED--	598	16
IT TROUBLED ME AS ONCE I WAS--	IT TROUBLED ME AS ONCE I	600	1
FOR I WAS ONCE A CHILD--	IT TROUBLED ME AS ONCE I	600	2
WITHOUT A BOLT--THAT I COULD PROVE--	IT TROUBLED ME AS ONCE I	600	7
SOME I SHALL KEEP [SAVE]--TO SOLVE	IT TROUBLED ME AS ONCE I	600	10
I THANK THESE KINSMEN OF THE SHELF--	UNTO MY BOOKS--SO GOOD	604	13
'TWAS MORE--I CANNOT MENTION--	THE TREES LIKE TASSELS--	606	25
AFRAID! OF WHOM AM I AFRAID?	AFRAID! OF WHOM AM I	608	1
OF LIFE? 'TWERE ODD I FEAR A THING	AFRAID! OF WHOM AM I	608	5
I YEARS HAD BEEN FROM HOME	I YEARS HAD BEEN FROM	609	1
I DARED NOT ENTER [OPEN], LEST A FACE	I YEARS HAD BEEN FROM	609	3
I NEVER SAW BEFORE	I YEARS HAD BEEN FROM	609	4
"MY BUSINESS BUT [JUST] A LIFE I LEFT	I YEARS HAD BEEN FROM	609	7
I LEANED UPON THE AWE--	I YEARS HAD BEEN FROM	609	9
I FUMBLED AT MY NERVE--	I YEARS HAD BEEN FROM	609	V 9
I LINGERED WITH BEFORE--	I YEARS HAD BEEN FROM	609	10
I SCANNED THE WINDOWS O'ER--	I YEARS HAD BEEN FROM	609	V 10
I LAUGHED A CRUMBLING [WOODEN] LAUGH	I YEARS HAD BEEN FROM	609	13
THAT I COULD FEAR A DOOR	I YEARS HAD BEEN FROM	609	14
I FITTED TO THE LATCH	I YEARS HAD BEEN FROM	609	17
THEN [I] MOVED MY FINGERS OFF	I YEARS HAD BEEN FROM	609	21
I SEE THEE BETTER--IN THE DARK--	I SEE THEE BETTER--IN	611	1
I DO NOT NEED A LIGHT--	I SEE THEE BETTER--IN	611	2
I SEE THEE BETTER FOR THE YEARS	I SEE THEE BETTER--IN	611	5
AND IN THE GRAVE--I SEE THEE BEST--	I SEE THEE BETTER--IN	611	9
I HELD SO HIGH, FOR THEE--	I SEE THEE BETTER--IN	611	12
TO LIVE [DINE] SO SMALL AS I--	IT WOULD HAVE STARVED A	612	2
AND YET I WAS A LIVING CHILD--	IT WOULD HAVE STARVED A	612	3
I COULD NO MORE REMOVE	IT WOULD HAVE STARVED A	612	6
THAN I COULD COAX A LEECH AWAY--[MODIFY A LEECH]	IT WOULD HAVE STARVED A	612	7
NOR LIKE THE GNAT--HAD I--	IT WOULD HAVE STARVED A	612	9
HOW MIGHTIER HE--THAN I--	IT WOULD HAVE STARVED A	612	12
AND LAUGH--NO MORE HAVE I--	THEY SHUT ME UP IN PROSE	613	12
I ROSE--BECAUSE HE SANK--	I ROSE--BECAUSE HE SANK	616	1
I THOUGHT IT WOULD BE OPPOSITE--	I ROSE--BECAUSE HE SANK	616	2
I CHEERED MY FAINTING PRINCE--	I ROSE--BECAUSE HE SANK	616	5
I SANG FIRM--EVEN--[STRAIGHT--STEADY] CHANTS--	I ROSE--BECAUSE HE SANK	616	6
I HELPED [STAYED] HIS FILM--WITH HYMN--	I ROSE--BECAUSE HE SANK	616	7
I MET [GAVE] HIM--	I ROSE--BECAUSE HE SANK	616	10
I TOLD HIM BEST--MUST PASS	I ROSE--BECAUSE HE SANK	616	12
I TOLD HIM WORLDS [A WORLD] I KNEW	I ROSE--BECAUSE HE SANK	616	16
I TOLD HIM WORLDS [A WORLD] I KNEW	I ROSE--BECAUSE HE SANK	616	16
AND WAYS I KNEW NOT THAT I KNEW--TILL THEN--	I ROSE--BECAUSE HE SANK	616	22
AND WAYS I KNEW NOT THAT I KNEW--TILL THEN--	I ROSE--BECAUSE HE SANK	616	22
I LIFTED HIM--	I ROSE--BECAUSE HE SANK	616	23
WHERE I PUT IT DOWN--	DONT PUT UP MY THREAD &	617	14
I CAN MAKE THE ZIGZAG STITCHES	DONT PUT UP MY THREAD &	617	15
STRAIGHT--WHEN I AM STRONG--	DONT PUT UP MY THREAD &	617	16
TILL THEN--DREAMING [DEEMING] I AM SOWING	DONT PUT UP MY THREAD &	617	17
FETCH THE SEAM I MISSED--	DONT PUT UP MY THREAD &	617	18
CLOSER--SO I--AT MY SLEEPING [SIGHING]--	DONT PUT UP MY THREAD &	617	19
STILL SURMISE I STITCH--	DONT PUT UP MY THREAD &	617	20
I ASKED NO OTHER THING--	I ASKED NO OTHER THING--	621	1
I OFFERED BEING--FOR IT--	I ASKED NO OTHER THING--	621	3
THE TINT I CANNOT TAKE--IS BEST--	THE TINT I CANNOT TAKE--	627	1
THAT I COULD SHOW IT IN BAZAAR--	THE TINT I CANNOT TAKE--	627	3

I (CONTINUED)	FIRST LINE	POEM	LINE
I ONLY SAW A SAPPHIRE [AN AMBER--] FARM--	THEY CALLED ME TO THE	628	3
AS EVEN WHILE I LOOKED--DISSOLVED--	THEY CALLED ME TO THE	628	7
AND WHEN I LOOKED AGAIN--	THEY CALLED ME TO THE	628	14
I WATCHED THE MOON AROUND THE HOUSE	I WATCHED THE MOON	629	1
I GAZED [TURNED]--AS AT A STRANGER--	I WATCHED THE MOON	629	5
AND NEXT--I MET HER ON A CLOUD--	I WATCHED THE MOON	629	33
I WEARIED--TOO--OF MINE--	OURSELVES WERE WED ONE	631	4
I--TOO--RECEIVED THE SIGN.	OURSELVES WERE WED ONE	631	8
WITHOUT A BUTTON--I C'D VOUCH--	YOU'LL KNOW HER--BY HER	634	7
I THINK THE LONGEST HOUR OF ALL	I THINK THE LONGEST HOUR	635	1
THEN I--MY TIMID SERVICE DONE--	I THINK THE LONGEST HOUR	635	13
THE WAY I READ A LETTER'S--THIS [SO]--	THE WAY I READ A	636	1
'TIS FIRST--I LOCK THE DOOR--	THE WAY I READ A	636	2
AND THEN I GO THE FURTHEST OFF	THE WAY I READ A	636	5
PERUSE HOW INFINITE I AM	THE WAY I READ A	636	13
I CANNOT LIVE WITH YOU--	I CANNOT LIVE WITH YOU--	640	1
I COULD NOT DIE--WITH YOU--	I CANNOT LIVE WITH YOU--	640	13
AND I--COULD I STAND BY	I CANNOT LIVE WITH YOU--	640	17
AND I--COULD I STAND BY	I CANNOT LIVE WITH YOU--	640	17
NOR COULD I RISE--WITH YOU--	I CANNOT LIVE WITH YOU--	640	21
I COULD NOT--	I CANNOT LIVE WITH YOU--	640	32
AND I HAD NO MORE EYES	I CANNOT LIVE WITH YOU--	640	34
AND WERE YOU LOST, I WOULD BE--	I CANNOT LIVE WITH YOU--	640	37
AND I--CONDEMNED TO BE	I CANNOT LIVE WITH YOU--	640	42
YOU THERE--I--HERE--	I CANNOT LIVE WITH YOU--	640	46
HAD I ART--	ME FROM MYSELF--TO	642	2
HOW HAVE I PEACE	ME FROM MYSELF--TO	642	6
I COULD SUFFICE FOR HIM, I KNEW--	I COULD SUFFICE FOR HIM,	643	1
I COULD SUFFICE FOR HIM, I KNEW--	I COULD SUFFICE FOR HIM,	643	1
"WOULD I BE WHOLE" HE SUDDEN BROACHED--	I COULD SUFFICE FOR HIM,	643	5
COULD I--DO ELSE--WITH MINE?	I COULD SUFFICE FOR HIM,	643	16
I THINK TO LIVE--MAY BE A BLISS [LIFE]	I THINK TO LIVE--MAY BE	646	1
I THINK THE HEART I FORMER WORE	I THINK TO LIVE--MAY BE	646	5
I THINK THE HEART I FORMER WORE	I THINK TO LIVE--MAY BE	646	5
I THINK THE DAYS--COULD EVERY ONE	I THINK TO LIVE--MAY BE	646	9
THAT I ESTEEM THE FICTION--REAL [TRUE]--	I THINK TO LIVE--MAY BE	646	23
'TIS THAT--I CANNOT SAY--	A LITTLE ROAD--NOT MADE	647	6
I ONLY KNOW [SIGH]--NO CURRICLE [VEHICLE] THAT RUMBLE THERE	A LITTLE ROAD--NOT MADE	647	7
HAD I NOT BEEN	PROMISE THIS--WHEN YOU	648	32
I COULD NOT CARE--TO GAIN	WITHOUT THIS--THERE IS	655	5
I WISHED A WAY [SORT] MIGHT BE	WITHOUT THIS--THERE IS	655	9
I DWELL IN POSSIBILITY--	I DWELL IN POSSIBILITY--	657	1
AND SAID THAT I WAS STRONG--	THAT FIRST DAY, WHEN YOU	659	2
AND COULD BE MIGHTY, IF I LIKED--	THAT FIRST DAY, WHEN YOU	659	3
COULD I BUT RIDE INDEFINITE	COULD I BUT RIDE	661	1
AND VISIT ONLY WHERE I LIKED	COULD I BUT RIDE	661	3
AND MARRY WHOM I MAY	COULD I BUT RIDE	661	6
I SAID "BUT JUST TO BE A BEE"	COULD I BUT RIDE	661	13
I FEEL THE OLD DEGREE--	AGAIN--HIS VOICE IS AT	663	2
I HEAR HIM ASK THE SERVANT	AGAIN--HIS VOICE IS AT	663	3
I TAKE A FLOWER--AS I GO--	AGAIN--HIS VOICE IS AT	663	5
I TAKE A FLOWER--AS I GO--	AGAIN--HIS VOICE IS AT	663	5
I MIGHT SURPRISE [NOT PLEASE] HIS EYE!	AGAIN--HIS VOICE IS AT	663	8
I CROSS THE HALL WITH MINGLED STEPS--	AGAIN--HIS VOICE IS AT	663	9
I--SILENT [SPEECHLESS]--PASS THE DOOR--	AGAIN--HIS VOICE IS AT	663	10
I LOOK ON ALL THIS WORLD CONTAINS--	AGAIN--HIS VOICE IS AT	663	11
WE WALK--I LEAVE MY DOG--AT HOME [BEHIND]--	AGAIN--HIS VOICE IS AT	663	18
I HAVE ELECTED--ONE--	OF ALL THE SOULS THAT	664	2
BEHOLD THE ATOM--I PREFERRED--	OF ALL THE SOULS THAT	664	11
SEED, HAD I, MY PURPLE SOWING	BLOOM UPON THE MOUNTAIN	667	5
WHILE I STATE--THE SOLEMN PETALS,	BLOOM UPON THE MOUNTAIN	667	13
IS BUT A FILAMENT, I KNOW,	THE LOVE A LIFE CAN SHOW	673	2
CONSCIOUS AM I IN MY CHAMBER,	CONSCIOUS AM I IN MY	679	1
NEITHER PLACE--NEED I PRESENT HIM--	CONSCIOUS AM I IN MY	679	5
DO HE DWELL--OR NAY--KNOW I--	CONSCIOUS AM I IN MY	679	18
BLOOM I STROVE TO RAISE--	SOIL OF FLINT, IF STEADY	681	V
BUT, BLOSSOM, WERE I,	'TWOULD EASE--A	682	5
I WOULD RATHER BE	'TWOULD EASE--A	682	6
FADE I UNTO DIVINITY--	'TWOULD EASE--A	682	11
UPON THE VILLAGE I PERCEIVED--	THE SUN KEPT SETTING--	692	3
HOW WELL I KNEW THE LIGHT BEFORE--	THE SUN KEPT SETTING--	692	13
I COULD NOT SEE IT NOW--	THE SUN KEPT SETTING--	692	14
'TIS DYING--I AM DOING--BUT	THE SUN KEPT SETTING--	692	15
I CHERISHED THEM FOR ALL--	SHELLS FROM THE COAST	693	2
WHEREFORE SO LATE--I MURMURED--	SHELLS FROM THE COAST	693	5
I'M FINITE--I CANT SEE--	THEIR HIGHT IN HEAVEN	696	4
THE WEALTH I HAD--CONTENTED ME--	THEIR HIGHT IN HEAVEN	696	9
THEN I HAD COUNTED IT UNTIL	THEIR HIGHT IN HEAVEN	696	11
KEEPS PLEADING--"I DONT KNOW."	THEIR HIGHT IN HEAVEN	696	16
I COULD BRING YOU JEWELS--HAD I A MIND TO--	I COULD BRING YOU JEWELS	697	1
I COULD BRING YOU JEWELS--HAD I A MIND TO--	I COULD BRING YOU JEWELS	697	1
I COULD BRING YOU ODORS FROM ST DOMINGO--	I COULD BRING YOU JEWELS	697	3
BERRIES OF THE BAHAMAS--HAVE I--	I COULD BRING YOU JEWELS	697	5
BETTER--COULD I BRING?	I COULD BRING YOU JEWELS	697	12
I ONLY ASK A TUNE	THE JUDGE IS LIKE THE	699	10
THAT I HAVE HAD BEFORE--	A THOUGHT WENT UP MY	701	2
I COULD NOT FIX THE YEAR--	A THOUGHT WENT UP MY	701	4
HAVE I THE ART TO SAY--	A THOUGHT WENT UP MY	701	8

I (CONTINUED)

	FIRST LINE	POEM	LINE
BUT SOMEWHERE--IN MY SOUL--I KNOW--	A THOUGHT WENT UP MY	701	9
I SHANT NEED IT--THEN--	NO MATTER--NOW--SWEET--	704	9
FOR I--INHABIT HER--	THE GRACE--MYSELF--MIGHT	707	4
I SOMETIMES DROP IT, FOR A QUICK--	I SOMETIMES DROP IT, FOR	708	1
BECAUSE I COULD NOT STOP FOR DEATH--	BECAUSE I COULD NOT STOP	712	1
AND I HAD PUT AWAY	BECAUSE I COULD NOT STOP	712	6
I FIRST SURMISED THE HORSES HEADS	BECAUSE I COULD NOT STOP	712	23
I MEANT TO FIND HER WHEN I CAME--	I MEANT TO FIND HER WHEN	718	1
I MEANT TO FIND HER WHEN I CAME--	I MEANT TO FIND HER WHEN	718	1
I MEANT TO TELL HER HOW I LONGED	I MEANT TO FIND HER WHEN	718	5
I MEANT TO TELL HER HOW I LONGED	I MEANT TO FIND HER WHEN	718	5
TURN ON ME--WHEN I FAIL--OR FEIGN,	SWEET MOUNTAINS--YE TELL	722	4
A LITTLE BRIG I KNEW--O'ERTOOK BY BLAST--	IT TOSSED--AND TOSSED--	723	2
I SCARCE ESTEEM LOCATION'S NAME--	WHERE THOU ART--THAT--IS	725	4
SO I MAY COME--	WHERE THOU ART--THAT--IS	725	5
THOUGH SHE FORGET THE NAME I BEAR--	PRECIOUS TO ME--SHE	727	2
THE FASHION OF THE GOWN I WEAR--	PRECIOUS TO ME--SHE	727	3
I DARED TO SHOW A TRESS OF THEIR'S	PRECIOUS TO ME--SHE	727	6
I KNOW THE WHOLE--OBSCURES THE PART--	PRECIOUS TO ME--SHE	727	9
I--THE GIRL AT SCHOOL--	LET US PLAY YESTERDAY--	728	2
LOGARITHM--HAD I--FOR DRINK--	LET US PLAY YESTERDAY--	728	7
WHEN I SLEPT--AT NIGHT--	LET US PLAY YESTERDAY--	728	22
I WILL--OF YOU--	ALTER! WHEN THE HILLS DO	729	8
DEFRAUDED I A BUTTERFLY--	DEFRAUDED I A BUTTERFLY	730	1
"I WANT"--IT PLEADED--ALL IT'S LIFE--	"I WANT"--IT PLEADED--	731	1
I WANT--WAS CHIEF IT SAID	"I WANT"--IT PLEADED--	731	2
I COULD NOT DEEM IT LATE--TO HEAR	"I WANT"--IT PLEADED--	731	5
IF HE WERE LIVING--DARE I ASK--	IF HE WERE LIVING--DARE	734	1
AND SO AROUND THE WORDS I WENT--	IF HE WERE LIVING--DARE	734	3
I HINTED CHANGES--LAPSE OF TIME--	IF HE WERE LIVING--DARE	734	5
I TOUCHED WITH CAUTION--LEST THEY CRACK [SLIT]--	IF HE WERE LIVING--DARE	734	7
WHEREVER I SUSPECTED GRAVES--	IF HE WERE LIVING--DARE	734	11
'TWAS PRUDENTER--I THOUGHT--	IF HE WERE LIVING--DARE	734	12
AND HE--I PUSHED--WITH SUDDEN FORCE--	IF HE WERE LIVING--DARE	734	13
THE LIKEST I HAVE KNOWN--	THE MOON WAS BUT A CHIN	737	8
YOU SAID THAT I "WAS GREAT"--ONE DAY--	YOU SAID THAT I "WAS	738	1
AND I MUST BE RHINOCEROS	YOU SAID THAT I "WAS	738	10
I SUIT THEE--	YOU SAID THAT I "WAS	738	18
I MANY TIMES THOUGHT PEACE HAD COME	I MANY TIMES THOUGHT	739	1
AS HOPELESSLY AS I--	I MANY TIMES THOUGHT	739	6
THIS--ALSO--I HAVE LEARNT--	YOU TAUGHT ME WAITING	740	4
BUT I AM DEAF--TODAY--	THE BIRDS REPORTED FROM	743	4
I REINFORCED [ONLY SEALED] THE DOOR--	THE BIRDS REPORTED FROM	743	6
GO BLOSSOM TO THE BEES--I SAID--	THE BIRDS REPORTED FROM	743	7
I RECOLLECTED [ROSE TO COMFORT--] HER--	THE BIRDS REPORTED FROM	743	16
SHE SUFFERED ME, FOR I HAD MOURNED--	THE BIRDS REPORTED FROM	743	17
I OFFERED HER NO WORD--	THE BIRDS REPORTED FROM	743	18
MY WITNESS--WAS THE CRAPE [BLACK] I BORE--	THE BIRDS REPORTED FROM	743	19
I [SHE] NEVER QUESTIONED HER [ME]--	THE BIRDS REPORTED FROM	743	22
NOR I--HERSELF--OUR COMPACT--	THE BIRDS REPORTED FROM	743	V 23
I HEARD IT HIT THE GROUND--	IT DROPPED SO LOW--IN MY	747	2
THAN I REVILED [DENOUNCED] MYSELF,	IT DROPPED SO LOW--IN MY	747	6
DYES--SAID HE--HAVE I--	AUTUMN--OVERLOOKED MY	748	2
SHOW ME THEM [GIVE THEM ME--]--SAID I--	AUTUMN--OVERLOOKED MY	748	4
COCHINEAL--I CHOSE--FOR DEEMING	AUTUMN--OVERLOOKED MY	748	5
LEST I SHOULD INSUFFICIENT PROVE [BE]	MY WORTHINESS IS ALL MY	751	5
SO I--THE UNDIVINE ABODE	MY WORTHINESS IS ALL MY	751	13
MY SOUL--ACCUSED ME--AND I QUAILED--	MY SOUL--ACCUSED ME--AND	753	1
ALL ELSE [THE WORLD] ACCUSED ME--AND I SMILED--	MY SOUL--ACCUSED ME--AND	753	3
AND EVERY TIME I SPEAK FOR HIM--	MY LIFE HAD STOOD--A	754	7
AND DO I SMILE, SUCH CORDIAL LIGHT	MY LIFE HAD STOOD--A	754	9
I GUARD MY MASTER'S HEAD--	MY LIFE HAD STOOD--A	754	14
ON WHOM I LAY A YELLOW EYE--	MY LIFE HAD STOOD--A	754	19
THOUGH I THAN HE--MAY LONGER LIVE	MY LIFE HAD STOOD--A	754	21
HE LONGER MUST--THAN I--	MY LIFE HAD STOOD--A	754	22
FOR I HAVE BUT THE POWER [ART] TO KILL,	MY LIFE HAD STOOD--A	754	23
ONE BLESSING HAD I THAN THE REST	ONE BLESSING HAD I THAN	756	1
THAT I STOPPED GUAGING--SATISFIED--	ONE BLESSING HAD I THAN	756	3
I KNEW NO MORE OF WANT--OR COLD--	ONE BLESSING HAD I THAN	756	9
I SPECULATE NO MORE--	ONE BLESSING HAD I THAN	756	20
COULD I SUCH A PLEA [FACE] WITHSTAND--	MOST SHE TOUCHED ME BY	760	8
I SUPPOSED--WHEN SUDDEN	MOST SHE TOUCHED ME BY	760	13
AFTERWARD I LEARNED	MOST SHE TOUCHED ME BY	760	18
I PUSHED MECHANIC FEET--	FROM BLANK TO BLANK--	761	3
IF END I GAINED [REACHED]	FROM BLANK TO BLANK--	761	6
I SHUT MY EYES--AND GROPED AS WELL	FROM BLANK TO BLANK--	761	9
I DEEMED ETERNITY	YOU CONSTITUTED TIME--	765	2
THAT I UNTO HIMSELF ADJUST	YOU CONSTITUTED TIME--	765	7
HOW DARE I, THEREFORE, STINT A FAITH	MY FAITH IS LARGER THAN	766	13
WHEN I HOPED, I RECOLLECT	WHEN I HOPED, I	768	1
WHEN I HOPED, I RECOLLECT	WHEN I HOPED, I	768	1
JUST THE PLACE I STOOD--	WHEN I HOPED, I	768	2
WHEN I FEARED--I RECOLLECT	WHEN I HOPED, I	768	9
WHEN I FEARED--I RECOLLECT	WHEN I HOPED, I	768	9
AND THE DAY THAT I DESPAIRED--	WHEN I HOPED, I	768	17
THIS--IF I FORGET	WHEN I HOPED, I	768	18
MEMORY AND I--	WHEN I HOPED, I	768	24

		FIRST LINE	POEM	LINE
I	(CONTINUED)			
	I LIVED ON DREAD--	I LIVED ON DREAD--	770	1
	I ENTERTAINED MYSELF--	DEPRIVED OF OTHER	773	2
	RED PILGRIM, HE AND I--	DEPRIVED OF OTHER	773	10
	I FEAR ME THIS--IS LONELINESS--	THE LONELINESS ONE DARE	777	13
	IS TENDEREST, I THINK--	THE SERVICE WITHOUT HOPE	779	2
	I COULD NOT COUNT THEIR FORCE--	THE BIRDS BEGUN AT FOUR	783	5
	THAT I COULD ASCERTAIN--	THE BIRDS BEGUN AT FOUR	783	14
	BEREAVED OF ALL, I WENT ABROAD--	BEREAVED OF ALL, I WENT	784	1
	NO LESS BEREAVED WAS I	BEREAVED OF ALL, I WENT	784	2
	AND WHEN I SOUGHT MY BED--	BEREAVED OF ALL, I WENT	784	6
	I WAKED, TO FIND IT FIRST AWAKE--	BEREAVED OF ALL, I WENT	784	9
	I ROSE--IT FOLLOWED ME--	BEREAVED OF ALL, I WENT	784	10
	I TRIED TO DROP [SHIFT] IT IN THE CROWD--	BEREAVED OF ALL, I WENT	784	11
	I--HASTENED TO DEMAND	SEVERER SERVICE OF	786	2
	I WORRIED NATURE WITH MY WHEELS	SEVERER SERVICE OF	786	5
	I STROVE TO WEARY BRAIN AND BONE--	SEVERER SERVICE OF	786	9
	THE HIGHT I RECOLLECT--	JOY TO HAVE MERITED THE	788	17
	I DARE NOT EAT IT--THO' I STARVE--	GOD GAVE A LOAF TO EVERY	791	3
	I DARE NOT EAT IT--THO' I STARVE--	GOD GAVE A LOAF TO EVERY	791	3
	I COULD NOT MISS AN EAR--	GOD GAVE A LOAF TO EVERY	791	10
	I WONDER HOW THE RICH--MAY FEEL--	GOD GAVE A LOAF TO EVERY	791	13
	I DEEM THAT I--WITH BUT A CRUMB--	GOD GAVE A LOAF TO EVERY	791	15
	I DEEM THAT I--WITH BUT A CRUMB--	GOD GAVE A LOAF TO EVERY	791	15
	BY MY WINDOW HAVE I FOR SCENERY	BY MY WINDOW HAVE I FOR	797	1
	OF SPICE--I INFER FROM THE ODORS BORNE--	BY MY WINDOW HAVE I FOR	797	12
	I SHALL MEET WITH CONVICTION I SOMEWHERE MET	BY MY WINDOW HAVE I FOR	797	20
	I SHALL MEET WITH CONVICTION I SOMEWHERE MET	BY MY WINDOW HAVE I FOR	797	20
	I PLAY AT RICHES--TO APPEASE	I PLAY AT RICHES--TO	801	1
	IT KEPT ME FROM A THIEF, I THINK,	I PLAY AT RICHES--TO	801	3
	I COULD [MIGHT] HAVE DONE A SIN	I PLAY AT RICHES--TO	801	6
	I DEEM MYSELF WHAT I WOULD BE--	I PLAY AT RICHES--TO	801	11
	I DEEM MYSELF WHAT I WOULD BE--	I PLAY AT RICHES--TO	801	11
	MY POVERTY AND I DERIVE--	I PLAY AT RICHES--TO	801	13
	HOW ['TIS] FITTER THEY WILL [I SHALL] BE--FOR [BY] WANT--	I PLAY AT RICHES--TO	801	21
	I KNOW NOT WHICH, DESIRE, OR GRANT [RIGHT / SIGHT]--	I PLAY AT RICHES--TO	801	23
	I FEAR ME THIS CIRCUMFERENCE	TIME FEELS SO VAST THAT	802	3
	SO I THE SHIPS MAY SEE	SO SET IT'S SUN IN THEE	808	4
	I DISSECT [REVIEW] THE PLAY	ONE DAY IS THERE OF THE	814	6
	I SCARCELY RECOLLECT TO STARVE	THE LUXURY TO APPREHEND	815	7
	SO FIRST AM I SUPPLIED--	THE LUXURY TO APPREHEND	815	8
	I COULD NOT DRINK IT, SWEET [SUE],	I COULD NOT DRINK IT,	818	1
	ALL I MAY, IF SMALL,	ALL I MAY, IF SMALL,	819	1
	AWAY FROM HOME ARE SOME [THEY] AND I--	AWAY FROM HOME ARE SOME	821	1
	"AS LARGE AS I"--RELATE THE SUN	LOVE RECKONS BY ITSELF--	826	2
	THE ONLY NEWS I KNOW	THE ONLY NEWS I KNOW	827	1
	THE ONLY SHOWS I SEE--	THE ONLY NEWS I KNOW	827	4
	THE ONLY ONE I MEET	THE ONLY NEWS I KNOW	827	7
	NATURE AND GOD--I NEITHER KNEW	NATURE AND GOD--I	835	1
	YET NEITHER TOLD--THAT I COULD LEARN--	NATURE AND GOD--I	835	5
	HOW WELL I KNEW HER NOT	HOW WELL I KNEW HER NOT	837	1
	I CANNOT BUY IT--'TIS NOT SOLD--	I CANNOT BUY IT--'TIS	840	1
	I WAS SO HAPPY I FORGOT	I CANNOT BUY IT--'TIS	840	4
	I WAS SO HAPPY I FORGOT	I CANNOT BUY IT--'TIS	840	4
	AND I AM ALL ALONE--	I CANNOT BUY IT--'TIS	840	6
	IF I COULD FIND IT ANYWHERE	I CANNOT BUY IT--'TIS	840	7
	I WOULD NOT MIND THE JOURNEY THERE	I CANNOT BUY IT--'TIS	840	8
	NATURE IS FOND, I SOMETIMES THINK,	A MOTH THE HUE OF THIS	841	5
	I MADE SLOW RICHES BUT MY GAIN	I MADE SLOW RICHES BUT	843	1
	ALL DAYS, I DID NOT EARN THE SAME	I MADE SLOW RICHES BUT	843	5
	I SING TO USE THE WAITING	I SING TO USE THE	850	1
	NO MORE TO DO HAVE I	I SING TO USE THE	850	4
	I MENTION IT TO YOU,	THIS CHASM, SWEET, UPON	858	2
	I SHOULD NOT MISS IN YIELDING, THOUGH	THIS CHASM, SWEET, UPON	858	15
	AND SO I BEAR IT BIG ABOUT	THIS CHASM, SWEET, UPON	858	17
	FOR THEE A BEE DO I BECOME	BECAUSE THE BEE MAY	869	2
	I THAT WAY WORSHIP THEE.	BECAUSE THE BEE MAY	869	12
	I, OF A FINER FAMINE	AS THE STARVED MAELSTROM	872	13
	WHEN I FORGET TO TEAZE--	THEY WONT FROWN ALWAYS--	874	2
	THEY'LL RECOLLECT HOW COLD I LOOKED	THEY WONT FROWN ALWAYS--	874	3
	AND HOW I JUST SAID "PLEASE."	THEY WONT FROWN ALWAYS--	874	4
	I STEPPED FROM PLANK TO PLANK	I STEPPED FROM PLANK TO	875	1
	THE STARS ABOUT MY HEAD I FELT	I STEPPED FROM PLANK TO	875	3
	I KNEW NOT BUT THE NEXT	I STEPPED FROM PLANK TO	875	5
	HAD I THE CURIOSITY	IT WAS A GRAVE, YET BORE	876	7
	TILL RESURRECTION, I MUST GUESS	IT WAS A GRAVE, YET BORE	876	9
	BUT EVERY TEAR I BORE	EACH SCAR I'LL KEEP FOR	877	5
	THAT I THE ANSWER MAY PURSUE	I'VE NONE TO TELL ME TO	881	11
	AS I OF HE, SO GOD OF ME	OUR LITTLE KINSMEN--	885	9
	I PONDERED, MAY HAVE JUDGED,	OUR LITTLE KINSMEN--	885	10
	WHEN I HAVE SEEN THE SUN EMERGE	WHEN I HAVE SEEN THE SUN	888	1
	I COULD NOT FIND A PRIVACY	TO MY QUICK EAR THE	891	3
	IN CAVE IF I PRESUMED TO HIDE	TO MY QUICK EAR THE	891	5
	A STRANGER I MUST JUDGE	WHO OCCUPIES THIS HOUSE?	892	2
	OR I SHOULD FEAR TO PAUSE	WHO OCCUPIES THIS HOUSE?	892	6
	WERE I COMPELLED TO BUILD	WHO OCCUPIES THIS HOUSE?	892	12
	HAD I BUT FURTHER SCANNED	A CLOUD WITHDREW FROM	895	5
	HAD I SECURED THE GLOW	A CLOUD WITHDREW FROM	895	6

I (CONTINUED)

I (CONTINUED)

	FIRST LINE	POEM		LINE
HOW SWEET I SHALL NOT LACK IN VAIN--	FITTER TO SEE HIM, I MAY	968		25
I COULD HOLD THE LATEST GLOWING--	ROBBED BY DEATH--BUT	971		3
THIS, TOO, I ENDURED--	ROBBED BY DEATH--BUT	971		6
I ONLY HAVE IT NOT TONIGHT	'TWAS AWKWARD, BUT IT	973		9
I HAVE ANOTHER TRUST"--	DEATH IS A DIALOGUE	976		4
I, PASSING, THOUGHT ANOTHER NOON	IT BLOOMED AND DROPT, A	978		3
HAD I BUT LINGERED YESTERDAY--	IT BLOOMED AND DROPT, A	978		11
THAT I, IN PASSING BY	IT BLOOMED AND DROPT, A	978		18
'TWAS NOT SO LARGE THAT I	THE MISSING ALL,	985		6
I MORE THAN ONCE AT NOON	A NARROW FELLOW IN THE	986		12
HAVE PASSED, I THOUGHT, A WHIP LASH	A NARROW FELLOW IN THE	986		13
I KNOW, AND THEY KNOW ME--	A NARROW FELLOW IN THE	986		18
I FEEL FOR THEM A TRANSPORT	A NARROW FELLOW IN THE	986		19
THE DUST BEHIND I STROVE TO JOIN	THE DUST BEHIND I STROVE	992		1
I KNOW THE FAMILY	PARTAKE AS DOTH THE BEE,	994	V	3
I LEFT HER I COULD FIND HER	WE'LL PASS WITHOUT THE	996		5
I LEFT HER I COULD FIND HER	WE'LL PASS WITHOUT THE	996		5
IF I TRIED--	WE'LL PASS WITHOUT THE	996		6
THIS WAY, I KEEP FROM MISSING	WE'LL PASS WITHOUT THE	996		7
WITH "I AM GREAT AND CANNOT WAIT	THE FINGERS OF THE LIGHT	1000		3
BUT SWEAR, AND I WILL LET YOU BY	THE FINGERS OF THE LIGHT	1000		7
BIND ME--I STILL CAN SING--	BIND ME--I STILL CAN	1005		1
FALSEHOOD OF THEE COULD I SUPPOSE	FALSEHOOD OF THEE COULD	1007		1
I WAS A PHEBE--NOTHING MORE--	I WAS A PHEBE--NOTHING	1009		1
I FITTED INTO PLACE--	I WAS A PHEBE--NOTHING	1009		4
I DWELT TOO LOW THAT ANY SEEK--	I WAS A PHEBE--NOTHING	1009		5
IF I PROVE IT STEEP--	UP LIFE'S HILL WITH MY	1010		2
I CANNOT HELP ESTEEM	WHICH IS BEST? HEAVEN--	1012		4
I OFFER EVEN THAT--	TOO SCANTY 'TWAS TO DIE	1013		4
I TENDERER COMMEND	MY SEASON'S FURTHEST	1019		2
BECAUSE I FOUND HER KINSMANLESS,	MY SEASON'S FURTHEST	1019		3
I MET SOMEBODY'S LITTLE BOY	TRUDGING TO EDEN,	1020		2
WOULD IT COMFORT--TO KNOW I MET HIM--	TRUDGING TO EDEN,	1020		5
I COULD'NT WEEP--FOR SO MANY SMILING	TRUDGING TO EDEN,	1020		7
I KNEW THAT I HAD GAINED	I KNEW THAT I HAD GAINED	1022		1
I KNEW THAT I HAD GAINED	I KNEW THAT I HAD GAINED	1022		1
AND YET I KNEW NOT HOW	I KNEW THAT I HAD GAINED	1022		2
THE LITTLE THAT I MAY	SO LARGE MY WILL	1024		2
I WAS OWNED OF THEE--	'TWAS MY ONE GLORY--	1028		4
WHERE I AM NOT AFRAID TO GO	HERE, WHERE THE DAISIES	1037		5
I MAY CONFIDE MY FLOWER--	HERE, WHERE THE DAISIES	1037		6
A SUMMER FURTHER I MUST WEAR,	HER LITTLE PARASOL TO	1038		5
I HEARD, AS IF I HAD NO EAR	I HEARD, AS IF I HAD NO	1039		1
I HEARD, AS IF I HAD NO EAR	I HEARD, AS IF I HAD NO	1039		1
AND THEN I KNEW I HEARD.	I HEARD, AS IF I HAD NO	1039		4
AND THEN I KNEW I HEARD.	I HEARD, AS IF I HAD NO	1039		4
I SAW, AS IF MY EYE WERE ON	I HEARD, AS IF I HAD NO	1039		5
AND NOW I KNOW 'TWAS LIGHT, BECAUSE	I HEARD, AS IF I HAD NO	1039		7
I DWELT, AS IF MYSELF WERE OUT,	I HEARD, AS IF I HAD NO	1039		9
I SIGHT THE APRILS--	SPRING COMES ON THE	1042		2
NOT DUMB--I HAD A SORT THAT MOVED--	I'VE DROPPED MY BRAIN--	1046		9
I CANNOT MEET THE SPRING UNMOVED--	I CANNOT MEET THE SPRING	1051		1
I FEEL THE OLD DESIRE--	I CANNOT MEET THE SPRING	1051		2
I SAW NO MORE OF HER.	I CANNOT MEET THE SPRING	1051		8
I NEVER SAW A MOOR--	I NEVER SAW A MOOR--	1052		1
I NEVER SAW THE SEA--	I NEVER SAW A MOOR--	1052		2
YET KNOW I HOW THE HEATHER LOOKS	I NEVER SAW A MOOR--	1052		3
I NEVER SPOKE WITH GOD	I NEVER SAW A MOOR--	1052		5
YET CERTAIN AM I OF THE SPOT	I NEVER SAW A MOOR--	1052		7
HE ASKED IF I WAS HIS--	IT WAS A QUIET WAY--	1053		2
I MADE NO ANSWER OF THE TONGUE	IT WAS A QUIET WAY--	1053		3
I HAD A DAILY BLISS	I HAD A DAILY BLISS	1057		1
I HALF INDIFFERENT VIEWED	I HAD A DAILY BLISS	1057		2
TILL SUDDEN I PERCEIVED IT STIR--	I HAD A DAILY BLISS	1057		3
IT GREW AS I PURSUED	I HAD A DAILY BLISS	1057		4
I LEARNED TO ESTIMATE.	I HAD A DAILY BLISS	1057		8
WHILE I REPEAT [RECITE] YOUR	SANG FROM THE HEART,	1059		15
THREE WEEKS PASSED SINCE I HAD SEEN HER--	THREE WEEKS PASSED SINCE	1061		1
I BEHELD HER NEXT	THREE WEEKS PASSED SINCE	1061		4
NOR KNOW I WHEN IT CEASE,	FURTHER IN SUMMER THAN	1068	V	
THAN THIS, I KNOW NO MORE.	FURTHER IN SUMMER THAN	1068	V	
HERE'S--WHAT I HAD TO "TELL YOU"--	TITLE DIVINE--IS MINE!	1072	V	
IS EVERY ONE I MEET	EXPERIMENT TO ME	1073		2
THE EARTH AND I, ALONE,	THE SUN WENT DOWN--NO	1079		2
THE EARTH AND I AND ONE	THE SUN WENT DOWN--NO	1079		6
I ALWAYS FEEL A DOUBT	WHEN THEY COME BACK--IF	1080		2
I ALWAYS HAD A FEAR	WHEN THEY COME BACK--IF	1080		6
I DID NOT TELL, IT WAS THEIR LAST EXPERIMENT	WHEN THEY COME BACK--IF	1080		7
IF I AM THERE--ONE DOES NOT KNOW	WHEN THEY COME BACK--IF	1080		13
TOMORROW, BUT IF I AM THERE	WHEN THEY COME BACK--IF	1080		15
I TAKE BACK ALL I SAY--	WHEN THEY COME BACK--IF	1080		16
I TAKE BACK ALL I SAY--	WHEN THEY COME BACK--IF	1080		16
I AM AFRAID TO OWN A BODY--	I AM AFRAID TO OWN A	1090		1
I AM AFRAID TO OWN A SOUL--	I AM AFRAID TO OWN A	1090		2
BECAUSE 'TWAS RICHES I COULD OWN,	BECAUSE 'TWAS RICHES I	1093		1
I KNEW THE DOLLARS BY THEIR NAMES--	BECAUSE 'TWAS RICHES I	1093		3
THEMSELF ARE ALL I HAVE--	THEMSELF ARE ALL I HAVE	1094		1
I THOUGHT YOU'D CHOOSE A VELVET CHEEK	THEMSELF ARE ALL I HAVE	1094		3
DEMEANS [DEGRADES] THE DRESS I WEAR--	MY COCOON TIGHTENS--	1099		4

I (CONTINUED)

	FIRST LINE	POEM	LINE
SO I MUST BAFFLE AT THE HINT	MY COCOON TIGHTENS--	1099	9
I TAKE THE CLUE DIVINE--	MY COCOON TIGHTENS--	1099	12
I KNOW FOR I HAVE TRIED	BETWEEN THE FORM OF LIFE	1101	8
I KNOW FOR I HAVE TRIED	BETWEEN THE FORM OF LIFE	1101	8
IF I COULD CRAWL BETWEEN	THE SPRY ARMS OF THE	1103	2
I HAVE AN ERRAND IMMINENT	THE SPRY ARMS OF THE	1103	3
I SHOULD NOT CARE TO STOP	THE SPRY ARMS OF THE	1103	5
REPUBLIC OF DELIGHT, I THOUGHT	THE BIRD DID PRANCE--THE	1107	7
I FIT FOR THEM--	I FIT FOR THEM--	1109	1
I SEEK THE DARK	I FIT FOR THEM--	1109	2
TILL I AM THOROUGH FIT.	I FIT FOR THEM--	1109	3
A PURER FOOD FOR THEM, IF I SUCCEED,	I FIT FOR THEM--	1109	7
IF NOT I HAD	I FIT FOR THEM--	1109	8
I HEARD IT'S AXLES GO	THIS SLOW DAY MOVED	1120	2
I TOLD MY SOUL TO COME--	THIS SLOW DAY MOVED	1120	5
I TELL IT GAY TO THOSE WHO SUFFER NOW--	TIME DOES GO ON--	1121	2
IF I SHOULD [SHALL] SPEND IT HERE--	'TIS MY FIRST NIGHT	1122	2
THAT [TILL] I MAY [CAN] GLOAT ON THEE--	OH SUMPTUOUS MOMENT	1125	3
NOW [SINCE] I [THAT] ABUNDANCE SEE--	OH SUMPTUOUS MOMENT	1125	5
SHALL I TAKE THEE, THE POET SAID	SHALL I TAKE THEE, THE	1126	1
TILL I HAVE FINER [VAINER / FURTHER] TRIED--	SHALL I TAKE THEE, THE	1126	4
HOWEVER, KNOW NOT I.	THE DUTIES OF THE WIND	1137	16
WHEN I SHALL LONG FOR EARTHLY PLAY	IN THY LONG PARADISE OF	1145	3
I NOTICED PEOPLE DISAPPEARED	I NOTICED PEOPLE	1149	1
NOW KNOW I--THEY BOTH VISITED	I NOTICED PEOPLE	1149	5
I REACHED THE STOLID BLISS	THROUGH WHAT TRANSPORTS	1153	2
I WON AS NEAR AS THIS	THROUGH WHAT TRANSPORTS	1153	6
AND SO MUCH MORE AT HOME THAN I	ALONE AND IN A	1167	5
I FELT MYSELF A [THE] VISITOR	ALONE AND IN A	1167	7
I FOUND IT QUIETLY ASSUMED	ALONE AND IN A	1167	11
I CAN RETURN THE BLOW--	ALONE AND IN A	1167	18
THAT I SHOULD SPECIFY.	ALONE AND IN A	1167	28
I THE DAY BEFORE	ON THE WORLD YOU COLORED	1171	6
WE [I] LIKE A HAIRBREADTH 'SCAPE	WE LIKE A HAIRBREADTH	1175	1
IF WE [I] HAD VENTURED LESS	WE LIKE A HAIRBREADTH	1175	5
I GIVE THEE GUARANTY.	"REMEMBER ME" IMPLORED	1180	4
WHEN I HOPED I FEARED--	WHEN I HOPED I FEARED--	1181	1
WHEN I HOPED I FEARED--	WHEN I HOPED I FEARED--	1181	1
SINCE I HOPED I DARED	WHEN I HOPED I FEARED--	1181	2
SINCE I HOPED I DARED	WHEN I HOPED I FEARED--	1181	2
OF SUCH A LITTLE DOG AM I	A LITTLE DOG THAT WAGS	1185	3
I HONESTLY SUPPOSE--	A LITTLE DOG THAT WAGS	1185	8
WHILE I DELAY [DELAYED] TO GUESS [DRESS]	OH SHADOW ON THE GRASS,	1187	6
HENCEFORTH I TAKE MY LIVING PLACE	SOMEHOW MYSELF SURVIVED	1194	5
I SHALL VOTE FOR LANDS WITH LOCKS	WHAT WE SEE WE KNOW	1195	5
GRANTED I CAN PICK 'EM--	WHAT WE SEE WE KNOW	1195	6
I SHOULD NOT DARE TO BE SO SAD	I SHOULD NOT DARE TO BE	1197	1
I KNOW 'TIS DRY--	BECAUSE MY BROOK IS	1200	2
I TRY TO FLEE	BECAUSE MY BROOK IS	1200	6
SO I PULL MY STOCKINGS OFF	SO I PULL MY STOCKINGS	1201	1
I FIND IT TO INFER.	THE FROST WAS NEVER SEEN	1202	20
I CHARGE HIM FLY [FLEE]	THE PAST IS SUCH A	1203	6
I WANT A BROOK--COME NOW"!	THE SEA SAID "COME" TO	1210	4
THE SEA SAID "I AM HE	THE SEA SAID "COME" TO	1210	6
I THINK, BECAUSE HIS EMPTY PLATE	A SPARROW TOOK A SLICE	1211	3
I SAY IT JUST	A WORD IS DEAD	1212	4
I BET WITH EVERY WIND THAT BLEW	I BET WITH EVERY WIND	1215	1
NOW I KNEW I LOST HER--	NOW I KNEW I LOST HER--	1219	1
NOW I KNEW I LOST HER--	NOW I KNEW I LOST HER--	1219	1
I HAD PAID SO MUCH FOR--	NOW I KNEW I LOST HER--	1219	15
OF NATURE I SHALL HAVE ENOUGH	OF NATURE I SHALL HAVE	1220	1
WHEN I HAVE ENTERED THESE	OF NATURE I SHALL HAVE	1220	2
I HEAR THE LEVEL BEE--	LIKE TRAINS OF CARS ON	1224	2
AND THEN I DROPPED MY VICTORY	MY TRIUMPH LASTED TILL	1227	3
AND THEN I HATED GLORY	MY TRIUMPH LASTED TILL	1227	7
BUT WHAT EXCUSE HAVE I?	SO MUCH OF HEAVEN HAS	1228	8
WHERE I FOR RIGHT TO BE [GO]--	SOMEWHERE UPON THE	1231	6
WOULD PAY [PAWN] EACH ATOM THAT I AM	SOMEWHERE UPON THE	1231	7
HAD I NOT SEEN THE SUN	HAD I NOT SEEN THE SUN	1233	1
I COULD HAVE BORNE THE SHADE	HAD I NOT SEEN THE SUN	1233	2
AND THEN I [WE] KNEW 'TWAS WIND--	LIKE RAIN IT SOUNDED	1235	2
AND I AFFRONTED [DISCOURAGED] GREW	MY HEART RAN SO TO THEE	1237	3
MENTIONED I THIS TO THEE--	MY HEART RAN SO TO THEE	1237	10
ERE I BE THERE--	MY HEART RAN SO TO THEE	1237	16
I EVER CARED TO EARN--	THE STARS ARE OLD, THAT	1249	4
WE [I] PONDERED WHEN A CHILD,	WHO WERE "THE FATHER AND	1258	2
WE [I] THOUGHT, AT LEAST THEY ARE NO WORSE	WHO WERE "THE FATHER AND	1258	7
DID WE [I] DEMAND TODAY	WHO WERE "THE FATHER AND	1258	10
WHEN WE [I] DESIRED TO KNOW,	WHO WERE "THE FATHER AND	1258	14
AND I, HOWEVER ABSOLUTE [ACCURATE]	BECAUSE THAT YOU ARE	1260	3
THE INSTANT I PERCEIVE	BECAUSE THAT YOU ARE	1260	14
A THING I NEVER KNEW--	BECAUSE THAT YOU ARE	1260	18
I RECOGNIZE YOUR OWN--	BECAUSE THAT YOU ARE	1260	24
OF HEAVEN AND HELL I ALSO YIELD	BECAUSE THAT YOU ARE	1260	29
I CANNOT SEE MY SOUL BUT KNOW 'TIS THERE	I CANNOT SEE MY SOUL BUT	1262	1
THAT I BE ADEQUATELY DRESSED,	I CANNOT SEE MY SOUL BUT	1262	6
WHERE I AM HOPING NOW.	THIS IS THE PLACE THEY	1264	2
THE MOST TRIUMPHANT BIRD I EVER KNEW OR MET	THE MOST TRIUMPHANT BIRD	1265	1
I FAMISH [PERISH] TO BEHOLD SO EMINENT	THE MOST TRIUMPHANT BIRD	1265	4

I (CONTINUED)

	FIRST LINE	POEM	LINE
A SIGHT [ANOTHER SUCH . . .			
I SAW THAT THE FLAKE WAS ON IT	I SAW THAT THE FLAKE WAS	1267	1
"UNCHANGED" I URGED WITH A CANDOR	I SAW THAT THE FLAKE WAS	1267	3
I WORKED FOR CHAFF AND EARNING WHEAT	I WORKED FOR CHAFF AND	1269	1
I TASTED WHEAT AND HATED CHAFF	I WORKED FOR CHAFF AND	1269	5
I TAKE THEE BY THE HAND--	THE SPIDER AS AN ARTIST	1275	8
WHILE WE WERE [I WAS] FEARING IT, IT CAME--	WHILE WE WERE FEARING IT	1277	1
ART THOU THE THING I WANTED?	ART THOU THE THING I	1282	1
I TELL THE WHILE I WAITED [FAMISHED]--	ART THOU THE THING I	1282	5
I TELL THE WHILE I WAITED [FAMISHED]--	ART THOU THE THING I	1282	5
INCREASED TILL I ABJURED IT	ART THOU THE THING I	1282	7
I KNOW SUSPENSE--IT STEPS SO TERSE	I KNOW SUSPENSE--IT	1285	1
WHEN I AM RIDING BY--	I KNOW SUSPENSE--IT	1285	4
THOUGH LATELY I DESCRY	I KNOW SUSPENSE--IT	1285	6
I THOUGHT THAT NATURE WAS ENOUGH	I THOUGHT THAT NATURE	1286	1
THE MOST PATHETIC THING I DO	THE MOST PATHETIC THING	1290	1
IS PLAY I HEAR FROM YOU--	THE MOST PATHETIC THING	1290	2
I MAKE BELIEVE UNTIL MY HEART	THE MOST PATHETIC THING	1290	3
BUT WHEN I BREAK IT WITH THE NEWS	THE MOST PATHETIC THING	1290	5
I WISH I HAD NOT BROKEN IT--	THE MOST PATHETIC THING	1290	7
I WISH I HAD NOT BROKEN IT--	THE MOST PATHETIC THING	1290	7
I FEEL [FELT] AS IF THE GRASS WAS PLEASED	THE MUSHROOM IS THE ELF	1298	13
I CANNOT WANT IT MORE--	I CANNOT WANT IT MORE--	1301	1
I CANNOT WANT IT LESS--	I CANNOT WANT IT MORE--	1301	2
I THINK THAT THE ROOT OF THE WIND IS WATER--	I THINK THAT THE ROOT OF	1302	1
I WON IT WITH A BUN--	THIS DIRTY--LITTLE--	1311	3
HOW GLAD I AM--	DEAR MARCH--COME IN--	1320	2
I HOPED [LOOKED] FOR YOU BEFORE--	DEAR MARCH--COME IN--	1320	3
I HAVE SO MUCH TO TELL--	DEAR MARCH--COME IN--	1320	10
I GOT YOUR LETTER, AND THE BIRDS--	DEAR MARCH--COME IN--	1320	11
THE MAPLES NEVER KNEW THAT YOU WERE COMING--TILL I CALLED	DEAR MARCH--COME IN--	1320	12
I DECLARE--HOW RED THEIR FACES GREW--	DEAR MARCH--COME IN--	1320	13
I WILL NOT BE PURSUED--	DEAR MARCH--COME IN--	1320	20
WHEN I AM OCCUPIED--	DEAR MARCH--COME IN--	1320	22
BUT I TELL YOU EVERY STEP IS A TROUGH [SLUICE]--	FLOSS WONT SAVE YOU FROM	1322	5
I NEVER HEAR THAT ONE IS DEAD [HAS DIED]	I NEVER HEAR THAT ONE IS	1323	1
I DO NOT KNOW THE MAN SO BOLD	I NEVER HEAR THAT ONE IS	1323	13
I SEND YOU A DECREPIT FLOWER	I SEND YOU A DECREPIT	1324	1
AND I DESIGNED TO STAY--	I SEND YOU A DECREPIT	1324	4
HARDENED [FASTENED] WITH I KNOW--	WHETHER THEY HAVE	1329	8
A BEE I PERSONALLY KNEW	A SINGLE CLOVER PLANK	1343	3
OTHERS--SHALL I SAY	NOT ANY MORE TO BE	1344	14
I OFTEN IN THE NIGHT [MY SLEEP]	ESCAPE IS SUCH A	1347	2
AND THAT IS WHY I LAY MY HEAD	ESCAPE IS SUCH A	1347	11
"I WILL GIVE" THE BASE PROVISO--	"FAITHFUL TO THE END"	1357	V
I SUED THE NEWS--YET FEARED--THE NEWS	I SUED THE NEWS--YET	1360	1
I [WE] KEEP ONE RAY	OF THEIR PECULIAR LIGHT	1362	2
PROMPT AS WHEN I LIT THEM	TRUSTY AS THE STARS	1369	3
I SUPPOSE THE TIME WILL COME	I SUPPOSE THE TIME WILL	1381	1
I SUPPOSE THE TIME WILL COME	I SUPPOSE THE TIME WILL	1381	5
I BELIEVE THE DAY WILL BE	I SUPPOSE THE TIME WILL	1381	9
I HAVE NO LIFE BUT THIS--[TO LIVE]	I HAVE NO LIFE BUT THIS	1398	1
I OFTEN WONDER HE	WHAT MYSTERY PERVADES A	1400	10
WHATEVER REALM I FORFEIT, LORD,	TO OWN A SUSAN OF MY OWN	1401	3
I MORE SHOULD MISS--	MY MAKER--LET ME BE	1403	4
I SHALL NOT MURMUR IF AT LAST	I SHALL NOT MURMUR IF AT	1410	1
THE ONES I LOVED BELOW	I SHALL NOT MURMUR IF AT	1410	2
FOR WHAT I SHUNNED THEM SO--	I SHALL NOT MURMUR IF AT	1410	4
I SHUN IT AS I DO DESPAIR	ONE JOY OF SO MUCH	1420	3
I SHUN IT AS I DO DESPAIR	ONE JOY OF SO MUCH	1420	3
THE FAIREST HOME I EVER KNEW	THE FAIREST HOME I EVER	1423	1
BY PARTIES ALSO THAT I KNEW	THE FAIREST HOME I EVER	1423	3
SINCE SHE AND I HAD MET AND PLAYED	A LITTLE SNOW WAS HERE	1444	3
I FIND ONE ON MY HAND	HOW SOFT A CATERPILLAR	1448	2
I THOUGHT THE TRAIN WOULD NEVER COME--	I THOUGHT THE TRAIN	1449	1
I DONT BELIEVE A PEEVISH BIRD	I THOUGHT THE TRAIN	1449	3
I TAUGHT MY HEART A HUNDRED TIMES	I THOUGHT THE TRAIN	1449	5
DESCRIED I--BY [IN] THE DISTANT [GAINING] LIGHT	THE ROAD WAS LIT WITH	1450	3
I WOULD NOT BE--	A COUNTERFEIT--A PLATED	1453	2
ONE THING OF IT WE [THEE I] BORROW	ONE THING OF IT WE	1464	1
ONE THING OF IT WE [THEE I] COVET--	ONE THING OF IT WE	1464	5
I NEVER THOUGHT THAT JASON SOUGHT	ONE OF THE ONES THAT	1466	21
BUT THEN I AM A RURAL MAN	ONE OF THE ONES THAT	1466	23
I NEVER MET IT NEAR	A WINGED SPARK DOTH SOAR	1468	2
SINCE HE AND I WERE BOYS	THE SAVIOR MUST HAVE	1487	6
ALL THAT I DO	ALL THAT I DO	1496	1
I KNOW HIS EYE	ALL THAT I DO	1496	4
WHERE E'ER I PLY	ALL THAT I DO	1496	5
AS YOU OR I [COWARDS DO]--	FACTS BY OUR SIDE ARE	1497	13
I SCANNED HIS NARROW REALM [GRANT]	IT CAME HIS TURN TO BEG	1500	5
I GAVE HIM LEAVE TO LIVE	IT CAME HIS TURN TO BEG	1500	6
LUXURY I	IT CAME HIS TURN TO BEG	1500	V
I SAW THE WIND WITHIN HER	I SAW THE WIND WITHIN	1502	1
I KNEW IT BLEW FOR ME--	I SAW THE WIND WITHIN	1502	2
I ASKED HUMILITY	I SAW THE WIND WITHIN	1502	4
I WATCHED [BOUGHT] THE FLUTTERING	I SAW THE WIND WITHIN	1502	V

I (CONTINUED)

	FIRST LINE	POEM		LINE
[VANQUISHED] SPIRIT				
I WATCHED THE PRECIOUS [SUBTLE] BEGGAR	I SAW THE WIND WITHIN	1502	V	
I CLING TO NOWHERE TILL I FALL--	MORE THAN THE GRAVE IS	1503		4
I CLING TO NOWHERE TILL I FALL--	MORE THAN THE GRAVE IS	1503		4
I STILL CAN REACH [TOUCH] THE TOP	THE PILE OF YEARS IS NOT	1507		6
AND CATCH ME ERE [WHEN / AS] I DROP	THE PILE OF YEARS IS NOT	1507		8
I HAVE AT LAST REVENGE--	MINE ENEMY IS GROWING	1509		2
IS JUST AS HIGH AS YOU AND I,	THE BUTTERFLY UPON THE	1521		5
AND HIGHER, I BELIEVE,	THE BUTTERFLY UPON THE	1521		6
I WANT TO SEND IT TO YOU	HE LIVED THE LIFE OF	1525	V	
I DARE NOT WRITE UNTIL I HEAR--	A PANG IS MORE	1530	V	
I DARE NOT WRITE UNTIL I HEAR--	A PANG IS MORE	1530	V	
SCATTERED--I SAY--TO PLACE [SEAT] THEM SIDE BY SIDE	ABOVE OBLIVION'S TIDE	1531		6
NOW I LAY THEE DOWN TO SLEEP--	NOW I LAY THEE DOWN TO	1539		1
I PRAY THE LORD THY DUST TO KEEP--	NOW I LAY THEE DOWN TO	1539		2
I PRAY THE LORD THY SOUL TO MAKE--	NOW I LAY THEE DOWN TO	1539		4
BUT I MUST DESIST--	THE BIBLE IS AN ANTIQUE	1545	V	10
I HAVE ONE BATTLE MORE--	MY WARS ARE LAID AWAY IN	1549		2
A FOE WHOM I HAVE NEVER SEEN	MY WARS ARE LAID AWAY IN	1549		3
HOW SWEET IF I AM NOT FORGOT	MY WARS ARE LAID AWAY IN	1549		9
I GIVE [SEND] MY DYING KISS--	"GO TELL IT"--WHAT A	1554		8
I GROPED FOR HIM BEFORE I KNEW	I GROPED FOR HIM BEFORE	1555		1
I GROPED FOR HIM BEFORE I KNEW	I GROPED FOR HIM BEFORE	1555		1
THOUGH I WITHIN SUPPOSE	I GROPED FOR HIM BEFORE	1555		6
OF DEATH I TRY TO THINK LIKE THIS--	OF DEATH I TRY TO THINK	1558		1
I DO REMEMBER WHEN A CHILD	OF DEATH I TRY TO THINK	1558		9
THAT DYING I MAY EARN THE LOOK [GAZE]	TRIED ALWAYS AND	1559		3
FOR WHICH I CEASE TO LIVE--	TRIED ALWAYS AND	1559		4
I WAS REGARDED [CONSIDERED] THEN	TO BE FORGOT BY THEE	1560		7
I FELT APOLOGY WERE DUE	NO BRIGADIER THROUGHOUT	1561		13
I CAN BUT KNOCK--	THE HEART HAS MANY DOORS	1567		2
THE FARTHEST THUNDER THAT I HEARD	THE FARTHEST THUNDER	1581		1
BUT [AND] I WOULD NOT EXCHANGE THE BOLT [FLASH]	THE FARTHEST THUNDER	1581		7
AND SO I SEND MY CRIMSON SCOUTS	WHERE ROSES WOULD NOT	1582		3
BUT HISTORY AND I	WITCHCRAFT WAS HUNG, IN	1583		2
AND THEN A [I] MUST	THERE ARE TWO MAYS	1618		2
AND THEN, PERHAPS, I SHALL.	THERE ARE TWO MAYS	1618	V	3
THAT INDICATES I WILL!	THERE ARE TWO MAYS	1618		5
I OPEN EVERY DOOR,	NOT KNOWING WHEN THE	1619		2
BACK FROM THE CORDIAL GRAVE I DRAG THEE	BACK FROM THE CORDIAL	1625		1
THE DEATH I NEVER FEARED	SO GIVE ME BACK TO DEATH	1632		2
IN MY OWN GRAVE I BREATHE	SO GIVE ME BACK TO DEATH	1632		5
THOUGH SLIPPING--SLIPPING I PERCEIVE	STILL OWN THEE--STILL	1633		3
WHICH QUESTION SHALL I CLUTCH--	STILL OWN THEE--STILL	1633		5
AND I AM RICHER THEN THAN ALL MY FELLOW MEN--	TAKE ALL AWAY FROM ME,	1640		2
I HAVE A NAVY IN THE WEST	"RED SEA," INDEED! TALK	1642		3
EXTOL THEE--COULD I--THEN I WILL	EXTOL THEE--COULD I--	1643		1
EXTOL THEE--COULD I--THEN I WILL	EXTOL THEE--COULD I--	1643		1
WHY SHOULD WE [I] HURRY--WHY INDEED	WHY SHOULD WE HURRY--WHY	1646		1
BUT HAVE I NOT MISTOOK	A WORD MADE FLESH IS	1651		4
BEAUTY CROWDS ME TILL I DIE	BEAUTY CROWDS ME TILL I	1654		1
BUT IF I EXPIRE TO-DAY	BEAUTY CROWDS ME TILL I	1654		3
GUEST AM I TO HAVE	GUEST AM I TO HAVE	1661		1
I MEET HIM WITH A START	HIS MIND OF MAN, A	1663		2
IN WHICH I HAVE NO PART	HIS MIND OF MAN, A	1663		4
OR EVEN IF I DEEM I DO	HIS MIND OF MAN, A	1663		5
OR EVEN IF I DEEM I DO	HIS MIND OF MAN, A	1663		5
I DID NOT REACH THEE	I DID NOT REACH THEE	1664		1
I SHALL NOT COUNT THE JOURNEY ONE	I DID NOT REACH THEE	1664		5
WHEN I AM TELLING THEE	I DID NOT REACH THEE	1664		6
I KNOW OF PEOPLE IN THE GRAVE	I KNOW OF PEOPLE IN THE	1665		1
TO KNOW THE NEWS I KNOW TO-NIGHT	I KNOW OF PEOPLE IN THE	1665		3
I SEE THEE CLEARER FOR THE GRAVE	I SEE THEE CLEARER FOR	1666		1
I KNOW THEE BETTER FOR THE ACT	I SEE THEE CLEARER FOR	1666		5
I WATCHED HER FACE TO SEE WHICH WAY	I WATCHED HER FACE TO	1667		1
IF I COULD TELL HOW GLAD I WAS	IF I COULD TELL HOW GLAD	1668		1
IF I COULD TELL HOW GLAD I WAS	IF I COULD TELL HOW GLAD	1668		1
I SHOULD NOT BE SO GLAD--	IF I COULD TELL HOW GLAD	1668		2
BUT WHEN I CANNOT MAKE THE FORCE	IF I COULD TELL HOW GLAD	1668		3
I KNOW IT IS A SIGN	IF I COULD TELL HOW GLAD	1668		5
I CAME UPON A WORM	IN WINTER IN MY ROOM	1670		2
I'D NOT BELIEVE IT IF I HEARD	IN WINTER IN MY ROOM	1670		12
I TIED HIM--TOO	IN WINTER IN MY ROOM	1670		19
I SHRANK--"HOW FAIR YOU ARE"!	IN WINTER IN MY ROOM	1670		22
THAT TIME I FLEW	IN WINTER IN MY ROOM	1670		32
I SET ME DOWN	IN WINTER IN MY ROOM	1670		38
FATHER I OBSERVED TO HEAVEN	LIGHTLY STEPPED A YELLOW	1672		7
DID I DISCLOSE	ON MY VOLCANO GROWS THE	1677		7
I FELT IT SECOND PAIN	THAT SHE FORGOT ME WAS	1683		2
THAT I WAS WORTHY TO FORGET	THAT SHE FORGOT ME WAS	1683		3
WAS MOST I THOUGHT UPON	THAT SHE FORGOT ME WAS	1683		4
FAITHFUL WAS ALL THAT I COULD BOAST	THAT SHE FORGOT ME WAS	1683		5
NO FRIEND HAVE I THAT SO PERSISTS	THE BLUNDER IS IN	1684		7
I ALMOST TOUCHED HER	TO-DAY OR THIS NOON	1702		3
I JUDGE FROM MY GEOGRAPHY	VOLCANOES BE IN SICILY	1705		3
AM I INCLINED TO CLIMB	VOLCANOES BE IN SICILY	1705		6
A CRATER I MAY CONTEMPLATE	VOLCANOES BE IN SICILY	1705		7

	FIRST LINE	POEM	LINE
I (CONTINUED)			
I DARE NOT ASK MY FEET--	A PIT--BUT HEAVEN OVER	1712	11
I ASCERTAIN IT WITH A SHOCK--	CONSULTING SUMMER'S	1715	3
I SHALL NOT LOOK AGAIN.	CONSULTING SUMMER'S	1715	4
THE TRUTH I DO NOT DARE TO KNOW	CONSULTING SUMMER'S	1715	7
I MUFFLE WITH A JEST.	CONSULTING SUMMER'S	1715	8
HAD I KNOWN THAT THE FIRST WAS THE LAST	HAD I KNOWN THAT THE	1720	1
I SHOULD HAVE KEPT IT LONGER.	HAD I KNOWN THAT THE	1720	2
HAD I KNOWN THAT THE LAST WAS THE FIRST	HAD I KNOWN THAT THE	1720	3
I SHOULD HAVE DRUNK [MIXED] IT STRONGER.	HAD I KNOWN THAT THE	1720	4
I NEVER TO THIS DAY	HE WAS MY HOST--HE WAS	1721	2
IF I INVITED HIM COULD TELL,	HE WAS MY HOST--HE WAS	1721	3
HIGH FROM THE EARTH I HEARD A BIRD!	HIGH FROM THE EARTH I	1723	1
I GATHERED FROM HIS TALK	HIGH FROM THE EARTH I	1723	10
I SUBSEQUENTLY LEARNED	HIGH FROM THE EARTH I	1723	14
I TOOK ONE DRAUGHT OF LIFE--	I TOOK ONE DRAUGHT OF	1725	1
I'LL TELL YOU WHAT I PAID--	I TOOK ONE DRAUGHT OF	1725	2
IF ALL THE GRIEFS I AM TO HAVE	IF ALL THE GRIEFS I AM	1726	1
I AM SO HAPPY I BELIEVE	IF ALL THE GRIEFS I AM	1726	3
I AM SO HAPPY I BELIEVE	IF ALL THE GRIEFS I AM	1726	3
IF ALL THE JOYS I AM TO HAVE	IF ALL THE GRIEFS I AM	1726	5
I THE DART REVERE.	I'VE GOT AN ARROW HERE.	1729	3
I PERCEIVE THE ROSE!	"LETHE" IN MY FLOWER,	1730	8
I DOUBT IF EVEN THAT	LOVE CAN DO ALL BUT	1731	2
I AM CONVINCED WAS THIS	NO MAN SAW AWE, NOR TO	1733	16
I NEVER KNEW THY POWER,	OH, HONEY OF AN HOUR,	1734	2
PROUD OF THE PAIN I DID NOT FEEL TILL THEE,	PROUD OF MY BROKEN HEART	1736	2
SEE! I USURPED THY CRUCIFIX TO HONOR MINE!	PROUD OF MY BROKEN HEART	1736	8
FOR I WEAR THE "THORNS" TILL SUNSET--	REARRANGE A "WIFE'S"	1737	15
I SAY GOODNIGHT BY DAY--	SOME SAY GOODNIGHT--AT	1739	2
GOODNIGHT, I STILL REPLY--	SOME SAY GOODNIGHT--AT	1739	4
I MAKE MY PARLOR ORDERLY	THE GRAVE MY LITTLE	1743	3
ALL OTHER HEARTS [THINGS] I KNEW.	TO LOSE THEE--SWEETER	1754	2
BUT THEN, I HAD THE DEW!	TO LOSE THEE--SWEETER	1754	4
"'TWAS ALL I HAD," SHE STRICKEN GASPED--	UPON THE GALLOWS HUNG A	1757	7
WITH "IF I COULD" ENDEAVORING	WHICH MISSES MOST,	1759	9
ICE			
BEFORE THE ICE IS IN THE POOLS--	BEFORE THE ICE IS IN THE	37	1
WHO CANNOT THANK THEM FOR THE ICE	THEY WONT FROWN ALWAYS--	874	7
ICES			
STILL--CLAD IN YOUR MAIL OF ICES--	AH, TENERIFFE!	666	6
ICICLE			
DRESSES EACH HOUSE IN CRAPE, AND ICICLE--	IT'S COMING--THE	390	7
GO MANACLE YOUR ICICLE	'TWAS HERE MY SUMMER	1756	7
ICICLES			
ICICLES--CRAWL FROM POLAR CAVERNS--	SAFE IN THEIR ALABASTER	216	V
ICICLES UPON MY SOUL	WHEN I HOPED, I	768	13
I'D			
I'D NOTICE NOBODY!	"SOWN IN DISHONOR"!	62	5
I'D RATHER CALL HIM "STAR."	"ARCTURUS" IS HIS OTHER	70	2
AND I'D LIKE TO LOOK A LITTLE MORE	GOING TO HEAVEN!	79	22
I THINK I'D SHOOT THE HUMAN RACE	MY FRIEND ATTACKS MY	118	7
I'D BRING THEM EVERY FLOWER THAT GROWS	IF I COULD BRIBE THEM BY	179	2
SO SURE I'D COME--SO SURE I'D COME--	I SHOULD NOT DARE TO	205	10
SO SURE I'D COME--SO SURE I'D COME--	I SHOULD NOT DARE TO	205	10
HIST! WHIST! I'D COME!	IS IT TRUE, DEAR SUE?	218	11
I'D HARASS GOD	SHOULD YOU BUT FAIL AT--	226	6
TO GAIN HIS GRACE--I'D DIE!	THE COURT IS FAR AWAY--	235	4
DO YOU THINK I'D STOP	AH, MOON--AND STAR!	240	5
I'D GIVE--I'D GIVE MY LIFE--OF COURSE--	WHAT WOULD I GIVE TO SEE	247	2
I'D GIVE--I'D GIVE MY LIFE--OF COURSE--	WHAT WOULD I GIVE TO SEE	247	2
I'D GIVE MY BIGGEST BOBOLINK!	WHAT WOULD I GIVE TO SEE	247	5
I'D GIVE HER--	WHAT WOULD I GIVE TO SEE	247	8
I'D SWEAR BY HIM--	THE ROBIN'S MY CRITERION	285	4
I'D DAISIES SPURN [CLOVERS--SCORN]--	THE ROBIN'S MY CRITERION	285	9
I'D RATHER SUIT MY FOOT	IS BLISS THEN, SUCH	340	4
I'D DO THIS WAY--	I'M SAYING EVERY DAY	373	3
I'D TUNNEL--TILL MY GROOVE	I HAD NOT MINDED--WALLS	398	5
I'D SO MUCH JOY--I TOLD IT--RED--	IT WOULD NEVER BE COMMON	430	9
I'D RATHER BE THE ONE	I WOULD NOT PAINT--A	505	2
I'D RATHER BE THE ONE	I WOULD NOT PAINT--A	505	10
I'D BRUSH THE SUMMER BY	IF YOU WERE COMING IN	511	2
I'D WIND THE MONTHS IN BALLS--	IF YOU WERE COMING IN	511	6
I'D COUNT THEM ON MY HAND,	IF YOU WERE COMING IN	511	10
I'D TOSS IT YONDER, LIKE A RIND,	IF YOU WERE COMING IN	511	15
AND TOLD HIM WHAT I'D LIKE, TODAY,	I PRAYED, AT FIRST, A	576	9
I'D GIVE--TO LIVE THAT HOUR--AGAIN--	AGAIN--HIS VOICE IS AT	663	26
I'D RATHER RECOLLECT A SETTING	I'D RATHER RECOLLECT A	1349	1
I'D NOT BELIEVE IT IF I HEARD	IN WINTER IN MY ROOM	1670	12
IDEA			
AS FAIR--AS OUR IDEA--	HEAVEN IS SO FAR OF THE	370	6
IDEAL			
TAKING UP THE FAIR IDEAL,	TAKING UP THE FAIR IDEAL	428	1
CHERISHING--OUR POOR IDEAL--	TAKING UP THE FAIR IDEAL	428	9
EACH--IT'S DIFFICULT [ABSOLUTE] IDEAL	GROWTH OF MAN--LIKE	750	5
IDEALS			
IDEALS ARE THE FAIRY OIL	IDEALS ARE THE FAIRY OIL	983	1
IDENTIFIED			
AT LAST, TO BE IDENTIFIED!	AT LAST, TO BE	174	1
THE OWNER PASSED--IDENTIFIED--	MY LIFE HAD STOOD--A	754	3

	FIRST LINE	POEM	LINE
IDENTIFY			
CEASE TO IDENTIFY--	THIS DUST, AND IT'S	936	4
IDENTITY			
IT'S OWN IDENTITY.	THIS CONSCIOUSNESS THAT	822	16
OF MY [AN] IDENTITY.	NATURE AND GOD--I	835	4
HIS TWIN IDENTITY	TRUTH--IS AS OLD AS GOD	836	2
IDENTITY TO QUESTION [HANDLE]	AS ONE DOES SICKNESS	957	11
BESIDES IDENTITY	THAT SACRED CLOSET WHEN	1273	6
BEFORE IDENTITY WAS CREASED [LEASED].	ESTRANGED FROM BEAUTY--	1474	4
IN ALL IDENTITY--	HOW FIRM ETERNITY MUST	1499	4
OR MANSION OF IDENTITY	THE LOOK OF THEE, WHAT	1689	3
IDLE			
WHEN LAST YEAR'S DISTAFF IDLE HUNG	THERE IS A MORN BY MEN	24	11
WILL IDLE LIE--IN AUBURN--	WHEN ROSES CEASE TO	32	7
SOME CHAFE IT'S IDLE HAND--	THERE'S SOMETHING	45	6
IDLE HIS VERMILLION	ON THE WORLD YOU COLORED	1171	3
IDLENESS			
THIS AUDIENCE OF IDLENESS	FROM COCOON FORTH A	354	20
WAS EVER IDLENESS [ARROGANCE] LIKE THIS?	A LONG--LONG SLEEP--A	654	5
HIS IDLENESS--A TUNE--	HIS FEET ARE SHOD WITH	916	6
OF IDLENESS AND SPRING--	HIS LITTLE HEARSE LIKE	1522	8
IDLY			
THE IDLY SWAYING PLANK	A SINGLE CLOVER PLANK	1343	9
IDOLATRY			
MY SLOW IDOLATRY--	YOU CONSTITUTED TIME--	765	8
OF IDOLATRY.	NOW I KNEW I LOST HER--	1219	20
IDOL'S			
A PENCIL IN AN IDOL'S [DAINTY] HAND	DEATH WARRANTS ARE	1375	4
I. E.			
I. E. GATHERED AWAY,	LIKE HER THE SAINTS	60	8
IGNIS			
BETTER AN IGNIS FATUUS	THOSE--DYING THEN,	1551	8
IGNITE			
A THING THAT CAN IGNITE	YOU CANNOT PUT A FIRE	530	2
IGNITED			
IGNITED THIS ABODE	THOUGH THE GREAT WATERS	1599	5
IGNITION			
THAT MAY FURNISH THE FUSE [IGNITION] UNTO A SPARK	A MAN MAY MAKE A REMARK	952	3
IGNOBLE			
THAT OUR IGNOBLE EYES	TWO--WERE IMMORTAL TWICE	800	5
OUR MOST IGNOBLE SERVICES	WHO GOES TO DINE MUST	1223	7
IGNOMINY			
WHEN THEY LET GO THE IGNOMINY--SMILING--	UNTO LIKE STORY--TROUBLE	295	7
T'IS IGNOMINY NOW	WHEN WE HAVE CEASED TO	1706	6
IGNOMINY'S			
OF IGNOMINY'S DUE	A RAT SURRENDERED HERE	1340	4
NOR IGNOMINY'S NAME--	TO HER DERIDED HOME	1586	4
IGNORANCE			
HIS IGNORANCE--THE ANGEL	NO MAN CAN COMPASS A	477	11
BE LIMITED BY IGNORANCE--	HE PARTS HIMSELF--LIKE	517	15
AN IGNORANCE [IMPOTENCE] A SUNSET	AN IGNORANCE A SUNSET	552	1
AN IGNORANCE BEHELD--	WE LEARNED THE WHOLE OF	568	6
UPON THE IGNORANCE STEALS--	"HEAVEN" HAS DIFFERENT	575	8
TO IGNORANCE REVEALED.	THE LIGHTNING IS A	1173	8
OUR IGNORANCE--OUR CUIRASS IS--	WE KNEW NOT THAT WE WERE	1462	3
RELISHED HIS IGNORANCE	THE EVENT WAS DIRECTLY	1686	4
IGNORANT			
THAT ONE SO SHY--SO IGNORANT	I HAV'NT TOLD MY GARDEN	50	7
PIPE THE SWEET BIRDS IN IGNORANT CADENCE--	SAFE IN THEIR ALABASTER	216	10
THO' IGNORANT OF A WORD	I GOT SO I COULD HEAR	293	19
IGNORANT IS IT LIFE OR DEATH	CRISIS IS A HAIR	889	7
WE IGNORANT MUST BE--	FROM US SHE WANDERED NOW	890	6
ARE IGNORANT OF IT'S CONCERN	DEATH LEAVES US HOMESICK	935	3
HOW IGNORANT I HAD BEEN	I LEARNED--AT LEAST--	944	2
WAS IGNORANT THAT NATURE CLOSED	IT BLOOMED AND DROPT, A	978	V 19
WAS INNOCENT [IGNORANT / NOT ENFORCED / UNENFORCED] OF WHEEL	ELIJAH'S WAGON KNEW NO	1254	2
OF BARNS FOR WINTER--BLAMELESS [IGNORANT]--	THOSE CATTLE SMALLER	1388	5
AS IGNORANT OF THEIR RESUMPTION	FACTS BY OUR SIDE ARE	1497	12
IGNORES			
IGNORES THE SOLEMN NEWS	MORE LIFE--WENT OUT--	422	18
IGNORES [EXCLUDES] THE POSSIBILITY	SIZE CIRCUMSCRIBES--IT	641	7
THE TIPPET THAT IGNORES [RESISTS] HIS VOICE	THE JAY HIS CASTANET HAS	1635	3
I'LL			
I'LL TAKE MY INDIA RUBBERS,	"SIC TRANSIT GLORIA	3	27
I'LL PUT A TRINKET ON.	THE MORNS ARE MEEKER	12	8
FOR THEE TO BLOOM, I'LL SKIP THE TOMB	SUMMER FOR THEE, GRANT I	31	5
I'LL DECK TRADITION'S BUTTONHOLE--	IF SHE HAD BEEN THE	44	7
I'LL INSTITUTE AN "ACTION"--	I HAD SOME THINGS THAT I	116	13
I'LL VINDICATE THE LAW--	I HAD SOME THINGS THAT I	116	14
I'LL BEAR IT BETTER NOW--	YOU LOVE ME--YOU ARE	156	15
I'LL FETCH [BRING] THEE BROOKS	MY RIVER RUNS TO THEE--	162	5
SO I AM HEARING HIM, I'LL DREAM,	MAKE ME A PICTURE OF THE	188	6
I'LL SEEK HIS ROYAL FEET--	THE COURT IS FAR AWAY--	235	5
I'LL SAY--REMEMBER--KING--	THE COURT IS FAR AWAY--	235	6
I'LL TELL YOU HOW THE SUN ROSE--	I'LL TELL YOU HOW THE	318	1
I'LL HAND IT TO THE ANGEL--	THE FACE I CARRY WITH ME	336	5
I'LL DWELL IN CALYX--GRAY--	I TEND MY FLOWERS FOR	339	24
I'LL UNROLL THEE--	MY REWARD FOR BEING, WAS	343	8

	FIRST LINE	POEM	LINE
I'LL (CONTINUED)			
SO GO YOUR WAY--AND I'LL GO MINE--	A MURMUR IN THE TREES--	416	19
I'LL CLUTCH--AND CLUTCH--	I'LL CLUTCH--AND CLUTCH	427	1
I'LL STRING YOU--IN FINE NECKLACE--	I'LL CLUTCH--AND CLUTCH	427	7
I'LL SHOW YOU AT THE COURT--	I'LL CLUTCH--AND CLUTCH	427	15
I'LL DO THY WILL--	FORGET! THE LADY WITH	438	16
I'LL BE CONTENTED--SO [NOW]--	IF I MAY HAVE IT, WHEN	577	2
I'LL TELL THEE ALL--HOW BALD [BLANK] IT GREW--	IF I MAY HAVE IT, WHEN	577	14
I'LL TELL YOU HOW I TRIED TO KEEP	IF I MAY HAVE IT, WHEN	577	22
I'LL BEGIN TO SOW	DONT PUT UP MY THREAD &	617	2
I'LL DO SEAMS--A QUEEN'S ENDEAVOR	DONT PUT UP MY THREAD &	617	7
I'LL SEND THE FEATHER FROM MY HAT!	I'LL SEND THE FEATHER	687	1
I'LL TELL IT YOU [SIGNIFY / TESTIFY]--	THE ONLY NEWS I KNOW	827	12
EACH SCAR I'LL KEEP FOR HIM	EACH SCAR I'LL KEEP FOR	877	1
INSTEAD I'LL SAY OF GEM	EACH SCAR I'LL KEEP FOR	877	2
I'LL MIS SUM THEM.	EACH SCAR I'LL KEEP FOR	877	8
AND WHOSE "I'LL MEET YOU" HESITATES	SUPERFLUOUS WERE THE SUN	999	7
I'LL SHIVER, SATISFIED.	I'VE DROPPED MY BRAIN--	1046	20
I'LL LET MY HEART BE JUST IN SIGHT--	THEY MIGHT NOT NEED ME--	1391	2
I'LL TELL YOU WHAT I PAID--	I TOOK ONE DRAUGHT OF	1725	2
ILL			
IT ILL BECOMETH ME--	I TEND MY FLOWERS FOR	339	23
HOW ILL THE CREATURES BEAR--	SHE DEALT HER PRETTY	479	8
MY FIRST WELL DAY--SINCE MANY ILL--	MY FIRST WELL DAY--SINCE	574	1
MYSELF FELT ILL--AND ODD--	I HAD BEEN HUNGRY, ALL	579	14
ILL FLUTTERED OUT--IN EVERLASTING WELL--	TO KNOW JUST HOW HE	622	17
ILL! WE HAVE BERRIES, FOR THE PARCHING!	WOULD YOU LIKE SUMMER?	691	3
FOR GREATNESS, THAT IS ILL AT EASE [COMPOSED]	WHO GIANTS KNOW, WITH	796	3
WERT THOU BUT ILL--THAT I MIGHT SHOW THEE	WERT THOU BUT ILL--THAT	961	1
ILL IT BECOMETH [IS IT BECOMING] ME TO DWELL SO WEALTHILY	TAKE ALL AWAY FROM ME,	1640	3
ILLEGIBLE			
A FORCE ILLEGIBLE.	ALL CIRCUMSTANCES ARE	820	8
ILLEGITIMATE			
ILLEGITIMATE--	SO MUCH SUMMER	651	3
ILLNESS			
A BRIEF, BUT PATIENT ILLNESS--	THE GENTIAN WEAVES HER	18	5
ILLOCALITY			
IS ILLOCALITY--	A NEARNESS TO	963	8
ILLUME			
THAN NO ILLUME AT ALL--	THOSE--DYING THEN,	1551	9
ILLUMINATE			
ILLUMINATE--[MAKE POPULATE-- / MAKE MANIFEST] OR SEAL--	THE LONELINESS ONE DARE	777	16
ILLUMINATE THE HOUSE!	"AND WITH WHAT BODY DO	1492	4
ILLUMINATION			
SUCH STRANGE ILLUMINATION	THE GLEAM OF AN HEROIC	1687	2
ILLUMINE			
NO MIRROR COULD ILLUMINE THEE	I SEE THEE CLEARER FOR	1666	3
ILLUMINES			
ILLUMINES [SUFFUSES] WITH A GLOW	OF WHOM SO DEAR	1504	3
ILLUSIVE			
HER BEES HAVE A FICTITIOUS [AN ILLUSIVE] HUM--	LIKE SOME OLD FASHIONED	302	9
A FOND--ILLUSIVE WAY--	MY FIRST WELL DAY--SINCE	574	12
ILLUSTRATION			
IT'S CORPOREAL ILLUSTRATION--SELL	PUBLICATION--IS THE	709	11
ILLUSTRIOUS			
THAT BUSTLE SO ILLUSTRIOUS	THAT SHORT--POTENTIAL	1307	3
IMPREGNABLE [ILLUSTRIOUS / INVINCIBLE / INVIOLATE] THE ROSE	A LITTLE SNOW WAS HERE	1444	6
I'M			
AND I'M A ROSE!	A SEPAL, PETAL, AND A	19	5
I HOPE I'M READY FOR "THE WORST"--	"ARCTURUS" IS HIS OTHER	70	24
INDEED I'M TOO ASTONISHED	GOING TO HEAVEN!	79	4
I'M GLAD I DONT BELIEVE IT	GOING TO HEAVEN!	79	20
AND HE WAS BAREFOOT, I'M AFRAID!	I MET A KING THIS	166	4
I'M THE LITTLE "HEART'S EASE"!	I'M THE LITTLE "HEART'S	176	1
YOU WILL KNOW I'M TRYING	IF I SHOULD'NT BE ALIVE	182	7
AND MAKE BELIEVE I'M GETTING WARM	MAKE ME A PICTURE OF THE	188	3
I'M "WIFE"--I'VE FINISHED THAT--	I'M "WIFE"--I'VE	199	1
I'M CZAR--I'M "WOMAN" NOW--	I'M "WIFE"--I'VE	199	3
I'M CZAR--I'M "WOMAN" NOW--	I'M "WIFE"--I'VE	199	3
I'M "WIFE"! STOP THERE!	I'M "WIFE"--I'VE	199	12
I'M PLEADING AT THE "COUNTER"--SIR--	I CAME TO BUY A SMILE--	223	7
I'M USED TO THAT--	I CAN WADE GRIEF--	252	3
IF I'M LOST--NOW--	IF I'M LOST--NOW--	256	1
I'M BANISHED--NOW--YOU KNOW IT--	IF I'M LOST--NOW--	256	10
THE SEASONS FLIT--I'M TAUGHT--	THE ROBIN'S MY CRITERION	285	12
I'M NOBODY! WHO ARE YOU?	I'M NOBODY! WHO ARE YOU?	288	1
I'M OLD ENOUGH, TODAY, I'M CERTAIN--THEN--	ONE YEAR AGO--JOTS WHAT?	296	33
I'M OLD ENOUGH, TODAY, I'M CERTAIN--THEN--	ONE YEAR AGO--JOTS WHAT?	296	33
I'M SURE 'TIS INDIA--ALL DAY--	YOUR RICHES--TAUGHT ME--	299	17
I'M SURE [I KNOW] IT IS GOLCONDA--	YOUR RICHES--TAUGHT ME--	299	21
I'M GOING, ALL ALONG.	SOME KEEP THE SABBATH	324	12
BUT THEN--I'M NOT SO STAID--AS HE--	FUNNY--TO BE A CENTURY--	345	4
I'M SOME ACCUSTOMED TO HIM GROWN,	I DREADED THAT FIRST	348	3
I'M SAYING EVERY DAY	I'M SAYING EVERY DAY	373	1
AND THO' I'M SCARCE ACCOUNTED,	WHEN DIAMONDS ARE A	397	5
I'M HARDLY JUSTIFIED	THE WINTERS ARE SO SHORT	403	2
I'M SO ACCUSTOMED TO MY FATE--	IT MIGHT BE LONELIER	405	3

	FIRST LINE	POEM	LINE
I'M (CONTINUED)			
"I'M MIDNIGHT"--NEED THE MIDNIGHT SAY--	YOU'LL KNOW IT--AS YOU	420	9
"I'M SUNRISE"--NEED THE MAJESTY?	YOU'LL KNOW IT--AS YOU	420	10
I'M COMING HOME--	GOOD MORNING--MIDNIGHT--	425	2
I'M DIVING--JUST A LITTLE LATE--	I'LL CLUTCH--AND CLUTCH	427	5
I'M OFTEN THIRSTY--BUT MY LIPS	I KNOW WHERE WELLS GROW	460	11
IT MUST MEAN THAT--I'M SURE--	I KNOW WHERE WELLS GROW	460	16
ETERNITY, I'M COMING--SIR,	A WIFE--AT DAYBREAK I	461	12
LET ME THINK--I'M SURE	I WAS THE SLIGHTEST IN	486	8
I'M KNOCKING--EVERYWHERE--	AT LEAST--TO PRAY--IS	502	4
AND NOW, I'M DIFFERENT FROM BEFORE,	HE TOUCHED ME, SO I LIVE	506	7
I'M CEDED--I'VE STOPPED BEING THEIR'S--	I'M CEDED--I'VE STOPPED	508	1
I'M SORRY FOR THE DEAD--TODAY--	I'M SORRY FOR THE DEAD--	529	1
I'M CONFIDENT THAT BRAVOES	WHEN I WAS SMALL, A	596	17
I'M SATISFIED--THE ROMANCE	IT ALWAYS FELT TO ME--A	597	7
I'M KNEELING--[WE'RE PLEADING] STILL--	AH, TENERIFFE!	666	10
I'M NOT AFRAID TO KNOW--	THE SUN KEPT SETTING--	692	16
I'M FINITE--I CANT SEE--	THEIR HIGHT IN HEAVEN	696	4
BUT WHEN I'M EARL--	NO MATTER--NOW--SWEET--	704	2
WHEN I'M EARL?	NO MATTER--NOW--SWEET--	704	8
NAY--I'M THE SIZE SUIT THEE--	YOU SAID THAT I "WAS	738	4
I'M THAT--OR NOUGHT--	YOU SAID THAT I "WAS	738	15
TO FOE OF HIS--I'M DEADLY FOE--	MY LIFE HAD STOOD--A	754	17
I'M NOT ASHAMED OF THAT	PERHAPS YOU THINK ME	833	2
I'M TEMPTED HALF TO STITCH IT UP	THIS CHASM, SWEET, UPON	858	13
I'M ANSWERED IN A LONESOME TONE--	OF TOLLING BELL I ASK	947	3
I'M THINKING ON THAT OTHER MORN--	'TIS ANGUISH GRANDER	984	V 5
BEE! I'M EXPECTING YOU!	BEE! I'M EXPECTING YOU!	1035	1
I'M SURE, AT MANY A WHIM	IF NATURE SMILES--THE	1085	2
I'M FEELING FOR THE AIR--	MY COCOON TIGHTENS--	1099	2
I'M NOT A PARTY TO--	IS HEAVEN A PHYSICIAN?	1270	8
IMAGE			
THAT IMAGE--SATISFIES--	A CHARM INVESTS A FACE	421	8
IMAGE [FELLOW] OF LIGHT, ADIEU--	IMAGE OF LIGHT, ADIEU--	1556	1
IMAGERY			
OF IMAGERY--	INCONCEIVABLY SOLEMN!	582	4
IMAGINATION			
BY THE IMAGINATION	THE GLEAM OF AN HEROIC	1687	4
IMITATE			
TO IMITATE HER LIFE	SHE HIDETH HER THE LAST	557	9
THENCEFORWARD IMITATE--	TILL DEATH--IS NARROW	907	8
TO IMITATE BE MINE.	HER LITTLE PARASOL TO	1038	4
TO IMITATE THESE NEIGHBORS FLEET	WHOSE PINK CAREER MAY	1394	3
COULD NOT IT IMITATE--	UPON HIS SADDLE SPRUNG A	1600	V 8
IMITATING			
IMITATING [MORE RESEMBLING] YOU--	PROMISE THIS--WHEN YOU	648	16
THAT IMITATING HER	WHO GOES TO DINE MUST	1223	6
IMITATION			
AN IMITATION OF A LIGHT	I MEASURE EVERY GRIEF I	561	15
IMMATERIAL			
IS IMMATERIAL.	HOW DARE THE ROBINS SING	1724	8
IMMEDIATELY			
OH LET ME IMMEDIATELY "FADE"!	IF THIS IS "FADING"	120	2
HE--COMPENSATES--IMMEDIATELY--	SOME--WORK FOR	406	3
IMMEDIATELY GREW	ALONE AND IN A	1167	6
IMMEDIATELY--THAT ANGUISH STOOPED	SO PROUD SHE WAS TO DIE	1272	7
IN DEATH'S IMMEDIATELY--	ONE JOY OF SO MUCH	1420	12
IMMENSE			
AND ATTAR SO IMMENSE	THIS WAS A POET--IT IS	448	4
IMMENSITY			
IT RENTS IMMENSITY--	A NEARNESS TO	963	V 8
TO MOUNT IMMENSITY--	A SPARROW TOOK A SLICE	1211	V 8
AND RODE IMMENSITY [DERIDING BY--]	A SPARROW TOOK A SLICE	1211	V 8
THIS--IS IMMENSITY--	ALL THINGS SWEPT SOLE	1512	2
IMMINENT			
MORE IMMINENT THAN PAIN--	THERE IS A LANGUOR OF	396	2
HOW IMMINENT THE VENTURE--	THE HEAVEN VESTS FOR	694	9
TOO IMMINENT THE CHANCE--	TOO LITTLE WAY THE HOUSE	911	6
I HAVE AN ERRAND IMMINENT	THE SPRY ARMS OF THE	1103	3
IMMORTAL			
BUT AN IMMORTAL HERO	"SIC TRANSIT GLORIA	3	55
OF OUR IMMORTAL MIND--	TO HANG OUR HEAD--	105	4
IMMORTAL ALPS LOOK DOWN--	IN LANDS I NEVER SAW--	124	2
AND THINE IMMORTAL WINE!	THESE ARE THE DAYS WHEN	130	18
WHOSE BUT HER SHY--IMMORTAL FACE	SHE BORE IT TILL THE	144	15
TO THE IMMORTAL TUNE--	THE ROSE DID CAPER ON	208	14
THERE BE IMMORTAL FRIENDS	BEREAVEMENT IN THEIR	645	6
TWO--WERE IMMORTAL TWICE--	TWO--WERE IMMORTAL TWICE	800	1
THAT WE'VE IMMORTAL PLACE	IT IS AN HONORABLE	946	5
THAT AN IMMORTAL BINDS.	OF PAUL AND SILAS IT IS	1166	8
IMMORTAL IS AN AMPLE WORD	IMMORTAL IS AN AMPLE	1205	1
LEFT IN IMMORTAL YOUTH	LEFT IN IMMORTAL YOUTH	1289	1
IN THAT IMMORTAL COPY	BELSHAZZAR HAD A LETTER	1459	5
IMMORTALITY			
TO IMMORTALITY.	THE FEET OF PEOPLE	7	16
IMMORTALITY!	AMBITION CANNOT FIND HIM	68	8
OF IMMORTALITY	THE SOUL'S SUPERIOR	306	16
SOME--WORK FOR IMMORTALITY--	SOME--WORK FOR	406	1
OF IMMORTALITY--	SOME--WORK FOR	406	8
OF IMMORTALITY--	I LIVE WITH HIM--I SEE	463	12

	FIRST LINE	POEM	LINE
IMMORTALITY (CONTINUED)			
IN IMMORTALITY?"	I AM ALIVE--I GUESS--	470	16
AND IMMORTALITY--CAN BE ALMOST--	IT'S THOUGHTS--AND JUST	495	27
AND LIFE HATH IMMORTALITY--	THAT I DID ALWAYS LOVE	549	8
IN IMMORTALITY--	AN IGNORANCE A SUNSET	552	12
IMMORTALITY--	CONSCIOUS AM I IN MY	679	20
WITH IMMORTALITY--	SUSPENSE--IS HOSTILER	705	8
AND IMMORTALITY.	BECAUSE I COULD NOT STOP	712	4
BEFORE ME--IMMORTALITY--	BEHIND ME--DIPS ETERNITY	721	2
TERMED IMMORTALITY--	WE THIRST AT FIRST--'TIS	726	8
THAT IMMORTALITY--	BY MY WINDOW HAVE I FOR	797	21
FOR LOVE IS IMMORTALITY,	UNABLE ARE THE LOVED TO	809	2
FOR LOVE REFORMS VITALITY [IS IMMORTALITY]	UNABLE ARE THE LOVED TO	809	5
FROM IMMORTALITY.	THE ONLY NEWS I KNOW	827	3
WITH IMMORTALITY	THE SOUL'S DISTINCT	974	2
TO IMMORTALITY.	SO LARGE MY WILL	1024	12
CERTIFICATE FOR IMMORTALITY.	THAT SUCH HAVE DIED	1030	4
IMMORTALITY CONTENTED	SATISFACTION--IS THE	1036	7
OF IMMORTALITY	A SPIDER SEWED AT NIGHT	1138	7
WITHOUT THE DATE, LIKE CONSCIOUSNESS OR IMMORTALITY--	LEST ANY DOUBT THAT WE	1156	3
WITH IMMORTALITY	TO DISAPPEAR ENHANCES--	1209	4
BUT IMMORTALITY--	SOMEWHERE UPON THE	1231	8
IS IMMORTALITY--	IF MY BARK SINK	1234	4
OF IMMORTALITY WHO DOUBTS	BECAUSE THAT YOU ARE	1260	25
IS LEFT--THE IMMORTALITY--	TAKE ALL AWAY--	1365	3
OF IMMORTALITY--	SUCH ARE THE INLETS OF	1421	4
FOR IMMORTALITY--	WITH PINIONS OF DISDAIN	1431	12
THE WHOLE OF IMMORTALITY INTRENCHED [SECRETED / DEPUTED]	HE LIVED THE LIFE OF	1525	7
UNFAIR AN IMMORTALITY	NO BRIGADIER THROUGHOUT	1561	23
THE WHOLE OF IMMORTALITY	WHO ABDICATED AMBUSH	1616	7
OF IMMORTALITY	EXTOL THEE--COULD I--	1643	8
BY IMMORTALITY	WHY SHOULD WE HURRY--WHY	1646	4
THE IMMORTALITY SHE GAVE	THE IMMORTALITY SHE GAVE	1648	1
RECALLS TO IMMORTALITY--	SUMMER BEGINS TO HAVE	1682	16
FOR IMMORTALITY--	THE BUTTERFLY OBTAINS	1685	12
BEGUILED OF IMMORTALITY	HOW DARE THE ROBINS SING	1724	11
IS IMMORTALITY A BANE	IS IMMORTALITY A BANE	1728	1
IF IMMORTALITY UNVEIL [DISCLOSE]	MY LIFE CLOSED TWICE	1732	3
IS IMMORTALITY.	THE RETICENT VOLCANO	1748	12
IMMURED			
IMMURED IN HEAVEN!	IMMURED IN HEAVEN!	1594	1
IMMURED THE WHOLE OF LIFE	OF GOD WE ASK ONE FAVOR,	1601	5
IMPAIR			
LET NOT MY WITNESS HINDER THEM [THEM IMPAIR--]	'TIS TRUE--THEY SHUT ME	538	5
ABRIDGE [IMPAIR / DEBAR / DEPRIVE] SOCIETY	WE MISS HER, NOT BECAUSE	993	4
IMPALED			
IMPALED HIM ON HER FIERCEST STAKES--	FATE SLEW HIM, BUT HE	1031	3
IMPALPABLE			
THE FINE--IMPALPABLE ARRAY--	THE TINT I CANNOT TAKE--	627	5
AFFLICTION FEELS IMPALPABLE	DESPAIR'S ADVANTAGE IS	799	11
IMPANELLED			
IMPANELLED FROM NO SUMMER BRIEF--	TO MY SMALL HEARTH HIS	638	5
IMPART			
IMPART--DEPART--	IMAGE OF LIGHT, ADIEU--	1556	6
IMPARTED			
DESCENDING [CONSENTING / ESTABLISHED / IMPARTED] TO ENAMOR US	THE FACE IN EVANESCENCE	1490	7
IMPARTS			
NATURE IMPARTS THE LITTLE BLUE-BIRD--ASSURED	AFTER ALL BIRDS HAVE	1395	2
IMPASSABLE			
UNTENABLE [IMPASSABLE / IMPERVIOUS] TO LOGIC	THE THINGS WE THOUGHT	1293	11
IMPASSIVE			
AND PAGEANTS AS IMPASSIVE	DEATH IS THE SUPPLE	1445	V 11
LIKE THAT IMPASSIVE STONE--	I SEE THEE CLEARER FOR	1666	4
IMPATIENT			
REFINING THESE IMPATIENT ORES	DARE YOU SEE A SOUL AT	365	13
IMPATIENT OF NO CHILD--	NATURE--THE GENTLEST	790	2
TILL MYSTERY IMPATIENT DREW	TWO TRAVELLERS PERISHING	933	13
IMPEACH			
LEST SKIES IMPEACH A WEALTH SO WONDERFUL--	I'LL CLUTCH--AND CLUTCH	427	23
AS SOON IMPEACH MY CROWN!	AFRAID! OF WHOM AM I	608	12
IMPEDE			
IMPEDING [IMPEDE THE] NAVIGATION BRIGHT [FAIR]	A STAGNANT PLEASURE LIKE	1281	5
IMPEDIMENT			
OF ECSTASY'S IMPEDIMENT--	THE FASCINATING CHILL	1480	3
IMPEDING			
IMPEDING [IMPEDE THE] NAVIGATION BRIGHT [FAIR]	A STAGNANT PLEASURE LIKE	1281	5
IMPEL			
THE DAISY WOULD IMPEL ME.	IF THOSE I LOVED WERE	29	6
IF AIMS IMPEL THESE ASTRAL ONES	THE MOON UPON HER FLUENT	1528	5
IMPELLED			
IMPELLED TO HARK--	THE HEART HAS MANY DOORS	1567	4
IMPENDING			
FOR HER [ONE] TO BE A [AN IMPENDING] BRIDE	ALL THAT I DO	1496	11
IMPERATIVE			
BEFORE IT WAS IMPERATIVE	LIVES HE IN ANY OTHER	1557	3
IMPERATOR			
WHEN THAT OLD IMPERATOR--DEATH--	TRIUMPH--MAY BE OF	455	3

	FIRST LINE	POEM	LINE
IMPERCEPTIBLE			
TOO IMPERCEPTIBLE TO NOTE--	A NIGHT--THERE LAY THE	471	7
TOO IMPERCEPTIBLE AT LAST	AS IMPERCEPTIBLY AS	1540	3
IMPERCEPTIBLY			
AS IMPERCEPTIBLY AS GRIEF	AS IMPERCEPTIBLY AS	1540	1
IMPERFECT			
AS MAKE OF [BREW FROM / MIX] OUR IMPERFECT [UNCOMELY / OBTUSER] . . .	SHE HIDETH HER THE LAST	557	11
'TWAS BEST IMPERFECT--AS IT WAS--	THEIR HIGHT IN HEAVEN	696	3
IMPERFECTLY			
IMPERFECTLY BEHELD--	A CHARM INVESTS A FACE	421	2
IMPERIAL			
IN HER IMPERIAL ROUND--	DELAYED TILL SHE HAD	58	15
I BROUGHT [BRING] THEE THE IMPERIAL [DEPARTED] HEART	SAVIOR! I'VE NO ONE ELSE	217	7
AN IMPERIAL AFFLICTION	THERE'S A CERTAIN SLANT	258	11
AND TURNED AWAY, IMPERIAL, ...	HE PUT THE BELT AROUND	273	3
DEALS--ONE--IMPERIAL--THUNDERBOLT-- . . .	HE FUMBLES AT YOUR SOUL	315	11
TO HER IMPERIAL SUN.	HE TOUCHED ME, SO I LIVE	506	18
OF THEIR IMPERIAL CONDUCT--	WHEN I WAS SMALL, A	596	11
IS AN IMPERIAL FRIEND--	THE SOUL UNTO ITSELF	683	2
TEARS OPEN HER IMPERIAL VEINS--	YOU'VE SEEN BALLOONS SET	700	15
SUPPORTS ME LIKE IMPERIAL DRAMS	THE STIMULUS, BEYOND THE	1001	3
TO AN IMPERIAL FEW--	MORNING IS DUE TO ALL--	1577	3
IMPERTINENCE			
IMPERTINENCE SUBORDINATE	THE WAY TO KNOW THE	1279	7
IMPERTINENTLY			
ASSIDUOUSLY [DELIBERATELY / DETERMINATELY / IMPERTINENTLY] CRAWLED	ALONE AND IN A	1167	4
IMPERVIOUS			
UNTENABLE [IMPASSABLE / IMPERVIOUS] TO LOGIC	THE THINGS WE THOUGHT	1293	11
IMPETUOUS			
OR TOO IMPETUOUS BIRD--	NATURE--THE GENTLEST	790	8
IMPETUS			
IN DANGER--OTHER IMPETUS	I LIVED ON DREAD--	770	4
HAS IMPETUS OF GAIN--	THE SERVICE WITHOUT HOPE	779	5
AND IMPETUS OF GOAL--	THE SERVICE WITHOUT HOPE	779	6
IMPLAUSIBLE SEE UNPLAUSIBLE			
IMPLEMENT			
MISFORTUNE HATH NO IMPLEMENT	REVERSE CANNOT BEFALL	395	7
PRAYER IS THE LITTLE IMPLEMENT	PRAYER IS THE LITTLE	437	1
NOR IMPLEMENT, BE SEEN--	AT HALF PAST THREE, A	1084	10
IMPLEMENTS			
WITH IMPLEMENTS TO FLY AWAY, ...	BRING ME THE SUNSET IN A	128	23
THE IMPLEMENTS OF BLISS ARE FEW--	NO LADDER NEEDS THE BIRD	1574	5
OF BLISS THE CODES [THE IMPLEMENTS OF BLISS] ARE FEW--	TO HER DERIDED HOME	1586	9
IMPLIES			
MEADOWS OF MAJESTY CONCEDES [IMPLIES] . .	MY COCOON TIGHTENS--	1099	7
IMPLORE			
IMPLORE A LARGER--THING--	THE COURT IS FAR AWAY--	235	8
DUNGEONS CAN [MAY] CALL--AND GUNS IMPLORE--	WHAT IF I SAY I SHALL	277	8
IMPLORED			
"REMEMBER ME" IMPLORED THE THIEF!	"REMEMBER ME" IMPLORED	1180	1
IMPLORING			
AND WE--IMPLORING DREW--	NO NOTICE GAVE SHE, BUT	804	18
IMPLY			
ECLIPSES--SUNS--IMPLY--	THE ZEROES--TAUGHT US--	689	V 6
NOT ANY VOICE IMPLY [DENOTE] IT HERE . . .	'TIS WHITER THAN AN	1482	5
IMPORT			
A VITAL KINSMANSHIP IMPORT	BEREAVEMENT IN THEIR	645	3
IT'S MEANING [IMPORT] IS EXTINCT--	HOW HUMAN NATURE DOTES	1417	4
IMPORTANT			
THE MOST IMPORTANT POPULATION	THE MOST IMPORTANT	1746	1
IMPORTED			
IMPORTED TO THE WOOD--	LIKE FLOWERS, THAT HEARD	513	9
IMPORTUNATE			
TOO EXORBITANT [EXTRAVAGANT / IMPORTUNATE] .	SO MUCH SUMMER	651	5
IMPORTUNED			
HAD IMPORTUNED TO SEE!	GOOD NIGHT! WHICH PUT	259	9
IT IMPORTUNED TO SEE	THE HEAVEN VESTS FOR	694	6
IMPORTUNES			
THE SHOPMAN IMPORTUNES IT--	A CLOCK STOPPED--	287	12
IMPORTUNITY			
THAT SUCH AN IMPORTUNITY	IF I COULD BRIBE THEM BY	179	15
THEIR DAPPLED IMPORTUNITY	THEIR DAPPLED	1611	1
IMPOSE			
THINE EYE IMPOSE ON ME--	THE MOON IS DISTANT FROM	429	12
IMPOSING			
AT SOME IMPOSING DOOR!	IN RAGS MYSTERIOUS AS	117	6
NATURE'S IMPOSING NEGATIVE	NATURE CAN DO NO MORE	1673	7
IMPOSSIBILITY			
IT'S BRIGHT [FAIR] IMPOSSIBILITY	I WOULD NOT PAINT--A	505	3
IMPOSSIBILITY, LIKE WINE	IMPOSSIBILITY, LIKE WINE	838	1
IMPOSSIBLE			
IMPOSSIBLE TO FEIGN	I LIKE A LOOK OF AGONY,	241	6
WERE AS IMPOSSIBLE AS HAND	THE WIND--TAPPED LIKE A	436	7
MORE FAIR--BECAUSE IMPOSSIBLE	DELIGHT--BECOMES	572	3
BUT HEAVEN MADE BOTH, IMPOSSIBLE	WE TALKED AS GIRLS DO--	586	15
A LOAD IS FIRST IMPOSSIBLE	I SHOULD NOT DARE TO BE	1197	3

	FIRST LINE	POEM	LINE
INCLEMENT			
WARM THIS INCLEMENT EAR	PRAISE IT--'TIS DEAD--	1384	3
INCLINE			
INHERENTLY INCLINE--	MY WORTHINESS IS ALL MY	751	10
INCLINED			
AM I INCLINED TO CLIMB	VOLCANOES BE IN SICILY	1705	6
INCLUDE			
THE ONE THE OTHER WILL CONTAIN [INCLUDE]	THE BRAIN--IS WIDER THAN	632	3
FOR DID NOT THIS INCLUDE THEMSELF--	WITHOUT THIS--THERE IS	655	7
AS SEAMS--INCLUDE THE BALL?	WITHOUT THIS--THERE IS	655	8
INCLUDE US [SCAN BETTER / CONVEY US]--AS THEY GO--	WE MISS HER, NOT BECAUSE	993	8
BUT LIVING, THIS INCLUDE	TOO SCANTY 'TWAS TO DIE	1013	6
INCLUDED			
BUT SINCE THE LAST--INCLUDED BOTH--	I MEANT TO HAVE BUT	476	5
INCLUDING			
TOOK HER OWN HEART, INCLUDING OUR'S,	THE PRETTY RAIN FROM	1426	3
INCOGNITO			
OH INCOGNITO!	GOOD NIGHT, BECAUSE WE	114	4
INCOME			
MY SOUL'S ENTIRE INCOME--	ONE LIFE OF SO MUCH	270	3
WITHIN MY INCOME--THESE COULD LIE	I MEANT TO HAVE BUT	476	3
AN INCOME IN THE AIR,	BECAUSE 'TWAS RICHES I	1093	6
INCOMPLETE			
ARE INCOMPLETE, AND SHY--	WHO GIANTS KNOW, WITH	796	2
INCOMPLETE--TO EYE--	UNFULFILLED TO	972	2
INCONCEIVABLY			
INCONCEIVABLY SOLEMN!	INCONCEIVABLY SOLEMN!	582	1
INCORPORATED			
WHEN FATE INCORPORATED US--	ESTRANGED FROM BEAUTY--	1474	V 4
INCORPOREAL			
STEPPING TO INCORPOREAL TUNES	HOW LONESOME THE WIND	1418	6
INCREASE			
HER EYES INCREASE TO BALLS--	SHE SIGHTS A BIRD--SHE	507	4
IS JUST DEATH, AND CANNOT INCREASE--	SUSPENSE--IS HOSTILER	705	3
IF AS THE DAYS RESUME [INCREASE]	AS FROST IS BEST	951	7
INCREASED			
INCREASED [ENLARGED] BEYOND MY UTMOST SCOPE	I HAD A DAILY BLISS	1057	7
INCREASED TILL I ABJURED IT	ART THOU THE THING I	1282	7
INCREDIBLE			
DEEM UNPLAUSIBLE [INCREDIBLE]	COLOR--CASTE--	970	16
INCREDULOUS			
INCREDULOUS OF OUGHT	LIKE EYES THAT LOOKED ON	458	2
WHO HEARS MAY BE INCREDULOUS,	HER FACE WAS IN A BED OF	1722	7
INCUR			
INCUR THE RISK	DOWN TIME'S QUAINT	1656	7
INCURRED			
MUST NOT BE INCURRED	RATHER ARID DELIGHT	1679	6
INDEBTEDNESS			
INDEBTEDNESS TO OXYGEN	THE FARTHEST THUNDER	1581	9
INDEED			
WHAT AND IF INDEED	IT DID NOT SURPRISE ME--	39	14
AH! INDEED!	"SOWN IN DISHONOR"!	62	2
INDEED I'M TOO ASTONISHED	GOING TO HEAVEN!	79	4
HUNDREDS HAVE LOST INDEED--	SOUL, WILT THOU TOSS	139	3
HE HAD NOT ON A CROWN INDEED,	I MET A KING THIS	166	2
INAUDIBLE, INDEED,	TO LEARN THE TRANSPORT	167	14
AND IF INDEED I FAIL,	'TIS SO MUCH JOY! 'TIS	172	9
THE GALES--INDEED--WERE DONE--	ON THIS LONG STORM THE	194	6
PARTAKEN--IT RELIEVES--INDEED--	UNDUE SIGNIFICANCE A	439	5
A DOUBT--IF IT BE FAIR--INDEED--	THE WORLD--STANDS--	493	5
OUR LORD--INDEED--MADE [BORE] COMPOUND WITNESS--	ONE CRUCIFIXION IS	553	13
GARLAND BE INDEED--	HER SWEET TURN TO LEAVE	649	12
IF THAT--INDEED [EVEN THAT]--REDEEM--	A PRISON GETS TO BE A	652	32
OLD, INDEED, THE EAST,	ALWAYS MINE!	839	7
BUT TENDERER INDEED	THERE IS A JUNE WHEN	930	4
LEST THIS BE HEAVEN INDEED	LEST THIS BE HEAVEN	1043	1
THAT WAS INDEED THE RAIN--	LIKE RAIN IT SOUNDED	1235	8
LUCRATIVE INDEED THE OFFER [THE PROPOSITION]	"FAITHFUL TO THE END"	1357	V
INDEED--'TWAS BUILT BY HIM--	HOW BRITTLE ARE THE	1433	6
MORE FLOWN INDEED	THAN HEAVEN MORE REMOTE,	1436	4
'TIS VERY COMFORTABLE INDEED	TO MEND EACH TATTERED	1442	7
"RED SEA," INDEED! TALK NOT TO ME	"RED SEA," INDEED! TALK	1642	1
WHY SHOULD WE [I] HURRY--WHY INDEED	WHY SHOULD WE HURRY--WHY	1646	1
GOD IS INDEED A JEALOUS GOD--	GOD IS INDEED A JEALOUS	1719	1
SO INTIMATE, INDEED,	HE WAS MY HOST--HE WAS	1721	6
INDEFINITE			
COULD I BUT RIDE INDEFINITE	COULD I BUT RIDE	661	1
INDEFINITE DISCLOSED--	FROM BLANK TO BLANK--	761	8
INDELIBLE			
FOR SUMMER TOO INDELIBLE [INSCRUTABLE]	A LITTLE SNOW WAS HERE	1444	7
INDEMNITY			
INDEMNITY TO FIND--	SHE SPED AS PETALS OF A	991	4
INDEMNITY FOR LONELINESS	OF SO DIVINE A LOSS	1179	3
INDEPENDANT			
AN INDEPENDANT ONE--	A LONG--LONG SLEEP--A	654	4
BUT INDEPENDANT EXTASY	THE BIRDS BEGUN AT FOUR	783	15
AN INDEPENDANT MAN--	I PLAY AT RICHES--TO	801	8

	FIRST LINE	POEM	LINE
INDEPENDENT			
DID INDEPENDENT, AMBER--	I WATCHED THE MOON	629	15
OF INDEPENDENT HUES	BEFORE YOU THOUGHT OF	1465	5
AND [WHO] INDEPENDENT AS THE SUN	HOW HAPPY IS THE LITTLE	1510	7
INDESTRUCTIBLE			
THAT INDESTRUCTIBLE ESTATE	YOU CANNOT TAKE ITSELF	1351	3
INDIA			
I'LL TAKE MY INDIA RUBBERS,	"SIC TRANSIT GLORIA	3	27
EAST INDIA--FOR YOU!	MY EYE IS FULLER THAN MY	202	4
I'M SURE 'TIS INDIA--ALL DAY--	YOUR RICHES--TAUGHT ME--	299	17
MY--DROP--OF INDIA?	IT WOULD NEVER BE COMMON	430	33
TO [FOR / OF] INDIA	HOW DESTITUTE IS HE	1477	8
INDIAMAN			
AN INDIAMAN--AN EARL--	GOD GAVE A LOAF TO EVERY	791	14
INDIAN SEE WEST-INDIAN			
AND INDIAN SUMMER NOON [SUN]--	EXCEPT THE SMALLER SIZE	1067	V
WHITE AS AN INDIAN PIPE	WHITE AS AN INDIAN PIPE	1250	1
'TIS WHITER THAN AN INDIAN PIPE--	'TIS WHITER THAN AN	1482	1
INDICATE			
AND SPICIEST AT FADING--INDICATE [CELEBRATE]--	THEY HAVE A LITTLE ODOR	785	3
NOR RIP, NOR WRINKLE INDICATE	TOO COLD IS THIS	1135	8
THOUGH NO APPEARANCE INDICATE--	TO MEND EACH TATTERED	1442	3
THEY INDICATE OR CAUSE	THEIR BARRICADE AGAINST	1471	6
INDICATES			
THAT INDICATES I WILL!	THERE ARE TWO MAYS	1618	5
INDICATING			
INDICATING, BY NO MUSCLE [FEATURE]--	BLOOM UPON THE MOUNTAIN	667	19
INDICATIVE			
INDICATIVE THAT SUNS GO DOWN--	PRESENTIMENT--IS THAT	764	2
INDIES			
FOR INDIES IN THE GROUND!	A MINE THERE IS NO MAN	1117	8
INDIFFERENCE			
IT MULTIPLIED INDIFFERENCE--	'TWAS WARM--AT FIRST--	519	11
A CHIEF INDIFFERENCE, AS FOREIGN	A SICKNESS OF THIS WORLD	1044	5
INDIFFERENT			
UNCERTAIN [INDIFFERENT]--TO RETURN BELOW--	HE PARTS HIMSELF--LIKE	517	11
INDIFFERENT TO HIM--	THE FUTURE--NEVER SPOKE	672	9
ALIKE INDIFFERENT--	FROM BLANK TO BLANK--	761	5
I HALF INDIFFERENT VIEWED	I HAD A DAILY BLISS	1057	2
INDIFFERENT HANGING [GATHERED] NOW--	HIS BILL IS CLASPED--HIS	1102	4
INDIFFERENT SEASONS DOUBTLESS PLAY	SOMEWHERE UPON THE	1231	5
INDIGENCE			
CANNOT BE [ENABLES] INDIGENCE	NONE CAN EXPERIENCE	771	8
INDIGNANT			
INDIGNANT [AFFRONTED]--THAT THE JOY WAS COME--	I THINK THE LONGEST HOUR	635	5
INDIGNATION			
WITH INDIGNATION,	AS FROM THE EARTH THE	1630	7
INDIGO			
OF INDIGO AND BROWN--	BEFORE YOU THOUGHT OF	1465	8
INDISCREET			
HOW FLEET--HOW INDISCREET AN ONE--	HOW FLEET--HOW	1771	1
INDIVIDUAL			
IT'S INDIVIDUAL DOOM	NO CROWD THAT HAS	515	14
HIS INDIVIDUAL ONE--	NO ROMANCE SOLD UNTO	669	4
OF INDIVIDUAL VOICE--	A SOUTH WIND--HAS A	719	2
BY SOBER INDIVIDUAL	AS IMPERCEPTIBLY AS	1540	V
INDIVIDUALS			
HIDING INDIVIDUALS FROM THE EARTH	ABSENCE DISEMBODIES--SO	860	2
LIKE INDIVIDUALS GO	DEATH LEAVES US HOMESICK	935	6
THE INDIVIDUALS DO	AS SLEIGH BELLS SEEM IN	981	4
INDOLENT			
INDOLENT HOUSEWIFE--IN DAISIES--LAIN!	HOW MANY TIMES THESE LOW	187	12
INDORSED			
SACRAMENT, SAINTS PARTOOK [INDORSED] BEFORE US--	TO PUT THIS WORLD DOWN,	527	12
WHO INDORSED [ENFORCED] THE CUP--	TO PUT THIS WORLD DOWN,	527	15
BUT HE INDORSED THE SHEEN [SCENE]--	THE ROAD WAS LIT WITH	1450	8
INDORSEMENT			
EXISTS AND IT'S INDORSEMENT	SPEECH IS ONE SYMPTOM OF	1681	5
INDUCED			
EVER BE INDUCED TO DO!	I'M THE LITTLE "HEART'S	176	14
INDUCES			
INDUCES MY BELIEF.	THESE ARE THE DAYS WHEN	130	9
INDURATED			
WAITS ANY INDURATED MATE	THAT ODD OLD MAN IS DEAD	1130	7
INDUSTRIES			
IS SOLEMNEST OF INDUSTRIES	THE BUSTLE IN A HOUSE	1078	3
BUT THOSE PECULIAR INDUSTRIES	THE THINGS WE THOUGHT	1293	3
INDUSTRIOUS			
INDUSTRIOUS! LACONIC!	DUST IS THE ONLY SECRET	153	9
GOD PERMITS INDUSTRIOUS ANGELS--	GOD PERMITS INDUSTRIOUS	231	1
INDUSTRIOUS UNTIL--	DEATH SETS A THING	360	8
WERE THEY INDUSTRIOUS?	WHAT DID THEY DO SINCE I	900	2
"AND YET THOU ART INDUSTRIOUS--	HAD I NOT THIS, OR THIS,	904	7
INDUSTRIOUSNESS			
IF TENDERER INDUSTRIOUSNESS	HER FINAL SUMMER WAS IT	795	3
INDUSTRY			
SOME INDUSTRY MUST BE--	I HAD NO TIME TO HATE--	478	9
UNTO THE SAINTS' SLOW DILIGENCE [INDUSTRY]--	EACH LIFE CONVERGES TO	680	15
IN HOMELY INDUSTRY ARRAYED [ATTIRED]--	THE BIRDS BEGUN AT FOUR	783	11

	FIRST LINE	POEM	LINE
INDUSTRY (CONTINUED)			
RETRIEVE THINE INDUSTRY--	'TIS SUNRISE--LITTLE	908	4
NOT ANY TRANCE OF INDUSTRY	A CHILLY PEACE INFESTS	1443	3
OF INDUSTRY AND MORALS [ETHICS]	HIS LITTLE HEARSE LIKE	1522	5
RESUMES HIS GAUDY INDUSTRY	SUMMER BEGINS TO HAVE	1682	12
OF MODEST INDUSTRY .	THE BUTTERFLY OBTAINS	1685	10
INEBRIATE			
INEBRIATE OF AIR--AM I--	I TASTE A LIQUOR NEVER	214	5
TO INTELLECTS INEBRIATE	WINTER IS GOOD--HIS HOAR	1316	3
INEBRIATE OUR OWN.	HOPE IS A STRANGE	1392	V 8
INEFFABLE			
EVENT INEFFABLE--	WHO WERE "THE FATHER AND	1258	22
LEST SIGHT'S [PROOF'S] INEFFABLE DISGRACE	WE SHUN BECAUSE WE PRIZE	1429	2
INERTIA			
INERTIA OR HASTE--	HIS MANSION IN THE POOL	1379	V
INFAMY			
JUST TO PARTAKE--THE INFAMY--	WERT THOU BUT ILL--THAT	961	12
LIKE GENTLE INFAMY--	SO LARGE MY WILL	1024	4
IN INFAMY OR URN--	ALL MEN FOR HONOR	1193	4
THE INFAMY OF TIME--	THE HARM OF YEARS IS ON	1280	2
WITH TENDER INFAMY .	THE DITCH IS DEAR TO THE	1645	V 8
INFANT			
UPON HIS INFANT FACE WAS SET	HE TOLD A HOMELY TALE	763	3
INFECTION			
INFECTION IN THE SENTENCE BREEDS	A WORD DROPPED CARELESS	1261	5
INFECTS			
INFECTS MY SIMPLE SPIRIT .	OF BRONZE--AND BLAZE--	290	8
INFER			
ALL SWINDLERS--BE--INFER--	I MEANT TO HAVE BUT	476	28
QUAINTLY INFER--EVE'S GREAT SURRENDER--	BETTER--THAN MUSIC! FOR	503	11
COULD I INFER HIS RESIDENCE--	MY PERIOD HAD COME FOR	564	11
OF SPICE--I INFER FROM THE ODORS BORNE--	BY MY WINDOW HAVE I FOR	797	12
ENABLED TO INFER.	THERE IS A FINISHED	856	8
I FIND IT TO INFER.	THE FROST WAS NEVER SEEN	1202	20
BUT IT'S VICINITY INFER,	OF PARADISE' EXISTENCE	1411	4
INFERENCE			
ONLY, YOUR INFERENCE THEREFROM!	AS IF SOME LITTLE ARCTIC	180	12
THIS TIME--BEYOND THE ESTIMATE [INFERENCE] .	SHE STAKED HER FEATHERS	798	3
PORTENTOUS INFERENCE.	THE LEAVES LIKE WOMEN,	987	4
OUR INFERENCE IS PREMATURE,	GOD MADE NO ACT WITHOUT	1163	3
WITH INFERENCE APPALLING [ALARMING]	WHO WERE "THE FATHER AND	1258	5
AN INFERENCE OF MEXICO	THEIR BARRICADE AGAINST	1471	7
NO RESPITE FROM THE INFERENCE [MIGHTINESS] .	WHY SHOULD WE HURRY--WHY	1646	5
INFERIOR			
OF OUR INFERIOR FACE--	AN IGNORANCE A SUNSET	552	8
LIT UP THE LOW--INFERIOR GRASS--	I THINK I WAS ENCHANTED	593	V 11
THAN AN INFERIOR KIND--	I THINK TO LIVE--MAY BE	646	12
BEHIND INFERIOR CLOUDS--OR ROUND	I MAKE HIS CRESCENT FILL	909	7
THEN HOVERS--AN INFERIOR GUARD--	LOVE--IS THAT LATER	924	9
A GRAVE--IS A RESTRICTED [AN INFERIOR] BREADTH--	A COFFIN--IS A SMALL	943	5
INFERRED			
BUT WHAT OUR LORD INFERS [INFERRED] WE WOULD	NOT WHAT WE DID, SHALL	823	3
INFERRED THE LESS BY GROWING THAN	I MADE SLOW RICHES BUT	843	7
AFFLICTION IS INFERRED	AS FROST IS BEST	951	3
OBLIGED TO BE INFERRED.	THE WAY TO KNOW THE	1279	4
THAT ANY, HEARING, HAD INFERRED	A LITTLE OVERFLOWING	1467	2
AUTUMN BEGINS TO BE INFERRED	SUMMER BEGINS TO HAVE	1682	5
INFERS			
BUT WHAT OUR LORD INFERS [INFERRED] WE WOULD	NOT WHAT WE DID, SHALL	823	3
AND ASSUMES [INFERS]--FROM HOME--	HE WHO IN HIMSELF	969	4
INFESTING			
TO KEEP IT FROM INFESTING EYES--	SHAME IS THE SHAWL OF	1412	3
INFESTS			
A CHILLY [LONESOME / WARNING] PEACE INFESTS THE GRASS	A CHILLY PEACE INFESTS	1443	1
INFIDEL			
TO FAIL--IS INFIDEL--	THE SWEETEST HERESY	387	8
AND YOU'RE AN INFIDEL--	YOU'LL KNOW HER--BY HER	634	V 28
IS IMPUDENT [RENEGADE / INFIDEL / ABLATIVE] TO NATURE	THE JAY HIS CASTANET HAS	1635	4
INFINITE			
AS INFINITE [BAGATELLES] TRADITION	LIKE SOME OLD FASHIONED	302	5
HAVE INFINITE WITHDRAWN--	THE SOUL'S SUPERIOR	306	4
THEY LEAVE US WITH THE INFINITE.	THEY LEAVE US WITH THE	350	1
TOO INFINITE ASLEEP	THE COLOR OF THE GRAVE	411	6
WERE INFINITE--TO ME--	I TIE MY HAT--I CREASE	443	4
HOW INFINITE--TO BE	I AM ALIVE--I GUESS--	470	26
IN FURTHER INFINITE--	HAD I PRESUMED TO HOPE--	522	8
NO DIFFERENT [AS INFINITE] OUR YEARS WOULD BE	FOREVER--IS COMPOSED OF	624	11
PERUSE HOW INFINITE I AM	THE WAY I READ A	636	13
IT'S INFINITE CONTAIN	PAIN--HAS AN ELEMENT OF	650	6
A SPECTRE--INFINITE--ACCOMPANYING--	ONE NEED NOT BE A	670	V 19
IT WERE INFINITE [TENDERER] ENACTED	DRAMA'S VITALLEST	741	12
TOO INFINITE FOR CONSCIOUSNESS'	SUCH IS THE FORCE OF	787	7
SO INFINITE--WHEN GONE--	JOY TO HAVE MERITED THE	788	14
WITH INFINITE AFFECTION--	NATURE--THE GENTLEST	790	21
FINITE--TO FAIL, BUT INFINITE TO VENTURE--	FINITE--TO FAIL, BUT	847	1
WITH THE INFINITE--	THE ADMIRATIONS--AND	906	12
TILL THE INFINITE AURORA	STRUCK, WAS I, NOR YET	925	23

	FIRST LINE	POEM	LINE
INSCRIBES			
INSCRIBES A SIMPLE NOON--	IT RISES--PASSES--ON OUR	1023	2
INSCRIBES UPON THE FLESH--	THE OVERTAKELESSNESS OF	1691	6
INSCRIPTION			
AND PERHAPS A PHRASE IN EGYPTIAN [LATIN INSCRIPTION]--	WE DREAM--IT IS GOOD WE	531	15
INSCRUTABLE			
IN THAT CAMPAIGN INSCRUTABLE	'TWAS FIGHTING FOR HIS	1188	7
IN FEATS INSCRUTABLE--	ELIJAH'S WAGON KNEW NO	1254	8
FOR SUMMER TOO INDELIBLE [INSCRUTABLE]	A LITTLE SNOW WAS HERE	1444	7
AN ARC ALIKE INSCRUTABLE	THE BAT IS DUN, WITH	1575	7
INSCRUTABLY			
EXTENDED INSCRUTABLY--	BY MY WINDOW HAVE I FOR	797	V 25
INSECT			
AND WHATSOEVER INSECT PASS--	THERE IS A FLOWER THAT	380	5
DEATH IS LIKE THE INSECT	DEATH IS LIKE THE INSECT	1716	1
INSECT'S			
IS AN INSECT'S FUTILE FORCES	PATIENCE--HAS A QUIET	926	3
INSECURE			
TO ME--SHOWS INSECURE--	THEIR HIGHT IN HEAVEN	696	8
HOW MIGHTY [MOMENTOUS] TO THE INSECURE	HOW FIRM ETERNITY MUST	1499	5
HOW INSECURE THE SOD	ON MY VOLCANO GROWS THE	1677	6
INSECURITY			
IN INSECURITY TO LIE	GO NOT TOO NEAR A HOUSE	1434	7
INSERT			
INSERT THE THING THAT CAUSED IT--	TO FILL A GAP	546	2
INSERTING			
PROCEED--INSERTING HERE--A SUN--	IT'S EASY TO INVENT A	724	11
INSIDE			
INSIDE A JACKET DULLER--	YOU'LL KNOW HER--BY HER	634	11
INSIDIOUS			
LIKE TIME'S INSIDIOUS [INVADING / PRESUMING / APPOINTED / . . .	LIKE TIME'S INSIDIOUS	1236	1
INSIGHT			
BEYOND THE BROKER'S INSIGHT--	SOME--WORK FOR	406	11
INSINUATES			
TILL CAVILER [PERJURY] INSINUATES	WHOEVER DISENCHANTS	1451	V 7
INSOLVENCY			
INSOLVENCY, SUBLIME!	"SIC TRANSIT GLORIA	3	44
INSOLVENT			
INSOLVENT--EVERY NOON--	I GAVE MYSELF TO HIM--	580	16
OR BE THAT MOST INSOLVENT THING	FAME IS THE ONE THAT	1475	5
INSPECT			
HIS QUAINT OPINIONS--TO INSPECT--	A PRECIOUS--MOULDERING	371	9
WHEN WE INSPECT--THAT'S AUDIBLE--	THE SPIRIT IS THE	733	3
COULD HOPE INSPECT HER [IT'S] BASIS	COULD HOPE INSPECT HER	1283	1
INSPECT THE ADMONITION	HOW KNOW IT FROM A	1364	7
WHOSE CRUMBS THE CROWS INSPECT	FAME IS A FICKLE FOOD	1659	6
INSPECTED			
AND YET--INSPECTED CLOSELY	HOPE IS A SUBTLE GLUTTON	1547	3
INSPECTING			
THEN VAIL MY TOO INSPECTING FACE	A SOMETHING IN A	122	10
WITH PLAIN INSPECTING FACE--	WHO IS IT SEEKS MY	1598	2
INSPECTION			
OMNIPOTENCE' INSPECTION [ANALYSIS]	AN IGNORANCE A SUNSET	552	7
INSPECTION'S			
FOR IT'S ENLARGED INSPECTION'S	THIS DUST, AND IT'S	936	7
INSPIRITING			
A PROMPT--EXECUTIVE [BOLD, INSPIRITING] BIRD IS THE JAY--	A PROMPT--EXECUTIVE BIRD	1177	1
INSPIRITING HABILIMENTS	BEFORE YOU THOUGHT OF	1465	7
INSTABILITY			
BY TRANSPORT'S INSTABILITY	A DEW SUFFICED ITSELF--	1437	15
INSTANCE			
BALKED IN THE VASTEST INSTANCE	COULD HOPE INSPECT HER	1283	5
INSTANCES			
STAMPED--OCCASIONALLY--[IN INSTANCES] FOREVER--	SO THE EYES ACCOST--AND	752	3
INSTANT			
FOR EACH EXTATIC INSTANT	FOR EACH EXTATIC INSTANT	125	1
THAT I WOULD INSTANT DIVE--	ONE LIFE OF SO MUCH	270	6
BETWEEN THE INSTANT OF A WRECK--	THE DIFFERENCE BETWEEN	305	3
AS IF THE CLOUD THAT INSTANT SLIT	IT STRUCK ME--EVERY DAY	362	3
AN INSTANT HAD FORGOT	SHE LAY AS IF AT PLAY	369	7
THE INSTANT THAT WE MEET--	I CROSS TILL I AM WEARY	550	21
BUT SLOWEST INSTANT--ENDS--	I THINK THE LONGEST HOUR	635	8
LET AN INSTANT PUSH	CRISIS IS A HAIR	889	9
THE INSTANT HOLDING IN IT'S CLAW	'TWAS CRISIS--ALL THE	948	5
THE DOOR AS INSTANT [SUDDEN] SHUT--AND I--	A DOOR JUST OPENED ON A	953	5
MORE DISTANT IN AN INSTANT	AS SLEIGH BELLS SEEM IN	981	7
HIS NOTICE SUDDEN [INSTANT] IS--	A NARROW FELLOW IN THE	986	4
FAIL IN AN INSTANT, NO MAN DID	CRUMBLING IS NOT AN	997	11
TO POSSESS, IS PAST THE INSTANT	SATISFACTION--IS THE	1036	5
OCCUPIED BY EACH AN INSTANT	PARADISE IS THAT OLD	1119	3
IS TINCTURED [GILDED] FOR AN INSTANT	TO DISAPPEAR ENHANCES--	1209	3
THIS INSTANT BE SUSPENDED [ABOLISHED]	BECAUSE THAT YOU ARE	1260	7
THE INSTANT I PERCEIVE	BECAUSE THAT YOU ARE	1260	14
AS SOON AS [THE INSTANT THAT] YOU HAVE COME	DEAR MARCH--COME IN--	1320	24
WOULD STRIKE US INSTANT DEAD	I NEVER HEAR THAT ONE IS	1323	12
AND INSTANT, TOO.	THAN HEAVEN MORE REMOTE,	1436	16

	FIRST LINE	POEM	LINE
INSTANT (CONTINUED)			
THAT VERY INSTANT PASSED--	THERE CAME A WIND LIKE A	1593	8
THAT FOR AN INSTANT	GLORY IS THAT BRIGHT	1660	2
THEY HAVE A HEAVEN EACH INSTANT [MINUTE]	THE MOST IMPORTANT	1746	3
INSTANTLY			
AND WINTER INSTANTLY BECOMES	THE DANDELION'S PALLID	1519	3
INSTANT'S			
'TIS AN INSTANT'S PLAY.	I KNOW THAT HE EXISTS.	338	5
UNFITTED BY AN INSTANT'S GRACE	I GAINED IT SO--	359	13
OTHERS--WHOSE INSTANT'S WANTING--	I KNOW LIVES, I COULD	372	3
WITHOUT AN INSTANT'S RESPITE--	I SOMETIMES DROP IT, FOR	708	7
AN INSTANT'S PUSH DEMOLISHES	THE HEART HAS NARROW	928	11
AN INSTANT'S WIDTH OF WARMTH DISCLOSED--	A DOOR JUST OPENED ON A	953	3
CRUMBLING IS NOT AN INSTANT'S ACT	CRUMBLING IS NOT AN	997	1
INSTANTS			
THE SOUL'S SUPERIOR INSTANTS	THE SOUL'S SUPERIOR	306	1
THE STOLID RAFTERS [CENTRES / HOURS / INSTANTS / SECONDS] GLOW	THE SMOULDERING EMBERS	1132	6
INSTEAD			
AND A DEAL OF SAD REFLECTION, AND WAILING INSTEAD OF SONG?	AWAKE YE MUSES NINE,	1	30
IN THE HEART INSTEAD?	IT DID NOT SURPRISE ME--	39	16
BUT CROWNS INSTEAD, AND COURTIERS--	SHE BORE IT TILL THE	144	13
AND INSTEAD OF TOLLING THE BELL, FOR CHURCH,	SOME KEEP THE SABBATH	324	7
SO INSTEAD OF GETTING TO HEAVEN, AT LAST--	SOME KEEP THE SABBATH	324	11
INSTEAD OF ONE--	LOVE--THOU ART HIGH--	453	10
BUT--THE INSTEAD--THE PINCHING FEAR	WHY MAKE IT DOUBT--IT	462	8
RAIMENT INSTEAD--OF POMPADOUR--	I AM ASHAMED--I HIDE--	473	11
INSTEAD OF PASSIVE CREATURES,	ENDOW THE LIVING--WITH	521	5
A LITTLE FURTHER REACHES--INSTEAD--	THE BLACK BERRY--WEARS A	554	11
INSTEAD OF KINGS--	THE CHILD'S FAITH IS NEW	637	24
INSTEAD I'LL SAY OF GEM	EACH SCAR I'LL KEEP FOR	877	2
INSTEAD OF MORNING--HAD'ST THOU BROACHED	'TIS SUNRISE--LITTLE	908	11
WOULD YOU--INSTEAD OF ME?	THEMSELF ARE ALL I HAVE	1094	5
THEY WERE NOT THERE INSTEAD.	OF PAUL AND SILAS IT IS	1166	4
HE BOWED TO HEAVEN INSTEAD OF EARTH [EVERY HEAVEN ABOVE / . . .	THE BOBOLINK IS GONE--	1591	6
INSTIGATES			
THIS INSTIGATES AN APPETITE	THAT IT WILL NEVER COME	1741	7
INSTIL			
THAT I INSTIL THE PAIN	AH, NECROMANCY SWEET!	177	4
INSTINCT			
AN INSTINCT [HUNGER] FOR THE HOAR [DREAR], THE BALD--	I THINK THE HEMLOCK	525	7
BUT [JUST] INSTINCT ESTEEM [REPORT] HIM	CONSCIOUS AM I IN MY	679	19
INSTINCT PICKING UP THE KEY	AFTER A HUNDRED YEARS	1147	11
INSTINCT PURSUES THE ADAMANT,	THE SPIRIT LASTS--BUT IN	1576	17
INSTINCTS			
INSTINCTS FOR DANCE--A CAPER PART--	I'VE DROPPED MY BRAIN--	1046	11
INSTITUTE			
I'LL INSTITUTE AN "ACTION"--	I HAD SOME THINGS THAT I	116	13
INSTITUTION			
FOR 'TIS HIS INSTITUTION--AND	REMORSE--IS MEMORY--	744	11
INSTRUCT			
THE LOVE, THO, WILL ARRAY [INSTRUCT] ME RIGHT	FITTER TO SEE HIM, I MAY	968	21
INSTRUCTED			
AND SO, INSTRUCTED BY MY OWN,	FOR LARGEST WOMAN'S	309	5
NO MAN INSTRUCTED ME--	I CANNOT DANCE UPON MY	326	2
INSTRUCTING			
INSTRUCTING BY THE SAME [ITSELF]--	WITH PINIONS OF DISDAIN	1431	9
INSTRUCTS			
INSTRUCTS TO THE DIVINE.	ESCAPING BACKWARD TO	867	8
INSTRUCTS US BY DEPARTING [DERISION] NOW [MORE]	THE SUMMER THAT WE DID	1773	3
INSUFFICIENT			
A HALF [TOO] UNCONSCIOUS [AN INSUFFICIENT] QUEEN--	I'M CEDED--I'VE STOPPED	508	16
LEST I SHOULD INSUFFICIENT PROVE [BE]	MY WORTHINESS IS ALL MY	751	5
AN INSUFFICIENT [INNUTRITIOUS] LOAF--	DEPRIVED OF OTHER	773	4
IT'S INSUFFICIENT AREA	THE HEART HAS NARROW	928	7
INSULATORS			
WITH INSULATORS--AND A GLOVE--	THE LIGHTNING PLAYETH--	630	5
INSULTED			
OFFENDED [INSULTED / ASSAULTED] BY THE WIND--	SHE SPED AS PETALS OF A	991	2
TO AN INSULTED SKY	NO BRIGADIER THROUGHOUT	1561	14
INSULTING			
INSULTING IS THE SUN	HOW DARE THE ROBINS SING	1724	9
INSURANCE			
. . . INSURANCE-- / TO THE HORIZON--]	THE LARGEST FIRE EVER	1114	7
INSURES			
COACH, IT INSURES, AND FOOTMEN--	ONE DIGNITY DELAYS FOR	98	5
SECURITY THE SAME INSURES	OF PAUL AND SILAS IT IS	1166	5
FOR HE INSURES TO NONE	I CANNOT SEE MY SOUL BUT	1262	7
INSURING			
IS JOY'S INSURING QUALITY.	GO NOT TOO NEAR A HOUSE	1434	8
INTACT			
INTACT--IN DIADEM!	ONE LIFE OF SO MUCH	270	12
INTACT, IN EVERLASTING FLAKE--	DOUBT ME! MY DIM	275	24
AND INTACT [DIRECT / DISTINCT] BELIEF--	GROWTH OF MAN--LIKE	750	12
ROBBED--WAS I--INTACT TO [YET MET NO] BANDIT--	STRUCK, WAS I, NOR YET	925	9

	FIRST LINE	POEM	LINE
INTEGRAL			
IS INTEGRAL [SUBSEQUENT]--AND THEREFORE . .	DEATH IS POTENTIAL TO	548	7
INTEGRITY			
HAS MORE INTEGRITY.	A SAUCER HOLDS A CUP	1374	V 16
ELEGY OF INTEGRITY.	AFTER ALL BIRDS HAVE	1395	8
COMPASSION FOR INTEGRITY	THE SWEETS OF PILLAGE,	1470	3
THE SAME OBLIQUE INTEGRITY, ...	THE ROBIN IS A GABRIEL	1483	7
INTELLECTS			
TO INTELLECTS INEBRIATE	WINTER IS GOOD--HIS HOAR	1316	3
INTELLIGENCE			
WHOSE WILL--A NUMB SIGNIFICANCE--[BLANK INTELLIGENCE]	DENIAL--IS THE ONLY FACT	965	3
INTEMPERANCE			
TO KNOW HER AN INTEMPERANCE [A DISPARAGEMENT / AN EMBARRASSMENT]	TO SEE HER IS A PICTURE	1568	3
IS A DIVINE INTEMPERANCE	THROUGH THOSE OLD	1753	3
INTENDING			
INTENDING TO RETURN--	SHE LAY AS IF AT PLAY	369	3
INTENSIFY			
ONLY TO AGGRAVATE [JUST TO INTENSIFY] THE DARK	FAIRER THROUGH FADING--	938	7
INTENT			
INTENT UPON THE [A] VISION	A POOR--TORN HEART-- A	78	7
ON SCHEMES INTENT	THE RAT IS THE CONCISEST	1356	4
INTENT UPON IT'S OWN CAREER [MISSION QUAINT / CIRCUIT QUAINT]	HOW SOFT A CATERPILLAR	1448	7
INTENTION			
IS MY INTENTION NOW.	A CLOUD WITHDREW FROM	895	12
INTENTIONED			
WHOSE CORPORATION [UNSUSPECTING / WELL INTENTIONED] COAT	AN ANTIQUATED TREE	1514	5
INTER			
OURSELVES WE DO INTER WITH SWEET DERISION. .	OURSELVES WE DO INTER	1144	1
THIS DOCILE ONE INTER	THIS DOCILE ONE INTER	1752	1
INTERCEDE			
TO INTERCEDE--FOR THEE--	THE COURT IS FAR AWAY--	235	12
BELIEVING IF IT INTERCEDE	LONGING IS LIKE THE SEED	1255	3
THAT WOULD NOT INTERCEDE	I SAW THE WIND WITHIN	1502	V
INTERCEDING			
WHEN THE LONG INTERCEDING LIPS	THERE COMES AN HOUR WHEN	1751	2
INTERCEPTING			
NO AUTUMN'S INTERCEPTING CHILL	NO AUTUMN'S INTERCEPTING	1516	1
INTERCEPTIVE			
NO AUTUMN'S INTERCEPTIVE CHILL, ...	HIS ORIENTAL HERESIES	1526	V 3
INTERCHANGE			
THE LEAVES LIKE WOMEN, INTERCHANGE . . .	THE LEAVES LIKE WOMEN,	987	1
INTERCOURSE			
A BOWING INTERCOURSE.	THE DUTIES OF THE WIND	1137	12
SO INFINITE OUR INTERCOURSE [INTERVIEW] . .	HE WAS MY HOST--HE WAS	1721	5
INTERDICT			
YET INTERDICT--MY BLOSSOM--	I ENVY SEAS, WHEREON HE	498	21
THE INTERDICT OF GOD--	ENDED, ERE IT BEGUN--	1088	8
INTERDICTED			
THE INTERDICTED LAND--	"HEAVEN"--IS WHAT I	239	6
THAT INTERDICTED WAY, ...	A TONGUE--TO TELL HIM I	400	6
INTEREST			
AS HERSCHEL'S PRIVATE INTEREST	NATURE AND GOD--I	835	7
INTERESTED			
WHAT INTERESTED SCHOLARS--MOST--	A PRECIOUS--MOULDERING	371	13
INTERESTS			
HIS INTERESTS OF FIRE	THE MOUNTAINS STOOD IN	1278	6
INTERFERE			
TO GO AND INTERFERE!	"ARCTURUS" IS HIS OTHER	70	4
INTERIOR			
WHOSE SOURCES ARE INTERIOR--	REVERSE CANNOT BEFALL	395	3
THAN IT'S [AN] INTERIOR CONFRONTING-- . .	ONE NEED NOT BE A	670	7
IS AN INTERIOR THING--	WHO COURT OBTAIN WITHIN	803	4
OF THE INTERIOR.	'TWAS FIGHTING FOR HIS	1188	8
INTERLOCUTORS			
OF OTHER INTERLOCUTORS	THAT SACRED CLOSET WHEN	1273	7
INTERMIT			
TO HAVE IT INTERMIT--	THE MUSHROOM IS THE ELF	1298	14
INTERMITTENT			
LIKE INTERMITTENT PLUSH, BE HEARD	THE NIGHT WAS WIDE, AND	589	11
INTERNAL			
BUT INTERNAL DIFFERENCE, ...	THERE'S A CERTAIN SLANT	258	7
WITH THE INTERNAL BAR.	THROUGH THOSE OLD	1753	8
INTERPOSED			
THERE INTERPOSED A FLY--	I HEARD A FLY BUZZ--WHEN	465	12
INTERROGATE			
A MOMENT TO INTERROGATE, ...	COCOON ABOVE! COCOON	129	10
INTERROGATES			
"WE DREAMED IT"? SHE INTERROGATES--	THE SYMPTOM OF THE GALE	1327	15
INTERRUPT			
WOULD INTERRUPT THE DARK--	IT MIGHT BE LONELIER	405	5
I SUPPOSE IT WILL INTERRUPT ME SOME	IT DONT SOUND SO	426	10
INTERRUPT--TO DIE--	SWEET--SAFE--HOUSES--	457	17
TO INTERRUPT HIS YELLOW PLAN	TO INTERRUPT HIS YELLOW	591	1
THAT INTERRUPT THE DAY	A PRISON GETS TO BE A	652	18
THAT INTERRUPT THE MORN	THE ROBIN IS THE ONE	828	2
INTERRUPT THIS GROUND--	AMPLE MAKE THIS BED--	829	8

	FIRST LINE	POEM	LINE
INTERRUPT (CONTINUED)			
TILL JEALOUS DAYLIGHT INTERRUPT--	WHAT I SEE NOT, I BETTER	939	11
WITH ONLY BIRDS [BLOOM] TO INTERRUPT	I LEARNED--AT LEAST--	944	11
NO SOLSTICE INTERRUPT--	THERE IS A ZONE WHOSE	1056	2
INTERRUPTED			
HE GAILY [BOLDLY] INTERRUPTED THAT OVERFLOWING DAY	THE BOBOLINK IS GONE--	1591	4
INTERRUPTING			
ITSELF, TOO GREAT [VAST], FOR INTERRUPTING--MORE--	I GOT SO I COULD HEAR	293	27
FOR INTERRUPTING TEARS--	DEATH SETS A THING	360	18
INTERRUPTION			
FOR LOWER RECOGNITION [INTERRUPTION]	THE SOUL'S SUPERIOR	306	7
INTERRUPTIONS			
IT'S MOSTLY, INTERRUPTIONS--	THE WINTERS ARE SO SHORT	403	9
INTERSECT			
DARKNESS INTERSECT HER FACE--	WHEN I HOPED, I	768	21
INTERSPERSED			
ALL INTERSPERSED WITH WEED,	ALL OVERGROWN BY CUNNING	148	2
INTERSPERSION			
TUCKS--OF DAINTY INTERSPERSION--	DONT PUT UP MY THREAD &	617	11
INTERVAL			
IS TRAVERSING THE INTERVAL	THIS CONSCIOUSNESS THAT	822	5
DISARMS THE LITTLE INTERVAL--	LOVE--IS THAT LATER	924	7
AS ACCENT FADES [WANES] TO INTERVAL	THE MURMURING OF BEES,	1115	11
SO SCANT AN INTERVAL--	THE SYMPTOM OF THE GALE	1327	12
DISCRETION IN THE INTERVAL	BEFORE YOU THOUGHT OF	1465	11
INTERVALS			
THE SUN SHONE WHOLE AT INTERVALS--	THE TREES LIKE TASSELS--	606	9
AT RARER INTERVALS--	THE LADY FEEDS HER	941	2
INTERVENE			
FOREVER INTERVENE!	OUR LIVES ARE SWISS--	80	10
AND FASHIONS--INTERVENE--	YOU KNOW THAT PORTRAIT	504	8
EXCEPT THERE INTERVENE	I CROSS TILL I AM WEARY	550	15
INTERVENED			
AND YOUR'S--THE JUDGMENT INTERVENED--	DID YOU EVER STAND IN A	590	11
INTERVIEW			
OUR INTERVIEW--WAS TRANSIENT--	THE ONLY GHOST I EVER	274	13
CONCLUDES HIS GLISTENING INTERVIEW--	A VISITOR IN MARL--	391	7
LEST INTERVIEW--ANNUL A WANT	A CHARM INVESTS A FACE	421	7
PAST INTERVIEW, AND VOW--	IF ANYBODY'S FRIEND BE	509	22
FOR INTERVIEW--HAD COME--	'TWAS A LONG PARTING--	625	2
WITHOUT A CORDIAL INTERVIEW	SPRING IS THE PERIOD	844	7
OUR FINAL INTERVIEW.	WERE IT TO BE THE LAST	1164	4
THIS LIVID INTERVIEW--	HIS VOICE DECREPIT WAS	1476	8
THANKS FOR THE INTERVIEW--	IMAGE OF LIGHT, ADIEU--	1556	2
SO INFINITE OUR INTERCOURSE [INTERVIEW]	HE WAS MY HOST--HE WAS	1721	5
INTIMATE			
MORE INTIMATE WITH US BECOME	THE MURMURING OF BEES,	1115	15
HIS [THIS] FIGURE INTIMATE	THESE ARE THE NIGHTS	1128	4
HOW INTIMATE, A [ORDERLY THE] TEMPEST PAST	THE WIND TOOK UP THE	1134	15
BUT INTIMATE [COMPETENT / ABSOLUTE / IMPUDENT] DELIGHT.	THE MOST TRIUMPHANT BIRD	1265	6
TOO INTIMATE WITH JOY--	THE WAY TO KNOW THE	1279	14
SO INTIMATE WITH MADNESS	HAD WE OUR SENSES	1284	3
ESTRANGED, HOWEVER INTIMATE--	WITHOUT A SMILE--WITHOUT	1330	5
. . . INTIMATE / AFFABLE / AFFLUENT / GRACIOUS] SO TO BE	YOUR THOUGHTS DONT HAVE	1452	6
OR INTIMATE [DESIGNATE] IT THERE	'TIS WHITER THAN AN	1482	6
AS INTIMATE [MAGICAL]--AS FUGITIVE	OF WHOM SO DEAR	1504	4
THE SNOW AND HE ARE INTIMATE--	NO BRIGADIER THROUGHOUT	1561	9
SO INTIMATE, INDEED,	HE WAS MY HOST--HE WAS	1721	6
SO INTIMATE HAVE WE BECOME	THE DISTANCE THAT THE	1742	7
INTIMATES			
IT INTIMATES THE FINER WANT--	WE THIRST AT FIRST--'TIS	726	5
INTONATIONS			
MEDITERRANEAN INTONATIONS--	I THINK THAT THE ROOT OF	1302	5
INTOXICATE			
SO ROYALLY INTOXICATE	EXHILIRATION--IS WITHIN	383	3
INTOXICATED			
INTOXICATED WITH THE PEACE	HIS ORIENTAL HERESIES	1526	V
INTOXICATION			
THE DIVINE INTOXICATION	EXULTATION IS THE GOING	76	7
ENACTS INTOXICATION	THE LONG SIGH OF THE	1359	3
INTRENCHED			
UNLESS CONCEALED IN [INTRENCHED IN / AFFIXED TO / INLAID IN] THEE	HOW FIRM ETERNITY MUST	1499	8
THE WHOLE OF IMMORTALITY INTRENCHED [SECRETED / DEPUTED]	HE LIVED THE LIFE OF	1525	7
INTRENCHMENT			
INTRENCHMENTS STIMULATE [INTRENCHMENT STIMULATE] A FRIEND	WHAT MYSTERY PERVADES A	1400	V
INTRENCHMENTS			
INTRENCHMENTS STIMULATE [INTRENCHMENT STIMULATE] A FRIEND	WHAT MYSTERY PERVADES A	1400	V
INTRICATE			
HOW INTRICATE THE DUST!	GOOD NIGHT, BECAUSE WE	114	2
INTRICATELY			
SO INTRICATELY DONE	BLOOM--IS RESULT--TO	1058	6

	FIRST LINE	POEM	LINE
INTRINSIC			
BECAUSE INTRINSIC SIZE	SIZE CIRCUMSCRIBES--IT	641	6
APART--INTRINSIC--STAND--	OF ALL THE SOULS THAT	664	6
TOO INTRINSIC FOR RENOWN--	LAY THIS LAUREL ON THE	1393	2
INTRO			
INTRO WITHOUT MY TRANS--	A PANG IS MORE	1530	V
INTRODUCE			
TO INTRODUCE HIS SOUL.	COULD LIVE--DID LIVE--	43	5
NOR INTRODUCE--MY SOUL--	I AM ASHAMED--I HIDE--	473	6
WE INTRODUCE OURSELVES	WE INTRODUCE OURSELVES	1214	1
INTRODUCED			
THE MIRACLE THAT INTRODUCED	THE BIRDS BEGUN AT FOUR	783	23
INTRODUCTION			
NEITHER INTRODUCTION	NEVER FOR SOCIETY	746	11
INTRODUCTIONS			
APPREHENSIONS--ARE GOD'S INTRODUCTIONS--	BY MY WINDOW HAVE I FOR	797	24
INTROSPECTIVE			
OF INTROSPECTIVE MINES--	TO TELL THE BEAUTY WOULD	1700	8
INTRUDE			
IT MIGHT INTRUDE UPON--	IT MIGHT BE LONELIER	405	10
WHEN THOU UPON THEIR CRYPTS INTRUDE	BECAUSE THE BEE MAY	869	8
BETTER THAN ON A DREAM INTRUDE	THE SUBURBS OF A SECRET	1245	3
INTRUSION			
BY HIS INTRUSION, GOD IS KNOWN--	WE KNEW NOT THAT WE WERE	1462	7
INTUITION			
THE INTUITION OF THE NEWS--	THERE'S BEEN A DEATH, IN	389	23
BY INTUITION, MIGHTIEST THINGS	YOU'LL KNOW IT--AS YOU	420	7
HOSPITABLE INTUITION	CONSCIOUS AM I IN MY	679	7
INTUITIONS			
OUR MINUTER INTUITIONS--	COLOR--CASTE--	970	15
INUNDATE			
DO ALL BUT [ALMOST] INUNDATE--	HOW MUCH THE PRESENT	1380	8
INUNDATION			
THE INUNDATION OF THE SPRING	THE INUNDATION OF THE	1425	1
OR INUNDATION OF A DEW	GO NOT TOO NEAR A HOUSE	1434	3
INURED			
INURED TO SLOWER [OTHER] THINGS	TO FLEE FROM MEMORY	1242	4
INVADES			
WHOSE AMPLITUDE NO END [CLOCK] INVADES--	WATER MAKES MANY BEDS	1428	7
INVADING			
LIKE TIME'S INSIDIOUS [INVADING / PRESUMING / APPOINTED / . . .	LIKE TIME'S INSIDIOUS	1236	1
INVALIDATE			
INVALIDATE [INVALIDATES] THE [A / HIS] SPELL--	LONG YEARS APART--CAN	1383	4
INVALIDATES			
INVALIDATES THE BALM OF THAT RELIGION	OURSELVES WE DO INTER	1144	3
INVALIDATE [INVALIDATES] THE [A / HIS] SPELL--	LONG YEARS APART--CAN	1383	4
INVENT			
IT'S EASY TO INVENT A LIFE--	IT'S EASY TO INVENT A	724	1
INVENTED			
INVENTED THIS [THAT] REPOSE	HOW SOFT THIS PRISON IS	1334	4
INVENTION			
"FAITH" IS A FINE INVENTION	"FAITH" IS A FINE	185	1
IF IT BE INVENTION	KNOWS HOW TO FORGET!	433	V
HOPE IS A STRANGE INVENTION--	HOPE IS A STRANGE	1392	1
INVEST			
TO INVEST EXISTENCE WITH A STATELY AIR,	TO VENERATE THE SIMPLE	57	7
THAN INVEST--OUR SNOW--	PUBLICATION--IS THE	709	8
INVEST THIS ALABASTER ZEST	PRAISE IT--'TIS DEAD--	1384	6
INVESTED			
SURFACES MAY [CAN] BE INVESTED [RELATED]	NONE WHO SAW IT EVER	1110	5
INVESTED SOMBRE PLACE--	AS IMPERCEPTIBLY AS	1540	V
INVESTIGATE			
WHILE WE SHREWDLY SPECULATE [SAGE INVESTIGATE / SHREWD INVESTIGATE]	YESTERDAY IS HISTORY,	1292	7
WHILE WE SHREWDLY SPECULATE [SAGE INVESTIGATE / SHREWD INVESTIGATE]	YESTERDAY IS HISTORY,	1292	7
INVESTIGATED			
AFTER ALL BIRDS HAVE BEEN INVESTIGATED AND LAID ASIDE--	AFTER ALL BIRDS HAVE	1395	1
INVESTIGATING			
INVESTIGATING MARCH,	HAVE ANY LIKE MYSELF	736	2
INVESTMENT'S			
INVESTMENT'S BEST EXPOSITOR	THE INCIDENTS OF LOVE	1248	3
INVESTS			
INVESTS SO MEAN A BROW!	WAIT TILL THE MAJESTY OF	171	2
A CHARM INVESTS A FACE	A CHARM INVESTS A FACE	421	1
INVIGORATED			
INVIGORATED, WADED [FULLY]	A SPARROW TOOK A SLICE	1211	5
INVINCIBLE			
INVINCIBLE [IMPREGNABLE] MY FORTRESS	ME FROM MYSELF--TO	642	3
IMPREGNABLE [ILLUSTRIOUS / INVINCIBLE / INVIOLATE] THE ROSE	A LITTLE SNOW WAS HERE	1444	6
HOW HAPPY IS [INVINCIBLE] THE LITTLE STONE	HOW HAPPY IS THE LITTLE	1510	1
INVINCIBLY			
WITHELD INVINCIBLY--	I SEND YOU A DECREPIT	1324	8
INVIOLABLE			
INVIOLABLE COMPACT	THE LEAVES LIKE WOMEN,	987	7
INVIOLATE			
BUT THAT GRATE INVIOLATE--	"SECRETS" IS A DAILY	1385	7

	FIRST LINE	POEM	LINE
ISHMAEL			
BUT--ISHMAEL--SINCE WE MET--'TIS LONG-- . .	YOU KNOW THAT PORTRAIT	504	7
ISLAND			
AN [SOME] ISLAND IN DISHONORED GRASS-- . .	OF BRONZE--AND BLAZE--	290	18
ISLES			
WHETHER TO ISLES ENCHANTED	WHETHER MY BARK WENT	52	3
RATHER THAN THE "SPICY ISLES--"	HOW SICK--TO WAIT--IN	368	11
STILL [HOW / SO] FABLE--IN THE ISLES OF SPICE--	I GAVE MYSELF TO HIM--	580	11
ISOLATE			
NOR ISOLATE IT SEEMS	THE GENTIAN HAS A	1424	9
ISOLATION			
ITS ISOLATION COVETED	ONE CROWN THAT NO ONE	1735	3
ISRAEL'S			
THE FAULT--WAS DOUBTLESS ISRAEL'S--	IT ALWAYS FELT TO ME--A	597	17
ISSUES			
STEADY--MY SOUL! WHAT ISSUES	A DAY! HELP! HELP!	42	7
ITALIC			
A SMALL--ITALIC SEED	THIS IS A BLOSSOM OF THE	945	2
EXCEPT FOR THE ITALIC FACE	THE HOLLOWS ROUND HIS	955	7
ITALIC FLAVOR YIELD--	WINTER IS GOOD--HIS HOAR	1316	2
IT IS THE PAST'S SUPREME ITALIC	GLASS WAS THE STREET--IN	1498	7
ITALICIZE			
ITALICIZE ITS SWEETNESS, ...	DID LIFE'S PENURIOUS	1717	2
ITALICIZED			
ITALICIZED--AS 'TWERE.	THE LAST NIGHT THAT SHE	1100	8
ITALY			
ITALY STANDS THE OTHER SIDE!	OUR LIVES ARE SWISS--	80	6
PUT HER DOWN--IN ITALY?	HER--"LAST POEMS"--	312	19
I'VE			
I'VE KNOWN PERMISSION GIVEN	A THROE UPON THE	71	7
I'VE HEARD THE HUNTER TELL--	A WOUNDED DEER--LEAPS	165	2
I'VE HEARD AN ORGAN TALK, SOMETIMES-- . .	I'VE HEARD AN ORGAN TALK	183	1
I'M "WIFE"--I'VE FINISHED THAT--	I'M "WIFE"--I'VE	199	1
SAVIOR! I'VE NO ONE ELSE TO TELL--	SAVIOR! I'VE NO ONE ELSE	217	1
I'VE DIAMONDS--ON MY FINGERS--	I CAME TO BUY A SMILE--	223	9
I'VE RUBIES--LIKE THE EVENING BLOOD-- . .	I CAME TO BUY A SMILE--	223	11
I'VE NOTHING ELSE--TO BRING, YOU KNOW-- . .	I'VE NOTHING ELSE--TO	224	1
I'VE KNOWN A HEAVEN, LIKE A TENT-- . . .	I'VE KNOWN A HEAVEN,	243	1
I'VE HEARD IT IN THE CHILLEST LAND-- . . .	"HOPE" IS THE THING WITH	254	9
I'VE KNOWN HER--FROM AN AMPLE NATION-- . .	THE SOUL SELECTS HER OWN	303	9
I'VE HEARD MEN SAY--	I'M SAYING EVERY DAY	373	11
SAVIOR [MASTER]--I'VE SEEN THE FACE--BEFORE!	A WIFE--AT DAYBREAK I	461	13
I'M CEDED--I'VE STOPPED BEING THEIR'S-- . .	I'M CEDED--I'VE STOPPED	508	1
I'VE FINISHED THREADING--TOO--	I'M CEDED--I'VE STOPPED	508	7
I'VE SEEN A DYING EYE	I'VE SEEN A DYING EYE	547	1
I'VE HEARD MY FATHER TELL--	THE JUDGE IS LIKE THE	699	2
I'VE MET THE THING BEFORE--	A THOUGHT WENT UP MY	701	10
I'VE SEEN?	YOU SAID THAT I "WAS	738	8
I'VE RANSOMED IT [FOUND IT--'TIS]--ALIVE-- .	HE TOLD A HOMELY TALE	763	16
I'VE NONE TO TELL ME TO BUT THEE	I'VE NONE TO TELL ME TO	881	1
A HOARY BOY, I'VE KNOWN TO DROP	NOT ALL DIE EARLY, DYING	990	5
I'VE DROPPED MY BRAIN--MY SOUL IS NUMB-- .	I'VE DROPPED MY BRAIN--	1046	1
I'VE STILL A CHANCE TO STRAIN	I'VE DROPPED MY BRAIN--	1046	16
I'VE KNOWN	NOT WITH A CLUB, THE	1304	4
I'VE OFTEN SEEN THEM PLAY	NO BRIGADIER THROUGHOUT	1561	10
I'VE GOT AN ARROW HERE.	I'VE GOT AN ARROW HERE.	1729	1
IVORY			
THE MEN OF IVORY--	THOSE FAIR--FICTITIOUS	499	4
OR ONE OF IVORY--	THEMSELF ARE ALL I HAVE	1094	4
JACKET			
IN JUST THE JACKET THAT HE WORE--	OF NEARNESS TO HER	607	9
INSIDE A JACKET DULLER--	YOU'LL KNOW HER--BY HER	634	11
WHOSE UNCLAIMED HAT AND JACKET	HOW THE WATERS CLOSED	923	7
BONNET [JACKET] DUE IN APRIL--	NOT AT HOME TO CALLERS	1590	3
JACKET'S			
BENEATH HIS FADED JACKET'S BLUE--	I MET A KING THIS	166	6
WITHIN THAT JACKET'S POCKET TOO!	I MET A KING THIS	166	8
JACOB			
AND JACOB, WAXING STRONG, ...	A LITTLE EAST OF JORDAN,	59	6
NOT SO, SAID CUNNING [QUOTH WILY] JACOB! .	A LITTLE EAST OF JORDAN,	59	9
JADED			
ALLURES [ENSNARES] HIS JADED EYE	HIS ORIENTAL HERESIES	1526	6
JAGGED			
A BELT OF JAGGED STONE--	I KNOW WHERE WELLS GROW	460	6
JAIL			
AND BAD MEN--"GO TO JAIL"--	YOU'RE RIGHT--"THE WAY	234	11
DITCHES FOR REALMS AND A TRIP TO JAIL . .	THE POPULAR HEART IS A	1226	7
JAILS			
FROM ALL THE JAILS THE BOYS AND GIRLS . .	FROM ALL THE JAILS THE	1532	1
JAMAICAS			
JAMAICAS OF REMEMBRANCE [PROSPECTIVE] STIR .	A DRUNKARD CANNOT MEET A	1628	5
JAMES			
AND CUSTOMS AT "ST. JAMES"!	THE MANNER OF IT'S DEATH	468	12
JANUARY			
JUNE NOON--AS JANUARY NIGHT--	WHAT CARE THE DEAD, FOR	592	19
A FEBUARY [JANUARY] DAY, ...	NO BRIGADIER THROUGHOUT	1561	6
THIS JANUARY DAY	A DRUNKARD CANNOT MEET A	1628	4
JAR SEE A/JAR			
CAUTIOUS--WE JAR EACH OTHER--	WE DREAM--IT IS GOOD WE	531	9

	FIRST LINE	POEM	LINE
JAR (CONTINUED)			
RESIDING IN A JAR	WHAT MYSTERY PERVADES A	1400	4
COULD NOT JAR OR SPILL.	BEES ARE BLACK, WITH	1405	8
BUT WHEN THE EARTH BEGAN TO JAR	IT WAS A QUIET SEEMING	1419	7
JARRED			
I JUDGED MY FEATURES--JARRED MY HAIR--	I FELT MY LIFE WITH BOTH	351	9
JASON			
JASON--SHAM--TOO.	FINDING IS THE FIRST ACT	870	8
I NEVER THOUGHT THAT JASON SOUGHT	ONE OF THE ONES THAT	1466	21
BUT IF THERE WERE A JASON,	ONE OF THE ONES THAT	1466	25
JASPER			
I SHANT WALK THE "JASPER"--BAREFOOT--	WHAT IS--"PARADISE"--	215	15
THAT ONCE--ON ME--THOSE JASPER GATES	IF I'M LOST--NOW--	256	4
JAWS			
HER JAWS STIR--TWITCHING [MOUTH STIRS--LONGING]--HUNGRY--	SHE SIGHTS A BIRD--SHE	507	5
JAY			
SHOW ME THE JAY!	ANSWER JULY--	386	13
QUIBBLED THE JAY--	ANSWER JULY--	386	14
A PROMPT--EXECUTIVE [BOLD, INSPIRITING] BIRD IS THE JAY--	A PROMPT--EXECUTIVE BIRD	1177	1
WHEN THE JAY WILL GIGGLE	I SUPPOSE THE TIME WILL	1381	10
SO CIVIC AS THE JAY--	NO BRIGADIER THROUGHOUT	1561	2
THE JAY HIS CASTANET HAS STRUCK	THE JAY HIS CASTANET HAS	1635	1
THE CURTNESS OF THE JAY--	THE ONES THAT	1690	4
JAYS			
IT HAS NO PORT, NOR A "LINE"--BUT THE JAYS--	BY MY WINDOW HAVE I FOR	797	5
JEALOUS			
A JEALOUS ZEPHYR--NOT A DOUBT--	GOOD NIGHT! WHICH PUT	259	2
LEST THE JEALOUS GRASS	PROMISE THIS--WHEN YOU	648	22
TILL JEALOUS DAYLIGHT INTERRUPT--	WHAT I SEE NOT, I BETTER	939	11
BECAUSE HE IS A "JEALOUS GOD"	BECAUSE THAT YOU ARE	1260	35
GOD IS INDEED A JEALOUS GOD--	GOD IS INDEED A JEALOUS	1719	1
JEALOUSIES			
OF CALUMNIES [JEALOUSIES]--OR FLIES.	SIZE CIRCUMSCRIBES--IT	641	8
JEALOUSY			
FOR PANG OF JEALOUSY--	THERE IS A FLOWER THAT	380	24
A JEALOUSY FOR HER AROSE	THE LAST NIGHT THAT SHE	1100	15
ALMOST TO JEALOUSY--	SO PROUD SHE WAS TO DIE	1272	8
JEHOVAH			
JEHOVAH--RECOLLECT--	NO OTHER CAN REDUCE	982	V 8
JEHOVAH TOLD TO HER	THE RETICENT VOLCANO	1748	6
JEHOVAH'S			
JEHOVAH'S WATCH--IS WRONG.	SUNSET AT NIGHT--IS	415	8
JEHOVAH'S COUNTENANCE--	TRIUMPH--MAY BE OF	455	16
A SMILE SUFFUSED JEHOVAH'S FACE--	I MEANT TO HAVE BUT	476	13
JEHOVAH'S ESTIMATE.	NO OTHER CAN REDUCE	982	8
JEHOVAHS			
THE JEHOVAHS--ARE NO BABBLERS--	ONLY GOD--DETECT THE	626	3
JEOPARDIZE			
TO JEOPARDIZE THE GAIN?	I CROSS TILL I AM WEARY	550	17
JEOPARDY			
THE MERRIMENT [JEOPARDY] OF MEN	THESE ARE THE NIGHTS	1128	6
JERUSALEM			
REBECCA, TO JERUSALEM,	HE TOUCHED ME, SO I LIVE	506	14
JESSAMINE			
BARE YOUR JESSAMINE--TO THE STORM--	KILL YOUR BALM--AND IT'S	238	2
JESSAMINES			
BASHFUL--SIP THY JESSAMINES--	COME SLOWLY--EDEN!	211	3
JEST			
WOULD NOT THE JEST--	I KNOW THAT HE EXISTS.	338	15
WE JEST AND SHUT THE DOOR--	WE NEVER KNOW WE GO WHEN	1523	2
I MUFFLE WITH A JEST.	CONSULTING SUMMER'S	1715	8
JESUIT			
THE JESUIT OF ORCHARDS	ONE OF THE ONES THAT	1466	13
JESUS			
BUT SINCE JESUS DARED--	"THEY HAVE NOT CHOSEN ME	85	6
AND "JESUS"! WHERE IS JESUS GONE?	DYING! DYING IN THE	158	5
AND "JESUS"! WHERE IS JESUS GONE?	DYING! DYING IN THE	158	5
THEY SAID THAT JESUS--ALWAYS CAME--	DYING! DYING IN THE	158	6
THIS WAY, JESUS, LET HIM PASS!	DYING! DYING IN THE	158	8
JESUS MERELY "LOOKED" AT PETER--	HE FORGOT--AND I--	203	7
JESUS! THY CRUCIFIX	JESUS! THY CRUCIFIX	225	1
JESUS! THY SECOND FACE	JESUS! THY CRUCIFIX	225	4
JUST SO--JESUS [CHRIST]--RAPS--	JUST SO--JESUS--RAPS--	317	1
'TWAS BASE AS JESUS--MOST!	'TWAS LOVE--NOT ME--	394	8
I SAY TO YOU, SAID JESUS--	DO PEOPLE MOULDER	432	9
IF JESUS WAS SINCERE--	DO PEOPLE MOULDER	432	12
AS WELL AS JESUS?	SO WELL THAT I CAN LIVE	456	3
JESUS--IT'S YOUR LITTLE "JOHN"!	HE STRAINED MY FAITH--	497	15
OH JESUS--IN THE AIR--	AT LEAST--TO PRAY--IS	502	2
SAY, JESUS CHRIST OF NAZARETH--	AT LEAST--TO PRAY--IS	502	7
"I AM JESUS--LATE OF JUDEA--	"UNTO ME?" I DO NOT KNOW	964	3
WHAT CONFUSION WOULD COVER THE INNOCENT JESUS	HE PREACHED UPON	1207	7
AS JESUS SAYS OF HIM,	NO LADDER NEEDS THE BIRD	1574	6
AS JESUS CITES [SAYS] OF HIM--	TO HER DERIDED HOME	1586	10
THOU CAN'ST NOT BOAST, LIKE JESUS, DRUNKEN WITHOUT COMPANION	PROUD OF MY BROKEN HEART	1736	5
JESUS'			
WOULD PUT OUT JESUS'--	I CANNOT LIVE WITH YOU--	640	23

	FIRST LINE	POEM	LINE
JEW			
'TWOULD BE "A BARGAIN" FOR A JEW!	I CAME TO BUY A SMILE--	223	13
MIGHT I--BUT BE THE JEW--	YOUR RICHES--TAUGHT ME--	299	20
THE ORCHARD SPARKLED LIKE A JEW--	THE DAY CAME SLOW--TILL	304	13
JEWEL			
AND GIVE HER WHAT SHE ASKETH, JEWEL, OR BIRD, OR FLOWER--	AWAKE YE MUSES NINE,	1	38
I HELD A JEWEL IN MY FINGERS--	I HELD A JEWEL IN MY	245	1
AND BORE MY JEWEL--HOME--	THE MALAY--TOOK THE	452	8
HAD I--THE JEWEL--GOT--	THE MALAY--TOOK THE	452	10
GLOWS CENTRAL--LIKE A JEWEL	THAT FIRST DAY, WHEN YOU	659	5
JEWELS			
I COULD BRING YOU JEWELS--HAD I A MIND TO--	I COULD BRING YOU JEWELS	697	1
JIB			
THEN AWAY UPON A JIB--HE GOES--	HE PARTS HIMSELF--LIKE	517	8
JIG			
ARE MARSHALLED FOR A JIG!	I COUNTED TILL THEY	36	8
JOCOSER			
THE BIRDS JOCOSER [REDOUBLED] SUNG--	A DROP FELL ON THE APPLE	794	10
JOCUND			
HOW CAN I BEAR THEIR JOCUND FACES	WHAT SHALL I DO WHEN THE	956	11
JOGGLE			
NOR THREATEN [JOGGLE / OGLE] A HAT--	THE WIND DID'NT COME	316	4
CARTS--JOGGLE BY--	I COULD DIE--TO KNOW--	570	4
JOGGLING			
FOR FEAR OF JOGGLING HIM!	IS IT TRUE, DEAR SUE?	218	4
JOHN			
OR LITTLE JOHN--OF LINCOLN GREEN--	LIKE SOME OLD FASHIONED	302	7
"MILES", AND "JOHN ALDEN" WERE SYNONYME--	GOD IS A DISTANT--	357	8
JESUS--IT'S YOUR LITTLE "JOHN"!	HE STRAINED MY FAITH--	497	15
JOIN			
PERMIT A CHILD TO JOIN.	THESE ARE THE DAYS WHEN	130	15
THE THOUGHT BEHIND, I STROVE [TRIED] TO JOIN	I FELT A CLEAVING IN MY	937	5
THE DUST BEHIND I STROVE TO JOIN	THE DUST BEHIND I STROVE	992	1
JOINS			
IT JOINS--BEHIND THE VAIL	FAITH--IS THE PIERLESS	915	8
HE JOINS ME IN MY RAMBLE	THE BLUNDER IS IN	1684	5
JOINT			
TO JOINT THIS AGATE WERE A WORK [FEAT]--	TOO COLD IS THIS	1135	4
JOINTED			
THE MORNING'S AMBER [LIGHTNING'S JOINTED] ROAD--	BEFORE I GOT MY EYE PUT	327	15
JOINTS			
ACRES OF JOINTS [SEAMS], WHERE HARVESTS WERE,	IT SIFTS FROM LEADEN	311	15
THE STUBBLE'S JOINTS BETWEEN--	'TWAS JUST THIS TIME,	445	10
JOKE			
WOULD NOT THE FUN [JOKE]	I KNOW THAT HE EXISTS.	338	13
JOLLY			
AND THEN THEY GREW SO JOLLY	I COUNTED TILL THEY	36	5
ASK THE JOLLY CLOVERS!	WE--BEE AND I--LIVE BY	230	7
JOLT			
IT--MAY JOLT THE HAND	CRISIS IS A HAIR	889	13
JORDAN			
A LITTLE EAST OF [OVER] JORDAN,	A LITTLE EAST OF JORDAN,	59	1
JOSTLE			
SOUTH WINDS JOSTLE THEM--	SOUTH WINDS JOSTLE THEM	86	1
JOSTLED			
TOO JOSTLED WERE OUR SOULS TO SPEAK	THE LAST NIGHT THAT SHE	1100	19
JOTS			
ONE YEAR AGO--JOTS WHAT?	ONE YEAR AGO--JOTS WHAT?	296	1
JOURNEY			
HASTENING FROM FAR JOURNEY--	NOBODY KNOWS THIS LITTLE	35	7
COULD CONTEMPLATE THE JOURNEY	COULD LIVE--DID LIVE--	43	8
WHAT IF THE BIRD FROM JOURNEY FAR--	NOT PROBABLE--THE BAREST	346	5
THAT GAZE UPON [GROW ALONG] HIS JOURNEY--	I ENVY SEAS, WHEREON HE	498	5
FOR JOURNEY--OR CRUSADE'S ACHIEVING--	ONE CRUCIFIXION IS	553	11
OUR JOURNEY HAD ADVANCED--	OUR JOURNEY HAD ADVANCED	615	1
JOURNEY OF DOWN--AND WHIP OF DIAMOND--	DROPPED INTO THE ETHER	665	7
I WOULD NOT MIND THE JOURNEY THERE	I CANNOT BUY IT--'TIS	840	8
WE JOURNEY TO THE DAY	I SING TO USE THE	850	6
THE ABSENCE [JOURNEY] OF AN EYE--	WE MISS HER, NOT BECAUSE	993	2
ELIJAH'S JOURNEY TO PORTRAY	ELIJAH'S WAGON KNEW NO	1254	5
IT'S JOURNEY NEVER WAKES MY HAND	HOW SOFT A CATERPILLAR	1448	V
THOUGH [BUT] JOYS--LIKE MEN--MAY SOMETIMES MAKE A JOURNEY--	THE THINGS THAT NEVER	1515	3
THEIR DAPPLED JOURNEY TO THEMSELVES	COSMOPOLITES WITHOUT A	1589	5
I SHALL NOT COUNT THE JOURNEY ONE	I DID NOT REACH THEE	1664	5
JOURNEYING			
CLEMATIS--JOURNEYING FAR--	'TIS CUSTOMARY AS WE	440	6
JOURNEYS			
ON SPANGLED JOURNEYS TO THE PEAK	THE PEDIGREE OF HONEY	1627	5
JOVE			
JOVE! CHOOSE YOUR COUNSEL--	I HAD SOME THINGS THAT I	116	15
JOY			
COULD BUT A CRIER OF THE JOY	DELAYED TILL SHE HAD	58	8
'TIS SO MUCH JOY! 'TIS SO MUCH JOY!	'TIS SO MUCH JOY! 'TIS	172	1
'TIS SO MUCH JOY! 'TIS SO MUCH JOY!	'TIS SO MUCH JOY! 'TIS	172	1
WILL NOT CRY WITH JOY "POMPEII"!	I HAVE NEVER SEEN	175	19
IF JOY--TO PUT MY PIECE AWAY	FOREVER AT HIS SIDE TO	246	8

	FIRST LINE	POEM	LINE
JOY (CONTINUED)			
BUT THE LEAST PUSH OF JOY	I CAN WADE GRIEF--	252	4
BUT THE PUSH [PAIN] OF JOY--	MANY A PHRASE HAS THE	276	14
I SHOULD HAVE HAD THE JOY	I SHOULD HAVE BEEN TOO	313	15
SINCE GRIEF AND JOY ARE DONE	SO GLAD WE ARE--A	329	6
AND FURTHER TO PARADE A JOY	THE MORNING AFTER WO--	364	7
TO HAVE THE JOY OF FEELING IT--AGAIN--	I'LL CLUTCH--AND CLUTCH	427	14
I'D SO MUCH JOY--I TOLD IT--RED--	IT WOULD NEVER BE COMMON	430	9
INDIGNANT [AFFRONTED]--THAT THE JOY WAS COME--	I THINK THE LONGEST HOUR	635	5
A GEOMETRIC JOY--	A PRISON GETS TO BE A	652	16
OF ALL CONCEIVED JOY--	'TIS GOOD--THE LOOKING	660	4
AS DIFFERENT FROM JOY--	THERE IS AN ARID	782	2
JOY TO HAVE MERITED THE PAIN--	JOY TO HAVE MERITED THE	788	1
JOY TO HAVE PERISHED EVERY STEP--	JOY TO HAVE MERITED THE	788	3
WE ACHIEVE THE JOY--	SATISFACTION--IS THE	1036	6
THE JOY THAT IN HIS HAPPY THROAT	HIS BILL IS CLASPED--HIS	1102	5
SO BLIND WITH [FULL OF] JOY HE COULD NOT CHOOSE	THE BIRD DID PRANCE--THE	1107	3
AS OLD AS BLISS [JOY]	AS OLD AS WOE--	1168	4
AND KNOWS NO OTHER JOY	A LITTLE DOG THAT WAGS	1185	2
PRECISELY AS THE JOY OF HIM--	THE WAY TO KNOW THE	1279	3
TOO INTIMATE WITH JOY--	THE WAY TO KNOW THE	1279	14
THE GERM [JOY] OF ALIBI--	THE MUSHROOM IS THE ELF	1298	10
MIGHT VILIFY THE JOY--	THE TREASON OF AN ACCENT	1358	V 2
WE FEEL A JOY--	IN MANY AND REPORTLESS	1382	2
BUT POMPOUS [SILLY / AWKWARD] JOY	MARCH IS THE MONTH OF	1404	6
ONE JOY [SOUND] OF SO MUCH ANGUISH	ONE JOY OF SO MUCH	1420	1
WHO NEVER WANTED--MADDEST JOY	WHO NEVER WANTED--	1430	1
AND SHOUTS FOR JOY TO NOBODY	BEFORE YOU THOUGHT OF	1465	15
HIS VOICE DECREPIT WAS WITH JOY--	HIS VOICE DECREPIT WAS	1476	1
FOR SUCH A FOE [SWEET / GLEE / DAWN / SCENE / DEW / JOY] AS THIS--	FROM ALL THE JAILS THE	1532	8
AFRAID OF JOY,	WE SHUN IT ERE IT COMES,	1580	2
NOT JOY, BUT A DECREE	EXPANSE CANNOT BE LOST--	1584	2
AND MORE ARE IN THE JOY--	A DRUNKARD CANNOT MEET A	1628	10
A LETTER IS A JOY OF EARTH--	A LETTER IS A JOY OF	1639	1
THOU SHALT GO AT SUCH A GAIT OF JOY	IN SNOW THOU COMEST	1669	6
NOT SO GOOD AS JOY--	RATHER ARID DELIGHT	1679	4
THE SECOND HALF OF JOY	CONSULTING SUMMER'S	1715	5
WOULD STAND SO DEEP IN JOY	DID LIFE'S PENURIOUS	1717	4
THE JOY THAT HAS NO STEM NOR CORE,	THE JOY THAT HAS NO STEM	1744	1
JOYFUL			
JOYFUL--TO WHOM THE SUNRISE	THE DOOMED--REGARD THE	294	9
JOYFUL--FOR WHOM THE MEADOW BIRD	THE DOOMED--REGARD THE	294	11
HER PANTING NOTE [JOYFUL CRY / CORDIAL NOTE] EXALTS US-- . . .	AFTER ALL BIRDS HAVE	1395	6
THE JOYFUL LITTLE DEITY	HOW FLEET--HOW	1771	3
JOYOUS			
A JOYOUS GOING FELLOW	HIGH FROM THE EARTH I	1723	9
JOY'S			
IS JOY'S INSURING QUALITY.	GO NOT TOO NEAR A HOUSE	1434	8
JOYS			
THOUGH [BUT] JOYS--LIKE MEN--MAY SOMETIMES MAKE A JOURNEY--	THE THINGS THAT NEVER	1515	3
IS PRECISELY THE FINEST OF JOYS--	TO DO A MAGNANIMOUS	1699	4
IF ALL THE JOYS I AM TO HAVE	IF ALL THE GRIEFS I AM	1726	5
JUBILEE			
FOR UTTER JUBILEE--	THE MORNING AFTER WO--	364	4
AS IF UNTO A JUBILEE [SACRAMENT]	I THINK I WAS ENCHANTED	593	19
JUDAS			
JUDAS--THE GREAT [FIRST] DEFAULTER--	THE BIBLE IS AN ANTIQUE	1545	7
JUDEA			
JUDEA--	ONE CRUCIFIXION IS	553	10
"I AM JESUS--LATE OF JUDEA--	"UNTO ME?" I DO NOT KNOW	964	3
JUDGE			
JUDGE TENDERLY--OF ME	THIS IS MY LETTER TO THE	441	8
THEY'D JUDGE US--HOW--	I CANNOT LIVE WITH YOU--	640	29
THE JUDGE IS LIKE THE OWL--	THE JUDGE IS LIKE THE	699	1
A STRANGER I MUST JUDGE	WHO OCCUPIES THIS HOUSE?	892	2
UNQUALIFIED TO JUDGE	THOSE CATTLE SMALLER	1388	14
I JUDGE FROM MY GEOGRAPHY	VOLCANOES BE IN SICILY	1705	3
JUDGED			
I JUDGED MY FEATURES--JARRED MY HAIR--	I FELT MY LIFE WITH BOTH	351	9
I PONDERED, MAY HAVE JUDGED,	OUR LITTLE KINSMEN--	885	10
WHEN THE JUDGED	JUDGEMENT IS JUSTEST	1671	2
JUDGMENT			
FOR WE MUST RIDE TO THE JUDGMENT--	TIE THE STRINGS TO MY	279	7
BUT THERE'S THE "JUDGMENT DAY"!	I NEVER FELT AT HOME--	413	16
BE JUDGMENT--WHAT IT MAY--	I LIVE WITH HIM--I SEE	463	16
THE JUDGMENT PUSH HIS PICTURE--	THE POWER TO BE TRUE TO	464	3
AND JUDGMENT--TWINKLED--TOO--	I MEANT TO HAVE BUT	476	20
DEPARTED--TO THE JUDGMENT--	DEPARTED--TO THE	524	1
AND YOUR'S--THE JUDGMENT INTERVENED--	DID YOU EVER STAND IN A	590	11
AUTO DA FE--AND JUDGMENT--	IT MAKES NO DIFFERENCE	620	9
BEFORE THE JUDGMENT SEAT OF GOD--	'TWAS A LONG PARTING--	625	3
THE JUDGMENT PERISHED--TOO--	ONE BLESSING HAD I THAN	756	16
IN IT WAIT TILL JUDGMENT BREAK	AMPLE MAKE THIS BED--	829	3
JUDGMENT IS JUSTEST	JUDGEMENT IS JUSTEST	1671	1
JUG			
AND LIQUOR IN THE JUG	BETWEEN THE FORM OF LIFE	1101	4

	FIRST LINE	POEM	LINE
JUG (CONTINUED)			
OF JULEPS, PART ARE IN THE JUG	A DRUNKARD CANNOT MEET A	1628	9
JUGGLER			
AND THE JUGGLER OF DAY IS GONE	BLAZING IN GOLD AND	228	8
GRIEF IS A JUGGLER--BOLDEST AT THE PLAY--	GRIEF IS A MOUSE--	793	9
UNTO A JUGGLER TURNED--	NATURE AFFECTS TO BE	1170	8
'TIS VEGETATION'S JUGGLER--	THE MUSHROOM IS THE ELF	1298	9
JUGGLER'S			
LIKE JUGGLER'S FLOWERS [FIGURES] SITUATES	IT SIFTS FROM LEADEN	311	V
THE JUGGLER'S HAT HER COUNTRY IS--	THE JUGGLER'S HAT HER	330	1
JUGS			
JUGS--A UNIVERSE'S FRACTURE [RUPTURE]	BEES ARE BLACK, WITH	1405	7
JUGULAR			
AS "BRANCH," [TRUNK] AND "JUGULAR."	THE VEINS OF OTHER	811	4
FOR HER JUGULAR DEFENCES--	ROBBED BY DEATH--BUT	971	5
JUICES			
'TIS NATURE'S BUOYANT JUICES	THE GENTIAN HAS A	1424	3
JUICY			
THE HOPES SO JUICY RIPENING--	SHE SIGHTS A BIRD--SHE	507	9
JULEP			
THE JULEP--OF THE BEE--	SHE HIDETH HER THE LAST	557	12
JULEPS			
OF JULEPS, PART ARE IN THE JUG	A DRUNKARD CANNOT MEET A	1628	9
JULIET			
OF HIS JULIET,	DRAMA'S VITALLEST	741	11
JULY			
ANSWER JULY--	ANSWER JULY--	386	1
AH, SAID JULY--	ANSWER JULY--	386	5
JUMBLED			
AND DIAMONDS--JUMBLED ON--	I KNOW WHERE WELLS GROW	460	8
JUMP			
TILL HE SHOULD JUMP PENINSULAS	COULD I BUT RIDE	661	11
JUNCTION			
MEET--AND THE JUNCTION BE [MEAN] ETERNITY	TO KNOW JUST HOW HE	622	26
JUNE			
AS BUMBLE BEE OF JUNE.	ONE SISTER HAVE I IN OUR	14	12
THE SWAMPS ARE PINK WITH JUNE.	ALL THESE MY BANNERS BE.	22	21
THE OLD--OLD SOPHISTRIES OF JUNE--	THESE ARE THE DAYS WHEN	130	5
BUT CERTAIN JUNE!	FOR THIS--ACCEPTED	195	12
YOU KNOW WHO "JUNE" IS--	WHAT WOULD I GIVE TO SEE	247	7
TO TELL YOUR [ONE'S] NAME--THE LIVELONG JUNE--	I'M NOBODY! WHO ARE YOU?	288	7
AND THE AFFAIRS OF JUNE	LIKE SOME OLD FASHIONED	302	4
HIS WAY--OF A JUNE DAY--	THE WIND DID'NT COME	316	16
OF A JUNE DAY	THE WIND DID'NT COME	316	V 16
LIKE THE JUNE BEE--BEFORE THE SCHOOL BOY,	THE NEAREST DREAM	319	3
SHE DOTH NOT WAIT FOR JUNE--	THERE IS A FLOWER THAT	380	13
WHEN SUDDENLY ACROSS THE JUNE	THEY DROPPED LIKE FLAKES	409	4
WHEN MEN--AND BOYS--AND CARTS [LARKS]--AND JUNE,	I'M SORRY FOR THE DEAD--	529	19
JUNE NOON--AS JANUARY NIGHT--	WHAT CARE THE DEAD, FOR	592	19
YOUR VISION--WAS IN JUNE--	OURSELVES WERE WED ONE	631	2
BUT YOU--WERE CROWNED [YOUR'S WAS FIRST--] IN JUNE--	OURSELVES WERE WED ONE	631	16
THERE IS A JUNE WHEN CORN IS CUT	THERE IS A JUNE WHEN	930	1
THE CENTURIES OF JUNE	THERE IS A ZONE WHOSE	1056	6
WHOSE GENESIS WAS JUNE.	THE MURMURING OF BEES,	1115	8
BEGINNING ONCE IN JUNE--	SUMMER HAS TWO	1422	2
AS INNOCENT [DANGEROUS] AS JUNE--	TO SEE HER IS A PICTURE	1568	4
JUNIOR			
OF JUNIOR OF FOURSCORE--'TWAS ACT	NOT ALL DIE EARLY, DYING	990	7
PAIN IS THE JUNIOR PARTY	PAIN HAS BUT ONE	1049	5
BECAUSE THAT JUNIOR FOLIAGE IS DISRESPECTFUL NOW	AN ANTIQUATED TREE	1514	3
JUPITER			
JUPITER! MY FATHER!	"LETHE" IN MY FLOWER,	1730	7
JURY			
THE JURY VOTED HIM--	I READ MY SENTENCE--	412	8
JUST			
BAFFLED FOR JUST A DAY OR TWO--	BAFFLED FOR JUST A DAY	17	1
AND JUST TO TURN AWAY,	DISTRUSTFUL OF THE	20	2
JUST AS THE DUSK WAS BROWN	ADRIFT! A LITTLE BOAT	30	6
JUST AS THE DAWN WAS RED	ADRIFT! A LITTLE BOAT	30	10
JUST A BRIDGE AWAY--	BEFORE THE ICE IS IN THE	37	12
THERE WERE JUST SUCH COFFIN	IT DID NOT SURPRISE ME--	39	15
LATER BY JUST AN HOUR THAN DEATH--	DELAYED TILL SHE HAD	58	5
SAVE JUST A LITTLE PLACE FOR ME	GOING TO HEAVEN!	79	14
AND JUST A BIT OF "CROWN"--	GOING TO HEAVEN!	79	17
WHY, I WILL LEND UNTIL JUST THEN,	PERHAPS YOU'D LIKE TO	134	9
BY JUST SUCH A HAZARD	SOUL, WILT THOU TOSS	139	2
IF YOU'LL JUST TELL ME SO--	YOU LOVE ME--YOU ARE	156	16
JUST LOST, WHEN I WAS SAVED!	JUST LOST, WHEN I WAS	160	1
JUST FELT [HEARD] THE WORLD GO BY!	JUST LOST, WHEN I WAS	160	2
JUST GIRT ME FOR THE ONSET WITH ETERNITY,	JUST LOST, WHEN I WAS	160	3
SHE LOOKS DOWN JUST AS OFTEN	MAMA NEVER FORGETS HER	164	3
AND JUST AS TENDERLY	MAMA NEVER FORGETS HER	164	4
JUST WHERE THE HECTIC STINGS!	A WOUNDED DEER--LEAPS	165	8
IT IS JUST AS WELL!	IF THE FOOLISH, CALL	168	4
THE HILLS JUST TELL THE ORCHARDS--	THE SKIES CANT KEEP	191	3
WE JUST SHUT OUR BROWN EYE	WE DONT CRY--TIM AND I,	196	11
THIS JUST MAKES OUT THE MORNING SKY.	A SLASH OF BLUE--	204	9

JUST (CONTINUED)	FIRST LINE	POEM	LINE
TO THINK JUST HOW THE FIRE WILL BURN--	THO' I GET HOME HOW LATE	207	9
JUST HOW LONG-CHEATED EYES WILL TURN--	THO' I GET HOME HOW LATE	207	10
JUST OPPOSITE--ANOTHER SPEECH	THE ROSE DID CAPER ON	208	11
AS LACES JUST REVEAL THE SURGE--	THE THOUGHT BENEATH SO	210	3
BUT JUST A SINGLE SMILE--	I CAME TO BUY A SMILE--	223	2
WILL SUIT ME JUST AS WELL--	I CAME TO BUY A SMILE--	223	4
JUST AS THE NIGHT KEEPS FETCHING STARS	I'VE NOTHING ELSE--TO	224	3
THE SUN--JUST TOUCHED THE MORNING--	THE SUN--JUST TOUCHED	232	1
'TIS JUST THE PRICE OF BREATH--	YOU'RE RIGHT--"THE WAY	234	6
SAY--THAT THE PULSE JUST LISPS--	IF HE DISSOLVE--THEN--	236	10
I THINK JUST HOW MY SHAPE WILL RISE--	I THINK JUST HOW MY	237	1
I THINK JUST HOW MY LIPS WILL WEIGH--	I THINK JUST HOW MY	237	5
JUST LAYING LIGHT--NO SOUL WILL WINK	WHEN WE STAND ON THE	242	5
BUT JUST THE MILES OF STARE--	I'VE KNOWN A HEAVEN,	243	6
DISCLOSES JUST A HUE--	I'VE KNOWN A HEAVEN,	243	15
JUST FINDING OUT--WHAT PUZZLED US--	FOREVER AT HIS SIDE TO	246	15
STOP JUST A MINUTE--LET ME THINK!	WHAT WOULD I GIVE TO SEE	247	4
JUST--ONCE--MORE--	WHY--DO THEY SHUT ME OUT	248	6
JUST--SEE--IF I TROUBLED THEM--	WHY--DO THEY SHUT ME OUT	248	7
TO DIE--TAKES JUST A LITTLE WHILE--	TO DIE--TAKES JUST A	255	1
MY EYES JUST TURNED TO SEE,	A SINGLE SCREW OF FLESH	263	10
JUST GRANTED, FOR THE PERIL'S SAKE--	A SINGLE SCREW OF FLESH	263	15
JUST ONE TIME!	DID WE DISOBEY HIM?	267	2
WOULD COST ME--JUST A LIFE!	ONE LIFE OF SO MUCH	270	8
BUT HALLOW JUST THE SNOW	DOUBT ME! MY DIM	275	23
JUST A LOOK AT THE HORSES--	TIE THE STRINGS TO MY	279	3
AND KISS THE HILLS, FOR ME, JUST ONCE--	TIE THE STRINGS TO MY	279	15
JUST LET GO THE BREATH--	'TIS SO APPALLING--IT	281	16
AND JUST--REVERE--	A MIEN TO MOVE A QUEEN--	283	25
JUST AS THE GRANITE CRUMB LET GO--	THAT AFTER HORROR--THAT	286	3
THAT JUST NOW DANGLED STILL--	A CLOCK STOPPED--	287	5
WITH JUST A CLOCK--	I KNOW SOME LONELY	289	14
A PAIR OF SPECTACLES AJAR JUST STIR--	I KNOW SOME LONELY	289	19
WHILE THE OLD COUPLE, JUST ASTIR,	I KNOW SOME LONELY	289	39
JUST A DOME OF ABYSS IS BOWING [NODDING]	HOW THE OLD MOUNTAINS	291	19
WAS'T GLORY? THAT--WILL DO ['TWAS JUST YOU]--	ONE YEAR AGO--JOTS WHAT?	296	4
BUT JUST THE NAMES, OF GEMS--	YOUR RICHES--TAUGHT ME--	299	10
ALTHO' I PROVE IT, JUST IN TIME	YOUR RICHES--TAUGHT ME--	299	27
WHILE JUST [YET] A GIRL AT SCHOOL.	YOUR RICHES--TAUGHT ME--	299	32
MORNING MEANS JUST RISK [CHANCE]--TO THE LOVER--	"MORNING"--MEANS	300	4
JUST REVELATION--TO THE BELOVED--	"MORNING"--MEANS	300	5
THE LADY JUST UNROLLED--	THE DAY CAME SLOW--TILL	304	8
JUST SO--JESUS [CHRIST]--RAPS--	JUST SO--JESUS--RAPS--	317	1
I JUST WEAR MY WINGS--	SOME KEEP THE SABBATH	324	6
SO SAFER GUESS--WITH JUST MY SOUL	BEFORE I GOT MY EYE PUT	327	18
AND JUST SIPPED--ME--	ALL THE LETTERS I CAN	334	8
THAT FACE--WILL JUST BE THINE--	THE FACE I CARRY WITH ME	336	4
JUST TO MAKE BLISS	I KNOW THAT HE EXISTS.	338	7
BUT BLISS, IS SOLD JUST ONCE.	IS BLISS THEN, SUCH	340	9
AND REALMS--JUST DROSS--	MY REWARD FOR BEING, WAS	343	5
THE BALLOTS OF ETERNITY, WILL SHOW JUST THAT.	MY REWARD FOR BEING, WAS	343	11
AND THIS WORN SHOE JUST FITS THE TRACK--	'TWAS THE OLD--ROAD--	344	15
MY BASKET HOLDS--JUST--FIRMAMENTS--	PERHAPS I ASKED TOO	352	5
JUST CONSUMMATED--NOW--	A HAPPY LIP--BREAKS	353	4
BUT JUST HIS EAR COULD KNOW	ALTHOUGH I PUT AWAY HIS	366	10
WITH JUST THE GRANT TO DO--	ALTHOUGH I PUT AWAY HIS	366	16
IN JUST THE DRESS HIS CENTURY WORE--	A PRECIOUS--MOULDERING	371	3
AND TANTALIZE--JUST SO--	A PRECIOUS--MOULDERING	371	28
THOUGH BUT FOR THE CRICKET--JUST,	I'M SAYING EVERY DAY	373	22
IS JUST A BOUGH OF APPLES--	THE ANGLE OF A LANDSCAPE	375	7
AND JUST THE STEEPLE'S FINGER--	THE ANGLE OF A LANDSCAPE	375	19
IN JUST A COUNTRY TOWN--	THERE'S BEEN A DEATH, IN	389	24
AND JUST BEFORE THE SUN--	A VISITOR IN MARL--	391	6
JUST HIM--NOT ME--	'TWAS LOVE--NOT ME--	394	4
MY BOND--HAVE JUST BEGUN--	A TONGUE--TO TELL HIM I	400	25
JUST TWO--THE BEARER--	UNIT, LIKE DEATH, FOR	408	7
AND SEAT--JUST ONE--	UNIT, LIKE DEATH, FOR	408	9
A TREMOR JUST, THAT ALL'S NOT SURE.	UNIT, LIKE DEATH, FOR	408	16
BUT JUST A DAISY--DEEP--	THE COLOR OF THE GRAVE	411	8
BUT JUST THE PRIMER--TO A LIFE--	NOT IN THIS WORLD TO SEE	418	4
AND LEAVE ME--JUST MY A--B--C--	NOT IN THIS WORLD TO SEE	418	11
A TEMPERATURE JUST ADEQUATE	MORE LIFE--WENT OUT--	422	7
MYSELF HAD JUST TO EARN--	REMOVED FROM ACCIDENT OF	424	4
SHIFT IT--JUST--	IT DONT SOUND SO	426	7
I'M DIVING--JUST A LITTLE LATE--	I'LL CLUTCH--AND CLUTCH	427	5
JUST AS HIGH--AS I--	I'LL CLUTCH--AND CLUTCH	427	19
JUST TO CAST HER DOWN	TAKING UP THE FAIR IDEAL	428	2
HE COMES JUST SO FAR--TOWARD THE TOWN--	THE MOON IS DISTANT FROM	429	7
JUST SO FAR--GOES AWAY--	THE MOON IS DISTANT FROM	429	8
BUT JUST BEFORE THE SNOWS	GOD MADE A LITTLE	442	4
'TWAS JUST THIS TIME, LAST YEAR, I DIED.	'TWAS JUST THIS TIME,	445	1
I THOUGHT JUST HOW RED--APPLES WEDGED	'TWAS JUST THIS TIME,	445	9
HOW JUST THIS TIME, SOME PERFECT YEAR--	'TWAS JUST THIS TIME,	445	23
JUST INFINITES OF NOUGHT--	LIKE EYES THAT LOOKED ON	458	5
JUST LOOKING ROUND TO SEE HOW FAR	WE DO NOT PLAY ON GRAVES	467	11
BUT JUST TO HEAR THE GRACE DEPART--	EXCEPT THE HEAVEN HAD	472	5
OUR SOULS SAW--JUST AS WELL--	THEY PUT US FAR APART--	474	12
CONDEMNED--BUT JUST--TO SEE--	THEY PUT US FAR APART--	474	16

JUST (CONTINUED)

	FIRST LINE	POEM	LINE
BUT JUST FOR ONE--TO STIPULATE--	I MEANT TO HAVE BUT	476	7
WHOSE OWN--HAS JUST BEGUN--	NO MAN CAN COMPASS A	477	10
JUST LOCKING UP--TO DIE.	SHE DEALT HER PRETTY	479	12
AND JUST MY BASKET--	I WAS THE SLIGHTEST IN	486	7
TELL HIM [HER] JUST HOW THE FINGERS HURRIED--	GOING TO HIM! HAPPY	494	6
TELL HIM [HER]--JUST HOW SHE SEALED YOU--CAUTIOUS!	GOING TO HIM! HAPPY	494	22
IT'S THOUGHTS--AND JUST ONE HEART--	IT'S THOUGHTS--AND JUST	495	1
IT'S THOUGHTS--AND JUST TWO HEART--	IT'S THOUGHTS--AND JUST	495	23
THAT JUST ABROAD HIS WINDOW	I ENVY SEAS, WHEREON HE	498	13
TO JUST VIBRATING BLOSSOMS!	WITHIN MY GARDEN, RIDES	500	19
MY LIPS JUST HOLD THE NAME--	YOU KNOW THAT PORTRAIT	504	10
WITH ONE SMALL [JUST ONE] DIADEM.	I'M CEDED--I'VE STOPPED	508	13
AND I CHOOSE, JUST A CROWN [THRONE]--	I'M CEDED--I'VE STOPPED	508	19
ACQUAINTANCE--JUST A FEW--	IF ANYBODY'S FRIEND BE	509	18
NOR FIRE--FOR JUST MY [TWO] MARBLE FEET	IT WAS NOT DEATH, FOR I	510	7
IF 'TWAS A DREAM--MADE SOLID--JUST	HER SWEET WEIGHT ON MY	518	5
JUST TO BE RICH--TO WASTE MY GUINEAS [GUINEA]	SWEET--YOU FORGOT--BUT I	523	9
JUST TO BE POOR--FOR BAREFOOT VISION [PLEASURE]	SWEET--YOU FORGOT--BUT I	523	11
LEST THE PHANTASM--PROVE THE [JUST] MISTAKE--	WE DREAM--IT IS GOOD WE	531	11
WITH JUST AN AGE--AND NAME--	WE DREAM--IT IS GOOD WE	531	14
AS JUST APPRENTICED TO THE AIR--	SHE'S HAPPY, WITH A NEW	535	4
OR WAS MYSELF [JUST MYSELF / ONLY ME / I]--TOO SMALL?	I TOOK MY POWER IN MY	540	8
JUST AT NOON--NO LATER--SWEET [THAN]--	SOME SUCH BUTTERFLY BE	541	3
AT LAST--THE GRACE [THE GRACE IS JUST] IN SIGHT--	I CROSS TILL I AM WEARY	550	18
HE OFFERS [SPICES / FLAVORS] HIS BERRY, JUST THE SAME	THE BLACK BERRY--WEARS A	554	3
OR DID IT JUST BEGIN--	I MEASURE EVERY GRIEF I	561	6
JUST OBVIATED BUD--	HE GAVE AWAY HIS LIFE--	567	14
A'BLOSSOM JUST WHEN I WENT IN	MY FIRST WELL DAY--SINCE	574	5
IF JUST AS SOON AS BREATH IS OUT	IF I MAY HAVE IT, WHEN	577	3
JUST MAKING SIGNS--ACROSS--[IT SEEMED] TO THEE--	IF I MAY HAVE IT, WHEN	577	20
JUST WHEN THE GRAVE AND I--	I CRIED AT PITY--NOT AT	588	22
AND JUST THE MEANEST [COMMON / FAINTEST] TUNES	I THINK I WAS ENCHANTED	593	12
FOR BRAVERIES JUST SEALED [PROVED] IN THIS	WHEN I WAS SMALL, A	596	V 19
JUST WINDING ROUND A STONE--	THE TREES LIKE TASSELS--	606	20
IN JUST THE JACKET THAT HE WORE--	OF NEARNESS TO HER	607	9
THEMSELF--HAD JUST REMAINED TILL WE REJOIN THEM--	OF NEARNESS TO HER	607	18
JUST AS THE CASE MAY BE--	AFRAID! OF WHOM AM I	608	8
"MY BUSINESS BUT [JUST] A LIFE I LEFT	I YEARS HAD BEEN FROM	609	7
TO STAY BEHIND--WITH JUST THE TOYS	YOU'LL FIND--IT WHEN YOU	610	15
BUT JUST THE PLACING PINS--	AT LEISURE IS THE SOUL	618	6
TO KNOW JUST HOW HE SUFFERED--WOULD BE DEAR--	TO KNOW JUST HOW HE	622	1
JUST HIS SIGH--ACCENTED--	TO KNOW JUST HOW HE	622	14
JUST AS [EQUAL] SURE--	ONLY GOD--DETECT THE	626	8
AS IF THEY JUST REPRESSED	THE TINT I CANNOT TAKE--	627	14
AND JUST A SINGLE HERD--	THEY CALLED ME TO THE	628	4
THE BRAIN IS JUST THE WEIGHT OF GOD--	THE BRAIN--IS WIDER THAN	632	9
WITH JUST THE DOOR AJAR	I CANNOT LIVE WITH YOU--	640	47
JUST RECTIFIED [QUALIFIED]--IN THEE	I THINK TO LIVE--MAY BE	646	28
JUST THAT YOU SHOULD SEE	PROMISE THIS--WHEN YOU	648	14
JUST [STILL] TO FOLLOW YOUR DEAR FEATURE--	PROMISE THIS--WHEN YOU	648	29
I SAID "BUT JUST TO BE A BEE"	COULD I BUT RIDE	661	13
JUST HIS FACE--NOTHING MORE!	AGAIN--HIS VOICE IS AT	663	12
JUST--HOW--DEEP--	AGAIN--HIS VOICE IS AT	663	16
GOES WITH US--JUST A LITTLE WAY--	AGAIN--HIS VOICE IS AT	663	20
BUT [JUST] INSTINCT ESTEEM [REPORT] HIM	CONSCIOUS AM I IN MY	679	19
JUST A DROP--	VICTORY COMES LATE--	690	6
JUST HIS OWN ENDORSEMENT--	LIFE--IS WHAT WE MAKE IT	698	7
THEIR RIBBONS JUST BEYOND THE EYE--	YOU'VE SEEN BALLOONS SET	700	9
IT JUST REMINDED ME--'TWAS ALL--	A THOUGHT WENT UP MY	701	11
TRIVIAL A WORD--JUST--	NO MATTER--NOW--SWEET--	704	5
WONT YOU WISH YOU'D SMILED--JUST--	NO MATTER--NOW--SWEET--	704	15
IS JUST DEATH, AND CANNOT INCREASE--	SUSPENSE--IS HOSTILER	705	3
BUT JUST ANEW TO DIE--	SUSPENSE--IS HOSTILER	705	6
THE CARRIAGE HELD BUT JUST OURSELVES--	BECAUSE I COULD NOT STOP	712	3
HER PETTICOAT--OF PURPLE PLAIN [JUST]--	THE DAY UNDRESSED--	716	3
FOR JUST THIS SINGLE [THIS PECULIAR / JUST THIS ONLY] TIME--	I MEANT TO FIND HER WHEN	718	6
FOR JUST THIS SINGLE [THIS PECULIAR / JUST THIS ONLY] TIME--	I MEANT TO FIND HER WHEN	718	6
JUST WE TWO--MEET--	WHERE THOU ART--THAT--IS	725	10
JUST LONG ENOUGH TO TASTE--	LET US PLAY YESTERDAY--	728	31
MY LIFE JUST HOLDS THE TRENCH--	IF HE WERE LIVING--DARE	734	16
WITH JUST THIS STIPULUS [RESERVATION]--	YOU SAID THAT I "WAS	738	17
JUST SUNRISE--	RENUNCIATION--IS A	745	6
THE SUN--WITH JUST [BROAD] DELIGHT	THE MOUNTAINS--GROW	757	6
JUST LONG ENOUGH FOR HOPE TO TEAZE [STIR]--	THE WHOLE OF IT CAME NOT	762	7
JUST THE PLACE I STOOD--	WHEN I HOPED, I	768	2
JUST THE DAY IT WAS--	WHEN I HOPED, I	768	10
LIFE--JUST--OR DEATH--	ONE AND ONE--ARE ONE--	769	5
FOR JUST A [SIMPLE] SCRUTINY--	THE LONELINESS ONE DARE	777	8
IF LOVE BE JUST BEYOND--	TO WAIT AN HOUR--IS LONG	781	2
MY OWN HAD JUST BEGUN.	SEVERER SERVICE OF	786	8

	FIRST LINE	POEM	LINE
JUST (CONTINUED)			
BUT JUST A CRUMB--TO ME--	GOD GAVE A LOAF TO EVERY	791	2
JUST A SEA--WITH A STEM--	BY MY WINDOW HAVE I FOR	797	2
JUST QUARTERING A TREE--	THE WIND BEGUN TO KNEAD	824	20
BUT JUST TO LOOK IT IN THE EYE--	I CANNOT BUY IT--'TIS	840	10
JUST AS HE SPOKE IT FROM HIS HANDS	JUST AS HE SPOKE IT FROM	848	1
WHEN IT HAS JUST CONTAINED A LIFE	THIS CHASM, SWEET, UPON	858	9
A JUST SUFFICIENT RING.	HE OUTSTRIPPED TIME WITH	865	8
AND HOW I JUST SAID "PLEASE."	THEY WONT FROWN ALWAYS--	874	4
JUST MEASURING UNCONSCIOUSNESS	EACH SECOND IS THE LAST	879	3
IT JUST HELD TWO, NOR THOSE IT HELD	I'VE NONE TO TELL ME TO	881	4
WOULD'ST THOU SEEK SO--JUST SAY	I'VE NONE TO TELL ME TO	881	10
NOT IF THE JUST SUSPECT ME	WHAT DID THEY DO SINCE I	900	13
STILL--JUST AS EASY, IF IT BE THY WILL	ONLY A SHRINE, BUT MINE	918	10
THE SUMMER OF THE JUST,	THERE IS A JUNE WHEN	930	10
ONLY TO AGGRAVATE [JUST TO INTENSIFY] THE DARK	FAIRER THROUGH FADING--	938	7
WHERE MORNING [SUNRISE] JUST BEGUN--	THE SUNSET STOPPED ON	950	6
A DOOR JUST [THERE] OPENED ON A STREET [TO A HOUSE]--	A DOOR JUST OPENED ON A	953	1
JUST TO PARTAKE--THE INFAMY--	WERT THOU BUT ILL--THAT	961	12
JUST A PALTRY ONE--	ALL FORGOT FOR	966	2
ALL FORSOOK, FOR JUST A STRANGER'S	ALL FORGOT FOR	966	3
JUST LAYING OFF FOR EVIDENCE	DEATH IS A DIALOGUE	976	7
THE PEARL--THE JUST--OUR THOUGHT.	BEST THINGS DWELL OUT OF	998	2
JUST SAVES IT FROM DESPAIR	SUPERFLUOUS WERE THE SUN	999	6
JUST GOING HOME FROM SCHOOL.	THE HILLS IN PURPLE	1016	4
WE JUST REVERSE THE ZODIAC	THE PRODUCTS OF MY FARM	1025	7
BY JUST A SECOND'S RIGHT--	PAIN HAS BUT ONE	1049	6
JUST ONCE! OH LEAST REQUEST!	JUST ONCE! OH LEAST	1076	1
"JUST ONCE" SWEET DEITY?	JUST ONCE! OH LEAST	1076	9
AND WAS [JUST / WHEN] ABOUT TO RING	SHALL I TAKE THEE, THE	1126	6
BUT JUST AN ASTERISK.	TOO COLD IS THIS	1135	9
JUST SUCH A RETROSPECT	THE PROPS ASSIST THE	1142	8
OH SUN--BUT JUST A SECOND'S RIGHT	MY GOD--HE SEES THEE--	1178	8
THAT JUST AS WE DISCERN	TO DISAPPEAR ENHANCES--	1209	14
I SAY IT JUST	A WORD IS DEAD	1212	4
RESERVING THAT BUT JUST TO PROVE	SOMEWHERE UPON THE	1231	9
HIS RESEARCH HAS BUT JUST BEGUN--	THE LILAC IS AN ANCIENT	1241	13
POSSESSION JUST AS LONG--	DOMINION LASTS UNTIL	1257	2
HOWEVER FIRST [TRUE / DUE / JUST] IT BE	BECAUSE THAT YOU ARE	1260	6
OF HUMAN NATURE JUST AWARE	I THOUGHT THAT NATURE	1286	5
THAT BLAME IS JUST AS DEAR AS PRAISE	DEAR MARCH--COME IN--	1320	25
BUILT OF BUT JUST A SYLLABLE	LOVE'S STRICKEN "WHY"	1368	3
I'LL LET MY HEART BE JUST IN SIGHT--	THEY MIGHT NOT NEED ME--	1391	2
BUT JUST HIS LID [LIP] OF GLASS--	WHAT MYSTERY PERVADES A	1400	6
WITHIN IT'S REACH [HOPE], THOUGH YET [AND JUST] UNGRASPED	WHO NEVER WANTED--	1430	5
IT'S SOUNDLESS TRAVELS JUST ARREST	HOW SOFT A CATERPILLAR	1448	5
AND HOLDS SCARCE [JUST] ONE.	THE ROAD TO PARADISE IS	1491	2
IS JUST AS HIGH AS YOU AND I,	THE BUTTERFLY UPON THE	1521	5
HE IS JUST AS [STILL MORE] HIGH--	FOLLOW WISE ORION	1538	4
FROM JUST A PURPLE FLOWER BEYOND	OF DEATH I TRY TO THINK	1558	13
THE CLOCK STRIKES ONE THAT JUST STRUCK TWO--	THE CLOCK STRIKES ONE	1569	1
BUT JUST THE ANTI FAIR--AVERRING--FAIREST-- TRUEST TRUTH	EXTOL THEE--COULD I--	1643	3
FOR JUST ONE PLAUDIT FAMISHING,	THE IMMORTALITY SHE GAVE	1648	3
ITS CIRCUIT JUST THE SAME	A PIT--BUT HEAVEN OVER	1712	15
BUT JUST THE SUMMER KNOWS.	THOSE FINAL CREATURES,--	1766	4
JUSTEST			
SHOW JUSTEST--THROUGH AN OPEN TOMB--	THE ADMIRATIONS--AND	906	2
JUDGMENT IS JUSTEST	JUDGEMENT IS JUSTEST	1671	1
JUSTICE			
TO BRINGING THEE TO JUSTICE, AND MARSHALLING THY SOUL:	AWAKE YE MUSES NINE,	1	26
BUT JUSTICE IS SUBLIMER	I HAD SOME THINGS THAT I	116	11
LET JUSTICE NOT MISTAKE--	'TWAS LOVE--NOT ME--	394	9
MY [ONE] JUSTICE BLEEDS--FOR THEE!	IT ALWAYS FELT TO ME--A	597	24
JUSTIFIED			
JUSTIFIED--THROUGH [BY] CALVARIES OF LOVE--	THERE CAME A DAY AT	322	28
NOR HOW OURSELVES BE JUSTIFIED--	SO GLAD WE ARE--A	329	5
BUT FOR THE JUSTIFIED PROCESSIONS	OVER AND OVER, LIKE A	367	7
I'M HARDLY JUSTIFIED	THE WINTERS ARE SO SHORT	403	2
TILL HE BE JUSTIFIED BY DEATH--	HAD I PRESUMED TO HOPE--	522	15
BUT NEVER STRANGER JUSTIFIED	I WATCHED THE MOON	629	9
WAS JUSTIFIED OF BIRD--	THIS BAUBLE WAS	805	4
EXCEPT THE FIRST HAD JUSTIFIED	THE FIRST WE KNEW OF HIM	1006	3
WHO JUSTIFIED [AUTHORIZED] ELIJAH [THE FORMER]	ELIJAH'S WAGON KNEW NO	1254	7
JUSTIFY			
WITHOUT THE FEAR--TO JUSTIFY--	I SHOULD HAVE BEEN TOO	313	16
TO JUSTIFY--DESPAIR.	IT WAS NOT DEATH, FOR I	510	24
JUSTIFY THE ROAD--	TO PUT THIS WORLD DOWN,	527	8
TO JUSTIFY THE DREAM--	I RECKON--WHEN I COUNT	569	16
A BOMB--TO JUSTIFY--	TO INTERRUPT HIS YELLOW	591	16
MY FACE TO JUSTIFY--	AGAIN--HIS VOICE IS AT	663	6
JUSTIFY HIM--THOUGH--	LIFE--IS WHAT WE MAKE IT	698	4
FAME OF MYSELF, TO JUSTIFY,	FAME OF MYSELF, TO	713	1
ITSELF TO JUSTIFY	RENUNCIATION--IS A	745	12
TO JUSTIFY OR SCOURGE--	THOSE CATTLE SMALLER	1388	16
JUSTIFYING			
POVERTY--BE JUSTIFYING	PUBLICATION--IS THE	709	3

	FIRST LINE	POEM	LINE
KATIE			
WHEN KATIE WALKS, THIS SIMPLE PAIR ACCOMPANY HER SIDE,	WHEN KATIE WALKS, THIS	222	1
WHEN KATIE RUNS UNWEARIED THEY FOLLOW ON THE ROAD,	WHEN KATIE WALKS, THIS	222	2
WHEN KATIE KNEELS, THEIR LOVING HANDS STILL CLASP HER PIOUS KNEE--	WHEN KATIE WALKS, THIS	222	3
AH! KATIE! SMILE AT FORTUNE, WITH TWO SO KNIT TO THEE!	WHEN KATIE WALKS, THIS	222	4
WHY, KATIE, TREASON HAS A VOICE--	I SHALL NOT MURMUR IF AT	1410	7
KEEL			
OR SERVICE OF A KEEL	AS IMPERCEPTIBLY AS	1540	14
KEEN			
IN KEEN AND QUIVERING RATIO	FOR EACH EXTATIC INSTANT	125	3
A FROST MORE NEEDLE KEEN	MORE LIFE--WENT OUT--	422	10
BE IT NE'ER SO KEEN--	SOMEWHAT, TO HOPE FOR,	1041	5
KEENEST			
BEHOLD THE KEENEST MARKSMAN!	THERE IS A WORD	8	15
KEEP			
WHETHER TO KEEP THE SECRET--	I NEVER TOLD THE BURIED	11	14
KEEP THEIR SERAPHIC MAY--	THERE IS A MORN BY MEN	24	3
I KEEP MY PLEDGE.	I KEEP MY PLEDGE.	46	1
AND BELLS KEEP SAYING "VICTORY"	I HAVE A KING, WHO DOES	103	11
ARE FORCED TO KEEP THEIR ROOMS--	WHERE BELLS NO MORE	112	4
CAN KEEP THE SOUL ALIVE--	A LITTLE BREAD--A CRUST	159	3
FEATURES KEEP THEIR PLACE--	I HAVE NEVER SEEN	175	12
THE SKIES CANT KEEP THEIR SECRET!	THE SKIES CANT KEEP	191	1
SO KEEP YOUR SECRET--FATHER!	THE SKIES CANT KEEP	191	13
SO I KEEP BRINGING THESE--	I'VE NOTHING ELSE--TO	224	2
I SAID "'TWILL KEEP"--	I HELD A JEWEL IN MY	245	4
I SHALL KEEP SINGING!	I SHALL KEEP SINGING!	250	1
THE PURPLE COULD NOT KEEP THE EAST--	THE DAY CAME SLOW--TILL	304	5
SOME KEEP THE SABBATH GOING TO CHURCH--	SOME KEEP THE SABBATH	324	1
I KEEP IT, STAYING AT HOME--	SOME KEEP THE SABBATH	324	2
SOME KEEP THE SABBATH IN SURPLICE--	SOME KEEP THE SABBATH	324	5
AND LIFE AND I--KEEP EVEN--	I MEANT TO HAVE BUT	476	4
SHE CANNOT KEEP HER PLACE.	"WHY DO I LOVE" YOU, SIR	480	5
FLOWERS--TO KEEP THE EYES--FROM GOING AWKWARD--	IT'S THOUGHTS--AND JUST	495	12
COULD KEEP A CHANCEL, COOL--	IT WAS NOT DEATH, FOR I	510	8
I'LL TELL YOU HOW I TRIED TO KEEP	IF I MAY HAVE IT, WHEN	577	22
TO KEEP THEIR PLACE--	IT CEASED TO HURT ME,	584	12
AND PUT A STONE TO KEEP IT WARM--	WHAT CARE THE DEAD, FOR	592	23
TO KEEP HERSELF IN CHEER--	I THINK I WAS ENCHANTED	593	14
LIKE DEITY--TO KEEP--	I THINK I WAS ENCHANTED	593	32
SOME I SHALL KEEP [SAVE]--TO SOLVE	IT TROUBLED ME AS ONCE I	600	10
TO KEEP THE OTHER--STILL--	YOU'LL KNOW HER--BY HER	634	28
GOD KEEP HIS OATH [VOW] TO SPARROWS--	VICTORY COMES LATE--	690	13
TO KEEP THE DARK AWAY.	I SING TO USE THE	850	8
EACH SCAR I'LL KEEP FOR HIM	EACH SCAR I'LL KEEP FOR	877	1
TO KEEP IT FROM EFFACING	AN EVERYWHERE OF SILVER	884	3
THE GARDEN [LANDSCAPE] KEEP [SHOW / OWN / HOLD] THE GASH--	AS FROST IS BEST	951	6
FROM THE MAPLE KEEP?	WHAT SHALL I DO WHEN THE	956	4
KEEP MAY!	BESIDES THIS MAY	977	10
THIS WAY, I KEEP FROM MISSING	WE'LL PASS WITHOUT THE	996	7
THE LATTER--EXCELLENT TO KEEP [HAVE]--	BETWEEN THE FORM OF LIFE	1101	5
A STRATEGIST SHOULD KEEP,	THE SUBURBS OF A SECRET	1245	2
AIRS NO OCEANS KEEP--	I THINK THAT THE ROOT OF	1302	4
NOT ANY HOUSE THE FLOWERS KEEP--	THE NOTICE THAT IS	1310	5
I [WE] KEEP ONE RAY	OF THEIR PECULIAR LIGHT	1362	2
TO KEEP IT FROM INFESTING EYES--	SHAME IS THE SHAWL OF	1412	3
THAT PRISON DOES'NT KEEP	FROM ALL THE JAILS THE	1532	4
I PRAY THE LORD THY DUST TO KEEP--	NOW I LAY THEE DOWN TO	1539	2
THE ONLY SECRET PEOPLE [NEIGHBORS] KEEP [SHUN]	THE RETICENT VOLCANO	1748	11
KEEPER			
NEED--A KEEPER--FROWN?	CIVILIZATION--SPURNS--	492	9
ONLY THE KEEPER OF THIS RING [THE SEAL]	GIVEN IN MARRIAGE UNTO	817	7
TO KEEPER OF THE SEED.	HE WAS MY HOST--HE WAS	1721	8
TILL THE DAY ITS WEARY KEEPER	REARRANGE A "WIFE'S"	1737	19
KEEPING			
WHERE "KEEPING HOUSE" FOR THEE	THE GRAVE MY LITTLE	1743	2
KEEPS			
TO HIM WHO KEEPS AN ORCHIS' HEART--	ALL THESE MY BANNERS BE.	22	20
AND KEEPS THE SOUL SERENE--	IF I SHOULD DIE,	54	16
HER ANNUAL SECRET KEEPS!	A LADY RED--AMID THE	74	2
JUST AS THE NIGHT KEEPS FETCHING STARS	I'VE NOTHING ELSE--TO	224	3
HE KEEPS HIS SECRETS SAFELY--VERY--	FUNNY--TO BE A CENTURY--	345	5
MY BRAIN KEEPS GIGGLING--STILL.	THE FIRST DAY'S NIGHT	410	16
THE SEXTON KEEPS THE KEY TO--	I CANNOT LIVE WITH YOU--	640	5
KEEPS PLEADING--"I DONT KNOW."	THEIR HIGHT IN HEAVEN	696	16
KEEPS WITH THE HILL--	THE SUNRISE RUNS FOR	710	3
'TIS [THAT'S] THIS--AND WITCHCRAFT--NATURE KEEPS [KNOWS / HAS]	THE COLOR OF A QUEEN, IS	776	7
KEEPS MAKING NOVEMBER DIFFICULT	HOW HAPPY I WAS IF I	898	5
IT KEEPS THE NERVES PROGRESSIVE [IN PROGRESS]	THESE ARE THE NIGHTS	1128	11
KEEPS ESOTERIC TIME	'TWAS LATER WHEN THE	1276	8
HIS CUTLERY--HE KEEPS	A SAUCER HOLDS A CUP	1374	9
THE RETICENT VOLCANO KEEPS	THE RETICENT VOLCANO	1748	1

	FIRST LINE	POEM	LINE
KEEPSAKE			
WILL LET IT'S KEEPSAKE--GO	A SINGLE SCREW OF FLESH	263	20
HERE'S A KEEPSAKE FOR THE HILLS	TIE THE STRINGS TO MY	279	V 15
IN EVERLASTING KEEPSAKE [CHILDHOOD]--	THOSE FAIR--FICTITIOUS	499	7
KEEPSAKES			
I WILLED MY KEEPSAKES--SIGNED AWAY	I HEARD A FLY BUZZ--WHEN	465	9
KENNEL			
HOW IT IS NIGHT--IN NEST AND KENNEL--	HOW THE OLD MOUNTAINS	291	17
KEPT			
I KEPT THE "HOUSE AT HAME."	I HAD A GUINEA GOLDEN--	23	16
THE SUN KEPT STOOPING--STOOPING--LOW!	THE SUN KEPT STOOPING--	152	1
THAT KEPT SO MANY WARM--	"HOPE" IS THE THING WITH	254	8
KEPT TREADING--TREADING--TILL IT SEEMED	I FELT A FUNERAL, IN MY	280	3
KEPT BEATING--BEATING--TILL I THOUGHT	I FELT A FUNERAL, IN MY	280	7
SUSPENSE KEPT SAWING SO--	'TIS SO APPALLING--IT	281	8
A SECRET--KEPT--	A SECRET TOLD--	381	3
KEPT NARROWING IT'S BOILING WHEEL	'TWAS LIKE A MAELSTROM,	414	3
KEPT MEASURING THE HOURS--	'TWAS LIKE A MAELSTROM,	414	11
I KEPT IT IN MY HAND--	IT WAS GIVEN TO ME BY	454	5
AND THE OLD CLOCK KEPT NEIGHING "DAY"!	GOING TO HIM! HAPPY	494	19
THE SUN KEPT SETTING--SETTING--STILL	THE SUN KEPT SETTING--	692	1
THE DUSK KEPT DROPPING--DROPPING--STILL	THE SUN KEPT SETTING--	692	5
MY FEET KEPT DROWSING--DROWSING--STILL	THE SUN KEPT SETTING--	692	9
APPOINTMENT STRICTLY KEPT--	YOU TAUGHT ME WAITING	740	2
HOPE IT WAS THAT KEPT ME WARM--	WHEN I HOPED, I	768	7
IT KEPT ME FROM A THIEF, I THINK,	I PLAY AT RICHES--TO	801	3
AS CHILDREN STRICTEST [STRICTLY] KEPT	CONTAINED IN THIS SHORT	1165	5
OH FAITHFUL FROST [SLEET] THAT KEPT THE DATE	IT CAME AT LAST BUT	1230	5
HE KEPT HIS WORD A TRILLION YEARS	OUR LITTLE SECRETS SLINK	1326	3
I SHOULD HAVE KEPT IT LONGER.	HAD I KNOWN THAT THE	1720	2
KERNEL			
THE CORN, HER FURTHEST KERNEL FILLED	MIDSUMMER, WAS IT, WHEN	962	5
AND SET MY KERNEL IN.	I HEARD, AS IF I HAD NO	1039	12
IF IT CONTAIN A KERNEL?	EXPERIMENT TO ME	1073	3
HOW WENT THE AGILE KERNEL OUT	TOO COLD IS THIS	1135	6
KEY			
WHO BAFFLE KEY--	ALONE, I CANNOT BE--	298	4
SOME KEY OF CALVARY--	THE MORNING AFTER WO--	364	16
AND TRY ANOTHER KEY--	I AM ALIVE--I GUESS--	470	24
AND COULD NOT BREATHE WITHOUT A KEY,	IT WAS NOT DEATH, FOR I	510	15
MYSELF--CAN OWN [HOLD] THE KEY--	IF I MAY HAVE IT, WHEN	577	8
THE SEXTON KEEPS THE KEY TO--	I CANNOT LIVE WITH YOU--	640	5
THE POSTURE OF THE KEY	A PRISON GETS TO BE A	652	17
INSTINCT PICKING UP THE KEY	AFTER A HUNDRED YEARS	1147	11
KEYLESS			
PERISH WITH HIM--THAT KEYLESS RHYME!	BETTER--THAN MUSIC! FOR	503	8
KEYS			
AS PLAYERS AT THE KEYS	HE FUMBLES AT YOUR SOUL	315	2
THE EARTH HAS MANY KEYS.	THE EARTH HAS MANY KEYS.	1775	1
KID			
THEIR COUNTENANCES KID	UNTO MY BOOKS--SO GOOD	604	14
KIDD			
"KIDD" WILL [MAY] SUDDEN SAIL--	I NEVER TOLD THE BURIED	11	17
BY THIS--WAS WILLIAM KIDD	TRUST IN THE UNEXPECTED	555	2
KIDDERMINSTER			
OF KIDDERMINSTER? NAY--	OF BRUSSELS--IT WAS NOT	602	2
KILL			
KILL YOUR BALM--AND IT'S ODORS BLESS YOU--	KILL YOUR BALM--AND IT'S	238	1
DYING--ANNULS THE POWER TO KILL.	IF ANY SINK, ASSURE THAT	358	8
BUT SINCE IT IS PLAYING--KILL US,	WE DREAM--IT IS GOOD WE	531	3
FOR I HAVE BUT THE POWER [ART] TO KILL,	MY LIFE HAD STOOD--A	754	23
ABRAHAM TO KILL HIM	ABRAHAM TO KILL HIM	1317	1
COMPETENT TO KILL IT,	DEATH IS LIKE THE INSECT	1716	3
KILLED			
THE MAN THAT WAS NOT LOST [WRECKED / ROBBED / KILLED]	HOW MANY SCHEMES MAY DIE	1150	5
KILLS			
IT AIMS ONCE--KILLS ONCE--CONQUERS ONCE--	'TWAS FIGHTING FOR HIS	1188	5
KIND			
WILT HAVE NO KIND COMPANION, THOU REAP'ST WHAT THOU HAST SOWN.	AWAKE YE MUSES NINE,	1	28
A POPE, OR SOMETHING OF THAT KIND!	I MET A KING THIS	166	12
THAT OTHER KIND--WAS PAIN--	I'M "WIFE"--I'VE	199	10
A KIND BEHIND THE DOOR--	'TIS NOT THAT DYING	335	4
AND THOUGH I MAY NOT GUESS THE KIND--	I MEASURE EVERY GRIEF I	561	33
THAN AN INFERIOR KIND--	I THINK TO LIVE--MAY BE	646	12
A KIND OF PLUMMET STRAIN--	AGAIN--HIS VOICE IS AT	663	14
WITH EXPLANATION KIND	TELL ALL THE TRUTH BUT	1129	6
HOW CRUEL ARE THE KIND--	HOW RUTHLESS ARE THE	1439	2
OF NO CORPOREAL KIND	TALK NOT TO ME OF SUMMER	1634	4
KINDER			
"THOU SHALT NOT" IS A KINDER SWORD	THERE COMES AN HOUR WHEN	1751	4
KINDLE			
WILD FLOWERS--KINDLE IN THE WOODS--	IT MAKES NO DIFFERENCE	620	5
KINDLY			
AND KINDLY ASK IT IN--	HE PUT THE BELT AROUND	273	14
PERHAPS 'TIS KINDLY--DONE US--	WE SEE--COMPARATIVELY--	534	9
HE KINDLY STOPPED FOR ME--	BECAUSE I COULD NOT STOP	712	2
LOOK BACK ON TIME, WITH KINDLY EYES--	LOOK BACK ON TIME, WITH	1478	1

	FIRST LINE	POEM	LINE
KINDRED			
AND KINDRED AS RESPONSIVE--	DEATH IS THE SUPPLE	1445	V 11
SO EASY [KINDRED / FULLY / FREE / AMPLE SEEMS / BOUNTEOUS / . . .	YOUR THOUGHTS DONT HAVE	1452	6
KINDS			
TRIUMPH--MAY BE OF SEVERAL KINDS--	TRIUMPH--MAY BE OF	455	1
KING			
THAT COULD NOT STOP TO BE A KING--	DELAYED TILL SHE HAD	58	17
I HAVE A KING, WHO DOES NOT SPEAK--	I HAVE A KING, WHO DOES	103	1
I MET A KING THIS AFTERNOON!	I MET A KING THIS	166	1
MEANWHILE--HER WHEELING KING--	THE SUN--JUST TOUCHED	232	8
I'LL SAY--REMEMBER--KING--	THE COURT IS FAR AWAY--	235	6
FOR THAT LAST ONSET--WHEN THE KING	I HEARD A FLY BUZZ--WHEN	465	7
SEES EVERY MAN A KING--	WHO COURT OBTAIN WITHIN	803	2
FOR FEAR TO BE A KING--	WE NEVER KNOW HOW HIGH	1176	8
HE IS KING [PRINCE] OF HARM--	WHEN I HOPED I FEARED--	1181	V 7
IS WHOLESOME EVEN FOR THE KING,	A LITTLE MADNESS IN THE	1333	2
NO DESPOT BUT THE KING OF DOWN	HOW SOFT THIS PRISON IS	1334	3
DEMANDS THE [MY] LITTLE KING	A SAUCER HOLDS A CUP	1374	6
KINGDOM			
RESERVE WITHIN THY KINGDOM	PAPA ABOVE!	61	4
PERHAPS THE "KINGDOM OF HEAVEN'S" CHANGED--	"ARCTURUS" IS HIS OTHER	70	26
AS IF A KINGDOM--CARED!	READ--SWEET--HOW OTHERS	260	7
A STRANGER PRESSED A KINGDOM,	AS IF I ASKED A COMMON	323	3
FOR THE SITE OF THE KINGDOM OF HEAVEN--	A LOSS OF SOMETHING EVER	959	16
KINGDOM'S			
MY KINGDOM'S WORTH OF BLISS!	WHAT WOULD I GIVE TO SEE	247	29
A KINGDOM'S TITLE DEED--	HE PUT THE BELT AROUND	273	6
KINGDOMS			
COURTIERS QUAINT, IN KINGDOMS	TAKEN FROM MEN--THIS	53	11
IN KINGDOMS--YOU HAVE HEARD THE RAISED--	THE FACE I CARRY WITH ME	336	7
'TIS KINGDOMS--AFTERWARD--THEY SAY--	BEHIND ME--DIPS ETERNITY	721	7
AND KINGDOMS, LIKE THE ORCHARD	IT IS AN HONORABLE	946	7
KINGS			
INSTEAD OF KINGS--	THE CHILD'S FAITH IS NEW	637	24
KINSMAN			
NOUGHT--THAT [YET, IF] WE--NO POET'S KINSMAN--	HER--"LAST POEMS"--	312	16
NEAR KINSMAN TO HERSELF--	THERE IS A FLOWER THAT	380	18
WE MISS A KINSMAN MORE	WE MISS A KINSMAN MORE	1087	1
A DUNGEON BUT A KINSMAN IS	HOW SOFT THIS PRISON IS	1334	7
KINSMANLESS			
BECAUSE I FOUND HER KINSMANLESS,	MY SEASON'S FURTHEST	1019	3
KINSMANSHIP			
A VITAL KINSMANSHIP IMPORT	BEREAVEMENT IN THEIR	645	3
AND OUR'S--A KINSMANSHIP EXPRESS [EXIST / SUBSIST / ARISE]--	A PRISON GETS TO BE A	652	3
KINSMEN			
HOW KINSMEN FELL--	UNTO LIKE STORY--TROUBLE	295	2
AND SO, AS KINSMEN, MET A NIGHT--	I DIED FOR BEAUTY--BUT	449	9
I THANK THESE KINSMEN OF THE SHELF--	UNTO MY BOOKS--SO GOOD	604	13
NEVER KINSMEN KNEELED	HER SWEET TURN TO LEAVE	649	10
OUR LITTLE KINSMEN--AFTER RAIN	OUR LITTLE KINSMEN--	885	1
THE KINSMEN OF THE WIND ARE PEAKS	THE DUTIES OF THE WIND	1137	9
AND KINSMEN AS DIVULGELESS	DEATH IS THE SUPPLE	1445	11
BY INFLUENTIAL KINSMEN	WITH SWEETNESS UNABATED	1709	7
KIRTLE			
GLOWING IS HER KIRTLE,	GLOWING IS HER BONNET,	72	3
KISS			
SOME TOUCH IT, AND SOME KISS IT--	THERE'S SOMETHING	45	5
AND KISS THE HILLS, FOR ME, JUST ONCE--	TIE THE STRINGS TO MY	279	15
NO OTHER KISS HAD KNOWN	HE TOLD A HOMELY TALE	763	6
REDEMPTION [THY TOTAL / THY BEING]--FOR A KISS--	GO SLOW, MY SOUL, TO	1297	8
I GIVE [SEND] MY DYING KISS--	"GO TELL IT"--WHAT A	1554	8
CONVEY MY DYING KISS--	"GO TELL IT"--WHAT A	1554	V 8
KISSED			
THAT EVER KISSED THE SPADE!	I NEVER TOLD THE BURIED	11	13
AND WHATSOEVER MOUTH HE KISSED--	A VISITOR IN MARL--	391	11
THEN SUNRISE KISSED MY CHRYSALIS--	THREE TIMES--WE PARTED--	598	15
A HALF A DOZEN KISSED THE EAVES--	A DROP FELL ON THE APPLE	794	3
KISSING			
KISSING HER [IT'S] BONNET TO THE MEADOW	BLAZING IN GOLD AND	228	7
KITCHEN			
STOOPING AS LOW AS [BENDING LOW AT] THE OTTER'S [KITCHEN / . . .	BLAZING IN GOLD AND	228	5
KITCHEN'D			
HOW ORDERLY THE KITCHEN'D LOOK, BY NIGHT,	I KNOW SOME LONELY	289	13
KNEAD			
THE WIND BEGUN TO KNEAD [ROCK] THE GRASS--	THE WIND BEGUN TO KNEAD	824	1
KNEE			
OR IF IT DARE--TO CLIMB YOUR DIZZY KNEE--	WHAT SHALL I DO--IT	186	10
WHEN KATIE KNEELS, THEIR LOVING HANDS STILL CLASP HER PIOUS KNEE--	WHEN KATIE WALKS, THIS	222	3
NOT UPON HER KNEE TO THANK ME	MOST SHE TOUCHED ME BY	760	9
AND FAINTING, ON HER YELLOW KNEE	THE LADY FEEDS HER	941	7
ABJECT IS HIS KNEE--	WHEN A LOVER IS A BEGGAR	1314	2
THAT BENDS A KNEE TO THEE	CIRCUMFERENCE THOU BRIDE	1620	V 4
KNEELED			
NEVER KINSMEN KNEELED	HER SWEET TURN TO LEAVE	649	10

	FIRST LINE	POEM	LINE
KNEELING			
UNMOVED--AN EMPEROR BE KNEELING	THE SOUL SELECTS HER OWN	303	7
I'M KNEELING--[WE'RE PLEADING] STILL--	AH, TENERIFFE!	666	10
KNEELS			
WHEN KATIE KNEELS, THEIR LOVING HANDS STILL CLASP HER PIOUS KNEE--	WHEN KATIE WALKS, THIS	222	3
KNEES			
IT WAS NOT FROST, FOR ON MY FLESH [KNEES]	IT WAS NOT DEATH, FOR I	510	5
THE SEASONS PLAYED AROUND HIS KNEES	THE MOUNTAIN SAT UPON	975	5
AND NOT THE KNEES.	THIS DIRTY--LITTLE--	1311	8
KNELL			
THE MOTHER THAT HAS NOT A KNELL	SHE COULD NOT LIVE UPON	1505	5
OF SWARTHY DAYS HE IS THE CLOSE [KNELL]	THE JAY HIS CASTANET HAS	1635	5
KNELT			
AND THEN WE KNELT IN PRAYER--	THE GENTIAN WEAVES HER	18	12
KNEW			
IS ALL THE REST I KNEW!	WENT UP A YEAR THIS	93	24
NOBODY KNEW "HIS FATHER"--	DUST IS THE ONLY SECRET	153	5
AH, FRIEND, YOU LITTLE KNEW	GOOD NIGHT! WHICH PUT	259	3
ALTHOUGH--I KNEW--TO TAKE IT--	ONE LIFE OF SO MUCH	270	7
I CEDED ALL OF DUST I KNEW--	DOUBT ME! MY DIM	275	11
FOR LARGEST WOMAN'S HEART I KNEW--	FOR LARGEST WOMAN'S	309	1
I KNEW SO PERFECT--YESTERDAY--	I SHOULD HAVE BEEN TOO	313	10
NOR ANY KNOW [KNEW] I KNOW THE ART	I CANNOT DANCE UPON MY	326	17
I KNEW LAST NIGHT--WHEN SOMEONE TRIED TO TWINE--	HOW SICK--TO WAIT--IN	368	2
ONES WE FORMER KNEW--	SMILING BACK FROM	385	6
WHOSE FATE--CONJECTURE KNEW--	A HOUSE UPON THE HIGHT--	399	9
THE NEGRO NEVER KNEW	THE MALAY--TOOK THE	452	14
AND ANY ONE I KNEW	I WAS THE SLIGHTEST IN	486	15
OF ALL TUNES I KNEW--AND MORE--	BETTER--THAN MUSIC! FOR	503	4
A PRANK NOBODY KNEW BUT THEM	IF ANYBODY'S FRIEND BE	509	7
AS THE STARS--YOU KNEW LAST NIGHT--	SOME SUCH BUTTERFLY BE	541	7
IT KNEW NO MEDICINE--	IT KNEW NO MEDICINE--	559	1
IT KNEW NO LAPSE, NOR DIMINUTION--	IT KNEW NO LAPSE, NOR	560	1
BUT ONLY KNEW BY LOOKING BACK--	IT CEASED TO HURT ME,	584	3
I WISH I KNEW THAT WOMAN'S NAME--	I CRIED AT PITY--NOT AT	588	17
AND KNEW ONE BIRD A TUNE--	WHAT CARE THE DEAD, FOR	592	12
I TOLD HIM WORLDS [A WORLD] I KNEW	I ROSE--BECAUSE HE SANK	616	16
AND WAYS I KNEW NOT THAT I KNEW--TILL THEN--	I ROSE--BECAUSE HE SANK	616	22
AND WAYS I KNEW NOT THAT I KNEW--TILL THEN--	I ROSE--BECAUSE HE SANK	616	22
I COULD SUFFICE FOR HIM, I KNEW--	I COULD SUFFICE FOR HIM,	643	1
THE LIBERTY WE KNEW	A PRISON GETS TO BE A	652	29
KNEW A PARTICLE--OF SPACE'S	CONSCIOUS AM I IN MY	679	15
HOW WELL I KNEW THE LIGHT BEFORE--	THE SUN KEPT SETTING--	692	13
WE SLOWLY DROVE--HE KNEW NO HASTE	BECAUSE I COULD NOT STOP	712	5
A LITTLE BRIG I KNEW--O'ERTOOK BY BLAST--	IT TOSSED--AND TOSSED--	723	2
NEVER KNEW SATIETY--	NEVER FOR SOCIETY	746	7
I KNEW NO MORE OF WANT--OR COLD--	ONE BLESSING HAD I THAN	756	9
THEY KNEW THE HAIR TO--	SEVERER SERVICE OF	786	15
AS SOME [US] SHE NEVER KNEW--	NO NOTICE GAVE SHE, BUT	804	20
WHO ONLY KNEW OF UNIVERSE--	THIS BAUBLE WAS	805	7
NATURE AND GOD--I NEITHER KNEW	NATURE AND GOD--I	835	1
YET BOTH SO WELL KNEW ME	NATURE AND GOD--I	835	2
HOW WELL I KNEW HER NOT	HOW WELL I KNEW HER NOT	837	1
I KNEW NOT BUT THE NEXT	I STEPPED FROM PLANK TO	875	5
WE KNEW BY CHANGE BETWEEN ITSELF	WE MET AS SPARKS--	958	7
BEREFT I WAS--OF WHAT I KNEW NOT	A LOSS OF SOMETHING EVER	959	3
SOME KNOW HIM [IT] WHOM WE KNEW--	BESIDES THIS MAY	977	6
A PARTY THAT [WHOM] WE KNEW--	AS SLEIGH BELLS SEEM IN	981	6
THE FIRST WE KNEW OF HIM WAS DEATH--	THE FIRST WE KNEW OF HIM	1006	1
I KNEW THAT I HAD GAINED	I KNEW THAT I HAD GAINED	1022	1
AND YET I KNEW NOT HOW	I KNEW THAT I HAD GAINED	1022	2
AND THEN I KNEW I HEARD.	I HEARD, AS IF I HAD NO	1039	4
A FALLACY, A FIGMENT, WE KNEW--	NOT SO THE INFINITE	1040	4
I KNEW THE DOLLARS BY THEIR NAMES--	BECAUSE 'TWAS RICHES I	1093	3
PROMETHEUS NEVER KNEW--[DID NOT KNOW]	THE SMOULDERING EMBERS	1132	8
WE STERN AND FORMER KNEW	THE SNOW THAT NEVER	1133	10
NOBODY KNOWS [KNEW] THE PLACE	AFTER A HUNDRED YEARS	1147	2
TELL HAD A SON--THE ONES THAT KNEW [HEARD] IT	TELL AS A MARKSMAN--WERE	1152	9
. . . KNEW HE WAS] NARROW--	HE PREACHED UPON	1207	1
NOW I KNEW I LOST HER--	NOW I KNEW I LOST HER--	1219	1
AND THEN I [WE] KNEW 'TWAS WIND--	LIKE RAIN IT SOUNDED	1235	2
ELIJAH'S WAGON KNEW [HAD] NO THILL	ELIJAH'S WAGON KNEW NO	1254	1
A THING I NEVER KNEW--	BECAUSE THAT YOU ARE	1260	18
THE MOST TRIUMPHANT BIRD I EVER KNEW OR MET	THE MOST TRIUMPHANT BIRD	1265	1
AND YET WE KNEW THAT GENTLE CLOCK	'TWAS LATER WHEN THE	1276	3
YOU KNEW IT [THAT] WAS NOT TRUE	THE MOST PATHETIC THING	1290	6
THE MAPLES NEVER KNEW THAT YOU WERE COMING--TILL I CALLED	DEAR MARCH--COME IN--	1320	12
THEY WORE [KNEW] NO LEXICONS--	"WAS NOT" WAS ALL THE	1342	4
A BEE I PERSONALLY KNEW	A SINGLE CLOVER PLANK	1343	3
THE SHAFT THAT NEVER KNEW--	SHE LAID HER DOCILE	1396	6
THE FAIREST HOME I EVER KNEW	THE FAIREST HOME I EVER	1423	1
BY PARTIES ALSO THAT I KNEW	THE FAIREST HOME I EVER	1423	3
KNEW WE OF THEE--	SPURN THE TEMERITY--	1432	4
WE KNEW NOT THAT WE WERE TO LIVE--	WE KNEW NOT THAT WE WERE	1462	1
PAUL KNEW THE MAN THAT KNEW THE NEWS--	"AND WITH WHAT BODY DO	1492	7
PAUL KNEW THE MAN THAT KNEW THE NEWS--	"AND WITH WHAT BODY DO	1492	7
I KNEW IT BLEW FOR ME--	I SAW THE WIND WITHIN	1502	2

	FIRST LINE	POEM	LINE
KNEW (CONTINUED)			
KNEW WHERE THEY WENT--	THOSE--DYING THEN,	1551	2
I GROPED FOR HIM BEFORE I KNEW	I GROPED FOR HIM BEFORE	1555	1
HE KNEW NO MORE THAT HE WAS POOR, ...	HE ATE AND DRANK THE	1587	3
. . . ALL THE SAINTS HE KNEW / EVERY GOD HE KNEW]	THE BOBOLINK IS GONE--	1591	6
. . . ALL THE SAINTS HE KNEW / EVERY GOD HE KNEW]	THE BOBOLINK IS GONE--	1591	6
WE THIS MOMENT KNEW--	IS IT TOO LATE TO TOUCH	1637	2
I NEVER KNEW THY POWER, ...	OH, HONEY OF AN HOUR,	1734	2
ALL OTHER HEARTS [THINGS] I KNEW.	TO LOSE THEE--SWEETER	1754	2
KNEWEST			
"OLD FRIEND, THOU KNOWEST [KNEWEST] ME," .	I HEARD, AS IF I HAD NO	1039	14
KNIFE			
WHEN THEY TAKE THE KNIFE!	SURGEONS MUST BE VERY	108	2
KNIGHT			
EARTH IS A MERRY DAMSEL, AND HEAVEN A KNIGHT SO TRUE,	AWAKE YE MUSES NINE,	1	23
POSSESSED BY EVERY HALLOWED KNIGHT . . .	CIRCUMFERENCE THOU BRIDE	1620	3
KNIT			
AH! KATIE! SMILE AT FORTUNE, WITH TWO SO KNIT TO THEE!	WHEN KATIE WALKS, THIS	222	4
THEN KNIT, AND SWEPT [PASSED]--	OF ALL THE SOUNDS	321	32
KNITS			
THERE KNITS A BOLDER ONE--	NO RACK CAN TORTURE ME--	384	4
AND DANCING SOFTLY TO HIMSELF [AS HE KNITS]	THE SPIDER HOLDS A	605	3
KNITTING			
AUTUMN--OVERLOOKED MY KNITTING--	AUTUMN--OVERLOOKED MY	748	1
KNOCK			
THEY HEAR MY UNEXPECTED KNOCK--	THO' I GET HOME HOW LATE	207	6
KNOCK--RECOLLECT--TO ME--	I HAD NO CAUSE TO BE	542	8
TO COUNTERACT A KNOCK--	THE WAY I READ A	636	6
KNOCK WITH TREMOR--	KNOCK WITH TREMOR--	1325	1
AUDACIOUS AS WITHOUT A KNOCK	THE LAST OF SUMMER IS	1353	7
I CAN BUT KNOCK--	THE HEART HAS MANY DOORS	1567	2
KNOCK AND IT SHALL BE OPENED	COSMOPOLITES WITHOUT A	1589	7
WALK BOLDLY UP AND KNOCK	T'WAS COMFORT IN HER	1703	4
KNOCKED			
DAY KNOCKED--AND WE MUST PART--	HE WAS WEAK, AND I WAS	190	9
AND THEY--WERE THE LITTLE HAND--THAT KNOCKED--	WHY--DO THEY SHUT ME OUT	248	11
KNOCKER			
LAST [FIRST]--AT THE KNOCKER--	JUST SO--JESUS--RAPS--	317	3
KNOCKING			
HEART! I AM KNOCKING--LOW AT THEE.	JUST SO--JESUS--RAPS--	317	11
I'M KNOCKING--EVERYWHERE--	AT LEAST--TO PRAY--IS	502	4
WITH A TO-MORROW KNOCKING	RATHER ARID DELIGHT	1679	7
KNOCKS			
A DEED KNOCKS FIRST AT THOUGHT	A DEED KNOCKS FIRST AT	1216	1
AND THEN--IT KNOCKS AT WILL--	A DEED KNOCKS FIRST AT	1216	2
WHO KNOCKS? THAT APRIL.	DEAR MARCH--COME IN--	1320	18
THE FOREIGNER BEFORE HE KNOCKS	WHERE EVERY BIRD IS BOLD	1758	3
KNOLL			
FOR EVERY LITTLE KNOLL--	ON SUCH A NIGHT, OR SUCH	146	18
OUR APPENINE--A KNOLL--	WE SEE--COMPARATIVELY--	534	8
KNOWN TO [OF] THE KNOLL--	PINK--SMALL--AND	1332	6
KNOT			
THE MONTHS HAVE ENDS--THE YEARS--A KNOT-- .	THE MONTHS HAVE ENDS--	423	1
TO THE SIGHTLESS KNOT--	DONT PUT UP MY THREAD &	617	10
KNOTS			
BRIGHT KNOTS OF APPARITIONS	OF NEARNESS TO HER	607	15
KNOW			
YET KNOW IT'S DRIPPING FEET	MY WHEEL IS IN THE DARK!	10	3
OF THE CROCUS KNOW--	ALL THESE MY BANNERS BE.	22	17
THE HILLSIDES MUST NOT KNOW IT--	I HAV'NT TOLD MY GARDEN	50	9
I DID NOT KNOW THE YEAR THEN--	I OFTEN PASSED THE	51	5
TIS SWEET TO KNOW THAT STOCKS WILL STAND .	IF I SHOULD DIE,	54	11
DELAYED TILL SHE HAD CEASED TO KNOW-- . .	DELAYED TILL SHE HAD	58	1
AFFECTION DOES'NT KNOW	AMBITION CANNOT FIND HIM	68	2
I DONT KNOW WHEN--	GOING TO HEAVEN!	79	2
FOR YOU KNOW WE DO NOT MIND OUR DRESS . .	GOING TO HEAVEN!	79	18
SOVREIGN! KNOW A DAISY	"THEY HAVE NOT CHOSEN ME	85	7
WHEN I HAVE LOST, YOU'LL KNOW BY THIS-- . .	WHERE I HAVE LOST, I	104	9
WHY, I HAVE LOST, THE PEOPLE KNOW	WHERE I HAVE LOST, I	104	13
I KNOW THE BUTTERFLY.	THE BEE IS NOT AFRAID OF	111	2
I WOULD GO, TO KNOW!	GOOD NIGHT, BECAUSE WE	114	3
BUT GALLANTER, I KNOW	TO FIGHT ALOUD, IS VERY	126	2
I DONT KNOW HIM; SNUGLY BUILT!	"HOUSES"--SO THE WISE	127	6
THE UNIVERSE TO KNOW!	COCOON ABOVE! COCOON	129	12
A FURTIVE LOOK YOU KNOW AS WELL--	AN ALTERED LOOK ABOUT	140	14
THAT NOBODY MIGHT KNOW	ON SUCH A NIGHT, OR SUCH	146	6
BE SURE YOU'RE SURE--YOU KNOW--	YOU LOVE ME--YOU ARE	156	14
PERHAPS HE DOES'NT KNOW THE HOUSE--	DYING! DYING IN THE	158	7
AT LEAST, TO KNOW THE WORST, IS SWEET! . .	'TIS SO MUCH JOY! 'TIS	172	10
YOU'LL KNOW IT BY THE ROW OF STARS . . .	I LOST A WORLD--THE	181	3
YOU WILL KNOW I'M TRYING	IF I SHOULD'NT BE ALIVE	182	7
YET--KNOW NOT WHAT WAS DONE TO ME	I'VE HEARD AN ORGAN TALK	183	7
THAT WAS ALL I CARED TO KNOW.	HE WAS WEAK, AND I WAS	190	8
IT'S FINER--NOT TO KNOW--	THE SKIES CANT KEEP	191	10
KNOW WHAT THE SAPPHIRE FELLOWS, DO, ...	THE SKIES CANT KEEP	191	15
I SHALL KNOW WHY--WHEN TIME IS OVER-- . .	I SHALL KNOW WHY--WHEN	193	1

	FIRST LINE	POEM	LINE
KNOW (CONTINUED)			
IT PUZZLED ME TO KNOW--	THE ROSE DID CAPER ON	208	8
DO THEY KNOW THAT THIS IS "AMHERST"--	WHAT IS--"PARADISE"--	215	5
YOU KNOW WHAT DIAMONDS ARE?	I CAME TO BUY A SMILE--	223	10
I'VE NOTHING ELSE--TO BRING, YOU KNOW--	I'VE NOTHING ELSE--TO	224	1
THE ONLY TRADE [ART] THEY KNOW--	A BURDOCK--CLAWED MY	229	8
BUT IT'S DIM CHAT OF THINGS BURGUND, WE KNOW--	WE--BEE AND I--LIVE BY	230 V	4
BECAUSE I KNOW IT'S TRUE--	I LIKE A LOOK OF AGONY,	241	2
ALL LIFE--TO KNOW EACH OTHER--	FOREVER AT HIS SIDE TO	246	10
YOU KNOW WHO "JUNE" IS--	WHAT WOULD I GIVE TO SEE	247	7
I COULD CLIMB--IF I TRIED, I KNOW--	OVER THE FENCE--	251	4
I'M BANISHED--NOW--YOU KNOW IT--	IF I'M LOST--NOW--	256	10
YOU'LL KNOW--SIR--WHEN THE SAVIOR'S FACE	IF I'M LOST--NOW--	256	12
THE LONESOME FOR THEY KNOW NOT WHAT--	THE LONESOME FOR THEY	262	1
THE SEA IS FULL--I KNOW IT!	ONE LIFE OF SO MUCH	270	9
THE LIFE IS THICK--I KNOW IT!	ONE LIFE OF SO MUCH	270	13
WHOSE INVITATION, KNOW YOU NOT [FOR THIS WORLD--]	HE PUT THE BELT AROUND	273	15
AND THE WORLD I USED TO KNOW--	TIE THE STRINGS TO MY	279	14
TO KNOW THE WORST, LEAVES NO DREAD MORE--	'TIS SO APPALLING--IT	281	4
BUT WE, WHO KNOW,	'TIS SO APPALLING--IT	281	13
DONT TELL! THEY'D BANISH US [ADVERTISE]--YOU KNOW!	I'M NOBODY! WHO ARE YOU?	288	4
I KNOW SOME LONELY HOUSES OFF THE ROAD	I KNOW SOME LONELY	289	1
WHOM NONE BUT DAISIES [BEETLES], KNOW.	OF BRONZE--AND BLAZE--	290	19
I DID NOT KNOW THE WINE	ONE YEAR AGO--JOTS WHAT?	296	13
AND COULD NOT KNOW HOW FONDNESS GREW	ONE YEAR AGO--JOTS WHAT?	296	19
BECAUSE IT WAS A CHILD, YOU KNOW--	ONE YEAR AGO--JOTS WHAT?	296	30
OF MINES, I LITTLE KNOW--MYSELF--	YOUR RICHES--TAUGHT ME--	299	9
HER GLORY I SHOULD KNOW--	YOUR RICHES--TAUGHT ME--	299	14
I'M SURE [I KNOW] IT IS GOLCONDA--	YOUR RICHES--TAUGHT ME--	299	21
AT LEAST, IT SOLACES TO KNOW	YOUR RICHES--TAUGHT ME--	299	25
WE KNOW [SAY] HE HAS CLIMBED A FIR--	THE WIND DID'NT COME	316	8
BUT HOW HE SET--I KNOW NOT--	I'LL TELL YOU HOW THE	318	9
NOR ANY KNOW [KNEW] I KNOW THE ART	I CANNOT DANCE UPON MY	326	17
NOR ANY KNOW [KNEW] I KNOW THE ART	I CANNOT DANCE UPON MY	326	17
AND KNOW NO OTHER WAY--	BEFORE I GOT MY EYE PUT	327	4
HE DID NOT KNOW I SAW--	A BIRD CAME DOWN THE	328	2
I KNOW A PLACE WHERE SUMMER STRIVES	I KNOW A PLACE WHERE	337	1
I KNOW THAT HE EXISTS.	I KNOW THAT HE EXISTS.	338	1
FOR DOUBT, THAT I SHOULD KNOW THE SOUND--	I FELT MY LIFE WITH BOTH	351	8
LIKE HAMMERS--DID THEY KNOW THEY FELL	THE MORNING AFTER WO--	364	11
BUT JUST HIS EAR COULD KNOW	ALTHOUGH I PUT AWAY HIS	366	10
A LITTLE BOOT I KNOW--	ALTHOUGH I PUT AWAY HIS	366	14
I KNOW LIVES, I COULD MISS	I KNOW LIVES, I COULD	372	1
WE KNOW NOT--	FOR DEATH--OR RATHER	382	11
THAT MAN AND WOMAN KNOW--	THE SWEETEST HERESY	387	2
I KNOW IT, BY THE NUMB LOOK	THERE'S BEEN A DEATH, IN	389	3
ENTERS--WITH A "YOU KNOW ME--SIR"?	IT'S COMING--THE	390	4
WITHOUT THE PRIVILEGE TO KNOW	HOW MANY FLOWERS FAIL IN	404	3
YOU WOULD NOT KNOW IT FROM THE FIELD--	THE COLOR OF THE GRAVE	411	3
YOU WOULD NOT KNOW IT FROM THE DRIFTS--	THE COLOR OF THE GRAVE	411	11
I SHALL NOT FEEL AT HOME--I KNOW--	I NEVER FELT AT HOME--	413	3
I WOULD NOT CHOOSE--A BOOK TO KNOW	NOT IN THIS WORLD TO SEE	418	8
YOU'LL KNOW IT--AS YOU KNOW 'TIS NOON--	YOU'LL KNOW IT--AS YOU	420	1
YOU'LL KNOW IT--AS YOU KNOW 'TIS NOON--	YOU'LL KNOW IT--AS YOU	420	1
KNOW GOD THE FATHER--AND THE SON.	YOU'LL KNOW IT--AS YOU	420	6
"HOW SHALL YOU KNOW"?	YOU'LL KNOW IT--AS YOU	420	14
I SHOULD LIKE TO KNOW--	KNOWS HOW TO FORGET!	433	4
GODS USED TO KNOW--	KNOWS HOW TO FORGET!	433	8
ENOUGH TO KNOW!	KNOWS HOW TO FORGET!	433 V	
TELESCOPES WOULD KNOW--	KNOWS HOW TO FORGET!	433 V	
DONT YOU KNOW?	KNOWS HOW TO FORGET!	433 V	
I KNOW I HEARD THE CORN,	'TWAS JUST THIS TIME,	445	2
EYES WERE NOT MEANT TO KNOW.	THE OUTER--FROM THE	451	16
THEY GIVE US PRESENTS MOST--YOU KNOW--	IT WAS GIVEN TO ME BY	454	3
I KNOW WHERE WELLS GROW--DROUGHTLESS WELLS--	I KNOW WHERE WELLS GROW	460	1
SO STRONG--TO KNOW--	WHY MAKE IT DOUBT--IT	462	3
SO VISITORS MAY KNOW	I AM ALIVE--I GUESS--	470	22
AND WE KNOW NOT--	"WHY DO I LOVE" YOU, SIR	480	8
BUT SOLEMNEST--TO KNOW	A SOLEMN THING WITHIN	483	13
FOR IT WOULD SPLIT HIS [HER] HEART, TO KNOW IT--	GOING TO HIM! HAPPY	494	16
DONT YOU KNOW--ME?	HE STRAINED MY FAITH--	497	16
PHILOSOPHY--DONT KNOW--	THIS WORLD IS NOT	501	6
I KNOW NOT WHICH THY CHAMBER IS [PALACES]--	AT LEAST--TO PRAY--IS	502	3
YOU KNOW THAT PORTRAIT IN THE MOON--	YOU KNOW THAT PORTRAIT	504	1
HE TOUCHED ME, SO I LIVE TO KNOW	HE TOUCHED ME, SO I LIVE	506	1
TOUCH LIBERTY--THEN KNOW NO MORE,	THE SOUL HAS BANDAGED	512	17
NO ONE [MAN] HE SEEMED TO KNOW--	I STARTED EARLY--TOOK MY	520	22
AND COULD [DID] NOT KNOW THE FEELING 'TWAS--	'TIS TRUE--THEY SHUT ME	538	3
FOREIGNERS [KNOW NOT YOU]--THIS MORNING--	SOME SUCH BUTTERFLY BE	541	8
I COULD [WOULD] DIE--TO KNOW--	I COULD DIE--TO KNOW--	570	1
I DID NOT KNOW THE AMPLE BREAD--	I HAD BEEN HUNGRY, ALL	579	9
YOU COULD NOT SPARE--YOU KNOW.	YOU'LL FIND--IT WHEN YOU	610	4
COULD HE--KNOW--THEY SOUGHT HIM--	IN FALLING TIMBERS	614	5
COULD THEY--KNOW--HE BREATHED [LIVED]--	IN FALLING TIMBERS	614	6
TO KNOW JUST HOW HE SUFFERED--WOULD BE DEAR--	TO KNOW JUST HOW HE	622	1
TO KNOW IF ANY HUMAN EYES WERE NEAR	TO KNOW JUST HOW HE	622	2
TO KNOW IF HE WAS PATIENT--PART CONTENT--	TO KNOW JUST HOW HE	622	5

KNOW (CONTINUED)

	FIRST LINE	POEM		LINE
MIGHT HE KNOW	TO KNOW JUST HOW HE	622		23
FOR FEAR THE SQUIRRELS--KNOW.	THE TINT I CANNOT TAKE--	627		20
YOU'LL KNOW HER--BY HER FOOT--	YOU'LL KNOW HER--BY HER	634		1
YOU'LL KNOW HER--BY HER VEST--	YOU'LL KNOW HER--BY HER	634		9
YOU'LL KNOW HER--BY HER VOICE--	YOU'LL KNOW HER--BY HER	634		21
TO NO ONE THAT YOU--KNOW--	THE WAY I READ A	636		14
FOR YOU--SERVED HEAVEN--YOU KNOW,	I CANNOT LIVE WITH YOU--	640		30
I ONLY KNOW [SIGH]--NO CURRICLE [VEHICLE] THAT RUMBLE THERE	A LITTLE ROAD--NOT MADE	647		7
LOOK--IF SHE SHOULD KNOW	SO MUCH SUMMER	651		8
WE LEARN TO KNOW THE PLANKS--	A PRISON GETS TO BE A	652		9
NATURE IS WHAT WE KNOW--	"NATURE" IS WHAT WE SEE	668		9
IS BUT A FILAMENT, I KNOW,	THE LOVE A LIFE CAN SHOW	673		2
DO HE DWELL--OR NAY--KNOW I--	CONSCIOUS AM I IN MY	679		18
WHO OF LITTLE LOVE--KNOW HOW TO STARVE--	VICTORY COMES LATE--	690		14
I'M NOT AFRAID TO KNOW--	THE SUN KEPT SETTING--	692		16
KEEPS PLEADING--"I DONT KNOW."	THEIR HIGHT IN HEAVEN	696		16
DEATH--WE DO NOT KNOW--	LIFE--IS WHAT WE MAKE IT	698		2
BUT SOMEWHERE--IN MY SOUL--I KNOW--	A THOUGHT WENT UP MY	701		9
ANONYMOUS DELIGHT TO KNOW--	I SOMETIMES DROP IT, FOR	708		3
THE SAILOR DOES'NT KNOW THE STROKE--	I SOMETIMES DROP IT, FOR	708		15
I KNOW THE WHOLE--OBSCURES THE PART--	PRECIOUS TO ME--SHE	727		9
THE HEAVEN YOU KNOW--TO UNDERSTAND	YOU TAUGHT ME WAITING	740		9
TO THOSE WHO KNOW	I LIVED ON DREAD--	770		2
POSSIBLY--IF THEY REFUSE--HOW THEN KNOW--	GRIEF IS A MOUSE--	793		16
WHO GIANTS KNOW, WITH LESSER MEN	WHO GIANTS KNOW, WITH	796		1
I KNOW NOT WHICH, DESIRE, OR GRANT [RIGHT / SIGHT]--	I PLAY AT RICHES--TO	801		23
UPON THE FURTHEST SLOPE YOU KNOW	A LIGHT EXISTS IN SPRING	812		11
THE ONLY NEWS I KNOW	THE ONLY NEWS I KNOW	827		1
WHOM NOT TO KNOW HAS BEEN	HOW WELL I KNEW HER NOT	837		2
GOOD TO KNOW, AND NOT TELL,	GOOD TO HIDE, AND HEAR	842		5
BEST, TO KNOW AND TELL,	GOOD TO HIDE, AND HEAR	842		6
WE ONLY KNOW WHAT TIME OF YEAR	FROM US SHE WANDERED NOW	890		7
AND ANGELS KNOW THE REST!	I HIDE MYSELF WITHIN MY	903	V	4
WE SHALL NEVER KNOW--	HOW THE WATERS CLOSED	923		2
FORBID THAT ANY KNOW--	HOW FAR IS IT TO HEAVEN?	929	V	8
THAT BELLS SHOULD RING TILL ALL SHOULD KNOW [HEAR]	OF TOLLING BELL I ASK	947		5
"UNTO ME?" I DO NOT KNOW YOU--	"UNTO ME?" I DO NOT KNOW	964		1
DOES NOT KNOW THEY ARE--	COLOR--CASTE--	970		4
WE KNOW	BESIDES THIS MAY	977		2
SOME KNOW HIM [IT] WHOM WE KNEW--	BESIDES THIS MAY	977		6
I KNOW, AND THEY KNOW ME--	A NARROW FELLOW IN THE	986		18
I KNOW, AND THEY KNOW ME--	A NARROW FELLOW IN THE	986		18
WE KNOW THAT THEIR SUPERIOR EYES	WE MISS HER, NOT BECAUSE	993		7
I KNOW THE FAMILY	PARTAKE AS DOTH THE BEE,	994	V	3
WOULD IT COMFORT--TO KNOW I MET HIM--	TRUDGING TO EDEN,	1020		5
WHO KNOW HIS MEED OF ALL.	SO LARGE MY WILL	1024		8
TO SOMEBODY YOU KNOW	BEE! I'M EXPECTING YOU!	1035		3
AND NOW I KNOW 'TWAS LIGHT, BECAUSE	I HEARD, AS IF I HAD NO	1039		7
YET KNOW I HOW THE HEATHER LOOKS	I NEVER SAW A MOOR--	1052		3
NOR KNOW I WHEN IT CEASE,	FURTHER IN SUMMER THAN	1068	V	
THAN THIS, I KNOW NO MORE.	FURTHER IN SUMMER THAN	1068	V	
IF I AM THERE--ONE DOES NOT KNOW	WHEN THEY COME BACK--IF	1080		13
I KNOW FOR I HAVE TRIED	BETWEEN THE FORM OF LIFE	1101		8
WE DO NOT KNOW THE TIME WE LOSE--	WE DO NOT KNOW THE TIME	1106		1
THAN PERSONS, THAT WE KNOW.	THE MURMURING OF BEES,	1115		16
PROMETHEUS NEVER KNEW--[DID NOT KNOW]	THE SMOULDERING EMBERS	1132		8
HOWEVER, KNOW NOT I.	THE DUTIES OF THE WIND	1137		16
NOW KNOW I--THEY BOTH VISITED	I NOTICED PEOPLE	1149		5
SURPASSES IT, WE KNOW, BECAUSE	THE LIFE WE HAVE IS VERY	1162		3
WE NEVER KNOW HOW HIGH WE ARE	WE NEVER KNOW HOW HIGH	1176		1
WHAT WE SEE WE KNOW SOMEWHAT	WHAT WE SEE WE KNOW	1195		1
I KNOW 'TIS DRY--	BECAUSE MY BROOK IS	1200		2
UNPROVED IS MUCH WE KNOW--	THE FROST WAS NEVER SEEN	1202		13
WE FUNDAMENTAL KNOW	IMMORTAL IS AN AMPLE	1205		6
NOT A TOMORROW TO KNOW IT'S NAME	THE POPULAR HEART IS A	1226		5
WHEN WE [I] DESIRED TO KNOW,	WHO WERE "THE FATHER AND	1258		14
I CANNOT SEE MY SOUL BUT KNOW 'TIS THERE	I CANNOT SEE MY SOUL BUT	1262		1
THE WAY TO KNOW THE BOBOLINK	THE WAY TO KNOW THE	1279		1
I KNOW SUSPENSE--IT STEPS SO TERSE	I KNOW SUSPENSE--IT	1285		1
I DO NOT KNOW THE MAN SO BOLD	I NEVER HEAR THAT ONE IS	1323		13
SAFER NOT TO KNOW--	WHETHER THEY HAVE	1329		4
HARDENED [FASTENED] WITH I KNOW--	WHETHER THEY HAVE	1329		8
NOT WHEN WE KNOW, THE POWER ACCOSTS--	LET ME NOT MAR THAT	1335		5
HOW KNOW IT FROM A SUMMER'S DAY?	HOW KNOW IT FROM A	1364		1
WE KNOW THAT WE ARE WISE--	HOW FITS HIS UMBER COAT	1371		9
IT MAY BE KNOW SO CERTAINLY	PERHAPS THEY DO NOT GO	1399		5
TO PITY THOSE THAT [WHO] KNOW HER NOT	WHAT MYSTERY PERVADES A	1400		21
THAT THOSE WHO KNOW HER, KNOW HER LESS	WHAT MYSTERY PERVADES A	1400		23
THAT THOSE WHO KNOW HER, KNOW HER LESS	WHAT MYSTERY PERVADES A	1400		23
THE THINGS WE DO NOT KNOW--	MARCH IS THE MONTH OF	1404		2
ALL WE KNOW	OF PARADISE' EXISTENCE	1411		2
THAT KNOWS--AND DOES NOT KNOW--	SWEET SKEPTICISM OF THE	1413		2
RESERVED FOR US TO KNOW	HOW HUMAN NATURE DOTES	1417		6
HIS OUTLETS--WOULD YOU SEE [KNOW]	SUCH ARE THE INLETS OF	1421		2
TRADITION OUGHT TO KNOW--	SO GAY A FLOWER	1456		5
TO KNOW THAT IT IS THEM!--	"AND WITH WHAT BODY DO	1492		6

	FIRST LINE	POEM	LINE
KNOW (CONTINUED)			
I KNOW HIS EYE	ALL THAT I DO	1496	4
WE NEVER KNOW--	FACTS BY OUR SIDE ARE	1497	6
THE PRESENT DID NOT KNOW HER	SHE COULD NOT LIVE UPON	1505	2
NOT SEEING, STILL WE KNOW--	NOT SEEING, STILL WE	1518	1
THAT DOES'NT KNOW ITS NAME	THE BUTTERFLY UPON THE	1521	2
WE NEVER KNOW WE GO WHEN WE ARE GOING--	WE NEVER KNOW WE GO WHEN	1523	1
AND WE ACCOST NO MORE--[WE KNOW]	WE NEVER KNOW WE GO WHEN	1523	4
THE ONES ALLOWED TO KNOW	THE MOON UPON HER FLUENT	1528	6
KNOW THAT WHICH MAKES THEM AS FORGOT	THE MOON UPON HER FLUENT	1528	7
TO KNOW HER AN INTEMPERANCE [A DISPARAGEMENT / AN EMBARRASSMENT]	TO SEE HER IS A PICTURE	1568	3
TO KNOW HER NOT--AFFLICTION--	TO SEE HER IS A PICTURE	1568	5
DOES THAT KNOW--NOW--OR DOES IT CEASE--	THE SPIRIT LASTS--BUT IN	1576	13
IT WOULD NOT KNOW IF IT WERE SPURNED,	IT WOULD NOT KNOW IF IT	1579	1
SHE DID NOT KNOW HER STATION LOW	TO HER DERIDED HOME	1586	3
FOR WHAT, HE IS PRESUMED TO KNOW--	OF GOD WE ASK ONE FAVOR,	1601	3
THE GOING FROM A WORLD WE KNOW	THE GOING FROM A WORLD	1603	1
SHE DOES NOT KNOW A ROUTE	QUITE EMPTY, QUITE AT	1606	3
IMPOSSIBLE TO KNOW--	A LANE OF YELLOW LED THE	1650	8
HE OTHERWISE MAY KNOW	HIS MIND OF MAN, A	1663	6
I KNOW OF PEOPLE IN THE GRAVE	I KNOW OF PEOPLE IN THE	1665	1
TO KNOW THE NEWS I KNOW TO-NIGHT	I KNOW OF PEOPLE IN THE	1665	3
TO KNOW THE NEWS I KNOW TO-NIGHT	I KNOW OF PEOPLE IN THE	1665	3
I KNOW THEE BETTER FOR THE ACT	I SEE THEE CLEARER FOR	1666	5
I KNOW IT IS A SIGN	IF I COULD TELL HOW GLAD	1668	5
THE TRUTH I DO NOT DARE TO KNOW	CONSULTING SUMMER'S	1715	7
VANQUISHED, MY SOUL WILL KNOW	I'VE GOT AN ARROW HERE.	1729	5
PARTING IS ALL WE KNOW OF HEAVEN,	MY LIFE CLOSED TWICE	1732	7
THEIR NAMES, UNLESS YOU KNOW THEM,	THE MOST IMPORTANT	1746	5
IS ALL WE KNOW OF LOVE;	THAT LOVE IS ALL THERE	1765	2
KNOWEST			
KNOWEST THOU THE SHORE	ON THIS WONDROUS SEA	4	4
THOU KNOWEST EVERY WO--	ONLY A SHRINE, BUT MINE	918	5
THOU KNOWEST, THOUGH, SO WHY TELL THEE?	ONLY A SHRINE, BUT MINE	918	12
"OLD FRIEND, THOU KNOWEST [KNEWEST] ME,"	I HEARD, AS IF I HAD NO	1039	14
KNOWING			
KNOWING THAT BIRD OF MINE	I HAVE A BIRD IN SPRING	5	8
KNOWING THAT BIRD OF MINE	I HAVE A BIRD IN SPRING	5	26
WITHOUT THE KNOWING WHY!	HEART, NOT SO HEAVY AS	83	16
AND FINISHED [GOT THROUGH--] KNOWING--THEN--	I FELT A FUNERAL, IN MY	280	20
THROUGH KNOWING--WHERE WE ONLY HOPE [GUESS]--	THOSE FAIR--FICTITIOUS	499	15
THERE IS A [GOOD] STRENGTH IN PROVING [KNOWING] THAT IT CAN BE . . .	THERE IS A STRENGTH IN	1113	1
LET MY FIRST KNOWING BE OF THEE	LET MY FIRST KNOWING BE	1218	1
'TIS HARDER KNOWING IT IS DUE	WHILE WE WERE FEARING IT	1277	7
THAN KNOWING IT IS HERE.	WHILE WE WERE FEARING IT	1277	8
WONDER--IS NOT PRECISELY KNOWING	WONDER--IS NOT PRECISELY	1331	1
AND NOT PRECISELY KNOWING NOT--	WONDER--IS NOT PRECISELY	1331	2
NOT KNOWING, GUESS--	NOT SEEING, STILL WE	1518	2
NOT KNOWING WHEN THE DAWN WILL [HERSELF MAY] COME,	NOT KNOWING WHEN THE	1619	1
KNOWLEDGE			
THAT HAD I BALLET KNOWLEDGE--	I CANNOT DANCE UPON MY	326	5
'TIS A TRIFLING KNOWLEDGE--	I COULD DIE--TO KNOW--	570	2
KNOWN			
I'VE KNOWN PERMISSION GIVEN	A THROE UPON THE	71	7
I'VE KNOWN A HEAVEN, LIKE A TENT--	I'VE KNOWN A HEAVEN,	243	1
THEIR COMING, MAY BE KNOWN	ALONE, I CANNOT BE--	298	9
I'VE KNOWN HER--FROM AN AMPLE NATION--	THE SOUL SELECTS HER OWN	303	9
THE HIMMALEH WAS KNOWN TO STOOP	THE HIMMALEH WAS KNOWN	481	1
CONTENTED, KNOWN, BEFORE--	LIKE FLOWERS, THAT HEARD	513	12
BUT ONLY TO HIMSELF--BE KNOWN	SHE ROSE TO HIS	732	11
THE LIKEST I HAVE KNOWN--	THE MOON WAS BUT A CHIN	737	8
GONE--AS SOON AS KNOWN--	SO THE EYES ACCOST--AND	752	8
BEST [ALL] HORIZON--GONE [KNOWN]--	NO BOBOLINK--REVERSE HIS	755	7
NO OTHER KISS HAD KNOWN	HE TOLD A HOMELY TALE	763	6
WHO BOUNTY--HAVE NOT KNOWN--	NONE CAN EXPERIENCE	771	2
A HOARY BOY, I'VE KNOWN TO DROP	NOT ALL DIE EARLY, DYING	990	5
THE LARGEST FIRE EVER KNOWN	THE LARGEST FIRE EVER	1114	1
HAD WE KNOWN THE TON [WEIGHT / LOAD] SHE BORE	HAD WE KNOWN THE TON SHE	1124	1
NATURE AFFECTS [WAS KNOWN] TO BE SEDATE	NATURE AFFECTS TO BE	1170	1
BUT ARE NOT KNOWN TO EARN--	ALL MEN FOR HONOR	1193	2
KNOWN ONLY TO THE DEW--	DOMINION LASTS UNTIL	1257	6
I'VE KNOWN	NOT WITH A CLUB, THE	1304	4
KNOWN TO [OF] THE KNOLL--	PINK--SMALL--AND	1332	6
NOT ANY MORE TO BE KNOWN--	NOT ANY MORE TO BE	1344	2
NOT ANYTHING IS KNOWN	HOPE IS A STRANGE	1392	6
NO PASSENGER WAS KNOWN TO FLEE--	NO PASSENGER WAS KNOWN	1406	1
BY HIS INTRUSION, GOD IS KNOWN--	WE KNEW NOT THAT WE WERE	1462	7
IT'S [THY] SWEETNESS TO HAVE KNOWN--	ONE THING OF IT WE	1464	4
THE SWEETS OF PILLAGE, CAN BE KNOWN	THE SWEETS OF PILLAGE,	1470	1
BUT HAVE SAGES KNOWN?	LOVE IS DONE WHEN LOVE'S	1485	3
PRECISELY HOW IT ENDED [IS IT KNOWN]	I SAW THE WIND WITHIN	1502	V
RECOUNTING NECTARS HE HAS KNOWN	HIS ORIENTAL HERESIES	1526	V
NOTWITHSTANDING IT NEVER BE KNOWN	TO DO A MAGNANIMOUS	1699	6
HAD I KNOWN THAT THE FIRST WAS THE LAST	HAD I KNOWN THAT THE	1720	1
HAD I KNOWN THAT THE LAST WAS THE FIRST	HAD I KNOWN THAT THE	1720	3
KNOWS			
NOBODY KNOWS THIS LITTLE ROSE--	NOBODY KNOWS THIS LITTLE	35	1

	FIRST LINE	POEM	LINE
KNOWS (CONTINUED)			
WHO KNOWS BUT THIS SURRENDERED FACE . . .	DELAYED TILL SHE HAD	58	11
WHO KNOWS?	GOING TO HEAVEN!	79	12
AND NOBODY KNOWS, SO STILL IT FLOWS, . . .	HAVE YOU GOT A BROOK IN	136	5
WHO KNOWS BUT SHE WOULD TELL?	THE SKIES CANT KEEP	191	8
SHE KNOWS HERSELF AN INCENSE [OFFERING] SMALL--	THE DROP, THAT WRESTLES	284	4
THAT KNOWS--IT CANNOT SEE--	THE DIFFERENCE BETWEEN	305	8
KNOWS HOW TO FORGET!	KNOWS HOW TO FORGET!	433	1
WHO KNOWS BUT WE--	LOVE--THOU ART HIGH--	453	4
WHO KNOWS--BUT WE'D REACH THE SUN? . . .	LOVE--THOU ART HIGH--	453	12
BECAUSE HE KNOWS--AND	"WHY DO I LOVE" YOU, SIR	480	6
BECAUSE HE KNOWS IT CANNOT SPEAK-- . . .	"WHY DO I LOVE" YOU, SIR	480	13
WHO KNOWS--BUT AT THE SIGHT OF THAT . . .	I'LL SEND THE FEATHER	687	2
'TIS [THAT'S] THIS--AND WITCHCRAFT--NATURE KEEPS [KNOWS / HAS]	THE COLOR OF A QUEEN, IS	776	7
THAT KNOWS NOT AN UNTIL--	THE SERVICE WITHOUT HOPE	779	8
SINCE NO ONE KNOWS HIS CIRCUMSTANCE-- . .	WHO OCCUPIES THIS HOUSE?	892	3
WHICH IS THE DESPOT, NEITHER KNOWS-- . . .	I MAKE HIS CRESCENT FILL	909	11
WHERE DAWN--KNOWS HOW TO BE--	I LEARNED--AT LEAST--	944	31
WHAT DEATH--KNOWS SO WELL--	COLOR--CASTE--	970	14
NOR DIFFERENCE IT KNOWS	FURTHER IN SUMMER THAN	1068	V
NATURE KNOWS AS WELL	HER SOVREIGN PEOPLE	1139	2
NOBODY KNOWS [KNEW] THE PLACE	AFTER A HUNDRED YEARS	1147	2
AND KNOWS NO OTHER JOY	A LITTLE DOG THAT WAGS	1185	2
KNOWS THE ADDER [ADDERS] TONGUE HIS COMING .	WE LIKE MARCH.	1213	6
UNTIL THE DESERT KNOWS	UNTIL THE DESERT KNOWS	1291	1
PORTENTOUS AS OUR OWN, WHO KNOWS?	WHOSE PINK CAREER MAY	1394	2
THAT KNOWS--AND DOES NOT KNOW--	SWEET SKEPTICISM OF THE	1413	2
NOR RAFTER--HAS [MARS / KNOWS] THAT EDIFICE	THE WAY HOPE BUILDS HIS	1481	3
AS EVERY PORTER KNOWS--	HER LOSSES MAKE OUR	1562	6
THAT ONLY CHILDHOOD KNOWS.	SWEET IS THE SWAMP WITH	1740	6
BUT JUST THE SUMMER KNOWS.	THOSE FINAL CREATURES,--	1766	4
KNOW'ST			
UNLESS THOU KNOW'ST THE TUNE	TOUCH LIGHTLY NATURE'S	1389	2
LABOR			
THEREFORE--WE DO LIFE'S LABOR--	I TIE MY HAT--I CREASE	443	30
MY LABOR AND MY LEISURE TOO, ...	BECAUSE I COULD NOT STOP	712	7
HIS LABOR IS A CHANT--	HIS FEET ARE SHOD WITH	916	5
YOUR PROBLEM [LABOR]--OF THE BRAIN--	I LEARNED--AT LEAST--	944	15
THE LABOR IS A SOBER ONE	I FIT FOR THEM--	1109	4
BUT LABOR VASTER THAN MYSELF	THE FROST WAS NEVER SEEN	1202	19
'TWILL BE A LABOR OF SURPRISE--	THAT SACRED CLOSET WHEN	1273	5
BUT WE MUST LABOR NOW	I DID NOT REACH THEE	1664	17
LABORED			
THE ANGELS--LABORED DILIGENT--	GOOD NIGHT! WHICH PUT	259	5
TO SINK, IF WE HAD LABORED, FOND	WHAT TWIGS WE HELD BY--	1086	12
LABORETH			
HE LABORETH AT EVERY TREE	HIS BILL AN AUGUR IS	1034	3
LABORING			
TILL LABORING TO FLEE	NO MAN SAW AWE, NOR TO	1733	6
LABORIOUS			
TO THIS LABORIOUS BOY--	HOW GOOD HIS LAVA BED,	1447	2
LABORS			
THOUGH WHERE IT'S LABORS LIE	WHY SHOULD WE HURRY--WHY	1646	7
LACE			
'TIS DIMMER THAN A LACE--	'TIS WHITER THAN AN	1482	2
LACERATING			
MAKES LACERATING TUNE--	UPON CONCLUDED LIVES	735	5
LACES			
AS LACES JUST REVEAL THE SURGE--	THE THOUGHT BENEATH SO	210	3
OR LACES--OR A TRAVELLING SHOW--	WHAT IF I SAY I SHALL	277	11
BONNET OF EVERLASTING LACES--	DROPPED INTO THE ETHER	665	3
LACK			
TO LACK--ENAMOR THEE--	'TIS OPPOSITES--ENTICE--	355	9
AND SIGH FOR LACK OF HEAVEN--BUT NOT . . .	THE WAY I READ A	636	15
FAME OF MYSELF TO LACK--ALTHOUGH	FAME OF MYSELF, TO	713	5
I MAKE HIS CRESCENT FILL OR LACK--	I MAKE HIS CRESCENT FILL	909	1
HOW SWEET I SHALL NOT LACK IN VAIN--	FITTER TO SEE HIM, I MAY	968	25
TO LACK OF IT IS WOE--	BEHOLD THIS LITTLE BANE	1438	5
LACKED			
NOT ANY MORE TO BE LACKED--	NOT ANY MORE TO BE	1344	1
LACONIC			
INDUSTRIOUS! LACONIC!	DUST IS THE ONLY SECRET	153	9
LAD			
LOVE THE DULL LAD--BEST--	DID WE DISOBEY HIM?	267	7
ANOTHER LAD--HELP THEE--	A TONGUE--TO TELL HIM I	400	17
THE BEGGAR LAD--DIES EARLY--	THE BEGGAR LAD--DIES	717	1
LAD OF ATHENS, FAITHFUL BE	LAD OF ATHENS, FAITHFUL	1768	1
LADDER			
NO LADDER NEEDS THE BIRD BUT SKIES . . .	NO LADDER NEEDS THE BIRD	1574	1
LADDER'S			
AND THEN THE LADDER'S THROWN AWAY, . . .	DOOM IS THE HOUSE	475	3
LADDERS			
THE MAKER'S LADDERS STOP--	A SOLEMN THING WITHIN	483	4
LADEN			
IS LADEN WITH A SINGLE CRUMB	THE LUXURY TO APPREHEND	815	15
FROM HEAVY LADEN LANDS [CLIMES] TO THEE . .	THE BIRD DID PRANCE--THE	1107	9
LADIES			
LADIES--WITH PARASOLS--	IT WILL BE SUMMER--	342	2

	FIRST LINE	POEM	LINE
LADIES (CONTINUED)			
OVAL--AS FEUDAL LADIES WORE--	I AM ASHAMED--I HIDE--	473	14
AS NEEDLES--LADIES SOFTLY PRESS	IT CEASED TO HURT ME,	584	10
THIS QUIET DUST WAS GENTLEMEN AND LADIES	THIS QUIET DUST WAS	813	1
LADS			
AND LADS AND GIRLS--	THIS QUIET DUST WAS	813	2
LADY			
TO SOME FASHIONABLE LADY	I CANT TELL YOU--BUT YOU	65	15
A LADY RED--AMID THE HILL	A LADY RED--AMID THE	74	1
A LADY WHITE, WITHIN THE FIELD	A LADY RED--AMID THE	74	3
THEN, FINER THAN A LADY,	A FUZZY FELLOW, WITHOUT	173	13
THE LADY JUST UNROLLED--	THE DAY CAME SLOW--TILL	304	8
THE LADY CROSS, OR NOT?	IS BLISS THEN, SUCH	340	13
AS LADY FROM HER DOOR	FROM COCOON FORTH A	354	2
REDEMPTION--BRITTLE LADY--	WHAT SOFT--CHERUBIC	401	11
THE LADY DARE NOT LIFT HER VAIL	A CHARM INVESTS A FACE	421	3
FORGET! THE LADY WITH THE AMULET	FORGET! THE LADY WITH	438	1
THE LADY WITH THE AMULET--WILL FADE--	FORGET! THE LADY WITH	438	9
I READ THAT FOREIGN LADY--	I THINK I WAS ENCHANTED	593	3
THE LADY IN THE TOWN	I WATCHED THE MOON	629	6
TO THE LADY	SO MUCH SUMMER	651	6
MAKE SUMMER--WHEN THE LADY LIE	ESSENTIAL OILS--ARE	675	7
THE LADY OF THE OCCIDENT	THE DAY UNDRESSED--	716	11
"SWEET LADY--CHARITY"--	THE BEGGAR LAD--DIES	717	8
WHEN THE LONE BRITISH LADY	WHEN THE ASTRONOMER	851	3
BUT IF THE LADY COME	THE BIRD MUST SING TO	880	6
THE LADY FEEDS HER LITTLE BIRD	THE LADY FEEDS HER	941	1
LADY, DID HE BELONG TO THEE?	TRUDGING TO EDEN,	1020	4
AS LADY FROM HER BOWER--	TO HER DERIDED HOME	1586	8
WERE NATURE MORTAL LADY	WERE NATURE MORTAL LADY	1762	1
LADY'S			
MIGHT HE BUT SPY THE LADY'S [HIDING] SOUL--	JUST SO--JESUS--RAPS--	317	6
UNTO THE LADY'S FACE--	I HAD NOT MINDED--WALLS	398	14
HEMS--TOO FINE FOR LADY'S TRACING	DONT PUT UP MY THREAD &	617	9
BUT [WHILE] THIS--IN LADY'S DRAWER	ESSENTIAL OILS--ARE	675	6
BUT LONG RECORDS THE LADY'S NAME	THE ROBIN FOR THE CRUMB	864	3
TO GAIN RENOWN OF LADY'S DRAWER	THE BIRD MUST SING TO	880	5
LAGGING			
HASTE! LEST WHILE YOU'RE LAGGING	HEART! WE WILL FORGET	47	7
OH LAGGING YESTERDAY!	DELAYED TILL SHE HAD	58	6
LAID			
LAID DOWN ON BUNKER HILL;	"SIC TRANSIT GLORIA	3	46
ALSO, WHO LAID THE RAINBOW'S PIERS,	BRING ME THE SUNSET IN A	128	13
IN QUIET "HAWORTH" LAID.	ALL OVERGROWN BY CUNNING	148	4
SHOULD BE A-DREAMING LAID.	I CAUTIOUS, SCANNED MY	178	4
LIKE [AS] LOWLY SPICES, LAIN TO SLEEP [GONE TO SLEEP / LAID . . .	THE GRASS SO LITTLE HAS	333	15
. . . ASLEEP / LAID TO SLEEP]--	THE GRASS SO LITTLE HAS	333	15
THE BEE--IN MAUSOLEUM LAID--	FORGET! THE LADY WITH	438	10
RETIRED [LAID DOWN] WITHOUT A CARE--	THE DAY UNDRESSED--	716	12
THEY WERE IN PRISON LAID	OF PAUL AND SILAS IT IS	1166	2
THE CLOUDS THEIR BACKS TOGETHER LAID	THE CLOUDS THEIR BACKS	1172	1
THAT EVER MASON LAID--	REMEMBRANCE HAS A	1182	6
HERE IS LAID AWAY	FORTITUDE INCARNATE	1217	2
THE TABLE IS NOT LAID WITHOUT	WHO GOES TO DINE MUST	1223	3
TILL IT IS LAID WITHIN.	WHO GOES TO DINE MUST	1223	4
SUMMER LAID HER SIMPLE HAT	SUMMER LAID HER SIMPLE	1363	1
SUMMER LAID HER SUPPLE GLOVE	SUMMER LAID HER SIMPLE	1363	5
AFTER ALL BIRDS HAVE BEEN INVESTIGATED AND LAID ASIDE--	AFTER ALL BIRDS HAVE	1395	1
SHE [HE] LAID HER [HIS] DOCILE CRESCENT DOWN	SHE LAID HER DOCILE	1396	1
MY WARS ARE LAID AWAY IN BOOKS--	MY WARS ARE LAID AWAY IN	1549	1
HIS ACTION LAID AWAY	JUDGEMENT IS JUSTEST	1671	3
A GRASP ON COMPREHENSION LAID	NO MAN SAW AWE, NOR TO	1733	7
LAIN			
LAIN SO LOW,	WHEN I COUNT THE SEEDS	40	5
THE BOSOMS WHERE THE FROST HAS LAIN	I BRING AN UNACCUSTOMED	132	12
INDOLENT HOUSEWIFE--IN DAISIES--LAIN!	HOW MANY TIMES THESE LOW	187	12
WHERE MIDNIGHT FROSTS--HAD LAIN!	I SHOULD NOT DARE TO	205	16
LIKE [AS] LOWLY SPICES, LAIN TO SLEEP [GONE TO SLEEP / LAID . . .	THE GRASS SO LITTLE HAS	333	15
WHEN ONE WHO DIED FOR TRUTH, WAS LAIN	I DIED FOR BEAUTY--BUT	449	3
IN DORMANT NATURE--LAIN--	A MAN MAY MAKE A REMARK	952	4
TODAY IN MEMORY LAIN	TO DISAPPEAR ENHANCES--	1209	6
LAIN IN NATURE--SO SUFFICE US	LAIN IN NATURE--SO	1288	1
THE FACE IN EVANESCENCE LAIN	THE FACE IN EVANESCENCE	1490	1
HAVE LAIN THEIR MISSILES BY--	THE FARTHEST THUNDER	1581	4
LAKE			
THE STAR'S WHOLE SECRET--IN THE LAKE--	THE OUTER--FROM THE	451	15
LAMB			
AT SUPPER OF THE LAMB.	THERE CAME A DAY AT	322	16
GOD BROKE HIS CONTRACT TO HIS LAMB	HOW RUTHLESS ARE THE	1439	3
LAMBS			
LAMBS FOR WHOM TIME HAD NOT A FOLD.	SOME, TOO FRAGILE FOR	141	12
LAME			
TILL YOU WASTE [FURL / LAME] YOUR EYE--	FOLLOW WISE ORION	1538	2
LAMP			
THE LAMP BURNS SURE--WITHIN--	THE LAMP BURNS SURE--	233	1
THE LAMP--BURNS GOLDEN--ON--	THE LAMP BURNS SURE--	233	6
IT MIGHT--HAVE BEEN THE WANING LAMP	GOOD NIGHT! WHICH PUT	259	10

	FIRST LINE	POEM	LINE
LAMP (CONTINUED)			
AS WHEN THE NEIGHBOR HOLDS THE LAMP . . .	WE GROW ACCUSTOMED TO	419	3
AT NIGHT, MY LITTLE LAMP, AND BOOK-- . . .	I WAS THE SLIGHTEST IN	486	3
THE MINER'S LAMP--SUFFICIENT BE--	I SEE THEE BETTER--IN	611	7
A LAMP FOR EACH--TO SET--	THE SUNRISE RUNS FOR	710	8
HIS FADED LAMP WENT OUT.	THAT ODD OLD MAN IS DEAD	1130	4
LAMPS			
AT LAST, THE LAMPS UPON THY [YOUR] SIDE . .	AT LAST, TO BE	174	2
AS WILL SUFFICE TO LIGHT HER LAMPS-- . . .	NATURE--THE GENTLEST	790	19
THE POETS LIGHT BUT LAMPS--	THE POETS LIGHT BUT	883	1
LAND			
LAND HO! ETERNITY!	ON THIS WONDROUS SEA	4	11
HELD IN A TRUER LAND	I HAVE A BIRD IN SPRING	5	14
AND POUNDS WERE IN THE LAND--	I HAD A GUINEA GOLDEN--	23	4
THERE MAY YET BE LAND!	ONCE MORE, MY NOW	48	8
OR WHAT CIRCASSIAN LAND?	SOME RAINBOW--COMING	64	24
OF THE FIRST LEAGUE OUT FROM LAND?	EXULTATION IS THE GOING	76	8
LAND--BY THE OCEANS PASSED.	WATER, IS TAUGHT BY	135	2
IN A STEADFAST LAND, ...	THO' MY DESTINY BE	163	14
WHEN ONE--TURNED SMILING TO THE LAND-- . .	TWO SWIMMERS WRESTLED ON	201	3
THE INTERDICTED LAND--	"HEAVEN"--IS WHAT I	239	6
I'VE HEARD IT IN THE CHILLEST LAND-- . . .	"HOPE" IS THE THING WITH	254	9
THIS--IS THE LAND--THE SUNSET WASHES-- . .	THIS--IS THE LAND--THE	266	1
TO FAIL--WITH LAND IN SIGHT--	IT MIGHT BE LONELIER	405	14
THEN--HIGHER THAN THE LAND	THE COLOR OF THE GRAVE	411	14
OR EVEN A REPORT OF LAND--	IT WAS NOT DEATH, FOR I	510	23
INTO VAN DIEMAN'S LAND.	IF YOU WERE COMING IN	511	12
UPHOLSTERER OF THE PINES [SEA / LAND / HILLS]--IS HE--	OF BRUSSELS--IT WAS NOT	602	15
FOUR--HAVE RECOVERED THE LAND--	GLEE--THE GREAT STORM IS	619	2
AS WRECKED MEN--DEEM THEY SIGHT THE LAND-- .	I MANY TIMES THOUGHT	739	3
WERE THERE FAMINE IN THE LAND--	MOST SHE TOUCHED ME BY	760	6
THE TRACK CALLED LAND.	AN EVERYWHERE OF SILVER	884	4
TO THE NATIVE LAND.	FAR FROM LOVE THE	1021	8
OSTENSIBLY, ON LAND	A GREAT HOPE FELL	1123	9
THE BROADEST LAND THAT GROWS	STEP LIGHTLY ON THIS	1183	2
THROUGHOUT A CHRISTIAN LAND--	THE SPIDER AS AN ARTIST	1275	6
ASCEND WITH ME THE EMINENCE [TABLE LAND] .	SUCH ARE THE INLETS OF	1421	3
HIS NATIVE LAND--	THE THINGS THAT NEVER	1515	13
ALIGHT IN EVERY LAND	COSMOPOLITES WITHOUT A	1589	2
WILL FEEL AS COOL AS LAND	I DID NOT REACH THEE	1664	11
BUT WITNESS FOR HER LAND, ...	THE EARTH HAS MANY KEYS.	1775	5
LANDING			
STREWS THE LANDING WITH OPAL BALES-- . . .	THIS--IS THE LAND--THE	266	7
LANDINGS			
AS ONE DETECT ON LANDINGS	A SOUTH WIND--HAS A	719	3
LANDLORD			
WHO IS THE LANDLORD?	WHAT INN IS THIS	115	4
NECROMANCER! LANDLORD!	WHAT INN IS THIS	115	9
LANDLORDS			
WHEN "LANDLORDS" TURN THE DRUNKEN BEE . .	I TASTE A LIQUOR NEVER	214	9
LANDS			
IN LANDS I NEVER SAW--THEY SAY	IN LANDS I NEVER SAW--	124	1
HAUNTED BY NATIVE LANDS, THE WHILE-- . . .	TO LEARN THE TRANSPORT	167	7
BOUND TO OPPOSING LANDS--	THERE CAME A DAY AT	322	20
AND LANDS HE LOOKS UPON	A COFFIN--IS A SMALL	943	8
FROM HEAVY LADEN LANDS [CLIMES] TO THEE . .	THE BIRD DID PRANCE--THE	1107	9
I SHALL VOTE FOR LANDS WITH LOCKS	WHAT WE SEE WE KNOW	1195	5
TO TAKE US [ONE] LANDS AWAY	THERE IS NO FRIGATE LIKE	1263	2
THE LANDS WE THOUGHT THAT WE SHOULD SEEK .	THE THINGS WE THOUGHT	1293	5
LANDSCAPE			
I "VIEW THE LANDSCAPE O'ER;"	"SIC TRANSIT GLORIA	3	22
AND YET, HOW STILL THE LANDSCAPE STANDS! .	A LADY RED--AMID THE	74	13
AND VIEW THE LANDSCAPE O'ER"	WHERE BELLS NO MORE	112	10
SCAN LIKE HIM, THE STATELY LANDSCAPE . . .	IF THE FOOLISH, CALL	168	11
WHEN IT COMES, THE LANDSCAPE LISTENS-- . .	THERE'S A CERTAIN SLANT	258	13
WILL TINT THE PALLID LANDSCAPE--	IT WILL BE SUMMER--	342	5
THE ANGLE OF A LANDSCAPE--	THE ANGLE OF A LANDSCAPE	375	1
A LANDSCAPE--NOT SO GREAT	IT'S THOUGHTS--AND JUST	495	17
THE GARDEN [LANDSCAPE] KEEP [SHOW / OWN / HOLD] THE GASH--	AS FROST IS BEST	951	6
AS LIGHTNING ON A LANDSCAPE	THE SOUL'S DISTINCT	974	5
MINUTER LANDSCAPE AS OURSELVES	LIKE MEN AND WOMEN	1105	7
LANDSCAPES			
THE EAGER LOOK--ON LANDSCAPES--	THE TINT I CANNOT TAKE--	627	13
LANE			
THROUGH LANE IT LAY--THRO' BRAMBLE--	THROUGH LANE IT LAY--	9	1
BY BOBOLINK FROM LANE.	I KEEP MY PLEDGE.	46	8
ONE GOSSIPPED IN THE LANE	THE TREES LIKE TASSELS--	606	18
A LANE OF YELLOW LED THE EYE	A LANE OF YELLOW LED THE	1650	1
LANES			
AND STRUGGLES IN THE LANES--	I KNOW A PLACE WHERE	337	6
AND TWILIGHT--IN THE LANES--	I LEARNED--AT LEAST--	944	19
LANGUAGE			
MANY A PHRASE HAS THE ENGLISH LANGUAGE-- .	MANY A PHRASE HAS THE	276	1
SAY IT AGAIN, SAXON [ENGLISH LANGUAGE]! . .	MANY A PHRASE HAS THE	276	15
FOR LANGUAGE, AND THE WIND	TWO TRAVELLERS PERISHING	933	8
WORDS ARE HANDED [LANGUAGE IS DRIVEN] AWAY--	WHATEVER IT IS--SHE HAS	1204	8
LIKE THIS CONSENT OF LANGUAGE	A WORD MADE FLESH IS	1651	15

	FIRST LINE	POEM	LINE
LANGUID			
AND [HE] PANTING [HEAVY / LANGUID] ON A CLOVER LEAN	THE BUTTERFLY'S NUMIDIAN	1387	5
LANGUOR			
THERE IS A LANGUOR OF THE LIFE	THERE IS A LANGUOR OF	396	1
LANK			
PINK LANK AND WARM	IN WINTER IN MY ROOM	1670	3
LAP			
AND HOLD THE SUNSHINE IN IT'S LAP	THE GRASS SO LITTLE HAS	333	7
INTO THE LAP OF ADAMANT--	I KNOW A PLACE WHERE	337	9
WHILE IT AND I LAP ONE AIR	WHILE IT IS ALIVE	491	3
I LIKE TO SEE [HEAR] IT LAP THE MILES--	I LIKE TO SEE IT LAP	585	1
LAPLAND'S			
LAPLAND'S--NESCESSITY--	I THINK THE HEMLOCK	525	8
LAPS			
PASSIVE--AS GRANITE--LAPS MY MUSIC--	PUT UP MY LUTE!	261	4
AS THE STARVED MAELSTROM LAPS THE NAVIES	AS THE STARVED MAELSTROM	872	1
LAPSE			
FAINT-GOING LIVES [EYES]--THEIR LAPSE FROM SIGHING--	"MORNING"--MEANS	300	9
THROUGH DECAY [FATIGUE / THE LAPSE] OF YOU--	SWEET--YOU FORGOT--BUT I	523	4
IT KNEW NO LAPSE, NOR DIMINUTION--	IT KNEW NO LAPSE, NOR	560	1
THAT HURT THEM EARLY--SUCH A LAPSE	I MEASURE EVERY GRIEF I	561	19
I HINTED CHANGES--LAPSE OF TIME--	IF HE WERE LIVING--DARE	734	5
AND CENTURIES OF AUGUST CEASE [FUSE / LAPSE / BLEND]	THERE IS A ZONE WHOSE	1056	7
PERHAPS COME [COMES] CLOSER, FOR THE LAPSE [FLIGHT]	PERHAPS THEY DO NOT GO	1399	3
LAPSED			
THE SUMMER LAPSED AWAY--	AS IMPERCEPTIBLY AS	1540	2
LAPWING'S			
OR THE LAPWING'S SHORE!	THE GUEST IS GOLD AND	15	10
LARCENY			
LARCENY--LEGACY--	THE FEET OF PEOPLE	7	14
THAT LARCENY OF TIME AND MIND	ALONE AND IN A	1167	25
THE ONLY THING WORTH LARCENY	TAKE ALL AWAY--	1365	2
LARDER			
A ROBIN'S LARDER	SO MUCH SUMMER	651	10
HIS LARDER--TERSE AND MILITANT--	NO BRIGADIER THROUGHOUT	1561	19
LARGE			
IS IT TOO LARGE FOR YOU?	SAVIOR! I'VE NO ONE ELSE	217	12
PERHAPS I ASKED TOO LARGE--	PERHAPS I ASKED TOO	352	1
A HEAVEN NOT SO LARGE AS YOUR'S,	I MEANT TO HAVE BUT	476	11
BUT LARGE ENOUGH--FOR ME--	I MEANT TO HAVE BUT	476	12
BE LARGE ENOUGH FOR ME--	I HAD NO TIME TO HATE--	478	12
WAS IT GOLIAH--WAS TOO LARGE--	I TOOK MY POWER IN MY	540	7
BUT LARGE--SERENE--	IT KNEW NO LAPSE, NOR	560	2
ALAS, THAT WISDOM IS SO LARGE--	WE LEARNED THE WHOLE OF	568	11
THE GNAT'S SUPREMACY IS LARGE AS THINE--	A TOAD, CAN DIE OF LIGHT	583	7
"AS LARGE AS I"--RELATE THE SUN	LOVE RECKONS BY ITSELF--	826	2
IT HOLDS AS LARGE A GLOW	LIGHT IS SUFFICIENT TO	862	6
A SMALLER [LESSER] THAN THE LARGE--	LOVE--IS THAT LATER	924	12
DEATH'S LARGE--DEMOCRATIC FINGERS	COLOR--CASTE--	970	7
'TWAS NOT SO LARGE THAT I	THE MISSING ALL,	985	6
SO LARGE MY WILL	SO LARGE MY WILL	1024	1
IT WAS NOT SAINT--IT WAS TOO LARGE--	IT WAS NOT SAINT--IT WAS	1092	1
AND LARGE [MOST] IN COURTESY--	THE MERCHANT OF THE	1131	6
WHEN LARGE ENOUGH TO RUN	THE THINGS WE THOUGHT	1293	6
LARGER			
LARGER THAN MINE--SERENER--	LOW AT MY PROBLEM	69	3
IMPLORE A LARGER--THING--	THE COURT IS FAR AWAY--	235	8
HOW LARGER--BE?	THE DROP, THAT WRESTLES	284	6
AND SO OF LARGER--DARKNESSES--	WE GROW ACCUSTOMED TO	419	9
THE LARGER, AS HER [MY] FACE WITHDREW--	I SHOWED HER HIGHTS SHE	446	11
ENLIGHTENED TO A LARGER PAIN--	I MEASURE EVERY GRIEF I	561	23
LIFE SET ME LARGER--PROBLEMS--	IT TROUBLED ME AS ONCE I	600	9
BE LARGER--AS THE SEA	'TIS GOOD--THE LOOKING	660	10
BETTER THAN LARGER VALUES--	THEIR HIGHT IN HEAVEN	696	13
WHEN LARGER FUNCTION--	RENUNCIATION--IS A	745	14
SO LARGER TO MY EYES	ONE BLESSING HAD I THAN	756	2
MY FAITH IS LARGER THAN THE HILLS--	MY FAITH IS LARGER THAN	766	1
LARGER FOR THE [IT'S] TOTALNESS--	ALL I MAY, IF SMALL,	819	3
LESS, THO LARGER, POOR.	ALL I MAY, IF SMALL,	819	8
THE LARGER GLORY FOR THE LESS	HE OUTSTRIPPED TIME WITH	865	7
IF NOTHING LARGER THAN A WORLD'S	THE MISSING ALL,	985	3
THE LARGER--SLOWER GROW	EXCEPT THE SMALLER SIZE	1067	5
A LARGER--IT IS WOE	THE FROST OF DEATH WAS	1136	21
LARGEST			
IF GRIEF--THE LARGEST PART--	FOREVER AT HIS SIDE TO	246	7
FOR LARGEST WOMAN'S HEART I KNEW--	FOR LARGEST WOMAN'S	309	1
AND YET THE LARGEST WOMAN'S HEART	FOR LARGEST WOMAN'S	309	3
LIKE OTHER NEW THINGS--SHOWS LARGEST--THEN--	IT DONT SOUND SO	426	12
WHAT LARGEST LOVER--HATH--	THE TEST OF LOVE--IS	573	3
LARGEST [NEWEST / FRESHEST] DEWS OF MORN	PROMISE THIS--WHEN YOU	648	20
THE LARGEST FIRE EVER KNOWN	THE LARGEST FIRE EVER	1114	1
LARK			
THE LARK IS NOT ASHAMED	FOR EVERY BIRD A NEST--	143	13
OF THE LARK--	AH, MOON--AND STAR!	240	9
CAN THE LARK RESUME THE SHELL--	LET US PLAY YESTERDAY--	728	25
SPLIT THE LARK--AND YOU'LL FIND THE MUSIC--	SPLIT THE LARK--AND	861	1

	FIRST LINE	POEM	LINE
LARK'S			
THE LARK'S PURE TERRITORY--	THE GUEST IS GOLD AND	15	9
LARKS			
WHEN MEN--AND BOYS--AND CARTS [LARKS]--AND JUNE,	I'M SORRY FOR THE DEAD--	529	19
LASH			
HAVE PASSED, I THOUGHT, A WHIP LASH	A NARROW FELLOW IN THE	986	13
TO LASH THE MAGIC CREATURE	NOT WITH A CLUB, THE	1304	5
LASSITUDES			
THE LASSITUDES OF CONTEMPLATION	THE LASSITUDES OF	1592	1
LAST			
ASHORE AT LAST!	ON THIS WONDROUS SEA	4	12
AND WORE MY LAST YEAR'S GOWN--	ONE SISTER HAVE I IN OUR	14	6
WHEN LAST YEAR'S DISTAFF IDLE HUNG	THERE IS A MORN BY MEN	24	11
OF LAST YEAR'S SUNDERED TUNE!	SOME RAINBOW--COMING	64	9
OH LAST COMMUNION IN THE HAZE--	THESE ARE THE DAYS WHEN	130	14
WHEN I AT LAST AWAKE.	I BRING AN UNACCUSTOMED	132	22
AT LAST, TO BE IDENTIFIED!	AT LAST, TO BE	174	1
AT LAST, THE LAMPS UPON THY [YOUR] SIDE	AT LAST, TO BE	174	2
FROM WHAT W'D LAST TILL HEADS LIKE MINE	I CAUTIOUS, SCANNED MY	178	3
MAY NOT AT LAST AVAIL?	IF I COULD BRIBE THEM BY	179	16
LEOPARD BREATHES--AT LAST!	WITH THEE, IN THE DESERT	209	4
LEST MY BESEECHING FACE--AT LAST--	COULD I--THEN--SHUT THE	220	2
NOON--OUR LAST CUP--	WE--BEE AND I--LIVE BY	230	15
OH, COULD YOU CATCH HER LAST REFRAIN--	KILL YOUR BALM--AND IT'S	238	6
"IF IT WOULD LAST"	DELIGHT IS AS THE FLIGHT	257	10
WITH LAST [LEAST] DELIGHT I OWN!	DOUBT ME! MY DIM	275	8
STRAIN TILL YOUR [HER] LAST SURMISE--	DOUBT ME! MY DIM	275	19
HER--"LAST POEMS"--	HER--"LAST POEMS"--	312	1
LAST [FIRST]--AT THE KNOCKER--	JUST SO--JESUS--RAPS--	317	3
DEPOSED--AT LENGTH [LAST], THE GRAVE--	THERE CAME A DAY AT	322	26
SO INSTEAD OF GETTING TO HEAVEN, AT LAST--	SOME KEEP THE SABBATH	324	11
THE FACE I CARRY WITH ME--LAST--	THE FACE I CARRY WITH ME	336	1
THERE--WHERE SHE--RESTED--LAST--	'TWAS THE OLD--ROAD--	344	6
WITH "THIS WAS LAST HER FINGERS DID"--	DEATH SETS A THING	360	7
I KNEW LAST NIGHT--WHEN SOMEONE TRIED TO TWINE--	HOW SICK--TO WAIT--IN	368	2
THE LAST--A SCANTY NUMBER--	I KNOW LIVES, I COULD	372	5
SURRENDERING--THE LAST--	THERE IS A FLOWER THAT	380	30
DID OUR BEST MOMENT LAST--	DID OUR BEST MOMENT LAST	393	1
FORGIVE IT--LAST--	'TWAS LOVE--NOT ME--	394	7
CAUGHT SUNRISE FIRST--AND SUNSET--LAST--	A HOUSE UPON THE HIGHT--	399	7
SAY--LAST I SAID--WAS THIS--	A TONGUE--TO TELL HIM I	400	22
THAT AT THE LAST, IT SHOULD NOT BE A NOVEL AGONY--	I READ MY SENTENCE--	412	10
'TWAS JUST THIS TIME, LAST YEAR, I DIED.	'TWAS JUST THIS TIME,	445	1
DUCAL--AT LAST--STAND UP BY THEE--	LOVE--THOU ART HIGH--	453	6
TO TELL THE VERY LAST THEY SAID	WHY MAKE IT DOUBT--IT	462	5
FOR THAT LAST ONSET--WHEN THE KING	I HEARD A FLY BUZZ--WHEN	465	7
BUT SINCE THE LAST--INCLUDED BOTH--	I MEANT TO HAVE BUT	476	5
AND THROUGH A RIDDLE, AT THE LAST--	THIS WORLD IS NOT	501	7
WHEN THE LAST SAINT--GOES UP THE AISLES--	BETTER--THAN MUSIC! FOR	503	18
SWEPT BY MY SEARCHING EYES--THE LAST--	ME PROVE IT NOW--WHOEVER	537	15
AS THE STARS--YOU KNEW LAST NIGHT--	SOME SUCH BUTTERFLY BE	541	7
AT LAST--THE GRACE [THE GRACE IS JUST] IN SIGHT--	I CROSS TILL I AM WEARY	550	18
SHE HIDETH HER THE LAST--	SHE HIDETH HER THE LAST	557	1
LAST--LEAST--	THE TEST OF LOVE--IS	573	11
WHAT LAST [FIRST]	TO KNOW JUST HOW HE	622	19
THE LAST--AND SECOND TIME	'TWAS A LONG PARTING--	625	4
'TWAS MY LAST GRATITUDE	LET US PLAY YESTERDAY--	728	21
WHEN SKILL ENTREATED IT--THE LAST--	"I WANT"--IT PLEADED--	731	3
LOOKS LONG--AND LAST--AND GOLDEN--	THE MOUNTAINS--GROW	757	7
HIS LAST DECADE [SLOW DECADES] AWAY,	JOY TO HAVE MERITED THE	788	22
AND HAUNTING ACTUALIZE--TO LAST	JOY TO HAVE MERITED THE	788	23
THE PEAKS, THAT LINGERED LAST	WHEN ONE HAS GIVEN UP	853	5
EACH SECOND IS THE LAST	EACH SECOND IS THE LAST	879	1
SUCCESSFUL CERTAIN, IF AT LAST,	HOW FORTUNATE THE GRAVE	897	3
NOT TILL THE LAST WAS ANSWERED	WHAT DID THEY DO SINCE I	900	7
THE LAST DAY THAT I WAS A LIFE	THE FIRST DAY THAT I WAS	902	3
WHEN FATE HATH TAUNTED LAST	THIS MERIT HATH THE	979	3
THE FROGS GOT HOME LAST WEEK--	BEE! I'M EXPECTING YOU!	1035	5
I DID NOT TELL, IT WAS THEIR LAST EXPERIMENT	WHEN THEY COME BACK--IF	1080	7
LAST YEAR,	WHEN THEY COME BACK--IF	1080	8
AND MAKE MUCH BLUNDER, IF AT LAST	MY COCOON TIGHTENS--	1099	11
THE LAST NIGHT THAT SHE LIVED	THE LAST NIGHT THAT SHE	1100	1
WERE IT TO BE THE LAST	WERE IT TO BE THE LAST	1164	1
IT CAME AT LAST BUT PROMPTER DEATH	IT CAME AT LAST BUT	1230	1
AT LAST.	A RAT SURRENDERED HERE	1340	12
THE LAST [CLOSE] OF SUMMER IS DELIGHT--[A TIME / RESULT--SURVEY]	THE LAST OF SUMMER IS	1353	1
IS LAST THAT LEAVES--	"TOMORROW"--WHOSE	1367	4
LAST TO ADHERE [AT THE SCENE] WHEN SUMMER CLEAVES [SUMMER . . .	AFTER ALL BIRDS HAVE	1395	7
I SHALL NOT MURMUR IF AT LAST	I SHALL NOT MURMUR IF AT	1410	1
THAT WINS AT LAST--	DEATH IS THE SUPPLE	1445	2
BUT BRAVE AT LAST WITH BUGLES	DEATH IS THE SUPPLE	1445	7
AND SO SHE SOUGHT THIS SWEET AT LAST	SHE COULD NOT LIVE UPON	1505	3
I HAVE AT LAST REVENGE--	MINE ENEMY IS GROWING	1509	2
FATIGUED AT LAST, A CLOVER PLAIN [LOW]	HIS ORIENTAL HERESIES	1526	5

	FIRST LINE	POEM	LINE
LAST (CONTINUED)			
TOO IMPERCEPTIBLE AT LAST	AS IMPERCEPTIBLY AS	1540	3
THE SEA COMES LAST--STEP MERRY FEET	I DID NOT REACH THEE	1664	14
THE LAST SHALL BE THE LIGHTEST LOAD	I DID NOT REACH THEE	1664	18
EACH HEAVIER THAN THE LAST	I WATCHED HER FACE TO	1667	6
HAD I KNOWN THAT THE FIRST WAS THE LAST	HAD I KNOWN THAT THE	1720	1
HAD I KNOWN THAT THE LAST WAS THE FIRST	HAD I KNOWN THAT THE	1720	3
EXPERIMENT ESCORTS [ACCOSTS] US LAST--	EXPERIMENT ESCORTS US	1770	1
LASTED			
MY TRIUMPH LASTED TILL THE DRUMS	MY TRIUMPH LASTED TILL	1227	1
LASTS			
THEIR SUMMER--LASTS A SOLID YEAR--	I RECKON--WHEN I COUNT	569	9
ONE [THIS] REQUISITE HAS FIRE THAT LASTS [EARTHLY FIRE / MORTAL FIRE]	THE SMOULDERING EMBERS	1132	7
DOMINION LASTS UNTIL OBTAINED--	DOMINION LASTS UNTIL	1257	1
THAT ONLY [MERELY] LASTS AN HOUR	IN THIS SHORT LIFE	1287	2
THE SPIRIT LASTS--BUT IN WHAT MODE--	THE SPIRIT LASTS--BUT IN	1576	1
AND YET IF YOU COMPARE THE LASTS,	A FLOWER WILL NOT	1621	2
LATCH			
CHOOSES IT'S LATCH, FROM ALL THE OTHER FASTENINGS--	IT'S COMING--THE	390	3
I FITTED TO THE LATCH	I YEARS HAD BEEN FROM	609	17
LATCH [BAR / BIND] THEM SOFTLY--	THESE--SAW VISIONS--	758	2
LATE			
WENDING LATE HOME--	HEART, NOT SO HEAVY AS	83	2
TOO LATE FOR STRIVING FINGERS	WITHIN MY REACH!	90	8
WHERE WE--WITH LATE--CELESTIAL FACE--	MUSICIANS WRESTLE	157	17
ON THIS LATE MORN--THE SUN--	ON THIS LONG STORM THE	194	2
WHILE I WAS GONE--AND I--TOO LATE--	I SHOULD NOT DARE TO	205	3
THO' I GET HOME HOW LATE--HOW LATE--	THO' I GET HOME HOW LATE	207	1
THO' I GET HOME HOW LATE--HOW LATE--	THO' I GET HOME HOW LATE	207	1
REACHING LATE HIS FLOWER,	COME SLOWLY--EDEN!	211	5
OR IT BE TOO LATE!	IF HE DISSOLVE--THEN--	236	9
THAT YOU--SO LATE--"CONSIDER" ME--	I THINK JUST HOW MY	237	7
LATE--WHEN I TAKE MY PLACE IN SUMMER--	I SHALL KEEP SINGING!	250	7
LATE--THE PRAISE--	HER--"LAST POEMS"--	312	11
AND HE WILL TELL YOU--SKILL IS LATE--	THERE IS A LANGUOR OF	396	13
I'M DIVING--JUST A LITTLE LATE--	I'LL CLUTCH--AND CLUTCH	427	5
SO LATE A DOWERLESS GIRL--	I AM ASHAMED--I HIDE--	473	3
FOND, AND LATE--	WE TALKED AS GIRLS DO--	586	2
'TIS LATE YOUR SUNRISE VEX THEIR FACE--	WHAT CARE THE DEAD, FOR	592	3
OLD MAN ON NEBO! LATE AS THIS--	IT ALWAYS FELT TO ME--A	597	23
IT WAS TOO LATE FOR MAN--	IT WAS TOO LATE FOR MAN	623	1
LATE--MY GARDEN [ACRE] OF A ROCK--	SOIL OF FLINT, IF STEADY	681	V
VICTORY COMES LATE--	VICTORY COMES LATE--	690	1
WHEREFORE SO LATE--I MURMURED--	SHELLS FROM THE COAST	693	5
I COULD NOT DEEM IT LATE--TO HEAR	"I WANT"--IT PLEADED--	731	5
"I AM JESUS--LATE OF JUDEA--	"UNTO ME?" I DO NOT KNOW	964	3
TOO LATE TO CHOOSE AGAIN.	WHICH IS BEST? HEAVEN--	1012	9
REVISITING MY LATE ABODE	ALONE AND IN A	1167	9
TO HIDE MY STRATEGY TOO LATE	I THOUGHT THE TRAIN	1449	9
HOW LATE THEIR FEATHERS BE!	HOW SLOW THE WIND--	1571	3
IS IT TOO LATE TO TOUCH YOU, DEAR?	IS IT TOO LATE TO TOUCH	1637	1
LATELY			
AS LATELY AS TODAY--	THERE'S BEEN A DEATH, IN	389	2
AS LATELY AS THE SNOW--	HAVE ANY LIKE MYSELF	736	6
THOUGH LATELY I DESCRY	I KNOW SUSPENSE--IT	1285	6
LATER			
LATER BY JUST AN HOUR THAN DEATH--	DELAYED TILL SHE HAD	58	5
AND LATER, IN AUGUST IT MAY BE--	HAVE YOU GOT A BROOK IN	136	13
LATER, HIS FAINT CONFEDERATES	TO PUT THIS WORLD DOWN,	527	7
JUST AT NOON--NO LATER--SWEET [THAN]--	SOME SUCH BUTTERFLY BE	541	3
GREENER LEAN--OR FONDER CLUSTER [LATER LINGER]	PROMISE THIS--WHEN YOU	648	23
AND LATER--WHEN WE DIE--	WE THIRST AT FIRST--'TIS	726	2
LOVE--IS THAT LATER THING THAN DEATH--	LOVE--IS THAT LATER	924	1
OR A LEAVING HOME, OR LATER,	THAT IS SOLEMN WE HAVE	934	5
LATER THAN LIGHT THY CONSCIOUSNESS ACCOST ME	AIR HAS NO RESIDENCE, NO	1060	7
AND LATER HANG--	EXCEPT THE SMALLER SIZE	1067	6
'TWAS LATER WHEN THE SUMMER WENT	'TWAS LATER WHEN THE	1276	1
LATEST			
FIRST--AT THE VAT--AND LATEST AT THE VINE--	WE--BEE AND I--LIVE BY	230	14
ON LUTE THE LEAST--THE LATEST--	ALTHOUGH I PUT AWAY HIS	366	9
MINE BELONG YOUR LATEST SIGHING--	PROMISE THIS--WHEN YOU	648	3
LONGEST [LATEST] ON YOUR SOUTH, TO LINGER,	PROMISE THIS--WHEN YOU	648	19
HER LATEST WORSHIP--WHEN THE DAY	SWEET MOUNTAINS--YE TELL	722	10
I COULD HOLD THE LATEST GLOWING--	ROBBED BY DEATH--BUT	971	3
THIS LATEST LEISURE EQUAL LULLS [CASTLE EQUAL HOLDS]	NOT ANY HIGHER STANDS	1256	5
LATHED			
LATHED--WITH DOWN--	I WENT TO HEAVEN--	374	4
LATIN			
PUT IT IN LATIN--LEFT OF MY SCHOOL--	IT DONT SOUND SO	426	3
AND PERHAPS A PHRASE IN EGYPTIAN [LATIN INSCRIPTION]--	WE DREAM--IT IS GOOD WE	531	15
LATITUDE			
ACCEPTS A BETTER LATITUDE--	'TIS NOT THAT DYING	335	7
NOR EASED--OF LATITUDE--	CONJECTURING A CLIMATE	562	8
AND LATITUDE OF HOME--	FOREVER--IS COMPOSED OF	624	4
OF ME--IN CHRIST'S BRIGHT AUDIENCE [LATITUDE]	YOU TAUGHT ME WAITING	740	11
A LATITUDE.	THESE TESTED OUR HORIZON	886	4

	FIRST LINE	POEM	LINE
LATITUDELESS			
LATITUDELESS PLACE.	NOW I KNEW I LOST HER--	1219	8
LATITUDES			
OF LATITUDES UNKNOWN.	A POOR--TORN HEART-- A	78	8
RETIRE TO OTHER LATITUDES--	ALL OVERGROWN BY CUNNING	148	7
WENT WANDERING DOWN THE LATITUDES	AS IF SOME LITTLE ARCTIC	180	3
AND DOWER LATITUDES FAR ON--	DELIGHT IS AS THE FLIGHT	257	23
LIFE'S LATITUDES LEANT OVER--FULL--	ONE BLESSING HAD I THAN	756	15
ALL LATITUDES EXIST FOR HIS	ALL CIRCUMSTANCES ARE	820	3
LATTER			
I PUT THE LATTER IN A BARN--	I CAUTIOUS, SCANNED MY	178	5
WHEN THE LATTER--IS PUT AWAY	BY MY WINDOW HAVE I FOR	797	19
THE LATTER--EXCELLENT TO KEEP [HAVE]--	BETWEEN THE FORM OF LIFE	1101	5
BUT THE LATTER, HER SIRE, IS HONORED	THE PARASOL IS THE	1747 V	7
LAUGH			
AND LAUGH AT ME--AND STARE--	"ARCTURUS" IS HIS OTHER	70	29
THE BROOKS LAUGH LOUDER WHEN I COME--	THE BEE IS NOT AFRAID OF	111	5
RANSOMED FOLKS--WONT LAUGH AT ME--	WHAT IS--"PARADISE"--	215	16
MY BRAIN--BEGUN TO LAUGH--	THE FIRST DAY'S NIGHT	410	13
AND LAUGH, A HOMELY SPECIES	I'M SORRY FOR THE DEAD--	529	7
I LAUGHED A CRUMBLING [WOODEN] LAUGH	I YEARS HAD BEEN FROM	609	13
AND LAUGH--NO MORE HAVE I--	THEY SHUT ME UP IN PROSE	613	12
AND MADE THE GABLES LAUGH--	A DROP FELL ON THE APPLE	794	4
WHEN NATURE'S LAUGH IS DONE	THE MURMURING OF BEES,	1115	6
THEY LAUGH AS WISE AS PLOTS OF WIT	THEY TALK AS SLOW AS	1697	5
THEY'D LAUGH AND RUN AWAY.	IF ALL THE GRIEFS I AM	1726	4
LAUGHED			
AND FAILED--AND ALL THE SUMMER LAUGHED--	GOD MADE A LITTLE	442	3
I LAUGHED A CRUMBLING [WOODEN] LAUGH	I YEARS HAD BEEN FROM	609	13
LAUGHS			
LIGHT LAUGHS THE BREEZE	SAFE IN THEIR ALABASTER	216	7
FAITH SLIPS--AND LAUGHS, AND RALLIES--	THIS WORLD IS NOT	501	13
LAUGHS--AT A SCRUPLE--	THE CHILD'S FAITH IS NEW	637	6
LAUGHTER			
HIS LAUGHTER, LIKE THE BREEZE	THE ONLY GHOST I EVER	274	10
LOW AS THE LAUGHTER OF THE CRICKET,	MANY A PHRASE HAS THE	276	3
AS LAUGHTER--WAS--AN HOUR AGO--	WHAT IF I SAY I SHALL	277	10
AS THE LAUGHTER--AND THE WHISPER--	SWEET--SAFE--HOUSES--	457	8
AND HEALTH, AND LAUGHTER, CURIOUS THINGS--	I CRIED AT PITY--NOT AT	588	7
WAS LAUGHTER AND ABILITY AND SIGHING	THIS QUIET DUST WAS	813	3
LAUNCH			
LAUNCH IT--THE AQUATIC	LIFT IT--WITH THE	1348	3
LAUNCHING			
WE WHO SAW THE LAUNCHING	COULD LIVE--DID LIVE--	43	12
LAUREATE			
A HABIT--OF A LAUREATE--	THEY HAVE A LITTLE ODOR	785	4
LAUREATES			
THESE ARE THE PATIENT "LAUREATES"	TO LEARN THE TRANSPORT	167	11
LAUREL			
LAY THIS LAUREL ON THE ONE	LAY THIS LAUREL ON THE	1393	1
LAUREL--VAIL YOUR [THY] DEATHLESS TREE--	LAY THIS LAUREL ON THE	1393	3
LAY THIS LAUREL ON THE ONE	LAY THIS LAUREL ON THE	1393 V	
LAUREL--FELL YOUR [THY] FUTILE TREE--	LAY THIS LAUREL ON THE	1393 V	
LAURELS			
LAURELS--FOR RARE DEGREE	GARLANDS FOR QUEENS, MAY	34	2
LAVA			
HOW GOOD HIS LAVA BED,	HOW GOOD HIS LAVA BED,	1447	1
A LAVA STEP AT ANY TIME	VOLCANOES BE IN SICILY	1705	5
LAVISHED			
ROBIN--UTTERED [PUBLISHED / LAVISHED] HALF THE TUNE--	HER--"LAST POEMS"--	312	8
LAW			
I'LL VINDICATE THE LAW--	I HAD SOME THINGS THAT I	116	14
A FILAMENT--A LAW--	I HAD NOT MINDED--WALLS	398	10
SLIPPING--IS CRASHE'S LAW.	CRUMBLING IS NOT AN	997	12
ACCORDING TO THE LAW	ALONE AND IN A	1167	20
AMENABLE TO LAW--	THE WAY TO KNOW THE	1279	10
TO LAW--SAID SWEET THERMOPYLAE	"GO TELL IT"--WHAT A	1554	7
TO WHICH THE LAW ENTITLED HIM.	UPON THE GALLOWS HUNG A	1757	3
LAWFUL			
UPON THE BROAD POSSESSION [LAWFUL MANOR--]	IT ALWAYS FELT TO ME--A	597	21
THE LAWFUL HEIR--FOR THEE--	DEFRAUDED I A BUTTERFLY	730	2
AS EACH WERE SPECIAL [LAWFUL / ONLY] HEIR--	ALONE AND IN A	1167	16
LAWFUL AS EQUILIBRIUM.	THE RAT IS THE CONCISEST	1356	10
THAT LAWFUL ORCHARDS [DAMSONS] MOCKS--	FORBIDDEN FRUIT A FLAVOR	1377	2
LAWN			
BACK TO THE LAWN AGAIN.	WE SHOULD NOT MIND SO	81	4
A DEEPER TWILIGHT ON THE LAWN--	AN ALTERED LOOK ABOUT	140	4
YET TAKE HER FROM THE LAWN	EXCEPT TO HEAVEN, SHE IS	154	10
A LONG--LONG YELLOW--ON THE LAWN--	A MURMUR IN THE TREES--	416	5
PRESENTIMENT--IS THAT LONG SHADOW--ON THE LAWN--	PRESENTIMENT--IS THAT	764	1
IT WAITS UPON THE LAWN,	A LIGHT EXISTS IN SPRING	812	9
LAWNS			
IT ALMOST TOUCHED THE LAWNS.	A CURIOUS CLOUD	1710	5
LAWS			
VICINITY TO LAWS	A NEARNESS TO	963	4
NO UNIVERSE--NO LAWS--	GREAT STREETS OF SILENCE	1159	4
FROM FUNDAMENTAL LAWS.	TWO LENGTHS HAS EVERY	1295	8
OR [AND] MORTISED WITH THE LAWS--	THE WAY HOPE BUILDS HIS	1481	8

	FIRST LINE	POEM	LINE
LAY			
THROUGH LANE IT LAY--THRO' BRAMBLE--	THROUGH LANE IT LAY--	9	1
HER LOVING BOSOM LAY--	DELAYED TILL SHE HAD	58	3
PARIS COULD NOT LAY THE FOLD	PIGMY SERAPHS--GONE	138	5
ON HER FOREHEAD LAY, ...	THO' MY DESTINY BE	163	10
AND THEN TO LAY THEM QUIET BACK--	IN EBON BOX, WHEN YEARS	169	17
BUT IT'S MANY A LAY OF THE DIM BURGUNDY-- .	WE--BEE AND I--LIVE BY	230	4
OR LAY A PRIMA, MAD, ...	I CANNOT DANCE UPON MY	326	8
SHE LAY AS IF AT PLAY	SHE LAY AS IF AT PLAY	369	1
A NIGHT--THERE LAY THE DAYS BETWEEN-- . .	A NIGHT--THERE LAY THE	471	1
'TIS TRUE--OUR FUTURES DIFFERENT LAY-- . .	OURSELVES WERE WED ONE	631	9
IT LAY UNMENTIONED--AS THE SEA	SHE ROSE TO HIS	732	9
ON WHOM I LAY A YELLOW EYE--	MY LIFE HAD STOOD--A	754	19
THE BUSY DARLING LAY--	HER FINAL SUMMER WAS IT	795	14
SOME THAT NEVER LAY	SNOW BENEATH WHOSE	942	2
AND LOWER LAY IN LOW WESTMINSTER	SHE ROSE AS HIGH AS HIS	1011	3
AND THAT IS WHY I LAY MY HEAD	ESCAPE IS SUCH A	1347	11
LAY THIS LAUREL ON THE ONE	LAY THIS LAUREL ON THE	1393	1
LAY THIS LAUREL ON THE ONE	LAY THIS LAUREL ON THE	1393	V
UPON IT'S FASTENED LIPS LAY WORDS-- . . .	OH GIVE IT MOTION--DECK	1527	3
NOW I LAY THEE DOWN TO SLEEP--	NOW I LAY THEE DOWN TO	1539	1
THE WELL IN WHICH THEY LAY US	OF DEATH I TRY TO THINK	1558	2
SUCH HINTS OF HONEY LAY	WITHIN THAT LITTLE HIVE	1607	2
AND LAY THE MARBLE TEA.	THE GRAVE MY LITTLE	1743	4
LAYING			
LAYING HER [IT'S] SPOTTED FACE TO DIE . .	BLAZING IN GOLD AND	228	4
JUST LAYING LIGHT--NO SOUL WILL WINK . . .	WHEN WE STAND ON THE	242	5
JUST LAYING OFF FOR EVIDENCE	DEATH IS A DIALOGUE	976	7
LAYS			
THE EARTH LAYS BACK THESE TIRED LIVES . .	THE MONTHS HAVE ENDS--	423	5
AND LAYS IT IN ITS PLACE--	THE BIRD HER PUNCTUAL	1585	2
LAZY			
AND RECOGNITION LAZY--	THE SUMMER THAT WE DID	1773	4
LE			
LESS SKILLFUL THAN LE VERRIERE	SHE WENT AS QUIET AS THE	149	7
MEEK [LOW] MY VIVE LE ROI, ...	MUTE THY CORONATION--	151	2
LEA			
THEN--SKIP--THE FROST--UPON THE LEA-- . .	MAKE ME A PICTURE OF THE	188	12
LEAD			
WHICH LEAD THE SEASONS BY, ...	TO VENERATE THE SIMPLE	57	2
LEAD THE WANDERING SAILS.	A POOR--TORN HEART-- A	78	16
PRAY LEAD ME TO HIS BED!	SEXTON! MY MASTER'S	96	2
SO HE LET ME LEAD HIM IN--	HE WAS WEAK, AND I WAS	190	2
SO I LET HIM LEAD ME--HOME.	HE WAS WEAK, AND I WAS	190	4
WITH THOSE SAME BOOTS OF LEAD, AGAIN, . .	I FELT A FUNERAL, IN MY	280	11
THIS IS THE HOUR OF LEAD--	AFTER GREAT PAIN, A	341	10
LIKE LITANIES OF LEAD--	THE MORNING AFTER WO--	364	12
TO LEAD HIM TO THE WELL	TO ONE DENIED TO DRINK	490	5
PRESUMING IT TO LEAD	EXPERIENCE IS THE ANGLED	910	4
BY THE LINE AND LEAD	GRATITUDE--IS NOT THE	989	6
TO [BUT] LEAD IT HERE--	I HAVE NO LIFE BUT THIS	1398	2
A CAP OF LEAD ACROSS THE SKY	A CAP OF LEAD ACROSS THE	1649	1
LEADEN			
IT SIFTS FROM LEADEN SIEVES--	IT SIFTS FROM LEADEN	311	1
LEADER			
WITH LEADER OF THE BAND--	'TIS ONE BY ONE--THE	545	14
LEADER'S			
NOR ANY LEADER'S GRIM BATON	NO LADDER NEEDS THE BIRD	1574	3
LEADING			
LEADING TO NO DAY--	DREAMS--ARE WELL--BUT	450	8
LEADS			
ALSO, WHO LEADS THE DOCILE SPHERES . . .	BRING ME THE SUNSET IN A	128	14
UNTO GUESSED CRESTS, MY MOANING FANCY, LEADS [LURES] ME,	UNTO LIKE STORY--TROUBLE	295	9
SHE--EACH YEAR--LEADS HER DAISIES BACK-- .	I KNOW A PLACE WHERE	337	3
SHE LEADS HIM--DOCILE AS A BOY--	THE MOON IS DISTANT FROM	429	3
THE MUSCLES GRAPPLED [STRUGGLED] AS WITH LEADS	'TWAS CRISIS--ALL THE	948	9
LEADS THE CHOSEN CHILD, ...	FAR FROM LOVE THE	1021	2
THAT LEADS AWAY FROM THEE--	OH FUTURE! THOU SECRETED	1631	4
LEADS IT THROUGH THE GRAVE TO THEE. . . .	REARRANGE A "WIFE'S"	1737	20
LEAF			
WHOSE LEAF IS EVER GREEN;	THERE IS ANOTHER SKY,	2	8
HURRIES A TIMID LEAF.	THESE ARE THE DAYS WHEN	130	12
AS OF BRIAR AND LEAF DISPLAYED	PIGMY SERAPHS--GONE	138	10
THE LEAF--AT LOVE--TURNED BACK--	'TWAS THE OLD--ROAD--	344	13
THOUGH NOT A LEAF	A WIND THAT ROSE	1259	2
AND SATISFIED A LEAF	A DEW SUFFICED ITSELF--	1437	2
WITHOUT A SINGLE LEAF	BEFORE YOU THOUGHT OF	1465	14
LEAFLETS			
SO HIDDEN IN HER LEAFLETS	SO BASHFUL WHEN I SPIED	91	3
LEAGUE			
WHO NEVER CLIMBED THE WEARY LEAGUE-- . . .	WHO NEVER LOST, ARE	73	5
OF THE FIRST LEAGUE OUT FROM LAND? . . .	EXULTATION IS THE GOING	76	8
OF RIVER OR OF RIDGE [OF FATHOM OR OF LEAGUE] BEYOND	HOW FAR IS IT TO HEAVEN?	929	3
A FURLONG THAN A LEAGUE	WE MISS A KINSMAN MORE	1087	5
LEAGUELESS			
IN LEAGUELESS OPPORTUNITY, ...	HOW NOTELESS MEN, AND	282	7
LEAGUES			
HOW MANY LEAGUES OF NOWHERE	AMBITION CANNOT FIND HIM	68	3

	FIRST LINE	POEM		LINE
LEAGUES (CONTINUED)				
AH, WHAT LEAGUES THERE WERE	AT LAST, TO BE	174		6
THAT CRAWLED LEAGUES OFF--I LIKED TO SEE--	THREE TIMES--WE PARTED--	598		9
AND HONOR LEAGUES AWAY	THE DITCH IS DEAR TO THE	1645		8
LEAK				
LIKE SAILORS FIGHTING WITH A LEAK	THE FROST OF DEATH WAS	1136		3
LEAKAGE				
THE BUNG OUT--OF [A LEAKAGE IN] AN ARTERY--	ONE ANGUISH--IN A CROWD	565		11
LEAKED				
AND SO WHEN ALL THE TIME HAD LEAKED [FAILED]--	THERE CAME A DAY AT	322		21
LEAKING				
IS LEAKING--RED--	IF HE DISSOLVE--THEN--	236		13
LEAN				
HE CAN LEAN AGAINST THE GRAVE,	IF YOUR NERVE, DENY YOU	292		3
AND LEAN--AND VIEW IT SIDEWISE--	I AM ALIVE--I GUESS--	470		13
GREENER LEAN--OR FONDER CLUSTER [LATER LINGER]	PROMISE THIS--WHEN YOU	648		23
AND MOUNTAINS--FEEBLE--LEAN--	THE TRUTH--IS STIRLESS--	780		6
LEAN FORWARD FOR A FINAL GLANCE--	POWER IS A FAMILIAR	1238		7
BUT IF THE HEART OMIT [BE LEAN / BE THIN / DECLINE]	THE MIND LIVES ON THE	1355		5
AND [HE] PANTING [HEAVY / LANGUID] ON A CLOVER LEAN	THE BUTTERFLY'S NUMIDIAN	1387		5
THE RIVERS LEAN TO SEE	THE HILLS ERECT THEIR	1688		2
LEANED				
I LEANED UPON THE AWE--	I YEARS HAD BEEN FROM	609		9
WHEN THESE--LEANED INTO [TWO--LEANED IN--] PERFECTNESS--	MIDSUMMER, WAS IT, WHEN	962		7
WHEN THESE--LEANED INTO [TWO--LEANED IN--] PERFECTNESS--	MIDSUMMER, WAS IT, WHEN	962		7
THE TWILIGHT STOOD [LEANED], AS STRANGERS DO	THE CRICKETS SANG	1104		6
SO LOW IT LEANED--THEN STATELIER DREW--	A CURIOUS CLOUD	1710		6
LEANETH				
OF ONE [HIM] THAT LEANETH FROM [IN] BALLOON	IT WAS A QUIET WAY--	1053		11
LEANING				
LEANING AGAINST THE--SUN--	I TASTE A LIQUOR NEVER	214	V	16
GREAT CLOUDS--LIKE USHERS--LEANING [PLACING]--	DEPARTED--TO THE	524		3
BUT LEANING TO THE SIGHT	TO DISAPPEAR ENHANCES--	1209		18
LEANS				
AND THEN HE LEANS WITH ALL HIS MIGHT	HE PARTS HIMSELF--LIKE	517	V	3
THE EVENING ON THE DAY LEANS	AS WILLING LID O'ER	1050		2
LEANT				
LIFE'S LATITUDES LEANT OVER--FULL--	ONE BLESSING HAD I THAN	756		15
LEAP				
LEAP SO HIGHLAND GAY,	SO FROM THE MOULD	66		8
AND BE WITH [LEAP TO] YOU--TONIGHT!	AH, MOON--AND STAR!	240		12
LEAP, PLASHLESS AS THEY SWIM.	A BIRD CAME DOWN THE	328		20
WOULD LEAP ABROAD LIKE ANTELOPE--	ALTHOUGH I PUT AWAY HIS	366		15
DID LEAP, FULL FLANKED, UPON THE HOST--	ONE ANGUISH--IN A CROWD	565		7
MAKE THE BLIND--LEAP--	LET US PLAY YESTERDAY--	728		12
THEY LEAP UPON THEIR SILVER FEET	HOW STILL THE BELLS IN	1008		3
ECSTATICALLY LEAP--	FROM ALL THE JAILS THE	1532		2
LEAPED				
THEIR SLIPPERS LEAPED THE TOWN,	I COUNTED TILL THEY	36		2
HER LIFE HAD LEAPED AWAY--	SHE LAY AS IF AT PLAY	369		2
SHE LEAPS, BUT ROBIN LEAPED THE FIRST--	SHE SIGHTS A BIRD--SHE	507		7
THE BOLDEST [BRAVEST] LEAPED, AND CLUTCHED IT--	OF DEATH I TRY TO THINK	1558		16
WHICH THOU HAST LEAPED ACROSS!	PASS TO THY RENDEZVOUS	1564		4
LOVE THAT NEVER LEAPED ITS SOCKET--	REARRANGE A "WIFE'S"	1737		9
LEAPING				
LEAPING LIKE LEOPARDS TO [IN] THE SKY	BLAZING IN GOLD AND	228		2
LEAPS				
TELL ME HOW FAR THE MORNING LEAPS--	BRING ME THE SUNSET IN A	128		4
A WOUNDED DEER--LEAPS HIGHEST--	A WOUNDED DEER--LEAPS	165		1
SHE LEAPS, BUT ROBIN LEAPED THE FIRST--	SHE SIGHTS A BIRD--SHE	507		7
LEARN				
TO LEARN THE TRANSPORT BY [THRO'] THE PAIN--	TO LEARN THE TRANSPORT	167		1
AS BLIND MEN LEARN THE SUN!	TO LEARN THE TRANSPORT	167		2
WHOM WE CAN NEVER LEARN--	FOREVER AT HIS SIDE TO	246		11
BUT WE COULD'NT LEARN!	DID WE DISOBEY HIM?	267		4
BUT WE MIGHT LEARN TO LIKE THE HEAVEN,	I FELT MY LIFE WITH BOTH	351		15
BUT AS THEY LEARN TO SEE--	WE GROW ACCUSTOMED TO	419		16
WHEN ONE LEARN HOW	KNOWS HOW TO FORGET!	433	V	
WE LEARN TO KNOW THE PLANKS--	A PRISON GETS TO BE A	652		9
YET NEITHER TOLD--THAT I COULD LEARN--	NATURE AND GOD--I	835		5
WE LEARN IN THE RETREATING	WE LEARN IN THE	1083		1
WE START--TO LEARN THAT WE BELIEVE	WHO WERE "THE FATHER AND	1258		17
LEARNED				
NOT PURSUED BY LEARNED ANGELS	IF THE FOOLISH, CALL	168		15
LEARNED GEM-TACTICS--	WE PLAY AT PASTE--	320		7
MIGHT SOME ONE ELSE--SO LEARNED--BE--	NOT IN THIS WORLD TO SEE	418		10
EDEN--A LEGEND--DIMLY TOLD [LEARNED / CROONED]--	BETTER--THAN MUSIC! FOR	503		14
WE LEARNED THE WHOLE OF LOVE--	WE LEARNED THE WHOLE OF	568		1
WE LEARNED TO LIKE THE FIRE	THE ZEROES--TAUGHT US--	689		2
AFTERWARD I LEARNED	MOST SHE TOUCHED ME BY	760		18
I LEARNED--AT LEAST--WHAT HOME COULD BE--	I LEARNED--AT LEAST--	944		1
I LEARNED TO ESTIMATE.	I HAD A DAILY BLISS	1057		8
THE STATUTE IS MY LEARNED FRIEND	ALONE AND IN A	1167		21
TO MEET [AT MEETING] SO ENABLED [LEARNED	HE PREACHED UPON	1207		8

	FIRST LINE	POEM	LINE
LEARNED (CONTINUED)			
/ RELIGIOUS / . . .			
YOU CHERISHED"--"LEARNED WATERS--	THE SEA SAID "COME" TO	1210	7
I SUBSEQUENTLY LEARNED	HIGH FROM THE EARTH I	1723	14
LEARNETH			
LEARNETH BEYOND THE SEA	I HAVE A BIRD IN SPRING	5	10
LEARNS			
THE HEART CONVULSIVE LEARNS	THE HEART HAS NARROW	928	8
LEARNT			
THIS--ALSO--I HAVE LEARNT--	YOU TAUGHT ME WAITING	740	4
LEASE			
HER LEASE OF SPOTTED HOURS,	SHE DIED AT PLAY,	75	3
UNCERTAIN LEASE--DEVELOPES LUSTRE	UNCERTAIN LEASE--	857	1
THAT HOLDS IN UNDISPUTED LEASE	TOO LITTLE WAY THE HOUSE	911	3
OMITTED IN THE LEASE--	'TWAS AWKWARD, BUT IT	973	12
LEASED			
BEFORE IDENTITY WAS CREASED [LEASED].	ESTRANGED FROM BEAUTY--	1474	4
LEASES			
BLISS IS FRUGAL OF HER LEASES	PARADISE IS THAT OLD	1119	5
LEAST			
AT LEAST, TO KNOW THE WORST, IS SWEET!	'TIS SO MUCH JOY! 'TIS	172	10
LEAST RIVERS--DOCILE TO SOME SEA.	LEAST RIVERS--DOCILE TO	212	1
BUT THE LEAST PUSH OF JOY	I CAN WADE GRIEF--	252	4
WITH LAST [LEAST] DELIGHT I OWN!	DOUBT ME! MY DIM	275	8
AT LEAST, IT SOLACES TO KNOW	YOUR RICHES--TAUGHT ME--	299	25
LEAST VILLAGE HAS [BOASTS] IT'S BLACKSMITH	DARE YOU SEE A SOUL AT	365	9
ON LUTE THE LEAST--THE LATEST--	ALTHOUGH I PUT AWAY HIS	366	9
LEAST FIGURE--ON THE ROAD--	A TONGUE--TO TELL HIM I	400	29
OBEDIENT TO THE LEAST COMMAND	THE MOON IS DISTANT FROM	429	11
AS THE VERY LEAST	I TIE MY HAT--I CREASE	443	3
I WONDERED WHICH WOULD MISS ME, LEAST,	'TWAS JUST THIS TIME,	445	13
AT LEAST--A COUNTERFEIT--	IT'S THOUGHTS--AND JUST	495	25
AT LEAST--TO PRAY--IS LEFT--IS LEFT--	AT LEAST--TO PRAY--IS	502	1
REGARDS LEAST CYPHERER ALIKE	'TIS ONE BY ONE--THE	545	13
WERE BUT MINE--THE CHARTER OF THE LEAST FLY--	I COULD DIE--TO KNOW--	570	6
LAST--LEAST--	THE TEST OF LOVE--IS	573	11
AT LEAST--'TIS MUTUAL--RISK--	I GAVE MYSELF TO HIM--	580	13
BE HORROR'S LEAST.	ONE NEED NOT BE A	670	16
LEAST BEE THAT BREW--	LEAST BEE THAT BREW--	676	1
HER LEAST ATTENTION RAISE ON ME--	'TWOULD EASE--A	682	14
BUT THE LEAST FAN	THE WORLD--FEELS DUSTY	715	6
THE LEAST--CAN LIFT A TON	SUCH IS THE FORCE OF	787	2
AT LEAST--ETERNITY--	JOY TO HAVE MERITED THE	788	24
AND THAT, SO LEAST DISPLAYS--	HER GRACE IS ALL SHE HAS	810	2
FOOT OF THE BOLD DID LEAST ATTEMPT IT--	THOSE WHO HAVE BEEN IN	922	5
I LEARNED--AT LEAST--WHAT HOME COULD BE--	I LEARNED--AT LEAST--	944	1
NOR THE LEAST SIGNAL, ME [MINE] ASSURE--	WERT THOU BUT ILL--THAT	961	4
I AM SMALL--"THE LEAST	"UNTO ME?" I DO NOT KNOW	964	10
JUST ONCE! OH LEAST REQUEST!	JUST ONCE! OH LEAST	1076	1
TO CHILDREN HE IS SMALL [LEAST] IN PRICE	THE MERCHANT OF THE	1131	5
WE [I] THOUGHT, AT LEAST THEY ARE NO WORSE	WHO WERE "THE FATHER AND	1258	7
THAN LEAST [BESIDE] VITALITY.	THE HARM OF YEARS IS ON	1280	8
AT LEAST WITHIN MY TREE	COME SHOW THY DURHAM	1542	5
WHOSE BUGLES CALL THE LEAST OF US	TALK NOT TO ME OF SUMMER	1634	7
T'IS THIS EXPANDS THE LEAST EVENT	I KNOW OF PEOPLE IN THE	1665	5
THAT SHE FORGOT ME WAS THE LEAST	THAT SHE FORGOT ME WAS	1683	1
BUT DEIGN THIS LEAST CERTIFICATE	THE LOOK OF THEE, WHAT	1689	11
LEAVE			
WITH YOUR MAJESTIC LEAVE!	GREAT CAESAR! CONDESCEND	102	4
I SHOULD NOT DARE TO LEAVE MY FRIEND,	I SHOULD NOT DARE TO	205	1
IF [WHEN] HE LEAVE A BUR AT THE DOOR	THE WIND DID'NT COME	316	7
THEY LEAVE US WITH THE INFINITE.	THEY LEAVE US WITH THE	350	1
TO LEAVE ME IN THE ATOM'S TOMB--	OF COURSE--I PRAYED--	376	9
AND LEAVE ME--JUST MY A--B--C--	NOT IN THIS WORLD TO SEE	418	11
HAVE SUMMER'S LEAVE TO PLAY--	I ENVY SEAS, WHEREON HE	498	14
AND LEAVE THE SOUL--ALONE--	DEPARTED--TO THE	524	8
BEGIN, AND LEAVE THEE OUT--	EMPTY MY HEART, OF THEE	587	3
AND LEAVE ME IN THE FLOOR--	I YEARS HAD BEEN FROM	609	20
LEAVE MY NEEDLE IN THE FURROW--	DONT PUT UP MY THREAD &	617	13
AND LEAVE IT WITH A DISCONTENT	THE TINT I CANNOT TAKE--	627	11
HER SWEET TURN TO LEAVE THE HOMESTEAD	HER SWEET TURN TO LEAVE	649	1
WE WALK--I LEAVE MY DOG--AT HOME [BEHIND]--	AGAIN--HIS VOICE IS AT	663	18
FOR HIS MEAN SAKE TO LEAVE THE ROW	THE HEAVEN VESTS FOR	694	11
THOUGH THE "ROMEO" LEFT [LEAVE] NO RECORD	DRAMA'S VITALLEST	741	10
FAME IS THE TINT THAT SCHOLARS LEAVE	FAME IS THE TINT THAT	866	1
AND LEAVE A DAY AT EVERY DOOR	WHEN I HAVE SEEN THE SUN	888	3
HE LEAVE OURSELVES A SPHERE BEHIND--	WE CAN BUT FOLLOW TO THE	920	3
AND LEAVE FOR THY SWEET MERCY'S [PATIENCE'] SAKE	SOME WRETCHED CREATURE,	1111	3
LEAVE ME NOT EVER THERE ALONE	REMEMBRANCE HAS A	1182	V 7
LEAVE US TO PRESUME	SOME WE SEE NO MORE,	1221	5
UNLESS YOU LEAVE HIM--THEN RETURN	SO MUCH OF HEAVEN HAS	1228	11
DID YOU LEAVE NATURE WELL--	DEAR MARCH--COME IN--	1320	8
I GAVE HIM LEAVE TO LIVE	IT CAME HIS TURN TO BEG	1500	6
TAKE ALL AWAY FROM ME, BUT LEAVE ME ECSTASY,	TAKE ALL AWAY FROM ME,	1640	1
REMEDILESSLY LEAVE	OF THIS IS DAY COMPOSED	1675	8
WRING THE TREE AND LEAVE IT,	DEATH IS LIKE THE INSECT	1716	11
LEAVES			
AND THEY MAKE MERRY WEDDING, WHOSE GUESTS ARE HUNDRED LEAVES!	AWAKE YE MUSES NINE,	1	14

	FIRST LINE	POEM	LINE
LEAVES (CONTINUED)			
DID COVER SUCH WITH LEAVES,	WHOSE CHEEK IS THIS?	82	7
AND LEAVES THE SHREDS BEHIND--	SHE SWEEPS WITH	219	2
TO KNOW THE WORST, LEAVES NO DREAD MORE--	'TIS SO APPALLING--IT	281	4
FAINTER LEAVES--TO FURTHER SEASONS--	NATURE--SOMETIMES SEARS	314	5
WITHDRAWS--AND LEAVES THE DAZZLED SOUL	DID OUR BEST MOMENT LAST	393	11
THE HAPPY--HAPPY LEAVES--	I ENVY SEAS, WHEREON HE	498	12
HE PARTS HIMSELF--LIKE LEAVES--	HE PARTS HIMSELF--LIKE	517	1
AND DROVE AWAY THE LEAVES	THE NIGHT WAS WIDE, AND	589	6
AND LEAVES ME WITH THE HILLS.	THE NAME--OF IT--IS	656	V 12
THE LEAVES UNHOOKED THEMSELVES FROM TREES--	THE WIND BEGUN TO KNEAD	824	5
TO MY QUICK EAR THE LEAVES--CONFERRED--	TO MY QUICK EAR THE	891	1
DEATH LEAVES US HOMESICK, WHO BEHIND,	DEATH LEAVES US HOMESICK	935	1
THE LEAVES LIKE WOMEN, INTERCHANGE	THE LEAVES LIKE WOMEN,	987	1
AND LEAVES US IN ANOTHER PLACE	EXHILIRATION IS THE	1118	3
THE LEAVES OBTAINED EXCUSE--	THE DAY GREW SMALL,	1140	6
BUT WHEN IT LEAVES US FOR A TIME	IMMORTAL IS AN AMPLE	1205	3
IS LAST THAT LEAVES--	"TOMORROW"--WHOSE	1367	4
BUT LEAVES A SUMPTUOUS [BLISSFUL] DESTITUTION--	IN MANY AND REPORTLESS	1382	7
BUT LEAVES THE WATER WHOLE--	THE INUNDATION OF THE	1425	4
THE FASCINATING CHILL THAT MUSIC LEAVES [OF MUSIC]	THE FASCINATING CHILL	1480	1
THAT LEAVES THIS NEIGHBOR [MAJOR] OUT--	NO BRIGADIER THROUGHOUT	1561	24
A GAIN UPON THE BACKWARD LEAVES	SUMMER BEGINS TO HAVE	1682	4
THAT TOTTERS IN THE LEAVES--	HER FACE WAS IN A BED OF	1722	6
AND LEAVES NO REMNANT BY--	TOO HAPPY TIME DISSOLVES	1774	2
LEAVING			
LEAVING NOOKS FOR DAISY	ALL THESE MY BANNERS BE.	22	14
LEAVING A NEW NESCESSITY!	THE SUN--JUST TOUCHED	232	11
THERE--LEAVING OUT A MAN--	IT'S EASY TO INVENT A	724	12
THE LEAVING LOVE BEHIND.	DYING! TO BE AFRAID OF	831	6
OR A LEAVING HOME, OR LATER,	THAT IS SOLEMN WE HAVE	934	5
LEAVING ON NATURE--A DEFAULT	SHE SPED AS PETALS OF A	991	5
LEAVING AN ATTITUDE [A MAGNITUDE] ON TIME	SHE SPED AS PETALS OF A	991	V 5
LED			
SO TO THE EYE PROSPECTIVE LED,	A SCIENCE--SO THE SAVANS	100	7
THE "MORNING STARS" THE TREBLE LED	MUSICIANS WRESTLE	157	11
AND LED THE FLOCK AWAY--	I'LL TELL YOU HOW THE	318	16
AND YOU WERE FROZEN LED	'TWAS LIKE A MAELSTROM,	414	19
WHEN, FELON LED ALONG,	THE SOUL HAS BANDAGED	512	20
OUR FEET--RELUCTANT--LED--	OUR JOURNEY HAD ADVANCED	615	6
'TIS TRUE, YOUR GARDEN LED THE BLOOM,	OURSELVES WERE WED ONE	631	13
LED ABSENT, WERE PROCURED [OBTAINED] OF HEAVEN	TWO TRAVELLERS PERISHING	933	15
ASK [TO] HIM UNTO THE GALLOWS LED [CALLED]--	OH SUMPTUOUS MOMENT	1125	8
GREAT STREETS OF SILENCE LED AWAY	GREAT STREETS OF SILENCE	1159	1
AS ONE COMMUTED LED--	SOMEHOW MYSELF SURVIVED	1194	6
WHO LED US WHILE HE STAYED.	NOT THAT HE GOES--WE	1435	2
A LANE OF YELLOW LED THE EYE	A LANE OF YELLOW LED THE	1650	1
LEDGE			
ROUND A LEDGE OF DREAM!	I CANT TELL YOU--BUT YOU	65	8
LEDGES			
AS IF IT WERE OF LEDGES SMIT	THE WAY HOPE BUILDS HIS	1481	7
LEECH			
A SMALL LEECH--ON THE VITALS--	ONE ANGUISH--IN A CROWD	565	9
THAN I COULD COAX A LEECH AWAY--[MODIFY A LEECH]	IT WOULD HAVE STARVED A	612	7
THAN I COULD COAX A LEECH AWAY--[MODIFY A LEECH]	IT WOULD HAVE STARVED A	612	7
LEFT			
I LEFT THEM IN THE GROUND.	GOING TO HEAVEN!	79	27
TO FIND THE SUNRISE LEFT--	YOU LOVE ME--YOU ARE	156	5
AND LEFT HIS PROCESS--SATISFIED--	HE PUT THE BELT AROUND	273	V 3
FANCY THE SUNRISE--LEFT THE DOOR AJAR!	I KNOW SOME LONELY	289	40
AND LEFT IT IN THE SKY--	IT STRUCK ME--EVERY DAY	362	12
WHERE EACH--HAS LEFT A FRIEND--	THE COLOR OF THE GRAVE	411	16
PUT IT IN LATIN--LEFT OF MY SCHOOL--	IT DONT SOUND SO	426	3
I LEFT THE PLACE, WITH ALL MY MIGHT--	I MEANT TO HAVE BUT	476	17
PITY--THE PARD--THAT LEFT HER ASIA--	CIVILIZATION--SPURNS--	492	10
AND LEFT THE VERB AND THE PRONOUN OUT--	GOING TO HIM! HAPPY	494	5
AT LEAST--TO PRAY--IS LEFT--IS LEFT--	AT LEAST--TO PRAY--IS	502	1
AT LEAST--TO PRAY--IS LEFT--IS LEFT--	AT LEAST--TO PRAY--IS	502	1
AND LEFT THE PROFILE--PLAINER--	IT KNEW NO MEDICINE--	559	7
IT LEFT THE LITTLE TINT	IT KNEW NO MEDICINE--	559	9
AND LEFT BRAZILIAN THREADS	MY FIRST WELL DAY--SINCE	574	20
IS LEFT--TO PUT AWAY--	EMPTY MY HEART, OF THEE	587	9
NOVEMBER LEFT--THEN CLAMBERED UP	THE NIGHT WAS WIDE, AND	589	7
"MY BUSINESS BUT [JUST] A LIFE I LEFT	I YEARS HAD BEEN FROM	609	7
YOU LEFT ME--SIRE [SWEET]--TWO LEGACIES--	YOU LEFT ME--SIRE--TWO	644	1
YOU LEFT ME BOUNDARIES OF PAIN--	YOU LEFT ME--SIRE--TWO	644	5
THOUGH THE "ROMEO" LEFT [LEAVE] NO RECORD	DRAMA'S VITALLEST	741	10
BUT HE--WAS LEFT [REMAINED] ALIVE BECAUSE	HE FOUGHT LIKE THOSE	759	11
YOUR LIFE HAD LEFT BEHIND--	SEVERER SERVICE OF	786	4
HAVE LEFT EXPOSED A FRIEND--	DYING! TO BE AFRAID OF	831	3
AND LEFT THE LITTLE ANGLE WORM	OUR LITTLE KINSMEN--	885	11
HOW FAR LEFT HAND THE SEPULCHRE	HOW FAR IS IT TO HEAVEN?	929	7
WHAT EITHER LEFT BEHIND	TWO TRAVELLERS PERISHING	933	6
AND THOSE THEY LEFT BEHIND	TWO TRAVELLERS PERISHING	933	14
IS ALL THAT'S LEFT THEM, NOW--	DEATH LEAVES US HOMESICK	935	8
HE LEFT BEHIND ONE DAY--SO LESS	FITTER TO SEE HIM, I MAY	968	13

	FIRST LINE	POEM	LINE
LEFT (CONTINUED)			
LOOKING BACK IS BEST THAT IS LEFT	THIS WAS IN THE WHITE OF	995	5
I LEFT HER I COULD FIND HER	WE'LL PASS WITHOUT THE	996	5
PHIALS LEFT, AND THE SUN!	DYING AT MY MUSIC!	1003	6
LEFT INACTIVE ON THE STALK	REVOLUTION IS THE POD	1082	9
NOTHING IS LEFT TO PRAY--	WHATEVER IT IS--SHE HAS	1204	6
ROSE [LEFT] SURREPTITIOUSLY--	A SPARROW TOOK A SLICE	1211	V 8
HAD LEFT THE DEAD ALONE	MY TRIUMPH LASTED TILL	1227	2
LEFT IN IMMORTAL YOUTH	LEFT IN IMMORTAL YOUTH	1289	1
ALL THOSE HILLS YOU LEFT FOR ME TO HUE-- .	DEAR MARCH--COME IN--	1320	15
IS LEFT--THE IMMORTALITY--	TAKE ALL AWAY--	1365	3
THE SAVED HAVE [LEFT] NO REMEMBRANCE . . .	I SAW THE WIND WITHIN	1502	V
OF GLORY NOT A BEAM IS LEFT	OF GLORY NOT A BEAM IS	1647	1
NATURE HAD LEFT BEHIND.	HIGH FROM THE EARTH I	1723	8
LEGACIES			
YOU LEFT ME--SIRE [SWEET]--TWO LEGACIES-- .	YOU LEFT ME--SIRE--TWO	644	1
A RAPTURE AS OF LEGACIES--	TO TELL THE BEAUTY WOULD	1700	7
LEGACY			
LARCENY--LEGACY--	THE FEET OF PEOPLE	7	14
A LEGACY OF LOVE	YOU LEFT ME--SIRE--TWO	644	2
WHAT NECKLACES [AFFLUENCE / LEGACY] COULD BE [FOR ME]--	A DROP FELL ON THE APPLE	794	8
. . . QUICK / SWIFT / WILD] EXPERIMENT [LEGACY / APOCALYPSE / . . .	A LITTLE MADNESS IN THE	1333	5
LEGEND			
WHEN DIAMONDS ARE A LEGEND, ...	WHEN DIAMONDS ARE A	397	1
BUT ARARAT'S A LEGEND--NOW--	THE WINTERS ARE SO SHORT	403	15
EDEN--A LEGEND--DIMLY TOLD [LEARNED / CROONED]--	BETTER--THAN MUSIC! FOR	503	14
LEGENDS			
THEY TALK AS SLOW AS LEGENDS GROW	THEY TALK AS SLOW AS	1697	1
LEGIBLE			
HAD BEEN LEGIBLE--TO ME--	TO KNOW JUST HOW HE	622	15
LEGIONS			
HOW MANY LEGIONS OVERCOME--	WHO NEVER LOST, ARE	73	9
AS LEGIONS OF ALARM	ONE ANGUISH--IN A CROWD	565	6
AS LEGIONS OF A NIGHT	THE BATTLE FOUGHT	594	10
LEGISLATURE			
UNTO THE LEGISLATURE	"SIC TRANSIT GLORIA	3	25
LEGITIMATE			
LEGITIMATE, AND RARE--	BEST THINGS DWELL OUT OF	998	4
LEISURE			
AT LEISURE IS THE SOUL	AT LEISURE IS THE SOUL	618	1
MY LABOR AND MY LEISURE TOO, ...	BECAUSE I COULD NOT STOP	712	7
TILL NATURE LEISURE HAS FOR TERMS	THE VEINS OF OTHER	811	3
THE LEISURE OF HIS WILL--	ALL CIRCUMSTANCES ARE	820	6
A LEISURE OF THE FUTURE--	THERE IS A FINISHED	856	3
. . . PLEASURE / LEISURE PLEASURE]--	STRUCK, WAS I, NOR YET	925	7
AND THEN AN AWFUL LEISURE WAS	THE LAST NIGHT THAT SHE	1100	27
THIS LATEST LEISURE EQUAL LULLS [CASTLE EQUAL HOLDS]	NOT ANY HIGHER STANDS	1256	5
AT LEISURE WAS THE SUN--	THE MOUNTAINS STOOD IN	1278	5
LEISURELY			
SO LEISURELY--WERE WE--	HER FINAL SUMMER WAS IT	795	16
LEND			
WHY, I WILL LEND UNTIL JUST THEN, ...	PERHAPS YOU'D LIKE TO	134	9
TO LEND AN AMPLE SINEW	TO OFFER BRAVE	767	5
LENGTH			
IF AT LENGTH, THE SMOULDERING ANGUISH . .	I HAVE NEVER SEEN	175	13
DEPOSED--AT LENGTH [LAST], THE GRAVE-- . .	THERE CAME A DAY AT	322	26
BUT, NOW, UNCERTAIN OF THE LENGTH	IF YOU WERE COMING IN	511	17
AT LENGTH, RENEW THEIR SMILE--	I MEASURE EVERY GRIEF I	561	14
AT LENGTH, A MOURNER, LIKE MYSELF, . . .	THE BIRDS REPORTED FROM	743	13
'TWAS CRISIS--ALL THE LENGTH HAD PASSED-- .	'TWAS CRISIS--ALL THE	948	1
AT LENGTH THE NOTICE CAME.	THE LAST NIGHT THAT SHE	1100	20
IT SHALL AT LENGTH BE FOUND.	LONGING IS LIKE THE SEED	1255	4
DID LIFE'S PENURIOUS LENGTH	DID LIFE'S PENURIOUS	1717	1
LENGTHS			
TWO LENGTHS HAS EVERY DAY--	TWO LENGTHS HAS EVERY	1295	1
LENS			
EACH AGE A LENS	THE POETS LIGHT BUT	883	6
LENSES			
WHAT TRIPLE LENSES BURN UPON	OF CONSCIOUSNESS, HER	894	7
LENT			
AN UNREALITY IS LENT, ...	A DOUBT IF IT BE US	859	5
BY HOPE OR HORROR LENT--	TWO LENGTHS HAS EVERY	1295	4
THE MAPLE LENT UNTO THE ROAD	AS IMPERCEPTIBLY AS	1540	V
LEONTODON			
LITTLE LEONTODON.	WHOSE ARE THE LITTLE	142	12
LEONTODON'S			
THE BUTTERCUP'S [LEONTODON'S] ESCUTSCHEON--	TO HER DERIDED HOME	1586	V
LEOPARD			
LEOPARD BREATHES--AT LAST!	WITH THEE, IN THE DESERT	209	4
CIVILIZATION--SPURNS--THE LEOPARD! . . .	CIVILIZATION--SPURNS--	492	1
WAS THE LEOPARD--BOLD?	CIVILIZATION--SPURNS--	492	2
LEOPARD'S			
THIS WAS THE LEOPARD'S NATURE--SIGNOR-- . .	CIVILIZATION--SPURNS--	492	8
LEOPARDS			
LEAPING LIKE LEOPARDS TO [IN] THE SKY . .	BLAZING IN GOLD AND	228	2

	FIRST LINE	POEM	LINE
LESS SEE SYLLABLE-LESS			
LESS SKILLFUL THAN LE VERRIERE	SHE WENT AS QUIET AS THE	149	7
I, A LESS DIVINE--	THO' MY DESTINY BE	163	4
TILL WE--ARE LESS AFRAID--	READ--SWEET--HOW OTHERS	260	4
AN ADMIRALTY, LESS--	MY REWARD FOR BEING, WAS	343	3
I TAKE--NO LESS THAN SKIES--	PERHAPS I ASKED TOO	352	2
MAY LESS APPEAR	TO LOVE THEE YEAR BY	434	2
WERE HAD FOR LESS--	MUST BE A WO--	571	10
THROUGH LESS INFINITY--	THE TEST OF LOVE--IS	573	6
LESS PAEANS--FEWER BELLS--	MY PORTION IS DEFEAT--	639	3
YET BLAMED THE FATE THAT FRACTURED--[FLUNG IT] LESS	IT DROPPED SO LOW--IN MY	747	5
NO LESS BEREAVED WAS I	BEREAVED OF ALL, I WENT	784	2
LESS, THO LARGER, POOR.	ALL I MAY, IF SMALL,	819	8
INFERRED THE LESS BY GROWING THAN	I MADE SLOW RICHES BUT	843	7
A TURRET MORE, A TURRET LESS	JUST AS HE SPOKE IT FROM	848	3
THE LARGER GLORY FOR THE LESS	HE OUTSTRIPPED TIME WITH	865	7
LESS ACCOUNTED THAN	ALL FORGOT FOR	966	6
HE LEFT BEHIND ONE DAY--SO LESS	FITTER TO SEE HIM, I MAY	968	13
A PHEBE--NOTHING LESS--	I WAS A PHEBE--NOTHING	1009	2
IF WE [I] HAD VENTURED LESS	WE LIKE A HAIRBREADTH	1175	5
LEST LOVE SHOULD VALUE LESS	HAD THIS ONE DAY NOT	1253	5
FOR HIS LESS PRICELESS FRIEND.	BECAUSE THAT YOU ARE	1260	32
BUT CAME WITH LESS OF FEAR	WHILE WE WERE FEARING IT	1277	2
IS THAT DELIGHT IS LESS	DELIGHT'S DESPAIR AT	1299	2
I CANNOT WANT IT LESS--	I CANNOT WANT IT MORE--	1301	2
THAT THOSE WHO KNOW HER, KNOW HER LESS	WHAT MYSTERY PERVADES A	1400	23
THAT THERE ARE LESS TO COME--	BIRTHDAY OF BUT A SINGLE	1488	2
ASCRIBE NO LESS THE PRAISE--	THE BAT IS DUN, WITH	1575	14
LESSER			
AT SUNSET, OR A LESSER GLOW	ME, CHANGE! ME, ALTER!	268	4
THE SPANGLED GOWNS, A LESSER RANK	OF TRIBULATION--THESE	325	3
WHEN LESSER FAMES INVITE--	I HAD THE GLORY--THAT	349	3
AS BOY--SHOULD DEAL WITH LESSER BOY--	IT ALWAYS FELT TO ME--A	597	15
A LESSER THAN THE WHOLE--	WITHOUT THIS--THERE IS	655	6
WHO GIANTS KNOW, WITH LESSER MEN	WHO GIANTS KNOW, WITH	796	1
A SMALLER [LESSER] THAN THE LARGE--	LOVE--IS THAT LATER	924	12
AND NOT A SMALLER [LESSER] MAN	I THOUGHT THAT NATURE	1286	12
LEST			
LEST I SH'D BE OLD FASHIONED	THE MORNS ARE MEEKER	12	7
HASTE! LEST WHILE YOU'RE LAGGING	HEART! WE WILL FORGET	47	7
LEST THAT SHOULD CONQUER ME.	I HAV'NT TOLD MY GARDEN	50	2
LEST ANYBODY FIND--	SO BASHFUL WHEN I SPIED	91	4
LEST SUCH A SUBTLE--SHIMMERING GRACE	A SOMETHING IN A	122	11
BEWARE, LEST THIS LITTLE BROOK OF LIFE,	HAVE YOU GOT A BROOK IN	136	15
LEST ANYBODY SPY THE BLOOD	A WOUNDED DEER--LEAPS	165	11
AND LEST I--CRY--	WE DONT CRY--TIM AND I,	196	16
LEST MY BESEECHING FACE--AT LAST--	COULD I--THEN--SHUT THE	220	2
LEST WE TOO AWKWARD SHOW	THERE CAME A DAY AT	322	15
BUT, LEST THE SOUL--LIKE FAIR "PRISCILLA"	GOD IS A DISTANT--	357	5
LEST IT FALL--	I GAINED IT SO--	359	11
LEST INTERVIEW--ANNUL A WANT	A CHARM INVESTS A FACE	421	7
LEST SKIES IMPEACH A WEALTH SO WONDERFUL--	I'LL CLUTCH--AND CLUTCH	427	23
LEST THEY--WONDER WHY--	SWEET--SAFE--HOUSES--	457	15
LEST NOON IN [DOWN] EVERLASTING NIGHT--	I ENVY SEAS, WHEREON HE	498	23
A TROUBLE LEST THEY'RE HOMESICK--	I'M SORRY FOR THE DEAD--	529	13
LEST THE PHANTASM--PROVE THE [JUST] MISTAKE--	WE DREAM--IT IS GOOD WE	531	11
I DARED NOT ENTER [OPEN], LEST A FACE	I YEARS HAD BEEN FROM	609	3
LEST BACK THE AWFUL DOOR SHOULD SPRING	I YEARS HAD BEEN FROM	609	19
NO NUMB ALARM--LEST DIFFERENCE COME--	I THINK TO LIVE--MAY BE	646	13
LEST THE JEALOUS GRASS	PROMISE THIS--WHEN YOU	648	22
I TOUCHED WITH CAUTION--LEST THEY CRACK [SLIT]--	IF HE WERE LIVING--DARE	734	7
LEST DAY--	RENUNCIATION--IS A	745	7
LEST I SHOULD INSUFFICIENT PROVE [BE]	MY WORTHINESS IS ALL MY	751	5
LEST FIRMAMENT [UNIVERSE / DEITY] SHOULD FAIL FOR ME--	MY FAITH IS LARGER THAN	766	15
IS LEST ITSELF SHOULD SEE--	THE LONELINESS ONE DARE	777	6
LEST IF HE FLINCH--THE EYE THAT WAY	GRIEF IS A MOUSE--	793	10
LEST THIS BELOVED CHARGE	LOVE--IS THAT LATER	924	10
LEST THIS BE HEAVEN INDEED	LEST THIS BE HEAVEN	1043	1
LEST IN A FACE SO BEAUTIFUL	WHEN THEY COME BACK--IF	1080	11
BEFRIEND THEM, LEST YOURSELF IN HEAVEN	THESE STRANGERS, IN A	1096	3
LEST SOME ONE ELSE SHOULD [RICHER PEOPLE] BUY	A DIAMOND ON THE HAND	1108	V 8
LEST ANY DOUBT THAT WE ARE GLAD THAT THEY WERE BORN TODAY	LEST ANY DOUBT THAT WE	1156	1
LEST THEY SHOULD COME--IS ALL MY FEAR	LEST THEY SHOULD COME--	1169	1
ONLY LEST SHE BE LONELY	WHATEVER IT IS--SHE HAS	1204	9
AND MY FIRST FEARING, LEST UNKNOWNS	LET MY FIRST KNOWING BE	1218	3
LEST LOVE SHOULD VALUE LESS	HAD THIS ONE DAY NOT	1253	5
LEST MEN SPECIFICAL ADORN	I CANNOT SEE MY SOUL BUT	1262	8
GO RAPID, LEST COMPETING DEATH	GO SLOW, MY SOUL, TO	1297	3
GO TIMID, LEST [SHOULD] HIS FINAL [TESTING / BLAZING / LOFTY] EYE	GO SLOW, MY SOUL, TO	1297	5
BUT LEST OUR SPECULATION	"WAS NOT" WAS ALL THE	1342	5
"THE SUMMER" THAN "THE AUTUMN," LEST	AS SUMMER INTO AUTUMN	1346	3
NOR ANY DEATH--BUT LEST	I HAVE NO LIFE BUT THIS	1398	3
LEST CERTAINTY BE SERE	SWEET SKEPTICISM OF THE	1413	6
LEST SIGHT'S [PROOF'S] INEFFABLE DISGRACE	WE SHUN BECAUSE WE PRIZE	1429	2
NO NEARER--LEST THE ACTUAL--[REALITY--	WHO NEVER WANTED--	1430	7

		FIRST LINE	POEM	LINE
LEST	(CONTINUED) / ITS PENURY-- / THE . . .			
	LEST GRATITUDE REVIVE THE SNAKE [MY THOUGHT]	IT CAME HIS TURN TO BEG	1500	7
	AND LEST IT FLY,	WE SHUN IT ERE IT COMES,	1580	4
	LEST HE PURSUE	IN WINTER IN MY ROOM	1670	34
LET				
	LET US GO WITH THEE!	THE GENTIAN WEAVES HER	18	16
	LET US CHANT IT SOFTLY--	ALL THESE MY BANNERS BE.	22	18
	"I WILL NOT LET THEE GO	A LITTLE EAST OF JORDAN,	59	10
	MODEST, LET US WALK AMONG IT	I CANT TELL YOU--BUT YOU	65	9
	OH LET ME IMMEDIATELY "FADE"!	IF THIS IS "FADING"	120	2
	MANSIONS CANNOT LET THE TEARS IN,	"HOUSES"--SO THE WISE	127	3
	WHO'LL LET ME OUT SOME GALA DAY	BRING ME THE SUNSET IN A	128	22
	THIS WAY, JESUS, LET HIM PASS!	DYING! DYING IN THE	158	8
	SO HE LET ME LEAD HIM IN--	HE WAS WEAK, AND I WAS	190	2
	SO I LET HIM LEAD ME--HOME.	HE WAS WEAK, AND I WAS	190	4
	UNTIL HE LET YOU IN!	SHOULD YOU BUT FAIL AT--	226	7
	STOP JUST A MINUTE--LET ME THINK!	WHAT WOULD I GIVE TO SEE	247	4
	LET NO PEBBLE--SMILE--	I CAN WADE GRIEF--	252	7
	WILL LET IT'S KEEPSAKE--GO	A SINGLE SCREW OF FLESH	263	20
	JUST LET GO THE BREATH--	'TIS SO APPALLING--IT	281	16
	LIKE LET OF SNOW--	A MIEN TO MOVE A QUEEN--	283	18
	JUST AS THE GRANITE CRUMB LET GO--	THAT AFTER HORROR--THAT	286	3
	WHERE HE TURNED SO, AND I TURNED--HOW [LET GO]--	I GOT SO I COULD HEAR	293	7
	WHEN THEY LET GO THE IGNOMINY--SMILING--	UNTO LIKE STORY--TROUBLE	295	7
	LET ME NOT SHAME THEIR SUBLIME DEPORTMENTS--	UNTO LIKE STORY--TROUBLE	295	21
	LET ME--CHOOSE!	ONE YEAR AGO--JOTS WHAT?	296	36
	TO LET A BEETLE PASS--	A BIRD CAME DOWN THE	328	8
	AND LET THE FIRE THROUGH--	IT STRUCK ME--EVERY DAY	362	4
	I NEVER WOULD LET GO--	ALTHOUGH I PUT AWAY HIS	366	12
	LET JUSTICE NOT MISTAKE--	'TWAS LOVE--NOT ME--	394	9
	AND LET YOU FROM A DREAM--	'TWAS LIKE A MAELSTROM,	414	9
	LET GO, THEN, OVERCOME--	'TWAS LIKE A MAELSTROM,	414	17
	LET GO A MUSIC--AS OF TUNES	THE WIND--TAPPED LIKE A	436	15
	MEEK--LET IT BE--TOO PROUD--FOR PRIDE--	I AM ASHAMED--I HIDE--	473	26
	LET ME THINK--I'M SURE	I WAS THE SLIGHTEST IN	486	8
	AND LET HIM HEAR IT DRIP	TO ONE DENIED TO DRINK	490	6
	LET ME NOT SPILL [LOSE / WASTE]--IT'S SMALLEST CADENCE--	BETTER--THAN MUSIC! FOR	503	21
	LET NOT MY WITNESS HINDER THEM [THEM IMPAIR--]	'TIS TRUE--THEY SHUT ME	538	5
	BUT LET A SPLINTER SWERVE--	THE BRAIN, WITHIN IT'S	556	3
	TO LET HIM SEE--THE CANAAN--	IT ALWAYS FELT TO ME--A	597	3
	TO LET THE ORCHARDS GROW--	THE TREES LIKE TASSELS--	606	16
	THE EASIER TO LET GO--	YOU'LL FIND--IT WHEN YOU	610	2
	LET MONTHS DISSOLVE IN FURTHER [OTHER] MONTHS--	FOREVER--IS COMPOSED OF	624	7
	AND WOULD NOT LET THE SECONDS BY--	I THINK THE LONGEST HOUR	635	7
	AT MIDNIGHT--LET THE OWL SELECT	THE JUDGE IS LIKE THE	699	11
	LET US PLAY YESTERDAY--	LET US PLAY YESTERDAY--	728	1
	LET IN--WITH LIGHT--	LET US PLAY YESTERDAY--	728	24
	HAD LET IT'S PLEASURE THROUGH--	MY LIFE HAD STOOD--A	754	12
	LET NO SUNRISE' YELLOW NOISE	AMPLE MAKE THIS BED--	829	7
	LET AN INSTANT PUSH	CRISIS IS A HAIR	889	9
	THAT WOULD NOT LET THE WILL--	'TWAS CRISIS--ALL THE	948	10
	LET US DIVIDE [DEPORT]--WITH SKILL--	A MAN MAY MAKE A REMARK	952	5
	LET US DISCOURSE [DISCLOSE]--WITH CARE--	A MAN MAY MAKE A REMARK	952	6
	WHEN CEREMENTS LET GO	'TIS ANGUISH GRANDER	984	6
	SO THEREFORE LET ME IN."	THE FINGERS OF THE LIGHT	1000	4
	BUT SWEAR, AND I WILL LET YOU BY	THE FINGERS OF THE LIGHT	1000	7
	LET IT BE	'TWAS MY ONE GLORY--	1028	2
	AND ONCE TO LET IT DOWN	HER LITTLE PARASOL TO	1038	2
	LET DOWN THE BARS, OH DEATH--	LET DOWN THE BARS, OH	1065	1
	LET BROOKS--RENEW OF BROOKS--	THE WELL UPON THE BROOK	1091	3
	AND LET NO WITNESS IN	A GREAT HOPE FELL	1123	5
	BUT LET OUR OBSERVATION SHUT [HALT]	NATURE AFFECTS TO BE	1170	3
	WE LET GO ALL OF TIME WITHOUT	THE DAYS THAT WE CAN	1184	7
	THE BROOK SAID "LET ME GROW"--	THE SEA SAID "COME" TO	1210	2
	LET MY FIRST KNOWING BE OF THEE	LET MY FIRST KNOWING BE	1218	1
	AND LET THE FLOODS ABROAD--	LIKE RAIN IT SOUNDED	1235	12
	AND SEATS ITSELF TO BE LET GO	RISK IS THE HAIR THAT	1239	7
	BUT LET NOT REVELATION	THE LILAC IS AN ANCIENT	1241	19
	UNCHALLENGED--LET IT LIE--	THAT SACRED CLOSET WHEN	1273	10
	BUT LET HIM ONCE SUSPECT	UNTIL THE DESERT KNOWS	1291	4
	LET ME NOT MAR THAT PERFECT DREAM	LET ME NOT MAR THAT	1335	1
	LET ALL ADDICTED TO	A RAT SURRENDERED HERE	1340	5
	THAT WOULD [WILL] NOT LET THE EYE DECIDE	THESE HELD THEIR WICK	1390	7
	I'LL LET MY HEART BE JUST IN SIGHT--	THEY MIGHT NOT NEED ME--	1391	2
	MY MAKER--LET ME BE	MY MAKER--LET ME BE	1403	1
	SO LET US GATHER--EVERY DAY--	TO EARN IT BY DISDAINING	1427	5
	LET HIM BE QUICK--THE VIAND FLITS [BANQUET COOLS]--	MINE ENEMY IS GROWING	1509	5
	AND SHOUTED [BUBBLED / GURGLED] LET US PRAY--	THE BOBOLINK IS GONE--	1591	7
	LET EVERY BONDAGE BE,	IMMURED IN HEAVEN!	1594	3
	LET IT BE IN SIGHT OF THEE--	BEAUTY CROWDS ME TILL I	1654	4
	AND LET HIS FLESH	THE EVENT WAS DIRECTLY	1686	7
	LET CHANGE TRANSFUSE ALL OTHER TRAITS	THE LOOK OF THEE, WHAT	1689	9
	LET EVERY BABBLER [PRATER] BE	THE RETICENT VOLCANO	1748	10
	LET ME NOT THIRST WITH THIS HOCK AT MY LIP,	LET ME NOT THIRST WITH	1772	1

	FIRST LINE	POEM	LINE
LETHARGIC			
LETHARGIC POOLS RESUME THE WHIRR	SOME RAINBOW--COMING	64	8
LETHE			
"LETHE" IN MY FLOWER,	"LETHE" IN MY FLOWER,	1730	1
LET'S			
LET'S PLAY THOSE--NEVER COME!	MAKE ME A PICTURE OF THE	188	14
LETS			
AND LETS THE MORNING GO--	AS WATCHERS HANG UPON	121	9
FEELS EASY, AS WHEN DAY LETS GO	WHEN ONE HAS GIVEN UP	853	3
LIGHTNING--LETS AWAY	STRUCK, WAS I, NOR YET	925	2
THAT LETS HIM OUT AGAIN.	WHO IS THE EAST?	1032	8
THAT LETS IT'S RUSHES GROW	A STAGNANT PLEASURE LIKE	1281	2
AND LETS THE BRAIN AWAY	IF EVER THE LID GETS OFF	1727	2
LETTER			
BY A FLOWER--BY A LETTER--	BY A FLOWER--BY A LETTER	109	1
TO HOLD A LETTER TO THE LIGHT--	IN EBON BOX, WHEN YEARS	169	5
THIS IS MY LETTER TO THE WORLD	THIS IS MY LETTER TO THE	441	1
AN AMPLE LETTER--HOW YOU MISS--	YOU LOVE THE LORD--YOU	487	5
GOING TO HIM [HER]! HAPPY LETTER!	GOING TO HIM! HAPPY	494	1
UNTIL TOMORROW [THE EVENING]--HAPPY LETTER! [AH! BE BASHFUL]	GOING TO HIM! HAPPY	494	24
THEN DRAW MY LITTLE LETTER FORTH	THE WAY I READ A	636	7
YOU'LL GET MY LETTER BY	BEE! I'M EXPECTING YOU!	1035	9
A LETTER CHIEF TO ME	MYSELF CAN READ THE	1089	2
I GOT YOUR LETTER, AND THE BIRDS--	DEAR MARCH--COME IN--	1320	11
BELSHAZZAR HAD A LETTER--	BELSHAZZAR HAD A LETTER	1459	1
A LETTER IS A JOY OF EARTH--	A LETTER IS A JOY OF	1639	1
LETTER'S			
THE WAY I READ A LETTER'S--THIS [SO]--	THE WAY I READ A	636	1
LETTERS			
IN WHICH HIS LETTERS GREW	I GOT SO I COULD HEAR	293	10
ALL THE LETTERS I CAN [COULD] WRITE	ALL THE LETTERS I CAN	334	1
LETTING			
FIRST--CHILL--THEN STUPOR--THEN THE LETTING GO--	AFTER GREAT PAIN, A	341	13
THAN LETTING HIM SURMISE?	TO ONE DENIED TO DRINK	490	4
THE LETTING GO	RENUNCIATION--IS A	745	2
LETTRES			
LOW AMID THAT GLAD BELLES LETTRES	IF THE FOOLISH, CALL	168	17
LEVEL			
I HEAR THE LEVEL BEE--	LIKE TRAINS OF CARS ON	1224	2
LEVELED			
WAS LEVELED, BUT FOR THAT TWOULD BE	THE SAVIOR MUST HAVE	1487	7
LEVELLED			
LOADED AND LEVELLED	THE EVENT WAS DIRECTLY	1686	6
LEVER			
THAT LEVER CANNOT PRY--	ON A COLUMNAR SELF--	789	5
LEXICON			
WITHOUT THE LEXICON!	FOREVER AT HIS SIDE TO	246	16
AT MY LEXICON--	LET US PLAY YESTERDAY--	728	6
LEXICONS			
THEY WORE [KNEW] NO LEXICONS--	"WAS NOT" WAS ALL THE	1342	4
LEXINGTON			
AS WHEN 'TWAS CUT AT LEXINGTON,	MY COUNTRY NEED NOT	1511	3
LIABLE			
HE'S [THAT'S / 'TIS] LIABLE WITH THEM	HAD WE OUR SENSES	1284	4
LIAR			
AND OF "TRUTH" UNTIL IT PROCLAIMED HIM A LIAR--	HE PREACHED UPON	1207	3
LIP WAS NOT THE LIAR.	HAD I KNOWN THAT THE	1720	6
LIBATION			
POURED LIKE THIS--MY WHOLE [BEST] LIBATION--	PROMISE THIS--WHEN YOU	648	13
LIBERTY			
AND STEP [WADE] IN LIBERTY!	WHAT IF I SAY I SHALL	277	6
IT SETS THE FRIGHT AT LIBERTY--	'TIS SO APPALLING--IT	281	22
MY SOUL--AT LIBERTY--	NO RACK CAN TORTURE ME--	384	2
SO'S LIBERTY.	NO RACK CAN TORTURE ME--	384	16
IN PAWN FOR LIBERTY--	IT FEELS A SHAME TO BE	444	8
TOUCH LIBERTY--THEN KNOW NO MORE,	THE SOUL HAS BANDAGED	512	17
THE PRIVILEGE [THE LIBERTY / AUTHORITY] TO SAY	HE PARTS HIMSELF--LIKE	517	14
THE PRIVILEGE [LIBERTY / LUXURY] TO DIE--	THE HEART ASKS PLEASURE	536	8
THE CHEEK OF LIBERTY--	A PRISON GETS TO BE A	652	20
THE LIBERTY WE KNEW	A PRISON GETS TO BE A	652	29
WHAT LIBERTY! SO CAPTIVES DEEM	COULD I BUT RIDE	661	17
WHERE LIBERTY--	NO PRISONER BE--	720	2
LIBERTY--COMMONER--	LET US PLAY YESTERDAY--	728	19
TAKE NOT MY LIBERTY	LET US PLAY YESTERDAY--	728	35
ROBBED BY LIBERTY	ROBBED BY DEATH--BUT	971	4
SO OF LIBERTY--	REVOLUTION IS THE POD	1082	8
AND USHER LIBERTY.	THE DUTIES OF THE WIND	1137	4
WAS BUT A BOOK--WHAT LIBERTY	HE ATE AND DRANK THE	1587	7
LIBERTY'S			
LIBERTY'S BEGUILE [FORESTALL]"	WOLFE DEMANDED DURING	678	8
LIBRARY			
TILL MY SMALL LIBRARY--	UNTO MY BOOKS--SO GOOD	604	8
LIBYAN SEE LYBIAN			
LICENSE			
THE LICENSE TO REVERE,	I WOULD NOT PAINT--A	505	20
THEN--THE LICENSE [VISION / PAGEANT] CLOSES--	SOME SUCH BUTTERFLY BE	541	4
WITH LIMIT [LICENSE] OF DECAY--	TO MY SMALL HEARTH HIS	638	6

	FIRST LINE	POEM	LINE
LICENSE (CONTINUED)			
PRESENCE--IS HIS FURTHEST LICENSE--	CONSCIOUS AM I IN MY	679	9
LICENSE TO THINK OF [CHERISH] US--	WHATEVER IT IS--SHE HAS	1204	12
LICENSED			
IS LICENSED TO BE STILL.	IT'S HOUR WITH ITSELF	1225	8
LICK			
AND LICK THE VALLEYS UP--	I LIKE TO SEE IT LAP	585	2
LICKED			
THAT LICKED IT FROM THE COAST--	'TWAS SUCH A LITTLE--	107	6
LID			
OPENS THE LID OF AMETHYST	AS WATCHERS HANG UPON	121	8
THOUGH GOD FORBID IT LIFT THE LID--	A TRANSPORT ONE CANNOT	184	3
BY STRETCH OF LIMB--OR STIR OF LID--	A LONG--LONG SLEEP--A	654	3
BUT, NO LID HAS MEMORY--	WHAT I SEE NOT, I BETTER	939	4
AS WILLING LID O'ER WEARY EYE	AS WILLING LID O'ER	1050	1
A CLOSING OF THE SIMPLE LID [GATE]	A GREAT HOPE FELL	1123	14
PUT ON THE PERFECT LID--	WHEN MEMORY IS FULL	1266	2
BUT JUST HIS LID [LIP] OF GLASS--	WHAT MYSTERY PERVADES A	1400	6
IF EVER THE LID GETS OFF MY HEAD	IF EVER THE LID GETS OFF	1727	1
LIDS			
THE CROCUS STIRS HER LIDS--	WHOSE ARE THE LITTLE	142	22
THEN--CLOSE THE VALVES [LIDS] OF HER ATTENTION--	THE SOUL SELECTS HER OWN	303	11
LIDS OF STEEL--ON LIDS OF MARBLE--	SWEET--SAFE--HOUSES--	457	4
LIDS OF STEEL--ON LIDS OF MARBLE--	SWEET--SAFE--HOUSES--	457	4
LIE			
THE VIOLETS LIE	ONE SISTER HAVE I IN OUR	14	21
ON EARS THAT DYING LIE--	DISTRUSTFUL OF THE	20	12
WILL IDLE LIE--IN AUBURN--	WHEN ROSES CEASE TO	32	7
ON IT'S BREAST TO LIE--	NOBODY KNOWS THIS LITTLE	35	8
WHEN WE WITH DAISIES LIE--	IF I SHOULD DIE,	54	12
LIE BETWEEN THEM NOW.	AMBITION CANNOT FIND HIM	68	4
WHEN THE MEADOWS PARCHING LIE,	HAVE YOU GOT A BROOK IN	136	14
WHICH IN THE VALLEYS LIE?	WHOSE ARE THE LITTLE	142	2
TOO SOUND ASLEEP DID LIE	ON SUCH A NIGHT, OR SUCH	146	12
SLEEP [LIE] THE MEEK MEMBERS OF THE RESURRECTION--	SAFE IN THEIR ALABASTER	216	4
OR DOOMED LIE--	SHOULD YOU BUT FAIL AT--	226	3
WINTER, WERE LIE--TO ME--	THE ROBIN'S MY CRITERION	285	14
FOR THE RATES--LIE HERE--	FOR DEATH--OR RATHER	382	12
AND THE GODS--A LIE--	TAKING UP THE FAIR IDEAL	428	6
WITHIN MY INCOME--THESE COULD LIE	I MEANT TO HAVE BUT	476	3
AND ALL THE DEAD, LIE DOWN--	IT WAS NOT DEATH, FOR I	510	2
HAD SCARCELY DEIGNED TO LIE--	HER SWEET WEIGHT ON MY	518	2
IT SEEMS SO STRAIGHT TO LIE AWAY	I'M SORRY FOR THE DEAD--	529	9
THE SUBTLE CARGOES--LIE--	I GAVE MYSELF TO HIM--	580	12
THE LIPS THAT NEVER LIE--	A STILL--VOLCANO--LIFE--	601	10
MAKE SUMMER--WHEN THE LADY LIE	ESSENTIAL OILS--ARE	675	7
BOTH LIE--	THE SUNRISE RUNS FOR	710	18
SWEET MOUNTAINS--YE TELL ME NO LIE--	SWEET MOUNTAINS--YE TELL	722	1
TOO LITTLE WAY THE HOUSE MUST LIE	TOO LITTLE WAY THE HOUSE	911	1
FRAUD [LIE] CANNOT PRESUME--	HE WHO IN HIMSELF	969	2
SHE HAD BEGUN TO LIE--	SHE SPED AS PETALS OF A	991	8
OUR PERIODS MAY LIE	SUPERFLUOUS WERE THE SUN	999	10
'TIS EASIEST TO LIE	HERE, WHERE THE DAISIES	1037	2
THOUGH SUNSET LIE BETWEEN--	COUNT NOT THAT FAR THAT	1074	2
IN SOFT DISTINCTION LIE	SOME DAYS RETIRED FROM	1157	2
ASSUREDLY WILL LIE	THE BUTTERFLY IN HONORED	1246	2
THE WRINKLED MAKER [AUTHOR] LIE	A WORD DROPPED CARELESS	1261	4
UNCHALLENGED--LET IT LIE--	THAT SACRED CLOSET WHEN	1273	10
WARM IN HER HAND THESE ACCENTS LIE	WARM IN HER HAND THESE	1313	1
MORE ELOQUENTLY LIE	THE FLAKE THE WIND	1361	2
DOUBTLESS SECRETS LIE--	"SECRETS" IS A DAILY	1385	6
IN INSECURITY TO LIE	GO NOT TOO NEAR A HOUSE	1434	7
HOW MEAGRE, WHAT AN EXILE--IS A LIE,	A COUNTERFEIT--A PLATED	1453	6
IS POETRY, THOUGH NEVER IN A BOOK IT LIE--	TO SEE THE SUMMER SKY	1472	2
ALAS--THAT FROWNS [DUSK] SHOULD LIE IN WAIT	FROM ALL THE JAILS THE	1532	7
THOUGH WHERE IT'S LABORS LIE	WHY SHOULD WE HURRY--WHY	1646	7
LIEF			
I HAD AS LIEF THEY BORE	I TEND MY FLOWERS FOR	339	19
LIES			
HOW FAR THE VILLAGE LIES--	THE FEET OF PEOPLE	7	18
UPON THE HILL--THAT LIES--	I NEVER TOLD THE BURIED	11	2
HOW STILL THE RIDDLE LIES!	SOME THINGS THAT FLY	89	9
WHERE THE PLACE CALLED "MORNING" LIES!	WILL THERE REALLY BE A	101	12
THAT ON THE ACRE LIES.	EXCEPT TO HEAVEN, SHE IS	154	8
THE VILLAGE LIES--TODAY--	IT WILL BE SUMMER--	342	8
HOW DUMB [STILL] THE DANCER LIES--	AS FAR FROM PITY, AS	496	10
IN AMBER--LIES--	DELIGHT--BECOMES	572	6
HEREIN A BLOSSOM LIES--	HEREIN A BLOSSOM LIES--	899	1
MY NERVE IN MARBLE LIES--	I'VE DROPPED MY BRAIN--	1046	6
AND ARTISAN LIES [SMALL ESTATE STANDS--] STILL--	DEW--IS THE FRESHET IN	1097	4
SUCCESS IN CIRCUIT LIES	TELL ALL THE TRUTH BUT	1129	2
WHAT DIFFERENCE IN SUBSTANCE LIES	THE VOICE THAT STANDS	1189	5
BEFORE THEM LIES ESCAPELESS SEA--	THIS IS THE PLACE THEY	1264	7
HOW LUSCIOUS LIES WITHIN THE POD	FORBIDDEN FRUIT A FLAVOR	1377	3
THE SUN RESPECTFUL LIES--	A CHILLY PEACE INFESTS	1443	2
WHAT OMNIPRESENCE LIES IN WAIT	ALL THAT I DO	1496	10
TO-NIGHT SHE LIES	TO-DAY OR THIS NOON	1702	4

		FIRST LINE	POEM	LINE
LIFE	SEE MOLD-LIFE,EGG-LIFE			
	THE LIFE DOTH PROVE THE PRECEPT, WHO OBEY SHALL HAPPY BE,	AWAKE YE MUSES NINE,	1	9
	MY LIFE HAD FORFEIT BEEN.	I NEVER TOLD THE BURIED	11	9
	THE WEB OF LIFE WOVEN--	BY SUCH AND SUCH AN	38	3
	MY VELVET LIFE TO CLOSE--	IF SHE HAD BEEN THE	44	4
	STIRS THE CULPRIT--LIFE!	SURGEONS MUST BE VERY	108	4
	AND YET YOUR LITTLE DRAUGHT OF LIFE	HAVE YOU GOT A BROOK IN	136	7
	BEWARE, LEST THIS LITTLE BROOK OF LIFE,	HAVE YOU GOT A BROOK IN	136	15
	I THINK IT THAT "NEW LIFE"!	MUSICIANS WRESTLE	157	6
	MUST SEEK THE NEIGHBORING LIFE!	A LITTLE BREAD--A CRUST	159	12
	LIFE IS BUT LIFE! AND DEATH, BUT DEATH!	'TIS SO MUCH JOY! 'TIS	172	7
	LIFE IS BUT LIFE! AND DEATH, BUT DEATH!	'TIS SO MUCH JOY! 'TIS	172	7
	THE REST OF LIFE TO SEE!	AT LAST, TO BE	174	3
	I CAUTIOUS, SCANNED MY LITTLE LIFE--	I CAUTIOUS, SCANNED MY	178	1
	HOW ODD THE GIRL'S LIFE LOOKS	I'M "WIFE"--I'VE	199	5
	LIFE HAS IT'S ALE--	WE--BEE AND I--LIVE BY	230	3
	AND LIFE WOULD ALL BE SPRING!	THE SUN--JUST TOUCHED	232	4
	SAY--THAT A LITTLE LIFE--FOR HIS--	IF HE DISSOLVE--THEN--	236	12
	ALL LIFE--TO KNOW EACH OTHER--	FOREVER AT HIS SIDE TO	246	10
	I'D GIVE--I'D GIVE MY LIFE--OF COURSE--	WHAT WOULD I GIVE TO SEE	247	2
	THAT MAKES TWO--HIM--AND LIFE!	WHAT WOULD I GIVE TO SEE	247	6
	ONE LIFE OF SO MUCH CONSEQUENCE!	ONE LIFE OF SO MUCH	270	1
	WOULD COST ME--JUST A LIFE!	ONE LIFE OF SO MUCH	270	8
	THE LIFE IS THICK--I KNOW IT!	ONE LIFE OF SO MUCH	270	13
	A TIMID [HALLOWED] THING--TO DROP A LIFE	A SOLEMN THING--IT WAS--	271	5
	AND THEN--THE SIZE OF THIS "SMALL" LIFE--	A SOLEMN THING--IT WAS--	271	13
	HE PUT THE BELT AROUND MY LIFE--	HE PUT THE BELT AROUND	273	1
	WITH BUT A FRACTION OF THE LIFE [LOVE]--	DOUBT ME! MY DIM	275	3
	TIE THE STRINGS TO MY LIFE, MY LORD,	TIE THE STRINGS TO MY	279	1
	GOODBYE TO THE LIFE I USED TO LIVE--	TIE THE STRINGS TO MY	279	13
	THE DIAL LIFE--	A CLOCK STOPPED--	287	17
	HE HAS HID HIS RARE LIFE	I KNOW THAT HE EXISTS.	338	3
	I FELT MY LIFE WITH BOTH MY HANDS	I FELT MY LIFE WITH BOTH	351	1
	ALTHOUGH I PUT AWAY HIS LIFE--	ALTHOUGH I PUT AWAY HIS	366	1
	HER LIFE HAD LEAPED AWAY--	SHE LAY AS IF AT PLAY	369	2
	MY REASON--LIFE--	OF COURSE--I PRAYED--	376	6
	INHERITED WITH LIFE--	TO LOSE ONE'S FAITH--	377	5
	SWEET LITIGANTS FOR LIFE--	THERE IS A FLOWER THAT	380	20
	WITH GIFTS OF LIFE	FOR DEATH--OR RATHER	382	9
	THERE IS A LANGUOR OF THE LIFE	THERE IS A LANGUOR OF	396	1
	BUT JUST THE PRIMER--TO A LIFE--	NOT IN THIS WORLD TO SEE	418	4
	AND LIFE STEPS ALMOST STRAIGHT.	WE GROW ACCUSTOMED TO	419	20
	MORE LIFE--WENT OUT--WHEN HE WENT	MORE LIFE--WENT OUT--	422	1
	WHOSE PEAT LIFE--AMPLY VIVID--	MORE LIFE--WENT OUT--	422	17
	AS LIFE--DISSOLVED BE--FOR US--	IT FEELS A SHAME TO BE	444	15
	AND THEN, I [HE] BRAKE MY [HIS] LIFE--AND LO,	I SHOWED HER HIGHTS SHE	446	9
	THAT LIFE LIKE THIS--IS STOPLESS--	I LIVE WITH HIM--I SEE	463	15
	WHEN CHOICE OF LIFE--IS PAST--	THE MANNER OF IT'S DEATH	468	5
	AND LIFE AND I--KEEP EVEN--	I MEANT TO HAVE BUT	476	4
	AND LIFE WAS NOT SO	I HAD NO TIME TO HATE--	478	4
	LOVE [FAITH] IS LIKE LIFE--MERELY [ONLY THE] LONGER	WHILE IT IS ALIVE	491	7
	AS IF MY LIFE WERE SHAVEN,	IT WAS NOT DEATH, FOR I	510	13
	IF CERTAIN, WHEN THIS LIFE WAS OUT--	IF YOU WERE COMING IN	511	13
	OH LOVER--LIFE COULD NOT CONVINCE--	ME PROVE IT NOW--WHOEVER	537	7
	THAT LOVE IS [BE] LIFE--	THAT I DID ALWAYS LOVE	549	7
	AND LIFE HATH IMMORTALITY--	THAT I DID ALWAYS LOVE	549	8
	TO IMITATE HER LIFE	SHE HIDETH HER THE LAST	557	9
	HE GAVE AWAY HIS LIFE--	HE GAVE AWAY HIS LIFE--	567	1
	TO HOLD MY LIFE [THE LIGHT] FOR ME	I PRAYED, AT FIRST, A	576	17
	AFTER A LIFE--A DEATH--WE'LL SAY--	IF I MAY HAVE IT, WHEN	577	11
	THE SOLEMN CONTRACT OF A LIFE	I GAVE MYSELF TO HIM--	580	3
	SWEET DEBT OF LIFE--EACH NIGHT TO OWE--	I GAVE MYSELF TO HIM--	580	15
	LIFE--IS A DIFFERENT [ANOTHER] THING--	A TOAD, CAN DIE OF LIGHT	583	8
	TO HOLD MY LIFE, AND HOLD MY EARS	I CRIED AT PITY--NOT AT	588	19
	LIFE SET ME LARGER--PROBLEMS--	IT TROUBLED ME AS ONCE I	600	9
	A STILL--VOLCANO [VOLCANIC]--LIFE--	A STILL--VOLCANO--LIFE--	601	1
	OF LIFE? 'TWERE ODD I FEAR A THING	AFRAID! OF WHOM AM I	608	5
	"MY BUSINESS BUT [JUST] A LIFE I LEFT	I YEARS HAD BEEN FROM	609	7
	THE WIDTH OF LIFE--BEFORE IT SPREADS [RUNS]	AT LEISURE IS THE SOUL	618	3
	AS HARASS US--LIKE LIFE--AND DEATH--	I WATCHED THE MOON	629	25
	IT WOULD BE LIFE--	I CANNOT LIVE WITH YOU--	640	2
	AND LIFE IS OVER THERE--	I CANNOT LIVE WITH YOU--	640	3
	OUR LIFE--HIS PORCELAIN--	I CANNOT LIVE WITH YOU--	640	7
	I THINK TO LIVE--MAY BE A BLISS [LIFE]	I THINK TO LIVE--MAY BE	646	1
	HAD ALL MY LIFE BUT BEEN [BEEN ONE / BEEN BLEAK] MISTAKE	I THINK TO LIVE--MAY BE	646	27
	IF THE LIFE BE TOO SURRENDERED--	PROMISE THIS--WHEN YOU	648	11
	LIFE OF MINE--RESTORE--	PROMISE THIS--WHEN YOU	648	12
	HE NEVER SAW ME--IN THIS LIFE--	AGAIN--HIS VOICE IS AT	663	7
	THE LOVE A LIFE [CHILD] CAN SHOW BELOW	THE LOVE A LIFE CAN SHOW	673	1
	EACH LIFE CONVERGES TO SOME CENTRE--	EACH LIFE CONVERGES TO	680	1
	THIS TIMID LIFE OF EVIDENCE	THEIR HIGHT IN HEAVEN	696	15
	LIFE--IS WHAT WE MAKE IT--	LIFE--IS WHAT WE MAKE IT	698	1
	LIFE, AND DEATH, AND GIANTS--	LIFE, AND DEATH, AND	706	1
	IT'S EASY TO INVENT A LIFE--	IT'S EASY TO INVENT A	724	1
	"I WANT"--IT PLEADED--ALL IT'S LIFE--	"I WANT"--IT PLEADED--	731	1
	THE PLAYTHINGS OF HER LIFE	SHE ROSE TO HIS	732	2
	MY LIFE JUST HOLDS THE TRENCH--	IF HE WERE LIVING--DARE	734	16

	FIRST LINE	POEM		LINE
LIFE (CONTINUED)				
THAN LIFE--HAD DONE--BEFORE IT--	YOU TAUGHT ME WAITING	740		7
OF A SILENT LIFE--	GROWTH OF MAN--LIKE	750		8
MY LIFE HAD STOOD--A LOADED GUN--	MY LIFE HAD STOOD--A	754		1
AS ONE WHO FOR A FURTHER LIFE	HE FOUGHT LIKE THOSE	759		3
A THRUST--AND THEN FOR LIFE A CHANCE--	THE WHOLE OF IT CAME NOT	762		3
LIFE--JUST--OR DEATH--	ONE AND ONE--ARE ONE--	769		5
YOUR LIFE HAD LEFT BEHIND--	SEVERER SERVICE OF	786		4
A FURTHER FORCE [FUND] OF LIFE	HER FINAL SUMMER WAS IT	795		5
A PLATED LIFE--DIVERSIFIED	A PLATED LIFE--	806		1
A DEATH BLOW IS A LIFE BLOW TO SOME	A DEATH BLOW IS A LIFE	816		1
WHEN ONE HAS GIVEN UP ONE'S LIFE	WHEN ONE HAS GIVEN UP	853		1
THIS CHASM, SWEET, UPON MY LIFE	THIS CHASM, SWEET, UPON	858		1
WHEN IT HAS JUST CONTAINED A LIFE	THIS CHASM, SWEET, UPON	858		9
A LIFE QUITE READY TO DEPART	THIS CHASM, SWEET, UPON	858		19
A NEEDLESS LIFE, IT SEEMED TO ME	OUR LITTLE KINSMEN--	885		5
IGNORANT IS IT LIFE OR DEATH	CRISIS IS A HAIR	889		7
THE FIRST DAY THAT I WAS A LIFE	THE FIRST DAY THAT I WAS	902		1
THE LAST DAY THAT I WAS A LIFE	THE FIRST DAY THAT I WAS	902		3
INADEQUATE--WERE LIFE--	HAD I NOT THIS, OR THIS,	904		4
YOUR LIFE TOO ABJECT FOR ITSELF	TILL DEATH--IS NARROW	907		7
LOVE--IS ANTERIOR TO LIFE--	LOVE--IS ANTERIOR TO	917		1
IF I CAN EASE ONE LIFE THE ACHING	IF I CAN STOP ONE HEART	919		3
MORE PREVIOUS--THAN LIFE--	LOVE--IS THAT LATER	924		2
SO DIFFER LIFE AND DEATH	AS PLAN FOR NOON AND	960		2
FOR LIFE--BE [IS / MEANS] LOVE--	WERT THOU BUT ILL--THAT	961		20
AND LIVE--WITHOUT THE LIFE	TO DIE--WITHOUT THE	1017		2
CAME ALL THE WAY FROM LIFE TO ME	I HEARD, AS IF I HAD NO	1039		3
AND WANDERED OUT OF LIFE.	HE SCANNED IT--STAGGERED	1062		9
BETWEEN THE FORM OF LIFE AND LIFE	BETWEEN THE FORM OF LIFE	1101		1
BETWEEN THE FORM OF LIFE AND LIFE	BETWEEN THE FORM OF LIFE	1101		1
MY EARTHLY HOUR [HUMAN LIFE] TO ME	SOME WRETCHED CREATURE,	1111	V	4
THAT ALL MY LIFE HAD ENTERED IT	A GREAT HOPE FELL	1123		12
OH LIFE, BEGUN IN FLUENT BLOOD	THAT ODD OLD MAN IS DEAD	1130		9
WE HATED DEATH AND HATED LIFE	THE FROST OF DEATH WAS	1136		18
HATH THE PERFECTED LIFE--	THE PROPS ASSIST THE	1142		9
THE LIFE WE HAVE IS VERY GREAT.	THE LIFE WE HAVE IS VERY	1162		1
THE LIFE THAT WE SHALL SEE	THE LIFE WE HAVE IS VERY	1162		2
CONTAINED [COMBINED / COMPRISED] IN THIS SHORT [PLAIN] LIFE	CONTAINED IN THIS SHORT	1165		1
'TWAS FIGHTING FOR HIS LIFE HE WAS--	'TWAS FIGHTING FOR HIS	1188		1
THE "LIFE THAT IS" WILL THEN HAVE BEEN	BECAUSE THAT YOU ARE	1260		17
THE "LIFE THAT IS TO BE," TO ME,	BECAUSE THAT YOU ARE	1260		21
THE NEED [FACT / LIFE] IS NOT OF [FOR] ME--	I KNOW SUSPENSE--IT	1285		8
IN THIS SHORT LIFE	IN THIS SHORT LIFE	1287		1
OF LIFE TO OWN--	OF LIFE TO OWN--	1294		1
FROM LIFE TO DRAW--	OF LIFE TO OWN--	1294		2
WITHOUT THE CHANCE OF LIFE	I NEVER HEAR THAT ONE IS	1323		2
THE REST OF LIFE IS DROPT--	ESCAPE IS SUCH A	1347		8
"CROWNS OF LIFE" ARE SERVILE PRIZES	"FAITHFUL TO THE END"	1357		5
SPARE YOUR "CROWN OF LIFE"--	"FAITHFUL TO THE END"	1357	V	
IN SORDID HUMAN LIFE	A SAUCER HOLDS A CUP	1374		2
I HAVE NO LIFE BUT THIS--[TO LIVE]	I HAVE NO LIFE BUT THIS	1398		1
"HOW TRIVIAL IS LIFE!"	A DEW SUFFICED ITSELF--	1437		4
IT IS THE SAME WITH LIFE--	WE KNEW NOT THAT WE WERE	1462		8
THE BEGGING FOR THE LIFE	IT CAME HIS TURN TO BEG	1500		2
LIFE IS SHORTER THAN SUMMER--	SUMMER IS SHORTER THAN	1506		2
HE LIVED THE LIFE OF AMBUSH	HE LIVED THE LIFE OF	1525		1
AND HONEYS, IF HIS LIFE BE SPARED,	HIS ORIENTAL HERESIES	1526	V	
THE LIFE THAT TIED TOO TIGHT ESCAPES	THE LIFE THAT TIED TOO	1535		1
FOR ALL THE REST OF LIFE--	THE FARTHEST THUNDER	1581		8
IMMURED THE WHOLE OF LIFE	OF GOD WE ASK ONE FAVOR,	1601		5
MAKE LIFE A SUDDEN PRICE.	MORNING THAT COMES BUT	1610		4
NO LIFE CAN POMPLESS PASS AWAY--	NO LIFE CAN POMPLESS	1626		1
AND NOW, BY LIFE DEPRIVED,	SO GIVE ME BACK TO DEATH	1632		4
TO POINT A HUMAN LIFE?	GO THY GREAT WAY!	1638		5
PAID ALL THAT LIFE HAD EARNED	HOW DARE THE ROBINS SING	1724		5
AND NOW, WHAT LIFE OR DEATH CAN DO	HOW DARE THE ROBINS SING	1724		7
I TOOK ONE DRAUGHT OF LIFE--	I TOOK ONE DRAUGHT OF	1725		1
MY LIFE CLOSED TWICE BEFORE ITS CLOSE;	MY LIFE CLOSED TWICE	1732		1
IS WHAT MAKES LIFE SO SWEET.	THAT IT WILL NEVER COME	1741		2
TILL EVERLASTING LIFE [RITE] UNITE	THE GRAVE MY LITTLE	1743		7
LIFELESS				
BUT STROVE TO STIR THE LIFELESS [FLICKERING] FAN	THREE TIMES--WE PARTED--	598		3
A LIFELESS DEITY.	TRUTH--IS AS OLD AS GOD	836		8
THE CLAWS THAT CLUNG, LIKE LIFELESS GLOVES	HIS BILL IS CLASPED--HIS	1102		3
LIFE'S				
IN LIFE'S DIVERSE BOQUET--	WENT UP A YEAR THIS	93		14
FOR LIFE'S ESTATE WITH YOU--	YOUR RICHES--TAUGHT ME--	299		8
OF LIFE'S PENURIOUS ROUND--	I SHOULD HAVE BEEN TOO	313		3
LIFE'S OPPORTUNITY--	FOR DEATH--OR RATHER	382		4
LIFE'S LITTLE DUTIES DO--PRECISELY--	I TIE MY HAT--I CREASE	443		2
THEREFORE--WE DO LIFE'S LABOR--	I TIE MY HAT--I CREASE	443		30
THOUGH LIFE'S REWARD--BE DONE--	I TIE MY HAT--I CREASE	443		31
BLISS OF DEATH--LIFE'S BLISS EXTOL THRO [SURPASS IN / EXCEL IN]	PROMISE THIS--WHEN YOU	648		15
UNGAINED--IT MAY BE--BY [IN] A LIFE'S LOW VENTURE--	EACH LIFE CONVERGES TO	680		17
THAN LIFE'S SWEET [NEW] CALCULATIONS--	UPON CONCLUDED LIVES	735		3

	FIRST LINE	POEM	LINE
LIFE'S (CONTINUED)			
LIFE'S LATITUDES LEANT OVER--FULL--	ONE BLESSING HAD I THAN	756	15
'TIS LIFE'S AWARD--TO DIE--	THE WHOLE OF IT CAME NOT	762	9
FOR TREASON NOT OF HIS, BUT LIFE'S,	THE SUNSET STOPPED ON	950	3
UP LIFE'S HILL WITH MY LITTLE BUNDLE	UP LIFE'S HILL WITH MY	1010	1
ESSENTIAL HOST, IN LIFE'S FAINT, WAILING INN,	AIR HAS NO RESIDENCE, NO	1060	6
WHEN LIFE'S SWIFT RIVER STRIVEN THROUGH	WHAT TWIGS WE HELD BY--	1086	3
BUT FROM LIFE'S CONSUMMATE CLUSTER--	DEATH'S WAYLAYING NOT	1296	7
OF LIFE'S DECLIVITY.	AS SUMMER INTO AUTUMN	1346	12
LIFE'S BOUQUET	TO EARN IT BY DISDAINING	1427	7
SHE [HE] BORE LIFE'S EMPTY PACK	HER LOSSES MAKE OUR	1562	2
LIFE'S EMPTY PACK IS HEAVIEST,	HER LOSSES MAKE OUR	1562	5
HOW [THAT] LIFE'S REVERBERATION	THE FARTHEST THUNDER	1581	19
ADVANCE IS LIFE'S CONDITION	ADVANCE IS LIFE'S	1652	1
DID LIFE'S PENURIOUS LENGTH	DID LIFE'S PENURIOUS	1717	1
LIFETIME			
YOU SEE I CANNOT SEE--YOUR LIFETIME--	YOU SEE I CANNOT SEE--	253	1
MY LIFETIME FOLDING UP--	HE PUT THE BELT AROUND	273	4
FROM OUR FAMILIAR LIFETIME [ADDRESS / GAZING / FINGERS / NOTICE]--	THOSE FAIR--FICTITIOUS	499	3
NO LIFETIME SET--ON THEM--	'TWAS A LONG PARTING--	625	9
AND WHEN YOUR LITTLE LIFETIME FAILED,	OURSELVES WERE WED ONE	631	3
AND DYING--LIFETIME--	'TWOULD EASE--A	682	12
LIFT			
AND LIFT IT UP TO THEE.	NOBODY KNOWS THIS LITTLE	35	4
WILL LIFT HIS LITTLE GIRL--	"ARCTURUS" IS HIS OTHER	70	31
A LORD, MIGHT DARE TO LIFT THE HAT	WAIT TILL THE MAJESTY OF	171	13
THOUGH GOD FORBID IT LIFT THE LID--	A TRANSPORT ONE CANNOT	184	3
TRY--CAN YOU LIFT THE HASPS OF STEEL!	HOW MANY TIMES THESE LOW	187	4
LIFT--IF YOU CARE--THE LISTLESS HAIR--	HOW MANY TIMES THESE LOW	187	6
AND THEN I HEARD THEM LIFT A BOX	I FELT A FUNERAL, IN MY	280	9
LIFT THE FLESH DOOR--	IF YOUR NERVE, DENY YOU	292	10
AND IT SHOULD LIFT IT'S PURPLE DIKES,	AS IF I ASKED A COMMON	323	7
LIFT, IN BEREAVED ACKNOWLEDGEMENT	I DREADED THAT FIRST	348	27
THE LADY DARE NOT LIFT HER VAIL	A CHARM INVESTS A FACE	421	3
THAT EVERY SIGH--MAY LIFT YOU	I'LL CLUTCH--AND CLUTCH	427	18
LIFT SUCH A CRUCIFIXAL SIGN	HE TOUCHED ME, SO I LIVE	506	17
TO LIFT HER GLASS--UPON--	I WATCHED THE MOON	629	8
TO LIFT HER BROWS ON YOU--	SWEET MOUNTAINS--YE TELL	722	12
ITSELF CAN REST [LIFT / BASE] UPON--	MY WORTHINESS IS ALL MY	751	12
THE LEAST--CAN LIFT A TON	SUCH IS THE FORCE OF	787	2
MAY LIFT A LOOK ON THINE, A MAID	BECAUSE THE BEE MAY	869	5
AND MAKES ONE LIFT ONE'S HAT	IT IS AN HONORABLE	946	2
COULD LIFT MY FOREHEAD FROM MY WORK	THE MISSING ALL,	985	7
HER LITTLE PARASOL TO LIFT	HER LITTLE PARASOL TO	1038	1
LIFT IT--WITH THE FEATHERS	LIFT IT--WITH THE	1348	1
THAT WILL NOT LIFT IT'S HAT--	OH GIVE IT MOTION--DECK	1527	8
NAY--LIFT THEMSELVES--FAME HAS NO ARMS--	ABOVE OBLIVION'S TIDE	1531	3
LIFTED			
TOO LIFTED--FOR THE SCANT DEGREE	I SHOULD HAVE BEEN TOO	313	2
I LIFTED HIM--	I ROSE--BECAUSE HE SANK	616	23
LIFTED ADORING--THEN--	THE BEGGAR LAD--DIES	717	14
IT LOOSENED ACRES, LIFTED SEAS	LIKE RAIN IT SOUNDED	1235	13
AND AN [THE] EFFACELESS "FEW" ARE LIFTED THERE--	ABOVE OBLIVION'S TIDE	1531	2
AND THEN HE LIFTED UP HIS THROAT	UPON HIS SADDLE SPRUNG A	1600	5
LIFTS			
WHERE NO AUTUMN LIFTS HER PENCIL--	THO' MY DESTINY BE	163	15
LIFTS [SPREADS] HIS LIGHT PINNACE--	THE NEAREST DREAM	319	8
THAT LIFTS US FROM THE GROUND	EXHILIRATION IS THE	1118	2
LIGHT			
IN A MORE GOLDEN LIGHT	I HAVE A BIRD IN SPRING	5	20
HERE TO LIGHT MEASURE, MOVE THE FEET	THERE IS A MORN BY MEN	24	7
I WILL FORGET THE LIGHT!	HEART! WE WILL FORGET	47	4
LIGHT SWUNG THE SILVER FLEECES	A LITTLE EAST OF JORDAN,	59	13
A TYRIAN LIGHT THE VILLAGE FILLS--	AN ALTERED LOOK ABOUT	140	2
WONT SOMEBODY BRING THE LIGHT	DYING! DYING IN THE	158	2
TO HOLD A LETTER TO THE LIGHT--	IN EBON BOX, WHEN YEARS	169	5
AFTER DINNER LIGHT--FOR FLOWERS--	MORNING--IS THE PLACE	197	3
LIGHT LAUGHS THE BREEZE	SAFE IN THEIR ALABASTER	216	7
JUST LAYING LIGHT--NO SOUL WILL WINK	WHEN WE STAND ON THE	242	5
THERE'S A CERTAIN SLANT OF LIGHT,	THERE'S A CERTAIN SLANT	258	1
IT MIGHT--HAVE BEEN THE LIGHT HOUSE SPARK--	GOOD NIGHT! WHICH PUT	259	7
TOWARD [TO] LIGHT--	UNTO LIKE STORY--TROUBLE	295	24
IT'S LIKE THE LIGHT--	IT'S LIKE THE LIGHT--	297	1
LIKE HINDERED RUBIES--OR THE LIGHT	THE DAY CAME SLOW--TILL	304	3
LIFTS [SPREADS] HIS LIGHT PINNACE--	THE NEAREST DREAM	319	8
WITHOUT A COLOR, BUT THE LIGHT	DARE YOU SEE A SOUL AT	365	7
UNTIL THE DESIGNATED LIGHT	DARE YOU SEE A SOUL AT	365	15
SO LIGHT--SO DEEP--	SHE LAY AS IF AT PLAY	369	16
WHEN LIGHT IS PUT AWAY--	WE GROW ACCUSTOMED TO	419	2
A LIGHT, FOR HER [ME], DID SOLEMN GLOW,	I SHOWED HER HIGHTS SHE	446	10
BETWEEN THE LIGHT--AND ME--	I HEARD A FLY BUZZ--WHEN	465	14
GAY--LIKE LIGHT--	I AM ASHAMED--I HIDE--	473	22
I ENVY LIGHT--THAT WAKES HIM--	I ENVY SEAS, WHEREON HE	498	17
AN IMITATION OF A LIGHT	I MEASURE EVERY GRIEF I	561	15
TO HOLD MY LIFE [THE LIGHT] FOR ME	I PRAYED, AT FIRST, A	576	17
A TOAD, CAN DIE OF LIGHT--	A TOAD, CAN DIE OF LIGHT	583	1
FOR VERY LUNACY OF LIGHT	I THINK I WAS ENCHANTED	593	7
HIS CONTINENTS [THEORIES] OF LIGHT--	THE SPIDER HOLDS A	605	10

	FIRST LINE	POEM		LINE
LIGHT (CONTINUED)				
I DO NOT NEED A LIGHT--	I SEE THEE BETTER--IN	611		2
AGLOW--ALL RUDDY--WITH THE LIGHT	I SEE THEE BETTER--IN	611		11
BY SOME ONE CARRYING A LIGHT--	OURSELVES WERE WED ONE	631		7
DID FAN AND ROCK, WITH SUDDEN LIGHT--	TO MY SMALL HEARTH HIS	638		3
HOW WELL I KNEW THE LIGHT BEFORE--	THE SUN KEPT SETTING--	692		13
LET IN--WITH LIGHT--	LET US PLAY YESTERDAY--	728		24
AND DO I SMILE, SUCH CORDIAL LIGHT	MY LIFE HAD STOOD--A	754		9
AS WILL SUFFICE TO LIGHT HER LAMPS--	NATURE--THE GENTLEST	790		19
A LIGHT EXISTS IN SPRING	A LIGHT EXISTS IN SPRING	812		1
THE LIGHT HIS ACTION, AND THE DARK	ALL CIRCUMSTANCES ARE	820		5
'TIS HEAVY AND 'TIS LIGHT.	BEFORE HE COMES WE WEIGH	834		2
TERM OF LIGHT THIS DAY BEGUN!	ALWAYS MINE!	839		3
DIVIDE LIGHT IF YOU DARE--	BANISH AIR FROM AIR--	854		2
LIGHT IS SUFFICIENT TO ITSELF--	LIGHT IS SUFFICIENT TO	862		1
THE POETS LIGHT BUT LAMPS--	THE POETS LIGHT BUT	883		1
IF VITAL LIGHT	THE POETS LIGHT BUT	883		4
LIGHT--ENABLING LIGHT--	THE ADMIRATIONS--AND	906		10
LIGHT--ENABLING LIGHT--	THE ADMIRATIONS--AND	906		10
AS SOMEONE HELD A LIGHT UNTO [UPON]	WHAT I SEE NOT, I BETTER	939		7
IN WHICH WE FIRST EXPERIENCED LIGHT	ON THAT DEAR FRAME THE	940		3
UNDER THE LIGHT, YET UNDER,	UNDER THE LIGHT, YET	949		1
OVER THE LIGHT, YET OVER,	UNDER THE LIGHT, YET	949		9
SUBSISTING ON THE LIGHT WE BORE	WE MET AS SPARKS--	958		5
THE FINGERS OF THE LIGHT	THE FINGERS OF THE LIGHT	1000		1
HELD UP HIS CUP FOR LIGHT.	THE FINGERS OF THE LIGHT	1000		16
THE EMIGRANT OF LIGHT, IT IS	WHO SAW NO SUNRISE	1018		5
AND NOW I KNOW 'TWAS LIGHT, BECAUSE	I HEARD, AS IF I HAD NO	1039		7
LATER THAN LIGHT THY CONSCIOUSNESS ACCOST ME	AIR HAS NO RESIDENCE, NO	1060		7
FIRE EXISTS THE FIRST IN LIGHT	ASHES DENOTE THAT FIRE	1063		5
HOW SCANT, BY EVERLASTING LIGHT	WHAT TWIGS WE HELD BY--	1086		14
BY THIS GREAT LIGHT UPON OUR MINDS	THE LAST NIGHT THAT SHE	1100		7
TO LIGHT, AND THEN RETURN--	THE SPRY ARMS OF THE	1103		12
WHO MISS HIS ANTIQUATED WICK [LIGHT]--	THAT ODD OLD MAN IS DEAD	1130		5
SOFT STIRS THE NEWS [STIR THE FLAKES] OF LIGHT	THE SMOULDERING EMBERS	1132		5
WITHOUT A LIGHT	A SPIDER SEWED AT NIGHT	1138		2
IN THY LONG PARADISE OF LIGHT	IN THY LONG PARADISE OF	1145		1
WITH MORNING'S WARMING LIGHT--	LET MY FIRST KNOWING BE	1218		2
BUT LIGHT A NEWER WILDERNESS	HAD I NOT SEEN THE SUN	1233		3
. . . THE / LUXURIOUS AS THE] LIGHT	YOU CANNOT TAKE ITSELF	1351		5
OF THEIR [HIS] PECULIAR LIGHT	OF THEIR PECULIAR LIGHT	1362		1
BY HER EXACTING LIGHT	UNWORTHY OF HER BREAST	1414		4
DESCRIED I--BY [IN] THE DISTANT [GAINING] LIGHT	THE ROAD WAS LIT WITH	1450		3
THE THRILL CAME SLOWLY LIKE A BOON [LIGHT] FOR	THE THRILL CAME SLOWLY	1495		1
OUR SUMMER MADE HER LIGHT ESCAPE	AS IMPERCEPTIBLY AS	1540		15
IMAGE [FELLOW] OF LIGHT, ADIEU--	IMAGE OF LIGHT, ADIEU--	1556		1
PASS TO THY RENDEZVOUS OF LIGHT,	PASS TO THY RENDEZVOUS	1564		1
THE AURORAL LIGHT.	MORNING IS DUE TO ALL--	1577		4
OF THAT WAYLAYING LIGHT--	THE FARTHEST THUNDER	1581		16
AS FROM THE EARTH THE LIGHT [FAIR] BALLOON	AS FROM THE EARTH THE	1630		1
LIGHT MY NORTHERN ROOM	GUEST AM I TO HAVE	1661		2
BY A DEPARTING [RETREATING / ABSCONDING] LIGHT	BY A DEPARTING LIGHT	1714		1
THAT FEEDS THE SACRED [CENTRAL] LIGHT.	HER FACE WAS IN A BED OF	1722		4
TO HIM WHOSE MORTAL LIGHT	HOW DARE THE ROBINS SING	1724		10
LIGHTED				
AND LIGHTED WITH A MATCH--	REMORSE--IS MEMORY--	744		6
THE TUNNEL IS NOT LIGHTED	ADVANCE IS LIFE'S	1652		5
LIGHTER				
BUT HER DISDAIN--'TWERE LIGHTER [COOLER] BEAR	MY SOUL--ACCUSED ME--AND	753		7
'TWAS LIGHTER [FIRMER]--TO BE BLIND--	FROM BLANK TO BLANK--	761		10
LIGHTEST				
THE LAST SHALL BE THE LIGHTEST LOAD	I DID NOT REACH THEE	1664		18
LIGHTLY				
POISED LIGHTLY ON HIS HAND,	THEY LEAVE US WITH THE	350		8
THEN LIGHTLY [SOFTLY] AS A REED	THE LAST NIGHT THAT SHE	1100		22
STEP LIGHTLY ON THIS NARROW SPOT--	STEP LIGHTLY ON THIS	1183		1
SPRANG LIGHTLY TO [ROSE SOFTLY IN / TURNED EASY IN] THE SKY	A SPARROW TOOK A SLICE	1211	V	6
TOUCH LIGHTLY NATURE'S SWEET GUITAR	TOUCH LIGHTLY NATURE'S	1389		1
TILL TREASON LIGHTLY PROPAGATES	WHOEVER DISENCHANTS	1451	V	7
AS LIGHTLY AS AN OPTION GOWN	WE KNEW NOT THAT WE WERE	1462		5
THEN SWEPT AS LIGHTLY FROM DISDAIN	TO HER DERIDED HOME	1586		7
LIGHTLY STEPPED A YELLOW STAR	LIGHTLY STEPPED A YELLOW	1672		1
LIGHTNING				
NO LIGHTNING, SCARES [DRIVES] AWAY--	WHEN WE STAND ON THE	242		8
THE LIGHTNING WAS AS NEW	IT STRUCK ME--EVERY DAY	362		2
HIS LISP--IS LIGHTNING--AND THE SUN--	YOU'LL KNOW IT--AS YOU	420		12
THE LIGHTNING--NEVER ASKED AN EYE	"WHY DO I LOVE" YOU, SIR	480		11
THE LIGHTNING PLAYETH--ALL THE WHILE--	THE LIGHTNING PLAYETH--	630		1
THE LIGHTNING SHOWED A YELLOW HEAD [BEAK]--	THE WIND BEGUN TO KNEAD	824		11
STRUCK, WAS I, NOR YET BY LIGHTNING--	STRUCK, WAS I, NOR YET	925		1
LIGHTNING--LETS AWAY	STRUCK, WAS I, NOR YET	925		2
AS LIGHTNING ON A LANDSCAPE	THE SOUL'S DISTINCT	974		5
AS LIGHTNING TO THE CHILDREN EASED	TELL ALL THE TRUTH BUT	1129		5
THE LIGHTNING PLAYED [SKIPPED] LIKE MICE	THE CLOUDS THEIR BACKS	1172		4
THE LIGHTNING IS A YELLOW FORK	THE LIGHTNING IS A	1173		1
FOR LIGHTNING IT IS OFT MISTOOK	A WINGED SPARK DOTH SOAR	1468		3
A LIGHTNING IN THE GERM--	FAME IS THE ONE THAT	1475		6

	FIRST LINE	POEM	LINE
LIGHTNING (CONTINUED)			
THE LIGHTNING THAT PRECEDED IT	THE FARTHEST THUNDER	1581	5
THE YELLOW LIGHTNING SHONE--	THE WIND DREW OFF	1694	6
LIGHTNING'S			
THE LIGHTNING'S POINARDS GLEAMED--	THROUGH LANE IT LAY--	9	10
THE MORNING'S AMBER [LIGHTNING'S JOINTED] ROAD--	BEFORE I GOT MY EYE PUT	327	15
LIGHTS			
LIKE MIGHTY FOOT LIGHTS--BURNED THE RED	LIKE MIGHTY FOOT LIGHTS	595	1
WHEN PEOPLE HAVE PUT OUT THE LIGHTS	HOW LONESOME THE WIND	1418	2
LIKE			
LIKE THEE TO DANCE--LIKE THEE TO SING--	THERE IS A MORN BY MEN	24	19
LIKE THEE TO DANCE--LIKE THEE TO SING--	THERE IS A MORN BY MEN	24	19
MORNS LIKE THESE--WE PARTED--	MORNS LIKE THESE--WE	27	1
NOONS LIKE THESE--SHE ROSE--	MORNS LIKE THESE--WE	27	2
LIKE HER THE SAINTS RETIRE,	LIKE HER THE SAINTS	60	1
LIKE HER THE EVENINGS STEAL	LIKE HER THE SAINTS	60	4
PEASANTS LIKE ME,	SO FROM THE MOULD	66	9
PEASANTS LIKE THEE	SO FROM THE MOULD	66	10
AND I'D LIKE TO LOOK A LITTLE MORE	GOING TO HEAVEN!	79	22
WHILE LIKE A GUARD BETWEEN--	OUR LIVES ARE SWISS--	80	7
BARBS HAS IT, LIKE A BEE!	MY FRIEND MUST BE A BIRD	92	5
HAS IT FEET LIKE WATER LILIES?	WILL THERE REALLY BE A	101	5
HAS IT FEATHERS LIKE A BIRD?	WILL THERE REALLY BE A	101	6
LIKE THIS!	WHERE I HAVE LOST, I	104	12
PERHAPS YOU'D LIKE TO BUY A FLOWER,	PERHAPS YOU'D LIKE TO	134	1
IF YOU WOULD LIKE TO BORROW,	PERHAPS YOU'D LIKE TO	134	3
FOR A SIMPLE BREAST LIKE MINE--	FLOWERS--WELL--IF	137	10
I HAD RATHER DWELL LIKE HER	PIGMY SERAPHS--GONE	138	14
NOT LIKE THE DEW, DID SHE RETURN	SHE WENT AS QUIET AS THE	149	3
BUILDS, LIKE A BIRD, TOO!	DUST IS THE ONLY SECRET	153	13
SCAN LIKE HIM, THE STATELY LANDSCAPE	IF THE FOOLISH, CALL	168	11
THAT QUICKENED US LIKE WINE!	IN EBON BOX, WHEN YEARS	169	8
FROM WHAT W'D LAST TILL HEADS LIKE MINE	I CAUTIOUS, SCANNED MY	178	3
LIKE MORNING GLORY!	POOR LITTLE HEART!	192	11
THE CLOUDS--LIKE LISTLESS ELEPHANTS--	ON THIS LONG STORM THE	194	3
MOST LIKE THEIR GLORY SHOW--	FOR THIS--ACCEPTED	195	16
HER PRETTY SPEECH--LIKE DRUNKEN MEN--	THE ROSE DID CAPER ON	208	3
THAT LIKE THE DRUNKARD GOES--	THE ROSE DID CAPER ON	208	12
A VEST THAT LIKE HER BODDICE, DANCED--	THE ROSE DID CAPER ON	208	13
I SHOULD'NT LIKE TO COME	IS IT TRUE, DEAR SUE?	218	3
I'VE RUBIES--LIKE THE EVENING BLOOD--	I CAME TO BUY A SMILE--	223	11
AND TOPAZ--LIKE THE STAR!	I CAME TO BUY A SMILE--	223	12
SOME LIKE "EMILY."	TEACH HIM--WHEN HE MAKES	227	9
LEAPING LIKE LEOPARDS TO [IN] THE SKY	BLAZING IN GOLD AND	228	2
I LIKE A LOOK OF AGONY,	I LIKE A LOOK OF AGONY,	241	1
AND LIKE THE TREES, LOOK DOWN--	WHEN WE STAND ON THE	242	2
THE SOUND ONES, LIKE THE HILLS--SHALL STAND [STAND UP]--	WHEN WE STAND ON THE	242	7
I'VE KNOWN A HEAVEN, LIKE A TENT--	I'VE KNOWN A HEAVEN,	243	1
LIKE A PANTHER IN THE GLOVE--	IT IS EASY TO WORK WHEN	244	8
AND LILY TUBES--LIKE WELLS--	WHAT WOULD I GIVE TO SEE	247	10
AND THEY'LL WILT, LIKE MEN--	I CAN WADE GRIEF--	252	14
LIKE HER TRANSLATED FACES--	YOU SEE I CANNOT SEE--	253	13
THAT OPPRESSES, LIKE THE HEFT	THERE'S A CERTAIN SLANT	258	3
WHEN IT GOES, 'TIS LIKE THE DISTANCE	THERE'S A CERTAIN SLANT	258	15
DIP--AND VANISH LIKE ORIOLES!	THIS--IS THE LAND--THE	266	9
SWELLED--LIKE HORIZONS--IN MY BREAST [VEST]--	A SOLEMN THING--IT WAS--	271	15
AND STEPPED LIKE FLAKES OF SNOW--	THE ONLY GHOST I EVER	274	4
HIS MIEN [GAIT], WAS SOUNDLESS, LIKE THE [A] BIRD--	THE ONLY GHOST I EVER	274	5
BUT RAPID--LIKE THE ROE--	THE ONLY GHOST I EVER	274	6
HIS LAUGHTER, LIKE THE BREEZE	THE ONLY GHOST I EVER	274	10
DROP, LIKE A TAPESTRY, AWAY,	DOUBT ME! MY DIM	275	20
MURMURING, LIKE OLD CASPIAN CHOIRS,	MANY A PHRASE HAS THE	276	5
LIKE A WHIPPOWIL--	MANY A PHRASE HAS THE	276	8
A SERVICE, LIKE A DRUM--	I FELT A FUNERAL, IN MY	280	6
A BONNET LIKE A DUKE--	A MIEN TO MOVE A QUEEN--	283	9
LIKE LET OF SNOW--	A MIEN TO MOVE A QUEEN--	283	18
THE QUEEN, DISCERNS LIKE ME--	THE ROBIN'S MY CRITERION	285	16
IS LIKE A FACE OF STEEL--	THAT AFTER HORROR--THAT	286	12
HOW PUBLIC--LIKE A FROG--	I'M NOBODY! WHO ARE YOU?	288	6
A ROBBER'D LIKE THE LOOK OF--	I KNOW SOME LONELY	289	2
THEN, HOW THE FIRE EBBS LIKE BILLOWS--	HOW THE OLD MOUNTAINS	291	9
UNTO LIKE STORY--TROUBLE HAS ENTICED ME--	UNTO LIKE STORY--TROUBLE	295	1
IT'S LIKE THE LIGHT--	IT'S LIKE THE LIGHT--	297	1
IT'S LIKE THE BEE--	IT'S LIKE THE LIGHT--	297	3
IT'S LIKE THE WOODS--	IT'S LIKE THE LIGHT--	297	5
PRIVATE--LIKE THE BREEZE--	IT'S LIKE THE LIGHT--	297	6
IT'S LIKE THE MORNING--	IT'S LIKE THE LIGHT--	297	9
LIKE GNOMES--	ALONE, I CANNOT BE--	298	8
LIKE SOME OLD FASHIONED MIRACLE	LIKE SOME OLD FASHIONED	302	1
HER BLOSSOMS, LIKE A DREAM--	LIKE SOME OLD FASHIONED	302	10
HER MEMORIES [MEMORY] LIKE STRAINS--REVIEW [ENCHANT]--	LIKE SOME OLD FASHIONED	302	13
LIKE STONE--	THE SOUL SELECTS HER OWN	303	12
LIKE HINDERED RUBIES--OR THE LIGHT	THE DAY CAME SLOW--TILL	304	3
LIKE BREADTHS OF TOPAZ--PACKED A NIGHT--	THE DAY CAME SLOW--TILL	304	7
THE ORCHARD SPARKLED LIKE A JEW--	THE DAY CAME SLOW--TILL	304	13
AND FEAR--IS LIKE THE ONE	THE DIFFERENCE BETWEEN	305	2

	FIRST LINE	POEM	LINE
LIKE (CONTINUED)			
BUT MAKE NO SYLLABLE--LIKE DEATH--	GIVE LITTLE ANGUISH--	310	6
THEN STILLS IT'S ARTISANS [MYRMIDONS]--LIKE GHOSTS [SWANS]--	IT SIFTS FROM LEADEN	311	19
IT SCATTERS LIKE THE BIRDS	IT SIFTS FROM LEADEN	311	V
CONDENSES LIKE A FLOCK	IT SIFTS FROM LEADEN	311	V
LIKE JUGGLER'S FLOWERS [FIGURES] SITUATES	IT SIFTS FROM LEADEN	311	V
THE NEWS, LIKE SQUIRRELS, RAN--	I'LL TELL YOU HOW THE	318	4
LIKE THE JUNE BEE--BEFORE THE SCHOOL BOY,	THE NEAREST DREAM	319	3
LIKE THAT OLD MEASURE IN THE BOUGHS--	OF ALL THE SOUNDS	321	3
THE WIND DOES--WORKING LIKE A HAND,	OF ALL THE SOUNDS	321	5
NOR HOPPED FOR [TO] AUDIENCES--LIKE BIRDS,	I CANNOT DANCE UPON MY	326	11
THEY LOOKED LIKE FRIGHTENED BEADS, I THOUGHT--	A BIRD CAME DOWN THE	328	11
LIKE ONE IN DANGER, CAUTIOUS,	A BIRD CAME DOWN THE	328	13
AND THREAD THE DEWS, ALL NIGHT, LIKE PEARLS [PEARL]--	THE GRASS SO LITTLE HAS	333	9
LIKE [AS] LOWLY SPICES, LAIN TO SLEEP [GONE TO SLEEP / LAID . . .	THE GRASS SO LITTLE HAS	333	15
THE NERVES SIT CEREMONIOUS, LIKE TOMBS--	AFTER GREAT PAIN, A	341	2
A QUARTZ CONTENTMENT, LIKE A STONE--	AFTER GREAT PAIN, A	341	9
BUT WE MIGHT LEARN TO LIKE THE HEAVEN,	I FELT MY LIFE WITH BOTH	351	15
SO PATIENT--LIKE A PAIN--	A HAPPY LIP--BREAKS	353	6
WAS LIKE THE OTHER DAYS--	THE DAY THAT I WAS	356	2
BUT, LEST THE SOUL--LIKE FAIR "PRISCILLA"	GOD IS A DISTANT--	357	5
FAILED LIKE THEMSELVES--AND CONSCIOUS THAT IT ROSE--	IF ANY SINK, ASSURE THAT	358	2
TO LOOK UPON HER LIKE--ALIVE--	I WENT TO THANK HER--	363	9
LIKE HAMMERS--DID THEY KNOW THEY FELL	THE MORNING AFTER WO--	364	11
LIKE LITANIES OF LEAD--	THE MORNING AFTER WO--	364	12
WOULD LEAP ABROAD LIKE ANTELOPE--	ALTHOUGH I PUT AWAY HIS	366	15
OVER AND OVER, LIKE A TUNE--	OVER AND OVER, LIKE A	367	1
ONE PORT--SUFFICES--FOR A BRIG--LIKE MINE--	HOW SICK--TO WAIT--IN	368	7
PEOPLE--LIKE THE MOTH--	I WENT TO HEAVEN--	374	9
LIKE A VENETIAN--WAITING--	THE ANGLE OF A LANDSCAPE	375	5
AFFORDS A BLISS LIKE MURDER--	REHEARSAL TO OURSELVES	379	3
A WINDOW OPENS LIKE A POD--	THERE'S BEEN A DEATH, IN	389	7
A DIMNESS LIKE A FOG	THERE IS A LANGUOR OF	396	6
A LIMIT LIKE THE VAIL	I HAD NOT MINDED--WALLS	398	13
UNIT, LIKE DEATH, FOR WHOM?	UNIT, LIKE DEATH, FOR	408	1
TRUE, LIKE THE TOMB,	UNIT, LIKE DEATH, FOR	408	2
THEY DROPPED LIKE FLAKES--	THEY DROPPED LIKE FLAKES	409	1
THEY DROPPED LIKE STARS--	THEY DROPPED LIKE FLAKES	409	2
LIKE PETALS FROM A ROSE--	THEY DROPPED LIKE FLAKES	409	3
I MUMBLED--LIKE A FOOL--	THE FIRST DAY'S NIGHT	410	14
I DONT LIKE PARADISE--	I NEVER FELT AT HOME--	413	4
'TWAS LIKE A MAELSTROM, WITH A NOTCH,	'TWAS LIKE A MAELSTROM,	414	1
LIKE OTHER NEW THINGS--SHOWS LARGEST--THEN--	IT DONT SOUND SO	426	12
HOW LIKE "A FIT"--THEN--	IT DONT SOUND SO	426	16
COMFORTS--SEARCH--LIKE THIS--	TAKING UP THE FAIR IDEAL	428	12
I SHOULD LIKE TO KNOW--	KNOWS HOW TO FORGET!	433	4
IS IT LIKE A PLANET?	KNOWS HOW TO FORGET!	433	V
THE WIND--TAPPED LIKE A TIRED MAN--	THE WIND--TAPPED LIKE A	436	1
AND LIKE A HOST--"COME IN"	THE WIND--TAPPED LIKE A	436	2
HIS SPEECH WAS LIKE THE PUSH	THE WIND--TAPPED LIKE A	436	10
THEN LIKE A TIMID MAN	THE WIND--TAPPED LIKE A	436	18
THAT LIVES--LIKE DOLLARS--MUST BE PILED	IT FEELS A SHAME TO BE	444	11
LIKE EYES THAT LOOKED ON WASTES--	LIKE EYES THAT LOOKED ON	458	1
I THINK A LITTLE WELL--LIKE MINE--	I KNOW WHERE WELLS GROW	460	19
THAT LIFE LIKE THIS--IS STOPLESS--	I LIVE WITH HIM--I SEE	463	15
WAS LIKE THE STILLNESS IN THE AIR--	I HEARD A FLY BUZZ--WHEN	465	3
SKILL--TO HOLD MY BROW LIKE AN EARL--	I AM ASHAMED--I HIDE--	473	16
PLEAD--LIKE A WHIPPOWIL--	I AM ASHAMED--I HIDE--	473	17
PROVE--LIKE A PEARL--	I AM ASHAMED--I HIDE--	473	18
QUICK--LIKE A LIQUOR--	I AM ASHAMED--I HIDE--	473	21
GAY--LIKE LIGHT--	I AM ASHAMED--I HIDE--	473	22
SHE DEALT HER PRETTY WORDS LIKE BLADES--	SHE DEALT HER PRETTY	479	1
MY GARDEN--LIKE THE BEACH--	MY GARDEN--LIKE THE	484	1
LOVE [FAITH] IS LIKE LIFE--MERELY [ONLY THE] LONGER	WHILE IT IS ALIVE	491	7
LOVE [FAITH] IS LIKE DEATH, DURING THE GRAVE	WHILE IT IS ALIVE	491	8
'TWAS'NT CONTAINED--LIKE OTHER STANZA--	BETTER--THAN MUSIC! FOR	503	5
SO TELL ME WHO 'TIS LIKE--	YOU KNOW THAT PORTRAIT	504	2
I WOULD NOT TALK, LIKE CORNETS--	I WOULD NOT PAINT--A	505	9
AND YET, IT TASTED, LIKE THEM ALL,	IT WAS NOT DEATH, FOR I	510	9
AND 'TWAS LIKE MIDNIGHT, SOME--	IT WAS NOT DEATH, FOR I	510	16
BUT, MOST, LIKE CHAOS--STOPLESS--COOL--	IT WAS NOT DEATH, FOR I	510	21
I'D TOSS IT YONDER, LIKE A RIND,	IF YOU WERE COMING IN	511	15
IT GOADS ME, LIKE THE GOBLIN BEE--	IF YOU WERE COMING IN	511	19
SHE DANCES LIKE A BOMB, ABROAD,	THE SOUL HAS BANDAGED	512	13
LIKE [AS] FLOWERS, THAT HEARD THE NEWS OF DEWS,	LIKE FLOWERS, THAT HEARD	513	1
HER SMILE WAS SHAPED LIKE OTHER SMILES--	HER SMILE WAS SHAPED	514	1
LIKE BEADS--AMONG THE BOG--	HER SMILE WAS SHAPED	514	8
HE PARTS HIMSELF--LIKE LEAVES--	HE PARTS HIMSELF--LIKE	517	1
AND DANGLES LIKE A MOTE	HE PARTS HIMSELF--LIKE	517	9
'TWAS WARM--AT FIRST--LIKE US--	'TWAS WARM--AT FIRST--	519	1
A CHILL--LIKE FROST UPON A GLASS--	'TWAS WARM--AT FIRST--	519	3
TO ACHE--AND LIKE A SKATER'S BROOK--	'TWAS WARM--AT FIRST--	519	7
'TWAS LOWERED, LIKE A WEIGHT [FREIGHT]--	'TWAS WARM--AT FIRST--	519	14
BUT DROPPED LIKE ADAMANT.	'TWAS WARM--AT FIRST--	519	16

LIKE (CONTINUED)	FIRST LINE	POEM	LINE
GREAT CLOUDS--LIKE USHERS--LEANING [PLACING]--	DEPARTED--TO THE	524	3
TWO [THE] WORLDS--LIKE AUDIENCES--DISPERSE [DISSOLVE / WITHDRAW / RETIRE]	DEPARTED--TO THE	524	7
TO PUT THIS WORLD DOWN, LIKE A BUNDLE--	TO PUT THIS WORLD DOWN,	527	1
THAT FEELS TO HER--LIKE SACRAMENT--	SHE'S HAPPY, WITH A NEW	535	2
I WONDER IF IT WEIGHS LIKE MINE--	I MEASURE EVERY GRIEF I	561	3
THAT SOME--ARE LIKE MY OWN--	I MEASURE EVERY GRIEF I	561	40
AN AWE IF IT SHOULD BE LIKE THAT	"HEAVEN" HAS DIFFERENT	575	7
AND TOLD HIM WHAT I'D LIKE, TODAY,	I PRAYED, AT FIRST, A	576	9
THAT IF THE SPIRIT--LIKE TO HIDE	THE BODY GROWS WITHOUT--	578	3
I LIKE TO SEE [HEAR] IT LAP THE MILES--	I LIKE TO SEE IT LAP	585	1
AND [THEN] NEIGH LIKE BOANERGES--	I LIKE TO SEE IT LAP	585	14
TO LOOK AT, LIKE A TOY--	I CRIED AT PITY--NOT AT	588	8
LIKE INTERMITTENT PLUSH, BE HEARD	THE NIGHT WAS WIDE, AND	589	11
HEAVES BALLS OF SPECKS, LIKE VICIOUS BOY	TO INTERRUPT HIS YELLOW	591	5
LIKE SANCTIFYING IN THE SOUL--	I THINK I WAS ENCHANTED	593	23
LIKE DEITY--TO KEEP--	I THINK I WAS ENCHANTED	593	32
LIKE MIGHTY FOOT LIGHTS--BURNED THE RED	LIKE MIGHTY FOOT LIGHTS	595	1
THEN CAUGHT ME--LIKE A BALL--	THREE TIMES--WE PARTED--	598	6
THE WINDS--LIKE CHILDREN--LULLED--	THREE TIMES--WE PARTED--	598	14
THE TREES LIKE TASSELS--HIT--AND SWUNG--	THE TREES LIKE TASSELS--	606	1
LIKE HINDERED FLAGS--SWEET HOISTED--	THE TREES LIKE TASSELS--	606	23
THE SECOND [SILENCE] LIKE AN OCEAN ROLLED	I YEARS HAD BEEN FROM	609	11
AND HELD MY EARS, AND LIKE A THIEF	I YEARS HAD BEEN FROM	609	23
UPON ME--LIKE A CLAW--	IT WOULD HAVE STARVED A	612	5
NOR LIKE THE GNAT--HAD I--	IT WOULD HAVE STARVED A	612	9
NOR LIKE HIMSELF--THE ART	IT WOULD HAVE STARVED A	612	13
LIKE THE GRACE--OF DEATH--	IN FALLING TIMBERS	614	16
LIKE A DOTTED DOT--	DONT PUT UP MY THREAD &	617	12
WAS BRIDAL--E'ER LIKE THIS?	'TWAS A LONG PARTING--	625	13
LIKE CLEOPATRA'S COMPANY--	THE TINT I CANNOT TAKE--	627	7
LIKE CHARIOTS--IN THE VEST--	THE TINT I CANNOT TAKE--	627	16
LIKE COLUMNS--IN THE BREAST--	THE TINT I CANNOT TAKE--	627	V 16
LIKE MINE--FOR NOT A FOOT--NOR HAND--	I WATCHED THE MOON	629	11
BUT LIKE A HEAD--A GUILLOTINE	I WATCHED THE MOON	629	13
OR LIKE A STEMLESS FLOWER--	I WATCHED THE MOON	629	17
AS HARASS US--LIKE LIFE--AND DEATH--	I WATCHED THE MOON	629	25
LIKE LITTLE SCHOLARS--LOUD--	I THINK THE LONGEST HOUR	635	10
WHOLE--LIKE HIS PRINCIPLE--	THE CHILD'S FAITH IS NEW	637	2
WIDE--LIKE THE SUNRISE	THE CHILD'S FAITH IS NEW	637	3
LIKE A CUP--	I CANNOT LIVE WITH YOU--	640	8
THE OTHER, LIKE THE LITTLE BANK	I THINK TO LIVE--MAY BE	646	7
POURED LIKE THIS--MY WHOLE [BEST] LIBATION--	PROMISE THIS--WHEN YOU	648	13
AVOIDED--LIKE [AS] A DREAM--	A PRISON GETS TO BE A	652	30
WAS EVER IDLENESS [ARROGANCE] LIKE THIS?	A LONG--LONG SLEEP--A	654	5
THEN--EDDIES LIKE A ROSE--AWAY--	THE NAME--OF IT--IS	656	11
GLOWS CENTRAL--LIKE A JEWEL	THAT FIRST DAY, WHEN YOU	659	5
IS SHIFTED--LIKE A SAND--	OF ALL THE SOULS THAT	664	8
NOR WILL HE--LIKE THE DUMB--	THE FUTURE--NEVER SPOKE	672	2
WE LEARNED TO LIKE THE FIRE	THE ZEROES--TAUGHT US--	689	2
WOULD YOU LIKE SUMMER? TASTE OF OURS.	WOULD YOU LIKE SUMMER?	691	1
THE JUDGE IS LIKE THE OWL--	THE JUDGE IS LIKE THE	699	1
COOLS--LIKE THE RAIN--	THE WORLD--FEELS DUSTY	715	8
SO LIKE THE MEADOWS--NOW--	PRECIOUS TO ME--SHE	727	5
HAVE ANY LIKE MYSELF	HAVE ANY LIKE MYSELF	736	1
HAVE ANY LIKE MYSELF	HAVE ANY LIKE MYSELF	736	9
HAVE ANY LIKE MYSELF	HAVE ANY LIKE MYSELF	736	17
TALL--LIKE THE STAG--WOULD THAT?	YOU SAID THAT I "WAS	738	5
OR LOWER--LIKE THE WREN--	YOU SAID THAT I "WAS	738	6
AT LENGTH, A MOURNER, LIKE MYSELF,	THE BIRDS REPORTED FROM	743	13
GROWTH OF MAN--LIKE GROWTH OF NATURE--	GROWTH OF MAN--LIKE	750	1
HE FOUGHT LIKE THOSE WHO'VE NOUGHT TO LOSE--	HE FOUGHT LIKE THOSE	759	1
HIS COMRADES, SHIFTED LIKE THE FLAKES	HE FOUGHT LIKE THOSE	759	9
LIKE HALLOWING OF HEAVEN,	THE HALLOWING OF PAIN	772	2
THERE IS NO DILIGENCE LIKE THAT	THE SERVICE WITHOUT HOPE	779	7
LIKE ELEMENT--ARE THEY--	THERE IS AN ARID	782	4
THE WORTHINESS [EXCELLENCE / QUALITY] OF SUFFERING LIKE	DESPAIR'S ADVANTAGE IS	799	5
AND WHEN ADJUSTED LIKE A SEED	NO NOTICE GAVE SHE, BUT	804	13
THEN CEASE [CEASED], LIKE THESE--	THIS QUIET DUST WAS	813	8
THE DUST DID SCOOP ITSELF LIKE HANDS--	THE WIND BEGUN TO KNEAD	824	7
ITSELF IS ALL THE LIKE IT HAS--	LOVE RECKONS BY ITSELF--	826	4
THEY STARTLED, LIKE EXECUTORS	NATURE AND GOD--I	835	3
IMPOSSIBILITY, LIKE WINE	IMPOSSIBILITY, LIKE WINE	838	1
LIKE GLOW WORMS, FLEE AWAY--	THE SUN AND MOON MUST	871	8
WE OUTGROW LOVE, LIKE OTHER THINGS	WE OUTGROW LOVE, LIKE	887	1
LIKE COSTUMES GRANDSIRES WORE.	WE OUTGROW LOVE, LIKE	887	4
LOSE MY WAY LIKE A LITTLE CHILD	HOW HAPPY I WAS IF I	898	7
IT MEASURES [PACES] LIKE THE SEA	THE HEART HAS NARROW	928	2
LIKE INDIVIDUALS GO	DEATH LEAVES US HOMESICK	935	6
LIKE BALLS--UPON A FLOOR.	I FELT A CLEAVING IN MY	937	8
RALLIES HER GLOW [THE WEST], LIKE A DYING FRIEND--	FAIRER THROUGH FADING--	938	5
WHOSE MEMORY DROWNS ME, LIKE THE DIP	I LEARNED--AT LEAST--	944	7
AND KINGDOMS, LIKE THE ORCHARD	IT IS AN HONORABLE	946	7
AND A SUSPICION, LIKE A FINGER	A LOSS OF SOMETHING EVER	959	13
LIKE CHILDREN ROUND A SIRE--	THE MOUNTAIN SAT UPON	975	6
LIKE THE REMEMBERING IT BE NOUGHT	NO OTHER CAN REDUCE	982	3
LIKE THE REMEMBERING IT EXIST--	NO OTHER CAN REDUCE	982	V

LIKE (CONTINUED)

	FIRST LINE	POEM		LINE
THE LEAVES LIKE WOMEN, INTERCHANGE	THE LEAVES LIKE WOMEN,	987		1
LIKE BALLS UPON A FLOOR--	THE DUST BEHIND I STROVE	992		4
SUPPORTS ME LIKE IMPERIAL DRAMS	THE STIMULUS, BEYOND THE	1001		3
LIKE GENTLE INFAMY--	SO LARGE MY WILL	1024		4
SPENDING SCARLET, LIKE A WOMAN	NATURE RARER USES YELLOW	1045		5
LIKE A LOVER'S WORDS.	NATURE RARER USES YELLOW	1045		8
BUT LIKE AN ORIENTAL TALE	REPORTLESS SUBJECTS, TO	1048		7
NATURE, LIKE US IS SOMETIMES CAUGHT	THE SKY IS LOW--THE	1075		7
LIKE SOMETHING SPIRITUAL--	IT WAS NOT SAINT--IT WAS	1092		4
IT FEELS LIKE POVERTY	BECAUSE 'TWAS RICHES I	1093		4
THE CLAWS THAT CLUNG, LIKE LIFELESS GLOVES	HIS BILL IS CLASPED--HIS	1102		3
LIKE MEN AND WOMEN SHADOWS WALK	LIKE MEN AND WOMEN	1105		1
LIKE WINTER AS A FACE	THE SNOW THAT NEVER	1133		9
LIKE WORMS BENEATH [BEFORE] THE POWER--	THE WIND TOOK UP THE	1134	V	8
LIKE SAILORS FIGHTING WITH A LEAK	THE FROST OF DEATH WAS	1136		3
WAGGONS LIKE MESSENGERS HURRY ABOUT	AFTER THE SUN COMES OUT	1148		3
WITHOUT THE DATE, LIKE CONSCIOUSNESS OR IMMORTALITY--	LEST ANY DOUBT THAT WE	1156		3
THE LIGHTNING PLAYED [SKIPPED] LIKE MICE	THE CLOUDS THEIR BACKS	1172		4
THE THUNDER CRUMBLED LIKE A STUFF	THE CLOUDS THEIR BACKS	1172		5
WE [I] LIKE A HAIRBREADTH 'SCAPE	WE LIKE A HAIRBREADTH	1175		1
LIKE PARAGRAPHS [ARTICLES] OF WIND	WE LIKE A HAIRBREADTH	1175		4
SITTING [RIDING] A BOUGH LIKE A BRIGADIER	A PROMPT--EXECUTIVE BIRD	1177		5
'TIS SOMETHING LIKE A HOUSE--	REMEMBRANCE HAS A	1182		2
WE LIKE MARCH.	WE LIKE MARCH.	1213		1
LIKE TRAINS OF CARS ON TRACKS OF PLUSH	LIKE TRAINS OF CARS ON	1224		1
LIKE RAIN IT SOUNDED TILL IT CURVED [SWELLED]	LIKE RAIN IT SOUNDED	1235		1
THEN LIKE ELIJAH RODE AWAY	LIKE RAIN IT SOUNDED	1235		15
LIKE TIME'S INSIDIOUS [INVADING / PRESUMING / APPOINTED / . . .	LIKE TIME'S INSIDIOUS	1236		1
BUT FOR THE GREED [VAUNT / LIKE] OF HIM--	MY HEART RAN SO TO THEE	1237		13
BESIDE US LIKE A BLAND ABYSS	POWER IS A FAMILIAR	1238		3
TO PILE LIKE THUNDER TO IT'S CLOSE	TO PILE LIKE THUNDER TO	1247		1
LIKE BROOMS OF STEEL	LIKE BROOMS OF STEEL	1252		1
LONGING IS LIKE THE SEED	LONGING IS LIKE THE SEED	1255		1
LIKE SEPARATION'S SWELL	A WIND THAT ROSE	1259		7
THERE IS NO [WAS NEVER] FRIGATE LIKE A BOOK	THERE IS NO FRIGATE LIKE	1263		1
NOR ANY COURSERS LIKE A PAGE	THERE IS NO FRIGATE LIKE	1263		3
DEPOSE HIM LIKE A FASHION	THE HARM OF YEARS IS ON	1280		3
A STAGNANT PLEASURE LIKE A POOL	A STAGNANT PLEASURE LIKE	1281		1
AND DINE [GROW] WITHOUT LIKE GOD--	ART THOU THE THING I	1282		8
SUBSISTING NOW [SINCE] LIKE GOD--	ART THOU THE THING I	1282	V	8
CANCELED LIKE DAWN	LEFT IN IMMORTAL YOUTH	1289		7
DOTH LIKE A BUBBLE ANTEDATE	THE MUSHROOM IS THE ELF	1298		11
AND LIKE A BUBBLE, HIE--	THE MUSHROOM IS THE ELF	1298		12
SURPRISE IS LIKE A THRILLING--PUNGENT--	SURPRISE IS LIKE A	1306		1
LIKE AN OBLOQUY--	WHEN A LOVER IS A BEGGAR	1314		8
'TWILL ENTER LIKE A DART!	HOW NEWS MUST FEEL WHEN	1319		4
'TWILL RIDDLE LIKE A SHOT.	HOW NEWS MUST FEEL WHEN	1319	V	4
WHEN SUING--LIKE HER ESSEX	ELIZABETH TOLD ESSEX	1321		7
BELIEFS ARE BANDAGED, LIKE THE TONGUE	I NEVER HEAR THAT ONE IS	1323		9
LIKE ANY PARASITE--	THE MIND LIVES ON THE	1355		2
LIKE DOG A BONE	THE MIND LIVES ON THE	1355	V	8
LIKE RAIMENT OF A DREAM--	HOW FITS HIS UMBER COAT	1371		4
THOUGH SHUTTING LIKE A DAPPLED FAN	THE BUTTERFLY'S NUMIDIAN	1387	V	4
. . . LIKE A FRIEND--	AFTER ALL BIRDS HAVE	1395		6
HER GALLANT NOTE ENDOWS US LIKE A FRIEND	AFTER ALL BIRDS HAVE	1395	V	6
LIKE LOOKING EVERY TIME YOU PLEASE	WHAT MYSTERY PERVADES A	1400		7
AND TOSSES LIKE A FLEET OF BALM--	SWEET SKEPTICISM OF THE	1413		3
LIKE AZURE DRIED	THE GENTIAN HAS A	1424		2
TO PUT OFF FILAMENTS LIKE THIS	WITH PINIONS OF DISDAIN	1431		11
HIS MIND LIKE FABRICS OF THE EAST	HIS MIND LIKE FABRICS OF	1446		1
LIKE SIGNAL ESOTERIC SIPS	YOUR THOUGHTS DONT HAVE	1452		3
DEPARTING LIKE A PAGEANT	ONE OF THE ONES THAT	1466		19
NO STATURE HAS IT, LIKE A FOG	'TIS WHITER THAN AN	1482		3
LIKE ONE THAT FED ON AWE.	HER SPIRIT ROSE TO SUCH	1486		3
THE THRILL CAME SLOWLY LIKE A BOON [LIGHT] FOR	THE THRILL CAME SLOWLY	1495		1
IT'S FITNESS GROWING LIKE THE FLOOD	THE THRILL CAME SLOWLY	1495		3
AND [BUT] THEN THEY SCARE US LIKE A SPECTRE	FACTS BY OUR SIDE ARE	1497		3
SHOT THE LITHE SLEDS LIKE SHOD VIBRATIONS	GLASS WAS THE STREET--IN	1498		5
TO CRUMBLING MEN LIKE ME [THEE]	HOW FIRM ETERNITY MUST	1499		2
REAL MEMORY, LIKE CEDAR FEET	YOU CANNOT MAKE	1508		7
THOUGH [BUT] JOYS--LIKE MEN--MAY SOMETIMES MAKE A JOURNEY--	THE THINGS THAT NEVER	1515		3
HIS LITTLE HEARSE LIKE FIGURE	HIS LITTLE HEARSE LIKE	1522		1
THERE COMES [CAME] A WARNING LIKE A SPY	THERE COMES A WARNING	1536		1
TO SEEM [FEEL] LIKE PERFIDY--	AS IMPERCEPTIBLY AS	1540		4
OF DEATH I TRY TO THINK LIKE THIS--	OF DEATH I TRY TO THINK	1558		1
LIKE FALLOW ARTICLE--	THE BAT IS DUN, WITH	1575		2
LIKE TIDES WITHIN THE SEA	THE SPIRIT LASTS--BUT IN	1576		10
BUT MEMORY LIKE MELODY	BLOSSOMS WILL RUN AWAY,	1578		3
LIKE OUR DISMAY AT THEE?	WE SHUN IT ERE IT COMES,	1580		8
THERE CAME A WIND LIKE A BUGLE--	THERE CAME A WIND LIKE A	1593		1
LIKE THAT WHICH RAVISHED THEE!	IMMURED IN HEAVEN!	1594		5
IS LIKE THE CHILD'S ADVERSITY	THE GOING FROM A WORLD	1603		3
WHICH LIKE THE MOON, SOME TURBID NIGHT,	EACH THAT WE LOSE TAKES	1605		3
OR HAS IT [SHE] FEATHERS, LIKE A BIRD,	NOT KNOWING WHEN THE	1619		3
OR BILLOWS, LIKE A SHORE--	NOT KNOWING WHEN THE	1619		4
THERE IS NO TRUMPET LIKE THE TOMB	THE IMMORTALITY SHE GAVE	1648	V	

	FIRST LINE	POEM	LINE
LIKE (CONTINUED)			
LIKE THIS CONSENT OF LANGUAGE	A WORD MADE FLESH IS	1651	15
WE STEP LIKE PLUSH	I DID NOT REACH THEE	1664	28
WE STAND LIKE SNOW	I DID NOT REACH THEE	1664	29
LIKE THAT IMPASSIVE STONE--	I SEE THEE CLEARER FOR	1666	4
A SOMETHING LIKE A SHAME	THAT SHE FORGOT ME WAS	1683	8
FITTED ITSELF TO HIMSELF LIKE A ROBE	THE EVENT WAS DIRECTLY	1686	3
THE LOOK OF THEE, WHAT IS IT LIKE	THE LOOK OF THEE, WHAT	1689	1
LIKE HUNGRY DOGS	THE WIND DREW OFF	1694	2
LIKE ANIMALS IN PAIN	THE WIND DREW OFF	1694	9
'TWAS LIKE A SHEET WITH HORNS!	A CURIOUS CLOUD	1710	2
AND TRAILED LIKE ROBES AWAY;	A CURIOUS CLOUD	1710	7
DEATH IS LIKE THE INSECT	DEATH IS LIKE THE INSECT	1716	1
LIKE AN ADVERSITY.	DROWNING IS NOT SO	1718	12
ANALYSIS AS [LIKE] CAPSULE SEEMED	HE WAS MY HOST--HE WAS	1721	7
LIKE FLOWERS IN A PLOT--	HER FACE WAS IN A BED OF	1722	2
THOU CAN'ST NOT BOAST, LIKE JESUS, DRUNKEN WITHOUT COMPANION	PROUD OF MY BROKEN HEART	1736	5
MAKE ME BEARDED LIKE A MAN!	REARRANGE A "WIFE'S"	1737	4
BUT GROWING LIKE A HURRICANE	THE MOB WITHIN THE HEART	1745	7
LIKED			
I LIKED AS WELL TO SEE--	BEFORE I GOT MY EYE PUT	327	2
FOR MINE--TO LOOK AT WHEN I LIKED--	BEFORE I GOT MY EYE PUT	327	16
I LIKED TO STAY--	GOOD MORNING--MIDNIGHT--	425	6
THAT CRAWLED LEAGUES OFF--I LIKED TO SEE--	THREE TIMES--WE PARTED--	598	9
BECAUSE THEY LIKED ME "STILL"--	THEY SHUT ME UP IN PROSE	613	4
AND COULD BE MIGHTY, IF I LIKED--	THAT FIRST DAY, WHEN YOU	659	3
AND VISIT ONLY WHERE I LIKED	COULD I BUT RIDE	661	3
AND WENT OR WAITED AS THEY LIKED	THE MOUNTAINS STOOD IN	1278	3
LIKENESS			
IS BUT THE LIKENESS OF THE BROOK	OF DEATH I TRY TO THINK	1558	3
LIKER			
IT'S LIKER SO--IT SEEMS--	DID YOU EVER STAND IN A	590	16
LIKES			
I THINK THE HEMLOCK LIKES TO STAND	I THINK THE HEMLOCK	525	1
HE LIKES A BOGGY ACRE	A NARROW FELLOW IN THE	986	9
LIKEST			
THE LIKEST TO THE DOWN	OF BEING IS A BIRD	653	2
THE LIKEST I HAVE KNOWN--	THE MOON WAS BUT A CHIN	737	8
LIKING			
LIKING THE QUIET OF THE PLACE	WHO OCCUPIES THIS HOUSE?	892	23
LILAC			
THE LILAC IS AN ANCIENT SHRUB	THE LILAC IS AN ANCIENT	1241	1
THE FIRMAMENTAL LILAC	THE LILAC IS AN ANCIENT	1241	3
UPON A LILAC SEA	UPON A LILAC SEA	1337	1
TO A DELUSIVE LILAC	HIS LITTLE HEARSE LIKE	1522	3
LILACS			
THE LILACS--BENDING MANY A YEAR--	IT WILL BE SUMMER--	342	9
LILIES			
HAS IT FEET LIKE WATER LILIES?	WILL THERE REALLY BE A	101	5
SPREADS THE POND HER BASE OF LILIES	HOW THE WATERS CLOSED	923	5
LILY			
IN PLACID [CHINTZ AND] LILY SLEEPS!	A LADY RED--AMID THE	74	4
OF ROSE AND LILY, MANIFOLD,	A SCIENCE--SO THE SAVANS	100	11
AND LILY TUBES--LIKE WELLS--	WHAT WOULD I GIVE TO SEE	247	10
THE LILY PASSES SURE--	THROUGH THE DARK SOD--AS	392	2
ART OF SNOW--OR TRICK OF LILY	HER SWEET TURN TO LEAVE	649	15
THE LILY--WAITING TO BE WED--	'TIS SUNRISE--LITTLE	908	7
LIMB			
UNTO A VELVET LIMB--	YOU'LL KNOW HER--BY HER	634	8
BY STRETCH OF LIMB--OR STIR OF LID--	A LONG--LONG SLEEP--A	654	3
LIMBS			
THEIR MANGLED LIMBS	THE WIND DREW OFF	1694	8
LIMIT			
LIMIT--HOW DEEP A BLEEDING GO!	BOUND--A TROUBLE--	269	3
STILL TO ANTICIPATE [CONJECTURE]--WERE NO LIMIT--	BOUND--A TROUBLE--	269	V
A LIMIT LIKE THE VAIL	I HAD NOT MINDED--WALLS	398	13
WHEN SWIFT [QUICK] IT SLIPPED IT'S LIMIT--	HE GAVE AWAY HIS LIFE--	567	7
WITH LIMIT [LICENSE] OF DECAY--	TO MY SMALL HEARTH HIS	638	6
BEYOND MY LIMIT TO CONCEIVE--	I THINK TO LIVE--MAY BE	646	3
HE [FIRST]--MUST PASS THE CRYSTAL ANGLE [LIMIT]	HER SWEET TURN TO LEAVE	649	25
IS REVELATION'S LIMIT [CAUTION],	EMBARRASSMENT OF ONE	662	3
IT WAS THE LIMIT OF MY DREAM--	ONE BLESSING HAD I THAN	756	5
WHEN DEATH LIT ALL THE SHORTNESS UP [LIMIT--UP / BREVITY]	HER FINAL SUMMER WAS IT	795	7
AND EVERY LIMIT A DECADE--	I'VE DROPPED MY BRAIN--	1046	19
AS LIMIT OF DOMINION	THE PUNGENT ATOM IN THE	1191	7
WITH THE EXTATIC LIMIT	TO DISAPPEAR ENHANCES--	1209	19
TO DIE DIVINELY ONCE A TWILIGHT--[AN EVENING / A LIMIT]	I'D RATHER RECOLLECT A	1349	7
WHOSE LIMIT NONE HAVE EVER SEEN,	WHAT MYSTERY PERVADES A	1400	5
LIMITATIONS			
THE LIMITATIONS OF THE WIND	THE DUTIES OF THE WIND	1137	13
LIMITED			
BE LIMITED BY IGNORANCE--	HE PARTS HIMSELF--LIKE	517	15
LIMITLESS			
THIS LIMITLESS HYPERBOLE	'TIS WHITER THAN AN	1482	9

	FIRST LINE	POEM	LINE
LIMITS			
AND BOROUGHS [LIMITS] WHERE WE LIVE--	LIKE MEN AND WOMEN	1105	8
LINCOLN			
OR LITTLE JOHN--OF LINCOLN GREEN--	LIKE SOME OLD FASHIONED	302	7
LINE			
CRUISING ROUND THE PURPLE LINE--	FLOWERS--WELL--IF	137	12
ODD SECRETS OF THE LINE TO TELL!	JUST LOST, WHEN I WAS	160	8
WHO STRAYED BEYOND THE AMBER LINE	THE LONESOME FOR THEY	262	3
EATS OFF THE BRITTLE LINE--	I SOMETIMES DROP IT, FOR	708	14
IT HAS NO PORT, NOR A "LINE"--BUT THE JAYS--	BY MY WINDOW HAVE I FOR	797	5
BY THE LINE AND LEAD	GRATITUDE--IS NOT THE	989	6
WARRANT [BUSINESS] IN EVERY LINE--	A PROMPT--EXECUTIVE BIRD	1177	4
THE CRICKET DROPS A SABLE LINE	THE JAY HIS CASTANET HAS	1635	7
THAT ALL ALONG THE LINE	"RED SEA," INDEED! TALK	1642	6
BETWEEN THE MARCH AND APRIL LINE--	THE SADDEST NOISE, THE	1764	5
LINEAGE			
NOR LINEAGE OF ECSTASY	THE PEDIGREE OF HONEY	1627	3
LINES			
ALONG MY GOLDEN LINES--	IT WOULD NEVER BE COMMON	430	29
NO CIRCUIT SAGE OF ALL THE COURSE [LINES]	OH FUTURE! THOU SECRETED	1631	5
LINGER			
IF THEY W'D LINGER FOR A BIRD	IF I COULD BRIBE THEM BY	179	7
LONGEST [LATEST] ON YOUR SOUTH, TO LINGER,	PROMISE THIS--WHEN YOU	648	19
GREENER LEAN--OR FONDER CLUSTER [LATER LINGER]	PROMISE THIS--WHEN YOU	648	23
NEED NOT LINGER [TARRY] HERE--	TELL AS A MARKSMAN--WERE	1152	10
LINGERED			
I LINGERED WITH BEFORE--	I YEARS HAD BEEN FROM	609	10
THE PEAKS, THAT LINGERED LAST	WHEN ONE HAS GIVEN UP	853	5
HAD I BUT LINGERED YESTERDAY--	IT BLOOMED AND DROPT, A	978	11
LINGERING			
THE LINGERING--AND THE STAIN--I MEAN--	THE ONE WHO COULD REPEAT	307	6
A HURRY WITH A LINGERING, MIXED,	I CANNOT MEET THE SPRING	1051	3
LINGERS			
LINGERS TO RECORD THEE--	SOUL, WILT THOU TOSS	139	6
LINNET			
AND THIS LINNET FLEW!	MORNS LIKE THESE--WE	27	12
LIP			
CLAPS MY MURMURING LIP!	IF I SHOULD CEASE TO	56	8
WITH MY GRANITE LIP!	IF I SHOULD'NT BE ALIVE	182	8
HAVE I THE LIP OF THE FLAMINGO	HOW THE OLD MOUNTAINS	291	7
HID, LIP, FOR THEE--	ALL THE LETTERS I CAN	334	6
A HAPPY LIP--BREAKS SUDDEN--	A HAPPY LIP--BREAKS	353	1
OF HIS CONDEMNED LIP?	TO ONE DENIED TO DRINK	490	8
BY BUT A LIP OF METAL--	I WOULD NOT PAINT--A	505	15
MY LIP--TO TESTIFY--	I THINK TO LIVE--MAY BE	646	4
HER GOLDEN FINGER ON HER LIP--	NATURE--THE GENTLEST	790	23
AS LIQUOR AT THE LIP BETWEEN	BETWEEN THE FORM OF LIFE	1101	3
BUT JUST HIS LID [LIP] OF GLASS--	WHAT MYSTERY PERVADES A	1400	6
COULD MORTAL LIP DIVINE	COULD MORTAL LIP DIVINE	1409	1
LIP WAS NOT THE LIAR.	HAD I KNOWN THAT THE	1720	6
NO, LIP IT WAS YOURS,	HAD I KNOWN THAT THE	1720	7
THE LIP THAT CAN,	WHICH MISSES MOST,	1759	7
LET ME NOT THIRST WITH THIS HOCK AT MY LIP,	LET ME NOT THIRST WITH	1772	1
LIPS			
THE LIPS AT HALLELUJAH	THE FEET OF PEOPLE	7	5
THOSE THIRSTY LIPS TO FLAGONS PRESSED,	AS WATCHERS HANG UPON	121	11
TO LIPS LONG PARCHING	I BRING AN UNACCUSTOMED	132	2
THE LIPS I W'D HAVE COOLED, ALAS--	I BRING AN UNACCUSTOMED	132	9
MY FLOWERS RAISE THEIR PRETTY LIPS--	AS CHILDREN BID THE	133	3
LIPS UNUSED TO THEE--	COME SLOWLY--EDEN!	211	2
ON HIS BABBLING--BERRY--LIPS--	TEACH HIM--WHEN HE MAKES	227	3
I THINK JUST HOW MY LIPS WILL WEIGH--	I THINK JUST HOW MY	237	5
UNTIL THE MOSS HAD REACHED OUR LIPS--	I DIED FOR BEAUTY--BUT	449	11
FROM LIPS AT CORNERS OF THE STREETS--	IT WAS GIVEN TO ME BY	454	11
I'M OFTEN THIRSTY--BUT MY LIPS	I KNOW WHERE WELLS GROW	460	11
MY LIPS JUST HOLD THE NAME--	YOU KNOW THAT PORTRAIT	504	10
SIP, GOBLIN, FROM THE VERY LIPS	THE SOUL HAS BANDAGED	512	7
THE LIPS THAT NEVER LIE--	A STILL--VOLCANO--LIFE--	601	10
BE MY LIPS--THE ONLY BUCKLE	PROMISE THIS--WHEN YOU	648	7
AND IS HELD LOW TO FREEZING LIPS--	VICTORY COMES LATE--	690	2
THE LIPS HAD PLACED AS WITH A "PLEASE"	"I WANT"--IT PLEADED--	731	7
HER LIPS OF AMBER NEVER PART--	THE MOON WAS BUT A CHIN	737	9
UNTO THE LIPS IT EDDIED THROUGH--	I'VE NONE TO TELL ME TO	881	12
THAT COULD THEIR LIPS REPLY	WHAT DID THEY DO SINCE I	900	6
HOW EVERLASTING ARE THE LIPS	DOMINION LASTS UNTIL	1257	5
WITHIN [BETWEEN] HIS RUSSET LIPS--	A SAUCER HOLDS A CUP	1374	10
TO MAKE LIPS ELDERLY	HIS VOICE DECREPIT WAS	1476	4
UPON IT'S FASTENED LIPS LAY WORDS--	OH GIVE IT MOTION--DECK	1527	3
AND NOT A SONG PERVADE HIS LIPS--	THE BAT IS DUN, WITH	1575	3
ADMONISHED BY HER BUCKLED LIPS	THE RETICENT VOLCANO	1748	9
WHEN THE LONG INTERCEDING LIPS	THERE COMES AN HOUR WHEN	1751	2
LIQUID			
THEIR LIQUID FEET GO SOFTLY OUT	YOU'VE SEEN BALLOONS SET	700	5
LIQUOR			
I TASTE A LIQUOR NEVER BREWED--	I TASTE A LIQUOR NEVER	214	1
'TWAS THE NEW LIQUOR--	I CAN WADE GRIEF--	252	8
QUICK--LIKE A LIQUOR--	I AM ASHAMED--I HIDE--	473	21
AS LIQUOR AT THE LIP BETWEEN	BETWEEN THE FORM OF LIFE	1101	3
AND LIQUOR IN THE JUG	BETWEEN THE FORM OF LIFE	1101	4

	FIRST LINE	POEM	LINE
LIQUORS			
YOUR CONNOISSEUR IN LIQUORS	A DRUNKARD CANNOT MEET A	1628	11
OF LIQUORS THAT ARE VENDED	THROUGH THOSE OLD	1753	5
LISP			
NEVER DID SHE LISP IT--	MORNS LIKE THESE--WE	27	5
NOR LISP IT AT THE TABLE--	I HAV'NT TOLD MY GARDEN	50	13
HIS LISP--IS LIGHTNING--AND THE SUN--	YOU'LL KNOW IT--AS YOU	420	12
LISPED			
AND WHAT IT WAS--WE NEVER LISPED--	A HOUSE UPON THE HIGHT--	399	11
ASKED HIM HIS NAME--HE LISPED ME "TROTWOOD"--	TRUDGING TO EDEN,	1020	3
LISPING			
THAT FILLED THE LISPING FULL.	THEY WONT FROWN ALWAYS--	874	8
LISPS			
SAY--THAT THE PULSE JUST LISPS--	IF HE DISSOLVE--THEN--	236	10
LIST			
ON HIS REPEALLESS--LIST.	THEY DROPPED LIKE FLAKES	409	9
AND THEN--THE LIST IS DONE--	I RECKON--WHEN I COUNT	569	4
AND HE AND HE IN MIGHTY LIST	HE OUTSTRIPPED TIME WITH	865	5
LIST EVEN UNTO ME.	BECAUSE THE BEE MAY	869	3
THAN PERISH FROM THE CHANCE'S LIST	EACH SECOND IS THE LAST	879	7
LISTENER			
THEIR WITNESSES WERE NOT--[LISTENER WAS NONE]	THE BIRDS BEGUN AT FOUR	783	9
WITHOUT A LISTENER?	THE RETICENT VOLCANO	1748	8
LISTENING			
IT LISTENING--LISTENING--WENT TO SLEEP--	I SHOULD NOT DARE TO	205	11
IT LISTENING--LISTENING--WENT TO SLEEP--	I SHOULD NOT DARE TO	205	11
WE WERE LISTENING TO [TOO ENGROSSED WITH] THE SECONDS . . .	WE TALKED WITH EACH	1473	3
THE TENT IS LISTENING,	EXPANSE CANNOT BE LOST--	1584	15
LISTENS			
WHEN IT COMES, THE LANDSCAPE LISTENS--	THERE'S A CERTAIN SLANT	258	13
LISTLESS			
LIFT--IF YOU CARE--THE LISTLESS HAIR--	HOW MANY TIMES THESE LOW	187	6
THE CLOUDS--LIKE LISTLESS ELEPHANTS--	ON THIS LONG STORM THE	194	3
LISTS			
ADVANCING ON CELESTIAL LISTS--	HAD I PRESUMED TO HOPE--	522	11
TO ALL THE LISTS OF CLAY!	OF ALL THE SOULS THAT	664	12
LIT			
THE MORNING LIT--THE BIRDS AROSE--	AN AWFUL TEMPEST MASHED	198	10
THAT LIT THE DRUMMER FROM THE CAMP	GOOD NIGHT! WHICH PUT	259	11
LIT--WITH A RUBY--	I WENT TO HEAVEN--	374	3
LIT WITH A FINER PHOSPHOR--	MORE LIFE--WENT OUT--	422	3
LIT UP THE LOW--INFERIOR GRASS--	I THINK I WAS ENCHANTED	593	V 11
WHEN DEATH LIT ALL THE SHORTNESS UP [LIMIT--UP / BREVITY]	HER FINAL SUMMER WAS IT	795	7
PROMPT AS WHEN I LIT THEM	TRUSTY AS THE STARS	1369	3
THE ROAD WAS LIT WITH [BY] MOON AND STAR--	THE ROAD WAS LIT WITH	1450	1
ALL OF EVENING SOFTLY LIT	LIGHTLY STEPPED A YELLOW	1672	5
THE POSSIBLE'S SLOW FUSE IS LIT	THE GLEAM OF AN HEROIC	1687	3
LITANIES			
LIKE LITANIES OF LEAD--	THE MORNING AFTER WO--	364	12
LITERATURE			
THE LITERATURE OF MAN--	A PRECIOUS--MOULDERING	371	12
LITHE			
SHOT THE LITHE SLEDS LIKE SHOD VIBRATIONS	GLASS WAS THE STREET--IN	1498	5
LITHEST			
SHOULD PROVE THE STRONGEST [SUPPLEST / LITHEST / STOUTEST] ONE.	MY FIRST WELL DAY--SINCE	574	8
LITIGANTS			
SWEET LITIGANTS FOR LIFE--	THERE IS A FLOWER THAT	380	20
LITTERED			
AND NOW YOU'VE LITTERED ALL THE EAST	SHE SWEEPS WITH	219	7
LITTLE			
HERE IS A LITTLE FOREST,	THERE IS ANOTHER SKY,	2	7
EACH LITTLE DOUBT AND FEAR,	I HAVE A BIRD IN SPRING	5	22
EACH LITTLE DISCORD HERE	I HAVE A BIRD IN SPRING	5	23
THOU LITTLE SPADE OF MINE	ALL THESE MY BANNERS BE.	22	13
ADRIFT! A LITTLE BOAT ADRIFT!	ADRIFT! A LITTLE BOAT	30	1
WILL NO ONE GUIDE A LITTLE BOAT	ADRIFT! A LITTLE BOAT	30	3
ONE LITTLE BOAT GAVE UP IT'S STRIFE	ADRIFT! A LITTLE BOAT	30	7
ONE LITTLE BOAT--O'ERSPENT WITH GALES--	ADRIFT! A LITTLE BOAT	30	11
NOBODY KNOWS THIS LITTLE ROSE--	NOBODY KNOWS THIS LITTLE	35	1
AH LITTLE ROSE--HOW EASY	NOBODY KNOWS THIS LITTLE	35	11
ONE LITTLE MAID--FROM PLAYMATES--	TAKEN FROM MEN--THIS	53	5
ONE LITTLE MIND FROM SCHOOL--	TAKEN FROM MEN--THIS	53	6
A LITTLE EAST OF [OVER] JORDAN,	A LITTLE EAST OF JORDAN,	59	1
WILL LIFT HIS LITTLE GIRL--	"ARCTURUS" IS HIS OTHER	70	31
IN SUCH A LITTLE WHILE!	A LADY RED--AMID THE	74	12
SAVE JUST A LITTLE PLACE FOR ME	GOING TO HEAVEN!	79	14
AND I'D LIKE TO LOOK A LITTLE MORE	GOING TO HEAVEN!	79	22
OUR LITTLE GARDEN THAT WE LOST	WE SHOULD NOT MIND SO	81	3
THAT WHOSO SEES THIS LITTLE FLOWER	WE SHOULD NOT MIND SO	81	9
PLEASE TO TELL A LITTLE PILGRIM	WILL THERE REALLY BE A	101	11
AND IF I DONT--THE LITTLE BIRD	I HAVE A KING, WHO DOES	103	13
A LITTLE TREMOR IN MY VOICE	WHERE I HAVE LOST, I	104	11
'TWAS SUCH A LITTLE--LITTLE BOAT	'TWAS SUCH A LITTLE--	107	1
'TWAS SUCH A LITTLE--LITTLE BOAT	'TWAS SUCH A LITTLE--	107	1
MY LITTLE CRAFT WAS LOST!	'TWAS SUCH A LITTLE--	107	8
WHO BUILT THIS LITTLE ALBAN HOUSE	BRING ME THE SUNSET IN A	128	19
A LITTLE THIS SIDE OF THE SNOW	BESIDES THE AUTUMN POETS	131	3

LITTLE (CONTINUED)

	FIRST LINE	POEM	LINE
"UNTO THE LITTLE, UNTO ME,"	I BRING-AN UNACCUSTOMED	132	21
HAVE YOU GOT A BROOK IN YOUR LITTLE HEART,	HAVE YOU GOT A BROOK IN	136	1
AND YET YOUR LITTLE DRAUGHT OF LIFE	HAVE YOU GOT A BROOK IN	136	7
WHY, LOOK OUT FOR THE LITTLE BROOK IN MARCH,	HAVE YOU GOT A BROOK IN	136	9
BEWARE, LEST THIS LITTLE BROOK OF LIFE,	HAVE YOU GOT A BROOK IN	136	15
FOR MY LITTLE DAMASK MAID--	PIGMY SERAPHS--GONE	138	11
WHOSE ARE THE LITTLE BEDS, I ASKED	WHOSE ARE THE LITTLE	142	1
A LITTLE FURTHER ON--	WHOSE ARE THE LITTLE	142	10
LITTLE LEONTODON.	WHOSE ARE THE LITTLE	142	12
SOME LITTLE WREN GOES SEEKING ROUND--	FOR EVERY BIRD A NEST--	143	3
THE LITTLE WREN DESIRES--	FOR EVERY BIRD A NEST--	143	9
IF SUCH A LITTLE FIGURE	ON SUCH A NIGHT, OR SUCH	146	3
BUT THAT THE LITTLE FIGURE	ON SUCH A NIGHT, OR SUCH	146	7
THAT SUCH A LITTLE FIGURE	ON SUCH A NIGHT, OR SUCH	146	11
THERE WAS A LITTLE FIGURE PLUMP	ON SUCH A NIGHT, OR SUCH	146	17
FOR EVERY LITTLE KNOLL--	ON SUCH A NIGHT, OR SUCH	146	18
THE LITTLE CAGE OF "CURRER BELL"	ALL OVERGROWN BY CUNNING	148	3
HER LITTLE FIGURE AT THE GATE	SHE DIED--THIS WAS THE	150	5
THAN WHEN--A LITTLE DULL BALM GROWN--	YOU LOVE ME--YOU ARE	156	17
A LITTLE BREAD--A CRUST--A CRUMB--	A LITTLE BREAD--A CRUST	159	1
A LITTLE TRUST--A DEMIJOHN--	A LITTLE BREAD--A CRUST	159	2
STILL, MY LITTLE GIPSEY BEING	THO' MY DESTINY BE	163	5
STILL, MY LITTLE SUNBURNT BOSOM	THO' MY DESTINY BE	163	7
AS WHEN HER LITTLE MORTAL NEST	MAMA NEVER FORGETS HER	164	5
A LITTLE PALMLEAF HAT WAS ALL,	I MET A KING THIS	166	3
AS IF THE LITTLE EBON BOX	IN EBON BOX, WHEN YEARS	169	19
I'M THE LITTLE "HEART'S EASE"!	I'M THE LITTLE "HEART'S	176	1
DEAR, OLD FASHIONED, LITTLE FLOWER!	I'M THE LITTLE "HEART'S	176	9
NOR WILL I, THE LITTLE HEART'S EASE--	I'M THE LITTLE "HEART'S	176	13
I CAUTIOUS, SCANNED MY LITTLE LIFE--	I CAUTIOUS, SCANNED MY	178	1
ART THOU WITHIN THE LITTLE BARN	I CAUTIOUS, SCANNED MY	178	19
AS IF SOME LITTLE ARCTIC FLOWER	AS IF SOME LITTLE ARCTIC	180	1
I SAY, AS IF THIS LITTLE FLOWER	AS IF SOME LITTLE ARCTIC	180	9
THIS LITTLE HOUND WITHIN THE HEART	WHAT SHALL I DO--IT	186	2
IT'S SUCH A LITTLE THING TO WEEP--	IT'S SUCH A LITTLE THING	189	1
IF I SHOULD BRIBE THE LITTLE BIRD--	THE SKIES CANT KEEP	191	7
POOR LITTLE HEART!	POOR LITTLE HEART!	192	1
PROUD LITTLE HEART!	POOR LITTLE HEART!	192	4
FRAIL LITTLE HEART!	POOR LITTLE HEART!	192	7
GAY LITTLE HEART--	POOR LITTLE HEART!	192	10
TIM--READS A LITTLE HYMN--	WE DONT CRY--TIM AND I,	196	17
A LITTLE PURPLE--SLIPPED BETWEEN--	A SLASH OF BLUE--	204	5
WHAT AILED SO SMART A LITTLE MAID--	THE ROSE DID CAPER ON	208	7
TILL THOSE TWO TROUBLED--LITTLE CLOCKS	THE ROSE DID CAPER ON	208	15
TO SEE THE LITTLE TIPPLER	I TASTE A LIQUOR NEVER	214	15
THAT WERE THE LITTLE LOAD--	SAVIOR! I'VE NO ONE ELSE	217	6
SAY--THAT A LITTLE LIFE--FOR HIS--	IF HE DISSOLVE--THEN--	236	12
HIS LITTLE SPANIEL--TELL HIM!	IF HE DISSOLVE--THEN--	236	14
BUT--I CAN SAY A LITTLE "MINOR"	WHY--DO THEY SHUT ME OUT	248	3
AND THEY--WERE THE LITTLE HAND--THAT KNOCKED--	WHY--DO THEY SHUT ME OUT	248	11
THAT COULD ABASH THE LITTLE BIRD	"HOPE" IS THE THING WITH	254	7
TO DIE--TAKES JUST A LITTLE WHILE--	TO DIE--TAKES JUST A	255	1
AH, FRIEND, YOU LITTLE KNEW	GOOD NIGHT! WHICH PUT	259	3
AND DO THE LITTLE TOILS	HE PUT THE BELT AROUND	273	10
THE VANE A LITTLE TO THE EAST--	A SHADY FRIEND--FOR	278	5
IN LITTLE WEALTHS, AS GIRLS COULD [CAN] BOAST	YOUR RICHES--TAUGHT ME--	299	3
OF MINES, I LITTLE KNOW--MYSELF--	YOUR RICHES--TAUGHT ME--	299	9
OR LITTLE JOHN--OF LINCOLN GREEN--	LIKE SOME OLD FASHIONED	302	7
'TIS LITTLE I CAN DO--	FOR LARGEST WOMAN'S	309	2
GIVE LITTLE ANGUISH--	GIVE LITTLE ANGUISH--	310	1
MY LITTLE CIRCUIT WOULD HAVE SHAMED	I SHOULD HAVE BEEN TOO	313	4
LITTLE BOYS HATS--AND STUBBLE--	THE WIND DID'NT COME	316	18
THAT [WHICH] LITTLE YELLOW BOYS AND GIRLS	I'LL TELL YOU HOW THE	318	11
OUR LITTLE SEXTON--SINGS.	SOME KEEP THE SABBATH	324	8
THE GRASS SO LITTLE HAS TO DO--	THE GRASS SO LITTLE HAS	333	1
THE GRASS SO LITTLE HAS TO DO	THE GRASS SO LITTLE HAS	333	19
AND LITTLE GIRLS--WITH DOLLS--	IT WILL BE SUMMER--	342	4
TOO LITTLE--DUST--	MY REWARD FOR BEING, WAS	343	V
THE LITTLE TRACKS--CLOSE PREST--	'TWAS THE OLD--ROAD--	344	8
WAIT! LOOK! HER LITTLE BOOK--	'TWAS THE OLD--ROAD--	344	12
HE HURTS A LITTLE, THOUGH--	I DREADED THAT FIRST	348	4
TO PONDER LITTLE WORKMANSHIPS	DEATH SETS A THING	360	5
THOUGH IT BE LITTLE AS A DAFFODIL--	WHAT I CAN DO--I WILL--	361	2
A LITTLE BOOT I KNOW--	ALTHOUGH I PUT AWAY HIS	366	14
AND SO I DECK, A LITTLE,	I'M SAYING EVERY DAY	373	4
HER STURDY LITTLE COUNTENANCE	THERE IS A FLOWER THAT	380	15
AND LITTLE BOYS--BESIDES--	THERE'S BEEN A DEATH, IN	389	16
AND CROWD THE LITTLE ROOM--	IT MIGHT BE LONELIER	405	6
THE LITTLE DWELLING HOUSES RISE	THE COLOR OF THE GRAVE	411	15
A HURRYING HOME OF LITTLE MEN	A MURMUR IN THE TREES--	416	9
THE BRAVEST--GROPE A LITTLE--	WE GROW ACCUSTOMED TO	419	13
TO STRETCH A LITTLE FURTHER	THE MONTHS HAVE ENDS--	423	3
BUT--PLEASE TAKE A LITTLE GIRL--	GOOD MORNING--MIDNIGHT--	425	15
TURN IT, A LITTLE--FULL IN THE FACE	IT DONT SOUND SO	426	5
I'M DIVING--JUST A LITTLE LATE--	I'LL CLUTCH--AND CLUTCH	427	5
PRAYER IS THE LITTLE IMPLEMENT	PRAYER IS THE LITTLE	437	1
BUT LONGER THAN THE LITTLE RILL--	FORGET! THE LADY WITH	438	12
GOD MADE A LITTLE GENTIAN--	GOD MADE A LITTLE	442	1
LIFE'S LITTLE DUTIES DO--PRECISELY--	I TIE MY HAT--I CREASE	443	2

LITTLE (CONTINUED)

	FIRST LINE	POEM	LINE
WHAT LITTLE OF HIM WE--POSSESSED	IT FEELS A SHAME TO BE	444	7
WHEN I WAS A LITTLE GIRL--	IT WAS GIVEN TO ME BY	454	2
I THINK A LITTLE WELL--LIKE MINE--	I KNOW WHERE WELLS GROW	460	19
SO BRAVE--UPON IT'S LITTLE BED	WHY MAKE IT DOUBT--IT	462	4
'TIS LITTLE I--COULD CARE FOR PEARLS--	'TIS LITTLE I--COULD	466	1
IT'S LITTLE FATE TO STIPULATE--	THE MANNER OF IT'S DEATH	468	7
THE LITTLE TOIL OF LOVE--	I HAD NO TIME TO HATE--	478	10
HE SHIFTS THE STEM--A LITTLE--	A SOLEMN THING WITHIN	483	11
A LITTLE NEARER--EVERY SUN	A SOLEMN THING WITHIN	483	15
AT NIGHT, MY LITTLE LAMP, AND BOOK--	I WAS THE SLIGHTEST IN	486	3
A LITTLE NOTE--WHEN YOU AWAKE--	YOU LOVE THE LORD--YOU	487	3
JESUS--IT'S YOUR LITTLE "JOHN"!	HE STRAINED MY FAITH--	497	15
BLAME THE LITTLE [EMPTY / CHILDISH] HAND	SWEET--YOU FORGOT--BUT I	523	6
AND THEN--THOSE LITTLE ANODYNES	THE HEART ASKS PLEASURE	536	3
A LITTLE FURTHER REACHES--INSTEAD--	THE BLACK BERRY--WEARS A	554	11
BUT LITTLE CARMINE HATH HER FACE--	BUT LITTLE CARMINE HATH	558	1
IT LEFT THE LITTLE TINT	IT KNEW NO MEDICINE--	559	9
THAT HAS SO LITTLE OIL--	I MEASURE EVERY GRIEF I	561	16
APPROACHED [POSSESSED]--THE AMBER FLITS [MOVES]--A LITTLE--	DELIGHT--BECOMES	572	7
I PRAYED, AT FIRST, A LITTLE GIRL,	I PRAYED, AT FIRST, A	576	1
THE WIND PURSUED THE LITTLE BUSH--	THE NIGHT WAS WIDE, AND	589	5
HER LITTLE ROCKING CHAIR TO DRAW--	THE NIGHT WAS WIDE, AND	589	15
WHEN FIRST A SOMBRE [LITTLE] GIRL--	I THINK I WAS ENCHANTED	593	2
'TWAS LITTLE--HE SHOULD SEE--	IT ALWAYS FELT TO ME--A	597	22
IT'S LITTLE PANELS BE	I SEE THEE BETTER--IN	611	10
TO GAD MY LITTLE BEING OUT--	IT WOULD HAVE STARVED A	612	15
AS WHEN A LITTLE GIRL	THEY SHUT ME UP IN PROSE	613	2
FOR LITTLE MYSTERIES	I WATCHED THE MOON	629	24
AND WHEN YOUR LITTLE LIFETIME FAILED,	OURSELVES WERE WED ONE	631	3
LIKE LITTLE SCHOLARS--LOUD--	I THINK THE LONGEST HOUR	635	10
TAKE UP MY LITTLE VIOLIN--	I THINK THE LONGEST HOUR	635	15
THEN DRAW MY LITTLE LETTER FORTH	THE WAY I READ A	636	7
THE OTHER, LIKE THE LITTLE BANK	I THINK TO LIVE--MAY BE	646	7
A LITTLE ROAD--NOT MADE OF MAN--	A LITTLE ROAD--NOT MADE	647	1
AND DWELL A LITTLE EVERYWHERE [GENERALLY]	COULD I BUT RIDE	661	7
GOES WITH US--JUST A LITTLE WAY--	AGAIN--HIS VOICE IS AT	663	20
CRUMBS--FIT SUCH LITTLE MOUTHS--	VICTORY COMES LATE--	690	10
WHO OF LITTLE LOVE--KNOW HOW TO STARVE--	VICTORY COMES LATE--	690	14
YET WHY SO LITTLE SOUND--MYSELF	THE SUN KEPT SETTING--	692	11
BUT THIS LITTLE BLAZE	I COULD BRING YOU JEWELS	697	6
A LITTLE BRIG I KNEW--O'ERTOOK BY BLAST--	IT TOSSED--AND TOSSED--	723	2
A LITTLE WATER SUPPLICATE--	WE THIRST AT FIRST--'TIS	726	3
A SPICY CHARGE, MY LITTLE POSTS [FRIENDS]--	THE BIRDS REPORTED FROM	743	3
AND THE LITTLE BORDER--DUSKER--	AUTUMN--OVERLOOKED MY	748	7
THEY HAVE A LITTLE ODOR--THAT TO ME	THEY HAVE A LITTLE ODOR	785	1
TO CALL THE LITTLE GIRL	THEY WONT FROWN ALWAYS--	874	6
IT WAS A LITTLE TIE--	I'VE NONE TO TELL ME TO	881	3
OUR LITTLE KINSMEN--AFTER RAIN	OUR LITTLE KINSMEN--	885	1
UNTIL A LITTLE BIRD	OUR LITTLE KINSMEN--	885	6
AND LEFT THE LITTLE ANGLE WORM	OUR LITTLE KINSMEN--	885	11
PURSUED OF LITTLE BOYS	WHEN I HAVE SEEN THE SUN	888	8
LOSE MY WAY LIKE A LITTLE CHILD	HOW HAPPY I WAS IF I	898	7
'TIS SUNRISE--LITTLE MAID--HAST THOU	'TIS SUNRISE--LITTLE	908	1
'TIS NOON--MY LITTLE MAID--	'TIS SUNRISE--LITTLE	908	5
MY LITTLE MAID--'TIS NIGHT--ALAS	'TIS SUNRISE--LITTLE	908	9
THY LITTLE PLAN TO DIE--	'TIS SUNRISE--LITTLE	908	12
TOO LITTLE WAY THE HOUSE MUST LIE	TOO LITTLE WAY THE HOUSE	911	1
DISARMS THE LITTLE INTERVAL--	LOVE--IS THAT LATER	924	7
THE LADY FEEDS HER LITTLE BIRD	THE LADY FEEDS HER	941	1
THE LITTLE BIRD WOULD NOT DISSENT [DEMUR]	THE LADY FEEDS HER	941	3
THE LITTLE NOTE THAT OTHERS DROPT	I WAS A PHEBE--NOTHING	1009	3
A PHEBE MAKES A LITTLE PRINT	I WAS A PHEBE--NOTHING	1009	7
UP LIFE'S HILL WITH MY LITTLE BUNDLE	UP LIFE'S HILL WITH MY	1010	1
TO LITTLE GROUPS OF CONTINENTS	THE HILLS IN PURPLE	1016	3
I MET SOMEBODY'S LITTLE BOY	TRUDGING TO EDEN,	1020	2
GUIDES THE LITTLE ONE PREDESTINED	FAR FROM LOVE THE	1021	7
THE LITTLE THAT I MAY	SO LARGE MY WILL	1024	2
THE DYING NEED BUT LITTLE, DEAR,	THE DYING NEED BUT	1026	1
MY HEART UPON A LITTLE PLATE	MY HEART UPON A LITTLE	1027	1
HER LITTLE PARASOL TO LIFT	HER LITTLE PARASOL TO	1038	1
A LITTLE NEWER FOR THE TERM	EXHILIRATION IS THE	1118	7
WHEN BUT A LITTLE CHILD--	I NOTICED PEOPLE	1149	2
A FACT WITHELD THE LITTLE CHILD--	I NOTICED PEOPLE	1149	8
A LITTLE DOG THAT WAGS HIS TAIL	A LITTLE DOG THAT WAGS	1185	1
OF SUCH A LITTLE DOG AM I	A LITTLE DOG THAT WAGS	1185	3
BECAUSE HE IS A LITTLE BOY	A LITTLE DOG THAT WAGS	1185	7
BESEECH [ADJURE] EACH LITTLE BOY--	A LITTLE DOG THAT WAGS	1185	16
BE IT BUT A LITTLE--	WHAT WE SEE WE KNOW	1195	2
UNTIL HIS LITTLE FIGURE	A SPARROW TOOK A SLICE	1211	7
THE WEST A LITTLE WORN--	THE STARS ARE OLD, THAT	1249	2
A LITTLE FROM REMARK WITHDRAWN--	THE MOUNTAINS STOOD IN	1278	7
HOW MUCH--HOW LITTLE--IS	IN THIS SHORT LIFE	1287	3
THIS DIRTY--LITTLE--HEART	THIS DIRTY--LITTLE--	1311	1
OUR LITTLE SECRETS SLINK AWAY--	OUR LITTLE SECRETS SLINK	1326	1
BOLD LITTLE BEAUTY	PINK--SMALL--AND	1332	9
A LITTLE MADNESS IN THE SPRING	A LITTLE MADNESS IN THE	1333	1
TO DIE--WAS LITTLE FATE--	TO HIS SIMPLICITY	1352	2
DEMANDS THE [MY] LITTLE KING	A SAUCER HOLDS A CUP	1374	6

	FIRST LINE	POEM	LINE
LITTLE (CONTINUED)			
HINDER IT A LITTLE	I SUPPOSE THE TIME WILL	1381	6
THAT, TOO, HALT A LITTLE--	I SUPPOSE THE TIME WILL	1381	12
NATURE IMPARTS THE LITTLE BLUE-BIRD--ASSURED	AFTER ALL BIRDS HAVE	1395	2
HOW LITTLE WORK [WHAT LITTLE ACT] IT BE--	WITH PINIONS OF DISDAIN	1431	10
HOW LITTLE WORK [WHAT LITTLE ACT] IT BE--	WITH PINIONS OF DISDAIN	1431	10
BEHOLD THIS LITTLE BANE--	BEHOLD THIS LITTLE BANE	1438	1
A LITTLE SNOW WAS HERE AND THERE	A LITTLE SNOW WAS HERE	1444	1
A LITTLE WEATHER WORN	BEFORE YOU THOUGHT OF	1465	6
A LITTLE OVERFLOWING WORD	A LITTLE OVERFLOWING	1467	1
FOR LITTLE FELLOWMEN--	THE SAVIOR MUST HAVE	1487	4
IT'S LITTLE ETHER HOOD	IT'S LITTLE ETHER HOOD	1501	1
BUT NOT THIS [MY] LITTLE MAID--	I SAW THE WIND WITHIN	1502	V
HOW HAPPY IS [INVINCIBLE] THE LITTLE STONE	HOW HAPPY IS THE LITTLE	1510	1
HIS LITTLE HEARSE LIKE FIGURE	HIS LITTLE HEARSE LIKE	1522	1
THIS GALLANT LITTLE FLOWER--	IT WOULD NOT KNOW IF IT	1579	2
WITHIN THAT LITTLE HIVE	WITHIN THAT LITTLE HIVE	1607	1
SAHARA IS TOO LITTLE PRICE	I DID NOT REACH THEE	1664	12
BUT LITTLE SYMPATHY	THE BUTTERFLY OBTAINS	1685	2
THE GRAVE MY LITTLE COTTAGE IS,	THE GRAVE MY LITTLE	1743	1
AND THEN ADJUSTED HIS LITTLE NOTES,	A TRAIN WENT THROUGH A	1761	5
WHO HAD SO LITTLE TIME	WERE NATURE MORTAL LADY	1762	2
THE JOYFUL LITTLE DEITY	HOW FLEET--HOW	1771	3
LITURGIES			
PAUSE IN YOUR LITURGIES--	SANG FROM THE HEART,	1059	13
LIVE			
COULD LIVE--DID LIVE--	COULD LIVE--DID LIVE--	43	1
COULD LIVE--DID LIVE--	COULD LIVE--DID LIVE--	43	1
AND YOU SHOULD LIVE--	IF I SHOULD DIE,	54	2
AND SUCH A WAGON! WHILE I LIVE	I MET A KING THIS	166	17
WHO LIVE THERE--	WHAT IS--"PARADISE"--	215	2
WE--BEE AND I--LIVE BY THE QUAFFING--	WE--BEE AND I--LIVE BY	230	1
GOODBYE TO THE LIFE I USED TO LIVE--	TIE THE STRINGS TO MY	279	13
I THOUGHT IF I COULD ONLY LIVE	I DREADED THAT FIRST	348	5
TO PERISH, OR TO LIVE?	'TWAS LIKE A MAELSTROM,	414	25
SO ANTHRACITE, TO LIVE--	MORE LIFE--WENT OUT--	422	8
AS POSITIVELY LIVE	DO PEOPLE MOULDER	432	4
IT MAY BE--A RENOWN TO LIVE--	IT FEELS A SHAME TO BE	444	17
SO WELL THAT I CAN LIVE WITHOUT--	SO WELL THAT I CAN LIVE	456	1
I LIVE WITH HIM--I SEE HIS FACE--	I LIVE WITH HIM--I SEE	463	1
I LIVE WITH HIM--I HEAR HIS VOICE--	I LIVE WITH HIM--I SEE	463	9
HOW SMALL IN THOSE WHO LIVE--	THE MANNER OF IT'S DEATH	468	8
I COULD NOT BEAR TO LIVE--ALOUD--	I WAS THE SLIGHTEST IN	486	12
SCOOPING UP THE DUST AND CHANTING "LIVE"!	WHILE IT IS ALIVE	491	10
HE TOUCHED ME, SO I LIVE TO KNOW	HE TOUCHED ME, SO I LIVE	506	1
THE DUST--CONNECT [ADJUST]--AND LIVE--	NO CROWD THAT HAS	515	8
I NEVER LIVED [DID NOT LIVE]--ENOUGH--	THAT I DID ALWAYS LOVE	549	4
I WONDER IF IT HURTS TO LIVE--	I MEASURE EVERY GRIEF I	561	9
TO LIVE [DINE] SO SMALL AS I--	IT WOULD HAVE STARVED A	612	2
I CANNOT LIVE WITH YOU--	I CANNOT LIVE WITH YOU--	640	1
I THINK TO LIVE--MAY BE A BLISS [LIFE]	I THINK TO LIVE--MAY BE	646	1
I'D GIVE--TO LIVE THAT HOUR--AGAIN--	AGAIN--HIS VOICE IS AT	663	26
BUT PERISHES--TO LIVE ANEW--	SUSPENSE--IS HOSTILER	705	5
THOUGH I THAN HE--MAY LONGER LIVE	MY LIFE HAD STOOD--A	754	21
TO HIM--TO LIVE--WAS DOOM--	HE FOUGHT LIKE THOSE	759	8
I SHALL NOT LIVE IN VAIN	IF I CAN STOP ONE HEART	919	2
I SHALL NOT LIVE IN VAIN.	IF I CAN STOP ONE HEART	919	7
THE PRIVILEGE TO LIVE	'TWAS CRISIS--ALL THE	948	6
TO DIE--OR LIVE--	WERT THOU BUT ILL--THAT	961	18
MIGHT THEY BUT LIVE, THEY WOULD!	WERE IT BUT ME THAT	1015	4
AND LIVE--WITHOUT THE LIFE	TO DIE--WITHOUT THE	1017	2
AND BOROUGHS [LIMITS] WHERE WE LIVE--	LIKE MEN AND WOMEN	1105	8
BEGINS TO LIVE	A WORD IS DEAD	1212	5
FOR NONE SEE GOD AND LIVE--	TO PILE LIKE THUNDER TO	1247	8
YOURSELF FORGOT TO LIVE--	BECAUSE THAT YOU ARE	1260	16
THAN WANE [LIVE] IS EASIER--	I'D RATHER RECOLLECT A	1349	8
IF DUTY LIVE--CONTENTED	TO HIS SIMPLICITY	1352	3
I HAVE NO LIFE BUT THIS--[TO LIVE]	I HAVE NO LIFE BUT THIS	1398	1
THOSE NOT LIVE YET	THOSE NOT LIVE YET	1454	1
WHO DOUBT TO LIVE AGAIN--	THOSE NOT LIVE YET	1454	2
WE KNEW NOT THAT WE WERE TO LIVE--	WE KNEW NOT THAT WE WERE	1462	1
I GAVE HIM LEAVE TO LIVE	IT CAME HIS TURN TO BEG	1500	6
SHE COULD NOT LIVE UPON THE PAST	SHE COULD NOT LIVE UPON	1505	1
AND IF THOU LIVE BEFORE THOU WAKE--	NOW I LAY THEE DOWN TO	1539	3
FOR WHICH I CEASE TO LIVE--	TRIED ALWAYS AND	1559	4
IT MIGHT HAVE BEEN TO LIVE	TO SEE HER IS A PICTURE	1568	V
THAT MAKE THE WATER LIVE, ESTRANGED	THE SPIRIT LASTS--BUT IN	1576	11
THAT MEN ANEW EMBARK TO LIVE	IN SNOW THOU COMEST	1669	7
THAT THESE COULD LIVE	T'WAS COMFORT IN HER	1703	8
THE MEN THAT DAILY LIVE	DID LIFE'S PENURIOUS	1717	3
IT IS POSSIBLE FOR SENSE TO LIVE	IF EVER THE LID GETS OFF	1727	7
WHILE WE WHO DARE TO LIVE	THIS DOCILE ONE INTER	1752	2
LIVED			
HE LIVED--WHERE DREAMS WERE BORN--	A PRECIOUS--MOULDERING	371	24
I NEVER LIVED [DID NOT LIVE]--ENOUGH--	THAT I DID ALWAYS LOVE	549	4
AND I STOOD UP--AND LIVED--	THREE TIMES--WE PARTED--	598	16
COULD THEY--KNOW--HE BREATHED [LIVED]--	IN FALLING TIMBERS	614	6
I LIVED ON DREAD--	I LIVED ON DREAD--	770	1
WHO HAD THEY LIVED, HAD DIED BUT WHEN	A DEATH BLOW IS A LIFE	816	3
NO EYE HATH SEEN AND LIVED	FROM US SHE WANDERED NOW	890	5

	FIRST LINE	POEM	LINE
LIVED (CONTINUED)			
THAT SUCH HAVE LIVED, ...	THAT SUCH HAVE DIED	1030	3
THE LAST NIGHT THAT SHE LIVED	THE LAST NIGHT THAT SHE	1100	1
THE SAME AS THOSE THAT LIVED	THAT THIS SHOULD FEEL	1112	2
WHOSE HAVING LIVED IS HELD BY US IN NOBLE HOLIDAY	LEST ANY DOUBT THAT WE	1156	2
BOY THAT LIVED FOR "OUGHT TO [OR'TER]" . .	SO I PULL MY STOCKINGS	1201	4
SIGNIFICANCE [OMNIPOTENCE] THAT EACH HAS LIVED	BECAUSE THAT YOU ARE	1260	9
LIVED TO TELL THE TALE--	ABRAHAM TO KILL HIM	1317	10
HE HAS NOT LIVED WHO HAS NOT FELT-- . . .	WONDER--IS NOT PRECISELY	1331	4
HE LIVED THE LIFE OF AMBUSH	HE LIVED THE LIFE OF	1525	1
THOSE LOOKED THAT LIVED--[THE LIVING LOOKED] THAT DAY--	THERE CAME A WIND LIKE A	1593	12
LIVELONG			
TO TELL YOUR [ONE'S] NAME--THE LIVELONG JUNE--	I'M NOBODY! WHO ARE YOU?	288	7
LIVERPOOL			
YESTERDAY [LIVERPOOL] IS OLD--	AFTER THE SUN COMES OUT	1148	4
LIVES			
OUR LIVES ARE SWISS--	OUR LIVES ARE SWISS--	80	1
TWO LIVES--ONE BEING--NOW--	FOREVER AT HIS SIDE TO	246	5
AND SO WITH LIVES--	DELIGHT IS AS THE FLIGHT	257	19
AND LIVES CAN [WILL] BEAR IT!	BOUND--A TROUBLE--	269	2
TO LIVES THAT [AS] STOOP TO NOTICE MINE-- .	HE PUT THE BELT AROUND	273	13
FAINT-GOING LIVES [EYES]--THEIR LAPSE FROM SIGHING--	"MORNING"--MEANS	300	9
LIVES WILL FRET--	GIVE LITTLE ANGUISH--	310	2
I KNOW LIVES, I COULD MISS	I KNOW LIVES, I COULD	372	1
THE EARTH LAYS BACK THESE TIRED LIVES . .	THE MONTHS HAVE ENDS--	423	5
THAT LIVES--LIKE DOLLARS--MUST BE PILED . .	IT FEELS A SHAME TO BE	444	11
THE SINGLE--TO SOME LIVES.	A SOLEMN THING WITHIN	483	16
TO LIVES THAT THOUGHT THE WORSHIPPING . .	LIKE FLOWERS, THAT HEARD	513	14
AND ALL THE NEIGHBOR'S LIVES--	I'M SORRY FOR THE DEAD--	529	16
REVERTED TO ADJOINING LIVES--	IF HE WERE LIVING--DARE	734	9
UPON CONCLUDED LIVES	UPON CONCLUDED LIVES	735	1
WASTES OF LIVES--RESOWN WITH COLORS . . .	ALL BUT DEATH, CAN BE	749	5
TO LIVES THAT STAND ALONE--	TO OFFER BRAVE	767	2
WHILE IT SUSPENDS THE LIVES.	A DOUBT IF IT BE US	859	8
SOME MINISTRY TO POORER LIVES--	I LEARNED--AT LEAST--	944	20
NO LIVES ARE ROUND--	EXCEPT THE SMALLER SIZE	1067	2
THE MIND LIVES ON THE HEART	THE MIND LIVES ON THE	1355	1
THE WATER LIVES SO FAR--	WHAT MYSTERY PERVADES A	1400	2
LIVES HE IN ANY OTHER WORLD	LIVES HE IN ANY OTHER	1557	1
WHILE PONTIUS PILATE LIVES	ONE CROWN THAT NO ONE	1735	5
LIVID			
AND THE LIVID SURPRISE	WE DREAM--IT IS GOOD WE	531	12
AND THEN A LIVID TOE [CLAW]--	THE WIND BEGUN TO KNEAD	824	12
THIS LIVID INTERVIEW--	HIS VOICE DECREPIT WAS	1476	8
OH, WHAT A LIVID BOON!	UPON THE GALLOWS HUNG A	1757	8
LIVING			
THE WORM DOTH WOO THE MORTAL, DEATH CLAIMS A LIVING BRIDE,	AWAKE YE MUSES NINE,	1	21
'TIS LIVING--HURTS US MORE--	'TIS NOT THAT DYING	335	2
WHEN SAPPHO--WAS A LIVING GIRL--	A PRECIOUS--MOULDERING	371	17
THE LIVING--TELL--	UNIT, LIKE DEATH, FOR	408	10
ENDOW THE LIVING--WITH THE TEARS--	ENDOW THE LIVING--WITH	521	1
AND YET I WAS A LIVING CHILD--	IT WOULD HAVE STARVED A	612	3
IF HE WERE LIVING--DARE I ASK--	IF HE WERE LIVING--DARE	734	1
THAT MAKES THE LIVING POSSIBLE	A DOUBT IF IT BE US	859	7
THE LIVING, SWEET, IS COSTLIER--	TOO SCANTY 'TWAS TO DIE	1013	3
BUT LIVING, THIS INCLUDE	TOO SCANTY 'TWAS TO DIE	1013	6
WHO GAMBOLS ALL THE LIVING DAY	A LITTLE DOG THAT WAGS	1185	5
HENCEFORTH I TAKE MY LIVING PLACE	SOMEHOW MYSELF SURVIVED	1194	5
FROM ANY HUMAN [LIVING] SOUL--	YOU CANNOT TAKE ITSELF	1351	2
THE HORSE THAT SCENTS THE LIVING GRASS . .	THE LIFE THAT TIED TOO	1535	5
THOSE LOOKED THAT LIVED--[THE LIVING LOOKED] THAT DAY--	THERE CAME A WIND LIKE A	1593	12
THE LIVING, FOR THE STARS--	OF GLORY NOT A BEAM IS	1647	4
TO HEAR THE LIVING CLOCK	T'WAS COMFORT IN HER	1703	2
LO			
LO, WHAT [THE] "AUGUSTAN" YEARS	IF PAIN FOR PEACE	63	2
LO, A TINT CASHMERE!	ARTISTS WRESTLED HERE!	110	2
LO, A ROSE!	ARTISTS WRESTLED HERE!	110	3
AND LO--MY PRICELESS HAY	I CAUTIOUS, SCANNED MY	178	8
AND THEN, I [HE] BRAKE MY [HIS] LIFE--AND LO,	I SHOWED HER HIGHTS SHE	446	9
AND LO, HER SILVER PRINCIPLE	AT HALF PAST THREE, A	1084	7
LOAD			
THAT WERE THE LITTLE LOAD--	SAVIOR! I'VE NO ONE ELSE	217	6
WILL SWAY WITH PURPLE LOAD--	IT WILL BE SUMMER--	342	10
COALS--FROM A ROLLING [PASSING] LOAD--RATTLE--HOW--NEAR--	I COULD DIE--TO KNOW--	570	9
HAD WE KNOWN THE TON [WEIGHT / LOAD] SHE BORE	HAD WE KNOWN THE TON SHE	1124	1
A LOAD IS FIRST IMPOSSIBLE	I SHOULD NOT DARE TO BE	1197	3
THE LAST SHALL BE THE LIGHTEST LOAD . . .	I DID NOT REACH THEE	1664	18
LOADED			
THAN DID LOADED [SWELLING] SEA	HER SWEET TURN TO LEAVE	649	6
MY LIFE HAD STOOD--A LOADED GUN--	MY LIFE HAD STOOD--A	754	1
THE LOW GRASS LOADED WITH THE DEW	THE CRICKETS SANG	1104	5
LOADED AND LEVELLED	THE EVENT WAS DIRECTLY	1686	6
HOME FLEW THE LOADED BEES	THE SUN RETIRED TO A	1693	6

	FIRST LINE	POEM	LINE
LOAF			
AN INSUFFICIENT [INNUTRITIOUS] LOAF--	DEPRIVED OF OTHER	773	4
GOD GAVE A LOAF TO EVERY BIRD--	GOD GAVE A LOAF TO EVERY	791	1
A SAUCER HOLDS A LOAF.	A SAUCER HOLDS A CUP	1374	4
LOAVES			
BEES--TO THEIR LOAVES OF HONEY	HE IS ALIVE, THIS	1160	5
LOCALITY			
FORGETS HER OWN LOCALITY--	THE DROP, THAT WRESTLES	284	2
IN LOCALITY--	UNFULFILLED TO	972	4
THE SAME LOCALITY--	IT BLOOMED AND DROPT, A	978	8
LOCATION			
IN ACRES--IT'S [ACRE--OR] LOCATION	A NEARNESS TO	963	7
LOCATION DOUBTLESS HE WOULD PLEAD [URGE]	SO MUCH OF HEAVEN HAS	1228	7
"TOMORROW"--WHOSE LOCATION	"TOMORROW"--WHOSE	1367	1
LOCATION'S			
LOCATION'S NARROW WAY IS FOR OURSELVES--	WE PRAY--TO HEAVEN--	489	7
I SCARCE ESTEEM LOCATION'S NAME--	WHERE THOU ART--THAT--IS	725	4
LOCATIONS			
FORETOLD LOCATIONS--	THE THINGS THAT NEVER	1515	10
LOCK			
UNTIL THEY LOCK IT IN THE GRAVE,	IF I MAY HAVE IT, WHEN	577	5
FOR THO' THEY LOCK THEE IN THE GRAVE,	IF I MAY HAVE IT, WHEN	577	7
'TIS FIRST--I LOCK THE DOOR--	THE WAY I READ A	636	2
AND SLOWLY [SLILY / SOFTLY] PICK THE LOCK--	THE WAY I READ A	636	8
AND BEING UNDER LOCK--	THE LONELINESS ONE DARE	777	12
LOCK THE DOOR--	DEAR MARCH--COME IN--	1320	19
LOCKED			
HIS BILL IS CLASPED [LOCKED]--HIS EYE FORSOOK [ESTRANGED]--	HIS BILL IS CLASPED--HIS	1102	1
LOCKING			
LOCKING BARE FEET OUT--	SWEET--SAFE--HOUSES--	457	5
JUST LOCKING UP--TO DIE.	SHE DEALT HER PRETTY	479	12
LOCKS			
I SHALL VOTE FOR LANDS WITH LOCKS	WHAT WE SEE WE KNOW	1195	5
THE PEA THAT DUTY LOCKS--	FORBIDDEN FRUIT A FLAVOR	1377	4
THE ROBIN LOCKS HER NEST, AND TRIES HER WINGS.	QUITE EMPTY, QUITE AT	1606	2
LODGE			
THE PORTER OF MY FATHER'S LODGE	AFRAID! OF WHOM AM I	608	3
AND YOU WILL [SHALL] LODGE A GIANT	I THOUGHT THAT NATURE	1286	11
LODGED			
THEY MIGHT AS WISE HAVE LODGED A BIRD	THEY SHUT ME UP IN PROSE	613	7
LODGED BY DESIGN OR HAPPENING	THIS IS A BLOSSOM OF THE	945	3
THAT [WHO] LODGED A NIGHT IN MEMORY--	NO PASSENGER WAS KNOWN	1406	2
LODGING			
NO LODGING CAN BE HAD	TOO FEW THE MORNINGS BE,	1186	3
LODGINGS			
OBTAINED [ENGROSSED] MY LODGINGS, ERE MYSELF--	BEREAVED OF ALL, I WENT	784	5
SHY AS THE WIND OF HIS CHAMBERS [LODGINGS]	THIS IS A BLOSSOM OF THE	945	5
LOFTY			
STEP LOFTY, FOR THIS NAME BE TOLD	STEP LIGHTLY ON THIS	1183	5
GO TIMID, LEST [SHOULD] HIS FINAL [TESTING / BLAZING / LOFTY] EYE	GO SLOW, MY SOUL, TO	1297	5
TO IT'S LOFTY PLACE	LIGHTLY STEPPED A YELLOW	1672	2
LOG			
HE RISES ON A LOG	HIS MANSION IN THE POOL	1379	3
UPON A SCARLET LOG--	THE SUN RETIRED TO A	1693	4
LOGARITHM			
NOR LOGARITHM SHOW	KNOWS HOW TO FORGET!	433	V
LOGARITHM--HAD I--FOR DRINK--	LET US PLAY YESTERDAY--	728	7
LOGIC			
UNTENABLE [IMPASSABLE / IMPERVIOUS] TO LOGIC	THE THINGS WE THOUGHT	1293	11
LOGICIAN			
BUT HE, THE BEST LOGICIAN,	WITHIN MY GARDEN, RIDES	500	17
LOINS			
AND GIRT HIS LOINS ANEW	A LITTLE EAST OF JORDAN,	59	V 10
LONE			
THOU ART A HUMAN SOLO, A BEING COLD, AND LONE,	AWAKE YE MUSES NINE,	1	27
EXCEPT FOR ANGELS--LONE.	EXCEPT TO HEAVEN, SHE IS	154	2
WHEN THE LONE BRITISH LADY	WHEN THE ASTRONOMER	851	3
AT THE LONE ORTHOGRAPHY	AFTER A HUNDRED YEARS	1147	7
PRESUMING ON THAT LONE RESULT	THE STARS ARE OLD, THAT	1249	5
A WIND THAT WOKE A LONE DELIGHT	A WIND THAT ROSE	1259	6
LONELIER			
IT MIGHT BE LONELIER	IT MIGHT BE LONELIER	405	1
I TRIED TO THINK A LONELIER THING	I TRIED TO THINK A	532	1
LONELINESS			
WITHOUT THE LONELINESS--	IT MIGHT BE LONELIER	405	2
THEN LONELINESS--LOOKS SO--	DID YOU EVER STAND IN A	590	8
THE LONELINESS ONE DARE NOT SOUND--	THE LONELINESS ONE DARE	777	1
THE LONELINESS WHOSE WORST ALARM	THE LONELINESS ONE DARE	777	5
I FEAR ME THIS--IS LONELINESS--	THE LONELINESS ONE DARE	777	13
ALMOST A LONELINESS.	I HIDE MYSELF WITHIN MY	903	4
ENLARGING LONELINESS.	FURTHER IN SUMMER THAN	1068	8
THERE IS ANOTHER LONELINESS	THERE IS ANOTHER	1116	1
REPAIRED OF ALL BUT LONELINESS	THE SNOW THAT NEVER	1133	11
INDEMNITY FOR LONELINESS	OF SO DIVINE A LOSS	1179	3
WOULD BURST THE LONELINESS--	COULD THAT SWEET	1493	4
LONELY			
UPON THE LONELY ROAD.	THROUGH LANE IT LAY--	9	4
I KNOW SOME LONELY HOUSES OFF THE ROAD	I KNOW SOME LONELY	289	1

	FIRST LINE	POEM	LINE
LONELY (CONTINUED)			
FORCES THE BROODS IN LONELY VALLEYS	AS THE STARVED MAELSTROM	872	3
ONLY LEST SHE BE LONELY	WHATEVER IT IS--SHE HAS	1204	9
HE DARE IN LONELY [LONESOME / SECRET] PLACE	I NEVER HEAR THAT ONE IS	1323	14
LONESOME			
MAYBE--"EDEN" A'NT SO LONESOME	WHAT IS--"PARADISE"--	215	17
THE LONESOME FOR THEY KNOW NOT WHAT--	THE LONESOME FOR THEY	262	1
AND EDEN'LL BE SO LONESOME	I NEVER FELT AT HOME--	413	7
DONT FEEL A LONESOME WAY--	I'M SORRY FOR THE DEAD--	529	18
IN LONESOME PLACE--	ONE NEED NOT BE A	670	12
IT IS A LONESOME GLEE--	IT IS A LONESOME GLEE--	774	1
I'M ANSWERED IN A LONESOME TONE--	OF TOLLING BELL I ASK	947	3
HE DARE IN LONELY [LONESOME / SECRET] PLACE	I NEVER HEAR THAT ONE IS	1323	14
THAT LONESOME GLORY	GATHERED INTO THE EARTH,	1370	4
HOW LONESOME THE WIND MUST FEEL NIGHTS--	HOW LONESOME THE WIND	1418	1
A CHILLY [LONESOME / WARNING] PEACE INFESTS THE GRASS	A CHILLY PEACE INFESTS	1443	1
WHO DROVE A LONESOME COW	A FADED BOY--IN SALLOW	1524	2
BOYS THAT "BELIEVE" ARE VERY LONESOME [BASTINADOED]--	THE BIBLE IS AN ANTIQUE	1545	11
LONG			
HAST NEVER SILENT HOURS, AND MINUTES ALL TOO LONG,	AWAKE YE MUSES NINE,	1	29
LONG YEARS OF PRACTISE BORE	THE FEET OF PEOPLE	7	6
AND ALL DAY LONG, WITH DANCE AND GAME,	THERE IS A MORN BY MEN	24	4
DID WRESTLE LONG AND HARD--	A LITTLE EAST OF JORDAN,	59	4
DIM--LONG EXPECTANT EYES,	MY NOSEGAYS ARE FOR	95	2
TO LIPS LONG PARCHING	I BRING AN UNACCUSTOMED	132	2
THIS HEART THAT BROKE SO LONG--	THIS HEART THAT BROKE SO	145	1
AND--WAKING--LONG BEFORE THE MORN--	MUSICIANS WRESTLE	157	4
UNWEARIED, ALL THE SUMMER LONG,	IF I COULD BRIBE THEM BY	179	10
ON THIS LONG STORM THE RAINBOW ROSE--	ON THIS LONG STORM THE	194	1
LONG AGO AS CHRIST AND PETER--	HE FORGOT--AND I--	203	3
THERE'S THAT LONG [THEN THERE'S THAT] TOWN OF WHITE--TO CROSS--	IT CANT BE "SUMMER"!	221	4
BY MY LONG BRIGHT--AND LONGER--TRUST--	I THINK JUST HOW MY	237	15
HOW LONG AT THAT CELESTIAL WICK	GOOD NIGHT! WHICH PUT	259	4
WHEN I, AM LONG AGO,	OF BRONZE--AND BLAZE--	290	17
AND THE SERMON IS NEVER LONG,	SOME KEEP THE SABBATH	324	10
WITH ONE LONG "NAY"--	I HAD THE GLORY--THAT	349	4
A LONG--LONG YELLOW--ON THE LAWN--	A MURMUR IN THE TREES--	416	5
A LONG--LONG YELLOW--ON THE LAWN--	A MURMUR IN THE TREES--	416	5
SOUNDS LONG--UNTIL I READ THE PLACE	NOT IN THIS WORLD TO SEE	418	2
LONG, AT IT'S GREEK--	KNOWS HOW TO FORGET!	433	5
WHEN TRUTH--AFFRONTED LONG--	TRIUMPH--MAY BE OF	455	6
SPARE THE TENANT--LONG ENO'--	IT'S THOUGHTS--AND JUST	495	8
BUT--ISHMAEL--SINCE WE MET--'TIS LONG--	YOU KNOW THAT PORTRAIT	504	7
SALUTE HER--WITH LONG FINGERS--	THE SOUL HAS BANDAGED	512	5
LONG DUNGEONED FROM HIS ROSE--	THE SOUL HAS BANDAGED	512	16
THE LONG RESTRICTED [SUBJECTED] GRAVE	NO CROWD THAT HAS	515	6
MINE--LONG AS [WHILE] AGES STEAL!	MINE--BY THE RIGHT OF	528	9
I WONDER IF THEY BORE IT LONG--	I MEASURE EVERY GRIEF I	561	5
I NOTE THAT SOME--GONE PATIENT LONG--	I MEASURE EVERY GRIEF I	561	13
SO LONG I FAINTED, TO MYSELF	I CRIED AT PITY--NOT AT	588	5
LONG BUTTONED IN THE MOLD	OF NEARNESS TO HER	607	10
'TWAS A LONG PARTING--BUT THE TIME	'TWAS A LONG PARTING--	625	1
THE VISION--PONDERED LONG--	I THINK TO LIVE--MAY BE	646	21
A LONG--LONG [VAST--VAST / BRAVE--BRAVE] SLEEP--A FAMOUS--SLEEP--	A LONG--LONG SLEEP--A	654	1
A LONG--LONG [VAST--VAST / BRAVE--BRAVE] SLEEP--A FAMOUS--SLEEP--	A LONG--LONG SLEEP--A	654	1
AND ROW IN NOWHERE ALL DAY LONG	COULD I BUT RIDE	661	15
CONFRONTING EYES LONG--COMFORTED--	I'LL SEND THE FEATHER	687	5
JUST LONG ENOUGH TO TASTE--	LET US PLAY YESTERDAY--	728	31
LOOKS LONG--AND LAST--AND GOLDEN--	THE MOUNTAINS--GROW	757	7
JUST LONG ENOUGH FOR HOPE TO TEAZE [STIR]--	THE WHOLE OF IT CAME NOT	762	7
PRESENTIMENT--IS THAT LONG SHADOW--ON THE LAWN--	PRESENTIMENT--IS THAT	764	1
TO WAIT AN HOUR--IS LONG--	TO WAIT AN HOUR--IS LONG	781	1
SHE TURNS AS LONG AWAY	NATURE--THE GENTLEST	790	18
OR IN THE LONG--UNEVEN TERM	I PLAY AT RICHES--TO	801	19
AND WILL ENDURE AS LONG AS HE	TRUTH--IS AS OLD AS GOD	836	3
BUT LONG RECORDS THE LADY'S NAME	THE ROBIN FOR THE CRUMB	864	3
IN HIS LONG ABSENCE WORN	EACH SCAR I'LL KEEP FOR	877	3
LONG STEPS ACROSS THE FEATURES TOOK	TWO TRAVELLERS PERISHING	933	9
WERE IT GIANT LONG,	UNDER THE LIGHT, YET	949	6
WERE THE DAY YEAR LONG,	UNDER THE LIGHT, YET	949	8
HOW LONG A DAY I COULD ENDURE	WERT THOU BUT ILL--THAT	961	2
FOR THE LONG HINDRANCE--GRACE--TO ME--	FITTER TO SEE HIM, I MAY	968	2
ARE LONG.	EXCEPT THE SMALLER SIZE	1067	8
THE SPRY [LONG] ARMS OF THE WIND	THE SPRY ARMS OF THE	1103	1
MY PROCESS IS NOT LONG	THE SPRY ARMS OF THE	1103	6
IN THY LONG PARADISE OF LIGHT	IN THY LONG PARADISE OF	1145	1
WHEN I SHALL LONG FOR EARTHLY PLAY	IN THY LONG PARADISE OF	1145	3
IN THY LONG RACE WITH HIM!	MY GOD--HE SEES THEE--	1178	9
NOT ANYTHING IS STALE SO LONG	THE RIDDLE WE CAN GUESS	1222	3
POSSESSION JUST AS LONG--	DOMINION LASTS UNTIL	1257	2
BECAUSE THAT FEARING IT SO LONG	WHILE WE WERE FEARING IT	1277	3
THAT HAS [WAS] NOT STARVED SO LONG	ART THOU THE THING I	1282	4
THOU DID'ST [COULD'ST] NOT GOAD SO LONG--	ART THOU THE THING I	1282 V	4

	FIRST LINE	POEM	LINE
LONG (CONTINUED)			
THE LONG SIGH OF THE FROG	THE LONG SIGH OF THE	1359	1
LONG YEARS APART--CAN MAKE NO	LONG YEARS APART--CAN	1383	1
AS LONG AS HE CAN BLUSH	HIS CHEEK IS HIS	1460	2
AS TWILIGHT LONG BEGUN,	AS IMPERCEPTIBLY AS	1540	6
SO LONG--SO SHORT--	IMAGE OF LIGHT, ADIEU--	1556	3
BESTOWED A SUMMER LONG	TO HER DERIDED HOME	1586	5
THAT FASTENED IT SO LONG	AS FROM THE EARTH THE	1630	6
WHEN THE LONG INTERCEDING LIPS	THERE COMES AN HOUR WHEN	1751	2
LONG-CHEATED			
JUST HOW LONG-CHEATED EYES WILL TURN--	THO' I GET HOME HOW LATE	207	10
LONGED			
I MEANT TO TELL HER HOW I LONGED	I MEANT TO FIND HER WHEN	718	5
ON THE LONGED FOR [SOLDERED] DEAD	LAIN IN NATURE--SO	1288	8
LONGER			
BY MY LONG BRIGHT--AND LONGER--TRUST--	I THINK JUST HOW MY	237	15
BUT LONGER THAN THE LITTLE RILL--	FORGET! THE LADY WITH	438	12
LOVE [FAITH] IS LIKE LIFE--MERELY [ONLY THE] LONGER	WHILE IT IS ALIVE	491	7
THOUGH I THAN HE--MAY LONGER LIVE	MY LIFE HAD STOOD--A	754	21
HE LONGER MUST--THAN I--	MY LIFE HAD STOOD--A	754	22
THE DEER ATTRACTS NO FURTHER [INVITES NO LONGER--]	THIS MERIT HATH THE	979	7
I SHOULD HAVE KEPT IT LONGER.	HAD I KNOWN THAT THE	1720	2
LONGEST			
THE LONGEST--FOR THE FRIEND--	DEATH IS POTENTIAL TO	548	6
I THINK THE LONGEST HOUR OF ALL	I THINK THE LONGEST HOUR	635	1
LONGEST [LATEST] ON YOUR SOUTH, TO LINGER,	PROMISE THIS--WHEN YOU	648	19
THOSE WHO HAVE BEEN IN THE GRAVE THE LONGEST--	THOSE WHO HAVE BEEN IN	922	1
OUR SALARY THE LONGEST DAY	THE NOTICE THAT IS	1310	7
THE LONGEST DAY THAT GOD APPOINTS	THE LONGEST DAY THAT GOD	1769	1
LONGING			
HER JAWS STIR--TWITCHING [MOUTH STIRS--LONGING]--HUNGRY--	SHE SIGHTS A BIRD--SHE	507	5
LONGING IS LIKE THE SEED	LONGING IS LIKE THE SEED	1255	1
THAN THE SUFFICING LONGING	DELIGHT'S DESPAIR AT	1299	3
SOME HAVE SOLACED THE LONGING	NOT ANY MORE TO BE	1344	11
OBEYED--A LURE--A LONGING?	"GO TELL IT"--WHAT A	1554	5
OR LONGING--AND IS THAT FOR US	THE LOOK OF THEE, WHAT	1689	7
IS EDIBLE TO LONGING,	THE JOY THAT HAS NO STEM	1744	3
CONVENIENT TO THE LONGING	THROUGH THOSE OLD	1753	15
LONGINGLY			
AND SHE WILL POINT UNDOUBTEDLY [YOU FONDLY-- / YOU LONGINGLY]	CRISIS IS SWEET AND YET	1416 V	7
LONGITUDE			
TO FILL THE AWFUL VACUUM [LONGITUDE]	SEVERER SERVICE OF	786	3
LOOK			
AND I'D LIKE TO LOOK A LITTLE MORE	GOING TO HEAVEN!	79	22
AND WE LOOK FARTHER ON!	OUR LIVES ARE SWISS--	80	5
WE MIGHT LOOK FOR HIM!	WENT UP A YEAR THIS	93	12
IMMORTAL ALPS LOOK DOWN--	IN LANDS I NEVER SAW--	124	2
TO TAKE A BACKWARD [FINAL / PARTING] LOOK.	THESE ARE THE DAYS WHEN	130	3
AND COME NEXT HOUR TO LOOK.	I BRING AN UNACCUSTOMED	132	7
WHY, LOOK OUT FOR THE LITTLE BROOK IN MARCH,	HAVE YOU GOT A BROOK IN	136	9
AN ALTERED LOOK ABOUT THE HILLS--	AN ALTERED LOOK ABOUT	140	1
A FURTIVE LOOK YOU KNOW AS WELL--	AN ALTERED LOOK ABOUT	140	14
BUILDING WHERE SCHOOLBOY DARE NOT LOOK,	SOME, TOO FRAGILE FOR	141	7
OH SEA--LOOK GRACIOUSLY--	MY RIVER RUNS TO THEE--	162	4
LOOK FURTHER ON!	A BURDOCK--CLAWED MY	229	13
I LIKE A LOOK OF AGONY,	I LIKE A LOOK OF AGONY,	241	1
AND LIKE THE TREES, LOOK DOWN--	WHEN WE STAND ON THE	242	2
ON THE LOOK OF DEATH--	THERE'S A CERTAIN SLANT	258	16
I PONDERED HOW THE BLISS WOULD LOOK--	A SOLEMN THING--IT WAS--	271	9
AND GOD FORBID I LOOK BEHIND--	THE ONLY GHOST I EVER	274	15
JUST A LOOK AT THE HORSES--	TIE THE STRINGS TO MY	279	3
A ROBBER'D LIKE THE LOOK OF--	I KNOW SOME LONELY	289	2
HOW ORDERLY THE KITCHEN'D LOOK, BY NIGHT,	I KNOW SOME LONELY	289	13
LOOK--FEED UPON EACH OTHER'S FACES--SO--	ONE YEAR AGO--JOTS WHAT?	296	9
TO THOSE WHO LOOK ON YOU--	YOUR RICHES--TAUGHT ME--	299	18
STRAIGHTEN--LOOK CAUTIOUS FOR THEIR BREATH--	GIVE LITTLE ANGUISH--	310	5
SO FACES ON TWO DECKS, LOOK BACK,	THERE CAME A DAY AT	322	19
FOR MINE--TO LOOK AT WHEN I LIKED--	BEFORE I GOT MY EYE PUT	327	16
LOOK TOO EXPENSIVE!	I KNOW THAT HE EXISTS.	338	14
WAIT! LOOK! HER LITTLE BOOK--	'TWAS THE OLD--ROAD--	344	12
COULD STRETCH--TO LOOK AT ME--	I DREADED THAT FIRST	348	16
LOOK, HOW I CLUTCH IT	I GAINED IT SO--	359	10
TO LOOK UPON HER LIKE--ALIVE--	I WENT TO THANK HER--	363	9
I KNOW IT, BY THE NUMB LOOK	THERE'S BEEN A DEATH, IN	389	3
THEN--LOOK FOR ME. BE SURE YOU SAY--	A TONGUE--TO TELL HIM I	400	28
I CAN LOOK--CANT I--	GOOD MORNING--MIDNIGHT--	425	9
I THOUGHT HOW YELLOW IT WOULD LOOK--	'TWAS JUST THIS TIME,	445	5
GRAVE SAINTS STOLE OUT TO LOOK AT ME--	I MEANT TO HAVE BUT	476	15
TO GIVE YOUR CORE--A LOOK--	A SOLEMN THING WITHIN	483	12
SHE RUNS WITHOUT THE LOOK OF FEET--	SHE SIGHTS A BIRD--SHE	507	3
AND STOP TO LOOK AT HER--	THE SOUL HAS BANDAGED	512	4
CAME OUT TO LOOK AT ME--	I STARTED EARLY--TOOK MY	520	4
AND BOWING--WITH A MIGHTY LOOK--	I STARTED EARLY--TOOK MY	520	23
THAT I MIGHT LOOK ON THEE?	MY PERIOD HAD COME FOR	564	16
THE OTHERS LOOK A NEEDLESS SHOW--	I RECKON--WHEN I COUNT	569	7
A MIGHTY LOOK RUNS ROUND THE WORLD	"HEAVEN" HAS DIFFERENT	575	5

	FIRST LINE	POEM	LINE
LOOK (CONTINUED)			
ALL WADED--WE LOOK BACK FOR PLAY,	IF I MAY HAVE IT, WHEN	577	24
FOR COVETING [EAGERNESS] TO LOOK AT THEE--	IF I MAY HAVE IT, WHEN	577	27
TO LOOK AT, LIKE A TOY--	I CRIED AT PITY--NOT AT	588	8
AND LOOK--AND SHUDDER, AND BLOCK YOUR BREATH--	DID YOU EVER STAND IN A	590	3
DID YOU EVER LOOK IN A CANNON'S FACE--	DID YOU EVER STAND IN A	590	9
TO LOOK AT HER--HOW SLOWLY	WHEN I WAS SMALL, A	596	5
LOOK DOWN UPON [ABOLISH HIS] CAPTIVITY--	THEY SHUT ME UP IN PROSE	613	11
THE EAGER LOOK--ON LANDSCAPES--	THE TINT I CANNOT TAKE--	627	13
LOOK--IF SHE SHOULD KNOW	SO MUCH SUMMER	651	8
WE COME TO LOOK WITH GRATITUDE [FONDNESS / PLEASURE]	A PRISON GETS TO BE A	652	5
NOR ONCE LOOK UP--FOR NOON?	A LONG--LONG SLEEP--A	654	8
I LOOK ON ALL THIS WORLD CONTAINS--	AGAIN--HIS VOICE IS AT	663	11
'TWOULD LOOK TOO FAR--TO DIE--	I SOMETIMES DROP IT, FOR	708	8
PARDON--TO LOOK UPON THY FACE--	JOY TO HAVE MERITED THE	788	5
TO LOOK AT THEE A SINGLE TIME	THE LUXURY TO APPREHEND	815	3
BUT JUST TO LOOK IT IN THE EYE--	I CANNOT BUY IT--'TIS	840	10
MAY LIFT A LOOK ON THINE, A MAID	BECAUSE THE BEE MAY	869	5
PATIENCE--LOOK WITHIN--	PATIENCE--HAS A QUIET	926	2
THROUGH AN [NATURE'S] EXPIRING--PERFECT--LOOK--	FAIRER THROUGH FADING--	938	8
AND THAT HE DID'NT LOOK AFRAID?	TRUDGING TO EDEN,	1020	6
HE MIGHT NOT LOOK AGAIN?	WHEN THEY COME BACK--IF	1080	12
MUCH IS THE MIEN [GOOD IS THE LOOK] OF HIM IN MARCH	A PROMPT--EXECUTIVE BIRD	1177	7
LOOK TO IT BY IT'S FATHOMS [CONTENTS]	REMEMBRANCE HAS A	1182	7
TO LOOK HER IN THE FACE	THE PAST IS SUCH A	1203	2
WE COULD NOT LOOK UPON THE EARTH [WORLD]--	HAD WE OUR SENSES	1284	7
BUT TRIFLES LOOK SO TRIVIAL	DEAR MARCH--COME IN--	1320	23
FOR A REPRIEVING LOOK--	ELIZABETH TOLD ESSEX	1321	8
DOES NOT LOOK AS WELL--	FLOSS WONT SAVE YOU FROM	1322 V	4
DELIBERATELY [LOOK SQUARELY IN THE] FACE--	I NEVER HEAR THAT ONE IS	1323	16
CAN STAND SO CLOSE AND LOOK SO BOLD	WHAT MYSTERY PERVADES A	1400	11
LOOK BEHIND--HE IS PURSUING THEE.	TO EARN IT BY DISDAINING	1427	4
LOOK BACK ON TIME, WITH KINDLY EYES--	LOOK BACK ON TIME, WITH	1478	1
UNTIL THEY LOOK AROUND	FACTS BY OUR SIDE ARE	1497	2
HOW FIRM ETERNITY MUST LOOK	HOW FIRM ETERNITY MUST	1499	1
WITH A PRUDENTIAL LOOK BEHIND	THE LIFE THAT TIED TOO	1535	3
THAT DYING I MAY EARN THE LOOK [GAZE]	TRIED ALWAYS AND	1559	3
AND GETS THE LOOK AT THEE--	I DID NOT REACH THEE	1664	34
SUMMER BEGINS TO HAVE THE LOOK	SUMMER BEGINS TO HAVE	1682	1
THE LOOK OF THEE, WHAT IS IT LIKE	THE LOOK OF THEE, WHAT	1689	1
TO LOOK UPON--	WHEN WE HAVE CEASED TO	1706	7
TO LOOK WOULD BE TO DROP--	A PIT--BUT HEAVEN OVER	1712	6
I SHALL NOT LOOK AGAIN.	CONSULTING SUMMER'S	1715	4
NOT DARING LOOK BEHIND:	THE WATERS CHASED HIM AS	1749	2
LOOKED			
THE OWL LOOKED PUZZLED DOWN--	THROUGH LANE IT LAY--	9	6
JESUS MERELY "LOOKED" AT PETER--	HE FORGOT--AND I--	203	7
BUT, HAD YOU LOOKED IN--	ONE YEAR AGO--JOTS WHAT?	296	22
THEY LOOKED LIKE FRIGHTENED BEADS, I THOUGHT--	A BIRD CAME DOWN THE	328	11
THINKING--PERHAPS--THAT I LOOKED TIRED--OR ALONE--	HOW SICK--TO WAIT--IN	368	3
WE TWO--LOOKED SO ALIKE--	'TWAS LOVE--NOT ME--	394	10
LIKE EYES THAT LOOKED ON WASTES--	LIKE EYES THAT LOOKED ON	458	1
SO LOOKED THE FACE I LOOKED UPON--	LIKE EYES THAT LOOKED ON	458	7
SO LOOKED THE FACE I LOOKED UPON--	LIKE EYES THAT LOOKED ON	458	7
SO LOOKED ITSELF--ON ME--	LIKE EYES THAT LOOKED ON	458	8
HOW PLEASED THEY WERE [LOOKED], AT WHAT YOU SAID--	IF ANYBODY'S FRIEND BE	509	13
I LOOKED AT SUNRISE--ONCE--	I HAD NO CAUSE TO BE	542	9
AND THEN I LOOKED AT THEM--	I HAD NO CAUSE TO BE	542	10
IF I BELIEVED [SUPPOSED] GOD LOOKED AROUND,	I PRAYED, AT FIRST, A	576	5
I LOOKED IN WINDOWS, FOR THE WEALTH [THINGS]	I HAD BEEN HUNGRY, ALL	579	7
AS EVEN WHILE I LOOKED--DISSOLVED--	THEY CALLED ME TO THE	628	7
AND WHEN I LOOKED AGAIN--	THEY CALLED ME TO THE	628	14
PERPLEXED! ESTATES OF VIOLET TROUBLE NE'ER LOOKED ON!	WOULD YOU LIKE SUMMER?	691	5
BECAUSE THEY LOOKED ON THEE BEFORE--	JOY TO HAVE MERITED THE	788	9
AND THOU HAST LOOKED ON THEM--	JOY TO HAVE MERITED THE	788	10
THOUGH ALL THE VILLAGE LOOKED--	NO NOTICE GAVE SHE, BUT	804	10
THEY'LL RECOLLECT HOW COLD I LOOKED	THEY WONT FROWN ALWAYS--	874	3
THE SUN WENT DOWN--NO MAN LOOKED ON--	THE SUN WENT DOWN--NO	1079	1
THE SUN WENT UP--NO MAN LOOKED ON--	THE SUN WENT DOWN--NO	1079	5
THE DAISY THAT HAS LOOKED BEHIND	THE CLOVER'S SIMPLE FAME	1232	7
I HOPED [LOOKED] FOR YOU BEFORE--	DEAR MARCH--COME IN--	1320	3
WHEN HEAVEN LOOKED UPON US ALL	NO BRIGADIER THROUGHOUT	1561	11
THOSE LOOKED THAT LIVED--[THE LIVING LOOKED] THAT DAY--	THERE CAME A WIND LIKE A	1593	12
THOSE LOOKED THAT LIVED--[THE LIVING LOOKED] THAT DAY--	THERE CAME A WIND LIKE A	1593	12
HOW PALTRY LOOKED MY CARES	CONFERRING WITH MYSELF	1655	5
LOOKETH			
THE WAVE WITH EYE SO PENSIVE, LOOKETH TO SEE THE MOON,	AWAKE YE MUSES NINE,	1	18
LOOKING			
LOOKING FOR HER FACE.	GLOWING IS HER BONNET,	72	10
SO LOOKING ON--THE NIGHT--THE MORN	A SOMETHING IN A	122	19
LOOKING AT DEATH, IS DYING--	'TIS SO APPALLING--IT	281	15

	FIRST LINE	POEM	LINE
LOOKING (CONTINUED)			
THE LOOKING IN HIS EYES--	I HAD NOT MINDED--WALLS	398	8
JUST LOOKING ROUND TO SEE HOW FAR	WE DO NOT PLAY ON GRAVES	467	11
CREATION--LOOKING ON--	DEPARTED--TO THE	524	4
BUT, LOOKING BACK--THE FIRST SO SEEMS	I RECKON--WHEN I COUNT	569	5
BUT ONLY KNEW BY LOOKING BACK--	IT CEASED TO HURT ME,	584	3
TOO STEEP FOR LOOKING UP--	A PRISON GETS TO BE A	652	28
'TIS GOOD [WELL]--THE LOOKING BACK ON GRIEF--	'TIS GOOD--THE LOOKING	660	1
LOOKING ON--IS THE DEPARTMENT	GROWTH OF MAN--LIKE	750	13
WHO SOMETHING LOST [DROPT], THE SEEKING [LOOKING] FOR	DEATH LEAVES US HOMESICK	935	7
THAT I AM LOOKING OPPOSITELY	A LOSS OF SOMETHING EVER	959	15
LOOKING BACK IS BEST THAT IS LEFT	THIS WAS IN THE WHITE OF	995	5
TRUDGING TO EDEN, LOOKING BACKWARD,	TRUDGING TO EDEN,	1020	1
LIKE LOOKING EVERY TIME YOU PLEASE	WHAT MYSTERY PERVADES A	1400	7
HOW FAIR ON LOOKING BACK THE DAY	EDEN IS THAT	1657	5
AND THE WORLD--IF THE WORLD BE LOOKING ON--	IF EVER THE LID GETS OFF	1727	5
LOOKS			
WHO LOOKS FOR HIM AT MORNING	THE GUEST IS GOLD AND	15	7
SHE LOOKS DOWN JUST AS OFTEN	MAMA NEVER FORGETS HER	164	3
HOW ODD THE GIRL'S LIFE LOOKS	I'M "WIFE"--I'VE	199	5
THAT SUDDENLY LOOKS INTO OUR'S	THAT AFTER HORROR--THAT	286	13
A TROUBLE LOOKS BITTEREST--	IT DONT SOUND SO	426	6
THEN LONELINESS--LOOKS SO--	DID YOU EVER STAND IN A	590	8
WHEN DIMNESS--LOOKS THE ODDITY--	OF NEARNESS TO HER	607	3
IT LOOKS TOO TAWDRY GRACE	YOU'LL FIND--IT WHEN YOU	610	14
LOOKS LONG--AND LAST--AND GOLDEN--	THE MOUNTAINS--GROW	757	7
THAT LOOKS A HARDER SKILL TO US--	ONLY A SHRINE, BUT MINE	918	9
AND LANDS HE LOOKS UPON	A COFFIN--IS A SMALL	943	8
IT LOOKS SO SMALL	SO LARGE MY WILL	1024	13
YET KNOW I HOW THE HEATHER LOOKS	I NEVER SAW A MOOR--	1052	3
AND NATURE LOOKS AROUND--	THE SYMPTOM OF THE GALE	1327	14
THE [IT'S] SPIRIT LOOKS UPON [TURNS UPON / GAZES AT / GLANCES ...	AS FROM THE EARTH THE	1630	5
LOOM			
SOME HAVE RESIGNED THE LOOM--	MY WHEEL IS IN THE DARK!	10	9
THE MAPLE'S LOOM IS RED--	THE GENTIAN WEAVES HER	18	2
LOOP			
SO I LOOP MY APRON, AGAINST THE MAJESTY	I'M SAYING EVERY DAY	373	12
LOOP UP A COUNTESS--WITH YOU--	I'LL CLUTCH--AND CLUTCH	427	10
DROPPED THE LOOP	HE SCANNED IT--STAGGERED	1062	2
LOOSE			
DID THE HAREBELL LOOSE HER GIRDLE	DID THE HAREBELL LOOSE	213	1
LOOSE THE FLOOD--YOU SHALL FIND IT PATENT--	SPLIT THE LARK--AND	861	5
AND THE SUN WILL FREE IT [LOOSE HIM]	FOLLOW WISE ORION	1538	V
LOOSED			
LOOSED THE MOON HER SILVER HAT	LIGHTLY STEPPED A YELLOW	1672	3
LOOSENED			
IT LOOSENED ACRES, LIFTED SEAS	LIKE RAIN IT SOUNDED	1235	13
A [THE] LOOSENED SPIRIT BRINGS--	HE ATE AND DRANK THE	1587	8
LORD			
"OH LORD--HOW FRAIL ARE WE"!	"ARCTURUS" IS HIS OTHER	70	8
GRANT ME, OH LORD, A SUNNY MIND--	BESIDES THE AUTUMN POETS	131	15
A LORD, MIGHT DARE TO LIFT THE HAT	WAIT TILL THE MAJESTY OF	171	13
SINCE THAT MY LORD, "THE LORD OF LORDS"	WAIT TILL THE MAJESTY OF	171	15
SINCE THAT MY LORD, "THE LORD OF LORDS"	WAIT TILL THE MAJESTY OF	171	15
TAKE US SIMULTANEOUS--LORD--	WE DONT CRY--TIM AND I,	196	27
TIE THE STRINGS TO MY LIFE, MY LORD,	TIE THE STRINGS TO MY	279	1
FAITH--THE EXPERIMENT OF OUR LORD--	"MORNING"--MEANS	300	10
THE WARDROBE--OF OUR LORD--	THERE CAME A DAY AT	322	12
HER LORD--AWAY!	I TEND MY FLOWERS FOR	339	22
THE STATEMENT OF THE LORD	DO PEOPLE MOULDER	432	14
OR OPPORTUNITY--HER LORD AWAY?	FORGET! THE LADY WITH	438	8
YOU LOVE THE LORD--YOU CANNOT SEE--	YOU LOVE THE LORD--YOU	487	1
FORGET IT--LORD [CHRIST]--OF THEM--	'TIS TRUE--THEY SHUT ME	538	4
OUR LORD--INDEED--MADE [BORE] COMPOUND WITNESS--	ONE CRUCIFIXION IS	553	13
OUR LORD--THOUGHT NO	MUST BE A WO--	571	13
OUR LORD--"SO LOVED"--IT SAITH--	THE TEST OF LOVE--IS	573	2
BUT WHAT OUR LORD INFERS [INFERRED] WE WOULD	NOT WHAT WE DID, SHALL	823	3
THE LORD ALONE IS BURNED--	THE SUN AND MOON MUST	871	4
THE LORD A CANDLE ENTERTAINS	THE SUN AND MOON MUST	871	12
THE FLOWER OF OUR LORD.	THIS IS A BLOSSOM OF THE	945	16
BY SPIDER, OR FORBID IT LORD	ALONE AND IN A	1167	27
WHATEVER REALM I FORFEIT, LORD,	TO OWN A SUSAN OF MY OWN	1401	3
I PRAY THE LORD THY DUST TO KEEP--	NOW I LAY THEE DOWN TO	1539	2
I PRAY THE LORD THY SOUL TO MAKE--	NOW I LAY THEE DOWN TO	1539	4
LORD'S			
AT THE LORD'S RIGHT HAND.	OVER AND OVER, LIKE A	367	8
LORDS			
SINCE THAT MY LORD, "THE LORD OF LORDS"	WAIT TILL THE MAJESTY OF	171	15
LORE			
ALL OTHER LORE--	KNOWS HOW TO FORGET!	433	14
IT'S ONLY LORE--IT'S STEADFASTNESS--	'TWAS AWKWARD, BUT IT	973	3
LOSE			
NO MORE HE SINGETH MOURNFUL, HER SADNESS SHE DOTH LOSE.	AWAKE YE MUSES NINE,	1	20
WE LOSE--BECAUSE WE WIN--	WE LOSE--BECAUSE WE WIN	21	1
TO LOSE--IF ONE CAN FIND AGAIN--	ALL THESE MY BANNERS BE.	22	8
SOME LOSE THEIR WAY!	OUR SHARE OF NIGHT TO	113	6

	FIRST LINE	POEM	LINE
LOSE (CONTINUED)			
TO LOSE ONE'S FAITH--SURPASS	TO LOSE ONE'S FAITH--	377	1
COUNT--HOARD--THEN LOSE--	I'LL CLUTCH--AND CLUTCH	427	12
LET ME NOT SPILL [LOSE / WASTE]--IT'S SMALLEST CADENCE--	BETTER--THAN MUSIC! FOR	503	21
HE FOUGHT LIKE THOSE WHO'VE NOUGHT TO LOSE--	HE FOUGHT LIKE THOSE	759	1
TO LOSE IT IN THE SEA--	BEREAVED OF ALL, I WENT	784	12
LOSE MY WAY LIKE A LITTLE CHILD	HOW HAPPY I WAS IF I	898	7
AND LOSE IT'S NEIGHBOR ONCE--	TOO LITTLE WAY THE HOUSE	911	8
WE DO NOT KNOW THE TIME WE LOSE--	WE DO NOT KNOW THE TIME	1106	1
EACH THAT WE LOSE TAKES PART OF US;	EACH THAT WE LOSE TAKES	1605	1
TO LOSE THEE--SWEETER THAN TO GAIN	TO LOSE THEE--SWEETER	1754	1
LOSES			
BUT ACCLIMATED--PINES NO MORE [GROPES NO MORE / LOSES SIGHT / . . .	THE INUNDATION OF THE	1425	7
MY WISDOM LOSES WAY	THE ONES THAT	1690	6
LOSS			
THE LOSS OF AN ESTATE--	TO LOSE ONE'S FAITH--	377	2
REMOVED FROM ACCIDENT OF LOSS	REMOVED FROM ACCIDENT OF	424	1
AFFLICTS ME WITH A DOUBLE LOSS--	EXCEPT THE HEAVEN HAD	472	7
THE LOSS HAD BEEN TO ME	HAD I PRESUMED TO HOPE--	522	2
THE ANGUISH--AND THE LOSS--	WE SEE--COMPARATIVELY--	534	10
A LOSS OR SO--	MUST BE A WO--	571	2
MY LOSS, BY SICKNESS--WAS IT LOSS?	MY FIRST WELL DAY--SINCE	574	25
MY LOSS, BY SICKNESS--WAS IT LOSS?	MY FIRST WELL DAY--SINCE	574	25
A QUALITY OF LOSS	A LIGHT EXISTS IN SPRING	812	17
THE SECOND, LOSS,	FINDING IS THE FIRST ACT	870	2
BUT HE WHOSE LOSS PROCURES YOU	TILL DEATH--IS NARROW	907	5
A LOSS OF SOMETHING EVER FELT I--	A LOSS OF SOMETHING EVER	959	1
BUT GAIN--THRO' LOSS--THROUGH GRIEF [PAIN]--OBTAIN--	FITTER TO SEE HIM, I MAY	968	26
WHO GUESS AT SEEING, GUESS AT LOSS	WHO SAW NO SUNRISE	1018	3
PRECISE [MORE OFT] THE OBJECT'S LOSS--	PERCEPTION OF AN OBJECT	1071	2
OF SO DIVINE A LOSS	OF SO DIVINE A LOSS	1179	1
WHAT LOSS WOULD VALUE MORE	HAD THIS ONE DAY NOT	1253	6
LOSSES			
HER [HIS] LOSSES MAKE OUR GAINS ASHAMED--	HER LOSSES MAKE OUR	1562	1
LOSSES'			
BEST GAINS--MUST HAVE THE LOSSES' TEST--	BEST GAINS--MUST HAVE	684	1
LOST			
I LOST IT IN THE SAND--	I HAD A GUINEA GOLDEN--	23	2
IF THOSE I LOVED WERE LOST	IF THOSE I LOVED WERE	29	1
I NEVER LOST AS MUCH BUT TWICE,	I NEVER LOST AS MUCH BUT	49	1
WHO NEVER LOST, ARE [IS] UNPREPARED	WHO NEVER LOST, ARE	73	1
CLOSE TO THE TWO I LOST--	GOING TO HEAVEN!	79	15
OUR LITTLE GARDEN THAT WE LOST	WE SHOULD NOT MIND SO	81	3
HAS LOST A BLUSH TODAY?	WHOSE CHEEK IS THIS?	82	3
AS FOR THE LOST WE GRAPPLE	AS BY THE DEAD WE LOVE	88	3
WHERE I HAVE LOST, I SOFTER TREAD--	WHERE I HAVE LOST, I	104	1
WHOM I HAVE LOST, I PIOUS GUARD	WHERE I HAVE LOST, I	104	5
WHEN I HAVE LOST, YOU'LL KNOW BY THIS--	WHERE I HAVE LOST, I	104	9
WHY, I HAVE LOST, THE PEOPLE KNOW	WHERE I HAVE LOST, I	104	13
MY LITTLE CRAFT WAS LOST!	'TWAS SUCH A LITTLE--	107	8
BELLES FROM SOME LOST SUMMER DAY--	PIGMY SERAPHS--GONE	138	3
HUNDREDS HAVE LOST INDEED--	SOUL, WILT THOU TOSS	139	3
AND SOMEBODY HAS LOST THE FACE	EXCEPT TO HEAVEN, SHE IS	154	11
JUST LOST, WHEN I WAS SAVED!	JUST LOST, WHEN I WAS	160	1
I LOST A WORLD--THE OTHER DAY!	I LOST A WORLD--THE	181	1
ALWAYS LOST THE WAY!	WE DONT CRY--TIM AND I,	196	20
ENTERS--AND IS LOST IN BALMS.	COME SLOWLY--EDEN!	211	8
SO IF I GET LOST--THERE--EVER--	WHAT IS--"PARADISE"--	215	13
IF I'M LOST--NOW--	IF I'M LOST--NOW--	256	1
THEN DROPPED [LOST] THE AIR--	ONE YEAR AGO--JOTS WHAT?	296	27
TILL IT IS LOST IN FLEECES--	IT SIFTS FROM LEADEN	311	11
RECORDING BRIEFLY--"LOST"--	I KNOW A PLACE WHERE	337	4
THE PATENT LOST	IS BLISS THEN, SUCH	340	10
THE LOST--DAY'S FACE--	'TIS OPPOSITES--ENTICE--	355	4
BUT NATURE LOST THE DATE OF THIS--	IT STRUCK ME--EVERY DAY	362	11
AND YOU DROPT, LOST,	'TWAS LIKE A MAELSTROM,	414	7
'TIS LOST--AND LOST TO ME--	EXCEPT THE HEAVEN HAD	472	8
'TIS LOST--AND LOST TO ME--	EXCEPT THE HEAVEN HAD	472	8
LOST, IN THE SEPULCHRE--	IF ANYBODY'S FRIEND BE	509	8
THEN LOST [STAKED / CHASED] THEMSELVES AND FOUND . . .	TWO BUTTERFLIES WENT OUT	533	V
. . . [LOST / CAUGHT] THEMSELVES	TWO BUTTERFLIES WENT OUT	533	V
AND WERE YOU LOST, I WOULD BE--	I CANNOT LIVE WITH YOU--	640	37
HAVE MISSED [LOST] A BAREFOOT CITIZEN--	HE TOLD A HOMELY TALE	763	15
ARE FOREVER LOST TO ME	A CLOUD WITHDREW FROM	895	4
SWEET [GOOD], TO HAVE HAD THEM LOST	SWEET, TO HAVE HAD THEM	901	1
WHO SOMETHING LOST [DROPT], THE SEEKING [LOOKING] FOR	DEATH LEAVES US HOMESICK	935	7
WHEN IT IS LOST, THAT DAY SHALL BE	THIS IS A BLOSSOM OF THE	945	13
I--LOST--WAS PASSING BY--	A DOOR JUST OPENED ON A	953	2
I--LOST--WAS PASSING BY--	A DOOR JUST OPENED ON A	953	6
LOST DOUBLY--BUT BY CONTRAST--MOST--	A DOOR JUST OPENED ON A	953	7
THAT NOUGHT BE LOST	THE CHEMICAL CONVICTION	954	2
THE MAN THAT WAS NOT LOST [WRECKED / ROBBED / KILLED]	HOW MANY SCHEMES MAY DIE	1150	5
NOW I KNEW I LOST HER--	NOW I KNEW I LOST HER--	1219	1
BEHOLD HIS LOST AGGRANDIZEMENT [EMOLUMENT]	ONE OF THE ONES THAT	1466	27

	FIRST LINE	POEM	LINE
LOST (CONTINUED)			
WHEN IT HAS LOST IT'S ROOT--	YOU CANNOT MAKE	1508	2
OTHER BOYS ARE "LOST"--	THE BIBLE IS AN ANTIQUE	1545	12
EXPANSE CANNOT BE LOST--	EXPANSE CANNOT BE LOST--	1584	1
THE BIRDS SHE LOST--	QUITE EMPTY, QUITE AT	1606	9
LOT			
A MODEST LOT--A FAME PETITE--	A LITTLE BREAD--A CRUST	159	7
HOME TO THE HUT! WHAT LOT	THE MALAY--TOOK THE	452	9
ON THE BLEAKNESS OF MY LOT	SOIL OF FLINT, IF STEADY	681	V
FOR LOT--EXHIBITED TO	A FIRST MUTE COMING--	702	7
BUT OFTEN AS MY LOT DISPLAYS	I PLAY AT RICHES--TO	801	9
OR CIRCUMSTANCE OF LOT	THERE IS ANOTHER	1116	4
OF HER DESIRELESS LOT	A LITTLE DOG THAT WAGS	1185	12
THE DOOM [LOT] TO BE ADORED	SUMMER--WE ALL HAVE SEEN	1386	V 9
IT'S LOT--WERE IT FORGOT--	THE GENTIAN HAS A	1424	14
LOTH			
THE SOUL RETURNING SOFT AT NIGHT [STILL BY DAWN / LOTH BY DAWN]	CONTAINED IN THIS SHORT	1165	3
LOTUS			
HIS LOTUS IS A CHESTNUT	THE JAY HIS CASTANET HAS	1635	6
LOUD			
'TWAS'NT LOUD, FOR HE SAID NOUGHT--	HE WAS WEAK, AND I WAS	190	7
DID I SING--TOO LOUD?	WHY--DO THEY SHUT ME OUT	248	2
LOUD, AS THE THUNDER'S TONGUE--	MANY A PHRASE HAS THE	276	4
NOT LOUD ENOUGH--FOR WIND--	A MURMUR IN THE TREES--	416	2
LIKE LITTLE SCHOLARS--LOUD--	I THINK THE LONGEST HOUR	635	10
MADE LOUD OBEISANCE AND THE GNAT	THE FINGERS OF THE LIGHT	1000	15
SECURITY IS LOUD--	WHEN ETNA BASKS AND	1146	4
LOUDER			
THE BROOKS LAUGH LOUDER WHEN I COME--	THE BEE IS NOT AFRAID OF	111	5
LOUDEST			
RANG LOUDEST	I CANNOT LIVE WITH YOU--	640	39
THANK GOD THE LOUDEST PLACE HE MADE	IT'S HOUR WITH ITSELF	1225	7
LOVE			
AS BY THE DEAD WE LOVE TO SIT,	AS BY THE DEAD WE LOVE	88	1
BECAUSE, SIR, LOVE IS SWEET!	THE DAISY FOLLOWS SOFT	106	6
BY A NIMBLE LOVE--	BY A FLOWER--BY A LETTER	109	2
REGARDS WITH PATRIOT LOVE--	TO FIGHT ALOUD, IS VERY	126	8
LOVE, BY MEMORIAL MOLD--	WATER, IS TAUGHT BY	135	5
YOU LOVE ME--YOU ARE SURE--	YOU LOVE ME--YOU ARE	156	1
LOVE PROVIDED THEE?	I CAUTIOUS, SCANNED MY	178	20
THAT BUT FOR LOVE OF US--	TO DIE--TAKES JUST A	255	10
SOME STRIDING--GIANT--LOVE--	A SINGLE SCREW OF FLESH	263	16
LOVE THE DULL LAD--BEST--	DID WE DISOBEY HIM?	267	7
WITH BUT A FRACTION OF THE LIFE [LOVE]--	DOUBT ME! MY DIM	275	3
JUSTIFIED--THROUGH [BY] CALVARIES OF LOVE--	THERE CAME A DAY AT	322	28
THE LEAF--AT LOVE--TURNED BACK--	'TWAS THE OLD--ROAD--	344	13
BECAUSE WE LOVE THE WOUND	REHEARSAL TO OURSELVES	379	6
'TWAS LOVE--NOT ME--	'TWAS LOVE--NOT ME--	394	1
SUCH GUILT--TO LOVE THEE--MOST!	'TWAS LOVE--NOT ME--	394	5
TO LOVE THEE YEAR BY YEAR--	TO LOVE THEE YEAR BY	434	1
FOR LOVE OF HER--SWEET--COUNTRYMEN--	THIS IS MY LETTER TO THE	441	7
LOVE--THOU ART HIGH--	LOVE--THOU ART HIGH--	453	1
LOVE--THOU ART DEEP--	LOVE--THOU ART HIGH--	453	7
LOVE--THOU ART VAILED--	LOVE--THOU ART HIGH--	453	13
I LOVE THEE--THEN HOW WELL IS THAT?	SO WELL THAT I CAN LIVE	456	2
AS I--LOVE THEE--	SO WELL THAT I CAN LIVE	456	6
THERE YET REMAINS A LOVE	THE MANNER OF IT'S DEATH	468	6
NOR HAD I TIME TO LOVE--	I HAD NO TIME TO HATE--	478	7
THE LITTLE TOIL OF LOVE--	I HAD NO TIME TO HATE--	478	10
"WHY DO I LOVE" YOU, SIR?	"WHY DO I LOVE" YOU, SIR	480	1
I LOVE THEE--	"WHY DO I LOVE" YOU, SIR	480	20
AND BLAME THE SCANTY LOVE	WE COVER THEE--SWEET	482	9
YOU LOVE THE LORD--YOU CANNOT SEE--	YOU LOVE THE LORD--YOU	487	1
LOVE [FAITH] IS LIKE LIFE--MERELY [ONLY THE] LONGER	WHILE IT IS ALIVE	491	7
LOVE [FAITH] IS LIKE DEATH, DURING THE GRAVE	WHILE IT IS ALIVE	491	8
LOVE [FAITH] IS THE FELLOW OF THE RESURRECTION	WHILE IT IS ALIVE	491	9
SO THAT THE SUM [LOVE] BE NEVER HINDERED	SWEET--YOU FORGOT--BUT I	523	3
OF HEAVENLY LOVE--FORGOT--	I TRIED TO THINK A	532	11
DOST RECOGNIZE THE LOVE?	ME PROVE IT NOW--WHOEVER	537	12
THAT I DID ALWAYS LOVE	THAT I DID ALWAYS LOVE	549	1
THAT I SHALL LOVE ALWAY--	THAT I DID ALWAYS LOVE	549	5
THAT LOVE IS [BE] LIFE--	THAT I DID ALWAYS LOVE	549	7
HER BEAUTY--IS THE LOVE SHE DOTH--	BUT LITTLE CARMINE HATH	558	3
IN CONTRAST WITH THE LOVE--	I MEASURE EVERY GRIEF I	561	24
WE LEARNED THE WHOLE OF LOVE--	WE LEARNED THE WHOLE OF	568	1
THE TEST OF LOVE--IS DEATH--	THE TEST OF LOVE--IS	573	1
THE DAILY OWN--OF LOVE	I GAVE MYSELF TO HIM--	580	8
THE FORMER LOVE--DISTINCTER GROWS--	YOU'LL FIND--IT WHEN YOU	610	11
THE LOVE OF THEE--A PRISM BE--	I SEE THEE BETTER--IN	611	3
TILL LOVE THAT WAS--AND LOVE TOO BEST TO BE--	TO KNOW JUST HOW HE	622	25
TILL LOVE THAT WAS--AND LOVE TOO BEST TO BE--	TO KNOW JUST HOW HE	622	25
THO' SERVICE 'TWAS, OF LOVE--	I THINK THE LONGEST HOUR	635	14
A LEGACY OF LOVE	YOU LEFT ME--SIRE--TWO	644	2
THE LOVE A LIFE [CHILD] CAN SHOW BELOW	THE LOVE A LIFE CAN SHOW	673	1
WHO OF LITTLE LOVE--KNOW HOW TO STARVE--	VICTORY COMES LATE--	690	14
IF LOVE BE JUST BEYOND--	TO WAIT AN HOUR--IS LONG	781	2
IF LOVE REWARD [BE AT] THE END--	TO WAIT AN HOUR--IS LONG	781	4
FOR LOVE IS IMMORTALITY,	UNABLE ARE THE LOVED TO	809	2

	FIRST LINE	POEM	LINE
LOVE (CONTINUED)			
UNABLE THEY THAT LOVE [ARE THE LOVED]--TO DIE	UNABLE ARE THE LOVED TO	809	4
FOR LOVE REFORMS VITALITY [IS IMMORTALITY]	UNABLE ARE THE LOVED TO	809	5
LOVE RECKONS BY ITSELF--ALONE--	LOVE RECKONS BY ITSELF--	826	1
THE LEAVING LOVE BEHIND.	DYING! TO BE AFRAID OF	831	6
TWO ARMIES, LOVE AND CERTAINTY	DYING! TO BE AFRAID OF	831	11
AND LOVE AND THE REVERSE.	DYING! TO BE AFRAID OF	831	12
OR LOVE ANNEALED OF LOVE	PERHAPS YOU THINK ME	833	6
OR LOVE ANNEALED OF LOVE	PERHAPS YOU THINK ME	833	6
SUPERSTITION HELPS, AS WELL AS LOVE--	ABSENCE DISEMBODIES--SO	860	3
WE OUTGROW LOVE, LIKE OTHER THINGS	WE OUTGROW LOVE, LIKE	887	1
EXHIBIT LOVE--SOMEWHAT--	TILL DEATH--IS NARROW	907	12
THE LOVE YOU OFFER--	I CANNOT BE ASHAMED	914	3
LOVE--IS ANTERIOR TO LIFE--	LOVE--IS ANTERIOR TO	917	1
LOVE--IS THAT LATER THING THAN DEATH--	LOVE--IS THAT LATER	924	1
MOST--I LOVE THE CAUSE THAT SLEW ME.	STRUCK, WAS I, NOR YET	925	17
THAT LOVE HAD TOUCHED THAT MORN	TWO TRAVELLERS PERISHING	933	10
ASSISTED FAINT [SLOW] OF LOVE.	AS PLAN FOR NOON AND	960	8
FOR LIFE--BE [IS / MEANS] LOVE--	WERT THOU BUT ILL--THAT	961	20
THE LOVE, THO, WILL ARRAY [INSTRUCT] ME RIGHT	FITTER TO SEE HIM, I MAY	968	21
IF LOVE INQUIRE "WHERE"?	SUPERFLUOUS WERE THE SUN	999	8
FAR FROM LOVE THE HEAVENLY FATHER	FAR FROM LOVE THE	1021	1
AND PUTTING LOVE AWAY	THE BUSTLE IN A HOUSE	1078	6
THESE ARE THE NIGHTS THAT BEETLES LOVE--	THESE ARE THE NIGHTS	1128	1
THE LOVE THAT WOULD NOT TRY	HOW MANY SCHEMES MAY DIE	1150	9
AWFUL FATHER [FOUNDER] OF LOVE--	WHATEVER IT IS--SHE HAS	1204	2
HAD LOVE AS PUNCTUAL BEEN	IT CAME AT LAST BUT	1230	6
LOVE IS ONE, NOT AGGREGATE--	SAFE DESPAIR IT IS THAT	1243	7
OR LOVE--THE TWO COEVAL COME--	TO PILE LIKE THUNDER TO	1247	5
THE INCIDENTS OF LOVE	THE INCIDENTS OF LOVE	1248	1
LEST LOVE SHOULD VALUE LESS	HAD THIS ONE DAY NOT	1253	5
IF "GOD IS LOVE" AS HE ADMITS	BECAUSE THAT YOU ARE	1260	33
IS ALL THAT LOVE CAN SPEAK--	LOVE'S STRICKEN "WHY"	1368	2
NOT THAT HE GOES--WE LOVE HIM MORE	NOT THAT HE GOES--WE	1435	1
THE NAME OF IT IS LOVE--	BEHOLD THIS LITTLE BANE	1438	4
HOW OLD THE NEWS OF LOVE MUST [SHOULD] BE	HIS VOICE DECREPIT WAS	1476	3
WHEN LOVE WITH BUT A PENCE	HOW DESTITUTE IS HE	1477	5
LOVE IS DONE WHEN LOVE'S BEGUN,	LOVE IS DONE WHEN LOVE'S	1485	1
WITH LOVE ALONE HAD [WERE] BENT,	'TIS NOT THE SWAYING	1597	4
LOVE MARINE AND LOVE TERRENE--	IS IT TOO LATE TO TOUCH	1637	3
LOVE MARINE AND LOVE TERRENE--	IS IT TOO LATE TO TOUCH	1637	3
LOVE CELESTIAL TOO--	IS IT TOO LATE TO TOUCH	1637	4
THE MIGHT OF HUMAN LOVE--	THE IMMORTALITY SHE GAVE	1648	4
FEW--LOVE AT ALL	SOMETIMES WITH THE HEART	1680	4
THESE ARE THE DAYS THAT REINDEER LOVE	THESE ARE THE DAYS THAT	1696	1
A FACE DEVOID OF LOVE OR GRACE,	A FACE DEVOID OF LOVE OR	1711	1
LOVE CAN DO ALL BUT RAISE THE DEAD	LOVE CAN DO ALL BUT	1731	1
BUT LOVE IS TIRED AND MUST SLEEP,	LOVE CAN DO ALL BUT	1731	5
LOVE THAT NEVER LEAPED ITS SOCKET--	REARRANGE A "WIFE'S"	1737	9
THAT LOVE IS ALL THERE IS,	THAT LOVE IS ALL THERE	1765	1
IS ALL WE KNOW OF LOVE;	THAT LOVE IS ALL THERE	1765	2
HOW ALWAYS WRONG IS LOVE--	HOW FLEET--HOW	1771	2
LOVED			
IF THOSE I LOVED WERE LOST	IF THOSE I LOVED WERE	29	1
IF THOSE I LOVED WERE FOUND	IF THOSE I LOVED WERE	29	3
DID THOSE I LOVED REPOSE	IF THOSE I LOVED WERE	29	5
THAT HE--LOVED MEN--	SO WELL THAT I CAN LIVE	456	5
THAT TILL I LOVED	THAT I DID ALWAYS LOVE	549	3
OUR LORD--"SO LOVED"--IT SAITH--	THE TEST OF LOVE--IS	573	2
UNABLE ARE THE LOVED TO DIE	UNABLE ARE THE LOVED TO	809	1
UNABLE THEY THAT LOVE [ARE THE LOVED]--TO DIE	UNABLE ARE THE LOVED TO	809	4
THE LOVED?	A SHADE UPON THE MIND	882	8
THE ONE THAT WE HAVE LOVED--	AS SUMMER INTO AUTUMN	1346	8
UNQUESTIONABLY LOVED--	SUMMER--WE ALL HAVE SEEN	1386	4
THE ONES I LOVED BELOW	I SHALL NOT MURMUR IF AT	1410	2
THIS LOVED PHILOLOGY	A WORD MADE FLESH IS	1651	16
LOVELINESS			
THE CLAMOR FOR THEIR LOVELINESS	COULD THAT SWEET	1493	3
LOVELY			
OF ONE HOWEVER LOVELY, NOT	AS SUMMER INTO AUTUMN	1346	7
LOVER			
FOR HER OLD LOVER--DON THE SUN!	SOME RAINBOW--COMING	64	17
TO THE LOVER BEE	DID THE HAREBELL LOOSE	213	2
MORNING MEANS JUST RISK [CHANCE]--TO THE LOVER--	"MORNING"--MEANS	300	4
GOD IS A DISTANT--STATELY LOVER--	GOD IS A DISTANT--	357	1
THE LOVER--HOVERED--O'ER--	THE SOUL HAS BANDAGED	512	8
OH LOVER--LIFE COULD NOT CONVINCE--	ME PROVE IT NOW--WHOEVER	537	7
WHAT LARGEST LOVER--HATH--	THE TEST OF LOVE--IS	573	3
THINK OF IT LOVER! I AND THEE	IF I MAY HAVE IT, WHEN	577	9
WHEN A LOVER IS A BEGGAR	WHEN A LOVER IS A BEGGAR	1314	1
WHEN A LOVER IS AN OWNER	WHEN A LOVER IS A BEGGAR	1314	3
PROVOKING LOVER, WHEN YOU CAME	I THOUGHT THE TRAIN	1449	7
THE HAPPY [THE CHEMIST / THE RANSOMED / A LOVER] MAY [CAN] REPAY,	THE FARTHEST THUNDER	1581	10
LOVER'S			
LIKE A LOVER'S WORDS.	NATURE RARER USES YELLOW	1045	8
BUT THE ARC OF A LOVER'S CONJECTURE	WE SHALL FIND THE CUBE	1484	3
LOVERS			
OH THE EARTH WAS MADE FOR LOVERS, FOR	AWAKE YE MUSES NINE,	1	3

	FIRST LINE	POEM	LINE
LOVERS (CONTINUED)			
DAMSEL, AND HOPELESS SWAIN,			
WHEN LOVERS BE AFAR--	'TIS CUSTOMARY AS WE	440	4
THESE FLESHLESS LOVERS MET--	'TWAS A LONG PARTING--	625	5
BASHFUL HEAVEN--THY LOVERS SMALL--	OUT OF SIGHT? WHAT OF	703	12
LOVE'S			
'TWAS LOVE'S--NOW STRIKE!	'TWAS LOVE--NOT ME--	394	12
PATIENCE--IS THE SMILE'S [MOUTH'S / LOVE'S] EXERTION	PATIENCE--HAS A QUIET	926	7
STOLID TO LOVE'S SUPREME [SUBLIME] ENTREATY	TELL AS A MARKSMAN--WERE	1152	20
BUT LOVE'S TRANSMIGRATION--	NOW I KNEW I LOST HER--	1219	11
LOVE'S STRICKEN "WHY"	LOVE'S STRICKEN "WHY"	1368	1
LOVE IS DONE WHEN LOVE'S BEGUN,	LOVE IS DONE WHEN LOVE'S	1485	1
OR LOVE'S CONVENIENT THINGS,	TO THE BRIGHT EAST SHE	1573	5
LOVES			
BECAUSE HE LOVES HER	BECAUSE HE LOVES HER	1229	1
HE LOVES [SEEKS] WHAT SPURNS [SHUNS] HIM--	TO EARN IT BY DISDAINING	1427	3
TO HER WHO LOVES THEE BEST,	COME SHOW THY DURHAM	1542	2
LOVEST			
AND SEIZE THE ONE THOU LOVEST, NOR CARE FOR SPACE, OR TIME!	AWAKE YE MUSES NINE,	1	36
LOVING			
NOR TELL THE LOVING FORESTS	I HAV'NT TOLD MY GARDEN	50	11
TRUST THE LOVING PROMISE	I OFTEN PASSED THE	51	15
HER LOVING BOSOM LAY--	DELAYED TILL SHE HAD	58	3
SAVE BY LOVING SUNRISE	GLOWING IS HER BONNET,	72	9
IF SOME LOVING ANTIQUARY,	I HAVE NEVER SEEN	175	17
WHEN KATIE KNEELS, THEIR LOVING HANDS STILL CLASP HER PIOUS KNEE--	WHEN KATIE WALKS, THIS	222	3
TILL DEATH--IS NARROW LOVING--	TILL DEATH--IS NARROW	907	1
THE REALM OF [LOVING] YOU--	I HAVE NO LIFE BUT THIS	1398	8
LOVING THE HAND THAT SENT IT	I'VE GOT AN ARROW HERE.	1729	2
LOW			
CROUCH LOW TO GUARD HIS PRIZE.	I NEVER TOLD THE BURIED	11	4
LAIN SO LOW,	WHEN I COUNT THE SEEDS	40	5
LOW AT MY PROBLEM BENDING,	LOW AT MY PROBLEM	69	1
MEEK [LOW] MY VIVE LE ROI,	MUTE THY CORONATION--	151	2
THE SUN KEPT STOOPING--STOOPING--LOW!	THE SUN KEPT STOOPING--	152	1
LOW AMID THAT GLAD BELLES LETTRES	IF THE FOOLISH, CALL	168	17
HOW MANY TIMES THESE LOW FEET STAGGERED--	HOW MANY TIMES THESE LOW	187	1
STOOPING AS LOW AS [BENDING LOW AT] THE OTTER'S [KITCHEN / . . .	BLAZING IN GOLD AND	228	5
STOOPING AS LOW AS [BENDING LOW AT] THE OTTER'S [KITCHEN / . . .	BLAZING IN GOLD AND	228	5
LOW AS THE LAUGHTER OF THE CRICKET,	MANY A PHRASE HAS THE	276	3
A VOICE THAT ALTERS--LOW	A MIEN TO MOVE A QUEEN--	283	16
AND WINDOWS HANGING LOW,	I KNOW SOME LONELY	289	4
AT HER LOW GATE--	THE SOUL SELECTS HER OWN	303	6
HEART! I AM KNOCKING--LOW AT THEE.	JUST SO--JESUS--RAPS--	317	11
LOW DAISIES--DOT--	I TEND MY FLOWERS FOR	339	6
FOR FOREHEAD LOW AS MINE, TO WEAR,	ALTHOUGH I PUT AWAY HIS	366	3
OF THE LOW GROUND?	IT IS DEAD--FIND IT--	417	6
UNTO THE DAISY LOW--	THE HIMMALEH WAS KNOWN	481	2
AND THEN, 'TWAS BRIEF AND LOW--	I WAS THE SLIGHTEST IN	486	11
AWAITED THEIR--LOW BROWS--	LIKE FLOWERS, THAT HEARD	513	3
IN LOW APARTMENTS IN THE SOD--	SHE HIDETH HER THE LAST	557	7
LIT UP THE LOW--INFERIOR GRASS--	I THINK I WAS ENCHANTED	593	V 11
THROUGH THIS LOW ARCH OF FLESH--	I ROSE--BECAUSE HE SANK	616	13
YOUR LOW [MEEK] EYES--DEMAND--	PROMISE THIS--WHEN YOU	648	8
TO DEMAND, IN YOUR LOW FAVOR	PROMISE THIS--WHEN YOU	648	21
UNGAINED--IT MAY BE--BY [IN] A LIFE'S LOW VENTURE--	EACH LIFE CONVERGES TO	680	17
AND IS HELD LOW TO FREEZING LIPS--	VICTORY COMES LATE--	690	2
IT DROPPED SO LOW--IN MY REGARD--	IT DROPPED SO LOW--IN MY	747	1
DEEP [LOW] PILLOW--TO HAVE SHARED--	MY LIFE HAD STOOD--A	754	16
WITH THREATENING TUNES AND LOW--	THE WIND BEGUN TO KNEAD	824	V 2
THE THUNDERS [THUNDER] GOSSIPED LOW--	THE WIND BEGUN TO KNEAD	824	10
UNTIL IT BEND AS LOW AS DEATH	PERHAPS YOU THINK ME	833	7
TO HIM WHO ON IT'S SMALL [LOW] REPOSE	A COFFIN--IS A SMALL	943	9
THE HOUSEWIFE IN THY LOW ATTENDANCE	WERT THOU BUT ILL--THAT	961	15
I DWELT TOO LOW THAT ANY SEEK--	I WAS A PHEBE--NOTHING	1009	5
AND LOWER LAY IN LOW WESTMINSTER	SHE ROSE AS HIGH AS HIS	1011	3
WHEN AUGUST BURNING LOW	FURTHER IN SUMMER THAN	1068	10
THE SKY IS LOW--THE CLOUDS ARE MEAN.	THE SKY IS LOW--THE	1075	1
HIS FEATHERS WILTED LOW--	HIS BILL IS CLASPED--HIS	1102	2
THE LOW GRASS LOADED WITH THE DEW	THE CRICKETS SANG	1104	5
ABOVE HIM IS TOO LOW A HIGHT	'TIS MY FIRST NIGHT	1122	3
ON THAT LOW PLAIN	LEFT IN IMMORTAL YOUTH	1289	2
AROMATIC--LOW--	PINK--SMALL--AND	1332	2
FATIGUED AT LAST, A CLOVER PLAIN [LOW]	HIS ORIENTAL HERESIES	1526	5
MY LOW [ONE / MEEK / WAN] RENOWN	TO BE FORGOT BY THEE	1560	V 12
SHE DID NOT KNOW HER STATION LOW	TO HER DERIDED HOME	1586	3
IN THAT LOW SUMMER OF THE WEST	A LANE OF YELLOW LED THE	1650	7
SO LOW IT LEANED--THEN STATELIER DREW--	A CURIOUS CLOUD	1710	6
LOWER			
BY HEADS REJECTED--IN THE LOWER COUNTRY--	UNTO LIKE STORY--TROUBLE	295	11
FOR LOWER RECOGNITION [INTERRUPTION]	THE SOUL'S SUPERIOR	306	7
TAUGHT ME--BY TIME--THE LOWER WAY--	I LIVE WITH HIM--I SEE	463	13
OR LOWER--LIKE THE WREN--	YOU SAID THAT I "WAS	738	6
AND LOWER LAY IN LOW WESTMINSTER	SHE ROSE AS HIGH AS HIS	1011	3

	FIRST LINE	POEM	LINE
LOWER (CONTINUED)			
THE LOWER METRES OF THE YEAR	THE MURMURING OF BEES,	1115	5
TO THE LOWER EYES--	LIFT IT--WITH THE	1348	6
LOWERED			
'TWAS LOWERED, LIKE A WEIGHT [FREIGHT]-- .	'TWAS WARM--AT FIRST--	519	14
LOWLIER			
DO LOWLIER--APPEAR--	MY WORTHINESS IS ALL MY	751	4
LOWLIEST			
THE LOWLIEST CAREER	NO LIFE CAN POMPLESS	1626	2
LOWLY			
THE HIGH DO SEEK THE LOWLY, THE GREAT DO SEEK THE SMALL,	AWAKE YE MUSES NINE,	1	11
LIKE [AS] LOWLY SPICES, LAIN TO SLEEP [GONE TO SLEEP / LAID . . .	THE GRASS SO LITTLE HAS	333	15
THAT LOWLY BREAST [HOMESTEAD SWEET] WHERE BUTTERFLIES	HIS ORIENTAL HERESIES	1526	7
LOYAL			
MORE LOYAL FOR THE EXODY	FROM HIS SLIM PALACE IN	1300	3
ABUNDANT [A FERVENT / A LOYAL / A GRACIOUS / AN AMPLE] END--	THE GENTIAN HAS A	1424	13
LOYALLY			
HOW LOYALLY AT PARTING	ONE DIGNITY DELAYS FOR	98	11
LUCK			
A PALER LUCK THAN VICTORY--	MY PORTION IS DEFEAT--	639	2
LUCK IS NOT CHANCE--	LUCK IS NOT CHANCE--	1350	1
LUCRATIVE			
LUCRATIVE INDEED THE OFFER [THE PROPOSITION]	"FAITHFUL TO THE END"	1357	V
LULL SEE A'/LULL			
AS IF FOR LULL OF SPORT--	SHE LAY AS IF AT PLAY	369	6
LULLABY			
HUMMING THE QUAINTEST LULLABY	WHOSE ARE THE LITTLE	142	19
OUR ONLY LULLABY--	I CRIED AT PITY--NOT AT	588	24
LULLED			
THE WINDS--LIKE CHILDREN--LULLED-- . . .	THREE TIMES--WE PARTED--	598	14
LULLS			
THE HAMMOCK'S MOTION LULLS THE HEADS . . .	I SOMETIMES DROP IT, FOR	708	11
THIS LATEST LEISURE EQUAL LULLS [CASTLE EQUAL HOLDS]	NOT ANY HIGHER STANDS	1256	5
LUNA			
TELL LUNA, TEA IS WAITING, ...	"SIC TRANSIT GLORIA	3	15
LUNACY			
FOR VERY LUNACY OF LIGHT	I THINK I WAS ENCHANTED	593	7
LUNG			
THE SLIVER, IN THE LUNG--	ONE ANGUISH--IN A CROWD	565	10
LUNGS			
THE LUNGS ARE STIRLESS--MUST DESCEND . . .	I BREATHED ENOUGH TO	272	5
AND FILL MY LUNGS, FOR WITNESS--	DO PEOPLE MOULDER	432	7
THE LUNGS--WITHIN--	IN FALLING TIMBERS	614	4
LURE			
OBEYED--A LURE--A LONGING?	"GO TELL IT"--WHAT A	1554	5
LURES			
UNTO GUESSED CRESTS, MY MOANING FANCY, LEADS [LURES] ME,	UNTO LIKE STORY--TROUBLE	295	9
LURK			
AGES COIL [LURK] WITHIN	PAIN--EXPANDS THE TIME--	967	2
LURKED			
A MOURNER WALKED [LURKED] AMONG THE CHILDREN	A LOSS OF SOMETHING EVER	959	5
LURKS			
THE SPIRIT LURKS WITHIN THE FLESH	THE SPIRIT LASTS--BUT IN	1576	9
LUSCIOUS			
HOW LUSCIOUS LIES WITHIN THE POD	FORBIDDEN FRUIT A FLAVOR	1377	3
IN BLISSFUL [LUSCIOUS / SUMPTUOUS] REVERY .	HIS ORIENTAL HERESIES	1526	V
LUSTRAL			
FROM HER LUSTRAL FACE	LIGHTLY STEPPED A YELLOW	1672	4
LUSTRE			
UNCERTAIN LEASE--DEVELOPES LUSTRE	UNCERTAIN LEASE--	857	1
LUSTROUS			
OF A TINT SO LUSTROUS MEEK--	PIGMY SERAPHS--GONE	138	8
LUTE			
PUT UP MY LUTE!	PUT UP MY LUTE!	261	1
ON LUTE THE LEAST--THE LATEST--	ALTHOUGH I PUT AWAY HIS	366	9
LUTES			
THE BREEZES BROUGHT DEJECTED LUTES-- . . .	A DROP FELL ON THE APPLE	794	13
SAVED FOR YOUR EAR WHEN LUTES BE OLD. . .	SPLIT THE LARK--AND	861	4
LUXURIES			
THO' SUCH--ARE LUXURIES--	IT'S THOUGHTS--AND JUST	495	22
LUXURIOUS			
. . . THE / LUXURIOUS AS THE] LIGHT . . .	YOU CANNOT TAKE ITSELF	1351	5
LUXURY			
OUR LUXURY!	WILD NIGHTS--WILD NIGHTS	249	4
MAY BE LUXURY--	SMILING BACK FROM	385	2
FROM DUNGEON'S LUXURY OF DOUBT	'TWAS LIKE A MAELSTROM,	414	20
A PRIVILEGE [LUXURY] SO AWFUL	I WOULD NOT PAINT--A	505	21
SUCH LUXURY--IT GREW--	I TRIED TO THINK A	532	17
THE PRIVILEGE [LIBERTY / LUXURY] TO DIE-- .	THE HEART ASKS PLEASURE	536	8
MY POIGNANT LUXURY--	GOD GAVE A LOAF TO EVERY	791	4
GRIEF IS A GOURMAND--SPARE HIS LUXURY-- . .	GRIEF IS A MOUSE--	793	12
THE LUXURY TO APPREHEND	THE LUXURY TO APPREHEND	815	1
THE LUXURY 'TWOULD BE	THE LUXURY TO APPREHEND	815	2
THE LUXURY TO MEDITATE	THE LUXURY TO APPREHEND	815	9

	FIRST LINE	POEM	LINE
LUXURY (CONTINUED)			
THE LUXURY IT WAS	THE LUXURY TO APPREHEND	815	10
LUXURY I	IT CAME HIS TURN TO BEG	1500	V
LYBIAN			
SEED OF PALM, BY LYBIAN SUN	SOIL OF FLINT, IF STEADY	681	3
LYING			
THE CREATURE LYING THERE--	THERE IS A LANGUOR OF	396	12
WORLDS WERE LYING OUT TO [SWIMMING IN THE / LYING IN THE] SUN--	WHEN I HOPED, I	768	11
WORLDS WERE LYING OUT TO [SWIMMING IN THE / LYING IN THE] SUN--	WHEN I HOPED, I	768	11
OURSELF AM LYING STRAIGHT WHEREIN	THIS CHASM, SWEET, UPON	858	7
A FIELD OF STUBBLE, LYING SERE	A FIELD OF STUBBLE,	1407	1
MACHINERY			
BEYOND MACHINERY	TOO COLD IS THIS	1135	V 5
MAD			
OR LAY A PRIMA, MAD,	I CANNOT DANCE UPON MY	326	8
AND CANNOT, BUT ARE MAD WITH [FOR] FEAR	A DIAMOND ON THE HAND	1108	7
MADAM			
"BUT--MADAM--IS THERE NOTHING ELSE--	I ASKED NO OTHER THING--	621	7
MADDER			
THE BREEZES MADDER PLAY;	THE BEE IS NOT AFRAID OF	111	6
SOME MADDER HOLIDAY--	THE LONESOME FOR THEY	262	4
AND MADDER--TO CONCIEVE--	I SOMETIMES DROP IT, FOR	708	4
MADDEST			
AND SHE WILL FLING HER MADDEST PERFUME--	KILL YOUR BALM--AND IT'S	238	3
THE NEAREST [MADDEST] DREAM RECEDES--UNREALIZED--	THE NEAREST DREAM	319	1
THE MADDEST--QUICKEST BY--	IT STRUCK ME--EVERY DAY	362	10
MADDEST HEART THAT GOD CREATED	LAIN IN NATURE--SO	1288	5
WHO NEVER WANTED--MADDEST JOY	WHO NEVER WANTED--	1430	1
THE MADDEST NOISE THAT GROWS,--	THE SADDEST NOISE, THE	1764	2
MADE			
OH THE EARTH WAS MADE FOR LOVERS, FOR DAMSEL, AND HOPELESS SWAIN,	AWAKE YE MUSES NINE,	1	3
FOR SIGHING, AND GENTLE WHISPERING, AND UNITY MADE OF TWAIN.	AWAKE YE MUSES NINE,	1	4
GOD HATH MADE NOTHING SINGLE BUT THEE IN HIS WORLD SO FAIR!	AWAKE YE MUSES NINE,	1	6
IS MADE A SECRET TO UNFOLD	A SCIENCE--SO THE SAVANS	100	4
AND NO ONE MADE REPLY.	WHOSE ARE THE LITTLE	142	4
THAT MADE EXISTENCE--HOME!	EXCEPT TO HEAVEN, SHE IS	154	12
CORN--IS MADE AT NOON--	MORNING--IS THE PLACE	197	2
SO NOTELESSLY--ARE MADE!	A SHADY FRIEND--FOR	278	12
BEST GIANT MADE--	IF YOUR NERVE, DENY YOU	292	8
WHERE MEN MADE HAY--	FROM COCOON FORTH A	354	11
AND MEN THAT MADE THE HAY--	FROM COCOON FORTH A	354	23
TO SEE THAT I MADE NO MISTAKE	I READ MY SENTENCE--	412	3
I MADE MY SOUL FAMILIAR--WITH HER EXTREMITY--	I READ MY SENTENCE--	412	9
GOD MADE A LITTLE GENTIAN--	GOD MADE A LITTLE	442	1
THE DIFFERENCE--MADE ME BOLD--	IT WAS GIVEN TO ME BY	454	16
IT'S MADE OF FATHOMS--AND A BELT--	I KNOW WHERE WELLS GROW	460	5
HAS MADE THE TOILETTE COOL	TO MAKE ONE'S TOILETTE--	485	2
IF 'TWAS A DREAM--MADE SOLID--JUST	HER SWEET WEIGHT ON MY	518	5
IT MADE NO SIGNAL, NOR DEMURRED,	'TWAS WARM--AT FIRST--	519	15
AND MADE AS HE WOULD EAT ME UP--	I STARTED EARLY--TOOK MY	520	13
OUR LORD--INDEED--MADE [BORE] COMPOUND WITNESS--	ONE CRUCIFIXION IS	553	13
BUT HEAVEN MADE BOTH, IMPOSSIBLE	WE TALKED AS GIRLS DO--	586	15
FOR CHILDREN, MADE OF GOLD--	I CRIED AT PITY--NOT AT	588	12
THEN MADE BLUE FACES IN MY FACE--	THREE TIMES--WE PARTED--	598	7
A LITTLE ROAD--NOT MADE OF MAN--	A LITTLE ROAD--NOT MADE	647	1
PROVE THE FEAT--THAT MADE THE PELLET MINE--	GOD GAVE A LOAF TO EVERY	791	6
AND MADE THE GABLES LAUGH--	A DROP FELL ON THE APPLE	794	4
IT MADE THE HURRY PLAIN--	HER FINAL SUMMER WAS IT	795	8
I MADE SLOW RICHES BUT MY GAIN	I MADE SLOW RICHES BUT	843	1
I MADE THE TAPER SHINE--	ONLY A SHRINE, BUT MINE	918	2
MADE LOUD OBEISANCE AND THE GNAT	THE FINGERS OF THE LIGHT	1000	15
NEW ACQUAINTANCE--THIS BABY MADE--	TRUDGING TO EDEN,	1020	8
I MADE NO ANSWER OF THE TONGUE	IT WAS A QUIET WAY--	1053	3
MADE NATURE DIFFERENT	THE LAST NIGHT THAT SHE	1100	4
GOD MADE NO ACT WITHOUT A CAUSE,	GOD MADE NO ACT WITHOUT	1163	1
THANK GOD THE LOUDEST PLACE HE MADE	IT'S HOUR WITH ITSELF	1225	7
MY WILDERNESS HAS MADE--	HAD I NOT SEEN THE SUN	1233	4
IT MADE US ALL ASHAMED [DEMEANED]	SO PROUD SHE WAS TO DIE	1272	2
HAD ALMOST MADE IT FAIR--	WHILE WE WERE FEARING IT	1277	4
"THE HOUSE NOT MADE WITH HANDS" IT WAS--	I SUED THE NEWS--YET	1360	3
FOR WHAT HE MOVED, HE MADE.	NOT THAT HE GOES--WE	1435	4
OUR SUMMER MADE HER LIGHT ESCAPE	AS IMPERCEPTIBLY AS	1540	15
SOEVER MADE IN VAIN,	WE SEND THE WAVE TO FIND	1604	6
AS MADE REALITY A DREAM	WITHIN THAT LITTLE HIVE	1607	3
A WORLD MADE PENNINILESS BY THAT [HIS] DEPARTURE	A WORLD MADE PENNINILESS	1623	1
A WORD MADE FLESH IS SELDOM	A WORD MADE FLESH IS	1651	1
"MADE FLESH AND DWELT AMONG US	A WORD MADE FLESH IS	1651	13
THAT MADE THEE FIRST UNKNOWN	I SEE THEE CLEARER FOR	1666	6
MADE NO DISTINCT REPLY.	THE WATERS CHASED HIM AS	1749	10
MADE CRUELLY MORE DEAR.	THE SADDEST NOISE, THE	1764	12
MADNESS			
COULD IT BE MADNESS--THIS?	THE FIRST DAY'S NIGHT	410	20

	FIRST LINE	POEM	LINE
MAIDS			
WHOSE MAIDS UPON REMOTER GREEN	THERE IS A MORN BY MEN	24	2
WHERE THE MAIDS?	WHAT-INN IS THIS	115	5
MAIL			
MIRTH IS THE MAIL OF ANGUISH--	A WOUNDED DEER--LEAPS	165	9
STILL--CLAD IN YOUR MAIL OF ICES--	AH, TENERIFFE!	666	6
WITHOUT CELESTIAL MAIL--	THE LAST OF SUMMER IS	1353	6
THE MAIL FROM TUNIS, PROBABLY,	A ROUTE OF EVANESCENCE	1463	7
MAILED SEE NEW-MAILED			
MAIMED			
MAIMED--WAS I--YET NOT BY VENTURE--	STRUCK, WAS I, NOR YET	925	5
THE MAIMED MAY PAUSE, AND BREATHE,	THIS MERIT HATH THE	979	5
MAIN			
THAT IS NOT OF MILE OR MAIN--	THAT DISTANCE WAS	863	2
SO GENIAL IN THE MAIN	A WILD BLUE SKY ABREAST	1415	6
MAINTAIN			
MAINTAIN--BY ACCIDENT THAT THEY PROCLAIM--	LIFE, AND DEATH, AND	706	6
MAINTAIN--	FOUR TREES--UPON A	742	4
AND FESTIVAL MAINTAIN	TO OWN THE ART WITHIN	855	4
MAINTAINING			
O'ERLOOKING [MAINTAINING] A SUPERIOR SPECTRE--	ONE NEED NOT BE A	670	19
MAISE			
YIELDED GRAPE--AND MAISE--	SOIL OF FLINT, IF STEADY	681	V
MAIZE			
WHERE BE THE MAIZE--	ANSWER JULY--	386	15
MAJESTIC			
WITH YOUR MAJESTIC LEAVE!	GREAT CAESAR! CONDESCEND	102	4
"SUNSET" SOUNDS MAJESTIC--	THERE'S THE BATTLE OF	1174	5
BUT BREAD IS THAT DIVINER [MAJESTIC] THING	THE BEGGAR AT THE DOOR	1240	3
MAJESTIC IS TO ME BEYOND	THE OVERTAKELESSNESS OF	1691	3
MAJESTIES			
WHAT MAJESTIES OF PEACE,	OH WHAT A GRACE IS THIS,	1615	2
THE MAJESTIES OF EARTH	THE OVERTAKELESSNESS OF	1691	4
MAJESTY			
WAIT TILL THE MAJESTY OF DEATH	WAIT TILL THE MAJESTY OF	171	1
WITH TAINTS OF MAJESTY--	OF BRONZE--AND BLAZE--	290	9
MYSELF AND IT, IN MAJESTY	THE DAY THAT I WAS	356	11
SO I LOOP MY APRON, AGAINST THE MAJESTY	I'M SAYING EVERY DAY	373	12
"I'M SUNRISE"--NEED THE MAJESTY?	YOU'LL KNOW IT--AS YOU	420	10
WITH TENDER MAJESTY	THIS IS MY LETTER TO THE	441	4
BUSY WITH MAJESTY--	TO INTERRUPT HIS YELLOW	591	8
AND MAJESTY--BE EASIER--	I THINK TO LIVE--MAY BE	646	11
WERE PRESENT AT THE MAJESTY--	THE SUN WENT DOWN--NO	1079	3
MEADOWS OF MAJESTY CONCEDES [IMPLIES]	MY COCOON TIGHTENS--	1099	7
AT TIMES TO MAJESTY.	THE WAY TO KNOW THE	1279	8
GIVEN FOR THE GIVING, SOLELY, [THE MAJESTY]	"FAITHFUL TO THE END"	1357	7
HAD NOT THE MAJESTY.	A CURIOUS CLOUD	1710	9
MAJOR			
'TWAS MAJOR ANDRE'S WAY--	THE MANNER OF IT'S DEATH	468	4
THAT LEAVES THIS NEIGHBOR [MAJOR] OUT--	NO BRIGADIER THROUGHOUT	1561	24
MAJORITY			
SOME SAY--THAT BRIGHT MAJORITY	MUSICIANS WRESTLE	157	14
TO [ON] HER DIVINE MAJORITY--	THE SOUL SELECTS HER OWN	303	3
'TIS THE MAJORITY	MUCH MADNESS IS DIVINEST	435	4
MAKE			
AND THEY MAKE MERRY WEDDING, WHOSE GUESTS ARE HUNDRED LEAVES;	AWAKE YE MUSES NINE,	1	14
THEIR SPIRITS MEET TOGETHER, THEY MAKE THEM SOLEMN VOWS,	AWAKE YE MUSES NINE,	1	19
MAKE ME A PICTURE OF THE SUN--	MAKE ME A PICTURE OF THE	188	1
AND MAKE BELIEVE I'M GETTING WARM	MAKE ME A PICTURE OF THE	188	3
OR MAKE HIM FAST	IS IT TRUE, DEAR SUE?	218	9
THAT MAKE THE CIRCUIT OF THE REST--	HE PUT THE BELT AROUND	273	11
TO MAKE SURE ALL'S ASLEEP--	I KNOW SOME LONELY	289	10
BUT MAKE NO SYLLABLE--LIKE DEATH--	GIVE LITTLE ANGUISH--	310	6
AND MAKE ITSELF SO FINE	THE GRASS SO LITTLE HAS	333	10
JUST TO MAKE BLISS	I KNOW THAT HE EXISTS.	338	7
WOMEN MAKE--TONIGHT--	'TWAS THE OLD--ROAD--	344	18
TO MAKE YOUR COTTAGE GAY--	ALTHOUGH I PUT AWAY HIS	366	29
A PASSAGE BACK--OR TWO--TO MAKE--	A PRECIOUS--MOULDERING	371	7
NOT ALL THE SNOWS C'D MAKE IT WHITE--	THE COLOR OF THE GRAVE	411	19
IF GOD COULD MAKE A VISIT--	I NEVER FELT AT HOME--	413	9
TIARAS--MAKE--OF SOME--	I'LL CLUTCH--AND CLUTCH	427	8
MAKE--A DIADEM--AND MEND MY OLD ONE--	I'LL CLUTCH--AND CLUTCH	427	11
TO MAKE AN EVEN SUM--	'TWAS JUST THIS TIME,	445	16
HOW SHORT IT TAKES TO MAKE IT BRIDE--	A WIFE--AT DAYBREAK I	461	4
WHY MAKE IT DOUBT--IT HURTS IT SO--	WHY MAKE IT DOUBT--IT	462	1
TRINKET--TO MAKE ME BEAUTIFUL--	I AM ASHAMED--I HIDE--	473	8
TO MAKE ONE'S TOILETTE--AFTER DEATH	TO MAKE ONE'S TOILETTE--	485	1
AND MAKE THE BODDICE GAY--	TO MAKE ONE'S TOILETTE--	485	6
MAKE FRUGAL--ONES--CONTENT--	IT'S THOUGHTS--AND JUST	495	3
WHOSE SPOKES A DIZZY MUSIC MAKE	WITHIN MY GARDEN, RIDES	500	3
MAKE HASTE--[COME NEAR] THE SCRUPLE! DEATH BE SCANT	ME PROVE IT NOW--WHOEVER	537	3
AS MAKE OF [BREW FROM / MIX] OUR IMPERFECT [UNCOMELY / OBTUSER]	SHE HIDETH HER THE LAST	557	11
'TIS UNITS--MAKE THE SWARM--	ONE ANGUISH--IN A CROWD	565	8
WHEN THEY TOGETHER VICTORY MAKE--	"HEAVEN" HAS DIFFERENT	575	11
OR MAKE A DRAGON--MOVE--	IT WOULD HAVE STARVED A	612	8
I CAN MAKE THE ZIGZAG STITCHES	DONT PUT UP MY THREAD &	617	15

	FIRST LINE	POEM	LINE
MAKE (CONTINUED)			
MAKE SUMMER--WHEN THE LADY LIE	ESSENTIAL OILS--ARE	675	7
UNTO MY SEEMING--MAKE?	THE SUN KEPT SETTING--	692	12
LIFE--IS WHAT WE MAKE IT--	LIFE--IS WHAT WE MAKE IT	698	1
MAKE THE BLIND--LEAP--	LET US PLAY YESTERDAY--	728	12
MAKE THAT APPEAR--	RENUNCIATION--IS A	745	15
ILLUMINATE--[MAKE POPULATE-- / MAKE MANIFEST] OR SEAL--	THE LONELINESS ONE DARE	777	16
ILLUMINATE--[MAKE POPULATE-- / MAKE MANIFEST] OR SEAL--	THE LONELINESS ONE DARE	777	16
OF SAVORS--MAKE US CONSCIOUS--	DESPAIR'S ADVANTAGE IS	799	9
SHALL MAKE DISCOVERY.	THIS CONSCIOUSNESS THAT	822	12
AMPLE MAKE THIS BED--	AMPLE MAKE THIS BED--	829	1
MAKE THIS BED WITH AWE--	AMPLE MAKE THIS BED--	829	2
NATURE'S EXPERIENCE WOULD MAKE	A MOTH THE HUE OF THIS	841	3
THE SUN AND MOON MUST MAKE THEIR HASTE--	THE SUN AND MOON MUST	871	1
HE HELPED TO MAKE TOO BRIGHT	THE SUN IS GAY OR STARK	878	6
TO MAKE ME VISIBLE--	TO MY QUICK EAR THE	891	8
I MAKE HIS CRESCENT FILL OR LACK--	I MAKE HIS CRESCENT FILL	909	1
WOULD IT MAKE THE DAISY,	IF IT HAD NO PENCIL	921	6
I FAILED TO MAKE [ELICIT NO] REPLY--	MY BEST ACQUAINTANCES	932	6
BUT COULD NOT MAKE THEM FIT.	I FELT A CLEAVING IN MY	937	4
MAKE THEIR FIRST REPOSE THIS WINTER	SNOW BENEATH WHOSE	942	3
BUT COULD NOT MAKE IT FEEL [TELL].	'TWAS CRISIS--ALL THE	948	12
A MAN MAY MAKE [DROP] A REMARK--	A MAN MAY MAKE A REMARK	952	1
TO MAKE ME FAIREST OF THE EARTH--	FITTER TO SEE HIM, I MAY	968	5
AND MAKE MUCH BLUNDER, IF AT LAST	MY COCOON TIGHTENS--	1099	11
DID MAKE [PRESUMED] AS TO DEVOUR	THE WIND TOOK UP THE	1134	6
MAKE OF HIS ONLY BOY A TARGET	TELL AS A MARKSMAN--WERE	1152	18
BUT NOT TO MAKE A "BIT OF NOISE"	A LITTLE DOG THAT WAGS	1185	15
GO MAKE THEE FAIR MY CANDIDATE	OH SHADOW ON THE GRASS,	1187	3
TO MAKE ROUTINE A STIMULUS	TO MAKE ROUTINE A	1196	1
AND MAKE THE WATER SLOW	A STAGNANT PLEASURE LIKE	1281	4
I MAKE BELIEVE UNTIL MY HEART	THE MOST PATHETIC THING	1290	3
THAT EACH CAN MAKE BUT ONCE--	THAT SHORT--POTENTIAL	1307	2
TO MAKE EACH OTHER STARE	OUR LITTLE SECRETS SLINK	1326	6
THE HEART AND THE MIND TOGETHER MAKE	THE HEART IS THE CAPITAL	1354	3
THAT MAKE US RICH AN HOUR--	DREAMS ARE THE SUBTLE	1376	2
LONG YEARS APART--CAN MAKE NO	LONG YEARS APART--CAN	1383	1
WITH THOUGHTS THAT MAKE FOR PEACE--	ONE OF THE ONES THAT	1466	24
TO MAKE LIPS ELDERLY	HIS VOICE DECREPIT WAS	1476	4
YOU CANNOT MAKE REMEMBRANCE GROW	YOU CANNOT MAKE	1508	1
THOUGH [BUT] JOYS--LIKE MEN--MAY SOMETIMES MAKE A JOURNEY--	THE THINGS THAT NEVER	1515	3
I PRAY THE LORD THY SOUL TO MAKE--	NOW I LAY THEE DOWN TO	1539	4
THEY MAKE THEIR CIRCUIT FAIR	NO MATTER WHERE THE	1541	2
HER [HIS] LOSSES MAKE OUR GAINS ASHAMED--	HER LOSSES MAKE OUR	1562	1
THAT MAKE THE WATER LIVE, ESTRANGED	THE SPIRIT LASTS--BUT IN	1576	11
COULD MAKE A DENT THEREON--	THE SPIRIT LASTS--BUT IN	1576	24
COULD MAKE A DENT THEREON--	EXPANSE CANNOT BE LOST--	1584	8
TO THOSE THAT MAGIC MAKE--	THE BIRD HER PUNCTUAL	1585	8
CAN [COULD] MAKE A [NO] DENT [CREASE / SEAM] THEREON [UPON]--	THIS ME--THAT WALKS AND	1588	8
THAT HIM REFRESH [MAKE HIM FRESH]--	THE LASSITUDES OF	1592	4
WE MAKE THE WISE DISTINCTION [SAGE DECISION] STILL,	WE SEND THE WAVE TO FIND	1604	5
MAKE LIFE A SUDDEN PRICE.	MORNING THAT COMES BUT	1610	4
BUT WHEN I CANNOT MAKE THE FORCE	IF I COULD TELL HOW GLAD	1668	3
MAKE AN ABSTEMIOUS ECSTASY	RATHER ARID DELIGHT	1679	3
MAKE ME BEARDED LIKE A MAN!	REARRANGE A "WIFE'S"	1737	4
I MAKE MY PARLOR ORDERLY	THE GRAVE MY LITTLE	1743	3
TO MAKE A PRAIRIE IT TAKES A CLOVER AND ONE BEE,	TO MAKE A PRAIRIE IT	1755	1
TO MAKE SOME TRIFLE FAIRER	WERE NATURE MORTAL LADY	1762	9
THE BIRDS, THEY MAKE IT IN THE SPRING,	THE SADDEST NOISE, THE	1764	3
MAKER			
HER MAKER--HER METROPOLIS--	SHE DWELLETH IN THE	671	3
THE MAKER [FURTHER]--OF OURSELVES--BE WHAT--	TO BE ALIVE--IS POWER--	677	7
THE MAKER OF THE SOUL	THE LONELINESS ONE DARE	777	14
THE WRINKLED MAKER [AUTHOR] LIE	A WORD DROPPED CARELESS	1261	4
MY MAKER--LET ME BE	MY MAKER--LET ME BE	1403	1
HE RECOGNIZED HIS MAKER--OVERTURNED THE DECALOGUE--	THE BOBOLINK IS GONE--	1591	8
MAKER'S			
THE MAKER'S LADDERS STOP--	A SOLEMN THING WITHIN	483	4
OF THE MAKER'S GIRL?	RIBBONS OF THE YEAR--	873	8
THE MAKER'S CORDIAL VISAGE,	DROWNING IS NOT SO	1718	9
MAKES			
IT MAKES THE PARTING TRANQUIL	IF I SHOULD DIE,	54	15
HOW MANY TRIPS THE TORTOISE MAKES--	BRING ME THE SUNSET IN A	128	10
THIS JUST MAKES OUT THE MORNING SKY.	A SLASH OF BLUE--	204	9
TEACH HIM--WHEN HE MAKES THE NAMES--	TEACH HIM--WHEN HE MAKES	227	1
MAKES WORK DIFFICULT--THEN--	IT IS EASY TO WORK WHEN	244	4
THAT MAKES TWO--HIM--AND LIFE!	WHAT WOULD I GIVE TO SEE	247	6
SUCH [SOME] SPIRIT MAKES [TELL] HER PERPETUAL MENTION,	UNTO LIKE STORY--TROUBLE	295	13
IT MAKES AN EVEN FACE	IT SIFTS FROM LEADEN	311	5
MAKES THE HEAVENS PORTABLE--	TAKING UP THE FAIR IDEAL	428	5
THAT--MAKES THE QUICK OF WO!	IF ANYBODY'S FRIEND BE	509	24
THAT MAKES THE FENCES SMILE--	I'M SORRY FOR THE DEAD--	529	8

	FIRST LINE	POEM	LINE
MAKES (CONTINUED)			
MAKES SCARCELY WORTH THE TOIL--	WE SEE--COMPARATIVELY--	534	6
IT MAKES NO DIFFERENCE ABROAD--	IT MAKES NO DIFFERENCE	620	1
THAT MAKES NO SHOW FOR MORN--	A LONG--LONG SLEEP--A	654	2
IT GATHERS RUDDY [STANDS IN--RUDDY / MAKES VERMILLION--] POOLS--	THE NAME--OF IT--IS	656	10
MAKES LACERATING TUNE--	UPON CONCLUDED LIVES	735	5
IN WHATSOEVER PRESENCE MAKES	THE LUXURY TO APPREHEND	815	5
ENCHANTMENT MAKES INGREDIENT	IMPOSSIBILITY, LIKE WINE	838	7
THAT MAKES THE LIVING POSSIBLE	A DOUBT IF IT BE US	859	7
AND MAKES ONE LIFT ONE'S HAT	IT IS AN HONORABLE	946	2
MAKES EFFORT AT CONCLUSION	AS PLAN FOR NOON AND	960	7
A PHEBE MAKES A LITTLE PRINT	I WAS A PHEBE--NOTHING	1009	7
AS MAKES ONE HIDE [HANG] IT'S HEAD	THAT THIS SHOULD FEEL	1112 V	4
THE FACE THAT MAKES THE MORNING MEAN	THE VOICE THAT STANDS	1189	3
MAKES HE MUD FOR DOG AND PEDDLER,	WE LIKE MARCH.	1213	4
MAKES HE FORESTS [FOREST] DRY.	WE LIKE MARCH.	1213	5
THAT MAKES OUR TRYING [RUNNING] POOR.	BECAUSE HE LOVES HER	1229	12
THAT MAKES THE HEART PUT UP IT'S FUN--	SEPTEMBER'S	1271	7
THAT MAKES THE EAR INORDINATE	THE LONG SIGH OF THE	1359	7
MAKES A WORLD'S SUSPENSE	TRUSTY AS THE STARS	1369	7
AND STATEMENTS MAKES--	HIS MANSION IN THE POOL	1379	4
WATER MAKES MANY BEDS	WATER MAKES MANY BEDS	1428	1
MAKES THAT FEROCIOUS ROOM	A DIMPLE IN THE TOMB	1489	2
MAKES THE [THIS] PRESENT [NEXT MOMENT] MEAN--	GLASS WAS THE STREET--IN	1498	8
'TIS STARVING MAKES IT FAT--	MINE ENEMY IS GROWING	1509	8
KNOW THAT WHICH MAKES THEM AS FORGOT	THE MOON UPON HER FLUENT	1528	7
MAKES THE BEHAVIOR SMALL--	THOSE--DYING THEN,	1551	7
MAKES MOCKERY OF MELODY	TO SEE HER IS A PICTURE	1568 V	
MAKES NOT AS MUCH OF SOUND	THE SUN IN REINING TO	1636	2
THAT MAKES IT HATED SO--	ADVANCE IS LIFE'S	1652	4
HIS MIND OF MAN, A SECRET MAKES	HIS MIND OF MAN, A	1663	1
BEFORE HE MAKES THE BEND	I DID NOT REACH THEE	1664	22
IS WHAT MAKES LIFE SO SWEET.	THAT IT WILL NEVER COME	1741	2
IT MAKES US THINK OF ALL THE DEAD	THE SADDEST NOISE, THE	1764	9
IT MAKES US THINK OF WHAT WE HAD,	THE SADDEST NOISE, THE	1764	13
MAKETH			
THAT [WHICH] MAKETH ALL THINGS NEW--	THERE CAME A DAY AT	322	8
MAKING			
WHILE HE--WAS MAKING ONE--	I SEND TWO SUNSETS--	308	4
MAKING THAT HOMELY, AND SEVERE,	LIKE FLOWERS, THAT HEARD	513	11
JUST MAKING SIGNS--ACROSS--[IT SEEMED] TO THEE--	IF I MAY HAVE IT, WHEN	577	20
MAKING [PAYING] GRATITUDE	MOST SHE TOUCHED ME BY	760	20
KEEPS MAKING NOVEMBER DIFFICULT	HOW HAPPY I WAS IF I	898	5
MAK'ST			
WHAT DIFFERENCE, AFTER ALL, THOU MAK'ST	THE SUNSET STOPPED ON	950	7
MALADY			
THERE WAS NO MALADY--	THEY SAY THAT "TIME	686	8
FOR BEING'S MALADY--	SEVERER SERVICE OF	786	24
MALARIA			
FROM THE MALARIA--	A WORD DROPPED CARELESS	1261	8
MALAY			
AS IS THE BROWN MALAY	REMOVED FROM ACCIDENT OF	424	6
THE MALAY--TOOK THE PEARL--	THE MALAY--TOOK THE	452	1
MALIGNITY			
NOT IN MALIGNITY	MY HEART RAN SO TO THEE	1237	9
EMPOWERED WITH WHAT MALIGNITY	THE BAT IS DUN, WITH	1575	11
MAMA			
MAMA NEVER FORGETS HER BIRDS,	MAMA NEVER FORGETS HER	164	1
MAN			
CAN PIERCE AN ARMED MAN--	THERE IS A WORD	8	3
OH SOME WISE MAN FROM THE SKIES!	WILL THERE REALLY BE A	101	10
NOR TAMBORIN--NOR MAN--	MUSICIANS WRESTLE	157	9
A RICH MAN--MIGHT NOT NOTICE IT--	I LOST A WORLD--THE	181	5
THE MAN--TO DIE--TOMORROW--	THE DOOMED--REGARD THE	294	5
NO MAN INSTRUCTED ME--	I CANNOT DANCE UPON MY	326	2
BUT HE--IS NOT A MAN--	THEY LEAVE US WITH THE	350	2
THE LITERATURE OF MAN--	A PRECIOUS--MOULDERING	371	12
AND SOPHOCLES--A MAN--	A PRECIOUS--MOULDERING	371	16
NO MAN DREW.	I WENT TO HEAVEN--	374	8
TO STIMULATE A MAN	EXHILIRATION--IS WITHIN	383	9
THAT MAN AND WOMAN KNOW--	THE SWEETEST HERESY	387	2
AND THEN THE MILLINER--AND THE MAN	THERE'S BEEN A DEATH, IN	389	17
THE WIND--TAPPED LIKE A TIRED MAN--	THE WIND--TAPPED LIKE A	436	1
THEN LIKE A TIMID MAN	THE WIND--TAPPED LIKE A	436	18
UNDUE SIGNIFICANCE A STARVING MAN ATTACHES	UNDUE SIGNIFICANCE A	439	1
AS A COMPLETED MAN	I TIE MY HAT--I CREASE	443	14
OF THIS--COULD MAN DEPRIVE ME--	THE POWER TO BE TRUE TO	464	5
NO MAN CAN COMPASS A DESPAIR--	NO MAN CAN COMPASS A	477	1
AGAINST THE MAN--PERSUADED--	MYSELF WAS FORMED--A	488	11
THE MAN--UPON THE WOMAN--BINDS--	THE WORLD--STANDS--	493	7
BUT NO MAN MOVED ME--TILL THE TIDE	I STARTED EARLY--TOOK MY	520	9
NO ONE [MAN] HE SEEMED TO KNOW--	I STARTED EARLY--TOOK MY	520	22
FOR THAT NO MAN OBTAIN	HAD I PRESUMED TO HOPE--	522	14
YOU CANNOT [NO MAN--] PUT A FIRE OUT--	YOU CANNOT PUT A FIRE	530	1
NO MAN CAN UNDERSTAND	THE PROVINCE OF THE	539	5
THAT MAN--BE QUALIFIED	THE PROVINCE OF THE	539	8
I FEAR A MAN OF FRUGAL [SCANTY] SPEECH--	I FEAR A MAN OF FRUGAL	543	1
I FEAR A SILENT MAN--	I FEAR A MAN OF FRUGAL	543	2

	FIRST LINE	POEM	LINE
MAN (CONTINUED)			
OF THIS MAN--I AM WARY--	I FEAR A MAN OF FRUGAL	543	7
DEATH IS POTENTIAL TO THAT MAN	DEATH IS POTENTIAL TO	548	1
A BEST DISGRACE--A BRAVE MAN FEELS--	THERE IS A SHAME OF	551	5
BUT NO MAN HEARD HIM CRY--	THE BLACK BERRY--WEARS A	554	2
AND NO MAN--IS THE ONE	THE BATTLE FOUGHT	594	2
OLD MAN ON NEBO! LATE AS THIS--	IT ALWAYS FELT TO ME--A	597	23
THERE BREATHED A MAN--	IN FALLING TIMBERS	614	2
IT WAS TOO LATE FOR MAN--	IT WAS TOO LATE FOR MAN	623	1
A LITTLE ROAD--NOT MADE OF MAN--	A LITTLE ROAD--NOT MADE	647	1
COULD SO ENTHRALL A MAN	NO ROMANCE SOLD UNTO	669	2
OF THE MIND OF MAN--	PUBLICATION--IS THE	709	2
THERE--LEAVING OUT A MAN--	IT'S EASY TO INVENT A	724	12
ON THE MAN--FREE--	LET US PLAY YESTERDAY--	728	30
BUT THE MAN WITHIN	NEVER FOR SOCIETY	746	6
GROWTH OF MAN--LIKE GROWTH OF NATURE--	GROWTH OF MAN--LIKE	750	1
TO HERSELF--AND MEN [MAN]--	MOST SHE TOUCHED ME BY	760	16
UNTO A NAMELESS MAN--	TO OFFER BRAVE	767	6
TRUTH STAYS HERSELF--AND EVERY MAN	THE TRUTH--IS STIRLESS--	780	11
EXCEPT OCCASIONAL MAN--	THE BIRDS BEGUN AT FOUR	783	10
FROM FURTHEST SPIRIT [FAITHFUL / GOOD MAN]--GOD--	ON A COLUMNAR SELF--	789	12
AN INDEPENDANT MAN--	I PLAY AT RICHES--TO	801	8
WE QUESTION IF THE MAN--	I PLAY AT RICHES--TO	801	14
SEES EVERY MAN A KING--	WHO COURT OBTAIN WITHIN	803	2
NO MAN [FATE] DEPOSE	WHO COURT OBTAIN WITHIN	803	5
EXHILIRATES THE MAN	IMPOSSIBILITY, LIKE WINE	838	2
THE MAN WHO WOULD POSSESS	THE GOOD WILL OF A	849	2
TILL HE MEET A MAN	AS THE STARVED MAELSTROM	872	6
'TWERE NOT APPEASED OF MEN [MAN]	IT WAS A GRAVE, YET BORE	876	8
PERHAPS, RECALLS THE MAN	EACH SECOND IS THE LAST	879	2
THE DISCIPLINE OF MAN--	EXPERIENCE IS THE ANGLED	910	6
A MAN MAY MAKE [DROP] A REMARK--	A MAN MAY MAKE A REMARK	952	1
FAIL IN AN INSTANT, NO MAN DID	CRUMBLING IS NOT AN	997	11
AWAKENED MAID AND MAN	THE FINGERS OF THE LIGHT	1000	12
ACKNOWLEDGED HIM A MAN.	FATE SLEW HIM, BUT HE	1031	8
THE YELLOW MAN	WHO IS THE EAST?	1032	2
THE PURPLE MAN	WHO IS THE EAST?	1032	6
THE SUN WENT DOWN--NO MAN LOOKED ON--	THE SUN WENT DOWN--NO	1079	1
THE SUN WENT UP--NO MAN LOOKED ON--	THE SUN WENT DOWN--NO	1079	5
A MINE THERE IS NO MAN WOULD OWN	A MINE THERE IS NO MAN	1117	1
OR EVERY MAN BE BLIND--	TELL ALL THE TRUTH BUT	1129	8
THAT ODD OLD MAN IS DEAD A YEAR--	THAT ODD OLD MAN IS DEAD	1130	1
THE MAN THAT WAS NOT LOST [WRECKED / ROBBED / KILLED]	HOW MANY SCHEMES MAY DIE	1150	5
BY THE TIME THAT MAN AND BEAST	THERE'S THE BATTLE OF	1174	3
. . . CONCLUSIVE] A MAN!	HE PREACHED UPON	1207	8
THE MAN THAT [WHO] RUNS AWAY	TO DISAPPEAR ENHANCES--	1209	2
FROM THE MIND OF MAN	TO FLEE FROM MEMORY	1242	8
AND NOT A SMALLER [LESSER] MAN	I THOUGHT THAT NATURE	1286	12
WHAT NEWS WILL DO WHEN EVERY MAN	HOW NEWS MUST FEEL WHEN	1319	9
I DO NOT KNOW THE MAN SO BOLD	I NEVER HEAR THAT ONE IS	1323	13
THAT EVERY MAN [ALL THE WORLD] BEHOLD	YOU CANNOT TAKE ITSELF	1351	6
BUT THEN I AM A RURAL MAN	ONE OF THE ONES THAT	1466	23
PAUL KNEW THE MAN THAT KNEW THE NEWS--	"AND WITH WHAT BODY DO	1492	7
THE SECRET OF THE MAN	BLISS IS THE PLAYTHING	1553	2
AS CART OF MAN IN ROAD BELOW	THE SUN IN REINING TO	1636	3
THE DITCH IS DEAR TO THE DRUNKEN MAN	THE DITCH IS DEAR TO THE	1645	1
HIS MIND OF MAN, A SECRET MAKES	HIS MIND OF MAN, A	1663	1
YET MAN HAS NOT OF ALL THE THRONG	THE HILLS ERECT THEIR	1688	3
BY ANY MAN BUT GOD--	TO THEIR APARTMENT DEEP	1701	4
THREE TIMES, 'TIS SAID, A SINKING MAN	DROWNING IS NOT SO	1718	3
NO MAN SAW AWE, NOR TO HIS HOUSE	NO MAN SAW AWE, NOR TO	1733	1
ADMITTED HE A MAN	NO MAN SAW AWE, NOR TO	1733	2
MAKE ME BEARDED LIKE A MAN!	REARRANGE A "WIFE'S"	1737	4
TO NO PRECARIOUS MAN.	THE RETICENT VOLCANO	1748	4
A PRUDENT MAN WOULD SHUN.	THROUGH THOSE OLD	1753	4
MANACLE			
GOD OF THE MANACLE	LET US PLAY YESTERDAY--	728	33
GO MANACLE YOUR ICICLE	'TWAS HERE MY SUMMER	1756	7
MANACLES			
MANACLES BE DIM--THEY SAY--	LET US PLAY YESTERDAY--	728	17
MANCHESTER			
DO BIRMINGHAM [MANCHESTER] ECLIPSE--	A SAUCER HOLDS A CUP	1374	12
MANDOLIN			
BANISH--MY MANDOLIN	BIND ME--I STILL CAN	1005	2
MANGLE			
MANGLE DAINTIER--TERRIBLER--	IT IS EASY TO WORK WHEN	244	7
HAD POWER TO MANGLE ME--	I DREADED THAT FIRST	348	8
MANGLED			
THEIR MANGLED LIMBS	THE WIND DREW OFF	1694	8
MANGLES			
THIS IS THE GNAT THAT MANGLES MEN--	WONDER--IS NOT PRECISELY	1331	8
MANIFEST			
ILLUMINATE--[MAKE POPULATE-- / MAKE MANIFEST] OR SEAL--	THE LONELINESS ONE DARE	777	16
MANIFOLD			
OF ROSE AND LILY, MANIFOLD,	A SCIENCE--SO THE SAVANS	100	11
AS MANIFOLD FOR ANGUISH--	A WEIGHT WITH NEEDLES ON	264	7
AND TRUTH--SO MANIFOLD!	WE LEARNED THE WHOLE OF	568	12

	FIRST LINE	POEM	LINE
MANKIND			
MINUTEST OF MANKIND SHOULD [MIGHT / COULD] BE--	THE ONE WHO COULD REPEAT	307	3
THIS ONE--BELOVED OF MANKIND	WHAT CARE THE DEAD, FOR	592	15
FRESH [NEW] AS MANKIND THAT HUMBLE STORY	TELL AS A MARKSMAN--WERE	1152	5
TO THINKING OF MANKIND.	BEST WITCHCRAFT IS	1158	4
BUT [THOUGH] ALL MANKIND DELIVER [CRUISE SOFTLY / ROW SOFTLY / . . .	A CHILLY PEACE INFESTS	1443	7
THOU ONLY CAMEST TO MANKIND	WITHIN THY GRAVE!	1552	3
BUT NATURE AND MANKIND MUST PAUSE	THE RIGHT TO PERISH	1692	7
MANNER			
THAT PUTS IT'S MANNER BY	A MIEN TO MOVE A QUEEN--	283	4
THE DATE, AND MANNER, OF THE SHAME--	I READ MY SENTENCE--	412	5
THE MANNER OF THE CHILDREN--	THE MONTHS HAVE ENDS--	423	9
THE MANNER OF IT'S DEATH	THE MANNER OF IT'S DEATH	468	1
SOME MANNER OF THE HAIR--	IF ANYBODY'S FRIEND BE	509	6
NOT A TROPIC [MANNER] OF A TWILIGHT--	BLOOM UPON THE MOUNTAIN	667	7
A COMPOUND MANNER,	TO THIS WORLD SHE	830	3
MANNERS			
TILL I TAKE VASTER ATTITUDES [MANNERS]--	OF BRONZE--AND BLAZE--	290	10
THEIR GRASPLESS MANNERS--MOCK US--	THE TINT I CANNOT TAKE--	627	21
THEIR REMOVING MANNERS	SOME WE SEE NO MORE,	1221	4
MANNERS MAY [WILL] PREVAIL.	ABRAHAM TO KILL HIM	1317	12
MANOR			
UPON THE BROAD POSSESSION [LAWFUL MANOR--] .	IT ALWAYS FELT TO ME--A	597	21
MAN'S			
THE GOOD MAN'S--"DIVIDEND"--	YOU'RE RIGHT--"THE WAY	234	10
BUT NONE WILL PASS THE [MAN'S] CATACOMB	THE BUTTERFLY IN HONORED	1246	3
MANSE			
A MANSE OF MECHLIN AND OF FLOSS [GLOSS / SUN]--	THE FAIREST HOME I EVER	1423	5
MANSION			
A "MANSION" FOR THE RAT!	PAPA ABOVE!	61	5
THIS PASSIVE PLACE A SUMMER'S NIMBLE MANSION	THIS QUIET DUST WAS	813	5
FROM MANSION OF THE UNIVERSE	TRUTH--IS AS OLD AS GOD	836	7
ALL MY MANSION TORN--	STRUCK, WAS I, NOR YET	925	10
PARADISE IS THAT OLD MANSION	PARADISE IS THAT OLD	1119	1
HIS MANSION IN THE POOL	HIS MANSION IN THE POOL	1379	1
OR MANSION OF IDENTITY	THE LOOK OF THEE, WHAT	1689	3
MANSIONS			
"MANSIONS"! MANSIONS MUST BE WARM!	"HOUSES"--SO THE WISE	127	2
"MANSIONS"! MANSIONS MUST BE WARM!	"HOUSES"--SO THE WISE	127	2
MANSIONS CANNOT LET THE TEARS IN,	"HOUSES"--SO THE WISE	127	3
MANSIONS MUST EXCLUDE THE STORM!	"HOUSES"--SO THE WISE	127	4
"MANY MANSIONS", BY "HIS FATHER",	"HOUSES"--SO THE WISE	127	5
OF MANSIONS NEVER QUITE DISCLOSED	THE LIGHTNING IS A	1173	5
MANTEL'S			
NOT THE MANTEL'S--	A CLOCK STOPPED--	287	2
MANUFACTORING			
THAT IS THE MANUFACTORING SPOT	A DEED KNOCKS FIRST AT	1216	3
MANY			
AND THO' FULL MANY A MORNING,	"SIC TRANSIT GLORIA	3	47
MANY THE SAILS AT REST--	ON THIS WONDROUS SEA	4	8
MOULDERED THIS MANY MAY.	ONE SISTER HAVE I IN OUR	14	22
WHO SANG FULL MANY A DAY	I HAD A GUINEA GOLDEN--	23	10
SO TIPTOED MANY A SLIPPER	SO HAS A DAISY VANISHED	28	3
MANY A BULB WILL RISE--	SO FROM THE MOULD	66	3
MANY A WORM	SO FROM THE MOULD	66	7
HOW MANY LEAGUES OF NOWHERE	AMBITION CANNOT FIND HIM	68	3
HOW MANY LEGIONS OVERCOME--	WHO NEVER LOST, ARE	73	9
HOW MANY COLORS TAKEN	WHO NEVER LOST, ARE	73	11
HOW MANY BULLETS BEAREST?	WHO NEVER LOST, ARE	73	13
MANY, WILL DOUBTLESS ASK ME,	SO BASHFUL WHEN I SPIED	91	11
MANY CROSS THE RHINE	MANY CROSS THE RHINE	123	1
"MANY MANSIONS", BY "HIS FATHER",	"HOUSES"--SO THE WISE	127	5
AND SAY HOW MANY DEW,	BRING ME THE SUNSET IN A	128	3
WRITE ME HOW MANY NOTES THERE BE	BRING ME THE SUNSET IN A	128	7
HOW MANY TRIPS THE TORTOISE MAKES--	BRING ME THE SUNSET IN A	128	10
HOW MANY CUPS THE BEE PARTAKES,	BRING ME THE SUNSET IN A	128	11
THE EYES OF MANY ELVES--	BESIDES THE AUTUMN POETS	131	12
MEANWHILE, AT MANY CRADLES	WHOSE ARE THE LITTLE	142	17
GATHERED FROM MANY WANDERINGS--	ALL OVERGROWN BY CUNNING	148	V
MANY SCIENCES,	IF THE FOOLISH, CALL	168	14
HOW MANY TIMES THESE LOW FEET STAGGERED--	HOW MANY TIMES THESE LOW	187	1
BUT IT'S MANY A LAY OF THE DIM BURGUNDY--	WE--BEE AND I--LIVE BY	230	4
HOW MANY TIMES IT ACHE FOR ME--TODAY--CONFESS--	YOU SEE I CANNOT SEE--	253	3
HOW MANY TIMES FOR MY FAR SAKE	YOU SEE I CANNOT SEE--	253	4
THAT KEPT SO MANY WARM--	"HOPE" IS THE THING WITH	254	8
HOW MANY TIMES THEY--BORE THE FAITHFUL WITNESS--	READ--SWEET--HOW OTHERS	260	5
SO--MANY--DROPS--OF VITAL SCARLET--	BOUND--A TROUBLE--	269	4
MANY A PHRASE HAS THE ENGLISH LANGUAGE--	MANY A PHRASE HAS THE	276	1
AND IT'S PARTLY [MANY A MILE], DOWN HILL--	TIE THE STRINGS TO MY	279	8
AND MANY HURT,	I REASON, EARTH IS SHORT	301	3
THE LILACS--BENDING MANY A YEAR--	IT WILL BE SUMMER--	342	9
WITH MANY A TURN--AND THORN--	'TWAS THE OLD--ROAD--	344	3
OF HOW MANY BE--	SMILING BACK FROM	385	10
HOW MANY FLOWERS FAIL IN WOOD--	HOW MANY FLOWERS FAIL IN	404	1
HOW MANY CAST A NAMELESS POD	HOW MANY FLOWERS FAIL IN	404	5

	FIRST LINE	POEM	LINE
MANY (CONTINUED)			
HOW MANY I ESPY	A MURMUR IN THE TREES--	416	14
"HOMESICK"? MANY MET IT--	IT IS DEAD--FIND IT--	417	7
MANY A BITTERNESS--HAD BEEN--	IT WOULD NEVER BE COMMON	430	3
HOW MANY BE	ONE CRUCIFIXION IS	553	2
AS MANY BE	ONE CRUCIFIXION IS	553	6
THE GRIEVED--ARE MANY--I AM TOLD--	I MEASURE EVERY GRIEF I	561	25
MY FIRST WELL DAY--SINCE MANY ILL--	MY FIRST WELL DAY--SINCE	574	1
MANY THINGS--ARE FRUITLESS--	IN FALLING TIMBERS	614	13
I MANY TIMES THOUGHT PEACE HAD COME . . .	I MANY TIMES THOUGHT	739	1
HOW MANY THE FICTITIOUS SHORES--	I MANY TIMES THOUGHT	739	7
SO MANY QUESTIONS TO PUT THEM	WHAT DID THEY DO SINCE I	900	3
HOW MANY THINGS THE DYING PLAY	WERE IT BUT ME THAT	1015	3
I COULD'NT WEEP--FOR SO MANY SMILING . . .	TRUDGING TO EDEN,	1020	7
I'M SURE, AT MANY A WHIM	IF NATURE SMILES--THE	1085	2
'TIS MANY A TINY MILL	DEW--IS THE FRESHET IN	1097	2
HOW MANY SIGHT AND SIGH	A DIAMOND ON THE HAND	1108	6
THAT MANY DIE WITHOUT--	THERE IS ANOTHER	1116	2
MANY OWNED BEFORE--	PARADISE IS THAT OLD	1119	2
HAST THOU SURVIVED SO MANY NIGHTS [YEARS]? .	THE SMOULDERING EMBERS	1132	3
HOW MANY SCHEMES MAY DIE	HOW MANY SCHEMES MAY DIE	1150	1
SO MANY YEARS AGAIN--	I SHOULD NOT DARE TO BE	1197	2
MANY WOULD FLY [SOAR]	TO FLEE FROM MEMORY	1242	3
IN MANY AND REPORTLESS PLACES	IN MANY AND REPORTLESS	1382	1
WATER MAKES MANY BEDS	WATER MAKES MANY BEDS	1428	1
THE HEART HAS MANY DOORS--	THE HEART HAS MANY DOORS	1567	1
FOR MANY AN ARDENT [A FRUITLESS] YEAR. . .	THE DISTANCE THAT THE	1742	4
THE EARTH HAS MANY KEYS.	THE EARTH HAS MANY KEYS.	1775	1
MANY-COLORED			
SHE SWEEPS WITH MANY-COLORED BROOMS-- . .	SHE SWEEPS WITH	219	1
MANY'S			
MANY'S THE GALLANT--OVERWHELMED CREATURE .	FINITE--TO FAIL, BUT	847	3
MANZANILLA			
FROM MANZANILLA COME!	I TASTE A LIQUOR NEVER	214	16
MAPLE			
THE MAPLE WEARS A GAYER SCARF--	THE MORNS ARE MEEKER	12	5
FROM THE MAPLE KEEP?	WHAT SHALL I DO WHEN THE	956	4
THE MAPLE LENT UNTO THE ROAD	AS IMPERCEPTIBLY AS	1540	V
MAPLE'S			
THE MAPLE'S LOOM IS RED--	THE GENTIAN WEAVES HER	18	2
MAPLES			
THE MAPLES NEVER KNEW THAT YOU WERE COMING--TILL I CALLED	DEAR MARCH--COME IN--	1320	12
MAPPED			
IS MAPPED AND CHARTED TOO.	"ARCTURUS" IS HIS OTHER	70	21
MAR			
COULD MAR IT--IF IT FOUND--	REVERSE CANNOT BEFALL	395	8
TO MAR [DARE]--	EACH LIFE CONVERGES TO	680	8
AND MAR THY PERFECTNESS--	WHAT I SEE NOT, I BETTER	939	12
LET ME NOT MAR THAT PERFECT DREAM	LET ME NOT MAR THAT	1335	1
OUR ADORATION STAIN [MAR / FLAW]	WE SHUN BECAUSE WE PRIZE	1429	3
MARAUDER			
WHEREFORE--MARAUDER--ART THOU HERE? . . .	THE DAISY FOLLOWS SOFT	106	5
MARAUDING			
EXCEPT FOR IT'S MARAUDING HAND	IMMORTAL IS AN AMPLE	1205	7
MARAUDS			
THERE MARAUDS A SORER ROBBER, ...	DEATH'S WAYLAYING NOT	1296	3
MARBLE			
MIDNIGHT IN MARBLE--REFUTES--THE SUNS-- . .	SAFE IN THEIR ALABASTER	216	V
TRIBES OF ECLIPSE--IN TENTS OF MARBLE-- . .	SAFE IN THEIR ALABASTER	216	V
WHO ONLY SHOWS HIS MARBLE DISC [GRANITE FACE]--	GIVE LITTLE ANGUISH--	310	7
LIDS OF STEEL--ON LIDS OF MARBLE--	SWEET--SAFE--HOUSES--	457	4
NOR FIRE--FOR JUST MY [TWO] MARBLE FEET . .	IT WAS NOT DEATH, FOR I	510	7
AS DID THEIR MARBLE NAMES	YOU'LL FIND--IT WHEN YOU	610	6
MY NERVE IN MARBLE LIES--	I'VE DROPPED MY BRAIN--	1046	6
AND LAY THE MARBLE TEA.	THE GRAVE MY LITTLE	1743	4
MARBLES			
I MISSED MINE--HOW DREARY--MARBLES-- . . .	GOD PERMITS INDUSTRIOUS	231	7
MARCH			
BARONIAL BEES--MARCH--ONE BY ONE--	SOME RAINBOW--COMING	64	11
WHY, LOOK OUT FOR THE LITTLE BROOK IN MARCH,	HAVE YOU GOT A BROOK IN	136	9
A SWEET ENDEAVOR--BUT AS MARCH	YOU'LL KNOW HER--BY HER	634	23
INVESTIGATING MARCH, ...	HAVE ANY LIKE MYSELF	736	2
EXCEPTING MARCH--'TIS THEN	HAVE ANY LIKE MYSELF	736	21
WHEN MARCH IS SCARCELY HERE	A LIGHT EXISTS IN SPRING	812	4
WHEN MARCH IS SCARCELY ON--	THE ROBIN IS THE ONE	828	4
BUT DURING MARCH AND APRIL	SPRING IS THE PERIOD	844	5
ESTABLISH MARCH, THE FLOODS ESCORT, ...	THE DUTIES OF THE WIND	1137	3
MUCH IS THE MIEN [GOOD IS THE LOOK] OF HIM IN MARCH	A PROMPT--EXECUTIVE BIRD	1177	7
WE LIKE MARCH.	WE LIKE MARCH.	1213	1
DEAR MARCH--COME IN--	DEAR MARCH--COME IN--	1320	1
DEAR MARCH, HOW ARE YOU, AND THE REST-- . .	DEAR MARCH--COME IN--	1320	7
OH MARCH, COME RIGHT UP STAIRS WITH ME-- .	DEAR MARCH--COME IN--	1320	9
BUT MARCH, FORGIVE ME--AND	DEAR MARCH--COME IN--	1320	14
FIRST AT THE MARCH--COMPETING WITH THE WIND--	AFTER ALL BIRDS HAVE	1395	5
MARCH IS THE MONTH OF EXPECTATION.	MARCH IS THE MONTH OF	1404	1
WHAT RUSSET HALTS IN NATURE'S MARCH	THEIR BARRICADE AGAINST	1471	5
PRECISELY AS IN MARCH IS HEARD	THE ONES THAT	1690	3

	FIRST LINE	POEM	LINE
MASQUERADE			
WHEN TIME'S BRIEF MASQUERADE WAS DONE . .	"ARCTURUS" IS HIS OTHER	70	20
MASS			
IT'S UNOBTRUSIVE MASS.	FURTHER IN SUMMER THAN	1068	4
MASSACRE			
SOFT AS THE MASSACRE [MASSACRES] OF SUNS .	SOFT AS THE MASSACRE OF	1127	1
THAT MASSACRE OF AIR--	THEIR BARRICADE AGAINST	1471	10
ANOTHER MASSACRE BEFORE	'TIS SEASONS SINCE THE	1529	5
MASSACRES			
SOFT AS THE MASSACRE [MASSACRES] OF SUNS .	SOFT AS THE MASSACRE OF	1127	1
MAST			
ON BALL OF MAST IN BOSPORUS [FOREIGN PORT]--	THE DAY UNDRESSED--	716	15
MASTER			
MASTER, IT WAS I--	MUTE THY CORONATION--	151	8
REVERSES NATURE--MASTER--	SUNSET AT NIGHT--IS	415	3
SAVIOR [MASTER]--I'VE SEEN THE FACE--BEFORE!	A WIFE--AT DAYBREAK I	461	13
OH, MASTER, THIS IS MISERY--	WHY MAKE IT DOUBT--IT	462	13
MASTERED			
BUT HE IS MASTERED, NOW, ...	I DREADED THAT FIRST	348	2
MASTER'S			
SEXTON! MY MASTER'S SLEEPING HERE.	SEXTON! MY MASTER'S	96	1
AS ONE THAT BORE HER MASTER'S NAME--	THE FACE I CARRY WITH ME	336	15
I GUARD MY MASTER'S HEAD--	MY LIFE HAD STOOD--A	754	14
MASTIFF			
MORAL--WITH A MASTIFF	ABRAHAM TO KILL HIM	1317	11
MASTS			
RETRIMMED IT'S MASTS--REDECKED IT'S SAILS--	ADRIFT! A LITTLE BOAT	30	12
ACRES OF MASTS ARE STANDING	HOW THE OLD MOUNTAINS	291	V 19
MAT			
BY YOUR CHAIR--OR, ON THE MAT--	WHAT SHALL I DO--IT	186	9
WAS IT THE MAT--WINKED, ...	I KNOW SOME LONELY	289	21
UPON HER [ON HER RUSH] MAT--	THE SOUL SELECTS HER OWN	303	8
PATIENT--UPON THE STEPS [MAT]--UNTIL THEN--	JUST SO--JESUS--RAPS--	317	10
MATCH			
TO MATCH THE GRANDMAMA--	I KNOW SOME LONELY	289	29
AND LIGHTED WITH A MATCH--	REMORSE--IS MEMORY--	744	6
MATCH ME THE SILVER [CRYSTAL] RETICENCE-- .	THIS THAT WOULD GREET--	778	7
MATCH ME THE SOLID CALM--	THIS THAT WOULD GREET--	778	8
I TRIED TO MATCH IT--SEAM BY SEAM--	I FELT A CLEAVING IN MY	937	3
MATCHED			
NEVER A FELLOW MATCHED THIS TOPAZ--	I COULD BRING YOU JEWELS	697	9
CAN NEVER BE FITTED [MATCHED] AGAIN?	OF THE HEART THAT GOES	1098	4
MATE			
OF CONSCIOUSNESS, HER AWFUL MATE	OF CONSCIOUSNESS, HER	894	1
WAITS ANY INDURATED MATE	THAT ODD OLD MAN IS DEAD	1130	7
MATERIAL			
MATERIAL [CORPOREAL] PLACE--	ONE NEED NOT BE A	670	4
MATES			
THESE WERE THE MATES--	THROUGH LANE IT LAY--	9	15
MATHEMATICS			
IN BROKEN MATHEMATICS	AS BY THE DEAD WE LOVE	88	5
IS NOT AFFIRMED OF MATHEMATICS--	ONE CRUCIFIXION IS	553	3
FROM MATHEMATICS FURTHER OFF	IF I COULD TELL HOW GLAD	1668	7
MATINS			
VESPERS--ARE SWEETER THAN MATINS--SIGNOR-- .	I SHALL KEEP SINGING!	250	9
MATTER			
AND THERE, THE MATTER ENDS--	I READ MY SENTENCE--	412	14
NO MATTER--NOW--SWEET--	NO MATTER--NOW--SWEET--	704	1
A MATTER OF THE SKIES.	IT IS A LONESOME GLEE--	774	8
NO MATTER WHERE THE SAINTS ABIDE, ...	NO MATTER WHERE THE	1541	1
MATTERS			
IT MATTERS NOT THE BUSY WICK--	THE LAMP BURNS SURE--	233	3
ON SILVER MATTERS CHARMED A SNAKE	THE TREES LIKE TASSELS--	606	19
IN MATTERS RATIFIED?	I WORKED FOR CHAFF AND	1269	4
MATTRASS			
SOMEBODY FLINGS A MATTRASS OUT--	THERE'S BEEN A DEATH, IN	389	9
MATTRESS			
BE IT'S MATTRESS STRAIGHT--	AMPLE MAKE THIS BED--	829	5
MATURED			
CHILDREN--MATURED [GROWN UP]--ARE WISER--MOSTLY--	BETTER--THAN MUSIC! FOR	503	13
MATURER			
SUSPENSE--IS HIS MATURER SISTER--	WONDER--IS NOT PRECISELY	1331	5
MATURING			
A HOMELIER MATURING--	THERE ARE TWO RIPENINGS	332	5
MATURITY			
HE CHOSE--MATURITY--	HE GAVE AWAY HIS LIFE--	567	12
MATURITY OF FATE	NOT ALL DIE EARLY, DYING	990	2
MAUSOLEUM			
THE BEE--IN MAUSOLEUM LAID--	FORGET! THE LADY WITH	438	10
MAY			
MOULDERED THIS MANY MAY.	ONE SISTER HAVE I IN OUR	14	22
IN MAY--	ALL THESE MY BANNERS BE.	22	3
WHERE IS THE MAY--	ANSWER JULY--	386	8
NAY--SAID THE MAY--	ANSWER JULY--	386	10
THE SLEET--THAN MAY, NO THEE--	THE NIGHT WAS WIDE, AND	589	20
BESIDES THIS MAY	BESIDES THIS MAY	977	1
KEEP MAY!	BESIDES THIS MAY	977	10
CANDID--IN MAY--	PINK--SMALL--AND	1332	4
FOREVER--UNTIL MAY--	SUMMER HAS TWO	1422	10

	FIRST LINE	POEM	LINE
MAYBE			
MAYBE--"EDEN" A'NT SO LONESOME	WHAT IS--"PARADISE"--	215	17
MAYBE, WE SHOULD'NT MIND THEM--	I'VE NOTHING ELSE--TO	224	5
THEN--MAYBE, IT WOULD PUZZLE US	I'VE NOTHING ELSE--TO	224	7
MAYBE--THAT--WOULD AWAKEN--THEM!	PUT UP MY LUTE!	261	10
YOU'VE SEEN THE COLOR--MAYBE--	THE COLOR OF THE GRAVE	411	21
MAYEST			
THINE EYES ARE SADLY BLINDED, BUT YET THOU MAYEST SEE	AWAKE YE MUSES NINE,	1	33
THAN MAYEST THOU--	NO RACK CAN TORTURE ME--	384	12
MAYS			
THERE ARE TWO MAYS	THERE ARE TWO MAYS	1618	1
MAZARIN			
OR NOON--IN MAZARIN?	I FOUND THE WORDS TO	581	8
ME			
AWAKE YE MUSES NINE, SING ME A STRAIN DIVINE,	AWAKE YE MUSES NINE,	1	1
AND COME AWAY WITH ME,	"SIC TRANSIT GLORIA	3	18
MY COUNTRY BIDS ME GO;	"SIC TRANSIT GLORIA	3	26
IT WAS ANNOUNCED TO ME	"SIC TRANSIT GLORIA	3	30
MY COUNTRY CALLETH ME;	"SIC TRANSIT GLORIA	3	58
ALLOW ME, SIR, AT PARTING,	"SIC TRANSIT GLORIA	3	59
MELODY NEW FOR ME	I HAVE A BIRD IN SPRING	5	11
BRIGHT MELODY FOR ME	I HAVE A BIRD IN SPRING	5	29
AND THE EARTH [WORLD]--THEY TELL ME--	FREQUENTLY THE WOODS ARE	6	9
MY FIGURES FAIL TO TELL ME	THE FEET OF PEOPLE	7	17
COULD A SHREWD ADVISE ME	I NEVER TOLD THE BURIED	11	18
SHOULD A SHREWD BETRAY ME--	I NEVER TOLD THE BURIED	11	20
BUT BOTH BELONG TO ME.	ONE SISTER HAVE I IN OUR	14	4
I SAT ME DOWN TO SIGH.	I HAD A GUINEA GOLDEN--	23	8
TIME BROUGHT ME OTHER ROBINS--	I HAD A GUINEA GOLDEN--	23	13
ANNOUNCING ME IN OTHER DELLS--	THERE IS A MORN BY MEN	24	23
REMEMBERED BUT BY ME.	SHE SLEPT BENEATH A TREE	25	2
IT WAS NOT FOR ME--	MORNS LIKE THESE--WE	27	6
THE CRIER'S VOICE W'D [WOULD] TELL ME--	IF THOSE I LOVED WERE	29	2
THE DAISY WOULD IMPEL ME.	IF THOSE I LOVED WERE	29	6
PRAY GATHER ME--	SUMMER FOR THEE, GRANT I	31	7
AH--BUT REMEMBERING ME--	GARLANDS FOR QUEENS, MAY	34	4
WILL ARRIVE TO ME!	BEFORE THE ICE IS IN THE	37	8
ANSWER ME TO WEAR?	BEFORE THE ICE IS IN THE	37	16
IT DID NOT SURPRISE ME--	IT DID NOT SURPRISE ME--	39	1
HAD DEPARTED ME?	IT DID NOT SURPRISE ME--	39	12
DEATH DID NOT NOTICE ME.	I KEEP MY PLEDGE.	46	3
WHEN YOU HAVE DONE, PRAY TELL ME	HEART! WE WILL FORGET	47	5
LEST THAT SHOULD CONQUER ME.	I HAV'NT TOLD MY GARDEN	50	2
FOR SHOPS W'D STARE AT ME--	I HAV'NT TOLD MY GARDEN	50	6
EXCEPT [UNTIL] THOU BLESS ME"--STRANGER [SIGNOR]!	A LITTLE EAST OF JORDAN,	59	11
NOR CAN YOU TELL ME--	I CANT TELL YOU--BUT YOU	65	2
NOT FOR ME--TO PRATE ABOUT IT!	I CANT TELL YOU--BUT YOU	65	13
PEASANTS LIKE ME,	SO FROM THE MOULD	66	9
AND LAUGH AT ME--AND STARE--	"ARCTURUS" IS HIS OTHER	70	29
PRAY DO NOT ASK ME HOW!	GOING TO HEAVEN!	79	3
SAVE JUST A LITTLE PLACE FOR ME	GOING TO HEAVEN!	79	14
THE SMALLEST "ROBE" WILL FIT ME	GOING TO HEAVEN!	79	16
"THEY HAVE NOT CHOSEN ME," HE SAID,	"THEY HAVE NOT CHOSEN ME	85	1
NOR THIS BEHOOVETH ME.	SOME THINGS THAT FLY	89	6
MANY, WILL DOUBTLESS ASK ME,	SO BASHFUL WHEN I SPIED	91	11
THOU PUZZLEST ME!	MY FRIEND MUST BE A BIRD	92	7
PRAY LEAD ME TO HIS BED!	SEXTON! MY MASTER'S	96	2
THE RAINBOW NEVER TELLS ME	THE RAINBOW NEVER TELLS	97	1
WHAT CATO COULD'NT PROVE ME	THE RAINBOW NEVER TELLS	97	7
THE BEE IS NOT AFRAID OF ME.	THE BEE IS NOT AFRAID OF	111	1
RECEIVE ME CORDIALLY--	THE BEE IS NOT AFRAID OF	111	4
TO ELUDE ME SO!	GOOD NIGHT, BECAUSE WE	114	6
FATHER! THEY WONT TELL ME,	GOOD NIGHT, BECAUSE WE	114	7
OH LET ME IMMEDIATELY "FADE"!	IF THIS IS "FADING"	120	2
BURY ME, IN SUCH A SHROUD OF RED!	IF THIS IS "FADING"	120	4
WHICH SOLEMNIZES ME.	A SOMETHING IN A	122	3
FLUTTER TOO FAR FOR ME--	A SOMETHING IN A	122	12
"HOUSES"--SO THE WISE MEN TELL ME--	"HOUSES"--SO THE WISE	127	1
BRING ME THE SUNSET IN A CUP,	BRING ME THE SUNSET IN A	128	1
TELL ME HOW FAR THE MORNING LEAPS--	BRING ME THE SUNSET IN A	128	4
TELL ME WHAT TIME THE WEAVER SLEEPS	BRING ME THE SUNSET IN A	128	5
WRITE ME HOW MANY NOTES THERE BE	BRING ME THE SUNSET IN A	128	7
WHO'LL LET ME OUT SOME GALA DAY	BRING ME THE SUNSET IN A	128	22
GRANT ME, OH LORD, A SUNNY MIND--	BESIDES THE AUTUMN POETS	131	15
TO WHOM THIS W'D HAVE POINTED ME	I BRING AN UNACCUSTOMED	132	15
IF, HAPLY, ANY SAY TO ME	I BRING AN UNACCUSTOMED	132	20
"UNTO THE LITTLE, UNTO ME,"	I BRING AN UNACCUSTOMED	132	21
ROYALTY ENOUGH FOR ME	PIGMY SERAPHS--GONE	138	16
A WITCHCRAFT--YIELDETH ME--	THE MURMUR OF A BEE	155	2
IF ANY ASK ME WHY--	THE MURMUR OF A BEE	155	3
IF ANY ASK ME HOW--	THE MURMUR OF A BEE	155	13
ARTIST--WHO DREW ME SO--	THE MURMUR OF A BEE	155	14
YOU LOVE ME--YOU ARE SURE--	YOU LOVE ME--YOU ARE	156	1
IF YOU'LL JUST TELL ME SO--	YOU LOVE ME--YOU ARE	156	16
JUST GIRT ME FOR THE ONSET WITH ETERNITY,	JUST LOST, WHEN I WAS	160	3
BLUE SEA! WILT WELCOME ME?	MY RIVER RUNS TO THEE--	162	2
SAY--SEA--TAKE ME!	MY RIVER RUNS TO THEE--	162	7
AS THEN TRANSPORTED ME!	I MET A KING THIS	166	20

		FIRST LINE	POEM	LINE
ME	(CONTINUED)			
	AND MIGHT EXTINGUISH ME!	'TIS SO MUCH JOY! 'TIS	172	18
	BY ME! BUT WHO AM I,	A FUZZY FELLOW, WITHOUT	173	18
	WHO'LL APOLOGIZE FOR ME?	I'M THE LITTLE "HEART'S	176	8
	TEACH ME THE SKILL,	AH, NECROMANCY SWEET!	177	3
	WHAT IF THEY HEAR ME!	IF I COULD BRIBE THEM BY	179	13
	OH FIND IT--SIR--FOR ME!	I LOST A WORLD--THE	181	8
	YET--KNOW NOT WHAT WAS DONE TO ME	I'VE HEARD AN ORGAN TALK	183	7
	WOULD YOU UNTIE IT, WERE YOU ME--	WHAT SHALL I DO--IT	186	5
	HE'LL TELL ME!	WHAT SHALL I DO--IT	186	15
	MAKE ME A PICTURE OF THE SUN--	MAKE ME A PICTURE OF THE	188	1
	DRAW ME A ROBIN--ON A STEM--	MAKE ME A PICTURE OF THE	188	5
	SO HE LET ME LEAD HIM IN--	HE WAS WEAK, AND I WAS	190	2
	SO I LET HIM LEAD ME--HOME.	HE WAS WEAK, AND I WAS	190	4
	COULD'ST CREDIT ME? COULD'ST CREDIT ME?	POOR LITTLE HEART!	192	9
	COULD'ST CREDIT ME? COULD'ST CREDIT ME?	POOR LITTLE HEART!	192	9
	HE WILL TELL ME WHAT "PETER" PROMISED--	I SHALL KNOW WHY--WHEN	193	5
	THAT SCALDS ME NOW--THAT SCALDS ME NOW!	I SHALL KNOW WHY--WHEN	193	8
	THAT SCALDS ME NOW--THAT SCALDS ME NOW!	I SHALL KNOW WHY--WHEN	193	8
	WHERE THIS ATTENDETH ME [THEE]--	FOR THIS--ACCEPTED	195	8
	NOR TO DREAM--HE AND ME--	WE DONT CRY--TIM AND I,	196	9
	I--"TIM"--AND--ME!	WE DONT CRY--TIM AND I,	196	28
	HE PARDONED ME!	I STOLE THEM FROM A BEE	200	4
	"NO"--SAID PETER, 'TWAS'NT ME--	HE FORGOT--AND I--	203	6
	SHOULD REACH THE HEART THAT WANTED ME--	I SHOULD NOT DARE TO	205	4
	THEY "NOTICED" ME--THEY NOTICED ME--	I SHOULD NOT DARE TO	205	8
	THEY "NOTICED" ME--THEY NOTICED ME--	I SHOULD NOT DARE TO	205	8
	THAT THEY HAVE DONE EXPECTING ME--	THO' I GET HOME HOW LATE	207	4
	AND WHAT ITSELF, WILL SAY TO ME--	THO' I GET HOME HOW LATE	207	12
	IT PUZZLED ME TO KNOW--	THE ROSE DID CAPER ON	208	8
	RANSOMED FOLKS--WONT LAUGH AT ME--	WHAT IS--"PARADISE"--	215	16
	DOST THOU REMEMBER ME?	SAVIOR! I'VE NO ONE ELSE	217	4
	WILL SUIT ME JUST AS WELL--	I CAME TO BUY A SMILE--	223	4
	IN SIGHT OF ME--	SHOULD YOU BUT FAIL AT--	226	2
	AS SHOULD SOUND--TO ME--	TEACH HIM--WHEN HE MAKES	227	4
	GRANT ME--THAT DAY--THE ROYALTY--	THE COURT IS FAR AWAY--	235	11
	THAT YOU--SO LATE--"CONSIDER" ME--	I THINK JUST HOW MY	237	7
	I MIND ME THAT OF ANGUISH--SENT--	I THINK JUST HOW MY	237	9
	THAT--"HEAVEN" IS--TO ME!	"HEAVEN"--IS WHAT I	239	4
	HE--IS MORE THAN A FIRMAMENT--FROM ME--	AH, MOON--AND STAR!	240	16
	STOP JUST A MINUTE--LET ME THINK!	WHAT WOULD I GIVE TO SEE	247	4
	BROUGHT ME--FROM FIRMAMENTAL SEAS--	WHAT WOULD I GIVE TO SEE	247	19
	SIGN ME THE BOND!	WHAT WOULD I GIVE TO SEE	247	23
	WHY--DO THEY SHUT ME OUT OF HEAVEN?	WHY--DO THEY SHUT ME OUT	248	1
	WOULD'NT THE ANGELS TRY ME--	WHY--DO THEY SHUT ME OUT	248	5
	BIRDS WILL PASS ME	I SHALL KEEP SINGING!	250	2
	HOW MANY TIMES IT ACHE FOR ME--TODAY--CONFESS--	YOU SEE I CANNOT SEE--	253	3
	IT ASKED A CRUMB--OF ME.	"HOPE" IS THE THING WITH	254	12
	THAT ONCE--ON ME--THOSE JASPER GATES	IF I'M LOST--NOW--	256	4
	AND TOUCHED ME WITH THEIR FLEECES,	IF I'M LOST--NOW--	256	8
	TEACH ME THE STRAIN	PUT UP MY LUTE!	261	7
	ME, CHANGE! ME, ALTER!	ME, CHANGE! ME, ALTER!	268	1
	ME, CHANGE! ME, ALTER!	ME, CHANGE! ME, ALTER!	268	1
	ONE PEARL--TO ME--SO SIGNAL-- [OF SUCH PROPORTION]	ONE LIFE OF SO MUCH	270	5
	WOULD COST ME--JUST A LIFE!	ONE LIFE OF SO MUCH	270	8
	AND WEAR--IF GOD SHOULD COUNT ME FIT--	A SOLEMN THING--IT WAS--	271	3
	OF ME, HIMSELF WAS SHY--	THE ONLY GHOST I EVER	274	14
	DOUBT ME! MY DIM [FAINT] COMPANION!	DOUBT ME! MY DIM	275	1
	THE WHOLE OF ME--FOREVER--	DOUBT ME! MY DIM	275	5
	NOT FOR THE SORROW, DONE ME--	MANY A PHRASE HAS THE	276	13
	HUSH--ONLY TO ME!	MANY A PHRASE HAS THE	276	16
	SEE WHERE IT HURT ME--THAT'S ENOUGH--	WHAT IF I SAY I SHALL	277	5
	THEY CANNOT TAKE ME [US]--ANY MORE!	WHAT IF I SAY I SHALL	277	7
	UNMEANING--NOW--TO ME--	WHAT IF I SAY I SHALL	277	9
	PUT ME IN ON THE FIRMEST [TIGHTEST / HIGHEST] SIDE--	TIE THE STRINGS TO MY	279	5
	AND KISS THE HILLS, FOR ME, JUST ONCE--	TIE THE STRINGS TO MY	279	15
	PLEADS--"ME"?	THE DROP, THAT WRESTLES	284	9
	WINTER, WERE LIE--TO ME--	THE ROBIN'S MY CRITERION	285	14
	THE QUEEN, DISCERNS LIKE ME--	THE ROBIN'S MY CRITERION	285	16
	TO UNIVERSE, OR ME--	OF BRONZE--AND BLAZE--	290	7
	UNTO LIKE STORY--TROUBLE HAS ENTICED ME--	UNTO LIKE STORY--TROUBLE	295	1
	UNTO GUESSED CRESTS, MY MOANING FANCY, LEADS [LURES] ME,	UNTO LIKE STORY--TROUBLE	295	9
	LET ME NOT SHAME THEIR SUBLIME DEPORTMENTS--	UNTO LIKE STORY--TROUBLE	295	21
	OH, HAD YOU TOLD ME SO--	ONE YEAR AGO--JOTS WHAT?	296	15
	LET ME--CHOOSE!	ONE YEAR AGO--JOTS WHAT?	296	36
	THE [FOR] HOSTS--DO VISIT ME--	ALONE, I CANNOT BE--	298	2
	YOUR RICHES--TAUGHT ME--POVERTY.	YOUR RICHES--TAUGHT ME--	299	1
	I TENDERER, TURN ME TO.	FOR LARGEST WOMAN'S	309	6
	TOO RESCUED--FEAR TOO DIM TO ME	I SHOULD HAVE BEEN TOO	313	8
	AND HEAVEN--NOT ENOUGH FOR ME--	I SHOULD HAVE BEEN TOO	313	14
	IT WILL BE AMPLE TIME FOR--ME--	JUST SO--JESUS--RAPS--	317	9
	THERE'S NOT A CHARGE TO ME	OF ALL THE SOUNDS	321	2
	PERMITTED GODS [MEN], AND ME--	OF ALL THE SOUNDS	321	8
	ENTIRELY FOR ME--	THERE CAME A DAY AT	322	2
	HAD IT FOR ME A MORN--	AS IF I ASKED A COMMON	323	6
	AND SHATTER [FLOOD] ME WITH DAWN!	AS IF I ASKED A COMMON	323	8

		FIRST LINE	POEM	LINE
ME	(CONTINUED)			
	NO MAN INSTRUCTED ME--	I CANNOT DANCE UPON MY	326	2
	A GLEE POSSESSETH ME,	I CANNOT DANCE UPON MY	326	4
	THE HOUSE ENCORE ME SO--	I CANNOT DANCE UPON MY	326	16
	NOR ANY PLACARD BOAST ME--	I CANNOT DANCE UPON MY	326	19
	BUT WERE IT TOLD TO ME--TODAY--	BEFORE I GOT MY EYE PUT	327	5
	WOULD SPLIT, FOR SIZE OF ME--	BEFORE I GOT MY EYE PUT	327	8
	THE NEWS WOULD STRIKE ME DEAD--	BEFORE I GOT MY EYE PUT	327	17
	AND JUST SIPPED--ME--	ALL THE LETTERS I CAN	334	8
	THE FACE I CARRY WITH ME--LAST--	THE FACE I CARRY WITH ME	336	1
	AND BEG ME PUT IT ON--	THE FACE I CARRY WITH ME	336	12
	AND THEN--HE'LL TURN ME ROUND AND ROUND--	THE FACE I CARRY WITH ME	336	13
	IT ILL BECOMETH ME--	I TEND MY FLOWERS FOR	339	23
	WITH "ME, MISS, ME"--	MY REWARD FOR BEING, WAS	343	7
	WITH "ME, MISS, ME"--	MY REWARD FOR BEING, WAS	343	7
	HAD POWER TO MANGLE ME--	I DREADED THAT FIRST	348	8
	WOULD PIERCE ME WITH A FASHION	I DREADED THAT FIRST	348	11
	COULD STRETCH--TO LOOK AT ME--	I DREADED THAT FIRST	348	16
	WHAT WORD HAD THEY, FOR ME?	I DREADED THAT FIRST	348	20
	IN GENTLE DEFERENCE TO ME--	I DREADED THAT FIRST	348	23
	EACH ONE SALUTES ME, AS HE GOES,	I DREADED THAT FIRST	348	25
	YOU FOR YOU, AND I, FOR YOU AND ME	THEY LEAVE US WITH THE	350	10
	CONVICTION MIGHT, OF ME--	I FELT MY LIFE WITH BOTH	351	12
	ME--	'TIS OPPOSITES--ENTICE--	355	12
	TO ME--SURPASSED THE CROWN	THE DAY THAT I WAS	356	14
	BETWEEN THE BLISS--AND ME--	I GAINED IT SO--	359	4
	IT STRUCK ME--EVERY DAY--	IT STRUCK ME--EVERY DAY	362	1
	IT BURNED ME--IN THE NIGHT--	IT STRUCK ME--EVERY DAY	362	5
	TO PARADISE, WITH ME--	ALTHOUGH I PUT AWAY HIS	366	31
	YOU, SIR, TAUGHT FIRST--TO ME.	ALTHOUGH I PUT AWAY HIS	366	33
	NONE ON ME, BEND SUPERCILIOUS--	I'M SAYING EVERY DAY	373	6
	RANK--OVERTAKE ME--	I'M SAYING EVERY DAY	373	15
	ONE ACCOST ME--	I'M SAYING EVERY DAY	373	25
	MEET ME IN ARRAGON--	I'M SAYING EVERY DAY	373	28
	FROM POLAR CASKETS--FETCHED ME--	THE ANGLE OF A LANDSCAPE	375	17
	AND CRIED "GIVE ME"--	OF COURSE--I PRAYED--	376	5
	TO LEAVE ME IN THE ATOM'S TOMB--	OF COURSE--I PRAYED--	376	9
	NO RACK CAN TORTURE ME--	NO RACK CAN TORTURE ME--	384	1
	ANSWER THEE--ME--	ANSWER JULY--	386	9
	SHOW ME THE SNOW--	ANSWER JULY--	386	11
	SHOW ME THE BELLS--	ANSWER JULY--	386	12
	SHOW ME THE JAY!	ANSWER JULY--	386	13
	ENTERS--WITH A "YOU KNOW ME--SIR"?	IT'S COMING--THE	390	4
	'TWAS LOVE--NOT ME--	'TWAS LOVE--NOT ME--	394	1
	JUST HIM--NOT ME--	'TWAS LOVE--NOT ME--	394	4
	THEN--LOOK FOR ME. BE SURE YOU SAY--	A TONGUE--TO TELL HIM I	400	28
	AND SO TO MEND HER--GAVE ME WORK	THE FIRST DAY'S NIGHT	410	7
	CLASPED YET--TO HIM--AND ME--	NOT IN THIS WORLD TO SEE	418	6
	AND YET--MY PRIMER SUITS ME SO	NOT IN THIS WORLD TO SEE	418	7
	AND LEAVE ME--JUST MY A--B--C--	NOT IN THIS WORLD TO SEE	418	11
	DAY--GOT TIRED OF ME--	GOOD MORNING--MIDNIGHT--	425	3
	BUT MORN--DID'NT WANT ME--NOW--	GOOD MORNING--MIDNIGHT--	425	7
	I SUPPOSE IT WILL INTERRUPT ME SOME	IT DONT SOUND SO	426	10
	AND BANISH ME--	I'LL CLUTCH--AND CLUTCH	427	24
	THINE EYE IMPOSE ON ME--	THE MOON IS DISTANT FROM	429	12
	UNNESCESSARY--NOW TO ME--	IT WOULD NEVER BE COMMON	430	15
	ME--COME! MY DAZZLED FACE	ME--COME! MY DAZZLED	431	1
	ME--HEAR! MY FOREIGN EAR	ME--COME! MY DAZZLED	431	3
	THAT THEY--REMEMBER ME--	ME--COME! MY DAZZLED	431	8
	HE TOLD ME, DEATH WAS DEAD--	DO PEOPLE MOULDER	432	16
	PRESENTS ME WITH A SINGLE CURL	'TIS CUSTOMARY AS WE	440	7
	THAT NEVER WROTE TO ME--	THIS IS MY LETTER TO THE	441	2
	JUDGE TENDERLY--OF ME	THIS IS MY LETTER TO THE	441	8
	WERE INFINITE--TO ME--	I TIE MY HAT--I CREASE	443	4
	I WONDERED WHICH WOULD MISS ME, LEAST,	'TWAS JUST THIS TIME,	445	13
	THE ALTITUDE OF ME--	'TWAS JUST THIS TIME,	445	20
	THEMSELF, SHOULD COME TO ME--	'TWAS JUST THIS TIME,	445	24
	I [HE] SHOWED HER [ME] HIGHTS SHE [I] NEVER SAW--	I SHOWED HER HIGHTS SHE	446	1
	"WITH ME--" I [HE] SAID--WITH ME?	I SHOWED HER HIGHTS SHE	446	4
	"WITH ME--" I [HE] SAID--WITH ME?	I SHOWED HER HIGHTS SHE	446	4
	I [HE] SHOWED HER [ME] SECRETS--MORNING'S NEST--	I SHOWED HER HIGHTS SHE	446	5
	AND NOW--"WOULD'ST HAVE ME FOR A GUEST?"	I SHOWED HER HIGHTS SHE	446	7
	A LIGHT, FOR HER [ME], DID SOLEMN GLOW,	I SHOWED HER HIGHTS SHE	446	10
	IT WAS GIVEN TO ME BY THE GODS--	IT WAS GIVEN TO ME BY	454	1
	THE DIFFERENCE--MADE ME BOLD--	IT WAS GIVEN TO ME BY	454	16
	PROVE IT ME	SO WELL THAT I CAN LIVE	456	4
	SO LOOKED ITSELF--ON ME--	LIKE EYES THAT LOOKED ON	458	8
	SUNRISE--HAST THOU A FLAG FOR ME?	A WIFE--AT DAYBREAK I	461	2
	AND THEY NO MORE REMEMBER ME--	WHY MAKE IT DOUBT--IT	462	11
	NOR EVER TURN TO TELL ME WHY--	WHY MAKE IT DOUBT--IT	462	12
	NO WEDLOCK--GRANTED ME--	I LIVE WITH HIM--I SEE	463	8
	TAUGHT ME--BY TIME--THE LOWER WAY--	I LIVE WITH HIM--I SEE	463	13
	OF THIS--COULD MAN DEPRIVE ME--	THE POWER TO BE TRUE TO	464	5
	WHAT PORTION OF ME BE	I HEARD A FLY BUZZ--WHEN	465	10
	BETWEEN THE LIGHT--AND ME--	I HEARD A FLY BUZZ--WHEN	465	14
	WITH RUBIES--PELTETH ME--	'TIS LITTLE I--COULD	466	4
	CONTINUAL UPON ME--	'TIS LITTLE I--COULD	466	8
	THE DISTANCE WOULD NOT HAUNT ME SO--	EXCEPT THE HEAVEN HAD	472	3

	FIRST LINE	POEM	LINE
ME (CONTINUED)			
AFFLICTS ME WITH A DOUBLE LOSS--	EXCEPT THE HEAVEN HAD	472	7
'TIS LOST--AND LOST TO ME--	EXCEPT THE HEAVEN HAD	472	8
NO ONE TO TEACH ME THAT NEW GRACE--	I AM ASHAMED--I HIDE--	473	5
ME TO ADORN--HOW--TELL--	I AM ASHAMED--I HIDE--	473	7
TRINKET--TO MAKE ME BEAUTIFUL--	I AM ASHAMED--I HIDE--	473	8
FOR ME--MY SOUL--TO WEAR--	I AM ASHAMED--I HIDE--	473	12
BRING ME MY BEST PRIDE--	I AM ASHAMED--I HIDE--	473	23
GREAT SPIRIT--GIVE TO ME	I MEANT TO HAVE BUT	476	10
BUT LARGE ENOUGH--FOR ME--	I MEANT TO HAVE BUT	476	12
GRAVE SAINTS STOLE OUT TO LOOK AT ME--	I MEANT TO HAVE BUT	476	15
THE GRAVE WOULD HINDER ME--	I HAD NO TIME TO HATE--	478	3
BE LARGE ENOUGH FOR ME--	I HAD NO TIME TO HATE--	478	12
THE SUNRISE--SIR--COMPELLETH ME--	"WHY DO I LOVE" YOU, SIR	480	17
SHE FETCHES--SUCH AS ME	MY GARDEN--LIKE THE	484	5
LET ME THINK--I'M SURE	I WAS THE SLIGHTEST IN	486	8
THE RACKET SHAMED ME SO--	I WAS THE SLIGHTEST IN	486	13
SHOW ME DIVISION [COULD] CAN SPLIT OR PARE--	WHILE IT IS ALIVE	491	6
THE WORLD--STANDS--SOLEMNER--TO ME--	THE WORLD--STANDS--	493	1
WRUNG ME--WITH ANGUISH--	HE STRAINED MY FAITH--	497	9
DONT YOU KNOW--ME?	HE STRAINED MY FAITH--	497	16
WHY--SLAY--ME?	HE STRAINED MY FAITH--	497	V 16
AS HEAVEN [EDEN]--UNTO ME!	I ENVY SEAS, WHEREON HE	498	8
COULD NOT OBTAIN FOR ME--	I ENVY SEAS, WHEREON HE	498	16
DROP GABRIEL--AND ME--	I ENVY SEAS, WHEREON HE	498	24
HAST THOU NO ARM FOR ME?	AT LEAST--TO PRAY--IS	502	8
LET ME NOT SPILL [LOSE / WASTE]--IT'S SMALLEST CADENCE--	BETTER--THAN MUSIC! FOR	503	21
SO TELL ME WHO 'TIS LIKE--	YOU KNOW THAT PORTRAIT	504	2
CUT THEE AWAY FROM ME--	YOU KNOW THAT PORTRAIT	504	14
HE TOUCHED ME, SO I LIVE TO KNOW	HE TOUCHED ME, SO I LIVE	506	1
IT WAS A BOUNDLESS PLACE TO ME	HE TOUCHED ME, SO I LIVE	506	4
REMINDED ME, OF MINE--	IT WAS NOT DEATH, FOR I	510	12
IT GOADS ME, LIKE THE GOBLIN BEE--	IF YOU WERE COMING IN	511	19
TO UNIVERSE--AND ME?	NO CROWD THAT HAS	515	20
WITH HIM REMAIN--WHO UNTO ME--	HER SWEET WEIGHT ON MY	518	9
CAME OUT TO LOOK AT ME--	I STARTED EARLY--TOOK MY	520	4
PRESUMING ME TO BE A MOUSE--	I STARTED EARLY--TOOK MY	520	7
BUT NO MAN MOVED ME--TILL THE TIDE	I STARTED EARLY--TOOK MY	520	9
AND MADE AS HE WOULD EAT ME UP--	I STARTED EARLY--TOOK MY	520	13
AT ME--THE SEA WITHDREW--	I STARTED EARLY--TOOK MY	520	24
THE LOSS HAD BEEN TO ME	HAD I PRESUMED TO HOPE--	522	2
YOU--SWEET [SIR]--SHUT ME OUT--	SWEET--YOU FORGOT--BUT I	523	12
THE SKEPTIC--SHOWETH ME--	TO HEAR AN ORIOLE SING	526	14
PERHAPS HE--PITIED ME--	I TRIED TO THINK A	532	19
HE--TOO--COULD PITY ME--	I TRIED TO THINK A	532	V 19
NO NOTICE--WAS--TO ME--	TWO BUTTERFLIES WENT OUT	533	12
REPORT WAS NOT--TO ME--	TWO BUTTERFLIES WENT OUT	533	V 12
ME PROVE IT NOW--WHOEVER [WHATEVER] DOUBT	ME PROVE IT NOW--WHOEVER	537	1
ME STOP TO PROVE IT--NOW--	ME PROVE IT NOW--WHOEVER	537	2
'TIS TRUE--THEY SHUT ME IN THE COLD--	'TIS TRUE--THEY SHUT ME	538	1
OR ELSE--FORGIVE NOT ME--	'TIS TRUE--THEY SHUT ME	538	12
ELSE--SAVIOR--BANISH ME--	'TIS TRUE--THEY SHUT ME	538	V 12
OR WAS MYSELF [JUST MYSELF / ONLY ME / I]--TOO SMALL?	I TOOK MY POWER IN MY	540	8
KNOCK--RECOLLECT--TO ME--	I HAD NO CAUSE TO BE	542	8
AND WISHFULNESS IN ME AROSE--	I HAD NO CAUSE TO BE	542	11
CORRECTLY--YET TO ME	I MEASURE EVERY GRIEF I	561	34
WAS COMPETENT TO ME--	I COULD NOT PROVE THE	563	10
CREATION STOPPED [THE HEAVENS PAUSED]--FOR ME--	MY PERIOD HAD COME FOR	564	18
OF WATER--AND OF ME--	A DYING TIGER--MOANED	566	8
"HEAVEN" HAS DIFFERENT SIGNS--TO ME--	"HEAVEN" HAS DIFFERENT	575	1
BECAUSE THEY TOLD ME TO--	I PRAYED, AT FIRST, A	576	2
HOW PRAYER WOULD FEEL [SOUND]--TO ME--	I PRAYED, AT FIRST, A	576	4
THAT BAFFLED ME--	I PRAYED, AT FIRST, A	576	11
TO HOLD MY LIFE [THE LIGHT] FOR ME	I PRAYED, AT FIRST, A	576	17
IT TAKES ME ALL THE WHILE TO POISE--	I PRAYED, AT FIRST, A	576	20
IT SHALL BELONG TO ME--	IF I MAY HAVE IT, WHEN	577	4
HOW MIDNIGHT FELT, AT FIRST--TO ME--	IF I MAY HAVE IT, WHEN	577	15
AND SUNSHINE PINCHED ME--'TWAS SO COLD--	IF I MAY HAVE IT, WHEN	577	17
THAT THIS WAY--THOU COULD'ST NOTICE [SPEAK TO] ME--	IF I MAY HAVE IT, WHEN	577	21
FORGIVE ME, IF THE GRAVE COME [SEEM] SLOW--	IF I MAY HAVE IT, WHEN	577	26
FORGIVE ME, IF TO STROKE [TOUCH / GREET] THY FROST	IF I MAY HAVE IT, WHEN	577	28
THE PLENTY HURT ME--'TWAS SO NEW--	I HAD BEEN HUNGRY, ALL	579	13
AND THAT--DEFIES ME--	I FOUND THE WORDS TO	581	3
IT CEASED TO HURT ME, THOUGH SO SLOW	IT CEASED TO HURT ME,	584	1
AND NOT ENOUGH OF ME	EMPTY MY HEART, OF THEE	587	8
THEE--THEN--NO ME--	EMPTY MY HEART, OF THEE	587	12
CONVINCED MYSELF OF ME--	I CRIED AT PITY--NOT AT	588	4
CONVICTED ME--OF ME--	I CRIED AT PITY--NOT AT	588	V 4
CONVICTED ME--OF ME--	I CRIED AT PITY--NOT AT	588	V 4
AND SO AND SO--HAD BEEN TO US [ME],	I CRIED AT PITY--NOT AT	588	15
IT ALWAYS FELT TO ME--A WRONG	IT ALWAYS FELT TO ME--A	597	1
THREE TIMES--THE BILLOWS THREW [TOSSED] ME UP--	THREE TIMES--WE PARTED--	598	5
THEN CAUGHT ME--LIKE A BALL--	THREE TIMES--WE PARTED--	598	6
IT TROUBLED ME AS ONCE I WAS--	IT TROUBLED ME AS ONCE I	600	1

		FIRST LINE	POEM	LINE
ME	(CONTINUED)			
	LIFE SET ME LARGER--PROBLEMS--	IT TROUBLED ME AS ONCE I	600	9
	WHAT SORER--PUZZLED ME--	IT TROUBLED ME AS ONCE I	600	14
	AND TUMBLE--BLUE--ON ME--	IT TROUBLED ME AS ONCE I	600	16
	THEY--SOLD [THEN--SELL] IT UNTO ME	OF BRUSSELS--IT WAS NOT	602	4
	AS MUCH ABASHETH ME!	AFRAID! OF WHOM AM I	608	4
	THAT COMPREHENDETH ME	AFRAID! OF WHOM AM I	608	6
	AND LEAVE ME IN THE FLOOR--	I YEARS HAD BEEN FROM	609	20
	UPON ME--LIKE A CLAW--	IT WOULD HAVE STARVED A	612	5
	THEY SHUT ME UP IN PROSE--	THEY SHUT ME UP IN PROSE	613	1
	THEY PUT ME IN THE CLOSET--	THEY SHUT ME UP IN PROSE	613	3
	BECAUSE THEY LIKED ME "STILL"--	THEY SHUT ME UP IN PROSE	613	4
	HAD BEEN LEGIBLE--TO ME--	TO KNOW JUST HOW HE	622	15
	THEY CALLED ME TO THE WINDOW, FOR	THEY CALLED ME TO THE	628	1
	WHERE YOU HAD PUT ME DOWN--	OURSELVES WERE WED ONE	631	6
	THE DRUMS DONT FOLLOW ME--WITH TUNES--	MY PORTION IS DEFEAT--	639	4
	THAT SELF--WERE HELL TO ME--	I CANNOT LIVE WITH YOU--	640	44
	ME FROM MYSELF--TO BANISH--	ME FROM MYSELF--TO	642	1
	BUT SINCE MYSELF--ASSAULT ME--	ME FROM MYSELF--TO	642	5
	ME--OF ME?	ME FROM MYSELF--TO	642	12
	ME--OF ME?	ME FROM MYSELF--TO	642	12
	HE--COULD SUFFICE FOR ME--	I COULD SUFFICE FOR HIM,	643	2
	YOU LEFT ME--SIRE [SWEET]--TWO LEGACIES--	YOU LEFT ME--SIRE--TWO	644	1
	YOU LEFT ME BOUNDARIES OF PAIN--	YOU LEFT ME--SIRE--TWO	644	5
	YOUR CONSCIOUSNESS--AND ME--	YOU LEFT ME--SIRE--TWO	644	8
	COULD WIDEN--TILL TO ME	I THINK TO LIVE--MAY BE	646	6
	BEAR [HOLD] ME--	A LITTLE ROAD--NOT MADE	647	8
	SOME SHALL [SOME ONE] SUMMON ME--	PROMISE THIS--WHEN YOU	648	2
	CHRIST--OMITTED--ME--	PROMISE THIS--WHEN YOU	648	28
	ME FOR SHOWING	SO MUCH SUMMER	651	2
	AND LEAVES ME WITH THE HILLS.	THE NAME--OF IT--IS	656	V 12
	THAT FIRST DAY, WHEN YOU PRAISED ME, SWEET,	THAT FIRST DAY, WHEN YOU	659	1
	AND NO ONE VISIT ME	COULD I BUT RIDE	661	4
	TO GET AWAY FROM ME--	COULD I BUT RIDE	661	12
	FOR SUCH AN ONE--AS ME--	AGAIN--HIS VOICE IS AT	663	4
	HE NEVER SAW ME--IN THIS LIFE--	AGAIN--HIS VOICE IS AT	663	7
	NEITHER HE TO ME	CONSCIOUS AM I IN MY	679	10
	IS ENOUGH FOR ME--	'TWOULD EASE--A	682	10
	HER LEAST ATTENTION RAISE ON ME--	'TWOULD EASE--A	682	14
	THEIR GLORY--NOUGHT TO ME--	THEIR HIGHT IN HEAVEN	696	2
	TO ME--SHOWS INSECURE--	THEIR HIGHT IN HEAVEN	696	8
	THE WEALTH I HAD--CONTENTED ME--	THEIR HIGHT IN HEAVEN	696	9
	SUITS ME--MORE THAN THOSE--	I COULD BRING YOU JEWELS	697	8
	THAT--SUFFICETH ME--	LIFE--IS WHAT WE MAKE IT	698	8
	THE SECOND TIME TO ME--	A THOUGHT WENT UP MY	701	6
	IT JUST REMINDED ME--'TWAS ALL--	A THOUGHT WENT UP MY	701	11
	ME UPON?	NO MATTER--NOW--SWEET--	704	16
	HE KINDLY STOPPED FOR ME--	BECAUSE I COULD NOT STOP	712	2
	TO MEMORY--AND ME.	I MEANT TO FIND HER WHEN	718	12
	BEHIND ME--DIPS ETERNITY--	BEHIND ME--DIPS ETERNITY	721	1
	BEFORE ME--IMMORTALITY--	BEHIND ME--DIPS ETERNITY	721	2
	'TIS MIRACLE BEFORE ME--THEN--	BEHIND ME--DIPS ETERNITY	721	13
	SWEET MOUNTAINS--YE TELL ME NO LIE--	SWEET MOUNTAINS--YE TELL	722	1
	NEVER DENY ME--NEVER FLY--	SWEET MOUNTAINS--YE TELL	722	2
	TURN ON ME--WHEN I FAIL--OR FEIGN,	SWEET MOUNTAINS--YE TELL	722	4
	THO' GABRIEL--PRAISE ME--SIR--	WHERE THOU ART--THAT--IS	725	14
	PRECIOUS TO ME--SHE STILL SHALL BE--	PRECIOUS TO ME--SHE	727	1
	NEVER COULD--TO ME--	LET US PLAY YESTERDAY--	728	20
	AWAY FROM ME--	LET US PLAY YESTERDAY--	728	36
	AND SHOW ME TO MY FEARS--	IF HE WERE LIVING--DARE	734	8
	YOU TAUGHT ME WAITING WITH MYSELF--	YOU TAUGHT ME WAITING	740	1
	YOU TAUGHT ME FORTITUDE OF FATE--	YOU TAUGHT ME WAITING	740	3
	OF ME--IN CHRIST'S BRIGHT AUDIENCE [LATITUDE]	YOU TAUGHT ME WAITING	740	11
	A NEWS EXPRESS TO ME--	THE BIRDS REPORTED FROM	743	2
	AND TROUBLE [HARASS] ME--NO MORE--	THE BIRDS REPORTED FROM	743	8
	SHE SUFFERED ME, FOR I HAD MOURNED--	THE BIRDS REPORTED FROM	743	17
	I [SHE] NEVER QUESTIONED HER [ME]--	THE BIRDS REPORTED FROM	743	22
	SHOW ME THEM [GIVE THEM ME--]--SAID I--	AUTUMN--OVERLOOKED MY	748	4
	SHOW ME THEM [GIVE THEM ME--]--SAID I--	AUTUMN--OVERLOOKED MY	748	4
	FOR RESEMBLING [THAT--RESEMBLE] ME--	AUTUMN--OVERLOOKED MY	748	8
	MY SOUL--ACCUSED ME--AND I QUAILED--	MY SOUL--ACCUSED ME--AND	753	1
	ALL ELSE [THE WORLD] ACCUSED ME--AND I SMILED--	MY SOUL--ACCUSED ME--AND	753	3
	AND CARRIED ME AWAY--	MY LIFE HAD STOOD--A	754	4
	MOST SHE TOUCHED ME BY HER MUTENESS--	MOST SHE TOUCHED ME BY	760	1
	MOST SHE WON ME BY THE WAY	MOST SHE TOUCHED ME BY	760	2
	NOT UPON HER KNEE TO THANK ME	MOST SHE TOUCHED ME BY	760	9
	LEST FIRMAMENT [UNIVERSE / DEITY] SHOULD FAIL FOR ME--	MY FAITH IS LARGER THAN	766	15
	NOT A SLEET COULD BITE ME--	WHEN I HOPED, I	768	5
	HOPE IT WAS THAT KEPT ME WARM--	WHEN I HOPED, I	768	7
	ONLY ME--[STILL MYSELF-- / ME ALONE] WAS STILL--	WHEN I HOPED, I	768	16
	ONLY ME--[STILL MYSELF-- / ME ALONE] WAS STILL--	WHEN I HOPED, I	768	16
	'TIS SUMPTUOUS ENOUGH FOR ME--	DEPRIVED OF OTHER	773	7
	IF BLAME BE MY SIDE--FORFEIT ME--	IF BLAME BE MY SIDE--	775	1
	BUT DOOM ME NOT TO FORFEIT THEE--	IF BLAME BE MY SIDE--	775	2
	I FEAR ME THIS--IS LONELINESS--	THE LONELINESS ONE DARE	777	13
	MATCH ME THE SILVER [CRYSTAL] RETICENCE--	THIS THAT WOULD GREET--	778	7

		FIRST LINE	POEM	LINE
ME	(CONTINUED)			
	MATCH ME THE SOLID CALM--	THIS THAT WOULD GREET--	778	8
	THE GRAVE PRECEDED ME--	BEREAVED OF ALL, I WENT	784	4
	I ROSE--IT FOLLOWED ME--	BEREAVED OF ALL, I WENT	784	10
	THEY HAVE A LITTLE ODOR--THAT TO ME	THEY HAVE A LITTLE ODOR	785	1
	PROVE ME--MY HAZEL [SWIMMING] WITNESSES	JOY TO HAVE MERITED THE	788	11
	BUT JUST A CRUMB--TO ME--	GOD GAVE A LOAF TO EVERY	791	2
	WHAT NECKLACES [AFFLUENCE / LEGACY] COULD BE [FOR ME]--	A DROP FELL ON THE APPLE	794	8
	IT KEPT ME FROM A THIEF, I THINK,	I PLAY AT RICHES--TO	801	3
	I FEAR ME THIS CIRCUMFERENCE	TIME FEELS SO VAST THAT	802	3
	WHAT DAY BE DARK TO ME	SO SET IT'S SUN IN THEE	808	2
	AN EPICURE OF ME	THE LUXURY TO APPREHEND	815	4
	WOULD IT TEACH ME NOW?	THE LUXURY TO APPREHEND	815	V
	BETWEEN A FEW, AND ME--	AN HOUR IS A SEA	825	2
	PERHAPS YOU THINK ME STOOPING	PERHAPS YOU THINK ME	833	1
	YET BOTH SO WELL KNEW ME	NATURE AND GOD--I	835	2
	APOLOGY FOR ME.	APOLOGY FOR HER	852	4
	CAN HARASS ME NO MORE--	THIS CHASM, SWEET, UPON	858	20
	PRECISELY, AS TO YOU [ME].	LIGHT IS SUFFICIENT TO	862	8
	LIST EVEN UNTO ME.	BECAUSE THE BEE MAY	869	3
	SO WINGS BESTOW ON ME	BECAUSE THE BEE MAY	869	9
	THIS GAVE ME THAT PRECARIOUS GAIT	I STEPPED FROM PLANK TO	875	7
	I'VE NONE TO TELL ME TO BUT THEE	I'VE NONE TO TELL ME TO	881	1
	IF THINGS WERE OPPOSITE--AND ME	I'VE NONE TO TELL ME TO	881	7
	AND ME IT WERE--THAT EBBED FROM THEE	I'VE NONE TO TELL ME TO	881	8
	A NEEDLESS LIFE, IT SEEMED TO ME	OUR LITTLE KINSMEN--	885	5
	AS I OF HE, SO GOD OF ME	OUR LITTLE KINSMEN--	885	9
	THE EARTH HAS SEEMED TO ME A DRUM,	WHEN I HAVE SEEN THE SUN	888	7
	TO MAKE ME VISIBLE--	TO MY QUICK EAR THE	891	8
	ARE MOSTLY SO--TO ME.	WHO OCCUPIES THIS HOUSE?	892	32
	ARE FOREVER LOST TO ME	A CLOUD WITHDREW FROM	895	4
	IT HAD AVAILED ME NOW.	A CLOUD WITHDREW FROM	895	8
	NOT IF TO TALK WITH ME	WHAT DID THEY DO SINCE I	900	10
	NOT IF THE JUST SUSPECT ME	WHAT DID THEY DO SINCE I	900	13
	YOU, UNSUSPECTING, FEEL FOR ME [WEAR ME TOO]--	I HIDE MYSELF WITHIN MY	903	3
	YOU, UNSUSPECTING, FEEL FOR ME [WEAR ME TOO]--	I HIDE MYSELF WITHIN MY	903	3
	"THOU HAST NOT ME, NOR ME"--IT SAID,	HAD I NOT THIS, OR THIS,	904	5
	"THOU HAST NOT ME, NOR ME"--IT SAID,	HAD I NOT THIS, OR THIS,	904	5
	TO THEE--GRANT ME--	ONLY A SHRINE, BUT MINE	918	11
	WHEN IT PLUCKED ME?	IF IT HAD NO PENCIL	921	8
	BE OF ME--AFRAID.	STRUCK, WAS I, NOR YET	925	16
	MOST--I LOVE THE CAUSE THAT SLEW ME.	STRUCK, WAS I, NOR YET	925	17
	HOLDS A SUN ON ME--	STRUCK, WAS I, NOR YET	925	20
	ESTEEMED ME NEVER RUDE	MY BEST ACQUAINTANCES	932	4
	WHOSE MEMORY DROWNS ME, LIKE THE DIP	I LEARNED--AT LEAST--	944	7
	AFFLICTS ME--AS A SETTING SUN--	I LEARNED--AT LEAST--	944	30
	WOULD SEEM TO ME THE MORE THE WAY	OF TOLLING BELL I ASK	947	7
	DEPARTED [ENTRUSTED] ME!	THE CHEMICAL CONVICTION	954	8
	DROP A TUNE ON ME--	WHAT SHALL I DO WHEN THE	956	6
	WHAT WILL BECOME OF ME?	WHAT SHALL I DO WHEN THE	956	8
	THOUGH THINE ATTENTION STOP NOT ON ME	WERT THOU BUT ILL--THAT	961	3
	NOR THE LEAST SIGNAL, ME [MINE] ASSURE--	WERT THOU BUT ILL--THAT	961	4
	CONVICTED--SENTENCED--ERMINE--NOT TO ME	WERT THOU BUT ILL--THAT	961	10
	CONTENTETH ME--	WERT THOU BUT ILL--THAT	961	16
	"UNTO ME?" I DO NOT KNOW YOU--	"UNTO ME?" I DO NOT KNOW	964	1
	WAGONS--HAVE YOU--TO CONVEY ME?	"UNTO ME?" I DO NOT KNOW	964	5
	PROVE [ASK]--ME--SWEET--IF I REGRET IT--	ALL FORGOT FOR	966	15
	FOR THE LONG HINDRANCE--GRACE--TO ME--	FITTER TO SEE HIM, I MAY	968	2
	TO MAKE ME FAIREST OF THE EARTH--	FITTER TO SEE HIM, I MAY	968	5
	THAT HE'LL [HE] MISTAKE--AND ASK FOR ME	FITTER TO SEE HIM, I MAY	968	16
	OF ME--WHEN FIRST UNTO THE DOOR	FITTER TO SEE HIM, I MAY	968	17
	THE LOVE, THO, WILL ARRAY [INSTRUCT] ME RIGHT	FITTER TO SEE HIM, I MAY	968	21
	'TWAS AWKWARD, BUT IT FITTED ME--	'TWAS AWKWARD, BUT IT	973	1
	PASSED [WENT] INFINITE BY ME--	IT BLOOMED AND DROPT, A	978	20
	THE MISSING ALL, PREVENTED ME	THE MISSING ALL,	985	1
	I KNOW, AND THEY KNOW ME--	A NARROW FELLOW IN THE	986	18
	SO THEREFORE LET ME IN."	THE FINGERS OF THE LIGHT	1000	4
	SUPPORTS ME LIKE IMPERIAL DRAMS	THE STIMULUS, BEYOND THE	1001	3
	HOLD ME TILL THE OCTAVE'S RUN!	DYING AT MY MUSIC!	1003	3
	BIND ME--I STILL CAN SING--	BIND ME--I STILL CAN	1005	1
	IF A DISCOURAGEMENT WITHOLD ME--	UP LIFE'S HILL WITH MY	1010	3
	THE "BUSH" MAY YIELD ME	WHICH IS BEST? HEAVEN--	1012	7
	WERE IT BUT ME THAT GAINED THE HIGHT--	WERE IT BUT ME THAT	1015	1
	ASKED HIM HIS NAME--HE LISPED ME "TROTWOOD"--	TRUDGING TO EDEN,	1020	3
	AFFRONT TO ME	SO LARGE MY WILL	1024	7
	NOR MOUNTAIN HINDER ME	NOR MOUNTAIN HINDER ME	1029	1
	"GIVE OF THINE AN ACRE UNTO ME."	SAID DEATH TO PASSION	1033	2
	OR BETTER, BE WITH ME--	BEE! I'M EXPECTING YOU!	1035	11
	IS SORRY, SOME, FOR ME.	HERE, WHERE THE DAISIES	1037	4
	WHO WAS NOT ENEMY OF ME	HERE, WHERE THE DAISIES	1037	7
	NOR SEPARATE, HERSELF AND ME	HERE, WHERE THE DAISIES	1037	9
	PRESENT ME FROM SEPULCHRAL CREASE	HER LITTLE PARASOL TO	1038	7
	CAME ALL THE WAY FROM LIFE TO ME	I HEARD, AS IF I HAD NO	1039	3
	UNTIL A MIGHT DETECTED ME	I HEARD, AS IF I HAD NO	1039	11
	"OLD FRIEND, THOU KNOWEST [KNEWEST] ME,"	I HEARD, AS IF I HAD NO	1039	14
	HUELESS TO ME UNTIL THOU COME	SPRING COMES ON THE	1042	3
	WHO WROUGHT CARRARA IN ME	I'VE DROPPED MY BRAIN--	1046	13
	AND THEN HE BORE ME ON [HIGH]	IT WAS A QUIET WAY--	1053	5
	LATER THAN LIGHT THY CONSCIOUSNESS ACCOST ME	AIR HAS NO RESIDENCE, NO	1060	7

		FIRST LINE	POEM	LINE
ME	(CONTINUED)			
	GRACIOUS NOW TO ME AS ANY--	THREE WEEKS PASSED SINCE	1061	7
	ACUTE DEGREE--CONFERRED ON ME--	TITLE DIVINE--IS MINE!	1072	3
	EXPERIMENT TO ME	EXPERIMENT TO ME	1073	1
	TO SQUIRRELS AND TO ME	EXPERIMENT TO ME	1073	8
	A LETTER CHIEF TO ME	MYSELF CAN READ THE	1089	2
	MYSELF HAD EARNED IT--ME,	BECAUSE 'TWAS RICHES I	1093	2
	WOULD YOU--INSTEAD OF ME?	THEMSELF ARE ALL I HAVE	1094	5
	PROTECTION ASKED OF ME--	THESE STRANGERS, IN A	1096	2
	GIVE ME THE CORKLESS	BETWEEN THE FORM OF LIFE	1101	V
	WHAT HINDERED ME	THE BIRD DID PRANCE--THE	1107	V
	THAT ABSTINENCE OF MINE [ME] PRODUCE	I FIT FOR THEM--	1109	6
	ANOTHER HOUR TO ME	SOME WRETCHED CREATURE,	1111	4
	MY EARTHLY HOUR [HUMAN LIFE] TO ME	SOME WRETCHED CREATURE,	1111	V 4
	ATTEST [REMIT] ME THIS AND THIS--	THROUGH WHAT TRANSPORTS	1153	4
	ABBREVIATE ME THIS	THROUGH WHAT TRANSPORTS	1153	8
	HIM--TO REGALE--ME--ONLY--	HE IS ALIVE, THIS	1160	7
	COME UNTO ME ENACTED [ACCOMPLISHED] HOW	CONTAINED IN THIS SHORT	1165	V
	IF ANY STRIKE ME ON THE STREET	ALONE AND IN A	1167	17
	"REMEMBER ME" IMPLORED THE THIEF!	"REMEMBER ME" IMPLORED	1180	1
	LEAVE ME NOT EVER THERE ALONE	REMEMBRANCE HAS A	1182	V 7
	ANOTHER CLASS REMIND ME [REMINDS ME OF]	A LITTLE DOG THAT WAGS	1185	13
	ANOTHER CLASS REMIND ME [REMINDS ME OF]	A LITTLE DOG THAT WAGS	1185	13
	THE VOICE THAT STANDS FOR FLOODS TO ME	THE VOICE THAT STANDS	1189	1
	THAT WHAT IS SUM TO ME	THE VOICE THAT STANDS	1189	6
	TO WHERE THE STRONG ASSURE ME	BECAUSE MY BROOK IS	1200	7
	MENAGERIE TO ME	THE SHOW IS NOT THE SHOW	1206	3
	THE BROOK SAID "LET ME GROW"--	THE SEA SAID "COME" TO	1210	2
	WISDOM IS STALE--TO ME"	THE SEA SAID "COME" TO	1210	8
	EMPLOYED A FACT TO VISIT ME	I BET WITH EVERY WIND	1215	3
	SUIT [PLEASE] ME AT A VENTURE	FORTITUDE INCARNATE	1217	11
	CONCLUSION TURNED ON ME	MY TRIUMPH LASTED TILL	1227	6
	THAT CONSECRATED ME--	SOMEWHERE UPON THE	1231	4
	IT WOULD NOT WAIT FOR ME	MY HEART RAN SO TO THEE	1237	2
	THE STARS ARE OLD, THAT STOOD FOR ME--	THE STARS ARE OLD, THAT	1249	1
	SUPPLANTING ME AND YOU	DOMINION LASTS UNTIL	1257	8
	AND WHAT HAD THEY TO DO WITH US [ME]	WHO WERE "THE FATHER AND	1258	3
	WOULD DOUBTLESS SPECIFY--[ANSWER ME]	WHO WERE "THE FATHER AND	1258	12
	THE "LIFE THAT IS TO BE," TO ME,	BECAUSE THAT YOU ARE	1260	21
	HE MAY EXCHANGE [CONFER] WITH ME	BECAUSE THAT YOU ARE	1260	26
	WHO HAS INVITED ME WITH HIM TO DWELL;	I CANNOT SEE MY SOUL BUT	1262	3
	THAT COST ME MY HONEST HEART--	I SAW THAT THE FLAKE WAS	1267	4
	THE NEED [FACT / LIFE] IS NOT OF [FOR] ME--	I KNOW SUSPENSE--IT	1285	8
	RECOLLECT THE FACE OF ME	RECOLLECT THE FACE OF ME	1305	1
	GIVEN TO ME WITHOUT THE SUIT	FRIGID AND SWEET HER	1318	5
	WHO WAS SHE TO WITHOLD FROM ME	FRIGID AND SWEET HER	1318	7
	OH MARCH, COME RIGHT UP STAIRS WITH ME--	DEAR MARCH--COME IN--	1320	9
	BUT MARCH, FORGIVE ME--AND	DEAR MARCH--COME IN--	1320	14
	ALL THOSE HILLS YOU LEFT FOR ME TO HUE--	DEAR MARCH--COME IN--	1320	15
	AFRESH ANNIHILATING ME	I NEVER HEAR THAT ONE IS	1323	3
	THAT NATURE SENT TO ME	I SEND YOU A DECREPIT	1324	2
	IF SENTIMENT FOR ME [IT BE]	I SEND YOU A DECREPIT	1324	6
	LET ME NOT MAR THAT PERFECT DREAM	LET ME NOT MAR THAT	1335	1
	FOR BUTTERFLIES AND ME--	WHAT TENEMENTS OF CLOVER	1338	4
	THROWN OPEN WIDE TO ME--	I SUED THE NEWS--YET	1360	4
	DEDUCTING ME--	HIS MANSION IN THE POOL	1379	6
	THEY MIGHT NOT NEED ME--YET THEY MIGHT--	THEY MIGHT NOT NEED ME--	1391	1
	AT WHAT IS AWE [DREAD] TO ME.	WHAT MYSTERY PERVADES A	1400	12
	CONTINUE ME IN THIS!	TO OWN A SUSAN OF MY OWN	1401	4
	MY MAKER--LET ME BE	MY MAKER--LET ME BE	1403	1
	THAT TOLD THE TRUTH [NEWS] TO ME--	COULD MORTAL LIP DIVINE	1409	V
	SWEET NATURE HAS FOR ME	ONE JOY OF SO MUCH	1420	2
	ASCEND WITH ME THE EMINENCE [TABLE LAND]	SUCH ARE THE INLETS OF	1421	3
	WHAT USE HAS IT FOR ME--	HOW SOFT A CATERPILLAR	1448	8
	TRADITION BEAR WITH [SUFFER] ME	ONE OF THE ONES THAT	1466	26
	NOT ME--NOR YOU--	THE ROAD TO PARADISE IS	1491	8
	TO CRUMBLING MEN LIKE ME [THEE]	HOW FIRM ETERNITY MUST	1499	2
	I KNEW IT BLEW FOR ME--	I SAW THE WIND WITHIN	1502	2
	MORE THAN THE GRAVE IS CLOSED TO ME--	MORE THAN THE GRAVE IS	1503	1
	AND CATCH ME ERE [WHEN / AS] I DROP	THE PILE OF YEARS IS NOT	1507	8
	SOCIETY FOR ME MY MISERY	SOCIETY FOR ME MY MISERY	1534	1
	COME NOT TO PLAY WITH ME--	CANDOR--MY TEPID FRIEND	1537	2
	AND IF IT BE NOT ME	COME SHOW THY DURHAM	1542	4
	CONFIDE IN ME.	SWEET PIRATE OF THE	1546	6
	BUT OFT HAS SCANNED ME O'ER--	MY WARS ARE LAID AWAY IN	1549	4
	AND HESITATED ME BETWEEN	MY WARS ARE LAID AWAY IN	1549	5
	BUT CHOSE THE BEST--NEGLECTING ME--TILL	MY WARS ARE LAID AWAY IN	1549	7
	TWAS ALL [ALL WAS] DISTINCT TO ME--	LIVES HE IN ANY OTHER	1557	4
	PERMIT [ALLOW / BESTOW] ME THIS REPRIEVE	TRIED ALWAYS AND	1559	2
	REPAST TO ME	THE HEART HAS MANY DOORS	1567	6
	"COME UNTO ME" THE MOIETY	NO LADDER NEEDS THE BIRD	1574	7
	BENEFICENT, BELIEVE ME,	THE BAT IS DUN, WITH	1575	15
	"COME UNTO ME" THE MOIETY	TO HER DERIDED HOME	1586	11
	THIS ME--THAT WALKS AND WORKS--MUST DIE,	THIS ME--THAT WALKS AND	1588	1
	AND NO ONE SWAGGERS NOW BUT ME--	THE BOBOLINK IS GONE--	1591	2
	THAT SEND ME REELING IN [ON]--	A DRUNKARD CANNOT MEET A	1628	6
	SO GIVE ME BACK TO DEATH--	SO GIVE ME BACK TO DEATH	1632	1
	TALK NOT TO ME OF SUMMER TREES	TALK NOT TO ME OF SUMMER	1634	1
	TAKE ALL AWAY FROM ME, BUT LEAVE ME ECSTASY,	TAKE ALL AWAY FROM ME,	1640	1
	TAKE ALL AWAY FROM ME, BUT LEAVE ME ECSTASY,	TAKE ALL AWAY FROM ME,	1640	1

	FIRST LINE	POEM	LINE
ME (CONTINUED)			
ILL IT BECOMETH [IS IT BECOMING] ME TO DWELL SO WEALTHILY	TAKE ALL AWAY FROM ME,	1640	3
"RED SEA," INDEED! TALK NOT TO ME	"RED SEA," INDEED! TALK	1642	1
BEAUTY CROWDS ME TILL I DIE	BEAUTY CROWDS ME TILL I	1654	1
BEAUTY MERCY HAVE ON ME	BEAUTY CROWDS ME TILL I	1654	2
OF ME"?	IN WINTER IN MY ROOM	1670	25
HE FATHOMED ME--	IN WINTER IN MY ROOM	1670	27
I SET ME DOWN	IN WINTER IN MY ROOM	1670	38
THAT SHE FORGOT ME WAS THE LEAST	THAT SHE FORGOT ME WAS	1683	1
HE JOINS ME IN MY RAMBLE	THE BLUNDER IS IN	1684	5
DIVIDES ABODE WITH ME	THE BLUNDER IS IN	1684	6
ONE SIDE OF ME THE NUTS ARE RIPE	THE ONES THAT	1690	7
MAJESTIC IS TO ME BEYOND	THE OVERTAKELESSNESS OF	1691	3
OR HE INVITED ME.	HE WAS MY HOST--HE WAS	1721	4
THEY WEIGHED ME, DUST BY DUST--	I TOOK ONE DRAUGHT OF	1725	5
THEN HANDED ME MY BEING'S WORTH--	I TOOK ONE DRAUGHT OF	1725	7
THAT HAPPENS TO ME NOW.	IF ALL THE GRIEFS I AM	1726	8
WITHOUT A HINT FROM ME, ...	IF EVER THE LID GETS OFF	1727	4
A THIRD EVENT TO ME, ...	MY LIFE CLOSED TWICE	1732	4
PROHIBIT ME	OH, HONEY OF AN HOUR,	1734	3
MAKE ME BEARDED LIKE A MAN!	REARRANGE A "WIFE'S"	1737	4
NONE SUSPECT ME OF THE CROWN, ...	REARRANGE A "WIFE'S"	1737	14
GOOD-BYE--THE GOING UTTER ME--	SOME SAY GOODNIGHT--AT	1739	3
"COME HOME WITH ME, MY FRIEND;	THE WATERS CHASED HIM AS	1749	4
LET ME NOT THIRST WITH THIS HOCK AT MY LIP,	LET ME NOT THIRST WITH	1772	1
OF ELEGY TO ME.	THE EARTH HAS MANY KEYS.	1775	8
MEAD			
THIS MEEKEST FLOWER OF THE MEAD	A SCIENCE--SO THE SAVANS	100	8
MEADOW			
FLEES SO THE PHANTOM MEADOW	DISTRUSTFUL OF THE	20	9
KISSING HER [IT'S] BONNET TO THE MEADOW . .	BLAZING IN GOLD AND	228	7
HARKS FOR [DETECTS] THE MEADOW BIRD-- . .	THE DOOMED--REGARD THE	294	6
JOYFUL--FOR WHOM THE MEADOW BIRD	THE DOOMED--REGARD THE	294	11
NOT IN ALL THE MEADOW--	I'M SAYING EVERY DAY	373	24
AFTERWARD--IN THE MEADOW--	THROUGH THE DARK SOD--AS	392	5
IN THE MEADOW--WHEN THE WIND	BEAUTY--BE NOT CAUSED--	516	5
AS DOTH THE MEADOW BEE	COULD I BUT RIDE	661	2
FLICKERING TO ITSELF--IN THE MEADOW-- . .	I COULD BRING YOU JEWELS	697	7
THAN THE MEADOW MILD.	FAR FROM LOVE THE	1021	4
HOW NULLIFIED THE MEADOW--	THE WAY TO KNOW THE	1279	23
THE BOBOLINK IS GONE--THE ROWDY OF THE MEADOW--	THE BOBOLINK IS GONE--	1591	1
MEADOWS			
AND ALL THE MEADOWS WIDE--	IT'S ALL I HAVE TO BRING	26	4
WITHIN THE MEADOWS GO--	WITHIN MY REACH!	90	7
WHEN THE MEADOWS PARCHING LIE, ...	HAVE YOU GOT A BROOK IN	136	14
THAT BROOKS IN MEADOWS RUN!	TO LEARN THE TRANSPORT	167	4
THE MEADOWS--MINE--	BEFORE I GOT MY EYE PUT	327	9
SO LIKE THE MEADOWS--NOW--	PRECIOUS TO ME--SHE	727	5
THE BUSHES [ORCHARDS / MEADOWS]--SPANGLES FLUNG--	A DROP FELL ON THE APPLE	794	12
MEADOWS OF MAJESTY CONCEDES [IMPLIES] . .	MY COCOON TIGHTENS--	1099	7
THE MORN WAS UP--THE MEADOWS OUT	THE BIRD DID PRANCE--THE	1107	5
MEAGRE			
WANT--IS A MEAGRE ART	NONE CAN EXPERIENCE	771	5
HOW MEAGRE, WHAT AN EXILE--IS A LIE, . . .	A COUNTERFEIT--A PLATED	1453	6
MEAGRES			
AND BUT ONE SMILE--THAT MEAGRES [HUMBLES] BALMS--	ABOVE OBLIVION'S TIDE	1531	4
MEAL			
IN DOUBTFUL MEAL, IF IT BE POSSIBLE . . .	ONE YEAR AGO--JOTS WHAT?	296	10
MEALS			
A FULL FED ROSE ON MEALS OF TINT	A FULL FED ROSE ON MEALS	1154	1
MEAN			
IT'S VERY MEAN OF SCIENCE	"ARCTURUS" IS HIS OTHER	70	3
INVESTS SO MEAN A BROW!	WAIT TILL THE MAJESTY OF	171	2
IF TO BE "ELDER"--MEAN MOST PAIN-- . . .	ONE YEAR AGO--JOTS WHAT?	296	32
THE LINGERING--AND THE STAIN--I MEAN-- . .	THE ONE WHO COULD REPEAT	307	6
THE OUTER GRAVE--I MEAN--	THE COLOR OF THE GRAVE	411	2
THE OUTER GRAVE--I MEAN--	THE COLOR OF THE GRAVE	411	10
THE DUPLICATE--I MEAN--	THE COLOR OF THE GRAVE	411	18
IT MUST MEAN THAT--I'M SURE--	I KNOW WHERE WELLS GROW	460	16
UNWORTHY, THAT A THOUGHT SO MEAN	THE SOUL HAS BANDAGED	512	9
HOW MEAN--TO THOSE THAT SEE--	THE TREES LIKE TASSELS--	606	26
MEET--AND THE JUNCTION BE [MEAN] ETERNITY .	TO KNOW JUST HOW HE	622	26
AND CAESAR--MEAN--	THE CHILD'S FAITH IS NEW	637	12
FOR HIS MEAN SAKE TO LEAVE THE ROW . . .	THE HEAVEN VESTS FOR	694	11
THEY SPURN THE AIR, AS 'TWERE TOO MEAN . .	YOU'VE SEEN BALLOONS SET	700	7
"DID'ST THOU?" "THOU DID'ST NOT MEAN," TO SAY,	I CANNOT BUY IT--'TIS	840	11
A NUTRITION MEAN	AS THE STARVED MAELSTROM	872	12
MEAN OF FORCES--STAND BY HER WING, . . .	PATIENCE--HAS A QUIET	926	V
THE SKY IS LOW--THE CLOUDS ARE MEAN. . . .	THE SKY IS LOW--THE	1075	1
THE FACE THAT MAKES THE MORNING MEAN . . .	THE VOICE THAT STANDS	1189	3
OR FIND THE BANQUET MEAN--	WHO GOES TO DINE MUST	1223	2
MAKES THE [THIS] PRESENT [NEXT MOMENT] MEAN--	GLASS WAS THE STREET--IN	1498	8
MEAN A	IT CAME HIS TURN TO BEG	1500	V
WHEN HE WAS MEAN AND NEW	IN WINTER IN MY ROOM	1670	20
MEANER			
IF 'TWAS A MEANER SIZE--	THEIR HIGHT IN HEAVEN	696	10

	FIRST LINE	POEM	LINE
MEANEST			
AND JUST THE MEANEST [COMMON / FAINTEST] TUNES	I THINK I WAS ENCHANTED	593	12
MEANING			
IT'S MEANING [IMPORT] IS EXTINCT--	HOW HUMAN NATURE DOTES	1417	4
MEANINGS			
WHERE THE MEANINGS, ARE--	THERE'S A CERTAIN SLANT	258	8
FROM ORDINARY MEANINGS--	THIS WAS A POET--IT IS	448	3
MEANS			
BY NO MEANS!	"SOWN IN DISHONOR"!	62 V	7
DEFEAT MEANS NOTHING BUT DEFEAT,	'TIS SO MUCH JOY! 'TIS	172	11
"MORNING"--MEANS "MILKING"--TO THE FARMER--	"MORNING"--MEANS	300	1
MORNING MEANS JUST RISK [CHANCE]--TO THE LOVER--	"MORNING"--MEANS	300	4
BY MEANS OF IT--IN GOD'S EAR--	PRAYER IS THE LITTLE	437	5
DEFEAT--A SOMEWHAT SLOWER--[SOMETHING DUMBER] MEANS--	MY PORTION IS DEFEAT--	639	5
TO ASK WHAT TREASON MEANS.	WHEN THE ASTRONOMER	851	8
FOR LIFE--BE [IS / MEANS] LOVE--	WERT THOU BUT ILL--THAT	961	20
HOW MUCH THE PRESENT MOMENT MEANS	HOW MUCH THE PRESENT	1380	1
MEANS DOMINION	GLORY IS THAT BRIGHT	1660	3
MEANT			
EYES WERE NOT MEANT TO KNOW.	THE OUTER--FROM THE	451	16
I MEANT TO HAVE BUT MODEST NEEDS--	I MEANT TO HAVE BUT	476	1
"MYSELF" MEANT THEE--	EMPTY MY HEART, OF THEE	587	10
I MEANT TO FIND HER WHEN I CAME--	I MEANT TO FIND HER WHEN	718	1
I MEANT TO TELL HER HOW I LONGED	I MEANT TO FIND HER WHEN	718	5
WHEN THE CRY IS MEANT	TELL AS A MARKSMAN--WERE	1152	25
MEANT NOUGHT BUT GOING HOME--	'TWAS LATER WHEN THE	1276	4
MEANWHILE			
MEANWHILE, AT MANY CRADLES	WHOSE ARE THE LITTLE	142	17
MEANWHILE--HER WHEELING KING--	THE SUN--JUST TOUCHED	232	8
MEANWHILE HE IS SO NEAR	THE BLUNDER IS IN	1684	4
MEASURE			
HERE TO LIGHT MEASURE, MOVE THE FEET	THERE IS A MORN BY MEN	24	7
LIKE THAT OLD MEASURE IN THE BOUGHS--	OF ALL THE SOUNDS	321	3
TO TAKE THE MEASURE OF THE HOUSE--	THERE'S BEEN A DEATH, IN	389	19
TO MEASURE OUR ATTAINMENTS--	MYSELF WAS FORMED--A	488	5
I MEASURE EVERY GRIEF I MEET	I MEASURE EVERY GRIEF I	561	1
SO MEASURE WINE--	A TOAD, CAN DIE OF LIGHT	583	9
BUT A DEMURER CIRCUIT [MEASURE]--	A PRISON GETS TO BE A	652	15
. . . MEASURE]--	EXPECTATION--IS	807	7
THIS MIND, AND IT'S MEASURE--	THIS DUST, AND IT'S	936	5
TO MEASURE OFF ANOTHER DAY	APPARENTLY WITH NO	1624	7
MEASURELESS			
A MUSIC NUMEROUS AS SPACE [MEASURELESS AS NOON]--	THE BIRDS BEGUN AT FOUR	783	3
MEASURES			
AND MEASURES WITH THE CLOUDS	OF BEING IS A BIRD	653	6
IT MEASURES [PACES] LIKE THE SEA	THE HEART HAS NARROW	928	2
REPORTLESS MEASURES, TO THE EAR	REPORTLESS SUBJECTS, TO	1048	5
MEASURING			
KEPT MEASURING THE HOURS--	'TWAS LIKE A MAELSTROM,	414	11
ONE EARNS [GETS] BY MEASURING THE GRAVE--	MY FIRST WELL DAY--SINCE	574	27
THEN--MEASURING THE SUN--	MY FIRST WELL DAY--SINCE	574	28
AS IN IT'S GRAVE GO PLUMBING [MEASURING]	THE LONELINESS ONE DARE	777	3
JUST MEASURING UNCONSCIOUSNESS	EACH SECOND IS THE LAST	879	3
MEAT			
BUT MEAT WITHIN, IS REQUISITE	EXPERIMENT TO ME	1073	7
UPON A TASTELESS MEAT	SURPRISE IS LIKE A	1306	2
IF THAT IS [BE] FULL OF MEAT	THE MIND LIVES ON THE	1355	3
IT IS A FADED [PHANTOM] MEAT--	MINE ENEMY IS GROWING	1509	6
DIVESTED OF IT'S MEAT	ENDANGER IT, AND THE	1658	8
MECHANIC			
I PUSHED MECHANIC FEET--	FROM BLANK TO BLANK--	761	3
AND THIS CONFIDING [MECHANIC / SUBJUNCTIVE] STONE	SHE LAID HER DOCILE	1396	2
MECHANICAL			
THE FEET, MECHANICAL, GO ROUND--	AFTER GREAT PAIN, A	341	5
MECHANICALLY			
ABRUPT--MECHANICALLY--	THERE'S BEEN A DEATH, IN	389	8
MECHLIN			
WAS DRESSED IN MECHLIN--SO--	THE ONLY GHOST I EVER	274	2
OF MECHLIN--FRAMES--	I WENT TO HEAVEN--	374	10
A MANSE OF MECHLIN AND OF FLOSS [GLOSS / SUN]--	THE FAIREST HOME I EVER	1423	5
MEDDLE			
DID MEDDLE [TAMPER]--ONE BY ONE--	'TIS GOOD--THE LOOKING	660	6
BUT STATUTES DO NOT MEDDLE	THROUGH THOSE OLD	1753	7
MEDDLED			
CLIMBING TO REACH [WHO "MEDDLED" WITH] THE COSTLY HEARTS	CLIMBING TO REACH THE	1566	1
MEDICINE			
IT KNEW NO MEDICINE--	IT KNEW NO MEDICINE--	559	1
EVEN FOR DEATH, A FAIRY MEDICINE.	WOULD YOU LIKE SUMMER?	691	8
BUT MEDICINE POSTHUMOUS	IS HEAVEN A PHYSICIAN?	1270	3
MEDITATE			
THE LUXURY TO MEDITATE	THE LUXURY TO APPREHEND	815	9
MEDITATION			
A MEDITATION CHASTENS SPEECH	SUMMER BEGINS TO HAVE	1682	10

	FIRST LINE	POEM	LINE
MEDITATIVE			
A MEDITATIVE SPOT--	ON MY VOLCANO GROWS THE	1677	2
MEDITERRANEAN			
NOR MEDITERRANEAN--	THEY CALLED ME TO THE	,628	16
MEDITERRANEAN INTONATIONS--	I THINK THAT THE ROOT OF	1302	5
MEED			
WHO KNOW HIS MEED OF ALL.	SO LARGE MY WILL	1024	8
MEEK			
SHOW THEM THIS MEEK APPARRELED THING	DELAYED TILL SHE HAD	58	16
PRESENT OUR MEEK ESCUTSCHEON	ONE DIGNITY DELAYS FOR	98	15
SO--WONDERING--THRO' THE HOURS MEEK	I HAVE A KING, WHO DOES	103	2
MEEK AT WHOSE EVERLASTING FEET	IN LANDS I NEVER SAW--	124	5
OF A TINT SO LUSTROUS MEEK--	PIGMY SERAPHS--GONE	138	8
MEEK [LOW] MY VIVE LE ROI,	MUTE THY CORONATION--	151	2
SLEEP [LIE] THE MEEK MEMBERS OF THE RESURRECTION--	SAFE IN THEIR ALABASTER	216	4
IN MEEK ARRAY--DISPLAY YOU--	I'LL CLUTCH--AND CLUTCH	427	21
MEEK--LET IT BE--TOO PROUD--FOR PRIDE--	I AM ASHAMED--I HIDE--	473	26
THAT HEAVEN PERMIT SO MEEK [FAINT] AS HER--	SHE'S HAPPY, WITH A NEW	535	7
YOUR LOW [MEEK] EYES--DEMAND--	PROMISE THIS--WHEN YOU	648	8
MY LOW [ONE / MEEK / WAN] RENOWN	TO BE FORGOT BY THEE	1560	V 12
MEEKER			
THE MORNS ARE MEEKER THAN THEY WERE--	THE MORNS ARE MEEKER	12	1
MEEKEST			
THIS MEEKEST FLOWER OF THE MEAD	A SCIENCE--SO THE SAVANS	100	8
MEEKLY			
BUT MEEKLY RECOGNIZE	THE LADY FEEDS HER	941	4
MEET			
THEIR SPIRITS MEET TOGETHER, THEY MAKE THEM SOLEMN VOWS,	AWAKE YE MUSES NINE,	1	19
TO MISS--IF ONE SHALL MEET--	ALL THESE MY BANNERS BE.	22	9
SHALL MEET THE EYE OF TRAITOR	I HAD A GUINEA GOLDEN--	23	31
AND I MEET, COMING THRO' THE DEWS	A SOMETHING IN A	122	21
AT TWILIGHT SOFT TO MEET--	SHE BORE IT TILL THE	144	10
YET NOT IN ALL THE NESTS I MEET--	ALL OVERGROWN BY CUNNING	148	11
THE HILLS TO MEET HIM ROSE!	THE SUN KEPT STOOPING--	152	2
SO MUCH, THAT DID I MEET THE QUEEN--	YOUR RICHES--TAUGHT ME--	299	13
I DARED NOT MEET THE DAFFODILS--	I DREADED THAT FIRST	348	9
TO MEET AN ANTIQUE BOOK--	A PRECIOUS--MOULDERING	371	2
MEET ME IN ARRAGON--	I'M SAYING EVERY DAY	373	28
DRESSED TO MEET YOU--	TAKE YOUR HEAVEN FURTHER	388	11
MEET TRANQUILLY, AS FRIENDS--	I READ MY SENTENCE--	412	12
AND MEET THE ROAD--ERECT--	WE GROW ACCUSTOMED TO	419	8
MEET US--WITH A SMILE--	TAKING UP THE FAIR IDEAL	428	17
THE INSTANT THAT WE MEET--	I CROSS TILL I AM WEARY	550	21
I MEASURE EVERY GRIEF I MEET	I MEASURE EVERY GRIEF I	561	1
MEET--AND THE JUNCTION BE [MEAN] ETERNITY	TO KNOW JUST HOW HE	622	26
SO WE MUST MEET APART--	I CANNOT LIVE WITH YOU--	640	45
RIDING TO MEET THE EARL--	DROPPED INTO THE ETHER	665	8
JUST WE TWO--MEET--	WHERE THOU ART--THAT--IS	725	10
THESE--ADJUST--THAT RAN TO MEET US--	THESE--SAW VISIONS--	758	12
I SHALL MEET WITH CONVICTION I SOMEWHERE MET	BY MY WINDOW HAVE I FOR	797	20
THE ONLY ONE I MEET	THE ONLY NEWS I KNOW	827	7
THEY'LL MEET	BANISH AIR FROM AIR--	854	3
OUR UNDERMINING FEET TO MEET	ESCAPING BACKWARD TO	867	7
TILL HE MEET A MAN	AS THE STARVED MAELSTROM	872	6
AND WHOSE "I'LL MEET YOU" HESITATES	SUPERFLUOUS WERE THE SUN	999	7
I CANNOT MEET THE SPRING UNMOVED--	I CANNOT MEET THE SPRING	1051	1
BLOOM--IS RESULT--TO MEET A FLOWER	BLOOM--IS RESULT--TO	1058	1
IS EVERY ONE I MEET	EXPERIMENT TO ME	1073	2
ALL MEN MEET [PASS / HASTE] AS IF	AFTER THE SUN COMES OUT	1148	5
UNARMED IF ANY MEET HER	THE PAST IS SUCH A	1203	5
TO MEET [AT MEETING] SO ENABLED [LEARNED / RELIGIOUS / . . .	HE PREACHED UPON	1207	8
TO MEET IT--NAMELESS AS IT IS--	THE LAST OF SUMMER IS	1353	5
IN AWE AND INNOCENCE, WERE MEET.	WHOSE PINK CAREER MAY	1394	4
HAVE FELT [THOUGHT] IT MEET TO DIE--	HIS ORIENTAL HERESIES	1526	8
A DRUNKARD CANNOT MEET A CORK	A DRUNKARD CANNOT MEET A	1628	1
I MEET HIM WITH A START	HIS MIND OF MAN, A	1663	2
AND MOURNERS MEET IT GOING OUT	WITCHCRAFT HAS NOT A	1708	3
UNTIL WE MEET A SNAKE;	SWEET IS THE SWAMP WITH	1740	2
DOUBTLESS, HE THOUGHT IT MEET OF HIM	A TRAIN WENT THROUGH A	1761	7
MEETING			
DO IN MEETING GOD!	I CANT TELL YOU--BUT YOU	65	12
FAR SAFER, OF A MIDNIGHT MEETING	ONE NEED NOT BE A	670	5
OF MEETING THEM--AFRAID--	IF HE WERE LIVING--DARE	734	4
THE MEETING BANDS OF SMITTEN FACE	'TIS ANGUISH GRANDER	984	3
TO MEET [AT MEETING] SO ENABLED [LEARNED / RELIGIOUS / . . .	HE PREACHED UPON	1207	8
MEETING BY ACCIDENT,	MEETING BY ACCIDENT,	1548	1
THE PRESBYTERIAN BIRDS CAN NOW RESUME THE MEETING	THE BOBOLINK IS GONE--	1591	3
MEETS			
THE SUN--UPON A MORNING MEETS THEM--	FOUR TREES--UPON A	742	5
MEETST			
THE STARS THOU MEETST	GO THY GREAT WAY!	1638	2
MELLOW			
OF [WITH] MELLOW--MURMURING THREAD--	A FEATHER FROM THE	161	6
IN HUE--A MELLOW DUN--	OF BRUSSELS--IT WAS NOT	602	10
. . . PUNGENT / WINNING / MELLOW] TELLER--	THE BIBLE IS AN ANTIQUE	1545	13

	FIRST LINE	POEM	LINE
MELODY			
MELODY NEW FOR ME	I HAVE A BIRD IN SPRING	5	11
BRIGHT MELODY FOR ME	I HAVE A BIRD IN SPRING	5	29
A DATELESS--MELODY--	IT'S LIKE THE LIGHT--	297	4
THAT PHRASELESS MELODY--	OF ALL THE SOUNDS	321	4
BUBBLED A BETTER--MELODY--	BETTER--THAN MUSIC! FOR	503	10
WITH BOLTS OF MELODY!	I WOULD NOT PAINT--A	505	24
NAY--NATURE IS HARMONY [MELODY]--	"NATURE" IS WHAT WE SEE	668	8
IS METRE [POESY]--NAY--'TIS MELODY--	THEY HAVE A LITTLE ODOR	785	2
THE DEFINITION OF MELODY--IS--	BY MY WINDOW HAVE I FOR	797	15
IN FRANTIC MELODY!	HOW STILL THE BELLS IN	1008	4
STROKING THE MELODY--	TITLE DIVINE--IS MINE!	1072	13
OF CAUTIOUS MELODY.	AT HALF PAST THREE, A	1084	4
FORTITUDE--FLANKED [STANCHED] WITH MELODY.	AFTER ALL BIRDS HAVE	1395 V	8
WITH DIRKS OF MELODY	ONE JOY OF SO MUCH	1420	8
MAKES MOCKERY OF MELODY	TO SEE HER IS A PICTURE	1568 V	
BUT MEMORY LIKE MELODY	BLOSSOMS WILL RUN AWAY,	1578	3
ARE PALTRY MELODY	THE WORDS THE HAPPY SAY	1750	2
WHERE MELODY IS NOT	THE EARTH HAS MANY KEYS.	1775	2
MELT			
COULD WASTE [MELT] THE SNOW BEFORE THEIR GATE--	WHAT CARE THE DEAD, FOR	592	11
AND CITIES--OOZE [SLIP / SLIDE / MELT] AWAY--	A STILL--VOLCANO--LIFE--	601	12
MEMBER			
A MEMBER OF THE CLOUD.	HE PUT THE BELT AROUND	273	8
MEMBERS			
SLEEP [LIE] THE MEEK MEMBERS OF THE RESURRECTION--	SAFE IN THEIR ALABASTER	216	4
MEMBERS OF THE INVISIBLE,	HOW NOTELESS MEN, AND	282	5
MEMENTO			
AND OH "MEMENTO MORI"	"SIC TRANSIT GLORIA	3	7
MEMNON			
WOULD BUT THE "MEMNON" OF THE DESERT--	PUT UP MY LUTE!	261	6
MEMORIAL			
LOVE, BY MEMORIAL MOLD--	WATER, IS TAUGHT BY	135	5
A MEMORIAL CRUMB.	IF I SHOULD'NT BE ALIVE	182	4
REMOTEST [MEMORIAL] SCRUTINY--	THIS DUST, AND IT'S	936	12
MEMORIES			
HER MEMORIES [MEMORY] LIKE STRAINS--REVIEW [ENCHANT]--	LIKE SOME OLD FASHIONED	302	13
MEMORIES--OF PALM--	CIVILIZATION--SPURNS--	492	11
MEMORY			
THE MEMORY OF MY ASHES	"SIC TRANSIT GLORIA	3	65
HER MEMORIES [MEMORY] LIKE STRAINS--REVIEW [ENCHANT]--	LIKE SOME OLD FASHIONED	302	13
SO MEMORY CAN STEP	THERE IS A PAIN--SO	599	4
WHEN MEMORY WAS A BOY--	A PRISON GETS TO BE A	652	14
TO MEMORY--AND ME.	I MEANT TO FIND HER WHEN	718	12
REMORSE--IS MEMORY--AWAKE--	REMORSE--IS MEMORY--	744	1
MEMORY AND I--	WHEN I HOPED, I	768	24
REMAINED IN MEMORY--	BEREAVED OF ALL, I WENT	784	16
PART IN MEMORY.	ONE DAY IS THERE OF THE	814	4
IN AN HERMETIC MEMORY	A CLOUD WITHDREW FROM	895	7
QUESTION MEMORY!	THE FIRST DAY THAT I WAS	902	16
BUT, NO LID HAS MEMORY--	WHAT I SEE NOT, I BETTER	939	4
WHOSE MEMORY DROWNS ME, LIKE THE DIP	I LEARNED--AT LEAST--	944	7
AS NEAR AS MEMORY--	THE SNOW THAT NEVER	1133	16
DROPPED BY MEMORY--	AFTER A HUNDRED YEARS	1147	12
TODAY IN MEMORY LAIN	TO DISAPPEAR ENHANCES--	1209	6
TO FLEE FROM MEMORY	TO FLEE FROM MEMORY	1242	1
WHEN MEMORY IS FULL	WHEN MEMORY IS FULL	1266	1
ENTITLED "MEMORY"--	THAT SACRED CLOSET WHEN	1273	2
THAT [WHO] LODGED A NIGHT IN MEMORY--	NO PASSENGER WAS KNOWN	1406	2
REAL MEMORY, LIKE CEDAR FEET	YOU CANNOT MAKE	1508	7
SURPASSES MEMORY	TO BE FORGOT BY THEE	1560	2
BUT MEMORY LIKE MELODY	BLOSSOMS WILL RUN AWAY,	1578	3
THROUGH THOSE OLD GROUNDS OF MEMORY,	THROUGH THOSE OLD	1753	1
MEM'RY			
THE MEM'RY OF THE SUN	THE SYMPTOM OF THE GALE	1327	9
MEN			
THERE IS A MORN BY MEN UNSEEN--	THERE IS A MORN BY MEN	24	1
TAKEN FROM MEN--THIS MORNING--	TAKEN FROM MEN--THIS	53	1
CARRIED BY MEN TODAY--	TAKEN FROM MEN--THIS	53	2
GOOD EVENING, GENTLE FELLOW MEN!	IF THIS IS "FADING"	120	8
"HOUSES"--SO THE WISE MEN TELL ME--	"HOUSES"--SO THE WISE	127	1
WITH WHICH FLOWERS HUMBLE MEN!	FLOWERS--WELL--IF	137	4
OF VANISHED DAMES--AND MEN!	MUSICIANS WRESTLE	157	15
AS BLIND MEN LEARN THE SUN!	TO LEARN THE TRANSPORT	167	2
BY MEN, YCLEPT CATERPILLAR!	A FUZZY FELLOW, WITHOUT	173	17
AND APPALLING MEN--	I HAVE NEVER SEEN	175	8
WE MEN AND WOMEN DIE!	IT'S SUCH A LITTLE THING	189	4
HER PRETTY SPEECH--LIKE DRUNKEN MEN--	THE ROSE DID CAPER ON	208	3
THE SPLASHING MEN!	A BURDOCK--CLAWED MY	229	9
AND BAD MEN--"GO TO JAIL"--	YOU'RE RIGHT--"THE WAY	234	11
MEN DO NOT SHAM CONVULSION,	I LIKE A LOOK OF AGONY,	241	3
MEN, AND FEATS--	I'VE KNOWN A HEAVEN,	243	12
RAPT NEIGHBORHOODS OF MEN--	FOREVER AT HIS SIDE TO	246	14
AND THEY'LL WILT, LIKE MEN--	I CAN WADE GRIEF--	252	14
BRAVE NAMES OF MEN--	READ--SWEET--HOW OTHERS	260	12
HOW NOTELESS MEN, AND PLEIADS, STAND,	HOW NOTELESS MEN, AND	282	1

	FIRST LINE	POEM		LINE
MEN (CONTINUED)				
AND SO MEN COMPROMISE--	A MIEN TO MOVE A QUEEN--	283		24
AND MEN--TOO BRIGADIER--	A MIEN TO MOVE A QUEEN--	283	V	24
DISDAINING MEN, AND OXYGEN,	OF BRONZE--AND BLAZE--	290		12
AND THE ODD FLAMBEAU, NO MEN CARRY	HOW THE OLD MOUNTAINS	291		15
PERMITTED GODS [MEN], AND ME--	OF ALL THE SOUNDS	321		8
HIS FISTS, THE SIZE OF MEN--	THEY LEAVE US WITH THE	350		4
WHERE MEN MADE HAY--	FROM COCOON FORTH A	354		11
AND MEN THAT MADE THE HAY--	FROM COCOON FORTH A	354		23
DEFORMED MEN--PONDER GRACE--	'TIS OPPOSITES--ENTICE--	355		2
I'VE HEARD MEN SAY--	I'M SAYING EVERY DAY	373		11
A HURRYING HOME OF LITTLE MEN	A MURMUR IN THE TREES--	416		9
THROUGH WHICH MEN REACH	PRAYER IS THE LITTLE	437		2
WHEN MEN SO BRAVE--ARE DEAD--	IT FEELS A SHAME TO BE	444		2
I THINK THE MEN WHO DIE--	IT FEELS A SHAME TO BE	444		18
THAT HE--LOVED MEN--	SO WELL THAT I CAN LIVE	456		5
THE MEN OF IVORY--	THOSE FAIR--FICTITIOUS	499		4
TO GAIN IT, MEN HAVE BORNE	THIS WORLD IS NOT	501		10
AND THEY WERE MEN AND WOMEN--NOW,	ENDOW THE LIVING--WITH	521		3
THAT MEN, MUST SLAKE IN WILDERNESS--	I THINK THE HEMLOCK	525		5
WHEN MEN--AND BOYS--AND CARTS [LARKS]--AND JUNE,	I'M SORRY FOR THE DEAD--	529		19
WHAT HARM? MEN DIE--EXTERNALLY--	WE DREAM--IT IS GOOD WE	531		5
SOME [MEN] SEEK IN ART--THE ART OF PEACE--	THE MARTYR POETS--DID	544		8
IT FAILED FROM MEN--	IT KNEW NO LAPSE, NOR	560		4
THAT MEN CALL "PARADISE"--	"HEAVEN" HAS DIFFERENT	575		16
OF TOADS AND MEN--	A TOAD, CAN DIE OF LIGHT	583		3
GIVE SPICES--UNTO MEN--	WHAT CARE THE DEAD, FOR	592		24
FAR FEET OF FAILING MEN--	UNTO MY BOOKS--SO GOOD	604		10
MEN--TO ANTICIPATE [PROPITIATE]	THE CHILD'S FAITH IS NEW	637		23
AND MEN TOO STRAIGHT TO STOOP [BEND] AGAIN,	MY PORTION IS DEFEAT--	639		8
THE EMPEROR [MIGHTIEST] OF MEN--	THE SOUL THAT HATH A	674		8
NATURE--AND SOME MEN--	RESTS AT NIGHT	714		3
REST AT NOON--SOME MEN--	RESTS AT NIGHT	714		4
NOT AFTERWARD--BY MEN--	HAVE ANY LIKE MYSELF	736		24
AS WRECKED MEN--DEEM THEY SIGHT THE LAND--	I MANY TIMES THOUGHT	739		3
CULTIVATE--OF MEN	NEVER FOR SOCIETY	746		4
WISER MEN [ONE / EAR] MAY WEARY--	NEVER FOR SOCIETY	746		5
TOWARD ARTIFICE OF TIME--OR MEN--	MY SOUL--ACCUSED ME--AND	753		6
AS OTHER MEN, WERE COY [SHY] OF DEATH--	HE FOUGHT LIKE THOSE	759		7
TO HERSELF--AND MEN [MAN]--	MOST SHE TOUCHED ME BY	760		16
FLING SUDDENLY ON MEN--	THE COLOR OF A QUEEN, IS	776		6
OF DEITY [UNIVERSE] AND MEN--	THE BIRDS BEGUN AT FOUR	783		16
WHO GIANTS KNOW, WITH LESSER MEN	WHO GIANTS KNOW, WITH	796		1
OF ENVY, OR OF MEN--	SHE STAKED HER FEATHERS	798		4
APPOINTED UNTO MEN--	THIS CONSCIOUSNESS THAT	822		8
'TWERE NOT APPEASED OF MEN [MAN]	IT WAS A GRAVE, YET BORE	876		8
TOWARD MEN--	THE FIRST DAY THAT I WAS	902		12
WHEN BEST MEN DIE.	A SICKNESS OF THIS WORLD	1044		2
LIKE MEN AND WOMEN SHADOWS WALK	LIKE MEN AND WOMEN	1105		1
CONSUMES AND NO [WITHOUT] REPORT TO MEN	THE LARGEST FIRE EVER	1114		5
THE MERRIMENT [JEOPARDY] OF MEN	THESE ARE THE NIGHTS	1128		6
ALL MEN MEET [PASS / HASTE] AS IF	AFTER THE SUN COMES OUT	1148		5
MEN EXPRESS AS IF	AFTER THE SUN COMES OUT	1148	V	5
ALL MEN FOR HONOR HARDEST WORK	ALL MEN FOR HONOR	1193		1
THE TYRANNIES OF MEN	MY TRIUMPH LASTED TILL	1227		12
OF MEN ESCAPING	TO FLEE FROM MEMORY	1242		7
FOR HEROES THAN FOR MEN--	NOT ANY HIGHER STANDS	1256		2
LEST MEN SPECIFICAL ADORN	I CANNOT SEE MY SOUL BUT	1262		8
THIS IS THE GNAT THAT MANGLES MEN--	WONDER--IS NOT PRECISELY	1331		8
ABOVE THE HAUNTS OF MEN--	A WINGED SPARK DOTH SOAR	1468		6
TO CRUMBLING MEN LIKE ME [THEE]	HOW FIRM ETERNITY MUST	1499		2
THOUGH [BUT] JOYS--LIKE MEN--MAY SOMETIMES MAKE A JOURNEY--	THE THINGS THAT NEVER	1515		3
WRITTEN BY FADED [UNKNOWN] MEN	THE BIBLE IS AN ANTIQUE	1545		2
DESCRIED BY CUNNING MEN	OH FUTURE! THOU SECRETED	1631		6
AND I AM RICHER THEN THAN ALL MY FELLOW MEN--	TAKE ALL AWAY FROM ME,	1640		2
MEN EAT OF IT AND DIE	FAME IS A FICKLE FOOD	1659		10
THAT MEN ANEW EMBARK TO LIVE	IN SNOW THOU COMEST	1669		7
THE MEN THAT DAILY LIVE	DID LIFE'S PENURIOUS	1717		3
WHEN MEN AND WOMEN HEAR	HOW DARE THE ROBINS SING	1724		2
THAT MEN ARE SO OPPRESSED?	IS IMMORTALITY A BANE	1728		2
TO SAY GOOD-BY TO MEN.	A TRAIN WENT THROUGH A	1761		8
MENACE				
HE THREW A MENACE AT THE EARTH--	THE WIND BEGUN TO KNEAD	824	V	3
A MENACE AT THE SKY.	THE WIND BEGUN TO KNEAD	824	V	4
NO ASSAULT, NOR ANY MENACE	DEATH'S WAYLAYING NOT	1296		5
MENACED				
THAT MENACED NOT TO SLAY US,	OF DEATH I TRY TO THINK	1558		4
MENACES				
BY MENACES OF AMETHYST	SUNSET THAT SCREENS,	1609		3
MENACING				
MENACING THE TREE,	DEATH IS LIKE THE INSECT	1716		2
MENAGERIE				
MY SPLENDORS, ARE MENAGERIE--	OF BRONZE--AND BLAZE--	290		14
MENAGERIE TO ME	THE SHOW IS NOT THE SHOW	1206		3
MEND				
AND SO TO MEND HER--GAVE ME WORK	THE FIRST DAY'S NIGHT	410		7
MAKE--A DIADEM--AND MEND MY OLD ONE--	I'LL CLUTCH--AND CLUTCH	427		11
TO MEND EACH TATTERED FAITH	TO MEND EACH TATTERED	1442		1

	FIRST LINE	POEM	LINE
MEND (CONTINUED)			
BUT DEVILS CANNOT MEND--	THE DEVIL--HAD HE	1479	4
MENDED			
TRANSFIGURED--MENDED--	TAKING UP THE FAIR IDEAL	428	16
NOT MENDED BY MORTALITY	THE HEALED HEART SHOWS	1440	3
MENTION			
AN ANGUISH AT THE MENTION	A THROE UPON THE	71	5
SUCH [SOME] SPIRIT MAKES [TELL] HER PERPETUAL MENTION,	UNTO LIKE STORY--TROUBLE	295	13
I MENTION--EASY--HERE--	I CANNOT DANCE UPON MY	326	18
'TWAS MORE--I CANNOT MENTION--	THE TREES LIKE TASSELS--	606	25
NOT A MENTION, WHOSE SMALL PEBBLE	ONE DAY IS THERE OF THE	814	13
I MENTION IT TO YOU,	THIS CHASM, SWEET, UPON	858	2
GRATITUDE--IS NOT THE MENTION	GRATITUDE--IS NOT THE	989	1
AND MENTION WHAT WE SAW.	DEW--IS THE FRESHET IN	1097	8
AND MENTION TO MY HORSES	I KNOW SUSPENSE--IT	1285	7
BECAUSE "GOD TOOK HIM" MENTION--[TELL US]	"WAS NOT" WAS ALL THE	1342	7
MENTIONED			
THEIR COMING, MENTIONED--BE--	TWO BUTTERFLIES WENT OUT	533	8
SHE MENTIONED, AND FORGOT--	THE LAST NIGHT THAT SHE	1100	21
MENTIONED I THIS TO THEE--	MY HEART RAN SO TO THEE	1237	10
THOUGH FAVORABLY MENTIONED	THE BUTTERFLY OBTAINS	1685	3
MERCHANT			
BUT TILL THE MERCHANT BUY--	I GAVE MYSELF TO HIM--	580	10
THE MIGHTY MERCHANT SNEERED [SMILED]--	I ASKED NO OTHER THING--	621	4
IN THE PARCEL--BE THE MERCHANT	PUBLICATION--IS THE	709	13
THE MERCHANT OF THE PICTURESQUE	THE MERCHANT OF THE	1131	1
MERCHANTMAN			
BY FRIGATE, OR BY MERCHANTMAN--	TWO BUTTERFLIES WENT OUT	533	11
MERCHANTMEN			
MERCHANTMEN--POISE UPON HORIZONS--	THIS--IS THE LAND--THE	266	8
MERCIFUL			
A MERCIFUL MIRAGE	A DOUBT IF IT BE US	859	6
A MERCIFUL [HAZARDOUS] MISTAKE	DEATH WARRANTS ARE	1375	3
MERCURY			
AND THEN HE SULKED IN MERCURY	THE SUN RETIRED TO A	1693	3
MERCURY'S			
OR MERCURY'S AFFAIR--	NATURE AND GOD--I	835	8
MERCY			
THAT "GOD HAVE MERCY" ON THE SOUL	I READ MY SENTENCE--	412	7
MERCY [POWER] OF THE ALMIGHTY BEGGING [ASKING]--	TELL AS A MARKSMAN--WERE	1152	22
WHEN SUPPLICATING MERCY	THE BOBOLINK IS GONE--	1591	10
BEAUTY MERCY HAVE ON ME	BEAUTY CROWDS ME TILL I	1654	2
MERCY'S			
AND LEAVE FOR THY SWEET MERCY'S [PATIENCE'] SAKE	SOME WRETCHED CREATURE,	1111	3
MERE			
AND PRAISE AS MERE AS BLAME--	DEAR MARCH--COME IN--	1320	26
MERELY			
JESUS MERELY "LOOKED" AT PETER--	HE FORGOT--AND I--	203	7
LOVE [FAITH] IS LIKE LIFE--MERELY [ONLY THE] LONGER	WHILE IT IS ALIVE	491	7
BUT NEARER [CLOSER / FURTHER / SIMPLY / MERELY] TO ADORE	BECAUSE HE LOVES HER	1229	10
THAT ONLY [MERELY] LASTS AN HOUR	IN THIS SHORT LIFE	1287	2
MERELY FLAKE OR PETAL	"LETHE" IN MY FLOWER,	1730	5
MEREST			
THE MEREST GREEK COULD THAT.	TOO SCANTY 'TWAS TO DIE	1013	2
MERIDIAN			
AT THE MERIDIAN?	I SEE THEE BETTER--IN	611	16
MIDSUMMER [MERIDIAN]--IN THE MIND--	I THINK TO LIVE--MAY BE	646	18
TO THE MERIDIAN--	BLOOM--IS RESULT--TO	1058	8
MERINO			
NOT MERINO SHAWL--	WHEN I HOPED, I	768	8
MERIT			
WHAT MERIT HAD THE GOAL--	I CROSS TILL I AM WEARY	550	14
HIS MERIT--ALL MY FEAR--	MY WORTHINESS IS ALL MY	751	2
TO MERIT THE RELEASE--	JOY TO HAVE MERITED THE	788	2
WHAT MERIT HAVE THE TUNE	THE BIRD MUST SING TO	880	2
FOR MERIT OF RETURN--	'TWAS AWKWARD, BUT IT	973	6
THIS MERIT HATH THE WORST--	THIS MERIT HATH THE	979	1
WITH SUPERSTITIOUS VALUE [MERIT / MOMENT]	TO DISAPPEAR ENHANCES--	1209	7
THOUGH HIS SURPASSING MERIT	THE SPIDER AS AN ARTIST	1275	3
THAN MERIT THE ETHEREAL SCORN	HER SPIRIT ROSE TO SUCH	1486	5
MERITED			
JOY TO HAVE MERITED THE PAIN--	JOY TO HAVE MERITED THE	788	1
MERMAIDS			
THE MERMAIDS IN THE BASEMENT	I STARTED EARLY--TOOK MY	520	3
MERRIER			
IF MERRY, HE IS MERRIER--	THE SUN IS GAY OR STARK	878	3
MERRIMENT			
WITH MERRIMENT--	A MIEN TO MOVE A QUEEN--	283	15
BUT THIS ONE, WEARS IT'S MERRIMENT	A HAPPY LIP--BREAKS	353	5
THE MERRIMENT [JEOPARDY] OF MEN	THESE ARE THE NIGHTS	1128	6
MERRY			
AND THEY MAKE MERRY WEDDING, WHOSE GUESTS ARE HUNDRED LEAVES;	AWAKE YE MUSES NINE,	1	14
EARTH IS A MERRY DAMSEL, AND HEAVEN A KNIGHT SO TRUE,	AWAKE YE MUSES NINE,	1	23

	FIRST LINE	POEM	LINE
MERRY (CONTINUED)			
AND IF TO MISS, WERE MERRY, ...	IF RECOLLECTING WERE	33	5
MERRY THAT IT IS MORN--	AS CHILDREN BID THE	133	6
I CANNOT VOUCH THE MERRY DUST	OF ALL THE SOUNDS	321	17
HER MERRY ARMS, HALF DROPT--	SHE LAY AS IF AT PLAY	369	5
MERRY, AND NOUGHT, AND GAY, AND NUMB-- . .	OF COURSE--I PRAYED--	376	10
IF MERRY, HE IS MERRIER--	THE SUN IS GAY OR STARK	878	3
FILLED WAS THE AIR WITH MERRY VENTURE . .	GLASS WAS THE STREET--IN	1498	3
THE SEA COMES LAST--STEP MERRY FEET	I DID NOT REACH THEE	1664	14
MESH			
BUT EVERY MESH--A CITADEL--	I HAD NOT MINDED--WALLS	398	15
BUT PEERS BEYOND HER MESH--	A CHARM INVESTS A FACE	421	5
MESMERIC			
MESMERIC FINGERS SOFTLY TOUCH	BESIDES THE AUTUMN POETS	131	11
MESSAGE			
ENLARGE MY MESSAGE--IF TOO VAST	A TONGUE--TO TELL HIM I	400	16
MY MESSAGE--MUST BE TOLD--	A TONGUE--TO TELL HIM I	400	21
HER MESSAGE IS COMMITTED	THIS IS MY LETTER TO THE	441	5
NO MESSAGE, BUT A SIGH--	NO NOTICE GAVE SHE, BUT	804	2
"GO TELL IT"--WHAT A MESSAGE--	"GO TELL IT"--WHAT A	1554	1
MESSENGER			
MESSENGER--	OF PARADISE' EXISTENCE	1411	6
THE MESSENGER ENAMORED TOO, ...	WE SEND THE WAVE TO FIND	1604	3
MESSENGERS			
WAGGONS LIKE MESSENGERS HURRY ABOUT . . .	AFTER THE SUN COMES OUT	1148	3
MET			
THROUGH FAITH IN ONE HE MET NOT, ...	COULD LIVE--DID LIVE--	43	4
WHETHER SHE MET WITH GALES--	WHETHER MY BARK WENT	52	2
MET BY THE GODS WITH BANNERS--	TAKEN FROM MEN--THIS	53	3
I MET A KING THIS AFTERNOON!	I MET A KING THIS	166	1
I MET ONE--FORGOT MY SCHOOLMATES--	GOD PERMITS INDUSTRIOUS	231	3
WHEN THAT YOU MET IT WITH BEFORE--	THE COLOR OF THE GRAVE	411	23
"HOMESICK"? MANY MET IT--	IT IS DEAD--FIND IT--	417	7
TO EVERY CREATURE--THAT I MET--	IT WOULD NEVER BE COMMON	430	19
AND SO, AS KINSMEN, MET A NIGHT--	I DIED FOR BEAUTY--BUT	449	9
BUT--ISHMAEL--SINCE WE MET--'TIS LONG-- . .	YOU KNOW THAT PORTRAIT	504	7
UNTIL WE MET THE SOLID TOWN--	I STARTED EARLY--TOOK MY	520	21
IF MET IN ETHER SEA	TWO BUTTERFLIES WENT OUT	533	10
ON EVERY SHOULDER THAT SHE MET [SHE COULD REACH]--	MY FIRST WELL DAY--SINCE	574	21
THAT OFTEN AS A CLOUD IT MET--	THE NIGHT WAS WIDE, AND	589	3
I MET [GAVE] HIM--	I ROSE--BECAUSE HE SANK	616	10
THESE FLESHLESS LOVERS MET--	'TWAS A LONG PARTING--	625	5
AND NEXT--I MET HER ON A CLOUD--	I WATCHED THE MOON	629	33
I'VE MET THE THING BEFORE--	A THOUGHT WENT UP MY	701	10
I SHALL MEET WITH CONVICTION I SOMEWHERE MET	BY MY WINDOW HAVE I FOR	797	20
AND MET THE GAZE--DIRECT--	NO NOTICE GAVE SHE, BUT	804	12
ROBBED--WAS I--INTACT TO [YET MET NO] BANDIT--	STRUCK, WAS I, NOR YET	925	9
AS ONE MET SUDDEN [ENCOUNTERED] GENTLEFOLK .	IT IS AN HONORABLE	946	3
WE MET AS SPARKS--DIVERGING FLINTS	WE MET AS SPARKS--	958	1
YOU MAY HAVE MET HIM--DID YOU NOT	A NARROW FELLOW IN THE	986	3
BUT NEVER MET THIS FELLOW	A NARROW FELLOW IN THE	986	21
I MET SOMEBODY'S LITTLE BOY	TRUDGING TO EDEN,	1020	2
WOULD IT COMFORT--TO KNOW I MET HIM-- . . .	TRUDGING TO EDEN,	1020	5
AND MET [UNTO] ETERNITY	I HEARD, AS IF I HAD NO	1039	16
IF MET, TOO RAPID PASSED, ...	THE FROST WAS NEVER SEEN	1202	2
THE MOST TRIUMPHANT BIRD I EVER KNEW OR MET	THE MOST TRIUMPHANT BIRD	1265	1
UNKNOWN--FOR ALL THE TIMES WE MET--	WITHOUT A SMILE--WITHOUT	1330	4
SINCE SHE AND I HAD MET AND PLAYED	A LITTLE SNOW WAS HERE	1444	3
I NEVER MET IT NEAR	A WINGED SPARK DOTH SOAR	1468	2
THAT WE HAVE NEVER MET, ...	PARTING WITH THEE	1614	2
METAL			
BY BUT A LIP OF METAL--	I WOULD NOT PAINT--A	505	15
METALLIC			
WITH A METALLIC GRIN--	THAT AFTER HORROR--THAT	286	14
AND HIS METALLIC PEACE--	IT CAME AT LAST BUT	1230	4
METEOR			
HARMLESS--AS STREAKS OF METEOR--	THROUGH THE STRAIT PASS	792	7
THE METEOR OF BIRDS, ...	ONE OF THE ONES THAT	1466	18
METRE			
THE MOWER'S METRE--STEALS	I'M SORRY FOR THE DEAD--	529	12
IS METRE [POESY]--NAY--'TIS MELODY--	THEY HAVE A LITTLE ODOR	785	2
METRES			
THE DAYS--TO MIGHTY METRES STEPT--	I THINK I WAS ENCHANTED	593	17
THE LOWER METRES OF THE YEAR	THE MURMURING OF BEES,	1115	5
METROPOLIS			
HER MAKER--HER METROPOLIS--	SHE DWELLETH IN THE	671	3
IN A METROPOLIS OF HOMES	AWAY FROM HOME ARE SOME	821	3
METTLE			
WHAT METTLE FAIR	THE LASSITUDES OF	1592	6
MEXICO			
AN INFERENCE OF MEXICO	THEIR BARRICADE AGAINST	1471	7
MICE			
AND MICE WONT BARK--	I KNOW SOME LONELY	289	16
THE LIGHTNING PLAYED [SKIPPED] LIKE MICE .	THE CLOUDS THEIR BACKS	1172	4
MICROSCOPES			
BUT MICROSCOPES ARE PRUDENT	"FAITH" IS A FINE	185	3
MICROSCOPIC			
AND THEN HIS FAIRY [MICROSCOPIC] GIG . . .	WITHIN MY GARDEN, RIDES	500	10

	FIRST LINE	POEM	LINE
MIDAS			
ONE OF THE ONES THAT MIDAS TOUCHED	ONE OF THE ONES THAT	1466	1
AS MIDAS IS OF GOLD--	MEETING BY ACCIDENT,	1548	8
MIDDLE			
AT MIDDLE [BOTTOM / CENTRE] OF THE HILL--	THE HALLOWING OF PAIN	772	6
WE MUST HAVE PASSED THE MIDDLE SEA	I DID NOT REACH THEE	1664	23
MIDGE			
OF EARL AND MIDGE	A TOAD, CAN DIE OF LIGHT	583	4
MIDNIGHT			
PAST MIDNIGHT! PAST THE MORNING STAR!	AT LAST, TO BE	174	4
WHERE MIDNIGHT FROSTS--HAD LAIN!	I SHOULD NOT DARE TO	205	16
MIDNIGHT IN MARBLE--REFUTES--THE SUNS--	SAFE IN THEIR ALABASTER	216	V
ECLIPSE--AT MIDNIGHT--	IF HE DISSOLVE--THEN--	236	2
FOR THAT OLD--FADED MIDNIGHT--	WHEN NIGHT IS ALMOST	347	7
NAY--MIDNIGHT--'TWAS--	A TONGUE--TO TELL HIM I	400	12
SINCE MIDNIGHT--HAPPENED--SAY--	A TONGUE--TO TELL HIM I	400	13
ADJUSTS ITSELF TO MIDNIGHT--	WE GROW ACCUSTOMED TO	419	19
"I'M MIDNIGHT"--NEED THE MIDNIGHT SAY--	YOU'LL KNOW IT--AS YOU	420	9
"I'M MIDNIGHT"--NEED THE MIDNIGHT SAY--	YOU'LL KNOW IT--AS YOU	420	9
GOOD MORNING--MIDNIGHT--	GOOD MORNING--MIDNIGHT--	425	1
YOU--ARE NOT SO FAIR--MIDNIGHT--	GOOD MORNING--MIDNIGHT--	425	13
IF ONE WAKE AT MIDNIGHT--BETTER--	DREAMS--ARE WELL--BUT	450	3
AT MIDNIGHT, I AM BUT [YET] A MAID,	A WIFE--AT DAYBREAK I	461	3
THEN--MIDNIGHT, I HAVE PASSED FROM THEE	A WIFE--AT DAYBREAK I	461	5
MIDNIGHT--GOOD NIGHT! I HEAR THEM CALL,	A WIFE--AT DAYBREAK I	461	7
AND 'TWAS LIKE MIDNIGHT, SOME--	IT WAS NOT DEATH, FOR I	510	16
HOW MIDNIGHT FELT, AT FIRST--TO ME--	IF I MAY HAVE IT, WHEN	577	15
FAR SAFER, OF A MIDNIGHT MEETING	ONE NEED NOT BE A	670	5
AT MIDNIGHT--LET THE OWL SELECT	THE JUDGE IS LIKE THE	699	11
WITH MIDNIGHT TO THE NORTH OF HER--	BEHIND ME--DIPS ETERNITY	721	16
AND MIDNIGHT TO THE SOUTH OF HER--	BEHIND ME--DIPS ETERNITY	721	17
THE MIDNIGHT TO CONFIRM--	SEVERER SERVICE OF	786	20
MIDNIGHT'S			
SO MIDNIGHT'S--DUE--AT NOON.	SUNSET AT NIGHT--IS	415	4
THE MIDNIGHT'S DUSKY ARMS	THE SUNRISE RUNS FOR	710	13
MIDNIGHT'S AWFUL PATTERN	ON THE WORLD YOU COLORED	1171	11
MIDNIGHTS			
WHAT MUST THE MIDNIGHTS--BE!	TO WHOM THE MORNINGS	1095	2
MIDST			
AND IN THE MIDST SO FAIR,	SHE BORE IT TILL THE	144	14
MIDSUMMER			
MIDSUMMER [MERIDIAN]--IN THE MIND--	I THINK TO LIVE--MAY BE	646	18
MIDSUMMER, WAS IT, WHEN THEY DIED--	MIDSUMMER, WAS IT, WHEN	962	1
MIEN			
HIS MIEN [GAIT], WAS SOUNDLESS, LIKE THE [A] BIRD--	THE ONLY GHOST I EVER	274	5
A MIEN TO MOVE A QUEEN--	A MIEN TO MOVE A QUEEN--	283	1
MUCH IS THE MIEN [GOOD IS THE LOOK] OF HIM IN MARCH	A PROMPT--EXECUTIVE BIRD	1177	7
MIGHT			
I LEFT THE PLACE, WITH ALL MY MIGHT--	I MEANT TO HAVE BUT	476	17
AS IF IT HELD BUT THE MIGHT OF A CHILD--	GOING TO HIM! HAPPY	494	13
AND THEN HE LEANS WITH ALL HIS MIGHT	HE PARTS HIMSELF--LIKE	517	V 3
PROCLAIM WITH THEIR REMAINING MIGHT--	ME PROVE IT NOW--WHOEVER	537	11
UNTIL A MIGHT DETECTED ME	I HEARD, AS IF I HAD NO	1039	11
OF MIGHT TO HELP, SO PITIFUL	WHAT TWIGS WE HELD BY--	1086	11
. . . A MIGHT / SO DELICATE A MIGHT / SO ADEQUATE A MIGHT / . . .	THE MOST TRIUMPHANT BIRD	1265	4
. . . A MIGHT / SO DELICATE A MIGHT / SO ADEQUATE A MIGHT / . . .	THE MOST TRIUMPHANT BIRD	1265	4
. . . A MIGHT / SO DELICATE A MIGHT / SO ADEQUATE A MIGHT / . . .	THE MOST TRIUMPHANT BIRD	1265	4
AND DURING IT'S ELECTRIC GALE [SPELL / STAY / MIGHT / ACT / SPAN]--	WITH PINIONS OF DISDAIN	1431	7
THE MIGHT OF HUMAN LOVE--	THE IMMORTALITY SHE GAVE	1648	4
SCARCER ONCE WITH THE MIGHT	SOMETIMES WITH THE HEART	1680	3
MIGHTIER			
A MIGHTIER THAN HE--	THERE IS A LANGUOR OF	396	14
HOW MIGHTIER HE--THAN I--	IT WOULD HAVE STARVED A	612	12
MIGHTIEST			
BY INTUITION, MIGHTIEST THINGS	YOU'LL KNOW IT--AS YOU	420	7
THE EMPEROR [MIGHTIEST] OF MEN--	THE SOUL THAT HATH A	674	8
WITH WHICH WE CITE THIS MIGHTIEST CASE	"REMEMBER ME" IMPLORED	1180	7
THAT MIGHTIEST BELIEF,	I NEVER HEAR THAT ONE IS	1323	4
MIGHTINESS			
NO RESPITE FROM THE INFERENCE [MIGHTINESS]	WHY SHOULD WE HURRY--WHY	1646	5
MIGHTY			
SINCE THE MIGHTY AUTUMN AFTERNOON	GOING TO HEAVEN!	79	26
HAD I A MIGHTY GUN	MY FRIEND ATTACKS MY	118	6
HOW MIGHTY 'TWAS--TO BE	THE DAY CAME SLOW--TILL	304	14
AND BOWING--WITH A MIGHTY LOOK--	I STARTED EARLY--TOOK MY	520	23
A MIGHTY AFTERNOON--	DEPARTED--TO THE	524	2
YET [BUT] MIGHTY--BY RELATION	ONE ANGUISH--IN A CROWD	565	13
HIS MIGHTY BALLS--IN DEATH WERE THICK--	A DYING TIGER--MOANED	566	5
A CHAPTER--THEN THE MIGHTY BOOK--	WE LEARNED THE WHOLE OF	568	3
A MIGHTY LOOK RUNS ROUND THE WORLD	"HEAVEN" HAS DIFFERENT	575	5
THE DAYS--TO MIGHTY METRES STEPT--	I THINK I WAS ENCHANTED	593	17
LIKE MIGHTY FOOT LIGHTS--BURNED THE RED	LIKE MIGHTY FOOT LIGHTS	595	1
THE MIGHTY MERCHANT SNEERED [SMILED]--	I ASKED NO OTHER THING--	621	4
AND COULD BE MIGHTY, IF I LIKED--	THAT FIRST DAY, WHEN YOU	659	3

	FIRST LINE	POEM	LINE
MIGHTY (CONTINUED)			
WE THOUGHT THE MIGHTY [MONSTROUS] FUNERAL--	'TIS GOOD--THE LOOKING	660	3
AND HE AND HE IN MIGHTY LIST	HE OUTSTRIPPED TIME WITH	865	5
HIS MIGHTY PLEASURE SUITS US NOT	THE SUN IS GAY OR STARK	878	7
A CLOUD THE MIGHTY SUN ENCLOSES	A SHADE UPON THE MIND	882	3
CREATION SEEMED A MIGHTY CRACK--	TO MY QUICK EAR THE	891	7
IN MIGHTY--UNREMITTING BASS	THE HEART HAS NARROW	928	3
WITH HERE AND THERE A MIGHTY BOW	LIKE MEN AND WOMEN	1105	3
THE MIND WAS BUILT FOR MIGHTY FREIGHT	A GREAT HOPE FELL	1123	6
STANDS THE SUN SO CLOSE AND MIGHTY	WE LIKE MARCH.	1213	8
WOULD SCAN THE MIGHTY [EAGER / BREATHLESS / HURRYING / • • •	TO FLEE FROM MEMORY	1242	6
TOO MIGHTY FOR THE DAILY MIND	I NEVER HEAR THAT ONE IS	1323	5
ON IT'S BOUNDLESS [MIGHTY / SUBTLE] SHELF--	SUMMER LAID HER SIMPLE	1363	2
• • • MIGHTY / GALLANT / SYLVAN / AMPLE / PERFECT] WAY	SUMMER--WE ALL HAVE SEEN	1386	6
HOW MIGHTY THE WIND MUST FEEL MORNS	HOW LONESOME THE WIND	1418	9
HOW MIGHTY [MOMENTOUS] TO THE INSECURE	HOW FIRM ETERNITY MUST	1499	5
ARE SO FOR THAT MOST FATAL [MIGHTY] CAUSE	DECLAIMING WATERS NONE	1595	3
SOME ONE PREPARED THIS MIGHTY SHOW	SOME ONE PREPARED THIS	1644	1
THIS MIGHTY NIGHT	WHY SHOULD WE HURRY--WHY	1646	10
WE COULD NOT FIND THE MIGHTY FACE	A CAP OF LEAD ACROSS THE	1649	3
THIS IS A MIGHTY ROOM;	SWEET HOURS HAVE	1767	2
MILD			
HER ADMONITION MILD--	NATURE--THE GENTLEST	790	4
THAN THE MEADOW MILD.	FAR FROM LOVE THE	1021	4
MILE			
AND IT'S PARTLY [MANY A MILE], DOWN HILL--	TIE THE STRINGS TO MY	279	8
REMEMBERED--AS THE MILE	OF TRIBULATION--THESE	325	12
NO FASTER THAN A MILE AT ONCE	NO MAN CAN COMPASS A	477	3
NO NEW MILE REMAINETH--	LIFE--IS WHAT WE MAKE IT	698	11
THAT IS NOT OF MILE OR MAIN--	THAT DISTANCE WAS	863	2
MILES			
WHICH SHORTENED ALL THE MILES--	ONE SISTER HAVE I IN OUR	14	16
BUT JUST THE MILES OF STARE--	I'VE KNOWN A HEAVEN,	243	6
"MILES", AND "PRISCILLA", WERE SUCH AN ONE--	GOD IS A DISTANT--	357	4
"MILES", AND "JOHN ALDEN" WERE SYNONYME--	GOD IS A DISTANT--	357	8
THERE MAY BE--MILES ON MILES OF NOUGHT--	I TIE MY HAT--I CREASE	443	17
THERE MAY BE--MILES ON MILES OF NOUGHT--	I TIE MY HAT--I CREASE	443	17
BUT MILES OF SPARKS--AT EVENING--	THE RED--BLAZE--IS THE	469	5
I LIKE TO SEE [HEAR] IT LAP THE MILES--	I LIKE TO SEE IT LAP	585	1
THE SUN RAN MILES AWAY	THE BIRD DID PRANCE--THE	1107	2
A RUGGED BILLION MILES--	THE SAVIOR MUST HAVE	1487	8
MILITANT			
HIS LARDER--TERSE AND MILITANT--	NO BRIGADIER THROUGHOUT	1561	19
MILKING			
"MORNING"--MEANS "MILKING"--TO THE FARMER--	"MORNING"--MEANS	300	1
MILL			
AND OTHER--WENT TO TURN THE MILL--	FORGET! THE LADY WITH	438	15
WHEN RICHARD WENT TO MILL--	'TWAS JUST THIS TIME,	445	6
PERHAPS--THE PROFILE OF A MILL	IT'S THOUGHTS--AND JUST	495	20
AS 'TWERE A TRAVELLING MILL--	WITHIN MY GARDEN, RIDES	500	4
MINOR--APPARATUS--HOPPER OF THE MILL--	LIFE, AND DEATH, AND	706	3
'TIS MANY A TINY MILL	DEW--IS THE FRESHET IN	1097	2
MILLER			
WORLDS [THE MILLER]--A FLOOD--	"MORNING"--MEANS	300	8
MILLINER			
AND THEN THE MILLINER--AND THE MAN	THERE'S BEEN A DEATH, IN	389	17
MILLINER'S			
REMEMBERED--AS THE MILLINER'S FLOWER	PRECIOUS TO ME--SHE	727	12
MILLINERY			
THE MILLINERY SUPPLE	IT'S LITTLE ETHER HOOD	1501	3
BY MILLINERY OF THE CLOUD	SUMMER BEGINS TO HAVE	1682	6
MILLIONAIRE			
MYSELF--A MILLIONAIRE	YOUR RICHES--TAUGHT ME--	299	2
MILLS			
AND TRODDEN OUT [BLOTTED OUT-- / SHOVED AWAY--] THE MILLS--	THE BRAIN, WITHIN IT'S	556	8
MIND			
NEVER MIND FADED FORESTS, AUSTIN,	THERE IS ANOTHER SKY,	2	5
NEVER MIND SILENT FIELDS--	THERE IS ANOTHER SKY,	2	6
MAY SEIZE UPON HIS MIND--	I HAD A GUINEA GOLDEN--	23	34
ONE LITTLE MIND FROM SCHOOL--	TAKEN FROM MEN--THIS	53	6
FOR YOU KNOW WE DO NOT MIND OUR DRESS	GOING TO HEAVEN!	79	18
WE SHOULD NOT MIND SO SMALL A FLOWER--	WE SHOULD NOT MIND SO	81	1
OF OUR IMMORTAL MIND--	TO HANG OUR HEAD--	105	4
NEVER MIND MY BREATHLESS ANVIL!	BY A FLOWER--BY A LETTER	109	5
NEVER MIND REPOSE!	BY A FLOWER--BY A LETTER	109	6
NEVER MIND THE SOOTY FACES	BY A FLOWER--BY A LETTER	109	7
GRANT ME, OH LORD, A SUNNY MIND--	BESIDES THE AUTUMN POETS	131	15
NOT PORTLY, MIND! BUT BREATHING--WARM--	A LITTLE BREAD--A CRUST	159	4
MAYBE, WE SHOULD'NT MIND THEM--	I'VE NOTHING ELSE--TO	224	5
MIND THEE IN PARADISE	JESUS! THY CRUCIFIX	225	5
I MIND ME THAT OF ANGUISH--SENT--	I THINK JUST HOW MY	237	9
FOR FRIGID--HOUR OF MIND--	A SHADY FRIEND--FOR	278	4
BUT NEVER I MIND THE STEEPEST [BRIDGES]--	TIE THE STRINGS TO MY	279	9
AND NEVER I MIND THE SEA--	TIE THE STRINGS TO MY	279	10
MY MIND WAS GOING NUMB--	I FELT A FUNERAL, IN MY	280	8
THE MIND IS SMOOTH--NO MOTION--	THE DIFFERENCE BETWEEN	305	5
BUT OFTENTIMES, AMONG MY MIND,	I CANNOT DANCE UPON MY	326	3

	FIRST LINE	POEM		LINE
MIND (CONTINUED)				
HEAVEN IS SO FAR OF THE MIND	HEAVEN IS SO FAR OF THE	370		1
THAT WERE THE MIND DISSOLVED--	HEAVEN IS SO FAR OF THE	370		2
ON THEMES CONCERN OUR MUTUAL MIND--	A PRECIOUS--MOULDERING	371		11
MOULD MY SLOW MIND TO THIS COMPREHENSION--	KNOWS HOW TO FORGET!	433		9
THERE'S TRIUMPH OF THE FINER MIND	TRIUMPH--MAY BE OF	455		5
WHEN CRESCENT--THOU ART WORN--I NOTE [MIND]--	YOU KNOW THAT PORTRAIT	504		11
A MOUNTAIN--IN MY MIND--	I CROSS TILL I AM WEARY	550		2
CONVERSION OF THE MIND	I THINK I WAS ENCHANTED	593		22
WHEN MY MIND--IS PLAIN	DONT PUT UP MY THREAD &	617		6
WHAT WAS HIS FURTHEST MIND--OF HOME--OR GOD--	TO KNOW JUST HOW HE	622		9
MIDSUMMER [MERIDIAN]--IN THE MIND--	I THINK TO LIVE--MAY BE	646		18
TO TAKE [MIND] IT--	VICTORY COMES LATE--	690		4
I COULD BRING YOU JEWELS--HAD I A MIND TO--	I COULD BRING YOU JEWELS	697		1
A THOUGHT WENT UP MY MIND TODAY--	A THOUGHT WENT UP MY	701		1
OF THE MIND OF MAN--	PUBLICATION--IS THE	709		2
OF AN HERMETIC MIND--	STRONG DRAUGHTS OF THEIR	711		8
AT BOTTOM OF MY MIND--	IT DROPPED SO LOW--IN MY	747		4
UPON MY THRONGING [CROWDED / HAPPY] MIND--	MY WORTHINESS IS ALL MY	751		8
YET SANCTIFIES THE MIND--	IT IS A LONESOME GLEE--	774		2
NO SETTLER HAD THE MIND.	SOTO! EXPLORE THYSELF!	832		4
I WOULD NOT MIND THE JOURNEY THERE	I CANNOT BUY IT--'TIS	840		8
ASSISTS THE STAGGERING MIND	A DOUBT IF IT BE US	859		2
A SHADE UPON THE MIND THERE PASSES	A SHADE UPON THE MIND	882		1
PREFERRED AGAINST THE MIND	EXPERIENCE IS THE ANGLED	910		2
BY--PARADOX--THE MIND ITSELF--	EXPERIENCE IS THE ANGLED	910		3
THIS MIND, AND IT'S MEASURE--	THIS DUST, AND IT'S	936		5
I FELT A CLEAVING IN MY MIND--	I FELT A CLEAVING IN MY	937		1
IN CONVALESCENT MIND,	AS ONE DOES SICKNESS	957		2
EXCEPT IT'S MIND ACCOMPANY	WE MISS HER, NOT BECAUSE	993		3
THE CAPSULE OF THE MIND	BEST THINGS DWELL OUT OF	998		6
HIS MIND WERE GOING BLIND--	HE SCANNED IT--STAGGERED	1062		5
RESEMBLES TO MY OUTRAGED MIND	HIS BILL IS CLASPED--HIS	1102		9
BUT HOARDED IN THE MIND	A MINE THERE IS NO MAN	1117		6
THE MIND WAS BUILT FOR MIGHTY FREIGHT	A GREAT HOPE FELL	1123		6
TO THE MAGICIAN'S MIND--	BEST WITCHCRAFT IS	1158		2
THAT LARCENY OF TIME AND MIND	ALONE AND IN A	1167		25
IT TINGLES IN THE MIND	WE LIKE A HAIRBREADTH	1175		2
FOR PATTERN IS THE MIND BESTOWED	WHO GOES TO DINE MUST	1223		5
FROM THE MIND OF MAN	TO FLEE FROM MEMORY	1242		8
TOO MIGHTY FOR THE DAILY MIND	I NEVER HEAR THAT ONE IS	1323		5
THE HEART IS THE CAPITAL OF THE MIND--	THE HEART IS THE CAPITAL	1354		1
THE MIND IS A SINGLE STATE--	THE HEART IS THE CAPITAL	1354		2
THE HEART AND THE MIND TOGETHER MAKE	THE HEART IS THE CAPITAL	1354		3
THE MIND LIVES ON THE HEART	THE MIND LIVES ON THE	1355		1
THE MIND IS FAT.	THE MIND LIVES ON THE	1355		4
THE BOLDEST MIND WILL PINE	THE MIND LIVES ON THE	1355	V	6
THE STOUTEST [FORTHWITH THE] MIND IS WAN	THE MIND LIVES ON THE	1355	V	6
SUCH [THESE] ARE THE INLETS OF THE MIND--	SUCH ARE THE INLETS OF	1421		1
HIS MIND LIKE FABRICS OF THE EAST	HIS MIND LIKE FABRICS OF	1446		1
BEREAVES THE MIND	SO GAY A FLOWER	1456		2
RECURRENT TO THE AFTER MIND [THOUGHT]	THEIR BARRICADE AGAINST	1471		9
TO HIS ENAMORED MIND	ALL THAT I DO	1496		3
THE MYRRHS, AND MOCHAS, OF THE MIND	CANDOR--MY TEPID FRIEND	1537		3
BEFORE MY MIND WAS SOWN,	THE SPIRIT LASTS--BUT IN	1576		22
BEFORE MY MIND [SOUL / BEAM] WAS BORN	THIS ME--THAT WALKS AND	1588		6
THE FOLIAGE OF THE MIND	TALK NOT TO ME OF SUMMER	1634		2
HIS MIND OF MAN, A SECRET MAKES	HIS MIND OF MAN, A	1663		1
NO MUSHROOM IS THEIR MIND	THEY TALK AS SLOW AS	1697		2
MINDED				
I HAD NOT MINDED--WALLS--	I HAD NOT MINDED--WALLS	398		1
EVER HE MINDED OCCUPYING	NO BOBOLINK--REVERSE HIS	755		3
MINDS				
STRONG DRAUGHTS OF THEIR REFRESHING MINDS	STRONG DRAUGHTS OF THEIR	711		1
BY THIS GREAT LIGHT UPON OUR MINDS	THE LAST NIGHT THAT SHE	1100		7
TO OUR ASSAULTED MINDS--	OF PAUL AND SILAS IT IS	1166		6
THAT OUR MINDS ARE HOT.	WE LIKE MARCH.	1213		9
THE TABERNACLES OF THE MINDS	COULD MORTAL LIP DIVINE	1409	V	
NOT BIRDS ENTIRELY--BUT MINDS--	A PANG IS MORE	1530		3
OF OTHER MINDS	TO BE FORGOT BY THEE	1560		3
SO MINDS PASS MINDS	AS WE PASS HOUSES MUSING	1653		3
SO MINDS PASS MINDS	AS WE PASS HOUSES MUSING	1653		3
MINE				
I STAY MINE ENEMY!	"SIC TRANSIT GLORIA	3		4
KNOWING THAT BIRD OF MINE	I HAVE A BIRD IN SPRING	5		8
ARE MINE--	I HAVE A BIRD IN SPRING	5		15
KNOWING THAT BIRD OF MINE	I HAVE A BIRD IN SPRING	5		26
THOU LITTLE SPADE OF MINE	ALL THESE MY BANNERS BE.	22		13
SINCE NONE OF THEM ARE MINE.	I HAD A GUINEA GOLDEN--	23		24
HER OATH, AND MINE--	I KEEP MY PLEDGE.	46		10
LARGER THAN MINE--SERENER--	LOW AT MY PROBLEM	69		3
HEART, NOT SO HEAVY AS MINE	HEART, NOT SO HEAVY AS	83		1
WHEREFORE MINE EYE THY SILVER MISTS,	THE BEE IS NOT AFRAID OF	111		7
I HAD SOME THINGS THAT I CALLED MINE--	I HAD SOME THINGS THAT I	116		1
IN THIS CUP OF MINE.	MANY CROSS THE RHINE	123		2
NEXT TO MINE,	I BRING AN UNACCUSTOMED	132		3
IF, HAPLY, MINE MAY BE THE DROP	I BRING AN UNACCUSTOMED	132		18
FOR A SIMPLE BREAST LIKE MINE--	FLOWERS--WELL--IF	137		10
FAR SUPERIOR TO MINE.	FLOWERS--WELL--IF	137		14
OVER THIS PAIN OF MINE--	YOU LOVE ME--YOU ARE	156		18

	FIRST LINE	POEM	LINE
MINE (CONTINUED)			
FROM WHAT W'D LAST TILL HEADS LIKE MINE	I CAUTIOUS, SCANNED MY	178	3
TILL MINE TOO HEAVY GREW--	SAVIOR! I'VE NO ONE ELSE	217	10
BUT MINE--	A BURDOCK--CLAWED MY	229	3
I MISSED MINE--HOW DREARY--MARBLES--	GOD PERMITS INDUSTRIOUS	231	7
MINE--GET SO DIM!	YOU SEE I CANNOT SEE--	253	7
THAT STANDS FOR DEITY, TO MINE,	A SINGLE SCREW OF FLESH	263	3
AS FAR FROM MINE, AS IF NO PLIGHT	A SINGLE SCREW OF FLESH	263	7
TO LIVES THAT [AS] STOOP TO NOTICE MINE--	HE PUT THE BELT AROUND	273	13
FEET, SMALL AS MINE--HAVE MARCHED IN REVOLUTION	UNTO LIKE STORY--TROUBLE	295	17
MINE--WAS AN ACORN'S BREAST--	ONE YEAR AGO--JOTS WHAT?	296	18
TO HAVE A SMILE FOR MINE--EACH DAY,	YOUR RICHES--TAUGHT ME--	299	23
MINE--IS THE MORE CONVENIENT	I SEND TWO SUNSETS--	308	7
FOR MINE--I TELL YOU THAT MY HEART	BEFORE I GOT MY EYE PUT	327	7
THE MEADOWS--MINE--	BEFORE I GOT MY EYE PUT	327	9
THE MOUNTAINS--MINE--	BEFORE I GOT MY EYE PUT	327	10
FOR MINE--TO LOOK AT WHEN I LIKED--	BEFORE I GOT MY EYE PUT	327	16
'TWAS EVEN THAT 'TWAS MINE--	THE DAY THAT I WAS	356	16
FOR FOREHEAD LOW AS MINE, TO WEAR,	ALTHOUGH I PUT AWAY HIS	366	3
ONE PORT--SUFFICES--FOR A BRIG--LIKE MINE--	HOW SICK--TO WAIT--IN	368	7
TO EARN A MINE--WOULD RUN	A TONGUE--TO TELL HIM I	400	5
ONE'S--MONEY--ONE'S--THE MINE--	SOME--WORK FOR	406	12
SO GO YOUR WAY--AND I'LL GO MINE--	A MURMUR IN THE TREES--	416	19
AND DOUBT THAT YOU ARE MINE--	I'LL CLUTCH--AND CLUTCH	427	13
AND MINE--THE DISTANT SEA--	THE MOON IS DISTANT FROM	429	10
BECAUSE THE CAUSE WAS MINE--	LIKE EYES THAT LOOKED ON	458	10
I THINK A LITTLE WELL--LIKE MINE--	I KNOW WHERE WELLS GROW	460	19
THE ONLY ONE--FORESTALLING MINE--	I LIVE WITH HIM--I SEE	463	5
WHICH DOOR IS MINE--AND NOT MISTAKE--	I AM ALIVE--I GUESS--	470	23
REMINDED ME, OF MINE--	IT WAS NOT DEATH, FOR I	510	12
THAT YOUR'S AND MINE, SHOULD BE--	IF YOU WERE COMING IN	511	14
MINE--BY THE RIGHT OF THE WHITE ELECTION!	MINE--BY THE RIGHT OF	528	1
MINE--BY THE ROYAL SEAL!	MINE--BY THE RIGHT OF	528	2
MINE--BY THE SIGN IN THE SCARLET PRISON--	MINE--BY THE RIGHT OF	528	3
MINE--HERE--IN VISION--AND IN VETO!	MINE--BY THE RIGHT OF	528	5
MINE--BY THE GRAVE'S REPEAL--	MINE--BY THE RIGHT OF	528	6
MINE--LONG AS [WHILE] AGES STEAL!	MINE--BY THE RIGHT OF	528	9
ITSELF--EXHIBIT [ENABLE / EMBOLDEN]--MINE--	BUT LITTLE CARMINE HATH	558	4
I WONDER IF IT WEIGHS LIKE MINE--	I MEASURE EVERY GRIEF I	561	3
I COULD NOT TELL THE DATE OF MINE--	I MEASURE EVERY GRIEF I	561	7
WERE BUT MINE--THE CHARTER OF THE LEAST FLY--	I COULD DIE--TO KNOW--	570	6
I COULD NOT HOPE--FOR MINE--[TO EARN]	I HAD BEEN HUNGRY, ALL	579	8
WHICH RUBY'S MINE?	A TOAD, CAN DIE OF LIGHT	583	12
STARE STOLID [VACANT / HORRID] INTO MINE	I YEARS HAD BEEN FROM	609	5
TO NULLIFY THE MINE--	I SEE THEE BETTER--IN	611	8
LIKE MINE--FOR NOT A FOOT--NOR HAND--	I WATCHED THE MOON	629	11
I WEARIED--TOO--OF MINE--	OURSELVES WERE WED ONE	631	4
ON EVERY SIDE OF MINE	OURSELVES WERE WED ONE	631	12
FOR MINE--IN FROSTS--WAS SOWN--	OURSELVES WERE WED ONE	631	14
COULD I--DO ELSE--WITH MINE?	I COULD SUFFICE FOR HIM,	643	16
MINE BELONG YOUR LATEST SIGHING--	PROMISE THIS--WHEN YOU	648	3
MINE--TO BELT YOUR EYE--	PROMISE THIS--WHEN YOU	648	4
MINE TO STAY--WHEN ALL HAVE WANDERED--	PROMISE THIS--WHEN YOU	648	9
LIFE OF MINE--RESTORE--	PROMISE THIS--WHEN YOU	648	12
MINE--TO GUARD YOUR NARROW PRECINCT--	PROMISE THIS--WHEN YOU	648	17
MINE TO SUPPLICATE MADONNA--	PROMISE THIS--WHEN YOU	648	25
CRUMB OF MINE	SO MUCH SUMMER	651	9
AND FETCH HER THEE--BE MINE--	SHE DWELLETH IN THE	671	8
TO DRINK--ENABLES MINE	STRONG DRAUGHTS OF THEIR	711	2
MINE BE THE MINISTRY	THE WORLD--FEELS DUSTY	715	9
AND THE SURRENDER [DISCOMFIT]--MINE--	I MEANT TO FIND HER WHEN	718	4
PROVE THE FEAT--THAT MADE THE PELLET MINE--	GOD GAVE A LOAF TO EVERY	791	6
CHANCE SOVREIGN ON A MINE--	I PLAY AT RICHES--TO	801	18
NEXT DOOR TO MINE THE PAIN.	HOW WELL I KNEW HER NOT	837	4
ALWAYS MINE!	ALWAYS MINE!	839	1
MINE WAS THE ONLY ONE	I CANNOT BUY IT--'TIS	840	3
BE MINE THE DOOM--	BE MINE THE DOOM--	845	1
OR A REDUCELESS MINE.	TO OWN THE ART WITHIN	855	8
ONLY A SHRINE, BUT MINE--	ONLY A SHRINE, BUT MINE	918	1
WOULD IT TRY MINE--	IF IT HAD NO PENCIL	921	2
WHO MINE ENEMY?	STRUCK, WAS I, NOR YET	925	8
AND MINE--SOME FOOLISHER EFFECT--	I LEARNED--AT LEAST--	944	16
NOR THE LEAST SIGNAL, ME [MINE] ASSURE--	WERT THOU BUT ILL--THAT	961	4
AND MINE--THE DOOR	WERT THOU BUT ILL--THAT	961	6
"ARMS OF MINE--SUFFICIENT PHAETON--	"UNTO ME?" I DO NOT KNOW	964	7
TO IMITATE BE MINE.	HER LITTLE PARASOL TO	1038	4
TILL IT DEPART, PERSUADING [CONVEYING] MINE--	AIR HAS NO RESIDENCE, NO	1060	8
TITLE DIVINE--IS MINE!	TITLE DIVINE--IS MINE!	1072	1
HAD IT BEEN MINE, TO PRINT!	ENDED, ERE IT BEGUN--	1088	5
AND HOLD THE WICK OF MINE TO IT	THE SPRY ARMS OF THE	1103	11
THAT ABSTINENCE OF MINE [ME] PRODUCE	I FIT FOR THEM--	1109	6
A MINE THERE IS NO MAN WOULD OWN	A MINE THERE IS NO MAN	1117	1
GUEST OF MINE ASSUREDLY--	RECOLLECT THE FACE OF ME	1305	4
IS FREELY MINE.	THIS DIRTY--LITTLE--	1311	2
THE FATHER OF THE MINE	LUCK IS NOT CHANCE--	1350	5
A SMILE SO SMALL AS MINE MIGHT BE	THEY MIGHT NOT NEED ME--	1391	3
BUT MINE--DISPELS--IN TEARS.	I SHALL NOT MURMUR IF AT	1410	8
FOR AN ALIGHTING MINE--	ONE OF THE ONES THAT	1466	8
MINE ENEMY [MY FOE] IS GROWING OLD--	MINE ENEMY IS GROWING	1509	1

	FIRST LINE	POEM	LINE
MIRACLE (CONTINUED)			
OF DEATH--			
'TIS MIRACLE BEFORE ME--THEN--	BEHIND ME--DIPS ETERNITY	721	13
'TIS MIRACLE BEHIND--BETWEEN--	BEHIND ME--DIPS ETERNITY	721	14
'TWAS THE FIRST MIRACLE	LET US PLAY YESTERDAY--	728	23
THE MIRACLE THAT INTRODUCED	THE BIRDS BEGUN AT FOUR	783	23
AND CREATURES CLAD IN MIRACLE [VICTORY]	'TIS ANGUISH GRANDER	984	7
THIS IS THE HARDEST MIRACLE	TO DIE--WITHOUT THE	1017	3
TO OWN THE MIRACLE--	WHO WERE "THE FATHER AND	1258	24
A MIRACLE FOR ALL!	NO LIFE CAN POMPLESS	1626	8
MIRACLES			
THEIR MIRACLES OF [UNSUSPECTING / UNSUSPICIOUS] TUNE--	HIS BILL IS CLASPED--HIS	1102	12
MIRACULOUS			
ARE MAGICAL [WERE WONDERFUL / ARE TERRIBLE / ARE MIRACULOUS / . . .	CONTAINED IN THIS SHORT	1165	2
MIRACULOUSLY			
MIRACULOUSLY FARED	CONFERRING WITH MYSELF	1655	4
MIRAGE			
A MERCIFUL MIRAGE	A DOUBT IF IT BE US	859	6
MIRROR			
NO MIRROR COULD ILLUMINE THEE	I SEE THEE CLEARER FOR	1666	3
MIRRORRS			
AND MIRRORRS ON THE SCENE--	WHEN WE STAND ON THE	242	4
MIRTH			
MIRTH IS THE MAIL OF ANGUISH--	A WOUNDED DEER--LEAPS	165	9
MISCELLANEOUS			
ON MISCELLANEOUS ENTERPRISE	FROM COCOON FORTH A	354	7
MISCONCEIVE			
MAY OVERLOOK [MISINFER / MISCONCEIVE] YOUR TRACK--	BECAUSE THAT YOU ARE	1260	4
MISERABLE			
SO MISERABLE A SOUND--AT FIRST--	A PRISON GETS TO BE A	652	11
MISERIES			
MISERIES OF CONJECTURE	WHETHER THEY HAVE	1329	5
FOR MISERIES SO HALCYON	I THOUGHT THE TRAIN	1449	11
MISER'S			
UNTO A MISER'S EAR--	BECAUSE 'TWAS RICHES I	1093	8
MISERS			
WHAT MISERS WRING THEIR HANDS TONIGHT	A MINE THERE IS NO MAN	1117	7
MISERY			
WHO WERE SUFFICIENT TO [COULD BEGIN ON--] MISERY?	BOUND--A TROUBLE--	269	V
AS MISERY--	I GOT SO I COULD HEAR	293	26
WITHOUT A MISERY--	I KNOW LIVES, I COULD	372	2
THAN THIS SMART MISERY.	OF COURSE--I PRAYED--	376	11
UNTO MISERY--	SMILING BACK FROM	385	12
A SKEIN OF MISERY--	THE MONTHS HAVE ENDS--	423	4
THE MISERY A COMPACT	LIKE EYES THAT LOOKED ON	458	11
OH, MASTER, THIS IS MISERY--	WHY MAKE IT DOUBT--IT	462	13
TO HIM--SUMS MISERY--	IT MAKES NO DIFFERENCE	620	12
A PRIVILEGE OF HURRICANE [MISERY]	I MEANT TO FIND HER WHEN	718	11
WHO MISERY--SUSTAIN--	SUCH IS THE FORCE OF	787	4
INFORMING [ENLIGHTENING / ENABLING]--MISERY--	A DOOR JUST OPENED ON A	953	8
MISERY, HOW FAIR	ON THE WORLD YOU COLORED	1171	8
SOCIETY FOR ME MY MISERY	SOCIETY FOR ME MY MISERY	1534	1
MISFORTUNE			
MISFORTUNE HATH NO IMPLEMENT	REVERSE CANNOT BEFALL	395	7
MISGIVES			
HER HEART MISGIVES HER, FOR HER VOW--	I KNOW A PLACE WHERE	337	7
MISGIVING			
OR OF ITSELF A [THE] NEW MISGIVING--	WONDER--IS NOT PRECISELY	1331	7
MISINFER			
MAY OVERLOOK [MISINFER / MISCONCEIVE] YOUR TRACK--	BECAUSE THAT YOU ARE	1260	4
MISS			
TO MISS--IF ONE SHALL MEET--	ALL THESE MY BANNERS BE.	22	9
AND IF TO MISS, WERE MERRY,	IF RECOLLECTING WERE	33	5
ONLY A BEE WILL MISS IT--	NOBODY KNOWS THIS LITTLE	35	5
THE ONE THAT NO ONE ELSE WOULD MISS	I CAME TO BUY A SMILE--	223	5
WHEN HEAVEN--WAS TOO COMMON--TO MISS--	THE LONESOME FOR THEY	262	11
TO MISS IT--BEGGARS SO--	YOUR RICHES--TAUGHT ME--	299	16
WITH "ME, MISS, ME"--	MY REWARD FOR BEING, WAS	343	7
I KNOW LIVES, I COULD MISS	I KNOW LIVES, I COULD	372	1
NO FEAR YOU'LL MISS THE ROAD.	A MURMUR IN THE TREES--	416	20
I WONDERED WHICH WOULD MISS ME, LEAST,	'TWAS JUST THIS TIME,	445	13
AN AMPLE LETTER--HOW YOU MISS--	YOU LOVE THE LORD--YOU	487	5
QUICK [SOON]--SWEET MOUTH--TO MISS THEE SO--	THESE--SAW VISIONS--	758	6
AND IF HIS YELLOW FEET SHOULD MISS--	MY FAITH IS LARGER THAN	766	9
I COULD NOT MISS AN EAR--	GOD GAVE A LOAF TO EVERY	791	10
I SHOULD NOT MISS IN YIELDING, THOUGH	THIS CHASM, SWEET, UPON	858	15
NEED [MISS]--ONCE IN AN ETERNITY--	LOVE--IS THAT LATER	924	11
WE MISS HER, NOT BECAUSE WE SEE--	WE MISS HER, NOT BECAUSE	993	1
WE MISS A KINSMAN MORE	WE MISS A KINSMAN MORE	1087	1
WE MISS HIS STATED HAT.	THAT ODD OLD MAN IS DEAD	1130	2
WHO MISS HIS ANTIQUATED WICK [LIGHT]--	THAT ODD OLD MAN IS DEAD	1130	5
THE FACE WE CHOOSE TO MISS--	THE FACE WE CHOOSE TO	1141	1
I MORE SHOULD MISS--	MY MAKER--LET ME BE	1403	4
'TIS NOT THE SWAYING FRAME WE MISS,	'TIS NOT THE SWAYING	1597	1
TO TRY TO SPEAK, AND MISS THE WAY	TO TRY TO SPEAK, AND	1617	1

	FIRST LINE	POEM	LINE
MISSED			
I MISSED MINE--HOW DREARY--MARBLES--	GOD PERMITS INDUSTRIOUS	231	7
TILL RAPTURE MISSED THEM [HER FOOTING-- / PENINSULA]	TWO BUTTERFLIES WENT OUT	533	V
MY TACTICS MISSED A RUDIMENT--	MY PERIOD HAD COME FOR	564	3
AND PAIN--IS MISSED--IN [FORGETS--FOR--] PRAISE--	UNTO MY BOOKS--SO GOOD	604	4
FETCH THE SEAM I MISSED--	DONT PUT UP MY THREAD &	617	18
IF OUGHT SHE MISSED IN HER NEW DAY,	SHE ROSE TO HIS	732	5
HAVE MISSED [LOST] A BAREFOOT CITIZEN--	HE TOLD A HOMELY TALE	763	15
THE DESOLATION ONLY MISSED	THE THRILL CAME SLOWLY	1495	5
MISSES			
HE NEVER MISSES A DEGREE--	THE MOON IS DISTANT FROM	429	5
WHICH MISSES MOST,	WHICH MISSES MOST,	1759	1
MISSILE			
NOR MISSILE [VENGEANCE] EVER COMES	THE CLOUDS THEIR BACKS	1172	8
MISSILES			
HAVE LAIN THEIR MISSILES BY--	THE FARTHEST THUNDER	1581	4
MISSING			
STILL, FOR MY MISSING TROUBADOUR	I HAD A GUINEA GOLDEN--	23	15
I HAVE A MISSING FRIEND--	I HAD A GUINEA GOLDEN--	23	26
THE MISSING ALL, PREVENTED ME	THE MISSING ALL,	985	1
FROM MISSING MINOR THINGS.	THE MISSING ALL,	985	2
THIS WAY, I KEEP FROM MISSING	WE'LL PASS WITHOUT THE	996	7
FOR THE MISSING SEED--	LAIN IN NATURE--SO	1288	4
MISSION			
INTENT UPON IT'S OWN CAREER [MISSION QUAINT / CIRCUIT QUAINT]	HOW SOFT A CATERPILLAR	1448	7
MISSIONARY			
THE MISSIONARY TO THE MOLE	SO MUCH OF HEAVEN HAS	1228	5
MIS SUM			
I'LL MIS SUM THEM	EACH SCAR I'LL KEEP FOR	877	8
MIST			
HERE A MIST, AND THERE A MIST,	OUR SHARE OF NIGHT TO	113	7
HERE A MIST, AND THERE A MIST,	OUR SHARE OF NIGHT TO	113	7
MISTAKE			
A BLUE AND GOLD MISTAKE.	THESE ARE THE DAYS WHEN	130	6
I SHALL NOT FEAR MISTAKE--	YOU LOVE ME--YOU ARE	156	2
LET JUSTICE NOT MISTAKE--	'TWAS LOVE--NOT ME--	394	9
TO SEE THAT I MADE NO MISTAKE	I READ MY SENTENCE--	412	3
WHICH DOOR IS MINE--AND NOT MISTAKE--	I AM ALIVE--I GUESS--	470	23
LEST THE PHANTASM--PROVE THE [JUST] MISTAKE--	WE DREAM--IT IS GOOD WE	531	11
MISTAKE DEFEAT FOR DEATH--EACH TIME--	THE PROVINCE OF THE	539	11
HAD ALL MY LIFE BUT BEEN [BEEN ONE / BEEN BLEAK] MISTAKE	I THINK TO LIVE--MAY BE	646	27
THAT HE'LL [HE] MISTAKE--AND ASK FOR ME	FITTER TO SEE HIM, I MAY	968	16
MISTAKE THE OUTSIDE FOR THE IN	DEW--IS THE FRESHET IN	1097	7
SAGACIOUS OF MY MISTAKE	I SAW THAT THE FLAKE WAS	1267	6
A MERCIFUL [HAZARDOUS] MISTAKE	DEATH WARRANTS ARE	1375	3
SO DAZZLING WE MISTAKE HIM	ONE OF THE ONES THAT	1466	7
MISTAKEN			
TO HOLD MISTAKEN	THE CHILD'S FAITH IS NEW	637	18
MISTAKEN OFT HAS BEEN	DELIGHT'S DESPAIR AT	1299	6
MISTAKING			
SHELLS FROM THE COAST MISTAKING--	SHELLS FROM THE COAST	693	1
MISTLETOE			
IF SHE HAD BEEN THE MISTLETOE	IF SHE HAD BEEN THE	44	1
OR HAPLY, MISTLETOE--	THE ONLY GHOST I EVER	274	8
MISTOOK			
FOR LIGHTNING IT IS OFT MISTOOK	A WINGED SPARK DOTH SOAR	1468	3
AND [THE] VENOMS HE MISTOOK FOR BALMS	ARROWS ENAMORED OF HIS	1629	3
BUT HAVE I NOT MISTOOK	A WORD MADE FLESH IS	1651	4
MISTRESS			
ONCE MORE HER MISTRESS, ON THE DEEP	ONCE MORE, MY NOW	48	3
MISTRESS IS "NOT AT HOME"--TO SAY--	THE FLOWER MUST NOT	206	5
MIST'S			
A MIST'S SLOW COLONNADE--	I MAKE HIS CRESCENT FILL	909	8
MISTS			
WHEREFORE MINE EYE THY SILVER MISTS,	THE BEE IS NOT AFRAID OF	111	7
OR MISTS--THE APPENINE--	THE THOUGHT BENEATH SO	210	4
AS MISTS--OBLITERATE A CRAG.	THERE IS A LANGUOR OF	396	8
AND MISTS--ARE CARVED AWAY,	OF ALL THE SOULS THAT	664	10
MITRED			
ONE MITRED AFTERNOON--	ONE DIGNITY DELAYS FOR	98	2
MITTENS			
HIS MITTENS AT HIS FEET	HIS MANSION IN THE POOL	1379	9
MIX			
AND DIP [MIX] YOUR FINGERS IN THE FROST--	IF ANYBODY'S FRIEND BE	509	15
AS MAKE OF [BREW FROM / MIX] OUR IMPERFECT [UNCOMELY / OBTUSER]	SHE HIDETH HER THE LAST	557	11
MIXED			
A HURRY WITH A LINGERING, MIXED,	I CANNOT MEET THE SPRING	1051	3
I SHOULD HAVE DRUNK [MIXED] IT STRONGER.	HAD I KNOWN THAT THE	1720	4
MIXING			
THE MIXING BELLS AND PALLS--	UPON CONCLUDED LIVES	735	4
MIXING FRESHER AIR.	IT SOUNDED AS IF THE	1397	8
MOAN			
AND PILES OF SOLID MOAN--	MY PORTION IS DEFEAT--	639	9
WITH CONFIDENTIAL MOAN--	THE HEALED HEART SHOWS	1440	2

	FIRST LINE	POEM	LINE
MOANED			
A DYING TIGER--MOANED FOR DRINK--	A DYING TIGER--MOANED	566	1
MOANING			
UNTO GUESSED CRESTS, MY MOANING FANCY, LEADS [LURES] ME,	UNTO LIKE STORY--TROUBLE	295	9
MOAT			
YIELD HER MOAT OF PEARL--	DID THE HAREBELL LOOSE	213	6
AND EVER SINCE--THE PURPLE MOAT	THE LONESOME FOR THEY	262	5
MOATS			
AND MOATS OF MYSTERY.	SUNSET THAT SCREENS,	1609	4
MOB			
A MOB OF SOLID BLISS--	FROM ALL THE JAILS THE	1532	6
ON A STRANGE [UPON A] MOB OF PANTING TREES	THERE CAME A WIND LIKE A	1593	9
THE MOB WITHIN THE HEART	THE MOB WITHIN THE HEART	1745	1
MOCCASIN			
THE DOOM'S ELECTRIC MOCCASIN	THERE CAME A WIND LIKE A	1593	7
MOCHAS			
THE MYRRHS, AND MOCHAS, OF THE MIND	CANDOR--MY TEPID FRIEND	1537	3
MOCK			
THEIR GRASPLESS MANNERS--MOCK US--	THE TINT I CANNOT TAKE--	627	21
MOCKERY			
AND MOCKERY--WAS STILL--	GOD MADE A LITTLE	442	8
MAKES MOCKERY OF MELODY	TO SEE HER IS A PICTURE	1568	V
MOCKING			
STARING--BEWILDERED [DEFRAUDED]--AT THE MOCKING SKY--	THE NEAREST DREAM	319	10
MOCKS			
THAT LAWFUL ORCHARDS [DAMSONS] MOCKS--	FORBIDDEN FRUIT A FLAVOR	1377	2
MODE			
THE SPIRIT LASTS--BUT IN WHAT MODE--	THE SPIRIT LASTS--BUT IN	1576	1
MODERATE			
THE MODERATE DRINKER OF DELIGHT	A DRUNKARD CANNOT MEET A	1628	7
MODERATELY			
THE TRUTH MUST DAZZLE GRADUALLY [MODERATELY]	TELL ALL THE TRUTH BUT	1129	7
MODERN			
BREATHE IN EAR MORE MODERN	IT DID NOT SURPRISE ME--	39	7
MODEST			
MODEST, LET US WALK AMONG IT	I CANT TELL YOU--BUT YOU	65	9
HER MODEST HOUSE--	FOR EVERY BIRD A NEST--	143	15
A MODEST LOT--A FAME PETITE--	A LITTLE BREAD--A CRUST	159	7
TO SUCH A MODEST CLAY,	WAIT TILL THE MAJESTY OF	171	14
I MEANT TO HAVE BUT MODEST NEEDS--	I MEANT TO HAVE BUT	476	1
SO MODEST AND SO VAIN--	'TIS SEASONS SINCE THE	1529	6
BUT ANGELS HAVE THAT MODEST WAY	FOREVER HONORED BE THE	1570	7
OF MODEST INDUSTRY	THE BUTTERFLY OBTAINS	1685	10
MODESTIES			
WITH MODESTIES ENLARGED.	OUR LITTLE KINSMEN--	885	12
MODESTLY			
HOW MODESTLY--ALWAY--	I TEND MY FLOWERS FOR	339	25
MODESTY			
A MODESTY BEFITS THE SOUL	THE WORLD--STANDS--	493	3
REVERSES MODESTY	I CANNOT BE ASHAMED	914	5
MODIFY			
THEY'D MODIFY THE GLEE	THE MORNING AFTER WO--	364	14
THAN I COULD COAX A LEECH AWAY--[MODIFY A LEECH]	IT WOULD HAVE STARVED A	612	7
MOIETY			
"COME UNTO ME" THE MOIETY	NO LADDER NEEDS THE BIRD	1574	7
"COME UNTO ME" THE MOIETY	TO HER DERIDED HOME	1586	11
MOLD SEE MOULD			
OF SOME RARE TENANT OF THE MOLD,	A SCIENCE--SO THE SAVANS	100	5
LOVE, BY MEMORIAL MOLD--	WATER, IS TAUGHT BY	135	5
LONG BUTTONED IN THE MOLD	OF NEARNESS TO HER	607	10
MOLD-LIFE			
THE MOLD-LIFE--ALL FORGOTTEN--NOW--	THROUGH THE DARK SOD--AS	392	7
MOLE			
THE MISSIONARY TO THE MOLE	SO MUCH OF HEAVEN HAS	1228	5
MOLESTED			
WE ARE MOLESTED EQUALLY	WHY SHOULD WE HURRY--WHY	1646	3
MOLTEN			
FROM INNS OF MOLTEN BLUE--	I TASTE A LIQUOR NEVER	214	8
MOMENT			
A MOMENT TO INTERROGATE,	COCOON ABOVE! COCOON	129	10
TRANSPORTING MUST THE MOMENT BE--	THO' I GET HOME HOW LATE	207	7
TELL THAT THE WORST, IS EASY IN A MOMENT--	IF ANY SINK, ASSURE THAT	358	5
DID OUR BEST MOMENT LAST--	DID OUR BEST MOMENT LAST	393	1
A MOMENT--WE UNCERTAIN STEP	WE GROW ACCUSTOMED TO	419	5
BUT WHERE MY MOMENT OF BROCADE--	IT WOULD NEVER BE COMMON	430	32
POSSIBLY, THIS MOMENT--	I COULD DIE--TO KNOW--	570	11
THY MOMENT	'TWOULD EASE--A	682	7
COOLED BY THE MORSEL FOR A MOMENT	AS THE STARVED MAELSTROM	872	9
IN MOMENT OF PROSPERITY--	HAD I NOT THIS, OR THIS,	904	3
IN MOMENT OF REVERSE--	HAD I NOT THIS, OR THIS,	904	6
CAJOLES A MOMENT WITH THE SPIRES	IT RISES--PASSES--ON OUR	1023	3
DUKE IN A MOMENT OF DEATHLESSNESS	I AM AFRAID TO OWN A	1090	7
THE AWFUL MOMENT IS	WE DO NOT KNOW THE TIME	1106	2
OH SUMPTUOUS MOMENT	OH SUMPTUOUS MOMENT	1125	1
NO MOMENT WILL THERE BE	IN THY LONG PARADISE OF	1145	2
WITH SUPERSTITIOUS VALUE [MERIT / MOMENT]	TO DISAPPEAR ENHANCES--	1209	7
THEIR MOMENT CONSUMMATED--	A BEE HIS BURNISHED	1339	9

	FIRST LINE	POEM	LINE
MOMENT (CONTINUED)			
HOW MUCH THE PRESENT MOMENT MEANS	HOW MUCH THE PRESENT	1380	1
WHICH RAPTURE [TRIUMPH / HOUR / MOMENT]-- SHE PREFERRED	CRISIS IS SWEET AND YET	1416	6
THE MOMENT THAT A PLOT IS PLUMBED	HOW HUMAN NATURE DOTES	1417	3
IN A MOMENT CONTRABAND--	"HEAVENLY FATHER"--TAKE	1461	4
THAT PURLED A MOMENT SINCE WITH GLEE-- . .	HIS VOICE DECREPIT WAS	1476	5
MAKES THE [THIS] PRESENT [NEXT MOMENT] MEAN--	GLASS WAS THE STREET--IN	1498	8
WE THIS MOMENT KNEW--	IS IT TOO LATE TO TOUCH	1637	2
IF THEY THIS MOMENT HAD	I KNOW OF PEOPLE IN THE	1665	8
THE MOMENT OF OUR DEATH--	WITCHCRAFT HAS NOT A	1708	4
FOR TRAINS THAT MOMENT [SEVERELY] OUT OF SIGHT,	THE SUMMER THAT WE DID	1773	7
MOMENTLY			
IF MOMENTLY [HER SWEET DOOR--] AJAR-- . .	IT KNEW NO MEDICINE--	559	13
MOMENTOUS			
HOW MIGHTY [MOMENTOUS] TO THE INSECURE . .	HOW FIRM ETERNITY MUST	1499	5
HOW RAPID, HOW MOMENTOUS--	WERE NATURE MORTAL LADY	1762	5
MOMENT'S			
WITHOUT A MOMENT'S BELL--	THAT AFTER HORROR--THAT	286	10
UPON A MOMENT'S SHALLOW [FICKLE] RIM . . .	HOW MUCH THE PRESENT	1380	5
MOMENTS			
THESE HEAVENLY MOMENTS ARE--	DID OUR BEST MOMENT LAST	393	8
THE SOUL HAS BANDAGED MOMENTS--	THE SOUL HAS BANDAGED	512	1
THE SOUL HAS MOMENTS OF ESCAPE--	THE SOUL HAS BANDAGED	512	11
THE SOUL'S RETAKEN MOMENTS--	THE SOUL HAS BANDAGED	512	19
AND THO' IN SOBERER MOMENTS--	IT ALWAYS FELT TO ME--A	597	5
THE MOMENTS OF DOMINION	THE TINT I CANNOT TAKE--	627	9
ALLOYS OUR FIRMER MOMENTS	THROUGH THOSE OLD	1753	13
MOMENTUM			
TO TAKE MOMENTUM--	WHAT TWIGS WE HELD BY--	1086	5
BUT [YET] IT'S UNIQUE MOMENTUM	HOPE IS A STRANGE	1392	7
MONAD			
OF MONAD OR OF FLY	SHE SPED AS PETALS OF A	991 V	6
MONARCH			
MY FRECKLED MONARCH HELD THE REIN-- . . .	I MET A KING THIS	166	14
AND SINCE WE'RE MUTUAL MONARCH	ME FROM MYSELF--TO	642	9
MONARCHS			
BUT MONARCHS--ARE PERCEPTIBLE--	ONE LIFE OF SO MUCH	270	15
WHERE EMPERORS [MONARCHS] GREW--	I ROSE--BECAUSE HE SANK	616	17
MONARCHY			
IN PERFECT--PAUSELESS MONARCHY--	BEHIND ME--DIPS ETERNITY	721	8
AND [SO / THE] POVERTY OF MONARCHY . . .	WHO COURT OBTAIN WITHIN	803	3
MONEY			
ONE'S--MONEY--ONE'S--THE MINE--	SOME--WORK FOR	406	12
'MONG			
'MONG SUCH UNIQUE	I WENT TO HEAVEN--	374	15
MONITION			
EXAMPLE--AND MONITION	TWO BUTTERFLIES WENT OUT	533 V	
THE NOTICE [MONITION] TO THE STARTLED GRASS	PRESENTIMENT--IS THAT	764	3
MONOTONY			
THAN MONOTONY	CONSCIOUS AM I IN MY	679	14
AND BLUE MONOTONY	THE HEART HAS NARROW	928	4
WITH MONOTONY.	NOT ANY MORE TO BE	1344	16
SO ABSOLUTE--MONOTONY	HIS MANSION IN THE POOL	1379 V	
MONSTER			
A MONSTER WITH A GLASS	"ARCTURUS" IS HIS OTHER	70	10
NO SPECTACLE [MONSTER THEN] IN SIGHT . . .	ESCAPE IS SUCH A	1347	4
EFFACE THE BURDEN [MONSTER / STATURE / SPECTRE / TROUBLE / . . .	THE PILE OF YEARS IS NOT	1507	7
MONSTER'S			
THE MONSTER'S FADED EYES	AN AWFUL TEMPEST MASHED	198	11
MONSTROUS			
HAD NATURE--IN HER MONSTROUS HOUSE . . .	A TONGUE--TO TELL HIM I	400	3
WE THOUGHT THE MIGHTY [MONSTROUS] FUNERAL--	'TIS GOOD--THE LOOKING	660	3
CONSOLES A WO SO MONSTROUS	I SOMETIMES DROP IT, FOR	708	5
MONTCALM			
MONTCALM, HIS OPPOSING SPIRIT	WOLFE DEMANDED DURING	678	5
MONTH			
IS BUT A MONTH FROM HERE [AWAY]--	THE NOTICE THAT IS	1310	2
MARCH IS THE MONTH OF EXPECTATION. . . .	MARCH IS THE MONTH OF	1404	1
MONTHS			
SO--TWELVE MONTHS AGO--	ONE YEAR AGO--JOTS WHAT?	296	25
THE MONTHS HAVE ENDS--THE YEARS--A KNOT-- .	THE MONTHS HAVE ENDS--	423	1
I'D WIND THE MONTHS IN BALLS--	IF YOU WERE COMING IN	511	6
LET MONTHS DISSOLVE IN FURTHER [OTHER] MONTHS--	FOREVER--IS COMPOSED OF	624	7
LET MONTHS DISSOLVE IN FURTHER [OTHER] MONTHS--	FOREVER--IS COMPOSED OF	624	7
MOOD			
AS IS THE CENTRAL MOOD--	THE OUTER--FROM THE	451	4
MOON			
ADAM, AND EVE, HIS CONSORT, THE MOON, AND THEN THE SUN!	AWAKE YE MUSES NINE,	1	8
THE WAVE WITH EYE SO PENSIVE, LOOKETH TO SEE THE MOON,	AWAKE YE MUSES NINE,	1	18
WHO FIRST OBSERVED THE MOON!	"SIC TRANSIT GLORIA	3	12
HATH PASSED BEYOND THE MOON, ...	"SIC TRANSIT GLORIA	3	64
AH, MOON--AND STAR!	AH, MOON--AND STAR!	240	1
BUT, MOON, AND STAR, ...	AH, MOON--AND STAR!	240	13

	FIRST LINE	POEM	LINE
MOON (CONTINUED)			
THE MOON--SLIDES DOWN THE STAIR,	I KNOW SOME LONELY	289	23
HER FACE BE ROUNDER THAN THE MOON	THERE IS A FLOWER THAT	380	9
WHEN NOT A MOON DISCLOSE A SIGN--	WE GROW ACCUSTOMED TO	419	11
THE MOON IS DISTANT FROM THE SEA--	THE MOON IS DISTANT FROM	429	1
YOU KNOW THAT PORTRAIT IN THE MOON--	YOU KNOW THAT PORTRAIT	504	1
OR SETTLE IN THE MOON--	HE PARTS HIMSELF--LIKE	517	12
I WATCHED THE MOON AROUND THE HOUSE	I WATCHED THE MOON	629	1
THE MOTION OF THE MOON--	I COULD SUFFICE FOR HIM,	643	14
A TENDER--THOUGHTFUL MOON	AGAIN--HIS VOICE IS AT	663	19
THE MOON WAS BUT A CHIN OF GOLD	THE MOON WAS BUT A CHIN	737	1
THE SUN AND MOON MUST MAKE THEIR HASTE--	THE SUN AND MOON MUST	871	1
FABULOUS AS A MOON AT NOON	WHITE AS AN INDIAN PIPE	1250	3
WHICH IS THE BEST--THE MOON OR THE CRESCENT?	WHICH IS THE BEST--THE	1315	1
NEITHER--SAID THE MOON--	WHICH IS THE BEST--THE	1315	2
AS ELIGIBLE [UNPERVERTED / UNDIVERTED / UNAVAILING] AS THE MOON	SUMMER--WE ALL HAVE SEEN	1386	7
THE ROAD WAS LIT WITH [BY] MOON AND STAR--	THE ROAD WAS LIT WITH	1450	1
THE MOON UPON HER FLUENT ROUTE	THE MOON UPON HER FLUENT	1528	1
WHICH LIKE THE MOON, SOME TURBID NIGHT,	EACH THAT WE LOSE TAKES	1605	3
LOOSED THE MOON HER SILVER HAT	LIGHTLY STEPPED A YELLOW	1672	3
MOONLESS			
THAN UNARMED [MOONLESS], ONE'S A'SELF ENCOUNTER--	ONE NEED NOT BE A	670	11
MOON'S			
WHEN MOON'S AT FULL--'TIS THOU--I SAY--	YOU KNOW THAT PORTRAIT	504	9
MOONS			
THE BUTTERFLIES--AS SWANS [MOONS]--	I THINK I WAS ENCHANTED	593	10
PROUD OF MY NIGHT, SINCE THOU WITH MOONS DOST SLAKE IT,	PROUD OF MY BROKEN HEART	1736	3
MOOR			
BY BECK, OR BURN, OR MOOR!	I WOULD DISTIL A CUP,	16	4
OF MORNING AND THE MOOR,	MY NOSEGAYS ARE FOR	95	6
MIGHT I BUT MOOR--TONIGHT--	WILD NIGHTS--WILD NIGHTS	249	11
I NEVER SAW A MOOR--	I NEVER SAW A MOOR--	1052	1
MOORING			
BY WHAT MYSTIC MOORING	WHETHER MY BARK WENT	52	5
RATHER THAN A MOORING--UNSHARED BY THEE.	HOW SICK--TO WAIT--IN	368	9
MOORINGS			
HANDS BUSTLED AT THE MOORINGS--	WENT UP A YEAR THIS	93	19
MORAL			
MY STORY HAS A MORAL--	I HAD A GUINEA GOLDEN--	23	25
MORAL--WITH A MASTIFF	ABRAHAM TO KILL HIM	1317	11
MORALS			
OF INDUSTRY AND MORALS [ETHICS]	HIS LITTLE HEARSE LIKE	1522	5
MORE			
NO MORE HE SINGETH MOURNFUL, HER SADNESS SHE DOTH LOSE.	AWAKE YE MUSES NINE,	1	20
IN A MORE GOLDEN LIGHT	I HAVE A BIRD IN SPRING	5	20
DRINKING TO HER NO MORE ASTIR,	I WOULD DISTIL A CUP,	16	3
"THERE IS NO MORE SNOW!"	ALL THESE MY BANNERS BE.	22	19
WHICH WALK NO MORE THE VILLAGE STREET--	THERE IS A MORN BY MEN	24	8
BREATHE IN EAR MORE MODERN	IT DID NOT SURPRISE ME--	39	7
ONCE MORE, MY NOW BEWILDERED DOVE	ONCE MORE, MY NOW	48	1
ONCE MORE HER MISTRESS, ON THE DEEP	ONCE MORE, MY NOW	48	3
I AM POOR ONCE MORE!	I NEVER LOST AS MUCH BUT	49	8
AND I'D LIKE TO LOOK A LITTLE MORE	GOING TO HEAVEN!	79	22
I PRAY YOU PASS [STROLL] ONCE MORE.	HEART, NOT SO HEAVY AS	83	20
YET IS SHE MORE CONVINCING	THE RAINBOW NEVER TELLS	97	3
WHERE BELLS NO MORE AFFRIGHT THE MORN--	WHERE BELLS NO MORE	112	1
COULD SCARE US ANY MORE!	WHERE BELLS NO MORE	112	12
BUT NOT AN HOUR MORE!	PERHAPS YOU'D LIKE TO	134	10
ALL THIS AND MORE I CANNOT TELL--	AN ALTERED LOOK ABOUT	140	13
NO MORE HER PATIENT FIGURE	SHE BORE IT TILL THE	144	9
NO MORE HER TIMID BONNET	SHE BORE IT TILL THE	144	11
AND NO MORE DOLLIE--MARK--	YOU LOVE ME--YOU ARE	156	12
A SOLDIER'S--BALLS! WHO ASKETH MORE,	A LITTLE BREAD--A CRUST	159	11
OF MORE ESTEEM THAN DUCATS--	I LOST A WORLD--THE	181	7
A MORE BERNARDINE GIRL--	I'VE HEARD AN ORGAN TALK	183	6
NEVER A THIMBLE--MORE--SHALL WEAR--	HOW MANY TIMES THESE LOW	187	8
TO PEOPLE--ANY MORE!	THE FLOWER MUST NOT	206	6
IS MORE DISTINCTLY SEEN--	THE THOUGHT BENEATH SO	210	2
I SHALL BUT DRINK THE MORE!	I TASTE A LIQUOR NEVER	214	12
IF HE DISSOLVE--THEN--THERE IS NOTHING--MORE--	IF HE DISSOLVE--THEN--	236	1
HE--IS MORE THAN A FIRMAMENT--FROM ME--	AH, MOON--AND STAR!	240	16
JUST--ONCE--MORE--	WHY--DO THEY SHUT ME OUT	248	6
MORE HANDS--TO HOLD--THESE ARE BUT TWO--	A SINGLE SCREW OF FLESH	263	13
ONE MORE NEW-MAILED NERVE	A SINGLE SCREW OF FLESH	263	14
WHAT MORE THE WOMAN CAN,	DOUBT ME! MY DIM	275	6
WHAT OPULENCE THE MORE	DOUBT ME! MY DIM	275	12
THEY CANNOT TAKE ME [US]--ANY MORE!	WHAT IF I SAY I SHALL	277	7
TO KNOW THE WORST, LEAVES NO DREAD MORE--	'TIS SO APPALLING--IT	281	4
A SEPULCHRE, FEARS FROST, NO MORE--	'TIS SO APPALLING--IT	281	V 4
A SECOND MORE, HAD DROPPED TOO DEEP	THAT AFTER HORROR--THAT	286	5
NOTHING MORE--	IF YOUR NERVE, DENY YOU	292	12
ITSELF, TOO GREAT [VAST], FOR INTERRUPTING--MORE--	I GOT SO I COULD HEAR	293	27
ONE--BIRTHDAY MORE--OR TEN?	ONE YEAR AGO--JOTS WHAT?	296	35
PRESENT [OBTRUDE] NO MORE--	THE SOUL SELECTS HER OWN	303	4
MINE--IS THE MORE CONVENIENT	I SEND TWO SUNSETS--	308	7

	FIRST LINE	POEM	LINE
MORE (CONTINUED)			
'TIS LIVING--HURTS US MORE--	'TIS NOT THAT DYING	335	2
NO CRIMSON--MORE--	I TEND MY FLOWERS FOR	339	20
NONE BUY IT ANY MORE--	IS BLISS THEN, SUCH	340	11
THEN--STEPPED MORE FAST--	'TWAS THE OLD--ROAD--	344	7
MORE IMMINENT THAN PAIN--	THERE IS A LANGUOR OF	396	2
IF ONCE MORE--PARDON--BOY--	A TONGUE--TO TELL HIM I	400	14
BUT DAPPERER--MORE SWEET--	A MURMUR IN THE TREES--	416	8
ALL THIS--AND MORE--IF I SHOULD TELL--	A MURMUR IN THE TREES--	416	11
MORE LIFE--WENT OUT--WHEN HE WENT	MORE LIFE--WENT OUT--	422	1
A FROST MORE NEEDLE KEEN	MORE LIFE--WENT OUT--	422	10
IT WOULD NEVER BE COMMON--MORE--I SAID--	IT WOULD NEVER BE COMMON	430	1
COULD--I DO MORE--FOR THEE--	COULD--I DO MORE--FOR	447	1
THOUGH SPOKES--SPIN--MORE CONSPICUOUS	THE OUTER--FROM THE	451	7
WHERE MOSSES GO NO MORE AWAY--	I KNOW WHERE WELLS GROW	460	3
THAT PEOPLE "THIRST NO MORE"--	I KNOW WHERE WELLS GROW	460	14
SO SOON TO BE A CHILD NO MORE--	A WIFE--AT DAYBREAK I	461	11
AND THEY NO MORE REMEMBER ME--	WHY MAKE IT DOUBT--IT	462	11
I GO NO MORE AWAY	I LIVE WITH HIM--I SEE	463	2
TILL IT BE NIGHT--NO MORE--	A NIGHT--THERE LAY THE	471	8
NEVER A GOWN OF DUN--MORE--	I AM ASHAMED--I HIDE--	473	10
NO MORE ASHAMED--	I AM ASHAMED--I HIDE--	473	24
NO MORE TO HIDE--	I AM ASHAMED--I HIDE--	473	25
THOU NOTICE US--NO MORE--	WE COVER THEE--SWEET	482	6
A PRAYER, THAT IT MORE ANGEL--PROVE--	THE WORLD--STANDS--	493	9
FOR NEEDING MORE--	IT'S THOUGHTS--AND JUST	495	11
OF ALL TUNES I KNEW--AND MORE--	BETTER--THAN MUSIC! FOR	503	4
TOUCH LIBERTY--THEN KNOW NO MORE,	THE SOUL HAS BANDAGED	512	17
SEEKING [SAVING] MORE--TO SPEND--	SWEET--YOU FORGOT--BUT I	523	8
WITH OTHER--AND 'TWILL YAWN THE MORE--	TO FILL A GAP	546	4
MORE MOUNTAINS--THEN A SEA--	I CROSS TILL I AM WEARY	550	3
MORE SEAS--AND THEN	I CROSS TILL I AM WEARY	550	4
ONE MORE--"YE BLESSED"--TO BE TOLD--	THERE IS A SHAME OF	551	7
MORE FAIR--BECAUSE IMPOSSIBLE	DELIGHT--BECOMES	572	3
THE MORE CONVENIENT WAY--	THE BODY GROWS WITHOUT--	578	2
'TWAS MORE--I CANNOT MENTION--	THE TREES LIKE TASSELS--	606	25
IN ONE OR TWO [MORE] EXISTENCES--	AFRAID! OF WHOM AM I	608	7
I COULD NO MORE REMOVE	IT WOULD HAVE STARVED A	612	6
AND LAUGH--NO MORE HAVE I--	THEY SHUT ME UP IN PROSE	613	12
DID THEY--COME BACK NO MORE?	GLEE--THE GREAT STORM IS	619	13
WOULD MORE AFFRONT THE SAND--	YOU'LL KNOW HER--BY HER	634	4
MORE ARDUOUS [DIFFICULT] THAN BALLS--	MY PORTION IS DEFEAT--	639	6
AND I HAD NO MORE EYES	I CANNOT LIVE WITH YOU--	640	34
REPUDIATES IT, ALL THE MORE--	SIZE CIRCUMSCRIBES--IT	641	5
TO DEVISE ONCE MORE	PROMISE THIS--WHEN YOU	648	10
IMITATING [MORE RESEMBLING] YOU--	PROMISE THIS--WHEN YOU	648	16
'TWAS MORE PITIFUL ENDEAVOR	HER SWEET TURN TO LEAVE	649	5
MORE NUMEROUS OF WINDOWS--	I DWELL IN POSSIBILITY--	657	3
JUST HIS FACE--NOTHING MORE!	AGAIN--HIS VOICE IS AT	663	12
OR MORE--	ONE NEED NOT BE A	670	20
MORE NEAR--	ONE NEED NOT BE A	670	V 20
SUITS ME--MORE THAN THOSE--	I COULD BRING YOU JEWELS	697	8
AND CAME MY WAY NO MORE--	A THOUGHT WENT UP MY	701	12
WOULD'NT BONDS HURT MORE	LET US PLAY YESTERDAY--	728	27
YET--THERE IS A SCIENCE MORE--	YOU TAUGHT ME WAITING	740	8
THIS--THE BEST ENACT [MORE EXERT]	DRAMA'S VITALLEST	741	5
AND TROUBLE [HARASS] ME--NO MORE--	THE BIRDS REPORTED FROM	743	8
I KNEW NO MORE OF WANT--OR COLD--	ONE BLESSING HAD I THAN	756	9
I SPECULATE NO MORE--	ONE BLESSING HAD I THAN	756	20
MORE [TWO]--WOULD BE TOO VAST	ONE AND ONE--ARE ONE--	769	7
THE MORE THEIR FEET RETIRE.	AWAY FROM HOME ARE SOME	821	8
NO MORE VACATION!	ALWAYS MINE!	839	2
AND EVERY NIGHT, IT NUMBERED MORE	I MADE SLOW RICHES BUT	843	3
A TURRET MORE, A TURRET LESS	JUST AS HE SPOKE IT FROM	848	3
NO MORE TO DO HAVE I	I SING TO USE THE	850	4
CAN HARASS ME NO MORE--	THIS CHASM, SWEET, UPON	858	20
HIS OWN WOULD FALL SO MORE	EACH SCAR I'LL KEEP FOR	877	7
ATTRACTED MORE UNTO--	WHO OCCUPIES THIS HOUSE?	892	24
AND WE BEHOLD--NO MORE	WE CAN BUT FOLLOW TO THE	920	8
MORE PREVIOUS--THAN LIFE--	LOVE--IS THAT LATER	924	2
WOULD SEEM TO ME THE MORE THE WAY	OF TOLLING BELL I ASK	947	7
HOW MORE THE FINISHED CREATURES	THE CHEMICAL CONVICTION	954	7
NO MORE--	WERT THOU BUT ILL--THAT	961	8
I GO--TO ELSEWHERE GO NO MORE--	FITTER TO SEE HIM, I MAY	968	18
WILL EQUAL GLOW, AND THOUGHT NO MORE	IT BLOOMED AND DROPT, A	978	5
MORE DISTANT IN AN INSTANT	AS SLEIGH BELLS SEEM IN	981	7
I MORE THAN ONCE AT NOON	A NARROW FELLOW IN THE	986	12
SOMETIMES, ALMOST MORE.	THIS WAS IN THE WHITE OF	995	8
I WAS A PHEBE--NOTHING MORE--	I WAS A PHEBE--NOTHING	1009	1
I SAW NO MORE OF HER.	I CANNOT MEET THE SPRING	1051	8
HER VISITOR, NO MORE--	THE SOUL SHOULD ALWAYS	1055	8
THAN THIS, I KNOW NO MORE.	FURTHER IN SUMMER THAN	1068	V
PRECISE [MORE OFT] THE OBJECT'S LOSS--	PERCEPTION OF AN OBJECT	1071	2
HOW DOUBLY MORE	WE LEARN IN THE	1083	6
THE DILIGENCE WERE NOT MORE BLIND	WHAT TWIGS WE HELD BY--	1086	13
WE MISS A KINSMAN MORE	WE MISS A KINSMAN MORE	1087	1
MORE INTIMATE WITH US BECOME	THE MURMURING OF BEES,	1115	15
NAPLES IS MORE AFRAID	WHEN ETNA BASKS AND	1146	2
TO BE ESTEEMED NO MORE	A FULL FED ROSE ON MEALS	1154	8
AND SO MUCH MORE AT HOME THAN I	ALONE AND IN A	1167	5

	FIRST LINE	POEM	LINE
MORE (CONTINUED)			
BECOME, ALAS, MORE FAIR--	TO MAKE ROUTINE A	1196	8
IS "NO MORE SEA"--	BECAUSE MY BROOK IS	1200	8
SOME WE SEE NO MORE, TENEMENTS OF WONDER	SOME WE SEE NO MORE,	1221	1
ARE MORE THAN IT'S EVENTS--	THE INCIDENTS OF LOVE	1248	2
WHAT LOSS WOULD VALUE MORE	HAD THIS ONE DAY NOT	1253	6
WISDOM IS MORE BECOMING VIEWED	I WORKED FOR CHAFF AND	1269	7
MORE LOYAL FOR THE EXODY	FROM HIS SLIM PALACE IN	1300	3
I CANNOT WANT IT MORE--	I CANNOT WANT IT MORE--	1301	1
NOT ANY MORE TO BE LACKED--	NOT ANY MORE TO BE	1344	1
NOT ANY MORE TO BE KNOWN--	NOT ANY MORE TO BE	1344	2
MORE ELOQUENTLY LIE	THE FLAKE THE WIND	1361	2
HAS MORE INTEGRITY.	A SAUCER HOLDS A CUP	1374	V 16
TO THOSE WHO'VE NOTHING MORE--	HOW MUCH THE PRESENT	1380	2
A FEW--THE MORE ASPIRING	SUMMER--WE ALL HAVE SEEN	1386	3
I MORE SHOULD MISS--	MY MAKER--LET ME BE	1403	4
BUT ACCLIMATED--PINES NO MORE [GROPES NO MORE / LOSES SIGHT / . . .	THE INUNDATION OF THE	1425	7
BUT ACCLIMATED--PINES NO MORE [GROPES NO MORE / LOSES SIGHT / . . .	THE INUNDATION OF THE	1425	7
. . . YEARNS NO MORE]	THE INUNDATION OF THE	1425	7
NOT THAT HE GOES--WE LOVE HIM MORE	NOT THAT HE GOES--WE	1435	1
THAN HEAVEN MORE REMOTE,	THAN HEAVEN MORE REMOTE,	1436	1
MORE FLOWN INDEED	THAN HEAVEN MORE REMOTE,	1436	4
MORE GENUINE WERE PERFIDY	THE HEALED HEART SHOWS	1440	7
WHOSE ALLIES GO NO MORE ASTRAY [ABROAD]	A CHILLY PEACE INFESTS	1443	5
MORE ARDUOUS THERE IS--	HIS MIND LIKE FABRICS OF	1446	6
MORE RESPECTFUL--"WE ARE DUST"--	"HEAVENLY FATHER"--TAKE	1461	6
THEIR ARMIES ARE NO MORE.	THEIR BARRICADE AGAINST	1471	4
MORE PRUDENT TO ASSAULT THE DAWN	HER SPIRIT ROSE TO SUCH	1486	4
IS MORE DISTINCT THAN OUR'S--	THE FACE IN EVANESCENCE	1490	2
IS MORE PREFERRED.	THE ROAD TO PARADISE IS	1491	6
MORE THAN THE GRAVE IS CLOSED TO ME--	MORE THAN THE GRAVE IS	1503	1
AND WE ACCOST NO MORE--[WE KNOW]	WE NEVER KNOW WE GO WHEN	1523	4
ACQUAINTED MORE WITH THAT	OH GIVE IT MOTION--DECK	1527	6
AND CENTURIES 'TWILL BE AND MORE	'TIS SEASONS SINCE THE	1529	4
A PANG IS MORE CONSPICUOUS IN SPRING	A PANG IS MORE	1530	1
HE IS JUST AS [STILL MORE] HIGH--	FOLLOW WISE ORION	1538	4
PERHAPS IS MORE ASTUTE	COME SHOW THY DURHAM	1542	8
I HAVE ONE BATTLE MORE--	MY WARS ARE LAID AWAY IN	1549	2
BEGUILE IT MORE AND MORE--	WE SHUN IT ERE IT COMES,	1580	5
BEGUILE IT MORE AND MORE--	WE SHUN IT ERE IT COMES,	1580	5
ESCAPE MORE SLOWLY	EXPANSE CANNOT BE LOST--	1584	13
HE KNEW NO MORE THAT HE WAS POOR,	HE ATE AND DRANK THE	1587	3
TO TWO--NOT ANY MORE--	THE AUCTIONEER OF	1612	8
A MORE ESSENTIAL THING.	THE PEDIGREE OF HONEY	1627	8
AND MORE ARE IN THE JOY--	A DRUNKARD CANNOT MEET A	1628	10
NO MORE FROM YOURS AT PRESENT	THE JAY HIS CASTANET HAS	1635	8
WHEN AT MY VERY DOOR ARE THOSE POSSESSING MORE,	TAKE ALL AWAY FROM ME,	1640	4
THAT ALL MAY THEM--IT--EXAMINE [WITNESS IT AND MORE]	SOME ONE PREPARED THIS	1644	5
BUT DISCOVER IT NO MORE	EDEN IS THAT	1657	8
NATURE CAN DO NO MORE	NATURE CAN DO NO MORE	1673	1
OR VALUES MORE SEVERE--	THE LOOK OF THEE, WHAT	1689	8
BUT WRONG THE MORE	T'WAS COMFORT IN HER	1703	7
HER TONGUE MORE TENDER [TIMID / MAGIC] THAN THE TUNE [TONE]	HER FACE WAS IN A BED OF	1722	5
MORE THAN WIFEHOOD EVER MAY!	REARRANGE A "WIFE'S"	1737	8
WE MORE THAN HALF SUSPECT,	THE DISTANCE THAT THE	1742	6
AND BY DEPARTURE MORE.	WERE NATURE MORTAL LADY	1762	12
MADE CRUELLY MORE DEAR.	THE SADDEST NOISE, THE	1764	12
WOULD GO AND SING NO MORE.	THE SADDEST NOISE, THE	1764	16
INSTRUCTS US BY DEPARTING [DERISION] NOW [MORE]	THE SUMMER THAT WE DID	1773	3
MORI			
AND OH "MEMENTO MORI"	"SIC TRANSIT GLORIA	3	7
MORN			
NIGHT UNTO DAY IS MARRIED, MORN UNTO EVENTIDE;	AWAKE YE MUSES NINE,	1	22
MORN IS SUPPOSED TO BE	SLEEP IS SUPPOSED TO BE	13	7
BUT TOOK THE MORN--	ONE SISTER HAVE I IN OUR	14	24
UPON A COMMON SUMMER'S MORN--	A SEPAL, PETAL, AND A	19	2
THERE IS A MORN BY MEN UNSEEN--	THERE IS A MORN BY MEN	24	1
I ASK, EACH NEW MAY MORN.	THERE IS A MORN BY MEN	24	21
AND MORN SH'D BEAM--	IF I SHOULD DIE,	54	4
A WAKING ON A MORN	A DARTING FEAR--A POMP--	87	2
WHERE BELLS NO MORE AFFRIGHT THE MORN--	WHERE BELLS NO MORE	112	1
SO LOOKING ON--THE NIGHT--THE MORN	A SOMETHING IN A	122	19
MERRY THAT IT IS MORN--	AS CHILDREN BID THE	133	6
A WIDER SUNRISE IN THE MORN--	AN ALTERED LOOK ABOUT	140	3
SOME GRINNING MORN--	YOU LOVE ME--YOU ARE	156	4
AND--WAKING--LONG BEFORE THE MORN--	MUSICIANS WRESTLE	157	4
ON RESUMPTION MORN,	I HAVE NEVER SEEN	175	18
ON THIS LATE MORN--THE SUN--	ON THIS LONG STORM THE	194	2
SOME SUDDEN MORN--	DELIGHT IS AS THE FLIGHT	257	24
SOME TRANSATLANTIC MORN--	THE LONESOME FOR THEY	262	10
HAD IT FOR ME A MORN--	AS IF I ASKED A COMMON	323	6
WITH EVERY MORN THAT CAME--	IT STRUCK ME--EVERY DAY	362	8
THAN DID NEXT MORN	I'M SAYING EVERY DAY	373	27
WHOSE WINDOWS--NIGHT AND MORN--	A HOUSE UPON THE HIGHT--	399	6

	FIRST LINE	POEM	LINE
MORNING (CONTINUED)			
MORNING THAT COMES BUT ONCE,	MORNING THAT COMES BUT	1610	1
A MORNING AND A NOON	OF THIS IS DAY COMPOSED	1675	2
MORNING'S			
NIGHT IS THE MORNING'S CANVAS	THE FEET OF PEOPLE	7	13
RECKON THE MORNING'S FLAGON'S UP	BRING ME THE SUNSET IN A	128	2
WERE USELESS AS NEXT MORNING'S SUN--	I SHOULD NOT DARE TO	205	15
THE MORNING'S AMBER [LIGHTNING'S JOINTED] ROAD--	BEFORE I GOT MY EYE PUT	327	15
I [HE] SHOWED HER [ME] SECRETS--MORNING'S NEST--	I SHOWED HER HIGHTS SHE	446	5
THIS MORNING'S FINER VERDICT--	WE SEE--COMPARATIVELY--	534	5
MORNING'S BOLD FACE--STARES IN THE WINDOW--	I COULD DIE--TO KNOW--	570	5
WITH MORNING'S WARMING LIGHT--	LET MY FIRST KNOWING BE	1218	2
THIS MORNING'S FINEST SYLLABLE	WHEN MEMORY IS FULL	1266	3
AN EASY MORNING'S RIDE--	A ROUTE OF EVANESCENCE	1463	8
MORNINGS			
A FEW INCISIVE MORNINGS--	BESIDES THE AUTUMN POETS	131	5
SINCE WE--OLD MORNINGS, CHILDREN--PLAYED--	OF NEARNESS TO HER	607	11
THE MORNINGS BLOSSOM INTO NOONS--	IT MAKES NO DIFFERENCE	620	3
WHAT MORNINGS IN OUR GARDEN--GUESSED--	I LEARNED--AT LEAST--	944	9
TO WHOM THE MORNINGS STAND FOR NIGHTS,	TO WHOM THE MORNINGS	1095	1
TOO FEW THE MORNINGS BE,	TOO FEW THE MORNINGS BE,	1186	1
MORNS			
THE MORNS ARE MEEKER THAN THEY WERE--	THE MORNS ARE MEEKER	12	1
MORNS LIKE THESE--WE PARTED--	MORNS LIKE THESE--WE	27	1
OR GRISLY FROSTS--FIRST AUTUMN MORNS,	IT WAS NOT DEATH, FOR I	510	19
HOW MIGHTY THE WIND MUST FEEL MORNS	HOW LONESOME THE WIND	1418	9
AND STOOD AMAZED BEFORE THE CHANGE [BOON / MORNS]	THE THRILL CAME SLOWLY	1495	7
MORROW SEE TO-MORROW, TOMORROW			
THE NIGHT'S TREMENDOUS MORROW	ON THAT SPECIFIC PILLOW	1533	3
MORSEL			
COOLED BY THE MORSEL FOR A MOMENT	AS THE STARVED MAELSTROM	872	9
MORTAL			
THE WORM DOTH WOO THE MORTAL, DEATH CLAIMS A LIVING BRIDE,	AWAKE YE MUSES NINE,	1	21
MORTAL SHALL NOT SEE--	WHEN I COUNT THE SEEDS	40	8
MORTAL, MY FRIEND MUST BE,	MY FRIEND MUST BE A BIRD	92	3
UPON THE MORTAL SIDE.	SHE DIED--THIS WAS THE	150	8
AS WHEN HER LITTLE MORTAL NEST	MAMA NEVER FORGETS HER	164	5
WHAT IF I FILE THIS MORTAL--OFF--	WHAT IF I SAY I SHALL	277	4
THIS MORTAL ABOLITION	THE SOUL'S SUPERIOR	306	9
BEHIND THIS MORTAL BONE	NO RACK CAN TORTURE ME--	384	3
THAT WHEN THEIR MORTAL NAME [FAME] BE NUMB--	THE MARTYR POETS--DID	544	3
THEIR MORTAL FATE--ENCOURAGE SOME--	THE MARTYR POETS--DID	544	4
OUR MORTAL CONSEQUENCE	NO OTHER CAN REDUCE	982	2
MORTAL CONSEQUENCE	NO OTHER CAN REDUCE	982 V	
BEFORE THIS MORTAL NOISE	IT WAS A QUIET WAY--	1053	6
BY MORTAL NUMERAL--	THERE IS ANOTHER	1116	8
ONE [THIS] REQUISITE HAS FIRE THAT LASTS [EARTHLY FIRE / MORTAL FIRE]	THE SMOULDERING EMBERS	1132	7
AND MORTAL COMPANY--	IN THY LONG PARADISE OF	1145	4
COULD MORTAL LIP DIVINE	COULD MORTAL LIP DIVINE	1409	1
TO HIM WHOSE MORTAL LIGHT	HOW DARE THE ROBINS SING	1724	10
WERE NATURE MORTAL LADY	WERE NATURE MORTAL LADY	1762	1
MORTALITY			
MORTALITY IS FATAL--	"SIC TRANSIT GLORIA	3	41
TERMED MORTALITY!	TO VENERATE THE SIMPLE	57	6
CONQUER MORTALITY--	GIVEN IN MARRIAGE UNTO	817	8
WE FOUGHT MORTALITY.	THE FROST OF DEATH WAS	1136	4
EACH BRIGHT MORTALITY	A FULL FED ROSE ON MEALS	1154	4
ABOVE MORTALITY--	BECAUSE THAT YOU ARE	1260	8
NOT MENDED BY MORTALITY	THE HEALED HEART SHOWS	1440	3
WE WEAR MORTALITY	WE KNEW NOT THAT WE WERE	1462	4
MORTALITY'S			
MORTALITY'S OLD CUSTOM--	SHE DEALT HER PRETTY	479	11
MORTALITY'S GROUND FLOOR	IF MY BARK SINK	1234	3
MORTALS			
CONFUSED BY SWEETS--AS MORTALS--ARE--	NOT PROBABLE--THE BAREST	346	6
MORTGAGED			
AND MORTGAGED HEAVEN	WHEN WE HAVE CEASED TO	1706	4
MORTISED			
COULD THRILL [PENETRATE] THEIR MORTISED EAR	WHAT CARE THE DEAD, FOR	592	13
MUFFLED [MORTISED]--IT REMITS [RESISTS] SURMISE--	"SECRETS" IS A DAILY	1385	3
OR [AND] MORTISED WITH THE LAWS--	THE WAY HOPE BUILDS HIS	1481	8
MOSAIC			
HIS FASHIONS, QUAINT, MOSAIC--	THE ONLY GHOST I EVER	274	7
MOSES			
"OH COULD WE CLIMB WHERE MOSES STOOD,	WHERE BELLS NO MORE	112	9
COULD WE STAND WITH THAT OLD "MOSES"--	IF THE FOOLISH, CALL	168	9
TO THAT OLD MOSES--DONE--	IT ALWAYS FELT TO ME--A	597	2
NO MOSES THERE CAN BE	IT ALWAYS FELT TO ME--A	597	6
ON MOSES--SEEMED TO FASTEN	IT ALWAYS FELT TO ME--A	597	13
AND USHERED GRAND OLD MOSES	IT ALWAYS FELT TO ME--A	597	19
MOSES WAS'NT FAIRLY USED--	SO I PULL MY STOCKINGS	1201	7
"AM NOT CONSUMED," OLD MOSES WROTE,	NO MAN SAW AWE, NOR TO	1733	13
MOSS			
ALL OVERGROWN BY CUNNING MOSS,	ALL OVERGROWN BY CUNNING	148	1

	FIRST LINE	POEM	LINE
MOSS (CONTINUED)			
UNTIL THE MOSS HAD REACHED OUR LIPS--	I DIED FOR BEAUTY--BUT	449	11
WITH MOSS--THEY NEVER GREW SO FULL--	YOU'LL FIND--IT WHEN YOU	610	7
DEAR TO THE MOSS--	PINK--SMALL--AND	1332	5
MOSSES			
BROUGHT OUT THEIR BURS AND MOSSES	I ROBBED THE WOODS--	41	4
WHERE MOSSES GO NO MORE AWAY--	I KNOW WHERE WELLS GROW	460	3
WHERE WATERS COOL AROUND THE MOSSES CRAWL--	THESE FEVERED DAYS--TO	1441	2
MOST			
THE MOST ACCOMPLISHED SHOT!	THERE IS A WORD	8	16
MOST LIKE THEIR GLORY SHOW--	FOR THIS--ACCEPTED	195	16
YOU SAID IT HURT YOU--MOST--	ONE YEAR AGO--JOTS WHAT?	296	17
IF TO BE "ELDER"--MEAN MOST PAIN--	ONE YEAR AGO--JOTS WHAT?	296	32
BUT THE ONES WHO OVERCAME MOST TIMES--	OF TRIBULATION--THESE	325	6
WHAT INTERESTED SCHOLARS--MOST--	A PRECIOUS--MOULDERING	371	13
SUCH GUILT--TO LOVE THEE--MOST!	'TWAS LOVE--NOT ME--	394	5
'TWAS BASE AS JESUS--MOST!	'TWAS LOVE--NOT ME--	394	8
'TIS THE ART, MOST OF ALL,	KNOWS HOW TO FORGET!	433	3
THEY GIVE US PRESENTS MOST--YOU KNOW--	IT WAS GIVEN TO ME BY	454	3
BUT, MOST, LIKE CHAOS--STOPLESS--COOL--	IT WAS NOT DEATH, FOR I	510	21
FOR BLISSFUL CAUSES--MOST OF ALL	SHE'S HAPPY, WITH A NEW	535	6
ACCEPT IT'S MOST [BEST]--	THE TEST OF LOVE--IS	573	9
THE HEAVENS WEIGHED THE MOST--BY FAR [WERE THE WEIGHTIEST--FAR]--	IT TROUBLED ME AS ONCE I	600	5
REMOTEST--WHEN MOST FAIR [NEAR]	THE TREES LIKE TASSELS--	606	8
THE UNOBTRUSIVE [MOST FAMILIAR] GUEST--	'TWAS A LONG PARTING--	625	16
MOST ENOUGH [AMPLEST]--DENIED?	PROMISE THIS--WHEN YOU	648	33
SHOULD STARTLE MOST--	ONE NEED NOT BE A	670	14
OR THE MOST AGONIZING SPY--	THE SOUL UNTO ITSELF	683	3
MOST SHE TOUCHED ME BY HER MUTENESS--	MOST SHE TOUCHED ME BY	760	1
MOST SHE WON ME BY THE WAY	MOST SHE TOUCHED ME BY	760	2
THE MOST UNWORTHY FLOWER--	NATURE--THE GENTLEST	790	16
AND MOST PROFOUND EXPERIMENT	THIS CONSCIOUSNESS THAT	822	7
ADVENTURE MOST UNTO ITSELF	THIS CONSCIOUSNESS THAT	822	13
IS THE MOST WE CAN	CRISIS IS A HAIR	889	6
MOST PRECIOUS ARE THE DEAD--	SWEET, TO HAVE HAD THEM	901	6
MOST AS BIG AS I WAS,	IF IT HAD NO PENCIL	921	7
MOST--I LOVE THE CAUSE THAT SLEW ME.	STRUCK, WAS I, NOR YET	925	17
LOST DOUBLY--BUT BY CONTRAST--MOST--	A DOOR JUST OPENED ON A	953	7
THE BEAUTY THAT REWARD HIM MOST [BEST]--	FITTER TO SEE HIM, I MAY	968	27
MOST SHUN THE PUBLIC AIR	BEST THINGS DWELL OUT OF	998	3
A SICKNESS OF THIS WORLD IT MOST OCCASIONS	A SICKNESS OF THIS WORLD	1044	1
BEHIND THE MOST UNCONSCIOUS [CONSUMMATE] CLOCK	NOT TO DISCOVER WEAKNESS	1054	7
AND LARGE [MOST] IN COURTESY--	THE MERCHANT OF THE	1131	6
TO THOSE THEY MOST CONCERN--	HOW MANY SCHEMES MAY DIE	1150	4
THAT THIS WAS DUE WHERE MOST [SOME] WE FEAR	"REMEMBER ME" IMPLORED	1180	11
OUR MOST IGNOBLE SERVICES	WHO GOES TO DINE MUST	1223	7
WHAT RAIMENT HONOR HIM THE MOST,	I CANNOT SEE MY SOUL BUT	1262	5
THE MOST TRIUMPHANT BIRD I EVER KNEW OR MET	THE MOST TRIUMPHANT BIRD	1265	1
THE MOST PATHETIC THING I DO	THE MOST PATHETIC THING	1290	1
THE MOST OBLIGING TRAP	A RAT SURRENDERED HERE	1340	7
THE ONES THAT [WHO] CITE HER MOST	WHAT MYSTERY PERVADES A	1400	18
ENAMORED MOST OF THEE--	MY MAKER--LET ME BE	1403	2
WHEN MOST IS PAST--IT COMES--	THE GENTIAN HAS A	1424	8
OR BE THAT MOST INSOLVENT THING	FAME IS THE ONE THAT	1475	5
REMOTEST [FANTASTIC / MOST GRACIOUS / MOST DUSKY / . . .	AN ANTIQUATED TREE	1514	7
REMOTEST [FANTASTIC / MOST GRACIOUS / MOST DUSKY / . . .	AN ANTIQUATED TREE	1514	7
. . . MOST POMPOUS] CONSULATE.	AN ANTIQUATED TREE	1514	7
ARE SO FOR THAT MOST FATAL [MIGHTY] CAUSE	DECLAIMING WATERS NONE	1595	3
AT MOST TO BE PERENNIAL	SUMMER BEGINS TO HAVE	1682	14
WAS MOST I THOUGHT UPON	THAT SHE FORGOT ME WAS	1683	4
BLISS WAS MOST TO BLAME.	HAD I KNOWN THAT THE	1720	8
THE MOST IMPORTANT POPULATION	THE MOST IMPORTANT	1746	1
WHICH MISSES MOST,	WHICH MISSES MOST,	1759	1
WHICH BLESSES MOST,	WHICH MISSES MOST,	1759	6
MOSTLY			
IT'S MOSTLY, INTERRUPTIONS--	THE WINTERS ARE SO SHORT	403	9
HOW "THEY ARE DYING MOSTLY--NOW"--	THE MANNER OF IT'S DEATH	468	11
CHILDREN--MATURED [GROWN UP]--ARE WISER--MOSTLY--	BETTER--THAN MUSIC! FOR	503	13
'TIS MOSTLY SLATE AND PENCIL--	'TIS ONE BY ONE--THE	545	9
AND HOW THEY'RE MOSTLY WORN--	I MEASURE EVERY GRIEF I	561	38
ARE MOSTLY SO--TO ME.	WHO OCCUPIES THIS HOUSE?	892	32
AND MOSTLY--SEE NOT	THE ADMIRATIONS--AND	906	7
'TIS MOSTLY--FOLLOWING--	WE CAN BUT FOLLOW TO THE	920	4
BIRDS, MOSTLY BACK--	BEE! I'M EXPECTING YOU!	1035	7
MOTE			
AND DANGLES LIKE A MOTE	HE PARTS HIMSELF--LIKE	517	9
MOTES			
IN OTHER MOTES--	PURSUING YOU IN YOUR	1602	2
MOTH			
PEOPLE--LIKE THE MOTH--	I WENT TO HEAVEN--	374	9
A MOTH THE HUE OF THIS	A MOTH THE HUE OF THIS	841	1
MOTHER			
IF MOTHER--IN THE GRAVE--	HE TOLD A HOMELY TALE	763	9
NATURE--THE GENTLEST MOTHER IS,	NATURE--THE GENTLEST	790	1
IF NATURE SMILES--THE MOTHER MUST	IF NATURE SMILES--THE	1085	1
THE TYPIC MOTHER SENDS	THE MURMURING OF BEES,	1115	10

	FIRST LINE	POEM	LINE
MOTHER (CONTINUED)			
IN OVENS GREEN OUR MOTHER BAKES,	THE WORK OF HER THAT	1143	3
WAS ALL OUR TIMID MOTHER WORE	LET ME NOT MAR THAT	1335	7
THE MOTHER THAT HAS NOT A KNELL	SHE COULD NOT LIVE UPON	1505	5
MOTION			
THE MIND IS SMOOTH--NO MOTION--	THE DIFFERENCE BETWEEN	305	5
THE MOTION OF THE MOON--	I COULD SUFFICE FOR HIM,	643	14
DISTANCE--BE HER ONLY MOTION [SIGNAL]--	HER SWEET TURN TO LEAVE	649	21
THE HAMMOCK'S MOTION LULLS THE HEADS	I SOMETIMES DROP IT, FOR	708	11
TO BEING, SOMEWHERE--MOTION--BREATH--	I'VE DROPPED MY BRAIN--	1046	17
THEY HATED MOTION SO--	THIS SLOW DAY MOVED	1120	4
MOTION, AND AM DUMB.	HE IS ALIVE, THIS	1160	8
OH GIVE IT MOTION--DECK IT SWEET	OH GIVE IT MOTION--DECK	1527	1
MOTIONED			
MOTIONED ITSELF TO DRILL	THE EVENT WAS DIRECTLY	1686	5
MOTIONLESS			
MOTIONLESS AS PEACE	AFTER A HUNDRED YEARS	1147	4
MOTIONS			
THE MOTIONS OF THE DIPPING BIRDS--	BEFORE I GOT MY EYE PUT	327	14
MOTIVE			
HER MOTIVE FOR [OBJECT IN] THE SOUVENIR	I SEND YOU A DECREPIT	1324	5
MOTTLES			
A SNAKE WITH MOTTLES RARE	IN WINTER IN MY ROOM	1670	14
MOULD SEE MOLD			
UNDERNEATH THE MOULD,	I OFTEN PASSED THE	51	16
SO FROM THE MOULD	SO FROM THE MOULD	66	1
AGES BENEATH THE MOULD--	I BRING AN UNACCUSTOMED	132	13
MOULD MY SLOW MIND TO THIS COMPREHENSION--	KNOWS HOW TO FORGET!	433	9
NOR MOULD IT INTO WORD	IF I COULD TELL HOW GLAD	1668	4
MOULDER			
DO PEOPLE MOULDER EQUALLY,	DO PEOPLE MOULDER	432	1
MOULDERED			
MOULDERED THIS MANY MAY.	ONE SISTER HAVE I IN OUR	14	22
MOULDERING			
BY GALLANT--MOULDERING HAND!	IN EBON BOX, WHEN YEARS	169	12
THAT PASSED THE MOULDERING PIER--	THAT AFTER HORROR--THAT	286	2
A PRECIOUS--MOULDERING PLEASURE--'TIS--	A PRECIOUS--MOULDERING	371	1
THE [OUR] MOULDERING PLAYMATE COMES--	OF NEARNESS TO HER	607	8
MOUND			
AND HINDERED BUT A MOUND	NO NOTICE GAVE SHE, BUT	804	16
MOUNT			
TO MOUNT IMMENSITY--	A SPARROW TOOK A SLICE	1211	V 8
MOUNTAIN			
TILL MORNING TOUCHING MOUNTAIN--	A LITTLE EAST OF JORDAN,	59	5
OF MOUNTAIN, AND OF PLAIN--	IT SIFTS FROM LEADEN	311	6
THE MOUNTAIN GORSE--THE BEE'S!	THE JUGGLER'S HAT HER	330	2
A MOUNTAIN--IN MY MIND--	I CROSS TILL I AM WEARY	550	2
THE MOUNTAIN--AT A GIVEN DISTANCE--	DELIGHT--BECOMES	572	5
AS BERRY--OF A MOUNTAIN BUSH--	I HAD BEEN HUNGRY, ALL	579	15
RETREATING [RECEDING] MOUNTAIN!	AH, TENERIFFE!	666	2
BLOOM UPON THE MOUNTAIN--STATED--	BLOOM UPON THE MOUNTAIN	667	1
WHO FOR TILLING--TO THE MOUNTAIN	BLOOM UPON THE MOUNTAIN	667	9
AND THE MOUNTAIN TO THE EVENING	BLOOM UPON THE MOUNTAIN	667	17
THE MOUNTAIN SAT UPON THE PLAIN	THE MOUNTAIN SAT UPON	975	1
NOR MOUNTAIN HINDER ME	NOR MOUNTAIN HINDER ME	1029	1
TO MOUNTAIN--TO THE SUN--	THE FROST OF DEATH WAS	1136	6
. . . MOUNTAIN] WITH YOUR FACE	THE PILE OF YEARS IS NOT	1507	7
MOUNTAINS			
BRED AS WE, AMONG THE MOUNTAINS,	EXULTATION IS THE GOING	76	5
COULD I SEE IT FROM THE MOUNTAINS	WILL THERE REALLY BE A	101	3
HOW THOSE OLD--PHLEGMATIC MOUNTAINS	I HAVE NEVER SEEN	175	3
HOW THE OLD MOUNTAINS DRIP WITH SUNSET	HOW THE OLD MOUNTAINS	291	1
THE MOUNTAINS--MINE--	BEFORE I GOT MY EYE PUT	327	10
MORE MOUNTAINS--THEN A SEA--	I CROSS TILL I AM WEARY	550	3
AROUND A PILE OF MOUNTAINS--	I LIKE TO SEE IT LAP	585	5
AS CREW OF MOUNTAINS--COULD AFFORD--	THEY CALLED ME TO THE	628	11
SWEET MOUNTAINS--YE TELL ME NO LIE--	SWEET MOUNTAINS--YE TELL	722	1
THE MOUNTAINS STRAIGHT REPLY--	MY LIFE HAD STOOD--A	754	8
THE MOUNTAINS--GROW UNNOTICED--	THE MOUNTAINS--GROW	757	1
AND MOUNTAINS--FEEBLE--LEAN--	THE TRUTH--IS STIRLESS--	780	6
THE MOUNTAINS STOOD IN HAZE--	THE MOUNTAINS STOOD IN	1278	1
MOUNTS			
AND MOUNTS TO BE TO ATOMS HURLED	RISK IS THE HAIR THAT	1239	V 7
MOURN			
AND TO MOURN, WERE GAY,	IF RECOLLECTING WERE	33	6
AND MOURN.	WHERE I HAVE LOST, I	104	4
FOR STRANGER--STRANGERS DO NOT MOURN--	BEREAVEMENT IN THEIR	645	5
WE DO NOT MOURN FOR TRAVELER, OR SAILOR,	THE THINGS THAT NEVER	1515	5
MOURNED			
THAT MOURNED.	OF NEARNESS TO HER	607	20
SHE SUFFERED ME, FOR I HAD MOURNED--	THE BIRDS REPORTED FROM	743	17
MOURNER			
THIS MOURNER--TO THE SKY	THE BLACK BERRY--WEARS A	554	10
AT LENGTH, A MOURNER, LIKE MYSELF,	THE BIRDS REPORTED FROM	743	13
A MOURNER WALKED [LURKED] AMONG THE CHILDREN	A LOSS OF SOMETHING EVER	959	5
MOURNERS			
AND MOURNERS TO AND FRO	I FELT A FUNERAL, IN MY	280	2
AND HE OWNED ALL THE MOURNERS--NOW--	THERE'S BEEN A DEATH, IN	389	15
AND MOURNERS MEET IT GOING OUT	WITCHCRAFT HAS NOT A	1708	3

	FIRST LINE	POEM	LINE
MOURNFUL			
THE STORM DOTH WALK THE SEASHORE HUMMING A MOURNFUL TUNE,	AWAKE YE MUSES NINE,	1	17
NO MORE HE SINGETH MOURNFUL, HER SADNESS SHE DOTH LOSE.	AWAKE YE MUSES NINE,	1	20
AND WHEN THIS MOURNFUL DITTY	I HAD A GUINEA GOLDEN--	23	29
MOUSE			
REGARD A MOUSE	PAPA ABOVE!	61	2
NARCOTICS CANNOT STILL THE TOOTH [MOUSE]	THIS WORLD IS NOT	501	19
PRESUMING ME TO BE A MOUSE--	I STARTED EARLY--TOOK MY	520	7
FOR FIRM CONVICTION OF A MOUSE	THE WAY I READ A	636	11
OR MOUSE	YOU SAID THAT I "WAS	738	11
THE CAT REPRIEVES THE MOUSE	THE WHOLE OF IT CAME NOT	762	5
GRIEF IS A MOUSE--	GRIEF IS A MOUSE--	793	1
FOR REFUSE AND THE MOUSE.	REMEMBRANCE HAS A	1182	4
THE MOUSE [RAT] BUT A TRADITION NOW	A LITTLE DOG THAT WAGS	1185	11
MOUTH			
ONLY THE SOLDERED MOUTH CAN TELL--	HOW MANY TIMES THESE LOW	187	2
AND WHATSOEVER MOUTH HE KISSED--	A VISITOR IN MARL--	391	11
ACROSS MY MOUTH--IT BLURS IT--	I AM ALIVE--I GUESS--	470	7
HER JAWS STIR--TWITCHING [MOUTH STIRS--LONGING]--HUNGRY--	SHE SIGHTS A BIRD--SHE	507	5
THE RIVER REACHES TO MY MOUTH--	ME PROVE IT NOW--WHOEVER	537	13
DID YOU EVER STAND IN A CAVERN'S MOUTH--	DID YOU EVER STAND IN A	590	1
QUICK [SOON]--SWEET MOUTH--TO MISS THEE SO--	THESE--SAW VISIONS--	758	6
AS CAN NO OTHER MOUTH	DESPAIR'S ADVANTAGE IS	799	8
AND OPENING HIS [IT'S] MOUTH	THE WIND TOOK UP THE	1134	4
MOUTH'S			
PATIENCE--IS THE SMILE'S [MOUTH'S / LOVE'S] EXERTION	PATIENCE--HAS A QUIET	926	7
MOUTHS			
CRUMBS--FIT SUCH LITTLE MOUTHS--	VICTORY COMES LATE--	690	10
MOVE			
HERE TO LIGHT MEASURE, MOVE THE FEET	THERE IS A MORN BY MEN	24	7
A MIEN TO MOVE A QUEEN--	A MIEN TO MOVE A QUEEN--	283	1
AND SO WE MOVE AS FAR	WE DO NOT PLAY ON GRAVES	467	9
OR MAKE A DRAGON--MOVE--	IT WOULD HAVE STARVED A	612	8
DOES'NT--ALWAYS--MOVE--	"SPEECH"--IS A PRANK OF	688	4
OTHER FORCE--MAY BE PRESUMED TO MOVE--	THE TRUTH--IS STIRLESS--	780	2
WHAT SKILFUL [ANXIOUS] POINTERS MOVE--	NOT TO DISCOVER WEAKNESS	1054	8
CANNOT MOVE A SOD	LAIN IN NATURE--SO	1288	6
TILL THEY HAD MOVED [COULD MOVE] A STONE--	A PANG IS MORE	1530	8
MOVED			
SOME DRIFTS WERE MOVED AWAY--	I THINK JUST HOW MY	237	10
SO YOU COULD SEE WHAT MOVED THEM SO--	GOING TO HIM! HAPPY	494	9
BUT NO MAN MOVED ME--TILL THE TIDE	I STARTED EARLY--TOOK MY	520	9
IT MOVED AWAY THE CHEEKS--	IT KNEW NO MEDICINE--	559	5
THEN [I] MOVED MY FINGERS OFF	I YEARS HAD BEEN FROM	609	21
IT ONLY MOVED [SWERVED] AS DO THE SUNS--	'TWAS AWKWARD, BUT IT	973	5
NOT DUMB--I HAD A SORT THAT MOVED--	I'VE DROPPED MY BRAIN--	1046	9
THIS SLOW DAY MOVED ALONG--	THIS SLOW DAY MOVED	1120	1
FOR WHAT HE MOVED, HE MADE.	NOT THAT HE GOES--WE	1435	4
TILL THEY HAD MOVED [COULD MOVE] A STONE--	A PANG IS MORE	1530	8
MOVES			
YOUR CHANCE IN HARVEST MOVES	A SOLEMN THING WITHIN	483	14
APPROACHED [POSSESSED]--THE AMBER FLITS [MOVES]--A LITTLE--	DELIGHT--BECOMES	572	7
MOVING			
AND MOVING INTO POD--	THE WINTERS ARE SO SHORT	403	4
MOWER			
THE MOWER IS TUNING HIS SCYTHE	BACK FROM THE CORDIAL	1625	V
MOWER'S			
THE MOWER'S METRE--STEALS	I'M SORRY FOR THE DEAD--	529	12
MOWERS			
THEN HE HAS BEEN WITH THE MOWERS--	THE WIND DID'NT COME	316	13
MOZART			
BUT THE COMPOSER--PERFECT MOZART--	BETTER--THAN MUSIC! FOR	503	7
MR			
TO MR. SO AND SO,	BY SUCH AND SUCH AN	38	2
GONE--MR BRYANT'S "GOLDEN ROD"--	BESIDES THE AUTUMN POETS	131	7
AND MR THOMSON'S "SHEAVES."	BESIDES THE AUTUMN POETS	131	8
MUCH			
I NEVER LOST AS MUCH BUT TWICE,	I NEVER LOST AS MUCH BUT	49	1
TOO MUCH PATHOS IN THEIR FACES	FLOWERS--WELL--IF	137	9
'TIS SO MUCH JOY! 'TIS SO MUCH JOY!	'TIS SO MUCH JOY! 'TIS	172	1
'TIS SO MUCH JOY! 'TIS SO MUCH JOY!	'TIS SO MUCH JOY! 'TIS	172	1
MUCH AS FORMERLY?	DID THE HAREBELL LOOSE	213	4
ONE LIFE OF SO MUCH CONSEQUENCE!	ONE LIFE OF SO MUCH	270	1
SO MUCH, THAT DID I MEET THE QUEEN--	YOUR RICHES--TAUGHT ME--	299	13
EARTH WOULD HAVE BEEN TOO MUCH--I SEE--	I SHOULD HAVE BEEN TOO	313	13
AS MUCH OF NOON AS I COULD TAKE	BEFORE I GOT MY EYE PUT	327	12
A SMILE TOO FEW--A WORD TOO MUCH	NOT PROBABLE--THE BAREST	346	2
HE CARED AS MUCH AS ON THE AIR	OF COURSE--I PRAYED--	376	3
I'D SO MUCH JOY--I TOLD IT--RED--	IT WOULD NEVER BE COMMON	430	9
MUCH MADNESS IS DIVINEST SENSE--	MUCH MADNESS IS DIVINEST	435	1
MUCH SENSE--THE STARKEST MADNESS--	MUCH MADNESS IS DIVINEST	435	3
I HAVE SO MUCH TO DO--	I TIE MY HAT--I CREASE	443	10
I--FEARED THE SEA--TOO MUCH	THE MALAY--TOOK THE	452	3
MUCH GESTURE, FROM THE PULPIT--	THIS WORLD IS NOT	501	17
BY SO MUCH--AS 'TWAS REAL--	HER SWEET WEIGHT ON MY	518	12

	FIRST LINE	POEM	LINE
MUCH (CONTINUED)			
'TWAS NOT SO MUCH AS DAVID--HAD--	I TOOK MY POWER IN MY	540	3
MUCH BILLOW HATH THE SEA--	EMPTY MY HEART, OF THEE	587	5
DOES NOT SO MUCH AS TURN HIS HEAD	TO INTERRUPT HIS YELLOW	591	7
AS MUCH ABASHETH ME!	AFRAID! OF WHOM AM I	608	4
NOR WE SO MUCH AS CHECK OUR SPEECH--	THE LIGHTNING PLAYETH--	630	11
SO MUCH SUMMER	SO MUCH SUMMER	651	1
BE WRINKLED--MUCH AS HER--	THE DAY UNDRESSED--	716	8
AND MUCH NOT UNDERSTOOD--	A SOUTH WIND--HAS A	719	6
AND NOVEL [SO MUCH] COMFORTING	I PLAY AT RICHES--TO	801	12
WHERE NOT SO MUCH AS HONEST DOG	WHO OCCUPIES THIS HOUSE?	892	7
WRITING MUCH TO THEE.	IF IT HAD NO PENCIL	921	4
MUCH FLOWERS OF THIS AND FURTHER ZONES	IT BLOOMED AND DROPT, A	978	13
AS MUCH THROUGH CONSCIOUSNESS [CONSCIOUS FAITH]	NOT TO DISCOVER WEAKNESS	1054	4
IF THE TUNE DRIP TOO MUCH	SANG FROM THE HEART,	1059	3
IS SHE SO MUCH TO BLAME?	IF NATURE SMILES--THE	1085	4
AND MAKE MUCH BLUNDER, IF AT LAST	MY COCOON TIGHTENS--	1099	11
AND SO MUCH MORE AT HOME THAN I	ALONE AND IN A	1167	5
MUCH IS THE MIEN [GOOD IS THE LOOK] OF HIM IN MARCH	A PROMPT--EXECUTIVE BIRD	1177	7
UNPROVED IS MUCH WE KNOW--	THE FROST WAS NEVER SEEN	1202	13
I HAD PAID SO MUCH FOR--	NOW I KNEW I LOST HER--	1219	15
SO MUCH OF HEAVEN HAS GONE FROM EARTH	SO MUCH OF HEAVEN HAS	1228	1
TOO MUCH OF PROOF AFFRONTS BELIEF	SO MUCH OF HEAVEN HAS	1228	9
HOW MUCH--HOW LITTLE--IS	IN THIS SHORT LIFE	1287	3
I HAVE SO MUCH TO TELL--	DEAR MARCH--COME IN--	1320	10
DID NOT SO MUCH AS WRING FROM HIM	A SINGLE CLOVER PLANK	1343	15
HOW MUCH THE PRESENT MOMENT MEANS	HOW MUCH THE PRESENT	1380	1
ONE JOY [SOUND] OF SO MUCH ANGUISH	ONE JOY OF SO MUCH	1420	1
HOW MUCH OF SOURCE ESCAPES WITH THEE--	HOW MUCH OF SOURCE	1517	1
HOW MUCH CAN COME	THERE CAME A WIND LIKE A	1593	15
AND MUCH CAN GO,	THERE CAME A WIND LIKE A	1593	16
MAKES NOT AS MUCH OF SOUND	THE SUN IN REINING TO	1636	2
OR TOO MUCH WEIGHT TO FLY--	TOO HAPPY TIME DISSOLVES	1774	4
MUD			
MAKES HE MUD FOR DOG AND PEDDLER,	WE LIKE MARCH.	1213	4
MUFF			
PUT ON YOUR MUFF [BELLS] FOR WINTER	THE JAY HIS CASTANET HAS	1635	2
MUFFLE			
I MUFFLE WITH A JEST.	CONSULTING SUMMER'S	1715	8
MUFFLED			
HUM BY--IN MUFFLED COACHES--	SWEET--SAFE--HOUSES--	457	14
MUFFLED [MORTISED]--IT REMITS [RESISTS] SURMISE--	"SECRETS" IS A DAILY	1385	3
MULTIFOLD			
THE DYING MULTIFOLD--WITHOUT	TOO SCANTY 'TWAS TO DIE	1013	7
MULTIPLIED			
IT MULTIPLIED INDIFFERENCE--	'TWAS WARM--AT FIRST--	519	11
MULTIPLY			
IF FATHER'D MULTIPLY THE PLATES--	'TWAS JUST THIS TIME,	445	15
THE SUMMER MULTIPLY--	LEAST BEE THAT BREW--	676	3
TO MULTIPLY [MAGNIFY] THE POND.	THE BIRDS BEGUN AT FOUR	783	8
MULTITUDE			
MULTITUDE BROCADE--	RIBBONS OF THE YEAR--	873	2
A PINK AND PULPY MULTITUDE	OUR LITTLE KINSMEN--	885	3
MULTITUDES			
BEHOLD! WHOSE MULTITUDES ARE THESE?	SOME RAINBOW--COMING	64	22
ALL MULTITUDES THAT WERE	NO CROWD THAT HAS	515	10
THE MULTITUDES OF NOON--	THE CRICKETS SANG	1104	V
SEDULOUS [TOO ELATE] OF HER MULTITUDES	NOT ANY MORE TO BE	1344	7
MUMBLED			
I MUMBLED--LIKE A FOOL--	THE FIRST DAY'S NIGHT	410	14
MUNDI			
"SIC TRANSIT GLORIA MUNDI,"	"SIC TRANSIT GLORIA	3	1
MUNIFICENCE			
TO THAT MUNIFICENCE, THAT CHOSE--	THE WORLD--STANDS--	493	11
UTMOST, IS MUNIFICENCE--	ALL I MAY, IF SMALL,	819	7
MURDER			
AFFORDS A BLISS LIKE MURDER--	REHEARSAL TO OURSELVES	379	3
MURDER--WEAR!	IT DONT SOUND SO	426	17
'TWAS MURDER BY DEGREES--	THE WHOLE OF IT CAME NOT	762	2
MURMUR			
I CAN MURMUR BROKEN,	MUTE THY CORONATION--	151	7
THE MURMUR [BUMBLE] OF A BEE	THE MURMUR OF A BEE	155	1
A MURMUR IN THE TREES--TO NOTE--	A MURMUR IN THE TREES--	416	1
THAT MURMUR SO--CHANT SO--FAR--	AGAIN--HIS VOICE IS AT	663	V 25
THE PERISHED PATTERNS MURMUR--	IT'S EASY TO INVENT A	724	9
I SHALL NOT MURMUR IF AT LAST	I SHALL NOT MURMUR IF AT	1410	1
NOT MURMUR--NOT ENDEARMENT--	"GO TELL IT"--WHAT A	1554	3
THE WATERS MURMUR NEW	I DID NOT REACH THEE	1664	30
MURMURED			
THE VALLEY MURMURED "COME"--	THROUGH LANE IT LAY--	9	14
MURMURED "RESURGAM"--"CENTIPEDE"!	"ARCTURUS" IS HIS OTHER	70	7
THAT NATURE MURMURED TO HERSELF	I THINK I WAS ENCHANTED	593	13
WHEREFORE SO LATE--I MURMURED--	SHELLS FROM THE COAST	693	5
MURMURED--IT HAS CEASED--	"SECRETS" IS A DAILY	1385	4
MURMURING			
CLAPS MY MURMURING LIP!	IF I SHOULD CEASE TO	56	8
IN MURMURING PLATOON!	SOME RAINBOW--COMING	64	12

	FIRST LINE	POEM	LINE
MURMURING (CONTINUED)			
OF [WITH] MELLOW--MURMURING THREAD--	A FEATHER FROM THE	161	6
MURMURING, LIKE OLD CASPIAN CHOIRS,	MANY A PHRASE HAS THE	276	5
THE MURMURING OF BEES, HAS CEASED	THE MURMURING OF BEES,	1115	1
BUT MURMURING OF SOME	THE MURMURING OF BEES,	1115	2
MUSCLE			
AS IF AN AXLE, [A MUSCLE--] HELD--	WHEN WE STAND ON THE	242	16
INDICATING, BY NO MUSCLE [FEATURE]--	BLOOM UPON THE MOUNTAIN	667	19
MUSCLES			
THE MUSCLES GRAPPLED [STRUGGLED] AS WITH LEADS	'TWAS CRISIS--ALL THE	948	9
MUSED			
CAROLLED, AND PAUSED [MUSED], AND CAROLLED--	HEART, NOT SO HEAVY AS	83	11
MUSES			
AWAKE YE MUSES NINE, SING ME A STRAIN DIVINE,	AWAKE YE MUSES NINE,	1	1
MUSHROOM			
THE MUSHROOM IS THE ELF OF PLANTS--	THE MUSHROOM IS THE ELF	1298	1
THAT MUSHROOM--IT IS HIM!	THE MUSHROOM IS THE ELF	1298	20
NO MUSHROOM IS THEIR MIND	THEY TALK AS SLOW AS	1697	2
MUSIC			
HERSELF TO HER A MUSIC	ONE SISTER HAVE I IN OUR	14	11
THY MUSIC STILL, WHEN WHIPPOWIL	SUMMER FOR THEE, GRANT I	31	3
WHAT OF--MY MUSIC!	PUT UP MY LUTE!	261	2
PASSIVE--AS GRANITE--LAPS MY MUSIC--	PUT UP MY LUTE!	261	4
BECAUSE IT'S MUSIC STIRS THE AXE	THE DOOMED--REGARD THE	294	7
BEFORE THEY DROP FULL MUSIC ON--	HE FUMBLES AT YOUR SOUL	315	3
LET GO A MUSIC--AS OF TUNES	THE WIND--TAPPED LIKE A	436	15
WHOSE SPOKES A DIZZY MUSIC MAKE	WITHIN MY GARDEN, RIDES	500	3
INVISIBLE, AS MUSIC--	THIS WORLD IS NOT	501	3
BETTER--THAN MUSIC! FOR I--WHO HEARD IT--	BETTER--THAN MUSIC! FOR	503	1
CONVULSIVE, WHILE THE MUSIC CRASHED [BROKE]--	HER SMILE WAS SHAPED	514	7
EXCEPT A WAKE OF MUSIC	OF BEING IS A BIRD	653	9
'TIS THIS--IN MUSIC--HINTS AND SWAYS--	THE LOVE A LIFE CAN SHOW	673	7
WHOSE MUSIC BE HIS	NO BOBOLINK--REVERSE HIS	755	8
A MUSIC NUMEROUS AS SPACE [MEASURELESS AS NOON]--	THE BIRDS BEGUN AT FOUR	783	3
SPLIT THE LARK--AND YOU'LL FIND THE MUSIC--	SPLIT THE LARK--AND	861	1
WHAT WHEN THE EGGS FLY OFF IN MUSIC	WHAT SHALL I DO WHEN THE	956	3
DYING AT MY MUSIC!	DYING AT MY MUSIC!	1003	1
THE FASCINATING CHILL THAT MUSIC LEAVES [OF MUSIC]	THE FASCINATING CHILL	1480	1
THE FASCINATING CHILL THAT MUSIC LEAVES [OF MUSIC]	THE FASCINATING CHILL	1480	1
THE MUSIC IN THE VIOLIN	THE SPIRIT LASTS--BUT IN	1576	5
THE BIRD HER PUNCTUAL MUSIC BRINGS	THE BIRD HER PUNCTUAL	1585	1
MUSICIANS			
MUSICIANS WRESTLE [WRESTLING] EVERYWHERE--	MUSICIANS WRESTLE	157	1
MUSIC'S			
MUSIC'S TRIUMPHANT--	INCONCEIVABLY SOLEMN!	582	12
MUSING			
AS WE PASS HOUSES MUSING SLOW	AS WE PASS HOUSES MUSING	1653	1
MUSKET			
EACH WITH A SOLEMN MUSKET	"SIC TRANSIT GLORIA	3	51
HIS MUSKET ON HIS BREAST--	BLESS GOD, HE WENT AS	147	2
A SUDDEN MUSKET--SPILLS--	THE DAY CAME SLOW--TILL	304	4
MUSLIN			
SCARES MUSLIN SOULS--AWAY--	A SHADY FRIEND--FOR	278	6
MUTE			
AND IS MUTE AGAIN--	THERE IS A WORD	8	5
I TOUCHED HER CRADLE MUTE--	SHE SLEPT BENEATH A TREE	25	3
SHE--WAS MUTE FROM TRANSPORT--	MORNS LIKE THESE--WE	27	7
MUTE THY CORONATION--	MUTE THY CORONATION--	151	1
WITH A MUTE POMP--	INCONCEIVABLY SOLEMN!	582	6
A FIRST MUTE COMING--	A FIRST MUTE COMING--	702	1
MUTENESS			
MOST SHE TOUCHED ME BY HER MUTENESS--	MOST SHE TOUCHED ME BY	760	1
MUTINEER			
NOT SUBJUGATE, THE MUTINEER	TO TRY TO SPEAK, AND	1617	7
MUTINY			
SOME SPICE'S MUTINY--	SWEET PIRATE OF THE	1546	4
MUTUAL			
FOR OUR MUTUAL HONOR,	AMBITION CANNOT FIND HIM	68	7
ON THEMES CONCERN OUR MUTUAL MIND--	A PRECIOUS--MOULDERING	371	11
AT LEAST--'TIS MUTUAL--RISK--	I GAVE MYSELF TO HIM--	580	13
SOME--FOUND IT--MUTUAL GAIN--	I GAVE MYSELF TO HIM--	580	14
DEATH IS THE COMMON [MUTUAL / EQUAL] RIGHT	A TOAD, CAN DIE OF LIGHT	583	2
AND SINCE WE'RE MUTUAL MONARCH	ME FROM MYSELF--TO	642	9
BUT SINCE WE HOLD A MUTUAL DISC--	I MAKE HIS CRESCENT FILL	909	9
AND FRONT A MUTUAL DAY--	I MAKE HIS CRESCENT FILL	909	10
OUR MUTUAL FRAME--THAT HAPLY	NO OTHER CAN REDUCE	982	V 7
RESUMING AT A MUTUAL DATE	THE SPIRIT LASTS--BUT IN	1576	15
MY			
UNWIND THE SOLEMN TWINE, AND TIE MY VALENTINE!	AWAKE YE MUSES NINE,	1	2
PRITHEE, MY BROTHER,	THERE IS ANOTHER SKY,	2	13
INTO MY GARDEN COME!	THERE IS ANOTHER SKY,	2	14
FROM OFF MY FATHER'S TREE!	"SIC TRANSIT GLORIA	3	20
MY COUNTRY BIDS ME GO;	"SIC TRANSIT GLORIA	3	26
I'LL TAKE MY INDIA RUBBERS,	"SIC TRANSIT GLORIA	3	27
DURING MY EDUCATION,	"SIC TRANSIT GLORIA	3	29
MY COUNTRY CALLETH ME;	"SIC TRANSIT GLORIA	3	58
TO WIPE MY WEEPING E'E.	"SIC TRANSIT GLORIA	3	60

		FIRST LINE	POEM	LINE
MY	(CONTINUED)			
	THE MEMORY OF MY ASHES	"SIC TRANSIT GLORIA	3	65
	TELL I MY DOUBTING HEART	I HAVE A BIRD IN SPRING	5	17
	BEHIND MY NATIVE TOWN.	FREQUENTLY THE WOODS ARE	6	4
	MY FIGURES FAIL TO TELL ME	THE FEET OF PEOPLE	7	17
	MY CLASSICS VAIL THEIR FACES--	THE FEET OF PEOPLE	7	21
	MY FAITH THAT DARK ADORES--	THE FEET OF PEOPLE	7	22
	MY WHEEL IS IN THE DARK!	MY WHEEL IS IN THE DARK!	10	1
	MY FOOT IS ON THE TIDE!	MY WHEEL IS IN THE DARK!	10	5
	MY LIFE HAD FORFEIT BEEN.	I NEVER TOLD THE BURIED	11	9
	AND WORE MY LAST YEAR'S GOWN--	ONE SISTER HAVE I IN OUR	14	6
	AND BEAR TO ALL MY FRIENDS, ...	I WOULD DISTIL A CUP,	16	2
	ENCOUNTER IN MY GARDEN	BAFFLED FOR JUST A DAY	17	3
	MY DEPARTING BLOSSOMS	THE GENTIAN WEAVES HER	18	3
	CHID MY PERFIDY--	DISTRUSTFUL OF THE	20	4
	WEARY FOR MY----	DISTRUSTFUL OF THE	20	5
	ALL THESE MY BANNERS BE.	ALL THESE MY BANNERS BE.	22	1
	I SOW MY PAGEANTRY	ALL THESE MY BANNERS BE.	22	2
	MY CHANCEL--ALL THE PLAIN	ALL THESE MY BANNERS BE.	22	6
	UNTO MY FRUGAL EYE--	I HAD A GUINEA GOLDEN--	23	6
	STILL, FOR MY MISSING TROUBADOUR	I HAD A GUINEA GOLDEN--	23	15
	MY STORY HAS A MORAL--	I HAD A GUINEA GOLDEN--	23	25
	THIS, AND MY HEART BESIDE--	IT'S ALL I HAVE TO BRING	26	2
	THIS, AND MY HEART, AND ALL THE FIELDS-- .	IT'S ALL I HAVE TO BRING	26	3
	THIS, AND MY HEART, AND ALL THE BEES	IT'S ALL I HAVE TO BRING	26	7
	I, MY RIDDLE BRING	IF THOSE I LOVED WERE	29	V 8
	AND ROW MY BLOSSOMS O'ER!	SUMMER FOR THEE, GRANT I	31	6
	THEN TAKE MY FLOWERS--PRAY!	WHEN ROSES CEASE TO	32	8
	AND TEN OF MY ONCE STATELY TOES	I COUNTED TILL THEY	36	7
	ONE WITHIN MY BOSOM	IT DID NOT SURPRISE ME--	39	11
	MY [HIS] FANTASY TO PLEASE.	I ROBBED THE WOODS--	41	5
	STEADY--MY SOUL: WHAT ISSUES	A DAY! HELP! HELP!	42	7
	MY VELVET LIFE TO CLOSE--	IF SHE HAD BEEN THE	44	4
	I KEEP MY PLEDGE.	I KEEP MY PLEDGE.	46	1
	I BRING MY ROSE.	I KEEP MY PLEDGE.	46	4
	ONCE MORE, MY NOW BEWILDERED DOVE	ONCE MORE, MY NOW	48	1
	COURAGE! MY BRAVE COLUMBA!	ONCE MORE, MY NOW	48	7
	REIMBURSED MY STORE--	I NEVER LOST AS MUCH BUT	49	6
	I HAV'NT TOLD MY GARDEN YET--	I HAV'NT TOLD MY GARDEN	50	1
	IN WHICH MY CALL WOULD COME--	I OFTEN PASSED THE	51	6
	WHETHER MY BARK WENT DOWN AT SEA--	WHETHER MY BARK WENT	52	1
	MY BUDS COMMEMORATE--	IF I SHOULD CEASE TO	56	6
	CLAPS MY MURMURING LIP!	IF I SHOULD CEASE TO	56	8
	LOW AT MY PROBLEM BENDING, ...	LOW AT MY PROBLEM	69	1
	I CHECK MY BUSY PENCIL, ...	LOW AT MY PROBLEM	69	5
	MY FIGURES FILE [CIPHERS STEAL] AWAY. . . .	LOW AT MY PROBLEM	69	6
	WHEREFORE, MY BAFFLED FINGERS	LOW AT MY PROBLEM	69	7
	AFORETIME IN MY HAT--	"ARCTURUS" IS HIS OTHER	70	14
	PRITHEE, MY PRETTY HOUSEWIVES!	A LADY RED--AMID THE	74	7
	BUT I TUG CHILDISH AT MY BARS	I NEVER HEAR THE WORD	77	7
	FOR IT W'D STOP MY BREATH--	GOING TO HEAVEN!	79	21
	MY SCRUTINY DECEIVES.	WHOSE CHEEK IS THIS?	82	10
	WHISTLING UNDER MY WINDOW	HEART, NOT SO HEAVY AS	83	T
	AS IT PASSED MY WINDOW	HEART, NOT SO HEAVY AS	83	3
	YET TO MY IRRITATED EAR	HEART, NOT SO HEAVY AS	83	7
	AH [OH] BUGLE! BY MY [THE] WINDOW	HEART, NOT SO HEAVY AS	83	19
	MY PERENNIAL NEST.	HER BREAST IS FIT FOR	84	8
	WITHIN MY REACH!	WITHIN MY REACH!	90	1
	MY FRIEND MUST BE A BIRD--	MY FRIEND MUST BE A BIRD	92	1
	MORTAL, MY FRIEND MUST BE, ...	MY FRIEND MUST BE A BIRD	92	3
	MY NOSEGAYS ARE FOR CAPTIVES--	MY NOSEGAYS ARE FOR	95	1
	SEXTON! MY MASTER'S SLEEPING HERE.	SEXTON! MY MASTER'S	96	1
	MY FLOWERS TURN FROM FORUMS--	THE RAINBOW NEVER TELLS	97	5
	NEW FEET WITHIN MY GARDEN GO--	NEW FEET WITHIN MY	99	1
	DID ROUND MY PILLOW ROLL, ...	I HAVE A KING, WHO DOES	103	9
	AND SHOUTS FILL ALL MY CHILDISH SKY, ...	I HAVE A KING, WHO DOES	103	10
	FROM STEEPLES IN MY SOUL!	I HAVE A KING, WHO DOES	103	12
	FOR MY WILL GOES THE OTHER WAY, ...	I HAVE A KING, WHO DOES	103	17
	A LITTLE TREMOR IN MY VOICE	WHERE I HAVE LOST, I	104	11
	MY LITTLE CRAFT WAS LOST!	'TWAS SUCH A LITTLE--	107	8
	NEVER MIND MY BREATHLESS ANVIL!	BY A FLOWER--BY A LETTER	109	5
	THE PROPERTY, MY GARDEN, ...	I HAD SOME THINGS THAT I	116	5
	MY FRIEND ATTACKS MY FRIEND!	MY FRIEND ATTACKS MY	118	1
	MY FRIEND ATTACKS MY FRIEND!	MY FRIEND ATTACKS MY	118	1
	I CLAP MY HANDS TO SEE--	A SOMETHING IN A	122	9
	THEN VAIL MY TOO INSPECTING FACE	A SOMETHING IN A	122	10
	FROM MY BROWN CIGAR.	MANY CROSS THE RHINE	123	4
	MY SPIRIT CANNOT SEE?	BRING ME THE SUNSET IN A	128	21
	INDUCES MY BELIEF.	THESE ARE THE DAYS WHEN	130	9
	MY SENTIMENTS TO SHARE--	BESIDES THE AUTUMN POETS	131	14
	I TURN MY BRIMMING EYES AWAY, ...	I BRING AN UNACCUSTOMED	132	6
	MY FLOWERS RAISE THEIR PRETTY LIPS--	AS CHILDREN BID THE	133	3
	MY FLOWERS FROM A HUNDRED CRIBS	AS CHILDREN BID THE	133	7
	FOR MY LITTLE DAMASK MAID--	PIGMY SERAPHS--GONE	138	11
	RAFFLE FOR MY SOUL!	SOUL, WILT THOU TOSS	139	8
	FROM OUT MY SUMMER'S EVE--	SHE WENT AS QUIET AS THE	149	6
	MEEK [LOW] MY VIVE LE ROI, ...	MUTE THY CORONATION--	151	2
	CHARGED, FROM MY CHIMNEY CORNER--	THE SUN KEPT STOOPING--	152	13
	TAKETH AWAY MY WILL--	THE MURMUR OF A BEE	155	7
	ADDETH TO MY DEGREE--	THE MURMUR OF A BEE	155	12

		FIRST LINE	POEM	LINE
MY	(CONTINUED)			
	MY RIVER RUNS TO THEE--	MY RIVER RUNS TO THEE--	162	1
	MY RIVER WAITS REPLY--	MY RIVER RUNS TO THEE--	162	3
	THO' MY DESTINY BE FUSTIAN--	THO' MY DESTINY BE	163	1
	STILL, MY LITTLE GIPSEY BEING	THO' MY DESTINY BE	163	5
	STILL, MY LITTLE SUNBURNT BOSOM	THO' MY DESTINY BE	163	7
	MY FRECKLED MONARCH HELD THE REIN--	I MET A KING THIS	166	14
	SINCE THAT MY LORD, "THE LORD OF LORDS" . . .	WAIT TILL THE MAJESTY OF	171	15
	I CAUTIOUS, SCANNED MY LITTLE LIFE--	I CAUTIOUS, SCANNED MY	178	1
	AND LO--MY PRICELESS HAY	I CAUTIOUS, SCANNED MY	178	8
	MY BUSINESS IS, TO FIND!	I CAUTIOUS, SCANNED MY	178	16
	MY BUSINESS WERE SO DEAR!	IF I COULD BRIBE THEM BY	179	6
	MY TAMBORIN WERE SOONEST HEARD	IF I COULD BRIBE THEM BY	179	8
	YET--TO MY FRUGAL EYE, ...	I LOST A WORLD--THE	181	6
	WITH MY GRANITE LIP!	IF I SHOULD'NT BE ALIVE	182	8
	YET HELD MY BREATH, THE WHILE--	I'VE HEARD AN ORGAN TALK	183	4
	SO I CAN HANG IT IN MY ROOM--	MAKE ME A PICTURE OF THE	188	2
	PUT MY PRETENSE--AWAY--	MAKE ME A PICTURE OF THE	188	8
	BY IT--MY TITLE TAKE--	FOR THIS--ACCEPTED	195	4
	TO MY NESCESSITY--STOOPED DOWN!	FOR THIS--ACCEPTED	195	6
	MY EYE IS FULLER THAN MY VASE--	MY EYE IS FULLER THAN MY	202	1
	MY EYE IS FULLER THAN MY VASE--	MY EYE IS FULLER THAN MY	202	1
	AND STILL--MY HEART--MY EYE OUTWEIGHS-- . .	MY EYE IS FULLER THAN MY	202	3
	AND STILL--MY HEART--MY EYE OUTWEIGHS-- . .	MY EYE IS FULLER THAN MY	202	3
	I SHOULD NOT DARE TO LEAVE MY FRIEND, . .	I SHOULD NOT DARE TO	205	1
	TELLING MY TARDY NAME--	I SHOULD NOT DARE TO	205	12
	MY HEART WOULD WISH IT BROKE BEFORE-- . .	I SHOULD NOT DARE TO	205	13
	THEY HEAR MY UNEXPECTED KNOCK--	THO' I GET HOME HOW LATE	207	6
	MY CASPIAN--THEE.	LEAST RIVERS--DOCILE TO	212	2
	THE HEART I CARRIED [CHERISHED] IN MY OWN--	SAVIOR! I'VE NO ONE ELSE	217	9
	LEST MY BESEECHING FACE--AT LAST--	COULD I--THEN--SHUT THE	220	2
	SO SUNSET SHUTS MY QUESTION DOWN	IT CANT BE "SUMMER"!	221	9
	I'VE DIAMONDS--ON MY FINGERS--	I CAME TO BUY A SMILE--	223	9
	WERE MY EAR--AS NEAR HIS NEST--	TEACH HIM--WHEN HE MAKES	227	5
	AS MY THOUGHT--TODAY--	TEACH HIM--WHEN HE MAKES	227	6
	A BURDOCK--CLAWED [TWITCHED] MY GOWN-- . .	A BURDOCK--CLAWED MY	229	1
	A BOG--AFFRONTS MY SHOE--	A BURDOCK--CLAWED MY	229	6
	I MET ONE--FORGOT MY SCHOOLMATES--	GOD PERMITS INDUSTRIOUS	231	3
	MY SOVREIGN IS OFFENDED--	THE COURT IS FAR AWAY--	235	3
	I THINK JUST HOW MY SHAPE WILL RISE-- . .	I THINK JUST HOW MY	237	1
	I THINK JUST HOW MY LIPS WILL WEIGH-- . .	I THINK JUST HOW MY	237	5
	BEFORE MY SIMPLE BOSOM--BROKE--	I THINK JUST HOW MY	237	11
	BY MY LONG BRIGHT--AND LONGER--TRUST-- . .	I THINK JUST HOW MY	237	15
	I DROP MY HEART--UNSHRIVEN!	I THINK JUST HOW MY	237	16
	I HELD A JEWEL IN MY FINGERS--	I HELD A JEWEL IN MY	245	1
	I WOKE--AND CHID MY HONEST FINGERS, . . .	I HELD A JEWEL IN MY	245	5
	IF JOY--TO PUT MY PIECE AWAY	FOREVER AT HIS SIDE TO	246	8
	I'D GIVE--I'D GIVE MY LIFE--OF COURSE-- . .	WHAT WOULD I GIVE TO SEE	247	2
	I'D GIVE MY BIGGEST BOBOLINK!	WHAT WOULD I GIVE TO SEE	247	5
	MY KINGDOM'S WORTH OF BLISS!	WHAT WOULD I GIVE TO SEE	247	29
	I--WITH MY REDBREAST--	I SHALL KEEP SINGING!	250	5
	AND MY RHYMES--	I SHALL KEEP SINGING!	250	6
	LATE--WHEN I TAKE MY PLACE IN SUMMER-- . .	I SHALL KEEP SINGING!	250	7
	BUT--IF I STAINED MY APRON--	OVER THE FENCE--	251	6
	BREAKS UP MY FEET--	I CAN WADE GRIEF--	252	5
	HOW MANY TIMES FOR MY FAR SAKE	YOU SEE I CANNOT SEE--	253	4
	MY OWN--SO PATIENT--COVETS--	YOU SEE I CANNOT SEE--	253	9
	MY TIMIDNESS ENFOLDS--	YOU SEE I CANNOT SEE--	253	11
	SHALL STILL MY TRANSPORT BE--	IF I'M LOST--NOW--	256	3
	THAT IN MY AWKWARD--GAZING--FACE--	IF I'M LOST--NOW--	256	6
	STRUCK UP MY CHILDISH	DELIGHT IS AS THE FLIGHT	257	13
	PUT UP MY LUTE!	PUT UP MY LUTE!	261	1
	WHAT OF--MY MUSIC!	PUT UP MY LUTE!	261	2
	PASSIVE--AS GRANITE--LAPS MY MUSIC-- . . .	PUT UP MY LUTE!	261	4
	UPON MY SIDE THE VAIL--	A SINGLE SCREW OF FLESH	263	4
	MY EYES JUST TURNED TO SEE, ...	A SINGLE SCREW OF FLESH	263	10
	WHEN IT WAS SMUGGLED BY MY SIGHT	A SINGLE SCREW OF FLESH	263	11
	MY SOUL'S ENTIRE INCOME--	ONE LIFE OF SO MUCH	270	3
	THAT--DOES NOT BLUR MY GEM!	ONE LIFE OF SO MUCH	270	10
	WHEN I COULD TAKE IT IN MY HAND--	A SOLEMN THING--IT WAS--	271	11
	SWELLED--LIKE HORIZONS--IN MY BREAST [VEST]--	A SOLEMN THING--IT WAS--	271	15
	HE PUT THE BELT AROUND MY LIFE--	HE PUT THE BELT AROUND	273	1
	MY LIFETIME FOLDING UP--	HE PUT THE BELT AROUND	273	4
	DOUBT ME! MY DIM [FAINT] COMPANION!	DOUBT ME! MY DIM	275	1
	IT CANNOT BE MY SPIRIT--	DOUBT ME! MY DIM	275	9
	ON MY SIMPLE SLEEP--	MANY A PHRASE HAS THE	276	10
	TIE THE STRINGS TO MY LIFE, MY LORD, . . .	TIE THE STRINGS TO MY	279	1
	TIE THE STRINGS TO MY LIFE, MY LORD, ...	TIE THE STRINGS TO MY	279	1
	BY MY OWN CHOICE, AND THEE--	TIE THE STRINGS TO MY	279	12
	I FELT A FUNERAL, IN MY BRAIN, ...	I FELT A FUNERAL, IN MY	280	1
	MY MIND WAS GOING NUMB--	I FELT A FUNERAL, IN MY	280	8
	AND CREAK ACROSS MY SOUL [BRAIN]	I FELT A FUNERAL, IN MY	280	10
	THE ROBIN'S MY CRITERION FOR TUNE--	THE ROBIN'S MY CRITERION	285	1
	THE BUTTERCUP'S, MY WHIM FOR BLOOM-- . . .	THE ROBIN'S MY CRITERION	285	6
	INFECTS MY SIMPLE SPIRIT	OF BRONZE--AND BLAZE--	290	8
	AND STRUT UPON MY STEM--	OF BRONZE--AND BLAZE--	290	11
	MY SPLENDORS, ARE MENAGERIE--	OF BRONZE--AND BLAZE--	290	14
	THAT STOP-SENSATION--ON MY SOUL--	I GOT SO I COULD HEAR	293	3
	WITHOUT THAT FORCING, IN MY BREATH--	I GOT SO I COULD HEAR	293	11
	AND SHAPE MY HANDS--	I GOT SO I COULD HEAR	293	17

		FIRST LINE	POEM	LINE
MY	(CONTINUED)			
	MY BUSINESS, WITH THE CLOUD,	I GOT SO I COULD HEAR	293	21
	UNTO GUESSED CRESTS, MY MOANING FANCY, LEADS [LURES] ME,	UNTO LIKE STORY--TROUBLE	295	9
	STEP MARTIAL--AT MY CRUCIFIXION--	UNTO LIKE STORY--TROUBLE	295	15
	BEYOND MY POWER TO DEEM [DREAM]--	YOUR RICHES--TAUGHT ME--	299	22
	THAT SLIPPED MY SIMPLE FINGERS THROUGH--	YOUR RICHES--TAUGHT ME--	299	31
	AND SO, INSTRUCTED BY MY OWN,	FOR LARGEST WOMAN'S	309	5
	MY LITTLE CIRCUIT WOULD HAVE SHAMED	I SHOULD HAVE BEEN TOO	313	4
	AND IN MY WONDERING HAND	AS IF I ASKED A COMMON	323	2
	I JUST WEAR MY WINGS--	SOME KEEP THE SABBATH	324	6
	I CANNOT DANCE UPON MY TOES--	I CANNOT DANCE UPON MY	326	1
	BUT OFTENTIMES, AMONG MY MIND,	I CANNOT DANCE UPON MY	326	3
	NO RINGLET, TO MY HAIR,	I CANNOT DANCE UPON MY	326	10
	NOR TOSSED MY SHAPE IN EIDER BALLS,	I CANNOT DANCE UPON MY	326	13
	BEFORE I GOT MY EYE PUT OUT	BEFORE I GOT MY EYE PUT	327	1
	FOR MINE--I TELL YOU THAT MY HEART	BEFORE I GOT MY EYE PUT	327	7
	BETWEEN MY FINITE EYES--	BEFORE I GOT MY EYE PUT	327	13
	SO SAFER GUESS--WITH JUST MY SOUL	BEFORE I GOT MY EYE PUT	327	18
	TO TAKE MY RANK--BY--IN THE WEST--	THE FACE I CARRY WITH ME	336	3
	THAT--SIR--WAS MY DEGREE--	THE FACE I CARRY WITH ME	336	6
	I TEND MY FLOWERS FOR THEE--	I TEND MY FLOWERS FOR	339	1
	MY FUSCHZIA'S CORAL SEAMS	I TEND MY FLOWERS FOR	339	3
	MY CACTUS--SPLITS HER BEARD	I TEND MY FLOWERS FOR	339	7
	UPON MY GARDEN FLOOR--	I TEND MY FLOWERS FOR	339	17
	I MUST NOT PUT MY FOOT AMISS	IS BLISS THEN, SUCH	340	2
	FOR FEAR I SPOIL MY SHOE?	IS BLISS THEN, SUCH	340	3
	I'D RATHER SUIT MY FOOT	IS BLISS THEN, SUCH	340	4
	THAN SAVE MY BOOT--	IS BLISS THEN, SUCH	340	5
	MY REWARD FOR BEING, WAS THIS.	MY REWARD FOR BEING, WAS	343	1
	MY PREMIUM--MY BLISS--	MY REWARD FOR BEING, WAS	343	2
	MY PREMIUM--MY BLISS--	MY REWARD FOR BEING, WAS	343	2
	WHEN THRONES ACCOST MY HANDS--	MY REWARD FOR BEING, WAS	343	6
	SO FOREIGN TO MY OWN--	I DREADED THAT FIRST	348	12
	AND I, MY CHILDISH PLUMES,	I DREADED THAT FIRST	348	26
	I FELT MY LIFE WITH BOTH MY HANDS	I FELT MY LIFE WITH BOTH	351	1
	I FELT MY LIFE WITH BOTH MY HANDS	I FELT MY LIFE WITH BOTH	351	1
	I HELD MY SPIRIT TO THE GLASS,	I FELT MY LIFE WITH BOTH	351	3
	I TURNED MY BEING ROUND AND ROUND	I FELT MY LIFE WITH BOTH	351	5
	I JUDGED MY FEATURES--JARRED MY HAIR--	I FELT MY LIFE WITH BOTH	351	9
	I JUDGED MY FEATURES--JARRED MY HAIR--	I FELT MY LIFE WITH BOTH	351	9
	I PUSHED MY DIMPLES BY, AND WAITED--	I FELT MY LIFE WITH BOTH	351	10
	BERRIES, IN MY NATIVE TOWN--	PERHAPS I ASKED TOO	352	4
	MY BASKET HOLDS--JUST--FIRMAMENTS--	PERHAPS I ASKED TOO	352	5
	THOSE--DANGLE EASY--ON MY ARM,	PERHAPS I ASKED TOO	352	6
	IT BLISTERED TO MY DREAM--	IT STRUCK ME--EVERY DAY	362	6
	IT SICKENED FRESH UPON MY SIGHT--	IT STRUCK ME--EVERY DAY	362	7
	BUT SAY MY APRON BRING THE STICKS	ALTHOUGH I PUT AWAY HIS	366	28
	SO I LOOP MY APRON, AGAINST THE MAJESTY	I'M SAYING EVERY DAY	373	12
	AND PERCH MY TONGUE	I'M SAYING EVERY DAY	373	16
	BUT THIS, MIGHT BE MY BRIEF TERM	I'M SAYING EVERY DAY	373	18
	PUT FROM MY SIMPLE SPEECH ALL PLAIN WORD--	I'M SAYING EVERY DAY	373	20
	MY OLD GOWN--ON--	I'M SAYING EVERY DAY	373	29
	BETWEEN MY CURTAIN AND THE WALL	THE ANGLE OF A LANDSCAPE	375	3
	ACCOSTS MY OPEN EYE--	THE ANGLE OF A LANDSCAPE	375	6
	THE SEASONS--SHIFT--MY PICTURE--	THE ANGLE OF A LANDSCAPE	375	13
	UPON MY EMERALD BOUGH,	THE ANGLE OF A LANDSCAPE	375	14
	MY REASON--LIFE--	OF COURSE--I PRAYED--	376	6
	MY SOUL--AT LIBERTY--	NO RACK CAN TORTURE ME--	384	2
	MY ART, A SUMMER DAY--HAD PATRONS--	WHEN DIAMONDS ARE A	397	6
	I'D TUNNEL--TILL MY GROOVE	I HAD NOT MINDED--WALLS	398	5
	THEN MY FACE TAKE HER RECOMPENSE--	I HAD NOT MINDED--WALLS	398	7
	ENLARGE MY MESSAGE--IF TOO VAST	A TONGUE--TO TELL HIM I	400	16
	MY MESSAGE--MUST BE TOLD--	A TONGUE--TO TELL HIM I	400	21
	MY BOND--HAVE JUST BEGUN--	A TONGUE--TO TELL HIM I	400	25
	AND THEN--IT'S TIME TO STRIKE MY TENT--	THE WINTERS ARE SO SHORT	403	7
	MY SUMMER--IS DESPOILED--	THE WINTERS ARE SO SHORT	403	10
	I'M SO ACCUSTOMED TO MY FATE--	IT MIGHT BE LONELIER	405	3
	THAN GAIN--MY BLUE PENINSULA--	IT MIGHT BE LONELIER	405	15
	I TOLD MY SOUL TO SING--	THE FIRST DAY'S NIGHT	410	4
	UNROLLED IT'S HORROR IN MY FACE--	THE FIRST DAY'S NIGHT	410	11
	UNTIL IT BLOCKED MY EYES--	THE FIRST DAY'S NIGHT	410	12
	MY BRAIN--BEGUN TO LAUGH--	THE FIRST DAY'S NIGHT	410	13
	MY BRAIN KEEPS GIGGLING--STILL.	THE FIRST DAY'S NIGHT	410	16
	I READ MY SENTENCE--STEADILY--	I READ MY SENTENCE--	412	1
	REVIEWED IT WITH MY EYES,	I READ MY SENTENCE--	412	2
	I MADE MY SOUL FAMILIAR--WITH HER EXTREMITY--	I READ MY SENTENCE--	412	9
	HOW COULD I BREAK MY WORD?	A MURMUR IN THE TREES--	416	18
	AND YET--MY PRIMER SUITS ME SO	NOT IN THIS WORLD TO SEE	418	7
	AND LEAVE ME--JUST MY A--B--C--	NOT IN THIS WORLD TO SEE	418	11
	BEFALLING NOT MY SIMPLE DAYS--	REMOVED FROM ACCIDENT OF	424	3
	PUT IT IN LATIN--LEFT OF MY SCHOOL--	IT DONT SOUND SO	426	3
	MAKE--A DIADEM--AND MEND MY OLD ONE--	I'LL CLUTCH--AND CLUTCH	427	11
	UPON MY SIMPLE CHEEK--	IT WOULD NEVER BE COMMON	430	10
	I FELT IT PUBLISH--IN MY EYE--	IT WOULD NEVER BE COMMON	430	11
	I WALKED--AS WINGS--MY BODY BORE--	IT WOULD NEVER BE COMMON	430	13
	I PUT MY PLEASURE ALL ABROAD--	IT WOULD NEVER BE COMMON	430	17
	WHEN--SUDDENLY--MY RICHES SHRANK--	IT WOULD NEVER BE COMMON	430	21
	A GOBLIN--DRANK MY DEW--	IT WOULD NEVER BE COMMON	430	22
	MY PALACES--DROPPED TENANTLESS--	IT WOULD NEVER BE COMMON	430	23

		FIRST LINE	POEM	LINE
MY	(CONTINUED)			
	ALONG MY GOLDEN LINES--	IT WOULD NEVER BE COMMON	430	29
	BUT WHERE MY MOMENT OF BROCADE--	IT WOULD NEVER BE COMMON	430	32
	MY--DROP--OF INDIA?	IT WOULD NEVER BE COMMON	430	33
	ME--COME! MY DAZZLED FACE	ME--COME! MY DAZZLED	431	1
	ME--HEAR! MY FOREIGN EAR	ME--COME! MY DAZZLED	431	3
	MY HOLIDAY, SHALL BE	ME--COME! MY DAZZLED	431	7
	MY PARADISE--THE FAME	ME--COME! MY DAZZLED	431	9
	THAT THEY--PRONOUNCE MY NAME--	ME--COME! MY DAZZLED	431	10
	AND FILL MY LUNGS, FOR WITNESS--	DO PEOPLE MOULDER	432	7
	FROM TANKS--ABOVE MY HEAD--	DO PEOPLE MOULDER	432	8
	MOULD MY SLOW MIND TO THIS COMPREHENSION--	KNOWS HOW TO FORGET!	433	9
	MY RESIDENCE WITHIN	THE WIND--TAPPED LIKE A	436	4
	THIS IS MY LETTER TO THE WORLD	THIS IS MY LETTER TO THE	441	1
	I TIE MY HAT--I CREASE MY SHAWL--	I TIE MY HAT--I CREASE	443	1
	I TIE MY HAT--I CREASE MY SHAWL--	I TIE MY HAT--I CREASE	443	1
	I PUSH A PETAL FROM MY GOWN	I TIE MY HAT--I CREASE	443	7
	STOPPED--STRUCK--MY TICKING--THROUGH--	I TIE MY HAT--I CREASE	443	12
	BUT SOMETHING HELD MY WILL.	'TWAS JUST THIS TIME,	445	8
	MY STOCKING HANG TOO HIGH	'TWAS JUST THIS TIME,	445	18
	SHE [I] COULD NOT FIND HER [MY] YES--	I SHOWED HER HIGHTS SHE	446	8
	AND THEN, I [HE] BRAKE MY [HIS] LIFE--AND LO,	I SHOWED HER HIGHTS SHE	446	9
	THE LARGER, AS HER [MY] FACE WITHDREW--	I SHOWED HER HIGHTS SHE	446	11
	AND BORE MY JEWEL--HOME--	THE MALAY--TOOK THE	452	8
	I KEPT IT IN MY HAND--	IT WAS GIVEN TO ME BY	454	5
	I'M OFTEN THIRSTY--BUT MY LIPS	I KNOW WHERE WELLS GROW	460	11
	SOFTLY MY FUTURE CLIMBS THE STAIR,	A WIFE--AT DAYBREAK I	461	9
	I FUMBLE AT MY CHILDHOOD'S PRAYER	A WIFE--AT DAYBREAK I	461	10
	UNTIL UPON MY FACE	THE POWER TO BE TRUE TO	464	2
	I WILLED MY KEEPSAKES--SIGNED AWAY	I HEARD A FLY BUZZ--WHEN	465	9
	THE BRANCHES ON MY HAND	I AM ALIVE--I GUESS--	470	2
	AND AT MY FINGER'S END--	I AM ALIVE--I GUESS--	470	4
	ACROSS MY MOUTH--IT BLURS IT--	I AM ALIVE--I GUESS--	470	7
	AND MARKED MY GIRLHOOD'S NAME--	I AM ALIVE--I GUESS--	470	21
	SO SEEMED TO CHOOSE MY DOOR--	EXCEPT THE HEAVEN HAD	472	2
	NOWHERE TO HIDE MY DAZZLED FACE--	I AM ASHAMED--I HIDE--	473	4
	NOR INTRODUCE--MY SOUL--	I AM ASHAMED--I HIDE--	473	6
	FOR ME--MY SOUL--TO WEAR--	I AM ASHAMED--I HIDE--	473	12
	FINGERS--TO FRAME MY ROUND HAIR	I AM ASHAMED--I HIDE--	473	13
	SKILL--TO HOLD MY BROW LIKE AN EARL--	I AM ASHAMED--I HIDE--	473	16
	FASHION MY SPIRIT QUAINT--WHITE--	I AM ASHAMED--I HIDE--	473	20
	BRING ME MY BEST PRIDE--	I AM ASHAMED--I HIDE--	473	23
	WITHIN MY INCOME--THESE COULD LIE	I MEANT TO HAVE BUT	476	3
	IT WOULD SUFFICE MY PRAYER	I MEANT TO HAVE BUT	476	6
	I LEFT THE PLACE, WITH ALL MY MIGHT--	I MEANT TO HAVE BUT	476	17
	I THREW MY PRAYER AWAY--	I MEANT TO HAVE BUT	476	18
	MY GARDEN--LIKE THE BEACH--	MY GARDEN--LIKE THE	484	1
	AT NIGHT, MY LITTLE LAMP, AND BOOK--	I WAS THE SLIGHTEST IN	486	3
	AND JUST MY BASKET--	I WAS THE SLIGHTEST IN	486	7
	MY PLANE--AND I, TOGETHER WROUGHT	MYSELF WAS FORMED--A	488	3
	MY TOOLS TOOK HUMAN--FACES--	MYSELF WAS FORMED--A	488	9
	AS IF MY TRADE WERE BONE--	AS FAR FROM PITY, AS	496	4
	HE STRAINED MY FAITH--	HE STRAINED MY FAITH--	497	1
	SHOOK MY STRONG TRUST--	HE STRAINED MY FAITH--	497	3
	HURLED MY BELIEF--	HE STRAINED MY FAITH--	497	5
	YET INTERDICT--MY BLOSSOM--	I ENVY SEAS, WHEREON HE	498	21
	AND ABROGATE--MY BEE--	I ENVY SEAS, WHEREON HE	498	22
	WITHIN MY GARDEN, RIDES A BIRD	WITHIN MY GARDEN, RIDES	500	1
	AND I REJOIN MY DOG,	WITHIN MY GARDEN, RIDES	500	12
	REFERS MY CLUMSY [DULLER] EYE--	WITHIN MY GARDEN, RIDES	500	18
	HUMMING--UNTIL MY FAINT REHEARSAL--	BETTER--THAN MUSIC! FOR	503	23
	MY LIPS JUST HOLD THE NAME--	YOU KNOW THAT PORTRAIT	504	10
	THE PIER TO MY PONTOON--	I WOULD NOT PAINT--A	505	16
	MY FEET, TOO, THAT HAD WANDERED SO--	HE TOUCHED ME, SO I LIVE	506	10
	MY GIPSY FACE--TRANSFIGURED NOW--	HE TOUCHED ME, SO I LIVE	506	11
	THE NAME THEY DROPPED UPON MY FACE	I'M CEDED--I'VE STOPPED	508	2
	AND THEY CAN PUT IT WITH MY DOLLS,	I'M CEDED--I'VE STOPPED	508	5
	MY CHILDHOOD, AND THE STRING OF SPOOLS,	I'M CEDED--I'VE STOPPED	508	6
	CALLED TO MY FULL--THE CRESCENT DROPPED--	I'M CEDED--I'VE STOPPED	508	11
	MY SECOND RANK--TOO SMALL THE FIRST--	I'M CEDED--I'VE STOPPED	508	14
	CROWNED--CROWING [WHIMPERING / DANGLING]--ON MY FATHER'S BREAST--	I'M CEDED--I'VE STOPPED	508	15
	IT WAS NOT FROST, FOR ON MY FLESH [KNEES]	IT WAS NOT DEATH, FOR I	510	5
	NOR FIRE--FOR JUST MY [TWO] MARBLE FEET	IT WAS NOT DEATH, FOR I	510	7
	AS IF MY LIFE WERE SHAVEN,	IT WAS NOT DEATH, FOR I	510	13
	I'D COUNT THEM ON MY HAND,	IF YOU WERE COMING IN	511	10
	SUBTRACTING, TILL MY FINGERS DROPPED	IF YOU WERE COMING IN	511	11
	HER SWEET WEIGHT ON MY HEART A NIGHT	HER SWEET WEIGHT ON MY	518	1
	MY BRIDE HAD SLIPPED AWAY--	HER SWEET WEIGHT ON MY	518	4
	I STARTED EARLY--TOOK MY DOG--	I STARTED EARLY--TOOK MY	520	1
	WENT PAST MY SIMPLE SHOE--	I STARTED EARLY--TOOK MY	520	10
	AND PAST MY APRON--AND MY BELT	I STARTED EARLY--TOOK MY	520	11
	AND PAST MY APRON--AND MY BELT	I STARTED EARLY--TOOK MY	520	11
	AND PAST MY BODDICE [BOSOM / BUCKLE]--TOO--	I STARTED EARLY--TOOK MY	520	12
	UPON MY ANCLE--THEN MY SHOES	I STARTED EARLY--TOOK MY	520	19
	UPON MY ANCLE--THEN MY SHOES	I STARTED EARLY--TOOK MY	520	19
	SAY IF I ERRED? ACCUSE MY FARTHINGS--	SWEET--YOU FORGOT--BUT I	523	5
	JUST TO BE RICH--TO WASTE MY GUINEAS [GUINEA]	SWEET--YOU FORGOT--BUT I	523	9
	MY DUPLICATE--TO BORROW--	I TRIED TO THINK A	532	6
	THE RIVER REACHES TO MY FEET--	ME PROVE IT NOW--WHOEVER	537	5

MY (CONTINUED)

	FIRST LINE	POEM	LINE
AS YET--MY HEART BE DRY--	ME PROVE IT NOW--WHOEVER	537	6
THE RIVER REACHES TO MY BREAST--	ME PROVE IT NOW--WHOEVER	537	9
STILL--STILL--MY HANDS ABOVE	ME PROVE IT NOW--WHOEVER	537	10
THE RIVER REACHES TO MY MOUTH--	ME PROVE IT NOW--WHOEVER	537	13
SWEPT BY MY SEARCHING EYES--THE LAST--	ME PROVE IT NOW--WHOEVER	537	15
LET NOT MY WITNESS HINDER THEM [THEM IMPAIR--]	'TIS TRUE--THEY SHUT ME	538	5
I TOOK MY POWER IN MY HAND--	I TOOK MY POWER IN MY	540	1
I TOOK MY POWER IN MY HAND--	I TOOK MY POWER IN MY	540	1
I AIMED MY PEBBLE--BUT MYSELF	I TOOK MY POWER IN MY	540	5
MY BEST--WAS GONE TO SLEEP--	I HAD NO CAUSE TO BE	542	2
A MOUNTAIN--IN MY MIND--	I CROSS TILL I AM WEARY	550	2
AND MY HORIZON BLOCKS	I CROSS TILL I AM WEARY	550	6
NOR THIS--DEFEAT MY PACE--	I CROSS TILL I AM WEARY	550	10
I SHOUT UNTO MY FEET--	I CROSS TILL I AM WEARY	550	19
THAT SOME--ARE LIKE MY OWN--	I MEASURE EVERY GRIEF I	561	40
I FIND MY FEET HAVE FURTHER GOALS--	I COULD NOT PROVE THE	563	5
MY PERIOD HAD COME FOR PRAYER--	MY PERIOD HAD COME FOR	564	1
MY TACTICS MISSED A RUDIMENT--	MY PERIOD HAD COME FOR	564	3
BUT AWED BEYOND MY ERRAND--	MY PERIOD HAD COME FOR	564	19
AND BORE IT IN MY HAND--	A DYING TIGER--MOANED	566	4
'TWAS NOT MY BLAME--WHO SPED TOO SLOW--	A DYING TIGER--MOANED	566	9
MY FIRST WELL DAY--SINCE MANY ILL--	MY FIRST WELL DAY--SINCE	574	1
AND TAKE THE SUNSHINE IN MY HANDS,	MY FIRST WELL DAY--SINCE	574	3
TO TAKE MY CHANCE [RISK] WITH PAIN--	MY FIRST WELL DAY--SINCE	574	6
MY LOSS, BY SICKNESS--WAS IT LOSS?	MY FIRST WELL DAY--SINCE	574	25
EACH TIME MY CHILDISH EYE	I PRAYED, AT FIRST, A	576	6
TO HOLD MY LIFE [THE LIGHT] FOR ME	I PRAYED, AT FIRST, A	576	17
TILL I COULD TAKE THE [CATCH MY] BALANCE	I PRAYED, AT FIRST, A	576	18
AS IF MY SOUL WERE DEAF AND DUMB--	IF I MAY HAVE IT, WHEN	577	19
MY NOON HAD COME--TO DINE--	I HAD BEEN HUNGRY, ALL	579	2
EMPTY MY HEART, OF THEE--	EMPTY MY HEART, OF THEE	587	1
TO HOLD MY LIFE, AND HOLD MY EARS	I CRIED AT PITY--NOT AT	588	19
TO HOLD MY LIFE, AND HOLD MY EARS	I CRIED AT PITY--NOT AT	588	19
PASS BACK AND FORTH, BEFORE MY BRAIN	WHEN I WAS SMALL, A	596	15
MY [ONE] JUSTICE BLEEDS--FOR THEE!	IT ALWAYS FELT TO ME--A	597	24
THEN MADE BLUE FACES IN MY FACE--	THREE TIMES--WE PARTED--	598	7
THEN SUNRISE KISSED MY CHRYSALIS--	THREE TIMES--WE PARTED--	598	15
HE FOUND MY BEING--SET IT UP--	HE FOUND MY BEING--SET	603	1
UNTO MY BOOKS--SO GOOD TO TURN--	UNTO MY BOOKS--SO GOOD	604	1
TILL MY SMALL LIBRARY--	UNTO MY BOOKS--SO GOOD	604	8
THE PORTER OF MY FATHER'S LODGE	AFRAID! OF WHOM AM I	608	3
AS SOON IMPEACH MY CROWN!	AFRAID! OF WHOM AM I	608	12
AND ASK MY BUSINESS THERE--	I YEARS HAD BEEN FROM	609	6
"MY BUSINESS BUT [JUST] A LIFE I LEFT	I YEARS HAD BEEN FROM	609	7
I FUMBLED AT MY NERVE--	I YEARS HAD BEEN FROM	609	V 9
AND BROKE [SMOTE] AGAINST MY EAR--	I YEARS HAD BEEN FROM	609	12
MY HAND, WITH TREMBLING CARE	I YEARS HAD BEEN FROM	609	18
THEN [I] MOVED MY FINGERS OFF	I YEARS HAD BEEN FROM	609	21
AND HELD MY EARS, AND LIKE A THIEF	I YEARS HAD BEEN FROM	609	23
TO GAD MY LITTLE BEING OUT--	IT WOULD HAVE STARVED A	612	15
AND SEEN MY BRAIN--GO ROUND--	THEY SHUT ME UP IN PROSE	613	6
MY SOUL GREW [FELT / BENT / STOOD] STRAIGHT.	I ROSE--BECAUSE HE SANK	616	4
I CHEERED MY FAINTING PRINCE--	I ROSE--BECAUSE HE SANK	616	5
DONT PUT UP MY THREAD & NEEDLE--	DONT PUT UP MY THREAD &	617	1
THESE WERE BENT--MY SIGHT GOT CROOKED--	DONT PUT UP MY THREAD &	617	5
WHEN MY MIND--IS PLAIN	DONT PUT UP MY THREAD &	617	6
LEAVE MY NEEDLE IN THE FURROW--	DONT PUT UP MY THREAD &	617	13
CLOSER--SO I--AT MY SLEEPING [SIGHING]--	DONT PUT UP MY THREAD &	617	19
WITHOUT A GLANCE MY WAY--	I ASKED NO OTHER THING--	621	6
WAS SCARCE UPON MY EYES	I WATCHED THE MOON	629	30
THEN I--MY TIMID SERVICE DONE--	I THINK THE LONGEST HOUR	635	13
TAKE UP MY LITTLE VIOLIN--	I THINK THE LONGEST HOUR	635	15
AND PUSH IT WITH MY FINGERS--NEXT--	THE WAY I READ A	636	3
THEN DRAW MY LITTLE LETTER FORTH	THE WAY I READ A	636	7
TO MY SMALL HEARTH HIS FIRE CAME--	TO MY SMALL HEARTH HIS	638	1
AND ALL MY HOUSE AGLOW	TO MY SMALL HEARTH HIS	638	2
MY PORTION IS DEFEAT--TODAY--	MY PORTION IS DEFEAT--	639	1
WITHOUT MY RIGHT OF FROST--	I CANNOT LIVE WITH YOU--	640	19
ON MY HOMESICK EYE--	I CANNOT LIVE WITH YOU--	640	26
THOUGH MY NAME	I CANNOT LIVE WITH YOU--	640	38
INVINCIBLE [IMPREGNABLE] MY FORTRESS	ME FROM MYSELF--TO	642	3
MY SYLLABLE REBELLED--	I COULD SUFFICE FOR HIM,	643	6
BEYOND MY LIMIT TO CONCEIVE--	I THINK TO LIVE--MAY BE	646	3
MY LIP--TO TESTIFY--	I THINK TO LIVE--MAY BE	646	4
HAD.ALL MY LIFE BUT BEEN [BEEN ONE / BEEN BLEAK] MISTAKE	I THINK TO LIVE--MAY BE	646	27
BE MY LIPS--THE ONLY BUCKLE	PROMISE THIS--WHEN YOU	648	7
POURED LIKE THIS--MY WHOLE [BEST] LIBATION--	PROMISE THIS--WHEN YOU	648	13
FOR MY HEAVEN--	PROMISE THIS--WHEN YOU	648	31
MY HEART TO SUBDIVIDE--	WITHOUT THIS--THERE IS	655	10
THE SPREADING WIDE MY NARROW HANDS	I DWELL IN POSSIBILITY--	657	11
MY FACE TO JUSTIFY--	AGAIN--HIS VOICE IS AT	663	6
WE WALK--I LEAVE MY DOG--AT HOME [BEHIND]--	AGAIN--HIS VOICE IS AT	663	18
THE PURPLE--IN MY VEIN--	AGAIN--HIS VOICE IS AT	663	27
MY PRICE FOR EVERY STAIN!	AGAIN--HIS VOICE IS AT	663	29
SEED, HAD I, MY PURPLE SOWING	BLOOM UPON THE MOUNTAIN	667	5
"SWEET" SAID HE "MY OWN SURRENDER	WOLFE DEMANDED DURING	678	7
CONSCIOUS AM I IN MY CHAMBER,	CONSCIOUS AM I IN MY	679	1
ON THE BLEAKNESS OF MY LOT	SOIL OF FLINT, IF STEADY	681	V

		FIRST LINE	POEM	LINE
MY	(CONTINUED)			
	LATE--MY GARDEN [ACRE] OF A ROCK--	SOIL OF FLINT, IF STEADY	681	V
	I'LL SEND THE FEATHER FROM MY HAT!	I'LL SEND THE FEATHER	687	1
	MY SOVREIGN WILL RELENT?	I'LL SEND THE FEATHER	687	3
	BUT ONLY ON MY FOREHEAD STOPPED--	THE SUN KEPT SETTING--	692	7
	AND WANDERED IN MY FACE--	THE SUN KEPT SETTING--	692	8
	MY FEET KEPT DROWSING--DROWSING--STILL	THE SUN KEPT SETTING--	692	9
	MY FINGERS WERE AWAKE--	THE SUN KEPT SETTING--	692	10
	UNTO MY SEEMING--MAKE?	THE SUN KEPT SETTING--	692	12
	MY NEED OF THEE--BE DONE--	SHELLS FROM THE COAST	693	6
	MY PERIOD BEGIN	SHELLS FROM THE COAST	693	8
	IT PLEASED MY NARROW EYES--	THEIR HIGHT IN HEAVEN	696	12
	I'VE HEARD MY FATHER TELL--	THE JUDGE IS LIKE THE	699	2
	THAT SLANTED IN MY PATH--	THE JUDGE IS LIKE THE	699	5
	A THOUGHT WENT UP MY MIND TODAY--	A THOUGHT WENT UP MY	701	1
	BUT SOMEWHERE--IN MY SOUL--I KNOW--	A THOUGHT WENT UP MY	701	9
	AND CAME MY WAY NO MORE--	A THOUGHT WENT UP MY	701	12
	EAGLES ON MY BUCKLES--	NO MATTER--NOW--SWEET--	704	11
	ON MY BELT--TOO--	NO MATTER--NOW--SWEET--	704	12
	ERMINE--MY FAMILIAR GOWN--	NO MATTER--NOW--SWEET--	704	13
	CONFER UPON MY FLOWER--	THE GRACE--MYSELF--MIGHT	707	2
	MY LABOR AND MY LEISURE TOO,	BECAUSE I COULD NOT STOP	712	7
	MY LABOR AND MY LEISURE TOO,	BECAUSE I COULD NOT STOP	712	7
	FOR ONLY GOSSAMER, MY GOWN--	BECAUSE I COULD NOT STOP	712	15
	MY TIPPET--ONLY TULLE--	BECAUSE I COULD NOT STOP	712	16
	MY NAME BE ELSE SUPREME--	FAME OF MYSELF, TO	713	6
	TO WANDER--NOW--IS MY REPOSE [ABODE]--	I MEANT TO FIND HER WHEN	718	9
	MY STRONG MADONNAS--CHERISH STILL--	SWEET MOUNTAINS--YE TELL	722	7
	THE VERY COLOR OF MY HAIR--	PRECIOUS TO ME--SHE	727	4
	EASING MY FAMINE	LET US PLAY YESTERDAY--	728	5
	AT MY LEXICON--	LET US PLAY YESTERDAY--	728	6
	'TWAS MY LAST GRATITUDE	LET US PLAY YESTERDAY--	728	21
	TAKE NOT MY LIBERTY	LET US PLAY YESTERDAY--	728	35
	AND SHOW ME TO MY FEARS--	IF HE WERE LIVING--DARE	734	8
	MY LIFE JUST HOLDS THE TRENCH--	IF HE WERE LIVING--DARE	734	16
	MY [THE] VILLAGES BE SEEN--	HAVE ANY LIKE MYSELF	736	22
	A SPICY CHARGE, MY LITTLE POSTS [FRIENDS]--	THE BIRDS REPORTED FROM	743	3
	MY WITNESS--WAS THE CRAPE [BLACK] I BORE--	THE BIRDS REPORTED FROM	743	19
	IT DROPPED SO LOW--IN MY REGARD--	IT DROPPED SO LOW--IN MY	747	1
	AT BOTTOM OF MY MIND--	IT DROPPED SO LOW--IN MY	747	4
	UPON MY SILVER SHELF--	IT DROPPED SO LOW--IN MY	747	8
	AUTUMN--OVERLOOKED MY KNITTING--	AUTUMN--OVERLOOKED MY	748	1
	MY WORTHINESS IS ALL MY DOUBT--	MY WORTHINESS IS ALL MY	751	1
	MY WORTHINESS IS ALL MY DOUBT--	MY WORTHINESS IS ALL MY	751	1
	HIS MERIT--ALL MY FEAR--	MY WORTHINESS IS ALL MY	751	2
	CONTRASTING WHICH, MY QUALITY	MY WORTHINESS IS ALL MY	751	3
	UPON MY THRONGING [CROWDED / HAPPY] MIND--	MY WORTHINESS IS ALL MY	751	8
	CONFORM MY SOUL--AS TWERE A CHURCH,	MY WORTHINESS IS ALL MY	751	15
	MY SOUL--ACCUSED ME--AND I QUAILED--	MY SOUL--ACCUSED ME--AND	753	1
	MY SOUL--THAT MORNING--WAS MY FRIEND--	MY SOUL--ACCUSED ME--AND	753	4
	MY SOUL--THAT MORNING--WAS MY FRIEND--	MY SOUL--ACCUSED ME--AND	753	4
	MY LIFE HAD STOOD--A LOADED GUN--	MY LIFE HAD STOOD--A	754	1
	I GUARD MY MASTER'S HEAD--	MY LIFE HAD STOOD--A	754	14
	SO LARGER TO MY EYES	ONE BLESSING HAD I THAN	756	2
	IT WAS THE LIMIT OF MY DREAM--	ONE BLESSING HAD I THAN	756	5
	THE FOCUS OF MY PRAYER--	ONE BLESSING HAD I THAN	756	6
	WERE A CRUMB MY WHOLE POSSESSION--	MOST SHE TOUCHED ME BY	760	5
	WERE IT MY RESOURCE FROM STARVING--	MOST SHE TOUCHED ME BY	760	7
	I SHUT MY EYES--AND GROPED AS WELL	FROM BLANK TO BLANK--	761	9
	MY SLOW IDOLATRY--	YOU CONSTITUTED TIME--	765	8
	MY FAITH IS LARGER THAN THE HILLS--	MY FAITH IS LARGER THAN	766	1
	MY FAITH MUST TAKE THE PURPLE WHEEL	MY FAITH IS LARGER THAN	766	3
	ICICLES UPON MY SOUL	WHEN I HOPED, I	768	13
	IF BLAME BE MY SIDE--FORFEIT ME--	IF BLAME BE MY SIDE--	775	1
	OBTAINED [ENGROSSED] MY LODGINGS, ERE MYSELF--	BEREAVED OF ALL, I WENT	784	5
	AND WHEN I SOUGHT MY BED--	BEREAVED OF ALL, I WENT	784	6
	THE PILLOW FOR MY HEAD--	BEREAVED OF ALL, I WENT	784	8
	I WORRIED NATURE WITH MY WHEELS	SEVERER SERVICE OF	786	5
	MY OWN HAD JUST BEGUN.	SEVERER SERVICE OF	786	8
	AS ALL MY STRATEGEM HAD BEEN	SEVERER SERVICE OF	786	19
	PROVE ME--MY HAZEL [SWIMMING] WITNESSES	JOY TO HAVE MERITED THE	788	11
	THE DEPTH UPON MY SOUL WAS NOTCHED--	JOY TO HAVE MERITED THE	788	19
	MY POIGNANT LUXURY--	GOD GAVE A LOAF TO EVERY	791	4
	TOO HAPPY--FOR [IN] MY SPARROW'S CHANCE--	GOD GAVE A LOAF TO EVERY	791	7
	SUCH PLENTY SMILES UPON MY BOARD--	GOD GAVE A LOAF TO EVERY	791	11
	MY GARNER SHOWS SO FAIR--	GOD GAVE A LOAF TO EVERY	791	12
	MY VISITOR IN PARADISE--	A DROP FELL ON THE APPLE	794	V
	BY MY WINDOW HAVE I FOR SCENERY	BY MY WINDOW HAVE I FOR	797	1
	WAS THE PINE AT MY WINDOW A "FELLOW	BY MY WINDOW HAVE I FOR	797	22
	BUT OFTEN AS MY LOT DISPLAYS	I PLAY AT RICHES--TO	801	9
	MY POVERTY AND I DERIVE--	I PLAY AT RICHES--TO	801	13
	TO WIN, BECOME THEIR [MY] TURN--	I PLAY AT RICHES--TO	801	20
	ENGROSS MY FINITY--	TIME FEELS SO VAST THAT	802	4
	SEEMS IT TO MY HOODED THINKING	ONE DAY IS THERE OF THE	814	7
	BRINGING STILL MY "PLEA FOR CULTURE."	THE LUXURY TO APPREHEND	815	V
	BUT OVERLOOKED MY FATHER'S HOUSE--	THE WIND BEGUN TO KNEAD	824	19
	OF MY [AN] IDENTITY.	NATURE AND GOD--I	835	4
	MY SECRET AS SECURE	NATURE AND GOD--I	835	6
	THOUGH IT TOOK ALL MY STORE	I CANNOT BUY IT--'TIS	840	9
	THEN, TURN MY FACE AWAY.	I CANNOT BUY IT--'TIS	840	12

MY (CONTINUED)

	FIRST LINE	POEM	LINE
I MADE SLOW RICHES BUT MY GAIN	I MADE SLOW RICHES BUT	843	1
BUT MY PERCEIVELESS GAIN	I MADE SLOW RICHES BUT	843	6
MY BONNET BUT TO TIE	I SING TO USE THE	850	2
AND SHUT THE DOOR UNTO MY HOUSE	I SING TO USE THE	850	3
THIS CHASM, SWEET, UPON MY LIFE	THIS CHASM, SWEET, UPON	858	1
MY BURIAL--BEFORE	THIS CHASM, SWEET, UPON	858	18
DEEM MY SUPPER DRY	AS THE STARVED MAELSTROM	872	14
THE STARS ABOUT MY HEAD I FELT	I STEPPED FROM PLANK TO	875	3
ABOUT MY FEET THE SEA.	I STEPPED FROM PLANK TO	875	4
WOULD BE MY FINAL INCH--	I STEPPED FROM PLANK TO	875	6
BEYOND MY BOUNDARY--	I'VE NONE TO TELL ME TO	881	6
TO MY QUICK EAR THE LEAVES--CONFERRED--	TO MY QUICK EAR THE	891	1
IS MY INTENTION NOW.	A CLOUD WITHDREW FROM	895	12
LOSE MY WAY LIKE A LITTLE CHILD	HOW HAPPY I WAS IF I	898	7
WOULD I RESTORE MY BOOTY	WHAT DID THEY DO SINCE I	900	15
THIS--WAS MY FINALLEST OCCASION--	THE FIRST DAY THAT I WAS	902	9
MY TENDERER EXPERIMENT	THE FIRST DAY THAT I WAS	902	11
I HIDE MYSELF WITHIN MY FLOWER,	I HIDE MYSELF WITHIN MY	903	1
MY NEED--WAS ALL I HAD--I SAID--	HAD I NOT THIS, OR THIS,	904	9
BETWEEN MY COUNTRY--AND THE OTHERS--	BETWEEN MY COUNTRY--AND	905	1
'TIS NOON--MY LITTLE MAID--	'TIS SUNRISE--LITTLE	908	5
MY LITTLE MAID--'TIS NIGHT--ALAS	'TIS SUNRISE--LITTLE	908	9
OR GROPES, AT MY COMMAND	I MAKE HIS CRESCENT FILL	909	6
AND THIS OF ALL MY HOPES	AND THIS OF ALL MY HOPES	913	1
BOUNTIFUL COLORED, MY MORNING ROSE	AND THIS OF ALL MY HOPES	913	3
ALL MY MANSION TORN--	STRUCK, WAS I, NOR YET	925	10
MY BEST ACQUAINTANCES ARE THOSE	MY BEST ACQUAINTANCES	932	1
MY CONSTANT--REVERENTIAL FACE	MY BEST ACQUAINTANCES	932	7
I FELT A CLEAVING IN MY MIND--	I FELT A CLEAVING IN MY	937	1
AS IF MY BRAIN HAD SPLIT--	I FELT A CLEAVING IN MY	937	2
THROUGH FAITH--MY HAZEL EYE	WHAT I SEE NOT, I BETTER	939	2
FOR FREQUENT [OFTEN], ALL MY SENSE OBSCURED	WHAT I SEE NOT, I BETTER	939	5
AND I ARISE--AND IN MY DREAM--	WHAT I SEE NOT, I BETTER	939	9
MY FRACTURED TRUST--	THE CHEMICAL CONVICTION	954	4
MY PERENNIAL THINGS?	WHAT SHALL I DO WHEN THE	956	16
FOR MY DELINQUENT PALACES--	A LOSS OF SOMETHING EVER	959	12
TOUCHES MY FOREHEAD NOW AND THEN	A LOSS OF SOMETHING EVER	959	14
OCCUPY MY HOUSE [BREAST]"--	"UNTO ME?" I DO NOT KNOW	964	12
DROPPED--MY FATE--A TIMID PEBBLE--	ALL FORGOT FOR	966	13
THE TURNING O'ER AND O'ER MY FACE	FITTER TO SEE HIM, I MAY	968	11
WAS MY RETRIEVELESS BLAME--	IT BLOOMED AND DROPT, A	978	12
HAVE PERISHED IN MY HANDS	IT BLOOMED AND DROPT, A	978	14
MY OPPORTUNITY	IT BLOOMED AND DROPT, A	978	V 20
COULD LIFT MY FOREHEAD FROM MY WORK	THE MISSING ALL,	985	7
COULD LIFT MY FOREHEAD FROM MY WORK	THE MISSING ALL,	985	7
"MY FACES ARE ASLEEP--	THE FINGERS OF THE LIGHT	1000	6
DYING AT MY MUSIC!	DYING AT MY MUSIC!	1003	1
BANISH--MY MANDOLIN	BIND ME--I STILL CAN	1005	2
SLAY--AND MY SOUL SHALL RISE	BIND ME--I STILL CAN	1005	4
TO WHICH MY FAITH PINNED BLOCK BY BLOCK	FALSEHOOD OF THEE COULD	1007	3
UP LIFE'S HILL WITH MY LITTLE BUNDLE	UP LIFE'S HILL WITH MY	1010	1
IF MY NEWEST STEP	UP LIFE'S HILL WITH MY	1010	4
MY SEASON'S FURTHEST FLOWER--	MY SEASON'S FURTHEST	1019	1
SO LARGE MY WILL	SO LARGE MY WILL	1024	1
THE PRODUCTS OF MY FARM ARE THESE	THE PRODUCTS OF MY FARM	1025	1
SUFFICIENT FOR MY OWN	THE PRODUCTS OF MY FARM	1025	2
MY HEART UPON A LITTLE PLATE	MY HEART UPON A LITTLE	1027	1
'TWAS MY ONE GLORY--	'TWAS MY ONE GLORY--	1028	1
YOU'LL GET MY LETTER BY	BEE! I'M EXPECTING YOU!	1035	9
HERE, WHERE THE DAISIES FIT MY HEAD	HERE, WHERE THE DAISIES	1037	1
I MAY CONFIDE MY FLOWER--	HERE, WHERE THE DAISIES	1037	6
I SAW, AS IF MY EYE WERE ON	I HEARD, AS IF I HAD NO	1039	5
MY BODY BUT WITHIN	I HEARD, AS IF I HAD NO	1039	10
AND SET MY KERNEL IN.	I HEARD, AS IF I HAD NO	1039	12
I'VE DROPPED MY BRAIN--MY SOUL IS NUMB--	I'VE DROPPED MY BRAIN--	1046	1
I'VE DROPPED MY BRAIN--MY SOUL IS NUMB--	I'VE DROPPED MY BRAIN--	1046	1
MY NERVE IN MARBLE LIES--	I'VE DROPPED MY BRAIN--	1046	6
AND CHISELLED ALL MY TUNE	I'VE DROPPED MY BRAIN--	1046	14
A COMPETITION IN MY SENSE	I CANNOT MEET THE SPRING	1051	5
IT WASTED FROM MY SIGHT	I HAD A DAILY BLISS	1057	6
INCREASED [ENLARGED] BEYOND MY UTMOST SCOPE	I HAD A DAILY BLISS	1057	7
DIPPED MY BEAK IN IT,	SANG FROM THE HEART,	1059	2
'TWAS'NT MY BLAME--	SANG FROM THE HEART,	1059	12
MY CRICKET	FURTHER IN SUMMER THAN	1068	T
"MY HUSBAND"--WOMEN SAY--	TITLE DIVINE--IS MINE!	1072	12
MY COCOON TIGHTENS--COLORS TEAZE--	MY COCOON TIGHTENS--	1099	1
RESEMBLES TO MY OUTRAGED MIND	HIS BILL IS CLASPED--HIS	1102	9
MY PROCESS IS NOT LONG	THE SPRY ARMS OF THE	1103	6
MY EARTHLY HOUR [HUMAN LIFE] TO ME	SOME WRETCHED CREATURE,	1111	V 4
I TOLD MY SOUL TO COME--	THIS SLOW DAY MOVED	1120	5
'TIS MY FIRST NIGHT BENEATH THE SUN	'TIS MY FIRST NIGHT	1122	1
THAT ALL MY LIFE HAD ENTERED IT	A GREAT HOPE FELL	1123	12
TO BREATHE MY BLANK WITHOUT THEE	THROUGH WHAT TRANSPORTS	1153	3
A SPIDER ON MY RETICENCE	ALONE AND IN A	1167	3
REVISITING MY LATE ABODE	ALONE AND IN A	1167	9
IF ANY TAKE [SEIZE] MY PROPERTY	ALONE AND IN A	1167	19
THE STATUTE IS MY LEARNED FRIEND	ALONE AND IN A	1167	21
LEST THEY SHOULD COME--IS ALL MY FEAR	LEST THEY SHOULD COME--	1169	1
BEHOLD OUR [MY / THIS] SPACIOUS CITIZEN	NATURE AFFECTS TO BE	1170	7

		FIRST LINE	POEM	LINE
MY	(CONTINUED)			
	MY GOD--HE SEES THEE--	MY GOD--HE SEES THEE--	1178	1
	MY GUEST "TODAY [VISITOR] IN PARADISE"	"REMEMBER ME" IMPLORED	1180	3
	GO MAKE THEE FAIR MY CANDIDATE	OH SHADOW ON THE GRASS,	1187	3
	MY NOMINATED HEART--	OH SHADOW ON THE GRASS,	1187	4
	HENCEFORTH I TAKE MY LIVING PLACE	SOMEHOW MYSELF SURVIVED	1194	5
	BECAUSE MY BROOK IS FLUENT	BECAUSE MY BROOK IS	1200	1
	BECAUSE MY BROOK IS SILENT	BECAUSE MY BROOK IS	1200	3
	SO I PULL MY STOCKINGS OFF	SO I PULL MY STOCKINGS	1201	1
	MY NEIGHBOR BE--	THE SHOW IS NOT THE SHOW	1206	4
	AND SCUTTLE MY BALLOON--	I BET WITH EVERY WIND	1215	4
	LET MY FIRST KNOWING BE OF THEE	LET MY FIRST KNOWING BE	1218	1
	AND MY FIRST FEARING, LEST UNKNOWNS	LET MY FIRST KNOWING BE	1218	3
	MY TRIUMPH LASTED TILL THE DRUMS	MY TRIUMPH LASTED TILL	1227	1
	AND THEN I DROPPED MY VICTORY	MY TRIUMPH LASTED TILL	1227	3
	MY WILDERNESS HAS MADE--	HAD I NOT SEEN THE SUN	1233	4
	IF MY BARK SINK	IF MY BARK SINK	1234	1
	MY HEART RAN SO TO THEE	MY HEART RAN SO TO THEE	1237	1
	FOR WHATSOE'ER MY PACE	MY HEART RAN SO TO THEE	1237	5
	BOASTING [WOOING] MY PREMIUM--	MY HEART RAN SO TO THEE	1237	14
	BUT VANQUISHED HER [HIM] WITH MY DEFEAT	THE STARS ARE OLD, THAT	1249	7
	UNLESS IN MY REDEEMER'S FACE	BECAUSE THAT YOU ARE	1260	23
	I CANNOT SEE MY SOUL BUT KNOW 'TIS THERE	I CANNOT SEE MY SOUL BUT	1262	1
	THAT COST ME MY HONEST HEART--	I SAW THAT THE FLAKE WAS	1267	4
	SAGACIOUS OF MY MISTAKE	I SAW THAT THE FLAKE WAS	1267	6
	BEGONE--MY TOOTH HAS GROWN--	ART THOU THE THING I	1282	2
	AND MENTION TO MY HORSES	I KNOW SUSPENSE--IT	1285	7
	I MAKE BELIEVE UNTIL MY HEART	THE MOST PATHETIC THING	1290	3
	GO SLOW, MY SOUL, TO FEED THYSELF	GO SLOW, MY SOUL, TO	1297	1
	MY HUMAN NATURE'S FULLEST FORCE	I CANNOT WANT IT MORE--	1301	3
	PUT UP MY HEART THY HOARY WORK	THE NOTICE THAT IS	1310	3
	FRIGID AND FLEET MY FEET--	FRIGID AND SWEET HER	1318	2
	BUT SO ADJUST MY DAILY NIGHT	LET ME NOT MAR THAT	1335	3
	I OFTEN IN THE NIGHT [MY SLEEP]	ESCAPE IS SUCH A	1347	2
	AND THAT IS WHY I LAY MY HEAD	ESCAPE IS SUCH A	1347	11
	DEMANDS THE [MY] LITTLE KING	A SAUCER HOLDS A CUP	1374	6
	I'LL LET MY HEART BE JUST IN SIGHT--	THEY MIGHT NOT NEED ME--	1391	2
	TO OWN A SUSAN OF MY OWN	TO OWN A SUSAN OF MY OWN	1401	1
	MY MAKER--LET ME BE	MY MAKER--LET ME BE	1403	1
	DIVULGING IT WOULD REST MY HEART	I SHALL NOT MURMUR IF AT	1410	5
	SHOULD STAB MY RAVISHED SPIRIT	ONE JOY OF SO MUCH	1420	7
	MY SOUL, TO FIND THEM, COME,	THAN HEAVEN MORE REMOTE,	1436	11
	I FIND ONE ON MY HAND	HOW SOFT A CATERPILLAR	1448	2
	MY SLOW--TERRESTRIAL EYE	HOW SOFT A CATERPILLAR	1448	6
	IT'S JOURNEY NEVER WAKES MY HAND	HOW SOFT A CATERPILLAR	1448	V
	I TAUGHT MY HEART A HUNDRED TIMES	I THOUGHT THE TRAIN	1449	5
	TO HIDE MY STRATEGY TOO LATE	I THOUGHT THE TRAIN	1449	9
	MY NATURE UNDERLIE--	A COUNTERFEIT--A PLATED	1453	4
	WHAT DOOR--WHAT HOUR--RUN--RUN--MY SOUL!	"AND WITH WHAT BODY DO	1492	3
	LEST GRATITUDE REVIVE THE SNAKE [MY THOUGHT]	IT CAME HIS TURN TO BEG	1500	7
	THOUGH SMUGGLED HIS [MY] REPRIEVE	IT CAME HIS TURN TO BEG	1500	8
	BUT SHE MUST BUY MY SHELTER	I SAW THE WIND WITHIN	1502	3
	BUT NOT THIS [MY] LITTLE MAID--	I SAW THE WIND WITHIN	1502	V
	BUT SHE MUST [MY PRICE / HUMILITY] PAY FOR SUCCOR	I SAW THE WIND WITHIN	1502	V
	AND WHILE BY STEPPING [STANDING] ON MY HEART	THE PILE OF YEARS IS NOT	1507	5
	MINE ENEMY [MY FOE] IS GROWING OLD--	MINE ENEMY IS GROWING	1509	1
	MY COUNTRY'S WARDROBE	MY COUNTRY NEED NOT	1511	T
	MY COUNTRY NEED NOT CHANGE HER GOWN,	MY COUNTRY NEED NOT	1511	1
	INTRO WITHOUT MY TRANS--	A PANG IS MORE	1530	V
	SOCIETY FOR ME MY MISERY	SOCIETY FOR ME MY MISERY	1534	1
	CANDOR--MY TEPID FRIEND--	CANDOR--MY TEPID FRIEND	1537	1
	AT LEAST WITHIN MY TREE	COME SHOW THY DURHAM	1542	5
	MY WARS ARE LAID AWAY IN BOOKS--	MY WARS ARE LAID AWAY IN	1549	1
	AND OTHERS AT MY SIDE,	MY WARS ARE LAID AWAY IN	1549	6
	I GIVE [SEND] MY DYING KISS--	"GO TELL IT"--WHAT A	1554	8
	CONVEY MY DYING KISS--	"GO TELL IT"--WHAT A	1554	V 8
	MY FAITH CANNOT REPLY	LIVES HE IN ANY OTHER	1557	2
	IS MY [THEIR] RENOWN	TO BE FORGOT BY THEE	1560	12
	MY LOW [ONE / MEEK / WAN] RENOWN	TO BE FORGOT BY THEE	1560	V 12
	BEFORE MY MIND WAS SOWN,	THE SPIRIT LASTS--BUT IN	1576	22
	AND SO I SEND MY CRIMSON SCOUTS	WHERE ROSES WOULD NOT	1582	3
	BEFORE MY BEAM WAS SOWN,	EXPANSE CANNOT BE LOST--	1584	6
	BEFORE MY MIND [SOUL / BEAM] WAS BORN	THIS ME--THAT WALKS AND	1588	6
	FROM THESE [THOSE] WITHIN MY HAND	COSMOPOLITES WITHOUT A	1589	4
	WHO IS IT SEEKS MY PILLOW NIGHTS--	WHO IS IT SEEKS MY	1598	1
	UPON MY WINCING HEAD--	WHO IS IT SEEKS MY	1598	6
	IN MY OWN GRAVE I BREATHE	SO GIVE ME BACK TO DEATH	1632	5
	AND I AM RICHER THEN THAN ALL MY FELLOW MEN--	TAKE ALL AWAY FROM ME,	1640	2
	WHEN AT MY VERY DOOR ARE THOSE POSSESSING MORE,	TAKE ALL AWAY FROM ME,	1640	4
	MY STRANGER DISAPPEARED	CONFERRING WITH MYSELF	1655	2
	HOW PALTRY LOOKED MY CARES	CONFERRING WITH MYSELF	1655	5
	MY PRACTISE HOW ABSURD	CONFERRING WITH MYSELF	1655	6
	SUPERFLUOUS MY WHOLE CAREER	CONFERRING WITH MYSELF	1655	7
	LIGHT MY NORTHERN ROOM	GUEST AM I TO HAVE	1661	2
	MY FIDELITY--	GUEST AM I TO HAVE	1661	7
	BUT MY FEET SLIP NEARER EVERY DAY	I DID NOT REACH THEE	1664	2
	NOW DEATH USURPS MY PREMIUM	I DID NOT REACH THEE	1664	33
	MY RIGHT TO WALK UPON THE EARTH	I KNOW OF PEOPLE IN THE	1665	7

		FIRST LINE	POEM	LINE
MY	(CONTINUED)			
	IN WINTER IN MY ROOM	IN WINTER IN MY ROOM	1670	1
	SURVEYED MY CHAMBER FLOOR	IN WINTER IN MY ROOM	1670	15
	ON MY VOLCANO GROWS THE GRASS	ON MY VOLCANO GROWS THE	1677	1
	WOULD POPULATE WITH AWE MY SOLITUDE	ON MY VOLCANO GROWS THE	1677	8
	HE JOINS ME IN MY RAMBLE	THE BLUNDER IS IN	1684	5
	MY WISDOM LOSES WAY	THE ONES THAT	1690	6
	MY WILL ENDEAVORS FOR IT'S WORD	TO TELL THE BEAUTY WOULD	1700	5
	I JUDGE FROM MY GEOGRAPHY	VOLCANOES BE IN SICILY	1705	3
	THAT HOLDS MY CHANCES UP.	A PIT--BUT HEAVEN OVER	1712	8
	THE DEPTH IS ALL MY THOUGHT--	A PIT--BUT HEAVEN OVER	1712	10
	I DARE NOT ASK MY FEET--	A PIT--BUT HEAVEN OVER	1712	11
	HE WAS MY HOST--HE WAS MY GUEST,	HE WAS MY HOST--HE WAS	1721	1
	HE WAS MY HOST--HE WAS MY GUEST,	HE WAS MY HOST--HE WAS	1721	1
	THEN HANDED ME MY BEING'S WORTH--	I TOOK ONE DRAUGHT OF	1725	7
	IF EVER THE LID GETS OFF MY HEAD	IF EVER THE LID GETS OFF	1727	1
	VANQUISHED, MY SOUL WILL KNOW	I'VE GOT AN ARROW HERE.	1729	5
	"LETHE" IN MY FLOWER,	"LETHE" IN MY FLOWER,	1730	1
	JUPITER! MY FATHER!	"LETHE" IN MY FLOWER,	1730	7
	MY LIFE CLOSED TWICE BEFORE ITS CLOSE;	MY LIFE CLOSED TWICE	1732	1
	TILL MY MINUTEST DOWER,	OH, HONEY OF AN HOUR,	1734	4
	MY UNFREQUENTED FLOWER	OH, HONEY OF AN HOUR,	1734	5
	PROUD OF MY BROKEN HEART, SINCE THOU DIDST BREAK IT,	PROUD OF MY BROKEN HEART	1736	1
	PROUD OF MY NIGHT, SINCE THOU WITH MOONS DOST SLAKE IT,	PROUD OF MY BROKEN HEART	1736	3
	NOT TO PARTAKE THY PASSION, MY HUMILITY.	PROUD OF MY BROKEN HEART	1736	4
	WHEN THEY DISLOCATE MY BRAIN!	REARRANGE A "WIFE'S"	1737	2
	AMPUTATE MY FRECKLED BOSOM!	REARRANGE A "WIFE'S"	1737	3
	BLUSH, MY SPIRIT, IN THY FASTNESS--	REARRANGE A "WIFE'S"	1737	5
	BLUSH, MY UNACKNOWLEDGED CLAY--	REARRANGE A "WIFE'S"	1737	6
	THEN--MY DIADEM PUT ON.	REARRANGE A "WIFE'S"	1737	16
	BIG MY SECRET BUT IT'S BANDAGED--	REARRANGE A "WIFE'S"	1737	17
	THE GRAVE MY LITTLE COTTAGE IS,	THE GRAVE MY LITTLE	1743	1
	I MAKE MY PARLOR ORDERLY	THE GRAVE MY LITTLE	1743	3
	"COME HOME WITH ME, MY FRIEND!	THE WATERS CHASED HIM AS	1749	4
	MY PARLOR IS OF SHRIVEN GLASS,	THE WATERS CHASED HIM AS	1749	5
	MY PANTRY HAS A FISH	THE WATERS CHASED HIM AS	1749	6
	'TWAS HERE MY SUMMER PAUSED	'TWAS HERE MY SUMMER	1756	1
	MY SENTENCE HAD BEGUN.	'TWAS HERE MY SUMMER	1756	4
	LET ME NOT THIRST WITH THIS HOCK AT MY LIP,	LET ME NOT THIRST WITH	1772	1
	NOR BEG, WITH DOMAINS IN MY POCKET--	LET ME NOT THIRST WITH	1772	2
MYRIAD				
	A MYRIAD DAISY PLAY--	IN LANDS I NEVER SAW--	124	6
MYRIADS				
	TO BALK THEE OF THY SACRED PREY--[THE INNOCENCE / THE MYRIADS]	OH FUTURE! THOU SECRETED	1631	7
MYRMIDONS				
	THEN STILLS IT'S ARTISANS [MYRMIDONS]--LIKE GHOSTS [SWANS]--	IT SIFTS FROM LEADEN	311	19
MYRRHS				
	THE MYRRHS, AND MOCHAS, OF THE MIND	CANDOR--MY TEPID FRIEND	1537	3
MYSELF				
	WHICH FOR MYSELF DOTH SING--	I HAVE A BIRD IN SPRING	5	2
	IF I WERE HALF SO FINE MYSELF	"SOWN IN DISHONOR"!	62	4
	TO WONDER WHAT MYSELF WILL SAY,	THO' I GET HOME HOW LATE	207	11
	NOR, FOR MYSELF, I CAME SO FAR--	SAVIOR! I'VE NO ONE ELSE	217	5
	FATHER--I BRING THEE--NOT MYSELF--	SAVIOR! I'VE NO ONE ELSE	217 V	5
	MYSELF--A MILLIONAIRE	YOUR RICHES--TAUGHT ME--	299	2
	OF MINES, I LITTLE KNOW--MYSELF--	YOUR RICHES--TAUGHT ME--	299	9
	THEN I SAID SOFTLY TO MYSELF--	I'LL TELL YOU HOW THE	318	7
	I TOLD MYSELF, "TAKE COURAGE, FRIEND--	I FELT MY LIFE WITH BOTH	351	13
	MYSELF AND IT, IN MAJESTY	THE DAY THAT I WAS	356	11
	I BROOCH AND EARRINGS FOR MYSELF,	WHEN DIAMONDS ARE A	397	3
	MYSELF--FOR SCARCELY SETTLED--	THE WINTERS ARE SO SHORT	403	5
	MYSELF WOULD RUN AWAY	I NEVER FELT AT HOME--	413	14
	MYSELF HAD JUST TO EARN--	REMOVED FROM ACCIDENT OF	424	4
	MYSELF--WAS BEGGARED--TOO--	IT WOULD NEVER BE COMMON	430	24
	BUT THIS SORT, GRIEVED MYSELF,	'TWAS JUST THIS TIME,	445	21
	RICH! 'TWAS MYSELF--WAS RICH--	IT WAS GIVEN TO ME BY	454	1[illegible]
	ENTITLED TO MYSELF--PRECISE--	I AM ALIVE--I GUESS--	470	19
	MYSELF WAS FORMED--A CARPENTER--	MYSELF WAS FORMED--A	488	1
	MYSELF--BE NOON TO HIM--	I ENVY SEAS, WHEREON HE	498	20
	MYSELF ENDUED [UPHELD / UPBORNE / SUSTAINED] BALLOON	I WOULD NOT PAINT--A	505	14
	HAD I THE ART TO STUN MYSELF	I WOULD NOT PAINT--A	505	23
	OR IF MYSELF WERE DREAMED OF HER--	HER SWEET WEIGHT ON MY	518	7
	THAT AS MYSELF--COULD PITY HIM--	I TRIED TO THINK A	532	18
	MYSELF--WHO BORE IT--DO--	'TIS TRUE--THEY SHUT ME	538	10
	FORGIVE THEM--EVEN AS MYSELF--	'TIS TRUE--THEY SHUT ME	538	11
	I AIMED MY PEBBLE--BUT MYSELF	I TOOK MY POWER IN MY	540	5
	OR WAS MYSELF [JUST MYSELF / ONLY ME / I]--TOO SMALL?	I TOOK MY POWER IN MY	540	8
	OR WAS MYSELF [JUST MYSELF / ONLY ME / I]--TOO SMALL?	I TOOK MY POWER IN MY	540	8
	UNCERTAIN IF MYSELF, OR HE,	MY FIRST WELL DAY--SINCE	574	7
	MYSELF--CAN OWN [HOLD] THE KEY--	IF I MAY HAVE IT, WHEN	577	8
	MYSELF FELT ILL--AND ODD--	I HAD BEEN HUNGRY, ALL	579	14
	I GAVE MYSELF TO HIM [HIM ALL MYSELF]--	I GAVE MYSELF TO HIM--	580	1
	I GAVE MYSELF TO HIM [HIM ALL MYSELF]--	I GAVE MYSELF TO HIM--	580	1

	FIRST LINE	POEM	LINE
MYSELF (CONTINUED)			
MYSELF A POORER PROVE	I GAVE MYSELF TO HIM--	580	6
"MYSELF" MEANT THEE--	EMPTY MY HEART, OF THEE	587	10
CONVINCED MYSELF OF ME--	I CRIED AT PITY--NOT AT	588	4
SO LONG I FAINTED, TO MYSELF	I CRIED AT PITY--NOT AT	588	5
MYSELF DISTINGUISHED GOD--	LIKE MIGHTY FOOT LIGHTS	595	8
MYSELF--HAD BANNED THE TRIBES--	IT ALWAYS FELT TO ME--A	597	18
AND SEEK [GAIN] A DINNER FOR MYSELF--	IT WOULD HAVE STARVED A	612	11
MYSELF TOO FAR BELOW	I WATCHED THE MOON	629	34
ME FROM MYSELF--TO BANISH--	ME FROM MYSELF--TO	642	1
BUT SINCE MYSELF--ASSAULT ME--	ME FROM MYSELF--TO	642	5
NOR MYSELF TO HIM--BY ACCENT--	CONSCIOUS AM I IN MY	679	11
YET WHY SO LITTLE SOUND--MYSELF	THE SUN KEPT SETTING--	692	11
THE GRACE--MYSELF--MIGHT NOT OBTAIN--	THE GRACE--MYSELF--MIGHT	707	1
FAME OF MYSELF, TO JUSTIFY,	FAME OF MYSELF, TO	713	1
FAME OF MYSELF TO LACK--ALTHOUGH	FAME OF MYSELF, TO	713	5
MYSELF--THE TERM BETWEEN--	BEHIND ME--DIPS ETERNITY	721	3
HAVE ANY LIKE MYSELF	HAVE ANY LIKE MYSELF	736	1
HAVE ANY LIKE MYSELF	HAVE ANY LIKE MYSELF	736	9
HAVE ANY LIKE MYSELF	HAVE ANY LIKE MYSELF	736	17
YOU TAUGHT ME WAITING WITH MYSELF--	YOU TAUGHT ME WAITING	740	1
AT LENGTH, A MOURNER, LIKE MYSELF,	THE BIRDS REPORTED FROM	743	13
THAN I REVILED [DENOUNCED] MYSELF,	IT DROPPED SO LOW--IN MY	747	6
ONLY ME--[STILL MYSELF-- / ME ALONE] WAS STILL--	WHEN I HOPED, I	768	16
I ENTERTAINED MYSELF--	DEPRIVED OF OTHER	773	2
OBTAINED [ENGROSSED] MY LODGINGS, ERE MYSELF--	BEREAVED OF ALL, I WENT	784	5
SEVERER SERVICE OF MYSELF	SEVERER SERVICE OF	786	1
MYSELF CONJECTURED [COMPUTED] WERE THEY PEARLS--	A DROP FELL ON THE APPLE	794	7
AND BEEN MYSELF THAT EASY [DISTANT] THING	I PLAY AT RICHES--TO	801	7
I DEEM MYSELF WHAT I WOULD BE--	I PLAY AT RICHES--TO	801	11
BEFORE MYSELF WAS BORN	WHO OCCUPIES THIS HOUSE?	892	17
I HIDE MYSELF WITHIN MY FLOWER,	I HIDE MYSELF WITHIN MY	903	1
APPEALING TO MYSELF,	HAD I NOT THIS, OR THIS,	904	2
I FIND MYSELF STILL SOFTLY SEARCHING	A LOSS OF SOMETHING EVER	959	11
ACCUSED--WERT THOU--AND MYSELF--TRIBUNAL--	WERT THOU BUT ILL--THAT	961	9
PROVE MYSELF--OF THEE--	ALL FORGOT FOR	966	16
I DWELT, AS IF MYSELF WERE OUT,	I HEARD, AS IF I HAD NO	1039	9
MYSELF CAN READ THE TELEGRAMS	MYSELF CAN READ THE	1089	1
MYSELF HAD EARNED IT--ME,	BECAUSE 'TWAS RICHES I	1093	2
MYSELF A FRECKLED--BE--	THEMSELF ARE ALL I HAVE	1094	2
I FELT MYSELF A [THE] VISITOR	ALONE AND IN A	1167	7
SOMEHOW MYSELF SURVIVED THE NIGHT	SOMEHOW MYSELF SURVIVED	1194	1
BUT LABOR VASTER THAN MYSELF	THE FROST WAS NEVER SEEN	1202	19
AND WISHED MYSELF WERE THEY.	MY TRIUMPH LASTED TILL	1227	8
CONSIDER IT UNTO MYSELF	ESCAPE IS SUCH A	1347	3
STRUCK NO ONE BUT MYSELF--	THE FARTHEST THUNDER	1581	6
CONFERRING WITH MYSELF	CONFERRING WITH MYSELF	1655	1
MYSTERIES			
FOR LITTLE MYSTERIES	I WATCHED THE MOON	629	24
MYSTERIOUS			
IN RAGS MYSTERIOUS AS THESE	IN RAGS MYSTERIOUS AS	117	1
OF THE MYSTERIOUS BARD [BAND]!	TO LEARN THE TRANSPORT	167	16
IN HER MYSTERIOUS DRAWERS--	THE MONTHS HAVE ENDS--	423	6
MYSTERY			
AND NICODEMUS' MYSTERY	AN ALTERED LOOK ABOUT	140	15
THESE--ARE THE WESTERN MYSTERY!	THIS--IS THE LAND--THE	266	4
HER BLAMELESS MYSTERY--	A SOLEMN THING--IT WAS--	271	4
THAT CUSHIONS MYSTERY WITH TULLE,	THE TINT I CANNOT TAKE--	627	19
THAT COVERS MYSTERY WITH BLONDE--	THE TINT I CANNOT TAKE--	627	V 19
WE TOOK THE MYSTERY.	FROM US SHE WANDERED NOW	890	8
TILL MYSTERY IMPATIENT DREW	TWO TRAVELLERS PERISHING	933	13
THE ARTIFICE [MYSTERY] OF STRENGTH--	NOT TO DISCOVER WEAKNESS	1054	2
THE MYSTERY OF FOOD	ART THOU THE THING I	1282	6
YESTERDAY IS MYSTERY--	YESTERDAY IS HISTORY,	1292	5
WHAT MYSTERY PERVADES A WELL!	WHAT MYSTERY PERVADES A	1400	1
WHO SLOWLY FORD THE MYSTERY	PASS TO THY RENDEZVOUS	1564	3
AND MOATS OF MYSTERY.	SUNSET THAT SCREENS,	1609	4
HOW CORDIAL IS THE MYSTERY!	NO LIFE CAN POMPLESS	1626	5
AND MYSTERY--	LAD OF ATHENS, FAITHFUL	1768	3
MYSTIC			
PEOPLE UPON THAT MYSTIC GREEN--	THERE IS A MORN BY MEN	24	20
BY WHAT MYSTIC MOORING	WHETHER MY BARK WENT	52	5
THE ABSENT--MYSTIC--CREATURE--	TO DIE--TAKES JUST A	255	9
INTO THE MYSTIC [PURPLE] WELL--	A SOLEMN THING--IT WAS--	271	6
TO TASTE HER MYSTIC BREAD--	THESE ARE THE SIGNS TO	1077	4
MYTHS			
OF OTHER MYTHS	PURSUING YOU IN YOUR	1602	3
NAIL			
OR RIP OF NAIL--OR CARPENTER--	I'VE KNOWN A HEAVEN,	243	5
THE SACKCLOTH--HANGS UPON THE NAIL--	IT WOULD NEVER BE COMMON	430	30
PERPETUAL NAIL IT DOWN--	A GREAT HOPE FELL	1123	17
UPON A NAIL OF PLUSH--	THE DAY GREW SMALL,	1140	8
A PAST [TIME / STATE] OF PLANK AND NAIL	THE PROPS ASSIST THE	1142	10
NAILS			
WHO DRILLS [NAILS] HIS WELCOME IN--	THAT AFTER HORROR--THAT	286	16
AND ONLY NAILS THE EYES--	I MEASURE EVERY GRIEF I	561	28
NAKED			
THAT SCALPS [PEELS] YOUR NAKED SOUL--	HE FUMBLES AT YOUR SOUL	315	12

	FIRST LINE	POEM	LINE
NAKED (CONTINUED)			
ACQUITTED--FROM THAT NAKED BAR--	TRIUMPH--MAY BE OF	455	15
NAKED OF FLASK--NAKED OF CASK--	A TOAD, CAN DIE OF LIGHT	583	10
NAKED OF FLASK--NAKED OF CASK--	A TOAD, CAN DIE OF LIGHT	583	10
SAYS THE NAKED TREE--	NOT AT HOME TO CALLERS	1590	2
NAME			
IN THE NAME OF THE BEE--	THE GENTIAN WEAVES HER	18	17
ONE "PLEIAD" WAS IT'S NAME--	I HAD A GUINEA GOLDEN--	23	18
"PLEIAD" IT'S NAME, AND ROBIN,	I HAD A GUINEA GOLDEN--	23	27
AND GAMBOL I MAY NEVER NAME--	THERE IS A MORN BY MEN	24	5
AND WILL NOT TELL IT'S NAME.	THERE'S SOMETHING	45	4
I WILL NOT NAME IT IN THE STREET	I HAV'NT TOLD MY GARDEN	50	5
"ARCTURUS" IS HIS OTHER NAME--	"ARCTURUS" IS HIS OTHER	70	1
TELLING MY TARDY NAME--	I SHOULD NOT DARE TO	205	12
IT'S NAME IS PUT AWAY	A SINGLE SCREW OF FLESH	263	6
AS SPECIES--BE--FOR NAME--	A WEIGHT WITH NEEDLES ON	264	8
TO TELL YOUR [ONE'S] NAME--THE LIVELONG JUNE--	I'M NOBODY! WHO ARE YOU?	288	7
I GOT SO I COULD HEAR [THINK / TAKE] HIS NAME--	I GOT SO I COULD HEAR	293	1
HIS NAME--REMAIN--	THE ONE WHO COULD REPEAT	307	9
AS ONE THAT BORE HER MASTER'S NAME--	THE FACE I CARRY WITH ME	336	15
TO ASK THE OWNER'S NAME--	I FELT MY LIFE WITH BOTH	351	7
AND A NAME--	FOR DEATH--OR RATHER	382	8
THAT THEY--PRONOUNCE MY NAME--	ME--COME! MY DAZZLED	431	10
TO TAKE THE NAME OF GOLD--	IT WAS GIVEN TO ME BY	454	14
AND MARKED MY GIRLHOOD'S NAME--	I AM ALIVE--I GUESS--	470	21
THAT BEARS ANOTHER'S--NAME--	THE WORLD--STANDS--	493	4
MY LIPS JUST HOLD THE NAME--	YOU KNOW THAT PORTRAIT	504	10
THE NAME THEY DROPPED UPON MY FACE	I'M CEDED--I'VE STOPPED	508	2
UNTO SUPREMEST NAME [TERM]--	I'M CEDED--I'VE STOPPED	508	10
OR BEES--THAT THOUGHT THE SUMMER'S NAME	LIKE FLOWERS, THAT HEARD	513	4
WITH JUST AN AGE--AND NAME--	WE DREAM--IT IS GOOD WE	531	14
THAT WHEN THEIR MORTAL NAME [FAME] BE NUMB--	THE MARTYR POETS--DID	544	3
THAT NEVER HAD A NAME--	IT KNEW NO MEDICINE--	559	10
I WISH I KNEW THAT WOMAN'S NAME--	I CRIED AT PITY--NOT AT	588	17
THEN CARVED [HE WROTE] HIS NAME--UPON IT--	HE FOUND MY BEING--SET	603	3
AND IF HE SPOKE--WHAT NAME WAS BEST--	TO KNOW JUST HOW HE	622	18
THOUGH MY NAME	I CANNOT LIVE WITH YOU--	640	38
THE NAME--OF IT--IS "AUTUMN"--	THE NAME--OF IT--IS	656	1
BLAMELESS OF A NAME--	BLOOM UPON THE MOUNTAIN	667	2
MY NAME BE ELSE SUPREME--	FAME OF MYSELF, TO	713	6
I SCARCE ESTEEM LOCATION'S NAME--	WHERE THOU ART--THAT--IS	725	4
THOUGH SHE FORGET THE NAME I BEAR--	PRECIOUS TO ME--SHE	727	2
TO FORFEIT THEE? THE VERY NAME	IF BLAME BE MY SIDE--	775	3
BUT LONG RECORDS THE LADY'S NAME	THE ROBIN FOR THE CRUMB	864	3
'TIS WELL THE NAME AND AGE	WHO OCCUPIES THIS HOUSE?	892	4
ASKED HIM HIS NAME--HE LISPED ME "TROTWOOD"--	TRUDGING TO EDEN,	1020	3
HALLOWED NAME--	SANG FROM THE HEART,	1059	16
A WISDOM, WITHOUT FACE, OR NAME,	THE CRICKETS SANG	1104	10
. . . [NAME HAS BEEN]	THE MURMURING OF BEES,	1115	V 13
STEP LOFTY, FOR THIS NAME BE TOLD	STEP LIGHTLY ON THIS	1183	5
NOT A TOMORROW TO KNOW IT'S NAME	THE POPULAR HEART IS A	1226	5
SILENCE--IS HIS NAME--	DEATH'S WAYLAYING NOT	1296	4
YET THAT WHIP'S NAME	NOT WITH A CLUB, THE	1304	7
RICHES AND NAME AND REALM--	FRIGID AND SWEET HER	1318	6
AND VANS WITHOUT A NAME	HOW KNOW IT FROM A	1364	6
WITHOUT A NAME--	IN MANY AND REPORTLESS	1382	8
THE NAME OF IT IS LOVE--	BEHOLD THIS LITTLE BANE	1438	4
THE NAME TO HEAR	OF WHOM SO DEAR	1504	2
THAT DOES'NT KNOW ITS NAME	THE BUTTERFLY UPON THE	1521	2
AND NOW AGAINST HIS SUBTLE NAME	HE LIVED THE LIFE OF	1525	3
NOR IGNOMINY'S NAME--	TO HER DERIDED HOME	1586	4
AND NOW AGAINST HIS SUBTLE NAME	WHO ABDICATED AMBUSH	1616	3
WARMS SOME POOR NAME	GLORY IS THAT BRIGHT	1660	4
YET BUT A NAME.	AS SUBTLE AS TOMORROW	1713	4
NAMED			
ALL THAT IS NAMED OF SUMMER DAYS	THE PUNGENT ATOM IN THE	1191	3
NAMELESS			
HOW MANY CAST A NAMELESS POD	HOW MANY FLOWERS FAIL IN	404	5
UNTO A NAMELESS MAN--	TO OFFER BRAVE	767	6
A NAMELESS BIRD--A STRANGER	THE SUN WENT DOWN--NO	1079	7
WHOSE NAMELESS FATHOMS SLINK AWAY	CONTAINED IN THIS SHORT	1165	7
WHOSE WATERS ARE THE BRAWLING [NAMELESS] BROOK	CONTAINED IN THIS SHORT	1165	V 7
TO MEET IT--NAMELESS AS IT IS--	THE LAST OF SUMMER IS	1353	5
WITH SOLEMN NAMELESS NEED	I GROPED FOR HIM BEFORE	1555	2
NAMES			
IF I SHOULD CEASE TO TAKE THE NAMES	IF I SHOULD CEASE TO	56	5
TEACH HIM--WHEN HE MAKES THE NAMES--	TEACH HIM--WHEN HE MAKES	227	1
BRAVE NAMES OF MEN--	READ--SWEET--HOW OTHERS	260	12
THEY HAVE NO ROBES, NOR NAMES--	ALONE, I CANNOT BE--	298	5
BUT JUST THE NAMES, OF GEMS--	YOUR RICHES--TAUGHT ME--	299	10
AND EIDER--NAMES--	I WENT TO HEAVEN--	374	12
AND COVERED UP--OUR NAMES--	I DIED FOR BEAUTY--BUT	449	12
AS DID THEIR MARBLE NAMES	YOU'LL FIND--IT WHEN YOU	610	6
YOU CHOSE THE NEWER NAMES [TIMES]--	YOU'LL FIND--IT WHEN YOU	610	8
OR TAKE THE ROYAL NAMES IN VAIN--	SWEET MOUNTAINS--YE TELL	722	5
UPON THEIR SETTING NAMES--	FAME IS THE TINT THAT	866	2
I KNEW THE DOLLARS BY THEIR NAMES--	BECAUSE 'TWAS RICHES I	1093	3
THEIR NAMES, UNLESS YOU KNOW THEM,	THE MOST IMPORTANT	1746	5

	FIRST LINE	POEM	LINE
NAP			
OR EVER TOOK A NAP--	I NEVER FELT AT HOME--	413	10
NAPLES			
BY NATURES THIS SIDE NAPLES--	A STILL--VOLCANO--LIFE--	601	7
NAPLES IS MORE AFRAID	WHEN ETNA BASKS AND	1146	2
NAPOLEON			
CONSCIOUS--AS OLD NAPOLEON, ...	A LITTLE BREAD--A CRUST	159	5
NARCOTIC			
CANNOT BE STIFLED--WITH NARCOTIC-- . . .	CIVILIZATION--SPURNS--	492	12
NARCOTICS			
NARCOTICS CANNOT STILL THE TOOTH [MOUSE] .	THIS WORLD IS NOT	501	19
NARRATES			
CORINTHIANS ONE. FIFTEEN. NARRATES . . .	"SOWN IN DISHONOR"!	62	9
NARROW			
STILL CHAFES IT'S NARROW BED--	A SOMETHING IN A	122	15
YOU'RE RIGHT--"THE WAY IS NARROW"-- . . .	YOU'RE RIGHT--"THE WAY	234	1
LOCATION'S NARROW WAY IS FOR OURSELVES-- .	WE PRAY--TO HEAVEN--	489	7
WITH NARROW, PROBING, [ANALYTIC] EYES-- . .	I MEASURE EVERY GRIEF I	561	2
APPROACHED--AND SPURNED THE NARROW GRASS-- .	I THINK I WAS ENCHANTED	593	11
THEN--GLANCING NARROW, AT THE WALL-- . . .	THE WAY I READ A	636	9
AND NARROW AT THE FLOOR [DOOR]	THE WAY I READ A	636	10
MINE--TO GUARD YOUR NARROW PRECINCT-- . .	PROMISE THIS--WHEN YOU	648	17
AND IN IT'S NARROW EYES--	A PRISON GETS TO BE A	652	4
THE NARROW ROUND--THE STINT--	A PRISON GETS TO BE A	652	25
THE SPREADING WIDE MY NARROW HANDS . . .	I DWELL IN POSSIBILITY--	657	11
IT PLEASED MY NARROW EYES--	THEIR HIGHT IN HEAVEN	696	12
TILL DEATH--IS NARROW LOVING--	TILL DEATH--IS NARROW	907	1
TOO NARROW IS THE RIGHT BETWEEN--	TOO LITTLE WAY THE HOUSE	911	5
THE HEART HAS NARROW BANKS	THE HEART HAS NARROW	928	1
THE TENANT OF THE NARROW COTTAGE, WERT THOU--	WERT THOU BUT ILL--THAT	961	13
A NARROW FELLOW IN THE GRASS	A NARROW FELLOW IN THE	986	1
A NARROW WIND COMPLAINS ALL DAY	THE SKY IS LOW--THE	1075	5
IT WAS A NARROW TIME--	THE LAST NIGHT THAT SHE	1100	18
YET [BUT] EASY AS THE [A] NARROW SNAKE . .	THE FROST OF DEATH WAS	1136	12
STEP LIGHTLY ON THIS NARROW SPOT-- . . .	STEP LIGHTLY ON THIS	1183	1
. . . KNEW HE WAS] NARROW--	HE PREACHED UPON	1207	1
I SCANNED HIS NARROW REALM [GRANT] . . .	IT CAME HIS TURN TO BEG	1500	5
TRUST ENTRENCHED IN NARROW PAIN--	REARRANGE A "WIFE'S"	1737	10
NARROWING			
KEPT NARROWING IT'S BOILING WHEEL	'TWAS LIKE A MAELSTROM,	414	3
NARROWLY			
WHY AVOID SO NARROWLY	GUEST AM I TO HAVE	1661	6
NATION			
I'VE KNOWN HER--FROM AN AMPLE NATION-- . .	THE SOUL SELECTS HER OWN	303	9
A MINOR NATION CELEBRATES	FURTHER IN SUMMER THAN	1068	3
THIS ECSTATIC NATION	THE HEART IS THE CAPITAL	1354	7
NATIONS			
WHO NOTIFIED THE NATIONS	"SIC TRANSIT GLORIA	3	39
THE FLAGS OF NATIONS SWANG.	A DAY! HELP! HELP!	42	6
WHO WIN, AND NATIONS DO NOT SEE--	TO FIGHT ALOUD, IS VERY	126	5
THIS WORLD, AND IT'S SPECIES [NATIONS / FASHIONS / SYMBOLS / . . .	THIS DUST, AND IT'S	936	9
IT'S TOILS [CORN] TO BRINDLED PEOPLE [NATIONS] THRUST [CAST]--	A FIELD OF STUBBLE,	1407	3
THE NATIONS AND THE DAYS--	SOME ONE PREPARED THIS	1644	3
OF BUMBLE-BEES AND OTHER NATIONS	THE MOST IMPORTANT	1746	7
NATIVE			
BEHIND MY NATIVE TOWN.	FREQUENTLY THE WOODS ARE	6	4
BACK TO HER NATIVE WOOD!	THERE'S SOMETHING	45	12
IN HIS "NATIVE TOWN."	DUST IS THE ONLY SECRET	153	4
HAUNTED BY NATIVE LANDS, THE WHILE-- . . .	TO LEARN THE TRANSPORT	167	7
TURNED SLOWLY TO HIS NATIVE COAST-- . . .	AN AWFUL TEMPEST MASHED	198	12
BERRIES, IN MY NATIVE TOWN--	PERHAPS I ASKED TOO	352	4
THERE'S BANISHMENT FROM NATIVE EYES-- . .	I MEASURE EVERY GRIEF I	561	31
IN SIGHT OF NATIVE AIR--	I MEASURE EVERY GRIEF I	561	32
TO THE NATIVE LAND.	FAR FROM LOVE THE	1021	8
WHICH WHILE YOU TASTE SO NATIVE [ADJACENT] SEEMS	YOUR THOUGHTS DONT HAVE	1452	5
HIS NATIVE LAND--	THE THINGS THAT NEVER	1515	13
NATURAL			
SUNSET AT NIGHT--IS NATURAL--	SUNSET AT NIGHT--IS	415	1
NATURE			
NATURE IN CHIVALRY--	GARLANDS FOR QUEENS, MAY	34	6
NATURE IN CHARITY--	GARLANDS FOR QUEENS, MAY	34	7
NATURE IN EQUITY--	GARLANDS FOR QUEENS, MAY	34	8
NATURE--SOMETIMES SEARS A SAPLING-- . . .	NATURE--SOMETIMES SEARS	314	1
PREPARES YOUR BRITTLE NATURE [SUBSTANCE] .	HE FUMBLES AT YOUR SOUL	315	5
BUT NATURE LOST THE DATE OF THIS-- . . .	IT STRUCK ME--EVERY DAY	362	11
AS NATURE DID NOT CARE--	THE MORNING AFTER WO--	364	5
HAD NATURE--IN HER MONSTROUS HOUSE . . .	A TONGUE--TO TELL HIM I	400	3
OF FRECKLED HUMAN NATURE--	WHAT SOFT--CHERUBIC	401	7
REVERSES NATURE--MASTER--	SUNSET AT NIGHT--IS	415	3
THE SIMPLE NEWS THAT NATURE TOLD-- . . .	THIS IS MY LETTER TO THE	441	3
THIS WAS THE LEOPARD'S NATURE--SIGNOR-- . .	CIVILIZATION--SPURNS--	492	8
THE HEMLOCK'S NATURE THRIVES--ON COLD-- . .	I THINK THE HEMLOCK	525	9
THAT NATURE MURMURED TO HERSELF	I THINK I WAS ENCHANTED	593	13
AT NEWS THAT HE CEASED HUMAN NATURE . . .	TO KNOW JUST HOW HE	622	11
NAY, NATURE, ['TWAS FURTHER--] IT WAS DAY--	TO MY SMALL HEARTH HIS	638	8
'TWAS FACE TO FACE WITH NATURE--FORCED-- .	I COULD SUFFICE FOR HIM,	643	7
"NATURE" IS WHAT WE SEE--	"NATURE" IS WHAT WE SEE	668	1

NATURE (CONTINUED)

	FIRST LINE	POEM	LINE
NAY--NATURE IS HEAVEN--	"NATURE" IS WHAT WE SEE	668	4
NATURE IS WHAT WE HEAR--	"NATURE" IS WHAT WE SEE	668	5
NAY--NATURE IS HARMONY [MELODY]--	"NATURE" IS WHAT WE SEE	668	8
NATURE IS WHAT WE KNOW--	"NATURE" IS WHAT WE SEE	668	9
EXISTS IN EVERY HUMAN NATURE	EACH LIFE CONVERGES TO	680	3
NATURE--AND SOME MEN--	RESTS AT NIGHT	714	3
WHILE NATURE	RESTS AT NIGHT	714	5
WHAT DEED IS THEIR'S [THEY BEAR] UNTO THE GENERAL NATURE--	FOUR TREES--UPON A	742	13
GROWTH OF MAN--LIKE GROWTH OF NATURE--	GROWTH OF MAN--LIKE	750	1
YET HOW NATURE FROZE--	WHEN I HOPED, I	768	12
NATURE WILL--THAT IT BE NIGHT	WHEN I HOPED, I	768	19
NATURE HESITATE--BEFORE	WHEN I HOPED, I	768	23
'TIS [THAT'S] THIS--AND WITCHCRAFT--NATURE KEEPS [KNOWS / HAS]	THE COLOR OF A QUEEN, IS	776	7
I WORRIED NATURE WITH MY WHEELS	SEVERER SERVICE OF	786	5
NATURE--THE GENTLEST MOTHER IS,	NATURE--THE GENTLEST	790	1
THEN ORIENT SHOWED [THE EAST PUT OUT / NATURE PUT OUT] A SINGLE FLAG,	A DROP FELL ON THE APPLE	794	15
THEN NATURE RAISED A COLORED HAND	A DROP FELL ON THE APPLE	794	V 15
A VALUE [NATURE] STRUGGLE--IT EXIST--	A PLATED LIFE--	806	5
TILL NATURE LEISURE HAS FOR TERMS	THE VEINS OF OTHER	811	3
BUT HUMAN NATURE FEELS.	A LIGHT EXISTS IN SPRING	812	8
NATURE AND GOD--I NEITHER KNEW	NATURE AND GOD--I	835	1
NATURE IS FOND, I SOMETIMES THINK,	A MOTH THE HUE OF THIS	841	5
NATURE, HAD'ST THOU NOT A BERRY	TWICE HAD SUMMER HER	846	7
DELIGHT OF NATURE--ABDICATE--	TILL DEATH--IS NARROW	907	11
HIS NATURE IS AT FULL	I MAKE HIS CRESCENT FILL	909	2
IN DORMANT NATURE--LAIN--	A MAN MAY MAKE A REMARK	952	4
NATURE--ALTERED SMALL--	ALL FORGOT FOR	966	10
A NATURE [SECTION] BE	BESIDES THIS MAY	977	8
WAS IGNORANT THAT NATURE CLOSED	IT BLOOMED AND DROPT, A	978	V 19
LEAVING ON NATURE--A DEFAULT	SHE SPED AS PETALS OF A	991	5
WHICH UTTERED, WOULD DISCOURAGE NATURE	THERE IS NO SILENCE IN	1004	3
NATURE RARER USES YELLOW	NATURE RARER USES YELLOW	1045	1
GREAT NATURE NOT TO DISAPPOINT	BLOOM--IS RESULT--TO	1058	13
ENHANCES NATURE NOW	FURTHER IN SUMMER THAN	1068	16
AND NATURE NOTHING WAITS TO DO	FURTHER IN SUMMER THAN	1068	V
NATURE, LIKE US IS SOMETIMES CAUGHT	THE SKY IS LOW--THE	1075	7
IF NATURE SMILES--THE MOTHER MUST	IF NATURE SMILES--THE	1085	1
MADE NATURE DIFFERENT	THE LAST NIGHT THAT SHE	1100	4
BUT NATURE, SOMETIMES, SOMETIMES THOUGHT	THERE IS ANOTHER	1116	5
AND NATURE VENTURED OUT--	THE WIND TOOK UP THE	1134	10
NATURE KNOWS AS WELL	HER SOVREIGN PEOPLE	1139	2
THOSE WHO DID [THAT DO] NOT TO HUMAN NATURE	TELL AS A MARKSMAN--WERE	1152	11
CAN [MAY] HUMAN NATURE HIDE	AS OLD AS WOE--	1168	10
NATURE AFFECTS [WAS KNOWN] TO BE SEDATE	NATURE AFFECTS TO BE	1170	1
OR FRIEND OR NATURE--STRANDED THEN	THE DAYS THAT WE CAN	1184	3
WAS HANDED NATURE TWICE--	A SPARROW TOOK A SLICE	1211	4
TILL NATURE IN CHAGRIN	I BET WITH EVERY WIND	1215	2
NATURE TOOK THE DAY	NOW I KNEW I LOST HER--	1219	14
OF NATURE I SHALL HAVE ENOUGH	OF NATURE I SHALL HAVE	1220	1
I THOUGHT THAT NATURE WAS ENOUGH	I THOUGHT THAT NATURE	1286	1
TILL HUMAN NATURE CAME	I THOUGHT THAT NATURE	1286	2
OF HUMAN NATURE JUST AWARE	I THOUGHT THAT NATURE	1286	5
LAIN IN NATURE--SO SUFFICE US	LAIN IN NATURE--SO	1288	1
HAD NATURE ANY SUPPLE [PLATED / OUTCAST] FACE	THE MUSHROOM IS THE ELF	1298	17
HAD NATURE AN APOSTATE--[ONE "ISCARIOT" / AN ISCARIOT,]	THE MUSHROOM IS THE ELF	1298	19
DID YOU LEAVE NATURE WELL--	DEAR MARCH--COME IN--	1320	8
THAT NATURE SENT TO ME	I SEND YOU A DECREPIT	1324	2
AND NATURE LOOKS AROUND--	THE SYMPTOM OF THE GALE	1327	14
NATURE FORSWEARS	PINK--SMALL--AND	1332	11
NATURE ASSIGNS THE SUN--	NATURE ASSIGNS THE SUN--	1336	1
NATURE CANNOT ENACT A FRIEND--	NATURE ASSIGNS THE SUN--	1336	3
EVEN NATURE HERSELF	NOT ANY MORE TO BE	1344	5
THIS NATURE--HOW UNDONE!	HOW FITS HIS UMBER COAT	1371	12
THE DITTY [SERMON] IS THAT NATURE SINGS--	THE WORTHLESSNESS OF	1373	2
REPORTLESS, ALSO, BUT SINCERE AS NATURE	IN MANY AND REPORTLESS	1382	3
TO NATURE WE REMAND THEM	THOSE CATTLE SMALLER	1388	15
NATURE IMPARTS THE LITTLE BLUE-BIRD--ASSURED	AFTER ALL BIRDS HAVE	1395	2
NATURE WAS IN AN OPAL [HER BERYL / HER BLUEST] APRON,	IT SOUNDED AS IF THE	1397	7
NATURE WAS IN THE BEST OF HUMORS	IT SOUNDED AS IF THE	1397	V 7
BUT NATURE [SUSAN] IS A STRANGER YET;	WHAT MYSTERY PERVADES A	1400	17
WHICH HELPLESS NATURE DROPS	SHAME IS THE SHAWL OF	1412	5
HOW HUMAN NATURE DOTES	HOW HUMAN NATURE DOTES	1417	1
AND HUMAN NATURE HID [POPULATION FLED]	IT WAS A QUIET SEEMING	1419	9
SWEET NATURE HAS FOR ME	ONE JOY OF SO MUCH	1420	2
MY NATURE UNDERLIE--	A COUNTERFEIT--A PLATED	1453	4
AND NATURE GENTLY [SOFTLY] OWNED HER	SHE COULD NOT LIVE UPON	1505	4
OR NATURE SPENDING WITH HERSELF	AS IMPERCEPTIBLY AS	1540	7
OH NATURE--NONE OF THIS--	"GO TELL IT"--WHAT A	1554	6
IN NATURE--THEY ARE FULL--	DECLAIMING WATERS NONE	1595	4
IS IMPUDENT [RENEGADE / INFIDEL / ABLATIVE] TO NATURE	THE JAY HIS CASTANET HAS	1635	4
BUT NATURE RELISHES THE PINKS	BETROTHED TO	1641	3
RECOVER IT TO NATURE	ENDANGER IT, AND THE	1658	5
NATURE CAN DO NO MORE	NATURE CAN DO NO MORE	1673	1

	FIRST LINE	POEM	LINE
NAZARETH			
SAY, JESUS CHRIST OF NAZARETH--	AT LEAST--TO PRAY--IS	502	7
NEAR			
HE STOOD AS NEAR	I NEVER TOLD THE BURIED	11	5
HOW NEAR I HAD FORGOT.	IF RECOLLECTING WERE	33	4
TAKE CARE--FOR GOD IS HERE [NEAR]--	THE MURMUR OF A BEE	155	9
'TWAS'NT FAR--THE DOOR WAS NEAR--	HE WAS WEAK, AND I WAS	190	5
WERE MY EAR--AS NEAR HIS NEST--	TEACH HIM--WHEN HE MAKES	227	5
WHO WENT TOO NEAR	A BURDOCK--CLAWED MY	229	4
YET NOT TOO FAR [NEAR ENOUGH--] TO COME AT CALL--	HE PUT THE BELT AROUND	273	9
WHEN NONE ARE NEAR	A MIEN TO MOVE A QUEEN--	283	6
AND SUNRISE GROWS SO NEAR	WHEN NIGHT IS ALMOST	347	2
NEAR KINSMAN TO HERSELF--	THERE IS A FLOWER THAT	380	18
IS NEAR AS I CAN GUESS--	I PAY--IN SATIN CASH--	402	4
NOR NEAR ENOUGH--TO FIND--	A MURMUR IN THE TREES--	416	4
EXCEPT THE HEAVEN HAD COME SO NEAR--	EXCEPT THE HEAVEN HAD	472	1
AS NEAR YOURSELF--TODAY--	AS FAR FROM PITY, AS	496	6
MAKE HASTE--[COME NEAR] THE SCRUPLE! DEATH BE SCANT	ME PROVE IT NOW--WHOEVER	537	3
TOO NEAR--	ONE CRUCIFIXION IS	553	12
TEMERITY--DREW NEAR--	IT KNEW NO MEDICINE--	559	14
COALS--FROM A ROLLING [PASSING] LOAD--RATTLE--HOW--NEAR--	I COULD DIE--TO KNOW--	570	9
I TREMBLING DREW THE TABLE NEAR--	I HAD BEEN HUNGRY, ALL	579	3
ARE DRUMS TOO NEAR--	INCONCEIVABLY SOLEMN!	582	15
REMOTEST--WHEN MOST FAIR [NEAR]	THE TREES LIKE TASSELS--	606	8
TO KNOW IF ANY HUMAN EYES WERE NEAR	TO KNOW JUST HOW HE	622	2
TO OUR ENDEAVOR--NOT SO REAL [TRUE / CLOSE / NEAR]	A PRISON GETS TO BE A	652	19
MORE NEAR--	ONE NEED NOT BE A	670	V 20
TOO NEAR TO GOD--TO PRAY--	THE DAY UNDRESSED--	716	9
TOO NEAR TO HEAVEN--TO FEAR--	THE DAY UNDRESSED--	716	10
TOO NEAR THOU ART FOR SEEKING THEE	LET DOWN THE BARS, OH	1065	7
TOO NEAR [CLOSE] THOU ART FOR FAME--	THE BIRD DID PRANCE--THE	1107	12
DO ONE ADVANCE [OBTAIN] SO NEAR	THE MERCHANT OF THE	1131	10
AS NEAR AS MEMORY--	THE SNOW THAT NEVER	1133	16
I WON AS NEAR AS THIS	THROUGH WHAT TRANSPORTS	1153	6
GO NOT TOO NEAR A HOUSE OF ROSE--	GO NOT TOO NEAR A HOUSE	1434	1
I NEVER MET IT NEAR	A WINGED SPARK DOTH SOAR	1468	2
A WARMTH AS NEAR [SURE / FINE] AS IF THE SUN	TO SEE HER IS A PICTURE	1568	7
SO NEAR THE WHOLE TO STAND	I DID NOT REACH THEE	1664	27
AND ROBINS NEAR	NOT ANY SUNNY TONE	1674	6
MEANWHILE HE IS SO NEAR	THE BLUNDER IS IN	1684	4
ALMOST TOO HEAVENLY NEAR.	THE SADDEST NOISE, THE	1764	8
SO DANGEROUSLY NEAR.	THE SADDEST NOISE, THE	1764	20
NEARER			
THE WONDROUS NEARER DREW--	WENT UP A YEAR THIS	93	18
WE NEARER STEAL TO THEE!	THE DAISY FOLLOWS SOFT	106	9
THEN NEARER--THEN SO SLOW	HE FUMBLES AT YOUR SOUL	315	8
NEARER TO YOUR COURTESIES	TAKE YOUR HEAVEN FURTHER	388	9
THAT NEARER, EVERY DAY,	'TWAS LIKE A MAELSTROM,	414	2
A LITTLE NEARER--EVERY SUN	A SOLEMN THING WITHIN	483	15
THERE'S NEWER--NEARER CRUCIFIXION	ONE CRUCIFIXION IS	553	15
NO NEARER NEIGHBOR--HAVE THEY--	FOUR TREES--UPON A	742	7
OBSCURED WITH RUDDIER [NEARER / COMELIER] BLUE--	ONE BLESSING HAD I THAN	756	14
THE NEARER THEY DEPARTED US	SWEET, TO HAVE HAD THEM	901	3
THE NEARER THEY, RESTORED,	SWEET, TO HAVE HAD THEM	901	4
BUT NEARER [CLOSER / FURTHER / SIMPLY / MERELY] TO ADORE	BECAUSE HE LOVES HER	1229	10
NOT ANY NEARER FOR THE CHILD	NOT ANY HIGHER STANDS	1256	3
THE NEARER HER THEY GET.	WHAT MYSTERY PERVADES A	1400	24
BUT NEARER THIS	MY MAKER--LET ME BE	1403	3
NO NEARER--LEST THE ACTUAL--[REALITY-- / ITS PENURY-- / THE ...	WHO NEVER WANTED--	1430	7
WAS NEARER THAN THE SKY	THE FARTHEST THUNDER	1581	2
BUT MY FEET SLIP NEARER EVERY DAY	I DID NOT REACH THEE	1664	2
VOLCANOES NEARER HERE	VOLCANOES BE IN SICILY	1705	4
NEAREST			
UNTO THE NEAREST TOWN?	ADRIFT! A LITTLE BOAT	30	4
NEAREST THE DOOR--TO WAKE THE FIRST--	WHOSE ARE THE LITTLE	142	11
THE NEAREST [MADDEST] DREAM RECEDES--UNREALIZED--	THE NEAREST DREAM	319	1
UPON THE NEAREST BREEZE--	HOW MANY FLOWERS FAIL IN	404	6
THE NEAREST NEIGHBOR TO--	HAVE ANY LIKE MYSELF	736	14
IN THE NEAREST ORCHARD DWELLING [WAITING]	STRUCK, WAS I, NOR YET	925	15
THE VERY NEAREST ROOM	ELYSIUM IS AS FAR AS TO	1760	2
NEARING			
TILL--THE EVENING NEARING	MORNS LIKE THESE--WE	27	9
NEARLY			
SO NEARLY INFINITE--	THE LAST NIGHT THAT SHE	1100	16
NEARNESS			
OF DEATH'S TREMENDOUS NEARNESS--	I TRIED TO THINK A	532	4
OF NEARNESS TO HER SUNDERED THINGS	OF NEARNESS TO HER	607	1
A NEARNESS TO TREMENDOUSNESS--	A NEARNESS TO	963	1
NEARS			
AND AS THE SUMMER NEARS--	I HAVE A BIRD IN SPRING	5	4
NEBO			
OLD MAN ON NEBO! LATE AS THIS--	IT ALWAYS FELT TO ME--A	597	23

	FIRST LINE	POEM	LINE
NECESSARY SEE NESCESSARY			
NECESSITY SEE NESCESSITY			
PRECISELY THEIR NECESSITY--	THEY MIGHT NOT NEED ME--	1391	4
NECKLACE			
I'LL STRING YOU--IN FINE NECKLACE--	I'LL CLUTCH--AND CLUTCH	427	7
NECKLACES			
WHAT NECKLACES [AFFLUENCE / LEGACY] COULD BE [FOR ME]--	A DROP FELL ON THE APPLE	794	8
NECROLOGY			
AND HOPE'S NECROLOGY	A DEW SUFFICED ITSELF--	1437	V 16
NECROMANCER			
NECROMANCER! LANDLORD!	WHAT INN IS THIS	115	9
NECROMANCY			
AH, NECROMANCY SWEET!	AH, NECROMANCY SWEET!	177	1
TO NECROMANCY AND THE TRADES	NATURE AFFECTS TO BE	1170	5
NECTAR			
TO COMPREHEND A NECTAR	SUCCESS IS COUNTED	67	3
"FOUND DEAD"--"OF NECTAR"--	WE--BEE AND I--LIVE BY	230	16
NECTARS			
COUNTS HIS NECTARS--	COME SLOWLY--EDEN!	211	7
RECOUNTING NECTARS HE HAS KNOWN	HIS ORIENTAL HERESIES	1526	V
NEED			
REQUIRES SOREST NEED.	SUCCESS IS COUNTED	67	4
I NEED NOT START--YOU'RE SURE--	YOU LOVE ME--YOU ARE	156	8
NEED THE WISER, TELL?	IF THE FOOLISH, CALL	168	2
"I'M MIDNIGHT"--NEED THE MIDNIGHT SAY--	YOU'LL KNOW IT--AS YOU	420	9
"I'M SUNRISE"--NEED THE MAJESTY?	YOU'LL KNOW IT--AS YOU	420	10
I NEED NO FURTHER ARGUE--	DO PEOPLE MOULDER	432	13
NEED--A KEEPER--FROWN?	CIVILIZATION--SPURNS--	492	9
THE ONLY RAIMENT I SHOULD NEED--	I HAD NO CAUSE TO BE	542	19
NOR ANY NEED OF SURGERY--	IT KNEW NO MEDICINE--	559	3
I DO NOT NEED A LIGHT--	I SEE THEE BETTER--IN	611	2
WHAT NEED OF DAY--	I SEE THEE BETTER--IN	611	13
ONE NEED NOT BE A CHAMBER--TO BE HAUNTED--	ONE NEED NOT BE A	670	1
ONE NEED NOT BE A HOUSE--	ONE NEED NOT BE A	670	2
OBLITERATE THE NEED--	THE SOUL THAT HATH A	674	4
NEITHER PLACE--NEED I PRESENT HIM--	CONSCIOUS AM I IN MY	679	5
MY NEED OF THEE--BE DONE--	SHELLS FROM THE COAST	693	6
I SHANT NEED IT--THEN--	NO MATTER--NOW--SWEET--	704	9
NEED YOU--UNTO HIM--	NEVER FOR SOCIETY	746	12
FOR HIS BELOVED NEED--	MY WORTHINESS IS ALL MY	751	6
NOR ROBINS, ROBINS NEED NOT HIDE	BECAUSE THE BEE MAY	869	7
NO NEED--HADST THOU--OF US"?	HAD I NOT THIS, OR THIS,	904	8
MY NEED--WAS ALL I HAD--I SAID--	HAD I NOT THIS, OR THIS,	904	9
THE NEED DID NOT REDUCE--	HAD I NOT THIS, OR THIS,	904	10
NEED [MISS]--ONCE IN AN ETERNITY--	LOVE--IS THAT LATER	924	11
THE DYING NEED BUT LITTLE, DEAR,	THE DYING NEED BUT	1026	1
BUT FOR EXTATIC NEED	BETWEEN THE FORM OF LIFE	1101	6
THAT THIS SHOULD FEEL THE NEED OF DEATH	THAT THIS SHOULD FEEL	1112	1
SHAME NEED NOT CROUCH	HOW MANY SCHEMES MAY DIE	1150	V
NEED NOT LINGER [TARRY] HERE--	TELL AS A MARKSMAN--WERE	1152	10
WHEN WHAT WE NEED IS BY	IMMORTAL IS AN AMPLE	1205	2
THE NEED [FACT / LIFE] IS NOT OF [FOR] ME--	I KNOW SUSPENSE--IT	1285	8
SHAME NEED NOT CROUCH	NOT WITH A CLUB, THE	1304	13
THEY MIGHT NOT NEED ME--YET THEY MIGHT--	THEY MIGHT NOT NEED ME--	1391	1
MY COUNTRY NEED NOT CHANGE HER GOWN,	MY COUNTRY NEED NOT	1511	1
WITH SOLEMN NAMELESS NEED	I GROPED FOR HIM BEFORE	1555	2
FIND ALL THE WITCHCRAFT THAT WE NEED	WITCHCRAFT WAS HUNG, IN	1583	3
AND ALL WE NEED OF HELL.	MY LIFE CLOSED TWICE	1732	8
NEEDING			
FOR NEEDING MORE--	IT'S THOUGHTS--AND JUST	495	11
NEEDLE			
HER NEEDLE WOULD NOT GO--	THE ROSE DID CAPER ON	208	6
A FROST MORE NEEDLE KEEN	MORE LIFE--WENT OUT--	422	10
DONT PUT UP MY THREAD & NEEDLE--	DONT PUT UP MY THREAD &	617	1
LEAVE MY NEEDLE IN THE FURROW--	DONT PUT UP MY THREAD &	617	13
THE NEEDLE--TO THE NORTH DEGREE--	THROUGH THE STRAIT PASS	792	11
WHEN TO HIS COVENANT NEEDLE	WHEN THE ASTRONOMER	851	5
THERE IS A NEEDLE FAIR	TO MEND EACH TATTERED	1442	2
NEEDLES			
BUSY NEEDLES, AND SPOOLS OF THREAD--	ON SUCH A NIGHT, OR SUCH	146	19
A WEIGHT WITH NEEDLES ON THE POUNDS--	A WEIGHT WITH NEEDLES ON	264	1
AS NEEDLES--LADIES SOFTLY PRESS	IT CEASED TO HURT ME,	584	10
NEEDLESS			
WAS NEEDLESS, AS AT SACRAMENT,	THERE CAME A DAY AT	322	11
'TWAS NEEDLESS--ANY SPEAK--	IT WOULD NEVER BE COMMON	430	12
THE OTHERS LOOK A NEEDLESS SHOW--	I RECKON--WHEN I COUNT	569	7
A NEEDLESS LIFE, IT SEEMED TO ME	OUR LITTLE KINSMEN--	885	5
NEEDLESS TO TELL THEE--SO--	ONLY A SHRINE, BUT MINE	918	6
NEEDS			
NEEDS BUT TO REMEMBER	TO VENERATE THE SIMPLE	57	3
NEEDS BUT TO REMEMBER	TO VENERATE THE SIMPLE	57	8
I MEANT TO HAVE BUT MODEST NEEDS--	I MEANT TO HAVE BUT	476	1
NO LADDER NEEDS THE BIRD BUT SKIES	NO LADDER NEEDS THE BIRD	1574	1
NEEDY			
THE UNIVERSE WAS NEEDY	I SAW THE WIND WITHIN	1502	V
NE'ER			
I NE'ER BEHELD BEFORE!	"SIC TRANSIT GLORIA	3	24
NE'ER SAW I SUCH A WONDROUS SCENE--	THERE IS A MORN BY MEN	24	13
NE'ER SUCH A RING ON SUCH A GREEN--	THERE IS A MORN BY MEN	24	14

	FIRST LINE	POEM	LINE
NE'ER (CONTINUED)			
NE'ER? WOULD	IF THOSE I LOVED WERE	29	V
BY THOSE WHO NE'ER SUCCEED.	SUCCESS IS COUNTED	67	2
BUT THEN I PROMISED NE'ER TO TELL--	A MURMUR IN THE TREES--	416	17
NE'ER SO FAR BEHIND--	PROMISE THIS--WHEN YOU	648	30
PERPLEXED! ESTATES OF VIOLET TROUBLE NE'ER LOOKED ON!	WOULD YOU LIKE SUMMER?	691	5
BE IT NE'ER SO FAR	SOMEWHAT, TO HOPE FOR,	1041	2
BE IT NE'ER SO KEEN--	SOMEWHAT, TO HOPE FOR,	1041	5
NEGATIVE			
BLOSSOMS STAND NEGATIVE,	SPRING COMES ON THE	1042	5
BUT IS WITHIN OR NEGATIVE	THE MERCHANT OF THE	1131	3
NATURE'S IMPOSING NEGATIVE	NATURE CAN DO NO MORE	1673	7
NEGLECT			
THE ALPS NEGLECT THEIR CURTAINS	OUR LIVES ARE SWISS--	80	4
NEGLECTED			
NEGLECTED SON OF GENIUS	THE SPIDER AS AN ARTIST	1275	7
NEGLECTING			
BUT CHOSE THE BEST--NEGLECTING ME--TILL	MY WARS ARE LAID AWAY IN	1549	7
NEGOTIATE			
BUT FLOWERS--NEGOTIATE BETWEEN US--	BETWEEN MY COUNTRY--AND	905	3
NEGOTIATION			
BUT THAT NEGOTIATION	IS HEAVEN A PHYSICIAN?	1270	7
NEGRO			
THE NEGRO NEVER KNEW	THE MALAY--TOOK THE	452	14
NEIGH			
AND [THEN] NEIGH LIKE BOANERGES--	I LIKE TO SEE IT LAP	585	14
NEIGHBOR			
NO OTHER NEIGHBOR--DID--	A HOUSE UPON THE HIGHT--	399	10
AS WHEN THE NEIGHBOR HOLDS THE LAMP	WE GROW ACCUSTOMED TO	419	3
NEIGHBOR--AND FRIEND--AND BRIDEGROOM--	GLEE--THE GREAT STORM IS	619	7
OF OUR OLD [NEW] NEIGHBOR--GOD--	IT WAS TOO LATE FOR MAN	623	8
THE NEAREST NEIGHBOR TO--	HAVE ANY LIKE MYSELF	736	14
NO NEARER NEIGHBOR--HAVE THEY--	FOUR TREES--UPON A	742	7
AND LOSE IT'S NEIGHBOR ONCE--	TOO LITTLE WAY THE HOUSE	911	8
BEARING THE NEIGHBOR OUT OF SOUND	PEACE IS A FICTION OF	912	3
BLANKET WEALTHIER THE NEIGHBOR	SNOW BENEATH WHOSE	942	5
WHERE SAINTS, AND OUR PLAIN GOING NEIGHBOR	BESIDES THIS MAY	977	9
THE NEIGHBOR IN THE POOL	THE FINGERS OF THE LIGHT	1000	13
AIR HAS NO RESIDENCE, NO NEIGHBOR,	AIR HAS NO RESIDENCE, NO	1060	1
A VASTNESS, AS A NEIGHBOR, CAME,	THE CRICKETS SANG	1104	9
MY NEIGHBOR BE--	THE SHOW IS NOT THE SHOW	1206	4
A NEIGHBOR FROM ANOTHER WORLD	WHAT MYSTERY PERVADES A	1400	3
THE HIGHT OF OUR PORTENTOUS [UNKNOWING] NEIGHBOR	FACTS BY OUR SIDE ARE	1497	5
A NEIGHBOR AND A WARRIOR TOO	NO BRIGADIER THROUGHOUT	1561	3
THAT LEAVES THIS NEIGHBOR [MAJOR] OUT--	NO BRIGADIER THROUGHOUT	1561	24
NEIGHBORHOOD			
PAST NEIGHBORHOOD	TO-DAY OR THIS NOON	1702	5
NEIGHBORHOODS			
RAPT NEIGHBORHOODS OF MEN--	FOREVER AT HIS SIDE TO	246	14
TO NEIGHBORHOODS OF PAUSE--	GREAT STREETS OF SILENCE	1159	2
NEIGHBORING			
MUST SEEK THE NEIGHBORING LIFE!	A LITTLE BREAD--A CRUST	159	12
IN A NEIGHBORING HORIZON--	SO THE EYES ACCOST--AND	752	7
BUT NEIGHBORING AS NOON--	THE BIRDS BEGUN AT FOUR	783	4
TO SOMETHING NEIGHBORING	IN WINTER IN MY ROOM	1670	8
NEIGHBORLY			
WE FELT HOW NEIGHBORLY A THING	THE MOUNTAINS STOOD IN	1278	11
BESIDES--SUSPENSE IS NEIGHBORLY	I KNOW SUSPENSE--IT	1285	3
HOWEVER NEIGHBORLY--	HIS MIND OF MAN, A	1663	8
NEIGHBOR'S			
AND ALL THE NEIGHBOR'S LIVES--	I'M SORRY FOR THE DEAD--	529	16
UNTO A NEIGHBOR'S BIN.	THE PRODUCTS OF MY FARM	1025	4
NEIGHBORS			
WHILE SIMPLE-HEARTED NEIGHBORS	THERE'S SOMETHING	45	13
THE NEIGHBORS DO NOT YET SUSPECT!	A LADY RED--AMID THE	74	9
THE NEIGHBORS RUSTLE IN AND OUT--	THERE'S BEEN A DEATH, IN	389	5
RELATE--WHEN NEIGHBORS DIE--	WE PRAY--TO HEAVEN--	489	3
OLD NEIGHBORS HAVE AT FENCES--	I'M SORRY FOR THE DEAD--	529	3
OF NEIGHBORS AND THE SUN	THIS CONSCIOUSNESS THAT	822	2
TO NEIGHBORS DOUBTLESS OF THEIR OWN	LIKE MEN AND WOMEN	1105	5
TO IMITATE THESE NEIGHBORS FLEET	WHOSE PINK CAREER MAY	1394	3
THE ONLY SECRET PEOPLE [NEIGHBORS] KEEP [SHUN]	THE RETICENT VOLCANO	1748	11
NEIGHING			
AND THE OLD CLOCK KEPT NEIGHING "DAY"!	GOING TO HIM! HAPPY	494	19
NEIGHS			
FOR WHOM THE SCAFFOLD NEIGHS--	I SOMETIMES DROP IT, FOR	708	10
NERVE			
BUT GIMBLETS--AMONG THE NERVE--	IT IS EASY TO WORK WHEN	244	6
ONE MORE NEW-MAILED NERVE	A SINGLE SCREW OF FLESH	263	14
IF YOUR NERVE, DENY YOU--	IF YOUR NERVE, DENY YOU	292	1
GO ABOVE YOUR NERVE--	IF YOUR NERVE, DENY YOU	292	2
AND EVERY ONE UNBARED A NERVE	SHE DEALT HER PRETTY	479	3
NOT A NERVE FAILED!	HE STRAINED MY FAITH--	497	8
THROUGH CENTURIES OF NERVE--	I MEASURE EVERY GRIEF I	561	22
THROUGH FAINTER NERVE--	THE TEST OF LOVE--IS	573	8
I FUMBLED AT MY NERVE--	I YEARS HAD BEEN FROM	609	V 9
"TEARS"--A TRICK OF THE NERVE--	"SPEECH"--IS A PRANK OF	688	2
MY NERVE IN MARBLE LIES--	I'VE DROPPED MY BRAIN--	1046	6

	FIRST LINE	POEM	LINE
NERVE (CONTINUED)			
AS PYRAMIDAL [ELEMENTAL / PLUPOTENTIAL] NERVE	NOT TO DISCOVER WEAKNESS	1054	6
NERVES			
THE NERVES SIT CEREMONIOUS, LIKE TOMBS--	AFTER GREAT PAIN, A	341	2
THE GLITTERING RETINUE OF NERVES--	SEVERER SERVICE OF	786	11
IT KEEPS THE NERVES PROGRESSIVE [IN PROGRESS]	THESE ARE THE NIGHTS	1128	11
NERVOUS			
OR A NERVOUS STAR?	I KNOW SOME LONELY	289	22
NESCESSARY			
IS NESCESSARY, TO REDUCE	MORE LIFE--WENT OUT--	422	11
NESCESSITY SEE NECESSITY			
TO MY NESCESSITY--STOOPED DOWN!	FOR THIS--ACCEPTED	195	6
LEAVING A NEW NESCESSITY!	THE SUN--JUST TOUCHED	232	11
LAPLAND'S--NESCESSITY--	I THINK THE HEMLOCK	525	8
WITH FOOD'S NESCESSITY	IT WOULD HAVE STARVED A	612	4
BEYOND NESCESSITY--	FAME OF MYSELF, TO	713	4
OF NESCESSITY	EXPECTATION--IS	807	4
A FIRST NESCESSITY.	FAITH--IS THE PIERLESS	915	12
'TIS A NESCESSITY.	IMMORTAL IS AN AMPLE	1205	4
NEST			
THE OTHER, AS A BIRD HER NEST,	ONE SISTER HAVE I IN OUR	14	7
AND THE NEST FORGOT,	IT DID NOT SURPRISE ME--	39	4
MY PERENNIAL NEST.	HER BREAST IS FIT FOR	84	8
I CAME TO BUILD THE BIRD'S NEST,	SEXTON! MY MASTER'S	96	3
NEVER THE TREASURES IN HER NEST	SOME, TOO FRAGILE FOR	141	5
FOR EVERY BIRD A NEST--	FOR EVERY BIRD A NEST--	143	1
NOR ANY SCHOOLBOY ROB THE NEST	THIS HEART THAT BROKE SO	145	7
CHRIST ROBS THE NEST--	DUST IS THE ONLY SECRET	153	14
IT IS NOT BIRD--IT HAS NO NEST--	MUSICIANS WRESTLE	157	7
WHOSE EMERALD NEST THE AGES SPIN	A FEATHER FROM THE	161	5
AS WHEN HER LITTLE MORTAL NEST	MAMA NEVER FORGETS HER	164	5
WERE MY EAR--AS NEAR HIS NEST--	TEACH HIM--WHEN HE MAKES	227	5
HOW IT IS NIGHT--IN NEST AND KENNEL--	HOW THE OLD MOUNTAINS	291	17
THE EAGLE OF HIS NEST	NO RACK CAN TORTURE ME--	384	9
I [HE] SHOWED HER [ME] SECRETS--MORNING'S NEST--	I SHOWED HER HIGHTS SHE	446	5
THAT SPEECHLESS FROM HER NEST	THE ROBIN IS THE ONE	828	10
UNTO HIS NEST AGAIN	IF I CAN STOP ONE HEART	919	6
THE ROBIN LOCKS HER NEST, AND TRIES HER WINGS.	QUITE EMPTY, QUITE AT	1606	2
THE STATURE OF THE EMPTY NEST	I SEE THEE CLEARER FOR	1666	7
NESTLED			
BUT NOT THE GRIEF--THAT NESTLED CLOSE	IT CEASED TO HURT ME,	584	9
NESTS			
YET NOT IN ALL THE NESTS I MEET--	ALL OVERGROWN BY CUNNING	148	11
THE BIRDS ROSE SMILING, IN THEIR NESTS--	ON THIS LONG STORM THE	194	5
I ENVY NESTS OF SPARROWS--	I ENVY SEAS, WHEREON HE	498	9
THE BIRDS PUT UP THE BARS TO NESTS--	THE WIND BEGUN TO KNEAD	824	13
NEUTRALIZED			
HE NEUTRALIZED THEM ALL--	FATE SLEW HIM, BUT HE	1031	4
NEVER			
HAST NEVER SILENT HOURS, AND MINUTES ALL TOO LONG,	AWAKE YE MUSES NINE,	1	29
NEVER MIND FADED FORESTS, AUSTIN,	THERE IS ANOTHER SKY,	2	5
NEVER MIND SILENT FIELDS--	THERE IS ANOTHER SKY,	2	6
I NEVER TOLD THE BURIED GOLD	I NEVER TOLD THE BURIED	11	1
I WAS NEVER IN!	BAFFLED FOR JUST A DAY	17	8
AND GAMBOL I MAY NEVER NAME--	THERE IS A MORN BY MEN	24	5
NEVER DID SHE LISP IT--	MORNS LIKE THESE--WE	27	5
NEVER SAILED THE BAY!	COULD LIVE--DID LIVE--	43	13
I NEVER LOST AS MUCH BUT TWICE,	I NEVER LOST AS MUCH BUT	49	1
WHO NEVER LOST, ARE [IS] UNPREPARED	WHO NEVER LOST, ARE	73	1
WHO NEVER THIRSTED	WHO NEVER LOST, ARE	73	3
WHO NEVER CLIMBED THE WEARY LEAGUE--	WHO NEVER LOST, ARE	73	5
I NEVER HEAR THE WORD "ESCAPE"	I NEVER HEAR THE WORD	77	1
I NEVER HEAR OF PRISONS BROAD	I NEVER HEAR THE WORD	77	5
WHOM I HAVE NEVER FOUND	GOING TO HEAVEN!	79	25
BUT I SHALL NEVER TELL!	SO BASHFUL WHEN I SPIED	91	12
THE RAINBOW NEVER TELLS ME	THE RAINBOW NEVER TELLS	97	1
OF WHICH I HAVE NEVER HEARD?	WILL THERE REALLY BE A	101	8
NEVER MIND MY BREATHLESS ANVIL!	BY A FLOWER--BY A LETTER	109	5
NEVER MIND REPOSE!	BY A FLOWER--BY A LETTER	109	6
NEVER MIND THE SOOTY FACES	BY A FLOWER--BY A LETTER	109	7
WHERE SCRABBLE NEVER COMES--	WHERE BELLS NO MORE	112	2
THE WIZARD FINGERS NEVER REST--	A SOMETHING IN A	122	13
IN LANDS I NEVER SAW--THEY SAY	IN LANDS I NEVER SAW--	124	1
BUT I COULD NEVER SELL--	PERHAPS YOU'D LIKE TO	134	2
NEVER SUCH AN AMBUSCADE	PIGMY SERAPHS--GONE	138	9
NEVER THE TREASURES IN HER NEST	SOME, TOO FRAGILE FOR	141	5
THESE FEET THAT NEVER FLAGGED--	THIS HEART THAT BROKE SO	145	2
SINCE I COULD NEVER FIND HER	SHE DIED--THIS WAS THE	150	7
NEVER WAS A BOY--	DUST IS THE ONLY SECRET	153	6
THAT NIGHT WILL NEVER BE--	YOU LOVE ME--YOU ARE	156	9
MAMA NEVER FORGETS HER BIRDS,	MAMA NEVER FORGETS HER	164	1
I HAVE NEVER SEEN "VOLCANOES"--	I HAVE NEVER SEEN	175	1
NEVER A THIMBLE--MORE--SHALL WEAR--	HOW MANY TIMES THESE LOW	187	8
LET'S PLAY THOSE--NEVER COME!	MAKE ME A PICTURE OF THE	188	14
I TASTE A LIQUOR NEVER BREWED--	I TASTE A LIQUOR NEVER	214	1
I--NEVER WED--	WE--BEE AND I--LIVE BY	230	9
SO I CAN NEVER [AND I CANNOT] GO!	AH, MOON--AND STAR!	240	17
WHOM WE CAN NEVER LEARN--	FOREVER AT HIS SIDE TO	246	11

NEVER (CONTINUED)	FIRST LINE	POEM	LINE
AND NEVER STOPS--AT ALL--	"HOPE" IS THE THING WITH	254	4
YET, NEVER, IN EXTREMITY,	"HOPE" IS THE THING WITH	254	11
SO I SHALL NEVER FALL--	TIE THE STRINGS TO MY	279	6
BUT NEVER I MIND THE STEEPEST [BRIDGES]--	TIE THE STRINGS TO MY	279	9
AND NEVER I MIND THE SEA--	TIE THE STRINGS TO MY	279	10
TITIAN--NEVER TOLD--	HOW THE OLD MOUNTAINS	291	22
NEVER ANY [ONE] BEND	IF YOUR NERVE, DENY YOU	292	6
FOR THEY'RE NEVER GONE--	ALONE, I CANNOT BE--	298	12
WHO [HE] NEVER HEARD THAT FLESHLESS CHANT--	OF ALL THE SOUNDS	321	27
AND THE SERMON IS NEVER LONG,	SOME KEEP THE SABBATH	324	10
AS GABRIEL--NEVER CAPERED AT--	THE FACE I CARRY WITH ME	336	11
I NEVER WOULD LET GO--	ALTHOUGH I PUT AWAY HIS	366	12
THESE--NEVER STIR AT ALL--	THE ANGLE OF A LANDSCAPE	375	20
THAT WAGON NEVER REACHED--	A HOUSE UPON THE HIGHT--	399	2
WHOSE CHIMNEY NEVER SMOKED--	A HOUSE UPON THE HIGHT--	399	5
AND WHAT IT WAS--WE NEVER LISPED--	A HOUSE UPON THE HIGHT--	399	11
BECAUSE HE--NEVER TOLD--	A HOUSE UPON THE HIGHT--	399	12
I NEVER FELT AT HOME--BELOW--	I NEVER FELT AT HOME--	413	1
AND RECESS--NEVER COMES--	I NEVER FELT AT HOME--	413	6
WOULD NEVER BE BELIEVED--	A MURMUR IN THE TREES--	416	12
HE NEVER MISSES A DEGREE--	THE MOON IS DISTANT FROM	429	5
IT WOULD NEVER BE COMMON--MORE--I SAID--	IT WOULD NEVER BE COMMON	430	1
THAT NEVER WROTE TO ME--	THIS IS MY LETTER TO THE	441	2
I [HE] SHOWED HER [ME] HIGHTS SHE [I] NEVER SAW--	I SHOWED HER HIGHTS SHE	446	1
NEVER GLADDENED TREE--	DREAMS--ARE WELL--BUT	450	6
THE NEGRO NEVER KNEW	THE MALAY--TOOK THE	452	14
I NEVER PUT IT DOWN--	IT WAS GIVEN TO ME BY	454	6
NEVER YET--CONSUMED--	THE RED--BLAZE--IS THE	469	8
I NEVER THOUGHT TO SEE--	EXCEPT THE HEAVEN HAD	472	6
NEVER A GOWN OF DUN--MORE--	I AM ASHAMED--I HIDE--	473	10
SHE NEVER DEEMED--SHE HURT--	SHE DEALT HER PRETTY	479	5
THE LIGHTNING--NEVER ASKED AN EYE	"WHY DO I LOVE" YOU, SIR	480	11
THAT NEVER CEASED TO FALL--	I WAS THE SLIGHTEST IN	486	6
I NEVER SPOKE--UNLESS ADDRESSED--	I WAS THE SLIGHTEST IN	486	10
DESERTS--NEVER REBUKED HER SATIN--	CIVILIZATION--SPURNS--	492	3
TELL HIM [HER] THE PAGE I DID'NT WRITE--[NEVER WROTE!]	GOING TO HIM! HAPPY	494	3
BUT I NEVER DOUBTED HIM--	HE STRAINED MY FAITH--	497	10
HE DID NEVER SAY--	HE STRAINED MY FAITH--	497	12
HE NEVER STOPS, BUT SLACKENS	WITHIN MY GARDEN, RIDES	500	5
BUT NEVER DEEMED THE DRIPPING PRIZE	LIKE FLOWERS, THAT HEARD	513	2
THAT YOU NEVER DO IT--	BEAUTY--BE NOT CAUSED--	516	8
SO THAT THE SUM [LOVE] BE NEVER HINDERED	SWEET--YOU FORGOT--BUT I	523	3
AND DRAMA--IS NEVER [SELDOM] DEAD--	WE DREAM--IT IS GOOD WE	531	8
THOUGH NEVER YET, IN ANY PORT--	TWO BUTTERFLIES WENT OUT	533	7
THE MARTYR PAINTERS--NEVER SPOKE--	THE MARTYR POETS--DID	544	5
I NEVER LIVED [DID NOT LIVE]--ENOUGH--	THAT I DID ALWAYS LOVE	549	4
THAT NEVER HAD A NAME--	IT KNEW NO MEDICINE--	559	10
IT NEVER DID BETRAY	THE BODY GROWS WITHOUT--	578	6
THE LIPS THAT NEVER LIE--	A STILL--VOLCANO--LIFE--	601	10
THEY NEVER YET DID SATISFY--	THE TREES LIKE TASSELS--	606	7
I NEVER SAW BEFORE	I YEARS HAD BEEN FROM	609	4
AND [BUT] NEVER WINCED [SHOOK / QUAKED] BEFORE.	I YEARS HAD BEEN FROM	609	16
WITH MOSS--THEY NEVER GREW SO FULL--	YOU'LL FIND--IT WHEN YOU	610	7
NEVER SLACKED THE DIGGERS--	IN FALLING TIMBERS	614	9
BUT NEVER STRANGER JUSTIFIED	I WATCHED THE MOON	629	9
NEVER HAD A DOUBT--	THE CHILD'S FAITH IS NEW	637	5
WHOM WE HAVE NEVER SEEN--	BEREAVEMENT IN THEIR	645	2
NEVER BRIDE HAD SUCH ASSEMBLING--	HER SWEET TURN TO LEAVE	649	9
NEVER KINSMEN KNEELED	HER SWEET TURN TO LEAVE	649	10
HE NEVER SAW ME--IN THIS LIFE--	AGAIN--HIS VOICE IS AT	663	7
THE FUTURE--NEVER SPOKE--	THE FUTURE--NEVER SPOKE	672	1
TIME NEVER DID ASSUAGE--	THEY SAY THAT "TIME	686	2
NEVER A FELLOW MATCHED THIS TOPAZ--	I COULD BRING YOU JEWELS	697	9
TO HIM WHOM NEVER RAGGED--COAT	THE BEGGAR LAD--DIES	717	15
NEVER DENY ME--NEVER FLY--	SWEET MOUNTAINS--YE TELL	722	2
NEVER DENY ME--NEVER FLY--	SWEET MOUNTAINS--YE TELL	722	2
NEVER COULD--TO ME--	LET US PLAY YESTERDAY--	728	20
HER LIPS OF AMBER NEVER PART--	THE MOON WAS BUT A CHIN	737	9
OWNER CANNOT [NEVER YET WAS] SHUT--	DRAMA'S VITALLEST	741	15
I [SHE] NEVER QUESTIONED HER [ME]--	THE BIRDS REPORTED FROM	743	22
NEVER FOR SOCIETY	NEVER FOR SOCIETY	746	1
NEVER KNEW SATIETY--	NEVER FOR SOCIETY	746	7
AS WE--WHO NEVER CAN--	I PLAY AT RICHES--TO	801	16
AS SOME [US] SHE NEVER KNEW--	NO NOTICE GAVE SHE, BUT	804	20
TO ONE WHO NEVER FELT IT BLAZE--	LOVE RECKONS BY ITSELF--	826	3
EQUATOR--NEVER CAN--	THAT DISTANCE WAS	863	4
NEVER TO PASS THE ANGEL	A CLOUD WITHDREW FROM	895	9
THAT NEVER DID ALIGHT.	PEACE IS A FICTION OF	912	4
NEVER BUD FROM A STEM	AND THIS OF ALL MY HOPES	913	5
NEVER A WORM SO CONFIDENT	AND THIS OF ALL MY HOPES	913	7
WE SHALL NEVER KNOW--	HOW THE WATERS CLOSED	923	2
ESTEEMED ME NEVER RUDE	MY BEST ACQUAINTANCES	932	4
SOME THAT NEVER LAY	SNOW BENEATH WHOSE	942	2
BUT NEVER MET THIS FELLOW	A NARROW FELLOW IN THE	986	21
I NEVER SAW A MOOR--	I NEVER SAW A MOOR--	1052	1
I NEVER SAW THE SEA--	I NEVER SAW A MOOR--	1052	2

	FIRST LINE	POEM		LINE
NEVER (CONTINUED)				
I NEVER SPOKE WITH GOD	I NEVER SAW A MOOR--	1052		5
FAME'S BOYS AND GIRLS, WHO NEVER DIE	FAME'S BOYS AND GIRLS,	1066		1
CAN NEVER BE FITTED [MATCHED] AGAIN?	OF THE HEART THAT GOES	1098		4
AS NEVER WAS ACHIEVED [BEHELD]--	THAT THIS SHOULD FEEL	1112		4
POTOSI NEVER TO BE SPENT	A MINE THERE IS NO MAN	1117		5
'TWILL NEVER BE THE SAME TO STARVE	OH SUMPTUOUS MOMENT	1125		4
PROMETHEUS NEVER KNEW--[DID NOT KNOW]	THE SMOULDERING EMBERS	1132		8
THE SNOW THAT NEVER DRIFTS--	THE SNOW THAT NEVER	1133		1
OF MANSIONS NEVER QUITE DISCLOSED	THE LIGHTNING IS A	1173		5
AND NEVER QUITE CONCEALED	THE LIGHTNING IS A	1173		6
WE NEVER KNOW HOW HIGH WE ARE	WE NEVER KNOW HOW HIGH	1176		1
AND WE WHO NEVER SAW	I SHOULD NOT DARE TO BE	1197		6
THE FROST WAS NEVER SEEN--	THE FROST WAS NEVER SEEN	1202		1
THAT NEVER COULD BE TRACED.	THE FROST WAS NEVER SEEN	1202		12
THE TRUTH NEVER FLAUNTED [HOISTED] A SIGN--	HE PREACHED UPON	1207		4
BUT "NEVER" FAR AS HONOR	TO DISAPPEAR ENHANCES--	1209		9
THE SPIRIT NEVER SHOWS.	IT'S HOUR WITH ITSELF	1225		2
TO ONE THAT NEVER DIED--	WHO WERE "THE FATHER AND	1258	V	6
AND NEVER COMING BACK	BECAUSE THAT YOU ARE	1260		2
A THING I NEVER KNEW--	BECAUSE THAT YOU ARE	1260		18
THERE IS NO [WAS NEVER] FRIGATE LIKE A BOOK	THERE IS NO FRIGATE LIKE	1263		1
HAS NEVER BEEN EMPLOYED--	THE SPIDER AS AN ARTIST	1275		2
HAVE NEVER BEEN BEGUN--	THE THINGS WE THOUGHT	1293		4
BUT NEVER TOUCH THE RESERVOIR--	OF LIFE TO OWN--	1294		3
WHICH NEVER WENT AWAY?	THE INFINITE A SUDDEN	1309		4
THE MAPLES NEVER KNEW THAT YOU WERE COMING--TILL I CALLED	DEAR MARCH--COME IN--	1320		12
I NEVER HEAR THAT ONE IS DEAD [HAS DIED]	I NEVER HEAR THAT ONE IS	1323		1
OR NEVER REMEMBERED--	WHETHER THEY HAVE	1329		3
YET NEVER WEARING OUT--	HOPE IS A STRANGE	1392		4
THE SHAFT THAT NEVER KNEW--	SHE LAID HER DOCILE	1396		6
HAVE NEVER PASSED [SCALED] HER HAUNTED HOUSE,	WHAT MYSTERY PERVADES A	1400		19
WHOSE AXIS [OWNER] NEVER COMES.	WATER MAKES MANY BEDS	1428		8
WHOSE MORNING NEVER HUMS--	WATER MAKES MANY BEDS	1428	V	8
WHO NEVER WANTED--MADDEST JOY	WHO NEVER WANTED--	1430		1
THAN ONES THAT NEVER WERE,	THAN HEAVEN MORE REMOTE,	1436		5
AS IF IT NEVER TORE	TO MEND EACH TATTERED	1442		6
IT'S JOURNEY NEVER WAKES MY HAND	HOW SOFT A CATERPILLAR	1448	V	
I THOUGHT THE TRAIN WOULD NEVER COME--	I THOUGHT THE TRAIN	1449		1
HE NEVER HAD BUT ONE--	BELSHAZZAR HAD A LETTER	1459		2
I NEVER THOUGHT THAT JASON SOUGHT	ONE OF THE ONES THAT	1466		21
I NEVER MET IT NEAR	A WINGED SPARK DOTH SOAR	1468		2
IS POETRY, THOUGH NEVER IN A BOOK IT LIE--	TO SEE THE SUMMER SKY	1472		2
FACTS BY OUR SIDE ARE NEVER SUDDEN	FACTS BY OUR SIDE ARE	1497		1
WE NEVER KNOW--	FACTS BY OUR SIDE ARE	1497		6
AND EXIGENCIES NEVER FEARS--	HOW HAPPY IS THE LITTLE	1510		4
THE THINGS THAT NEVER CAN COME BACK, ARE SEVERAL--	THE THINGS THAT NEVER	1515		1
SO SOAR AWAY AND NEVER SIGH	THE BUTTERFLY UPON THE	1521		7
WE NEVER KNOW WE GO WHEN WE ARE GOING--	WE NEVER KNOW WE GO WHEN	1523		1
THAT NEVER SEATS BUT ONE--	HOPE IS A SUBTLE GLUTTON	1547		6
A FOE WHOM I HAVE NEVER SEEN	MY WARS ARE LAID AWAY IN	1549		3
WAS NEVER BLOWN AWAY--	NO BRIGADIER THROUGHOUT	1561		8
WHICH NEVER TO RECEIVE	TO SEE HER IS A PICTURE	1568	V	
APART, IT NEVER TALKS--	THE SPIRIT LASTS--BUT IN	1576		4
THE PRISM NEVER HELD THE HUES,	PURSUING YOU IN YOUR	1602		5
THAT WE HAVE NEVER MET,	PARTING WITH THEE	1614		2
DOES NOT DESERVE THE [HAS NEVER TASTED] SPRING--	A DRUNKARD CANNOT MEET A	1628		8
THE DEATH I NEVER FEARED	SO GIVE ME BACK TO DEATH	1632		2
THAT NEVER FELT THE SUN	GLORY IS THAT BRIGHT	1660		5
NOTWITHSTANDING IT NEVER BE KNOWN	TO DO A MAGNANIMOUS	1699		6
THAT NEVER CAME,	AS SUBTLE AS TOMORROW	1713		2
I NEVER TO THIS DAY	HE WAS MY HOST--HE WAS	1721		2
I NEVER KNEW THY POWER,	OH, HONEY OF AN HOUR,	1734		2
LOVE THAT NEVER LEAPED ITS SOCKET--	REARRANGE A "WIFE'S"	1737		9
IT WILL NEVER GET AWAY	REARRANGE A "WIFE'S"	1737		18
THAT IT WILL NEVER COME AGAIN	THAT IT WILL NEVER COME	1741		1
HIS NEVER SLUMBERING PLAN;	THE RETICENT VOLCANO	1748		2
NEVERMORE				
NODDING IN NAVIES NEVERMORE--	FINITE--TO FAIL, BUT	847		4
NEW				
MELODY NEW FOR ME	I HAVE A BIRD IN SPRING	5		11
SOME WITH NEW--STATELY FEET--	MY WHEEL IS IN THE DARK!	10		12
I ASK, EACH NEW MAY MORN.	THERE IS A MORN BY MEN	24		21
WONT BE "NEW FASHIONED" WHEN I COME--	"ARCTURUS" IS HIS OTHER	70		28
TALKED SOFTLY OF NEW SPECIES	WENT UP A YEAR THIS	93		15
TO COUNTENANCES NEW!	WENT UP A YEAR THIS	93		22
NEW FEET WITHIN MY GARDEN GO--	NEW FEET WITHIN MY	99		1
NEW FINGERS STIR THE SOD--	NEW FEET WITHIN MY	99		2
NEW CHILDREN PLAY UPON THE GREEN--	NEW FEET WITHIN MY	99		5
NEW WEARY SLEEP BELOW--	NEW FEET WITHIN MY	99		6
IN THE NEW ROBIN'S EXTASY	BRING ME THE SUNSET IN A	128		8
I THINK IT THAT "NEW LIFE"!	MUSICIANS WRESTLE	157		6
GET SAINTS--WITH NEW--UNSTEADY TONGUE--	FOR THIS--ACCEPTED	195		14
DO THEY WEAR "NEW SHOES"--IN "EDEN"--	WHAT IS--"PARADISE"--	215		7
AS NEW ENGLAND USED TO BE!	WHAT IS--"PARADISE"--	215		18
LEAVING A NEW NESCESSITY!	THE SUN--JUST TOUCHED	232		11
'TWAS THE NEW LIQUOR--	I CAN WADE GRIEF--	252		8

	FIRST LINE	POEM	LINE
NEW (CONTINUED)			
SAYING ITSELF IN NEW INFLECTION--	MANY A PHRASE HAS THE	276	7
BECAUSE I SEE--NEW ENGLANDLY--	THE ROBIN'S MY CRITERION	285	15
SOME NEW EQUATION, GIVEN--	I REASON, EARTH IS SHORT	301	11
THIS NEW CIRCUMFERENCE--HAVE BLAMED--	I SHOULD HAVE BEEN TOO	313	5
AND OUR NEW HANDS	WE PLAY AT PASTE--	320	6
THAT [WHICH] MAKETH ALL THINGS NEW--	THERE CAME A DAY AT	322	8
TO THAT NEW MARRIAGE [FONDNESS],	THERE CAME A DAY AT	322	27
THE CAPTIVE--STRANGLES NEW--	'TIS OPPOSITES--ENTICE--	355	7
THE LIGHTNING WAS AS NEW	IT STRUCK ME--EVERY DAY	362	2
LIKE OTHER NEW THINGS--SHOWS LARGEST--THEN--	IT DONT SOUND SO	426	12
I PUT NEW BLOSSOMS IN THE GLASS--	I TIE MY HAT--I CREASE	443	5
WHEN WE ARE NEW--AND SMALL.	IT WAS GIVEN TO ME BY	454	4
NO ONE TO TEACH ME THAT NEW GRACE--	I AM ASHAMED--I HIDE--	473	5
THOSE FAIR [NEW]--FICTITIOUS PEOPLE--	THOSE FAIR--FICTITIOUS	499	1
SHE'S HAPPY, WITH A NEW CONTENT--	SHE'S HAPPY, WITH A NEW	535	1
TO THOSE WHO FAILING NEW--	THE PROVINCE OF THE	539	10
AND MORN A NEW POLITENESS TOOK--	I HAD NO CAUSE TO BE	542	3
THE PLENTY HURT ME--'TWAS SO NEW--	I HAD BEEN HUNGRY, ALL	579	13
OF OUR OLD [NEW] NEIGHBOR--GOD--	IT WAS TOO LATE FOR MAN	623	8
APPARELED AS THE NEW	'TWAS A LONG PARTING--	625	10
THE CHILD'S FAITH IS NEW--	THE CHILD'S FAITH IS NEW	637	1
THAT NEW GRACE	I CANNOT LIVE WITH YOU--	640	24
NEW PERIODS--OF PAIN.	PAIN--HAS AN ELEMENT OF	650	8
NO NEW MILE REMAINETH--	LIFE--IS WHAT WE MAKE IT	698	11
TO THE NEW FREE--	LET US PLAY YESTERDAY--	728	18
THEN--DOOMED NEW--	LET US PLAY YESTERDAY--	728	32
IF OUGHT SHE MISSED IN HER NEW DAY,	SHE ROSE TO HIS	732	5
THAN LIFE'S SWEET [NEW] CALCULATIONS--	UPON CONCLUDED LIVES	735	3
NEW HOUSES ON THE HILL DESCRIED--	HAVE ANY LIKE MYSELF	736	3
FOR THIS NEW VALUE [FORTUNE / PORTION] IN THE SOUL--	ONE BLESSING HAD I THAN	756	11
UPON A NEW PENINSULA--	BEREAVED OF ALL, I WENT	784	3
BETTER THAN NEW--COULD BE--FOR THAT--	JOY TO HAVE MERITED THE	788	7
OLD THE GRACE, BUT NEW THE SUBJECTS--	ALWAYS MINE!	839	6
WE SO NEW BESTOW	SNOW BENEATH WHOSE	942	6
ROUND OUR NEW FIRESIDE--BUT FOR THIS--	I LEARNED--AT LEAST--	944	5
A NEW--DIVINER--CARE--	I LEARNED--AT LEAST--	944	24
NEW ACCOMPANYING--	ALL FORGOT FOR	966	4
I ONLY MUST NOT GROW SO NEW	FITTER TO SEE HIM, I MAY	968	15
NEW HORIZONS--THEY EMBELLISH [REPLENISH]--	UNFULFILLED TO	972	7
NEW ACQUAINTANCE--THIS BABY MADE--	TRUDGING TO EDEN,	1020	8
THE CONTINENTS WERE NEW--	IT WAS A QUIET WAY--	1053	14
WITH HAT IN HAND, POLITE AND NEW	THE CRICKETS SANG	1104	7
FRESH [NEW] AS MANKIND THAT HUMBLE STORY	TELL AS A MARKSMAN--WERE	1152	5
HE IS NEW AND HIGH--	WE LIKE MARCH.	1213	3
IN A NEW ENGLAND TOWN--	THE BUTTERFLY'S	1244	6
THE MORNING IT IS NEW	WHILE WE WERE FEARING IT	1277	10
NO TERRITORY NEW IS STAKED--	TWO LENGTHS HAS EVERY	1295	11
OR OF ITSELF A [THE] NEW MISGIVING--	WONDER--IS NOT PRECISELY	1331	7
IN GENESIS' NEW HOUSE,	TRUSTY AS THE STARS	1369	4
AT HIS NEW WHITE HOUSE THE EARTH	I SUPPOSE THE TIME WILL	1381	11
NOR ACTION [WISDOMS] NEW--	I HAVE NO LIFE BUT THIS	1398	6
ON OUR NEW ENGLAND FARMS--	A FIELD OF STUBBLE,	1407	8
OF THE NEW ENGLAND FARMER--	THE ROBIN IS A GABRIEL	1483	6
TO SITUATIONS [EXHIBITION / COMPREHENSION] NEW	ON THAT SPECIFIC PILLOW	1533	6
BY SAYING NOTHING NEW--	EXTOL THEE--COULD I--	1643	2
THE WATERS MURMUR NEW	I DID NOT REACH THEE	1664	30
THAT NEW DILEMMA BE	IF I COULD TELL HOW GLAD	1668	6
WHEN HE WAS MEAN AND NEW	IN WINTER IN MY ROOM	1670	20
NEWER			
AND NEWER FASHIONS BLOW--	THERE IS A FLOWER THAT	380	22
THERE'S NEWER--NEARER CRUCIFIXION	ONE CRUCIFIXION IS	553	15
YOU CHOSE THE NEWER NAMES [TIMES]--	YOU'LL FIND--IT WHEN YOU	610	8
A NEWER SEVRES PLEASES--	I CANNOT LIVE WITH YOU--	640	11
A LITTLE NEWER FOR THE TERM	EXHILIRATION IS THE	1118	7
BUT LIGHT A NEWER WILDERNESS	HAD I NOT SEEN THE SUN	1233	3
YET NEWER GLOWS THE ONLY GOLD	THE STARS ARE OLD, THAT	1249	3
. . . [NEWEST / NEWER] ONE.	I'D RATHER RECOLLECT A	1349	4
NEWEST			
LARGEST [NEWEST / FRESHEST] DEWS OF MORN	PROMISE THIS--WHEN YOU	648	20
AND YET THE NEWEST STAR--	THE DAY UNDRESSED--	716	6
HIS SERVICE TO THE NEWEST GRACE	OF SILKEN SPEECH AND	896	3
IF MY NEWEST STEP	UP LIFE'S HILL WITH MY	1010	4
. . . [NEWEST / NEWER] ONE.	I'D RATHER RECOLLECT A	1349	4
NEW-FASHIONED			
IN YOUR NEW-FASHIONED WORLD!	THE SKIES CANT KEEP	191	16
NEWLY			
AND WHEN SO NEWLY DEAD--	"I WANT"--IT PLEADED--	731	4
SOME--NEWLY RAISED THIS AFTERNOON,	WHO OCCUPIES THIS HOUSE?	892	11
NEW-MAILED			
ONE MORE NEW-MAILED NERVE	A SINGLE SCREW OF FLESH	263	14
NEWNESS			
FOR NEWNESS OF THE NIGHT--	WE GROW ACCUSTOMED TO	419	6
NEWS			
THE NEWS, LIKE SQUIRRELS, RAN--	I'LL TELL YOU HOW THE	318	4
THE NEWS WOULD STRIKE ME DEAD--	BEFORE I GOT MY EYE PUT	327	17
THE INTUITION OF THE NEWS--	THERE'S BEEN A DEATH, IN	389	23
IGNORES THE SOLEMN NEWS	MORE LIFE--WENT OUT--	422	18
THE SIMPLE NEWS THAT NATURE TOLD--	THIS IS MY LETTER TO THE	441	3

	FIRST LINE	POEM	LINE
NEWS (CONTINUED)			
LIKE [AS] FLOWERS, THAT HEARD THE NEWS OF DEWS,	LIKE FLOWERS, THAT HEARD	513	1
NO NEWS OF IT IS HAD ABROAD--	THE BATTLE FOUGHT	594	5
AT NEWS THAT HE CEASED HUMAN NATURE . . .	TO KNOW JUST HOW HE	622	11
CONTINUAL--WITH THE NEWS--	THE LIGHTNING PLAYETH--	630	10
'TWAS NOON--WITHOUT THE NEWS [REPORT] OF NIGHT--	TO MY SMALL HEARTH HIS	638	7
WHOM DEATH SEE FIRST--'TIS NEWS OF THIS . .	BEREAVEMENT IN THEIR	645	7
BUT WHEN THE NEWS BE RIPE--	THE FUTURE--NEVER SPOKE	672	5
A NEWS EXPRESS TO ME--	THE BIRDS REPORTED FROM	743	2
THE ONLY NEWS I KNOW	THE ONLY NEWS I KNOW	827	1
IF OTHER NEWS THERE BE--	THE ONLY NEWS I KNOW	827	10
FOR NEWS THAT THEY BE SAVED--	SWEET, TO HAVE HAD THEM	901	2
EACH OTHER WITH THE WORDS [NEWS]	TWO TRAVELLERS PERISHING	933	4
A GOOD NEWS SHOULD BE GIVEN.	OF TOLLING BELL I ASK	947	8
AND TIME WENT OUT TO TELL THE NEWS . . .	I HEARD, AS IF I HAD NO	1039	15
'TIS NEWS AS NULL AS NOTHING, ...	MYSELF CAN READ THE	1089	7
SOFT STIRS THE NEWS [STIR THE FLAKES] OF LIGHT	THE SMOULDERING EMBERS	1132	5
EACH FORECLOSED A NEWS--	AFTER THE SUN COMES OUT	1148	6
NEWS IS HE OF ALL THE OTHERS--	WE LIKE MARCH.	1213	10
BUT WHEN I BREAK IT WITH THE NEWS	THE MOST PATHETIC THING	1290	5
HOW NEWS MUST FEEL WHEN TRAVELLING . . .	HOW NEWS MUST FEEL WHEN	1319	1
IF NEWS HAVE ANY HEART	HOW NEWS MUST FEEL WHEN	1319	2
WHAT NEWS MUST THINK WHEN PONDERING . . .	HOW NEWS MUST FEEL WHEN	1319	5
IF NEWS HAVE ANY THOUGHT	HOW NEWS MUST FEEL WHEN	1319	6
WHAT NEWS WILL DO WHEN EVERY MAN	HOW NEWS MUST FEEL WHEN	1319	9
THAN A FACT [NEWS] OF IRON	WHETHER THEY HAVE	1329	7
I SUED THE NEWS--YET FEARED--THE NEWS . .	I SUED THE NEWS--YET	1360	1
I SUED THE NEWS--YET FEARED--THE NEWS . .	I SUED THE NEWS--YET	1360	1
THE NEWS THAT SHE [HE] IS GONE--	SHE LAID HER DOCILE	1396	4
THAT TOLD THE TRUTH [NEWS] TO ME-- . . .	COULD MORTAL LIP DIVINE	1409	V
HOW OLD THE NEWS OF LOVE MUST [SHOULD] BE .	HIS VOICE DECREPIT WAS	1476	3
PAUL KNEW THE MAN THAT KNEW THE NEWS-- . .	"AND WITH WHAT BODY DO	1492	7
TO KNOW THE NEWS I KNOW TO-NIGHT	I KNOW OF PEOPLE IN THE	1665	3
SHE TOOK THE AWFUL NEWS	I WATCHED HER FACE TO	1667	2
NEWS-BOYS			
NEWS-BOYS SALUTE THE DOOR--	I COULD DIE--TO KNOW--	570	3
NEXT			
NEXT BLISS!	WHERE I HAVE LOST, I	104	16
NEXT TO MINE, ...	I BRING AN UNACCUSTOMED	132	3
AND COME NEXT HOUR TO LOOK.	I BRING AN UNACCUSTOMED	132	7
NEXT TIME, TO STAY!	JUST LOST, WHEN I WAS	160	12
NEXT TIME, THE THINGS TO SEE	JUST LOST, WHEN I WAS	160	13
NEXT TIME, TO TARRY, ...	JUST LOST, WHEN I WAS	160	16
WERE USELESS AS NEXT MORNING'S SUN-- . . .	I SHOULD NOT DARE TO	205	15
NEXT SUN--TO DIE--	SHOULD YOU BUT FAIL AT--	226	4
INTO [BACK OF / AT THE / AFTER / UNTO / NEXT TO] SOLITUDE--	HOW THE OLD MOUNTAINS	291	20
BECAUSE--WHEN NEXT IT BURNS ABROAD . . .	THE DOOMED--REGARD THE	294	3
THAN DID NEXT MORN	I'M SAYING EVERY DAY	373	27
NEXT--ONE--MIGHT BE THE GOLDEN TOUCH-- . .	I'LL CLUTCH--AND CLUTCH	427	2
AND NEXT--I MET HER ON A CLOUD--	I WATCHED THE MOON	629	33
AND PUSH IT WITH MY FINGERS--NEXT-- . . .	THE WAY I READ A	636	3
NEXT DOOR TO MINE THE PAIN.	HOW WELL I KNEW HER NOT	837	4
I KNEW NOT BUT THE NEXT	I STEPPED FROM PLANK TO	875	5
NEXT PRECIOUS	SWEET, TO HAVE HAD THEM	901	7
THE GRACE NEXT TO IT--HEAL?	ONLY A SHRINE, BUT MINE	918	8
I BEHELD HER NEXT	THREE WEEKS PASSED SINCE	1061	4
REBUILT ANOTHER MORNING [IN TIME NEXT MORNING / WITHOUT . . .	THE LARGEST FIRE EVER	1114	7
NEXT TO THE ROBIN	PINK--SMALL--AND	1332	7
THE SEDGE STANDS NEXT THE SEA--	WHAT MYSTERY PERVADES A	1400	14
DEPARTING THEN [NEXT]--FOREVER--	SUMMER HAS TWO	1422	9
MAKES THE [THIS] PRESENT [NEXT MOMENT] MEAN--	GLASS WAS THE STREET--IN	1498	8
FOR ANGELS RENT THE HOUSE NEXT OUR'S, . .	WHO HAS NOT FOUND THE	1544	3
NIBBLE			
TO NIBBLE ALL THE DAY, ...	PAPA ABOVE!	61	7
NIBBLES			
THAT NIBBLES AT THE SOUL--	THIS WORLD IS NOT	501	20
NICE			
BERRIES ARE NICE!	OVER THE FENCE--	251	5
AND THOUGHT IT VERY NICE	A SPARROW TOOK A SLICE	1211	2
NICELY			
NICELY BALANCING.	CRISIS IS A HAIR	889	8
NICKNAMED			
NICKNAMED BY GOD--	LOVE--THOU ART HIGH--	453	17
NICODEMUS'			
AND NICODEMUS' MYSTERY	AN ALTERED LOOK ABOUT	140	15
OLD NICODEMUS' PHANTOM	THE BONE THAT HAS NO	1274	11
NIGGARD			
NIGGARD GRACE!	WHAT WOULD I GIVE TO SEE	247	28
NIGGARDLY			
BUT FOR THE NIGGARDLY DELIGHT	OUR LITTLE SECRETS SLINK	1326	5
ALL OTHER BOUNTY SUDDEN CHAFF [NIGGARDLY] .	I GROPED FOR HIM BEFORE	1555	3
NIGHT SEE TO-NIGHT			
NIGHT UNTO DAY IS MARRIED, MORN UNTO EVENTIDE;	AWAKE YE MUSES NINE,	1	22
NIGHT IS THE MORNING'S CANVAS	THE FEET OF PEOPLE	7	13
AND ALL THE NIGHT ASHINE--	I HAD A GUINEA GOLDEN--	23	22
AS IF THE STARS SOME SUMMER NIGHT	THERE IS A MORN BY MEN	24	16

	FIRST LINE	POEM	LINE
NIGHT (CONTINUED)			
AND NIGHT IS COMING DOWN!	ADRIFT! A LITTLE BOAT	30	2
IF NIGHT STANDS FIRST--THEN NOON	IF PAIN FOR PEACE	63	7
NOR NOTICED NIGHT DID SOFT DESCEND--	A POOR--TORN HEART-- A	78	5
AS SURE AS FLOCKS GO HOME AT NIGHT	GOING TO HEAVEN!	79	9
TOMORROW, NIGHT WILL COME AGAIN--	HEART, NOT SO HEAVY AS	83	17
HALF GLAD WHEN IT IS NIGHT, AND SLEEP,	I HAVE A KING, WHO DOES	103	4
OUR SHARE OF NIGHT TO BEAR--	OUR SHARE OF NIGHT TO	113	1
GOOD NIGHT, BECAUSE WE MUST,	GOOD NIGHT, BECAUSE WE	114	1
WHERE FOR THE NIGHT	WHAT INN IS THIS	115	2
ON SUCH A NIGHT	IF THIS IS "FADING"	120	6
AND STILL WITHIN A SUMMER'S NIGHT	A SOMETHING IN A	122	7
SO LOOKING ON--THE NIGHT--THE MORN	A SOMETHING IN A	122	19
WHO COUNTS THE WAMPUM OF THE NIGHT	BRING ME THE SUNSET IN A	128	17
AS CHILDREN BID THE GUEST "GOOD NIGHT"	AS CHILDREN BID THE	133	1
ON SUCH A NIGHT, OR SUCH A NIGHT,	ON SUCH A NIGHT, OR SUCH	146	1
ON SUCH A NIGHT, OR SUCH A NIGHT,	ON SUCH A NIGHT, OR SUCH	146	1
THAT NIGHT WILL NEVER BE--	YOU LOVE ME--YOU ARE	156	9
DYING! DYING IN THE NIGHT!	DYING! DYING IN THE	158	1
THE NIGHT BEFORE THE CROWN!	A LITTLE BREAD--A CRUST	159	6
I WOULD NOT STOP FOR NIGHT, OR STORM--	IF I COULD BRIBE THEM BY	179	4
ALL DAY AND NIGHT WITH BARK AND START--	WHAT SHALL I DO--IT	186	3
WHEN NIGHT--DESCENDING--DUMB--AND DARK--	THO' I GET HOME HOW LATE	207	5
JUST AS THE NIGHT KEEPS FETCHING STARS	I'VE NOTHING ELSE--TO	224	3
HAPLY--YOUR SUMMER NIGHT TO CHARM--	KILL YOUR BALM--AND IT'S	238	4
GOOD NIGHT! WHICH PUT THE CANDLE OUT?	GOOD NIGHT! WHICH PUT	259	1
NIGHT AFTER NIGHT	THIS--IS THE LAND--THE	266	5
NIGHT AFTER NIGHT	THIS--IS THE LAND--THE	266	5
HOW ORDERLY THE KITCHEN'D LOOK, BY NIGHT,	I KNOW SOME LONELY	289	13
HOW IT IS NIGHT--IN NEST AND KENNEL--	HOW THE OLD MOUNTAINS	291	17
LIKE BREADTHS OF TOPAZ--PACKED A NIGHT--	THE DAY CAME SLOW--TILL	304	7
WHEN NIGHT DEVOURED THE ROAD--	OF TRIBULATION--THESE	325	14
AND THREAD THE DEWS, ALL NIGHT, LIKE PEARLS [PEARL]--	THE GRASS SO LITTLE HAS	333	9
FOR OUR HOARSE GOOD NIGHT--	'TWAS THE OLD--ROAD--	344	21
WHEN NIGHT IS ALMOST DONE--	WHEN NIGHT IS ALMOST	347	1
IT BURNED ME--IN THE NIGHT--	IT STRUCK ME--EVERY DAY	362	5
I KNEW LAST NIGHT--WHEN SOMEONE TRIED TO TWINE--	HOW SICK--TO WAIT--IN	368	2
WHO VISITS IN THE NIGHT--	A VISITOR IN MARL--	391	5
WHOSE WINDOWS--NIGHT AND MORN--	A HOUSE UPON THE HIGHT--	399	6
THAT NIGHT--BEGUN--	A TONGUE--TO TELL HIM I	400	11
THE FIRST DAY'S NIGHT HAD COME--	THE FIRST DAY'S NIGHT	410	1
SUNSET AT NIGHT--IS NATURAL--	SUNSET AT NIGHT--IS	415	1
FOR NEWNESS OF THE NIGHT--	WE GROW ACCUSTOMED TO	419	6
BUT STARS--GO SLOW--FOR NIGHT--	I'LL CLUTCH--AND CLUTCH	427	6
AND SO, AS KINSMEN, MET A NIGHT--	I DIED FOR BEAUTY--BUT	449	9
DIVERSIFIED BY NIGHT--	LIKE EYES THAT LOOKED ON	458	4
MIDNIGHT--GOOD NIGHT! I HEAR THEM CALL,	A WIFE--AT DAYBREAK I	461	7
A NIGHT--THERE LAY THE DAYS BETWEEN--	A NIGHT--THERE LAY THE	471	1
AND NOW--'TWAS NIGHT--WAS HERE--	A NIGHT--THERE LAY THE	471	4
SLOW--NIGHT--THAT MUST BE WATCHED AWAY--	A NIGHT--THERE LAY THE	471	5
TILL IT BE NIGHT--NO MORE--	A NIGHT--THERE LAY THE	471	8
AT NIGHT, MY LITTLE LAMP, AND BOOK--	I WAS THE SLIGHTEST IN	486	3
TELL HIM [HER]--NIGHT [DAY] FINISHED--BEFORE WE FINISHED--	GOING TO HIM! HAPPY	494	18
LEST NOON IN [DOWN] EVERLASTING NIGHT--	I ENVY SEAS, WHEREON HE	498	23
AND WHEN--SOME NIGHT--BOLD--SLASHING CLOUDS	YOU KNOW THAT PORTRAIT	504	13
IT WAS NOT NIGHT, FOR ALL THE BELLS	IT WAS NOT DEATH, FOR I	510	3
WHAT COME OF HIM--AT NIGHT--	HE PARTS HIMSELF--LIKE	517	13
HER SWEET WEIGHT ON MY HEART A NIGHT	HER SWEET WEIGHT ON MY	518	1
UPON THE SLOWEST NIGHT--	YOU CANNOT PUT A FIRE	530	4
AS THE STARS--YOU KNEW LAST NIGHT--	SOME SUCH BUTTERFLY BE	541	7
HER NIGHT DOTH HARDLY RECOMPENSE	SHE HIDETH HER THE LAST	557	3
SWEET DEBT OF LIFE--EACH NIGHT TO OWE--	I GAVE MYSELF TO HIM--	580	15
I HUNG UPON THE PEG, AT NIGHT.	IT CEASED TO HURT ME,	584	8
BEFORE ANOTHER NIGHT.	WE TALKED AS GIRLS DO--	586	16
THE NIGHT WAS WIDE, AND FURNISHED SCANT	THE NIGHT WAS WIDE, AND	589	1
JUNE NOON--AS JANUARY NIGHT--	WHAT CARE THE DEAD, FOR	592	19
AND WHETHER IT WAS NOON AT NIGHT--	I THINK I WAS ENCHANTED	593	5
AS LEGIONS OF A NIGHT	THE BATTLE FOUGHT	594	10
THAT FLICKERED IN THE NIGHT--	A STILL--VOLCANO--LIFE--	601	2
BUT HOLIDAY--EXCLUDES THE NIGHT--	UNTO MY BOOKS--SO GOOD	604	11
'TWAS NOON--WITHOUT THE NEWS [REPORT] OF NIGHT--	TO MY SMALL HEARTH HIS	638	7
WHOSE FEATURES--DAY AND NIGHT--	A PRISON GETS TO BE A	652	22
TOO WIDE FOR ANY NIGHT BUT HEAVEN--	A PRISON GETS TO BE A	652	31
NOR DOES THE NIGHT FORGET	THE SUNRISE RUNS FOR	710	7
RESTS AT NIGHT	RESTS AT NIGHT	714	1
AH, BRIG--GOOD NIGHT	IT TOSSED--AND TOSSED--	723	9
WHEN I SLEPT--AT NIGHT--	LET US PLAY YESTERDAY--	728	22
A NIGHT OR TWO AGO--	THE MOON WAS BUT A CHIN	737	2
AND WHEN AT NIGHT--OUR GOOD DAY DONE--	MY LIFE HAD STOOD--A	754	13
FOR FELLOWSHIP [SYMPATHY]--AT NIGHT--	THE MOUNTAINS--GROW	757	8
NATURE WILL--THAT IT BE NIGHT	WHEN I HOPED, I	768	19
AND WHEN AT NIGHT--AURORAN WIDTHS	THE COLOR OF A QUEEN, IS	776	5
AND EVERY NIGHT, IT NUMBERED MORE	I MADE SLOW RICHES BUT	843	3
MY LITTLE MAID--'TIS NIGHT--ALAS	'TIS SUNRISE--LITTLE	908	9
THAT NIGHT SHOULD BE TO THEE	'TIS SUNRISE--LITTLE	908	10
THE BELLS A WINTER NIGHT	PEACE IS A FICTION OF	912	2

	FIRST LINE	POEM	LINE
NIGHT (CONTINUED)			
AND THEN RETURN--AND NIGHT [TRUST]--AND HOME--	I LEARNED--AT LEAST--	944	22
AS PLAN FOR NOON AND PLAN FOR NIGHT	AS PLAN FOR NOON AND	960	1
FRONTING US--WITH [TURNING US--THEIR] NIGHT.	UNFULFILLED TO	972	8
IN AGES, OR A NIGHT--	NOT ALL DIE EARLY, DYING	990	4
IT WAS NOT NIGHT NOR MORN [NOON]--	IT WAS A QUIET WAY--	1053	18
TO THE PARISH NIGHT--	THREE WEEKS PASSED SINCE	1061	10
THINE IS THE STILLEST NIGHT	LET DOWN THE BARS, OH	1065	5
THE LAST NIGHT THAT SHE LIVED	THE LAST NIGHT THAT SHE	1100	1
IT WAS A COMMON NIGHT	THE LAST NIGHT THAT SHE	1100	2
AND SO THE NIGHT BECAME.	THE CRICKETS SANG	1104	12
'TIS MY FIRST NIGHT BENEATH THE SUN	'TIS MY FIRST NIGHT	1122	1
AT NIGHT BENEATH [BELOW] THE STAR	THE SNOW THAT NEVER	1133	6
A SPIDER SEWED AT NIGHT	A SPIDER SEWED AT NIGHT	1138	1
BY EARLY, STOOPING NIGHT--	THE DAY GREW SMALL,	1140	2
BY CLOCKS, 'TWAS MORNING, AND FOR NIGHT	GREAT STREETS OF SILENCE	1159	5
THE SOUL RETURNING SOFT AT NIGHT [STILL BY DAWN / LOTH BY DAWN]	CONTAINED IN THIS SHORT	1165	3
SOMEHOW MYSELF SURVIVED THE NIGHT	SOMEHOW MYSELF SURVIVED	1194	1
TILL SOME RETRIEVELESS NIGHT	THE FROST WAS NEVER SEEN	1202	9
ENGULPH THEE IN THE NIGHT--	LET MY FIRST KNOWING BE	1218	4
BUT SO ADJUST MY DAILY NIGHT	LET ME NOT MAR THAT	1335	3
I OFTEN IN THE NIGHT [MY SLEEP]	ESCAPE IS SUCH A	1347	2
HIS HEART WAS DARKER THAN THE STARLESS NIGHT	HIS HEART WAS DARKER	1378	1
THAT [WHO] LODGED A NIGHT IN MEMORY--	NO PASSENGER WAS KNOWN	1406	2
TO REND IT WITH GOOD NIGHT--	WITHIN THY GRAVE!	1552	4
TO SOME--THE NIGHT--	MORNING IS DUE TO ALL--	1577	2
WHICH LIKE THE MOON, SOME TURBID NIGHT,	EACH THAT WE LOSE TAKES	1605	3
THIS MIGHTY NIGHT	WHY SHOULD WE HURRY--WHY	1646	10
THAT IS NIGHT	I DID NOT REACH THEE	1664	21
BEQUEATHS HIM TO THE NIGHT.	HOW DARE THE ROBINS SING	1724	12
PROUD OF MY NIGHT, SINCE THOU WITH MOONS DOST SLAKE IT,	PROUD OF MY BROKEN HEART	1736	3
SOME SAY GOODNIGHT--AT NIGHT--	SOME SAY GOODNIGHT--AT	1739	1
FOR PARTING, THAT IS NIGHT,	SOME SAY GOODNIGHT--AT	1739	5
NIGHTFALL			
HE REACHES [COMES TO] TOWN AT NIGHTFALL--	THE GUEST IS GOLD AND	15	5
OR ANY CHEEK AT NIGHTFALL	BEFORE THE ICE IS IN THE	37	3
NIGHTGOWNS			
THEN PUT THEIR NIGHTGOWNS ON.	AS CHILDREN BID THE	133	4
WHOSE NIGHTGOWNS COULD NOT HIDE THE WINGS--	A MURMUR IN THE TREES--	416	15
NIGHTINGALE			
CAN NIGHTINGALE BE SEEN--	ALL OVERGROWN BY CUNNING	148	12
NIGHT'S			
FROM OUT THE WIDE NIGHT'S NUMBERS--	ONE SISTER HAVE I IN OUR	14	26
NIGHT'S POSSIBILITY!	THE DAISY FOLLOWS SOFT	106	12
THE NIGHT'S TREMENDOUS MORROW	ON THAT SPECIFIC PILLOW	1533	3
AT NIGHT'S DELICIOUS CLOSE.	THE SADDEST NOISE, THE	1764	4
NIGHTS			
WILD NIGHTS--WILD NIGHTS!	WILD NIGHTS--WILD NIGHTS	249	1
WILD NIGHTS--WILD NIGHTS!	WILD NIGHTS--WILD NIGHTS	249	1
WILD NIGHTS SHOULD BE	WILD NIGHTS--WILD NIGHTS	249	3
THE ROPE THE NIGHTS WERE PUT ACROSS--	I SHOWED HER HIGHTS SHE	446	6
TO WHOM THE MORNINGS STAND FOR NIGHTS,	TO WHOM THE MORNINGS	1095	1
THESE ARE THE NIGHTS THAT BEETLES LOVE--	THESE ARE THE NIGHTS	1128	1
HAST THOU SURVIVED SO MANY NIGHTS [YEARS]?	THE SMOULDERING EMBERS	1132	3
TOO SCANT THE NIGHTS.	TOO FEW THE MORNINGS BE,	1186	2
HOW LONESOME THE WIND MUST FEEL NIGHTS--	HOW LONESOME THE WIND	1418	1
WHEN NIGHTS ARE HOT AND SERE--	A WINGED SPARK DOTH SOAR	1468	4
WHO IS IT SEEKS MY PILLOW NIGHTS--	WHO IS IT SEEKS MY	1598	1
NIMBLE			
BY A NIMBLE LOVE--	BY A FLOWER--BY A LETTER	109	2
WHERE VERY NIMBLE GENTLEMEN	WHERE BELLS NO MORE	112	3
THIS PASSIVE PLACE A SUMMER'S NIMBLE MANSION	THIS QUIET DUST WAS	813	5
WHAT RESIDENCES NIMBLE	WHAT TENEMENTS OF CLOVER	1338	5
NINE			
AWAKE YE MUSES NINE, SING ME A STRAIN DIVINE,	AWAKE YE MUSES NINE,	1	1
NOAH			
AND NO ONE CREDITS NOAH--	THE WINTERS ARE SO SHORT	403	16
NOBLE			
WHOSE HAVING LIVED IS HELD BY US IN NOBLE HOLIDAY	LEST ANY DOUBT THAT WE	1156	2
TOO NOBLE THEN TO TELL.	NOT WITH A CLUB, THE	1304	8
NOBLENESS			
THERE IS A SHAME OF NOBLENESS--	THERE IS A SHAME OF	551	1
NOBODY			
NOBODY KNOWS THIS LITTLE ROSE--	NOBODY KNOWS THIS LITTLE	35	1
I'D NOTICE NOBODY!	"SOWN IN DISHONOR"!	62	5
AND NOBODY KNOWS, SO STILL IT FLOWS,	HAVE YOU GOT A BROOK IN	136	5
THAT NOBODY MIGHT KNOW	ON SUCH A NIGHT, OR SUCH	146	6
BUT NOBODY WAS THERE!	THE SUN KEPT STOOPING--	152	14
NOBODY KNEW "HIS FATHER"--	DUST IS THE ONLY SECRET	153	5
I'M NOBODY! WHO ARE YOU?	I'M NOBODY! WHO ARE YOU?	288	1
ARE YOU--NOBODY--TOO?	I'M NOBODY! WHO ARE YOU?	288	2
A PRANK NOBODY KNEW BUT THEM	IF ANYBODY'S FRIEND BE	509	7
SO WHEN THOU FAILEST, NOBODY.	I'VE NONE TO TELL ME TO	881	2
HAD NOBODY A PANG	WHEN THEY COME BACK--IF	1080	10
NOBODY KNOWS [KNEW] THE PLACE	AFTER A HUNDRED YEARS	1147	2
AND SHOUTS FOR JOY TO NOBODY	BEFORE YOU THOUGHT OF	1465	15

	FIRST LINE	POEM	LINE
NOD			
SO SPICY HER CARNATIONS NOD--	WE SHOULD NOT MIND SO	81	5
NODDING			
JUST A DOME OF ABYSS IS BOWING [NODDING] .	HOW THE OLD MOUNTAINS	291	19
NODDING IN NAVIES NEVERMORE--	FINITE--TO FAIL, BUT	847	4
NODS			
SHE NODS, AND ALL BEGIN--	BAFFLED FOR JUST A DAY	17	6
NODS [STARES] FROM THE GILDED POINTERS-- .	A CLOCK STOPPED--	287	14
NODS FROM THE SECONDS SLIM--	A CLOCK STOPPED--	287	15
SOMEWHAT OF NODS AND SOMEWHAT	THE LEAVES LIKE WOMEN,	987	3
NOISE			
FROM ALL THE NOISE [SOUND] OF FIELDS-- . .	I'M SORRY FOR THE DEAD--	529	10
LET NO SUNRISE' YELLOW NOISE	AMPLE MAKE THIS BED--	829	7
OR ACCIDENT OF NOISE--	WHEN I HAVE SEEN THE SUN	888	6
BEFORE THIS MORTAL NOISE	IT WAS A QUIET WAY--	1053	6
YOU HEARD NO NOISE [CRASH]	A GREAT HOPE FELL	1123	2
BUT NOT TO MAKE A "BIT OF NOISE"	A LITTLE DOG THAT WAGS	1185	15
AND WHEN THE NOISE IS CAUGHT	THE SYMPTOM OF THE GALE	1327	13
THE SADDEST NOISE, THE SWEETEST NOISE, . .	THE SADDEST NOISE, THE	1764	1
THE SADDEST NOISE, THE SWEETEST NOISE, . .	THE SADDEST NOISE, THE	1764	1
THE MADDEST NOISE THAT GROWS,--	THE SADDEST NOISE, THE	1764	2
NOISELESS			
THERE IS IT'S NOISELESS ONSET--	THERE IS A WORD	8	13
NOISY			
THEMSELF--THE NOISY PLAYTHING	THE MONTHS HAVE ENDS--	423	11
TO STILL IT'S NOISY [HELP IT'S VACANT] HANDS--	AT LEISURE IS THE SOUL	618	8
NOMINATED			
MY NOMINATED HEART--	OH SHADOW ON THE GRASS,	1187	4
NOMINATION			
NOT UNTO NOMINATION	SHALL I TAKE THEE, THE	1126	11
NONCHALANCE			
THE QUIET NONCHALANCE OF DEATH--	ON THIS LONG STORM THE	194	9
NONCHALANT			
HOW NONCHALANT THE HEDGE!	A LADY RED--AMID THE	74	14
NONE			
NONE CANNOT FIND WHO SEEKETH, ON THIS TERRESTIAL BALL:	AWAKE YE MUSES NINE,	1	12
SINCE NONE OF THEM ARE MINE.	I HAD A GUINEA GOLDEN--	23	24
NONE CAN AVOID THIS PURPLE--	ONE DIGNITY DELAYS FOR	98	3
NONE EVADE THIS CROWN!	ONE DIGNITY DELAYS FOR	98	4
WHO FALL--AND NONE OBSERVE--	TO FIGHT ALOUD, IS VERY	126	6
TO SEE THAT NONE IS DUE?	BRING ME THE SUNSET IN A	128	18
QUITE NONE?	YOU LOVE ME--YOU ARE	156	13
WERE NONE OF OUR AFFAIR!	IN EBON BOX, WHEN YEARS	169	20
NONE MAY TEACH IT--ANY--	THERE'S A CERTAIN SLANT	258	9
WHEN NONE ARE NEAR	A MIEN TO MOVE A QUEEN--	283	6
NONE BUT THE NUT--OCTOBER FIT--	THE ROBIN'S MY CRITERION	285	10
NONE--WILL--	I KNOW SOME LONELY	289	18
WHOM NONE BUT DAISIES [BEETLES], KNOW. . .	OF BRONZE--AND BLAZE--	290	19
AH, SIR, NONE!	ONE YEAR AGO--JOTS WHAT?	296	37
NONE BUY IT ANY MORE--	IS BLISS THEN, SUCH	340	11
NONE ON ME, BEND SUPERCILIOUS--	I'M SAYING EVERY DAY	373	6
THE COY DEAD--NONE--	UNIT, LIKE DEATH, FOR	408	12
AND AFTER THAT--IS NONE--	THE RED--BLAZE--IS THE	469	4
OR WHETHER IT BE NONE [DIN]	TO HEAR AN ORIOLE SING	526	11
OF OUR'S, NONE AFFAIR--	WE TALKED AS GIRLS DO--	586	4
AND NONE COULD SEE THE STONE.	'TIS GOOD--THE LOOKING	660	8
NONE SAW--	ONE NEED NOT BE A	670	V 20
WHOSE PRINCE--IS SON OF NONE--	BEHIND ME--DIPS ETERNITY	721	9
NONE STIR [HARM] THE SECOND TIME--	MY LIFE HAD STOOD--A	754	18
NONE CAN EXPERIENCE STINT	NONE CAN EXPERIENCE	771	1
THEIR WITNESSES WERE NOT--[LISTENER WAS NONE]	THE BIRDS BEGUN AT FOUR	783	9
THOUGH NONE BE ON OUR SIDE--	ON A COLUMNAR SELF--	789	8
THAT DEFINITION IS NONE--	BY MY WINDOW HAVE I FOR	797	16
ITSELF UNTO ITSELF AND NONE	THIS CONSCIOUSNESS THAT	822	11
NONE STIR ABROAD	SPRING IS THE PERIOD	844	6
I'VE NONE TO TELL ME TO BUT THEE	I'VE NONE TO TELL ME TO	881	1
THAT DEFINITION IS NONE--	THE DEFINITION OF BEAUTY	988	2
GRACIOUS UNTO NONE--	THREE WEEKS PASSED SINCE	1061	8
BUT SWEETER SO--THAN NONE.	MYSELF CAN READ THE	1089	8
NONE [THEY] WHO SAW IT EVER TOLD IT . . .	NONE WHO SAW IT EVER	1110	1
REDUCES IT TO NONE.	THE LIFE WE HAVE IS VERY	1162	8
THAT NONE CAN PUNISH HIM	LIKE TIME'S INSIDIOUS	1236	8
BUT NONE WILL PASS THE [MAN'S] CATACOMB . .	THE BUTTERFLY IN HONORED	1246	3
FOR NONE SEE GOD AND LIVE--	TO PILE LIKE THUNDER TO	1247	8
FOR HE INSURES TO NONE	I CANNOT SEE MY SOUL BUT	1262	7
WHERE NONE OF US SHOULD [WOULD] BE	SO PROUD SHE WAS TO DIE	1272	6
OR IT HAS [SHE IS] NONE--	COULD HOPE INSPECT HER	1283	4
WHOSE LIMIT NONE HAVE EVER SEEN, ...	WHAT MYSTERY PERVADES A	1400	5
CONTRIVES THAT NONE GO OUT AGAIN--	NO PASSENGER WAS KNOWN	1406	4
YET [AND] NONE HATH SUCH A CROWD.	HOW BRITTLE ARE THE	1433	4
ESTRANGED FROM BEAUTY--NONE CAN BE-- . . .	ESTRANGED FROM BEAUTY--	1474	1
OH NATURE--NONE OF THIS--	"GO TELL IT"--WHAT A	1554	6
OR NONE PERCEPTIBLE.	THE BAT IS DUN, WITH	1575	4
DECLAIMING WATERS NONE MAY DREAD--	DECLAIMING WATERS NONE	1595	1
THAT NONE CAN UNDERSTAND	BACK FROM THE CORDIAL	1625	4
IS HEARD OF NONE	SPEECH IS ONE SYMPTOM OF	1681	4
NONE SUSPECT ME OF THE CROWN, ...	REARRANGE A "WIFE'S"	1737	14
NOOKS			
LEAVING NOOKS FOR DAISY	ALL THESE MY BANNERS BE.	22	14

	FIRST LINE	POEM	LINE
NOOKS (CONTINUED)			
FROM SPOTTED [DAPPLED] NOOKS--	MY RIVER RUNS TO THEE--	162	6
NOON			
AND NOON SHOULD BURN--	IF I SHOULD DIE,	54	5
IF NIGHT STANDS FIRST--THEN NOON	IF PAIN FOR PEACE	63	7
THRO' CENTURIES OF NOON	WHERE BELLS NO MORE	112	6
A SOMETHING IN A SUMMER'S NOON--	A SOMETHING IN A	122	4
SOME BURNING NOON GO DRY!	HAVE YOU GOT A BROOK IN	136	16
SAY IF IT'S REALLY--WARM AT NOON--	MAKE ME A PICTURE OF THE	188	9
NO DESERT NOON--	FOR THIS--ACCEPTED	195	9
CORN--IS MADE AT NOON--	MORNING--IS THE PLACE	197	2
AND UNTOUCHED BY NOON--	SAFE IN THEIR ALABASTER	216	3
NOON--OUR LAST CUP--	WE--BEE AND I--LIVE BY	230	15
WHERE OTHERS, DARE NOT GO [WALK] AT NOON,	WHEN WE STAND ON THE	242	11
MORNING--ONLY THE SEED OF NOON--	I SHALL KEEP SINGING!	250	10
THE ODE FAMILIAR--RULES THE NOON--	THE ROBIN'S MY CRITERION	285	5
INTO DEGREELESS NOON--	A CLOCK STOPPED--	287	9
CHIME [STRIKE]--NOON!	IT'S LIKE THE LIGHT--	297	12
AS MUCH OF NOON AS I COULD TAKE	BEFORE I GOT MY EYE PUT	327	12
OR BUTTERFLIES, OFF BANKS OF NOON	A BIRD CAME DOWN THE	328	19
HER PUBLIC--BE THE NOON--	THERE IS A FLOWER THAT	380	25
SO MIDNIGHT'S--DUE--AT NOON.	SUNSET AT NIGHT--IS	415	4
YOU'LL KNOW IT--AS YOU KNOW 'TIS NOON--	YOU'LL KNOW IT--AS YOU	420	1
THE VIOLET--IS NOON--	THE RED--BLAZE--IS THE	469	2
TO TELL HIM IT IS NOON, ABROAD--	I ENVY SEAS, WHEREON HE	498	19
MYSELF--BE NOON TO HIM--	I ENVY SEAS, WHEREON HE	498	20
LEST NOON IN [DOWN] EVERLASTING NIGHT--	I ENVY SEAS, WHEREON HE	498	23
PUT OUT THEIR TONGUES, FOR NOON.	IT WAS NOT DEATH, FOR I	510	4
BUT NOON, AND PARADISE--	THE SOUL HAS BANDAGED	512	18
SUSPENDED IN THE NOON--	HE PARTS HIMSELF--LIKE	517	10
TWO BUTTERFLIES WENT OUT AT NOON--	TWO BUTTERFLIES WENT OUT	533	1
AND BOTH WERE WRECKED [DROWNED / QUENCHED / WHELMED] IN NOON--	TWO BUTTERFLIES WENT OUT	533	V
AND THEY WERE HURLED FROM NOON--	TWO BUTTERFLIES WENT OUT	533	V
JUST AT NOON--NO LATER--SWEET [THAN]--	SOME SUCH BUTTERFLY BE	541	3
SOMETIMES, I THINK THAT NOON	"HEAVEN" HAS DIFFERENT	575	2
MY NOON HAD COME--TO DINE--	I HAD BEEN HUNGRY, ALL	579	2
INSOLVENT--EVERY NOON--	I GAVE MYSELF TO HIM--	580	16
OR NOON--IN MAZARIN?	I FOUND THE WORDS TO	581	8
JUNE NOON--AS JANUARY NIGHT--	WHAT CARE THE DEAD, FOR	592	19
AND WHETHER IT WAS NOON AT NIGHT--	I THINK I WAS ENCHANTED	593	5
OR ONLY HEAVEN--AT NOON--	I THINK I WAS ENCHANTED	593	6
'TWAS NOON--WITHOUT THE NEWS [REPORT] OF NIGHT--	TO MY SMALL HEARTH HIS	638	7
BUT CERTAINTIES OF SUN [NOON]--	I THINK TO LIVE--MAY BE	646	17
NOR ONCE LOOK UP--FOR NOON?	A LONG--LONG SLEEP--A	654	8
THAT FAINTS UPON THE FACE OF NOON--	THE LOVE A LIFE CAN SHOW	673	4
FROM HOUSE TO HOUSE 'TWAS NOON--	THE SUN KEPT SETTING--	692	4
THE NOON UNWINDS HER BLUE	THE SUNRISE RUNS FOR	710	4
REST AT NOON--SOME MEN--	RESTS AT NIGHT	714	4
NOT SO ARROGANT--THIS NOON--	THESE--SAW VISIONS--	758	11
BERYL--AND THIS, AT NOON--	THE COLOR OF A QUEEN, IS	776	4
HAD IT A NOTICE [SUMMONS] FROM THE NOON	THIS THAT WOULD GREET--	778	5
A MUSIC NUMEROUS AS SPACE [MEASURELESS AS NOON]--	THE BIRDS BEGUN AT FOUR	783	3
BUT NEIGHBORING AS NOON--	THE BIRDS BEGUN AT FOUR	783	4
DID NOON--ENAMEL [ENABLE / EMBELLISH]--IN HERSELF	THIS BAUBLE WAS	805	5
THAT OVERFLOW THE NOON	THE ROBIN IS THE ONE	828	6
AS WHEN ON NOON	A SHADE UPON THE MIND	882	2
'TIS NOON--MY LITTLE MAID--	'TIS SUNRISE--LITTLE	908	5
OF CLOVERS, AND OF NOON!	HIS FEET ARE SHOD WITH	916	8
EMERGE A SINGLE NOON	THERE IS A JUNE WHEN	930	6
NOON--IS THE HINGE OF DAY--	NOON--IS THE HINGE OF	931	1
WHEN THE BEE HANGS ALL NOON IN THE BUTTERCUP	WHAT SHALL I DO WHEN THE	956	7
AS PLAN FOR NOON AND PLAN FOR NIGHT	AS PLAN FOR NOON AND	960	1
IT BLOOMED AND DROPT, A SINGLE NOON--	IT BLOOMED AND DROPT, A	978	1
I, PASSING, THOUGHT ANOTHER NOON	IT BLOOMED AND DROPT, A	978	3
I MORE THAN ONCE AT NOON	A NARROW FELLOW IN THE	986	12
INSCRIBES A SIMPLE NOON--	IT RISES--PASSES--ON OUR	1023	2
IT WAS NOT NIGHT NOR MORN [NOON]--	IT WAS A QUIET WAY--	1053	18
WHOSE SUN CONSTRUCTS PERPETUAL NOON	THERE IS A ZONE WHOSE	1056	3
AND CONSCIOUSNESS--IS NOON.	THERE IS A ZONE WHOSE	1056	8
AND INDIAN SUMMER NOON [SUN]--	EXCEPT THE SMALLER SIZE	1067	V
ANTIQUEST [ANTIQUER] FELT AT NOON	FURTHER IN SUMMER THAN	1068	9
THE MULTITUDES OF NOON--	THE CRICKETS SANG	1104	V
IN PROCESS OF THE NOON BECAME--	A FULL FED ROSE ON MEALS	1154	3
FABULOUS AS A MOON AT NOON	WHITE AS AN INDIAN PIPE	1250	3
SHE DOES NOT ASK FOR NOON--	QUITE EMPTY, QUITE AT	1606	6
AND WINDS DO GO THAT WAY AT NOON [TIMES]	TALK NOT TO ME OF SUMMER	1634	5
OUR NOON BECAME A WELL	A CAP OF LEAD ACROSS THE	1649	6
A MORNING AND A NOON	OF THIS IS DAY COMPOSED	1675	2
TO-DAY OR THIS NOON	TO-DAY OR THIS NOON	1702	1
NOONS			
NOONS LIKE THESE--SHE ROSE--	MORNS LIKE THESE--WE	27	2
NOONS BLAZE!	IF PAIN FOR PEACE	63	12
THE MORNINGS BLOSSOM INTO NOONS--	IT MAKES NO DIFFERENCE	620	3
OR NOONS REPORT AWAY	A LIGHT EXISTS IN SPRING	812	14
HOW POMPOUS THE WIND MUST FEEL NOONS	HOW LONESOME THE WIND	1418	5
HE SPENDS THE EVENING OF HIS DAYS [NOONS]	HIS ORIENTAL HERESIES	1526	V

	FIRST LINE	POEM		LINE
NOONS (CONTINUED)				
AND RUMBLES STILL, THOUGH TORRID NOONS	THE FARTHEST THUNDER	1581		3
NORMAL				
WOULD BE A NORMAL [DAILY] THING	WE NEVER KNOW HOW HIGH	1176		6
NORSEMAN'S				
GOOD AS A NORSEMAN'S HYMN--	A PROMPT--EXECUTIVE BIRD	1177	V	2
NORTH				
IN NORTH AMERICA--	I'VE KNOWN A HEAVEN,	243		8
THE NORTH--TONIGHT--	OF BRONZE--AND BLAZE--	290		2
UNTIL THE NORTH--INVOKE IT--	GOD MADE A LITTLE	442		11
AND SO I STEPPED [STOOD] UPON THE NORTH	MY PERIOD HAD COME FOR	564		7
THE NORTH CANNOT DETECT	A STILL--VOLCANO--LIFE--	601		8
WHILE OCEANS--AND THE NORTH MUST BE-- [DID PLAY]	OURSELVES WERE WED ONE	631		11
AND FURTHER NORTH--REMOVE.	I THINK THE LONGEST HOUR	635		16
FAR AS NORTH--AND EAST,	BLOOM UPON THE MOUNTAIN	667		14
THE NORTH--HER BLAZING SIGN	THE SUNRISE RUNS FOR	710		10
WITH MIDNIGHT TO THE NORTH OF HER--	BEHIND ME--DIPS ETERNITY	721		16
THE NEEDLE--TO THE NORTH DEGREE--	THROUGH THE STRAIT PASS	792		11
THE NORTH AND SOUTH WHEN HE	THE SUN AND MOON MUST	871		6
AND IN THE NORTH, THE STAR--	THESE ARE THE SIGNS TO	1077		12
THE NORTH BEGUN TO PUSH	THE CLOUDS THEIR BACKS	1172		2
NORTHERN				
FROSTS UNHOOK--IN THE NORTHERN ZONES--	SAFE IN THEIR ALABASTER	216	V	
THE GNASH OF NORTHERN WINDS	I THINK THE HEMLOCK	525		10
THE WIND TOOK UP THE NORTHERN THINGS	THE WIND TOOK UP THE	1134		1
LIGHT MY NORTHERN ROOM	GUEST AM I TO HAVE	1661		2
AND PRANKS THE NORTHERN STAR	THESE ARE THE DAYS THAT	1696		2
NORWEGIAN				
HIS BEST [GOOD] NORWEGIAN WINES--	I THINK THE HEMLOCK	525		12
NOSEGAYS				
MY NOSEGAYS ARE FOR CAPTIVES--	MY NOSEGAYS ARE FOR	95		1
WITH NOSEGAYS AT THE HEAD AND FOOT--	I WENT TO THANK HER--	363		4
NOTABILITY				
OF NOTABILITY [NOTORIETY].	THE CLOVER'S SIMPLE FAME	1232		4
NOTCH				
'TWAS LIKE A MAELSTROM, WITH A NOTCH,	'TWAS LIKE A MAELSTROM,	414		1
NOTCHED				
HAD NOTCHED THE PLACE THAT PLEASED HIM--	DEATH SETS A THING	360		15
THE DEPTH UPON MY SOUL WAS NOTCHED--	JOY TO HAVE MERITED THE	788		19
NOTCHING				
NOTCHING THE FALL OF THE EVEN SUN!	BOUND--A TROUBLE--	269		10
NOTE				
TO NOTE THE REBELS DOWN.	I COUNTED TILL THEY	36		4
A MURMUR IN THE TREES--TO NOTE--	A MURMUR IN THE TREES--	416		1
TOO IMPERCEPTIBLE TO NOTE--	A NIGHT--THERE LAY THE	471		7
A LITTLE NOTE--WHEN YOU AWAKE--	YOU LOVE THE LORD--YOU	487		3
WHEN CRESCENT--THOU ART WORN--I NOTE [MIND]--	YOU KNOW THAT PORTRAIT	504		11
I NOTE THAT SOME--GONE PATIENT LONG--	I MEASURE EVERY GRIEF I	561		13
TO NOTE THE FASHIONS--OF THE CROSS--	I MEASURE EVERY GRIEF I	561		37
AND WHEN WE TURNED TO NOTE THE GROWTH--	HE GAVE AWAY HIS LIFE--	567		15
THE LITTLE NOTE THAT OTHERS DROPT	I WAS A PHEBE--NOTHING	1009		3
HER PANTING NOTE [JOYFUL CRY / CORDIAL NOTE] EXALTS US-- . . .	AFTER ALL BIRDS HAVE	1395		6
HER PANTING NOTE [JOYFUL CRY / CORDIAL NOTE] EXALTS US-- . . .	AFTER ALL BIRDS HAVE	1395		6
HER ZEALOUS NOTE DELIGHTS IT TO ASCEND.	AFTER ALL BIRDS HAVE	1395	V	6
HER GALLANT NOTE ENDOWS US LIKE A FRIEND	AFTER ALL BIRDS HAVE	1395	V	6
AND SQUANDERED SUCH A NOTE	UPON HIS SADDLE SPRUNG A	1600		6
NOTED				
GOD PREACHES, A NOTED CLERGYMAN--	SOME KEEP THE SABBATH	324		9
NOTELESS				
HOW NOTELESS MEN, AND PLEIADS, STAND,	HOW NOTELESS MEN, AND	282		1
HOW NOTELESS--I COULD DIE--	I WAS THE SLIGHTEST IN	486		17
NOTELESSLY				
SO NOTELESSLY--ARE MADE!	A SHADY FRIEND--FOR	278		12
NOTES				
WRITE ME HOW MANY NOTES THERE BE	BRING ME THE SUNSET IN A	128		7
UNMOVED--SHE NOTES THE CHARIOTS--PAUSING--	THE SOUL SELECTS HER OWN	303		5
IT NOTES [GAINS] DELIGHT	MUST BE A WO--	571		6
AND THEN ADJUSTED HIS LITTLE NOTES,	A TRAIN WENT THROUGH A	1761		5
NOTHING				
GOD HATH MADE NOTHING SINGLE BUT THEE IN HIS WORLD SO FAIR!	AWAKE YE MUSES NINE,	1		6
WERE NOTHING VERY STRANGE!	A LADY RED--AMID THE	74		16
DEFEAT MEANS NOTHING BUT DEFEAT,	'TIS SO MUCH JOY! 'TIS	172		11
WHAT THEN? WHY NOTHING,	AS IF SOME LITTLE ARCTIC	180		11
I'VE NOTHING ELSE--TO BRING, YOU KNOW--	I'VE NOTHING ELSE--TO	224		1
IF HE DISSOLVE--THEN--THERE IS NOTHING--MORE--	IF HE DISSOLVE--THEN--	236		1
NOTHING MORE--	IF YOUR NERVE, DENY YOU	292		12
WEAR NOTHING COMMONER THAN SNOW--	OF TRIBULATION--THESE	325		7
AND THEN DOES NOTHING--	HE PARTS HIMSELF--LIKE	517		7
NOTHING TO SHOW	THAT I DID ALWAYS LOVE	549		11
ARE NOTHING TO THE BEE--	IT MAKES NO DIFFERENCE	620		10
"BUT--MADAM--IS THERE NOTHING ELSE--	I ASKED NO OTHER THING--	621		7
IS NOTHING THAT IS CHIEF,	EMBARRASSMENT OF ONE	662		5
JUST HIS FACE--NOTHING MORE!	AGAIN--HIS VOICE IS AT	663		12
THERE'S NOTHING COOLER FALLS--	UPON CONCLUDED LIVES	735		2
FOR NOTHING HIGHER THAN ITSELF	MY WORTHINESS IS ALL MY	751		11
WHEN NOTHING WAS TO SEE	HER FINAL SUMMER WAS IT	795		10

	FIRST LINE	POEM	LINE
NOTHING (CONTINUED)			
IF NOTHING LARGER THAN A WORLD'S	THE MISSING ALL,	985	3
I WAS A PHEBE--NOTHING MORE--	I WAS A PHEBE--NOTHING	1009	1
A PHEBE--NOTHING LESS--	I WAS A PHEBE--NOTHING	1009	2
AND NATURE NOTHING WAITS TO DO	FURTHER IN SUMMER THAN	1068	V
'TIS NEWS AS NULL AS NOTHING, ...	MYSELF CAN READ THE	1089	7
NOTHING IS LEFT TO PRAY--	WHATEVER IT IS--SHE HAS	1204	6
IS NOTHING TO THE DEAD.	MY TRIUMPH LASTED TILL	1227	16
AND SANG FOR NOTHING SCRUTABLE [IN THE WORLD]	THE MOST TRIUMPHANT BIRD	1265	5
AND YET IT NOTHING IS	I CANNOT WANT IT MORE--	1301	5
IS NOTHING BUT A BIER.	THE NOTICE THAT IS	1310	8
AND NOTHING IN THE COUNTENANCE	HOW KNOW IT FROM A	1364	3
TO THOSE WHO'VE NOTHING MORE--	HOW MUCH THE PRESENT	1380	2
NOTHING WITH A TONGUE OR EAR--[AN EAR OR TONGUE--]	"SECRETS" IS A DAILY	1385	9
NOTHING AFFRONT THY SECRECY.	TO THE STANCH DUST	1402	V 7
A NOTHING AT A TIME--	IT'S LITTLE ETHER HOOD	1501	6
THE [A] CRASH OF NOTHING, YET [AND] OF ALL--	MORE THAN THE GRAVE IS	1503	5
OF NOTHING--	BY HOMELY GIFT AND	1563	3
"NOTHING" IS THE FORCE	BY HOMELY GIFT AND	1563	4
REFORMED TO NOTHING BUT DELIGHT WHICH . .	ARROWS ENAMORED OF HIS	1629	V
ASKS NOTHING BUT RELEASE--[IT'S FLIGHT] . .	AS FROM THE EARTH THE	1630	2
BY SAYING NOTHING NEW--	EXTOL THEE--COULD I--	1643	2
NOTICE			
DEATH DID NOT NOTICE ME.	I KEEP MY PLEDGE.	46	3
I'D NOTICE NOBODY!	"SOWN IN DISHONOR"!	62	5
A RICH MAN--MIGHT NOT NOTICE IT--	I LOST A WORLD--THE	181	5
TO LIVES THAT [AS] STOOP TO NOTICE MINE-- .	HE PUT THE BELT AROUND	273	13
THOU NOTICE US--NO MORE--	WE COVER THEE--SWEET	482	6
FROM OUR FAMILIAR LIFETIME [ADDRESS / GAZING / FINGERS / NOTICE]--	THOSE FAIR--FICTITIOUS	499	3
NO NOTICE--WAS--TO ME--	TWO BUTTERFLIES WENT OUT	533	12
THAT THIS WAY--THOU COULD'ST NOTICE [SPEAK TO] ME--	IF I MAY HAVE IT, WHEN	577	21
OR ORDER, OR APPARENT ACTION [SIGNAL / NOTICE]--	FOUR TREES--UPON A	742	3
THE SUMMER GRACE, FOR NOTICE STROVE-- . .	THE BIRDS REPORTED FROM	743	9
THE NOTICE [MONITION] TO THE STARTLED GRASS	PRESENTIMENT--IS THAT	764	3
HAD IT A NOTICE [SUMMONS] FROM THE NOON . .	THIS THAT WOULD GREET--	778	5
NO NOTICE GAVE SHE, BUT A CHANGE-- . . .	NO NOTICE GAVE SHE, BUT	804	1
THAT SOME THERE BE TOO NUMB TO NOTICE . .	A SHADE UPON THE MIND	882	5
HIS NOTICE SUDDEN [INSTANT] IS--	A NARROW FELLOW IN THE	986	4
AT LENGTH THE NOTICE CAME.	THE LAST NIGHT THAT SHE	1100	20
HERE WAS NO NOTICE--NO DISSENT	GREAT STREETS OF SILENCE	1159	3
THE FLOWERS NOTICE FIRST	THE FROST WAS NEVER SEEN	1202	4
NOT HOPING FOR HIS NOTICE VAST [FAR / FINE]	BECAUSE HE LOVES HER	1229	9
THE NOTICE THAT IS CALLED THE SPRING . . .	THE NOTICE THAT IS	1310	1
NOTICED			
NOR NOTICED THAT THE EBBING DAY	A POOR--TORN HEART-- A	78	3
NOR NOTICED NIGHT DID SOFT DESCEND-- . . .	A POOR--TORN HEART-- A	78	5
THEY "NOTICED" ME--THEY NOTICED ME-- . . .	I SHOULD NOT DARE TO	205	8
THEY "NOTICED" ME--THEY NOTICED ME-- . . .	I SHOULD NOT DARE TO	205	8
NOT EITHER--NOTICED DEATH--	THEY PUT US FAR APART--	474	21
NEITHER WITNESSED [NOTICED] RISE	STRUCK, WAS I, NOR YET	925	22
WE NOTICED SMALLEST THINGS--	THE LAST NIGHT THAT SHE	1100	5
I NOTICED PEOPLE DISAPPEARED	I NOTICED PEOPLE	1149	1
NOTICES			
SHE "NOTICES," ABOVE.	MAMA NEVER FORGETS HER	164	8
NOTICING			
FOR SUCH A NOTICING--	THE GRASS SO LITTLE HAS	333	12
NOTIFIED			
WHO NOTIFIED THE NATIONS	"SIC TRANSIT GLORIA	3	39
NOTORIETY			
TO NOTORIETY.	THE LEAVES LIKE WOMEN,	987	8
OF NOTABILITY [NOTORIETY].	THE CLOVER'S SIMPLE FAME	1232	4
NOTWITHSTANDING			
AND NOTWITHSTANDING BEE--THAT WORKED-- . .	FROM COCOON FORTH A	354	18
I NOTWITHSTANDING WENT [STOLE] ABOUT . . .	A LOSS OF SOMETHING EVER	959	6
OWN [DWELL] IN EDEN NOTWITHSTANDING . . .	PARADISE IS OF THE	1069	3
NOTWITHSTANDING [TO BE SURE] A ROPE FOR A SOUVENIR	FLOSS WONT SAVE YOU FROM	1322	3
NOTWITHSTANDING [TO RETAIN] DESPAIR-- . .	NOT ANY MORE TO BE	1344	8
NOTWITHSTANDING IT NEVER BE KNOWN	TO DO A MAGNANIMOUS	1699	6
NOTWITHSTANDING IT COST US EXISTENCE ONCE .	TO DO A MAGNANIMOUS	1699	7
NOUGHT			
EXCEPT TO HEAVEN, SHE IS NOUGHT.	EXCEPT TO HEAVEN, SHE IS	154	1
'TWAS'NT LOUD, FOR HE SAID NOUGHT-- . . .	HE WAS WEAK, AND I WAS	190	7
NOUGHT--THAT [YET, IF] WE--NO POET'S KINSMAN--	HER--"LAST POEMS"--	312	16
MERRY, AND NOUGHT, AND GAY, AND NUMB-- . .	OF COURSE--I PRAYED--	376	10
THERE MAY BE--MILES ON MILES OF NOUGHT-- .	I TIE MY HAT--I CREASE	443	17
NOUGHT BUT BOQUET?	COULD--I DO MORE--FOR	447	4
JUST INFINITES OF NOUGHT--	LIKE EYES THAT LOOKED ON	458	5
TO SATIN RACES--HE IS NOUGHT--	I THINK THE HEMLOCK	525	13
HE PLIES FROM NOUGHT TO NOUGHT--	THE SPIDER HOLDS A	605	5
HE PLIES FROM NOUGHT TO NOUGHT--	THE SPIDER HOLDS A	605	5
RULER OF NOUGHT, ...	THE CHILD'S FAITH IS NEW	637	15
WITHOUT THIS--THERE IS NOUGHT--	WITHOUT THIS--THERE IS	655	1
THEIR GLORY--NOUGHT TO ME--	THEIR HIGHT IN HEAVEN	696	2
I'M THAT--OR NOUGHT--	YOU SAID THAT I "WAS	738	15
HE FOUGHT LIKE THOSE WHO'VE NOUGHT TO LOSE--	HE FOUGHT LIKE THOSE	759	1

	FIRST LINE	POEM	LINE
NOUGHT (CONTINUED)			
THAT NOUGHT BE LOST	THE CHEMICAL CONVICTION	954	2
LIKE THE REMEMBERING IT BE NOUGHT	NO OTHER CAN REDUCE	982	3
COTEMPORANEOUS NOUGHT	NO OTHER CAN REDUCE	982	6
THE OBJECT ABSOLUTE--IS NOUGHT--	PERCEPTION OF AN OBJECT	1071	5
BELIEF [WITH NOUGHT / OUR FAITH] TO REGULATE--	THE LAST NIGHT THAT SHE	1100	28
MEANT NOUGHT BUT GOING HOME--	'TWAS LATER WHEN THE	1276	4
RESPONSIBLE TO NOUGHT	A SINGLE CLOVER PLANK	1343	10
NOVEL			
SOME SAILOR, SKIRTING FOREIGN [NOVEL] SHORES--	JUST LOST, WHEN I WAS	160	9
THAT AT THE LAST, IT SHOULD NOT BE A NOVEL AGONY--	I READ MY SENTENCE--	412	10
OUR NOVEL [ROMANCE]--WHEN 'TIS SMALL ENOUGH	NO ROMANCE SOLD UNTO	669	6
AND NOVEL [SO MUCH] COMFORTING	I PLAY AT RICHES--TO	801	12
NOVEMBER			
NOVEMBER LEFT--THEN CLAMBERED UP	THE NIGHT WAS WIDE, AND	589	7
NOT A FROST COULD [NO NOVEMBER] COOL--	WHEN I HOPED, I	768	6
KEEPS MAKING NOVEMBER DIFFICULT	HOW HAPPY I WAS IF I	898	5
NOVEMBER HUNG HIS GRANITE HAT	THE DAY GREW SMALL,	1140	7
NOWHERE			
HOW MANY LEAGUES OF NOWHERE	AMBITION CANNOT FIND HIM	68	3
THE PERFECT, NOWHERE BE AFRAID--	WHEN WE STAND ON THE	242	9
TO NOWHERE--SEEMED TO GO	FROM COCOON FORTH A	354	15
NOWHERE TO HIDE MY DAZZLED FACE--	I AM ASHAMED--I HIDE--	473	4
AND ROW IN NOWHERE ALL DAY LONG	COULD I BUT RIDE	661	15
AND NOWHERE WAS TO GO--	THE FROST OF DEATH WAS	1136	19
I CLING TO NOWHERE TILL I FALL--	MORE THAN THE GRAVE IS	1503	4
NOWS			
FOREVER--IS COMPOSED OF NOWS--	FOREVER--IS COMPOSED OF	624	1
NULL			
'TIS NEWS AS NULL AS NOTHING,	MYSELF CAN READ THE	1089	7
NULLIFIED			
HOW NULLIFIED THE MEADOW--	THE WAY TO KNOW THE	1279	23
NULLIFY			
TO NULLIFY THE MINE--	I SEE THEE BETTER--IN	611	8
NULLS			
NULLS OPPORTUNITY--	NATURE CAN DO NO MORE	1673	8
NUMB			
HOAR--IS THE WINDOW--AND NUMB--THE DOOR--	SAFE IN THEIR ALABASTER	216	V
HOW NUMB [COOL], THE BELLOWS FEELS!	I BREATHED ENOUGH TO	272	8
MY MIND WAS GOING NUMB--	I FELT A FUNERAL, IN MY	280	8
PUTS RECOLLECTION NUMB--	THAT AFTER HORROR--THAT	286	8
WHEN SPEECH WENT NUMB--	UNTO LIKE STORY--TROUBLE	295	20
AND EAR--AND HEAVEN--NUMB--	LIKE SOME OLD FASHIONED	302	16
MERRY, AND NOUGHT, AND GAY, AND NUMB--	OF COURSE--I PRAYED--	376	10
I KNOW IT, BY THE NUMB LOOK	THERE'S BEEN A DEATH, IN	389	3
AND SENSE WAS SETTING NUMB--	'TWAS LIKE A MAELSTROM,	414	15
AS NUMB TO REVELATION	AS FAR FROM PITY, AS	496	3
AUGUST--ABSORBED--NUMB--[RESISTLESS--DUMB]	NO CROWD THAT HAS	515	16
THAT WHEN THEIR MORTAL NAME [FAME] BE NUMB--	THE MARTYR POETS--DID	544	3
NO NUMB ALARM--LEST DIFFERENCE COME--	I THINK TO LIVE--MAY BE	646	13
PARALYSIS--OUR PRIMER--DUMB [NUMB]--	THE ZEROES--TAUGHT US--	689	7
IS NUMB--AND VITALLESS--	I LIVED ON DREAD--	770	5
THAT SOME THERE BE TOO NUMB TO NOTICE	A SHADE UPON THE MIND	882	5
WHOSE WILL--A NUMB SIGNIFICANCE--[BLANK INTELLIGENCE]	DENIAL--IS THE ONLY FACT	965	3
I'VE DROPPED MY BRAIN--MY SOUL IS NUMB--	I'VE DROPPED MY BRAIN--	1046	1
THAN NUMB THREE SCORE AND TEN--	NOT ANY HIGHER STANDS	1256	4
NUMBER			
THE LAST--A SCANTY NUMBER--	I KNOW LIVES, I COULD	372	5
NUMBERED			
AND EVERY NIGHT, IT NUMBERED MORE	I MADE SLOW RICHES BUT	843	3
NUMBER'S			
TILL NUMBER'S EMPERY--	PRECIOUS TO ME--SHE	727	11
NUMBERS			
FROM OUT THE WIDE NIGHT'S NUMBERS--	ONE SISTER HAVE I IN OUR	14	26
FOR FEAR THE NUMBERS FUSE--	IF YOU WERE COMING IN	511	8
THEIR VOICES [NUMBERS] DID EXPEND	THE BIRDS BEGUN AT FOUR	783	6
NUMERAL			
BY MORTAL NUMERAL--	THERE IS ANOTHER	1116	8
NUMERALS			
THEN NUMERALS ARE DOWERED BACK--	'TIS ONE BY ONE--THE	545	7
NUMEROUS			
OF NUMEROUS HUMMING BIRDS AT ONCE	THE WIND--TAPPED LIKE A	436	11
MORE NUMEROUS OF WINDOWS--	I DWELL IN POSSIBILITY--	657	3
A MUSIC NUMEROUS AS SPACE [MEASURELESS AS NOON]--	THE BIRDS BEGUN AT FOUR	783	3
NUMEROUS ENOUGH--	THE HEART IS THE CAPITAL	1354	6
NUMIDIAN			
THE BUTTERFLY'S NUMIDIAN GOWN	THE BUTTERFLY'S NUMIDIAN	1387	1
NUN			
THE WAYWARD NUN--BENEATH THE HILL--	SWEET MOUNTAINS--YE TELL	722	8
REGARD A NUN--	ONLY A SHRINE, BUT MINE	918	4
NUPTIAL			
THY NUPTIAL SO MINUTE	COME SHOW THY DURHAM	1542	7
NURSE			
OR DO WHAT THE NURSE CALLS "DIE"--	WHAT IS--"PARADISE"--	215	14
'TIS "CONSCIENCE"--CHILDHOOD'S NURSE--	WHO IS IT SEEKS MY	1598	4
NURTURED			
TO RACES--NURTURED IN THE DARK--	I FOUND THE WORDS TO	581	5

	FIRST LINE	POEM	LINE
NUT			
NONE BUT THE NUT--OCTOBER FIT--	THE ROBIN'S MY CRITERION	285	10
SHE DEALT A [THE] FASHION TO THE NUT--	MY FIRST WELL DAY--SINCE	574	17
THE FIGURE OF A NUT	EXPERIMENT TO ME	1073	4
THE TAILOR OF THE NUT?	HOW FITS HIS UMBER COAT	1371	2
NUTRIMENT			
IS SWEETEST NUTRIMENT--TO HIM--	I THINK THE HEMLOCK	525	11
WHOSE POMPOUS FROWN WAS NUTRIMENT	NO BRIGADIER THROUGHOUT	1561	15
NUTRITION			
AT FIRST--A SCANT NUTRITION--[PLAIN REGALING]	DEPRIVED OF OTHER	773	3
A NUTRITION MEAN	AS THE STARVED MAELSTROM	872	12
NUTS			
THE NUTS ARE GETTING BROWN--	THE MORNS ARE MEEKER	12	2
PLAYMATES, AND HOLIDAYS, AND NUTS--	ON SUCH A NIGHT, OR SUCH	146	21
ONE SIDE OF ME THE NUTS ARE RIPE	THE ONES THAT	1690	7
O'			
IT'S TIME O' YEAR FOR HAY.	I'M SORRY FOR THE DEAD--	529	4
OAK			
WHAT WILL THE OAK [FIR] TREE SAY?	I ROBBED THE WOODS--	41	9
OAKS			
AND OWLS DO BUILD IN OAKS--	THE JUDGE IS LIKE THE	699	3
AND OAKS UNTWIST [UNKNOT / UNKNIT / UNCLINCH] THEIR FISTS--	THE TRUTH--IS STIRLESS--	780	5
OAR			
IT'S FERVOR THE ELECTRIC OAR,	'TIS NOT THE SWAYING	1597	5
WITHOUT AN OAR	DOWN TIME'S QUAINT	1656	2
OARS			
A PLASH OF OARS, A GAIETY--	I'VE KNOWN A HEAVEN,	243	16
THAN OARS DIVIDE THE OCEAN,	A BIRD CAME DOWN THE	328	17
OATH			
HER OATH, AND MINE--	I KEEP MY PLEDGE.	46	10
GOD KEEP HIS OATH [VOW] TO SPARROWS--	VICTORY COMES LATE--	690	13
THE CROWD--RETIRE WITH AN OATH--	YOU'VE SEEN BALLOONS SET	700	17
OBDURATE			
TOO OBDURATE [COMPETENT / SUMPTUOUS] FOR SNOWS--	A LITTLE SNOW WAS HERE	1444	8
OBEDIENT			
OBEDIENT TO HER EYE	THE MOON IS DISTANT FROM	429	6
OBEDIENT TO THE LEAST COMMAND	THE MOON IS DISTANT FROM	429	11
OBEISANCE			
MADE LOUD OBEISANCE AND THE GNAT	THE FINGERS OF THE LIGHT	1000	15
FLATTERED BY OBEISANCE	ABRAHAM TO KILL HIM	1317	7
OBELISK			
WHEN OBELISK DECAYS	AN HONEST TEAR	1192	8
OBEY			
THE LIFE DOTH PROVE THE PRECEPT, WHO OBEY SHALL HAPPY BE,	AWAKE YE MUSES NINE,	1	9
A SWEETER TO OBEY,	ALTHOUGH I PUT AWAY HIS	366	18
OBEYED			
BUT SIMPLY--WE--OBEYED--	"GO TELL IT"--WHAT A	1554	4
OBEYED--A LURE--A LONGING?	"GO TELL IT"--WHAT A	1554	5
OBJECT			
PERCEPTION OF AN OBJECT COSTS	PERCEPTION OF AN OBJECT	1071	1
THE OBJECT ABSOLUTE--IS NOUGHT--	PERCEPTION OF AN OBJECT	1071	5
HER MOTIVE FOR [OBJECT IN] THE SOUVENIR	I SEND YOU A DECREPIT	1324	5
THE OBJECT FLOATING AT HIS SIDE	THE WATERS CHASED HIM AS	1749	9
OBJECTION			
THEY FOUND TO OUR OBJECTION [ABHORRENCE]--	THOSE CATTLE SMALLER	1388	7
OBJECTIVE			
THIS IS THE SUN'S OBJECTIVE	THESE ARE THE DAYS THAT	1696	3
OBJECT'S			
PRECISE [MORE OFT] THE OBJECT'S LOSS--	PERCEPTION OF AN OBJECT	1071	2
OBLIGATION			
HE HAS OBLIGATION	LIFT IT--WITH THE	1348	7
REPUDIATES THE OBLIGATION--	THE RAT IS THE CONCISEST	1356	3
BUT NOT THE OBLIGATION	THE FARTHEST THUNDER	1581	11
OBLIGATIONS			
A BONE HAS OBLIGATIONS--	THE BONE THAT HAS NO	1274	5
OBLIGED			
HE WILL NOT BE OBLIGED TO WAIT	THE SOUL SHOULD ALWAYS	1055	3
OR WAS OBLIGED TO DIE	SOME DAYS RETIRED FROM	1157	4
OBLIGED TO BE INFERRED.	THE WAY TO KNOW THE	1279	4
OBLIGING			
WHILE THAT DELUSIVE [OBLIGING / ENCHANTING] HAIR	RISK IS THE HAIR THAT	1239	10
THE MOST OBLIGING TRAP	A RAT SURRENDERED HERE	1340	7
OBLIQUE			
THAT OBLIQUE BELIEF WHICH WE CALL CONJECTURE	SOME WE SEE NO MORE,	1221	6
THE SAME OBLIQUE INTEGRITY,	THE ROBIN IS A GABRIEL	1483	7
OBLIQUITY			
HAD HE OBLIQUITY	MY HEART RAN SO TO THEE	1237	11
BY OUR OBLIQUITY.	SUMMER--WE ALL HAVE SEEN	1386	V 8
OBLITERATE			
OBLITERATE THE ETCHINGS	DEATH SETS A THING	360	19
AS MISTS--OBLITERATE A CRAG.	THERE IS A LANGUOR OF	396	8
SUFFICIENT TO OBLITERATE	MORE LIFE--WENT OUT--	422	15
OBLITERATE THE NEED--	THE SOUL THAT HATH A	674	4
OBLIVION			
TO PASTURES OF OBLIVION--	A FADED BOY--IN SALLOW	1524	3
RAISED FROM OBLIVION	TO BE FORGOT BY THEE	1560	8

	FIRST LINE	POEM	LINE
OBLIVION (CONTINUED)			
OBLIVION BENDING OVER [ENFOLDING] HIM . . .	THE DITCH IS DEAR TO THE	1645	7
IN OBLIVION--	GLORY IS THAT BRIGHT	1660	7
OBLIVION'S			
WOULD DECORATE OBLIVION'S	AN ANTIQUATED TREE	1514	6
ABOVE OBLIVION'S TIDE THERE IS A PIER . .	ABOVE OBLIVION'S TIDE	1531	1
OBLIVIONS			
WHOLE CHAOSES [OBLIVIONS] ON HIM--	A PLATED LIFE--	806	8
OBLOQUIES			
THE OBLOQUIES OF ETIQUETTE	THEIR DAPPLED	1611	3
OBLOQUY			
LIKE AN OBLOQUY--	WHEN A LOVER IS A BEGGAR	1314	8
OBSCURE			
AND THEN--OBSCURE WITH FOG--	I'VE SEEN A DYING EYE	547	5
THAT OBSCURE [DIVIDE] HER FACE--	HER SWEET TURN TO LEAVE	649	26
REMOTE [ASTUTE / OBSCURE] TO UNDERSTAND . .	NATURE AFFECTS TO BE	1170	6
OBSCURED			
THAT SOMETHING--HAD OBSCURED [BEMUMBED] THE TRACK--	IT CEASED TO HURT ME,	584	4
OBSCURED WITH RUDDIER [NEARER / COMELIER] BLUE--	ONE BLESSING HAD I THAN	756	14
FOR FREQUENT [OFTEN], ALL MY SENSE OBSCURED	WHAT I SEE NOT, I BETTER	939	5
BY BLESSED HEALTH OBSCURED--	AS ONE DOES SICKNESS	957	4
OBSCURES			
I KNOW THE WHOLE--OBSCURES THE PART-- . .	PRECIOUS TO ME--SHE	727	9
OBSCURING			
THEY EMERGE FROM HIS OBSCURING--	COLOR--CASTE--	970	13
CURTAILED BY YOUR OBSCURING [REMOVING] FACE	BECAUSE THAT YOU ARE	1260	27
OBSEQUIOUS			
OBSEQUIOUS ANGELS WAIT!	WAIT TILL THE MAJESTY OF	171	10
OBSERVATION			
UNFULFILLED TO OBSERVATION--	UNFULFILLED TO	972	1
HIS OBSERVATION OMNIFOLD, ...	THE MOUNTAIN SAT UPON	975	3
REPEALED FROM OBSERVATION--	AS SLEIGH BELLS SEEM IN	981	5
BUT LET OUR OBSERVATION SHUT [HALT] . . .	NATURE AFFECTS TO BE	1170	3
OBSERVE			
WHO FALL--AND NONE OBSERVE--	TO FIGHT ALOUD, IS VERY	126	6
OBSERVE--"'TWAS ONLY A BALLOON"--	YOU'VE SEEN BALLOONS SET	700	20
OBSERVED			
WHO FIRST OBSERVED THE MOON!	"SIC TRANSIT GLORIA	3	12
OR SUN'S EXTINCTION, BE OBSERVED	THE MISSING ALL,	985	5
FATHER I OBSERVED TO HEAVEN	LIGHTLY STEPPED A YELLOW	1672	7
OBSERVING			
THIS BIRD--OBSERVING OTHERS	ALL OVERGROWN BY CUNNING	148	5
OBSOLETE			
ARE OBSOLETE TO BLISS--	THEIR DAPPLED	1611	4
OBSTACLE			
AN OBSTACLE IS GIVEN	LEST THIS BE HEAVEN	1043	2
WITH FORTITUDE OF OBSTACLE	TO UNDERTAKE IS TO	1070	3
OBSTRUCTS			
TILL DUSK OBSTRUCTS THE DILIGENCE-- . . .	SHE SWEEPS WITH	219	V 11
OBTAIN			
BEFORE WE MAY OBTAIN?	IT FEELS A SHAME TO BE	444	12
COULD NOT OBTAIN FOR ME--	I ENVY SEAS, WHEREON HE	498	16
THE FROST--POSSESS [OBTAIN] THE WORLD-- . .	HE PARTS HIMSELF--LIKE	517	17
FOR THAT NO MAN OBTAIN	HAD I PRESUMED TO HOPE--	522	14
TO OBTAIN THE SKY--	HER SWEET TURN TO LEAVE	649	20
"WHICH OBTAIN [CONTROLLED / CONTROL] THE DAY"?	WOLFE DEMANDED DURING	678	2
THE GRACE--MYSELF--MIGHT NOT OBTAIN-- . .	THE GRACE--MYSELF--MIGHT	707	1
TO SOME DULL COMFORT THOSE OBTAIN	SEVERER SERVICE OF	786	13
WHO COURT OBTAIN WITHIN HIMSELF	WHO COURT OBTAIN WITHIN	803	1
ALL PRIZES TO OBTAIN--	HOW FORTUNATE THE GRAVE	897	2
BUT GAIN--THRO' LOSS--THROUGH GRIEF [PAIN]--OBTAIN--	FITTER TO SEE HIM, I MAY	968	26
OBTAIN IT'S RIGHT OF DEW--	BLOOM--IS RESULT--TO	1058	10
OBTAIN "ADMISSION" AS A CHILD	DEW--IS THE FRESHET IN	1097	11
DO ONE ADVANCE [OBTAIN] SO NEAR	THE MERCHANT OF THE	1131	10
A FUNCTION FRESH OBTAIN?	THE BONE THAT HAS NO	1274	10
OBTAINED			
THROUGH SKILL OBTAINED IN THEMSELVES-- . .	THE PROVINCE OF THE	539	3
AND SATISFY--OBTAINED--	UNTO MY BOOKS--SO GOOD	604	16
OBTAINED [ENGROSSED] MY LODGINGS, ERE MYSELF--	BEREAVED OF ALL, I WENT	784	5
ETERNITY--OBTAINED--IN TIME--	TWO--WERE IMMORTAL TWICE	800	3
LED ABSENT, WERE PROCURED [OBTAINED] OF HEAVEN	TWO TRAVELLERS PERISHING	933	15
THE LEAVES OBTAINED EXCUSE--	THE DAY GREW SMALL,	1140	6
DOMINION LASTS UNTIL OBTAINED--	DOMINION LASTS UNTIL	1257	1
BUT TIME HAD ADDED NOT OBTAINED	A LITTLE SNOW WAS HERE	1444	5
OBTAINING			
OBTAINING BUT OUR [HIS] OWN EXTENT . . .	OBTAINING BUT OUR OWN	1543	1
OBTAINS			
OBTAINS AT A CORPOREAL COST--	THE HALLOWING OF PAIN	772	3
HE FATHOMS WHO OBTAINS.	I CANNOT WANT IT MORE--	1301	8
THE BUTTERFLY OBTAINS	THE BUTTERFLY OBTAINS	1685	1
OBTRUDE			
PRESENT [OBTRUDE] NO MORE--	THE SOUL SELECTS HER OWN	303	4
OBTUSER			
AS MAKE OF [BREW FROM / MIX] OUR IMPERFECT [UNCOMELY / OBTUSER] . . .	SHE HIDETH HER THE LAST	557	11
OBVIATE			
OBVIATE PARADE.	THE GENTIAN WEAVES HER	18	4

	FIRST LINE	POEM	LINE
OBVIATED			
NOT OBVIATED OF DEGREE--	CONJECTURING A CLIMATE	562	7
JUST OBVIATED BUD--	HE GAVE AWAY HIS LIFE--	567	14
OCCASION			
WHEN FRIEND--AND EARTH'S OCCASION	THE SOUL'S SUPERIOR	306	3
THIS--WAS MY FINALLEST OCCASION--	THE FIRST DAY THAT I WAS	902	9
SHE ROSE AS HIGH AS HIS OCCASION	SHE ROSE AS HIGH AS HIS	1011	1
FOR DREAD OCCASION PLANNED	A GREAT HOPE FELL	1123	7
UPON OCCASION, GRAND	NATURE AFFECTS TO BE	1170	2
OCCASIONAL			
AND DEAL OCCASIONAL SMILES	HE PUT THE BELT AROUND	273	12
WITH AN OCCASIONAL STEEPLE--	THE WIND DID'NT COME	316	19
BUT THAT'S--OCCASIONAL--	THE ANGLE OF A LANDSCAPE	375	12
EXCEPT OCCASIONAL MAN--	THE BIRDS BEGUN AT FOUR	783	10
OCCASIONALLY			
THE STARS DARE SHINE OCCASIONALLY	WHEN WE STAND ON THE	242	13
IT IS--OCCASIONALLY--	WE DO NOT PLAY ON GRAVES	467	12
STAMPED--OCCASIONALLY--[IN INSTANCES] FOREVER--	SO THE EYES ACCOST--AND	752	3
OCCASIONALLY RIDES--	A NARROW FELLOW IN THE	986	2
OCCASIONS			
A SICKNESS OF THIS WORLD IT MOST OCCASIONS	A SICKNESS OF THIS WORLD	1044	1
NOT WANT OF FRIEND OCCASIONS IT	THERE IS ANOTHER	1116	3
OCCIDENT			
AND OCCIDENT--BECOME UNKNOWN--	THE ONE WHO COULD REPEAT	307	8
THE LADY OF THE OCCIDENT	THE DAY UNDRESSED--	716	11
THE IRIS NOT OF OCCIDENT	FAME IS THE TINT THAT	866	3
THE FLOWER OF OCCIDENT.	THE LILAC IS AN ANCIENT	1241	8
OCCIDENTAL			
AN OCCIDENTAL TOWN,	THE LARGEST FIRE EVER	1114	6
OCCUPANT			
IT'S OCCUPANT MUST DIE	FAME IS THE ONE THAT	1475	2
EACH OCCUPANT AN EARL	NO LIFE CAN POMPLESS	1626	V 8
OCCUPANTS			
THE OCCUPANTS OF THESE ABODES--	HAVE ANY LIKE MYSELF	736	11
OCCUPATION			
FOR OCCUPATION--THIS--	I DWELL IN POSSIBILITY--	657	10
OCCUPIED			
OCCUPIED WITH SHOT	PAIN--EXPANDS THE TIME--	967	6
OCCUPIED BY EACH AN INSTANT	PARADISE IS THAT OLD	1119	3
HAD OCCUPIED THE HOUSE--	IT CAME AT LAST BUT	1230	2
WHEN I AM OCCUPIED--	DEAR MARCH--COME IN--	1320	22
IF THEY BE OCCUPIED	AS WE PASS HOUSES MUSING	1653	2
IF THEY BE OCCUPIED	AS WE PASS HOUSES MUSING	1653	4
OCCUPIES			
WHO OCCUPIES THIS HOUSE?	WHO OCCUPIES THIS HOUSE?	892	1
OCCUPY			
WE--OCCUPY--DEGREE [TOO--PARTAKE]--	WE TALKED AS GIRLS DO--	586	12
OCCUPY MY HOUSE [BREAST]"--	"UNTO ME?" I DO NOT KNOW	964	12
TO OCCUPY.	A SICKNESS OF THIS WORLD	1044	4
OCCUPY TO US THOUGH PERHAPS TO THEM	SOME WE SEE NO MORE,	1221	2
OCCUPYING			
EVER HE MINDED OCCUPYING	NO BOBOLINK--REVERSE HIS	755	3
OCCUR			
OCCUR TO HER--ALONE--	THE SOUL'S SUPERIOR	306	2
OCCURRED			
MORNING HAS NOT OCCURRED!	SLEEP IS SUPPOSED TO BE	13	10
NO CROWD THAT HAS OCCURRED	NO CROWD THAT HAS	515	1
A THING OCCURRED	IN WINTER IN MY ROOM	1670	11
OCCURS			
OCCURS EACH AFTERNOON--	THE LARGEST FIRE EVER	1114	2
OCEAN			
THE OCEAN--SMILES--AT HER CONCEIT--	THE DROP, THAT WRESTLES	284	7
THAN OARS DIVIDE THE OCEAN,	A BIRD CAME DOWN THE	328	17
THE WAVES GREW SLEEPY--[THE OCEAN--TIRED-- / THE OCEAN-- . . .	THREE TIMES--WE PARTED--	598	13
THE WAVES GREW SLEEPY--[THE OCEAN--TIRED-- / THE OCEAN-- . . .	THREE TIMES--WE PARTED--	598	13
THE SECOND [SILENCE] LIKE AN OCEAN ROLLED	I YEARS HAD BEEN FROM	609	11
EDIFICE [ARCHITECT] OF OCEAN	FORTITUDE INCARNATE	1217	9
OCEAN'S			
THE OCEAN'S HEART TOO SMOOTH--TOO BLUE--	IT TOSSED--AND TOSSED--	723	11
OCEANS			
LAND--BY THE OCEANS PASSED.	WATER, IS TAUGHT BY	135	2
WHILE OCEANS--AND THE NORTH MUST BE-- [DID PLAY]	OURSELVES WERE WED ONE	631	11
THAT OCEANS ARE--AND PRAYER--	I CANNOT LIVE WITH YOU--	640	48
THAN WHEN WITHELD OF OCEANS	WE MISS A KINSMAN MORE	1087	3
AIRS NO OCEANS KEEP--	I THINK THAT THE ROOT OF	1302	4
O'CLOCK			
THE DAY CAME SLOW--TILL FIVE O'CLOCK--	THE DAY CAME SLOW--TILL	304	1
THE TIME 'TWILL BE TILL SIX O'CLOCK	I TIE MY HAT--I CREASE	443	9
AT WHAT O'CLOCK TO HEAVEN--THEY FLED--	WE PRAY--TO HEAVEN--	489	4
THE BIRDS BEGUN AT FOUR O'CLOCK--	THE BIRDS BEGUN AT FOUR	783	1
OCTAVE'S			
HOLD ME TILL THE OCTAVE'S RUN!	DYING AT MY MUSIC!	1003	3
OCTOBER			
NONE BUT THE NUT--OCTOBER FIT--	THE ROBIN'S MY CRITERION	285	10
IN [ON] FAR [STILL] OCTOBER AIR.	THERE ARE TWO RIPENINGS	332	8
BEGINNING IN OCTOBER	SUMMER HAS TWO	1422	3

	FIRST LINE	POEM	LINE
ODD			
TILL SOME ODD AFTERNOON	OUR LIVES ARE SWISS--	80	3
ODD SECRETS OF THE LINE TO TELL!	JUST LOST, WHEN I WAS	160	8
HOW ODD THE GIRL'S LIFE LOOKS	I'M "WIFE"--I'VE	199	5
AND THE ODD FLAMBEAU, NO MEN CARRY	HOW THE OLD MOUNTAINS	291	15
IN SOME ODD FASHION [PATTERN] OF IT'S OWN,	OF ALL THE SOUNDS	321	19
AND SOMETHING'S ODD--WITHIN--	THE FIRST DAY'S NIGHT	410	17
BUT SOMETHING AWKWARD IN [ODD ABOUT] THE FIT--	I COULD NOT PROVE THE	563	11
MYSELF FELT ILL--AND ODD--	I HAD BEEN HUNGRY, ALL	579	14
OF LIFE? 'TWERE ODD I FEAR A THING	AFRAID! OF WHOM AM I	608	5
TO THAT ODD FORK IN BEING'S ROAD--	OUR JOURNEY HAD ADVANCED	615	3
OF OPPOSITE--TO BALANCE ODD [EQUAL OUGHT]--	THE ZEROES--TAUGHT US--	689	5
THAT ODD OLD MAN IS DEAD A YEAR--	THAT ODD OLD MAN IS DEAD	1130	1
ODDEST			
ODDEST OF SCIENCES--BOOK EVER BORE--	KNOWS HOW TO FORGET!	433	10
ODDITY			
I--SHOULD DIE OF THE ODDITY--	FUNNY--TO BE A CENTURY--	345	3
BLISS--WERE AN ODDITY--WITHOUT THEE--	LOVE--THOU ART HIGH--	453	16
WHEN DIMNESS--LOOKS THE ODDITY--	OF NEARNESS TO HER	607	3
ODE			
THE ODE FAMILIAR--RULES THE NOON--	THE ROBIN'S MY CRITERION	285	5
ODIOUSER			
OR ODIOUSER [FATALLER / OTHERWISE] OFFEND--	THOSE CATTLE SMALLER	1388	12
ODOR			
THEY HAVE A LITTLE ODOR--THAT TO ME	THEY HAVE A LITTLE ODOR	785	1
ODORLESS			
AS CASUAL [ODORLESS / INNOCENT] AS RAIN	THE GENTIAN HAS A	1424	6
ODORS			
FERN ODORS ON UNTRAVELLED ROADS--	AN ALTERED LOOK ABOUT	140	12
KILL YOUR BALM--AND IT'S ODORS BLESS YOU--	KILL YOUR BALM--AND IT'S	238	1
IF HE BRING ODORS OF CLOVERS--	THE WIND DID'NT COME	316	11
IN ODORS SO DIVINE--	THE GRASS SO LITTLE HAS	333	14
AND ODORS FALL	I TEND MY FLOWERS FOR	339	13
I COULD BRING YOU ODORS FROM ST DOMINGO--	I COULD BRING YOU JEWELS	697	3
OF SPICE--I INFER FROM THE ODORS BORNE--	BY MY WINDOW HAVE I FOR	797	12
ODORS RETURN WHOLE	BANISH AIR FROM AIR--	854	8
O'ER			
I "VIEW THE LANDSCAPE O'ER;"	"SIC TRANSIT GLORIA	3	22
A SAILING O'ER THE TIDE,	"SIC TRANSIT GLORIA	3	38
AND ROW MY BLOSSOMS O'ER!	SUMMER FOR THEE, GRANT I	31	6
HER GHOST STROLLED SOFTLY O'ER THE HILL	SHE DIED AT PLAY,	75	6
AND VIEW THE LANDSCAPE O'ER"	WHERE BELLS NO MORE	112	10
THE LOVER--HOVERED--O'ER--	THE SOUL HAS BANDAGED	512	8
I SCANNED THE WINDOWS O'ER--	I YEARS HAD BEEN FROM	609	V 10
O'ER THE CURLS ATTEMPT TO CAPER	HER SWEET TURN TO LEAVE	649	7
WERE HE TO COUNT THEM O'ER	EACH SCAR I'LL KEEP FOR	877	6
THE TURNING O'ER AND O'ER MY FACE	FITTER TO SEE HIM, I MAY	968	11
THE TURNING O'ER AND O'ER MY FACE	FITTER TO SEE HIM, I MAY	968	11
AS WILLING LID O'ER WEARY EYE	AS WILLING LID O'ER	1050	1
CREATION O'ER--	THE GENTIAN HAS A	1424	17
THAT SEPULTURE IS O'ER.	THE DANDELION'S PALLID	1519	8
BUT OFT HAS SCANNED ME O'ER--	MY WARS ARE LAID AWAY IN	1549	4
OER			
WHERE THE STORM IS OER?	ON THIS WONDROUS SEA	4	6
TO CON THEE OER AND OER--	WE COVER THEE--SWEET	482	8
TO CON THEE OER AND OER--	WE COVER THEE--SWEET	482	8
O'ERLOOKING			
O'ERLOOKING [MAINTAINING] A SUPERIOR SPECTRE--	ONE NEED NOT BE A	670	19
O'ERPOWERED			
O'ERPOWERED BY THE CAT!	PAPA ABOVE!	61	3
O'ERSPENT			
ONE LITTLE BOAT--O'ERSPENT WITH GALES--	ADRIFT! A LITTLE BOAT	30	11
O'ERTAKELESS			
O'ERTAKELESS, AS THE AIR--	HOW NOTELESS MEN, AND	282	8
O'ERTOOK			
A LITTLE BRIG I KNEW--O'ERTOOK BY BLAST--	IT TOSSED--AND TOSSED--	723	2
OFF			
FROM OFF MY FATHER'S TREE!	"SIC TRANSIT GLORIA	3	20
FROM OFF HIS CHAMBER DOOR--	SEXTON! MY MASTER'S	96	6
WHAT IF I FILE THIS MORTAL--OFF--	WHAT IF I SAY I SHALL	277	4
I KNOW SOME LONELY HOUSES OFF THE ROAD	I KNOW SOME LONELY	289	1
OFF [ON] DESERTS, IN THE SKY,	OF ALL THE SOUNDS	321	30
OR BUTTERFLIES, OFF BANKS OF NOON	A BIRD CAME DOWN THE	328	19
DRUMS OFF THE PHANTOM BATTLEMENTS	OVER AND OVER, LIKE A	367	3
FAR OFF--HE SIGHS--AND THEREFORE--HOPELESS--	UNDUE SIGNIFICANCE A	439	3
SO SHORT WAY OFF IT SEEMS--	IF ANYBODY'S FRIEND BE	509	11
THAT CRAWLED LEAGUES OFF--I LIKED TO SEE--	THREE TIMES--WE PARTED--	598	9
THEN [I] MOVED MY FINGERS OFF	I YEARS HAD BEEN FROM	609	21
AND WHEN THE DEWS DREW OFF	I ROSE--BECAUSE HE SANK	616	8
WHAT ONE BROKE OFF WITH	TO KNOW JUST HOW HE	622	20
SHE'D PASS FOR BAREHEAD--SHORT WAY OFF--	YOU'LL KNOW HER--BY HER	634	15
AND THEN I GO THE FURTHEST OFF	THE WAY I READ A	636	5
AND ANCHOR "OFF THE BAR"	COULD I BUT RIDE	661	16
EATS OFF THE BRITTLE LINE--	I SOMETIMES DROP IT, FOR	708	14
AND THAT ASSEMBLY [COMPANION]--NOT FAR OFF	ON A COLUMNAR SELF--	789	11
WHAT WHEN THE EGGS FLY OFF IN MUSIC	WHAT SHALL I DO WHEN THE	956	3
JUST LAYING OFF FOR EVIDENCE	DEATH IS A DIALOGUE	976	7
WHERE TAX ASLEEP AND TITLE OFF	ALONE AND IN A	1167	13
SO I PULL MY STOCKINGS OFF	SO I PULL MY STOCKINGS	1201	1
TO PUT OFF FILAMENTS LIKE THIS	WITH PINIONS OF DISDAIN	1431	11

	FIRST LINE	POEM	LINE
OFF (CONTINUED)			
TILL ASKED TO TAKE IT OFF--	WE KNEW NOT THAT WE WERE	1462	6
TO MEASURE OFF ANOTHER DAY	APPARENTLY WITH NO	1624	7
WERE FURTHER OFF	I DID NOT REACH THEE	1664	25
FROM MATHEMATICS FURTHER OFF	IF I COULD TELL HOW GLAD	1668	7
THE WIND DREW OFF	THE WIND DREW OFF	1694	1
IF EVER THE LID GETS OFF MY HEAD	IF EVER THE LID GETS OFF	1727	1
OFFENCE			
ENTOMBED BY WHOM, FOR WHAT OFFENCE	IT WAS A GRAVE, YET BORE	876	5
WITHOUT OFFENCE [OPPRESS] OF TOLL--	THERE IS NO FRIGATE LIKE	1263	6
OFFEND			
OFFEND THE VISION--AND IT FLEE--	WHY MAKE IT DOUBT--IT	462	10
OR ODIOUSER [FATALLER / OTHERWISE] OFFEND--	THOSE CATTLE SMALLER	1388	12
OFFENDED			
MY SOVREIGN IS OFFENDED--	THE COURT IS FAR AWAY--	235	3
OFFENDED [INSULTED / ASSAULTED] BY THE WIND--	SHE SPED AS PETALS OF A	991	2
OFFENSE			
FOR AN OFFENSE NOR HERE NOR THERE [ANYWHERE]	ALONE AND IN A	1167	23
OFFER			
TO OFFER WHOM A CHAIR	THE WIND--TAPPED LIKE A	436	6
I ARGUE [OFFER] THEE	THAT I DID ALWAYS LOVE	549	6
I OFFER THEM THE WHOLE [HALF] OF HEAVEN	I CROSS TILL I AM WEARY	550	20
HAD HE THE OFFER OF--	YOU LEFT ME--SIRE--TWO	644	4
TO OFFER BRAVE ASSISTANCE	TO OFFER BRAVE	767	1
AND OFFER A REWARD	WHAT DID THEY DO SINCE I	900	14
THE LOVE YOU OFFER--	I CANNOT BE ASHAMED	914	3
I OFFER EVEN THAT--	TOO SCANTY 'TWAS TO DIE	1013	4
SHIPS--OFFER THESE--	EXCEPT THE SMALLER SIZE	1067	V
LUCRATIVE INDEED THE OFFER [THE PROPOSITION]	"FAITHFUL TO THE END"	1357	V
OFFERED			
I OFFERED HIM A CRUMB	A BIRD CAME DOWN THE	328	14
I OFFERED IT NO HELP--	LIKE EYES THAT LOOKED ON	458	9
I OFFERED BEING--FOR IT--	I ASKED NO OTHER THING--	621	3
I OFFERED HER NO WORD--	THE BIRDS REPORTED FROM	743	18
THEN OFFERED AS A BUTTERFLY	BLOOM--IS RESULT--TO	1058	7
ARKS OF REPRIEVE HE OFFERED [OPENED] TO US--	WE TALKED WITH EACH	1473	7
OFFERING			
BY SUCH AND SUCH AN OFFERING	BY SUCH AND SUCH AN	38	1
SHE KNOWS HERSELF AN INCENSE [OFFERING] SMALL--	THE DROP, THAT WRESTLES	284	4
EXHALE IN OFFERING.	EXHILIRATION--IS WITHIN	383	12
OFFERS			
HE OFFERS [SPICES / FLAVORS] HIS BERRY, JUST THE SAME	THE BLACK BERRY--WEARS A	554	3
OFFICE			
HIS OFFICE--BUT TO EXECUTE	THE FUTURE--NEVER SPOKE	672	11
OFFICERS			
WILL CONCENTRATE IT'S OFFICERS--	THE RIGHT TO PERISH	1692	5
OFT			
OFT A HEAD IS CRESTED	FREQUENTLY THE WOODS ARE	6	5
AND AS OFT A CRANNY	FREQUENTLY THE WOODS ARE	6	7
AS OFT AS HE GO DOWN	WE CAN BUT FOLLOW TO THE	920	2
PRECISE [MORE OFT] THE OBJECT'S LOSS--	PERCEPTION OF AN OBJECT	1071	2
MISTAKEN OFT HAS BEEN	DELIGHT'S DESPAIR AT	1299	6
A DEVOTEE HAS OFT [COOL / BLAND] CONSIGNED	DEATH WARRANTS ARE	1375	5
FOR LIGHTNING IT IS OFT MISTOOK	A WINGED SPARK DOTH SOAR	1468	3
BUT OFT HAS SCANNED ME O'ER--	MY WARS ARE LAID AWAY IN	1549	4
OFTEN			
BANDITTI OFTEN PASSED US	THROUGH LANE IT LAY--	9	3
I OFTEN PASSED THE VILLAGE	I OFTEN PASSED THE	51	1
AND THE BRIDGES OFTEN GO--	HAVE YOU GOT A BROOK IN	136	12
EARLY AGED, AND OFTEN COLD,	SOME, TOO FRAGILE FOR	141	10
SHE LOOKS DOWN JUST AS OFTEN	MAMA NEVER FORGETS HER	164	3
STROKE THE COOL FOREHEAD--HOT SO OFTEN--	HOW MANY TIMES THESE LOW	187	5
TOO OFTEN AT HER DOOR--	THE FLOWER MUST NOT	206	3
SOMETIMES--NOT OFTEN--IN ETERNITY--	ONE YEAR AGO--JOTS WHAT?	296	7
I'M OFTEN THIRSTY--BUT MY LIPS	I KNOW WHERE WELLS GROW	460	11
WERE GOING--I HAD OFTEN THOUGHT	I WAS THE SLIGHTEST IN	486	16
AND OFTEN SINCE, IN DANGER,	I PRAYED, AT FIRST, A	576	14
THE BIRDS AND I, HAD OFTEN SHARED	I HAD BEEN HUNGRY, ALL	579	11
THAT OFTEN AS A CLOUD IT MET--	THE NIGHT WAS WIDE, AND	589	3
FOR OFTEN, OVERBOLD	I PLAY AT RICHES--TO	801	4
BUT OFTEN AS MY LOT DISPLAYS	I PLAY AT RICHES--TO	801	9
SETTLERS OFTEN DO	WHO OCCUPIES THIS HOUSE?	892	22
OFTEN AS I DIE	STRUCK, WAS I, NOR YET	925	18
FOR FREQUENT [OFTEN], ALL MY SENSE OBSCURED	WHAT I SEE NOT, I BETTER	939	5
HOW OFTEN FOUNDERING AT SEA	A GREAT HOPE FELL	1123	8
I OFTEN IN THE NIGHT [MY SLEEP]	ESCAPE IS SUCH A	1347	2
I OFTEN WONDER HE	WHAT MYSTERY PERVADES A	1400	10
IS OFTEN SEEN--BUT SELDOM FELT,	A FIELD OF STUBBLE,	1407	7
AS OFTEN AS A CENTURY	MEETING BY ACCIDENT,	1548	3
I'VE OFTEN SEEN THEM PLAY	NO BRIGADIER THROUGHOUT	1561	10
OFTENER			
DIE OFTENER--NOT SO VITALLY--	NATURE--SOMETIMES SEARS	314	8
THE SHORTER FATE--IS OFTENER THE CHIEFEST	UNCERTAIN LEASE--	857	5
OFTENER THROUGH REALM OF BRIAR	FAR FROM LOVE THE	1021	3
OFTENER BY THE CLAW OF DRAGON	FAR FROM LOVE THE	1021	5
OFTENTIMES			
BUT OFTENTIMES, AMONG MY MIND,	I CANNOT DANCE UPON MY	326	3

	FIRST LINE	POEM	LINE
OGLE			
NOR THREATEN [JOGGLE / OGLE] A HAT--	THE WIND DID'NT COME	316	4
OH			
OH THE EARTH WAS MADE FOR LOVERS, FOR DAMSEL, AND HOPELESS SWAIN,	AWAKE YE MUSES NINE,	1	3
OH "VENI, VIDI, VICI!"	"SIC TRANSIT GLORIA	3	5
OH CAPUT CAP-A-PIE!	"SIC TRANSIT GLORIA	3	6
AND OH "MEMENTO MORI"	"SIC TRANSIT GLORIA	3	7
IF RECOLLECTING [OH IF REMEMBERING] WERE FORGETTING,	IF RECOLLECTING WERE	33	1
YOUR PRAYERS, OH PASSER BY!	A DAY! HELP! HELP!	42	2
OH LAGGING YESTERDAY!	DELAYED TILL SHE HAD	58	6
OH IF THERE MAY DEPARTING [REMAINING] BE	DELAYED TILL SHE HAD	58	13
"OH LORD--HOW FRAIL ARE WE"!	"ARCTURUS" IS HIS OTHER	70	8
AH [OH] BUGLE! BY MY [THE] WINDOW	HEART, NOT SO HEAVY AS	83	19
OH SOME SCHOLAR! OH SOME SAILOR!	WILL THERE REALLY BE A	101	9
OH SOME SCHOLAR! OH SOME SAILOR!	WILL THERE REALLY BE A	101	9
OH SOME WISE MAN FROM THE SKIES!	WILL THERE REALLY BE A	101	10
WHEREFORE, OH SUMMER'S DAY?	THE BEE IS NOT AFRAID OF	111	8
"OH COULD WE CLIMB WHERE MOSES STOOD,	WHERE BELLS NO MORE	112	9
OH INCOGNITO!	GOOD NIGHT, BECAUSE WE	114	4
OH BATTLE PICTURESQUE!	MY FRIEND ATTACKS MY	118	2
OH LET ME IMMEDIATELY "FADE"!	IF THIS IS "FADING"	120	2
OH FRAUD THAT CANNOT CHEAT THE BEE--	THESE ARE THE DAYS WHEN	130	7
OH SACRAMENT OF SUMMER DAYS,	THESE ARE THE DAYS WHEN	130	13
OH LAST COMMUNION IN THE HAZE--	THESE ARE THE DAYS WHEN	130	14
GRANT ME, OH LORD, A SUNNY MIND--	BESIDES THE AUTUMN POETS	131	15
SO QUIET--OH HOW QUIET,	ON SUCH A NIGHT, OR SUCH	146	5
OH WHAT AN AFTERNOON FOR HEAVEN,	ALL OVERGROWN BY CUNNING	148	V
OH SEA--LOOK GRACIOUSLY--	MY RIVER RUNS TO THEE--	162	4
AND IF I GAIN! OH GUN AT SEA!	'TIS SO MUCH JOY! 'TIS	172	13
OH BELLS, THAT IN THE STEEPLES BE!	'TIS SO MUCH JOY! 'TIS	172	14
OH FIND IT--SIR--FOR ME!	I LOST A WORLD--THE	181	8
BUT, OH, SO HIGH!	WE DONT CRY--TIM AND I,	196	14
OH GOD! THE OTHER ONE!	TWO SWIMMERS WRESTLED ON	201	4
OH HOUSEWIFE IN THE EVENING WEST--	SHE SWEEPS WITH	219	3
OH, COULD YOU CATCH HER LAST REFRAIN--	KILL YOUR BALM--AND IT'S	238	6
OH, IF I--WERE THE GENTLEMAN	WHY--DO THEY SHUT ME OUT	248	9
OH, DEAR,--I GUESS IF HE WERE A BOY--	OVER THE FENCE--	251	8
OH, WOULDN'T YOU?	DID WE DISOBEY HIM?	267	8
OH, CAVILER, FOR YOU!	DOUBT ME! MY DIM	275	25
OH, HAD YOU TOLD ME SO--	ONE YEAR AGO--JOTS WHAT?	296	15
OH, GROPING FEET--	NOT PROBABLE--THE BAREST	346	9
OH PHANTOM QUEEN!	NOT PROBABLE--THE BAREST	346	10
OH PUNISH--PRAY--	'TWAS LOVE--NOT ME--	394	2
OH, SIGNOR, THINE, THE AMBER HAND--	THE MOON IS DISTANT FROM	429	9
OH, MASTER, THIS IS MISERY--	WHY MAKE IT DOUBT--IT	462	13
OH JESUS--IN THE AIR--	AT LEAST--TO PRAY--IS	502	2
OH LOVER--LIFE COULD NOT CONVINCE--	ME PROVE IT NOW--WHOEVER	537	7
OH, REWARD [RECOMPENSE] OF ANGUISH,	IN FALLING TIMBERS	614	11
AND OH, THE SHOWER OF STAIN--	THE NAME--OF IT--IS	656	6
OH MAGNANIMITY--	A DROP FELL ON THE APPLE	794	V
OH THOU CELESTIAL HOST--	GIVEN IN MARRIAGE UNTO	817	2
OH POOR AND FAR--	THE SUN AND MOON MUST	871	9
OH HINDERED EYE	THE SUN AND MOON MUST	871	10
OH GOD	A SHADE UPON THE MIND	882	6
OH, FOR A BEE'S EXPERIENCE	HIS FEET ARE SHOD WITH	916	7
OH FOR A DISC TO THE DISTANCE	UNDER THE LIGHT, YET	949	15
OH, WHEN THE SQUIRREL FILLS HIS POCKETS	WHAT SHALL I DO WHEN THE	956	9
OH, HAPPY AIR!	AIR HAS NO RESIDENCE, NO	1060	4
LET DOWN THE BARS, OH DEATH--	LET DOWN THE BARS, OH	1065	1
JUST ONCE! OH LEAST REQUEST!	JUST ONCE! OH LEAST	1076	1
OH THE VIEW	WHAT TWIGS WE HELD BY--	1086	2
OH THE AUDACITY [POMPOSITY]--	THAT THIS SHOULD FEEL	1112	7
OH CUNNING WRECK THAT TOLD NO TALE	A GREAT HOPE FELL	1123	4
OH SUMPTUOUS MOMENT	OH SUMPTUOUS MOMENT	1125	1
OH LIFE, BEGUN IN FLUENT BLOOD	THAT ODD OLD MAN IS DEAD	1130	9
OH CHEEK [HEART] WITHIN THE COAL	THE SMOULDERING EMBERS	1132	2
OH SUN--BUT JUST A SECOND'S RIGHT	MY GOD--HE SEES THEE--	1178	8
OH HOSPITALITY [MAGNANIMITY]!	"REMEMBER ME" IMPLORED	1180	2
OH THOU ALMIGHTY GOD!	REMEMBRANCE HAS A	1182	V 8
OH SHADOW ON THE GRASS,	OH SHADOW ON THE GRASS,	1187	1
OH SHADOW ON THE GRASS	OH SHADOW ON THE GRASS,	1187	5
OH UNELECTED FACE--	OH SHADOW ON THE GRASS,	1187	8
OH FAITHFUL FROST [SLEET] THAT KEPT THE DATE	IT CAME AT LAST BUT	1230	5
OH GOD OF WIDTH, DO NOT FOR US	SOMEWHERE UPON THE	1231	11
OH, THOU UNKNOWN RENOWN	THAT SHORT--POTENTIAL	1307	6
OH DISPARITY--	WHEN A LOVER IS A BEGGAR	1314	6
OH MARCH, COME RIGHT UP STAIRS WITH ME--	DEAR MARCH--COME IN--	1320	9
OH, SUBSIDY OF BALM!	UNTO THE WHOLE--HOW ADD?	1341	4
OH GIVE IT MOTION--DECK IT SWEET	OH GIVE IT MOTION--DECK	1527	1
OH NO, BUT ON SOME OTHER FLIGHT--	WITHIN THY GRAVE!	1552	2
OH NATURE--NONE OF THIS--	"GO TELL IT"--WHAT A	1554	6
OH WHAT A GRACE IS THIS,	OH WHAT A GRACE IS THIS,	1615	1
OH FUTURE! THOU SECRETED PEACE	OH FUTURE! THOU SECRETED	1631	1
OH, HONEY OF AN HOUR,	OH, HONEY OF AN HOUR,	1734	1
OH, WHAT A LIVID BOON!	UPON THE GALLOWS HUNG A	1757	8
OIL			
THO' SERFS--SUPPLY THE OIL--	THE LAMP BURNS SURE--	233	2
UNCONSCIOUS THAT THE OIL IS OUT--	THE LAMP BURNS SURE--	233	7

		FIRST LINE	POEM	LINE
OIL	(CONTINUED)			
	THAT HAS SO LITTLE OIL--	I MEASURE EVERY GRIEF I	561	16
	IDEALS ARE THE FAIRY OIL	IDEALS ARE THE FAIRY OIL	983	1
	THE EYE REJECTS THE OIL.	IDEALS ARE THE FAIRY OIL	983	4
OILS				
	ESSENTIAL OILS--ARE WRUNG--	ESSENTIAL OILS--ARE	675	1
OLD				
	LEST I SH'D BE OLD FASHIONED	THE MORNS ARE MEEKER	12	7
	GOD'S OLD FASHIONED VOWS--	IT DID NOT SURPRISE ME--	39	8
	FROM SOME OLD FORTRESS ON THE SUN	SOME RAINBOW--COMING	64	10
	FOR HER OLD LOVER--DON THE SUN!	SOME RAINBOW--COMING	64	17
	OLD FASHIONED--NAUGHTY--EVERYTHING-- . . .	"ARCTURUS" IS HIS OTHER	70	32
	SIP OLD FRANKFORT AIR	MANY CROSS THE RHINE	123	3
	THE OLD--OLD SOPHISTRIES OF JUNE-- . . .	THESE ARE THE DAYS WHEN	130	5
	THE OLD--OLD SOPHISTRIES OF JUNE-- . . .	THESE ARE THE DAYS WHEN	130	5
	CONSCIOUS--AS OLD NAPOLEON, ...	A LITTLE BREAD--A CRUST	159	5
	COULD WE STAND WITH THAT OLD "MOSES"-- . .	IF THE FOOLISH, CALL	168	9
	HOW THOSE OLD--PHLEGMATIC MOUNTAINS . . .	I HAVE NEVER SEEN	175	3
	DEAR, OLD FASHIONED, LITTLE FLOWER! . . .	I'M THE LITTLE "HEART'S	176	9
	EDEN IS OLD FASHIONED, TOO!	I'M THE LITTLE "HEART'S	176	10
	IN THAT OLD CHAPEL AISLE.	I'VE HEARD AN ORGAN TALK	183	8
	THEN AT THE FEET OF THE OLD HORIZON . . .	BLAZING IN GOLD AND	228	3
	MURMURING, LIKE OLD CASPIAN CHOIRS, . . .	MANY A PHRASE HAS THE	276	5
	OLD FASHIONED EYES--	I KNOW SOME LONELY	289	11
	WHILE THE OLD COUPLE, JUST ASTIR, ...	I KNOW SOME LONELY	289	39
	HOW THE OLD MOUNTAINS DRIP WITH SUNSET . .	HOW THE OLD MOUNTAINS	291	1
	HOW THE OLD STEEPLES HAND THE SCARLET . .	HOW THE OLD MOUNTAINS	291	5
	I'M OLD ENOUGH, TODAY, I'M CERTAIN--THEN-- .	ONE YEAR AGO--JOTS WHAT?	296	33
	AS OLD AS THEE--HOW SOON?	ONE YEAR AGO--JOTS WHAT?	296	34
	LIKE SOME OLD FASHIONED MIRACLE	LIKE SOME OLD FASHIONED	302	1
	THE REEFS IN OLD GETHSEMANE	I SHOULD HAVE BEEN TOO	313	20
	LIKE THAT OLD MEASURE IN THE BOUGHS-- . .	OF ALL THE SOUNDS	321	3
	'TWAS THE OLD--ROAD--THROUGH PAIN-- . . .	'TWAS THE OLD--ROAD--	344	1
	FOR THAT OLD--FADED MIDNIGHT--	WHEN NIGHT IS ALMOST	347	7
	AS WELL AS OUR OLD HOME!"	I FELT MY LIFE WITH BOTH	351	16
	OLD VOLUMES SHAKE THEIR VELLUM HEADS . . .	A PRECIOUS--MOULDERING	371	27
	MY OLD GOWN--ON--	I'M SAYING EVERY DAY	373	29
	MAKE--A DIADEM--AND MEND MY OLD ONE-- . .	I'LL CLUTCH--AND CLUTCH	427	11
	BUT THAT OLD SORT--WAS DONE--	IT WOULD NEVER BE COMMON	430	4
	AND THROW THE OLD--AWAY--	I TIE MY HAT--I CREASE	443	6
	WHEN THAT OLD IMPERATOR--DEATH--	TRIUMPH--MAY BE OF	455	3
	I READ IN AN OLD FASHIONED BOOK	I KNOW WHERE WELLS GROW	460	13
	MORTALITY'S OLD CUSTOM--	SHE DEALT HER PRETTY	479	11
	AND THE OLD CLOCK KEPT NEIGHING "DAY"! . .	GOING TO HIM! HAPPY	494	19
	AND OLD SUNSHINE--ABOUT--	IT'S THOUGHTS--AND JUST	495	2
	FLAVORS OF THAT OLD CRUCIFIXION--	TO PUT THIS WORLD DOWN,	527	9
	OLD NEIGHBORS HAVE AT FENCES--	I'M SORRY FOR THE DEAD--	529	3
	THROUGH THIS--THE OLD PHILOSOPHER-- . . .	TRUST IN THE UNEXPECTED	555	5
	IT FEELS SO OLD A PAIN--	I MEASURE EVERY GRIEF I	561	8
	AT THOSE OLD TIMES--IN CALVARY.	IF I MAY HAVE IT, WHEN	577	25
	TO THAT OLD MOSES--DONE--	IT ALWAYS FELT TO ME--A	597	2
	AND USHERED GRAND OLD MOSES	IT ALWAYS FELT TO ME--A	597	19
	OLD MAN ON NEBO! LATE AS THIS--	IT ALWAYS FELT TO ME--A	597	23
	SINCE WE--OLD MORNINGS, CHILDREN--PLAYED-- .	OF NEARNESS TO HER	607	11
	OF OUR OLD [NEW] NEIGHBOR--GOD--	IT WAS TOO LATE FOR MAN	623	8
	OLD ONES CRACK--	I CANNOT LIVE WITH YOU--	640	12
	I FEEL THE OLD DEGREE--	AGAIN--HIS VOICE IS AT	663	2
	HER DIMITIES--AS OLD	THE DAY UNDRESSED--	716	4
	WITH THESE OLD FASHIONED EYES--	JOY TO HAVE MERITED THE	788	6
	THAN THINE OLD ARROW IS A SHOT	DYING! TO BE AFRAID OF	831	4
	TRUTH--IS AS OLD AS GOD--	TRUTH--IS AS OLD AS GOD	836	1
	OLD THE GRACE, BUT NEW THE SUBJECTS-- . .	ALWAYS MINE!	839	6
	OLD, INDEED, THE EAST, ...	ALWAYS MINE!	839	7
	SAVED FOR YOUR EAR WHEN LUTES BE OLD. . . .	SPLIT THE LARK--AND	861	4
	SOME HOUSES VERY OLD, ...	WHO OCCUPIES THIS HOUSE?	892	10
	WITH THAT OLD CODICIL OF DOUBT?	WHICH IS BEST? HEAVEN--	1012	3
	"OLD FRIEND, THOU KNOWEST [KNEWEST] ME," .	I HEARD, AS IF I HAD NO	1039	14
	I FEEL THE OLD DESIRE--	I CANNOT MEET THE SPRING	1051	2
	PARADISE IS THAT OLD MANSION	PARADISE IS THAT OLD	1119	1
	THAT ODD OLD MAN IS DEAD A YEAR--	THAT ODD OLD MAN IS DEAD	1130	1
	YESTERDAY [LIVERPOOL] IS OLD--	AFTER THE SUN COMES OUT	1148	4
	AS OLD AS WOE--	AS OLD AS WOE--	1168	1
	HOW OLD IS THAT?	AS OLD AS WOE--	1168	2
	AS OLD AS BLISS [JOY]	AS OLD AS WOE--	1168	4
	HOW OLD IS THAT	AS OLD AS WOE--	1168	5
	BUT THE SEA [DEEP] IS OLD	FORTITUDE INCARNATE	1217	8
	THE STARS ARE OLD, THAT STOOD FOR ME-- . .	THE STARS ARE OLD, THAT	1249	1
	OLD NICODEMUS' PHANTOM	THE BONE THAT HAS NO	1274	11
	ABRAHAM WAS OLD--	ABRAHAM TO KILL HIM	1317	4
	IT IS AS OLD AS GOD--	HOW BRITTLE ARE THE	1433	5
	HOW OLD THE NEWS OF LOVE MUST [SHOULD] BE .	HIS VOICE DECREPIT WAS	1476	3
	MINE ENEMY [MY FOE] IS GROWING OLD-- . . .	MINE ENEMY IS GROWING	1509	1
	BUT DESTINY IS OLD	MEETING BY ACCIDENT,	1548	6
	OLD SUITOR HEAVEN, ...	WE SHUN IT ERE IT COMES,	1580	7
	AS WERE THEY OLD ACQUAINTANCES--	A FACE DEVOID OF LOVE OR	1711	5
	"AM NOT CONSUMED," OLD MOSES WROTE, ...	NO MAN SAW AWE, NOR TO	1733	13
	THROUGH THOSE OLD GROUNDS OF MEMORY, . . .	THROUGH THOSE OLD	1753	1
OLDER				
	OLDER FEEL THAN THE HOPE THAT PROMPTED-- .	UP LIFE'S HILL WITH MY	1010	5

	FIRST LINE	POEM	LINE
OLDEST			
WHEN OLDEST CEDARS SWERVE--	THE TRUTH--IS STIRLESS--	780	4
POSSESS THE OLDEST ONE--	OPINION IS A FLITTING	1455	4
OLD-FASHIONED			
IS THAT OLD-FASHIONED COIN	LUCK IS NOT CHANCE--	1350	6
EDEN IS THAT OLD-FASHIONED HOUSE	EDEN IS THAT	1657	1
OMEN			
SOME POLAR EXPIATION--AN OMEN IN THE BONE	I TRIED TO THINK A	532	3
THAT HATH NO OMEN HERE--BUT AWE--	GATHERED INTO THE EARTH,	1370	5
OMINOUS			
SO OMINOUS DID PASS	THERE CAME A WIND LIKE A	1593	4
OMIT			
AND I OMIT TO PRAY	I HAVE A KING, WHO DOES	103	15
BUT IF THE HEART OMIT [BE LEAN / BE THIN / DECLINE]	THE MIND LIVES ON THE	1355	5
OMITTED			
CHRIST--OMITTED--ME--	PROMISE THIS--WHEN YOU	648	28
OMITTED IN THE LEASE--	'TWAS AWKWARD, BUT IT	973	12
OMNIFOLD			
HIS OBSERVATION OMNIFOLD,	THE MOUNTAIN SAT UPON	975	3
OMNIPOTENCE			
OMNIPOTENCE--HAD NOT A TONGUE--	YOU'LL KNOW IT--AS YOU	420	11
OMNIPOTENCE--ENOUGH--	TO BE ALIVE--IS POWER--	677	4
TRUST OMNIPOTENCE"--	"UNTO ME?" I DO NOT KNOW	964	8
EXCEPT OMNIPOTENCE	CONTAINED IN THIS SHORT	1165	V
SIGNIFICANCE [OMNIPOTENCE] THAT EACH HAS LIVED	BECAUSE THAT YOU ARE	1260	9
OMNIPOTENCE'			
OMNIPOTENCE' INSPECTION [ANALYSIS]	AN IGNORANCE A SUNSET	552	7
OMNIPOTENT			
THAN HER OMNIPOTENT--	THE SOUL'S SUPERIOR	306	8
OMNIPOTENT--ACUTE--	REHEARSAL TO OURSELVES	379	4
STOP--DOCILE AND OMNIPOTENT	I LIKE TO SEE IT LAP	585	16
OMNIPRESENCE			
WHERE--OMNIPRESENCE--FLY?	WE PRAY--TO HEAVEN--	489	11
WHAT OMNIPRESENCE LIES IN WAIT	ALL THAT I DO	1496	10
ONCE			
WAS ONCE SUPPOSED TO TURN,	"SIC TRANSIT GLORIA	3	34
PEDESTRIAN ONCE--AS WE--	THE FEET OF PEOPLE	7	12
AND TEN OF MY ONCE STATELY TOES	I COUNTED TILL THEY	36	7
ONCE MORE, MY NOW BEWILDERED DOVE	ONCE MORE, MY NOW	48	1
ONCE MORE HER MISTRESS, ON THE DEEP	ONCE MORE, MY NOW	48	3
I AM POOR ONCE MORE!	I NEVER LOST AS MUCH BUT	49	8
WHAT ONCE WAS "HEAVEN"	"ARCTURUS" IS HIS OTHER	70	17
I PRAY YOU PASS [STROLL] ONCE MORE.	HEART, NOT SO HEAVY AS	83	20
WHO ONCE THE COCKADE WORE--	THE SUN KEPT STOOPING--	152	12
THE EYES GLAZE ONCE--AND THAT IS DEATH--	I LIKE A LOOK OF AGONY,	241	5
JUST--ONCE--MORE--	WHY--DO THEY SHUT ME OUT	248	6
THAT ONCE--ON ME--THOSE JASPER GATES	IF I'M LOST--NOW--	256	4
ONCE WITNESSED OF THE GAUZE--	A SINGLE SCREW OF FLESH	263	5
AND KISS THE HILLS, FOR ME, JUST ONCE--	TIE THE STRINGS TO MY	279	15
CAME ONCE A WORLD--DID YOU?	ONE YEAR AGO--JOTS WHAT?	296	14
BUT BLISS, IS SOLD JUST ONCE.	IS BLISS THEN, SUCH	340	9
BELIEF--BUT ONCE--CAN BE--	TO LOSE ONE'S FAITH--	377	6
ONCE--IT WAS A QUEEN--	WHEN DIAMONDS ARE A	397	7
AND ONCE--A BUTTERFLY--	WHEN DIAMONDS ARE A	397	8
IF ONCE MORE--PARDON--BOY--	A TONGUE--TO TELL HIM I	400	14
BECAUSE THERE WAS A WINTER--ONCE--	THE WINTERS ARE SO SHORT	403	11
OF NUMEROUS HUMMING BIRDS AT ONCE	THE WIND--TAPPED LIKE A	436	11
NO FASTER THAN A MILE AT ONCE	NO MAN CAN COMPASS A	477	3
I LOOKED AT SUNRISE--ONCE--	I HAD NO CAUSE TO BE	542	9
DEATH--IS BUT ONE--AND COMES BUT ONCE--	I MEASURE EVERY GRIEF I	561	27
WHEN ONCE IT HAS BEGUN--	ONE ANGUISH--IN A CROWD	565	16
BUT--ONCE ASLANT	MUST BE A WO--	571	5
IT TROUBLED ME AS ONCE I WAS--	IT TROUBLED ME AS ONCE I	600	1
FOR I WAS ONCE A CHILD--	IT TROUBLED ME AS ONCE I	600	2
TO DEVISE ONCE MORE	PROMISE THIS--WHEN YOU	648	10
NOR ONCE LOOK UP--FOR NOON?	A LONG--LONG SLEEP--A	654	8
AT ONCE--FOR THEE--	YOU SAID THAT I "WAS	738	12
THE WHOLE OF IT CAME NOT AT ONCE--	THE WHOLE OF IT CAME NOT	762	1
CONTENTEDER IF ONCE--	THE WHOLE OF IT CAME NOT	762	10
WHERE WAS ONCE A ROOM--	ONE DAY IS THERE OF THE	814	12
WORN TO NATURE'S PARTY ONCE	RIBBONS OF THE YEAR--	873	3
BUT ONCE A CENTURY, THE ROSE	THE BIRD MUST SING TO	880	7
AND LOSE IT'S NEIGHBOR ONCE--	TOO LITTLE WAY THE HOUSE	911	8
ONCE TO ACHIEVE, ANNULS THE POWER	THOSE WHO HAVE BEEN IN	922	7
ONCE TO COMMUNICATE--	THOSE WHO HAVE BEEN IN	922	8
NEED [MISS]--ONCE IN AN ETERNITY--	LOVE--IS THAT LATER	924	11
I MORE THAN ONCE AT NOON	A NARROW FELLOW IN THE	986	12
BUT ONCE WITHIN THE TOWN	THE FINGERS OF THE LIGHT	1000	10
AND ONCE TO LET IT DOWN	HER LITTLE PARASOL TO	1038	2
JUST ONCE! OH LEAST REQUEST!	JUST ONCE! OH LEAST	1076	1
"JUST ONCE" SWEET DEITY?	JUST ONCE! OH LEAST	1076	9
WHEN ONCE THE ART IS OUT--	WHEN THEY COME BACK--IF	1080	4
BANKRUPT ONCE THROUGH HIS EXCESSES--	PARADISE IS THAT OLD	1119	7
THE CHANNEL OF THE DUST WHO ONCE ACHIEVES	OURSELVES WE DO INTER	1144	2
IT AIMS ONCE--KILLS ONCE--CONQUERS ONCE--	'TWAS FIGHTING FOR HIS	1188	5
IT AIMS ONCE--KILLS ONCE--CONQUERS ONCE--	'TWAS FIGHTING FOR HIS	1188	5
IT AIMS ONCE--KILLS ONCE--CONQUERS ONCE--	'TWAS FIGHTING FOR HIS	1188	5
BUT ONCE--ENTIRELY--	WHO WERE "THE FATHER AND	1258	18
BUT LET HIM ONCE SUSPECT	UNTIL THE DESERT KNOWS	1291	4

		FIRST LINE	POEM	LINE
ONCE (CONTINUED)				
	THAT EACH CAN MAKE BUT ONCE--	THAT SHORT--POTENTIAL	1307	2
	HAD MADNESS, HAD IT ONCE OR TWICE	I NEVER HEAR THAT ONE IS	1323	7
	TO DIE DIVINELY ONCE A TWILIGHT--[AN EVENING / A LIMIT]	I'D RATHER RECOLLECT A	1349	7
	NOR WE WHO HAVING ONCE INHALED [WAYLAID] IT--	IN MANY AND REPORTLESS	1382	11
	WILL EMERGE [DECAMP] BUT ONCE--AND DUMB [ARMED]--	"SECRETS" IS A DAILY	1385	11
	BEGINNING ONCE IN JUNE--	SUMMER HAS TWO	1422	2
	BE ONCE DISCLOSED TO US	COULD THAT SWEET	1493	2
	WHEN IT SHALL ONCE HAVE GROWN--	YOU CANNOT MAKE	1508	10
	MORNING THAT COMES BUT ONCE, ...	MORNING THAT COMES BUT	1610	1
	WHOSE TABLE ONCE A	FAME IS A FICKLE FOOD	1659	3
	SCARCER ONCE WITH THE MIGHT	SOMETIMES WITH THE HEART	1680	3
	NOTWITHSTANDING IT COST US EXISTENCE ONCE .	TO DO A MAGNANIMOUS	1699	7
ONE	SEE SOMEONE			
	THE BRIDE, AND THEN THE BRIDEGROOM, THE TWO, AND THEN THE ONE,	AWAKE YE MUSES NINE,	1	7
	AND SEIZE THE ONE THOU LOVEST, NOR CARE FOR SPACE, OR TIME!	AWAKE YE MUSES NINE,	1	36
	ONE WITH THE BANNER GAY--	SLEEP IS SUPPOSED TO BE	13	13
	ONE IN THE RED ARRAY--	SLEEP IS SUPPOSED TO BE	13	14
	ONE SISTER HAVE I IN OUR HOUSE, ...	ONE SISTER HAVE I IN OUR	14	1
	AND ONE, A HEDGE AWAY.	ONE SISTER HAVE I IN OUR	14	2
	THERE'S ONLY ONE RECORDED, ...	ONE SISTER HAVE I IN OUR	14	3
	ONE CAME THE ROAD THAT I CAME--	ONE SISTER HAVE I IN OUR	14	5
	AND ONE BELOW, THIS MORNING	THE GENTIAN WEAVES HER	18	7
	TO LOSE--IF ONE CAN FIND AGAIN--	ALL THESE MY BANNERS BE.	22	8
	TO MISS--IF ONE SHALL MEET--	ALL THESE MY BANNERS BE.	22	9
	ONE "PLEIAD" WAS IT'S NAME--	I HAD A GUINEA GOLDEN--	23	18
	SOME ONE THE SUM COULD TELL--	IT'S ALL I HAVE TO BRING	26	6
	ONE THE CURTAINS DREW--	MORNS LIKE THESE--WE	27	10
	WILL NO ONE GUIDE A LITTLE BOAT	ADRIFT! A LITTLE BOAT	30	3
	ONE LITTLE BOAT GAVE UP IT'S STRIFE	ADRIFT! A LITTLE BOAT	30	7
	ONE LITTLE BOAT--O'ERSPENT WITH GALES-- . .	ADRIFT! A LITTLE BOAT	30	11
	WHEN THERE'S NO ONE HERE--	BEFORE THE ICE IS IN THE	37	14
	ONE WITHIN MY BOSOM	IT DID NOT SURPRISE ME--	39	11
	THROUGH FAITH IN ONE HE MET NOT, ...	COULD LIVE--DID LIVE--	43	4
	SUCH TRUST HAD ONE AMONG US, ...	COULD LIVE--DID LIVE--	43	10
	HOW RUDE IN ONE TO SOB!	THERE'S SOMETHING	45	10
	THAT ONE SO SHY--SO IGNORANT	I HAV'NT TOLD MY GARDEN	50	7
	ONE WILL WALK TODAY--	I HAV'NT TOLD MY GARDEN	50	16
	ONE LITTLE MAID--FROM PLAYMATES--	TAKEN FROM MEN--THIS	53	5
	ONE LITTLE MIND FROM SCHOOL--	TAKEN FROM MEN--THIS	53	6
	ONE MIGHT DEPART AT OPTION	IF I SHOULD DIE,	54	9
	CORINTHIANS ONE. FIFTEEN. NARRATES	"SOWN IN DISHONOR"!	62	9
	BARONIAL BEES--MARCH--ONE BY ONE--	SOME RAINBOW--COMING	64	11
	BARONIAL BEES--MARCH--ONE BY ONE--	SOME RAINBOW--COMING	64	11
	NOT ONE OF ALL THE PURPLE HOST	SUCCESS IS COUNTED	67	5
	TO FIND THAT WHAT ONE WAKED FOR, ...	A DARTING FEAR--A POMP--	87	3
	ONE DIGNITY DELAYS FOR ALL--	ONE DIGNITY DELAYS FOR	98	1
	ONE MITRED AFTERNOON--	ONE DIGNITY DELAYS FOR	98	2
	AND NO ONE MADE REPLY.	WHOSE ARE THE LITTLE	142	4
	DEATH, THE ONLY ONE	DUST IS THE ONLY SECRET	153	2
	THEREFORE, AS ONE RETURNED, I FEEL, ...	JUST LOST, WHEN I WAS	160	7
	I WENT ONE WINTER MORNING	I CAUTIOUS, SCANNED MY	178	7
	GIVE THE ONE IN RED CRAVAT, ...	IF I SHOULD'NT BE ALIVE	182	3
	A TRANSPORT ONE CANNOT CONTAIN	A TRANSPORT ONE CANNOT	184	1
	WHEN ONE--TURNED SMILING TO THE LAND-- . .	TWO SWIMMERS WRESTLED ON	201	3
	OH GOD! THE OTHER ONE!	TWO SWIMMERS WRESTLED ON	201	4
	TICKED SOFTLY INTO ONE.	THE ROSE DID CAPER ON	208	16
	SAVIOR! I'VE NO ONE ELSE TO TELL--	SAVIOR! I'VE NO ONE ELSE	217	1
	I AM THE ONE FORGOT THEE SO--	SAVIOR! I'VE NO ONE ELSE	217	3
	THE SMALLEST ONE UPON YOUR FACE [CHEEK] . .	I CAME TO BUY A SMILE--	223	3
	THE ONE THAT NO ONE ELSE WOULD MISS . . .	I CAME TO BUY A SMILE--	223	5
	THE ONE THAT NO ONE ELSE WOULD MISS . . .	I CAME TO BUY A SMILE--	223	5
	SUCH AN ONE--TO SAY--	TEACH HIM--WHEN HE MAKES	227	2
	I MET ONE--FORGOT MY SCHOOLMATES--	GOD PERMITS INDUSTRIOUS	231	3
	HENCEFORTH--HER ONLY ONE!	THE SUN--JUST TOUCHED	232	16
	THOU SHALT--THYSELF--ONE DAY--A CHILD-- . .	THE COURT IS FAR AWAY--	235	7
	BUT WERE NO ONE	AH, MOON--AND STAR!	240	3
	THERE IS ONE--FARTHER THAN YOU--	AH, MOON--AND STAR!	240	15
	TWO LIVES--ONE BEING--NOW--	FOREVER AT HIS SIDE TO	246	5
	ONE HOUR--OF HER SOVREIGN'S FACE"!	WHAT WOULD I GIVE TO SEE	247	26
	ONE MORE NEW-MAILED NERVE	A SINGLE SCREW OF FLESH	263	14
	JUST ONE TIME!	DID WE DISOBEY HIM?	267	2
	ONE LIFE OF SO MUCH CONSEQUENCE!	ONE LIFE OF SO MUCH	270	1
	ONE PEARL--TO ME--SO SIGNAL-- [OF SUCH PROPORTION]	ONE LIFE OF SO MUCH	270	5
	THAT ONE, TO BE QUITE SURE--	I BREATHED ENOUGH TO	272	4
	I HAVE HEARD BUT ONE--	MANY A PHRASE HAS THE	276	2
	THAN ONE OF HIGHER TEMPERATURE	A SHADY FRIEND--FOR	278	3
	REVEALS THE FACT THAT ONE IS RAPT	HOW NOTELESS MEN, AND	282	3
	ONE--HAND THE TOOLS--	I KNOW SOME LONELY	289	8
	NEVER ANY [ONE] BEND	IF YOUR NERVE, DENY YOU	292	6
	ONE YEAR AGO--JOTS WHAT?	ONE YEAR AGO--JOTS WHAT?	296	1
	ONE--BIRTHDAY MORE--OR TEN?	ONE YEAR AGO--JOTS WHAT?	296	35
	CHOOSE ONE--	THE SOUL SELECTS HER OWN	303	10
	AND FEAR--IS LIKE THE ONE	THE DIFFERENCE BETWEEN	305	2
	THE ONE WHO [THAT] COULD REPEAT	THE ONE WHO COULD REPEAT	307	1

ONE (CONTINUED)	FIRST LINE	POEM	LINE
THE SUMMER DAY--			
WHILE HE--WAS MAKING ONE--	I SEND TWO SUNSETS--	308	4
THAT SCALDING ONE--SABACTHINI--	I SHOULD HAVE BEEN TOO	313	11
DEALS--ONE--IMPERIAL--THUNDERBOLT--	HE FUMBLES AT YOUR SOUL	315	11
ONE CLAW UPON THE AIR,	I CANNOT DANCE UPON MY	326	12
LIKE ONE IN DANGER, CAUTIOUS,	A BIRD CAME DOWN THE	328	13
THERE ARE TWO RIPENINGS--ONE--OF SIGHT--	THERE ARE TWO RIPENINGS	332	1
AS ONE THAT BORE HER MASTER'S NAME--	THE FACE I CARRY WITH ME	336	15
THAT UNFREQUENTED--ONE--	'TWAS THE OLD--ROAD--	344	2
ANOTHER BED--A SHORT ONE--	'TWAS THE OLD--ROAD--	344	17
HE'D BE TOO TALL, THE TALLEST ONE	I DREADED THAT FIRST	348	15
EACH ONE SALUTES ME, AS HE GOES,	I DREADED THAT FIRST	348	25
WITH ONE LONG "NAY"--	I HAD THE GLORY--THAT	349	4
BUT THIS ONE, WEARS IT'S MERRIMENT	A HAPPY LIP--BREAKS	353	5
ARE ONE--AND YET THE FORMER	THE DAY THAT I WAS	356	7
"MILES", AND "PRISCILLA", WERE SUCH AN ONE--	GOD IS A DISTANT--	357	4
ONE PORT--SUFFICES--FOR A BRIG--LIKE MINE--	HOW SICK--TO WAIT--IN	368	7
AS ONE SHOULD COME TO TOWN--	A PRECIOUS--MOULDERING	371	22
ONE ACCOST ME--	I'M SAYING EVERY DAY	373	25
THAT--CAN APPAL BUT ONE--	A SECRET TOLD--	381	4
THERE KNITS A BOLDER ONE--	NO RACK CAN TORTURE ME--	384	4
BIND ONE--THE OTHER FLY--	NO RACK CAN TORTURE ME--	384	8
AND CARRIES ONE--OUT OF IT--TO GOD--	IT'S COMING--THE	390	8
THE REAL ONE DIED FOR THEE--	'TWAS LOVE--NOT ME--	394	3
WERE UNIVERSE--ONE ROCK--	I HAD NOT MINDED--WALLS	398	2
ONE WOULD AS SOON ASSAULT A PLUSH--	WHAT SOFT--CHERUBIC	401	3
AND NO ONE CREDITS NOAH--	THE WINTERS ARE SO SHORT	403	16
AND SEAT--JUST ONE--	UNIT, LIKE DEATH, FOR	408	9
AND THIS ONE--DO NOT FEEL THE SAME--	THE FIRST DAY'S NIGHT	410	19
BUT DO ONE FACE US SUDDENLY--	SUNSET AT NIGHT--IS	415	7
MIGHT SOME ONE ELSE--SO LEARNED--BE--	NOT IN THIS WORLD TO SEE	418	10
I SHALL HAVE WADED DOWN ONE DAY".	IT DONT SOUND SO	426	9
NEXT--ONE--MIGHT BE THE GOLDEN TOUCH--	I'LL CLUTCH--AND CLUTCH	427	2
MAKE--A DIADEM--AND MEND MY OLD ONE--	I'LL CLUTCH--AND CLUTCH	427	11
WHEN ONE LEARN HOW	KNOWS HOW TO FORGET!	433	V
ONE ENVIES THE DISTINGUISHED DUST--	IT FEELS A SHAME TO BE	444	3
WHEN ONE WHO DIED FOR TRUTH, WAS LAIN	I DIED FOR BEAUTY--BUT	449	3
"AND I--FOR TRUTH--THEMSELF ARE ONE--	I DIED FOR BEAUTY--BUT	449	7
IF ONE WAKE AT MORN--	DREAMS--ARE WELL--BUT	450	2
IF ONE WAKE AT MIDNIGHT--BETTER--	DREAMS--ARE WELL--BUT	450	3
ALIKE TO HIM--ONE--	THE MALAY--TOOK THE	452	17
INSTEAD OF ONE--	LOVE--THOU ART HIGH--	453	10
ONE EYE UPON THE HEAVEN RENOUNCED--	TRIUMPH--MAY BE OF	455	11
AND ONE--UPON THE RACK--	TRIUMPH--MAY BE OF	455	12
THE ONLY ONE--FORESTALLING MINE--	I LIVE WITH HIM--I SEE	463	5
AND FITTING NO ONE ELSE--	I AM ALIVE--I GUESS--	470	20
AND DAY THAT WAS BEHIND--WERE ONE--	A NIGHT--THERE LAY THE	471	3
NO ONE TO TEACH ME THAT NEW GRACE--	I AM ASHAMED--I HIDE--	473	5
BUT JUST FOR ONE--TO STIPULATE--	I MEANT TO HAVE BUT	476	7
THAT ONE SO HONEST--BE EXTANT--	I MEANT TO HAVE BUT	476	21
SO ACCURATE THE ONE	NO MAN CAN COMPASS A	477	8
AND EVERY ONE UNBARED A NERVE	SHE DEALT HER PRETTY	479	3
AND ONE GERANIUM--	I WAS THE SLIGHTEST IN	486	4
AND ANY ONE I KNEW	I WAS THE SLIGHTEST IN	486	15
TO ONE DENIED TO DRINK	TO ONE DENIED TO DRINK	490	1
WHILE IT AND I LAP ONE AIR	WHILE IT IS ALIVE	491	3
DWELL IN ONE BLOOD	WHILE IT IS ALIVE	491	4
UNDER ONE SACRAMENT [FIRMAMENT]	WHILE IT IS ALIVE	491	5
IT'S THOUGHTS--AND JUST ONE HEART--	IT'S THOUGHTS--AND JUST	495	1
NO ONE COULD PLAY IT--THE SECOND TIME--	BETTER--THAN MUSIC! FOR	503	6
I'D RATHER BE THE ONE	I WOULD NOT PAINT--A	505	2
I'D RATHER BE THE ONE	I WOULD NOT PAINT--A	505	10
AND FLED WITH EVERY ONE--	SHE SIGHTS A BIRD--SHE	507	12
WITH ONE SMALL [JUST ONE] DIADEM.	I'M CEDED--I'VE STOPPED	508	13
WITH ONE SMALL [JUST ONE] DIADEM.	I'M CEDED--I'VE STOPPED	508	13
NO ONE [MAN] HE SEEMED TO KNOW--	I STARTED EARLY--TOOK MY	520	22
THERE DWELLS ONE OTHER CREATURE	I TRIED TO THINK A	532	10
AS ONE SHOULD PRY THE WALLS--	I TRIED TO THINK A	532	13
WAS ALL THE ONE THAT FELL--	I TOOK MY POWER IN MY	540	6
'TIS ONE BY ONE--THE FATHER COUNTS--	'TIS ONE BY ONE--THE	545	1
'TIS ONE BY ONE--THE FATHER COUNTS--	'TIS ONE BY ONE--THE	545	1
ONE HURRYING TO REST--	I CROSS TILL I AM WEARY	550	13
ONE MORE--"YE BLESSED"--TO BE TOLD--	THERE IS A SHAME OF	551	7
ONE CRUCIFIXION IS RECORDED--ONLY--	ONE CRUCIFIXION IS	553	1
ONE CALVARY--EXHIBITED TO STRANGER--	ONE CRUCIFIXION IS	553	5
AS ONE HAD TESTIFIED--	TRUST IN THE UNEXPECTED	555	4
DEATH--IS BUT ONE--AND COMES BUT ONCE--	I MEASURE EVERY GRIEF I	561	27
ONE ANGUISH--IN A CROWD--	ONE ANGUISH--IN A CROWD	565	1
SHOULD PROVE THE STRONGEST [SUPPLEST / LITHEST / STOUTEST] ONE,	MY FIRST WELL DAY--SINCE	574	8
ONE EARNS [GETS] BY MEASURING THE GRAVE--	MY FIRST WELL DAY--SINCE	574	27
I EVER HAD--BUT ONE--	I FOUND THE WORDS TO	581	2
EVER WENT BY ONE--	INCONCEIVABLY SOLEMN!	582	10
ONE BALTIC--THEY--	EMPTY MY HEART, OF THEE	587	6
AND KNEW ONE BIRD A TUNE--	WHAT CARE THE DEAD, FOR	592	12
THIS ONE--BELOVED OF MANKIND	WHAT CARE THE DEAD, FOR	592	15
AND NO MAN--IS THE ONE	THE BATTLE FOUGHT	594	2
BY FAR THE GREATER ONE--	THE BATTLE FOUGHT	594	4
MY [ONE] JUSTICE BLEEDS--FOR THEE!	IT ALWAYS FELT TO ME--A	597	24

ONE (CONTINUED)

	FIRST LINE	POEM	LINE
AS ONE WITHIN A SWOON--	THERE IS A PAIN--SO	599	6
ONE GOSSIPPED IN THE LANE	THE TREES LIKE TASSELS--	606	18
IN ONE OR TWO [MORE] EXISTENCES--	AFRAID! OF WHOM AM I	608	7
WHAT ONE BROKE OFF WITH	TO KNOW JUST HOW HE	622	20
OF ONE ANOTHER'S EYES--	'TWAS A LONG PARTING--	625	8
"'TWAS SUNSET"--SOME ONE SAID--	THEY CALLED ME TO THE	628	2
OURSELVES WERE WED ONE SUMMER--DEAR--	OURSELVES WERE WED ONE	631	1
BY SOME ONE CARRYING A LIGHT--	OURSELVES WERE WED ONE	631	7
AND YET, ONE SUMMER, WE WERE QUEENS [WED]--	OURSELVES WERE WED ONE	631	15
THE ONE THE OTHER WILL CONTAIN [INCLUDE]	THE BRAIN--IS WIDER THAN	632	3
THE ONE THE OTHER WILL ABSORB--	THE BRAIN--IS WIDER THAN	632	7
TO NO ONE THAT YOU--KNOW--	THE WAY I READ A	636	14
TO HIM WHO HAS IT--AND THE ONE	MY PORTION IS DEFEAT--	639	17
FOR ONE MUST WAIT	I CANNOT LIVE WITH YOU--	640	14
I THINK THE DAYS--COULD EVERY ONE	I THINK TO LIVE--MAY BE	646	9
HAD ALL MY LIFE BUT BEEN [BEEN ONE / BEEN BLEAK] MISTAKE	I THINK TO LIVE--MAY BE	646	27
SOME SHALL [SOME ONE] SUMMON ME--	PROMISE THIS--WHEN YOU	648	2
AN INDEPENDANT ONE--	A LONG--LONG SLEEP--A	654	4
THE MINOR ONE--THAT GLEAMED [SHONE] BEHIND--	THAT FIRST DAY, WHEN YOU	659	7
AND VASTER [THIS ONE / DIFFERENT]--OF THE WORLD'S.	THAT FIRST DAY, WHEN YOU	659	8
DID MEDDLE [TAMPER]--ONE BY ONE--	'TIS GOOD--THE LOOKING	660	6
DID MEDDLE [TAMPER]--ONE BY ONE--	'TIS GOOD--THE LOOKING	660	6
THEY PROVE ONE CHEMISTRY--	'TIS GOOD--THE LOOKING	660	V 12
AND NO ONE VISIT ME	COULD I BUT RIDE	661	4
EMBARRASSMENT OF ONE ANOTHER	EMBARRASSMENT OF ONE	662	1
FOR SUCH AN ONE--AS ME--	AGAIN--HIS VOICE IS AT	663	4
THE OTHER'S ONE [FOOT]--HAD BEEN--	AGAIN--HIS VOICE IS AT	663	17
I HAVE ELECTED--ONE--	OF ALL THE SOULS THAT	664	2
HIS INDIVIDUAL ONE--	NO ROMANCE SOLD UNTO	669	4
ONE NEED NOT BE A CHAMBER--TO BE HAUNTED--	ONE NEED NOT BE A	670	1
ONE NEED NOT BE A HOUSE--	ONE NEED NOT BE A	670	2
AS ONE SHOULD SUE A STAR--	THE HEAVEN VESTS FOR	694	10
BUT WONT YOU WISH YOU'D SPARED ONE	NO MATTER--NOW--SWEET--	704	7
TILL ONE BREADTH COVER TWO--	THE SUNRISE RUNS FOR	710	5
UPON HER BOSOM--ONE--	THE SUNRISE RUNS FOR	710	16
AND ONE UPON HER HEM--	THE SUNRISE RUNS FOR	710	17
TO GO ELASTIC--OR AS ONE	STRONG DRAUGHTS OF THEIR	711	5
AS ONE DETECT ON LANDINGS	A SOUTH WIND--HAS A	719	3
AS ONE THAT DRUNKEN--STEPT--	IT TOSSED--AND TOSSED--	723	6
BE THE PERFECT ONE--	ALTER! WHEN THE HILLS DO	729	4
YOU SAID THAT I "WAS GREAT"--ONE DAY--	YOU SAID THAT I "WAS	738	1
WISER MEN [ONE / EAR] MAY WEARY--	NEVER FOR SOCIETY	746	5
COUNTENANCE OF ONE	SO THE EYES ACCOST--AND	752	6
ONE BLESSING HAD I THAN THE REST	ONE BLESSING HAD I THAN	756	1
AS ONE WHO FOR A FURTHER LIFE	HE FOUGHT LIKE THOSE	759	3
WHEN ONE [YOU] HAS FAILED TO STOP THEM--	TO OFFER BRAVE	767	3
ONE AND ONE--ARE ONE--	ONE AND ONE--ARE ONE--	769	1
ONE AND ONE--ARE ONE--	ONE AND ONE--ARE ONE--	769	1
ONE AND ONE--ARE ONE--	ONE AND ONE--ARE ONE--	769	1
THE LONELINESS ONE DARE NOT SOUND--	THE LONELINESS ONE DARE	777	1
YET ONE--REJOICES FLOWERS--	THERE IS AN ARID	782	5
AND ONE--THE FLOWERS ABHOR--	THERE IS AN ARID	782	6
POUNCE ON HIS BRUISES--ONE--SAY--OR THREE--	GRIEF IS A MOUSE--	793	11
ONE MUST REVERSE HAVE [ITSELF HAVE / HAVE PREVIOUS] BORE--	DESPAIR'S ADVANTAGE IS	799	4
ONE ART TO RECOGNIZE, MUST BE,	HER GRACE IS ALL SHE HAS	810	3
ONE DAY IS THERE OF THE SERIES	ONE DAY IS THERE OF THE	814	1
WILL BE THE ONE AWARE OF DEATH	THIS CONSCIOUSNESS THAT	822	3
THEN CAME ONE DROP OF GIANT RAIN--	THE WIND BEGUN TO KNEAD	824	15
TO ONE WHO NEVER FELT IT BLAZE--	LOVE RECKONS BY ITSELF--	826	3
THE ONLY ONE I MEET	THE ONLY NEWS I KNOW	827	7
THE ROBIN IS THE ONE	THE ROBIN IS THE ONE	828	1
THE ROBIN IS THE ONE	THE ROBIN IS THE ONE	828	5
THE ROBIN IS THE ONE	THE ROBIN IS THE ONE	828	9
ONE MUST TO THINE ARTILLERY	DYING! TO BE AFRAID OF	831	2
MINE WAS THE ONLY ONE	I CANNOT BUY IT--'TIS	840	3
IF ONE CARE TO, THAT IS,	GOOD TO HIDE, AND HEAR	842	3
CAN ONE FIND THE RARE EAR	GOOD TO HIDE, AND HEAR	842	7
THAN THE PRECEDING ONE	I MADE SLOW RICHES BUT	843	4
FOR THE ONE SHIP THAT STRUTS THE SHORE	FINITE--TO FAIL, BUT	847	2
WHEN ONE HAS GIVEN UP ONE'S LIFE	WHEN ONE HAS GIVEN UP	853	1
POSSESSION IS TO ONE	TO OWN THE ART WITHIN	855	6
A COSTLIER ONE	EACH SCAR I'LL KEEP FOR	877	4
SINCE NO ONE KNOWS HIS CIRCUMSTANCE--	WHO OCCUPIES THIS HOUSE?	892	3
IF I CAN STOP ONE HEART FROM BREAKING	IF I CAN STOP ONE HEART	919	1
IF I CAN EASE ONE LIFE THE ACHING	IF I CAN STOP ONE HEART	919	3
OR COOL ONE PAIN	IF I CAN STOP ONE HEART	919	4
OR HELP ONE FAINTING ROBIN	IF I CAN STOP ONE HEART	919	5
'SCAPING ONE--AGAINST THE OTHER	PATIENCE--HAS A QUIET	926	5
THAT WE BUT RECOLLECT THE ONE	THERE IS A JUNE WHEN	930	15
AND MAKES ONE LIFT ONE'S HAT	IT IS AN HONORABLE	946	2
AS ONE MET SUDDEN [ENCOUNTERED] GENTLEFOLK	IT IS AN HONORABLE	946	3
AS ONE DOES SICKNESS OVER	AS ONE DOES SICKNESS	957	1
AS ONE REWALKS A PRECIPICE	AS ONE DOES SICKNESS	957	5
AS ONE BEMOANING A DOMINION	A LOSS OF SOMETHING EVER	959	7
JUST A PALTRY ONE--	ALL FORGOT FOR	966	2
HE LEFT BEHIND ONE DAY--SO LESS	FITTER TO SEE HIM, I MAY	968	13

ONE (CONTINUED)

	FIRST LINE	POEM	LINE
HE'LL SIGH--"THE OTHER--[REAL ONE] SHE--IS WHERE?"	FITTER TO SEE HIM, I MAY	968	20
SINCE HEAVEN AND HE ARE ONE.	THE DEFINITION OF BEAUTY	988	4
SUPERIOR TO THE ONE	WHICH IS BEST? HEAVEN--	1012	6
GUIDES THE LITTLE ONE PREDESTINED	FAR FROM LOVE THE	1021	7
AND CERTAINTY THAT ONE	THE DYING NEED BUT	1026	6
'TWAS MY ONE GLORY--	'TWAS MY ONE GLORY--	1028	1
PAIN HAS BUT ONE ACQUAINTANCE	PAIN HAS BUT ONE	1049	1
EACH ONE UNTO THE OTHER	PAIN HAS BUT ONE	1049	3
OF ONE [HIM] THAT LEANETH FROM [IN] BALLOON	IT WAS A QUIET WAY--	1053	11
WOULD CAUSE ONE SCARCELY TO SUSPECT	BLOOM--IS RESULT--TO	1058	3
IS EVERY ONE I MEET	EXPERIMENT TO ME	1073	2
HOW SOME ONE [PARTIES] TREATED HIM	THE SKY IS LOW--THE	1075	6
THE EARTH AND I AND ONE	THE SUN WENT DOWN--NO	1079	6
IF I AM THERE--ONE DOES NOT KNOW	WHEN THEY COME BACK--IF	1080	13
WHAT PARTY--ONE MAY BE	WHEN THEY COME BACK--IF	1080	14
HOW VAST AN ONE	WE LEARN IN THE	1083	2
OR ONE OF IVORY--	THEMSELF ARE ALL I HAVE	1094	4
AND WORKMEN FINISHED ONE BY ONE	THE CRICKETS SANG	1104	3
AND WORKMEN FINISHED ONE BY ONE	THE CRICKETS SANG	1104	3
LEST SOME ONE ELSE SHOULD [RICHER PEOPLE] BUY	A DIAMOND ON THE HAND	1108	V 8
THE LABOR IS A SOBER ONE	I FIT FOR THEM--	1109	4
AS MAKES ONE HIDE [HANG] IT'S HEAD	THAT THIS SHOULD FEEL	1112	V 4
DO ONE ADVANCE [OBTAIN] SO NEAR	THE MERCHANT OF THE	1131	10
ONE [THIS] REQUISITE HAS FIRE THAT LASTS [EARTHLY FIRE / MORTAL FIRE]	THE SMOULDERING EMBERS	1132	7
IN ONE SHORT AFTERNOON	HOW MANY SCHEMES MAY DIE	1150	2
AS ONE COMMUTED LED--	SOMEHOW MYSELF SURVIVED	1194	6
WITHDRAWS THE WORTHLESS THING [ONE]	TO DISAPPEAR ENHANCES--	1209	10
RISK IS THE HAIR THAT HOLDS THE TUN [ONE]	RISK IS THE HAIR THAT	1239	1
OF ONE COROLLA IS THE WEST--	THE LILAC IS AN ANCIENT	1241	9
LOVE IS ONE, NOT AGGREGATE--	SAFE DESPAIR IT IS THAT	1243	7
WAS ALL THE ONE THAT PLAYED.	LIKE BROOMS OF STEEL	1252	11
HAD THIS ONE DAY NOT BEEN,	HAD THIS ONE DAY NOT	1253	1
TO ONE THAT NEVER DIED--	WHO WERE "THE FATHER AND	1258	V 6
TO TAKE US [ONE] LANDS AWAY	THERE IS NO FRIGATE LIKE	1263	2
FELLED BY BUT ONE ASSASSIN--	COULD HOPE INSPECT HER	1283	7
BUT POSSIBLY THE ONE--	THE THINGS WE THOUGHT	1293	12
OR COULD SHE ONE CONTEMN--	THE MUSHROOM IS THE ELF	1298	18
HAD NATURE AN APOSTATE--[ONE "ISCARIOT" / AN ISCARIOT,]	THE MUSHROOM IS THE ELF	1298	19
NOT ONE BY HEAVEN DEFRAUDED STAY--	NOT ONE BY HEAVEN	1303	1
SHALL COMPREHEND [SCRUTINIZE] AS ONE	HOW NEWS MUST FEEL WHEN	1319	10
I NEVER HEAR THAT ONE IS DEAD [HAS DIED]	I NEVER HEAR THAT ONE IS	1323	1
BY ONE DEFAULTING [HEROIC] FACE	THE VASTEST EARTHLY DAY	1328	3
OF ONE HOWEVER LOVELY, NOT	AS SUMMER INTO AUTUMN	1346	7
THE ONE THAT WE HAVE LOVED--	AS SUMMER INTO AUTUMN	1346	8
ON ONE ATTEMPTING SHY	AS SUMMER INTO AUTUMN	1346	10
THOUGH ONE IS BEAUTIFUL FORGETTING [SECESSION]--	I'D RATHER RECOLLECT A	1349	3
... [NEWEST / NEWER] ONE.	I'D RATHER RECOLLECT A	1349	4
ONE--IS THE POPULATION--	THE HEART IS THE CAPITAL	1354	5
I [WE] KEEP ONE RAY	OF THEIR PECULIAR LIGHT	1362	2
THE SUN IS ONE--AND ON THE TARE	THE SUN IS ONE--AND ON	1372	1
LAY THIS LAUREL ON THE ONE	LAY THIS LAUREL ON THE	1393	1
LAY THIS LAUREL ON THE ONE	LAY THIS LAUREL ON THE	1393	V
A STROLLING HUE, ONE WOULD HAVE SAID	IT WAS A QUIET SEEMING	1419	5
ONE JOY [SOUND] OF SO MUCH ANGUISH	ONE JOY OF SO MUCH	1420	1
THAT ONE SHOULD COMPREHEND THE WORTH	HIS MIND LIKE FABRICS OF	1446	7
I FIND ONE ON MY HAND	HOW SOFT A CATERPILLAR	1448	2
BUT THIS--IS ONE--	THOSE NOT LIVE YET	1454	4
POSSESS THE OLDEST ONE--	OPINION IS A FLITTING	1455	4
HE NEVER HAD BUT ONE--	BELSHAZZAR HAD A LETTER	1459	2
ONE THING OF IT WE [THEE I] BORROW	ONE THING OF IT WE	1464	1
ONE THING OF IT WE [THEE I] COVET--	ONE THING OF IT WE	1464	5
ONE OF THE ONES THAT MIDAS TOUCHED	ONE OF THE ONES THAT	1466	1
TO NO ONE BUT THE THIEF--	THE SWEETS OF PILLAGE,	1470	2
FAME IS THE ONE THAT DOES NOT STAY--	FAME IS THE ONE THAT	1475	1
EACH ONE OF US SHALL BE--	'TIS WHITER THAN AN	1482	10
LIKE ONE THAT FED ON AWE.	HER SPIRIT ROSE TO SUCH	1486	3
AND HOLDS SCARCE [JUST] ONE.	THE ROAD TO PARADISE IS	1491	2
FOR HER [ONE] TO BE A [AN IMPENDING] BRIDE	ALL THAT I DO	1496	11
REDEMPTION IS THE ONE [PRINCIPALLY]	I SAW THE WIND WITHIN	1502	V
NOT ONE OF US WILL OWN	I SAW THE WIND WITHIN	1502	V
SUMMER IS SHORTER THAN ANY ONE--	SUMMER IS SHORTER THAN	1506	1
THAN WITH THIS HORIZONTAL ONE	OH GIVE IT MOTION--DECK	1527	7
AND BUT ONE SMILE--THAT MEAGRES [HUMBLES] BALMS--	ABOVE OBLIVION'S TIDE	1531	4
THAT NEVER SEATS BUT ONE--	HOPE IS A SUBTLE GLUTTON	1547	6
I HAVE ONE BATTLE MORE--	MY WARS ARE LAID AWAY IN	1549	2
FOR ONE MUST RECOLLECT	TO BE FORGOT BY THEE	1560	V 10
MY LOW [ONE / MEEK / WAN] RENOWN	TO BE FORGOT BY THEE	1560	V 12
THE CLOCK STRIKES ONE THAT JUST STRUCK TWO--	THE CLOCK STRIKES ONE	1569	1
WITH EVERY FUTURE ONE?	THE SPIRIT LASTS--BUT IN	1576	16
IF ONE WOULD TAMPER THERE.	IT WOULD NOT KNOW IF IT	1579	4
STRUCK NO ONE BUT MYSELF--	THE FARTHEST THUNDER	1581	6
AND NO ONE SWAGGERS NOW BUT ME--	THE BOBOLINK IS GONE--	1591	2
ENOUGH IS ONE--	FEW, YET ENOUGH,	1596	2
HAVE NOT EACH ONE OF US THE RIGHT	FEW, YET ENOUGH,	1596	4

	FIRST LINE	POEM	LINE
ONE (CONTINUED)			
OF GOD WE ASK ONE FAVOR,	OF GOD WE ASK ONE FAVOR,	1601	1
TO ONE A WONDER STILL	THE GOING FROM A WORLD	1603	2
CRUMBLESS AND HOMELESS, OF BUT ONE REQUEST--	QUITE EMPTY, QUITE AT	1606	8
SOME ONE PREPARED THIS MIGHTY SHOW	SOME ONE PREPARED THIS	1644	1
FOR JUST ONE PLAUDIT FAMISHING,	THE IMMORTALITY SHE GAVE	1648	3
EACH ONE OF US HAS TASTED	A WORD MADE FLESH IS	1651	5
ONE DESERT AND A SEA	I DID NOT REACH THEE	1664	4
I SHALL NOT COUNT THE JOURNEY ONE	I DID NOT REACH THEE	1664	5
ONE DESERT CROSSED--	I DID NOT REACH THEE	1664	9
THE SECOND ONE	I DID NOT REACH THEE	1664	10
SPEECH IS ONE SYMPTOM OF AFFECTION	SPEECH IS ONE SYMPTOM OF	1681	1
AND SILENCE ONE--	SPEECH IS ONE SYMPTOM OF	1681	2
ONE SIDE OF ME THE NUTS ARE RIPE	THE ONES THAT	1690	7
NO OTHER ONE MAY GO	UNTO A BROKEN HEART	1704	2
IN ONE CONSUMMATE BILL,	HOW DARE THE ROBINS SING	1724	6
I TOOK ONE DRAUGHT OF LIFE--	I TOOK ONE DRAUGHT OF	1725	1
ONE CROWN THAT NO ONE SEEKS [NOT ANY SEEK]	ONE CROWN THAT NO ONE	1735	1
ONE CROWN THAT NO ONE SEEKS [NOT ANY SEEK]	ONE CROWN THAT NO ONE	1735	1
IN STRONG [ONE] SOCIETY.	THE GRAVE MY LITTLE	1743	8
THIS DOCILE ONE INTER	THIS DOCILE ONE INTER	1752	1
TO MAKE A PRAIRIE IT TAKES A CLOVER AND ONE BEE,	TO MAKE A PRAIRIE IT	1755	1
ONE CLOVER, AND A BEE,	TO MAKE A PRAIRIE IT	1755	2
THE ONE WHO BORE HIM TOTTERED IN,--	UPON THE GALLOWS HUNG A	1757	5
HOW FLEET--HOW INDISCREET AN ONE--	HOW FLEET--HOW	1771	1
ONE'S			
TO TELL YOUR [ONE'S] NAME--THE LIVELONG JUNE--	I'M NOBODY! WHO ARE YOU?	288	7
TO LOSE ONE'S FAITH--SURPASS	TO LOSE ONE'S FAITH--	377	1
ONE'S--MONEY--ONE'S--THE MINE--	SOME--WORK FOR	406	12
ONE'S--MONEY--ONE'S--THE MINE--	SOME--WORK FOR	406	12
TO MAKE ONE'S TOILETTE--AFTER DEATH	TO MAKE ONE'S TOILETTE--	485	1
THAN UNARMED [MOONLESS], ONE'S A'SELF ENCOUNTER--	ONE NEED NOT BE A	670	11
WHEN ONE HAS GIVEN UP ONE'S LIFE	WHEN ONE HAS GIVEN UP	853	1
AND MAKES ONE LIFT ONE'S HAT	IT IS AN HONORABLE	946	2
WERE SHINING IN YOUR [ONE'S] HAND.	TO SEE HER IS A PICTURE	1568	8
ONES			
THE SOUND ONES, LIKE THE HILLS--SHALL STAND [STAND UP]--	WHEN WE STAND ON THE	242	7
BUT THE ONES WHO OVERCAME MOST TIMES--	OF TRIBULATION--THESE	325	6
ONES WE FORMER KNEW--	SMILING BACK FROM	385	6
MAKE FRUGAL--ONES--CONTENT--	IT'S THOUGHTS--AND JUST	495	3
AND REDDER CHEEKED ONES--IN THEIR STEAD [PLACE]--	MY FIRST WELL DAY--SINCE	574	11
OLD ONES CRACK--	I CANNOT LIVE WITH YOU--	640	12
OR OTHER HIGHTS OF OTHER ONES	YOU SAID THAT I "WAS	738	7
YIELD GROUPS OF ONES--	EXCEPT THE SMALLER SIZE	1067	V
TELL HAD A SON--THE ONES THAT KNEW [HEARD] IT	TELL AS A MARKSMAN--WERE	1152	9
OF THE ONES THAT PURSUED IT	NOT ANY MORE TO BE	1344	9
THE ONES THAT [WHO] CITE HER MOST	WHAT MYSTERY PERVADES A	1400	18
THE ONES I LOVED BELOW	I SHALL NOT MURMUR IF AT	1410	2
THAN ONES THAT NEVER WERE,	THAN HEAVEN MORE REMOTE,	1436	5
ONE OF THE ONES THAT MIDAS TOUCHED	ONE OF THE ONES THAT	1466	1
IF AIMS IMPEL THESE ASTRAL ONES	THE MOON UPON HER FLUENT	1528	5
THE ONES ALLOWED TO KNOW	THE MOON UPON HER FLUENT	1528	6
THE ONES THAT DISAPPEARED ARE BACK	THE ONES THAT	1690	1
ONESELF			
AND TAKE ONESELF BY SURPRISE	TO DO A MAGNANIMOUS	1699	2
IF ONESELF IS NOT IN THE HABIT OF HIM	TO DO A MAGNANIMOUS	1699	3
ONLY			
THERE'S ONLY ONE RECORDED,	ONE SISTER HAVE I IN OUR	14	3
ONLY A BEE WILL MISS IT--	NOBODY KNOWS THIS LITTLE	35	5
ONLY A BUTTERFLY,	NOBODY KNOWS THIS LITTLE	35	6
ONLY A BIRD WILL WONDER--	NOBODY KNOWS THIS LITTLE	35	9
ONLY A BREEZE WILL SIGH--	NOBODY KNOWS THIS LITTLE	35	10
WHAT IS ONLY WALKING	BEFORE THE ICE IS IN THE	37	11
ONLY TO FAIL AGAIN!	I NEVER HEAR THE WORD	77	8
DUST IS THE ONLY SECRET--	DUST IS THE ONLY SECRET	153	1
DEATH, THE ONLY ONE	DUST IS THE ONLY SECRET	153	2
ONLY TO BREAK IN WILDER SONG	IF I COULD BRIBE THEM BY	179	11
ONLY, YOUR INFERENCE THEREFROM!	AS IF SOME LITTLE ARCTIC	180	12
ONLY THE SOLDERED MOUTH CAN TELL--	HOW MANY TIMES THESE LOW	187	2
THE ONLY TRADE [ART] THEY KNOW--	A BURDOCK--CLAWED MY	229	8
HENCEFORTH--HER ONLY ONE!	THE SUN--JUST TOUCHED	232	16
MORNING--ONLY THE SEED OF NOON--	I SHALL KEEP SINGING!	250	10
POWER IS ONLY PAIN--	I CAN WADE GRIEF--	252	10
IT--ONLY--CAN SUFFICE!	YOU SEE I CANNOT SEE--	253	15
IT'S ONLY FAINTER--BY DEGREES--	TO DIE--TAKES JUST A	255	3
THE ONLY GHOST I EVER SAW	THE ONLY GHOST I EVER	274	1
HUSH--ONLY TO ME!	MANY A PHRASE HAS THE	276	16
WHO ONLY SHOWS HIS MARBLE DISC [GRANITE FACE]--	GIVE LITTLE ANGUISH--	310	7
WITH ONLY BUTTERFLIES TO BROOD	THE GRASS SO LITTLE HAS	333	3
I THOUGHT IF I COULD ONLY LIVE	I DREADED THAT FIRST	348	5
BE ONLY	'TIS OPPOSITES--ENTICE--	355	11
HER GOD--HER ONLY THRONG--	TRIUMPH--MAY BE OF	455	8
THE ONLY ONE--FORESTALLING MINE--	I LIVE WITH HIM--I SEE	463	5
OF ONLY TASTE WE CARED TO PLEASE	TO MAKE ONE'S TOILETTE--	485	3
LOVE [FAITH] IS LIKE LIFE--MERELY [ONLY	WHILE IT IS ALIVE	491	7

ONLY (CONTINUED)

	FIRST LINE	POEM	LINE
THE] LONGER			
TELL HIM [HER]--I ONLY SAID THE SYNTAX--	GOING TO HIM! HAPPY	494	4
THROUGH KNOWING--WHERE WE ONLY HOPE [GUESS]--	THOSE FAIR--FICTITIOUS	499	15
IF ONLY CENTURIES, DELAYED,	IF YOU WERE COMING IN	511	9
OR ONLY A DIVINE.	TO HEAR AN ORIOLE SING	526	3
OR WAS MYSELF [JUST MYSELF / ONLY ME / I]--TOO SMALL?	I TOOK MY POWER IN MY	540	8
THE ONLY RAIMENT I SHOULD NEED--	I HAD NO CAUSE TO BE	542	19
ONE CRUCIFIXION IS RECORDED--ONLY--	ONE CRUCIFIXION IS	553	1
AND ONLY NAILS THE EYES--	I MEASURE EVERY GRIEF I	561	28
BUT ONLY KNEW BY LOOKING BACK--	IT CEASED TO HURT ME,	584	3
OUR ONLY LULLABY--	I CRIED AT PITY--NOT AT	588	24
OR ONLY HEAVEN--AT NOON--	I THINK I WAS ENCHANTED	593	6
TODAY--HER ONLY BOY	WHEN I WAS SMALL, A	596	2
FOR THESE--WERE ONLY PUT TO DEATH--	IT ALWAYS FELT TO ME--A	597	11
AND ONLY THE SEA--REPLY--	GLEE--THE GREAT STORM IS	619	17
ONLY GOD--DETECT THE SORROW [POSSESS THE SECRET]--	ONLY GOD--DETECT THE	626	1
ONLY GOD--	ONLY GOD--DETECT THE	626	2
I ONLY SAW A SAPPHIRE [AN AMBER--] FARM--	THEY CALLED ME TO THE	628	3
WHO, VITAL ONLY TO OUR THOUGHT--	BEREAVEMENT IN THEIR	645	9
I ONLY KNOW [SIGH]--NO CURRICLE [VEHICLE] THAT RUMBLE THERE	A LITTLE ROAD--NOT MADE	647	7
BE MY LIPS--THE ONLY BUCKLE	PROMISE THIS--WHEN YOU	648	7
DISTANCE--BE HER ONLY MOTION [SIGNAL]--	HER SWEET TURN TO LEAVE	649	21
AND VISIT ONLY WHERE I LIKED	COULD I BUT RIDE	661	3
BUT ONLY ON MY FOREHEAD STOPPED--	THE SUN KEPT SETTING--	692	7
I ONLY ASK A TUNE	THE JUDGE IS LIKE THE	699	10
OBSERVE--"'TWAS ONLY A BALLOON"--	YOU'VE SEEN BALLOONS SET	700	20
FOR ONLY GOSSAMER, MY GOWN--	BECAUSE I COULD NOT STOP	712	15
MY TIPPET--ONLY TULLE--	BECAUSE I COULD NOT STOP	712	16
FOR JUST THIS SINGLE [THIS PECULIAR / JUST THIS ONLY] TIME--	I MEANT TO FIND HER WHEN	718	6
BUT ONLY TO HIMSELF--BE KNOWN	SHE ROSE TO HIS	732	11
THE OTHER--ONLY--HEAR--	THE SPIRIT IS THE	733	8
ONLY THEATRE RECORDED	DRAMA'S VITALLEST	741	14
I REINFORCED [ONLY SEALED] THE DOOR--	THE BIRDS REPORTED FROM	743	6
WHEN THE ONLY TREE	NO BOBOLINK--REVERSE HIS	755	2
ONLY ANODYNE--	NO BOBOLINK--REVERSE HIS	755	9
PARADISE--THE ONLY PALACE	THESE--SAW VISIONS--	758	14
ONLY ME--[STILL MYSELF-- / ME ALONE] WAS STILL--	WHEN I HOPED, I	768	16
IS NATURE'S ONLY PHARMACY	SEVERER SERVICE OF	786	23
WHO ONLY KNEW OF UNIVERSE--	THIS BAUBLE WAS	805	7
ONLY THE KEEPER OF THIS RING [THE SEAL]	GIVEN IN MARRIAGE UNTO	817	7
THE ONLY NEWS I KNOW	THE ONLY NEWS I KNOW	827	1
THE ONLY SHOWS I SEE--	THE ONLY NEWS I KNOW	827	4
THE ONLY ONE I MEET	THE ONLY NEWS I KNOW	827	7
IS GOD--THE ONLY STREET--	THE ONLY NEWS I KNOW	827	8
MINE WAS THE ONLY ONE	I CANNOT BUY IT--'TIS	840	3
WE ONLY KNOW WHAT TIME OF YEAR	FROM US SHE WANDERED NOW	890	7
ONLY A SHRINE, BUT MINE--	ONLY A SHRINE, BUT MINE	918	1
ONLY TO AGGRAVATE [JUST TO INTENSIFY] THE DARK	FAIRER THROUGH FADING--	938	7
WITH ONLY BIRDS [BLOOM] TO INTERRUPT	I LEARNED--AT LEAST--	944	11
ITSELF THE ONLY PRINCE CAST OUT--	A LOSS OF SOMETHING EVER	959	8
DENIAL--IS THE ONLY FACT	DENIAL--IS THE ONLY FACT	965	1
I ONLY MUST NOT GROW SO NEW	FITTER TO SEE HIM, I MAY	968	15
I ONLY MUST NOT CHANGE SO FAIR	FITTER TO SEE HIM, I MAY	968	19
IT'S ONLY LORE--IT'S STEADFASTNESS--	'TWAS AWKWARD, BUT IT	973	3
IT ONLY MOVED [SWERVED] AS DO THE SUNS--	'TWAS AWKWARD, BUT IT	973	5
I ONLY HAVE IT NOT TONIGHT	'TWAS AWKWARD, BUT IT	973	9
OUR SINGLE [ONLY] COMPETITION	NO OTHER CAN REDUCE	982	7
OR ONLY HEAVEN TO COME	WHICH IS BEST? HEAVEN--	1012	2
ONLY SCANTLY AND SELECTLY	NATURE RARER USES YELLOW	1045	7
ONLY THE CHEMIST CAN DISCLOSE	ASHES DENOTE THAT FIRE	1063	7
IT ONLY HELD ITSELF ALOOF	IT WAS NOT SAINT--IT WAS	1092	3
MAKE OF HIS ONLY BOY A TARGET	TELL AS A MARKSMAN--WERE	1152	18
HIM--TO REGALE--ME--ONLY--	HE IS ALIVE, THIS	1160	7
AS EACH WERE SPECIAL [LAWFUL / ONLY] HEIR--	ALONE AND IN A	1167	16
BUT IF THEY ONLY STAY	ARE FRIENDS DELIGHT OR	1199	4
THE GARDEN GETS THE ONLY SHOT	THE FROST WAS NEVER SEEN	1202	11
ONLY LEST SHE BE LONELY	WHATEVER IT IS--SHE HAS	1204	9
THAT ONLY TO THE EAR OF GOD	A DEED KNOCKS FIRST AT	1216	7
IF ONLY TO ENCLOSE THE SAINTS	SO MUCH OF HEAVEN HAS	1228	3
YET NEWER GLOWS THE ONLY GOLD	THE STARS ARE OLD, THAT	1249	3
KNOWN ONLY TO THE DEW--	DOMINION LASTS UNTIL	1257	6
THAT ONLY [MERELY] LASTS AN HOUR	IN THIS SHORT LIFE	1287	2
NOT THE ONLY SEA--	LIFT IT--WITH THE	1348	4
THE ONLY THING WORTH LARCENY	TAKE ALL AWAY--	1365	2
NOT ONLY MUST CONFIRM US	THE FACT THAT EARTH IS	1408	5
THE ONLY VESSEL THAT IS SHUNNED	IF WRECKED UPON THE	1469	3
BUT ONLY PINNACLE--	THE WAY HOPE BUILDS HIS	1481	4
THE DESOLATION ONLY MISSED	THE THRILL CAME SLOWLY	1495	5
THE ONLY ADAMANT ESTATE	HOW FIRM ETERNITY MUST	1499	3
AS AN ONLY DOLLAR--	SUMMER IS SHORTER THAN	1506	4
BELOVED ONLY AFTERNOON	FROM ALL THE JAILS THE	1532	3
THOU ONLY CAMEST TO MANKIND	WITHIN THY GRAVE!	1552	3
THE ONLY FOOD THAT GROWS	I GROPED FOR HIM BEFORE	1555	8
IT ONLY SWEETER GROWS.	HER LOSSES MAKE OUR	1562	8

	FIRST LINE	POEM	LINE
ONLY (CONTINUED)			
IT ONLY HEARD THEM PLAY--	PURSUING YOU IN YOUR	1602	6
THE SAGEST [ONLY] TIME TO DAM THE SEA IS WHEN THE SEA IS GONE--	WE SEND THE WAVE TO FIND	1604	7
HE ONLY SELLS THE WILDERNESS,	THE AUCTIONEER OF	1612	5
WOULD ONLY COME TODAY,	IF ALL THE GRIEFS I AM	1726	2
WOULD ONLY COME TODAY,	IF ALL THE GRIEFS I AM	1726	6
FOR BREATHING IS THE ONLY WORK	NO MAN SAW AWE, NOR TO	1733	11
THAT ONLY CHILDHOOD KNOWS.	SWEET IS THE SWAMP WITH	1740	6
THE ONLY SECRET PEOPLE [NEIGHBORS] KEEP [SHUN]	THE RETICENT VOLCANO	1748	11
ONSET			
THERE IS IT'S NOISELESS ONSET--	THERE IS A WORD	8	13
JUST GIRT ME FOR THE ONSET WITH ETERNITY,	JUST LOST, WHEN I WAS	160	3
FOR THAT LAST ONSET--WHEN THE KING	I HEARD A FLY BUZZ--WHEN	465	7
ONYX			
HIS BREAST, A SINGLE ONYX	HIS FEET ARE SHOD WITH	916	3
OOZE			
AND CITIES--OOZE [SLIP / SLIDE / MELT] AWAY--	A STILL--VOLCANO--LIFE--	601	12
OOZED			
OOZED SO IN CRIMSON BUBBLES	SO HAS A DAISY VANISHED	28	5
OPAL			
AN OPAL GUEST AND GRAY--	THE GUEST IS GOLD AND	15	2
STREWS THE LANDING WITH OPAL BALES--	THIS--IS THE LAND--THE	266	7
OF OPAL CATTLE--FEEDING FAR	THEY CALLED ME TO THE	628	5
NOR FARM--NOR OPAL HERD--WAS THERE--	THEY CALLED ME TO THE	628	15
NATURE WAS IN AN OPAL [HER BERYL / HER BLUEST] APRON,	IT SOUNDED AS IF THE	1397	7
OPAQUE			
OF HIS PROFOUND [OPAQUE] TO COME--	THE FUTURE--NEVER SPOKE	672	4
OPAQUEST			
AND THEIR OPAQUEST ADAMANT--	THEY PUT US FAR APART--	474	11
OPEN			
BLAZED OPEN--SUDDENLY--	IF I'M LOST--NOW--	256	5
ACCOSTS MY OPEN EYE--	THE ANGLE OF A LANDSCAPE	375	6
AND OPEN HOUSE--AGAIN--	THE WINTERS ARE SO SHORT	403	8
AND EITHER--OPEN THE [IT'S] EYES--	WE DREAM--IT IS GOOD WE	531	10
GOES SAFELY [STEADY]--WHERE AN OPEN EYE--	THERE IS A PAIN--SO	599	7
I DARED NOT ENTER [OPEN], LEST A FACE	I YEARS HAD BEEN FROM	609	3
TEARS OPEN HER IMPERIAL VEINS--	YOU'VE SEEN BALLOONS SET	700	15
SHOW JUSTEST--THROUGH AN OPEN TOMB--	THE ADMIRATIONS--AND	906	2
THROWN OPEN WIDE TO ME--	I SUED THE NEWS--YET	1360	4
IT'S AWFUL CHAMBER OPEN STANDS--	WATER MAKES MANY BEDS	1428	3
I OPEN EVERY DOOR,	NOT KNOWING WHEN THE	1619	2
OPENED			
A DOOR JUST [THERE] OPENED ON A STREET [TO A HOUSE]--	A DOOR JUST OPENED ON A	953	1
THAT OPENED TO THE SUN	A GREAT HOPE FELL	1123	15
ARKS OF REPRIEVE HE OFFERED [OPENED] TO US--	WE TALKED WITH EACH	1473	7
THE WORLD THAT THOU HAST OPENED	EXPANSE CANNOT BE LOST--	1584	9
KNOCK AND IT SHALL BE OPENED	COSMOPOLITES WITHOUT A	1589	7
OPENING			
THE OPENING AND THE CLOSE	THE OPENING AND THE	1047	1
AND OPENING HIS [IT'S] MOUTH	THE WIND TOOK UP THE	1134	4
WHEN OPENING THE SABBATH IN THEIR AFFLICTIVE WAY	THE BOBOLINK IS GONE--	1591	5
THE OPENING OF A DOOR--	ELYSIUM IS AS FAR AS TO	1760	8
OPENS			
OPENS THE LID OF AMETHYST	AS WATCHERS HANG UPON	121	8
A WINDOW OPENS LIKE A POD--	THERE'S BEEN A DEATH, IN	389	7
AND OPENS FURTHER ON--	A NARROW FELLOW IN THE	986	8
THAT OPENS WITH AN EQUAL WIDTH	THESE ARE THE SIGNS TO	1077	7
OPERA			
WHOSE OPERA--[STANZAS, ARE] THE SPRINGS--	A FEATHER FROM THE	161	4
IT'S FULL AS OPERA--	I CANNOT DANCE UPON MY	326	20
TITANIC OPERA--	I THINK I WAS ENCHANTED	593	16
OPHIR			
BROTHER OF INGOTS--[SISTER OF OPHIR--] AH PERU--	BROTHER OF INGOTS--AH	1366	1
BROTHER OF OPHIR, BRIGHT ADIEU,	BROTHER OF INGOTS--AH	1366	V 1
OPINION			
THE OPINION WILL DO [SERVE]--FOR THEM--	BY MY WINDOW HAVE I FOR	797	4
IN THE OPINION FAIR	CONFIRMING ALL WHO	1268	2
OPINION IS A FLITTING THING,	OPINION IS A FLITTING	1455	1
OPINIONS			
HIS QUAINT OPINIONS--TO INSPECT--	A PRECIOUS--MOULDERING	371	9
OPPORTUNITY			
IN LEAGUELESS OPPORTUNITY,	HOW NOTELESS MEN, AND	282	7
LIFE'S OPPORTUNITY--	FOR DEATH--OR RATHER	382	4
OR OPPORTUNITY--HER LORD AWAY?	FORGET! THE LADY WITH	438	8
FOR OPPORTUNITY--	ME PROVE IT NOW--WHOEVER	537	4
WITH WANT, AND OPPORTUNITY--	I PLAY AT RICHES--TO	801	5
MY OPPORTUNITY	IT BLOOMED AND DROPT, A	978	V 20
NULLS OPPORTUNITY--	NATURE CAN DO NO MORE	1673	8
AN OPPORTUNITY	EXPERIMENT ESCORTS US	1770	4
OPPOSE			
TO PACK THE BUD--OPPOSE THE WORM--	BLOOM--IS RESULT--TO	1058	9
OPPOSING			
BOUND TO OPPOSING LANDS--	THERE CAME A DAY AT	322	20
WITH AN OPPOSING CLOUD--	FROM COCOON FORTH A	354	13
WITHIN OPPOSING CELLS--	I TRIED TO THINK A	532	15

	FIRST LINE	POEM	LINE
OPPOSING (CONTINUED)			
MONTCALM, HIS OPPOSING SPIRIT	WOLFE DEMANDED DURING	678	5
PATIENCE OF OPPOSING FORCES--	GROWTH OF MAN--LIKE	750	11
OPPOSITE			
TILL OPPOSITE--I SPIED A CHEEK	THE ROSE DID CAPER ON	208	9
JUST OPPOSITE--ANOTHER SPEECH	THE ROSE DID CAPER ON	208	11
THERE'S BEEN A DEATH, IN THE OPPOSITE HOUSE,	THERE'S BEEN A DEATH, IN	389	1
UNTO THE SOFA OPPOSITE--	THE NIGHT WAS WIDE, AND	589	19
I THOUGHT IT WOULD BE OPPOSITE--	I ROSE--BECAUSE HE SANK	616	2
HEARD [HELD] OPPOSITE THE SEA--	WITHOUT THIS--THERE IS	655	4
OF OPPOSITE--TO BALANCE ODD [EQUAL OUGHT]--	THE ZEROES--TAUGHT US--	689	5
IF THINGS WERE OPPOSITE--AND ME	I'VE NONE TO TELL ME TO	881	7
QUITE OPPOSITE--HOW COMPLICATE	EXPERIENCE IS THE ANGLED	910	5
TO OUR OPPOSITE--	UNFULFILLED TO	972	6
UPON THE OPPOSITE	THE RIGHT TO PERISH	1692	4
PRECISELY OPPOSITE.	THAT IT WILL NEVER COME	1741	8
OPPOSITELY			
THAT I AM LOOKING OPPOSITELY	A LOSS OF SOMETHING EVER	959	15
OPPOSITES			
'TIS OPPOSITES--ENTICE--	'TIS OPPOSITES--ENTICE--	355	1
OPPRESS			
WITHOUT OFFENCE [OPPRESS] OF TOLL--	THERE IS NO FRIGATE LIKE	1263	6
OPPRESSED			
THAT MEN ARE SO OPPRESSED?	IS IMMORTALITY A BANE	1728	2
OPPRESSES			
THAT OPPRESSES, LIKE THE HEFT	THERE'S A CERTAIN SLANT	258	3
OPPROBRIUM			
PERDITION IS OPPROBRIUM--	HIS CHEEK IS HIS	1460	3
OPTION			
ONE MIGHT DEPART AT OPTION	IF I SHOULD DIE,	54	9
PARADISE IS OF THE OPTION.	PARADISE IS OF THE	1069	1
AS LIGHTLY AS AN OPTION GOWN	WE KNEW NOT THAT WE WERE	1462	5
OPTIONAL			
AS IF HIMSELF WERE OPTIONAL	THE TREES LIKE TASSELS--	606	11
IS OPTIONAL WITH US--	DID WE ABOLISH FROST	1014	4
POSSESSION, NOT OPTIONAL--	I AM AFRAID TO OWN A	1090	4
THE STAPLE MUST BE OPTIONAL	OF PAUL AND SILAS IT IS	1166	7
OPTIZAN			
SO SIMILAR--AN OPTIZAN	SO GLAD WE ARE--A	329	7
OPULENCE			
WHAT OPULENCE THE MORE	DOUBT ME! MY DIM	275	12
WHO OWN--ESTEEM THE OPULENCE--	I PLAY AT RICHES--TO	801	15
OPULENT			
IMPREGNABLE AS [AS OPULENT IT / EXTRAVAGANT AS / ABUNDANT AS . . .	YOU CANNOT TAKE ITSELF	1351	5
ORANGE			
TIGHT FITTING--ORANGE--BROWN--	YOU'LL KNOW HER--BY HER	634	10
ORATOR			
THE ORATOR OF APRIL	HIS MANSION IN THE POOL	1379	7
ORATORIO			
BETIMES AN ORATORIO--	ONE OF THE ONES THAT	1466	11
ORBIT			
FOR THE AUTHENTIC ORBIT	DELIGHT'S DESPAIR AT	1299	7
ORCHARD			
ORCHARD, AND BUTTERCUP, AND BIRD--	A LADY RED--AMID THE	74	11
WITHIN THE ORCHARD, IS NOT HEARD,	I HAVE A KING, WHO DOES	103	14
OR GIDDY BIRD IN ORCHARD--	ON SUCH A NIGHT, OR SUCH	146	15
BECAUSE, WE'RE ORCHARD SPRUNG--	THE ROBIN'S MY CRITERION	285	7
THE ORCHARD SPARKLED LIKE A JEW--	THE DAY CAME SLOW--TILL	304	13
THE WIND DID'NT COME FROM THE ORCHARD--TODAY--	THE WIND DID'NT COME	316	1
AND AN ORCHARD, FOR A DOME--	SOME KEEP THE SABBATH	324	4
AND IN THE ORCHARD FAR BELOW--	A SOLEMN THING WITHIN	483	5
THE ORCHARD, WHEN THE SUN IS ON--	"HEAVEN" HAS DIFFERENT	575	9
IN THE NEAREST ORCHARD DWELLING [WAITING]	STRUCK, WAS I, NOR YET	925	15
AND KINGDOMS, LIKE THE ORCHARD	IT IS AN HONORABLE	946	7
ORCHARDS			
AND ORCHARDS--UNBEREFT--	YOU LOVE ME--YOU ARE	156	6
AND WHEN THE ORCHARDS STOP THEIR TUNE--	MAKE ME A PICTURE OF THE	188	7
THE HILLS JUST TELL THE ORCHARDS--	THE SKIES CANT KEEP	191	3
TRAILED--SLOW--ALONG THE ORCHARDS--	THE SUN--JUST TOUCHED	232	9
TO LET THE ORCHARDS GROW--	THE TREES LIKE TASSELS--	606	16
THE BUSHES [ORCHARDS / MEADOWS]--SPANGLES FLUNG--	A DROP FELL ON THE APPLE	794	12
OVER REALMS OF ORCHARDS	ON THE WORLD YOU COLORED	1171	5
THAT LAWFUL ORCHARDS [DAMSONS] MOCKS--	FORBIDDEN FRUIT A FLAVOR	1377	2
THE JESUIT OF ORCHARDS	ONE OF THE ONES THAT	1466	13
IN THE FADELESS ORCHARDS	"LETHE" IN MY FLOWER,	1730	3
ORCHESTRA			
WHEN [THO'] ORCHESTRA IS [BE] DUMB--	LIKE SOME OLD FASHIONED	302	14
TO BEAR THEM ORCHESTRA.	OF ALL THE SOUNDS	321	24
ORCHIS			
THE ORCHIS BINDS HER FEATHER ON	SOME RAINBOW--COMING	64	16
OF ORCHIS IN THE PASTURE--	THERE IS A FLOWER THAT	380	11
ORCHIS'			
TO HIM WHO KEEPS AN ORCHIS' HEART--	ALL THESE MY BANNERS BE.	22	20
ORDAIN			
WHOM FATE [TRAIT] ORDAIN--	WHO COURT OBTAIN WITHIN	803	6
ORDAINED			
THE ROSE ORDAINED!	GARLANDS FOR QUEENS, MAY	34	9
ORDAINED TO SUFFERING--	IT MIGHT BE LONELIER	405	12

	FIRST LINE	POEM	LINE
ORDAINED (CONTINUED)			
'TWERE SUDDENLY CONFIRMED [ORDAINED]-- . .	I THINK I WAS ENCHANTED	593	20
FUZZ ORDAINED--NOT FUZZ CONTINGENT-- . . .	BEES ARE BLACK, WITH	1405	5
ORDER			
THEIR FAR PARADES--ORDER [HALT] ON THE EYE .	INCONCEIVABLY SOLEMN!	582	5
OR ORDER, OR APPARENT ACTION [SIGNAL / NOTICE]--	FOUR TREES--UPON A	742	3
AND DISTANT AS AN ORDER DONE	THE CRICKETS SANG	1104	V
TO PACK HER TRUNK AND ORDER	WERE NATURE MORTAL LADY	1762	3
ORDERLY			
HOW ORDERLY THE KITCHEN'D LOOK, BY NIGHT, .	I KNOW SOME LONELY	289	13
TILL THEY ARE ORDERLY AS BUSTS--	A VISITOR IN MARL--	391	3
SET ORDERLY, FOR BURIAL, ...	IT WAS NOT DEATH, FOR I	510	11
HOW INTIMATE, A [ORDERLY THE] TEMPEST PAST .	THE WIND TOOK UP THE	1134	15
I MAKE MY PARLOR ORDERLY	THE GRAVE MY LITTLE	1743	3
ORDINANCE			
NO ORDINANCE BE SEEN	FURTHER IN SUMMER THAN	1068	5
ORDINARY			
THAN ORDINARY BREATH--	MORE LIFE--WENT OUT--	422	2
FROM ORDINARY MEANINGS--	THIS WAS A POET--IT IS	448	3
HIS ORDINARY ACTS ARE FEATS	BEST WITCHCRAFT IS	1158	3
ORDINATION			
THAT ORDINATION--UTTERS--	I GOT SO I COULD HEAR	293	20
IN ORDINATION STAND--	I THINK TO LIVE--MAY BE	646	10
ORDNANCE			
BEAR WITHIN--APPALLING ORDNANCE, ...	I HAVE NEVER SEEN	175	5
THE ORDNANCE OF VITALITY	'TWAS FIGHTING FOR HIS	1188	3
ORE			
BUT WHEN THE VIVID [QUICKENED] ORE . . .	DARE YOU SEE A SOUL AT	365	4
TO PROVE THE PRESENCE OF THE ORE	A PLATED LIFE--	806	3
ORES			
REFINING THESE IMPATIENT ORES	DARE YOU SEE A SOUL AT	365	13
ORGAN			
I'VE HEARD AN ORGAN TALK, SOMETIMES-- . .	I'VE HEARD AN ORGAN TALK	183	1
ORGANDY			
THAN THOSE OF ORGANDY--	A SHADY FRIEND--FOR	278	8
ORGANIZED			
ARE ORGANIZED DECAYS.	CRUMBLING IS NOT AN	997	4
ORIEL			
. . . ORIEL] WINDOW	BLAZING IN GOLD AND	228	5
ORIENT			
WHEN ORIENT HAVE BEEN OUTGROWN--	THE ONE WHO COULD REPEAT	307	7
AS IF I ASKED THE ORIENT	AS IF I ASKED A COMMON	323	5
THEN ORIENT SHOWED [THE EAST PUT OUT / NATURE PUT OUT] A SINGLE FLAG,	A DROP FELL ON THE APPLE	794	15
ORIENTAL			
EXIST AN [FULFILLED THEIR] ORIENTAL CIRCUIT	THIS QUIET DUST WAS	813	7
BUT LIKE AN ORIENTAL TALE	REPORTLESS SUBJECTS, TO	1048	7
HIS ORIENTAL HERESIES	HIS ORIENTAL HERESIES	1526	1
ORIENT'S			
AN ORIENT'S APPARITION--	JOY TO HAVE MERITED THE	788	15
ORIOLE			
AND ORIOLE--ARE DONE!	SUMMER FOR THEE, GRANT I	31	4
TO HEAR AN ORIOLE SING	TO HEAR AN ORIOLE SING	526	1
THE ORIOLE	ONE OF THE ONES THAT	1466	T
THE REELING [BLISSFUL] ORIOLE--	ONE OF THE ONES THAT	1466	4
ORIOLES			
DIP--AND VANISH LIKE ORIOLES!	THIS--IS THE LAND--THE	266	9
ORION			
FOLLOW WISE [FINE] ORION	FOLLOW WISE ORION	1538	1
ORLEANS			
AN ORLEANS IN THE EYE	A MIEN TO MOVE A QUEEN--	283	3
ORNAMENT			
NO ORNAMENT--BUT PALMS--	OF TRIBULATION--THESE	325	8
AN ORNAMENT TOO GRAND	ALTHOUGH I PUT AWAY HIS	366	2
BEAR YOU--FOR ORNAMENT	I'LL CLUTCH--AND CLUTCH	427	16
CONTENT, SOE'ER, IT ORNAMENT	JUST AS HE SPOKE IT FROM	848	7
ORNITHOLOGY			
IN [BY] ORNITHOLOGY--	WITH PINIONS OF DISDAIN	1431	4
ORPHEUS'			
ORPHEUS' SERMON CAPTIVATED--	THE BIBLE IS AN ANTIQUE	1545	15
OR'TER			
BOY THAT LIVED FOR "OUGHT TO [OR'TER]" . .	SO I PULL MY STOCKINGS	1201	4
ORTHOGRAPHY			
BREAKING IN BRIGHT ORTHOGRAPHY	MANY A PHRASE HAS THE	276	9
AT THE LONE ORTHOGRAPHY	AFTER A HUNDRED YEARS	1147	7
OSTENSIBLE			
ABOVE OSTENSIBLE VICISSITUDE.	AFTER ALL BIRDS HAVE	1395	4
OSTENSIBLY			
TO HANG OUR HEAD--OSTENSIBLY--	TO HANG OUR HEAD--	105	1
OSTENSIBLY, ON LAND	A GREAT HOPE FELL	1123	9
OSTENTATION			
RIDE ABROAD IN OSTENTATION	BEES ARE BLACK, WITH	1405	3
OTHERWISE			
AND THEN--'TWAS OTHERWISE--	THE DAY THAT I WAS	356	4
OR ODIOUSER [FATALLER / OTHERWISE] OFFEND--	THOSE CATTLE SMALLER	1388	12
HE OTHERWISE MAY KNOW	HIS MIND OF MAN, A	1663	6
BUT OTHERWISE WITHHELD.	THROUGH THOSE OLD	1753	16
OTTER'S			
STOOPING AS LOW AS [BENDING LOW AT] THE	BLAZING IN GOLD AND	228	5

	FIRST LINE	POEM	LINE
OTTER'S (CONTINUED)			
OTTER'S [KITCHEN / . . .			
OUGHT			
HAS OUGHT BUT ELEGY!	THE DOOMED--REGARD THE	294	12
OF GROUND, OR AIR, OR OUGHT--	AFTER GREAT PAIN, A	341	6
INCREDULOUS OF OUGHT	LIKE EYES THAT LOOKED ON	458	2
OF OPPOSITE--TO BALANCE ODD [EQUAL OUGHT]--	THE ZEROES--TAUGHT US--	689	5
IF OUGHT SHE MISSED IN HER NEW DAY,	SHE ROSE TO HIS	732	5
BOY THAT LIVED FOR "OUGHT TO [OR'TER]"	SO I PULL MY STOCKINGS	1201	4
TRADITION OUGHT TO KNOW--	SO GAY A FLOWER	1456	5
OUR			
OUR FATHERS BEING WEARY,	"SIC TRANSIT GLORIA	3	45
IN TOKEN OF OUR FRIENDSHIP	"SIC TRANSIT GLORIA	3	61
DEATH, BUT OUR RAPT ATTENTION	THE FEET OF PEOPLE	7	15
THE TEMPESTS TOUCHED OUR GARMENTS--	THROUGH LANE IT LAY--	9	9
ONE SISTER HAVE I IN OUR HOUSE,	ONE SISTER HAVE I IN OUR	14	1
BUILDED OUR HEARTS AMONG.	ONE SISTER HAVE I IN OUR	14	8
OUR DEPARTED ARE.	TAKEN FROM MEN--THIS	53	12
OUR FEET AWAIT!	IF PAIN FOR PEACE	63	3
ON OUR DEVELOPED EYES	IF PAIN FOR PEACE	63	11
SOLVE OUR APRIL DAY!	I CANT TELL YOU--BUT YOU	65	4
WITH OUR FACES VAILED--	I CANT TELL YOU--BUT YOU	65	10
FOR OUR MUTUAL HONOR,	AMBITION CANNOT FIND HIM	68	7
FOR YOU KNOW WE DO NOT MIND OUR DRESS	GOING TO HEAVEN!	79	18
OUR LIVES ARE SWISS--	OUR LIVES ARE SWISS--	80	1
OUR LITTLE GARDEN THAT WE LOST	WE SHOULD NOT MIND SO	81	3
WE ESTIMATE OUR PRIZE	AS BY THE DEAD WE LOVE	88	6
TO OUR PENURIOUS EYES!	AS BY THE DEAD WE LOVE	88	8
ASCENDED FROM OUR VISION	WENT UP A YEAR THIS	93	21
PRESENT OUR MEEK ESCUTSCHEON	ONE DIGNITY DELAYS FOR	98	15
TO HANG OUR HEAD--OSTENSIBLY--	TO HANG OUR HEAD--	105	1
OF OUR IMMORTAL MIND--	TO HANG OUR HEAD--	105	4
OUR SHARE OF NIGHT TO BEAR--	OUR SHARE OF NIGHT TO	113	1
OUR SHARE OF MORNING--	OUR SHARE OF NIGHT TO	113	2
OUR BLANK IN BLISS TO FILL	OUR SHARE OF NIGHT TO	113	3
OUR BLANK IN SCORNING--	OUR SHARE OF NIGHT TO	113	4
OUR CONSTANCY FORGOT--	IN EBON BOX, WHEN YEARS	169	14
WERE NONE OF OUR AFFAIR!	IN EBON BOX, WHEN YEARS	169	20
BETWEEN OUR FEET, AND DAY!	AT LAST, TO BE	174	7
THEN WE HIDE OUR BRAVE FACE	WE DONT CRY--TIM AND I,	196	5
DEEP IN OUR HAND--	WE DONT CRY--TIM AND I,	196	6
WE JUST SHUT OUR BROWN EYE	WE DONT CRY--TIM AND I,	196	11
TO OUR FAMILIAR EYES--	I'VE NOTHING ELSE--TO	224	4
TO FIND OUR WAY HOME--	I'VE NOTHING ELSE--TO	224	8
DO WE "BEAT" OUR "WIFE"?	WE--BEE AND I--LIVE BY	230	8
NOON--OUR LAST CUP--	WE--BEE AND I--LIVE BY	230	15
OUR LUXURY!	WILD NIGHTS--WILD NIGHTS	249	4
OUR PORTION--IN THE FASHION--	DELIGHT IS AS THE FLIGHT	257	25
OUR INTERVIEW--WAS TRANSIENT--	THE ONLY GHOST I EVER	274	13
SWEEP BY OUR DISAPPOINTED HEADS	HOW NOTELESS MEN, AND	282	11
OUR SAVIOR, BY A HAIR--	THAT AFTER HORROR--THAT	286	4
AND ALL OUR SINEW TORE--	I GOT SO I COULD HEAR	293	8
FAITH--THE EXPERIMENT OF OUR LORD--	"MORNING"--MEANS	300	10
AND OUR NEW HANDS	WE PLAY AT PASTE--	320	6
AS IF NO SOUL THE [WHILE OUR TWO SOULS THAT] SOLSTICE PASSED	THERE CAME A DAY AT	322	7
THE WARDROBE--OF OUR LORD--	THERE CAME A DAY AT	322	12
OUR LITTLE SEXTON--SINGS.	SOME KEEP THE SABBATH	324	8
OUR PANTING ANCLE BARELY PASSED [GAINED],	OF TRIBULATION--THESE	325	13
PERSUADE OUR FEATHERS HOME	'TIS NOT THAT DYING	335	12
FROM OUR GROSS EYES.	I KNOW THAT HE EXISTS.	338	4
FOR OUR HOARSE GOOD NIGHT--	'TWAS THE OLD--ROAD--	344	21
AS WELL AS OUR OLD HOME!"	I FELT MY LIFE WITH BOTH	351	16
'TIS VAST--AS OUR CAPACITY--	HEAVEN IS SO FAR OF THE	370	5
AS FAIR--AS OUR IDEA--	HEAVEN IS SO FAR OF THE	370	6
AND WARMING IN OUR OWN--	A PRECIOUS--MOULDERING	371	6
ON THEMES CONCERN OUR MUTUAL MIND--	A PRECIOUS--MOULDERING	371	11
DID OUR BEST MOMENT LAST--	DID OUR BEST MOMENT LAST	393	1
THEN--FIT OUR VISION TO THE DARK--	WE GROW ACCUSTOMED TO	419	7
CHERISHING--OUR POOR IDEAL--	TAKING UP THE FAIR IDEAL	428	9
OUR BASHFUL FEET--	ME--COME! MY DAZZLED	431	6
AND HELD IT IN OUR BOSOM--	I TIE MY HAT--I CREASE	443	28
TO HOLD OUR SENSES--ON--	I TIE MY HAT--I CREASE	443	33
UNTIL THE MOSS HAD REACHED OUR LIPS--	I DIED FOR BEAUTY--BUT	449	11
AND COVERED UP--OUR NAMES--	I DIED FOR BEAUTY--BUT	449	12
A TOOTH UPON OUR PEACE	A TOOTH UPON OUR PEACE	459	1
AND CRUSH OUR PRETTY PLAY--	WE DO NOT PLAY ON GRAVES	467	8
THEY TOOK AWAY OUR EYES--	THEY PUT US FAR APART--	474	5
OUR SOULS SAW--JUST AS WELL--	THEY PUT US FAR APART--	474	12
WE STOOD UPON OUR STAPLED FEET--	THEY PUT US FAR APART--	474	15
WE TURNED OUR BACKS UPON THE SUN	THEY PUT US FAR APART--	474	19
TO MEASURE OUR ATTAINMENTS--	MYSELF WAS FORMED--A	488	5
TO OUR--EAR--	IT'S THOUGHTS--AND JUST	495	16
FROM OUR FAMILIAR LIFETIME [ADDRESS / GAZING / FINGERS / NOTICE]--	THOSE FAIR--FICTITIOUS	499	3
BEYOND OUR FAINT [SMALL] CONJECTURE--	THOSE FAIR--FICTITIOUS	499	11
OUR DIZZY [SCANTY] ESTIMATE--	THOSE FAIR--FICTITIOUS	499	12
I PLUCKED AT OUR PARTITION	I TRIED TO THINK A	532	12
A FURROW--OUR CORDILLERA--	WE SEE--COMPARATIVELY--	534	7
OUR APPENINE--A KNOLL--	WE SEE--COMPARATIVELY--	534	8

OUR (CONTINUED)	FIRST LINE	POEM	LINE
OUR GIANTS--FURTHER ON--	WE SEE--COMPARATIVELY--	534	16
OF OUR INFERIOR FACE--	AN IGNORANCE A SUNSET	552	8
OUR LORD--INDEED--MADE [BORE] COMPOUND WITNESS--	ONE CRUCIFIXION IS	553	13
AS MAKE OF [BREW FROM / MIX] OUR IMPERFECT [UNCOMELY / OBTUSER] . . .	SHE HIDETH HER THE LAST	557	11
OUR LORD--THOUGHT NO	MUST BE A WO--	571	13
OUR LORD--"SO LOVED"--IT SAITH--	THE TEST OF LOVE--IS	573	2
FROM OUR UNFITTED [UNFURNISHED] EYES.	MY FIRST WELL DAY--SINCE	574	24
NOT YET, OUR EYES CAN SEE--	"HEAVEN" HAS DIFFERENT	575	20
TO OUR AUTHORITY--	WE TALKED AS GIRLS DO--	586	8
OUR ONLY LULLABY--	I CRIED AT PITY--NOT AT	588	24
SUPPLANTS OUR TAPESTRIES WITH HIS--	THE SPIDER HOLDS A	605	7
THE [OUR] MOULDERING PLAYMATE COMES--	OF NEARNESS TO HER	607	8
THE YEARS, OUR PILFERED THINGS--	OF NEARNESS TO HER	607	14
OUR JOURNEY HAD ADVANCED--	OUR JOURNEY HAD ADVANCED	615	1
OUR FEET WERE ALMOST COME	OUR JOURNEY HAD ADVANCED	615	2
OUR PACE TOOK SUDDEN AWE--	OUR JOURNEY HAD ADVANCED	615	5
OUR FEET--RELUCTANT--LED--	OUR JOURNEY HAD ADVANCED	615	6
BUT PRAYER--REMAINED--OUR SIDE--	IT WAS TOO LATE FOR MAN	623	4
OF OUR OLD [NEW] NEIGHBOR--GOD--	IT WAS TOO LATE FOR MAN	623	8
NO DIFFERENT [AS INFINITE] OUR YEARS WOULD BE	FOREVER--IS COMPOSED OF	624	11
UPON THE ROPES--ABOVE OUR HEAD--	THE LIGHTNING PLAYETH--	630	9
NOR WE SO MUCH AS CHECK OUR SPEECH--	THE LIGHTNING PLAYETH--	630	11
'TIS TRUE--OUR FUTURES DIFFERENT LAY--	OURSELVES WERE WED ONE	631	9
OUR LIFE--HIS PORCELAIN--	I CANNOT LIVE WITH YOU--	640	7
OUR SOUL AND THEIR'S--BETWEEN--	BEREAVEMENT IN THEIR	645	4
WHO, VITAL ONLY TO OUR THOUGHT--	BEREAVEMENT IN THEIR	645	9
IN DYING--'TIS AS IF OUR SOULS [WORLD / SELVES / SUN]	BEREAVEMENT IN THEIR	645	11
IT DEAL US [FURNISH]--STATED AS OUR FOOD--	A PRISON GETS TO BE A	652	7
THAT ANSWER TO OUR FEET--	A PRISON GETS TO BE A	652	10
TO OUR ENDEAVOR--NOT SO REAL [TRUE / CLOSE / NEAR]	A PRISON GETS TO BE A	652	19
ARE PRESENT TO US--AS OUR OWN--	A PRISON GETS TO BE A	652	23
SO IMPOTENT OUR WISDOM IS [BE]	"NATURE" IS WHAT WE SEE	668	11
OUR NOVEL [ROMANCE]--WHEN 'TIS SMALL ENOUGH	NO ROMANCE SOLD UNTO	669	6
ASSASSIN HID IN OUR APARTMENT	ONE NEED NOT BE A	670	15
BUT OUR UNFURNISHED EYES--	NOT "REVELATION"--'TIS--	685	2
PARALYSIS--OUR PRIMER--DUMB [NUMB]--	THE ZEROES--TAUGHT US--	689	7
FROM OUR GARRET GO	PUBLICATION--IS THE	709	6
THAN INVEST--OUR SNOW--	PUBLICATION--IS THE	709	8
OUR CONTRACT	THE BIRDS REPORTED FROM	743	23
NOR I--HERSELF--OUR COMPACT--	THE BIRDS REPORTED FROM	743	V 23
AND WHEN AT NIGHT--OUR GOOD DAY DONE--	MY LIFE HAD STOOD--A	754	13
THESE--WE HELD AMONG [FONDLED IN] OUR OWN--	THESE--SAW VISIONS--	758	9
A BERRY FROM OUR TABLE	DEPRIVED OF OTHER	773	11
THOUGH NONE BE ON OUR SIDE--	ON A COLUMNAR SELF--	789	8
WE WONDERED AT OUR BLINDNESS	HER FINAL SUMMER WAS IT	795	9
AT OUR STUPIDITY--	HER FINAL SUMMER WAS IT	795	12
WHEN DULLER THAN OUR DULLNESS	HER FINAL SUMMER WAS IT	795	13
IT--SUGGESTS TO OUR FAITH--	BY MY WINDOW HAVE I FOR	797	17
THEY--SUGGEST TO OUR SIGHT--	BY MY WINDOW HAVE I FOR	797	18
THAT OUR IGNOBLE EYES	TWO--WERE IMMORTAL TWICE	800	5
REMOVED OUR INVITATION BY	NO NOTICE GAVE SHE, BUT	804	19
AFFECTING OUR CONTENT	A LIGHT EXISTS IN SPRING	812	18
BUT WHAT OUR LORD INFERS [INFERRED] WE WOULD	NOT WHAT WE DID, SHALL	823	3
OUR REDDEST SECOND PALE.	A MOTH THE HUE OF THIS	841	4
THE SEA UPON OUR PLACE--	ESCAPING BACKWARD TO	867	2
OUR UNDERMINING FEET TO MEET	ESCAPING BACKWARD TO	867	7
THEY ASK BUT OUR DELIGHT--	THEY ASK BUT OUR DELIGHT	868	1
ACCORDING TO OUR DEED.	THE SUN IS GAY OR STARK	878	2
IT MAGNIFIES OUR FREIGHT	THE SUN IS GAY OR STARK	878	8
OUR LITTLE KINSMEN--AFTER RAIN	OUR LITTLE KINSMEN--	885	1
THESE TESTED OUR HORIZON--	THESE TESTED OUR HORIZON	886	1
OUR RETROSPECTION OF THEM	THESE TESTED OUR HORIZON	886	5
BUT OUR ANTICIPATION	THESE TESTED OUR HORIZON	886	7
SHALL STAND TO OUR RIGHT HAND--	SWEET, TO HAVE HAD THEM	901	5
PEACE IS A FICTION OF OUR FAITH--	PEACE IS A FICTION OF	912	1
TO OUR FAR, VASCILLATING FEET	FAITH--IS THE PIERLESS	915	11
EQUALLY PERISH FROM OUR PRACTISE--	THOSE WHO HAVE BEEN IN	922	3
MAY NOT OUR SECOND WITH IT'S FIRST	THERE IS A JUNE WHEN	930	13
SHOULD SOFTLY PLACE WITHIN OUR OWN	ON THAT DEAR FRAME THE	940	7
ROUND OUR NEW FIRESIDE--BUT FOR THIS--	I LEARNED--AT LEAST--	944	5
WHAT MORNINGS IN OUR GARDEN--GUESSED--	I LEARNED--AT LEAST--	944	9
THE RIPPLE OF OUR THEME--	I LEARNED--AT LEAST--	944	12
SEEN POOREST--THRO' OUR GAINS--	I LEARNED--AT LEAST--	944	21
THE FLOWER OF OUR LORD.	THIS IS A BLOSSOM OF THE	945	16
THE SPOILER OF OUR HOME?	DENIAL--IS THE ONLY FACT	965	8
OUR MINUTER INTUITIONS--	COLOR--CASTE--	970	15
STAKING OUR ENTIRE [DIVINE] POSSESSION	ROBBED BY DEATH--BUT	971	13
TO OUR OPPOSITE--	UNFULFILLED TO	972	6
OUR SPECULATIONS OF THE FOREIGNER!	BESIDES THIS MAY	977	5
WHERE SAINTS, AND OUR PLAIN GOING NEIGHBOR	BESIDES THIS MAY	977	9
OUR MORTAL CONSEQUENCE	NO OTHER CAN REDUCE	982	2
OUR SINGLE [ONLY] COMPETITION	NO OTHER CAN REDUCE	982	7
OUR MUTUAL FRAME--THAT HAPLY	NO OTHER CAN REDUCE	982	V 7
NO OTHER CAN EXALT OUR	NO OTHER CAN REDUCE	982	V
THE PEARL--THE JUST--OUR THOUGHT.	BEST THINGS DWELL OUT OF	998	2

OUR (CONTINUED)

	FIRST LINE	POEM		LINE
OUR PERIODS MAY LIE	SUPERFLUOUS WERE THE SUN	999		10
IT RISES--PASSES--ON OUR SOUTH	IT RISES--PASSES--ON OUR	1023		1
AT OUR CONCEIT	SO LARGE MY WILL	1024		15
TILL OF ALL OUR NATURE'S HOUSE	AS WILLING LID O'ER	1050		3
AND A COMPANY--OUR PLEASURE	THREE WEEKS PASSED SINCE	1061		5
TO HELP OUR BLEAKER PARTS	TO HELP OUR BLEAKER	1064		1
OUR PROPS DISCLOSE	WHAT TWIGS WE HELD BY--	1086		9
THE DISCS THAT SATISFIED OUR SIGHT--	WHAT TWIGS WE HELD BY--	1086		15
THAT IT WAS NOT OUR PRIVILEGE	ENDED, ERE IT BEGUN--	1088		7
TURNS UNPERCEIVED BENEATH OUR FEET	DEW--IS THE FRESHET IN	1097		3
BY THIS GREAT LIGHT UPON OUR MINDS	THE LAST NIGHT THAT SHE	1100		7
TOO JOSTLED WERE OUR SOULS TO SPEAK	THE LAST NIGHT THAT SHE	1100		19
BELIEF [WITH NOUGHT / OUR FAITH] TO REGULATE--	THE LAST NIGHT THAT SHE	1100		28
SMILED TOO BRAVE FOR THE DETECTING [OUR DETECTION]	HAD WE KNOWN THE TON SHE	1124	V	3
TOO BRIGHT [BOLD] FOR OUR INFIRM DELIGHT	TELL ALL THE TRUTH BUT	1129		3
OUR PASSIVE FLOWER WE HELD TO SEA--	THE FROST OF DEATH WAS	1136		5
AND THEN OUR WRATH BEGUN [BEGAN]--	THE FROST OF DEATH WAS	1136		15
IN OVENS GREEN OUR MOTHER BAKES,	THE WORK OF HER THAT	1143		3
SUBMITTING FOR OUR UNKNOWN SAKE	A FULL FED ROSE ON MEALS	1154		7
OUR INFERENCE IS PREMATURE,	GOD MADE NO ACT WITHOUT	1163		3
OUR PREMISES TO BLAME.	GOD MADE NO ACT WITHOUT	1163		4
OUR FINAL INTERVIEW.	WERE IT TO BE THE LAST	1164		4
TO OUR ASSAULTED MINDS--	OF PAUL AND SILAS IT IS	1166		6
BUT LET OUR OBSERVATION SHUT [HALT]	NATURE AFFECTS TO BE	1170		3
BEHOLD OUR [MY / THIS] SPACIOUS CITIZEN	NATURE AFFECTS TO BE	1170		7
THAT REACHES TO OUR UTMOST HAIR	WE LIKE A HAIRBREADTH	1175		7
OUR STATURES TOUCH THE SKIES--	WE NEVER KNOW HOW HIGH	1176		4
IN OUR ECONOMY	THE DAYS THAT WE CAN	1184		4
OUR ESTIMATES A SCHEME [FORSOOK]--	THE DAYS THAT WE CAN	1184		5
OUR ULTIMATES A SHAM--	THE DAYS THAT WE CAN	1184		6
OUR AFFLUENCE A WHIM	THE DAYS THAT WE CAN	1184	V	6
RELINQUISHED OUR ESTATE--	THE PUNGENT ATOM IN THE	1191		4
OUR VIGILANCE AT WASTE	THE FROST WAS NEVER SEEN	1202		10
OUR OWN POSSESSIONS--THOUGH OUR OWN--	OUR OWN POSSESSIONS--	1208		1
OUR OWN POSSESSIONS--THOUGH OUR OWN--	OUR OWN POSSESSIONS--	1208		1
THAT OUR MINDS ARE HOT.	WE LIKE MARCH.	1213		9
OUR MOST IGNOBLE SERVICES	WHO GOES TO DINE MUST	1223		7
THAT MAKES OUR TRYING [RUNNING] POOR.	BECAUSE HE LOVES HER	1229		12
OUR CONFISCATED GODS--	BECAUSE THAT YOU ARE	1260		40
HAD WE OUR SENSES	HAD WE OUR SENSES	1284		1
HAD WE THE EYES WITHIN OUR HEAD [HEADS]--	HAD WE OUR SENSES	1284		5
WITHIN OUR POWER	IN THIS SHORT LIFE	1287		4
OUR SALARY THE LONGEST DAY	THE NOTICE THAT IS	1310		7
OUR LITTLE SECRETS SLINK AWAY--	OUR LITTLE SECRETS SLINK	1326		1
A [DO / OUR] SUMMER'S [NATURE'S] SOFT ASSEMBLIES GO	WITHOUT A SMILE--WITHOUT	1330		2
WAS ALL OUR TIMID MOTHER WORE	LET ME NOT MAR THAT	1335		7
BUT LEST OUR SPECULATION	"WAS NOT" WAS ALL THE	1342		5
WE AND OUR PLOTTING HEART [GAUDY HEART / SCHEMING TINSEL / . . .	AN ANTIQUATED GRACE	1345		5
BALKING OUR WIT	THE RAT IS THE CONCISEST	1356		5
OF OUR MINUTIAE	A SAUCER HOLDS A CUP	1374		14
TO THE [A / OUR] TEMERITY [EXTREMITY / ADVERSITY]--	SUMMER--WE ALL HAVE SEEN	1386		8
BY OUR OBLIQUITY.	SUMMER--WE ALL HAVE SEEN	1386	V	8
THEY FOUND TO OUR OBJECTION [ABHORRENCE]--	THOSE CATTLE SMALLER	1388		7
INEBRIATE OUR OWN.	HOPE IS A STRANGE	1392	V	8
PORTENTOUS AS OUR OWN, WHO KNOWS?	WHOSE PINK CAREER MAY	1394		2
ON OUR NEW ENGLAND FARMS--	A FIELD OF STUBBLE,	1407		8
OUR ADORATION STAIN [MAR / FLAW]	WE SHUN BECAUSE WE PRIZE	1429		3
ON WHICH OUR FAITH DOTH TREAD--	HOW BRITTLE ARE THE	1433		2
OUR FAITH DOTH DAILY TREAD--	HOW BRITTLE ARE THE	1433	V	2
OUR IGNORANCE--OUR CUIRASS IS--	WE KNEW NOT THAT WE WERE	1462		3
OUR IGNORANCE--OUR CUIRASS IS--	WE KNEW NOT THAT WE WERE	1462		3
PAUSING IN FRONT OF [AGAINST] OUR PALSIED [SENTENCED / . . .	WE TALKED WITH EACH	1473		5
BUT NOT TO OUR CREATOR--	THE FASCINATING CHILL	1480		8
FACTS BY OUR SIDE ARE NEVER SUDDEN	FACTS BY OUR SIDE ARE	1497		1
THE HIGHT OF OUR PORTENTOUS [UNKNOWING] NEIGHBOR	FACTS BY OUR SIDE ARE	1497		5
IN OUR COMPETING DAYS	I SAW THE WIND WITHIN	1502	V	
OUR PROJECTS FLIT AWAY--	ON THAT SPECIFIC PILLOW	1533		2
OUR SUMMER MADE HER LIGHT ESCAPE	AS IMPERCEPTIBLY AS	1540		15
IS OUR PROPENSITY	COME SHOW THY DURHAM	1542		11
OBTAINING BUT OUR [HIS] OWN EXTENT	OBTAINING BUT OUR OWN	1543		1
HER [HIS] LOSSES MAKE OUR GAINS ASHAMED--	HER LOSSES MAKE OUR	1562		1
WE WEAR OUR SOBER DRESSES WHEN WE DIE,	WE WEAR OUR SOBER	1572		1
LIKE OUR DISMAY AT THEE?	WE SHUN IT ERE IT COMES,	1580		8
OUR NOON BECAME A WELL	A CAP OF LEAD ACROSS THE	1649		6
TO OUR SPECIFIC STRENGTH--	A WORD MADE FLESH IS	1651		8
OUR PORT A SECRET	DOWN TIME'S QUAINT	1656		4
OUR PERCHANCE A GALE	DOWN TIME'S QUAINT	1656		5
WITHOUT SUSPECTING OUR ABODE	EDEN IS THAT	1657		3
UNCONSCIOUS OUR RETURNING	EDEN IS THAT	1657		7
T'IS EARLY AS OUR BREATH	WITCHCRAFT HAS NOT A	1708		2
THE MOMENT OF OUR DEATH--	WITCHCRAFT HAS NOT A	1708		4
PROTECTS OUR SANITY.	DID LIFE'S PENURIOUS	1717		8
SO INFINITE OUR INTERCOURSE [INTERVIEW]	HE WAS MY HOST--HE WAS	1721		5

	FIRST LINE	POEM	LINE
OUR (CONTINUED)			
A CONTRAST TO OUR RESPITES.	HIGH FROM THE EARTH I	1723	19
AND OUR DEPARTURE TAKE	SWEET IS THE SWAMP WITH	1740	4
ALLOYS OUR FIRMER MOMENTS	THROUGH THOSE OLD	1753	13
OUR'S			
OF OUR'S!	JESUS! THY CRUCIFIX	225	6
THAT SUDDENLY LOOKS INTO OUR'S.	THAT AFTER HORROR--THAT	286	13
AND THAT IS HIS BUSINESS--NOT OUR'S--	THE WIND DID'NT COME	316	12
THIS BASHFUL GLOBE OF OUR'S WOULD BE--	FUNNY--TO BE A CENTURY--	345	7
OUR'S BE THE TOSSING--WILD THOUGH THE SEA--	HOW SICK--TO WAIT--IN	368	8
OUR'S BE THE CARGO--UNLADEN--HERE--	HOW SICK--TO WAIT--IN	368	10
NOT AUDIBLE--AS OUR'S--TO US--	A MURMUR IN THE TREES--	416	7
FOR THEIR--SAKE--NOT FOR OUR'S--	I TIE MY HAT--I CREASE	443	24
OF OUR'S, NONE AFFAIR--	WE TALKED AS GIRLS DO--	586	4
AND OUR'S--A KINSMANSHIP EXPRESS [EXIST / SUBSIST / ARISE]--	A PRISON GETS TO BE A	652	3
AND THIS OF OUR'S, DIVERSIFIED	THERE IS A JUNE WHEN	930	11
IS NOT OUR'S THE CHASTISING--	WHATEVER IT IS--SHE HAS	1204	3
IN SUCH AN EARTH AS OUR'S--	NOT WITH A CLUB, THE	1304	14
TOOK HER OWN HEART, INCLUDING OUR'S,	THE PRETTY RAIN FROM	1426	3
IS MORE DISTINCT THAN OUR'S--	THE FACE IN EVANESCENCE	1490	2
AND OUR'S SURRENDERED [CONSIDERED] FOR IT'S SAKE	THE FACE IN EVANESCENCE	1490	3
FOR ANGELS RENT THE HOUSE NEXT OUR'S,	WHO HAS NOT FOUND THE	1544	3
OURS			
'TIS OURS--TO WINCE--AND WEEP--	HE GAVE AWAY HIS LIFE--	567	9
WOULD YOU LIKE SUMMER? TASTE OF OURS.	WOULD YOU LIKE SUMMER?	691	1
AND THIS OF OURS MUST DIE	T'WAS COMFORT IN HER	1703	9
OURSELF			
WHAT, AND IF, OURSELF A BRIDEGROOM--	HER--"LAST POEMS"--	312	18
AND DEEM OURSELF A FOOL--	WE PLAY AT PASTE--	320	4
WE CANNOT PUT OURSELF AWAY	I TIE MY HAT--I CREASE	443	13
THE WAY OURSELF, MUST COME--	THOSE FAIR--FICTITIOUS	499	24
PAST WHAT OURSELF CAN ESTIMATE [UNDERSTAND]--	IF ANYBODY'S FRIEND BE	509	23
BUT HOW OURSELF, SHALL BE	"HEAVEN" HAS DIFFERENT	575	18
BUT FONDEST, DWELT UPON OURSELF	WE TALKED AS GIRLS DO--	586	9
OURSELF CANNOT DECIDE--	WHEN I WAS SMALL, A	596	10
AND 'TWAS THEY, AND NOT OURSELF	OF NEARNESS TO HER	607	19
OURSELF BEHIND OURSELF, CONCEALED--	ONE NEED NOT BE A	670	13
OURSELF BEHIND OURSELF, CONCEALED--	ONE NEED NOT BE A	670	13
OURSELF--AND RECTITUDE--	ON A COLUMNAR SELF--	789	10
OURSELF AM LYING STRAIGHT WHEREIN	THIS CHASM, SWEET, UPON	858	7
BETWEEN OURSELF AND HEAVEN.	LEST THIS BE HEAVEN	1043	4
OURSELVES			
NOR HOW OURSELVES BE JUSTIFIED--	SO GLAD WE ARE--A	329	5
REHEARSAL TO OURSELVES	REHEARSAL TO OURSELVES	379	1
WHEN OURSELVES WERE ALSO DUSTY--	SMILING BACK FROM	385	7
WE WONDER IT WAS NOT OURSELVES	THIS WAS A POET--IT IS	448	7
LOCATION'S NARROW WAY IS FOR OURSELVES--	WE PRAY--TO HEAVEN--	489	7
REMEMBERING OURSELVES, WE TRUST--	THOSE FAIR--FICTITIOUS	499	13
HAVE SOBBED OURSELVES ALMOST TO SLEEP,	I CRIED AT PITY--NOT AT	588	23
WOULD DEEM OURSELVES--THE BUSIER	TO INTERRUPT HIS YELLOW	591	13
OURSELVES ARE CONSCIOUS HE EXIST--	THE LIGHTNING PLAYETH--	630	3
NOR STOP TO CROSS OURSELVES--	THE LIGHTNING PLAYETH--	630	12
OURSELVES WERE WED ONE SUMMER--DEAR--	OURSELVES WERE WED ONE	631	1
THAT PARALYZE OURSELVES--	BEREAVEMENT IN THEIR	645	8
THE MAKER [FURTHER]--OF OURSELVES--BE WHAT--	TO BE ALIVE--IS POWER--	677	7
THE CARRIAGE HELD BUT JUST OURSELVES--	BECAUSE I COULD NOT STOP	712	3
AS DID OURSELVES PARTAKE--	DESPAIR'S ADVANTAGE IS	799	10
UNTIL OURSELVES ARE STRUCK--	DESPAIR'S ADVANTAGE IS	799	12
HE LEAVE OURSELVES A SPHERE BEHIND--	WE CAN BUT FOLLOW TO THE	920	3
BETWEEN OURSELVES AND THE DEAD!	UNDER THE LIGHT, YET	949	16
OURSELVES--ASLEEP BELOW--	WE MISS HER, NOT BECAUSE	993	6
MINUTER LANDSCAPE AS OURSELVES	LIKE MEN AND WOMEN	1105	7
OURSELVES WE WEDGED	THE FROST OF DEATH WAS	1136	10
OURSELVES WE DO INTER WITH SWEET DERISION.	OURSELVES WE DO INTER	1144	1
DID NOT OURSELVES THE CUBITS WARP	WE NEVER KNOW HOW HIGH	1176	7
OURSELVES BE NOT PURSUED--	REMEMBRANCE HAS A	1182	8
NOT FOR OURSELVES, PETITION--	WHATEVER IT IS--SHE HAS	1204	5
WE INTRODUCE OURSELVES	WE INTRODUCE OURSELVES	1214	1
BUT WITH OURSELVES	WE INTRODUCE OURSELVES	1214	3
WE COMMEND OURSELVES TO THEE	RECOLLECT THE FACE OF ME	1305	7
OURSELVES, DENIED THE PRIVILEGE,	'TIS NOT THE SWAYING	1597	7
THAT WE DESIRE WITH OURSELVES	GOD IS INDEED A JEALOUS	1719 V	3
OUT			
THE ROSE IS OUT OF TOWN.	THE MORNS ARE MEEKER	12	4
FROM OUT THE WIDE NIGHT'S NUMBERS--	ONE SISTER HAVE I IN OUR	14	26
BROUGHT OUT THEIR BURS AND MOSSES	I ROBBED THE WOODS--	41	4
OUT UPON THE BAY.	WHETHER MY BARK WENT	52	8
OF THE FIRST LEAGUE OUT FROM LAND?	EXULTATION IS THE GOING	76	8
FROM OUT A HUNDRED TREES--	WE SHOULD NOT MIND SO	81	8
WHO'LL LET ME OUT SOME GALA DAY	BRING ME THE SUNSET IN A	128	22
WHY, LOOK OUT FOR THE LITTLE BROOK IN MARCH,	HAVE YOU GOT A BROOK IN	136	9
FROM OUT MY SUMMER'S EVE--	SHE WENT AS QUIET AS THE	149	6
YOU CANNOT FIND OUT ALL ABOUT	DUST IS THE ONLY SECRET	153	3
THIS JUST MAKES OUT THE MORNING SKY.	A SLASH OF BLUE--	204	9
OUT OF THE FOXGLOVE'S DOOR--	I TASTE A LIQUOR NEVER	214	10
UNCONSCIOUS THAT THE OIL IS OUT--	THE LAMP BURNS SURE--	233	7
ARE OUT OF SIGHT--IN HEAVEN--	I THINK JUST HOW MY	237	4
JUST FINDING OUT--WHAT PUZZLED US--	FOREVER AT HIS SIDE TO	246	15

OUT (CONTINUED)

	FIRST LINE	POEM	LINE
WHY--DO THEY SHUT ME OUT OF HEAVEN?	WHY--DO THEY SHUT ME OUT	248	1
AND THEN--IT'S OUT OF SIGHT--	TO DIE--TAKES JUST A	255	4
GOOD NIGHT! WHICH PUT THE CANDLE OUT?	GOOD NIGHT! WHICH PUT	259	1
PASSED OUT--OF RECORD	READ--SWEET--HOW OTHERS	260	14
THEN QUIVERED OUT OF DECIMALS--	A CLOCK STOPPED--	287	8
AND A HOARSE "GET OUT OF THE WAY, I SAY,"	THE WIND DID'NT COME	316	20
TILL I WAS OUT OF SIGHT, IN SOUND,	I CANNOT DANCE UPON MY	326	15
BEFORE I GOT MY EYE PUT OUT	BEFORE I GOT MY EYE PUT	327	1
WHEN I GO OUT OF TIME--	THE FACE I CARRY WITH ME	336	2
PUTS OUT A RUFFLED HEAD--	I TEND MY FLOWERS FOR	339	12
TOO OUT OF SIGHT--THOUGH--	'TWAS THE OLD--ROAD--	344	20
WENT OUT UPON CIRCUMFERENCE--	I SAW NO WAY--THE	378	7
THE NEIGHBORS RUSTLE IN AND OUT--	THERE'S BEEN A DEATH, IN	389	5
SOMEBODY FLINGS A MATTRASS OUT--	THERE'S BEEN A DEATH, IN	389	9
AND CARRIES ONE--OUT OF IT--TO GOD--	IT'S COMING--THE	390	8
HAS FURROWED OUT THE AISLES--	THE COLOR OF THE GRAVE	411	13
OUT OF SOUND--OUT OF SIGHT--	IT IS DEAD--FIND IT--	417	2
OUT OF SOUND--OUT OF SIGHT--	IT IS DEAD--FIND IT--	417	2
OR STAR--COME OUT--WITHIN--	WE GROW ACCUSTOMED TO	419	12
MORE LIFE--WENT OUT--WHEN HE WENT	MORE LIFE--WENT OUT--	422	1
AND THEN, I WANTED TO GET OUT,	'TWAS JUST THIS TIME,	445	7
LOCKING BARE FEET OUT--	SWEET--SAFE--HOUSES--	457	5
GRAVE SAINTS STOLE OUT TO LOOK AT ME--	I MEANT TO HAVE BUT	476	15
HUNG OUT IT'S FLAGS OF SNOW--	THE HIMMALEH WAS KNOWN	481	6
AND LEFT THE VERB AND THE PRONOUN OUT--	GOING TO HIM! HAPPY	494	5
AND OUT [BY], AND EASY ON--	I WOULD NOT PAINT--A	505	12
PUT OUT THEIR TONGUES, FOR NOON,	IT WAS NOT DEATH, FOR I	510	4
IF CERTAIN, WHEN THIS LIFE WAS OUT--	IF YOU WERE COMING IN	511	13
CAME OUT TO LOOK AT ME--	I STARTED EARLY--TOOK MY	520	4
YOU--SWEET [SIR]--SHUT ME OUT--	SWEET--YOU FORGOT--BUT I	523	12
YOU CANNOT [NO MAN--] PUT A FIRE OUT--	YOU CANNOT PUT A FIRE	530	1
BECAUSE THE WINDS WOULD FIND IT OUT--	YOU CANNOT PUT A FIRE	530	7
TWO BUTTERFLIES WENT OUT AT NOON--	TWO BUTTERFLIES WENT OUT	533	1
AND TRODDEN OUT [BLOTTED OUT-- / SHOVED AWAY--] THE MILLS--	THE BRAIN, WITHIN IT'S	556	8
AND TRODDEN OUT [BLOTTED OUT-- / SHOVED AWAY--] THE MILLS--	THE BRAIN, WITHIN IT'S	556	8
THE BUNG OUT--OF [A LEAKAGE IN] AN ARTERY--	ONE ANGUISH--IN A CROWD	565	11
IF JUST AS SOON AS BREATH IS OUT	IF I MAY HAVE IT, WHEN	577	3
OUTVISIONS [OUT FABLES] PARADISE!	IF I MAY HAVE IT, WHEN	577	29
BEGIN, AND LEAVE THEE OUT--	EMPTY MY HEART, OF THEE	587	3
BLEW OUT ITSELF--FOR FEAR--	THE NIGHT WAS WIDE, AND	589	4
WIDTHS OUT OF THE SUN--	DID YOU EVER STAND IN A	590	2
TO GAD MY LITTLE BEING OUT--	IT WOULD HAVE STARVED A	612	15
RETREAT--WAS OUT OF HOPE--	OUR JOURNEY HAD ADVANCED	615	9
ILL FLUTTERED OUT--IN EVERLASTING WELL--	TO KNOW JUST HOW HE	622	17
SHE VAULTED OUT OF GAZE--	I WATCHED THE MOON	629	32
WOULD PUT OUT JESUS'--	I CANNOT LIVE WITH YOU--	640	23
THEIR LIQUID FEET GO SOFTLY OUT	YOU'VE SEEN BALLOONS SET	700	5
OUT OF SIGHT? WHAT OF THAT?	OUT OF SIGHT? WHAT OF	703	1
THERE--LEAVING OUT A MAN--	IT'S EASY TO INVENT A	724	12
ADROITLY TURNING OUT	IF HE WERE LIVING--DARE	734	10
THE PUTTING OUT OF EYES--	RENUNCIATION--IS A	745	5
WORLDS WERE LYING OUT TO [SWIMMING IN THE / LYING IN THE] SUN--	WHEN I HOPED, I	768	11
AND PUT OUT HER EYE--	WHEN I HOPED, I	768	22
A FEW WENT OUT TO HELP THE BROOK	A DROP FELL ON THE APPLE	794	5
THEN ORIENT SHOWED [THE EAST PUT OUT / NATURE PUT OUT] A SINGLE FLAG,	A DROP FELL ON THE APPLE	794	15
THEN ORIENT SHOWED [THE EAST PUT OUT / NATURE PUT OUT] A SINGLE FLAG,	A DROP FELL ON THE APPLE	794	15
TO SHUT THE DOOR AND IT WENT OUT	I CANNOT BUY IT--'TIS	840	5
THEMSELVES--GO OUT--	THE POETS LIGHT BUT	883	2
BEARING THE NEIGHBOR OUT OF SOUND	PEACE IS A FICTION OF	912	3
BUT SEQUENCE RAVELLED OUT OF SOUND [REACH]	I FELT A CLEAVING IN MY	937	7
ITSELF THE ONLY PRINCE CAST OUT--	A LOSS OF SOMETHING EVER	959	8
OUT OF PLUMB OF SPEECH.	GRATITUDE--IS NOT THE	989	4
BUT SEQUENCE RAVELLED OUT OF SOUND	THE DUST BEHIND I STROVE	992	3
BEST THINGS DWELL OUT OF SIGHT	BEST THINGS DWELL OUT OF	998	1
THAT LETS HIM OUT AGAIN.	WHO IS THE EAST?	1032	8
I DWELT, AS IF MYSELF WERE OUT,	I HEARD, AS IF I HAD NO	1039	9
AND TIME WENT OUT TO TELL THE NEWS	I HEARD, AS IF I HAD NO	1039	15
WHICH BE OUT OF SIGHT?	THREE WEEKS PASSED SINCE	1061	12
AND WANDERED OUT OF LIFE.	HE SCANNED IT--STAGGERED	1062	9
WHEN ONCE THE ART IS OUT--	WHEN THEY COME BACK--IF	1080	4
AN EARLDOM OUT OF SIGHT TO HOLD,	BECAUSE 'TWAS RICHES I	1093	5
AS WE WENT OUT AND IN	THE LAST NIGHT THAT SHE	1100	9
THE MORN WAS UP--THE MEADOWS OUT	THE BIRD DID PRANCE--THE	1107	5
AND IT WAS OUT OF SIGHT	THIS SLOW DAY MOVED	1120	8
HIS FADED LAMP WENT OUT.	THAT ODD OLD MAN IS DEAD	1130	4
AND NATURE VENTURED OUT--	THE WIND TOOK UP THE	1134	10
HOW WENT THE AGILE KERNEL OUT	TOO COLD IS THIS	1135	6
THE WINDS WENT OUT THEIR MARTIAL WAYS	THE DAY GREW SMALL,	1140	5
AFTER THE SUN COMES OUT	AFTER THE SUN COMES OUT	1148	1
BUT WHEN THEY WENT TO TAKE THEM OUT	OF PAUL AND SILAS IT IS	1166	3
IT THEN GOES OUT AN ACT	A DEED KNOCKS FIRST AT	1216	5
THE SUN SENT OUT	LIKE BROOMS OF STEEL	1252	5
HOW OUT OF BREATH YOU ARE--	DEAR MARCH--COME IN--	1320	6
AND OUT OF STORY--	GATHERED INTO THE EARTH,	1370	2

	FIRST LINE	POEM	LINE
OUT (CONTINUED)			
OUT OF THE PURPLE DOOR	DREAMS ARE THE SUBTLE	1376	4
YET NEVER WEARING OUT--	HOPE IS A STRANGE	1392	4
BY AND BY--THE BOLDEST STOLE OUT OF HIS COVERT	IT SOUNDED AS IF THE	1397	5
CONTRIVES THAT NONE GO OUT AGAIN-- . . .	NO PASSENGER WAS KNOWN	1406	4
WHEN PEOPLE HAVE PUT OUT THE LIGHTS . . .	HOW LONESOME THE WIND	1418	2
THE SUN WENT OUT TO WORK--	A DEW SUFFICED ITSELF--	1437	5
THE DAY WENT OUT TO PLAY	A DEW SUFFICED ITSELF--	1437	6
OR OUT OF SIGHT OF ESTIMATE	FAME IS THE ONE THAT	1475	3
ELUDES THE FINDING OUT.	WE SHALL FIND THE CUBE	1484	4
THAT LEAVES THIS NEIGHBOR [MAJOR] OUT-- . .	NO BRIGADIER THROUGHOUT	1561	24
TO PUT IT OUT--	THOUGH THE GREAT WATERS	1599	6
AND MOURNERS MEET IT GOING OUT	WITCHCRAFT HAS NOT A	1708	3
OUT OF REACH OF SKILL--	DEATH IS LIKE THE INSECT	1716	10
TILL IT IS OUT OF GAZE.	LOVE CAN DO ALL BUT	1731	8
FOR TRAINS THAT MOMENT [SEVERELY] OUT OF SIGHT,	THE SUMMER THAT WE DID	1773	7
OUTCAST			
IF SUCH AN OUTCAST BE--	OF ALL THE SOUNDS	321	26
HAD NATURE ANY SUPPLE [PLATED / OUTCAST] FACE	THE MUSHROOM IS THE ELF	1298	17
OUTCAST'S			
ETHERIAL GUEST AT E'EN AN OUTCAST'S PILLOW--	AIR HAS NO RESIDENCE, NO	1060	5
OUTER			
THERE CAN NO OUTER WINE	EXHILIRATION--IS WITHIN	383	2
THE OUTER GRAVE--I MEAN--	THE COLOR OF THE GRAVE	411	2
THE OUTER GRAVE--I MEAN--	THE COLOR OF THE GRAVE	411	10
THE OUTER--FROM THE INNER	THE OUTER--FROM THE	451	1
THE INNER--PAINTS THE OUTER--	THE OUTER--FROM THE	451	9
PATIENCE--HAS A QUIET OUTER--	PATIENCE--HAS A QUIET	926	1
OF YELLOW WAS THE OUTER SKY	OF YELLOW WAS THE OUTER	1676	1
OUTGLOW			
OUTGLOW--	RENUNCIATION--IS A	745	V 9
OUTGROW			
COULD EASILY OUTGROW--	I KNOW LIVES, I COULD	372	8
WE OUTGROW LOVE, LIKE OTHER THINGS . . .	WE OUTGROW LOVE, LIKE	887	1
OUTGROWN			
WHEN ORIENT HAVE BEEN OUTGROWN--	THE ONE WHO COULD REPEAT	307	7
"DEFEAT", AN OUTGROWN ANGUISH, ...	OF TRIBULATION--THESE	325	11
PROVES THAT--OUTGROWN--I SEE--	I COULD NOT PROVE THE	563	12
OUTLASTS			
BUT TRUTH, OUTLASTS THE SUN--	OPINION IS A FLITTING	1455	2
OUTLETS			
HIS OUTLETS--WOULD YOU SEE [KNOW]	SUCH ARE THE INLETS OF	1421	2
OUTLIVED			
REMEMBERED, IF OUTLIVED, ...	AFTER GREAT PAIN, A	341	11
OUTRAGED			
RESEMBLES TO MY OUTRAGED MIND	HIS BILL IS CLASPED--HIS	1102	9
OUTSHOW			
OUTSHOW--	RENUNCIATION--IS A	745	V 9
OUTSIDE			
OF WHAT THEY DO OUTSIDE--	DOOM IS THE HOUSE	475	6
THE BODY GROWS WITHOUT [OUTSIDE]-- . . .	THE BODY GROWS WITHOUT--	578	1
OF PERSONS [CREATURES] OUTSIDE WINDOWS-- .	I HAD BEEN HUNGRY, ALL	579	19
OUTSIDE [WITHOUT]--THE SPADES--WERE PLYING--	IN FALLING TIMBERS	614	3
OUTSIDE THE CASTLE [CENTRE / CITY]--THAT CONTAIN [PRESENT]--	THE SPIRIT IS THE	733	7
AND EVERY GRASS THAT PLAYS OUTSIDE . . .	HERE, WHERE THE DAISIES	1037	3
MISTAKE THE OUTSIDE FOR THE IN	DEW--IS THE FRESHET IN	1097	7
OUTSTARING			
OUTSTARING [DEFYING / APPALLING / ABASHING] MASONRY--	TOO COLD IS THIS	1135	5
OUTSTRIPPED			
HE OUTSTRIPPED TIME WITH BUT A BOUT, ...	HE OUTSTRIPPED TIME WITH	865	1
HE OUTSTRIPPED STARS AND SUN	HE OUTSTRIPPED TIME WITH	865	2
OUTVIE			
OUTVIE	RENUNCIATION--IS A	745	9
OUTVISIONS			
OUTVISIONS [OUT FABLES] PARADISE!	IF I MAY HAVE IT, WHEN	577	29
OUTWEIGHS			
AND STILL--MY HEART--MY EYE OUTWEIGHS-- . .	MY EYE IS FULLER THAN MY	202	3
OVAL			
OVAL--AS FEUDAL LADIES WORE--	I AM ASHAMED--I HIDE--	473	14
OVENS			
IN OVENS GREEN OUR MOTHER BAKES, ...	THE WORK OF HER THAT	1143	3
OVER			
A LITTLE EAST OF [OVER] JORDAN, ...	A LITTLE EAST OF JORDAN,	59	1
OVER THE STILE OF "PEARL".	"ARCTURUS" IS HIS OTHER	70	33
OVER THIS PAIN OF MINE--	YOU LOVE ME--YOU ARE	156	18
I SHALL KNOW WHY--WHEN TIME IS OVER-- . .	I SHALL KNOW WHY--WHEN	193	1
OVER THE FENCE--	OVER THE FENCE--	251	1
OVER THE FENCE--	OVER THE FENCE--	251	3
SO OVER HORROR, IT HALF CAPTIVATES [DUMB FASCINATES]--	'TIS SO APPALLING--IT	281	2
OVER AND OVER, LIKE A TUNE--	OVER AND OVER, LIKE A	367	1
OVER AND OVER, LIKE A TUNE--	OVER AND OVER, LIKE A	367	1
I RUN IT OVER--"DEAD", BRAIN, "DEAD." . .	IT DONT SOUND SO	426	2
UNTO [OVER] THE EAST, AND VICTORY-- . . .	A WIFE--AT DAYBREAK I	461	6
GLEE--THE GREAT STORM IS OVER--	GLEE--THE GREAT STORM IS	619	1
THERE'S SOMEWHAT [SOMETHING] PROUDER, OVER THERE--	MY PORTION IS DEFEAT--	639	14

	FIRST LINE	POEM	LINE
OVERWHELMED			
MANY'S THE GALLANT--OVERWHELMED CREATURE	FINITE--TO FAIL, BUT	847	3
OWE			
SWEET DEBT OF LIFE--EACH NIGHT TO OWE--	I GAVE MYSELF TO HIM--	580	15
THEY SPEAK OF WHAT WE OWE--	IS HEAVEN A PHYSICIAN?	1270	6
OWL			
THE OWL LOOKED PUZZLED DOWN--	THROUGH LANE IT LAY--	9	6
THE JUDGE IS LIKE THE OWL--	THE JUDGE IS LIKE THE	699	1
AT MIDNIGHT--LET THE OWL SELECT	THE JUDGE IS LIKE THE	699	11
OWLS			
AND OWLS DO BUILD IN OAKS--	THE JUDGE IS LIKE THE	699	3
OWN			
TO REJOIN IT'S OWN.	A THROE UPON THE	71	8
THE HEART I CARRIED [CHERISHED] IN MY OWN--	SAVIOR! I'VE NO ONE ELSE	217	9
IS ALL I OWN--	I HELD A JEWEL IN MY	245	8
MY OWN--SO PATIENT--COVETS--	YOU SEE I CANNOT SEE--	253	9
WITH LAST [LEAST] DELIGHT I OWN!	DOUBT ME! MY DIM	275	8
BY MY OWN CHOICE, AND THEE--	TIE THE STRINGS TO MY	279	12
FORGETS HER OWN LOCALITY--	THE DROP, THAT WRESTLES	284	2
THE SOUL SELECTS HER OWN SOCIETY--	THE SOUL SELECTS HER OWN	303	1
HIS OWN WAS [IS] AMPLER--BUT AS I .	I SEND TWO SUNSETS--	308	5
AND SO, INSTRUCTED BY MY OWN,	FOR LARGEST WOMAN'S	309	5
IN SOME ODD FASHION [PATTERN] OF IT'S OWN,	OF ALL THE SOUNDS	321	19
EARN HER OWN SURPRISE!	I KNOW THAT HE EXISTS.	338	8
SO FOREIGN TO MY OWN--	I DREADED THAT FIRST	348	12
THE WORLD, WILL HAVE IT'S OWN--TO DO--	ALTHOUGH I PUT AWAY HIS	366	24
AND WARMING IN OUR OWN--	A PRECIOUS--MOULDERING	371	6
EXCEPT IT OWN A STONE--	THE COLOR OF THE GRAVE	411	4
AND GOLD TO OWN--IN SOLID BARS--	IT WAS GIVEN TO ME BY	454	15
WHO OWN THE AMPLE SEA--	'TIS LITTLE I--COULD	466	2
I DO NOT OWN A HOUSE--	I AM ALIVE--I GUESS--	470	18
WHOSE OWN--HAS JUST BEGUN--	NO MAN CAN COMPASS A	477	10
IT'S FINER--OWN THE EAR--	I WOULD NOT PAINT--A	505	18
IT SUITS HIS OWN AUSTERITY--	I THINK THE HEMLOCK	525	3
THAT SOME--ARE LIKE MY OWN--	I MEASURE EVERY GRIEF I	561	40
A TRIFLE--IN HIS OWN ESTEEM [ESTIMATE]--	HE GAVE AWAY HIS LIFE--	567	3
FIXED FULL, AND STEADY, ON HIS OWN	I PRAYED, AT FIRST, A	576	7
MYSELF--CAN OWN [HOLD] THE KEY--	IF I MAY HAVE IT, WHEN	577	8
THE DAILY OWN--OF LOVE	I GAVE MYSELF TO HIM--	580	8
HOW WOULD YOUR OWN--BEGIN?	I FOUND THE WORDS TO	581	6
AT IT'S OWN STABLE DOOR--	I LIKE TO SEE IT LAP	585	17
WOULD NOT BLUSH TO OWN--	DONT PUT UP MY THREAD &	617	8
ARE PRESENT TO US--AS OUR OWN--	A PRISON GETS TO BE A	652	23
"SWEET" SAID HE "MY OWN SURRENDER	WOLFE DEMANDED DURING	678	7
SECURE AGAINST IT'S OWN--	THE SOUL UNTO ITSELF	683	5
JUST HIS OWN ENDORSEMENT--	LIFE--IS WHAT WE MAKE IT	698	7
WHO HIS OWN ACQUAINTANCE	NEVER FOR SOCIETY	746	3
THESE--WE HELD AMONG [FONDLED IN] OUR OWN--	THESE--SAW VISIONS--	758	9
MY OWN HAD JUST BEGUN.	SEVERER SERVICE OF	786	8
TO OWN IT--TOUCH IT--	GOD GAVE A LOAF TO EVERY	791	5
WHO OWN--ESTEEM THE OPULENCE--	I PLAY AT RICHES--TO	801	15
CONSPIRE AGAINST [REPUDIATE] HIS OWN	WHO COURT OBTAIN WITHIN	803	9
IT'S OWN IDENTITY.	THIS CONSCIOUSNESS THAT	822	16
TO OWN THE ART WITHIN THE SOUL	TO OWN THE ART WITHIN	855	1
HIS OWN WOULD FALL SO MORE	EACH SCAR I'LL KEEP FOR	877	7
SHOULD SOFTLY PLACE WITHIN OUR OWN	ON THAT DEAR FRAME THE	940	7
THE GARDEN [LANDSCAPE] KEEP [SHOW / OWN / HOLD] THE GASH--	AS FROST IS BEST	951	6
SUFFICIENT FOR MY OWN	THE PRODUCTS OF MY FARM	1025	2
OWN [DWELL] IN EDEN NOTWITHSTANDING	PARADISE IS OF THE	1069	3
HONOR--IS IT'S OWN PAWN--	TITLE DIVINE--IS MINE!	1072	V
I AM AFRAID TO OWN A BODY--	I AM AFRAID TO OWN A	1090	1
I AM AFRAID TO OWN A SOUL--	I AM AFRAID TO OWN A	1090	2
BECAUSE 'TWAS RICHES I COULD OWN,	BECAUSE 'TWAS RICHES I	1093	1
TO NEIGHBORS DOUBTLESS OF THEIR OWN	LIKE MEN AND WOMEN	1105	5
A MINE THERE IS NO MAN WOULD OWN	A MINE THERE IS NO MAN	1117	1
OUR OWN POSSESSIONS--THOUGH OUR OWN--	OUR OWN POSSESSIONS--	1208	1
OUR OWN POSSESSIONS--THOUGH OUR OWN--	OUR OWN POSSESSIONS--	1208	1
FOR IT'S OWN PERUSAL.	SAFE DESPAIR IT IS THAT	1243	4
TO OWN THE MIRACLE--	WHO WERE "THE FATHER AND	1258	24
I RECOGNIZE YOUR OWN--	BECAUSE THAT YOU ARE	1260	24
OF LIFE TO OWN--	OF LIFE TO OWN--	1294	1
AS IF IT WERE HIS OWN!	A LITTLE MADNESS IN THE	1333	6
THAN OWN A RISING SUN	I'D RATHER RECOLLECT A	1349	2
EMBELLISH ALL WE OWN--	HOPE IS A STRANGE	1392	8
INEBRIATE OUR OWN.	HOPE IS A STRANGE	1392	V 8
PORTENTOUS AS OUR OWN, WHO KNOWS?	WHOSE PINK CAREER MAY	1394	2
TO OWN A SUSAN OF MY OWN	TO OWN A SUSAN OF MY OWN	1401	1
TO OWN A SUSAN OF MY OWN	TO OWN A SUSAN OF MY OWN	1401	1
TOOK HER OWN HEART, INCLUDING OUR'S,	THE PRETTY RAIN FROM	1426	3
TO OWN OF IT IS WOUND--	BEHOLD THIS LITTLE BANE	1438	6
INTENT UPON IT'S OWN CAREER [MISSION QUAINT / CIRCUIT QUAINT]	HOW SOFT A CATERPILLAR	1448	7
IF THEN WE CANNOT OWN THEM BOTH--	OPINION IS A FLITTING	1455	3
BEGINNING NOT TO OWN--	IT STOLE ALONG SO	1457	4
FOR THINE OWN DUPLICITY--	"HEAVENLY FATHER"--TAKE	1461	8
NOT ONE OF US WILL OWN	I SAW THE WIND WITHIN	1502	V
OBTAINING BUT OUR [HIS] OWN EXTENT	OBTAINING BUT OUR OWN	1543	1
'TWAS CHRIST'S OWN PERSONAL EXPANSE	OBTAINING BUT OUR OWN	1543	3
TO OWN HER FOR A FRIEND	TO SEE HER IS A PICTURE	1568	6

	FIRST LINE	POEM	LINE
OWN (CONTINUED)			
IN MY OWN GRAVE I BREATHE	SO GIVE ME BACK TO DEATH	1632	5
STILL OWN THEE--STILL THOU ART	STILL OWN THEE--STILL	1633	1
AS IF IT WERE HER OWN--	THIS DOCILE ONE INTER	1752	8
OWNED			
AND HE OWNED ALL THE MOURNERS--NOW--	THERE'S BEEN A DEATH, IN	389	15
AND HAD [OWNED] ESTATES OF CLOUD	THE TREES LIKE TASSELS--	606	12
I WAS OWNED OF THEE--	'TWAS MY ONE GLORY--	1028	4
MANY OWNED BEFORE--	PARADISE IS THAT OLD	1119	2
THAT OWNED IT ALL--	THE VASTEST EARTHLY DAY	1328	V 4
POSSESSED [ABHORRED / WE OWNED] BEFORE--	DREAMS ARE THE SUBTLE	1376	6
AND NATURE GENTLY [SOFTLY] OWNED HER	SHE COULD NOT LIVE UPON	1505	4
OWNER			
AS IF THEIR OWNER WERE	SHE LAY AS IF AT PLAY	369	10
OWNER CANNOT [NEVER YET WAS] SHUT--	DRAMA'S VITALLEST	741	15
THE OWNER PASSED--IDENTIFIED--	MY LIFE HAD STOOD--A	754	3
THE OWNER OF THIS HOUSE	WHO OCCUPIES THIS HOUSE?	892	29
WHEN A LOVER IS AN OWNER	WHEN A LOVER IS A BEGGAR	1314	3
WHOSE AXIS [OWNER] NEVER COMES.	WATER MAKES MANY BEDS	1428	8
OWNER'S			
TO ASK THE OWNER'S NAME--	I FELT MY LIFE WITH BOTH	351	7
OWNEST			
OR OWNEST WHERE?	"TOMORROW"--WHOSE	1367	8
OWNS			
TO HIM WHO EASY OWNS--	I CANNOT WANT IT MORE--	1301	6
OXYGEN			
DISDAINING MEN, AND OXYGEN,	OF BRONZE--AND BLAZE--	290	12
THE POLTROON WANTS OXYGEN--	IF YOUR NERVE, DENY YOU	292	11
INDEBTEDNESS TO OXYGEN	THE FARTHEST THUNDER	1581	9
PACE			
A PACE HAD BEEN BETWEEN--	I NEVER TOLD THE BURIED	11	7
HAD NOT THE BLISS SO SLOW A PACE	DELAYED TILL SHE HAD	58	10
NOR THIS--DEFEAT MY PACE--	I CROSS TILL I AM WEARY	550	10
OUR PACE TOOK SUDDEN AWE--	OUR JOURNEY HAD ADVANCED	615	5
TO FOLLOW HER SUPERIOR ROAD [PACE]--	I WATCHED THE MOON	629	35
IN EASY--EVEN--DAZZLING PACE--	OF BEING IS A BIRD	653	7
IT WILL NOT HARM HER MAGIC PACE	BECAUSE HE LOVES HER	1229	5
FOR WHATSOE'ER MY PACE	MY HEART RAN SO TO THEE	1237	5
PACES			
IT MEASURES [PACES] LIKE THE SEA	THE HEART HAS NARROW	928	2
PACK			
TO PACK THE BUD--OPPOSE THE WORM--	BLOOM--IS RESULT--TO	1058	9
SHE [HE] BORE LIFE'S EMPTY PACK	HER LOSSES MAKE OUR	1562	2
LIFE'S EMPTY PACK IS HEAVIEST,	HER LOSSES MAKE OUR	1562	5
TO PACK HER TRUNK AND ORDER	WERE NATURE MORTAL LADY	1762	3
PACKED			
LIKE BREADTHS OF TOPAZ--PACKED A NIGHT--	THE DAY CAME SLOW--TILL	304	7
PAEANS			
LESS PAEANS--FEWER BELLS--	MY PORTION IS DEFEAT--	639	3
PAGE			
TELL HIM [HER] THE PAGE I DID'NT WRITE--[NEVER WROTE!]	GOING TO HIM! HAPPY	494	3
OR PAGE--PLEASE THEE--	YOU SAID THAT I "WAS	738	14
A WORD DROPPED CARELESS ON A PAGE	A WORD DROPPED CARELESS	1261	1
NOR ANY COURSERS LIKE A PAGE	THERE IS NO FRIGATE LIKE	1263	3
PAGEANT			
TILL THE PAGEANT BY,	MUTE THY CORONATION--	151	6
THEN--THE LICENSE [VISION / PAGEANT] CLOSES--	SOME SUCH BUTTERFLY BE	541	4
IS A MINUTER [DENUDED] PAGEANT	THE HARM OF YEARS IS ON	1280	7
DEPARTING LIKE A PAGEANT	ONE OF THE ONES THAT	1466	19
TO THE SAME PAGEANT WENDS ITS WAY	NO LIFE CAN POMPLESS	1626	3
PAGEANTRY			
I SOW MY PAGEANTRY	ALL THESE MY BANNERS BE.	22	2
A PLEADING PAGEANTRY--	INCONCEIVABLY SOLEMN!	582	7
PAGEANTS			
AND PAGEANTS AS IMPASSIVE	DEATH IS THE SUPPLE	1445	V 11
PAGES			
AND THEN YOU WISHED YOU HAD EYES IN YOUR PAGES--	GOING TO HIM! HAPPY	494	8
WERE PAGES WHERE TO READ	THE HOLLOWS ROUND HIS	955	2
PAID			
THE PRICE IS GREAT--SUBLIMELY PAID--	IT FEELS A SHAME TO BE	444	9
PAID AFTER THEY HAVE CEASED TO WORK	ALL MEN FOR HONOR	1193	3
I HAD PAID SO MUCH FOR--	NOW I KNEW I LOST HER--	1219	15
PAID ALL THAT LIFE HAD EARNED	HOW DARE THE ROBINS SING	1724	5
I'LL TELL YOU WHAT I PAID--	I TOOK ONE DRAUGHT OF	1725	2
PAID'ST			
GO [BUT] BOLDLY--FOR THOU PAID'ST HIS PRICE	GO SLOW, MY SOUL, TO	1297	7
PAIN			
IF PAIN FOR PEACE PREPARES	IF PAIN FOR PEACE	63	1
OVER THIS PAIN OF MINE--	YOU LOVE ME--YOU ARE	156	18
TO LEARN THE TRANSPORT BY [THRO'] THE PAIN--	TO LEARN THE TRANSPORT	167	1
WHEN UPON A PAIN TITANIC	I HAVE NEVER SEEN	175	11
THAT I INSTIL THE PAIN	AH, NECROMANCY SWEET!	177	4
THAT OTHER KIND--WAS PAIN--	I'M "WIFE"--I'VE	199	10
BUT WHEN THE SOUL IS IN PAIN--	IT IS EASY TO WORK WHEN	244	2
POWER IS ONLY PAIN--	I CAN WADE GRIEF--	252	10
SING--AT IT'S PAIN--AS ANY WORKMAN--	BOUND--A TROUBLE--	269	9
BUT THE PUSH [PAIN] OF JOY--	MANY A PHRASE HAS THE	276	14
THE FIGURES HUNCHED, WITH PAIN--	A CLOCK STOPPED--	287	7

	FIRST LINE	POEM	LINE
PAIN (CONTINUED)			
IF TO BE "ELDER"--MEAN MOST PAIN--	ONE YEAR AGO--JOTS WHAT?	296	32
AFTER GREAT PAIN, A FORMAL FEELING COMES--	AFTER GREAT PAIN, A	341	1
'TWAS THE OLD--ROAD--THROUGH PAIN--	'TWAS THE OLD--ROAD--	344	1
SO PATIENT--LIKE A PAIN--	A HAPPY LIP--BREAKS	353	6
OR SMOOTHED A HOMELY PAIN,	ALTHOUGH I PUT AWAY HIS	366	6
OR BREAKING--ALMOST--WITH UNSPOKEN PAIN--	HOW SICK--TO WAIT--IN	368	4
MORE IMMINENT THAN PAIN--	THERE IS A LANGUOR OF	396	2
THE SURGEON--DOES NOT BLANCH--AT PAIN--	THERE IS A LANGUOR OF	396	9
'TWOULD GIVE AN EASIER--PAIN--	IT WOULD NEVER BE COMMON	430	8
AT ESTIMATING PAIN--	NO MAN CAN COMPASS A	477	9
WITH TRANSPORT, THAT WOULD BE A PAIN	THOSE FAIR--FICTITIOUS	499	19
AND THEN--EXCUSE FROM PAIN--	THE HEART ASKS PLEASURE	536	2
AND THEREFORE--'TWAS NOT PAIN--	IT KNEW NO MEDICINE--	559	4
IT FEELS SO OLD A PAIN--	I MEASURE EVERY GRIEF I	561	8
ENLIGHTENED TO A LARGER PAIN--	I MEASURE EVERY GRIEF I	561	23
WHEN VIEWED THROUGH PAIN--	DELIGHT--BECOMES	572	2
TO TAKE MY CHANCE [RISK] WITH PAIN--	MY FIRST WELL DAY--SINCE	574	6
I CRIED AT PITY--NOT AT PAIN--	I CRIED AT PITY--NOT AT	588	1
THERE IS A PAIN--SO UTTER--	THERE IS A PAIN--SO	599	1
AND PAIN--IS MISSED--IN [FORGETS--FOR--] PRAISE--	UNTO MY BOOKS--SO GOOD	604	4
YOU LEFT ME BOUNDARIES OF PAIN--	YOU LEFT ME--SIRE--TWO	644	5
PAIN--HAS AN ELEMENT OF BLANK--	PAIN--HAS AN ELEMENT OF	650	1
NEW PERIODS--OF PAIN.	PAIN--HAS AN ELEMENT OF	650	8
DISTILS UNCERTAIN PAIN--	THE LOVE A LIFE CAN SHOW	673	9
UNTIL HE'S PAST THE PAIN--	I SOMETIMES DROP IT, FOR	708	16
THE HALLOWING OF PAIN	THE HALLOWING OF PAIN	772	1
JOY TO HAVE MERITED THE PAIN--	JOY TO HAVE MERITED THE	788	1
WITH GOLD AND SILVER PAIN	A PLATED LIFE--	806	2
NEXT DOOR TO MINE THE PAIN.	HOW WELL I KNEW HER NOT	837	4
HIS PREAPPOINTED PAIN--	EXPERIENCE IS THE ANGLED	910	8
OR COOL ONE PAIN	IF I CAN STOP ONE HEART	919	4
OF UNOBTRUSIVE PAIN	THE HOLLOWS ROUND HIS	955	6
PAIN--EXPANDS THE TIME--	PAIN--EXPANDS THE TIME--	967	1
PAIN CONTRACTS--THE TIME--	PAIN--EXPANDS THE TIME--	967	5
I SHALL IMPUTE WITH HALF A PAIN	FITTER TO SEE HIM, I MAY	968	7
BUT GAIN--THRO' LOSS--THROUGH GRIEF [PAIN]--OBTAIN--	FITTER TO SEE HIM, I MAY	968	26
'TIS RESURRECTION PAIN--	'TIS ANGUISH GRANDER	984	2
PAIN HAS BUT ONE ACQUAINTANCE	PAIN HAS BUT ONE	1049	1
PAIN IS THE JUNIOR PARTY	PAIN HAS BUT ONE	1049	5
INFLICTS A PRICKLIER PAIN,	WE MISS A KINSMAN MORE	1087	6
ARE FRIENDS DELIGHT OR PAIN?	ARE FRIENDS DELIGHT OR	1199	1
WHETHER ADULT DELIGHT IS [BE] PAIN	WONDER--IS NOT PRECISELY	1331	6
I FELT IT SECOND PAIN	THAT SHE FORGOT ME WAS	1683	2
LIKE ANIMALS IN PAIN	THE WIND DREW OFF	1694	9
PROUD OF THE PAIN I DID NOT FEEL TILL THEE,	PROUD OF MY BROKEN HEART	1736	2
TRUST ENTRENCHED IN NARROW PAIN--	REARRANGE A "WIFE'S"	1737	10
PAIN'S			
'TIS PAIN'S SUCCESSOR--WHEN THE SOUL	THERE IS A LANGUOR OF	396	3
PAINT			
I WOULD NOT PAINT--A PICTURE--	I WOULD NOT PAINT--A	505	1
PAINTED			
BUT WHEN THE WOODS WERE PAINTED,	I HAD A GUINEA GOLDEN--	23	11
MORNING PAINTED ROSE--	ON THE WORLD YOU COLORED	1171	2
PAINTERS			
THE MARTYR PAINTERS--NEVER SPOKE--	THE MARTYR POETS--DID	544	5
PAINTS			
THE INNER--PAINTS THE OUTER--	THE OUTER--FROM THE	451	9
PAIR			
WHEN KATIE WALKS, THIS SIMPLE PAIR ACCOMPANY HER SIDE,	WHEN KATIE WALKS, THIS	222	1
THEN THERE'S A PAIR OF US!	I'M NOBODY! WHO ARE YOU?	288	3
A PAIR OF SPECTACLES AJAR JUST STIR--	I KNOW SOME LONELY	289	19
FOR YET TO BUY ANOTHER PAIR	IS BLISS THEN, SUCH	340	6
AND GRACE WOULD GRANT THE PAIR--	I MEANT TO HAVE BUT	476	8
PAIRS			
AS YESTERDAYS IN PAIRS,	THE FIRST DAY'S NIGHT	410	10
PALACE			
BESIDE YOUR PALACE [TWINKLING / GLIMMERING] DOOR--	THE MOON WAS BUT A CHIN	737	16
PARADISE--THE ONLY PALACE	THESE--SAW VISIONS--	758	14
FROM HIS SLIM PALACE IN THE DUST	FROM HIS SLIM PALACE IN	1300	1
PALACES			
MY PALACES--DROPPED TENANTLESS--	IT WOULD NEVER BE COMMON	430	23
I KNOW NOT WHICH THY CHAMBER IS [PALACES]--	AT LEAST--TO PRAY--IS	502	3
FOR MY DELINQUENT PALACES--	A LOSS OF SOMETHING EVER	959	12
PALATE			
A ROBIN'S FAMINE [PALATE / HUNGER] ABLE--	DEPRIVED OF OTHER	773	9
HER PALATE TO DELIGHT	MY HEART UPON A LITTLE	1027	2
. . . THE] MINOR PALATE	ART THOU THE THING I	1282	3
THE PALATE OF THE HATE DEPARTS--	MINE ENEMY IS GROWING	1509	3
FOR EVERY PALATE IN THE YEAR,"--	THE WATERS CHASED HIM AS	1749	7
PALATES			
BY FUNDAMENTAL PALATES	THE JOY THAT HAS NO STEM	1744	5
PALE			
SOME PALE REPORTER, FROM THE AWFUL DOORS	JUST LOST, WHEN I WAS	160	10
OUR REDDEST SECOND PALE.	A MOTH THE HUE OF THIS	841	4

	FIRST LINE	POEM	LINE
PALER			
A PALER LUCK THAN VICTORY--	MY PORTION IS DEFEAT--	639	2
PALL			
AND WHICH THE PALL	WHOSE CHEEK IS THIS?	82	9
BEHIND A PALL--	THE VASTEST EARTHLY DAY	1328	4
THE HOSPITABLE PALL	NO LIFE CAN POMPLESS	1626	6
PALLIATE			
TO PALLIATE A COLD--	CONJECTURING A CLIMATE	562	6
OR TAKE AWAY [PALLIATE] A BRIAR.	IT WAS A GRAVE, YET BORE	876	12
PALLID			
WILL TINT THE PALLID LANDSCAPE--	IT WILL BE SUMMER--	342	5
HIS PALLID FURNITURE ARRANGED	IT CAME AT LAST BUT	1230	3
BY PALLID INNUENDOES	DEATH IS THE SUPPLE	1445	5
THE DANDELION'S PALLID TUBE	THE DANDELION'S PALLID	1519	1
PALLS			
THE MIXING BELLS AND PALLS--	UPON CONCLUDED LIVES	735	4
PALM			
THE PALM--WITHOUT THE CALVARY--	I SHOULD HAVE BEEN TOO	313	17
MEMORIES--OF PALM--	CIVILIZATION--SPURNS--	492	11
AS THE PALM--THAT SERVE THE DESERT--	HER SWEET TURN TO LEAVE	649	19
SEED OF PALM, BY LYBIAN SUN	SOIL OF FLINT, IF STEADY	681	3
PALMLEAF			
A LITTLE PALMLEAF HAT WAS ALL,	I MET A KING THIS	166	3
PALMS			
NO ORNAMENT--BUT PALMS--	OF TRIBULATION--THESE	325	8
PALPITATING			
AND THE PALPITATING VINEYARD	I HAVE NEVER SEEN	175	15
PALSIED			
STOP PALSIED--'TIS PARALYSIS	I'VE DROPPED MY BRAIN--	1046	3
PAUSING IN FRONT OF [AGAINST] OUR PALSIED [SENTENCED / . . .	WE TALKED WITH EACH	1473	5
PALTRY			
JUST A PALTRY ONE--	ALL FORGOT FOR	966	2
REMOVES THE PALTRY THING	TO DISAPPEAR ENHANCES--	1209	V 10
HOW PALTRY LOOKED MY CARES	CONFERRING WITH MYSELF	1655	5
ARE PALTRY MELODY	THE WORDS THE HAPPY SAY	1750	2
PAMPAS			
ON BRAZILIAN PAMPAS--	SOME SUCH BUTTERFLY BE	541	2
PANE			
A FLIPPANT FLY UPON THE PANE--	AN ALTERED LOOK ABOUT	140	7
UPON THE WINDOW PANE--	THE SUN KEPT STOOPING--	152	6
BRAVE--SHINES THE SUN THROUGH THE FRECKLED PANE--	HOW MANY TIMES THESE LOW	187	10
UPON THE WINDOW PANE--	BEFORE I GOT MY EYE PUT	327	19
THEN--HELD AN EMPTY PANE--	A HOUSE UPON THE HIGHT--	399	8
THE WEALTHY [HAPPY] FLY, UPON HIS PANE--	I ENVY SEAS, WHEREON HE	498	11
UPON THE WINDOW PANE	IT WOULD HAVE STARVED A	612	14
UNTIL UPON A PANE--	I WATCHED THE MOON	629	2
AND DOME [SPIRE / CHURCH]--AND WINDOW PANE--	THE DAY UNDRESSED--	716	16
THE FROST OF DEATH WAS ON THE PANE--	THE FROST OF DEATH WAS	1136	1
PANELS			
IT'S LITTLE PANELS BE	I SEE THEE BETTER--IN	611	10
AND THEN THE PANELS ARE REVERSED--	WE CAN BUT FOLLOW TO THE	920	7
PANES			
IT CAN BE HAD ON WINDOW PANES	LIGHT IS SUFFICIENT TO	862	3
PANG			
FOR PANG OF JEALOUSY--	THERE IS A FLOWER THAT	380	24
BUT WROUGHT THEIR PANG IN SYLLABLE--	THE MARTYR POETS--DID	544	2
HAD NOBODY A PANG	WHEN THEY COME BACK--IF	1080	10
WE BUY WITH CONTRAST--PANG IS GOOD	THE SNOW THAT NEVER	1133	15
BIRTHDAY OF BUT A SINGLE PANG	BIRTHDAY OF BUT A SINGLE	1488	1
A PANG IS MORE CONSPICUOUS IN SPRING	A PANG IS MORE	1530	1
PANGLESS			
PANGLESS EXCEPT FOR US--	PASS TO THY RENDEZVOUS	1564	2
PANTHER			
LIKE A PANTHER IN THE GLOVE--	IT IS EASY TO WORK WHEN	244	8
PANTING			
THAT FLUTTERED PANTING, HERE--	THIS HEART THAT BROKE SO	145	6
OUR PANTING ANCLE BARELY PASSED [GAINED],	OF TRIBULATION--THESE	325	13
AND [HE] PANTING [HEAVY / LANGUID] ON A CLOVER LEAN	THE BUTTERFLY'S NUMIDIAN	1387	5
HER PANTING NOTE [JOYFUL CRY / CORDIAL NOTE] EXALTS US-- . . .	AFTER ALL BIRDS HAVE	1395	6
ON A STRANGE [UPON A] MOB OF PANTING TREES	THERE CAME A WIND LIKE A	1593	9
PANTOMIME			
AND TOUCH THE PANTOMIME--HIMSELF,	I BREATHED ENOUGH TO	272	7
PANTRY			
MY PANTRY HAS A FISH	THE WATERS CHASED HIM AS	1749	6
PAPA			
PAPA ABOVE!	PAPA ABOVE!	61	1
PARADE			
OBVIATE PARADE.	THE GENTIAN WEAVES HER	18	4
AND FURTHER TO PARADE A JOY	THE MORNING AFTER WO--	364	7
THERE'LL BE THAT DARK PARADE--	THERE'S BEEN A DEATH, IN	389	20
IT'S SWEET PARADE--BLASPHEME THE PLACE--	IT MIGHT BE LONELIER	405	11
NOR WAS IT FOR APPLAUSE [PARADE / RESULT]--	THE BIRDS BEGUN AT FOUR	783	13
PARADES			
THEIR FAR PARADES--ORDER [HALT] ON THE EYE	INCONCEIVABLY SOLEMN!	582	5
PARADISE			
TO PARADISE AWAY--	SO HAS A DAISY VANISHED	28	4

	FIRST LINE	POEM	LINE
PARADISE (CONTINUED)			
PATIENT TILL PARADISE.	MY NOSEGAYS ARE FOR	95	4
AND PEACE--WAS PARADISE!	AN AWFUL TEMPEST MASHED	198	13
DID THE "PARADISE"--PERSUADED--	DID THE HAREBELL LOOSE	213	5
WHAT IS--"PARADISE"--	WHAT IS--"PARADISE"--	215	1
MIND THEE IN PARADISE	JESUS! THY CRUCIFIX	225	5
OR RAP--AT PARADISE--UNHEARD	SHOULD YOU BUT FAIL AT--	226	5
THERE--PARADISE--IS FOUND!	"HEAVEN"--IS WHAT I	239	8
THE TAPESTRIES OF PARADISE	A SHADY FRIEND--FOR	278	11
THE SOUL SO CLOSE ON PARADISE--	NOT PROBABLE--THE BAREST	346	4
TO PARADISE, WITH ME--	ALTHOUGH I PUT AWAY HIS	366	31
CORNETS OF PARADISE--	OVER AND OVER, LIKE A	367	4
I DONT LIKE PARADISE--	I NEVER FELT AT HOME--	413	4
MY PARADISE--THE FAME	ME--COME! MY DAZZLED	431	9
OF PARADISE--AWARE--	THEY PUT US FAR APART--	474	22
BUT NOON, AND PARADISE--	THE SOUL HAS BANDAGED	512	18
NO PARADISE COULD BE--CONFERRED	'TIS TRUE--THEY SHUT ME	538	7
WAS PARADISE--TO BLAME--	IT KNEW NO MEDICINE--	559	12
THAT MEN CALL "PARADISE"--	"HEAVEN" HAS DIFFERENT	575	16
OUTVISIONS [OUT FABLES] PARADISE!	IF I MAY HAVE IT, WHEN	577	29
IF PRIDE SHALL BE IN PARADISE--	WHEN I WAS SMALL, A	596	9
UNTIL IT SETTLED BROAD [FULL / FIRM]--ON PARADISE--	TO KNOW JUST HOW HE	622	4
A PARADISE--THE HOST--	'TWAS A LONG PARTING--	625	14
BUT PARADISE--	THE CHILD'S FAITH IS NEW	637	8
AS PARADISE	I CANNOT LIVE WITH YOU--	640	36
EQUAL PARADISE--	HER SWEET TURN TO LEAVE	649	28
TO GATHER PARADISE--	I DWELL IN POSSIBILITY--	657	12
THEN--FLINGS IN PARADISE--	THE LOVE A LIFE CAN SHOW	673	16
FAR AS PARADISE--	LIFE--IS WHAT WE MAKE IT	698	12
SO CLOSE ON PARADISE--	I SOMETIMES DROP IT, FOR	708	12
WHY PARADISE DEFER [DEMUR]--	ONE BLESSING HAD I THAN	756	18
PARADISE--THE ONLY PALACE	THESE--SAW VISIONS--	758	14
NO BELLS HAVE PARADISE--	MY FAITH IS LARGER THAN	766	12
HAD IT A GUEST FROM PARADISE--	THIS THAT WOULD GREET--	778	3
TO COMPASS PARADISE--	JOY TO HAVE MERITED THE	788	4
THOUGH BOUGHT IN PARADISE--	JOY TO HAVE MERITED THE	788	8
MY VISITOR IN PARADISE--	A DROP FELL ON THE APPLE	794	V
OF PARADISE SUPERLATIVE--	TWO--WERE IMMORTAL TWICE	800	7
FOR IN THE ZONES OF PARADISE	THE SUN AND MOON MUST	871	3
A CITIZEN [RUDIMENT] OF PARADISE	A COFFIN--IS A SMALL	943	3
NOW--OF PARADISE"--	"UNTO ME?" I DO NOT KNOW	964	4
CHANTING TO PARADISE--	BIND ME--I STILL CAN	1005	5
YESTERDAY--ENDOWED WITH PARADISE.	I'VE DROPPED MY BRAIN--	1046	8
PARADISE IS OF THE OPTION.	PARADISE IS OF THE	1069	1
SUBSIST TILL PARADISE.	SUPERIORITY TO FATE	1081	8
PARADISE IS THAT OLD MANSION	PARADISE IS THAT OLD	1119	1
IN THY LONG PARADISE OF LIGHT	IN THY LONG PARADISE OF	1145	1
MY GUEST "TODAY [VISITOR] IN PARADISE"	"REMEMBER ME" IMPLORED	1180	3
AS PARADISE FICTITIOUS	BECAUSE THAT YOU ARE	1260	19
DUE IN PARADISE TODAY	RECOLLECT THE FACE OF ME	1305	3
AT HOME--IN PARADISE.	LET ME NOT MAR THAT	1335	8
WHO HAS PARADISE--	LIFT IT--WITH THE	1348	8
NOT ELSEWHERE--IF IN PARADISE	BEHOLD THIS LITTLE BANE	1438	7
THE ROAD TO PARADISE IS PLAIN,	THE ROAD TO PARADISE IS	1491	1
THE BELLES [GUESTS] OF PARADISE ARE FEW--	THE ROAD TO PARADISE IS	1491	7
BROTHERS OF PARADISE	TO THE BRIGHT EAST SHE	1573	2
THE COMPLIMENTS OF PARADISE	COSMOPOLITES WITHOUT A	1589	3
PARADISE'			
OF PARADISE' EXISTENCE	OF PARADISE' EXISTENCE	1411	1
PARADOX			
BY--PARADOX--THE MIND ITSELF--	EXPERIENCE IS THE ANGLED	910	3
PARAGON			
PARAGON OF CHIVALRY.	RECOLLECT THE FACE OF ME	1305	8
PARAGRAPH			
A PETAL, FOR A PARAGRAPH	I PAY--IN SATIN CASH--	402	3
PARAGRAPHS			
LIKE PARAGRAPHS [ARTICLES] OF WIND	WE LIKE A HAIRBREADTH	1175	4
PARALLAX			
AS PARALLAX [FIRMAMENT] A FLAME--	I THOUGHT THAT NATURE	1286	4
PARALLEL			
WHAT PARALLEL [SCENERY] CAN BE--	NO CROWD THAT HAS	515	18
GO PARALLEL, PERFECTED	THE OPENING AND THE	1047	7
PARALYSIS			
PARALYSIS--OUR PRIMER--DUMB [NUMB]--	THE ZEROES--TAUGHT US--	689	7
STOP PALSIED--'TIS PARALYSIS	I'VE DROPPED MY BRAIN--	1046	3
PARALYZE			
THAT PARALYZE OURSELVES--	BEREAVEMENT IN THEIR	645	8
PARALYZED			
PARALYZED, WITH GOLD--	HOW THE OLD MOUNTAINS	291	24
PARALYZING			
A PERFECT--PARALYZING BLISS--	ONE BLESSING HAD I THAN	756	7
PARASITE			
LIKE ANY PARASITE--	THE MIND LIVES ON THE	1355	2
PARASOL			
HER PRETTY PARASOL BE SEEN	FROM COCOON FORTH A	354	9
HER LITTLE PARASOL TO LIFT	HER LITTLE PARASOL TO	1038	1
THE PARASOL IS THE UMBRELLA'S DAUGHTER,	THE PARASOL IS THE	1747	1
PARASOLS			
LADIES--WITH PARASOLS--	IT WILL BE SUMMER--	342	2

	FIRST LINE	POEM	LINE
PARCEL			
AND SEE THE PARCEL ROLLED--	I CRIED AT PITY--NOT AT	588	10
IN THE PARCEL--BE THE MERCHANT	PUBLICATION--IS THE	709	13
PARCHED			
PARCHED THE FLOWERS THEY BEAR ALONG.	ANGELS, IN THE EARLY	94	8
THE GENTIAN HAS A PARCHED COROLLA--	THE GENTIAN HAS A	1424	1
PARCHING			
TO LIPS LONG PARCHING	I BRING AN UNACCUSTOMED	132	2
WHEN THE MEADOWS PARCHING LIE,	HAVE YOU GOT A BROOK IN	136	14
'TIS THIRSTING [PARCHING]--VITALIZES WINE--	I SHOULD HAVE BEEN TOO	313	23
SHALL WE REMEMBER PARCHING--THEN?	I KNOW WHERE WELLS GROW	460	17
ILL! WE HAVE BERRIES, FOR THE PARCHING!	WOULD YOU LIKE SUMMER?	691	3
PARD			
PITY--THE PARD--THAT LEFT HER ASIA--	CIVILIZATION--SPURNS--	492	10
PARDON			
IF ONCE MORE--PARDON--BOY--	A TONGUE--TO TELL HIM I	400	14
PARDON--TO LOOK UPON THY FACE--	JOY TO HAVE MERITED THE	788	5
I AM SPOTTED--"I AM PARDON"--	"UNTO ME?" I DO NOT KNOW	964	9
PARDON THE COCHINEAL--	SANG FROM THE HEART,	1059	5
PARDONED			
HE PARDONED ME!	I STOLE THEM FROM A BEE	200	4
PARE			
SHOW ME DIVISION [COULD] CAN SPLIT OR PARE--	WHILE IT IS ALIVE	491	6
AND THEN A QUARRY PARE	I LIKE TO SEE IT LAP	585	8
PARIAN			
THO' DRIFTED DEEP, IN PARIAN--	IT WILL BE SUMMER--	342	7
PARIS			
PARIS COULD NOT LAY THE FOLD	PIGMY SERAPHS--GONE	138	5
PARISH			
TO THE PARISH NIGHT--	THREE WEEKS PASSED SINCE	1061	10
A PORTRAIT OF THE PARISH	A FIELD OF STUBBLE,	1407	T
PARISHES			
OF PARISHES, COMPLAIN.	WE MISS A KINSMAN MORE	1087	8
PARLEY			
HURRAH FOR PETER PARLEY!	"SIC TRANSIT GLORIA	3	9
RATHER--HEAVEN'S "PETER PARLEY"!	I CANT TELL YOU--BUT YOU	65	17
PARLIAMENT			
"SPEECH"--IS A PRANK OF PARLIAMENT--	"SPEECH"--IS A PRANK OF	688	1
HERSELF, WITHOUT A PARLIAMENT	APOLOGY FOR HER	852	3
PARLOR			
THE PARLOR--OF THE DAY--	THE DAY CAME SLOW--TILL	304	16
THE PARLOR--COMMONLY--IT IS--	I AM ALIVE--I GUESS--	470	11
I MAKE MY PARLOR ORDERLY	THE GRAVE MY LITTLE	1743	3
MY PARLOR IS OF SHRIVEN GLASS,	THE WATERS CHASED HIM AS	1749	5
PARLORS			
IN PARLORS, SHUT BY DAY.	I HAVE A KING, WHO DOES	103	6
NO BALD DEATH--AFFRONT THEIR PARLORS--	SWEET--SAFE--HOUSES--	457	10
PART			
ON HIS SIDE [PART], WHAT TRANSACTION!	THE SUN KEPT STOOPING--	152	3
ON THEIR SIDE [PART], WHAT REPOSE!	THE SUN KEPT STOOPING--	152	4
DAY KNOCKED--AND WE MUST PART--	HE WAS WEAK, AND I WAS	190	9
IF GRIEF--THE LARGEST PART--	FOREVER AT HIS SIDE TO	246	7
THE CHIEFER PART, FOR TIME--	SOME--WORK FOR	406	2
'TIS CUSTOMARY AS WE PART	'TIS CUSTOMARY AS WE	440	1
WHOSE HISSING CORALS PART--AND SHUT--	A STILL--VOLCANO--LIFE--	601	11
TO KNOW IF HE WAS PATIENT--PART CONTENT--	TO KNOW JUST HOW HE	622	5
AS IF THE SEA SHOULD PART	AS IF THE SEA SHOULD	695	1
I KNOW THE WHOLE--OBSCURES THE PART--	PRECIOUS TO ME--SHE	727	9
HER LIPS OF AMBER NEVER PART--	THE MOON WAS BUT A CHIN	737	9
THAN DYING HALF [PART]--THEN RALLYING	THE WHOLE OF IT CAME NOT	762	11
CELEBRATED PART AT TABLE	ONE DAY IS THERE OF THE	814	3
PART IN MEMORY.	ONE DAY IS THERE OF THE	814	4
INSTINCTS FOR DANCE--A CAPER PART--	I'VE DROPPED MY BRAIN--	1046	11
ENJOINING US TO PART	AN ANTIQUATED GRACE	1345	4
IS PART OF AN INQUIRY	ONE JOY OF SO MUCH	1420	9
"ALL" ROGUES "SHALL HAVE THEIR PART IN" WHAT--	WHO IS IT SEEKS MY	1598	7
EACH THAT WE LOSE TAKES PART OF US;	EACH THAT WE LOSE TAKES	1605	1
OF JULEPS, PART ARE IN THE JUG	A DRUNKARD CANNOT MEET A	1628	9
IN WHICH I HAVE NO PART	HIS MIND OF MAN, A	1663	4
WHERE HOPE AND HE PART COMPANY--	DROWNING IS NOT SO	1718	7
PARTAKE			
THY SACRED EMBLEMS TO PARTAKE--	THESE ARE THE DAYS WHEN	130	16
WE--OCCUPY--DEGREE [TOO--PARTAKE]--	WE TALKED AS GIRLS DO--	586	12
AS DID OURSELVES PARTAKE--	DESPAIR'S ADVANTAGE IS	799	10
JUST TO PARTAKE--THE INFAMY--	WERT THOU BUT ILL--THAT	961	12
PARTAKE AS DOTH THE BEE,	PARTAKE AS DOTH THE BEE,	994	1
NOT TO PARTAKE THY PASSION, MY HUMILITY.	PROUD OF MY BROKEN HEART	1736	4
PARTAKEN			
PARTAKEN--IT RELIEVES--INDEED--	UNDUE SIGNIFICANCE A	439	5
PARTAKES			
HOW MANY CUPS THE BEE PARTAKES,	BRING ME THE SUNSET IN A	128	11
PARTAKES WITHOUT ALIGHTING	WITHIN MY GARDEN, RIDES	500	7
AND PARTAKES--HIS TONGUE	AS THE STARVED MAELSTROM	872	8
PARTAKING			
PARTAKING THEE A GUARANTY	EXTOL THEE--COULD I--	1643	7
PARTED			
MORNS LIKE THESE--WE PARTED--	MORNS LIKE THESE--WE	27	1
WHEN FARTHER [SHARPER] PARTED, THAN THE COMMON WO--	ONE YEAR AGO--JOTS WHAT?	296	8
HAD PARTED [BROKEN] RANK,	OF ALL THE SOUNDS	321	31

	FIRST LINE	POEM	LINE
PARTED (CONTINUED)			
WE PARTED WITH A CONTRACT	WE TALKED AS GIRLS DO--	586	13
THREE TIMES--WE PARTED--BREATH--AND I--	THREE TIMES--WE PARTED--	598	1
THAT HELD THE DAMS--HAD PARTED HOLD--	THE WIND BEGUN TO KNEAD	824	17
WE PARTED AS THE CENTRAL FLINT	WE MET AS SPARKS--	958	3
PARTICLE			
KNEW A PARTICLE--OF SPACE'S	CONSCIOUS AM I IN MY	679	15
PARTICLES			
IN PARTICLES--'TIS WHEN	A PLATED LIFE--	806	4
PARTIES			
THE STATION OF THE PARTIES	I HAD SOME THINGS THAT I	116	9
WHERE PARTIES--PHANTOM AS HERSELF--	FROM COCOON FORTH A	354	14
HER PARTIES ALL [COMPANIES] ASTIR--	REMORSE--IS MEMORY--	744	2
THE PARTIES IN BOTH CASES	THE LEAVES LIKE WOMEN,	987	5
OF THE SEPARATED PARTIES [PEOPLE]	THREE WEEKS PASSED SINCE	1061	11
HOW SOME ONE [PARTIES] TREATED HIM	THE SKY IS LOW--THE	1075	6
BY PARTIES ALSO THAT I KNEW	THE FAIREST HOME I EVER	1423	3
PARTING			
ALLOW ME, SIR, AT PARTING,	"SIC TRANSIT GLORIA	3	59
IT MAKES THE PARTING TRANQUIL	IF I SHOULD DIE,	54	15
AN EXTASY OF PARTING	A THROE UPON THE	71	3
HOW LOYALLY AT PARTING	ONE DIGNITY DELAYS FOR	98	11
ENAMORED OF THE PARTING WEST--	THE DAISY FOLLOWS SOFT	106	10
TO TAKE A BACKWARD [FINAL / PARTING] LOOK.	THESE ARE THE DAYS WHEN	130	3
PUT UP--TO HIDE [HOLD] HER PARTING GRACE	MY FIRST WELL DAY--SINCE	574	23
'TWAS A LONG PARTING--BUT THE TIME	'TWAS A LONG PARTING--	625	1
HEEDLESS [PASSIVE]--ALIKE--OF [TO] POMP--OR [AND] PARTING	AH, TENERIFFE!	666	8
THE PARTING WITH THE REST	WHEN ONE HAS GIVEN UP	853	2
PARTING WITH A WORLD	THAT IS SOLEMN WE HAVE	934	6
WE'LL PASS WITHOUT THE PARTING	WE'LL PASS WITHOUT THE	996	1
FRIGID AND SWEET HER PARTING FACE--	FRIGID AND SWEET HER	1318	1
AT PARTING--SHE WAS GOING SOUTH	I SEND YOU A DECREPIT	1324	3
THE AUCTIONEER OF PARTING	THE AUCTIONEER OF	1612	1
PARTING WITH THEE RELUCTANTLY,	PARTING WITH THEE	1614	1
PARTING IS ALL WE KNOW OF HEAVEN,	MY LIFE CLOSED TWICE	1732	7
FOR PARTING, THAT IS NIGHT,	SOME SAY GOODNIGHT--AT	1739	5
PARTITION			
I PLUCKED AT OUR PARTITION	I TRIED TO THINK A	532	12
HORRID SAND PARTITION--	IN FALLING TIMBERS	614	7
PARTITIONS			
IN THE SWIFT PARTITIONS	FORTITUDE INCARNATE	1217	3
PARTLY			
AND IT'S PARTLY [MANY A MILE], DOWN HILL--	TIE THE STRINGS TO MY	279	8
PARTOOK			
HIS ROYAL STATE PARTOOK!	I MET A KING THIS	166	22
SACRAMENT, SAINTS PARTOOK [INDORSED] BEFORE US--	TO PUT THIS WORLD DOWN,	527	12
BUT THE CRUMB PARTOOK--DEPARTED--	MOST SHE TOUCHED ME BY	760	11
WE TRUST THAT SHE PARTOOK	ELIZABETH TOLD ESSEX	1321	6
AND TREMBLINGLY PARTOOK	A WORD MADE FLESH IS	1651	2
AND BADINAGE PARTOOK.	HIGH FROM THE EARTH I	1723	12
PARTRIDGE			
TO PARTRIDGE--AND TO BOY--	THE BLACK BERRY--WEARS A	554	4
PARTS			
HE PARTS HIMSELF--LIKE LEAVES--	HE PARTS HIMSELF--LIKE	517	1
AND PARTS OF HIS FAR PLAN	I PRAYED, AT FIRST, A	576	10
TO HELP OUR BLEAKER PARTS	TO HELP OUR BLEAKER	1064	1
PARTY			
AND GOD, A QUIET PARTY	WE TALKED AS GIRLS DO--	586	7
WORN TO NATURE'S PARTY ONCE	RIBBONS OF THE YEAR--	873	3
NOT IF THEIR PARTY WERE WAITING,	WHAT DID THEY DO SINCE I	900	9
A PARTY THAT [WHOM] WE KNEW--	AS SLEIGH BELLS SEEM IN	981	6
PAIN IS THE JUNIOR PARTY	PAIN HAS BUT ONE	1049	5
WHAT PARTY--ONE MAY BE	WHEN THEY COME BACK--IF	1080	14
I'M NOT A PARTY TO--	IS HEAVEN A PHYSICIAN?	1270	8
PASS			
PASS ROYAL THRO' THE GATE--	MY WHEEL IS IN THE DARK!	10	13
I PRAY YOU PASS [STROLL] ONCE MORE.	HEART, NOT SO HEAVY AS	83	20
AN HOUR IN CHRYSALIS TO PASS,	COCOON ABOVE! COCOON	129	7
THIS WAY, JESUS, LET HIM PASS!	DYING! DYING IN THE	158	8
BIRDS WILL PASS ME	I SHALL KEEP SINGING!	250	2
AND PASS ESCAPED--TO THEE!	WHAT IF I SAY I SHALL	277	3
THE POSSIBILITY--TO PASS	THAT AFTER HORROR--THAT	286	9
TO LET A BEETLE PASS--	A BIRD CAME DOWN THE	328	8
AND EVEN WHEN IT DIES [DIE]--TO PASS	THE GRASS SO LITTLE HAS	333	13
AND WHATSOEVER INSECT PASS--	THERE IS A FLOWER THAT	380	5
SALUTE, AND PASS, WITHOUT A HINT--	I READ MY SENTENCE--	412	13
EXPERIENCED--WHO PASS	TRIUMPH--MAY BE OF	455	14
TO ANSWER--WHEREFORE WHEN HE PASS	"WHY DO I LOVE" YOU, SIR	480	4
SOME SUCH SPICE [ROSE]--EXPRESS AND PASS--	SOME SUCH BUTTERFLY BE	541	5
PASS BACK AND FORTH, BEFORE MY BRAIN	WHEN I WAS SMALL, A	596	15
I TOLD HIM BEST--MUST PASS	I ROSE--BECAUSE HE SANK	616	12
MAY PASS--AND COUNTERPASS--	THE LIGHTNING PLAYETH--	630	8
SHE'D PASS FOR BAREHEAD--SHORT WAY OFF--	YOU'LL KNOW HER--BY HER	634	15
HE [FIRST]--MUST PASS THE CRYSTAL ANGLE [LIMIT]	HER SWEET TURN TO LEAVE	649	25
I--SILENT [SPEECHLESS]--PASS THE DOOR--	AGAIN--HIS VOICE IS AT	663	10
THAT DARKNESS--IS ABOUT TO PASS--	PRESENTIMENT--IS THAT	764	4
THROUGH THE STRAIT [STRAIGHT] PASS OF	THROUGH THE STRAIT PASS	792	1

	FIRST LINE	POEM	LINE
PASS (CONTINUED)			
SUFFERING--			
WE PASS, AND SHE ABIDES.	THE VEINS OF OTHER	811	5
NEVER TO PASS THE ANGEL	A CLOUD WITHDREW FROM	895	9
TASTES'DEATH--THE FIRST--TO HAND [PASS / PROVE] THE STING	LOVE--IS THAT LATER	924	5
AND THEN AWAY TO YOU TO PASS--	I LEARNED--AT LEAST--	944	23
WE'LL PASS WITHOUT THE PARTING	WE'LL PASS WITHOUT THE	996	1
OR PASS	THE BIRD DID PRANCE--THE	1107	V
IS SUCH A FEAT [STROKE / HIGHT / PASS] OF IRONY	THAT THIS SHOULD FEEL	1112	3
ALL MEN MEET [PASS / HASTE] AS IF	AFTER THE SUN COMES OUT	1148	5
BUT NONE WILL PASS THE [MAN'S] CATACOMB . .	THE BUTTERFLY IN HONORED	1246	3
THOUGH GENERATIONS PASS AWAY, ...	A LITTLE OVERFLOWING	1467	4
PASS TO THY RENDEZVOUS OF LIGHT, ...	PASS TO THY RENDEZVOUS	1564	1
SO OMINOUS DID PASS	THERE CAME A WIND LIKE A	1593	4
NO LIFE CAN POMPLESS PASS AWAY--	NO LIFE CAN POMPLESS	1626	1
DISPLAYED [PASS SLOW] BEFORE THE SIMPLEST [HUMBLEST] DOOR	SOME ONE PREPARED THIS	1644	4
AS WE PASS HOUSES MUSING SLOW	AS WE PASS HOUSES MUSING	1653	1
SO MINDS PASS MINDS	AS WE PASS HOUSES MUSING	1653	3
PASSAGE			
ON THEIR PASSAGE CASHMERE--	SOUTH WINDS JOSTLE THEM	86	6
A PASSAGE BACK--OR TWO--TO MAKE--	A PRECIOUS--MOULDERING	371	7
PASSED			
HATH PASSED BEYOND THE MOON, ...	"SIC TRANSIT GLORIA	3	64
BANDITTI OFTEN PASSED US	THROUGH LANE IT LAY--	9	3
HAVE PASSED BEYOND THE SUN--	WHEN ROSES CEASE TO	32	4
I OFTEN PASSED THE VILLAGE	I OFTEN PASSED THE	51	1
AS IT PASSED MY WINDOW	HEART, NOT SO HEAVY AS	83	3
THAT PASSED, AN HOUR AGO!	WITHIN MY REACH!	90	9
SO BREATHLESS TILL I PASSED HER--	SO BASHFUL WHEN I SPIED	91	5
YOU HAVE PASSED ENFRANCHIZED FEET!	TALK WITH PRUDENCE TO A	119	6
LAND--BY THE OCEANS PASSED.	WATER, IS TAUGHT BY	135	2
PASSED OUT--OF RECORD	READ--SWEET--HOW OTHERS	260	14
THAT PASSED THE MOULDERING PIER--	THAT AFTER HORROR--THAT	286	2
AS A DUCHESS PASSED--	HOW THE OLD MOUNTAINS	291	12
THEN KNIT, AND SWEPT [PASSED]--	OF ALL THE SOUNDS	321	32
AS IF NO SOUL THE [WHILE OUR TWO SOULS THAT] SOLSTICE PASSED	THERE CAME A DAY AT	322	7
OUR PANTING ANCLE BARELY PASSED [GAINED], .	OF TRIBULATION--THESE	325	13
THIS--WAS THE TOWN--SHE PASSED--	'TWAS THE OLD--ROAD--	344	5
HOW WEAKNESS PASSED--OR FORCE--AROSE-- . . .	IF ANY SINK, ASSURE THAT	358	4
HIS FINGERS, AS HE PASSED	THE WIND--TAPPED LIKE A	436	14
THEN--MIDNIGHT, I HAVE PASSED FROM THEE . .	A WIFE--AT DAYBREAK I	461	5
AND PASSED THEIR CURTAINS BY--	I HAD NO CAUSE TO BE	542	6
AND HE PASSED [WENT] QUICKLY [SOFTLY] ROUND--	WHEN I WAS SMALL, A	596	8
WE PASSED THE SCHOOL, WHERE CHILDREN STROVE	BECAUSE I COULD NOT STOP	712	9
WE PASSED THE FIELDS OF GAZING GRAIN-- . .	BECAUSE I COULD NOT STOP	712	11
WE PASSED THE SETTING SUN--	BECAUSE I COULD NOT STOP	712	12
OR RATHER--HE PASSED US--	BECAUSE I COULD NOT STOP	712	13
THE OWNER PASSED--IDENTIFIED--	MY LIFE HAD STOOD--A	754	3
'TWAS CRISIS--ALL THE LENGTH HAD PASSED-- .	'TWAS CRISIS--ALL THE	948	1
BIOGRAPHY TO ALL WHO PASSED	THE HOLLOWS ROUND HIS	955	5
PASSED [WENT] INFINITE BY ME--	IT BLOOMED AND DROPT, A	978	20
HAVE PASSED, I THOUGHT, A WHIP LASH . . .	A NARROW FELLOW IN THE	986	13
THREE WEEKS PASSED SINCE I HAD SEEN HER-- .	THREE WEEKS PASSED SINCE	1061	1
WE WAITED WHILE SHE PASSED--	THE LAST NIGHT THAT SHE	1100	17
IF MET, TOO RAPID PASSED, ...	THE FROST WAS NEVER SEEN	1202	2
HAVE NEVER PASSED [SCALED] HER HAUNTED HOUSE,	WHAT MYSTERY PERVADES A	1400	19
HE PASSED THROUGH BETHLEHEM--	"AND WITH WHAT BODY DO	1492	8
AND SUMMER IS [SUMMER PASSED / SUMMERS ARE] AWAY--	THERE COMES A WARNING	1536	4
BY CHUMS THAT PASSED AWAY--	MY WARS ARE LAID AWAY IN	1549	10
THAT VERY INSTANT PASSED--	THERE CAME A WIND LIKE A	1593	8
WE MUST HAVE PASSED THE MIDDLE SEA	I DID NOT REACH THEE	1664	23
THREE RIVERS AND THE HILL ARE PASSED . . .	I DID NOT REACH THEE	1664	31
PASSENGER			
DECOYS IT'S TRAVELLER [PASSENGER]	RISK IS THE HAIR THAT	1239	12
PASSENGER--OF INFINITY--	TO THE STANCH DUST	1402	7
NO PASSENGER WAS KNOWN TO FLEE--	NO PASSENGER WAS KNOWN	1406	1
PASSENGERS			
TOO UNCERTAIN PASSENGERS	THE BIRD DID PRANCE--THE	1107	V
PASSER			
YOUR PRAYERS, OH PASSER BY!	A DAY! HELP! HELP!	42	2
UPON THE PASSER-BY!	A FUZZY FELLOW, WITHOUT	173	8
THEY--HIM--ATTENTION OF PASSER BY--	FOUR TREES--UPON A	742	10
UPON THE REVERY--[PASSER BY]	THE LONG SIGH OF THE	1359	4
PASSES			
THE LILY PASSES SURE--	THROUGH THE DARK SOD--AS	392	2
IT PASSES AND WE STAY--	A LIGHT EXISTS IN SPRING	812	16
A SHADE UPON THE MIND THERE PASSES	A SHADE UPON THE MIND	882	1
IT RISES--PASSES--ON OUR SOUTH	IT RISES--PASSES--ON OUR	1023	1
THE BLONDE ASSASSIN PASSES ON--	APPARENTLY WITH NO	1624	5
PASSING			
A "SAVAN" PASSING BY	"ARCTURUS" IS HIS OTHER	70	6
PASSING POMPOSITY?	BRING ME THE SUNSET IN A	128	24
THE STRAY SHIPS--PASSING--	TWO SWIMMERS WRESTLED ON	201	5
IN PASSING CALVARY--	I MEASURE EVERY GRIEF I	561	36
COALS--FROM A ROLLING [PASSING]	I COULD DIE--TO KNOW--	570	9

	FIRST LINE	POEM	LINE
PASSING (CONTINUED)			
LOAD--RATTLE--HOW--NEAR--			
TO THE VERY SQUARE--HIS FOOT IS PASSING--	I COULD DIE--TO KNOW--	570	10
YET ANY PASSING BY	TO INTERRUPT HIS YELLOW	591	12
FOR PASSING CALVARY--	IT MAKES NO DIFFERENCE	620	8
I--LOST--WAS PASSING BY--	A DOOR JUST OPENED ON A	953	2
I--LOST--WAS PASSING BY--	A DOOR JUST OPENED ON A	953	6
THOU PAUSED AT, FOR A PASSING [DOUBTFUL] BOUNTY--	WERT THOU BUT ILL--THAT	961	7
SOME PASSING YEAR--A TRAIT [CHARM] BESTOW	FITTER TO SEE HIM, I MAY	968	4
I, PASSING, THOUGHT ANOTHER NOON	IT BLOOMED AND DROPT, A	978	3
THAT I, IN PASSING BY	IT BLOOMED AND DROPT, A	978	18
WHOSE TILLAGE [PASTURE] IS THE PASSING [WANDERING] CRUMB--	THOSE CATTLE SMALLER	1388	3
INTO THE SEA IN PASSING	A DEW SUFFICED ITSELF--	1437	11
A PASSING UNIVERSE PUT ON,	HOW HAPPY IS THE LITTLE	1510	6
PASSION			
SAID DEATH TO PASSION	SAID DEATH TO PASSION	1033	1
SAID PASSION, THROUGH CONTRACTING BREATHS	SAID DEATH TO PASSION	1033	3
BORE DEATH FROM PASSION	SAID DEATH TO PASSION	1033	5
NOT TO PARTAKE THY PASSION, MY HUMILITY.	PROUD OF MY BROKEN HEART	1736	4
PASSIVE			
PASSIVE--AS GRANITE--LAPS MY MUSIC--	PUT UP MY LUTE!	261	4
INSTEAD OF PASSIVE CREATURES,	ENDOW THE LIVING--WITH	521	5
HEEDLESS [PASSIVE]--ALIKE--OF [TO] POMP--OR [AND] PARTING	AH, TENERIFFE!	666	8
THIS PASSIVE PLACE A SUMMER'S NIMBLE MANSION	THIS QUIET DUST WAS	813	5
OUR PASSIVE FLOWER WE HELD TO SEA--	THE FROST OF DEATH WAS	1136	5
THE MAGIC PASSIVE BUT EXTANT	SOMEWHERE UPON THE	1231	3
PASSIVER			
FOR SOMETHING PASSIVER--CONTENT	A PRISON GETS TO BE A	652	27
PAST			
PAST THE HOUSES--PAST THE HEADLANDS--	EXULTATION IS THE GOING	76	3
PAST THE HOUSES--PAST THE HEADLANDS--	EXULTATION IS THE GOING	76	3
PAST MIDNIGHT! PAST THE MORNING STAR!	AT LAST, TO BE	174	4
PAST MIDNIGHT! PAST THE MORNING STAR!	AT LAST, TO BE	174	4
PAST SUNRISE!	AT LAST, TO BE	174	5
WHEN CHOICE OF LIFE--IS PAST--	THE MANNER OF IT'S DEATH	468	5
PAST BOWS, AND INVITATIONS--	IF ANYBODY'S FRIEND BE	509	21
PAST INTERVIEW, AND VOW--	IF ANYBODY'S FRIEND BE	509	22
PAST WHAT OURSELF CAN ESTIMATE [UNDERSTAND]--	IF ANYBODY'S FRIEND BE	509	23
WENT PAST MY SIMPLE SHOE--	I STARTED EARLY--TOOK MY	520	10
AND PAST MY APRON--AND MY BELT	I STARTED EARLY--TOOK MY	520	11
AND PAST MY BODDICE [BOSOM / BUCKLE]--TOO--	I STARTED EARLY--TOOK MY	520	12
AM I, FROM SYMPTOMS THAT ARE PAST	I COULD NOT PROVE THE	563	3
IT'S PAST--ENLIGHTENED TO PERCEIVE	PAIN--HAS AN ELEMENT OF	650	7
UNTIL HE'S PAST THE PAIN--	I SOMETIMES DROP IT, FOR	708	16
AND SHE HAD PAST, WITH [FLED WITH / TRUSTED / HEARKENED] HIM--	I MEANT TO FIND HER WHEN	718	8
IT'S PAST--SET DOWN BEFORE THE SOUL	REMORSE--IS MEMORY--	744	5
PAST WHICH FORCES RETROGRADE	CRISIS IS A HAIR	889	3
THE DYING, IS A TRIFLE, PAST,	TOO SCANTY 'TWAS TO DIE	1013	5
TO POSSESS, IS PAST THE INSTANT	SATISFACTION--IS THE	1036	5
TO PAST OR PERIOD--	HE SCANNED IT--STAGGERED	1062	3
AT HALF PAST THREE, A SINGLE BIRD	AT HALF PAST THREE, A	1084	1
AT HALF PAST FOUR, EXPERIMENT	AT HALF PAST THREE, A	1084	5
AT HALF PAST SEVEN, ELEMENT	AT HALF PAST THREE, A	1084	9
HOW INTIMATE, A [ORDERLY THE] TEMPEST PAST	THE WIND TOOK UP THE	1134	15
A PAST [TIME / STATE] OF PLANK AND NAIL	THE PROPS ASSIST THE	1142	10
THE PAST IS SUCH A CURIOUS CREATURE	THE PAST IS SUCH A	1203	1
NOR A PAST TO STARE--	THE POPULAR HEART IS A	1226	6
WHEN MOST IS PAST--IT COMES--	THE GENTIAN HAS A	1424	8
PAST THAT, HE SINS IN PEACE--	HIS CHEEK IS HIS	1460	4
SHE COULD NOT LIVE UPON THE PAST	SHE COULD NOT LIVE UPON	1505	1
FLAP PAST IT TO THE	FAME IS A FICKLE FOOD	1659	8
PAST NEIGHBORHOOD	TO-DAY OR THIS NOON	1702	5
NOW PAST SURMISE	TO-DAY OR THIS NOON	1702	7
HER RESIDUE BE PAST--	WITH SWEETNESS UNABATED	1709	12
PASTE			
WE PLAY AT PASTE--	WE PLAY AT PASTE--	320	1
THEN, DROP THE PASTE--	WE PLAY AT PASTE--	320	3
PASTED			
PASTED BY THE SIMPLE SUMMER	LAIN IN NATURE--SO	1288	7
PAST'S			
IT IS THE PAST'S SUPREME ITALIC	GLASS WAS THE STREET--IN	1498	7
PASTURE			
OF ORCHIS IN THE PASTURE--	THERE IS A FLOWER THAT	380	11
WHOSE TILLAGE [PASTURE] IS THE PASSING [WANDERING] CRUMB--	THOSE CATTLE SMALLER	1388	3
PASTURES			
TO PASTURES OF OBLIVION--	A FADED BOY--IN SALLOW	1524	3
AND SEES [SPIES] THE PASTURES SMILE	THE LIFE THAT TIED TOO	1535	6
PATCHES			
SOME SCARLET PATCHES ON THE WAY,	A SLASH OF BLUE--	204	3
PATCHWORK			
OR HUMBLEST PATCHWORK--CHILDREN DO [MAY]--	AT LEISURE IS THE SOUL	618	7
PATENT			
THE PATENT LOST	IS BLISS THEN, SUCH	340	10
IT MUST HAVE A PATENT.	KNOWS HOW TO FORGET!	433	V
PATENT, EVERY DROP,	TO PUT THIS WORLD DOWN,	527	13

	FIRST LINE	POEM	LINE
PAUSE (CONTINUED)			
THE MAIMED MAY PAUSE, AND BREATHE,	THIS MERIT HATH THE	979	5
A FUNDAMENTAL PAUSE	CRUMBLING IS NOT AN	997	2
PAUSE IN YOUR LITURGIES--	SANG FROM THE HEART,	1059	13
OF CADENCE OR OF PAUSE	FURTHER IN SUMMER THAN	1068	V
WE PAUSE BEFORE A FURTHER PLUNGE	WHAT TWIGS WE HELD BY--	1086	4
TO NEIGHBORHOODS OF PAUSE--	GREAT STREETS OF SILENCE	1159	2
THE HEAVEN, IN WHICH WE HOPED TO PAUSE	THE THINGS WE THOUGHT	1293	9
VELOCITY OR PAUSE	TWO LENGTHS HAS EVERY	1295	6
NOR ANY FLIGHT [PAUSE]	ALL THAT I DO	1496	8
BUT NATURE AND MANKIND MUST PAUSE	THE RIGHT TO PERISH	1692	7
PAUSED			
THE HAND THAT PAUSED TO GATHER	WHEN ROSES CEASE TO	32	5
CAROLLED, AND PAUSED [MUSED], AND CAROLLED--	HEART, NOT SO HEAVY AS	83	11
AND PAUSED AT EVERY POUND	I FELT MY LIFE WITH BOTH	351	6
CREATION STOPPED [THE HEAVENS PAUSED]--FOR ME--	MY PERIOD HAD COME FOR	564	18
WE PAUSED BEFORE A HOUSE THAT SEEMED	BECAUSE I COULD NOT STOP	712	17
THOU PAUSED AT, FOR A PASSING [DOUBTFUL] BOUNTY--	WERT THOU BUT ILL--THAT	961	7
'TWAS HERE MY SUMMER PAUSED	'TWAS HERE MY SUMMER	1756	1
PAUSELESS			
IN PERFECT--PAUSELESS MONARCHY--	BEHIND ME--DIPS ETERNITY	721	8
PAUSES			
TO SWEET PAUSES OF HAY--	THE WIND DID'NT COME	316	15
PAUSING			
PAUSING AT THE PLACE.	GLOWING IS HER BONNET,	72	12
UNMOVED--SHE NOTES THE CHARIOTS--PAUSING--	THE SOUL SELECTS HER OWN	303	5
TRAVERSED SHE THOUGH PAUSING	NOW I KNEW I LOST HER--	1219	7
PAUSING IN FRONT OF [AGAINST] OUR PALSIED [SENTENCED / . . .	WE TALKED WITH EACH	1473	5
PAWN			
IN PAWN FOR LIBERTY--	IT FEELS A SHAME TO BE	444	8
HONOR--IS IT'S OWN PAWN--	TITLE DIVINE--IS MINE!	1072	V
WOULD PAY [PAWN] EACH ATOM THAT I AM	SOMEWHERE UPON THE	1231	7
PAWS			
WHEN WINDS TAKE [HOLD] FORESTS IN THEIR PAWS--	HE FUMBLES AT YOUR SOUL	315	13
WEIGH, HELPLESS, IN HIS PAWS--	'TWAS LIKE A MAELSTROM,	414	13
PAY			
WE MUST AN ANGUISH PAY	FOR EACH EXTATIC INSTANT	125	2
"I VOW TO PAY	WHAT WOULD I GIVE TO SEE	247	24
YET I--FOR IT--WOULD PAY--	ONE LIFE OF SO MUCH	270	2
THY PAY--IN DIAMONDS--BE--	A TONGUE--TO TELL HIM I	400	18
I PAY--IN SATIN CASH--	I PAY--IN SATIN CASH--	402	1
TO PAY--A CROSS--	MUST BE A WO--	571	15
AND TOOK HIMSELF, FOR PAY,	I GAVE MYSELF TO HIM--	580	2
WOULD PAY [PAWN] EACH ATOM THAT I AM	SOMEWHERE UPON THE	1231	7
BUT SHE MUST [MY PRICE / HUMILITY] PAY FOR SUCCOR	I SAW THE WIND WITHIN	1502	V
AND HAS'NT ANY TAX TO PAY	THE BUTTERFLY UPON THE	1521	3
TO PAY FOR THY RIGHT HAND	I DID NOT REACH THEE	1664	13
TO PAY YOU SCRUTINY--	THE RIGHT TO PERISH	1692	8
PAYING			
MAKING [PAYING] GRATITUDE	MOST SHE TOUCHED ME BY	760	20
PAYS			
HE PAYS NO RENT.	THE RAT IS THE CONCISEST	1356	2
PEA			
THE PEA THAT DUTY LOCKS--	FORBIDDEN FRUIT A FLAVOR	1377	4
PEACE			
IF PAIN FOR PEACE PREPARES	IF PAIN FOR PEACE	63	1
THE PEACE--THE FLIGHT--THE AMETHYST--	THE DAISY FOLLOWS SOFT	106	11
PEACE--BY IT'S BATTLES TOLD--	WATER, IS TAUGHT BY	135	4
AND PEACE--WAS PARADISE!	AN AWFUL TEMPEST MASHED	198	13
PERHAPS THE OTHER--PEACE--	IT MIGHT BE LONELIER	405	4
A TOOTH UPON OUR PEACE	A TOOTH UPON OUR PEACE	459	1
THE PEACE CANNOT DEFACE--	A TOOTH UPON OUR PEACE	459	2
'TWAS SUCH AN AMPLE PEACE--	I HAD NO CAUSE TO BE	542	13
SOME [MEN] SEEK IN ART--THE ART OF PEACE--	THE MARTYR POETS--DID	544	8
IT'S BETTER--ALMOST PEACE--	IT CEASED TO HURT ME,	584	15
HOW HAVE I PEACE	ME FROM MYSELF--TO	642	6
I MANY TIMES THOUGHT PEACE HAD COME	I MANY TIMES THOUGHT	739	1
WHEN PEACE WAS FAR AWAY--	I MANY TIMES THOUGHT	739	2
PEACE IS A FICTION OF OUR FAITH--	PEACE IS A FICTION OF	912	1
A PEACE, AS HEMISPHERES AT HOME	THE CRICKETS SANG	1104	11
MOTIONLESS AS PEACE	AFTER A HUNDRED YEARS	1147	4
AND HIS METALLIC PEACE--	IT CAME AT LAST BUT	1230	4
SUBSTANTIATES A PEACE	THE LONG SIGH OF THE	1359	6
A CHILLY [LONESOME / WARNING] PEACE INFESTS THE GRASS	A CHILLY PEACE INFESTS	1443	1
PAST THAT, HE SINS IN PEACE--	HIS CHEEK IS HIS	1460	4
WITH THOUGHTS THAT MAKE FOR PEACE--	ONE OF THE ONES THAT	1466	24
INTOXICATED WITH THE PEACE	HIS ORIENTAL HERESIES	1526	V
A PEACE AS PURE AS IF THE SKY	TO SEE HER IS A PICTURE	1568	V 7
WHAT MAJESTIES OF PEACE,	OH WHAT A GRACE IS THIS,	1615	2
AND WRECKS IN PEACE A PURPLE TAR,	A SLOOP OF AMBER SLIPS	1622	3
OH FUTURE! THOU SECRETED PEACE	OH FUTURE! THOU SECRETED	1631	1
IS AUTHORIZED AS PEACE	THE MOB WITHIN THE HEART	1745	4
PEACEFUL			
IN THE PEACEFUL [SILENT] WEST	ON THIS WONDROUS SEA	4	7

	FIRST LINE	POEM	LINE
PEACOCK			
PEACOCK PRESUMES TO DIE!	IF THIS IS "FADING"	120	9
PEACOCK'S			
OR ELSE A PEACOCK'S PURPLE TRAIN	SOME RAINBOW--COMING	64	4
PEAK			
ON SPANGLED JOURNEYS TO THE PEAK	THE PEDIGREE OF HONEY	1627	5
PEAKS			
THE PEAKS, THAT LINGERED LAST	WHEN ONE HAS GIVEN UP	853	5
THE KINSMEN OF THE WIND ARE PEAKS	THE DUTIES OF THE WIND	1137	9
PEAL			
BEFORE THE QUICK [RIPE / PEAL / DRUM / DRUMS / BELLS / BOMB / . . .	ONE JOY OF SO MUCH	1420	6
PEARL			
OVER THE STILE OF "PEARL".	"ARCTURUS" IS HIS OTHER	70	33
YIELD HER MOAT OF PEARL--	DID THE HAREBELL LOOSE	213	6
FROM TANKARDS SCOOPED IN PEARL--	I TASTE A LIQUOR NEVER	214	2
ONE PEARL--TO ME--SO SIGNAL-- [OF SUCH PROPORTION]	ONE LIFE OF SO MUCH	270	5
AND ESTIMATE THE PEARL--	YOUR RICHES--TAUGHT ME--	299	30
TILL QUALIFIED, FOR PEARL--	WE PLAY AT PASTE--	320	2
AND THREAD THE DEWS, ALL NIGHT, LIKE PEARLS [PEARL]--	THE GRASS SO LITTLE HAS	333	9
THAT SUCH ENORMOUS PEARL	IT FEELS A SHAME TO BE	444	14
THE MALAY--TOOK THE PEARL--	THE MALAY--TOOK THE	452	1
FROM THEIR PEOPLE PEARL--	SWEET--SAFE--HOUSES--	457	9
PROVE--LIKE A PEARL--	I AM ASHAMED--I HIDE--	473	18
TO WEAR THAT PERFECT--PEARL--	THE WORLD--STANDS--	493	6
WOULD OVERFLOW WITH PEARL--	I STARTED EARLY--TOOK MY	520	20
HIS YARN [COIL] OF PEARL--UNWINDS [EXPENDS]--	THE SPIDER HOLDS A	605	4
SUCH THRENODIES [EXTACIES / REVENUES / ARGUMENTS] OF PEARL--	YOU'LL KNOW HER--BY HER	634	26
BAGGAGE A [OF] STRAPPED PEARL--	DROPPED INTO THE ETHER	665	6
TO ENTERTAIN A PEARL--	SHELLS FROM THE COAST	693	4
THEREFORE--THE PEARL RESPONDED--	SHELLS FROM THE COAST	693	7
DEVELOPE PEARL, AND WEED,	SHE ROSE TO HIS	732	10
PEARL--FOR [THE] STOCKING--PEARL FOR SHOE--	THESE--SAW VISIONS--	758	13
PEARL--FOR [THE] STOCKING--PEARL FOR SHOE--	THESE--SAW VISIONS--	758	13
OR A WRINKLED PEARL--	RIBBONS OF THE YEAR--	873	6
THE PEARL--THE JUST--OUR THOUGHT.	BEST THINGS DWELL OUT OF	998	2
PEARLS			
PEARLS ARE THE DIVER'S FARTHINGS	THE FEET OF PEOPLE	7	9
HER BREAST IS FIT FOR PEARLS,	HER BREAST IS FIT FOR	84	1
AND THREAD THE DEWS, ALL NIGHT, LIKE PEARLS [PEARL]--	THE GRASS SO LITTLE HAS	333	9
OF PEARLS IN EASTERN WATERS,	REMOVED FROM ACCIDENT OF	424	7
'TIS LITTLE I--COULD CARE FOR PEARLS--	'TIS LITTLE I--COULD	466	1
SUCH AS THESE--THE PEARLS	MY GARDEN--LIKE THE	484	4
MYSELF CONJECTURED [COMPUTED] WERE THEY PEARLS--	A DROP FELL ON THE APPLE	794	7
PEARLY			
PURSUES HIS PEARLY STRANDS--	THE SPIDER HOLDS A	605 V	4
PEASANTRY			
BEING'S PEASANTRY--	SMILING BACK FROM	385	4
PEASANTS			
WHOSE PEASANTS ARE THE ANGELS--	THE FEET OF PEOPLE	7	19
PEASANTS LIKE ME,	SO FROM THE MOULD	66	9
PEASANTS LIKE THEE	SO FROM THE MOULD	66	10
THE INMATES [PEASANTS] OF THE AIR	ALONE AND IN A	1167	14
PEAT			
WHOSE PEAT LIFE--AMPLY VIVID--	MORE LIFE--WENT OUT--	422	17
PEBBLE			
LET NO PEBBLE--SMILE--	I CAN WADE GRIEF--	252	7
IF HE FLING SAND [DUST], AND PEBBLE--	THE WIND DID'NT COME	316	17
OR PUSHED THE PEBBLE FROM HIS PATH--	ALTHOUGH I PUT AWAY HIS	366	7
AND PEBBLE--SAFELY PLAYS--	I KNOW WHERE WELLS GROW	460	4
I AIMED MY PEBBLE--BUT MYSELF	I TOOK MY POWER IN MY	540	5
NOT A MENTION, WHOSE SMALL PEBBLE	ONE DAY IS THERE OF THE	814	13
DROPPED--MY FATE--A TIMID PEBBLE--	ALL FORGOT FOR	966	13
A PEBBLE	HOW HAPPY IS THE LITTLE	1510	T
PECULIAR			
PECULIAR TRAVELLER COMES?	WHAT INN IS THIS	115	3
FOR JUST THIS SINGLE [THIS PECULIAR / JUST THIS ONLY] TIME--	I MEANT TO FIND HER WHEN	718	6
IN HIS ECCENTRIC [PECULIAR] STYLE	ELIJAH'S WAGON KNEW NO	1254 V	8
BUT THOSE PECULIAR INDUSTRIES	THE THINGS WE THOUGHT	1293	3
OF THEIR [HIS] PECULIAR LIGHT	OF THEIR PECULIAR LIGHT	1362	1
OF THEIR PECULIAR CALLING	THOSE CATTLE SMALLER	1388	13
PECULIARLY			
THAT WE DEPLORE PECULIARLY	A WILD BLUE SKY ABREAST	1415	7
PEDANTIC			
TO A FINE, PEDANTIC SUNSHINE--	PORTRAITS ARE TO DAILY	170	3
PEDDLER			
MAKES HE MUD FOR DOG AND PEDDLER,	WE LIKE MARCH.	1213	4
PEDDLER'S			
NO PEDDLER'S CART--APPROACHED--	A HOUSE UPON THE HIGHT--	399	4
PEDESTRIAN			
PEDESTRIAN ONCE--AS WE--	THE FEET OF PEOPLE	7	12
PEDIGREE			
THAN ARMS, OR PEDIGREE.	I HAD SOME THINGS THAT I	116	12
THE PEDIGREE OF HONEY	THE PEDIGREE OF HONEY	1627	1

	FIRST LINE	POEM	LINE
PEDIGREE (CONTINUED)			
WITCHCRAFT HAS NOT A PEDIGREE	WITCHCRAFT HAS NOT A	1708	1
PEELS			
THAT SCALPS [PEELS] YOUR NAKED SOUL--	HE FUMBLES AT YOUR SOUL	315	12
PEEP			
IF, HAPLY, THRO' A DREAM, TO PEEP	I HAVE A KING, WHO DOES	103	5
WILL PEEP, AND PRANCE AGAIN.	AS CHILDREN BID THE	133	8
THE OTHER PEEP--	I KNOW SOME LONELY	289	9
PEEPED			
STILL! COULD THEMSELF HAVE PEEPED--	THEY SHUT ME UP IN PROSE	613	5
PEER			
TO REVERENTLY PEER,	IN EBON BOX, WHEN YEARS	169	2
TO PEER THIS GRACE--	MY REWARD FOR BEING, WAS	343	V
AND SUPERCILIOUS PEER	I LIKE TO SEE IT LAP	585	6
PEERED			
THE ANGELS--SOFTLY PEERED--	IF I'M LOST--NOW--	256	7
PEERING			
THE WOLF CAME PEERING CURIOUS--	THROUGH LANE IT LAY--	9	5
PEERLESS			
THOU CAN'ST NOT PIERCE TRADITION WITH THE PEERLESS PUNCTURE,	PROUD OF MY BROKEN HEART	1736	7
PEERS			
BUT PEERS BEYOND HER MESH--	A CHARM INVESTS A FACE	421	5
PEEVISH			
UNTIL THE PEEVISH STUDENT	'TIS ONE BY ONE--THE	545	5
I DONT BELIEVE A PEEVISH BIRD	I THOUGHT THE TRAIN	1449	3
PEG			
I HUNG UPON THE PEG, AT NIGHT.	IT CEASED TO HURT ME,	584	8
PELF			
CONFRONTING SUDDEN PELF--	THERE IS A SHAME OF	551	2
PELLET			
PROVE THE FEAT--THAT MADE THE PELLET MINE--	GOD GAVE A LOAF TO EVERY	791	6
PELLETS			
OR PELLETS OF SHAPE	BANISH AIR FROM AIR--	854	5
PELTETH			
WITH RUBIES--PELTETH ME--	'TIS LITTLE I--COULD	466	4
PENALTY			
WERE DOOM ITSELF THE PENALTY--	OF DEATH I TRY TO THINK	1558	V 15
PENCE			
THE CHILDISH HANDS THAT TEAZED FOR PENCE	THE BEGGAR LAD--DIES	717	13
WHEN LOVE WITH BUT A PENCE	HOW DESTITUTE IS HE	1477	5
PENCIL			
AND THEN I TOOK A PENCIL	I COUNTED TILL THEY	36	3
SAINTS, WITH RAVISHED SLATE AND PENCIL	I CANT TELL YOU--BUT YOU	65	3
I CHECK MY BUSY PENCIL,	LOW AT MY PROBLEM	69	5
WHERE NO AUTUMN LIFTS HER PENCIL--	THO' MY DESTINY BE	163	15
DOMENICHINO DROPPED HIS PENCIL--	HOW THE OLD MOUNTAINS	291	23
WHOSE PENCIL--HERE AND THERE--	DEATH SETS A THING	360	14
'TIS MOSTLY SLATE AND PENCIL--	'TIS ONE BY ONE--THE	545	9
IF IT HAD NO PENCIL	IF IT HAD NO PENCIL	921	1
A PENCIL IN AN IDOL'S [DAINTY] HAND	DEATH WARRANTS ARE	1375	4
PENDULUM			
THIS PENDULUM OF SNOW--	A CLOCK STOPPED--	287	11
THE PENDULUM BEGINS TO COUNT--	I THINK THE LONGEST HOUR	635	9
YET THAT PATHETIC PENDULUM	'TWAS LATER WHEN THE	1276	7
HAS WRECKED THE PENDULUM--	THE CLOCK STRIKES ONE	1569	4
PENETRATE			
COULD THRILL [PENETRATE] THEIR MORTISED EAR	WHAT CARE THE DEAD, FOR	592	13
PENIEL			
"PENIEL" HILLS BEYOND [AMONG],	A LITTLE EAST OF JORDAN,	59	14
PENINSULA			
THAN GAIN--MY BLUE PENINSULA--	IT MIGHT BE LONELIER	405	15
AND HER UNSOWN PENINSULA--	THEY PUT US FAR APART--	474	3
TILL RAPTURE MISSED THEM [HER FOOTING-- / PENINSULA]	TWO BUTTERFLIES WENT OUT	533	V
UPON A NEW PENINSULA--	BEREAVED OF ALL, I WENT	784	3
OR A SQUIRREL, WHOSE GIDDY PENINSULA	BY MY WINDOW HAVE I FOR	797	7
FOR THAT PENINSULA--	THE INUNDATION OF THE	1425	8
IS THE UNKNOWN PENINSULA.	THE EARTH HAS MANY KEYS.	1775	3
PENINSULAR			
OF AUGHT PENINSULAR--	THE INUNDATION OF THE	1425	V 8
PENINSULAS			
AS PERSONS--OR PENINSULAS--	ONE CRUCIFIXION IS	553	7
TILL HE SHOULD JUMP PENINSULAS	COULD I BUT RIDE	661	11
PENNILESS			
A SCEPTRE--PENNILESS--	MY REWARD FOR BEING, WAS	343	4
PENNINILESS			
A WORLD MADE PENNINILESS BY THAT [HIS] DEPARTURE	A WORLD MADE PENNINILESS	1623	1
PENSIVE			
THE WAVE WITH EYE SO PENSIVE, LOOKETH TO SEE THE MOON,	AWAKE YE MUSES NINE,	1	18
AND STILL THE PENSIVE SPRING RETURNS--	NEW FEET WITHIN MY	99	7
AMONG THE PENSIVE [SMILING] TREES--	THE ONLY GHOST I EVER	274	12
A [GENTLE] PENSIVE CUSTOM IT BECOMES	FURTHER IN SUMMER THAN	1068	7
PENTATEUCHAL			
IN PENTATEUCHAL ROBES	IT ALWAYS FELT TO ME--A	597	20
PENURIOUS			
TO OUR PENURIOUS EYES!	AS BY THE DEAD WE LOVE	88	8
OF LIFE'S PENURIOUS ROUND--	I SHOULD HAVE BEEN TOO	313	3

	FIRST LINE	POEM	LINE
PENURIOUS (CONTINUED)			
FOR A PENURIOUS SMILE.	THEY ASK BUT OUR DELIGHT	868	4
DID LIFE'S PENURIOUS LENGTH	DID LIFE'S PENURIOUS	1717	1
PENURY			
HIS IS PENURY	NOW I KNEW I LOST HER--	1219	16
PENURY [HEMISPHERE] AND HOME?	FRIGID AND SWEET HER	1318	8
NO NEARER--LEST THE ACTUAL--[REALITY-- / ITS PENURY-- / THE . . .	WHO NEVER WANTED--	1430	7
'TIS PENURY IN CHIEF--	IT CAME HIS TURN TO BEG	1500	4
AND PENURY FOR GLORY	OF THIS IS DAY COMPOSED	1675	7
PEOPLE			
THE FEET OF PEOPLE WALKING HOME	THE FEET OF PEOPLE	7	1
BY PEOPLE OF DEGREE	SLEEP IS SUPPOSED TO BE	13	8
PEOPLE UPON THAT MYSTIC GREEN--	THERE IS A MORN BY MEN	24	20
WHEN I CON THE PEOPLE	WHEN I COUNT THE SEEDS	40	4
WHY, I HAVE LOST, THE PEOPLE KNOW	WHERE I HAVE LOST, I	104	13
THE PRETTY PEOPLE IN THE WOODS	THE BEE IS NOT AFRAID OF	111	3
VELVET PEOPLE FROM VEVAY--	PIGMY SERAPHS--GONE	138	2
TO PEOPLE--ANY MORE!	THE FLOWER MUST NOT	206	6
HER GREEN PEOPLE RECOLLECT IT	NATURE--SOMETIMES SEARS	314	3
AND SEE THE PEOPLE--GOING BY--	FUNNY--TO BE A CENTURY--	345	2
PEOPLE--LIKE THE MOTH--	I WENT TO HEAVEN--	374	9
DO PEOPLE MOULDER EQUALLY,	DO PEOPLE MOULDER	432	1
FROM THEIR PEOPLE PEARL--	SWEET--SAFE--HOUSES--	457	9
THAT PEOPLE "THIRST NO MORE"--	I KNOW WHERE WELLS GROW	460	14
AND PEOPLE COME--	WE DO NOT PLAY ON GRAVES	467	4
THOSE FAIR [NEW]--FICTITIOUS PEOPLE--	THOSE FAIR--FICTITIOUS	499	1
TO SOMETIMES HEAR "RICH PEOPLE" BUY	I CRIED AT PITY--NOT AT	588	9
SEVERAL OF NATURE'S PEOPLE	A NARROW FELLOW IN THE	986	17
OF THE SEPARATED PARTIES [PEOPLE]	THREE WEEKS PASSED SINCE	1061	11
LEST SOME ONE ELSE SHOULD [RICHER PEOPLE] BUY	A DIAMOND ON THE HAND	1108	V 8
HER SOVREIGN PEOPLE	HER SOVREIGN PEOPLE	1139	1
I NOTICED PEOPLE DISAPPEARED	I NOTICED PEOPLE	1149	1
IT'S TOILS [CORN] TO BRINDLED PEOPLE [NATIONS] THRUST [CAST]--	A FIELD OF STUBBLE,	1407	3
WHEN PEOPLE HAVE PUT OUT THE LIGHTS	HOW LONESOME THE WIND	1418	2
I KNOW OF PEOPLE IN THE GRAVE	I KNOW OF PEOPLE IN THE	1665	1
THE ONLY SECRET PEOPLE [NEIGHBORS] KEEP [SHUN]	THE RETICENT VOLCANO	1748	11
PEOPLES			
A HINT OF PORTS AND PEOPLES--	A SOUTH WIND--HAS A	719	5
PER			
IS THE MINUTE PER CENTS--	THE INCIDENTS OF LOVE	1248	4
PERADVENTURE			
NOR A SPORTSMAN'S PERADVENTURE [RUTHLESS PLEASURE / WANTON . . .	STRUCK, WAS I, NOR YET	925	7
TRUST ADJUSTS HER "PERADVENTURE"--	TRUST ADJUSTS HER	1161	1
THAT HATH NOR RETROSPECTION [PERADVENTURE]	LEFT IN IMMORTAL YOUTH	1289	3
PERCEIVE			
IT'S PAST--ENLIGHTENED TO PERCEIVE	PAIN--HAS AN ELEMENT OF	650	7
THE QUALITY CONCEIVE [PERCEIVE]	TWO--WERE IMMORTAL TWICE	800	6
ESCAPING BACKWARD TO PERCEIVE	ESCAPING BACKWARD TO	867	1
POWER TO PERCEIVE HIS PROCESS	STRUCK, WAS I, NOR YET	925	3
IF HE PERCEIVE THE OTHER TRUTH--	FITTER TO SEE HIM, I MAY	968	23
PERCEIVE, WHEN YOU ARE GONE.	THE DYING NEED BUT	1026	8
NOT QUICKENED TO PERCEIVE	LIKE MEN AND WOMEN	1105	6
THE INSTANT I PERCEIVE	BECAUSE THAT YOU ARE	1260	14
THOUGH SLIPPING--SLIPPING I PERCEIVE	STILL OWN THEE--STILL	1633	3
I PERCEIVE THE ROSE!	"LETHE" IN MY FLOWER,	1730	8
PERCEIVE THEIR PRAYER IS VAIN.	THERE COMES AN HOUR WHEN	1751	3
PERCEIVED			
UPON THE VILLAGE I PERCEIVED--	THE SUN KEPT SETTING--	692	3
PERCEIVED BY THE DENIED--	DENIAL--IS THE ONLY FACT	965	2
TILL SUDDEN I PERCEIVED IT STIR--	I HAD A DAILY BLISS	1057	3
A SPECK OF RAPTURE--FIRST PERCEIVED	A WINGED SPARK DOTH SOAR	1468	7
PERCEIVELESS			
BUT MY PERCEIVELESS GAIN	I MADE SLOW RICHES BUT	843	6
OF IT'S PERCEIVELESS FREIGHT!	HOW NEWS MUST FEEL WHEN	1319	8
OF SOME PERCEIVELESS THING--	THE PEDIGREE OF HONEY	1627	6
PERCEIVES			
AND WHEN A SOUL PERCEIVES ITSELF	PURPLE--IS FASHIONABLE	980	3
RENOWN PERCEIVES ITSELF	THE CLOVER'S SIMPLE FAME	1232	5
RELUCTANTLY BUT SURE PERCEIVES	SUMMER BEGINS TO HAVE	1682	3
PERCEIVING			
'TWAS BETTER--THE PERCEIVING NOT--	TRUST IN THE UNEXPECTED	555	15
PERCEIVING THEE IS EVIDENCE	EXTOL THEE--COULD I--	1643	5
PERCEPTIBLE			
BUT MONARCHS--ARE PERCEPTIBLE--	ONE LIFE OF SO MUCH	270	15
OR NONE PERCEPTIBLE.	THE BAT IS DUN, WITH	1575	4
PERCEPTION			
PERCEPTION OF AN OBJECT COSTS	PERCEPTION OF AN OBJECT	1071	1
PERCEPTION IN ITSELF A GAIN	PERCEPTION OF AN OBJECT	1071	3
PERCEPTION SETS IT FAIR	PERCEPTION OF AN OBJECT	1071	6
PERCH			
AND PERCH MY TONGUE	I'M SAYING EVERY DAY	373	16
PERCHANCE			
A CHEEK--PERCHANCE A BROW--	THE OUTER--FROM THE	451	14
PERCHANCE [THREE--WITH / AND SOME] ETERNITY--	THE ONLY NEWS I KNOW	827	6
OUR PERCHANCE A GALE	DOWN TIME'S QUAINT	1656	5
PERCHED			
YOUR SECRET, PERCHED IN EXTASY	COCOON ABOVE! COCOON	129	5

	FIRST LINE	POEM	LINE
PERCHES			
THAT PERCHES IN THE SOUL--	"HOPE" IS THE THING WITH	254	2
PERDITION			
THAT HELD HIM FROM PERDITION	AS ONE DOES SICKNESS	957	7
PERSUASIVE AS PERDITION,	RISK IS THE HAIR THAT	1239	11
PERDITION IS OPPROBRIUM--	HIS CHEEK IS HIS	1460	3
FOR THE DIVINE PERDITION	HIS LITTLE HEARSE LIKE	1522	7
PERENNIAL			
MY PERENNIAL NEST.	HER BREAST IS FIT FOR	84	8
HAUNT THE PERENNIAL BLOOM--	FOR THIS--ACCEPTED	195	11
PERENNIAL BEHOLDS US--	I NEVER FELT AT HOME--	413	13
MY PERENNIAL THINGS?	WHAT SHALL I DO WHEN THE	956	16
AT MOST TO BE PERENNIAL	SUMMER BEGINS TO HAVE	1682	14
PERFECT			
THE PERFECT, NOWHERE BE AFRAID--	WHEN WE STAND ON THE	242	9
I KNEW SO PERFECT--YESTERDAY--	I SHOULD HAVE BEEN TOO	313	10
HOW JUST THIS TIME, SOME PERFECT YEAR--	'TWAS JUST THIS TIME,	445	23
TO WEAR THAT PERFECT--PEARL--	THE WORLD--STANDS--	493	6
BUT THE COMPOSER--PERFECT MOZART--	BETTER--THAN MUSIC! FOR	503	7
BROKE--PERFECT--FROM THE POD--	HE GAVE AWAY HIS LIFE--	567	16
IN PERFECT--PAUSELESS MONARCHY--	BEHIND ME--DIPS ETERNITY	721	8
BE THE PERFECT ONE--	ALTER! WHEN THE HILLS DO	729	4
AND NOW SHE TURNS HER PERFECT FACE	THE MOON WAS BUT A CHIN	737	3
A PERFECT--PARALYZING BLISS--	ONE BLESSING HAD I THAN	756	7
UNTIL--RESEMBLANCE PERFECT--	TILL DEATH--IS NARROW	907	9
THROUGH AN [NATURE'S] EXPIRING--PERFECT--LOOK--	FAIRER THROUGH FADING--	938	8
A FULL, AND PERFECT TIME--	MIDSUMMER, WAS IT, WHEN	962	2
I SHALL BE PERFECT--IN HIS SIGHT--	FITTER TO SEE HIM, I MAY	968	22
ON NATURE'S PERFECT [GENERAL] SUM--	IT BLOOMED AND DROPT, A	978	10
WHOSE PERFECT SEASONS WAIT--	THERE IS A ZONE WHOSE	1056	4
PUT ON THE PERFECT LID--	WHEN MEMORY IS FULL	1266	2
LET ME NOT MAR THAT PERFECT DREAM	LET ME NOT MAR THAT	1335	1
. . . MIGHTY / GALLANT / SYLVAN / AMPLE / PERFECT] WAY	SUMMER--WE ALL HAVE SEEN	1386	6
DESIRE'S PERFECT GOAL--	WHO NEVER WANTED--	1430	6
PERFECTED			
GO PARALLEL, PERFECTED	THE OPENING AND THE	1047	7
HATH THE PERFECTED LIFE--	THE PROPS ASSIST THE	1142	9
PERFECTER			
WE TRUST--IN PLACES PERFECTER--	THOSE FAIR--FICTITIOUS	499	9
DONE PERFECTER ON STONE.	I'VE DROPPED MY BRAIN--	1046	4
PERFECTEST			
THE PERFECTEST COMMUNICATION	SPEECH IS ONE SYMPTOM OF	1681	3
PERFECTNESS			
AND MAR THY PERFECTNESS--	WHAT I SEE NOT, I BETTER	939	12
WHEN THESE--LEANED INTO [TWO--LEANED IN--] PERFECTNESS--	MIDSUMMER, WAS IT, WHEN	962	7
UNCONSCIOUSNESS OF PERFECTNESS	AURORA IS THE EFFORT	1002	3
AND THEN UPBRAIDS A PERFECTNESS	PERCEPTION OF AN OBJECT	1071	7
PERFIDIOUS			
BY THAT PERFIDIOUS HAIR--	RISK IS THE HAIR THAT	1239	8
PERFIDY			
CHID MY PERFIDY--	DISTRUSTFUL OF THE	20	4
MORE GENUINE WERE PERFIDY	THE HEALED HEART SHOWS	1440	7
PERFIDY IS THE VIRTUE	THE DEVIL--HAD HE	1479	5
TO SEEM [FEEL] LIKE PERFIDY--	AS IMPERCEPTIBLY AS	1540	4
SOME ATTAR'S PERFIDY?	SWEET PIRATE OF THE	1546	5
THE TRANQUIL PERFIDY	THROUGH THOSE OLD	1753	12
PERFORMED			
BY BUT TWELVE PERFORMED!	FREQUENTLY THE WOODS ARE	6	12
PERFUME			
A DEPTH--AN AZURE--A PERFUME--	A SOMETHING IN A	122	5
AND SHE WILL FLING HER MADDEST PERFUME--	KILL YOUR BALM--AND IT'S	238	3
PERHAPS			
PERHAPS THE "KINGDOM OF HEAVEN'S" CHANGED--	"ARCTURUS" IS HIS OTHER	70	26
PERHAPS YOU'RE GOING TOO!	GOING TO HEAVEN!	79	11
PERHAPS, WEARY [TIRED] AND SORE--	HEART, NOT SO HEAVY AS	83	18
PERHAPS A SQUIRREL MAY REMAIN--	BESIDES THE AUTUMN POETS	131	13
PERHAPS YOU'D LIKE TO BUY A FLOWER,	PERHAPS YOU'D LIKE TO	134	1
PERHAPS THEY DID NOT HEAR, I SAID,	WHOSE ARE THE LITTLE	142	5
PERHAPS A HOME TOO HIGH--	FOR EVERY BIRD A NEST--	143	7
PERHAPS OF TWIG SO FINE--	FOR EVERY BIRD A NEST--	143	10
PERHAPS HE DOES'NT KNOW THE HOUSE--	DYING! DYING IN THE	158	7
PERHAPS A FLOWER'S SHRIVELLED CHEEK	IN EBON BOX, WHEN YEARS	169	9
A CURL, PERHAPS, FROM FOREHEADS	IN EBON BOX, WHEN YEARS	169	13
PERHAPS, AN ANTIQUE TRINKET--	IN EBON BOX, WHEN YEARS	169	15
PERHAPS--I COULD'NT--	ONE YEAR AGO--JOTS WHAT?	296	21
PERHAPS I ASKED TOO LARGE--	PERHAPS I ASKED TOO	352	1
THINKING--PERHAPS--THAT I LOOKED TIRED--OR ALONE--	HOW SICK--TO WAIT--IN	368	3
PERHAPS THE OTHER--PEACE--	IT MIGHT BE LONELIER	405	4
A HILL--PERHAPS--	IT'S THOUGHTS--AND JUST	495	19
PERHAPS--THE PROFILE OF A MILL	IT'S THOUGHTS--AND JUST	495	20
AND PERHAPS A PHRASE IN EGYPTIAN [LATIN INSCRIPTION]--	WE DREAM--IT IS GOOD WE	531	15
PERHAPS HE--PITIED ME--	I TRIED TO THINK A	532	19
PERHAPS 'TIS KINDLY--DONE US--	WE SEE--COMPARATIVELY--	534	9
SKIRTS THE ACRES OF PERHAPS--	THEIR HIGHT IN HEAVEN	696	7
PERHAPS YOU THINK ME STOOPING	PERHAPS YOU THINK ME	833	1

	FIRST LINE	POEM		LINE
PERHAPS (CONTINUED)				
PERHAPS, RECALLS THE MAN	EACH SECOND IS THE LAST	879		2
A FLINT UNTO THIS DAY--PERHAPS--	WE MET AS SPARKS--	958	V	7
A FAN, PERHAPS, A FRIEND'S REGRET	THE DYING NEED BUT	1026		5
WENT TO HEAVEN PERHAPS AT DEATH	SO I PULL MY STOCKINGS	1201		5
AND PERHAPS HE DID'NT	SO I PULL MY STOCKINGS	1201		6
TO ANALYZE PERHAPS	THE FROST WAS NEVER SEEN	1202		17
OCCUPY TO US THOUGH PERHAPS TO THEM	SOME WE SEE NO MORE,	1221		2
WE BETTER FRIENDS HAD BEEN, PERHAPS,	WHO WERE "THE FATHER AND	1258		15
BUT [THO'] PERHAPS 'TIS WELL THEY'RE NOT AT HOME	HAD WE OUR SENSES	1284		2
PERHAPS--THE COMPREHENSION--	"WAS NOT" WAS ALL THE	1342		3
PERHAPS THEY DO [SHE DOES] NOT GO SO FAR	PERHAPS THEY DO NOT GO	1399		1
PERHAPS COME [COMES] CLOSER, FOR THE LAPSE [FLIGHT]	PERHAPS THEY DO NOT GO	1399		3
WITHOUT, PERHAPS, THE RIOT	SUMMER HAS TWO	1422		5
DECEIVES PERHAPS THE UNIVERSE	YOU CANNOT MAKE	1508		5
PERHAPS IS MORE ASTUTE	COME SHOW THY DURHAM	1542		8
AND THEN, PERHAPS, I SHALL.	THERE ARE TWO MAYS	1618	V	3
NOR THEN PERHAPS REPORTED	A WORD MADE FLESH IS	1651		3
PERIHELION				
ENCHANTMENT'S PERIHELION	DELIGHT'S DESPAIR AT	1299		5
PERIL				
GLASS WAS THE STREET--IN TINSEL PERIL	GLASS WAS THE STREET--IN	1498		1
PERIL AS A POSSESSION	PERIL AS A POSSESSION	1678		1
PERIL'S				
JUST GRANTED, FOR THE PERIL'S SAKE--	A SINGLE SCREW OF FLESH	263		15
PERIOD				
AT PERIOD OF GOING DOWN--	THE ONE WHO COULD REPEAT	307		5
MY PERIOD HAD COME FOR PRAYER--	MY PERIOD HAD COME FOR	564		1
IN HALF THE PERIOD--	THE SPIDER HOLDS A	605		8
MY PERIOD BEGIN	SHELLS FROM THE COAST	693		8
THEIR PERIOD FOR DAWN--	THE BIRDS BEGUN AT FOUR	783		2
AT ANY OTHER PERIOD--	A LIGHT EXISTS IN SPRING	812		3
SPRING IS THE PERIOD	SPRING IS THE PERIOD	844		1
A PERIOD FROM HENCE	NO OTHER CAN REDUCE	982		4
A PERIOD FROM HENCE--	NO OTHER CAN REDUCE	982	V	
NOT PERIOD--THAT DIED.	NOT ALL DIE EARLY, DYING	990		8
TO PAST OR PERIOD--	HE SCANNED IT--STAGGERED	1062		3
FOR PERIOD EXHALED.	GREAT STREETS OF SILENCE	1159		8
PERIODS				
NEW PERIODS--OF PAIN.	PAIN--HAS AN ELEMENT OF	650		8
OF PERIODS OF SEAS--	AS IF THE SEA SHOULD	695		5
HAS PERIODS OF SHUTTING--	WHAT I SEE NOT, I BETTER	939		3
OUR PERIODS MAY LIE	SUPERFLUOUS WERE THE SUN	999		10
PERIPHERY				
• • • EXPERIENCE / ASTONISHMENT / PERIPHERY] OF GREEN--	A LITTLE MADNESS IN THE	1333		5
PERIPHRASIS				
WE--PRONE TO PERIPHRASIS,	THERE'S SOMETHING	45		15
PERISH				
AND PERISH--BUT A BOUGH BETWEEN--	NOT PROBABLE--THE BAREST	346		8
OR PERISH FROM THE HILL--	HOW MANY FLOWERS FAIL IN	404		2
TO PERISH--OF DELIGHT--	IT MIGHT BE LONELIER	405		16
TO PERISH, OR TO LIVE?	'TWAS LIKE A MAELSTROM,	414		25
WE PERISH--THO' WE REIGN--	LIKE EYES THAT LOOKED ON	458		16
PERISH WITH HIM--THAT KEYLESS RHYME!	BETTER--THAN MUSIC! FOR	503		8
THEY PERISH [STAGGER]--DO WE DIE--	I CROSS TILL I AM WEARY	550		23
THEN DANGLE FROM [PERISH BY] THE HOUSEWIFE'S BROOM--	THE SPIDER HOLDS A	605		11
PERISH IN THE RECITATION--	DRAMA'S VITALLEST	741		4
TO STOP--OR PERISH--OR ADVANCE--	FROM BLANK TO BLANK--	761		4
AND PERISH FROM BEFORE ITSELF	THE LONELINESS ONE DARE	777		7
AND PERISH ON THE DAY	TRUTH--IS AS OLD AS GOD	836		5
TO PERISH IN HER HAND!	BE MINE THE DOOM--	845		3
IT PERISH, OR ENDURE--	JUST AS HE SPOKE IT FROM	848		6
THAN PERISH FROM THE CHANCE'S LIST	EACH SECOND IS THE LAST	879		7
AND PERISH OF THE COLD.	HOW HAPPY I WAS IF I	898		8
EQUALLY PERISH FROM OUR PRACTISE--	THOSE WHO HAVE BEEN IN	922		3
CANNOT PERISH, THOUGH IT FAIL	HE WHO IN HIMSELF	969		5
IF SEASONS PERISH OR PREVAIL	DID WE ABOLISH FROST	1014		3
BEGIN TO PERISH NOW.	I SHOULD NOT DARE TO BE	1197		8
I FAMISH [PERISH] TO BEHOLD SO EMINENT A SIGHT [ANOTHER SUCH • • •	THE MOST TRIUMPHANT BIRD	1265		4
PERISH AND REJOICE.	TRUSTY AS THE STARS	1369		8
TO DARE AND PERISH THERE?	IT WOULD NOT KNOW IF IT	1579		8
THE RIGHT TO PERISH MIGHT BE THO'T	THE RIGHT TO PERISH	1692		1
PERISHED				
ELSE PERISHED IN THE STONE--	A SCIENCE--SO THE SAVANS	100		6
AH, WHAT SAGACITY PERISHED HERE!	SAFE IN THEIR ALABASTER	216		11
SILVER--PERISHED--WITH HER TONGUE--	HER--"LAST POEMS"--	312		3
EXCEPT A PERISHED CREATURE	DEATH SETS A THING	360		3
THEY PERISHED IN THE SEAMLESS GRASS--	THEY DROPPED LIKE FLAKES	409		6
THAT PERISHED BY THE DOOR--	THIS WAS A POET--IT IS	448		6
I GROPED [PERISHED / DWELT] UPON HIS BREAST--	HE TOUCHED ME, SO I LIVE	506		3
AS WE--IT WERE--THAT PERISHED--	OF NEARNESS TO HER	607		17
THE PERISHED PATTERNS MURMUR--	IT'S EASY TO INVENT A	724		9
THE JUDGMENT PERISHED--TOO--	ONE BLESSING HAD I THAN	756		16
JOY TO HAVE PERISHED EVERY STEP--	JOY TO HAVE MERITED THE	788		3
HAVE PERISHED IN MY HANDS	IT BLOOMED AND DROPT, A	978		14

	FIRST LINE	POEM	LINE
PERISHED (CONTINUED)			
A PERISHED SUN	WE LEARN IN THE	1083	4
WHEN THE PREFACE PERISHED FROM CONSCIOUSNESS	ENDED, ERE IT BEGUN--	1088	3
THE BEE HAD PERISHED FROM THE SCENE	THE CRICKETS SANG	1104	V
SWEET HOURS HAVE PERISHED HERE;	SWEET HOURS HAVE	1767	1
PERISHES			
BUT PERISHES--TO LIVE ANEW--	SUSPENSE--IS HOSTILER	705	5
PERISHING			
OR SPIKENARDS, PERISHING [AMULETS OF PINE]--	THE GRASS SO LITTLE HAS	333	16
BEFORE THE PERISHING!	EACH SECOND IS THE LAST	879	8
TWO TRAVELLERS PERISHING IN SNOW	TWO TRAVELLERS PERISHING	933	1
HINDERING--HAUNTING--PERISHING--	FAIRER THROUGH FADING--	938	4
PERJURY			
AND IT WERE PERJURY!	I HAVE A KING, WHO DOES	103	18
FOR HIS PERJURY!	TAKING UP THE FAIR IDEAL	428	8
FOR PERJURY OF THAT--	THEY PUT US FAR APART--	474	20
TILL CAVILER [PERJURY] INSINUATES	WHOEVER DISENCHANTS	1451	V 7
ALL THE REST IS PERJURY--	LAD OF ATHENS, FAITHFUL	1768	4
PERMANENCE			
THESE ARE THE BRIDES OF PERMANENCE	DOMINION LASTS UNTIL	1257	7
PERMISSION			
THE ANGEL BEGGED PERMISSION	A LITTLE EAST OF JORDAN,	59	7
I'VE KNOWN PERMISSION GIVEN	A THROE UPON THE	71	7
PERMISSION TO RECANT--	THEY PUT US FAR APART--	474	17
PERMISSION TO FORGET--	THEY PUT US FAR APART--	474	18
PERMISSION HAVE TO UNDERSTAND	I SHALL NOT MURMUR IF AT	1410	3
PERMIT			
PERMIT A CHILD TO JOIN.	THESE ARE THE DAYS WHEN	130	15
THAT HEAVEN PERMIT SO MEEK [FAINT] AS HER--	SHE'S HAPPY, WITH A NEW	535	7
PERMIT TO BE	WERT THOU BUT ILL--THAT	961	14
PERMIT [ALLOW / BESTOW] ME THIS REPRIEVE	TRIED ALWAYS AND	1559	2
PERMITS			
GOD PERMITS INDUSTRIOUS ANGELS--	GOD PERMITS INDUSTRIOUS	231	1
PERMITTED			
PERMITTED GODS [MEN], AND ME--	OF ALL THE SOUNDS	321	8
PERMITTED TO COMMUNE THIS--TIME--	THERE CAME A DAY AT	322	14
PERMITTED--SUCH A HEAD--	IT FEELS A SHAME TO BE	444	4
THAT SUCH A DAY, PERMITTED [PERSUADED / ACCEPTED] SO,	HE TOUCHED ME, SO I LIVE	506	2
PERMITTED--FACE TO FACE TO BE--	IF I MAY HAVE IT, WHEN	577	10
PERMITTED TO REVERE	TO UNDERTAKE IS TO	1070	6
PERMITTING			
PERMITTING TO PURSUE	THROUGH THOSE OLD	1753	10
PERNICIOUS			
PERNICIOUS AS THE SUNSET	THROUGH THOSE OLD	1753	9
PERPENDICULAR			
DRIVES PONDEROUS PERPENDICULAR	THESE ARE THE NIGHTS	1128	3
PERPENDICULARS			
TO [IN] MAGIC PERPENDICULARS	THE ROAD WAS LIT WITH	1450	5
PERPETUAL			
SUCH [SOME] SPIRIT MAKES [TELL] HER PERPETUAL MENTION,	UNTO LIKE STORY--TROUBLE	295	13
PERPETUAL BREAK [BE / GO] ABROAD	WHEN I WAS SMALL, A	596	18
AS AN ESTATE PERPETUAL	TO OWN THE ART WITHIN	855	7
OR BIRDS--CONFIRMED PERPETUAL	'TWAS AWKWARD, BUT IT	973	7
WHOSE SUN CONSTRUCTS PERPETUAL NOON	THERE IS A ZONE WHOSE	1056	3
PERPETUAL NAIL IT DOWN--	A GREAT HOPE FELL	1123	17
PERPETUAL PRESUMPTION [COMPLACENCE] TOOK	ALONE AND IN A	1167	15
WHEN FOLDED IN PERPETUAL SEAM	A WORD DROPPED CARELESS	1261	3
PROCURING HIM PERPETUAL DREST	I CANNOT SEE MY SOUL BUT	1262	9
PERPLEX			
AND HE AND I, PERPLEX US	WITHIN MY GARDEN, RIDES	500	13
PERPLEXED			
OR PERPLEXED--OR COLD--	I OFTEN PASSED THE	51	14
PERPLEXED! ESTATES OF VIOLET TROUBLE NE'ER LOOKED ON!	WOULD YOU LIKE SUMMER?	691	5
PERPLEXEDLY			
GAZE PERPLEXEDLY!	SO FROM THE MOULD	66	11
PERPLEXITY			
THY PERPLEXITY?	LOW AT MY PROBLEM	69	8
PERQUISITE			
WITHOUT THE STERILE PERQUISITE,	TO LOSE THEE--SWEETER	1754	7
PERSEVERED			
YET PERSEVERED TOWARD--SURER [STRICTER]--FOR THE DISTANCE--	EACH LIFE CONVERGES TO	680	13
PERSIAN			
NOR PERSIAN, BAFFLED AT HER SHRINE	HE TOUCHED ME, SO I LIVE	506	16
PERSISTS			
NO FRIEND HAVE I THAT SO PERSISTS	THE BLUNDER IS IN	1684	7
PERSON			
YOU ARE SURE THERE'S SUCH A PERSON	WHAT IS--"PARADISE"--	215	11
THAT PERSON THAT I WAS--	THE FIRST DAY'S NIGHT	410	18
NO PERSON TESTIFIED--	WHEN I WAS SMALL, A	596	12
HE--MUST HAVE ACHIEVED IN PERSON	HER SWEET TURN TO LEAVE	649	27
TO THAT BOLD PERSON, GOD--	WHAT DID THEY DO SINCE I	900	16
GOD IT IS SAID REPLIES IN PERSON	TELL AS A MARKSMAN--WERE	1152	24
A COUNTERFEIT--A PLATED PERSON--	A COUNTERFEIT--A PLATED	1453	1
PERSONAL			
'TWAS CHRIST'S OWN PERSONAL EXPANSE	OBTAINING BUT OUR OWN	1543	3

	FIRST LINE	POEM	LINE
PERSONALLY			
A BEE I PERSONALLY KNEW	A SINGLE CLOVER PLANK	1343	3
PERSONS			
AS FREEZING PERSONS, RECOLLECT THE SNOW--	AFTER GREAT PAIN, A	341	12
AS PERSONS--OR PENINSULAS--	ONE CRUCIFIXION IS	553	7
OF PERSONS [CREATURES] OUTSIDE WINDOWS--	I HAD BEEN HUNGRY, ALL	579	19
THAN PERSONS, THAT WE KNOW.	THE MURMURING OF BEES,	1115	16
THE PERSONS [TRANSPORTS / TREASURES / ASPECTS] OF PROGNOSTICATION	MARCH IS THE MONTH OF	1404	3
PERSPICACITY			
THE GUESTS OF PERSPICACITY	THE ROBIN IS A GABRIEL	1483	11
PERSUADE			
PERSUADE OUR FEATHERS HOME	'TIS NOT THAT DYING	335	12
TO SEDUCE [ENTICE / PERSUADE] THE SUN	PROMISE THIS--WHEN YOU	648	18
PERSUADED			
DID THE "PARADISE"--PERSUADED--	DID THE HAREBELL LOOSE	213	5
AGAINST THE MAN--PERSUADED--	MYSELF WAS FORMED--A	488	11
THAT SUCH A DAY, PERMITTED [PERSUADED / ACCEPTED] SO,	HE TOUCHED ME, SO I LIVE	506	2
PERSUADED OF THE BURIED GOLD--	TRUST IN THE UNEXPECTED	555	3
PERSUADING			
TILL IT DEPART, PERSUADING [CONVEYING] MINE--	AIR HAS NO RESIDENCE, NO	1060	8
PERSUASIVE			
PERSUASIVE AS PERDITION,	RISK IS THE HAIR THAT	1239	11
PERTURBATION			
WHICH IN A PERTURBATION	HIGH FROM THE EARTH I	1723	7
PERTURBED			
A SMALLER, COULD NOT BE PERTURBED--	WHO GIANTS KNOW, WITH	796	5
PERTURBLESS			
BUT HIS PERTURBLESS PLAN	IT'S EASY TO INVENT A	724	10
PERU			
AND PURPLE--FROM PERU--	WHAT WOULD I GIVE TO SEE	247	20
A DIFFERENT PERU--	YOUR RICHES--TAUGHT ME--	299	6
BROTHER OF INGOTS--[SISTER OF OPHIR--] AH PERU--	BROTHER OF INGOTS--AH	1366	1
PERUKE			
AND YET A WREN'S PERUKE	A MIEN TO MOVE A QUEEN--	283	10
PERUSAL			
AS THE PERUSAL OF	NO ROMANCE SOLD UNTO	669	3
PERUSAL--TO FACILITATE--	REMORSE--IS MEMORY--	744	7
FOR IT'S OWN PERUSAL.	SAFE DESPAIR IT IS THAT	1243	4
PERUSE			
PERUSE HOW INFINITE I AM	THE WAY I READ A	636	13
PERUSER			
PERUSER OF ENCHANTING BOOK	SUMMER BEGINS TO HAVE	1682	2
PERVADE			
AND NOT A SONG PERVADE HIS LIPS--	THE BAT IS DUN, WITH	1575	3
PERVADED			
PERVADED HER, WE THOUGHT	HER FINAL SUMMER WAS IT	795	4
PERVADES			
WHAT MYSTERY PERVADES A WELL!	WHAT MYSTERY PERVADES A	1400	1
PERVERSE			
THE FRUIT PERVERSE TO PLUCKING,	TO DISAPPEAR ENHANCES--	1209	17
PERVERSITY			
WHAT A POMPOSITY [AN ABSURDITY / A PERVERSITY]	THAT THIS SHOULD FEEL	1112	V 7
PETAL			
A SEPAL, PETAL, AND A THORN	A SEPAL, PETAL, AND A	19	1
A PETAL, FOR A PARAGRAPH	I PAY--IN SATIN CASH--	402	3
I PUSH A PETAL FROM MY GOWN	I TIE MY HAT--I CREASE	443	7
MERELY FLAKE OR PETAL	"LETHE" IN MY FLOWER,	1730	5
PETALS			
LIKE PETALS FROM A ROSE--	THEY DROPPED LIKE FLAKES	409	3
WHILE I STATE--THE SOLEMN PETALS,	BLOOM UPON THE MOUNTAIN	667	13
UPON HER BOSOM [PETALS / SOFTNESS] PILED--	NO NOTICE GAVE SHE, BUT	804	8
OR PETALS, OR A DOWER OF BUZZ	BECAUSE THE BEE MAY	869	10
SHE SPED AS PETALS OF [FROM] A ROSE	SHE SPED AS PETALS OF A	991	1
PETER			
HURRAH FOR PETER PARLEY!	"SIC TRANSIT GLORIA	3	9
PETER, PUT UP THE SUNSHINE;	"SIC TRANSIT GLORIA	3	13
RATHER--HEAVEN'S "PETER PARLEY"!	I CANT TELL YOU--BUT YOU	65	17
HE WILL TELL ME WHAT "PETER" PROMISED--	I SHALL KNOW WHY--WHEN	193	5
LONG AGO AS CHRIST AND PETER--	HE FORGOT--AND I--	203	3
"NO"--SAID PETER, 'TWAS'NT ME--	HE FORGOT--AND I--	203	6
JESUS MERELY "LOOKED" AT PETER--	HE FORGOT--AND I--	203	7
PETITE			
A MODEST LOT--A FAME PETITE--	A LITTLE BREAD--A CRUST	159	7
'TWAS POSSIBLY A CZAR PETITE--	I MET A KING THIS	166	11
PETITION			
NOT FOR OURSELVES, PETITION--	WHATEVER IT IS--SHE HAS	1204	5
PETITION'S			
PETITION'S WAY,	I GOT SO I COULD HEAR	293	18
PETTICOAT			
HER PETTICOAT--OF PURPLE PLAIN [JUST]--	THE DAY UNDRESSED--	716	3
PETTY			
FOR PETTY FURNITURE--	SIZE CIRCUMSCRIBES--IT	641	2
PHAETON			
"ARMS OF MINE--SUFFICIENT PHAETON--	"UNTO ME?" I DO NOT KNOW	964	7
PHANTASM			
LEST THE PHANTASM--PROVE THE [JUST] MISTAKE--	WE DREAM--IT IS GOOD WE	531	11
AS THIS PHANTASM [COMPANION] STEEL--	A PRISON GETS TO BE A	652	21

	FIRST LINE	POEM	LINE
PHANTASMS			
PHANTASMS [FICTITIOUS] BOTH BECOME	ONE BLESSING HAD I THAN	756	10
PHANTOM			
FLEES SO THE PHANTOM MEADOW	DISTRUSTFUL OF THE	20	9
OH PHANTOM QUEEN!	NOT PROBABLE--THE BAREST	346	10
WHERE PARTIES--PHANTOM AS HERSELF--	FROM COCOON FORTH A	354	14
DRUMS OFF THE PHANTOM BATTLEMENTS	OVER AND OVER, LIKE A	367	3
OLD NICODEMUS' PHANTOM	THE BONE THAT HAS NO	1274	11
IT IS A FADED [PHANTOM] MEAT--	MINE ENEMY IS GROWING	1509	6
PHANTOMS			
PHANTOMS ENTERED "AND NOT YOU."	TRUST ADJUSTS HER	1161	2
PHARAOH			
OF PURPLE PHARAOH--	"RED SEA," INDEED! TALK	1642	2
PHARMACY			
IS NATURE'S ONLY PHARMACY	SEVERER SERVICE OF	786	23
PHEBE			
I WAS A PHEBE--NOTHING MORE--	I WAS A PHEBE--NOTHING	1009	1
A PHEBE--NOTHING LESS--	I WAS A PHEBE--NOTHING	1009	2
A PHEBE MAKES A LITTLE PRINT	I WAS A PHEBE--NOTHING	1009	7
THE PHEBE AND THE CROW	THE ONES THAT	1690	2
PHEBES			
THE PHEBES HAVE BEGUN--	THE WINTERS ARE SO SHORT	403	6
PHIALS			
PHIALS LEFT, AND THE SUN!	DYING AT MY MUSIC!	1003	6
PHILIP			
PHILIP--WHEN BEWILDERED [QUESTIONED EAGER]	IF THOSE I LOVED WERE	29	7
A PHILIP WOULD PREFER	THE FROST WAS NEVER SEEN	1202	18
PHILOLOGY			
THE POET SEARCHED [PROBED] PHILOLOGY	SHALL I TAKE THEE, THE	1126	5
THAT WAS PHILOLOGY--	"WAS NOT" WAS ALL THE	1342	8
THIS LOVED PHILOLOGY	A WORD MADE FLESH IS	1651	16
PHILOSOPHER			
SAY--SOME--PHILOSOPHER!	KNOWS HOW TO FORGET!	433	V
THROUGH THIS--THE OLD PHILOSOPHER--	TRUST IN THE UNEXPECTED	555	5
THAN BIND PHILOSOPHER--	I WATCHED THE MOON	629	20
AND TURN PHILOSOPHER.	SEPTEMBER'S	1271	8
ELATE PHILOSOPHER.	THE BAT IS DUN, WITH	1575	8
PHILOSOPHY			
THAN PHILOSOPHY.	THE RAINBOW NEVER TELLS	97	4
PHILOSOPHY--DONT KNOW--	THIS WORLD IS NOT	501	6
'TIS PHILOSOPHY--	YESTERDAY IS HISTORY,	1292	4
IS THEIR THEOLOGY [PHILOSOPHY]	COSMOPOLITES WITHOUT A	1589	8
PHLEGMATIC			
HOW THOSE OLD--PHLEGMATIC MOUNTAINS	I HAVE NEVER SEEN	175	3
PHOEBE SEE PHEBE			
PHOSPHOR			
LIT WITH A FINER PHOSPHOR--	MORE LIFE--WENT OUT--	422	3
PHOSPHORIC			
AT HER PHOSPHORIC TOIL!	THE LAMP BURNS SURE--	233	4
PHOSPHORUS			
THE ZEROES--TAUGHT US--PHOSPHORUS--	THE ZEROES--TAUGHT US--	689	1
THE PHOSPHORUS OF GOD--	WHO IS IT SEEKS MY	1598	8
PHRASE			
MANY A PHRASE HAS THE ENGLISH LANGUAGE--	MANY A PHRASE HAS THE	276	1
AND PERHAPS A PHRASE IN EGYPTIAN [LATIN INSCRIPTION]--	WE DREAM--IT IS GOOD WE	531	15
I FOUND THE WORDS [PHRASE] TO EVERY THOUGHT	I FOUND THE WORDS TO	581	1
PHRASELESS			
PHRASELESS--YET IT STIRS	IT'S LIKE THE LIGHT--	297	7
THAT PHRASELESS MELODY--	OF ALL THE SOUNDS	321	4
PHYSICIAN			
IS HEAVEN A PHYSICIAN?	IS HEAVEN A PHYSICIAN?	1270	1
PHYSICIAN'S			
PHYSICIAN'S--PROOF OF BREATH--	I AM ALIVE--I GUESS--	470	8
PHYSIOGNOMY			
WAS PHYSIOGNOMY.	A SPIDER SEWED AT NIGHT	1138	9
BY PHYSIOGNOMY	A DEW SUFFICED ITSELF--	1437	8
THY PHYSIOGNOMY	HOW FIRM ETERNITY MUST	1499	6
THAT VERY PHYSIOGNOMY	NO MAN SAW AWE, NOR TO	1733	15
PIANOS			
NOT ALL PIANOS IN THE WOODS	I DREADED THAT FIRST	348	7
PICK			
PICK BY FAITH IT'S BLOSSOM	WHEN I COUNT THE SEEDS	40	9
TO PICK ANOTHER DAY;	WENT UP A YEAR THIS	93	16
AND BEES--PICK UP--	I TEND MY FLOWERS FOR	339	10
AND SLOWLY [SLILY / SOFTLY] PICK THE LOCK--	THE WAY I READ A	636	8
GRANTED I CAN PICK 'EM--	WHAT WE SEE WE KNOW	1195	6
PICKED			
THE QUIET AGES PICKED IT UP--	I MEANT TO HAVE BUT	476	19
ETERNITY'S VAST [WIDE] POCKET, PICKED--	EMPTY MY HEART, OF THEE	587	14
PICKING			
INSTINCT PICKING UP THE KEY	AFTER A HUNDRED YEARS	1147	11
PICTORIAL			
DELIGHT--BECOMES PICTORIAL--	DELIGHT--BECOMES	572	1
PICTURE			
MAKE ME A PICTURE OF THE SUN--	MAKE ME A PICTURE OF THE	188	1
THE SEASONS--SHIFT--MY PICTURE--	THE ANGLE OF A LANDSCAPE	375	13
IT'S PICTURE PUBLISHES--PRECISE--	THE OUTER--FROM THE	451	11
THE JUDGMENT PUSH HIS PICTURE--	THE POWER TO BE TRUE TO	464	3
A PICTURE--IF IT CARE--	IT'S THOUGHTS--AND JUST	495	9

	FIRST LINE	POEM		LINE
PICTURE (CONTINUED)				
I WOULD NOT PAINT--A PICTURE--	I WOULD NOT PAINT--A	505		1
TO SEE HER IS A PICTURE--	TO SEE HER IS A PICTURE	1568		1
PICTURES				
PORTRAITS [PICTURES] ARE TO DAILY FACES	PORTRAITS ARE TO DAILY	170		1
BEAUTIFUL--AS PICTURES--	I WENT TO HEAVEN--	374		7
OF PICTURES, THE DISCLOSER--	THIS WAS A POET--IT IS	448		9
PICTURESQUE				
OH BATTLE PICTURESQUE!	MY FRIEND ATTACKS MY	118		2
THE MERCHANT OF THE PICTURESQUE	THE MERCHANT OF THE	1131		1
PIECE				
IF JOY--TO PUT MY PIECE AWAY	FOREVER AT HIS SIDE TO	246		8
PIECED				
AND SO I PIECED IT, WITH A FLOWER, NOW.	TO LOVE THEE YEAR BY	434		6
PIECES				
AND GO TO PIECES ON THE STONES [IN THE DITCH]	IT DROPPED SO LOW--IN MY	747		3
PIER				
THAT PASSED THE MOULDERING PIER--	THAT AFTER HORROR--THAT	286		2
THE PIER TO MY PONTOON--	I WOULD NOT PAINT--A	505		16
ABOVE OBLIVION'S TIDE THERE IS A PIER	ABOVE OBLIVION'S TIDE	1531		1
PIERCE				
CAN PIERCE AN ARMED MAN--	THERE IS A WORD	8		3
TO PUSH, AND PIERCE, BESIDES--	A WEIGHT WITH NEEDLES ON	264		2
WOULD PIERCE ME WITH A FASHION	I DREADED THAT FIRST	348		11
NOR PIERCE WITH CIMITAR--	NO RACK CAN TORTURE ME--	384		6
PIERCE--BY THE VERY PRESS	INCONCEIVABLY SOLEMN!	582		3
WOULD PIERCE HIS COLUMNS THRO'--	"RED SEA," INDEED! TALK	1642		4
THOU CAN'ST NOT PIERCE TRADITION WITH THE PEERLESS PUNCTURE,	PROUD OF MY BROKEN HEART	1736		7
PIERCES				
THAT CORONATION PIERCES HIM	ONE CROWN THAT NO ONE	1735		7
PIERCING				
PROVE PIERCING EARNEST--	I KNOW THAT HE EXISTS.	338		10
A PIERCING COMFORT IT AFFORDS	I MEASURE EVERY GRIEF I	561		35
RENUNCIATION--IS A PIERCING VIRTUE--	RENUNCIATION--IS A	745		1
PIERLESS				
FAITH--IS THE PIERLESS BRIDGE	FAITH--IS THE PIERLESS	915		1
PIERS				
ALSO, WHO LAID THE RAINBOW'S PIERS,	BRING ME THE SUNSET IN A	128		13
HOW BRITTLE ARE THE PIERS	HOW BRITTLE ARE THE	1433		1
UPON WHAT BRITTLE [FICKLE / TRIFLING] PIERS	HOW BRITTLE ARE THE	1433	V	1
PIGMY				
PIGMY SERAPHS--GONE ASTRAY--	PIGMY SERAPHS--GONE	138		1
PILATE				
FILAMENTS OF BLOOM, PONTIUS PILATE SOWED--	TO PUT THIS WORLD DOWN,	527		10
WHILE PONTIUS PILATE LIVES	ONE CROWN THAT NO ONE	1735		5
PILE				
AROUND A PILE OF MOUNTAINS--	I LIKE TO SEE IT LAP	585		5
THAT HUNCH [PILE] THEMSELVES BETWEEN--	I SEE THEE BETTER--IN	611		6
ALTHOUGH ANNIHILATION PILE	A PLATED LIFE--	806		7
REVERE [RESPECT] THE GRAYEST PILE	ASHES DENOTE THAT FIRE	1063		2
TO PILE LIKE THUNDER TO IT'S CLOSE	TO PILE LIKE THUNDER TO	1247		1
THE PILE OF YEARS IS NOT SO HIGH	THE PILE OF YEARS IS NOT	1507		1
UPON A PILE OF WIND	HIGH FROM THE EARTH I	1723		6
PILED				
AND PILED HER BLOSSOMS ON--	THE MORNING AFTER WO--	364		6
THAT LIVES--LIKE DOLLARS--MUST BE PILED	IT FEELS A SHAME TO BE	444		11
I WONDER IF WHEN YEARS HAVE PILED--	I MEASURE EVERY GRIEF I	561		17
UPON HER BOSOM [PETALS / SOFTNESS] PILED--	NO NOTICE GAVE SHE, BUT	804		8
AND PILED THEM IN [SHOWED THEM TO] THE SOUTH--	THE WIND TOOK UP THE	1134		2
PILES				
AND PILES OF SOLID MOAN--	MY PORTION IS DEFEAT--	639		9
PILFERED				
THE YEARS, OUR PILFERED THINGS--	OF NEARNESS TO HER	607		14
PILGRIM				
IT MIGHT A PILGRIM BE	NOBODY KNOWS THIS LITTLE	35		2
PLEASE TO TELL A LITTLE PILGRIM	WILL THERE REALLY BE A	101		11
SOME PILGRIM THIRST TO SLAKE--	I BRING AN UNACCUSTOMED	132		19
PILGRIM BE FOUND?	FOR EVERY BIRD A NEST--	143		6
RED PILGRIM, HE AND I--	DEPRIVED OF OTHER	773		10
PILLAGE				
"HAVE ALTERED--ACCEPT THE PILLAGE	I SAW THAT THE FLAKE WAS	1267		7
THE PILLAGE OF [IRREVERENCED--IN] THE SEA	COULD MORTAL LIP DIVINE	1409	V	
THE SWEETS OF PILLAGE, CAN BE KNOWN	THE SWEETS OF PILLAGE,	1470		1
PILLOW				
DID ROUND MY PILLOW ROLL,	I HAVE A KING, WHO DOES	103		9
FEELING AS IF THEIR PILLOW HEARD,	WHERE I HAVE LOST, I	104		7
AND NOT THE PILLOW AT YOUR CHEEK	'TIS SO APPALLING--IT	281		17
DEEP [LOW] PILLOW--TO HAVE SHARED--	MY LIFE HAD STOOD--A	754		16
THE PILLOW FOR MY HEAD--	BEREAVED OF ALL, I WENT	784		8
BE IT'S PILLOW ROUND--	AMPLE MAKE THIS BED--	829		6
ETHERIAL GUEST AT E'EN AN OUTCAST'S PILLOW--	AIR HAS NO RESIDENCE, NO	1060		5
ON THAT SPECIFIC PILLOW	ON THAT SPECIFIC PILLOW	1533		1
THE PILLOW OF THIS DARING HEAD	NO BRIGADIER THROUGHOUT	1561		17
WHO IS IT SEEKS MY PILLOW NIGHTS--	WHO IS IT SEEKS MY	1598		1
PILOT				
HO! PILOT, HO!	ON THIS WONDROUS SEA	4		3
THITHER I PILOT THEE--	ON THIS WONDROUS SEA	4		10
THAT PILOT HIM ALONG--	NO MAN CAN COMPASS A	477		12

	FIRST LINE	POEM	LINE
PIN			
OR TIE HIM TO A PIN	IS IT TRUE, DEAR SUE?	218	7
PINCHED			
AND SUNSHINE PINCHED ME--'TWAS SO COLD-- .	IF I MAY HAVE IT, WHEN	577	17
PINCHING			
BUT--THE INSTEAD--THE PINCHING FEAR . . .	WHY MAKE IT DOUBT--IT	462	8
PINE			
PINE BOUGH	A FEATHER FROM THE	161	T
OR SPIKENARDS, PERISHING [AMULETS OF PINE]--	THE GRASS SO LITTLE HAS	333	16
IF [GRANT] THE BIRD AND THE FARMER--DEEM IT A "PINE"--	BY MY WINDOW HAVE I FOR	797	3
WAS THE PINE AT MY WINDOW A "FELLOW . . .	BY MY WINDOW HAVE I FOR	797	22
THE BOLDEST MIND WILL PINE	THE MIND LIVES ON THE	1355	V 6
PINES			
UPHOLSTERER OF THE PINES [SEA / LAND / HILLS]--IS HE--	OF BRUSSELS--IT WAS NOT	602	15
BUT ACCLIMATED--PINES NO MORE [GROPES NO MORE / LOSES SIGHT / . . .	THE INUNDATION OF THE	1425	7
PINIONS			
PINIONS--THE SERAPH'S WAGON	THE FEET OF PEOPLE	7	11
SHE WILL STIR HER PINIONS	IT DID NOT SURPRISE ME--	39	3
WITH PINIONS OF DISDAIN	WITH PINIONS OF DISDAIN	1431	1
PINK			
FREQUENTLY THE WOODS ARE PINK--	FREQUENTLY THE WOODS ARE	6	1
THE SWAMPS ARE PINK WITH JUNE.	ALL THESE MY BANNERS BE.	22	21
A PINK AND PULPY MULTITUDE	OUR LITTLE KINSMEN--	885	3
PINK--SMALL--AND PUNCTUAL--	PINK--SMALL--AND	1332	1
AND IN CHINTZ [RED / PINK] THE APPLE . . .	I SUPPOSE THE TIME WILL	1381	8
WHOSE PINK CAREER MAY HAVE A CLOSE . . .	WHOSE PINK CAREER MAY	1394	1
SHAME IS THE SHAWL OF PINK	SHAME IS THE SHAWL OF	1412	1
. . . BURST / FLAGS / STEP / TICK / SHOUTS / PINK / RED / . . .	ONE JOY OF SO MUCH	1420	6
OF A DESPATCH OF PINK.	THE STEM OF A DEPARTED	1520	4
TO THAT PINK STRANGER WE CALL DUST-- . . .	OH GIVE IT MOTION--DECK	1527	5
EACH WAS TO EACH THE PINK REDOUBT-- . . .	'TIS SEASONS SINCE THE	1529	8
IS PINK ETERNALLY.	BLOSSOMS WILL RUN AWAY,	1578	4
PINK LANK AND WARM	IN WINTER IN MY ROOM	1670	3
CONFIDED ARE HIS PROJECTS PINK	THE RETICENT VOLCANO	1748	3
PINKS			
BUT NATURE RELISHES THE PINKS	BETROTHED TO	1641	3
PINNACE			
LIFTS [SPREADS] HIS LIGHT PINNACE--	THE NEAREST DREAM	319	8
PINNACLE			
BUT ONLY PINNACLE--	THE WAY HOPE BUILDS HIS	1481	4
PINNED			
TO WHICH MY FAITH PINNED BLOCK BY BLOCK . .	FALSEHOOD OF THEE COULD	1007	3
PINS			
IS ALL THAT PINS THE SOUL	A SINGLE SCREW OF FLESH	263	2
WITH BRIGHT PINS OF BUTTERCUP--	I'M SAYING EVERY DAY	373	13
BUT JUST THE PLACING PINS--	AT LEISURE IS THE SOUL	618	6
PIONEER			
TENDER PIONEER--	LIFE--IS WHAT WE MAKE IT	698	14
UNTIL A PIONEER, AS	WHO OCCUPIES THIS HOUSE?	892	21
PIOUS			
WHOM I HAVE LOST, I PIOUS GUARD	WHERE I HAVE LOST, I	104	5
WHEN KATIE KNEELS, THEIR LOVING HANDS STILL CLASP HER PIOUS KNEE--	WHEN KATIE WALKS, THIS	222	3
AND THEN THE PIOUS FORM	I READ MY SENTENCE--	412	6
PIPE			
PIPE THE SWEET BIRDS IN IGNORANT CADENCE-- .	SAFE IN THEIR ALABASTER	216	10
WHITE AS AN INDIAN PIPE	WHITE AS AN INDIAN PIPE	1250	1
'TIS WHITER THAN AN INDIAN PIPE--	'TIS WHITER THAN AN	1482	1
PIPPIN			
SO SHALT THOU HAVE A PIPPIN	"SIC TRANSIT GLORIA	3	19
PIRATE			
SWEET PIRATE OF THE HEART, ...	SWEET PIRATE OF THE	1546	1
NOT PIRATE OF THE SEA, ...	SWEET PIRATE OF THE	1546	2
PIROUETTE			
IN PIROUETTE TO BLANCH A TROUPE--	I CANNOT DANCE UPON MY	326	7
PIT			
A PIT--BUT HEAVEN OVER IT--	A PIT--BUT HEAVEN OVER	1712	1
AND YET A PIT--	A PIT--BUT HEAVEN OVER	1712	3
AH! PIT! WITH HEAVEN OVER IT!	A PIT--BUT HEAVEN OVER	1712	9
IT WAS A PIT--WITH FATHOMS UNDER IT . . .	A PIT--BUT HEAVEN OVER	1712	14
PITIED			
YOU ALMOST PITIED IT--YOU--IT WORKED SO-- .	GOING TO HIM! HAPPY	494	14
PERHAPS HE--PITIED ME--	I TRIED TO THINK A	532	19
PITIFUL			
DID STAGGER PITIFUL--	THE ROSE DID CAPER ON	208	4
'TWAS MORE PITIFUL ENDEAVOR	HER SWEET TURN TO LEAVE	649	5
OF MIGHT TO HELP, SO PITIFUL	WHAT TWIGS WE HELD BY--	1086	11
DROWNING IS NOT SO PITIFUL	DROWNING IS NOT SO	1718	1
PITTANCE			
A PITTANCE AT A TIME	SUPERIORITY TO FATE	1081	5
PITTANCES			
SHARP PITTANCES OF YEARS--	FOR EACH EXTATIC INSTANT	125	6
PITY			
AH, PITY--THEN!	A BURDOCK--CLAWED MY	229	10
PITY--THE PARD--THAT LEFT HER ASIA-- . . .	CIVILIZATION--SPURNS--	492	10
AS FAR FROM PITY, AS COMPLAINT--	AS FAR FROM PITY, AS	496	1

	FIRST LINE	POEM	LINE
PITY (CONTINUED)			
THAT AS MYSELF--COULD PITY HIM--	I TRIED TO THINK A	532	18
HE--TOO--COULD PITY ME--	I TRIED TO THINK A	532	V 19
I CRIED AT PITY--NOT AT PAIN--	I CRIED AT PITY--NOT AT	588	1
TO PITY THOSE THAT [WHO] KNOW HER NOT	WHAT MYSTERY PÈRVADES A	1400	21
T'IS EASIER TO PITY THOSE WHEN DEAD	T'IS EASIER TO PITY	1698	1
THAT WHICH PITY PREVIOUS	T'IS EASIER TO PITY	1698	2
PITYING			
WE STIPULATE--TILL PITYING SNOWS	'TIS NOT THAT DYING	335	11
PIZARRO			
THE EAR RINGS OF PIZARRO	I ENVY SEAS, WHEREON HE	498	15
PIZARRO'S			
ON PIZARRO'S SHORE?	WHO NEVER LOST, ARE	73	8
PLACARD			
NOR ANY PLACARD BOAST ME--	I CANNOT DANCE UPON MY	326	19
PLACE			
PAUSING AT THE PLACE.	GLOWING IS HER BONNET,	72	12
SAVE JUST A LITTLE PLACE FOR ME	GOING TO HEAVEN!	79	14
WHERE THE PLACE CALLED "MORNING" LIES!	WILL THERE REALLY BE A	101	12
THIS PLACE IS BLISS--THIS TOWN IS HEAVEN--	WHERE BELLS NO MORE	112	7
HOW MARTIAL IS THIS PLACE!	MY FRIEND ATTACKS MY	118	5
SOME--THINK IT SERVICE IN THE PLACE	MUSICIANS WRESTLE	157	16
FEATURES KEEP THEIR PLACE--	I HAVE NEVER SEEN	175	12
MORNING--IS THE PLACE FOR DEW--	MORNING--IS THE PLACE	197	1
LATE--WHEN I TAKE MY PLACE IN SUMMER--	I SHALL KEEP SINGING!	250	7
A GUEST IN THIS STUPENDOUS PLACE--	THE DAY CAME SLOW--TILL	304	15
I KNOW A PLACE WHERE SUMMER STRIVES	I KNOW A PLACE WHERE	337	1
HAD NOTCHED THE PLACE THAT PLEASED HIM--	DEATH SETS A THING	360	15
HOW SICK--TO WAIT--IN ANY PLACE--BUT THINE--	HOW SICK--TO WAIT--IN	368	1
BEGGED IN THE MARKET PLACE--	I'M SAYING EVERY DAY	373	8
COURT IS A STATELY PLACE--	I'M SAYING EVERY DAY	373	10
IT'S SWEET PARADE--BLASPHEME THE PLACE--	IT MIGHT BE LONELIER	405	11
NO EYE COULD FIND THE PLACE--	THEY DROPPED LIKE FLAKES	409	7
SOUNDS LONG--UNTIL I READ THE PLACE	NOT IN THIS WORLD TO SEE	418	2
SUNSHINE WAS A SWEET PLACE--	GOOD MORNING--MIDNIGHT--	425	5
IN SUCH A SHINING PLACE!	ME--COME! MY DAZZLED	431	2
AND EVERY SIGN BEFORE THE PLACE	A TOOTH UPON OUR PEACE	459	7
PRESUMPTUOUS OF YOUR PLACE--	THE POWER TO BE TRUE TO	464	4
I LEFT THE PLACE, WITH ALL MY MIGHT--	I MEANT TO HAVE BUT	476	17
SHE CANNOT KEEP HER PLACE.	"WHY DO I LOVE" YOU, SIR	480	5
IS HEAVEN A PLACE--A SKY--A TREE?	WE PRAY--TO HEAVEN--	489	6
IT WAS A BOUNDLESS PLACE TO ME	HE TOUCHED ME, SO I LIVE	506	4
ON ATOMS--FEATURES PLACE--	NO CROWD THAT HAS	515	9
AND IN THE PLACE [STEAD] OF BLOOM	IT KNEW NO MEDICINE--	559	8
AND REDDER CHEEKED ONES--IN THEIR STEAD [PLACE]--	MY FIRST WELL DAY--SINCE	574	11
IS BUT A SYMBOL OF THE PLACE--	"HEAVEN" HAS DIFFERENT	575	3
ALL THESE--REMIND US OF THE PLACE	"HEAVEN" HAS DIFFERENT	575	15
TO KEEP THEIR PLACE--	IT CEASED TO HURT ME,	584	12
IN SUCH A PLACE, WHAT HORROR,	DID YOU EVER STAND IN A	590	5
AND BIND ASTRONOMY, IN PLACE, [FROM BLAME]	TO INTERRUPT HIS YELLOW	591	11
ADJUSTED IT TO PLACE--	HE FOUND MY BEING--SET	603	2
WE BOUGHT--TO EASE THEIR PLACE--	YOU'LL FIND--IT WHEN YOU	610	16
DID PLACE ABOUT THE WEST--TONIGHT--	WHOLE GULFS--OF RED, AND	658	3
MATERIAL [CORPOREAL] PLACE--	ONE NEED NOT BE A	670	4
IN LONESOME PLACE--	ONE NEED NOT BE A	670	12
NEITHER PLACE--NEED I PRESENT HIM--	CONSCIOUS AM I IN MY	679	5
BY SHUNNING CAREFULLY THE PLACE [SPOT / SITE]	HAVE ANY LIKE MYSELF	736	19
THE ACRE GIVES THEM--PLACE--	FOUR TREES--UPON A	742	9
JUST THE PLACE I STOOD--	WHEN I HOPED, I	768	2
THIS PASSIVE PLACE A SUMMER'S NIMBLE MANSION	THIS QUIET DUST WAS	813	5
THE SEA UPON OUR PLACE--	ESCAPING BACKWARD TO	867	2
A DEED, IN EVERY PLACE--	WHEN I HAVE SEEN THE SUN	888	4
LIKING THE QUIET OF THE PLACE	WHO OCCUPIES THIS HOUSE?	892	23
ABSENT PLACE--AN APRIL DAY--	ABSENT PLACE--AN APRIL	927	1
SHOULD SOFTLY PLACE WITHIN OUR OWN	ON THAT DEAR FRAME THE	940	7
BUT WHAT THAT PLACE COULD BE--	I LEARNED--AT LEAST--	944	29
THAT WE'VE IMMORTAL PLACE	IT IS AN HONORABLE	946	5
IN IT'S ESTABLISHED PLACE--	'TWAS AWKWARD, BUT IT	973	10
EXHIBITS [DEVELOPES] SHEETS OF PLACE--	THE SOUL'S DISTINCT	974	6
THE SUN IN PLACE--NO OTHER FRAUD	IT BLOOMED AND DROPT, A	978	9
I FITTED INTO PLACE--	I WAS A PHEBE--NOTHING	1009	4
BUT [FOR] SUNRISE STOPPED UPON THE PLACE	IT WAS A QUIET WAY--	1053	19
AND PLACE WAS WHERE THE PRESENCE WAS	AT HALF PAST THREE, A	1084	11
AND TAKES IT'S FUNDAMENTAL PLACE	WE DO NOT KNOW THE TIME	1106	3
AND LEAVES US IN ANOTHER PLACE	EXHILIRATION IS THE	1118	3
HER SUBJECTS SCATTERED INTO PLACE	THE WIND TOOK UP THE	1134	11
NOBODY KNOWS [KNEW] THE PLACE	AFTER A HUNDRED YEARS	1147	2
HENCEFORTH I TAKE MY LIVING PLACE	SOMEHOW MYSELF SURVIVED	1194	5
LATITUDELESS PLACE.	NOW I KNEW I LOST HER--	1219	8
THANK GOD THE LOUDEST PLACE HE MADE	IT'S HOUR WITH ITSELF	1225	7
THIS IS THE PLACE THEY HOPED BEFORE,	THIS IS THE PLACE THEY	1264	1
SO SOFT UPON THE SCENE [PLACE]	THE MOUNTAINS STOOD IN	1278	9
AND YET IT'S WHOLE CAREER [ALIEN PLACE / COVERT PLACE]	THE MUSHROOM IS THE ELF	1298	6
AND YET IT'S WHOLE CAREER [ALIEN PLACE / COVERT PLACE]	THE MUSHROOM IS THE ELF	1298	6
HE DARE IN LONELY [LONESOME / SECRET] PLACE	I NEVER HEAR THAT ONE IS	1323	14
TO DWELL IN SUCH A PLACE--	THE FACT THAT EARTH IS	1408	8
WHEN YOU APPROACH THE PLACE--	'TIS WHITER THAN AN	1482	4

	FIRST LINE	POEM	LINE
PLACE (CONTINUED)			
SCATTERED--I SAY--TO PLACE [SEAT] THEM SIDE BY SIDE	ABOVE OBLIVION'S TIDE	1531	6
INVESTED SOMBRE PLACE--	AS IMPERCEPTIBLY AS	1540	V
AND LAYS IT IN ITS PLACE--	THE BIRD HER PUNCTUAL	1585	2
IT'S PLACE IS IN THE HUMAN HEART	THE BIRD HER PUNCTUAL	1585	3
TO IT'S LOFTY PLACE	LIGHTLY STEPPED A YELLOW	1672	2
PLACED			
THE LIPS HAD PLACED AS WITH A "PLEASE"	"I WANT"--IT PLEADED--	731	7
AND WE--WE PLACED THE HAIR--	THE LAST NIGHT THAT SHE	1100	25
PLACES			
AND BIRDS TAKE PLACES, OVERHEAD,	OF ALL THE SOUNDS	321	23
WE TRUST--IN PLACES PERFECTER--	THOSE FAIR--FICTITIOUS	499	9
AND THOUGH THEIR PLACES SOMEWHAT FILLED--	YOU'LL FIND--IT WHEN YOU	610	5
THROUGH ALL THEIR [IT'S] FORMER PLACES, WE	DEATH LEAVES US HOMESICK	935	5
IN MANY AND REPORTLESS PLACES	IN MANY AND REPORTLESS	1382	1
PLACID			
IN PLACID [CHINTZ AND] LILY SLEEPS!	A LADY RED--AMID THE	74	4
WHERE TIRED CHILDREN PLACID SLEEP	WHERE BELLS NO MORE	112	5
PLACING			
GREAT CLOUDS--LIKE USHERS--LEANING [PLACING]--	DEPARTED--TO THE	524	3
BUT JUST THE PLACING PINS--	AT LEISURE IS THE SOUL	618	6
PLAIN			
MY CHANCEL--ALL THE PLAIN	ALL THESE MY BANNERS BE.	22	6
FEATHER BY FEATHER--ON THE PLAIN	SOME RAINBOW--COMING	64	5
SO THICK UPON THE PLAIN?	WHOSE ARE THE LITTLE	142	8
NOR HERB OF ALL THE PLAIN	AH, NECROMANCY SWEET!	177	6
OF MOUNTAIN, AND OF PLAIN--	IT SIFTS FROM LEADEN	311	6
I ROSE, AND ALL WAS PLAIN--	THE DAY THAT I WAS	356	9
THAT NOT TOO PLAIN--	I'M SAYING EVERY DAY	373	14
PUT FROM MY SIMPLE SPEECH ALL PLAIN WORD--	I'M SAYING EVERY DAY	373	20
AND TELL HIM--CHARGE THEE SPEAK IT PLAIN--	A TONGUE--TO TELL HIM I	400	7
AND HOLD NO HIGHER THAN THE PLAIN--	A TONGUE--TO TELL HIM I	400	24
WHEN MY MIND--IS PLAIN	DONT PUT UP MY THREAD &	617	6
GLOW PLAIN--AND FOREIGN	I CANNOT LIVE WITH YOU--	640	25
HER PETTICOAT--OF PURPLE PLAIN [JUST]--	THE DAY UNDRESSED--	716	3
AT FIRST--A SCANT NUTRITION--[PLAIN REGALING]	DEPRIVED OF OTHER	773	3
IT MADE THE HURRY PLAIN--	HER FINAL SUMMER WAS IT	795	8
HE FLUNG A HAND FULL AT THE PLAIN--	THE WIND BEGUN TO KNEAD	824	3
PROFFERED TO THE PLAIN--	TWICE HAD SUMMER HER	846	2
THE MOUNTAIN SAT UPON THE PLAIN	THE MOUNTAIN SAT UPON	975	1
WHERE SAINTS, AND OUR PLAIN GOING NEIGHBOR	BESIDES THIS MAY	977	9
CONTAINED [COMBINED / COMPRISED] IN THIS SHORT [PLAIN] LIFE	CONTAINED IN THIS SHORT	1165	1
TO SOME REMOTEST PLAIN	LIKE RAIN IT SOUNDED	1235	6
A RESIDENCE TOO PLAIN	BECAUSE THAT YOU ARE	1260	22
ON THAT LOW PLAIN	LEFT IN IMMORTAL YOUTH	1289	2
THE ROAD TO PARADISE IS PLAIN,	THE ROAD TO PARADISE IS	1491	1
FATIGUED AT LAST, A CLOVER PLAIN [LOW]	HIS ORIENTAL HERESIES	1526	5
WITH PLAIN INSPECTING FACE--	WHO IS IT SEEKS MY	1598	2
PLAINER			
AND LEFT THE PROFILE--PLAINER--	IT KNEW NO MEDICINE--	559	7
ON [TO] PLAINER DAYS, WHOSE TABLE FAR	THE LUXURY TO APPREHEND	815	13
PLAN			
AND PARTS OF HIS FAR PLAN	I PRAYED, AT FIRST, A	576	10
TO INTERRUPT HIS YELLOW PLAN	TO INTERRUPT HIS YELLOW	591	1
BUT HIS PERTURBLESS PLAN	IT'S EASY TO INVENT A	724	10
WHAT PLAN	FOUR TREES--UPON A	742	14
THY LITTLE PLAN TO DIE--	'TIS SUNRISE--LITTLE	908	12
HOW AWKWARD AT THE HYMN [PLAN]	I LEARNED--AT LEAST--	944	4
AS PLAN FOR NOON AND PLAN FOR NIGHT	AS PLAN FOR NOON AND	960	1
AS PLAN FOR NOON AND PLAN FOR NIGHT	AS PLAN FOR NOON AND	960	1
AND THEN IF WE ARE TRUE TO PLAN [GROWTH]	WE NEVER KNOW HOW HIGH	1176	3
HIS NEVER SLUMBERING PLAN;	THE RETICENT VOLCANO	1748	2
PLANE			
UPON A PLANE OF GAUZE!	TO HANG OUR HEAD--	105	8
MY PLANE--AND I, TOGETHER WROUGHT	MYSELF WAS FORMED--A	488	3
IN IT'S DIMINISHED PLANE.	A COFFIN--IS A SMALL	943	4
PLANET			
IS IT LIKE A PLANET?	KNOWS HOW TO FORGET!	433	V
PLANETARY			
I COULD [DID] NOT DEEM THESE [THAT] PLANETARY FORCES	IT KNEW NO LAPSE, NOR	560	5
PLANET'S			
UPON A PLANET'S BOND--	THROUGH THE STRAIT PASS	792	8
PLANETS			
TO PLANETS AND TO FLOWERS	WE INTRODUCE OURSELVES	1214	2
PLANK			
AND THEN A PLANK IN REASON, BROKE,	I FELT A FUNERAL, IN MY	280	17
I STEPPED FROM PLANK TO PLANK	I STEPPED FROM PLANK TO	875	1
I STEPPED FROM PLANK TO PLANK	I STEPPED FROM PLANK TO	875	1
A PAST [TIME / STATE] OF PLANK AND NAIL	THE PROPS ASSIST THE	1142	10
THAT WALK THIS PLANK OF BALM--	THIS IS THE PLACE THEY	1264	6
A SINGLE CLOVER PLANK [SPAR]	A SINGLE CLOVER PLANK	1343	1
THE IDLY SWAYING PLANK	A SINGLE CLOVER PLANK	1343	9
HE SENT HIS SON TO TEST THE PLANK,	HOW BRITTLE ARE THE	1433	7
PLANKS			
WE LEARN TO KNOW THE PLANKS--	A PRISON GETS TO BE A	652	9
AND ROSE AND FELL THE MAGIC PLANKS	A SOFT SEA WASHED AROUND	1198	3

	FIRST LINE	POEM	LINE
PLANNED			
FOR DREAD OCCASION PLANNED	A GREAT HOPE FELL	1123	7
PLANT			
BEQUEATHES THIS FINAL PLANT	THE LILAC IS AN ANCIENT	1241	6
BUT NOT RETRIEVES THE PLANT--	YOU CANNOT MAKE	1508	6
PLANTED			
THE SEEDS OF SMILES ARE PLANTED--	BY CHIVALRIES AS TINY,	55	3
PLANTS			
THE MUSHROOM IS THE ELF OF PLANTS-- . . .	THE MUSHROOM IS THE ELF	1298	1
PLASH			
A PLASH OF OARS, A GAIETY--	I'VE KNOWN A HEAVEN,	243	16
PLASHING			
AS PLASHING IN THE POOLS--	A PRISON GETS TO BE A	652	13
PLASHLESS			
LEAP, PLASHLESS AS THEY SWIM.	A BIRD CAME DOWN THE	328	20
PLATE			
MY HEART UPON A LITTLE PLATE	MY HEART UPON A LITTLE	1027	1
I THINK, BECAUSE HIS EMPTY PLATE	A SPARROW TOOK A SLICE	1211	3
UPON A SHIFTING PLATE	FAME IS A FICKLE FOOD	1659	2
PLATED			
ANNIHILATION--PLATED FRESH	SUSPENSE--IS HOSTILER	705	7
FOR ENTERTAINING PLATED WARES	IT DROPPED SO LOW--IN MY	747	7
A PLATED LIFE--DIVERSIFIED	A PLATED LIFE--	806	1
HAD NATURE ANY SUPPLE [PLATED / OUTCAST] FACE	THE MUSHROOM IS THE ELF	1298	17
PLATED THE RESIDUE OF ADZ	NOT ANY MORE TO BE	1344	15
A COUNTERFEIT--A PLATED PERSON--	A COUNTERFEIT--A PLATED	1453	1
PLATES			
IF FATHER'D MULTIPLY THE PLATES--	'TWAS JUST THIS TIME,	445	15
PLATO			
WHEN PLATO--WAS A CERTAINTY--	A PRECIOUS--MOULDERING	371	15
PLATOON			
IN MURMURING PLATOON!	SOME RAINBOW--COMING	64	12
PLAUDIT			
ALL OTHER PLAUDIT BE	FAME OF MYSELF, TO	713	2
FOR JUST ONE PLAUDIT FAMISHING, ...	THE IMMORTALITY SHE GAVE	1648	3
PLAUSIBILITY			
ALMOST THY PLAUSIBILITY	THESE ARE THE DAYS WHEN	130	8
'TIS FICTION'S--TO DILUTE [CONTRACT] TO PLAUSIBILITY [CREDIBILITY]	NO ROMANCE SOLD UNTO	669	5
PLAUSIBLE			
SO PLAUSIBLE [EXQUISITE]--THEY SEEM-- . .	LIKE SOME OLD FASHIONED	302	12
SO PLAUSIBLE [TANGIBLE / POSITIVE] BECOMES [APPEARS]	I THINK TO LIVE--MAY BE	646	22
PLAUSIBLY			
EQUALLY PLAUSIBLY	EXPERIMENT TO ME	1073	6
PLAY			
SHE DIED AT PLAY, ...	SHE DIED AT PLAY,	75	1
NEW CHILDREN PLAY UPON THE GREEN--	NEW FEET WITHIN MY	99	5
THE BREEZES MADDER PLAY;	THE BEE IS NOT AFRAID OF	111	6
A MYRIAD DAISY PLAY--	IN LANDS I NEVER SAW--	124	6
SOME--SAY--IT IS "THE SPHERES"--AT PLAY! .	MUSICIANS WRESTLE	157	13
LET'S PLAY THOSE--NEVER COME!	MAKE ME A PICTURE OF THE	188	14
AFTERNOONS--TO PLAY--	GOD PERMITS INDUSTRIOUS	231	2
IT IS EASY TO WORK WHEN THE SOUL IS AT PLAY--	IT IS EASY TO WORK WHEN	244	1
NOR STOP TO PLAY WITH THE HAY--	THE WIND DID'NT COME	316	3
WE PLAY AT PASTE--	WE PLAY AT PASTE--	320	1
DO NOT ARISE AND PLAY	OF ALL THE SOUNDS	321	18
PLAY IT WERE A HUMMING BIRD--	ALL THE LETTERS I CAN	334	7
'TIS AN INSTANT'S PLAY.	I KNOW THAT HE EXISTS.	338	5
BUT--SHOULD THE PLAY	I KNOW THAT HE EXISTS.	338	9
FOR DEEMING--BEGGARS--PLAY--	'TIS OPPOSITES--ENTICE--	355	8
SHE LAY AS IF AT PLAY	SHE LAY AS IF AT PLAY	369	1
FOR PRIVILEGE OF PLAY	FORGET! THE LADY WITH	438	6
WE DO NOT PLAY ON GRAVES--	WE DO NOT PLAY ON GRAVES	467	1
AND CRUSH OUR PRETTY PLAY--	WE DO NOT PLAY ON GRAVES	467	8
WHERE SQUIRRELS PLAY--AND BERRIES DIE-- . .	DOOM IS THE HOUSE	475	7
OR SUNSET'S YELLOW PLAY	AS FAR FROM PITY, AS	496	8
HAVE SUMMER'S LEAVE TO PLAY--	I ENVY SEAS, WHEREON HE	498	14
NO ONE COULD PLAY IT--THE SECOND TIME-- . .	BETTER--THAN MUSIC! FOR	503	6
BENEATH HIS TABERNACLES, PLAY, ...	I THINK THE HEMLOCK	525	15
ALL WADED--WE LOOK BACK FOR PLAY, ...	IF I MAY HAVE IT, WHEN	577	24
SUBTRACT THYSELF, IN PLAY, ...	EMPTY MY HEART, OF THEE	587	7
WITH [IN] TANTALIZING PLAY	IT ALWAYS FELT TO ME--A	597	14
WHILE OCEANS--AND THE NORTH MUST BE-- [DID PLAY]	OURSELVES WERE WED ONE	631	11
BONDAGE AS PLAY--BE SWEET--	WHERE THOU ART--THAT--IS	725	7
LET US PLAY YESTERDAY--	LET US PLAY YESTERDAY--	728	1
GRIEF IS A JUGGLER--BOLDEST AT THE PLAY-- .	GRIEF IS A MOUSE--	793	9
I PLAY AT RICHES--TO APPEASE	I PLAY AT RICHES--TO	801	1
I DISSECT [REVIEW] THE PLAY	ONE DAY IS THERE OF THE	814	6
BE IT BUT A PLAY	THAT IS SOLEMN WE HAVE	934	2
WHEN PLAY BE DONE--	I LEARNED--AT LEAST--	944	14
HOW MANY THINGS THE DYING PLAY	WERE IT BUT ME THAT	1015	3
THE BIRD DID PRANCE--THE BEE [BIRD] DID PLAY--	THE BIRD DID PRANCE--THE	1107	1
WHEN I SHALL LONG FOR EARTHLY PLAY	IN THY LONG PARADISE OF	1145	3
TILL EVERY CUBIT PLAY WITH THEE	MY GOD--HE SEES THEE--	1178	4
WHO NEITHER PLEASE NOR PLAY	A LITTLE DOG THAT WAGS	1185	14
FAIR PLAY--	THE SHOW IS NOT THE SHOW	1206	5
INDIFFERENT SEASONS DOUBTLESS PLAY	SOMEWHERE UPON THE	1231	5
IS PLAY I HEAR FROM YOU--	THE MOST PATHETIC THING	1290	2

	FIRST LINE	POEM	LINE
PLEASE (CONTINUED)			
OF ONLY TASTE WE CARED TO PLEASE	TO MAKE ONE'S TOILETTE--	485	3
I MIGHT SURPRISE [NOT PLEASE] HIS EYE!	AGAIN--HIS VOICE IS AT	663	8
THE LIPS HAD PLACED AS WITH A "PLEASE"	"I WANT"--IT PLEADED--	731	7
THEN "GREAT" IT BE--IF THAT PLEASE THEE--	YOU SAID THAT I "WAS	738	2
OR PAGE--PLEASE THEE--	YOU SAID THAT I "WAS	738	14
AND HOW I JUST SAID "PLEASE."	THEY WONT FROWN ALWAYS--	874	4
WHO NEITHER PLEASE NOR PLAY	A LITTLE DOG THAT WAGS	1185	14
SUIT [PLEASE] ME AT A VENTURE	FORTITUDE INCARNATE	1217	11
LIKE LOOKING EVERY TIME YOU PLEASE	WHAT MYSTERY PERVADES A	1400	7
HIS FANTASY DID PLEASE	UPON HIS SADDLE SPRUNG A	1600	4
PLEASED			
HAD NOTCHED THE PLACE THAT PLEASED HIM--	DEATH SETS A THING	360	15
HOW PLEASED THEY WERE [LOOKED], AT WHAT YOU SAID--	IF ANYBODY'S FRIEND BE	509	13
IT PLEASED MY NARROW EYES--	THEIR HIGHT IN HEAVEN	696	12
IT FILLED THE WELLS, IT PLEASED THE POOLS	LIKE RAIN IT SOUNDED	1235	9
SO PROUD [PLEASED / FAIN] SHE WAS TO DIE	SO PROUD SHE WAS TO DIE	1272	1
I FEEL [FELT] AS IF THE GRASS WAS PLEASED	THE MUSHROOM IS THE ELF	1298	13
PLEASES			
A NEWER SEVRES PLEASES--	I CANNOT LIVE WITH YOU--	640	11
PLEASING			
CONDUCT THE PLEASING SCENE!	IF I SHOULD DIE,	54	18
PLEASURE			
A PRECIOUS--MOULDERING PLEASURE--'TIS--	A PRECIOUS--MOULDERING	371	1
I PUT MY PLEASURE ALL ABROAD--	IT WOULD NEVER BE COMMON	430	17
JUST TO BE POOR--FOR BAREFOOT VISION [PLEASURE]	SWEET--YOU FORGOT--BUT I	523	11
THE HEART ASKS PLEASURE [BLESSING]--FIRST--	THE HEART ASKS PLEASURE	536	1
WE COME TO LOOK WITH GRATITUDE [FONDNESS / PLEASURE]	A PRISON GETS TO BE A	652	5
HAD LET IT'S PLEASURE THROUGH--	MY LIFE HAD STOOD--A	754	12
THERE IS AN ARID PLEASURE--	THERE IS AN ARID	782	1
OF AN AUSTERE TRAIT IN PLEASURE--	EXPECTATION--IS	807	5
HIS MIGHTY PLEASURE SUITS US NOT	THE SUN IS GAY OR STARK	878	7
NOR A SPORTSMAN'S PERADVENTURE [RUTHLESS PLEASURE / WANTON ...	STRUCK, WAS I, NOR YET	925	7
... PLEASURE / LEISURE PLEASURE]--	STRUCK, WAS I, NOR YET	925	7
... PLEASURE / LEISURE PLEASURE]--	STRUCK, WAS I, NOR YET	925	7
AND A COMPANY--OUR PLEASURE	THREE WEEKS PASSED SINCE	1061	5
DOUBLE ESTATE--ENTAILED AT PLEASURE	I AM AFRAID TO OWN A	1090	5
A STAGNANT PLEASURE LIKE A POOL	A STAGNANT PLEASURE LIKE	1281	1
PLEASURES			
THE PLEASURES OF THE WIND ARE BROAD,	THE DUTIES OF THE WIND	1137	5
PLEDGE			
I KEEP MY PLEDGE.	I KEEP MY PLEDGE.	46	1
PLEDGES			
BEE--PLEDGES HIS--IN MINUTE FLAGONS--	WE--BEE AND I--LIVE BY	230	10
TO HER--WHO PLEDGES THIS--	WHAT WOULD I GIVE TO SEE	247	25
PLEIAD			
ONE "PLEIAD" WAS IT'S NAME--	I HAD A GUINEA GOLDEN--	23	18
"PLEIAD" IT'S NAME, AND ROBIN,	I HAD A GUINEA GOLDEN--	23	27
I FOUND HER--"PLEIAD"--IN THE WOODS	WHOSE CHEEK IS THIS?	82	4
PLEIAD'S			
FOR HIS PLEIAD'S FACE--	WHEN THE ASTRONOMER	851	2
PLEIADS			
HOW NOTELESS MEN, AND PLEIADS, STAND,	HOW NOTELESS MEN, AND	282	1
PLENTY			
IS PLENTY! IS ENOUGH!	A LITTLE BREAD--A CRUST	159	9
THE PLENTY HURT ME--'TWAS SO NEW--	I HAD BEEN HUNGRY, ALL	579	13
WHAT PLENTY--IT WOULD BE--	I THINK TO LIVE--MAY BE	646	26
SUCH PLENTY SMILES UPON MY BOARD--	GOD GAVE A LOAF TO EVERY	791	11
IN PLENTY MAY BE SEEN,	OUR LITTLE KINSMEN--	885	2
PLIANT			
SO EASY [SUPPLE / PLIANT] TO REPAIR.	SOFTENED BY TIME'S	1738	8
PLIED			
HER BUSY FOOT SHE PLIED--	WHOSE ARE THE LITTLE	142	18
PLIES			
AND STILL, SHE PLIES HER SPOTTED BROOMS, [THRIFT]	SHE SWEEPS WITH	219	9
HE PLIES FROM NOUGHT TO NOUGHT--	THE SPIDER HOLDS A	605	5
PLIGHT			
I PLIGHT AGAIN,	I KEEP MY PLEDGE.	46	5
AS FAR FROM MINE, AS IF NO PLIGHT	A SINGLE SCREW OF FLESH	263	7
PLODDING			
HIS AMPLE--PLODDING STEED	LIKE BROOMS OF STEEL	1252	9
IS PUSHING [ROAMING / PLODDING / STARING / AMBLING] CLOSE BEHIND	ALL THAT I DO	1496	6
PLOT			
THE MOMENT THAT A PLOT IS PLUMBED	HOW HUMAN NATURE DOTES	1417	3
LIKE FLOWERS IN A PLOT--	HER FACE WAS IN A BED OF	1722	2
PLOTS			
THEY LAUGH AS WISE AS PLOTS OF WIT	THEY TALK AS SLOW AS	1697	5
PLOTTED			
BUT PLOTTED WITH TIME TO DISPUTE--	I SAW THAT THE FLAKE WAS	1267	2
PLOTTING			
WE AND OUR PLOTTING HEART [GAUDY HEART / SCHEMING TINSEL / ...	AN ANTIQUATED GRACE	1345	5
PLOVER			
THOUGH WINTER FIRE--SING CLEAR AS PLOVER--	IT'S THOUGHTS--AND JUST	495	15

	FIRST LINE	POEM	LINE
PLUCK			
PLUCK UP IT'S STAKES, AND DISAPPEAR-- . .	I'VE KNOWN A HEAVEN,	243	3
THE FIRMAMENT'S--TO PLUCK HER--	SHE DWELLETH IN THE	671	7
PLUCKED			
AND WHEN THE HAND THAT PLUCKED IT	"SIC TRANSIT GLORIA	3	63
PLUCKED FAR AWAY, SOME MORNING-- . . .	IN EBON BOX, WHEN YEARS	169	11
THE WOMEN--PLUCKED [SLIPPED] AWAY . . .	THOSE FAIR--FICTITIOUS	499	2
I PLUCKED AT OUR PARTITION	I TRIED TO THINK A	532	12
WHEN IT PLUCKED ME?	IF IT HAD NO PENCIL	921	8
PLUCKING			
I--SOFTLY PLUCKING, ...	SOUTH WINDS JOSTLE THEM	86	7
STOOPING--PLUCKING--SMILING--FLYING-- . .	ANGELS, IN THE EARLY	94	3
STOOPING--PLUCKING--SIGHING--FLYING-- . .	ANGELS, IN THE EARLY	94	7
FINGERS DENIED THE PLUCKING, ...	MY NOSEGAYS ARE FOR	95	3
SUBJECT [PRESENT] TO YOUR PLUCKING-- . . .	SOME SUCH BUTTERFLY BE	541	6
THE FRUIT PERVERSE TO PLUCKING, ...	TO DISAPPEAR ENHANCES--	1209	17
PLUCKS			
PLUCKS AT A TWIG OF EVIDENCE--	THIS WORLD IS NOT	501	15
PLUG			
YOU CANNOT SOLDER AN ABYSS [PLUG A SEPULCHRE]	TO FILL A GAP	546	5
PLUMB			
FOR FISHERMAN TO PLUMB--	THAT AFTER HORROR--THAT	286	6
OUT OF PLUMB OF SPEECH.	GRATITUDE--IS NOT THE	989	4
PLUMBED			
THE MOMENT THAT A PLOT IS PLUMBED	HOW HUMAN NATURE DOTES	1417	3
PLUMBING			
AS IN IT'S GRAVE GO PLUMBING [MEASURING] .	THE LONELINESS ONE DARE	777	3
PLUMED			
WE TRUST, IN PLUMED PROCESSION	TO FIGHT ALOUD, IS VERY	126	9
WITH SHACKLES [IRONS] ON THE PLUMED FEET, .	THE SOUL HAS BANDAGED	512	21
PLUMES			
VAILING THE PURPLE, AND THE PLUMES-- . . .	IN RAGS MYSTERIOUS AS	117	3
AND I, MY CHILDISH PLUMES, ...	I DREADED THAT FIRST	348	26
PLUMMET			
A KIND OF PLUMMET STRAIN--	AGAIN--HIS VOICE IS AT	663	14
PLUMMETLESS			
TOO PLUMMETLESS--THAT IT COME BACK [RETURN]--	A SOLEMN THING--IT WAS--	271	7
PLUMP			
THERE WAS A LITTLE FIGURE PLUMP	ON SUCH A NIGHT, OR SUCH	146	17
PLUMPER			
THE BERRY'S CHEEK IS PLUMPER--	THE MORNS ARE MEEKER	12	3
PLUNDER			
I SAW THE SUN--HIS PLUNDER DONE	I NEVER TOLD THE BURIED	11	3
THERE'S PLUNDER--WHERE--	I KNOW SOME LONELY	289	25
PLUNGE			
AND HIT A WORLD, AT EVERY PLUNGE [CRASH], .	I FELT A FUNERAL, IN MY	280	19
WE PAUSE BEFORE A FURTHER PLUNGE	WHAT TWIGS WE HELD BY--	1086	4
PLUPOTENTIAL			
AS PYRAMIDAL [ELEMENTAL / PLUPOTENTIAL] NERVE	NOT TO DISCOVER WEAKNESS	1054	6
PLUSH			
FROM WHICH HE DOTH DESCEND IN PLUSH . . .	A FUZZY FELLOW, WITHOUT	173	7
SENTENCES OF PLUSH, ...	ALL THE LETTERS I CAN	334	4
ONE WOULD AS SOON ASSAULT A PLUSH-- . . .	WHAT SOFT--CHERUBIC	401	3
BROOKS OF PLUSH--IN BANKS OF SATIN . . .	SWEET--SAFE--HOUSES--	457	6
LIKE INTERMITTENT PLUSH, BE HEARD	THE NIGHT WAS WIDE, AND	589	11
UPON A NAIL OF PLUSH--	THE DAY GREW SMALL,	1140	8
LIKE TRAINS OF CARS ON TRACKS OF PLUSH . .	LIKE TRAINS OF CARS ON	1224	1
HIS PLUSH ALARM	UPON A LILAC SEA	1337	3
WE STEP LIKE PLUSH	I DID NOT REACH THEE	1664	28
SOFTENED BY TIME'S CONSUMMATE PLUSH, . . .	SOFTENED BY TIME'S	1738	1
PLUSHES			
SUCH PLUSHES AT COMMAND	HOW SOFT A CATERPILLAR	1448	4
PLY			
THAT PLY BETWEEN IT AND THE SKY	BY MY WINDOW HAVE I FOR	797 V	6
CORRODELESS PLY.	THE COMPETITIONS OF THE	1494	2
WHERE E'ER I PLY	ALL THAT I DO	1496	5
PLYING			
OUTSIDE [WITHOUT]--THE SPADES--WERE PLYING--	IN FALLING TIMBERS	614	3
POCKET			
WITHIN THAT JACKET'S POCKET TOO!	I MET A KING THIS	166	8
ETERNITY'S VAST [WIDE] POCKET, PICKED-- . .	EMPTY MY HEART, OF THEE	587	14
NOR BEG, WITH DOMAINS IN MY POCKET-- . . .	LET ME NOT THIRST WITH	1772	2
POCKETS			
OH, WHEN THE SQUIRREL FILLS HIS POCKETS . .	WHAT SHALL I DO WHEN THE	956	9
POD			
A WINDOW OPENS LIKE A POD--	THERE'S BEEN A DEATH, IN	389	7
AND MOVING INTO POD--	THE WINTERS ARE SO SHORT	403	4
HOW MANY CAST A NAMELESS POD	HOW MANY FLOWERS FAIL IN	404	5
BROKE--PERFECT--FROM THE POD--	HE GAVE AWAY HIS LIFE--	567	16
AND SEE THE THINGS IN POD--	MY FIRST WELL DAY--SINCE	574	4
REVOLUTION IS THE POD	REVOLUTION IS THE POD	1082	1
THE ENCHANTLESS POD	LAIN IN NATURE--SO	1288	2
HOW LUSCIOUS LIES WITHIN THE POD	FORBIDDEN FRUIT A FLAVOR	1377	3
AND PATENTED BY POD.	THE JOY THAT HAS NO STEM	1744	8
PODS			
AND SPLIT THEIR PODS OF FLAME--	IT MAKES NO DIFFERENCE	620	4
POEMS			
HER--"LAST POEMS"--	HER--"LAST POEMS"--	312	1
TRUE POEMS FLEE--	TO SEE THE SUMMER SKY	1472	3

	FIRST LINE	POEM		LINE
POESY				
IS METRE [POESY]--NAY--'TIS MELODY--	THEY HAVE A LITTLE ODOR	785		2
POET				
THIS WAS A POET--IT IS THAT	THIS WAS A POET--IT IS	448		1
THE POET--IT IS HE--	THIS WAS A POET--IT IS	448		10
NOR WOULD I BE A POET--	I WOULD NOT PAINT--A	505		17
SHALL I TAKE THEE, THE POET SAID	SHALL I TAKE THEE, THE	1126		1
THE POET SEARCHED [PROBED] PHILOLOGY	SHALL I TAKE THEE, THE	1126		5
POETRY				
THIS--WOULD BE POETRY--	TO PILE LIKE THUNDER TO	1247		4
OF PRANCING POETRY--	THERE IS NO FRIGATE LIKE	1263		4
YESTERDAY IS POETRY--	YESTERDAY IS HISTORY,	1292		3
IS POETRY, THOUGH NEVER IN A BOOK IT LIE--	TO SEE THE SUMMER SKY	1472		2
POET'S				
NOUGHT--THAT [YET, IF] WE--NO POET'S KINSMAN--	HER--"LAST POEMS"--	312		16
POETS				
BESIDES THE AUTUMN POETS SING	BESIDES THE AUTUMN POETS	131		1
POETS--ENDED--	HER--"LAST POEMS"--	312		2
THE MARTYR POETS--DID NOT TELL--	THE MARTYR POETS--DID	544		1
FIRST--POETS--THEN THE SUN--	I RECKON--WHEN I COUNT	569		2
SO I WRITE--POETS--ALL--	I RECKON--WHEN I COUNT	569		8
THE POETS LIGHT BUT LAMPS--	THE POETS LIGHT BUT	883		1
POIGNANCY				
ADDS [GIVES] POIGNANCY TO WINTER--	CONJECTURING A CLIMATE	562		3
POIGNANT				
MY POIGNANT LUXURY--	GOD GAVE A LOAF TO EVERY	791		4
POINARDS				
THE LIGHTNING'S POINARDS GLEAMED--	THROUGH LANE IT LAY--	9		10
POINT				
DAISIES POINT THE WAY THERE--	SEXTON! MY MASTER'S	96		7
SAY, FOOT, DECIDE THE POINT--	IS BLISS THEN, SUCH	340		12
IN POINT OF INJURY--	IT ALWAYS FELT TO ME--A	597		8
OR EVERY BIRD WILL POINT AT THEE	TOUCH LIGHTLY NATURE'S	1389		3
AND SHE WILL POINT UNDOUBTEDLY [YOU FONDLY-- / YOU LONGINGLY]	CRISIS IS SWEET AND YET	1416	V	7
TO POINT A HUMAN LIFE?	GO THY GREAT WAY!	1638		5
THE POINT WITH BLAND PREVISION	THEY TALK AS SLOW AS	1697		7
POINTED				
TO WHOM THIS W'D HAVE POINTED ME	I BRING AN UNACCUSTOMED	132		15
POINTERS				
NODS [STARES] FROM THE GILDED POINTERS--	A CLOCK STOPPED--	287		14
WHAT SKILFUL [ANXIOUS] POINTERS MOVE--	NOT TO DISCOVER WEAKNESS	1054		8
POISE				
MERCHANTMEN--POISE UPON HORIZONS--	THIS--IS THE LAND--THE	266		8
IT TAKES ME ALL THE WHILE TO POISE--	I PRAYED, AT FIRST, A	576		20
POISED				
POISED LIGHTLY ON HIS HAND,	THEY LEAVE US WITH THE	350		8
THE SECOND POISED--DEBATED--SHOT--	'TWAS CRISIS--ALL THE	948		13
POISING				
TILL POISING FOR A TURN	HOW SOFT A CATERPILLAR	1448	V	
POLAR				
UPON THE POLAR HEM--	AS IF SOME LITTLE ARCTIC	180		2
ICICLES--CRAWL FROM POLAR CAVERNS--	SAFE IN THEIR ALABASTER	216	V	
FROM POLAR CASKETS--FETCHED ME--	THE ANGLE OF A LANDSCAPE	375		17
SOME POLAR EXPIATION--AN OMEN IN THE BONE	I TRIED TO THINK A	532		3
HER POLAR TIME--BEHIND--	I THINK TO LIVE--MAY BE	646		20
WADES--SO--THRO' POLAR AIR!	THROUGH THE STRAIT PASS	792		12
THAT POLAR PRIVACY	THERE IS A SOLITUDE OF	1695		6
POLES				
WHAT IF THE POLES SH'D FRISK ABOUT	"ARCTURUS" IS HIS OTHER	70		22
POLICE				
WITH NO POLICE TO FOLLOW	COULD I BUT RIDE	661		9
POLICE CANNOT SUPPRESS	THE MOB WITHIN THE HEART	1745		2
POLITE				
AS THEY SAY POLITE ARCHANGELS	I CANT TELL YOU--BUT YOU	65		11
THAN THIS SUFFERER POLITE--	TAKE YOUR HEAVEN FURTHER	388		10
TO ACHE IS HUMAN--NOT POLITE--	SHE DEALT HER PRETTY	479		9
WITH HAT IN HAND, POLITE AND NEW	THE CRICKETS SANG	1104		7
SORROW [AROMA]--NOW--IS POLITE [COURTEOUS]--AND STAYS--	SUMMER IS SHORTER THAN	1506		5
POLITENESS				
AND MORN A NEW POLITENESS TOOK--	I HAD NO CAUSE TO BE	542		3
POLLUTES				
AND THAT PROFANES [POLLUTES / DEFILES] THE POWER	THE CLOVER'S SIMPLE FAME	1232	V	6
POLTROON				
THE POLTROON WANTS OXYGEN--	IF YOUR NERVE, DENY YOU	292		11
POMP				
A DARTING FEAR--A POMP--A TEAR--	A DARTING FEAR--A POMP--	87		1
HOW POMP SURPASSING ERMINE	ONE DIGNITY DELAYS FOR	98		13
WITH A MUTE POMP--	INCONCEIVABLY SOLEMN!	582		6
HEEDLESS [PASSIVE]--ALIKE--OF [TO] POMP--OR [AND] PARTING	AH, TENERIFFE!	666		8
THE POMP OF SUMMER [ETHIOPIAN] DAYS	SOME ONE PREPARED THIS	1644		6
POMPADOUR				
RAIMENT INSTEAD--OF POMPADOUR--	I AM ASHAMED--I HIDE--	473		11
POMPEII				
WILL NOT CRY WITH JOY "POMPEII"!	I HAVE NEVER SEEN	175		19
POMPLESS				
NO LIFE CAN POMPLESS PASS AWAY--	NO LIFE CAN POMPLESS	1626		1

	FIRST LINE	POEM	LINE
POMPOSITY			
PASSING POMPOSITY?	BRING ME THE SUNSET IN A	128	24
OH THE AUDACITY [POMPOSITY]--	THAT THIS SHOULD FEEL	1112	7
WHAT A POMPOSITY [AN ABSURDITY / A PERVERSITY]	THAT THIS SHOULD FEEL	1112	V 7
POMPOUS			
BUT POMPOUS [SILLY / AWKWARD] JOY	MARCH IS THE MONTH OF	1404	6
HOW POMPOUS THE WIND MUST FEEL NOONS	HOW LONESOME THE WIND	1418	5
. . . MOST POMPOUS] CONSULATE.	AN ANTIQUATED TREE	1514	7
WHOSE POMPOUS FROWN WAS NUTRIMENT	NO BRIGADIER THROUGHOUT	1561	15
POMPOUSLY			
WHEEL SOLEMNLY [POMPOUSLY] AWAY!	PAPA ABOVE!	61	9
POMPS			
WHOSE POMPS ALLURE AND SPURN	OF THIS IS DAY COMPOSED	1675	5
POND			
COME BACK, AND DUST THE POND!	SHE SWEEPS WITH	219	4
UPHOLSTERER--OF THE POND--	OF BRUSSELS--IT WAS NOT	602	16
TO MULTIPLY [MAGNIFY] THE POND.	THE BIRDS BEGUN AT FOUR	783	8
SPREADS THE POND HER BASE OF LILIES	HOW THE WATERS CLOSED	923	5
PONDER			
WHETHER AS [WHILE] I PONDER	I NEVER TOLD THE BURIED	11	16
DEFORMED MEN--PONDER GRACE--	'TIS OPPOSITES--ENTICE--	355	2
TO PONDER LITTLE WORKMANSHIPS	DEATH SETS A THING	360	5
HER FROSTS TO PONDER--THEN IT WAS	THE BIRDS REPORTED FROM	743	15
PONDERED			
I PONDERED HOW THE BLISS WOULD LOOK--	A SOLEMN THING--IT WAS--	271	9
THE VISION--PONDERED LONG--	I THINK TO LIVE--MAY BE	646	21
I PONDERED, MAY HAVE JUDGED,	OUR LITTLE KINSMEN--	885	10
WE [I] PONDERED WHEN A CHILD,	WHO WERE "THE FATHER AND	1258	2
PONDERING			
WHAT NEWS MUST THINK WHEN PONDERING	HOW NEWS MUST FEEL WHEN	1319	5
PONDEROUS			
BETWEEN IT'S PONDEROUS FACE	A PRISON GETS TO BE A	652	2
DRIVES PONDEROUS PERPENDICULAR	THESE ARE THE NIGHTS	1128	3
TOO PONDEROUS TO SUSPECT THE SNARE	RISK IS THE HAIR THAT	1239	5
PONDERS			
WHO PONDERS THIS TREMENDOUS SCENE--	A LITTLE MADNESS IN THE	1333	4
PONIARDS SEE POINARDS			
PONTIUS			
FILAMENTS OF BLOOM, PONTIUS PILATE SOWED--	TO PUT THIS WORLD DOWN,	527	10
WHILE PONTIUS PILATE LIVES	ONE CROWN THAT NO ONE	1735	5
PONTOON			
THE PIER TO MY PONTOON--	I WOULD NOT PAINT--A	505	16
POOL			
THE NEIGHBOR IN THE POOL	THE FINGERS OF THE LIGHT	1000	13
A STAGNANT PLEASURE LIKE A POOL	A STAGNANT PLEASURE LIKE	1281	1
HIS MANSION IN THE POOL	HIS MANSION IN THE POOL	1379	1
POOLS			
BEFORE THE ICE IS IN THE POOLS--	BEFORE THE ICE IS IN THE	37	1
LETHARGIC POOLS RESUME THE WHIRR	SOME RAINBOW--COMING	64	8
WHOLE POOLS OF IT--	I CAN WADE GRIEF--	252	2
BUT WHEN THE SOUTH WIND STIRS THE POOLS	I KNOW A PLACE WHERE	337	5
AS PLASHING IN THE POOLS--	A PRISON GETS TO BE A	652	13
IT GATHERS RUDDY [STANDS IN--RUDDY / MAKES VERMILLION--] POOLS--	THE NAME--OF IT--IS	656	10
IT FILLED THE WELLS, IT PLEASED THE POOLS	LIKE RAIN IT SOUNDED	1235	9
POOR			
I AM POOR ONCE MORE!	I NEVER LOST AS MUCH BUT	49	8
A POOR--TORN HEART--A TATTERED HEART--	A POOR--TORN HEART-- A	78	1
AND YET, AS POOR AS I,	'TIS SO MUCH JOY! 'TIS	172	3
POOR LITTLE HEART!	POOR LITTLE HEART!	192	1
CHERISHING--OUR POOR IDEAL--	TAKING UP THE FAIR IDEAL	428	9
JUST TO BE POOR--FOR BAREFOOT VISION [PLEASURE]	SWEET--YOU FORGOT--BUT I	523	11
"POOR CHILD"--AND SOMETHING IN HER VOICE	I CRIED AT PITY--NOT AT	588	3
AND SHIVER FOR [RECOLLECT] THE POOR--	THE NIGHT WAS WIDE, AND	589	16
LESS, THO LARGER, POOR.	ALL I MAY, IF SMALL,	819	8
OH POOR AND FAR--	THE SUN AND MOON MUST	871	9
THAT MAKES OUR TRYING [RUNNING] POOR.	BECAUSE HE LOVES HER	1229	12
THEN FLING US POOR	DREAMS ARE THE SUBTLE	1376	3
HE KNEW NO MORE THAT HE WAS POOR,	HE ATE AND DRANK THE	1587	3
WARMS SOME POOR NAME	GLORY IS THAT BRIGHT	1660	4
POORER			
MYSELF A POORER PROVE	I GAVE MYSELF TO HIM--	580	6
SOME MINISTRY TO POORER LIVES--	I LEARNED--AT LEAST--	944	20
POOREST			
THE POOREST--COULD AFFORD--	OF BRUSSELS--IT WAS NOT	602	6
SEEN POOREST--THRO' OUR GAINS--	I LEARNED--AT LEAST--	944	21
OF THE POOREST BIRD.	SANG FROM THE HEART,	1059	8
THIS TRAVEL [TRAVERSE] MAY THE POOREST TAKE	THERE IS NO FRIGATE LIKE	1263	5
POPE			
A POPE, OR SOMETHING OF THAT KIND!	I MET A KING THIS	166	12
POPOCATAPEL			
THAT POPOCATAPEL EXISTS--	MORE LIFE--WENT OUT--	422	19
POPPY			
THE POPPY [WARRANT] IN THE CLOUD	IT WAS A QUIET SEEMING	1419	12
POPULAR			
THE POPULAR HEART IS A CANNON FIRST--	THE POPULAR HEART IS A	1226	1
POPULATE			
ILLUMINATE--[MAKE POPULATE-- / MAKE MANIFEST] OR SEAL--	THE LONELINESS ONE DARE	777	16

	FIRST LINE	POEM	LINE
POPULATE (CONTINUED)			
WOULD POPULATE WITH AWE MY SOLITUDE . . .	ON MY VOLCANO GROWS THE	1677	8
POPULATES			
AND ALL THE SEAS HE POPULATES	A COFFIN--IS A SMALL	943	7
POPULATION			
ONE--IS THE POPULATION--	THE HEART IS THE CAPITAL	1354	5
AND HUMAN NATURE HID [POPULATION FLED] . .	IT WAS A QUIET SEEMING	1419	9
THE MOST IMPORTANT POPULATION	THE MOST IMPORTANT	1746	1
POPULOUS			
TIS POPULOUS WITH BONE AND STAIN-- . . .	MY PORTION IS DEFEAT--	639	7
PORCELAIN			
OUR LIFE--HIS PORCELAIN--	I CANNOT LIVE WITH YOU--	640	7
AS PORCELAIN	DEATH IS THE SUPPLE	1445	V 12
PORCH			
OR PORCH OF GNOME--	DRAB HABITATION OF WHOM?	893	4
AS CONTENTED [FEARLESS] IN THE PORCH OF DEATH	THIS DOCILE ONE INTER	1752	V 7
PORE			
THAT NOT A PORE BE OVERLOOKED	A WEIGHT WITH NEEDLES ON	264	5
PORED			
I--WHO PORED--PATIENT--	KNOWS HOW TO FORGET!	433	6
PORT			
TO A HEART IN PORT--	WILD NIGHTS--WILD NIGHTS	249	6
ONE PORT--SUFFICES--FOR A BRIG--LIKE MINE--	HOW SICK--TO WAIT--IN	368	7
INTO THIS PORT, IF I MIGHT COME, ...	HE TOUCHED ME, SO I LIVE	506	13
THOUGH NEVER YET, IN ANY PORT--	TWO BUTTERFLIES WENT OUT	533	7
ON BALL OF MAST IN BOSPORUS [FOREIGN PORT]--	THE DAY UNDRESSED--	716	15
IT HAS NO PORT, NOR A "LINE"--BUT THE JAYS--	BY MY WINDOW HAVE I FOR	797	5
NOT ANY PORT	ALL THAT I DO	1496	7
OUR PORT A SECRET	DOWN TIME'S QUAINT	1656	4
PORTABLE			
MAKES THE HEAVENS PORTABLE--	TAKING UP THE FAIR IDEAL	428	5
PORTENTOUS			
PORTENTOUS INFERENCE.	THE LEAVES LIKE WOMEN,	987	4
AND WHEN PORTENTOUS [IN TERROR] TOLD . . .	WHO WERE "THE FATHER AND	1258	4
PORTENTOUS AS OUR OWN, WHO KNOWS?	WHOSE PINK CAREER MAY	1394	2
THE HIGHT OF OUR PORTENTOUS [UNKNOWING] NEIGHBOR	FACTS BY OUR SIDE ARE	1497	5
IN A PORTENTOUS WAY--	THE BOBOLINK IS GONE--	1591	11
PORTENTOUSLY			
PORTENTOUSLY UNTOLD	THEY TALK AS SLOW AS	1697	8
PORTER			
THE PORTER OF MY FATHER'S LODGE	AFRAID! OF WHOM AM I	608	3
AS EVERY PORTER KNOWS--	HER LOSSES MAKE OUR	1562	6
PORTICO			
A PORTICO, ...	I KNOW SOME LONELY	289	6
PORTION			
OUR PORTION--IN THE FASHION--	DELIGHT IS AS THE FLIGHT	257	25
OF PORTION--SO UNCONSCIOUS--	THIS WAS A POET--IT IS	448	13
WHAT PORTION OF ME BE	I HEARD A FLY BUZZ--WHEN	465	10
MY PORTION IS DEFEAT--TODAY--	MY PORTION IS DEFEAT--	639	1
FOR THIS NEW VALUE [FORTUNE / PORTION] IN THE SOUL--	ONE BLESSING HAD I THAN	756	11
THAT PORTION OF THE VISION	SHALL I TAKE THEE, THE	1126	9
PORTLY			
NOT PORTLY, MIND! BUT BREATHING--WARM-- . .	A LITTLE BREAD--A CRUST	159	4
PORTRAIT			
YOU KNOW THAT PORTRAIT IN THE MOON-- . . .	YOU KNOW THAT PORTRAIT	504	1
A PORTRAIT OF THE PARISH	A FIELD OF STUBBLE,	1407	T
PORTRAITS			
PORTRAITS [PICTURES] ARE TO DAILY FACES . .	PORTRAITS ARE TO DAILY	170	1
PORTRAY			
ELIJAH'S JOURNEY TO PORTRAY	ELIJAH'S WAGON KNEW NO	1254	5
PORTS			
A HINT OF PORTS AND PEOPLES--	A SOUTH WIND--HAS A	719	5
POSITIVE			
IF POSITIVE, 'TWERE WE--	WITHIN MY GARDEN, RIDES	500	14
BUT POSITIVE, AS SOUND--	THIS WORLD IS NOT	501	4
THE POSITIVE [TRANSITIVE]--OF BELLS-- . .	WHEN BELLS STOP RINGING	633	2
SO PLAUSIBLE [TANGIBLE / POSITIVE] BECOMES [APPEARS]	I THINK TO LIVE--MAY BE	646	22
IN POSITIVE PROSPECTIVE--	AS PLAN FOR NOON AND	960	3
AS POSITIVE ARE WE	THE PUNGENT ATOM IN THE	1191	6
POSITIVELY			
AS POSITIVELY LIVE	DO PEOPLE MOULDER	432	4
POSSESS			
POSSESS EACH SEPARATE CONSCIOUSNESS-- . .	NO CROWD THAT HAS	515	15
THE FROST--POSSESS [OBTAIN] THE WORLD-- . .	HE PARTS HIMSELF--LIKE	517	17
ONLY GOD--DETECT THE SORROW [POSSESS THE SECRET]--	ONLY GOD--DETECT THE	626	1
THE MAN WHO WOULD POSSESS	THE GOOD WILL OF A	849	2
TO POSSESS, IS PAST THE INSTANT	SATISFACTION--IS THE	1036	5
POSSESS THE OLDEST ONE--	OPINION IS A FLITTING	1455	4
POSSESSED			
WHAT LITTLE OF HIM WE--POSSESSED	IT FEELS A SHAME TO BE	444	7
APPROACHED [POSSESSED]--THE AMBER FLITS [MOVES]--A LITTLE--	DELIGHT--BECOMES	572	7
POSSESSED [ABHORRED / WE OWNED] BEFORE-- .	DREAMS ARE THE SUBTLE	1376	6
A BETTER COAT IF HE POSSESSED	TO TRY TO SPEAK, AND	1617	5
POSSESSED BY EVERY HALLOWED KNIGHT . . .	CIRCUMFERENCE THOU BRIDE	1620	3

	FIRST LINE	POEM	LINE
POSSESSETH			
A GLEE POSSESSETH ME,	I CANNOT DANCE UPON MY	326	4
POSSESSING			
AN UNKNOWN ESTEEM [CONTENT] POSSESSING--	ALL FORGOT FOR	966	7
POSSESSING THOU SHALT BE	CIRCUMFERENCE THOU BRIDE	1620	2
WHEN AT MY VERY DOOR ARE THOSE POSSESSING MORE,	TAKE ALL AWAY FROM ME,	1640	4
POSSESSION			
UPON THE BROAD POSSESSION [LAWFUL MANOR--]	IT ALWAYS FELT TO ME--A	597	21
WERE A CRUMB MY WHOLE POSSESSION--	MOST SHE TOUCHED ME BY	760	5
IS A TOO ESTABLISHED FORTUNE [SECURE POSSESSION / CONTENDED . . .	EXPECTATION--IS	807	7
POSSESSION IS TO ONE	TO OWN THE ART WITHIN	855	6
STAKING OUR ENTIRE [DIVINE] POSSESSION	ROBBED BY DEATH--BUT	971	13
POSSESSION, NOT OPTIONAL--	I AM AFRAID TO OWN A	1090	4
POSSESSION--HAS A SWEETER CHINK	BECAUSE 'TWAS RICHES I	1093	7
POSSESSION JUST AS LONG--	DOMINION LASTS UNTIL	1257	2
PERIL AS A POSSESSION	PERIL AS A POSSESSION	1678	1
POSSESSIONS			
OUR OWN POSSESSIONS--THOUGH OUR OWN--	OUR OWN POSSESSIONS--	1208	1
POSSIBILITY			
NIGHT'S POSSIBILITY!	THE DAISY FOLLOWS SOFT	106	12
THE POSSIBILITY--TO PASS	THAT AFTER HORROR--THAT	286	9
TIME'S POSSIBILITY.	I HAD THE GLORY--THAT	349	7
UNKNOWN TO POSSIBILITY--	WHAT I CAN DO--I WILL--	361	4
IGNORES [EXCLUDES] THE POSSIBILITY	SIZE CIRCUMSCRIBES--IT	641	7
I DWELL IN POSSIBILITY--	I DWELL IN POSSIBILITY--	657	1
WHO TASTES IT; POSSIBILITY	IMPOSSIBILITY, LIKE WINE	838	3
FROM POSSIBILITY	WE MISS A KINSMAN MORE	1087	4
OF POSSIBILITY.	OUR OWN POSSESSIONS--	1208	4
POSSIBLE			
IN DOUBTFUL MEAL, IF IT BE POSSIBLE	ONE YEAR AGO--JOTS WHAT?	296	10
IS POSSIBLE,	IS BLISS THEN, SUCH	340	7
AS IMPOTENT [POSSIBLE] WOULD BE	SHE HIDETH HER THE LAST	557	10
THAT MAKES THE LIVING POSSIBLE	A DOUBT IF IT BE US	859	7
AND BOYS WERE POSSIBLE.	WHO OCCUPIES THIS HOUSE?	892	16
BUT POSSIBLE TO EARN	SUPERIORITY TO FATE	1081	4
IF "ALL IS POSSIBLE WITH" HIM	BECAUSE THAT YOU ARE	1260	37
. . . POSSIBLE / VICINITY--]	WHO NEVER WANTED--	1430	7
IT IS POSSIBLE FOR SENSE TO LIVE	IF EVER THE LID GETS OFF	1727	7
THEIR COMING BACK SEEMS POSSIBLE	THE DISTANCE THAT THE	1742	3
POSSIBLER			
TO PROVE IT POSSIBLER--	I FELT MY LIFE WITH BOTH	351	4
POSSIBLE'S			
THE POSSIBLE'S SLOW FUSE IS LIT	THE GLEAM OF AN HEROIC	1687	3
POSSIBLY			
'TWAS POSSIBLY A CZAR PETITE--	I MET A KING THIS	166	11
REFER TO--POSSIBLY.	THE FACE I CARRY WITH ME	336	8
POSSIBLY, E'EN YOU HAD SEEN	TAKE YOUR HEAVEN FURTHER	388	4
REQUIRES ENERGY--POSSIBLY AGONY--	TO PUT THIS WORLD DOWN,	527	3
POSSIBLY, THIS MOMENT--	I COULD DIE--TO KNOW--	570	11
POSSIBLY BESTOW	HER SWEET TURN TO LEAVE	649	16
POSSIBLY--BUT WE--WOULD RATHER	PUBLICATION--IS THE	709	5
AND POSSIBLY A CHURCH--	HAVE ANY LIKE MYSELF	736	4
AND POSSIBLY A STEEPLE--	HAVE ANY LIKE MYSELF	736	23
POSSIBLY--IF THEY REFUSE--HOW THEN KNOW--	GRIEF IS A MOUSE--	793	16
IS EASY [COMMON], POSSIBLY--	AWAY FROM HOME ARE SOME	821	4
"EYE HATH NOT SEEN" MAY POSSIBLY	THE LILAC IS AN ANCIENT	1241	17
OR, HAPPILY [POSSIBLY], RENOWN--	THE WAY TO KNOW THE	1279	20
BUT POSSIBLY THE ONE--	THE THINGS WE THOUGHT	1293	12
POST			
BUT HER CARRARA GUIDE POST--	HER FINAL SUMMER WAS IT	795	11
POSTERIOR			
POSTERIOR--TO DEATH--	LOVE--IS ANTERIOR TO	917	2
POSTERIOR, PROPHETIC,	THE MURMURING OF BEES,	1115	3
POSTHUMOUS			
BUT MEDICINE POSTHUMOUS	IS HEAVEN A PHYSICIAN?	1270	3
IN A POSTHUMOUS SUN	JUDGEMENT IS JUSTEST	1671	7
POSTPONELESS			
IT'S COMING--THE POSTPONELESS CREATURE--	IT'S COMING--THE	390	1
POSTS			
IT RUFFLES WRISTS OF POSTS	IT SIFTS FROM LEADEN	311	17
A SPICY CHARGE, MY LITTLE POSTS [FRIENDS]--	THE BIRDS REPORTED FROM	743	3
POSTULATE			
ENCHANTMENT'S SYNDICATE [POSTULATE / TESTAMENT].	THE LAST OF SUMMER IS	1353	4
POSTULATED			
WE COMPREHENDED [POSTULATED / RECOLLECTED] BY THE AWE	IT WAS A QUIET SEEMING	1419	10
POSTURE			
THAT SUCH WAS NOT THE POSTURE	TO HANG OUR HEAD--	105	3
THAT'S A STEADY POSTURE--	IF YOUR NERVE, DENY YOU	292	5
OR POSTURE--TO REDEEM!	THE WORLD--STANDS--	493	16
THE POSTURE OF THE KEY	A PRISON GETS TO BE A	652	17
HE DOTH NOT ATTEST BY POSTURE--	CONSCIOUS AM I IN MY	679	3
POTENTIAL			
DEATH IS POTENTIAL TO THAT MAN	DEATH IS POTENTIAL TO	548	1
THAT SHORT--POTENTIAL STIR	THAT SHORT--POTENTIAL	1307	1
POTOMAC			
WENT UP FROM THE POTOMAC--	WHEN I WAS SMALL, A	596	3

	FIRST LINE	POEM	LINE
POTOSI			
OF "POTOSI," AND THE MINES!	TALK WITH PRUDENCE TO A	119	2
POTOSI NEVER TO BE SPENT	A MINE THERE IS NO MAN	1117	5
POUNCE			
POUNCE ON HIS BRUISES--ONE--SAY--OR THREE--	GRIEF IS A MOUSE--	793	11
POUND			
AND PAUSED AT EVERY POUND	I FELT MY LIFE WITH BOTH	351	6
EXPEND THEIR FURTHEST [INMOST] POUND--	I FEAR A MAN OF FRUGAL	543	6
FOR TREASON--IN THE POUND--	THEY SHUT ME UP IN PROSE	613	8
FOR--HEFT THEM--POUND FOR POUND--	THE BRAIN--IS WIDER THAN	632	10
FOR--HEFT THEM--POUND FOR POUND--	THE BRAIN--IS WIDER THAN	632	10
POUNDS			
AND POUNDS WERE IN THE LAND--	I HAD A GUINEA GOLDEN--	23	4
A WEIGHT WITH NEEDLES ON THE POUNDS--	A WEIGHT WITH NEEDLES ON	264	1
POUR			
POUR AS BLANK ON THEM	WHAT CARE THE DEAD, FOR	592	5
POURED			
POURED THEE, WITHOUT A STINT--	DOUBT ME! MY DIM	275	4
POURED LIKE THIS--MY WHOLE [BEST] LIBATION--	PROMISE THIS--WHEN YOU	648	13
WAS WAITING [ASSEMBLED] TO BE POURED	HIS BILL IS CLASPED--HIS	1102	6
POURS			
SUCH RESURRECTION POURS.	THE FEET OF PEOPLE	7	24
AND SHE POURS SOFT REFRAINS	I KNOW A PLACE WHERE	337	8
POUTING			
I DONT CARE FOR POUTING SKIES!	I'M THE LITTLE "HEART'S	176	2
. . . POUTING HEART]	AN ANTIQUATED GRACE	1345	5
POVERTY			
IF I SHOULD FAIL, WHAT POVERTY!	'TIS SO MUCH JOY! 'TIS	172	2
YOUR RICHES--TAUGHT ME--POVERTY.	YOUR RICHES--TAUGHT ME--	299	1
AND I ESTEEMED ALL POVERTY	YOUR RICHES--TAUGHT ME--	299	7
TO CEASELESS POVERTY--	THIS WAS A POET--IT IS	448	12
POVERTY--BE JUSTIFYING	PUBLICATION--IS THE	709	3
THE POVERTY THAT WAS NOT WEALTH--	NONE CAN EXPERIENCE	771	7
IT IS THAT POVERTY WAS WEALTH	NONE CAN EXPERIENCE	771	V 7
MY POVERTY AND I DERIVE--	I PLAY AT RICHES--TO	801	13
AND [SO / THE] POVERTY OF MONARCHY	WHO COURT OBTAIN WITHIN	803	3
IT FEELS LIKE POVERTY	BECAUSE 'TWAS RICHES I	1093	4
EXCLUSIVE POVERTY!	THE VOICE THAT STANDS	1189	8
IS GRATITUDE'S SWEET POVERTY,	TO TRY TO SPEAK, AND	1617	3
IN ABJECT [BOUNDLESS] POVERTY--	TAKE ALL AWAY FROM ME,	1640	5
POWDER			
POWDER EXISTS IN CHARCOAL [ELEMENTS / SULPHURETS]--	A MAN MAY MAKE A REMARK	952	7
POWDERED			
ALMOST A POWDERED FOOTMAN	WAIT TILL THE MAJESTY OF	171	3
POWDERS			
IT POWDERS ALL THE WOOD [FIELD].	IT SIFTS FROM LEADEN	311	2
POWER			
I HAD NOT STRENGTH [POWER] TO HOLD--	SAVIOR! I'VE NO ONE ELSE	217	8
POWER IS ONLY PAIN--	I CAN WADE GRIEF--	252	10
IF ANY POWER BEHIND IT, BE,	I GOT SO I COULD HEAR	293	22
BEYOND MY POWER TO DEEM [DREAM]--	YOUR RICHES--TAUGHT ME--	299	22
HAD POWER TO MANGLE ME--	I DREADED THAT FIRST	348	8
DYING--ANNULS THE POWER TO KILL.	IF ANY SINK, ASSURE THAT	358	8
A POWER OF RENOWNED COLD,	MORE LIFE--WENT OUT--	422	5
NO POWER CAN UNTIE	THE MONTHS HAVE ENDS--	423	2
HAD HE THE POWER TO DREAM	REMOVED FROM ACCIDENT OF	424	10
THE POWER TO BE TRUE TO YOU,	THE POWER TO BE TRUE TO	464	1
WITH WILL [POWER] TO CHOOSE, OR TO REJECT,	I'M CEDED--I'VE STOPPED	508	18
THE POWER [WISDOM] TO PRESUME--	HER SWEET WEIGHT ON MY	518	8
WITH FAINT--TERRESTRIAL POWER--	HAD I PRESUMED TO HOPE--	522	12
I TOOK MY POWER IN MY HAND--	I TOOK MY POWER IN MY	540	1
I HAD NOT POWER TO TELL--	I THINK I WAS ENCHANTED	593	8
BUT WHEN HIS POWER DROPPED [BENT]--	I ROSE--BECAUSE HE SANK	616	3
TO BE ALIVE--IS POWER--	TO BE ALIVE--IS POWER--	677	1
AND TINDER--GUESSED--BY POWER	THE ZEROES--TAUGHT US--	689	4
FOR I HAVE BUT THE POWER [ART] TO KILL,	MY LIFE HAD STOOD--A	754	23
WITHOUT--THE POWER TO DIE--	MY LIFE HAD STOOD--A	754	24
A POWER--WILL PROCLAIM	A PLATED LIFE--	806	6
ONCE TO ACHIEVE, ANNULS THE POWER	THOSE WHO HAVE BEEN IN	922	7
POWER TO PERCEIVE HIS PROCESS	STRUCK, WAS I, NOR YET	925	3
A POWER OF BUTTERFLY MUST BE--	MY COCOON TIGHTENS--	1099	5
BEHIND THE AWFUL POWER--	THE WIND TOOK UP THE	1134	8
LIKE WORMS BENEATH [BEFORE] THE POWER--	THE WIND TOOK UP THE	1134	V 8
MERCY [POWER] OF THE ALMIGHTY BEGGING [ASKING]--	TELL AS A MARKSMAN--WERE	1152	22
THAT POWER TO REPAIR	TO MAKE ROUTINE A	1196	6
AND THAT PROFANES [POLLUTES / DEFILES] THE POWER	THE CLOVER'S SIMPLE FAME	1232	V 6
HAS COMPROMISED IT'S POWER--	THE CLOVER'S SIMPLE FAME	1232	8
POWER IS A FAMILIAR GROWTH--	POWER IS A FAMILIAR	1238	1
THE POWER TO CONTAIN	I THOUGHT THAT NATURE	1286	8
WITHIN OUR POWER	IN THIS SHORT LIFE	1287	4
HAD HE THE POWER TO SPURN--	THAT SHORT--POTENTIAL	1307	8
NOT WHEN WE KNOW, THE POWER ACCOSTS--	LET ME NOT MAR THAT	1335	5
THE POWER TO FORGET--	ONE THING OF IT WE	1464	6
AND POWER TO BE FINITE CEASED	ESTRANGED FROM BEAUTY--	1474	3
IN ACCIDENTAL POWER--	APPARENTLY WITH NO	1624	4
HAS NOT THE POWER TO DIE	A WORD MADE FLESH IS	1651	10
BUT RINGED WITH POWER	IN WINTER IN MY ROOM	1670	17

	FIRST LINE	POEM	LINE
POWER (CONTINUED)			
I NEVER KNEW THY POWER,	OH, HONEY OF AN HOUR,	1734	2
POWERFUL			
HOW POWERFUL THE STIMULUS	STRONG DRAUGHTS OF THEIR	711	7
POWERLESS			
POWERLESS TO UNFOLD--	HOW THE OLD MOUNTAINS	291	V 24
CREATION--POWERLESS--	MY REWARD FOR BEING, WAS	343	V
PRACTICES			
HER PRACTICES [QUALITIES] EXTEND	NATURE AFFECTS TO BE	1170	4
PRACTICING			
PRACTICING SANDS--	WE PLAY AT PASTE--	320	8
PRACTISE			
LONG YEARS OF PRACTISE BORE	THE FEET OF PEOPLE	7	6
WHEN, WITH A SILVER PRACTISE--	I WATCHED THE MOON	629	31
EQUALLY PERISH FROM OUR PRACTISE--	THOSE WHO HAVE BEEN IN	922	3
MY PRACTISE HOW ABSURD	CONFERRING WITH MYSELF	1655	6
PRACTISED			
WITH SUCH A PRACTISED FROST--	I KNOW A PLACE WHERE	337	2
TELL HIM [HER]--IT WAS'NT A PRACTISED WRITER--	GOING TO HIM! HAPPY	494	10
PRACTISING			
I TOOK FOR GIANTS--PRACTISING	I THINK I WAS ENCHANTED	593	15
PRAIRIE			
TO MAKE A PRAIRIE IT TAKES A CLOVER AND ONE BEE,	TO MAKE A PRAIRIE IT	1755	1
PRAIRIES			
VAST [WIDE] PRAIRIES OF AIR	MY PERIOD HAD COME FOR	564	12
PRAISE			
LATE--THE PRAISE--	HER--"LAST POEMS"--	312	11
AND PAIN--IS MISSED--IN [FORGETS--FOR--] PRAISE--	UNTO MY BOOKS--SO GOOD	604	4
THO' GABRIEL--PRAISE ME--SIR--	WHERE THOU ART--THAT--IS	725	14
SUCH A PRAISE BEGAN	MOST SHE TOUCHED ME BY	760	14
ANOTHER ART, TO PRAISE.	HER GRACE IS ALL SHE HAS	810	4
THAT BLAME IS JUST AS DEAR AS PRAISE	DEAR MARCH--COME IN--	1320	25
AND PRAISE AS MERE AS BLAME--	DEAR MARCH--COME IN--	1320	26
PRAISE IT--'TIS DEAD--	PRAISE IT--'TIS DEAD--	1384	1
THEY CANNOT PRAISE.	THAN HEAVEN MORE REMOTE,	1436	10
BUT THEIR'S FORGET IN PRAISE	I SAW THE WIND WITHIN	1502	V
ASCRIBE NO LESS THE PRAISE--	THE BAT IS DUN, WITH	1575	14
PRAISED			
THAT FIRST DAY, WHEN YOU PRAISED ME, SWEET,	THAT FIRST DAY, WHEN YOU	659	1
PRAISES			
AND PRAISES AS HE GOES,	WITHIN MY GARDEN, RIDES	500	8
PRAISING			
BIRD WENT PRAISING EVERYWHERE--	WHEN I HOPED, I	768	15
PRANCE			
WILL PEEP, AND PRANCE AGAIN.	AS CHILDREN BID THE	133	8
THE BIRD DID PRANCE--THE BEE [BIRD] DID PLAY--	THE BIRD DID PRANCE--THE	1107	1
PRANCING			
OF PRANCING POETRY--	THERE IS NO FRIGATE LIKE	1263	4
PRANK			
WHATEVER PRANK BETIDES!	"ARCTURUS" IS HIS OTHER	70	25
A PRANK NOBODY KNEW BUT THEM	IF ANYBODY'S FRIEND BE	509	7
THAT OTHER PRANK--OF SNOW--	THE TINT I CANNOT TAKE--	627	18
"SPEECH"--IS A PRANK OF PARLIAMENT--	"SPEECH"--IS A PRANK OF	688	1
PRANKS			
AND PRANKS THE NORTHERN STAR	THESE ARE THE DAYS THAT	1696	2
PRATE			
NOT FOR ME--TO PRATE ABOUT IT!	I CANT TELL YOU--BUT YOU	65	13
THEN PRATE ABOUT "PREFERMENT"--	WAIT TILL THE MAJESTY OF	171	7
WE PRATE--OF HEAVEN--	WE PRAY--TO HEAVEN--	489	2
PRATER			
LET EVERY BABBLER [PRATER] BE	THE RETICENT VOLCANO	1748	10
PRATTLE			
SMILE--AND ALTER--AND PRATTLE--AND DIE--	LOVE--THOU ART HIGH--	453	15
PRAY			
I PRAY HIM TOO--EXPLORE	THE GUEST IS GOLD AND	15	8
PRAY GATHER ME--	SUMMER FOR THEE, GRANT I	31	7
THEN TAKE MY FLOWERS--PRAY!	WHEN ROSES CEASE TO	32	8
WHEN YOU HAVE DONE, PRAY TELL ME	HEART! WE WILL FORGET	47	5
PRAY DO NOT ASK ME HOW!	GOING TO HEAVEN!	79	3
I PRAY YOU PASS [STROLL] ONCE MORE.	HEART, NOT SO HEAVY AS	83	20
PRAY LEAD ME TO HIS BED!	SEXTON! MY MASTER'S	96	2
AND I OMIT TO PRAY	I HAVE A KING, WHO DOES	103	15
AND WE BOTH PRAY--	WE DONT CRY--TIM AND I,	196	18
OH PUNISH--PRAY--	'TWAS LOVE--NOT ME--	394	2
WE PRAY--TO HEAVEN--	WE PRAY--TO HEAVEN--	489	1
RECEIVING [BEHOLDING]--WHERE WE--PRAY--	THOSE FAIR--FICTITIOUS	499	16
AT LEAST--TO PRAY--IS LEFT--IS LEFT--	AT LEAST--TO PRAY--IS	502	1
GOD GROWS ABOVE--SO THOSE WHO PRAY	MY PERIOD HAD COME FOR	564	5
I WORSHIPPED--DID NOT "PRAY"--	MY PERIOD HAD COME FOR	564	20
TOO NEAR TO GOD--TO PRAY--	THE DAY UNDRESSED--	716	9
NOTHING IS LEFT TO PRAY--	WHATEVER IT IS--SHE HAS	1204	6
I PRAY THE LORD THY DUST TO KEEP--	NOW I LAY THEE DOWN TO	1539	2
I PRAY THE LORD THY SOUL TO MAKE--	NOW I LAY THEE DOWN TO	1539	4
AND SHOUTED [BUBBLED / GURGLED] LET US PRAY--	THE BOBOLINK IS GONE--	1591	7
PRAYED			
OF COURSE--I PRAYED--	OF COURSE--I PRAYED--	376	1
AND SO--UPON THIS WISE--I PRAYED--	I MEANT TO HAVE BUT	476	9
I PRAYED, AT FIRST, A LITTLE GIRL,	I PRAYED, AT FIRST, A	576	1

	FIRST LINE	POEM	LINE
PRAYER			
AND THEN WE KNELT IN PRAYER--	THE GENTIAN WEAVES HER	18	12
AND I, NO OTHER PRAYER.	MY NOSEGAYS ARE FOR	95	8
WITH SHAPELESS--QUIVERING--PRAYER--	I THINK JUST HOW MY	237	6
WE SHOW THEM--PRAYER--	'TIS SO APPALLING--IT	281	12
THAT I COULD SPELL THE PRAYER	I SHOULD HAVE BEEN TOO	313	9
PRAYER IS THE LITTLE IMPLEMENT	PRAYER IS THE LITTLE	437	1
COMPRISED IN PRAYER--	PRAYER IS THE LITTLE	437	8
I FUMBLE AT MY CHILDHOOD'S PRAYER	A WIFE--AT DAYBREAK I	461	10
IT WOULD SUFFICE MY PRAYER	I MEANT TO HAVE BUT	476	6
I THREW MY PRAYER AWAY--	I MEANT TO HAVE BUT	476	18
A PRAYER, THAT IT MORE ANGEL--PROVE--	THE WORLD--STANDS--	493	9
AND TAKING BUT A PRAYER--	I HAD NO CAUSE TO BE	542	18
MY PERIOD HAD COME FOR PRAYER--	MY PERIOD HAD COME FOR	564	1
HOW PRAYER WOULD FEEL [SOUND]--TO ME--	I PRAYED, AT FIRST, A	576	4
BUT PRAYER--REMAINED--OUR SIDE--	IT WAS TOO LATE FOR MAN	623	4
AND SCRAPS [SHREDS] OF PRAYER--	MY PORTION IS DEFEAT--	639	11
THAT OCEANS ARE--AND PRAYER--	I CANNOT LIVE WITH YOU--	640	48
THE FOCUS OF MY PRAYER--	ONE BLESSING HAD I THAN	756	6
INCITE THE TIMID PRAYER	NATURE--THE GENTLEST	790	14
PERCEIVE THEIR PRAYER IS VAIN.	THERE COMES AN HOUR WHEN	1751	3
PRAYERS			
YOUR PRAYERS, OH PASSER BY!	A DAY! HELP! HELP!	42	2
PRAYING			
PRAYING THAT I MIGHT BE	THE MALAY--TOOK THE	452	5
PREACHED			
HE PREACHED UPON [ABOUT] "BREADTH" TILL IT ARGUED HIM [WE . . .	HE PREACHED UPON	1207	1
PREACHES			
GOD PREACHES, A NOTED CLERGYMAN--	SOME KEEP THE SABBATH	324	9
PREAPPOINTED			
HIS PREAPPOINTED PAIN--	EXPERIENCE IS THE ANGLED	910	8
PRECARIOUS			
THIS GAVE ME THAT PRECARIOUS GAIT	I STEPPED FROM PLANK TO	875	7
PROFOUND--PRECARIOUS PROPERTY--	I AM AFRAID TO OWN A	1090	3
TO NO PRECARIOUS MAN.	THE RETICENT VOLCANO	1748	4
PRECEDED			
THE GRAVE PRECEDED ME--	BEREAVED OF ALL, I WENT	784	4
THE LIGHTNING THAT PRECEDED IT	THE FARTHEST THUNDER	1581	5
PRECEDES			
PRECEDES ENAMORED--DAY--	THE DOOMED--REGARD THE	294	10
PRECEDING			
HIS SURE FOOT PRECEDING--	LIFE--IS WHAT WE MAKE IT	698	13
THAN THE PRECEDING ONE	I MADE SLOW RICHES BUT	843	4
PRECEPT			
THE LIFE DOTH PROVE THE PRECEPT, WHO OBEY SHALL HAPPY BE,	AWAKE YE MUSES NINE,	1	9
PRECEPTOR			
PRECEPTOR OF THE WHOLE--	IMAGE OF LIGHT, ADIEU--	1556	4
PRECINCT			
MINE--TO GUARD YOUR NARROW PRECINCT--	PROMISE THIS--WHEN YOU	648	17
INTO THE PRECINCT [MINUTE] RAW	DREAMS ARE THE SUBTLE	1376	5
PRECINCTS			
WITHIN ITS PRECINCTS HOPES HAVE PLAYED,--	SWEET HOURS HAVE	1767	3
PRECIOUS			
STRANGE THAT THE FEET SO PRECIOUS CHARGED	ON SUCH A NIGHT, OR SUCH	146	23
A PRECIOUS--MOULDERING PLEASURE--'TIS--	A PRECIOUS--MOULDERING	371	1
PRECIOUS TO ME--SHE STILL SHALL BE--	PRECIOUS TO ME--SHE	727	1
MOST PRECIOUS ARE THE DEAD--	SWEET, TO HAVE HAD THEM	901	6
NEXT PRECIOUS	SWEET, TO HAVE HAD THEM	901	7
YET PRECIOUS AS THE HOUSE	ON THAT DEAR FRAME THE	940	2
PRECIOUS! IT WAS CONCEIVELESS FAIR	ON THAT DEAR FRAME THE	940	5
I WATCHED THE PRECIOUS [SUBTLE] BEGGAR	I SAW THE WIND WITHIN	1502	V
HE ATE AND DRANK THE PRECIOUS WORDS--	HE ATE AND DRANK THE	1587	1
PRECIPICE			
AS ONE REWALKS A PRECIPICE	AS ONE DOES SICKNESS	957	5
SIN--A DISTINGUISHED PRECIPICE	THE BIBLE IS AN ANTIQUE	1545	9
PRECISE			
IT'S PICTURE PUBLISHES--PRECISE--	THE OUTER--FROM THE	451	11
ENTITLED TO MYSELF--PRECISE--	I AM ALIVE--I GUESS--	470	19
PRECISE [MORE OFT] THE OBJECT'S LOSS--	PERCEPTION OF AN OBJECT	1071	2
PRECISELY			
LIFE'S LITTLE DUTIES DO--PRECISELY--	I TIE MY HAT--I CREASE	443	2
EXACTLY [PRECISELY]--AS THE WORLD--	THE DAY UNDRESSED--	716	5
PRECISELY, AS TO YOU [ME].	LIGHT IS SUFFICIENT TO	862	8
PRECISELY AS THE CALLS--	THE MERCHANT OF THE	1131	4
PRECISELY AS THE JOY OF HIM--	THE WAY TO KNOW THE	1279	3
PRECISELY AS THE CANDIDATE [CHARACTER]	TWO LENGTHS HAS EVERY	1295	V 7
WONDER--IS NOT PRECISELY KNOWING	WONDER--IS NOT PRECISELY	1331	1
AND NOT PRECISELY KNOWING NOT--	WONDER--IS NOT PRECISELY	1331	2
PRECISELY THEIR NECESSITY--	THEY MIGHT NOT NEED ME--	1391	4
PRECISELY WHAT TO SAY--	I THOUGHT THE TRAIN	1449	6
PRECISELY HOW IT ENDED [IS IT KNOWN]	I SAW THE WIND WITHIN	1502	V
PRECISELY AS IN MARCH IS HEARD	THE ONES THAT	1690	3
IS PRECISELY THE FINEST OF JOYS--	TO DO A MAGNANIMOUS	1699	4
PRECISELY AN EXISTENCE--	I TOOK ONE DRAUGHT OF	1725	3
PRECISELY OPPOSITE.	THAT IT WILL NEVER COME	1741	8
PRECISER			
PRECISER WHAT WE ARE	THERE IS A FINISHED	856	6

	FIRST LINE	POEM	LINE
PRESENT (CONTINUED)			
UNTO THIS PRESENT, RUN,	HE OUTSTRIPPED TIME WITH	865	6
PRESENT CONTINUALLY	OF SILKEN SPEECH AND	896	4
OR WARRANT TO REPORT [PRESENT] THE SOUL	'TWAS CRISIS--ALL THE	948	7
PRESENT ME FROM SEPULCHRAL CREASE	HER LITTLE PARASOL TO	1038	7
PRESENT THE AWKWARD RIND--	EXCEPT THE SMALLER SIZE	1067 V	
WERE PRESENT AT THE MAJESTY--	THE SUN WENT DOWN--NO	1079	3
HOW MUCH THE PRESENT MOMENT MEANS	HOW MUCH THE PRESENT	1380	1
MAKES THE [THIS] PRESENT [NEXT MOMENT] MEAN--	GLASS WAS THE STREET--IN	1498	8
TO WHOM NOT ANY FACE COHERE [PRESENT / PROPOUND]--	HOW FIRM ETERNITY MUST	1499	7
THE PRESENT DID NOT KNOW HER	SHE COULD NOT LIVE UPON	1505	2
NO MORE FROM YOURS AT PRESENT	THE JAY HIS CASTANET HAS	1635	8
PRESENTED			
SHE PRESENTED HER SMALL FIGURE--	MOST SHE TOUCHED ME BY	760	3
PRESENTIMENT			
PRESENTIMENT--IS THAT LONG SHADOW--ON THE LAWN--	PRESENTIMENT--IS THAT	764	1
PRESENTING			
FROM PRESENTING--HERE--	CRISIS IS A HAIR	889	16
PRESENTS			
PRESENTS ME WITH A SINGLE CURL	'TIS CUSTOMARY AS WE	440	7
THEY GIVE US PRESENTS MOST--YOU KNOW--	IT WAS GIVEN TO ME BY	454	3
PRESENTS A CLAIM INVISIBLE--	I LIVE WITH HIM--I SEE	463	7
PRESENTS IT--IN THE ACT--	THE FUTURE--NEVER SPOKE	672	6
PRESENTS UPON A TREE	EXPERIMENT TO ME	1073	5
AND PRESENTS [BEGETS] HER SPOT--	WE LIKE MARCH.	1213	7
PRESERVED			
PRESERVED THE CHARM [VISION SURE / VISION CLEAR] SECURE	HAVE ANY LIKE MYSELF	736	18
PRESIDE			
BUT HE DOTH THERE PRESIDE	ALL THAT I DO	1496	9
WHERE HE DOES NOT [FIRST] PRESIDE	ALL THAT I DO	1496 V	9
PRESS			
ANY--FOR THE PRESS OF SMILING--	SWEET--SAFE--HOUSES--	457	16
PIERCE--BY THE VERY PRESS	INCONCEIVABLY SOLEMN!	582	3
AS NEEDLES--LADIES SOFTLY PRESS	IT CEASED TO HURT ME,	584	10
OR AN ATOM PRESS	CRISIS IS A HAIR	889	10
PRESSED			
THOSE THIRSTY LIPS TO FLAGONS PRESSED,	AS WATCHERS HANG UPON	121	11
A STRANGER PRESSED A KINGDOM,	AS IF I ASKED A COMMON	323	3
PREST			
THE LITTLE TRACKS--CLOSE PREST--	'TWAS THE OLD--ROAD--	344	8
PRESUME			
DARE I PRESUME TO SEE	I MET A KING THIS	166	18
THE POWER [WISDOM] TO PRESUME--	HER SWEET WEIGHT ON MY	518	8
STILL FASCINATED TO PRESUME	I MEASURE EVERY GRIEF I	561	39
TO WHAT, COULD WE PRESUME	FAITH--IS THE PIERLESS	915	9
FRAUD [LIE] CANNOT PRESUME--	HE WHO IN HIMSELF	969	2
LEAVE US TO PRESUME	SOME WE SEE NO MORE,	1221	5
BUT WE PRESUME	THE ROAD TO PARADISE IS	1491	4
CONSOLELESSLY PRESUME--	'TIS NOT THE SWAYING	1597	8
OR FLOWER PRESUME TO SHOW	A LANE OF YELLOW LED THE	1650	6
AND WORMS PRESUME	IN WINTER IN MY ROOM	1670	5
PRESUMED			
HAD I PRESUMED TO HOPE--	HAD I PRESUMED TO HOPE--	522	1
HAD I PRESUMED TO GAIN	HAD I PRESUMED TO HOPE--	522	5
OTHER FORCE--MAY BE PRESUMED TO MOVE--	THE TRUTH--IS STIRLESS--	780	2
IN CAVE IF I PRESUMED TO HIDE	TO MY QUICK EAR THE	891	5
DID MAKE [PRESUMED] AS TO DEVOUR	THE WIND TOOK UP THE	1134	6
FOR WHAT, HE IS PRESUMED TO KNOW--	OF GOD WE ASK ONE FAVOR,	1601	3
PRESUMES			
PEACOCK PRESUMES TO DIE!	IF THIS IS "FADING"	120	9
PRESUMING			
PRESUMING ME TO BE A MOUSE--	I STARTED EARLY--TOOK MY	520	7
PRESUMING IT TO LEAD	EXPERIENCE IS THE ANGLED	910	4
LIKE TIME'S INSIDIOUS [INVADING / PRESUMING / APPOINTED / . . .	LIKE TIME'S INSIDIOUS	1236	1
PRESUMING ON THAT LONE RESULT	THE STARS ARE OLD, THAT	1249	5
PRESUMPTION			
AFFORDS THE SLY PRESUMPTION	TO HANG OUR HEAD--	105	5
FOR CREDIBILITY'S PRESUMPTION [TEMERITY]	EACH LIFE CONVERGES TO	680	7
BUT A PRESUMPTION BE--	AS IF THE SEA SHOULD	695	4
PRESUMPTION IS VITALITY	AS FROST IS BEST	951	11
PERPETUAL PRESUMPTION [COMPLACENCE] TOOK	ALONE AND IN A	1167	15
ETERNITY, PRESUMPTION	BECAUSE THAT YOU ARE	1260	13
RESERVING THE PRESUMPTION	THOSE CATTLE SMALLER	1388	9
PRESUMPTION WAS--HIS ANCESTORS	AS IMPERCEPTIBLY AS	1540 V	
PRESUMPTUOUS			
PRESUMPTUOUS OF YOUR PLACE--	THE POWER TO BE TRUE TO	464	4
A TOO PRESUMPTUOUS PSALM--	LIKE FLOWERS, THAT HEARD	513	15
PRESUMPTUOUS EVENING SAID--	WHEN MEMORY IS FULL	1266	4
PRETENSE			
PUT MY PRETENSE--AWAY--	MAKE ME A PICTURE OF THE	188	8
PRETTY			
PRITHEE, MY PRETTY HOUSEWIVES!	A LADY RED--AMID THE	74	7
SO PRETTY--SO ASHAMED!	SO BASHFUL WHEN I SPIED	91	2
THE PRETTY PEOPLE IN THE WOODS	THE BEE IS NOT AFRAID OF	111	3
PLEASE, PATER, PRETTY SOON!	WHERE BELLS NO MORE	112	8
HE CLAIMS THE PRETTY ACRE,	I HAD SOME THINGS THAT I	116	7

	FIRST LINE	POEM	LINE
PRETTY (CONTINUED)			
MY FLOWERS RAISE THEIR PRETTY LIPS--	AS CHILDREN BID THE	133	3
TO TELL THE PRETTY SECRET	A FUZZY FELLOW, WITHOUT	173	19
HER PRETTY SPEECH--LIKE DRUNKEN MEN--	THE ROSE DID CAPER ON	208	3
AND THEN THE PRETTY SUNSHINE COMES--	TO DIE--TAKES JUST A	255	7
AND STIR ALL DAY TO PRETTY TUNES	THE GRASS SO LITTLE HAS	333	5
HER PRETTY PARASOL BE SEEN	FROM COCOON FORTH A	354	9
AND CRUSH OUR PRETTY PLAY--	WE DO NOT PLAY ON GRAVES	467	8
SHE DEALT HER PRETTY WORDS LIKE BLADES--	SHE DEALT HER PRETTY	479	1
HIS PRETTY ESTIMATES	THE CHILD'S FAITH IS NEW	637	19
OF PRETTY WAYS OF COVENANT--	I LEARNED--AT LEAST--	944	3
THE PRETTY RAIN FROM THOSE SWEET EAVES	THE PRETTY RAIN FROM	1426	1
PREVAIL			
IN THIS, AS ALL, PREVAIL--	MUCH MADNESS IS DIVINEST	435	5
SOLEMNITY--PREVAIL--	NO CROWD THAT HAS	515	13
IF SEASONS PERISH OR PREVAIL	DID WE ABOLISH FROST	1014	3
SCARCELY WOULD [COULD] PREVAIL--	TELL AS A MARKSMAN--WERE	1152	8
PREVAIL UPON THE COACH--	GO SLOW, MY SOUL, TO	1297	4
MANNERS MAY [WILL] PREVAIL.	ABRAHAM TO KILL HIM	1317	12
PREVAILING			
IS THE PREVAILING [SUPERIOR] FREIGHT.	BEFORE HE COMES WE WEIGH	834	4
PREVAILS			
AND STILL THE APRONS FLY, [SCENE PREVAILS]	SHE SWEEPS WITH	219	10
PREVALENT			
OF ALL THE BATTLES PREVALENT--	THE BATTLE FOUGHT	594	3
PREVENT			
TO PREVENT A FRIEND--	WE DONT CRY--TIM AND I,	196	4
IF WILDERNESS PREVENT HER FEET	FROM US SHE WANDERED NOW	890	3
PREVENTED			
THE MISSING ALL, PREVENTED ME	THE MISSING ALL,	985	1
PREVIOUS			
ONE MUST REVERSE HAVE [ITSELF HAVE / HAVE PREVIOUS] BORE--	DESPAIR'S ADVANTAGE IS	799	4
MORE PREVIOUS--THAN LIFE--	LOVE--IS THAT LATER	924	2
THAT WHICH PITY PREVIOUS	T'IS EASIER TO PITY	1698	2
PREVISION			
THE POINT WITH BLAND PREVISION	THEY TALK AS SLOW AS	1697	7
PREY			
THE CERTAIN PREY TO TEAZE--	THE WHOLE OF IT CAME NOT	762	V 4
THE PREY OF [IN SPANS IN] UNKNOWN ZONES--	COULD MORTAL LIP DIVINE	1409	V
TO BALK THEE OF THY SACRED PREY--[THE INNOCENCE / THE MYRIADS]	OH FUTURE! THOU SECRETED	1631	7
PRICE			
'TIS JUST THE PRICE OF BREATH--	YOU'RE RIGHT--"THE WAY	234	6
YOU DID NOT STATE--YOUR PRICE--	I PAY--IN SATIN CASH--	402	2
THE PRICE IS GREAT--SUBLIMELY PAID--	IT FEELS A SHAME TO BE	444	9
THE PRICE--IS	MUST BE A WO--	571	11
IT WAS A GENTLE PRICE--	OF BRUSSELS--IT WAS NOT	602	5
MY PRICE FOR EVERY STAIN!	AGAIN--HIS VOICE IS AT	663	29
ABOUT THE PRICE--'TIS SMALL--	THE JUDGE IS LIKE THE	699	9
TO DISGRACE OF PRICE--	PUBLICATION--IS THE	709	16
ALL--IS THE PRICE OF ALL--	THE HALLOWING OF PAIN	772	8
REPLYING TO IT'S PRICE--	PERCEPTION OF AN OBJECT	1071	4
TO CHILDREN HE IS SMALL [LEAST] IN PRICE	THE MERCHANT OF THE	1131	5
GO [BUT] BOLDLY--FOR THOU PAID'ST HIS PRICE	GO SLOW, MY SOUL, TO	1297	7
FOR THOUGH HIS [THE] PRICE WAS NOT OF GOLD--	HIS MIND LIKE FABRICS OF	1446	5
WAS ALL THE PRICE [TERMS] THERE WAS--	HIS MIND LIKE FABRICS OF	1446	8
YOU CANNOT COMPREHEND ITS PRICE [WORTH]	YOUR THOUGHTS DONT HAVE	1452	7
BUT SHE MUST [MY PRICE / HUMILITY] PAY FOR SUCCOR	I SAW THE WIND WITHIN	1502	V
MAKE LIFE A SUDDEN PRICE.	MORNING THAT COMES BUT	1610	4
SAHARA IS TOO LITTLE PRICE	I DID NOT REACH THEE	1664	12
THE MARKET PRICE, THEY SAID.	I TOOK ONE DRAUGHT OF	1725	4
PRICELESS			
AND LO--MY PRICELESS HAY	I CAUTIOUS, SCANNED MY	178	8
FOR HIS LESS PRICELESS FRIEND.	BECAUSE THAT YOU ARE	1260	32
PRICES			
PRICES REASONABLE--	FLOSS WONT SAVE YOU FROM	1322	8
THE PRICES OF DESPAIR	THE AUCTIONEER OF	1612	6
PRICK			
YOU CANNOT PRICK WITH SAW--	NO RACK CAN TORTURE ME--	384	5
PRICKLED			
PRICKLED BLUE [RAW] AND COOL--	WHEN I HOPED, I	768	14
PRICKLIER			
INFLICTS A PRICKLIER PAIN,	WE MISS A KINSMAN MORE	1087	6
PRICKLY			
OF PRICKLY THINGS	THE CHILD'S FAITH IS NEW	637	20
PRICKS			
PRICKS HIS EAR--REPORT TO HEAR	GRIEF IS A MOUSE--	793	6
PRIDE			
HER PRIDE ASPIRES--	FOR EVERY BIRD A NEST--	143	12
BRING ME MY BEST PRIDE--	I AM ASHAMED--I HIDE--	473	23
MEEK--LET IT BE--TOO PROUD--FOR PRIDE--	I AM ASHAMED--I HIDE--	473	26
AS PRIDE WERE ALL IT COULD--	'TWAS WARM--AT FIRST--	519	12
IF PRIDE SHALL BE IN PARADISE--	WHEN I WAS SMALL, A	596	9
PRIED			
WE PRIED HIM BACK	THE FROST OF DEATH WAS	1136	9
PRIESTS			
OR PRIESTS--ADJUST THE SYMBOLS--	IT WILL BE SUMMER--	342	19

	FIRST LINE	POEM	LINE
PRIG			
I DID RESIGN THE PRIG,	I COUNTED TILL THEY	36	6
PRIMA			
OR LAY A PRIMA, MAD,	I CANNOT DANCE UPON MY	326	8
PRIME			
AND TAKES THE WIND AT PRIME--	'TIS MY FIRST NIGHT	1122	6
DISHEVELS EVERY PRIME	LIKE TIME'S INSIDIOUS	1236	6
AS WELL AS [BETTER THAN] PRIME	AN ANTIQUATED GRACE	1345	3
PRIMER			
BUT JUST THE PRIMER--TO A LIFE--	NOT IN THIS WORLD TO SEE	418	4
AND YET--MY PRIMER SUITS ME SO	NOT IN THIS WORLD TO SEE	418	7
PARALYSIS--OUR PRIMER--DUMB [NUMB]--	THE ZEROES--TAUGHT US--	689	7
PRIMEVAL			
IN THOSE PRIMEVAL CLOTHES--	HOW FITS HIS UMBER COAT	1371	8
PRIMOGENITURE			
ASSERT HER VITAL PRIVILEGE--[HIS PRIMOGENITURE]	NO CROWD THAT HAS	515	7
PRIMROSE			
THEN I HAVE "SHARES" IN PRIMROSE "BANKS"--	WHAT WOULD I GIVE TO SEE	247	15
PRINCE			
ARRANGED THEMSELVES AROUND THEIR PRINCE	THE DAY CAME SLOW--TILL	304	11
THE WIND--IS PRINCE OF THOSE--	THE DAY CAME SLOW--TILL	304	12
OR GOLD--WHO AM THE PRINCE OF MINES--	'TIS LITTLE I--COULD	466	5
I CHEERED MY FAINTING PRINCE--	I ROSE--BECAUSE HE SANK	616	5
WHOSE PRINCE--IS SON OF NONE--	BEHIND ME--DIPS ETERNITY	721	9
ITSELF THE ONLY PRINCE CAST OUT--	A LOSS OF SOMETHING EVER	959	8
HE IS KING [PRINCE] OF HARM--	WHEN I HOPED I FEARED--	1181 V	7
PRINCES			
TWO OTHER RAGGED PRINCES	I MET A KING THIS	166	21
PRINCIPALLY			
BUT, PRINCIPALLY--OF SUN--	OF BRUSSELS--IT WAS NOT	602	12
REDEMPTION IS THE ONE [PRINCIPALLY]	I SAW THE WIND WITHIN	1502 V	
PRINCIPLE			
WHOLE--LIKE HIS PRINCIPLE--	THE CHILD'S FAITH IS NEW	637	2
AND LO, HER SILVER PRINCIPLE	AT HALF PAST THREE, A	1084	7
PRINT			
A PRINT OF A VERMILLION FOOT--	AN ALTERED LOOK ABOUT	140	5
A PHEBE MAKES A LITTLE PRINT	I WAS A PHEBE--NOTHING	1009	7
HAD IT BEEN MINE, TO PRINT!	ENDED, ERE IT BEGUN--	1088	5
PRINTED			
HAD PRINTED YESTERDAY,	A SINGLE SCREW OF FLESH	263	8
PRISCILLA			
"MILES", AND "PRISCILLA", WERE SUCH AN ONE--	GOD IS A DISTANT--	357	4
BUT, LEST THE SOUL--LIKE FAIR "PRISCILLA"	GOD IS A DISTANT--	357	5
PRISM			
THE LOVE OF THEE--A PRISM BE--	I SEE THEE BETTER--IN	611	3
ASSERTING FROM HIS PRISM	LIKE TIME'S INSIDIOUS	1236	7
HE IS PRISM BORN.	WHICH IS THE BEST--THE	1315	8
THE PRISM NEVER HELD THE HUES,	PURSUING YOU IN YOUR	1602	5
PRISON			
MINE--BY THE SIGN IN THE SCARLET PRISON--	MINE--BY THE RIGHT OF	528	3
A PRISON GETS TO BE A FRIEND--	A PRISON GETS TO BE A	652	1
IS HEAVEN THEN A PRISON?	OF TOLLING BELL I ASK	947	4
THEY WERE IN PRISON LAID	OF PAUL AND SILAS IT IS	1166	2
HOW SOFT THIS [HIS] PRISON IS	HOW SOFT THIS PRISON IS	1334	1
THAT PRISON DOES'NT KEEP	FROM ALL THE JAILS THE	1532	4
WITHIN A MAGIC PRISON	OF GOD WE ASK ONE FAVOR,	1601	6
PRISONER			
NO PRISONER BE--	NO PRISONER BE--	720	1
PRISONS			
I NEVER HEAR OF PRISONS BROAD	I NEVER HEAR THE WORD	77	5
PRITHEE			
PRITHEE, MY BROTHER,	THERE IS ANOTHER SKY,	2	13
PRITHEE, MY PRETTY HOUSEWIVES!	A LADY RED--AMID THE	74	7
PRIVACY			
DEATH'S SINGLE PRIVACY	I LIVE WITH HIM--I SEE	463	4
I COULD NOT FIND A PRIVACY	TO MY QUICK EAR THE	891	3
THAT POLAR PRIVACY	THERE IS A SOLITUDE OF	1695	6
PRIVATE			
PRIVATE--LIKE THE BREEZE--	IT'S LIKE THE LIGHT--	297	6
AS HERSCHEL'S PRIVATE INTEREST	NATURE AND GOD--I	835	7
PRIVATELY			
AS WORTHILY [PRIVATELY] AS WE.	SHE HIDETH HER THE LAST	557	8
PRIVILEGE			
A PRIVILEGE--I THINK--	A PRECIOUS--MOULDERING	371	4
FOR PRIVILEGE OF SOD AND SUN--	THERE IS A FLOWER THAT	380	19
WITHOUT THE PRIVILEGE TO KNOW	HOW MANY FLOWERS FAIL IN	404	3
FOR PRIVILEGE OF PLAY	FORGET! THE LADY WITH	438	6
'TIS DEEMED A PRIVILEGE TO CHOOSE--	THE MANNER OF IT'S DEATH	468	3
A PRIVILEGE [LUXURY] SO AWFUL	I WOULD NOT PAINT--A	505	21
ASSERT HER VITAL PRIVILEGE--[HIS PRIMOGENITURE]	NO CROWD THAT HAS	515	7
THE PRIVILEGE [THE LIBERTY / AUTHORITY] TO SAY	HE PARTS HIMSELF--LIKE	517	14
THE PRIVILEGE [LIBERTY / LUXURY] TO DIE--	THE HEART ASKS PLEASURE	536	8
THE PRIVILEGE--	A TOAD, CAN DIE OF LIGHT	583	5
THE PRIVILEGE TO FLY	IT WOULD HAVE STARVED A	612	10
A HEAVEN OF HEAVENS--THE PRIVILEGE	'TWAS A LONG PARTING--	625	7
SHE STOPPED--A TRAVELLER'S PRIVILEGE--FOR REST--	I WATCHED THE MOON	629	3
THE PRIVILEGE TO SCRUTINIZE	I WATCHED THE MOON	629	29

	FIRST LINE	POEM	LINE
PRIVILEGE (CONTINUED)			
DEATH'S PRIVILEGE?	I CANNOT LIVE WITH YOU--	640	20
AND THAT WHITE SUSTENANCE--[EXERCISE / PRIVILEGE]	I CANNOT LIVE WITH YOU--	640	49
A PRIVILEGE OF HURRICANE [MISERY]	I MEANT TO FIND HER WHEN	718	11
AND WHAT A PRIVILEGE TO BE	THE MOON WAS BUT A CHIN	737	13
THE PRIVILEGE OF FEW--	TWO--WERE IMMORTAL TWICE	800	2
WILL HOLD YOU TILL YOUR PRIVILEGE	TILL DEATH--IS NARROW	907	3
THE PRIVILEGE TO LIVE	'TWAS CRISIS--ALL THE	948	6
THAT IT WAS NOT OUR PRIVILEGE	ENDED, ERE IT BEGUN--	1088	7
THY PRIVILEGE OF DYING	THROUGH WHAT TRANSPORTS	1153	7
HAD IT THE STRICKEN PRIVILEGE, ...	HAD THIS ONE DAY NOT	1253	7
OURSELVES, DENIED THE PRIVILEGE, ...	'TIS NOT THE SWAYING	1597	7
PRIZE			
CROUCH LOW TO GUARD HIS PRIZE.	I NEVER TOLD THE BURIED	11	4
WE ESTIMATE OUR PRIZE	AS BY THE DEAD WE LOVE	88	6
BUT NEVER DEEMED THE DRIPPING PRIZE . . .	LIKE FLOWERS, THAT HEARD	513	2
PRIZE--	UNCERTAIN LEASE--	857	8
WE SHUN BECAUSE WE PRIZE HER FACE	WE SHUN BECAUSE WE PRIZE	1429	1
THE SUMMER THAT WE DID NOT PRIZE, ...	THE SUMMER THAT WE DID	1773	1
PRIZES			
ALL PRIZES TO OBTAIN--	HOW FORTUNATE THE GRAVE	897	2
"CROWNS OF LIFE" ARE SERVILE PRIZES . . .	"FAITHFUL TO THE END"	1357	5
PROBABILITY			
A PROBABILITY--	THAT SACRED CLOSET WHEN	1273	8
PROBABLE			
NOT PROBABLE--THE BAREST CHANCE--	NOT PROBABLE--THE BAREST	346	1
PROBABLY			
THE MAIL FROM TUNIS, PROBABLY, ...	A ROUTE OF EVANESCENCE	1463	7
PROBED			
I PROBED RETRIEVELESS THINGS	I TRIED TO THINK A	532	5
THE POET SEARCHED [PROBED] PHILOLOGY . . .	SHALL I TAKE THEE, THE	1126	5
PROBING			
WITH NARROW, PROBING, [ANALYTIC] EYES-- . .	I MEASURE EVERY GRIEF I	561	2
PROBITY			
FORFEIT PROBITY--	CONSCIOUS AM I IN MY	679	12
REPUGNANT TO HER PROBITY--	SHAME IS THE SHAWL OF	1412	7
PROBLEM			
FLINGING THE PROBLEM BACK	MY WHEEL IS IN THE DARK!	10	14
LOW AT MY PROBLEM BENDING, ...	LOW AT MY PROBLEM	69	1
ANOTHER PROBLEM COMES--	LOW AT MY PROBLEM	69	2
YOUR PROBLEM [LABOR]--OF THE BRAIN--	I LEARNED--AT LEAST--	944	15
PROBLEMS			
LIFE SET ME LARGER--PROBLEMS--	IT TROUBLED ME AS ONCE I	600	9
PROCEED			
THE TRAVELLER PROCEED--	NO MAN CAN COMPASS A	477	4
PROCEED--INSERTING HERE--A SUN--	IT'S EASY TO INVENT A	724	11
WITHOUT DIMINUET PROCEED!	OH WHAT A GRACE IS THIS,	1615	5
CAN HUMAN NATURE NOT SURVIVE [PROCEED] . .	THE RETICENT VOLCANO	1748	7
PROCEEDS			
PROCEEDS WITHOUT CONCERN--	THE LARGEST FIRE EVER	1114	4
THE SUN PROCEEDS UNMOVED	APPARENTLY WITH NO	1624	6
PROCESS			
AND LEFT HIS PROCESS--SATISFIED--	HE PUT THE BELT AROUND	273	V 3
A PROCESS IN THE BUR--	THERE ARE TWO RIPENINGS	332	6
BY BLOSSOMS GRADUAL [COMMON] PROCESS-- . .	HE GAVE AWAY HIS LIFE--	567	11
POWER TO PERCEIVE HIS PROCESS	STRUCK, WAS I, NOR YET	925	3
IT'S PROCESS IS UNKNOWN.	THIS IS A BLOSSOM OF THE	945	8
MY PROCESS IS NOT LONG	THE SPRY ARMS OF THE	1103	6
IN PROCESS OF THE NOON BECAME--	A FULL FED ROSE ON MEALS	1154	3
PROCESSES			
BY PROCESSES [RUDIMENTS / PREFACES] OF SIZE	TIME FEELS SO VAST THAT	802	6
DELAPIDATION'S PROCESSES	CRUMBLING IS NOT AN	997	3
PROCESSION			
IT WAS A SHORT PROCESSION, ...	THE GENTIAN WEAVES HER	18	9
WE TRUST, IN PLUMED PROCESSION	TO FIGHT ALOUD, IS VERY	126	9
RECOGNIZING IN PROCESSION	SMILING BACK FROM	385	5
PROCESSIONS			
BUT FOR THE JUSTIFIED PROCESSIONS	OVER AND OVER, LIKE A	367	7
PROCLAIM			
PROCLAIM WITH THEIR REMAINING MIGHT-- . .	ME PROVE IT NOW--WHOEVER	537	11
MAINTAIN--BY ACCIDENT THAT THEY PROCLAIM-- .	LIFE, AND DEATH, AND	706	6
A POWER--WILL PROCLAIM	A PLATED LIFE--	806	6
PROCLAIMED			
HER PROGRESS--BY THE BEE--PROCLAIMED-- . .	THERE IS A FLOWER THAT	380	27
AND OF "TRUTH" UNTIL IT PROCLAIMED HIM A LIAR--	HE PREACHED UPON	1207	3
PROCLAIMING			
PROCLAIMING TO THE GLOOM	NOT ANY SUNNY TONE	1674	8
PROCLAMATION			
THE PROCLAMATION OF THE SUNS	THE DANDELION'S PALLID	1519	7
PROCURE			
A FEW--AND THEY BY RISK--PROCURE-- . . .	DID OUR BEST MOMENT LAST	393	3
PROCURED			
LED ABSENT, WERE PROCURED [OBTAINED] OF HEAVEN	TWO TRAVELLERS PERISHING	933	15
PROCURES			
BUT HE WHOSE LOSS PROCURES YOU	TILL DEATH--IS NARROW	907	5
AN AGONY PROCURES--	A NEARNESS TO	963	2
PROCURING			
PROCURING HIM PERPETUAL DREST	I CANNOT SEE MY SOUL BUT	1262	9

	FIRST LINE	POEM	LINE
PRODIGAL			
PRODIGAL OF BLUE	NATURE RARER USES YELLOW	1045	4
WAS THAT CONFIDING PRODIGAL [MINUTE DOMINGO]	ONE OF THE ONES THAT	1466	3
PRODIGIOUS			
AND THEN--PRODIGIOUS STEP	I LIKE TO SEE IT LAP	585	4
PRODUCE			
THAT ABSTINENCE OF MINE [ME] PRODUCE	I FIT FOR THEM--	1109	6
PRODUCT			
UNTIL THE VELVET PRODUCT	THERE ARE TWO RIPENINGS	332	3
WERE IT A FIRMAMENTAL PRODUCT--	I THINK THAT THE ROOT OF	1302	3
PRODUCTS			
THE PRODUCTS OF MY FARM ARE THESE	THE PRODUCTS OF MY FARM	1025	1
THOSE PRODUCTS ARE PREFERRED	THE JOY THAT HAS NO STEM	1744	6
PROFANE			
PROFANE IT BY A SEARCH [PURSUIT]--WE CANNOT	IN MANY AND REPORTLESS	1382	9
PROFANED			
THE TIME WAS SCARCE PROFANED, BY SPEECH--	THERE CAME A DAY AT	322	9
BY THESES BE DETAINED [PROFANED]--	THE LILAC IS AN ANCIENT	1241	20
PROFANES			
AND THAT DEGRADES [PROFANES] THE FLOWER--	THE CLOVER'S SIMPLE FAME	1232	6
AND THAT PROFANES [POLLUTES / DEFILES] THE POWER	THE CLOVER'S SIMPLE FAME	1232	V 6
PROFFERED			
PROFFERED TO THE PLAIN--	TWICE HAD SUMMER HER	846	2
PROFILE			
THE VERY PROFILE OF THE THOUGHT	THAT AFTER HORROR--THAT	286	7
PERHAPS--THE PROFILE OF A MILL	IT'S THOUGHTS--AND JUST	495	20
AND LEFT THE PROFILE--PLAINER--	IT KNEW NO MEDICINE--	559	7
PROFOUND			
PROFOUND!	LIKE HER THE SAINTS	60	12
STARS, AMID PROFOUND GALAXIES--	IF THE FOOLISH, CALL	168	19
OF HIS PROFOUND [OPAQUE] TO COME--	THE FUTURE--NEVER SPOKE	672	4
AND MOST PROFOUND EXPERIMENT	THIS CONSCIOUSNESS THAT	822	7
TO BE A FLOWER, IS PROFOUND	BLOOM--IS RESULT--TO	1058	15
PROFOUND--PRECARIOUS PROPERTY--	I AM AFRAID TO OWN A	1090	3
PROFOUNDER			
COMPARED WITH THAT PROFOUNDER SITE	THERE IS A SOLITUDE OF	1695	5
PROGENITOR			
DAY'S GREAT PROGENITOR--	RENUNCIATION--IS A	745	8
PROGNOSTICATION			
THE PERSONS [TRANSPORTS / TREASURES / ASPECTS] OF PROGNOSTICATION	MARCH IS THE MONTH OF	1404	3
PROGNOSTIC'S			
NOT EVEN A PROGNOSTIC'S PUSH	THE SPIRIT LASTS--BUT IN	1576	23
NOT EVEN A PROGNOSTIC'S PUSH	EXPANSE CANNOT BE LOST--	1584	7
NOT [THAT] EVEN A PROGNOSTIC'S PUSH [FOOT]	THIS ME--THAT WALKS AND	1588	7
PROGRAMME			
YET UPON HIS PURPLE PROGRAMME	ALWAYS MINE!	839	8
PROGRESS			
HER PROGRESS--BY THE BEE--PROCLAIMED--	THERE IS A FLOWER THAT	380	27
BE SETTING ON HIS PROGRESS--	NO MAN CAN COMPASS A	477	7
IT KEEPS THE NERVES PROGRESSIVE [IN PROGRESS]	THESE ARE THE NIGHTS	1128	11
PROGRESS'			
FOR THE PROGRESS' SAKE"--	I SAW THAT THE FLAKE WAS	1267	8
PROGRESSIVE			
IT KEEPS THE NERVES PROGRESSIVE [IN PROGRESS]	THESE ARE THE NIGHTS	1128	11
PROHIBIT			
NEITHER [OR] DECREE PROHIBIT HIM--	THE RAT IS THE CONCISEST	1356	9
PROHIBIT ME	OH, HONEY OF AN HOUR,	1734	3
PROJECTED			
PROJECTED HIM.	IN WINTER IN MY ROOM	1670	31
PROJECTS			
OUR PROJECTS FLIT AWAY--	ON THAT SPECIFIC PILLOW	1533	2
CONFIDED ARE HIS PROJECTS PINK	THE RETICENT VOLCANO	1748	3
PROMETHEUS			
PROMETHEUS NEVER KNEW--[DID NOT KNOW]	THE SMOULDERING EMBERS	1132	8
PROMISE			
TRUST THE LOVING PROMISE	I OFTEN PASSED THE	51	15
THAT I MAY TAKE THAT PROMISE	ALTHOUGH I PUT AWAY HIS	366	30
HUMMING--FOR PROMISE--WHEN ALONE--	BETTER--THAN MUSIC! FOR	503	22
PROMISE THIS--WHEN YOU BE DYING--	PROMISE THIS--WHEN YOU	648	1
AND PROMISE TO RETURN--	ONE THING OF IT WE	1464	2
PROMISED			
HE WILL TELL ME WHAT "PETER" PROMISED--	I SHALL KNOW WHY--WHEN	193	5
BUT THEN I PROMISED NE'ER TO TELL--	A MURMUR IN THE TREES--	416	17
PROMOTE			
THEY SEVERALLY--RETARD--OR FURTHER [PROMOTE--OR HINDER]--	FOUR TREES--UPON A	742	15
PROMOTED			
ANGELS! WRITE [MARK] "PROMOTED"	WHO NEVER LOST, ARE	73	15
PROMPT			
A PROMPT--EXECUTIVE [BOLD, INSPIRITING] BIRD IS THE JAY--	A PROMPT--EXECUTIVE BIRD	1177	1
PROMPT AS WHEN I LIT THEM	TRUSTY AS THE STARS	1369	3
PROMPTED			
OLDER FEEL THAN THE HOPE THAT PROMPTED--	UP LIFE'S HILL WITH MY	1010	5
PROMPTER			
THEN--PROMPTER THAN [PUNCTUAL AS] A STAR	I LIKE TO SEE IT LAP	585	15
IT CAME AT LAST BUT PROMPTER DEATH	IT CAME AT LAST BUT	1230	1

	FIRST LINE	POEM	LINE
PROMPTLY			
GOD CALLS HOME--THE ANGELS--PROMPTLY--	GOD PERMITS INDUSTRIOUS	231	5
DUE--PROMPTLY--AS A DRAMA--	WHOLE GULFS--OF RED, AND	658	7
PROMPTNESS			
AND SCANS WITH [WITH WHAT A] FATAL PROMPTNESS	THE SUMMER THAT WE DID	1773	6
PRONE			
WE--PRONE TO PERIPHRASIS,	THERE'S SOMETHING	45	15
BUT [YET] PRONE TO SHUT IT'S [HIS] SPOTTED [SUBTLE] FAN	THE BUTTERFLY'S NUMIDIAN	1387	4
TO PLAY TOGETHER WE ARE PRONE	I DID NOT REACH THEE	1664	16
PRONOUN			
AND LEFT THE VERB AND THE PRONOUN OUT--	GOING TO HIM! HAPPY	494	5
PRONOUNCE			
THAT THEY--PRONOUNCE MY NAME--	ME--COME! MY DAZZLED	431	10
PRONOUNCED			
AS IF YOUR SENTENCE STOOD--PRONOUNCED--	'TWAS LIKE A MAELSTROM,	414	18
WHEN DEITY ASSURED [PRONOUNCED]	TRUST IN THE UNEXPECTED	555	14
AND HE PRONOUNCED IT FIRM.	HOW BRITTLE ARE THE	1433	8
AND FIRST PRONOUNCED "A FIT."	MY COUNTRY NEED NOT	1511	4
PRONOUNCING			
PRONOUNCING EVERY WORD	THE MORNING AFTER WO--	364	10
AFFIRMING [PRONOUNCING] IT A SOUL.	THE PROPS ASSIST THE	1142	12
PROOF			
AND SUNS, GO SURER, FOR THEIR PROOF,	WHEN WE STAND ON THE	242	15
PHYSICIAN'S--PROOF OF BREATH--	I AM ALIVE--I GUESS--	470	8
I BRING THEE PROOF	THAT I DID ALWAYS LOVE	549	2
OF HEAVEN ABOVE THE FIRMEST PROOF	IMMORTAL IS AN AMPLE	1205	5
TOO MUCH OF PROOF AFFRONTS BELIEF	SO MUCH OF HEAVEN HAS	1228	9
IS PROOF AGAINST THE SUN	THE BUTTERFLY'S NUMIDIAN	1387	3
PROOF'S			
LEST SIGHT'S [PROOF'S] INEFFABLE DISGRACE	WE SHUN BECAUSE WE PRIZE	1429	2
PROP			
THAT HOLDS WITHOUT A PROP--	THE TRUTH--IS STIRLESS--	780	10
TO DREAM--TO SAP THE PROP	A PIT--BUT HEAVEN OVER	1712	7
PROPAGATES			
TILL TREASON LIGHTLY PROPAGATES	WHOEVER DISENCHANTS	1451	V 7
PROPENSITY			
IS OUR PROPENSITY	COME SHOW THY DURHAM	1542	11
PROPER			
AND WEARS A PROPER COAT	THE BUTTERFLY OBTAINS	1685	6
PROPERTIES			
IT'S PROPERTIES SHALL BE	THIS CONSCIOUSNESS THAT	822	10
PROPERTY			
THE PROPERTY, MY GARDEN,	I HAD SOME THINGS THAT I	116	5
PROFOUND--PRECARIOUS PROPERTY--	I AM AFRAID TO OWN A	1090	3
IF ANY TAKE [SEIZE] MY PROPERTY	ALONE AND IN A	1167	19
PROPHETIC			
POSTERIOR, PROPHETIC,	THE MURMURING OF BEES,	1115	3
PROPITIATE			
MEN--TO ANTICIPATE [PROPITIATE]	THE CHILD'S FAITH IS NEW	637	23
HER DISTANCES [ELEMENT] PROPITIATE	BECAUSE HE LOVES HER	1229	7
PROPITIATE THIS DEMOCRAT	NOT ANY HIGHER STANDS	1256	7
PROPITIATION'S			
PROPITIATION'S CLAW--	IN WINTER IN MY ROOM	1670	23
PROPITIOUS			
WHEN, WERE THE GALES PROPITIOUS--	WENT UP A YEAR THIS	93	11
PROPORTION			
ONE PEARL--TO ME--SO SIGNAL-- [OF SUCH PROPORTION]	ONE LIFE OF SO MUCH	270	5
PROPORTIONED			
PROPORTIONED TO HIS SEVERAL DEARTH	THERE IS A FLOWER THAT	380	7
PROPORTIONED TO THE CHANCE--	HAD I NOT THIS, OR THIS,	904	14
PROPORTIONED TO THE GROOVE.	THAT LOVE IS ALL THERE	1765	4
PROPOSED			
WHERE I PROPOSED TO GO	"ARCTURUS" IS HIS OTHER	70	19
HEART THAT PROPOSED AS HEART THAT ACCEPTED	UP LIFE'S HILL WITH MY	1010	7
PROPOSITION			
LUCRATIVE INDEED THE OFFER [THE PROPOSITION]	"FAITHFUL TO THE END"	1357	V
PROPOUND			
"GOOD MORNING"--WE PROPOUND?	THE SYMPTOM OF THE GALE	1327	16
TO WHOM NOT ANY FACE COHERE [PRESENT / PROPOUND]--	HOW FIRM ETERNITY MUST	1499	7
PROPOUNDED			
PROPOUNDED TO BELIEF.	TO DIE--WITHOUT THE	1017	4
PROPOUNDED BUT A SINGLE TERM	AT HALF PAST THREE, A	1084	3
TO THE PROPOUNDED WORD?	SHALL I TAKE THEE, THE	1126	2
PROPOUNDETH			
CONTINUAL BAN PROPOUNDETH HE	OF SILKEN SPEECH AND	896	8
PROPRIETY			
AS OF FRUGALITY [VELOCITY / AMENITY / PROPRIETY]--	A SPARROW TOOK A SLICE	1211	V 8
PROPS			
OUR PROPS DISCLOSE	WHAT TWIGS WE HELD BY--	1086	9
THE PROPS ASSIST THE HOUSE	THE PROPS ASSIST THE	1142	1
AND THEN THE PROPS WITHDRAW	THE PROPS ASSIST THE	1142	3
PROSAIC			
A FEW PROSAIC DAYS	BESIDES THE AUTUMN POETS	131	2
PROSE			
THEY SHUT ME UP IN PROSE--	THEY SHUT ME UP IN PROSE	613	1
A FAIRER HOUSE THAN PROSE--	I DWELL IN POSSIBILITY--	657	2

	FIRST LINE	POEM	LINE
PROSPECT			
SUCH TRANSCENDENTAL PROSPECT, ...	"SIC TRANSIT GLORIA	3	23
WITH PROSPECT, AND WITH FROST--	THERE IS A JUNE WHEN	930	12
COULD PROSPECT TASTE OF RETROSPECT . . .	MY TRIUMPH LASTED TILL	1227	11
PROSPECTIVE			
SO TO THE EYE PROSPECTIVE LED, ...	A SCIENCE--SO THE SAVANS	100	7
THUNDERING IT'S PROSPECTIVE--	MANY A PHRASE HAS THE	276	11
ENAMOR--IN PROSPECTIVE--	UNTO MY BOOKS--SO GOOD	604	15
OR FIRST PROSPECTIVE--OR THE GOLD	SHE ROSE TO HIS	732	7
A BOUNTY IN PROSPECTIVE, NOW	HOW WELL I KNEW HER NOT	837	3
IN POSITIVE PROSPECTIVE--	AS PLAN FOR NOON AND	960	3
HAS DOWERS OF PROSPECTIVE	CRISIS IS SWEET AND YET	1416	3
PROSPECTIVE IS EXTINCT.	HOW HUMAN NATURE DOTES	1417	V 4
PROSPECTIVE IS THE FRIEND	HOW HUMAN NATURE DOTES	1417	5
IF SUCH PROSPECTIVE BE--	THE MOON UPON HER FLUENT	1528	V
JAMAICAS OF REMEMBRANCE [PROSPECTIVE] STIR .	A DRUNKARD CANNOT MEET A	1628	5
PROSPECT'S			
RETROSPECTION IS PROSPECT'S HALF, ...	THIS WAS IN THE WHITE OF	995	7
PROSPERITY			
THAT FINE PROSPERITY	REVERSE CANNOT BEFALL	395	2
IN MOMENT OF PROSPERITY--	HAD I NOT THIS, OR THIS,	904	3
PROSPERITY--	COULD HOPE INSPECT HER	1283	8
WILD PROSPERITY, ...	THE SPIRIT LASTS--BUT IN	1576	20
OR WILD PROSPERITY	THIS ME--THAT WALKS AND	1588	4
PROSY			
THE DAY WAS WARM, AND WINDS WERE PROSY-- .	I HELD A JEWEL IN MY	245	3
PROTECT			
"SECURE [PROTECT] YOUR FLOWER" SAID HE. . .	THE FROST OF DEATH WAS	1136	2
PROTECTED			
PROTECTED BY THEIR DEEDS--	WHEN WE STAND ON THE	242	12
PROTECTION			
PROTECTION ASKED OF ME--	THESE STRANGERS, IN A	1096	2
PROTECTS			
PROTECTS OUR SANITY.	DID LIFE'S PENURIOUS	1717	8
PROTRACTED			
PROTRACTED AS THE BREEZE	OF SILKEN SPEECH AND	896	7
OR IN PROTRACTED BRUISE	I WATCHED HER FACE TO	1667	4
PROTRUDING			
PROTRUDING FROM THE GROUND--	FACTS BY OUR SIDE ARE	1497	4
PROUD			
HOW PROUD TO SHUT THE EYE!	IF THIS IS "FADING"	120	7
PROUD LITTLE HEART!	POOR LITTLE HEART!	192	4
MEEK--LET IT BE--TOO PROUD--FOR PRIDE-- . .	I AM ASHAMED--I HIDE--	473	26
BUT, PROUD IN APPARITION--	WHEN I WAS SMALL, A	596	13
AND I CANNOT BE PROUD	I CANNOT BE ASHAMED	914	6
SO PROUD [PLEASED / FAIN] SHE WAS TO DIE .	SO PROUD SHE WAS TO DIE	1272	1
PROUD OF MY BROKEN HEART, SINCE THOU DIDST BREAK IT,	PROUD OF MY BROKEN HEART	1736	1
PROUD OF THE PAIN I DID NOT FEEL TILL THEE,	PROUD OF MY BROKEN HEART	1736	2
PROUD OF MY NIGHT, SINCE THOU WITH MOONS DOST SLAKE IT,	PROUD OF MY BROKEN HEART	1736	3
PROUDER			
THERE'S SOMEWHAT [SOMETHING] PROUDER, OVER THERE--	MY PORTION IS DEFEAT--	639	14
PROUDEST			
THE PROUDEST TREES--	IT'S LIKE THE LIGHT--	297	8
INQUIRE OF THE PROUDEST [FULLEST / CLOSING] ROSE	CRISIS IS SWEET AND YET	1416	5
PROVE			
THE LIFE DOTH PROVE THE PRECEPT, WHO OBEY SHALL HAPPY BE,	AWAKE YE MUSES NINE,	1	9
WHAT CATO COULD'NT PROVE ME	THE RAINBOW NEVER TELLS	97	7
ALTHO' I PROVE IT, JUST IN TIME	YOUR RICHES--TAUGHT ME--	299	27
PROVE PIERCING EARNEST--	I KNOW THAT HE EXISTS.	338	10
TO PROVE IT POSSIBLER--	I FELT MY LIFE WITH BOTH	351	4
PROVE IT ME	SO WELL THAT I CAN LIVE	456	4
PROVE--LIKE A PEARL--	I AM ASHAMED--I HIDE--	473	18
A PRAYER, THAT IT MORE ANGEL--PROVE-- . .	THE WORLD--STANDS--	493	9
TOO BEAUTIFUL--FOR SHAPE TO PROVE-- . . .	THE WORLD--STANDS--	493	15
TO GUESS [PROVE] IT, PUZZLES SCHOLARS-- . .	THIS WORLD IS NOT	501	9
LEST THE PHANTASM--PROVE THE [JUST] MISTAKE--	WE DREAM--IT IS GOOD WE	531	11
ME PROVE IT NOW--WHOEVER [WHATEVER] DOUBT .	ME PROVE IT NOW--WHOEVER	537	1
ME STOP TO PROVE IT--NOW--	ME PROVE IT NOW--WHOEVER	537	2
I COULD NOT PROVE THE YEARS HAD FEET-- . .	I COULD NOT PROVE THE	563	1
SHOULD PROVE THE STRONGEST [SUPPLEST / LITHEST / STOUTEST] ONE.	MY FIRST WELL DAY--SINCE	574	8
MYSELF A POORER PROVE	I GAVE MYSELF TO HIM--	580	6
TO PROVE ABILITY. [SHOW SUPREMACY] . . .	IT ALWAYS FELT TO ME--A	597	16
WITHOUT A BOLT--THAT I COULD PROVE-- . . .	IT TROUBLED ME AS ONCE I	600	7
THEY PROVE ONE CHEMISTRY--	'TIS GOOD--THE LOOKING	660	V 12
IF SUCH IT PROVE, IT PROVE TOO	THEY SAY THAT "TIME	686	7
IF SUCH IT PROVE, IT PROVE TOO	THEY SAY THAT "TIME	686	7
AND STRUGGLE SLACKER--BUT TO PROVE . . .	I MANY TIMES THOUGHT	739	5
LEST I SHOULD INSUFFICIENT PROVE [BE] . .	MY WORTHINESS IS ALL MY	751	5
PROVE ME--MY HAZEL [SWIMMING] WITNESSES . .	JOY TO HAVE MERITED THE	788	11
PROVE THE FEAT--THAT MADE THE PELLET MINE--	GOD GAVE A LOAF TO EVERY	791	6
TO PROVE THE PRESENCE OF THE ORE	A PLATED LIFE--	806	3
TENDERNESS DECREASES AS WE PROVE-- . . .	ABSENCE DISEMBODIES--SO	860	4
TASTES DEATH--THE FIRST--TO HAND [PASS / PROVE] THE STING	LOVE--IS THAT LATER	924	5

	FIRST LINE	POEM	LINE
PROVE (CONTINUED)			
PROVE [ASK]--ME--SWEET--IF I REGRET IT--	ALL FORGOT FOR	966	15
PROVE MYSELF--OF THEE--	ALL FORGOT FOR	966	16
IF I PROVE IT STEEP--	UP LIFE'S HILL WITH MY	1010	2
TILL WHAT WE COULD NOT SEE [FACE / CHOOSE / PROVE] HAS COME . . .	THE MURMURING OF BEES,	1115	V 13
MUST PROVE THERE IS A SKY	SO MUCH OF HEAVEN HAS	1228	6
RESERVING THAT BUT JUST TO PROVE	SOMEWHERE UPON THE	1231	9
WE BOTH AND NEITHER PROVE--	TO PILE LIKE THUNDER TO	1247	6
NOR PROVE, NOR WOO,	THAN HEAVEN MORE REMOTE,	1436	13
PROVED			
HAVE SOMETIMES PROVED DEADLY SWEET!	TALK WITH PRUDENCE TO A	119	8
COULD NOT AGAIN BE PROVED--	HEAVEN IS SO FAR OF THE	370	4
FOR BRAVERIES JUST SEALED [PROVED] IN THIS	WHEN I WAS SMALL, A	596	V 19
OR SIMPLER PROVED--ABOVE--	IT TROUBLED ME AS ONCE I	600	12
THE FIRST--SWEET, PROVED I, [THAT WAS] ERE I SAW THEE--	WERT THOU BUT ILL--THAT	961	19
PROVES			
BUT PROVES US	UNDUE SIGNIFICANCE A	439	6
PROVES THAT--OUTGROWN--I SEE--	I COULD NOT PROVE THE	563	12
FLITS--GLIMMERS--PROVES--DISSOLVES--	THE LOVE A LIFE CAN SHOW	673	14
PROVES IT THERE'S NO SEA, OR RATHER	GRATITUDE--IS NOT THE	989	7
PROVIDE			
A VISION TO PROVIDE	THAN HEAVEN MORE REMOTE,	1436	8
PROVIDED			
LOVE PROVIDED THEE?	I CAUTIOUS, SCANNED MY	178	20
PROVIDED IT DO HOPELESS--HANG--	"HEAVEN"--IS WHAT I	239	3
PROVIDED IT BELIEVED--	TRUST IN THE UNEXPECTED	555	16
PROVIDENCE			
HER PROVIDENCE--THE SUN--	THERE IS A FLOWER THAT	380	26
PROVINCE			
THE PROVINCE OF THE SAVED	THE PROVINCE OF THE	539	1
IS BUT A PROVINCE--IN THE BEING'S [HUMAN] CENTRE--	ONE CRUCIFIXION IS	553	9
PROVINCIAL			
EXCEPT FOR WINDS--PROVINCIAL.	EXCEPT TO HEAVEN, SHE IS	154	5
PROVINCIALLY			
PROVINCIALLY--	THE ROBIN'S MY CRITERION	285	17
PROVING			
THERE IS A [GOOD] STRENGTH IN PROVING [KNOWING] THAT IT CAN BE . . .	THERE IS A STRENGTH IN	1113	1
PROVISO			
CONSTANCY WITH A PROVISO .	"FAITHFUL TO THE END"	1357	3
"I WILL GIVE" THE BASE PROVISO--	"FAITHFUL TO THE END"	1357	V
PROVOKES			
EVOKES [PROVOKES] SO SWEET A TORMENT--	I WOULD NOT PAINT--A	505	7
PROVOKING			
PROVOKING LOVER, WHEN YOU CAME	I THOUGHT THE TRAIN	1449	7
PROWESS			
THROUGH THE SOLITARY PROWESS	GROWTH OF MAN--LIKE	750	7
PROWLING			
ESCAPE THE PROWLING BEE	BLOOM--IS RESULT--TO	1058	12
PRUDENCE			
TALK WITH PRUDENCE TO A BEGGAR	TALK WITH PRUDENCE TO A	119	1
PRUDENT			
BUT MICROSCOPES ARE PRUDENT	"FAITH" IS A FINE	185	3
THE BODY--BORROWS [THE PRUDENT--CARRIES] A [THE] REVOLVER--	ONE NEED NOT BE A	670	17
HOW WELL THAT [PRUDENT] WE ARE BLIND--	HAD WE OUR SENSES	1284	6
MORE PRUDENT TO ASSAULT THE DAWN	HER SPIRIT ROSE TO SUCH	1486	4
A PRUDENT MAN WOULD SHUN.	THROUGH THOSE OLD	1753	4
PRUDENTER			
IT'S PRUDENTER--TO DREAM--	WE DREAM--IT IS GOOD WE	531	16
'TWAS PRUDENTER--I THOUGHT--	IF HE WERE LIVING--DARE	734	12
PRUDENTIAL			
OR CIRCUMSTANCE PRUDENTIAL	I SEND YOU A DECREPIT	1324	7
WITH A PRUDENTIAL LOOK BEHIND	THE LIFE THAT TIED TOO	1535	3
PRUDENTLY			
IS HITHERTO [PRUDENTLY] UNKNOWN	I SAW THE WIND WITHIN	1502	V
PRY			
AS ONE SHOULD PRY THE WALLS--	I TRIED TO THINK A	532	13
THAT LEVER CANNOT PRY--	ON A COLUMNAR SELF--	789	5
WE WILL PRY AND SEE IF SHE IS FAIR	BECAUSE HE LOVES HER	1229	2
PSALM			
SOBBING--WILL SUIT--AS WELL AS PSALM!	PUT UP MY LUTE!	261	5
A TOO PRESUMPTUOUS PSALM--	LIKE FLOWERS, THAT HEARD	513	15
PSALTERIES			
FAR PSALTERIES OF SUMMER--	THE TREES LIKE TASSELS--	606	5
PUBLIC			
HOW PUBLIC--LIKE A FROG--	I'M NOBODY! WHO ARE YOU?	288	6
HER PUBLIC--BE THE NOON--	THERE IS A FLOWER THAT	380	25
BURN HIM IN THE PUBLIC SQUARE--	GRIEF IS A MOUSE--	793	14
MOST SHUN THE PUBLIC AIR	BEST THINGS DWELL OUT OF	998	3
PUBLICATION			
PUBLICATION--IS THE AUCTION	PUBLICATION--IS THE	709	1
PUBLICITY			
FORBIDS PUBLICITY,	I HAD SOME THINGS THAT I	116	10
SO DAINTY OF PUBLICITY--	FUNNY--TO BE A CENTURY--	345	8
PUBLISH			
I FELT IT PUBLISH--IN MY EYE--	IT WOULD NEVER BE COMMON	430	11

	FIRST LINE	POEM	LINE
PUBLISHED			
ROBIN--UTTERED [PUBLISHED / LAVISHED] HALF THE TUNE--	HER--"LAST POEMS"--	312	8
PUBLISHES			
THERE PUBLISHES [BUSTLES BUT] A TEAR--	SO GLAD WE ARE--A	329	4
IT'S PICTURE PUBLISHES--PRECISE--	THE OUTER--FROM THE	451	11
PUCK'S			
OR PUCK'S APOSTACY.	THE WAY TO KNOW THE	1279	12
PULL			
I PULL A FLOWER FROM THE WOODS--	"ARCTURUS" IS HIS OTHER	70	9
SO I PULL MY STOCKINGS OFF	SO I PULL MY STOCKINGS	1201	1
PULLED			
IT PULLED THE SPIGOT FROM THE HILLS	LIKE RAIN IT SOUNDED	1235	11
PULPIT			
IT IS NOT HYMN FROM PULPIT READ--	MUSICIANS WRESTLE	157	10
MUCH GESTURE, FROM THE PULPIT--	THIS WORLD IS NOT	501	17
PULPY			
A PINK AND PULPY MULTITUDE	OUR LITTLE KINSMEN--	885	3
PULSE			
SAY--THAT THE PULSE JUST LISPS--	IF HE DISSOLVE--THEN--	236	10
PUMPKINS			
TO TAKE THE PUMPKINS IN--	'TWAS JUST THIS TIME,	445	12
IT'S TRIUMPHS [PUMPKINS]--TO THE BIN--	A FIELD OF STUBBLE,	1407	4
PUNCTUAL			
AND STILL THE PUNCTUAL SNOW!	NEW FEET WITHIN MY	99	8
PUNCTUAL! SEDATE!	DUST IS THE ONLY SECRET	153	10
FOR, WHEN FROSTS, THEIR PUNCTUAL FINGERS	THO' MY DESTINY BE	163	9
THEN--PROMPTER THAN [PUNCTUAL AS] A STAR	I LIKE TO SEE IT LAP	585	15
HAD LOVE AS PUNCTUAL BEEN	IT CAME AT LAST BUT	1230	6
PINK--SMALL--AND PUNCTUAL--	PINK--SMALL--AND	1332	1
HE DOTH AS PUNCTUAL CALL	THE SUN IS ONE--AND ON	1372	2
THE BIRD HER PUNCTUAL MUSIC BRINGS	THE BIRD HER PUNCTUAL	1585	1
YOU ARE PUNCTUAL--	LIGHTLY STEPPED A YELLOW	1672	8
PUNCTUALITY			
HE HAS THE PUNCTUALITY	THE ROBIN IS A GABRIEL	1483	5
PUNCTUATE			
TO PUNCTUATE THE WALL,	THE DYING NEED BUT	1026	4
PUNCTUATION			
AND SYLVAN PUNCTUATION--	THE ROBIN IS A GABRIEL	1483	16
PUNCTURE			
THE PUNCTURE--COOLLY TRIES--	A WEIGHT WITH NEEDLES ON	264	4
THOU CAN'ST NOT PIERCE TRADITION WITH THE PEERLESS PUNCTURE,	PROUD OF MY BROKEN HEART	1736	7
PUNGENT			
THE PUNGENT ATOM IN THE AIR	THE PUNGENT ATOM IN THE	1191	1
SURPRISE IS LIKE A THRILLING--PUNGENT--	SURPRISE IS LIKE A	1306	1
. . . PUNGENT / WINNING / MELLOW] TELLER--	THE BIBLE IS AN ANTIQUE	1545	13
IS PUNGENT EVERGREENS--	NO BRIGADIER THROUGHOUT	1561	18
HIS PUNGENT COMPANY	EXPERIMENT ESCORTS US	1770	2
PUNISH			
OH PUNISH--PRAY--	'TWAS LOVE--NOT ME--	394	2
THAT NONE CAN PUNISH HIM	LIKE TIME'S INSIDIOUS	1236	8
IN VAIN TO PUNISH HONEY--	HER LOSSES MAKE OUR	1562	7
PUNISHMENT			
HE [AND] BROKE THEM, FEARING PUNISHMENT	CLIMBING TO REACH THE	1566	3
PUPPET			
CANT PUT THE PUPPET BOWING--	A CLOCK STOPPED--	287	4
PURCHASE			
SUBTLE THE SUM THAT PURCHASE YOU--	BROTHER OF INGOTS--AH	1366	V 2
PURCHASED			
EMPTY THE HEARTS THAT PURCHASED YOU--	BROTHER OF INGOTS--AH	1366	2
PURCHASER			
THAN THIS GREAT PURCHASER SUSPECT,	I GAVE MYSELF TO HIM--	580	7
AN HUMBLE PURCHASER--	HIS MIND LIKE FABRICS OF	1446	4
PURCHASING			
IN PURCHASING.	SO LARGE MY WILL	1024	16
PURE			
THE LARK'S PURE TERRITORY--	THE GUEST IS GOLD AND	15	9
A PEACE AS PURE AS IF THE SKY	TO SEE HER IS A PICTURE	1568	V 7
PURER			
TO PURER REVEILLE!	GOOD NIGHT! WHICH PUT	259	12
TILL IN PURER DRESS--	TAKING UP THE FAIR IDEAL	428	10
A PURER FOOD FOR THEM, IF I SUCCEED,	I FIT FOR THEM--	1109	7
PUREST			
WHO DRESSED IN FROCKS OF PUREST SNOW	WHERE I HAVE LOST, I	104	14
PURLED			
THAT PURLED A MOMENT SINCE WITH GLEE--	HIS VOICE DECREPIT WAS	1476	5
PURPLE			
PURPLE AND COCHINEAL	LIKE HER THE SAINTS	60	5
OR ELSE A PEACOCK'S PURPLE TRAIN	SOME RAINBOW--COMING	64	4
NOT ONE OF ALL THE PURPLE HOST	SUCCESS IS COUNTED	67	5
THE PURPLE TERRITORIES	WHO NEVER LOST, ARE	73	7
NONE CAN AVOID THIS PURPLE--	ONE DIGNITY DELAYS FOR	98	3
VAILING THE PURPLE, AND THE PLUMES--	IN RAGS MYSTERIOUS AS	117	3
THE PURPLE BROOK WITHIN THE BREAST	A SOMETHING IN A	122	14
CRUISING ROUND THE PURPLE LINE--	FLOWERS--WELL--IF	137	12
A PURPLE FINGER ON THE SLOPE--	AN ALTERED LOOK ABOUT	140	6
THE PURPLE CRAYONS STAND.	SHE BORE IT TILL THE	144	4
FULL PURPLE IS HIS STATE!	WAIT TILL THE MAJESTY OF	171	12
A LITTLE PURPLE--SLIPPED BETWEEN--	A SLASH OF BLUE--	204	5

	FIRST LINE	POEM	LINE
PURPLE (CONTINUED)			
YOU DROPPED A PURPLE RAVELLING IN--	SHE SWEEPS WITH	219	5
BLAZING IN GOLD AND QUENCHING IN PURPLE	BLAZING IN GOLD AND	228	1
AND PURPLE--FROM PERU--	WHAT WOULD I GIVE TO SEE	247	20
AND EVER SINCE--THE PURPLE MOAT	THE LONESOME FOR THEY	262	5
WHERE SHIPS OF PURPLE--GENTLY TOSS--	WHERE SHIPS OF PURPLE--	265	1
HER PURPLE TRAFFIC	THIS--IS THE LAND--THE	266	6
A SMALLER PURPLE GROWS--	ME, CHANGE! ME, ALTER!	268	3
INTO THE MYSTIC [PURPLE] WELL--	A SOLEMN THING--IT WAS--	271	6
THE PURPLE COULD NOT KEEP THE EAST--	THE DAY CAME SLOW--TILL	304	5
THERE SEEMED A PURPLE STILE	I'LL TELL YOU HOW THE	318	10
AND IT SHOULD LIFT IT'S PURPLE DIKES,	AS IF I ASKED A COMMON	323	7
WILL SWAY WITH PURPLE LOAD--	IT WILL BE SUMMER--	342	10
TO GAIN THE PURPLE DEMOCRAT	THERE IS A FLOWER THAT	380	3
THERE ROSE A PURPLE CREATURE--	GOD MADE A LITTLE	442	5
SHE DOTH HER PURPLE WORK--	SHE HIDETH HER THE LAST	557	5
AND PURPLE RIBALDRY--OF MORNING	WHAT CARE THE DEAD, FOR	592	4
THE PURPLE--IN MY VEIN--	AGAIN--HIS VOICE IS AT	663	27
SEED, HAD I, MY PURPLE SOWING	BLOOM UPON THE MOUNTAIN	667	5
THE EAST--HER PURPLE TROTH	THE SUNRISE RUNS FOR	710	2
HER PETTICOAT--OF PURPLE PLAIN [JUST]--	THE DAY UNDRESSED--	716	3
THEIR PURPLE FIGURES RISE	THE MOUNTAINS--GROW	757	2
MY FAITH MUST TAKE THE PURPLE WHEEL	MY FAITH IS LARGER THAN	766	3
PURPLE--	THE COLOR OF A QUEEN, IS	776	T
YET UPON HIS PURPLE PROGRAMME	ALWAYS MINE!	839	8
PURPLE--IS FASHIONABLE TWICE--	PURPLE--IS FASHIONABLE	980	1
THE HILLS IN PURPLE SYLLABLES	THE HILLS IN PURPLE	1016	1
WHO MAY BE PURPLE IF HE CAN	WHO IS THE EAST?	1032	3
THE PURPLE MAN	WHO IS THE EAST?	1032	6
THE PURPLE IN THE EAST IS SET	THESE ARE THE SIGNS TO	1077	11
ALL IT'S PURPLE FLED	REVOLUTION IS THE POD	1082	10
HIS SHOES ARE PURPLE--	WE LIKE MARCH.	1213	2
THERE WAS NO PURPLE SUITABLE--	DEAR MARCH--COME IN--	1320	16
OUT OF THE PURPLE DOOR	DREAMS ARE THE SUBTLE	1376	4
FROM JUST A PURPLE FLOWER BEYOND	OF DEATH I TRY TO THINK	1558	13
AND WRECKS IN PEACE A PURPLE TAR,	A SLOOP OF AMBER SLIPS	1622	3
OF PURPLE PHARAOH--	"RED SEA," INDEED! TALK	1642	2
UNTO A PURPLE WOOD	A LANE OF YELLOW LED THE	1650	2
THE HILLS ERECT THEIR PURPLE HEADS	THE HILLS ERECT THEIR	1688	1
THE SOUTH UNROLLED A PURPLE FAN	THE SUN RETIRED TO A	1693	7
IN SUPPLEMENTS OF PURPLE	WITH SWEETNESS UNABATED	1709	9
ITSELF, THE PURPLE ON THE HIGHT	SOME SAY GOODNIGHT--AT	1739	7
PURPLES			
'TIS COSTLY--SO ARE PURPLES!	YOU'RE RIGHT--"THE WAY	234	5
HER TEAZING PURPLES--AFTERNOONS--	"HEAVEN"--IS WHAT I	239	9
PURPLES OF AGES--PAUSE [HALT] FOR YOU--	AH, TENERIFFE!	666	3
PURPOSELESS			
IN PURPOSELESS CIRCUMFERENCE--	FROM COCOON FORTH A	354	16
PURPOSES			
FOR OTHER SERVICES [PURPOSES]--AS SOUND--	THE SPIRIT IS THE	733	5
THE EPICURE OF FIRMAMENTS [VEHICLES / COURTESY / PURPOSES]	A SPARROW TOOK A SLICE	1211	V 7
PURRS			
WHEN ETNA BASKS AND PURRS	WHEN ETNA BASKS AND	1146	1
PURSE			
IT WAS WITHIN THE FRUGAL PURSE	OF BRUSSELS--IT WAS NOT	602	7
PURSUE			
THAT I THE ANSWER MAY PURSUE	I'VE NONE TO TELL ME TO	881	11
LEST HE PURSUE	IN WINTER IN MY ROOM	1670	34
PERMITTING TO PURSUE	THROUGH THOSE OLD	1753	10
PURSUED			
NOT PURSUED BY LEARNED ANGELS	IF THE FOOLISH, CALL	168	15
THE WIND PURSUED THE LITTLE BUSH--	THE NIGHT WAS WIDE, AND	589	5
PURSUED OF LITTLE BOYS	WHEN I HAVE SEEN THE SUN	888	8
IT GREW AS I PURSUED	I HAD A DAILY BLISS	1057	4
OURSELVES BE NOT PURSUED--	REMEMBRANCE HAS A	1182	8
I WILL NOT BE PURSUED--	DEAR MARCH--COME IN--	1320	20
OF THE ONES THAT PURSUED IT	NOT ANY MORE TO BE	1344	9
PURSUES			
PURSUES HIS PEARLY STRANDS--	THE SPIDER HOLDS A	605	V 4
IT'S TWINKLING TRAVELS IT PURSUES	A WINGED SPARK DOTH SOAR	1468	5
INSTINCT PURSUES THE ADAMANT,	THE SPIRIT LASTS--BUT IN	1576	17
PURSUING			
AND FLY, AS 'TWERE PURSUING YOU?	DID YOU EVER STAND IN A	590	7
LOOK BEHIND--HE IS PURSUING THEE.	TO EARN IT BY DISDAINING	1427	4
PURSUING [SUBDUING] WINDS THAT CENSURE [SUNDER] US	NO BRIGADIER THROUGHOUT	1561	5
PURSUING YOU IN YOUR TRANSITIONS,	PURSUING YOU IN YOUR	1602	1
PURSUIT			
YOURSELF, FOR HIS PURSUIT	TILL DEATH--IS NARROW	907	10
PROFANE IT BY A SEARCH [PURSUIT]--WE CANNOT	IN MANY AND REPORTLESS	1382	9
AND WHAT IS THY PURSUIT	THE LOOK OF THEE, WHAT	1689	4
PUSH			
BUT THE LEAST PUSH OF JOY	I CAN WADE GRIEF--	252	4
TO PUSH, AND PIERCE, BESIDES--	A WEIGHT WITH NEEDLES ON	264	2
BUT THE PUSH [PAIN] OF JOY--	MANY A PHRASE HAS THE	276	14
HIS SPEECH WAS LIKE THE PUSH	THE WIND--TAPPED LIKE A	436	10
I PUSH A PETAL FROM MY GOWN	I TIE MY HAT--I CREASE	443	7
THE JUDGMENT PUSH HIS PICTURE--	THE POWER TO BE TRUE TO	464	3
AND PUSH IT WITH MY FINGERS--NEXT--	THE WAY I READ A	636	3

	FIRST LINE	POEM	LINE
PUSH (CONTINUED)			
AND WITH A BLONDE PUSH	BANISH AIR FROM AIR--	854	10
LET AN INSTANT PUSH	CRISIS IS A HAIR	889	9
AN INSTANT'S PUSH DEMOLISHES	THE HEART HAS NARROW	928	11
THE NORTH BEGUN TO PUSH	THE CLOUDS THEIR BACKS	1172	2
NOT EVEN A PROGNOSTIC'S PUSH	THE SPIRIT LASTS--BUT IN	1576	23
NOT EVEN A PROGNOSTIC'S PUSH	EXPANSE CANNOT BE LOST--	1584	7
NOT [THAT] EVEN A PROGNOSTIC'S PUSH [FOOT]	THIS ME--THAT WALKS AND	1588	7
PUSHED			
I PUSHED MY DIMPLES BY, AND WAITED--	I FELT MY LIFE WITH BOTH	351	10
OR PUSHED THE PEBBLE FROM HIS PATH--	ALTHOUGH I PUT AWAY HIS	366	7
PUSHED SUDDEN THRO' TO HIS--	I HAD NOT MINDED--WALLS	398	6
UNTIL A ZEPHYR PUSHED [CHASED / FLUNG / SPURNED / SCOURGED] THEM	TWO BUTTERFLIES WENT OUT	533	V
AND PUSHED AWAY A SAIL	THREE TIMES--WE PARTED--	598	8
AND HE--I PUSHED--WITH SUDDEN FORCE--	IF HE WERE LIVING--DARE	734	13
I PUSHED MECHANIC FEET--	FROM BLANK TO BLANK--	761	3
SHORED [PUSHED] THE SUN AWAY	ON THE WORLD YOU COLORED	1171	10
WHEN IT HAD PUSHED ITSELF AWAY	LIKE RAIN IT SOUNDED	1235	5
WHEN PUSHED UPON A SCENE	SHAME IS THE SHAWL OF	1412	6
PUSHING			
SOME SECRET--THAT WAS PUSHING	THE TINT I CANNOT TAKE--	627	15
IS PUSHING [ROAMING / PLODDING / STARING / AMBLING] CLOSE BEHIND	ALL THAT I DO	1496	6
PUSSY			
AH, PUSSY, OF THE SAND,	SHE SIGHTS A BIRD--SHE	507	8
NEITHER PATRIARCH NOR PUSSY [ANCESTOR NOR URCHIN]	ONE DAY IS THERE OF THE	814	5
PUT			
PETER, PUT UP THE SUNSHINE!	"SIC TRANSIT GLORIA	3	13
PUT DOWN THE APPLE, ADAM,	"SIC TRANSIT GLORIA	3	17
I'LL PUT A TRINKET ON.	THE MORNS ARE MEEKER	12	8
PUT ON HER CARMINE SUIT	SHE SLEPT BENEATH A TREE	25	5
THEN PUT THEIR NIGHTGOWNS ON.	AS CHILDREN BID THE	133	4
I PUT THE LATTER IN A BARN--	I CAUTIOUS, SCANNED MY	178	5
PUT MY PRETENSE--AWAY--	MAKE ME A PICTURE OF THE	188	8
THE HEARING HIM PUT HIS PLAYTHINGS UP	IT IS EASY TO WORK WHEN	244	3
IF JOY--TO PUT MY PIECE AWAY	FOREVER AT HIS SIDE TO	246	8
GOOD NIGHT! WHICH PUT THE CANDLE OUT?	GOOD NIGHT! WHICH PUT	259	1
PUT UP MY LUTE!	PUT UP MY LUTE!	261	1
IT'S NAME IS PUT AWAY	A SINGLE SCREW OF FLESH	263	6
HE PUT THE BELT AROUND MY LIFE--	HE PUT THE BELT AROUND	273	1
PUT ME IN ON THE FIRMEST [TIGHTEST / HIGHEST] SIDE--	TIE THE STRINGS TO MY	279	5
CANT PUT THE PUPPET BOWING--	A CLOCK STOPPED--	287	4
PUT HER DOWN--IN ITALY?	HER--"LAST POEMS"--	312	19
PUT GENTLY UP THE EVENING BARS--	I'LL TELL YOU HOW THE	318	15
WOULD PUT ITSELF ABROAD	I CANNOT DANCE UPON MY	326	6
BEFORE I GOT MY EYE PUT OUT	BEFORE I GOT MY EYE PUT	327	1
WHERE OTHER CREATURES PUT THEIR EYES--	BEFORE I GOT MY EYE PUT	327	20
AND BEG ME PUT IT ON--	THE FACE I CARRY WITH ME	336	12
I MUST NOT PUT MY FOOT AMISS	IS BLISS THEN, SUCH	340	2
AND THEN 'TWAS PUT AMONG THE DUST	DEATH SETS A THING	360	11
ALTHOUGH I PUT AWAY HIS LIFE--	ALTHOUGH I PUT AWAY HIS	366	1
PUT FROM MY SIMPLE SPEECH ALL PLAIN WORD--	I'M SAYING EVERY DAY	373	20
THIS--PUT AWAY	FOR DEATH--OR RATHER	382	3
AN ETERNITY--PUT ON--	TAKE YOUR HEAVEN FURTHER	388	5
WHEN LIGHT IS PUT AWAY--	WE GROW ACCUSTOMED TO	419	2
THEY CANNOT PUT AWAY--	THE MONTHS HAVE ENDS--	423	12
PUT IT IN LATIN--LEFT OF MY SCHOOL--	IT DONT SOUND SO	426	3
PUT THE THOUGHT IN ADVANCE--A YEAR--	IT DONT SOUND SO	426	15
I PUT MY PLEASURE ALL ABROAD--	IT WOULD NEVER BE COMMON	430	17
I PUT NEW BLOSSOMS IN THE GLASS--	I TIE MY HAT--I CREASE	443	5
WE CANNOT PUT OURSELF AWAY	I TIE MY HAT--I CREASE	443	13
THIS SPARTAN PUT AWAY	IT FEELS A SHAME TO BE	444	6
THE ROPE THE NIGHTS WERE PUT ACROSS--	I SHOWED HER HIGHTS SHE	446	6
I NEVER PUT IT DOWN--	IT WAS GIVEN TO ME BY	454	6
AND PUT A FLOWER ON IT--	WE DO NOT PLAY ON GRAVES	467	5
THEY PUT US FAR APART--	THEY PUT US FAR APART--	474	1
AND THEY CAN PUT IT WITH MY DOLLS,	I'M CEDED--I'VE STOPPED	508	5
PUT OUT THEIR TONGUES, FOR NOON,	IT WAS NOT DEATH, FOR I	510	4
AND PUT THEM EACH IN SEPARATE DRAWERS,	IF YOU WERE COMING IN	511	7
TO PUT THIS WORLD DOWN, LIKE A BUNDLE--	TO PUT THIS WORLD DOWN,	527	1
SET SEPARATE [PUT QUIET--] FROM THE FARMING--	I'M SORRY FOR THE DEAD--	529	15
YOU CANNOT [NO MAN--] PUT A FIRE OUT--	YOU CANNOT PUT A FIRE	530	1
AND PUT IT IN A DRAWER--	YOU CANNOT PUT A FIRE	530	6
TO PUT A CURRENT [THE WATERS] BACK--	THE BRAIN, WITHIN IT'S	556	5
SHE PUT SOME FLOWERS AWAY--	MY FIRST WELL DAY--SINCE	574	10
PUT UP--TO HIDE [HOLD] HER PARTING GRACE	MY FIRST WELL DAY--SINCE	574	23
IS LEFT--TO PUT AWAY--	EMPTY MY HEART, OF THEE	587	9
AND PUT A STONE TO KEEP IT WARM--	WHAT CARE THE DEAD, FOR	592	23
FOR THESE--WERE ONLY PUT TO DEATH--	IT ALWAYS FELT TO ME--A	597	11
THEY PUT ME IN THE CLOSET--	THEY SHUT ME UP IN PROSE	613	3
DONT PUT UP MY THREAD & NEEDLE--	DONT PUT UP MY THREAD &	617	1
WHERE I PUT IT DOWN--	DONT PUT UP MY THREAD &	617	14
WHERE YOU HAD PUT ME DOWN--	OURSELVES WERE WED ONE	631	6
FOR--PUT THEM SIDE BY SIDE--	THE BRAIN--IS WIDER THAN	632	2
WOULD PUT OUT JESUS'--	I CANNOT LIVE WITH YOU--	640	23
AN EASY BREEZE DO PUT AFLOAT	OF BEING IS A BIRD	653	3
AND I HAD PUT AWAY	BECAUSE I COULD NOT STOP	712	6

	FIRST LINE	POEM	LINE
PUT (CONTINUED)			
AND PUT OUT HER EYE--	WHEN I HOPED, I	768	22
WHEN SHE HAD PUT AWAY HER WORK	SEVERER SERVICE OF	786	7
WHO PUT A HEAD AWAY	SEVERER SERVICE OF	786	14
THEN ORIENT SHOWED [THE EAST PUT OUT / NATURE PUT OUT] A SINGLE FLAG,	A DROP FELL ON THE APPLE	794	15
THEN ORIENT SHOWED [THE EAST PUT OUT / NATURE PUT OUT] A SINGLE FLAG,	A DROP FELL ON THE APPLE	794	15
WHEN THE LATTER--IS PUT AWAY	BY MY WINDOW HAVE I FOR	797	19
THE BIRDS PUT UP THE BARS TO NESTS--	THE WIND BEGUN TO KNEAD	824	13
AND PUT IT IN THE DRAWER--	WE OUTGROW LOVE, LIKE	887	2
SO MANY QUESTIONS TO PUT THEM	WHAT DID THEY DO SINCE I	900	3
WAS SOMEWHERE PUT IN TWAIN.	AS FROST IS BEST	951	12
TENETS--PUT BEHIND--	COLOR--CASTE--	970	6
IF HE PUT AWAY	COLOR--CASTE--	970	10
SO SCANTY PUT,	JUST ONCE! OH LEAST	1076	4
PUT THEIR WORK AWAY	THERE'S THE BATTLE OF	1174	4
WHEN WE HAVE PUT IT DOWN--	I SHOULD NOT DARE TO BE	1197	4
THIS AFTERNOON PUT ON--	THE BUTTERFLY'S	1244	3
PUT ON THE PERFECT LID--	WHEN MEMORY IS FULL	1266	2
THAT MAKES THE HEART PUT UP IT'S FUN--	SEPTEMBER'S	1271	7
PUT UP MY HEART THY HOARY WORK	THE NOTICE THAT IS	1310	3
PUT DOWN YOUR HAT--	DEAR MARCH--COME IN--	1320	4
WHEN PEOPLE HAVE PUT OUT THE LIGHTS	HOW LONESOME THE WIND	1418	2
TO PUT OFF FILAMENTS LIKE THIS	WITH PINIONS OF DISDAIN	1431	11
A PASSING UNIVERSE PUT ON,	HOW HAPPY IS THE LITTLE	1510	6
TO PUT IT OUT--	THOUGH THE GREAT WATERS	1599	6
NOR PUT HIS SPACIOUS ARM AROUND THEE	BACK FROM THE CORDIAL	1625	3
PUT ON YOUR MUFF [BELLS] FOR WINTER	THE JAY HIS CASTANET HAS	1635	2
THEN--MY DIADEM PUT ON.	REARRANGE A "WIFE'S"	1737	16
PUTS			
THAT PUTS IT'S MANNER BY	A MIEN TO MOVE A QUEEN--	283	4
PUTS RECOLLECTION NUMB--	THAT AFTER HORROR--THAT	286	8
PUTS OUT A RUFFLED HEAD--	I TEND MY FLOWERS FOR	339	12
THAT PUTS THE HEART--ABROAD--	GOOD MORNING--MIDNIGHT--	425	12
PUTS MINOR STREAMS TO REST.	HE TOUCHED ME, SO I LIVE	506	6
RUNS [PUTS] HIS FINGERS THRO' IT--	BEAUTY--BE NOT CAUSED--	516	6
PUTS ITSELF SEVERE AWAY	SAFE DESPAIR IT IS THAT	1243	3
BUT PUTS HER CRAFT ABOUT	QUITE EMPTY, QUITE AT	1606	4
BESTIRS ITSELF--PUTS ON IT'S COAT,	THE SUMMER THAT WE DID	1773	5
PUTTETH			
AND PUTTETH HER AWAY	SHE HIDETH HER THE LAST	557	6
PUTTING			
PUTTING UP	I CANNOT LIVE WITH YOU--	640	6
THE PUTTING OUT OF EYES--	RENUNCIATION--IS A	745	5
AND PUTTING LOVE AWAY	THE BUSTLE IN A HOUSE	1078	6
PUZZLE			
THEN--MAYBE, IT WOULD PUZZLE US	I'VE NOTHING ELSE--TO	224	7
PUZZLED			
THE OWL LOOKED PUZZLED DOWN--	THROUGH LANE IT LAY--	9	6
BESTIRS HER PUZZLED WINGS	ONCE MORE, MY NOW	48	2
UPON HER PUZZLED EAR--	ALL OVERGROWN BY CUNNING	148	V
UNTIL IT PUZZLED CAME	AS IF SOME LITTLE ARCTIC	180	4
IT PUZZLED ME TO KNOW--	THE ROSE DID CAPER ON	208	8
JUST FINDING OUT--WHAT PUZZLED US--	FOREVER AT HIS SIDE TO	246	15
WHAT SORER--PUZZLED ME--	IT TROUBLED ME AS ONCE I	600	14
PUZZLES			
TO GUESS [PROVE] IT, PUZZLES SCHOLARS--	THIS WORLD IS NOT	501	9
PUZZLEST			
THOU PUZZLEST ME!	MY FRIEND MUST BE A BIRD	92	7
PYRAMIDAL			
AS PYRAMIDAL [ELEMENTAL / PLUPOTENTIAL] NERVE	NOT TO DISCOVER WEAKNESS	1054	6
PYRAMIDS			
THOUGH PYRAMIDS DECAY	IT IS AN HONORABLE	946	6
PYRITES			
AS GOLD THE [A] PYRITES WOULD SHUN--	HE PREACHED UPON	1207	6
PYRRHENEES			
TILL WE, WHO SMILED AT PYRRHENEES--	WE MISS A KINSMAN MORE	1087	7
QUAFFING			
WE--BEE AND I--LIVE BY THE QUAFFING--	WE--BEE AND I--LIVE BY	230	1
QUAILED			
MY SOUL--ACCUSED ME--AND I QUAILED--	MY SOUL--ACCUSED ME--AND	753	1
QUAINT			
FIND QUAINT EMPLOY--	MY WHEEL IS IN THE DARK!	10	11
COURTIERS QUAINT, IN KINGDOMS	TAKEN FROM MEN--THIS	53	11
HIS FASHIONS, QUAINT, MOSAIC--	THE ONLY GHOST I EVER	274	7
HIS QUAINT OPINIONS--TO INSPECT--	A PRECIOUS--MOULDERING	371	9
FASHION MY SPIRIT QUAINT--WHITE--	I AM ASHAMED--I HIDE--	473	20
THAN THIS QUAINT CREATURE'S BOOT--	YOU'LL KNOW HER--BY HER	634	5
QUAINT--OR BROKE--	I CANNOT LIVE WITH YOU--	640	10
INTENT UPON IT'S OWN CAREER [MISSION QUAINT / CIRCUIT QUAINT]	HOW SOFT A CATERPILLAR	1448	7
INTENT UPON IT'S OWN CAREER [MISSION QUAINT / CIRCUIT QUAINT]	HOW SOFT A CATERPILLAR	1448	7
REKINDLED BY SOME ACTION QUAINT	A WINGED SPARK DOTH SOAR	1468	9
DOWN TIME'S QUAINT STREAM	DOWN TIME'S QUAINT	1656	1
QUAINTER			
SOME QUAINTER HOLIDAY,	OF ALL THE SOUNDS	321	20
WEARINESS OF HIM, WERE QUAINTER	CONSCIOUS AM I IN MY	679	13

	FIRST LINE	POEM		LINE
QUAINTEST				
HUMMING THE QUAINTEST LULLABY	WHOSE ARE THE LITTLE	142		19
A SEPULCHRE OF QUAINTEST FLOSS--	HE PARTS HIMSELF--LIKE	517		19
IS QUAINTEST DISTANCE [STIFFNESS]--NOW--	THIS THAT WOULD GREET--	778		2
QUAINTLY				
QUAINTLY INFER--EVE'S GREAT SURRENDER--	BETTER--THAN MUSIC! FOR	503		11
HIS SMALL UMBRELLA QUAINTLY HALVED	THE BAT IS DUN, WITH	1575		5
QUAKE				
AND QUAKE--AND TURN AWAY,	NOT SEEING, STILL WE	1518		5
QUAKED				
AND [BUT] NEVER WINCED [SHOOK / QUAKED] BEFORE.	I YEARS HAD BEEN FROM	609		16
QUALIFIED				
TILL QUALIFIED, FOR PEARL--	WE PLAY AT PASTE--	320		2
THAT MAN--BE QUALIFIED	THE PROVINCE OF THE	539		8
BUT STOPPED, WHEN QUALIFIED TO GUESS	I PRAYED, AT FIRST, A	576		3
JUST RECTIFIED [QUALIFIED]--IN THEE	I THINK TO LIVE--MAY BE	646		28
QUALIFY				
TO QUALIFY--	I'M SAYING EVERY DAY	373		19
TO QUALIFY DESPAIR	THE PROVINCE OF THE	539		9
TO QUALIFY THE WIND--	HOW RUTHLESS ARE THE	1439		4
QUALITIES				
NATURE'S QUALITIES--	AFTER THE SUN COMES OUT	1148		8
HER PRACTICES [QUALITIES] EXTEND	NATURE AFFECTS TO BE	1170		4
QUALITY				
CONTRASTING WHICH, MY QUALITY	MY WORTHINESS IS ALL MY	751		3
WITH OTHER QUALITY--	WHO GIANTS KNOW, WITH	796	V	4
THE WORTHINESS [EXCELLENCE / QUALITY] OF SUFFERING LIKE	DESPAIR'S ADVANTAGE IS	799		5
THE QUALITY CONCEIVE [PERCEIVE]	TWO--WERE IMMORTAL TWICE	800		6
A QUALITY OF LOSS	A LIGHT EXISTS IN SPRING	812		17
BRITTLE AND BRIEF IN QUALITY--	A PROMPT--EXECUTIVE BIRD	1177		3
THE EXCELLENCE [QUALITY] DEFIES US--	TO DISAPPEAR ENHANCES--	1209		15
IS JOY'S INSURING QUALITY.	GO NOT TOO NEAR A HOUSE	1434		8
QUANTITY				
OF UNCONJECTURED QUANTITY--	I CROSS TILL I AM WEARY	550		8
THE AMBER QUANTITY--	LEAST BEE THAT BREW--	676		5
WITH HER CHERUBIC QUANTITY--	THE ROBIN IS THE ONE	828		7
QUARRY				
AND THEN A QUARRY PARE	I LIKE TO SEE IT LAP	585		8
GENERIC AS A QUARRY	WINTER IS GOOD--HIS HOAR	1316		5
QUARTER				
OR QUARTER--AS I SIGNIFY--	I MAKE HIS CRESCENT FILL	909		3
QUARTERING				
JUST QUARTERING A TREE--	THE WIND BEGUN TO KNEAD	824		20
QUARTZ				
THAT STIFFENS QUIETLY TO QUARTZ--	I KNOW A PLACE WHERE	337		11
A QUARTZ CONTENTMENT, LIKE A STONE--	AFTER GREAT PAIN, A	341		9
QUEEN				
A MIEN TO MOVE A QUEEN--	A MIEN TO MOVE A QUEEN--	283		1
THE QUEEN, DISCERNS LIKE ME--	THE ROBIN'S MY CRITERION	285		16
SO MUCH, THAT DID I MEET THE QUEEN--	YOUR RICHES--TAUGHT ME--	299		13
AS ANKLES OF A QUEEN--	IT SIFTS FROM LEADEN	311		18
OH PHANTOM QUEEN!	NOT PROBABLE--THE BAREST	346		10
THE QUEEN OF CALVARY--	I DREADED THAT FIRST	348		24
"IF I SHOULD BE A QUEEN, TOMORROW"--	I'M SAYING EVERY DAY	373		2
ONCE--IT WAS A QUEEN--	WHEN DIAMONDS ARE A	397		7
SINCE FOR THE QUEEN, HAVE I--	COULD--I DO MORE--FOR	447		3
NEITHER WOULD BE A QUEEN	LIKE EYES THAT LOOKED ON	458		14
SO UNADORNED--A QUEEN--	THE WORLD--STANDS--	493		12
A HALF [TOO] UNCONSCIOUS [AN INSUFFICIENT] QUEEN--	I'M CEDED--I'VE STOPPED	508		16
SO SAY--IF QUEEN IT BE--	YOU SAID THAT I "WAS	738		13
THE COLOR OF A QUEEN, IS THIS--	THE COLOR OF A QUEEN, IS	776		1
THE BEGGAR AND HIS QUEEN	NOT ANY HIGHER STANDS	1256		6
A QUEEN ADOWN A SATIN AISLE,	A CURIOUS CLOUD	1710		8
QUEEN'S				
I'LL DO SEAMS--A QUEEN'S ENDEAVOR	DONT PUT UP MY THREAD &	617		7
QUEENS				
GARLANDS FOR QUEENS, MAY BE--	GARLANDS FOR QUEENS, MAY	34		1
AND YET, ONE SUMMER, WE WERE QUEENS [WED]--	OURSELVES WERE WED ONE	631		15
QUENCH				
REQUIRING IN THE QUENCH--	MORE LIFE--WENT OUT--	422		4
QUENCHED				
AND BOTH WERE WRECKED [DROWNED / QUENCHED / WHELMED] IN NOON--	TWO BUTTERFLIES WENT OUT	533	V	
QUENCHING				
BLAZING IN GOLD AND QUENCHING IN PURPLE	BLAZING IN GOLD AND	228		1
QUEST				
WHEREFORE IN TIMID QUEST	FOR EVERY BIRD A NEST--	143		2
AND BAFFLES QUEST--	GRIEF IS A MOUSE--	793		4
QUESTION				
HER TROUBLED QUESTION FLINGS--	ONCE MORE, MY NOW	48		4
I QUESTION IF THE ROYAL COACH	I MET A KING THIS	166		25
SO SUNSET SHUTS MY QUESTION DOWN	IT CANT BE "SUMMER"!	221		9
THE QUESTION OF "TO DIE"--	DID YOU EVER STAND IN A	590		12
AND THE CHILDREN--NO FURTHER QUESTION--	GLEE--THE GREAT STORM IS	619		16
QUESTION IF HIS GLORY	ALTER! WHEN THE HILLS DO	729		3
WE QUESTION IF THE MAN--	I PLAY AT RICHES--TO	801		14
QUESTION MEMORY!	THE FIRST DAY THAT I WAS	902		16

	FIRST LINE	POEM	LINE
QUESTION (CONTINUED)			
IDENTITY TO QUESTION [HANDLE]	AS ONE DOES SICKNESS	957	11
THE DEVIL--WITHOUT QUESTION [SO AMENDED--]	THE DEVIL--HAD HE	1479	7
WHICH QUESTION SHALL I CLUTCH--	STILL OWN THEE--STILL	1633	5
QUESTIONED			
PHILIP--WHEN BEWILDERED [QUESTIONED EAGER]	IF THOSE I LOVED WERE	29	7
HE QUESTIONED SOFTLY "WHY I FAILED"?	I DIED FOR BEAUTY--BUT	449	5
I [SHE] NEVER QUESTIONED HER [ME]--	THE BIRDS REPORTED FROM	743	22
WE QUESTIONED TO, AGAIN.	'TIS ANGUISH GRANDER	984	4
QUESTIONING			
A QUESTIONING--DISSOLVES.	THE HEART HAS NARROW	928	12
QUESTIONS			
THE STIFF HEART QUESTIONS WAS IT HE, THAT BORE,	AFTER GREAT PAIN, A	341	3
SO MANY QUESTIONS TO PUT THEM	WHAT DID THEY DO SINCE I	900	3
QUIBBLE			
TELL HIM [HER]--NO--YOU MAY QUIBBLE THERE--	GOING TO HIM! HAPPY	494	15
QUIBBLED			
QUIBBLED THE JAY--	ANSWER JULY--	386	14
QUICK			
QUICK! A SHARPER RUSTLING!	MORNS LIKE THESE--WE	27	11
SAY QUICK, THAT I MAY [SO I CAN] DOWER THEE	DOUBT ME! MY DIM	275	7
AND QUICK ENOUGH, IF TRUE.	THEY LEAVE US WITH THE	350	12
QUICK--LIKE A LIQUOR--	I AM ASHAMED--I HIDE--	473	21
THAT--MAKES THE QUICK OF WO!	IF ANYBODY'S FRIEND BE	509	24
THEMSELVES WERE QUICK--WITH THEE!	ME PROVE IT NOW--WHOEVER	537	16
ACQUIRE THE QUICK OF SKILL--	'TIS ONE BY ONE--THE	545	6
WHEN SWIFT [QUICK] IT SLIPPED IT'S LIMIT--	HE GAVE AWAY HIS LIFE--	567	7
I SOMETIMES DROP IT, FOR A QUICK--	I SOMETIMES DROP IT, FOR	708	1
QUICK [SOON]--SWEET MOUTH--TO MISS THEE SO--	THESE--SAW VISIONS--	758	6
GRIEF IS A THIEF--QUICK STARTLED--	GRIEF IS A MOUSE--	793	5
HER WARM [STRAIGHT / GOOD / QUICK / SAFE] RETURN, IF SO SHE . . .	NO NOTICE GAVE SHE, BUT	804	17
TO MY QUICK EAR THE LEAVES--CONFERRED--	TO MY QUICK EAR THE	891	1
OR QUICK CALAMITY--	THE SOUL'S DISTINCT	974	4
QUICK! BURST THE WINDOWS!	DYING AT MY MUSIC!	1003	4
REPORTLESS SUBJECTS, TO THE QUICK	REPORTLESS SUBJECTS, TO	1048	1
. . . QUICK / SWIFT / WILD] EXPERIMENT [LEGACY / APOCALYPSE / . . .	A LITTLE MADNESS IN THE	1333	5
BEFORE THE QUICK [RIPE / PEAL / DRUM / DRUMS / BELLS / BOMB / . . .	ONE JOY OF SO MUCH	1420	6
SEVENTY YEARS IS SPENT AS QUICK	SUMMER IS SHORTER THAN	1506	3
LET HIM BE QUICK--THE VIAND FLITS [BANQUET COOLS]--	MINE ENEMY IS GROWING	1509	5
QUICKENED			
THAT QUICKENED US LIKE WINE!	IN EBON BOX, WHEN YEARS	169	8
BUT WHEN THE VIVID [QUICKENED] ORE	DARE YOU SEE A SOUL AT	365	4
THE WAGONS QUICKENED ON THE STREET [STREETS]--	THE WIND BEGUN TO KNEAD	824	9
NOT QUICKENED TO PERCEIVE	LIKE MEN AND WOMEN	1105	6
QUICKENING			
AND QUICKENING [RIPENING]--AS WE SOWED--	HE GAVE AWAY HIS LIFE--	567	13
QUICKER			
WITHOUT A QUICKER BLOOD,	I NEVER HEAR THE WORD	77	2
QUICKEST			
THE MADDEST--QUICKEST BY--	IT STRUCK ME--EVERY DAY	362	10
QUICKLY			
AND HE PASSED [WENT] QUICKLY [SOFTLY] ROUND--	WHEN I WAS SMALL, A	596	8
AS QUICKLY AS A SPEAR,	THE SADDEST NOISE, THE	1764	18
QUIET			
MIGHT SCARE THE QUIET FAIRY	THERE'S SOMETHING	45	11
EXCEPT IT QUIET BRING	WE SHOULD NOT MIND SO	81	2
TILL PLEADING, ROUND HER QUIET EYES	SHE BORE IT TILL THE	144	3
SLIPPED QUIET FROM IT'S CHAIR--	ON SUCH A NIGHT, OR SUCH	146	4
SO QUIET--OH HOW QUIET,	ON SUCH A NIGHT, OR SUCH	146	5
SO QUIET--OH HOW QUIET,	ON SUCH A NIGHT, OR SUCH	146	5
IN QUIET "HAWORTH" LAID.	ALL OVERGROWN BY CUNNING	148	4
SHE WENT AS QUIET AS THE DEW	SHE WENT AS QUIET AS THE	149	1
AND THEN TO LAY THEM QUIET BACK--	IN EBON BOX, WHEN YEARS	169	17
AROUND THIS QUIET COURTIER	WAIT TILL THE MAJESTY OF	171	9
THE QUIET NONCHALANCE OF DEATH--	ON THIS LONG STORM THE	194	9
THE QUIET AGES PICKED IT UP--	I MEANT TO HAVE BUT	476	19
SET SEPARATE [PUT QUIET--] FROM THE FARMING--	I'M SORRY FOR THE DEAD--	529	15
AND GOD, A QUIET PARTY	WE TALKED AS GIRLS DO--	586	7
A QUIET--EARTHQUAKE STYLE--	A STILL--VOLCANO--LIFE--	601	5
THIS QUIET DUST WAS GENTLEMEN AND LADIES	THIS QUIET DUST WAS	813	1
LIKING THE QUIET OF THE PLACE	WHO OCCUPIES THIS HOUSE?	892	23
PATIENCE--HAS A QUIET OUTER--	PATIENCE--HAS A QUIET	926	1
IN ITSELF--A QUIET [TRANQUIL] THING	A MAN MAY MAKE A REMARK	952	2
CONTENTMENT'S QUIET SUBURB--	A NEARNESS TO	963	5
WANT--A QUIET COMISSARY	SATISFACTION--IS THE	1036	3
IT WAS A QUIET WAY--	IT WAS A QUIET WAY--	1053	1
IT WAS A QUIET SEEMING DAY--	IT WAS A QUIET SEEMING	1419	1
THE THOUGHT IS [SCENE WAS] QUIET AS A FLAKE--	THE FARTHEST THUNDER	1581	17
QUIETER			
THERE'S SOMETHING QUIETER THAN SLEEP	THERE'S SOMETHING	45	1
QUIETLY			
QUIETLY DID THE SAME--	ALL OVERGROWN BY CUNNING	148	8
THAT STIFFENS QUIETLY TO QUARTZ--	I KNOW A PLACE WHERE	337	11
I FOUND IT QUIETLY ASSUMED	ALONE AND IN A	1167	11

	FIRST LINE	POEM	LINE
QUIETNESS			
A QUIETNESS DISTILLED	AS IMPERCEPTIBLY AS	1540	5
QUIT			
WHO QUIT THEIR SHINING WORKING	TRUSTY AS THE STARS	1369	2
QUITE			
AND EARTH IS QUITE COQUETTISH, AND BESEEMETH IN VAIN TO SUE.	AWAKE YE MUSES NINE,	1	24
I HAV'NT QUITE THE STRENGTH NOW	I HAV'NT TOLD MY GARDEN	50	3
QUITE NONE?	YOU LOVE ME--YOU ARE	156	13
THAT ONE, TO BE QUITE SURE--	I BREATHED ENOUGH TO	272	4
IT DONT SOUND SO TERRIBLE--QUITE--AS IT DID--	IT DONT SOUND SO	426	1
NOT QUITE--CONTENT--	IT'S THOUGHTS--AND JUST	495	28
AND AS ESCAPELESS--QUITE--	A PRISON GETS TO BE A	652	24
A LIFE QUITE READY TO DEPART	THIS CHASM, SWEET, UPON	858	19
QUITE OPPOSITE--HOW COMPLICATE	EXPERIENCE 'S THE ANGLED	910	5
WHILE SHE MUST FINISH QUITE	THE LAST NIGHT THAT SHE	1100	14
OF MANSIONS NEVER QUITE DISCLOSED	THE LIGHTNING IS A	1173	5
AND NEVER QUITE CONCEALED	THE LIGHTNING IS A	1173	6
QUITE EMPTY, QUITE AT REST,	QUITE EMPTY, QUITE AT	1606	1
QUITE EMPTY, QUITE AT REST,	QUITE EMPTY, QUITE AT	1606	1
NOT QUITE WITH HIM AT HOME	IN WINTER IN MY ROOM	1670	6
WE SEE ACUTER [DISTINCTER / SINCERER], QUITE,	BY A DEPARTING LIGHT	1714	2
QUIVER			
THEN QUIVER DOWN--WITH TUFTS OF TUNE--	OF ALL THE SOUNDS	321	7
QUIVERED			
THEN QUIVERED OUT OF DECIMALS--	A CLOCK STOPPED--	287	8
IT QUIVERED THROUGH [BUBBLED IN] THE GRASS	THERE CAME A WIND LIKE A	1593	2
AND TRILLED, AND QUIVERED, AND SHOOK HIS THROAT	A TRAIN WENT THROUGH A	1761	3
QUIVERING			
IN KEEN AND QUIVERING RATIO	FOR EACH EXTATIC INSTANT	125	3
WITH SHAPELESS--QUIVERING--PRAYER--	I THINK JUST HOW MY	237	6
THE DEWS DREW QUIVERING AND CHILL--	BECAUSE I COULD NOT STOP	712	14
THROUGH THE QUIVERING--	PATIENCE--HAS A QUIET	926	8
QUIVERS			
IT [SHE] QUIVERS FROM THE FORGE	DARE YOU SEE A SOUL AT	365	6
QUOTH			
"THOU WERT WITH HIM"--QUOTH "THE DAMSEL"?	HE FORGOT--AND I--	203	5
RABBI			
RABBI OF THE WISE BOOK	KNOWS HOW TO FORGET!	433	V
RACE			
I THINK I'D SHOOT THE HUMAN RACE	MY FRIEND ATTACKS MY	118	7
HELD FAST IN EVERLASTING RACE--	TIE THE STRINGS TO MY	279	11
AND I, AND SILENCE, SOME STRANGE RACE	I FELT A FUNERAL, IN MY	280	15
INVITES THE RACE--	THE NEAREST DREAM	319	4
FORSAKES THE ARCTIC RACE	WHEN THE ASTRONOMER	851	4
IN THY LONG RACE WITH HIM!	MY GOD--HE SEES THEE--	1178	9
AS A FOREIGN RACE--	NOW I KNEW I LOST HER--	1219	6
AT DAY BREAK TO BEGIN HIS RACE	HE WENT BY SLEEP THAT	1662	3
RACES			
TO SATIN RACES--HE IS NOUGHT--	I THINK THE HEMLOCK	525	13
TO RACES--NURTURED IN THE DARK--	I FOUND THE WORDS TO	581	5
. . . [SECOND'S] RACES	WE TALKED WITH EACH	1473	3
RACK			
NO RACK CAN TORTURE ME--	NO RACK CAN TORTURE ME--	384	1
AND ONE--UPON THE RACK--	TRIUMPH--MAY BE OF	455	12
SINCE A RACK COULD'NT COAX A SYLLABLE [AN ANSWER]--NOW	GRIEF IS A MOUSE--	793	17
RACKED			
RACKED--WITH SUSPENSE--	HE STRAINED MY FAITH--	497	7
RACKET			
THE RACKET SHAMED ME SO--	I WAS THE SLIGHTEST IN	486	13
RAFFLE			
RAFFLE FOR MY SOUL!	SOUL, WILT THOU TOSS	139	8
RAFT			
UPON A RAFT OF AIR	COULD I BUT RIDE	661	14
RAFTER			
RAFTER OF SATIN,	SAFE IN THEIR ALABASTER	216	5
NOR RAFTER--HAS [MARS / KNOWS] THAT EDIFICE	THE WAY HOPE BUILDS HIS	1481	3
RAFTERS			
THE STOLID RAFTERS [CENTRES / HOURS / INSTANTS / SECONDS] GLOW	THE SMOULDERING EMBERS	1132	6
RAGGED			
TWO OTHER RAGGED PRINCES	I MET A KING THIS	166	21
A SINGLE RAGGED CHILD--	A TONGUE--TO TELL HIM I	400	4
TO HIM WHOM NEVER RAGGED--COAT	THE BEGGAR LAD--DIES	717	15
RAGS			
IN RAGS MYSTERIOUS AS THESE	IN RAGS MYSTERIOUS AS	117	1
RAIL			
IT WRAPS IT RAIL BY RAIL	IT SIFTS FROM LEADEN	311	10
IT WRAPS IT RAIL BY RAIL	IT SIFTS FROM LEADEN	311	10
ENCLOSED 'TWAS NOT OF RAIL	IT WAS A GRAVE, YET BORE	876	2
RAIMENT			
RAIMENT INSTEAD--OF POMPADOUR--	I AM ASHAMED--I HIDE--	473	11
THE ONLY RAIMENT I SHOULD NEED--	I HAD NO CAUSE TO BE	542	19
WERE HOPELESS, AS THE [A] RAINBOW'S RAIMENT	EACH LIFE CONVERGES TO	680	11
WHAT RAIMENT HONOR HIM THE MOST,	I CANNOT SEE MY SOUL BUT	1262	5
LIKE RAIMENT OF A DREAM--	HOW FITS HIS UMBER COAT	1371	4
RAIN			
FLUNG COLORED, AFTER RAIN,	DELIGHT IS AS THE FLIGHT	257	6

	FIRST LINE	POEM	LINE
RAIN (CONTINUED)			
AND SPILL [TIP] THE SCARLET RAIN--	THE NAME--OF IT--IS	656	8
COOLS--LIKE THE RAIN--	THE WORLD--FEELS DUSTY	715	8
THEN CAME ONE DROP OF GIANT RAIN--	THE WIND BEGUN TO KNEAD	824	15
OUR LITTLE KINSMEN--AFTER RAIN	OUR LITTLE KINSMEN--	885	1
LIKE RAIN IT SOUNDED TILL IT CURVED [SWELLED]	LIKE RAIN IT SOUNDED	1235	1
THAT WAS INDEED THE RAIN--	LIKE RAIN IT SOUNDED	1235	8
AS CASUAL [ODORLESS / INNOCENT] AS RAIN	THE GENTIAN HAS A	1424	6
THE PRETTY RAIN FROM THOSE SWEET EAVES	THE PRETTY RAIN FROM	1426	1
AND ABRIDGES THE RAIN.	THE PARASOL IS THE	1747	4
RAINBOW			
SOME RAINBOW--COMING FROM THE FAIR!	SOME RAINBOW--COMING	64	1
THE RAINBOW NEVER TELLS ME	THE RAINBOW NEVER TELLS	97	1
ON THIS LONG STORM THE RAINBOW ROSE--	ON THIS LONG STORM THE	194	1
NO COLOR IN THE RAINBOW	THE DYING NEED BUT	1026	7
WE SHALL FIND THE CUBE OF THE RAINBOW.	WE SHALL FIND THE CUBE	1484	1
RAINBOW'S			
ALSO, WHO LAID THE RAINBOW'S PIERS,	BRING ME THE SUNSET IN A	128	13
THE RAINBOW'S WAY--	DELIGHT IS AS THE FLIGHT	257	4
AS CHILDREN, TO THE RAINBOW'S SCARF--	AS FAR FROM PITY, AS	496	7
WERE HOPELESS, AS THE [A] RAINBOW'S RAIMENT	EACH LIFE CONVERGES TO	680	11
RAINBOWS			
TOOK RAINBOWS, AS THE COMMON WAY,	DELIGHT IS AS THE FLIGHT	257	16
TO FADE [DIE]--TOMORROW--RAINBOWS HELD [THRUST]	MY FIRST WELL DAY--SINCE	574	15
RAINS			
AS ASIATIC RAINS--	I CROSS TILL I AM WEARY	550	9
THE WEATHER--HOW THE RAINS	MYSELF CAN READ THE	1089	5
RAISE			
THEIR HUNDRED HATS THEY RAISE!	ONE DIGNITY DELAYS FOR	98	12
MY FLOWERS RAISE THEIR PRETTY LIPS--	AS CHILDREN BID THE	133	3
DO SOW, AND RAISE FOR SALE--	WHEN DIAMONDS ARE A	397	4
BLOOM I STROVE TO RAISE--	SOIL OF FLINT, IF STEADY	681	V
HER LEAST ATTENTION RAISE ON ME--	'TWOULD EASE--A	682	14
LOVE CAN DO ALL BUT RAISE THE DEAD	LOVE CAN DO ALL BUT	1731	1
RAISED			
WITH EYES IN DEATH--STILL BEGGING RAISED--	TWO SWIMMERS WRESTLED ON	201	8
A RAISED--ETHERIAL THING!	THE SUN--JUST TOUCHED	232	6
IN KINGDOMS--YOU HAVE HEARD THE RAISED--	THE FACE I CARRY WITH ME	336	7
RAISED SOFTLY TO THE CEILINGS [HORIZONS]--	I WOULD NOT PAINT--A	505	11
WHEN GIRLS TO WOMEN, SOFTLY RAISED	WE TALKED AS GIRLS DO--	586	11
THEN NATURE RAISED A COLORED HAND	A DROP FELL ON THE APPLE	794	V 15
SOME--NEWLY RAISED THIS AFTERNOON,	WHO OCCUPIES THIS HOUSE?	892	11
RAISED FROM OBLIVION	TO BE FORGOT BY THEE	1560	8
RALLIES			
FAITH SLIPS--AND LAUGHS, AND RALLIES--	THIS WORLD IS NOT	501	13
RALLIES HER GLOW [THE WEST], LIKE A DYING FRIEND--	FAIRER THROUGH FADING--	938	5
RALLYING			
THAN DYING HALF [PART]--THEN RALLYING	THE WHOLE OF IT CAME NOT	762	11
RAMBLE			
HE JOINS ME IN MY RAMBLE	THE BLUNDER IS IN	1684	5
RAMBLED			
WHERE I HAVE RAMBLED SO--	I HAV'NT TOLD MY GARDEN	50	10
RAMBLES			
THAT RAMBLES IN THE ROAD ALONE,	HOW HAPPY IS THE LITTLE	1510	2
RAMPANT			
RESTRAINING RAMPANT SQUIRREL--	NATURE--THE GENTLEST	790	7
RAN			
DAY AND I--IN COMPETITION RAN--	I SEND TWO SUNSETS--	308	2
THE NEWS, LIKE SQUIRRELS, RAN--	I'LL TELL YOU HOW THE	318	4
WHAT COMPETITIONS RAN--	A PRECIOUS--MOULDERING	371	14
THE DIMPLES RAN ALONG--	HER SMILE WAS SHAPED	514	2
THESE--ADJUST--THAT RAN TO MEET US--	THESE--SAW VISIONS--	758	12
THE SUN RAN MILES AWAY	THE BIRD DID PRANCE--THE	1107	2
THE FENCES ALL BUT RAN,	THE BIRD DID PRANCE--THE	1107	6
MY HEART RAN SO TO THEE	MY HEART RAN SO TO THEE	1237	1
HE [SHE] RAN AWAY FROM EARTH--	CLIMBING TO REACH THE	1566	4
AND RIVERS WHERE THE HOUSES RAN	THERE CAME A WIND LIKE A	1593	11
RANG			
RANG LOUDEST	I CANNOT LIVE WITH YOU--	640	39
TILL ALL THE CHURCHYARD RANG;	A TRAIN WENT THROUGH A	1761	4
RANGE			
RANGE FROM A SINGLE HUMAN HEART	THE AUCTIONEER OF	1612	7
RANGED			
HER SYSTEMS RANGED [STOLE] ABOUT	THE WIND TOOK UP THE	1134	12
WEEDS TRIUMPHANT RANGED	AFTER A HUNDRED YEARS	1147	5
RANGES			
AFFLICTION RANGES BOUNDLESSNESS--	A NEARNESS TO	963	3
RANK			
AND CLAIM THE RANK TO DIE!	ONE DIGNITY DELAYS FOR	98	16
RANK AFTER RANK, WITH EVEN FEET--	TO FIGHT ALOUD, IS VERY	126	11
RANK AFTER RANK, WITH EVEN FEET--	TO FIGHT ALOUD, IS VERY	126	11
HAD PARTED [BROKEN] RANK,	OF ALL THE SOUNDS	321	31
THE SPANGLED GOWNS, A LESSER RANK	OF TRIBULATION--THESE	325	3
TO TAKE MY RANK--BY--IN THE WEST--	THE FACE I CARRY WITH ME	336	3
RANK--OVERTAKE ME--	I'M SAYING EVERY DAY	373	15
MY SECOND RANK--TOO SMALL THE FIRST--	I'M CEDED--I'VE STOPPED	508	14
A RANK--FOR [THE RANK OF / AN AWE OF--] IODINE--	THE COLOR OF A QUEEN, IS	776	8

	FIRST LINE	POEM	LINE
RANK (CONTINUED)			
A RANK--FOR [THE RANK OF / AN AWE OF--] IODINE--	THE COLOR OF A QUEEN, IS	776	8
GRACE OF RANK--AND GRACE OF FORTUNE	ALL FORGOT FOR	966	V 5
HAS STILL A SILENT RANK.	THE STEM OF A DEPARTED	1520	2
RANKLE			
FORGOT TO RANKLE [ENTER] THERE	ARROWS ENAMORED OF HIS	1629	2
DISDAINED [REFUSED] TO RANKLE THERE--	ARROWS ENAMORED OF HIS	1629	4
RANKS			
TILL RANKS OF SEEDS THEIR WITNESS BEAR--	THESE ARE THE DAYS WHEN	130	10
RANSACK			
SO I BEGIN TO RANSACK!	I CAUTIOUS, SCANNED MY	178	17
RANSOM			
THERE'S RANSOM IN A VOICE--	SILENCE IS ALL WE DREAD.	1251	2
RANSOMED			
RANSOMED FOLKS--WONT LAUGH AT ME--	WHAT IS--"PARADISE"--	215	16
I'VE RANSOMED IT [FOUND IT--'TIS]--ALIVE--	HE TOLD A HOMELY TALE	763	16
RANSOMED FROM YEARS--	LEFT IN IMMORTAL YOUTH	1289	5
THE HAPPY [THE CHEMIST / THE RANSOMED / A LOVER] MAY [CAN] REPAY,	THE FARTHEST THUNDER	1581	10
RAP			
OR RAP--AT PARADISE--UNHEARD	SHOULD YOU BUT FAIL AT--	226	5
RAPID			
BUT RAPID--LIKE THE ROE--	THE ONLY GHOST I EVER	274	6
RAPID! THAT WILL DO!	TIE THE STRINGS TO MY	279	4
HE GLANCED WITH RAPID EYES	A BIRD CAME DOWN THE	328	9
A RAPID--FOOTLESS GUEST--	THE WIND--TAPPED LIKE A	436	5
IF MET, TOO RAPID PASSED,	THE FROST WAS NEVER SEEN	1202	2
GO RAPID, LEST COMPETING DEATH	GO SLOW, MY SOUL, TO	1297	3
HOW RAPID, HOW MOMENTOUS--	WERE NATURE MORTAL LADY	1762	5
RAPIDS			
IN EDDIES OF [FATHOMS IN / RAPIDS OF / GAMBOLS WITH / . . .	TWO BUTTERFLIES WENT OUT	533	V
RAPS			
JUST SO--JESUS [CHRIST]--RAPS--	JUST SO--JESUS--RAPS--	317	1
RAPT			
DEATH, BUT OUR RAPT ATTENTION	THE FEET OF PEOPLE	7	15
RAPT NEIGHBORHOODS OF MEN--	FOREVER AT HIS SIDE TO	246	14
REVEALS THE FACT THAT ONE IS RAPT	HOW NOTELESS MEN, AND	282	3
TOO RAPT WITH FROST	VICTORY COMES LATE--	690	3
RAPTURE			
A DIAGRAM--OF RAPTURE!	A TRANSPORT ONE CANNOT	184	5
TILL RAPTURE MISSED THEM [HER FOOTING-- / PENINSULA]	TWO BUTTERFLIES WENT OUT	533	V
THE RAPTURE OF A FINISHED [CONCLUDED] DAY--	"HEAVEN" HAS DIFFERENT	575	13
THE TRANSPORT [RAPTURE / TRIUMPH / RIOT] OF THE BIRD--	THE WIND TOOK UP THE	1134	16
REMAINED FOR HER--OF RAPTURE	A BEE HIS BURNISHED	1339	11
TO BREATHE--CORRODE THE RAPTURE	THE TREASON OF AN ACCENT	1358	V
WHICH RAPTURE [TRIUMPH / HOUR / MOMENT]-- SHE PREFERRED	CRISIS IS SWEET AND YET	1416	6
THE TRANSPORT [RAPTURE] OF THE BUD	CRISIS IS SWEET AND YET	1416	V 8
A SPECK OF RAPTURE--FIRST PERCEIVED	A WINGED SPARK DOTH SOAR	1468	7
WHILE RAPTURE CHANGED IT'S DRESS	THE THRILL CAME SLOWLY	1495	6
IT'S SOARING [RAPTURE] RESIDENCE.	AS FROM THE EARTH THE	1630	4
IS RAPTURE HERSELF SPURN--	TO DO A MAGNANIMOUS	1699	8
A RAPTURE AS OF LEGACIES--	TO TELL THE BEAUTY WOULD	1700	7
RAPTURE'S			
'TIS RAPTURE'S GERMINATION	THE FASCINATING CHILL	1480	4
BUT RAPTURE'S EXPENSE	RATHER ARID DELIGHT	1679	5
RARE			
LAURELS--FOR RARE DEGREE	GARLANDS FOR QUEENS, MAY	34	2
OF SOME RARE TENANT OF THE MOLD,	A SCIENCE--SO THE SAVANS	100	5
THAT BREWS THAT RARE VARIETY!	THE NEAREST DREAM	319	13
HE HAS HID HIS RARE LIFE	I KNOW THAT HE EXISTS.	338	3
UNOPENED--RARE--UPON THE SHELF--	NOT IN THIS WORLD TO SEE	418	5
ITSELF--A GALLERY [VATICAN] TOO RARE--	IT'S THOUGHTS--AND JUST	495	10
WHOSE RARE--CELESTIAL--STIR--	I WOULD NOT PAINT--A	505	6
CAN ONE FIND THE RARE EAR	GOOD TO HIDE, AND HEAR	842	7
LEGITIMATE, AND RARE--	BEST THINGS DWELL OUT OF	998	4
UPON HIS RARE APPROACH--	GO SLOW, MY SOUL, TO	1297	2
A SNAKE WITH MOTTLES RARE	IN WINTER IN MY ROOM	1670	14
RARER			
AT RARER INTERVALS--	THE LADY FEEDS HER	941	2
NATURE RARER USES YELLOW	NATURE RARER USES YELLOW	1045	1
RASCALITY			
RASCALITY, HEROIC,	"SIC TRANSIT GLORIA	3	43
RASHNESS			
RASHNESS OF CALVARY--	SPURN THE TEMERITY--	1432	2
RAT			
A "MANSION" FOR THE RAT!	PAPA ABOVE!	61	5
THE MOUSE [RAT] BUT A TRADITION NOW	A LITTLE DOG THAT WAGS	1185	11
A RAT SURRENDERED HERE	A RAT SURRENDERED HERE	1340	1
THE RAT IS THE CONCISEST TENANT.	THE RAT IS THE CONCISEST	1356	1
RATES			
FOR THE RATES--LIE HERE--	FOR DEATH--OR RATHER	382	12
RATHER			
RATHER--HEAVEN'S "PETER PARLEY"!	I CANT TELL YOU--BUT YOU	65	17
I'D RATHER CALL HIM "STAR."	"ARCTURUS" IS HIS OTHER	70	2
I HAD RATHER WEAR HER GRACE	PIGMY SERAPHS--GONE	138	12

	FIRST LINE	POEM	LINE
RATHER (CONTINUED)			
I HAD RATHER DWELL LIKE HER	PIGMY SERAPHS--GONE	138	14
I'D RATHER SUIT MY FOOT	IS BLISS THEN, SUCH	340	4
RATHER THAN A MOORING--UNSHARED BY THEE.	HOW SICK--TO WAIT--IN	368	9
RATHER THAN THE "SPICY ISLES--"	HOW SICK--TO WAIT--IN	368	11
ON TWIGS OF SINGING--RATHER HIGH--	I'M SAYING EVERY DAY	373	17
FOR DEATH--OR RATHER	FOR DEATH--OR RATHER	382	1
I'D RATHER BE THE ONE	I WOULD NOT PAINT--A	505	2
I'D RATHER BE THE ONE	I WOULD NOT PAINT--A	505	10
BEQUEATHING--RATHER--TO THEIR WORK--	THE MARTYR POETS--DID	544	6
I WOULD RATHER BE	'TWOULD EASE--A	682	6
POSSIBLY--BUT WE--WOULD RATHER	PUBLICATION--IS THE	709	5
OR RATHER--HE PASSED US--	BECAUSE I COULD NOT STOP	712	13
PROVES IT THERE'S NO SEA, OR RATHER	GRATITUDE--IS NOT THE	989	7
BETTER [RATHER] THAN THE TOMBS	FORTITUDE INCARNATE	1217	12
I'D RATHER RECOLLECT A SETTING	I'D RATHER RECOLLECT A	1349	1
RATHER ARID DELIGHT	RATHER ARID DELIGHT	1679	1
THAT WE HAD RATHER NOT WITH HIM	GOD IS INDEED A JEALOUS	1719	3
RATIFIED			
WAS RATIFIED, THIS WAY--	I GAVE MYSELF TO HIM--	580	4
IN MATTERS RATIFIED?	I WORKED FOR CHAFF AND	1269	4
THAN ANY FEATHER SPECIFIED [RATIFIED / CERTIFIED]	WITH PINIONS OF DISDAIN	1431	3
IS RATIFIED BY DESTINY,	MEETING BY ACCIDENT,	1548	5
RATIO			
VAST--IN IT'S FADING RATIO	AS BY THE DEAD WE LOVE	88	7
IN KEEN AND QUIVERING RATIO	FOR EACH EXTATIC INSTANT	125	3
OR IN THE RATIO OF IT,	DELIGHT IS AS THE FLIGHT	257	2
RATTLE			
COALS--FROM A ROLLING [PASSING] LOAD--RATTLE--HOW--NEAR--	I COULD DIE--TO KNOW--	570	9
SYSTEMS RATTLE FROM	REVOLUTION IS THE POD	1082	2
RATTLES			
DAY--RATTLES--TOO	I KNOW SOME LONELY	289	31
RAVAGE			
BUT IT WOULD RAVAGE THEIR'S--	I SHALL NOT MURMUR IF AT	1410	6
RAVELLED			
BUT SEQUENCE RAVELLED OUT OF SOUND [REACH]	I FELT A CLEAVING IN MY	937	7
BUT SEQUENCE RAVELLED OUT OF SOUND	THE DUST BEHIND I STROVE	992	3
RAVELLING			
YOU DROPPED A PURPLE RAVELLING IN--	SHE SWEEPS WITH	219	5
RAVES			
SAFE DESPAIR IT IS THAT RAVES--	SAFE DESPAIR IT IS THAT	1243	1
RAVINE			
WE HUNTED HIM TO HIS RAVINE	THE FROST OF DEATH WAS	1136	16
RAVISHED			
SAINTS, WITH RAVISHED SLATE AND PENCIL	I CANT TELL YOU--BUT YOU	65	3
THAT RAVISHED ALL THE HILL--	GOD MADE A LITTLE	442	6
WOULD NOT SO RAVISHED TURN--	HE TOUCHED ME, SO I LIVE	506	15
SHOULD STAB MY RAVISHED SPIRIT	ONE JOY OF SO MUCH	1420	7
IN RAVISHED [DAZZLING / SIMPLE] HOLINESS--	THE THRILL CAME SLOWLY	1495	8
LIKE THAT WHICH RAVISHED THEE!	IMMURED IN HEAVEN!	1594	5
RAW			
AND ATE THE FELLOW, RAW,	A BIRD CAME DOWN THE	328	4
PRICKLED BLUE [RAW] AND COOL--	WHEN I HOPED, I	768	14
INTO THE PRECINCT [MINUTE] RAW	DREAMS ARE THE SUBTLE	1376	5
RAY			
I [WE] KEEP ONE RAY	OF THEIR PECULIAR LIGHT	1362	2
RAYS			
AND DECKS [BRIMS / FILLS / SWELLS] THE RAYS	BY A DEPARTING LIGHT	1714	6
REACH			
WITHIN MY REACH!	WITHIN MY REACH!	90	1
SHOULD REACH SO SMALL A GOAL!	ON SUCH A NIGHT, OR SUCH	146	24
SHOULD REACH THE HEART THAT WANTED ME--	I SHOULD NOT DARE TO	205	4
"HEAVEN"--IS WHAT I CANNOT REACH!	"HEAVEN"--IS WHAT I	239	1
THROUGH WHICH MEN REACH	PRAYER IS THE LITTLE	437	2
FOR ANY SANTA CLAUS TO REACH	'TWAS JUST THIS TIME,	445	19
WHO KNOWS--BUT WE'D REACH THE SUN?	LOVE--THOU ART HIGH--	453	12
YOU TRY TO TOUCH [REACH] THE SMILE	IF ANYBODY'S FRIEND BE	509	14
TO SEE [REACH / TOUCH] THIS CURIOUS FRIEND--	MY PERIOD HAD COME FOR	564	8
ON EVERY SHOULDER THAT SHE MET [SHE COULD REACH]--	MY FIRST WELL DAY--SINCE	574	21
TO REACH	EACH LIFE CONVERGES TO	680	10
SEE THE BIRD--REACH IT!	OUT OF SIGHT? WHAT OF	703	2
AND HELP BELIEF TO STRETCH [REACH]--	REMORSE--IS MEMORY--	744	8
BUT SEQUENCE RAVELLED OUT OF SOUND [REACH]	I FELT A CLEAVING IN MY	937	7
WHERE NATURE'S TEMPER CANNOT [COULD NOT] REACH	THE CLOUDS THEIR BACKS	1172	7
WITHIN IT'S REACH [HOPE], THOUGH YET [AND JUST] UNGRASPED	WHO NEVER WANTED--	1430	5
I STILL CAN REACH [TOUCH] THE TOP	THE PILE OF YEARS IS NOT	1507	6
CLIMBING TO REACH [WHO "MEDDLED" WITH] THE COSTLY HEARTS	CLIMBING TO REACH THE	1566	1
I DID NOT REACH THEE	I DID NOT REACH THEE	1664	1
OUT OF REACH OF SKILL--	DEATH IS LIKE THE INSECT	1716	10
REACHED			
SHE REACHED THE ASPHODEL!	ALL OVERGROWN BY CUNNING	148	V
TILL WHEN THEY REACHED THE OTHER SIDE,	I'LL TELL YOU HOW THE	318	13
THAT WAGON NEVER REACHED--	A HOUSE UPON THE HIGHT--	399	2
UNTIL THE MOSS HAD REACHED OUR LIPS--	I DIED FOR BEAUTY--BUT	449	11
IF END I GAINED [REACHED]	FROM BLANK TO BLANK--	761	6

	FIRST LINE	POEM	LINE
REACHED (CONTINUED)			
MAY BE EASIER REACHED [BETTER ATTAINED / EASIER GAINED]--THIS WAY--	BY MY WINDOW HAVE I FOR	797	8
I REACHED THE STOLID BLISS	THROUGH WHAT TRANSPORTS	1153	2
REACHES			
HE REACHES [COMES TO] TOWN AT NIGHTFALL--	THE GUEST IS GOLD AND	15	5
IT REACHES TO THE FENCE--	IT SIFTS FROM LEADEN	311	9
THE RIVER REACHES TO MY FEET--	ME PROVE IT NOW--WHOEVER	537	5
THE RIVER REACHES TO MY BREAST--	ME PROVE IT NOW--WHOEVER	537	9
THE RIVER REACHES TO MY MOUTH--	ME PROVE IT NOW--WHOEVER	537	13
A LITTLE FURTHER REACHES--INSTEAD--	THE BLACK BERRY--WEARS A	554	11
THAT REACHES TO OUR UTMOST HAIR	WE LIKE A HAIRBREADTH	1175	7
REACHING			
REACHING LATE HIS FLOWER,	COME SLOWLY--EDEN!	211	5
WHILE I WAS REACHING HIM--	A DYING TIGER--MOANED	566	11
READ			
IT IS NOT HYMN FROM PULPIT READ--	MUSICIANS WRESTLE	157	10
THOSE WHO READ THE "REVELATIONS"	IF THE FOOLISH, CALL	168	5
THOSE WHO READ THE SAME EDITION--	IF THE FOOLISH, CALL	168	7
READ--SWEET--HOW OTHERS--STROVE--	READ--SWEET--HOW OTHERS	260	1
READ THEN--OF FAITH--	READ--SWEET--HOW OTHERS	260	8
NOW--WHEN I READ--I READ NOT--	DEATH SETS A THING	360	17
NOW--WHEN I READ--I READ NOT--	DEATH SETS A THING	360	17
I READ MY SENTENCE--STEADILY--	I READ MY SENTENCE--	412	1
SOUNDS LONG--UNTIL I READ THE PLACE	NOT IN THIS WORLD TO SEE	418	2
I READ IN AN OLD FASHIONED BOOK	I KNOW WHERE WELLS GROW	460	13
I READ THAT FOREIGN LADY--	I THINK I WAS ENCHANTED	593	3
THE WAY I READ A LETTER'S--THIS [SO]--	THE WAY I READ A	636	1
WERE PAGES WHERE TO READ	THE HOLLOWS ROUND HIS	955	2
HAD IT BEEN YOUR'S, TO READ!	ENDED, ERE IT BEGUN--	1088	6
MYSELF CAN READ THE TELEGRAMS	MYSELF CAN READ THE	1089	1
CAN READ WITHOUT IT'S GLASSES	BELSHAZZAR HAD A LETTER	1459	7
READINESS			
BUT HAD THEY THE FELICITY [HAD THE READINESS]	WHO WERE "THE FATHER AND	1258	13
READING			
NOW TO THE APPLICATION, TO THE READING OF THE ROLL,	AWAKE YE MUSES NINE,	1	25
READS			
TIM--READS A LITTLE HYMN--	WE DONT CRY--TIM AND I,	196	17
READY			
I HOPE I'M READY FOR "THE WORST"--	"ARCTURUS" IS HIS OTHER	70	24
THEN, I AM READY TO GO!	TIE THE STRINGS TO MY	279	2
THEN [NOW]--I AM READY TO GO!	TIE THE STRINGS TO MY	279	16
AND GET THE DIMPLES READY--	WHEN NIGHT IS ALMOST	347	5
BETTER TO BE READY--	I'M SAYING EVERY DAY	373	26
A LIFE QUITE READY TO DEPART	THIS CHASM, SWEET, UPON	858	19
BUT NATURE WILL BE READY	WERE NATURE MORTAL LADY	1762	7
REAL			
THEIR BANQUET'S REAL [TRUE]--	ONE YEAR AGO--JOTS WHAT?	296	11
THE REAL ONE DIED FOR THEE--	'TWAS LOVE--NOT ME--	394	3
BY SO MUCH--AS 'TWAS REAL--	HER SWEET WEIGHT ON MY	518	12
THAT I ESTEEM THE FICTION--REAL [TRUE]--	I THINK TO LIVE--MAY BE	646	23
THE REAL [TRUTH]--FICTITIOUS SEEMS--	I THINK TO LIVE--MAY BE	646	24
TO OUR ENDEAVOR--NOT SO REAL [TRUE / CLOSE / NEAR]	A PRISON GETS TO BE A	652	19
HE'LL SIGH--"THE OTHER--[REAL ONE] SHE--IS WHERE?"	FITTER TO SEE HIM, I MAY	968	20
AND TRUE [BEST / REAL / BLAND / FINE / FAIR] THE OTHER . . .	I'D RATHER RECOLLECT A	1349	4
"BODY!" THEN REAL--A FACE AND EYES--	"AND WITH WHAT BODY DO	1492	5
REAL MEMORY, LIKE CEDAR FEET	YOU CANNOT MAKE	1508	7
REALITY			
NO NEARER--LEST THE ACTUAL--[REALITY-- / ITS PENURY-- / THE . . .	WHO NEVER WANTED--	1430	7
AS MADE REALITY A DREAM	WITHIN THAT LITTLE HIVE	1607	3
AND DREAMS, REALITY--	WITHIN THAT LITTLE HIVE	1607	4
REALLY			
WILL THERE REALLY BE A "MORNING"?	WILL THERE REALLY BE A	101	1
SAY IF IT'S REALLY--WARM AT NOON--	MAKE ME A PICTURE OF THE	188	9
REALM			
AS TONE OF REALM	A MIEN TO MOVE A QUEEN--	283	20
OFTENER THROUGH REALM OF BRIAR	FAR FROM LOVE THE	1021	3
DISTANCE--IS NOT THE REALM OF FOX	DISTANCE--IS NOT THE	1155	1
BEYOND THE REALM OF BIRD--	A WIND THAT ROSE	1259	5
UNTIL THE REALM OF YOU--	BECAUSE THAT YOU ARE	1260	20
HE RELEGATES THE REALM,	FROM HIS SLIM PALACE IN	1300	2
RICHES AND NAME AND REALM--	FRIGID AND SWEET HER	1318	6
HAS HE NO ADDED REALM	HOW SOFT THIS PRISON IS	1334	6
HAS "ALL" A FURTHER REALM--	UNTO THE WHOLE--HOW ADD?	1341	2
THAT SUCH A REALM COULD BE--	I SUED THE NEWS--YET	1360	2
THE REALM OF [LOVING] YOU--	I HAVE NO LIFE BUT THIS	1398	8
WHATEVER REALM I FORFEIT, LORD,	TO OWN A SUSAN OF MY OWN	1401	3
I SCANNED HIS NARROW REALM [GRANT]	IT CAME HIS TURN TO BEG	1500	5
IN WHATSOEVER REALM--	OBTAINING BUT OUR OWN	1543	2
THAT DEVASTATED CHILDHOOD'S REALM,	SOFTENED BY TIME'S	1738	7
ITS OTHER REALM OF SEA.	TO LOSE THEE--SWEETER	1754	6
REALMS			
AND REALMS--JUST DROSS--	MY REWARD FOR BEING, WAS	343	5
OVER REALMS OF ORCHARDS	ON THE WORLD YOU COLORED	1171	5
DITCHES FOR REALMS AND A TRIP TO JAIL	THE POPULAR HEART IS A	1226	7

	FIRST LINE	POEM	LINE
REALMS (CONTINUED)			
IS BETTER [SWEETER] THAN ENAMELED REALMS	THE CLOVER'S SIMPLE FAME	1232	3
TO UNDEPICTED [UNREPORTED] REALMS	TALK NOT TO ME OF SUMMER	1634	8
THY FELLOWS ARE THEY REALMS OR THEMES	THE LOOK OF THEE, WHAT	1689	5
THE CASPIAN HAS ITS REALMS OF SAND,	TO LOSE THEE--SWEETER	1754	5
REAPERS			
AND NO REAPERS STAND!	THO' MY DESTINY BE	163	16
REAP'ST			
WILT HAVE NO KIND COMPANION, THOU REAP'ST WHAT THOU HAST SOWN.	AWAKE YE MUSES NINE,	1	28
REAR			
AN HOUR TO REAR SUPREME	THE SPIDER HOLDS A	605	9
REMEMBRANCE HAS A REAR AND FRONT--	REMEMBRANCE HAS A	1182	1
REARED			
REARED BY ITSELF--	AN HONEST TEAR	1192	5
REARRANGE			
REARRANGE A "WIFE'S" AFFECTION!	REARRANGE A "WIFE'S"	1737	1
REARS			
STILL REARS THE EAST HER AMBER FLAG--	A SOMETHING IN A	122	16
REASON			
AND THEN A PLANK IN REASON, BROKE,	I FELT A FUNERAL, IN MY	280	17
I REASON, EARTH IS SHORT--	I REASON, EARTH IS SHORT	301	1
I REASON, WE COULD [SHOULD] DIE--	I REASON, EARTH IS SHORT	301	5
I REASON, THAT IN HEAVEN--	I REASON, EARTH IS SHORT	301	9
MY REASON--LIFE--	OF COURSE--I PRAYED--	376	6
OF THAT REVOLVING REASON	DID LIFE'S PENURIOUS	1717	6
REASONABLE			
PRICES REASONABLE--	FLOSS WONT SAVE YOU FROM	1322	8
REASONS			
REASONS THE DAFFODIL	LIKE HER THE SAINTS	60	11
AND REASONS NOT CONTAINED--	"WHY DO I LOVE" YOU, SIR	480	14
DEATH DOUBTS IT--ARGUES [REASONS] FROM THE GROUND--	DEATH IS A DIALOGUE	976	5
REBECCA			
REBECCA, TO JERUSALEM,	HE TOUCHED ME, SO I LIVE	506	14
REBELLED			
MY SYLLABLE REBELLED--	I COULD SUFFICE FOR HIM,	643	6
REBELS			
TO NOTE THE REBELS DOWN.	I COUNTED TILL THEY	36	4
REBUILT			
REBUILT ANOTHER MORNING [IN TIME NEXT MORNING / WITHOUT . . .	THE LARGEST FIRE EVER	1114	7
REBUKE			
REBUKE IT IF WE CAN	BLISS IS THE PLAYTHING	1553	4
REBUKED			
DESERTS--NEVER REBUKED HER SATIN--	CIVILIZATION--SPURNS--	492	3
RECALL			
NOT ANY CAN RECALL--	THE SYMPTOM OF THE GALE	1327	10
RECALLLESS			
IN THE RECALLLESS SEA?	STILL OWN THEE--STILL	1633	8
RECALLS			
PERHAPS, RECALLS THE MAN	EACH SECOND IS THE LAST	879	2
RECALLS TO IMMORTALITY--	SUMMER BEGINS TO HAVE	1682	16
RECANT			
PERMISSION TO RECANT--	THEY PUT US FAR APART--	474	17
RECEDE			
I HEARD RECEDE THE DISAPPOINTED TIDE!	JUST LOST, WHEN I WAS	160	6
RECEDED			
THESE RECEDED TO ACCOSTAL	KNOCK WITH TREMOR--	1325	V 6
RECEDES			
THE NEAREST [MADDEST] DREAM RECEDES--UNREALIZED--	THE NEAREST DREAM	319	1
RECEDING			
THEN GAY ABOVE RECEDING GRASS	COCOON ABOVE! COCOON	129	8
RETREATING [RECEDING] MOUNTAIN!	AH, TENERIFFE!	666	2
BUT HIS RECEDING SWELL	THE LONG SIGH OF THE	1359	5
TO HER RESCINDED [SURRENDERED / RECEDING / DEPARTED / . . .	CRISIS IS SWEET AND YET	1416	8
RECEIPT			
IN THE RECEIPT--IT WAS THE DISTANCE--	UNDUE SIGNIFICANCE A	439	8
A TRANSPORT MAY [MIGHT] RECEIPT US	THE PAST IS SUCH A	1203	3
RECEIPTED			
. . . RECEIPTED / EXPENDED] BUD	CRISIS IS SWEET AND YET	1416	8
WERE A RECEIPTED BLISS	THE ECSTASY TO GUESS	1608	2
RECEIPTED WITH ENCORES	TALK NOT TO ME OF SUMMER	1634	V
RECEIVE			
THE DAISY, TO RECEIVE,	GREAT CAESAR! CONDESCEND	102	2
RECEIVE ME CORDIALLY--	THE BEE IS NOT AFRAID OF	111	4
THAT WILL RECEIVE [DELAYING ITS] REPLY	ONE JOY OF SO MUCH	1420	10
WHICH NEVER TO RECEIVE	TO SEE HER IS A PICTURE	1568	V
RECEIVED SEE RECIEVED			
TO BE RECEIVED AS HIGH--	WHEN I COUNT THE SEEDS	40	6
I--TOO--RECEIVED THE SIGN.	OURSELVES WERE WED ONE	631	8
THE ROSE RECEIVED HIS VISIT	A BEE HIS BURNISHED	1339	5
RECEIVES			
THE BEE DOTH COURT THE FLOWER, THE FLOWER HIS SUIT RECEIVES,	AWAKE YE MUSES NINE,	1	13
RECEIVES IT'S ANNUAL REPLY!	AN ALTERED LOOK ABOUT	140	16
RECEIVES UNBLUSHINGLY!	WAIT TILL THE MAJESTY OF	171	16

	FIRST LINE	POEM	LINE
RECEIVING			
RECEIVING [BEHOLDING]--WHERE WE--PRAY--	THOSE FAIR--FICTITIOUS	499	16
RECENTLY			
TILL, RECENTLY A RIVAL CLAIM	I HAD SOME THINGS THAT I	116	3
WAS RECENTLY AMONG US--	WE LEARN IN THE	1083	3
RECEPTACLE			
BUT IN THIS BLACK RECEPTACLE	HIS HEART WAS DARKER	1378	3
RECEPTION			
FIT FOR HER RECEPTION--NOW--	THESE--SAW VISIONS--	758	15
RECESS			
IN "RECESS"--OVERHEAD!	A FEATHER FROM THE	161	8
AND RECESS--NEVER COMES--	I NEVER FELT AT HOME--	413	6
AT RECESS--IN THE RING--	BECAUSE I COULD NOT STOP	712	10
RECIEVED			
THE SWEETEST HERESY RECIEVED	THE SWEETEST HERESY	387	1
RECITATION			
TO SUBLIMER RECITATION	I CANT TELL YOU--BUT YOU	65	19
PERISH IN THE RECITATION--	DRAMA'S VITALLEST	741	4
RECITE			
WHILE I REPEAT [RECITE] YOUR	SANG FROM THE HEART,	1059	15
THE HEROISM WE RECITE	WE NEVER KNOW HOW HIGH	1176	5
RECITED			
RECITED FLUENT--HERE--	I SHOULD HAVE BEEN TOO	313	12
RECKON			
RECKON THE MORNING'S FLAGON'S UP	BRING ME THE SUNSET IN A	128	2
I RECKON--WHEN I COUNT AT ALL--	I RECKON--WHEN I COUNT	569	1
RECKONED			
BE RECKONED UP?	IF PAIN FOR PEACE	63	6
RECKONS			
LOVE RECKONS BY ITSELF--ALONE--	LOVE RECKONS BY ITSELF--	826	1
RECOGNITION			
FOR LOWER RECOGNITION [INTERRUPTION]	THE SOUL'S SUPERIOR	306	7
SIMPLE SALUTE--AND CERTAIN RECOGNITION--	IT'S COMING--THE	390	5
SUN--WITHDRAWN TO RECOGNITION--	STRUCK, WAS I, NOR YET	925	11
IT'S [THAT] BELOVED RECOGNITION	STRUCK, WAS I, NOR YET	925	19
TILL SUMMONED TO HIS RECOGNITION	FACTS BY OUR SIDE ARE	1497	7
AND RECOGNITION LAZY--	THE SUMMER THAT WE DID	1773	4
RECOGNIZE			
YOU'D SCARCE RECOGNIZE HIM!	A FUZZY FELLOW, WITHOUT	173	16
DOST RECOGNIZE THE LOVE?	ME PROVE IT NOW--WHOEVER	537	12
ONE ART TO RECOGNIZE, MUST BE,	HER GRACE IS ALL SHE HAS	810	3
BUT MEEKLY RECOGNIZE	THE LADY FEEDS HER	941	4
I RECOGNIZE YOUR OWN--	BECAUSE THAT YOU ARE	1260	24
RECOGNIZED			
SHE RECOGNIZED THE FOOT--	SHE SLEPT BENEATH A TREE	25	4
HE RECOGNIZED HIS MAKER--OVERTURNED THE DECALOGUE--	THE BOBOLINK IS GONE--	1591	8
RECOGNIZING			
RECOGNIZING IN PROCESSION	SMILING BACK FROM	385	5
RECOLLECT			
I RECOLLECT IT WELL!	WENT UP A YEAR THIS	93	2
COULD DIMLY RECOLLECT A GRACE [FORCE]--	I GOT SO I COULD HEAR	293	13
HER GREEN PEOPLE RECOLLECT IT	NATURE--SOMETIMES SEARS	314	3
AS FREEZING PERSONS, RECOLLECT THE SNOW--	AFTER GREAT PAIN, A	341	12
THEN RECOLLECT A BALL, SHE GOT--	HER SMILE WAS SHAPED	514	5
KNOCK--RECOLLECT--TO ME--	I HAD NO CAUSE TO BE	542	8
TO CHERISH, AND [RECOLLECT] TO WRITE	WE TALKED AS GIRLS DO--	586	14
AND SHIVER FOR [RECOLLECT] THE POOR--	THE NIGHT WAS WIDE, AND	589	16
IT CANNOT RECOLLECT	PAIN--HAS AN ELEMENT OF	650	2
TO RECOLLECT HOW BUSY GRASS	'TIS GOOD--THE LOOKING	660	5
WHEN I HOPED, I RECOLLECT	WHEN I HOPED, I	768	1
WHEN I FEARED--I RECOLLECT	WHEN I HOPED, I	768	9
THE HIGHT I RECOLLECT--	JOY TO HAVE MERITED THE	788	17
I SCARCELY RECOLLECT TO STARVE	THE LUXURY TO APPREHEND	815	7
THEY'LL RECOLLECT HOW COLD I LOOKED	THEY WONT FROWN ALWAYS--	874	3
I RECOLLECT IT--HOW STILL--	THE FIRST DAY THAT I WAS	902	2
I RECOLLECT IT--AS WELL--	THE FIRST DAY THAT I WAS	902	4
THAT WE BUT RECOLLECT THE ONE	THERE IS A JUNE WHEN	930	15
THE FIRST THAT I COULD RECOLLECT	A LOSS OF SOMETHING EVER	959	2
JEHOVAH--RECOLLECT--	NO OTHER CAN REDUCE	982 V	8
AND CEASE TO RECOLLECT	THE PROPS ASSIST THE	1142	6
RECOLLECT THE WAY--	AFTER A HUNDRED YEARS	1147	10
RECOLLECT THE FACE OF ME	RECOLLECT THE FACE OF ME	1305	1
I'D RATHER RECOLLECT A SETTING	I'D RATHER RECOLLECT A	1349	1
FOR ONE MUST RECOLLECT	TO BE FORGOT BY THEE	1560 V	10
RECOLLECTED			
WHO RECOLLECTED US	I ROSE--BECAUSE HE SANK	616	18
I RECOLLECTED [ROSE TO COMFORT--] HER--	THE BIRDS REPORTED FROM	743	16
WE COMPREHENDED [POSTULATED / RECOLLECTED] BY THE AWE	IT WAS A QUIET SEEMING	1419	10
RECOLLECTING			
GAMBLERS--RECOLLECTING WHICH	WE LOSE--BECAUSE WE WIN	21	2
IF RECOLLECTING [OH IF REMEMBERING] WERE FORGETTING,	IF RECOLLECTING WERE	33	1
AND IF FORGETTING, RECOLLECTING,	IF RECOLLECTING WERE	33	3
FOR RECOLLECTING SUCH AS WENT--	YOU'LL FIND--IT WHEN YOU	610	3
BUT THE RECOLLECTING OF BLOOM	HOW HAPPY I WAS IF I	898	4
ALL FORGOT FOR [THROUGH] RECOLLECTING	ALL FORGOT FOR	966	1
RECOLLECTION			
PUTS RECOLLECTION NUMB--	THAT AFTER HORROR--THAT	286	8

	FIRST LINE	POEM	LINE
RECOLLECTION (CONTINUED)			
SEEMS SUMMER'S RECOLLECTION	LIKE SOME OLD FASHIONED	302	3
THE RECOLLECTION PLAYS--	OVER AND OVER, LIKE A	367	2
RECOLLECTION'S			
FROM RECOLLECTION'S FLOOR	THE PILE OF YEARS IS NOT	1507	4
RECOLLECTS			
HE RECOLLECTS IT WELL.	ONE CROWN THAT NO ONE	1735	8
RECOMPENSE			
THEN MY FACE TAKE HER RECOMPENSE-- . . .	I HAD NOT MINDED--WALLS	398	7
HER NIGHT DOTH HARDLY RECOMPENSE	SHE HIDETH HER THE LAST	557	3
OH, REWARD [RECOMPENSE] OF ANGUISH, . . .	IN FALLING TIMBERS	614	11
RECORD			
EVANGELISTS [AS GENESIS] RECORD, ...	A LITTLE EAST OF JORDAN,	59	2
LINGERS TO RECORD THEE--	SOUL, WILT THOU TOSS	139	6
PASSED OUT--OF RECORD	READ--SWEET--HOW OTHERS	260	14
NOT ON RECORD--BUBBLED OTHER, ...	HER--"LAST POEMS"--	312	4
NOR HISTORY--RECORD IT--	THE BATTLE FOUGHT	594	9
THOUGH THE "ROMEO" LEFT [LEAVE] NO RECORD .	DRAMA'S VITALLEST	741	10
RECORDED			
THERE'S ONLY ONE RECORDED, ...	ONE SISTER HAVE I IN OUR	14	3
ONE CRUCIFIXION IS RECORDED--ONLY-- . . .	ONE CRUCIFIXION IS	553	1
ONLY THEATRE RECORDED	DRAMA'S VITALLEST	741	14
RECORDING			
RECORDING BRIEFLY--"LOST"--	I KNOW A PLACE WHERE	337	4
RECORDLESS			
RECORDLESS COMPANY--	ALONE, I CANNOT BE--	298	3
RECORDLESS, BUT FOR THEM--	IT SIFTS FROM LEADEN	311	16
RECORDS			
BUT LONG RECORDS THE LADY'S NAME	THE ROBIN FOR THE CRUMB	864	3
RECOUNTING			
RECOUNTING NECTARS HE HAS KNOWN	HIS ORIENTAL HERESIES	1526	V
RECOVER			
RECOVER IT TO NATURE	ENDANGER IT, AND THE	1658	5
RECOVERED			
FOUR--HAVE RECOVERED THE LAND--	GLEE--THE GREAT STORM IS	619	2
RECOVERER			
IS NO RECOVERER--	THE TREASON OF AN ACCENT	1358	4
RECTIFIED			
JUST RECTIFIED [QUALIFIED]--IN THEE . . .	I THINK TO LIVE--MAY BE	646	28
RECTITUDE			
OURSELF--AND RECTITUDE--	ON A COLUMNAR SELF--	789	10
TILL RECTITUDE IS SUFFOCATE	THE WORTHLESSNESS OF	1373	V 4
RECURRENT			
FOREVER IS DECIDUOUS [RECURRENT]-- . . .	SUMMER HAS TWO	1422	11
RECURRENT TO THE AFTER MIND [THOUGHT] . .	THEIR BARRICADE AGAINST	1471	9
RECUSANCE			
IN RECUSANCE AUGUST.	PRAISE IT--'TIS DEAD--	1384	9
RED			
ONE IN THE RED ARRAY--	SLEEP IS SUPPOSED TO BE	13	14
THE MAPLE'S LOOM IS RED--	THE GENTIAN WEAVES HER	18	2
JUST AS THE DAWN WAS RED	ADRIFT! A LITTLE BOAT	30	10
A LADY RED--AMID THE HILL	A LADY RED--AMID THE	74	1
BURY ME, IN SUCH A SHROUD OF RED!	IF THIS IS "FADING"	120	4
HIS CARAVAN OF RED--	A SOMETHING IN A	122	18
BARTSIA, IN THE BLANKET RED--	WHOSE ARE THE LITTLE	142	15
WHEN APRIL WOODS ARE RED.	WHOSE ARE THE LITTLE	142	28
THE RED UPON THE HILL	THE MURMUR OF A BEE	155	6
GIVE THE ONE IN RED CRAVAT, ...	IF I SHOULD'NT BE ALIVE	182	3
IS LEAKING--RED--	IF HE DISSOLVE--THEN--	236	13
RED--IS THE FIRE'S COMMON TINT--	DARE YOU SEE A SOUL AT	365	3
WHEN THE EAST IS RED?	GOOD MORNING--MIDNIGHT--	425	10
I'D SO MUCH JOY--I TOLD IT--RED--	IT WOULD NEVER BE COMMON	430	9
I THOUGHT JUST HOW RED--APPLES WEDGED . .	'TWAS JUST THIS TIME,	445	9
THE RED--BLAZE--IS THE MORNING--	THE RED--BLAZE--IS THE	469	1
LIKE MIGHTY FOOT LIGHTS--BURNED THE RED .	LIKE MIGHTY FOOT LIGHTS	595	1
WHOLE GULFS--OF RED, AND FLEETS--OF RED-- .	WHOLE GULFS--OF RED, AND	658	1
WHOLE GULFS--OF RED, AND FLEETS--OF RED-- .	WHOLE GULFS--OF RED, AND	658	1
DAY--DROPS YOU HER [HIS] RED ADIEU! . . .	AH, TENERIFFE!	666	5
IF WHITE--A RED--MUST BE!	THE ZEROES--TAUGHT US--	689	6
RED PILGRIM, HE AND I--	DEPRIVED OF OTHER	773	10
THE FLOWER--DISTINCT AND RED--	IT BLOOMED AND DROPT, A	978	2
HAVE A TINT TOO RED	SANG FROM THE HEART,	1059	4
RED AS A CARDINAL FLOWER	WHITE AS AN INDIAN PIPE	1250	2
I DECLARE--HOW RED THEIR FACES GREW-- . .	DEAR MARCH--COME IN--	1320	13
AND IN CHINTZ [RED / PINK] THE APPLE . . .	I SUPPOSE THE TIME WILL	1381	8
TILL WHEN THE RED DECLINED--	THESE HELD THEIR WICK	1390	2
THERE STRAYED AN ACCIDENTAL RED	IT WAS A QUIET SEEMING	1419	4
. . . BURST / FLAGS / STEP / TICK / SHOUTS / PINK / RED / . . .	ONE JOY OF SO MUCH	1420	6
"RED SEA," INDEED! TALK NOT TO ME	"RED SEA," INDEED! TALK	1642	1
HOW RED THE FIRE ROCKS BELOW	ON MY VOLCANO GROWS THE	1677	5
REDBREAST			
I--WITH MY REDBREAST--	I SHALL KEEP SINGING!	250	5
THE REDBREAST OF THE BARN--	HE TOLD A HOMELY TALE	763	8
REDDEN			
THE WILD ROSE--REDDEN IN THE BOG--	IT WILL BE SUMMER--	342	13
REDDER			
A CHEEK IS ALWAYS REDDER	A WOUNDED DEER--LEAPS	165	7
AND REDDER CHEEKED ONES--IN THEIR STEAD [PLACE]--	MY FIRST WELL DAY--SINCE	574	11

	FIRST LINE	POEM	LINE
REDDEST			
OUR REDDEST SECOND PALE.	A MOTH THE HUE OF THIS	841	4
REDECKED			
RETRIMMED IT'S MASTS--REDECKED IT'S SAILS--	ADRIFT! A LITTLE BOAT	30	12
REDEEM			
OR POSTURE--TO REDEEM!	THE WORLD--STANDS--	493	16
IF THAT--INDEED [EVEN THAT]--REDEEM-- . .	A PRISON GETS TO BE A	652	32
REDEEMED			
AMONG REDEEMED CHILDREN	THE BEGGAR LAD--DIES	717	9
REDEEMER'S			
UNLESS IN MY REDEEMER'S FACE	BECAUSE THAT YOU ARE	1260	23
REDEMPTION			
REDEMPTION--BRITTLE LADY--	WHAT SOFT--CHERUBIC	401	11
WHEN THE REDEMPTION STRIKES [SHAKES] HER BELLS--	BETTER--THAN MUSIC! FOR	503	20
REDEMPTION [THY TOTAL / THY BEING]--FOR A KISS--	GO SLOW, MY SOUL, TO	1297	8
REDEMPTION IS THE ONE [PRINCIPALLY] . . .	I SAW THE WIND WITHIN	1502	V
IS DEARER THAN REDEMPTION--	TO SEE HER IS A PICTURE	1568	V
REDIGNIFIED			
REDIGNIFIED [RE-ROYALIZED], ABOVE? . . .	PERHAPS YOU THINK ME	833	8
REDOUBLED			
THE BIRDS JOCOSER [REDOUBLED] SUNG-- . . .	A DROP FELL ON THE APPLE	794	10
REDOUBT			
EACH WAS TO EACH THE PINK REDOUBT-- . . .	'TIS SEASONS SINCE THE	1529	8
HIS CHANCES [DOCTRINES / DOGMAS] A REDOUBT--	NO BRIGADIER THROUGHOUT	1561	V 22
REDOUBTABLEST			
REDOUBTABLEST IS THIS	HOW HUMAN NATURE DOTES	1417	10
REDRESS			
BUT WHAT REDRESS CAN BE	ALONE AND IN A	1167	22
REDS			
CUNNING REDS OF MORNING	LET US PLAY YESTERDAY--	728	11
REDUCE			
IS NESCESSARY, TO REDUCE	MORE LIFE--WENT OUT--	422	11
AND NOT REDUCE--THE GOLD--	WITHOUT THIS--THERE IS	655	12
BUT REDUCE NO HUMAN SPIRIT	PUBLICATION--IS THE	709	15
THE NEED DID NOT REDUCE--	HAD I NOT THIS, OR THIS,	904	10
NO OTHER CAN REDUCE	NO OTHER CAN REDUCE	982	1
REDUCED			
WHOSE INVITATION--YOUR'S REDUCED	THE POWER TO BE TRUE TO	464	7
REDUCELESS			
OR A REDUCELESS MINE.	TO OWN THE ART WITHIN	855	8
REDUCES			
REDUCES IT TO NONE.	THE LIFE WE HAVE IS VERY	1162	8
REED			
THEN LIGHTLY [SOFTLY] AS A REED	THE LAST NIGHT THAT SHE	1100	22
REEF			
A REEF--CRAWLED EASY FROM THE SEA	I SOMETIMES DROP IT, FOR	708	13
REEFS			
THE REEFS IN OLD GETHSEMANE	I SHOULD HAVE BEEN TOO	313	20
REEL			
SO DRUNKEN, REEL HER BEES--	WE SHOULD NOT MIND SO	81	6
REELING			
REELING--THRO ENDLESS SUMMER DAYS-- . . .	I TASTE A LIQUOR NEVER	214	7
THE REELING [BLISSFUL] ORIOLE--	ONE OF THE ONES THAT	1466	4
THAT SEND ME REELING IN [ON]--	A DRUNKARD CANNOT MEET A	1628	6
REELS			
REELS IN REMOTER ATMOSPHERES--	WITHIN MY GARDEN, RIDES	500	11
RE-ENDURE			
TO RE-ENDURE A DAY--	'TIS GOOD--THE LOOKING	660	2
REFER			
REFER TO--POSSIBLY.	THE FACE I CARRY WITH ME	336	8
REFERS			
REFERS MY CLUMSY [DULLER] EYE--	WITHIN MY GARDEN, RIDES	500	18
REFINED			
A HORROR SO REFINED	WHAT SOFT--CHERUBIC	401	6
REFINING			
REFINING THESE IMPATIENT ORES	DARE YOU SEE A SOUL AT	365	13
REFLECTION			
AND A DEAL OF SAD REFLECTION, AND WAILING INSTEAD OF SONG?	AWAKE YE MUSES NINE,	1	30
REFLEX			
REFLEX HOLIDAY.	ONE DAY IS THERE OF THE	814	8
REFORMED			
REFORMED TO NOTHING BUT DELIGHT WHICH . .	ARROWS ENAMORED OF HIS	1629	V
REFORMS			
FOR LOVE REFORMS VITALITY [IS IMMORTALITY] .	UNABLE ARE THE LOVED TO	809	5
REFRACTED			
REFRACTED BUT A COUNTENANCE--	THE GRACE--MYSELF--MIGHT	707	3
REFRAIN			
OH, COULD YOU CATCH HER LAST REFRAIN-- . .	KILL YOUR BALM--AND IT'S	238	6
HIS FAVORITE REFRAIN.	THE JUDGE IS LIKE THE	699	12
REFRAINS			
AND SHE POURS SOFT REFRAINS	I KNOW A PLACE WHERE	337	8
REFRESH			
THAT HIM REFRESH [MAKE HIM FRESH]-- . . .	THE LASSITUDES OF	1592	4
REFRESHING			
STRONG DRAUGHTS OF THEIR REFRESHING MINDS .	STRONG DRAUGHTS OF THEIR	711	1
UNKNOWN--REFRESHING THINGS--	NO BRIGADIER THROUGHOUT	1561	20

	FIRST LINE	POEM	LINE
REFUGEE			
BE FOUND A REFUGEE--	THESE STRANGERS, IN A	1096	4
REFUND			
WILL REFUND [REWARD / REPAY] THE HAND-- . .	SOIL OF FLINT, IF STEADY	681	2
HE WILL REFUND US FINALLY	BECAUSE THAT YOU ARE	1260	39
REFUSE			
POSSIBLY--IF THEY REFUSE--HOW THEN KNOW-- .	GRIEF IS A MOUSE--	793	16
COULD ADAMANT REFUSE	JUST ONCE! OH LEAST	1076	2
FOR REFUSE AND THE MOUSE.	REMEMBRANCE HAS A	1182	4
REFUSED			
REFUSED TOO UTTERLY--	THE BIRDS REPORTED FROM	743	12
DISDAINED [REFUSED] TO RANKLE THERE-- . .	ARROWS ENAMORED OF HIS	1629	4
REFUTES			
MIDNIGHT IN MARBLE--REFUTES--THE SUNS-- . .	SAFE IN THEIR ALABASTER	216	V
REGALE			
HIM--TO REGALE--ME--ONLY--	HE IS ALIVE, THIS	1160	7
REGALING			
AT FIRST--A SCANT NUTRITION--[PLAIN REGALING]	DEPRIVED OF OTHER	773	3
REGARD			
REGARD A MOUSE	PAPA ABOVE!	61	2
THE DOOMED--REGARD THE SUNRISE	THE DOOMED--REGARD THE	294	1
COULD BEHOLD [REGARD] SO FAR [SMALL / DIM / SCARCE] A CREATURE--	PROMISE THIS--WHEN YOU	648	27
IT DROPPED SO LOW--IN MY REGARD--	IT DROPPED SO LOW--IN MY	747	1
REGARD A NUN--	ONLY A SHRINE, BUT MINE	918	4
REGARDED			
AND HE--UNMOVED REGARDED HER--	FATE SLEW HIM, BUT HE	1031	7
I WAS REGARDED [CONSIDERED] THEN	TO BE FORGOT BY THEE	1560	7
REGARDLESS			
REGARDLESS GROWN, ...	AFTER GREAT PAIN, A	341	8
REGARDS			
REGARDS WITH PATRIOT LOVE--	TO FIGHT ALOUD, IS VERY	126	8
REGARDS LEAST CYPHERER ALIKE	'TIS ONE BY ONE--THE	545	13
REGIMENT			
SUNSET--REVIEWS HER SAPPHIRE REGIMENT [REGIMENTS]--	AH, TENERIFFE!	666	4
REGIMENTS			
THE REGIMENTS OF WOOD AND HILL	SOME RAINBOW--COMING	64	20
SUNSET--REVIEWS HER SAPPHIRE REGIMENT [REGIMENTS]--	AH, TENERIFFE!	666	4
REGIONS			
OR SETTLED REGIONS WILD--	I NOTICED PEOPLE	1149	4
AND SETTLED REGIONS WILD	I NOTICED PEOPLE	1149	6
REGISTER			
TO ASCERTAIN [REGISTER] THE SIZE-- . . .	THE LONELINESS ONE DARE	777	4
REGISTERED			
THEY REGISTERED IN NATURE'S BOOK	FOREVER HONORED BE THE	1570	5
REGRET			
REMAIN IN HER REGRET	WHEN ONE HAS GIVEN UP	853	6
PROVE [ASK]--ME--SWEET--IF I REGRET IT-- .	ALL FORGOT FOR	966	15
A FAN, PERHAPS, A FRIEND'S REGRET	THE DYING NEED BUT	1026	5
IS HELPED [SOOTHED] BY THE REGRET	WHAT MYSTERY PERVADES A	1400	22
REGULATE			
BELIEF [WITH NOUGHT / OUR FAITH] TO REGULATE--	THE LAST NIGHT THAT SHE	1100	28
REGULATES			
THAT REGULATES THE WHEEL--	THE OUTER--FROM THE	451	6
REHEARSAL			
REHEARSAL TO OURSELVES	REHEARSAL TO OURSELVES	379	1
HUMMING--UNTIL MY FAINT REHEARSAL-- . . .	BETTER--THAN MUSIC! FOR	503	23
REIGN			
WE PERISH--THO' WE REIGN--	LIKE EYES THAT LOOKED ON	458	16
DO REIGN--	FOUR TREES--UPON A	742	V 4
CAKES REIGN BUT A DAY, ...	BLOSSOMS WILL RUN AWAY,	1578	2
REIMBURSE			
HER CRESCENT REIMBURSE	NATURE CAN DO NO MORE	1673	5
REIMBURSED			
REIMBURSED MY STORE--	I NEVER LOST AS MUCH BUT	49	6
REIN			
MY FRECKLED MONARCH HELD THE REIN-- . . .	I MET A KING THIS	166	14
AND SPECTRES OF THE REIN--	THE LIFE THAT TIED TOO	1535	4
REINDEER			
THESE ARE THE DAYS THAT REINDEER LOVE . .	THESE ARE THE DAYS THAT	1696	1
REINFORCED			
I REINFORCED [ONLY SEALED] THE DOOR-- . .	THE BIRDS REPORTED FROM	743	6
REINING			
THE SUN IN REINING TO THE WEST	THE SUN IN REINING TO	1636	1
REJECT			
WITH WILL [POWER] TO CHOOSE, OR TO REJECT, .	I'M CEDED--I'VE STOPPED	508	18
REJECTED			
REJECTED--BE--OF HER?	COULD I--THEN--SHUT THE	220	3
BY HEADS REJECTED--IN THE LOWER COUNTRY-- .	UNTO LIKE STORY--TROUBLE	295	11
REJECTS			
THE EYE REJECTS THE OIL.	IDEALS ARE THE FAIRY OIL	983	4
REJOICE			
DOES SO REJOICE?	FOR EVERY BIRD A NEST--	143	18
WHEN THE BELLS REJOICE--	A FIRST MUTE COMING--	702	4
WHEN IT IS FOUND, A FEW REJOICE	THIS IS A BLOSSOM OF THE	945	9
PERISH AND REJOICE.	TRUSTY AS THE STARS	1369	8
THEN THEY DO COME--REJOICE!	"AND WITH WHAT BODY DO	1492	2

	FIRST LINE	POEM	LINE
REJOICES			
YET ONE--REJOICES FLOWERS--	THERE IS AN ARID	782	5
REJOIN			
TO REJOIN IT'S OWN.	A THROE UPON THE	71	8
AND I REJOIN MY DOG,	WITHIN MY GARDEN, RIDES	500	12
THEMSELF--HAD JUST REMAINED TILL WE REJOIN THEM--	OF NEARNESS TO HER	607	18
REKINDLED			
REKINDLED BY SOME ACTION QUAINT	A WINGED SPARK DOTH SOAR	1468	9
REKNOWN			
A FUGITIVE REKNOWN--	THE ROBIN IS A GABRIEL	1483	V
RELATE			
RELATE--WHEN NEIGHBORS DIE--	WE PRAY--TO HEAVEN--	489	3
"AS LARGE AS I"--RELATE THE SUN	LOVE RECKONS BY ITSELF--	826	2
RELATED			
SURFACES MAY [CAN] BE INVESTED [RELATED]	NONE WHO SAW IT EVER	1110	5
RELATED SOMEHOW THEY MAY BE,	WHAT MYSTERY PERVADES A	1400	13
RELATION			
YET [BUT] MIGHTY--BY RELATION	ONE ANGUISH--IN A CROWD	565	13
RELATIONS			
NOT SO THE INFINITE RELATIONS--BELOW	NOT SO THE INFINITE	1040	1
RELATIVE			
THE RELATIVE AWAY--	YOU CONSTITUTED TIME--	765	6
UTMOST IS RELATIVE--	UNTIL THE DESERT KNOWS	1291	7
RELAY			
NOR BY RELAY OF BIRD	DISTANCE--IS NOT THE	1155	2
THE GRAVE BUT A RELAY	ADVANCE IS LIFE'S	1652	2
RELEASE			
TO MERIT THE RELEASE--	JOY TO HAVE MERITED THE	788	2
FOR CORPORAL RELEASE--	THE LONG SIGH OF THE	1359	8
ASKS NOTHING BUT RELEASE--[IT'S FLIGHT]	AS FROM THE EARTH THE	1630	2
RELEGATES			
HE RELEGATES THE REALM,	FROM HIS SLIM PALACE IN	1300	2
RELENT			
MY SOVREIGN WILL RELENT?	I'LL SEND THE FEATHER	687	3
RELIEF			
CIRCUMFERENCE WITHOUT RELIEF--	A COFFIN--IS A SMALL	943	11
A SHORT RELIEF TO HAVE THE WIND	T'WAS COMFORT IN HER	1703	3
RELIEVES			
PARTAKEN--IT RELIEVES--INDEED--	UNDUE SIGNIFICANCE A	439	5
RELIGION			
INVALIDATES THE BALM OF THAT RELIGION	OURSELVES WE DO INTER	1144	3
THE BUMBLE BEE'S RELIGION	HIS LITTLE HEARSE LIKE	1522	T
RELIGIOUS			
TO MEET [AT MEETING] SO ENABLED [LEARNED / RELIGIOUS / . . .	HE PREACHED UPON	1207	8
RELINQUISHED			
RELINQUISHED OUR ESTATE--	THE PUNGENT ATOM IN THE	1191	4
RELISHED			
RELISHED HIS IGNORANCE	THE EVENT WAS DIRECTLY	1686	4
RELISHES			
BUT NATURE RELISHES THE PINKS	BETROTHED TO	1641	3
RELUCTANT			
AND THEN RELUCTANT TURN--	AS CHILDREN BID THE	133	2
FOR WHOSE RELUCTANT CRUMB--	'TIS NOT THAT DYING	335	10
AND THEN--RELUCTANT--TURN AWAY	WE COVER THEE--SWEET	482	7
OUR FEET--RELUCTANT--LED--	OUR JOURNEY HAD ADVANCED	615	6
RELUCTANT TO BE TOLD	ALONE AND IN A	1167	2
RELUCTANTLY			
PARTING WITH THEE RELUCTANTLY,	PARTING WITH THEE	1614	1
RELUCTANTLY BUT SURE PERCEIVES	SUMMER BEGINS TO HAVE	1682	3
RELY			
RELY ON THAT--	THE WIND DID'NT COME	316	6
HOW AMPLE TO RELY	ON A COLUMNAR SELF--	789	2
REMAIN			
A COWARD WILL REMAIN, SIR,	"SIC TRANSIT GLORIA	3	53
PERHAPS A SQUIRREL MAY REMAIN--	BESIDES THE AUTUMN POETS	131	13
HIS NAME--REMAIN--	THE ONE WHO COULD REPEAT	307	9
WITH HIM REMAIN--WHO UNTO ME--	HER SWEET WEIGHT ON MY	518	9
FOR WHOM, THE TIME DID NOT SUFFICE [REMAIN]	NO NOTICE GAVE SHE, BUT	804	3
AS CHILDREN, WHO REMAIN IN FACE	AWAY FROM HOME ARE SOME	821	7
THIS EDIFICE REMAIN--	JUST AS HE SPOKE IT FROM	848	2
REMAIN IN HER REGRET	WHEN ONE HAS GIVEN UP	853	6
REMAIN--'TIS BUT A RIND.	HEREIN A BLOSSOM LIES--	899	4
REMAIN, OR WANDER,	THE DUTIES OF THE WIND	1137	7
THAT COURTESY WILL FAIR REMAIN	"REMEMBER ME" IMPLORED	1180	5
AS A CHURCH REMAIN--	WHEN I HOPED I FEARED--	1181	4
COULD BOUNTY BUT REMAIN	ARE FRIENDS DELIGHT OR	1199	2
WITH HIM THE SKILL [RIGHT / ART] REMAIN	ELIJAH'S WAGON KNEW NO	1254	V 6
REMAIN THOU AS THOU ART.	TWO LENGTHS HAS EVERY	1295	12
A THING TO TELL REMAIN?	HOW NEWS MUST FEEL WHEN	1319	12
THE SAME AMOUNT REMAIN--	HOPE IS A SUBTLE GLUTTON	1547	8
AND YET ABIDE [REMAIN] THE WORLD!	THERE CAME A WIND LIKE A	1593	17
OR EVER TO REMAIN--	HE WENT BY SLEEP THAT	1662	4
BUT HALF THE HOURS REMAIN.	CONSULTING SUMMER'S	1715	2
NO WILDERNESS REMAIN [RETAIN]	THIS DOCILE ONE INTER	1752	6
REMAINED			
HAD IT REMAINED TO SPEAK--	I BRING AN UNACCUSTOMED	132	16
THEMSELF--HAD JUST REMAINED TILL WE REJOIN THEM--	OF NEARNESS TO HER	607	18

	FIRST LINE	POEM	LINE
REMAINED (CONTINUED)			
BUT PRAYER--REMAINED--OUR SIDE--	IT WAS TOO LATE FOR MAN	623	4
BUT HE--WAS LEFT [REMAINED] ALIVE BECAUSE .	HE FOUGHT LIKE THOSE	759	11
REMAINED IN MEMORY--	BEREAVED OF ALL, I WENT	784	16
REMAINED FOR HIM--TO FLEE--	A BEE HIS BURNISHED	1339	10
REMAINED FOR HER--OF RAPTURE	A BEE HIS BURNISHED	1339	11
TRIUMPHED AND REMAINED UNKNOWN--	LAY THIS LAUREL ON THE	1393	V
REMAINED A FEW SLOW YEARS WITH US	I WATCHED HER FACE TO	1667	5
REMAINETH			
NO NEW MILE REMAINETH--	LIFE--IS WHAT WE MAKE IT	698	11
REMAINING			
OH IF THERE MAY DEPARTING [REMAINING] BE .	DELAYED TILL SHE HAD	58	13
PROCLAIM WITH THEIR REMAINING MIGHT-- . .	ME PROVE IT NOW--WHOEVER	537	11
WAS SUCH REMAINING [STILL DWELLING] THERE?"	I YEARS HAD BEEN FROM	609	8
WITH A REMAINING BREATH	THIS CHASM, SWEET, UPON	858	14
WITH IT'S [A] REMAINING CHARM	THESE ARE THE NIGHTS	1128	16
THAN A REMAINING FACE--	SUMMER HAS TWO	1422	8
ENCHANTING BY REMAINING, ...	WERE NATURE MORTAL LADY	1762	11
REMAINS			
THERE YET REMAINS A LOVE	THE MANNER OF IT'S DEATH	468	6
REMAINS BUT BALCONY	AS WILLING LID O'ER	1050	4
REMAINS TO HIM UNKNOWN--	WHO NEVER WANTED--	1430	2
IT YET REMAINS TO SEE	MY LIFE CLOSED TWICE	1732	2
REMAND			
TO NATURE WE REMAND THEM	THOSE CATTLE SMALLER	1388	15
REMANDED			
REMANDED OF THE MORN--	JOY TO HAVE MERITED THE	788	16
REMANDED TO A BALLAD'S BARN	A FADED BOY--IN SALLOW	1524	7
REMARK			
REMARK THAT BIRDS HAVE FLED!	THERE'S SOMETHING	45	16
A MAN MAY MAKE [DROP] A REMARK--	A MAN MAY MAKE A REMARK	952	1
A LITTLE FROM REMARK WITHDRAWN--	THE MOUNTAINS STOOD IN	1278	7
REMEDILESSLY			
REMEDILESSLY LEAVE	OF THIS IS DAY COMPOSED	1675	8
REMEDY			
BUT NOT A REMEDY--	THEY SAY THAT "TIME	686	6
HIS REMEDY FOR CARE,--	HIGH FROM THE EARTH I	1723	18
REMEMBER			
THEN I REMEMBER NOT.	IF RECOLLECTING WERE	33	2
I REMEMBER HIM!	HEART! WE WILL FORGET	47	8
NEEDS BUT TO REMEMBER	TO VENERATE THE SIMPLE	57	3
NEEDS BUT TO REMEMBER	TO VENERATE THE SIMPLE	57	8
DOST THOU REMEMBER ME?	SAVIOR! I'VE NO ONE ELSE	217	4
I'LL SAY--REMEMBER--KING--	THE COURT IS FAR AWAY--	235	6
THAT THEY--REMEMBER ME--	ME--COME! MY DAZZLED	431	8
SHALL WE REMEMBER PARCHING--THEN?	I KNOW WHERE WELLS GROW	460	17
AND THEY NO MORE REMEMBER ME--	WHY MAKE IT DOUBT--IT	462	11
REMEMBER--AS THOU GO--	WE COVER THEE--SWEET	482	4
THAT DONT REMEMBER YOU--	IF ANYBODY'S FRIEND BE	509	20
REMEMBER--WHEN THE SEA	ME PROVE IT NOW--WHOEVER	537	14
IF YOU REMEMBER, AND WERE SAVED--	DID YOU EVER STAND IN A	590	15
TO REMEMBER HOW SAD I AM	HOW HAPPY I WAS IF I	898	2
"REMEMBER ME" IMPLORED THE THIEF!	"REMEMBER ME" IMPLORED	1180	1
REMEMBER IT CAN CEASE--	TO MAKE ROUTINE A	1196	2
HENCEFORTH TO REMEMBER	NOW I KNEW I LOST HER--	1219	13
I DO REMEMBER WHEN A CHILD	OF DEATH I TRY TO THINK	1558	9
REMEMBERED			
REMEMBERED BUT BY ME.	SHE SLEPT BENEATH A TREE	25	2
HE FORGOT--AND I--REMEMBERED--	HE FORGOT--AND I--	203	1
REMEMBERED--AS THE MILE	OF TRIBULATION--THESE	325	12
REMEMBERED, IF OUTLIVED, ...	AFTER GREAT PAIN, A	341	11
WHEN GOD--REMEMBERED--AND THE FIEND . . .	'TWAS LIKE A MAELSTROM,	414	16
SWEET--YOU FORGOT--BUT I REMEMBERED . . .	SWEET--YOU FORGOT--BUT I	523	1
REMEMBERED--AS THE MILLINER'S FLOWER . . .	PRECIOUS TO ME--SHE	727	12
REMEMBERED	'TWAS MY ONE GLORY--	1028	3
REMEMBERED OF THE COW--	THE CLOVER'S SIMPLE FAME	1232	2
OR NEVER REMEMBERED--	WHETHER THEY HAVE	1329	3
TO BE REMEMBERED WHAT--	TO BE FORGOT BY THEE	1560	10
REMEMBERING			
IF RECOLLECTING [OH IF REMEMBERING] WERE FORGETTING,	IF RECOLLECTING WERE	33	1
AH--BUT REMEMBERING ME--	GARLANDS FOR QUEENS, MAY	34	4
AH--BUT REMEMBERING THEE--	GARLANDS FOR QUEENS, MAY	34	5
REMEMBERING OURSELVES, WE TRUST--	THOSE FAIR--FICTITIOUS	499	13
REMEMBERING	A SHADE UPON THE MIND	882	4
LIKE THE REMEMBERING IT BE NOUGHT	NO OTHER CAN REDUCE	982	3
LIKE THE REMEMBERING IT EXIST--	NO OTHER CAN REDUCE	982	V
REMEMBERING THE DIMENSIONS	OUR OWN POSSESSIONS--	1208	3
REMEMBERS			
OF THESE TWO--GOD REMEMBERS	DEATH IS POTENTIAL TO	548	5
REMEMBERS IT FORGOT--	PARTING WITH THEE	1614	4
REMEMBRANCE			
AND NOW, AN AMETHYST REMEMBRANCE	I HELD A JEWEL IN MY	245	7
REMEMBRANCE HAS A REAR AND FRONT--	REMEMBRANCE HAS A	1182	1
THE SAVED HAVE [LEFT] NO REMEMBRANCE . . .	I SAW THE WIND WITHIN	1502	V
NOR HAVE THE SAVED REMEMBRANCE	I SAW THE WIND WITHIN	1502	V
YOU CANNOT MAKE REMEMBRANCE GROW	YOU CANNOT MAKE	1508	1
NOR CAN YOU CUT REMEMBRANCE DOWN	YOU CANNOT MAKE	1508	9
JAMAICAS OF REMEMBRANCE [PROSPECTIVE] STIR .	A DRUNKARD CANNOT MEET A	1628	5

	FIRST LINE	POEM	LINE
REMIND			
REMIND US THAT WE DIED.	REHEARSAL TO OURSELVES	379	8
REMIND HIM, WOULD IT NOT, SOMEWHAT	TO ONE DENIED TO DRINK	490	7
ALL THESE--REMIND US OF THE PLACE	"HEAVEN" HAS DIFFERENT	575	15
ANOTHER CLASS REMIND ME [REMINDS ME OF]	A LITTLE DOG THAT WAGS	1185	13
REMINDED			
REMINDED ME, OF MINE--	IT WAS NOT DEATH, FOR I	510	12
IT JUST REMINDED ME--'TWAS ALL--	A THOUGHT WENT UP MY	701	11
REMINDED BY A BOY	A LITTLE DOG THAT WAGS	1185	4
REMINDS			
ANOTHER CLASS REMIND ME [REMINDS ME OF]	A LITTLE DOG THAT WAGS	1185	13
REMISS			
WITH NO REMISS OF TRIUMPH	WITH SWEETNESS UNABATED	1709	3
REMIT			
REMIT AS YET NO GRACE	FURTHER IN SUMMER THAN	1068	13
ATTEST [REMIT] ME THIS AND THIS--	THROUGH WHAT TRANSPORTS	1153	4
REMIT HER HOME,	TO THE BRIGHT EAST SHE	1573	3
REMITS			
MUFFLED [MORTISED]--IT REMITS [RESISTS] SURMISE--	"SECRETS" IS A DAILY	1385	3
REMITTED			
REMITTED--SINCE IT FLITTED IT	PRAISE IT--'TIS DEAD--	1384	8
REMNANT			
AND LEAVES NO REMNANT BY--	TOO HAPPY TIME DISSOLVES	1774	2
REMORSE			
REMORSE--IS MEMORY--AWAKE--	REMORSE--IS MEMORY--	744	1
REMORSE IS CURELESS--THE DISEASE	REMORSE--IS MEMORY--	744	9
AND AS [WHEN] SHE VANISHES, REMORSE	I CANNOT MEET THE SPRING	1051	7
REMOTE			
TO TOO REMOTE A HIGHT	THE SOUL'S SUPERIOR	306	6
A FAVOR SO REMOTE--	HAD I PRESUMED TO HOPE--	522	6
FOR BRAVERIES, REMOTE AS THIS [HIS]	WHEN I WAS SMALL, A	596	19
THE COLOR TOO REMOTE	THE TINT I CANNOT TAKE--	627	2
REMOTE--HER BEST ARRAY--	THE BIRDS REPORTED FROM	743	10
AFAR [REMOTE / ASTRAY] UPON THE WIND	IT IS A LONESOME GLEE--	774	4
AS DOWN HIS HEAVEN DROPT REMOTE [ECHOED FAINT]	JUST ONCE! OH LEAST	1076	8
FROM EMINENCE REMOTE	THESE ARE THE NIGHTS	1128	2
SUPPOSED THEY VISITED REMOTE	I NOTICED PEOPLE	1149	3
REMOTE [ASTUTE / OBSCURE] TO UNDERSTAND	NATURE AFFECTS TO BE	1170	6
THAN HEAVEN MORE REMOTE,	THAN HEAVEN MORE REMOTE,	1436	1
REMOTELY			
IN VILLAGES REMOTELY SET	THE FROST WAS NEVER SEEN	1202	7
REMOTENESS			
BUT REMOTENESS TRAVELLED	NOW I KNEW I LOST HER--	1219	3
REMOTER			
WHOSE MAIDS UPON REMOTER GREEN	THERE IS A MORN BY MEN	24	2
IT CARE, IN SOME REMOTER WAY,	I GOT SO I COULD HEAR	293	24
REELS IN REMOTER ATMOSPHERES--	WITHIN MY GARDEN, RIDES	500	11
A REMOTER BED?	GRATITUDE--IS NOT THE	989	8
REMOTEST			
REMOTEST--WHEN MOST FAIR [NEAR]	THE TREES LIKE TASSELS--	606	8
REMOTEST--STILL--	THE SUNRISE RUNS FOR	710	6
BUT THE REMOTEST STAR--	THE MOON WAS BUT A CHIN	737	14
REMOTEST [MEMORIAL] SCRUTINY--	THIS DUST, AND IT'S	936	12
TO SOME REMOTEST PLAIN	LIKE RAIN IT SOUNDED	1235	6
REMOTEST [FANTASTIC / MOST GRACIOUS / MOST DUSKY / . . .	AN ANTIQUATED TREE	1514	7
REMOVE			
I COULD NO MORE REMOVE	IT WOULD HAVE STARVED A	612	6
REMOVE THE DATES--TO THESE--	FOREVER--IS COMPOSED OF	624	6
AND FURTHER NORTH--REMOVE.	I THINK THE LONGEST HOUR	635	16
WHEREVER WE REMOVE--	WHO HAS NOT FOUND THE	1544	4
TO WINTER TO REMOVE	'TWAS HERE MY SUMMER	1756	5
REMOVED			
REMOVED.	I HAVE A BIRD IN SPRING	5	24
AND NOW, REMOVED FROM AIR--	I BREATHED ENOUGH TO	272	2
REMOVED FROM ACCIDENT OF LOSS	REMOVED FROM ACCIDENT OF	424	1
CENTURIES REMOVED	ALL BUT DEATH, CAN BE	749	V 4
THE ABSOLUTE--REMOVED [WITHDREW]	YOU CONSTITUTED TIME--	765	5
REMOVED OUR INVITATION BY	NO NOTICE GAVE SHE, BUT	804	19
REMOVES			
REMOVES THE PALTRY THING	TO DISAPPEAR ENHANCES--	1209	V 10
REMOVING			
THEIR REMOVING MANNERS	SOME WE SEE NO MORE,	1221	4
CURTAILED BY YOUR OBSCURING [REMOVING] FACE	BECAUSE THAT YOU ARE	1260	27
REND			
SHOULD THEY REND YOU WITH "HOW ARE YOU"	KNOCK WITH TREMOR--	1325	8
TO REND IT WITH GOOD NIGHT--	WITHIN THY GRAVE!	1552	4
RENDERED			
RENDERED WITH A SMILE	WOLFE DEMANDED DURING	678	6
BE RENDERED BY THE BEE--	APOLOGY FOR HER	852	2
RENDEZVOUS			
PASS TO THY RENDEZVOUS OF LIGHT,	PASS TO THY RENDEZVOUS	1564	1
RENEGADE			
IS IMPUDENT [RENEGADE / INFIDEL / ABLATIVE] TO NATURE	THE JAY HIS CASTANET HAS	1635	4
RENEW			
AT LENGTH, RENEW THEIR SMILE--	I MEASURE EVERY GRIEF I	561	14
LET BROOKS--RENEW OF BROOKS--	THE WELL UPON THE BROOK	1091	3
BUT TO RENEW--	COULD HOPE INSPECT HER	1283	6

	FIRST LINE	POEM	LINE
RENEWING			
. . . RENEWING] WHEEL--	A ROUTE OF EVANESCENCE	1463	2
RENOUNCE			
WHEN BUTTERFLIES--RENOUNCE THEIR "DRAMS"--	I TASTE A LIQUOR NEVER	214	11
RENOUNCED			
WHAT THEY--RENOUNCED--	READ--SWEET--HOW OTHERS	260	3
ONE EYE UPON THE HEAVEN RENOUNCED--	TRIUMPH--MAY BE OF	455	11
RENOUNCHED			
RENOUNCHED THEIR CHARACTER	ARROWS ENAMORED OF HIS	1629	V 4
RENOVATES			
THAT RENOVATES THE WORLD--	BY HOMELY GIFT AND	1563	5
RENOWN			
INTO--RENOWN!	READ--SWEET--HOW OTHERS	260	15
IT MAY BE--A RENOWN TO LIVE--	IT FEELS A SHAME TO BE	444	17
TO TENDERER RENOWN--	HE TOUCHED ME, SO I LIVE	506	12
WHOSE BE HER [THIS] RENOWN, OR FADING,	BLOOM UPON THE MOUNTAIN	667	11
AND FAIRNESS--AND RENOWN--	SHE DWELLETH IN THE	671	6
TO GAIN RENOWN OF LADY'S DRAWER	THE BIRD MUST SING TO	880	5
THE SECOND--WAS--RENOWN--	THE FIRST WE KNEW OF HIM	1006	2
RENOWN PERCEIVES ITSELF	THE CLOVER'S SIMPLE FAME	1232	5
OR, HAPPILY [POSSIBLY], RENOWN--	THE WAY TO KNOW THE	1279	20
OH, THOU UNKNOWN RENOWN	THAT SHORT--POTENTIAL	1307	6
TOO INTRINSIC FOR RENOWN--	LAY THIS LAUREL ON THE	1393	2
IS MY [THEIR] RENOWN	TO BE FORGOT BY THEE	1560	12
MY LOW [ONE / MEEK / WAN] RENOWN	TO BE FORGOT BY THEE	1560	V 12
TO SCREEN THEM FROM RENOWN.	FOREVER HONORED BE THE	1570	8
RENOWNED			
RENOWNED TO EASE [STIR] EXTREMITY--	I GOT SO I COULD HEAR	293	15
A POWER OF RENOWNED COLD,	MORE LIFE--WENT OUT--	422	5
FOR CREATURES SO RENOWNED--	YOU'VE SEEN BALLOONS SET	700	8
RENT			
HE PAYS NO RENT.	THE RAT IS THE CONCISEST	1356	2
FOR ANGELS RENT THE HOUSE NEXT OUR'S,	WHO HAS NOT FOUND THE	1544	3
AND THE RENT UNPAID--	RATHER ARID DELIGHT	1679	8
RENTS			
IT RENTS IMMENSITY--	A NEARNESS TO	963	V 8
RENUNCIATION			
TRODDEN WITH STRAIGHT RENUNCIATION	TO PUT THIS WORLD DOWN,	527	5
RENUNCIATION--IS A PIERCING VIRTUE--	RENUNCIATION--IS A	745	1
RENUNCIATION--IS THE CHOOSING	RENUNCIATION--IS A	745	10
REORGANIZES			
REORGANIZES ESTIMATE	THE ADMIRATIONS--AND	906	4
REPAIR			
THAT POWER TO REPAIR	TO MAKE ROUTINE A	1196	6
SO EASY [SUPPLE / PLIANT] TO REPAIR.	SOFTENED BY TIME'S	1738	8
REPAIRED			
DYNASTIES REPAIRED--	ALL BUT DEATH, CAN BE	749	2
REPAIRED OF ALL BUT LONELINESS	THE SNOW THAT NEVER	1133	11
REPAIRING			
REPAIRING EVERYWHERE--	FROM COCOON FORTH A	354	4
REPAIRS			
TOO COSTLY FOR REPAIRS.	DEATH SETS A THING	360	20
REPAST			
REPAST TO ME	THE HEART HAS MANY DOORS	1567	6
AN ADEQUATE REPAST	WITH SWEETNESS UNABATED	1709	10
REPAY			
WILL REFUND [REWARD / REPAY] THE HAND--	SOIL OF FLINT, IF STEADY	681	2
THE HAPPY [THE CHEMIST / THE RANSOMED / A LOVER] MAY [CAN] REPAY,	THE FARTHEST THUNDER	1581	10
REPEAL			
REPEAL THE BEATING GROUND--	IT WAS NOT DEATH, FOR I	510	20
MINE--BY THE GRAVE'S REPEAL--	MINE--BY THE RIGHT OF	528	6
ADAM AND REPEAL.	PARADISE IS OF THE	1069	4
REPEALED			
REPEALED FROM OBSERVATION--	AS SLEIGH BELLS SEEM IN	981	5
REPEALING			
. . . FORECLOSING / REPEALING] WRINKLE	LIKE TIME'S INSIDIOUS	1236	1
REPEALLESS			
ON HIS REPEALLESS--LIST.	THEY DROPPED LIKE FLAKES	409	9
TO THAT REPEALLESS THING--	ONE ANGUISH--IN A CROWD	565	14
REPEAT			
AT FIRST, REPEAT IT SLOW!	'TIS SO MUCH JOY! 'TIS	172	15
THE ONE WHO [THAT] COULD REPEAT THE SUMMER DAY--	THE ONE WHO COULD REPEAT	307	1
WHILE I REPEAT [RECITE] YOUR	SANG FROM THE HEART,	1059	15
WHOSE BLEATING CEASES TO REPEAT	LET DOWN THE BARS, OH	1065	3
REPEATED			
REPEATED--IN THE SKY--	THE TINT I CANNOT TAKE--	627	8
THOUGH THEIR REPEATED GRACE	MY BEST ACQUAINTANCES	932	V 5
REPELS			
REPELS THE HEALTHY BEE--	THERE IS AN ARID	782	V 8
REPENTANCE			
GRANT THAT REPENTANCE SOLEMN	I HAD A GUINEA GOLDEN--	23	33
REPETITION			
GROWN IN [BY] THE REPETITION HOARY	TELL AS A MARKSMAN--WERE	1152	7
REPINE			
YET DO I NOT REPINE	I HAVE A BIRD IN SPRING	5	7
THEN WILL I NOT REPINE,	I HAVE A BIRD IN SPRING	5	25
REPLACED			
THE VIOLIN IN BAIZE REPLACED--	LIKE SOME OLD FASHIONED	302	15

	FIRST LINE	POEM	LINE
REPLACED (CONTINUED)			
THE DUST REPLACED, IN HOISTED ROADS-- . .	A DROP FELL ON THE APPLE	794	9
REPLACING			
GENTLY REPLACING	GLORY IS THAT BRIGHT	1660	6
REPLENISH			
NEW HORIZONS--THEY EMBELLISH [REPLENISH]-- .	UNFULFILLED TO	972	7
REPLENISHED			
REPLENISHED--FAITH CANNOT--	TO LOSE ONE'S FAITH--	377	4
REPLEVYS			
AND ESTIMATES [ENFORCES / COMMENCES / REPLEVYS / CONFISCATES] . . .	PERHAPS THEY DO NOT GO	1399	8
REPLIED			
"FOR BEAUTY", I REPLIED--	I DIED FOR BEAUTY--BUT	449	6
"YOU'RE SOON," THE TOWN REPLIED, ...	THE FINGERS OF THE LIGHT	1000	5
REPLIES			
GOD IT IS SAID REPLIES IN PERSON	TELL AS A MARKSMAN--WERE	1152	24
REPLY			
RECEIVES IT'S ANNUAL REPLY!	AN ALTERED LOOK ABOUT	140	16
AND NO ONE MADE REPLY.	WHOSE ARE THE LITTLE	142	4
MY RIVER WAITS REPLY--	MY RIVER RUNS TO THEE--	162	3
AN EXQUISITE REPLY!	WITHIN MY GARDEN, RIDES	500	20
AND ONLY THE SEA--REPLY--	GLEE--THE GREAT STORM IS	619	17
THE MOUNTAINS STRAIGHT REPLY--	MY LIFE HAD STOOD--A	754	8
THAT COULD THEIR LIPS REPLY	WHAT DID THEY DO SINCE I	900	6
I FAILED TO MAKE [ELICIT NO] REPLY--	MY BEST ACQUAINTANCES	932	6
THE SEVENTEENTH; REPLY	BEE! I'M EXPECTING YOU!	1035	10
MIGHT YET [STILL] REPLY [DESTROY].	THE PAST IS SUCH A	1203	8
IS [WAS] SHORTER THAN A [THE] SNAKE'S DELAY [EVENT / REPLY]	THE MUSHROOM IS THE ELF	1298	7
THAT WILL RECEIVE [DELAYING ITS] REPLY . .	ONE JOY OF SO MUCH	1420	10
MY FAITH CANNOT REPLY	LIVES HE IN ANY OTHER	1557	2
EXACTING THIS REPLY--	THE SPIRIT LASTS--BUT IN	1576	18
GOODNIGHT, I STILL REPLY--	SOME SAY GOODNIGHT--AT	1739	4
MADE NO DISTINCT REPLY.	THE WATERS CHASED HIM AS	1749	10
REPLYING			
REPLYING TO IT'S PRICE--	PERCEPTION OF AN OBJECT	1071	4
REPORT			
OR EVEN A REPORT OF LAND--	IT WAS NOT DEATH, FOR I	510	23
REPORT WAS NOT--TO ME--	TWO BUTTERFLIES WENT OUT	533	V 12
'TWAS NOON--WITHOUT THE NEWS [REPORT] OF NIGHT--	TO MY SMALL HEARTH HIS	638	7
REPORT BY SIGN A CIRCUMSTANCE	THE FUTURE--NEVER SPOKE	672	V 3
BUT [JUST] INSTINCT ESTEEM [REPORT] HIM . .	CONSCIOUS AM I IN MY	679	19
PRICKS HIS EAR--REPORT TO HEAR	GRIEF IS A MOUSE--	793	6
OR NOONS REPORT AWAY	A LIGHT EXISTS IN SPRING	812	14
OR WARRANT TO REPORT [PRESENT] THE SOUL . .	'TWAS CRISIS--ALL THE	948	7
AND DOUBTFUL AS REPORT UPON	THE CRICKETS SANG	1104	V
CONSUMES AND NO [WITHOUT] REPORT TO MEN . .	THE LARGEST FIRE EVER	1114	5
REPORTED			
THE BIRDS REPORTED FROM THE SOUTH--	THE BIRDS REPORTED FROM	743	1
NOR THEN PERHAPS REPORTED	A WORD MADE FLESH IS	1651	3
REPORTER			
SOME PALE REPORTER, FROM THE AWFUL DOORS .	JUST LOST, WHEN I WAS	160	10
REPORTLESS			
REPORTLESS SUBJECTS, TO THE QUICK	REPORTLESS SUBJECTS, TO	1048	1
REPORTLESS MEASURES, TO THE EAR	REPORTLESS SUBJECTS, TO	1048	5
IN MANY AND REPORTLESS PLACES	IN MANY AND REPORTLESS	1382	1
REPORTLESS, ALSO, BUT SINCERE AS NATURE . .	IN MANY AND REPORTLESS	1382	3
TO THY REPORTLESS GRAVE--	STILL OWN THEE--STILL	1633	4
REPORTS			
WITH HURRIED--FEW--EXPRESS REPORTS	THE ROBIN IS THE ONE	828	3
BETRAYS [REPORTS] US, AS HIS FIRST BETROTHAL	MARCH IS THE MONTH OF	1404	7
REPOSE			
TO HER FAIR REPOSE.	MORNS LIKE THESE--WE	27	4
DID THOSE I LOVED REPOSE	IF THOSE I LOVED WERE	29	5
TRANQUIL--AS TO REPOSE--	WENT UP A YEAR THIS	93	6
NEVER MIND REPOSE!	BY A FLOWER--BY A LETTER	109	6
SAY REPOSE!	ARTISTS WRESTLED HERE!	110	6
ON THEIR SIDE [PART], WHAT REPOSE!	THE SUN KEPT STOOPING--	152	4
AN ULTIMATE REPOSE--	THE MONTHS HAVE ENDS--	423	8
TO WANDER--NOW--IS MY REPOSE [ABODE]-- . .	I MEANT TO FIND HER WHEN	718	9
MAKE THEIR FIRST REPOSE THIS WINTER . . .	SNOW BENEATH WHOSE	942	3
TO HIM WHO ON IT'S SMALL [LOW] REPOSE . .	A COFFIN--IS A SMALL	943	9
REPOSE TO TYPIFY	FURTHER IN SUMMER THAN	1068	12
INVENTED THIS [THAT] REPOSE	HOW SOFT THIS PRISON IS	1334	4
REPOSED			
THE GRAVE IT WAS REPOSED UPON	BEREAVED OF ALL, I WENT	784	7
REPREHEND			
THE RIGHT TO REPREHEND	BECAUSE THAT YOU ARE	1260	30
REPREIVE			
A CREATURE GASPED "REPREIVE"!	'TWAS LIKE A MAELSTROM,	414	23
REPRESENTATIVE			
STANDS REPRESENTATIVE IN GOLD	A SCIENCE--SO THE SAVANS	100	10
REPRESSED			
AS IF THEY JUST REPRESSED	THE TINT I CANNOT TAKE--	627	14
REPRIEVE SEE REPREIVE			
CAPTIVE! WE BRING REPRIEVE OF ROSES!	WOULD YOU LIKE SUMMER?	691	6
ARKS OF REPRIEVE HE OFFERED [OPENED] TO US--	WE TALKED WITH EACH	1473	7
THOUGH SMUGGLED HIS [MY] REPRIEVE	IT CAME HIS TURN TO BEG	1500	8
PERMIT [ALLOW / BESTOW] ME THIS REPRIEVE .	TRIED ALWAYS AND	1559	2

	FIRST LINE	POEM	LINE
REPRIEVES			
THE CAT REPRIEVES THE MOUSE	THE WHOLE OF IT CAME NOT	762	5
REPRIEVING			
FOR A REPRIEVING LOOK--	ELIZABETH TOLD ESSEX	1321	8
REPRIMAND			
WE REPRIMAND THE HAPPINESS	OF GOD WE ASK ONE FAVOR,	1601	7
REPRODUCE			
AND HE--COULD REPRODUCE THE SUN--	THE ONE WHO COULD REPEAT	307	4
REPRODUCED			
REPRODUCED--THE SAME--	BLOOM UPON THE MOUNTAIN	667	4
REPUBLIC			
REPUBLIC OF DELIGHT, I THOUGHT	THE BIRD DID PRANCE--THE	1107	7
REPUDIATE			
REPUDIATE THE FORGE--	DARE YOU SEE A SOUL AT	365	16
CONSPIRE AGAINST [REPUDIATE] HIS OWN	WHO COURT OBTAIN WITHIN	803	9
REPUDIATES			
REPUDIATES IT, ALL THE MORE--	SIZE CIRCUMSCRIBES--IT	641	5
REPUDIATES THE OBLIGATION--	THE RAT IS THE CONCISEST	1356	3
REPUGNANT			
REPUGNANT TO HER PROBITY--	SHAME IS THE SHAWL OF	1412	7
REPUGNANTLY			
REPUGNANTLY RESIGNED	A RAT SURRENDERED HERE	1340	11
REPULSE			
NOT SADDENED BY REPULSE,	THE HEART HAS MANY DOORS	1567	5
REQUEST			
SMILING, AS THEY REQUEST AN ALMS--	IN RAGS MYSTERIOUS AS	117	5
THE CROSS'--REQUEST--	THE TEST OF LOVE--IS	573	12
JUST ONCE! OH LEAST REQUEST!	JUST ONCE! OH LEAST	1076	1
CRUMBLESS AND HOMELESS, OF BUT ONE REQUEST--	QUITE EMPTY, QUITE AT	1606	8
REQUIRE			
THE WIND DOES NOT REQUIRE THE GRASS	"WHY DO I LOVE" YOU, SIR	480	3
REQUIRED			
REQUIRED A BLOW AS VAST--	TO BREAK SO VAST A HEART	1312	2
REQUIREMENT			
SHE ROSE TO HIS REQUIREMENT--DROPT	SHE ROSE TO HIS	732	1
REQUIREMENTS			
REQUIREMENTS	I CANNOT BE ASHAMED	914	9
REQUIRES			
REQUIRES SOREST NEED.	SUCCESS IS COUNTED	67	4
REQUIRES ENERGY--POSSIBLY AGONY--	TO PUT THIS WORLD DOWN,	527	3
TO WALK ON SEAS [TIDES] REQUIRES CEDAR FEET	THERE IS A STRENGTH IN	1113	6
REQUIRING			
REQUIRING IN THE QUENCH--	MORE LIFE--WENT OUT--	422	4
REQUISITE			
BUT MEAT WITHIN, IS REQUISITE	EXPERIMENT TO ME	1073	7
ONE [THIS] REQUISITE HAS FIRE THAT LASTS [EARTHLY FIRE / MORTAL FIRE]	THE SMOULDERING EMBERS	1132	7
REQUISITION			
YOUR REQUISITION BE.	PURSUING YOU IN YOUR	1602	4
RE-ROYALIZED			
REDIGNIFIED [RE-ROYALIZED], ABOVE?	PERHAPS YOU THINK ME	833	8
RESCINDED			
SOME--RESCINDED THE WRENCH--	NOT ANY MORE TO BE	1344	13
TO HER RESCINDED [SURRENDERED / RECEDING / DEPARTED / . . .	CRISIS IS SWEET AND YET	1416	8
RESCUED			
TOO RESCUED--FEAR TOO DIM TO ME	I SHOULD HAVE BEEN TOO	313	8
RESEARCH			
HIS RESEARCH HAS BUT JUST BEGUN--	THE LILAC IS AN ANCIENT	1241	13
RESEMBLANCE			
UNTIL--RESEMBLANCE PERFECT--	TILL DEATH--IS NARROW	907	9
FOR SEEKING IT'S RESEMBLANCE [SIMILITUDE]--	IT BLOOMED AND DROPT, A	978	15
RESEMBLE			
IT [THAT] RESEMBLE THEE--	AUTUMN--OVERLOOKED MY	748	6
FOR RESEMBLING [THAT--RESEMBLE] ME--	AUTUMN--OVERLOOKED MY	748	8
RESEMBLES			
RESEMBLES TO MY OUTRAGED MIND	HIS BILL IS CLASPED--HIS	1102	9
RESEMBLING			
IMITATING [MORE RESEMBLING] YOU--	PROMISE THIS--WHEN YOU	648	16
FOR RESEMBLING [THAT--RESEMBLE] ME--	AUTUMN--OVERLOOKED MY	748	8
RESENT			
THOUGH [WHILE / BUT] WE RESENT THE CREASE	LIKE TIME'S INSIDIOUS	1236	4
RESENTS			
BREAD OF HEAVEN RESENTS BESTOWAL	WHEN A LOVER IS A BEGGAR	1314	7
RESERVATION			
WITH JUST THIS STIPULUS [RESERVATION]--	YOU SAID THAT I "WAS	738	17
RESERVE			
RESERVE WITHIN THY KINGDOM	PAPA ABOVE!	61	4
OR STUPOR--THE RESERVE--	DID OUR BEST MOMENT LAST	393	7
RESERVE--FOR CHARITY--	DEPRIVED OF OTHER	773	12
RESERVED			
GUSH AFTER GUSH, RESERVED FOR YOU--	SPLIT THE LARK--AND	861	6
SECRETED [RESERVED] UTTERLY	I SEND YOU A DECREPIT	1324 V	8
RESERVED FOR US TO KNOW	HOW HUMAN NATURE DOTES	1417	6
RESERVING			
RESERVING THAT BUT JUST TO PROVE	SOMEWHERE UPON THE	1231	9
RESERVING THE PRESUMPTION	THOSE CATTLE SMALLER	1388	9
RESERVOIR			
BUT NEVER TOUCH THE RESERVOIR--	OF LIFE TO OWN--	1294	3

	FIRST LINE	POEM	LINE
RESIDE			
OF WHERE I WOULD RESIDE!	"SIC TRANSIT GLORIA	3	40
RESIDENCE			
HE TAKETH DAMASK RESIDENCE--	A FUZZY FELLOW, WITHOUT	173	11
MY RESIDENCE WITHIN	THE WIND--TAPPED LIKE A	436	4
COULD I INFER HIS RESIDENCE--	MY PERIOD HAD COME FOR	564	11
AIR HAS NO RESIDENCE, NO NEIGHBOR, ...	AIR HAS NO RESIDENCE, NO	1060	1
A RESIDENCE TOO PLAIN	BECAUSE THAT YOU ARE	1260	22
A SMALL BUT STURDY RESIDENCE, ...	THE ROBIN IS A GABRIEL	1483	9
IT'S SOARING [RAPTURE] RESIDENCE.	AS FROM THE EARTH THE	1630	4
THOUGH BY HIS AWFUL RESIDENCE	NO MAN SAW AWE, NOR TO	1733	3
RESIDENCES			
WHAT RESIDENCES NIMBLE	WHAT TENEMENTS OF CLOVER	1338	5
RESIDING			
RESIDING IN A JAR	WHAT MYSTERY PERVADES A	1400	4
RESIDUE			
PLATED THE RESIDUE OF ADZ	NOT ANY MORE TO BE	1344	15
HER RESIDUE BE PAST--	WITH SWEETNESS UNABATED	1709	12
RESIGN			
I DID RESIGN THE PRIG, ...	I COUNTED TILL THEY	36	6
THAT WOULD BUT HE RESIGN	THE DEVIL--HAD HE	1479	6
RESIGNED			
SOME HAVE RESIGNED THE LOOM--	MY WHEEL IS IN THE DARK!	10	9
ENDURED, UNHELPED [RESIGNED]--UNKNOWN. . .	THE HOLLOWS ROUND HIS	955	8
REPUGNANTLY RESIGNED	A RAT SURRENDERED HERE	1340	11
RESIST			
THAT IF THE FLESH RESIST THE HEFT--	A WEIGHT WITH NEEDLES ON	264	3
CANNOT RESIST--	A RAT SURRENDERED HERE	1340	9
OF SUBJECTS THAT RESIST	HOW HUMAN NATURE DOTES	1417	9
OTHERS MUST RESIST--	THE BIBLE IS AN ANTIQUE	1545	10
RESISTLESS			
AUGUST--ABSORBED--NUMB--[RESISTLESS--DUMB] .	NO CROWD THAT HAS	515	16
RESISTS			
THAN IT RESISTS [EVADES / ELUDES]--THE HOUND--	THIS MERIT HATH THE	979	8
MUFFLED [MORTISED]--IT REMITS [RESISTS] SURMISE--	"SECRETS" IS A DAILY	1385	3
THE TIPPET THAT IGNORES [RESISTS] HIS VOICE	THE JAY HIS CASTANET HAS	1635	3
RESITUATED			
RESITUATED IN THE WEST	SAID DEATH TO PASSION	1033	8
RESOLUTE			
BUT CONFIDENT [DILIGENT / RESOLUTE] DESPAIR--	HAD I PRESUMED TO HOPE--	522	10
RESOLUTER			
I, MUST RESOLUTER BE!	I'M THE LITTLE "HEART'S	176	7
RESONANCE			
IT'S TENTACLES [RESONANCE] DIVINE.	WE LIKE A HAIRBREADTH	1175	8
A RESONANCE OF EMERALD--	A ROUTE OF EVANESCENCE	1463	3
RESOURCE			
WERE IT MY RESOURCE FROM STARVING--	MOST SHE TOUCHED ME BY	760	7
RESOWN			
WASTES OF LIVES--RESOWN WITH COLORS	ALL BUT DEATH, CAN BE	749	5
RESPECT			
REVERE [RESPECT] THE GRAYEST PILE	ASHES DENOTE THAT FIRE	1063	2
RESPECTFUL			
THE CROWD RESPECTFUL GREW--	WENT UP A YEAR THIS	93	20
THE SUN RESPECTFUL LIES--	A CHILLY PEACE INFESTS	1443	2
MORE RESPECTFUL--"WE ARE DUST"--	"HEAVENLY FATHER"--TAKE	1461	6
RESPITE			
WITHOUT AN INSTANT'S RESPITE--	I SOMETIMES DROP IT, FOR	708	7
THE RESPITE TO BE DEAD.	TOO SCANTY 'TWAS TO DIE	1013	8
WHAT RESPITE FROM HER THRILLING TOIL . . .	THE BIRD HER PUNCTUAL	1585	5
NO RESPITE FROM THE INFERENCE [MIGHTINESS] .	WHY SHOULD WE HURRY--WHY	1646	5
RESPITES			
A CONTRAST TO OUR RESPITES.	HIGH FROM THE EARTH I	1723	19
RESPLENDENT			
AS THAT EXALTED [THOSE RESPLENDENT] HERE-- .	NO LIFE CAN POMPLESS	1626	4
RESPONDED			
"I SEE THEE" EACH RESPONDED STRAIGHT . . .	THEY PUT US FAR APART--	474	7
THEREFORE--THE PEARL RESPONDED--	SHELLS FROM THE COAST	693	7
RESPONSIBILITY			
HER WHOLE RESPONSIBILITY--	HER LITTLE PARASOL TO	1038	3
RESPONSIBILITY--	BLOOM--IS RESULT--TO	1058	16
RESPONSIBLE			
RESPONSIBLE TO NOUGHT	A SINGLE CLOVER PLANK	1343	10
RESPONSIVE			
AND KINDRED AS RESPONSIVE--	DEATH IS THE SUPPLE	1445	V 11
REST			
MANY THE SAILS AT REST--	ON THIS WONDROUS SEA	4	8
THAN THE REST HAVE GONE.	I OFTEN PASSED THE	51	8
THAT SAT IT DOWN TO REST--	A POOR--TORN HEART-- A	78	2
HER HEART IS FIT FOR HOME [REST]--	HER BREAST IS FIT FOR	84	5
THO' ALL THE REST ARE HERE--	AS BY THE DEAD WE LOVE	88	4
IS ALL THE REST I KNEW!	WENT UP A YEAR THIS	93	24
THE WIZARD FINGERS NEVER REST--	A SOMETHING IN A	122	13
THERE TO REST REVERING	MUTE THY CORONATION--	151	5
SMUGGLED TO REST!	DUST IS THE ONLY SECRET	153	16
AND "STATION", AND THE REST!	WAIT TILL THE MAJESTY OF	171	8
THE REST OF LIFE TO SEE!	AT LAST, TO BE	174	3
THAT MAKE THE CIRCUIT OF THE REST--	HE PUT THE BELT AROUND	273	11
AND FAR FROM HEAVEN AS THE REST--	NOT PROBABLE--THE BAREST	346	3
AT REST--HIS FINGERS ARE--	DEATH SETS A THING	360	16

	FIRST LINE	POEM	LINE
REST (CONTINUED)			
DOOM IT BEYOND THE REST--	'TWAS LOVE--NOT ME--	394	6
PUTS MINOR STREAMS TO REST.	HE TOUCHED ME, SO I LIVE	506	6
BUT HE WHO WEIGHETH--WHILE THE REST--	I FEAR A MAN OF FRUGAL	543	5
ONE HURRYING TO REST--	I CROSS TILL I AM WEARY	550	13
SHE STOPPED--A TRAVELLER'S PRIVILEGE--FOR REST--	I WATCHED THE MOON	629	3
CULMINATE--IN REST--	BLOOM UPON THE MOUNTAIN	667	16
REST AT NOON--SOME MEN--	RESTS AT NIGHT	714	4
TO REST [PAUSE]--TO REST [PAUSE / STAY / DWELL] WOULD BE	I MEANT TO FIND HER WHEN	718	10
TO REST [PAUSE]--TO REST [PAUSE / STAY / DWELL] WOULD BE	I MEANT TO FIND HER WHEN	718	10
ITSELF CAN REST [LIFT / BASE] UPON--	MY WORTHINESS IS ALL MY	751	12
ONE BLESSING HAD I THAN THE REST	ONE BLESSING HAD I THAN	756	1
THE PARTING WITH THE REST	WHEN ONE HAS GIVEN UP	853	2
AND ANGELS KNOW THE REST!	I HIDE MYSELF WITHIN MY	903	V 4
THE BEAUTY OF DEMAND [BELIEF]--AT REST--	FITTER TO SEE HIM, I MAY	968	28
OF DANES, UNTO THE REST.	REPORTLESS SUBJECTS, TO	1048	4
SUPPLANTED ALL THE REST.	AT HALF PAST THREE, A	1084	8
SOME DAYS RETIRED FROM THE REST	SOME DAYS RETIRED FROM	1157	1
DEAR MARCH, HOW ARE YOU, AND THE REST--	DEAR MARCH--COME IN--	1320	7
THE REST OF LIFE IS DROPT--	ESCAPE IS SUCH A	1347	8
DIVULGING IT WOULD REST MY HEART	I SHALL NOT MURMUR IF AT	1410	5
ABHORRENT IS THE REST	WATER MAKES MANY BEDS	1428	5
AND ASIATIC REST.	NO AUTUMN'S INTERCEPTING	1516	4
ALL THE REST, HAVE DIED--	MY WARS ARE LAID AWAY IN	1549	8
FOR ALL THE REST OF LIFE--	THE FARTHEST THUNDER	1581	8
BUT WORK MIGHT BE ELECTRIC REST	THE BIRD HER PUNCTUAL	1585	7
QUITE EMPTY, QUITE AT REST,	QUITE EMPTY, QUITE AT	1606	1
ALL THE REST IS PERJURY--	LAD OF ATHENS, FAITHFUL	1768	4
RESTED			
THERE--WHERE SHE--RESTED--LAST--	'TWAS THE OLD--ROAD--	344	6
AND RESTED, ON A BEAM--	TWO BUTTERFLIES WENT OUT	533	4
RESTING			
THERE ARE THAT RESTING, RISE.	SOME THINGS THAT FLY	89	7
RESTITUTES			
HE RESTITUTES IN SOME SWEET WAY	NOT ONE BY HEAVEN	1303	3
RESTITUTION			
BUT THE RESTITUTION	NOW I KNEW I LOST HER--	1219	19
RESTORE			
LIFE OF MINE--RESTORE--	PROMISE THIS--WHEN YOU	648	12
WOULD I RESTORE MY BOOTY	WHAT DID THEY DO SINCE I	900	15
RESTORED			
THE NEARER THEY, RESTORED,	SWEET, TO HAVE HAD THEM	901	4
RESTORED IN ARCTIC CONFIDENCE	A WIND THAT ROSE	1259	8
RESTRAINING			
RESTRAINING RAMPANT SQUIRREL--	NATURE--THE GENTLEST	790	7
RESTRICTED			
THE LONG RESTRICTED [SUBJECTED] GRAVE	NO CROWD THAT HAS	515	6
A GRAVE--IS A RESTRICTED [AN INFERIOR] BREADTH--	A COFFIN--IS A SMALL	943	5
RESTS			
RESTS AT NIGHT	RESTS AT NIGHT	714	1
RESULT			
NOR WAS IT FOR APPLAUSE [PARADE / RESULT]--	THE BIRDS BEGUN AT FOUR	783	13
BY FORCE OF [SCANNING] IT'S RESULT--	AS FROST IS BEST	951	2
FAITH IS CONSTANCY'S RESULT--	HE WHO IN HIMSELF	969	3
ON A HAIR'S RESULT--	ROBBED BY DEATH--BUT	971	14
BLOOM--IS RESULT--TO MEET A FLOWER	BLOOM--IS RESULT--TO	1058	1
PRESUMING ON THAT LONE RESULT	THE STARS ARE OLD, THAT	1249	5
THE LAST [CLOSE] OF SUMMER IS DELIGHT--[A TIME / RESULT--SURVEY]	THE LAST OF SUMMER IS	1353	1
IF DOOM ITSELF WERE THE RESULT,	OF DEATH I TRY TO THINK	1558	15
RESUME			
LETHARGIC POOLS RESUME THE WHIRR	SOME RAINBOW--COMING	64	8
THESE ARE THE DAYS WHEN SKIES RESUME	THESE ARE THE DAYS WHEN	130	4
CAN THE LARK RESUME THE SHELL--	LET US PLAY YESTERDAY--	728	25
IF AS THE DAYS RESUME [INCREASE]	AS FROST IS BEST	951	7
THE PRESBYTERIAN BIRDS CAN NOW RESUME THE MEETING	THE BOBOLINK IS GONE--	1591	3
RESUMED			
THE DAY CONTROLLED [RESUMED] THE WORLD--	THE BIRDS BEGUN AT FOUR	783	22
THE DAY ABROAD WAS HEARD--[RESUMED ABROAD]	THE WIND TOOK UP THE	1134	14
RETIRED, AND RESUMED HIS TRANSITIVE ESTATE--	THE MOST TRIUMPHANT BIRD	1265	7
RESUMES			
RESUMES HIS GAUDY INDUSTRY	SUMMER BEGINS TO HAVE	1682	12
RESUMING			
BIRDS ARE RESUMING FOR HIM--	HE IS ALIVE, THIS	1160	3
RESUMING AT A MUTUAL DATE	THE SPIRIT LASTS--BUT IN	1576	15
THOU SHALT GO WITH THE RESUMING GROUND	IN SNOW THOU COMEST	1669	2
RESUMPTION			
ON RESUMPTION MORN,	I HAVE NEVER SEEN	175	18
AS IGNORANT OF THEIR RESUMPTION	FACTS BY OUR SIDE ARE	1497	12
RESURGAM			
MURMURED "RESURGAM"--"CENTIPEDE"!	"ARCTURUS" IS HIS OTHER	70	7
RESURRECTION			
SUCH RESURRECTION POURS.	THE FEET OF PEOPLE	7	24
AS IF THE "RESURRECTION"	A LADY RED--AMID THE	74	15
SLEEP [LIE] THE MEEK MEMBERS OF	SAFE IN THEIR ALABASTER	216	4

	FIRST LINE	POEM	LINE
RESURRECTION (CONTINUED)			
THE RESURRECTION-- LOVE [FAITH] IS THE FELLOW OF THE RESURRECTION	WHILE IT IS ALIVE	491	9
THAT RESURRECTION--DOES--	NO CROWD THAT HAS	515	4
OF RESURRECTION? IS THE EAST	AFRAID! OF WHOM AM I	608	9
TILL RESURRECTION, I MUST GUESS	IT WAS A GRAVE, YET BORE	876	9
'TIS RESURRECTION PAIN--	'TIS ANGUISH GRANDER	984	2
WHY, RESURRECTION HAD TO WAIT	A PANG IS MORE	1530	7
RESURRECTIONS			
WHERE RESURRECTIONS [REVELATIONS]--BE--	THERE CAME A DAY AT	322	4
RETAIN			
I RETAIN "SHAW"!	I HAD SOME THINGS THAT I	116	16
WHY DID'NT WE DETAIN [RETAIN] THEM [IT]?	HOW NOTELESS MEN, AND	282	9
NOTWITHSTANDING [TO RETAIN] DESPAIR--	NOT ANY MORE TO BE	1344	8
EQUALLY RETAIN HIM--	SUMMER IS SHORTER THAN	1506	8
NO WILDERNESS REMAIN [RETAIN]	THIS DOCILE ONE INTER	1752	6
RETAKEN			
THE SOUL'S RETAKEN MOMENTS--	THE SOUL HAS BANDAGED	512	19
WILL BE RETAKEN WITH A SHOT	THE LIFE THAT TIED TOO	1535	7
RETARD			
THEY SEVERALLY--RETARD--OR FURTHER [PROMOTE--OR HINDER]--	FOUR TREES--UPON A	742	15
RETARDED			
AS FLAVORS--CHEER RETARDED GUESTS	UNTO MY BOOKS--SO GOOD	604	5
RETARDS			
INVITES AND THEN RETARDS THE TRUTH	SWEET SKEPTICISM OF THE	1413	5
RETICENCE			
MATCH ME THE SILVER [CRYSTAL] RETICENCE--	THIS THAT WOULD GREET--	778	7
A SPIDER ON MY RETICENCE	ALONE AND IN A	1167	3
RETICENT			
A FOE SO RETICENT--	THE RAT IS THE CONCISEST	1356	8
THE RETICENT VOLCANO KEEPS	THE RETICENT VOLCANO	1748	1
RETINA			
A VISION ON THE RETINA	A DYING TIGER--MOANED	566	7
RETINUE			
FULL ROYAL IS HIS RETINUE!	WAIT TILL THE MAJESTY OF	171	11
THE GLITTERING RETINUE OF NERVES--	SEVERER SERVICE OF	786	11
RETIRE			
LIKE HER THE SAINTS RETIRE,	LIKE HER THE SAINTS	60	1
RETIRE TO OTHER LATITUDES--	ALL OVERGROWN BY CUNNING	148	7
TWO [THE] WORLDS--LIKE AUDIENCES--DISPERSE [DISSOLVE / WITHDRAW / RETIRE]	DEPARTED--TO THE	524	7
THE CROWD--RETIRE WITH AN OATH--	YOU'VE SEEN BALLOONS SET	700	17
THE MORE THEIR FEET RETIRE.	AWAY FROM HOME ARE SOME	821	8
RETIRED			
RETIRED [LAID DOWN] WITHOUT A CARE--	THE DAY UNDRESSED--	716	12
SOME DAYS RETIRED FROM THE REST	SOME DAYS RETIRED FROM	1157	1
RETIRED, AND RESUMED HIS TRANSITIVE ESTATE--	THE MOST TRIUMPHANT BIRD	1265	7
THE SUN RETIRED TO A CLOUD	THE SUN RETIRED TO A	1693	1
RETIRES			
WHEN HE--RETIRES--	JUST SO--JESUS--RAPS--	317	7
RETRACT			
DOTH NOT RETRACT A SINGLE SPICE	THERE IS A FLOWER THAT	380	23
RETREAT			
THAT SIGNALIZE A SHOW'S RETREAT--	I'VE KNOWN A HEAVEN,	243	7
RETREAT--WAS OUT OF HOPE--	OUR JOURNEY HAD ADVANCED	615	9
RETREATING			
RETREATING [RECEDING] MOUNTAIN!	AH, TENERIFFE!	666	2
RETREATING UP, A BILLOW'S HIGHT	ESCAPING BACKWARD TO	867	5
RETREATING BLINDED DOWN	ESCAPING BACKWARD TO	867	6
WE LEARN IN THE RETREATING	WE LEARN IN THE	1083	1
BY A DEPARTING [RETREATING / ABSCONDING] LIGHT	BY A DEPARTING LIGHT	1714	1
RETRIEVE			
RETRIEVE THINE INDUSTRY--	'TIS SUNRISE--LITTLE	908	4
RETRIEVELESS			
I PROBED RETRIEVELESS THINGS	I TRIED TO THINK A	532	5
WAS MY RETRIEVELESS BLAME--	IT BLOOMED AND DROPT, A	978	12
TILL SOME RETRIEVELESS NIGHT	THE FROST WAS NEVER SEEN	1202	9
RETRIEVER			
TOMORROW--THOU RETRIEVER	"TOMORROW"--WHOSE	1367	5
RETRIEVES			
BUT NOT RETRIEVES THE PLANT--	YOU CANNOT MAKE	1508	6
RETRIMMED			
RETRIMMED IT'S MASTS--REDECKED IT'S SAILS--	ADRIFT! A LITTLE BOAT	30	12
RETROGRADE			
PAST WHICH FORCES RETROGRADE	CRISIS IS A HAIR	889	3
TO FEED UPON THE RETROGRADE--	HAD I NOT THIS, OR THIS,	904	15
THE STOCK'S ADVANCE AND RETROGRADE	MYSELF CAN READ THE	1089	3
RETROSPECT			
JUST SUCH A RETROSPECT	THE PROPS ASSIST THE	1142	8
OF RETROSPECT THE ARROW	TO MAKE ROUTINE A	1196	5
COULD PROSPECT TASTE OF RETROSPECT	MY TRIUMPH LASTED TILL	1227	11
DETERRED BY [FOR CHASTENED / SUBDUED TO] RETROSPECT.	THE LAST OF SUMMER IS	1353	2
OR CLOVER'S RETROSPECT--	A FADED BOY--IN SALLOW	1524	8
WITH THEIR DEAR RETROSPECT.	THE DISTANCE THAT THE	1742	8
RETROSPECTION			
OUR RETROSPECTION OF THEM	THESE TESTED OUR HORIZON	886	5
RETROSPECTION IS PROSPECT'S HALF,	THIS WAS IN THE WHITE OF	995	7
THAT HATH NOR RETROSPECTION [PERADVENTURE]	LEFT IN IMMORTAL YOUTH	1289	3

	FIRST LINE	POEM	LINE
RETROSPECTS			
OF CRICKETS--CROWS--AND RETROSPECTS	SEPTEMBER'S	1271	3
RETURN			
AND WILL RETURN.	I HAVE A BIRD IN SPRING	5	12
RETURN.	I HAVE A BIRD IN SPRING	5	30
TO BREAKFAST--TO [AND] RETURN--	A LITTLE EAST OF JORDAN,	59	8
NOT LIKE THE DEW, DID SHE RETURN	SHE WENT AS QUIET AS THE	149	3
TO THE HILLS RETURN!	I HAVE NEVER SEEN	175	20
TOO PLUMMETLESS--THAT IT COME BACK [RETURN]--	A SOLEMN THING--IT WAS--	271	7
RETURN--WITH SUCH A CROWN	THE FACE I CARRY WITH ME	336	10
INTENDING TO RETURN--	SHE LAY AS IF AT PLAY	369	3
UNCERTAIN [INDIFFERENT]--TO RETURN BELOW--	HE PARTS HIMSELF--LIKE	517	11
HER WARM [STRAIGHT / GOOD / QUICK / SAFE] RETURN, IF SO SHE	NO NOTICE GAVE SHE, BUT	804	17
ODORS RETURN WHOLE	BANISH AIR FROM AIR--	854	8
AFFECT US, AND RETURN--	THERE IS A JUNE WHEN	930	8
AND THEN RETURN--AND NIGHT [TRUST]--AND HOME--	I LEARNED--AT LEAST--	944	22
FOR MERIT OF RETURN--	'TWAS AWKWARD, BUT IT	973	6
WHEN THE SEA RETURN NO ANSWER	GRATITUDE--IS NOT THE	989	5
WHEN IT IS MAY, IF MAY RETURN,	WHEN THEY COME BACK--IF	1080	9
TO LIGHT, AND THEN RETURN--	THE SPRY ARMS OF THE	1103	12
I CAN RETURN THE BLOW--	ALONE AND IN A	1167	18
UNLESS YOU LEAVE HIM--THEN RETURN	SO MUCH OF HEAVEN HAS	1228	11
AND PROMISE TO RETURN--	ONE THING OF IT WE	1464	2
FORGETTING TO RETURN,	WE SEND THE WAVE TO FIND	1604	4
INVITED TO RETURN	WITH SWEETNESS UNABATED	1709	8
AND THEN IT MUST RETURN.	THE LONGEST DAY THAT GOD	1769	4
RETURNED			
THE PATRIARCH'S BIRD RETURNED,	ONCE MORE, MY NOW	48	6
THEREFORE, AS ONE RETURNED, I FEEL,	JUST LOST, WHEN I WAS	160	7
AND RETURNED ON HIGH--	MOST SHE TOUCHED ME BY	760	12
TO THIS WORLD SHE RETURNED.	TO THIS WORLD SHE	830	1
BUT "YOU"--SHE RETURNED WITH VALOR	I SAW THAT THE FLAKE WAS	1267	5
RETURNING			
DID NOT TALK OF RETURNING!	WENT UP A YEAR THIS	93	9
BUT DIFFERED IN RETURNING--	ALL OVERGROWN BY CUNNING	148	9
RETURNING TO THE WEST--	"HEAVEN" HAS DIFFERENT	575	14
THE SOUL RETURNING SOFT AT NIGHT [STILL BY DAWN / LOTH BY DAWN]	CONTAINED IN THIS SHORT	1165	3
RETURNING HERE--	THE THINGS THAT NEVER	1515	8
UNCONSCIOUS OUR RETURNING	EDEN IS THAT	1657	7
RETURNING IS A DIFFERENT ROUTE	NO MAN SAW AWE, NOR TO	1733	9
RETURNS			
AND STILL THE PENSIVE SPRING RETURNS--	NEW FEET WITHIN MY	99	7
RETURNS--SUGGESTS--CONVICTS--ENCHANTS--	THE LOVE A LIFE CAN SHOW	673	15
RETURNS NO SYLLABLE	THE ROBIN FOR THE CRUMB	864	2
RETURNS US NOT, BUT AFTER TIME	EXHILIRATION IS THE	1118	5
REVEAL			
WHETHER TO REVEAL--	I NEVER TOLD THE BURIED	11	15
AS LACES JUST REVEAL THE SURGE--	THE THOUGHT BENEATH SO	210	3
REVEAL THE WIDTH THAT BURNED--	THE RED--BLAZE--IS THE	469	6
REVEAL BY SIGN--A SYLLABLE	THE FUTURE--NEVER SPOKE	672	3
IF WHEN [AS] THE SUN REVEAL,	AS FROST IS BEST	951	5
THE CHERUBIM REVEAL--	SHALL I TAKE THEE, THE	1126	12
REVEALED			
IS RICHER THAN COULD BE REVEALED	THERE IS ANOTHER	1116	7
TO IGNORANCE REVEALED.	THE LIGHTNING IS A	1173	8
'TIS ECSTASY'S REVEALED [DIVINE / SUBLIME / REVERED] REVIEW--	THE LAST OF SUMMER IS	1353	3
REVEALS			
REVEALS THE FACT THAT ONE IS RAPT	HOW NOTELESS MEN, AND	282	3
SUNSET THAT SCREENS, REVEALS--	SUNSET THAT SCREENS,	1609	1
REVEILLE			
TO PURER REVEILLE!	GOOD NIGHT! WHICH PUT	259	12
REVEL			
AND REVEL TILL THE DAY--	THERE IS A MORN BY MEN	24	18
AS BEGGARS REVEL AT A FEAST	AS WATCHERS HANG UPON	121	2
HE AND I--REVEL--	WE--BEE AND I--LIVE BY	230	13
REVELATION			
JUST REVELATION--TO THE BELOVED--	"MORNING"--MEANS	300	5
AS NUMB TO REVELATION	AS FAR FROM PITY, AS	496	3
IT'S AMBER REVELATION	AN IGNORANCE A SUNSET	552	5
THEN--REVELATION CLOSED--	WE LEARNED THE WHOLE OF	568	4
NOT "REVELATION"--'TIS--THAT WAITS,	NOT "REVELATION"--'TIS--	685	1
A REVELATION OF YOURSELF--	YOU CONSTITUTED TIME--	765	3
BUT LET NOT REVELATION	THE LILAC IS AN ANCIENT	1241	19
REVELATION'S			
IS REVELATION'S LIMIT [CAUTION],	EMBARRASSMENT OF ONE	662	3
ON REVELATION'S WALL--	BELSHAZZAR HAD A LETTER	1459	8
REVELATIONS			
THOSE WHO READ THE "REVELATIONS"	IF THE FOOLISH, CALL	168	5
WHERE RESURRECTIONS [REVELATIONS]--BE--	THERE CAME A DAY AT	322	4
WHILE COLOR'S REVELATIONS BREAK--	AS FAR FROM PITY, AS	496	11
THE REVELATIONS OF THE BOOK	THE MURMURING OF BEES,	1115	7
REVELRY			
IS ALMOST REVELRY [ECSTASY]--	THE SYMPTOM OF THE GALE	1327	4
SURPASSING REVELRY,	HIS ORIENTAL HERESIES	1526	V
A REVELRY UNSPEAKABLE	OF THIS IS DAY COMPOSED	1675	3
REVENGE			
I HAVE AT LAST REVENGE--	MINE ENEMY IS GROWING	1509	2

	FIRST LINE	POEM	LINE
REVENUES			
SUCH THRENODIES [EXTACIES / REVENUES / ARGUMENTS] OF PEARL--	YOU'LL KNOW HER--BY HER	634	26
REVERBERATION			
HOW [THAT] LIFE'S REVERBERATION	THE FARTHEST THUNDER	1581	19
REVERE			
AND JUST--REVERE--	A MIEN TO MOVE A QUEEN--	283	25
THE LICENSE TO REVERE,	I WOULD NOT PAINT--A	505	20
REVERE [RESPECT] THE GRAYEST PILE	ASHES DENOTE THAT FIRE	1063	2
PERMITTED TO REVERE	TO UNDERTAKE IS TO	1070	6
I THE DART REVERE.	I'VE GOT AN ARROW HERE.	1729	3
REVERED			
'TIS ECSTASY'S REVEALED [DIVINE / SUBLIME / REVERED] REVIEW--	THE LAST OF SUMMER IS	1353	3
REVERENT			
THEN TURNING FROM THEM REVERENT--	WHOSE ARE THE LITTLE	142	25
REVERENTIAL			
MY CONSTANT--REVERENTIAL FACE	MY BEST ACQUAINTANCES	932	7
WITH REVERENTIAL HYACINTH--	TWO TRAVELLERS PERISHING	933	11
SELECT A REVERENTIAL BROOM--	THAT SACRED CLOSET WHEN	1273	3
REVERENTLY			
REVERENTLY, TO THE HUNGRY	TALK WITH PRUDENCE TO A	119	3
TO REVERENTLY PEER,	IN EBON BOX, WHEN YEARS	169	2
REVERING			
THERE TO REST REVERING	MUTE THY CORONATION--	151	5
TO A REVERING--EYE	THE SOUL'S SUPERIOR	306	V 14
REVERSE			
REVERSE CANNOT BEFALL	REVERSE CANNOT BEFALL	395	1
NO BOBOLINK--REVERSE HIS SINGING	NO BOBOLINK--REVERSE HIS	755	1
WHEN GUSTS REVERSE THE SNOW--	HE FOUGHT LIKE THOSE	759	10
ACQUIRED BY REVERSE--	NONE CAN EXPERIENCE	771	6
TO BE ASSISTED OF REVERSE	DESPAIR'S ADVANTAGE IS	799	3
ONE MUST REVERSE HAVE [ITSELF HAVE / HAVE PREVIOUS] BORE--	DESPAIR'S ADVANTAGE IS	799	4
AND LOVE AND THE REVERSE.	DYING! TO BE AFRAID OF	831	12
IN MOMENT OF REVERSE--	HAD I NOT THIS, OR THIS,	904	6
HALF THE CONDITION [DISTINCTION], THY REVERSE--TO FOLLOW--	WERT THOU BUT ILL--THAT	961	11
WE JUST REVERSE THE ZODIAC	THE PRODUCTS OF MY FARM	1025	7
REVERSED			
THE EARTH REVERSED HER HEMISPHERES--	I SAW NO WAY--THE	378	3
'TWAS SABBATH--WITH THE BELLS DIVORCED [REVERSED]--	I HAD NO CAUSE TO BE	542	15
REVERSED--IN VICTORY?	I CROSS TILL I AM WEARY	550	25
REVERSED DIVINITY--	TWO--WERE IMMORTAL TWICE	800	4
AND THEN THE PANELS ARE REVERSED--	WE CAN BUT FOLLOW TO THE	920	7
THEN REVERSED THE DOOR--	PARADISE IS THAT OLD	1119	4
REVERSES			
REVERSES NATURE--MASTER--	SUNSET AT NIGHT--IS	415	3
REVERSES MODESTY	I CANNOT BE ASHAMED	914	5
REVERTED			
REVERTED TO ADJOINING LIVES--	IF HE WERE LIVING--DARE	734	9
REVERY			
UPON THE REVERY--[PASSER BY]	THE LONG SIGH OF THE	1359	4
IN BLISSFUL [LUSCIOUS / SUMPTUOUS] REVERY	HIS ORIENTAL HERESIES	1526	V
WITHOUT A REVERY--	A DRUNKARD CANNOT MEET A	1628	2
AND REVERY.	TO MAKE A PRAIRIE IT	1755	3
THE REVERY ALONE WILL DO,	TO MAKE A PRAIRIE IT	1755	4
REVIEW			
HER MEMORIES [MEMORY] LIKE STRAINS--REVIEW [ENCHANT]--	LIKE SOME OLD FASHIONED	302	13
I DISSECT [REVIEW] THE PLAY	ONE DAY IS THERE OF THE	814	6
'TIS ECSTASY'S REVEALED [DIVINE / SUBLIME / REVERED] REVIEW--	THE LAST OF SUMMER IS	1353	3
IS IN REVIEW	ALL THAT I DO	1496	2
REVIEWED			
REVIEWED IT WITH MY EYES,	I READ MY SENTENCE--	412	2
REVIEWING			
IN HEAVENLY REVIEWING	WITH SWEETNESS UNABATED	1709	11
REVIEWS			
SUNSET--REVIEWS HER SAPPHIRE REGIMENT [REGIMENTS]--	AH, TENERIFFE!	666	4
REVILED			
THAN I REVILED [DENOUNCED] MYSELF,	IT DROPPED SO LOW--IN MY	747	6
AS TONGUES [THRONGS / EYES] OF DIAMOND HAD REVILED	MY SOUL--ACCUSED ME--AND	753	2
REVISITING			
REVISITING THE BOG!	SOME RAINBOW--COMING	64	18
REVISITING MY LATE ABODE	ALONE AND IN A	1167	9
IRRESOLUTE OF [REVISITING FOR] ALMS--	A FIELD OF STUBBLE,	1407	6
REVIVE			
LEST GRATITUDE REVIVE THE SNAKE [MY THOUGHT]	IT CAME HIS TURN TO BEG	1500	7
REVOLTING			
TO THIS REVOLTING BLISS	THE WATERS CHASED HIM AS	1749	8
REVOLUTION			
ON REVOLUTION DAY?	WHO NEVER LOST, ARE	73	12
FEET, SMALL AS MINE--HAVE MARCHED IN REVOLUTION	UNTO LIKE STORY--TROUBLE	295	17
BUT TO FAITH--A REVOLUTION	UNFULFILLED TO	972	3
REVOLUTION IS THE POD	REVOLUTION IS THE POD	1082	1

	FIRST LINE	POEM	LINE
REVOLUTION (CONTINUED)			
REVOLUTION SHAKES IT FOR	REVOLUTION IS THE POD	1082	11
REVOLVER			
THE BODY--BORROWS [THE PRUDENT--CARRIES] A [THE] REVOLVER--	ONE NEED NOT BE A	670	17
REVOLVING			
WITH A REVOLVING [DELUSIVE / DISSEMBLING / DISSOLVING / . . .	A ROUTE OF EVANESCENCE	1463	2
OF THAT REVOLVING REASON	DID LIFE'S PENURIOUS	1717	6
REWALKS			
AS ONE REWALKS A PRECIPICE	AS ONE DOES SICKNESS	957	5
REWARD			
MY REWARD FOR BEING, WAS THIS.	MY REWARD FOR BEING, WAS	343	1
THOUGH LIFE'S REWARD--BE DONE--	I TIE MY HAT--I CREASE	443	31
OH, REWARD [RECOMPENSE] OF ANGUISH, . . .	IN FALLING TIMBERS	614	11
SHOULD ENDOW [ADDRESS / REWARD] THE DAY-- .	BLOOM UPON THE MOUNTAIN	667	6
WILL REFUND [REWARD / REPAY] THE HAND-- . .	SOIL OF FLINT, IF STEADY	681	2
IF LOVE REWARD [BE AT] THE END--	TO WAIT AN HOUR--IS LONG	781	4
AND OFFER A REWARD	WHAT DID THEY DO SINCE I	900	14
THE BEAUTY THAT REWARD HIM MOST [BEST]-- .	FITTER TO SEE HIM, I MAY	968	27
REWARDED			
BY STINT [END]--REWARDED WORK--	THE SERVICE WITHOUT HOPE	779	4
RHINE			
MANY CROSS THE RHINE	MANY CROSS THE RHINE	123	1
NOT ALL THE FRANKFORT BERRIES [VATS UPON THE RHINE]	I TASTE A LIQUOR NEVER	214	3
WHILE RUNS THE RHINE--	WE--BEE AND I--LIVE BY	230	12
WHO HATH THE AMPLE RHINE	EXHILIRATION--IS WITHIN	383	10
BARE RHINE--	A TOAD, CAN DIE OF LIGHT	583	11
RHINOCEROS			
AND I MUST BE RHINOCEROS	YOU SAID THAT I "WAS	738	10
RHODODENDRON			
OR RHODODENDRON--WORN--	THERE IS A FLOWER THAT	380	12
RHODORA'S			
RHODORA'S CHEEK IS CRIMSON, ...	WHOSE ARE THE LITTLE	142	23
RHYME			
PERISH WITH HIM--THAT KEYLESS RHYME! . . .	BETTER--THAN MUSIC! FOR	503	8
RHYMES			
AND MY RHYMES--	I SHALL KEEP SINGING!	250	6
RHYTHM			
THEN TO A RHYTHM SLIM	IN WINTER IN MY ROOM	1670	28
RHYTHMIC			
WITHOUT A RHYTHMIC RUMOR	WHAT TENEMENTS OF CLOVER	1338	7
RIBALDRY			
AND PURPLE RIBALDRY--OF MORNING	WHAT CARE THE DEAD, FOR	592	4
NO RIBALDRY MAY CREEP	TO THEIR APARTMENT DEEP	1701	2
RIBBON			
A DARKER RIBBON--FOR A DAY--	TO DIE--TAKES JUST A	255	5
A RIBBON AT A TIME--	I'LL TELL YOU HOW THE	318	2
RIBBON'S			
HE VARIED BY A RIBBON'S WIDTH	HOW MANY SCHEMES MAY DIE	1150	7
RIBBONS			
THEIR RIBBONS JUST BEYOND THE EYE-- . . .	YOU'VE SEEN BALLOONS SET	700	9
RIBBONS OF THE YEAR--	RIBBONS OF THE YEAR--	873	1
RIBIN			
UNOBSERVED--A RIBIN SLIPT, ...	SUMMER LAID HER SIMPLE	1363	3
RIBS			
TO FIT IT'S SIDES [RIBS]	I LIKE TO SEE IT LAP	585	9
RICH			
A RICH MAN--MIGHT NOT NOTICE IT--	I LOST A WORLD--THE	181	5
STILL TO SHOW--HOW RICH I GO--	I'LL CLUTCH--AND CLUTCH	427	22
I HEARD SUCH WORDS AS "RICH"--	IT WAS GIVEN TO ME BY	454	9
RICH! 'TWAS MYSELF--WAS RICH--	IT WAS GIVEN TO ME BY	454	13
RICH! 'TWAS MYSELF--WAS RICH--	IT WAS GIVEN TO ME BY	454	13
IT HAS NO BUCKET--WERE I RICH	I KNOW WHERE WELLS GROW	460	9
JUST TO BE RICH--TO WASTE MY GUINEAS [GUINEA]	SWEET--YOU FORGOT--BUT I	523	9
TO SOMETIMES HEAR "RICH PEOPLE" BUY . . .	I CRIED AT PITY--NOT AT	588	9
I WONDER HOW THE RICH--MAY FEEL--	GOD GAVE A LOAF TO EVERY	791	13
THAT MAKE US RICH AN HOUR--	DREAMS ARE THE SUBTLE	1376	2
RICHARD			
WHEN RICHARD WENT TO MILL--	'TWAS JUST THIS TIME,	445	6
RICHER			
LEST SOME ONE ELSE SHOULD [RICHER PEOPLE] BUY	A DIAMOND ON THE HAND	1108 V	8
IS RICHER THAN COULD BE REVEALED	THERE IS ANOTHER	1116	7
AND I AM RICHER THEN THAN ALL MY FELLOW MEN--	TAKE ALL AWAY FROM ME,	1640	2
RICHES			
YOUR RICHES--TAUGHT ME--POVERTY.	YOUR RICHES--TAUGHT ME--	299	1
OF RICHES--AS UNCONSCIOUS	REMOVED FROM ACCIDENT OF	424	5
WHEN--SUDDENLY--MY RICHES SHRANK--	IT WOULD NEVER BE COMMON	430	21
ALL OTHER RICHES BE	WITHOUT THIS--THERE IS	655	2
I PLAY AT RICHES--TO APPEASE	I PLAY AT RICHES--TO	801	1
I MADE SLOW RICHES BUT MY GAIN	I MADE SLOW RICHES BUT	843	1
BECAUSE 'TWAS RICHES I COULD OWN, ...	BECAUSE 'TWAS RICHES I	1093	1
RICHES WERE GOOD--	ARE FRIENDS DELIGHT OR	1199	3
RICHES ARE SAD.	ARE FRIENDS DELIGHT OR	1199	6
RICHES AND NAME AND REALM--	FRIGID AND SWEET HER	1318	6
RID			
THE SOUL CANNOT BE RID--	OF CONSCIOUSNESS, HER	894	2
RIDDLE			
BORE HIS RIDDLE IN!	IF THOSE I LOVED WERE	29	8

	FIRST LINE	POEM		LINE
RIDDLE (CONTINUED)				
I, MY RIDDLE BRING	IF THOSE I LOVED WERE	29	V	8
HINT THAT WITHIN THE RIDDLE	I HAV'NT TOLD MY GARDEN	50		15
HOW STILL THE RIDDLE LIES!	SOME THINGS THAT FLY	89		9
AND THROUGH A RIDDLE, AT THE LAST--	THIS WORLD IS NOT	501		7
FURTHER THAN RIDDLE RIDE--	UNDER THE LIGHT, YET	949		14
THE RIDDLE WE CAN [THAT WE] GUESS	THE RIDDLE WE CAN GUESS	1222		1
'TWILL RIDDLE LIKE A SHOT.	HOW NEWS MUST FEEL WHEN	1319	V	4
RIDE				
AS WE RIDE GRAND ALONG!	ONE DIGNITY DELAYS FOR	98		8
FOR WE MUST RIDE TO THE JUDGMENT--	TIE THE STRINGS TO MY	279		7
AND CAUGHT A RIDE [TOOK A BOUT] WITH HIM	TWO BUTTERFLIES WENT OUT	533	V	4
COULD I BUT RIDE INDEFINITE	COULD I BUT RIDE	661		1
THAT BEE TO RIDE, OR FLOWER OF FURZE	BECAUSE THE BEE MAY	869		11
FURTHER THAN RIDDLE RIDE--	UNDER THE LIGHT, YET	949		14
AND RIDE AWAY.	TOO FEW THE MORNINGS BE,	1186		7
RIDE ABROAD IN OSTENTATION	BEES ARE BLACK, WITH	1405		3
AN EASY MORNING'S RIDE--	A ROUTE OF EVANESCENCE	1463		8
WHAT BUCCANEER WOULD RIDE	DOWN TIME'S QUAINT	1656		8
RIDES				
I ENVY SEAS, WHEREON HE RIDES--[THAT BEAR HIM]	I ENVY SEAS, WHEREON HE	498		1
WITHIN MY GARDEN, RIDES A BIRD	WITHIN MY GARDEN, RIDES	500		1
THAT RIDES--EMITS [SUPPORTS] A THUNDER--	TO INTERRUPT HIS YELLOW	591		15
OCCASIONALLY RIDES--	A NARROW FELLOW IN THE	986		2
RIDGE				
A ROSE UPON IT'S RIDGE TO SOW	IT WAS A GRAVE, YET BORE	876		11
OF RIVER OR OF RIDGE [OF FATHOM OR OF LEAGUE] BEYOND	HOW FAR IS IT TO HEAVEN?	929		3
RIDING				
RIDING TO MEET THE EARL--	DROPPED INTO THE ETHER	665		8
SITTING [RIDING] A BOUGH LIKE A BRIGADIER	A PROMPT--EXECUTIVE BIRD	1177		5
WHEN I AM RIDING BY--	I KNOW SUSPENSE--IT	1285		4
RIGHT				
AT THAT GRAND "RIGHT HAND"!	IF THE FOOLISH, CALL	168		20
YOU'RE RIGHT--"THE WAY IS NARROW"--	YOU'RE RIGHT--"THE WAY	234		1
AT THE LORD'S RIGHT HAND.	OVER AND OVER, LIKE A	367		8
THAT RIGHT--WAS THINE--	HOW SICK--TO WAIT--IN	368		6
AND THAT--BY RIGHT THAT HE	I LIVE WITH HIM--I SEE	463		6
WHAT RIGHT HAVE I--TO BE A BRIDE--	I AM ASHAMED--I HIDE--	473		2
MINE--BY THE RIGHT OF THE WHITE ELECTION!	MINE--BY THE RIGHT OF	528		1
'TIS BLISS [WEALTH / RIGHT] I CANNOT WEIGH--	IF I MAY HAVE IT, WHEN	577		6
DEATH IS THE COMMON [MUTUAL / EQUAL] RIGHT	A TOAD, CAN DIE OF LIGHT	583		2
WITHOUT MY RIGHT OF FROST--	I CANNOT LIVE WITH YOU--	640		19
I KNOW NOT WHICH, DESIRE, OR GRANT [RIGHT / SIGHT]--	I PLAY AT RICHES--TO	801		23
SHALL STAND TO OUR RIGHT HAND--	SWEET, TO HAVE HAD THEM	901		5
TOO NARROW IS THE RIGHT BETWEEN--	TOO LITTLE WAY THE HOUSE	911		5
THE LOVE, THO, WILL ARRAY [INSTRUCT] ME RIGHT	FITTER TO SEE HIM, I MAY	968		21
BY JUST A SECOND'S RIGHT--	PAIN HAS BUT ONE	1049		6
OBTAIN IT'S RIGHT OF DEW--	BLOOM--IS RESULT--TO	1058		10
OH SUN--BUT JUST A SECOND'S RIGHT	MY GOD--HE SEES THEE--	1178		8
WHERE I FOR RIGHT TO BE [GO]--	SOMEWHERE UPON THE	1231		6
WITH HIM THE SKILL [RIGHT / ART] REMAIN	ELIJAH'S WAGON KNEW NO	1254	V	6
THE RIGHT TO REPREHEND	BECAUSE THAT YOU ARE	1260		30
WHAT RIGHT HAD FIELDS TO ARBITRATE	I WORKED FOR CHAFF AND	1269		3
OH MARCH, COME RIGHT UP STAIRS WITH ME--	DEAR MARCH--COME IN--	1320		9
THEY WENT TO GOD'S RIGHT HAND--	THOSE--DYING THEN,	1551		3
HAVE NOT EACH ONE OF US THE RIGHT	FEW, YET ENOUGH,	1596		4
THE FINE--ENSUING RIGHT	OH WHAT A GRACE IS THIS,	1615		4
THE RIGHT OF WAY TO TRIPOLI	THE PEDIGREE OF HONEY	1627		7
TO PAY FOR THY RIGHT HAND	I DID NOT REACH THEE	1664		13
MY RIGHT TO WALK UPON THE EARTH	I KNOW OF PEOPLE IN THE	1665		7
THE RIGHT TO PERISH MIGHT BE THO'T	THE RIGHT TO PERISH	1692		1
AN UNDISPUTED RIGHT	THE RIGHT TO PERISH	1692		2
RIGHTEOUS				
AND EVERY RIGHTEOUS [FOUNDED] THING	HIS LITTLE HEARSE LIKE	1522		6
RIGHTEOUSNESS				
BETROTHED TO RIGHTEOUSNESS MIGHT BE	BETROTHED TO	1641		1
RIGID				
HOARY [EVIL / RIGID / WRINKLED / ARID / SHRUNKEN] THE FRUITION	FORTITUDE INCARNATE	1217		7
RIGOR				
A RIGOR UNRELIEVED	I KNEW THAT I HAD GAINED	1022		5
RILL				
SAVE BY TEARFUL RILL--	GLOWING IS HER BONNET,	72		8
BUT LONGER THAN THE LITTLE RILL--	FORGET! THE LADY WITH	438		12
RIM				
EXISTENCE'S WHOLE ARC, [WHOLE EYE / WHOLE RIM / SURMISE] FILLED UP,	I'M CEDED--I'VE STOPPED	508		12
UPON A MOMENT'S SHALLOW [FICKLE] RIM	HOW MUCH THE PRESENT	1380		5
RIME				
THOUGH RIME BY RIME, THE STEADY FROST	NO NOTICE GAVE SHE, BUT	804		7
THOUGH RIME BY RIME, THE STEADY FROST	NO NOTICE GAVE SHE, BUT	804		7
RIND				
IT IS SIMPLE, TO ACHE IN THE BONE, OR THE RIND--	IT IS EASY TO WORK WHEN	244		5
I'D TOSS IT YONDER, LIKE A RIND,	IF YOU WERE COMING IN	511		15
REMAIN--'TIS BUT A RIND.	HEREIN A BLOSSOM LIES--	899		4
PRESENT THE AWKWARD RIND--	EXCEPT THE SMALLER SIZE	1067	V	

	FIRST LINE	POEM	LINE
RING SEE WRING			
NE'ER SUCH A RING ON SUCH A GREEN--	THERE IS A MORN BY MEN	24	14
THE BELLS OF GHENT W'D RING--	IF THOSE I LOVED WERE	29	4
NO RING--NO MARVEL--	I'VE KNOWN A HEAVEN,	243	11
WHOSE ANVIL'S EVEN RING	DARE YOU SEE A SOUL AT	365	10
NOW--TO RING A DOOR BEYOND	TAKE YOUR HEAVEN FURTHER	388	6
AND BELLS--THAT BOLDLY RING [COME]	I ENVY SEAS, WHEREON HE	498	18
RING--FOR THE SCANT SALVATION--	GLEE--THE GREAT STORM IS	619	5
AT RECESS--IN THE RING--	BECAUSE I COULD NOT STOP	712	10
ONLY THE KEEPER OF THIS RING [THE SEAL]	GIVEN IN MARRIAGE UNTO	817	7
A JUST SUFFICIENT RING.	HE OUTSTRIPPED TIME WITH	865	8
THAT BELLS SHOULD RING TILL ALL SHOULD KNOW [HEAR]	OF TOLLING BELL I ASK	947	5
THOUGH THE RING IS UNWHOLE, AND THE COMPANY BROKE	OF THE HEART THAT GOES	1098	3
AND WAS [JUST / WHEN] ABOUT TO RING	SHALL I TAKE THEE, THE	1126	6
RINGED			
BUT RINGED WITH POWER	IN WINTER IN MY ROOM	1670	17
RINGING			
WHEN BELLS STOP RINGING--CHURCH--BEGINS--	WHEN BELLS STOP RINGING	633	1
RINGLET			
NO RINGLET, TO MY HAIR,	I CANNOT DANCE UPON MY	326	10
RINGS			
THE EAR RINGS OF PIZARRO	I ENVY SEAS, WHEREON HE	498	15
RIOT			
THE TRANSPORT [RAPTURE / TRIUMPH / RIOT] OF THE BIRD--	THE WIND TOOK UP THE	1134	16
WITHOUT, PERHAPS, THE RIOT	SUMMER HAS TWO	1422	5
THE RIOT GIVEN AT THE FIRST	THE MOB WITHIN THE HEART	1745	3
RIP			
OR RIP OF NAIL--OR CARPENTER--	I'VE KNOWN A HEAVEN,	243	5
RIP--WHILE THE SOWER--DREAMS--	I TEND MY FLOWERS FOR	339	4
NOR RIP, NOR WRINKLE INDICATE	TOO COLD IS THIS	1135	8
RIPE			
TO FEEL ITSELF GET RIPE--	A SOLEMN THING WITHIN	483	2
BUT WHEN THE NEWS BE RIPE--	THE FUTURE--NEVER SPOKE	672	5
WHAT, WHEN THE ROSE IS RIPE--	WHAT SHALL I DO WHEN THE	956	2
BEFORE THE QUICK [RIPE / PEAL / DRUM / DRUMS / BELLS / BOMB / . . .	ONE JOY OF SO MUCH	1420	6
ONE SIDE OF ME THE NUTS ARE RIPE	THE ONES THAT	1690	7
RIPEN			
TRADITIONS RIPEN AND DECAY,	A LITTLE OVERFLOWING	1467	5
RIPENESS			
WHAT RIPENESS AFTER THEN	'TWAS HERE MY SUMMER	1756	2
RIPENING			
THE HOPES SO JUICY RIPENING--	SHE SIGHTS A BIRD--SHE	507	9
AND QUICKENING [RIPENING]--AS WE SOWED--	HE GAVE AWAY HIS LIFE--	567	13
RIPENINGS			
THERE ARE TWO RIPENINGS--ONE--OF SIGHT--	THERE ARE TWO RIPENINGS	332	1
RIPEST			
ABOVE THE RIPEST ROSE--	WITHIN MY GARDEN, RIDES	500	6
RIPPLE			
THE RIPPLE OF OUR THEME--	I LEARNED--AT LEAST--	944	12
RIPPLES			
OF SHADOWS [RIPPLES] GOING DOWN	A STAGNANT PLEASURE LIKE	1281	6
RISE			
IN DREAMS I SEE THEM RISE,	"SIC TRANSIT GLORIA	3	50
IF SPRINGS FROM WINTER RISE,	IF PAIN FOR PEACE	63	4
MANY A BULB WILL RISE--	SO FROM THE MOULD	66	3
THERE ARE THAT RESTING, RISE.	SOME THINGS THAT FLY	89	7
I THINK JUST HOW MY SHAPE WILL RISE--	I THINK JUST HOW MY	237	1
RISE--SOLEMN--ON [IN] THE TREE,	OF ALL THE SOUNDS	321	28
SUFFICIENT TROTH, THAT WE SHALL [SHE WILL] RISE--	THERE CAME A DAY AT	322	25
THE LITTLE DWELLING HOUSES RISE	THE COLOR OF THE GRAVE	411	15
RISE--STILL THE DUNCE--	KNOWS HOW TO FORGET!	433	7
AND IS THE FIRST, TO RISE--	SHE HIDETH HER THE LAST	557	2
THERE SEEMED TO RISE A TUNE	THE TREES LIKE TASSELS--	606	2
NOR COULD I RISE--WITH YOU--	I CANNOT LIVE WITH YOU--	640	21
THEIR PURPLE FIGURES RISE	THE MOUNTAINS--GROW	757	2
NEITHER WITNESSED [NOTICED] RISE	STRUCK, WAS I, NOR YET	925	22
SLAY--AND MY SOUL SHALL RISE	BIND ME--I STILL CAN	1005	4
TILL WE ARE ASKED [CALLED] TO RISE	WE NEVER KNOW HOW HIGH	1176	2
AS THE ATTEMPT TO RISE.	DROWNING IS NOT SO	1718	2
RISEN			
AND RISEN UP--AND GONE AWAY,	I'VE HEARD AN ORGAN TALK	183	5
RISES			
THE CROCUS--TILL SHE RISES	THE FEET OF PEOPLE	7	3
IT RISES TRAIN BY TRAIN--	ALL THESE MY BANNERS BE.	22	4
IT RISES--PASSES--ON OUR SOUTH	IT RISES--PASSES--ON OUR	1023	1
HE RISES ON A LOG	HIS MANSION IN THE POOL	1379	3
RISING			
AND STARTLED AT IT'S SWELLING [RISING]	BECAUSE MY BROOK IS	1200	5
THAN OWN A RISING SUN	I'D RATHER RECOLLECT A	1349	2
BUT IT IS RISING [HIGHER / FURTHER] EVERY DAY	THE PILE OF YEARS IS NOT	1507	3
RISK			
MORNING MEANS JUST RISK [CHANCE]--TO THE LOVER--	"MORNING"--MEANS	300	4
A FEW--AND THEY BY RISK--PROCURE--	DID OUR BEST MOMENT LAST	393	3
TO TAKE MY CHANCE [RISK] WITH PAIN--	MY FIRST WELL DAY--SINCE	574	6

	FIRST LINE	POEM	LINE
RISK (CONTINUED)			
AT LEAST--'TIS MUTUAL--RISK--	I GAVE MYSELF TO HIM--	580	13
SOUL, TAKE THY RISK [RISKS / CHANCE],	SOUL, TAKE THY RISK,	1151	1
RISK IS THE HAIR THAT HOLDS THE TUN [ONE]	RISK IS THE HAIR THAT	1239	1
WHAT HEART WOULD RISK [COULD FIND] THE WAY--	WHERE ROSES WOULD NOT	1582	2
INCUR THE RISK	DOWN TIME'S QUAINT	1656	7
RISKS			
SOUL, TAKE THY RISK [RISKS / CHANCE],	SOUL, TAKE THY RISK,	1151	1
RITARDANDO			
RITARDANDO!	DYING AT MY MUSIC!	1003	5
RITE			
TILL EVERLASTING LIFE [RITE] UNITE	THE GRAVE MY LITTLE	1743	7
RITES			
THESE ARE THE RITES OF NATURE'S HOUSE--	THESE ARE THE SIGNS TO	1077	5
RITUAL			
THE RITUAL--SO SMALL--	THE SWEETEST HERESY	387	6
RIVAL			
TILL, RECENTLY A RIVAL CLAIM	I HAD SOME THINGS THAT I	116	3
RIVER			
MY RIVER RUNS TO THEE--	MY RIVER RUNS TO THEE--	162	1
MY RIVER WAITS REPLY--	MY RIVER RUNS TO THEE--	162	3
THE RIVER COULD NOT DROWN--	READ--SWEET--HOW OTHERS	260	11
THE RIVER REACHES TO MY FEET--	ME PROVE IT NOW--WHOEVER	537	5
THE RIVER REACHES TO MY BREAST--	ME PROVE IT NOW--WHOEVER	537	9
THE RIVER REACHES TO MY MOUTH--	ME PROVE IT NOW--WHOEVER	537	13
OF RIVER OR OF RIDGE [OF FATHOM OR OF LEAGUE] BEYOND	HOW FAR IS IT TO HEAVEN?	929	3
WHEN LIFE'S SWIFT RIVER STRIVEN THROUGH	WHAT TWIGS WE HELD BY--	1086	3
THE RIVER AND THE SKY.	THE MOUNTAINS STOOD IN	1278	4
RIVERS			
WHEN THE RIVERS OVERFLOW,	HAVE YOU GOT A BROOK IN	136	10
LEAST RIVERS--DOCILE TO SOME SEA.	LEAST RIVERS--DOCILE TO	212	1
ON THE RIVERS BEEN--	TWICE HAD SUMMER HER	846	4
AND RIVERS WHERE THE HOUSES RAN	THERE CAME A WIND LIKE A	1593	11
THREE RIVERS AND A HILL TO CROSS	I DID NOT REACH THEE	1664	3
THREE RIVERS AND THE HILL ARE PASSED	I DID NOT REACH THEE	1664	31
THE RIVERS LEAN TO SEE	THE HILLS ERECT THEIR	1688	2
RIVET			
IF I WELD THE RIVET FASTER--	BY A FLOWER--BY A LETTER	109	3
TRY--CAN YOU STIR THE AWFUL RIVET--	HOW MANY TIMES THESE LOW	187	3
THE RIVET IN THE BANDS	MY FAITH IS LARGER THAN	766	16
RIVETS			
AND STAPLES [RIVETS], IN THE SONG,	THE SOUL HAS BANDAGED	512	22
ROAD			
UPON THE LONELY ROAD.	THROUGH LANE IT LAY--	9	4
THIS WAS THE ROAD	THROUGH LANE IT LAY--	9	16
AN UNFREQUENTED ROAD--	MY WHEEL IS IN THE DARK!	10	6
ONE CAME THE ROAD THAT I CAME--	ONE SISTER HAVE I IN OUR	14	5
WHEN KATIE RUNS UNWEARIED THEY FOLLOW ON THE ROAD,	WHEN KATIE WALKS, THIS	222	2
FAR DOWN THE DUSTIEST ROAD!	ONE LIFE OF SO MUCH	270	16
I KNOW SOME LONELY HOUSES OFF THE ROAD	I KNOW SOME LONELY	289	1
THE WRINKLES OF THE ROAD--	IT SIFTS FROM LEADEN	311	4
WHEN NIGHT DEVOURED THE ROAD--	OF TRIBULATION--THESE	325	14
THE MORNING'S AMBER [LIGHTNING'S JOINTED] ROAD--	BEFORE I GOT MY EYE PUT	327	15
'TWAS THE OLD--ROAD--THROUGH PAIN--	'TWAS THE OLD--ROAD--	344	1
LEAST FIGURE--ON THE ROAD--	A TONGUE--TO TELL HIM I	400	29
NO FEAR YOU'LL MISS THE ROAD.	A MURMUR IN THE TREES--	416	20
AND MEET THE ROAD--ERECT--	WE GROW ACCUSTOMED TO	419	8
AS ROUND A GOALLESS ROAD	NO MAN CAN COMPASS A	477	2
JUSTIFY THE ROAD--	TO PUT THIS WORLD DOWN,	527	8
TRANSPLANTED--TO THE ROAD--	I HAD BEEN HUNGRY, ALL	579	16
TO THAT ODD FORK IN BEING'S ROAD--	OUR JOURNEY HAD ADVANCED	615	3
TO FOLLOW HER SUPERIOR ROAD [PACE]--	I WATCHED THE MOON	629	35
A LITTLE ROAD--NOT MADE OF MAN--	A LITTLE ROAD--NOT MADE	647	1
A VEIN--ALONG THE ROAD--	THE NAME--OF IT--IS	656	4
SALUTING [CONFRONTING / CONTRASTING]--IN THE ROAD--	UPON CONCLUDED LIVES	735	8
AND THROW [THREW] AWAY THE ROAD--	THE WIND BEGUN TO KNEAD	824	8
EXPERIENCE IS THE ANGLED ROAD	EXPERIENCE IS THE ANGLED	910	1
IT WARBLED IN THE ROAD--	LIKE RAIN IT SOUNDED	1235	10
ON THE FAMILIAR ROAD	UNTIL THE DESERT KNOWS	1291	11
THE ROAD WAS LIT WITH [BY] MOON AND STAR--	THE ROAD WAS LIT WITH	1450	1
THE ROAD TO BETHLEHEM	THE SAVIOR MUST HAVE	1487	5
THE ROAD TO PARADISE IS PLAIN,	THE ROAD TO PARADISE IS	1491	1
A DIMPLED [FLORID / DAPPLED] ROAD	THE ROAD TO PARADISE IS	1491	5
HEARTY WITH BOYS THE ROAD--	GLASS WAS THE STREET--IN	1498	4
THAT RAMBLES IN THE ROAD ALONE,	HOW HAPPY IS THE LITTLE	1510	2
DEFIANT OF A ROAD--	THE MOON UPON HER FLUENT	1528	2
THE MAPLE LENT UNTO THE ROAD	AS IMPERCEPTIBLY AS	1540	V
AS CART OF MAN IN ROAD BELOW	THE SUN IN REINING TO	1636	3
ROADS			
YET HAVE ALL ROADS	MY WHEEL IS IN THE DARK!	10	7
FERN ODORS ON UNTRAVELLED ROADS--	AN ALTERED LOOK ABOUT	140	12
IN SHANTIES--BY THE SIDES OF ROADS--	I LIKE TO SEE IT LAP	585	7
THE DUST REPLACED, IN HOISTED ROADS--	A DROP FELL ON THE APPLE	794	9
ROAM			
AND NOW WE ROAM IN [THE] SOVREIGN WOODS--	MY LIFE HAD STOOD--A	754	5
THEREAFTER ROAM.	IN MANY AND REPORTLESS	1382	12

	FIRST LINE	POEM	LINE
ROAMING			
IS PUSHING [ROAMING / PLODDING / STARING / AMBLING] CLOSE BEHIND	ALL THAT I DO	1496	6
ROAMS			
WHEREVER ROAMS THE DAY--	THERE IS A WORD	8	12
ROAR			
WHERE NO BREAKERS ROAR--	ON THIS WONDROUS SEA	4	5
AND HOUSES VANISHED WITH A ROAR	IT WAS A QUIET SEEMING	1419	8
ROARING			
WITHHELD US BY IT'S ROARING	OF DEATH I TRY TO THINK	1558	12
ROASTED			
WITH SPOTS OF BURNISH ROASTED ON	THE BUTTERFLY'S NUMIDIAN	1387	2
ROB			
THE BURGLAR CANNOT ROB--THEN--	ALL THESE MY BANNERS BE.	22	10
NOR ANY SCHOOLBOY ROB THE NEST	THIS HEART THAT BROKE SO	145	7
ROBBED			
I [WHO] ROBBED THE WOODS--	I ROBBED THE WOODS--	41	1
FOR WHOM I ROBBED THE DINGLE--	SO BASHFUL WHEN I SPIED	91	9
ROBBED--WAS I--INTACT TO [YET MET NO] BANDIT--	STRUCK, WAS I, NOR YET	925	9
ROBBED BY DEATH--BUT THAT WAS EASY--	ROBBED BY DEATH--BUT	971	1
ROBBED BY LIBERTY	ROBBED BY DEATH--BUT	971	4
THE MAN THAT WAS NOT LOST [WRECKED / ROBBED / KILLED]	HOW MANY SCHEMES MAY DIE	1150	5
ROBBER			
BY ROBBER, SINCE THE GAIN	OF ALL THE SOUNDS	321	12
THERE MARAUDS A SORER ROBBER,	DEATH'S WAYLAYING NOT	1296	3
ROBBER'D			
A ROBBER'D LIKE THE LOOK OF--	I KNOW SOME LONELY	289	2
ROBBERIES			
THE GRAVE YIELDS BACK HER ROBBERIES--	OF NEARNESS TO HER	607	13
ROBBING			
THE ROBBING--COULD NOT HARM--	THIS WAS A POET--IT IS	448	14
ROBE			
THE SMALLEST "ROBE" WILL FIT ME	GOING TO HEAVEN!	79	16
IN THE "WHITE ROBE"--	WHY--DO THEY SHUT ME OUT	248	10
FITTED ITSELF TO HIMSELF LIKE A ROBE	THE EVENT WAS DIRECTLY	1686	3
ROBES			
WAIT TILL IN EVERLASTING ROBES	WAIT TILL THE MAJESTY OF	171	5
THEY HAVE NO ROBES, NOR NAMES--	ALONE, I CANNOT BE--	298	5
IN PENTATEUCHAL ROBES	IT ALWAYS FELT TO ME--A	597	20
AND TRAILED LIKE ROBES AWAY;	A CURIOUS CLOUD	1710	7
ROBIN			
ROBIN IS GONE.	I HAVE A BIRD IN SPRING	5	6
I HAD A CRIMSON ROBIN--	I HAD A GUINEA GOLDEN--	23	9
"PLEIAD" IT'S NAME, AND ROBIN,	I HAD A GUINEA GOLDEN--	23	27
ROBIN AFTER ROBIN	DUST IS THE ONLY SECRET	153	15
ROBIN AFTER ROBIN	DUST IS THE ONLY SECRET	153	15
DRAW ME A ROBIN--ON A STEM--	MAKE ME A PICTURE OF THE	188	5
ROBIN--UTTERED [PUBLISHED / LAVISHED] HALF THE TUNE--	HER--"LAST POEMS"--	312	8
I DREADED THAT FIRST ROBIN, SO,	I DREADED THAT FIRST	348	1
SHE LEAPS, BUT ROBIN LEAPED THE FIRST--	SHE SIGHTS A BIRD--SHE	507	7
YOU BEG THE ROBIN IN YOUR BRAIN	YOU'LL KNOW HER--BY HER	634	27
DENY SHE IS A ROBIN--NOW--	YOU'LL KNOW HER--BY HER	634	V 27
THE ROBIN IS THE ONE	THE ROBIN IS THE ONE	828	1
THE ROBIN IS THE ONE	THE ROBIN IS THE ONE	828	5
THE ROBIN IS THE ONE	THE ROBIN IS THE ONE	828	9
THE ROBIN FOR THE CRUMB	THE ROBIN FOR THE CRUMB	864	1
OR HELP ONE FAINTING ROBIN	IF I CAN STOP ONE HEART	919	5
'TWOULD'NT AFFLICT A ROBIN--	WHAT SHALL I DO WHEN THE	956	13
CONQUERED WITH THE ROBIN--	ON THE WORLD YOU COLORED	1171	7
NEXT TO THE ROBIN	PINK--SMALL--AND	1332	7
THE ROBIN IS A GABRIEL [TROUBADOUR]	THE ROBIN IS A GABRIEL	1483	1
FOR EITHER DUKE OR ROBIN	SHE COULD NOT LIVE UPON	1505	6
DELICIOUS ROBIN--	COME SHOW THY DURHAM	1542	3
AS ROBINS [ROBIN]--SIRE AND SON--	FOREVER HONORED BE THE	1570	6
THE ROBIN LOCKS HER NEST, AND TRIES HER WINGS.	QUITE EMPTY, QUITE AT	1606	2
ROBIN'S			
IN THE NEW ROBIN'S EXTASY	BRING ME THE SUNSET IN A	128	8
EACH--WITH A ROBIN'S EXPECTATION--	I SHALL KEEP SINGING!	250	4
THE ROBIN'S MY CRITERION FOR TUNE--	THE ROBIN'S MY CRITERION	285	1
A ROBIN'S LARDER	SO MUCH SUMMER	651	10
A ROBIN'S FAMINE [PALATE / HUNGER] ABLE--	DEPRIVED OF OTHER	773	9
ROBINS			
TIME BROUGHT ME OTHER ROBINS--	I HAD A GUINEA GOLDEN--	23	13
THE ROBINS STAND AS THICK TODAY	SOME RAINBOW--COMING	64	13
ROBINS, IN THE TRADITION	WHOSE CHEEK IS THIS?	82	6
WHEN THE ROBINS COME,	IF I SHOULD'NT BE ALIVE	182	2
BECAUSE I GROW--WHERE ROBINS DO--	THE ROBIN'S MY CRITERION	285	2
OF ROBINS IN THE TRUNDLE BED	A MURMUR IN THE TREES--	416	13
SWEETER--THE SURMISING ROBINS--	DREAMS--ARE WELL--BUT	450	5
CHERRIES--SUIT ROBINS--	VICTORY COMES LATE--	690	11
NOR ROBINS, ROBINS NEED NOT HIDE	BECAUSE THE BEE MAY	869	7
NOR ROBINS, ROBINS NEED NOT HIDE	BECAUSE THE BEE MAY	869	7
WHEN THEY BEGIN, IF ROBINS MAY,	WHEN THEY COME BACK--IF	1080	5
AS ROBINS [ROBIN]--SIRE AND SON--	FOREVER HONORED BE THE	1570	6
AND ROBINS NEAR	NOT ANY SUNNY TONE	1674	6
HOW DARE THE ROBINS SING,	HOW DARE THE ROBINS SING	1724	1
ROBS			
CHRIST ROBS THE NEST--	DUST IS THE ONLY SECRET	153	14

	FIRST LINE	POEM		LINE
ROBUST				
HIS SPIRIT GREW ROBUST--	HE ATE AND DRANK THE	1587		2
ROCK				
THE SMITTEN ROCK THAT GUSHES!	A WOUNDED DEER--LEAPS	165		5
WERE UNIVERSE--ONE ROCK--	I HAD NOT MINDED--WALLS	398		2
OR CLASPS A ROCK, WITH BOTH HIS HANDS-- . .	THE BLACK BERRY--WEARS A	554		7
I CAUGHT THE DRIPPING OF A ROCK	A DYING TIGER--MOANED	566		3
DID FAN AND ROCK, WITH SUDDEN LIGHT-- . .	TO MY SMALL HEARTH HIS	638		3
LATE--MY GARDEN [ACRE] OF A ROCK-- . . .	SOIL OF FLINT, IF STEADY	681	V	
THE WIND BEGUN TO KNEAD [ROCK] THE GRASS-- .	THE WIND BEGUN TO KNEAD	824		1
ROCKED				
THAT EVER ROCKED A CHILD.	WHOSE ARE THE LITTLE	142		20
ROCKED SOFTER--TO AND FRO--	ON SUCH A NIGHT, OR SUCH	146		8
AS IT WERE ROCKED IN STEEL	FAITH--IS THE PIERLESS	915		6
ROCKING				
HER LITTLE ROCKING CHAIR TO DRAW-- . . .	THE NIGHT WAS WIDE, AND	589		15
ROCKS				
HOW RED THE FIRE ROCKS BELOW	ON MY VOLCANO GROWS THE	1677		5
ROD				
GONE--MR BRYANT'S "GOLDEN ROD"--	BESIDES THE AUTUMN POETS	131		7
RODE				
WHEN IT HAS RODE AWAY.	THE FACE WE CHOOSE TO	1141		4
AND BOLDLY RODE AWAY--	A SPARROW TOOK A SLICE	1211	V	8
AND RODE IMMENSITY [DERIDING BY--]	A SPARROW TOOK A SLICE	1211	V	8
THEN LIKE ELIJAH RODE AWAY	LIKE RAIN IT SOUNDED	1235		15
WHERE RODE THE BIRD	LIKE BROOMS OF STEEL	1252		7
ROE				
BUT RAPID--LIKE THE ROE--	THE ONLY GHOST I EVER	274		6
ROGUES				
"ALL" ROGUES "SHALL HAVE THEIR PART IN" WHAT--	WHO IS IT SEEKS MY	1598		7
ROI				
MEEK [LOW] MY VIVE LE ROI, ...	MUTE THY CORONATION--	151		2
ROLL				
NOW TO THE APPLICATION, TO THE READING OF THE ROLL,	AWAKE YE MUSES NINE,	1		25
DID ROUND MY PILLOW ROLL, ...	I HAVE A KING, WHO DOES	103		9
I FELT THE WILDERNESS ROLL BACK	IT WOULD NEVER BE COMMON	430		28
STRONG [SURE] HALLELUJAHS ROLL--	THIS WORLD IS NOT	501		18
ROLLED				
AS TRUMPETS--ROLLED--	UNTO LIKE STORY--TROUBLE	295		16
NOR ROLLED ON WHEELS OF SNOW	I CANNOT DANCE UPON MY	326		14
AND SEE THE PARCEL ROLLED--	I CRIED AT PITY--NOT AT	588		10
THE SECOND [SILENCE] LIKE AN OCEAN ROLLED .	I YEARS HAD BEEN FROM	609		11
BULB AFTER BULB, IN SILVER ROLLED-- . . .	SPLIT THE LARK--AND	861		2
ROLLING				
COALS--FROM A ROLLING [PASSING] LOAD--RATTLE--HOW--NEAR--	I COULD DIE--TO KNOW--	570		9
UPHELD IN ROLLING AIR	I WATCHED THE MOON	629		18
ROMANCE				
I'M SATISFIED--THE ROMANCE	IT ALWAYS FELT TO ME--A	597		7
NO ROMANCE SOLD UNTO	NO ROMANCE SOLD UNTO	669		1
OUR NOVEL [ROMANCE]--WHEN 'TIS SMALL ENOUGH	NO ROMANCE SOLD UNTO	669		6
ROMEO				
THOUGH THE "ROMEO" LEFT [LEAVE] NO RECORD .	DRAMA'S VITALLEST	741		10
ROOF				
ON FENCE--AND ROOF--AND TWIG!	SOME RAINBOW--COMING	64		15
AND ROOF OF STONE.	SAFE IN THEIR ALABASTER	216		6
TOUCHING THE ROOF [FLOODING THE STEEPLE] AND TINTING THE BARN	BLAZING IN GOLD AND	228		6
AND FOR AN EVERLASTING ROOF	I DWELL IN POSSIBILITY--	657		7
THE ROOF WAS SCARCELY VISIBLE--	BECAUSE I COULD NOT STOP	712		19
ANOTHER--ON THE ROOF--	A DROP FELL ON THE APPLE	794		2
ROOFS				
THE CREATURES CHUCKLED ON THE ROOFS-- . .	AN AWFUL TEMPEST MASHED	198		5
ROOM				
WITHIN THIS INNER ROOM!	THERE'S SOMETHING	45		2
SO I CAN HANG IT IN MY ROOM--	MAKE ME A PICTURE OF THE	188		2
AND THUNDER--IN THE ROOM--	I GOT SO I COULD HEAR	293		4
A SUMMER'S [THE SUMMERS] EMPTY ROOM-- . .	IT SIFTS FROM LEADEN	311		14
ARE ROOM--	FOR DEATH--OR RATHER	382		6
AND CROWD THE LITTLE ROOM--	IT MIGHT BE LONELIER	405		6
IN AN ADJOINING ROOM--	I DIED FOR BEAUTY--BUT	449		4
THERE'S TRIUMPH IN THE ROOM	TRIUMPH--MAY BE OF	455		2
THE STILLNESS IN THE ROOM	I HEARD A FLY BUZZ--WHEN	465		2
BE WITNESSED--IN THE ROOM--	I HEARD A FLY BUZZ--WHEN	465		8
BECAUSE THERE IS'NT ROOM--	WE DO NOT PLAY ON GRAVES	467		2
I AM NOT IN A ROOM--	I AM ALIVE--I GUESS--	470		10
I TOOK THE SMALLEST ROOM--	I WAS THE SLIGHTEST IN	486		2
RUN ROUND AND ROUND A ROOM--	I'VE SEEN A DYING EYE	547		2
IN NATURE'S--DINING ROOM--	I HAD BEEN HUNGRY, ALL	579		12
BUT IN THEIR ROOM [STEAD]--A SEA--DISPLAYED--	THEY CALLED ME TO THE	628		9
SIZE CIRCUMSCRIBES--IT HAS NO ROOM . . .	SIZE CIRCUMSCRIBES--IT	641		1
WHERE WAS ONCE A ROOM--	ONE DAY IS THERE OF THE	814		12
BETWEEN HER FINAL ROOM	THE LAST NIGHT THAT SHE	1100		10
AND THERE WERE [WAS] TROUGHS [SPACE / ROOM] BESIDE	A GREAT HOPE FELL	1123		13
AND GIVE DOMINION ROOM.	THE HARM OF YEARS IS ON	1280		4
BUT GIVE A GIANT ROOM	I THOUGHT THAT NATURE	1286		10
HIS DINING ROOM DO [DOTH] SWING.	A SAUCER HOLDS A CUP	1374		8
MAKES THAT FEROCIOUS ROOM	A DIMPLE IN THE TOMB	1489		2

	FIRST LINE	POEM	LINE
ROOM (CONTINUED)			
NOT THAT IT IS NOT FIRM [HAS NOT ROOM]	THE ROAD TO PARADISE IS	1491	3
LIGHT MY NORTHERN ROOM	GUEST AM I TO HAVE	1661	2
IN WINTER IN MY ROOM	IN WINTER IN MY ROOM	1670	1
T'WAS COMFORT IN HER DYING ROOM	T'WAS COMFORT IN HER	1703	1
THE VERY NEAREST ROOM	ELYSIUM IS AS FAR AS TO	1760	2
IF IN THAT ROOM A FRIEND AWAIT	ELYSIUM IS AS FAR AS TO	1760	3
THIS IS A MIGHTY ROOM;	SWEET HOURS HAVE	1767	2
ROOMS			
ALL THE ROOMS ARE FULL--	TAKEN FROM MEN--THIS	53	8
ARE FORCED TO KEEP THEIR ROOMS--	WHERE BELLS NO MORE	112	4
BEHOLD, WHAT CURIOUS ROOMS!	WHAT INN IS THIS	115	6
IN HER UNFURNISHED ROOMS--	DID OUR BEST MOMENT LAST	393	12
WE TALKED BETWEEN THE ROOMS--	I DIED FOR BEAUTY--BUT	449	10
FAMILIAR, IN THE ROOMS--	OF NEARNESS TO HER	607	6
AND CLERKS IN COUNTING ROOMS	YOU'VE SEEN BALLOONS SET	700	19
AND ROOMS WHERE THOSE TO BE ALIVE	THE LAST NIGHT THAT SHE	1100	11
THY TUMULTUOUS ROOMS	FORTITUDE INCARNATE	1217	10
IN UNDULATING ROOMS	WATER MAKES MANY BEDS	1428	6
ROOT			
ERASE THE ROOT--NO TREE--	EMPTY MY HEART, OF THEE	587	11
CLOVE TO THE ROOT [CORE]--	NO BOBOLINK--REVERSE HIS	755	5
BORED AT SO BRAVE A ROOT	AND THIS OF ALL MY HOPES	913	8
UNDER THE CLOVER'S ROOT [FOOT],	UNDER THE LIGHT, YET	949	4
I THINK THAT THE ROOT OF THE WIND IS WATER--	I THINK THAT THE ROOT OF	1302	1
THE HOUSES FIRMER ROOT--	THE SYMPTOM OF THE GALE	1327	5
FOR HEAVEN IS THE ROOT,	THAN HEAVEN MORE REMOTE,	1436	2
WHEN IT HAS LOST IT'S ROOT--	YOU CANNOT MAKE	1508	2
ROPE			
THE ROPE THE NIGHTS WERE PUT ACROSS--	I SHOWED HER HIGHTS SHE	446	6
BUT A ROPE WILL--	FLOSS WONT SAVE YOU FROM	1322	2
NOTWITHSTANDING [TO BE SURE] A ROPE FOR A SOUVENIR	FLOSS WONT SAVE YOU FROM	1322	3
NOW WILL YOU HAVE THE ROPE OR THE FLOSS?	FLOSS WONT SAVE YOU FROM	1322	7
ROPES			
UPON THE ROPES--ABOVE OUR HEAD--	THE LIGHTNING PLAYETH--	630	9
WITH ROPES OF SAND	AN EVERYWHERE OF SILVER	884	2
ROSE			
AND AS THE ROSE APPEARS,	I HAVE A BIRD IN SPRING	5	5
THE ROSE IS OUT OF TOWN.	THE MORNS ARE MEEKER	12	4
AND I'M A ROSE!	A SEPAL, PETAL, AND A	19	5
NOONS LIKE THESE--SHE ROSE--	MORNS LIKE THESE--WE	27	2
THE ROSE ORDAINED!	GARLANDS FOR QUEENS, MAY	34	9
NOBODY KNOWS THIS LITTLE ROSE--	NOBODY KNOWS THIS LITTLE	35	1
AH LITTLE ROSE--HOW EASY	NOBODY KNOWS THIS LITTLE	35	11
AND I HAD BEEN THE ROSE--	IF SHE HAD BEEN THE	44	2
AND SEND THE ROSE TO YOU.	IF SHE HAD BEEN THE	44	8
I BRING MY ROSE.	I KEEP MY PLEDGE.	46	4
IF I SHOULD CEASE TO BRING A ROSE	IF I SHOULD CEASE TO	56	1
TWILL BE BECAUSE BEYOND THE ROSE	IF I SHOULD CEASE TO	56	3
THIS HUMBLE TOURIST ROSE!	WENT UP A YEAR THIS	93	8
OF ROSE AND LILY, MANIFOLD,	A SCIENCE--SO THE SAVANS	100	11
LO, A ROSE!	ARTISTS WRESTLED HERE!	110	3
THE HILLS TO MEET HIM ROSE!	THE SUN KEPT STOOPING--	152	2
IF I COULD BRIBE THEM BY A ROSE	IF I COULD BRIBE THEM BY	179	1
ON THIS LONG STORM THE RAINBOW ROSE--	ON THIS LONG STORM THE	194	1
THE BIRDS ROSE SMILING, IN THEIR NESTS--	ON THIS LONG STORM THE	194	5
THE ROSE DID CAPER ON HER CHEEK--	THE ROSE DID CAPER ON	208	1
HER BODDICE ROSE AND FELL--	THE ROSE DID CAPER ON	208	2
THAT BORE ANOTHER ROSE--	THE ROSE DID CAPER ON	208	10
WHERE IT ROSE--OR WHITHER IT RUSHES--	THIS--IS THE LAND--THE	266	3
I'LL TELL YOU HOW THE SUN ROSE--	I'LL TELL YOU HOW THE	318	1
THE WILD ROSE--REDDEN IN THE BOG--	IT WILL BE SUMMER--	342	13
I ROSE, AND ALL WAS PLAIN--	THE DAY THAT I WAS	356	9
FAILED LIKE THEMSELVES--AND CONSCIOUS THAT IT ROSE--	IF ANY SINK, ASSURE THAT	358	2
SURPASSES ALL THAT ROSE BEFORE--	THE MORNING AFTER WO--	364	3
LIKE PETALS FROM A ROSE--	THEY DROPPED LIKE FLAKES	409	3
DENY! DID ROSE HER BEE--	FORGET! THE LADY WITH	438	5
IT TRIED--TO BE A ROSE--	GOD MADE A LITTLE	442	2
THERE ROSE A PURPLE CREATURE--	GOD MADE A LITTLE	442	5
ABOVE THE RIPEST ROSE--	WITHIN MY GARDEN, RIDES	500	6
LONG DUNGEONED FROM HIS ROSE--	THE SOUL HAS BANDAGED	512	16
AND OVERSETS [OVERTURNS] A ROSE--	HE PARTS HIMSELF--LIKE	517	6
SOME SUCH SPICE [ROSE]--EXPRESS AND PASS--	SOME SUCH BUTTERFLY BE	541	5
I ROSE--BECAUSE HE SANK--	I ROSE--BECAUSE HE SANK	616	1
HIS SEPARATION FROM HIS ROSE--	IT MAKES NO DIFFERENCE	620	11
THEN--EDDIES LIKE A ROSE--AWAY--	THE NAME--OF IT--IS	656	11
THE ATTAR FROM THE ROSE	ESSENTIAL OILS--ARE	675	2
THE GENERAL ROSE--DECAY--	ESSENTIAL OILS--ARE	675	5
SHE ROSE TO HIS REQUIREMENT--DROPT	SHE ROSE TO HIS	732	1
I RECOLLECTED [ROSE TO COMFORT--] HER--	THE BIRDS REPORTED FROM	743	16
I ROSE--IT FOLLOWED ME--	BEREAVED OF ALL, I WENT	784	10
DEBATED--ROSE AGAIN--	SHE STAKED HER FEATHERS	798	2
A ROSE UPON IT'S RIDGE TO SOW	IT WAS A GRAVE, YET BORE	876	11
THE ROSE CONTENT MAY BLOOM	THE BIRD MUST SING TO	880	4
BUT ONCE A CENTURY, THE ROSE	THE BIRD MUST SING TO	880	7
THOSE THAT ROSE [TURNED] TO GO--	SWEET, TO HAVE HAD THEM	901	8
BOUNTIFUL COLORED, MY MORNING ROSE	AND THIS OF ALL MY HOPES	913	3
WHAT, WHEN THE ROSE IS RIPE--	WHAT SHALL I DO WHEN THE	956	2

	FIRST LINE	POEM	LINE
ROSE (CONTINUED)			
SHE SPED AS PETALS OF [FROM] A ROSE	SHE SPED AS PETALS OF A	991	1
THE [A] ROSE IS AN ESTATE--	PARTAKE AS DOTH THE BEE,	994	3
SHE ROSE AS HIGH AS HIS OCCASION	SHE ROSE AS HIGH AS HIS	1011	1
AGAIN THE SMOKE FROM DWELLINGS ROSE [CURLED]	THE WIND TOOK UP THE	1134	13
A FULL FED ROSE ON MEALS OF TINT	A FULL FED ROSE ON MEALS	1154	1
MORNING PAINTED ROSE--	ON THE WORLD YOU COLORED	1171	2
AND ROSE AND FELL THE MAGIC PLANKS	A SOFT SEA WASHED AROUND	1198	3
SPRANG LIGHTLY TO [ROSE SOFTLY IN / TURNED EASY IN] THE SKY	A SPARROW TOOK A SLICE	1211	V 6
ROSE [LEFT] SURREPTITIOUSLY--	A SPARROW TOOK A SLICE	1211	V 8
A WIND THAT ROSE	A WIND THAT ROSE	1259	1
AND HEARTY--AS A ROSE--	WINTER IS GOOD--HIS HOAR	1316	6
DROVE BOLDLY TO A ROSE--	A BEE HIS BURNISHED	1339	2
THE ROSE RECEIVED HIS VISIT	A BEE HIS BURNISHED	1339	5
INQUIRE OF THE PROUDEST [FULLEST / CLOSING] ROSE	CRISIS IS SWEET AND YET	1416	5
GO NOT TOO NEAR A HOUSE OF ROSE--	GO NOT TOO NEAR A HOUSE	1434	1
IMPREGNABLE [ILLUSTRIOUS / INVINCIBLE / INVIOLATE] THE ROSE	A LITTLE SNOW WAS HERE	1444	6
HER SPIRIT ROSE TO SUCH A HIGHT	HER SPIRIT ROSE TO SUCH	1486	1
I PERCEIVE THE ROSE!	"LETHE" IN MY FLOWER,	1730	8
ROSEMARY			
IN CEASELESS ROSEMARY--	ESSENTIAL OILS--ARE	675	8
ROSES			
WHEN ROSES CEASE TO BLOOM, SIR,	WHEN ROSES CEASE TO	32	1
WAS GRATEFUL FOR THE ROSES	WENT UP A YEAR THIS	93	13
ROSES OF A STEADFAST SUMMER	THO' MY DESTINY BE	163	13
ROSES A DAY FROM ZENZIBAR--	WHAT WOULD I GIVE TO SEE	247	9
GLOBE ROSES--BREAK THEIR SATIN FLAKE--	I TEND MY FLOWERS FOR	339	16
CAPTIVE! WE BRING REPRIEVE OF ROSES!	WOULD YOU LIKE SUMMER?	691	6
AND ROSES IN THE SEED--	THERE IS A JUNE WHEN	930	2
WHERE ROSES WOULD NOT DARE TO GO,	WHERE ROSES WOULD NOT	1582	1
ROSIER			
TO HER ROSIER,	THO' MY DESTINY BE	163	8
ROSY			
WHAT ROSY FACE	WHOSE CHEEK IS THIS?	82	2
AND TAKE A ROSY CHAIR.	THE NOTICE THAT IS	1310	4
ROTATION			
WONDERFUL ROTATION!	FREQUENTLY THE WOODS ARE	6	11
FAILLESS AS THE FAIR ROTATION	ALWAYS MINE!	839	4
ROUGE			
IT'S TOO ROUGE--	IT CANT BE "SUMMER"!	221	7
ROUGHEST			
ROUGHEST AIR--WAS GOOD--	WHEN I HOPED, I	768	4
ROUND			
GO ROUND AND ROUND.	MY WHEEL IS IN THE DARK!	10	4
GO ROUND AND ROUND.	MY WHEEL IS IN THE DARK!	10	4
IN HER IMPERIAL ROUND--	DELAYED TILL SHE HAD	58	15
ROUND A LEDGE OF DREAM!	I CANT TELL YOU--BUT YOU	65	8
DID ROUND MY PILLOW ROLL,	I HAVE A KING, WHO DOES	103	9
CRUISING ROUND THE PURPLE LINE--	FLOWERS--WELL--IF	137	12
SOME LITTLE WREN GOES SEEKING ROUND--	FOR EVERY BIRD A NEST--	143	3
TILL PLEADING, ROUND HER QUIET EYES	SHE BORE IT TILL THE	144	3
ROUND WHICH THE FOOTMEN WAIT	I MET A KING THIS	166	26
ROUND HER CHAMBER HUMS--	COME SLOWLY--EDEN!	211	6
OF LIFE'S PENURIOUS ROUND--	I SHOULD HAVE BEEN TOO	313	3
WHEN WINDS GO ROUND AND ROUND IN BANDS--	OF ALL THE SOUNDS	321	21
WHEN WINDS GO ROUND AND ROUND IN BANDS--	OF ALL THE SOUNDS	321	21
WHOSE FORCES SPHERIC WIND [ROUND]	THERE ARE TWO RIPENINGS	332	2
THE SHIVERERS ROUND FARMER'S DOORS--	'TIS NOT THAT DYING	335	9
AND THEN--HE'LL TURN ME ROUND AND ROUND--	THE FACE I CARRY WITH ME	336	13
AND THEN--HE'LL TURN ME ROUND AND ROUND--	THE FACE I CARRY WITH ME	336	13
THE FEET, MECHANICAL, GO ROUND--	AFTER GREAT PAIN, A	341	5
I TURNED MY BEING ROUND AND ROUND	I FELT MY LIFE WITH BOTH	351	5
I TURNED MY BEING ROUND AND ROUND	I FELT MY LIFE WITH BOTH	351	5
AND CARTS WENT STOOPING ROUND THE FIELDS	'TWAS JUST THIS TIME,	445	11
JUST LOOKING ROUND TO SEE HOW FAR	WE DO NOT PLAY ON GRAVES	467	11
FINGERS--TO FRAME MY ROUND HAIR	I AM ASHAMED--I HIDE--	473	13
AS ROUND A GOALLESS ROAD	NO MAN CAN COMPASS A	477	2
RUN ROUND AND ROUND A ROOM--	I'VE SEEN A DYING EYE	547	2
RUN ROUND AND ROUND A ROOM--	I'VE SEEN A DYING EYE	547	2
A MIGHTY LOOK RUNS ROUND THE WORLD	"HEAVEN" HAS DIFFERENT	575	5
AND HE PASSED [WENT] QUICKLY [SOFTLY] ROUND--	WHEN I WAS SMALL, A	596	8
JUST WINDING ROUND A STONE--	THE TREES LIKE TASSELS--	606	20
AND SEEN MY BRAIN--GO ROUND--	THEY SHUT ME UP IN PROSE	613	6
ROUND SOME OTHER FACE--	PROMISE THIS--WHEN YOU	648	24
THE NARROW ROUND--THE STINT--	A PRISON GETS TO BE A	652	25
ROUND THE STEEP AIR--	OUT OF SIGHT? WHAT OF	703	4
CONVULSION--PLAYING ROUND--	THROUGH THE STRAIT PASS	792	6
BE IT'S PILLOW ROUND--	AMPLE MAKE THIS BED--	829	6
BEHIND INFERIOR CLOUDS--OR ROUND	I MAKE HIS CRESCENT FILL	909	7
ROUND OUR NEW FIRESIDE--BUT FOR THIS--	I LEARNED--AT LEAST--	944	5
THE HOLLOWS ROUND HIS EAGER EYES	THE HOLLOWS ROUND HIS	955	1
AND ALL THE EARTH STROVE COMMON ROUND--	DENIAL--IS THE ONLY FACT	965	5
LIKE CHILDREN ROUND A SIRE--	THE MOUNTAIN SAT UPON	975	6
AND GLANCE SECURELY ROUND--	THIS MERIT HATH THE	979	6
NO LIVES ARE ROUND--	EXCEPT THE SMALLER SIZE	1067	2
A STRANGER HOVERING ROUND	THE FROST WAS NEVER SEEN	1202	5
ADROITLY TURNING ROUND	THE SUN IN REINING TO	1636	4

	FIRST LINE	POEM		LINE
ROUNDER				
HER FACE BE ROUNDER THAN THE MOON	THERE IS A FLOWER THAT	380		9
ROUSE				
YET EVEN THIS SHALL ROUSE [STIR] ITSELF	A STAGNANT PLEASURE LIKE	1281		7
ROUTE				
BEHIND--A SEALED ROUTE--	OUR JOURNEY HAD ADVANCED	615		10
THAT SPLIT THEIR ROUTE TO THE SKY--	BY MY WINDOW HAVE I FOR	797		6
FROM HIS ACCUSTOMED ROUTE--	HOW MANY SCHEMES MAY DIE	1150		8
HONOR, THE SHORTEST ROUTE TO YOU.	BROTHER OF INGOTS--AH	1366	V	2
A ROUTE OF EVANESCENCE	A ROUTE OF EVANESCENCE	1463		1
THE MOON UPON HER FLUENT ROUTE	THE MOON UPON HER FLUENT	1528		1
SHE DOES NOT KNOW A ROUTE	QUITE EMPTY, QUITE AT	1606		3
IS THERE NO WANDERING ROUTE OF GRACE	OH FUTURE! THOU SECRETED	1631		3
HE WENT BY SLEEP THAT DROWSY ROUTE	HE WENT BY SLEEP THAT	1662		1
RETURNING IS A DIFFERENT ROUTE	NO MAN SAW AWE, NOR TO	1733		9
ROUTES				
AS SLIGHTLY [SCARCELY] AS THE ROUTES [FLIGHTS] OF STARS--	WE MISS HER, NOT BECAUSE	993		5
BY ROUTES OF ECSTASY	"GO TRAVELING WITH US!"	1513		3
THEIR ROUTES ARE FAIR--	THE THINGS THAT NEVER	1515		6
ROUTINE				
TO MAKE ROUTINE A STIMULUS	TO MAKE ROUTINE A	1196		1
ROW				
AND ROW MY BLOSSOMS O'ER!	SUMMER FOR THEE, GRANT I	31		6
YOU'LL KNOW IT BY THE ROW OF STARS	I LOST A WORLD--THE	181		3
AND FIRMAMENTS--ROW--	SAFE IN THEIR ALABASTER	216	V	
IT BURNS--DISTINCT FROM ALL THE ROW--	ONE LIFE OF SO MUCH	270		11
AS ON THE TIER [ROW] OF WALL	WHAT CARE THE DEAD, FOR	592		6
AND ROW IN NOWHERE ALL DAY LONG	COULD I BUT RIDE	661		15
FOR HIS MEAN SAKE TO LEAVE THE ROW	THE HEAVEN VESTS FOR	694		11
THO' BANDS OF SPICES--ROW--	WHERE THOU ART--THAT--IS	725		12
BUT [THOUGH] ALL MANKIND DELIVER [CRUISE SOFTLY / ROW SOFTLY / . . .	A CHILLY PEACE INFESTS	1443		7
ROWDY				
THE BOBOLINK IS GONE--THE ROWDY OF THE MEADOW--	THE BOBOLINK IS GONE--	1591		1
ROWED				
AND ROWED HIM SOFTER HOME--	A BIRD CAME DOWN THE	328		16
ROWER				
ROWER, AND YACHT--SOME SOVREIGN SUMMER--	LOVE--THOU ART HIGH--	453		11
ROWING				
ROWING IN EDEN--	WILD NIGHTS--WILD NIGHTS	249		9
SOME SAILOR--ROWING IN THE DARK--	GOOD NIGHT! WHICH PUT	259		8
ROWS				
UNTIL THE BEES, FROM CLOVER ROWS	PERHAPS YOU'D LIKE TO	134		7
THE BIRDS--IN DOCILE ROWS	THE DAY CAME SLOW--TILL	304		10
ROYAL				
PASS ROYAL THRO' THE GATE--	MY WHEEL IS IN THE DARK!	10		13
HAST THOU THE ROYAL SCAR?	WHO NEVER LOST, ARE	73		14
HIS ROYAL STATE PARTOOK!	I MET A KING THIS	166		22
I QUESTION IF THE ROYAL COACH	I MET A KING THIS	166		25
FULL ROYAL IS HIS RETINUE!	WAIT TILL THE MAJESTY OF	171		11
AH, WHAT A ROYAL SAKE	FOR THIS--ACCEPTED	195		5
GET GABRIEL--TO TELL--THE ROYAL SYLLABLE--	FOR THIS--ACCEPTED	195		13
I'LL SEEK HIS ROYAL FEET--	THE COURT IS FAR AWAY--	235		5
THEN--TO THE ROYAL CLOUDS	THE NEAREST DREAM	319		7
OR BRUSHED A ROYAL GOWN--	HE TOUCHED ME, SO I LIVE	506		9
MINE--BY THE ROYAL SEAL!	MINE--BY THE RIGHT OF	528		2
ENABLED BY HIS ROYAL DRESS--	LIKE MIGHTY FOOT LIGHTS	595		7
WHEN FIGURES SHOW THEIR ROYAL FRONT--	OF ALL THE SOULS THAT	664		9
THE ROYAL AIR--	PUBLICATION--IS THE	709		12
OR TAKE THE ROYAL NAMES IN VAIN--	SWEET MOUNTAINS--YE TELL	722		5
OF THE ROYAL" INFINITY?	BY MY WINDOW HAVE I FOR	797		23
ROYAL--ALL BUT THE CROWN!	TITLE DIVINE--IS MINE!	1072		5
A SINGLE [ROYAL / SIGNAL / HALLOWED] TIME	TO BE FORGOT BY THEE	1560		9
ROYALIZED SEE RE-ROYALIZED				
ROYALLY				
SO ROYALLY INTOXICATE	EXHILIRATION--IS WITHIN	383		3
ROYALTY				
ROYALTY ENOUGH FOR ME	PIGMY SERAPHS--GONE	138		16
GRANT ME--THAT DAY--THE ROYALTY--	THE COURT IS FAR AWAY--	235		11
SUFFICIENT ROYALTY!	THE FACE I CARRY WITH ME	336		16
RUB				
RUB AWAY THE BRAND--	COLOR--CASTE--	970		8
RUBBED				
THIS--TOO--THE SHOWMAN RUBBED AWAY--	THEY CALLED ME TO THE	628		13
RUBBERS				
I'LL TAKE MY INDIA RUBBERS,	"SIC TRANSIT GLORIA	3		27
RUBIES				
I'VE RUBIES--LIKE THE EVENING BLOOD--	I CAME TO BUY A SMILE--	223		11
LIKE HINDERED RUBIES--OR THE LIGHT	THE DAY CAME SLOW--TILL	304		3
SAY RUBIES--IF HE HESITATE--	A TONGUE--TO TELL HIM I	400		20
WITH RUBIES--PELTETH ME--	'TIS LITTLE I--COULD	466		4
RUBY				
SOME RUBY TROWSERS HURRIED ON--	A SLASH OF BLUE--	204		6
DEPTHS OF RUBY, UNDRAINED,	ALL THE LETTERS I CAN	334		5
LIT--WITH A RUBY--	I WENT TO HEAVEN--	374		3
RUBY'S				
WHICH RUBY'S MINE?	A TOAD, CAN DIE OF LIGHT	583		12

	FIRST LINE	POEM	LINE
RUDDIER			
AND RUDDIER THAN THE GOWN	THERE IS A FLOWER THAT	380	10
OBSCURED WITH RUDDIER [NEARER / COMELIER] BLUE--	ONE BLESSING HAD I THAN	756	14
RUDDY			
NO RUDDY FIRES ON THE HEARTH--	WHAT INN IS THIS	115	7
AGLOW--ALL RUDDY--WITH THE LIGHT	I SEE THEE BETTER--IN	611	11
IT GATHERS RUDDY [STANDS IN--RUDDY / MAKES VERMILLION--] POOLS--	THE NAME--OF IT--IS	656	10
IT GATHERS RUDDY [STANDS IN--RUDDY / MAKES VERMILLION--] POOLS--	THE NAME--OF IT--IS	656	10
RUDDY AS THAT COEVAL APPLE	TELL AS A MARKSMAN--WERE	1152	3
RUDE			
HOW RUDE IN ONE TO SOB!	THERE'S SOMETHING	45	10
ESTEEMED ME NEVER RUDE	MY BEST ACQUAINTANCES	932	4
RUDIMENT			
MY TACTICS MISSED A RUDIMENT--	MY PERIOD HAD COME FOR	564	3
A CITIZEN [RUDIMENT] OF PARADISE	A COFFIN--IS A SMALL	943	3
RUDIMENTS			
BY PROCESSES [RUDIMENTS / PREFACES] OF SIZE	TIME FEELS SO VAST THAT	802	6
RUFF			
IF RUFF IT WAS OF DAME	A SPIDER SEWED AT NIGHT	1138	4
RUFFLE			
A RUFFLE [THIMBLE]--OR A TUNE--	I LEARNED--AT LEAST--	944	17
RUFFLED			
PUTS OUT A RUFFLED HEAD--	I TEND MY FLOWERS FOR	339	12
RUFFLES			
IT RUFFLES WRISTS OF POSTS	IT SIFTS FROM LEADEN	311	17
RUGGED			
A RUGGED BILLION MILES--	THE SAVIOR MUST HAVE	1487	8
RUIN			
RUIN IS FORMAL--DEVILS WORK	CRUMBLING IS NOT AN	997	9
THE RUIN [HAVOC / DAMAGE] WAS WITHIN	A GREAT HOPE FELL	1123	3
RULE			
SEEMS IT DONT SHRIEK SO--UNDER RULE.	IT DONT SOUND SO	426	4
ADORNING ALL THE RULE--	'TIS ONE BY ONE--THE	545	8
STILL THE ETERNAL RULE	'TIS ONE BY ONE--THE	545	12
RULER			
RULER OF NOUGHT,	THE CHILD'S FAITH IS NEW	637	15
RULES			
THE ODE FAMILIAR--RULES THE NOON--	THE ROBIN'S MY CRITERION	285	5
RUM			
AND AN AFTERWARD OF RUM--	THE POPULAR HEART IS A	1226	4
RUMBLE			
I ONLY KNOW [SIGH]--NO CURRICLE [VEHICLE] THAT RUMBLE THERE	A LITTLE ROAD--NOT MADE	647	7
RUMBLES			
AND RUMBLES STILL, THOUGH TORRID NOONS	THE FARTHEST THUNDER	1581	3
RUMOR			
SOME RUMOR OF DELIRIUM,	LIKE FLOWERS, THAT HEARD	513	5
BETWEEN IT'S RUMOR AND IT'S FACE--	THE SYMPTOM OF THE GALE	1327	3
WITHOUT A RHYTHMIC RUMOR	WHAT TENEMENTS OF CLOVER	1338	7
RUMORED			
FOR RUMORED SPRINGS--	QUITE EMPTY, QUITE AT	1606	5
RUMOR'S			
THE RUMOR'S GATE WAS SHUT SO TIGHT	THE SPIRIT LASTS--BUT IN	1576	21
WHOSE RUMOR'S GATE WAS SHUT SO TIGHT	EXPANSE CANNOT BE LOST--	1584	5
THE RUMOR'S GATE WAS SHUT SO TIGHT	THIS ME--THAT WALKS AND	1588	5
RUN			
WILL TAKE HIS HAT, AND RUN!	"SIC TRANSIT GLORIA	3	56
AND THEN TO GLORY RUN!	MY FRIEND ATTACKS MY	118	8
WHEN FRIGHTENED--HOME TO THEE I RUN--	YOU LOVE ME--YOU ARE	156	10
SOMEBODY RUN TO THE GREAT GATE	DYING! DYING IN THE	158	9
BUT NOT AT ALL DISPOSED TO RUN!	I MET A KING THIS	166	16
THAT BROOKS IN MEADOWS RUN!	TO LEARN THE TRANSPORT	167	4
YET DOTH EXCEEDING RUN!	A FUZZY FELLOW, WITHOUT	173	2
OR--SOMETIMES AT YOUR SIDE TO RUN--	WHAT SHALL I DO--IT	186	11
AND SAINTS--TO WINDOWS RUN--	I TASTE A LIQUOR NEVER	214	14
AND WHERE HIS FEET HAVE RUN--	A VISITOR IN MARL--	391	10
TO EARN A MINE--WOULD RUN	A TONGUE--TO TELL HIM I	400	5
MYSELF WOULD RUN AWAY	I NEVER FELT AT HOME--	413	14
I RUN IT OVER--"DEAD", BRAIN, "DEAD."	IT DONT SOUND SO	426	2
AND DNIEPER WRESTLERS, RUN.	I THINK THE HEMLOCK	525	16
RUN ROUND AND ROUND A ROOM--	I'VE SEEN A DYING EYE	547	2
YET CONFIDENT THEY RUN	I COULD NOT PROVE THE	563	2
OR BETTER, RUN AWAY	COULD I BUT RIDE	661	8
WHEN HER'S HAD CEASED TO RUN--	SEVERER SERVICE OF	786	6
UNTO THIS PRESENT, RUN,	HE OUTSTRIPPED TIME WITH	865	6
HOLD ME TILL THE OCTAVE'S RUN!	DYING AT MY MUSIC!	1003	3
THE VEINS THAT USED TO RUN	I'VE DROPPED MY BRAIN--	1046	2
WHEN LARGE ENOUGH TO RUN	THE THINGS WE THOUGHT	1293	6
AND EVERY BREEZE THAT RUN ALONG	A SAUCER HOLDS A CUP	1374	7
THAT THREATENED IT--DID RUN	A WILD BLUE SKY ABREAST	1415	2
WHAT DOOR--WHAT HOUR--RUN--RUN--MY SOUL!	"AND WITH WHAT BODY DO	1492	3
WHAT DOOR--WHAT HOUR--RUN--RUN--MY SOUL!	"AND WITH WHAT BODY DO	1492	3
WILL EVER AFTER RUN	THE LIFE THAT TIED TOO	1535	2
BLOSSOMS WILL RUN AWAY,	BLOSSOMS WILL RUN AWAY,	1578	1
NOR EVER CEASED TO RUN	IN WINTER IN MY ROOM	1670	35
THEY'D LAUGH AND RUN AWAY.	IF ALL THE GRIEFS I AM	1726	4

	FIRST LINE	POEM	LINE
RUNE			
SO WHETHER IT BE RUNE,	TO HEAR AN ORIOLE SING	526	10
RUNNING			
THAT MAKES OUR TRYING [RUNNING] POOR.	BECAUSE HE LOVES HER	1229	12
IT SOUNDED AS IF THE STREETS [AIR] WERE RUNNING	IT SOUNDED AS IF THE	1397	1
RUNS			
WHEREVER RUNS THE BREATHLESS SUN--	THERE IS A WORD	8	11
MY RIVER RUNS TO THEE--	MY RIVER RUNS TO THEE--	162	1
WHEN KATIE RUNS UNWEARIED THEY FOLLOW ON THE ROAD,	WHEN KATIE WALKS, THIS	222	2
WHILE RUNS THE RHINE--	WE--BEE AND I--LIVE BY	230	12
SHE RUNS WITHOUT THE LOOK OF FEET--	SHE SIGHTS A BIRD--SHE	507	3
RUNS [PUTS] HIS FINGERS THRO' IT--	BEAUTY--BE NOT CAUSED--	516	6
AND THEN HE RUNS AGAINST	HE PARTS HIMSELF--LIKE	517	5
RUNS EVENLY--AND TRUE--	THE BRAIN, WITHIN IT'S	556	2
A MIGHTY LOOK RUNS ROUND THE WORLD	"HEAVEN" HAS DIFFERENT	575	5
THE WIDTH OF LIFE--BEFORE IT SPREADS [RUNS]	AT LEISURE IS THE SOUL	618	3
THE SUNRISE RUNS FOR BOTH--	THE SUNRISE RUNS FOR	710	1
THE MAN THAT [WHO] RUNS AWAY	TO DISAPPEAR ENHANCES--	1209	2
RUPTURE			
JUGS--A UNIVERSE'S FRACTURE [RUPTURE]	BEES ARE BLACK, WITH	1405	7
RURAL			
BUT THEN I AM A RURAL MAN	ONE OF THE ONES THAT	1466	23
RUSH			
UPON HER [ON HER RUSH] MAT--	THE SOUL SELECTS HER OWN	303	8
A RUSH OF COCHINEAL--	A ROUTE OF EVANESCENCE	1463	4
RUSHES			
WHERE IT ROSE--OR WHITHER IT RUSHES--	THIS--IS THE LAND--THE	266	3
THAT LETS IT'S RUSHES GROW	A STAGNANT PLEASURE LIKE	1281	2
RUSSET			
AND SKIP THE RUSSET--ON THE TREE--	MAKE ME A PICTURE OF THE	188	13
BUT EXCEPT IT'S RUSSET BASE	REVOLUTION IS THE POD	1082	5
WITHIN [BETWEEN] HIS RUSSET LIPS--	A SAUCER HOLDS A CUP	1374	10
WHAT RUSSET HALTS IN NATURE'S MARCH	THEIR BARRICADE AGAINST	1471	5
RUSSETLY			
FLIT RUSSETLY AWAY	IT IS AN HONORABLE	946	8
RUSSIAN			
WILT THOU, AUSTERE [RUSSIAN] SNOW?	SNOW BENEATH WHOSE	942	8
RUST			
AN ELEMENTAL RUST--	CRUMBLING IS NOT AN	997	8
RUSTICS			
RUSTICS--WEAR--	I'M SAYING EVERY DAY	373	31
RUSTLE			
THE NEIGHBORS RUSTLE IN AND OUT--	THERE'S BEEN A DEATH, IN	389	5
RUSTLING			
QUICK! A SHARPER RUSTLING!	MORNS LIKE THESE--WE	27	11
RUSTY			
HER FADED [RUSTY] AMMUNITION	THE PAST IS SUCH A	1203	7
RUT			
ACROSS A BARN OR THROUGH A RUT	THE SKY IS LOW--THE	1075	3
RUTHLESS			
FROM ACCENT HARSH, OR RUTHLESS WORD--	WHERE I HAVE LOST, I	104	6
NOR A SPORTSMAN'S PERADVENTURE [RUTHLESS PLEASURE / WANTON . . .	STRUCK, WAS I, NOR YET	925	7
HOW RUTHLESS ARE THE GENTLE--	HOW RUTHLESS ARE THE	1439	1
SABACTHINI			
THAT SCALDING ONE--SABACTHINI--	I SHOULD HAVE BEEN TOO	313	11
SABBATH			
SOME KEEP THE SABBATH GOING TO CHURCH--	SOME KEEP THE SABBATH	324	1
SOME KEEP THE SABBATH IN SURPLICE--	SOME KEEP THE SABBATH	324	5
'TWAS SABBATH--WITH THE BELLS DIVORCED [REVERSED]--	I HAD NO CAUSE TO BE	542	15
WHEN OPENING THE SABBATH IN THEIR AFFLICTIVE WAY	THE BOBOLINK IS GONE--	1591	5
SABLE			
THE CRICKET DROPS A SABLE LINE	THE JAY HIS CASTANET HAS	1635	7
SABRE			
BY EVENING'S SABRES [SABRE] SLAIN	SOFT AS THE MASSACRE OF	1127	2
SABRES			
BY EVENING'S SABRES [SABRE] SLAIN	SOFT AS THE MASSACRE OF	1127	2
SACKCLOTH			
THE SACKCLOTH--HANGS UPON THE NAIL--	IT WOULD NEVER BE COMMON	430	30
SACRAMENT			
OH SACRAMENT OF SUMMER DAYS,	THESE ARE THE DAYS WHEN	130	13
WAS NEEDLESS, AS AT SACRAMENT,	THERE CAME A DAY AT	322	11
WHEN SACRAMENT--IS DONE--	IT WILL BE SUMMER--	342	20
FOR VISITER--OR SACRAMENT--	EXHILIRATION--IS WITHIN	383	7
THE SACRAMENT--OF HIM--	IT MIGHT BE LONELIER	405	8
UNDER ONE SACRAMENT [FIRMAMENT]	WHILE IT IS ALIVE	491	5
CROWDED--AS SACRAMENT--	IT'S THOUGHTS--AND JUST	495	6
SACRAMENT, SAINTS PARTOOK [INDORSED] BEFORE US--	TO PUT THIS WORLD DOWN,	527	12
THAT FEELS TO HER--LIKE SACRAMENT--	SHE'S HAPPY, WITH A NEW	535	2
AS IF UNTO A JUBILEE [SACRAMENT]	I THINK I WAS ENCHANTED	593	19
AND SENTENCE--SACRAMENT--	WHERE THOU ART--THAT--IS	725	9
UNTO HER SACRAMENT--	MY WORTHINESS IS ALL MY	751	16
UPON A SACRAMENT.	A LIGHT EXISTS IN SPRING	812	20
DO THOSE AT SACRAMENT	PERHAPS YOU THINK ME	833	4

	FIRST LINE	POEM	LINE
SACRAMENTAL			
OF THE COMMUNION [SACRAMENTAL] WINE	YOUR THOUGHTS DONT HAVE	1452	4
SACRED			
THY SACRED EMBLEMS TO PARTAKE--	THESE ARE THE DAYS WHEN	130	16
THAT IS SOLEMN [TENDER / SACRED] WE HAVE ENDED	THAT IS SOLEMN WE HAVE	934	1
THAT SACRED CLOSET WHEN YOU SWEEP--	THAT SACRED CLOSET WHEN	1273	1
THE SACRED STEALTH [HAPPY GUILT] OF BOY AND GIRL	BLISS IS THE PLAYTHING	1553	3
TO BALK THEE OF THY SACRED PREY--[THE INNOCENCE / THE MYRIADS]	OH FUTURE! THOU SECRETED	1631	7
THAT FEEDS THE SACRED [CENTRAL] LIGHT.	HER FACE WAS IN A BED OF	1722	4
SACRIFICE			
SACRIFICE FOR SCIENCE	KNOWS HOW TO FORGET!	433	V
THAN SACRIFICE, AND CEASE--	TO LOVE THEE YEAR BY	434	3
IS GILT WITH SACRIFICE--	A TOOTH UPON OUR PEACE	459	8
SACRIFICIAL			
OR SACRIFICIAL FLOWER--	IT WAS A GRAVE, YET BORE	876	V 12
SAD			
AND A DEAL OF SAD REFLECTION, AND WAILING INSTEAD OF SONG?	AWAKE YE MUSES NINE,	1	30
TO REMEMBER HOW SAD I AM	HOW HAPPY I WAS IF I	898	2
I SHOULD NOT DARE TO BE SO SAD	I SHOULD NOT DARE TO BE	1197	1
RICHES ARE SAD.	ARE FRIENDS DELIGHT OR	1199	6
SADDENED			
NOT SADDENED BY REPULSE,	THE HEART HAS MANY DOORS	1567	5
SADDEST			
THE SADDEST NOISE, THE SWEETEST NOISE,	THE SADDEST NOISE, THE	1764	1
SADDLE			
AS A FAMILIAR STIRRUP [SADDLE]	A SPARROW TOOK A SLICE	1211	V 7
UPON HIS SADDLE SPRUNG A [SPRANG THE] BIRD	UPON HIS SADDLE SPRUNG A	1600	1
SADLY			
THINE EYES ARE SADLY BLINDED, BUT YET THOU MAYEST SEE	AWAKE YE MUSES NINE,	1	33
SADNESS			
NO MORE HE SINGETH MOURNFUL, HER SADNESS SHE DOTH LOSE.	AWAKE YE MUSES NINE,	1	20
SAFE			
AND BORE HER SAFE AWAY.	WHOSE CHEEK IS THIS?	82	5
SAFE IN THEIR ALABASTER CHAMBERS--	SAFE IN THEIR ALABASTER	216	1
SWEET--SAFE--HOUSES--	SWEET--SAFE--HOUSES--	457	1
HER WARM [STRAIGHT / GOOD / QUICK / SAFE] RETURN, IF SO SHE	NO NOTICE GAVE SHE, BUT	804	17
HOW GOOD [SAFE / FIRM / CALM] TO BE IN TOMBS	THE CLOUDS THEIR BACKS	1172	6
SAFE DESPAIR IT IS THAT RAVES--	SAFE DESPAIR IT IS THAT	1243	1
WE SAFE [SOFT] COMMIT THEE--	TO THE STANCH DUST	1402	2
IS SAFE--SIMPLICITY--	IF WRECKED UPON THE	1469	4
HOW THEREFORE SAFE TO BE A FLOWER	IT WOULD NOT KNOW IF IT	1579	3
HOW SAFE HIS FALLEN HEAD	THE DITCH IS DEAR TO THE	1645	4
SAFELY			
HE KEEPS HIS SECRETS SAFELY--VERY--	FUNNY--TO BE A CENTURY--	345	5
AND PEBBLE--SAFELY PLAYS--	I KNOW WHERE WELLS GROW	460	4
GOES SAFELY [STEADY]--WHERE AN OPEN EYE--	THERE IS A PAIN--SO	599	7
SAFER			
FAST IN A SAFER HAND	I HAVE A BIRD IN SPRING	5	13
IT'S SAFER SO--	I'M "WIFE"--I'VE	199	4
SO SAFER GUESS--WITH JUST MY SOUL	BEFORE I GOT MY EYE PUT	327	18
FAR SAFER, OF A MIDNIGHT MEETING	ONE NEED NOT BE A	670	5
FAR SAFER, THROUGH AN ABBEY GALLOP,	ONE NEED NOT BE A	670	9
SAFER NOT TO KNOW--	WHETHER THEY HAVE	1329	4
SAFEST			
HONOR IS THEN THE SAFEST HUE	JUDGEMENT IS JUSTEST	1671	6
SAFETY			
TRUTH IS GOOD HEALTH--AND SAFETY, AND THE SKY.	A COUNTERFEIT--A PLATED	1453	5
SAFFRON			
TILL SAFFRON IN VERMILLION SLID	OF YELLOW WAS THE OUTER	1676	3
SAGACIOUS			
FROM SAGACIOUS EYES.	SO FROM THE MOULD	66	5
SAGACIOUS [EXCLUSIVE] CONFIDENCE--	THE LEAVES LIKE WOMEN,	987	2
SAGACIOUS OF MY MISTAKE	I SAW THAT THE FLAKE WAS	1267	6
OF THE SAGACIOUS GOD--	IT'S LITTLE ETHER HOOD	1501	4
SAGACITY			
AH, WHAT SAGACITY PERISHED HERE!	SAFE IN THEIR ALABASTER	216	11
SAGACITY, MUST GO--	THIS WORLD IS NOT	501	8
SAGE			
WHILE WE SHREWDLY SPECULATE [SAGE INVESTIGATE / SHREWD INVESTIGATE]	YESTERDAY IS HISTORY,	1292	7
THE SAGE [WISE] CANNOT CONJECTURE	FACTS BY OUR SIDE ARE	1497	10
WE MAKE THE WISE DISTINCTION [SAGE DECISION] STILL,	WE SEND THE WAVE TO FIND	1604	5
NO CIRCUIT SAGE OF ALL THE COURSE [LINES]	OH FUTURE! THOU SECRETED	1631	5
SAGES			
THE SAGES--CALL IT SMALL--	A SOLEMN THING--IT WAS--	271	14
SAGES SAY,	LOVE IS DONE WHEN LOVE'S	1485	2
BUT HAVE SAGES KNOWN?	LOVE IS DONE WHEN LOVE'S	1485	3
SAGEST			
THE SAGEST [ONLY] TIME TO DAM THE SEA IS WHEN THE SEA IS GONE--	WE SEND THE WAVE TO FIND	1604	7
SAHARA			
SAHARA [CONTENTMENT / CREATION / HIS STATUS] DIES	UNTIL THE DESERT KNOWS	1291	6

	FIRST LINE	POEM	LINE
SAHARA (CONTINUED)			
SAHARA IS TOO LITTLE PRICE	I DID NOT REACH THEE	1664	12
SAID			
SO I SAID--OR THOUGHT--	IT DID NOT SURPRISE ME--	39	2
NOT SO, SAID CUNNING [QUOTH WILY] "JACOB!	A LITTLE EAST OF JORDAN,	59	9
"THEY HAVE NOT CHOSEN ME," HE SAID,	"THEY HAVE NOT CHOSEN ME	85	1
PERHAPS THEY DID NOT HEAR, I SAID,	WHOSE ARE THE LITTLE	142	5
THEIR BEDTIME 'TIS, SHE SAID--	WHOSE ARE THE LITTLE	142	26
THEY SAID THAT JESUS--ALWAYS CAME--	DYING! DYING IN THE	158	6
AND UNDERSTOOD NO WORD IT SAID--	I'VE HEARD AN ORGAN TALK	183	3
'TWAS'NT LOUD, FOR HE SAID NOUGHT--	HE WAS WEAK, AND I WAS	190	7
"NO"--SAID PETER, 'TWAS'NT ME--	HE FORGOT--AND I--	203	6
I SAID "'TWILL KEEP"--	I HELD A JEWEL IN MY	245	4
A SOLEMN THING--IT WAS--I SAID--	A SOLEMN THING--IT WAS--	271	1
YOU SAID IT HURT YOU--MOST--	ONE YEAR AGO--JOTS WHAT?	296	17
THEN I SAID SOFTLY TO MYSELF--	I'LL TELL YOU HOW THE	318	7
AND ALL WE SAID--WAS	OF TRIBULATION--THESE	325	16
I SAID I GAINED IT--	I GAINED IT SO--	359	8
AH, SAID JULY--	ANSWER JULY--	386	5
NAY--SAID THE MAY--	ANSWER JULY--	386	10
HERE--SAID THE YEAR--	ANSWER JULY--	386	18
SAY--LAST I SAID--WAS THIS--	A TONGUE--TO TELL HIM I	400	22
SHE SAID HER STRINGS WERE SNAPT--	THE FIRST DAY'S NIGHT	410	5
WHERE THIS--IS SAID TO BE	NOT IN THIS WORLD TO SEE	418	3
IT WOULD NEVER BE COMMON--MORE--I SAID--	IT WOULD NEVER BE COMMON	430	1
I SAY TO YOU, SAID JESUS--	DO PEOPLE MOULDER	432	9
"WOULD'ST CLIMB," I [HE] SAID?	I SHOWED HER HIGHTS SHE	446	2
SHE [I] SAID--"NOT SO"--	I SHOWED HER HIGHTS SHE	446	3
"WITH ME--" I [HE] SAID--WITH ME?	I SHOWED HER HIGHTS SHE	446	4
WE BRETHEREN, ARE", HE SAID--	I DIED FOR BEAUTY--BUT	449	8
TO TELL THE VERY LAST THEY SAID	WHY MAKE IT DOUBT--IT	462	5
WE--TEMPLES BUILD--I SAID--	MYSELF WAS FORMED--A	488	12
TELL HIM [HER]--I ONLY SAID THE SYNTAX--	GOING TO HIM! HAPPY	494	4
HOW PLEASED THEY WERE [LOOKED], AT WHAT YOU SAID--	IF ANYBODY'S FRIEND BE	509	13
HOW PLEASANTER--SAID SHE	THE NIGHT WAS WIDE, AND	589	18
"'TWAS SUNSET"--SOME ONE SAID--	THEY CALLED ME TO THE	628	2
AND SAID THAT I WAS STRONG--	THAT FIRST DAY, WHEN YOU	659	2
I SAID "BUT JUST TO BE A BEE"	COULD I BUT RIDE	661	13
"SWEET" SAID HE "MY OWN SURRENDER	WOLFE DEMANDED DURING	678	7
I WANT--WAS CHIEF IT SAID	"I WANT"--IT PLEADED--	731	2
YOU SAID THAT I "WAS GREAT"--ONE DAY--	YOU SAID THAT I "WAS	738	1
GO BLOSSOM TO THE BEES--I SAID--	THE BIRDS REPORTED FROM	743	7
DYES--SAID HE--HAVE I--	AUTUMN--OVERLOOKED MY	748	2
SHOW ME THEM [GIVE THEM ME--]--SAID I--	AUTUMN--OVERLOOKED MY	748	4
AND HOW I JUST SAID "PLEASE."	THEY WONT FROWN ALWAYS--	874	4
HAD I NOT THIS, OR THIS, I SAID,	HAD I NOT THIS, OR THIS,	904	1
"THOU HAST NOT ME, NOR ME"--IT SAID,	HAD I NOT THIS, OR THIS,	904	5
MY NEED--WAS ALL I HAD--I SAID--	HAD I NOT THIS, OR THIS,	904	9
TWO SEASONS, IT IS SAID, EXIST--	THERE IS A JUNE WHEN	930	9
AS THOSE FIRST FURNISHED, SAID--	TWO TRAVELLERS PERISHING	933	16
FOR EVERY DAY BE SAID	SUPERFLUOUS WERE THE SUN	999	4
SAID DEATH TO PASSION	SAID DEATH TO PASSION	1033	1
SAID PASSION, THROUGH CONTRACTING BREATHS	SAID DEATH TO PASSION	1033	3
AND SPIRIT TURNED [THE SPIRIT SAID] UNTO THE DUST	I HEARD, AS IF I HAD NO	1039	13
SHALL I TAKE THEE, THE POET SAID	SHALL I TAKE THEE, THE	1126	1
"SECURE [PROTECT] YOUR FLOWER" SAID HE.	THE FROST OF DEATH WAS	1136	2
GOD IT IS SAID REPLIES IN PERSON	TELL AS A MARKSMAN--WERE	1152	24
OF PAUL AND SILAS IT IS SAID	OF PAUL AND SILAS IT IS	1166	1
THE SEA SAID "COME" TO THE BROOK--	THE SEA SAID "COME" TO	1210	1
THE BROOK SAID "LET ME GROW"--	THE SEA SAID "COME" TO	1210	2
THE SEA SAID "THEN YOU WILL BE A SEA--	THE SEA SAID "COME" TO	1210	3
THE SEA SAID "GO" TO THE SEA--	THE SEA SAID "COME" TO	1210	5
THE SEA SAID "I AM HE	THE SEA SAID "COME" TO	1210	6
WHEN IT IS SAID,	A WORD IS DEAD	1212	2
PRESUMPTUOUS EVENING SAID--	WHEN MEMORY IS FULL	1266	4
NEITHER--SAID THE MOON--	WHICH IS THE BEST--THE	1315	2
A STROLLING HUE, ONE WOULD HAVE SAID	IT WAS A QUIET SEEMING	1419	5
TO LAW--SAID SWEET THERMOPYLAE	"GO TELL IT"--WHAT A	1554	7
BEHOLD SAID THE APOSTLE	SPEECH IS ONE SYMPTOM OF	1681	7
THREE TIMES, 'TIS SAID, A SINKING MAN	DROWNING IS NOT SO	1718	3
THE MARKET PRICE, THEY SAID.	I TOOK ONE DRAUGHT OF	1725	4
SAIL			
"KIDD" WILL [MAY] SUDDEN SAIL--	I NEVER TOLD THE BURIED	11	17
AND PUSHED AWAY A SAIL	THREE TIMES--WE PARTED--	598	8
UNCONSCIOUS THAT HIS SINGLE FLEET [BULK / SAIL]	WHO GIANTS KNOW, WITH	796	7
. . . SAIL SOFTLY / DO ANCHOR] HERE	A CHILLY PEACE INFESTS	1443	7
WE ARE ENFORCED TO SAIL	DOWN TIME'S QUAINT	1656	3
SAILED			
NEVER SAILED THE BAY!	COULD LIVE--DID LIVE--	43	13
NAVIES OF BUTTERFLIES--SAILED THRO'--	WHAT WOULD I GIVE TO SEE	247	13
THAT SAILED WITHOUT A CARE--	A SOFT SEA WASHED AROUND	1198	4
SAILING SEE A SAILING			
SAILING SILENTLY,	ON THIS WONDROUS SEA	4	2
SAILOR			
CAN THE SAILOR UNDERSTAND	EXULTATION IS THE GOING	76	6
OH SOME SCHOLAR! OH SOME SAILOR!	WILL THERE REALLY BE A	101	9
SOME SAILOR, SKIRTING FOREIGN [NOVEL] SHORES--	JUST LOST, WHEN I WAS	160	9

	FIRST LINE	POEM	LINE
SAILOR (CONTINUED)			
SOME SAILOR--ROWING IN THE DARK--	GOOD NIGHT! WHICH PUT	259	8
THE SAILOR DOES'NT KNOW THE STROKE--	I SOMETIMES DROP IT, FOR	708	15
THE SAILOR DOUBTING TURNS--	WHEN THE ASTRONOMER	851	6
WE DO NOT MOURN FOR TRAVELER, OR SAILOR,	THE THINGS THAT NEVER	1515	5
SAILOR'S			
A SAILOR'S BUSINESS IS THE SHORE!	A LITTLE BREAD--A CRUST	159	10
SAILORS			
SO SAILORS SAY--ON YESTERDAY--	ADRIFT! A LITTLE BOAT	30	5
FANTASTIC SAILORS--MINGLE--	WHERE SHIPS OF PURPLE--	265	3
LIKE SAILORS FIGHTING WITH A LEAK	THE FROST OF DEATH WAS	1136	3
SAILS			
MANY THE SAILS AT REST--	ON THIS WONDROUS SEA	4	8
RETRIMMED IT'S MASTS--REDECKED IT'S SAILS--	ADRIFT! A LITTLE BOAT	30	12
SHE BENT HER DOCILE SAILS--	WHETHER MY BARK WENT	52	4
LEAD THE WANDERING SAILS.	A POOR--TORN HEART-- A	78	16
NOR EVER GUESSED THE STATELY SAILS	'TWAS SUCH A LITTLE--	107	7
SAINT SEE ST			
WHEN THE LAST SAINT--GOES UP THE AISLES--	BETTER--THAN MUSIC! FOR	503	18
IT WAS NOT SAINT--IT WAS TOO LARGE--	IT WAS NOT SAINT--IT WAS	1092	1
SAINTED			
BY EVERY SAINTED BEE--	I KEEP MY PLEDGE.	46	6
SAINTS			
LIKE HER THE SAINTS RETIRE,	LIKE HER THE SAINTS	60	1
SAINTS, WITH RAVISHED SLATE AND PENCIL	I CANT TELL YOU--BUT YOU	65	3
AND WITH THE SAINTS SAT DOWN.	SHE BORE IT TILL THE	144	8
GET SAINTS--WITH NEW--UNSTEADY TONGUE--	FOR THIS--ACCEPTED	195	14
AND SAINTS--TO WINDOWS RUN--	I TASTE A LIQUOR NEVER	214	14
I THOUGHT THAT SUCH WERE FOR THE SAINTS,	THERE CAME A DAY AT	322	3
THE SAINTS FORGET	ME--COME! MY DAZZLED	431	5
GRAVE SAINTS STOLE OUT TO LOOK AT ME--	I MEANT TO HAVE BUT	476	15
SACRAMENT, SAINTS PARTOOK [INDORSED] BEFORE US--	TO PUT THIS WORLD DOWN,	527	12
WHERE SAINTS, AND OUR PLAIN GOING NEIGHBOR	BESIDES THIS MAY	977	9
IF ONLY TO ENCLOSE THE SAINTS	SO MUCH OF HEAVEN HAS	1228	3
NO MATTER WHERE THE SAINTS ABIDE,	NO MATTER WHERE THE	1541	1
. . . ALL THE SAINTS HE KNEW / EVERY GOD HE KNEW]	THE BOBOLINK IS GONE--	1591	6
SAINTS'			
UNTO THE SAINTS' SLOW DILIGENCE [INDUSTRY]--	EACH LIFE CONVERGES TO	680	15
SAITH			
OUR LORD--"SO LOVED"--IT SAITH--	THE TEST OF LOVE--IS	573	2
SAKE			
AH, WHAT A ROYAL SAKE	FOR THIS--ACCEPTED	195	5
HOW MANY TIMES FOR MY FAR SAKE	YOU SEE I CANNOT SEE--	253	4
JUST GRANTED, FOR THE PERIL'S SAKE--	A SINGLE SCREW OF FLESH	263	15
WHICH WAS THE GUILTY SAKE--	'TWAS LOVE--NOT ME--	394	11
FOR THEIR--SAKE--NOT FOR OUR'S--	I TIE MY HAT--I CREASE	443	24
FOR THAT DEAR--DISTANT--DANGEROUS--SAKE--	WHY MAKE IT DOUBT--IT	462	7
A-FOG FOR--SAY--WHOSE SAKE?	YOU KNOW THAT PORTRAIT	504	4
A VALUE--FOR THE GREATNESS' SAKE--	HAD I PRESUMED TO HOPE--	522	3
FOR HIS MEAN SAKE TO LEAVE THE ROW	THE HEAVEN VESTS FOR	694	11
FOR THE DEPARTED CREATURE'S SAKE	ASHES DENOTE THAT FIRE	1063	3
AND LEAVE FOR THY SWEET MERCY'S [PATIENCE'] SAKE	SOME WRETCHED CREATURE,	1111	3
SUBMITTING FOR OUR UNKNOWN SAKE	A FULL FED ROSE ON MEALS	1154	7
BLOSSOMS--DRESS FOR HIS SAKE.	HE IS ALIVE, THIS	1160	4
FOR THE DISOBEDIENCE' SAKE	SO I PULL MY STOCKINGS	1201	3
FOR THE PROGRESS' SAKE"--	I SAW THAT THE FLAKE WAS	1267	8
THE GRACE SO AWKWARD FOR HER SAKE	WARM IN HER HAND THESE	1313	3
AND OUR'S SURRENDERED [CONSIDERED] FOR IT'S SAKE	THE FACE IN EVANESCENCE	1490	3
SALARY			
IN CEASELESS--SALARY--	ONE LIFE OF SO MUCH	270	4
OUR SALARY THE LONGEST DAY	THE NOTICE THAT IS	1310	7
SALE			
DO SOW, AND RAISE FOR SALE--	WHEN DIAMONDS ARE A	397	4
SALES			
A COUNTER HAS AND SALES	THE MERCHANT OF THE	1131	2
SALLOW			
A FADED BOY--IN SALLOW CLOTHES	A FADED BOY--IN SALLOW	1524	1
SALUBRIOUS			
SALUBRIOUS HOURS ARE GIVEN	TO HELP OUR BLEAKER	1064	2
SALUTE			
SIMPLE SALUTE--AND CERTAIN RECOGNITION--	IT'S COMING--THE	390	5
SALUTE, AND PASS, WITHOUT A HINT--	I READ MY SENTENCE--	412	13
SALUTE HER--WITH LONG FINGERS--	THE SOUL HAS BANDAGED	512	5
BUT AS AN ENEMY'S SALUTE	I CROSS TILL I AM WEARY	550	12
NEWS-BOYS SALUTE THE DOOR--	I COULD DIE--TO KNOW--	570	3
SALUTE US, WITH THEIR WINGS--	OF NEARNESS TO HER	607	16
TO SALUTE SO FAIR A FOREHEAD--	HER SWEET TURN TO LEAVE	649	11
AND FIRMAMENT SALUTE THEE,	TO THE STANCH DUST	1402	V 6
SALUTES			
EACH ONE SALUTES ME, AS HE GOES,	I DREADED THAT FIRST	348	25
SALUTING			
SALUTING [CONFRONTING / CONTRASTING]--IN THE ROAD--	UPON CONCLUDED LIVES	735	8
SALVATION			
RING--FOR THE SCANT SALVATION--	GLEE--THE GREAT STORM IS	619	5

	FIRST LINE	POEM	LINE
SAME			
THEIR BALLADS WERE THE SAME--	I HAD A GUINEA GOLDEN--	23	14
IT WANDERED FROM THE SAME.	I HAD A GUINEA GOLDEN--	23	20
AS THAT SAME WATCHER, WHEN THE EAST	AS WATCHERS HANG UPON	121	7
QUIETLY DID THE SAME--	ALL OVERGROWN BY CUNNING	148	8
THOSE WHO READ THE SAME EDITION--	IF THE FOOLISH, CALL	168	7
WITH THOSE SAME BOOTS OF LEAD, AGAIN,	I FELT A FUNERAL, IN MY	280	11
AND THIS ONE--DO NOT FEEL THE SAME--	THE FIRST DAY'S NIGHT	410	19
BUT--THERE--THE GOLDEN SAME--	YOU KNOW THAT PORTRAIT	504	12
WHO SINGS THE SAME, UNHEARD,	TO HEAR AN ORIOLE SING	526	5
FOR CIRCUMSTANCE THE SAME--	I HAD NO CAUSE TO BE	542	12
HE OFFERS [SPICES / FLAVORS] HIS BERRY, JUST THE SAME	THE BLACK BERRY--WEARS A	554	3
THE SAME--AFFLICTED THOMAS--	TRUST IN THE UNEXPECTED	555	13
THE SEASONS--FIT--THE SAME--	IT MAKES NO DIFFERENCE	620	2
AND HUNGERED FOR--THE SAME--	A PRISON GETS TO BE A	652	8
REPRODUCED--THE SAME--	BLOOM UPON THE MOUNTAIN	667	4
DEATH--HAD THE SAME DESIGN--	I MEANT TO FIND HER WHEN	718	2
THOSE SAME UNVARYING EYES	SWEET MOUNTAINS--YE TELL	722	3
CASHMERE--OR CALVARY--THE SAME--	WHERE THOU ART--THAT--IS	725	2
THE FEATURES ARE THE SAME--	JOY TO HAVE MERITED THE	788	12
ALL DAYS, I DID NOT EARN THE SAME	I MADE SLOW RICHES BUT	843	5
THE SAME LOCALITY--	IT BLOOMED AND DROPT, A	978	8
THE SAME AS THOSE THAT LIVED	THAT THIS SHOULD FEEL	1112	2
THE SMALL MUST [DO] DIE, THE SAME [AS WELL] AS HE--	THAT THIS SHOULD FEEL	1112	6
'TWILL NEVER BE THE SAME TO STARVE	OH SUMPTUOUS MOMENT	1125	4
SECURITY THE SAME INSURES	OF PAUL AND SILAS IT IS	1166	5
UNIVERSE THE SAME	NOW I KNEW I LOST HER--	1219	10
A BEING HAS THE SAME--	THE BONE THAT HAS NO	1274	6
BUT SCINTILLATES THE SAME--	HOW KNOW IT FROM A	1364	4
DISSOLVES [ABATES / EXHALES]--THE SAME--	IN MANY AND REPORTLESS	1382	6
INSTRUCTING BY THE SAME [ITSELF]--	WITH PINIONS OF DISDAIN	1431	9
IT IS THE SAME WITH LIFE--	WE KNEW NOT THAT WE WERE	1462	8
THE SMALL [SAME] STALE SUM--	HOW DESTITUTE IS HE	1477	4
THE SAME OBLIQUE INTEGRITY,	THE ROBIN IS A GABRIEL	1483	7
THE SAME AMOUNT REMAIN--	HOPE IS A SUBTLE GLUTTON	1547	8
TO THE SAME FLOWER HESPERIAN,	OF DEATH I TRY TO THINK	1558	7
TO THE SAME PAGEANT WENDS ITS WAY	NO LIFE CAN POMPLESS	1626	3
THAT THOU SHALT BE THE SAME--	THE LOOK OF THEE, WHAT	1689	12
ITS CIRCUIT JUST THE SAME	A PIT--BUT HEAVEN OVER	1712	15
SANCTIFIES			
YET SANCTIFIES THE MIND--	IT IS A LONESOME GLEE--	774	2
SANCTIFYING			
LIKE SANCTIFYING IN THE SOUL--	I THINK I WAS ENCHANTED	593	23
SANCTION			
. . . IT / SANCTION IT / FASTEN IT] YOURSELF.	SUMMER LAID HER SIMPLE	1363	4
SANCTITY			
AND SANCTITY, ARE BEST	THE ROBIN IS THE ONE	828	12
OF SANCTITY TO BE--	THE TREASON OF AN ACCENT	1358	V
AND SANCTITY--ENFORCE THEE--	TO THE STANCH DUST	1402	6
IN HER DISHEVELED SANCTITY--	THE DITCH IS DEAR TO THE	1645	5
SAND			
I LOST IT IN THE SAND--	I HAD A GUINEA GOLDEN--	23	2
AND GUINEA IN THE SAND.	I HAD A GUINEA GOLDEN--	23	28
IF HE FLING SAND [DUST], AND PEBBLE--	THE WIND DID'NT COME	316	17
AH, PUSSY, OF THE SAND,	SHE SIGHTS A BIRD--SHE	507	8
I HUNTED [WORRIED] ALL THE SAND--	A DYING TIGER--MOANED	566	2
HORRID SAND PARTITION--	IN FALLING TIMBERS	614	7
INTO THE BOILING SAND--	GLEE--THE GREAT STORM IS	619	4
WOULD MORE AFFRONT THE SAND--	YOU'LL KNOW HER--BY HER	634	4
IS SHIFTED--LIKE A SAND--	OF ALL THE SOULS THAT	664	8
FRUCTIFIED IN SAND--	SOIL OF FLINT, IF STEADY	681	4
WITH ROPES OF SAND	AN EVERYWHERE OF SILVER	884	2
WHOSE SUBSTANCES ARE SAND--	WE DO NOT KNOW THE TIME	1106	8
BUT SWEPT AS DRY AS SAND--	LIKE RAIN IT SOUNDED	1235	4
SO THAT WILL HELP THE SAND	I DID NOT REACH THEE	1664	8
THE CASPIAN HAS ITS REALMS OF SAND,	TO LOSE THEE--SWEETER	1754	5
SANDAL			
HE HAD [WORE] NO SANDAL ON HIS FOOT--	THE ONLY GHOST I EVER	274	3
SANDALS			
WITH GAYER SANDALS GO--	THE FEET OF PEOPLE	7	2
THERE--SANDALS FOR THE BAREFOOT--	A POOR--TORN HEART-- A	78	13
WHOSE SANDALS TOUCH THE TOWN--	IN LANDS I NEVER SAW--	124	4
SANDS			
MAY BE SEEN THE SANDS AMONG,	ANGELS, IN THE EARLY	94	6
PRACTICING SANDS--	WE PLAY AT PASTE--	320	8
ALONG APPOINTED SANDS--	THE MOON IS DISTANT FROM	429	4
AGROUND--UPON THE SANDS--	I STARTED EARLY--TOOK MY	520	8
HIS SANDS SUFFICE	UNTIL THE DESERT KNOWS	1291	3
SANE			
ASSENT--AND YOU ARE SANE--	MUCH MADNESS IS DIVINEST	435	6
THE DANGER [SORROW] TO BE SANE	I THINK I WAS ENCHANTED	593	26
SANG			
WHO SANG FULL MANY A DAY	I HAD A GUINEA GOLDEN--	23	10
I SANG FIRM--EVEN--[STRAIGHT--STEADY] CHANTS--	I ROSE--BECAUSE HE SANK	616	6
SANG FROM THE HEART, SIRE,	SANG FROM THE HEART,	1059	1
THE CRICKETS SANG	THE CRICKETS SANG	1104	1
AND SANG FOR NOTHING SCRUTABLE [IN THE WORLD]	THE MOST TRIUMPHANT BIRD	1265	5
HOW SLOW THE WHISTLE SANG--	I THOUGHT THE TRAIN	1449	2

	FIRST LINE	POEM	LINE
SANG (CONTINUED)			
A BIRD BROKE FORTH AND SANG, ...	A TRAIN WENT THROUGH A	1761	2
AND BOWED AND SANG AGAIN.	A TRAIN WENT THROUGH A	1761	6
SANITY			
BY SOULS OF SANITY	SLEEP IS SUPPOSED TO BE	13	2
PROTECTS OUR SANITY.	DID LIFE'S PENURIOUS	1717	8
SANK			
THEN SANK AS GAILY AS A TURK	SHE DIED AT PLAY,	75	4
I ROSE--BECAUSE HE SANK--	I ROSE--BECAUSE HE SANK	616	1
SANK THIS [THE] BEGGAR FROM THE SKY-- . .	MOST SHE TOUCHED ME BY	760	10
SANTA			
FOR ANY SANTA CLAUS TO REACH	'TWAS JUST THIS TIME,	445	19
SAP			
TO DREAM--TO SAP THE PROP	A PIT--BUT HEAVEN OVER	1712	7
SAPLING			
NATURE--SOMETIMES SEARS A SAPLING-- . . .	NATURE--SOMETIMES SEARS	314	1
SAPPED			
SHE STUNG HIM--SAPPED HIS FIRM ADVANCE-- .	FATE SLEW HIM, BUT HE	1031	5
SAPPHIRE			
KNOW WHAT THE SAPPHIRE FELLOWS, DO, . . .	THE SKIES CANT KEEP	191	15
WITH A DEPARTING--SAPPHIRE--FEATURE-- . .	HOW THE OLD MOUNTAINS	291	11
I ONLY SAW A SAPPHIRE [AN AMBER--] FARM-- .	THEY CALLED ME TO THE	628	3
SUNSET--REVIEWS HER SAPPHIRE REGIMENT [REGIMENTS]--	AH, TENERIFFE!	666	4
SAPPHO			
WHEN SAPPHO--WAS A LIVING GIRL--	A PRECIOUS--MOULDERING	371	17
SARAH			
THERE'S SARAH, AND ELIZA, AND EMELINE SO FAIR,	AWAKE YE MUSES NINE,	1	31
SAT			
I SAT ME DOWN TO SIGH.	I HAD A GUINEA GOLDEN--	23	8
THAT SAT IT DOWN TO REST--	A POOR--TORN HEART-- A	78	2
AND WITH THE SAINTS SAT DOWN.	SHE BORE IT TILL THE	144	8
A BIRD SAT CARELESS ON THE FENCE--	THE TREES LIKE TASSELS--	606	17
'TWAS AS SPACE SAT SINGING	MOST SHE TOUCHED ME BY	760	15
THE MOUNTAIN SAT UPON THE PLAIN	THE MOUNTAIN SAT UPON	975	1
WAS [SAT] THE DEFIANT SUN--	A WILD BLUE SKY ABREAST	1415	4
SATAN			
SATAN--THE BRIGADIER--	THE BIBLE IS AN ANTIQUE	1545	6
SATED			
HAS VANQUISHED [SATED] FLAME'S CONDITIONS, .	DARE YOU SEE A SOUL AT	365	5
SMALLER--THAT COVERED [FLOODED / SATED] VISION--HERE--	RENUNCIATION--IS A	745	16
SATIETY			
NEVER KNEW SATIETY--	NEVER FOR SOCIETY	746	7
GAIN--SATIETY--	EXPECTATION--IS	807	2
BUT SATIETY--CONVICTION	EXPECTATION--IS	807	3
OF SATIETY--	SATISFACTION--IS THE	1036	2
DANGER DISINTEGRATES SATIETY	PERIL AS A POSSESSION	1678	3
SATIN			
THE SERPENT'S SATIN FIGURE	THROUGH LANE IT LAY--	9	7
IN A SATIN VEST!	PORTRAITS ARE TO DAILY	170	4
RAFTER OF SATIN, ...	SAFE IN THEIR ALABASTER	216	5
GLOBE ROSES--BREAK THEIR SATIN FLAKE-- . .	I TEND MY FLOWERS FOR	339	16
I PAY--IN SATIN CASH--	I PAY--IN SATIN CASH--	402	1
BROOKS OF PLUSH--IN BANKS OF SATIN	SWEET--SAFE--HOUSES--	457	6
DESERTS--NEVER REBUKED HER SATIN--	CIVILIZATION--SPURNS--	492	3
TO SATIN RACES--HE IS NOUGHT--	I THINK THE HEMLOCK	525	13
UNNUMBERED SATIN--	THESE--SAW VISIONS--	758	8
THE SHIP MIGHT BE OF SATIN HAD IT NOT TO FIGHT--	THERE IS A STRENGTH IN	1113	5
A QUEEN ADOWN A SATIN AISLE, ...	A CURIOUS CLOUD	1710	8
SATIRIST			
AND HE TURNS SATIRIST!	MY FRIEND ATTACKS MY	118	4
SATISFACTION			
SATISFACTION--IS THE AGENT	SATISFACTION--IS THE	1036	1
SATISFIED			
AND LEFT HIS PROCESS--SATISFIED--	HE PUT THE BELT AROUND	273 V	3
I'M SATISFIED--THE ROMANCE	IT ALWAYS FELT TO ME--A	597	7
THAT I STOPPED GUAGING--SATISFIED-- . . .	ONE BLESSING HAD I THAN	756	3
I'LL SHIVER, SATISFIED.	I'VE DROPPED MY BRAIN--	1046	20
THE DISCS THAT SATISFIED OUR SIGHT--	WHAT TWIGS WE HELD BY--	1086	15
NOT SATISFIED TO APE THE GREAT IN HIS SIMPLICITY	THAT THIS SHOULD FEEL	1112	5
SO SATISFIED TO GO	SO PROUD SHE WAS TO DIE	1272	5
AND SATISFIED A LEAF	A DEW SUFFICED ITSELF--	1437	2
SATISFIES			
THAT IMAGE--SATISFIES--	A CHARM INVESTS A FACE	421	8
AND SATISFIES AN AWE	I THINK THE HEMLOCK	525	4
SATISFY			
AND SATISFY--OBTAINED--	UNTO MY BOOKS--SO GOOD	604	16
THEY NEVER YET DID SATISFY--	THE TREES LIKE TASSELS--	606	7
SATURATED			
BECAUSE YOU SATURATED SIGHT--	I CANNOT LIVE WITH YOU--	640	33
SATURN'S			
HOW DIMMER THAN A SATURN'S BAR	WHAT TWIGS WE HELD BY--	1086	16
SATYR'S			
AS COOL [DISTINCT] AS SATYR'S DRUMS-- . .	DID YOU EVER STAND IN A	590	14
SATYRS			
THE SATYRS FINGERS BECKONED--	THROUGH LANE IT LAY--	9	13

	FIRST LINE	POEM	LINE
SAUCER			
A SAUCER HOLDS A CUP	A SAUCER HOLDS A CUP	1374	1
A SAUCER HOLDS A LOAF.	A SAUCER HOLDS A CUP	1374	4
SAUCY			
SAUCY, SAUCY SERAPH	GOOD NIGHT, BECAUSE WE	114	5
SAUCY, SAUCY SERAPH	GOOD NIGHT, BECAUSE WE	114	5
SAUNTERED			
SOFT SAUNTERED THRO' THE VILLAGE--	WITHIN MY REACH!	90	4
SAUNTERED AS SOFT AWAY!	WITHIN MY REACH!	90	5
WE SAUNTERED FROM THE DOOR	EDEN IS THAT	1657	6
THAT SAUNTERED WITH US HERE, ...	THE SADDEST NOISE, THE	1764	10
SAUNTERING			
SAUNTERING THIS WAY	HEART, NOT SO HEAVY AS	83	10
SAUNTERING GENTLEMEN--WITH CANES--	IT WILL BE SUMMER--	342	3
THE SAUNTERING ALONE	THROUGH THOSE OLD	1753	2
SAVAN			
A "SAVAN" PASSING BY	"ARCTURUS" IS HIS OTHER	70	6
SAVANS			
A SCIENCE--SO THE SAVANS SAY, ...	A SCIENCE--SO THE SAVANS	100	1
IF THE SAVANS "CLASSIFY" THEM	IF THE FOOLISH, CALL	168	3
SAVE			
SAVE BY TEARFUL RILL--	GLOWING IS HER BONNET,	72	8
SAVE BY LOVING SUNRISE	GLOWING IS HER BONNET,	72	9
SAVE BY FEET UNNUMBERED	GLOWING IS HER BONNET,	72	11
SAVE JUST A LITTLE PLACE FOR ME	GOING TO HEAVEN!	79	14
THAN SAVE MY BOOT--	IS BLISS THEN, SUCH	340	5
SHOULD BE THE ART [EXCLUSIVELY]--TO SAVE-- .	THE PROVINCE OF THE	539	2
SOME I SHALL KEEP [SAVE]--TO SOLVE . . .	IT TROUBLED ME AS ONCE I	600	10
FLOSS WONT SAVE YOU FROM AN ABYSS	FLOSS WONT SAVE YOU FROM	1322	1
SAVED			
THE SAVED WILL TELL	THERE IS A WORD	8	7
JUST LOST, WHEN I WAS SAVED!	JUST LOST, WHEN I WAS	160	1
I SHOULD HAVE BEEN TOO SAVED--I SEE-- . .	I SHOULD HAVE BEEN TOO	313	7
SAVED!	OF TRIBULATION--THESE	325	17
THE PROVINCE OF THE SAVED	THE PROVINCE OF THE	539	1
IF YOU REMEMBER, AND WERE SAVED--	DID YOU EVER STAND IN A	590	15
AND WERE YOU--SAVED--	I CANNOT LIVE WITH YOU--	640	41
SAVED FOR YOUR EAR WHEN LUTES BE OLD. . .	SPLIT THE LARK--AND	861	4
FOR NEWS THAT THEY BE SAVED--	SWEET, TO HAVE HAD THEM	901	2
THAT IT BE SAVED THE SAVED SUFFICE . . .	SOMEHOW MYSELF SURVIVED	1194	3
THAT IT BE SAVED THE SAVED SUFFICE . . .	SOMEHOW MYSELF SURVIVED	1194	3
WAS ALL THAT SAVED [ALONE SUSTAINED-- / ALONE UPHELD--] A BEE	A SINGLE CLOVER PLANK	1343	2
IT IS TO BE THE SAVED--	ESCAPE IS SUCH A	1347	10
THE SAVED HAVE [LEFT] NO REMEMBRANCE . . .	I SAW THE WIND WITHIN	1502	V
NOR HAVE THE SAVED REMEMBRANCE	I SAW THE WIND WITHIN	1502	V
WOULD HAVE SAVED	T'IS EASIER TO PITY	1698	3
SAVES			
JUST SAVES IT FROM DESPAIR	SUPERFLUOUS WERE THE SUN	999	6
SAVES SHE ALL OF THAT FOR SUNSETS	NATURE RARER USES YELLOW	1045	3
SAVING			
SEEKING [SAVING] MORE--TO SPEND--	SWEET--YOU FORGOT--BUT I	523	8
SAVIOR			
SAVIOR! I'VE NO ONE ELSE TO TELL-- . . .	SAVIOR! I'VE NO ONE ELSE	217	1
OUR SAVIOR, BY A HAIR--	THAT AFTER HORROR--THAT	286	4
SO SAVIOR--CRUCIFY--	I SHOULD HAVE BEEN TOO	313	18
SAVIOR [MASTER]--I'VE SEEN THE FACE--BEFORE!	A WIFE--AT DAYBREAK I	461	13
ELSE--SAVIOR--BANISH ME--	'TIS TRUE--THEY SHUT ME	538	V 12
SOME WRETCHED CREATURE, SAVIOR TAKE . . .	SOME WRETCHED CREATURE,	1111	1
'TIS NOT TO SIGHT THE SAVIOR--	ESCAPE IS SUCH A	1347	9
THE SAVIOR MUST HAVE BEEN	THE SAVIOR MUST HAVE	1487	1
SAVIOR'S			
YOU'LL KNOW--SIR--WHEN THE SAVIOR'S FACE .	IF I'M LOST--NOW--	256	12
SAVIORS			
THOSE UNSUSTAINED--SAVIORS--	IT FEELS A SHAME TO BE	444	19
SAVORS			
OF SAVORS--MAKE US CONSCIOUS--	DESPAIR'S ADVANTAGE IS	799	9
SAVORY			
BY SAVORY FANCY SPREAD--	AS WATCHERS HANG UPON	121	3
WAS SAVORY--	UNDUE SIGNIFICANCE A	439	9
SAW			
I SAW THE SUN--HIS PLUNDER DONE	I NEVER TOLD THE BURIED	11	3
NE'ER SAW I SUCH A WONDROUS SCENE-- . . .	THERE IS A MORN BY MEN	24	13
WE WHO SAW THE LAUNCHING	COULD LIVE--DID LIVE--	43	12
IN LANDS I NEVER SAW--THEY SAY	IN LANDS I NEVER SAW--	124	1
THE ONLY GHOST I EVER SAW	THE ONLY GHOST I EVER	274	1
HE DID NOT KNOW I SAW--	A BIRD CAME DOWN THE	328	2
I SAW NO WAY--THE HEAVENS WERE STITCHED-- .	I SAW NO WAY--THE	378	1
YOU CANNOT PRICK WITH SAW--	NO RACK CAN TORTURE ME--	384	5
I [HE] SHOWED HER [ME] HIGHTS SHE [I] NEVER SAW--	I SHOWED HER HIGHTS SHE	446	1
OUR SOULS SAW--JUST AS WELL--	THEY PUT US FAR APART--	474	12
EACH OTHER'S SETTING--SAW--	THEY PUT US FAR APART--	474	24
WHO SAW THEM--WHEREFORE FLY?	WE PRAY--TO HEAVEN--	489	5
FOR SOMEWHAT THAT [WHATSOE'ER] IT SAW? . .	IT KNEW NO MEDICINE--	559	16
I NEVER SAW BEFORE	I YEARS HAD BEEN FROM	609	4
I ONLY SAW A SAPPHIRE [AN AMBER--] FARM-- .	THEY CALLED ME TO THE	628	3
HE NEVER SAW ME--IN THIS LIFE--	AGAIN--HIS VOICE IS AT	663	7
NONE SAW--	ONE NEED NOT BE A	670	V 20
THESE--SAW VISIONS--	THESE--SAW VISIONS--	758	1

	FIRST LINE	POEM	LINE
SAW (CONTINUED)			
WHAT DID THEY DO SINCE I SAW THEM?	WHAT DID THEY DO SINCE I	900	1
AND WHAT WE SAW NOT	THE ADMIRATIONS--AND	906	5
WHAT WE SAW BEFORE--	THE ADMIRATIONS--AND	906	8
THE FIRST--SWEET, PROVED I, [THAT WAS] ERE I SAW THEE--	WERT THOU BUT ILL--THAT	961	19
WHO SAW NO SUNRISE CANNOT SAY	WHO SAW NO SUNRISE	1018	1
I SAW, AS IF MY EYE WERE ON	I HEARD, AS IF I HAD NO	1039	5
I SAW NO MORE OF HER.	I CANNOT MEET THE SPRING	1051	8
I NEVER SAW A MOOR--	I NEVER SAW A MOOR--	1052	1
I NEVER SAW THE SEA--	I NEVER SAW A MOOR--	1052	2
AND MENTION WHAT WE SAW.	DEW--IS THE FRESHET IN	1097	8
NONE [THEY] WHO SAW IT EVER TOLD IT	NONE WHO SAW IT EVER	1110	1
AND WE WHO NEVER SAW	I SHOULD NOT DARE TO BE	1197	6
NOR EVER SAW HIS HOUSE NOR FURNITURE,	I CANNOT SEE MY SOUL BUT	1262	2
I SAW THAT THE FLAKE WAS ON IT	I SAW THAT THE FLAKE WAS	1267	1
AS THOSE THAT DISSOLUTION SAW	IT WAS A QUIET SEEMING	1419	11
I SAW THE WIND WITHIN HER	I SAW THE WIND WITHIN	1502	1
SEEK IT WITH THE SAW,	DEATH IS LIKE THE INSECT	1716	6
NO MAN SAW AWE, NOR TO HIS HOUSE	NO MAN SAW AWE, NOR TO	1733	1
"YET SAW HIM FACE TO FACE"--	NO MAN SAW AWE, NOR TO	1733	14
SAWING			
SUSPENSE KEPT SAWING SO--	'TIS SO APPALLING--IT	281	8
SAXON			
SAY IT AGAIN, SAXON [ENGLISH LANGUAGE]!	MANY A PHRASE HAS THE	276	15
SAY			
SO SAILORS SAY--ON YESTERDAY--	ADRIFT! A LITTLE BOAT	30	5
SO ANGELS SAY--ON YESTERDAY--	ADRIFT! A LITTLE BOAT	30	9
WHAT WILL THE OAK [FIR] TREE SAY?	I ROBBED THE WOODS--	41	9
"DEPARTED"--BOTH--THEY SAY!	LIKE HER THE SAINTS	60	7
AS THEY SAY POLITE ARCHANGELS	I CANT TELL YOU--BUT YOU	65	11
NOT FOR YOU--TO SAY	I CANT TELL YOU--BUT YOU	65	14
THE EMPEROR WILL SAY?	WHO NEVER LOST, ARE	73	10
A SCIENCE--SO THE SAVANS SAY,	A SCIENCE--SO THE SAVANS	100	1
SAY REPOSE!	ARTISTS WRESTLED HERE!	110	6
IN LANDS I NEVER SAW--THEY SAY	IN LANDS I NEVER SAW--	124	1
AND SAY HOW MANY DEW,	BRING ME THE SUNSET IN A	128	3
IF, HAPLY, ANY SAY TO ME	I BRING AN UNACCUSTOMED	132	20
SOME--SAY--IT IS "THE SPHERES"--AT PLAY!	MUSICIANS WRESTLE	157	13
SOME SAY--THAT BRIGHT MAJORITY	MUSICIANS WRESTLE	157	14
SAY--SEA--TAKE ME!	MY RIVER RUNS TO THEE--	162	7
WHO SHALL SAY	IF I COULD BRIBE THEM BY	179	14
THEY MAY NOT FINALLY SAY, YES--	IF I COULD BRIBE THEM BY	179	18
I SAY, AS IF THIS LITTLE FLOWER	AS IF SOME LITTLE ARCTIC	180	9
SAY IF IT'S REALLY--WARM AT NOON--	MAKE ME A PICTURE OF THE	188	9
TO SAY WHAT TRANCE BELOW	FOR THIS--ACCEPTED	195	15
CLERGYMEN SAY--	WE DONT CRY--TIM AND I,	196	22
MISTRESS IS "NOT AT HOME"--TO SAY--	THE FLOWER MUST NOT	206	5
TO WONDER WHAT MYSELF WILL SAY,	THO' I GET HOME HOW LATE	207	11
AND WHAT ITSELF, WILL SAY TO ME--	THO' I GET HOME HOW LATE	207	12
SAY--MAY I HAVE IT--SIR?	I CAME TO BUY A SMILE--	223	14
SUCH AN ONE--TO SAY--	TEACH HIM--WHEN HE MAKES	227	2
I'LL SAY--REMEMBER--KING--	THE COURT IS FAR AWAY--	235	6
AS SMALL--THEY SAY--AS I--	THE COURT IS FAR AWAY--	235	10
SAY--THAT THE PULSE JUST LISPS--	IF HE DISSOLVE--THEN--	236	10
SAY--THAT A LITTLE LIFE--FOR HIS--	IF HE DISSOLVE--THEN--	236	12
"SHYLOCK"? SAY!	WHAT WOULD I GIVE TO SEE	247	22
BUT--I CAN SAY A LITTLE "MINOR"	WHY--DO THEY SHUT ME OUT	248	3
THEY SAY IT DOES'NT HURT--	TO DIE--TAKES JUST A	255	2
AS THE SCHOOLS WOULD SAY--	DELIGHT IS AS THE FLIGHT	257	3
SAY QUICK, THAT I MAY [SO I CAN] DOWER THEE	DOUBT ME! MY DIM	275	7
SAY IT AGAIN, SAXON [ENGLISH LANGUAGE]!	MANY A PHRASE HAS THE	276	15
WHAT IF I SAY I SHALL NOT WAIT!	WHAT IF I SAY I SHALL	277	1
DEFEAT WHETS VICTORY--THEY SAY--	I SHOULD HAVE BEEN TOO	313	19
WE KNOW [SAY] HE HAS CLIMBED A FIR--	THE WIND DID'NT COME	316	8
AND A HOARSE "GET OUT OF THE WAY, I SAY,"	THE WIND DID'NT COME	316	20
WOULD YOU--SAY--	THE WIND DID'NT COME	316	22
SAY, FOOT, DECIDE THE POINT--	IS BLISS THEN, SUCH	340	12
BUT SAY MY APRON BRING THE STICKS	ALTHOUGH I PUT AWAY HIS	366	28
I'VE HEARD MEN SAY--	I'M SAYING EVERY DAY	373	11
SINCE MIDNIGHT--HAPPENED--SAY--	A TONGUE--TO TELL HIM I	400	13
SAY RUBIES--IF HE HESITATE--	A TONGUE--TO TELL HIM I	400	20
SAY--LAST I SAID--WAS THIS--	A TONGUE--TO TELL HIM I	400	22
THEN--LOOK FOR ME. BE SURE YOU SAY--	A TONGUE--TO TELL HIM I	400	28
SO NOT TO SEE US--BUT THEY SAY	I NEVER FELT AT HOME--	413	11
"I'M MIDNIGHT"--NEED THE MIDNIGHT SAY--	YOU'LL KNOW IT--AS YOU	420	9
SAY "WHEN TOMORROW COMES THIS WAY--	IT DONT SOUND SO	426	8
I SAY TO YOU, SAID JESUS--	DO PEOPLE MOULDER	432	9
EASIEST OF ARTS, THEY SAY	KNOWS HOW TO FORGET!	433	V
SAY--SOME--PHILOSOPHER!	KNOWS HOW TO FORGET!	433	V
WHAT COULD IT HINDER SO--TO SAY?	GOING TO HIM! HAPPY	494	21
HE DID NEVER SAY--	HE STRAINED MY FAITH--	497	12
SAY, JESUS CHRIST OF NAZARETH--	AT LEAST--TO PRAY--IS	502	7
A-FOG FOR--SAY--WHOSE SAKE?	YOU KNOW THAT PORTRAIT	504	4
WHEN MOON'S AT FULL--'TIS THOU--I SAY--	YOU KNOW THAT PORTRAIT	504	9
THE PRIVILEGE [THE LIBERTY / AUTHORITY] TO SAY	HE PARTS HIMSELF--LIKE	517	14
SAY IF I ERRED? ACCUSE MY FARTHINGS--	SWEET--YOU FORGOT--BUT I	523	5
AFTER A LIFE--A DEATH--WE'LL SAY--	IF I MAY HAVE IT, WHEN	577	11
NOR WHEN IT ALTERED, I COULD SAY,	IT CEASED TO HURT ME,	584	5
I HEARD A WOMAN SAY	I CRIED AT PITY--NOT AT	588	2

	FIRST LINE	POEM	LINE
SAY (CONTINUED)			
FOR FEAR I HEAR HER SAY	I CRIED AT PITY--NOT AT	588	20
AS DYING--SAY IT DOES--	YOU'LL FIND--IT WHEN YOU	610	10
OR WHAT THE DISTANT SAY--	TO KNOW JUST HOW HE	622	10
'TIS THAT--I CANNOT SAY--	A LITTLE ROAD--NOT MADE	647	6
YET [BUT] HAVE NO ART TO SAY--	"NATURE" IS WHAT WE SEE	668	10
THEY SAY THAT "TIME ASSUAGES"--	THEY SAY THAT "TIME	686	1
HAVE I THE ART TO SAY--	A THOUGHT WENT UP MY	701	8
SAY--SWEET--THEN	NO MATTER--NOW--SWEET--	704	14
'TIS KINGDOMS--AFTERWARD--THEY SAY--	BEHIND ME--DIPS ETERNITY	721	7
MANACLES BE DIM--THEY SAY--	LET US PLAY YESTERDAY--	728	17
SO SAY--IF QUEEN IT BE--	YOU SAID THAT I "WAS	738	13
POUNCE ON HIS BRUISES--ONE--SAY--OR THREE--	GRIEF IS A MOUSE--	793	11
"DID'ST THOU?" "THOU DID'ST NOT MEAN," TO SAY,	I CANNOT BUY IT--'TIS	840	11
INSTEAD I'LL SAY OF GEM	EACH SCAR I'LL KEEP FOR	877	2
WOULD'ST THOU SEEK SO--JUST SAY	I'VE NONE TO TELL ME TO	881	10
'TWAS SETTLED, SO THEY SAY,	WHO OCCUPIES THIS HOUSE?	892	18
THAT--I CANNOT SAY--	THE FIRST DAY THAT I WAS	902	14
WHO SAW NO SUNRISE CANNOT SAY	WHO SAW NO SUNRISE	1018	1
"MY HUSBAND"--WOMEN SAY--	TITLE DIVINE--IS MINE!	1072	12
I TAKE BACK ALL I SAY--	WHEN THEY COME BACK--IF	1080	16
AND WHAT THE MARKETS SAY	MYSELF CAN READ THE	1089	4
SOME SAY.	A WORD IS DEAD	1212	3
I SAY IT JUST	A WORD IS DEAD	1212	4
THE "FOOLISH TUN" THE CRITICS SAY--	RISK IS THE HAIR THAT	1239	9
THEY SAY THAT HE CAN HEAL--	IS HEAVEN A PHYSICIAN?	1270	2
OTHERS--SHALL I SAY	NOT ANY MORE TO BE	1344	14
AND YET WE SOONER SAY	AS SUMMER INTO AUTUMN	1346	2
PRECISELY WHAT TO SAY--	I THOUGHT THE TRAIN	1449	6
SAGES SAY,	LOVE IS DONE WHEN LOVE'S	1485	2
SCATTERED--I SAY--TO PLACE [SEAT] THEM SIDE BY SIDE	ABOVE OBLIVION'S TIDE	1531	6
WE SAY AS OF A STATION	THE BLUNDER IS IN	1684	3
FELL, THEY WILL SAY, IN "SKIRMISH"!	I'VE GOT AN ARROW HERE.	1729	4
SOME SAY GOODNIGHT--AT NIGHT--	SOME SAY GOODNIGHT--AT	1739	1
I SAY GOODNIGHT BY DAY--	SOME SAY GOODNIGHT--AT	1739	2
THE WORDS THE HAPPY SAY	THE WORDS THE HAPPY SAY	1750	1
TO SAY GOOD-BY TO MEN.	A TRAIN WENT THROUGH A	1761	8
SAYING			
AND BELLS KEEP SAYING "VICTORY"	I HAVE A KING, WHO DOES	103	11
SAYING ITSELF IN NEW INFLECTION--	MANY A PHRASE HAS THE	276	7
WAS SAYING TO A FRIEND--	I SEND TWO SUNSETS--	308	6
I'M SAYING EVERY DAY	I'M SAYING EVERY DAY	373	1
WAS SAYING YESTERDAY	BEE! I'M EXPECTING YOU!	1035	2
BY SAYING NOTHING NEW--	EXTOL THEE--COULD I--	1643	2
SAYS			
"DISSOLVE" SAYS DEATH--THE SPIRIT "SIR	DEATH IS A DIALOGUE	976	3
WHO SAYS THE ABSENCE OF A WITCH	LONG YEARS APART--CAN	1383	V 4
AS JESUS SAYS OF HIM,	NO LADDER NEEDS THE BIRD	1574	6
AS JESUS CITES [SAYS] OF HIM--	TO HER DERIDED HOME	1586	10
SAYS THE NAKED TREE--	NOT AT HOME TO CALLERS	1590	2
SCAFFOLD			
WAS NOT UPON THE "SCAFFOLD"--	I CAUTIOUS, SCANNED MY	178	9
BENT TO THE SCAFFOLD, OR IN DUNGEONS--CHANTED [WAITED]--	UNTO LIKE STORY--TROUBLE	295	5
FOR WHOM THE SCAFFOLD NEIGHS--	I SOMETIMES DROP IT, FOR	708	10
THE AUGUR [SCAFFOLD] AND THE CARPENTER--	THE PROPS ASSIST THE	1142	7
SCAFFOLDS			
AND SLOWNESS--THEN THE SCAFFOLDS DROP [SCAFFOLDS CLEAVE / . . .	THE PROPS ASSIST THE	1142	11
AND SLOWNESS--THEN THE SCAFFOLDS DROP [SCAFFOLDS CLEAVE / . . .	THE PROPS ASSIST THE	1142	11
SCALDING			
THAT SCALDING ONE--SABACTHINI--	I SHOULD HAVE BEEN TOO	313	11
SCALDS			
THAT SCALDS ME NOW--THAT SCALDS ME NOW!	I SHALL KNOW WHY--WHEN	193	8
THAT SCALDS ME NOW--THAT SCALDS ME NOW!	I SHALL KNOW WHY--WHEN	193	8
SCALED			
HAVE NEVER PASSED [SCALED] HER HAUNTED HOUSE,	WHAT MYSTERY PERVADES A	1400	19
SCALPS			
SOMETIMES--SCALPS A TREE--	NATURE--SOMETIMES SEARS	314	2
THAT SCALPS [PEELS] YOUR NAKED SOUL--	HE FUMBLES AT YOUR SOUL	315	12
SCAN			
SCAN LIKE HIM, THE STATELY LANDSCAPE	IF THE FOOLISH, CALL	168	11
TO SCAN A GHOST, IS FAINT--	'TIS SO APPALLING--IT	281	5
HE'LL TAKE IT--SCAN IT--STEP ASIDE--	THE FACE I CARRY WITH ME	336	9
UNQUALIFIED, TO SCAN--	A HAPPY LIP--BREAKS	353	8
BUT I, GROWN SHREWDER--SCAN THE SKIES	I MEANT TO HAVE BUT	476	25
INCLUDE US [SCAN BETTER / CONVEY US]--AS THEY GO--	WE MISS HER, NOT BECAUSE	993	8
WOULD SCAN THE MIGHTY [EAGER / BREATHLESS / HURRYING / . . .	TO FLEE FROM MEMORY	1242	6
SCANNED			
I [HE] SCANNED THEIR TRINKETS CURIOUS--	I ROBBED THE WOODS--	41	6
I CAUTIOUS, SCANNED MY LITTLE LIFE--	I CAUTIOUS, SCANNED MY	178	1
I SCANNED THE WINDOWS O'ER--	I YEARS HAD BEEN FROM	609	V 10
HAD I BUT FURTHER SCANNED	A CLOUD WITHDREW FROM	895	5
HE SCANNED IT--STAGGERED--	HE SCANNED IT--STAGGERED	1062	1
I SCANNED HIS NARROW REALM [GRANT]	IT CAME HIS TURN TO BEG	1500	5
BUT OFT HAS SCANNED ME O'ER--	MY WARS ARE LAID AWAY IN	1549	4

	FIRST LINE	POEM	LINE
SCANNING			
BY FORCE OF [SCANNING] IT'S RESULT-- . . .	AS FROST IS BEST	951	2
SCANS			
AND SCANS WITH [WITH WHAT A] FATAL PROMPTNESS	THE SUMMER THAT WE DID	1773	6
SCANT			
TOO LIFTED--FOR THE SCANT DEGREE	I SHOULD HAVE BEEN TOO	313	2
TOO SCANT--BY CUBITS--TO CONTAIN	IT MIGHT BE LONELIER	405	7
MAKE HASTE--[COME NEAR] THE SCRUPLE! DEATH BE SCANT	ME PROVE IT NOW--WHOEVER	537	3
OF EMERALD SCANT--HER GOWN--	BUT LITTLE CARMINE HATH	558	2
THE NIGHT WAS WIDE, AND FURNISHED SCANT . .	THE NIGHT WAS WIDE, AND	589	1
RING--FOR THE SCANT SALVATION--	GLEE--THE GREAT STORM IS	619	5
AT FIRST--A SCANT NUTRITION--[PLAIN REGALING]	DEPRIVED OF OTHER	773	3
AND SCANT TO HIM THE CROWD--	OF CONSCIOUSNESS, HER	894	6
SO SCANT, SO EMINENTLY SMALL	WHAT TWIGS WE HELD BY--	1086	10
HOW SCANT, BY EVERLASTING LIGHT	WHAT TWIGS WE HELD BY--	1086	14
TOO SCANT THE NIGHTS.	TOO FEW THE MORNINGS BE,	1186	2
SO SCANT AN INTERVAL--	THE SYMPTOM OF THE GALE	1327	12
SCANTEST			
THE SCANTEST HEART EXTANT	TILL DEATH--IS NARROW	907	2
AND SWELLS THE SCANTEST DEED	I KNOW OF PEOPLE IN THE	1665	6
SCANTILY			
WHY BLISS SO SCANTILY [CAUTIOUSLY] DISBURSE [EXPRESS / AFFORD]--	ONE BLESSING HAD I THAN	756	17
SCANTILY DEALT TO THE SUMMER MORNING . . .	SPLIT THE LARK--AND	861	3
SCANTLY			
ONLY SCANTLY AND SELECTLY	NATURE RARER USES YELLOW	1045	7
SCANTY			
THE LAST--A SCANTY NUMBER--	I KNOW LIVES, I COULD	372	5
AND BLAME THE SCANTY LOVE	WE COVER THEE--SWEET	482	9
OUR DIZZY [SCANTY] ESTIMATE--	THOSE FAIR--FICTITIOUS	499	12
I FEAR A MAN OF FRUGAL [SCANTY] SPEECH-- .	I FEAR A MAN OF FRUGAL	543	1
TOO SCANTY 'TWAS TO DIE FOR YOU, ...	TOO SCANTY 'TWAS TO DIE	1013	1
IS BUT A SCANTY TOY--	SO LARGE MY WILL	1024	10
SO SCANTY PUT, ...	JUST ONCE! OH LEAST	1076	4
'SCAPE			
WE [I] LIKE A HAIRBREADTH 'SCAPE	WE LIKE A HAIRBREADTH	1175	1
'SCAPING			
'SCAPING ONE--AGAINST THE OTHER	PATIENCE--HAS A QUIET	926	5
SCAR			
HAST THOU THE ROYAL SCAR?	WHO NEVER LOST, ARE	73	14
WE CAN FIND NO SCAR, ...	THERE'S A CERTAIN SLANT	258	6
EACH SCAR I'LL KEEP FOR HIM	EACH SCAR I'LL KEEP FOR	877	1
THE HEALED HEART SHOWS IT'S SHALLOW SCAR .	THE HEALED HEART SHOWS	1440	1
THE WOUND THAT WAS NOT WOUND NOR SCAR-- . .	THEIR BARRICADE AGAINST	1471	11
SCARCE			
YOU'D SCARCE RECOGNIZE HIM!	A FUZZY FELLOW, WITHOUT	173	16
AND SCARCE OF DIADEMS--	YOUR RICHES--TAUGHT ME--	299	12
THE TIME WAS SCARCE PROFANED, BY SPEECH-- .	THERE CAME A DAY AT	322	9
AND THO' I'M SCARCE ACCOUNTED, ...	WHEN DIAMONDS ARE A	397	5
I DIED FOR BEAUTY--BUT WAS SCARCE	I DIED FOR BEAUTY--BUT	449	1
ARE SCARCE ACCOUNTED [COMPUTED]--HARMS-- .	ONE ANGUISH--IN A CROWD	565	12
WAS SCARCE UPON MY EYES	I WATCHED THE MOON	629	30
COULD BEHOLD [REGARD] SO FAR [SMALL / DIM / SCARCE] A CREATURE--	PROMISE THIS--WHEN YOU	648	27
COULD SCARCE AFFORD ETERNITY	IT'S EASY TO INVENT A	724	7
I SCARCE ESTEEM LOCATION'S NAME--	WHERE THOU ART--THAT--IS	725	4
BENT TO THE WATER, STRUGGLED [SHIVERED] SCARCE--	THE LAST NIGHT THAT SHE	1100	23
AND HOLDS SCARCE [JUST] ONE.	THE ROAD TO PARADISE IS	1491	2
SO STRAIGHT YOU'D SCARCE SUSPECT	A PIT--BUT HEAVEN OVER	1712	13
SCARCELY			
'TWOULD SCARCELY FILL A TWO--	I KNOW LIVES, I COULD	372	6
MYSELF--FOR SCARCELY SETTLED--	THE WINTERS ARE SO SHORT	403	5
HAD SCARCELY DEIGNED TO LIE--	HER SWEET WEIGHT ON MY	518	2
MAKES SCARCELY WORTH THE TOIL--	WE SEE--COMPARATIVELY--	534	6
EMBODIED [ADMITTED] SCARCELY TO ITSELF--IT MAY BE--	EACH LIFE CONVERGES TO	680	5
THE ROOF WAS SCARCELY VISIBLE--	BECAUSE I COULD NOT STOP	712	19
WHEN MARCH IS SCARCELY HERE	A LIGHT EXISTS IN SPRING	812	4
I SCARCELY RECOLLECT TO STARVE	THE LUXURY TO APPREHEND	815	7
WHEN MARCH IS SCARCELY ON--	THE ROBIN IS THE ONE	828	4
AS SCARCELY AS THE IODINE	WHEN ONE HAS GIVEN UP	853	7
AS SLIGHTLY [SCARCELY] AS THE ROUTES [FLIGHTS] OF STARS--	WE MISS HER, NOT BECAUSE	993	5
WOULD CAUSE ONE SCARCELY TO SUSPECT	BLOOM--IS RESULT--TO	1058	3
THE TITLE WAS SCARCELY TOLD	ENDED, ERE IT BEGUN--	1088	2
SCARCELY WOULD [COULD] PREVAIL--	TELL AS A MARKSMAN--WERE	1152	8
AND SCARCELY HAD THE HILL--	AS IMPERCEPTIBLY AS	1540	V
SCARCER			
SCARCER ONCE WITH THE MIGHT	SOMETIMES WITH THE HEART	1680	3
SCARCITY			
ARE SUCH A SCARCITY--	MY WARS ARE LAID AWAY IN	1549	12
SCARE			
MIGHT SCARE THE QUIET FAIRY	THERE'S SOMETHING	45	11
COULD SCARE US ANY MORE!	WHERE BELLS NO MORE	112	12
AND [BUT] THEN THEY SCARE US LIKE A SPECTRE	FACTS BY OUR SIDE ARE	1497	3
SCARES			
NO LIGHTNING, SCARES [DRIVES] AWAY--	WHEN WE STAND ON THE	242	8
SCARES MUSLIN SOULS--AWAY--	A SHADY FRIEND--FOR	278	6

	FIRST LINE	POEM	LINE
SCARF			
THE MAPLE WEARS A GAYER SCARF--	THE MORNS ARE MEEKER	12	5
AS CHILDREN, TO THE RAINBOW'S SCARF--	AS FAR FROM PITY, AS	496	7
SCARLET			
THE FIELD A SCARLET GOWN--	THE MORNS ARE MEEKER	12	6
SCARLET AND GOLD	SO FROM THE MOULD	66	2
NOR "BAND"--IN BRASS AND SCARLET--DREST--	MUSICIANS WRESTLE	157	8
SOME SCARLET PATCHES ON THE WAY,	A SLASH OF BLUE--	204	3
SO--MANY--DROPS--OF VITAL SCARLET--	BOUND--A TROUBLE--	269	4
HOW THE OLD STEEPLES HAND THE SCARLET	HOW THE OLD MOUNTAINS	291	5
UNCONSCIOUS OF THE SCARLET FREIGHT--	HOW MANY FLOWERS FAIL IN	404	7
'TIS THE SCARLET WAY	TO PUT THIS WORLD DOWN,	527	4
MINE--BY THE SIGN IN THE SCARLET PRISON--	MINE--BY THE RIGHT OF	528	3
IN YONDER [SCARLET] MARYLAND--	WHEN I WAS SMALL, A	596	20
AND SPILL [TIP] THE SCARLET RAIN--	THE NAME--OF IT--IS	656	8
THE SCARLET FLOWERS ARE	THE VEINS OF OTHER	811	2
SCARLET EXPERIMENT! SCEPTIC THOMAS!	SPLIT THE LARK--AND	861	7
BY BUT A CRUMB OF BLOOD, FASTS SCARLET	AS THE STARVED MAELSTROM	872	5
SPENDING SCARLET, LIKE A WOMAN	NATURE RARER USES YELLOW	1045	5
YET [BUT] EVEN ON HIS SCARLET SHELF	THE FROST OF DEATH WAS	1136	7
UPON A SCARLET LOG--	THE SUN RETIRED TO A	1693	4
SCARLETS			
OR ETNA'S SCARLETS, CHOOSE--	MORE LIFE--WENT OUT--	422	20
SCATHING			
THOUGH BY THAT SCATHING TEST	UNWORTHY OF HER BREAST	1414	2
SCATTERED			
WHEN THE AUDIENCE IS SCATTERED	DRAMA'S VITALLEST	741	6
SENT VARIOUS--SCATTERED WAYS--	WE MET AS SPARKS--	958	2
HER SUBJECTS SCATTERED INTO PLACE	THE WIND TOOK UP THE	1134	11
ARE SCATTERED THERE.	ABOVE OBLIVION'S TIDE	1531	5
SCATTERED--I SAY--TO PLACE [SEAT] THEM SIDE BY SIDE	ABOVE OBLIVION'S TIDE	1531	6
SCATTERS			
IT SCATTERS LIKE THE BIRDS	IT SIFTS FROM LEADEN	311	V
THE SUNRISE SCATTERS--THESE ENDURE--	THE BATTLE FOUGHT	594	11
SCENE			
NE'ER SAW I SUCH A WONDROUS SCENE--	THERE IS A MORN BY MEN	24	13
COULD GO FROM SCENE FAMILIAR	COULD LIVE--DID LIVE--	43	6
CONDUCT THE PLEASING SCENE!	IF I SHOULD DIE,	54	18
AND STILL THE APRONS FLY, [SCENE PREVAILS]	SHE SWEEPS WITH	219	10
AND MIRRORRS ON THE SCENE--	WHEN WE STAND ON THE	242	4
TILL ALL THE SCENE--BE GONE.	'TWAS WARM--AT FIRST--	519	4
UNTO THE SCENE THAT WE DO NOT--	FAITH--IS THE PIERLESS	915	3
TILL SUNRISE TAKE [CALL] US BACK TO SCENE--	I LEARNED--AT LEAST--	944	25
THE BEE HAD PERISHED FROM THE SCENE	THE CRICKETS SANG	1104	V
IN THAT UNCOMMON [CONSUMMATE] SCENE--	ELIJAH'S WAGON KNEW NO	1254	V 8
SO SOFT UPON THE SCENE [PLACE]	THE MOUNTAINS STOOD IN	1278	9
WHO PONDERS THIS TREMENDOUS SCENE--	A LITTLE MADNESS IN THE	1333	4
LAST TO ADHERE [AT THE SCENE] WHEN SUMMER CLEAVES [SUMMER . . .	AFTER ALL BIRDS HAVE	1395	7
WHEN PUSHED UPON A SCENE	SHAME IS THE SHAWL OF	1412	6
BUT HE INDORSED THE SHEEN [SCENE]--	THE ROAD WAS LIT WITH	1450	8
FOR SUCH A FOE [SWEET / GLEE / DAWN / SCENE / DEW / JOY] AS THIS--	FROM ALL THE JAILS THE	1532	8
THE THOUGHT IS [SCENE WAS] QUIET AS A FLAKE--	THE FARTHEST THUNDER	1581	17
HIS SCENE, INFINITY--	EXPANSE CANNOT BE LOST--	1584	4
NOR DOUBT OF SCENE TO COME,	NOT SICKNESS STAINS THE	1613	3
UNCERTIFIED [NOT CERTIFIED] OF SCENE	THE MOB WITHIN THE HEART	1745	5
TO OTHER [ANY] SCENE OR OTHER SOUL	'TWAS HERE MY SUMMER	1756	3
SCENERY			
WHAT PARALLEL [SCENERY] CAN BE--	NO CROWD THAT HAS	515	18
BY MY WINDOW HAVE I FOR SCENERY	BY MY WINDOW HAVE I FOR	797	1
AND CLARIFYING SCENERY	HOW LONESOME THE WIND	1418	8
SCENES			
THE SOUL CAME HOME FROM TRIPS [FROM TOWNS / FROM SCENES / TO SLEEP]	CONTAINED IN THIS SHORT	1165	V
SCENTS			
THE HORSE THAT SCENTS THE LIVING GRASS	THE LIFE THAT TIED TOO	1535	5
SCEPTIC SEE SKEPTIC			
SCARLET EXPERIMENT! SCEPTIC THOMAS!	SPLIT THE LARK--AND	861	7
SCEPTRE			
A SCEPTRE--PENNILESS--	MY REWARD FOR BEING, WAS	343	4
SCHEDULE			
DEEP IS THE SCHEDULE	THOSE NOT LIVE YET	1454	8
OR SCHEDULE OF THE TIDE--	DOWN TIME'S QUAINT	1656	10
SCHEME			
OUR ESTIMATES A SCHEME [FORSOOK]--	THE DAYS THAT WE CAN	1184	5
SCHEMES			
HOW MANY SCHEMES MAY DIE	HOW MANY SCHEMES MAY DIE	1150	1
ON SCHEMES INTENT	THE RAT IS THE CONCISEST	1356	4
SCHEMING			
WE AND OUR PLOTTING HEART [GAUDY HEART / SCHEMING TINSEL / . . .	AN ANTIQUATED GRACE	1345	5
SCHISM			
SOME SCHISM IN THE SUM--	THE CLOCK STRIKES ONE	1569	2
SCHOLAR			
OH SOME SCHOLAR! OH SOME SAILOR!	WILL THERE REALLY BE A	101	9
SCHOLARS			
TO US--THE DULLER SCHOLARS [CORNETS]	TO LEARN THE TRANSPORT	167	15
WHAT INTERESTED SCHOLARS--MOST--	A PRECIOUS--MOULDERING	371	13

	FIRST LINE	POEM	LINE
SCHOLARS (CONTINUED)			
TO GUESS [PROVE] IT, PUZZLES SCHOLARS--	THIS WORLD IS NOT	501	9
LIKE LITTLE SCHOLARS--LOUD--	I THINK THE LONGEST HOUR	635	10
FAME IS THE TINT THAT SCHOLARS LEAVE	FAME IS THE TINT THAT	866	1
SCHOLASTIC			
IN SCHOLASTIC SKIES!	IF THE FOOLISH, CALL	168	16
SCHOOL			
WHEN GOING HOME FROM SCHOOL--	I OFTEN PASSED THE	51	2
ONE LITTLE MIND FROM SCHOOL--	TAKEN FROM MEN--THIS	53	6
AND TRUDGING FEET FROM SCHOOL--	ON SUCH A NIGHT, OR SUCH	146	20
WHOSE BERYL EGG, WHAT SCHOOL BOYS HUNT	A FEATHER FROM THE	161	7
WHILE JUST [YET] A GIRL AT SCHOOL.	YOUR RICHES--TAUGHT ME--	299	32
LIKE THE JUNE BEE--BEFORE THE SCHOOL BOY,	THE NEAREST DREAM	319	3
PUT IT IN LATIN--LEFT OF MY SCHOOL--	IT DONT SOUND SO	426	3
I WENT TO SCHOOL	KNOWS HOW TO FORGET!	433	V
WHEN HURRYING TO SCHOOL--	IT WAS GIVEN TO ME BY	454	10
AND DARKNESS ON THE SCHOOL	'TIS ONE BY ONE--THE	545	10
WE PASSED THE SCHOOL, WHERE CHILDREN STROVE	BECAUSE I COULD NOT STOP	712	9
I--THE GIRL AT SCHOOL--	LET US PLAY YESTERDAY--	728	2
JUST GOING HOME FROM SCHOOL.	THE HILLS IN PURPLE	1016	4
SCHOOLBOY			
BUILDING WHERE SCHOOLBOY DARE NOT LOOK,	SOME, TOO FRAGILE FOR	141	7
NOR ANY SCHOOLBOY ROB THE NEST	THIS HEART THAT BROKE SO	145	7
SCHOOLMATES			
I MET ONE--FORGOT MY SCHOOLMATES--	GOD PERMITS INDUSTRIOUS	231	3
SCHOOLROOM			
IN THE FAIR SCHOOLROOM OF THE SKY--	I SHALL KNOW WHY--WHEN	193	4
SCHOOLS			
AS THE SCHOOLS WOULD SAY--	DELIGHT IS AS THE FLIGHT	257	3
WELL ENOUGH FOR SCHOOLS--	ONE AND ONE--ARE ONE--	769	3
SCIENCE			
I CLIMB THE "HILL OF SCIENCE,"	"SIC TRANSIT GLORIA	3	21
IT'S VERY MEAN OF SCIENCE	"ARCTURUS" IS HIS OTHER	70	3
A SCIENCE--SO THE SAVANS SAY,	A SCIENCE--SO THE SAVANS	100	1
AND SCIENCE BOWS THEM IN--	SUNSET AT NIGHT--IS	415	6
SACRIFICE FOR SCIENCE	KNOWS HOW TO FORGET!	433	V
FROM SCIENCE--AND FROM SURGERY--	I TIE MY HAT--I CREASE	443	21
THE SCIENCE OF THE GRAVE	THE PROVINCE OF THE	539	4
YET--THERE IS A SCIENCE MORE--	YOU TAUGHT ME WAITING	740	8
THAT SCIENCE CANNOT OVERTAKE	A LIGHT EXISTS IN SPRING	812	7
SCIENCES			
MANY SCIENCES,	IF THE FOOLISH, CALL	168	14
ODDEST OF SCIENCES--BOOK EVER BORE--	KNOWS HOW TO FORGET!	433	10
SCIENTIST			
THE SCIENTIST OF FAITH	THE LILAC IS AN ANCIENT	1241	12
SCIMITAR SEE CIMITAR			
SCINTILLATES			
BUT SCINTILLATES THE SAME--	HOW KNOW IT FROM A	1364	4
SCION			
THIS SURREPTITIOUS SCION	THE MUSHROOM IS THE ELF	1298	15
SCOLD			
WONT THEY SCOLD US--WHEN WE'RE HUNGRY [HOMESICK]--	WHAT IS--"PARADISE"--	215	9
GOD WOULD CERTAINLY SCOLD!	OVER THE FENCE--	251	7
SCOOP			
WORLDS SCOOP THEIR ARCS--	SAFE IN THEIR ALABASTER	216	V
THE DUST DID SCOOP ITSELF LIKE HANDS--	THE WIND BEGUN TO KNEAD	824	7
SCOOPED			
FROM TANKARDS SCOOPED IN PEARL--	I TASTE A LIQUOR NEVER	214	2
AND SCOOPED A TURNPIKE FOR THEMSELVES--	THE BRAIN, WITHIN IT'S	556	7
SCOOPING			
SCOOPING UP THE DUST AND CHANTING "LIVE"!	WHILE IT IS ALIVE	491	10
SCOPE			
INCREASED [ENLARGED] BEYOND MY UTMOST SCOPE	I HAD A DAILY BLISS	1057	7
SCORE			
WAS SUMMER TO A SCORE	THIS BAUBLE WAS	805	6
THAN NUMB THREE SCORE AND TEN--	NOT ANY HIGHER STANDS	1256	4
SCORN			
I'D DAISIES SPURN [CLOVERS--SCORN]--	THE ROBIN'S MY CRITERION	285	9
AND SHAME [SCORN] WENT STILL [DUMB]--	UNTO LIKE STORY--TROUBLE	295	8
WITH DEATH'S ETHERIAL SCORN--	ENDOW THE LIVING--WITH	521	8
THAN MERIT THE ETHEREAL SCORN	HER SPIRIT ROSE TO SUCH	1486	5
SCORNING			
OUR BLANK IN SCORNING--	OUR SHARE OF NIGHT TO	113	4
SCOURGE			
TO JUSTIFY OR SCOURGE--	THOSE CATTLE SMALLER	1388	16
SCOURGED			
UNTIL A ZEPHYR PUSHED [CHASED / FLUNG / SPURNED / SCOURGED] THEM	TWO BUTTERFLIES WENT OUT	533	V
WE ARE NOT SCOURGED TO SERVE--	HOW FLEET--HOW	1771	4
SCOUTS			
AND SO I SEND MY CRIMSON SCOUTS	WHERE ROSES WOULD NOT	1582	3
SCOWLED			
DOUBTLESS--"ADAM"--SCOWLED AT EDEN--	TAKING UP THE FAIR IDEAL	428	7
SCRABBLE			
WHERE SCRABBLE NEVER COMES--	WHERE BELLS NO MORE	112	2
SCRAPS			
SHE DROPPED BRIGHT SCRAPS OF TINT, ABOUT--	MY FIRST WELL DAY--SINCE	574	19
AND SCRAPS [SHREDS] OF PRAYER--	MY PORTION IS DEFEAT--	639	11

	FIRST LINE	POEM	LINE
SCREAMED			
THE HUNGRY VULTURE SCREAMED--	THROUGH LANE IT LAY--	9	12
SCREAMS			
SCREAMS CHANTICLEER	I KNOW SOME LONELY	289	35
SCREEN			
TO SCREEN THEM FROM RENOWN.	FOREVER HONORED BE THE	1570	8
SCREENS			
SUNSET THAT SCREENS, REVEALS--	SUNSET THAT SCREENS,	1609	1
SCREW			
A SINGLE SCREW OF FLESH	A SINGLE SCREW OF FLESH	263	1
SCREWS			
IT IS THE GIFT OF SCREWS--	ESSENTIAL OILS--ARE	675	4
SCRUPLE			
MAKE HASTE--[COME NEAR] THE SCRUPLE! DEATH BE SCANT	ME PROVE IT NOW--WHOEVER	537	3
LAUGHS--AT A SCRUPLE--	THE CHILD'S FAITH IS NEW	637	6
SCRUPULOUS			
WITH SCRUPULOUS EXACTNESS--	I TIE MY HAT--I CREASE	443	32
NOR SCRUPULOUS OF COLD	NO NOTICE GAVE SHE, BUT	804	6
SCRUTABLE			
AND SANG FOR NOTHING SCRUTABLE [IN THE WORLD]	THE MOST TRIUMPHANT BIRD	1265	5
SCRUTINIZE			
THE PRIVILEGE TO SCRUTINIZE	I WATCHED THE MOON	629	29
TO SCRUTINIZE THE SLEEP.	THE SUBURBS OF A SECRET	1245	4
SHALL COMPREHEND [SCRUTINIZE] AS ONE	HOW NEWS MUST FEEL WHEN	1319	10
THESE [THE] SHADOWS SCRUTINIZE--	A CHILLY PEACE INFESTS	1443	4
SCRUTINY			
MY SCRUTINY DECEIVES.	WHOSE CHEEK IS THIS?	82	10
FOR JUST A [SIMPLE] SCRUTINY--	THE LONELINESS ONE DARE	777	8
REMOTEST [MEMORIAL] SCRUTINY--	THIS DUST, AND IT'S	936	12
HIS SCRUTINY OF CHANCES	AS ONE DOES SICKNESS	957	3
THAT SCRUTINY CAN BURN--	JUDGEMENT IS JUSTEST	1671	9
TO PAY YOU SCRUTINY--	THE RIGHT TO PERISH	1692	8
SCUTCHEON			
HAD HE THE HOMELY SCUTCHEON	THE BUTTERFLY OBTAINS	1685	9
SCUTTLE			
AND SCUTTLE MY BALLOON--	I BET WITH EVERY WIND	1215	4
SCYTHE			
THE MOWER IS TUNING HIS SCYTHE	BACK FROM THE CORDIAL	1625	V
SEA			
ALL THINGS DO GO A COURTING, IN EARTH, OR SEA, OR AIR,	AWAKE YE MUSES NINE,	1	5
ON THIS WONDROUS SEA	ON THIS WONDROUS SEA	4	1
LEARNETH BEYOND THE SEA	I HAVE A BIRD IN SPRING	5	10
EXTORTED FROM THE SEA--	THE FEET OF PEOPLE	7	10
WHETHER MY BARK WENT DOWN AT SEA--	WHETHER MY BARK WENT	52	1
OF AN INLAND SOUL TO SEA, ...	EXULTATION IS THE GOING	76	2
'TWAS SUCH A GALLANT--GALLANT SEA	'TWAS SUCH A LITTLE--	107	3
BLUE SEA! WILT WELCOME ME?	MY RIVER RUNS TO THEE--	162	2
OH SEA--LOOK GRACIOUSLY--	MY RIVER RUNS TO THEE--	162	4
SAY--SEA--TAKE ME!	MY RIVER RUNS TO THEE--	162	7
AND IF I GAIN! OH GUN AT SEA!	'TIS SO MUCH JOY! 'TIS	172	13
LEAST RIVERS--DOCILE TO SOME SEA.	LEAST RIVERS--DOCILE TO	212	1
SHOULD YOU BUT FAIL AT--SEA--	SHOULD YOU BUT FAIL AT--	226	1
AH, THE SEA!	WILD NIGHTS--WILD NIGHTS	249	10
AND ON THE STRANGEST SEA--	"HOPE" IS THE THING WITH	254	10
THESE--ARE THE BANKS OF THE YELLOW SEA-- .	THIS--IS THE LAND--THE	266	2
THE SEA IS FULL--I KNOW IT!	ONE LIFE OF SO MUCH	270	9
AND NEVER I MIND THE SEA--	TIE THE STRINGS TO MY	279	10
THE DROP, THAT WRESTLES IN THE SEA--	THE DROP, THAT WRESTLES	284	1
EXTINGUISHED--IN THE SEA--	FROM COCOON FORTH A	354	25
'TWAS SHORT--TO CROSS THE SEA--	I WENT TO THANK HER--	363	8
OUR'S BE THE TOSSING--WILD THOUGH THE SEA--	HOW SICK--TO WAIT--IN	368	8
HIS CONVERSATION--WITH THE SEA--	YOU'LL KNOW IT--AS YOU	420	13
THE MOON IS DISTANT FROM THE SEA--	THE MOON IS DISTANT FROM	429	1
AND MINE--THE DISTANT SEA--	THE MOON IS DISTANT FROM	429	10
WHILE OTHER--WENT THE SEA TO FILL--	FORGET! THE LADY WITH	438	14
I--FEARED THE SEA--TOO MUCH	THE MALAY--TOOK THE	452	3
WHO OWN THE AMPLE SEA--	'TIS LITTLE I--COULD	466	2
AS SEPARATE AS SEA	THEY PUT US FAR APART--	474	2
DENOTES THERE BE--A SEA--	MY GARDEN--LIKE THE	484	2
AND MAELSTROM, IN THE SEA--	AT LEAST--TO PRAY--IS	502	6
AND SILENCED, AS THE AWFUL SEA	HE TOUCHED ME, SO I LIVE	506	5
AND VISITED THE SEA--	I STARTED EARLY--TOOK MY	520	2
AT ME--THE SEA WITHDREW--	I STARTED EARLY--TOOK MY	520	24
UPON A SHINING SEA--	TWO BUTTERFLIES WENT OUT	533	6
IF MET IN ETHER SEA	TWO BUTTERFLIES WENT OUT	533	10
REMEMBER--WHEN THE SEA	ME PROVE IT NOW--WHOEVER	537	14
MORE MOUNTAINS--THEN A SEA--	I CROSS TILL I AM WEARY	550	3
MUCH BILLOW HATH THE SEA--	EMPTY MY HEART, OF THEE	587	5
AND MAGNETIZE THE SEA--	TO INTERRUPT HIS YELLOW	591	10
UPHOLSTERER OF THE PINES [SEA / LAND / HILLS]--IS HE--	OF BRUSSELS--IT WAS NOT	602	15
AND ONLY THE SEA--REPLY--	GLEE--THE GREAT STORM IS	619	17
BUT IN THEIR ROOM [STEAD]--A SEA--DISPLAYED--	THEY CALLED ME TO THE	628	9
THE BRAIN IS DEEPER THAN THE SEA--	THE BRAIN--IS WIDER THAN	632	5
THE ANSWER OF THE SEA UNTO	I COULD SUFFICE FOR HIM,	643	13
CAPACIOUS AS THE SEA--	YOU LEFT ME--SIRE--TWO	644	6
APPEAR--UNTO THE SEA--	I THINK TO LIVE--MAY BE	646	8
THAN DID LOADED [SWELLING] SEA	HER SWEET TURN TO LEAVE	649	6

	FIRST LINE	POEM	LINE
SEA (CONTINUED)			
HEARD [HELD] OPPOSITE THE SEA--	WITHOUT THIS--THERE IS	655	4
BE LARGER--AS THE SEA	'TIS GOOD--THE LOOKING	660	10
THE BOBOLINK--THE SEA--	"NATURE" IS WHAT WE SEE	668	6
AS IF THE SEA SHOULD PART	AS IF THE SEA SHOULD	695	1
AND SHOW A FURTHER SEA--	AS IF THE SEA SHOULD	695	2
UPON A SEA OF BLONDE--	YOU'VE SEEN BALLOONS SET	700	6
AND TUMBLES IN THE SEA--	YOU'VE SEEN BALLOONS SET	700	16
A REEF--CRAWLED EASY FROM THE SEA	I SOMETIMES DROP IT, FOR	708	13
A CRESCENT IN THE SEA--	BEHIND ME--DIPS ETERNITY	721	15
IT LAY UNMENTIONED--AS THE SEA	SHE ROSE TO HIS	732	9
AT CENTRE OF THE SEA--	I MANY TIMES THOUGHT	739	4
OR FATHER--ON THE SEA--	HE TOLD A HOMELY TALE	763	10
TO LOSE IT IN THE SEA--	BEREAVED OF ALL, I WENT	784	12
THAT [WHO] WENT TO HELP THE SEA--	A DROP FELL ON THE APPLE	794	6
AND BATHED THEM IN THE GLEE [SEA]--	A DROP FELL ON THE APPLE	794	14
JUST A SEA--WITH A STEM--	BY MY WINDOW HAVE I FOR	797	2
WRINKLED ANY SEA,	ONE DAY IS THERE OF THE	814	14
AN HOUR IS A SEA	AN HOUR IS A SEA	825	1
THE SEA UPON OUR PLACE--	ESCAPING BACKWARD TO	867	2
ABOUT MY FEET THE SEA.	I STEPPED FROM PLANK TO	875	4
THE SEA AND SPAR BETWEEN.	EACH SECOND IS THE LAST	879	4
THERE IS A SEA--	BETWEEN MY COUNTRY--AND	905	2
IT MEASURES [PACES] LIKE THE SEA	THE HEART HAS NARROW	928	2
OF A CELESTIAL SEA--	I LEARNED--AT LEAST--	944	8
IN THY BOLDER SEA--	ALL FORGOT FOR	966	14
WHEN THE SEA RETURN NO ANSWER	GRATITUDE--IS NOT THE	989	5
PROVES IT THERE'S NO SEA, OR RATHER	GRATITUDE--IS NOT THE	989	7
NOR SEA--	NOR MOUNTAIN HINDER ME	1029	2
I NEVER SAW THE SEA--	I NEVER SAW A MOOR--	1052	2
HOW OFTEN FOUNDERING AT SEA	A GREAT HOPE FELL	1123	8
OUR PASSIVE FLOWER WE HELD TO SEA--	THE FROST OF DEATH WAS	1136	5
THAN SEA AND CONTINENT THERE IS	THE FROST OF DEATH WAS	1136	20
TO CAST THE SHIPS, AT SEA,	THE DUTIES OF THE WIND	1137	2
TURN [TAKE] SOONEST [SOONER] TO THE SEA	CONTAINED IN THIS SHORT	1165	6
A SOFT SEA WASHED AROUND THE HOUSE	A SOFT SEA WASHED AROUND	1198	1
A SEA OF SUMMER AIR	A SOFT SEA WASHED AROUND	1198	2
IT IS THE SEA--	BECAUSE MY BROOK IS	1200	4
IS "NO MORE SEA"--	BECAUSE MY BROOK IS	1200	8
THE SEA SAID "COME" TO THE BROOK--	THE SEA SAID "COME" TO	1210	1
THE SEA SAID "THEN YOU WILL BE A SEA--	THE SEA SAID "COME" TO	1210	3
THE SEA SAID "THEN YOU WILL BE A SEA--	THE SEA SAID "COME" TO	1210	3
THE SEA SAID "GO" TO THE SEA--	THE SEA SAID "COME" TO	1210	5
THE SEA SAID "GO" TO THE SEA--	THE SEA SAID "COME" TO	1210	5
THE SEA SAID "I AM HE	THE SEA SAID "COME" TO	1210	6
OF THE AWFUL [SWINGING] SEA--	FORTITUDE INCARNATE	1217	4
BUT THE SEA [DEEP] IS OLD	FORTITUDE INCARNATE	1217	8
'TIS TO ANOTHER SEA--	IF MY BARK SINK	1234	2
BEFORE THEM LIES ESCAPELESS SEA--	THIS IS THE PLACE THEY	1264	7
UPON A LILAC SEA	UPON A LILAC SEA	1337	1
NOT THE ONLY SEA--	LIFT IT--WITH THE	1348	4
THE SEDGE STANDS NEXT THE SEA--	WHAT MYSTERY PERVADES A	1400	14
THE PILLAGE OF [IRREVERENCED--IN] THE SEA	COULD MORTAL LIP DIVINE	1409	V
INTO THE SEA IN PASSING	A DEW SUFFICED ITSELF--	1437	11
FROM WHATSOEVER SEA--	A CHILLY PEACE INFESTS	1443	8
DEATH--SO--THE HYPHEN OF THE SEA--	THOSE NOT LIVE YET	1454	7
HOW IS IT WITH THE SEA?	IF WRECKED UPON THE	1469	2
TO EVENING'S SEA--	"GO TRAVELING WITH US!"	1513	4
NOT PIRATE OF THE SEA,	SWEET PIRATE OF THE	1546	2
TO WHERE A BROOK THAT SEEMED A SEA	OF DEATH I TRY TO THINK	1558	11
HOW SLOW THE SEA--	HOW SLOW THE WIND--	1571	2
LIKE TIDES WITHIN THE SEA	THE SPIRIT LASTS--BUT IN	1576	10
THE SAGEST [ONLY] TIME TO DAM THE SEA IS WHEN THE SEA IS GONE--	WE SEND THE WAVE TO FIND	1604	7
THE SAGEST [ONLY] TIME TO DAM THE SEA IS WHEN THE SEA IS GONE--	WE SEND THE WAVE TO FIND	1604	7
UPON AN ETHER SEA,	A SLOOP OF AMBER SLIPS	1622	2
IN THE RECALLLESS SEA?	STILL OWN THEE--STILL	1633	8
"RED SEA," INDEED! TALK NOT TO ME	"RED SEA," INDEED! TALK	1642	1
ONE DESERT AND A SEA	I DID NOT REACH THEE	1664	4
THE SEA COMES LAST--STEP MERRY FEET	I DID NOT REACH THEE	1664	14
WE MUST HAVE PASSED THE MIDDLE SEA	I DID NOT REACH THEE	1664	23
TWO DESERTS AND THE SEA!	I DID NOT REACH THEE	1664	32
A SOLITUDE OF SEA	THERE IS A SOLITUDE OF	1695	2
THERE IS A SYLLABLE-LESS SEA	TO TELL THE BEAUTY WOULD	1700	3
ITS OTHER REALM OF SEA.	TO LOSE THEE--SWEETER	1754	6
AND WITNESS FOR HER SEA,	THE EARTH HAS MANY KEYS.	1775	6
SEAL			
BEFORE THE SEAL!	JUST LOST, WHEN I WAS	160	11
'TIS THE SEAL DESPAIR--	THERE'S A CERTAIN SLANT	258	10
MINE--BY THE ROYAL SEAL!	MINE--BY THE RIGHT OF	528	2
DIVINITY DWELLS UNDER SEAL.	EMBARRASSMENT OF ONE	662	7
ILLUMINATE--[MAKE POPULATE-- / MAKE MANIFEST] OR SEAL--	THE LONELINESS ONE DARE	777	16
ONLY THE KEEPER OF THIS RING [THE SEAL]	GIVEN IN MARRIAGE UNTO	817	7
SEALED			
SEALED ARE THE SPICY VALVES--	BESIDES THE AUTUMN POETS	131	10
EACH WAS TO EACH THE SEALED CHURCH,	THERE CAME A DAY AT	322	13
SEALED SO STATELY TIGHT--	SWEET--SAFE--HOUSES--	457	3
TELL HIM [HER]--JUST HOW SHE SEALED	GOING TO HIM! HAPPY	494	22

	FIRST LINE	POEM	LINE
SEALED (CONTINUED)			
YOU--CAUTIOUS! FOR BRAVERIES JUST SEALED [PROVED] IN THIS .	WHEN I WAS SMALL, A	596	V 19
BEHIND--A SEALED ROUTE--	OUR JOURNEY HAD ADVANCED	615	10
AS BORE IT SEALED WINE--	STRONG DRAUGHTS OF THEIR	711	4
I REINFORCED [ONLY SEALED] THE DOOR-- . .	THE BIRDS REPORTED FROM	743	6
SEALS			
SPRINGS--SHAKE THE SILLS [SEALS]-- . . .	SAFE IN THEIR ALABASTER	216	V
SEAM			
TOO SILVER FOR A SEAM--	A BIRD CAME DOWN THE	328	18
FETCH THE SEAM I MISSED--	DONT PUT UP MY THREAD &	617	18
YOU CANNOT FEEL THE SEAM--	YOU'LL KNOW HER--BY HER	634	18
I TRIED TO MATCH IT--SEAM BY SEAM-- . . .	I FELT A CLEAVING IN MY	937	3
I TRIED TO MATCH IT--SEAM BY SEAM-- . . .	I FELT A CLEAVING IN MY	937	3
THEIR SEAM [SEAMS] THE DAY UPON.	THE CRICKETS SANG	1104	4
WHEN FOLDED IN PERPETUAL SEAM	A WORD DROPPED CARELESS	1261	3
COMBINED WITHOUT A SEAM	HOW FITS HIS UMBER COAT	1371	3
CAN [COULD] MAKE A [NO] DENT [CREASE / SEAM] THEREON [UPON]--	THIS ME--THAT WALKS AND	1588	8
WHOSE SEAM COULD NOT BE SHEWN--	OF YELLOW WAS THE OUTER	1676	4
SEAMLESS			
IN SEAMLESS COMPANY--	OF ALL THE SOUNDS	321	33
THEY PERISHED IN THE SEAMLESS GRASS-- . .	THEY DROPPED LIKE FLAKES	409	6
SEAMS			
ACRES OF JOINTS [SEAMS], WHERE HARVESTS WERE,	IT SIFTS FROM LEADEN	311	15
MY FUSCHZIA'S CORAL SEAMS	I TEND MY FLOWERS FOR	339	3
I'LL DO SEAMS--A QUEEN'S ENDEAVOR	DONT PUT UP MY THREAD &	617	7
AS SEAMS--INCLUDE THE BALL?	WITHOUT THIS--THERE IS	655	8
THEIR SEAM [SEAMS] THE DAY UPON.	THE CRICKETS SANG	1104	4
THESE EMERALD SEAMS ENCLOSE.	STEP LIGHTLY ON THIS	1183	4
SEAR SEE SERE			
AN INNUENDO SEAR	SEPTEMBER'S	1271	6
SEARCH			
COMFORTS--SEARCH--LIKE THIS--	TAKING UP THE FAIR IDEAL	428	12
IN SEARCH OF SOMETHING [SOMEWHAT]--AS IT SEEMED--	I'VE SEEN A DYING EYE	547	3
TO SEARCH [SEEK] FOR THE ACCOMPLISHED GUEST,	THE SOUL SHOULD ALWAYS	1055	7
BUT SEARCH EFFACES HIM	THE FROST WAS NEVER SEEN	1202	8
PROFANE IT BY A SEARCH [PURSUIT]--WE CANNOT	IN MANY AND REPORTLESS	1382	9
SEARCHED			
THE POET SEARCHED [PROBED] PHILOLOGY . . .	SHALL I TAKE THEE, THE	1126	5
SEARCHES			
THAT SEARCHES HUMAN NATURE'S CREASES . . .	PERIL AS A POSSESSION	1678	6
SEARCHING			
SWEPT BY MY SEARCHING EYES--THE LAST-- . .	ME PROVE IT NOW--WHOEVER	537	15
BUT SEARCHING--I COULD SEE	A DYING TIGER--MOANED	566	6
I FIND MYSELF STILL SOFTLY SEARCHING . . .	A LOSS OF SOMETHING EVER	959	11
SEARS			
NATURE--SOMETIMES SEARS A SAPLING-- . . .	NATURE--SOMETIMES SEARS	314	1
SEAS			
THE CHILDREN OF WHOSE TURBANED SEAS-- . .	SOME RAINBOW--COMING	64	23
BROUGHT ME--FROM FIRMAMENTAL SEAS-- . . .	WHAT WOULD I GIVE TO SEE	247	19
ON SEAS OF DAFFODIL--	WHERE SHIPS OF PURPLE--	265	2
I ENVY SEAS, WHEREON HE RIDES--[THAT BEAR HIM]	I ENVY SEAS, WHEREON HE	498	1
MORE SEAS--AND THEN	I CROSS TILL I AM WEARY	550	4
OF PERIODS OF SEAS--	AS IF THE SEA SHOULD	695	5
THEMSELVES THE VERGE OF SEAS TO BE-- . . .	AS IF THE SEA SHOULD	695	7
AND ALL THE SEAS HE POPULATES	A COFFIN--IS A SMALL	943	7
WERE SEAS TO CROSS TO COME	THE BIRD DID PRANCE--THE	1107	10
TO WALK ON SEAS [TIDES] REQUIRES CEDAR FEET	THERE IS A STRENGTH IN	1113	6
IT LOOSENED ACRES, LIFTED SEAS	LIKE RAIN IT SOUNDED	1235	13
SEASHORE			
THE STORM DOTH WALK THE SEASHORE HUMMING A MOURNFUL TUNE,	AWAKE YE MUSES NINE,	1	17
SEASON			
TO A FICTITIOUS COUNTRY [SUMMER / SEASON] .	CONJECTURING A CLIMATE	562	5
THIS SEASON OF THE YEAR, ...	PURPLE--IS FASHIONABLE	980	2
SEASON'S			
MY SEASON'S FURTHEST FLOWER--	MY SEASON'S FURTHEST	1019	1
SEASONS			
WHICH LEAD THE SEASONS BY, ...	TO VENERATE THE SIMPLE	57	2
THE SEASONS FLIT--I'M TAUGHT--	THE ROBIN'S MY CRITERION	285	12
FAINTER LEAVES--TO FURTHER SEASONS-- . . .	NATURE--SOMETIMES SEARS	314	5
THE SEASONS--SHIFT--MY PICTURE--	THE ANGLE OF A LANDSCAPE	375	13
THE SEASONS MUST HAVE TURNED	WHEN I WAS SMALL, A	596	6
THE SEASONS--FIT--THE SAME--	IT MAKES NO DIFFERENCE	620	2
ALL SEASONS OF THE YEAR, ...	HAVE ANY LIKE MYSELF	736	20
OF THE SEASONS AND THE SUN.	ALWAYS MINE!	839	5
AMONG THE OTHER SEASONS	SPRING IS THE PERIOD	844	3
TWO SEASONS, IT IS SAID, EXIST--	THERE IS A JUNE WHEN	930	9
THE SEASONS PLAYED AROUND HIS KNEES . . .	THE MOUNTAIN SAT UPON	975	5
IF SEASONS PERISH OR PREVAIL	DID WE ABOLISH FROST	1014	3
NO SEASONS WERE TO US--	IT WAS A QUIET WAY--	1053	17
WHOSE PERFECT SEASONS WAIT--	THERE IS A ZONE WHOSE	1056	4
INDIFFERENT SEASONS DOUBTLESS PLAY . . .	SOMEWHERE UPON THE	1231	5
BY SEASONS OR HIS CHILDREN--	THE WAY TO KNOW THE	1279	17
'TIS SEASONS SINCE THE DIMPLED WAR . . .	'TIS SEASONS SINCE THE	1529	1
SEAT			
AND SEAT--JUST ONE--	UNIT, LIKE DEATH, FOR	408	9
BEFORE THE JUDGMENT SEAT OF GOD--	'TWAS A LONG PARTING--	625	3

	FIRST LINE	POEM	LINE
SEAT (CONTINUED)			
AND DECKS--TO SEAT THE SKIES--	THEY CALLED ME TO THE	628	12
SCATTERED--I SAY--TO PLACE [SEAT] THEM SIDE BY SIDE	ABOVE OBLIVION'S TIDE	1531	6
THERE IS A WORLD [TOMB / CHAIR / SEAT] FOR ALL	NO LIFE CAN POMPLESS	1626	V 8
SEATED			
AND WHEN THEY ALL WERE SEATED,	I FELT A FUNERAL, IN MY	280	5
SEATS			
AND SEATS ITSELF TO BE LET GO	RISK IS THE HAIR THAT	1239	7
THAT NEVER SEATS BUT ONE--	HOPE IS A SUBTLE GLUTTON	1547	6
SECEDED			
THESE SECEDED FROM YOUR SUMMONS [SUMMITS / SUBJECTS / SUBSTANCE]	KNOCK WITH TREMOR--	1325	6
SECESSION			
THOUGH ONE IS BEAUTIFUL FORGETTING [SECESSION]--	I'D RATHER RECOLLECT A	1349	3
SECOND			
JESUS! THY SECOND FACE	JESUS! THY CRUCIFIX	225	4
A SECOND MORE, HAD DROPPED TOO DEEP	THAT AFTER HORROR--THAT	286	5
UNTIL YOU FELT YOUR SECOND	'TWAS LIKE A MAELSTROM,	414	12
NO ONE COULD PLAY IT--THE SECOND TIME--	BETTER--THAN MUSIC! FOR	503	6
MY SECOND RANK--TOO SMALL THE FIRST--	I'M CEDED--I'VE STOPPED	508	14
THIS--IS THE SECOND GAIN--	HAD I PRESUMED TO HOPE--	522	16
THE SECOND [SILENCE] LIKE AN OCEAN ROLLED	I YEARS HAD BEEN FROM	609	11
THE LAST--AND SECOND TIME	'TWAS A LONG PARTING--	625	4
THE SECOND TIME TO ME--	A THOUGHT WENT UP MY	701	6
NONE STIR [HARM] THE SECOND TIME--	MY LIFE HAD STOOD--A	754	18
OUR REDDEST SECOND PALE.	A MOTH THE HUE OF THIS	841	4
THE SECOND, LOSS,	FINDING IS THE FIRST ACT	870	2
EACH SECOND IS THE LAST	EACH SECOND IS THE LAST	879	1
THE SECOND--TO IT'S FRIEND--	LOVE--IS THAT LATER	924	6
MAY NOT OUR SECOND WITH IT'S FIRST	THERE IS A JUNE WHEN	930	13
WILL IN A SECOND FUTURE [BEING]--	THIS DUST, AND IT'S	936	3
THE SECOND POISED--DEBATED--SHOT--	'TWAS CRISIS--ALL THE	948	13
EVERY SECOND TIME--	HE WHO IN HIMSELF	969	6
THE SECOND--WAS--RENOWN--	THE FIRST WE KNEW OF HIM	1006	2
THE SECOND HAD NOT BEEN.	THE FIRST WE KNEW OF HIM	1006	4
THERE IS NO SECOND WAR	'TWAS FIGHTING FOR HIS	1188	6
THE SECOND OF DISMAY--	THE SYMPTOM OF THE GALE	1327	2
BREACH A SECOND CANNOT FILL--	LONG YEARS APART--CAN	1383	2
BENEATH THE SECOND SUN--	A FIELD OF STUBBLE,	1407	2
THE SECOND TIME IS SET	FAME IS A FICKLE FOOD	1659	5
THE SECOND ONE	I DID NOT REACH THEE	1664	10
I FELT IT SECOND PAIN	THAT SHE FORGOT ME WAS	1683	2
THE SECOND HALF OF JOY	CONSULTING SUMMER'S	1715	5
SECONDARY			
THAT SECONDARY SUCCOR	ELIZABETH TOLD ESSEX	1321	5
SECOND'S			
BY JUST A SECOND'S RIGHT--	PAIN HAS BUT ONE	1049	6
OH SUN--BUT JUST A SECOND'S RIGHT	MY GOD--HE SEES THEE--	1178	8
. . . [SECOND'S] RACES	WE TALKED WITH EACH	1473	3
SECONDS			
NODS FROM THE SECONDS SLIM--	A CLOCK STOPPED--	287	15
AND WOULD NOT LET THE SECONDS BY--	I THINK THE LONGEST HOUR	635	7
THE STOLID RAFTERS [CENTRES / HOURS / INSTANTS / SECONDS] GLOW	THE SMOULDERING EMBERS	1132	6
WE WERE LISTENING TO [TOO ENGROSSED WITH] THE SECONDS . . .	WE TALKED WITH EACH	1473	3
SECRECY			
ENJOINING SECRECY--	THE LEAVES LIKE WOMEN,	987	6
NOTHING AFFRONT THY SECRECY.	TO THE STANCH DUST	1402	V 7
SECRET			
WHETHER TO KEEP THE SECRET--	I NEVER TOLD THE BURIED	11	14
YOU AND I THE SECRET	ALL THESE MY BANNERS BE.	22	16
HER ANNUAL SECRET KEEPS!	A LADY RED--AMID THE	74	2
IS MADE A SECRET TO UNFOLD	A SCIENCE--SO THE SAVANS	100	4
YOUR SECRET, PERCHED IN EXTASY	COCOON ABOVE! COCOON	129	5
DUST IS THE ONLY SECRET--	DUST IS THE ONLY SECRET	153	1
TO TELL THE PRETTY SECRET	A FUZZY FELLOW, WITHOUT	173	19
THE SKIES CANT KEEP THEIR SECRET!	THE SKIES CANT KEEP	191	1
SO KEEP YOUR SECRET--FATHER!	THE SKIES CANT KEEP	191	13
FORGET THE SECRET OF HIS WING	NOT PROBABLE--THE BAREST	346	7
A SECRET TOLD--	A SECRET TOLD--	381	1
CEASES TO BE A SECRET--THEN--	A SECRET TOLD--	381	2
A SECRET--KEPT--	A SECRET TOLD--	381	3
WHO TELLS NO SECRET	UNIT, LIKE DEATH, FOR	408	3
THE STAR'S WHOLE SECRET--IN THE LAKE--	THE OUTER--FROM THE	451	15
ONLY GOD--DETECT THE SORROW [POSSESS THE SECRET]--	ONLY GOD--DETECT THE	626	1
SOME SECRET--THAT WAS PUSHING	THE TINT I CANNOT TAKE--	627	15
MY SECRET AS SECURE	NATURE AND GOD--I	835	6
THE SUBURBS OF A SECRET	THE SUBURBS OF A SECRET	1245	1
HE DARE IN LONELY [LONESOME / SECRET] PLACE	I NEVER HEAR THAT ONE IS	1323	14
THE SECRET OF THE MAN	BLISS IS THE PLAYTHING	1553	2
BUT WILL THE SECRET COMPENSATE	THE GOING FROM A WORLD	1603	7
OUR PORT A SECRET	DOWN TIME'S QUAINT	1656	4
HIS MIND OF MAN, A SECRET MAKES	HIS MIND OF MAN, A	1663	1
BIG MY SECRET BUT IT'S BANDAGED--	REARRANGE A "WIFE'S"	1737	17
THE ONLY SECRET PEOPLE [NEIGHBORS] KEEP [SHUN]	THE RETICENT VOLCANO	1748	11

	FIRST LINE	POEM	LINE
SECRETED			
SECRETED IN HIS WILL--	NOT ONE BY HEAVEN	1303	4
SECRETED [RESERVED] UTTERLY	I SEND YOU A DECREPIT	1324	V 8
THE WHOLE OF IMMORTALITY INTRENCHED [SECRETED / DEPUTED]	HE LIVED THE LIFE OF	1525	7
SECRETED IN A STAR.	WHO ABDICATED AMBUSH	1616	8
OH FUTURE! THOU SECRETED PEACE	OH FUTURE! THOU SECRETED	1631	1
SECRETED IN HIS FORM	IN WINTER IN MY ROOM	1670	29
SECRETING			
AS EASY THE SECRETING HER	OF CONSCIOUSNESS, HER	894	3
SECRETS			
ODD SECRETS OF THE LINE TO TELL!	JUST LOST, WHEN I WAS	160	8
HE KEEPS HIS SECRETS SAFELY--VERY--	FUNNY--TO BE A CENTURY--	345	5
I [HE] SHOWED HER [ME] SECRETS--MORNING'S NEST--	I SHOWED HER HIGHTS SHE	446	5
OF SECRETS IS [TRAVELLERS] THE AIR--	THE FROST WAS NEVER SEEN	1202	16
OUR LITTLE SECRETS SLINK AWAY--	OUR LITTLE SECRETS SLINK	1326	1
"SECRETS" IS A DAILY WORD	"SECRETS" IS A DAILY	1385	1
DOUBTLESS SECRETS LIE--	"SECRETS" IS A DAILY	1385	6
SECRETS STAPLED THERE	"SECRETS" IS A DAILY	1385	10
SWEET IS THE SWAMP WITH ITS SECRETS,	SWEET IS THE SWAMP WITH	1740	1
SECTION			
A NATURE [SECTION] BE	BESIDES THIS MAY	977	8
SECURE			
THE SOUL STARES AFTER IT, SECURE--	'TIS SO APPALLING--IT	281	3
AJAR--SECURE--INVITING--	THE BODY GROWS WITHOUT--	578	5
STILL SECURE--	ONLY GOD--DETECT THE	626	6
SECURE AGAINST IT'S OWN--	THE SOUL UNTO ITSELF	683	5
PRESERVED THE CHARM [VISION SURE / VISION CLEAR] SECURE	HAVE ANY LIKE MYSELF	736	18
IS A TOO ESTABLISHED FORTUNE [SECURE POSSESSION / CONTENDED . . .	EXPECTATION--IS	807	7
MY SECRET AS SECURE	NATURE AND GOD--I	835	6
WHEN STOOPING TO SECURE IT	A NARROW FELLOW IN THE	986	15
"SECURE [PROTECT] YOUR FLOWER" SAID HE.	THE FROST OF DEATH WAS	1136	2
SECURED			
HAD I SECURED THE GLOW	A CLOUD WITHDREW FROM	895	6
SECURED HIM BY A STRING	IN WINTER IN MY ROOM	1670	7
SECURELY			
AND GLANCE SECURELY ROUND--	THIS MERIT HATH THE	979	6
SECURER			
TO STEAL SECURER [AT SUNRISE] THENCE	CONTAINED IN THIS SHORT	1165	4
SECURES			
THAT SECURES ETERNITY	CRISIS IS A HAIR	889	15
SECURES APPLAUSE	T'IS EASIER TO PITY	1698	5
SECUREST			
THINE THE SECUREST [PATERNAL] FOLD	LET DOWN THE BARS, OH	1065	6
SECUREST GATHERED THEN	TO DISAPPEAR ENHANCES--	1209	16
SECURITY			
SECURITY IS LOUD--	WHEN ETNA BASKS AND	1146	4
SECURITY THE SAME INSURES	OF PAUL AND SILAS IT IS	1166	5
SEDATE			
PUNCTUAL! SEDATE!	DUST IS THE ONLY SECRET	153	10
NATURE AFFECTS [WAS KNOWN] TO BE SEDATE	NATURE AFFECTS TO BE	1170	1
SEDGE			
THE SEDGE STANDS NEXT THE SEA--	WHAT MYSTERY PERVADES A	1400	14
SEDITIOUS			
OF SENTIMENTS SEDITIOUS	THE WAY TO KNOW THE	1279	9
SEDUCE			
TO SEDUCE [ENTICE / PERSUADE] THE SUN	PROMISE THIS--WHEN YOU	648	18
SEDUCTIVE			
SEDUCTIVE IN THE AIR--	RISK IS THE HAIR THAT	1239	2
SEDULOUS			
SEDULOUS [TOO ELATE] OF HER MULTITUDES	NOT ANY MORE TO BE	1344	7
SEE			
THE WAVE WITH EYE SO PENSIVE, LOOKETH TO SEE THE MOON,	AWAKE YE MUSES NINE,	1	18
THINE EYES ARE SADLY BLINDED, BUT YET THOU MAYEST SEE	AWAKE YE MUSES NINE,	1	33
IN DREAMS I SEE THEM RISE,	"SIC TRANSIT GLORIA	3	50
I SEE	I HAVE A BIRD IN SPRING	5	21
I WAS WONT TO SEE--	FREQUENTLY THE WOODS ARE	6	6
I CANNOT SEE A SPOKE	MY WHEEL IS IN THE DARK!	10	2
AND SEE!	SHE SLEPT BENEATH A TREE	25	6
MORTAL SHALL NOT SEE--	WHEN I COUNT THE SEEDS	40	8
I CONFIDENTLY SEE!	SOME RAINBOW--COMING	64	3
COULD I SEE IT FROM THE MOUNTAINS	WILL THERE REALLY BE A	101	3
I CLAP MY HANDS TO SEE--	A SOMETHING IN A	122	9
WHO WIN, AND NATIONS DO NOT SEE--	TO FIGHT ALOUD, IS VERY	126	5
TO SEE THAT NONE IS DUE?	BRING ME THE SUNSET IN A	128	18
MY SPIRIT CANNOT SEE?	BRING ME THE SUNSET IN A	128	21
SO I CAN SEE WHICH WAY TO GO	DYING! DYING IN THE	158	3
AND SEE IF DOLLIE'S COMING! WAIT!	DYING! DYING IN THE	158	10
NEXT TIME, THE THINGS TO SEE	JUST LOST, WHEN I WAS	160	13
DARE I PRESUME TO SEE	I MET A KING THIS	166	18
THE REST OF LIFE TO SEE!	AT LAST, TO BE	174	3
WHEN GENTLEMEN CAN [FOR GENTLEMEN WHO] SEE--	"FAITH" IS A FINE	185	2
TO SEE TO THE END--	WE DONT CRY--TIM AND I,	196	12
TIM--SEE COTTAGES--	WE DONT CRY--TIM AND I,	196	13
THAT HUNTED--HUNTED SO--TO SEE--	I SHOULD NOT DARE TO	205	6

SEE (CONTINUED)

	FIRST LINE	POEM	LINE
TO SEE THE LITTLE TIPPLER	I TASTE A LIQUOR NEVER	214	15
WHAT WOULD I GIVE TO SEE HIS FACE?	WHAT WOULD I GIVE TO SEE	247	1
JUST--SEE--IF I TROUBLED THEM--	WHY--DO THEY SHUT ME OUT	248	7
YOU SEE I CANNOT SEE--YOUR LIFETIME--	YOU SEE I CANNOT SEE--	253	1
YOU SEE I CANNOT SEE--YOUR LIFETIME--	YOU SEE I CANNOT SEE--	253	1
HAD IMPORTUNED TO SEE!	GOOD NIGHT! WHICH PUT	259	9
MY EYES JUST TURNED TO SEE,	A SINGLE SCREW OF FLESH	263	10
SEE WHERE IT HURT ME--THAT'S ENOUGH--	WHAT IF I SAY I SHALL	277	5
BECAUSE I SEE--NEW ENGLANDLY--	THE ROBIN'S MY CRITERION	285	15
TO SEE WHO'S THERE!	I KNOW SOME LONELY	289	24
THAT KNOWS--IT CANNOT SEE--	THE DIFFERENCE BETWEEN	305	8
I SHOULD HAVE BEEN TOO GLAD, I SEE--	I SHOULD HAVE BEEN TOO	313	1
I SHOULD HAVE BEEN TOO SAVED--I SEE--	I SHOULD HAVE BEEN TOO	313	7
EARTH WOULD HAVE BEEN TOO MUCH--I SEE--	I SHOULD HAVE BEEN TOO	313	13
I LIKED AS WELL TO SEE--	BEFORE I GOT MY EYE PUT	327	2
AND SEE THE PEOPLE--GOING BY--	FUNNY--TO BE A CENTURY--	345	2
SO--WHEN 'TWAS TIME TO SEE--	I DREADED THAT FIRST	348	14
TO SEE IF IT WAS THERE--	I FELT MY LIFE WITH BOTH	351	2
ENOUGH ESTATE--TO SEE--	'TIS OPPOSITES--ENTICE--	355	6
DARE YOU SEE A SOUL AT THE WHITE HEAT?	DARE YOU SEE A SOUL AT	365	1
SEE--IN WHITE!	TAKE YOUR HEAVEN FURTHER	388	12
TO SEE THAT I MADE NO MISTAKE	I READ MY SENTENCE--	412	3
SO NOT TO SEE US--BUT THEY SAY	I NEVER FELT AT HOME--	413	11
NOT IN THIS WORLD TO SEE HIS FACE--	NOT IN THIS WORLD TO SEE	418	1
BUT AS THEY LEARN TO SEE--	WE GROW ACCUSTOMED TO	419	16
TO HANDS I CANNOT SEE--	THIS IS MY LETTER TO THE	441	6
AS FAR AS IT COULD SEE--	LIKE EYES THAT LOOKED ON	458	6
ARE SO HIGH UP--YOU SEE--	I KNOW WHERE WELLS GROW	460	12
I LIVE WITH HIM--I SEE HIS FACE--	I LIVE WITH HIM--I SEE	463	1
I COULD NOT SEE TO SEE--	I HEARD A FLY BUZZ--WHEN	465	16
I COULD NOT SEE TO SEE--	I HEARD A FLY BUZZ--WHEN	465	16
JUST LOOKING ROUND TO SEE HOW FAR	WE DO NOT PLAY ON GRAVES	467	11
I NEVER THOUGHT TO SEE--	EXCEPT THE HEAVEN HAD	472	6
WE SIGNIFIED "THESE SEE"--	THEY PUT US FAR APART--	474	4
"I SEE THEE" EACH RESPONDED STRAIGHT	THEY PUT US FAR APART--	474	7
CONDEMNED--BUT JUST--TO SEE--	THEY PUT US FAR APART--	474	16
BECAUSE HE'S SUNRISE--AND I SEE--	"WHY DO I LOVE" YOU, SIR	480	18
YOU LOVE THE LORD--YOU CANNOT SEE--	YOU LOVE THE LORD--YOU	487	1
AND WOULD DELIGHT TO SEE--	YOU LOVE THE LORD--YOU	487	6
AND MINE'S--IN HEAVEN--YOU SEE.	YOU LOVE THE LORD--YOU	487	8
SO YOU COULD SEE WHAT MOVED THEM SO--	GOING TO HIM! HAPPY	494	9
HOW EASY ALL CAN SEE	I ENVY SEAS, WHEREON HE	498	6
BLUSHES, IF ANY SEE--	THIS WORLD IS NOT	501	14
IF I COULD SEE YOU IN A YEAR,	IF YOU WERE COMING IN	511	5
DEITY WILL SEE TO IT	BEAUTY--BE NOT CAUSED--	516	7
WE SEE--COMPARATIVELY--	WE SEE--COMPARATIVELY--	534	1
PROVES THAT--OUTGROWN--I SEE--	I COULD NOT PROVE THE	563	12
TO SEE [REACH / TOUCH] THIS CURIOUS FRIEND--	MY PERIOD HAD COME FOR	564	8
WERE ALL THAT I COULD SEE--	MY PERIOD HAD COME FOR	564	14
BUT SEARCHING--I COULD SEE	A DYING TIGER--MOANED	566	6
AND SEE THE THINGS IN POD--	MY FIRST WELL DAY--SINCE	574	4
NOT YET, OUR EYES CAN SEE--	"HEAVEN" HAS DIFFERENT	575	20
I COULD NOT SEE [FEEL] THE TROUBLE [ANGUISH] GO--	IT CEASED TO HURT ME,	584	2
I LIKE TO SEE [HEAR] IT LAP THE MILES--	I LIKE TO SEE IT LAP	585	1
AND SEE THE PARCEL ROLLED--	I CRIED AT PITY--NOT AT	588	10
TO LET HIM SEE--THE CANAAN--	IT ALWAYS FELT TO ME--A	597	3
'TWAS LITTLE--HE SHOULD SEE--	IT ALWAYS FELT TO ME--A	597	22
BUT TITLED HIM--TO SEE--	IT ALWAYS FELT TO ME--A	597	V 22
THAT CRAWLED LEAGUES OFF--I LIKED TO SEE--	THREE TIMES--WE PARTED--	598	9
HOW MEAN--TO THOSE THAT SEE--	THE TREES LIKE TASSELS--	606	26
I SEE THEE BETTER--IN THE DARK--	I SEE THEE BETTER--IN	611	1
I SEE THEE BETTER FOR THE YEARS	I SEE THEE BETTER--IN	611	5
AND IN THE GRAVE--I SEE THEE BEST--	I SEE THEE BETTER--IN	611	9
ANOTHER WAY--TO SEE--	THE TINT I CANNOT TAKE--	627	24
AND SEE YOU--FREEZE--	I CANNOT LIVE WITH YOU--	640	18
WHOM DEATH SEE FIRST--'TIS NEWS OF THIS	BEREAVEMENT IN THEIR	645	7
JUST THAT YOU SHOULD SEE	PROMISE THIS--WHEN YOU	648	14
AND NONE COULD SEE THE STONE.	'TIS GOOD--THE LOOKING	660	8
"NATURE" IS WHAT WE SEE--	"NATURE" IS WHAT WE SEE	668	1
I COULD NOT SEE IT NOW--	THE SUN KEPT SETTING--	692	14
IT IMPORTUNED TO SEE	THE HEAVEN VESTS FOR	694	6
I'M FINITE--I CANT SEE--	THEIR HIGHT IN HEAVEN	696	4
SEE THE BIRD--REACH IT!	OUT OF SIGHT? WHAT OF	703	2
SEEK--FRIEND--AND SEE--	OUT OF SIGHT? WHAT OF	703	10
TILL BOTH--CAN SEE--	THE SUNRISE RUNS FOR	710	12
'TIS FIRST [YOU SEE] HE STEPS UPON THE VANE--	MY FAITH IS LARGER THAN	766	5
IS LEST ITSELF SHOULD SEE--	THE LONELINESS ONE DARE	777	6
WHEN NOTHING WAS TO SEE	HER FINAL SUMMER WAS IT	795	10
SO I THE SHIPS MAY SEE	SO SET IT'S SUN IN THEE	808	4
AS CERTAINTY CAN SEE	THE LUXURY TO APPREHEND	815	14
THE ONLY SHOWS I SEE--	THE ONLY NEWS I KNOW	827	4
IF OTHERS WANT TO SEE	LIGHT IS SUFFICIENT TO	862	2
AND MOSTLY--SEE NOT	THE ADMIRATIONS--AND	906	7
BECAUSE I CANNOT SEE	I CANNOT BE ASHAMED	914	2
SUPPORTING WHAT WE SEE	FAITH--IS THE PIERLESS	915	2
WHAT [WHEN] I SEE NOT, I BETTER SEE--	WHAT I SEE NOT, I BETTER	939	1
WHAT [WHEN] I SEE NOT, I BETTER SEE--	WHAT I SEE NOT, I BETTER	939	1
IF I SHALL SEE	THE CHEMICAL CONVICTION	954	6

	FIRST LINE	POEM	LINE
SEE (CONTINUED)			
FITTER TO SEE HIM, I MAY BE	FITTER TO SEE HIM, I MAY	968	1
WE MISS HER, NOT BECAUSE WE SEE--	WE MISS HER, NOT BECAUSE	993	1
HIS COUNTENANCE TO SEE	THE STIMULUS, BEYOND THE	1001	2
GROPED UP, TO SEE IF GOD WERE [WAS] THERE--	HE SCANNED IT--STAGGERED	1062	6
WHEN WARRANTED TO SEE	WE MISS A KINSMAN MORE	1087	2
TILL WHAT WE COULD NOT SEE [FACE / CHOOSE / PROVE] HAS COME	THE MURMURING OF BEES,	1115	V 13
NOW [SINCE] I [THAT] ABUNDANCE SEE--	OH SUMPTUOUS MOMENT	1125	5
THE LIFE THAT WE SHALL SEE	THE LIFE WE HAVE IS VERY	1162	2
WHAT WE SEE WE KNOW SOMEWHAT	WHAT WE SEE WE KNOW	1195	1
BOTH WENT TO SEE--	THE SHOW IS NOT THE SHOW	1206	6
SOME WE SEE NO MORE, TENEMENTS OF WONDER	SOME WE SEE NO MORE,	1221	1
WE WILL PRY AND SEE IF SHE IS FAIR	BECAUSE HE LOVES HER	1229	2
FOR NONE SEE GOD AND LIVE--	TO PILE LIKE THUNDER TO	1247	8
BEFORE IT SEE THE SUN!	LONGING IS LIKE THE SEED	1255	8
I CANNOT SEE MY SOUL BUT KNOW 'TIS THERE	I CANNOT SEE MY SOUL BUT	1262	1
A WHIP SO SMALL YOU COULD NOT SEE IT	NOT WITH A CLUB, THE	1304	3
TO SEE IT FLASHING WHEN HE DINES	A SAUCER HOLDS A CUP	1374	11
ECLIPSE--WAS ALL WE COULD SEE AT THE WINDOW	IT SOUNDED AS IF THE	1397	3
TO SEE IF TIME WAS [WERE] THERE--	IT SOUNDED AS IF THE	1397	6
HIS OUTLETS--WOULD YOU SEE [KNOW]	SUCH ARE THE INLETS OF	1421	2
SO SHAMELESS IS TO SEE	THE HEALED HEART SHOWS	1440	6
YOU SEE--GOD BLESS HIS SUDDENNESS--	BEFORE YOU THOUGHT OF	1465	3
TO SEE THE SUMMER SKY	TO SEE THE SUMMER SKY	1472	1
SEE HOW WELL WE SPURN HIM--	SUMMER IS SHORTER THAN	1506	6
TO SEE HER IS A PICTURE--	TO SEE HER IS A PICTURE	1568	1
ENHANCING WHAT WE SEE	SUNSET THAT SCREENS,	1609	2
I SEE THEE CLEARER FOR THE GRAVE	I SEE THEE CLEARER FOR	1666	1
I WATCHED HER FACE TO SEE WHICH WAY	I WATCHED HER FACE TO	1667	1
THE RIVERS LEAN TO SEE	THE HILLS ERECT THEIR	1688	2
WE SEE ACUTER [DISTINCTER / SINCERER], QUITE,	BY A DEPARTING LIGHT	1714	2
HOWEVER GOOD TO SEE,	DROWNING IS NOT SO	1718	10
HE CANNOT BEAR TO SEE	GOD IS INDEED A JEALOUS	1719	2
WILL SEE HOW FAR FROM HOME	IF EVER THE LID GETS OFF	1727	6
IT YET REMAINS TO SEE	MY LIFE CLOSED TWICE	1732	2
SEE! I USURPED THY CRUCIFIX TO HONOR MINE!	PROUD OF MY BROKEN HEART	1736	8
SEED			
AND SOW THE EARLY SEED--	SEXTON! MY MASTER'S	96	4
MORNING--ONLY THE SEED OF NOON--	I SHALL KEEP SINGING!	250	10
WHERE IS THE SEED--	ANSWER JULY--	386	6
SEED, HAD I, MY PURPLE SOWING	BLOOM UPON THE MOUNTAIN	667	5
SEED OF PALM, BY LYBIAN SUN	SOIL OF FLINT, IF STEADY	681	3
AND WHEN ADJUSTED LIKE A SEED	NO NOTICE GAVE SHE, BUT	804	13
AND ROSES IN THE SEED--	THERE IS A JUNE WHEN	930	2
A SMALL--ITALIC SEED	THIS IS A BLOSSOM OF THE	945	2
THAT FROM AN EQUAL SEED	THE OPENING AND THE	1047	5
LONGING IS LIKE THE SEED	LONGING IS LIKE THE SEED	1255	1
THE SEED OF DISAPPOINTMENT GREW	THIS IS THE PLACE THEY	1264	3
FOR THE MISSING SEED--	LAIN IN NATURE--SO	1288	4
BUT THESE THE FLITTED SEED,	THAN HEAVEN MORE REMOTE,	1436	3
SEED--SUMMER--TOMB--	A PIT--BUT HEAVEN OVER	1712	16
TO KEEPER OF THE SEED.	HE WAS MY HOST--HE WAS	1721	8
NOR SEED THAT WE CAN SOW,	THE JOY THAT HAS NO STEM	1744	2
SEEDS			
WHEN I COUNT THE SEEDS	WHEN I COUNT THE SEEDS	40	1
THE SEEDS OF SMILES ARE PLANTED--	BY CHIVALRIES AS TINY,	55	3
TILL RANKS OF SEEDS THEIR WITNESS BEAR--	THESE ARE THE DAYS WHEN	130	10
SHE TIED THE HOODS TO SEEDS--	MY FIRST WELL DAY--SINCE	574	18
THE CAPSULES BURNISHED SEEDS THE STARS--	THE LILAC IS AN ANCIENT	1241	11
SEEING			
'TWAS BLESSEDER--THE SEEING NOT--	TRUST IN THE UNEXPECTED	555	V 15
WHO GUESS AT SEEING, GUESS AT LOSS	WHO SAW NO SUNRISE	1018	3
NOT SEEING, STILL WE KNOW--	NOT SEEING, STILL WE	1518	1
SEEK			
THE HIGH DO SEEK THE LOWLY, THE GREAT DO SEEK THE SMALL,	AWAKE YE MUSES NINE,	1	11
THE HIGH DO SEEK THE LOWLY, THE GREAT DO SEEK THE SMALL,	AWAKE YE MUSES NINE,	1	11
MUST SEEK THE NEIGHBORING LIFE!	A LITTLE BREAD--A CRUST	159	12
I'LL SEEK HIS ROYAL FEET--	THE COURT IS FAR AWAY--	235	5
THAN "HIDE AND SEEK"--	ALTHOUGH I PUT AWAY HIS	366	19
A STAR--NOT FAR ENOUGH TO SEEK--	A MURMUR IN THE TREES--	416	3
SOME [MEN] SEEK IN ART--THE ART OF PEACE--	THE MARTYR POETS--DID	544	8
AND SEEK [GAIN] A DINNER FOR MYSELF--	IT WOULD HAVE STARVED A	612	11
HE SHALL SEEK AS HIGH	HER SWEET TURN TO LEAVE	649	18
SEEK--FRIEND--AND SEE--	OUT OF SIGHT? WHAT OF	703	10
HE SHALL SEEK IN VAIN--	NEVER FOR SOCIETY	746	2
WOULD'ST THOU SEEK SO--JUST SAY	I'VE NONE TO TELL ME TO	881	10
HE SEEK CONVICTION, THAT--BE THIS--	FITTER TO SEE HIM, I MAY	968	14
I DWELT TOO LOW THAT ANY SEEK--	I WAS A PHEBE--NOTHING	1009	5
TO SEARCH [SEEK] FOR THE ACCOMPLISHED GUEST,	THE SOUL SHOULD ALWAYS	1055	7
I SEEK THE DARK	I FIT FOR THEM--	1109	2
WOULD YOU SERVE [SEEK] IT SO?	NONE WHO SAW IT EVER	1110	8
THE LANDS WE THOUGHT THAT WE SHOULD SEEK	THE THINGS WE THOUGHT	1293	5
SEEK--IT IS YOURSELF.	THE HEART IS THE CAPITAL	1354	8
TO SEEK THEM [HIM] BY--	OF THEIR PECULIAR LIGHT	1362	4
NOT TO SEEK THEM	HE LIVED THE LIFE OF	1525	V
SEEK IT WITH THE SAW,	DEATH IS LIKE THE INSECT	1716	6
ONE CROWN THAT NO ONE SEEKS [NOT ANY SEEK]	ONE CROWN THAT NO ONE	1735	1

	FIRST LINE	POEM	LINE
SEEKETH			
NONE CANNOT FIND WHO SEEKETH, ON THIS TERRESTIAL BALL!	AWAKE YE MUSES NINE,	1	12
THAT SEEKETH HIS FELICITY	THE FLOWER MUST NOT	206	2
SEEKING			
SOME LITTLE WREN GOES SEEKING ROUND-- . .	FOR EVERY BIRD A NEST--	143	3
SEEKING [SAVING] MORE--TO SPEND--	SWEET--YOU FORGOT--BUT I	523	8
WHEN THE ASTRONOMER STOPS SEEKING	WHEN THE ASTRONOMER	851	1
WHO SOMETHING LOST [DROPT], THE SEEKING [LOOKING] FOR	DEATH LEAVES US HOMESICK	935	7
FOR SEEKING IT'S RESEMBLANCE [SIMILITUDE]--	IT BLOOMED AND DROPT, A	978	15
TOO NEAR THOU ART FOR SEEKING THEE . . .	LET DOWN THE BARS, OH	1065	7
SEEKS			
SEEKS FAINTLY [SOFTLY / FURTIVE] FOR IT'S SHORE	THE INUNDATION OF THE	1425	6
HE LOVES [SEEKS] WHAT SPURNS [SHUNS] HIM-- .	TO EARN IT BY DISDAINING	1427	3
WHO IS IT SEEKS MY PILLOW NIGHTS-- . . .	WHO IS IT SEEKS MY	1598	1
ONE CROWN THAT NO ONE SEEKS [NOT ANY SEEK] .	ONE CROWN THAT NO ONE	1735	1
SEEM			
SO PLAUSIBLE [EXQUISITE]--THEY SEEM-- . .	LIKE SOME OLD FASHIONED	302	12
FORGIVE ME, IF THE GRAVE COME [SEEM] SLOW--	IF I MAY HAVE IT, WHEN	577	26
TWOULD SEEM THAT GOD SHOULD BE	HAVE ANY LIKE MYSELF	736	13
WOULD SEEM TO ME THE MORE THE WAY	OF TOLLING BELL I ASK	947	7
THE WAITING--THEN--WILL SEEM SO WORTH . .	FITTER TO SEE HIM, I MAY	968	6
AS SLEIGH BELLS SEEM [SOUND] IN SUMMER . .	AS SLEIGH BELLS SEEM IN	981	1
ALTHOUGH HE SEEM TO STEAL	NOT ONE BY HEAVEN	1303	2
THOUGH TO TRUST US--SEEM TO US	"HEAVENLY FATHER"--TAKE	1461	5
TO SEEM [FEEL] LIKE PERFIDY--	AS IMPERCEPTIBLY AS	1540	4
SEEMED			
KEPT TREADING--TREADING--TILL IT SEEMED . .	I FELT A FUNERAL, IN MY	280	3
THERE SEEMED A PURPLE STILE	I'LL TELL YOU HOW THE	318	10
TO NOWHERE--SEEMED TO GO	FROM COCOON FORTH A	354	15
SO SEEMED TO CHOOSE MY DOOR--	EXCEPT THE HEAVEN HAD	472	2
NO ONE [MAN] HE SEEMED TO KNOW--	I STARTED EARLY--TOOK MY	520	22
IN SEARCH OF SOMETHING [SOMEWHAT]--AS IT SEEMED--	I'VE SEEN A DYING EYE	547	3
TO CHEAT HERSELF, IT SEEMED SHE TRIED-- . .	MY FIRST WELL DAY--SINCE	574	13
JUST MAKING SIGNS--ACROSS--[IT SEEMED] TO THEE--	IF I MAY HAVE IT, WHEN	577	20
IT SEEMED THE COMMON WAY, ...	I CRIED AT PITY--NOT AT	588	6
ON MOSES--SEEMED TO FASTEN	IT ALWAYS FELT TO ME--A	597	13
THERE SEEMED TO RISE A TUNE	THE TREES LIKE TASSELS--	606	2
BUT SEEMED ENGROSSED TO ABSOLUTE-- . . .	I WATCHED THE MOON	629	27
WE PAUSED BEFORE A HOUSE THAT SEEMED . . .	BECAUSE I COULD NOT STOP	712	17
A NEEDLESS LIFE, IT SEEMED TO ME	OUR LITTLE KINSMEN--	885	5
THE EARTH HAS SEEMED TO ME A DRUM, . . .	WHEN I HAVE SEEN THE SUN	888	7
CREATION SEEMED A MIGHTY CRACK--	TO MY QUICK EAR THE	891	7
TO HER DESIRE SEEMED--	SO PROUD SHE WAS TO DIE	1272	4
TO WHERE A BROOK THAT SEEMED A SEA . . .	OF DEATH I TRY TO THINK	1558	11
ANALYSIS AS [LIKE] CAPSULE SEEMED	HE WAS MY HOST--HE WAS	1721	7
SEEMING			
UNTO MY SEEMING--MAKE?	THE SUN KEPT SETTING--	692	12
IT WAS A QUIET SEEMING DAY--	IT WAS A QUIET SEEMING	1419	1
SEEMS			
SEEMS SUMMER'S RECOLLECTION	LIKE SOME OLD FASHIONED	302	3
SEEMS IT DONT SHRIEK SO--UNDER RULE. . . .	IT DONT SOUND SO	426	4
SO SHORT WAY OFF IT SEEMS--	IF ANYBODY'S FRIEND BE	509	11
IT SEEMS SO STRAIGHT TO LIE AWAY	I'M SORRY FOR THE DEAD--	529	9
BUT, LOOKING BACK--THE FIRST SO SEEMS . .	I RECKON--WHEN I COUNT	569	5
IT'S LIKER SO--IT SEEMS--	DID YOU EVER STAND IN A	590	16
DISTINCTNESS--EASY--SEEMS--	OF NEARNESS TO HER	607	4
IT SEEMS AS THOUGH THE TIME	I THINK THE LONGEST HOUR	635	4
THE REAL [TRUTH]--FICTITIOUS SEEMS-- . . .	I THINK TO LIVE--MAY BE	646	24
BUT THE SUCCESS--WAS HIS--IT SEEMS-- . . .	I MEANT TO FIND HER WHEN	718	3
SEEMS IT TO MY HOODED THINKING	ONE DAY IS THERE OF THE	814	7
IT SEEMS A CURIOUS TOWN--	WHO OCCUPIES THIS HOUSE?	892	9
THIS SEEMS A HOME--	I LEARNED--AT LEAST--	944	27
TOO WISE HE SEEMS FOR WAKELESSNESS, . . .	THE DUTIES OF THE WIND	1137	15
NOR ISOLATE IT SEEMS	THE GENTIAN HAS A	1424	9
SEEMS IT SOMETIMES THIS WOULD BE ALL-- . .	THESE FEVERED DAYS--TO	1441	4
WHICH WHILE YOU TASTE SO NATIVE [ADJACENT] SEEMS	YOUR THOUGHTS DONT HAVE	1452	5
SO EASY [KINDRED / FULLY / FREE / AMPLE SEEMS / BOUNTEOUS / . . .	YOUR THOUGHTS DONT HAVE	1452	6
TOO GREAT IT SEEMS	I DID NOT REACH THEE	1664	26
THEIR COMING BACK SEEMS POSSIBLE	THE DISTANCE THAT THE	1742	3
SEEN			
MAY BE SEEN THE DEWS AMONG, ...	ANGELS, IN THE EARLY	94	2
MAY BE SEEN THE SANDS AMONG, ...	ANGELS, IN THE EARLY	94	6
CAN NIGHTINGALE BE SEEN--	ALL OVERGROWN BY CUNNING	148	12
I HAVE NEVER SEEN "VOLCANOES"--	I HAVE NEVER SEEN	175	1
IS MORE DISTINCTLY SEEN--	THE THOUGHT BENEATH SO	210	2
SEEN MAGIC--THROUGH THE FRIGHT	DELIGHT IS AS THE FLIGHT	257	21
AS HOVERING [GLIMMERING]--SEEN--THROUGH FOG--	A SOLEMN THING--IT WAS--	271	12
HER PRETTY PARASOL BE SEEN	FROM COCOON FORTH A	354	9
AGAINST THE WIND--BE SEEN--	THERE IS A FLOWER THAT	380	16
POSSIBLY, E'EN YOU HAD SEEN	TAKE YOUR HEAVEN FURTHER	388	4
YOU'VE SEEN THE COLOR--MAYBE--	THE COLOR OF THE GRAVE	411	21
SAVIOR [MASTER]--I'VE SEEN THE FACE--BEFORE!	A WIFE--AT DAYBREAK I	461	13
THE FIGURES I HAVE SEEN	IT WAS NOT DEATH, FOR I	510	10

	FIRST LINE	POEM	LINE
SEEN (CONTINUED)			
THAN ANY I HAD SEEN--	I TRIED TO THINK A	532	2
SOME SUCH BUTTERFLY BE SEEN	SOME SUCH BUTTERFLY BE	541	1
I'VE SEEN A DYING EYE	I'VE SEEN A DYING EYE	547	1
'TWERE BLESSED TO HAVE SEEN--	I'VE SEEN A DYING EYE	547	8
YOU'VE SEEN IT ON A CAST'S FACE [CHEEK]--	IT KNEW NO MEDICINE--	559	11
'TWAS THIS ON TABLES I HAD SEEN--	I HAD BEEN HUNGRY, ALL	579	5
AND SEEN MY BRAIN--GO ROUND--	THEY SHUT ME UP IN PROSE	613	6
WHOM WE HAVE NEVER SEEN--	BEREAVEMENT IN THEIR	645	2
YOU'VE SEEN BALLOONS SET--HAV'NT YOU?	YOU'VE SEEN BALLOONS SET	700	1
THE FLICKERING BE SEEN	THE DAY UNDRESSED--	716	14
MY [THE] VILLAGES BE SEEN--	HAVE ANY LIKE MYSELF	736	22
I'VE SEEN?	YOU SAID THAT I "WAS	738	8
HER STEADY BOAT BE SEEN--	SHE STAKED HER FEATHERS	798	6
IN PLENTY MAY BE SEEN,	OUR LITTLE KINSMEN--	885	2
WHEN I HAVE SEEN THE SUN EMERGE	WHEN I HAVE SEEN THE SUN	888	1
NO EYE HATH SEEN AND LIVED	FROM US SHE WANDERED NOW	890	5
SEEN POOREST--THRO' OUR GAINS--	I LEARNED--AT LEAST--	944	21
A SPOTTED SHAFT IS SEEN--	A NARROW FELLOW IN THE	986	6
AS DAISIES NOW TO BE SEEN--	THIS WAS IN THE WHITE OF	995	4
THREE WEEKS PASSED SINCE I HAD SEEN HER--	THREE WEEKS PASSED SINCE	1061	1
NO ORDINANCE BE SEEN	FURTHER IN SUMMER THAN	1068	5
NOR IMPLEMENT, BE SEEN--	AT HALF PAST THREE, A	1084	10
TOO DISTANT [SUBTLE] TO BE SEEN	CONTAINED IN THIS SHORT	1165	V
THE FROST WAS NEVER SEEN--	THE FROST WAS NEVER SEEN	1202	1
HAD I NOT SEEN THE SUN	HAD I NOT SEEN THE SUN	1233	1
"EYE HATH NOT SEEN" MAY POSSIBLY	THE LILAC IS AN ANCIENT	1241	17
SUMMER--WE ALL HAVE SEEN--	SUMMER--WE ALL HAVE SEEN	1386	1
WHOSE LIMIT NONE HAVE EVER SEEN,	WHAT MYSTERY PERVADES A	1400	5
IS OFTEN SEEN--BUT SELDOM FELT,	A FIELD OF STUBBLE,	1407	7
AND [BUT] NOT AGAIN THAT DEW BE SEEN	A DEW SUFFICED ITSELF--	1437	7
A FOE WHOM I HAVE NEVER SEEN	MY WARS ARE LAID AWAY IN	1549	3
I'VE OFTEN SEEN THEM PLAY	NO BRIGADIER THROUGHOUT	1561	10
YET HAD NOT SEEN!	SPEECH IS ONE SYMPTOM OF	1681	8
SEES			
THAT WHOSO SEES THIS LITTLE FLOWER	WE SHOULD NOT MIND SO	81	9
SEES EVERY MAN A KING--	WHO COURT OBTAIN WITHIN	803	2
MY GOD--HE SEES THEE--	MY GOD--HE SEES THEE--	1178	1
TO HIM WHO SEES	THIS DIRTY--LITTLE--	1311	6
AND SEES [SPIES] THE PASTURES SMILE	THE LIFE THAT TIED TOO	1535	6
SEESAW			
IF YOUR SOUL SEESAW [STAGGER]--	IF YOUR NERVE, DENY YOU	292	9
SEESAWING			
THEN--SEESAWING--COOLLY--ON IT--	ROBBED BY DEATH--BUT	971	15
SEGMENT			
WE COULD NOT GRASP IT'S SEGMENT [ANGLE]	WE SEE--COMPARATIVELY--	534	3
SEIZE			
AND SEIZE THE ONE THOU LOVEST, NOR CARE FOR SPACE, OR TIME!	AWAKE YE MUSES NINE,	1	36
MAY SEIZE UPON HIS MIND--	I HAD A GUINEA GOLDEN--	23	34
IF ANY TAKE [SEIZE] MY PROPERTY	ALONE AND IN A	1167	19
SNATCH IT FOR [COVET IT / TIE IT FOR / SEIZE IT FOR / SUMMON ...	SUMMER LAID HER SIMPLE	1363	4
SELDOM			
HIS CONVERSATION--SELDOM--	THE ONLY GHOST I EVER	274	9
IS SELDOM--BUT AS FAIR	THE SOUL'S SUPERIOR	306	10
AND DRAMA--IS NEVER [SELDOM] DEAD--	WE DREAM--IT IS GOOD WE	531	8
DOTH SELDOM GO ABROAD--	THE SOUL THAT HATH A	674	2
AND ARE TOO SELDOM BORN--	FAME'S BOYS AND GIRLS,	1066	2
BUT [THO] SELDOM SIDE BY SIDE	AS OLD AS WOE--	1168	8
IS OFTEN SEEN--BUT SELDOM FELT,	A FIELD OF STUBBLE,	1407	7
A WORD MADE FLESH IS SELDOM	A WORD MADE FLESH IS	1651	1
SELDOM WITH THE SOUL	SOMETIMES WITH THE HEART	1680	2
TOO SELDOM DOES	T'IS EASIER TO PITY	1698	7
SELDOMLY			
THAT TOUCH HOW SELDOMLY	SO SET IT'S SUN IN THEE	808	5
SELECT			
AT MIDNIGHT--LET THE OWL SELECT	THE JUDGE IS LIKE THE	699	11
SELECT A REVERENTIAL BROOM--	THAT SACRED CLOSET WHEN	1273	3
SELECTLY			
ONLY SCANTLY AND SELECTLY	NATURE RARER USES YELLOW	1045	7
SELECTS			
THE SOUL SELECTS HER OWN SOCIETY--	THE SOUL SELECTS HER OWN	303	1
SELF SEE A'SELF			
I DO NOT DOUBT THE SELF I WAS	I COULD NOT PROVE THE	563	9
THAT SELF--WERE HELL TO ME--	I CANNOT LIVE WITH YOU--	640	44
ON A COLUMNAR SELF--	ON A COLUMNAR SELF--	789	1
THAT IT WAS FEBUARY'S FOOT [FACE / SELF]	THE SNOW THAT NEVER	1133	7
BUT HIS SERAPHIC SELF--	BEFORE YOU THOUGHT OF	1465	16
A SELF DENYING HOUSEHOLD,	THE ROBIN IS A GABRIEL	1483	10
SELL			
BUT I COULD NEVER SELL--	PERHAPS YOU'D LIKE TO	134	2
COULD YOU AFFORD TO SELL--	I CAME TO BUY A SMILE--	223	8
THEY--SOLD [THEN--SELL] IT UNTO ME	OF BRUSSELS--IT WAS NOT	602	4
IT'S CORPOREAL ILLUSTRATION--SELL	PUBLICATION--IS THE	709	11
FATE HAS BOTH TO SELL--	FLOSS WONT SAVE YOU FROM	1322	V 8
SELLER'S			
WITHIN A SELLER'S SHRINE	A DIAMOND ON THE HAND	1108	5
SELLS			
HE ONLY SELLS THE WILDERNESS,	THE AUCTIONEER OF	1612	5

	FIRST LINE	POEM	LINE
SELVES			
IN DYING--'TIS AS IF OUR SOULS [WORLD / SELVES / SUN]	BEREAVEMENT IN THEIR	645	11
SEND			
AND SEND THE ROSE TO YOU.	IF SHE HAD BEEN THE	44	8
I SEND TWO SUNSETS--	I SEND TWO SUNSETS--	308	1
AN ENEMY--COULD SEND--	THE SOUL UNTO ITSELF	683	4
I'LL SEND THE FEATHER FROM MY HAT!	I'LL SEND THE FEATHER	687	1
I SEND YOU A DECREPIT FLOWER	I SEND YOU A DECREPIT	1324	1
I WANT TO SEND IT TO YOU	HE LIVED THE LIFE OF	1525	V
I GIVE [SEND] MY DYING KISS--	"GO TELL IT"--WHAT A	1554	8
AND SO I SEND MY CRIMSON SCOUTS	WHERE ROSES WOULD NOT	1582	3
WE SEND THE WAVE TO FIND THE WAVE--	WE SEND THE WAVE TO FIND	1604	1
THAT SEND ME REELING IN [ON]--	A DRUNKARD CANNOT MEET A	1628	6
SENDING			
IN SENDING ALL THE BIRDS AWAY--	THE WINTERS ARE SO SHORT	403	3
SENDS			
AND SENDS A BAILIFF THERE.	I HAD SOME THINGS THAT I	116	8
GOD SENDS [GIVES] US WOMEN--	TITLE DIVINE--IS MINE!	1072	7
THE TYPIC MOTHER SENDS	THE MURMURING OF BEES,	1115	10
SENSATION SEE STOP-SENSATION			
SENSE			
THAT SENSE WAS BREAKING THROUGH--	I FELT A FUNERAL, IN MY	280	4
AND SENSE WAS SETTING NUMB--	'TWAS LIKE A MAELSTROM,	414	15
MUCH MADNESS IS DIVINEST SENSE--	MUCH MADNESS IS DIVINEST	435	1
MUCH SENSE--THE STARKEST MADNESS--	MUCH MADNESS IS DIVINEST	435	3
DISTILLS AMAZING SENSE	THIS WAS A POET--IT IS	448	2
WHEN SENSE FROM SPIRIT--FILES AWAY--	OF ALL THE SOULS THAT	664	3
FOR FREQUENT [OFTEN], ALL MY SENSE OBSCURED	WHAT I SEE NOT, I BETTER	939	5
A SENSE THAT SMOTE AND STIRRED--	I'VE DROPPED MY BRAIN--	1046	10
A COMPETITION IN MY SENSE	I CANNOT MEET THE SPRING	1051	5
CAUGHT HELPLESS AT A SENSE AS IF	HE SCANNED IT--STAGGERED	1062	4
THAT WOULD TO [UN TO] SENSE HAVE DAZZLED	CONTAINED IN THIS SHORT	1165	V
UNMANIFEST TO [UNWITNESSED OF THE / AS DOTH THE TIRED] SENSE	CONTAINED IN THIS SHORT	1165	V
IT IS POSSIBLE FOR SENSE TO LIVE	IF EVER THE LID GETS OFF	1727	7
SENSES			
TO HOLD OUR SENSES--ON--	I TIE MY HAT--I CREASE	443	33
HAD WE OUR SENSES	HAD WE OUR SENSES	1284	1
SENT			
I SENT IT--EVEN NOW?	WHAT SHALL I DO--IT	186	7
I MIND ME THAT OF ANGUISH--SENT--	I THINK JUST HOW MY	237	9
SENT US OF THE AIR--	THERE'S A CERTAIN SLANT	258	12
SENT VARIOUS--SCATTERED WAYS--	WE MET AS SPARKS--	958	2
TELL HIS ARROW SENT--	TELL AS A MARKSMAN--WERE	1152	23
THE SUN SENT OUT	LIKE BROOMS OF STEEL	1252	5
THAT NATURE SENT TO ME	I SEND YOU A DECREPIT	1324	2
HE SENT HIS SON TO TEST THE PLANK,	HOW BRITTLE ARE THE	1433	7
LOVING THE HAND THAT SENT IT	I'VE GOT AN ARROW HERE.	1729	2
SENTENCE			
I READ MY SENTENCE--STEADILY--	I READ MY SENTENCE--	412	1
AS IF YOUR SENTENCE STOOD--PRONOUNCED--	'TWAS LIKE A MAELSTROM,	414	18
YOU GUESSED--FROM THE WAY THE SENTENCE TOILED--	GOING TO HIM! HAPPY	494	11
AND SENTENCE--SACRAMENT--	WHERE THOU ART--THAT--IS	725	9
IS SENTENCE [EXILE] FROM BELIEF--AND HOME--	IF BLAME BE MY SIDE--	775	4
INFECTION IN THE SENTENCE BREEDS	A WORD DROPPED CARELESS	1261	5
MY SENTENCE HAD BEGUN.	'TWAS HERE MY SUMMER	1756	4
SENTENCED			
CONVICTED--SENTENCED--ERMINE--NOT TO ME	WERT THOU BUT ILL--THAT	961	10
PAUSING IN FRONT OF [AGAINST] OUR PALSIED [SENTENCED / . . .	WE TALKED WITH EACH	1473	5
SENTENCES			
SENTENCES OF PLUSH,	ALL THE LETTERS I CAN	334	4
SENTIMENT			
IF SENTIMENT FOR ME [IT BE]	I SEND YOU A DECREPIT	1324	6
SENTIMENTS			
MY SENTIMENTS TO SHARE--	BESIDES THE AUTUMN POETS	131	14
OF SENTIMENTS SEDITIOUS	THE WAY TO KNOW THE	1279	9
SENTINELS			
FROM NATURE'S SENTINELS--	TO MY QUICK EAR THE	891	4
SEPAL			
A SEPAL, PETAL, AND A THORN	A SEPAL, PETAL, AND A	19	1
SEPARATE			
CHRIST WILL EXPLAIN EACH SEPARATE ANGUISH	I SHALL KNOW WHY--WHEN	193	3
AS SEPARATE AS SEA	THEY PUT US FAR APART--	474	2
AND PUT THEM EACH IN SEPARATE DRAWERS,	IF YOU WERE COMING IN	511	7
POSSESS EACH SEPARATE CONSCIOUSNESS--	NO CROWD THAT HAS	515	15
SET SEPARATE [PUT QUIET--] FROM THE FARMING--	I'M SORRY FOR THE DEAD--	529	15
AND EVERY SEPARATE URCHIN'S SUM--	'TIS ONE BY ONE--THE	545	15
NOR SEPARATE, HERSELF AND ME	HERE, WHERE THE DAISIES	1037	9
SEPARATED			
OF THE SEPARATED PARTIES [PEOPLE]	THREE WEEKS PASSED SINCE	1061	11
SEPARATING			
WITH SEPARATING FRIENDS	THE MURMURING OF BEES,	1115	12
SEPARATION			
HIS SEPARATION FROM HIS ROSE--	IT MAKES NO DIFFERENCE	620	11
SEPARATION'S			
LIKE SEPARATION'S SWELL	A WIND THAT ROSE	1259	7
BY SEPARATION'S SORCERY	THE SADDEST NOISE, THE	1764	11

	FIRST LINE	POEM	LINE
SEPTEMBER'S			
SEPTEMBER'S BACCALAUREATE	SEPTEMBER'S	1271	1
SEPULCHRAL			
WHOSE SHORT--SEPULCHRAL BASS	THE LIGHTNING PLAYETH--	630	6
PRESENT ME FROM SEPULCHRAL CREASE	HER LITTLE PARASOL TO	1038	7
SEPULCHRE			
A SEPULCHRE, FEARS FROST, NO MORE--	'TIS SO APPALLING--IT	281	V 4
TO EYELIDS IN THE SEPULCHRE--	AS FAR FROM PITY, AS	496	9
LOST, IN THE SEPULCHRE--	IF ANYBODY'S FRIEND BE	509	8
A SEPULCHRE OF QUAINTEST FLOSS--	HE PARTS HIMSELF--LIKE	517	19
A WONDER IF THE SEPULCHRE	I'M SORRY FOR THE DEAD--	529	17
YOU CANNOT SOLDER AN ABYSS [PLUG A SEPULCHRE]	TO FILL A GAP	546	5
THE SEPULCHRE, COULD HIDE.	MY FIRST WELL DAY--SINCE	574	16
UNTARNISHED BY THE SEPULCHRE,	OF NEARNESS TO HER	607	7
NO BANKRUPTCY [SEPULCHRE / WILDERNESS]--NO DOOM--	I THINK TO LIVE--MAY BE	646	16
IN SPICELESS SEPULCHRE.	ESSENTIAL OILS--ARE	675	V 8
A SEPULCHRE, BETWEEN--	HEREIN A BLOSSOM LIES--	899	2
HOW FAR LEFT HAND THE SEPULCHRE	HOW FAR IS IT TO HEAVEN?	929	7
TO THE SEPULCHRE--	"SECRETS" IS A DAILY	1385	12
SEPULTURE			
THAT SEPULTURE IS O'ER.	THE DANDELION'S PALLID	1519	8
SEQUEL			
A SPECIES [SEQUEL] STANDS BEYOND--	THIS WORLD IS NOT	501	2
SEQUENCE			
BUT SEQUENCE RAVELLED OUT OF SOUND [REACH]	I FELT A CLEAVING IN MY	937	7
BUT SEQUENCE RAVELLED OUT OF SOUND	THE DUST BEHIND I STROVE	992	3
SEQUESTERED			
SEQUESTERED FROM DECAY	LEFT IN IMMORTAL YOUTH	1289	6
SEQUESTERED AFTERNOON--	AS IMPERCEPTIBLY AS	1540	8
SERAPH			
SUMMER--SISTER--SERAPH!	THE GENTIAN WEAVES HER	18	15
SAUCY, SAUCY SERAPH	GOOD NIGHT, BECAUSE WE	114	5
SERAPHIC			
KEEP THEIR SERAPHIC MAY--	THERE IS A MORN BY MEN	24	3
SNUG IN SERAPHIC CUPBOARDS	PAPA ABOVE!	61	6
OR THAT ETHERIAL [SERAPHIC] GAIN	MY FIRST WELL DAY--SINCE	574	26
BUT HIS SERAPHIC SELF--	BEFORE YOU THOUGHT OF	1465	16
SERAPHIC FEAR--	NOT SEEING, STILL WE	1518	6
SERAPHIM			
AND CHERUBIM--AND SERAPHIM--	'TWAS A LONG PARTING--	625	15
THAT WAFTS THE SERAPHIM--	TO HER DERIDED HOME	1586	12
SERAPH'S			
PINIONS--THE SERAPH'S WAGON	THE FEET OF PEOPLE	7	11
SERAPHS			
PIGMY SERAPHS--GONE ASTRAY--	PIGMY SERAPHS--GONE	138	1
TILL SERAPHS SWING THEIR SNOWY HATS--	I TASTE A LIQUOR NEVER	214	13
SERE SEE SEAR			
OF SUNSHINE--AND OF SERE--COMPOSED--	OF BRUSSELS--IT WAS NOT	602	11
EARLY AND SERE, IT'S END	AND THIS OF ALL MY HOPES	913	4
A FIELD OF STUBBLE, LYING SERE	A FIELD OF STUBBLE,	1407	1
LEST CERTAINTY BE SERE	SWEET SKEPTICISM OF THE	1413	6
WHEN NIGHTS ARE HOT AND SERE--	A WINGED SPARK DOTH SOAR	1468	4
SERENE			
EVER SERENE AND FAIR,	THERE IS ANOTHER SKY,	2	2
NOR SO SERENE ARRAY--	THERE IS A MORN BY MEN	24	15
AND KEEPS THE SOUL SERENE--	IF I SHOULD DIE,	54	16
BUT LARGE--SERENE--	IT KNEW NO LAPSE, NOR	560	2
IN HER SERENE DISPLAY;	THE PARASOL IS THE	1747	6
SERENER			
IN A SERENER BRIGHT,	I HAVE A BIRD IN SPRING	5	19
LARGER THAN MINE--SERENER--	LOW AT MY PROBLEM	69	3
SERFS			
THO' SERFS--SUPPLY THE OIL--	THE LAMP BURNS SURE--	233	2
SERIES			
AND SERIES THAT ARE DONE--	I COULD NOT PROVE THE	563	4
ONE DAY IS THERE OF THE SERIES	ONE DAY IS THERE OF THE	814	1
SERMON			
AND THE SERMON IS NEVER LONG,	SOME KEEP THE SABBATH	324	10
THE DITTY [SERMON] IS THAT NATURE SINGS--	THE WORTHLESSNESS OF	1373	2
CUPID'S SERMON	MINE ENEMY IS GROWING	1509	T
ORPHEUS' SERMON CAPTIVATED--	THE BIBLE IS AN ANTIQUE	1545	15
SERPENT			
SERPENT CANNOT [MAY NOT] CHARM--	WHEN I HOPED I FEARED--	1181	6
SERPENT'S			
THE SERPENT'S SATIN FIGURE	THROUGH LANE IT LAY--	9	7
SERVANT			
YOUR SERVANT, SIR, WILL WEARY--	ALTHOUGH I PUT AWAY HIS	366	22
I HEAR HIM ASK THE SERVANT	AGAIN--HIS VOICE IS AT	663	3
SERVE			
WHO WILL NOT SERVE THE SOVREIGN, BE HANGED ON FATAL TREE.	AWAKE YE MUSES NINE,	1	10
AS THE PALM--THAT SERVE THE DESERT--	HER SWEET TURN TO LEAVE	649	19
AND IF IT SERVE YOU FOR A HOUSE--	THE JUDGE IS LIKE THE	699	7
THE OPINION WILL DO [SERVE]--FOR THEM--	BY MY WINDOW HAVE I FOR	797	4
IN HIM EXISTENCE SERVE OR SET	ALL CIRCUMSTANCES ARE	820	7
WOULD YOU SERVE [SEEK] IT SO?	NONE WHO SAW IT EVER	1110	8
WE ARE NOT SCOURGED TO SERVE--	HOW FLEET--HOW	1771	4
SERVED			
FOR YOU--SERVED HEAVEN--YOU KNOW,	I CANNOT LIVE WITH YOU--	640	30

	FIRST LINE	POEM	LINE
SERVED (CONTINUED)			
WHY FLOODS BE SERVED TO US--IN BOWLS--	ONE BLESSING HAD I THAN	756	19
SERVICE			
WHAT SERVICE WHEN WE PAUSE!	ONE DIGNITY DELAYS FOR	98	10
SOME--THINK IT SERVICE IN THE PLACE	MUSICIANS WRESTLE	157	16
A SERVICE, LIKE A DRUM--	I FELT A FUNERAL, IN MY	280	6
THEN I--MY TIMID SERVICE DONE--	I THINK THE LONGEST HOUR	635	13
THO' SERVICE 'TWAS, OF LOVE--	I THINK THE LONGEST HOUR	635	14
WHOSE SERVICE--IS TO YOU--	SWEET MOUNTAINS--YE TELL	722	9
THE SERVICE WITHOUT HOPE--	THE SERVICE WITHOUT HOPE	779	1
SEVERER SERVICE OF MYSELF	SEVERER SERVICE OF	786	1
HIS SERVICE TO THE NEWEST GRACE	OF SILKEN SPEECH AND	896	3
NO SERVICE HAST THOU, I WOULD NOT ACHIEVE [ATTEMPT] IT--	WERT THOU BUT ILL--THAT	961	17
THE SERVICE EMPHASIZE;	FURTHER IN SUMMER THAN	1068	V
FOR SERVICE [HONOR / WELCOME] OR FOR GLEE--	A CHILLY PEACE INFESTS	1443	6
OR SERVICE OF A KEEL	AS IMPERCEPTIBLY AS	1540	14
SERVICES			
FOR OTHER SERVICES [PURPOSES]--AS SOUND--	THE SPIRIT IS THE	733	5
AND SERVICES OF SNOW.	I CANNOT BE ASHAMED	914	10
OUR MOST IGNOBLE SERVICES	WHO GOES TO DINE MUST	1223	7
SERVILE			
"CROWNS OF LIFE" ARE SERVILE PRIZES	"FAITHFUL TO THE END"	1357	5
SESSION			
ELDER, TODAY, A SESSION WISER	A LOSS OF SOMETHING EVER	959	9
THE HOUR [SESSION] OF HER BUD--	CRISIS IS SWEET AND YET	1416	V 8
SESSIONS			
HOW CHIEF THY SESSIONS BE--	HOW MUCH OF SOURCE	1517	2
SET			
SET BLEEDING FEET TO MINUETS	HEART, NOT SO HEAVY AS	83	15
IN VANISHED FASHIONS SET!	IN EBON BOX, WHEN YEARS	169	16
BUT HOW HE SET--I KNOW NOT--	I'LL TELL YOU HOW THE	318	9
THEIR EVERLASTING FASHIONS--SET--	WHILE ASTERS--	331	3
HER EVERLASTING FASHION--SET--	IT WILL BE SUMMER--	342	15
TO DRINK--OR SET AWAY	EXHILIRATION--IS WITHIN	383	6
SET ORDERLY, FOR BURIAL,	IT WAS NOT DEATH, FOR I	510	11
SET SEPARATE [PUT QUIET--] FROM THE FARMING--	I'M SORRY FOR THE DEAD--	529	15
SET CYPHERLESS--TO TEACH THE EYE	'TIS ONE BY ONE--THE	545	3
LIFE SET ME LARGER--PROBLEMS--	IT TROUBLED ME AS ONCE I	600	9
HE FOUND MY BEING--SET IT UP--	HE FOUND MY BEING--SET	603	1
NO LIFETIME SET--ON THEM--	'TWAS A LONG PARTING--	625	9
YOU'VE SEEN BALLOONS SET--HAV'NT YOU?	YOU'VE SEEN BALLOONS SET	700	1
A LAMP FOR EACH--TO SET--	THE SUNRISE RUNS FOR	710	8
THAT ARISE AND SET ABOUT US--	DRAMA'S VITALLEST	741	2
IT'S PAST--SET DOWN BEFORE THE SOUL	REMORSE--IS MEMORY--	744	5
UPON HIS INFANT FACE WAS SET	HE TOLD A HOMELY TALE	763	3
AFTER SUN HAS [WHEN THE SUN IS] SET--	WHEN I HOPED, I	768	20
SO SET IT'S SUN IN THEE	SO SET IT'S SUN IN THEE	808	1
IN WHICH HIS FACE IS SET--	ALL CIRCUMSTANCES ARE	820	2
IN HIM EXISTENCE SERVE OR SET	ALL CIRCUMSTANCES ARE	820	7
AND SET MY KERNEL IN.	I HEARD, AS IF I HAD NO	1039	12
WHOSE [WHERE] SUMMER SET IN SUMMER, TILL	THERE IS A ZONE WHOSE	1056	5
THE PURPLE IN THE EAST IS SET	THESE ARE THE SIGNS TO	1077	11
AND SET THE SUN	THE CRICKETS SANG	1104	2
IN VILLAGES REMOTELY SET	THE FROST WAS NEVER SEEN	1202	7
AND TILL DOMINION SET	THE MOST TRIUMPHANT BIRD	1265	3
THE SECOND TIME IS SET	FAME IS A FICKLE FOOD	1659	5
I SET ME DOWN	IN WINTER IN MY ROOM	1670	38
SETS			
IT SETS THE FRIGHT AT LIBERTY--	'TIS SO APPALLING--IT	281	22
DEATH SETS A THING SIGNIFICANT	DEATH SETS A THING	360	1
AND WHEN THIS WORLD--SETS FURTHER BACK--	YOU'LL FIND--IT WHEN YOU	610	9
PERCEPTION SETS IT FAIR	PERCEPTION OF AN OBJECT	1071	6
SETTEST			
THOU SETTEST [STIRREST] EARTHQUAKE IN THE SOUTH--	AT LEAST--TO PRAY--IS	502	5
SETTING			
DUKES--FOR SETTING SUN!	MORNING--IS THE PLACE	197	4
AT THE SETTING SUN--	GOD PERMITS INDUSTRIOUS	231	6
BY THE WIZARD [SETTING] SUN--	HOW THE OLD MOUNTAINS	291	4
AND SENSE WAS SETTING NUMB--	'TWAS LIKE A MAELSTROM,	414	15
EACH OTHER'S SETTING--SAW--	THEY PUT US FAR APART--	474	24
BE SETTING ON HIS PROGRESS--	NO MAN CAN COMPASS A	477	7
THE SUN KEPT SETTING--SETTING--STILL	THE SUN KEPT SETTING--	692	1
THE SUN KEPT SETTING--SETTING--STILL	THE SUN KEPT SETTING--	692	1
WE PASSED THE SETTING SUN--	BECAUSE I COULD NOT STOP	712	12
AT SETTING--THIS AND AMBER--	THE COLOR OF A QUEEN, IS	776	3
UPON THEIR SETTING NAMES--	FAME IS THE TINT THAT	866	2
BEST--AT SETTING--AS IS NATURE'S--	STRUCK, WAS I, NOR YET	925	21
AFFLICTS ME--AS A SETTING SUN--	I LEARNED--AT LEAST--	944	30
DELIGHT'S DESPAIR AT SETTING	DELIGHT'S DESPAIR AT	1299	1
I'D RATHER RECOLLECT A SETTING	I'D RATHER RECOLLECT A	1349	1
TILL WITH THE SETTING [CLOSING] SUN	IT WAS A QUIET SEEMING	1419	3
AND SETTING IT UPRIGHT	YOU CANNOT MAKE	1508	4
SETTLE			
OR SETTLE IN THE MOON--	HE PARTS HIMSELF--LIKE	517	12
SETTLED			
MYSELF--FOR SCARCELY SETTLED--	THE WINTERS ARE SO SHORT	403	5
UNTIL IT SETTLED BROAD [FULL / FIRM]--ON PARADISE--	TO KNOW JUST HOW HE	622	4

	FIRST LINE	POEM	LINE
SETTLED (CONTINUED)			
SYSTEMS--SETTLED IN THEIR SOCKETS--	ALL BUT DEATH, CAN BE	749	3
'TWAS SETTLED, SO THEY SAY, ...	WHO OCCUPIES THIS HOUSE?	892	18
ARE SETTLED, AND AT WORK--	BEE! I'M EXPECTING YOU!	1035	6
OR SETTLED REGIONS WILD--	I NOTICED PEOPLE	1149	4
AND SETTLED REGIONS WILD	I NOTICED PEOPLE	1149	6
HAVE SETTLED WITH THE YEAR!--	HOW DARE THE ROBINS SING	1724	4
SETTLEMENT			
AND FROM A SETTLEMENT	WHO OCCUPIES THIS HOUSE?	892	25
SETTLER			
UNBROKEN BY A SETTLER--	MY PERIOD HAD COME FOR	564	13
NO SETTLER HAD THE MIND.	SOTO! EXPLORE THYSELF!	832	4
SETTLERS			
SETTLERS OFTEN DO	WHO OCCUPIES THIS HOUSE?	892	22
SETTLES			
AND SETTLES IN THE HILLS--	"HEAVEN" HAS DIFFERENT	575	6
SEVEN			
AT HALF PAST SEVEN, ELEMENT	AT HALF PAST THREE, A	1084	9
SEVEN YEARS OF TROTH HAVE TAUGHT THEE . .	REARRANGE A "WIFE'S"	1737	7
SEVENTEENTH			
THE SEVENTEENTH; REPLY	BEE! I'M EXPECTING YOU!	1035	10
SEVENTY			
SEVENTY YEARS IS SPENT AS QUICK	SUMMER IS SHORTER THAN	1506	3
SEVERAL			
I FINISHED TWO--AND SEVERAL STARS--	I SEND TWO SUNSETS--	308	3
PROPORTIONED TO HIS SEVERAL DEARTH . . .	THERE IS A FLOWER THAT	380	7
TRIUMPH--MAY BE OF SEVERAL KINDS-- . . .	TRIUMPH--MAY BE OF	455	1
SEVERAL OF NATURE'S PEOPLE	A NARROW FELLOW IN THE	986	17
THE THINGS THAT NEVER CAN COME BACK, ARE SEVERAL--	THE THINGS THAT NEVER	1515	1
SEVERALLY			
THEY SEVERALLY--RETARD--OR FURTHER [PROMOTE--OR HINDER]--	FOUR TREES--UPON A	742	15
SEVERE			
HIS HABIT--IS SEVERE--	THERE IS A LANGUOR OF	396	10
MAKING THAT HOMELY, AND SEVERE, ...	LIKE FLOWERS, THAT HEARD	513	11
TO HIM WHO STRIVES SEVERE	THE HALLOWING OF PAIN	772	5
PUTS ITSELF SEVERE AWAY	SAFE DESPAIR IT IS THAT	1243	3
OR VALUES MORE SEVERE--	THE LOOK OF THEE, WHAT	1689	8
SEVERELY			
FOR TRAINS THAT MOMENT [SEVERELY] OUT OF SIGHT,	THE SUMMER THAT WE DID	1773	7
SEVERER			
SEVERER TRIUMPH--BY HIMSELF	TRIUMPH--MAY BE OF	455	13
SEVERER SERVICE OF MYSELF	SEVERER SERVICE OF	786	1
SEVEREST			
WITH THAT SEVEREST GOLD	THROUGH THOSE OLD	1753	14
SEVERITY			
WITH SUCH SEVERITY	NO BRIGADIER THROUGHOUT	1561	12
SEVRES			
A NEWER SEVRES PLEASES--	I CANNOT LIVE WITH YOU--	640	11
SEWED			
A SPIDER SEWED AT NIGHT	A SPIDER SEWED AT NIGHT	1138	1
SEWING			
AND STRUTS IN SEWING SILK!	A FUZZY FELLOW, WITHOUT	173	12
SEXTON			
SEXTON! MY MASTER'S SLEEPING HERE.	SEXTON! MY MASTER'S	96	1
OUR LITTLE SEXTON--SINGS.	SOME KEEP THE SABBATH	324	8
THE SEXTON KEEPS THE KEY TO--	I CANNOT LIVE WITH YOU--	640	5
SHACKLES			
WITH SHACKLES [IRONS] ON THE PLUMED FEET, .	THE SOUL HAS BANDAGED	512	21
SHADE			
A SHADE UPON THE MIND THERE PASSES . . .	A SHADE UPON THE MIND	882	1
I COULD HAVE BORNE THE SHADE	HAD I NOT SEEN THE SUN	1233	2
AND SHADE IS ALL THAT DEVASTATES THE STILLNESS	THESE FEVERED DAYS--TO	1441	3
SHADOW			
OF SHADOW, OR OF SQUIRREL, HAPLY--	FOUR TREES--UPON A	742	11
PRESENTIMENT--IS THAT LONG SHADOW--ON THE LAWN--	PRESENTIMENT--IS THAT	764	1
OH SHADOW ON THE GRASS, ...	OH SHADOW ON THE GRASS,	1187	1
OH SHADOW ON THE GRASS	OH SHADOW ON THE GRASS,	1187	5
SHADOWS			
AND SHADOWS TREMBLE SO--	HAVE YOU GOT A BROOK IN	136	4
SHADOWS--HOLD THEIR BREATH--	THERE'S A CERTAIN SLANT	258	14
LIKE MEN AND WOMEN SHADOWS WALK	LIKE MEN AND WOMEN	1105	1
OF SHADOWS [RIPPLES] GOING DOWN	A STAGNANT PLEASURE LIKE	1281	6
THESE [THE] SHADOWS SCRUTINIZE--	A CHILLY PEACE INFESTS	1443	4
NOW SHADOWS IN THE TOMB.	SWEET HOURS HAVE	1767	4
SHADY			
A SHADY FRIEND--FOR TORRID DAYS--	A SHADY FRIEND--FOR	278	1
SHAFT			
A SPOTTED SHAFT IS SEEN--	A NARROW FELLOW IN THE	986	6
THE CIRCUMVENTION OF THE SHAFT [THOUGHT / SITE / FACT]	AS SUMMER INTO AUTUMN	1346	11
THE SHAFT THAT NEVER KNEW--	SHE LAID HER DOCILE	1396	6
A CHILL CAME UP AS FROM A SHAFT	A CAP OF LEAD ACROSS THE	1649	5
SHAFTS			
COOL US TO SHAFTS OF GRANITE--	WE DREAM--IT IS GOOD WE	531	13
SHAGGIER			
IN SHAGGIER VEST--	ONE YEAR AGO--JOTS WHAT?	296	20

	FIRST LINE	POEM	LINE
SHARPEST (CONTINUED)			
DEATH'S WAYLAYING NOT THE SHARPEST . . .	DEATH'S WAYLAYING NOT	1296	1
SHATTER			
AND SHATTER [FLOOD] ME WITH DAWN!	AS IF I ASKED A COMMON	323	8
BUT--DID HE SHATTER--IT?	HE STRAINED MY FAITH--	497	6
SHATTERED			
SUN--IF SHONE--OR STORM--IF SHATTERED-- . .	ALL FORGOT FOR	966	11
SHAVEN			
AS IF MY LIFE WERE SHAVEN, ...	IT WAS NOT DEATH, FOR I	510	13
SHAW			
I RETAIN "SHAW"!	I HAD SOME THINGS THAT I	116	16
SHAWL			
I TIE MY HAT--I CREASE MY SHAWL--	I TIE MY HAT--I CREASE	443	1
NOT MERINO SHAWL--	WHEN I HOPED, I	768	8
SHAME IS THE SHAWL OF PINK	SHAME IS THE SHAWL OF	1412	1
OR DEEPER COLOR IN THE SHAWL	SUMMER BEGINS TO HAVE	1682	7
A WOMAN'S SHAWL AS BIG	THE SUN RETIRED TO A	1693	2
SHE			
NO MORE HE SINGETH MOURNFUL, HER SADNESS SHE DOTH LOSE.	AWAKE YE MUSES NINE,	1	20
AND HARRIET, AND SUSAN, AND SHE WITH CURLING HAIR!	AWAKE YE MUSES NINE,	1	32
AND GIVE HER WHAT SHE ASKETH, JEWEL, OR BIRD, OR FLOWER--	AWAKE YE MUSES NINE,	1	38
THE CROCUS--TILL SHE RISES	THE FEET OF PEOPLE	7	3
SHE DID NOT SING AS WE DID--	ONE SISTER HAVE I IN OUR	14	9
SHE BECKONS, AND THE WOODS START--	BAFFLED FOR JUST A DAY	17	5
SHE NODS, AND ALL BEGIN--	BAFFLED FOR JUST A DAY	17	6
WE TRUST THAT SHE WAS WILLING--	THE GENTIAN WEAVES HER	18	13
SHE SLEPT BENEATH A TREE--	SHE SLEPT BENEATH A TREE	25	1
SHE RECOGNIZED THE FOOT--	SHE SLEPT BENEATH A TREE	25	4
NOONS LIKE THESE--SHE ROSE--	MORNS LIKE THESE--WE	27	2
NEVER DID SHE LISP IT--	MORNS LIKE THESE--WE	27	5
SHE--WAS MUTE FROM TRANSPORT--	MORNS LIKE THESE--WE	27	7
SHE WILL STIR HER PINIONS	IT DID NOT SURPRISE ME--	39	3
IF SHE HAD BEEN THE MISTLETOE	IF SHE HAD BEEN THE	44	1
AND SHE IS OF THE DEW--	IF SHE HAD BEEN THE	44	6
WHETHER SHE MET WITH GALES--	WHETHER MY BARK WENT	52	2
SHE BENT HER DOCILE SAILS--	WHETHER MY BARK WENT	52	4
SHE IS HELD TODAY--	WHETHER MY BARK WENT	52	6
DELAYED TILL SHE HAD CEASED TO KNOW-- . .	DELAYED TILL SHE HAD	58	1
COULD SHE HAVE GUESSED THAT IT WOULD BE-- .	DELAYED TILL SHE HAD	58	7
MARTIAL AS SHE!	LIKE HER THE SAINTS	60	3
YET SHE CANNOT SPEAK.	GLOWING IS HER BONNET,	72	4
SHE DIED AT PLAY, ...	SHE DIED AT PLAY,	75	1
YET IS SHE MORE CONVINCING	THE RAINBOW NEVER TELLS	97	3
HER BUSY FOOT SHE PLIED--	WHOSE ARE THE LITTLE	142	18
THEIR BEDTIME 'TIS, SHE SAID--	WHOSE ARE THE LITTLE	142	26
SHE BORE IT TILL THE SIMPLE VEINS	SHE BORE IT TILL THE	144	1
AND THEN SHE CEASED TO BEAR IT--	SHE BORE IT TILL THE	144	7
SHE REACHED THE ASPHODEL!	ALL OVERGROWN BY CUNNING	148	V
SHE WENT AS QUIET AS THE DEW	SHE WENT AS QUIET AS THE	149	1
NOT LIKE THE DEW, DID SHE RETURN	SHE WENT AS QUIET AS THE	149	3
SHE DROPT AS SOFTLY AS A STAR	SHE WENT AS QUIET AS THE	149	5
SHE DIED--THIS WAS THE WAY SHE DIED. . . .	SHE DIED--THIS WAS THE	150	1
SHE DIED--THIS WAS THE WAY SHE DIED. . . .	SHE DIED--THIS WAS THE	150	1
EXCEPT TO HEAVEN, SHE IS NOUGHT.	EXCEPT TO HEAVEN, SHE IS	154	1
THO' SHE WEAR A SILVER APRON--	THO' MY DESTINY BE	163	3
SHE LOOKS DOWN JUST AS OFTEN	MAMA NEVER FORGETS HER	164	3
WITH CUNNING CARE SHE WOVE--	MAMA NEVER FORGETS HER	164	6
SHE "NOTICES," ABOVE.	MAMA NEVER FORGETS HER	164	8
WHO KNOWS BUT SHE WOULD TELL?	THE SKIES CANT KEEP	191	8
SHE SWEEPS WITH MANY-COLORED BROOMS-- . .	SHE SWEEPS WITH	219	1
AND STILL, SHE PLIES HER SPOTTED BROOMS, [THRIFT]	SHE SWEEPS WITH	219	9
SHE FELT HERSELF SUPREMER--	THE SUN--JUST TOUCHED	232	5
AND SHE WILL FLING HER MADDEST PERFUME-- .	KILL YOUR BALM--AND IT'S	238	3
WAS--THAT SHE MIGHT--	DOUBT ME! MY DIM	275	15
SHE KNOWS HERSELF AN INCENSE [OFFERING] SMALL--	THE DROP, THAT WRESTLES	284	4
YET SMALL--SHE SIGHS--IF ALL--IS ALL-- . .	THE DROP, THAT WRESTLES	284	5
BUT SHE, FORGETTING AMPHITRITE--	THE DROP, THAT WRESTLES	284	8
UNMOVED--SHE NOTES THE CHARIOTS--PAUSING-- .	THE SOUL SELECTS HER OWN	303	5
OR SHE--HERSELF--ASCENDED	THE SOUL'S SUPERIOR	306	5
SUFFICIENT TROTH, THAT WE SHALL [SHE WILL] RISE--	THERE CAME A DAY AT	322	25
SHE--EACH YEAR--LEADS HER DAISIES BACK-- .	I KNOW A PLACE WHERE	337	3
AND SHE POURS SOFT REFRAINS	I KNOW A PLACE WHERE	337	8
THIS--WAS THE TOWN--SHE PASSED--	'TWAS THE OLD--ROAD--	344	5
THERE--WHERE SHE--RESTED--LAST--	'TWAS THE OLD--ROAD--	344	6
BUT SHE SLEPT--	I WENT TO THANK HER--	363	2
BUT SHE SLEPT--	I WENT TO THANK HER--	363	7
IT [SHE] QUIVERS FROM THE FORGE	DARE YOU SEE A SOUL AT	365	6
SHE LAY AS IF AT PLAY	SHE LAY AS IF AT PLAY	369	1
WITH "THIS WAS SHE--	I'M SAYING EVERY DAY	373	7
SHE DOTH NOT WAIT FOR JUNE--	THERE IS A FLOWER THAT	380	13
SHE SAID HER STRINGS WERE SNAPT--	THE FIRST DAY'S NIGHT	410	5
BUT SHE, AND DEATH, ACQUAINTED--	I READ MY SENTENCE--	412	11
SHE LEADS HIM--DOCILE AS A BOY--	THE MOON IS DISTANT FROM	429	3
BUT--COULD SHE [IT] TEACH--IT?	KNOWS HOW TO FORGET!	433	2

SHE (CONTINUED)

	FIRST LINE	POEM	LINE
FORGOT SHE WORE IT AT HER HEART	FORGET! THE LADY WITH	438	2
BECAUSE SHE BREATHED AGAINST	FORGET! THE LADY WITH	438	3
I [HE] SHOWED HER [ME] HIGHTS SHE [I] NEVER SAW--	I SHOWED HER HIGHTS SHE	446	1
SHE [I] SAID--"NOT SO"--	I SHOWED HER HIGHTS SHE	446	3
SHE [I] COULD NOT FIND HER [MY] YES--	I SHOWED HER HIGHTS SHE	446	8
AND COULD SHE [I], FURTHER, "NO"?	I SHOWED HER HIGHTS SHE	446	12
SHE DEALT HER PRETTY WORDS LIKE BLADES--	SHE DEALT HER PRETTY	479	1
SHE NEVER DEEMED--SHE HURT--	SHE DEALT HER PRETTY	479	5
SHE NEVER DEEMED--SHE HURT--	SHE DEALT HER PRETTY	479	5
SHE CANNOT KEEP HER PLACE.	"WHY DO I LOVE" YOU, SIR	480	5
SHE FETCHES--SUCH AS ME	MY GARDEN--LIKE THE	484	5
SHE WAS CONSCIOUS--	CIVILIZATION--SPURNS--	492	6
TELL HIM [HER]--JUST HOW SHE SEALED YOU--CAUTIOUS!	GOING TO HIM! HAPPY	494	22
BUT--IF HE [SHE] ASK WHERE YOU ARE HID	GOING TO HIM! HAPPY	494	23
SHE SIGHTS A BIRD--SHE CHUCKLES--	SHE SIGHTS A BIRD--SHE	507	1
SHE SIGHTS A BIRD--SHE CHUCKLES--	SHE SIGHTS A BIRD--SHE	507	1
SHE FLATTENS--THEN SHE CRAWLS--	SHE SIGHTS A BIRD--SHE	507	2
SHE FLATTENS--THEN SHE CRAWLS--	SHE SIGHTS A BIRD--SHE	507	2
SHE RUNS WITHOUT THE LOOK OF FEET--	SHE SIGHTS A BIRD--SHE	507	3
SHE LEAPS, BUT ROBIN LEAPED THE FIRST--	SHE SIGHTS A BIRD--SHE	507	7
SHE FEELS SOME GHASTLY FRIGHT COME UP	THE SOUL HAS BANDAGED	512	3
SHE DANCES LIKE A BOMB, ABROAD,	THE SOUL HAS BANDAGED	512	13
THEN RECOLLECT A BALL, SHE GOT--	HER SMILE WAS SHAPED	514	5
SHE'S TEARFUL--IF SHE WEEP AT ALL--	SHE'S HAPPY, WITH A NEW	535	5
SHE HIDETH HER THE LAST--	SHE HIDETH HER THE LAST	557	1
SHE DOTH HER PURPLE WORK--	SHE HIDETH HER THE LAST	557	5
HER BEAUTY--IS THE LOVE SHE DOTH--	BUT LITTLE CARMINE HATH	558	3
SHE PUT SOME FLOWERS AWAY--	MY FIRST WELL DAY--SINCE	574	10
TO CHEAT HERSELF, IT SEEMED SHE TRIED--	MY FIRST WELL DAY--SINCE	574	13
SHE DEALT A [THE] FASHION TO THE NUT--	MY FIRST WELL DAY--SINCE	574	17
SHE TIED THE HOODS TO SEEDS--	MY FIRST WELL DAY--SINCE	574	18
SHE DROPPED BRIGHT SCRAPS OF TINT, ABOUT--	MY FIRST WELL DAY--SINCE	574	19
ON EVERY SHOULDER THAT SHE MET [SHE COULD REACH]--	MY FIRST WELL DAY--SINCE	574	21
ON EVERY SHOULDER THAT SHE MET [SHE COULD REACH]--	MY FIRST WELL DAY--SINCE	574	21
SO WHEN SHE COMES THIS WAY,	I CRIED AT PITY--NOT AT	588	18
HOW PLEASANTER--SAID SHE	THE NIGHT WAS WIDE, AND	589	18
SHE STOPPED--A TRAVELLER'S PRIVILEGE--FOR REST--	I WATCHED THE MOON	629	3
NOR FORMULA--HAD SHE--	I WATCHED THE MOON	629	12
NO HUNGER--HAD SHE--NOR AN INN--	I WATCHED THE MOON	629	21
SHE VAULTED OUT OF GAZE--	I WATCHED THE MOON	629	32
SHE WORE WHEN SHE WAS BORN--	YOU'LL KNOW HER--BY HER	634	12
SHE WORE WHEN SHE WAS BORN--	YOU'LL KNOW HER--BY HER	634	12
BUT AS SHE CLOSER STANDS--	YOU'LL KNOW HER--BY HER	634	16
SHE SQUANDERS ON YOUR HEAD [EAR]	YOU'LL KNOW HER--BY HER	634	25
DENY SHE IS A ROBIN--NOW--	YOU'LL KNOW HER--BY HER	634	V 27
LOOK--IF SHE SHOULD KNOW	SO MUCH SUMMER	651	8
SHE DWELLETH IN THE GROUND--	SHE DWELLETH IN THE	671	1
AND SHE HAD PAST, WITH [FLED WITH / TRUSTED / HEARKENED] HIM--	I MEANT TO FIND HER WHEN	718	8
PRECIOUS TO ME--SHE STILL SHALL BE--	PRECIOUS TO ME--SHE	727	1
THOUGH SHE FORGET THE NAME I BEAR--	PRECIOUS TO ME--SHE	727	2
IF HAPLY--SHE MIGHT NOT DESPISE	PRECIOUS TO ME--SHE	727	7
SHE ROSE TO HIS REQUIREMENT--DROPT	SHE ROSE TO HIS	732	1
IF OUGHT SHE MISSED IN HER NEW DAY,	SHE ROSE TO HIS	732	5
AND NOW SHE TURNS HER PERFECT FACE	THE MOON WAS BUT A CHIN	737	3
UPON HER FRIEND SHE COULD CONFER [BESTOW]	THE MOON WAS BUT A CHIN	737	11
FOR CERTAINTY SHE TAKE HER WAY	THE MOON WAS BUT A CHIN	737	15
SHE DREW AWAY AUSTERE--	THE BIRDS REPORTED FROM	743	14
SHE SUFFERED ME, FOR I HAD MOURNED--	THE BIRDS REPORTED FROM	743	17
I [SHE] NEVER QUESTIONED HER [ME]--	THE BIRDS REPORTED FROM	743	22
MOST SHE TOUCHED ME BY HER MUTENESS--	MOST SHE TOUCHED ME BY	760	1
MOST SHE WON ME BY THE WAY	MOST SHE TOUCHED ME BY	760	2
SHE PRESENTED HER SMALL FIGURE--	MOST SHE TOUCHED ME BY	760	3
SHE EASES FROM HER TEETH	THE WHOLE OF IT CAME NOT	762	6
WHEN SHE HAD PUT AWAY HER WORK	SEVERER SERVICE OF	786	7
SHE TURNS AS LONG AWAY	NATURE--THE GENTLEST	790	18
SO BUSY WAS SHE--FINISHING--	HER FINAL SUMMER WAS IT	795	15
SHE STAKED HER FEATHERS--GAINED AN ARC--	SHE STAKED HER FEATHERS	798	1
SHE STAKED HER WINGS--AND GAINED A BUSH--	SHE STAKED HER FEATHERS	798	V 1
THE BOUGH WHERE SHE WAS BORN--	SHE STAKED HER FEATHERS	798	8
NO NOTICE GAVE SHE, BUT A CHANGE--	NO NOTICE GAVE SHE, BUT	804	1
THAT SHE SHOULD [COULD] SPECIFY.	NO NOTICE GAVE SHE, BUT	804	4
SHE WAS NOT WARM, THOUGH SUMMER SHONE	NO NOTICE GAVE SHE, BUT	804	5
OF SHRINKING WAYS--SHE DID NOT [FOREBORE HER] FRIGHT	NO NOTICE GAVE SHE, BUT	804	9
HER WARM [STRAIGHT / GOOD / QUICK / SAFE] RETURN, IF SO SHE . . .	NO NOTICE GAVE SHE, BUT	804	17
AS SOME [US] SHE NEVER KNEW--	NO NOTICE GAVE SHE, BUT	804	20
HER GRACE IS ALL SHE HAS--	HER GRACE IS ALL SHE HAS	810	1
WE PASS, AND SHE ABIDES.	THE VEINS OF OTHER	811	5
WHILE SHE CREATES AND FEDERATES	THE VEINS OF OTHER	811	7
TO THIS WORLD SHE RETURNED.	TO THIS WORLD SHE	830	1
FROM US SHE WANDERED NOW A YEAR,	FROM US SHE WANDERED NOW	890	1
HE'LL SIGH--"THE OTHER--[REAL ONE]	FITTER TO SEE HIM, I MAY	968	20

	FIRST LINE	POEM	LINE
SHE (CONTINUED)			
SHE--IS WHERE?"			
SHE SPED AS PETALS OF [FROM] A ROSE	SHE SPED AS PETALS OF A	991	1
SHE HAD BEGUN TO LIE--	SHE SPED AS PETALS OF A	991	8
SHE ROSE AS HIGH AS HIS OCCASION	SHE ROSE AS HIGH AS HIS	1011	1
SHE FELLED--HE DID NOT FALL--	FATE SLEW HIM, BUT HE	1031	2
SHE STUNG HIM--SAPPED HIS FIRM ADVANCE--	FATE SLEW HIM, BUT HE	1031	5
SAVES SHE ALL OF THAT FOR SUNSETS	NATURE RARER USES YELLOW	1045	3
YELLOW SHE AFFORDS	NATURE RARER USES YELLOW	1045	6
AND AS [WHEN] SHE VANISHES, REMORSE	I CANNOT MEET THE SPRING	1051	7
IS SHE SO MUCH TO BLAME?	IF NATURE SMILES--THE	1085	4
THE LAST NIGHT THAT SHE LIVED	THE LAST NIGHT THAT SHE	1100	1
WHILE SHE MUST FINISH QUITE	THE LAST NIGHT THAT SHE	1100	14
WE WAITED WHILE SHE PASSED--	THE LAST NIGHT THAT SHE	1100	17
SHE MENTIONED, AND FORGOT--	THE LAST NIGHT THAT SHE	1100	21
HAD WE KNOWN THE TON [WEIGHT / LOAD] SHE BORE	HAD WE KNOWN THE TON SHE	1124	1
BUT SHE STRAIGHTER WALKED FOR FREIGHT	HAD WE KNOWN THE TON SHE	1124	3
THAN WHEN SHE SHOWS HER GARNET TOOTH--	WHEN ETNA BASKS AND	1146	3
WHATEVER IT IS [BE]--SHE HAS TRIED IT--	WHATEVER IT IS--SHE HAS	1204	1
ONLY LEST SHE BE LONELY	WHATEVER IT IS--SHE HAS	1204	9
NOT THAT SHE WAS GONE--	NOW I KNEW I LOST HER--	1219	2
TRAVERSED SHE THOUGH PAUSING	NOW I KNEW I LOST HER--	1219	7
WE WILL PRY AND SEE IF SHE IS FAIR	BECAUSE HE LOVES HER	1229	2
BUT "YOU"--SHE RETURNED WITH VALOR	I SAW THAT THE FLAKE WAS	1267	5
SO PROUD [PLEASED / FAIN] SHE WAS TO DIE	SO PROUD SHE WAS TO DIE	1272	1
OR IT HAS [SHE IS] NONE--	COULD HOPE INSPECT HER	1283	4
OR COULD SHE ONE CONTEMN--	THE MUSHROOM IS THE ELF	1298	18
COULD SHE A SON CONTEMN	THE MUSHROOM IS THE ELF	1298	V 18
THE DAY SHE GOES	THE DAY SHE GOES	1308	1
OR DAY SHE STAYS	THE DAY SHE GOES	1308	2
WHO WAS SHE TO WITHOLD FROM ME	FRIGID AND SWEET HER	1318	7
THAT SHE [HERSELF] COULD NOT FORGIVE	ELIZABETH TOLD ESSEX	1321	2
WE TRUST THAT SHE PARTOOK	ELIZABETH TOLD ESSEX	1321	6
AT PARTING--SHE WAS GOING SOUTH	I SEND YOU A DECREPIT	1324	3
"WE DREAMED IT"? SHE INTERROGATES--	THE SYMPTOM OF THE GALE	1327	15
WHERESOE'ER, OR WAS SHE--[SHE IS / OR AS WAS SHE]	SUMMER LAID HER SIMPLE	1363	7
WHERESOE'ER, OR WAS SHE--[SHE IS / OR AS WAS SHE]	SUMMER LAID HER SIMPLE	1363	7
WHERESOE'ER, OR WAS SHE--[SHE IS / OR AS WAS SHE]	SUMMER LAID HER SIMPLE	1363	7
SHE TAKES [GOES] HER GRACIOUS [SPACIOUS / SUBTLE / SIMPLE / . . .	SUMMER--WE ALL HAVE SEEN	1386	6
SHE [HE] LAID HER [HIS] DOCILE CRESCENT DOWN	SHE LAID HER DOCILE	1396	1
THE NEWS THAT SHE [HE] IS GONE--	SHE LAID HER DOCILE	1396	4
PERHAPS THEY DO [SHE DOES] NOT GO SO FAR	PERHAPS THEY DO NOT GO	1399	1
WHICH RAPTURE [TRIUMPH / HOUR / MOMENT]--SHE PREFERRED	CRISIS IS SWEET AND YET	1416	6
AND SHE WOULD TELL YOU [ANSWER] SIGHING--	CRISIS IS SWEET AND YET	1416	7
AND SHE WILL POINT UNDOUBTEDLY [YOU FONDLY-- / YOU LONGINGLY]	CRISIS IS SWEET AND YET	1416	V 7
SINCE SHE AND I HAD MET AND PLAYED	A LITTLE SNOW WAS HERE	1444	3
BUT SHE MUST BUY MY SHELTER	I SAW THE WIND WITHIN	1502	3
BUT SHE MUST [MY PRICE / HUMILITY] PAY FOR SUCCOR	I SAW THE WIND WITHIN	1502	V
SHE COULD NOT LIVE UPON THE PAST	SHE COULD NOT LIVE UPON	1505	1
AND SO SHE SOUGHT THIS SWEET AT LAST	SHE COULD NOT LIVE UPON	1505	3
SHE [HE] BORE LIFE'S EMPTY PACK	HER LOSSES MAKE OUR	1562	2
TO WHICH HE [SHE] GAVE THE WORTH,	CLIMBING TO REACH THE	1566	2
HE [SHE] RAN AWAY FROM EARTH--	CLIMBING TO REACH THE	1566	4
TO THE BRIGHT EAST SHE FLIES,	TO THE BRIGHT EAST SHE	1573	1
FASHIONING WHAT SHE IS,	TO THE BRIGHT EAST SHE	1573	7
FATHOMING WHAT SHE WAS,	TO THE BRIGHT EAST SHE	1573	8
SHE DID NOT KNOW HER STATION LOW	TO HER DERIDED HOME	1586	3
WITH MARTIAL HAND SHE STROKES THE HAIR	WHO IS IT SEEKS MY	1598	5
SHE DOES NOT KNOW A ROUTE	QUITE EMPTY, QUITE AT	1606	3
SHE DOES NOT ASK FOR NOON--	QUITE EMPTY, QUITE AT	1606	6
SHE DOES NOT ASK FOR BOON,	QUITE EMPTY, QUITE AT	1606	7
THE BIRDS SHE LOST--	QUITE EMPTY, QUITE AT	1606	9
OR HAS IT [SHE] FEATHERS, LIKE A BIRD,	NOT KNOWING WHEN THE	1619	3
WHICH SHE WAS TAUGHT TO EAT--	BETROTHED TO	1641	4
THE IMMORTALITY SHE GAVE	THE IMMORTALITY SHE GAVE	1648	1
SHE TOOK THE AWFUL NEWS	I WATCHED HER FACE TO	1667	2
WHETHER SHE DIED BEFORE SHE HEARD	I WATCHED HER FACE TO	1667	3
WHETHER SHE DIED BEFORE SHE HEARD	I WATCHED HER FACE TO	1667	3
SHE HAS FULFILLED HER DYES	NATURE CAN DO NO MORE	1673	2
THAT SHE FORGOT ME WAS THE LEAST	THAT SHE FORGOT ME WAS	1683	1
SHE DWELT SO CLOSE	TO-DAY OR THIS NOON	1702	2
TO-NIGHT SHE LIES	TO-DAY OR THIS NOON	1702	4
"'TWAS ALL I HAD," SHE STRICKEN GASPED--	UPON THE GALLOWS HUNG A	1757	7
SHEAVES			
AND MR THOMSON'S "SHEAVES."	BESIDES THE AUTUMN POETS	131	8
SHE'D			
SHE'D PASS FOR BAREHEAD--SHORT WAY OFF--	YOU'LL KNOW HER--BY HER	634	15
SHEEN			
YOU EFFACE THE SHEEN.	WHICH IS THE BEST--THE	1315	4
WITHOUT A VAUNT OR SHEEN	THE GENTIAN HAS A	1424	5
BUT HE INDORSED THE SHEEN [SCENE]--	THE ROAD WAS LIT WITH	1450	8
OR IS IT THE CONFIDING SHEEN	THE FACE IN EVANESCENCE	1490	5
FOR SHEEN MUST HAVE A DISK	THE PATTERN OF THE SUN	1550	3

	FIRST LINE	POEM	LINE
SHEEN (CONTINUED)			
TO THY TRACTS OF SHEEN--	EXPANSE CANNOT BE LOST--	1584	14
SHEET			
'TWAS LIKE A SHEET WITH HORNS;	A CURIOUS CLOUD	1710	2
THE SHEET WAS BLUE--	A CURIOUS CLOUD	1710	3
SHEETS			
EXHIBITS [DEVELOPES] SHEETS OF PLACE--	THE SOUL'S DISTINCT	974	6
SHELF			
UNOPENED--RARE--UPON THE SHELF--	NOT IN THIS WORLD TO SEE	418	5
I THANK THESE KINSMEN OF THE SHELF--	UNTO MY BOOKS--SO GOOD	604	13
BEHIND THE SHELF	I CANNOT LIVE WITH YOU--	640	4
UPON MY SILVER SHELF--	IT DROPPED SO LOW--IN MY	747	8
YET [BUT] EVEN ON HIS SCARLET SHELF	THE FROST OF DEATH WAS	1136	7
ON IT'S BOUNDLESS [MIGHTY / SUBTLE] SHELF--	SUMMER LAID HER SIMPLE	1363	2
SHELL			
CHAFING THE SHELL--	LET US PLAY YESTERDAY--	728	14
CAN THE LARK RESUME THE SHELL--	LET US PLAY YESTERDAY--	728	25
SHELLS			
SHELLS FROM THE COAST MISTAKING--	SHELLS FROM THE COAST	693	1
SHELTER			
THE SOUL THAT ASKED IT'S SHELTER	THE BODY GROWS WITHOUT--	578	7
BUT SHE MUST BUY MY SHELTER	I SAW THE WIND WITHIN	1502	3
SHELVES			
UPON THE CLOSET SHELVES--	DEATH SETS A THING	360	12
SHEPHERD'S			
UNTO THE SHEPHERD'S ARM!	GOING TO HEAVEN!	79	10
SHERRY			
THEIR HOCK, AND SHERRY, DRAW,	PERHAPS YOU'D LIKE TO	134	8
SHE'S			
SHE'S DREAMING OF THE WOODS!	WHOSE ARE THE LITTLE	142	24
SHE'S HAPPY, WITH A NEW CONTENT--	SHE'S HAPPY, WITH A NEW	535	1
SHE'S BUSY--WITH AN ALTERED CARE--	SHE'S HAPPY, WITH A NEW	535	3
SHE'S TEARFUL--IF SHE WEEP AT ALL--	SHE'S HAPPY, WITH A NEW	535	5
SHE'S "SORRY I AM DEAD"--AGAIN--	I CRIED AT PITY--NOT AT	588	21
SHEWN			
WHOSE SEAM COULD NOT BE SHEWN--	OF YELLOW WAS THE OUTER	1676	4
SHIELD			
THE DANDELION'S SHIELD	TO HER DERIDED HOME	1586	V
SHIFT			
OR SHIFT SUPREME--	A MIEN TO MOVE A QUEEN--	283	19
THE SEASONS--SHIFT--MY PICTURE--	THE ANGLE OF A LANDSCAPE	375	13
SHIFT IT--JUST--	IT DONT SOUND SO	426	7
SHOW [SHIFT] ITSELF AWAY--	BLOOM UPON THE MOUNTAIN	667	8
I TRIED TO DROP [SHIFT] IT IN THE CROWD--	BEREAVED OF ALL, I WENT	784	11
SHIFTED			
THE FLESH--SURRENDERED--CANCELLED [SHIFTED]--	DEPARTED--TO THE	524	5
IS SHIFTED--LIKE A SAND--	OF ALL THE SOULS THAT	664	8
HIS COMRADES, SHIFTED LIKE THE FLAKES	HE FOUGHT LIKE THOSE	759	9
SHIFTING			
UPON A SHIFTING PLATE	FAME IS A FICKLE FOOD	1659	2
SHIFTS			
HE SHIFTS THE STEM--A LITTLE--	A SOLEMN THING WITHIN	483	11
IT SOARS--AND SHIFTS--AND WHIRLS--	OF BEING IS A BIRD	653	5
SHILY			
SITS SHILY AT HIS FEET--	THE DAISY FOLLOWS SOFT	106	3
EACH--SOUNDING--SHILY--	AGAIN--HIS VOICE IS AT	663	15
SHIMMERING			
LEST SUCH A SUBTLE--SHIMMERING GRACE	A SOMETHING IN A	122	11
UNKNOWN HIS SHIMMERING [GIDDY / DAZZLING] ULTIMATE--	THE ROAD WAS LIT WITH	1450	7
SHINE SEE ASHINE			
THE STARS DARE SHINE OCCASIONALLY	WHEN WE STAND ON THE	242	13
I MADE THE TAPER SHINE--	ONLY A SHRINE, BUT MINE	918	2
SHINE THY BEST--	MY GOD--HE SEES THEE--	1178	2
SHINES			
BRAVE--SHINES THE SUN THROUGH THE FRECKLED PANE--	HOW MANY TIMES THESE LOW	187	10
SHINING			
THE SHINING COURTIERS GO--	IN RAGS MYSTERIOUS AS	117	2
TO WRAP IT'S SHINING YARDS--	I'VE KNOWN A HEAVEN,	243	2
IN SUCH A SHINING PLACE!	ME--COME! MY DAZZLED	431	2
UPON A SHINING SEA--	TWO BUTTERFLIES WENT OUT	533	6
WITH SHINING--AND THE SKY--	I WATCHED THE MOON	629	28
THE SUN FROM SHINING,	RESTS AT NIGHT	714	2
FURTHEST SHINING--DONE--	STRUCK, WAS I, NOR YET	925	12
WHO QUIT THEIR SHINING WORKING	TRUSTY AS THE STARS	1369	2
WERE SHINING IN YOUR [ONE'S] HAND.	TO SEE HER IS A PICTURE	1568	8
AND SO ABETS THE SHINING FLEET	LOVE CAN DO ALL BUT	1731	7
SHIP			
FOR THE ONE SHIP THAT STRUTS THE SHORE	FINITE--TO FAIL, BUT	847	2
THE SHIP MIGHT BE OF SATIN HAD IT NOT TO FIGHT--	THERE IS A STRENGTH IN	1113	5
THE SHIP BENEATH THE DRAW	THOSE NOT LIVE YET	1454	5
SHIPS			
THE STRAY SHIPS--PASSING--	TWO SWIMMERS WRESTLED ON	201	5
WHERE SHIPS OF PURPLE--GENTLY TOSS--	WHERE SHIPS OF PURPLE--	265	1
AND SHIPS--OF SUCH A SIZE	THEY CALLED ME TO THE	628	10
SO I THE SHIPS MAY SEE	SO SET IT'S SUN IN THEE	808	4
SHIPS--OFFER THESE--	EXCEPT THE SMALLER SIZE	1067	V
TO CAST THE SHIPS, AT SEA,	THE DUTIES OF THE WIND	1137	2

	FIRST LINE	POEM	LINE
SHIVER			
AND SHIVER FOR [RECOLLECT] THE POOR--	THE NIGHT WAS WIDE, AND	589	16
I'LL SHIVER, SATISFIED.	I'VE DROPPED MY BRAIN--	1046	20
SHIVERED			
BENT TO THE WATER, STRUGGLED [SHIVERED] SCARCE--	THE LAST NIGHT THAT SHE	1100	23
SHIVERERS			
THE SHIVERERS ROUND FARMER'S DOORS--	'TIS NOT THAT DYING	335	9
SHIVERING			
THE SHIVERING [FREEZING] FANCY TURNS	CONJECTURING A CLIMATE	562	4
SHOAL			
IF WRECKED UPON THE SHOAL [WHARF / CAPE / DOCK / BAY] OF THOUGHT	IF WRECKED UPON THE	1469	1
SHOALS			
SPINNING UPON THE SHOALS--	GLEE--THE GREAT STORM IS	619	8
SHOCK			
I ASCERTAIN IT WITH A SHOCK--	CONSULTING SUMMER'S	1715	3
SHOD			
HIS FEET ARE SHOD WITH GAUZE--	HIS FEET ARE SHOD WITH	916	1
SHOT THE LITHE SLEDS LIKE SHOD VIBRATIONS	GLASS WAS THE STREET--IN	1498	5
IS SHOD WITH ADAMANT--	YOU CANNOT MAKE	1508	8
SHOE			
A BOG--AFFRONTS MY SHOE--	A BURDOCK--CLAWED MY	229	6
UPON HER AMBER SHOE--	I KNOW A PLACE WHERE	337	12
FOR FEAR I SPOIL MY SHOE?	IS BLISS THEN, SUCH	340	3
AND THIS WORN SHOE JUST FITS THE TRACK--	'TWAS THE OLD--ROAD--	344	15
GIBRALTAR'S EVERLASTING SHOE	THEY LEAVE US WITH THE	350	7
WENT PAST MY SIMPLE SHOE--	I STARTED EARLY--TOOK MY	520	10
THE UNIVERSE--[THE VALLEYS--ARE] HER SHOE--	THE MOON WAS BUT A CHIN	737	18
PEARL--FOR [THE] STOCKING--PEARL FOR SHOE--	THESE--SAW VISIONS--	758	13
OF SILKEN SPEECH AND SPECIOUS SHOE	OF SILKEN SPEECH AND	896	1
SHOES			
DO THEY WEAR "NEW SHOES"--IN "EDEN"--	WHAT IS--"PARADISE"--	215	7
UPON MY ANCLE--THEN MY SHOES	I STARTED EARLY--TOOK MY	520	19
HIS SHOES ARE PURPLE--	WE LIKE MARCH.	1213	2
SHONE			
ON WHOM THE SUMMER SHONE!	ON THIS LONG STORM THE	194	8
IT SHONE SO VERY SMALL--	I CAME TO BUY A SMILE--	223	6
THAT SHONE ABOVE THE FAGOT--	READ--SWEET--HOW OTHERS	260	9
HOW GLITTERING THEY SHONE--	SHE DEALT HER PRETTY	479	2
THE SUN SHONE WHOLE AT INTERVALS--	THE TREES LIKE TASSELS--	606	9
SHONE CLOSER BY--	I CANNOT LIVE WITH YOU--	640	28
THE MINOR ONE--THAT GLEAMED [SHONE] BEHIND--	THAT FIRST DAY, WHEN YOU	659	7
SHE WAS NOT WARM, THOUGH SUMMER SHONE	NO NOTICE GAVE SHE, BUT	804	5
SUN--IF SHONE--OR STORM--IF SHATTERED--	ALL FORGOT FOR	966	11
THE MORNING FOREIGN SHONE--	AS IMPERCEPTIBLY AS	1540	10
THE YELLOW LIGHTNING SHONE--	THE WIND DREW OFF	1694	6
SHOOK			
SOME SHOOK THEIR HEADS, AND OTHERS SMILED--	WHOSE ARE THE LITTLE	142	3
WHEN WINTER SHOOK THE BOUGHS!	IF I COULD BRIBE THEM BY	179	12
AND SHOOK THEIR FISTS--	AN AWFUL TEMPEST MASHED	198	7
THE SUNRISE SHOOK ABROAD	THE DAY CAME SLOW--TILL	304	6
HE BIT [SHOOK] AN ANGLEWORM IN HALVES	A BIRD CAME DOWN THE	328	3
SHOOK MY STRONG TRUST--	HE STRAINED MY FAITH--	497	3
AND [BUT] NEVER WINCED [SHOOK / QUAKED] BEFORE.	I YEARS HAD BEEN FROM	609	16
THE SPIRIT SHOOK THE ADAMANT--	'TWAS CRISIS--ALL THE	948	11
TIME'S DECISION SHOOK--	WE TALKED WITH EACH	1473	V 6
AND TRILLED, AND QUIVERED, AND SHOOK HIS THROAT	A TRAIN WENT THROUGH A	1761	3
SHOOT			
I THINK I'D SHOOT THE HUMAN RACE	MY FRIEND ATTACKS MY	118	7
SHOPMAN			
THE SHOPMAN IMPORTUNES IT--	A CLOCK STOPPED--	287	12
SHOPS			
FOR SHOPS W'D STARE AT ME--	I HAV'NT TOLD MY GARDEN	50	6
SHORE			
KNOWEST THOU THE SHORE	ON THIS WONDROUS SEA	4	4
WALKED SINGING ON THE SHORE.	THE FEET OF PEOPLE	7	8
OR THE LAPWING'S SHORE!	THE GUEST IS GOLD AND	15	10
ON PIZARRO'S SHORE?	WHO NEVER LOST, ARE	73	8
A SAILOR'S BUSINESS IS THE SHORE!	A LITTLE BREAD--A CRUST	159	10
UPON A FOREIGN SHORE--	TO LEARN THE TRANSPORT	167	6
ENDEAR THE SHORE [COAST] BEYOND--	I SHOULD HAVE BEEN TOO	313	21
AS GRAINS UPON A SHORE--	A NIGHT--THERE LAY THE	471	6
THY SHORE?	SO SET IT'S SUN IN THEE	808	6
FOR THE ONE SHIP THAT STRUTS THE SHORE	FINITE--TO FAIL, BUT	847	2
ON SOME UNANSWERING SHORE--	I'VE NONE TO TELL ME TO	881	9
SEEKS FAINTLY [SOFTLY / FURTIVE] FOR IT'S SHORE	THE INUNDATION OF THE	1425	6
OR BILLOWS, LIKE A SHORE--	NOT KNOWING WHEN THE	1619	4
SHORED			
SHORED [PUSHED] THE SUN AWAY	ON THE WORLD YOU COLORED	1171	10
SHORES			
SOME SAILOR, SKIRTING FOREIGN [NOVEL] SHORES--	JUST LOST, WHEN I WAS	160	9
UNVISITED OF SHORES--	AS IF THE SEA SHOULD	695	6
HOW MANY THE FICTITIOUS SHORES--	I MANY TIMES THOUGHT	739	7
SHORT			
IT WAS A SHORT PROCESSION,	THE GENTIAN WEAVES HER	18	9
SO SHORT A THING TO SIGH--	IT'S SUCH A LITTLE THING	189	2

	FIRST LINE	POEM	LINE
SHORT (CONTINUED)			
I REASON, EARTH IS SHORT--	I REASON, EARTH IS SHORT	301	1
ANOTHER BED--A SHORT ONE--	'TWAS THE OLD--ROAD--	344	17
'TWAS SHORT--TO CROSS THE SEA--	I WENT TO THANK HER--	363	8
THE WINTERS ARE SO SHORT--	THE WINTERS ARE SO SHORT	403	1
FOREVER MIGHT BE SHORT, I THOUGHT TO SHOW--	TO LOVE THEE YEAR BY	434	5
HOW SHORT IT TAKES TO MAKE IT BRIDE--	A WIFE--AT DAYBREAK I	461	4
SO SHORT WAY OFF IT SEEMS--	IF ANYBODY'S FRIEND BE	509	11
THE HARM THEY DID--WAS SHORT [BRIEF]--AND SINCE	'TIS TRUE--THEY SHUT ME	538	9
WHOSE SHORT--SEPULCHRAL BASS	THE LIGHTNING PLAYETH--	630	6
SHE'D PASS FOR BAREHEAD--SHORT WAY OFF--	YOU'LL KNOW HER--BY HER	634	15
TO WAIT ETERNITY--IS SHORT--	TO WAIT AN HOUR--IS LONG	781	3
IN ONE SHORT AFTERNOON	HOW MANY SCHEMES MAY DIE	1150	2
CONTAINED [COMBINED / COMPRISED] IN THIS SHORT [PLAIN] LIFE	CONTAINED IN THIS SHORT	1165	1
IN THIS SHORT LIFE	IN THIS SHORT LIFE	1287	1
THAT SHORT--POTENTIAL STIR	THAT SHORT--POTENTIAL	1307	1
HOW SHORT WE HAVE TO FEAR	PERHAPS THEY DO NOT GO	1399	6
SO LONG--SO SHORT--	IMAGE OF LIGHT, ADIEU--	1556	3
SO SHORT WE HAVE TO GO	I DID NOT REACH THEE	1664	15
A SHORT RELIEF TO HAVE THE WIND	T'WAS COMFORT IN HER	1703	3
SHORTENED			
WHICH SHORTENED ALL THE MILES--	ONE SISTER HAVE I IN OUR	14	16
SHORTER			
FEELS SHORTER THAN THE DAY	BECAUSE I COULD NOT STOP	712	22
THE SHORTER FATE--IS OFTENER THE CHIEFEST	UNCERTAIN LEASE--	857	5
IS [WAS] SHORTER THAN A [THE] SNAKE'S DELAY [EVENT / REPLY]	THE MUSHROOM IS THE ELF	1298	7
SUMMER IS SHORTER THAN ANY ONE--	SUMMER IS SHORTER THAN	1506	1
LIFE IS SHORTER THAN SUMMER--	SUMMER IS SHORTER THAN	1506	2
A SHORTER BREATH OF DAY	THERE COMES A WARNING	1536	2
IS SHORTER THAN THE FIRST.	CONSULTING SUMMER'S	1715	6
SHORTEST			
'TIS DAISY, IN THE SHORTEST--	WHOSE ARE THE LITTLE	142	9
HIS--SHORTEST CONSCIOUSNESS--	NO OTHER CAN REDUCE	982	V
HONOR, THE SHORTEST ROUTE TO YOU.	BROTHER OF INGOTS--AH	1366	V 2
SHORTNESS			
WHEN DEATH LIT ALL THE SHORTNESS UP [LIMIT--UP / BREVITY]	HER FINAL SUMMER WAS IT	795	7
IT'S YELLOW SHORTNESS DROPT--	THE DAY GREW SMALL,	1140	4
SHOT			
THE MOST ACCOMPLISHED SHOT!	THERE IS A WORD	8	16
AND SHOT--EXULTANT ON!	ADRIFT! A LITTLE BOAT	30	13
THAN THINE OLD ARROW IS A SHOT	DYING! TO BE AFRAID OF	831	4
THE SECOND POISED--DEBATED--SHOT--	'TWAS CRISIS--ALL THE	948	13
OCCUPIED WITH SHOT	PAIN--EXPANDS THE TIME--	967	6
THE GARDEN GETS THE ONLY SHOT	THE FROST WAS NEVER SEEN	1202	11
'TWILL RIDDLE LIKE A SHOT.	HOW NEWS MUST FEEL WHEN	1319	V 4
SHOT THE LITHE SLEDS LIKE SHOD VIBRATIONS	GLASS WAS THE STREET--IN	1498	5
WILL BE RETAKEN WITH A SHOT	THE LIFE THAT TIED TOO	1535	7
SHOULDER			
A FEATHER ON EACH SHOULDER!	A FUZZY FELLOW, WITHOUT	173	15
ON EVERY SHOULDER THAT SHE MET [SHE COULD REACH]--	MY FIRST WELL DAY--SINCE	574	21
SHOULDERS			
WITH THEIR BRICK SHOULDERS--	I COULD DIE--TO KNOW--	570	8
SHOUT			
TILL THAT FIRST SHOUT GOT BY--	I DREADED THAT FIRST	348	6
I SHOUT UNTO MY FEET--	I CROSS TILL I AM WEARY	550	19
SHOUTED			
AND SHOUTED [BUBBLED / GURGLED] LET US PRAY--	THE BOBOLINK IS GONE--	1591	7
SHOUTING			
AND THEN A SHOUTING FLOWER,--	THE DANDELION'S PALLID	1519	6
SHOUTS			
AND SHOUTS FILL ALL MY CHILDISH SKY,	I HAVE A KING, WHO DOES	103	10
. . . BURST / FLAGS / STEP / TICK / SHOUTS / PINK / RED / . . .	ONE JOY OF SO MUCH	1420	6
AND SHOUTS FOR JOY TO NOBODY	BEFORE YOU THOUGHT OF	1465	15
SHOUTS EVEN FROM THE CRUCIFIX,	THE AUCTIONEER OF	1612	3
SHOVED			
AND TRODDEN OUT [BLOTTED OUT-- / SHOVED AWAY--] THE MILLS--	THE BRAIN, WITHIN IT'S	556	8
SHOW			
SO MARTYRS ALBUMS SHOW!	BY SUCH AND SUCH AN	38	4
SHOW THEM THIS MEEK APPARRELED THING	DELAYED TILL SHE HAD	58	16
VÉNICE COULD NOT SHOW A CHEEK	PIGMY SERAPHS--GONE	138	7
A SIXPENCE AT A SHOW--	A TRANSPORT ONE CANNOT	184	6
MOST LIKE THEIR GLORY SHOW--	FOR THIS--ACCEPTED	195	16
SO GREATER THAN THE GODS CAN SHOW,	A SINGLE SCREW OF FLESH	263	17
OR LACES--OR A TRAVELLING SHOW--	WHAT IF I SAY I SHALL	277	11
WE SHOW THEM--PRAYER--	'TIS SO APPALLING--IT	281	12
BUT THEIR COMPETELESS SHOW	OF BRONZE--AND BLAZE--	290	15
LEST WE TOO AWKWARD SHOW	THERE CAME A DAY AT	322	15
TO SHOW HER THROAT--	I TEND MY FLOWERS FOR	339	8
THE BALLOTS OF ETERNITY, WILL SHOW JUST THAT.	MY REWARD FOR BEING, WAS	343	11
AS 'TWERE A TROPIC SHOW--	FROM COCOON FORTH A	354	17
SHOW ME THE SNOW--	ANSWER JULY--	386	11
SHOW ME THE BELLS--	ANSWER JULY--	386	12
SHOW ME THE JAY!	ANSWER JULY--	386	13

	FIRST LINE	POEM	LINE
SHOW (CONTINUED)			
I'LL SHOW YOU AT THE COURT--	I'LL CLUTCH--AND CLUTCH	427	15
STILL TO SHOW--HOW RICH I GO--	I'LL CLUTCH--AND CLUTCH	427	22
NOR LOGARITHM SHOW	KNOWS HOW TO FORGET!	433	V
FOREVER MIGHT BE SHORT, I THOUGHT TO SHOW--	TO LOVE THEE YEAR BY	434	5
WE WERE CONTENT TO SHOW--	WE COVER THEE--SWEET	482	10
SHOW ME DIVISION [COULD] CAN SPLIT OR PARE--	WHILE IT IS ALIVE	491	6
NOTHING TO SHOW	THAT I DID ALWAYS LOVE	549	11
THE OTHERS LOOK A NEEDLESS SHOW--	I RECKON--WHEN I COUNT	569	7
A SMILE, TO SHOW YOU, WHEN THIS DEEP	IF I MAY HAVE IT, WHEN	577	23
TO PROVE ABILITY. [SHOW SUPREMACY]	IT ALWAYS FELT TO ME--A	597	16
WHEN IT WAS DARK ENOUGH TO DO [SHOW]	A STILL--VOLCANO--LIFE--	601	3
THAT WE CAN SHOW--TODAY?"	I ASKED NO OTHER THING--	621	8
THAT I COULD SHOW IT IN BAZAAR--	THE TINT I CANNOT TAKE--	627	3
THAT MAKES NO SHOW FOR MORN--	A LONG--LONG SLEEP--A	654	2
WHEN FIGURES SHOW THEIR ROYAL FRONT--	OF ALL THE SOULS THAT	664	9
SHOW [SHIFT] ITSELF AWAY--	BLOOM UPON THE MOUNTAIN	667	8
THE LOVE A LIFE [CHILD] CAN SHOW BELOW	THE LOVE A LIFE CAN SHOW	673	1
AND SHOW A FURTHER SEA--	AS IF THE SEA SHOULD	695	2
THAT SHOW HOWEVER TRUE--	THEIR HIGHT IN HEAVEN	696	14
I DARED TO SHOW A TRESS OF THEIR'S	PRECIOUS TO ME--SHE	727	6
AND SHOW ME TO MY FEARS--	IF HE WERE LIVING--DARE	734	8
FOR SHOW, OR COMPANY--	HAVE ANY LIKE MYSELF	736	16
SHOW ME THEM [GIVE THEM ME--]--SAID I--	AUTUMN--OVERLOOKED MY	748	4
TO SHOW THE SUN THE WAY--	MY FAITH IS LARGER THAN	766	4
AND SIGNED THE FETE [SHOW / VAN] AWAY--	A DROP FELL ON THE APPLE	794	16
OR ADMIRABLER SHOW--	THE ONLY NEWS I KNOW	827	11
SHOW JUSTEST--THROUGH AN OPEN TOMB--	THE ADMIRATIONS--AND	906	2
A TOO CONCLUDED SHOW	THIS DUST, AND IT'S	936	10
THE GARDEN [LANDSCAPE] KEEP [SHOW / OWN / HOLD] THE GASH--	AS FROST IS BEST	951	6
WERT THOU BUT ILL--THAT I MIGHT SHOW THEE	WERT THOU BUT ILL--THAT	961	1
ARE [FLIT / SHOW] AS THEY WERE NOT--	PAIN--EXPANDS THE TIME--	967	8
OR BEES, AT CHRISTMAS SHOW--	AS SLEIGH BELLS SEEM IN	981	2
AND SHOW AND END--	EXCEPT THE SMALLER SIZE	1067	4
THE TENTS TO NATURE'S SHOW	DEW--IS THE FRESHET IN	1097	6
AND THOUGHTS WE WILL NOT SHOW	THE MURMURING OF BEES,	1115	14
THE SHOW IS NOT THE SHOW	THE SHOW IS NOT THE SHOW	1206	1
THE SHOW IS NOT THE SHOW	THE SHOW IS NOT THE SHOW	1206	1
WHAT HAVE YOU TO SHOW?	KNOCK WITH TREMOR--	1325	9
WE TRY TO SHOW BECOMING FIRMNESS [CALMNESS]--	MARCH IS THE MONTH OF	1404	5
COME SHOW THY DURHAM BREAST	COME SHOW THY DURHAM	1542	1
SOME ONE PREPARED THIS MIGHTY SHOW	SOME ONE PREPARED THIS	1644	1
OR FLOWER PRESUME TO SHOW	A LANE OF YELLOW LED THE	1650	6
THE SPIRIT COULD NOT SHOW	NO MAN SAW AWE, NOR TO	1733	10
BUT ABLATIVE TO SHOW.	THE JOY THAT HAS NO STEM	1744	4
SHOWED			
OR--IF IT SOMETIME--SHOWED--AS 'TWILL--	IT WOULD NEVER BE COMMON	430	5
I [HE] SHOWED HER [ME] HIGHTS SHE [I] NEVER SAW--	I SHOWED HER HIGHTS SHE	446	1
I [HE] SHOWED HER [ME] SECRETS--MORNING'S NEST--	I SHOWED HER HIGHTS SHE	446	5
UNTIL IT SHOWED TOO SMALL--	THE POWER TO BE TRUE TO	464	8
AND SHOWED THEIR DIMPLES--TOO--	I MEANT TO HAVE BUT	476	16
THEN ORIENT SHOWED [THE EAST PUT OUT / NATURE PUT OUT] A SINGLE FLAG,	A DROP FELL ON THE APPLE	794	15
THE LIGHTNING SHOWED A YELLOW HEAD [BEAK]--	THE WIND BEGUN TO KNEAD	824	11
AND PILED THEM IN [SHOWED THEM TO] THE SOUTH--	THE WIND TOOK UP THE	1134	2
SHOWER			
AND OH, THE SHOWER OF STAIN--	THE NAME--OF IT--IS	656	6
SHOWETH			
THE SKEPTIC--SHOWETH ME--	TO HEAR AN ORIOLE SING	526	14
SHOWING			
DIADEM--OR DUCAL SHOWING [SYMBOL / TOKEN]--	HER--"LAST POEMS"--	312	14
ME FOR SHOWING	SO MUCH SUMMER	651	2
SHOWMAN			
THIS--TOO--THE SHOWMAN RUBBED AWAY--	THEY CALLED ME TO THE	628	13
SHOWN			
AND CRUCIFIXION, SHOWN--	THIS WORLD IS NOT	501	12
IN CABINETS--BE SHOWN--	HE PARTS HIMSELF--LIKE	517	18
CAN BLAZE BE SHOWN [DONE] IN COCHINEAL--	I FOUND THE WORDS TO	581	7
AND ALL DOMINION SHOWN	THE LIFE WE HAVE IS VERY	1162	6
SHOW'S			
THAT SIGNALIZE A SHOW'S RETREAT--	I'VE KNOWN A HEAVEN,	243	7
SHOWS			
WHO ONLY SHOWS HIS MARBLE DISC [GRANITE FACE]--	GIVE LITTLE ANGUISH--	310	7
LIKE OTHER NEW THINGS--SHOWS LARGEST--THEN--	IT DONT SOUND SO	426	12
TO ME--SHOWS INSECURE--	THEIR HIGHT IN HEAVEN	696	8
MY GARNER SHOWS SO FAIR--	GOD GAVE A LOAF TO EVERY	791	12
IT SHOWS THE FURTHEST TREE	A LIGHT EXISTS IN SPRING	812	10
THE ONLY SHOWS I SEE--	THE ONLY NEWS I KNOW	827	4
TILL IT AN ANTIQUE FASHION SHOWS--	WE OUTGROW LOVE, LIKE	887	3
UPON A FORMER GARMENT SHOWS	WHAT TWIGS WE HELD BY--	1086	7
THAN WHEN SHE SHOWS HER GARNET TOOTH--	WHEN ETNA BASKS AND	1146	3
THOUGH IT SHOWS SO FICKLE	WHAT WE SEE WE KNOW	1195	4
THE SPIRIT NEVER SHOWS.	IT'S HOUR WITH ITSELF	1225	2
THE HEALED HEART SHOWS IT'S SHALLOW SCAR	THE HEALED HEART SHOWS	1440	1
SHRANK			
WHEN--SUDDENLY--MY RICHES SHRANK--	IT WOULD NEVER BE COMMON	430	21

	FIRST LINE	POEM	LINE
SHRANK (CONTINUED)			
I SHRANK--"HOW FAIR YOU ARE"!	IN WINTER IN MY ROOM	1670	22
SHREDS			
AND LEAVES THE SHREDS BEHIND--	SHE SWEEPS WITH	219	2
AND SCRAPS [SHREDS] OF PRAYER--	MY PORTION IS DEFEAT--	639	11
SHREWD			
COULD A SHREWD ADVISE ME	I NEVER TOLD THE BURIED	11	18
SHOULD A SHREWD BETRAY ME--	I NEVER TOLD THE BURIED	11	20
WHILE WE SHREWDLY SPECULATE [SAGE INVESTIGATE / SHREWD INVESTIGATE]	YESTERDAY IS HISTORY,	1292	7
SHREWDER			
IT'S SHREWDER THEN	IT DONT SOUND SO	426	14
BUT I, GROWN SHREWDER--SCAN THE SKIES	I MEANT TO HAVE BUT	476	25
SHREWDLY			
WHILE WE SHREWDLY SPECULATE [SAGE INVESTIGATE / SHREWD INVESTIGATE]	YESTERDAY IS HISTORY,	1292	7
SHRIEK			
SEEMS IT DONT SHRIEK SO--UNDER RULE.	IT DONT SOUND SO	426	4
AND WE ARE PLAYING--SHRIEK--	WE DREAM--IT IS GOOD WE	531	4
SHRILL			
AN AXE SHRILL SINGING IN THE WOODS--	AN ALTERED LOOK ABOUT	140	11
WITH SHRILL FELICITY	NO BRIGADIER THROUGHOUT	1561	4
SHRINE			
NOR PERSIAN, BAFFLED AT HER SHRINE	HE TOUCHED ME, SO I LIVE	506	16
ONLY A SHRINE, BUT MINE--	ONLY A SHRINE, BUT MINE	918	1
WITHIN A SELLER'S SHRINE	A DIAMOND ON THE HAND	1108	5
A FRECKLED SHRINE--	THIS DIRTY--LITTLE--	1311	4
SHRINKING			
TO SPARE THESE STRIDING SPIRITS [SHRINKING SPIRITS / . . .	WE SEE--COMPARATIVELY--	534	13
HALF SHRINKING FROM THE GLORY	THE HEAVEN VESTS FOR	694	5
OF SHRINKING WAYS--SHE DID NOT [FOREBORE HER] FRIGHT	NO NOTICE GAVE SHE, BUT	804	9
SHRIVELLED			
PERHAPS A FLOWER'S SHRIVELLED CHEEK	IN EBON BOX, WHEN YEARS	169	9
IS SHRUNKEN [SHRIVELLED / DWINDLED / CHASTENED] SMALL	THE VASTEST EARTHLY DAY	1328	2
SHRIVEN			
A STATELY--SHRIVEN--COMPANY--	THROUGH THE STRAIT PASS	792	5
MY PARLOR IS OF SHRIVEN GLASS,	THE WATERS CHASED HIM AS	1749	5
SHROUD			
BURY ME, IN SUCH A SHROUD OF RED!	IF THIS IS "FADING"	120	4
OR SHROUD OF GNOME	A SPIDER SEWED AT NIGHT	1138	5
SHROUDED			
BORN--BRIDALLED--SHROUDED--	TITLE DIVINE--IS MINE!	1072	10
SHRUB			
THE LILAC IS AN ANCIENT SHRUB	THE LILAC IS AN ANCIENT	1241	1
SHRUNKEN			
HOARY [EVIL / RIGID / WRINKLED / ARID / SHRUNKEN] THE FRUITION	FORTITUDE INCARNATE	1217	7
IS SHRUNKEN [SHRIVELLED / DWINDLED / CHASTENED] SMALL	THE VASTEST EARTHLY DAY	1328	2
SHUDDER			
AND LOOK--AND SHUDDER, AND BLOCK YOUR BREATH--	DID YOU EVER STAND IN A	590	3
SHUDDER TO ATTAIN.	WHICH IS THE BEST--THE	1315	6
SHUN			
MOST SHUN THE PUBLIC AIR	BEST THINGS DWELL OUT OF	998	3
AS GOLD THE [A] PYRITES WOULD SHUN--	HE PREACHED UPON	1207	6
I SHUN IT AS I DO DESPAIR	ONE JOY OF SO MUCH	1420	3
WE SHUN BECAUSE WE PRIZE HER FACE	WE SHUN BECAUSE WE PRIZE	1429	1
WE SHUN IT ERE IT COMES,	WE SHUN IT ERE IT COMES,	1580	1
THE ONLY SECRET PEOPLE [NEIGHBORS] KEEP [SHUN]	THE RETICENT VOLCANO	1748	11
A PRUDENT MAN WOULD SHUN.	THROUGH THOSE OLD	1753	4
SHUNNED			
WE SHALL HAVE SHUNNED UNTIL ASHAMED	WHO WERE "THE FATHER AND	1258	23
FOR WHAT I SHUNNED THEM SO--	I SHALL NOT MURMUR IF AT	1410	4
THE ONLY VESSEL THAT IS SHUNNED	IF WRECKED UPON THE	1469	3
IS SHUNNED, WE MUST ADMIT IT,	DROWNING IS NOT SO	1718	11
SHUNNING			
BY SHUNNING CAREFULLY THE PLACE [SPOT / SITE]	HAVE ANY LIKE MYSELF	736	19
SHUNS			
HE LOVES [SEEKS] WHAT SPURNS [SHUNS] HIM--	TO EARN IT BY DISDAINING	1427	3
SHUT			
IN PARLORS, SHUT BY DAY.	I HAVE A KING, WHO DOES	103	6
HOW PROUD TO SHUT THE EYE!	IF THIS IS "FADING"	120	7
AND SHUT THE WINDOWS DOWN SO CLOSE	BRING ME THE SUNSET IN A	128	20
WE JUST SHUT OUR BROWN EYE	WE DONT CRY--TIM AND I,	196	11
AND COULD NOT BEAR TO SHUT UNTIL	I SHOULD NOT DARE TO	205	7
IF I COULD SHUT HIM UP	IS IT TRUE, DEAR SUE?	218	5
COULD I--THEN--SHUT THE DOOR--	COULD I--THEN--SHUT THE	220	1
WHY--DO THEY SHUT ME OUT OF HEAVEN?	WHY--DO THEY SHUT ME OUT	248	1
BUT DONT--SHUT THE DOOR!	WHY--DO THEY SHUT ME OUT	248	8
WHEREFORE IT SHUT--WHEN HE WAS BY--	"WHY DO I LOVE" YOU, SIR	480	12
YOU--SWEET [SIR]--SHUT ME OUT--	SWEET--YOU FORGOT--BUT I	523	12
'TIS TRUE--THEY SHUT ME IN THE COLD--	'TIS TRUE--THEY SHUT ME	538	1
WHOSE HISSING CORALS PART--AND SHUT--	A STILL--VOLCANO--LIFE--	601	11
THEY SHUT ME UP IN PROSE--	THEY SHUT ME UP IN PROSE	613	1
TO SHUT THE OTHER'S GAZE DOWN--	I CANNOT LIVE WITH YOU--	640	15
AND THE BOXES SHUT--	DRAMA'S VITALLEST	741	7
OWNER CANNOT [NEVER YET WAS] SHUT--	DRAMA'S VITALLEST	741	15

	FIRST LINE	POEM	LINE
SHUT (CONTINUED)			
I SHUT MY EYES--AND GROPED AS WELL	FROM BLANK TO BLANK--	761	9
TO SHUT THE DOOR AND IT WENT OUT	I CANNOT BUY IT--'TIS	840	5
AND SHUT THE DOOR UNTO MY HOUSE	I SING TO USE THE	850	3
THE DOOR AS INSTANT [SUDDEN] SHUT--AND I--	A DOOR JUST OPENED ON A	953	5
BUT LET OUR OBSERVATION SHUT [HALT]	NATURE AFFECTS TO BE	1170	3
BUT [YET] PRONE TO SHUT IT'S [HIS] SPOTTED [SUBTLE] FAN	THE BUTTERFLY'S NUMIDIAN	1387	4
WE JEST AND SHUT THE DOOR--	WE NEVER KNOW WE GO WHEN	1523	2
THE RUMOR'S GATE WAS SHUT SO TIGHT	THE SPIRIT LASTS--BUT IN	1576	21
WHOSE RUMOR'S GATE WAS SHUT SO TIGHT	EXPANSE CANNOT BE LOST--	1584	5
THE RUMOR'S GATE WAS SHUT SO TIGHT	THIS ME--THAT WALKS AND	1588	5
SHUTS			
SO SUNSET SHUTS MY QUESTION DOWN	IT CANT BE "SUMMER"!	221	9
THEN--SHUTS THE DOOR--	THE SOUL SELECTS HER OWN	303	2
SHUTS ARROGANTLY--IN THE GRAVE--	THE TINT I CANNOT TAKE--	627	23
SHUTS FOR THEE,	EXPANSE CANNOT BE LOST--	1584	10
SHUTTER			
CLOSES THE [HIS] SHUTTER AND GOES IN--	HOW LONESOME THE WIND	1418	4
SHUTTING			
THE SHUTTING OF THE EYE.	SLEEP IS SUPPOSED TO BE	13	3
HAS PERIODS OF SHUTTING--	WHAT I SEE NOT, I BETTER	939	3
THOUGH SHUTTING LIKE A DAPPLED FAN	THE BUTTERFLY'S NUMIDIAN	1387	V 4
SHY			
THAT ONE SO SHY--SO IGNORANT	I HAV'NT TOLD MY GARDEN	50	7
WHOSE BUT HER SHY--IMMORTAL FACE	SHE BORE IT TILL THE	144	15
TIM--WAS--SO--SHY?	WE DONT CRY--TIM AND I,	196	26
OF ME, HIMSELF WAS SHY--	THE ONLY GHOST I EVER	274	14
WERE NOT SO SHY	A MIEN TO MOVE A QUEEN--	283	11
HEAVEN IS SHY OF EARTH--THAT'S ALL--	OUT OF SIGHT? WHAT OF	703	11
AS OTHER MEN, WERE COY [SHY] OF DEATH--	HE FOUGHT LIKE THOSE	759	7
FOR HIS SHY HOUSE--	GRIEF IS A MOUSE--	793	3
ARE INCOMPLETE, AND SHY--	WHO GIANTS KNOW, WITH	796	2
NOT FOR ITSELF, THE DUST IS SHY,	DYING! TO BE AFRAID OF	831	7
SHY AS THE WIND OF HIS CHAMBERS [LODGINGS]	THIS IS A BLOSSOM OF THE	945	5
TOO SHY, THAT ANY BLAME--	I WAS A PHEBE--NOTHING	1009	6
OR SHY OF TROUBLING HER	THE SOUL SHOULD ALWAYS	1055	4
OF COUNTERFEITS HE IS SO SHY	THE MERCHANT OF THE	1131	9
ON ONE ATTEMPTING SHY	AS SUMMER INTO AUTUMN	1346	10
SHYLOCK			
"SHYLOCK"? SAY!	WHAT WOULD I GIVE TO SEE	247	22
SHYLY SEE SHILY			
SIC			
"SIC TRANSIT GLORIA MUNDI,"	"SIC TRANSIT GLORIA	3	1
SICILY			
IN SICILY [TRIPOLI].	PARTAKE AS DOTH THE BEE,	994	4
VOLCANOES BE IN SICILY	VOLCANOES BE IN SICILY	1705	1
SICK			
HOW SICK--TO WAIT--IN ANY PLACE--BUT THINE--	HOW SICK--TO WAIT--IN	368	1
SO SICK--TO GUESS--	WHY MAKE IT DOUBT--IT	462	2
SICKENED			
IT SICKENED FRESH UPON MY SIGHT--	IT STRUCK ME--EVERY DAY	362	7
AND SICKENED--EVER AFTERWARD	IT KNEW NO MEDICINE--	559	15
SICKER			
OF ACTION--SICKER FAR--	I TIE MY HAT--I CREASE	443	18
SICKNESS			
NO BOLD SICKNESS COME	SWEET--SAFE--HOUSES--	457	11
IT WAS NOT SICKNESS--THEN--	IT KNEW NO MEDICINE--	559	2
MY LOSS, BY SICKNESS--WAS IT LOSS?	MY FIRST WELL DAY--SINCE	574	25
AS ONE DOES SICKNESS OVER	AS ONE DOES SICKNESS	957	1
A SICKNESS OF THIS WORLD IT MOST OCCASIONS	A SICKNESS OF THIS WORLD	1044	1
NOT SICKNESS STAINS THE BRAVE,	NOT SICKNESS STAINS THE	1613	1
SIDE			
ITALY STANDS THE OTHER SIDE!	OUR LIVES ARE SWISS--	80	6
A LITTLE THIS SIDE OF THE SNOW	BESIDES THE AUTUMN POETS	131	3
AND THAT SIDE OF THE HAZE--	BESIDES THE AUTUMN POETS	131	4
UPON THE MORTAL SIDE.	SHE DIED--THIS WAS THE	150	8
ON HIS SIDE [PART], WHAT TRANSACTION!	THE SUN KEPT STOOPING--	152	3
ON THEIR SIDE [PART], WHAT REPOSE!	THE SUN KEPT STOOPING--	152	4
AND ON THE OTHER SIDE	JUST LOST, WHEN I WAS	160	5
ON THE OTHER SIDE--	IF THE FOOLISH, CALL	168	12
THIS SIDE THE VICTORY!	'TIS SO MUCH JOY! 'TIS	172	6
AT LAST, THE LAMPS UPON THY [YOUR] SIDE	AT LAST, TO BE	174	2
OR--SOMETIMES AT YOUR SIDE TO RUN--	WHAT SHALL I DO--IT	186	11
WHEN KATIE WALKS, THIS SIMPLE PAIR ACCOMPANY HER SIDE,	WHEN KATIE WALKS, THIS	222	1
FOREVER AT HIS SIDE TO WALK--	FOREVER AT HIS SIDE TO	246	1
UPON MY SIDE THE VAIL--	A SINGLE SCREW OF FLESH	263	4
PUT ME IN ON THE FIRMEST [TIGHTEST / HIGHEST] SIDE--	TIE THE STRINGS TO MY	279	5
TILL WHEN THEY REACHED THE OTHER SIDE,	I'LL TELL YOU HOW THE	318	13
THE OTHER SIDE THE BLOCK--	I HAD NOT MINDED--WALLS	398	4
THE BLACK BERRY--WEARS A THORN IN HIS SIDE--	THE BLACK BERRY--WEARS A	554	1
THE MINGLED [UNDER / FURTHER] SIDE	I PRAYED, AT FIRST, A	576	12
BY NATURES THIS SIDE NAPLES--	A STILL--VOLCANO--LIFE--	601	7
BUT PRAYER--REMAINED--OUR SIDE--	IT WAS TOO LATE FOR MAN	623	4
ON EVERY SIDE OF MINE	OURSELVES WERE WED ONE	631	12
FOR--PUT THEM SIDE BY SIDE--	THE BRAIN--IS WIDER THAN	632	2
FOR--PUT THEM SIDE BY SIDE--	THE BRAIN--IS WIDER THAN	632	2
TO EARS THE DYING SIDE--	UPON CONCLUDED LIVES	735	6

	FIRST LINE	POEM	LINE
SIDE (CONTINUED)			
IF BLAME BE MY SIDE--FORFEIT ME--	IF BLAME BE MY SIDE--	775	1
THOUGH NONE BE ON OUR SIDE--	ON A COLUMNAR SELF--	789	8
FOR INLANDS--THE EARTH IS THE UNDER SIDE--	BY MY WINDOW HAVE I FOR	797	9
AND THE UPPER SIDE--IS THE SUN--	BY MY WINDOW HAVE I FOR	797	10
WITH ARMS OF STEEL AT EITHER SIDE--	FAITH--IS THE PIERLESS	915	7
THE OTHER SIDE THE GRAVE.	'TWAS CRISIS--ALL THE	948	8
WHOLE STATURED--BY THE SIDE	NOT ALL DIE EARLY, DYING	990	6
BUT [THO] SELDOM SIDE BY SIDE	AS OLD AS WOE--	1168	8
BUT [THO] SELDOM SIDE BY SIDE	AS OLD AS WOE--	1168	8
THE GIANT AT THE OTHER SIDE	I SHOULD NOT DARE TO BE	1197	7
UPON THE HITHER SIDE	CRISIS IS SWEET AND YET	1416	2
WHAT MADNESS, BY THEIR SIDE,	THAN HEAVEN MORE REMOTE,	1436	7
FACTS BY OUR SIDE ARE NEVER SUDDEN	FACTS BY OUR SIDE ARE	1497	1
SCATTERED--I SAY--TO PLACE [SEAT] THEM SIDE BY SIDE	ABOVE OBLIVION'S TIDE	1531	6
SCATTERED--I SAY--TO PLACE [SEAT] THEM SIDE BY SIDE	ABOVE OBLIVION'S TIDE	1531	6
AND OTHERS AT MY SIDE,	MY WARS ARE LAID AWAY IN	1549	6
ONE SIDE OF ME THE NUTS ARE RIPE	THE ONES THAT	1690	7
THE OTHER SIDE IS MAY.	THE ONES THAT	1690	8
THE OBJECT FLOATING AT HIS SIDE	THE WATERS CHASED HIM AS	1749	9
SIDES			
IN SHANTIES--BY THE SIDES OF ROADS--	I LIKE TO SEE IT LAP	585	7
TO FIT IT'S SIDES [RIBS]	I LIKE TO SEE IT LAP	585	9
IF WE DEMUR, IT'S GAPING SIDES	THIS CHASM, SWEET, UPON	858	5
SIDEWISE			
AND THEN HOPPED SIDEWISE TO THE WALL	A BIRD CAME DOWN THE	328	7
AND LEAN--AND VIEW IT SIDEWISE--	I AM ALIVE--I GUESS--	470	13
SOWN SIDEWISE IN THE CRAG	AS ONE DOES SICKNESS	957	8
SIEVES			
IT SIFTS FROM LEADEN SIEVES--	IT SIFTS FROM LEADEN	311	1
SIFT			
SIFT HER, FROM BROW TO BAREFOOT!	DOUBT ME! MY DIM	275	18
SIFTS			
IT SIFTS FROM LEADEN SIEVES--	IT SIFTS FROM LEADEN	311	1
SIGH			
I SAT ME DOWN TO SIGH.	I HAD A GUINEA GOLDEN--	23	8
ONLY A BREEZE WILL SIGH--	NOBODY KNOWS THIS LITTLE	35	10
WOULD ANYBODY SIGH	ON SUCH A NIGHT, OR SUCH	146	10
SO SHORT A THING TO SIGH--	IT'S SUCH A LITTLE THING	189	2
THAT EVERY SIGH--MAY LIFT YOU	I'LL CLUTCH--AND CLUTCH	427	18
IT COULD NOT HOLD A SIGH--	I HAD NO CAUSE TO BE	542	14
OR THINK OF, WITH A SIGH--	I CRIED AT PITY--NOT AT	588	14
JUST HIS SIGH--ACCENTED--	TO KNOW JUST HOW HE	622	14
AND SIGH FOR LACK OF HEAVEN--BUT NOT	THE WAY I READ A	636	15
I ONLY KNOW [SIGH]--NO CURRICLE [VEHICLE] THAT RUMBLE THERE	A LITTLE ROAD--NOT MADE	647	7
THAT SINGLE--STEADFAST SIGH--	"I WANT"--IT PLEADED--	731	6
NO MESSAGE, BUT A SIGH--	NO NOTICE GAVE SHE, BUT	804	2
HE'LL SIGH--"THE OTHER--[REAL ONE] SHE--IS WHERE?"	FITTER TO SEE HIM, I MAY	968	20
BE CONSCIOUS OF A SIGH	JUST ONCE! OH LEAST	1076	7
HOW MANY SIGHT AND SIGH	A DIAMOND ON THE HAND	1108	6
THE LONG SIGH OF THE FROG	THE LONG SIGH OF THE	1359	1
SO SOAR AWAY AND NEVER SIGH	THE BUTTERFLY UPON THE	1521	7
ADJOURNS HER SIGH--	WE WEAR OUR SOBER	1572	3
THE EYE INQUIRES WITH A SIGH	"RED SEA," INDEED! TALK	1642	9
OF TICKETS FOR A SIGH	ENDANGER IT, AND THE	1658	2
'TIS THEN WE SIGH FOR HOUSES,	SWEET IS THE SWAMP WITH	1740	3
SIGHING			
FOR SIGHING, AND GENTLE WHISPERING, AND UNITY MADE OF TWAIN.	AWAKE YE MUSES NINE,	1	4
STOOPING--PLUCKING--SIGHING--FLYING--	ANGELS, IN THE EARLY	94	7
FAINT-GOING LIVES [EYES]--THEIR LAPSE FROM SIGHING--	"MORNING"--MEANS	300	9
CLOSER--SO I--AT MY SLEEPING [SIGHING]--	DONT PUT UP MY THREAD &	617	19
MINE BELONG YOUR LATEST SIGHING--	PROMISE THIS--WHEN YOU	648	3
WAS LAUGHTER AND ABILITY AND SIGHING	THIS QUIET DUST WAS	813	3
AND SHE WOULD TELL YOU [ANSWER] SIGHING--	CRISIS IS SWEET AND YET	1416	7
SIGHS			
YET SMALL--SHE SIGHS--IF ALL--IS ALL--	THE DROP, THAT WRESTLES	284	5
FAR OFF--HE SIGHS--AND THEREFORE--HOPELESS--	UNDUE SIGNIFICANCE A	439	3
SIGHT			
IN SIGHT OF ME--	SHOULD YOU BUT FAIL AT--	226	2
ARE OUT OF SIGHT--IN HEAVEN--	I THINK JUST HOW MY	237	4
AND THEN--IT'S OUT OF SIGHT--	TO DIE--TAKES JUST A	255	4
THAT THEY WILL CHEAT THE SIGHT--	DELIGHT IS AS THE FLIGHT	257	22
WHEN IT WAS SMUGGLED BY MY SIGHT	A SINGLE SCREW OF FLESH	263	11
TILL I WAS OUT OF SIGHT, IN SOUND,	I CANNOT DANCE UPON MY	326	15
THERE ARE TWO RIPENINGS--ONE--OF SIGHT--	THERE ARE TWO RIPENINGS	332	1
TOO OUT OF SIGHT--THOUGH--	'TWAS THE OLD--ROAD--	344	20
IT SICKENED FRESH UPON MY SIGHT--	IT STRUCK ME--EVERY DAY	362	7
TO FAIL--WITH LAND IN SIGHT--	IT MIGHT BE LONELIER	405	14
OUT OF SOUND--OUT OF SIGHT--	IT IS DEAD--FIND IT--	417	2
OR SOMETHING IN THE SIGHT	WE GROW ACCUSTOMED TO	419	18
AT LAST--THE GRACE [THE GRACE IS JUST] IN SIGHT--	I CROSS TILL I AM WEARY	550	18
IN SIGHT OF NATIVE AIR--	I MEASURE EVERY GRIEF I	561	32
FLAGS, ARE A BRAVE SIGHT--	INCONCEIVABLY SOLEMN!	582	8

	FIRST LINE	POEM	LINE
SIGHT (CONTINUED)			
WITHOUT ERASING [ENDANGERING] SIGHT--	A STILL--VOLCANO--LIFE--	601	4
THESE WERE BENT--MY SIGHT GOT CROOKED--	DONT PUT UP MY THREAD &	617	5
A GUINEA AT A SIGHT--	THE TINT I CANNOT TAKE--	627	4
BECAUSE YOU SATURATED SIGHT--	I CANNOT LIVE WITH YOU--	640	33
WHO KNOWS--BUT AT THE SIGHT OF THAT	I'LL SEND THE FEATHER	687	2
OUT OF SIGHT? WHAT OF THAT?	OUT OF SIGHT? WHAT OF	703	1
THEN DROPPED FROM SIGHT--	IT TOSSED--AND TOSSED--	723	8
AS WRECKED MEN--DEEM THEY SIGHT THE LAND--	I MANY TIMES THOUGHT	739	3
THEY--SUGGEST TO OUR SIGHT--	BY MY WINDOW HAVE I FOR	797	18
I KNOW NOT WHICH, DESIRE, OR GRANT [RIGHT / SIGHT]--	I PLAY AT RICHES--TO	801	23
I SHALL BE PERFECT--IN HIS SIGHT--	FITTER TO SEE HIM, I MAY	968	22
BEST THINGS DWELL OUT OF SIGHT	BEST THINGS DWELL OUT OF	998	1
I SIGHT THE APRILS--	SPRING COMES ON THE	1042	2
AND THEN ABSCONDS FROM SIGHT.	PAIN HAS BUT ONE	1049	8
IT WASTED FROM MY SIGHT	I HAD A DAILY BLISS	1057	6
WHICH BE OUT OF SIGHT?	THREE WEEKS PASSED SINCE	1061	12
THE DISCS THAT SATISFIED OUR SIGHT--	WHAT TWIGS WE HELD BY--	1086	15
AN EARLDOM OUT OF SIGHT TO HOLD,	BECAUSE 'TWAS RICHES I	1093	5
HOW MANY SIGHT AND SIGH	A DIAMOND ON THE HAND	1108	6
AND IT WAS OUT OF SIGHT	THIS SLOW DAY MOVED	1120	8
BUT LEANING TO THE SIGHT	TO DISAPPEAR ENHANCES--	1209	18
I FAMISH [PERISH] TO BEHOLD SO EMINENT A SIGHT [ANOTHER SUCH . . .	THE MOST TRIUMPHANT BIRD	1265	4
. . . SO COMPETENT A SIGHT]	THE MOST TRIUMPHANT BIRD	1265	4
NO SPECTACLE [MONSTER THEN] IN SIGHT	ESCAPE IS SUCH A	1347	4
'TIS NOT TO SIGHT THE SAVIOR--	ESCAPE IS SUCH A	1347	9
TO CLARIFY THE SIGHT	OF THEIR PECULIAR LIGHT	1362	3
I'LL LET MY HEART BE JUST IN SIGHT--	THEY MIGHT NOT NEED ME--	1391	2
BUT ACCLIMATED--PINES NO MORE [GROPES NO MORE / LOSES SIGHT / . . .	THE INUNDATION OF THE	1425	7
OR OUT OF SIGHT OF ESTIMATE	FAME IS THE ONE THAT	1475	3
BESETS THE SIGHT	WHY SHOULD WE HURRY--WHY	1646	9
LET IT BE IN SIGHT OF THEE--	BEAUTY CROWDS ME TILL I	1654	4
THAT CLARIFIES THE SIGHT	BY A DEPARTING LIGHT	1714	5
FOR TRAINS THAT MOMENT [SEVERELY] OUT OF SIGHT,	THE SUMMER THAT WE DID	1773	7
SIGHTED			
THE DEEPEST HID IS SIGHTED FIRST	OF CONSCIOUSNESS, HER	894	5
SIGHTLESS			
TO THE SIGHTLESS KNOT--	DONT PUT UP MY THREAD &	617	10
SIGHT'S			
LEST SIGHT'S [PROOF'S] INEFFABLE DISGRACE	WE SHUN BECAUSE WE PRIZE	1429	2
SIGHTS			
SHE SIGHTS A BIRD--SHE CHUCKLES--	SHE SIGHTS A BIRD--SHE	507	1
SIGN			
SIGN ME THE BOND!	WHAT WOULD I GIVE TO SEE	247	23
BE IT'S GRAVE--SUFFICIENT SIGN--	HER--"LAST POEMS"--	312	15
IT'S EASY AS A SIGN--	THERE'S BEEN A DEATH, IN	389	22
WHEN NOT A MOON DISCLOSE A SIGN--	WE GROW ACCUSTOMED TO	419	11
AND EVERY SIGN BEFORE THE PLACE	A TOOTH UPON OUR PEACE	459	7
LIFT SUCH A CRUCIFIXAL SIGN	HE TOUCHED ME, SO I LIVE	506	17
MINE--BY THE SIGN IN THE SCARLET PRISON--	MINE--BY THE RIGHT OF	528	3
HIS HOUSE WAS NOT--NO SIGN HAD HE--	MY PERIOD HAD COME FOR	564	9
I--TOO--RECEIVED THE SIGN.	OURSELVES WERE WED ONE	631	8
REVEAL BY SIGN--A SYLLABLE	THE FUTURE--NEVER SPOKE	672	3
REPORT BY SIGN A CIRCUMSTANCE	THE FUTURE--NEVER SPOKE	672 V	3
THE NORTH--HER BLAZING SIGN	THE SUNRISE RUNS FOR	710	10
THE WIFE--WITHOUT THE SIGN!	TITLE DIVINE--IS MINE!	1072	2
COULD COMMENTATORS ON THE SIGN	DEW--IS THE FRESHET IN	1097	9
AND CIPHER AT THE SIGN	MY COCOON TIGHTENS--	1099	10
THE TRUTH NEVER FLAUNTED [HOISTED] A SIGN--	HE PREACHED UPON	1207	4
I KNOW IT IS A SIGN	IF I COULD TELL HOW GLAD	1668	5
OF WHICH IT IS THE SIGN	TO TELL THE BEAUTY WOULD	1700	4
SIGNAL			
THIS--THE SIGNAL WO!	TO LEARN THE TRANSPORT	167	10
ONE PEARL--TO ME--SO SIGNAL-- [OF SUCH PROPORTION]	ONE LIFE OF SO MUCH	270	5
OR WIND'S BRIGHT SIGNAL TO THE EAR--	LIKE FLOWERS, THAT HEARD	513	10
IT MADE NO SIGNAL, NOR DEMURRED,	'TWAS WARM--AT FIRST--	519	15
DISTANCE--BE HER ONLY MOTION [SIGNAL]--	HER SWEET TURN TO LEAVE	649	21
AS 'TWERE SPECIFIC [A SIGNAL] GROUND--	WHOLE GULFS--OF RED, AND	658	4
OR ORDER, OR APPARENT ACTION [SIGNAL / NOTICE]--	FOUR TREES--UPON A	742	3
NOR THE LEAST SIGNAL, ME [MINE] ASSURE--	WERT THOU BUT ILL--THAT	961	4
LIKE SIGNAL ESOTERIC SIPS	YOUR THOUGHTS DONT HAVE	1452	3
THE TUBE UPLIFTS A SIGNAL BUD	THE DANDELION'S PALLID	1519	5
A SINGLE [ROYAL / SIGNAL / HALLOWED] TIME	TO BE FORGOT BY THEE	1560	9
SIGNALIZE			
THAT SIGNALIZE A SHOW'S RETREAT--	I'VE KNOWN A HEAVEN,	243	7
ITSELF TO SIGNALIZE--	A TOOTH UPON OUR PEACE	459	6
SIGNALS			
AT FUNDAMENTAL SIGNALS	TWO LENGTHS HAS EVERY	1295	7
SIGNED			
I WILLED MY KEEPSAKES--SIGNED AWAY	I HEARD A FLY BUZZ--WHEN	465	9
AND SIGNED THE FETE [SHOW / VAN] AWAY--	A DROP FELL ON THE APPLE	794	16
. . . CHOSE [SIGNED]--	NO NOTICE GAVE SHE, BUT	804	17
SIGNIFICANCE			
HAS THE SIGNIFICANCE, ON HIGH,	I MET A KING THIS	166	27

	FIRST LINE	POEM	LINE
SIGNIFICANCE (CONTINUED)			
UNDUE SIGNIFICANCE A STARVING MAN ATTACHES .	UNDUE SIGNIFICANCE A	439	1
OF THE SIGNIFICANCE [STUPENDOUSNESS] OF THIS--	NO CROWD THAT HAS	515	19
WHOSE WILL--A NUMB SIGNIFICANCE--[BLANK INTELLIGENCE]	DENIAL--IS THE ONLY FACT	965	3
SUBSIDES FROM IT'S SIGNIFICANCE	A DIAMOND ON THE HAND	1108	3
SIGNIFICANCE [OMNIPOTENCE] THAT EACH HAS LIVED	BECAUSE THAT YOU ARE	1260	9
DENIZEN OF SIGNIFICANCE	NOT ANY MORE TO BE	1344	3
SIGNIFICANT			
DEATH SETS A THING SIGNIFICANT	DEATH SETS A THING	360	1
SIGNIFIED			
WE SIGNIFIED "THESE SEE"--	THEY PUT US FAR APART--	474	4
OR SIGNIFIED OF SOUND	THE MOB WITHIN THE HEART	1745	6
SIGNIFY			
I'LL TELL IT YOU [SIGNIFY / TESTIFY]--	THE ONLY NEWS I KNOW	827	12
OR QUARTER--AS I SIGNIFY--	I MAKE HIS CRESCENT FILL	909	3
SIGNIFYING			
AND IS AS FOND OF SIGNIFYING	HER SOVREIGN PEOPLE	1139	3
SIGNOR			
EXCEPT [UNLESS] THOU BLESS ME"--STRANGER [SIGNOR]!	A LITTLE EAST OF JORDAN,	59	11
VESPERS--ARE SWEETER THAN MATINS--SIGNOR--	I SHALL KEEP SINGING!	250	9
OH, SIGNOR, THINE, THE AMBER HAND--	THE MOON IS DISTANT FROM	429	9
THIS WAS THE LEOPARD'S NATURE--SIGNOR--	CIVILIZATION--SPURNS--	492	8
SIGNS			
THROUGH TELEGRAPHIC SIGNS--	THEY PUT US FAR APART--	474	8
"HEAVEN" HAS DIFFERENT SIGNS--TO ME--	"HEAVEN" HAS DIFFERENT	575	1
JUST MAKING SIGNS--ACROSS--[IT SEEMED] TO THEE--	IF I MAY HAVE IT, WHEN	577	20
THESE ARE THE SIGNS TO NATURE'S INNS--	THESE ARE THE SIGNS TO	1077	1
SILAS			
OF PAUL AND SILAS IT IS SAID	OF PAUL AND SILAS IT IS	1166	1
SILENCE			
BUT--THE ECHOES--STIFFEN [SILENCE--STIFFENS]--	SAFE IN THEIR ALABASTER	216	V
AND I, AND SILENCE, SOME STRANGE RACE	I FELT A FUNERAL, IN MY	280	15
SOMEWHERE--IN SILENCE--	I KNOW THAT HE EXISTS.	338	2
WHEN THE BALL ENTERS, ENTERS SILENCE--	IF ANY SINK, ASSURE THAT	358	7
NOT SUCH A STANZA SPLITS THE SILENCE--	BETTER--THAN MUSIC! FOR	503	19
THE SILENCE CONDESCENDED--	MY PERIOD HAD COME FOR	564	17
THE SECOND [SILENCE] LIKE AN OCEAN ROLLED	I YEARS HAD BEEN FROM	609	11
AND A SILENCE--THE TELLER'S EYE--	GLEE--THE GREAT STORM IS	619	15
WILLS SILENCE--EVERYWHERE--	NATURE--THE GENTLEST	790	24
WITH SILENCE AS A COMPANY	TO OWN THE ART WITHIN	855	3
THERE IS NO SILENCE IN THE EARTH--SO SILENT	THERE IS NO SILENCE IN	1004	1
GREAT STREETS OF SILENCE LED AWAY	GREAT STREETS OF SILENCE	1159	1
SILENCE IS ALL WE DREAD.	SILENCE IS ALL WE DREAD.	1251	1
BUT SILENCE IS INFINITY.	SILENCE IS ALL WE DREAD.	1251	3
THE SILENCE TIED	LIKE BROOMS OF STEEL	1252	8
BUT IT CAN SILENCE YOU--	THAT SACRED CLOSET WHEN	1273	12
SILENCE--IS HIS NAME--	DEATH'S WAYLAYING NOT	1296	4
THE BARD TO SILENCE BORN--	TOUCH LIGHTLY NATURE'S	1389	V 4
SILENCE--DENOTE--	TO THE STANCH DUST	1402	5
IF BIRD THE SILENCE CONTRADICT	A LANE OF YELLOW LED THE	1650	5
AND SILENCE ONE--	SPEECH IS ONE SYMPTOM OF	1681	2
SILENCED			
AND SILENCED, AS THE AWFUL SEA	HE TOUCHED ME, SO I LIVE	506	5
SILENT			
HAST NEVER SILENT HOURS, AND MINUTES ALL TOO LONG,	AWAKE YE MUSES NINE,	1	29
NEVER MIND SILENT FIELDS--	THERE IS ANOTHER SKY,	2	6
IN THE PEACEFUL [SILENT] WEST	ON THIS WONDROUS SEA	4	7
I FEAR A SILENT MAN--	I FEAR A MAN OF FRUGAL	543	2
I--SILENT [SPEECHLESS]--PASS THE DOOR--	AGAIN--HIS VOICE IS AT	663	10
A WISER [WORDLESS / SILENT / SPEECHLESS] SYMPATHY	THE BIRDS REPORTED FROM	743	24
OF A SILENT LIFE--	GROWTH OF MAN--LIKE	750	8
THIS, IS THE SILENT END	AND THIS OF ALL MY HOPES	913	2
THERE IS NO SILENCE IN THE EARTH--SO SILENT	THERE IS NO SILENCE IN	1004	1
UNTO A SILENT SKY	AT HALF PAST THREE, A	1084	2
BECAUSE MY BROOK IS SILENT	BECAUSE MY BROOK IS	1200	3
HAS STILL A SILENT RANK.	THE STEM OF A DEPARTED	1520	2
BUT THOSE THE SILENT FEEL	THE WORDS THE HAPPY SAY	1750	3
SILENTER			
AND THEN YOU AND I, WERE SILENTER.	GOING TO HIM! HAPPY	494	17
SILENTLY			
SAILING SILENTLY,	ON THIS WONDROUS SEA	4	2
DRILL SILENTLY [ARRANGE THE HEART] FOR HEAVEN--	TO HELP OUR BLEAKER	1064	4
AND DO IT SILENTLY.	THAT SACRED CLOSET WHEN	1273	4
SILK			
AND STRUTS IN SEWING SILK!	A FUZZY FELLOW, WITHOUT	173	12
WHEN THE CORN IN SILK [GILT] WILL DRESS	I SUPPOSE THE TIME WILL	1381	7
SILKEN			
OF SILKEN SPEECH AND SPECIOUS SHOE	OF SILKEN SPEECH AND	896	1
SILL			
SO HERE'S AN AMBER SILL--	THE JUDGE IS LIKE THE	699	4
MORNING--THE EAST COMPELLING THE SILL	NOON--IS THE HINGE OF	931	3
'TWOULD UNDERMINE THE SILL	FALSEHOOD OF THEE COULD	1007	2
IT IS NOT WITH A SILL--	THE WAY HOPE BUILDS HIS	1481	2

	FIRST LINE	POEM	LINE
SILLS			
SPRINGS--SHAKE THE SILLS [SEALS]--	SAFE IN THEIR ALABASTER	216	V
SILLY			
BUT POMPOUS [SILLY / AWKWARD] JOY	MARCH IS THE MONTH OF	1404	6
SILVER			
LIGHT SWUNG THE SILVER FLEECES	A LITTLE EAST OF JORDAN,	59	13
HER VESTMENTS AS THE SILVER FLEECE--	SHE DIED AT PLAY,	75	8
FLOWED SILVER TO THE WEST--	A POOR--TORN HEART-- A	78	4
SO SILVER STEAL A HUNDRED FLUTES	WE SHOULD NOT MIND SO	81	7
WHEREFORE MINE EYE THY SILVER MISTS,	THE BEE IS NOT AFRAID OF	111	7
I HEAR THE SILVER STRIFE--	MUSICIANS WRESTLE	157	3
THO' SHE WEAR A SILVER APRON--	THO' MY DESTINY BE	163	3
AND A CHAMOIS' SILVER BOOT--	AH, MOON--AND STAR!	240	10
SILVER--PERISHED--WITH HER TONGUE--	HER--"LAST POEMS"--	312	3
TOO SILVER FOR A SEAM--	A BIRD CAME DOWN THE	328	18
AND FAR I HEARD HIS SILVER CALL	I HAD NOT MINDED--WALLS	398	3
I FELT HIS SILVER HEEL	I STARTED EARLY--TOOK MY	520	18
THE SPIDER HOLDS A SILVER BALL	THE SPIDER HOLDS A	605	1
ON SILVER MATTERS CHARMED A SNAKE	THE TREES LIKE TASSELS--	606	19
WHEN, WITH A SILVER PRACTISE--	I WATCHED THE MOON	629	31
HORSES OF BLONDE--AND COACH OF SILVER--	DROPPED INTO THE ETHER	665	5
WERE SUCH HER SILVER WILL--	THE MOON WAS BUT A CHIN	737	12
UPON MY SILVER SHELF--	IT DROPPED SO LOW--IN MY	747	8
MATCH ME THE SILVER [CRYSTAL] RETICENCE--	THIS THAT WOULD GREET--	778	7
WITH GOLD AND SILVER PAIN	A PLATED LIFE--	806	2
TWICE A WINTER'S SILVER FRACTURE	TWICE HAD SUMMER HER	846	3
BULB AFTER BULB, IN SILVER ROLLED--	SPLIT THE LARK--AND	861	2
IN SILVER CHRONICLE.	THE ROBIN FOR THE CRUMB	864	4
AN EVERYWHERE OF SILVER	AN EVERYWHERE OF SILVER	884	1
THEY LEAP UPON THEIR SILVER FEET	HOW STILL THE BELLS IN	1008	3
AND LO, HER SILVER PRINCIPLE	AT HALF PAST THREE, A	1084	7
LOOSED THE MOON HER SILVER HAT	LIGHTLY STEPPED A YELLOW	1672	3
SIMILAR			
THE SHAPES--THOUGH--WERE SIMILAR--	WE PLAY AT PASTE--	320	5
SO SIMILAR--AN OPTIZAN	SO GLAD WE ARE--A	329	7
HOW SIMILAR APPEARS--	MORE THAN THE GRAVE IS	1503	6
SIMILITUDE			
FOR SEEKING IT'S RESEMBLANCE [SIMILITUDE]--	IT BLOOMED AND DROPT, A	978	15
SIMPLE			
AND THO' THE SUM WAS SIMPLE	I HAD A GUINEA GOLDEN--	23	3
FROM MARSHALLINGS AS SIMPLE	A DAY! HELP! HELP!	42	5
IT HAS A SIMPLE GRAVITY	THERE'S SOMETHING	45	7
TO VENERATE THE SIMPLE DAYS	TO VENERATE THE SIMPLE	57	1
HER SIMPLE HAUNTS BEYOND!	SO BASHFUL WHEN I SPIED	91	8
WHEN SIMPLE YOU, AND I,	ONE DIGNITY DELAYS FOR	98	14
FOR A SIMPLE BREAST LIKE MINE--	FLOWERS--WELL--IF	137	10
SHE BORE IT TILL THE SIMPLE VEINS	SHE BORE IT TILL THE	144	1
TOOK UP HER SIMPLE WARDROBE	SHE DIED--THIS WAS THE	150	3
WHEN KATIE WALKS, THIS SIMPLE PAIR ACCOMPANY HER SIDE,	WHEN KATIE WALKS, THIS	222	1
BEFORE MY SIMPLE BOSOM--BROKE--	I THINK JUST HOW MY	237	11
IT IS SIMPLE, TO ACHE IN THE BONE, OR THE RIND--	IT IS EASY TO WORK WHEN	244	5
ON MY SIMPLE SLEEP--	MANY A PHRASE HAS THE	276	10
INFECTS MY SIMPLE SPIRIT	OF BRONZE--AND BLAZE--	290	8
THAT SLIPPED MY SIMPLE FINGERS THROUGH--	YOUR RICHES--TAUGHT ME--	299	31
A SPHERE OF SIMPLE GREEN--	THE GRASS SO LITTLE HAS	333	2
PUT FROM MY SIMPLE SPEECH ALL PLAIN WORD--	I'M SAYING EVERY DAY	373	20
SIMPLE SALUTE--AND CERTAIN RECOGNITION--	IT'S COMING--THE	390	5
BEFALLING NOT MY SIMPLE DAYS--	REMOVED FROM ACCIDENT OF	424	3
UPON MY SIMPLE CHEEK--	IT WOULD NEVER BE COMMON	430	10
THE SIMPLE NEWS THAT NATURE TOLD--	THIS IS MY LETTER TO THE	441	3
WENT PAST MY SIMPLE SHOE--	I STARTED EARLY--TOOK MY	520	10
FOR EASE OF [FOR SIMPLE / BECAUSE OF] GIANTURE--	SIZE CIRCUMSCRIBES--IT	641	4
FOR JUST A [SIMPLE] SCRUTINY--	THE LONELINESS ONE DARE	777	8
INSCRIBES A SIMPLE NOON--	IT RISES--PASSES--ON OUR	1023	2
A CLOSING OF THE SIMPLE LID [GATE]	A GREAT HOPE FELL	1123	14
THE [A] CLOVER'S SIMPLE FAME	THE CLOVER'S SIMPLE FAME	1232	1
PASTED BY THE SIMPLE SUMMER	LAIN IN NATURE--SO	1288	7
SUMMER LAID HER SIMPLE HAT	SUMMER LAID HER SIMPLE	1363	1
SHE TAKES [GOES] HER GRACIOUS [SPACIOUS / SUBTLE / SIMPLE / ...	SUMMER--WE ALL HAVE SEEN	1386	6
THE WRESTLE IN HER SIMPLE THROAT	THE PRETTY RAIN FROM	1426	5
IN RAVISHED [DAZZLING / SIMPLE] HOLINESS--	THE THRILL CAME SLOWLY	1495	8
BY BUT A SIMPLE ARROW	I'VE GOT AN ARROW HERE.	1729	6
SIMPLE-HEARTED			
WHILE SIMPLE-HEARTED NEIGHBORS	THERE'S SOMETHING	45	13
SIMPLER			
OR SIMPLER PROVED--ABOVE--	IT TROUBLED ME AS ONCE I	600	12
SIMPLER ARE THE DAYS THAN THE SUPPOSITION	SOME WE SEE NO MORE,	1221	3
SIMPLEST			
DISPLAYED [PASS SLOW] BEFORE THE SIMPLEST [HUMBLEST] DOOR	SOME ONE PREPARED THIS	1644	4
SIMPLICITY			
TO HER SIMPLICITY [SINCERITY]	"NATURE" IS WHAT WE SEE	668	12
NOT SATISFIED TO APE THE GREAT IN HIS SIMPLICITY	THAT THIS SHOULD FEEL	1112	5
SIMPLICITY FLED FROM HIS COUNTERFEIT PRESENCE	HE PREACHED UPON	1207	5
TO HIS SIMPLICITY	TO HIS SIMPLICITY	1352	1

	FIRST LINE	POEM	LINE
SIMPLICITY (CONTINUED)			
IS SAFE--SIMPLICITY--	IF WRECKED UPON THE	1469	4
IN CASUAL [COMPETENT] SIMPLICITY--	HOW HAPPY IS THE LITTLE	1510	10
SIMPLIFIED			
NOR SIMPLIFIED [COMPROMISED] HER GHOST.	WHAT MYSTERY PERVADES A	1400	20
SIMPLY			
SIMPLY EXTINCTION'S DATE--	EMPTY MY HEART, OF THEE	587	4
BUT NEARER [CLOSER / FURTHER / SIMPLY / MERELY] TO ADORE	BECAUSE HE LOVES HER	1229	10
BUT SIMPLY--WE--OBEYED--	"GO TELL IT"--WHAT A	1554	4
AND PRESENCE, SIMPLY DAWN--	SOME SAY GOODNIGHT--AT	1739	6
SIMULATE			
NOR SIMULATE, A THROE--	I LIKE A LOOK OF AGONY,	241	4
I SIMULATE THE BREATH, SO WELL--	I BREATHED ENOUGH TO	272	3
TO SIMULATE--IS STINGING WORK--	I TIE MY HAT--I CREASE	443	19
TO SIMULATE, TO US.	AURORA IS THE EFFORT	1002	4
SIMULTANEOUS			
TAKE US SIMULTANEOUS--LORD--	WE DONT CRY--TIM AND I,	196	27
BUT SIMULTANEOUS AS SOUND	FURTHER IN SUMMER THAN	1068	V
HAS SIMULTANEOUS COME.	THE MURMURING OF BEES,	1115	4
SIMULTANEOUSLY			
AND SIMULTANEOUSLY, A SOUL	'TWAS CRISIS--ALL THE	948	15
SIN			
I COULD [MIGHT] HAVE DONE A SIN	I PLAY AT RICHES--TO	801	6
SIN--A DISTINGUISHED PRECIPICE	THE BIBLE IS AN ANTIQUE	1545	9
SINCE			
SINCE NONE OF THEM ARE MINE.	I HAD A GUINEA GOLDEN--	23	24
SINCE I AM OF THE DRUID,	IF SHE HAD BEEN THE	44	5
SINCE THE MIGHTY AUTUMN AFTERNOON	GOING TO HEAVEN!	79	26
BUT SINCE JESUS DARED--	"THEY HAVE NOT CHOSEN ME	85	6
SINCE YORKSHIRE HILLS ARE GREEN--	ALL OVERGROWN BY CUNNING	148	10
SINCE I COULD NEVER FIND HER	SHE DIED--THIS WAS THE	150	7
SINCE THAT MY LORD, "THE LORD OF LORDS"	WAIT TILL THE MAJESTY OF	171	15
SINCE BREAKING THEN--SINCE BREAKING THEN--	I SHOULD NOT DARE TO	205	14
SINCE BREAKING THEN--SINCE BREAKING THEN--	I SHOULD NOT DARE TO	205	14
YET--STRANGEST--HEAVIER SINCE IT WENT--	SAVIOR! I'VE NO ONE ELSE	217	11
SINCE THE SOLE EAR I CARED TO CHARM--	PUT UP MY LUTE!	261	3
AND EVER SINCE--THE PURPLE MOAT	THE LONESOME FOR THEY	262	5
SINCE THAT APPALLING DAY!	THE ONLY GHOST I EVER	274	16
BY ROBBER, SINCE THE GAIN	OF ALL THE SOUNDS	321	12
SINCE GRIEF AND JOY ARE DONE	SO GLAD WE ARE--A	329	6
SINCE MIDNIGHT--HAPPENED--SAY--	A TONGUE--TO TELL HIM I	400	13
BUT SINCE WE GOT A BOMB--	I TIE MY HAT--I CREASE	443	27
SINCE FOR THE QUEEN, HAVE I--	COULD--I DO MORE--FOR	447	3
BUT SINCE THE LAST--INCLUDED BOTH--	I MEANT TO HAVE BUT	476	5
BUT SINCE	I HAD NO TIME TO HATE--	478	8
SINCE I WAS WED--TO HIM--	THE WORLD--STANDS--	493	2
BUT--ISHMAEL--SINCE WE MET--'TIS LONG--	YOU KNOW THAT PORTRAIT	504	7
BUT SINCE IT IS PLAYING--KILL US,	WE DREAM--IT IS GOOD WE	531	3
THE HARM THEY DID--WAS SHORT [BRIEF]--AND SINCE	'TIS TRUE--THEY SHUT ME	538	9
MY FIRST WELL DAY--SINCE MANY ILL--	MY FIRST WELL DAY--SINCE	574	1
AND OFTEN SINCE, IN DANGER,	I PRAYED, AT FIRST, A	576	14
SINCE WE--OLD MORNINGS, CHILDREN--PLAYED--	OF NEARNESS TO HER	607	11
BUT SINCE MYSELF--ASSAULT ME--	ME FROM MYSELF--TO	642	5
AND SINCE WE'RE MUTUAL MONARCH	ME FROM MYSELF--TO	642	9
SINCE THEN--'TIS CENTURIES--AND YET	BECAUSE I COULD NOT STOP	712	21
SINCE A RACK COULD'NT COAX A SYLLABLE [AN ANSWER]--NOW	GRIEF IS A MOUSE--	793	17
SINCE SOMEWHERE THY SWEET FACE HAS SPILLED	I'VE NONE TO TELL ME TO	881	5
SINCE NO ONE KNOWS HIS CIRCUMSTANCE--	WHO OCCUPIES THIS HOUSE?	892	3
WHAT DID THEY DO SINCE I SAW THEM?	WHAT DID THEY DO SINCE I	900	1
BUT SINCE WE HOLD A MUTUAL DISC--	I MAKE HIS CRESCENT FILL	909	9
SINCE HEAVEN AND HE ARE ONE.	THE DEFINITION OF BEAUTY	988	4
THREE WEEKS PASSED SINCE I HAD SEEN HER--	THREE WEEKS PASSED SINCE	1061	1
NOW [SINCE] I [THAT] ABUNDANCE SEE--	OH SUMPTUOUS MOMENT	1125	5
SINCE I HOPED I DARED	WHEN I HOPED I FEARED--	1181	2
SUBSISTING NOW [SINCE] LIKE GOD--	ART THOU THE THING I	1282	V 8
SINCE IT WAS GATHERED [TETHERED] HERE--	PRAISE IT--'TIS DEAD--	1384	5
REMITTED--SINCE IT FLITTED IT	PRAISE IT--'TIS DEAD--	1384	8
SINCE SHE AND I HAD MET AND PLAYED	A LITTLE SNOW WAS HERE	1444	3
THAT PURLED A MOMENT SINCE WITH GLEE--	HIS VOICE DECREPIT WAS	1476	5
SINCE HE AND I WERE BOYS	THE SAVIOR MUST HAVE	1487	6
'TIS SEASONS SINCE THE DIMPLED WAR	'TIS SEASONS SINCE THE	1529	1
SINCE GIFT OF THEE--	SOCIETY FOR ME MY MISERY	1534	2
SINCE PLAYMATES AT THREESCORE AND TEN	MY WARS ARE LAID AWAY IN	1549	11
WHO SINCE THEY WENT TO THEIR ACCOUNT	HOW DARE THE ROBINS SING	1724	3
PROUD OF MY BROKEN HEART, SINCE THOU DIDST BREAK IT,	PROUD OF MY BROKEN HEART	1736	1
PROUD OF MY NIGHT, SINCE THOU WITH MOONS DOST SLAKE IT,	PROUD OF MY BROKEN HEART	1736	3
SINCERE			
IF JESUS WAS SINCERE--	DO PEOPLE MOULDER	432	12
REPORTLESS, ALSO, BUT SINCERE AS NATURE	IN MANY AND REPORTLESS	1382	3
SINCERER			
WE SEE ACUTER [DISTINCTER / SINCERER], QUITE,	BY A DEPARTING LIGHT	1714	2
SINCERITY			
TO HER SIMPLICITY [SINCERITY]	"NATURE" IS WHAT WE SEE	668	12
BUT HIS SINCERITY	JUDGEMENT IS JUSTEST	1671	5

	FIRST LINE	POEM	LINE
SINEW			
AND ALL OUR SINEW TORE--	I GOT SO I COULD HEAR	293	8
AND NOT A SINEW--STIRRED--COULD HELP,	'TWAS LIKE A MAELSTROM,	414	14
AND SINEW FROM WITHIN--	I ROSE--BECAUSE HE SANK	616	21
TO LEND AN AMPLE SINEW	TO OFFER BRAVE	767	5
NO SINEW CAN AFFORD--	SUCH IS THE FORCE OF	787	5
SINEWS			
AS SINEWS DO, WITH AGE--	THEY SAY THAT "TIME	686	4
WHAT ARE THE SINEWS OF SUCH CORDAGE FOR	THERE IS A STRENGTH IN	1113	3
SING			
AWAKE YE MUSES NINE, SING ME A STRAIN DIVINE,	AWAKE YE MUSES NINE,	1	1
WHICH FOR MYSELF DOTH SING--	I HAVE A BIRD IN SPRING	5	2
SHE DID NOT SING AS WE DID--	ONE SISTER HAVE I IN OUR	14	9
LIKE THEE TO DANCE--LIKE THEE TO SING--	THERE IS A MORN BY MEN	24	19
BESIDES THE AUTUMN POETS SING	BESIDES THE AUTUMN POETS	131	1
BEFORE THE BLACKBIRDS SING!	IT CANT BE "SUMMER"!	221	5
DID I SING--TOO LOUD?	WHY--DO THEY SHUT ME OUT	248	2
SING--AT IT'S PAIN--AS ANY WORKMAN--	BOUND--A TROUBLE--	269	9
I TOLD MY SOUL TO SING--	THE FIRST DAY'S NIGHT	410	4
THOUGH WINTER FIRE--SING CLEAR AS PLOVER--	IT'S THOUGHTS--AND JUST	495	15
DID HOIST HERSELF, TO SING,	HER SMILE WAS SHAPED	514	4
TO HEAR AN ORIOLE SING	TO HEAR AN ORIOLE SING	526	1
I SING TO USE THE WAITING	I SING TO USE THE	850	1
THE BIRD MUST SING TO EARN THE CRUMB	THE BIRD MUST SING TO	880	1
BIND ME--I STILL CAN SING--	BIND ME--I STILL CAN	1005	1
IN CONTRAST WITH THE [THOSE] THINGS THAT SING	A PANG IS MORE	1530	2
HOW DARE THE ROBINS SING,	HOW DARE THE ROBINS SING	1724	1
WOULD GO AND SING NO MORE.	THE SADDEST NOISE, THE	1764	16
SINGETH			
NO MORE HE SINGETH MOURNFUL, HER SADNESS SHE DOTH LOSE.	AWAKE YE MUSES NINE,	1	20
BUT WHEN HE SINGETH--THEN--	THE LIGHTNING PLAYETH--	630	2
SINGING			
WALKED SINGING ON THE SHORE.	THE FEET OF PEOPLE	7	8
I WILL SINGING GO--	DISTRUSTFUL OF THE	20	6
AN AXE SHRILL SINGING IN THE WOODS--	AN ALTERED LOOK ABOUT	140	11
I SHALL KEEP SINGING!	I SHALL KEEP SINGING!	250	1
ON TWIGS OF SINGING--RATHER HIGH--	I'M SAYING EVERY DAY	373	17
NO BOBOLINK--REVERSE HIS SINGING	NO BOBOLINK--REVERSE HIS	755	1
'TWAS AS SPACE SAT SINGING	MOST SHE TOUCHED ME BY	760	15
'TWAS WITH TEXT AND VILLAGE [ANTIQUE] SINGING	THREE WEEKS PASSED SINCE	1061	3
SINGING UNTO THE STONE	NOT WITH A CLUB, THE	1304	11
SINGLE			
GOD HATH MADE NOTHING SINGLE BUT THEE IN HIS WORLD SO FAIR!	AWAKE YE MUSES NINE,	1	6
I CHOSE THIS SINGLE STAR	ONE SISTER HAVE I IN OUR	14	25
BY WHICH A SINGLE BONE--	A SCIENCE--SO THE SAVANS	100	3
UNNOTICED AS A SINGLE DEW	EXCEPT TO HEAVEN, SHE IS	154	7
BUT JUST A SINGLE SMILE--	I CAME TO BUY A SMILE--	223	2
A SINGLE SCREW OF FLESH	A SINGLE SCREW OF FLESH	263	1
ANNIHILATE A SINGLE CLAUSE--	TO LOSE ONE'S FAITH--	377	7
DOTH NOT RETRACT A SINGLE SPICE	THERE IS A FLOWER THAT	380	23
BUT 'TIS A SINGLE HAIR--	I HAD NOT MINDED--WALLS	398	9
A SINGLE RAGGED CHILD--	A TONGUE--TO TELL HIM I	400	4
PRESENTS ME WITH A SINGLE CURL	'TIS CUSTOMARY AS WE	440	7
DEATH'S SINGLE PRIVACY	I LIVE WITH HIM--I SEE	463	4
THE SINGLE--TO SOME LIVES.	A SOLEMN THING WITHIN	483	16
UPON A SINGLE WHEEL--	WITHIN MY GARDEN, RIDES	500	2
AND YET, UNTO THE SINGLE DOE	ONE ANGUISH--IN A CROWD	565	3
IT'S SINGLE [GIANT] ARTERY--	EMPTY MY HEART, OF THEE	587	2
WITH BUT A SINGLE STAR--	THE NIGHT WAS WIDE, AND	589	2
AND JUST A SINGLE HERD--	THEY CALLED ME TO THE	628	4
FLOWER OF A SINGLE SUNSET--	BLOOM UPON THE MOUNTAIN	667	V 3
FOR JUST THIS SINGLE [THIS PECULIAR / JUST THIS ONLY] TIME--	I MEANT TO FIND HER WHEN	718	6
THAT SINGLE--STEADFAST SIGH--	"I WANT"--IT PLEADED--	731	6
THEN ORIENT SHOWED [THE EAST PUT OUT / NATURE PUT OUT] A SINGLE FLAG,	A DROP FELL ON THE APPLE	794	15
UNCONSCIOUS THAT HIS SINGLE FLEET [BULK / SAIL]	WHO GIANTS KNOW, WITH	796	7
TO LOOK AT THEE A SINGLE TIME	THE LUXURY TO APPREHEND	815	3
IS LADEN WITH A SINGLE CRUMB	THE LUXURY TO APPREHEND	815	15
ATTENDED BY A SINGLE HOUND	THIS CONSCIOUSNESS THAT	822	15
HIS BREAST, A SINGLE ONYX	HIS FEET ARE SHOD WITH	916	3
EMERGE A SINGLE NOON	THERE IS A JUNE WHEN	930	6
BESTOWS [CONFERRED] A SINGLE FRIEND--	A COFFIN--IS A SMALL	943	10
BUT FOR THAT SINGLE SPARK.	WE MET AS SPARKS--	958	V 8
OF A SINGLE BRAIN--	PAIN--EXPANDS THE TIME--	967	4
IT BLOOMED AND DROPT, A SINGLE NOON--	IT BLOOMED AND DROPT, A	978	1
THE SINGLE FLOWER OF THE EARTH	IT BLOOMED AND DROPT, A	978	17
OUR SINGLE [ONLY] COMPETITION	NO OTHER CAN REDUCE	982	7
A SINGLE BLOOM WE CONSTITUTE	HERE, WHERE THE DAISIES	1037	11
AT HALF PAST THREE, A SINGLE BIRD	AT HALF PAST THREE, A	1084	1
PROPOUNDED BUT A SINGLE TERM	AT HALF PAST THREE, A	1084	3
THAT COMES A SINGLE TIME A YEAR	THE SNOW THAT NEVER	1133	3
A SINGLE CLOVER PLANK [SPAR]	A SINGLE CLOVER PLANK	1343	1
THE MIND IS A SINGLE STATE--	THE HEART IS THE CAPITAL	1354	2
A SINGLE CONTINENT--	THE HEART IS THE CAPITAL	1354	4
A SINGLE HUMAN SOUL	WHOEVER DISENCHANTS	1451	2
THEY COME A SINGLE TIME	YOUR THOUGHTS DONT HAVE	1452	2

	FIRST LINE	POEM	LINE
SINGLE (CONTINUED)			
WITHOUT A SINGLE LEAF .	BEFORE YOU THOUGHT OF	1465	14
BIRTHDAY OF BUT A SINGLE PANG	BIRTHDAY OF BUT A SINGLE	1488	1
A SINGLE [ROYAL / SIGNAL / HALLOWED] TIME	TO BE FORGOT BY THEE	1560	9
TWO DAWNS UPON A SINGLE MORN,	MORNING THAT COMES BUT	1610	3
RANGE FROM A SINGLE HUMAN HEART	THE AUCTIONEER OF	1612	7
A SINGLE DRAM OF HEAVEN!	I TOOK ONE DRAUGHT OF	1725	8
SINGS			
THAT WHICH SINGS SO--SPEAKS SO--	BEFORE THE ICE IS IN THE	37	13
THAT EVERLASTING--SINGS!	A FEATHER FROM THE	161	2
AND SINGS THE TUNE WITHOUT THE WORDS--	"HOPE" IS THE THING WITH	254	3
OUR LITTLE SEXTON--SINGS.	SOME KEEP THE SABBATH	324	8
WHO SINGS THE SAME, UNHEARD,	TO HEAR AN ORIOLE SING	526	5
THE DITTY [SERMON] IS THAT NATURE SINGS--	THE WORTHLESSNESS OF	1373	2
ARRAIGNS IT AS IT SINGS.	NO LADDER NEEDS THE BIRD	1574	4
SINISTER			
TILL THE SUGGESTION SINISTER	WHOEVER DISENCHANTS	1451	7
SINK			
IF ANY SINK, ASSURE THAT THIS, NOW STANDING--	IF ANY SINK, ASSURE THAT	358	1
TO SINK, IF WE HAD LABORED, FOND	WHAT TWIGS WE HELD BY--	1086	12
IF MY BARK SINK	IF MY BARK SINK	1234	1
SINKING			
FROM SINKING [IN CRISIS / IN HAZARD] IN THE SKY--	A SINGLE CLOVER PLANK	1343	4
THREE TIMES, 'TIS SAID, A SINKING MAN	DROWNING IS NOT SO	1718	3
SINKS			
HOW SOFTLY SINKS THAT [HIS] TREMBLING SUN	LOOK BACK ON TIME, WITH	1478	3
SINS			
PAST THAT, HE SINS IN PEACE--	HIS CHEEK IS HIS	1460	4
SIP			
SIP OLD FRANKFORT AIR	MANY CROSS THE RHINE	123	3
BASHFUL--SIP THY JESSAMINES--	COME SLOWLY--EDEN!	211	3
SIP, GOBLIN, FROM THE VERY LIPS	THE SOUL HAS BANDAGED	512	7
SIPPED			
AND JUST SIPPED--ME--	ALL THE LETTERS I CAN	334	8
SIPS			
LIKE SIGNAL ESOTERIC SIPS	YOUR THOUGHTS DONT HAVE	1452	3
SIR			
THREE CHEERS, SIR, FOR THE GENTLEMAN	"SIC TRANSIT GLORIA	3	11
THE TRUMPET, SIR, SHALL WAKE THEM,	"SIC TRANSIT GLORIA	3	49
A COWARD WILL REMAIN, SIR,	"SIC TRANSIT GLORIA	3	53
GOOD BYE, SIR, I AM GOING;	"SIC TRANSIT GLORIA	3	57
ALLOW ME, SIR, AT PARTING,	"SIC TRANSIT GLORIA	3	59
AND FAREWELL, SIR, TO THEE!	"SIC TRANSIT GLORIA	3	68
WHEN ROSES CEASE TO BLOOM, SIR,	WHEN ROSES CEASE TO	32	1
BECAUSE, SIR, LOVE IS SWEET!	THE DAISY FOLLOWS SOFT	106	6
WHICH, SIR, ARE YOU AND WHICH AM I	IN LANDS I NEVER SAW--	124	7
'TIS IRIS, SIR, AND ASTER--	WHOSE ARE THE LITTLE	142	13
IN THINE ERMINE, SIR,	MUTE THY CORONATION--	151	4
OH FIND IT--SIR--FOR ME!	I LOST A WORLD--THE	181	8
PLEASE, SIR, I AND TIM--	WE DONT CRY--TIM AND I,	196	19
I'M PLEADING AT THE "COUNTER"--SIR--	I CAME TO BUY A SMILE--	223	7
SAY--MAY I HAVE IT--SIR?	I CAME TO BUY A SMILE--	223	14
YOU'LL KNOW--SIR--WHEN THE SAVIOR'S FACE	IF I'M LOST--NOW--	256	12
AH, SIR, NONE!	ONE YEAR AGO--JOTS WHAT?	296	37
THAT--SIR--WAS MY DEGREE--	THE FACE I CARRY WITH ME	336	6
YOUR SERVANT, SIR, WILL WEARY--	ALTHOUGH I PUT AWAY HIS	366	22
YOU, SIR, TAUGHT FIRST--TO ME.	ALTHOUGH I PUT AWAY HIS	366	33
ENTERS--WITH A "YOU KNOW ME--SIR"?	IT'S COMING--THE	390	4
ETERNITY, I'M COMING--SIR,	A WIFE--AT DAYBREAK I	461	12
"WHY DO I LOVE" YOU, SIR?	"WHY DO I LOVE" YOU, SIR	480	1
THE SUNRISE--SIR--COMPELLETH ME--	"WHY DO I LOVE" YOU, SIR	480	17
YOU--SWEET [SIR]--SHUT ME OUT--	SWEET--YOU FORGOT--BUT I	523	12
"NO SIR! IN THEE!"	TO HEAR AN ORIOLE SING	526	15
BUT, WHICH IS IT, SIR?	WOULD YOU LIKE SUMMER?	691	9
THO' GABRIEL--PRAISE ME--SIR--	WHERE THOU ART--THAT--IS	725	14
EVEN AS HERSELF--SIR--	ALTER! WHEN THE HILLS DO	729	7
"DISSOLVE" SAYS DEATH--THE SPIRIT "SIR	DEATH IS A DIALOGUE	976	3
SIRE			
YOU LEFT ME--SIRE [SWEET]--TWO LEGACIES--	YOU LEFT ME--SIRE--TWO	644	1
LIKE CHILDREN ROUND A SIRE--	THE MOUNTAIN SAT UPON	975	6
SANG FROM THE HEART, SIRE,	SANG FROM THE HEART,	1059	1
AS ROBINS [ROBIN]--SIRE AND SON--	FOREVER HONORED BE THE	1570	6
BUT THE LATTER, HER SIRE, IS HONORED	THE PARASOL IS THE	1747	V 7
SIREN			
THE SIREN ALPS	OUR LIVES ARE SWISS--	80	9
THE FORMER ASSISTS A SIREN	THE PARASOL IS THE	1747	5
WE ALMOST WISH THOSE SIREN THROATS	THE SADDEST NOISE, THE	1764	15
SIROCCOS			
I FELT SIROCCOS--CRAWL--	IT WAS NOT DEATH, FOR I	510	6
SISTER			
ONE SISTER HAVE I IN OUR HOUSE,	ONE SISTER HAVE I IN OUR	14	1
SUMMER--SISTER--SERAPH!	THE GENTIAN WEAVES HER	18	15
SUSPENSE--IS HIS MATURER SISTER--	WONDER--IS NOT PRECISELY	1331	5
BROTHER OF INGOTS--[SISTER OF OPHIR--] AH PERU--	BROTHER OF INGOTS--AH	1366	1
SISTERS			
BROTHERS AND SISTERS--WHO PREFERRED THE GLORY--	UNTO LIKE STORY--TROUBLE	295	3

	FIRST LINE	POEM	LINE
SIT			
AS BY THE DEAD WE LOVE TO SIT,	AS BY THE DEAD WE LOVE	88	1
THE NERVES SIT CEREMONIOUS, LIKE TOMBS--	AFTER GREAT PAIN, A	341	2
DOTH SIT UPON IT'S HEAD--	IT'S LITTLE ETHER HOOD	1501	2
'TWOULD START US WHERE WE SIT	A PIT--BUT HEAVEN OVER	1712	12
SITE			
THE SITE--OF IT--BY ARCHITECT	HEAVEN IS SO FAR OF THE	370	3
BY SHUNNING CAREFULLY THE PLACE [SPOT / SITE]	HAVE ANY LIKE MYSELF	736	19
FOR THE SITE OF THE KINGDOM OF HEAVEN--	A LOSS OF SOMETHING EVER	959	16
THE CIRCUMVENTION OF THE SHAFT [THOUGHT / SITE / FACT]	AS SUMMER INTO AUTUMN	1346	11
COMPARED WITH THAT PROFOUNDER SITE	THERE IS A SOLITUDE OF	1695	5
SITELESS			
OR FAME ERECT HER SITELESS CITADEL	SOCIETY FOR ME MY MISERY	1534	V
SITES			
THE SITES OF CENTRES STIRRED	LIKE RAIN IT SOUNDED	1235	14
SITS			
HE SITS ERECT IN "CABINETS"--	"ARCTURUS" IS HIS OTHER	70	15
SITS SHILY AT HIS FEET--	THE DAISY FOLLOWS SOFT	106	3
THE CAT THAT IN THE CORNER DWELLS [SITS]	A LITTLE DOG THAT WAGS	1185	9
SITTING			
SIX TRUE, AND COMELY MAIDENS SITTING UPON THE TREE;	AWAKE YE MUSES NINE,	1	34
SITTING [RIDING] A BOUGH LIKE A BRIGADIER	A PROMPT--EXECUTIVE BIRD	1177	5
SITUATE			
TO SITUATE ITS WINGS,	NO LADDER NEEDS THE BIRD	1574	2
SITUATED			
AND SITUATED SOFTLY	HIGH FROM THE EARTH I	1723	5
SITUATES			
LIKE JUGGLER'S FLOWERS [FIGURES] SITUATES	IT SIFTS FROM LEADEN	311	V
THE WILL IT IS THAT SITUATES--	THAT DISTANCE WAS	863	3
THAT SITUATES SO FAR--	PERCEPTION OF AN OBJECT	1071	8
SITUATIONS			
TO SITUATIONS [EXHIBITION / COMPREHENSION] NEW	ON THAT SPECIFIC PILLOW	1533	6
SIX			
SIX TRUE, AND COMELY MAIDENS SITTING UPON THE TREE;	AWAKE YE MUSES NINE,	1	34
THE TIME 'TWILL BE TILL SIX O'CLOCK	I TIE MY HAT--I CREASE	443	9
BY SIX, THE FLOOD [GUSH] HAD DONE--	THE BIRDS BEGUN AT FOUR	783	17
SIXPENCE			
A SIXPENCE AT A SHOW--	A TRANSPORT ONE CANNOT	184	6
SIZE			
AND YET--BY TRADES--THE SIZE OF THESE	IT'S SUCH A LITTLE THING	189	3
THE SMALLER SIZE!	JESUS! THY CRUCIFIX	225	3
AND THEN--THE SIZE OF THIS "SMALL" LIFE--	A SOLEMN THING--IT WAS--	271	13
WOULD SPLIT, FOR SIZE OF ME--	BEFORE I GOT MY EYE PUT	327	8
HIS FINGERS ARE THE SIZE OF FISTS--	THEY LEAVE US WITH THE	350	3
HIS FISTS, THE SIZE OF MEN--	THEY LEAVE US WITH THE	350	4
OR HAS AN EASIER SIZE.	I MEASURE EVERY GRIEF I	561	4
AND SHIPS--OF SUCH A SIZE	THEY CALLED ME TO THE	628	10
SIZE CIRCUMSCRIBES--IT HAS NO ROOM	SIZE CIRCUMSCRIBES--IT	641	1
BECAUSE INTRINSIC SIZE	SIZE CIRCUMSCRIBES--IT	641	6
IF 'TWAS A MEANER SIZE--	THEIR HIGHT IN HEAVEN	696	10
OR SMALL--OR ANY SIZE AT ALL--	YOU SAID THAT I "WAS	738	3
NAY--I'M THE SIZE SUIT THEE--	YOU SAID THAT I "WAS	738	4
FOR THIS ENCHANTED SIZE--	ONE BLESSING HAD I THAN	756	4
TO SO ESTEEMED A SIZE	DEPRIVED OF OTHER	773	6
TO ASCERTAIN [REGISTER] THE SIZE--	THE LONELINESS ONE DARE	777	4
BY PROCESSES [RUDIMENTS / PREFACES] OF SIZE	TIME FEELS SO VAST THAT	802	6
A WILDERNESS OF SIZE.	THERE IS A FINISHED	856	4
EXCEPT THE SMALLER SIZE	EXCEPT THE SMALLER SIZE	1067	1
AND ESTIMATE IT'S SIZE--	SO GIVE ME BACK TO DEATH	1632	6
IT'S SIZE IS ALL THAT HELL CAN GUESS--	SO GIVE ME BACK TO DEATH	1632	7
SKATER'S			
TO ACHE--AND LIKE A SKATER'S BROOK--	'TWAS WARM--AT FIRST--	519	7
SKATERS			
BEFORE THE SKATERS GO,	BEFORE THE ICE IS IN THE	37	2
SKEIN			
A SKEIN	DELIGHT IS AS THE FLIGHT	257	5
A SKEIN OF MISERY--	THE MONTHS HAVE ENDS--	423	4
SKEPTIC SEE SCEPTIC			
THE SKEPTIC--SHOWETH ME--	TO HEAR AN ORIOLE SING	526	14
SKEPTICISM			
SWEET SKEPTICISM OF THE HEART--	SWEET SKEPTICISM OF THE	1413	1
SKIES			
A MARCHING TO THE SKIES!	"SIC TRANSIT GLORIA	3	52
WHOSE CANTONS DOT THE SKIES--	THE FEET OF PEOPLE	7	20
AND THO' THE SKIES ARE CROWDED--	I HAD A GUINEA GOLDEN--	23	21
WHEN FROM A THOUSAND SKIES	IF PAIN FOR PEACE	63	10
I HOPE THE FATHER IN THE SKIES	"ARCTURUS" IS HIS OTHER	70	30
CAN I EXPOUND THE SKIES?	SOME THINGS THAT FLY	89	8
OH SOME WISE MAN FROM THE SKIES!	WILL THERE REALLY BE A	101	10
THESE ARE THE DAYS WHEN SKIES RESUME	THESE ARE THE DAYS WHEN	130	4
IN SCHOLASTIC SKIES!	IF THE FOOLISH, CALL	168	16
I DONT CARE FOR POUTING SKIES!	I'M THE LITTLE "HEART'S	176	2
THE SKIES CANT KEEP THEIR SECRET!	THE SKIES CANT KEEP	191	1
AND EMPTY SKIES	DELIGHT IS AS THE FLIGHT	257	17
I TAKE--NO LESS THAN SKIES--	PERHAPS I ASKED TOO	352	2
TO THE SKIES--APOLOGIZE--	TAKE YOUR HEAVEN FURTHER	388	8
AND IN THE HANDSOME SKIES	I NEVER FELT AT HOME--	413	2

	FIRST LINE	POEM	LINE
SKIES (CONTINUED)			
HIMSELF--COULD HAVE THE SKIES--	NOT IN THIS WORLD TO SEE	418	12
LEST SKIES IMPEACH A WEALTH SO WONDERFUL--	I'LL CLUTCH--AND CLUTCH	427	23
BUT I, GROWN SHREWDER--SCAN THE SKIES	I MEANT TO HAVE BUT	476	25
AND THAT'S--THE SKIES--	DELIGHT--BECOMES	572	8
AND DECKS--TO SEAT THE SKIES--	THEY CALLED ME TO THE	628	12
A MATTER OF THE SKIES.	IT IS A LONESOME GLEE--	774	8
DO NOT COMPRISE THE SKIES--	WHO GIANTS KNOW, WITH	796	8
THAT CHIEFER TO THE SKIES	TO THIS WORLD SHE	830	6
WHAT SHALL I DO WHEN THE SKIES A'CHIRRUP	WHAT SHALL I DO WHEN THE	956	5
OUR STATURES TOUCH THE SKIES--	WE NEVER KNOW HOW HIGH	1176	4
A FELLOW IN THE SKIES	BEFORE YOU THOUGHT OF	1465	4
NO LADDER NEEDS THE BIRD BUT SKIES	NO LADDER NEEDS THE BIRD	1574	1
THE GODS [STARS / HEAVENS / SKIES / SUNS] BUT DREGS	A WORLD MADE PENNINILESS	1623	4
COMES UP TO FACE THE SKIES,	DROWNING IS NOT SO	1718	4
SKILFUL			
WHAT SKILFUL [ANXIOUS] POINTERS MOVE--	NOT TO DISCOVER WEAKNESS	1054	8
SKILL			
TEACH ME THE SKILL,	AH, NECROMANCY SWEET!	177	3
GENEVA'S FARTHEST SKILL	A CLOCK STOPPED--	287	3
AND HE WILL TELL YOU--SKILL IS LATE--	THERE IS A LANGUOR OF	396	13
SKILL--TO HOLD MY BROW LIKE AN EARL--	I AM ASHAMED--I HIDE--	473	16
BUT THROUGH THEIR THICKEST SKILL--	THEY PUT US FAR APART--	474	10
THROUGH SKILL OBTAINED IN THEMSELVES--	THE PROVINCE OF THE	539	3
ACQUIRE THE QUICK OF SKILL--	'TIS ONE BY ONE--THE	545	6
HE GAINS THE SKILL	THE CHILD'S FAITH IS NEW	637	21
WHEN SKILL ENTREATED IT--THE LAST--	"I WANT"--IT PLEADED--	731	3
WE CONJUGATE HER SKILL	THE VEINS OF OTHER	811	6
ACCORDING AS HIS SKILL PREFER	JUST AS HE SPOKE IT FROM	848	5
THAT LOOKS A HARDER SKILL TO US--	ONLY A SHRINE, BUT MINE	918	9
LET US DIVIDE [DEPORT]--WITH SKILL--	A MAN MAY MAKE A REMARK	952	5
EXPIRE WITH HIM THE SKILL	ELIJAH'S WAGON KNEW NO	1254	6
WITH HIM THE SKILL [RIGHT / ART] REMAIN	ELIJAH'S WAGON KNEW NO	1254	V 6
OUT OF REACH OF SKILL--	DEATH IS LIKE THE INSECT	1716	10
SKILLFUL			
LESS SKILLFUL THAN LE VERRIERE	SHE WENT AS QUIET AS THE	149	7
SKIM			
WHETHER IT'S BUTTERCUPS--THAT "SKIM"--	MAKE ME A PICTURE OF THE	188	10
SKIP			
FOR THEE TO BLOOM, I'LL SKIP THE TOMB	SUMMER FOR THEE, GRANT I	31	5
THEN--SKIP--THE FROST--UPON THE LEA--	MAKE ME A PICTURE OF THE	188	12
AND SKIP THE RUSSET--ON THE TREE--	MAKE ME A PICTURE OF THE	188	13
OR SKIP TO FLUTES--	ALTHOUGH I PUT AWAY HIS	366	20
SKIPPED			
THE LIGHTNING PLAYED [SKIPPED] LIKE MICE	THE CLOUDS THEIR BACKS	1172	4
SKIPPER			
WHAT SKIPPER WOULD	DOWN TIME'S QUAINT	1656	6
SKIRMISH			
FELL, THEY WILL SAY, IN "SKIRMISH"!	I'VE GOT AN ARROW HERE.	1729	4
SKIRTED			
BUT SKIRTED IN THE DARK--	THE LONELINESS ONE DARE	777	10
SKIRTING			
SOME SAILOR, SKIRTING FOREIGN [NOVEL] SHORES--	JUST LOST, WHEN I WAS	160	9
SKIRTS			
SKIRTS THE ACRES OF PERHAPS--	THEIR HIGHT IN HEAVEN	696	7
SKY			
THERE IS ANOTHER SKY,	THERE IS ANOTHER SKY,	2	1
AND SHOUTS FILL ALL MY CHILDISH SKY,	I HAVE A KING, WHO DOES	103	10
IN THE FAIR SCHOOLROOM OF THE SKY--	I SHALL KNOW WHY--WHEN	193	4
COMPOSE AN EVENING SKY--	A SLASH OF BLUE--	204	4
THIS JUST MAKES OUT THE MORNING SKY.	A SLASH OF BLUE--	204	9
AS "A FATHER"--IN THE SKY--	WHAT IS--"PARADISE"--	215	12
LEAPING LIKE LEOPARDS TO [IN] THE SKY	BLAZING IN GOLD AND	228	2
UNTIL A SUDDEN SKY	HOW NOTELESS MEN, AND	282	2
STARING--BEWILDERED [DEFRAUDED]--AT THE MOCKING SKY--	THE NEAREST DREAM	319	10
WHOSE FINGERS COMB [BRUSH] THE SKY--	OF ALL THE SOUNDS	321	6
OFF [ON] DESERTS, IN THE SKY,	OF ALL THE SOUNDS	321	30
THAT I MIGHT HAVE THE SKY	BEFORE I GOT MY EYE PUT	327	6
TO AN ADMIRING SKY--	THE FACE I CARRY WITH ME	336	14
DISDAINED THEM, FROM THE SKY--	FROM COCOON FORTH A	354	21
AS WELL THE SKY	I GAINED IT SO--	359	6
AND LEFT IT IN THE SKY--	IT STRUCK ME--EVERY DAY	362	12
HELD SLANTING, IN THE SKY--	THE ANGLE OF A LANDSCAPE	375	8
AND GAIN THE SKY	NO RACK CAN TORTURE ME--	384	11
IS HEAVEN A PLACE--A SKY--A TREE?	WE PRAY--TO HEAVEN--	489	6
THIS MOURNER--TO THE SKY	THE BLACK BERRY--WEARS A	554	10
AS EVEN IN THE SKY--	WHEN I WAS SMALL, A	596	16
REPEATED--IN THE SKY--	THE TINT I CANNOT TAKE--	627	8
SUSTAIN HER IN THE SKY--	I WATCHED THE MOON	629	16
WITH SHINING--AND THE SKY--	I WATCHED THE MOON	629	28
THE BRAIN--IS WIDER THAN THE SKY--	THE BRAIN--IS WIDER THAN	632	1
'TWAS SUNRISE--'TWAS THE SKY--	TO MY SMALL HEARTH HIS	638	4
TO OBTAIN THE SKY--	HER SWEET TURN TO LEAVE	649	20
THE GAMBRELS [GABLES] OF THE SKY--	I DWELL IN POSSIBILITY--	657	8
FIRST TIME THEY TRY THE SKY!	AGAIN--HIS VOICE IS AT	663	23
THE SKY--	EACH LIFE CONVERGES TO	680	16
AND MAELSTROM--IN THE SKY--	BEHIND ME--DIPS ETERNITY	721	18
EASIER--FOR THE SKY--	LET US PLAY YESTERDAY--	728	26

	FIRST LINE	POEM	LINE
SKY (CONTINUED)			
SO EASY TO THE SKY--	HAVE ANY LIKE MYSELF	736	12
SANK THIS [THE] BEGGAR FROM THE SKY-- . .	MOST SHE TOUCHED ME BY	760	10
OVERTAKE THE SKY--	WHEN I HOPED, I	768	V 22
THEN BENDING [STOOPING] FROM THE SKY-- . .	NATURE--THE GENTLEST	790	20
THAT SPLIT THEIR ROUTE TO THE SKY-- . . .	BY MY WINDOW HAVE I FOR	797	6
THAT PLY BETWEEN IT AND THE SKY	BY MY WINDOW HAVE I FOR	797	V 6
THE HABIT OF A FOREIGN SKY	AWAY FROM HOME ARE SOME	821	5
A HAND FULL AT THE SKY--	THE WIND BEGUN TO KNEAD	824	4
A MENACE AT THE SKY.	THE WIND BEGUN TO KNEAD	824	V 4
THE WATERS WRECKED THE SKY--	THE WIND BEGUN TO KNEAD	824	18
A CLOUD WITHDREW FROM THE SKY	A CLOUD WITHDREW FROM	895	1
SHOULD THEY START FOR THE SKY.	WHAT DID THEY DO SINCE I	900	8
HE HOLDS SUPERIOR IN THE SKY	I MAKE HIS CRESCENT FILL	909	5
FROM AN ABUNDANT SKY.	SUPERFLUOUS WERE THE SUN	999	12
TILL SWOLLEN WITH THE SKY	HOW STILL THE BELLS IN	1008	2
THE SKY IS LOW--THE CLOUDS ARE MEAN. . . .	THE SKY IS LOW--THE	1075	1
UNTO A SILENT SKY	AT HALF PAST THREE, A	1084	2
AND EASY SWEEPS OF SKY--	MY COCOON TIGHTENS--	1099	8
WITH [BY] MORNING IN THE SKY	OH SUMPTUOUS MOMENT	1125	9
FROM TABLES IN THE SKY	THE LIGHTNING IS A	1173	2
IN ALL THE DEEPEST SKY	A SPARROW TOOK A SLICE	1211	6
SPRANG LIGHTLY TO [ROSE SOFTLY IN / TURNED EASY IN] THE SKY	A SPARROW TOOK A SLICE	1211	V 6
ON HIS BRITISH SKY.	WE LIKE MARCH.	1213	13
MUST PROVE THERE IS A SKY	SO MUCH OF HEAVEN HAS	1228	6
THE RIVER AND THE SKY.	THE MOUNTAINS STOOD IN	1278	4
THE HEAVENS [TREES / SKY / FIELD] CANNOT BE FOUND--	THE SYMPTOM OF THE GALE	1327	6
FROM SINKING [IN CRISIS / IN HAZARD] IN THE SKY--	A SINGLE CLOVER PLANK	1343	4
A WILD BLUE SKY ABREAST OF WINDS	A WILD BLUE SKY ABREAST	1415	1
CORRECTING ERRORS OF THE SKY	HOW LONESOME THE WIND	1418	7
THERE WAS NO HARM IN EARTH OR SKY-- . . .	IT WAS A QUIET SEEMING	1419	2
TRUTH IS GOOD HEALTH--AND SAFETY, AND THE SKY.	A COUNTERFEIT--A PLATED	1453	5
THEIR BARRICADE AGAINST THE SKY	THEIR BARRICADE AGAINST	1471	1
TO SEE THE SUMMER SKY	TO SEE THE SUMMER SKY	1472	1
THE COMPETITIONS OF THE SKY	THE COMPETITIONS OF THE	1494	1
THE BUTTERFLY UPON THE SKY, ...	THE BUTTERFLY UPON THE	1521	1
AND FILLING ALL THE EARTH AND AIR [SKY] . .	HIS ORIENTAL HERESIES	1526	3
TO AN INSULTED SKY	NO BRIGADIER THROUGHOUT	1561	14
A PEACE AS PURE AS IF THE SKY	TO SEE HER IS A PICTURE	1568	V 7
ENTICED TO BREAKFAST FROM THE SKY	FOREVER HONORED BE THE	1570	3
WAS NEARER THAN THE SKY	THE FARTHEST THUNDER	1581	2
THAT WE ARE OF THE SKY	EXTOL THEE--COULD I--	1643	6
ABOVE HIM IS THE SKY--[BENEATH]	THE DITCH IS DEAR TO THE	1645	6
A CAP OF LEAD ACROSS THE SKY	A CAP OF LEAD ACROSS THE	1649	1
OF YELLOW WAS THE OUTER SKY	OF YELLOW WAS THE OUTER	1676	1
A CURIOUS CLOUD SURPRISED THE SKY, ...	A CURIOUS CLOUD	1710	1
SLACKED			
NEVER SLACKED THE DIGGERS--	IN FALLING TIMBERS	614	9
SLACKENS			
HE NEVER STOPS, BUT SLACKENS	WITHIN MY GARDEN, RIDES	500	5
SLACKER			
AND STRUGGLE SLACKER--BUT TO PROVE . . .	I MANY TIMES THOUGHT	739	5
SLAIN			
BY EVENING'S SABRES [SABRE] SLAIN	SOFT AS THE MASSACRE OF	1127	2
'TWAS VICTORY WAS SLAIN.	THE STARS ARE OLD, THAT	1249	8
AND EACH OF US WERE SLAIN	'TIS SEASONS SINCE THE	1529	3
TO CAPTIVATE THE SLAIN--	A PANG IS MORE	1530	V
SLAKE			
SOME PILGRIM THIRST TO SLAKE--	I BRING AN UNACCUSTOMED	132	19
THAT MEN, MUST SLAKE IN WILDERNESS-- . . .	I THINK THE HEMLOCK	525	5
PROUD OF MY NIGHT, SINCE THOU WITH MOONS DOST SLAKE IT,	PROUD OF MY BROKEN HEART	1736	3
SLAM			
THE BROOKS SLAM [BRAG]--ALL THE DAY-- . .	IT MAKES NO DIFFERENCE	620	6
SLANT			
THERE'S A CERTAIN SLANT OF LIGHT, ...	THERE'S A CERTAIN SLANT	258	1
AND THEY'LL SLANT--	GIVE LITTLE ANGUISH--	310	4
TELL ALL THE TRUTH BUT TELL IT SLANT-- . .	TELL ALL THE TRUTH BUT	1129	1
SLANTED			
THAT SLANTED IN MY PATH--	THE JUDGE IS LIKE THE	699	5
SLANTING			
HELD SLANTING, IN THE SKY--	THE ANGLE OF A LANDSCAPE	375	8
SLANTS			
BESIDES--IT ISN'T EVEN--IT SLANTS	WE DO NOT PLAY ON GRAVES	467	3
SLASH			
A SLASH OF BLUE--	A SLASH OF BLUE--	204	1
SLASHING			
AND WHEN--SOME NIGHT--BOLD--SLASHING CLOUDS	YOU KNOW THAT PORTRAIT	504	13
SLATE			
SAINTS, WITH RAVISHED SLATE AND PENCIL . .	I CANT TELL YOU--BUT YOU	65	3
'TIS MOSTLY SLATE AND PENCIL--	'TIS ONE BY ONE--THE	545	9
SLAVE			
THE SLAVE--FORGETS--TO FILL--	THE LAMP BURNS SURE--	233	5
AS THAT THE SLAVE--IS GONE.	THE LAMP BURNS SURE--	233	8
SLAY			
WHY--SLAY--ME?	HE STRAINED MY FAITH--	497	V 16
SLAY--AND MY SOUL SHALL RISE	BIND ME--I STILL CAN	1005	4

	FIRST LINE	POEM	LINE
SLAY (CONTINUED)			
DISPERSE IT--SLAY IT--	YOU CANNOT MAKE	1508	V
THAT MENACED NOT TO SLAY US,	OF DEATH I TRY TO THINK	1558	4
SOME ARROWS SLAY BUT WHOM THEY STRIKE--	SOME ARROWS SLAY BUT	1565	1
SLEDS			
SHOT THE LITHE SLEDS LIKE SHOD VIBRATIONS	GLASS WAS THE STREET--IN	1498	5
SLEEK			
HOW SLEEK THE WOE APPEARS	SOFTENED BY TIME'S	1738	2
SLEEP			
SLEEP IS SUPPOSED TO BE	SLEEP IS SUPPOSED TO BE	13	1
SLEEP IS THE STATION GRAND	SLEEP IS SUPPOSED TO BE	13	4
THERE'S SOMETHING QUIETER THAN SLEEP	THERE'S SOMETHING	45	1
NEW WEARY SLEEP BELOW--	NEW FEET WITHIN MY	99	6
HALF GLAD WHEN IT IS NIGHT, AND SLEEP,	I HAVE A KING, WHO DOES	103	4
WHERE TIRED CHILDREN PLACID SLEEP	WHERE BELLS NO MORE	112	5
IF THIS IS "SLEEP,"	IF THIS IS "FADING"	120	5
IT LISTENING--LISTENING--WENT TO SLEEP--	I SHOULD NOT DARE TO	205	11
SLEEP [LIE] THE MEEK MEMBERS OF THE RESURRECTION--	SAFE IN THEIR ALABASTER	216	4
AND WENT TO SLEEP--	I HELD A JEWEL IN MY	245	2
HAD GONE TO SLEEP--THAT SOUNDEST TIME--	TO DIE--TAKES JUST A	255	11
ON MY SIMPLE SLEEP--	MANY A PHRASE HAS THE	276	10
TO GUAGE THE SLEEP--	I KNOW SOME LONELY	289	V 10
LIKE [AS] LOWLY SPICES, LAIN TO SLEEP [GONE TO SLEEP / LAID . . .	THE GRASS SO LITTLE HAS	333	15
LIKE [AS] LOWLY SPICES, LAIN TO SLEEP [GONE TO SLEEP / LAID . . .	THE GRASS SO LITTLE HAS	333	15
. . . ASLEEP / LAID TO SLEEP]--	THE GRASS SO LITTLE HAS	333	15
TO FORCE HER SLEEP--	SHE LAY AS IF AT PLAY	369	15
I DID NOT DARE TO EAT--OR SLEEP--	IT WAS GIVEN TO ME BY	454	7
AND THEN--TO GO TO SLEEP--	THE HEART ASKS PLEASURE	536	5
MY BEST--WAS GONE TO SLEEP--	I HAD NO CAUSE TO BE	542	2
HAVE SOBBED OURSELVES ALMOST TO SLEEP,	I CRIED AT PITY--NOT AT	588	23
A LONG--LONG [VAST--VAST / BRAVE--BRAVE] SLEEP--A FAMOUS--SLEEP--	A LONG--LONG SLEEP--A	654	1
A LONG--LONG [VAST--VAST / BRAVE--BRAVE] SLEEP--A FAMOUS--SLEEP--	A LONG--LONG SLEEP--A	654	1
DREAMS TINT THE SLEEP--	LET US PLAY YESTERDAY--	728	10
THE FLOWERS WOULD SLUMBER ON [SLEEP UPON--] THEIR STEMS--	MY FAITH IS LARGER THAN	766	11
WHEN ALL THE CHILDREN SLEEP--	NATURE--THE GENTLEST	790	17
IF IT COME IN SLEEP	CRISIS IS A HAIR	889	4
AS IN SLEEP--ALL HUE FORGOTTEN--	COLOR--CASTE--	970	5
THE SOUL CAME HOME FROM TRIPS [FROM TOWNS / FROM SCENES / TO SLEEP]	CONTAINED IN THIS SHORT	1165	V
TO SCRUTINIZE THE SLEEP.	THE SUBURBS OF A SECRET	1245	4
I OFTEN IN THE NIGHT [MY SLEEP]	ESCAPE IS SUCH A	1347	2
FOR THOSE AVERSE TO SLEEP--	WATER MAKES MANY BEDS	1428	2
AND WHETHER SLEEP WILL STAY	ON THAT SPECIFIC PILLOW	1533	4
NOW I LAY THEE DOWN TO SLEEP--	NOW I LAY THEE DOWN TO	1539	1
THOUGH THE GREAT WATERS SLEEP,	THOUGH THE GREAT WATERS	1599	1
HE WENT BY SLEEP THAT DROWSY ROUTE	HE WENT BY SLEEP THAT	1662	1
BUT LOVE IS TIRED AND MUST SLEEP,	LOVE CAN DO ALL BUT	1731	5
OR THAT THAT WENT TO SLEEP	WHICH MISSES MOST,	1759	8
SLEEPING			
YET THEY ARE SLEEPING STILL,--	"SIC TRANSIT GLORIA	3	48
SEXTON! MY MASTER'S SLEEPING HERE.	SEXTON! MY MASTER'S	96	1
STAID SLEEPING--THERE--	I KNOW SOME LONELY	289	30
CLOSER--SO I--AT MY SLEEPING [SIGHING]--	DONT PUT UP MY THREAD &	617	19
ALAS--AND ART THOU SLEEPING YET?	'TIS SUNRISE--LITTLE	908	6
SLEEPS			
THEN SLEEPS IN STATE AGAIN--	ALL THESE MY BANNERS BE.	22	5
IN PLACID [CHINTZ AND] LILY SLEEPS!	A LADY RED--AMID THE	74	4
TELL ME WHAT TIME THE WEAVER SLEEPS	BRING ME THE SUNSET IN A	128	5
SLEEPY			
AND YOU--GOT SLEEPY--AND BEGGED TO BE ENDED--	GOING TO HIM! HAPPY	494	20
THEN HOW THE GRIEF GOT SLEEPY--SOME--	IF I MAY HAVE IT, WHEN	577	18
THE WAVES GREW SLEEPY--[THE OCEAN--TIRED-- / THE OCEAN-- . . .	THREE TIMES--WE PARTED--	598	13
AND DRESS [CURL] THE SLEEPY DAY--	HOW GOOD HIS LAVA BED,	1447	4
SLEET			
I SHALL NOT FEEL THE SLEET--THEN--	DISTRUSTFUL OF THE	20	7
THE SLEET--THAN MAY, NO THEE--	THE NIGHT WAS WIDE, AND	589	20
THE SLEET--THE BITTER WIND--	THE BEGGAR LAD--DIES	717	12
NOT A SLEET COULD BITE ME--	WHEN I HOPED, I	768	5
OH FAITHFUL FROST [SLEET] THAT KEPT THE DATE	IT CAME AT LAST BUT	1230	5
SLEEVE			
UPON A DANDELION'S SLEEVE--	I STARTED EARLY--TOOK MY	520	15
SLEIGH			
AS SLEIGH BELLS SEEM [SOUND] IN SUMMER	AS SLEIGH BELLS SEEM IN	981	1
SLENDER			
BUT GROWN BY SLENDER ADDINGS	DEPRIVED OF OTHER	773	5
TOO SLENDER FOR THE EYE	FAITH--IS THE PIERLESS	915	4
SLEPT			
SHE SLEPT BENEATH A TREE--	SHE SLEPT BENEATH A TREE	25	1
BUT SHE SLEPT--	I WENT TO THANK HER--	363	2
BUT SHE SLEPT--	I WENT TO THANK HER--	363	7
WHEN I SLEPT--AT NIGHT--	LET US PLAY YESTERDAY--	728	22
SLEW			
I SLEW A WORM THE OTHER DAY--	"ARCTURUS" IS HIS OTHER	70	5

	FIRST LINE	POEM	LINE
SLEW (CONTINUED)			
MOST--I LOVE THE CAUSE THAT SLEW ME.	STRUCK, WAS I, NOR YET	925	17
FATE SLEW HIM, BUT HE DID NOT DROP--	FATE SLEW HIM, BUT HE	1031	1
BUT THIS SLEW ALL BUT HIM--	SOME ARROWS SLAY BUT	1565	2
SLICE			
A SPARROW TOOK A SLICE OF TWIG	A SPARROW TOOK A SLICE	1211	1
SLID			
THE HOURS SLID FAST--AS HOURS WILL, ...	THERE CAME A DAY AT	322	17
AND BACK IT SLID--AND I ALONE--	I SAW NO WAY--THE	378	5
SLID CARELESSLY AWAY--	I WATCHED THE MOON	629	14
DEPART, BEFORE THE HOST HAVE SLID	THE SOUL SHOULD ALWAYS	1055	5
TILL SAFFRON IN VERMILLION SLID	OF YELLOW WAS THE OUTER	1676	3
SLIDE			
AND CITIES--OOZE [SLIP / SLIDE / MELT] AWAY--	A STILL--VOLCANO--LIFE--	601	12
SLIDES			
THE MOON--SLIDES DOWN THE STAIR, ...	I KNOW SOME LONELY	289	23
SLIGHT			
THE THOUGHT BENEATH SO SLIGHT A FILM-- . .	THE THOUGHT BENEATH SO	210	1
AND HANDS--SO SLIGHT--	A MIEN TO MOVE A QUEEN--	283	13
WHICH OTHERS TASTE AND SPURN AND SNEER [SLIGHT]--	I GROPED FOR HIM BEFORE	1555	5
SLIGHTEST			
I WAS THE SLIGHTEST IN THE HOUSE--	I WAS THE SLIGHTEST IN	486	1
SLIGHTLY			
AS SLIGHTLY [SCARCELY] AS THE ROUTES [FLIGHTS] OF STARS--	WE MISS HER, NOT BECAUSE	993	5
SLILY			
AND SLOWLY [SLILY / SOFTLY] PICK THE LOCK--	THE WAY I READ A	636	8
SLIM			
NODS FROM THE SECONDS SLIM--	A CLOCK STOPPED--	287	15
FINGERS OF THE SLIM AURORA--	THESE--SAW VISIONS--	758	10
FROM HIS SLIM PALACE IN THE DUST	FROM HIS SLIM PALACE IN	1300	1
THEN TO A RHYTHM SLIM	IN WINTER IN MY ROOM	1670	28
SLINK			
THEY SLINK BEFORE THE CLAY, ...	A SINGLE SCREW OF FLESH	263	18
WHOSE NAMELESS FATHOMS SLINK AWAY	CONTAINED IN THIS SHORT	1165	7
OUR LITTLE SECRETS SLINK AWAY--	OUR LITTLE SECRETS SLINK	1326	1
SLIP			
AND CITIES--OOZE [SLIP / SLIDE / MELT] AWAY--	A STILL--VOLCANO--LIFE--	601	12
TILL WHEN IT [AND THEN DOTH] SLIP AWAY . .	IT'S LITTLE ETHER HOOD	1501	5
BUT MY FEET SLIP NEARER EVERY DAY	I DID NOT REACH THEE	1664	2
TO STIR WOULD BE TO SLIP--	A PIT--BUT HEAVEN OVER	1712	5
SLIPPED			
SLIPPED QUIET FROM IT'S CHAIR--	ON SUCH A NIGHT, OR SUCH	146	4
A LITTLE PURPLE--SLIPPED BETWEEN--	A SLASH OF BLUE--	204	5
THAT SLIPPED MY SIMPLE FINGERS THROUGH-- .	YOUR RICHES--TAUGHT ME--	299	31
THE WOMEN--PLUCKED [SLIPPED] AWAY	THOSE FAIR--FICTITIOUS	499	2
MY BRIDE HAD SLIPPED AWAY--	HER SWEET WEIGHT ON MY	518	4
WHEN SWIFT [QUICK] IT SLIPPED IT'S LIMIT-- .	HE GAVE AWAY HIS LIFE--	567	7
IT SLIPPED--AND SLIPPED--	IT TOSSED--AND TOSSED--	723	5
IT SLIPPED--AND SLIPPED--	IT TOSSED--AND TOSSED--	723	5
SLIPPER			
SO TIPTOED MANY A SLIPPER	SO HAS A DAISY VANISHED	28	3
SLIPPERS			
THEIR SLIPPERS LEAPED THE TOWN, ...	I COUNTED TILL THEY	36	2
SLIPPING			
SLIPPING--IS CRASHE'S LAW.	CRUMBLING IS NOT AN	997	12
THOUGH SLIPPING--SLIPPING I PERCEIVE	STILL OWN THEE--STILL	1633	3
THOUGH SLIPPING--SLIPPING I PERCEIVE	STILL OWN THEE--STILL	1633	3
SLIPS			
FAITH SLIPS--AND LAUGHS, AND RALLIES-- . .	THIS WORLD IS NOT	501	13
THAT TIPS SO FREQUENT, [SLIPS SO EASY] NOW,	I PRAYED, AT FIRST, A	576	19
AS SUMMER INTO AUTUMN SLIPS	AS SUMMER INTO AUTUMN	1346	1
A SLOOP OF AMBER SLIPS AWAY	A SLOOP OF AMBER SLIPS	1622	1
SLIPT			
UNOBSERVED--A RIBIN SLIPT, ...	SUMMER LAID HER SIMPLE	1363	3
SLIT			
AS IF THE CLOUD THAT INSTANT SLIT	IT STRUCK ME--EVERY DAY	362	3
WHEN FLOODS HAVE SLIT THE HILLS--	THE BRAIN, WITHIN IT'S	556	6
BRIGHT FLOWERS SLIT A CALYX	THE TREES LIKE TASSELS--	606	21
I TOUCHED WITH CAUTION--LEST THEY CRACK [SLIT]--	IF HE WERE LIVING--DARE	734	7
SLIVER			
THE SLIVER, IN THE LUNG--	ONE ANGUISH--IN A CROWD	565	10
SLOOP			
A SLOOP OF AMBER SLIPS AWAY	A SLOOP OF AMBER SLIPS	1622	1
SLOPE			
A PURPLE FINGER ON THE SLOPE--	AN ALTERED LOOK ABOUT	140	6
UPON THE FURTHEST SLOPE YOU KNOW	A LIGHT EXISTS IN SPRING	812	11
SLOW			
HAD NOT THE BLISS SO SLOW A PACE	DELAYED TILL SHE HAD	58	10
BY WHICH CHILDREN SLOW	I CANT TELL YOU--BUT YOU	65	18
THEN BUBBLED SLOW AWAY!	HEART, NOT SO HEAVY AS	83	12
AS SLOW HER FLAMBEAUX BURN AWAY	A SOMETHING IN A	122	2
SLOW TRAMP THE CENTURIES, ...	JUST LOST, WHEN I WAS	160	18
AT FIRST, REPEAT IT SLOW!	'TIS SO MUCH JOY! 'TIS	172	15
THE SLOW--ARCHANGEL'S SYLLABLES	ON THIS LONG STORM THE	194	11
TRAILED--SLOW--ALONG THE ORCHARDS--	THE SUN--JUST TOUCHED	232	9
STEALTH'S--SLOW--	I KNOW SOME LONELY	289	32
THE DAY CAME SLOW--TILL FIVE O'CLOCK-- . .	THE DAY CAME SLOW--TILL	304	1

	FIRST LINE	POEM	LINE
SLOW (CONTINUED)			
THEN NEARER--THEN SO SLOW	HE FUMBLES AT YOUR SOUL	315	8
SLOW--SLOW--AS FEET DID WEARY--GROW--	'TWAS THE OLD--ROAD--	344	10
SLOW--SLOW--AS FEET DID WEARY--GROW--	'TWAS THE OLD--ROAD--	344	10
BY CLIMBING SLOW--	I GAINED IT SO--	359	2
BUT TURNING BACK--'TWAS SLOW--	I WENT TO THANK HER--	363	10
SLOW GOLD--BUT EVERLASTING--	SOME--WORK FOR	406	5
WOULD STIR HIS SLOW CONCEPTION--	REMOVED FROM ACCIDENT OF	424	9
BUT STARS--GO SLOW--FOR NIGHT--	I'LL CLUTCH--AND CLUTCH	427	6
MOULD MY SLOW MIND TO THIS COMPREHENSION--	KNOWS HOW TO FORGET!	433	9
SLOW--NIGHT--THAT MUST BE WATCHED AWAY--	A NIGHT--THERE LAY THE	471	5
THEN--HOW THEY WADED [STAMMERED]--SLOW--SLOW--	GOING TO HIM! HAPPY	494	7
THEN--HOW THEY WADED [STAMMERED]--SLOW--SLOW--	GOING TO HIM! HAPPY	494	7
'TWAS NOT MY BLAME--WHO SPED TOO SLOW--	A DYING TIGER--MOANED	566	9
FORGIVE ME, IF THE GRAVE COME [SEEM] SLOW--	IF I MAY HAVE IT, WHEN	577	26
IT CEASED TO HURT ME, THOUGH SO SLOW	IT CEASED TO HURT ME,	584	1
THE SLOW EXCHANGE OF HOPE--	A PRISON GETS TO BE A	652	26
UNTO THE SAINTS' SLOW DILIGENCE [INDUSTRY]--	EACH LIFE CONVERGES TO	680	15
THEIR FAR--SLOW--VIOLET GAZE--	SWEET MOUNTAINS--YE TELL	722	6
SMOOTH THEM SLOW--	THESE--SAW VISIONS--	758	4
MY SLOW IDOLATRY--	YOU CONSTITUTED TIME--	765	8
SLOW CAPABILITIES.	SUCH IS THE FORCE OF	787	8
HIS LAST DECADE [SLOW DECADES] AWAY,	JOY TO HAVE MERITED THE	788	22
THE THUNDER HURRIED SLOW--	THE WIND BEGUN TO KNEAD	824	V 10
I MADE SLOW RICHES BUT MY GAIN	I MADE SLOW RICHES BUT	843	1
A SLOW AND CAUTIOUS WAY	I STEPPED FROM PLANK TO	875	2
A MIST'S SLOW COLONNADE--	I MAKE HIS CRESCENT FILL	909	8
ASSISTED FAINT [SLOW] OF LOVE.	AS PLAN FOR NOON AND	960	8
CONSECUTIVE AND SLOW--	CRUMBLING IS NOT AN	997	10
THIS SLOW DAY MOVED ALONG--	THIS SLOW DAY MOVED	1120	1
AND MAKE THE WATER SLOW	A STAGNANT PLEASURE LIKE	1281	4
GO SLOW, MY SOUL, TO FEED THYSELF	GO SLOW, MY SOUL, TO	1297	1
BEYOND IT'S DULL [SLOW]--CONTROL	WITH PINIONS OF DISDAIN	1431	6
MY SLOW--TERRESTRIAL EYE	HOW SOFT A CATERPILLAR	1448	6
HOW SLOW THE WHISTLE SANG--	I THOUGHT THE TRAIN	1449	2
HOW SLOW THE WIND--	HOW SLOW THE WIND--	1571	1
HOW SLOW THE SEA--	HOW SLOW THE WIND--	1571	2
DISPLAYED [PASS SLOW] BEFORE THE SIMPLEST [HUMBLEST] DOOR	SOME ONE PREPARED THIS	1644	4
AS WE PASS HOUSES MUSING SLOW	AS WE PASS HOUSES MUSING	1653	1
REMAINED A FEW SLOW YEARS WITH US	I WATCHED HER FACE TO	1667	5
THE POSSIBLE'S SLOW FUSE IS LIT	THE GLEAM OF AN HEROIC	1687	3
THEY TALK AS SLOW AS LEGENDS GROW	THEY TALK AS SLOW AS	1697	1
SLOWER			
SPELL SLOWER--GLORY--	ONE YEAR AGO--JOTS WHAT?	296	5
DEFEAT--A SOMEWHAT SLOWER--[SOMETHING DUMBER] MEANS--	MY PORTION IS DEFEAT--	639	5
THE LARGER--SLOWER GROW	EXCEPT THE SMALLER SIZE	1067	5
SLOWER GO	OH SUMPTUOUS MOMENT	1125	2
INURED TO SLOWER [OTHER] THINGS	TO FLEE FROM MEMORY	1242	4
SLOWEST			
UPON THE SLOWEST NIGHT--	YOU CANNOT PUT A FIRE	530	4
BUT SLOWEST INSTANT--ENDS--	I THINK THE LONGEST HOUR	635	8
SLOWLY			
THAT WHEN THE SNOW CREEPS SLOWLY	SEXTON! MY MASTER'S	96	5
TURNED SLOWLY TO HIS NATIVE COAST--	AN AWFUL TEMPEST MASHED	198	12
COME SLOWLY--EDEN!	COME SLOWLY--EDEN!	211	1
BE SLOWLY HANDED BACK--	TRIUMPH--MAY BE OF	455	10
TO LOOK AT HER--HOW SLOWLY	WHEN I WAS SMALL, A	596	5
AND SLOWLY [SLILY / SOFTLY] PICK THE LOCK--	THE WAY I READ A	636	8
WE SLOWLY DROVE--HE KNEW NO HASTE	BECAUSE I COULD NOT STOP	712	5
THE THRILL CAME SLOWLY LIKE A BOON [LIGHT] FOR	THE THRILL CAME SLOWLY	1495	1
WHO SLOWLY FORD THE MYSTERY	PASS TO THY RENDEZVOUS	1564	3
ESCAPE MORE SLOWLY	EXPANSE CANNOT BE LOST--	1584	13
SLOWNESS			
AND SLOWNESS--THEN THE SCAFFOLDS DROP [SCAFFOLDS CLEAVE / . . .	THE PROPS ASSIST THE	1142	11
SLUICE			
BUT I TELL YOU EVERY STEP IS A TROUGH [SLUICE]--	FLOSS WONT SAVE YOU FROM	1322	5
SLUMBER			
THE FLOWERS WOULD SLUMBER ON [SLEEP UPON--] THEIR STEMS--	MY FAITH IS LARGER THAN	766	11
SLUMBERETH			
SO SLUMBERETH--	'TIS SO APPALLING--IT	281	18
SLUMBERING			
HIS NEVER SLUMBERING PLAN;	THE RETICENT VOLCANO	1748	2
SLUNK			
WHILE EVERYTHING TO CORNERS SLUNK	THE WIND TOOK UP THE	1134	7
SLY			
AFFORDS THE SLY PRESUMPTION	TO HANG OUR HEAD--	105	5
SLYLY SEE SLILY			
SMALL			
THE HIGH DO SEEK THE LOWLY, THE GREAT DO SEEK THE SMALL,	AWAKE YE MUSES NINE,	1	11
WE SHOULD NOT MIND SO SMALL A FLOWER--	WE SHOULD NOT MIND SO	81	1
AND VISIONS VAST AND SMALL--	ON SUCH A NIGHT, OR SUCH	146	22
SHOULD REACH SO SMALL A GOAL!	ON SUCH A NIGHT, OR SUCH	146	24
IT SHONE SO VERY SMALL--	I CAME TO BUY A SMILE--	223	6
AS SMALL--THEY SAY--AS I--	THE COURT IS FAR AWAY--	235	10

	FIRST LINE	POEM	LINE
SMALL (CONTINUED)			
AND THEN--THE SIZE OF THIS "SMALL" LIFE-- .	A SOLEMN THING--IT WAS--	271	13
THE SAGES--CALL IT SMALL--	A SOLEMN THING--IT WAS--	271	14
AND I SNEERED--SOFTLY--"SMALL"!	A SOLEMN THING--IT WAS--	271	16
TOO SMALL--TO FEAR--	A MIEN TO MOVE A QUEEN--	283	22
SHE KNOWS HERSELF AN INCENSE [OFFERING] SMALL--	THE DROP, THAT WRESTLES	284	4
YET SMALL--SHE SIGHS--IF ALL--IS ALL-- . .	THE DROP, THAT WRESTLES	284	5
HOW A SMALL DUSK CRAWLS ON THE VILLAGE . .	HOW THE OLD MOUNTAINS	291	13
FEET, SMALL AS MINE--HAVE MARCHED IN REVOLUTION	UNTO LIKE STORY--TROUBLE	295	17
FROM FLASKS--SO SMALL--	I TEND MY FLOWERS FOR	339	14
'TWAS A SMALL TOWN--	I WENT TO HEAVEN--	374	2
THE RITUAL--SO SMALL--	THE SWEETEST HERESY	387	6
CRITERION--BE SMALL--	IF WHAT WE COULD--WERE	407	2
WHEN WE ARE NEW--AND SMALL.	IT WAS GIVEN TO ME BY	454	4
UNTIL IT SHOWED TOO SMALL--	THE POWER TO BE TRUE TO	464	8
HOW SMALL IN THOSE WHO LIVE--	THE MANNER OF IT'S DEATH	468	8
BEYOND OUR FAINT [SMALL] CONJECTURE-- . .	THOSE FAIR--FICTITIOUS	499	11
WITH ONE SMALL [JUST ONE] DIADEM.	I'M CEDED--I'VE STOPPED	508	13
MY SECOND RANK--TOO SMALL THE FIRST-- . .	I'M CEDED--I'VE STOPPED	508	14
OR WAS MYSELF [JUST MYSELF / ONLY ME / I]--TOO SMALL?	I TOOK MY POWER IN MY	540	8
A SMALL LEECH--ON THE VITALS--	ONE ANGUISH--IN A CROWD	565	9
WHEN I WAS SMALL, A WOMAN DIED--	WHEN I WAS SMALL, A	596	1
OF SMALL AND SPICY YARDS [BREADTHS]-- . .	OF BRUSSELS--IT WAS NOT	602	9
TILL MY SMALL LIBRARY--	UNTO MY BOOKS--SO GOOD	604	8
TO LIVE [DINE] SO SMALL AS I--	IT WOULD HAVE STARVED A	612	2
HER CAP IS SMALL--AND SNUG--	YOU'LL KNOW HER--BY HER	634	13
TO MY SMALL HEARTH HIS FIRE CAME-- . . .	TO MY SMALL HEARTH HIS	638	1
COULD BEHOLD [REGARD] SO FAR [SMALL / DIM / SCARCE] A CREATURE--	PROMISE THIS--WHEN YOU	648	27
OUR NOVEL [ROMANCE]--WHEN 'TIS SMALL ENOUGH	NO ROMANCE SOLD UNTO	669	6
IN THAT SMALL DEITY	THE HEAVEN VESTS FOR	694	2
ABOUT THE PRICE--'TIS SMALL--	THE JUDGE IS LIKE THE	699	9
BASHFUL HEAVEN--THY LOVERS SMALL-- . . .	OUT OF SIGHT? WHAT OF	703	12
OR SMALL--OR ANY SIZE AT ALL--	YOU SAID THAT I "WAS	738	3
SHE PRESENTED HER SMALL FIGURE--	MOST SHE TOUCHED ME BY	760	3
NOT A MENTION, WHOSE SMALL PEBBLE	ONE DAY IS THERE OF THE	814	13
ALL I MAY, IF SMALL, ...	ALL I MAY, IF SMALL,	819	1
DENIED THE SMALL DESIRE	IT WAS A GRAVE, YET BORE	876	10
A COFFIN--IS A SMALL DOMAIN, ...	A COFFIN--IS A SMALL	943	1
TO HIM WHO ON IT'S SMALL [LOW] REPOSE . .	A COFFIN--IS A SMALL	943	9
A SMALL--ITALIC SEED	THIS IS A BLOSSOM OF THE	945	2
I AM SMALL--"THE LEAST	"UNTO ME?" I DO NOT KNOW	964	10
NATURE--ALTERED SMALL--	ALL FORGOT FOR	966	10
FOR WHOM THE WHOLE WERE SMALL	SO LARGE MY WILL	1024	6
IT LOOKS SO SMALL	SO LARGE MY WILL	1024	13
SO SMALL A GRACE	JUST ONCE! OH LEAST	1076	3
SO SCANT, SO EMINENTLY SMALL	WHAT TWIGS WE HELD BY--	1086	10
NOR SNOW--IT WAS TOO SMALL--	IT WAS NOT SAINT--IT WAS	1092	2
AND ARTISAN LIES [SMALL ESTATE STANDS--] STILL--	DEW--IS THE FRESHET IN	1097	4
THE SMALL MUST [DO] DIE, THE SAME [AS WELL] AS HE--	THAT THIS SHOULD FEEL	1112	6
TO CHILDREN HE IS SMALL [LEAST] IN PRICE .	THE MERCHANT OF THE	1131	5
THE DAY GREW SMALL, SURROUNDED TIGHT . . .	THE DAY GREW SMALL,	1140	1
A WHIP SO SMALL YOU COULD NOT SEE IT . . .	NOT WITH A CLUB, THE	1304	3
IS SHRUNKEN [SHRIVELLED / DWINDLED / CHASTENED] SMALL	THE VASTEST EARTHLY DAY	1328	2
PINK--SMALL--AND PUNCTUAL--	PINK--SMALL--AND	1332	1
A SMILE SO SMALL AS MINE MIGHT BE	THEY MIGHT NOT NEED ME--	1391	3
THE SMALL [SAME] STALE SUM--	HOW DESTITUTE IS HE	1477	4
A SMALL BUT STURDY RESIDENCE, ...	THE ROBIN IS A GABRIEL	1483	9
MAKES THE BEHAVIOR SMALL--	THOSE--DYING THEN,	1551	7
HIS SMALL UMBRELLA QUAINTLY HALVED . . .	THE BAT IS DUN, WITH	1575	5
A FLOWER WILL NOT TROUBLE HER, IT HAS SO SMALL A FOOT,	A FLOWER WILL NOT	1621	1
SMALLER			
THE SMALLER SIZE!	JESUS! THY CRUCIFIX	225	3
THE SMALLER OF THE TWO!	FOREVER AT HIS SIDE TO	246	2
A SMALLER PURPLE GROWS--	ME, CHANGE! ME, ALTER!	268	3
BUT SMALLER BUNDLES--CRAM.	PERHAPS I ASKED TOO	352	7
AND SMALLER, BY HABIT--	IT DONT SOUND SO	426	13
IF SMALLER PATIENCE--BE--	THE TEST OF LOVE--IS	573	5
THERE HANGS A SMALLER [MINOR] EAR	THE SPIRIT IS THE	733	6
SMALLER--THAT COVERED [FLOODED / SATED] VISION--HERE--	RENUNCIATION--IS A	745	16
A SMALLER, COULD NOT BE PERTURBED-- . . .	WHO GIANTS KNOW, WITH	796	5
A SMALLER [LESSER] THAN THE LARGE-- . . .	LOVE--IS THAT LATER	924	12
EXCEPT THE SMALLER SIZE	EXCEPT THE SMALLER SIZE	1067	1
AND NOT A SMALLER [LESSER] MAN	I THOUGHT THAT NATURE	1286	12
THOSE CATTLE SMALLER THAN A BEE	THOSE CATTLE SMALLER	1388	1
SMALLEST			
THE SMALLEST "ROBE" WILL FIT ME	GOING TO HEAVEN!	79	16
THE SMALLEST HOUSEWIFE IN THE GRASS, . . .	EXCEPT TO HEAVEN, SHE IS	154	9
THE SMALLEST ONE UPON YOUR FACE [CHEEK] . .	I CAME TO BUY A SMILE--	223	3
I TOOK THE SMALLEST ROOM--	I WAS THE SLIGHTEST IN	486	2
LET ME NOT SPILL [LOSE / WASTE]--IT'S SMALLEST CADENCE--	BETTER--THAN MUSIC! FOR	503	21

	FIRST LINE	POEM	LINE
SMALLEST (CONTINUED)			
THE SMALLEST [FINEST] GAMBOGE HAND	YOU'LL KNOW HER--BY HER	634	2
CONTENT HER SMALLEST FRACTION HELP	LEAST BEE THAT BREW--	676	4
NOT THE SMALLEST BIRD	STRUCK, WAS I, NOR YET	925	14
WE NOTICED SMALLEST THINGS--	THE LAST NIGHT THAT SHE	1100	5
THE SMALLEST HUMAN HEART'S EXTENT	THE LIFE WE HAVE IS VERY	1162	7
THE SMALLEST CITIZEN THAT FLIES	A SAUCER HOLDS A CUP	1374	15
HER'S IS THE SMALLEST BOOT--	A FLOWER WILL NOT	1621	3
SMART			
WHAT AILED SO SMART A LITTLE MAID-- . . .	THE ROSE DID CAPER ON	208	7
THAN THIS SMART MISERY.	OF COURSE--I PRAYED--	376	11
SMARTNESS			
UNCONSCIOUS [DISDAINFUL] OF HIS SMARTNESS. .	THE SUMMER THAT WE DID	1773	8
SMILE			
COULD SMILE UPON THE WHOLE	COULD LIVE--DID LIVE--	43	3
THE WOODS EXCHANGE A SMILE!	A LADY RED--AMID THE	74	10
AH! KATIE! SMILE AT FORTUNE, WITH TWO SO KNIT TO THEE!	WHEN KATIE WALKS, THIS	222	4
I CAME TO BUY A SMILE--TODAY--	I CAME TO BUY A SMILE--	223	1
BUT JUST A SINGLE SMILE--	I CAME TO BUY A SMILE--	223	2
LET NO PEBBLE--SMILE--	I CAN WADE GRIEF--	252	7
THE HEAVENS WITH A SMILE, ...	HOW NOTELESS MEN, AND	282	10
TO HAVE A SMILE FOR MINE--EACH DAY, ...	YOUR RICHES--TAUGHT ME--	299	23
A SMILE TOO FEW--A WORD TOO MUCH	NOT PROBABLE--THE BAREST	346	2
MEET US--WITH A SMILE--	TAKING UP THE FAIR IDEAL	428	17
SMILE--AND ALTER--AND PRATTLE--AND DIE-- .	LOVE--THOU ART HIGH--	453	15
AND WRESTLED WITH A SMILE.	IT WAS GIVEN TO ME BY	454	12
UNTO ITSELF--AND SMILE--AND SHAKE--	WHY MAKE IT DOUBT--IT	462	6
A SMILE SUFFUSED JEHOVAH'S FACE--	I MEANT TO HAVE BUT	476	13
YOU TRY TO TOUCH [REACH] THE SMILE	IF ANYBODY'S FRIEND BE	509	14
WITH HALF A SMILE, AND HALF A SPURN, ...	IF YOU WERE COMING IN	511	3
HER SMILE WAS SHAPED LIKE OTHER SMILES-- .	HER SMILE WAS SHAPED	514	1
THAT MAKES THE FENCES SMILE--	I'M SORRY FOR THE DEAD--	529	8
AT LENGTH, RENEW THEIR SMILE--	I MEASURE EVERY GRIEF I	561	14
I SMILE UPON THE AIMS	I COULD NOT PROVE THE	563	6
A SMILE, TO SHOW YOU, WHEN THIS DEEP . . .	IF I MAY HAVE IT, WHEN	577	23
RENDERED WITH A SMILE	WOLFE DEMANDED DURING	678	6
TRIVIAL--A SMILE--	NO MATTER--NOW--SWEET--	704	6
BUT WHAT MUST BE THE SMILE	THE MOON WAS BUT A CHIN	737	10
AND DO I SMILE, SUCH CORDIAL LIGHT	MY LIFE HAD STOOD--A	754	9
FOR A PENURIOUS SMILE.	THEY ASK BUT OUR DELIGHT	868	4
THE SMOULDERING EMBERS SMILE--	THE SMOULDERING EMBERS	1132	4
WITHOUT A SMILE--WITHOUT A THROE	WITHOUT A SMILE--WITHOUT	1330	1
FORTUNE'S EXPENSIVE SMILE	LUCK IS NOT CHANCE--	1350	3
A SMILE SO SMALL AS MINE MIGHT BE	THEY MIGHT NOT NEED ME--	1391	3
NOT GUESSING, SMILE AND HIDE	NOT SEEING, STILL WE	1518	3
AND BUT ONE SMILE--THAT MEAGRES [HUMBLES] BALMS--	ABOVE OBLIVION'S TIDE	1531	4
AND A CHILL [BLEAK] SMILE INLAID WITH BALMS--	ABOVE OBLIVION'S TIDE	1531 V	4
AND SEES [SPIES] THE PASTURES SMILE	THE LIFE THAT TIED TOO	1535	6
SMILED			
SOME SHOOK THEIR HEADS, AND OTHERS SMILED--	WHOSE ARE THE LITTLE	142	3
THE MIGHTY MERCHANT SNEERED [SMILED]-- . .	I ASKED NO OTHER THING--	621	4
WONT YOU WISH YOU'D SMILED--JUST--	NO MATTER--NOW--SWEET--	704	15
ALL ELSE [THE WORLD] ACCUSED ME--AND I SMILED--	MY SOUL--ACCUSED ME--AND	753	3
TILL WE, WHO SMILED AT PYRRHENEES--	WE MISS A KINSMAN MORE	1087	7
SMILED TOO BRAVE FOR THE DETECTING [OUR DETECTION]	HAD WE KNOWN THE TON SHE	1124 V	3
SMILE'S			
WOULD A SMILE'S MINUTE BESTOWING	SO MUCH SUMMER	651	4
PATIENCE--IS THE SMILE'S [MOUTH'S / LOVE'S] EXERTION	PATIENCE--HAS A QUIET	926	7
SMILES			
THE SEEDS OF SMILES ARE PLANTED--	BY CHIVALRIES AS TINY,	55	3
AND DEAL OCCASIONAL SMILES	HE PUT THE BELT AROUND	273	12
THE OCEAN--SMILES--AT HER CONCEIT--	THE DROP, THAT WRESTLES	284	7
HER SMILE WAS SHAPED LIKE OTHER SMILES-- .	HER SMILE WAS SHAPED	514	1
SUCH PLENTY SMILES UPON MY BOARD--	GOD GAVE A LOAF TO EVERY	791	11
IF NATURE SMILES--THE MOTHER MUST	IF NATURE SMILES--THE	1085	1
SMILING			
STOOPING--PLUCKING--SMILING--FLYING-- . .	ANGELS, IN THE EARLY	94	3
SMILING, AS THEY REQUEST AN ALMS--	IN RAGS MYSTERIOUS AS	117	5
SMILING WHEN WE WALK BAREFOOT	IN RAGS MYSTERIOUS AS	117	7
THE BIRDS ROSE SMILING, IN THEIR NESTS-- .	ON THIS LONG STORM THE	194	5
WHEN ONE--TURNED SMILING TO THE LAND-- . .	TWO SWIMMERS WRESTLED ON	201	3
AMONG THE PENSIVE [SMILING] TREES--	THE ONLY GHOST I EVER	274	12
WHEN THEY LET GO THE IGNOMINY--SMILING-- .	UNTO LIKE STORY--TROUBLE	295	7
IT CONTEMPLATED--SMILING--	A HAPPY LIP--BREAKS	353	3
SMILING BACK FROM CORONATION	SMILING BACK FROM	385	1
ANY--FOR THE PRESS OF SMILING--	SWEET--SAFE--HOUSES--	457	16
THE CRUEL--SMILING--BOWING WORLD--	THE BEGGAR LAD--DIES	717	5
I COULD'NT WEEP--FOR SO MANY SMILING . . .	TRUDGING TO EDEN,	1020	7
SMIT			
AS IF IT WERE OF LEDGES SMIT	THE WAY HOPE BUILDS HIS	1481	7
SMITES			
AND SMITES THE TINDER IN THE SUN--	THE LOVE A LIFE CAN SHOW	673	5
SMITTEN			
THE SMITTEN ROCK THAT GUSHES!	A WOUNDED DEER--LEAPS	165	5
THE MEETING BANDS OF SMITTEN FACE	'TIS ANGUISH GRANDER	984	3

	FIRST LINE	POEM	LINE
SMITTEN (CONTINUED)			
HOW SMITTEN, HOW SUPERFLUOUS,	HAD THIS ONE DAY NOT	1253	3
SMOKE			
FIRE, AND SMOKE, AND GUN,	I HAVE NEVER SEEN	175	6
THE SMOKE ALL CLEARED AWAY FROM IT--	WHEN WE STAND ON THE	242	3
AGAIN THE SMOKE FROM DWELLINGS ROSE [CURLED]	THE WIND TOOK UP THE	1134	13
SMOKED			
WHOSE CHIMNEY NEVER SMOKED--	A HOUSE UPON THE HIGHT--	399	5
SMOOTH			
THE MIND IS SMOOTH--NO MOTION--	THE DIFFERENCE BETWEEN	305	5
IT'S TIME TO SMOOTH THE HAIR--	WHEN NIGHT IS ALMOST	347	4
THE OCEAN'S HEART TOO SMOOTH--TOO BLUE--	IT TOSSED--AND TOSSED--	723	11
SMOOTH THEM SLOW--	THESE--SAW VISIONS--	758	4
SMOOTHED			
OR SMOOTHED A HOMELY PAIN,	ALTHOUGH I PUT AWAY HIS	366	6
SMOTE			
AND BROKE [SMOTE] AGAINST MY EAR--	I YEARS HAD BEEN FROM	609	12
A SENSE THAT SMOTE AND STIRRED--	I'VE DROPPED MY BRAIN--	1046	10
SMOULDERING			
IF AT LENGTH, THE SMOULDERING ANGUISH	I HAVE NEVER SEEN	175	13
TOO SUBTLE [SMOULDERING] TO SUSPECT	A STILL--VOLCANO--LIFE--	601	6
THE SMOULDERING EMBERS BLUSH--	THE SMOULDERING EMBERS	1132	1
THE SMOULDERING EMBERS SMILE--	THE SMOULDERING EMBERS	1132	4
SMUGGLED			
SMUGGLED TO REST!	DUST IS THE ONLY SECRET	153	16
WHEN IT WAS SMUGGLED BY MY SIGHT	A SINGLE SCREW OF FLESH	263	11
THOUGH SMUGGLED HIS [MY] REPRIEVE	IT CAME HIS TURN TO BEG	1500	8
SNAKE			
DID BUT A SNAKE BISECT THE BRAKE	I NEVER TOLD THE BURIED	11	8
ON SILVER MATTERS CHARMED A SNAKE	THE TREES LIKE TASSELS--	606	19
YET [BUT] EASY AS THE [A] NARROW SNAKE	THE FROST OF DEATH WAS	1136	12
LEST GRATITUDE REVIVE THE SNAKE [MY THOUGHT]	IT CAME HIS TURN TO BEG	1500	7
A SNAKE WITH MOTTLES RARE	IN WINTER IN MY ROOM	1670	14
UNTIL WE MEET A SNAKE;	SWEET IS THE SWAMP WITH	1740	2
A SNAKE IS SUMMER'S [NATURE'S] TREASON [DRAMA],	SWEET IS THE SWAMP WITH	1740	7
SNAKE'S			
IS [WAS] SHORTER THAN A [THE] SNAKE'S DELAY [EVENT / REPLY]	THE MUSHROOM IS THE ELF	1298	7
SNAP			
I HEARD THE BUCKLE SNAP--	HE PUT THE BELT AROUND	273	2
IT'S TENDENCY TO SNAP	A RAT SURRENDERED HERE	1340	8
SNAPT			
SHE SAID HER STRINGS WERE SNAPT--	THE FIRST DAY'S NIGHT	410	5
SNARE			
TOO PONDEROUS TO SUSPECT THE SNARE	RISK IS THE HAIR THAT	1239	5
SNATCH			
A CARELESS SNATCH--A BALLAD--	HEART, NOT SO HEAVY AS	83	5
THAT COULD I SNATCH THEIR FACES	WHAT DID THEY DO SINCE I	900	5
SNATCH IT FOR [COVET IT / TIE IT FOR / SEIZE IT FOR / SUMMON . . .	SUMMER LAID HER SIMPLE	1363	4
SNATCHES			
SNATCHES, FROM BAPTIZED GENERATIONS--	OVER AND OVER, LIKE A	367	5
SNEER			
IF ANYBODY SNEER--	THE MURMUR OF A BEE	155	8
SNEER--"WHERE"!	I KNOW SOME LONELY	289	38
WITH A SNEER AT YOU--	FOLLOW WISE ORION	1538	V
WHICH OTHERS TASTE AND SPURN AND SNEER [SLIGHT]--	I GROPED FOR HIM BEFORE	1555	5
SNEERED			
AND I SNEERED--SOFTLY--"SMALL"!	A SOLEMN THING--IT WAS--	271	16
THE MIGHTY MERCHANT SNEERED [SMILED]--	I ASKED NO OTHER THING--	621	4
SNOW			
THE VASSAL OF THE SNOW--	THE FEET OF PEOPLE	7	4
I SHALL NOT FEAR THE SNOW.	DISTRUSTFUL OF THE	20	8
"THERE IS NO MORE SNOW!"	ALL THESE MY BANNERS BE.	22	19
SNOW FLAKES	I COUNTED TILL THEY	36	T
IS TARNISHED BY THE SNOW--	BEFORE THE ICE IS IN THE	37	4
DELAYED TILL IN IT'S VEST OF SNOW	DELAYED TILL SHE HAD	58	2
AS FLAKES OF SNOW STOOD [DID] YESTERDAY--	SOME RAINBOW--COMING	64	14
THAT WHEN THE SNOW CREEPS SLOWLY	SEXTON! MY MASTER'S	96	5
AND STILL THE PUNCTUAL SNOW!	NEW FEET WITHIN MY	99	8
WHO DRESSED IN FROCKS OF PUREST SNOW	WHERE I HAVE LOST, I	104	14
AND UNIFORMS OF SNOW.	TO FIGHT ALOUD, IS VERY	126	12
A LITTLE THIS SIDE OF THE SNOW	BESIDES THE AUTUMN POETS	131	3
BIRDS, BY THE SNOW.	WATER, IS TAUGHT BY	135	6
INTO THE EVERLASTING SNOW?	DYING! DYING IN THE	158	4
WHAT SORCERY HAD SNOW?	THE SKIES CANT KEEP	191	12
SOUNDLESS AS DOTS--ON A DISC OF SNOW--	SAFE IN THEIR ALABASTER	216	V
AND STEPPED LIKE FLAKES OF SNOW--	THE ONLY GHOST I EVER	274	4
BUT HALLOW JUST THE SNOW	DOUBT ME! MY DIM	275	23
LIKE LET OF SNOW--	A MIEN TO MOVE A QUEEN--	283	18
THIS PENDULUM OF SNOW--	A CLOCK STOPPED--	287	11
SNOW	IT SIFTS FROM LEADEN	311	T
WEAR NOTHING COMMONER THAN SNOW--	OF TRIBULATION--THESE	325	7
NOR ROLLED ON WHEELS OF SNOW	I CANNOT DANCE UPON MY	326	14
AS FREEZING PERSONS, RECOLLECT THE SNOW--	AFTER GREAT PAIN, A	341	12
THEN--DIAMONDS--WHICH THE SNOW	THE ANGLE OF A LANDSCAPE	375	16
SHOW ME THE SNOW--	ANSWER JULY--	386	11
HUNG OUT IT'S FLAGS OF SNOW--	THE HIMMALEH WAS KNOWN	481	6

	FIRST LINE	POEM		LINE
SNOW (CONTINUED)				
UPON A MARGE OF SNOW--	I THINK THE HEMLOCK	525		2
AND EVEN WHEN THE SNOW	TO INTERRUPT HIS YELLOW	591		4
COULD WASTE [MELT] THE SNOW BEFORE THEIR GATE--	WHAT CARE THE DEAD, FOR	592		11
THAT OTHER PRANK--OF SNOW--	THE TINT I CANNOT TAKE--	627		18
ART OF SNOW--OR TRICK OF LILY	HER SWEET TURN TO LEAVE	649		15
THAN INVEST--OUR SNOW--	PUBLICATION--IS THE	709		8
AS LATELY AS THE SNOW--	HAVE ANY LIKE MYSELF	736		6
WHEN GUSTS REVERSE THE SNOW--	HE FOUGHT LIKE THOSE	759		10
THAN FLAKE OF SNOW, DIVIDED WITH [IMPRINTED SWIFT]	HE TOLD A HOMELY TALE	763		7
AND SERVICES OF SNOW.	I CANNOT BE ASHAMED	914		10
TO THE [UNTO] SOULS THAT SNOW--	ABSENT PLACE--AN APRIL	927		4
TWO TRAVELLERS PERISHING IN SNOW	TWO TRAVELLERS PERISHING	933		1
SNOW BENEATH WHOSE CHILLY SOFTNESS	SNOW BENEATH WHOSE	942		1
WILT THOU, AUSTERE [RUSSIAN] SNOW?	SNOW BENEATH WHOSE	942		8
A TRAVELLING FLAKE OF SNOW	THE SKY IS LOW--THE	1075		2
NOR SNOW--IT WAS TOO SMALL--	IT WAS NOT SAINT--IT WAS	1092		2
THE SNOW THAT NEVER DRIFTS--	THE SNOW THAT NEVER	1133		1
THE TRANSIENT, FRAGRANT SNOW	THE SNOW THAT NEVER	1133		2
WERE EVERY STORM [GALE / SNOW] SO SPICE [FAIR / SWEET]	THE SNOW THAT NEVER	1133		13
THE SNOW AND WIND	LIKE BROOMS OF STEEL	1252		2
AFFRONTED BY THE SNOW--	SWEET SKEPTICISM OF THE	1413		4
A LITTLE SNOW WAS HERE AND THERE	A LITTLE SNOW WAS HERE	1444		1
AS SUNSET ON THE SNOW--	OF WHOM SO DEAR	1504		5
THE SNOW AND HE ARE INTIMATE--	NO BRIGADIER THROUGHOUT	1561		9
WE STAND LIKE SNOW.	I DID NOT REACH THEE	1664		29
IN SNOW THOU COMEST	IN SNOW THOU COMEST	1669		1
SNOW'S				
WITHOUT THE SNOW'S TABLEAU	THE ROBIN'S MY CRITERION	285		13
SNOWS				
AND THE SNOWS COME HURRYING FROM THE HILLS,	HAVE YOU GOT A BROOK IN	136		11
WE STIPULATE--TILL PITYING SNOWS	'TIS NOT THAT DYING	335		11
NOT ALL THE SNOWS C'D MAKE IT WHITE--	THE COLOR OF THE GRAVE	411		19
BUT JUST BEFORE THE SNOWS	GOD MADE A LITTLE	442		4
WHEN IT SNOWS--	IT'S THOUGHTS--AND JUST	495		13
TOO OBDURATE [COMPETENT / SUMPTUOUS] FOR SNOWS--	A LITTLE SNOW WAS HERE	1444		8
SNOWY				
TILL SERAPHS SWING THEIR SNOWY HATS--	I TASTE A LIQUOR NEVER	214		13
SNUG				
SNUG IN SERAPHIC CUPBOARDS	PAPA ABOVE!	61		6
HER CAP IS SMALL--AND SNUG--	YOU'LL KNOW HER--BY HER	634		13
THE APPLE IN THE CELLAR SNUG	LIKE BROOMS OF STEEL	1252		10
SNUGLY				
I DONT KNOW HIM; SNUGLY BUILT!	"HOUSES"--SO THE WISE	127		6
SOAR				
MANY WOULD FLY [SOAR]	TO FLEE FROM MEMORY	1242		3
HER CONSCIENTIOUS VOICE WILL SOAR UNMOVED	AFTER ALL BIRDS HAVE	1395		3
A WINGED SPARK DOTH SOAR ABOUT--	A WINGED SPARK DOTH SOAR	1468		1
SO SOAR AWAY AND NEVER SIGH	THE BUTTERFLY UPON THE	1521		7
FOR SO TO SOAR AWAY	COME SHOW THY DURHAM	1542		10
SOARED				
AND [OR] SOARED UPON A STEM	THE TREES LIKE TASSELS--	606		22
SOARING				
THEN SOARING TO HIS TEMPLE [TURRET] TALL--	HOW LONESOME THE WIND	1418		12
IT'S SOARING [RAPTURE] RESIDENCE.	AS FROM THE EARTH THE	1630		4
SOARS				
IT SOARS--AND SHIFTS--AND WHIRLS--	OF BEING IS A BIRD	653		5
SOB				
HOW RUDE IN ONE TO SOB!	THERE'S SOMETHING	45		10
SOBBED				
HAVE SOBBED OURSELVES ALMOST TO SLEEP,	I CRIED AT PITY--NOT AT	588		23
SOBBING				
SOBBING--WILL SUIT--AS WELL AS PSALM!	PUT UP MY LUTE!	261		5
SOBER				
THE LABOR IS A SOBER ONE	I FIT FOR THEM--	1109		4
WITH USUALLY [GENERALLY] A SOBER BIRD--	A FIELD OF STUBBLE,	1407	V	5
BY SOBER INDIVIDUAL	AS IMPERCEPTIBLY AS	1540	V	
WE WEAR OUR SOBER DRESSES WHEN WE DIE,	WE WEAR OUR SOBER	1572		1
SOBERER				
AND THO' IN SOBERER MOMENTS--	IT ALWAYS FELT TO ME--A	597		5
SOBERLY				
WE SOBERLY DESCEND	EXHILIRATION IS THE	1118		6
SOBRIETY				
SOBRIETY INHERED	AS IMPERCEPTIBLY AS	1540	V	
SOCIALLY				
HIS DRESS DENOTES HIM SOCIALLY,	THE ROBIN IS A GABRIEL	1483		3
SOCIETY				
THE SOUL SELECTS HER OWN SOCIETY--	THE SOUL SELECTS HER OWN	303		1
SOCIETY--	I WENT TO HEAVEN--	374		16
VAST SOCIETY--	CONSCIOUS AM I IN MY	679		16
NEVER FOR SOCIETY	NEVER FOR SOCIETY	746		1
ABRIDGE [IMPAIR / DEBAR / DEPRIVE] SOCIETY	WE MISS HER, NOT BECAUSE	993		4
SOCIETY ENOUGH.	PAIN HAS BUT ONE	1049		4
SOCIETY FOR ME MY MISERY	SOCIETY FOR ME MY MISERY	1534		1
SOCIETY SHALL BE	THERE IS A SOLITUDE OF	1695		4
IN STRONG [ONE] SOCIETY.	THE GRAVE MY LITTLE	1743		8

	FIRST LINE	POEM	LINE
SOCKET			
LOVE THAT NEVER LEAPED ITS SOCKET--	REARRANGE A "WIFE'S"	1737	9
SOCKETS			
SYSTEMS--SETTLED IN THEIR SOCKETS--	ALL BUT DEATH, CAN BE	749	3
SOD			
AND THAT WAS IN THE SOD.	I NEVER LOST AS MUCH BUT	49	2
NEW FINGERS STIR THE SOD--	NEW FEET WITHIN MY	99	2
FOR PRIVILEGE OF SOD AND SUN--	THERE IS A FLOWER THAT	380	19
THROUGH THE DARK SOD--AS EDUCATION--	THROUGH THE DARK SOD--AS	392	1
IN LOW APARTMENTS IN THE SOD--	SHE HIDETH HER THE LAST	557	7
WEARING THE SOD GOWN--	DROPPED INTO THE ETHER	665	2
AS A SOD	TO THIS WORLD SHE	830	4
CANNOT MOVE A SOD	LAIN IN NATURE--SO	1288	6
HOW INSECURE THE SOD	ON MY VOLCANO GROWS THE	1677	6
SOE'ER			
CONTENT, SOE'ER, IT ORNAMENT	JUST AS HE SPOKE IT FROM	848	7
SOEVER			
SOEVER MADE IN VAIN,	WE SEND THE WAVE TO FIND	1604	6
SOFA			
A SOFA TO THE AIR--	THE WIND--TAPPED LIKE A	436	8
UNTO THE SOFA OPPOSITE--	THE NIGHT WAS WIDE, AND	589	19
SOFT			
NOR NOTICED NIGHT DID SOFT DESCEND--	A POOR--TORN HEART-- A	78	5
SOFT SAUNTERED THRO' THE VILLAGE--	WITHIN MY REACH!	90	4
SAUNTERED AS SOFT AWAY!	WITHIN MY REACH!	90	5
THE DAISY FOLLOWS SOFT THE SUN--	THE DAISY FOLLOWS SOFT	106	1
AT TWILIGHT SOFT TO MEET--	SHE BORE IT TILL THE	144	10
SOFT FALL THE SOUNDS OF EDEN	ALL OVERGROWN BY CUNNING	148	V
SOFT OVERHEARS THE WHOLE--	THE SKIES CANT KEEP	191	6
BEHIND THIS SOFT ECLIPSE--	I'M "WIFE"--I'VE	199	6
AND SHE POURS SOFT REFRAINS	I KNOW A PLACE WHERE	337	8
WHAT SOFT--CHERUBIC CREATURES--	WHAT SOFT--CHERUBIC	401	1
TAPPED SOFT UPON THE TOWN	THE FINGERS OF THE LIGHT	1000	2
SOFT AS THE MASSACRE [MASSACRES] OF SUNS	SOFT AS THE MASSACRE OF	1127	1
SOFT STIRS THE NEWS [STIR THE FLAKES] OF LIGHT	THE SMOULDERING EMBERS	1132	5
IN SOFT DISTINCTION LIE	SOME DAYS RETIRED FROM	1157	2
THE SOUL RETURNING SOFT AT NIGHT [STILL BY DAWN / LOTH BY DAWN]	CONTAINED IN THIS SHORT	1165	3
A SOFT SEA WASHED AROUND THE HOUSE	A SOFT SEA WASHED AROUND	1198	1
SO SOFT UPON THE SCENE [PLACE]	THE MOUNTAINS STOOD IN	1278	9
A [DO / OUR] SUMMER'S [NATURE'S] SOFT ASSEMBLIES GO	WITHOUT A SMILE--WITHOUT	1330	2
HOW SOFT THIS [HIS] PRISON IS	HOW SOFT THIS PRISON IS	1334	1
WE SAFE [SOFT] COMMIT THEE--	TO THE STANCH DUST	1402	2
HOW SOFT A CATERPILLAR STEPS--	HOW SOFT A CATERPILLAR	1448	1
WHOSE SOFT INHABITANTS TO BE	A LANE OF YELLOW LED THE	1650	3
SOFTENED			
SOFTENED BY TIME'S CONSUMMATE PLUSH,	SOFTENED BY TIME'S	1738	1
SOFTER			
WHERE I HAVE LOST, I SOFTER TREAD--	WHERE I HAVE LOST, I	104	1
ROCKED SOFTER--TO AND FRO--	ON SUCH A NIGHT, OR SUCH	146	8
AND ROWED HIM SOFTER HOME--	A BIRD CAME DOWN THE	328	16
ARE A SOFTER WO	WHETHER THEY HAVE	1329	6
SOFTLY			
LET US CHANT IT SOFTLY--	ALL THESE MY BANNERS BE.	22	18
HER GHOST STROLLED SOFTLY O'ER THE HILL	SHE DIED AT PLAY,	75	6
I--SOFTLY PLUCKING,	SOUTH WINDS JOSTLE THEM	86	7
TALKED SOFTLY OF NEW SPECIES	WENT UP A YEAR THIS	93	15
AND SOFTLY [SWIFTLY] THRO' THE ALTERED AIR	THESE ARE THE DAYS WHEN	130	11
MESMERIC FINGERS SOFTLY TOUCH	BESIDES THE AUTUMN POETS	131	11
SHE DROPT AS SOFTLY AS A STAR	SHE WENT AS QUIET AS THE	149	5
TICKED SOFTLY INTO ONE.	THE ROSE DID CAPER ON	208	16
TILL BROOMS FADE SOFTLY INTO STARS--	SHE SWEEPS WITH	219	11
THE ANGELS--SOFTLY PEERED--	IF I'M LOST--NOW--	256	7
AND I SNEERED--SOFTLY--"SMALL"!	A SOLEMN THING--IT WAS--	271	16
THEN I SAID SOFTLY TO MYSELF--	I'LL TELL YOU HOW THE	318	7
HE QUESTIONED SOFTLY "WHY I FAILED"?	I DIED FOR BEAUTY--BUT	449	5
NOT SO SOFTLY FALL	SWEET--SAFE--HOUSES--	457	7
SOFTLY MY FUTURE CLIMBS THE STAIR,	A WIFE--AT DAYBREAK I	461	9
RAISED SOFTLY TO THE CEILINGS [HORIZONS]--	I WOULD NOT PAINT--A	505	11
AS NEEDLES--LADIES SOFTLY PRESS	IT CEASED TO HURT ME,	584	10
WHEN GIRLS TO WOMEN, SOFTLY RAISED	WE TALKED AS GIRLS DO--	586	11
AND HE PASSED [WENT] QUICKLY [SOFTLY] ROUND--	WHEN I WAS SMALL, A	596	8
AND DANCING SOFTLY TO HIMSELF [AS HE KNITS]	THE SPIDER HOLDS A	605	3
AND SLOWLY [SLILY / SOFTLY] PICK THE LOCK--	THE WAY I READ A	636	8
THEIR LIQUID FEET GO SOFTLY OUT	YOU'VE SEEN BALLOONS SET	700	5
LATCH [BAR / BIND] THEM SOFTLY--	THESE--SAW VISIONS--	758	2
SHOULD SOFTLY PLACE WITHIN OUR OWN	ON THAT DEAR FRAME THE	940	7
FALL SOFTLY, AND ADORE--	THE LADY FEEDS HER	941	8
I FIND MYSELF STILL SOFTLY SEARCHING	A LOSS OF SOMETHING EVER	959	11
THEN LIGHTLY [SOFTLY] AS A REED	THE LAST NIGHT THAT SHE	1100	22
IS SOFTLY DRIVING NOW--	THE SNOW THAT NEVER	1133	4
SPRANG LIGHTLY TO [ROSE SOFTLY IN / TURNED EASY IN] THE SKY	A SPARROW TOOK A SLICE	1211 V	6
SEEKS FAINTLY [SOFTLY / FURTIVE] FOR IT'S SHORE	THE INUNDATION OF THE	1425	6
BUT [THOUGH] ALL MANKIND DELIVER [CRUISE SOFTLY / ROW SOFTLY / . . .	A CHILLY PEACE INFESTS	1443	7
BUT [THOUGH] ALL MANKIND DELIVER [CRUISE SOFTLY / ROW SOFTLY / . . .	A CHILLY PEACE INFESTS	1443	7

	FIRST LINE	POEM	LINE
SOFTLY (CONTINUED)			
. . . SAIL SOFTLY / DO ANCHOR] HERE	A CHILLY PEACE INFESTS	1443	7
HOW SOFTLY SINKS THAT [HIS] TREMBLING SUN	LOOK BACK ON TIME, WITH	1478	3
AND NATURE GENTLY [SOFTLY] OWNED HER	SHE COULD NOT LIVE UPON	1505	4
SOFTLY CLIMB	THE PILE OF YEARS IS NOT	1507	V
ALL OF EVENING SOFTLY LIT	LIGHTLY STEPPED A YELLOW	1672	5
AND SITUATED SOFTLY	HIGH FROM THE EARTH I	1723	5
SOFTNESS			
THEN A SOFTNESS--SUFFUSE THE STORY--	GLEE--THE GREAT STORM IS	619	14
UPON HER BOSOM [PETALS / SOFTNESS] PILED--	NO NOTICE GAVE SHE, BUT	804	8
SNOW BENEATH WHOSE CHILLY SOFTNESS	SNOW BENEATH WHOSE	942	1
SOIL			
ON THIS SUPERIOR SOIL--	OF TRIBULATION--THESE	325	10
NOR CATTLE WERE--NOR SOIL--	THEY CALLED ME TO THE	628	8
SOIL OF FLINT, IF STEADY [STEADFAST] TILLED--	SOIL OF FLINT, IF STEADY	681	1
THE DARLINGS OF THE SOIL	THEY ASK BUT OUR DELIGHT	868	2
IN TIMID AND TUMULTUOUS SOIL	THE FASCINATING CHILL	1480	5
THE TIGHTENING THE SOIL AROUND	YOU CANNOT MAKE	1508	3
SOLACED			
SOME HAVE SOLACED THE LONGING	NOT ANY MORE TO BE	1344	11
SOLACES			
AT LEAST, IT SOLACES TO KNOW	YOUR RICHES--TAUGHT ME--	299	25
SOLD			
BUT BLISS, IS SOLD JUST ONCE.	IS BLISS THEN, SUCH	340	9
THEY--SOLD [THEN--SELL] IT UNTO ME	OF BRUSSELS--IT WAS NOT	602	4
NO ROMANCE SOLD UNTO	NO ROMANCE SOLD UNTO	669	1
I CANNOT BUY IT--'TIS NOT SOLD--	I CANNOT BUY IT--'TIS	840	1
SOLDER			
YOU CANNOT SOLDER AN ABYSS [PLUG A SEPULCHRE]	TO FILL A GAP	546	5
SOLDERED			
ONLY THE SOLDERED MOUTH CAN TELL--	HOW MANY TIMES THESE LOW	187	2
AND THEN--BE SOLDERED DOWN	I'VE SEEN A DYING EYE	547	6
ON THE LONGED FOR [SOLDERED] DEAD	LAIN IN NATURE--SO	1288	8
SOLDIER			
THEN I TURN SOLDIER TOO,	MY FRIEND ATTACKS MY	118	3
SOLDIER'S			
ON THIS SOLDIER'S BROW!	WHO NEVER LOST, ARE	73	16
A SOLDIER'S--BALLS! WHO ASKETH MORE,	A LITTLE BREAD--A CRUST	159	11
SOLDIERS			
BY SOLDIERS BATTERED DOWN,	I NEVER HEAR THE WORD	77	6
BLESS GOD, HE WENT AS SOLDIERS,	BLESS GOD, HE WENT AS	147	1
SOLE			
SINCE THE SOLE EAR I CARED TO CHARM--	PUT UP MY LUTE!	261	3
EFFORT--IS THE SOLE CONDITION--	GROWTH OF MAN--LIKE	750	9
ALL THINGS SWEPT SOLE AWAY	ALL THINGS SWEPT SOLE	1512	1
SOLELY			
GIVEN FOR THE GIVING, SOLELY, [THE MAJESTY]	"FAITHFUL TO THE END"	1357	7
SOLEMN			
UNWIND THE SOLEMN TWINE, AND TIE MY VALENTINE!	AWAKE YE MUSES NINE,	1	2
THEIR SPIRITS MEET TOGETHER, THEY MAKE THEM SOLEMN VOWS,	AWAKE YE MUSES NINE,	1	19
EACH WITH A SOLEMN MUSKET	"SIC TRANSIT GLORIA	3	51
WHICH FROM IT'S SOLEMN ABBEYS	THE FEET OF PEOPLE	7	23
GRANT THAT REPENTANCE SOLEMN	I HAD A GUINEA GOLDEN--	23	33
WHEN BUMBLEBEES IN SOLEMN FLIGHT	WHEN ROSES CEASE TO	32	3
WHAT WILL THE SOLEMN HEMLOCK--	I ROBBED THE WOODS--	41	8
THE SOLEMN ALPS--	OUR LIVES ARE SWISS--	80	8
IN TENDER--SOLEMN ALPHABET,	A SINGLE SCREW OF FLESH	263	9
A SOLEMN THING--IT WAS--I SAID--	A SOLEMN THING--IT WAS--	271	1
RISE--SOLEMN--ON [IN] THE TREE,	OF ALL THE SOUNDS	321	28
IGNORES THE SOLEMN NEWS	MORE LIFE--WENT OUT--	422	18
A LIGHT, FOR HER [ME], DID SOLEMN GLOW,	I SHOWED HER HIGHTS SHE	446	10
A SOLEMN THING WITHIN THE SOUL	A SOLEMN THING WITHIN	483	1
AND WHEN THE SOLEMN FEATURES	AN IGNORANCE A SUNSET	552	9
IN CHILDISH [SOLEMN] HONESTY--	I PRAYED, AT FIRST, A	576	8
IN SOLEMN [TIMID] HONESTY	THE BODY GROWS WITHOUT--	578	8
THE SOLEMN CONTRACT OF A LIFE	I GAVE MYSELF TO HIM--	580	3
INCONCEIVABLY SOLEMN!	INCONCEIVABLY SOLEMN!	582	1
THE SOLEMN--TORRID--SYMBOL--	A STILL--VOLCANO--LIFE--	601	9
WHILE I STATE--THE SOLEMN PETALS,	BLOOM UPON THE MOUNTAIN	667	13
AND THEN THE CHEER TOO SOLEMN GREW	TWO TRAVELLERS PERISHING	933	7
THAT IS SOLEMN [TENDER / SACRED] WE HAVE ENDED	THAT IS SOLEMN WE HAVE	934	1
THE AWFUL [SOLEMN] CUTLERY	THE LIGHTNING IS A	1173	4
BUT THAT SOLEMN WAR	THERE'S THE BATTLE OF	1174	6
WITH SOLEMN NAMELESS NEED	I GROPED FOR HIM BEFORE	1555	2
SOLEMNER			
THE WORLD--STANDS--SOLEMNER--TO ME--	THE WORLD--STANDS--	493	1
SOLEMNEST			
BUT SOLEMNEST--TO KNOW	A SOLEMN THING WITHIN	483	13
IS SOLEMNEST OF INDUSTRIES	THE BUSTLE IN A HOUSE	1078	3
SOLEMNITY			
SOLEMNITY--PREVAIL--	NO CROWD THAT HAS	515	13
SOLEMNIZES			
WHICH SOLEMNIZES ME.	A SOMETHING IN A	122	3
SOLEMNLY			
WHEEL SOLEMNLY [POMPOUSLY] AWAY!	PAPA ABOVE!	61	9
SOLID			
AND HIS--IN SOLID GOLD--	A TONGUE--TO TELL HIM I	400	19
THAN A SOLID DAWN--CONFRONTING--	DREAMS--ARE WELL--BUT	450	7
AND GOLD TO OWN--IN SOLID BARS--	IT WAS GIVEN TO ME BY	454	15

	FIRST LINE	POEM	LINE
SOLID (CONTINUED)			
IF 'TWAS A DREAM--MADE SOLID--JUST	HER SWEET WEIGHT ON MY	518	5
UNTIL WE MET THE SOLID TOWN--	I STARTED EARLY--TOOK MY	520	21
THEIR SUMMER--LASTS A SOLID YEAR--	I RECKON--WHEN I COUNT	569	9
TO TOMES OF SOLID WITCHCRAFT--	I THINK I WAS ENCHANTED	593	29
YET BLUE--AND SOLID [EASY]--STOOD--	IT TROUBLED ME AS ONCE I	600	6
AND PILES OF SOLID MOAN--	MY PORTION IS DEFEAT--	639	9
AND CREWS--OF SOLID BLOOD--	WHOLE GULFS--OF RED, AND	658	2
MATCH ME THE SOLID CALM--	THIS THAT WOULD GREET--	778	8
A MOB OF SOLID BLISS--	FROM ALL THE JAILS THE	1532	6
SOLIDITIES			
THE SPECTRE OF SOLIDITIES	WE DO NOT KNOW THE TIME	1106	7
SOLITARY			
WRECKED, SOLITARY, HERE--	I FELT A FUNERAL, IN MY	280	16
FOUR TREES--UPON A SOLITARY ACRE--	FOUR TREES--UPON A	742	1
THROUGH THE SOLITARY PROWESS	GROWTH OF MAN--LIKE	750	7
ON SOLITARY FIELDS	A LIGHT EXISTS IN SPRING	812	6
SOLITUDE			
BETRAYS THE SOLITUDE.	NEW FEET WITHIN MY	99	4
INTO [BACK OF / AT THE / AFTER / UNTO / NEXT TO] SOLITUDE--	HOW THE OLD MOUNTAINS	291	20
IN SUMPTUOUS SOLITUDE--	THE THRILL CAME SLOWLY	1495	4
SURPASSES SOLITUDE	A LANE OF YELLOW LED THE	1650	4
WOULD POPULATE WITH AWE MY SOLITUDE	ON MY VOLCANO GROWS THE	1677	8
THERE IS A SOLITUDE OF SPACE	THERE IS A SOLITUDE OF	1695	1
A SOLITUDE OF SEA	THERE IS A SOLITUDE OF	1695	2
A SOLITUDE OF DEATH, BUT THESE	THERE IS A SOLITUDE OF	1695	3
SOLO			
THOU ART A HUMAN SOLO, A BEING COLD, AND LONE,	AWAKE YE MUSES NINE,	1	27
SOLSTICE			
AS IF NO SOUL THE [WHILE OUR TWO SOULS THAT] SOLSTICE PASSED	THERE CAME A DAY AT	322	7
THE SOLSTICE HAD NO SUN	WHAT CARE THE DEAD, FOR	592	10
NO SOLSTICE INTERRUPT--	THERE IS A ZONE WHOSE	1056	2
SOLVE			
SOLVE OUR APRIL DAY!	I CANT TELL YOU--BUT YOU	65	4
SOME I SHALL KEEP [SAVE]--TO SOLVE	IT TROUBLED ME AS ONCE I	600	10
SOMBRE			
WHEN FIRST A SOMBRE [LITTLE] GIRL--	I THINK I WAS ENCHANTED	593	2
INVESTED SOMBRE PLACE--	AS IMPERCEPTIBLY AS	1540	V
SOME			
SOME EPAULETTED BROTHER	THERE IS A WORD	8	9
SOME HAVE RESIGNED THE LOOM--	MY WHEEL IS IN THE DARK!	10	9
SOME IN THE BUSY TOMB	MY WHEEL IS IN THE DARK!	10	10
SOME WITH NEW--STATELY FEET--	MY WHEEL IS IN THE DARK!	10	12
AS IF THE STARS SOME SUMMER NIGHT	THERE IS A MORN BY MEN	24	16
SOME ONE THE SUM COULD TELL--	IT'S ALL I HAVE TO BRING	26	6
SOME TOUCH IT, AND SOME KISS IT--	THERE'S SOMETHING	45	5
SOME TOUCH IT, AND SOME KISS IT--	THERE'S SOMETHING	45	5
SOME CHAFE IT'S IDLE HAND--	THERE'S SOMETHING	45	6
SOME RAINBOW--COMING FROM THE FAIR!	SOME RAINBOW--COMING	64	1
SOME VISION OF THE WORLD CASHMERE--	SOME RAINBOW--COMING	64	2
FROM SOME OLD FORTRESS ON THE SUN	SOME RAINBOW--COMING	64	10
TO SOME FASHIONABLE LADY	I CANT TELL YOU--BUT YOU	65	15
TILL SOME ODD AFTERNOON	OUR LIVES ARE SWISS--	80	3
SOME THINGS THAT FLY THERE BE--	SOME THINGS THAT FLY	89	1
SOME THINGS THAT STAY THERE BE--	SOME THINGS THAT FLY	89	4
OF SOME RARE TENANT OF THE MOLD,	A SCIENCE--SO THE SAVANS	100	5
OH SOME SCHOLAR! OH SOME SAILOR!	WILL THERE REALLY BE A	101	9
OH SOME SCHOLAR! OH SOME SAILOR!	WILL THERE REALLY BE A	101	9
OH SOME WISE MAN FROM THE SKIES!	WILL THERE REALLY BE A	101	10
SOME LOSE THEIR WAY!	OUR SHARE OF NIGHT TO	113	6
I HAD SOME THINGS THAT I CALLED MINE--	I HAD SOME THINGS THAT I	116	1
AT SOME IMPOSING DOOR!	IN RAGS MYSTERIOUS AS	117	6
SOME, WOULD EVEN TRUDGE TONIGHT!	"HOUSES"--SO THE WISE	127	8
WHO'LL LET ME OUT SOME GALA DAY	BRING ME THE SUNSET IN A	128	22
SOME OTHER THIRSTY THERE MAY BE	I BRING AN UNACCUSTOMED	132	14
SOME PILGRIM THIRST TO SLAKE--	I BRING AN UNACCUSTOMED	132	19
SOME BURNING NOON GO DRY!	HAVE YOU GOT A BROOK IN	136	16
BELLES FROM SOME LOST SUMMER DAY--	PIGMY SERAPHS--GONE	138	3
SOME, TOO FRAGILE FOR WINTER WINDS	SOME, TOO FRAGILE FOR	141	1
SOME SHOOK THEIR HEADS, AND OTHERS SMILED--	WHOSE ARE THE LITTLE	142	3
SOME LITTLE WREN GOES SEEKING ROUND--	FOR EVERY BIRD A NEST--	143	3
EXCEPT TO SOME WIDE-WANDERING BEE	EXCEPT TO HEAVEN, SHE IS	154	3
SOME GRINNING MORN--	YOU LOVE ME--YOU ARE	156	4
SOME--SAY--IT IS "THE SPHERES"--AT PLAY!	MUSICIANS WRESTLE	157	13
SOME SAY--THAT BRIGHT MAJORITY	MUSICIANS WRESTLE	157	14
SOME--THINK IT SERVICE IN THE PLACE	MUSICIANS WRESTLE	157	16
SOME SAILOR, SKIRTING FOREIGN [NOVEL] SHORES--	JUST LOST, WHEN I WAS	160	9
SOME PALE REPORTER, FROM THE AWFUL DOORS	JUST LOST, WHEN I WAS	160	10
PLUCKED FAR AWAY, SOME MORNING--	IN EBON BOX, WHEN YEARS	169	11
IF SOME LOVING ANTIQUARY,	I HAVE NEVER SEEN	175	17
AS IF SOME LITTLE ARCTIC FLOWER	AS IF SOME LITTLE ARCTIC	180	1
SOME SCARLET PATCHES ON THE WAY,	A SLASH OF BLUE--	204	3
SOME RUBY TROWSERS HURRIED ON--	A SLASH OF BLUE--	204	6
LEAST RIVERS--DOCILE TO SOME SEA.	LEAST RIVERS--DOCILE TO	212	1
SOME LIKE "EMILY."	TEACH HIM--WHEN HE MAKES	227	9
WOULD BUT SOME GOD--INFORM HIM--	IF HE DISSOLVE--THEN--	236	8
SOME DRIFTS WERE MOVED AWAY--	I THINK JUST HOW MY	237	10
BUBBLE! "FORGIVE"--"SOME BETTER"--BUBBLE!	KILL YOUR BALM--AND IT'S	238	7

	FIRST LINE	POEM	LINE
SOME (CONTINUED)			
SOME SUDDEN MORN--	DELIGHT IS AS THE FLIGHT	257	24
SOME SAILOR--ROWING IN THE DARK--	GOOD NIGHT! WHICH PUT	259	8
SOME MADDER HOLIDAY--	THE LONESOME FOR THEY	262	4
SOME TRANSATLANTIC MORN--	THE LONESOME FOR THEY	262	10
SOME STRIDING--GIANT--LOVE--	A SINGLE SCREW OF FLESH	263	16
SOME DISTANT HEAVEN,	DOUBT ME! MY DIM	275	16
AND I, AND SILENCE, SOME STRANGE RACE	I FELT A FUNERAL, IN MY	280	15
I KNOW SOME LONELY HOUSES OFF THE ROAD	I KNOW SOME LONELY	289	1
A WATCH--SOME ANCIENT [ANTIQUE] BROOCH	I KNOW SOME LONELY	289	28
AN [SOME] ISLAND IN DISHONORED GRASS--	OF BRONZE--AND BLAZE--	290	18
IT CARE, IN SOME REMOTER WAY,	I GOT SO I COULD HEAR	293	24
SUCH [SOME] SPIRIT MAKES [TELL] HER PERPETUAL MENTION,	UNTO LIKE STORY--TROUBLE	295	13
SOME NEW EQUATION, GIVEN--	I REASON, EARTH IS SHORT	301	11
LIKE SOME OLD FASHIONED MIRACLE	LIKE SOME OLD FASHIONED	302	1
IN SOME ODD FASHION [PATTERN] OF IT'S OWN,	OF ALL THE SOUNDS	321	19
SOME QUAINTER HOLIDAY,	OF ALL THE SOUNDS	321	20
AS IF SOME CARAVAN OF SOUND	OF ALL THE SOUNDS	321	29
SOME KEEP THE SABBATH GOING TO CHURCH--	SOME KEEP THE SABBATH	324	1
SOME KEEP THE SABBATH IN SURPLICE--	SOME KEEP THE SABBATH	324	5
I'M SOME ACCUSTOMED TO HIM GROWN,	I DREADED THAT FIRST	348	3
TO FIT SOME CRUCIFIXAL CLEF--	THE MORNING AFTER WO--	364	15
SOME KEY OF CALVARY--	THE MORNING AFTER WO--	364	16
SOME FEBUARY DAY,	ALTHOUGH I PUT AWAY HIS	366	27
SOME--WORK FOR IMMORTALITY--	SOME--WORK FOR	406	1
MIGHT SOME ONE ELSE--SO LEARNED--BE--	NOT IN THIS WORLD TO SEE	418	10
FOR SOME--AN AMPLER ZERO--	MORE LIFE--WENT OUT--	422	9
I SUPPOSE IT WILL INTERRUPT ME SOME	IT DONT SOUND SO	426	10
TIARAS--MAKE--OF SOME--	I'LL CLUTCH--AND CLUTCH	427	8
SAY--SOME--PHILOSOPHER!	KNOWS HOW TO FORGET!	433	V
AND YET--EXISTENCE--SOME WAY BACK--	I TIE MY HAT--I CREASE	443	11
HOW JUST THIS TIME, SOME PERFECT YEAR--	'TWAS JUST THIS TIME,	445	23
ROWER, AND YACHT--SOME SOVREIGN SUMMER--	LOVE--THOU ART HIGH--	453	11
SOME INDUSTRY MUST BE--	I HAD NO TIME TO HATE--	478	9
THE SINGLE--TO SOME LIVES.	A SOLEMN THING WITHIN	483	16
AND WHEN--SOME NIGHT--BOLD--SLASHING CLOUDS	YOU KNOW THAT PORTRAIT	504	13
SOME MANNER OF THE HAIR--	IF ANYBODY'S FRIEND BE	509	6
AND 'TWAS LIKE MIDNIGHT, SOME--	IT WAS NOT DEATH, FOR I	510	16
SHE FEELS SOME GHASTLY FRIGHT COME UP	THE SOUL HAS BANDAGED	512	3
SOME RUMOR OF DELIRIUM,	LIKE FLOWERS, THAT HEARD	513	5
BY TROPIC HINT--SOME TRAVELLED BIRD	LIKE FLOWERS, THAT HEARD	513	8
AND STILL IT HURT YOU, AS SOME BIRD	HER SMILE WAS SHAPED	514	3
SOME POLAR EXPIATION--AN OMEN IN THE BONE	I TRIED TO THINK A	532	3
SOME MORNING OF CHAGRIN--	WE SEE--COMPARATIVELY--	534	14
SOME SUCH BUTTERFLY BE SEEN	SOME SUCH BUTTERFLY BE	541	1
SOME SUCH SPICE [ROSE]--EXPRESS AND PASS--	SOME SUCH BUTTERFLY BE	541	5
THEIR MORTAL FATE--ENCOURAGE SOME--	THE MARTYR POETS--DID	544	4
SOME [MEN] SEEK IN ART--THE ART OF PEACE--	THE MARTYR POETS--DID	544	8
I NOTE THAT SOME--GONE PATIENT LONG--	I MEASURE EVERY GRIEF I	561	13
SOME THOUSANDS--ON THE HARM--	I MEASURE EVERY GRIEF I	561	18
THAT SOME--ARE LIKE MY OWN--	I MEASURE EVERY GRIEF I	561	40
SHE PUT SOME FLOWERS AWAY--	MY FIRST WELL DAY--SINCE	574	10
SOME CARNIVALS OF CLOUDS--	"HEAVEN" HAS DIFFERENT	575	12
THEN HOW THE GRIEF GOT SLEEPY--SOME--	IF I MAY HAVE IT, WHEN	577	18
SOME--FOUND IT--MUTUAL GAIN--	I GAVE MYSELF TO HIM--	580	14
SOME I SHALL KEEP [SAVE]--TO SOLVE	IT TROUBLED ME AS ONCE I	600	10
SOME SECRET--THAT WAS PUSHING	THE TINT I CANNOT TAKE--	627	15
"'TWAS SUNSET"--SOME ONE SAID--	THEY CALLED ME TO THE	628	2
BY SOME ONE CARRYING A LIGHT--	OURSELVES WERE WED ONE	631	7
SOME SHALL [SOME ONE] SUMMON ME--	PROMISE THIS--WHEN YOU	648	2
SOME SHALL [SOME ONE] SUMMON ME--	PROMISE THIS--WHEN YOU	648	2
ROUND SOME OTHER FACE--	PROMISE THIS--WHEN YOU	648	24
EACH LIFE CONVERGES TO SOME CENTRE--	EACH LIFE CONVERGES TO	680	1
SOME BASHFUL SUMMER'S DAY--	THE HEAVEN VESTS FOR	694	4
THEY STRUGGLE--SOME--FOR BREATH--	YOU'VE SEEN BALLOONS SET	700	10
BUT DID NOT FINISH--SOME WAY BACK--	A THOUGHT WENT UP MY	701	3
NATURE--AND SOME MEN--	RESTS AT NIGHT	714	3
REST AT NOON--SOME MEN--	RESTS AT NIGHT	714	4
TO SOME DULL COMFORT THOSE OBTAIN	SEVERER SERVICE OF	786	13
AS SOME [US] SHE NEVER KNEW--	NO NOTICE GAVE SHE, BUT	804	20
A DEATH BLOW IS A LIFE BLOW TO SOME	A DEATH BLOW IS A LIFE	816	1
AWAY FROM HOME ARE SOME [THEY] AND I--	AWAY FROM HOME ARE SOME	821	1
PERCHANCE [THREE--WITH / AND SOME] ETERNITY--	THE ONLY NEWS I KNOW	827	6
SOME HOURS IN [OF] THE DAY.	LIGHT IS SUFFICIENT TO	862	4
THEY WONT FROWN ALWAYS--SOME SWEET DAY	THEY WONT FROWN ALWAYS--	874	1
SOME CALL EXPERIENCE.	I STEPPED FROM PLANK TO	875	8
ON SOME UNANSWERING SHORE--	I'VE NONE TO TELL ME TO	881	9
THAT SOME THERE BE TOO NUMB TO NOTICE	A SHADE UPON THE MIND	882	5
SOME HOUSES VERY OLD,	WHO OCCUPIES THIS HOUSE?	892	10
SOME--NEWLY RAISED THIS AFTERNOON,	WHO OCCUPIES THIS HOUSE?	892	11
OR SOME ELF'S CATACOMB?	DRAB HABITATION OF WHOM?	893	5
SOME THAT NEVER LAY	SNOW BENEATH WHOSE	942	2
AND MINE--SOME FOOLISHER EFFECT--	I LEARNED--AT LEAST--	944	16
SOME MINISTRY TO POORER LIVES--	I LEARNED--AT LEAST--	944	20
SOME PASSING YEAR--A TRAIT [CHARM] BESTOW	FITTER TO SEE HIM, I MAY	968	4
FOR SOME OTHER [ANOTHER] SHAME--	HE WHO IN HIMSELF	969	8
SOME KNOW HIM [IT] WHOM WE KNEW--	BESIDES THIS MAY	977	6
IS SORRY, SOME, FOR ME.	HERE, WHERE THE DAISIES	1037	4
SOME DISEASE HAD VEXT	THREE WEEKS PASSED SINCE	1061	2

	FIRST LINE	POEM	LINE
SOME (CONTINUED)			
HOW SOME ONE [PARTIES] TREATED HIM . . .	THE SKY IS LOW--THE	1075	6
SOME WEDNESDAY AFTERNOON.	DEW--IS THE FRESHET IN	1097	12
LEST SOME ONE ELSE SHOULD [RICHER PEOPLE] BUY	A DIAMOND ON THE HAND	1108	V 8
SOME WRETCHED CREATURE, SAVIOR TAKE . . .	SOME WRETCHED CREATURE,	1111	1
BUT MURMURING OF SOME	THE MURMURING OF BEES,	1115	2
[SOME] IT MUST BE COMPETITIONS	HOW MANY SCHEMES MAY DIE	1150	11
SOME UNSUSPECTING HORSE WAS TIED	HOW MANY SCHEMES MAY DIE	1150	12
SOME DAYS RETIRED FROM THE REST	SOME DAYS RETIRED FROM	1157	1
SOME EIGHTEEN THOUSAND YEARS--	AS OLD AS WOE--	1168	3
THAT THIS WAS DUE WHERE MOST [SOME] WE FEAR	"REMEMBER ME" IMPLORED	1180	11
SOME OTHER THOU WILT [DID'ST] CONSECRATE-- .	OH SHADOW ON THE GRASS,	1187	7
IS STERILE BORNE TO SOME--	THE VOICE THAT STANDS	1189	2
TILL SOME RETRIEVELESS NIGHT	THE FROST WAS NEVER SEEN	1202	9
SOME SAY.	A WORD IS DEAD	1212	3
SOME WE SEE NO MORE, TENEMENTS OF WONDER .	SOME WE SEE NO MORE,	1221	1
TO SOME REMOTEST PLAIN	LIKE RAIN IT SOUNDED	1235	6
SUPPLY THE [INVITE SOME / ENDOW SOME / AFFRONT A / AFFRONT . . .	ART THOU THE THING I	1282	3
SUPPLY THE [INVITE SOME / ENDOW SOME / AFFRONT A / AFFRONT . . .	ART THOU THE THING I	1282	3
HE RESTITUTES IN SOME SWEET WAY	NOT ONE BY HEAVEN	1303	3
SOME HAVE SOLACED THE LONGING	NOT ANY MORE TO BE	1344	11
SOME--RESCINDED THE WRENCH--	NOT ANY MORE TO BE	1344	13
WHEN DOWN SOME AWFUL BATTLEMENT	ESCAPE IS SUCH A	1347	7
SOME CONFLICT WITH THOSE UPPER FRIENDS . .	A WILD BLUE SKY ABREAST	1415	5
TO SOME SUPERIOR TREE	BEFORE YOU THOUGHT OF	1465	13
REKINDLED BY SOME ACTION QUAINT	A WINGED SPARK DOTH SOAR	1468	9
FULFILLING ABSOLUTE [SOME EXPRESS] DECREE .	HOW HAPPY IS THE LITTLE	1510	9
CHILDHOOD--SOME FORMS OF HOPE--THE DEAD-- .	THE THINGS THAT NEVER	1515	2
SOME SPICE'S MUTINY--	SWEET PIRATE OF THE	1546	4
SOME ATTAR'S PERFIDY?	SWEET PIRATE OF THE	1546	5
OH NO, BUT ON SOME OTHER FLIGHT--	WITHIN THY GRAVE!	1552	2
SOME ARROWS SLAY BUT WHOM THEY STRIKE-- . .	SOME ARROWS SLAY BUT	1565	1
SOME SCHISM IN THE SUM--	THE CLOCK STRIKES ONE	1569	2
TO SOME--THE NIGHT--	MORNING IS DUE TO ALL--	1577	2
SOME FAIR OR STORMY DAY, ...	THIS ME--THAT WALKS AND	1588	2
WHICH LIKE THE MOON, SOME TURBID NIGHT, . .	EACH THAT WE LOSE TAKES	1605	3
OF SOME PERCEIVELESS THING--	THE PEDIGREE OF HONEY	1627	6
SOME ONE PREPARED THIS MIGHTY SHOW . . .	SOME ONE PREPARED THIS	1644	1
WARMS SOME POOR NAME	GLORY IS THAT BRIGHT	1660	4
SOME DYER OF A DISTANT TREE	SUMMER BEGINS TO HAVE	1682	11
SOME SAY GOODNIGHT--AT NIGHT--	SOME SAY GOODNIGHT--AT	1739	1
TO MAKE SOME TRIFLE FAIRER	WERE NATURE MORTAL LADY	1762	9
SOMEBODY			
AND SOMEBODY HAS LOST THE FACE	EXCEPT TO HEAVEN, SHE IS	154	11
WONT SOMEBODY BRING THE LIGHT	DYING! DYING IN THE	158	2
SOMEBODY RUN TO THE GREAT GATE	DYING! DYING IN THE	158	9
HOW DREARY--TO BE--SOMEBODY!	I'M NOBODY! WHO ARE YOU?	288	5
SOMEBODY FLINGS A MATTRASS OUT--	THERE'S BEEN A DEATH, IN	389	9
TO SOMEBODY YOU KNOW	BEE! I'M EXPECTING YOU!	1035	3
SOMEBODY'S			
I MET SOMEBODY'S LITTLE BOY	TRUDGING TO EDEN,	1020	2
SOMEHOW			
SOMEHOW, IT WILL BE EVEN--	I REASON, EARTH IS SHORT	301	10
SOMEHOW MYSELF SURVIVED THE NIGHT	SOMEHOW MYSELF SURVIVED	1194	1
SOMEHOW THIS HAD COME--	NOW I KNEW I LOST HER--	1219	12
RELATED SOMEHOW THEY MAY BE, ...	WHAT MYSTERY PERVADES A	1400	13
SOMEONE			
I KNEW LAST NIGHT--WHEN SOMEONE TRIED TO TWINE--	HOW SICK--TO WAIT--IN	368	2
AS SOMEONE HELD A LIGHT UNTO [UPON] . . .	WHAT I SEE NOT, I BETTER	939	7
SOMETHING			
THERE'S SOMETHING QUIETER THAN SLEEP . . .	THERE'S SOMETHING	45	1
A SOMETHING IN A SUMMER'S DAY	A SOMETHING IN A	122	1
A SOMETHING IN A SUMMER'S NOON--	A SOMETHING IN A	122	4
A SOMETHING SO TRANSPORTING BRIGHT . . .	A SOMETHING IN A	122	8
A POPE, OR SOMETHING OF THAT KIND! . . .	I MET A KING THIS	166	12
WHEN SOMETHING BROKE--	'TWAS LIKE A MAELSTROM,	414	8
OR SOMETHING IN THE SIGHT	WE GROW ACCUSTOMED TO	419	18
BUT SOMETHING HELD MY WILL.	'TWAS JUST THIS TIME,	445	8
THAT SOMETHING--IT DID DO--OR DARE-- . . .	WHY MAKE IT DOUBT--IT	462	9
IN SEARCH OF SOMETHING [SOMEWHAT]--AS IT SEEMED--	I'VE SEEN A DYING EYE	547	3
BUT SOMETHING AWKWARD IN [ODD ABOUT] THE FIT--	I COULD NOT PROVE THE	563	11
THAT SOMETHING--HAD OBSCURED [BEMUMBED] THE TRACK--	IT CEASED TO HURT ME,	584	4
"POOR CHILD"--AND SOMETHING IN HER VOICE .	I CRIED AT PITY--NOT AT	588	3
DEFEAT--A SOMEWHAT SLOWER--[SOMETHING DUMBER] MEANS--	MY PORTION IS DEFEAT--	639	5
THERE'S SOMEWHAT [SOMETHING] PROUDER, OVER THERE--	MY PORTION IS DEFEAT--	639	14
FOR SOMETHING PASSIVER--CONTENT	A PRISON GETS TO BE A	652	27
WHO SOMETHING LOST [DROPT], THE SEEKING [LOOKING] FOR	DEATH LEAVES US HOMESICK	935	7
A LOSS OF SOMETHING EVER FELT I--	A LOSS OF SOMETHING EVER	959	1
WITH SOMETHING HID IN HER--	I CANNOT MEET THE SPRING	1051	6
LIKE SOMETHING SPIRITUAL--	IT WAS NOT SAINT--IT WAS	1092	4
'TIS SOMETHING LIKE A HOUSE--	REMEMBRANCE HAS A	1182	2
TO SOMETHING UPPER WOOING US	THE FASCINATING CHILL	1480	7

	FIRST LINE	POEM	LINE
SOMETHING (CONTINUED)			
THERE'S SOMETHING IN THEIR ATTITUDE . . .	MY COUNTRY NEED NOT	1511	7
TO SOMETHING NEIGHBORING	IN WINTER IN MY ROOM	1670	8
A SOMETHING LIKE A SHAME	THAT SHE FORGOT ME WAS	1683	8
THERE'S SOMETHING IN THE FLIGHT	BY A DEPARTING LIGHT	1714	4
SOMETHING'S			
AND SOMETHING'S ODD--WITHIN--	THE FIRST DAY'S NIGHT	410	17
SOMETIME			
SOMETIME, HE DWELLETH IN THE GRASS! . . .	A FUZZY FELLOW, WITHOUT	173	5
SOMETIME, UPON A BOUGH, ...	A FUZZY FELLOW, WITHOUT	173	6
OR--IF IT SOMETIME--SHOWED--AS 'TWILL-- . .	IT WOULD NEVER BE COMMON	430	5
SOMETIMES			
HAVE SOMETIMES PROVED DEADLY SWEET! . . .	TALK WITH PRUDENCE TO A	119	8
I'VE HEARD AN ORGAN TALK, SOMETIMES-- . .	I'VE HEARD AN ORGAN TALK	183	1
OR--SOMETIMES AT YOUR SIDE TO RUN-- . . .	WHAT SHALL I DO--IT	186	11
SOMETIMES--NOT OFTEN--IN ETERNITY-- . . .	ONE YEAR AGO--JOTS WHAT?	296	7
NATURE--SOMETIMES SEARS A SAPLING-- . . .	NATURE--SOMETIMES SEARS	314	1
SOMETIMES--SCALPS A TREE--	NATURE--SOMETIMES SEARS	314	2
SOMETIMES--A VANE'S FOREFINGER--	THE ANGLE OF A LANDSCAPE	375	11
AND SOMETIMES HIT A TREE	WE GROW ACCUSTOMED TO	419	14
HE SOMETIMES HOLDS UPON THE FENCE-- . . .	THE BLACK BERRY--WEARS A	554	5
IF BRAVO, SOMETIMES SWERVE--	THE TEST OF LOVE--IS	573	7
SOMETIMES, I THINK THAT NOON	"HEAVEN" HAS DIFFERENT	575	2
TO SOMETIMES HEAR "RICH PEOPLE" BUY . . .	I CRIED AT PITY--NOT AT	588	9
I SOMETIMES DROP IT, FOR A QUICK-- . . .	I SOMETIMES DROP IT, FOR	708	1
NATURE IS FOND, I SOMETIMES THINK, . . .	A MOTH THE HUE OF THIS	841	5
SOMETIMES, ALMOST MORE.	THIS WAS IN THE WHITE OF	995	8
NATURE, LIKE US IS SOMETIMES CAUGHT . . .	THE SKY IS LOW--THE	1075	7
BUT NATURE, SOMETIMES, SOMETIMES THOUGHT .	THERE IS ANOTHER	1116	5
BUT NATURE, SOMETIMES, SOMETIMES THOUGHT .	THERE IS ANOTHER	1116	5
SEEMS IT SOMETIMES THIS WOULD BE ALL-- . .	THESE FEVERED DAYS--TO	1441	4
THOUGH [BUT] JOYS--LIKE MEN--MAY SOMETIMES MAKE A JOURNEY--	THE THINGS THAT NEVER	1515	3
A HEART SOMETIMES A FOREIGNER, ...	PARTING WITH THEE	1614	3
SOMETIMES WITH THE HEART	SOMETIMES WITH THE HEART	1680	1
SOMEWHAT			
REMIND HIM, WOULD IT NOT, SOMEWHAT . . .	TO ONE DENIED TO DRINK	490	7
IN SEARCH OF SOMETHING [SOMEWHAT]--AS IT SEEMED--	I'VE SEEN A DYING EYE	547	3
FOR SOMEWHAT THAT [WHATSOE'ER] IT SAW? . .	IT KNEW NO MEDICINE--	559	16
AND THOUGH THEIR PLACES SOMEWHAT FILLED-- .	YOU'LL FIND--IT WHEN YOU	610	5
DEFEAT--A SOMEWHAT SLOWER--[SOMETHING DUMBER] MEANS--	MY PORTION IS DEFEAT--	639	5
THERE'S SOMEWHAT [SOMETHING] PROUDER, OVER THERE--	MY PORTION IS DEFEAT--	639	14
IT'S SOMEWHAT IN THE COLD--	THE BEGGAR LAD--DIES	717	2
AND SOMEWHAT IN THE TRUDGING FEET-- . . .	THE BEGGAR LAD--DIES	717	3
SOMEWHAT DIFFERENT--MUST BE--	LET US PLAY YESTERDAY--	728	9
EXHIBIT LOVE--SOMEWHAT--	TILL DEATH--IS NARROW	907	12
SOMEWHAT OF NODS AND SOMEWHAT	THE LEAVES LIKE WOMEN,	987	3
SOMEWHAT OF NODS AND SOMEWHAT	THE LEAVES LIKE WOMEN,	987	3
SOMEWHAT, TO HOPE FOR, ...	SOMEWHAT, TO HOPE FOR,	1041	1
SOMEWHAT, TO SUFFER, ...	SOMEWHAT, TO HOPE FOR,	1041	4
WHAT WE SEE WE KNOW SOMEWHAT	WHAT WE SEE WE KNOW	1195	1
SOMEWHERE			
SOMEWHERE--IN SILENCE--	I KNOW THAT HE EXISTS.	338	2
FROM THE BELIEF THAT SOMEWHERE--	I TRIED TO THINK A	532	8
BUT SOMEWHERE--IN MY SOUL--I KNOW--	A THOUGHT WENT UP MY	701	9
I SHALL MEET WITH CONVICTION I SOMEWHERE MET	BY MY WINDOW HAVE I FOR	797	20
SINCE SOMEWHERE THY SWEET FACE HAS SPILLED .	I'VE NONE TO TELL ME TO	881	5
WAS SOMEWHERE PUT IN TWAIN.	AS FROST IS BEST	951	12
TO BEING, SOMEWHERE--MOTION--BREATH-- . .	I'VE DROPPED MY BRAIN--	1046	17
SOMEWHERE UPON THE GENERAL EARTH	SOMEWHERE UPON THE	1231	1
FOR THAT THERE IS A [SOMEWHERE IS] MORN . .	HIS HEART WAS DARKER	1378	2
THAT SOMEWHERE, THERE EXISTS, ...	THE HEART HAS MANY DOORS	1567	7
SON			
AND THE FATHER FOND DEMANDETH THE MAIDEN FOR HIS SON.	AWAKE YE MUSES NINE,	1	16
WOOS, AS HE STATES US--BY HIS SON--	GOD IS A DISTANT--	357	2
KNOW GOD THE FATHER--AND THE SON.	YOU'LL KNOW IT--AS YOU	420	6
BY THE SON OF GOD--	TO PUT THIS WORLD DOWN,	527	6
GOD THE SON--CONFIDE [DISCLOSE] IT--	ONLY GOD--DETECT THE	626	5
WHOSE PRINCE--IS SON OF NONE--	BEHIND ME--DIPS ETERNITY	721	9
BRIDE OF THE FATHER AND THE SON	GIVEN IN MARRIAGE UNTO	817	3
TELL HAD A SON--THE ONES THAT KNEW [HEARD] IT	TELL AS A MARKSMAN--WERE	1152	9
WHO WERE "THE FATHER AND THE SON"	WHO WERE "THE FATHER AND	1258	1
WHO ARE "THE FATHER AND THE SON"	WHO WERE "THE FATHER AND	1258	9
"THE FATHER AND THE SON" HIMSELF	WHO WERE "THE FATHER AND	1258	11
NEGLECTED SON OF GENIUS	THE SPIDER AS AN ARTIST	1275	7
TO SPECULATION'S SON--	THE THINGS WE THOUGHT	1293	8
COULD SHE A SON CONTEMN	THE MUSHROOM IS THE ELF	1298	V 18
HE SENT HIS SON TO TEST THE PLANK, ...	HOW BRITTLE ARE THE	1433	7
AS ROBINS [ROBIN]--SIRE AND SON--	FOREVER HONORED BE THE	1570	6
THE SON [A WOE] OF ECSTASY--	A SLOOP OF AMBER SLIPS	1622	4
FOR THIS WAS WOMAN'S SON.	UPON THE GALLOWS HUNG A	1757	6
SONG			
AND A DEAL OF SAD REFLECTION, AND WAILING INSTEAD OF SONG?	AWAKE YE MUSES NINE,	1	30
ONLY TO BREAK IN WILDER SONG	IF I COULD BRIBE THEM BY	179	11
AND STAPLES [RIVETS], IN THE SONG, ...	THE SOUL HAS BANDAGED	512	22

	FIRST LINE	POEM	LINE
SONG (CONTINUED)			
WITH SPECIMENS OF SONG	BEFORE YOU THOUGHT OF	1465	9
AND NOT A SONG PERVADE HIS LIPS--	THE BAT IS DUN, WITH	1575	3
DEFRAUDED OF IT'S SONG.	AS FROM THE EARTH THE	1630	9
IT HAS A SONG--	FAME IS A BEE.	1763	2
SOON			
PLEASE, PATER, PRETTY SOON!	WHERE BELLS NO MORE	112	8
I W'D AS SOON ATTEMPT TO WARM	I BRING AN UNACCUSTOMED	132	11
AS OLD AS THEE--HOW SOON?	ONE YEAR AGO--JOTS WHAT?	296	34
BUT NOT SO SOON--	SHE LAY AS IF AT PLAY	369	4
OF TASSELS--AND OF COACHES--SOON--	THERE'S BEEN A DEATH, IN	389	21
AS SOON--ADVERSITY	REVERSE CANNOT BEFALL	395	4
ONE WOULD AS SOON ASSAULT A PLUSH--	WHAT SOFT--CHERUBIC	401	3
SO SOON TO BE A CHILD NO MORE--	A WIFE--AT DAYBREAK I	461	11
IF JUST AS SOON AS BREATH IS OUT	IF I MAY HAVE IT, WHEN	577	3
AS SOON THE SOUTH--HER BREEZE	WHAT CARE THE DEAD, FOR	592	20
AS SOON IMPEACH MY CROWN!	AFRAID! OF WHOM AM I	608	12
GONE--AS SOON AS KNOWN--	SO THE EYES ACCOST--AND	752	8
QUICK [SOON]--SWEET MOUTH--TO MISS THEE SO--	THESE--SAW VISIONS--	758	6
AND WOULD AS SOON SURMISE	THE LONELINESS ONE DARE	777	2
"YOU'RE SOON," THE TOWN REPLIED,	THE FINGERS OF THE LIGHT	1000	5
AS SOON AS [THE INSTANT THAT] YOU HAVE COME	DEAR MARCH--COME IN--	1320	24
BECAUSE [THAT WERT] A BARD TOO SOON--	TOUCH LIGHTLY NATURE'S	1389	4
TO WISER BE [GROW] TOO SOON--	I THOUGHT THE TRAIN	1449	10
ANGER AS SOON AS FED IS DEAD--	MINE ENEMY IS GROWING	1509	7
SOONER			
TURN [TAKE] SOONEST [SOONER] TO THE SEA	CONTAINED IN THIS SHORT	1165	6
'TWAS SOONER WHEN THE CRICKET WENT	'TWAS LATER WHEN THE	1276	5
AND YET WE SOONER SAY	AS SUMMER INTO AUTUMN	1346	2
SOONEST			
MY TAMBORIN WERE SOONEST HEARD	IF I COULD BRIBE THEM BY	179	8
TURN [TAKE] SOONEST [SOONER] TO THE SEA	CONTAINED IN THIS SHORT	1165	6
SOONEST TO SHARE [SPARE]	MY HEART RAN SO TO THEE	1237	12
SOOTHED			
IS HELPED [SOOTHED] BY THE REGRET	WHAT MYSTERY PERVADES A	1400	22
SOOTY			
NEVER MIND THE SOOTY FACES	BY A FLOWER--BY A LETTER	109	7
SOPHISTRIES			
THE OLD--OLD SOPHISTRIES OF JUNE--	THESE ARE THE DAYS WHEN	130	5
HIS BOUNDARIES [SOPHISTRIES]--FORGOT--	THE SPIDER HOLDS A	605	12
SOPHOCLES			
AND SOPHOCLES--A MAN--	A PRECIOUS--MOULDERING	371	16
SORCERER			
HER SORCERER WITHDRAWN!	THE WAY TO KNOW THE	1279	24
A VAGABOND [SORCERER] FROM GENESIS	THE CLOCK STRIKES ONE	1569	3
SORCERY			
WHAT SORCERY HAD SNOW?	THE SKIES CANT KEEP	191	12
BEHIND THE HILL IS SORCERY	THE GOING FROM A WORLD	1603	5
BY SEPARATION'S SORCERY	THE SADDEST NOISE, THE	1764	11
SORDID			
FOR SORDID EXCELLENCE [CONSEQUENCE]	I CANNOT LIVE WITH YOU--	640	35
IN SORDID HUMAN LIFE	A SAUCER HOLDS A CUP	1374	2
IT WAFTS THIS SORDID FLESH	WITH PINIONS OF DISDAIN	1431	5
SORE			
PERHAPS, WEARY [TIRED] AND SORE--	HEART, NOT SO HEAVY AS	83	18
AND SORE MUST BE THE STORM--	"HOPE" IS THE THING WITH	254	6
SORER			
IT'S SORER TO BELIEVE!	SHE WENT AS QUIET AS THE	149	8
WHAT SORER--PUZZLED ME--	IT TROUBLED ME AS ONCE I	600	14
WOULD'NT DUNGEONS SORER GRATE	LET US PLAY YESTERDAY--	728	29
THERE MARAUDS A SORER ROBBER,	DEATH'S WAYLAYING NOT	1296	3
SOREST			
REQUIRES SOREST NEED.	SUCCESS IS COUNTED	67	4
SORROW			
NOT FOR THE SORROW, DONE ME--	MANY A PHRASE HAS THE	276	13
THE DANGER [SORROW] TO BE SANE	I THINK I WAS ENCHANTED	593	26
ONLY GOD--DETECT THE SORROW [POSSESS THE SECRET]--	ONLY GOD--DETECT THE	626	1
THE BOOTY AND THE SORROW	ONE THING OF IT WE	1464	3
SORROW [AROMA]--NOW--IS POLITE [COURTEOUS]--AND STAYS--	SUMMER IS SHORTER THAN	1506	5
SORROWFUL			
SORROWFUL--AS CERTAIN--	THE CHILD'S FAITH IS NEW	637	22
SORRY			
'TWAS SORRY, THAT WE WERE--	SO GLAD WE ARE--A	329	2
WERE HE TO TELL--EXTREMELY SORRY	FUNNY--TO BE A CENTURY--	345	6
I'M SORRY FOR THE DEAD--TODAY--	I'M SORRY FOR THE DEAD--	529	1
SHE'S "SORRY I AM DEAD"--AGAIN--	I CRIED AT PITY--NOT AT	588	21
IS SORRY, SOME, FOR ME.	HERE, WHERE THE DAISIES	1037	4
SORT			
HENCEFORTH, A DEDICATED SORT--	HE PUT THE BELT AROUND	273	7
SUBLIMER SORT [THING / WAY]--THAN SPEECH--	GIVE LITTLE ANGUISH--	310	8
"SURRENDER"--IS A SORT UNKNOWN	OF TRIBULATION--THESE	325	9
SO THIS SORT--ARE NOT GIVEN--	DID OUR BEST MOMENT LAST	393	4
BUT THAT OLD SORT--WAS DONE--	IT WOULD NEVER BE COMMON	430	4
A SORT, THAT SHALL NOT TASTE OF DEATH--	DO PEOPLE MOULDER	432	11
BUT THIS SORT, GRIEVED MYSELF,	'TWAS JUST THIS TIME,	445	21
A SORT THEY CALL "DESPAIR"--	I MEASURE EVERY GRIEF I	561	30
I WISHED A WAY [SORT] MIGHT BE	WITHOUT THIS--THERE IS	655	9
NOT DUMB--I HAD A SORT THAT MOVED--	I'VE DROPPED MY BRAIN--	1046	9

	FIRST LINE	POEM	LINE
SORT (CONTINUED)			
THAT SORT ACCOMPLISH WELL--	'TWAS FIGHTING FOR HIS	1188	2
SOTO			
SOTO! EXPLORE THYSELF!	SOTO! EXPLORE THYSELF!	832	1
SOUGHT			
HERE ARE THE BIRDS THAT SOUGHT THE SUN	THERE IS A MORN BY MEN	24	10
COULD HE--KNOW--THEY SOUGHT HIM--	IN FALLING TIMBERS	614	5
OR SOUGHT TO--	I CANNOT LIVE WITH YOU--	640	31
AND WHEN I SOUGHT MY BED--	BEREAVED OF ALL, I WENT	784	6
THEN SOUGHT THE DUST--	SHE ROSE AS HIGH AS HIS	1011	2
I NEVER THOUGHT THAT JASON SOUGHT	ONE OF THE ONES THAT	1466	21
AND SO SHE SOUGHT THIS SWEET AT LAST	SHE COULD NOT LIVE UPON	1505	3
SOUL			
TO BRINGING THEE TO JUSTICE, AND MARSHALLING THY SOUL:	AWAKE YE MUSES NINE,	1	26
IS A SOUL "FORGOT!"	THERE IS A WORD	8	18
OF SOUL OR SWORD.	GARLANDS FOR QUEENS, MAY	34	3
STEADY--MY SOUL: WHAT ISSUES	A DAY! HELP! HELP!	42	7
TO INTRODUCE HIS SOUL.	COULD LIVE--DID LIVE--	43	5
AND KEEPS THE SOUL SERENE--	IF I SHOULD DIE,	54	16
OF AN INLAND SOUL TO SEA,	EXULTATION IS THE GOING	76	2
FROM STEEPLES IN MY SOUL!	I HAVE A KING, WHO DOES	103	12
SOUL, WILT THOU TOSS AGAIN?	SOUL, WILT THOU TOSS	139	1
RAFFLE FOR MY SOUL!	SOUL, WILT THOU TOSS	139	8
CAN KEEP THE SOUL ALIVE--	A LITTLE BREAD--A CRUST	159	3
JUST LAYING LIGHT--NO SOUL WILL WINK	WHEN WE STAND ON THE	242	5
IT IS EASY TO WORK WHEN THE SOUL IS AT PLAY--	IT IS EASY TO WORK WHEN	244	1
BUT WHEN THE SOUL IS IN PAIN--	IT IS EASY TO WORK WHEN	244	2
THAT PERCHES IN THE SOUL--	"HOPE" IS THE THING WITH	254	2
IS ALL THAT PINS THE SOUL	A SINGLE SCREW OF FLESH	263	2
DEAL WITH THE SOUL	BOUND--A TROUBLE--	269	5
AND CREAK ACROSS MY SOUL [BRAIN]	I FELT A FUNERAL, IN MY	280	10
THE SOUL STARES AFTER IT, SECURE--	'TIS SO APPALLING--IT	281	3
IF YOUR SOUL SEESAW [STAGGER]--	IF YOUR NERVE, DENY YOU	292	9
THAT STOP-SENSATION--ON MY SOUL--	I GOT SO I COULD HEAR	293	3
THE SOUL SELECTS HER OWN SOCIETY--	THE SOUL SELECTS HER OWN	303	1
HE FUMBLES AT YOUR SOUL	HE FUMBLES AT YOUR SOUL	315	1
THAT SCALPS [PEELS] YOUR NAKED SOUL--	HE FUMBLES AT YOUR SOUL	315	12
MIGHT HE BUT SPY THE LADY'S [HIDING] SOUL--	JUST SO--JESUS--RAPS--	317	6
AS IF NO SOUL THE [WHILE OUR TWO SOULS THAT] SOLSTICE PASSED	THERE CAME A DAY AT	322	7
SO SAFER GUESS--WITH JUST MY SOUL	BEFORE I GOT MY EYE PUT	327	18
THE SOUL SO CLOSE ON PARADISE--	NOT PROBABLE--THE BAREST	346	4
BUT, LEST THE SOUL--LIKE FAIR "PRISCILLA"	GOD IS A DISTANT--	357	5
DARE YOU SEE A SOUL AT THE WHITE HEAT?	DARE YOU SEE A SOUL AT	365	1
THE SOUL ACHIEVES--HERSELF--	EXHILIRATION--IS WITHIN	383	5
MY SOUL--AT LIBERTY--	NO RACK CAN TORTURE ME--	384	2
WITHDRAWS--AND LEAVES THE DAZZLED SOUL	DID OUR BEST MOMENT LAST	393	11
'TIS PAIN'S SUCCESSOR--WHEN THE SOUL	THERE IS A LANGUOR OF	396	3
I TOLD MY SOUL TO SING--	THE FIRST DAY'S NIGHT	410	4
THAT "GOD HAVE MERCY" ON THE SOUL	I READ MY SENTENCE--	412	7
I MADE MY SOUL FAMILIAR--WITH HER EXTREMITY--	I READ MY SENTENCE--	412	9
NOR INTRODUCE--MY SOUL--	I AM ASHAMED--I HIDE--	473	6
FOR ME--MY SOUL--TO WEAR--	I AM ASHAMED--I HIDE--	473	12
A SOLEMN THING WITHIN THE SOUL	A SOLEMN THING WITHIN	483	1
A MODESTY BEFITS THE SOUL	THE WORLD--STANDS--	493	3
TO CLASP HER SOUL--FOR ALL--	THE WORLD--STANDS--	493	8
THAT NIBBLES AT THE SOUL--	THIS WORLD IS NOT	501	20
THE SOUL HAS BANDAGED MOMENTS--	THE SOUL HAS BANDAGED	512	1
THE SOUL HAS MOMENTS OF ESCAPE--	THE SOUL HAS BANDAGED	512	11
AND LEAVE THE SOUL--ALONE--	DEPARTED--TO THE	524	8
AS IF MY SOUL WERE DEAF AND DUMB--	IF I MAY HAVE IT, WHEN	577	19
THE SOUL THAT ASKED IT'S SHELTER	THE BODY GROWS WITHOUT--	578	7
LIKE SANCTIFYING IN THE SOUL--	I THINK I WAS ENCHANTED	593	23
THE BATTLE FOUGHT BETWEEN THE SOUL	THE BATTLE FOUGHT	594	1
THE SOUL HAS SPECIAL TIMES--	OF NEARNESS TO HER	607	2
MY SOUL GREW [FELT / BENT / STOOD] STRAIGHT.	I ROSE--BECAUSE HE SANK	616	4
AT LEISURE IS THE SOUL	AT LEISURE IS THE SOUL	618	1
THAT HAPPEN ON THE SOUL	THE TINT I CANNOT TAKE--	627	10
OUR SOUL AND THEIR'S--BETWEEN--	BEREAVEMENT IN THEIR	645	4
A STEADFAST SOUTH--UPON THE SOUL--	I THINK TO LIVE--MAY BE	646	19
THE SOUL THAT HATH A GUEST	THE SOUL THAT HATH A	674	1
THE SOUL UNTO ITSELF	THE SOUL UNTO ITSELF	683	1
THE SOUL SHOULD STAND [BE] IN AWE--	THE SOUL UNTO ITSELF	683	8
BUT SOMEWHERE--IN MY SOUL--I KNOW--	A THOUGHT WENT UP MY	701	9
IT'S PAST--SET DOWN BEFORE THE SOUL	REMORSE--IS MEMORY--	744	5
CONFORM MY SOUL--AS TWERE A CHURCH,	MY WORTHINESS IS ALL MY	751	15
MY SOUL--ACCUSED ME--AND I QUAILED--	MY SOUL--ACCUSED ME--AND	753	1
MY SOUL--THAT MORNING--WAS MY FRIEND--	MY SOUL--ACCUSED ME--AND	753	4
FOR THIS NEW VALUE [FORTUNE / PORTION] IN THE SOUL--	ONE BLESSING HAD I THAN	756	11
ICICLES UPON MY SOUL	WHEN I HOPED, I	768	13
AS 'TWERE A SPUR--UPON THE SOUL--	I LIVED ON DREAD--	770	6
THE MAKER OF THE SOUL	THE LONELINESS ONE DARE	777	14
THE DEPTH UPON MY SOUL WAS NOTCHED--	JOY TO HAVE MERITED THE	788	19
THE SOUL CONDEMNED TO BE--	THIS CONSCIOUSNESS THAT	822	14
TO OWN THE ART WITHIN THE SOUL	TO OWN THE ART WITHIN	855	1
THE SOUL TO ENTERTAIN	TO OWN THE ART WITHIN	855	2
IT HELD A HUMAN SOUL.	IT WAS A GRAVE, YET BORE	876	4
THE SOUL CANNOT BE RID--	OF CONSCIOUSNESS, HER	894	2

	FIRST LINE	POEM	LINE
SOUL (CONTINUED)			
IT BEARS THE SOUL AS BOLD	FAITH--IS THE PIERLESS	915	5
SO OF THE FLOWER OF THE SOUL	THIS IS A BLOSSOM OF THE	945	7
UPON HIS BREAST, A CLOSING SOUL	THIS IS A BLOSSOM OF THE	945	15
"A SOUL HAS GONE TO HEAVEN"	OF TOLLING BELL I ASK	947	2
A SOUL HAD GONE TO HEAVEN	OF TOLLING BELL I ASK	947	6
OR WARRANT TO REPORT [PRESENT] THE SOUL	'TWAS CRISIS--ALL THE	948	7
AND SIMULTANEOUSLY, A SOUL	'TWAS CRISIS--ALL THE	948	15
A CUSTOM [HABIT] OF THE SOUL	AS ONE DOES SICKNESS	957	9
AND WHEN A SOUL PERCEIVES ITSELF	PURPLE--IS FASHIONABLE	980	3
'TIS FIRST A COBWEB ON THE SOUL	CRUMBLING IS NOT AN	997	5
SLAY--AND MY SOUL SHALL RISE	BIND ME--I STILL CAN	1005	4
I'VE DROPPED MY BRAIN--MY SOUL IS NUMB--	I'VE DROPPED MY BRAIN--	1046	1
THE SOUL SHOULD ALWAYS STAND AJAR	THE SOUL SHOULD ALWAYS	1055	1
THE SOUL WITH STRICT ECONOMY	SUPERIORITY TO FATE	1081	7
I AM AFRAID TO OWN A SOUL--	I AM AFRAID TO OWN A	1090	2
AND IS THE SOUL AT HOME	THE SPRY ARMS OF THE	1103	10
I TOLD MY SOUL TO COME--	THIS SLOW DAY MOVED	1120	5
AFFIRMING [PRONOUNCING] IT A SOUL.	THE PROPS ASSIST THE	1142	12
SOUL, TAKE THY RISK [RISKS / CHANCE],	SOUL, TAKE THY RISK,	1151	1
THE SOUL RETURNING SOFT AT NIGHT [STILL BY DAWN / LOTH BY DAWN]	CONTAINED IN THIS SHORT	1165	3
THE SOUL CAME HOME FROM TRIPS [FROM TOWNS / FROM SCENES / TO SLEEP]	CONTAINED IN THIS SHORT	1165	V
THE CELLARS OF THE SOUL--	IT'S HOUR WITH ITSELF	1225	6
GARRISONED NO SOUL CAN BE	SAFE DESPAIR IT IS THAT	1243	5
I CANNOT SEE MY SOUL BUT KNOW 'TIS THERE	I CANNOT SEE MY SOUL BUT	1262	1
THAT BEARS THE HUMAN SOUL.	THERE IS NO FRIGATE LIKE	1263	8
GO SLOW, MY SOUL, TO FEED THYSELF	GO SLOW, MY SOUL, TO	1297	1
THE VISAGE OF THE SOUL	THIS DIRTY--LITTLE--	1311	7
IN EVERY HUMAN SOUL--	PINK--SMALL--AND	1332	8
FROM ANY HUMAN [LIVING] SOUL--	YOU CANNOT TAKE ITSELF	1351	2
IN WHICH WE WRAP THE SOUL	SHAME IS THE SHAWL OF	1412	2
WHAT SOUL SURVIVE?	UNWORTHY OF HER BREAST	1414	3
ENLARGES [SUBMERGES] EVERY SOUL--	THE INUNDATION OF THE	1425	2
IN WHICH THE SOUL AT FIRST ESTRANGED [ALARMED / SUBMERGED]--	THE INUNDATION OF THE	1425	5
SHOULD DISENTHRALL THY SOUL--	WHO NEVER WANTED--	1430	8
THE SOUL CAN FARTHER FLY	WITH PINIONS OF DISDAIN	1431	2
THE BODY IS A SOUL--	WITH PINIONS OF DISDAIN	1431	8
MY SOUL, TO FIND THEM, COME,	THAN HEAVEN MORE REMOTE,	1436	11
A SINGLE HUMAN SOUL	WHOEVER DISENCHANTS	1451	2
WHAT DOOR--WHAT HOUR--RUN--RUN--MY SOUL!	"AND WITH WHAT BODY DO	1492	3
IS ALL THE SOUL CAN DO.	ON THAT SPECIFIC PILLOW	1533	8
I PRAY THE LORD THY SOUL TO MAKE--	NOW I LAY THEE DOWN TO	1539	4
BEFORE MY MIND [SOUL / BEAM] WAS BORN	THIS ME--THAT WALKS AND	1588	6
WHOSE TITLE IS [DISCREETLY CALLED] "THE SOUL."	TO TRY TO SPEAK, AND	1617	8
SELDOM WITH THE SOUL	SOMETIMES WITH THE HEART	1680	2
CENTURIES FROM HIS SOUL	THE EVENT WAS DIRECTLY	1686	8
THE SOUL HER "NOT AT HOME"	THE OVERTAKELESSNESS OF	1691	5
A SOUL ADMITTED TO ITSELF--	THERE IS A SOLITUDE OF	1695	7
THE SOUL THERE--ALL THE TIME.	IF EVER THE LID GETS OFF	1727	8
VANQUISHED, MY SOUL WILL KNOW	I'VE GOT AN ARROW HERE.	1729	5
TO OTHER [ANY] SCENE OR OTHER SOUL	'TWAS HERE MY SUMMER	1756	3
WHAT FORTITUDE THE SOUL CONTAINS,	ELYSIUM IS AS FAR AS TO	1760	5
SOUL'S			
MY SOUL'S ENTIRE INCOME--	ONE LIFE OF SO MUCH	270	3
THE SOUL'S SUPERIOR INSTANTS	THE SOUL'S SUPERIOR	306	1
THE SOUL'S RETAKEN MOMENTS--	THE SOUL HAS BANDAGED	512	19
FOR THE SOUL'S COMPRISING--	ONE AND ONE--ARE ONE--	769	8
THE SOUL'S DISTINCT CONNECTION	THE SOUL'S DISTINCT	974	1
AND IF THE SOUL'S WITHIN	THE SPRY ARMS OF THE	1103	V 10
SOULS			
BY SOULS OF SANITY	SLEEP IS SUPPOSED TO BE	13	2
SCARES MUSLIN SOULS--AWAY--	A SHADY FRIEND--FOR	278	6
WE--WHO HAVE THE SOULS--	NATURE--SOMETIMES SEARS	314	7
AS IF NO SOUL THE [WHILE OUR TWO SOULS THAT] SOLSTICE PASSED	THERE CAME A DAY AT	322	7
OUR SOULS SAW--JUST AS WELL--	THEY PUT US FAR APART--	474	12
TOLL--FOR THE BONNIE SOULS--	GLEE--THE GREAT STORM IS	619	6
IN DYING--'TIS AS IF OUR SOULS [WORLD / SELVES / SUN]	BEREAVEMENT IN THEIR	645	11
OF ALL THE SOULS THAT STAND CREATE--	OF ALL THE SOULS THAT	664	1
TO THE [UNTO] SOULS THAT SNOW--	ABSENT PLACE--AN APRIL	927	4
TOO JOSTLED WERE OUR SOULS TO SPEAK	THE LAST NIGHT THAT SHE	1100	19
SOUND			
TOO SOUND ASLEEP DID LIE	ON SUCH A NIGHT, OR SUCH	146	12
AS SHOULD SOUND--TO ME--	TEACH HIM--WHEN HE MAKES	227	4
AS SHOULD SOUND--	TEACH HIM--WHEN HE MAKES	227	7
THE SOUND ONES, LIKE THE HILLS--SHALL STAND [STAND UP]--	WHEN WE STAND ON THE	242	7
WITHOUT THE SOUND OF BOARDS	I'VE KNOWN A HEAVEN,	243	4
AS IF SOME CARAVAN OF SOUND	OF ALL THE SOUNDS	321	29
WITHOUT EXTERNAL SOUND	THERE CAME A DAY AT	322	22
TILL I WAS OUT OF SIGHT, IN SOUND,	I CANNOT DANCE UPON MY	326	15
FOR DOUBT, THAT I SHOULD KNOW THE SOUND--	I FELT MY LIFE WITH BOTH	351	8
OUT OF SOUND--OUT OF SIGHT--	IT IS DEAD--FIND IT--	417	2
IT DONT SOUND SO TERRIBLE--QUITE--AS IT DID--	IT DONT SOUND SO	426	1
THOSE WATERS SOUND SO GRAND--	I KNOW WHERE WELLS GROW	460	18
BUT POSITIVE, AS SOUND--	THIS WORLD IS NOT	501	4

	FIRST LINE	POEM	LINE
SOUND (CONTINUED)			
FROM ALL THE NOISE [SOUND] OF FIELDS--	I'M SORRY FOR THE DEAD--	529	10
HOW PRAYER WOULD FEEL [SOUND]--TO ME--	I PRAYED, AT FIRST, A	576	4
AS SYLLABLE FROM SOUND--	THE BRAIN--IS WIDER THAN	632	12
SO MISERABLE A SOUND--AT FIRST--	A PRISON GETS TO BE A	652	11
YET WHY SO LITTLE SOUND--MYSELF	THE SUN KEPT SETTING--	692	11
FOR OTHER SERVICES [PURPOSES]--AS SOUND--	THE SPIRIT IS THE	733	5
THE LONELINESS ONE DARE NOT SOUND--	THE LONELINESS ONE DARE	777	1
WITHOUT THE FORMULA OF SOUND	A LIGHT EXISTS IN SPRING	812	15
BEARING THE NEIGHBOR OUT OF SOUND	PEACE IS A FICTION OF	912	3
BUT SEQUENCE RAVELLED OUT OF SOUND [REACH]	I FELT A CLEAVING IN MY	937	7
AS SLEIGH BELLS SEEM [SOUND] IN SUMMER	AS SLEIGH BELLS SEEM IN	981	1
BUT SEQUENCE RAVELLED OUT OF SOUND	THE DUST BEHIND I STROVE	992	3
BUT SIMULTANEOUS AS SOUND	FURTHER IN SUMMER THAN	1068	V
IT WOULD NOT SOUND SO DEEP	I THINK THAT THE ROOT OF	1302	2
TO SOUND OR CIRCUMVENT--	THE RAT IS THE CONCISEST	1356	6
ONE JOY [SOUND] OF SO MUCH ANGUISH	ONE JOY OF SO MUCH	1420	1
A SYMPTOM THAT IS NOT A SOUND	THERE COMES A WARNING	1536	V 3
A CRASH WITHOUT A SOUND,	THE FARTHEST THUNDER	1581	18
TO SOUND [TEST] THE ENEMY--	WHERE ROSES WOULD NOT	1582	4
MAKES NOT AS MUCH OF SOUND	THE SUN IN REINING TO	1636	2
AND GLEE'S ADVANCING SOUND	IN SNOW THOU COMEST	1669	4
OR SIGNIFIED OF SOUND	THE MOB WITHIN THE HEART	1745	6
SOUNDED			
LIKE RAIN IT SOUNDED TILL IT CURVED [SWELLED]	LIKE RAIN IT SOUNDED	1235	1
IT SOUNDED AS IF THE STREETS [AIR] WERE RUNNING	IT SOUNDED AS IF THE	1397	1
SOUNDEST			
HAD GONE TO SLEEP--THAT SOUNDEST TIME--	TO DIE--TAKES JUST A	255	11
SOUNDING			
EACH--SOUNDING--SHILY--	AGAIN--HIS VOICE IS AT	663	15
SOUNDLESS			
SOUNDLESS AS DOTS--ON A DISC OF SNOW--	SAFE IN THEIR ALABASTER	216	V
HIS MIEN [GAIT], WAS SOUNDLESS, LIKE THE [A] BIRD--	THE ONLY GHOST I EVER	274	5
THAT SOUNDLESS TUGS--WITHIN--	DARE YOU SEE A SOUL AT	365	12
IT'S SOUNDLESS TRAVELS JUST ARREST	HOW SOFT A CATERPILLAR	1448	5
SOUNDS			
HOW DIM IT SOUNDS!	GOING TO HEAVEN!	79	7
SOFT FALL THE SOUNDS OF EDEN	ALL OVERGROWN BY CUNNING	148	V
OF ALL THE SOUNDS DESPATCHED ABROAD,	OF ALL THE SOUNDS	321	1
SOUNDS LONG--UNTIL I READ THE PLACE	NOT IN THIS WORLD TO SEE	418	2
I CLUTCHED AT SOUNDS--	IT WOULD NEVER BE COMMON	430	25
THE SOUNDS OF WELCOME--THERE!	ME--COME! MY DAZZLED	431	4
A MINOR THING--IT SOUNDS--	ONE ANGUISH--IN A CROWD	565	2
"SUNSET" SOUNDS MAJESTIC--	THERE'S THE BATTLE OF	1174	5
SOURCE			
HOW MUCH OF SOURCE ESCAPES WITH THEE--	HOW MUCH OF SOURCE	1517	1
SOURCES			
WHOSE SOURCES ARE INTERIOR--	REVERSE CANNOT BEFALL	395	3
CRITERION SOURCES [NATURES] HERE	TO UNDERTAKE IS TO	1070	8
SOUTH			
SOUTH WINDS JOSTLE THEM--	SOUTH WINDS JOSTLE THEM	86	1
BUT WHEN THE SOUTH WIND STIRS THE POOLS	I KNOW A PLACE WHERE	337	5
THOU SETTEST [STIRREST] EARTHQUAKE IN THE SOUTH--	AT LEAST--TO PRAY--IS	502	5
AS SOON THE SOUTH--HER BREEZE	WHAT CARE THE DEAD, FOR	592	20
A STEADFAST SOUTH--UPON THE SOUL--	I THINK TO LIVE--MAY BE	646	19
LONGEST [LATEST] ON YOUR SOUTH, TO LINGER,	PROMISE THIS--WHEN YOU	648	19
FAR AS SOUTH AND WEST--EXPANDING [DISCLOSING]--	BLOOM UPON THE MOUNTAIN	667	15
A SOUTH WIND--HAS A PATHOS	A SOUTH WIND--HAS A	719	1
AND MIDNIGHT TO THE SOUTH OF HER--	BEHIND ME--DIPS ETERNITY	721	17
THE BIRDS REPORTED FROM THE SOUTH--	THE BIRDS REPORTED FROM	743	1
THE NORTH AND SOUTH WHEN HE	THE SUN AND MOON MUST	871	6
IT RISES--PASSES--ON OUR SOUTH	IT RISES--PASSES--ON OUR	1023	1
AND PILED THEM IN [SHOWED THEM TO] THE SOUTH--	THE WIND TOOK UP THE	1134	2
AT PARTING--SHE WAS GOING SOUTH	I SEND YOU A DECREPIT	1324	3
THE SOUTH UNROLLED A PURPLE FAN	THE SUN RETIRED TO A	1693	7
AND SOUTH AMERICA	VOLCANOES BE IN SICILY	1705	2
SOUTHERN			
THE SOUTHERN CUSTOM--OF THE BIRD--	'TIS NOT THAT DYING	335	5
SOUVENIR			
FOR A SOUVENIR	THE POPULAR HEART IS A	1226	8
NOTWITHSTANDING [TO BE SURE] A ROPE FOR A SOUVENIR	FLOSS WONT SAVE YOU FROM	1322	3
HER MOTIVE FOR [OBJECT IN] THE SOUVENIR	I SEND YOU A DECREPIT	1324	5
SOVREIGN			
WHO WILL NOT SERVE THE SOVREIGN, BE HANGED ON FATAL TREE.	AWAKE YE MUSES NINE,	1	10
SOVREIGN! KNOW A DAISY	"THEY HAVE NOT CHOSEN ME	85	7
THIS IS THE SOVREIGN ANGUISH!	TO LEARN THE TRANSPORT	167	9
MY SOVREIGN IS OFFENDED--	THE COURT IS FAR AWAY--	235	3
AN UNCONCERN SO SOVREIGN	OF BRONZE--AND BLAZE--	290	6
AND THEN, IN SOVREIGN BARNS TO DWELL--	THE GRASS SO LITTLE HAS	333	17
IN SOVREIGN--SWERVELESS TUNE--	THERE IS A FLOWER THAT	380	28
ROWER, AND YACHT--SOME SOVREIGN SUMMER--	LOVE--THOU ART HIGH--	453	11
ITSELF--IT'S SOVREIGN--OF ITSELF	THE SOUL UNTO ITSELF	683	7
MY SOVREIGN WILL RELENT?	I'LL SEND THE FEATHER	687	3
AND NOW WE ROAM IN [THE] SOVREIGN WOODS--	MY LIFE HAD STOOD--A	754	5

	FIRST LINE	POEM	LINE
SOVREIGN (CONTINUED)			
AM SOVREIGN OF THEM ALL--	GOD GAVE A LOAF TO EVERY	791	16
CHANCE SOVREIGN ON A MINE--	I PLAY AT RICHES--TO	801	18
HE--SOVREIGN AS THE SUN	SAID DEATH TO PASSION	1033	7
UNTIL THE TENDER CARPENTER [SOVREIGN CARPENTER / UNSUSPECTING . . .	A GREAT HOPE FELL	1123	16
HER SOVREIGN PEOPLE	HER SOVREIGN PEOPLE	1139	1
SOVREIGN'S			
ONE HOUR--OF HER SOVREIGN'S FACE"!	WHAT WOULD I GIVE TO SEE	247	26
SOVREIGNS			
THESE SOVREIGNS EVER TOOK!	I MET A KING THIS	166	24
SOVREIGNTIES			
BROADEST OF SOVREIGNTIES--	THE CHILD'S FAITH IS NEW	637	11
SOW			
I SOW MY PAGEANTRY	ALL THESE MY BANNERS BE.	22	2
AND SOW THE EARLY SEED--	SEXTON! MY MASTER'S	96	4
I SOW SWEET FLOWER FROM GARDEN BED--	WHERE I HAVE LOST, I	104	2
DO SOW, AND RAISE FOR SALE--	WHEN DIAMONDS ARE A	397	4
I'LL BEGIN TO SOW	DONT PUT UP MY THREAD &	617	2
A ROSE UPON IT'S RIDGE TO SOW	IT WAS A GRAVE, YET BORE	876	11
NOR SEED THAT WE CAN SOW,	THE JOY THAT HAS NO STEM	1744	2
SOWED			
THAT SOWED THE FLOWER, HE PREFERRED--	ALTHOUGH I PUT AWAY HIS	366	5
FILAMENTS OF BLOOM, PONTIUS PILATE SOWED--	TO PUT THIS WORLD DOWN,	527	10
AND QUICKENING [RIPENING]--AS WE SOWED--	HE GAVE AWAY HIS LIFE--	567	13
SOWER			
RIP--WHILE THE SOWER--DREAMS--	I TEND MY FLOWERS FOR	339	4
SOWING			
TILL THEN--DREAMING [DEEMING] I AM SOWING	DONT PUT UP MY THREAD &	617	17
SEED, HAD I, MY PURPLE SOWING	BLOOM UPON THE MOUNTAIN	667	5
SOWN			
WILT HAVE NO KIND COMPANION, THOU REAP'ST WHAT THOU HAST SOWN.	AWAKE YE MUSES NINE,	1	28
THAT ARE SOWN BENEATH,	WHEN I COUNT THE SEEDS	40	2
"SOWN IN DISHONOR"!	"SOWN IN DISHONOR"!	62	1
"SOWN IN CORRUPTION"!	"SOWN IN DISHONOR"!	62	6
WHICH HAVING SOWN WITH CARE,	I HAD SOME THINGS THAT I	116	6
FOR MINE--IN FROSTS--WAS SOWN--	OURSELVES WERE WED ONE	631	14
SOWN SIDEWISE IN THE CRAG	AS ONE DOES SICKNESS	957	8
BEFORE MY MIND WAS SOWN,	THE SPIRIT LASTS--BUT IN	1576	22
BEFORE MY BEAM WAS SOWN,	EXPANSE CANNOT BE LOST--	1584	6
SPACE			
AND SEIZE THE ONE THOU LOVEST, NOR CARE FOR SPACE, OR TIME!	AWAKE YE MUSES NINE,	1	36
THEN SPACE--BEGAN TO TOLL,	I FELT A FUNERAL, IN MY	280	12
AND SPACE STARES ALL AROUND--	IT WAS NOT DEATH, FOR I	510	18
'TWAS AS SPACE SAT SINGING	MOST SHE TOUCHED ME BY	760	15
A MUSIC NUMEROUS AS SPACE [MEASURELESS AS NOON]--	THE BIRDS BEGUN AT FOUR	783	3
AND THERE WERE [WAS] TROUGHS [SPACE / ROOM] BESIDE	A GREAT HOPE FELL	1123	13
BUT WHEN ALL SPACE HAS BEEN BEHELD	THE LIFE WE HAVE IS VERY	1162	5
THERE IS A SOLITUDE OF SPACE	THERE IS A SOLITUDE OF	1695	1
SPACE'S			
KNEW A PARTICLE--OF SPACE'S	CONSCIOUS AM I IN MY	679	15
SPACES			
THAT WE CAN TOUCH THE SPACES--	WHEN NIGHT IS ALMOST	347	3
SPACIOUS			
HIS SPACIOUS FUTURE--	NO BOBOLINK--REVERSE HIS	755	6
BEHOLD OUR [MY / THIS] SPACIOUS CITIZEN	NATURE AFFECTS TO BE	1170	7
SHE TAKES [GOES] HER GRACIOUS [SPACIOUS / SUBTLE / SIMPLE / . . .	SUMMER--WE ALL HAVE SEEN	1386	6
AND SPACIOUS AS BEFORE--	TO MEND EACH TATTERED	1442	8
. . . BONNIE / SPACIOUS / TROPIC / ARDENT / FRIENDLY / MAGIC / . . .	THE BIBLE IS AN ANTIQUE	1545	13
NOR PUT HIS SPACIOUS ARM AROUND THEE	BACK FROM THE CORDIAL	1625	3
SPACIOUSLY			
A "THIS WAY" BECKONS SPACIOUSLY--	NO LIFE CAN POMPLESS	1626	7
SPADE			
THAT EVER KISSED THE SPADE!	I NEVER TOLD THE BURIED	11	13
THOU LITTLE SPADE OF MINE	ALL THESE MY BANNERS BE.	22	13
THE GRAVE--WAS FINISHED--BUT THE SPADE	BEREAVED OF ALL, I WENT	784	15
SPADES			
OUTSIDE [WITHOUT]--THE SPADES--WERE PLYING--	IN FALLING TIMBERS	614	3
BUT WHEN SPADES HAD DONE--	IN FALLING TIMBERS	614	10
SPAN			
FOR A SPAN SO WORN--	NOT ANY MORE TO BE	1344	4
AND DURING IT'S ELECTRIC GALE [SPELL / STAY / MIGHT / ACT / SPAN]--	WITH PINIONS OF DISDAIN	1431	7
ON [OF] HER DEPARTING SPAN	THIS DOCILE ONE INTER	1752	5
SPANGLED			
HIS HAUGHTY--SPANGLED HEMS--	THE SUN--JUST TOUCHED	232	10
THE SPANGLED GOWNS, A LESSER RANK	OF TRIBULATION--THESE	325	3
ON SPANGLED JOURNEYS TO THE PEAK	THE PEDIGREE OF HONEY	1627	5
SPANGLES			
THE BUSHES [ORCHARDS / MEADOWS]--SPANGLES FLUNG--	A DROP FELL ON THE APPLE	794	12
SPANIEL			
HIS LITTLE SPANIEL--TELL HIM!	IF HE DISSOLVE--THEN--	236	14

	FIRST LINE	POEM	LINE
SPANS			
THE PREY OF [IN SPANS IN] UNKNOWN ZONES--	COULD MORTAL LIP DIVINE	1409	V
SPAR			
TWO SWIMMERS WRESTLED ON THE SPAR--	TWO SWIMMERS WRESTLED ON	201	1
WITHOUT A CHANCE, OR SPAR--	IT WAS NOT DEATH, FOR I	510	22
THE SEA AND SPAR BETWEEN.	EACH SECOND IS THE LAST	879	4
A SINGLE CLOVER PLANK [SPAR]	A SINGLE CLOVER PLANK	1343	1
SPARE			
I CAN SPARE THIS SUMMER, UNRELUCTANTLY.	WHEN I COUNT THE SEEDS	40	11
SPARE THE TENANT--LONG ENO'--	IT'S THOUGHTS--AND JUST	495	8
TO SPARE THESE STRIDING SPIRITS [SHRINKING SPIRITS / . . .	WE SEE--COMPARATIVELY--	534	13
YOU COULD NOT SPARE--YOU KNOW.	YOU'LL FIND--IT WHEN YOU	610	4
GRIEF IS A GOURMAND--SPARE HIS LUXURY--	GRIEF IS A MOUSE--	793	12
SO TO SPARE	WE'LL PASS WITHOUT THE	996	2
THE DAYS THAT WE CAN SPARE	THE DAYS THAT WE CAN	1184	1
SOONEST TO SHARE [SPARE]	MY HEART RAN SO TO THEE	1237	12
WITH HUNDRED WEIGHTS--TO SPARE--	RISK IS THE HAIR THAT	1239	4
HAS NOT A VOICE TO SPARE--	CONFIRMING ALL WHO	1268	4
SPARE YOUR "CROWN OF LIFE"--	"FAITHFUL TO THE END"	1357	V
AND HAVE AN HOUR TO SPARE.	WERE NATURE MORTAL LADY	1762	8
SPARED			
BUT WONT YOU WISH YOU'D SPARED ONE	NO MATTER--NOW--SWEET--	704	7
AND HONEYS, IF HIS LIFE BE SPARED,	HIS ORIENTAL HERESIES	1526	V
HOW ARCHLY SPARED THE HEAVEN "TO COME"--	THE MOON UPON HER FLUENT	1528	V
SPARK			
IT MIGHT--HAVE BEEN THE LIGHT HOUSE SPARK--	GOOD NIGHT! WHICH PUT	259	7
THAT MAY FURNISH THE FUSE [IGNITION] UNTO A SPARK	A MAN MAY MAKE A REMARK	952	3
AND THAT ETHERIAL SPARK.	WE MET AS SPARKS--	958	8
BUT FOR THAT SINGLE SPARK.	WE MET AS SPARKS--	958	V 8
A WINGED SPARK DOTH SOAR ABOUT--	A WINGED SPARK DOTH SOAR	1468	1
SPARKLED			
THE ORCHARD SPARKLED LIKE A JEW--	THE DAY CAME SLOW--TILL	304	13
THAT SPARKLED TO [SPARKLES IN] THE GRAVE	THIS DOCILE ONE INTER	1752	4
SPARKLES			
THAT SPARKLED TO [SPARKLES IN] THE GRAVE	THIS DOCILE ONE INTER	1752	4
SPARKLING			
STILL SPARKLING THROUGH	SHE LAY AS IF AT PLAY	369	11
SPARKS			
BUT MILES OF SPARKS--AT EVENING--	THE RED--BLAZE--IS THE	469	5
WE MET AS SPARKS--DIVERGING FLINTS	WE MET AS SPARKS--	958	1
SPARROW			
I--A SPARROW--BUILD THERE	HER BREAST IS FIT FOR	84	6
THE "SPARROW" OF YOUR CARE--	I THINK JUST HOW MY	237	8
A SPARROW TOOK A SLICE OF TWIG	A SPARROW TOOK A SLICE	1211	1
SPARROW'S			
TOO HAPPY--FOR [IN] MY SPARROW'S CHANCE--	GOD GAVE A LOAF TO EVERY	791	7
SPARROWS			
SPARROWS, UNNOTICED BY THE FATHER--	SOME, TOO FRAGILE FOR	141	11
IF EITHER OF HER "SPARROWS FALL",	MAMA NEVER FORGETS HER	164	7
I ENVY NESTS OF SPARROWS--	I ENVY SEAS, WHEREON HE	498	9
GOD KEEP HIS OATH [VOW] TO SPARROWS--	VICTORY COMES LATE--	690	13
SPARTAN			
THIS SPARTAN PUT AWAY	IT FEELS A SHAME TO BE	444	6
SPEAK			
YET SHE CANNOT SPEAK.	GLOWING IS HER BONNET,	72	4
I HAVE A KING, WHO DOES NOT SPEAK--	I HAVE A KING, WHO DOES	103	1
HAD IT REMAINED TO SPEAK--	I BRING AN UNACCUSTOMED	132	16
AND TELL HIM--CHARGE THEE SPEAK IT PLAIN--	A TONGUE--TO TELL HIM I	400	7
'TWAS NEEDLESS--ANY SPEAK--	IT WOULD NEVER BE COMMON	430	12
BECAUSE HE KNOWS IT CANNOT SPEAK--	"WHY DO I LOVE" YOU, SIR	480	13
THAT THIS WAY--THOU COULD'ST NOTICE [SPEAK TO] ME--	IF I MAY HAVE IT, WHEN	577	21
AND EVERY TIME I SPEAK FOR HIM--	MY LIFE HAD STOOD--A	754	7
TOO JOSTLED WERE OUR SOULS TO SPEAK	THE LAST NIGHT THAT SHE	1100	19
THEY SPEAK OF WHAT WE OWE--	IS HEAVEN A PHYSICIAN?	1270	6
IS ALL THAT LOVE CAN SPEAK--	LOVE'S STRICKEN "WHY"	1368	2
TO TRY TO SPEAK, AND MISS THE WAY	TO TRY TO SPEAK, AND	1617	1
SPEAKS			
THAT WHICH SINGS SO--SPEAKS SO--	BEFORE THE ICE IS IN THE	37	13
IT ALMOST SPEAKS TO YOU.	A LIGHT EXISTS IN SPRING	812	12
BELOW, THE BODY SPEAKS,	THE SPIRIT LASTS--BUT IN	1576	2
SPEAR			
AS QUICKLY AS A SPEAR,	THE SADDEST NOISE, THE	1764	18
SPECIAL			
THE SOUL HAS SPECIAL TIMES--	OF NEARNESS TO HER	607	2
AS EACH WERE SPECIAL [LAWFUL / ONLY] HEIR--	ALONE AND IN A	1167	16
SPECIES			
TALKED SOFTLY OF NEW SPECIES	WENT UP A YEAR THIS	93	15
AS SPECIES--BE--FOR NAME--	A WEIGHT WITH NEEDLES ON	264	8
I DO BELIEVE A SPECIES	DO PEOPLE MOULDER	432	3
FROM THE FAMILIAR SPECIES	THIS WAS A POET--IT IS	448	5
A SPECIES [SEQUEL] STANDS BEYOND--	THIS WORLD IS NOT	501	2
AND LAUGH, A HOMELY SPECIES	I'M SORRY FOR THE DEAD--	529	7
THIS WORLD, AND IT'S SPECIES [NATIONS / FASHIONS / SYMBOLS / . . .	THIS DUST, AND IT'S	936	9
TO FIND THE SPECIES DISAPPEARED--	IT BLOOMED AND DROPT, A	978	7
SPECIFIC			
AS 'TWERE SPECIFIC [A SIGNAL] GROUND--	WHOLE GULFS--OF RED, AND	658	4

	FIRST LINE	POEM	LINE
SPECIFIC (CONTINUED)			
BUT DEATH HAD TOLD HER SO THE [SPECIFIC TOLD HER / ENAMORED . . .	I MEANT TO FIND HER WHEN	718	7
HAD FOR THAT SPECIFIC TREASURE	NONE WHO SAW IT EVER	1110	3
IS A SPECIFIC GRACE--	TO MAKE ROUTINE A	1196	4
OF THAT SPECIFIC SPOT	THE FACT THAT EARTH IS	1408	4
ON THAT SPECIFIC PILLOW	ON THAT SPECIFIC PILLOW	1533	1
TO OUR SPECIFIC STRENGTH--	A WORD MADE FLESH IS	1651	8
SPECIFICAL			
LEST MEN SPECIFICAL ADORN	I CANNOT SEE MY SOUL BUT	1262	8
SPECIFIED			
THAN ANY FEATHER SPECIFIED [RATIFIED / CERTIFIED]	WITH PINIONS OF DISDAIN	1431	3
TO WHOM--IS SPECIFIED--	"GO TELL IT"--WHAT A	1554	2
SPECIFY			
THAT SHE SHOULD [COULD] SPECIFY.	NO NOTICE GAVE SHE, BUT	804	4
THAT I SHOULD SPECIFY.	ALONE AND IN A	1167	28
WOULD DOUBTLESS SPECIFY--[ANSWER ME]	WHO WERE "THE FATHER AND	1258	12
SPECIMENS			
WITH SPECIMENS OF SONG	BEFORE YOU THOUGHT OF	1465	9
SPECIOUS			
OF SILKEN SPEECH AND SPECIOUS SHOE	OF SILKEN SPEECH AND	896	1
SPECK			
A SPECK UPON A BALL--	I SAW NO WAY--THE	378	6
A SPECK OF RAPTURE--FIRST PERCEIVED	A WINGED SPARK DOTH SOAR	1468	7
SPECKS			
HEAVES BALLS OF SPECKS, LIKE VICIOUS BOY	TO INTERRUPT HIS YELLOW	591	5
SPECTACLE			
TO CONTEMPLATION--[TO SPECTACLE, BUT] NOT TO TOUCH--	THE LILAC IS AN ANCIENT	1241	7
NO SPECTACLE [MONSTER THEN] IN SIGHT	ESCAPE IS SUCH A	1347	4
SPECTACLES			
A PAIR OF SPECTACLES AJAR JUST STIR--	I KNOW SOME LONELY	289	19
SPECTRAL			
ARISE THIS SPECTRAL CANTICLE	FURTHER IN SUMMER THAN	1068	11
SPECTRE			
O'ERLOOKING [MAINTAINING] A SUPERIOR SPECTRE--	ONE NEED NOT BE A	670	19
A SPECTRE--INFINITE--ACCOMPANYING--	ONE NEED NOT BE A	670	V 19
THE SPECTRE OF SOLIDITIES	WE DO NOT KNOW THE TIME	1106	7
SPECTRE CANNOT HARM--	WHEN I HOPED I FEARED--	1181	5
AND [BUT] THEN THEY SCARE US LIKE A SPECTRE	FACTS BY OUR SIDE ARE	1497	3
EFFACE THE BURDEN [MONSTER / STATURE / SPECTRE / TROUBLE / . . .	THE PILE OF YEARS IS NOT	1507	7
SPECTRE'S			
A BLACK--AS OF A SPECTRE'S CLOAK	AN AWFUL TEMPEST MASHED	198	3
TO GO WITHOUT THE SPECTRE'S AID [HELP]	I LIVED ON DREAD--	770	8
SPECTRES			
AND SPECTRES OF THE REIN--	THE LIFE THAT TIED TOO	1535	4
AT THE SUGGESTION OF HOLY SPECTRES--	THE BIBLE IS AN ANTIQUE	1545	3
BY THE DIRECTION OF HALLOWED SPECTRES--	THE BIBLE IS AN ANTIQUE	1545	V 3
SPECULATE			
I SPECULATE NO MORE--	ONE BLESSING HAD I THAN	756	20
TILL WHAT WE SPECULATE, HAS BEEN	THE MURMURING OF BEES,	1115	13
SPECULATE, OR FORESTS ENTERTAIN.	THE DUTIES OF THE WIND	1137	8
WHILE WE SHREWDLY SPECULATE [SAGE INVESTIGATE / SHREWD INVESTIGATE]	YESTERDAY IS HISTORY,	1292	7
SPECULATED			
WE SPECULATED FAIR, ON EVERY SUBJECT, BUT THE GRAVE--	WE TALKED AS GIRLS DO--	586	3
SPECULATION			
AFFLICTION BUT A SPECULATION--AND WO	NOT SO THE INFINITE	1040	3
BY SPECULATION CEDED	THE THINGS WE THOUGHT	1293	7
BUT LEST OUR SPECULATION	"WAS NOT" WAS ALL THE	1342	5
SPECULATION'S			
TO SPECULATION'S SON--	THE THINGS WE THOUGHT	1293	8
SPECULATIONS			
OUR SPECULATIONS OF THE FOREIGNER!	BESIDES THIS MAY	977	5
AS SPECULATIONS FLEE	A SPARROW TOOK A SLICE	1211	V 6
SPED			
'TWAS NOT MY BLAME--WHO SPED TOO SLOW--	A DYING TIGER--MOANED	566	9
SHE SPED AS PETALS OF [FROM] A ROSE	SHE SPED AS PETALS OF A	991	1
SPED BY AN ARCHER'S BOW.	I'VE GOT AN ARROW HERE.	1729	7
SPEECH			
HER PRETTY SPEECH--LIKE DRUNKEN MEN--	THE ROSE DID CAPER ON	208	3
JUST OPPOSITE--ANOTHER SPEECH	THE ROSE DID CAPER ON	208	11
WHEN SPEECH WENT NUMB--	UNTO LIKE STORY--TROUBLE	295	20
SUBLIMER SORT [THING / WAY]--THAN SPEECH--	GIVE LITTLE ANGUISH--	310	8
THE TIME WAS SCARCE PROFANED, BY SPEECH--	THERE CAME A DAY AT	322	9
PUT FROM MY SIMPLE SPEECH ALL PLAIN WORD--	I'M SAYING EVERY DAY	373	20
HIS SPEECH WAS LIKE THE PUSH	THE WIND--TAPPED LIKE A	436	10
THEY FLING THEIR SPEECH	PRAYER IS THE LITTLE	437	4
AS COOL TO SPEECH--AS STONE--	AS FAR FROM PITY, AS	496	2
I FEAR A MAN OF FRUGAL [SCANTY] SPEECH--	I FEAR A MAN OF FRUGAL	543	1
NOR WE SO MUCH AS CHECK OUR SPEECH--	THE LIGHTNING PLAYETH--	630	11
BEFORE DECISION--STOOPED TO SPEECH--	I COULD SUFFICE FOR HIM,	643	11
"SPEECH"--IS A PRANK OF PARLIAMENT--	"SPEECH"--IS A PRANK OF	688	1
OF SILKEN SPEECH AND SPECIOUS SHOE	OF SILKEN SPEECH AND	896	1
OUT OF PLUMB OF SPEECH.	GRATITUDE--IS NOT THE	989	4
THE WORDS ARE WITHERED [SPEECH IS STOLEN] AWAY	WHATEVER IT IS--SHE HAS	1204	V 8
SPEECH IS ONE SYMPTOM OF AFFECTION	SPEECH IS ONE SYMPTOM OF	1681	1

	FIRST LINE	POEM	LINE
SPIDER (CONTINUED)			
A SPIDER AND A FLOWER--	THE FAIREST HOME I EVER	1423	4
SPIED			
SO BASHFUL WHEN I SPIED HER!	SO BASHFUL WHEN I SPIED	91	1
THE ANGELS MUST HAVE SPIED,	SHE DIED--THIS WAS THE	150	6
SPIED A FACE--	TWO SWIMMERS WRESTLED ON	201	6
TILL OPPOSITE--I SPIED A CHEEK	THE ROSE DID CAPER ON	208	9
AND THEN HE SPIED A BREEZE,	HIGH FROM THE EARTH I	1723	4
SPIES			
AND SEES [SPIES] THE PASTURES SMILE	THE LIFE THAT TIED TOO	1535	6
SPIGOT			
IT PULLED THE SPIGOT FROM THE HILLS	LIKE RAIN IT SOUNDED	1235	11
SPIKENARDS			
OR SPIKENARDS, PERISHING [AMULETS OF PINE]--	THE GRASS SO LITTLE HAS	333	16
SPILL			
LET ME NOT SPILL [LOSE / WASTE]--IT'S SMALLEST CADENCE--	BETTER--THAN MUSIC! FOR	503	21
WOULD DROP [SPILL] HIM--BONE BY BONE.	THERE IS A PAIN--SO	599	8
AND SPILL [TIP] THE SCARLET RAIN--	THE NAME--OF IT--IS	656	8
COULD NOT JAR OR SPILL.	BEES ARE BLACK, WITH	1405	8
SPILLED			
SINCE SOMEWHERE THY SWEET FACE HAS SPILLED	I'VE NONE TO TELL ME TO	881	5
SPILLS			
A SUDDEN MUSKET--SPILLS--	THE DAY CAME SLOW--TILL	304	4
SPILT			
I SPILT THE DEW--	ONE SISTER HAVE I IN OUR	14	23
SPIN			
WHOSE EMERALD NEST THE AGES SPIN	A FEATHER FROM THE	161	5
THOUGH SPOKES--SPIN--MORE CONSPICUOUS	THE OUTER--FROM THE	451	7
SPINNING			
SPINNING UPON THE SHOALS--	GLEE--THE GREAT STORM IS	619	8
SPINS			
THE GILDED CREATURE STRAINS--AND SPINS--	YOU'VE SEEN BALLOONS SET	700	13
SPIRE			
AND DOME [SPIRE / CHURCH]--AND WINDOW PANE--	THE DAY UNDRESSED--	716	16
THE TWILIGHT SPOKE THE SPIRE,	THE MOUNTAINS STOOD IN	1278	8
SPIRES			
BURN SO THE EVENING SPIRES	DISTRUSTFUL OF THE	20	13
CAJOLES A MOMENT WITH THE SPIRES	IT RISES--PASSES--ON OUR	1023	3
SPIRIT			
MY SPIRIT CANNOT SEE?	BRING ME THE SUNSET IN A	128	21
IT CANNOT BE MY SPIRIT--	DOUBT ME! MY DIM	275	9
INFECTS MY SIMPLE SPIRIT	OF BRONZE--AND BLAZE--	290	8
SUCH [SOME] SPIRIT MAKES [TELL] HER PERPETUAL MENTION,	UNTO LIKE STORY--TROUBLE	295	13
I HELD MY SPIRIT TO THE GLASS,	I FELT MY LIFE WITH BOTH	351	3
FASHION MY SPIRIT QUAINT--WHITE--	I AM ASHAMED--I HIDE--	473	20
GREAT SPIRIT--GIVE TO ME	I MEANT TO HAVE BUT	476	10
THAT IF THE SPIRIT--LIKE TO HIDE	THE BODY GROWS WITHOUT--	578	3
WHEN SENSE FROM SPIRIT--FILES AWAY--	OF ALL THE SOULS THAT	664	3
MONTCALM, HIS OPPOSING SPIRIT	WOLFE DEMANDED DURING	678	5
BUT REDUCE NO HUMAN SPIRIT	PUBLICATION--IS THE	709	15
THE SPIRIT IS THE CONSCIOUS EAR.	THE SPIRIT IS THE	733	1
FROM FURTHEST SPIRIT [FAITHFUL / GOOD MAN]--GOD--	ON A COLUMNAR SELF--	789	12
HOW HE STRETCHED HIS ANGUISH [SPIRIT] TO US	HOW THE WATERS CLOSED	923	3
THE SPIRIT FRUCTIFIED--	THIS IS A BLOSSOM OF THE	945	4
THE SPIRIT SHOOK THE ADAMANT--	'TWAS CRISIS--ALL THE	948	11
THE SPIRIT AND THE DUST.	DEATH IS A DIALOGUE	976	2
"DISSOLVE" SAYS DEATH--THE SPIRIT "SIR	DEATH IS A DIALOGUE	976	3
THE SPIRIT TURNS AWAY	DEATH IS A DIALOGUE	976	6
AND SPIRIT TURNED [THE SPIRIT SAID] UNTO THE DUST	I HEARD, AS IF I HAD NO	1039	13
AND SPIRIT TURNED [THE SPIRIT SAID] UNTO THE DUST	I HEARD, AS IF I HAD NO	1039	13
THE SPIRIT NEVER SHOWS.	IT'S HOUR WITH ITSELF	1225	2
SHOULD STAB MY RAVISHED SPIRIT	ONE JOY OF SO MUCH	1420	7
WHEN [TILL] FLESH AND SPIRIT SUNDER	ONE JOY OF SO MUCH	1420	11
A SPIRIT--HOW DOTH IT ACCOST--	'TIS WHITER THAN AN	1482	7
HER SPIRIT ROSE TO SUCH A HIGHT	HER SPIRIT ROSE TO SUCH	1486	1
I WATCHED [BOUGHT] THE FLUTTERING [VANQUISHED] SPIRIT	I SAW THE WIND WITHIN	1502	V
THE SPIRIT DOES NOT STAND--	THE THINGS THAT NEVER	1515	11
THE SPIRIT LASTS--BUT IN WHAT MODE--	THE SPIRIT LASTS--BUT IN	1576	1
BUT AS THE SPIRIT FURNISHES--	THE SPIRIT LASTS--BUT IN	1576	3
THE SPIRIT LURKS WITHIN THE FLESH	THE SPIRIT LASTS--BUT IN	1576	9
HIS SPIRIT GREW ROBUST--	HE ATE AND DRANK THE	1587	2
A [THE] LOOSENED SPIRIT BRINGS--	HE ATE AND DRANK THE	1587	8
BUT SUSTENANCE IS OF THE SPIRIT	A WORLD MADE PENNINILESS	1623	3
THE [IT'S] SPIRIT LOOKS UPON [TURNS UPON / GAZES AT / GLANCES . . .	AS FROM THE EARTH THE	1630	5
COHESIVE AS THE SPIRIT	A WORD MADE FLESH IS	1651	11
THE SPIRIT COULD NOT SHOW	NO MAN SAW AWE, NOR TO	1733	10
BLUSH, MY SPIRIT, IN THY FASTNESS--	REARRANGE A "WIFE'S"	1737	5
SPIRIT'S			
GOD THE SPIRIT'S HONOR--	ONLY GOD--DETECT THE	626	7
SPIRITS			
THEIR SPIRITS MEET TOGETHER, THEY MAKE THEM SOLEMN VOWS,	AWAKE YE MUSES NINE,	1	19
TO SPARE THESE STRIDING SPIRITS	WE SEE--COMPARATIVELY--	534	13

	FIRST LINE	POEM	LINE
SPIRITS (CONTINUED)			
[SHRINKING SPIRITS / . . .			
TO SPARE THESE STRIDING SPIRITS	WE SEE--COMPARATIVELY--	534	13
[SHRINKING SPIRITS / . . .			
THEY ARE THE SPIRITS STILL VACATION . . .	THE LASSITUDES OF	1592	3
SPIRITUAL			
LIKE SOMETHING SPIRITUAL--	IT WAS NOT SAINT--IT WAS	1092	4
SPLASHING			
THE SPLASHING MEN!	A BURDOCK--CLAWED MY	229	9
SPLENDOR			
THE SPLENDOR OF A BURMAH	ONE OF THE ONES THAT	1466	17
SPLENDORS			
MY SPLENDORS, ARE MENAGERIE--	OF BRONZE--AND BLAZE--	290	14
SPLINTER			
BUT LET A SPLINTER SWERVE--	THE BRAIN, WITHIN IT'S	556	3
SPLINTERED			
OR A SPLINTERED CROWN--	TAKING UP THE FAIR IDEAL	428	4
SPLIT			
WOULD SPLIT, FOR SIZE OF ME--	BEFORE I GOT MY EYE PUT	327	8
SHOW ME DIVISION [COULD] CAN SPLIT OR PARE--	WHILE IT IS ALIVE	491	6
FOR IT WOULD SPLIT HIS [HER] HEART, TO KNOW IT--	GOING TO HIM! HAPPY	494	16
AND SPLIT THEIR PODS OF FLAME--	IT MAKES NO DIFFERENCE	620	4
THAT SPLIT THEIR ROUTE TO THE SKY-- . . .	BY MY WINDOW HAVE I FOR	797	6
SPLIT THE LARK--AND YOU'LL FIND THE MUSIC--	SPLIT THE LARK--AND	861	1
AS IF MY BRAIN HAD SPLIT--	I FELT A CLEAVING IN MY	937	2
TRYING IF IT SPLIT--	ROBBED BY DEATH--BUT	971	16
SPLITS			
MY CACTUS--SPLITS HER BEARD	I TEND MY FLOWERS FOR	339	7
NOT SUCH A STANZA SPLITS THE SILENCE-- . .	BETTER--THAN MUSIC! FOR	503	19
SPOIL			
FOR FEAR I SPOIL MY SHOE?	IS BLISS THEN, SUCH	340	3
SPOILER			
THE SPOILER OF OUR HOME?	DENIAL--IS THE ONLY FACT	965	8
SPOKE			
I CANNOT SEE A SPOKE	MY WHEEL IS IN THE DARK!	10	2
I NEVER SPOKE--UNLESS ADDRESSED--	I WAS THE SLIGHTEST IN	486	10
THE MARTYR PAINTERS--NEVER SPOKE--	THE MARTYR POETS--DID	544	5
AND IF HE SPOKE--WHAT NAME WAS BEST-- . .	TO KNOW JUST HOW HE	622	18
THE FUTURE--NEVER SPOKE--	THE FUTURE--NEVER SPOKE	672	1
JUST AS HE SPOKE IT FROM HIS HANDS . . .	JUST AS HE SPOKE IT FROM	848	1
WITH WHOM I SPOKE NO WORD--	MY BEST ACQUAINTANCES	932	2
I NEVER SPOKE WITH GOD	I NEVER SAW A MOOR--	1052	5
THE TWILIGHT SPOKE THE SPIRE, ...	THE MOUNTAINS STOOD IN	1278	8
THOUGH NEITHER OF US SPOKE--	WE TALKED WITH EACH	1473	2
THE CRICKET SPOKE SO CLEAR	AS IMPERCEPTIBLY AS	1540	V
SPOKEN			
IF SPOKEN BY THE DISTANT BIRD--	TWO BUTTERFLIES WENT OUT	533	9
WONT YOU WISH YOU'D SPOKEN	NO MATTER--NOW--SWEET--	704	3
SPOKES			
THOUGH SPOKES--SPIN--MORE CONSPICUOUS . .	THE OUTER--FROM THE	451	7
I ENVY SPOKES OF WHEELS	I ENVY SEAS, WHEREON HE	498	2
WHOSE SPOKES A DIZZY MUSIC MAKE	WITHIN MY GARDEN, RIDES	500	3
SPONGES			
AS SPONGES--BUCKETS--DO--	THE BRAIN--IS WIDER THAN	632	8
SPONTANEITY			
TO SPONTANEITY--	IT'S EASY TO INVENT A	724	8
SPOOLS			
BUSY NEEDLES, AND SPOOLS OF THREAD--	ON SUCH A NIGHT, OR SUCH	146	19
MY CHILDHOOD, AND THE STRING OF SPOOLS, . .	I'M CEDED--I'VE STOPPED	508	6
SPOON			
TANKARD, OR SPOON--	I KNOW SOME LONELY	289	26
SPORT			
AS IF FOR LULL OF SPORT--	SHE LAY AS IF AT PLAY	369	6
SPORTSMAN			
AND SPORTSMAN IS NOT BOLD.	SOME, TOO FRAGILE FOR	141	8
SPORTSMAN'S			
NOR A SPORTSMAN'S PERADVENTURE [RUTHLESS PLEASURE / WANTON . . .	STRUCK, WAS I, NOR YET	925	7
SPOT			
TO AN UNTRAVERSED SPOT--	COULD LIVE--DID LIVE--	43	7
GERANIUMS--TINT--AND SPOT--	I TEND MY FLOWERS FOR	339	5
BY SHUNNING CAREFULLY THE PLACE [SPOT / SITE]	HAVE ANY LIKE MYSELF	736	19
CAREFULLY CHERISHING THE SPOT	THIS IS A BLOSSOM OF THE	945	11
YET CERTAIN AM I OF THE SPOT	I NEVER SAW A MOOR--	1052	7
STEP LIGHTLY ON THIS NARROW SPOT--	STEP LIGHTLY ON THIS	1183	1
AND PRESENTS [BEGETS] HER SPOT--	WE LIKE MARCH.	1213	7
THAT IS THE MANUFACTORING SPOT	A DEED KNOCKS FIRST AT	1216	3
IT STOP UPON A SPOT	THE MUSHROOM IS THE ELF	1298	4
OF THAT SPECIFIC SPOT	THE FACT THAT EARTH IS	1408	4
A MEDITATIVE SPOT--	ON MY VOLCANO GROWS THE	1677	2
SPOTLESS			
SPOTLESS BE FROM BLAME	UP LIFE'S HILL WITH MY	1010	6
SPOTS			
WITH SPOTS OF BURNISH ROASTED ON	THE BUTTERFLY'S NUMIDIAN	1387	2
SPOTTED			
HER LEASE OF SPOTTED HOURS, ...	SHE DIED AT PLAY,	75	3
FROM SPOTTED [DAPPLED] NOOKS--	MY RIVER RUNS TO THEE--	162	6
AND STILL, SHE PLIES HER SPOTTED BROOMS, [THRIFT]	SHE SWEEPS WITH	219	9

	FIRST LINE	POEM	LINE
SPOTTED (CONTINUED)			
LAYING HER [IT'S] SPOTTED FACE TO DIE	BLAZING IN GOLD AND	228	4
UPON A SPOTTED WORLD--	WHEN WE STAND ON THE	242	14
SPOTTED--HER DUN GOWN--	CIVILIZATION--SPURNS--	492	7
AND SPOTTED IT WITH TEARS--	HE TOLD A HOMELY TALE	763	2
I AM SPOTTED--"I AM PARDON"--	"UNTO ME?" I DO NOT KNOW	964	9
A SPOTTED SHAFT IS SEEN--	A NARROW FELLOW IN THE	986	6
BUT [YET] PRONE TO SHUT IT'S [HIS] SPOTTED [SUBTLE] FAN	THE BUTTERFLY'S NUMIDIAN	1387	4
SPRANG			
THEN SPRANG BEFORE THE HILLS	THE DAY CAME SLOW--TILL	304	2
SPRANG LIGHTLY TO [ROSE SOFTLY IN / TURNED EASY IN] THE SKY	A SPARROW TOOK A SLICE	1211 V	6
UPON HIS SADDLE SPRUNG A [SPRANG THE] BIRD	UPON HIS SADDLE SPRUNG A	1600	1
SPRAY			
HER COUNTENANCE AS SPRAY.	SHE DIED AT PLAY,	75	9
SPREAD			
BY SAVORY FANCY SPREAD--	AS WATCHERS HANG UPON	121	3
AND SPREAD IT ON THE GROUND--	OF BRUSSELS--IT WAS NOT	602	14
HIS TABLE'S SPREAD TOO HIGH FOR US--	VICTORY COMES LATE--	690	8
SPREADING			
THE SPREADING WIDE MY NARROW HANDS	I DWELL IN POSSIBILITY--	657	11
SPREADS			
LIFTS [SPREADS] HIS LIGHT PINNACE--	THE NEAREST DREAM	319	8
THE WIDTH OF LIFE--BEFORE IT SPREADS [RUNS]	AT LEISURE IS THE SOUL	618	3
SPREADS THE POND HER BASE OF LILIES	HOW THE WATERS CLOSED	923	5
SPRIG			
IT WEARS A SPRIG UPON IT'S BREAST--	THERE'S SOMETHING	45	3
SPRIGHTLY			
THAT GENTLEMEN SO SPRIGHTLY	IF I SHOULD DIE,	54	17
SPRING			
I HAVE A BIRD IN SPRING	I HAVE A BIRD IN SPRING	5	1
THE SPRING DECOYS.	I HAVE A BIRD IN SPRING	5	3
AND STILL THE PENSIVE SPRING RETURNS--	NEW FEET WITHIN MY	99	7
EMERGES IN THE SPRING!	A FUZZY FELLOW, WITHOUT	173	14
IT'S EARLY--YET--FOR "SPRING"!	IT CANT BE "SUMMER"!	221	3
AND LIFE WOULD ALL BE SPRING!	THE SUN--JUST TOUCHED	232	4
LEST BACK THE AWFUL DOOR SHOULD SPRING	I YEARS HAD BEEN FROM	609	19
UNTO THE EVERLASTING SPRING	NO NOTICE GAVE SHE, BUT	804	15
A LIGHT EXISTS IN SPRING	A LIGHT EXISTS IN SPRING	812	1
SPRING IS THE PERIOD	SPRING IS THE PERIOD	844	1
SPRING COMES ON THE WORLD--	SPRING COMES ON THE	1042	1
I CANNOT MEET THE SPRING UNMOVED--	I CANNOT MEET THE SPRING	1051	1
THE NOTICE THAT IS CALLED THE SPRING	THE NOTICE THAT IS	1310	1
A LITTLE MADNESS IN THE SPRING	A LITTLE MADNESS IN THE	1333	1
WHO FLEEING FROM THE SPRING	UPON A LILAC SEA	1337	4
THE SPRING AVENGING FLING	UPON A LILAC SEA	1337	5
THE INUNDATION OF THE SPRING	THE INUNDATION OF THE	1425	1
SO WHIMPERED FOR THE SPRING--	I THOUGHT THE TRAIN	1449	4
BEFORE YOU THOUGHT OF SPRING	BEFORE YOU THOUGHT OF	1465	1
OF IDLENESS AND SPRING--	HIS LITTLE HEARSE LIKE	1522	8
A PANG IS MORE CONSPICUOUS IN SPRING	A PANG IS MORE	1530	1
DOES NOT DESERVE THE [HAS NEVER TASTED] SPRING--	A DRUNKARD CANNOT MEET A	1628	8
BE THIS AN AUTUMN OR A SPRING	THE ONES THAT	1690	5
IS AS ARABLE AS SPRING	WINTER UNDER CULTIVATION	1707	2
THE BIRDS, THEY MAKE IT IN THE SPRING,	THE SADDEST NOISE, THE	1764	3
SPRINGS			
IF SPRINGS FROM WINTER RISE,	IF PAIN FOR PEACE	63	4
WHOSE OPERA--[STANZAS, ARE] THE SPRINGS--	A FEATHER FROM THE	161	4
THE TRAMPLED STEEL THAT SPRINGS!	A WOUNDED DEER--LEAPS	165	6
SPRINGS--SHAKE THE SILLS [SEALS]--	SAFE IN THEIR ALABASTER	216 V	
A HAGGARD COMFORT SPRINGS	I TRIED TO THINK A	532	7
BY SUCCEEDING [SUPREMER] SPRINGS--	ALL BUT DEATH, CAN BE	749	6
FOR RUMORED SPRINGS--	QUITE EMPTY, QUITE AT	1606	5
SPRINKLED			
SUMMERS HAVE SPRINKLED THERE!	IN EBON BOX, WHEN YEARS	169	4
SPRINKLES			
IT SPRINKLES BONNETS--FAR BELOW--	THE NAME--OF IT--IS	656	9
SPRITE			
THEY WOULD ELATE A SPRITE	A MIEN TO MOVE A QUEEN--	283	14
SPROUT			
IT'S IRON BUDS WILL SPROUT ANEW [AFRESH]	YOU CANNOT MAKE	1508	11
SPRUNG			
BECAUSE, WE'RE ORCHARD SPRUNG--	THE ROBIN'S MY CRITERION	285	7
UPON HIS SADDLE SPRUNG A [SPRANG THE] BIRD	UPON HIS SADDLE SPRUNG A	1600	1
SPRY			
THE SPRY [LONG] ARMS OF THE WIND	THE SPRY ARMS OF THE	1103	1
SPUN			
WHO SPUN THE BREADTHS OF BLUE!	BRING ME THE SUNSET IN A	128	6
IT SPUN--AND SPUN--	IT TOSSED--AND TOSSED--	723	3
IT SPUN--AND SPUN--	IT TOSSED--AND TOSSED--	723	3
WHO SPUN THE AUBURN CLOTH?	HOW FITS HIS UMBER COAT	1371	5
SPUR			
AS 'TWERE A SPUR--UPON THE SOUL--	I LIVED ON DREAD--	770	6
SPURN			
I'D DAISIES SPURN [CLOVERS--SCORN]--	THE ROBIN'S MY CRITERION	285	9
CHOOSE THE ENVOY--AND SPURN THE GROOM--	GOD IS A DISTANT--	357	6
WITH HALF A SMILE, AND HALF A SPURN,	IF YOU WERE COMING IN	511	3
IT SPURN THE GRAVE--	I ROSE--BECAUSE HE SANK	616	15

	FIRST LINE	POEM	LINE
SPURN (CONTINUED)			
THEY SPURN THE AIR, AS 'TWERE TOO MEAN	YOU'VE SEEN BALLOONS SET	700	7
HAD HE THE POWER TO SPURN--	THAT SHORT--POTENTIAL	1307	8
SPURN THE TEMERITY--	SPURN THE TEMERITY--	1432	1
SEE HOW WELL WE SPURN HIM--	SUMMER IS SHORTER THAN	1506	6
WHICH OTHERS TASTE AND SPURN AND SNEER [SLIGHT]--	I GROPED FOR HIM BEFORE	1555	5
WHOSE POMPS ALLURE AND SPURN	OF THIS IS DAY COMPOSED	1675	5
IS RAPTURE HERSELF SPURN--	TO DO A MAGNANIMOUS	1699	8
SPURNED			
THAT SPURNED US--YESTERDAY!	"HEAVEN"--IS WHAT I	239	12
UNTIL A ZEPHYR PUSHED [CHASED / FLUNG / SPURNED / SCOURGED] THEM	TWO BUTTERFLIES WENT OUT	533	V
APPROACHED--AND SPURNED THE NARROW GRASS--	I THINK I WAS ENCHANTED	593	11
WE SPURNED [DISOWNED]--	LUCK IS NOT CHANCE--	1350	7
IT WOULD NOT KNOW IF IT WERE SPURNED,	IT WOULD NOT KNOW IF IT	1579	1
SPURNING			
ESPOUSING EACH AND SPURNING ALL	HOW LONESOME THE WIND	1418	11
SPURNS			
CIVILIZATION--SPURNS--THE LEOPARD!	CIVILIZATION--SPURNS--	492	1
HE LOVES [SEEKS] WHAT SPURNS [SHUNS] HIM--	TO EARN IT BY DISDAINING	1427	3
SPY			
LEST ANYBODY SPY THE BLOOD	A WOUNDED DEER--LEAPS	165	11
MIGHT HE BUT SPY THE LADY'S [HIDING] SOUL--	JUST SO--JESUS--RAPS--	317	6
OR THE MOST AGONIZING SPY--	THE SOUL UNTO ITSELF	683	3
WE SPY THE FORESTS AND THE HILLS	DEW--IS THE FRESHET IN	1097	5
THERE COMES [CAME] A WARNING LIKE A SPY	THERE COMES A WARNING	1536	1
SQUANDER			
YOU SQUANDER ON [SPEND UPON] THE DEAD,	ENDOW THE LIVING--WITH	521	2
SQUANDERED			
AND SQUANDERED SUCH A NOTE	UPON HIS SADDLE SPRUNG A	1600	6
SQUANDERING			
ON ANGELS--SQUANDERING FOR YOU	HIS BILL IS CLASPED--HIS	1102	11
SQUANDERS			
SHE SQUANDERS ON YOUR HEAD [EAR]	YOU'LL KNOW HER--BY HER	634	25
SQUARE			
TO THE VERY SQUARE--HIS FOOT IS PASSING--	I COULD DIE--TO KNOW--	570	10
BURN HIM IN THE PUBLIC SQUARE--	GRIEF IS A MOUSE--	793	14
SQUARELY			
DELIBERATELY [LOOK SQUARELY IN THE] FACE--	I NEVER HEAR THAT ONE IS	1323	16
SQUIRREL			
PERHAPS A SQUIRREL MAY REMAIN--	BESIDES THE AUTUMN POETS	131	13
NO SQUIRREL WENT ABROAD--	THE NIGHT WAS WIDE, AND	589	9
SQUIRREL--ECLIPSE--THE BUMBLE BEE--	"NATURE" IS WHAT WE SEE	668	3
OF SHADOW, OR OF SQUIRREL, HAPLY--	FOUR TREES--UPON A	742	11
RESTRAINING RAMPANT SQUIRREL--	NATURE--THE GENTLEST	790	7
OR A SQUIRREL, WHOSE GIDDY PENINSULA	BY MY WINDOW HAVE I FOR	797	7
TWO FULL AUTUMNS FOR THE SQUIRREL	TWICE HAD SUMMER HER	846	5
TO SQUIRREL IN THE HIMMALEH	LIGHT IS SUFFICIENT TO	862	7
OH, WHEN THE SQUIRREL FILLS HIS POCKETS	WHAT SHALL I DO WHEN THE	956	9
SQUIRREL'S			
BUT IN A SQUIRREL'S ESTIMATE	A SAUCER HOLDS A CUP	1374	3
SQUIRRELS			
THE NEWS, LIKE SQUIRRELS, RAN--	I'LL TELL YOU HOW THE	318	4
WHERE SQUIRRELS PLAY--AND BERRIES DIE--	DOOM IS THE HOUSE	475	7
FOR FEAR THE SQUIRRELS--KNOW.	THE TINT I CANNOT TAKE--	627	20
AND SQUIRRELS, FORMERLY.	WHO OCCUPIES THIS HOUSE?	892	20
TO SQUIRRELS AND TO ME	EXPERIMENT TO ME	1073	8
ST			
BUTTERFLIES FROM ST DOMINGO	FLOWERS--WELL--IF	137	11
AND CUSTOMS AT "ST. JAMES"!	THE MANNER OF IT'S DEATH	468	12
I COULD BRING YOU ODORS FROM ST DOMINGO--	I COULD BRING YOU JEWELS	697	3
STAB			
IF I SHOULD STAB THE PATIENT FAITH	I SHOULD NOT DARE TO	205	9
STAB THE BIRD--THAT BUILT IN YOUR BOSOM--	KILL YOUR BALM--AND IT'S	238	5
SHOULD STAB MY RAVISHED SPIRIT	ONE JOY OF SO MUCH	1420	7
STABBED			
STABBED--WHILE I SUED	HE STRAINED MY FAITH--	497	13
STABILITY			
AND THEN ELUDE STABILITY	SUMMER BEGINS TO HAVE	1682	15
STABLE			
AT IT'S OWN STABLE DOOR--	I LIKE TO SEE IT LAP	585	17
STACK			
TO [ON] STUMP, AND STACK--AND STEM--	IT SIFTS FROM LEADEN	311	13
STAG			
TALL--LIKE THE STAG--WOULD THAT?	YOU SAID THAT I "WAS	738	5
STAGGER			
DID STAGGER PITIFUL--	THE ROSE DID CAPER ON	208	4
IF YOUR SOUL SEESAW [STAGGER]--	IF YOUR NERVE, DENY YOU	292	9
THEY PERISH [STAGGER]--DO WE DIE--	I CROSS TILL I AM WEARY	550	23
STAGGERED			
HOW MANY TIMES THESE LOW FEET STAGGERED--	HOW MANY TIMES THESE LOW	187	1
THE MORNING--FLUTTERED--STAGGERED--	THE SUN--JUST TOUCHED	232	13
HE SCANNED IT--STAGGERED--	HE SCANNED IT--STAGGERED	1062	1
STAGGERING			
THAT GETS A STAGGERING BLOW--	AT LEISURE IS THE SOUL	618	2
ASSISTS THE STAGGERING MIND	A DOUBT IF IT BE US	859	2
STAGINGS			
. . . STAGINGS DROP]	THE PROPS ASSIST THE	1142	11

	FIRST LINE	POEM	LINE
STAGNANT			
A STAGNANT PLEASURE LIKE A POOL	A STAGNANT PLEASURE LIKE	1281	1
STAID			
STAID SLEEPING--THERE--	I KNOW SOME LONELY	289	30
BUT THEN--I'M NOT SO STAID--AS HE--	FUNNY--TO BE A CENTURY--	345	4
STAIN			
DEEPER AND DEEPER GREW THE STAIN	THE SUN KEPT STOOPING--	152	5
THE LINGERING--AND THE STAIN--I MEAN--	THE ONE WHO COULD REPEAT	307	6
TIS POPULOUS WITH BONE AND STAIN--	MY PORTION IS DEFEAT--	639	7
AND OH, THE SHOWER OF STAIN--	THE NAME--OF IT--IS	656	6
MY PRICE FOR EVERY STAIN!	AGAIN--HIS VOICE IS AT	663	29
OR COUNTERACT THE STAIN--	AS FROST IS BEST	951	10
BY AN AURORAL STAIN	LET ME NOT MAR THAT	1335	2
OUR ADORATION STAIN [MAR / FLAW]	WE SHUN BECAUSE WE PRIZE	1429	3
STAINED			
BUT--IF I STAINED MY APRON--	OVER THE FENCE--	251	6
STAINS			
STAINS--ALL WASHED--	TAKING UP THE FAIR IDEAL	428	15
NOT SICKNESS STAINS THE BRAVE,	NOT SICKNESS STAINS THE	1613	1
STAIR			
I HEAR HER FEET UPON THE STAIR!	DYING! DYING IN THE	158	11
THE MOON--SLIDES DOWN THE STAIR,	I KNOW SOME LONELY	289	23
SOFTLY MY FUTURE CLIMBS THE STAIR,	A WIFE--AT DAYBREAK I	461	9
STAIRS			
OH MARCH, COME RIGHT UP STAIRS WITH ME--	DEAR MARCH--COME IN--	1320	9
STAKE			
TO CRUCIFIX OR BLOCK [STAKE]	DEATH WARRANTS ARE	1375	6
STAKE AN ENTIRE STORE	HOW MUCH THE PRESENT	1380	4
ANGUISH CAN TRAVEL TO ITS STAKE,	THE LONGEST DAY THAT GOD	1769	3
STAKED			
THEN LOST [STAKED / CHASED] THEMSELVES AND FOUND . . .	TWO BUTTERFLIES WENT OUT	533	V
SHE STAKED HER FEATHERS--GAINED AN ARC--	SHE STAKED HER FEATHERS	798	1
SHE STAKED HER WINGS--AND GAINED A BUSH--	SHE STAKED HER FEATHERS	798	V 1
NO TERRITORY NEW IS STAKED--	TWO LENGTHS HAS EVERY	1295	11
STAKES			
PLUCK UP IT'S STAKES, AND DISAPPEAR--	I'VE KNOWN A HEAVEN,	243	3
IMPALED HIM ON HER FIERCEST STAKES--	FATE SLEW HIM, BUT HE	1031	3
STAKING			
STAKING OUR ENTIRE [DIVINE] POSSESSION	ROBBED BY DEATH--BUT	971	13
STALACTITE			
WHOSE FINGERS STRING THE STALACTITE--	BRING ME THE SUNSET IN A	128	16
AS STALACTITE [VIOLET]--	MUST BE A WO--	571	8
STALE			
WISDOM IS STALE--TO ME"	THE SEA SAID "COME" TO	1210	8
NOT ANYTHING IS STALE SO LONG	THE RIDDLE WE CAN GUESS	1222	3
THE SMALL [SAME] STALE SUM--	HOW DESTITUTE IS HE	1477	4
STALK			
AS BLOOM UPON A STALK.	THE OPENING AND THE	1047	4
LEFT INACTIVE ON THE STALK	REVOLUTION IS THE POD	1082	9
STALLS			
EXTEMPORANEOUS STALLS	THOSE CATTLE SMALLER	1388	6
STAMENS			
COMPUTES THE STAMENS IN A BREATH--	"ARCTURUS" IS HIS OTHER	70	11
STAMMERED			
THEN--HOW THEY WADED [STAMMERED]--SLOW--SLOW--	GOING TO HIM! HAPPY	494	7
STAMP			
WITH THE BRAND [STAMP] OF THE GENTILE DRINKER	TO PUT THIS WORLD DOWN,	527	14
STAMPED			
A BIRD--HAD STAMPED HER FOOT--	OF COURSE--I PRAYED--	376	4
STAMPED VISIBLE--IN STONE--	MY PORTION IS DEFEAT--	639	13
STAMPED--OCCASIONALLY--[IN INSTANCES] FOREVER--	SO THE EYES ACCOST--AND	752	3
STANCH			
TO THE STANCH [UNWILLING] DUST	TO THE STANCH DUST	1402	1
STANCHED			
FORTITUDE--FLANKED [STANCHED] WITH MELODY.	AFTER ALL BIRDS HAVE	1395	V 8
STAND			
THE HOSTS OF WITNESS STAND!	SLEEP IS SUPPOSED TO BE	13	6
TIS SWEET TO KNOW THAT STOCKS WILL STAND	IF I SHOULD DIE,	54	11
THE ROBINS STAND AS THICK TODAY	SOME RAINBOW--COMING	64	13
IN BRIGHT DETACHMENT [DETACHMENTS] STAND!	SOME RAINBOW--COMING	64	21
AND STAND UPON THEIR HEADS!	"ARCTURUS" IS HIS OTHER	70	23
THE PURPLE CRAYONS STAND.	SHE BORE IT TILL THE	144	4
AND NO REAPERS STAND!	THO' MY DESTINY BE	163	16
COULD WE STAND WITH THAT OLD "MOSES"--	IF THE FOOLISH, CALL	168	9
GRANT THAT WE MAY STAND,	IF THE FOOLISH, CALL	168	18
WHEN WE STAND ON THE TOPS OF THINGS--	WHEN WE STAND ON THE	242	1
THE SOUND ONES, LIKE THE HILLS--SHALL STAND [STAND UP]--	WHEN WE STAND ON THE	242	7
THE SOUND ONES, LIKE THE HILLS--SHALL STAND [STAND UP]--	WHEN WE STAND ON THE	242	7
HOW NOTELESS MEN, AND PLEIADS, STAND,	HOW NOTELESS MEN, AND	282	1
AND I, BEWILDERED, STAND--	AS IF I ASKED A COMMON	323	4
AS HIMMALEH, SHALL STAND--	THEY LEAVE US WITH THE	350	6
DUCAL--AT LAST--STAND UP BY THEE--	LOVE--THOU ART HIGH--	453	6
I STAND ALIVE--TODAY--	I LIVE WITH HIM--I SEE	463	10
HER TEETH CAN HARDLY STAND--	SHE SIGHTS A BIRD--SHE	507	6
I THINK THE HEMLOCK LIKES TO STAND	I THINK THE HEMLOCK	525	1
DID YOU EVER STAND IN A CAVERN'S MOUTH--	DID YOU EVER STAND IN A	590	1

	FIRST LINE	POEM	LINE
STAND (CONTINUED)			
AND I--COULD I STAND BY	I CANNOT LIVE WITH YOU--	640	17
IN ORDINATION STAND--	I THINK TO LIVE--MAY BE	646	10
OF ALL THE SOULS THAT STAND CREATE--	OF ALL THE SOULS THAT	664	1
APART--INTRINSIC--STAND--	OF ALL THE SOULS THAT	664	6
THE SOUL SHOULD STAND [BE] IN AWE--	THE SOUL UNTO ITSELF	683	8
IF TRUDGING FEET MAY STAND--	THE BEGGAR LAD--DIES	717	10
TO LIVES THAT STAND ALONE--	TO OFFER BRAVE	767	2
SHALL STAND TO OUR RIGHT HAND--	SWEET, TO HAVE HAD THEM	901	5
MEAN OF FORCES--STAND BY HER WING,	PATIENCE--HAS A QUIET	926	V
HOW STILL THE BELLS IN STEEPLES STAND	HOW STILL THE BELLS IN	1008	1
BLOSSOMS STAND NEGATIVE,	SPRING COMES ON THE	1042	5
THE SOUL SHOULD ALWAYS STAND AJAR	THE SOUL SHOULD ALWAYS	1055	1
TO WHOM THE MORNINGS STAND FOR NIGHTS,	TO WHOM THE MORNINGS	1095	1
SHAME--STAND ERECT--	NOT WITH A CLUB, THE	1304	15
CAN STAND SO CLOSE AND LOOK SO BOLD	WHAT MYSTERY PERVADES A	1400	11
THE SPIRIT DOES NOT STAND--	THE THINGS THAT NEVER	1515	11
SO NEAR THE WHOLE TO STAND	I DID NOT REACH THEE	1664	27
WE STAND LIKE SNOW	I DID NOT REACH THEE	1664	29
WOULD STAND SO DEEP IN JOY	DID LIFE'S PENURIOUS	1717	4
STANDARD			
STANDARD DENIES	UNTIL THE DESERT KNOWS	1291	V 6
STANDARDS			
• • • / STANDARDS]	THIS DUST, AND IT'S	936	9
DEPARTED STANDARDS AND THE FEW	TO UNDERTAKE IS TO	1070	7
STANDING			
ACRES OF MASTS ARE STANDING	HOW THE OLD MOUNTAINS	291	V 19
THEN--ON DIVINEST TIPTOE--STANDING--	JUST SO--JESUS--RAPS--	317	5
IF ANY SINK, ASSURE THAT THIS, NOW STANDING--	IF ANY SINK, ASSURE THAT	358	1
THAT THERE BE STANDING HERE--	DO PEOPLE MOULDER	432	10
AND WHILE BY STEPPING [STANDING] ON MY HEART	THE PILE OF YEARS IS NOT	1507	5
STANDS			
IF NIGHT STANDS FIRST--THEN NOON	IF PAIN FOR PEACE	63	7
AND YET, HOW STILL THE LANDSCAPE STANDS!	A LADY RED--AMID THE	74	13
ITALY STANDS THE OTHER SIDE!	OUR LIVES ARE SWISS--	80	6
STANDS REPRESENTATIVE IN GOLD	A SCIENCE--SO THE SAVANS	100	10
THAT STANDS FOR DEITY, TO MINE,	A SINGLE SCREW OF FLESH	263	3
STANDS SYMBOL FOR THE FINER FORGE	DARE YOU SEE A SOUL AT	365	11
THE WORLD--STANDS--SOLEMNER--TO ME--	THE WORLD--STANDS--	493	1
A SPECIES [SEQUEL] STANDS BEYOND--	THIS WORLD IS NOT	501	2
THEN STANDS UPON THE BONNET	HE PARTS HIMSELF--LIKE	517	3
IT'S TEMPLE [CLOSET] STANDS, ALWAY,	THE BODY GROWS WITHOUT--	578	4
BUT AS SHE CLOSER STANDS--	YOU'LL KNOW HER--BY HER	634	16
IT GATHERS RUDDY [STANDS IN--RUDDY / MAKES VERMILLION--] POOLS--	THE NAME--OF IT--IS	656	10
STANDS WITHOUT A BONE--	THE TRUTH--IS STIRLESS--	780	8
A COLOR STANDS ABROAD	A LIGHT EXISTS IN SPRING	812	5
BUT UNAPPROACHED IT STANDS--	IT BLOOMED AND DROPT, A	978	16
AND ARTISAN LIES [SMALL ESTATE STANDS--] STILL--	DEW--IS THE FRESHET IN	1097	4
BUT AFFIDAVIT STANDS	"REMEMBER ME" IMPLORED	1180	10
THE VOICE THAT STANDS FOR FLOODS TO ME	THE VOICE THAT STANDS	1189	1
STANDS THE SUN SO CLOSE AND MIGHTY	WE LIKE MARCH.	1213	8
NOT ANY HIGHER STANDS THE GRAVE	NOT ANY HIGHER STANDS	1256	1
THE SEDGE STANDS NEXT THE SEA--	WHAT MYSTERY PERVADES A	1400	14
IT'S AWFUL CHAMBER OPEN STANDS--	WATER MAKES MANY BEDS	1428	3
THERE STANDS AN ASTERISK	HE LIVED THE LIFE OF	1525	4
THERE STANDS AN ASTERISK	WHO ABDICATED AMBUSH	1616	4
STANZA			
WHOSE VOICES--TRAINED--[STANZA, HUSHED,] BELOW--	TO LEARN THE TRANSPORT	167	12
'TWAS'NT CONTAINED--LIKE OTHER STANZA--	BETTER--THAN MUSIC! FOR	503	5
NOT SUCH A STANZA SPLITS THE SILENCE--	BETTER--THAN MUSIC! FOR	503	19
IN HORRID--HOOTING STANZA--	I LIKE TO SEE IT LAP	585	12
STANZAS			
WHOSE OPERA--[STANZAS, ARE] THE SPRINGS--	A FEATHER FROM THE	161	4
STAPLE			
THE STAPLE MUST BE OPTIONAL	OF PAUL AND SILAS IT IS	1166	7
STAPLED			
WE STOOD UPON OUR STAPLED FEET--	THEY PUT US FAR APART--	474	15
SECRETS STAPLED THERE	"SECRETS" IS A DAILY	1385	10
STAPLES			
STAPLES OF AGES--HAVE BUCKLED THERE--	SAFE IN THEIR ALABASTER	216	V
AS STAPLES--DRIVEN THROUGH--	I GOT SO I COULD HEAR	293	12
AND STAPLES [RIVETS], IN THE SONG,	THE SOUL HAS BANDAGED	512	22
STAR			
I CHOSE THIS SINGLE STAR	ONE SISTER HAVE I IN OUR	14	25
I HAD A STAR IN HEAVEN--	I HAD A GUINEA GOLDEN--	23	17
DIM--AS THE BORDER STAR--	TAKEN FROM MEN--THIS	53	10
I'D RATHER CALL HIM "STAR."	"ARCTURUS" IS HIS OTHER	70	2
HERE A STAR, AND THERE A STAR,	OUR SHARE OF NIGHT TO	113	5
HERE A STAR, AND THERE A STAR,	OUR SHARE OF NIGHT TO	113	5
THIS FAITH THAT WATCHED FOR STAR IN VAIN,	THIS HEART THAT BROKE SO	145	3
SHE DROPT AS SOFTLY AS A STAR	SHE WENT AS QUIET AS THE	149	5
PAST MIDNIGHT! PAST THE MORNING STAR!	AT LAST, TO BE	174	4
AND TOPAZ--LIKE THE STAR!	I CAME TO BUY A SMILE--	223	12
FAINT STAR OF BETHLEHEM--	IF HE DISSOLVE--THEN--	236	6
AH, MOON--AND STAR!	AH, MOON--AND STAR!	240	1
BUT, MOON, AND STAR,	AH, MOON--AND STAR!	240	13
OR A NERVOUS STAR?	I KNOW SOME LONELY	289	22

	FIRST LINE	POEM	LINE
STAR (CONTINUED)			
OR VIOLATE A STAR--	WHAT SOFT--CHERUBIC	401	4
A STAR--NOT FAR ENOUGH TO SEEK--	A MURMUR IN THE TREES--	416	3
OR STAR--COME OUT--WITHIN--	WE GROW ACCUSTOMED TO	419	12
AS SUNS--DISSOLVE [ANNUL] A STAR--	NO CROWD THAT HAS	515	12
THEN--PROMPTER THAN [PUNCTUAL AS] A STAR	I LIKE TO SEE IT LAP	585	15
WITH BUT A SINGLE STAR--	THE NIGHT WAS WIDE, AND	589	2
AND EASY AS A STAR	THEY SHUT ME UP IN PROSE	613	10
WITHDREW THE FURTHEST STAR	I COULD SUFFICE FOR HIM,	643	10
AS ONE SHOULD SUE A STAR--	THE HEAVEN VESTS FOR	694	10
AND YET THE NEWEST STAR--	THE DAY UNDRESSED--	716	6
BUT THE REMOTEST STAR--	THE MOON WAS BUT A CHIN	737	14
AND WITHOLD A STAR--	ALL I MAY, IF SMALL,	819	6
AND IN THE NORTH, THE STAR--	THESE ARE THE SIGNS TO	1077	12
AT NIGHT BENEATH [BELOW] THE STAR	THE SNOW THAT NEVER	1133	6
THE ROAD WAS LIT WITH [BY] MOON AND STAR--	THE ROAD WAS LIT WITH	1450	1
AS GRAPHIC AS A STAR	WHOEVER DISENCHANTS	1451	6
WITHIN [IN / TO] A STAR--	HE LIVED THE LIFE OF	1525	8
ACCOMPANIES A STAR.	NO MATTER WHERE THE	1541	4
IS VALID AS A STAR--	TO HER DERIDED HOME	1586	V
SECRETED IN A STAR.	WHO ABDICATED AMBUSH	1616	8
LIGHTLY STEPPED A YELLOW STAR	LIGHTLY STEPPED A YELLOW	1672	1
AND PRANKS THE NORTHERN STAR	THESE ARE THE DAYS THAT	1696	2
STARE			
FOR SHOPS W'D STARE AT ME--	I HAV'NT TOLD MY GARDEN	50	6
AND LAUGH AT ME--AND STARE--	"ARCTURUS" IS HIS OTHER	70	29
BUT JUST THE MILES OF STARE--	I'VE KNOWN A HEAVEN,	243	6
EXISTING, WHILE WE STARE,	HOW NOTELESS MEN, AND	282	6
IN DEATH'S--STIFF--STARE--	I KNOW THAT HE EXISTS.	338	12
STARE STOLID [VACANT / HORRID] INTO MINE	I YEARS HAD BEEN FROM	609	5
AND THE BERRIES STARE	WHAT SHALL I DO WHEN THE	956	10
YOU WOULD CHASTENED STARE--	THERE'S THE BATTLE OF	1174	8
NOR A PAST TO STARE--	THE POPULAR HEART IS A	1226	6
TO MAKE EACH OTHER STARE	OUR LITTLE SECRETS SLINK	1326	6
STARED			
HER VICTIM STARED UPON--	THE MORNING AFTER WO--	364	8
STARES			
THE SOUL STARES AFTER IT, SECURE--	'TIS SO APPALLING--IT	281	3
NODS [STARES] FROM THE GILDED POINTERS--	A CLOCK STOPPED--	287	14
AND SPACE STARES ALL AROUND--	IT WAS NOT DEATH, FOR I	510	18
MORNING'S BOLD FACE--STARES IN THE WINDOW--	I COULD DIE--TO KNOW--	570	5
STARING			
STARING--BEWILDERED [DEFRAUDED]--AT THE MOCKING SKY--	THE NEAREST DREAM	319	10
IS PUSHING [ROAMING / PLODDING / STARING / AMBLING] CLOSE BEHIND	ALL THAT I DO	1496	6
STARK			
THE SUN IS GAY OR STARK	THE SUN IS GAY OR STARK	878	1
STARKEST			
MUCH SENSE--THE STARKEST MADNESS--	MUCH MADNESS IS DIVINEST	435	3
STARLESS			
HIS HEART WAS DARKER THAN THE STARLESS NIGHT	HIS HEART WAS DARKER	1378	1
STAR'S			
THE STAR'S WHOLE SECRET--IN THE LAKE--	THE OUTER--FROM THE	451	15
THE STAR'S ETRUSCAN ARGUMENT	THE MOON UPON HER FLUENT	1528	3
STARS			
PATTIE, ARRANGE THE STARS;	"SIC TRANSIT GLORIA	3	14
AS IF THE STARS SOME SUMMER NIGHT	THERE IS A MORN BY MEN	24	16
THE "MORNING STARS" THE TREBLE LED	MUSICIANS WRESTLE	157	11
STARS, AMID PROFOUND GALAXIES--	IF THE FOOLISH, CALL	168	19
YOU'LL KNOW IT BY THE ROW OF STARS	I LOST A WORLD--THE	181	3
TILL BROOMS FADE SOFTLY INTO STARS--	SHE SWEEPS WITH	219	11
JUST AS THE NIGHT KEEPS FETCHING STARS	I'VE NOTHING ELSE--TO	224	3
THE STARS DARE SHINE OCCASIONALLY	WHEN WE STAND ON THE	242	13
I FINISHED TWO--AND SEVERAL STARS--	I SEND TWO SUNSETS--	308	3
ALL FORESTS--STINTLESS STARS--	BEFORE I GOT MY EYE PUT	327	11
THEY DROPPED LIKE STARS--	THEY DROPPED LIKE FLAKES	409	2
BUT STARS--GO SLOW--FOR NIGHT--	I'LL CLUTCH--AND CLUTCH	427	6
AS THE STARS--YOU KNEW LAST NIGHT--	SOME SUCH BUTTERFLY BE	541	7
THE STARS--THE TRINKETS AT HER BELT--	THE MOON WAS BUT A CHIN	737	19
HE OUTSTRIPPED STARS AND SUN	HE OUTSTRIPPED TIME WITH	865	2
THE STARS EXPRESS AROUND	THE SUN AND MOON MUST	871	2
THE STARS ABOUT MY HEAD I FELT	I STEPPED FROM PLANK TO	875	3
THE STARS THAT STATED COME TO TOWN	MY BEST ACQUAINTANCES	932	3
AS SLIGHTLY [SCARCELY] AS THE ROUTES [FLIGHTS] OF STARS--	WE MISS HER, NOT BECAUSE	993	5
AS STARS THAT DROP ANONYMOUS	SUPERFLUOUS WERE THE SUN	999	11
THE CAPSULES BURNISHED SEEDS THE STARS--	THE LILAC IS AN ANCIENT	1241	11
THE STARS ARE OLD, THAT STOOD FOR ME--	THE STARS ARE OLD, THAT	1249	1
TRUSTY AS THE STARS	TRUSTY AS THE STARS	1369	1
GREAT BRITAIN DISAPPROVES, "THE STARS";	MY COUNTRY NEED NOT	1511	5
A GLEE AS SWEET AS IF THE STARS	TO SEE HER IS A PICTURE	1568	V 7
THE GODS [STARS / HEAVENS / SKIES / SUNS] BUT DREGS	A WORLD MADE PENNINILESS	1623	4
THE STARS THOU MEETST	GO THY GREAT WAY!	1638	2
FOR WHAT ARE STARS BUT ASTERISKS	GO THY GREAT WAY!	1638	4
THE LIVING, FOR THE STARS--	OF GLORY NOT A BEAM IS	1647	4
START			
SHE BECKONS, AND THE WOODS START--	BAFFLED FOR JUST A DAY	17	5
I NEED NOT START--YOU'RE SURE--	YOU LOVE ME--YOU ARE	156	8

	FIRST LINE	POEM	LINE
START (CONTINUED)			
ALL DAY AND NIGHT WITH BARK AND START--	WHAT SHALL I DO--IT	186	3
TILL I STIR [GROPE / START], AND WEEP--	MANY A PHRASE HAS THE	276	12
THE TRICK TO START--	SHE LAY AS IF AT PLAY	369	8
'TWOULD START THEM--	I TIE MY HAT--I CREASE	443	25
WE START--AS IF DETECTED	AN IGNORANCE A SUNSET	552	11
NO START [CLICK] IN APPREHENSION'S EAR,	I THINK TO LIVE--MAY BE	646	15
SHOULD THEY START FOR THE SKY.	WHAT DID THEY DO SINCE I	900	8
WE START--TO LEARN THAT WE BELIEVE	WHO WERE "THE FATHER AND	1258	17
I MEET HIM WITH A START	HIS MIND OF MAN, A	1663	2
'TWOULD START US WHERE WE SIT	A PIT--BUT HEAVEN OVER	1712	12
STARTED			
AND STARTED FOR THE SUN.	SHE DIED--THIS WAS THE	150	4
ON THE HEADS THAT STARTED WITH US--	SMILING BACK FROM	385	3
I STARTED EARLY--TOOK MY DOG--	I STARTED EARLY--TOOK MY	520	1
AND THEN--I STARTED--TOO--	I STARTED EARLY--TOOK MY	520	16
AND STARTED ALL ABROAD--	THE WIND BEGUN TO KNEAD	824	6
THE AUTUMN STARTED HOME--	WITH SWEETNESS UNABATED	1709	4
STARTLE			
SHOULD STARTLE MOST--	ONE NEED NOT BE A	670	14
STARTLED			
THE NOTICE [MONITION] TO THE STARTLED GRASS	PRESENTIMENT--IS THAT	764	3
GRIEF IS A THIEF--QUICK STARTLED--	GRIEF IS A MOUSE--	793	5
THEY STARTLED, LIKE EXECUTORS	NATURE AND GOD--I	835	3
AND STARTLED AT IT'S SWELLING [RISING]	BECAUSE MY BROOK IS	1200	5
STARVE			
WHO OF LITTLE LOVE--KNOW HOW TO STARVE--	VICTORY COMES LATE--	690	14
I DARE NOT EAT IT--THO' I STARVE--	GOD GAVE A LOAF TO EVERY	791	3
I SCARCELY RECOLLECT TO STARVE	THE LUXURY TO APPREHEND	815	7
'TWILL NEVER BE THE SAME TO STARVE	OH SUMPTUOUS MOMENT	1125	4
STARVED			
AND ALL THE CATTLE--STARVED--	THE WINTERS ARE SO SHORT	403	12
IT WOULD HAVE STARVED A GNAT--	IT WOULD HAVE STARVED A	612	1
AS THE STARVED MAELSTROM LAPS THE NAVIES	AS THE STARVED MAELSTROM	872	1
THAT HAS [WAS] NOT STARVED SO LONG	ART THOU THE THING I	1282	4
STARVING			
UNDUE SIGNIFICANCE A STARVING MAN ATTACHES	UNDUE SIGNIFICANCE A	439	1
WERE IT MY RESOURCE FROM STARVING--	MOST SHE TOUCHED ME BY	760	7
'TIS STARVING MAKES IT FAT--	MINE ENEMY IS GROWING	1509	8
STATE			
THEN SLEEPS IN STATE AGAIN--	ALL THESE MY BANNERS BE.	22	5
CHAMBER, AND STATE, AND THRONG--	ONE DIGNITY DELAYS FOR	98	6
HIS ROYAL STATE PARTOOK!	I MET A KING THIS	166	22
FULL PURPLE IS HIS STATE!	WAIT TILL THE MAJESTY OF	171	12
THAT OTHER STATE--	I'M "WIFE"--I'VE	199	2
TELL [STATE] IT THE AGES--TO A CYPHER--	BOUND--A TROUBLE--	269	7
EMPIRE--STATE--	MY REWARD FOR BEING, WAS	343	V
IT DOES'NT STATE YOU HOW	A HAPPY LIP--BREAKS	353	2
YOU DID NOT STATE--YOUR PRICE--	I PAY--IN SATIN CASH--	402	2
BUT STATE--ENDOWAL--FOCUS--	WE PRAY--TO HEAVEN--	489	10
THAT WILL NOT STATE--IT'S STING.	IF YOU WERE COMING IN	511	20
WHILE I STATE--THE SOLEMN PETALS,	BLOOM UPON THE MOUNTAIN	667	13
A PAST [TIME / STATE] OF PLANK AND NAIL	THE PROPS ASSIST THE	1142	10
THE MIND IS A SINGLE STATE--	THE HEART IS THE CAPITAL	1354	2
BUT STATE WITH CREEPING BLOOD	IN WINTER IN MY ROOM	1670	13
TO STATE THE SPELL DEMEAN	TO TELL THE BEAUTY WOULD	1700	2
STATED			
SURPASSES SHARPER STATED--	IT ALWAYS FELT TO ME--A	597	9
IT DEAL US [FURNISH]--STATED AS OUR FOOD--	A PRISON GETS TO BE A	652	7
BLOOM UPON THE MOUNTAIN--STATED--	BLOOM UPON THE MOUNTAIN	667	1
THE STARS THAT STATED COME TO TOWN	MY BEST ACQUAINTANCES	932	3
WE MISS HIS STATED HAT.	THAT ODD OLD MAN IS DEAD	1130	2
EXISTENCE HAS A STATED WIDTH	THE DAY SHE GOES	1308	4
STATELIER SEE STATLIER			
INVOLVING STATELIER SUMS.	LOW AT MY PROBLEM	69	4
SO LOW IT LEANED--THEN STATELIER DREW--	A CURIOUS CLOUD	1710	6
STATELY			
SOME WITH NEW--STATELY FEET--	MY WHEEL IS IN THE DARK!	10	12
AND TEN OF MY ONCE STATELY TOES	I COUNTED TILL THEY	36	7
TO INVEST EXISTENCE WITH A STATELY AIR,	TO VENERATE THE SIMPLE	57	7
NOR EVER GUESSED THE STATELY SAILS	'TWAS SUCH A LITTLE--	107	7
FOR 'TWAS TOO STATELY FOR AN EARL--	I MET A KING THIS	166	9
SCAN LIKE HIM, THE STATELY LANDSCAPE	IF THE FOOLISH, CALL	168	11
GOD IS A DISTANT--STATELY LOVER--	GOD IS A DISTANT--	357	1
COURT IS A STATELY PLACE--	I'M SAYING EVERY DAY	373	10
SEALED SO STATELY TIGHT--	SWEET--SAFE--HOUSES--	457	3
TO DEFACE THEIR STATELY TREASURES--	SWEET--SAFE--HOUSES--	457	12
SO STATELY THEY ASCEND--	YOU'VE SEEN BALLOONS SET	700	2
A STATELY--SHRIVEN--COMPANY--	THROUGH THE STRAIT PASS	792	5
TO THE STATELY HEART,	"FAITHFUL TO THE END"	1357	6
STATEMENT			
BRAVE--BROKEN HEARTED STATEMENT--	"THEY HAVE NOT CHOSEN ME	85	3
THE STATEMENT OF THE LORD	DO PEOPLE MOULDER	432	14
WHOSE STATEMENT IS NOT FOUND--	EXHILIRATION IS THE	1118	4
"WAS NOT" WAS ALL THE STATEMENT.	"WAS NOT" WAS ALL THE	1342	1
STATEMENTS			
AND STATEMENTS MAKES--	HIS MANSION IN THE POOL	1379	4
STATES			
WOOS, AS HE STATES US--BY HIS SON--	GOD IS A DISTANT--	357	2
STILL STATES TO DATES THAT HAVE FORGOT	SHE LAID HER DOCILE	1396	3

	FIRST LINE	POEM	LINE
STATESMAN'S			
A STATESMAN'S EMBRYO--	A FADED BOY--IN SALLOW	1524	4
STATION			
SLEEP IS THE STATION GRAND	SLEEP IS SUPPOSED TO BE	13	4
THE STATION OF THE PARTIES	I HAD SOME THINGS THAT I	116	9
AND "STATION", AND THE REST!	WAIT TILL THE MAJESTY OF	171	8
NO STATION IN THE DAY?	'TIS SUNRISE--LITTLE	908	2
GRACE OF WEALTH, AND GRACE OF STATION	ALL FORGOT FOR	966	5
SHE DID NOT KNOW HER STATION LOW	TO HER DERIDED HOME	1586	3
WE SAY AS OF A STATION	THE BLUNDER IS IN	1684	3
STATIONED			
SO STATIONED I COULD CATCH THE MINT	I WAS THE SLIGHTEST IN	486	5
BE STATIONED WITH THE CANDIDATES	SHALL I TAKE THEE, THE	1126	3
STATLIER			
THOUGH [WHILE] A STATLIER TALE	TELL AS A MARKSMAN--WERE	1152	6
STATURE			
NO STATURE HAS IT, LIKE A FOG	'TIS WHITER THAN AN	1482	3
EFFACE THE BURDEN [MONSTER / STATURE / SPECTRE / TROUBLE / . . .	THE PILE OF YEARS IS NOT	1507	7
THE STATURE OF THE EMPTY NEST	I SEE THEE CLEARER FOR	1666	7
STATURED			
WHOLE STATURED--BY THE SIDE	NOT ALL DIE EARLY, DYING	990	6
STATURES			
OUR STATURES TOUCH THE SKIES--	WE NEVER KNOW HOW HIGH	1176	4
STATUS			
SAHARA [CONTENTMENT / CREATION / HIS STATUS] DIES	UNTIL THE DESERT KNOWS	1291	6
STATUTE			
THE STATUTE IS MY LEARNED FRIEND	ALONE AND IN A	1167	21
STATUTES			
BUT STATUTES DO NOT MEDDLE	THROUGH THOSE OLD	1753	7
STAUNCH			
FOR SURETIES OF HER STAUNCH ESTATE	THESE ARE THE SIGNS TO	1077	9
STAY			
I STAY MINE ENEMY!	"SIC TRANSIT GLORIA	3	4
SOME THINGS THAT STAY THERE BE--	SOME THINGS THAT FLY	89	4
NEXT TIME, TO STAY!	JUST LOST, WHEN I WAS	160	12
TO STAY THE HOMESICK--HOMESICK FEET	TO LEARN THE TRANSPORT	167	5
CAN I, THEREFORE, STAY AWAY?	I'M THE LITTLE "HEART'S	176	4
IN HIS CHIMNEY CORNER STAY,	I'M THE LITTLE "HEART'S	176	6
WHO'D BE THE FOOL TO STAY?	THE WIND DID'NT COME	316	21
WOULD YOU BE THE FOOL TO STAY?	THE WIND DID'NT COME	316	23
WE--ARE THE BIRDS--THAT STAY.	'TIS NOT THAT DYING	335	8
I WISHED THEY'D STAY AWAY	I DREADED THAT FIRST	348	18
SO BABBLER, AND BOHEA--STAY THERE--	UNIT, LIKE DEATH, FOR	408	14
I LIKED TO STAY--	GOOD MORNING--MIDNIGHT--	425	6
WHO STAY [DWELL] UPON THE WALL	THOSE FAIR--FICTITIOUS	499	6
AND THEN--IT DOES'NT STAY--	I PRAYED, AT FIRST, A	576	21
THE WATERS--STROVE TO STAY.	THREE TIMES--WE PARTED--	598	4
TO STAY BEHIND--WITH JUST THE TOYS	YOU'LL FIND--IT WHEN YOU	610	15
MINE TO STAY--WHEN ALL HAVE WANDERED--	PROMISE THIS--WHEN YOU	648	9
TO REST [PAUSE]--TO REST [PAUSE / STAY / DWELL] WOULD BE	I MEANT TO FIND HER WHEN	718	10
IT PASSES AND WE STAY--	A LIGHT EXISTS IN SPRING	812	16
AFFLICTION CANNOT STAY	A NEARNESS TO	963	6
TO STAY AS IF, OR GO.	THE CRICKETS SANG	1104	8
THAT COME TO EARTH TO STAY,	TOO FEW THE MORNINGS BE,	1186	5
BUT IF THEY ONLY STAY	ARE FRIENDS DELIGHT OR	1199	4
NOT ONE BY HEAVEN DEFRAUDED STAY--	NOT ONE BY HEAVEN	1303	1
AND I DESIGNED TO STAY--	I SEND YOU A DECREPIT	1324	4
AS WE [YOU] WHO STAY, SUPPOSE--	PERHAPS THEY DO NOT GO	1399	2
AND DURING IT'S ELECTRIC GALE [SPELL / STAY / MIGHT / ACT / SPAN]--	WITH PINIONS OF DISDAIN	1431	7
FAME IS THE ONE THAT DOES NOT STAY--	FAME IS THE ONE THAT	1475	1
AND WHETHER SLEEP WILL STAY	ON THAT SPECIFIC PILLOW	1533	4
STAYED			
NO BLOSSOM STAYED AWAY	I DREADED THAT FIRST	348	22
I HELPED [STAYED] HIS FILM--WITH HYMN--	I ROSE--BECAUSE HE SANK	616	7
THEN THOUGHT OF US, AND STAYED.	SWEET, TO HAVE HAD THEM	901	9
HE STAYED AWAY A YEAR TO CALL	DEAR MARCH--COME IN--	1320	21
WHO LED US WHILE HE STAYED.	NOT THAT HE GOES--WE	1435	2
STAYING			
I KEEP IT, STAYING AT HOME--	SOME KEEP THE SABBATH	324	2
STAYING CANNOT [COULD NOT] CONFER	I'D RATHER RECOLLECT A	1349	6
STAYS			
DISPERSES, WHILE [AS] IT STAYS	IT SIFTS FROM LEADEN	311	V
TRUTH STAYS HERSELF--AND EVERY MAN	THE TRUTH--IS STIRLESS--	780	11
OR DAY SHE STAYS	THE DAY SHE GOES	1308	2
SORROW [AROMA]--NOW--IS POLITE [COURTEOUS]--AND STAYS--	SUMMER IS SHORTER THAN	1506	5
THAN BY A [THE] WICK THAT STAYS.	BY A DEPARTING LIGHT	1714	3
STEAD			
AND IN THE PLACE [STEAD] OF BLOOM	IT KNEW NO MEDICINE--	559	8
AND REDDER CHEEKED ONES--IN THEIR STEAD [PLACE]--	MY FIRST WELL DAY--SINCE	574	11
BUT IN THEIR ROOM [STEAD]--A SEA--DISPLAYED--	THEY CALLED ME TO THE	628	9
ANOTHER IN IT'S STEAD	IT BLOOMED AND DROPT, A	978	4
STEADFAST			
ROSES OF A STEADFAST SUMMER	THO' MY DESTINY BE	163	13
IN A STEADFAST LAND,	THO' MY DESTINY BE	163	14

	FIRST LINE	POEM	LINE
STEADFAST (CONTINUED)			
HOMESICK FOR STEADFAST HONEY--	THE NEAREST DREAM	319	11
A STEADFAST SOUTH--UPON THE SOUL--	I THINK TO LIVE--MAY BE	646	19
SOIL OF FLINT, IF STEADY [STEADFAST] TILLED--	SOIL OF FLINT, IF STEADY	681	1
THAT SINGLE--STEADFAST SIGH--	"I WANT"--IT PLEADED--	731	6
IT IS THE STEADFAST HEART,	'TIS NOT THE SWAYING	1597	2
STEADFASTNESS			
IT'S ONLY LORE--IT'S STEADFASTNESS--	'TWAS AWKWARD, BUT IT	973	3
STEADILY			
I READ MY SENTENCE--STEADILY--	I READ MY SENTENCE--	412	1
STEADILY--	INCONCEIVABLY SOLEMN!	582	11
STEADY			
STEADY--MY SOUL! WHAT ISSUES	A DAY! HELP! HELP!	42	7
THAT'S A STEADY POSTURE--	IF YOUR NERVE, DENY YOU	292	5
TILL SUNDOWN CREPT--A STEADY TIDE--	FROM COCOON FORTH A	354	22
BUT BLANK--AND STEADY WILDERNESS--	LIKE EYES THAT LOOKED ON	458	3
AND WALK STEADY, AWAY,	TO PUT THIS WORLD DOWN,	527	2
WITH STEADY--DRIFTING--[SUDDEN--BLINDING] GRAINS	I CROSS TILL I AM WEARY	550	7
FIXED FULL, AND STEADY, ON HIS OWN	I PRAYED, AT FIRST, A	576	7
IT ISN'T STEADY--THO'--	I PRAYED, AT FIRST, A	576	V 21
GOES SAFELY [STEADY]--WHERE AN OPEN EYE--	THERE IS A PAIN--SO	599	7
I SANG FIRM--EVEN--[STRAIGHT--STEADY] CHANTS--	I ROSE--BECAUSE HE SANK	616	6
SOIL OF FLINT, IF STEADY [STEADFAST] TILLED--	SOIL OF FLINT, IF STEADY	681	1
THE MARTYRS--EVEN [STEADY]--TROD.	THROUGH THE STRAIT PASS	792	2
HER STEADY BOAT BE SEEN--	SHE STAKED HER FEATHERS	798	6
THOUGH RIME BY RIME, THE STEADY FROST	NO NOTICE GAVE SHE, BUT	804	7
WAS STEADY AS THE SUN	I MADE SLOW RICHES BUT	843	2
STEAL			
LIKE HER THE EVENINGS STEAL	LIKE HER THE SAINTS	60	4
MY FIGURES FILE [CIPHERS STEAL] AWAY.	LOW AT MY PROBLEM	69	6
SO SILVER STEAL A HUNDRED FLUTES	WE SHOULD NOT MIND SO	81	7
WE NEARER STEAL TO THEE!	THE DAISY FOLLOWS SOFT	106	9
WHILE THE AGES STEAL--	JUST LOST, WHEN I WAS	160	17
MINE--LONG AS [WHILE] AGES STEAL!	MINE--BY THE RIGHT OF	528	9
TO STEAL SECURER [AT SUNRISE] THENCE	CONTAINED IN THIS SHORT	1165	4
ALTHOUGH HE SEEM TO STEAL	NOT ONE BY HEAVEN	1303	2
STEALING			
A STEALING THAT IS NOT A STEALTH	THERE COMES A WARNING	1536	3
STEALS			
THE MOWER'S METRE--STEALS	I'M SORRY FOR THE DEAD--	529	12
UPON THE IGNORANCE STEALS--	"HEAVEN" HAS DIFFERENT	575	8
STEALTH			
A STEALING THAT IS NOT A STEALTH	THERE COMES A WARNING	1536	3
THE SACRED STEALTH [HAPPY GUILT] OF BOY AND GIRL	BLISS IS THE PLAYTHING	1553	3
WITH ECSTASIES OF STEALTH	A WORD MADE FLESH IS	1651	6
STEALTHILY			
GLID STEALTHILY ALONG--	THROUGH LANE IT LAY--	9	8
TO STEALTHILY BELONG?	FEW, YET ENOUGH,	1596	5
STEALTH'S			
STEALTH'S--SLOW--	I KNOW SOME LONELY	289	32
STEALTHY			
STEALTHY COCOON, WHY HIDE YOU SO	COCOON ABOVE! COCOON	129	2
IT IS A STEALTHY WOOING	DEATH IS THE SUPPLE	1445	3
IT STOLE ALONG SO STEALTHY	IT STOLE ALONG SO	1457	1
STEAM			
FLITS STEAM.	BANISH AIR FROM AIR--	854	12
STEED			
HIS AMPLE--PLODDING STEED	LIKE BROOMS OF STEEL	1252	9
STEEL			
THE TRAMPLED STEEL THAT SPRINGS!	A WOUNDED DEER--LEAPS	165	6
TRY--CAN YOU LIFT THE HASPS OF STEEL!	HOW MANY TIMES THESE LOW	187	4
IS LIKE A FACE OF STEEL--	THAT AFTER HORROR--THAT	286	12
LIDS OF STEEL--ON LIDS OF MARBLE--	SWEET--SAFE--HOUSES--	457	4
AS THIS PHANTASM [COMPANION] STEEL--	A PRISON GETS TO BE A	652	21
THIGH [EYE] OF GRANITE--AND THEW [EAR]--OF STEEL--	AH, TENERIFFE!	666	7
AS IT WERE ROCKED IN STEEL	FAITH--IS THE PIERLESS	915	6
WITH ARMS OF STEEL AT EITHER SIDE--	FAITH--IS THE PIERLESS	915	7
LIKE BROOMS OF STEEL	LIKE BROOMS OF STEEL	1252	1
STEEL'S			
THAT--IS NOT STEEL'S AFFAIR--	SHE DEALT HER PRETTY	479	6
STEEP			
TOO STEEP FOR LOOKING UP--	A PRISON GETS TO BE A	652	28
ROUND THE STEEP AIR--	OUT OF SIGHT? WHAT OF	703	4
TO STEEP IT'S SHAPE AWAY--	BEREAVED OF ALL, I WENT	784	14
IF I PROVE IT STEEP--	UP LIFE'S HILL WITH MY	1010	2
STEEPEST			
BUT NEVER I MIND THE STEEPEST [BRIDGES]--	TIE THE STRINGS TO MY	279	9
STEEPLE			
TOUCHING THE ROOF [FLOODING THE STEEPLE] AND TINTING THE BARN	BLAZING IN GOLD AND	228	6
WITH AN OCCASIONAL STEEPLE--	THE WIND DID'NT COME	316	19
AND POSSIBLY A STEEPLE--	HAVE ANY LIKE MYSELF	736	23
THE BELL WITHIN THE STEEPLE WILD	THERE CAME A WIND LIKE A	1593	13
AND BOUGH AND STEEPLE	TO-DAY OR THIS NOON	1702	6
STEEPLE'S			
AND JUST THE STEEPLE'S FINGER--	THE ANGLE OF A LANDSCAPE	375	19

	FIRST LINE	POEM	LINE
STEEPLES			
FROM STEEPLES IN MY SOUL!	I HAVE A KING, WHO DOES	103	12
OH BELLS, THAT IN THE STEEPLES BE!	'TIS SO MUCH JOY! 'TIS	172	14
HOW THE OLD STEEPLES HAND THE SCARLET	HOW THE OLD MOUNTAINS	291	5
THE STEEPLES SWAM IN AMETHYST--	I'LL TELL YOU HOW THE	318	3
HOW STILL THE BELLS IN STEEPLES STAND	HOW STILL THE BELLS IN	1008	1
STEERSMAN			
FOR HELMSMAN [STEERSMAN] WAS THE BEE	A SOFT SEA WASHED AROUND	1198	6
STEM			
DRAW ME A ROBIN--ON A STEM--	MAKE ME A PICTURE OF THE	188	5
AND STRUT UPON MY STEM--	OF BRONZE--AND BLAZE--	290	11
TO [ON] STUMP, AND STACK--AND STEM--	IT SIFTS FROM LEADEN	311	13
HE SHIFTS THE STEM--A LITTLE--	A SOLEMN THING WITHIN	483	11
AND [OR] SOARED UPON A STEM	THE TREES LIKE TASSELS--	606	22
ADJUSTED BY A STEM--	YOU'LL KNOW HER--BY HER	634	6
JUST A SEA--WITH A STEM--	BY MY WINDOW HAVE I FOR	797	2
NEVER BUD FROM A STEM	AND THIS OF ALL MY HOPES	913	5
AND STEM [STEMS] AN ENEMY	WHAT MYSTERY PERVADES A	1400	V
EXPIRES IN A STEM.	IT'S LITTLE ETHER HOOD	1501	8
THE STEM OF A DEPARTED FLOWER	THE STEM OF A DEPARTED	1520	1
THE JOY THAT HAS NO STEM NOR CORE,	THE JOY THAT HAS NO STEM	1744	1
STEMLESS			
OR LIKE A STEMLESS FLOWER--	I WATCHED THE MOON	629	17
STEMS			
THE FLOWERS WOULD SLUMBER ON [SLEEP UPON--] THEIR STEMS--	MY FAITH IS LARGER THAN	766	11
AND STEM [STEMS] AN ENEMY	WHAT MYSTERY PERVADES A	1400	V
STEP			
AND STEP [WADE] IN LIBERTY!	WHAT IF I SAY I SHALL	277	6
STEP MARTIAL--AT MY CRUCIFIXION--	UNTO LIKE STORY--TROUBLE	295	15
HE'LL TAKE IT--SCAN IT--STEP ASIDE--	THE FACE I CARRY WITH ME	336	9
A MOMENT--WE UNCERTAIN STEP	WE GROW ACCUSTOMED TO	419	5
BUT THEN HIS HOUSE--IS BUT A STEP--	YOU LOVE THE LORD--YOU	487	7
AND THEN--PRODIGIOUS STEP	I LIKE TO SEE IT LAP	585	4
SO MEMORY CAN STEP	THERE IS A PAIN--SO	599	4
JOY TO HAVE PERISHED EVERY STEP--	JOY TO HAVE MERITED THE	788	3
THEN AS HORIZONS STEP	A LIGHT EXISTS IN SPRING	812	13
TILL HIS BEST STEP APPROACHING	I SING TO USE THE	850	5
IF MY NEWEST STEP	UP LIFE'S HILL WITH MY	1010	4
STEP LIGHTLY ON THIS NARROW SPOT--	STEP LIGHTLY ON THIS	1183	1
STEP LOFTY, FOR THIS NAME BE TOLD	STEP LIGHTLY ON THIS	1183	5
ART THOU A STEP OR NOT?	OH SHADOW ON THE GRASS,	1187	2
BUT I TELL YOU EVERY STEP IS A TROUGH [SLUICE]--	FLOSS WONT SAVE YOU FROM	1322	5
. . . BURST / FLAGS / STEP / TICK / SHOUTS / PINK / RED / . . .	ONE JOY OF SO MUCH	1420	6
THE SEA COMES LAST--STEP MERRY FEET	I DID NOT REACH THEE	1664	14
WE STEP LIKE PLUSH	I DID NOT REACH THEE	1664	28
A LAVA STEP AT ANY TIME	VOLCANOES BE IN SICILY	1705	5
STEPHEN			
OF STEPHEN--OR OF PAUL--	IT ALWAYS FELT TO ME--A	597	10
STEPPED			
AND STEPPED LIKE FLAKES OF SNOW--	THE ONLY GHOST I EVER	274	4
THEN--STEPPED MORE FAST--	'TWAS THE OLD--ROAD--	344	7
AND "WAS IT CONSCIOUS--WHEN IT STEPPED	I AM ALIVE--I GUESS--	470	15
THEN STEPPED STRAIGHT THROUGH THE FIRMAMENT	TWO BUTTERFLIES WENT OUT	533	3
AND SO I STEPPED [STOOD] UPON THE NORTH	MY PERIOD HAD COME FOR	564	7
I STEPPED FROM PLANK TO PLANK	I STEPPED FROM PLANK TO	875	1
STEPPED WITH SO GAY A FOOT	AND THIS OF ALL MY HOPES	913	6
LIGHTLY STEPPED A YELLOW STAR	LIGHTLY STEPPED A YELLOW	1672	1
STEPPING			
STEPPING TO INCORPOREAL TUNES	HOW LONESOME THE WIND	1418	6
AND WHILE BY STEPPING [STANDING] ON MY HEART	THE PILE OF YEARS IS NOT	1507	5
STEPS			
PATIENT--UPON THE STEPS [MAT]--UNTIL THEN--	JUST SO--JESUS--RAPS--	317	10
AND LIFE STEPS ALMOST STRAIGHT.	WE GROW ACCUSTOMED TO	419	20
THE STEPS GROW THICKER--IN THE HALL--	I THINK THE LONGEST HOUR	635	11
I CROSS THE HALL WITH MINGLED STEPS--	AGAIN--HIS VOICE IS AT	663	9
'TIS FIRST [YOU SEE] HE STEPS UPON THE VANE--	MY FAITH IS LARGER THAN	766	5
LONG STEPS ACROSS THE FEATURES TOOK	TWO TRAVELLERS PERISHING	933	9
I KNOW SUSPENSE--IT STEPS SO TERSE	I KNOW SUSPENSE--IT	1285	1
HOW SOFT A CATERPILLAR STEPS--	HOW SOFT A CATERPILLAR	1448	1
STEPT			
THE DAYS--TO MIGHTY METRES STEPT--	I THINK I WAS ENCHANTED	593	17
AS ONE THAT DRUNKEN--STEPT--	IT TOSSED--AND TOSSED--	723	6
STERILE			
IS STERILE BORNE TO SOME--	THE VOICE THAT STANDS	1189	2
WITHOUT THE STERILE PERQUISITE,	TO LOSE THEE--SWEETER	1754	7
STERILITY			
BUT FOLIAGE OF STERILITY	THEY TALK AS SLOW AS	1697	3
STERLING			
ALTHOUGH BY NATURE'S STERLING WATCH	THE SYMPTOM OF THE GALE	1327	11
STERN			
AND WE APPROACH [ACCOST] HIM--STERN--	THE LIGHTNING PLAYETH--	630	4
WE STERN AND FORMER KNEW	THE SNOW THAT NEVER	1133	10
STERNEST			
OF DEATH THE STERNEST [SHARPEST] FUNCTION [FEATURE]	TO DISAPPEAR ENHANCES--	1209	13
STERNLY			
FIGHT STERNLY IN A DYING EYE	DYING! TO BE AFRAID OF	831	10

	FIRST LINE	POEM	LINE
STICKS			
BUT SAY MY APRON BRING THE STICKS	ALTHOUGH I PUT AWAY HIS	366	28
STIFF			
IN DEATH'S--STIFF--STARE--	I KNOW THAT HE EXISTS.	338	12
THE STIFF HEART QUESTIONS WAS IT HE, THAT BORE,	AFTER GREAT PAIN, A	341	3
THAT HELD HIS FOREHEAD STIFF--	I ROSE--BECAUSE HE SANK	616	9
'TWAS SUCH AN EVENING BRIGHT AND STIFF	THAT ODD OLD MAN IS DEAD	1130	3
TOO STIFF TO BENDED BE,	TOO COLD IS THIS	1135	3
STIFFEN			
BUT--THE ECHOES--STIFFEN [SILENCE--STIFFENS]--	SAFE IN THEIR ALABASTER	216	V
STIFFENS			
BUT--THE ECHOES--STIFFEN [SILENCE--STIFFENS]--	SAFE IN THEIR ALABASTER	216	V
THAT STIFFENS QUIETLY TO QUARTZ--	I KNOW A PLACE WHERE	337	11
STIFFLY			
THE MINISTER--GOES STIFFLY IN--	THERE'S BEEN A DEATH, IN	389	13
STIFFNESS			
IS QUAINTEST DISTANCE [STIFFNESS]--NOW--	THIS THAT WOULD GREET--	778	2
STIFLED			
CANNOT BE STIFLED--WITH NARCOTIC--	CIVILIZATION--SPURNS--	492	12
STIGMA			
ITS STIGMA [FORFEIT] DEIFIED	ONE CROWN THAT NO ONE	1735	4
STILE			
OVER THE STILE OF "PEARL".	"ARCTURUS" IS HIS OTHER	70	33
THERE SEEMED A PURPLE STILE	I'LL TELL YOU HOW THE	318	10
STILL			
YET THEY ARE SLEEPING STILL,--	"SIC TRANSIT GLORIA	3	48
AND STILL HER HUM	ONE SISTER HAVE I IN OUR	14	17
STILL IN HER EYE	ONE SISTER HAVE I IN OUR	14	20
STILL, HAD IT SUCH A VALUE	I HAD A GUINEA GOLDEN--	23	5
STILL, FOR MY MISSING TROUBADOUR	I HAD A GUINEA GOLDEN--	23	15
THY MUSIC STILL, WHEN WHIPPOWIL	SUMMER FOR THEE, GRANT I	31	3
AND WHY IT WAS SO STILL--	I OFTEN PASSED THE	51	4
WERE UNDEFEATED STILL?	DELAYED TILL SHE HAD	58	12
ARGUES THE ASTER STILL--	LIKE HER THE SAINTS	60	10
WITHOUT COMMANDER! COUNTLESS! STILL!	SOME RAINBOW--COMING	64	19
AND YET, HOW STILL THE LANDSCAPE STANDS!	A LADY RED--AMID THE	74	13
SO STILL--SO COOL--	OUR LIVES ARE SWISS--	80	2
HOW STILL THE RIDDLE LIES!	SOME THINGS THAT FLY	89	9
AND STILL THE PENSIVE SPRING RETURNS--	NEW FEET WITHIN MY	99	7
AND STILL THE PUNCTUAL SNOW!	NEW FEET WITHIN MY	99	8
AND STILL WITHIN A SUMMER'S NIGHT	A SOMETHING IN A	122	7
STILL CHAFES IT'S NARROW BED--	A SOMETHING IN A	122	15
STILL REARS THE EAST HER AMBER FLAG--	A SOMETHING IN A	122	16
GUIDES STILL THE SUN ALONG THE CRAG	A SOMETHING IN A	122	17
STILL, IS THE BUSTLE IN THE BROOK--	BESIDES THE AUTUMN POETS	131	9
THE HANDS STILL HUG THE TARDY GLASS--	I BRING AN UNACCUSTOMED	132	8
AND NOBODY KNOWS, SO STILL IT FLOWS,	HAVE YOU GOT A BROOK IN	136	5
STILL, MY LITTLE GIPSEY BEING	THO' MY DESTINY BE	163	5
STILL, MY LITTLE SUNBURNT BOSOM	THO' MY DESTINY BE	163	7
AND THEN THE BRAKE IS STILL!	A WOUNDED DEER--LEAPS	165	4
USUALLY SO STILL--	I HAVE NEVER SEEN	175	4
WITH EYES IN DEATH--STILL BEGGING RAISED--	TWO SWIMMERS WRESTLED ON	201	8
AND STILL--MY HEART--MY EYE OUTWEIGHS--	MY EYE IS FULLER THAN MY	202	3
AND STILL, SHE PLIES HER SPOTTED BROOMS, [THRIFT]	SHE SWEEPS WITH	219	9
AND STILL THE APRONS FLY, [SCENE PREVAILS]	SHE SWEEPS WITH	219	10
WHEN KATIE KNEELS, THEIR LOVING HANDS STILL CLASP HER PIOUS KNEE--	WHEN KATIE WALKS, THIS	222	3
SHALL STILL MY TRANSPORT BE--	IF I'M LOST--NOW--	256	3
AND THEN--THE WHARF IS STILL!	WHERE SHIPS OF PURPLE--	265	4
STILL TO ANTICIPATE [CONJECTURE]--WERE NO LIMIT--	BOUND--A TROUBLE--	269	V
THAT JUST NOW DANGLED STILL--	A CLOCK STOPPED--	287	5
AND SHAME [SCORN] WENT STILL [DUMB]--	UNTO LIKE STORY--TROUBLE	295	8
THE UNIVERSE--IS [FIRMAMENTS--ARE] STILL--	HE FUMBLES AT YOUR SOUL	315	14
IN [ON] FAR [STILL] OCTOBER AIR.	THERE ARE TWO RIPENINGS	332	8
STILL SPARKLING THROUGH	SHE LAY AS IF AT PLAY	369	11
MY BRAIN KEEPS GIGGLING--STILL.	THE FIRST DAY'S NIGHT	410	16
STILL TO SHOW--HOW RICH I GO--	I'LL CLUTCH--AND CLUTCH	427	22
RISE--STILL THE DUNCE--	KNOWS HOW TO FORGET!	433	7
HE VISITED--STILL FLITTING--	THE WIND--TAPPED LIKE A	436	17
AND MOCKERY--WAS STILL--	GOD MADE A LITTLE	442	8
STILL TOILING AT THE CHEEK	A SOLEMN THING WITHIN	483	8
IS DIFFICULT, AND STILL--	TO MAKE ONE'S TOILETTE--	485	4
HOW DUMB [STILL] THE DANCER LIES--	AS FAR FROM PITY, AS	496	10
NARCOTICS CANNOT STILL THE TOOTH [MOUSE]	THIS WORLD IS NOT	501	19
AND STILL IT HURT YOU, AS SOME BIRD	HER SMILE WAS SHAPED	514	3
STILL--STILL--MY HANDS ABOVE	ME PROVE IT NOW--WHOEVER	537	10
STILL--STILL--MY HANDS ABOVE	ME PROVE IT NOW--WHOEVER	537	10
STILL THE ETERNAL RULE	'TIS ONE BY ONE--THE	545	12
DISCERNED--STILL WITHOLDEN	TRUST IN THE UNEXPECTED	555	7
OR WOULD THEY GO ON ACHING STILL	I MEASURE EVERY GRIEF I	561	21
STILL FASCINATED TO PRESUME	I MEASURE EVERY GRIEF I	561	39
STILL [HOW / SO] FABLE--IN THE ISLES OF SPICE--	I GAVE MYSELF TO HIM--	580	11
A STILL--VOLCANO [VOLCANIC]--LIFE--	A STILL--VOLCANO--LIFE--	601	1
WAS SUCH REMAINING [STILL DWELLING] THERE?"	I YEARS HAD BEEN FROM	609	8
BECAUSE THEY LIKED ME "STILL"--	THEY SHUT ME UP IN PROSE	613	4
STILL! COULD THEMSELF HAVE PEEPED--	THEY SHUT ME UP IN PROSE	613	5

	FIRST LINE	POEM	LINE
STILL (CONTINUED)			
STILL SURMISE I STITCH--	DONT PUT UP MY THREAD &	617	20
TO STILL IT'S NOISY [HELP IT'S VACANT] HANDS--	AT LEISURE IS THE SOUL	618	8
STILL SECURE--	ONLY GOD--DETECT THE	626	6
TO KEEP THE OTHER--STILL--	YOU'LL KNOW HER--BY HER	634	28
JUST [STILL] TO FOLLOW YOUR DEAR FEATURE--	PROMISE THIS--WHEN YOU	648	29
BUT STILL,	EMBARRASSMENT OF ONE	662	6
STILL--CLAD IN YOUR MAIL OF ICES--	AH, TENERIFFE!	666	6
I'M KNEELING--[WE'RE PLEADING] STILL--	AH, TENERIFFE!	666	10
EXPRESSED--OR STILL--	EACH LIFE CONVERGES TO	680	2
THE SUN KEPT SETTING--SETTING--STILL	THE SUN KEPT SETTING--	692	1
THE DUSK KEPT DROPPING--DROPPING--STILL	THE SUN KEPT SETTING--	692	5
MY FEET KEPT DROWSING--DROWSING--STILL	THE SUN KEPT SETTING--	692	9
SUCH AS THESE--ARE STILL--	LIFE, AND DEATH, AND	706	2
REMOTEST--STILL--	THE SUNRISE RUNS FOR	710	6
MY STRONG MADONNAS--CHERISH STILL--	SWEET MOUNTAINS--YE TELL	722	7
PRECIOUS TO ME--SHE STILL SHALL BE--	PRECIOUS TO ME--SHE	727	1
STILL AT THE EGG-LIFE--	LET US PLAY YESTERDAY--	728	13
ONLY ME--[STILL MYSELF-- / ME ALONE] WAS STILL--	WHEN I HOPED, I	768	16
ONLY ME--[STILL MYSELF-- / ME ALONE] WAS STILL--	WHEN I HOPED, I	768	16
BRINGING STILL MY "PLEA FOR CULTURE."	THE LUXURY TO APPREHEND	815	V
INHABITANTS SO STILL	WHO OCCUPIES THIS HOUSE?	892	14
I RECOLLECT IT--HOW STILL--	THE FIRST DAY THAT I WAS	902	2
WAS STILL--	THE FIRST DAY THAT I WAS	902	6
STILL--JUST AS EASY, IF IT BE THY WILL	ONLY A SHRINE, BUT MINE	918	10
STILL [YET] TO BE EXPLAINED.	THAT IS SOLEMN WE HAVE	934	8
I FIND MYSELF STILL SOFTLY SEARCHING	A LOSS OF SOMETHING EVER	959	11
NOT YET SUSPECTED--[STILL UNSUSPECTED] BUT FOR FLASH [FORK]--	THE SOUL'S DISTINCT	974	7
BUT IT'S STILL APPRECIATION	GRATITUDE--IS NOT THE	989	3
BIND ME--I STILL CAN SING--	BIND ME--I STILL CAN	1005	1
STILL THINE.	BIND ME--I STILL CAN	1005	6
HOW STILL THE BELLS IN STEEPLES STAND	HOW STILL THE BELLS IN	1008	1
I'VE STILL A CHANCE TO STRAIN	I'VE DROPPED MY BRAIN--	1046	16
AND ARTISAN LIES [SMALL ESTATE STANDS--] STILL--	DEW--IS THE FRESHET IN	1097	4
A FIRM APPEARANCE STILL INFLATES	WE DO NOT KNOW THE TIME	1106	5
THE SOUL RETURNING SOFT AT NIGHT [STILL BY DAWN / LOTH BY DAWN]	CONTAINED IN THIS SHORT	1165	3
MIGHT YET [STILL] REPLY [DESTROY].	THE PAST IS SUCH A	1203	8
OR IS ENTOMBED SO STILL	A DEED KNOCKS FIRST AT	1216	6
IS LICENSED TO BE STILL.	IT'S HOUR WITH ITSELF	1225	8
STILL STATES TO DATES THAT HAVE FORGOT	SHE LAID HER DOCILE	1396	3
AND THEN--THE STREETS [AIR] STOOD STILL--	IT SOUNDED AS IF THE	1397	2
THE TREES WERE BRIGHT AND STILL--	THE ROAD WAS LIT WITH	1450	2
TIS [IT] STILL IS AN ASSISTANCE	I SAW THE WIND WITHIN	1502	V
I STILL CAN REACH [TOUCH] THE TOP	THE PILE OF YEARS IS NOT	1507	6
AND STILL ABIDE--	THE THINGS THAT NEVER	1515	4
NOT SEEING, STILL WE KNOW--	NOT SEEING, STILL WE	1518	1
HAS STILL A SILENT RANK.	THE STEM OF A DEPARTED	1520	2
HE IS JUST AS [STILL MORE] HIGH--	FOLLOW WISE ORION	1538	4
AND RUMBLES STILL, THOUGH TORRID NOONS	THE FARTHEST THUNDER	1581	3
THEY ARE THE SPIRITS STILL VACATION	THE LASSITUDES OF	1592	3
BUT WATERS THAT ARE STILL	DECLAIMING WATERS NONE	1595	2
THAT THEY ARE STILL THE DEEP,	THOUGH THE GREAT WATERS	1599	2
TO ONE A WONDER STILL	THE GOING FROM A WORLD	1603	2
WE MAKE THE WISE DISTINCTION [SAGE DECISION] STILL,	WE SEND THE WAVE TO FIND	1604	5
A CRESCENT STILL ABIDES,	EACH THAT WE LOSE TAKES	1605	2
STILL OWN THEE--STILL THOU ART	STILL OWN THEE--STILL	1633	1
STILL OWN THEE--STILL THOU ART	STILL OWN THEE--STILL	1633	1
GOODNIGHT, I STILL REPLY--	SOME SAY GOODNIGHT--AT	1739	4
STILLER			
IT'S STILLER THAN THE SUNDOWN.	I OFTEN PASSED THE	51	9
STILLER [SWIFTER] THAN A FLEET!	DUST IS THE ONLY SECRET	153	12
STILLER--THAN THE FIELDS	I WENT TO HEAVEN--	374	5
'TWAS STILLER--THOUGH THE FIRST	THE FIRST DAY THAT I WAS	902	5
STILLEST			
THINE IS THE STILLEST NIGHT	LET DOWN THE BARS, OH	1065	5
STILLNESS			
IF THE STILLNESS IS VOLCANIC	I HAVE NEVER SEEN	175	9
THE STILLNESS IN THE ROOM	I HEARD A FLY BUZZ--WHEN	465	2
WAS LIKE THE STILLNESS IN THE AIR--	I HEARD A FLY BUZZ--WHEN	465	3
AND SHADE IS ALL THAT DEVASTATES THE STILLNESS	THESE FEVERED DAYS--TO	1441	3
STILLS			
THEN STILLS IT'S ARTISANS [MYRMIDONS]--LIKE GHOSTS [SWANS]--	IT SIFTS FROM LEADEN	311	19
STIMULANTS			
EXCEPT AS STIMULANTS--IN	DID OUR BEST MOMENT LAST	393	5
STIMULATE			
TO STIMULATE A MAN	EXHILIRATION--IS WITHIN	383	9
IT HELPS TO STIMULATE THE FAITH	'TIS CUSTOMARY AS WE	440	3
'TIS HIS TO STIMULATE THE EARTH--	TO INTERRUPT HIS YELLOW	591	9
SO SPICES--STIMULATE THE TIME	UNTO MY BOOKS--SO GOOD	604	7
THE HEART--TO STIMULATE THE EYE	THE BIRDS REPORTED FROM	743	11
THE WICKS THEY STIMULATE--	THE POETS LIGHT BUT	883	3
MAY STIMULATE [CONSECRATE] AN EYE	A WORD DROPPED CARELESS	1261	2
INTRENCHMENTS STIMULATE [INTRENCHMENT	WHAT MYSTERY PERVADES A	1400	V

	FIRST LINE	POEM	LINE
STIMULATE (CONTINUED)			
STIMULATE] A FRIEND			
INTRENCHMENTS STIMULATE [INTRENCHMENT STIMULATE] A FRIEND	WHAT MYSTERY PERVADES A	1400	V
STIMULATED			
STIMULATED--BY THE CONTRAST--	SMILING BACK FROM	385	11
STIMULUS			
HOW POWERFUL THE STIMULUS	STRONG DRAUGHTS OF THEIR	711	7
THE STIMULUS THERE IS	I LIVED ON DREAD--	770	3
ASSISTED BY IT'S STIMULUS--	SUCH IS THE FORCE OF	787	3
THE STIMULUS, BEYOND THE GRAVE	THE STIMULUS, BEYOND THE	1001	1
SUSCEPTIVE--STIMULUS--	REPORTLESS SUBJECTS, TO	1048	6
TO MAKE ROUTINE A STIMULUS	TO MAKE ROUTINE A	1196	1
STING			
YOU STING--AGAIN!	YOU LOVE ME--YOU ARE	156	19
A BRIEF CAMPAIGN OF STING AND SWEET	A LITTLE BREAD--A CRUST	159	8
THAT WILL NOT STATE--IT'S STING.	IF YOU WERE COMING IN	511	20
TASTES DEATH--THE FIRST--TO HAND [PASS / PROVE] THE STING	LOVE--IS THAT LATER	924	5
IT HAS A STING--	FAME IS A BEE.	1763	3
STINGING			
TO SIMULATE--IS STINGING WORK--	I TIE MY HAT--I CREASE	443	19
STINGS			
JUST WHERE THE HECTIC STINGS!	A WOUNDED DEER--LEAPS	165	8
STINT			
POURED THEE, WITHOUT A STINT--	DOUBT ME! MY DIM	275	4
WITHOUT A STINT--WITHOUT A BLAME,	YOUR RICHES--TAUGHT ME--	299	19
THE NARROW ROUND--THE STINT--	A PRISON GETS TO BE A	652	25
HOW DARE I, THEREFORE, STINT A FAITH	MY FAITH IS LARGER THAN	766	13
NONE CAN EXPERIENCE STINT	NONE CAN EXPERIENCE	771	1
BY STINT [END]--REWARDED WORK--	THE SERVICE WITHOUT HOPE	779	4
THE STINT NOR THE DIVINITY	YOUR THOUGHTS DONT HAVE	1452	V 8
STINTLESS			
ALL FORESTS--STINTLESS STARS--	BEFORE I GOT MY EYE PUT	327	11
STIPULATE			
WE STIPULATE--TILL PITYING SNOWS	'TIS NOT THAT DYING	335	11
IT'S LITTLE FATE TO STIPULATE--	THE MANNER OF IT'S DEATH	468	7
BUT JUST FOR ONE--TO STIPULATE--	I MEANT TO HAVE BUT	476	7
STIPULUS			
WITH JUST THIS STIPULUS [RESERVATION]--	YOU SAID THAT I "WAS	738	17
STIR			
SHE WILL STIR HER PINIONS	IT DID NOT SURPRISE ME--	39	3
NEW FINGERS STIR THE SOD--	NEW FEET WITHIN MY	99	2
TRY--CAN YOU STIR THE AWFUL RIVET--	HOW MANY TIMES THESE LOW	187	3
TILL I STIR [GROPE / START], AND WEEP--	MANY A PHRASE HAS THE	276	12
IT WILL NOT STIR FOR DOCTOR'S--	A CLOCK STOPPED--	287	10
A PAIR OF SPECTACLES AJAR JUST STIR--	I KNOW SOME LONELY	289	19
I GOT SO I COULD STIR THE BOX--	I GOT SO I COULD HEAR	293	9
RENOWNED TO EASE [STIR] EXTREMITY--	I GOT SO I COULD HEAR	293	15
AND STIR ALL DAY TO PRETTY TUNES	THE GRASS SO LITTLE HAS	333	5
THESE--NEVER STIR AT ALL--	THE ANGLE OF A LANDSCAPE	375	20
WOULD STIR HIS SLOW CONCEPTION--	REMOVED FROM ACCIDENT OF	424	9
WHOSE RARE--CELESTIAL--STIR--	I WOULD NOT PAINT--A	505	6
HER JAWS STIR--TWITCHING [MOUTH STIRS--LONGING]--HUNGRY--	SHE SIGHTS A BIRD--SHE	507	5
WHEN TOO APPALLED TO STIR--	THE SOUL HAS BANDAGED	512	2
BUT STROVE TO STIR THE LIFELESS [FLICKERING] FAN	THREE TIMES--WE PARTED--	598	3
BY STRETCH OF LIMB--OR STIR OF LID--	A LONG--LONG SLEEP--A	654	3
BUT IT STIR--ALONE--	GROWTH OF MAN--LIKE	750	4
NONE STIR [HARM] THE SECOND TIME--	MY LIFE HAD STOOD--A	754	18
JUST LONG ENOUGH FOR HOPE TO TEAZE [STIR]--	THE WHOLE OF IT CAME NOT	762	7
NONE STIR ABROAD	SPRING IS THE PERIOD	844	6
TILL SUDDEN I PERCEIVED IT STIR--	I HAD A DAILY BLISS	1057	3
SOFT STIRS THE NEWS [STIR THE FLAKES] OF LIGHT	THE SMOULDERING EMBERS	1132	5
YET EVEN THIS SHALL ROUSE [STIR] ITSELF	A STAGNANT PLEASURE LIKE	1281	7
THAT SHORT--POTENTIAL STIR	THAT SHORT--POTENTIAL	1307	1
WILL GLEAM [STIR] AND UNDERSTAND	LONG YEARS APART--CAN	1383	8
THEY WILL NOT STIR FOR BLOWS--	TIME'S WILY CHARGERS	1458	4
JAMAICAS OF REMEMBRANCE [PROSPECTIVE] STIR	A DRUNKARD CANNOT MEET A	1628	5
TO STIR WOULD BE TO SLIP--	A PIT--BUT HEAVEN OVER	1712	5
STIRLESS			
THE LUNGS ARE STIRLESS--MUST DESCEND	I BREATHED ENOUGH TO	272	5
THE TRUTH--IS STIRLESS--	THE TRUTH--IS STIRLESS--	780	1
STIRRED			
HE STIRRED HIS VELVET HEAD	A BIRD CAME DOWN THE	328	12
AND NOT A SINEW--STIRRED--COULD HELP,	'TWAS LIKE A MAELSTROM,	414	14
OR ARCTIC CREATURES, DIMLY STIRRED--	LIKE FLOWERS, THAT HEARD	513	7
STIRRED BY A FRIEND'S HAND--	THE WORLD--FEELS DUSTY	715	7
A SENSE THAT SMOTE AND STIRRED--	I'VE DROPPED MY BRAIN--	1046	10
WHEN THE WINDS OF WILL ARE STIRRED	REVOLUTION IS THE POD	1082	3
THE SITES OF CENTRES STIRRED	LIKE RAIN IT SOUNDED	1235	14
IN ANY FOREST STIRRED	A WIND THAT ROSE	1259	3
STIRREST			
THOU SETTEST [STIRREST] EARTHQUAKE IN THE SOUTH--	AT LEAST--TO PRAY--IS	502	5
STIRRING			
OR STIRRING HOUSE BELOW--	ON SUCH A NIGHT, OR SUCH	146	14
WHEN, STIRRING, FOR BELIEF'S DELIGHT,	HER SWEET WEIGHT ON MY	518	3

	FIRST LINE	POEM	LINE
STONES			
THE STONES A'CHASE--	ONE NEED NOT BE A	670	10
AND GO TO PIECES ON THE STONES [IN THE DITCH]	IT DROPPED SO LOW--IN MY	747	3
STOOD			
HE STOOD AS NEAR	I NEVER TOLD THE BURIED	11	5
AS STOOD YOU HERE--	I NEVER TOLD THE BURIED	11	6
TWICE HAVE I STOOD A BEGGAR	I NEVER LOST AS MUCH BUT	49	3
AS FLAKES OF SNOW STOOD [DID] YESTERDAY--	SOME RAINBOW--COMING	64	14
"OH COULD WE CLIMB WHERE MOSES STOOD,	WHERE BELLS NO MORE	112	9
THICKER AND THICKER STOOD THE FEET	THE SUN KEPT STOOPING--	152	7
BUT WE--STOOD--WHISPERING IN THE HOUSE--	OF TRIBULATION--THESE	325	15
AS IF YOUR SENTENCE STOOD--PRONOUNCED--	'TWAS LIKE A MAELSTROM,	414	18
WE STOOD UPON OUR STAPLED FEET--	THEY PUT US FAR APART--	474	15
IT WAS NOT DEATH, FOR I STOOD UP,	IT WAS NOT DEATH, FOR I	510	1
AND SO I STEPPED [STOOD] UPON THE NORTH	MY PERIOD HAD COME FOR	564	7
AND I STOOD UP--AND LIVED--	THREE TIMES--WE PARTED--	598	16
YET BLUE--AND SOLID [EASY]--STOOD--	IT TROUBLED ME AS ONCE I	600	6
MY SOUL GREW [FELT / BENT / STOOD] STRAIGHT.	I ROSE--BECAUSE HE SANK	616	4
MY LIFE HAD STOOD--A LOADED GUN--	MY LIFE HAD STOOD--A	754	1
JUST THE PLACE I STOOD--	WHEN I HOPED, I	768	2
THE TWILIGHT STOOD [LEANED], AS STRANGERS DO	THE CRICKETS SANG	1104	6
THE STARS ARE OLD, THAT STOOD FOR ME--	THE STARS ARE OLD, THAT	1249	1
THE MOUNTAINS STOOD IN HAZE--	THE MOUNTAINS STOOD IN	1278	1
AND THEN--THE STREETS [AIR] STOOD STILL--	IT SOUNDED AS IF THE	1397	2
AND STOOD AMAZED BEFORE THE CHANGE [BOON / MORNS]	THE THRILL CAME SLOWLY	1495	7
AND STOOD BEFORE THE SUDDENNESS	THE THRILL CAME SLOWLY	1495 V	7
TREE AND TRAVELLER STOOD--	GLASS WAS THE STREET--IN	1498	2
THE DROPS ON NATURE'S FOREHEAD STOOD	THE SUN RETIRED TO A	1693	5
STOOP			
TO LIVES THAT [AS] STOOP TO NOTICE MINE--	HE PUT THE BELT AROUND	273	13
THE HIMMALEH WAS KNOWN TO STOOP	THE HIMMALEH WAS KNOWN	481	1
AND MEN TOO STRAIGHT TO STOOP [BEND] AGAIN,	MY PORTION IS DEFEAT--	639	8
'TIS TRUE--THAT DEITY TO STOOP	MY WORTHINESS IS ALL MY	751	9
A FRIEND TOO STRAIGHT TO STOOP	CONTAINED IN THIS SHORT	1165 V	
STOOPED			
TO MY NESCESSITY--STOOPED DOWN!	FOR THIS--ACCEPTED	195	6
BEFORE DECISION--STOOPED TO SPEECH--	I COULD SUFFICE FOR HIM,	643	11
CHRIST--STOOPED UNTIL HE TOUCHED THE GRAVE--	PERHAPS YOU THINK ME	833	3
IMMEDIATELY--THAT ANGUISH STOOPED	SO PROUD SHE WAS TO DIE	1272	7
STOOPING			
STOOPING--PLUCKING--SMILING--FLYING--	ANGELS, IN THE EARLY	94	3
STOOPING--PLUCKING--SIGHING--FLYING--	ANGELS, IN THE EARLY	94	7
THE SUN KEPT STOOPING--STOOPING--LOW!	THE SUN KEPT STOOPING--	152	1
THE SUN KEPT STOOPING--STOOPING--LOW!	THE SUN KEPT STOOPING--	152	1
STOOPING AS LOW AS [BENDING LOW AT] THE OTTER'S [KITCHEN / ...	BLAZING IN GOLD AND	228	5
AND CARTS WENT STOOPING ROUND THE FIELDS	'TWAS JUST THIS TIME,	445	11
THE VERY BROW--THE STOOPING EYES--	YOU KNOW THAT PORTRAIT	504	3
THEN BENDING [STOOPING] FROM THE SKY--	NATURE--THE GENTLEST	790	20
PERHAPS YOU THINK ME STOOPING	PERHAPS YOU THINK ME	833	1
WHEN STOOPING TO SECURE IT	A NARROW FELLOW IN THE	986	15
BY EARLY, STOOPING NIGHT--	THE DAY GREW SMALL,	1140	2
STOOPS			
STOOPS--TO AN EASY CLOVER--	THE NEAREST DREAM	319	5
STOP			
THAT COULD NOT STOP TO BE A KING--	DELAYED TILL SHE HAD	58	17
FOR IT W'D STOP MY BREATH--	GOING TO HEAVEN!	79	21
I WOULD NOT STOP FOR NIGHT, OR STORM--	IF I COULD BRIBE THEM BY	179	4
WOULD IT STOP WHINING--IF TO THEE--	WHAT SHALL I DO--IT	186	6
AND WHEN THE ORCHARDS STOP THEIR TUNE--	MAKE ME A PICTURE OF THE	188	7
I'M "WIFE"! STOP THERE!	I'M "WIFE"--I'VE	199	12
DO YOU THINK I'D STOP	AH, MOON--AND STAR!	240	5
STOP JUST A MINUTE--LET ME THINK!	WHAT WOULD I GIVE TO SEE	247	4
STOP HOPING, NOW--	'TIS SO APPALLING--IT	281	14
NOR STOP TO PLAY WITH THE HAY--	THE WIND DID'NT COME	316	3
TO STOP AND TELL THEM WHERE IT IS--	THE COLOR OF THE GRAVE	411	7
THE MAKER'S LADDERS STOP--	A SOLEMN THING WITHIN	483	4
AND STOP TO LOOK AT HER--	THE SOUL HAS BANDAGED	512	4
ME STOP TO PROVE IT--NOW--	ME PROVE IT NOW--WHOEVER	537	2
A BEING--IMPOTENT TO END [STOP]--	ONE ANGUISH--IN A CROWD	565	15
AND STOP TO FEED ITSELF AT TANKS--	I LIKE TO SEE IT LAP	585	3
STOP--DOCILE AND OMNIPOTENT	I LIKE TO SEE IT LAP	585	16
NOR STOP TO CROSS OURSELVES--	THE LIGHTNING PLAYETH--	630	12
WHEN BELLS STOP RINGING--CHURCH--BEGINS--	WHEN BELLS STOP RINGING	633	1
WHEN COGS--STOP--THAT'S CIRCUMFERENCE--	WHEN BELLS STOP RINGING	633	3
BECAUSE I COULD NOT STOP FOR DEATH--	BECAUSE I COULD NOT STOP	712	1
WHEN WE STOP TO DIE--	THE WORLD--FEELS DUSTY	715	2
TO STOP--OR PERISH--OR ADVANCE--	FROM BLANK TO BLANK--	761	4
WHEN ONE [YOU] HAS FAILED TO STOP THEM--	TO OFFER BRAVE	767	3
IF I CAN STOP ONE HEART FROM BREAKING	IF I CAN STOP ONE HEART	919	1
THOUGH THINE ATTENTION STOP NOT ON ME	WERT THOU BUT ILL--THAT	961	3
STOP PALSIED--'TIS PARALYSIS	I'VE DROPPED MY BRAIN--	1046	3
I SHOULD NOT CARE TO STOP	THE SPRY ARMS OF THE	1103	5
IT STOP UPON A SPOT	THE MUSHROOM IS THE ELF	1298	4
AND EVERY STOP A WELL--	FLOSS WONT SAVE YOU FROM	1322	6
STOPLESS			
THAT LIFE LIKE THIS--IS STOPLESS--	I LIVE WITH HIM--I SEE	463	15
BUT, MOST, LIKE CHAOS--STOPLESS--COOL--	IT WAS NOT DEATH, FOR I	510	21

	FIRST LINE	POEM	LINE
STOPPED			
A CLOCK STOPPED--	A CLOCK STOPPED--	287	1
THEN--STOPPED--NO OTHER TRACK!	'TWAS THE OLD--ROAD--	344	11
THE STITCHES STOPPED--THEMSELVES--	DEATH SETS A THING	360	10
STOPPED--STRUCK--MY TICKING--THROUGH--	I TIE MY HAT--I CREASE	443	12
I'M CEDED--I'VE STOPPED BEING THEIR'S--	I'M CEDED--I'VE STOPPED	508	1
WHEN EVERYTHING THAT TICKED--HAS STOPPED--	IT WAS NOT DEATH, FOR I	510	17
CREATION STOPPED [THE HEAVENS PAUSED]--FOR ME--	MY PERIOD HAD COME FOR	564	18
BUT STOPPED, WHEN QUALIFIED TO GUESS	I PRAYED, AT FIRST, A	576	3
HOW ALL THE CLOCKS STOPPED IN THE WORLD--	IF I MAY HAVE IT, WHEN	577	16
SHE STOPPED--A TRAVELLER'S PRIVILEGE--FOR REST--	I WATCHED THE MOON	629	3
BUT ONLY ON MY FOREHEAD STOPPED--	THE SUN KEPT SETTING--	692	7
HE KINDLY STOPPED FOR ME--	BECAUSE I COULD NOT STOP	712	2
THAT I STOPPED GUAGING--SATISFIED--	ONE BLESSING HAD I THAN	756	3
NO OTHER--STOPPED [CARED] TO EARN--	TO OFFER BRAVE	767	8
THE SUNSET STOPPED [DROPPED] ON COTTAGES	THE SUNSET STOPPED ON	950	1
THE SUNSET STOPPED ON COTTAGES	THE SUNSET STOPPED ON	950	5
BUT [FOR] SUNRISE STOPPED UPON THE PLACE	IT WAS A QUIET WAY--	1053	19
THE VALLEYS STOPPED BELOW	THE MOUNTAINS STOOD IN	1278	2
STOPS			
HE STOPS AT EVERY DOOR--	THE GUEST IS GOLD AND	15	6
AND NEVER STOPS--AT ALL--	"HOPE" IS THE THING WITH	254	4
THAT STOPS--AT HEAVEN--	'TWAS THE OLD--ROAD--	344	4
HE NEVER STOPS, BUT SLACKENS	WITHIN MY GARDEN, RIDES	500	5
WHEN THE ASTRONOMER STOPS SEEKING	WHEN THE ASTRONOMER	851	1
THERE COMES AN HOUR WHEN BEGGING STOPS,	THERE COMES AN HOUR WHEN	1751	1
STOP-SENSATION			
THAT STOP-SENSATION--ON MY SOUL--	I GOT SO I COULD HEAR	293	3
STORE			
REIMBURSED MY STORE--	I NEVER LOST AS MUCH BUT	49	6
AT ANY STORE--	IS BLISS THEN, SUCH	340	8
THOUGH IT TOOK ALL MY STORE	I CANNOT BUY IT--'TIS	840	9
STAKE AN ENTIRE STORE	HOW MUCH THE PRESENT	1380	4
STORES			
AMONG IT'S STORES TO FIND--	IN EBON BOX, WHEN YEARS	169	10
STORM			
THE STORM DOTH WALK THE SEASHORE HUMMING A MOURNFUL TUNE,	AWAKE YE MUSES NINE,	1	17
WHERE THE STORM IS OER?	ON THIS WONDROUS SEA	4	6
THAT GUST AND STORM ARE BY,	THE RAINBOW NEVER TELLS	97	2
MANSIONS MUST EXCLUDE THE STORM!	"HOUSES"--SO THE WISE	127	4
I WOULD NOT STOP FOR NIGHT, OR STORM--	IF I COULD BRIBE THEM BY	179	4
ON THIS LONG STORM THE RAINBOW ROSE--	ON THIS LONG STORM THE	194	1
BARE YOUR JESSAMINE--TO THE STORM--	KILL YOUR BALM--AND IT'S	238	2
AND SORE MUST BE THE STORM--	"HOPE" IS THE THING WITH	254	6
I THOUGHT THAT STORM--WAS BRIEF--	IT STRUCK ME--EVERY DAY	362	9
BETWEEN THE HEAVES OF STORM--	I HEARD A FLY BUZZ--WHEN	465	4
GLEE--THE GREAT STORM IS OVER--	GLEE--THE GREAT STORM IS	619	1
THUNDER STORM	THE WIND BEGUN TO KNEAD	824	T
SUN--IF SHONE--OR STORM--IF SHATTERED--	ALL FORGOT FOR	966	11
WERE EVERY STORM [GALE / SNOW] SO SPICE [FAIR / SWEET]	THE SNOW THAT NEVER	1133	13
THEY STORM THE EARTH AND STUN THE AIR,	FROM ALL THE JAILS THE	1532	5
A THUNDER STORM COMBINES THE CHARMS	A CAP OF LEAD ACROSS THE	1649	7
STORMY			
SOME FAIR OR STORMY DAY,	THIS ME--THAT WALKS AND	1588	2
STORY			
MY STORY HAS A MORAL--	I HAD A GUINEA GOLDEN--	23	25
THIS WAS BUT A STORY--	IT DID NOT SURPRISE ME--	39	13
UNTO LIKE STORY--TROUBLE HAS ENTICED ME--	UNTO LIKE STORY--TROUBLE	295	1
EVE--AND THE ANGUISH--GRANDAME'S STORY--	BETTER--THAN MUSIC! FOR	503	15
HOW THEY WILL TELL THE STORY--	GLEE--THE GREAT STORM IS	619	9
THEN A SOFTNESS--SUFFUSE THE STORY--	GLEE--THE GREAT STORM IS	619	14
THE STORY, UNREVEALED--	ENDED, ERE IT BEGUN--	1088	4
FRESH [NEW] AS MANKIND THAT HUMBLE STORY	TELL AS A MARKSMAN--WERE	1152	5
AND OUT OF STORY--	GATHERED INTO THE EARTH,	1370	2
STOUT			
HANDS--NOT SO STOUT--HOISTED THEM--IN WITNESS--	UNTO LIKE STORY--TROUBLE	295	19
STOUTER			
TILL WE--ARE STOUTER--	READ--SWEET--HOW OTHERS	260	2
STOUTEST			
SHOULD PROVE THE STRONGEST [SUPPLEST / LITHEST / STOUTEST] ONE.	MY FIRST WELL DAY--SINCE	574	8
THE STOUTEST [FORTHWITH THE] MIND IS WAN	THE MIND LIVES ON THE	1355	V 6
STOW			
WOULD [COULD] SUFFICE TO STOW--	SO MUCH SUMMER	651	11
STRAGGLED			
HORIZONS--STRAGGLED DOWN--	ON THIS LONG STORM THE	194	4
STRAIGHT			
THAT I MAY STRAIGHT BEGIN!	HEART! WE WILL FORGET	47	6
AND LIFE STEPS ALMOST STRAIGHT.	WE GROW ACCUSTOMED TO	419	20
"I SEE THEE" EACH RESPONDED STRAIGHT	THEY PUT US FAR APART--	474	7
TRODDEN WITH STRAIGHT RENUNCIATION	TO PUT THIS WORLD DOWN,	527	5
IT SEEMS SO STRAIGHT TO LIE AWAY	I'M SORRY FOR THE DEAD--	529	9
THEN STEPPED STRAIGHT THROUGH THE FIRMAMENT	TWO BUTTERFLIES WENT OUT	533	3
MY SOUL GREW [FELT / BENT / STOOD] STRAIGHT.	I ROSE--BECAUSE HE SANK	616	4
I SANG FIRM--EVEN--[STRAIGHT--STEADY] CHANTS--	I ROSE--BECAUSE HE SANK	616	6

	FIRST LINE	POEM	LINE
STRAIGHT (CONTINUED)			
STRAIGHT--WHEN I AM STRONG--	DONT PUT UP MY THREAD &	617	16
AND MEN TOO STRAIGHT TO STOOP [BEND] AGAIN,	MY PORTION IS DEFEAT--	639	8
THE MOUNTAINS STRAIGHT REPLY--	MY LIFE HAD STOOD--A	754	8
THROUGH THE STRAIT [STRAIGHT] PASS OF SUFFERING--	THROUGH THE STRAIT PASS	792	1
HER WARM [STRAIGHT / GOOD / QUICK / SAFE] RETURN, IF SO SHE	NO NOTICE GAVE SHE, BUT	804	17
BE IT'S MATTRESS STRAIGHT--	AMPLE MAKE THIS BED--	829	5
OURSELF AM LYING STRAIGHT WHEREIN	THIS CHASM, SWEET, UPON	858	7
A FRIEND TOO STRAIGHT TO STOOP	CONTAINED IN THIS SHORT	1165	V
CONFIDENT AND STRAIGHT--	A PROMPT--EXECUTIVE BIRD	1177	6
NO ZEPHYR FELLED THIS CEDAR STRAIGHT--	TO BREAK SO VAST A HEART	1312	3
SO STRAIGHT YOU'D SCARCE SUSPECT	A PIT--BUT HEAVEN OVER	1712	13
STRAIGHTEN			
STRAIGHTEN--LOOK CAUTIOUS FOR THEIR BREATH--	GIVE LITTLE ANGUISH--	310	5
YOUR BREATH HAS TIME [CHANCE] TO STRAIGHTEN--	HE FUMBLES AT YOUR SOUL	315	9
STRAIGHTENED			
IT STRAIGHTENED--THAT WAS ALL--	'TWAS WARM--AT FIRST--	519	9
A FLOWER TO HELP HIS STRAIGHTENED FACE	AS IMPERCEPTIBLY AS	1540	V
STRAIGHTER			
DELIVERED STRAIGHTER TO THE HEART	DYING! TO BE AFRAID OF	831	5
BUT SHE STRAIGHTER WALKED FOR FREIGHT	HAD WE KNOWN THE TON SHE	1124	3
STRAIGHTWAY			
ALL--FOR HIM--STRAIGHTWAY--	GOD PERMITS INDUSTRIOUS	231	4
DEMUR--YOU'RE STRAIGHTWAY DANGEROUS--	MUCH MADNESS IS DIVINEST	435	7
STRAIN			
AWAKE YE MUSES NINE, SING ME A STRAIN DIVINE,	AWAKE YE MUSES NINE,	1	1
TEACH ME THE STRAIN	PUT UP MY LUTE!	261	7
DO FUMBLE AT THE STRAIN--	THE LONESOME FOR THEY	262	8
STRAIN TILL YOUR [HER] LAST SURMISE--	DOUBT ME! MY DIM	275	19
NOT SUCH A STRAIN--THE CHURCH--BAPTIZES--	BETTER--THAN MUSIC! FOR	503	17
A KIND OF PLUMMET STRAIN--	AGAIN--HIS VOICE IS AT	663	14
FIT [STRAIN] HIS COUNTENANCE--	BLOOM UPON THE MOUNTAIN	667	18
I'VE STILL A CHANCE TO STRAIN	I'VE DROPPED MY BRAIN--	1046	16
STRAINED			
HE STRAINED MY FAITH--	HE STRAINED MY FAITH--	497	1
STRAINS			
THE DISTANT STRAINS OF TRIUMPH	SUCCESS IS COUNTED	67	11
CLEAR STRAINS OF HYMN	READ--SWEET--HOW OTHERS	260	10
HER MEMORIES [MEMORY] LIKE STRAINS--REVIEW [ENCHANT]--	LIKE SOME OLD FASHIONED	302	13
THE GILDED CREATURE STRAINS--AND SPINS--	YOU'VE SEEN BALLOONS SET	700	13
AT DISTANCE, AND ACHIEVEMENT, STRAINS,	AS PLAN FOR NOON AND	960	5
STRAIT			
THROUGH THE STRAIT [STRAIGHT] PASS OF SUFFERING--	THROUGH THE STRAIT PASS	792	1
STRAITS			
STRAITS OF BLUE	WHAT WOULD I GIVE TO SEE	247	12
STRANDED			
STRANDED, THRO' DISCIPLINE,	I CAN WADE GRIEF--	252	11
OR FRIEND OR NATURE--STRANDED THEN	THE DAYS THAT WE CAN	1184	3
STRANDS			
PURSUES HIS PEARLY STRANDS--	THE SPIDER HOLDS A	605	V 4
STRANGE			
WERE NOTHING VERY STRANGE!	A LADY RED--AMID THE	74	16
STRANGE THAT THE FEET SO PRECIOUS CHARGED	ON SUCH A NIGHT, OR SUCH	146	23
TO STRANGE, BRIGHT CROWDS OF FLOWERS--	AS IF SOME LITTLE ARCTIC	180	7
AND I, AND SILENCE, SOME STRANGE RACE	I FELT A FUNERAL, IN MY	280	15
GATHERED TO THAT STRANGE FAME--	GATHERED INTO THE EARTH,	1370	3
HOPE IS A STRANGE INVENTION--	HOPE IS A STRANGE	1392	1
ON A STRANGE [UPON A] MOB OF PANTING TREES	THERE CAME A WIND LIKE A	1593	9
SUCH STRANGE ILLUMINATION	THE GLEAM OF AN HEROIC	1687	2
STRANGER			
EXCEPT [UNLESS] THOU BLESS ME"--STRANGER [SIGNOR]!	A LITTLE EAST OF JORDAN,	59	11
A STRANGER PRESSED A KINGDOM,	AS IF I ASKED A COMMON	323	3
ONE CALVARY--EXHIBITED TO STRANGER--	ONE CRUCIFIXION IS	553	5
I GAZED [TURNED]--AS AT A STRANGER--	I WATCHED THE MOON	629	5
BUT NEVER STRANGER JUSTIFIED	I WATCHED THE MOON	629	9
FOR STRANGER--STRANGERS DO NOT MOURN--	BEREAVEMENT IN THEIR	645	5
HE--WOULD TRUST NO STRANGER--	LIFE--IS WHAT WE MAKE IT	698	5
A STRANGER I MUST JUDGE	WHO OCCUPIES THIS HOUSE?	892	2
A STRANGER HE MUST BE--	WHO OCCUPIES THIS HOUSE?	892	30
WERT THOU BUT STRANGER IN UNGRACIOUS COUNTRY--	WERT THOU BUT ILL--THAT	961	5
A NAMELESS BIRD--A STRANGER	THE SUN WENT DOWN--NO	1079	7
A STRANGER HOVERING ROUND	THE FROST WAS NEVER SEEN	1202	5
THAT AWFUL STRANGER CONSCIOUSNESS	I NEVER HEAR THAT ONE IS	1323	15
BUT NATURE [SUSAN] IS A STRANGER YET;	WHAT MYSTERY PERVADES A	1400	17
TO THAT PINK STRANGER WE CALL DUST--	OH GIVE IT MOTION--DECK	1527	5
OR USHER US--A STRANGER--	ON THAT SPECIFIC PILLOW	1533	5
MY STRANGER DISAPPEARED	CONFERRING WITH MYSELF	1655	2
STRANGER'D			
SO GLAD WE ARE--A STRANGER'D DEEM	SO GLAD WE ARE--A	329	1
STRANGER'S			
IN THE STRANGER'S HOUSE--	A FIRST MUTE COMING--	702	2
ALL FORSOOK, FOR JUST A STRANGER'S	ALL FORGOT FOR	966	3
STRANGERS			
FOR STRANGER--STRANGERS DO NOT MOURN--	BEREAVEMENT IN THEIR	645	5
THESE STRANGERS, IN A FOREIGN WORLD,	THESE STRANGERS, IN A	1096	1

	FIRST LINE	POEM	LINE
STRANGERS (CONTINUED)			
THE TWILIGHT STOOD [LEANED], AS STRANGERS DO	THE CRICKETS SANG	1104	6
STRANGERS STROLLED AND SPELLED	AFTER A HUNDRED YEARS	1147	6
OF STRANGERS IS THE EARTH THE INN	THE FROST WAS NEVER SEEN	1202	15
STRANGEST			
YET--STRANGEST--HEAVIER SINCE IT WENT--	SAVIOR! I'VE NO ONE ELSE	217	11
AND ON THE STRANGEST SEA--	"HOPE" IS THE THING WITH	254	10
STRANGLES			
THE CAPTIVE--STRANGLES NEW--	'TIS OPPOSITES--ENTICE--	355	7
THE EAGLE'S GOLDEN BREAKFAST STRANGLES [DAZZLES]--THEM--	VICTORY COMES LATE--	690	12
STRAPPED			
BAGGAGE A [OF] STRAPPED PEARL--	DROPPED INTO THE ETHER	665	6
STRATA			
WHATEVER STRATA OF INIQUITY	A COUNTERFEIT--A PLATED	1453	3
STRATEGEM			
AS ALL MY STRATEGEM HAD BEEN	SEVERER SERVICE OF	786	19
STRATEGIST			
A STRATEGIST SHOULD KEEP,	THE SUBURBS OF A SECRET	1245	2
STRATEGY			
ATTEMPT BY STRATEGY--	I GAINED IT SO--	359	7
HIS STRATEGY	A SPIDER SEWED AT NIGHT	1138	8
TO HIDE MY STRATEGY TOO LATE	I THOUGHT THE TRAIN	1449	9
STRAW			
A BATTLEMENT--OF STRAW--	I HAD NOT MINDED--WALLS	398	12
STRAWBERRIES			
STRAWBERRIES--GROW--	OVER THE FENCE--	251	2
STRAY			
THE STRAY SHIPS--PASSING--	TWO SWIMMERS WRESTLED ON	201	5
EXCEPT TO STRAY ABROAD	FROM COCOON FORTH A	354	6
STRAYED			
WHO STRAYED BEYOND THE AMBER LINE	THE LONESOME FOR THEY	262	3
THERE STRAYED AN ACCIDENTAL RED	IT WAS A QUIET SEEMING	1419	4
STRAYING			
WITH BOLDER PLAYMATES STRAYING	OF DEATH I TRY TO THINK	1558	10
STRAYS			
THROUGH WHICH EXISTENCE STRAYS	TO THE BRIGHT EAST SHE	1573	11
STREAKS			
HARMLESS--AS STREAKS OF METEOR--	THROUGH THE STRAIT PASS	792	7
STREAM			
DOWN TIME'S QUAINT STREAM	DOWN TIME'S QUAINT	1656	1
STREAMS			
PUTS MINOR STREAMS TO REST.	HE TOUCHED ME, SO I LIVE	506	6
STREET			
WHICH WALK NO MORE THE VILLAGE STREET--	THERE IS A MORN BY MEN	24	8
I WILL NOT NAME IT IN THE STREET	I HAV'NT TOLD MY GARDEN	50	5
A DITTY OF THE STREET--	HEART, NOT SO HEAVY AS	83	6
UPON THE VILLAGE STREET--	SHE BORE IT TILL THE	144	12
GLIMMER ON THE STREET--	HOW THE OLD MOUNTAINS	291	16
ADOWN THE EMPTY STREET--	THE NIGHT WAS WIDE, AND	589	12
THE WAGONS QUICKENED ON THE STREET [STREETS]--	THE WIND BEGUN TO KNEAD	824	9
IS GOD--THE ONLY STREET--	THE ONLY NEWS I KNOW	827	8
UPON A DAILY STREET	IT IS AN HONORABLE	946	4
A DOOR JUST [THERE] OPENED ON A STREET [TO A HOUSE]--	A DOOR JUST OPENED ON A	953	1
UPON AN ETHER STREET.	IT WAS A QUIET WAY--	1053	12
IF ANY STRIKE ME ON THE STREET	ALONE AND IN A	1167	17
WHAT TERROR WOULD ENTHRALL THE STREET	IT'S HOUR WITH ITSELF	1225	3
HAD SWEPT THE WINTER STREET--	LIKE BROOMS OF STEEL	1252	3
GLASS WAS THE STREET--IN TINSEL PERIL	GLASS WAS THE STREET--IN	1498	1
STREETS			
FROM LIPS AT CORNERS OF THE STREETS--	IT WAS GIVEN TO ME BY	454	11
THE DUST IN STREETS--GO DOWN--	YOU'VE SEEN BALLOONS SET	700	18
THE WAGONS QUICKENED ON THE STREET [STREETS]--	THE WIND BEGUN TO KNEAD	824	9
GREAT STREETS OF SILENCE LED AWAY	GREAT STREETS OF SILENCE	1159	1
IT SOUNDED AS IF THE STREETS [AIR] WERE RUNNING	IT SOUNDED AS IF THE	1397	1
AND THEN--THE STREETS [AIR] STOOD STILL--	IT SOUNDED AS IF THE	1397	2
STRENGTH			
I HAV'NT QUITE THE STRENGTH NOW	I HAV'NT TOLD MY GARDEN	50	3
I HAD NOT STRENGTH [POWER] TO HOLD--	SAVIOR! I'VE NO ONE ELSE	217	8
TOO FAR--THE STRENGTH--	YOU SEE I CANNOT SEE--	253	10
SUCH IS THE FORCE [STRENGTH] OF HAPPINESS--	SUCH IS THE FORCE OF	787	1
THE ARTIFICE [MYSTERY] OF STRENGTH--	NOT TO DISCOVER WEAKNESS	1054	2
THERE IS A [GOOD] STRENGTH IN PROVING [KNOWING] THAT IT CAN BE . . .	THERE IS A STRENGTH IN	1113	1
TO OUR SPECIFIC STRENGTH--	A WORD MADE FLESH IS	1651	8
WITHOUT THE STRENGTH TO SHAPE?	WHICH MISSES MOST,	1759	10
STRENGTHENING			
TOGETHER HEARD THEM STRENGTHENING	TWO TRAVELLERS PERISHING	933	3
STRENGTHENS			
AN ACTUAL SUFFERING STRENGTHENS	THEY SAY THAT "TIME	686	3
STRESS			
IN STRESS OF BURIAL--	AS IMPERCEPTIBLY AS	1540	V
STRETCH			
COULD STRETCH--TO LOOK AT ME--	I DREADED THAT FIRST	348	16
TO STRETCH A LITTLE FURTHER	THE MONTHS HAVE ENDS--	423	3
BY STRETCH OF LIMB--OR STIR OF LID--	A LONG--LONG SLEEP--A	654	3
AND HELP BELIEF TO STRETCH [REACH]--	REMORSE--IS MEMORY--	744	8
FURTHER THAN ARM COULD STRETCH	UNDER THE LIGHT, YET	949	5

	FIRST LINE	POEM	LINE
STRETCHED			
HOW HE STRETCHED HIS ANGUISH [SPIRIT] TO US	HOW THE WATERS CLOSED	923	3
STREWS			
STREWS THE LANDING WITH OPAL BALES--	THIS--IS THE LAND--THE	266	7
STRICKEN			
HAD IT THE STRICKEN PRIVILEGE,	HAD THIS ONE DAY NOT	1253	7
LOVE'S STRICKEN "WHY"	LOVE'S STRICKEN "WHY"	1368	1
IS STRICKEN BY IT YET--	UPON HIS SADDLE SPRUNG A	1600	8
"'TWAS ALL I HAD," SHE STRICKEN GASPED--	UPON THE GALLOWS HUNG A	1757	7
STRICT			
THE GRAVE IS STRICT--	UNIT, LIKE DEATH, FOR	408	5
THE SOUL WITH STRICT ECONOMY	SUPERIORITY TO FATE	1081	7
STRICTER			
YET PERSEVERED TOWARD--SURER [STRICTER]--FOR THE DISTANCE--	EACH LIFE CONVERGES TO	680	13
STRICTEST			
AS CHILDREN STRICTEST [STRICTLY] KEPT	CONTAINED IN THIS SHORT	1165	5
STRICTLY			
APPOINTMENT STRICTLY KEPT--	YOU TAUGHT ME WAITING	740	2
AS CHILDREN STRICTEST [STRICTLY] KEPT	CONTAINED IN THIS SHORT	1165	5
STRIDING			
SOME STRIDING--GIANT--LOVE--	A SINGLE SCREW OF FLESH	263	16
TO SPARE THESE STRIDING SPIRITS [SHRINKING SPIRITS / . . .	WE SEE--COMPARATIVELY--	534	13
STRIFE			
ONE LITTLE BOAT GAVE UP IT'S STRIFE	ADRIFT! A LITTLE BOAT	30	7
I HEAR THE SILVER STRIFE--	MUSICIANS WRESTLE	157	3
STRIKE			
CHIME [STRIKE]--NOON!	IT'S LIKE THE LIGHT--	297	12
THE NEWS WOULD STRIKE ME DEAD--	BEFORE I GOT MY EYE PUT	327	17
'TWAS LOVE'S--NOW STRIKE!	'TWAS LOVE--NOT ME--	394	12
AND THEN--IT'S TIME TO STRIKE MY TENT--	THE WINTERS ARE SO SHORT	403	7
IF ANY STRIKE ME ON THE STREET	ALONE AND IN A	1167	17
WOULD STRIKE US INSTANT DEAD	I NEVER HEAR THAT ONE IS	1323	12
SOME ARROWS SLAY BUT WHOM THEY STRIKE--	SOME ARROWS SLAY BUT	1565	1
STRIKES			
WHEN THE REDEMPTION STRIKES [SHAKES] HER BELLS--	BETTER--THAN MUSIC! FOR	503	20
STRIKES TRUE WITHIN--	BIND ME--I STILL CAN	1005	3
THE CLOCK STRIKES ONE THAT JUST STRUCK TWO--	THE CLOCK STRIKES ONE	1569	1
STRING			
WHOSE FINGERS STRING THE STALACTITE--	BRING ME THE SUNSET IN A	128	16
I'LL STRING YOU--IN FINE NECKLACE--	I'LL CLUTCH--AND CLUTCH	427	7
MY CHILDHOOD, AND THE STRING OF SPOOLS,	I'M CEDED--I'VE STOPPED	508	6
SECURED HIM BY A STRING	IN WINTER IN MY ROOM	1670	7
THE VERY STRING WITH WHICH	IN WINTER IN MY ROOM	1670	18
THAT STRING WAS THERE--	IN WINTER IN MY ROOM	1670	21
STRINGS			
TIE THE STRINGS TO MY LIFE, MY LORD,	TIE THE STRINGS TO MY	279	1
SHE SAID HER STRINGS WERE SNAPT--	THE FIRST DAY'S NIGHT	410	5
DEATH TWISTS THE STRINGS--	SANG FROM THE HEART,	1059	11
STRIPE			
WHEN THAT BENT STRIPE	DELIGHT IS AS THE FLIGHT	257	12
STRIPPED			
THE HEAVENS STRIPPED--	EMPTY MY HEART, OF THEE	587	13
STRIVE			
THEY STRIVE TO CLIMB--IN VAIN--	THE LONESOME FOR THEY	262	6
THEY STRIVE--AND YET DELAY--	I CROSS TILL I AM WEARY	550	22
STRIVEN			
WHEN LIFE'S SWIFT RIVER STRIVEN THROUGH	WHAT TWIGS WE HELD BY--	1086	3
STRIVES			
I KNOW A PLACE WHERE SUMMER STRIVES	I KNOW A PLACE WHERE	337	1
TO HIM WHO STRIVES SEVERE	THE HALLOWING OF PAIN	772	5
STRIVING			
TOO LATE FOR STRIVING FINGERS	WITHIN MY REACH!	90	8
STROKE			
STROKE THE COOL FOREHEAD--HOT SO OFTEN--	HOW MANY TIMES THESE LOW	187	5
FORGIVE ME, IF TO STROKE [TOUCH / GREET] THY FROST	IF I MAY HAVE IT, WHEN	577	28
THE SAILOR DOES'NT KNOW THE STROKE--	I SOMETIMES DROP IT, FOR	708	15
IS SUCH A FEAT [STROKE / HIGHT / PASS] OF IRONY	THAT THIS SHOULD FEEL	1112	3
STROKED			
THIS--WE STROKED--	THESE--SAW VISIONS--	758	7
STROKES			
WITH MARTIAL HAND SHE STROKES THE HAIR	WHO IS IT SEEKS MY	1598	5
STROKING			
STROKING THE MELODY--	TITLE DIVINE--IS MINE!	1072	13
STROLL			
I PRAY YOU PASS [STROLL] ONCE MORE.	HEART, NOT SO HEAVY AS	83	20
OR STROLL THE TOWN AMONG.	THE SPRY ARMS OF THE	1103	8
STROLLED			
HER GHOST STROLLED SOFTLY O'ER THE HILL	SHE DIED AT PLAY,	75	6
STRANGERS STROLLED AND SPELLED	AFTER A HUNDRED YEARS	1147	6
STROLLING			
A STROLLING HUE, ONE WOULD HAVE SAID	IT WAS A QUIET SEEMING	1419	5
STRONG			
AND JACOB, WAXING STRONG,	A LITTLE EAST OF JORDAN,	59	6
HE WAS WEAK, AND I WAS STRONG--THEN--	HE WAS WEAK, AND I WAS	190	1
I WAS WEAK, AND HE WAS STRONG THEN--	HE WAS WEAK, AND I WAS	190	3

	FIRST LINE	POEM	LINE
STRONG (CONTINUED)			
SO STRONG--TO KNOW--	WHY MAKE IT DOUBT--IT	462	3
SHOOK MY STRONG TRUST--	HE STRAINED MY FAITH--	497	3
STRONG [SURE] HALLELUJAHS ROLL--	THIS WORLD IS NOT	501	18
STRONG CLUSTERS, FROM BARABBAS' TOMB--	TO PUT THIS WORLD DOWN,	527	11
TO HAVE A GOD SO STRONG AS THAT	I PRAYED, AT FIRST, A	576	16
STRAIGHT--WHEN I AM STRONG--	DONT PUT UP MY THREAD &	617	16
AND SAID THAT I WAS STRONG--	THAT FIRST DAY, WHEN YOU	659	2
STRONG DRAUGHTS OF THEIR REFRESHING MINDS	STRONG DRAUGHTS OF THEIR	711	1
MY STRONG MADONNAS--CHERISH STILL--	SWEET MOUNTAINS--YE TELL	722	7
TO WHERE THE STRONG ASSURE ME	BECAUSE MY BROOK IS	1200	7
WAS THE STRONG CUP OF ANGUISH BREWED FOR THE NAZARENE	PROUD OF MY BROKEN HEART	1736	6
IN STRONG [ONE] SOCIETY.	THE GRAVE MY LITTLE	1743	8
STRONGER			
I SHOULD HAVE DRUNK [MIXED] IT STRONGER.	HAD I KNOWN THAT THE	1720	4
STRONGEST			
NEITHER--WAS STRONGEST--NOW--	HE WAS WEAK, AND I WAS	190	10
SHOULD PROVE THE STRONGEST [SUPPLEST / LITHEST / STOUTEST] ONE.	MY FIRST WELL DAY--SINCE	574	8
STROVE			
HE STROVE--AND I STROVE--TOO--	HE WAS WEAK, AND I WAS	190	11
HE STROVE--AND I STROVE--TOO--	HE WAS WEAK, AND I WAS	190	11
READ--SWEET--HOW OTHERS--STROVE--	READ--SWEET--HOW OTHERS	260	1
I ALMOST STROVE TO CLASP HIS HAND,	I TRIED TO THINK A	532	16
THE SUMMER DEEPENED, WHILE WE STROVE--	MY FIRST WELL DAY--SINCE	574	9
BUT STROVE TO STIR THE LIFELESS [FLICKERING] FAN	THREE TIMES--WE PARTED--	598	3
THE WATERS--STROVE TO STAY.	THREE TIMES--WE PARTED--	598	4
BLOOM I STROVE TO RAISE--	SOIL OF FLINT, IF STEADY	681	V
WE PASSED THE SCHOOL, WHERE CHILDREN STROVE	BECAUSE I COULD NOT STOP	712	9
THE SUMMER GRACE, FOR NOTICE STROVE--	THE BIRDS REPORTED FROM	743	9
I STROVE TO WEARY BRAIN AND BONE--	SEVERER SERVICE OF	786	9
THE THOUGHT BEHIND, I STROVE [TRIED] TO JOIN	I FELT A CLEAVING IN MY	937	5
AND ALL THE EARTH STROVE COMMON ROUND--	DENIAL--IS THE ONLY FACT	965	5
THE DUST BEHIND I STROVE TO JOIN	THE DUST BEHIND I STROVE	992	1
STRUCK			
STRUCK UP MY CHILDISH	DELIGHT IS AS THE FLIGHT	257	13
IT STRUCK ME--EVERY DAY--	IT STRUCK ME--EVERY DAY	362	1
STOPPED--STRUCK--MY TICKING--THROUGH--	I TIE MY HAT--I CREASE	443	12
UNTIL OURSELVES ARE STRUCK--	DESPAIR'S ADVANTAGE IS	799	12
STRUCK, WAS I, NOR YET BY LIGHTNING--	STRUCK, WAS I, NOR YET	925	1
THE CLOCK STRIKES ONE THAT JUST STRUCK TWO--	THE CLOCK STRIKES ONE	1569	1
STRUCK NO ONE BUT MYSELF--	THE FARTHEST THUNDER	1581	6
THE JAY HIS CASTANET HAS STRUCK	THE JAY HIS CASTANET HAS	1635	1
STRUGGLE			
THEY STRUGGLE--SOME--FOR BREATH--	YOU'VE SEEN BALLOONS SET	700	10
AND STRUGGLE SLACKER--BUT TO PROVE	I MANY TIMES THOUGHT	739	5
A VALUE [NATURE] STRUGGLE--IT EXIST--	A PLATED LIFE--	806	5
BRIEF STRUGGLE FOR CAPACITY	I THOUGHT THAT NATURE	1286	7
STRUGGLED			
I STRUGGLED--AND WAS THERE--	I HAD NO CAUSE TO BE	542	20
THE MUSCLES GRAPPLED [STRUGGLED] AS WITH LEADS	'TWAS CRISIS--ALL THE	948	9
BENT TO THE WATER, STRUGGLED [SHIVERED] SCARCE--	THE LAST NIGHT THAT SHE	1100	23
STRUGGLES			
AND STRUGGLES IN THE LANES--	I KNOW A PLACE WHERE	337	6
OR STRUGGLES TO A TREE--	THE BLACK BERRY--WEARS A	554	6
STRUGGLING			
AND BORE HER STRUGGLING, BLUSHING,	SO BASHFUL WHEN I SPIED	91	7
THEN STRUGGLING HARD	FROM COCOON FORTH A	354	12
STRUNG			
BY HOMELY ANGUISH STRUNG.	I LIKE A LOOK OF AGONY,	241	8
STRUT			
AN ADDED STRUT IN CHANTICLEER--	AN ALTERED LOOK ABOUT	140	9
AND STRUT UPON MY STEM--	OF BRONZE--AND BLAZE--	290	11
STRUTS			
AND STRUTS IN SEWING SILK!	A FUZZY FELLOW, WITHOUT	173	12
FOR THE ONE SHIP THAT STRUTS THE SHORE	FINITE--TO FAIL, BUT	847	2
STUBBLE			
LITTLE BOYS HATS--AND STUBBLE--	THE WIND DID'NT COME	316	18
A FIELD OF STUBBLE, LYING SERE	A FIELD OF STUBBLE,	1407	1
STUBBLE'S			
THE STUBBLE'S JOINTS BETWEEN--	'TWAS JUST THIS TIME,	445	10
STUBBORN			
GRAPPLES WITH A THEME STUBBORN AS SUBLIME	SOME WE SEE NO MORE,	1221	7
STUDENT			
STUDENT OF THE YEAR!	ARTISTS WRESTLED HERE!	110	4
UNTIL THE PEEVISH STUDENT	'TIS ONE BY ONE--THE	545	5
STUFF			
THE THUNDER CRUMBLED LIKE A STUFF	THE CLOUDS THEIR BACKS	1172	5
STUMBLING			
THAT GRAVITATION, STUMBLING,	"SIC TRANSIT GLORIA	3	31
WITH BLUE--UNCERTAIN STUMBLING BUZZ--	I HEARD A FLY BUZZ--WHEN	465	13
STUMP			
TO [ON] STUMP, AND STACK--AND STEM--	IT SIFTS FROM LEADEN	311	13
STUN			
HAD I THE ART TO STUN MYSELF	I WOULD NOT PAINT--A	505	23
THEY STORM THE EARTH AND STUN THE AIR,	FROM ALL THE JAILS THE	1532	5

	FIRST LINE	POEM	LINE
STUNG			
SHE STUNG HIM--SAPPED HIS FIRM ADVANCE-- .	FATE SLEW HIM, BUT HE	1031	5
STUNS			
HE STUNS YOU BY DEGREES--	HE FUMBLES AT YOUR SOUL	315	4
THE UNPRETENSION STUNS--	"WAS NOT" WAS ALL THE	1342	2
STUPENDOUS			
A GUEST IN THIS STUPENDOUS PLACE--	THE DAY CAME SLOW--TILL	304	15
FOR THE STUPENDOUS VISION [VOLUME]	TIME FEELS SO VAST THAT	802	7
BUT HOW CAN THAT STUPENDOUS COME	THE INFINITE A SUDDEN	1309	3
THAN A STUPENDOUS TOMB	NOT ANY SUNNY TONE	1674	7
STUPENDOUSNESS			
OF THE SIGNIFICANCE [STUPENDOUSNESS] OF THIS--	NO CROWD THAT HAS	515	19
CONCERNING THE STUPENDOUSNESS	HOW NEWS MUST FEEL WHEN	1319	7
STUPIDITY			
AT OUR STUPIDITY--	HER FINAL SUMMER WAS IT	795	12
STUPOR			
FIRST--CHILL--THEN STUPOR--THEN THE LETTING GO--	AFTER GREAT PAIN, A	341	13
OR STUPOR--THE RESERVE--	DID OUR BEST MOMENT LAST	393	7
STURDY			
HER STURDY LITTLE COUNTENANCE	THERE IS A FLOWER THAT	380	15
A SMALL BUT STURDY RESIDENCE, ...	THE ROBIN IS A GABRIEL	1483	9
STYLE			
A QUIET--EARTHQUAKE STYLE--	A STILL--VOLCANO--LIFE--	601	5
IN HIS ECCENTRIC [PECULIAR] STYLE	ELIJAH'S WAGON KNEW NO	1254	V 8
STYLES			
WITH BABBLE OF THE STYLES--	THE MANNER OF IT'S DEATH	468	10
SUBDIVIDE			
MY HEART TO SUBDIVIDE--	WITHOUT THIS--THERE IS	655	10
SUBDUE			
TO SUBDUE THE BUMBLEBEE.	PIGMY SERAPHS--GONE	138	17
SUBDUED			
DETERRED BY [FOR CHASTENED / SUBDUED TO] RETROSPECT.	THE LAST OF SUMMER IS	1353	2
SUBDUING			
PURSUING [SUBDUING] WINDS THAT CENSURE [SUNDER] US	NO BRIGADIER THROUGHOUT	1561	5
SUBJECT			
NOT SUBJECT TO [SUPREMER THAN / SUPERIOR TO] DESPAIR--	I GOT SO I COULD HEAR	293	23
AS APPARITION--SUBJECT	THE SOUL'S SUPERIOR	306	11
SUBJECT [PRESENT] TO YOUR PLUCKING--	SOME SUCH BUTTERFLY BE	541	6
WE SPECULATED FAIR, ON EVERY SUBJECT, BUT THE GRAVE--	WE TALKED AS GIRLS DO--	586	3
WHEN A [THE] SUBJECT IS FINISHED [ENDED / TAKEN]--	WHATEVER IT IS--SHE HAS	1204	7
SUBJECTED			
THE LONG RESTRICTED [SUBJECTED] GRAVE . .	NO CROWD THAT HAS	515	6
SUBJECTION			
IT'S FOND SUBJECTION WEAR--	WARM IN HER HAND THESE	1313	4
SUBJECTS			
ON SUBJECTS DIADEM--	A MIEN TO MOVE A QUEEN--	283	21
OLD THE GRACE, BUT NEW THE SUBJECTS-- . .	ALWAYS MINE!	839	6
REPORTLESS SUBJECTS, TO THE QUICK	REPORTLESS SUBJECTS, TO	1048	1
HER SUBJECTS SCATTERED INTO PLACE	THE WIND TOOK UP THE	1134	11
THESE SECEDED FROM YOUR SUMMONS [SUMMITS / SUBJECTS / SUBSTANCE]	KNOCK WITH TREMOR--	1325	6
OF SUBJECTS THAT RESIST	HOW HUMAN NATURE DOTES	1417	9
SUBJECTS--BETHLEHEM--	THE BIBLE IS AN ANTIQUE	1545	4
SUBJUGATE			
NOT SUBJUGATE, THE MUTINEER	TO TRY TO SPEAK, AND	1617	7
SUBJUGATED			
HAD SUBJUGATED TEST	AT HALF PAST THREE, A	1084	6
SUBJUGATING			
EXCEPT BY SUBJUGATING	ME FROM MYSELF--TO	642	7
SUBJUNCTIVE			
AND THIS CONFIDING [MECHANIC / SUBJUNCTIVE] STONE	SHE LAID HER DOCILE	1396	2
SUBLIME			
INSOLVENCY, SUBLIME!	"SIC TRANSIT GLORIA	3	44
LET ME NOT SHAME THEIR SUBLIME DEPORTMENTS--	UNTO LIKE STORY--TROUBLE	295	21
STOLID TO LOVE'S SUPREME [SUBLIME] ENTREATY	TELL AS A MARKSMAN--WERE	1152	20
GRAPPLES WITH A THEME STUBBORN AS SUBLIME .	SOME WE SEE NO MORE,	1221	7
'TIS ECSTASY'S REVEALED [DIVINE / SUBLIME / REVERED] REVIEW--	THE LAST OF SUMMER IS	1353	3
SUBLIMELY			
THE PRICE IS GREAT--SUBLIMELY PAID--	IT FEELS A SHAME TO BE	444	9
SUBLIMER			
TO SUBLIMER RECITATION	I CANT TELL YOU--BUT YOU	65	19
BUT JUSTICE IS SUBLIMER	I HAD SOME THINGS THAT I	116	11
SUBLIMER SORT [THING / WAY]--THAN SPEECH-- .	GIVE LITTLE ANGUISH--	310	8
SUBLIMEST			
TIME'S SUBLIMEST TARGET	THERE IS A WORD	8	17
SUBMERGED			
IN WHICH THE SOUL AT FIRST ESTRANGED [ALARMED / SUBMERGED]--	THE INUNDATION OF THE	1425	5
SUBMERGES			
ENLARGES [SUBMERGES] EVERY SOUL--	THE INUNDATION OF THE	1425	2
SUBMIT			
SUBMIT THAT HOME--AND CERTAINTY	THE ROBIN IS THE ONE	828	11

	FIRST LINE	POEM		LINE
SUBMITTING				
SUBMITTING FOR OUR UNKNOWN SAKE	A FULL FED ROSE ON MEALS	1154		7
SUBORDINATE				
IMPERTINENCE SUBORDINATE	THE WAY TO KNOW THE	1279		7
SUBSCRIBE				
WILL [WOULD] SUBSCRIBE A TEAR--	TELL AS A MARKSMAN--WERE	1152		12
SUBSEQUENT				
AND SUBSEQUENT, TO FIND	TO HANG OUR HEAD--	105		2
IS INTEGRAL [SUBSEQUENT]--AND THEREFORE	DEATH IS POTENTIAL TO	548		7
BY SUBSEQUENT EFFECT--	AS FROST IS BEST	951		4
SUBSEQUENT A DRUM--	THE POPULAR HEART IS A	1226		2
SUBSEQUENTLY				
I SUBSEQUENTLY LEARNED	HIGH FROM THE EARTH I	1723		14
SUBSIDES				
SUBSIDES FROM IT'S SIGNIFICANCE	A DIAMOND ON THE HAND	1108		3
SUBSIDING				
THE SUN SUBSIDING ON HIS COURSE	THE LILAC IS AN ANCIENT	1241		5
SUBSIDY				
OH, SUBSIDY OF BALM!	UNTO THE WHOLE--HOW ADD?	1341		4
SUBSIST				
AND OUR'S--A KINSMANSHIP EXPRESS [EXIST / SUBSIST / ARISE]--	A PRISON GETS TO BE A	652		3
SUBSIST TILL PARADISE.	SUPERIORITY TO FATE	1081		8
OR FLAG SUBSIST OR FAME EXPORT	STEP LIGHTLY ON THIS	1183		7
AND SUBSIST ON FUZZ.	BEES ARE BLACK, WITH	1405		4
SUBSISTING				
SUBSISTING ON THE LIGHT WE BORE	WE MET AS SPARKS--	958		5
SUBSISTING NOW [SINCE] LIKE GOD--	ART THOU THE THING I	1282	V	8
SUBSTANCE				
OF THE COLOSSAL SUBSTANCE	THE SOUL'S SUPERIOR	306		15
PREPARES YOUR BRITTLE NATURE [SUBSTANCE]	HE FUMBLES AT YOUR SOUL	315		5
IT SWALLOWS SUBSTANCE [BEING] UP--	THERE IS A PAIN--SO	599		2
WHAT DIFFERENCE IN SUBSTANCE LIES	THE VOICE THAT STANDS	1189		5
THESE SECEDED FROM YOUR SUMMONS [SUMMITS / SUBJECTS / SUBSTANCE]	KNOCK WITH TREMOR--	1325		6
SUBSTANCES				
WHOSE SUBSTANCES ARE SAND--	WE DO NOT KNOW THE TIME	1106		8
SUBSTANTIATE				
SUBSTANTIATE A GOD--	THE MOON UPON HER FLUENT	1528		4
SUBSTANTIATES				
SUBSTANTIATES A PEACE	THE LONG SIGH OF THE	1359		6
SUBSTITUTE				
ESCAPE--OR SUBSTITUTE--	THE FUTURE--NEVER SPOKE	672		8
SUBTERFUGE				
AND SUBTERFUGE--IS DONE--	OF ALL THE SOULS THAT	664		4
SUBTERRANEAN				
THE SUBTERRANEAN FREIGHT	IT'S HOUR WITH ITSELF	1225		5
THAT WILY--SUBTERRANEAN [UNSUBSTANTIAL] INN	NO PASSENGER WAS KNOWN	1406		3
OR SUBTERRANEAN [UNSUSPECTED] WO--	OH FUTURE! THOU SECRETED	1631		2
SUBTLE				
LEST SUCH A SUBTLE--SHIMMERING GRACE	A SOMETHING IN A	122		11
THE SUBTLE CARGOES--LIE--	I GAVE MYSELF TO HIM--	580		12
TOO SUBTLE [SMOULDERING] TO SUSPECT	A STILL--VOLCANO--LIFE--	601		6
TOO DISTANT [SUBTLE] TO BE SEEN	CONTAINED IN THIS SHORT	1165	V	
ON IT'S BOUNDLESS [MIGHTY / SUBTLE] SHELF--	SUMMER LAID HER SIMPLE	1363		2
SUBTLE THE SUM THAT PURCHASE YOU--	BROTHER OF INGOTS--AH	1366	V	2
DREAMS ARE THE SUBTLE DOWER	DREAMS ARE THE SUBTLE	1376		1
SHE TAKES [GOES] HER GRACIOUS [SPACIOUS / SUBTLE / SIMPLE / . . .	SUMMER--WE ALL HAVE SEEN	1386		6
BUT [YET] PRONE TO SHUT IT'S [HIS] SPOTTED [SUBTLE] FAN	THE BUTTERFLY'S NUMIDIAN	1387		4
I WATCHED THE PRECIOUS [SUBTLE] BEGGAR	I SAW THE WIND WITHIN	1502	V	
AND NOW AGAINST HIS SUBTLE NAME	HE LIVED THE LIFE OF	1525		3
HOPE IS A SUBTLE GLUTTON--	HOPE IS A SUBTLE GLUTTON	1547		1
AND NOW AGAINST HIS SUBTLE NAME	WHO ABDICATED AMBUSH	1616		3
AS SUBTLE AS TOMORROW	AS SUBTLE AS TOMORROW	1713		1
SUBTRACT				
SUBTRACT THYSELF, IN PLAY,	EMPTY MY HEART, OF THEE	587		7
SUBTRACTING				
SUBTRACTING, TILL MY FINGERS DROPPED	IF YOU WERE COMING IN	511		11
SUBTRACTION				
HAD THERE BEEN NO SHARP SUBTRACTION	ONE DAY IS THERE OF THE	814		9
SUBURB				
CONTENTMENT'S QUIET SUBURB--	A NEARNESS TO	963		5
SUBURBS				
THE SUBURBS OF A SECRET	THE SUBURBS OF A SECRET	1245		1
SUCCEED				
BY THOSE WHO NE'ER SUCCEED.	SUCCESS IS COUNTED	67		2
A PURER FOOD FOR THEM, IF I SUCCEED,	I FIT FOR THEM--	1109		7
SUCCEEDING				
BY SUCCEEDING [SUPREMER] SPRINGS--	ALL BUT DEATH, CAN BE	749		6
SUCCESS				
SUCCESS IS COUNTED SWEETEST	SUCCESS IS COUNTED	67		1
BUT THE SUCCESS--WAS HIS--IT SEEMS--	I MEANT TO FIND HER WHEN	718		3
SUCCESS IN CIRCUIT LIES	TELL ALL THE TRUTH BUT	1129		2
SUCCESSFUL				
SUCCESSFUL CERTAIN, IF AT LAST,	HOW FORTUNATE THE GRAVE	897		3
A HATEFUL, HARD, SUCCESSFUL FACE,	A FACE DEVOID OF LOVE OR	1711		2
SUCCESSOR				
'TIS PAIN'S SUCCESSOR--WHEN THE SOUL	THERE IS A LANGUOR OF	396		3

	FIRST LINE	POEM	LINE
SUCCOR			
THAT SECONDARY SUCCOR	ELIZABETH TOLD ESSEX	1321	5
BUT SHE MUST [MY PRICE / HUMILITY] PAY FOR SUCCOR	I SAW THE WIND WITHIN	1502	V
SUCH			
SUCH TRANSCENDENTAL PROSPECT,	"SIC TRANSIT GLORIA	3	23
SUCH RESURRECTION POURS.	THE FEET OF PEOPLE	7	24
SURELY, SUCH A COUNTRY	BAFFLED FOR JUST A DAY	17	7
STILL, HAD IT SUCH A VALUE	I HAD A GUINEA GOLDEN--	23	5
NE'ER SAW I SUCH A WONDROUS SCENE--	THERE IS A MORN BY MEN	24	13
NE'ER SUCH A RING ON SUCH A GREEN--	THERE IS A MORN BY MEN	24	14
NE'ER SUCH A RING ON SUCH A GREEN--	THERE IS A MORN BY MEN	24	14
FOR SUCH AS THEE TO DIE!	NOBODY KNOWS THIS LITTLE	35	12
BY SUCH AND SUCH AN OFFERING	BY SUCH AND SUCH AN	38	1
BY SUCH AND SUCH AN OFFERING	BY SUCH AND SUCH AN	38	1
THERE WERE JUST SUCH COFFIN	IT DID NOT SURPRISE ME--	39	15
FROM SUCH A COMMON BALL AS THIS	A DAY! HELP! HELP!	42	3
SUCH TRUST HAD ONE AMONG US,	COULD LIVE--DID LIVE--	43	10
CAN SUCH A FOOT EXPLORE	WHO NEVER LOST, ARE	73	6
IN SUCH A LITTLE WHILE!	A LADY RED--AMID THE	74	12
AT SUCH A CURIOUS EARTH!	GOING TO HEAVEN!	79	23
DID COVER SUCH WITH LEAVES,	WHOSE CHEEK IS THIS?	82	7
TO SUCH, IF THEY SH'D WHISPER	MY NOSEGAYS ARE FOR	95	5
IS THERE SUCH A THING AS "DAY"?	WILL THERE REALLY BE A	101	2
THAT SUCH WAS NOT THE POSTURE	TO HANG OUR HEAD--	105	3
'TWAS SUCH A LITTLE--LITTLE BOAT	'TWAS SUCH A LITTLE--	107	1
'TWAS SUCH A GALLANT--GALLANT SEA	'TWAS SUCH A LITTLE--	107	3
'TWAS SUCH A GREEDY, GREEDY WAVE	'TWAS SUCH A LITTLE--	107	5
BURY ME, IN SUCH A SHROUD OF RED!	IF THIS IS "FADING"	120	4
ON SUCH A NIGHT	IF THIS IS "FADING"	120	6
LEST SUCH A SUBTLE--SHIMMERING GRACE	A SOMETHING IN A	122	11
FOR SUCH, THE ANGELS GO--	TO FIGHT ALOUD, IS VERY	126	10
NEVER SUCH AN AMBUSCADE	PIGMY SERAPHS--GONE	138	9
BY JUST SUCH A HAZARD	SOUL, WILT THOU TOSS	139	2
ON SUCH A NIGHT, OR SUCH A NIGHT,	ON SUCH A NIGHT, OR SUCH	146	1
ON SUCH A NIGHT, OR SUCH A NIGHT,	ON SUCH A NIGHT, OR SUCH	146	1
IF SUCH A LITTLE FIGURE	ON SUCH A NIGHT, OR SUCH	146	3
ON SUCH A DAWN, OR SUCH A DAWN--	ON SUCH A NIGHT, OR SUCH	146	9
ON SUCH A DAWN, OR SUCH A DAWN--	ON SUCH A NIGHT, OR SUCH	146	9
THAT SUCH A LITTLE FIGURE	ON SUCH A NIGHT, OR SUCH	146	11
SUCH TRANSPORT BREAKS UPON THE TOWN	MUSICIANS WRESTLE	157	5
AND SUCH A WAGON! WHILE I LIVE	I MET A KING THIS	166	17
ANOTHER SUCH A VEHICLE	I MET A KING THIS	166	19
TO SUCH A MODEST CLAY,	WAIT TILL THE MAJESTY OF	171	14
THAT SUCH AN IMPORTUNITY	IF I COULD BRIBE THEM BY	179	15
IT'S SUCH A LITTLE THING TO WEEP--	IT'S SUCH A LITTLE THING	189	1
YIELD SUCH AN ALCOHOL!	I TASTE A LIQUOR NEVER	214	4
YOU ARE SURE THERE'S SUCH A PERSON	WHAT IS--"PARADISE"--	215	11
SUCH AN ONE--TO SAY--	TEACH HIM--WHEN HE MAKES	227	2
WERE HIMSELF--SUCH A DUNCE--	DID WE DISOBEY HIM?	267	5
ONE PEARL--TO ME--SO SIGNAL-- [OF SUCH PROPORTION]	ONE LIFE OF SO MUCH	270	5
SUCH [SOME] SPIRIT MAKES [TELL] HER PERPETUAL MENTION,	UNTO LIKE STORY--TROUBLE	295	13
SUCH ANNIVERSARY SHALL BE--	ONE YEAR AGO--JOTS WHAT?	296	6
IF SUCH AN OUTCAST BE--	OF ALL THE SOUNDS	321	26
I THOUGHT THAT SUCH WERE FOR THE SAINTS,	THERE CAME A DAY AT	322	3
FOR SUCH A NOTICING--	THE GRASS SO LITTLE HAS	333	12
RETURN--WITH SUCH A CROWN	THE FACE I CARRY WITH ME	336	10
WITH SUCH A PRACTISED FROST--	I KNOW A PLACE WHERE	337	2
IS BLISS THEN, SUCH ABYSS,	IS BLISS THEN, SUCH	340	1
"MILES", AND "PRISCILLA", WERE SUCH AN ONE--	GOD IS A DISTANT--	357	4
TAKE OTHER ACCENTS, AS SUCH I HEARD	I'M SAYING EVERY DAY	373	21
'MONG SUCH UNIQUE	I WENT TO HEAVEN--	374	15
SUCH HOUSES HAVE--ALWAY--	THERE'S BEEN A DEATH, IN	389	4
SUCH GUILT--TO LOVE THEE--MOST!	'TWAS LOVE--NOT ME--	394	5
SUCH DIMITY CONVICTIONS--	WHAT SOFT--CHERUBIC	401	5
IT'S SUCH A COMMON--GLORY--	WHAT SOFT--CHERUBIC	401	9
SUCH BLISS--HAD I--FOR ALL THE YEARS--	IT WOULD NEVER BE COMMON	430	7
IN SUCH A SHINING PLACE!	ME--COME! MY DAZZLED	431	2
PERMITTED--SUCH A HEAD--	IT FEELS A SHAME TO BE	444	4
THAT SUCH ENORMOUS PEARL	IT FEELS A SHAME TO BE	444	14
I HEARD SUCH WORDS AS "RICH"--	IT WAS GIVEN TO ME BY	454	9
SUCH AS CONTENT--AND HEAVEN--	I MEANT TO HAVE BUT	476	2
THAT SUCH A DOLL SHOULD GROW	THE HIMMALEH WAS KNOWN	481	4
SUCH AS THESE--THE PEARLS	MY GARDEN--LIKE THE	484	4
SHE FETCHES--SUCH AS ME	MY GARDEN--LIKE THE	484	5
A GRATITUDE--THAT SUCH BE TRUE--	THE WORLD--STANDS--	493	13
THO' SUCH--ARE LUXURIES--	IT'S THOUGHTS--AND JUST	495	22
NOT SUCH A STRAIN--THE CHURCH--BAPTIZES--	BETTER--THAN MUSIC! FOR	503	17
NOT SUCH A STANZA SPLITS THE SILENCE--	BETTER--THAN MUSIC! FOR	503	19
SUCH SUMPTUOUS--DESPAIR--	I WOULD NOT PAINT--A	505	8
THAT SUCH A DAY, PERMITTED [PERSUADED / ACCEPTED] SO,	HE TOUCHED ME, SO I LIVE	506	2
LIFT SUCH A CRUCIFIXAL SIGN	HE TOUCHED ME, SO I LIVE	506	17
AT SUCH AND SUCH A TIME--	IF ANYBODY'S FRIEND BE	509	4
AT SUCH AND SUCH A TIME--	IF ANYBODY'S FRIEND BE	509	4
HOW WARM, THEY WERE, ON SUCH A DAY,	IF ANYBODY'S FRIEND BE	509	9
IT'S SUCH CONGENIAL TIMES [WAY]	I'M SORRY FOR THE DEAD--	529	2
SUCH LUXURY--IT GREW--	I TRIED TO THINK A	532	17

	FIRST LINE	POEM	LINE
SUCH (CONTINUED)			
TO SUCH A FATE--TO MINISTER.	SHE'S HAPPY, WITH A NEW	535	8
SOME SUCH BUTTERFLY BE SEEN	SOME SUCH BUTTERFLY BE	541	1
SOME SUCH SPICE [ROSE]--EXPRESS AND PASS--	SOME SUCH BUTTERFLY BE	541	5
'TWAS SUCH AN AMPLE PEACE--	I HAD NO CAUSE TO BE	542	13
THAT HURT THEM EARLY--SUCH A LAPSE	I MEASURE EVERY GRIEF I	561	19
IN SUCH A PLACE, WHAT HORROR,	DID YOU EVER STAND IN A	590	5
WAS SUCH REMAINING [STILL DWELLING] THERE?"	I YEARS HAD BEEN FROM	609	8
FOR RECOLLECTING SUCH AS WENT--	YOU'LL FIND--IT WHEN YOU	610	3
SUCH A DAY--	TO KNOW JUST HOW HE	622	12
AND SHIPS--OF SUCH A SIZE	THEY CALLED ME TO THE	628	10
SUCH THRENODIES [EXTACIES / REVENUES / ARGUMENTS] OF PEARL--	YOU'LL KNOW HER--BY HER	634	26
SUCH PRESENCE BEAR AWAY	BEREAVEMENT IN THEIR	645	10
NEVER BRIDE HAD SUCH ASSEMBLING--	HER SWEET TURN TO LEAVE	649	9
FOR SUCH AN ONE--AS ME--	AGAIN--HIS VOICE IS AT	663	4
SUCH BEING FINITUDE!	TO BE ALIVE--IS POWER--	677	8
IF SUCH IT PROVE, IT PROVE TOO	THEY SAY THAT "TIME	686	7
CRUMBS--FIT SUCH LITTLE MOUTHS--	VICTORY COMES LATE--	690	10
SUCH AS THESE--ARE STILL--	LIFE, AND DEATH, AND	706	2
WERE SUCH HER SILVER WILL--	THE MOON WAS BUT A CHIN	737	12
AND DO I SMILE, SUCH CORDIAL LIGHT	MY LIFE HAD STOOD--A	754	9
COULD I SUCH A PLEA [FACE] WITHSTAND--	MOST SHE TOUCHED ME BY	760	8
SUCH A PRAISE BEGAN	MOST SHE TOUCHED ME BY	760	14
SUCH IS THE FORCE [STRENGTH] OF HAPPINESS--	SUCH IS THE FORCE OF	787	1
SUCH PLENTY SMILES UPON MY BOARD--	GOD GAVE A LOAF TO EVERY	791	11
UNTO SUCH, WERE SUCH ASSEMBLY	ONE DAY IS THERE OF THE	814	15
UNTO SUCH, WERE SUCH ASSEMBLY	ONE DAY IS THERE OF THE	814	15
SUCH DESTITUTION THAT	TILL DEATH--IS NARROW	907	6
THAT SUCH HAVE DIED ENABLE US	THAT SUCH HAVE DIED	1030	1
THAT SUCH HAVE LIVED,	THAT SUCH HAVE DIED	1030	3
SUCH AGONIZING TERMS?	JUST ONCE! OH LEAST	1076	5
IS SUCH A FEAT [STROKE / HIGHT / PASS] OF IRONY	THAT THIS SHOULD FEEL	1112	3
WHAT ARE THE SINEWS OF SUCH CORDAGE FOR	THERE IS A STRENGTH IN	1113	3
'TWAS SUCH AN EVENING BRIGHT AND STIFF	THAT ODD OLD MAN IS DEAD	1130	3
JUST SUCH A RETROSPECT	THE PROPS ASSIST THE	1142	8
THAT SUCH A BLISS HAS BEEN.	OF SO DIVINE A LOSS	1179	4
OF SUCH A LITTLE DOG AM I	A LITTLE DOG THAT WAGS	1185	3
THE PAST IS SUCH A CURIOUS CREATURE	THE PAST IS SUCH A	1203	1
I FAMISH [PERISH] TO BEHOLD SO EMINENT A SIGHT [ANOTHER SUCH . . .	THE MOST TRIUMPHANT BIRD	1265	4
IN SUCH AN EARTH AS OUR'S--	NOT WITH A CLUB, THE	1304	14
ESCAPE IS SUCH A THANKFUL WORD	ESCAPE IS SUCH A	1347	1
THAT SUCH A REALM COULD BE--	I SUED THE NEWS--YET	1360	2
SUCH A VICTOR COULD NOT [CANNOT] BE--	LAY THIS LAUREL ON THE	1393	V
TO DWELL IN SUCH A PLACE--	THE FACT THAT EARTH IS	1408	8
SUCH [THESE] ARE THE INLETS OF THE MIND--	SUCH ARE THE INLETS OF	1421	1
YET [AND] NONE HATH SUCH A CROWD.	HOW BRITTLE ARE THE	1433	4
THAN SUCH FIDELITY.	THE HEALED HEART SHOWS	1440	8
FROM SUCH A VELVET WORLD IT COMES [CAME]	HOW SOFT A CATERPILLAR	1448	3
SUCH PLUSHES AT COMMAND	HOW SOFT A CATERPILLAR	1448	4
HER SPIRIT ROSE TO SUCH A HIGHT	HER SPIRIT ROSE TO SUCH	1486	1
IF SUCH PROSPECTIVE BE--	THE MOON UPON HER FLUENT	1528	V
FOR SUCH A FOE [SWEET / GLEE / DAWN / SCENE / DEW / JOY] AS THIS--	FROM ALL THE JAILS THE	1532	8
ARE SUCH A SCARCITY--	MY WARS ARE LAID AWAY IN	1549	12
WITH SUCH SEVERITY	NO BRIGADIER THROUGHOUT	1561	12
AND SQUANDERED SUCH A NOTE	UPON HIS SADDLE SPRUNG A	1600	6
SUCH HINTS OF HONEY LAY	WITHIN THAT LITTLE HIVE	1607	2
GUILELESS, YET OF SUCH GLORY FINE	"RED SEA," INDEED! TALK	1642	5
THOU SHALT GO AT SUCH A GAIT OF JOY	IN SNOW THOU COMEST	1669	6
SUCH STRANGE ILLUMINATION	THE GLEAM OF AN HEROIC	1687	2
FROM SUCH A GIANT [BEGGAR] WERE WITHHELD	LOVE CAN DO ALL BUT	1731	3
SUDDEN			
"KIDD" WILL [MAY] SUDDEN SAIL--	I NEVER TOLD THE BURIED	11	17
A SUDDEN EXPECTATION,	I NEVER HEAR THE WORD	77	3
CONJECTURED, AND WAKED SUDDEN IN--	'TIS SO MUCH JOY! 'TIS	172	17
SOME SUDDEN MORN--	DELIGHT IS AS THE FLIGHT	257	24
UNTIL A SUDDEN SKY	HOW NOTELESS MEN, AND	282	2
A SUDDEN MUSKET--SPILLS--	THE DAY CAME SLOW--TILL	304	4
A HAPPY LIP--BREAKS SUDDEN--	A HAPPY LIP--BREAKS	353	1
PUSHED SUDDEN THRO' TO HIS--	I HAD NOT MINDED--WALLS	398	6
WITH STEADY--DRIFTING--[SUDDEN--BLINDING] GRAINS	I CROSS TILL I AM WEARY	550	7
CONFRONTING SUDDEN PELF--	THERE IS A SHAME OF	551	2
OUR PACE TOOK SUDDEN AWE--	OUR JOURNEY HAD ADVANCED	615	5
DID FAN AND ROCK, WITH SUDDEN LIGHT--	TO MY SMALL HEARTH HIS	638	3
"WOULD I BE WHOLE" HE SUDDEN BROACHED--	I COULD SUFFICE FOR HIM,	643	5
AND HE--I PUSHED--WITH SUDDEN FORCE--	IF HE WERE LIVING--DARE	734	13
I SUPPOSED--WHEN SUDDEN	MOST SHE TOUCHED ME BY	760	13
AS ONE MET SUDDEN [ENCOUNTERED] GENTLEFOLK	IT IS AN HONORABLE	946	3
THE DOOR AS INSTANT [SUDDEN] SHUT--AND I--	A DOOR JUST OPENED ON A	953	5
HIS NOTICE SUDDEN [INSTANT] IS--	A NARROW FELLOW IN THE	986	4
TILL SUDDEN I PERCEIVED IT STIR--	I HAD A DAILY BLISS	1057	3
BY DATING IT A SUDDEN FEAST.	I CANNOT SEE MY SOUL BUT	1262	10
THE INFINITE A SUDDEN GUEST	THE INFINITE A SUDDEN	1309	1
THIS WHOLE [SUDDEN / FAIR / GAY / BRIGHT / FLEET / SWEET / . . .	A LITTLE MADNESS IN THE	1333	5
A SUDDEN FREIGHT OF WIND ASSUMED [TOOK ON--]	A SINGLE CLOVER PLANK	1343	11

	FIRST LINE	POEM	LINE
SUDDEN (CONTINUED)			
WAS FERVOR'S SUDDEN CROWN--	THE PRETTY RAIN FROM	1426	8
FACTS BY OUR SIDE ARE NEVER SUDDEN	FACTS BY OUR SIDE ARE	1497	1
ALL OTHER BOUNTY SUDDEN CHAFF [NIGGARDLY]	I GROPED FOR HIM BEFORE	1555	3
MAKE LIFE A SUDDEN PRICE.	MORNING THAT COMES BUT	1610	4
SUDDENLY			
BLAZED OPEN--SUDDENLY--	IF I'M LOST--NOW--	256	5
THAT SUDDENLY LOOKS INTO OUR'S	THAT AFTER HORROR--THAT	286	13
WHEN SUDDENLY ACROSS THE JUNE	THEY DROPPED LIKE FLAKES	409	4
BUT DO ONE FACE US SUDDENLY--	SUNSET AT NIGHT--IS	415	7
WHEN--SUDDENLY--MY RICHES SHRANK--	IT WOULD NEVER BE COMMON	430	21
'TWERE SUDDENLY CONFIRMED [ORDAINED]--	I THINK I WAS ENCHANTED	593	20
ABSCONDED--SUDDENLY--	BEREAVEMENT IN THEIR	645	12
FLING SUDDENLY ON MEN--	THE COLOR OF A QUEEN, IS	776	6
AS TRADE HAD SUDDENLY ENCROACHED	A LIGHT EXISTS IN SPRING	812	19
TO SUDDENLY DESCEND	THOSE CATTLE SMALLER	1388	10
AS SUDDENLY BE WORN	AS IMPERCEPTIBLY AS	1540	V
SUDDENNESS			
AND CLICK [BOLT]--AND SUDDENNESS.	THE SOUL'S DISTINCT	974	8
YOU SEE--GOD BLESS HIS SUDDENNESS--	BEFORE YOU THOUGHT OF	1465	3
AND STOOD BEFORE THE SUDDENNESS	THE THRILL CAME SLOWLY	1495	V 7
SUE			
AND EARTH IS QUITE COQUETTISH, AND BESEEMETH IN VAIN TO SUE.	AWAKE YE MUSES NINE,	1	24
SUE--FOREVERMORE!	ONE SISTER HAVE I IN OUR	14	27
IS IT TRUE, DEAR SUE?	IS IT TRUE, DEAR SUE?	218	1
AS ONE SHOULD SUE A STAR--	THE HEAVEN VESTS FOR	694	10
I COULD NOT DRINK IT, SWEET [SUE],	I COULD NOT DRINK IT,	818	1
THEN SUE IT TO DELAY	WE SHUN IT ERE IT COMES,	1580	3
SUED			
STABBED--WHILE I SUED	HE STRAINED MY FAITH--	497	13
I SUED THE NEWS--YET FEARED--THE NEWS	I SUED THE NEWS--YET	1360	1
SUFFER			
SOMEWHAT, TO SUFFER,	SOMEWHAT, TO HOPE FOR,	1041	4
SUFFER THE VERMILLION--	SANG FROM THE HEART,	1059	6
I TELL IT GAY TO THOSE WHO SUFFER NOW--	TIME DOES GO ON--	1121	2
TRADITION BEAR WITH [SUFFER] ME	ONE OF THE ONES THAT	1466	26
SUFFERED			
HAS SUFFERED ALL IT CAN--	THERE IS A LANGUOR OF	396	4
BUT SUFFERED AN [ABSENT THROUGH] EXCHANGE OF TERRITORY--	IT KNEW NO LAPSE, NOR	560	7
TO KNOW JUST HOW HE SUFFERED--WOULD BE DEAR--	TO KNOW JUST HOW HE	622	1
SHE SUFFERED ME, FOR I HAD MOURNED--	THE BIRDS REPORTED FROM	743	17
WHO HATH SUFFERED HIM--	WHEN I HOPED I FEARED--	1181	8
ITSELF HATH SUFFERED TOO	UNTO A BROKEN HEART	1704	4
SUFFERER			
THAN THIS SUFFERER POLITE--	TAKE YOUR HEAVEN FURTHER	388	10
SUFFERING			
ORDAINED TO SUFFERING--	IT MIGHT BE LONELIER	405	12
THAT DEADEN SUFFERING--	THE HEART ASKS PLEASURE	536	4
AN ACTUAL SUFFERING STRENGTHENS	THEY SAY THAT "TIME	686	3
THROUGH THE STRAIT [STRAIGHT] PASS OF SUFFERING--	THROUGH THE STRAIT PASS	792	1
BY SUFFERING--DESPAIR--	DESPAIR'S ADVANTAGE IS	799	2
THE WORTHINESS [EXCELLENCE / QUALITY] OF SUFFERING LIKE	DESPAIR'S ADVANTAGE IS	799	5
FAR AFTER SUFFERING	AS ONE DOES SICKNESS	957	10
SUFFICE			
IT--ONLY--CAN SUFFICE!	YOU SEE I CANNOT SEE--	253	15
IT WOULD SUFFICE MY PRAYER	I MEANT TO HAVE BUT	476	6
HER TOILETTE--TO SUFFICE--	I WATCHED THE MOON	629	22
I COULD SUFFICE FOR HIM, I KNEW--	I COULD SUFFICE FOR HIM,	643	1
HE--COULD SUFFICE FOR ME--	I COULD SUFFICE FOR HIM,	643	2
A HEAVENLY FATHER WOULD SUFFICE [CONTENT]	YOU LEFT ME--SIRE--TWO	644	3
WOULD [COULD] SUFFICE TO STOW--	SO MUCH SUMMER	651	11
AND ALMOST TO SUFFICE	DEPRIVED OF OTHER	773	8
SUFFICE US--FOR A CROWD--	ON A COLUMNAR SELF--	789	9
AS WILL SUFFICE TO LIGHT HER LAMPS--	NATURE--THE GENTLEST	790	19
FOR WHOM, THE TIME DID NOT SUFFICE [REMAIN]	NO NOTICE GAVE SHE, BUT	804	3
NO DEPUTY SUFFICE--	AN HONEST TEAR	1192	6
THAT IT BE SAVED THE SAVED SUFFICE	SOMEHOW MYSELF SURVIVED	1194	3
LAIN IN NATURE--SO SUFFICE US	LAIN IN NATURE--SO	1288	1
HIS SANDS SUFFICE	UNTIL THE DESERT KNOWS	1291	3
SUFFICED			
A DEW SUFFICED ITSELF--	A DEW SUFFICED ITSELF--	1437	1
SUFFICES			
ONE PORT--SUFFICES--FOR A BRIG--LIKE MINE--	HOW SICK--TO WAIT--IN	368	7
SUFFICETH			
THAT--SUFFICETH ME--	LIFE--IS WHAT WE MAKE IT	698	8
SUFFICIENCY			
'TIS GLORY'S FAR SUFFICIENCY [OVERTAKELESSNESS]	BECAUSE HE LOVES HER	1229	11
SUFFICIENT			
WHO WERE SUFFICIENT TO [COULD BEGIN ON--] MISERY?	BOUND--A TROUBLE--	269	V
BE IT'S GRAVE--SUFFICIENT SIGN--	HER--"LAST POEMS"--	312	15
SUFFICIENT TROTH, THAT WE SHALL [SHE WILL] RISE--	THERE CAME A DAY AT	322	25
SUFFICIENT ROYALTY!	THE FACE I CARRY WITH ME	336	16
SUFFICIENT DYNASTY--	MY REWARD FOR BEING, WAS	343	V

	FIRST LINE	POEM	LINE
SUFFICIENT (CONTINUED)			
SUFFICIENT TO OBLITERATE	MORE LIFE--WENT OUT--	422	15
ARE WE THAT WAIT--SUFFICIENT WORTH-- . . .	IT FEELS A SHAME TO BE	444	13
SUFFICIENT TO ENFOLD HIM	THE TREES LIKE TASSELS--	606	13
THE MINER'S LAMP--SUFFICIENT BE--	I SEE THEE BETTER--IN	611	7
SUFFICIENT CONTINENT--	ALL CIRCUMSTANCES ARE	820	4
SUFFICIENT FAME--	BE MINE THE DOOM--	845	2
LIGHT IS SUFFICIENT TO ITSELF--	LIGHT IS SUFFICIENT TO	862	1
A JUST SUFFICIENT RING.	HE OUTSTRIPPED TIME WITH	865	8
SUFFICIENT COURTESY.	MY BEST ACQUAINTANCES	932	8
"ARMS OF MINE--SUFFICIENT PHAETON-- . . .	"UNTO ME?" I DO NOT KNOW	964	7
SUFFICIENT FOR MY OWN	THE PRODUCTS OF MY FARM	1025	2
WITH THIS SUFFICIENT SWEET	I FIT FOR THEM--	1109	V 5
SUFFICIENTLY			
SUFFICIENTLY DEVELOPED--HE'D HIRE US . . .	MYSELF WAS FORMED--A	488	7
SUFFICING			
THAN THE SUFFICING LONGING	DELIGHT'S DESPAIR AT	1299	3
SUFFOCATE			
SUFFOCATE--WITH EASY WO--	HER--"LAST POEMS"--	312	17
TO SUFFOCATE THE EYE--	IT'S THOUGHTS--AND JUST	495	18
TILL RECTITUDE IS SUFFOCATE	THE WORTHLESSNESS OF	1373	V 4
SUFFUSE			
THEN A SOFTNESS--SUFFUSE THE STORY-- . . .	GLEE--THE GREAT STORM IS	619	14
SUFFUSED			
A SMILE SUFFUSED JEHOVAH'S FACE--	I MEANT TO HAVE BUT	476	13
SUFFUSES			
ILLUMINES [SUFFUSES] WITH A GLOW	OF WHOM SO DEAR	1504	3
SUGGEST			
THEY--SUGGEST TO OUR SIGHT--	BY MY WINDOW HAVE I FOR	797	18
SUGGESTION			
TILL THE SUGGESTION SINISTER	WHOEVER DISENCHANTS	1451	7
AT THE SUGGESTION OF HOLY SPECTRES-- . . .	THE BIBLE IS AN ANTIQUE	1545	3
SUGGESTS			
RETURNS--SUGGESTS--CONVICTS--ENCHANTS-- . .	THE LOVE A LIFE CAN SHOW	673	15
IT--SUGGESTS TO OUR FAITH--	BY MY WINDOW HAVE I FOR	797	17
SUING			
WHEN SUING--LIKE HER ESSEX	ELIZABETH TOLD ESSEX	1321	7
SUING IT NOT TO GO	NOT ANY MORE TO BE	1344	10
THAN VASTER SUING--	COME SHOW THY DURHAM	1542	9
SUIT			
THE BEE DOTH COURT THE FLOWER, THE FLOWER HIS SUIT RECEIVES,	AWAKE YE MUSES NINE,	1	13
PUT ON HER CARMINE SUIT	SHE SLEPT BENEATH A TREE	25	5
WILL SUIT ME JUST AS WELL--	I CAME TO BUY A SMILE--	223	4
WOULD SUIT AS BRIGHT, ...	DELIGHT IS AS THE FLIGHT	257	7
SOBBING--WILL SUIT--AS WELL AS PSALM! . .	PUT UP MY LUTE!	261	5
I'D RATHER SUIT MY FOOT	IS BLISS THEN, SUCH	340	4
CHERRIES--SUIT ROBINS--	VICTORY COMES LATE--	690	11
NAY--I'M THE SIZE SUIT THEE--	YOU SAID THAT I "WAS	738	4
I SUIT THEE--	YOU SAID THAT I "WAS	738	18
HIS SUIT A CHANCE	OF SILKEN SPEECH AND	896	5
SUIT [PLEASE] ME AT A VENTURE	FORTITUDE INCARNATE	1217	11
GIVEN TO ME WITHOUT THE SUIT	FRIGID AND SWEET HER	1318	5
HER TRIPLE SUIT AS SWEET	MY COUNTRY NEED NOT	1511	2
SUITABLE			
THERE WAS NO PURPLE SUITABLE--	DEAR MARCH--COME IN--	1320	16
SUITOR			
FIRST SUITOR NOT IN VAIN.	HOW FORTUNATE THE GRAVE	897	4
DEATH IS THE SUPPLE SUITOR	DEATH IS THE SUPPLE	1445	1
OLD SUITOR HEAVEN, ...	WE SHUN IT ERE IT COMES,	1580	7
SUITS			
AND YET--MY PRIMER SUITS ME SO	NOT IN THIS WORLD TO SEE	418	7
IT SUITS HIS OWN AUSTERITY--	I THINK THE HEMLOCK	525	3
SUITS ME--MORE THAN THOSE--	I COULD BRING YOU JEWELS	697	8
HIS MIGHTY PLEASURE SUITS US NOT	THE SUN IS GAY OR STARK	878	7
IT SUITS HIM BETTER THAN A CHECK	THE MERCHANT OF THE	1131	7
SULKED			
AND THEN HE SULKED IN MERCURY	THE SUN RETIRED TO A	1693	3
SULLEN			
HOW SWEET THESE [THOSE] SULLEN BARS . . .	HOW SOFT THIS PRISON IS	1334	2
SULLIED			
TOO SULLIED FOR THE HELL	UPON THE GALLOWS HUNG A	1757	2
SULPHURETS			
POWDER EXISTS IN CHARCOAL [ELEMENTS / SULPHURETS]--	A MAN MAY MAKE A REMARK	952	7
SUM SEE MIS SUM			
AND THO' THE SUM WAS SIMPLE	I HAD A GUINEA GOLDEN--	23	3
SOME ONE THE SUM COULD TELL--	IT'S ALL I HAVE TO BRING	26	6
I CANNOT TELL THE SUM, ...	SHE BORE IT TILL THE	144	6
TO MAKE AN EVEN SUM--	'TWAS JUST THIS TIME,	445	16
SO THAT THE SUM [LOVE] BE NEVER HINDERED .	SWEET--YOU FORGOT--BUT I	523	3
AND EVERY SEPARATE URCHIN'S SUM--	'TIS ONE BY ONE--THE	545	15
TO US--GIGANTIC SUM--	HE GAVE AWAY HIS LIFE--	567	2
SUPREMEST EARTHLY SUM--	ONE BLESSING HAD I THAN	756	12
DANGER--DEEPENS SUM--	EXPECTATION--IS	807	8
FROM THE EARLY SUM--	ONE DAY IS THERE OF THE	814	10
THE SUM THAT IT HAD GROWN.	I MADE SLOW RICHES BUT	843	8
OF SUM--	UNCERTAIN LEASE--	857	4
I'LL MIS SUM THEM.	EACH SCAR I'LL KEEP FOR	877	8
SUM THE HISTORY--	HOW THE WATERS CLOSED	923	8

	FIRST LINE	POEM	LINE
SUM (CONTINUED)			
ON NATURE'S PERFECT [GENERAL] SUM--	IT BLOOMED AND DROPT, A	978	10
THAT WHAT IS SUM TO ME	THE VOICE THAT STANDS	1189	6
SUBTLE THE SUM THAT PURCHASE YOU--	BROTHER OF INGOTS--AH	1366	V 2
THE SMALL [SAME] STALE SUM--	HOW DESTITUTE IS HE	1477	4
SOME SCHISM IN THE SUM--	THE CLOCK STRIKES ONE	1569	2
SUMMER			
AND AS THE SUMMER NEARS--	I HAVE A BIRD IN SPRING	5	4
SUMMER--SISTER--SERAPH!	THE GENTIAN WEAVES HER	18	15
AS IF THE STARS SOME SUMMER NIGHT	THERE IS A MORN BY MEN	24	16
SUMMER FOR THEE, GRANT I MAY BE	SUMMER FOR THEE, GRANT I	31	1
WHEN SUMMER DAYS ARE FLOWN!	SUMMER FOR THEE, GRANT I	31	2
I CAN SPARE THIS SUMMER, UNRELUCTANTLY.	WHEN I COUNT THE SEEDS	40	11
FROM THE SUMMER HILL	GLOWING IS HER BONNET,	72	6
OH SACRAMENT OF SUMMER DAYS,	THESE ARE THE DAYS WHEN	130	13
BELLES FROM SOME LOST SUMMER DAY--	PIGMY SERAPHS--GONE	138	3
ROSES OF A STEADFAST SUMMER	THO' MY DESTINY BE	163	13
ALL THIS IN SUMMER.	A FUZZY FELLOW, WITHOUT	173	9
UNWEARIED, ALL THE SUMMER LONG,	IF I COULD BRIBE THEM BY	179	10
TO CONTINENTS OF SUMMER--	AS IF SOME LITTLE ARCTIC	180	5
IF SUMMER WERE AN AXIOM--	THE SKIES CANT KEEP	191	11
ON WHOM THE SUMMER SHONE!	ON THIS LONG STORM THE	194	8
REELING--THRO ENDLESS SUMMER DAYS--	I TASTE A LIQUOR NEVER	214	7
IT CANT BE "SUMMER"!	IT CANT BE "SUMMER"!	221	1
HAPLY--YOUR SUMMER NIGHT TO CHARM--	KILL YOUR BALM--AND IT'S	238	4
LATE--WHEN I TAKE MY PLACE IN SUMMER--	I SHALL KEEP SINGING!	250	7
THE ONE WHO [THAT] COULD REPEAT THE SUMMER DAY--	THE ONE WHO COULD REPEAT	307	1
NOT UNTO [UPON] IT'S SUMMER--MORNING	HER--"LAST POEMS"--	312	7
I CRAVE HIM GRACE OF SUMMER BOUGHS,	OF ALL THE SOUNDS	321	25
I KNOW A PLACE WHERE SUMMER STRIVES	I KNOW A PLACE WHERE	337	1
IT WILL BE SUMMER--EVENTUALLY.	IT WILL BE SUMMER--	342	1
TILL SUMMER FOLDS HER MIRACLE--	IT WILL BE SUMMER--	342	17
EMERGED--A SUMMER AFTERNOON--	FROM COCOON FORTH A	354	3
MY ART, A SUMMER DAY--HAD PATRONS--	WHEN DIAMONDS ARE A	397	6
MY SUMMER--IS DESPOILED--	THE WINTERS ARE SO SHORT	403	10
AND FAILED--AND ALL THE SUMMER LAUGHED--	GOD MADE A LITTLE	442	3
AND SUMMER HID HER FOREHEAD--	GOD MADE A LITTLE	442	7
ROWER, AND YACHT--SOME SOVREIGN SUMMER--	LOVE--THOU ART HIGH--	453	11
DEEP DUG--FOR SUMMER DAYS--	I KNOW WHERE WELLS GROW	460	2
THAT'S SUMMER--	MY GARDEN--LIKE THE	484	3
I'D BRUSH THE SUMMER BY	IF YOU WERE COMING IN	511	2
NO SUMMER--COULD--FOR THEM--	LIKE FLOWERS, THAT HEARD	513	6
TO A FICTITIOUS COUNTRY [SUMMER / SEASON]	CONJECTURING A CLIMATE	562	5
THEN SUMMER--THEN THE HEAVEN OF GOD--	I RECKON--WHEN I COUNT	569	3
THEIR SUMMER--LASTS A SOLID YEAR--	I RECKON--WHEN I COUNT	569	9
THE SUMMER DEEPENED, WHILE WE STROVE--	MY FIRST WELL DAY--SINCE	574	9
WHAT CARE THE DEAD FOR SUMMER?	WHAT CARE THE DEAD, FOR	592	9
FAR PSALTERIES OF SUMMER--	THE TREES LIKE TASSELS--	606	5
OF NATURE'S--SUMMER DAY!	THE TREES LIKE TASSELS--	606	28
THE PLEADING OF THE SUMMER--	THE TINT I CANNOT TAKE--	627	17
OURSELVES WERE WED ONE SUMMER--DEAR--	OURSELVES WERE WED ONE	631	1
AND YET, ONE SUMMER, WE WERE QUEENS [WED]--	OURSELVES WERE WED ONE	631	15
IMPANELLED FROM NO SUMMER BRIEF--	TO MY SMALL HEARTH HIS	638	5
SO MUCH SUMMER	SO MUCH SUMMER	651	1
TILL ALL THE GRIEF WITH SUMMER--WAVED [BLEW]	'TIS GOOD--THE LOOKING	660	7
AND FAR ABROAD ON SUMMER DAYS--	THE LOVE A LIFE CAN SHOW	673	8
MAKE SUMMER--WHEN THE LADY LIE	ESSENTIAL OILS--ARE	675	7
THE SUMMER MULTIPLY--	LEAST BEE THAT BREW--	676	3
WOULD YOU LIKE SUMMER? TASTE OF OURS.	WOULD YOU LIKE SUMMER?	691	1
HER EYE UNTO THE SUMMER DEW	THE MOON WAS BUT A CHIN	737	7
THE SUMMER GRACE, FOR NOTICE STROVE--	THE BIRDS REPORTED FROM	743	9
A SUMMER AFTERNOON--	NATURE--THE GENTLEST	790	10
HER FINAL SUMMER WAS IT--	HER FINAL SUMMER WAS IT	795	1
THE SUMMER GNAT DISPLAYS--	WHO GIANTS KNOW, WITH	796	6
SHE WAS NOT WARM, THOUGH SUMMER SHONE	NO NOTICE GAVE SHE, BUT	804	5
WAS SUMMER TO A SCORE	THIS BAUBLE WAS	805	6
TWICE HAD SUMMER HER FAIR VERDURE	TWICE HAD SUMMER HER	846	1
SCANTILY DEALT TO THE SUMMER MORNING	SPLIT THE LARK--AND	861	3
A SUMMER BRIEFER THAN THE FIRST	THERE IS A JUNE WHEN	930	3
THE SUMMER OF THE JUST,	THERE IS A JUNE WHEN	930	10
WHAT SHALL I DO WHEN THE SUMMER TROUBLES--	WHAT SHALL I DO WHEN THE	956	1
THE SUMMER CLOSED UPON ITSELF	MIDSUMMER, WAS IT, WHEN	962	3
AS SLEIGH BELLS SEEM [SOUND] IN SUMMER	AS SLEIGH BELLS SEEM IN	981	1
THE SUMMER WOULD NOT CEASE--	DID WE ABOLISH FROST	1014	2
A SUMMER FURTHER I MUST WEAR,	HER LITTLE PARASOL TO	1038	5
WHOSE [WHERE] SUMMER SET IN SUMMER, TILL	THERE IS A ZONE WHOSE	1056	5
WHOSE [WHERE] SUMMER SET IN SUMMER, TILL	THERE IS A ZONE WHOSE	1056	5
AND INDIAN SUMMER NOON [SUN]--	EXCEPT THE SMALLER SIZE	1067	V
FURTHER IN SUMMER THAN THE BIRDS	FURTHER IN SUMMER THAN	1068	1
EVERY SUMMER BE	REVOLUTION IS THE POD	1082	6
TOO DEAR THE [WERE] SUMMER EVENING	THESE ARE THE NIGHTS	1128	13
WINDS OF SUMMER FIELDS	AFTER A HUNDRED YEARS	1147	9
ALL THAT IS NAMED OF SUMMER DAYS	THE PUNGENT ATOM IN THE	1191	3
A SEA OF SUMMER AIR	A SOFT SEA WASHED AROUND	1198	2
'TWAS LATER WHEN THE SUMMER WENT	'TWAS LATER WHEN THE	1276	1
PASTED BY THE SIMPLE SUMMER	LAIN IN NATURE--SO	1288	7
WITH SUMMER, OR THE WORLD--	WINTER IS GOOD--HIS HOAR	1316	4
AS SUMMER INTO AUTUMN SLIPS	AS SUMMER INTO AUTUMN	1346	1
"THE SUMMER" THAN "THE AUTUMN," LEST	AS SUMMER INTO AUTUMN	1346	3

	FIRST LINE	POEM	LINE
SUMMER (CONTINUED)			
THE LAST [CLOSE] OF SUMMER IS DELIGHT--[A TIME / RESULT--SURVEY]	THE LAST OF SUMMER IS	1353	1
SUMMER LAID HER SIMPLE HAT	SUMMER LAID HER SIMPLE	1363	1
SUMMER LAID HER SUPPLE GLOVE	SUMMER LAID HER SIMPLE	1363	5
SUMMER--WE ALL HAVE SEEN--	SUMMER--WE ALL HAVE SEEN	1386	1
BUT SUMMER DOES NOT CARE--	SUMMER--WE ALL HAVE SEEN	1386	5
LAST TO ADHERE [AT THE SCENE] WHEN SUMMER CLEAVES [SUMMER . . .	AFTER ALL BIRDS HAVE	1395	7
LAST TO ADHERE [AT THE SCENE] WHEN SUMMER CLEAVES [SUMMER . . .	AFTER ALL BIRDS HAVE	1395	7
WHY BIRDS, A SUMMER MORNING	ONE JOY OF SO MUCH	1420	5
SUMMER HAS TWO BEGINNINGS--	SUMMER HAS TWO	1422	1
FOR SUMMER TOO INDELIBLE [INSCRUTABLE]	A LITTLE SNOW WAS HERE	1444	7
TO SEE THE SUMMER SKY	TO SEE THE SUMMER SKY	1472	1
SUMMER IS SHORTER THAN ANY ONE--	SUMMER IS SHORTER THAN	1506	1
LIFE IS SHORTER THAN SUMMER--	SUMMER IS SHORTER THAN	1506	2
AND SUMMER IS [SUMMER PASSED / SUMMERS ARE] AWAY--	THERE COMES A WARNING	1536	4
AND SUMMER IS [SUMMER PASSED / SUMMERS ARE] AWAY--	THERE COMES A WARNING	1536	4
THE SUMMER LAPSED AWAY--	AS IMPERCEPTIBLY AS	1540	2
OUR SUMMER MADE HER LIGHT ESCAPE	AS IMPERCEPTIBLY AS	1540	15
BUT SUMMER, FRILLED AS FOR A HOLIDAY	WE WEAR OUR SOBER	1572	2
A WEED OF SUMMER CAME--	TO HER DERIDED HOME	1586	2
BESTOWED A SUMMER LONG	TO HER DERIDED HOME	1586	5
TALK NOT TO ME OF SUMMER TREES	TALK NOT TO ME OF SUMMER	1634	1
THE POMP OF SUMMER [ETHIOPIAN] DAYS	SOME ONE PREPARED THIS	1644	6
IN THAT LOW SUMMER OF THE WEST	A LANE OF YELLOW LED THE	1650	7
OF OTHER SUMMER DAYS	NATURE CAN DO NO MORE	1673	4
SUMMER BEGINS TO HAVE THE LOOK	SUMMER BEGINS TO HAVE	1682	1
SEED--SUMMER--TOMB--	A PIT--BUT HEAVEN OVER	1712	16
'TWAS HERE MY SUMMER PAUSED	'TWAS HERE MY SUMMER	1756	1
BEYOND WHICH SUMMER HESITATES,	THE SADDEST NOISE, THE	1764	7
BUT JUST THE SUMMER KNOWS.	THOSE FINAL CREATURES,--	1766	4
THE SUMMER THAT WE DID NOT PRIZE,	THE SUMMER THAT WE DID	1773	1
SUMMER'S			
UPON A COMMON SUMMER'S MORN--	A SEPAL, PETAL, AND A	19	2
AND SUMMER'S BROWS WERE BOUND.	THERE IS A MORN BY MEN	24	12
UPON THIS SUMMER'S DAY	WHEN ROSES CEASE TO	32	6
ON A SUMMER'S DAY--	BEFORE THE ICE IS IN THE	37	10
WHEREFORE, OH SUMMER'S DAY?	THE BEE IS NOT AFRAID OF	111	8
A SOMETHING IN A SUMMER'S DAY	A SOMETHING IN A	122	1
A SOMETHING IN A SUMMER'S NOON--	A SOMETHING IN A	122	4
AND STILL WITHIN A SUMMER'S NIGHT	A SOMETHING IN A	122	7
ANOTHER SUMMER'S DAY!	A SOMETHING IN A	122	22
FROM OUT MY SUMMER'S EVE--	SHE WENT AS QUIET AS THE	149	6
SEEMS SUMMER'S RECOLLECTION	LIKE SOME OLD FASHIONED	302	3
A SUMMER'S [THE SUMMERS] EMPTY ROOM--	IT SIFTS FROM LEADEN	311	14
THERE CAME A DAY AT SUMMER'S FULL,	THERE CAME A DAY AT	322	1
HAVE SUMMER'S LEAVE TO PLAY--	I ENVY SEAS, WHEREON HE	498	14
OR BEES--THAT THOUGHT THE SUMMER'S NAME	LIKE FLOWERS, THAT HEARD	513	4
SOME BASHFUL SUMMER'S DAY--	THE HEAVEN VESTS FOR	694	4
WHEN SUMMER'S EVERLASTING DOWER--	PRECIOUS TO ME--SHE	727	13
THIS PASSIVE PLACE A SUMMER'S NIMBLE MANSION	THIS QUIET DUST WAS	813	5
A SUMMER'S AFTERNOON--	NOT ANY HIGHER STANDS	1256	8
OF SUMMER'S CIRCUMSPECT.	THE MUSHROOM IS THE ELF	1298	16
A [DO / OUR] SUMMER'S [NATURE'S] SOFT ASSEMBLIES GO	WITHOUT A SMILE--WITHOUT	1330	2
UPON A SUMMER'S DAY	THE LONG SIGH OF THE	1359	2
HOW KNOW IT FROM A SUMMER'S DAY?	HOW KNOW IT FROM A	1364	1
CONSULTING SUMMER'S CLOCK,	CONSULTING SUMMER'S	1715	1
A SNAKE IS SUMMER'S [NATURE'S] TREASON [DRAMA],	SWEET IS THE SWAMP WITH	1740	7
SUMMERS			
SUMMERS HAVE SPRINKLED THERE!	IN EBON BOX, WHEN YEARS	169	4
A SUMMER'S [THE SUMMERS] EMPTY ROOM--	IT SIFTS FROM LEADEN	311	14
NOT ALL THE SUMMERS--GREEN--	THE COLOR OF THE GRAVE	411	20
WITH SUMMERS, AND WITH WINTERS, GROW,	FITTER TO SEE HIM, I MAY	968	3
THE SUMMERS OF [IN] HESPERIDES	EXCEPT THE SMALLER SIZE	1067	7
. . . SWERVES / SUMMERS SWERVE] AWAY--	AFTER ALL BIRDS HAVE	1395	7
AND SUMMER IS [SUMMER PASSED / SUMMERS ARE] AWAY--	THERE COMES A WARNING	1536	4
IF OTHER SUMMERS BE	NATURE CAN DO NO MORE	1673	6
SUMMERTIME			
WHEN SUMMERTIME IS DONE--	LIKE SOME OLD FASHIONED	302	2
SUMMIT			
THE SUMMIT IS NOT GIVEN	THE HALLOWING OF PAIN	772	4
SUMMITS			
THESE SECEDED FROM YOUR SUMMONS [SUMMITS / SUBJECTS / SUBSTANCE]	KNOCK WITH TREMOR--	1325	6
SUMMON			
AND SUMMON THEM TO DRINK;	I BRING AN UNACCUSTOMED	132	4
BUT GOD CAN SUMMON EVERY FACE	THEY DROPPED LIKE FLAKES	409	8
SOME SHALL [SOME ONE] SUMMON ME--	PROMISE THIS--WHEN YOU	648	2
SNATCH IT FOR [COVET IT / TIE IT FOR / SEIZE IT FOR / SUMMON . . .	SUMMER LAID HER SIMPLE	1363	4
SUMMONED			
SUMMONED--UNEXPECTEDLY--	I'M SAYING EVERY DAY	373	32
THEY SUMMONED US TO DIE--	THEY PUT US FAR APART--	474	13

	FIRST LINE	POEM	LINE
SUMMONED (CONTINUED)			
TILL SUMMONED TO HIS RECOGNITION	FACTS BY OUR SIDE ARE	1497	7
IS SUMMONED BY THE TIDES.	EACH THAT WE LOSE TAKES	1605	4
SUMMONS			
HAD IT A NOTICE [SUMMONS] FROM THE NOON	THIS THAT WOULD GREET--	778	5
THESE SECEDED FROM YOUR SUMMONS [SUMMITS / SUBJECTS / SUBSTANCE]	KNOCK WITH TREMOR--	1325	6
SUMPTUOUS			
SUCH SUMPTUOUS--DESPAIR--	I WOULD NOT PAINT--A	505	8
'TIS SUMPTUOUS ENOUGH FOR ME--	DEPRIVED OF OTHER	773	7
OH SUMPTUOUS MOMENT	OH SUMPTUOUS MOMENT	1125	1
BUT LEAVES A SUMPTUOUS [BLISSFUL] DESTITUTION--	IN MANY AND REPORTLESS	1382	7
TOO OBDURATE [COMPETENT / SUMPTUOUS] FOR SNOWS--	A LITTLE SNOW WAS HERE	1444	8
IN SUMPTUOUS SOLITUDE--	THE THRILL CAME SLOWLY	1495	4
IN BLISSFUL [LUSCIOUS / SUMPTUOUS] REVERY	HIS ORIENTAL HERESIES	1526	V
SUMPTUOUSNESS			
A SUMPTUOUSNESS BESTOWS [SUPPLIES]	THE LUXURY TO APPREHEND	815	12
SUMS			
INVOLVING STATELIER SUMS.	LOW AT MY PROBLEM	69	4
THIS SUMS THE APPARATUS	PRAYER IS THE LITTLE	437	7
TO HIM--SUMS MISERY--	IT MAKES NO DIFFERENCE	620	12
ADJACENT SUMS	UNTIL THE DESERT KNOWS	1291	9
SUN			
ADAM, AND EVE, HIS CONSORT, THE MOON, AND THEN THE SUN;	AWAKE YE MUSES NINE,	1	8
IN HONOR OF THE SUN!	"SIC TRANSIT GLORIA	3	36
WHEREVER RUNS THE BREATHLESS SUN--	THERE IS A WORD	8	11
I SAW THE SUN--HIS PLUNDER DONE	I NEVER TOLD THE BURIED	11	3
BENEATH THE SUN MAY FIND.	I HAD A GUINEA GOLDEN--	23	36
HERE ARE THE BIRDS THAT SOUGHT THE SUN	THERE IS A MORN BY MEN	24	10
HAVE PASSED BEYOND THE SUN--	WHEN ROSES CEASE TO	32	4
TO GIRD US FOR THE SUN,	IF PAIN FOR PEACE	63	8
FROM SOME OLD FORTRESS ON THE SUN	SOME RAINBOW--COMING	64	10
FOR HER OLD LOVER--DON THE SUN!	SOME RAINBOW--COMING	64	17
ANGELS, WHEN THE SUN IS HOTTEST	ANGELS, IN THE EARLY	94	5
THE DAISY FOLLOWS SOFT THE SUN--	THE DAISY FOLLOWS SOFT	106	1
WE ARE THE FLOWER--THOU THE SUN!	THE DAISY FOLLOWS SOFT	106	7
GUIDES STILL THE SUN ALONG THE CRAG	A SOMETHING IN A	122	17
DANCING AROUND THE SUN	FOR EVERY BIRD A NEST--	143	17
AND STARTED FOR THE SUN.	SHE DIED--THIS WAS THE	150	4
THE SUN KEPT STOOPING--STOOPING--LOW!	THE SUN KEPT STOOPING--	152	1
AS BLIND MEN LEARN THE SUN!	TO LEARN THE TRANSPORT	167	2
TO FIRMAMENTS OF SUN--	AS IF SOME LITTLE ARCTIC	180	6
BRAVE--SHINES THE SUN THROUGH THE FRECKLED PANE--	HOW MANY TIMES THESE LOW	187	10
MAKE ME A PICTURE OF THE SUN--	MAKE ME A PICTURE OF THE	188	1
WIND AND SUN--WILT THEE ARRAY!	POOR LITTLE HEART!	192	12
ON THIS LATE MORN--THE SUN--	ON THIS LONG STORM THE	194	2
DUKES--FOR SETTING SUN!	MORNING--IS THE PLACE	197	4
UNTIL THE MORNING SUN--	TWO SWIMMERS WRESTLED ON	201	2
WERE USELESS AS NEXT MORNING'S SUN--	I SHOULD NOT DARE TO	205	15
LEANING AGAINST THE--SUN--	I TASTE A LIQUOR NEVER	214	V 16
NEXT SUN--TO DIE--	SHOULD YOU BUT FAIL AT--	226	4
AT THE SETTING SUN--	GOD PERMITS INDUSTRIOUS	231	6
THE SUN--JUST TOUCHED THE MORNING--	THE SUN--JUST TOUCHED	232	1
NOTCHING THE FALL OF THE EVEN SUN!	BOUND--A TROUBLE--	269	10
THE SUN HAS GOT AS FAR	I KNOW SOME LONELY	289	33
BY THE WIZARD [SETTING] SUN--	HOW THE OLD MOUNTAINS	291	4
AND HE--COULD REPRODUCE THE SUN--	THE ONE WHO COULD REPEAT	307	4
I'LL TELL YOU HOW THE SUN ROSE--	I'LL TELL YOU HOW THE	318	1
"THAT MUST HAVE BEEN THE SUN"!	I'LL TELL YOU HOW THE	318	8
THE SUN, AS COMMON, WENT ABROAD,	THERE CAME A DAY AT	322	5
INCAUTIOUS--OF THE SUN--	BEFORE I GOT MY EYE PUT	327	21
FOR PRIVILEGE OF SOD AND SUN--	THERE IS A FLOWER THAT	380	19
HER PROVIDENCE--THE SUN--	THERE IS A FLOWER THAT	380	26
AND JUST BEFORE THE SUN--	A VISITOR IN MARL--	391	6
IN WINTER--TILL THE SUN--	THE COLOR OF THE GRAVE	411	12
AS YOU DO THE SUN--	YOU'LL KNOW IT--AS YOU	420	3
HIS LISP--IS LIGHTNING--AND THE SUN--	YOU'LL KNOW IT--AS YOU	420	12
WHO KNOWS--BUT WE'D REACH THE SUN?	LOVE--THOU ART HIGH--	453	12
WE TURNED OUR BACKS UPON THE SUN	THEY PUT US FAR APART--	474	19
'TIS ENTERED FROM THE SUN--	DOOM IS THE HOUSE	475	2
UNCONSCIOUS THAT THE SUN	NO MAN CAN COMPASS A	477	6
A WONDERFUL--TO FEEL THE SUN	A SOLEMN THING WITHIN	483	7
A LITTLE NEARER--EVERY SUN	A SOLEMN THING WITHIN	483	15
TO HER IMPERIAL SUN.	HE TOUCHED ME, SO I LIVE	506	18
. . . GAMBOLS OF] THE SUN--	TWO BUTTERFLIES WENT OUT	533	V
FOR FRENZY OF [FRENZIES OF / ANTICS IN / ANTICS WITH] THE SUN--	TWO BUTTERFLIES WENT OUT	533	V
FIRST--POETS--THEN THE SUN--	I RECKON--WHEN I COUNT	569	2
THEY CAN AFFORD A SUN	I RECKON--WHEN I COUNT	569	10
THEN--MEASURING THE SUN--	MY FIRST WELL DAY--SINCE	574	28
THE ORCHARD, WHEN THE SUN IS ON--	"HEAVEN" HAS DIFFERENT	575	9
AS A HAND DID TRY TO CHALK THE SUN	I FOUND THE WORDS TO	581	4
WIDTHS OUT OF THE SUN--	DID YOU EVER STAND IN A	590	2
THE SUN DOES NOT ALLOW	TO INTERRUPT HIS YELLOW	591	2
THE SOLSTICE HAD NO SUN	WHAT CARE THE DEAD, FOR	592	10
BUT, PRINCIPALLY--OF SUN--	OF BRUSSELS--IT WAS NOT	602	12

	FIRST LINE	POEM	LINE
SUN (CONTINUED)			
ACCOMPANYING THE SUN--	THE TREES LIKE TASSELS--	606	4
THE SUN SHONE WHOLE AT INTERVALS--	THE TREES LIKE TASSELS--	606	9
TO THOSE WHOSE DARK--HATH SO--SURPASSING SUN--	I SEE THEE BETTER--IN	611	14
YOUR COTTAGE--FACED THE SUN--	OURSELVES WERE WED ONE	631	10
WITHDREW THE SUN--TO OTHER WESTS--	I COULD SUFFICE FOR HIM,	643	9
IN DYING--'TIS AS IF OUR SOULS [WORLD / SELVES / SUN]	BEREAVEMENT IN THEIR	645	11
BUT CERTAINTIES OF SUN [NOON]--	I THINK TO LIVE--MAY BE	646	17
TO SEDUCE [ENTICE / PERSUADE] THE SUN	PROMISE THIS--WHEN YOU	648	18
AND SMITES THE TINDER IN THE SUN--	THE LOVE A LIFE CAN SHOW	673	5
SEED OF PALM, BY LYBIAN SUN	SOIL OF FLINT, IF STEADY	681	3
THE SUN KEPT SETTING--SETTING--STILL	THE SUN KEPT SETTING--	692	1
WE PASSED THE SETTING SUN--	BECAUSE I COULD NOT STOP	712	12
THE SUN FROM SHINING,	RESTS AT NIGHT	714	2
AND THE SUN--GO ON--	RESTS AT NIGHT	714	6
PROCEED--INSERTING HERE--A SUN--	IT'S EASY TO INVENT A	724	11
FALTER! WHEN THE SUN	ALTER! WHEN THE HILLS DO	729	2
THE SUN--UPON A MORNING MEETS THEM--	FOUR TREES--UPON A	742	5
ATMOSPHERE, AND SUN ENDORSE [CONFIRM] IT--	GROWTH OF MAN--LIKE	750	3
THE SUN--WITH JUST [BROAD] DELIGHT	THE MOUNTAINS--GROW	757	6
TO SHOW THE SUN THE WAY--	MY FAITH IS LARGER THAN	766	4
WORLDS WERE LYING OUT TO [SWIMMING IN THE / LYING IN THE] SUN--	WHEN I HOPED, I	768	11
AFTER SUN HAS [WHEN THE SUN IS] SET--	WHEN I HOPED, I	768	20
AFTER SUN HAS [WHEN THE SUN IS] SET--	WHEN I HOPED, I	768	20
THE COLOR OF A SUN	THE COLOR OF A QUEEN, IS	776	2
THE SUN ENGROSSED THE EAST--	THE BIRDS BEGUN AT FOUR	783	21
AND WHEN THE SUN GO DOWN--	NATURE--THE GENTLEST	790	12
AND THE UPPER SIDE--IS THE SUN--	BY MY WINDOW HAVE I FOR	797	10
SO SET IT'S SUN IN THEE	SO SET IT'S SUN IN THEE	808	1
OF NEIGHBORS AND THE SUN	THIS CONSCIOUSNESS THAT	822	2
"AS LARGE AS I"--RELATE THE SUN	LOVE RECKONS BY ITSELF--	826	2
OF THE SEASONS AND THE SUN.	ALWAYS MINE!	839	5
WAS STEADY AS THE SUN	I MADE SLOW RICHES BUT	843	2
HE OUTSTRIPPED STARS AND SUN	HE OUTSTRIPPED TIME WITH	865	2
THE SUN AND MOON MUST MAKE THEIR HASTE--	THE SUN AND MOON MUST	871	1
THE SUN IS GAY OR STARK	THE SUN IS GAY OR STARK	878	1
A CLOUD THE MIGHTY SUN ENCLOSES	A SHADE UPON THE MIND	882	3
WHEN I HAVE SEEN THE SUN EMERGE	WHEN I HAVE SEEN THE SUN	888	1
WE CAN BUT FOLLOW TO THE SUN--	WE CAN BUT FOLLOW TO THE	920	1
SUN--WITHDRAWN TO RECOGNITION--	STRUCK, WAS I, NOR YET	925	11
HOLDS A SUN ON ME--	STRUCK, WAS I, NOR YET	925	20
HALF HER COMPLEXION OF THE SUN--	FAIRER THROUGH FADING--	938	3
YET AMPLER THAN THE SUN--	A COFFIN--IS A SMALL	943	6
AFFLICTS ME--AS A SETTING SUN--	I LEARNED--AT LEAST--	944	30
THOU SUPERCILIOUS SUN?	THE SUNSET STOPPED ON	950	8
IF WHEN [AS] THE SUN REVEAL,	AS FROST IS BEST	951	5
SUN--IF SHONE--OR STORM--IF SHATTERED--	ALL FORGOT FOR	966	11
THE SUN IN PLACE--NO OTHER FRAUD	IT BLOOMED AND DROPT, A	978	9
UNBRAIDING IN THE SUN	A NARROW FELLOW IN THE	986	14
SUPERFLUOUS WERE THE SUN	SUPERFLUOUS WERE THE SUN	999	1
PHIALS LEFT, AND THE SUN!	DYING AT MY MUSIC!	1003	6
THAT CARRIES IN THE SUN.	WHO IS THE EAST?	1032	4
HE--SOVREIGN AS THE SUN	SAID DEATH TO PASSION	1033	7
WHOSE SUN CONSTRUCTS PERPETUAL NOON	THERE IS A ZONE WHOSE	1056	3
AND INDIAN SUMMER NOON [SUN]--	EXCEPT THE SMALLER SIZE	1067	V
IS FURTHER THAN THE SUN.	COUNT NOT THAT FAR THAT	1074	4
THE SUN WENT DOWN--NO MAN LOOKED ON--	THE SUN WENT DOWN--NO	1079	1
THE SUN WENT UP--NO MAN LOOKED ON--	THE SUN WENT DOWN--NO	1079	5
A PERISHED SUN	WE LEARN IN THE	1083	4
AND SET THE SUN	THE CRICKETS SANG	1104	2
THE SUN RAN MILES AWAY	THE BIRD DID PRANCE--THE	1107	2
THERE IS A SUN--	TIME DOES GO ON--	1121	4
'TIS MY FIRST NIGHT BENEATH THE SUN	'TIS MY FIRST NIGHT	1122	1
THAT OPENED TO THE SUN	A GREAT HOPE FELL	1123	15
TO WARM WITH SUN--	TOO COLD IS THIS	1135	2
TO MOUNTAIN--TO THE SUN--	THE FROST OF DEATH WAS	1136	6
BY FIRES OF THE SUN.	THE WORK OF HER THAT	1143	4
AFTER THE SUN COMES OUT	AFTER THE SUN COMES OUT	1148	1
SHORED [PUSHED] THE SUN AWAY	ON THE WORLD YOU COLORED	1171	10
OH SUN--BUT JUST A SECOND'S RIGHT	MY GOD--HE SEES THEE--	1178	8
THE SUN AND FOG CONTESTED	THE SUN AND FOG	1190	1
THE SUN TOOK DOWN HIS YELLOW WHIP	THE SUN AND FOG	1190	3
STANDS THE SUN SO CLOSE AND MIGHTY	WE LIKE MARCH.	1213	8
HAD I NOT SEEN THE SUN	HAD I NOT SEEN THE SUN	1233	1
THE SUN SUBSIDING ON HIS COURSE	THE LILAC IS AN ANCIENT	1241	5
UNROLLS UPON THE SUN	THE BUTTERFLY'S	1244	V 3
THE SUN SENT OUT	LIKE BROOMS OF STEEL	1252	5
BEFORE IT SEE THE SUN!	LONGING IS LIKE THE SEED	1255	8
AT LEISURE WAS THE SUN--	THE MOUNTAINS STOOD IN	1278	5
OF IT'S ANTERIOR SUN.	DELIGHT'S DESPAIR AT	1299	8
IS THERE NO SWEET BENEATH THE SUN	OUR LITTLE SECRETS SLINK	1326	7
THE MEM'RY OF THE SUN	THE SYMPTOM OF THE GALE	1327	9
NATURE ASSIGNS THE SUN--	NATURE ASSIGNS THE SUN--	1336	1
WE TURN THE SUN [SPELL] AWAY,	AS SUMMER INTO AUTUMN	1346	4
THAN OWN A RISING SUN	I'D RATHER RECOLLECT A	1349	2
THE SUN IS ONE--AND ON THE TARE	THE SUN IS ONE--AND ON	1372	1
IS PROOF AGAINST THE SUN	THE BUTTERFLY'S NUMIDIAN	1387	3
BENEATH THE SECOND SUN--	A FIELD OF STUBBLE,	1407	2

	FIRST LINE	POEM	LINE
SUN (CONTINUED)			
WAS [SAT] THE DEFIANT SUN--	A WILD BLUE SKY ABREAST	1415	4
TILL WITH THE SETTING [CLOSING] SUN	IT WAS A QUIET SEEMING	1419	3
A MANSE OF MECHLIN AND OF FLOSS [GLOSS / SUN]--	THE FAIREST HOME I EVER	1423	5
THE SUN WENT OUT TO WORK--	A DEW SUFFICED ITSELF--	1437	5
OR EMPTIED BY THE SUN	A DEW SUFFICED ITSELF--	1437	10
THE SUN RESPECTFUL LIES--	A CHILLY PEACE INFESTS	1443	2
BUT TRUTH, OUTLASTS THE SUN--	OPINION IS A FLITTING	1455	2
HOW SOFTLY SINKS THAT [HIS] TREMBLING SUN	LOOK BACK ON TIME, WITH	1478	3
AND [WHO] INDEPENDENT AS THE SUN	HOW HAPPY IS THE LITTLE	1510	7
AND THE SUN WILL FREE IT [LOOSE HIM]	FOLLOW WISE ORION	1538	V
THE PATTERN OF THE SUN	THE PATTERN OF THE SUN	1550	1
TO BE A SUN--	THE PATTERN OF THE SUN	1550	4
A WARMTH AS NEAR [SURE / FINE] AS IF THE SUN	TO SEE HER IS A PICTURE	1568	7
THE SUN PROCEEDS UNMOVED	APPARENTLY WITH NO	1624	6
THE SUN IN REINING TO THE WEST	THE SUN IN REINING TO	1636	1
THAT NEVER FELT THE SUN	GLORY IS THAT BRIGHT	1660	5
THE SUN GOES CROOKED--	I DID NOT REACH THEE	1664	20
IN A POSTHUMOUS SUN	JUDGEMENT IS JUSTEST	1671	7
THE SUN RETIRED TO A CLOUD	THE SUN RETIRED TO A	1693	1
INSULTING IS THE SUN	HOW DARE THE ROBINS SING	1724	9
WILL FINISH WITH THE SUN.	THE LONGEST DAY THAT GOD	1769	2
SUNBURNED			
AND BROAD--SUNBURNED ACQUAINTANCE	I'M SORRY FOR THE DEAD--	529	5
SUNBURNT			
STILL, MY LITTLE SUNBURNT BOSOM	THO' MY DESTINY BE	163	7
SUNDAY			
BECAUSE IT'S SUNDAY--ALL THE TIME--	I NEVER FELT AT HOME--	413	5
THEIR COSTUME, OF A SUNDAY,	IF ANYBODY'S FRIEND BE	509	5
SUNDER			
SO THE EYES ACCOST--AND SUNDER	SO THE EYES ACCOST--AND	752	1
AND SUNDER AS THEY CAME--	HOW KNOW IT FROM A	1364	8
WHEN [TILL] FLESH AND SPIRIT SUNDER	ONE JOY OF SO MUCH	1420	11
PURSUING [SUBDUING] WINDS THAT CENSURE [SUNDER] US	NO BRIGADIER THROUGHOUT	1561	5
SUNDERED			
OF LAST YEAR'S SUNDERED TUNE!	SOME RAINBOW--COMING	64	9
OF NEARNESS TO HER SUNDERED THINGS	OF NEARNESS TO HER	607	1
SUNDOWN			
IT'S STILLER THAN THE SUNDOWN.	I OFTEN PASSED THE	51	9
TILL SUNDOWN CREPT--A STEADY TIDE--	FROM COCOON FORTH A	354	22
FOR VISITER--OR SUNDOWN--	I LIVE WITH HIM--I SEE	463	3
'TWAS SUNSET [SUNDOWN]--ALL THE DAY--	I HAD NO CAUSE TO BE	542	16
SUNG			
THE BIRDS JOCOSER [REDOUBLED] SUNG--	A DROP FELL ON THE APPLE	794	10
AND TELL EACH OTHER HOW WE SUNG	I SING TO USE THE	850	7
WHEN WHAT THEY SUNG FOR IS UNDONE	A PANG IS MORE	1530	5
SUNNY			
GRANT ME, OH LORD, A SUNNY MIND--	BESIDES THE AUTUMN POETS	131	15
NOT ANY SUNNY TONE	NOT ANY SUNNY TONE	1674	1
ARRAIGN THE SUNNY BREVITY	THIS DOCILE ONE INTER	1752	3
SUNRISE			
SAVE BY LOVING SUNRISE	GLOWING IS HER BONNET,	72	9
A WIDER SUNRISE IN THE MORN--	AN ALTERED LOOK ABOUT	140	3
TO FIND THE SUNRISE LEFT--	YOU LOVE ME--YOU ARE	156	5
WHOSE GALLERIES--ARE SUNRISE--	A FEATHER FROM THE	161	3
PAST SUNRISE!	AT LAST, TO BE	174	5
WHEN HE--SURRENDERED TO THE SUNRISE--	PUT UP MY LUTE!	261	9
FANCY THE SUNRISE--LEFT THE DOOR AJAR!	I KNOW SOME LONELY	289	40
THE DOOMED--REGARD THE SUNRISE	THE DOOMED--REGARD THE	294	1
JOYFUL--TO WHOM THE SUNRISE	THE DOOMED--REGARD THE	294	9
THE SUNRISE SHOOK ABROAD	THE DAY CAME SLOW--TILL	304	6
AND SUNRISE GROWS SO NEAR	WHEN NIGHT IS ALMOST	347	2
CAUGHT SUNRISE FIRST--AND SUNSET--LAST--	A HOUSE UPON THE HIGHT--	399	7
"I'M SUNRISE"--NEED THE MAJESTY?	YOU'LL KNOW IT--AS YOU	420	10
SUNRISE--HAST THOU A FLAG FOR ME?	A WIFE--AT DAYBREAK I	461	2
THE SUNRISE--SIR--COMPELLETH ME--	"WHY DO I LOVE" YOU, SIR	480	17
BECAUSE HE'S SUNRISE--AND I SEE--	"WHY DO I LOVE" YOU, SIR	480	18
I LOOKED AT SUNRISE--ONCE--	I HAD NO CAUSE TO BE	542	9
'TIS LATE YOUR SUNRISE VEX THEIR FACE--	WHAT CARE THE DEAD, FOR	592	3
THE SUNRISE SCATTERS--THESE ENDURE--	THE BATTLE FOUGHT	594	11
THEN SUNRISE KISSED MY CHRYSALIS--	THREE TIMES--WE PARTED--	598	15
WIDE--LIKE THE SUNRISE	THE CHILD'S FAITH IS NEW	637	3
'TWAS SUNRISE--'TWAS THE SKY--	TO MY SMALL HEARTH HIS	638	4
THE SUNRISE RUNS FOR BOTH--	THE SUNRISE RUNS FOR	710	1
JUST SUNRISE--	RENUNCIATION--IS A	745	6
WHEN SUNRISE THROUGH A FISSURE DROP	THIS CHASM, SWEET, UPON	858	3
'TIS SUNRISE--LITTLE MAID--HAST THOU	'TIS SUNRISE--LITTLE	908	1
TILL SUNRISE TAKE [CALL] US BACK TO SCENE--	I LEARNED--AT LEAST--	944	25
WHERE MORNING [SUNRISE] JUST BEGUN--	THE SUNSET STOPPED ON	950	6
WHO SAW NO SUNRISE CANNOT SAY	WHO SAW NO SUNRISE	1018	1
BUT [FOR] SUNRISE STOPPED UPON THE PLACE	IT WAS A QUIET WAY--	1053	19
WHEN SUNRISE IS, THAT IS IT NOT.	FURTHER IN SUMMER THAN	1068	V
TO STEAL SECURER [AT SUNRISE] THENCE	CONTAINED IN THIS SHORT	1165	4
SUNRISE'			
LET NO SUNRISE' YELLOW NOISE	AMPLE MAKE THIS BED--	829	7
SUN'S			
OR SUN'S EXTINCTION, BE OBSERVED	THE MISSING ALL,	985	5
THIS IS THE SUN'S OBJECTIVE	THESE ARE THE DAYS THAT	1696	3

	FIRST LINE	POEM	LINE
SUPERIOR (CONTINUED)			
THE SOUL'S SUPERIOR INSTANTS	THE SOUL'S SUPERIOR	306	1
ON THIS SUPERIOR SOIL--	OF TRIBULATION--THESE	325	10
FROM A SUPERIOR BUSH--	THE WIND--TAPPED LIKE A	436	12
AS IF I BREATHED SUPERIOR AIR--	HE TOUCHED ME, SO I LIVE	506	8
ADORNED, FOR A SUPERIOR GRACE--	"HEAVEN" HAS DIFFERENT	575	19
TO FOLLOW HER SUPERIOR ROAD [PACE]--	I WATCHED THE MOON	629	35
SUPERIOR--FOR DOORS--	I DWELL IN POSSIBILITY--	657	4
O'ERLOOKING [MAINTAINING] A SUPERIOR SPECTRE--	ONE NEED NOT BE A	670	19
IS THE PREVAILING [SUPERIOR] FREIGHT.	BEFORE HE COMES WE WEIGH	834	4
SUPERIOR GLORY BE	A CLOUD WITHDREW FROM	895	2
HE HOLDS SUPERIOR IN THE SKY	I MAKE HIS CRESCENT FILL	909	5
WE KNOW THAT THEIR SUPERIOR EYES	WE MISS HER, NOT BECAUSE	993	7
SUPERIOR TO THE ONE	WHICH IS BEST? HEAVEN--	1012	6
THE CORKLESS IS SUPERIOR--	BETWEEN THE FORM OF LIFE	1101	7
AND AREA SUPERIOR	TWO LENGTHS HAS EVERY	1295	3
TO SOME SUPERIOR TREE	BEFORE YOU THOUGHT OF	1465	13
SUPERIORITY			
SUPERIORITY TO FATE	SUPERIORITY TO FATE	1081	1
SUPERLATIVE			
OF PARADISE SUPERLATIVE--	TWO--WERE IMMORTAL TWICE	800	7
SUPERSEDE			
'TWOULD SUPERSEDE THE HEAVEN--	DID OUR BEST MOMENT LAST	393	2
YOU CANNOT SUPERSEDE ITSELF	THAT SACRED CLOSET WHEN	1273	11
SUPERSEDES			
AND SUPERSEDES THE FRESH--	YOU'LL FIND--IT WHEN YOU	610	12
SUPERSEDING			
A FICTION SUPERSEDING FAITH--	HER SWEET WEIGHT ON MY	518	11
BY SUPERSEDING DESTINY	THE MOON UPON HER FLUENT	1528	V
SUPERSTITION			
SUPERSTITION HELPS, AS WELL AS LOVE--	ABSENCE DISEMBODIES--SO	860	3
SUPERSTITIOUS			
WITH SUPERSTITIOUS VALUE [MERIT / MOMENT]	TO DISAPPEAR ENHANCES--	1209	7
SUPPER			
AT SUPPER OF THE LAMB.	THERE CAME A DAY AT	322	16
DEEM MY SUPPER DRY	AS THE STARVED MAELSTROM	872	14
SUPPLANTED			
SUPPLANTED ALL THE REST.	AT HALF PAST THREE, A	1084	8
SUPPLANTING			
SUPPLANTING ME AND YOU	DOMINION LASTS UNTIL	1257	8
SUPPLANTS			
SUPPLANTS OUR TAPESTRIES WITH HIS--	THE SPIDER HOLDS A	605	7
HE SUPPLANTS THE BALM.	DEATH'S WAYLAYING NOT	1296	8
SUPPLE			
BY WITHES OF SUPPLE BLUE?	BRING ME THE SUNSET IN A	128	15
DID HE FIND IT SUPPLE?	HE STRAINED MY FAITH--	497	2
HAD NATURE ANY SUPPLE [PLATED / OUTCAST] FACE	THE MUSHROOM IS THE ELF	1298	17
SUMMER LAID HER SUPPLE GLOVE	SUMMER LAID HER SIMPLE	1363	5
DEATH IS THE SUPPLE SUITOR	DEATH IS THE SUPPLE	1445	1
THE MILLINERY SUPPLE	IT'S LITTLE ETHER HOOD	1501	3
SO EASY [SUPPLE / PLIANT] TO REPAIR.	SOFTENED BY TIME'S	1738	8
SUPPLEMENTS			
IN SUPPLEMENTS OF PURPLE	WITH SWEETNESS UNABATED	1709	9
SUPPLEST			
SHOULD PROVE THE STRONGEST [SUPPLEST / LITHEST / STOUTEST] ONE.	MY FIRST WELL DAY--SINCE	574	8
SUPPLICATE			
MINE TO SUPPLICATE MADONNA--	PROMISE THIS--WHEN YOU	648	25
DID SUPPLICATE IN VAIN--	THE BEGGAR LAD--DIES	717	16
A LITTLE WATER SUPPLICATE--	WE THIRST AT FIRST--'TIS	726	3
SUPPLICATING			
WHEN SUPPLICATING MERCY	THE BOBOLINK IS GONE--	1591	10
SUPPLIED			
SO FIRST AM I SUPPLIED--	THE LUXURY TO APPREHEND	815	8
SUPPLIED BY ENTOMOLOGY	THESE ARE THE NIGHTS	1128	15
WERE EASILY SUPPLIED	THE BEGGAR AT THE DOOR	1240	2
SUPPLIES			
A SUMPTUOUSNESS BESTOWS [SUPPLIES]	THE LUXURY TO APPREHEND	815	12
SUPPLY			
THO' SERFS--SUPPLY THE OIL--	THE LAMP BURNS SURE--	233	2
WHOSE ADEQUATE SUPPLY	WE THIRST AT FIRST--'TIS	726	6
SUPPLY THE [INVITE SOME / ENDOW SOME / AFFRONT A / AFFRONT ...	ART THOU THE THING I	1282	3
SUPPORT			
THE HOUSE SUPPORT [SUSTAIN] ITSELF	THE PROPS ASSIST THE	1142	5
SUPPORTING			
SUPPORTING WHAT WE SEE	FAITH--IS THE PIERLESS	915	2
SUPPORTS			
THAT RIDES--EMITS [SUPPORTS] A THUNDER--	TO INTERRUPT HIS YELLOW	591	15
SUPPORTS ME LIKE IMPERIAL DRAMS	THE STIMULUS, BEYOND THE	1001	3
SUPPOSE			
I SUPPOSE IT WILL INTERRUPT ME SOME	IT DONT SOUND SO	426	10
EXHIBIT--I SUPPOSE	NO CROWD THAT HAS	515	2
ITSELF BE FAIRER--WE SUPPOSE--	"HEAVEN" HAS DIFFERENT	575	17
AND CARRIED, WE SUPPOSE--[I SUPPOSED] TO HEAVEN,	I CRIED AT PITY--NOT AT	588	11
FALSEHOOD OF THEE COULD I SUPPOSE	FALSEHOOD OF THEE COULD	1007	1
I HONESTLY SUPPOSE--	A LITTLE DOG THAT WAGS	1185	8
I SUPPOSE THE TIME WILL COME	I SUPPOSE THE TIME WILL	1381	1
I SUPPOSE THE TIME WILL COME	I SUPPOSE THE TIME WILL	1381	5

	FIRST LINE	POEM	LINE
SUPPOSE (CONTINUED)			
AS WE [YOU] WHO STAY, SUPPOSE--	PERHAPS THEY DO NOT GO	1399	2
THOUGH I WITHIN SUPPOSE	I GROPED FOR HIM BEFORE	1555	6
SUPPOSED			
WAS ONCE SUPPOSED TO TURN,	"SIC TRANSIT GLORIA	3	34
SLEEP IS SUPPOSED TO BE	SLEEP IS SUPPOSED TO BE	13	1
MORN IS SUPPOSED TO BE	SLEEP IS SUPPOSED TO BE	13	7
SUPPOSED THAT HE HAD COME TO DWELL--	THE SUN--JUST TOUCHED	232	3
IF I BELIEVED [SUPPOSED] GOD LOOKED AROUND,	I PRAYED, AT FIRST, A	576	5
AND CARRIED, WE SUPPOSE--[I SUPPOSED] TO HEAVEN,	I CRIED AT PITY--NOT AT	588	11
I SUPPOSED--WHEN SUDDEN	MOST SHE TOUCHED ME BY	760	13
AS SHOULD A FACE SUPPOSED THE GRAVE'S	THERE IS A JUNE WHEN	930	5
SUPPOSED THEY VISITED REMOTE	I NOTICED PEOPLE	1149	3
DEATH WARRANTS ARE SUPPOSED [BELIEVED] TO BE	DEATH WARRANTS ARE	1375	1
SUPPOSED TO BE A TERMINUS	ADVANCE IS LIFE'S	1652	3
SUPPOSITION			
THE HOUSE OF SUPPOSITION--	THEIR HIGHT IN HEAVEN	696	5
SIMPLER ARE THE DAYS THAN THE SUPPOSITION	SOME WE SEE NO MORE,	1221	3
SUPPRESS			
POLICE CANNOT SUPPRESS	THE MOB WITHIN THE HEART	1745	2
SUPPRESSED			
NOR SUPPRESSED--WITH BALM--	CIVILIZATION--SPURNS--	492	13
SUPREMACY			
THE GNAT'S SUPREMACY IS LARGE AS THINE--	A TOAD, CAN DIE OF LIGHT	583	7
TO PROVE ABILITY. [SHOW SUPREMACY]	IT ALWAYS FELT TO ME--A	597	16
SUPREMACY--	THE HEART HAS MANY DOORS	1567	8
SUPREME			
OR SHIFT SUPREME--	A MIEN TO MOVE A QUEEN--	283	19
ADVANCE UNMOVED--TO HER SUPREME--	TRIUMPH--MAY BE OF	455	7
AN HOUR TO REAR SUPREME	THE SPIDER HOLDS A	605	9
MY NAME BE ELSE SUPREME--	FAME OF MYSELF, TO	713	6
STOLID TO LOVE'S SUPREME [SUBLIME] ENTREATY	TELL AS A MARKSMAN--WERE	1152	20
ARE EQUALLY SUPREME--	THE DAY SHE GOES	1308	3
THE SUPREME INIQUITY	"HEAVENLY FATHER"--TAKE	1461	2
ABODE IN AS SUPREME	THE WAY HOPE BUILDS HIS	1481	5
IT IS THE PAST'S SUPREME ITALIC	GLASS WAS THE STREET--IN	1498	7
SUPREMER			
SHE FELT HERSELF SUPREMER--	THE SUN--JUST TOUCHED	232	5
NOT SUBJECT TO [SUPREMER THAN / SUPERIOR TO] DESPAIR--	I GOT SO I COULD HEAR	293	23
BY SUCCEEDING [SUPREMER] SPRINGS--	ALL BUT DEATH, CAN BE	749	6
SUPREMEST			
UNTO SUPREMEST NAME [TERM]--	I'M CEDED--I'VE STOPPED	508	10
SUPREMEST EARTHLY SUM--	ONE BLESSING HAD I THAN	756	12
SURCINGLES			
BEES ARE BLACK, WITH GILT SURCINGLES--	BEES ARE BLACK, WITH	1405	1
SURE			
BE SURE YOU COUNT--SH'D I FORGET	IT'S ALL I HAVE TO BRING	26	5
AS SURE AS FLOCKS GO HOME AT NIGHT	GOING TO HEAVEN!	79	9
YOU LOVE ME--YOU ARE SURE--	YOU LOVE ME--YOU ARE	156	1
I NEED NOT START--YOU'RE SURE--	YOU LOVE ME--YOU ARE	156	8
BE SURE YOU'RE SURE--YOU KNOW--	YOU LOVE ME--YOU ARE	156	14
BE SURE YOU'RE SURE--YOU KNOW--	YOU LOVE ME--YOU ARE	156	14
BUT SURE I AM HE ERMINE WORE	I MET A KING THIS	166	5
AND SURE I AM, THE CREST HE BORE	I MET A KING THIS	166	7
SO SURE I'D COME--SO SURE I'D COME--	I SHOULD NOT DARE TO	205	10
SO SURE I'D COME--SO SURE I'D COME--	I SHOULD NOT DARE TO	205	10
YOU ARE SURE THERE'S SUCH A PERSON	WHAT IS--"PARADISE"--	215	11
THE LAMP BURNS SURE--WITHIN--	THE LAMP BURNS SURE--	233	1
TOO SURE--TO DOTE UPON!	THE LONESOME FOR THEY	262	12
THAT ONE, TO BE QUITE SURE--	I BREATHED ENOUGH TO	272	4
IF ANY ARE NOT SURE--	'TIS SO APPALLING--IT	281	11
TO MAKE SURE ALL'S ASLEEP--	I KNOW SOME LONELY	289	10
I'M SURE 'TIS INDIA--ALL DAY--	YOUR RICHES--TAUGHT ME--	299	17
I'M SURE [I KNOW] IT IS GOLCONDA--	YOUR RICHES--TAUGHT ME--	299	21
DEVISING, I AM SURE--	SHE LAY AS IF AT PLAY	369	14
THE LILY PASSES SURE--	THROUGH THE DARK SOD--AS	392	2
THEN--LOOK FOR ME. BE SURE YOU SAY--	A TONGUE--TO TELL HIM I	400	28
A TREMOR JUST, THAT ALL'S NOT SURE.	UNIT, LIKE DEATH, FOR	408	16
IT MUST MEAN THAT--I'M SURE--	I KNOW WHERE WELLS GROW	460	16
LET ME THINK--I'M SURE	I WAS THE SLIGHTEST IN	486	8
STRONG [SURE] HALLELUJAHS ROLL--	THIS WORLD IS NOT	501	18
JUST AS [EQUAL] SURE--	ONLY GOD--DETECT THE	626	8
FOR TRANSPORT IT BE SURE--	THE WAY I READ A	636	4
CARRIAGES--BE SURE--AND GUESTS--TRUE [TOO]--	HER SWEET TURN TO LEAVE	649	3
HIS SURE FOOT PRECEDING--	LIFE--IS WHAT WE MAKE IT	698	13
THAT WERE NOT, WE ARE SURE--	HAVE ANY LIKE MYSELF	736	5
PRESERVED THE CHARM [VISION SURE / VISION CLEAR] SECURE	HAVE ANY LIKE MYSELF	736	18
THEIR EXPECTATION--FAIR [SURE]--	THROUGH THE STRAIT PASS	792	10
I'M SURE, AT MANY A WHIM	IF NATURE SMILES--THE	1085	2
NOTWITHSTANDING [TO BE SURE] A ROPE FOR A SOUVENIR	FLOSS WONT SAVE YOU FROM	1322	3
A WARMTH AS NEAR [SURE / FINE] AS IF THE SUN	TO SEE HER IS A PICTURE	1568	7
RELUCTANTLY BUT SURE PERCEIVES	SUMMER BEGINS TO HAVE	1682	3
SURELY			
SURELY, SUCH A COUNTRY	BAFFLED FOR JUST A DAY	17	7
WILL SURELY COME AGAIN.	I KEEP MY PLEDGE.	46	11

	FIRST LINE	POEM	LINE
SURER			
AND SUNS, GO SURER, FOR THEIR PROOF,	WHEN WE STAND ON THE	242	15
YET PERSEVERED TOWARD--SURER [STRICTER]--FOR THE DISTANCE--	EACH LIFE CONVERGES TO	680	13
SURETIES			
FOR SURETIES OF HER STAUNCH ESTATE	THESE ARE THE SIGNS TO	1077	9
SURETY			
WITHOUT A SURETY FROM THE WIND	DOWN TIME'S QUAINT	1656	9
SURFACES			
THE SURFACES OF YEARS--	IF HE WERE LIVING--DARE	734	6
SURFACES MAY [CAN] BE INVESTED [RELATED]	NONE WHO SAW IT EVER	1110	5
THE UPPER SURFACES OF THINGS	THE SYMPTOM OF THE GALE	1327	7
SURFEIT			
SURFEIT! WHEN THE DAFFODIL	ALTER! WHEN THE HILLS DO	729	5
SURGE			
AS LACES JUST REVEAL THE SURGE--	THE THOUGHT BENEATH SO	210	3
SURGEON			
THE SURGEON, WILL NOT COME--	ALTHOUGH I PUT AWAY HIS	366	23
THE SURGEON--DOES NOT BLANCH--AT PAIN--	THERE IS A LANGUOR OF	396	9
SURGEONS			
SURGEONS MUST BE VERY CAREFUL	SURGEONS MUST BE VERY	108	1
SURGEONS ASSUAGE IN VAIN,	AH, NECROMANCY SWEET!	177	5
WHAT SURGEONS CALL ALIVE--	STILL OWN THEE--STILL	1633	2
SURGERY			
FROM SCIENCE--AND FROM SURGERY--	I TIE MY HAT--I CREASE	443	21
NOR ANY NEED OF SURGERY--	IT KNEW NO MEDICINE--	559	3
SURLY			
HEAVEN THE BALM OF A SURLY TECHNICALITY!	HOW HAPPY IS THE LITTLE	1510	V
WAS TIGHT AND SURLY DRAWN	A CAP OF LEAD ACROSS THE	1649	2
SURMISE			
STRAIN TILL YOUR [HER] LAST SURMISE--	DOUBT ME! MY DIM	275	19
IT'S FAR--FAR TREASURE TO SURMISE--	YOUR RICHES--TAUGHT ME--	299	29
THAN LETTING HIM SURMISE?	TO ONE DENIED TO DRINK	490	4
EXISTENCE'S WHOLE ARC, [WHOLE EYE / WHOLE RIM / SURMISE] FILLED UP,	I'M CEDED--I'VE STOPPED	508	12
STILL SURMISE I STITCH--	DONT PUT UP MY THREAD &	617	20
AND WOULD AS SOON SURMISE	THE LONELINESS ONE DARE	777	2
WHAT WE DONT SURMISE WE DO	WHAT WE SEE WE KNOW	1195	3
MUFFLED [MORTISED]--IT REMITS [RESISTS] SURMISE--	"SECRETS" IS A DAILY	1385	3
EXCEPT AS A SURMISE	BEFORE YOU THOUGHT OF	1465	2
EFFACES THE SURMISE--	THEIR BARRICADE AGAINST	1471	8
AND ALL THAT HEAVEN WAS [SURMISE]--	SO GIVE ME BACK TO DEATH	1632	8
NOW PAST SURMISE	TO-DAY OR THIS NOON	1702	7
SURMISED			
I FIRST SURMISED THE HORSES HEADS	BECAUSE I COULD NOT STOP	712	23
SURMISING			
SWEETER--THE SURMISING ROBINS--	DREAMS--ARE WELL--BUT	450	5
TO THE SURMISING INN--	HE WENT BY SLEEP THAT	1662	2
SURPASS			
TO LOSE ONE'S FAITH--SURPASS	TO LOSE ONE'S FAITH--	377	1
BLISS OF DEATH--LIFE'S BLISS EXTOL THRO [SURPASS IN / EXCEL IN]	PROMISE THIS--WHEN YOU	648	15
SURPASSED			
TO ME--SURPASSED THE CROWN	THE DAY THAT I WAS	356	14
SURPASSES			
SURPASSES ALL THAT ROSE BEFORE--	THE MORNING AFTER WO--	364	3
SURPASSES SHARPER STATED--	IT ALWAYS FELT TO ME--A	597	9
THAT SURPASSES DEATH--	TELL AS A MARKSMAN--WERE	1152	19
SURPASSES IT, WE KNOW, BECAUSE	THE LIFE WE HAVE IS VERY	1162	3
DEFACES [DEBASES / SURPASSES] THAT OF WINE--	WHO NEVER WANTED--	1430	4
SURPASSES MEMORY	TO BE FORGOT BY THEE	1560	2
SURPASSES SOLITUDE	A LANE OF YELLOW LED THE	1650	4
SURPASSING			
HOW POMP SURPASSING ERMINE	ONE DIGNITY DELAYS FOR	98	13
TO THOSE WHOSE DARK--HATH SO--SURPASSING SUN--	I SEE THEE BETTER--IN	611	14
THE BRAIN HAS CORRIDORS--SURPASSING	ONE NEED NOT BE A	670	3
THOUGH HIS SURPASSING MERIT	THE SPIDER AS AN ARTIST	1275	3
SURPASSING REVELRY,	HIS ORIENTAL HERESIES	1526	V
SURPLICE			
A BONNET BLACK--A DUSK SURPLICE--	WHERE I HAVE LOST, I	104	10
SOME KEEP THE SABBATH IN SURPLICE--	SOME KEEP THE SABBATH	324	5
SURPRISE			
IT DID NOT SURPRISE ME--	IT DID NOT SURPRISE ME--	39	1
NOT EASY TO SURPRISE!	I KNOW SOME LONELY	289	12
EARN HER OWN SURPRISE!	I KNOW THAT HE EXISTS.	338	8
AND THE LIVID SURPRISE	WE DREAM--IT IS GOOD WE	531	12
AND DEATH'S SURPRISE,	MY PORTION IS DEFEAT--	639	12
I MIGHT SURPRISE [NOT PLEASE] HIS EYE!	AGAIN--HIS VOICE IS AT	663	8
IT'S [THE] FIRST--DELIGHT--AND THEN--SURPRISE--	FITTER TO SEE HIM, I MAY	968	10
UNTIL TO HER SURPRISE	SUPERIORITY TO FATE	1081	6
DISCOVERED IS WITHOUT SURPRISE	THE LARGEST FIRE EVER	1114	3
THE TRUTH'S SUPERB SURPRISE	TELL ALL THE TRUTH BUT	1129	4
AS YESTERDAY'S SURPRISE--	THE RIDDLE WE CAN GUESS	1222	4
BIRDS WITH DISMAY [SURPRISE]	TO FLEE FROM MEMORY	1242	5
'TWILL BE A LABOR OF SURPRISE--	THAT SACRED CLOSET WHEN	1273	5
SURPRISE IS LIKE A THRILLING--PUNGENT--	SURPRISE IS LIKE A	1306	1
THE GARMENT OF SURPRISE	LET ME NOT MAR THAT	1335	6
ACCOMPLISHED IN SURPRISE--	HOW FITS HIS UMBER COAT	1371	10

	FIRST LINE	POEM	LINE
SURPRISE (CONTINUED)			
BY INNOCENT [ELOQUENT / HALLOWED / HEAVENLY / DIFFIDENT] SURPRISE--	THE PRETTY RAIN FROM	1426	4
APPARENTLY WITH NO SURPRISE	APPARENTLY WITH NO	1624	1
AND TAKE ONESELF BY SURPRISE	TO DO A MAGNANIMOUS	1699	2
SURPRISED			
AND THE SURPRISED AIR	I'M SAYING EVERY DAY	373	30
A CURIOUS CLOUD SURPRISED THE SKY,	A CURIOUS CLOUD	1710	1
SURRENDER			
DIADEMS--DROP--AND DOGES--SURRENDER--	SAFE IN THEIR ALABASTER	216	V
"SURRENDER"--IS A SORT UNKNOWN	OF TRIBULATION--THESE	325	9
QUAINTLY INFER--EVE'S GREAT SURRENDER--	BETTER--THAN MUSIC! FOR	503	11
"SWEET" SAID HE "MY OWN SURRENDER	WOLFE DEMANDED DURING	678	7
AND THE SURRENDER [DISCOMFIT]--MINE--	I MEANT TO FIND HER WHEN	718	4
GIBRALTAR COULD SURRENDER	I SAW THE WIND WITHIN	1502	V
SURRENDERED			
WHO KNOWS BUT THIS SURRENDERED FACE	DELAYED TILL SHE HAD	58	11
WHEN HE--SURRENDERED TO THE SUNRISE--	PUT UP MY LUTE!	261	9
THE FLESH--SURRENDERED--CANCELLED [SHIFTED]--	DEPARTED--TO THE	524	5
IF THE LIFE BE TOO SURRENDERED--	PROMISE THIS--WHEN YOU	648	11
A RAT SURRENDERED HERE	A RAT SURRENDERED HERE	1340	1
SURRENDERED BY THE TRIED--	CRISIS IS SWEET AND YET	1416	V 4
TO HER RESCINDED [SURRENDERED / RECEDING / DEPARTED / . . .	CRISIS IS SWEET AND YET	1416	8
AND OUR'S SURRENDERED [CONSIDERED] FOR IT'S SAKE	THE FACE IN EVANESCENCE	1490	3
SURRENDERING			
SURRENDERING--THE LAST--	THERE IS A FLOWER THAT	380	30
SURREPTITIOUS			
THIS SURREPTITIOUS SCION	THE MUSHROOM IS THE ELF	1298	15
GAY FROM AN UNANNOINTED [SWEET FROM A SURREPTITIOUS] TWIG	THE BOBOLINK IS GONE--	1591	12
SURREPTITIOUSLY			
ROSE [LEFT] SURREPTITIOUSLY--	A SPARROW TOOK A SLICE	1211	V 8
SURROGATE			
THEN WISER THAN A "SURROGATE",	COCOON ABOVE! COCOON	129	11
SURROUNDED			
THE DAY GREW SMALL, SURROUNDED TIGHT	THE DAY GREW SMALL,	1140	1
SURVEY			
THE LAST [CLOSE] OF SUMMER IS DELIGHT--[A TIME / RESULT--SURVEY]	THE LAST OF SUMMER IS	1353	1
SURVEYED			
SURVEYED [DELAYED / DEFERRED] INFINITY--	I COULD SUFFICE FOR HIM,	643	4
THE HORROR [CHASM] NOT TO BE SURVEYED--	THE LONELINESS ONE DARE	777	9
SURVEYED MY CHAMBER FLOOR	IN WINTER IN MY ROOM	1670	15
SURVEYING			
[THAT] SURVEYING HIS DESPAIR	HOW MANY SCHEMES MAY DIE	1150	13
SURVIVE			
THEY SHALL SURVIVE--	TIME DOES GO ON--	1121	3
HOWEVER--MIGHT SURVIVE--	ELIZABETH TOLD ESSEX	1321	4
WHAT SOUL SURVIVE?	UNWORTHY OF HER BREAST	1414	3
CAN HUMAN NATURE NOT SURVIVE [PROCEED]	THE RETICENT VOLCANO	1748	7
SURVIVED			
HAST THOU SURVIVED SO MANY NIGHTS [YEARS]?	THE SMOULDERING EMBERS	1132	3
SOMEHOW MYSELF SURVIVED THE NIGHT	SOMEHOW MYSELF SURVIVED	1194	1
SURVIVING			
TO ALL SURVIVING BUTTERFLIES	TWO BUTTERFLIES WENT OUT	533	V
SUSAN			
AND HARRIET, AND SUSAN, AND SHE WITH CURLING HAIR!	AWAKE YE MUSES NINE,	1	32
BUT NATURE [SUSAN] IS A STRANGER YET!	WHAT MYSTERY PERVADES A	1400	17
TO OWN A SUSAN OF MY OWN	TO OWN A SUSAN OF MY OWN	1401	1
SUSCEPTIVE			
SUSCEPTIVE--STIMULUS--	REPORTLESS SUBJECTS, TO	1048	6
SUSPECT			
THE NEIGHBORS DO NOT YET SUSPECT!	A LADY RED--AMID THE	74	9
WHAT ALL THE WORLD SUSPECT?	COCOON ABOVE! COCOON	129	3
THAN THIS GREAT PURCHASER SUSPECT,	I GAVE MYSELF TO HIM--	580	7
TOO SUBTLE [SMOULDERING] TO SUSPECT	A STILL--VOLCANO--LIFE--	601	6
NOT IF THE JUST SUSPECT ME	WHAT DID THEY DO SINCE I	900	13
TOO YOUNG THAT ANY SHOULD SUSPECT	A LOSS OF SOMETHING EVER	959	4
WOULD CAUSE ONE SCARCELY TO SUSPECT	BLOOM--IS RESULT--TO	1058	3
WHAT WE DID NOT SUSPECT WAS MARKED--	WERE IT TO BE THE LAST	1164	3
TOO PONDEROUS TO SUSPECT THE SNARE	RISK IS THE HAIR THAT	1239	5
BUT LET HIM ONCE SUSPECT	UNTIL THE DESERT KNOWS	1291	4
SO STRAIGHT YOU'D SCARCE SUSPECT	A PIT--BUT HEAVEN OVER	1712	13
NONE SUSPECT ME OF THE CROWN,	REARRANGE A "WIFE'S"	1737	14
WE MORE THAN HALF SUSPECT,	THE DISTANCE THAT THE	1742	6
SUSPECTED			
WHEREVER I SUSPECTED GRAVES--	IF HE WERE LIVING--DARE	734	11
YET WE SUSPECTED NOT	HER FINAL SUMMER WAS IT	795	V 2
NOT YET SUSPECTED--[STILL UNSUSPECTED] BUT FOR FLASH [FORK]--	THE SOUL'S DISTINCT	974	7
SUSPECTING			
TO DIE OF THIRST--SUSPECTING	TO LEARN THE TRANSPORT	167	3
WITHOUT SUSPECTING OUR ABODE	EDEN IS THAT	1657	3
SUSPEND			
TO SUSPEND THE BREATH	CRISIS IS A HAIR	889	5
SUSPENDED			
SUSPENDED IN THE NOON--	HE PARTS HIMSELF--LIKE	517	10

	FIRST LINE	POEM	LINE
SUSPENDED (CONTINUED)			
WITH CONSCIOUSNESS SUSPENDED--	THE LONELINESS ONE DARE	777	11
FOR THE SUSPENDED CANDIDATE	SHALL I TAKE THEE, THE	1126	7
THIS INSTANT BE SUSPENDED [ABOLISHED]	BECAUSE THAT YOU ARE	1260	7
SUSPENDS			
WHILE IT SUSPENDS THE LIVES.	A DOUBT IF IT BE US	859	8
SUSPENSE			
SUSPENSE KEPT SAWING SO--	'TIS SO APPALLING--IT	281	8
RACKED--WITH SUSPENSE--	HE STRAINED MY FAITH--	497	7
SUSPENSE--IS HOSTILER THAN DEATH--	SUSPENSE--IS HOSTILER	705	1
SUSPENSE--DOES NOT CONCLUDE--	SUSPENSE--IS HOSTILER	705	4
IN FACE OF THE SUSPENSE--	IF HE WERE LIVING--DARE	734	14
I KNOW SUSPENSE--IT STEPS SO TERSE	I KNOW SUSPENSE--IT	1285	1
BESIDES--SUSPENSE IS NEIGHBORLY	I KNOW SUSPENSE--IT	1285	3
SUSPENSE--IS HIS MATURER SISTER--	WONDER--IS NOT PRECISELY	1331	5
MAKES A WORLD'S SUSPENSE	TRUSTY AS THE STARS	1369	7
SUSPENSE'S			
IT IS BOUNTY--TO SUSPENSE'S	ROBBED BY DEATH--BUT	971	11
SUSPICION			
AND A SUSPICION, LIKE A FINGER	A LOSS OF SOMETHING EVER	959	13
THAT FINE SUSPICION, NATURES MUST	TO UNDERTAKE IS TO	1070	5
SUSPICION IT WAS DONE	IT STOLE ALONG SO	1457	2
SUSPICIOUS			
WITH A SUSPICIOUS AIR--	I MEANT TO HAVE BUT	476	26
SUSTAIN			
SUSTAIN HER IN THE SKY--	I WATCHED THE MOON	629	16
WHO MISERY--SUSTAIN--	SUCH IS THE FORCE OF	787	4
THE HOUSE SUPPORT [SUSTAIN] ITSELF	THE PROPS ASSIST THE	1142	5
SUSTAINED			
MYSELF ENDUED [UPHELD / UPBORNE / SUSTAINED] BALLOON	I WOULD NOT PAINT--A	505	14
WAS ALL THAT SAVED [ALONE SUSTAINED-- / ALONE UPHELD--] A BEE	A SINGLE CLOVER PLANK	1343	2
SUSTAINS			
SUSTAINS HIM [HER] ANYWHERE--	TO HER DERIDED HOME	1586	V
SUSTENANCE			
AND THAT WHITE SUSTENANCE--[EXERCISE / PRIVILEGE]	I CANNOT LIVE WITH YOU--	640	49
BUT SUSTENANCE IS OF THE SPIRIT	A WORLD MADE PENNINILESS	1623	3
SWAGGER			
WHY SWAGGER, THEN?	A TOAD, CAN DIE OF LIGHT	583	6
SWAGGERS			
THAT SWAGGERS ON THE EYE	THE TINT I CANNOT TAKE--	627	6
AND NO ONE SWAGGERS NOW BUT ME--	THE BOBOLINK IS GONE--	1591	2
SWAIN			
OH THE EARTH WAS MADE FOR LOVERS, FOR DAMSEL, AND HOPELESS SWAIN,	AWAKE YE MUSES NINE,	1	3
SWALLOWED			
THEN SWALLOWED UP, OF VIEW.	I'VE KNOWN A HEAVEN,	243	17
SWALLOWS			
IT SWALLOWS SUBSTANCE [BEING] UP--	THERE IS A PAIN--SO	599	2
SWAM			
THE STEEPLES SWAM IN AMETHYST--	I'LL TELL YOU HOW THE	318	3
THE SWARTHY FELLOW SWAM--	THE MALAY--TOOK THE	452	7
SWAMP			
SWEET IS THE SWAMP WITH ITS SECRETS,	SWEET IS THE SWAMP WITH	1740	1
SWAMPS			
THE SWAMPS ARE PINK WITH JUNE.	ALL THESE MY BANNERS BE.	22	21
SWANG			
THE FLAGS OF NATIONS SWANG.	A DAY! HELP! HELP!	42	6
SWANS			
THEN STILLS IT'S ARTISANS [MYRMIDONS]--LIKE GHOSTS [SWANS]--	IT SIFTS FROM LEADEN	311	19
THE BUTTERFLIES--AS SWANS [MOONS]--	I THINK I WAS ENCHANTED	593	10
IT IS AS SWANS--DISCARDED YOU,	YOU'VE SEEN BALLOONS SET	700	3
SWARM			
'TIS UNITS--MAKE THE SWARM--	ONE ANGUISH--IN A CROWD	565	8
SWARTHY			
THE SWARTHY FELLOW SWAM--	THE MALAY--TOOK THE	452	7
OF SWARTHY DAYS HE IS THE CLOSE [KNELL]	THE JAY HIS CASTANET HAS	1635	5
SWAY			
WILL SWAY WITH PURPLE LOAD--	IT WILL BE SUMMER--	342	10
SWAYING			
YET SWAYING ALL--	THE CHILD'S FAITH IS NEW	637	16
THE IDLY SWAYING PLANK	A SINGLE CLOVER PLANK	1343	9
'TIS NOT THE SWAYING FRAME WE MISS,	'TIS NOT THE SWAYING	1597	1
SWAYS			
'TIS THIS--IN MUSIC--HINTS AND SWAYS--	THE LOVE A LIFE CAN SHOW	673	7
SWEAR			
I'D SWEAR BY HIM--	THE ROBIN'S MY CRITERION	285	4
BUT SWEAR, AND I WILL LET YOU BY	THE FINGERS OF THE LIGHT	1000	7
EXPERIENCE WOULD [COULD] SWEAR--	THE SNOW THAT NEVER	1133	8
YOU'D THINK [SWEAR] HE TOOK A DEED	HOW DESTITUTE IS HE	1477 V	7
SWEEP			
SWEEP VALE--AND HILL--AND TREE!	A LADY RED--AMID THE	74	6
A SWEEP OF GRAY--	A SLASH OF BLUE--	204	2
SWEEP BY OUR DISAPPOINTED HEADS	HOW NOTELESS MEN, AND	282	11
CURVE BY CURVE--SWEEP BY SWEEP--	OUT OF SIGHT? WHAT OF	703	3
CURVE BY CURVE--SWEEP BY SWEEP--	OUT OF SIGHT? WHAT OF	703	3
THAT SACRED CLOSET WHEN YOU SWEEP--	THAT SACRED CLOSET WHEN	1273	1

	FIRST LINE	POEM	LINE
SWEEP (CONTINUED)			
IT'S CURTAINS BLANDLY SWEEP--	WATER MAKES MANY BEDS	1428	4
SWEEPING			
THE SWEEPING UP THE HEART	THE BUSTLE IN A HOUSE	1078	5
OR TRAILING [SWEEPING] COURTESY	LIKE MEN AND WOMEN	1105	4
WERE SWEEPING HIM AWAY--	A SINGLE CLOVER PLANK	1343	8
SWEEPS			
SHE SWEEPS WITH MANY-COLORED BROOMS--	SHE SWEEPS WITH	219	1
AND EASY SWEEPS OF SKY--	MY COCOON TIGHTENS--	1099	8
IT SWEEPS THE TENEMENT [TENEMENTS] AWAY	THE INUNDATION OF THE	1425	3
SWEET			
TIS SWEET TO KNOW THAT STOCKS WILL STAND	IF I SHOULD DIE,	54	11
AN ANODYNE SO SWEET--	HEART, NOT SO HEAVY AS	83	8
SWEET OF TWIGS AND TWINE	HER BREAST IS FIT FOR	84	7
I SOW SWEET FLOWER FROM GARDEN BED--	WHERE I HAVE LOST, I	104	2
BECAUSE, SIR, LOVE IS SWEET!	THE DAISY FOLLOWS SOFT	106	6
HAVE SOMETIMES PROVED DEADLY SWEET!	TALK WITH PRUDENCE TO A	119	8
AS BROOKS IN DESERTS BABBLE SWEET	AS WATCHERS HANG UPON	121	4
A BRIEF CAMPAIGN OF STING AND SWEET	A LITTLE BREAD--A CRUST	159	8
AT LEAST, TO KNOW THE WORST, IS SWEET!	'TIS SO MUCH JOY! 'TIS	172	10
AH, NECROMANCY SWEET!	AH, NECROMANCY SWEET!	177	1
SWEET PLEA--	I STOLE THEM FROM A BEE	200	3
PIPE THE SWEET BIRDS IN IGNORANT CADENCE--	SAFE IN THEIR ALABASTER	216	10
READ--SWEET--HOW OTHERS--STROVE--	READ--SWEET--HOW OTHERS	260	1
TO SWEET PAUSES OF HAY--	THE WIND DID'NT COME	316	15
SWEET LITIGANTS FOR LIFE--	THERE IS A FLOWER THAT	380	20
IT'S SWEET PARADE--BLASPHEME THE PLACE--	IT MIGHT BE LONELIER	405	11
BUT DAPPERER--MORE SWEET--	A MURMUR IN THE TREES--	416	8
SUNSHINE WAS A SWEET PLACE--	GOOD MORNING--MIDNIGHT--	425	5
FOR LOVE OF HER--SWEET--COUNTRYMEN--	THIS IS MY LETTER TO THE	441	7
SWEET--SAFE--HOUSES--	SWEET--SAFE--HOUSES--	457	1
WITH SWEET ALACRITY	THEY PUT US FAR APART--	474	14
WE COVER THEE--SWEET FACE--	WE COVER THEE--SWEET	482	1
AUGMENTED--SWEET--A HUNDRED FOLD--	WE COVER THEE--SWEET	482	11
HIS SWEET FORGIVENESS--	HE STRAINED MY FAITH--	497	14
EVOKES [PROVOKES] SO SWEET A TORMENT--	I WOULD NOT PAINT--A	505	7
HER SWEET WEIGHT ON MY HEART A NIGHT	HER SWEET WEIGHT ON MY	518	1
SWEET--YOU FORGOT--BUT I REMEMBERED	SWEET--YOU FORGOT--BUT I	523	1
YOU--SWEET [SIR]--SHUT ME OUT--	SWEET--YOU FORGOT--BUT I	523	12
JUST AT NOON--NO LATER--SWEET [THAN]--	SOME SUCH BUTTERFLY BE	541	3
SWEET MORNING--WHEN I OVERSLEEP--	I HAD NO CAUSE TO BE	542	7
THIS--DOST THOU DOUBT--SWEET--	THAT I DID ALWAYS LOVE	549	9
IF MOMENTLY [HER SWEET DOOR--] AJAR--	IT KNEW NO MEDICINE--	559	13
SWEET DEBT OF LIFE--EACH NIGHT TO OWE--	I GAVE MYSELF TO HIM--	580	15
LIKE HINDERED FLAGS--SWEET HOISTED--	THE TREES LIKE TASSELS--	606	23
A SWEET ENDEAVOR--BUT AS MARCH	YOU'LL KNOW HER--BY HER	634	23
YOU LEFT ME--SIRE [SWEET]--TWO LEGACIES--	YOU LEFT ME--SIRE--TWO	644	1
HER SWEET TURN TO LEAVE THE HOMESTEAD	HER SWEET TURN TO LEAVE	649	1
NOR EVEN NOW--SO SWEET--	A PRISON GETS TO BE A	652	12
THAT FIRST DAY, WHEN YOU PRAISED ME, SWEET,	THAT FIRST DAY, WHEN YOU	659	1
"SWEET" SAID HE "MY OWN SURRENDER	WOLFE DEMANDED DURING	678	7
HOW SWEET IT WOULD HAVE TASTED--	VICTORY COMES LATE--	690	5
NO MATTER--NOW--SWEET--	NO MATTER--NOW--SWEET--	704	1
SAY--SWEET--THEN	NO MATTER--NOW--SWEET--	704	14
"SWEET LADY--CHARITY"--	THE BEGGAR LAD--DIES	717	8
SWEET MOUNTAINS--YE TELL ME NO LIE--	SWEET MOUNTAINS--YE TELL	722	1
BONDAGE AS PLAY--BE SWEET--	WHERE THOU ART--THAT--IS	725	7
THAN LIFE'S SWEET [NEW] CALCULATIONS--	UPON CONCLUDED LIVES	735	3
QUICK [SOON]--SWEET MOUTH--TO MISS THEE SO--	THESE--SAW VISIONS--	758	6
I COULD NOT DRINK IT, SWEET [SUE],	I COULD NOT DRINK IT,	818	1
THIS CHASM, SWEET, UPON MY LIFE	THIS CHASM, SWEET, UPON	858	1
THEY WONT FROWN ALWAYS--SOME SWEET DAY	THEY WONT FROWN ALWAYS--	874	1
SINCE SOMEWHERE THY SWEET FACE HAS SPILLED	I'VE NONE TO TELL ME TO	881	5
SWEET [GOOD], TO HAVE HAD THEM LOST	SWEET, TO HAVE HAD THEM	901	1
DISSUADE THEE, IF I C'D NOT, SWEET,	'TIS SUNRISE--LITTLE	908	13
WORN--NOW--AND DULL--SWEET,	IF IT HAD NO PENCIL	921	3
THE FIRST--SWEET, PROVED I, [THAT WAS] ERE I SAW THEE--	WERT THOU BUT ILL--THAT	961	19
PROVE [ASK]--ME--SWEET--IF I REGRET IT--	ALL FORGOT FOR	966	15
HOW SWEET I SHALL NOT LACK IN VAIN--	FITTER TO SEE HIM, I MAY	968	25
SWEET WONDER--	BESIDES THIS MAY	977	7
THE LIVING, SWEET, IS COSTLIER--	TOO SCANTY 'TWAS TO DIE	1013	3
"JUST ONCE" SWEET DEITY?	JUST ONCE! OH LEAST	1076	9
WITH THE [AN / THIS] AUSTERER SWEET--	I FIT FOR THEM--	1109	5
WITH THIS SUFFICIENT SWEET	I FIT FOR THEM--	1109 V	5
AND LEAVE FOR THY SWEET MERCY'S [PATIENCE'] SAKE	SOME WRETCHED CREATURE,	1111	3
WERE EVERY STORM [GALE / SNOW] SO SPICE [FAIR / SWEET]	THE SNOW THAT NEVER	1133	13
OURSELVES WE DO INTER WITH SWEET DERISION.	OURSELVES WE DO INTER	1144	1
WHEN SWEET INCARCERATED HERE	LEST THEY SHOULD COME--	1169	2
WITHSTANDS UNTIL THE SWEET ASSAULT	LIKE TRAINS OF CARS ON	1224	5
HE RESTITUTES IN SOME SWEET WAY	NOT ONE BY HEAVEN	1303	3
FRIGID AND SWEET HER PARTING FACE--	FRIGID AND SWEET HER	1318	1
IS THERE NO SWEET BENEATH THE SUN	OUR LITTLE SECRETS SLINK	1326	7
THIS WHOLE [SUDDEN / FAIR / GAY / BRIGHT / FLEET / SWEET / . . .	A LITTLE MADNESS IN THE	1333	5
HOW SWEET THESE [THOSE] SULLEN BARS	HOW SOFT THIS PRISON IS	1334	2
TOUCH LIGHTLY NATURE'S SWEET GUITAR	TOUCH LIGHTLY NATURE'S	1389	1
SWEET SKEPTICISM OF THE HEART--	SWEET SKEPTICISM OF THE	1413	1

	FIRST LINE	POEM	LINE
SWEET (CONTINUED)			
CRISIS IS SWEET AND YET THE HEART	CRISIS IS SWEET AND YET	1416	1
SWEET NATURE HAS FOR ME	ONE JOY OF SO MUCH	1420	2
THE PRETTY RAIN FROM THOSE SWEET EAVES	THE PRETTY RAIN FROM	1426	1
COULD THAT SWEET DARKNESS WHERE THEY DWELL	COULD THAT SWEET	1493	1
AND SO SHE SOUGHT THIS SWEET AT LAST	SHE COULD NOT LIVE UPON	1505	3
HER TRIPLE SUIT AS SWEET	MY COUNTRY NEED NOT	1511	2
THAT LOWLY BREAST [HOMESTEAD SWEET] WHERE BUTTERFLIES	HIS ORIENTAL HERESIES	1526	7
SWEET HOMESTEAD WHERE THE BUTTERFLY	HIS ORIENTAL HERESIES	1526 V	7
OH GIVE IT MOTION--DECK IT SWEET	OH GIVE IT MOTION--DECK	1527	1
FOR SUCH A FOE [SWEET / GLEE / DAWN / SCENE / DEW / JOY] AS THIS--	FROM ALL THE JAILS THE	1532	8
SWEET PIRATE OF THE HEART,	SWEET PIRATE OF THE	1546	1
HOW SWEET IF I AM NOT FORGOT	MY WARS ARE LAID AWAY IN	1549	9
TO LAW--SAID SWEET THERMOPYLAE	"GO TELL IT"--WHAT A	1554	7
FOR ANY SWEET "COME IN"	THE HEART HAS MANY DOORS	1567	3
A GLEE AS SWEET AS IF THE STARS	TO SEE HER IS A PICTURE	1568 V	7
GAY FROM AN UNANNOINTED [SWEET FROM A SURREPTITIOUS] TWIG	THE BOBOLINK IS GONE--	1591	12
IS GRATITUDE'S SWEET POVERTY,	TO TRY TO SPEAK, AND	1617	3
THE SWEET DERISION OF THE CROW	IN SNOW THOU COMEST	1669	3
SWEET IS THE SWAMP WITH ITS SECRETS,	SWEET IS THE SWAMP WITH	1740	1
IS WHAT MAKES LIFE SO SWEET.	THAT IT WILL NEVER COME	1741	2
SWEET HOURS HAVE PERISHED HERE!	SWEET HOURS HAVE	1767	1
SWEETER			
SWEETER THAN A VANISHED FROLIC	I CANT TELL YOU--BUT YOU	65	5
VESPERS--ARE SWEETER THAN MATINS--SIGNOR--	I SHALL KEEP SINGING!	250	9
A SWEETER TO OBEY,	ALTHOUGH I PUT AWAY HIS	366	18
THAN THAT--BE SWEETER WISE--	NOT IN THIS WORLD TO SEE	418	9
SWEETER--THE SURMISING ROBINS--	DREAMS--ARE WELL--BUT	450	5
BUT SWEETER SO--THAN NONE.	MYSELF CAN READ THE	1089	8
POSSESSION--HAS A SWEETER CHINK	BECAUSE 'TWAS RICHES I	1093	7
IS BETTER [SWEETER] THAN ENAMELED REALMS	THE CLOVER'S SIMPLE FAME	1232	3
IT ONLY SWEETER GROWS.	HER LOSSES MAKE OUR	1562	8
TO LOSE THEE--SWEETER THAN TO GAIN	TO LOSE THEE--SWEETER	1754	1
SWEETEST			
SUCCESS IS COUNTED SWEETEST	SUCCESS IS COUNTED	67	1
AND SWEETEST--IN THE GALE--IS HEARD--	"HOPE" IS THE THING WITH	254	5
THE SWEETEST HERESY RECIEVED	THE SWEETEST HERESY	387	1
IS SWEETEST NUTRIMENT--TO HIM--	I THINK THE HEMLOCK	525	11
THOU SWEETEST OF THE UNIVERSE,	IMMURED IN HEAVEN!	1594	4
THAT THOU ART TRITEST--BRIGHTEST [SWEETEST] TRUTH--	EXTOL THEE--COULD I--	1643 V	4
THE SADDEST NOISE, THE SWEETEST NOISE,	THE SADDEST NOISE, THE	1764	1
SWEETNESS			
IT'S [THY] SWEETNESS TO HAVE KNOWN--	ONE THING OF IT WE	1464	4
WHICH IS THE ZEST OF SWEETNESS	OF DEATH I TRY TO THINK	1558	6
WITH SWEETNESS UNABATED	WITH SWEETNESS UNABATED	1709	1
ITALICIZE ITS SWEETNESS,	DID LIFE'S PENURIOUS	1717	2
SWEETS			
CONFUSED BY SWEETS--AS MORTALS--ARE--	NOT PROBABLE--THE BAREST	346	6
THE SWEETS OF PILLAGE, CAN BE KNOWN	THE SWEETS OF PILLAGE,	1470	1
SWELL			
LIKE SEPARATION'S SWELL	A WIND THAT ROSE	1259	7
BUT HIS RECEDING SWELL	THE LONG SIGH OF THE	1359	5
SWELLED			
SWELLED--LIKE HORIZONS--IN MY BREAST [VEST]--	A SOLEMN THING--IT WAS--	271	15
LIKE RAIN IT SOUNDED TILL IT CURVED [SWELLED]	LIKE RAIN IT SOUNDED	1235	1
SWELLING			
THAN DID LOADED [SWELLING] SEA	HER SWEET TURN TO LEAVE	649	6
A SWELLING OF THE GROUND--	BECAUSE I COULD NOT STOP	712	18
AND STARTLED AT IT'S SWELLING [RISING]	BECAUSE MY BROOK IS	1200	5
SWELLS			
AND SWELLS THE SCANTEST DEED	I KNOW OF PEOPLE IN THE	1665	6
AND DECKS [BRIMS / FILLS / SWELLS] THE RAYS	BY A DEPARTING LIGHT	1714	6
SWEPT			
THEN KNIT, AND SWEPT [PASSED]--	OF ALL THE SOUNDS	321	32
AND SWEPT THE WORLD AWAY--	THE WINTERS ARE SO SHORT	403	14
SWEPT BY MY SEARCHING EYES--THE LAST--	ME PROVE IT NOW--WHOEVER	537	15
THAT SWEPT HIS BEING--BACK--	GRIEF IS A MOUSE--	793	8
BUT SWEPT AS DRY AS SAND--	LIKE RAIN IT SOUNDED	1235	4
HAD SWEPT THE WINTER STREET--	LIKE BROOMS OF STEEL	1252	3
ALL THINGS SWEPT SOLE AWAY	ALL THINGS SWEPT SOLE	1512	1
THEN SWEPT AS LIGHTLY FROM DISDAIN	TO HER DERIDED HOME	1586	7
SWERVE			
IF HE FEAR TO SWERVE--	IF YOUR NERVE, DENY YOU	292	4
BUT LET A SPLINTER SWERVE--	THE BRAIN, WITHIN IT'S	556	3
IF BRAVO, SOMETIMES SWERVE--	THE TEST OF LOVE--IS	573	7
WHEN OLDEST CEDARS SWERVE--	THE TRUTH--IS STIRLESS--	780	4
. . . SWERVES / SUMMERS SWERVE] AWAY--	AFTER ALL BIRDS HAVE	1395	7
SWERVED			
IT ONLY MOVED [SWERVED] AS DO THE SUNS--	'TWAS AWKWARD, BUT IT	973	5
SWERVELESS			
IN SOVREIGN--SWERVELESS TUNE--	THERE IS A FLOWER THAT	380	28
SWERVES			
. . . SWERVES / SUMMERS SWERVE] AWAY--	AFTER ALL BIRDS HAVE	1395	7
SWIFT			
THEN--NOT SO SWIFT--	'TWAS THE OLD--ROAD--	344	9
WHEN SWIFT [QUICK] IT SLIPPED IT'S LIMIT--	HE GAVE AWAY HIS LIFE--	567	7

	FIRST LINE	POEM	LINE
SWIFT (CONTINUED)			
THAN FLAKE OF SNOW, DIVIDED WITH [IMPRINTED SWIFT]	HE TOLD A HOMELY TALE	763	7
SWIFT AS A FRESHET'S TONGUE	THIS IS A BLOSSOM OF THE	945	6
WHEN LIFE'S SWIFT RIVER STRIVEN THROUGH	WHAT TWIGS WE HELD BY--	1086	3
IN THE SWIFT PARTITIONS	FORTITUDE INCARNATE	1217	3
. . . QUICK / SWIFT / WILD] EXPERIMENT [LEGACY / APOCALYPSE / . . .	A LITTLE MADNESS IN THE	1333	5
SWIFTER			
SWIFTER THAN THE HOOFS OF HORSEMEN	I CANT TELL YOU--BUT YOU	65	7
STILLER [SWIFTER] THAN A FLEET!	DUST IS THE ONLY SECRET	153	12
SWIFTLY			
AND SOFTLY [SWIFTLY] THRO' THE ALTERED AIR	THESE ARE THE DAYS WHEN	130	11
SWIFTNESS			
WITH SWIFTNESS, AS OF CHARIOTS	IT WAS A QUIET WAY--	1053	7
SWIM			
LEAP, PLASHLESS AS THEY SWIM.	A BIRD CAME DOWN THE	328	20
UPON HIS ATOM SWIM--	MY GOD--HE SEES THEE--	1178	7
AS PATTERNS SWIM	IN WINTER IN MY ROOM	1670	30
SWIMMERS			
TWO SWIMMERS WRESTLED ON THE SPAR--	TWO SWIMMERS WRESTLED ON	201	1
SWIMMING			
WORLDS WERE LYING OUT TO [SWIMMING IN THE / LYING IN THE] SUN--	WHEN I HOPED, I	768	11
PROVE ME--MY HAZEL [SWIMMING] WITNESSES	JOY TO HAVE MERITED THE	788	11
SWINDLED			
AS CHILDREN--SWINDLED FOR THE FIRST	I MEANT TO HAVE BUT	476	27
SWINDLERS			
ALL SWINDLERS--BE--INFER--	I MEANT TO HAVE BUT	476	28
SWING			
SHOULD SWING THEIR CUPS OF CHRYSOLITE--	THERE IS A MORN BY MEN	24	17
TILL SERAPHS SWING THEIR SNOWY HATS--	I TASTE A LIQUOR NEVER	214	13
AND HIS EMERALD SWING--	I COULD BRING YOU JEWELS	697	10
HIS DINING ROOM DO [DOTH] SWING.	A SAUCER HOLDS A CUP	1374	8
SWINGING			
SWINGING HER BERYL BELL--	THROUGH THE DARK SOD--AS	392	6
OF THE AWFUL [SWINGING] SEA--	FORTITUDE INCARNATE	1217	4
WERE SWINGING AT HER [HIS] BACK.	HER LOSSES MAKE OUR	1562	4
SWINGS			
FEARLESS--THE COBWEB SWINGS FROM THE CEILING--	HOW MANY TIMES THESE LOW	187	11
AND SWINGS UPON THE HOURS,	THE SOUL HAS BANDAGED	512	14
SWISS			
OUR LIVES ARE SWISS--	OUR LIVES ARE SWISS--	80	1
SWOLLEN			
TILL SWOLLEN WITH THE SKY	HOW STILL THE BELLS IN	1008	2
SWOON			
AS ONE WITHIN A SWOON--	THERE IS A PAIN--SO	599	6
BETROTHED--WITHOUT THE SWOON	TITLE DIVINE--IS MINE!	1072	6
SWORD			
WHICH BEARS A SWORD	THERE IS A WORD	8	2
OF SOUL OR SWORD.	GARLANDS FOR QUEENS, MAY	34	3
"THOU SHALT NOT" IS A KINDER SWORD	THERE COMES AN HOUR WHEN	1751	4
SWUNG SEE SWANG			
LIGHT SWUNG THE SILVER FLEECES	A LITTLE EAST OF JORDAN,	59	13
AND SWUNG THEIR FRENZIED HAIR.	AN AWFUL TEMPEST MASHED	198	9
THE TREES LIKE TASSELS--HIT--AND SWUNG--	THE TREES LIKE TASSELS--	606	1
HE SWUNG UPON THE DECALOGUE	THE BOBOLINK IS GONE--	1591	9
SYCAMORE			
AS THE THIRD SYCAMORE--	I KNOW SOME LONELY	289	34
OF SYCAMORE--OR CINNAMON--	WHAT CARE THE DEAD, FOR	592	21
SYLLABLE			
GET GABRIEL--TO TELL--THE ROYAL SYLLABLE--	FOR THIS--ACCEPTED	195	13
WITHOUT A [BUT DEIGN NO] SYLLABLE--	HOW NOTELESS MEN, AND	282	12
BUT MAKE NO SYLLABLE--LIKE DEATH--	GIVE LITTLE ANGUISH--	310	6
THE DYING--BUT A SYLLABLE--	UNIT, LIKE DEATH, FOR	408	11
BUT WROUGHT THEIR PANG IN SYLLABLE--	THE MARTYR POETS--DID	544	2
AS SYLLABLE FROM SOUND--	THE BRAIN--IS WIDER THAN	632	12
MY SYLLABLE REBELLED--	I COULD SUFFICE FOR HIM,	643	6
REVEAL BY SIGN--A SYLLABLE	THE FUTURE--NEVER SPOKE	672	3
SINCE A RACK COULD'NT COAX A SYLLABLE [AN ANSWER]--NOW	GRIEF IS A MOUSE--	793	17
WITHOUT A SYLLABLE.	THE VEINS OF OTHER	811	8
RETURNS NO SYLLABLE	THE ROBIN FOR THE CRUMB	864	2
THAT SYLLABLE WHOSE FAITH	SUPERFLUOUS WERE THE SUN	999	5
HER DEATHLESS SYLLABLE.	STEP LIGHTLY ON THIS	1183	8
THIS MORNING'S FINEST SYLLABLE	WHEN MEMORY IS FULL	1266	3
BUILT OF BUT JUST A SYLLABLE	LOVE'S STRICKEN "WHY"	1368	3
OF A [ITS] DELIVERED SYLLABLE	COULD MORTAL LIP DIVINE	1409	3
SYLLABLE-LESS			
THERE IS A SYLLABLE-LESS SEA	TO TELL THE BEAUTY WOULD	1700	3
SYLLABLES			
IT HURLS IT'S BARBED SYLLABLES	THERE IS A WORD	8	4
TO CON THE FADED SYLLABLES	IN EBON BOX, WHEN YEARS	169	7
THE SLOW--ARCHANGEL'S SYLLABLES	ON THIS LONG STORM THE	194	11
SYLLABLES OF VELVET--	ALL THE LETTERS I CAN	334	3
THE HILLS IN PURPLE SYLLABLES	THE HILLS IN PURPLE	1016	1
SYLVAN			
IN IT'S SYLVAN DRAWER--	SUMMER LAID HER SIMPLE	1363	6
. . . MIGHTY / GALLANT / SYLVAN / AMPLE / PERFECT] WAY	SUMMER--WE ALL HAVE SEEN	1386	6

	FIRST LINE	POEM	LINE
TAKE (CONTINUED)			
YET TAKE HER FROM THE LAWN	EXCEPT TO HEAVEN, SHE IS	154	10
TAKE CARE--FOR GOD IS HERE [NEAR]-- . . .	THE MURMUR OF A BEE	155	9
SAY--SEA--TAKE ME!	MY RIVER RUNS TO THEE--	162	7
BY IT--MY TITLE TAKE--	FOR THIS--ACCEPTED	195	4
TAKE US SIMULTANEOUS--LORD--	WE DONT CRY--TIM AND I,	196	27
LATE--WHEN I TAKE MY PLACE IN SUMMER-- . .	I SHALL KEEP SINGING!	250	7
ALTHOUGH--I KNEW--TO TAKE IT--	ONE LIFE OF SO MUCH	270	7
WHEN I COULD TAKE IT IN MY HAND--	A SOLEMN THING--IT WAS--	271	11
I BREATHED ENOUGH TO TAKE THE TRICK-- . .	I BREATHED ENOUGH TO	272	1
THEY CANNOT TAKE ME [US]--ANY MORE! . . .	WHAT IF I SAY I SHALL	277	7
TILL I TAKE VASTER ATTITUDES [MANNERS]-- .	OF BRONZE--AND BLAZE--	290	10
I GOT SO I COULD HEAR [THINK / TAKE] HIS NAME--	I GOT SO I COULD HEAR	293	1
WHEN WINDS TAKE [HOLD] FORESTS IN THEIR PAWS--	HE FUMBLES AT YOUR SOUL	315	13
BEYOND THE TRAIT TO TAKE AWAY	OF ALL THE SOUNDS	321	11
AND BIRDS TAKE PLACES, OVERHEAD, ...	OF ALL THE SOUNDS	321	23
AS MUCH OF NOON AS I COULD TAKE	BEFORE I GOT MY EYE PUT	327	12
TO TAKE MY RANK--BY--IN THE WEST--	THE FACE I CARRY WITH ME	336	3
HE'LL TAKE IT--SCAN IT--STEP ASIDE--	THE FACE I CARRY WITH ME	336	9
I TOLD MYSELF, "TAKE COURAGE, FRIEND-- . .	I FELT MY LIFE WITH BOTH	351	13
I TAKE--NO LESS THAN SKIES--	PERHAPS I ASKED TOO	352	2
THAT I MAY TAKE THAT PROMISE	ALTHOUGH I PUT AWAY HIS	366	30
HIS VENERABLE HAND TO TAKE--	A PRECIOUS--MOULDERING	371	5
TAKE OTHER ACCENTS, AS SUCH I HEARD . . .	I'M SAYING EVERY DAY	373	21
TAKE YOUR HEAVEN FURTHER ON--	TAKE YOUR HEAVEN FURTHER	388	1
TO TAKE THE MEASURE OF THE HOUSE--	THERE'S BEEN A DEATH, IN	389	19
THEN MY FACE TAKE HER RECOMPENSE--	I HAD NOT MINDED--WALLS	398	7
BUT--PLEASE TAKE A LITTLE GIRL--	GOOD MORNING--MIDNIGHT--	425	15
COULD TAKE IT--	I'LL CLUTCH--AND CLUTCH	427	3
TO TAKE THE PUMPKINS IN--	'TWAS JUST THIS TIME,	445	12
TO TAKE THE NAME OF GOLD--	IT WAS GIVEN TO ME BY	454	14
IT TAKE THE TALE FOR TRUE--	I MEANT TO HAVE BUT	476	22
IF THOU WOULD'ST TAKE IT--NOW--	WE COVER THEE--SWEET	482	12
AND TAKE [TASTE] ETERNITY--	IF YOU WERE COMING IN	511	16
AND TAKE THE SUNSHINE IN MY HANDS, ...	MY FIRST WELL DAY--SINCE	574	3
TO TAKE MY CHANCE [RISK] WITH PAIN--	MY FIRST WELL DAY--SINCE	574	6
TILL I COULD TAKE THE [CATCH MY] BALANCE .	I PRAYED, AT FIRST, A	576	18
THAT TIME--TO TAKE IT HOME--	HE FOUND MY BEING--SET	603	8
THE TINT I CANNOT TAKE--IS BEST--	THE TINT I CANNOT TAKE--	627	1
TAKE UP MY LITTLE VIOLIN--	I THINK THE LONGEST HOUR	635	15
I TAKE A FLOWER--AS I GO--	AGAIN--HIS VOICE IS AT	663	5
TO TAKE [MIND] IT--	VICTORY COMES LATE--	690	4
OR TAKE THE ROYAL NAMES IN VAIN--	SWEET MOUNTAINS--YE TELL	722	5
TAKE NOT MY LIBERTY	LET US PLAY YESTERDAY--	728	35
TO TAKE THE HONORABLE WORK	SHE ROSE TO HIS	732	3
FOR CERTAINTY SHE TAKE HER WAY	THE MOON WAS BUT A CHIN	737	15
MY FAITH MUST TAKE THE PURPLE WHEEL	MY FAITH IS LARGER THAN	766	3
OR TAKE AWAY [PALLIATE] A BRIAR.	IT WAS A GRAVE, YET BORE	876	12
WHY GIVE IF THOU MUST TAKE AWAY	A SHADE UPON THE MIND	882	7
TILL SUNRISE TAKE [CALL] US BACK TO SCENE--	I LEARNED--AT LEAST--	944	25
I TAKE BACK ALL I SAY--	WHEN THEY COME BACK--IF	1080	16
TO TAKE MOMENTUM--	WHAT TWIGS WE HELD BY--	1086	5
I TAKE THE CLUE DIVINE--	MY COCOON TIGHTENS--	1099	12
SOME WRETCHED CREATURE, SAVIOR TAKE	SOME WRETCHED CREATURE,	1111	1
SHALL I TAKE THEE, THE POET SAID	SHALL I TAKE THEE, THE	1126	1
SOUL, TAKE THY RISK [RISKS / CHANCE], . . .	SOUL, TAKE THY RISK,	1151	1
TURN [TAKE] SOONEST [SOONER] TO THE SEA . .	CONTAINED IN THIS SHORT	1165	6
BUT WHEN THEY WENT TO TAKE THEM OUT . . .	OF PAUL AND SILAS IT IS	1166	3
IF ANY TAKE [SEIZE] MY PROPERTY	ALONE AND IN A	1167	19
HENCEFORTH I TAKE MY LIVING PLACE	SOMEHOW MYSELF SURVIVED	1194	5
WHO GOES TO DINE MUST TAKE HIS FEAST . . .	WHO GOES TO DINE MUST	1223	1
TO TAKE US [ONE] LANDS AWAY	THERE IS NO FRIGATE LIKE	1263	2
THIS TRAVEL [TRAVERSE] MAY THE POOREST TAKE	THERE IS NO FRIGATE LIKE	1263	5
I TAKE THEE BY THE HAND--	THE SPIDER AS AN ARTIST	1275	8
AND TAKE A ROSY CHAIR.	THE NOTICE THAT IS	1310	4
TAKE COVERT IN THE GROUND--	THE SYMPTOM OF THE GALE	1327	8
YOU CANNOT TAKE ITSELF	YOU CANNOT TAKE ITSELF	1351	1
BUT TAKE AWAY AS DIFFICULT [IMPOTENT / EASILY]	YOU CANNOT TAKE ITSELF	1351	7
TAKE ALL AWAY--	TAKE ALL AWAY--	1365	1
THESE FEVERED DAYS--TO TAKE THEM TO THE FOREST	THESE FEVERED DAYS--TO	1441	1
"HEAVENLY FATHER"--TAKE TO THEE	"HEAVENLY FATHER"--TAKE	1461	1
TILL ASKED TO TAKE IT OFF--	WE KNEW NOT THAT WE WERE	1462	6
DID BEAUTY EVER TAKE--	THE BIRD HER PUNCTUAL	1585	6
HE SHALL NOT TAKE THY HAND	BACK FROM THE CORDIAL	1625	2
TAKE ALL AWAY FROM ME, BUT LEAVE ME ECSTASY,	TAKE ALL AWAY FROM ME,	1640	1
AND TAKE ONESELF BY SURPRISE	TO DO A MAGNANIMOUS	1699	2
AND OUR DEPARTURE TAKE	SWEET IS THE SWAMP WITH	1740	4
TAKEN			
TAKEN FROM MEN--THIS MORNING--	TAKEN FROM MEN--THIS	53	1
HOW MANY COLORS TAKEN	WHO NEVER LOST, ARE	73	11
WHEN A [THE] SUBJECT IS FINISHED [ENDED / TAKEN]--	WHATEVER IT IS--SHE HAS	1204	7
TAKES			
TO DIE--TAKES JUST A LITTLE WHILE--	TO DIE--TAKES JUST A	255	1
HOW SHORT IT TAKES TO MAKE IT BRIDE-- . . .	A WIFE--AT DAYBREAK I	461	4
IT TAKES ME ALL THE WHILE TO POISE--	I PRAYED, AT FIRST, A	576	20
THE ENTERING--TAKES AWAY--	I HAD BEEN HUNGRY, ALL	579	20
AND TAKES IT'S FUNDAMENTAL PLACE	WE DO NOT KNOW THE TIME	1106	3
AND TAKES THE WIND AT PRIME--	'TIS MY FIRST NIGHT	1122	6

	FIRST LINE	POEM	LINE
TAKES (CONTINUED)			
SHE TAKES [GOES] HER GRACIOUS [SPACIOUS / SUBTLE / SIMPLE / . . .	SUMMER--WE ALL HAVE SEEN	1386	6
EACH THAT WE LOSE TAKES PART OF US!	EACH THAT WE LOSE TAKES	1605	1
AND TAKES HER FAIR AERIAL GAIT .	THE OVERTAKELESSNESS OF	1691	7
TO MAKE A PRAIRIE IT TAKES A CLOVER AND ONE BEE,	TO MAKE A PRAIRIE IT	1755	1
TAKETH			
TAKETH AWAY MY WILL--	THE MURMUR OF A BEE	155	7
HE TAKETH DAMASK RESIDENCE--	A FUZZY FELLOW, WITHOUT	173	11
TAKING			
TAKING VILLAGES FOR BREAKFAST,	I HAVE NEVER SEEN	175	7
TAKING UP THE FAIR IDEAL,	TAKING UP THE FAIR IDEAL	428	1
TAKING TURNS--AT THE CHIMBORAZO--	LOVE--THOU ART HIGH--	453	5
AND TAKING BUT A PRAYER--	I HAD NO CAUSE TO BE	542	18
TALE			
AND DIADEMS--A TALE--	WHEN DIAMONDS ARE A	397	2
IT TAKE THE TALE FOR TRUE--	I MEANT TO HAVE BUT	476	22
UNTOLD TALE--	LET US PLAY YESTERDAY--	728	4
HE TOLD A HOMELY TALE	HE TOLD A HOMELY TALE	763	1
BUT LIKE AN ORIENTAL TALE	REPORTLESS SUBJECTS, TO	1048	7
OH CUNNING WRECK THAT TOLD NO TALE	A GREAT HOPE FELL	1123	4
THOUGH [WHILE] A STATLIER TALE	TELL AS A MARKSMAN--WERE	1152	6
LIVED TO TELL THE TALE--	ABRAHAM TO KILL HIM	1317	10
HAD BUT THE TALE A WARBLING [THRILLING / TYPIC / HEARTY / . . .	THE BIBLE IS AN ANTIQUE	1545	13
IF NATURE WILL NOT TELL THE TALE	THE RETICENT VOLCANO	1748	5
TALELESS			
THE TALELESS DAYS WENT ON	TWO TRAVELLERS PERISHING	933	12
TALISMANIC			
HIS TALISMANIC STONE	TRUST IN THE UNEXPECTED	555	6
TALK			
DID NOT TALK OF RETURNING!	WENT UP A YEAR THIS	93	9
TALK WITH PRUDENCE TO A BEGGAR	TALK WITH PRUDENCE TO A	119	1
I'VE HEARD AN ORGAN TALK, SOMETIMES--	I'VE HEARD AN ORGAN TALK	183	1
IT IS THE ULTIMATE OF TALK--	IF WHAT WE COULD--WERE	407	3
--OF TALK--	"WHY DO I LOVE" YOU, SIR	480	15
I WOULD NOT TALK, LIKE CORNETS--	I WOULD NOT PAINT--A	505	9
WE TALK IN CARELESS [VENTURE]--AND IN TOSS--	AGAIN--HIS VOICE IS AT	663	13
NOT IF TO TALK WITH ME	WHAT DID THEY DO SINCE I	900	10
IF GRACE COULD TALK.	THE ECSTASY TO GUESS	1608	3
TALK NOT TO ME OF SUMMER TREES	TALK NOT TO ME OF SUMMER	1634	1
"RED SEA," INDEED! TALK NOT TO ME	"RED SEA," INDEED! TALK	1642	1
THEY TALK AS SLOW AS LEGENDS GROW	THEY TALK AS SLOW AS	1697	1
I GATHERED FROM HIS TALK	HIGH FROM THE EARTH I	1723	10
TALKED			
TALKED SOFTLY OF NEW SPECIES	WENT UP A YEAR THIS	93	15
WE TALKED BETWEEN THE ROOMS--	I DIED FOR BEAUTY--BUT	449	10
WE TALKED AS GIRLS DO--	WE TALKED AS GIRLS DO--	586	1
WE TALKED WITH EACH OTHER ABOUT EACH OTHER	WE TALKED WITH EACH	1473	1
TALKS			
APART, IT NEVER TALKS--	THE SPIRIT LASTS--BUT IN	1576	4
TALL			
IF I WERE AS TALL AS THEY?	WILL THERE REALLY BE A	101	4
HE'D BE TOO TALL, THE TALLEST ONE	I DREADED THAT FIRST	348	15
TALL--LIKE THE STAG--WOULD THAT?	YOU SAID THAT I "WAS	738	5
THEN SOARING TO HIS TEMPLE [TURRET] TALL--	HOW LONESOME THE WIND	1418	12
TALLEST			
HE'D BE TOO TALL, THE TALLEST ONE	I DREADED THAT FIRST	348	15
TAMARIND			
FLAGONS, AND COOLING TAMARIND!	WHO NEVER LOST, ARE	73	4
WITH THEE IN THE TAMARIND WOOD--	WITH THEE, IN THE DESERT	209	3
TAMBORIN			
NOR TAMBORIN--NOR MAN--	MUSICIANS WRESTLE	157	9
MY TAMBORIN WERE SOONEST HEARD	IF I COULD BRIBE THEM BY	179	8
TAMPER			
DID MEDDLE [TAMPER]--ONE BY ONE--	'TIS GOOD--THE LOOKING	660	6
WE TAMPER WITH "AGAIN"	TO DISAPPEAR ENHANCES--	1209	8
IF ONE WOULD TAMPER THERE.	IT WOULD NOT KNOW IF IT	1579	4
TANGIBLE			
SO PLAUSIBLE [TANGIBLE / POSITIVE] BECOMES [APPEARS]	I THINK TO LIVE--MAY BE	646	22
TANKARD			
TANKARD, OR SPOON--	I KNOW SOME LONELY	289	26
TANKARDS			
NO BRIMMING TANKARDS FLOW--	WHAT INN IS THIS	115	8
FROM TANKARDS SCOOPED IN PEARL--	I TASTE A LIQUOR NEVER	214	2
TANKS			
FROM TANKS--ABOVE MY HEAD--	DO PEOPLE MOULDER	432	8
AND STOP TO FEED ITSELF AT TANKS--	I LIKE TO SEE IT LAP	585	3
TANTALIZE			
AND TANTALIZE--JUST SO--	A PRECIOUS--MOULDERING	371	28
TANTALIZING			
WITH [IN] TANTALIZING PLAY	IT ALWAYS FELT TO ME--A	597	14
TANTAMOUNT			
IT'S TANTAMOUNT BE FOUND--	BEHOLD THIS LITTLE BANE	1438	8
TAPER			
I MADE THE TAPER SHINE--	ONLY A SHRINE, BUT MINE	918	2
TAPESTRIES			
THE TAPESTRIES OF PARADISE	A SHADY FRIEND--FOR	278	11

	FIRST LINE	POEM	LINE
TAPESTRIES (CONTINUED)			
SUPPLANTS OUR TAPESTRIES WITH HIS-- . . .	THE SPIDER HOLDS A	605	7
TAPESTRY			
DROP, LIKE A TAPESTRY, AWAY, ...	DOUBT ME! MY DIM	275	20
TAPPED			
THE WIND--TAPPED LIKE A TIRED MAN-- . . .	THE WIND--TAPPED LIKE A	436	1
AGAIN, HE TAPPED--'TWAS FLURRIEDLY-- . . .	THE WIND--TAPPED LIKE A	436	19
TAPPED SOFT UPON THE TOWN	THE FINGERS OF THE LIGHT	1000	2
TAR			
AND WRECKS IN PEACE A PURPLE TAR, ...	A SLOOP OF AMBER SLIPS	1622	3
TARDY			
THE HANDS STILL HUG THE TARDY GLASS-- . .	I BRING AN UNACCUSTOMED	132	8
TELLING MY TARDY NAME--	I SHOULD NOT DARE TO	205	12
TARE			
AND FLEETER THAN A TARE--	THE MUSHROOM IS THE ELF	1298	8
OF EVERY TARE--	"TOMORROW"--WHOSE	1367	6
THE SUN IS ONE--AND ON THE TARE	THE SUN IS ONE--AND ON	1372	1
TARGET			
TIME'S SUBLIMEST TARGET	THERE IS A WORD	8	17
MAKE OF HIS ONLY BOY A TARGET	TELL AS A MARKSMAN--WERE	1152	18
TARNISHED			
IS TARNISHED BY THE SNOW--	BEFORE THE ICE IS IN THE	37	4
TARRIED			
AS IF IT TARRIED ALWAYS	THE MUSHROOM IS THE ELF	1298	5
TARRY			
NEXT TIME, TO TARRY, ...	JUST LOST, WHEN I WAS	160	16
TO TARRY AN ETERNITY--	NO OTHER CAN REDUCE	982	V
NEED NOT LINGER [TARRY] HERE--	TELL AS A MARKSMAN--WERE	1152	10
TARRYING			
HER TARRYING, UNKNOWN, ...	FROM US SHE WANDERED NOW	890	2
TASK			
OR EARLY TASK TO DO?	ON SUCH A NIGHT, OR SUCH	146	16
THE HOUSEWIFE'S GENTLE TASK--	THE NIGHT WAS WIDE, AND	589	17
AND TASK FOR BOTH--	I LEARNED--AT LEAST--	944	13
TASSELS			
OF TASSELS--AND OF COACHES--SOON-- . . .	THERE'S BEEN A DEATH, IN	389	21
IT HAD THE TASSELS ON--	'TWAS JUST THIS TIME,	445	4
THE TREES LIKE TASSELS--HIT--AND SWUNG-- .	THE TREES LIKE TASSELS--	606	1
TASTE			
I TASTE A LIQUOR NEVER BREWED--	I TASTE A LIQUOR NEVER	214	1
FOREVER OF HIS FATE TO TASTE--	FOREVER AT HIS SIDE TO	246	6
A SORT, THAT SHALL NOT TASTE OF DEATH-- . .	DO PEOPLE MOULDER	432	11
'TIS VARIOUS--AS THE VARIOUS TASTE-- . . .	'TIS CUSTOMARY AS WE	440	5
OF ONLY TASTE WE CARED TO PLEASE	TO MAKE ONE'S TOILETTE--	485	3
AND TAKE [TASTE] ETERNITY--	IF YOU WERE COMING IN	511	16
WOULD YOU LIKE SUMMER? TASTE OF OURS. . .	WOULD YOU LIKE SUMMER?	691	1
HONORS--TASTE DRY--	THE WORLD--FEELS DUSTY	715	4
JUST LONG ENOUGH TO TASTE--	LET US PLAY YESTERDAY--	728	31
TO TASTE HER MYSTIC BREAD--	THESE ARE THE SIGNS TO	1077	4
COULD PROSPECT TASTE OF RETROSPECT . . .	MY TRIUMPH LASTED TILL	1227	11
WHICH WHILE YOU TASTE SO NATIVE [ADJACENT] SEEMS	YOUR THOUGHTS DONT HAVE	1452	5
WHICH OTHERS TASTE AND SPURN AND SNEER [SLIGHT]--	I GROPED FOR HIM BEFORE	1555	5
TASTED			
I TASTED--CARELESS--THEN--	ONE YEAR AGO--JOTS WHAT?	296	12
TILL EVERY SPICE IS TASTED--	WITHIN MY GARDEN, RIDES	500	9
AND YET, IT TASTED, LIKE THEM ALL, ...	IT WAS NOT DEATH, FOR I	510	9
HOW SWEET IT WOULD HAVE TASTED--	VICTORY COMES LATE--	690	5
TILL YOU HAD TASTED FIRST, ...	I COULD NOT DRINK IT,	818	2
I TASTED WHEAT AND HATED CHAFF	I WORKED FOR CHAFF AND	1269	5
DOES NOT DESERVE THE [HAS NEVER TASTED] SPRING--	A DRUNKARD CANNOT MEET A	1628	8
EACH ONE OF US HAS TASTED	A WORD MADE FLESH IS	1651	5
TASTELESS			
UPON A TASTELESS MEAT	SURPRISE IS LIKE A	1306	2
TASTES			
WHO TASTES IT; POSSIBILITY	IMPOSSIBILITY, LIKE WINE	838	3
TASTES DEATH--THE FIRST--TO HAND [PASS / PROVE] THE STING	LOVE--IS THAT LATER	924	5
TASTING			
IS ASCERTAINED BY TASTING [TESTING]-- . .	DESPAIR'S ADVANTAGE IS	799	7
TATTERED			
A POOR--TORN HEART--A TATTERED HEART-- . .	A POOR--TORN HEART-- A	78	1
TO MEND EACH TATTERED FAITH	TO MEND EACH TATTERED	1442	1
TATTERS			
THE TATTERS THAT HE WEARS--	TO TRY TO SPEAK, AND	1617	4
TAUGHT			
WATER, IS TAUGHT BY THIRST.	WATER, IS TAUGHT BY	135	1
THE BLESSED ETHER--TAUGHT THEM--	THE LONESOME FOR THEY	262	9
THE SEASONS FLIT--I'M TAUGHT--	THE ROBIN'S MY CRITERION	285	12
YOUR RICHES--TAUGHT ME--POVERTY.	YOUR RICHES--TAUGHT ME--	299	1
YOU, SIR, TAUGHT FIRST--TO ME.	ALTHOUGH I PUT AWAY HIS	366	33
TAUGHT ME--BY TIME--THE LOWER WAY-- . . .	I LIVE WITH HIM--I SEE	463	13
THE ZEROES--TAUGHT US--PHOSPHORUS-- . . .	THE ZEROES--TAUGHT US--	689	1
YOU TAUGHT ME WAITING WITH MYSELF-- . . .	YOU TAUGHT ME WAITING	740	1
YOU TAUGHT ME FORTITUDE OF FATE--	YOU TAUGHT ME WAITING	740	3
ADAM TAUGHT HER THRIFT	PARADISE IS THAT OLD	1119	6
I TAUGHT MY HEART A HUNDRED TIMES	I THOUGHT THE TRAIN	1449	5
WHICH SHE WAS TAUGHT TO EAT--	BETROTHED TO	1641	4

	FIRST LINE	POEM	LINE
TAUGHT (CONTINUED)			
SEVEN YEARS OF TROTH HAVE TAUGHT THEE	REARRANGE A "WIFE'S"	1737	7
TAUNTED			
WHEN FATE HATH TAUNTED LAST	THIS MERIT HATH THE	979	3
TAUNTING			
TEAZING [TAUNTING] WITH GLITTERING AMEND--	FAIRER THROUGH FADING--	938	6
TAUNTS			
THAT TAUNTS HER BAYONET.	MY COUNTRY NEED NOT	1511	8
TAWDRY			
IT LOOKS TOO TAWDRY GRACE	YOU'LL FIND--IT WHEN YOU	610	14
TAWNY			
GROWN TAWNY NOW, WITH TIME--	IN EBON BOX, WHEN YEARS	169	6
TAWNY--HER CUSTOMS--	CIVILIZATION--SPURNS--	492	5
TAX			
WHERE TAX ASLEEP AND TITLE OFF	ALONE AND IN A	1167	13
AND HAS'NT ANY TAX TO PAY	THE BUTTERFLY UPON THE	1521	3
TEA			
TELL LUNA, TEA IS WAITING,	"SIC TRANSIT GLORIA	3	15
NO CHATTER--HERE--NO TEA--	UNIT, LIKE DEATH, FOR	408	13
YOU ASKED THE COMPANY TO TEA--	IF ANYBODY'S FRIEND BE	509	17
AND LAY THE MARBLE TEA.	THE GRAVE MY LITTLE	1743	4
TEACH			
TEACH ME THE SKILL,	AH, NECROMANCY SWEET!	177	3
BUT TEACH THE FOOTMAN FROM VEVAY--	THE FLOWER MUST NOT	206	4
TEACH HIM--WHEN HE MAKES THE NAMES--	TEACH HIM--WHEN HE MAKES	227	1
NONE MAY TEACH IT--ANY--	THERE'S A CERTAIN SLANT	258	9
TEACH ME THE STRAIN	PUT UP MY LUTE!	261	7
TO TEACH THE ANGELS, AVARICE,	ALTHOUGH I PUT AWAY HIS	366	32
BUT--COULD SHE [IT] TEACH--IT?	KNOWS HOW TO FORGET!	433	2
GLOBE DID NOT TEACH IT	KNOWS HOW TO FORGET!	433	V
NO ONE TO TEACH ME THAT NEW GRACE--	I AM ASHAMED--I HIDE--	473	5
SET CYPHERLESS--TO TEACH THE EYE	'TIS ONE BY ONE--THE	545	3
WOULD IT TEACH ME NOW?	THE LUXURY TO APPREHEND	815	V
TEAM			
OR IN TOO UNSUBSTANTIAL TEAM--	THE FROST WAS NEVER SEEN	1202	3
TEAR			
ACCOMPANIED WITH TEAR--	I HAD A GUINEA GOLDEN--	23	30
A DARTING FEAR--A POMP--A TEAR--	A DARTING FEAR--A POMP--	87	1
EVEN A TEAR--	A MIEN TO MOVE A QUEEN--	283	7
THERE PUBLISHES [BUSTLES BUT] A TEAR--	SO GLAD WE ARE--A	329	4
THAT DID IT TEAR ALL DAY,	I SOMETIMES DROP IT, FOR	708	6
BUT EVERY TEAR I BORE	EACH SCAR I'LL KEEP FOR	877	5
ALTHOUGH IT TEAR--	THERE IS A STRENGTH IN	1113	2
WILL [WOULD] SUBSCRIBE A TEAR--	TELL AS A MARKSMAN--WERE	1152	12
AN HONEST TEAR	AN HONEST TEAR	1192	1
TEARFUL			
SAVE BY TEARFUL RILL--	GLOWING IS HER BONNET,	72	8
SHE'S TEARFUL--IF SHE WEEP AT ALL--	SHE'S HAPPY, WITH A NEW	535	5
TEARS			
AND COFFERS HEAPED WITH TEARS!	FOR EACH EXTATIC INSTANT	125	8
MANSIONS CANNOT LET THE TEARS IN,	"HOUSES"--SO THE WISE	127	3
FOR INTERRUPTING TEARS--	DEATH SETS A THING	360	18
ENDOW THE LIVING--WITH THE TEARS--	ENDOW THE LIVING--WITH	521	1
"TEARS"--A TRICK OF THE NERVE--	"SPEECH"--IS A PRANK OF	688	2
TEARS OPEN HER IMPERIAL VEINS--	YOU'VE SEEN BALLOONS SET	700	15
AND SPOTTED IT WITH TEARS--	HE TOLD A HOMELY TALE	763	2
BUT MINE--DISPELS--IN TEARS.	I SHALL NOT MURMUR IF AT	1410	8
FOR ARDOR OR FOR TEARS,	A LITTLE OVERFLOWING	1467	3
AND ASK IT OF THE TEARS,	TO TRY TO SPEAK, AND	1617	2
MUST THRUST THE TEARS AWAY.	WHERE EVERY BIRD IS BOLD	1758	4
TEASE			
IT SHOULD NOT TEASE YOU--	WHAT SHALL I DO--IT	186	8
TEAZE			
THE MIRACLE TO TEAZE	THE MANNER OF IT'S DEATH	468	9
THE CERTAIN PREY TO TEAZE--	THE WHOLE OF IT CAME NOT	762	V 4
JUST LONG ENOUGH FOR HOPE TO TEAZE [STIR]--	THE WHOLE OF IT CAME NOT	762	7
WHEN I FORGET TO TEAZE--	THEY WONT FROWN ALWAYS--	874	2
MY COCOON TIGHTENS--COLORS TEAZE--	MY COCOON TIGHTENS--	1099	1
TEAZED			
THE CHILDISH HANDS THAT TEAZED FOR PENCE	THE BEGGAR LAD--DIES	717	13
AS THE VULTURE TEAZED	AS THE STARVED MAELSTROM	872	2
TEAZES			
DIPS--EVADES--TEAZES--DEPLOYS--	THE NEAREST DREAM	319	6
TEAZING			
HER TEAZING PURPLES--AFTERNOONS--	"HEAVEN"--IS WHAT I	239	9
TEAZING THE WANT--	YOU SEE I CANNOT SEE--	253	14
TEAZING [TAUNTING] WITH GLITTERING AMEND--	FAIRER THROUGH FADING--	938	6
TECHNICALITY			
FOR TECHNICALITY OF DEATH--	'TWAS AWKWARD, BUT IT	973	11
HEAVEN THE BALM OF A SURLY TECHNICALITY!	HOW HAPPY IS THE LITTLE	1510	V
TEETH			
AND GNASHED THEIR TEETH--	AN AWFUL TEMPEST MASHED	198	8
THAT [WHICH] TEETH OF FROSTS ALONE DISCLOSE	THERE ARE TWO RIPENINGS	332	7
HER TEETH CAN HARDLY STAND--	SHE SIGHTS A BIRD--SHE	507	6
SHE EASES FROM HER TEETH	THE WHOLE OF IT CAME NOT	762	6
TELEGRAM			
FATE'S--TELEGRAM--TO HIM--	THE FUTURE--NEVER SPOKE	672	12
TELEGRAMS			
MYSELF CAN READ THE TELEGRAMS	MYSELF CAN READ THE	1089	1

	FIRST LINE	POEM	LINE
TELEGRAPHIC			
THROUGH TELEGRAPHIC SIGNS--	THEY PUT US FAR APART--	474	8
TELESCOPE			
HIMSELF--A TELESCOPE	I NEVER FELT AT HOME--	413	12
TELESCOPES			
TELESCOPES WOULD KNOW--	KNOWS HOW TO FORGET!	433	V
TELESCOPIC			
TOO TELESCOPIC EYES	I TIE MY HAT--I CREASE	443	22
TELL			
TELL LUNA, TEA IS WAITING,	"SIC TRANSIT GLORIA	3	15
TELL I MY DOUBTING HEART	I HAVE A BIRD IN SPRING	5	17
AND THE EARTH [WORLD]--THEY TELL ME--	FREQUENTLY THE WOODS ARE	6	9
MY FIGURES FAIL TO TELL ME	THE FEET OF PEOPLE	7	17
THE SAVED WILL TELL	THERE IS A WORD	8	7
SOME ONE THE SUM COULD TELL--	IT'S ALL I HAVE TO BRING	26	6
THE CRIER'S VOICE W'D [WOULD] TELL ME--	IF THOSE I LOVED WERE	29	2
AND WILL NOT TELL IT'S NAME.	THERE'S SOMETHING	45	4
WHEN YOU HAVE DONE, PRAY TELL ME	HEART! WE WILL FORGET	47	5
NOR TELL THE LOVING FORESTS	I HAV'NT TOLD MY GARDEN	50	11
I CANT TELL YOU--BUT YOU FEEL IT--	I CANT TELL YOU--BUT YOU	65	1
NOR CAN YOU TELL ME--	I CANT TELL YOU--BUT YOU	65	2
CAN TELL THE DEFINITION	SUCCESS IS COUNTED	67	7
BUT I SHALL NEVER TELL!	SO BASHFUL WHEN I SPIED	91	12
THE BYSTANDERS WILL TELL!	WENT UP A YEAR THIS	93	4
PLEASE TO TELL A LITTLE PILGRIM	WILL THERE REALLY BE A	101	11
FATHER! THEY WONT TELL ME,	GOOD NIGHT, BECAUSE WE	114	7
WONT YOU TELL THEM TO?	GOOD NIGHT, BECAUSE WE	114	8
"HOUSES"--SO THE WISE MEN TELL ME--	"HOUSES"--SO THE WISE	127	1
TELL ME HOW FAR THE MORNING LEAPS--	BRING ME THE SUNSET IN A	128	4
TELL ME WHAT TIME THE WEAVER SLEEPS	BRING ME THE SUNSET IN A	128	5
ALL THIS AND MORE I CANNOT TELL--	AN ALTERED LOOK ABOUT	140	13
I CANNOT TELL THE SUM,	SHE BORE IT TILL THE	144	6
GETHSEMANE CAN TELL	ALL OVERGROWN BY CUNNING	148	V
THAN TELL--	THE MURMUR OF A BEE	155	5
MUST TELL!	THE MURMUR OF A BEE	155	15
IF YOU'LL JUST TELL ME SO--	YOU LOVE ME--YOU ARE	156	16
ODD SECRETS OF THE LINE TO TELL!	JUST LOST, WHEN I WAS	160	8
I'VE HEARD THE HUNTER TELL--	A WOUNDED DEER--LEAPS	165	2
IF I MUST TELL YOU, OF A HORSE	I MET A KING THIS	166	13
NEED THE WISER, TELL?	IF THE FOOLISH, CALL	168	2
TO TELL THE PRETTY SECRET	A FUZZY FELLOW, WITHOUT	173	19
BUT, WHEN TRAVELLERS TELL	I HAVE NEVER SEEN	175	2
TELL CARLO--	WHAT SHALL I DO--IT	186	14
HE'LL TELL ME!	WHAT SHALL I DO--IT	186	15
ONLY THE SOLDERED MOUTH CAN TELL--	HOW MANY TIMES THESE LOW	187	2
THEY TELL IT TO THE HILLS--	THE SKIES CANT KEEP	191	2
THE HILLS JUST TELL THE ORCHARDS--	THE SKIES CANT KEEP	191	3
WHO KNOWS BUT SHE WOULD TELL?	THE SKIES CANT KEEP	191	8
HE WILL TELL ME WHAT "PETER" PROMISED--	I SHALL KNOW WHY--WHEN	193	5
GET GABRIEL--TO TELL--THE ROYAL SYLLABLE--	FOR THIS--ACCEPTED	195	13
OR TELL GOD--HOW CROSS WE ARE--	WHAT IS--"PARADISE"--	215	10
SAVIOR! I'VE NO ONE ELSE TO TELL--	SAVIOR! I'VE NO ONE ELSE	217	1
HIS LITTLE SPANIEL--TELL HIM!	IF HE DISSOLVE--THEN--	236	14
TELL [STATE] IT THE AGES--TO A CYPHER--	BOUND--A TROUBLE--	269	7
DONT TELL! THEY'D BANISH US [ADVERTISE]--YOU KNOW!	I'M NOBODY! WHO ARE YOU?	288	4
TO TELL YOUR [ONE'S] NAME--THE LIVELONG JUNE--	I'M NOBODY! WHO ARE YOU?	288	7
AND SO THE WALLS--DONT TELL--	I KNOW SOME LONELY	289	17
THAT I DARE TO TELL?	HOW THE OLD MOUNTAINS	291	8
SUCH [SOME] SPIRIT MAKES [TELL] HER PERPETUAL MENTION,	UNTO LIKE STORY--TROUBLE	295	13
I'LL TELL YOU HOW THE SUN ROSE--	I'LL TELL YOU HOW THE	318	1
FOR MINE--I TELL YOU THAT MY HEART	BEFORE I GOT MY EYE PUT	327	7
WERE HE TO TELL--EXTREMELY SORRY	FUNNY--TO BE A CENTURY--	345	6
TELL THAT THE WORST, IS EASY IN A MOMENT--	IF ANY SINK, ASSURE THAT	358	5
AND TELL YOU ALL YOUR DREAMS--WERE TRUE--	A PRECIOUS--MOULDERING	371	23
BUT TELL HIM THAT IT CEASED TO FEEL--	THERE IS A LANGUOR OF	396	11
AND HE WILL TELL YOU--SKILL IS LATE--	THERE IS A LANGUOR OF	396	13
A TONGUE--TO TELL HIM I AM TRUE!	A TONGUE--TO TELL HIM I	400	1
AND TELL HIM--CHARGE THEE SPEAK IT PLAIN--	A TONGUE--TO TELL HIM I	400	7
THE IMPOTENCE TO TELL--	IF WHAT WE COULD--WERE	407	4
THE LIVING--TELL--	UNIT, LIKE DEATH, FOR	408	10
TO STOP AND TELL THEM WHERE IT IS--	THE COLOR OF THE GRAVE	411	7
ALL THIS--AND MORE--IF I SHOULD TELL--	A MURMUR IN THE TREES--	416	11
BUT THEN I PROMISED NE'ER TO TELL--	A MURMUR IN THE TREES--	416	17
TO TELL THE VERY LAST THEY SAID	WHY MAKE IT DOUBT--IT	462	5
NOR EVER TURN TO TELL ME WHY--	WHY MAKE IT DOUBT--IT	462	12
ME TO ADORN--HOW--TELL--	I AM ASHAMED--I HIDE--	473	7
TO TELL WHAT WATER IS	TO ONE DENIED TO DRINK	490	2
TELL HIM [HER]--	GOING TO HIM! HAPPY	494	2
TELL HIM [HER] THE PAGE I DID'NT WRITE--[NEVER WROTE!]	GOING TO HIM! HAPPY	494	3
TELL HIM [HER]--I ONLY SAID THE SYNTAX--	GOING TO HIM! HAPPY	494	4
TELL HIM [HER] JUST HOW THE FINGERS HURRIED--	GOING TO HIM! HAPPY	494	6
TELL HIM [HER]--IT WAS'NT A PRACTISED WRITER--	GOING TO HIM! HAPPY	494	10
TELL HIM [HER]--NO--YOU MAY QUIBBLE THERE--	GOING TO HIM! HAPPY	494	15
TELL HIM [HER]--NIGHT [DAY] FINISHED--BEFORE WE FINISHED--	GOING TO HIM! HAPPY	494	18
TELL HIM [HER]--JUST HOW SHE SEALED YOU--CAUTIOUS!	GOING TO HIM! HAPPY	494	22

	FIRST LINE	POEM	LINE
TELL (CONTINUED)			
TO TELL HIM IT IS NOON, ABROAD--	I ENVY SEAS, WHEREON HE	498	19
CAN ANYBODY TELL?	THOSE FAIR--FICTITIOUS	499	8
WHERE ARE THEY--CAN YOU TELL--	THOSE FAIR--FICTITIOUS	499	V 8
SO TELL ME WHO 'TIS LIKE--	YOU KNOW THAT PORTRAIT	504	2
WHEN WAS IT--CAN YOU TELL--	IF ANYBODY'S FRIEND BE	509	16
AND TELL YOUR CEDAR FLOOR--	YOU CANNOT PUT A FIRE	530	8
THE MARTYR POETS--DID NOT TELL--	THE MARTYR POETS--DID	544	1
WE--TELL A HURT--TO COOL IT--	THE BLACK BERRY--WEARS A	554	9
I COULD NOT TELL THE DATE OF MINE--	I MEASURE EVERY GRIEF I	561	7
I'LL TELL THEE ALL--HOW BALD [BLANK] IT GREW--	IF I MAY HAVE IT, WHEN	577	14
I'LL TELL YOU HOW I TRIED TO KEEP	IF I MAY HAVE IT, WHEN	577	22
I HAD NOT POWER TO TELL--	I THINK I WAS ENCHANTED	593	8
HOW THEY WILL TELL THE STORY--	GLEE--THE GREAT STORM IS	619	9
TOO EXQUISITE--TO TELL--	THE TINT I CANNOT TAKE--	627	12
THE TRUMPETS TELL IT TO THE AIR--	MY PORTION IS DEFEAT--	639	15
I'VE HEARD MY FATHER TELL--	THE JUDGE IS LIKE THE	699	2
I MEANT TO TELL HER HOW I LONGED	I MEANT TO FIND HER WHEN	718	5
SWEET MOUNTAINS--YE TELL ME NO LIE--	SWEET MOUNTAINS--YE TELL	722	1
TELL WHICH--IT'S DULL TO GUESS--	YOU SAID THAT I "WAS	738	9
BEST GRIEF IS TONGUELESS--BEFORE HE'LL TELL--	GRIEF IS A MOUSE--	793	13
I'LL TELL IT YOU [SIGNIFY / TESTIFY]--	THE ONLY NEWS I KNOW	827	12
GOOD TO KNOW, AND NOT TELL,	GOOD TO HIDE, AND HEAR	842	5
BEST, TO KNOW AND TELL,	GOOD TO HIDE, AND HEAR	842	6
AND TELL EACH OTHER HOW WE SUNG	I SING TO USE THE	850	7
I'VE NONE TO TELL ME TO BUT THEE	I'VE NONE TO TELL ME TO	881	1
THE WALLS--BEGUN TO TELL--	TO MY QUICK EAR THE	891	6
NEEDLESS TO TELL THEE--SO--	ONLY A SHRINE, BUT MINE	918	6
THOU KNOWEST, THOUGH, SO WHY TELL THEE?	ONLY A SHRINE, BUT MINE	918	12
BUT COULD NOT MAKE IT FEEL [TELL].	'TWAS CRISIS--ALL THE	948	12
THE DAY'S ADVENTURES TELL	THE HILLS IN PURPLE	1016	2
AND TIME WENT OUT TO TELL THE NEWS	I HEARD, AS IF I HAD NO	1039	15
HERE'S--WHAT I HAD TO "TELL YOU"--	TITLE DIVINE--IS MINE!	1072	V
YOU WILL TELL NO OTHER?	TITLE DIVINE--IS MINE!	1072	V
I DID NOT TELL, IT WAS THEIR LAST EXPERIMENT	WHEN THEY COME BACK--IF	1080	7
I TELL IT GAY TO THOSE WHO SUFFER NOW--	TIME DOES GO ON--	1121	2
TELL ALL THE TRUTH BUT TELL IT SLANT--	TELL ALL THE TRUTH BUT	1129	1
TELL ALL THE TRUTH BUT TELL IT SLANT--	TELL ALL THE TRUTH BUT	1129	1
TELL AS A MARKSMAN--WERE FORGOTTEN	TELL AS A MARKSMAN--WERE	1152	1
TELL--THIS DAY [TILL NOW] ENDURES	TELL AS A MARKSMAN--WERE	1152	2
TELL HAD A SON--THE ONES THAT KNEW [HEARD] IT	TELL AS A MARKSMAN--WERE	1152	9
TELL WOULD NOT BARE HIS HEAD	TELL AS A MARKSMAN--WERE	1152	13
TELL HIS ARROW SENT--	TELL AS A MARKSMAN--WERE	1152	23
I TELL THE WHILE I WAITED [FAMISHED]--	ART THOU THE THING I	1282	5
TOO NOBLE THEN TO TELL.	NOT WITH A CLUB, THE	1304	8
LIVED TO TELL THE TALE--	ABRAHAM TO KILL HIM	1317	10
A THING TO TELL REMAIN?	HOW NEWS MUST FEEL WHEN	1319	12
I HAVE SO MUCH TO TELL--	DEAR MARCH--COME IN--	1320	10
BUT I TELL YOU EVERY STEP IS A TROUGH [SLUICE]--	FLOSS WONT SAVE YOU FROM	1322	5
BESIDE GOD'S SHALL [WILL] NOT TELL--	OUR LITTLE SECRETS SLINK	1326	2
BECAUSE "GOD TOOK HIM" MENTION--[TELL US]	"WAS NOT" WAS ALL THE	1342	7
AND SHE WOULD TELL YOU [ANSWER] SIGHING--	CRISIS IS SWEET AND YET	1416	7
BUT THINK ENLARGED OF ALL THAT THEY WILL TELL US	THE THINGS THAT NEVER	1515	7
"GO TELL IT"--WHAT A MESSAGE--	"GO TELL IT"--WHAT A	1554	1
IF I COULD TELL HOW GLAD I WAS	IF I COULD TELL HOW GLAD	1668	1
TO TELL THE BEAUTY WOULD DECREASE	TO TELL THE BEAUTY WOULD	1700	1
IF I INVITED HIM COULD TELL,	HE WAS MY HOST--HE WAS	1721	3
I'LL TELL YOU WHAT I PAID--	I TOOK ONE DRAUGHT OF	1725	2
'TWERE USELESS TELL.	THE MOST IMPORTANT	1746	6
IF NATURE WILL NOT TELL THE TALE	THE RETICENT VOLCANO	1748	5
TELLER			
. . . PUNGENT / WINNING / MELLOW] TELLER--	THE BIBLE IS AN ANTIQUE	1545	13
TELLER'S			
AND A SILENCE--THE TELLER'S EYE--	GLEE--THE GREAT STORM IS	619	15
TELLING			
TELLING MY TARDY NAME--	I SHOULD NOT DARE TO	205	12
BUT--I WAS TELLING A TUNE--I HEARD--	BETTER--THAN MUSIC! FOR	503	16
WHEN I AM TELLING THEE	I DID NOT REACH THEE	1664	6
TELLS			
THE RAINBOW NEVER TELLS ME	THE RAINBOW NEVER TELLS	97	1
WHO TELLS NO SECRET	UNIT, LIKE DEATH, FOR	408	3
THE STONE--THAT TELLS DEFENDING WHOM	IT FEELS A SHAME TO BE	444	5
HE TELLS US CERTAINLY	BECAUSE THAT YOU ARE	1260	36
TEMERITY			
TEMERITY--DREW NEAR--	IT KNEW NO MEDICINE--	559	14
FOR CREDIBILITY'S PRESUMPTION [TEMERITY]	EACH LIFE CONVERGES TO	680	7
TO THE [A / OUR] TEMERITY [EXTREMITY / ADVERSITY]--	SUMMER--WE ALL HAVE SEEN	1386	8
SPURN THE TEMERITY--	SPURN THE TEMERITY--	1432	1
TO THEIR TEMERITY--	NO BRIGADIER THROUGHOUT	1561	16
TEMPER			
WHERE NATURE'S TEMPER CANNOT [COULD NOT] REACH	THE CLOUDS THEIR BACKS	1172	7
TEMPERATURE			
THAN ONE OF HIGHER TEMPERATURE	A SHADY FRIEND--FOR	278	3
A TEMPERATURE JUST ADEQUATE	MORE LIFE--WENT OUT--	422	7
TEMPEST			
AN AWFUL TEMPEST MASHED THE AIR--	AN AWFUL TEMPEST MASHED	198	1
HOW INTIMATE, A [ORDERLY THE] TEMPEST PAST	THE WIND TOOK UP THE	1134	15

	FIRST LINE	POEM	LINE
TEMPEST (CONTINUED)			
WHILE HER FATHER ABUTS THE TEMPEST . . .	THE PARASOL IS THE	1747	3
TEMPESTS			
THE TEMPESTS TOUCHED OUR GARMENTS-- . . .	THROUGH LANE IT LAY--	9	9
TEMPLE			
"WARMED THEM" AT THE "TEMPLE FIRE". . . .	HE FORGOT--AND I--	203	4
IT'S TEMPLE [CLOSET] STANDS, ALWAY, . . .	THE BODY GROWS WITHOUT--	578	4
THEN SOARING TO HIS TEMPLE [TURRET] TALL-- .	HOW LONESOME THE WIND	1418	12
TEMPLES			
WE--TEMPLES BUILD--I SAID--	MYSELF WAS FORMED--A	488	12
TEMPTATION			
THEIR FEET--UPON TEMPTATION--	THROUGH THE STRAIT PASS	792	3
TEMPTATION IS THE FRIEND	A RAT SURRENDERED HERE	1340	10
TEMPTATION'S			
A TRIUMPH--WHEN TEMPTATION'S BRIBE . . .	TRIUMPH--MAY BE OF	455	9
TEMPTED			
I'M TEMPTED HALF TO STITCH IT UP	THIS CHASM, SWEET, UPON	858	13
TEN			
AND TEN OF MY ONCE STATELY TOES	I COUNTED TILL THEY	36	7
ONE--BIRTHDAY MORE--OR TEN?	ONE YEAR AGO--JOTS WHAT?	296	35
THE VALUE OF IT'S TEN--	'TIS ONE BY ONE--THE	545	4
THAN NUMB THREE SCORE AND TEN--	NOT ANY HIGHER STANDS	1256	4
SINCE PLAYMATES AT THREESCORE AND TEN . .	MY WARS ARE LAID AWAY IN	1549	11
TENANT			
OF SOME RARE TENANT OF THE MOLD, ...	A SCIENCE--SO THE SAVANS	100	5
SPARE THE TENANT--LONG ENO'--	IT'S THOUGHTS--AND JUST	495	8
THE TENANT OF THE NARROW COTTAGE, WERT THOU--	WERT THOU BUT ILL--THAT	961	13
A GIANT IS YOUR TENANT	I THOUGHT THAT NATURE	1286	V 11
THE RAT IS THE CONCISEST TENANT.	THE RAT IS THE CONCISEST	1356	1
TENANTLESS			
MY PALACES--DROPPED TENANTLESS--	IT WOULD NEVER BE COMMON	430	23
TEND			
I TEND MY FLOWERS FOR THEE--	I TEND MY FLOWERS FOR	339	1
TENDENCY			
IT'S TENDENCY TO SNAP	A RAT SURRENDERED HERE	1340	8
TENDER			
IN TENDER--SOLEMN ALPHABET, ...	A SINGLE SCREW OF FLESH	263	9
WITH TENDER MAJESTY	THIS IS MY LETTER TO THE	441	4
A TENDER--THOUGHTFUL MOON	AGAIN--HIS VOICE IS AT	663	19
TENDER PIONEER--	LIFE--IS WHAT WE MAKE IT	698	14
THAT IS SOLEMN [TENDER / SACRED] WE HAVE ENDED	THAT IS SOLEMN WE HAVE	934	1
TOO TENDER, TO BE TOLD.	LET DOWN THE BARS, OH	1065	8
UNTIL THE TENDER CARPENTER [SOVREIGN CARPENTER / UNSUSPECTING . . .	A GREAT HOPE FELL	1123	16
WITH TENDER INFAMY	THE DITCH IS DEAR TO THE	1645	V 8
HER TONGUE MORE TENDER [TIMID / MAGIC] THAN THE TUNE [TONE]	HER FACE WAS IN A BED OF	1722	5
TENDERER			
I TENDERER, TURN ME TO.	FOR LARGEST WOMAN'S	309	6
TO TENDERER RENOWN--	HE TOUCHED ME, SO I LIVE	506	12
IT WERE INFINITE [TENDERER] ENACTED . . .	DRAMA'S VITALLEST	741	12
IF TENDERER INDUSTRIOUSNESS	HER FINAL SUMMER WAS IT	795	3
MY TENDERER EXPERIMENT	THE FIRST DAY THAT I WAS	902	11
BUT TENDERER INDEED	THERE IS A JUNE WHEN	930	4
I TENDERER COMMEND	MY SEASON'S FURTHEST	1019	2
WERE TENDERER--DIVINER	MY TRIUMPH LASTED TILL	1227	13
TENDEREST			
IS TENDEREST, I THINK--	THE SERVICE WITHOUT HOPE	779	2
. . . ARE TENDEREST--/ WERE EXQUISITE] EXTENTS	CONTAINED IN THIS SHORT	1165	2
TENDERLY			
TENDERLY TOOK IT UP FROM TOIL	A POOR--TORN HEART-- A	78	11
TENDERLY TUCKING THEM IN FROM FROST . . .	SOME, TOO FRAGILE FOR	141	3
AND JUST AS TENDERLY	MAMA NEVER FORGETS HER	164	4
ENTREAT US TENDERLY	DEATH SETS A THING	360	4
TOO TENDERLY, THAT ANY DOUBT	THE MONTHS HAVE ENDS--	423	7
JUDGE TENDERLY--OF ME	THIS IS MY LETTER TO THE	441	8
DEATH TENDERLY ASSISTS HIM	PAIN HAS BUT ONE	1049	7
TENDERNESS			
TENDERNESS BUILDED THERE.	THIS HEART THAT BROKE SO	145	8
TENDERNESS DECREASES AS WE PROVE--	ABSENCE DISEMBODIES--SO	860	4
OF A TENDERNESS, ...	GRATITUDE--IS NOT THE	989	2
TENDS			
THE HAND THAT TENDS, ...	WHICH MISSES MOST,	1759	2
TENEMENT			
IT SWEEPS THE TENEMENT [TENEMENTS] AWAY . .	THE INUNDATION OF THE	1425	3
TENEMENTS			
SOME WE SEE NO MORE, TENEMENTS OF WONDER .	SOME WE SEE NO MORE,	1221	1
WHAT TENEMENTS OF CLOVER	WHAT TENEMENTS OF CLOVER	1338	1
IT SWEEPS THE TENEMENT [TENEMENTS] AWAY . .	THE INUNDATION OF THE	1425	3
TENERIFFE			
DAWN--TO THE TENERIFFE [APPENINE]--	"MORNING"--MEANS	300	2
AH, TENERIFFE!	AH, TENERIFFE!	666	1
AH, TENERIFFE!	AH, TENERIFFE!	666	9
TENERIFFE'S			
TENERIFFE'S ADVENTURE	THE JAY HIS CASTANET HAS	1635	V
TENETS			
TENETS--PUT BEHIND--	COLOR--CASTE--	970	6
TENS			
BUT TENS HAVE WON AN ALL--	SOUL, WILT THOU TOSS	139	4

	FIRST LINE	POEM	LINE
TENT			
I'VE KNOWN A HEAVEN, LIKE A TENT-- . . .	I'VE KNOWN A HEAVEN,	243	1
AND THEN--IT'S TIME TO STRIKE MY TENT-- . .	THE WINTERS ARE SO SHORT	403	7
WHERE TENT BY TENT--HER UNIVERSE	THE HIMMALEH WAS KNOWN	481	5
WHERE TENT BY TENT--HER UNIVERSE	THE HIMMALEH WAS KNOWN	481	5
THE TENT IS LISTENING, ...	EXPANSE CANNOT BE LOST--	1584	15
TENTACLES			
IT'S TENTACLES [RESONANCE] DIVINE.	WE LIKE A HAIRBREADTH	1175	8
TENTS			
TRIBES OF ECLIPSE--IN TENTS OF MARBLE-- . .	SAFE IN THEIR ALABASTER	216	V
THE TENTS TO NATURE'S SHOW	DEW--IS THE FRESHET IN	1097	6
TENURE			
INHERITORS UPON A TENURE	UNCERTAIN LEASE--	857	7
TEPID			
THE TEPID GROUND UPON.	OUR LITTLE KINSMEN--	885	4
CANDOR--MY TEPID FRIEND--	CANDOR--MY TEPID FRIEND	1537	1
TERM			
BUT THIS, MIGHT BE MY BRIEF TERM	I'M SAYING EVERY DAY	373	18
UNTO SUPREMEST NAME [TERM]--	I'M CEDED--I'VE STOPPED	508	10
ETERNITY--BY TERM--	OUR JOURNEY HAD ADVANCED	615	4
MYSELF--THE TERM BETWEEN--	BEHIND ME--DIPS ETERNITY	721	3
OR IN THE LONG--UNEVEN TERM	I PLAY AT RICHES--TO	801	19
TERM OF LIGHT THIS DAY BEGUN!	ALWAYS MINE!	839	3
HIS TROTH A TERM	OF SILKEN SPEECH AND	896	6
PROPOUNDED BUT A SINGLE TERM	AT HALF PAST THREE, A	1084	3
A LITTLE NEWER FOR THE TERM	EXHILIRATION IS THE	1118	7
TERMED			
TERMED MORTALITY!	TO VENERATE THE SIMPLE	57	6
TERMED BY THE BROKERS--"DEATH"!	YOU'RE RIGHT--"THE WAY	234	8
TERMED IMMORTALITY--	WE THIRST AT FIRST--'TIS	726	8
TERMED THANKSGIVING DAY.	ONE DAY IS THERE OF THE	814	2
TERMINABLE			
IF TERMINABLE, MAY BE BORNE.	SOMEWHAT, TO HOPE FOR,	1041	6
TERMINATE			
ENACT--AND TERMINATE [DISSIPATE]-- . . .	THE BATTLE FOUGHT	594	12
BUT TERMINATE IN TUNE;	FURTHER IN SUMMER THAN	1068	V
CAPACITY TO TERMINATE	TO MAKE ROUTINE A	1196	3
TERMINATES			
ESTABLISHES, AND TERMINATES--	THE BATTLE FOUGHT	594	7
TERMINUS			
SUPPOSED TO BE A TERMINUS	ADVANCE IS LIFE'S	1652	3
TERMS			
ASSERT THEMSELVES--AND NOT BY TERMS-- . .	YOU'LL KNOW IT--AS YOU	420	8
TILL NATURE LEISURE HAS FOR TERMS	THE VEINS OF OTHER	811	3
SUCH AGONIZING TERMS?	JUST ONCE! OH LEAST	1076	5
WAS ALL THE PRICE [TERMS] THERE WAS-- . .	HIS MIND LIKE FABRICS OF	1446	8
TERRENE			
ASCENDING, THOUGH TERRENE--	THE ROAD WAS LIT WITH	1450	6
LOVE MARINE AND LOVE TERRENE--	IS IT TOO LATE TO TOUCH	1637	3
TERRESTIAL			
NONE CANNOT FIND WHO SEEKETH, ON THIS TERRESTIAL BALL;	AWAKE YE MUSES NINE,	1	12
TERRESTRIAL			
WITH FAINT--TERRESTRIAL POWER--	HAD I PRESUMED TO HOPE--	522	12
MY SLOW--TERRESTRIAL EYE	HOW SOFT A CATERPILLAR	1448	6
TERRIBLE			
SO TERRIBLE--HAD BEEN ENDURED--	THE FIRST DAY'S NIGHT	410	3
IT DONT SOUND SO TERRIBLE--QUITE--AS IT DID--	IT DONT SOUND SO	426	1
ARE MAGICAL [WERE WONDERFUL / ARE TERRIBLE / ARE MIRACULOUS / . . .	CONTAINED IN THIS SHORT	1165	2
THROUGH ACCENTS TERRIBLE AS DEATH	WHO WERE "THE FATHER AND	1258	V 5
TERRIBLER			
MANGLE DAINTIER--TERRIBLER--	IT IS EASY TO WORK WHEN	244	7
HOW TERRIBLER A THING	EACH SECOND IS THE LAST	879	6
IS TERRIBLER THAN WEARING IT	WHILE WE WERE FEARING IT	1277	11
TERRITORIES			
THE PURPLE TERRITORIES	WHO NEVER LOST, ARE	73	7
TERRITORY			
THE LARK'S PURE TERRITORY--	THE GUEST IS GOLD AND	15	9
THE TERRITORY ARGENT--THAT	THE RED--BLAZE--IS THE	469	7
OF TERRITORY--COLOR--	AN IGNORANCE A SUNSET	552	3
BUT SUFFERED AN [ABSENT THROUGH] EXCHANGE OF TERRITORY--	IT KNEW NO LAPSE, NOR	560	7
A TERRITORY FOR THE GHOSTS--	WHO OCCUPIES THIS HOUSE?	892	19
NO TERRITORY NEW IS STAKED--	TWO LENGTHS HAS EVERY	1295	11
TERROR			
TIS TERROR AS CONSUMMATE	ONE ANGUISH--IN A CROWD	565	5
WE HAD HELPED THE TERROR	HAD WE KNOWN THE TON SHE	1124	2
THE TERROR [TRANSPORT] OF THE CHILDREN . .	THESE ARE THE NIGHTS	1128	5
WHAT TERROR WOULD ENTHRALL THE STREET . .	IT'S HOUR WITH ITSELF	1225	3
AND WHEN PORTENTOUS [IN TERROR] TOLD . . .	WHO WERE "THE FATHER AND	1258	4
WHEN TERROR WERE IT TOLD	I NEVER HEAR THAT ONE IS	1323	10
OR TERROR--THAT DO DECORATE [CELEBRATE / GENERATE]	HIS VOICE DECREPIT WAS	1476	7
TERROR'S			
AND TERROR'S FREE--	'TIS SO APPALLING--IT	281	23
TERSE			
I KNOW SUSPENSE--IT STEPS SO TERSE . . .	I KNOW SUSPENSE--IT	1285	1
HIS LARDER--TERSE AND MILITANT--	NO BRIGADIER THROUGHOUT	1561	19

	FIRST LINE	POEM	LINE
TEST			
THE TEST OF LOVE--IS DEATH--	THE TEST OF LOVE--IS	573	1
BEST GAINS--MUST HAVE THE LOSSES' TEST--	BEST GAINS--MUST HAVE	684	1
TIME IS A TEST OF TROUBLE--	THEY SAY THAT "TIME	686	5
NOT WHAT WE DID, SHALL BE THE TEST	NOT WHAT WE DID, SHALL	823	1
TEST IF IT BE DEAD.	REVOLUTION IS THE POD	1082	12
HAD SUBJUGATED TEST	AT HALF PAST THREE, A	1084	6
THOUGH BY THAT SCATHING TEST	UNWORTHY OF HER BREAST	1414	2
HE SENT HIS SON TO TEST THE PLANK,	HOW BRITTLE ARE THE	1433	7
TO SOUND [TEST] THE ENEMY--	WHERE ROSES WOULD NOT	1582	4
TESTAMENT			
ENCHANTMENT'S SYNDICATE [POSTULATE / TESTAMENT].	THE LAST OF SUMMER IS	1353	4
TESTED			
THESE TESTED OUR HORIZON--	THESE TESTED OUR HORIZON	886	1
TESTIFIED			
AS ONE HAD TESTIFIED--	TRUST IN THE UNEXPECTED	555	4
NO PERSON TESTIFIED--	WHEN I WAS SMALL, A	596	12
TESTIFY			
DUMBLY TESTIFY--	NATURE--SOMETIMES SEARS	314	6
CANNOT TESTIFY--	IT IS DEAD--FIND IT--	417	9
AS I, WHO TESTIFY IT	DO PEOPLE MOULDER	432	5
MY LIP--TO TESTIFY--	I THINK TO LIVE--MAY BE	646	4
I'LL TELL IT YOU [SIGNIFY / TESTIFY]--	THE ONLY NEWS I KNOW	827	12
TESTING			
IS ASCERTAINED BY TASTING [TESTING]--	DESPAIR'S ADVANTAGE IS	799	7
GO TIMID, LEST [SHOULD] HIS FINAL [TESTING / BLAZING / LOFTY] EYE	GO SLOW, MY SOUL, TO	1297	5
TETHERED			
SINCE IT WAS GATHERED [TETHERED] HERE--	PRAISE IT--'TIS DEAD--	1384	5
TEXT			
'TWAS WITH TEXT AND VILLAGE [ANTIQUE] SINGING	THREE WEEKS PASSED SINCE	1061	3
THANK			
IF I COULD'NT THANK YOU,	IF I SHOULD'NT BE ALIVE	182	5
I WENT TO THANK HER--	I WENT TO THANK HER--	363	1
WHO WENT TO THANK HER--	I WENT TO THANK HER--	363	6
I THANK THESE KINSMEN OF THE SHELF--	UNTO MY BOOKS--SO GOOD	604	13
NOT UPON HER KNEE TO THANK ME	MOST SHE TOUCHED ME BY	760	9
WHO CANNOT THANK THEM FOR THE ICE	THEY WONT FROWN ALWAYS--	874	7
THANK GOD THE LOUDEST PLACE HE MADE	IT'S HOUR WITH ITSELF	1225	7
THANKED			
AND THANKED THE AMPLE FRIEND--	I WORKED FOR CHAFF AND	1269	6
THE COWS THAT FED AND THANKED	A FADED BOY--IN SALLOW	1524	6
THANKFUL			
ESCAPE IS SUCH A THANKFUL WORD	ESCAPE IS SUCH A	1347	1
THANKS			
THANKS FOR THE INTERVIEW--	IMAGE OF LIGHT, ADIEU--	1556	2
THANKSGIVING			
AND WHEN THANKSGIVING, CAME,	'TWAS JUST THIS TIME,	445	14
TERMED THANKSGIVING DAY.	ONE DAY IS THERE OF THE	814	2
TWERE THANKSGIVING DAY.	ONE DAY IS THERE OF THE	814	16
THEATRE			
ONLY THEATRE RECORDED	DRAMA'S VITALLEST	741	14
THEATRICALS			
THE FAR THEATRICALS OF DAY	LIKE MIGHTY FOOT LIGHTS	595	3
THEE			
GOD HATH MADE NOTHING SINGLE BUT THEE IN HIS WORLD SO FAIR!	AWAKE YE MUSES NINE,	1	6
TO BRINGING THEE TO JUSTICE, AND MARSHALLING THY SOUL!	AWAKE YE MUSES NINE,	1	26
WHEN I AM FAR FROM THEE!	"SIC TRANSIT GLORIA	3	8
AND FAREWELL, SIR, TO THEE!	"SIC TRANSIT GLORIA	3	68
THITHER I PILOT THEE--	ON THIS WONDROUS SEA	4	10
LET US GO WITH THEE!	THE GENTIAN WEAVES HER	18	16
LIKE THEE TO DANCE--LIKE THEE TO SING--	THERE IS A MORN BY MEN	24	19
LIKE THEE TO DANCE--LIKE THEE TO SING--	THERE IS A MORN BY MEN	24	19
SUMMER FOR THEE, GRANT I MAY BE	SUMMER FOR THEE, GRANT I	31	1
FOR THEE TO BLOOM, I'LL SKIP THE TOMB	SUMMER FOR THEE, GRANT I	31	5
AH--BUT REMEMBERING THEE--	GARLANDS FOR QUEENS, MAY	34	5
AND LIFT IT UP TO THEE.	NOBODY KNOWS THIS LITTLE	35	4
FOR SUCH AS THEE TO DIE!	NOBODY KNOWS THIS LITTLE	35	12
"I WILL NOT LET THEE GO	A LITTLE EAST OF JORDAN,	59	10
PEASANTS LIKE THEE	SO FROM THE MOULD	66	10
WE NEARER STEAL TO THEE!	THE DAISY FOLLOWS SOFT	106	9
LINGERS TO RECORD THEE--	SOUL, WILT THOU TOSS	139	6
WHEN FRIGHTENED--HOME TO THEE I RUN--	YOU LOVE ME--YOU ARE	156	10
MY RIVER RUNS TO THEE--	MY RIVER RUNS TO THEE--	162	1
I'LL FETCH [BRING] THEE BROOKS	MY RIVER RUNS TO THEE--	162	5
HOW IS IT HEARTS, WITH THEE?	I CAUTIOUS, SCANNED MY	178	18
LOVE PROVIDED THEE?	I CAUTIOUS, SCANNED MY	178	20
WOULD IT STOP WHINING--IF TO THEE--	WHAT SHALL I DO--IT	186	6
DID THEY FORGET THEE?	POOR LITTLE HEART!	192	2
DID THEY FORSAKE THEE?	POOR LITTLE HEART!	192	5
I WOULD NOT BREAK THEE--	POOR LITTLE HEART!	192	8
WIND AND SUN--WILT THEE ARRAY!	POOR LITTLE HEART!	192	12
WHERE THIS ATTENDETH ME [THEE]--	FOR THIS--ACCEPTED	195	8
BECAUSE--THEE--	I STOLE THEM FROM A BEE	200	2
COULD I DO AUGHT ELSE--TO THEE?	HE FORGOT--AND I--	203	8
WITH THEE, IN THE DESERT--	WITH THEE, IN THE DESERT	209	1
WITH THEE IN THE THIRST--	WITH THEE, IN THE DESERT	209	2

THEE (CONTINUED)

	FIRST LINE	POEM		LINE
WITH THEE IN THE TAMARIND WOOD--	WITH THEE, IN THE DESERT	209		3
LIPS UNUSED TO THEE--	COME SLOWLY--EDEN!	211		2
MY CASPIAN--THEE.	LEAST RIVERS--DOCILE TO	212		2
AND SO I TROUBLE THEE.	SAVIOR! I'VE NO ONE ELSE	217		2
I AM THE ONE FORGOT THEE SO--	SAVIOR! I'VE NO ONE ELSE	217		3
FATHER--I BRING THEE--NOT MYSELF--	SAVIOR! I'VE NO ONE ELSE	217	V	5
I BROUGHT [BRING] THEE THE IMPERIAL [DEPARTED] HEART	SAVIOR! I'VE NO ONE ELSE	217		7
AH! KATIE! SMILE AT FORTUNE, WITH TWO SO KNIT TO THEE!	WHEN KATIE WALKS, THIS	222		4
ENABLE THEE TO GUESS	JESUS! THY CRUCIFIX	225		2
MIND THEE IN PARADISE	JESUS! THY CRUCIFIX	225		5
TO INTERCEDE--FOR THEE--	THE COURT IS FAR AWAY--	235		12
WERE I WITH THEE	WILD NIGHTS--WILD NIGHTS	249		2
IN THEE!	WILD NIGHTS--WILD NIGHTS	249		12
POURED THEE, WITHOUT A STINT--	DOUBT ME! MY DIM	275		4
SAY QUICK, THAT I MAY [SO I CAN] DOWER THEE	DOUBT ME! MY DIM	275		7
DWELL TIMIDLY, WITH THEE!	DOUBT ME! MY DIM	275		17
AND PASS ESCAPED--TO THEE!	WHAT IF I SAY I SHALL	277		3
BY MY OWN CHOICE, AND THEE--	TIE THE STRINGS TO MY	279		12
AS I--TOWARD [IN] THEE--	THE DROP, THAT WRESTLES	284		3
AS OLD AS THEE--HOW SOON?	ONE YEAR AGO--JOTS WHAT?	296		34
HEART! I AM KNOCKING--LOW AT THEE.	JUST SO--JESUS--RAPS--	317		11
HID, LIP, FOR THEE--	ALL THE LETTERS I CAN	334		6
I TEND MY FLOWERS FOR THEE--	I TEND MY FLOWERS FOR	339		1
DRAPED FOR THEE!	I TEND MY FLOWERS FOR	339		27
I'LL UNROLL THEE--	MY REWARD FOR BEING, WAS	343		8
TO LACK--ENAMOR THEE--	'TIS OPPOSITES--ENTICE--	355		9
RATHER THAN A MOORING--UNSHARED BY THEE.	HOW SICK--TO WAIT--IN	368		9
ANSWER THEE--ME--	ANSWER JULY--	386		9
THE REAL ONE DIED FOR THEE--	'TWAS LOVE--NOT ME--	394		3
SUCH GUILT--TO LOVE THEE--MOST!	'TWAS LOVE--NOT ME--	394		5
AND TELL HIM--CHARGE THEE SPEAK IT PLAIN--	A TONGUE--TO TELL HIM I	400		7
ANOTHER LAD--HELP THEE--	A TONGUE--TO TELL HIM I	400		17
BE SO--ASHAMED OF THEE--	WHAT SOFT--CHERUBIC	401		12
TO LOVE THEE YEAR BY YEAR--	TO LOVE THEE YEAR BY	434		1
COULD--I DO MORE--FOR THEE--	COULD--I DO MORE--FOR	447		1
I CANNOT CLIMB THEE--	LOVE--THOU ART HIGH--	453		2
DUCAL--AT LAST--STAND UP BY THEE--	LOVE--THOU ART HIGH--	453		6
I CANNOT CROSS THEE--	LOVE--THOU ART HIGH--	453		8
A FEW--BEHOLD THEE--	LOVE--THOU ART HIGH--	453		14
BLISS--WERE AN ODDITY--WITHOUT THEE--	LOVE--THOU ART HIGH--	453		16
I LOVE THEE--THEN HOW WELL IS THAT?	SO WELL THAT I CAN LIVE	456		2
AS I--LOVE THEE--	SO WELL THAT I CAN LIVE	456		6
THEN--MIDNIGHT, I HAVE PASSED FROM THEE	A WIFE--AT DAYBREAK I	461		5
AND THIS--BESIDES, IN--THEE!	I AM ALIVE--I GUESS--	470		28
"I SEE THEE" EACH RESPONDED STRAIGHT	THEY PUT US FAR APART--	474		7
I LOVE THEE--	"WHY DO I LOVE" YOU, SIR	480		20
WE COVER THEE--SWEET FACE--	WE COVER THEE--SWEET	482		1
NOT THAT WE TIRE OF THEE--	WE COVER THEE--SWEET	482		2
WE FOLLOW THEE UNTIL	WE COVER THEE--SWEET	482		5
TO CON THEE OER AND OER--	WE COVER THEE--SWEET	482		8
CUT THEE AWAY FROM ME--	YOU KNOW THAT PORTRAIT	504		14
"NO SIR! IN THEE!"	TO HEAR AN ORIOLE SING	526		15
MIGHT DEATH--ENABLE THEE--	ME PROVE IT NOW--WHOEVER	537		8
THEMSELVES WERE QUICK--WITH THEE!	ME PROVE IT NOW--WHOEVER	537		16
I BRING THEE PROOF	THAT I DID ALWAYS LOVE	549		2
I ARGUE [OFFER] THEE	THAT I DID ALWAYS LOVE	549		6
THAT I MIGHT LOOK ON THEE?	MY PERIOD HAD COME FOR	564		16
FOR THO' THEY LOCK THEE IN THE GRAVE,	IF I MAY HAVE IT, WHEN	577		7
THINK OF IT LOVER! I AND THEE	IF I MAY HAVE IT, WHEN	577		9
AND THIS--IS THEE--	IF I MAY HAVE IT, WHEN	577		13
I'LL TELL THEE ALL--HOW BALD [BLANK] IT GREW--	IF I MAY HAVE IT, WHEN	577		14
JUST MAKING SIGNS--ACROSS--[IT SEEMED] TO THEE--	IF I MAY HAVE IT, WHEN	577		20
FOR COVETING [EAGERNESS] TO LOOK AT THEE--	IF I MAY HAVE IT, WHEN	577		27
EMPTY MY HEART, OF THEE--	EMPTY MY HEART, OF THEE	587		1
BEGIN, AND LEAVE THEE OUT--	EMPTY MY HEART, OF THEE	587		3
"MYSELF" MEANT THEE--	EMPTY MY HEART, OF THEE	587		10
THEE--THEN--NO ME--	EMPTY MY HEART, OF THEE	587		12
THE SLEET--THAN MAY, NO THEE--	THE NIGHT WAS WIDE, AND	589		20
MY [ONE] JUSTICE BLEEDS--FOR THEE!	IT ALWAYS FELT TO ME--A	597		24
I SEE THEE BETTER--IN THE DARK--	I SEE THEE BETTER--IN	611		1
THE LOVE OF THEE--A PRISM BE--	I SEE THEE BETTER--IN	611		3
I SEE THEE BETTER FOR THE YEARS	I SEE THEE BETTER--IN	611		5
AND IN THE GRAVE--I SEE THEE BEST--	I SEE THEE BETTER--IN	611		9
I HELD SO HIGH, FOR THEE--	I SEE THEE BETTER--IN	611		12
JUST RECTIFIED [QUALIFIED]--IN THEE	I THINK TO LIVE--MAY BE	646		28
AND FETCH HER THEE--BE MINE--	SHE DWELLETH IN THE	671		8
MY NEED OF THEE--BE DONE--	SHELLS FROM THE COAST	693		6
HIDE--TOO--FROM THEE--	OUT OF SIGHT? WHAT OF	703		13
HIMSELF--ABIDE WITH THEE--	NO PRISONER BE--	720		3
THE LAWFUL HEIR--FOR THEE--	DEFRAUDED I A BUTTERFLY	730		2
THEN "GREAT" IT BE--IF THAT PLEASE THEE--	YOU SAID THAT I "WAS	738		2
NAY--I'M THE SIZE SUIT THEE--	YOU SAID THAT I "WAS	738		4
AT ONCE--FOR THEE--	YOU SAID THAT I "WAS	738		12
OR PAGE--PLEASE THEE--	YOU SAID THAT I "WAS	738		14
I SUIT THEE--	YOU SAID THAT I "WAS	738		18
IT [THAT] RESEMBLE THEE--	AUTUMN--OVERLOOKED MY	748		6

THEE (CONTINUED)

	FIRST LINE	POEM		LINE
QUICK [SOON]--SWEET MOUTH--TO MISS THEE SO--	THESE--SAW VISIONS--	758		6
BUT DOOM ME NOT TO FORFEIT THEE--	IF BLAME BE MY SIDE--	775		2
TO FORFEIT THEE? THE VERY NAME	IF BLAME BE MY SIDE--	775		3
BECAUSE THEY LOOKED ON THEE BEFORE--	JOY TO HAVE MERITED THE	788		9
SO SET IT'S SUN IN THEE	SO SET IT'S SUN IN THEE	808		1
TO LOOK AT THEE A SINGLE TIME	THE LUXURY TO APPREHEND	815		3
THE CONSCIOUSNESS OF THEE.	THE LUXURY TO APPREHEND	815		16
GIVEN IN MARRIAGE UNTO THEE	GIVEN IN MARRIAGE UNTO	817		1
DYING! TO BE AFRAID OF THEE	DYING! TO BE AFRAID OF	831		1
FOR THEE A BEE DO I BECOME	BECAUSE THE BEE MAY	869		2
I THAT WAY WORSHIP THEE.	BECAUSE THE BEE MAY	869		12
ENTIRELY FOR THEE--	THE SUN AND MOON MUST	871		13
I'VE NONE TO TELL ME TO BUT THEE	I'VE NONE TO TELL ME TO	881		1
AND ME IT WERE--THAT EBBED FROM THEE	I'VE NONE TO TELL ME TO	881		8
SO--OVERTAKING THEE--	I'VE NONE TO TELL ME TO	881		13
THAT NIGHT SHOULD BE TO THEE	'TIS SUNRISE--LITTLE	908		10
DISSUADE THEE, IF I C'D NOT, SWEET,	'TIS SUNRISE--LITTLE	908		13
I MIGHT HAVE AIDED--THEE--	'TIS SUNRISE--LITTLE	908		14
NEEDLESS TO TELL THEE--SO--	ONLY A SHRINE, BUT MINE	918		6
TO THEE--GRANT ME--	ONLY A SHRINE, BUT MINE	918		11
THOU KNOWEST, THOUGH, SO WHY TELL THEE?	ONLY A SHRINE, BUT MINE	918		12
WRITING MUCH TO THEE.	IF IT HAD NO PENCIL	921		4
DO THEE DISTINGUISHED GRACE--	WHAT I SEE NOT, I BETTER	939		10
I ADMONISH THEE	SNOW BENEATH WHOSE	942		4
WERT THOU BUT ILL--THAT I MIGHT SHOW THEE	WERT THOU BUT ILL--THAT	961		1
THE FIRST--SWEET, PROVED I, [THAT WAS] ERE I SAW THEE--	WERT THOU BUT ILL--THAT	961		19
PROVE MYSELF--OF THEE--	ALL FORGOT FOR	966		16
FALSEHOOD OF THEE COULD I SUPPOSE	FALSEHOOD OF THEE COULD	1007		1
LADY, DID HE BELONG TO THEE?	TRUDGING TO EDEN,	1020		4
I WAS OWNED OF THEE--	'TWAS MY ONE GLORY--	1028		4
"A THOUSAND TIMES THEE NAY."	SAID DEATH TO PASSION	1033		4
TOO NEAR THOU ART FOR SEEKING THEE	LET DOWN THE BARS, OH	1065		7
FROM HEAVY LADEN LANDS [CLIMES] TO THEE	THE BIRD DID PRANCE--THE	1107		9
THAT [TILL] I MAY [CAN] GLOAT ON THEE--	OH SUMPTUOUS MOMENT	1125		3
SHALL I TAKE THEE, THE POET SAID	SHALL I TAKE THEE, THE	1126		1
ACHIEVEMENT CONTEMPLATING THEE [THIS / HERE]--	THAT ODD OLD MAN IS DEAD	1130		11
WITH THEE	SOUL, TAKE THY RISK,	1151		4
TO BREATHE MY BLANK WITHOUT THEE	THROUGH WHAT TRANSPORTS	1153		3
MY GOD--HE SEES THEE--	MY GOD--HE SEES THEE--	1178		1
TILL EVERY CUBIT PLAY WITH THEE	MY GOD--HE SEES THEE--	1178		4
I GIVE THEE GUARANTY.	"REMEMBER ME" IMPLORED	1180		4
GO MAKE THEE FAIR MY CANDIDATE	OH SHADOW ON THE GRASS,	1187		3
LET MY FIRST KNOWING BE OF THEE	LET MY FIRST KNOWING BE	1218		1
ENGULPH THEE IN THE NIGHT--	LET MY FIRST KNOWING BE	1218		4
ANOTHER DATE OF THEE--	SOMEWHERE UPON THE	1231		10
MY HEART RAN SO TO THEE	MY HEART RAN SO TO THEE	1237		1
MENTIONED I THIS TO THEE--	MY HEART RAN SO TO THEE	1237		10
I TAKE THEE BY THE HAND--	THE SPIDER AS AN ARTIST	1275		8
DETERMINE THEE AMISS--	GO SLOW, MY SOUL, TO	1297		6
WE COMMEND OURSELVES TO THEE	RECOLLECT THE FACE OF ME	1305		7
BEDECKED WITH THEE	PINK--SMALL--AND	1332		10
OR EVERY BIRD WILL POINT AT THEE	TOUCH LIGHTLY NATURE'S	1389		3
WE SAFE [SOFT] COMMIT THEE--	TO THE STANCH DUST	1402		2
INVIOLATE TO THEE--	TO THE STANCH DUST	1402		4
AND SANCTITY--ENFORCE THEE--	TO THE STANCH DUST	1402		6
AND FIRMAMENT SALUTE THEE,	TO THE STANCH DUST	1402	V	6
ENAMORED MOST OF THEE--	MY MAKER--LET ME BE	1403		2
A FENCE [WORLD] OR TWO FROM THEE--	MY MAKER--LET ME BE	1403	V	2
LOOK BEHIND--HE IS PURSUING THEE.	TO EARN IT BY DISDAINING	1427		4
KNEW WE OF THEE--	SPURN THE TEMERITY--	1432		4
"HEAVENLY FATHER"--TAKE TO THEE	"HEAVENLY FATHER"--TAKE	1461		1
WE APOLOGIZE TO THEE	"HEAVENLY FATHER"--TAKE	1461		7
ONE THING OF IT WE [THEE I] BORROW	ONE THING OF IT WE	1464		1
ONE THING OF IT WE [THEE I] COVET--	ONE THING OF IT WE	1464		5
TO CRUMBLING MEN LIKE ME [THEE]	HOW FIRM ETERNITY MUST	1499		2
UNLESS CONCEALED IN [INTRENCHED IN / AFFIXED TO / INLAID IN] THEE	HOW FIRM ETERNITY MUST	1499		8
HOW MUCH OF SOURCE ESCAPES WITH THEE--	HOW MUCH OF SOURCE	1517		1
SINCE GIFT OF THEE--	SOCIETY FOR ME MY MISERY	1534		2
NOW I LAY THEE DOWN TO SLEEP--	NOW I LAY THEE DOWN TO	1539		1
TO HER WHO LOVES THEE BEST,	COME SHOW THY DURHAM	1542		2
WHAT WRECKETH THEE?	SWEET PIRATE OF THE	1546		3
TRIED ALWAYS AND CONDEMNED BY THEE	TRIED ALWAYS AND	1559		1
TO BE FORGOT BY THEE	TO BE FORGOT BY THEE	1560		1
LIKE OUR DISMAY AT THEE?	WE SHUN IT ERE IT COMES,	1580		8
SHUTS FOR THEE,	EXPANSE CANNOT BE LOST--	1584		10
WE ALL HAVE FOLLOWED THEE--	EXPANSE CANNOT BE LOST--	1584		12
LIKE THAT WHICH RAVISHED THEE!	IMMURED IN HEAVEN!	1594		5
PARTING WITH THEE RELUCTANTLY,	PARTING WITH THEE	1614		1
THAT DARES [FEARS] TO COVET THEE	CIRCUMFERENCE THOU BRIDE	1620		4
THAT BENDS A KNEE TO THEE	CIRCUMFERENCE THOU BRIDE	1620	V	4
BACK FROM THE CORDIAL GRAVE I DRAG THEE	BACK FROM THE CORDIAL	1625		1
NOR PUT HIS SPACIOUS ARM AROUND THEE	BACK FROM THE CORDIAL	1625		3
THAT LEADS AWAY FROM THEE--	OH FUTURE! THOU SECRETED	1631		4
TO BALK THEE OF THY SACRED PREY--[THE INNOCENCE / THE MYRIADS]	OH FUTURE! THOU SECRETED	1631		7
EXCEPT THAT IT DEPRIVED OF THEE--	SO GIVE ME BACK TO DEATH	1632		3
STILL OWN THEE--STILL THOU ART	STILL OWN THEE--STILL	1633		1

	FIRST LINE	POEM	LINE
THEE (CONTINUED)			
WHAT ANSWER [TIDINGS] WREST FROM THEE	STILL OWN THEE--STILL	1633	6
EXTOL THEE--COULD I--THEN I WILL	EXTOL THEE--COULD I--	1643	1
PERCEIVING THEE IS EVIDENCE	EXTOL THEE--COULD I--	1643	5
PARTAKING THEE A GUARANTY	EXTOL THEE--COULD I--	1643	7
LET IT BE IN SIGHT OF THEE--	BEAUTY CROWDS ME TILL I	1654	4
I DID NOT REACH THEE	I DID NOT REACH THEE	1664	1
WHEN I AM TELLING THEE	I DID NOT REACH THEE	1664	6
AND GETS THE LOOK AT THEE--	I DID NOT REACH THEE	1664	34
I SEE THEE CLEARER FOR THE GRAVE	I SEE THEE CLEARER FOR	1666	1
NO MIRROR COULD ILLUMINE THEE	I SEE THEE CLEARER FOR	1666	3
I KNOW THEE BETTER FOR THE ACT	I SEE THEE CLEARER FOR	1666	5
THAT MADE THEE FIRST UNKNOWN	I SEE THEE CLEARER FOR	1666	6
UPON THE DEPTH OF THEE--	IN SNOW THOU COMEST	1669	8
THE LOOK OF THEE, WHAT IS IT LIKE	THE LOOK OF THEE, WHAT	1689	1
PROUD OF THE PAIN I DID NOT FEEL TILL THEE,	PROUD OF MY BROKEN HEART	1736	2
SEVEN YEARS OF TROTH HAVE TAUGHT THEE	REARRANGE A "WIFE'S"	1737	7
LEADS IT THROUGH THE GRAVE TO THEE.	REARRANGE A "WIFE'S"	1737	20
WHERE "KEEPING HOUSE" FOR THEE	THE GRAVE MY LITTLE	1743	2
TO LOSE THEE--SWEETER THAN TO GAIN	TO LOSE THEE--SWEETER	1754	1
THEFTS			
OF THE THEFTS OF TIME--	DEATH'S WAYLAYING NOT	1296	2
THEME			
IT'S SHARPEST OF THE THEME	IF ANYBODY'S FRIEND BE	509	2
ACCOST A THEME--SO--FAIR--	THE SOUL HAS BANDAGED	512	10
THE RIPPLE OF OUR THEME--	I LEARNED--AT LEAST--	944	12
GRAPPLES WITH A THEME STUBBORN AS SUBLIME	SOME WE SEE NO MORE,	1221	7
DIVERSION FROM THE DYING THEME	T'WAS COMFORT IN HER	1703	5
THEMES			
ON THEMES CONCERN OUR MUTUAL MIND--	A PRECIOUS--MOULDERING	371	11
THY FELLOWS ARE THEY REALMS OR THEMES	THE LOOK OF THEE, WHAT	1689	5
THENCE			
THIS IS FAR FROM THENCE--	"UNTO ME?" I DO NOT KNOW	964	6
TO STEAL SECURER [AT SUNRISE] THENCE	CONTAINED IN THIS SHORT	1165	4
THENCEFORWARD			
THENCEFORWARD--WE--TOGETHER DWELT [WALKED]--	THE BIRDS REPORTED FROM	743	21
THENCEFORWARD IMITATE--	TILL DEATH--IS NARROW	907	8
THEOLOGY			
IS THEIR THEOLOGY [PHILOSOPHY]	COSMOPOLITES WITHOUT A	1589	8
THEORIES			
HIS CONTINENTS [THEORIES] OF LIGHT--	THE SPIDER HOLDS A	605	10
THEREAFTER			
THEREAFTER ROAM.	IN MANY AND REPORTLESS	1382	12
THEREAT			
THAT "ENTER IN--THEREAT"--	YOU'RE RIGHT--"THE WAY	234	4
THEREFROM			
ONLY, YOUR INFERENCE THEREFROM!	AS IF SOME LITTLE ARCTIC	180	12
THEREIN			
THEREIN THYSELF SHALT FIND	SOTO! EXPLORE THYSELF!	832	2
THEREON			
COULD MAKE A DENT THEREON--	THE SPIRIT LASTS--BUT IN	1576	24
COULD MAKE A DENT THEREON--	EXPANSE CANNOT BE LOST--	1584	8
CAN [COULD] MAKE A [NO] DENT [CREASE / SEAM] THEREON [UPON]--	THIS ME--THAT WALKS AND	1588	8
THERMOPYLAE			
TO LAW--SAID SWEET THERMOPYLAE	"GO TELL IT"--WHAT A	1554	7
THESES			
BY THESES BE DETAINED [PROFANED]--	THE LILAC IS AN ANCIENT	1241	20
THESSALY			
DEWS OF THESSALY, TO FETCH--	THE WORLD--FEELS DUSTY	715	11
THEW			
THIGH [EYE] OF GRANITE--AND THEW [EAR]--OF STEEL--	AH, TENERIFFE!	666	7
THEWS			
AND SO WITH THEWS OF HYMN--	I ROSE--BECAUSE HE SANK	616	20
THICK			
THE ROBINS STAND AS THICK TODAY	SOME RAINBOW--COMING	64	13
SO THICK UPON THE PLAIN?	WHOSE ARE THE LITTLE	142	8
THE LIFE IS THICK--I KNOW IT!	ONE LIFE OF SO MUCH	270	13
FOR EARTHS, GROW THICK AS	PERHAPS I ASKED TOO	352	3
HIS MIGHTY BALLS--IN DEATH WERE THICK--	A DYING TIGER--MOANED	566	5
THE CLOVER WARM AND THICK--	BEE! I'M EXPECTING YOU!	1035	8
THICKER			
THICKER AND THICKER STOOD THE FEET	THE SUN KEPT STOOPING--	152	7
THICKER AND THICKER STOOD THE FEET	THE SUN KEPT STOOPING--	152	7
THE STEPS GROW THICKER--IN THE HALL--	I THINK THE LONGEST HOUR	635	11
THICKEST			
BUT THROUGH THEIR THICKEST SKILL--	THEY PUT US FAR APART--	474	10
THIEF			
WHETHER A THIEF DID IT--	I CAUTIOUS, SCANNED MY	178	13
AND HELD MY EARS, AND LIKE A THIEF	I YEARS HAD BEEN FROM	609	23
GRIEF IS A THIEF--QUICK STARTLED--	GRIEF IS A MOUSE--	793	5
IT KEPT ME FROM A THIEF, I THINK,	I PLAY AT RICHES--TO	801	3
"REMEMBER ME" IMPLORED THE THIEF!	"REMEMBER ME" IMPLORED	1180	1
AN EPICURE--A THIEF--	ONE OF THE ONES THAT	1466	10
TO NO ONE BUT THE THIEF--	THE SWEETS OF PILLAGE,	1470	2
THIGH			
THIGH [EYE] OF GRANITE--AND THEW [EAR]--OF STEEL--	AH, TENERIFFE!	666	7

	FIRST LINE	POEM	LINE
THILL			
ACCESSIBLE TO THILL OF BEE--	A LITTLE ROAD--NOT MADE	647	3
ELIJAH'S WAGON KNEW [HAD] NO THILL	ELIJAH'S WAGON KNEW NO	1254	1
THIMBLE			
NEVER A THIMBLE--MORE--SHALL WEAR--	HOW MANY TIMES THESE LOW	187	8
THE THIMBLE WEIGHED TOO HEAVY--	DEATH SETS A THING	360	9
A RUFFLE [THIMBLE]--OR A TUNE--	I LEARNED--AT LEAST--	944	17
THIN			
BUT IF THE HEART OMIT [BE LEAN / BE THIN / DECLINE]	THE MIND LIVES ON THE	1355	5
THINE			
THINE EYES ARE SADLY BLINDED, BUT YET THOU MAYEST SEE	AWAKE YE MUSES NINE,	1	33
THEY'RE THINE.	I HAVE A BIRD IN SPRING	5	18
UPON THINE ARROW HANG!	A DAY! HELP! HELP!	42	8
THINE [THY] EXTREMITY	LOW AT MY PROBLEM	69	V 8
AND THINE IMMORTAL WINE!	THESE ARE THE DAYS WHEN	130	18
IN THINE ERMINE, SIR,	MUTE THY CORONATION--	151	4
FOR THAT WAS THINE, BEFORE--	DOUBT ME! MY DIM	275	10
THAT FACE--WILL JUST BE THINE--	THE FACE I CARRY WITH ME	336	4
HOW SICK--TO WAIT--IN ANY PLACE--BUT THINE--	HOW SICK--TO WAIT--IN	368	1
THAT RIGHT--WAS THINE--	HOW SICK--TO WAIT--IN	368	6
THINE ENEMY--	NO RACK CAN TORTURE ME--	384	14
OH, SIGNOR, THINE, THE AMBER HAND--	THE MOON IS DISTANT FROM	429	9
THINE EYE IMPOSE ON ME--	THE MOON IS DISTANT FROM	429	12
THE GNAT'S SUPREMACY IS LARGE AS THINE--	A TOAD, CAN DIE OF LIGHT	583	7
ONE MUST TO THINE ARTILLERY	DYING! TO BE AFRAID OF	831	2
THAN THINE OLD ARROW IS A SHOT	DYING! TO BE AFRAID OF	831	4
MAY LIFT A LOOK ON THINE, A MAID	BECAUSE THE BEE MAY	869	5
RETRIEVE THINE INDUSTRY--	'TIS SUNRISE--LITTLE	908	4
THAN THINE ACCLIMATED CREATURE	SNOW BENEATH WHOSE	942	7
THOUGH THINE ATTENTION STOP NOT ON ME	WERT THOU BUT ILL--THAT	961	3
STILL THINE.	BIND ME--I STILL CAN	1005	6
"GIVE OF THINE AN ACRE UNTO ME."	SAID DEATH TO PASSION	1033	2
THINE IS THE STILLEST NIGHT	LET DOWN THE BARS, OH	1065	5
THINE THE SECUREST [PATERNAL] FOLD	LET DOWN THE BARS, OH	1065	6
BESIDE [TO THINE] INFINITY	CONTAINED IN THIS SHORT	1165	8
FOR THINE OWN DUPLICITY--	"HEAVENLY FATHER"--TAKE	1461	8
THING			
SHOW THEM THIS MEEK APPARRELED THING	DELAYED TILL SHE HAD	58	16
IS THERE SUCH A THING AS "DAY"?	WILL THERE REALLY BE A	101	2
FOR HEAVEN IS A DIFFERENT THING,	'TIS SO MUCH JOY! 'TIS	172	16
IT'S SUCH A LITTLE THING TO WEEP--	IT'S SUCH A LITTLE THING	189	1
SO SHORT A THING TO SIGH--	IT'S SUCH A LITTLE THING	189	2
THE MORNING--HAPPY THING--	THE SUN--JUST TOUCHED	232	2
A RAISED--ETHERIAL THING!	THE SUN--JUST TOUCHED	232	6
IMPLORE A LARGER--THING--	THE COURT IS FAR AWAY--	235	8
AND SO I CON THAT THING--"FORGIVEN"--	I THINK JUST HOW MY	237	13
NO TRACE--NO FIGMENT OF THE THING	I'VE KNOWN A HEAVEN,	243	9
"HOPE" IS THE THING WITH FEATHERS--	"HOPE" IS THE THING WITH	254	1
A SOLEMN THING--IT WAS--I SAID--	A SOLEMN THING--IT WAS--	271	1
A TIMID [HALLOWED] THING--TO DROP A LIFE	A SOLEMN THING--IT WAS--	271	5
SUBLIMER SORT [THING / WAY]--THAN SPEECH--	GIVE LITTLE ANGUISH--	310	8
DEATH SETS A THING SIGNIFICANT	DEATH SETS A THING	360	1
AND GRATEFUL THAT A THING	THE FIRST DAY'S NIGHT	410	2
DO WE DESERVE--A THING--	IT FEELS A SHAME TO BE	444	10
A SOLEMN THING WITHIN THE SOUL	A SOLEMN THING WITHIN	483	1
AND CHATTED CLOSE WITH THIS GRAND THING	IF ANYBODY'S FRIEND BE	509	19
MAY BE A COMMON THING--	TO HEAR AN ORIOLE SING	526	2
A THING THAT CAN IGNITE	YOU CANNOT PUT A FIRE	530	2
I TRIED TO THINK A LONELIER THING	I TRIED TO THINK A	532	1
THE THING SO TOWERING HIGH	WE SEE--COMPARATIVELY--	534	2
THE THING BELONGED TO US--	WE SEE--COMPARATIVELY--	534	12
INSERT THE THING THAT CAUSED IT--	TO FILL A GAP	546	2
A MINOR THING--IT SOUNDS--	ONE ANGUISH--IN A CROWD	565	2
TO THAT REPEALLESS THING--	ONE ANGUISH--IN A CROWD	565	14
LIFE--IS A DIFFERENT [ANOTHER] THING--	A TOAD, CAN DIE OF LIGHT	583	8
HOW PLEASANT TO BEHOLD A THING	THREE TIMES--WE PARTED--	598	11
OF LIFE? 'TWERE ODD I FEAR A THING	AFRAID! OF WHOM AM I	608	5
WITHOUT A THING TO DO--	AT LEISURE IS THE SOUL	618	4
I ASKED NO OTHER THING--	I ASKED NO OTHER THING--	621	1
OF THAT DIVINER THING	THE LOVE A LIFE CAN SHOW	673	3
I'VE MET THE THING BEFORE--	A THOUGHT WENT UP MY	701	10
FOR SO FOUL A THING	PUBLICATION--IS THE	709	4
OR OTHER THING--IF OTHER THING THERE BE--	YOU SAID THAT I "WAS	738	16
OR OTHER THING--IF OTHER THING THERE BE--	YOU SAID THAT I "WAS	738	16
AND BEEN MYSELF THAT EASY [DISTANT] THING	I PLAY AT RICHES--TO	801	7
IS AN INTERIOR THING--	WHO COURT OBTAIN WITHIN	803	4
GROWS A FIERCER THING	AS THE STARVED MAELSTROM	872	10
HOW TERRIBLER A THING	EACH SECOND IS THE LAST	879	6
LOVE--IS THAT LATER THING THAN DEATH--	LOVE--IS THAT LATER	924	1
IN ITSELF--A QUIET [TRANQUIL] THING	A MAN MAY MAKE A REMARK	952	2
ANOTHER, TILL A THING	I HEARD, AS IF I HAD NO	1039	6
IS AN IMPROVING THING--	THESE ARE THE NIGHTS	1128	10
WOULD BE A NORMAL [DAILY] THING	WE NEVER KNOW HOW HIGH	1176	6
WITHDRAWS THE WORTHLESS THING [ONE]	TO DISAPPEAR ENHANCES--	1209	10
REMOVES THE PALTRY THING	TO DISAPPEAR ENHANCES--	1209	V 10
BUT BREAD IS THAT DIVINER [MAJESTIC] THING	THE BEGGAR AT THE DOOR	1240	3
A THING I NEVER KNEW--	BECAUSE THAT YOU ARE	1260	18
WE FELT HOW NEIGHBORLY A THING	THE MOUNTAINS STOOD IN	1278	11

	FIRST LINE	POEM		LINE
THING (CONTINUED)				
ART THOU THE THING I WANTED?	ART THOU THE THING I	1282		1
THE MOST PATHETIC THING I DO	THE MOST PATHETIC THING	1290		1
A THING TO TELL REMAIN?	HOW NEWS MUST FEEL WHEN	1319		12
THE ONLY THING WORTH LARCENY	TAKE ALL AWAY--	1365		2
OPINION IS A FLITTING THING,	OPINION IS A FLITTING	1455		1
ONE THING OF IT WE [THEE I] BORROW	ONE THING OF IT WE	1464		1
ONE THING OF IT WE [THEE I] COVET--	ONE THING OF IT WE	1464		5
OR BE THAT MOST INSOLVENT THING	FAME IS THE ONE THAT	1475		5
AND THIS--THIS UNSURMISED [APOCALYPTIC] THING--	'TIS WHITER THAN AN	1482	V	9
AND EVERY RIGHTEOUS [FOUNDED] THING	HIS LITTLE HEARSE LIKE	1522		6
OF SOME PERCEIVELESS THING--	THE PEDIGREE OF HONEY	1627		6
A MORE ESSENTIAL THING.	THE PEDIGREE OF HONEY	1627		8
GLORY IS THAT BRIGHT TRAGIC THING	GLORY IS THAT BRIGHT	1660		1
A THING OCCURRED	IN WINTER IN MY ROOM	1670		11
TO DO A MAGNANIMOUS THING	TO DO A MAGNANIMOUS	1699		1
NOT TO DO A MAGNANIMOUS THING	TO DO A MAGNANIMOUS	1699		5
THINGS				
ALL THINGS DO GO A COURTING, IN EARTH, OR SEA, OR AIR,	AWAKE YE MUSES NINE,	1		5
SOME THINGS THAT FLY THERE BE--	SOME THINGS THAT FLY	89		1
SOME THINGS THAT STAY THERE BE--	SOME THINGS THAT FLY	89		4
I HAD SOME THINGS THAT I CALLED MINE--	I HAD SOME THINGS THAT I	116		1
NEXT TIME, THE THINGS TO SEE	JUST LOST, WHEN I WAS	160		13
BUT IT'S DIM CHAT OF THINGS BURGUND, WE KNOW--	WE--BEE AND I--LIVE BY	230	V	4
WHEN WE STAND ON THE TOPS OF THINGS--	WHEN WE STAND ON THE	242		1
THAT [WHICH] MAKETH ALL THINGS NEW--	THERE CAME A DAY AT	322		8
FOR THE THINGS 'TWOULD BUY--	FOR DEATH--OR RATHER	382		2
THE THINGS THAT DEATH WILL BUY	FOR DEATH--OR RATHER	382		5
BY INTUITION, MIGHTIEST THINGS	YOU'LL KNOW IT--AS YOU	420		7
LIKE OTHER NEW THINGS--SHOWS LARGEST--THEN--	IT DONT SOUND SO	426		12
I PROBED RETRIEVELESS THINGS	I TRIED TO THINK A	532		5
AND SEE THE THINGS IN POD--	MY FIRST WELL DAY--SINCE	574		4
I LOOKED IN WINDOWS, FOR THE WEALTH [THINGS]	I HAD BEEN HUNGRY, ALL	579		7
THINGS SO [TOO] GAY	INCONCEIVABLY SOLEMN!	582		2
AND HEALTH, AND LAUGHTER, CURIOUS THINGS--	I CRIED AT PITY--NOT AT	588		7
OF NEARNESS TO HER SUNDERED THINGS	OF NEARNESS TO HER	607		1
THE YEARS, OUR PILFERED THINGS--	OF NEARNESS TO HER	607		14
MANY THINGS--ARE FRUITLESS--	IN FALLING TIMBERS	614		13
OF PRICKLY THINGS	THE CHILD'S FAITH IS NEW	637		20
IF THINGS WERE OPPOSITE--AND ME	I'VE NONE TO TELL ME TO	881		7
WE OUTGROW LOVE, LIKE OTHER THINGS	WE OUTGROW LOVE, LIKE	887		1
MY PERENNIAL THINGS?	WHAT SHALL I DO WHEN THE	956		16
FROM MISSING MINOR THINGS.	THE MISSING ALL,	985		2
BEST THINGS DWELL OUT OF SIGHT	BEST THINGS DWELL OUT OF	998		1
HOW MANY THINGS THE DYING PLAY	WERE IT BUT ME THAT	1015		3
THE THINGS ESTEEMED, FOR THINGS THAT ARE!	WHAT TWIGS WE HELD BY--	1086		17
THE THINGS ESTEEMED, FOR THINGS THAT ARE!	WHAT TWIGS WE HELD BY--	1086		17
WE NOTICED SMALLEST THINGS--	THE LAST NIGHT THAT SHE	1100		5
THINGS OVERLOOKED BEFORE	THE LAST NIGHT THAT SHE	1100		6
THE WIND TOOK UP THE NORTHERN THINGS	THE WIND TOOK UP THE	1134		1
INURED TO SLOWER [OTHER] THINGS	TO FLEE FROM MEMORY	1242		4
THE THINGS WE THOUGHT THAT WE SHOULD DO	THE THINGS WE THOUGHT	1293		1
WE OTHER THINGS HAVE DONE	THE THINGS WE THOUGHT	1293		2
THE UPPER SURFACES OF THINGS	THE SYMPTOM OF THE GALE	1327		7
THE WORTHLESSNESS [EMPTINESS] OF EARTHLY THINGS	THE WORTHLESSNESS OF	1373		1
THE THINGS WE DO NOT KNOW--	MARCH IS THE MONTH OF	1404		2
THINGS ARE NOT WHAT THEY ARE--	WHOEVER DISENCHANTS	1451		8
BUT UNSUSPECTED THINGS--	THE ROAD TO PARADISE IS	1491		9
ALL THINGS SWEPT SOLE AWAY	ALL THINGS SWEPT SOLE	1512		1
THE THINGS THAT NEVER CAN COME BACK, ARE SEVERAL--	THE THINGS THAT NEVER	1515		1
IN CONTRAST WITH THE [THOSE] THINGS THAT SING	A PANG IS MORE	1530		2
UNKNOWN--REFRESHING THINGS--	NO BRIGADIER THROUGHOUT	1561		20
OR LOVE'S CONVENIENT THINGS,	TO THE BRIGHT EAST SHE	1573		5
ALL OTHER HEARTS [THINGS] I KNEW.	TO LOSE THEE--SWEETER	1754		2
THINK				
TO THINK OF ANSWERING YOU!	GOING TO HEAVEN!	79		5
I THINK I'D SHOOT THE HUMAN RACE	MY FRIEND ATTACKS MY	118		7
I THINK IT THAT "NEW LIFE"!	MUSICIANS WRESTLE	157		6
SOME--THINK IT SERVICE IN THE PLACE	MUSICIANS WRESTLE	157		16
I THINK I WONT--HOWEVER--	THE SKIES CANT KEEP	191		9
I THINK THAT EARTH FEELS SO	I'M "WIFE"--I'VE	199		7
TO THINK JUST HOW THE FIRE WILL BURN--	THO' I GET HOME HOW LATE	207		9
I THINK JUST HOW MY SHAPE WILL RISE--	I THINK JUST HOW MY	237		1
I THINK JUST HOW MY LIPS WILL WEIGH--	I THINK JUST HOW MY	237		5
DO YOU THINK I'D STOP	AH, MOON--AND STAR!	240		5
STOP JUST A MINUTE--LET ME THINK!	WHAT WOULD I GIVE TO SEE	247		4
I GOT SO I COULD HEAR [THINK / TAKE] HIS NAME--	I GOT SO I COULD HEAR	293		1
I THINK, THEY CALL IT "GOD"--	I GOT SO I COULD HEAR	293		14
A PRIVILEGE--I THINK--	A PRECIOUS--MOULDERING	371		4
I THINK THE MEN WHO DIE--	IT FEELS A SHAME TO BE	444		18
I THINK A LITTLE WELL--LIKE MINE--	I KNOW WHERE WELLS GROW	460		19
LET ME THINK--I'M SURE	I WAS THE SLIGHTEST IN	486		8
I THINK THE HEMLOCK LIKES TO STAND	I THINK THE HEMLOCK	525		1
I TRIED TO THINK A LONELIER THING	I TRIED TO THINK A	532		1
SOMETIMES, I THINK THAT NOON	"HEAVEN" HAS DIFFERENT	575		2

	FIRST LINE	POEM	LINE
THINK (CONTINUED)			
THINK OF IT LOVER! I AND THEE	IF I MAY HAVE IT, WHEN	577	9
OR THINK OF, WITH A SIGH--	I CRIED AT PITY--NOT AT	588	14
I THINK I WAS ENCHANTED	I THINK I WAS ENCHANTED	593	1
DOTH THINK NO INCIVILITY	I WATCHED THE MOON	629	7
I THINK THE LONGEST HOUR OF ALL	I THINK THE LONGEST HOUR	635	1
I THINK TO LIVE--MAY BE A BLISS [LIFE]	I THINK TO LIVE--MAY BE	646	1
I THINK THE HEART I FORMER WORE	I THINK TO LIVE--MAY BE	646	5
I THINK THE DAYS--COULD EVERY ONE	I THINK TO LIVE--MAY BE	646	9
IS TENDEREST, I THINK--	THE SERVICE WITHOUT HOPE	779	2
IT KEPT ME FROM A THIEF, I THINK,	I PLAY AT RICHES--TO	801	3
PERHAPS YOU THINK ME STOOPING	PERHAPS YOU THINK ME	833	1
NATURE IS FOND, I SOMETIMES THINK,	A MOTH THE HUE OF THIS	841	5
DRIFTS WERE AS DIFFICULT THEN TO THINK	THIS WAS IN THE WHITE OF	995	3
LICENSE TO THINK OF [CHERISH] US--	WHATEVER IT IS--SHE HAS	1204	12
I THINK, BECAUSE HIS EMPTY PLATE	A SPARROW TOOK A SLICE	1211	3
WE THINK THAT HE MUST BE	BECAUSE THAT YOU ARE	1260	34
I THINK THAT THE ROOT OF THE WIND IS WATER--	I THINK THAT THE ROOT OF	1302	1
WHAT NEWS MUST THINK WHEN PONDERING	HOW NEWS MUST FEEL WHEN	1319	5
YOU'D THINK [SWEAR] HE TOOK A DEED	HOW DESTITUTE IS HE	1477	V 7
BUT THINK ENLARGED OF ALL THAT THEY WILL TELL US	THE THINGS THAT NEVER	1515	7
OF DEATH I TRY TO THINK LIKE THIS--	OF DEATH I TRY TO THINK	1558	1
IT MAKES US THINK OF ALL THE DEAD	THE SADDEST NOISE, THE	1764	9
IT MAKES US THINK OF WHAT WE HAD,	THE SADDEST NOISE, THE	1764	13
THINKING			
THINKING--PERHAPS--THAT I LOOKED TIRED--OR ALONE--	HOW SICK--TO WAIT--IN	368	3
THE THINKING HOW THEY WALKED ALIVE--	IF ANYBODY'S FRIEND BE	509	3
FOR THINKING--WHILE I DIE--	THREE TIMES--WE PARTED--	598	10
SEEMS IT TO MY HOODED THINKING	ONE DAY IS THERE OF THE	814	7
I'M THINKING ON THAT OTHER MORN--	'TIS ANGUISH GRANDER	984	V 5
TO THINKING OF MANKIND.	BEST WITCHCRAFT IS	1158	4
THIRD			
AS THE THIRD SYCAMORE--	I KNOW SOME LONELY	289	34
THIRD, EXPEDITION FOR	FINDING IS THE FIRST ACT	870	3
A THIRD EVENT TO ME,	MY LIFE CLOSED TWICE	1732	4
THIRST			
SOME PILGRIM THIRST TO SLAKE--	I BRING AN UNACCUSTOMED	132	19
WATER, IS TAUGHT BY THIRST.	WATER, IS TAUGHT BY	135	1
TO DIE OF THIRST--SUSPECTING	TO LEARN THE TRANSPORT	167	3
WITH THEE IN THE THIRST--	WITH THEE, IN THE DESERT	209	2
THIS THIRST WOULD BLISTER--EASIER--NOW--	ONE YEAR AGO--JOTS WHAT?	296	16
THAT PEOPLE "THIRST NO MORE"--	I KNOW WHERE WELLS GROW	460	14
WHEN THY THIRST COMES--	THE WORLD--FEELS DUSTY	715	10
WE THIRST AT FIRST--'TIS NATURE'S ACT--	WE THIRST AT FIRST--'TIS	726	1
THE THOUGHTFULNESS OF THIRST.	I COULD NOT DRINK IT,	818	4
LET ME NOT THIRST WITH THIS HOCK AT MY LIP,	LET ME NOT THIRST WITH	1772	1
THIRSTED			
WHO NEVER THIRSTED	WHO NEVER LOST, ARE	73	3
THIRSTING			
'TIS THIRSTING [PARCHING]--VITALIZES WINE--	I SHOULD HAVE BEEN TOO	313	23
THIRSTY			
THOSE THIRSTY LIPS TO FLAGONS PRESSED,	AS WATCHERS HANG UPON	121	11
SOME OTHER THIRSTY THERE MAY BE	I BRING AN UNACCUSTOMED	132	14
I'M OFTEN THIRSTY--BUT MY LIPS	I KNOW WHERE WELLS GROW	460	11
THITHER			
THITHER I PILOT THEE--	ON THIS WONDROUS SEA	4	10
THOMAS			
THE SAME--AFFLICTED THOMAS--	TRUST IN THE UNEXPECTED	555	13
SCARLET EXPERIMENT! SCEPTIC THOMAS!	SPLIT THE LARK--AND	861	7
THOMSON'S			
AND MR THOMSON'S "SHEAVES."	BESIDES THE AUTUMN POETS	131	8
THORN			
A SEPAL, PETAL, AND A THORN	A SEPAL, PETAL, AND A	19	1
WITH MANY A TURN--AND THORN--	'TWAS THE OLD--ROAD--	344	3
THE BLACK BERRY--WEARS A THORN IN HIS SIDE--	THE BLACK BERRY--WEARS A	554	1
THORNS			
FOR I WEAR THE "THORNS" TILL SUNSET--	REARRANGE A "WIFE'S"	1737	15
THOROUGH			
TILL I AM THOROUGH FIT.	I FIT FOR THEM--	1109	3
SO THOROUGH IN THE TREE	THE SNOW THAT NEVER	1133	5
THOROUGHLY			
WERE THOROUGHLY [DURABLY] DIVINE	THE DEVIL--HAD HE	1479	8
WOULD FEEL AS THOROUGHLY AT EASE	A FACE DEVOID OF LOVE OR	1711	4
THO'T			
THE RIGHT TO PERISH MIGHT BE THO'T	THE RIGHT TO PERISH	1692	1
THOU SEE THOU'RT			
THOU ART A HUMAN SOLO, A BEING COLD, AND LONE,	AWAKE YE MUSES NINE,	1	27
WILT HAVE NO KIND COMPANION, THOU REAP'ST WHAT THOU HAST SOWN.	AWAKE YE MUSES NINE,	1	28
WILT HAVE NO KIND COMPANION, THOU REAP'ST WHAT THOU HAST SOWN.	AWAKE YE MUSES NINE,	1	28
THINE EYES ARE SADLY BLINDED, BUT YET THOU MAYEST SEE	AWAKE YE MUSES NINE,	1	33
AND SEIZE THE ONE THOU LOVEST, NOR CARE FOR SPACE, OR TIME!	AWAKE YE MUSES NINE,	1	36
SO SHALT THOU HAVE A PIPPIN	"SIC TRANSIT GLORIA	3	19
KNOWEST THOU THE SHORE	ON THIS WONDROUS SEA	4	4
THOU LITTLE SPADE OF MINE	ALL THESE MY BANNERS BE.	22	13

	FIRST LINE	POEM	LINE
THOU (CONTINUED)			
EXCEPT [UNTIL] THOU BLESS ME"--STRANGER [SIGNOR]!	A LITTLE EAST OF JORDAN,	59	11
HAST THOU THE ROYAL SCAR?	WHO NEVER LOST, ARE	73	14
THOU PUZZLEST ME!	MY FRIEND MUST BE A BIRD	92	7
WHEREFORE--MARAUDER--ART THOU HERE?	THE DAISY FOLLOWS SOFT	106	5
WE ARE THE FLOWER--THOU THE SUN!	THE DAISY FOLLOWS SOFT	106	7
SOUL, WILT THOU TOSS AGAIN?	SOUL, WILT THOU TOSS	139	1
ART THOU WITHIN THE LITTLE BARN	I CAUTIOUS, SCANNED MY	178	19
"THOU WERT WITH HIM"--QUOTH "THE DAMSEL"? .	HE FORGOT--AND I--	203	5
DOST THOU REMEMBER ME?	SAVIOR! I'VE NO ONE ELSE	217	4
THOU SHALT--THYSELF--ONE DAY--A CHILD-- . .	THE COURT IS FAR AWAY--	235	7
YET--THOU--NOT THERE--	I TEND MY FLOWERS FOR	339	18
AND THOU--NOT THERE--	HOW SICK--TO WAIT--IN	368	12
THAN MAYEST THOU--	NO RACK CAN TORTURE ME--	384	12
THE MAGNITUDE THOU MAY	A TONGUE--TO TELL HIM I	400	15
WERT THOU A BUMBLE BEE--	COULD--I DO MORE--FOR	447	2
LOVE--THOU ART HIGH--	LOVE--THOU ART HIGH--	453	1
LOVE--THOU ART DEEP--	LOVE--THOU ART HIGH--	453	7
LOVE--THOU ART VAILED--	LOVE--THOU ART HIGH--	453	13
SUNRISE--HAST THOU A FLAG FOR ME?	A WIFE--AT DAYBREAK I	461	2
REMEMBER--AS THOU GO--	WE COVER THEE--SWEET	482	4
THOU NOTICE US--NO MORE--	WE COVER THEE--SWEET	482	6
IF THOU WOULD'ST TAKE IT--NOW--	WE COVER THEE--SWEET	482	12
THOU SETTEST [STIRREST] EARTHQUAKE IN THE SOUTH--	AT LEAST--TO PRAY--IS	502	5
HAST THOU NO ARM FOR ME?	AT LEAST--TO PRAY--IS	502	8
WHEN MOON'S AT FULL--'TIS THOU--I SAY-- . .	YOU KNOW THAT PORTRAIT	504	9
WHEN CRESCENT--THOU ART WORN--I NOTE [MIND]--	YOU KNOW THAT PORTRAIT	504	11
THIS--DOST THOU DOUBT--SWEET--	THAT I DID ALWAYS LOVE	549	9
INFINITUDE--HAD'ST THOU NO FACE	MY PERIOD HAD COME FOR	564	15
THAT THIS WAY--THOU COULD'ST NOTICE [SPEAK TO] ME--	IF I MAY HAVE IT, WHEN	577	21
WHERE THOU ART--THAT--IS HOME--	WHERE THOU ART--THAT--IS	725	1
WHAT THOU DOST--IS DELIGHT--	WHERE THOU ART--THAT--IS	725	6
WHERE THOU ART NOT--IS WO--	WHERE THOU ART--THAT--IS	725	11
WHAT THOU DOST NOT--DESPAIR--	WHERE THOU ART--THAT--IS	725	13
AND THOU HAST LOOKED ON THEM--	JOY TO HAVE MERITED THE	788	10
SO FLEET THOU WERT, WHEN PRESENT--	JOY TO HAVE MERITED THE	788	13
OH THOU CELESTIAL HOST--	GIVEN IN MARRIAGE UNTO	817	2
"DID'ST THOU?" "THOU DID'ST NOT MEAN," TO SAY,	I CANNOT BUY IT--'TIS	840	11
"DID'ST THOU?" "THOU DID'ST NOT MEAN," TO SAY,	I CANNOT BUY IT--'TIS	840	11
NATURE, HAD'ST THOU NOT A BERRY	TWICE HAD SUMMER HER	846	7
WHEN THOU UPON THEIR CRYPTS INTRUDE . . .	BECAUSE THE BEE MAY	869	8
SO WHEN THOU FAILEST, NOBODY.	I'VE NONE TO TELL ME TO	881	2
WOULD'ST THOU SEEK SO--JUST SAY	I'VE NONE TO TELL ME TO	881	10
WHY GIVE IF THOU MUST TAKE AWAY	A SHADE UPON THE MIND	882	7
"THOU HAST NOT ME, NOR ME"--IT SAID, ...	HAD I NOT THIS, OR THIS,	904	5
"AND YET THOU ART INDUSTRIOUS--	HAD I NOT THIS, OR THIS,	904	7
NO NEED--HADST THOU--OF US"?	HAD I NOT THIS, OR THIS,	904	8
'TIS SUNRISE--LITTLE MAID--HAST THOU . . .	'TIS SUNRISE--LITTLE	908	1
ALAS--AND ART THOU SLEEPING YET?	'TIS SUNRISE--LITTLE	908	6
THE BEE--HAST THOU FORGOT?	'TIS SUNRISE--LITTLE	908	8
INSTEAD OF MORNING--HAD'ST THOU BROACHED .	'TIS SUNRISE--LITTLE	908	11
THOU KNOWEST EVERY WO--	ONLY A SHRINE, BUT MINE	918	5
BUT CAN'ST THOU DO	ONLY A SHRINE, BUT MINE	918	7
THOU KNOWEST, THOUGH, SO WHY TELL THEE? . .	ONLY A SHRINE, BUT MINE	918	12
WILT THOU, AUSTERE [RUSSIAN] SNOW?	SNOW BENEATH WHOSE	942	8
WHAT DIFFERENCE, AFTER ALL, THOU MAK'ST . .	THE SUNSET STOPPED ON	950	7
THOU SUPERCILIOUS SUN?	THE SUNSET STOPPED ON	950	8
THOU FROM HERE, SO FAR?	WHAT SHALL I DO WHEN THE	956	12
WERT THOU BUT ILL--THAT I MIGHT SHOW THEE .	WERT THOU BUT ILL--THAT	961	1
WERT THOU BUT STRANGER IN UNGRACIOUS COUNTRY--	WERT THOU BUT ILL--THAT	961	5
THOU PAUSED AT, FOR A PASSING [DOUBTFUL] BOUNTY--	WERT THOU BUT ILL--THAT	961	7
ACCUSED--WERT THOU--AND MYSELF--TRIBUNAL-- .	WERT THOU BUT ILL--THAT	961	9
THE TENANT OF THE NARROW COTTAGE, WERT THOU--	WERT THOU BUT ILL--THAT	961	13
NO SERVICE HAST THOU, I WOULD NOT ACHIEVE [ATTEMPT] IT--	WERT THOU BUT ILL--THAT	961	17
"OLD FRIEND, THOU KNOWEST [KNEWEST] ME," .	I HEARD, AS IF I HAD NO	1039	14
HUELESS TO ME UNTIL THOU COME	SPRING COMES ON THE	1042	3
TOO NEAR THOU ART FOR SEEKING THEE . . .	LET DOWN THE BARS, OH	1065	7
TOO NEAR [CLOSE] THOU ART FOR FAME-- . . .	THE BIRD DID PRANCE--THE	1107	12
HAST THOU SURVIVED SO MANY NIGHTS [YEARS]? .	THE SMOULDERING EMBERS	1132	3
OH THOU ALMIGHTY GOD!	REMEMBRANCE HAS A	1182	V 8
ART THOU A STEP OR NOT?	OH SHADOW ON THE GRASS,	1187	2
SOME OTHER THOU WILT [DID'ST] CONSECRATE-- .	OH SHADOW ON THE GRASS,	1187	7
ART THOU THE THING I WANTED?	ART THOU THE THING I	1282	1
THOU DID'ST [COULD'ST] NOT GOAD SO LONG-- .	ART THOU THE THING I	1282	V 4
REMAIN THOU AS THOU ART.	TWO LENGTHS HAS EVERY	1295	12
REMAIN THOU AS THOU ART.	TWO LENGTHS HAS EVERY	1295	12
GO [BUT] BOLDLY--FOR THOU PAID'ST HIS PRICE	GO SLOW, MY SOUL, TO	1297	7
OH, THOU UNKNOWN RENOWN	THAT SHORT--POTENTIAL	1307	6
TOMORROW--THOU RETRIEVER	"TOMORROW"--WHOSE	1367	5
OF ALIBI ART THOU	"TOMORROW"--WHOSE	1367	7
UNLESS THOU KNOW'ST THE TUNE	TOUCH LIGHTLY NATURE'S	1389	2
HIM YOU CHASTEN, [THOU CHASTENEST-- / YOU CHASTENED] THAT IS [WAS] HE!	LAY THIS LAUREL ON THE	1393	4
FOR THOU HAST BORNE A UNIVERSE	HOW MUCH OF SOURCE	1517	3
AND IF THOU LIVE BEFORE THOU WAKE-- . . .	NOW I LAY THEE DOWN TO	1539	3

	FIRST LINE	POEM	LINE
THOU (CONTINUED)			
AND IF THOU LIVE BEFORE THOU WAKE--	NOW I LAY THEE DOWN TO	1539	3
THOU ONLY CAMEST TO MANKIND	WITHIN THY GRAVE!	1552	3
WHICH THOU HAST LEAPED ACROSS!	PASS TO THY RENDEZVOUS	1564	4
THE WORLD THAT THOU HAST OPENED	EXPANSE CANNOT BE LOST--	1584	9
THOU SWEETEST OF THE UNIVERSE,	IMMURED IN HEAVEN!	1594	4
CIRCUMFERENCE THOU BRIDE OF AWE	CIRCUMFERENCE THOU BRIDE	1620	1
POSSESSING THOU SHALT BE	CIRCUMFERENCE THOU BRIDE	1620	2
OH FUTURE! THOU SECRETED PEACE	OH FUTURE! THOU SECRETED	1631	1
STILL OWN THEE--STILL THOU ART	STILL OWN THEE--STILL	1633	1
BEFORE THOU DOST EXUDE [DISSOLVE] AWAY	STILL OWN THEE--STILL	1633	7
THE STARS THOU MEETST	GO THY GREAT WAY!	1638	2
THAT THOU ART HEAVENLY	EXTOL THEE--COULD I--	1643	4
THAT THOU ART TRITEST--BRIGHTEST [SWEETEST] TRUTH--	EXTOL THEE--COULD I--	1643	V 4
THAT THOU ART THAT TRITEST EULOGY	EXTOL THEE--COULD I--	1643	V 4
IN SNOW THOU COMEST	IN SNOW THOU COMEST	1669	1
THOU SHALT GO WITH THE RESUMING GROUND	IN SNOW THOU COMEST	1669	2
IN FEAR THOU COMEST	IN SNOW THOU COMEST	1669	5
THOU SHALT GO AT SUCH A GAIT OF JOY	IN SNOW THOU COMEST	1669	6
HAST THOU A HAND OR FOOT	THE LOOK OF THEE, WHAT	1689	2
HAST THOU DELIGHT OR FEAR	THE LOOK OF THEE, WHAT	1689	6
THAT THOU SHALT BE THE SAME--	THE LOOK OF THEE, WHAT	1689	12
PROUD OF MY BROKEN HEART, SINCE THOU DIDST BREAK IT,	PROUD OF MY BROKEN HEART	1736	1
PROUD OF MY NIGHT, SINCE THOU WITH MOONS DOST SLAKE IT,	PROUD OF MY BROKEN HEART	1736	3
THOU CAN'ST NOT BOAST, LIKE JESUS, DRUNKEN WITHOUT COMPANION	PROUD OF MY BROKEN HEART	1736	5
THOU CAN'ST NOT PIERCE TRADITION WITH THE PEERLESS PUNCTURE,	PROUD OF MY BROKEN HEART	1736	7
"THOU SHALT NOT" IS A KINDER SWORD	THERE COMES AN HOUR WHEN	1751	4
THOUGHT SEE THO'T, BETHOUGHT			
SO I SAID--OR THOUGHT--	IT DID NOT SURPRISE ME--	39	2
THE THOUGHT BENEATH SO SLIGHT A FILM--	THE THOUGHT BENEATH SO	210	1
AS MY THOUGHT--TODAY--	TEACH HIM--WHEN HE MAKES	227	6
KEPT BEATING--BEATING--TILL I THOUGHT	I FELT A FUNERAL, IN MY	280	7
THE VERY PROFILE OF THE THOUGHT	THAT AFTER HORROR--THAT	286	7
I THOUGHT THAT SUCH WERE FOR THE SAINTS,	THERE CAME A DAY AT	322	3
THEY LOOKED LIKE FRIGHTENED BEADS, I THOUGHT--	A BIRD CAME DOWN THE	328	11
I THOUGHT IF I COULD ONLY LIVE	I DREADED THAT FIRST	348	5
AN HONOR, THOUGHT CAN TURN HER TO	I HAD THE GLORY--THAT	349	2
I THOUGHT THAT STORM--WAS BRIEF--	IT STRUCK ME--EVERY DAY	362	9
HIS THOUGHT TO ASCERTAIN	A PRECIOUS--MOULDERING	371	10
PUT THE THOUGHT IN ADVANCE--A YEAR--	IT DONT SOUND SO	426	15
FOREVER MIGHT BE SHORT, I THOUGHT TO SHOW--	TO LOVE THEE YEAR BY	434	5
I THOUGHT HOW YELLOW IT WOULD LOOK--	'TWAS JUST THIS TIME,	445	5
I THOUGHT JUST HOW RED--APPLES WEDGED	'TWAS JUST THIS TIME,	445	9
AND SO, I THOUGHT THE OTHER WAY,	'TWAS JUST THIS TIME,	445	22
I NEVER THOUGHT TO SEE--	EXCEPT THE HEAVEN HAD	472	6
I THOUGHT	I HAD NO TIME TO HATE--	478	11
YOU THOUGHT WAS FINISHED--	A SOLEMN THING WITHIN	483	9
WERE GOING--I HAD OFTEN THOUGHT	I WAS THE SLIGHTEST IN	486	16
UNWORTHY, THAT A THOUGHT SO MEAN	THE SOUL HAS BANDAGED	512	9
OR BEES--THAT THOUGHT THE SUMMER'S NAME	LIKE FLOWERS, THAT HEARD	513	4
TO LIVES THAT THOUGHT THE WORSHIPPING	LIKE FLOWERS, THAT HEARD	513	14
WITHIN THE CLUTCH OF THOUGHT--	I TRIED TO THINK A	532	9
OUR LORD--THOUGHT NO	MUST BE A WO--	571	13
I FOUND THE WORDS [PHRASE] TO EVERY THOUGHT	I FOUND THE WORDS TO	581	1
AND THOUGHT OF THEM--SO FAIR INVITES--	YOU'LL FIND--IT WHEN YOU	610	13
I THOUGHT IT WOULD BE OPPOSITE--	I ROSE--BECAUSE HE SANK	616	2
WAS DYING AS HE THOUGHT--OR DIFFERENT--	TO KNOW JUST HOW HE	622	6
WHO, VITAL ONLY TO OUR THOUGHT--	BEREAVEMENT IN THEIR	645	9
WE THOUGHT THE MIGHTY [MONSTROUS] FUNERAL--	'TIS GOOD--THE LOOKING	660	3
A THOUGHT WENT UP MY MIND TODAY--	A THOUGHT WENT UP MY	701	1
THE THOUGHT TO BE ALIVE--	I SOMETIMES DROP IT, FOR	708	2
THOUGHT BELONG TO HIM WHO GAVE IT--	PUBLICATION--IS THE	709	9
'TWAS PRUDENTER--I THOUGHT--	IF HE WERE LIVING--DARE	734	12
I MANY TIMES THOUGHT PEACE HAD COME	I MANY TIMES THOUGHT	739	1
PERVADED HER, WE THOUGHT	HER FINAL SUMMER WAS IT	795	4
THEN THOUGHT OF US, AND STAYED.	SWEET, TO HAVE HAD THEM	901	9
THE THOUGHT BEHIND, I STROVE [TRIED] TO JOIN	I FELT A CLEAVING IN MY	937	5
UNTO THE THOUGHT BEFORE--	I FELT A CLEAVING IN MY	937	6
IT IS AN HONORABLE THOUGHT	IT IS AN HONORABLE	946	1
I, PASSING, THOUGHT ANOTHER NOON	IT BLOOMED AND DROPT, A	978	3
WILL EQUAL GLOW, AND THOUGHT NO MORE	IT BLOOMED AND DROPT, A	978	5
HAVE PASSED, I THOUGHT, A WHIP LASH	A NARROW FELLOW IN THE	986	13
THE PEARL--THE JUST--OUR THOUGHT.	BEST THINGS DWELL OUT OF	998	2
I THOUGHT YOU'D CHOOSE A VELVET CHEEK	THEMSELF ARE ALL I HAVE	1094	3
REPUBLIC OF DELIGHT, I THOUGHT	THE BIRD DID PRANCE--THE	1107	7
BUT NATURE, SOMETIMES, SOMETIMES THOUGHT	THERE IS ANOTHER	1116	5
AND THOUGHT IT VERY NICE	A SPARROW TOOK A SLICE	1211	2
A DEED KNOCKS FIRST AT THOUGHT	A DEED KNOCKS FIRST AT	1216	1
WE [I] THOUGHT, AT LEAST THEY ARE NO WORSE	WHO WERE "THE FATHER AND	1258	7
I THOUGHT THAT NATURE WAS ENOUGH	I THOUGHT THAT NATURE	1286	1
THE THINGS WE THOUGHT THAT WE SHOULD DO	THE THINGS WE THOUGHT	1293	1
THE LANDS WE THOUGHT THAT WE SHOULD SEEK	THE THINGS WE THOUGHT	1293	5
IF NEWS HAVE ANY THOUGHT	HOW NEWS MUST FEEL WHEN	1319	6
THE CIRCUMVENTION OF THE SHAFT [THOUGHT / SITE / FACT]	AS SUMMER INTO AUTUMN	1346	11

	FIRST LINE	POEM	LINE
THOUGHT (CONTINUED)			
AND FELT [THOUGHT] "HOW VAST A DESTINY"-- .	A DEW SUFFICED ITSELF--	1437	3
I THOUGHT THE TRAIN WOULD NEVER COME-- . .	I THOUGHT THE TRAIN	1449	1
BEFORE YOU THOUGHT OF SPRING	BEFORE YOU THOUGHT OF	1465	1
I NEVER THOUGHT THAT JASON SOUGHT	ONE OF THE ONES THAT	1466	21
IF WRECKED UPON THE SHOAL [WHARF / CAPE / DOCK / BAY] OF THOUGHT	IF WRECKED UPON THE	1469	1
RECURRENT TO THE AFTER MIND [THOUGHT] . .	THEIR BARRICADE AGAINST	1471	9
LEST GRATITUDE REVIVE THE SNAKE [MY THOUGHT]	IT CAME HIS TURN TO BEG	1500	7
HAVE FELT [THOUGHT] IT MEET TO DIE-- . . .	HIS ORIENTAL HERESIES	1526	8
THE THOUGHT IS [SCENE WAS] QUIET AS A FLAKE--	THE FARTHEST THUNDER	1581	17
WOULD BE THE GENERAL THOUGHT--	ON MY VOLCANO GROWS THE	1677	4
WAS MOST I THOUGHT UPON	THAT SHE FORGOT ME WAS	1683	4
THE DEPTH IS ALL MY THOUGHT--	A PIT--BUT HEAVEN OVER	1712	10
DOUBTLESS, HE THOUGHT IT MEET OF HIM . . .	A TRAIN WENT THROUGH A	1761	7
THOUGHTFUL			
THE THOUGHTFUL GRAVE ENCLOSES--	SOME, TOO FRAGILE FOR	141	2
A TENDER--THOUGHTFUL MOON	AGAIN--HIS VOICE IS AT	663	19
THOUGHTFULNESS			
THE THOUGHTFULNESS OF THIRST.	I COULD NOT DRINK IT,	818	4
THOUGHTS			
IT'S THOUGHTS--AND JUST ONE HEART-- . . .	IT'S THOUGHTS--AND JUST	495	1
IT'S THOUGHTS--AND JUST TWO HEART-- . . .	IT'S THOUGHTS--AND JUST	495	23
AND THOUGHTS WE WILL NOT SHOW	THE MURMURING OF BEES,	1115	14
YOUR THOUGHTS DONT HAVE WORDS EVERY DAY . .	YOUR THOUGHTS DONT HAVE	1452	1
WITH THOUGHTS THAT MAKE FOR PEACE-- . . .	ONE OF THE ONES THAT	1466	24
THOU'RT			
THOU'RT NEITHER--	'TWOULD EASE--A	682	3
THOUSAND			
WHEN FROM A THOUSAND SKIES	IF PAIN FOR PEACE	63	10
"A THOUSAND TIMES THEE NAY."	SAID DEATH TO PASSION	1033	4
SOME EIGHTEEN THOUSAND YEARS--	AS OLD AS WOE--	1168	3
THE EMBERS OF A THOUSAND YEARS	LONG YEARS APART--CAN	1383	5
ENCAMPING ON A THOUSAND DAWNS	HOW LONESOME THE WIND	1418	10
THAT HAD IT BEAT A THOUSAND YEARS, . . .	'TIS NOT THE SWAYING	1597	3
AND CROSSED A THOUSAND TREES	UPON HIS SADDLE SPRUNG A	1600	2
THOUSANDS			
SOME THOUSANDS--ON THE HARM--	I MEASURE EVERY GRIEF I	561	18
THREAD			
BUSY NEEDLES, AND SPOOLS OF THREAD--	ON SUCH A NIGHT, OR SUCH	146	19
OF [WITH] MELLOW--MURMURING THREAD--	A FEATHER FROM THE	161	6
YOU DROPPED AN AMBER THREAD--	SHE SWEEPS WITH	219	6
AH, THE BEWILDERING THREAD!	A SHADY FRIEND--FOR	278	10
AND THREAD THE DEWS, ALL NIGHT, LIKE PEARLS [PEARL]--	THE GRASS SO LITTLE HAS	333	9
DONT PUT UP MY THREAD & NEEDLE--	DONT PUT UP MY THREAD &	617	1
THREADED			
'TIS THREADED IN THE AIR--	TO MEND EACH TATTERED	1442	4
THREADING			
I'VE FINISHED THREADING--TOO--	I'M CEDED--I'VE STOPPED	508	7
THREADLESS			
A THREADLESS WAY [COURSE]	FROM BLANK TO BLANK--	761	2
THREADS			
AND LEFT BRAZILIAN THREADS	MY FIRST WELL DAY--SINCE	574	20
THREATEN			
NOR THREATEN [JOGGLE / OGLE] A HAT--	THE WIND DID'NT COME	316	4
THREATENED			
THREATENED FOR THAT WITH DEATH--BY GESSLER--	TELL AS A MARKSMAN--WERE	1152	16
THAT THREATENED IT--DID RUN	A WILD BLUE SKY ABREAST	1415	2
THAT THREATENED CHILDHOOD'S CITADEL . . .	SOFTENED BY TIME'S	1738	3
THREATENING			
WITH THREATENING TUNES AND LOW--	THE WIND BEGUN TO KNEAD	824	V 2
THREE			
THREE CHEERS, SIR, FOR THE GENTLEMAN . . .	"SIC TRANSIT GLORIA	3	11
AND TWO OR THREE--FOR COMPANY--	IT'S THOUGHTS--AND JUST	495	4
THREE TIMES--WE PARTED--BREATH--AND I-- . .	THREE TIMES--WE PARTED--	598	1
THREE TIMES--HE WOULD NOT GO--	THREE TIMES--WE PARTED--	598	2
THREE TIMES--THE BILLOWS THREW [TOSSED] ME UP--	THREE TIMES--WE PARTED--	598	5
AND THAT--A FURTHER--AND THE THREE	AS IF THE SEA SHOULD	695	3
POUNCE ON HIS BRUISES--ONE--SAY--OR THREE--	GRIEF IS A MOUSE--	793	11
PERCHANCE [THREE--WITH / AND SOME] ETERNITY--	THE ONLY NEWS I KNOW	827	6
THREE WEEKS PASSED SINCE I HAD SEEN HER-- .	THREE WEEKS PASSED SINCE	1061	1
AT HALF PAST THREE, A SINGLE BIRD	AT HALF PAST THREE, A	1084	1
THAN NUMB THREE SCORE AND TEN--	NOT ANY HIGHER STANDS	1256	4
THREE RIVERS AND A HILL TO CROSS	I DID NOT REACH THEE	1664	3
THREE RIVERS AND THE HILL ARE PASSED . .	I DID NOT REACH THEE	1664	31
THREE TIMES, 'TIS SAID, A SINKING MAN . .	DROWNING IS NOT SO	1718	3
THREESCORE			
SINCE PLAYMATES AT THREESCORE AND TEN . .	MY WARS ARE LAID AWAY IN	1549	11
THRENODIES			
SUCH THRENODIES [EXTACIES / REVENUES / ARGUMENTS] OF PEARL--	YOU'LL KNOW HER--BY HER	634	26
THRESHOLD			
ARE ALL THAT CROSS HIS THRESHOLD--	THE ROBIN IS A GABRIEL	1483	12
THREW			
I THREW MY PRAYER AWAY--	I MEANT TO HAVE BUT	476	18
THREE TIMES--THE BILLOWS THREW [TOSSED] ME UP--	THREE TIMES--WE PARTED--	598	5
THE SUNSHINE THREW HIS HAT AWAY--	A DROP FELL ON THE APPLE	794	11

	FIRST LINE	POEM	LINE
THREW (CONTINUED)			
HE THREW A MENACE AT THE EARTH--	THE WIND BEGUN TO KNEAD	824	V 3
AND THROW [THREW] AWAY THE ROAD--	THE WIND BEGUN TO KNEAD	824	8
THRICE			
THRICE TO THE FLOATING CASEMENT	ONCE MORE, MY NOW	48	5
THRIFT			
AND STILL, SHE PLIES HER SPOTTED BROOMS, [THRIFT]	SHE SWEEPS WITH	219	9
ADAM TAUGHT HER THRIFT	PARADISE IS THAT OLD	1119	6
THRIFTY			
THE THRIFTY DEITY	IT'S EASY TO INVENT A	724	6
THRILL			
COULD THRILL [PENETRATE] THEIR MORTISED EAR	WHAT CARE THE DEAD, FOR	592	13
IT CANNOT GLOW [THRILL / BLUSH]--	PRAISE IT--'TIS DEAD--	1384	2
THE THRILL CAME SLOWLY LIKE A BOON [LIGHT] FOR	THE THRILL CAME SLOWLY	1495	1
THRILLED			
OF TRANSPORT THRILLED WITH FEAR--	SWEET SKEPTICISM OF THE	1413	8
THRILLING			
. . . THRILLING / FLUTTERING / COWERING] VAN	TO FLEE FROM MEMORY	1242	6
SURPRISE IS LIKE A THRILLING--PUNGENT-- . .	SURPRISE IS LIKE A	1306	1
HAD BUT THE TALE A WARBLING [THRILLING / TYPIC / HEARTY / . . .	THE BIBLE IS AN ANTIQUE	1545	13
WHAT RESPITE FROM HER THRILLING TOIL . . .	THE BIRD HER PUNCTUAL	1585	5
THRILLS			
'TIS TRANSPORT WILD AS THRILLS THE GRAVES .	'TIS ANGUISH GRANDER	984	5
THRIVES			
THE HEMLOCK'S NATURE THRIVES--ON COLD-- . .	I THINK THE HEMLOCK	525	9
THRIVING			
AND FROM A THRIVING FARMER--	I CAUTIOUS, SCANNED MY	178	11
THROAT			
TO SHOW HER THROAT--	I TEND MY FLOWERS FOR	339	8
THE JOY THAT IN HIS HAPPY THROAT	HIS BILL IS CLASPED--HIS	1102	5
THE WRESTLE IN HER SIMPLE THROAT	THE PRETTY RAIN FROM	1426	5
AND THEN HE LIFTED UP HIS THROAT	UPON HIS SADDLE SPRUNG A	1600	5
AND TRILLED, AND QUIVERED, AND SHOOK HIS THROAT	A TRAIN WENT THROUGH A	1761	3
THROATS			
WE ALMOST WISH THOSE SIREN THROATS . . .	THE SADDEST NOISE, THE	1764	15
THROE			
A THROE UPON THE FEATURES--	A THROE UPON THE	71	1
TRANSPORT--BY THROE--	WATER, IS TAUGHT BY	135	3
NOR SIMULATE, A THROE--	I LIKE A LOOK OF AGONY,	241	4
WITHOUT A SMILE--WITHOUT A THROE	WITHOUT A SMILE--WITHOUT	1330	1
COMPARED WITH THE DELICIOUS THROE	SWEET SKEPTICISM OF THE	1413	7
THRONE			
THE BOBOLINKS AROUND THE THRONE	WE SHOULD NOT MIND SO	81	11
DROP INTO TUNE--AROUND THE THRONE--	BETTER--THAN MUSIC! FOR	503	24
AND I CHOOSE, JUST A CROWN [THRONE]-- . .	I'M CEDED--I'VE STOPPED	508	19
IN PRESENCE OF THE THRONE.	HE OUTSTRIPPED TIME WITH	865	4
THRONES			
HER BROW IS FIT FOR THRONES	HER BREAST IS FIT FOR	84	3
WHEN THRONES ACCOST MY HANDS--	MY REWARD FOR BEING, WAS	343	6
THRONG			
CHAMBER, AND STATE, AND THRONG--	ONE DIGNITY DELAYS FOR	98	6
YET WHO OF ALL THE THRONG	FOR EVERY BIRD A NEST--	143	16
HER GOD--HER ONLY THRONG--	TRIUMPH--MAY BE OF	455	8
THE FLOWERS--APPEALED--A TIMID THRONG-- . .	THE BIRDS REPORTED FROM	743	5
TO THAT ETHERIAL THRONG	FEW, YET ENOUGH,	1596	3
YET MAN HAS NOT OF ALL THE THRONG	THE HILLS ERECT THEIR	1688	3
THRONGING			
UPON MY THRONGING [CROWDED / HAPPY] MIND-- .	MY WORTHINESS IS ALL MY	751	8
THRONGS			
AS TONGUES [THRONGS / EYES] OF DIAMOND HAD REVILED	MY SOUL--ACCUSED ME--AND	753	2
AS THRONGS [CLANS] OF DOWN--	DEATH IS THE SUPPLE	1445	12
THROUGHOUT			
THROUGHOUT A CHRISTIAN LAND--	THE SPIDER AS AN ARTIST	1275	6
NO BRIGADIER THROUGHOUT THE YEAR	NO BRIGADIER THROUGHOUT	1561	1
THROW			
HAVE VENTURED ALL UPON A THROW!	'TIS SO MUCH JOY! 'TIS	172	4
AND THROW THE OLD--AWAY--	I TIE MY HAT--I CREASE	443	6
AND THROW [THREW] AWAY THE ROAD--	THE WIND BEGUN TO KNEAD	824	8
THROW [GIVE / CAST] NOT TO THE DIVINE . .	THE MIND LIVES ON THE	1355	V 7
THROWN			
IN THE DUST, BE THROWN?	I HAVE NEVER SEEN	175	16
AND HANDS--BESEECHING--THROWN!	TWO SWIMMERS WRESTLED ON	201	9
THAT TRAVELLERS--HAD THROWN--	I WENT TO THANK HER--	363	5
AND THEN THE LADDER'S THROWN AWAY, ...	DOOM IS THE HOUSE	475	3
AND THROWN HER FURTHEST STONE--	THIS MERIT HATH THE	979	4
THROWN OPEN WIDE TO ME--	I SUED THE NEWS--YET	1360	4
FIRST TIME TOGETHER THROWN.	A FACE DEVOID OF LOVE OR	1711	6
THRUM			
AND THRUM UPON THE DOOR, ...	OF ALL THE SOUNDS	321	22
THRUST			
TO FADE [DIE]--TOMORROW--RAINBOWS HELD [THRUST]	MY FIRST WELL DAY--SINCE	574	15
A THRUST--AND THEN FOR LIFE A CHANCE-- . . .	THE WHOLE OF IT CAME NOT	762	3
IT'S TOILS [CORN] TO BRINDLED PEOPLE [NATIONS] THRUST [CAST]--	A FIELD OF STUBBLE,	1407	3
MUST THRUST THE TEARS AWAY.	WHERE EVERY BIRD IS BOLD	1758	4

	FIRST LINE	POEM	LINE
THUMB			
OR AN EMPHATIC THUMB--	MY LIFE HAD STOOD--A	754	20
THUNDER			
AND THUNDER--IN THE ROOM--	I GOT SO I COULD HEAR	293	4
THAT RIDES--EMITS [SUPPORTS] A THUNDER--	TO INTERRUPT HIS YELLOW	591	15
THUNDER--THE CRICKET--	"NATURE" IS WHAT WE SEE	668	7
THUNDER STORM	THE WIND BEGUN TO KNEAD	824	T
THE THUNDERS [THUNDER] GOSSIPED LOW--	THE WIND BEGUN TO KNEAD	824	10
THE THUNDER HURRIED SLOW--	THE WIND BEGUN TO KNEAD	824	V 10
DEPOSITING HIS THUNDER	THESE ARE THE NIGHTS	1128	7
THE THUNDER CRUMBLED LIKE A STUFF	THE CLOUDS THEIR BACKS	1172	5
TO PILE LIKE THUNDER TO IT'S CLOSE	TO PILE LIKE THUNDER TO	1247	1
THE FARTHEST THUNDER THAT I HEARD	THE FARTHEST THUNDER	1581	1
A THUNDER STORM COMBINES THE CHARMS	A CAP OF LEAD ACROSS THE	1649	7
THUNDERBOLT			
DEALS--ONE--IMPERIAL--THUNDERBOLT--	HE FUMBLES AT YOUR SOUL	315	11
THUNDERING			
THUNDERING IT'S PROSPECTIVE--	MANY A PHRASE HAS THE	276	11
THUNDER'S			
LOUD, AS THE THUNDER'S TONGUE--	MANY A PHRASE HAS THE	276	4
THUNDERS			
THE THUNDERS [THUNDER] GOSSIPED LOW--	THE WIND BEGUN TO KNEAD	824	10
THWARTED			
THEY THWARTED US WITH GUNS--	THEY PUT US FAR APART--	474	6
THY			
TO BRINGING THEE TO JUSTICE, AND MARSHALLING THY SOUL!	AWAKE YE MUSES NINE,	1	26
I WAIT THY FAR, FANTASTIC BELLS--	THERE IS A MORN BY MEN	24	22
THY MUSIC STILL, WHEN WHIPPOWIL	SUMMER FOR THEE, GRANT I	31	3
THY FLOWER--FOREVERMORE!	SUMMER FOR THEE, GRANT I	31	9
RESERVE WITHIN THY KINGDOM	PAPA ABOVE!	61	4
THY PERPLEXITY?	LOW AT MY PROBLEM	69	8
THINE [THY] EXTREMITY	LOW AT MY PROBLEM	69	V 8
THY DISHONOR SHARED!	"THEY HAVE NOT CHOSEN ME	85	8
"FATHER, THY WILL BE DONE" TODAY	I HAVE A KING, WHO DOES	103	16
WHEREFORE MINE EYE THY SILVER MISTS,	THE BEE IS NOT AFRAID OF	111	7
ALMOST THY PLAUSIBILITY	THESE ARE THE DAYS WHEN	130	8
THY SACRED EMBLEMS TO PARTAKE--	THESE ARE THE DAYS WHEN	130	16
THY CONSECRATED BREAD TO TAKE	THESE ARE THE DAYS WHEN	130	17
THY WINDY WILL TO BEAR!	BESIDES THE AUTUMN POETS	131	16
MUTE THY CORONATION--	MUTE THY CORONATION--	151	1
AT LAST, THE LAMPS UPON THY [YOUR] SIDE	AT LAST, TO BE	174	2
BASHFUL--SIP THY JESSAMINES--	COME SLOWLY--EDEN!	211	3
JESUS! THY CRUCIFIX	JESUS! THY CRUCIFIX	225	1
JESUS! THY SECOND FACE	JESUS! THY CRUCIFIX	225	4
THY FLOWER--BE GAY--	I TEND MY FLOWERS FOR	339	21
THY DAISY--	I TEND MY FLOWERS FOR	339	26
THY PAY--IN DIAMONDS--BE--	A TONGUE--TO TELL HIM I	400	18
I'LL DO THY WILL--	FORGET! THE LADY WITH	438	16
I KNOW NOT WHICH THY CHAMBER IS [PALACES]--	AT LEAST--TO PRAY--IS	502	3
FORGIVE ME, IF TO STROKE [TOUCH / GREET] THY FROST	IF I MAY HAVE IT, WHEN	577	28
NEITHER--THY CAPACITY--	'TWOULD EASE--A	682	4
THY MOMENT	'TWOULD EASE--A	682	7
BASHFUL HEAVEN--THY LOVERS SMALL--	OUT OF SIGHT? WHAT OF	703	12
WHEN THY THIRST COMES--	THE WORLD--FEELS DUSTY	715	10
PARDON--TO LOOK UPON THY FACE--	JOY TO HAVE MERITED THE	788	5
THY SHORE?	SO SET IT'S SUN IN THEE	808	6
TO BANQUET ON THY COUNTENANCE	THE LUXURY TO APPREHEND	815	11
THY BATTERIES DIVORCE.	DYING! TO BE AFRAID OF	831	9
FOR THY WANDERING BIRD?	TWICE HAD SUMMER HER	846	8
SINCE SOMEWHERE THY SWEET FACE HAS SPILLED	I'VE NONE TO TELL ME TO	881	5
'TWAS NOT THY WONT, TO HINDER SO--	'TIS SUNRISE--LITTLE	908	3
THY LITTLE PLAN TO DIE--	'TIS SUNRISE--LITTLE	908	12
STILL--JUST AS EASY, IF IT BE THY WILL	ONLY A SHRINE, BUT MINE	918	10
AND MAR THY PERFECTNESS--	WHAT I SEE NOT, I BETTER	939	12
HALF THE CONDITION [DISTINCTION], THY REVERSE--TO FOLLOW--	WERT THOU BUT ILL--THAT	961	11
THE HOUSEWIFE IN THY LOW ATTENDANCE	WERT THOU BUT ILL--THAT	961	15
IN THY BOLDER SEA--	ALL FORGOT FOR	966	14
LATER THAN LIGHT THY CONSCIOUSNESS ACCOST ME	AIR HAS NO RESIDENCE, NO	1060	7
AND LEAVE FOR THY SWEET MERCY'S [PATIENCE'] SAKE	SOME WRETCHED CREATURE,	1111	3
IN THY LONG PARADISE OF LIGHT	IN THY LONG PARADISE OF	1145	1
SOUL, TAKE THY RISK [RISKS / CHANCE],	SOUL, TAKE THY RISK,	1151	1
THY PRIVILEGE OF DYING	THROUGH WHAT TRANSPORTS	1153	7
SHINE THY BEST--	MY GOD--HE SEES THEE--	1178	2
FLING UP THY BALLS OF GOLD	MY GOD--HE SEES THEE--	1178	3
IN THY LONG RACE WITH HIM!	MY GOD--HE SEES THEE--	1178	9
IN THY BEAUTIFUL HOUSE	WHATEVER IT IS--SHE HAS	1204	10
THY TUMULTUOUS ROOMS	FORTITUDE INCARNATE	1217	10
HE FIRST ACHIEVE [ESPOUSE] THY FACE	MY HEART RAN SO TO THEE	1237	6
REDEMPTION [THY TOTAL / THY BEING]--FOR A KISS--	GO SLOW, MY SOUL, TO	1297	8
REDEMPTION [THY TOTAL / THY BEING]--FOR A KISS--	GO SLOW, MY SOUL, TO	1297	8
WHEN IN THY FELICITY,	RECOLLECT THE FACE OF ME	1305	2
PUT UP MY HEART THY HOARY WORK	THE NOTICE THAT IS	1310	3
LAUREL--VAIL YOUR [THY] DEATHLESS TREE--	LAY THIS LAUREL ON THE	1393	3
LAUREL--FELL YOUR [THY] FUTILE TREE--	LAY THIS LAUREL ON THE	1393	V

	FIRST LINE	POEM	LINE
THY (CONTINUED)			
NOTHING AFFRONT THY SECRECY.	TO THE STANCH DUST	1402	V 7
SHOULD DISENTHRALL THY SOUL--	WHO NEVER WANTED--	1430	8
FASHIONED BY THY CANDID HAND	"HEAVENLY FATHER"--TAKE	1461	3
IT'S [THY] SWEETNESS TO HAVE KNOWN--	ONE THING OF IT WE	1464	4
THY PHYSIOGNOMY	HOW FIRM ETERNITY MUST	1499	6
HOW CHIEF THY SESSIONS BE--	HOW MUCH OF SOURCE	1517	2
I PRAY THE LORD THY DUST TO KEEP--	NOW I LAY THEE DOWN TO	1539	2
I PRAY THE LORD THY SOUL TO MAKE--	NOW I LAY THEE DOWN TO	1539	4
COME SHOW THY DURHAM BREAST	COME SHOW THY DURHAM	1542	1
DO THE [THY] AVOWING--	COME SHOW THY DURHAM	1542	6
THY NUPTIAL SO MINUTE	COME SHOW THY DURHAM	1542	7
WITHIN THY GRAVE!	WITHIN THY GRAVE!	1552	1
PASS TO THY RENDEZVOUS OF LIGHT,	PASS TO THY RENDEZVOUS	1564	1
TO THY TRACTS OF SHEEN--	EXPANSE CANNOT BE LOST--	1584	14
HE SHALL NOT TAKE THY HAND	BACK FROM THE CORDIAL	1625	2
TO BALK THEE OF THY SACRED PREY--[THE INNOCENCE / THE MYRIADS]	OH FUTURE! THOU SECRETED	1631	7
ADVANCING [DEPUTED] TO THY DEN--	OH FUTURE! THOU SECRETED	1631	8
TO THY REPORTLESS GRAVE--	STILL OWN THEE--STILL	1633	4
GO THY GREAT WAY!	GO THY GREAT WAY!	1638	1
TO PAY FOR THY RIGHT HAND	I DID NOT REACH THEE	1664	13
THAT TOOK THY FACE BETWEEN	I SEE THEE CLEARER FOR	1666	2
AND WHAT IS THY PURSUIT	THE LOOK OF THEE, WHAT	1689	4
THY FELLOWS ARE THEY REALMS OR THEMES	THE LOOK OF THEE, WHAT	1689	5
I NEVER KNEW THY POWER,	OH, HONEY OF AN HOUR,	1734	2
NOT TO PARTAKE THY PASSION, MY HUMILITY.	PROUD OF MY BROKEN HEART	1736	4
SEE! I USURPED THY CRUCIFIX TO HONOR MINE!	PROUD OF MY BROKEN HEART	1736	8
BLUSH, MY SPIRIT, IN THY FASTNESS--	REARRANGE A "WIFE'S"	1737	5
THYME SEE BY-THYME			
THYSELF			
THOU SHALT--THYSELF--ONE DAY--A CHILD--	THE COURT IS FAR AWAY--	235	7
EXCEPT THYSELF MAY BE	NO RACK CAN TORTURE ME--	384	13
BUT THAT THYSELF FATIGUE OF US--	WE COVER THEE--SWEET	482	3
SUBTRACT THYSELF, IN PLAY,	EMPTY MY HEART, OF THEE	587	7
SOTO! EXPLORE THYSELF!	SOTO! EXPLORE THYSELF!	832	1
THEREIN THYSELF SHALT FIND	SOTO! EXPLORE THYSELF!	832	2
UNTIL THYSELF, BELOVED.	DISTANCE--IS NOT THE	1155	4
GO SLOW, MY SOUL, TO FEED THYSELF	GO SLOW, MY SOUL, TO	1297	1
ARE EVEN AS THYSELF--	GO THY GREAT WAY!	1638	3
TO THYSELF,	LAD OF ATHENS, FAITHFUL	1768	2
TIARAS			
TIARAS--MAKE--OF SOME--	I'LL CLUTCH--AND CLUTCH	427	8
TICK			
BUT THEY COULD GAG THE TICK--	I KNOW SOME LONELY	289	15
. . . BURST / FLAGS / STEP / TICK / SHOUTS / PINK / RED / . . .	ONE JOY OF SO MUCH	1420	6
TICKED			
TICKED SOFTLY INTO ONE.	THE ROSE DID CAPER ON	208	16
WHEN EVERYTHING THAT TICKED--HAS STOPPED--	IT WAS NOT DEATH, FOR I	510	17
TICKET			
TO WHICH WITHOUT A TICKET GO	SOME ONE PREPARED THIS	1644	2
TICKETS			
TICKETS ADMIT	UNIT, LIKE DEATH, FOR	408	6
OF TICKETS FOR A SIGH	ENDANGER IT, AND THE	1658	2
TICKING			
STOPPED--STRUCK--MY TICKING--THROUGH--	I TIE MY HAT--I CREASE	443	12
TIDE			
A SAILING O'ER THE TIDE,	"SIC TRANSIT GLORIA	3	38
MY FOOT IS ON THE TIDE!	MY WHEEL IS IN THE DARK!	10	5
DAY'S DEPARTING TIDE--	SO HAS A DAISY VANISHED	28	6
I HEARD RECEDE THE DISAPPOINTED TIDE!	JUST LOST, WHEN I WAS	160	6
TILL SUNDOWN CREPT--A STEADY TIDE--	FROM COCOON FORTH A	354	22
BUT NO MAN MOVED ME--TILL THE TIDE	I STARTED EARLY--TOOK MY	520	9
ABOVE OBLIVION'S TIDE THERE IS A PIER	ABOVE OBLIVION'S TIDE	1531	1
OR SCHEDULE OF THE TIDE--	DOWN TIME'S QUAINT	1656	10
TIDE'S			
WHEN THE TIDE'S A' LULL--	MANY A PHRASE HAS THE	276	6
TIDES			
HERSELF ADJUST HER TIDES--UNTO--	I COULD SUFFICE FOR HIM,	643	15
HIS TIDES--DO I CONTROL--	I MAKE HIS CRESCENT FILL	909	4
TO WALK ON SEAS [TIDES] REQUIRES CEDAR FEET	THERE IS A STRENGTH IN	1113	6
LIKE TIDES WITHIN THE SEA	THE SPIRIT LASTS--BUT IN	1576	10
IS SUMMONED BY THE TIDES.	EACH THAT WE LOSE TAKES	1605	4
TIDINGS			
THE FLYING TIDINGS TOLD--	THERE CAME A WIND LIKE A	1593	14
WHAT ANSWER [TIDINGS] WREST FROM THEE	STILL OWN THEE--STILL	1633	6
TIDY			
THE TIDY BREEZES, WITH THEIR BROOMS--	A LADY RED--AMID THE	74	5
TIE			
UNWIND THE SOLEMN TWINE, AND TIE MY VALENTINE!	AWAKE YE MUSES NINE,	1	2
OR TIE HIM TO A PIN	IS IT TRUE, DEAR SUE?	218	7
TIE THE STRINGS TO MY LIFE, MY LORD,	TIE THE STRINGS TO MY	279	1
I TIE MY HAT--I CREASE MY SHAWL--	I TIE MY HAT--I CREASE	443	1
MY BONNET BUT TO TIE	I SING TO USE THE	850	2
IT WAS A LITTLE TIE--	I'VE NONE TO TELL ME TO	881	3
SNATCH IT FOR [COVET IT / TIE IT FOR / SEIZE IT FOR / SUMMON . . .	SUMMER LAID HER SIMPLE	1363	4
NOR TIE TO EARTHS TO COME--	I HAVE NO LIFE BUT THIS	1398	5
NOR TRY TO TIE THE BUTTERFLY,	GO NOT TOO NEAR A HOUSE	1434	5

	FIRST LINE	POEM	LINE
TIED			
SHE TIED THE HOODS TO SEEDS--	MY FIRST WELL DAY--SINCE	574	18
SOME UNSUSPECTING HORSE WAS TIED	HOW MANY SCHEMES MAY DIE	1150	12
THE SILENCE TIED	LIKE BROOMS OF STEEL	1252	8
THE LIFE THAT TIED TOO TIGHT ESCAPES	THE LIFE THAT TIED TOO	1535	1
I TIED HIM--TOO	IN WINTER IN MY ROOM	1670	19
TIER			
AS ON THE TIER [ROW] OF WALL	WHAT CARE THE DEAD, FOR	592	6
TIGER			
A DYING TIGER--MOANED FOR DRINK--	A DYING TIGER--MOANED	566	1
AS THE TIGER EASED	AS THE STARVED MAELSTROM	872	4
TIGHT			
BUT WE BOLT THE DOOR TIGHT	WE DONT CRY--TIM AND I,	196	3
CLUTCHED TIGHT, BY GREEDY HANDS--	THERE CAME A DAY AT	322	18
SEALED SO STATELY TIGHT--	SWEET--SAFE--HOUSES--	457	3
TIGHT FITTING--ORANGE--BROWN--	YOU'LL KNOW HER--BY HER	634	10
WHO TIGHT IN DUNGEONS ARE.	COULD I BUT RIDE	661	18
THE DAY GREW SMALL, SURROUNDED TIGHT	THE DAY GREW SMALL,	1140	1
THE LIFE THAT TIED TOO TIGHT ESCAPES	THE LIFE THAT TIED TOO	1535	1
THE RUMOR'S GATE WAS SHUT SO TIGHT	THE SPIRIT LASTS--BUT IN	1576	21
WHOSE RUMOR'S GATE WAS SHUT SO TIGHT	EXPANSE CANNOT BE LOST--	1584	5
THE RUMOR'S GATE WAS SHUT SO TIGHT	THIS ME--THAT WALKS AND	1588	5
WAS TIGHT AND SURLY DRAWN	A CAP OF LEAD ACROSS THE	1649	2
TIGHTENING			
THE TIGHTENING THE SOIL AROUND	YOU CANNOT MAKE	1508	3
TIGHTENS			
MY COCOON TIGHTENS--COLORS TEAZE--	MY COCOON TIGHTENS--	1099	1
TIGHTER			
I HELD HER HAND THE TIGHTER--	ONE SISTER HAVE I IN OUR	14	15
WITHOUT A TIGHTER BREATHING	A NARROW FELLOW IN THE	986	23
WE CLUTCH THE GRACE THE TIGHTER	LIKE TIME'S INSIDIOUS	1236	3
TIGHTEST			
PUT ME IN ON THE FIRMEST [TIGHTEST / HIGHEST] SIDE--	TIE THE STRINGS TO MY	279	5
THE COLD WILL FORCE YOUR TIGHTEST DOOR	ALTHOUGH I PUT AWAY HIS	366	26
TILL			
THE CROCUS--TILL SHE RISES	THE FEET OF PEOPLE	7	3
TILL BYE AND BYE THESE BARGEMEN	THE FEET OF PEOPLE	7	7
AND REVEL TILL THE DAY--	THERE IS A MORN BY MEN	24	18
TILL--THE EVENING NEARING	MORNS LIKE THESE--WE	27	9
I COUNTED TILL THEY DANCED SO	I COUNTED TILL THEY	36	1
DELAYED TILL SHE HAD CEASED TO KNOW--	DELAYED TILL SHE HAD	58	1
DELAYED TILL IN IT'S VEST OF SNOW	DELAYED TILL SHE HAD	58	2
TILL MORNING TOUCHING MOUNTAIN--	A LITTLE EAST OF JORDAN,	59	5
TILL SOME ODD AFTERNOON	OUR LIVES ARE SWISS--	80	3
SO BREATHLESS TILL I PASSED HER--	SO BASHFUL WHEN I SPIED	91	5
PATIENT TILL PARADISE.	MY NOSEGAYS ARE FOR	95	4
TILL, RECENTLY A RIVAL CLAIM	I HAD SOME THINGS THAT I	116	3
TILL RANKS OF SEEDS THEIR WITNESS BEAR--	THESE ARE THE DAYS WHEN	130	10
SHE BORE IT TILL THE SIMPLE VEINS	SHE BORE IT TILL THE	144	1
TILL PLEADING, ROUND HER QUIET EYES	SHE BORE IT TILL THE	144	3
TILL DAFFODILS HAD COME AND GONE	SHE BORE IT TILL THE	144	5
TILL THE PAGEANT BY,	MUTE THY CORONATION--	151	6
WAIT TILL THE MAJESTY OF DEATH	WAIT TILL THE MAJESTY OF	171	1
WAIT TILL IN EVERLASTING ROBES	WAIT TILL THE MAJESTY OF	171	5
FROM WHAT W'D LAST TILL HEADS LIKE MINE	I CAUTIOUS, SCANNED MY	178	3
TILL OPPOSITE--I SPIED A CHEEK	THE ROSE DID CAPER ON	208	9
TILL THOSE TWO TROUBLED--LITTLE CLOCKS	THE ROSE DID CAPER ON	208	15
TILL SERAPHS SWING THEIR SNOWY HATS--	I TASTE A LIQUOR NEVER	214	13
TILL MINE TOO HEAVY GREW--	SAVIOR! I'VE NO ONE ELSE	217	10
TILL I GOT IN--	IS IT TRUE, DEAR SUE?	218	8
TILL BROOMS FADE SOFTLY INTO STARS--	SHE SWEEPS WITH	219	11
TILL DUSK OBSTRUCTS THE DILIGENCE--	SHE SWEEPS WITH	219	V 11
TILL HAIR--AND EYES--AND TIMID HEAD--	I THINK JUST HOW MY	237	3
TILL WEIGHTS--WILL HANG--	I CAN WADE GRIEF--	252	12
TILL WE--ARE STOUTER--	READ--SWEET--HOW OTHERS	260	2
TILL WE--ARE LESS AFRAID--	READ--SWEET--HOW OTHERS	260	4
TILL WE--ARE HELPED--	READ--SWEET--HOW OTHERS	260	6
STRAIN TILL YOUR [HER] LAST SURMISE--	DOUBT ME! MY DIM	275	19
TILL I STIR [GROPE / START], AND WEEP--	MANY A PHRASE HAS THE	276	12
KEPT TREADING--TREADING--TILL IT SEEMED	I FELT A FUNERAL, IN MY	280	3
KEPT BEATING--BEATING--TILL I THOUGHT	I FELT A FUNERAL, IN MY	280	7
TILL I TAKE VASTER ATTITUDES [MANNERS]--	OF BRONZE--AND BLAZE--	290	10
TILL THE BALL IS FULL--	HOW THE OLD MOUNTAINS	291	6
TILL THE HOUSES BLOT	HOW THE OLD MOUNTAINS	291	14
TILL GOD'S FULL TIME [WHOLE--WILL]--	UNTO LIKE STORY--TROUBLE	295	6
TILL BROAD AS BUENOS AYRE--	YOUR RICHES--TAUGHT ME--	299	4
ELATE US--TILL WE ALMOST WEEP--	LIKE SOME OLD FASHIONED	302	11
THE DAY CAME SLOW--TILL FIVE O'CLOCK--	THE DAY CAME SLOW--TILL	304	1
TILL IT IS LOST IN FLEECES--	IT SIFTS FROM LEADEN	311	11
TILL WHEN THEY REACHED THE OTHER SIDE,	I'LL TELL YOU HOW THE	318	13
TILL QUALIFIED, FOR PEARL--	WE PLAY AT PASTE--	320	2
TILL I WAS OUT OF SIGHT, IN SOUND,	I CANNOT DANCE UPON MY	326	15
WE STIPULATE--TILL PITYING SNOWS	'TIS NOT THAT DYING	335	11
TILL SUMMER FOLDS HER MIRACLE--	IT WILL BE SUMMER--	342	17
TILL THAT FIRST SHOUT GOT BY--	I DREADED THAT FIRST	348	6
TILL SUNDOWN CREPT--A STEADY TIDE--	FROM COCOON FORTH, A	354	22
TILL THEY ARE ORDERLY AS BUSTS--	A VISITOR IN MARL--	391	3
I'D TUNNEL--TILL MY GROOVE	I HAD NOT MINDED--WALLS	398	5
IN WINTER--TILL THE SUN--	THE COLOR OF THE GRAVE	411	12

TILL (CONTINUED)

	FIRST LINE	POEM	LINE
TILL I GET ACCUSTOMED--BUT THEN THE TOMB	IT DONT SOUND SO	426	11
TILL IN PURER DRESS--	TAKING UP THE FAIR IDEAL	428	10
TILL THE BROKEN CREATURES--	TAKING UP THE FAIR IDEAL	428	13
THE TIME 'TWILL BE TILL SIX O'CLOCK	I TIE MY HAT--I CREASE	443	9
TILL IT BE NIGHT--NO MORE--	A NIGHT--THERE LAY THE	471	8
TILL EVERY SPICE IS TASTED--	WITHIN MY GARDEN, RIDES	500	9
SUBTRACTING, TILL MY FINGERS DROPPED	IF YOU WERE COMING IN	511	11
TILL ALL THE SCENE--BE GONE.	'TWAS WARM--AT FIRST--	519	4
BUT NO MAN MOVED ME--TILL THE TIDE	I STARTED EARLY--TOOK MY	520	9
TILL THEY--THE CHERISHING DENY--	ENDOW THE LIVING--WITH	521	7
TILL HE BE JUSTIFIED BY DEATH--	HAD I PRESUMED TO HOPE--	522	15
TILL RAPTURE MISSED THEM [HER FOOTING-- / PENINSULA]	TWO BUTTERFLIES WENT OUT	533	V
TILL GRAVITATION CHASED [HUMBLED / EJECTED / FOUNDERED / . . .	TWO BUTTERFLIES WENT OUT	533	V
TILL ACCLIMATED--TO--	THE PROVINCE OF THE	539	12
THAT TILL I LOVED	THAT I DID ALWAYS LOVE	549	3
I CROSS TILL I AM WEARY	I CROSS TILL I AM WEARY	550	1
WHEN [TILL] GENOA--WITHDREW	TRUST IN THE UNEXPECTED	555	10
TILL I COULD TAKE THE [CATCH MY] BALANCE	I PRAYED, AT FIRST, A	576	18
BUT TILL THE MERCHANT BUY--	I GAVE MYSELF TO HIM--	580	10
TILL BULLETS CLIPT AN ANGLE	WHEN I WAS SMALL, A	596	7
TILL [WHERE] ALGEBRA IS EASIER--	IT TROUBLED ME AS ONCE I	600	11
TILL MY SMALL LIBRARY--	UNTO MY BOOKS--SO GOOD	604	8
THEMSELF--HAD JUST REMAINED TILL WE REJOIN THEM--	OF NEARNESS TO HER	607	18
AND WAYS I KNEW NOT THAT I KNEW--TILL THEN--	I ROSE--BECAUSE HE SANK	616	22
TILL THEN--DREAMING [DEEMING] I AM SOWING	DONT PUT UP MY THREAD &	617	17
TILL THE CHILDREN URGE [ASK]--	GLEE--THE GREAT STORM IS	619	11
TILL LOVE THAT WAS--AND LOVE TOO BEST TO BE--	TO KNOW JUST HOW HE	622	25
COULD WIDEN--TILL TO ME	I THINK TO LIVE--MAY BE	646	6
TILL ALL THE GRIEF WITH SUMMER--WAVED [BLEW]	'TIS GOOD--THE LOOKING	660	7
TILL HE SHOULD JUMP PENINSULAS	COULD I BUT RIDE	661	11
TILL THESE FAINT TABERNACLES DROP	THE HEAVEN VESTS FOR	694	7
TILL ONE BREADTH COVER TWO--	THE SUNRISE RUNS FOR	710	5
TILL BOTH--CAN SEE--	THE SUNRISE RUNS FOR	710	12
TILL NUMBER'S EMPERY--	PRECIOUS TO ME--SHE	727	11
IN CORNERS--TILL A DAY	MY LIFE HAD STOOD--A	754	2
TO HAUNT--TILL TIME HAVE DROPPED	JOY TO HAVE MERITED THE	788	21
TILL NATURE LEISURE HAS FOR TERMS	THE VEINS OF OTHER	811	3
TILL FOR A FURTHER FOOD	THE LUXURY TO APPREHEND	815	6
WHO TILL THEY DIED, DID NOT ALIVE BECOME--	A DEATH BLOW IS A LIFE	816	2
TILL YOU HAD TASTED FIRST,	I COULD NOT DRINK IT,	818	2
IN IT WAIT TILL JUDGMENT BREAK	AMPLE MAKE THIS BED--	829	3
TILL HIS BEST STEP APPROACHING	I SING TO USE THE	850	5
TILL HE MEET A MAN	AS THE STARVED MAELSTROM	872	6
TILL HE ESTEEM HIS DATES AND COCOA	AS THE STARVED MAELSTROM	872	11
TILL RESURRECTION, I MUST GUESS	IT WAS A GRAVE, YET BORE	876	9
TILL IT AN ANTIQUE FASHION SHOWS--	WE OUTGROW LOVE, LIKE	887	3
TILL I AM FIRM IN HEAVEN	A CLOUD WITHDREW FROM	895	11
TILL I WHO WAS ALMOST BOLD	HOW HAPPY I WAS IF I	898	6
NOT TILL THE LAST WAS ANSWERED	WHAT DID THEY DO SINCE I	900	7
TILL DEATH--IS NARROW LOVING--	TILL DEATH--IS NARROW	907	1
WILL HOLD YOU TILL YOUR PRIVILEGE	TILL DEATH--IS NARROW	907	3
TILL THE INFINITE AURORA	STRUCK, WAS I, NOR YET	925	23
TILL HURRICANE BISECT	THE HEART HAS NARROW	928	5
TILL ALL THE WORLD IS AJAR--	NOON--IS THE HINGE OF	931	4
TILL MYSTERY IMPATIENT DREW	TWO TRAVELLERS PERISHING	933	13
TILL JEALOUS DAYLIGHT INTERRUPT--	WHAT I SEE NOT, I BETTER	939	11
TILL SUNRISE TAKE [CALL] US BACK TO SCENE--	I LEARNED--AT LEAST--	944	25
THAT BELLS SHOULD RING TILL ALL SHOULD KNOW [HEAR]	OF TOLLING BELL I ASK	947	5
HOLD ME TILL THE OCTAVE'S RUN!	DYING AT MY MUSIC!	1003	3
TILL SWOLLEN WITH THE SKY	HOW STILL THE BELLS IN	1008	2
ANOTHER, TILL A THING	I HEARD, AS IF I HAD NO	1039	6
AS, TILL THE BEE	SPRING COMES ON THE	1042	4
TILL OF ALL OUR NATURE'S HOUSE	AS WILLING LID O'ER	1050	3
WHOSE [WHERE] SUMMER SET IN SUMMER, TILL	THERE IS A ZONE WHOSE	1056	5
TILL SUDDEN I PERCEIVED IT STIR--	I HAD A DAILY BLISS	1057	3
TILL WHEN AROUND A HIGHT	I HAD A DAILY BLISS	1057	5
TILL IT DEPART, PERSUADING [CONVEYING] MINE--	AIR HAS NO RESIDENCE, NO	1060	8
SUBSIST TILL PARADISE.	SUPERIORITY TO FATE	1081	8
TILL WE, WHO SMILED AT PYRRHENEES--	WE MISS A KINSMAN MORE	1087	7
TILL I AM THOROUGH FIT.	I FIT FOR THEM--	1109	3
TILL WHAT WE SPECULATE, HAS BEEN	THE MURMURING OF BEES,	1115	13
TILL WHAT WE COULD NOT SEE [FACE / CHOOSE / PROVE] HAS COME . . .	THE MURMURING OF BEES,	1115	V 13
TILL ARRESTED [DISCOVERED] HERE	HAD WE KNOWN THE TON SHE	1124	V 4
THAT [TILL] I MAY [CAN] GLOAT ON THEE--	OH SUMPTUOUS MOMENT	1125	3
TILL I HAVE FINER [VAINER / FURTHER] TRIED--	SHALL I TAKE THEE, THE	1126	4
TILL ALL HER HELPLESS BEAUTY BENT	THE FROST OF DEATH WAS	1136	14
TELL--THIS DAY [TILL NOW] ENDURES	TELL AS A MARKSMAN--WERE	1152	2
TILL YOUR WRINKLED FINGER	ON THE WORLD YOU COLORED	1171	9
THE FORESTS GALLOPED TILL THEY FELL	THE CLOUDS THEIR BACKS	1172	3
TILL WE ARE ASKED [CALLED] TO RISE	WE NEVER KNOW HOW HIGH	1176	2
TILL EVERY CUBIT PLAY WITH THEE	MY GOD--HE SEES THEE--	1178	4
TILL SOME RETRIEVELESS NIGHT	THE FROST WAS NEVER SEEN	1202	9
HE PREACHED UPON [ABOUT] "BREADTH" TILL IT ARGUED HIM [WE . . .	HE PREACHED UPON	1207	1

	FIRST LINE	POEM	LINE
TILL (CONTINUED)			
TILL NATURE IN CHAGRIN	I BET WITH EVERY WIND	1215	2
TILL IT IS LAID WITHIN.	WHO GOES TO DINE MUST	1223	4
MY TRIUMPH LASTED TILL THE DRUMS	MY TRIUMPH LASTED TILL	1227	1
LIKE RAIN IT SOUNDED TILL IT CURVED [SWELLED]	LIKE RAIN IT SOUNDED	1235	1
AND TILL DOMINION SET .	THE MOST TRIUMPHANT BIRD	1265	3
INCREASED TILL I ABJURED IT .	ART THOU THE THING I	1282	7
TILL HUMAN NATURE CAME	I THOUGHT THAT NATURE	1286	2
TILL IT FELL,	NOT WITH A CLUB, THE	1304	6
THE MAPLES NEVER KNEW THAT YOU WERE COMING--TILL I CALLED	DEAR MARCH--COME IN--	1320	12
TILL SYNODS ARE [ZION IS] INORDINATE--	THE WORTHLESSNESS OF	1373	4
TILL RECTITUDE IS SUFFOCATE .	THE WORTHLESSNESS OF	1373	V 4
TILL WHEN THE RED DECLINED--	THESE HELD THEIR WICK	1390	2
TILL WITH THE SETTING [CLOSING] SUN	IT WAS A QUIET SEEMING	1419	3
WHEN [TILL] FLESH AND SPIRIT SUNDER	ONE JOY OF SO MUCH	1420	11
TILL POISING FOR A TURN	HOW SOFT A CATERPILLAR	1448	V
TILL THE SUGGESTION SINISTER	WHOEVER DISENCHANTS	1451	7
TILL TREASON LIGHTLY PROPAGATES	WHOEVER DISENCHANTS	1451	V 7
TILL CAVILER [PERJURY] INSINUATES .	WHOEVER DISENCHANTS	1451	V 7
TILL ASKED TO TAKE IT OFF-- .	WE KNEW NOT THAT WE WERE	1462	6
TILL SUMMONED TO HIS RECOGNITION	FACTS BY OUR SIDE ARE	1497	7
ADIEU FOR WHENCE [TILL WHEN]	FACTS BY OUR SIDE ARE	1497	9
TILL WHEN IT [AND THEN DOTH] SLIP AWAY	IT'S LITTLE ETHER HOOD	1501	5
I CLING TO NOWHERE TILL I FALL--	MORE THAN THE GRAVE IS	1503	4
TILL THEY HAD MOVED [COULD MOVE] A STONE-- .	A PANG IS MORE	1530	8
TILL YOU WASTE [FURL / LAME] YOUR EYE-- .	FOLLOW WISE ORION	1538	2
BUT CHOSE THE BEST--NEGLECTING ME--TILL .	MY WARS ARE LAID AWAY IN	1549	7
BEAUTY CROWDS ME TILL I DIE .	BEAUTY CROWDS ME TILL I	1654	1
TILL IN A DISTANT TOWN	IN WINTER IN MY ROOM	1670	36
TILL SAFFRON IN VERMILLION SLID	OF YELLOW WAS THE OUTER	1676	3
TILL IT IS OUT OF GAZE.	LOVE CAN DO ALL BUT	1731	8
TILL LABORING TO FLEE .	NO MAN SAW AWE, NOR TO	1733	6
TILL MY MINUTEST DOWER,	OH, HONEY OF AN HOUR,	1734	4
PROUD OF THE PAIN I DID NOT FEEL TILL THEE,	PROUD OF MY BROKEN HEART	1736	2
FOR I WEAR THE "THORNS" TILL SUNSET--	REARRANGE A "WIFE'S"	1737	15
TILL THE DAY ITS WEARY KEEPER	REARRANGE A "WIFE'S"	1737	19
TILL EVERLASTING LIFE [RITE] UNITE	THE GRAVE MY LITTLE	1743	7
TILL ALL THE CHURCHYARD RANG;	A TRAIN WENT THROUGH A	1761	4
TILLAGE			
WHOSE TILLAGE [PASTURE] IS THE PASSING [WANDERING] CRUMB--	THOSE CATTLE SMALLER	1388	3
TILLED			
SOIL OF FLINT, IF STEADY [STEADFAST] TILLED--	SOIL OF FLINT, IF STEADY	681	1
TILLING			
WHO FOR TILLING--TO THE MOUNTAIN	BLOOM UPON THE MOUNTAIN	667	9
THAT TILLING IT'S ABYSS, .	I NEVER HEAR THAT ONE IS	1323	6
TILTS			
WHILE HE, VICTORIOUS TILTS AWAY	LIKE TRAINS OF CARS ON	1224	7
TIM			
WE DONT CRY--TIM AND I,	WE DONT CRY--TIM AND I,	196	1
NOT TO CRY--TIM AND I--	WE DONT CRY--TIM AND I,	196	7
TIM--SEE COTTAGES--	WE DONT CRY--TIM AND I,	196	13
THEN--WE SHAKE--TIM AND I-- .	WE DONT CRY--TIM AND I,	196	15
TIM--READS A LITTLE HYMN--	WE DONT CRY--TIM AND I,	196	17
PLEASE, SIR, I AND TIM-- .	WE DONT CRY--TIM AND I,	196	19
TIM--SHALL--IF I--DO--	WE DONT CRY--TIM AND I,	196	23
TIM--WAS--SO--SHY? .	WE DONT CRY--TIM AND I,	196	26
I--"TIM"--AND--ME! .	WE DONT CRY--TIM AND I,	196	28
TIMBERS			
IN FALLING [CRASHING] TIMBERS BURIED--	IN FALLING TIMBERS	614	1
TIMBRELS			
THE HAPPY WINDS--THEIR TIMBRELS TOOK--	THE DAY CAME SLOW--TILL	304	9
TIMBUCTOO			
THAN DAWN IN [ON] TIMBUCTOO.	AS SLEIGH BELLS SEEM IN	981	8
TIME SEE SUMMERTIME			
AND SEIZE THE ONE THOU LOVEST, NOR CARE FOR SPACE, OR TIME!	AWAKE YE MUSES NINE,	1	36
TIME BROUGHT ME OTHER ROBINS-- .	I HAD A GUINEA GOLDEN--	23	13
AND TIME SH'D GURGLE ON--	IF I SHOULD DIE,	54	3
ALLUDED TO NO TIME .	WENT UP A YEAR THIS	93	10
TELL ME WHAT TIME THE WEAVER SLEEPS	BRING ME THE SUNSET IN A	128	5
LAMBS FOR WHOM TIME HAD NOT A FOLD.	SOME, TOO FRAGILE FOR	141	12
NEXT TIME, TO STAY!	JUST LOST, WHEN I WAS	160	12
NEXT TIME, THE THINGS TO SEE	JUST LOST, WHEN I WAS	160	13
NEXT TIME, TO TARRY,	JUST LOST, WHEN I WAS	160	16
GROWN TAWNY NOW, WITH TIME--	IN EBON BOX, WHEN YEARS	169	6
I SHALL KNOW WHY--WHEN TIME IS OVER--	I SHALL KNOW WHY--WHEN	193	1
HAD GONE TO SLEEP--THAT SOUNDEST TIME-- .	TO DIE--TAKES JUST A	255	11
JUST ONE TIME! .	DID WE DISOBEY HIM?	267	2
TILL GOD'S FULL TIME [WHOLE--WILL]-- .	UNTO LIKE STORY--TROUBLE	295	6
ALTHO' I PROVE IT, JUST IN TIME	YOUR RICHES--TAUGHT ME--	299	27
THE HOMELIER TIME BEHIND.	I SHOULD HAVE BEEN TOO	313	6
YOUR BREATH HAS TIME [CHANCE] TO STRAIGHTEN--	HE FUMBLES AT YOUR SOUL	315	9
IT WILL BE AMPLE TIME FOR--ME--	JUST SO--JESUS--RAPS--	317	9
A RIBBON AT A TIME--	I'LL TELL YOU HOW THE	318	2
THE TIME WAS SCARCE PROFANED, BY SPEECH--	THERE CAME A DAY AT	322	9
PERMITTED TO COMMUNE THIS--TIME-- .	THERE CAME A DAY AT	322	14
AND SO WHEN ALL THE TIME HAD LEAKED [FAILED]--	THERE CAME A DAY AT	322	21
WHEN I GO OUT OF TIME--	THE FACE I CARRY WITH ME	336	2

TIME (CONTINUED)

	FIRST LINE	POEM	LINE
IT'S TIME TO SMOOTH THE HAIR--	WHEN NIGHT IS ALMOST	347	4
SO--WHEN 'TWAS TIME TO SEE--	I DREADED THAT FIRST	348	14
THAT--WAS A FORMER TIME--	I FELT MY LIFE WITH BOTH	351	14
THAT EVERY TIME I WAKE--	THE ANGLE OF A LANDSCAPE	375	2
AND THEN--IT'S TIME TO STRIKE MY TENT--	THE WINTERS ARE SO SHORT	403	7
THE CHIEFER PART, FOR TIME--	SOME--WORK FOR	406	2
BECAUSE IT'S SUNDAY--ALL THE TIME--	I NEVER FELT AT HOME--	413	5
THE TIME 'TWILL BE TILL SIX O'CLOCK	I TIE MY HAT--I CREASE	443	9
'TWAS JUST THIS TIME, LAST YEAR, I DIED.	'TWAS JUST THIS TIME,	445	1
HOW JUST THIS TIME, SOME PERFECT YEAR--	'TWAS JUST THIS TIME,	445	23
EXTERIOR--TO TIME--	THIS WAS A POET--IT IS	448	16
TAUGHT ME--BY TIME--THE LOWER WAY--	I LIVE WITH HIM--I SEE	463	13
I HAD NO TIME TO HATE--	I HAD NO TIME TO HATE--	478	1
NOR HAD I TIME TO LOVE--	I HAD NO TIME TO HATE--	478	7
AN UNPRETENDING TIME	MYSELF WAS FORMED--A	488	2
AS FAR FROM TIME--AS HISTORY--	AS FAR FROM PITY, AS	496	5
NO ONE COULD PLAY IT--THE SECOND TIME--	BETTER--THAN MUSIC! FOR	503	6
BUT THIS TIME, CONSCIOUSLY, OF GRACE--	I'M CEDED--I'VE STOPPED	508	9
BUT THIS TIME--ADEQUATE--ERECT,	I'M CEDED--I'VE STOPPED	508	17
AT SUCH AND SUCH A TIME--	IF ANYBODY'S FRIEND BE	509	4
EVERY TIME--FOR TWO--	SWEET--YOU FORGOT--BUT I	523	2
IT'S TIME O' YEAR FOR HAY.	I'M SORRY FOR THE DEAD--	529	4
MISTAKE DEFEAT FOR DEATH--EACH TIME--	THE PROVINCE OF THE	539	11
A DIMPLE AT A TIME--	IT KNEW NO MEDICINE--	559	6
EACH TIME MY CHILDISH EYE	I PRAYED, AT FIRST, A	576	6
THAT TIME--TO TAKE IT HOME--	HE FOUND MY BEING--SET	603	8
SO SPICES--STIMULATE THE TIME	UNTO MY BOOKS--SO GOOD	604	7
'TIS NOT A DIFFERENT TIME--	FOREVER--IS COMPOSED OF	624	2
'TWAS A LONG PARTING--BUT THE TIME	'TWAS A LONG PARTING--	625	1
THE LAST--AND SECOND TIME	'TWAS A LONG PARTING--	625	4
IT SEEMS AS THOUGH THE TIME	I THINK THE LONGEST HOUR	635	4
BETWEEN ETERNITY AND TIME--	YOU LEFT ME--SIRE--TWO	644	7
HER POLAR TIME--BEHIND--	I THINK TO LIVE--MAY BE	646	20
A TIME [DAY] WHEN IT WAS NOT--	PAIN--HAS AN ELEMENT OF	650	4
FIRST TIME THEY TRY THE SKY!	AGAIN--HIS VOICE IS AT	663	23
THEY SAY THAT "TIME ASSUAGES"--	THEY SAY THAT "TIME	686	1
TIME NEVER DID ASSUAGE--	THEY SAY THAT "TIME	686	2
TIME IS A TEST OF TROUBLE--	THEY SAY THAT "TIME	686	5
THE SECOND TIME TO ME--	A THOUGHT WENT UP MY	701	6
THE BAREFOOT TIME FORGOTTEN--SO--	THE BEGGAR LAD--DIES	717	11
FOR JUST THIS SINGLE [THIS PECULIAR / JUST THIS ONLY] TIME--	I MEANT TO FIND HER WHEN	718	6
I HINTED CHANGES--LAPSE OF TIME--	IF HE WERE LIVING--DARE	734	5
TOWARD ARTIFICE OF TIME--OR MEN--	MY SOUL--ACCUSED ME--AND	753	6
AND EVERY TIME I SPEAK FOR HIM--	MY LIFE HAD STOOD--A	754	7
NONE STIR [HARM] THE SECOND TIME--	MY LIFE HAD STOOD--A	754	18
YOU CONSTITUTED TIME--	YOU CONSTITUTED TIME--	765	1
TO HAUNT--TILL TIME HAVE DROPPED	JOY TO HAVE MERITED THE	788	21
THIS TIME--BEYOND THE ESTIMATE [INFERENCE]	SHE STAKED HER FEATHERS	798	3
ETERNITY--OBTAINED--IN TIME--	TWO--WERE IMMORTAL TWICE	800	3
TIME FEELS SO VAST THAT WERE IT NOT	TIME FEELS SO VAST THAT	802	1
FOR WHOM, THE TIME DID NOT SUFFICE [REMAIN]	NO NOTICE GAVE SHE, BUT	804	3
TO LOOK AT THEE A SINGLE TIME	THE LUXURY TO APPREHEND	815	3
BEFORE HE COMES WE WEIGH THE TIME!	BEFORE HE COMES WE WEIGH	834	1
ON TIME	UNCERTAIN LEASE--	857	2
HE OUTSTRIPPED TIME WITH BUT A BOUT,	HE OUTSTRIPPED TIME WITH	865	1
WE ONLY KNOW WHAT TIME OF YEAR	FROM US SHE WANDERED NOW	890	7
THE ADMIRATIONS--AND CONTEMPTS--OF TIME--	THE ADMIRATIONS--AND	906	1
BACK--TOWARD TIME--	THE ADMIRATIONS--AND	906	14
THAT DULL--BENUMBING TIME	'TWAS CRISIS--ALL THE	948	2
A FULL, AND PERFECT TIME--	MIDSUMMER, WAS IT, WHEN	962	2
PAIN--EXPANDS THE TIME--	PAIN--EXPANDS THE TIME--	967	1
PAIN CONTRACTS--THE TIME--	PAIN--EXPANDS THE TIME--	967	5
TIME [TIME'S] TO ANTICIPATE HIS GAZE--	FITTER TO SEE HIM, I MAY	968	9
EVERY SECOND TIME--	HE WHO IN HIMSELF	969	6
A FRAIL [FLEET / BRIEF] ARISTOCRAT OF TIME	SHE SPED AS PETALS OF A	991	3
LEAVING AN ATTITUDE [A MAGNITUDE] ON TIME	SHE SPED AS PETALS OF A	991	V 5
AND TIME WENT OUT TO TELL THE NEWS	I HEARD, AS IF I HAD NO	1039	15
A PITTANCE AT A TIME	SUPERIORITY TO FATE	1081	5
IT WAS A NARROW TIME--	THE LAST NIGHT THAT SHE	1100	18
WE DO NOT KNOW THE TIME WE LOSE--	WE DO NOT KNOW THE TIME	1106	1
REBUILT ANOTHER MORNING [IN TIME NEXT MORNING / WITHOUT . . .	THE LARGEST FIRE EVER	1114	7
RETURNS US NOT, BUT AFTER TIME	EXHILIRATION IS THE	1118	5
TIME DOES GO ON--	TIME DOES GO ON--	1121	1
THAT COMES A SINGLE TIME A YEAR	THE SNOW THAT NEVER	1133	3
A PAST [TIME / STATE] OF PLANK AND NAIL	THE PROPS ASSIST THE	1142	10
THAT LARCENY OF TIME AND MIND	ALONE AND IN A	1167	25
BY THE TIME THAT MAN AND BEAST	THERE'S THE BATTLE OF	1174	3
WE LET GO ALL OF TIME WITHOUT	THE DAYS THAT WE CAN	1184	7
HER MARTIAL DAY [TIME] FORGOT	A LITTLE DOG THAT WAGS	1185	10
BUT WHEN IT LEAVES US FOR A TIME	IMMORTAL IS AN AMPLE	1205	3
THAN TIME ENSUE TO BE--	WHO WERE "THE FATHER AND	1258	16
BUT PLOTTED WITH TIME TO DISPUTE--	I SAW THAT THE FLAKE WAS	1267	2
KEEPS ESOTERIC TIME	'TWAS LATER WHEN THE	1276	8
THE INFAMY OF TIME--	THE HARM OF YEARS IS ON	1280	2
OF THE THEFTS OF TIME--	DEATH'S WAYLAYING NOT	1296	2
GOOD FRIENDS WITH TIME	AN ANTIQUATED GRACE	1345	6
THE LAST [CLOSE] OF SUMMER IS DELIGHT--[A	THE LAST OF SUMMER IS	1353	1

	FIRST LINE	POEM		LINE
TIME (CONTINUED)				
TIME / RESULT--SURVEY]				
I SUPPOSE THE TIME WILL COME	I SUPPOSE THE TIME WILL	1381		1
I SUPPOSE THE TIME WILL COME	I SUPPOSE THE TIME WILL	1381		5
TO SEE IF TIME WAS [WERE] THERE--	IT SOUNDED AS IF THE	1397		6
LIKE LOOKING EVERY TIME YOU PLEASE	WHAT MYSTERY PERVADES A	1400		7
BUT TIME HAD ADDED NOT OBTAINED	A LITTLE SNOW WAS HERE	1444		5
THEY COME A SINGLE TIME	YOUR THOUGHTS DONT HAVE	1452		2
TIME COMPASSION TOOK--	WE TALKED WITH EACH	1473		6
WHO FINDS IT EVERY TIME	HOW DESTITUTE IS HE	1477		3
LOOK BACK ON TIME, WITH KINDLY EYES--	LOOK BACK ON TIME, WITH	1478		1
A NOTHING AT A TIME--	IT'S LITTLE ETHER HOOD	1501		6
A SINGLE [ROYAL / SIGNAL / HALLOWED] TIME	TO BE FORGOT BY THEE	1560		9
THE SAGEST [ONLY] TIME TO DAM THE SEA IS WHEN THE SEA IS GONE--	WE SEND THE WAVE TO FIND	1604		7
A CLOVER, ANY TIME, TO HIM,	THE PEDIGREE OF HONEY	1627	V	3
THE SECOND TIME IS SET	FAME IS A FICKLE FOOD	1659		5
THAT TIME I FLEW	IN WINTER IN MY ROOM	1670		32
A LAVA STEP AT ANY TIME	VOLCANOES BE IN SICILY	1705		5
FIRST TIME TOGETHER THROWN.	A FACE DEVOID OF LOVE OR	1711		6
THE SOUL THERE--ALL THE TIME.	IF EVER THE LID GETS OFF	1727		8
WHO HAD SO LITTLE TIME	WERE NATURE MORTAL LADY	1762		2
TOO HAPPY TIME DISSOLVES ITSELF	TOO HAPPY TIME DISSOLVES	1774		1
TIME'S				
TIME'S SUBLIMEST TARGET	THERE IS A WORD	8		17
WHEN TIME'S BRIEF MASQUERADE WAS DONE	"ARCTURUS" IS HIS OTHER	70		20
ON TIME'S FIRST AFTERNOON!	MUSICIANS WRESTLE	157		12
TIME'S POSSIBILITY.	I HAD THE GLORY--THAT	349		7
TIME [TIME'S] TO ANTICIPATE HIS GAZE--	FITTER TO SEE HIM, I MAY	968		9
THESE--ARE TIME'S AFFAIR--	COLOR--CASTE--	970		2
LIKE TIME'S INSIDIOUS [INVADING / PRESUMING / APPOINTED / . . .	LIKE TIME'S INSIDIOUS	1236		1
TO TIME'S ANALYSIS--	THE LILAC IS AN ANCIENT	1241		16
TIME'S WILY CHARGERS WILL NOT WAIT	TIME'S WILY CHARGERS	1458		1
TIME'S DECISION SHOOK--	WE TALKED WITH EACH	1473	V	6
DOWN TIME'S QUAINT STREAM	DOWN TIME'S QUAINT	1656		1
SOFTENED BY TIME'S CONSUMMATE PLUSH,	SOFTENED BY TIME'S	1738		1
TIMES				
HOW MANY TIMES THESE LOW FEET STAGGERED--	HOW MANY TIMES THESE LOW	187		1
HOW MANY TIMES IT ACHE FOR ME--TODAY--CONFESS--	YOU SEE I CANNOT SEE--	253		3
HOW MANY TIMES FOR MY FAR SAKE	YOU SEE I CANNOT SEE--	253		4
HOW MANY TIMES THEY--BORE THE FAITHFUL WITNESS--	READ--SWEET--HOW OTHERS	260		5
BUT THE ONES WHO OVERCAME MOST TIMES--	OF TRIBULATION--THESE	325		6
TO TIMES WHEN HE--WAS YOUNG--	A PRECIOUS--MOULDERING	371		8
IT'S SUCH CONGENIAL TIMES [WAY]	I'M SORRY FOR THE DEAD--	529		2
AT THOSE OLD TIMES--IN CALVARY.	IF I MAY HAVE IT, WHEN	577		25
THREE TIMES--WE PARTED--BREATH--AND I--	THREE TIMES--WE PARTED--	598		1
THREE TIMES--HE WOULD NOT GO--	THREE TIMES--WE PARTED--	598		2
THREE TIMES--THE BILLOWS THREW [TOSSED] ME UP--	THREE TIMES--WE PARTED--	598		5
THE SOUL HAS SPECIAL TIMES--	OF NEARNESS TO HER	607		2
YOU CHOSE THE NEWER NAMES [TIMES]--	YOU'LL FIND--IT WHEN YOU	610		8
I MANY TIMES THOUGHT PEACE HAD COME	I MANY TIMES THOUGHT	739		1
"A THOUSAND TIMES THEE NAY."	SAID DEATH TO PASSION	1033		4
AT TIMES TO MAJESTY.	THE WAY TO KNOW THE	1279		8
UNKNOWN--FOR ALL THE TIMES WE MET--	WITHOUT A SMILE--WITHOUT	1330		4
I TAUGHT MY HEART A HUNDRED TIMES	I THOUGHT THE TRAIN	1449		5
AND WINDS DO GO THAT WAY AT NOON [TIMES]	TALK NOT TO ME OF SUMMER	1634		5
THREE TIMES, 'TIS SAID, A SINKING MAN	DROWNING IS NOT SO	1718		3
TIMID				
HURRIES A TIMID LEAF.	THESE ARE THE DAYS WHEN	130		12
WHEREFORE IN TIMID QUEST	FOR EVERY BIRD A NEST--	143		2
NO MORE HER TIMID BONNET	SHE BORE IT TILL THE	144		11
TILL HAIR--AND EYES--AND TIMID HEAD--	I THINK JUST HOW MY	237		3
TIMID AS A BIRD!	WHY--DO THEY SHUT ME OUT	248		4
A TIMID [HALLOWED] THING--TO DROP A LIFE	A SOLEMN THING--IT WAS--	271		5
THEN LIKE A TIMID MAN	THE WIND--TAPPED LIKE A	436		18
IN SOLEMN [TIMID] HONESTY	THE BODY GROWS WITHOUT--	578		8
THEN I--MY TIMID SERVICE DONE--	I THINK THE LONGEST HOUR	635		13
THIS TIMID LIFE OF EVIDENCE	THEIR HIGHT IN HEAVEN	696		15
NOR HEARD THE TIMID CRY FOR "BREAD"--	THE BEGGAR LAD--DIES	717		7
THE FLOWERS--APPEALED--A TIMID THRONG--	THE BIRDS REPORTED FROM	743		5
INCITE THE TIMID PRAYER	NATURE--THE GENTLEST	790		14
DROPPED--MY FATE--A TIMID PEBBLE--	ALL FORGOT FOR	966		13
GO TIMID, LEST [SHOULD] HIS FINAL [TESTING / BLAZING / LOFTY] EYE	GO SLOW, MY SOUL, TO	1297		5
WAS ALL OUR TIMID MOTHER WORE	LET ME NOT MAR THAT	1335		7
ACCOSTED BY A TIMID BIRD	A FIELD OF STUBBLE,	1407		5
IN TIMID AND TUMULTUOUS SOIL	THE FASCINATING CHILL	1480		5
IT IS A TIMID BULWARK	I SAW THE WIND WITHIN	1502	V	
HER TONGUE MORE TENDER [TIMID / MAGIC] THAN THE TUNE [TONE]	HER FACE WAS IN A BED OF	1722		5
TIMIDITY				
AND DOES NO TIMIDITY BETRAY	WHAT MYSTERY PERVADES A	1400		16
TIMIDLY				
DWELL TIMIDLY, WITH THEE!	DOUBT ME! MY DIM	275		17
ATTEMPTED TO [DID TIMIDLY] EXPOUND	WE LEARNED THE WHOLE OF	568		9

	FIRST LINE	POEM	LINE
TIMIDNESS			
MY TIMIDNESS ENFOLDS--	YOU SEE I CANNOT SEE--	253	11
TINCTURE			
A CHANCE'S FAINTEST TINCTURE	IMPOSSIBILITY, LIKE WINE	838	5
TINCTURED			
IS TINCTURED [GILDED] FOR AN INSTANT	TO DISAPPEAR ENHANCES--	1209	3
TINDER			
AND SMITES THE TINDER IN THE SUN--	THE LOVE A LIFE CAN SHOW	673	5
AND TINDER--GUESSED--BY POWER	THE ZEROES--TAUGHT US--	689	4
TINGE			
BUT WITH A TINGE OF THAT--	TO THIS WORLD SHE	830	2
TINGLES			
THE CARMINE--TINGLES WARM--	I AM ALIVE--I GUESS--	470	5
IT TINGLES IN THE MIND	WE LIKE A HAIRBREADTH	1175	2
TINSEL			
HOW THE DUN BRAKE IS DRAPED IN CINDER [TIPPED IN TINSEL]	HOW THE OLD MOUNTAINS	291	3
WE AND OUR PLOTTING HEART [GAUDY HEART / SCHEMING TINSEL / . . .	AN ANTIQUATED GRACE	1345	5
GLASS WAS THE STREET--IN TINSEL PERIL	GLASS WAS THE STREET--IN	1498	1
TINT			
LO, A TINT CASHMERE!	ARTISTS WRESTLED HERE!	110	2
OF A TINT SO LUSTROUS MEEK--	PIGMY SERAPHS--GONE	138	8
GERANIUMS--TINT--AND SPOT--	I TEND MY FLOWERS FOR	339	5
WILL TINT THE PALLID LANDSCAPE--	IT WILL BE SUMMER--	342	5
RED--IS THE FIRE'S COMMON TINT--	DARE YOU SEE A SOUL AT	365	3
IT LEFT THE LITTLE TINT	IT KNEW NO MEDICINE--	559	9
SHE DROPPED BRIGHT SCRAPS OF TINT, ABOUT--	MY FIRST WELL DAY--SINCE	574	19
THE TINT I CANNOT TAKE--IS BEST--	THE TINT I CANNOT TAKE--	627	1
DREAMS TINT THE SLEEP--	LET US PLAY YESTERDAY--	728	10
FAME IS THE TINT THAT SCHOLARS LEAVE	FAME IS THE TINT THAT	866	1
HAVE A TINT TOO RED	SANG FROM THE HEART,	1059	4
A FULL FED ROSE ON MEALS OF TINT	A FULL FED ROSE ON MEALS	1154	1
SHAME IS THE TINT DIVINE.	SHAME IS THE SHAWL OF	1412	8
TINTING			
TOUCHING THE ROOF [FLOODING THE STEEPLE] AND TINTING THE BARN	BLAZING IN GOLD AND	228	6
TINTS			
AND TINTS THE TRANSIT IN THE WEST	THE LOVE A LIFE CAN SHOW	673	11
TINY			
BY CHIVALRIES AS TINY,	BY CHIVALRIES AS TINY,	55	1
WHOSE ARE THE BEDS--THE TINY BEDS	WHOSE ARE THE LITTLE	142	7
FOLD A TINY COURTIER	MUTE THY CORONATION--	151	3
'TIS MANY A TINY MILL	DEW--IS THE FRESHET IN	1097	2
TIP			
AND I TIP--DRUNKEN--	I CAN WADE GRIEF--	252	6
CARNATIONS--TIP THEIR SPICE--	I TEND MY FLOWERS FOR	339	9
AND SPILL [TIP] THE SCARLET RAIN--	THE NAME--OF IT--IS	656	8
TIPPED			
HOW THE DUN BRAKE IS DRAPED IN CINDER [TIPPED IN TINSEL]	HOW THE OLD MOUNTAINS	291	3
TIPPET			
MY TIPPET--ONLY TULLE--	BECAUSE I COULD NOT STOP	712	16
THE TIPPET THAT IGNORES [RESISTS] HIS VOICE	THE JAY HIS CASTANET HAS	1635	3
TIPPLER			
TO SEE THE LITTLE TIPPLER	I TASTE A LIQUOR NEVER	214	15
TIPS			
THAT TIPS SO FREQUENT, [SLIPS SO EASY] NOW,	I PRAYED, AT FIRST, A	576	19
TIPTOE			
THEN--ON DIVINEST TIPTOE--STANDING--	JUST SO--JESUS--RAPS--	317	5
UNLESS [EXCEPT] WE DINE ON TIPTOE--	VICTORY COMES LATE--	690	9
TIPTOED			
SO TIPTOED MANY A SLIPPER	SO HAS A DAISY VANISHED	28	3
TIRE			
NOT THAT WE TIRE OF THEE--	WE COVER THEE--SWEET	482	2
TIRED			
SO WHEN YOU ARE TIRED--	I OFTEN PASSED THE	51	13
PERHAPS, WEARY [TIRED] AND SORE--	HEART, NOT SO HEAVY AS	83	18
WHERE TIRED CHILDREN PLACID SLEEP	WHERE BELLS NO MORE	112	5
HEAVEN BEGUILES THE TIRED.	AS WATCHERS HANG UPON	121	6
THINKING--PERHAPS--THAT I LOOKED TIRED--OR ALONE--	HOW SICK--TO WAIT--IN	368	3
THE EARTH LAYS BACK THESE TIRED LIVES	THE MONTHS HAVE ENDS--	423	5
DAY--GOT TIRED OF ME--	GOOD MORNING--MIDNIGHT--	425	3
THE WIND--TAPPED LIKE A TIRED MAN--	THE WIND--TAPPED LIKE A	436	1
THE WAVES GREW SLEEPY--[THE OCEAN--TIRED-- / THE OCEAN-- . . .	THREE TIMES--WE PARTED--	598	13
FAR ENDS OF TIRED [HOMELY] DAYS--	UNTO MY BOOKS--SO GOOD	604	2
THE TIRED FLOCKS COME IN	LET DOWN THE BARS, OH	1065	2
UNMANIFEST TO [UNWITNESSED OF THE / AS DOTH THE TIRED] SENSE	CONTAINED IN THIS SHORT	1165	V
BUT LOVE IS TIRED AND MUST SLEEP,	LOVE CAN DO ALL BUT	1731	5
TISSUE			
EVENING--THE TISSUE [FOLDING] DOOR--	NOON--IS THE HINGE OF	931	2
TISSUES			
DAINTY ADORNED WITH VEINS AND TISSUES	AS THE STARVED MAELSTROM	872	7
TITANIC			
WHEN UPON A PAIN TITANIC	I HAVE NEVER SEEN	175	11
TITANIC OPERA--	I THINK I WAS ENCHANTED	593	16

	FIRST LINE	POEM	LINE
TITIAN			
TITIAN--NEVER TOLD--	HOW THE OLD MOUNTAINS	291	22
TITLE			
BY IT--MY TITLE TAKE--	FOR THIS--ACCEPTED	195	4
A KINGDOM'S TITLE DEED--	HE PUT THE BELT AROUND	273	6
TITLE DIVINE--IS MINE!	TITLE DIVINE--IS MINE!	1072	1
THE TITLE WAS SCARCELY TOLD	ENDED, ERE IT BEGUN--	1088	2
WHERE TAX ASLEEP AND TITLE OFF	ALONE AND IN A	1167	13
WHOSE TITLE IS [DISCREETLY CALLED] "THE SOUL."	TO TRY TO SPEAK, AND	1617	8
TITLED			
TITLED--CONFIRMED--	MINE--BY THE RIGHT OF	528	7
BUT TITLED HIM--TO SEE--	IT ALWAYS FELT TO ME--A	597	V 22
TOAD			
A TOAD, CAN DIE OF LIGHT--	A TOAD, CAN DIE OF LIGHT	583	1
TOADS			
OF TOADS AND MEN--	A TOAD, CAN DIE OF LIGHT	583	3
TOBY'S			
TO "TOBY'S" FIST--	IS IT TRUE, DEAR SUE?	218	10
TODAY			
TODAY IS FAR FROM CHILDHOOD--	ONE SISTER HAVE I IN OUR	14	13
TODAY.	ALL THESE MY BANNERS BE.	22	7
IT'S ALL I HAVE TO BRING TODAY--	IT'S ALL I HAVE TO BRING	26	1
FROM THE FIELDS TODAY--	SO HAS A DAISY VANISHED	28	2
THAT [WHO] GATHERED THIS [THESE], TODAY!	IF RECOLLECTING WERE	33	8
AMONG US NOT TODAY--	COULD LIVE--DID LIVE--	43	11
ONE WILL WALK TODAY--	I HAV'NT TOLD MY GARDEN	50	16
SHE IS HELD TODAY--	WHETHER MY BARK WENT	52	6
CARRIED BY MEN TODAY--	TAKEN FROM MEN--THIS	53	2
THE ROBINS STAND AS THICK TODAY	SOME RAINBOW--COMING	64	13
WHO TOOK THE FLAG TODAY	SUCCESS IS COUNTED	67	6
EMINENT TODAY	AMBITION CANNOT FIND HIM	68	6
YESTERDAY, AND TODAY,	SHE DIED AT PLAY,	75	7
HAS LOST A BLUSH TODAY?	WHOSE CHEEK IS THIS?	82	3
"FATHER, THY WILL BE DONE" TODAY	I HAVE A KING, WHO DOES	103	16
I CAME TO BUY A SMILE--TODAY--	I CAME TO BUY A SMILE--	223	1
AS MY THOUGHT--TODAY--	TEACH HIM--WHEN HE MAKES	227	6
HOW MANY TIMES IT ACHE FOR ME--TODAY--CONFESS--	YOU SEE I CANNOT SEE--	253	3
I'M OLD ENOUGH, TODAY, I'M CERTAIN--THEN--	ONE YEAR AGO--JOTS WHAT?	296	33
THE WIND DID'NT COME FROM THE ORCHARD--TODAY--	THE WIND DID'NT COME	316	1
BUT WERE IT TOLD TO ME--TODAY--	BEFORE I GOT MY EYE PUT	327	5
THE VILLAGE LIES--TODAY--	IT WILL BE SUMMER--	342	8
AS LATELY AS TODAY--	THERE'S BEEN A DEATH, IN	389	2
THE BULLION OF TODAY--	SOME--WORK FOR	406	6
I STAND ALIVE--TODAY--	I LIVE WITH HIM--I SEE	463	10
AS NEAR YOURSELF--TODAY--	AS FAR FROM PITY, AS	496	6
I'M SORRY FOR THE DEAD--TODAY--	I'M SORRY FOR THE DEAD--	529	1
AND TOLD HIM WHAT I'D LIKE, TODAY,	I PRAYED, AT FIRST, A	576	9
TODAY--HER ONLY BOY	WHEN I WAS SMALL, A	596	2
THAT WE CAN SHOW--TODAY?"	I ASKED NO OTHER THING--	621	8
MY PORTION IS DEFEAT--TODAY--	MY PORTION IS DEFEAT--	639	1
AND THOUGH THE WO YOU HAVE TODAY	'TIS GOOD--THE LOOKING	660	9
A THOUGHT WENT UP MY MIND TODAY--	A THOUGHT WENT UP MY	701	1
AND ARE TODAY--IF WE EXIST--	HAVE ANY LIKE MYSELF	736	7
BUT I AM DEAF--TODAY--	THE BIRDS REPORTED FROM	743	4
TOMORROW AND TODAY--	THE ONLY NEWS I KNOW	827	5
THOSE WHO BEGIN TODAY--	THOSE WHO HAVE BEEN IN	922	2
ACCREDITED--TODAY--	THIS DUST, AND IT'S	936	2
GONE WESTERLY, TODAY--	THE SUNSET STOPPED ON	950	4
ELDER, TODAY, A SESSION WISER	A LOSS OF SOMETHING EVER	959	9
UPON THE HILLS TODAY--	LIKE MEN AND WOMEN	1105	2
LEST ANY DOUBT THAT WE ARE GLAD THAT THEY WERE BORN TODAY	LEST ANY DOUBT THAT WE	1156	1
MY GUEST "TODAY [VISITOR] IN PARADISE"	"REMEMBER ME" IMPLORED	1180	3
TODAY IN MEMORY LAIN	TO DISAPPEAR ENHANCES--	1209	6
ITSELF EXIST TODAY--	SOMEWHERE UPON THE	1231	2
DID WE [I] DEMAND TODAY	WHO WERE "THE FATHER AND	1258	10
EMBARKED UPON A TWIG TODAY	THE MOST TRIUMPHANT BIRD	1265	2
WHERE IT IS TODAY	YESTERDAY IS HISTORY,	1292	6
DUE IN PARADISE TODAY	RECOLLECT THE FACE OF ME	1305	3
IS HOARSE TODAY--	HIS MANSION IN THE POOL	1379	8
AND DWELLING THERE TODAY--	THE MOON UPON HER FLUENT	1528	V
WOULD ONLY COME TODAY,	IF ALL THE GRIEFS I AM	1726	2
WOULD ONLY COME TODAY,	IF ALL THE GRIEFS I AM	1726	6
TO-DAY			
BUT IF I EXPIRE TO-DAY	BEAUTY CROWDS ME TILL I	1654	3
TO-DAY OR THIS NOON	TO-DAY OR THIS NOON	1702	1
TODAY'S			
TODAY'S--HAVE VASTER CLAIMS [FORM]--	I COULD NOT PROVE THE	563	8
TODDLED			
THAT TODDLED DOWN THE BAY!	'TWAS SUCH A LITTLE--	107	2
TOE			
AND THEN A LIVID TOE [CLAW]--	THE WIND BEGUN TO KNEAD	824	12
TOES			
AND TEN OF MY ONCE STATELY TOES	I COUNTED TILL THEY	36	7
I CANNOT DANCE UPON MY TOES--	I CANNOT DANCE UPON MY	326	1
WHEN BLISS DISCLOSED A HUNDRED TOES [WINGS]--	SHE SIGHTS A BIRD--SHE	507	11
WITH FINGERS--WHERE THE TOES SHOULD BE--	YOU'LL KNOW HER--BY HER	634	3
TOGETHER			
THEIR SPIRITS MEET TOGETHER, THEY MAKE	AWAKE YE MUSES NINE,	1	19

	FIRST LINE	POEM	LINE
TOGETHER (CONTINUED)			
THEM SOLEMN VOWS,			
MY PLANE--AND I, TOGETHER WROUGHT	MYSELF WAS FORMED--A	488	3
AND THEN--TOGETHER BORE AWAY	TWO BUTTERFLIES WENT OUT	533	5
WHEN THEY TOGETHER VICTORY MAKE--	"HEAVEN" HAS DIFFERENT	575	11
FORTY--GONE DOWN TOGETHER--	GLEE--THE GREAT STORM IS	619	3
THENCEFORWARD--WE--TOGETHER DWELT [WALKED]--	THE BIRDS REPORTED FROM	743	21
TOGETHER HEARD THEM STRENGTHENING	TWO TRAVELLERS PERISHING	933	3
THE AFTERNOONS--TOGETHER SPENT--	I LEARNED--AT LEAST--	944	18
TOGETHER CHIEFEST [CHIEFLY] THEY ARE FOUND	AS OLD AS WOE--	1168	7
THE CLOUDS THEIR BACKS TOGETHER LAID	THE CLOUDS THEIR BACKS	1172	1
THE HEART AND THE MIND TOGETHER MAKE	THE HEART IS THE CAPITAL	1354	3
TO PLAY TOGETHER WE ARE PRONE	I DID NOT REACH THEE	1664	16
FIRST TIME TOGETHER THROWN.	A FACE DEVOID OF LOVE OR	1711	6
TOIL			
TENDERLY TOOK IT UP FROM TOIL	A POOR--TORN HEART-- A	78	11
AT HER PHOSPHORIC TOIL!	THE LAMP BURNS SURE--	233	4
THE LITTLE TOIL OF LOVE--	I HAD NO TIME TO HATE--	478	10
DISCOURSE BETWEEN THE TOIL--	I'M SORRY FOR THE DEAD--	529	6
MAKES SCARCELY WORTH THE TOIL--	WE SEE--COMPARATIVELY--	534	6
THE TOIL OF FELLOWS DONE--	THE WORK OF HER THAT	1143	2
IT'S ['TIS] TOIL--	LUCK IS NOT CHANCE--	1350	2
WHAT RESPITE FROM HER THRILLING TOIL	THE BIRD HER PUNCTUAL	1585	5
TOILED			
THE BENCH, WHERE WE HAD TOILED--	MYSELF WAS FORMED--A	488	10
YOU GUESSED--FROM THE WAY THE SENTENCE TOILED--	GOING TO HIM! HAPPY	494	11
TOILETTE			
TO MAKE ONE'S TOILETTE--AFTER DEATH	TO MAKE ONE'S TOILETTE--	485	1
HAS MADE THE TOILETTE COOL	TO MAKE ONE'S TOILETTE--	485	2
HER TOILETTE--TO SUFFICE--	I WATCHED THE MOON	629	22
TOILING			
STILL TOILING AT THE CHEEK	A SOLEMN THING WITHIN	483	8
TOILS			
AND DO THE LITTLE TOILS	HE PUT THE BELT AROUND	273	10
NOT WHO TOILS FOR FREEDOM	NOW I KNEW I LOST HER--	1219	17
IT'S TOILS [CORN] TO BRINDLED PEOPLE [NATIONS] THRUST [CAST]--	A FIELD OF STUBBLE,	1407	3
TOILSOME			
UPON A [THE] DUSTY [TOILSOME] WAY--	HEART, NOT SO HEAVY AS	83	14
TOKEN			
IN TOKEN OF OUR FRIENDSHIP	"SIC TRANSIT GLORIA	3	61
DIADEM--OR DUCAL SHOWING [SYMBOL / TOKEN]--	HER--"LAST POEMS"--	312	14
TOLD			
I NEVER TOLD THE BURIED GOLD	I NEVER TOLD THE BURIED	11	1
I HAV'NT TOLD MY GARDEN YET--	I HAV'NT TOLD MY GARDEN	50	1
I COULD NOT HAVE TOLD IT,	"THEY HAVE NOT CHOSEN ME	85	5
PEACE--BY IT'S BATTLES TOLD--	WATER, IS TAUGHT BY	135	4
TITIAN--NEVER TOLD--	HOW THE OLD MOUNTAINS	291	22
OH, HAD YOU TOLD ME SO--	ONE YEAR AGO--JOTS WHAT?	296	15
BUT WERE IT TOLD TO ME--TODAY--	BEFORE I GOT MY EYE PUT	327	5
I TOLD MYSELF, "TAKE COURAGE, FRIEND--	I FELT MY LIFE WITH BOTH	351	13
A SECRET TOLD--	A SECRET TOLD--	381	1
AND WHOM YOU TOLD IT TO--BESIDE--	A SECRET TOLD--	381	7
BECAUSE HE--NEVER TOLD--	A HOUSE UPON THE HIGHT--	399	12
MY MESSAGE--MUST BE TOLD--	A TONGUE--TO TELL HIM I	400	21
TOLD TO HIM--	UNIT, LIKE DEATH, FOR	408	4
I TOLD MY SOUL TO SING--	THE FIRST DAY'S NIGHT	410	4
I'D SO MUCH JOY--I TOLD IT--RED--	IT WOULD NEVER BE COMMON	430	9
HE TOLD ME, DEATH WAS DEAD--	DO PEOPLE MOULDER	432	16
THE SIMPLE NEWS THAT NATURE TOLD--	THIS IS MY LETTER TO THE	441	3
SO--CHILDREN--TOLD HOW [ASSURED THAT] BROOKS IN EDEN--	BETTER--THAN MUSIC! FOR	503	9
EDEN--A LEGEND--DIMLY TOLD [LEARNED / CROONED]--	BETTER--THAN MUSIC! FOR	503	14
ONE MORE--"YE BLESSED"--TO BE TOLD--	THERE IS A SHAME OF	551	7
THE GRIEVED--ARE MANY--I AM TOLD--	I MEASURE EVERY GRIEF I	561	25
BECAUSE THEY TOLD ME TO--	I PRAYED, AT FIRST, A	576	2
AND TOLD HIM WHAT I'D LIKE, TODAY,	I PRAYED, AT FIRST, A	576	9
I TOLD HIM BEST--MUST PASS	I ROSE--BECAUSE HE SANK	616	12
I TOLD HIM WORLDS [A WORLD] I KNEW	I ROSE--BECAUSE HE SANK	616	16
BUT DEATH HAD TOLD HER SO THE [SPECIFIC TOLD HER / ENAMORED . . .	I MEANT TO FIND HER WHEN	718	7
BUT DEATH HAD TOLD HER SO THE [SPECIFIC TOLD HER / ENAMORED . . .	I MEANT TO FIND HER WHEN	718	7
. . . TOLD HER] FIRST--	I MEANT TO FIND HER WHEN	718	7
HE TOLD A HOMELY TALE	HE TOLD A HOMELY TALE	763	1
YET NEITHER TOLD--THAT I COULD LEARN--	NATURE AND GOD--I	835	5
TOO TENDER, TO BE TOLD.	LET DOWN THE BARS, OH	1065	8
THE TITLE WAS SCARCELY TOLD	ENDED, ERE IT BEGUN--	1088	2
NONE [THEY] WHO SAW IT EVER TOLD IT	NONE WHO SAW IT EVER	1110	1
I TOLD MY SOUL TO COME--	THIS SLOW DAY MOVED	1120	5
OH CUNNING WRECK THAT TOLD NO TALE	A GREAT HOPE FELL	1123	4
RELUCTANT TO BE TOLD	ALONE AND IN A	1167	2
STEP LOFTY, FOR THIS NAME BE TOLD	STEP LIGHTLY ON THIS	1183	5
AND WHEN PORTENTOUS [IN TERROR] TOLD	WHO WERE "THE FATHER AND	1258	4
WAS DISTINCTLY [DIRECTLY] TOLD--	ABRAHAM TO KILL HIM	1317	2
ELIZABETH TOLD ESSEX	ELIZABETH TOLD ESSEX	1321	1
WHEN TERROR WERE IT TOLD	I NEVER HEAR THAT ONE IS	1323	10
THAT TOLD THE TRUTH [NEWS] TO ME--	COULD MORTAL LIP DIVINE	1409	V

	FIRST LINE	POEM	LINE
TOLD (CONTINUED)			
THE HUMAN HEART IS TOLD	BY HOMELY GIFT AND	1563	2
THE FLYING TIDINGS TOLD--	THERE CAME A WIND LIKE A	1593	14
JEHOVAH TOLD TO HER	THE RETICENT VOLCANO	1748	6
TOLERATES			
THE GIANT TOLERATES [ENTERTAINS] NO GNAT	SIZE CIRCUMSCRIBES--IT	641	3
TOLL			
THEN SPACE--BEGAN TO TOLL,	I FELT A FUNERAL, IN MY	280	12
TOLL--FOR THE BONNIE SOULS--	GLEE--THE GREAT STORM IS	619	6
WITHOUT OFFENCE [OPPRESS] OF TOLL--	THERE IS NO FRIGATE LIKE	1263	6
TOLLING			
AND INSTEAD OF TOLLING THE BELL, FOR CHURCH,	SOME KEEP THE SABBATH	324	7
OF TOLLING BELL I ASK THE CAUSE?	OF TOLLING BELL I ASK	947	1
TOMB			
SOME IN THE BUSY TOMB	MY WHEEL IS IN THE DARK!	10	10
FOR THEE TO BLOOM, I'LL SKIP THE TOMB	SUMMER FOR THEE, GRANT I	31	5
TO LEAVE ME IN THE ATOM'S TOMB--	OF COURSE--I PRAYED--	376	9
TRUE, LIKE THE TOMB,	UNIT, LIKE DEATH, FOR	408	2
TILL I GET ACCUSTOMED--BUT THEN THE TOMB	IT DONT SOUND SO	426	11
ADJUSTED IN THE TOMB	I DIED FOR BEAUTY--BUT	449	2
ANGUISH--AND THE TOMB--	SWEET--SAFE--HOUSES--	457	13
STRONG CLUSTERS, FROM BARABBAS' TOMB--	TO PUT THIS WORLD DOWN,	527	11
DISCLOSE AS 'TWERE A TOMB	THIS CHASM, SWEET, UPON	858	6
TABERNACLE OR TOMB--	DRAB HABITATION OF WHOM?	893	2
SHOW JUSTEST--THROUGH AN OPEN TOMB--	THE ADMIRATIONS--AND	906	2
TO ENLIST THE TOMB.	SOME WE SEE NO MORE,	1221	10
A DIMPLE IN THE TOMB	A DIMPLE IN THE TOMB	1489	1
THAT BORE HIM FROM THE TOMB--	OBTAINING BUT OUR OWN	1543	4
TOO TRACKLESS FOR A TOMB--	SOME ARROWS SLAY BUT	1565	4
THAT BORE IT THROUGH THE TOMB,	'TIS NOT THE SWAYING	1597	6
THERE IS A WORLD [TOMB / CHAIR / SEAT] FOR ALL	NO LIFE CAN POMPLESS	1626 V	8
THERE IS NO TRUMPET LIKE THE TOMB	THE IMMORTALITY SHE GAVE	1648 V	
THAN A STUPENDOUS TOMB	NOT ANY SUNNY TONE	1674	7
SEED--SUMMER--TOMB--	A PIT--BUT HEAVEN OVER	1712	16
NOW SHADOWS IN THE TOMB.	SWEET HOURS HAVE	1767	4
TOMBS			
THE NERVES SIT CEREMONIOUS, LIKE TOMBS--	AFTER GREAT PAIN, A	341	2
HOW GOOD [SAFE / FIRM / CALM] TO BE IN TOMBS	THE CLOUDS THEIR BACKS	1172	6
BETTER [RATHER] THAN THE TOMBS	FORTITUDE INCARNATE	1217	12
TOMES			
TO TOMES OF SOLID WITCHCRAFT--	I THINK I WAS ENCHANTED	593	29
TOMORROW			
TOMORROW, NIGHT WILL COME AGAIN--	HEART, NOT SO HEAVY AS	83	17
THE MAN--TO DIE--TOMORROW--	THE DOOMED--REGARD THE	294	5
"IF I SHOULD BE A QUEEN, TOMORROW"--	I'M SAYING EVERY DAY	373	2
SAY "WHEN TOMORROW COMES THIS WAY--	IT DONT SOUND SO	426	8
UNTIL TOMORROW [THE EVENING]--HAPPY LETTER! [AH! BE BASHFUL]	GOING TO HIM! HAPPY	494	24
TO FADE [DIE]--TOMORROW--RAINBOWS HELD [THRUST]	MY FIRST WELL DAY--SINCE	574	15
TOMORROW AND TODAY--	THE ONLY NEWS I KNOW	827	5
TOMORROW, BUT IF I AM THERE	WHEN THEY COME BACK--IF	1080	15
TOMORROW WERE, A BLAME	THE LAST NIGHT THAT SHE	1100	12
NOT A TOMORROW TO KNOW IT'S NAME	THE POPULAR HEART IS A	1226	5
"TOMORROW"--WHOSE LOCATION	"TOMORROW"--WHOSE	1367	1
TOMORROW--THOU RETRIEVER	"TOMORROW"--WHOSE	1367	5
AS SUBTLE AS TOMORROW	AS SUBTLE AS TOMORROW	1713	1
TO-MORROW			
WITH A TO-MORROW KNOCKING	RATHER ARID DELIGHT	1679	7
TON			
THE LEAST--CAN LIFT A TON	SUCH IS THE FORCE OF	787	2
HAD WE KNOWN THE TON [WEIGHT / LOAD] SHE BORE	HAD WE KNOWN THE TON SHE	1124	1
TONE			
AS TONE OF REALM	A MIEN TO MOVE A QUEEN--	283	20
AT FIRST--A DOUBTFUL TONE--	YOU'LL KNOW HER--BY HER	634	22
I'M ANSWERED IN A LONESOME TONE--	OF TOLLING BELL I ASK	947	3
IN ANY TONE COMMENSURATE	I NEVER HEAR THAT ONE IS	1323	11
NOT ANY SUNNY TONE	NOT ANY SUNNY TONE	1674	1
HER TONGUE MORE TENDER [TIMID / MAGIC] THAN THE TUNE [TONE]	HER FACE WAS IN A BED OF	1722	5
TONGUE			
AND BIRDS, OF FOREIGN TONGUE!	AS IF SOME LITTLE ARCTIC	180	8
GET SAINTS--WITH NEW--UNSTEADY TONGUE--	FOR THIS--ACCEPTED	195	14
LOUD, AS THE THUNDER'S TONGUE--	MANY A PHRASE HAS THE	276	4
SILVER--PERISHED--WITH HER TONGUE--	HER--"LAST POEMS"--	312	3
AND PERCH MY TONGUE	I'M SAYING EVERY DAY	373	16
A TONGUE--TO TELL HIM I AM TRUE!	A TONGUE--TO TELL HIM I	400	1
OMNIPOTENCE--HAD NOT A TONGUE--	YOU'LL KNOW IT--AS YOU	420	11
YOU ALMOST BATHED YOUR TONGUE--	SHE SIGHTS A BIRD--SHE	507	10
THESE, ARE NOT BRAYED OF TONGUE--	THE SOUL HAS BANDAGED	512	24
AND PARTAKES--HIS TONGUE	AS THE STARVED MAELSTROM	872	8
SWIFT AS A FRESHET'S TONGUE	THIS IS A BLOSSOM OF THE	945	6
I MADE NO ANSWER OF THE TONGUE	IT WAS A QUIET WAY--	1053	3
KNOWS THE ADDER [ADDERS] TONGUE HIS COMING	WE LIKE MARCH.	1213	6
ON HER FACE AND TONGUE.	NOW I KNEW I LOST HER--	1219	4
BELIEFS ARE BANDAGED, LIKE THE TONGUE	I NEVER HEAR THAT ONE IS	1323	9
NOTHING WITH A TONGUE OR EAR--[AN EAR OR TONGUE--]	"SECRETS" IS A DAILY	1385	9
NOTHING WITH A TONGUE OR EAR--[AN EAR OR TONGUE--]	"SECRETS" IS A DAILY	1385	9

	FIRST LINE	POEM		LINE
TONGUE (CONTINUED)				
TONGUE [GUILE] IF IT HATH,	TO THE STANCH DUST	1402		3
HER TONGUE MORE TENDER [TIMID / MAGIC] THAN THE TUNE [TONE]	HER FACE WAS IN A BED OF	1722		5
TONGUELESS				
BEST GRIEF IS TONGUELESS--BEFORE HE'LL TELL--	GRIEF IS A MOUSE--	793		13
TONGUES				
PUT OUT THEIR TONGUES, FOR NOON.	IT WAS NOT DEATH, FOR I	510		4
AS TONGUES [THRONGS / EYES] OF DIAMOND HAD REVILED	MY SOUL--ACCUSED ME--AND	753		2
TONIC				
HIS CHARACTER--A TONIC--	NO BRIGADIER THROUGHOUT	1561		21
TONIGHT				
YOU AND I--TONIGHT!	HEART! WE WILL FORGET	47		2
SOME, WOULD EVEN TRUDGE TONIGHT!	"HOUSES"--SO THE WISE	127		8
AND BE WITH [LEAP TO] YOU--TONIGHT!	AH, MOON--AND STAR!	240		12
MIGHT I BUT MOOR--TONIGHT--	WILD NIGHTS--WILD NIGHTS	249		11
THE NORTH--TONIGHT--	OF BRONZE--AND BLAZE--	290		2
WOMEN MAKE--TONIGHT--	'TWAS THE OLD--ROAD--	344		18
DID PLACE ABOUT THE WEST--TONIGHT--	WHOLE GULFS--OF RED, AND	658		3
I ONLY HAVE IT NOT TONIGHT	'TWAS AWKWARD, BUT IT	973		9
WHAT MISERS WRING THEIR HANDS TONIGHT	A MINE THERE IS NO MAN	1117		7
UPON THE HILL TONIGHT--	THE LILAC IS AN ANCIENT	1241		4
TO-NIGHT				
TO KNOW THE NEWS I KNOW TO-NIGHT	I KNOW OF PEOPLE IN THE	1665		3
TO-NIGHT SHE LIES	TO-DAY OR THIS NOON	1702		4
TOOK				
BUT TOOK THE MORN--	ONE SISTER HAVE I IN OUR	14		24
AND THEN I TOOK A PENCIL	I COUNTED TILL THEY	36		3
WHO TOOK THE FLAG TODAY	SUCCESS IS COUNTED	67		6
WHEREAS I TOOK THE BUTTERFLY	"ARCTURUS" IS HIS OTHER	70		13
TENDERLY TOOK IT UP FROM TOIL	A POOR--TORN HEART-- A	78		11
TOOK UP HER SIMPLE WARDROBE	SHE DIED--THIS WAS THE	150		3
THESE SOVREIGNS EVER TOOK!	I MET A KING THIS	166		24
TOOK RAINBOWS, AS THE COMMON WAY,	DELIGHT IS AS THE FLIGHT	257		16
THE HAPPY WINDS--THEIR TIMBRELS TOOK--	THE DAY CAME SLOW--TILL	304		9
OR EVER TOOK A NAP--	I NEVER FELT AT HOME--	413		10
THE MALAY--TOOK THE PEARL--	THE MALAY--TOOK THE	452		1
THEY TOOK AWAY OUR EYES--	THEY PUT US FAR APART--	474		5
I TOOK THE SMALLEST ROOM--	I WAS THE SLIGHTEST IN	486		2
MY TOOLS TOOK HUMAN--FACES--	MYSELF WAS FORMED--A	488		9
I STARTED EARLY--TOOK MY DOG--	I STARTED EARLY--TOOK MY	520		1
AND CAUGHT A RIDE [TOOK A BOUT] WITH HIM	TWO BUTTERFLIES WENT OUT	533	V	4
I TOOK MY POWER IN MY HAND--	I TOOK MY POWER IN MY	540		1
AND MORN A NEW POLITENESS TOOK--	I HAD NO CAUSE TO BE	542		3
AND TOOK HIMSELF, FOR PAY,	I GAVE MYSELF TO HIM--	580		2
I TOOK FOR GIANTS--PRACTISING	I THINK I WAS ENCHANTED	593		15
OUR PACE TOOK SUDDEN AWE--	OUR JOURNEY HAD ADVANCED	615		5
THAT TOOK IT'S CAMBRIC WAY--	THE BEGGAR LAD--DIES	717		6
THOUGH IT TOOK ALL MY STORE	I CANNOT BUY IT--'TIS	840		9
WE TOOK THE MYSTERY.	FROM US SHE WANDERED NOW	890		8
LONG STEPS ACROSS THE FEATURES TOOK	TWO TRAVELLERS PERISHING	933		9
THE WIND TOOK UP THE NORTHERN THINGS	THE WIND TOOK UP THE	1134		1
PERPETUAL PRESUMPTION [COMPLACENCE] TOOK	ALONE AND IN A	1167		15
THE SUN TOOK DOWN HIS YELLOW WHIP	THE SUN AND FOG	1190		3
A SPARROW TOOK A SLICE OF TWIG	A SPARROW TOOK A SLICE	1211		1
NATURE TOOK THE DAY	NOW I KNEW I LOST HER--	1219		14
YOU TOOK IT ALL WITH YOU--	DEAR MARCH--COME IN--	1320		17
BECAUSE "GOD TOOK HIM" MENTION--[TELL US]	"WAS NOT" WAS ALL THE	1342		7
A SUDDEN FREIGHT OF WIND ASSUMED [TOOK ON--]	A SINGLE CLOVER PLANK	1343		11
TOOK HER OWN HEART, INCLUDING OUR'S,	THE PRETTY RAIN FROM	1426		3
TIME COMPASSION TOOK--	WE TALKED WITH EACH	1473		6
ARARATS--WE TOOK--	WE TALKED WITH EACH	1473		8
YOU'D THINK [SWEAR] HE TOOK A DEED	HOW DESTITUTE IS HE	1477	V	7
THAT TOOK THY FACE BETWEEN	I SEE THEE CLEARER FOR	1666		2
SHE TOOK THE AWFUL NEWS	I WATCHED HER FACE TO	1667		2
I TOOK ONE DRAUGHT OF LIFE--	I TOOK ONE DRAUGHT OF	1725		1
TOOLS				
ONE--HAND THE TOOLS--	I KNOW SOME LONELY	289		8
MY TOOLS TOOK HUMAN--FACES--	MYSELF WAS FORMED--A	488		9
TOOTH				
A TOOTH UPON OUR PEACE	A TOOTH UPON OUR PEACE	459		1
THEN WHEREFORE BE THE TOOTH?	A TOOTH UPON OUR PEACE	459		3
NARCOTICS CANNOT STILL THE TOOTH [MOUSE]	THIS WORLD IS NOT	501		19
THAN WHEN SHE SHOWS HER GARNET TOOTH--	WHEN ETNA BASKS AND	1146		3
BEGONE--MY TOOTH HAS GROWN--	ART THOU THE THING I	1282		2
TOP				
BUT HE WHO HAS ACHIEVED THE TOP [CREST]--	THE HALLOWING OF PAIN	772		7
I STILL CAN REACH [TOUCH] THE TOP	THE PILE OF YEARS IS NOT	1507		6
TOPAZ				
AND TOPAZ--LIKE THE STAR!	I CAME TO BUY A SMILE--	223		12
LIKE BREADTHS OF TOPAZ--PACKED A NIGHT--	THE DAY CAME SLOW--TILL	304		7
NEVER A FELLOW MATCHED THIS TOPAZ--	I COULD BRING YOU JEWELS	697		9
TOPOGRAPHY				
DEFIES TOPOGRAPHY.	HOW FAR IS IT TO HEAVEN?	929		8
TOPS				
WHEN WE STAND ON THE TOPS OF THINGS--	WHEN WE STAND ON THE	242		1
I TOUCHED THE TOPS OF FILMS--	IT WOULD NEVER BE COMMON	430		27
TORE				
AND ALL OUR SINEW TORE--	I GOT SO I COULD HEAR	293		8

	FIRST LINE	POEM	LINE
TORE (CONTINUED)			
AS IF IT NEVER TORE	TO MEND EACH TATTERED	1442	6
TORMENT			
HOW EASY, TORMENT, NOW--	'TIS SO APPALLING--IT	281	7
EVOKES [PROVOKES] SO SWEET A TORMENT--	I WOULD NOT PAINT--A	505	7
DEPARTED WITH THE TORMENT	TO MAKE ROUTINE A	1196	7
TORN			
A POOR--TORN HEART--A TATTERED HEART--	A POOR--TORN HEART-- A	78	1
ALL MY MANSION TORN--	STRUCK, WAS I, NOR YET	925	10
ARE FABRICS TRULY TORN--	THE HEALED HEART SHOWS	1440	4
TORRENTS			
THE TORRENTS [WATERS] OF ETERNITY	HOW MUCH THE PRESENT	1380	7
TORRID			
A SHADY FRIEND--FOR TORRID DAYS--	A SHADY FRIEND--FOR	278	1
THE SOLEMN--TORRID--SYMBOL--	A STILL--VOLCANO--LIFE--	601	9
AND A TORRID EYE.	AS THE STARVED MAELSTROM	872	16
AND RUMBLES STILL, THOUGH TORRID NOONS	THE FARTHEST THUNDER	1581	3
TORTOISE			
HOW MANY TRIPS THE TORTOISE MAKES--	BRING ME THE SUNSET IN A	128	10
TORTURE			
NO RACK CAN TORTURE ME--	NO RACK CAN TORTURE ME--	384	1
TOSS			
TOSS THEIR DICE AGAIN!	WE LOSE--BECAUSE WE WIN	21	3
SOUL, WILT THOU TOSS AGAIN?	SOUL, WILT THOU TOSS	139	1
WHERE SHIPS OF PURPLE--GENTLY TOSS--	WHERE SHIPS OF PURPLE--	265	1
I'D TOSS IT YONDER, LIKE A RIND,	IF YOU WERE COMING IN	511	15
WE TALK IN CARELESS [VENTURE]--AND IN TOSS--	AGAIN--HIS VOICE IS AT	663	13
TO TOSS INCESSANTLY	UPON A LILAC SEA	1337	2
TOSSED			
NOR TOSSED MY SHAPE IN EIDER BALLS,	I CANNOT DANCE UPON MY	326	13
THREE TIMES--THE BILLOWS THREW [TOSSED] ME UP--	THREE TIMES--WE PARTED--	598	5
IT TOSSED--AND TOSSED--	IT TOSSED--AND TOSSED--	723	1
IT TOSSED--AND TOSSED--	IT TOSSED--AND TOSSED--	723	1
TOSSES			
AND TOSSES LIKE A FLEET OF BALM--	SWEET SKEPTICISM OF THE	1413	3
TOSSING			
OUR'S BE THE TOSSING--WILD THOUGH THE SEA--	HOW SICK--TO WAIT--IN	368	8
TOTAL			
THERE IS A FITTING--A [TOTAL IN] DISMAY--	WHILE WE WERE FEARING IT	1277	5
REDEMPTION [THY TOTAL / THY BEING]--FOR A KISS--	GO SLOW, MY SOUL, TO	1297	8
TOTALLER			
FOR CONSCIOUSER [TOTALLER] ECLIPSE--	THE WHOLE OF IT CAME NOT	762	12
TOTALNESS			
LARGER FOR THE [IT'S] TOTALNESS--	ALL I MAY, IF SMALL,	819	3
TOTTER			
NO BRIDGE BELOW DOTH TOTTER SO--	HOW BRITTLE ARE THE	1433	3
HER WORDS DID TOTTER SO	HIS VOICE DECREPIT WAS	1476	2
TOTTERED			
THE ONE WHO BORE HIM TOTTERED IN,--	UPON THE GALLOWS HUNG A	1757	5
TOTTERS			
THAT TOTTERS IN THE LEAVES--	HER FACE WAS IN A BED OF	1722	6
TOUCH			
WHAT WE TOUCH THE HEMS OF	BEFORE THE ICE IS IN THE	37	9
SOME TOUCH IT, AND SOME KISS IT--	THERE'S SOMETHING	45	5
WHOSE BONNETS TOUCH THE FIRMAMENT--	IN LANDS I NEVER SAW--	124	3
WHOSE SANDALS TOUCH THE TOWN--	IN LANDS I NEVER SAW--	124	4
MESMERIC FINGERS SOFTLY TOUCH	BESIDES THE AUTUMN POETS	131	11
MIGHT DARE TO TOUCH IT NOW!	WAIT TILL THE MAJESTY OF	171	4
THE FELLOW CANNOT TOUCH THIS CROWN--	FOR THIS--ACCEPTED	195	3
AND TOUCH THE PANTOMIME--HIMSELF,	I BREATHED ENOUGH TO	272	7
TO TOUCH HER HEAD!	'TWAS THE OLD--ROAD--	344	22
THAT WE CAN TOUCH THE SPACES--	WHEN NIGHT IS ALMOST	347	3
NEXT--ONE--MIGHT BE THE GOLDEN TOUCH--	I'LL CLUTCH--AND CLUTCH	427	2
UNSANCTIFIED--TO TOUCH--	THE MALAY--TOOK THE	452	4
YOU TRY TO TOUCH [REACH] THE SMILE	IF ANYBODY'S FRIEND BE	509	14
TOUCH LIBERTY--THEN KNOW NO MORE,	THE SOUL HAS BANDAGED	512	17
TO SEE [REACH / TOUCH] THIS CURIOUS FRIEND--	MY PERIOD HAD COME FOR	564	8
FORGIVE ME, IF TO STROKE [TOUCH / GREET] THY FROST	IF I MAY HAVE IT, WHEN	577	28
BUT NOT TO TOUCH, OR WISH FOR,	I CRIED AT PITY--NOT AT	588	13
TO TOUCH--	EACH LIFE CONVERGES TO	680	12
TO OWN IT--TOUCH IT--	GOD GAVE A LOAF TO EVERY	791	5
THAT TOUCH HOW SELDOMLY	SO SET IT'S SUN IN THEE	808	5
OUR STATURES TOUCH THE SKIES--	WE NEVER KNOW HOW HIGH	1176	4
AS FORESTS [BRANCHES] TOUCH THE WIND	BECAUSE HE LOVES HER	1229	8
TO CONTEMPLATION--[TO SPECTACLE, BUT] NOT TO TOUCH--	THE LILAC IS AN ANCIENT	1241	7
BUT NEVER TOUCH THE RESERVOIR--	OF LIFE TO OWN--	1294	3
TOUCH LIGHTLY NATURE'S SWEET GUITAR	TOUCH LIGHTLY NATURE'S	1389	1
WHO FAILED TO TOUCH US ALL	ONE OF THE ONES THAT	1466	2
I STILL CAN REACH [TOUCH] THE TOP	THE PILE OF YEARS IS NOT	1507	6
BUT ARM IN ARM WITH TOUCH, YET TOUCH	THE SPIRIT LASTS--BUT IN	1576	7
BUT ARM IN ARM WITH TOUCH, YET TOUCH	THE SPIRIT LASTS--BUT IN	1576	7
IS IT TOO LATE TO TOUCH YOU, DEAR?	IS IT TOO LATE TO TOUCH	1637	1
BEYOND THE HOPE OF TOUCH	THE OVERTAKELESSNESS OF	1691	8
TOUCHED			
THE TEMPESTS TOUCHED OUR GARMENTS--	THROUGH LANE IT LAY--	9	9
I TOUCHED HER CRADLE MUTE--	SHE SLEPT BENEATH A TREE	25	3

	FIRST LINE	POEM	LINE
TOUCHED (CONTINUED)			
I COULD HAVE TOUCHED!	WITHIN MY REACH!	90	2
THE SUN--JUST TOUCHED THE MORNING--	THE SUN--JUST TOUCHED	232	1
AND TOUCHED ME WITH THEIR FLEECES,	IF I'M LOST--NOW--	256	8
I TOUCHED THE UNIVERSE--	I SAW NO WAY--THE	378	4
BUT WHOM HIS FINGERS TOUCHED--	A VISITOR IN MARL--	391	9
I TOUCHED THE TOPS OF FILMS--	IT WOULD NEVER BE COMMON	430	27
HE TOUCHED ME, SO I LIVE TO KNOW	HE TOUCHED ME, SO I LIVE	506	1
AND TOUCHED THE CURIOUS WINE--	I HAD BEEN HUNGRY, ALL	579	4
I TOUCHED WITH CAUTION--LEST THEY CRACK [SLIT]--	IF HE WERE LIVING--DARE	734	7
MOST SHE TOUCHED ME BY HER MUTENESS--	MOST SHE TOUCHED ME BY	760	1
CHRIST--STOOPED UNTIL HE TOUCHED THE GRAVE--	PERHAPS YOU THINK ME	833	3
THAT LOVE HAD TOUCHED THAT MORN	TWO TRAVELLERS PERISHING	933	10
TOUCHED TO CONDITIONS	SPRING COMES ON THE	1042	6
ONE OF THE ONES THAT MIDAS TOUCHED	ONE OF THE ONES THAT	1466	1
I ALMOST TOUCHED HER	TO-DAY OR THIS NOON	1702	3
IT ALMOST TOUCHED THE LAWNS.	A CURIOUS CLOUD	1710	5
TOUCHES			
UNTIL DEATH TOUCHES IT	WHILE IT IS ALIVE	491	2
TOUCHES MY FOREHEAD NOW AND THEN	A LOSS OF SOMETHING EVER	959	14
TOUCHING			
TILL MORNING TOUCHING MOUNTAIN--	A LITTLE EAST OF JORDAN,	59	5
TOUCHING THE ROOF [FLOODING THE STEEPLE] AND TINTING THE BARN	BLAZING IN GOLD AND	228	6
TOUCHING ALL THE GRASS	HOW THE OLD MOUNTAINS	291	10
TOURIST			
THIS HUMBLE TOURIST ROSE!	WENT UP A YEAR THIS	93	8
TOWARD			
AS I--TOWARD [IN] THEE--	THE DROP, THAT WRESTLES	284	3
TOWARD [TO] LIGHT--	UNTO LIKE STORY--TROUBLE	295	24
HE COMES JUST SO FAR--TOWARD THE TOWN--	THE MOON IS DISTANT FROM	429	7
YET PERSEVERED TOWARD--SURER [STRICTER]--FOR THE DISTANCE--	EACH LIFE CONVERGES TO	680	13
WERE TOWARD ETERNITY--	BECAUSE I COULD NOT STOP	712	24
TOWARD ETERNITY--	"I WANT"--IT PLEADED--	731	8
TOWARD ARTIFICE OF TIME--OR MEN--	MY SOUL--ACCUSED ME--AND	753	6
TOWARD WHICH FORCES CREEP	CRISIS IS A HAIR	889	2
TOWARD MEN--	THE FIRST DAY THAT I WAS	902	12
BACK--TOWARD TIME--	THE ADMIRATIONS--AND	906	14
TOWARD THE GOD OF HIM--	THE ADMIRATIONS--AND	906	16
AND TOWARD ENCOURAGEMENT	TO UNDERTAKE IS TO	1070	4
THE TRANSITIVE TOWARD.	MY TRIUMPH LASTED TILL	1227	14
TOWARD HUMAN NATURE'S HOME	NOT ANY SUNNY TONE	1674	5
TOWERING			
THE THING SO TOWERING HIGH	WE SEE--COMPARATIVELY--	534	2
TOWN			
BEHIND MY NATIVE TOWN.	FREQUENTLY THE WOODS ARE	6	4
THE ROSE IS OUT OF TOWN.	THE MORNS ARE MEEKER	12	4
HE REACHES [COMES TO] TOWN AT NIGHTFALL--	THE GUEST IS GOLD AND	15	5
UNTO THE NEAREST TOWN?	ADRIFT! A LITTLE BOAT	30	4
THEIR SLIPPERS LEAPED THE TOWN,	I COUNTED TILL THEY	36	2
THIS PLACE IS BLISS--THIS TOWN IS HEAVEN--	WHERE BELLS NO MORE	112	7
WHOSE SANDALS TOUCH THE TOWN--	IN LANDS I NEVER SAW--	124	4
IN HIS "NATIVE TOWN."	DUST IS THE ONLY SECRET	153	4
SUCH TRANSPORT BREAKS UPON THE TOWN	MUSICIANS WRESTLE	157	5
THERE'S THAT LONG [THEN THERE'S THAT] TOWN OF WHITE--TO CROSS--	IT CANT BE "SUMMER"!	221	4
THIS--WAS THE TOWN--SHE PASSED--	'TWAS THE OLD--ROAD--	344	5
BERRIES, IN MY NATIVE TOWN--	PERHAPS I ASKED TOO	352	4
AS ONE SHOULD COME TO TOWN--	A PRECIOUS--MOULDERING	371	22
'TWAS A SMALL TOWN--	I WENT TO HEAVEN--	374	2
IN JUST A COUNTRY TOWN--	THERE'S BEEN A DEATH, IN	389	24
HE COMES JUST SO FAR--TOWARD THE TOWN--	THE MOON IS DISTANT FROM	429	7
UNTIL WE MET THE SOLID TOWN--	I STARTED EARLY--TOOK MY	520	21
THE LADY IN THE TOWN	I WATCHED THE MOON	629	6
IF TOWN IT HAVE--BEYOND [BESIDES] ITSELF--	A LITTLE ROAD--NOT MADE	647	5
WHEN HURRYING TO THE TOWN	HE TOLD A HOMELY TALE	763 V	8
IT SEEMS A CURIOUS TOWN--	WHO OCCUPIES THIS HOUSE?	892	9
THE STARS THAT STATED COME TO TOWN	MY BEST ACQUAINTANCES	932	3
TAPPED SOFT UPON THE TOWN	THE FINGERS OF THE LIGHT	1000	2
"YOU'RE SOON," THE TOWN REPLIED,	THE FINGERS OF THE LIGHT	1000	5
BUT ONCE WITHIN THE TOWN	THE FINGERS OF THE LIGHT	1000	10
OR STROLL THE TOWN AMONG.	THE SPRY ARMS OF THE	1103	8
AN OCCIDENTAL TOWN,	THE LARGEST FIRE EVER	1114	6
IN A NEW ENGLAND TOWN--	THE BUTTERFLY'S	1244	6
TO WESTWARD [UPPER] OF THE TOWN--	IT WAS A QUIET SEEMING	1419	6
TILL IN A DISTANT TOWN	IN WINTER IN MY ROOM	1670	36
TOWNS			
THE SOUL CAME HOME FROM TRIPS [FROM TOWNS / FROM SCENES / TO SLEEP]	CONTAINED IN THIS SHORT	1165 V	
TOWNS ON FROM MINE	IN WINTER IN MY ROOM	1670	37
TOY			
TO LOOK AT, LIKE A TOY--	I CRIED AT PITY--NOT AT	588	8
IS BUT A SCANTY TOY--	SO LARGE MY WILL	1024	10
TOYED			
TOYED COOLLY WITH THE FINAL INCH	'TWAS LIKE A MAELSTROM,	414	5
TOYS			
TO STAY BEHIND--WITH JUST THE TOYS	YOU'LL FIND--IT WHEN YOU	610	15

	FIRST LINE	POEM	LINE
TRACE			
NO TRACE--NO FIGMENT OF THE THING	I'VE KNOWN A HEAVEN,	243	9
WITHOUT DESIGN--THAT I COULD TRACE . . .	FROM COCOON FORTH A	354	5
NOR WHAT CONSOLED IT, I COULD TRACE-- . .	IT CEASED TO HURT ME,	584	13
TRACED			
TRACED AZURE ON HER HAND--	SHE BORE IT TILL THE	144	2
THAT NEVER COULD BE TRACED.	THE FROST WAS NEVER SEEN	1202	12
TRACING			
HEMS--TOO FINE FOR LADY'S TRACING	DONT PUT UP MY THREAD &	617	9
TRACK			
THEN--STOPPED--NO OTHER TRACK!	'TWAS THE OLD--ROAD--	344	11
AND THIS WORN SHOE JUST FITS THE TRACK-- .	'TWAS THE OLD--ROAD--	344	15
THAT SOMETHING--HAD OBSCURED [BEMUMBED] THE TRACK--	IT CEASED TO HURT ME,	584	4
THE TRACK CALLED LAND.	AN EVERYWHERE OF SILVER	884	4
MAY OVERLOOK [MISINFER / MISCONCEIVE] YOUR TRACK--	BECAUSE THAT YOU ARE	1260	4
TRACKLESS			
TOO TRACKLESS FOR A TOMB--	SOME ARROWS SLAY BUT	1565	4
TRACKS			
THE LITTLE TRACKS--CLOSE PREST--	'TWAS THE OLD--ROAD--	344	8
LIKE TRAINS OF CARS ON TRACKS OF PLUSH . .	LIKE TRAINS OF CARS ON	1224	1
TRACT			
A TRACT OF CITIZEN--	MORE LIFE--WENT OUT--	422	16
AND THEN A TRACT BETWEEN	'TIS ONE BY ONE--THE	545	2
TRACTS			
TO THY TRACTS OF SHEEN--	EXPANSE CANNOT BE LOST--	1584	14
TRADE			
A SPIDER AT HIS TRADE AGAIN--	AN ALTERED LOOK ABOUT	140	8
THE ONLY TRADE [ART] THEY KNOW--	A BURDOCK--CLAWED MY	229	8
OF THE APPALLING TRADE--	THERE'S BEEN A DEATH, IN	389	18
AS IF MY TRADE WERE BONE--	AS FAR FROM PITY, AS	496	4
IN UNSUBSTANTIAL TRADE--	THE SPIDER HOLDS A	605	6
AS TRADE HAD SUDDENLY ENCROACHED	A LIGHT EXISTS IN SPRING	812	19
TRADES			
AND TRADES AS BRISKLY FLY--	IF I SHOULD DIE,	54	14
AND YET--BY TRADES--THE SIZE OF THESE . .	IT'S SUCH A LITTLE THING	189	3
TO NECROMANCY AND THE TRADES	NATURE AFFECTS TO BE	1170	5
TRADITION			
ROBINS, IN THE TRADITION	WHOSE CHEEK IS THIS?	82	6
AS INFINITE [BAGATELLES] TRADITION	LIKE SOME OLD FASHIONED	302	5
THE TRADITION [HEROISM] BEARS--	TELL AS A MARKSMAN--WERE	1152	4
THE MOUSE [RAT] BUT A TRADITION NOW . . .	A LITTLE DOG THAT WAGS	1185	11
TRADITION OUGHT TO KNOW--	SO GAY A FLOWER	1456	5
TRADITION BEAR WITH [SUFFER] ME	ONE OF THE ONES THAT	1466	26
THOU CAN'ST NOT PIERCE TRADITION WITH THE PEERLESS PUNCTURE,	PROUD OF MY BROKEN HEART	1736	7
TRADITION'S			
I'LL DECK TRADITION'S BUTTONHOLE--	IF SHE HAD BEEN THE	44	7
TRADITIONS			
TRADITIONS RIPEN AND DECAY, ...	A LITTLE OVERFLOWING	1467	5
TRAFFIC			
HER PURPLE TRAFFIC	THIS--IS THE LAND--THE	266	6
TRAFFICKING			
BEYOND EARTH'S TRAFFICKING FRONTIER, . . .	NOT THAT HE GOES--WE	1435	3
TRAGEDY			
AND THIS BRIEF TRAGEDY OF [DRAMA IN THE] FLESH--	OF ALL THE SOULS THAT	664	7
OTHER TRAGEDY	DRAMA'S VITALLEST	741	3
THAT AWFUL TRAGEDY	A DEW SUFFICED ITSELF--	1437	14
IT BE NOT TRAGEDY--	'TIS WHITER THAN AN	1482	12
TRAGEDY	WHY SHOULD WE HURRY--WHY	1646	V
A TRAGEDY ENACTED	T'IS EASIER TO PITY	1698	4
THAT TRAGEDY ENACTING	T'IS EASIER TO PITY	1698	6
TRAGIC			
GLORY IS THAT BRIGHT TRAGIC THING	GLORY IS THAT BRIGHT	1660	1
TRAILED			
TRAILED--SLOW--ALONG THE ORCHARDS-- . . .	THE SUN--JUST TOUCHED	232	9
AND TRAILED LIKE ROBES AWAY;	A CURIOUS CLOUD	1710	7
TRAILING			
OR TRAILING [SWEEPING] COURTESY	LIKE MEN AND WOMEN	1105	4
TRAIN			
IT RISES TRAIN BY TRAIN--	ALL THESE MY BANNERS BE.	22	4
IT RISES TRAIN BY TRAIN--	ALL THESE MY BANNERS BE.	22	4
OR ELSE A PEACOCK'S PURPLE TRAIN	SOME RAINBOW--COMING	64	4
I THOUGHT THE TRAIN WOULD NEVER COME-- . .	I THOUGHT THE TRAIN	1449	1
A TRAIN WENT THROUGH A BURIAL GATE, . . .	A TRAIN WENT THROUGH A	1761	1
TRAINED			
WHOSE VOICES--TRAINED--[STANZA, HUSHED,] BELOW--	TO LEARN THE TRANSPORT	167	12
TRAINS			
AND ECHOES--TRAINS AWAY, ...	I KNOW SOME LONELY	289	37
LIKE TRAINS OF CARS ON TRACKS OF PLUSH . .	LIKE TRAINS OF CARS ON	1224	1
FOR TRAINS THAT MOMENT [SEVERELY] OUT OF SIGHT,	THE SUMMER THAT WE DID	1773	7
TRAIT			
BEYOND THE TRAIT TO TAKE AWAY	OF ALL THE SOUNDS	321	11
THE CAMEL'S TRAIT--ATTAINED--	STRONG DRAUGHTS OF THEIR	711	6
WHOM FATE [TRAIT] ORDAIN--	WHO COURT OBTAIN WITHIN	803	6
OF AN AUSTERE TRAIT IN PLEASURE--	EXPECTATION--IS	807	5

	FIRST LINE	POEM	LINE
TRAIT (CONTINUED)			
SOME PASSING YEAR--A TRAIT [CHARM] BESTOW	FITTER TO SEE HIM, I MAY	968	4
TRAITOR			
SHALL MEET THE EYE OF TRAITOR	I HAD A GUINEA GOLDEN--	23	31
A TRAITOR IS THE BEE	OF SILKEN SPEECH AND	896	2
TRAITS			
LET CHANGE TRANSFUSE ALL OTHER TRAITS	THE LOOK OF THEE, WHAT	1689	9
TRAMP			
SLOW TRAMP THE CENTURIES,	JUST LOST, WHEN I WAS	160	18
THE FOP--THE CARP--[THE DOG--THE TRAMP--]THE ATHEIST--	HOW MUCH THE PRESENT	1380	3
TRAMPLED			
THE TRAMPLED STEEL THAT SPRINGS!	A WOUNDED DEER--LEAPS	165	6
TRANCE			
TO SAY WHAT TRANCE BELOW	FOR THIS--ACCEPTED	195	15
THEN COVERS THE ABYSS WITH TRANCE--	THERE IS A PAIN--SO	599	3
NOT ANY TRANCE OF INDUSTRY	A CHILLY PEACE INFESTS	1443	3
TRANQUIL			
IT MAKES THE PARTING TRANQUIL	IF I SHOULD DIE,	54	15
TRANQUIL--AS TO REPOSE--	WENT UP A YEAR THIS	93	6
THEY BEAR THEIR DAUNTLESS [FEARLESS / TRANQUIL] HEADS,	WHEN WE STAND ON THE	242	10
WAS HE AFRAID--OR TRANQUIL--	TO KNOW JUST HOW HE	622	22
IN ITSELF--A QUIET [TRANQUIL] THING	A MAN MAY MAKE A REMARK	952	2
THE TRANQUIL PERFIDY	THROUGH THOSE OLD	1753	12
TRANQUILITY			
WITH FRANK TRANQUILITY	A BEE HIS BURNISHED	1339	6
TRANQUILLER			
THE TRANQUILLER TO DIE--	THAT SUCH HAVE DIED	1030	2
TRANQUILLY			
MEET TRANQUILLY, AS FRIENDS--	I READ MY SENTENCE--	412	12
TRANS			
INTRO WITHOUT MY TRANS--	A PANG IS MORE	1530	V
TRANSACTION			
ON HIS SIDE [PART], WHAT TRANSACTION!	THE SUN KEPT STOOPING--	152	3
BUT TRANSACTION--IS ASSISTED	GROWTH OF MAN--LIKE	750	15
TRANSATLANTIC			
SOME TRANSATLANTIC MORN--	THE LONESOME FOR THEY	262	10
TRANSCENDENTAL			
SUCH TRANSCENDENTAL PROSPECT,	"SIC TRANSIT GLORIA	3	23
TRANSCENDING			
TRANSCENDING EXTASY.	A SOMETHING IN A	122	6
TRANSFER			
MIGHT ECSTASY TRANSFER--	THE TREASON OF AN ACCENT	1358	2
TRANSFIGURED			
TRANSFIGURED--MENDED--	TAKING UP THE FAIR IDEAL	428	16
MY GIPSY FACE--TRANSFIGURED NOW--	HE TOUCHED ME, SO I LIVE	506	11
TRANSFUSE			
LET CHANGE TRANSFUSE ALL OTHER TRAITS	THE LOOK OF THEE, WHAT	1689	9
TRANSGRESSION			
GIVE HER FOR HER TRANSGRESSION	WHATEVER IT IS--SHE HAS	1204	11
TRANSIENT			
OUR INTERVIEW--WAS TRANSIENT--	THE ONLY GHOST I EVER	274	13
THE TRANSIENT, FRAGRANT SNOW	THE SNOW THAT NEVER	1133	2
TRANSIT			
"SIC TRANSIT GLORIA MUNDI,"	"SIC TRANSIT GLORIA	3	1
AND TINTS THE TRANSIT IN THE WEST	THE LOVE A LIFE CAN SHOW	673	11
IMPREGNABLE TO TRANSIT	THE JOY THAT HAS NO STEM	1744	7
TRANSITIONS			
PURSUING YOU IN YOUR TRANSITIONS,	PURSUING YOU IN YOUR	1602	1
TRANSITIVE			
HE'S A TRANSITIVE FELLOW--VERY--	THE WIND DID'NT COME	316	5
THE POSITIVE [TRANSITIVE]--OF BELLS--	WHEN BELLS STOP RINGING	633	2
FEELS TRANSITIVE AND COOL.	THAT ODD OLD MAN IS DEAD	1130	12
THE TRANSITIVE TOWARD.	MY TRIUMPH LASTED TILL	1227	14
RETIRED, AND RESUMED HIS TRANSITIVE ESTATE--	THE MOST TRIUMPHANT BIRD	1265	7
TRANSLATED			
LIKE HER TRANSLATED FACES--	YOU SEE I CANNOT SEE--	253	13
TRANSLATION			
THIS--WAS DIFFERENT--'TWAS TRANSLATION--	BETTER--THAN MUSIC! FOR	503	3
TRANSMIGRATION			
BUT LOVE'S TRANSMIGRATION--	NOW I KNEW I LOST HER--	1219	11
TRANSMUTED			
TRANSMUTED--VIVIDER--	I LEARNED--AT LEAST--	944	26
TRANSPIRING			
TRANSPIRING IN THE GRASS	A SINGLE CLOVER PLANK	1343	14
TRANSPLANTED			
TRANSPLANTED--TO THE ROAD--	I HAD BEEN HUNGRY, ALL	579	16
TRANSPORT			
SHE--WAS MUTE FROM TRANSPORT--	MORNS LIKE THESE--WE	27	7
TRANSPORT--BY THROE--	WATER, IS TAUGHT BY	135	3
HALF A TRANSPORT--HALF A TROUBLE--	FLOWERS--WELL--IF	137	3
SUCH TRANSPORT BREAKS UPON THE TOWN	MUSICIANS WRESTLE	157	5
TO LEARN THE TRANSPORT BY [THRO'] THE PAIN--	TO LEARN THE TRANSPORT	167	1
A TRANSPORT ONE CANNOT CONTAIN	A TRANSPORT ONE CANNOT	184	1
MAY YET, A TRANSPORT BE--	A TRANSPORT ONE CANNOT	184	2
SHALL STILL MY TRANSPORT BE--	IF I'M LOST--NOW--	256	3
WITH TRANSPORT, THAT WOULD BE A PAIN	THOSE FAIR--FICTITIOUS	499	19
FOR TRANSPORT IT BE SURE--	THE WAY I READ A	636	4
'TIS TRANSPORT WILD AS THRILLS THE GRAVES	'TIS ANGUISH GRANDER	984	5

	FIRST LINE	POEM	LINE
TRANSPORT (CONTINUED)			
I FEEL FOR THEM A TRANSPORT	A NARROW FELLOW IN THE	986	19
THE TRANSPORT OF HIS COUNTENANCE	THE FINGERS OF THE LIGHT	1000	11
THE TRANSPORT OF THE AIM--	I FIT FOR THEM--	1109	9
THE TERROR [TRANSPORT] OF THE CHILDREN	THESE ARE THE NIGHTS	1128	5
THE TRANSPORT [RAPTURE / TRIUMPH / RIOT] OF THE BIRD--	THE WIND TOOK UP THE	1134	16
A TRANSPORT MAY [MIGHT] RECEIPT US	THE PAST IS SUCH A	1203	3
AS HERESIES OF TRANSPORT	THE WAY TO KNOW THE	1279	11
ADVANCING ON THE TRANSPORT	HOW NEWS MUST FEEL WHEN	1319	V 3
OF TRANSPORT THRILLED WITH FEAR--	SWEET SKEPTICISM OF THE	1413	8
THE TRANSPORT [RAPTURE] OF THE BUD	CRISIS IS SWEET AND YET	1416	V 8
AND THIS UNTOWARD TRANSPORT	HIGH FROM THE EARTH I	1723	17
TRANSPORTED			
AS THEN TRANSPORTED ME!	I MET A KING THIS	166	20
TRANSPORTED WITH COMPASSION	THE HIMMALEH WAS KNOWN	481	3
TRANSPORTING			
A SOMETHING SO TRANSPORTING BRIGHT	A SOMETHING IN A	122	8
THRO' WHAT TRANSPORTING ANGUISH	ALL OVERGROWN BY CUNNING	148	V
TRANSPORTING MUST THE MOMENT BE--	THO' I GET HOME HOW LATE	207	7
TRANSPORT'S			
TRANSPORT'S DOUBTFUL DIVIDEND	WHAT WE SEE WE KNOW	1195	7
TRANSPORT'S DECOMPOSITION FOLLOWS--	WHICH IS THE BEST--THE	1315	7
BY TRANSPORT'S INSTABILITY	A DEW SUFFICED ITSELF--	1437	15
IN TRANSPORT'S EXEGESIS	A DEW SUFFICED ITSELF--	1437	V 15
OF TRANSPORT'S WORKING CLASSES--	THE ROBIN IS A GABRIEL	1483	4
TRANSPORTS			
THROUGH WHAT TRANSPORTS OF PATIENCE	THROUGH WHAT TRANSPORTS	1153	1
THE PERSONS [TRANSPORTS / TREASURES / ASPECTS] OF PROGNOSTICATION	MARCH IS THE MONTH OF	1404	3
TRAP			
THE MOST OBLIGING TRAP	A RAT SURRENDERED HERE	1340	7
CATCH [TRAP / BIND] A DROP OF DEW	FOLLOW WISE ORION	1538	V
TRAVEL			
THIS TRAVEL [TRAVERSE] MAY THE POOREST TAKE	THERE IS NO FRIGATE LIKE	1263	5
ANGUISH CAN TRAVEL TO ITS STAKE,	THE LONGEST DAY THAT GOD	1769	3
TRAVELER			
WE DO NOT MOURN FOR TRAVELER, OR SAILOR,	THE THINGS THAT NEVER	1515	5
TRAVELING			
"GO TRAVELING WITH US!"	"GO TRAVELING WITH US!"	1513	1
TRAVELLED			
BY TROPIC HINT--SOME TRAVELLED BIRD	LIKE FLOWERS, THAT HEARD	513	8
BUT REMOTENESS TRAVELLED	NOW I KNEW I LOST HER--	1219	3
TRAVELLER			
PECULIAR TRAVELLER COMES?	WHAT INN IS THIS	115	3
THE TRAVELLER PROCEED--	NO MAN CAN COMPASS A	477	4
BY TRAVELLER--BE HEARD--	NATURE--THE GENTLEST	790	6
DECOYS IT'S TRAVELLER [PASSENGER]	RISK IS THE HAIR THAT	1239	12
A TRAVELLER [HORSEMAN] ON A HILL--	THE ROAD WAS LIT WITH	1450	4
TREE AND TRAVELLER STOOD--	GLASS WAS THE STREET--IN	1498	2
TRAVELLER'S			
SHE STOPPED--A TRAVELLER'S PRIVILEGE--FOR REST--	I WATCHED THE MOON	629	3
TRAVELLERS			
BUT, WHEN TRAVELLERS TELL	I HAVE NEVER SEEN	175	2
THAT TRAVELLERS--HAD THROWN--	I WENT TO THANK HER--	363	5
TWO TRAVELLERS PERISHING IN SNOW	TWO TRAVELLERS PERISHING	933	1
OF SECRETS IS [TRAVELLERS] THE AIR--	THE FROST WAS NEVER SEEN	1202	16
TRAVELLING			
OR LACES--OR A TRAVELLING SHOW--	WHAT IF I SAY I SHALL	277	11
AS 'TWERE A TRAVELLING MILL--	WITHIN MY GARDEN, RIDES	500	4
A TRAVELLING FLAKE OF SNOW	THE SKY IS LOW--THE	1075	2
HOW NEWS MUST FEEL WHEN TRAVELLING	HOW NEWS MUST FEEL WHEN	1319	1
BESIDE THIS TRAVELLING BIRD	CONFERRING WITH MYSELF	1655	8
TRAVELS			
IT'S SOUNDLESS TRAVELS JUST ARREST	HOW SOFT A CATERPILLAR	1448	5
IT'S TWINKLING TRAVELS IT PURSUES	A WINGED SPARK DOTH SOAR	1468	5
HER TRAVELS DAILY BE	"GO TRAVELING WITH US!"	1513	2
BECAUSE HE TRAVELS FREELY	THE BUTTERFLY OBTAINS	1685	5
TRAVERSE			
TRAVERSE BROADER FORESTS--	IT DID NOT SURPRISE ME--	39	5
THIS TRAVEL [TRAVERSE] MAY THE POOREST TAKE	THERE IS NO FRIGATE LIKE	1263	5
IT'S TRAVERSE	HOW SOFT A CATERPILLAR	1448	V
TRAVERSED			
HE HATH TRAVERSED FIRST--	LIFE--IS WHAT WE MAKE IT	698	10
EXISTENCE--THIS TRAVERSED	THE ONLY NEWS I KNOW	827	9
TRAVERSED SHE THOUGH PAUSING	NOW I KNEW I LOST HER--	1219	7
TRAVERSES			
IT TRAVERSES--YET HALTS--	IT SIFTS FROM LEADEN	311	V
HE TRAVERSES--FAMILIAR--	A PRECIOUS--MOULDERING	371	21
TRAVERSING			
IS TRAVERSING THE INTERVAL	THIS CONSCIOUSNESS THAT	822	5
TREAD			
WHERE I HAVE LOST, I SOFTER TREAD--	WHERE I HAVE LOST, I	104	1
ON WHICH OUR FAITH DOTH TREAD--	HOW BRITTLE ARE THE	1433	2
OUR FAITH DOTH DAILY TREAD--	HOW BRITTLE ARE THE	1433	V 2
TREADING			
KEPT TREADING--TREADING--TILL IT SEEMED	I FELT A FUNERAL, IN MY	280	3
KEPT TREADING--TREADING--TILL IT SEEMED	I FELT A FUNERAL, IN MY	280	3

	FIRST LINE	POEM	LINE
TREASON			
WAS TREASON TWIXT?	FORGET! THE LADY WITH	438	4
FOR TREASON--IN THE POUND--	THEY SHUT ME UP IN PROSE	613	8
NO TREASON IT CAN FEAR--	THE SOUL UNTO ITSELF	683	6
TO ASK WHAT TREASON MEANS.	WHEN THE ASTRONOMER	851	8
FOR TREASON NOT OF HIS, BUT LIFE'S,	THE SUNSET STOPPED ON	950	3
BECAUSE THAT DEATH IS FINAL [TREASON / DIFFERENT],	BECAUSE THAT YOU ARE	1260	5
THE TREASON OF AN ACCENT	THE TREASON OF AN ACCENT	1358	1
WHY, KATIE, TREASON HAS A VOICE--	I SHALL NOT MURMUR IF AT	1410	7
TILL TREASON LIGHTLY PROPAGATES	WHOEVER DISENCHANTS	1451	V 7
A SNAKE IS SUMMER'S [NATURE'S] TREASON [DRAMA],	SWEET IS THE SWAMP WITH	1740	7
TREASURE			
IT'S FAR--FAR TREASURE TO SURMISE--	YOUR RICHES--TAUGHT ME--	299	29
HAD FOR THAT SPECIFIC TREASURE	NONE WHO SAW IT EVER	1110	3
TREASURES			
NEVER THE TREASURES IN HER NEST	SOME, TOO FRAGILE FOR	141	5
TO DEFACE THEIR STATELY TREASURES--	SWEET--SAFE--HOUSES--	457	12
THE PERSONS [TRANSPORTS / TREASURES / ASPECTS] OF PROGNOSTICATION	MARCH IS THE MONTH OF	1404	3
HER TREASURES WERE SO EASY	THE SUMMER THAT WE DID	1773	2
TREATED			
HOW SOME ONE [PARTIES] TREATED HIM	THE SKY IS LOW--THE	1075	6
TREATISE			
IT'S TREATISE FLEW AWAY	I THOUGHT THE TRAIN	1449	8
TREBLE			
THE "MORNING STARS" THE TREBLE LED	MUSICIANS WRESTLE	157	11
TREE			
WHO WILL NOT SERVE THE SOVREIGN, BE HANGED ON FATAL TREE.	AWAKE YE MUSES NINE,	1	10
SIX TRUE, AND COMELY MAIDENS SITTING UPON THE TREE;	AWAKE YE MUSES NINE,	1	34
APPROACH THAT TREE WITH CAUTION, THEN UP IT BOLDLY CLIMB,	AWAKE YE MUSES NINE,	1	35
FROM OFF MY FATHER'S TREE!	"SIC TRANSIT GLORIA	3	20
FELL FROM AN APPLE TREE!	"SIC TRANSIT GLORIA	3	32
SHALL IN A DISTANT TREE	I HAVE A BIRD IN SPRING	5	28
SHE SLEPT BENEATH A TREE--	SHE SLEPT BENEATH A TREE	25	1
BEFORE THE CHRISTMAS TREE,	BEFORE THE ICE IS IN THE	37	6
WHAT WILL THE OAK [FIR] TREE SAY?	I ROBBED THE WOODS--	41	9
SWEEP VALE--AND HILL--AND TREE!	A LADY RED--AMID THE	74	6
AN HOUR, AND GAY ON EVERY TREE	COCOON ABOVE! COCOON	129	4
HOUSEHOLDS IN EVERY TREE--	FOR EVERY BIRD A NEST--	143	5
THOUGH IN ANOTHER TREE--	MAMA NEVER FORGETS HER	164	2
AND SKIP THE RUSSET--ON THE TREE--	MAKE ME A PICTURE OF THE	188	13
THE APPLE ON THE TREE--	"HEAVEN"--IS WHAT I	239	2
SOMETIMES--SCALPS A TREE--	NATURE--SOMETIMES SEARS	314	2
RISE--SOLEMN--ON [IN] THE TREE,	OF ALL THE SOUNDS	321	28
AND SOMETIMES HIT A TREE	WE GROW ACCUSTOMED TO	419	14
NEVER GLADDENED TREE--	DREAMS--ARE WELL--BUT	450	6
IS HEAVEN A PLACE--A SKY--A TREE?	WE PRAY--TO HEAVEN--	489	6
THE "TUNE IS IN THE TREE--"	TO HEAR AN ORIOLE SING	526	13
OR STRUGGLES TO A TREE--	THE BLACK BERRY--WEARS A	554	6
ERASE THE ROOT--NO TREE--	EMPTY MY HEART, OF THEE	587	11
TRIPS FRANTIC IN A TREE--	YOU'VE SEEN BALLOONS SET	700	14
WHEN THE ONLY TREE	NO BOBOLINK--REVERSE HIS	755	2
A DROP FELL ON THE APPLE TREE--	A DROP FELL ON THE APPLE	794	1
IT SHOWS THE FURTHEST TREE	A LIGHT EXISTS IN SPRING	812	10
JUST QUARTERING A TREE--	THE WIND BEGUN TO KNEAD	824	20
HE LABORETH AT EVERY TREE	HIS BILL AN AUGUR IS	1034	3
PRESENTS UPON A TREE	EXPERIMENT TO ME	1073	5
SO THOROUGH IN THE TREE	THE SNOW THAT NEVER	1133	5
A TABLE OF A TREE	A SAUCER HOLDS A CUP	1374	5
WHEN THE BIRD WILL CROWD THE TREE	I SUPPOSE THE TIME WILL	1381	3
LAUREL--VAIL YOUR [THY] DEATHLESS TREE--	LAY THIS LAUREL ON THE	1393	3
LAUREL--FELL YOUR [THY] FUTILE TREE--	LAY THIS LAUREL ON THE	1393	V
TO SOME SUPERIOR TREE	BEFORE YOU THOUGHT OF	1465	13
UPON THE APPLE TREE--	ONE OF THE ONES THAT	1466	28
TREE AND TRAVELLER STOOD--	GLASS WAS THE STREET--IN	1498	2
AN ANTIQUATED TREE	AN ANTIQUATED TREE	1514	1
AT LEAST WITHIN MY TREE	COME SHOW THY DURHAM	1542	5
FOREVER HONORED [CHERISHED] BE THE TREE	FOREVER HONORED BE THE	1570	1
SAYS THE NAKED TREE--	NOT AT HOME TO CALLERS	1590	2
SOME DYER OF A DISTANT TREE	SUMMER BEGINS TO HAVE	1682	11
MENACING THE TREE,	DEATH IS LIKE THE INSECT	1716	2
WRING THE TREE AND LEAVE IT,	DEATH IS LIKE THE INSECT	1716	11
TREES			
A BREEZE--A CAPER IN THE TREES--	A SEPAL, PETAL, AND A	19	4
THE UNSUSPECTING TREES	I ROBBED THE WOODS--	41	3
FROM OUT A HUNDRED TREES--	WE SHOULD NOT MIND SO	81	8
AND LIKE THE TREES, LOOK DOWN--	WHEN WE STAND ON THE	242	2
AMONG THE PENSIVE [SMILING] TREES--	THE ONLY GHOST I EVER	274	12
THE PROUDEST TREES--	IT'S LIKE THE LIGHT--	297	8
A MURMUR IN THE TREES--TO NOTE--	A MURMUR IN THE TREES--	416	1
AT BASES OF THE TREES--	LIKE MIGHTY FOOT LIGHTS	595	2
THE TREES LIKE TASSELS--HIT--AND SWUNG--	THE TREES LIKE TASSELS--	606	1
FOUR TREES--UPON A SOLITARY ACRE--	FOUR TREES--UPON A	742	1
THE LEAVES UNHOOKED THEMSELVES FROM TREES--	THE WIND BEGUN TO KNEAD	824	5
THE HEAVENS [TREES / SKY / FIELD] CANNOT	THE SYMPTOM OF THE GALE	1327	6

	FIRST LINE	POEM	LINE
TREES (CONTINUED)			
BE FOUND--			
THE TREES WERE BRIGHT AND STILL--	THE ROAD WAS LIT WITH	1450	2
THE MARTIAL TREES WITHDRAW	THEIR BARRICADE AGAINST	1471	2
ON A STRANGE [UPON A] MOB OF PANTING TREES .	THERE CAME A WIND LIKE A	1593	9
AND CROSSED A THOUSAND TREES	UPON HIS SADDLE SPRUNG A	1600	2
TALK NOT TO ME OF SUMMER TREES	TALK NOT TO ME OF SUMMER	1634	1
AND HANDED TO THE TREES	THE SUN RETIRED TO A	1693	8
THE TREES HELD UP	THE WIND DREW OFF	1694	7
HE TROD UPON THE TREES	HIGH FROM THE EARTH I	1723	2
TREMBLE			
AND SHADOWS TREMBLE SO--	HAVE YOU GOT A BROOK IN	136	4
WE--COULD TREMBLE--	I TIE MY HAT--I CREASE	443	26
TREMBLING			
I TREMBLING DREW THE TABLE NEAR--	I HAD BEEN HUNGRY, ALL	579	3
MY HAND, WITH TREMBLING CARE	I YEARS HAD BEEN FROM	609	18
HOW SOFTLY SINKS THAT [HIS] TREMBLING SUN .	LOOK BACK ON TIME, WITH	1478	3
TREMBLINGLY			
AND TREMBLINGLY PARTOOK	A WORD MADE FLESH IS	1651	2
TREMENDOUS			
WITHOUT--TREMENDOUS GAIN--	I GOT SO I COULD HEAR	293	2
OF DEATH'S TREMENDOUS NEARNESS--	I TRIED TO THINK A	532	4
IN HIS TREMENDOUS [ETERNAL / ENORMOUS] CHAIR--	THE MOUNTAIN SAT UPON	975	2
WHO PONDERS THIS TREMENDOUS SCENE-- . . .	A LITTLE MADNESS IN THE	1333	4
THE NIGHT'S TREMENDOUS MORROW	ON THAT SPECIFIC PILLOW	1533	3
TREMENDOUSNESS			
A NEARNESS TO TREMENDOUSNESS--	A NEARNESS TO	963	1
TREMOR			
A LITTLE TREMOR IN MY VOICE	WHERE I HAVE LOST, I	104	11
A TREMOR JUST, THAT ALL'S NOT SURE.	UNIT, LIKE DEATH, FOR	408	16
KNOCK WITH TREMOR--	KNOCK WITH TREMOR--	1325	1
TREMULOUS			
BLOWN TREMULOUS IN GLASS--	THE WIND--TAPPED LIKE A	436	16
TRENCH			
MY LIFE JUST HOLDS THE TRENCH--	IF HE WERE LIVING--DARE	734	16
TREPIDATION			
FEELS HER WHITE FOOT--NO TREPIDATION-- . .	THROUGH THE DARK SOD--AS	392	3
TRESS			
DAINTY--AS THE TRESS--ON HER DEFT HEAD-- .	WE--BEE AND I--LIVE BY	230	11
I DARED TO SHOW A TRESS OF THEIR'S	PRECIOUS TO ME--SHE	727	6
TRI			
TRI VICTORY--	TITLE DIVINE--IS MINE!	1072	V
TRIBES			
TRIBES OF ECLIPSE--IN TENTS OF MARBLE-- . .	SAFE IN THEIR ALABASTER	216	V
MYSELF--HAD BANNED THE TRIBES--	IT ALWAYS FELT TO ME--A	597	18
TRIBULATION			
OF TRIBULATION--THESE ARE THEY, ...	OF TRIBULATION--THESE	325	1
TRIBUNAL			
ACCUSED--WERT THOU--AND MYSELF--TRIBUNAL-- .	WERT THOU BUT ILL--THAT	961	9
TRICK			
I BREATHED ENOUGH TO TAKE THE TRICK-- . .	I BREATHED ENOUGH TO	272	1
THE TRICK TO START--	SHE LAY AS IF AT PLAY	369	8
ART OF SNOW--OR TRICK OF LILY	HER SWEET TURN TO LEAVE	649	15
"TEARS"--A TRICK OF THE NERVE--	"SPEECH"--IS A PRANK OF	688	2
TRIED			
I COULD CLIMB--IF I TRIED, I KNOW--	OVER THE FENCE--	251	4
I KNEW LAST NIGHT--WHEN SOMEONE TRIED TO TWINE--	HOW SICK--TO WAIT--IN	368	2
IT TRIED--TO BE A ROSE--	GOD MADE A LITTLE	442	2
I TRIED TO THINK A LONELIER THING	I TRIED TO THINK A	532	1
TO CHEAT HERSELF, IT SEEMED SHE TRIED-- . .	MY FIRST WELL DAY--SINCE	574	13
I'LL TELL YOU HOW I TRIED TO KEEP	IF I MAY HAVE IT, WHEN	577	22
I TRIED TO DROP [SHIFT] IT IN THE CROWD-- .	BEREAVED OF ALL, I WENT	784	11
I TRIED TO MATCH IT--SEAM BY SEAM--	I FELT A CLEAVING IN MY	937	3
THE THOUGHT BEHIND, I STROVE [TRIED] TO JOIN	I FELT A CLEAVING IN MY	937	5
IF I TRIED--	WE'LL PASS WITHOUT THE	996	6
I KNOW FOR I HAVE TRIED	BETWEEN THE FORM OF LIFE	1101	8
TILL I HAVE FINER [VAINER / FURTHER] TRIED--	SHALL I TAKE THEE, THE	1126	4
WHATEVER IT IS [BE]--SHE HAS TRIED IT-- . .	WHATEVER IT IS--SHE HAS	1204	1
SURRENDERED BY THE TRIED--	CRISIS IS SWEET AND YET	1416	V 4
TRIED ALWAYS AND CONDEMNED BY THEE	TRIED ALWAYS AND	1559	1
TRIES			
THE PUNCTURE--COOLLY TRIES--	A WEIGHT WITH NEEDLES ON	264	4
THE ROBIN LOCKS HER NEST, AND TRIES HER WINGS.	QUITE EMPTY, QUITE AT	1606	2
TRIFLE			
THEY MAY TAKE THE TRIFLE	TO VENERATE THE SIMPLE	57	5
A TRIFLE--IN HIS OWN ESTEEM [ESTIMATE]-- .	HE GAVE AWAY HIS LIFE--	567	3
THE DYING, IS A TRIFLE, PAST, ...	TOO SCANTY 'TWAS TO DIE	1013	5
A TRIFLE AFTERWARD	IN WINTER IN MY ROOM	1670	10
TO MAKE SOME TRIFLE FAIRER	WERE NATURE MORTAL LADY	1762	9
TRIFLES			
BUT TRIFLES LOOK SO TRIVIAL	DEAR MARCH--COME IN--	1320	23
AS HE ESTEEMED THEM TRIFLES, ...	HIGH FROM THE EARTH I	1723	3
TRIFLING			
'TIS A TRIFLING KNOWLEDGE--	I COULD DIE--TO KNOW--	570	2
UPON WHAT BRITTLE [FICKLE / TRIFLING] PIERS	HOW BRITTLE ARE THE	1433	V 1
TRIGGER			
CARESSED A TRIGGER ABSENTLY	HE SCANNED IT--STAGGERED	1062	8
TRILLED			
AND TRILLED, AND QUIVERED, AND SHOOK	A TRAIN WENT THROUGH A	1761	3

	FIRST LINE	POEM	LINE
TROTH			
SUFFICIENT TROTH, THAT WE SHALL [SHE WILL] RISE--	THERE CAME A DAY AT	322	25
THE EAST--HER PURPLE TROTH	THE SUNRISE RUNS FOR	710	2
THEIR FAITH--THE EVERLASTING TROTH--	THROUGH THE STRAIT PASS	792	9
HIS TROTH A TERM	OF SILKEN SPEECH AND	896	6
TO TROTH UNKNOWN	DEATH IS THE SUPPLE	1445	10
SEVEN YEARS OF TROTH HAVE TAUGHT THEE	REARRANGE A "WIFE'S"	1737	7
TROTWOOD			
ASKED HIM HIS NAME--HE LISPED ME "TROTWOOD"--	TRUDGING TO EDEN,	1020	3
TROUBADOUR			
STILL, FOR MY MISSING TROUBADOUR	I HAD A GUINEA GOLDEN--	23	15
AND THE TROUBADOUR.	SEXTON! MY MASTER'S	96	8
A TROUBADOUR UPON THE ELM	NEW FEET WITHIN MY	99	3
THE ROBIN IS A GABRIEL [TROUBADOUR]	THE ROBIN IS A GABRIEL	1483	1
DAVID--THE TROUBADOUR--	THE BIBLE IS AN ANTIQUE	1545	8
TROUBLE			
HALF A TRANSPORT--HALF A TROUBLE--	FLOWERS--WELL--IF	137	3
AND SO I TROUBLE THEE.	SAVIOR! I'VE NO ONE ELSE	217	2
BOUND--A TROUBLE--	BOUND--A TROUBLE--	269	1
UNTO LIKE STORY--TROUBLE HAS ENTICED ME--	UNTO LIKE STORY--TROUBLE	295	1
A TROUBLE LOOKS BITTEREST--	IT DONT SOUND SO	426	6
A TROUBLE LEST THEY'RE HOMESICK--	I'M SORRY FOR THE DEAD--	529	13
I COULD NOT SEE [FEEL] THE TROUBLE [ANGUISH] GO--	IT CEASED TO HURT ME,	584	2
TIME IS A TEST OF TROUBLE--	THEY SAY THAT "TIME	686	5
PERPLEXED! ESTATES OF VIOLET TROUBLE NE'ER LOOKED ON!	WOULD YOU LIKE SUMMER?	691	5
AND TROUBLE [HARASS] ME--NO MORE--	THE BIRDS REPORTED FROM	743	8
THE DARKNESS [TROUBLE] BRACED AS FIRM	SEVERER SERVICE OF	786	18
IN THE FRONT OF TROUBLE--	SAFE DESPAIR IT IS THAT	1243	6
EFFACE THE BURDEN [MONSTER / STATURE / SPECTRE / TROUBLE / . . .	THE PILE OF YEARS IS NOT	1507	7
A FLOWER WILL NOT TROUBLE HER, IT HAS SO SMALL A FOOT,	A FLOWER WILL NOT	1621	1
TROUBLED			
HER TROUBLED QUESTION FLINGS--	ONCE MORE, MY NOW	48	4
TILL THOSE TWO TROUBLED--LITTLE CLOCKS	THE ROSE DID CAPER ON	208	15
JUST--SEE--IF I TROUBLED THEM--	WHY--DO THEY SHUT ME OUT	248	7
IT TROUBLED ME AS ONCE I WAS--	IT TROUBLED ME AS ONCE I	600	1
WHEN YOU TROUBLED THE ELLIPSE--	LET US PLAY YESTERDAY--	728	15
TROUBLES			
WHAT SHALL I DO WHEN THE SUMMER TROUBLES--	WHAT SHALL I DO WHEN THE	956	1
TROUBLING			
OR SHY OF TROUBLING HER	THE SOUL SHOULD ALWAYS	1055	4
TROUGH			
BUT I TELL YOU EVERY STEP IS A TROUGH [SLUICE]--	FLOSS WONT SAVE YOU FROM	1322	5
TROUGHS			
AND THERE WERE [WAS] TROUGHS [SPACE / ROOM] BESIDE	A GREAT HOPE FELL	1123	13
TROUPE			
IN PIROUETTE TO BLANCH A TROUPE--	I CANNOT DANCE UPON MY	326	7
TROWSERS			
SOME RUBY TROWSERS HURRIED ON--	A SLASH OF BLUE--	204	6
TRUDGE			
I TRUDGE THE DAY AWAY--	I HAVE A KING, WHO DOES	103	3
SOME, WOULD EVEN TRUDGE TONIGHT!	"HOUSES"--SO THE WISE	127	8
TRUDGING			
AND TRUDGING FEET FROM SCHOOL--	ON SUCH A NIGHT, OR SUCH	146	20
HER TRUDGING FEET ESPIED--	SHE DIED--THIS WAS THE	150 V	6
AND SOMEWHAT IN THE TRUDGING FEET--	THE BEGGAR LAD--DIES	717	3
IF TRUDGING FEET MAY STAND--	THE BEGGAR LAD--DIES	717	10
TRUDGING TO EDEN, LOOKING BACKWARD,	TRUDGING TO EDEN,	1020	1
TRUE			
EARTH IS A MERRY DAMSEL, AND HEAVEN A KNIGHT SO TRUE,	AWAKE YE MUSES NINE,	1	23
SIX TRUE, AND COMELY MAIDENS SITTING UPON THE TREE;	AWAKE YE MUSES NINE,	1	34
HEAVEN TO US, IF TRUE.	AS WATCHERS HANG UPON	121	12
IS IT TRUE, DEAR SUE?	IS IT TRUE, DEAR SUE?	218	1
BECAUSE I KNOW IT'S TRUE--	I LIKE A LOOK OF AGONY,	241	2
THEIR BANQUET'S REAL [TRUE]--	ONE YEAR AGO--JOTS WHAT?	296	11
AND QUICK ENOUGH, IF TRUE.	THEY LEAVE US WITH THE	350	12
AND TELL YOU ALL YOUR DREAMS--WERE TRUE--	A PRECIOUS--MOULDERING	371	23
A TONGUE--TO TELL HIM I AM TRUE!	A TONGUE--TO TELL HIM I	400	1
THAT SO FAR--TRUTH IS TRUE?	A TONGUE--TO TELL HIM I	400	8
TRUE, LIKE THE TOMB,	UNIT, LIKE DEATH, FOR	408	2
THE POWER TO BE TRUE TO YOU,	THE POWER TO BE TRUE TO	464	1
IT TAKE THE TALE FOR TRUE--	I MEANT TO HAVE BUT	476	22
A GRATITUDE--THAT SUCH BE TRUE--	THE WORLD--STANDS--	493	13
'TIS TRUE--THEY SHUT ME IN THE COLD--	'TIS TRUE--THEY SHUT ME	538	1
RUNS EVENLY--AND TRUE--	THE BRAIN, WITHIN IT'S	556	2
BUT NO TRUE EYE	INCONCEIVABLY SOLEMN!	582	9
IF WE WERE TRUE--	I ROSE--BECAUSE HE SANK	616	19
'TIS TRUE--OUR FUTURES DIFFERENT LAY--	OURSELVES WERE WED ONE	631	9
'TIS TRUE, YOUR GARDEN LED THE BLOOM,	OURSELVES WERE WED ONE	631	13
THAT I ESTEEM THE FICTION--REAL [TRUE]--	I THINK TO LIVE--MAY BE	646	23
CARRIAGES--BE SURE--AND GUESTS--TRUE [TOO]--	HER SWEET TURN TO LEAVE	649	3
TO OUR ENDEAVOR--NOT SO REAL [TRUE /	A PRISON GETS TO BE A	652	19

	FIRST LINE	POEM	LINE
TRUE (CONTINUED)			
CLOSE / NEAR]			
TO CREDIT [COMPASS]--'TIS'NT TRUE!	NO ROMANCE SOLD UNTO	669	7
THAT SHOW HOWEVER TRUE--	THEIR HIGHT IN HEAVEN	696	14
'TIS TRUE--THAT DEITY TO STOOP	MY WORTHINESS IS ALL MY	751	9
NOW, DO YOU DOUBT THAT YOUR BIRD WAS TRUE?	SPLIT THE LARK--AND	861	8
STRIKES TRUE WITHIN--	BIND ME--I STILL CAN	1005	3
IT MUST AT FIRST BE TRUE--	THE SMOULDERING EMBERS	1132 V	8
AND THEN IF WE ARE TRUE TO PLAN [GROWTH]	WE NEVER KNOW HOW HIGH	1176	3
HOWEVER FIRST [TRUE / DUE / JUST] IT BE	BECAUSE THAT YOU ARE	1260	6
YOU KNEW IT [THAT] WAS NOT TRUE	THE MOST PATHETIC THING	1290	6
AND TRUE [BEST / REAL / BLAND / FINE / FAIR] THE OTHER	I'D RATHER RECOLLECT A	1349	4
TRUE POEMS FLEE--	TO SEE THE SUMMER SKY	1472	3
'TIS TRUE THE DROUGHT IS DESTITUTE,	TO LOSE THEE--SWEETER	1754	3
TRUER			
HELD IN A TRUER LAND	I HAVE A BIRD IN SPRING	5	14
TRUEST			
BUT JUST THE ANTI FAIR--AVERRING--FAIREST-- TRUEST TRUTH	EXTOL THEE--COULD I--	1643	3
TRUFFLED			
AT MORNING, IN A TRUFFLED HUT	THE MUSHROOM IS THE ELF	1298	3
TRULY			
ARE FABRICS TRULY TORN--	THE HEALED HEART SHOWS	1440	4
TRUMPET			
AND BRING THE FIFE, AND TRUMPET, AND BEAT UPON THE DRUM--	AWAKE YE MUSES NINE,	1	39
THE TRUMPET, SIR, SHALL WAKE THEM,	"SIC TRANSIT GLORIA	3	49
THERE IS NO TRUMPET LIKE THE TOMB	THE IMMORTALITY SHE GAVE	1648 V	
TRUMPETS			
AS TRUMPETS--ROLLED--	UNTO LIKE STORY--TROUBLE	295	16
THE TRUMPETS TELL IT TO THE AIR--	MY PORTION IS DEFEAT--	639	15
TRUNDLE			
OF ROBINS IN THE TRUNDLE BED	A MURMUR IN THE TREES--	416	13
TRUNK			
AS "BRANCH," [TRUNK] AND "JUGULAR."	THE VEINS OF OTHER	811	4
TO PACK HER TRUNK AND ORDER	WERE NATURE MORTAL LADY	1762	3
TRUST			
WE TRUST THAT SHE WAS WILLING--	THE GENTIAN WEAVES HER	18	13
SUCH TRUST HAD ONE AMONG US,	COULD LIVE--DID LIVE--	43	10
TRUST THE LOVING PROMISE	I OFTEN PASSED THE	51	15
WE TRUST, IN PLUMED PROCESSION	TO FIGHT ALOUD, IS VERY	126	9
A LITTLE TRUST--A DEMIJOHN--	A LITTLE BREAD--A CRUST	159	2
BY MY LONG BRIGHT--AND LONGER--TRUST--	I THINK JUST HOW MY	237	15
SO TRUST HIM, COMRADE--	THEY LEAVE US WITH THE	350	9
SHOOK MY STRONG TRUST--	HE STRAINED MY FAITH--	497	3
WE TRUST--IN PLACES PERFECTER--	THOSE FAIR--FICTITIOUS	499	9
REMEMBERING OURSELVES, WE TRUST--	THOSE FAIR--FICTITIOUS	499	13
TRUST IN THE UNEXPECTED--	TRUST IN THE UNEXPECTED	555	1
FOR [TO] THOSE WHO WORSHIP [TRUST IN / ASK OF] THEM--	I RECKON--WHEN I COUNT	569	14
AFRAID TO TRUST THE MORN	AFRAID! OF WHOM AM I	608	10
HE--WOULD TRUST NO STRANGER--	LIFE--IS WHAT WE MAKE IT	698	5
AND THEN RETURN--AND NIGHT [TRUST]--AND HOME--	I LEARNED--AT LEAST--	944	22
MY FRACTURED TRUST--	THE CHEMICAL CONVICTION	954	4
TRUST OMNIPOTENCE"--	"UNTO ME?" I DO NOT KNOW	964	8
I HAVE ANOTHER TRUST"--	DEATH IS A DIALOGUE	976	4
TRUST ADJUSTS HER "PERADVENTURE"--	TRUST ADJUSTS HER	1161	1
OF COMPENSATED TRUST.	"REMEMBER ME" IMPLORED	1180	8
WE TRUST THAT SHE PARTOOK	ELIZABETH TOLD ESSEX	1321	6
SO CONSTANT TO IT'S STOLID TRUST,	SHE LAID HER DOCILE	1396	5
THOUGH TO TRUST US--SEEM TO US	"HEAVENLY FATHER"--TAKE	1461	5
TRUST ENTRENCHED IN NARROW PAIN--	REARRANGE A "WIFE'S"	1737	10
TRUSTED			
AND SHE HAD PAST, WITH [FLED WITH / TRUSTED / HEARKENED] HIM--	I MEANT TO FIND HER WHEN	718	8
TRUSTING			
THE TRUSTING WOODS.	I ROBBED THE WOODS--	41	2
TRUSTS			
THAT TRUSTS HER--BOLDLY UP--	THE TRUTH--IS STIRLESS--	780	12
TRUSTY			
UPON THIS TRUSTY WORD--	ESCAPE IS SUCH A	1347	12
TRUSTY AS THE STARS	TRUSTY AS THE STARS	1369	1
TRUTH			
THE TRUTH, IS BALD, AND COLD--	'TIS SO APPALLING--IT	281	9
THAT SO FAR--TRUTH IS TRUE?	A TONGUE--TO TELL HIM I	400	8
WHEN ONE WHO DIED FOR TRUTH, WAS LAIN	I DIED FOR BEAUTY--BUT	449	3
"AND I--FOR TRUTH--THEMSELF ARE ONE--	I DIED FOR BEAUTY--BUT	449	7
WHEN TRUTH--AFFRONTED LONG--	TRIUMPH--MAY BE OF	455	6
IT IS A TRUTH [FACT]--OF BLOOD--	WE DREAM--IT IS GOOD WE	531	6
AND TRUTH--SO MANIFOLD!	WE LEARNED THE WHOLE OF	568	12
THE REAL [TRUTH]--FICTITIOUS SEEMS--	I THINK TO LIVE--MAY BE	646	24
THE TRUTH--IS STIRLESS--	THE TRUTH--IS STIRLESS--	780	1
TRUTH STAYS HERSELF--AND EVERY MAN	THE TRUTH--IS STIRLESS--	780	11
TRUTH--IS AS OLD AS GOD--	TRUTH--IS AS OLD AS GOD	836	1
IF HE PERCEIVE THE OTHER TRUTH--	FITTER TO SEE HIM, I MAY	968	23
TELL ALL THE TRUTH BUT TELL IT SLANT--	TELL ALL THE TRUTH BUT	1129	1
THE TRUTH MUST DAZZLE GRADUALLY [MODERATELY]	TELL ALL THE TRUTH BUT	1129	7
AND OF "TRUTH" UNTIL IT PROCLAIMED HIM A LIAR--	HE PREACHED UPON	1207	3

	FIRST LINE	POEM		LINE
TRUTH (CONTINUED)				
THE TRUTH NEVER FLAUNTED [HOISTED] A SIGN--	HE PREACHED UPON	1207		4
THAT TOLD THE TRUTH [NEWS] TO ME-- . . .	COULD MORTAL LIP DIVINE	1409	V	
INVITES AND THEN RETARDS THE TRUTH . . .	SWEET SKEPTICISM OF THE	1413		5
THIS TRUTH ENDEAR [DECLARE]--	THE GENTIAN HAS A	1424		15
TRUTH IS GOOD HEALTH--AND SAFETY, AND THE SKY.	A COUNTERFEIT--A PLATED	1453		5
BUT TRUTH, OUTLASTS THE SUN--	OPINION IS A FLITTING	1455		2
TRUTH ADJOURN YOUR BOON	LOVE IS DONE WHEN LOVE'S	1485		4
BUT JUST THE ANTI FAIR--AVERRING--FAIREST-- TRUEST TRUTH	EXTOL THEE--COULD I--	1643		3
THAT THOU ART TRITEST--BRIGHTEST [SWEETEST] TRUTH--	EXTOL THEE--COULD I--	1643	V	4
THE TRUTH I DO NOT DARE TO KNOW	CONSULTING SUMMER'S	1715		7
TRUTH'S				
THE TRUTH'S SUPERB SURPRISE	TELL ALL THE TRUTH BUT	1129		4
TRY				
TRY--CAN YOU STIR THE AWFUL RIVET-- . . .	HOW MANY TIMES THESE LOW	187		3
TRY--CAN YOU LIFT THE HASPS OF STEEL! . .	HOW MANY TIMES THESE LOW	187		4
WOULD'NT THE ANGELS TRY ME--	WHY--DO THEY SHUT ME OUT	248		5
ALTHOUGH I HEARD THEM TRY--	A MURMUR IN THE TREES--	416		16
AND TRY ANOTHER KEY--	I AM ALIVE--I GUESS--	470		24
YOU TRY TO TOUCH [REACH] THE SMILE . . .	IF ANYBODY'S FRIEND BE	509		14
AND IF THEY HAVE TO TRY--	I MEASURE EVERY GRIEF I	561		10
AS A HAND DID TRY TO CHALK THE SUN . . .	I FOUND THE WORDS TO	581		4
YOU'LL FIND--IT WHEN YOU TRY TO DIE-- . .	YOU'LL FIND--IT WHEN YOU	610		1
TO THOSE WHO DARE [ALLOWED] TO TRY-- . . .	I THINK TO LIVE--MAY BE	646		2
FIRST TIME THEY TRY THE SKY!	AGAIN--HIS VOICE IS AT	663		23
WOULD IT TRY MINE--	IF IT HAD NO PENCIL	921		2
THE LOVE THAT WOULD NOT TRY	HOW MANY SCHEMES MAY DIE	1150		9
FROM NEITHER OF THEM THO' HE TRY	AS OLD AS WOE--	1168		9
I TRY TO FLEE	BECAUSE MY BROOK IS	1200		6
THE TURTLE WILL NOT TRY	SO MUCH OF HEAVEN HAS	1228		10
TRY IT ON YOURSELF--	"FAITHFUL TO THE END"	1357	V	
WE TRY TO SHOW BECOMING FIRMNESS [CALMNESS]--	MARCH IS THE MONTH OF	1404		5
NOR TRY TO TIE THE BUTTERFLY, ...	GO NOT TOO NEAR A HOUSE	1434		5
OF DEATH I TRY TO THINK LIKE THIS-- . . .	OF DEATH I TRY TO THINK	1558		1
TO TRY TO SPEAK, AND MISS THE WAY	TO TRY TO SPEAK, AND	1617		1
TRYING				
YOU WILL KNOW I'M TRYING	IF I SHOULD'NT BE ALIVE	182		7
TRYING IF IT SPLIT--	ROBBED BY DEATH--BUT	971		16
THAT MAKES OUR TRYING [RUNNING] POOR. . .	BECAUSE HE LOVES HER	1229		12
THE TRYING ON THE [AN] UTMOST	WHILE WE WERE FEARING IT	1277		9
TUBE				
THE DANDELION'S PALLID TUBE	THE DANDELION'S PALLID	1519		1
THE TUBE UPLIFTS A SIGNAL BUD	THE DANDELION'S PALLID	1519		5
TUBES				
AND LILY TUBES--LIKE WELLS--	WHAT WOULD I GIVE TO SEE	247		10
TUCKING				
TENDERLY TUCKING THEM IN FROM FROST . . .	SOME, TOO FRAGILE FOR	141		3
TUCKS				
TUCKS--OF DAINTY INTERSPERSION--	DONT PUT UP MY THREAD &	617		11
TUFTS				
THEN QUIVER DOWN--WITH TUFTS OF TUNE-- . .	OF ALL THE SOUNDS	321		7
TUG				
BUT I TUG CHILDISH AT MY BARS	I NEVER HEAR THE WORD	77		7
YOU COULD HEAR THE BODDICE TUG, BEHIND YOU--	GOING TO HIM! HAPPY	494		12
TUGGING				
TUGGING AT THE FORGE!	BY A FLOWER--BY A LETTER	109		8
TUGS				
THAT SOUNDLESS TUGS--WITHIN--	DARE YOU SEE A SOUL AT	365		12
TULLE				
THAT CUSHIONS MYSTERY WITH TULLE, ...	THE TINT I CANNOT TAKE--	627		19
MY TIPPET--ONLY TULLE--	BECAUSE I COULD NOT STOP	712		16
TUMBLE				
AS BIRDS--THAT TUMBLE FROM THE CLOUDS . .	THE LONESOME FOR THEY	262		7
AND TUMBLE--BLUE--ON ME--	IT TROUBLED ME AS ONCE I	600		16
UNTIL THEY HEEDLESS TUMBLE IN	A STAGNANT PLEASURE LIKE	1281		3
TUMBLED				
ADJUSTS IT'S TUMBLED HEAD--	A ROUTE OF EVANESCENCE	1463		6
TUMBLES				
AND TUMBLES IN THE SEA--	YOU'VE SEEN BALLOONS SET	700		16
TUMULT				
NO TUMULT THERE HAD BEEN	THE BIRDS BEGUN AT FOUR	783		18
IN TUMULT--OR EXTREMITY--	ON A COLUMNAR SELF--	789		3
TUMULTUOUS				
THY TUMULTUOUS ROOMS	FORTITUDE INCARNATE	1217		10
IN TIMID AND TUMULTUOUS SOIL	THE FASCINATING CHILL	1480		5
TUN				
RISK IS THE HAIR THAT HOLDS THE TUN [ONE] .	RISK IS THE HAIR THAT	1239		1
THAT TUN IS HOLLOW--BUT THE TUN--	RISK IS THE HAIR THAT	1239		3
THAT TUN IS HOLLOW--BUT THE TUN--	RISK IS THE HAIR THAT	1239		3
THE "FOOLISH TUN" THE CRITICS SAY--	RISK IS THE HAIR THAT	1239		9
TUNE				
THE STORM DOTH WALK THE SEASHORE HUMMING A MOURNFUL TUNE,	AWAKE YE MUSES NINE,	1		17
IT WAS A DIFFERENT TUNE--	ONE SISTER HAVE I IN OUR	14		10
OF LAST YEAR'S SUNDERED TUNE!	SOME RAINBOW--COMING	64		9
WHISTLED ITSELF A TUNE--	HEART, NOT SO HEAVY AS	83		4
AND WHEN THE ORCHARDS STOP THEIR TUNE-- . .	MAKE ME A PICTURE OF THE	188		7
TO THE IMMORTAL TUNE--	THE ROSE DID CAPER ON	208		14

	FIRST LINE	POEM	LINE
TUNE (CONTINUED)			
BUT--I SHALL BRING A FULLER TUNE--	I SHALL KEEP SINGING!	250	8
AND SINGS THE TUNE WITHOUT THE WORDS--	"HOPE" IS THE THING WITH	254	3
THE ROBIN'S MY CRITERION FOR TUNE--	THE ROBIN'S MY CRITERION	285	1
ROBIN--UTTERED [PUBLISHED / LAVISHED] HALF THE TUNE--	HER--"LAST POEMS"--	312	8
THEN QUIVER DOWN--WITH TUFTS OF TUNE--	OF ALL THE SOUNDS	321	7
THE BEES--WILL NOT DESPISE THE TUNE--	IT WILL BE SUMMER--	342	11
OR PLAYED HIS CHOSEN TUNE--	ALTHOUGH I PUT AWAY HIS	366	8
OVER AND OVER, LIKE A TUNE--	OVER AND OVER, LIKE A	367	1
IN SOVREIGN--SWERVELESS TUNE--	THERE IS A FLOWER THAT	380	28
BUT--I WAS TELLING A TUNE--I HEARD--	BETTER--THAN MUSIC! FOR	503	16
DROP INTO TUNE--AROUND THE THRONE--	BETTER--THAN MUSIC! FOR	503	24
THE "TUNE IS IN THE TREE--"	TO HEAR AN ORIOLE SING	526	13
AND KNEW ONE BIRD A TUNE--	WHAT CARE THE DEAD, FOR	592	12
THERE SEEMED TO RISE A TUNE	THE TREES LIKE TASSELS--	606	2
AS DID [SHOULD] THE DOWN EMIT A TUNE--	OF BEING IS A BIRD	653	11
I ONLY ASK A TUNE	THE JUDGE IS LIKE THE	699	10
MAKES LACERATING TUNE--	UPON CONCLUDED LIVES	735	5
WHAT MERIT HAVE THE TUNE	THE BIRD MUST SING TO	880	2
HIS IDLENESS--A TUNE--	HIS FEET ARE SHOD WITH	916	6
A RUFFLE [THIMBLE]--OR A TUNE--	I LEARNED--AT LEAST--	944	17
DROP A TUNE ON ME--	WHAT SHALL I DO WHEN THE	956	6
AND CHISELLED ALL MY TUNE	I'VE DROPPED MY BRAIN--	1046	14
IF THE TUNE DRIP TOO MUCH	SANG FROM THE HEART,	1059	3
BUT TERMINATE IN TUNE!	FURTHER IN SUMMER THAN	1068	V
THEIR MIRACLES OF [UNSUSPECTING / UNSUSPICIOUS] TUNE--	HIS BILL IS CLASPED--HIS	1102	12
UNLESS THOU KNOW'ST THE TUNE	TOUCH LIGHTLY NATURE'S	1389	2
WHO CARES ABOUT A BLUE BIRD'S TUNE--	A PANG IS MORE	1530	6
TO HEAR HER IS A TUNE--	TO SEE HER IS A PICTURE	1568	2
ALONE--IS NOT A TUNE--	THE SPIRIT LASTS--BUT IN	1576	8
HER TONGUE MORE TENDER [TIMID / MAGIC] THAN THE TUNE [TONE]	HER FACE WAS IN A BED OF	1722	5
TUNES			
OF CATHEDRAL TUNES--	THERE'S A CERTAIN SLANT	258	4
AND STIR ALL DAY TO PRETTY TUNES	THE GRASS SO LITTLE HAS	333	5
THE BIRDS DECLAIM THEIR TUNES--	THE MORNING AFTER WO--	364	9
LET GO A MUSIC--AS OF TUNES	THE WIND--TAPPED LIKE A	436	15
OF ALL TUNES I KNEW--AND MORE--	BETTER--THAN MUSIC! FOR	503	4
AND JUST THE MEANEST [COMMON / FAINTEST] TUNES	I THINK I WAS ENCHANTED	593	12
THE DRUMS DONT FOLLOW ME--WITH TUNES--	MY PORTION IS DEFEAT--	639	4
WITH THREATENING TUNES AND LOW--	THE WIND BEGUN TO KNEAD	824	V 2
STEPPING TO INCORPOREAL TUNES	HOW LONESOME THE WIND	1418	6
TUNING			
THE MOWER IS TUNING HIS SCYTHE	BACK FROM THE CORDIAL	1625	V
TUNIS			
THE MAIL FROM TUNIS, PROBABLY,	A ROUTE OF EVANESCENCE	1463	7
TUNNEL			
I'D TUNNEL--TILL MY GROOVE	I HAD NOT MINDED--WALLS	398	5
THE TUNNEL IS NOT LIGHTED	ADVANCE IS LIFE'S	1652	5
TURBANED			
THE CHILDREN OF WHOSE TURBANED SEAS--	SOME RAINBOW--COMING	64	23
TURBID			
WHICH LIKE THE MOON, SOME TURBID NIGHT,	EACH THAT WE LOSE TAKES	1605	3
TURBULENT			
SO TURBULENT IT GROWS	THIS CHASM, SWEET, UPON	858	12
TURK			
THEN SANK AS GAILY AS A TURK	SHE DIED AT PLAY,	75	4
TURN			
WAS ONCE SUPPOSED TO TURN,	"SIC TRANSIT GLORIA	3	34
AND JUST TO TURN AWAY,	DISTRUSTFUL OF THE	20	2
MY FLOWERS TURN FROM FORUMS--	THE RAINBOW NEVER TELLS	97	5
THEN I TURN SOLDIER TOO,	MY FRIEND ATTACKS MY	118	3
I TURN MY BRIMMING EYES AWAY,	I BRING AN UNACCUSTOMED	132	6
AND THEN RELUCTANT TURN--	AS CHILDREN BID THE	133	2
JUST HOW LONG-CHEATED EYES WILL TURN--	THO' I GET HOME HOW LATE	207	10
WHEN "LANDLORDS" TURN THE DRUNKEN BEE	I TASTE A LIQUOR NEVER	214	9
I TENDERER, TURN ME TO.	FOR LARGEST WOMAN'S	309	6
AND THEN--HE'LL TURN ME ROUND AND ROUND--	THE FACE I CARRY WITH ME	336	13
WITH MANY A TURN--AND THORN--	'TWAS THE OLD--ROAD--	344	3
AN HONOR, THOUGHT CAN TURN HER TO	I HAD THE GLORY--THAT	349	2
TURN IT, A LITTLE--FULL IN THE FACE	IT DONT SOUND SO	426	5
AND OTHER--WENT TO TURN THE MILL--	FORGET! THE LADY WITH	438	15
NOR EVER TURN TO TELL ME WHY--	WHY MAKE IT DOUBT--IT	462	12
AND THEN--RELUCTANT--TURN AWAY	WE COVER THEE--SWEET	482	7
WOULD NOT SO RAVISHED TURN--	HE TOUCHED ME, SO I LIVE	506	15
DOES NOT SO MUCH AS TURN HIS HEAD	TO INTERRUPT HIS YELLOW	591	7
'TIS ANTIDOTE TO TURN--	I THINK I WAS ENCHANTED	593	28
UNTO MY BOOKS--SO GOOD TO TURN--	UNTO MY BOOKS--SO GOOD	604	1
HER SWEET TURN TO LEAVE THE HOMESTEAD	HER SWEET TURN TO LEAVE	649	1
TURN ON ME--WHEN I FAIL--OR FEIGN,	SWEET MOUNTAINS--YE TELL	722	4
TO WIN, BECOME THEIR [MY] TURN--	I PLAY AT RICHES--TO	801	20
THEN, TURN MY FACE AWAY.	I CANNOT BUY IT--'TIS	840	12
TURN [TAKE] SOONEST [SOONER] TO THE SEA	CONTAINED IN THIS SHORT	1165	6
AND TURN PHILOSOPHER.	SEPTEMBER'S	1271	8
WE TURN THE SUN [SPELL] AWAY,	AS SUMMER INTO AUTUMN	1346	4
TILL POISING FOR A TURN	HOW SOFT A CATERPILLAR	1448	V
AND WITH A FLAG AT EVERY TURN	THEIR BARRICADE AGAINST	1471	3
IT CAME HIS TURN TO BEG--	IT CAME HIS TURN TO BEG	1500	1

	FIRST LINE	POEM	LINE
TURN (CONTINUED)			
AND QUAKE--AND TURN AWAY,	NOT SEEING, STILL WE	1518	5
TURNED			
ON IT'S AXIS TURNED!	FREQUENTLY THE WOODS ARE	6	10
SO HELPLESS WHEN I TURNED	SO BASHFUL WHEN I SPIED	91	6
TURNED SLOWLY TO HIS NATIVE COAST--	AN AWFUL TEMPEST MASHED	198	12
WHEN ONE--TURNED SMILING TO THE LAND--	TWO SWIMMERS WRESTLED ON	201	3
MY EYES JUST TURNED TO SEE,	A SINGLE SCREW OF FLESH	263	10
AND TURNED AWAY, IMPERIAL,	HE PUT THE BELT AROUND	273	3
WHERE HE TURNED SO, AND I TURNED--HOW [LET GO]--	I GOT SO I COULD HEAR	293	7
WHERE HE TURNED SO, AND I TURNED--HOW [LET GO]--	I GOT SO I COULD HEAR	293	7
THE LEAF--AT LOVE--TURNED BACK--	'TWAS THE OLD--ROAD--	344	13
I TURNED MY BEING ROUND AND ROUND	I FELT MY LIFE WITH BOTH	351	5
AND I TURNED--DUCAL--	HOW SICK--TO WAIT--IN	368	5
HE TURNED AWAY!	GOOD MORNING--MIDNIGHT--	425	16
WE TURNED OUR BACKS UPON THE SUN	THEY PUT US FAR APART--	474	19
TURNED BY THE WIND--	IT'S THOUGHTS--AND JUST	495	21
AND WHEN WE TURNED TO NOTE THE GROWTH--	HE GAVE AWAY HIS LIFE--	567	15
THE SEASONS MUST HAVE TURNED	WHEN I WAS SMALL, A	596	6
I GAZED [TURNED]--AS AT A STRANGER--	I WATCHED THE MOON	629	5
THOSE THAT ROSE [TURNED] TO GO--	SWEET, TO HAVE HAD THEM	901	8
AND SPIRIT TURNED [THE SPIRIT SAID] UNTO THE DUST	I HEARD, AS IF I HAD NO	1039	13
UNTO A JUGGLER TURNED--	NATURE AFFECTS TO BE	1170	8
SPRANG LIGHTLY TO [ROSE SOFTLY IN / TURNED EASY IN] THE SKY	A SPARROW TOOK A SLICE	1211 V	6
CONCLUSION TURNED ON ME	MY TRIUMPH LASTED TILL	1227	6
TURNING			
THEN TURNING FROM THEM REVERENT--	WHOSE ARE THE LITTLE	142	25
BUT TURNING BACK--'TWAS SLOW--	I WENT TO THANK HER--	363	10
WHEN TURNING, HUNGRY, HOME	I HAD BEEN HUNGRY, ALL	579	6
ADROITLY TURNING OUT	IF HE WERE LIVING--DARE	734	10
THE TURNING O'ER AND O'ER MY FACE	FITTER TO SEE HIM, I MAY	968	11
FRONTING US--WITH [TURNING US--THEIR] NIGHT.	UNFULFILLED TO	972	8
ADROITLY TURNING ROUND	THE SUN IN REINING TO	1636	4
TURNPIKE			
AND SCOOPED A TURNPIKE FOR THEMSELVES--	THE BRAIN, WITHIN IT'S	556	7
TURNS			
AND HE TURNS SATIRIST!	MY FRIEND ATTACKS MY	118	4
TURNS SO--AWAY FROM YOU--	IF I'M LOST--NOW--	256	13
TAKING TURNS--AT THE CHIMBORAZO--	LOVE--THOU ART HIGH--	453	5
THE SHIVERING [FREEZING] FANCY TURNS	CONJECTURING A CLIMATE	562	4
AND NOW SHE TURNS HER PERFECT FACE	THE MOON WAS BUT A CHIN	737	3
SHE TURNS AS LONG AWAY	NATURE--THE GENTLEST	790	18
THE SAILOR DOUBTING TURNS--	WHEN THE ASTRONOMER	851	6
THE SPIRIT TURNS AWAY	DEATH IS A DIALOGUE	976	6
BUT WHEN THE VITAL AXLE TURNS	IDEALS ARE THE FAIRY OIL	983	3
TURNS UNPERCEIVED BENEATH OUR FEET	DEW--IS THE FRESHET IN	1097	3
AND TURNS SO WEAK AWAY--	I KNOW SUSPENSE--IT	1285	2
THE [IT'S] SPIRIT LOOKS UPON [TURNS UPON / GAZES AT / GLANCES . . .	AS FROM THE EARTH THE	1630	5
TURRET			
A TURRET MORE, A TURRET LESS	JUST AS HE SPOKE IT FROM	848	3
A TURRET MORE, A TURRET LESS	JUST AS HE SPOKE IT FROM	848	3
THEN SOARING TO HIS TEMPLE [TURRET] TALL--	HOW LONESOME THE WIND	1418	12
TURTLE			
THE TURTLE WILL NOT TRY	SO MUCH OF HEAVEN HAS	1228	10
TUSCARORA			
THEN, FAREWELL, TUSCARORA,	"SIC TRANSIT GLORIA	3	67
TWAIN			
FOR SIGHING, AND GENTLE WHISPERING, AND UNITY MADE OF TWAIN.	AWAKE YE MUSES NINE,	1	4
WAS SOMEWHERE PUT IN TWAIN.	AS FROST IS BEST	951	12
TWELVE			
BY BUT TWELVE PERFORMED!	FREQUENTLY THE WOODS ARE	6	12
SO--TWELVE MONTHS AGO--	ONE YEAR AGO--JOTS WHAT?	296	25
TWICE			
I NEVER LOST AS MUCH BUT TWICE,	I NEVER LOST AS MUCH BUT	49	1
TWICE HAVE I STOOD A BEGGAR	I NEVER LOST AS MUCH BUT	49	3
ANGELS--TWICE DESCENDING	I NEVER LOST AS MUCH BUT	49	5
BUT I--WAS TWICE AS BOLD--	I TOOK MY POWER IN MY	540	4
TWO--WERE IMMORTAL TWICE--	TWO--WERE IMMORTAL TWICE	800	1
TWICE HAD SUMMER HER FAIR VERDURE	TWICE HAD SUMMER HER	846	1
TWICE A WINTER'S SILVER FRACTURE	TWICE HAD SUMMER HER	846	3
PURPLE--IS FASHIONABLE TWICE--	PURPLE--IS FASHIONABLE	980	1
WAS HANDED NATURE TWICE--	A SPARROW TOOK A SLICE	1211	4
HAD MADNESS, HAD IT ONCE OR TWICE	I NEVER HEAR THAT ONE IS	1323	7
"AGAIN" IS OF A TWICE	THOSE NOT LIVE YET	1454	3
CONSIDERS COMING TWICE--	MORNING THAT COMES BUT	1610	2
MY LIFE CLOSED TWICE BEFORE ITS CLOSE!	MY LIFE CLOSED TWICE	1732	1
AS THESE THAT TWICE BEFEL.	MY LIFE CLOSED TWICE	1732	6
'TIS TWICE AS HEAVY AS IT WAS	WHICH MISSES MOST,	1759	4
TWIG			
ON FENCE--AND ROOF--AND TWIG!	SOME RAINBOW--COMING	64	15
PERHAPS OF TWIG SO FINE--	FOR EVERY BIRD A NEST--	143	10
PLUCKS AT A TWIG OF EVIDENCE--	THIS WORLD IS NOT	501	15
AND HOLD UPON THE TWIG,	HER SMILE WAS SHAPED	514	6
AND WHITTLES AT THE TWIG	AS ONE DOES SICKNESS	957	6

	FIRST LINE	POEM	LINE
TWIG (CONTINUED)			
A SPARROW TOOK A SLICE OF TWIG	A SPARROW TOOK A SLICE	1211	1
EMBARKED UPON A TWIG TODAY	THE MOST TRIUMPHANT BIRD	1265	2
GAY FROM AN UNANNOINTED [SWEET FROM A SURREPTITIOUS] TWIG	THE BOBOLINK IS GONE--	1591	12
TWIGS			
SWEET OF TWIGS AND TWINE	HER BREAST IS FIT FOR	84	7
BY CATCHING AT THE TWIGS THAT GROW	I GAINED IT SO--	359	3
ON TWIGS OF SINGING--RATHER HIGH--	I'M SAYING EVERY DAY	373	17
WHAT TWIGS WE HELD BY--	WHAT TWIGS WE HELD BY--	1086	1
TWILIGHT			
A DEEPER TWILIGHT ON THE LAWN--	AN ALTERED LOOK ABOUT	140	4
AT TWILIGHT SOFT TO MEET--	SHE BORE IT TILL THE	144	10
NOT A TROPIC [MANNER] OF A TWILIGHT--	BLOOM UPON THE MOUNTAIN	667	7
INTO THE DARKNESS [TWILIGHT / EVENING] DIPS AWAY--	FAIRER THROUGH FADING--	938	2
AND TWILIGHT--IN THE LANES--	I LEARNED--AT LEAST--	944	19
THE TWILIGHT STOOD [LEANED], AS STRANGERS DO	THE CRICKETS SANG	1104	6
THE TWILIGHT SPOKE THE SPIRE,	THE MOUNTAINS STOOD IN	1278	8
TO DIE DIVINELY ONCE A TWILIGHT--[AN EVENING / A LIMIT]	I'D RATHER RECOLLECT A	1349	7
AS TWILIGHT LONG BEGUN,	AS IMPERCEPTIBLY AS	1540	6
TWIN			
BETWEEN HIMSELF--AND HORROR'S TWIN--	I TRIED TO THINK A	532	14
HIS TWIN IDENTITY	TRUTH--IS AS OLD AS GOD	836	2
TWINE			
UNWIND THE SOLEMN TWINE, AND TIE MY VALENTINE!	AWAKE YE MUSES NINE,	1	2
SWEET OF TWIGS AND TWINE	HER BREAST IS FIT FOR	84	7
OF TWINE E'EN SUPERFINE,	FOR EVERY BIRD A NEST--	143	11
I KNEW LAST NIGHT--WHEN SOMEONE TRIED TO TWINE--	HOW SICK--TO WAIT--IN	368	2
TWINKLED			
IF THEY--TWINKLED BACK--	I FELT MY LIFE WITH BOTH	351	11
AND JUDGMENT--TWINKLED--TOO--	I MEANT TO HAVE BUT	476	20
TWINKLING			
BESIDE YOUR PALACE [TWINKLING / GLIMMERING] DOOR--	THE MOON WAS BUT A CHIN	737	16
IT'S TWINKLING TRAVELS IT PURSUES	A WINGED SPARK DOTH SOAR	1468	5
TWIRLED			
BRAZIL? HE TWIRLED A BUTTON--	I ASKED NO OTHER THING--	621	5
TWISTS			
DEATH TWISTS THE STRINGS--	SANG FROM THE HEART,	1059	11
TWITCHED			
A BURDOCK--CLAWED [TWITCHED] MY GOWN--	A BURDOCK--CLAWED MY	229	1
TWITCHING			
HER JAWS STIR--TWITCHING [MOUTH STIRS--LONGING]--HUNGRY--	SHE SIGHTS A BIRD--SHE	507	5
TWITTER			
AS IS THE TWITTER OF A BIRD--	WITHOUT THIS--THERE IS	655	3
'WIXT			
WAS TREASON TWIXT?	FORGET! THE LADY WITH	438	4
TWIXT FIRMAMENT ABOVE	A SINGLE CLOVER PLANK	1343	5
WO			
THE BRIDE, AND THEN THE BRIDEGROOM, THE TWO, AND THEN THE ONE,	AWAKE YE MUSES NINE,	1	7
BAFFLED FOR JUST A DAY OR TWO--	BAFFLED FOR JUST A DAY	17	1
A FLASK OF DEW--A BEE OR TWO--	A SEPAL, PETAL, AND A	19	3
A CIRCUMSTANCE OR TWO!	"SOWN IN DISHONOR"!	62	10
CLOSE TO THE TWO I LOST--	GOING TO HEAVEN!	79	15
A VERY FEW--A BIRD OR TWO--	THESE ARE THE DAYS WHEN	130	2
TWO OTHER RAGGED PRINCES	I MET A KING THIS	166	21
TWO SWIMMERS WRESTLED ON THE SPAR--	TWO SWIMMERS WRESTLED ON	201	1
TILL THOSE TWO TROUBLED--LITTLE CLOCKS	THE ROSE DID CAPER ON	208	15
ARE THERE TWO?	IS IT TRUE, DEAR SUE?	218	2
AH! KATIE! SMILE AT FORTUNE, WITH TWO SO KNIT TO THEE!	WHEN KATIE WALKS, THIS	222	4
THE SMALLER OF THE TWO!	FOREVER AT HIS SIDE TO	246	2
TWO LIVES--ONE BEING--NOW--	FOREVER AT HIS SIDE TO	246	5
THAT MAKES TWO--HIM--AND LIFE!	WHAT WOULD I GIVE TO SEE	247	6
MORE HANDS--TO HOLD--THESE ARE BUT TWO--	A SINGLE SCREW OF FLESH	263	13
WHERE TWO COULD CREEP--	I KNOW SOME LONELY	289	7
I SEND TWO SUNSETS--	I SEND TWO SUNSETS--	308	1
I FINISHED TWO--AND SEVERAL STARS--	I SEND TWO SUNSETS--	308	3
AS IF NO SOUL THE [WHILE OUR TWO SOULS THAT] SOLSTICE PASSED	THERE CAME A DAY AT	322	7
SO FACES ON TWO DECKS, LOOK BACK,	THERE CAME A DAY AT	322	19
THERE ARE TWO RIPENINGS--ONE--OF SIGHT--	THERE ARE TWO RIPENINGS	332	1
A PASSAGE BACK--OR TWO--TO MAKE--	A PRECIOUS--MOULDERING	371	7
'TWOULD SCARCELY FILL A TWO--	I KNOW LIVES, I COULD	372	6
TWO BODIES--THEREFORE BE--	NO RACK CAN TORTURE ME--	384	7
THOUGH THE FAITH ACCOMMODATE BUT TWO--	THE SWEETEST HERESY	387	4
WE TWO--LOOKED SO ALIKE--	'TWAS LOVE--NOT ME--	394	10
JUST TWO--THE BEARER--	UNIT, LIKE DEATH, FOR	408	7
BUT, WERE IT TWO--	LOVE--THOU ART HIGH--	453	3
BUT, WERE THERE TWO	LOVE--THOU ART HIGH--	453	9
AND TWO OR THREE--FOR COMPANY--	IT'S THOUGHTS--AND JUST	495	4
IT'S THOUGHTS--AND JUST TWO HEART--	IT'S THOUGHTS--AND JUST	495	23
NOR FIRE--FOR JUST MY [TWO] MARBLE FEET	IT WAS NOT DEATH, FOR I	510	7
EVERY TIME--FOR TWO--	SWEET--YOU FORGOT--BUT I	523	2
TWO [THE] WORLDS--LIKE AUDIENCES--DISPERSE	DEPARTED--TO THE	524	7

	FIRST LINE	POEM	LINE
UNALTERED			
ELEMENTS UNALTERED--	NOW I KNEW I LOST HER--	1219	9
UNANNOINTED			
HER UNANNOINTED FOREHEAD--	THE SUN--JUST TOUCHED	232	15
OF UNANNOINTED BLAZE.	DARE YOU SEE A SOUL AT	365	8
GAY FROM AN UNANNOINTED [SWEET FROM A SURREPTITIOUS] TWIG	THE BOBOLINK IS GONE--	1591	12
UNANSWERING			
ON SOME UNANSWERING SHORE--	I'VE NONE TO TELL ME TO	881	9
UNAPPROACHED			
BUT UNAPPROACHED IT STANDS--	IT BLOOMED AND DROPT, A	978	16
UNARMED			
THAN UNARMED [MOONLESS], ONE'S A'SELF ENCOUNTER--	ONE NEED NOT BE A	670	11
UNARMED IF ANY MEET HER	THE PAST IS SUCH A	1203	5
UNATTEMPTED			
OF UNATTEMPTED GAUZE	THE HEART HAS NARROW	928	10
UNAVAILABLE			
IS UNAVAILABLE--	IS HEAVEN A PHYSICIAN?	1270	4
UNAVAILING			
AS ELIGIBLE [UNPERVERTED / UNDIVERTED / UNAVAILING] AS THE MOON	SUMMER--WE ALL HAVE SEEN	1386	7
UNAVOIDABLE			
THE GRACE SO UNAVOIDABLE--	THE SWEETEST HERESY	387	7
UNBARED			
AND EVERY ONE UNBARED A NERVE	SHE DEALT HER PRETTY	479	3
UNBEREFT			
AND ORCHARDS--UNBEREFT--	YOU LOVE ME--YOU ARE	156	6
UNBLUSHINGLY			
RECEIVES UNBLUSHINGLY!	WAIT TILL THE MAJESTY OF	171	16
UNBORN			
UNBORN--EXCEPT THEY HAD BEHELD--	'TWAS A LONG PARTING--	625	11
UNBRAIDING			
UNBRAIDING IN THE SUN	A NARROW FELLOW IN THE	986	14
UNBROKEN			
UNBROKEN FOREHEAD FROM THE EAST	IT SIFTS FROM LEADEN	311	7
UNBROKEN BY A SETTLER--	MY PERIOD HAD COME FOR	564	13
UNCERTAIN			
A MOMENT--WE UNCERTAIN STEP	WE GROW ACCUSTOMED TO	419	5
WITH BLUE--UNCERTAIN STUMBLING BUZZ--	I HEARD A FLY BUZZ--WHEN	465	13
BUT, NOW, UNCERTAIN OF THE LENGTH	IF YOU WERE COMING IN	511	17
UNCERTAIN [INDIFFERENT]--TO RETURN BELOW--	HE PARTS HIMSELF--LIKE	517	11
UNCERTAIN IF MYSELF, OR HE,	MY FIRST WELL DAY--SINCE	574	7
DISTILS UNCERTAIN PAIN--	THE LOVE A LIFE CAN SHOW	673	9
UNCERTAIN LEASE--DEVELOPES LUSTRE	UNCERTAIN LEASE--	857	1
UNCERTAIN GRASP, APPRECIATION	UNCERTAIN LEASE--	857	3
TOO UNCERTAIN PASSENGERS	THE BIRD DID PRANCE--THE	1107 V	
IS THE UNCERTAIN CERTAINTY--	OF PARADISE' EXISTENCE	1411	3
UNCERTAINTY			
A BLAND UNCERTAINTY	WHY SHOULD WE HURRY--WHY	1646	8
UNCERTIFIED			
UNCERTIFIED [NOT CERTIFIED] OF SCENE	THE MOB WITHIN THE HEART	1745	5
UNCHALLENGED			
UNCHALLENGED--LET IT LIE--	THAT SACRED CLOSET WHEN	1273	10
UNCHANGED			
"UNCHANGED" I URGED WITH A CANDOR	I SAW THAT THE FLAKE WAS	1267	3
UNCLAIMED			
WHOSE UNCLAIMED HAT AND JACKET	HOW THE WATERS CLOSED	923	7
UNCLINCH			
AND OAKS UNTWIST [UNKNOT / UNKNIT / UNCLINCH] THEIR FISTS--	THE TRUTH--IS STIRLESS--	780	5
UNCOMELY			
AS MAKE OF [BREW FROM / MIX] OUR IMPERFECT [UNCOMELY / OBTUSER]	SHE HIDETH HER THE LAST	557	11
UNCOMMON			
IN THAT UNCOMMON [CONSUMMATE] SCENE--	ELIJAH'S WAGON KNEW NO	1254 V	8
UNCONCERN			
AN UNCONCERN SO SOVREIGN	OF BRONZE--AND BLAZE--	290	6
UNCONJECTURED			
OF UNCONJECTURED QUANTITY--	I CROSS TILL I AM WEARY	550	8
UNCONSCIOUS			
UNCONSCIOUS THAT THE OIL IS OUT--	THE LAMP BURNS SURE--	233	7
UNCONSCIOUS OF THE SCARLET FREIGHT--	HOW MANY FLOWERS FAIL IN	404	7
OF RICHES--AS UNCONSCIOUS	REMOVED FROM ACCIDENT OF	424	5
OF PORTION--SO UNCONSCIOUS--	THIS WAS A POET--IT IS	448	13
UNCONSCIOUS OF THE WIDTH--	NO MAN CAN COMPASS A	477	5
UNCONSCIOUS THAT THE SUN	NO MAN CAN COMPASS A	477	6
A HALF [TOO] UNCONSCIOUS [AN INSUFFICIENT] QUEEN--	I'M CEDED--I'VE STOPPED	508	16
UNCONSCIOUS THAT HIS SINGLE FLEET [BULK / SAIL]	WHO GIANTS KNOW, WITH	796	7
UNCONSCIOUS WAS--GREAT NATURE'S FACE	IT BLOOMED AND DROPT, A	978	19
BEHIND THE MOST UNCONSCIOUS [CONSUMMATE] CLOCK	NOT TO DISCOVER WEAKNESS	1054	7
UNCONSCIOUS OUR RETURNING	EDEN IS THAT	1657	7
UNCONSCIOUS [DISDAINFUL] OF HIS SMARTNESS.	THE SUMMER THAT WE DID	1773	8
UNCONSCIOUSNESS			
JUST MEASURING UNCONSCIOUSNESS	EACH SECOND IS THE LAST	879	3
UNCONSCIOUSNESS OF PERFECTNESS	AURORA IS THE EFFORT	1002	3
UNCONSPICUOUS			
BEYOND THAT--UNCONSPICUOUS	DEATH IS POTENTIAL TO	548	3

	FIRST LINE	POEM	LINE
UNCOVERED			
UNCOVERED BY THE HAND	LONG YEARS APART--CAN	1383	6
UNDECAYING			
HER UNDECAYING CHEER	THESE ARE THE SIGNS TO	1077	10
UNDEFEATED			
WERE UNDEFEATED STILL?	DELAYED TILL SHE HAD	58	12
UNDEPICTED			
TO UNDEPICTED [UNREPORTED] REALMS	TALK NOT TO ME OF SUMMER	1634	8
UNDER			
WHISTLING UNDER MY WINDOW	HEART, NOT SO HEAVY AS	83	T
SEEMS IT DONT SHRIEK SO--UNDER RULE.	IT DONT SOUND SO	426	4
UNDER ONE SACRAMENT [FIRMAMENT]	WHILE IT IS ALIVE	491	5
THE MINGLED [UNDER / FURTHER] SIDE	I PRAYED, AT FIRST, A	576	12
DIVINITY DWELLS UNDER SEAL.	EMBARRASSMENT OF ONE	662	7
AND BEING UNDER LOCK--	THE LONELINESS ONE DARE	777	12
FOR INLANDS--THE EARTH IS THE UNDER SIDE--	BY MY WINDOW HAVE I FOR	797	9
UNDER THE LIGHT, YET UNDER,	UNDER THE LIGHT, YET	949	1
UNDER THE LIGHT, YET UNDER,	UNDER THE LIGHT, YET	949	1
UNDER THE GRASS AND THE DIRT,	UNDER THE LIGHT, YET	949	2
UNDER THE BEETLE'S CELLAR	UNDER THE LIGHT, YET	949	3
UNDER THE CLOVER'S ROOT [FOOT],	UNDER THE LIGHT, YET	949	4
WINTER UNDER CULTIVATION	WINTER UNDER CULTIVATION	1707	1
IT WAS A PIT--WITH FATHOMS UNDER IT	A PIT--BUT HEAVEN OVER	1712	14
UNDERLIE			
MY NATURE UNDERLIE--	A COUNTERFEIT--A PLATED	1453	4
UNDERMINE			
'TWOULD UNDERMINE THE SILL	FALSEHOOD OF THEE COULD	1007	2
UNDERMINED			
AND UNDERMINED THE YEARS.	SOFTENED BY TIME'S	1738	4
UNDERMINING			
OUR UNDERMINING FEET TO MEET	ESCAPING BACKWARD TO	867	7
UNDERNEATH			
UNDERNEATH THE MOULD,	I OFTEN PASSED THE	51	16
UNDERNEATH THEIR FINE INCISIONS	SURGEONS MUST BE VERY	108	3
UNDERSTAND			
I DO NOT UNDERSTAND!	THERE'S SOMETHING	45	8
CAN THE SAILOR UNDERSTAND	EXULTATION IS THE GOING	76	6
FAITH BLEATS [FAINTS] TO UNDERSTAND--	I SHOULD HAVE BEEN TOO	313	24
DEARER TO UNDERSTAND--	I KNOW WHERE WELLS GROW	460	20
PAST WHAT OURSELF CAN ESTIMATE [UNDERSTAND]--	IF ANYBODY'S FRIEND BE	509	23
NO MAN CAN UNDERSTAND	THE PROVINCE OF THE	539	5
WOULD [DID / MIGHT] GIANTS--UNDERSTAND?	IT TROUBLED ME AS ONCE I	600	8
THE HEAVEN YOU KNOW--TO UNDERSTAND	YOU TAUGHT ME WAITING	740	9
REMOTE [ASTUTE / OBSCURE] TO UNDERSTAND	NATURE AFFECTS TO BE	1170	6
WILL GLEAM [STIR] AND UNDERSTAND	LONG YEARS APART--CAN	1383	8
PERMISSION HAVE TO UNDERSTAND	I SHALL NOT MURMUR IF AT	1410	3
THAT NONE CAN UNDERSTAND	BACK FROM THE CORDIAL	1625	4
UNDERSTANDING			
GREW BY THE FACT, AND NOT THE UNDERSTANDING	IF ANY SINK, ASSURE THAT	358	3
UNDERSTOOD			
AND UNDERSTOOD NO WORD IT SAID--	I'VE HEARD AN ORGAN TALK	183	3
THE CLOVERS--UNDERSTOOD--	FROM COCOON FORTH A	354	8
WHAT NEITHER--UNDERSTOOD--	WE LEARNED THE WHOLE OF	568	10
AND MUCH NOT UNDERSTOOD--	A SOUTH WIND--HAS A	719	6
WE HAVE UNDERSTOOD FOR BETTER	THAT IS SOLEMN WE HAVE	934	7
UNDERTAKE			
TO UNDERTAKE IS TO ACHIEVE	TO UNDERTAKE IS TO	1070	1
UNDERTAKING			
BE UNDERTAKING BLENT	TO UNDERTAKE IS TO	1070	2
UNDESERVED			
'TWAS UNDESERVED BLAST--	TO BREAK SO VAST A HEART	1312	4
UNDEVELOPED			
EXCEEDS IT'S UNREMEMBERED [UNDEVELOPED] DROP--	'TIS GOOD--THE LOOKING	660	11
THE UNDEVELOPED [ELEMENTAL] FREIGHT	COULD MORTAL LIP DIVINE	1409	2
UNDISCOVERED			
THE "UNDISCOVERED CONTINENT"--	SOTO! EXPLORE THYSELF!	832	3
AS UNDISCOVERED GOLD--	YOU CANNOT TAKE ITSELF	1351	8
UNDISPUTED			
THAT HOLDS IN UNDISPUTED LEASE	TOO LITTLE WAY THE HOUSE	911	3
AN UNDISPUTED RIGHT	THE RIGHT TO PERISH	1692	2
UNDISTINGUISHED			
YESTERDAY, UNDISTINGUISHED!	AMBITION CANNOT FIND HIM	68	5
UNDIVERTED			
AS ELIGIBLE [UNPERVERTED / UNDIVERTED / UNAVAILING] AS THE MOON	SUMMER--WE ALL HAVE SEEN	1386	7
UNDIVINE			
TO EFFORT UNDIVINE--	TRUST IN THE UNEXPECTED	555	8
SO I--THE UNDIVINE ABODE	MY WORTHINESS IS ALL MY	751	13
UNDONE			
TO GAIN, OR BE UNDONE--	THE MALAY--TOOK THE	452	16
THIS NATURE--HOW UNDONE!	HOW FITS HIS UMBER COAT	1371	12
AS IF IT [HE] WERE [AS FREQUENTLY] UNDONE--	THE BUTTERFLY'S NUMIDIAN	1387	6
WHEN WHAT THEY SUNG FOR IS UNDONE	A PANG IS MORE	1530	5
BY WHICH TO BE UNDONE	TO SEE HER IS A PICTURE	1568	V
UNDOUBTEDLY			
AND SHE WILL POINT UNDOUBTEDLY [YOU FONDLY-- / YOU LONGINGLY]	CRISIS IS SWEET AND YET	1416	V 7
UNDRAINED			
DEPTHS OF RUBY, UNDRAINED,	ALL THE LETTERS I CAN	334	5

	FIRST LINE	POEM	LINE
UNDRESS			
FREQUENTLY THE HILLS UNDRESS	FREQUENTLY THE WOODS ARE	6	3
UNDRESSED			
THE DAY UNDRESSED--HERSELF--	THE DAY UNDRESSED--	716	1
UNDUE			
UNDUE SIGNIFICANCE A STARVING MAN ATTACHES	UNDUE SIGNIFICANCE A	439	1
UNDULATING			
IN UNDULATING ROOMS	WATER MAKES MANY BEDS	1428	6
UNELECTED			
OH UNELECTED FACE--	OH SHADOW ON THE GRASS,	1187	8
UNENFORCED			
WAS INNOCENT [IGNORANT / NOT ENFORCED / UNENFORCED] OF WHEEL	ELIJAH'S WAGON KNEW NO	1254	2
UNERUDITE			
IN CHANGE--UNERUDITE--	'TWAS AWKWARD, BUT IT	973	4
UNEVEN			
OR IN THE LONG--UNEVEN TERM	I PLAY AT RICHES--TO	801	19
UNEXPECTED			
AN UNEXPECTED MAID.	BAFFLED FOR JUST A DAY	17	4
THEY HEAR MY UNEXPECTED KNOCK--	THO' I GET HOME HOW LATE	207	6
THE HEAVEN--UNEXPECTED COME,	LIKE FLOWERS, THAT HEARD	513	13
TRUST IN THE UNEXPECTED--	TRUST IN THE UNEXPECTED	555	1
BE [ARE] UNEXPECTED FRIENDS.	"REMEMBER ME" IMPLORED	1180	12
UNEXPECTEDLY			
SUMMONED--UNEXPECTEDLY--	I'M SAYING EVERY DAY	373	32
UNFADING			
IN ITS UNFADING FLOWERS	THERE IS ANOTHER SKY,	2	11
UNFAIR			
UNFAIR AN IMMORTALITY	NO BRIGADIER THROUGHOUT	1561	23
UNFITTED			
UNFITTED BY AN INSTANT'S GRACE	I GAINED IT SO--	359	13
FROM OUR UNFITTED [UNFURNISHED] EYES.	MY FIRST WELL DAY--SINCE	574	24
UNFOLD			
IS MADE A SECRET TO UNFOLD	A SCIENCE--SO THE SAVANS	100	4
POWERLESS TO UNFOLD--	HOW THE OLD MOUNTAINS	291	V 24
PREDESTINED TO UNFOLD	THEY TALK AS SLOW AS	1697	6
UNFORESEEN			
OR UNFORESEEN AGGRANDIZEMENT	THE WAY TO KNOW THE	1279	19
UNFREQUENTED			
AN UNFREQUENTED ROAD--	MY WHEEL IS IN THE DARK!	10	6
THAT UNFREQUENTED--ONE--	'TWAS THE OLD--ROAD--	344	2
MY UNFREQUENTED FLOWER	OH, HONEY OF AN HOUR,	1734	5
UNFULFILLED			
UNFULFILLED TO OBSERVATION--	UNFULFILLED TO	972	1
UNFURNISHED			
IN HER UNFURNISHED ROOMS--	DID OUR BEST MOMENT LAST	393	12
FROM OUR UNFITTED [UNFURNISHED] EYES.	MY FIRST WELL DAY--SINCE	574	24
BUT OUR UNFURNISHED EYES--	NOT "REVELATION"--'TIS--	685	2
IS AN UNFURNISHED CIRCUMSTANCE	TO OWN THE ART WITHIN	855	5
UNGAINED			
UNGAINED--IT MAY BE--BY [IN] A LIFE'S LOW VENTURE--	EACH LIFE CONVERGES TO	680	17
UNGRACIOUS			
WERT THOU BUT STRANGER IN UNGRACIOUS COUNTRY--	WERT THOU BUT ILL--THAT	961	5
UNGRASPED			
WITHIN IT'S REACH [HOPE], THOUGH YET [AND JUST] UNGRASPED	WHO NEVER WANTED--	1430	5
UNHEARD			
BY EAR UNHEARD,	JUST LOST, WHEN I WAS	160	14
OR RAP--AT PARADISE--UNHEARD	SHOULD YOU BUT FAIL AT--	226	5
WHO SINGS THE SAME, UNHEARD,	TO HEAR AN ORIOLE SING	526	5
UNHELPED			
ENDURED, UNHELPED [RESIGNED]--UNKNOWN.	THE HOLLOWS ROUND HIS	955	8
UNHOOK			
FROSTS UNHOOK--IN THE NORTHERN ZONES--	SAFE IN THEIR ALABASTER	216	V
UNHOOKED			
THE LEAVES UNHOOKED THEMSELVES FROM TREES--	THE WIND BEGUN TO KNEAD	824	5
UNIFORMS			
AND UNIFORMS OF SNOW.	TO FIGHT ALOUD, IS VERY	126	12
UNIMPEACHABLE			
THE FLORA UNIMPEACHABLE	THE LILAC IS AN ANCIENT	1241	15
UNINTENDING			
HER UNINTENDING EYES--	THE PRETTY RAIN FROM	1426	2
UNIQUE			
'MONG SUCH UNIQUE	I WENT TO HEAVEN--	374	15
ELIJAH'S HORSES AS UNIQUE	ELIJAH'S WAGON KNEW NO	1254	3
BUT [YET] IT'S UNIQUE MOMENTUM	HOPE IS A STRANGE	1392	7
UNIT			
UNIT, LIKE DEATH, FOR WHOM?	UNIT, LIKE DEATH, FOR	408	1
BOOKS--WHEN THE UNIT--	IT'S THOUGHTS--AND JUST	495	7
UNITE			
TILL EVERLASTING LIFE [RITE] UNITE	THE GRAVE MY LITTLE	1743	7
UNITS			
'TIS UNITS--MAKE THE SWARM--	ONE ANGUISH--IN A CROWD	565	8
UNITY			
FOR SIGHING, AND GENTLE WHISPERING, AND UNITY MADE OF TWAIN.	AWAKE YE MUSES NINE,	1	4
UNIVERSE			
THE UNIVERSE TO KNOW!	COCOON ABOVE! COCOON	129	12
THE UNIVERSE WOULD GO!	A TRANSPORT ONE CANNOT	184	8

	FIRST LINE	POEM	LINE
UNIVERSE (CONTINUED)			
TO UNIVERSE, OR ME--	OF BRONZE--AND BLAZE--	290	7
THE UNIVERSE--IS [FIRMAMENTS--ARE] STILL--	HE FUMBLES AT YOUR SOUL	315	14
I TOUCHED THE UNIVERSE--	I SAW NO WAY--THE	378	4
WERE UNIVERSE--ONE ROCK--	I HAD NOT MINDED--WALLS	398	2
WHERE TENT BY TENT--HER UNIVERSE	THE HIMMALEH WAS KNOWN	481	5
TO UNIVERSE--AND ME?	NO CROWD THAT HAS	515	20
'TWAS UNIVERSE--THAT DID APPLAUD [ATTEND]--	LIKE MIGHTY FOOT LIGHTS	595	5
THE UNIVERSE--HER MAID--	SHE DWELLETH IN THE	671	4
THE UNIVERSE--[THE VALLEYS--ARE] HER SHOE--	THE MOON WAS BUT A CHIN	737	18
LEST FIRMAMENT [UNIVERSE / DEITY] SHOULD FAIL FOR ME--	MY FAITH IS LARGER THAN	766	15
OF DEITY [UNIVERSE] AND MEN--	THE BIRDS BEGUN AT FOUR	783	16
WHO ONLY KNEW OF UNIVERSE--	THIS BAUBLE WAS	805	7
FROM MANSION OF THE UNIVERSE	TRUTH--IS AS OLD AS GOD	836	7
A UNIVERSE BESIDE--	A MINE THERE IS NO MAN	1117	4
NO UNIVERSE--NO LAWS--	GREAT STREETS OF SILENCE	1159	4
AND AN ENTIRE UNIVERSE	A SOFT SEA WASHED AROUND	1198	7
UNIVERSE THE SAME	NOW I KNEW I LOST HER--	1219	10
THE UNIVERSE IS YOUR'S.	NOT WITH A CLUB, THE	1304	16
AND NOT IN ALL THE UNIVERSE	HOW NEWS MUST FEEL WHEN	1319	11
THE UNIVERSE WAS NEEDY	I SAW THE WIND WITHIN	1502	V
DECEIVES PERHAPS THE UNIVERSE	YOU CANNOT MAKE	1508	5
A PASSING UNIVERSE PUT ON,	HOW HAPPY IS THE LITTLE	1510	6
FOR THOU HAST BORNE A UNIVERSE	HOW MUCH OF SOURCE	1517	3
THE BROTHER OF THE UNIVERSE	NO BRIGADIER THROUGHOUT	1561	7
THOU SWEETEST OF THE UNIVERSE,	IMMURED IN HEAVEN!	1594	4
A UNIVERSE THAT OVERHEARD	UPON HIS SADDLE SPRUNG A	1600	7
ATTEMPT IT, AND THE UNIVERSE	THE RIGHT TO PERISH	1692	3
UNIVERSE'S			
JUGS--A UNIVERSE'S FRACTURE [RUPTURE]	BEES ARE BLACK, WITH	1405	7
A UNIVERSE'S UTTER ART	UPON HIS SADDLE SPRUNG A	1600	V 7
UNJADED			
AND THEN, UNJADED, CHALLENGED GOD	HE OUTSTRIPPED TIME WITH	865	3
UNKNIT			
AND OAKS UNTWIST [UNKNOT / UNKNIT / UNCLINCH] THEIR FISTS--	THE TRUTH--IS STIRLESS--	780	5
UNKNOT			
AND OAKS UNTWIST [UNKNOT / UNKNIT / UNCLINCH] THEIR FISTS--	THE TRUTH--IS STIRLESS--	780	5
UNKNOWING			
THE HIGHT OF OUR PORTENTOUS [UNKNOWING] NEIGHBOR	FACTS BY OUR SIDE ARE	1497	5
UNKNOWN			
OF LATITUDES UNKNOWN.	A POOR--TORN HEART-- A	78	8
AND OCCIDENT--BECOME UNKNOWN--	THE ONE WHO COULD REPEAT	307	8
"SURRENDER"--IS A SORT UNKNOWN	OF TRIBULATION--THESE	325	9
UNKNOWN TO POSSIBILITY--	WHAT I CAN DO--I WILL--	361	4
INVISIBLE--UNKNOWN--	THE BATTLE FOUGHT	594	8
UNKNOWN--	FOUR TREES--UPON A	742	16
HER TARRYING, UNKNOWN,	FROM US SHE WANDERED NOW	890	2
IT'S PROCESS IS UNKNOWN.	THIS IS A BLOSSOM OF THE	945	8
ENDURED, UNHELPED [RESIGNED]--UNKNOWN.	THE HOLLOWS ROUND HIS	955	8
AN UNKNOWN ESTEEM [CONTENT] POSSESSING--	ALL FORGOT FOR	966	7
THE GEM WERE BEST UNKNOWN--	A DIAMOND ON THE HAND	1108	4
ENTIRELY UNKNOWN	HOW MANY SCHEMES MAY DIE	1150	3
SUBMITTING FOR OUR UNKNOWN SAKE	A FULL FED ROSE ON MEALS	1154	7
UNKNOWN THE WORST WE FEAR--	THE FROST WAS NEVER SEEN	1202	14
EACH CIRCUMSTANCE UNKNOWN,	LONGING IS LIKE THE SEED	1255	6
THAT WHAT WE CHERISHED, SO UNKNOWN [VALUED SO DEVOID / HOARDED . . .	SO PROUD SHE WAS TO DIE	1272	3
. . . SO UNKNOWN]	SO PROUD SHE WAS TO DIE	1272	3
OH, THOU UNKNOWN RENOWN	THAT SHORT--POTENTIAL	1307	6
UNKNOWN--FOR ALL THE TIMES WE MET--	WITHOUT A SMILE--WITHOUT	1330	4
UNKNOWN AS TO AN ECSTASY	SUMMER--WE ALL HAVE SEEN	1386	11
TRIUMPHED AND REMAINED UNKNOWN--	LAY THIS LAUREL ON THE	1393	V
THE PREY OF [IN SPANS IN] UNKNOWN ZONES--	COULD MORTAL LIP DIVINE	1409	V
REMAINS TO HIM UNKNOWN--	WHO NEVER WANTED--	1430	2
ETERNALLY UNKNOWN	A DEW SUFFICED ITSELF--	1437	12
AS COMMON AS IT IS UNKNOWN	BEHOLD THIS LITTLE BANE	1438	3
TO TROTH UNKNOWN	DEATH IS THE SUPPLE	1445	10
UNKNOWN HIS SHIMMERING [GIDDY / DAZZLING] ULTIMATE--	THE ROAD WAS LIT WITH	1450	7
IS HITHERTO [PRUDENTLY] UNKNOWN	I SAW THE WIND WITHIN	1502	V
WRITTEN BY FADED [UNKNOWN] MEN	THE BIBLE IS AN ANTIQUE	1545	2
UNKNOWN--REFRESHING THINGS--	NO BRIGADIER THROUGHOUT	1561	20
AND EVERYTHING UNKNOWN,	THE GOING FROM A WORLD	1603	6
THAT MADE THEE FIRST UNKNOWN	I SEE THEE CLEARER FOR	1666	6
AND THEN A GAY UNKNOWN	OF THIS IS DAY COMPOSED	1675	4
IS THE UNKNOWN PENINSULA.	THE EARTH HAS MANY KEYS.	1775	3
UNKNOWNS			
AND MY FIRST FEARING, LEST UNKNOWNS	LET MY FIRST KNOWING BE	1218	3
UNLADEN			
OUR'S BE THE CARGO--UNLADEN--HERE--	HOW SICK--TO WAIT--IN	368	10
UNLESS			
UNLESS THEY DID'NT COME--	I'VE NOTHING ELSE--TO	224	6
I NEVER SPOKE--UNLESS ADDRESSED--	I WAS THE SLIGHTEST IN	486	10
UNLESS [EXCEPT] WE DINE ON TIPTOE--	VICTORY COMES LATE--	690	9
UNLESS YOU LEAVE HIM--THEN RETURN	SO MUCH OF HEAVEN HAS	1228	11
UNLESS IN MY REDEEMER'S FACE	BECAUSE THAT YOU ARE	1260	23

	FIRST LINE	POEM	LINE
UNLESS (CONTINUED)			
UNLESS THOU KNOW'ST THE TUNE	TOUCH LIGHTLY NATURE'S	1389	2
UNLESS CONCEALED IN [INTRENCHED IN / AFFIXED TO / INLAID IN] THEE	HOW FIRM ETERNITY MUST	1499	8
UNLESS [UNTIL] IT CONTEMPLATE	TO BE FORGOT BY THEE	1560	5
THEIR NAMES, UNLESS YOU KNOW THEM,	THE MOST IMPORTANT	1746	5
UNLIKE			
'TWAS SO UNLIKE THE CRUMB	I HAD BEEN HUNGRY, ALL	579	10
UNMANIFEST			
UNMANIFEST TO [UNWITNESSED OF THE / AS DOTH THE TIRED] SENSE	CONTAINED IN THIS SHORT	1165	V
UNMEANING			
UNMEANING--NOW--TO ME--	WHAT IF I SAY I SHALL	277	9
UNMENTIONED			
IT LAY UNMENTIONED--AS THE SEA	SHE ROSE TO HIS	732	9
UNMOVED			
UNMOVED--SHE NOTES THE CHARIOTS--PAUSING--	THE SOUL SELECTS HER OWN	303	5
UNMOVED--AN EMPEROR BE KNEELING	THE SOUL SELECTS HER OWN	303	7
ADVANCE UNMOVED--TO HER SUPREME--	TRIUMPH--MAY BE OF	455	7
AND HE--UNMOVED REGARDED HER--	FATE SLEW HIM, BUT HE	1031	7
I CANNOT MEET THE SPRING UNMOVED--	I CANNOT MEET THE SPRING	1051	1
SO UTTERLY UNMOVED--	HAD WE OUR SENSES	1284	8
HER CONSCIENTIOUS VOICE WILL SOAR UNMOVED	AFTER ALL BIRDS HAVE	1395	3
THE SUN PROCEEDS UNMOVED	APPARENTLY WITH NO	1624	6
UNNESCESSARY			
UNNESCESSARY--NOW TO ME--	IT WOULD NEVER BE COMMON	430	15
UNNOTICED			
SPARROWS, UNNOTICED BY THE FATHER--	SOME, TOO FRAGILE FOR	141	11
UNNOTICED AS A SINGLE DEW	EXCEPT TO HEAVEN, SHE IS	154	7
THE MOUNTAINS--GROW UNNOTICED--	THE MOUNTAINS--GROW	757	1
UNNOTICED DWELL,	THE MOST IMPORTANT	1746	2
UNNUMBERED			
SAVE BY FEET UNNUMBERED	GLOWING IS HER BONNET,	72	11
UNNUMBERED SATIN--	THESE--SAW VISIONS--	758	8
UNOBSERVED			
UNOBSERVED--A RIBIN SLIPT,	SUMMER LAID HER SIMPLE	1363	3
UNOBTAINED			
OF UNOBTAINED DELIGHT----	TO DISAPPEAR ENHANCES--	1209	20
UNOBTRUSIVE			
THE UNOBTRUSIVE [MOST FAMILIAR] GUEST--	'TWAS A LONG PARTING--	625	16
OF UNOBTRUSIVE PAIN	THE HOLLOWS ROUND HIS	955	6
A FLOWER'S UNOBTRUSIVE FACE	THE DYING NEED BUT	1026	3
IT'S UNOBTRUSIVE MASS.	FURTHER IN SUMMER THAN	1068	4
UNOBTRUSIVE BLOSSOM	FOLLOW WISE ORION	1538	V
UNOPENED			
UNOPENED--RARE--UPON THE SHELF--	NOT IN THIS WORLD TO SEE	418	5
UNPAID			
AND THE RENT UNPAID--	RATHER ARID DELIGHT	1679	8
UNPERCEIVED			
TO HOUSES UNPERCEIVED--	A MURMUR IN THE TREES--	416	10
IN UNPERCEIVED HANDS--	THE SPIDER HOLDS A	605	2
TURNS UNPERCEIVED BENEATH OUR FEET	DEW--IS THE FRESHET IN	1097	3
UNPERVERTED			
AS ELIGIBLE [UNPERVERTED / UNDIVERTED / UNAVAILING] AS THE MOON	SUMMER--WE ALL HAVE SEEN	1386	7
UNPLAUSIBLE			
DEEM UNPLAUSIBLE [INCREDIBLE]	COLOR--CASTE--	970	16
UNPREPARED			
WHO NEVER LOST, ARE [IS] UNPREPARED	WHO NEVER LOST, ARE	73	1
UNPRETENDING			
AN UNPRETENDING TIME	MYSELF WAS FORMED--A	488	2
UNPRETENSION			
THE UNPRETENSION STUNS--	"WAS NOT" WAS ALL THE	1342	2
UNPROVED			
UNPROVED IS MUCH WE KNOW--	THE FROST WAS NEVER SEEN	1202	13
UNPUZZLED			
WITH UNPUZZLED HEART--	COULD LIVE--DID LIVE--	43	9
UNQUALIFIED			
UNQUALIFIED, TO SCAN--	A HAPPY LIP--BREAKS	353	8
UNQUALIFIED TO JUDGE	THOSE CATTLE SMALLER	1388	14
UNQUESTIONABLY			
UNQUESTIONABLY LOVED--	SUMMER--WE ALL HAVE SEEN	1386	4
UNREALITY			
AN UNREALITY IS LENT,	A DOUBT IF IT BE US	859	5
UNREALIZED			
THE NEAREST [MADDEST] DREAM RECEDES--UNREALIZED--	THE NEAREST DREAM	319	1
UNRECORDED			
VANISH UNRECORDED	GLOWING IS HER BONNET,	72	7
UNRELIEVED			
A RIGOR UNRELIEVED	I KNEW THAT I HAD GAINED	1022	5
UNRELUCTANTLY			
I CAN SPARE THIS SUMMER, UNRELUCTANTLY.	WHEN I COUNT THE SEEDS	40	11
UNREMEMBERED			
EXCEEDS IT'S UNREMEMBERED [UNDEVELOPED] DROP--	'TIS GOOD--THE LOOKING	660	11
UNREMITTING			
IN MIGHTY--UNREMITTING BASS	THE HEART HAS NARROW	928	3
IN UNREMITTING ACTION	HOPE IS A STRANGE	1392	3
UNREPORTED			
TO UNDEPICTED [UNREPORTED] REALMS	TALK NOT TO ME OF SUMMER	1634	8

	FIRST LINE	POEM	LINE
UNTIL (CONTINUED)			
UNTIL THE DAFFODIL	PERHAPS YOU'D LIKE TO	134	4
UNTIL THE BEES, FROM CLOVER ROWS	PERHAPS YOU'D LIKE TO	134	7
WHY, I WILL LEND UNTIL JUST THEN,	PERHAPS YOU'D LIKE TO	134	9
UNTIL THE TYRIAN	THE SUN KEPT STOOPING--	152	8
UNTIL IT PUZZLED CAME	AS IF SOME LITTLE ARCTIC	180	4
UNTIL THE MORNING SUN--	TWO SWIMMERS WRESTLED ON	201	2
AND COULD NOT BEAR TO SHUT UNTIL	I SHOULD NOT DARE TO	205	7
UNTIL HE LET YOU IN!	SHOULD YOU BUT FAIL AT--	226	7
UNTIL--DELIRIOUS--BORNE--	I THINK JUST HOW MY	237	14
ETERNITY--UNTIL--	A SOLEMN THING--IT WAS--	271	8
UNTIL A SUDDEN SKY	HOW NOTELESS MEN, AND	282	2
PATIENT--UPON THE STEPS [MAT]--UNTIL THEN--	JUST SO--JESUS--RAPS--	317	10
UNTIL THE VELVET PRODUCT	THERE ARE TWO RIPENINGS	332	3
UNTIL THE CORONATION CAME--	THE DAY THAT I WAS	356	3
INDUSTRIOUS UNTIL--	DEATH SETS A THING	360	8
UNTIL THE DESIGNATED LIGHT	DARE YOU SEE A SOUL AT	365	15
UNTIL ANOTHER MORN--	THE FIRST DAY'S NIGHT	410	8
UNTIL IT BLOCKED MY EYES--	THE FIRST DAY'S NIGHT	410	12
UNTIL THE AGONY	'TWAS LIKE A MAELSTROM,	414	4
UNTIL YOU FELT YOUR SECOND	'TWAS LIKE A MAELSTROM,	414	12
SOUNDS LONG--UNTIL I READ THE PLACE	NOT IN THIS WORLD TO SEE	418	2
UNTIL THE NORTH--INVOKE IT--	GOD MADE A LITTLE	442	11
UNTIL THE MOSS HAD REACHED OUR LIPS--	I DIED FOR BEAUTY--BUT	449	11
UNTIL UPON MY FACE	THE POWER TO BE TRUE TO	464	2
UNTIL IT SHOWED TOO SMALL--	THE POWER TO BE TRUE TO	464	8
WE FOLLOW THEE UNTIL	WE COVER THEE--SWEET	482	5
UNTIL DEATH TOUCHES IT	WHILE IT IS ALIVE	491	2
UNTIL TOMORROW [THE EVENING]--HAPPY LETTER! [AH! BE BASHFUL]	GOING TO HIM! HAPPY	494	24
HUMMING--UNTIL MY FAINT REHEARSAL--	BETTER--THAN MUSIC! FOR	503	23
UNTIL THERE CREPT UPON	'TWAS WARM--AT FIRST--	519	2
UNTIL WE MET THE SOLID TOWN--	I STARTED EARLY--TOOK MY	520	21
UNTIL A ZEPHYR PUSHED [CHASED / FLUNG / SPURNED / SCOURGED] THEM	TWO BUTTERFLIES WENT OUT	533	V
UNTIL THE PEEVISH STUDENT	'TIS ONE BY ONE--THE	545	5
BURNED [GLOWED] ON--UNTIL THROUGH DISSOLUTION--	IT KNEW NO LAPSE, NOR	560	3
UNTIL IT BURST THE HEARTS	HE GAVE AWAY HIS LIFE--	567	5
UNTIL THEY LOCK IT IN THE GRAVE,	IF I MAY HAVE IT, WHEN	577	5
UNTIL IT SETTLED BROAD [FULL / FIRM]--ON PARADISE--	TO KNOW JUST HOW HE	622	4
AND WAS HE CONFIDENT UNTIL	TO KNOW JUST HOW HE	622	16
UNTIL THE CHEATED EYE	THE TINT I CANNOT TAKE--	627	22
UNTIL UPON A PANE--	I WATCHED THE MOON	629	2
THEN I HAD COUNTED IT UNTIL	THEIR HIGHT IN HEAVEN	696	11
UNTIL HE'S PAST THE PAIN--	I SOMETIMES DROP IT, FOR	708	16
THAT KNOWS NOT AN UNTIL--	THE SERVICE WITHOUT HOPE	779	8
UNTIL OURSELVES ARE STRUCK--	DESPAIR'S ADVANTAGE IS	799	12
CHRIST--STOOPED UNTIL HE TOUCHED THE GRAVE--	PERHAPS YOU THINK ME	833	3
UNTIL IT BEND AS LOW AS DEATH	PERHAPS YOU THINK ME	833	7
UNTIL IT FOOTING FIND.	A DOUBT IF IT BE US	859	4
UNTIL A LITTLE BIRD	OUR LITTLE KINSMEN--	885	6
UNTIL A PIONEER, AS	WHO OCCUPIES THIS HOUSE?	892	21
UNTIL--RESEMBLANCE PERFECT--	TILL DEATH--IS NARROW	907	9
UNTIL A VITAL WORD	I HEARD, AS IF I HAD NO	1039	2
UNTIL A MIGHT DETECTED ME	I HEARD, AS IF I HAD NO	1039	11
HUELESS TO ME UNTIL THOU COME	SPRING COMES ON THE	1042	3
UNTIL ETERNITY.	THE BUSTLE IN A HOUSE	1078	8
UNTIL TO HER SURPRISE	SUPERIORITY TO FATE	1081	6
UNTIL IT GREW SO WIDE	A GREAT HOPE FELL	1123	11
UNTIL THE TENDER CARPENTER [SOVREIGN CARPENTER / UNSUSPECTING . . .	A GREAT HOPE FELL	1123	16
UNTIL THE HOUSE IS BUILT	THE PROPS ASSIST THE	1142	2
UNTIL THYSELF, BELOVED.	DISTANCE--IS NOT THE	1155	4
AND OF "TRUTH" UNTIL IT PROCLAIMED HIM A LIAR--	HE PREACHED UPON	1207	3
UNTIL HIS LITTLE FIGURE	A SPARROW TOOK A SLICE	1211	7
WITHSTANDS UNTIL THE SWEET ASSAULT	LIKE TRAINS OF CARS ON	1224	5
DOMINION LASTS UNTIL OBTAINED--	DOMINION LASTS UNTIL	1257	1
WE SHALL HAVE SHUNNED UNTIL ASHAMED	WHO WERE "THE FATHER AND	1258	23
UNTIL THE REALM OF YOU--	BECAUSE THAT YOU ARE	1260	20
UNTIL ALLURED AWAY	THE WAY TO KNOW THE	1279	16
UNTIL THEY HEEDLESS TUMBLE IN	A STAGNANT PLEASURE LIKE	1281	3
I MAKE BELIEVE UNTIL MY HEART	THE MOST PATHETIC THING	1290	3
UNTIL THE DESERT KNOWS	UNTIL THE DESERT KNOWS	1291	1
FOREVER--UNTIL MAY--	SUMMER HAS TWO	1422	10
UNTIL THEY LOOK AROUND	FACTS BY OUR SIDE ARE	1497	2
I DARE NOT WRITE UNTIL I HEAR--	A PANG IS MORE	1530	V
UNTIL CONSTRAINED TO CLUTCH IT	OF DEATH I TRY TO THINK	1558	14
UNLESS [UNTIL] IT CONTEMPLATE	TO BE FORGOT BY THEE	1560	5
UNTIL WE DRIVE AWAY	EDEN IS THAT	1657	4
UNTIL WE MEET A SNAKE;	SWEET IS THE SWAMP WITH	1740	2
UNTO			
NIGHT UNTO DAY IS MARRIED, MORN UNTO EVENTIDE;	AWAKE YE MUSES NINE,	1	22
NIGHT UNTO DAY IS MARRIED, MORN UNTO EVENTIDE;	AWAKE YE MUSES NINE,	1	22
UNTO THE LEGISLATURE	"SIC TRANSIT GLORIA	3	25
UNTO MY FRUGAL EYE--	I HAD A GUINEA GOLDEN--	23	6
UNTO THE DIFFERENT DAWN!	THERE IS A MORN BY MEN	24	24
UNTO THE NEAREST TOWN?	ADRIFT! A LITTLE BOAT	30	4

UNTO (CONTINUED)

	FIRST LINE	POEM	LINE
AFTER [UNTO] THE DAY!	LIKE HER THE SAINTS	60	6
UNTO THE SHEPHERD'S ARM!	GOING TO HEAVEN!	79	10
"UNTO THE LITTLE, UNTO ME,"	I BRING AN UNACCUSTOMED	132	21
"UNTO THE LITTLE, UNTO ME,"	I BRING AN UNACCUSTOMED	132	21
UNTO IT'S EXTASY!	A TRANSPORT ONE CANNOT	184	4
INTO [BACK OF / AT THE / AFTER / UNTO / NEXT TO] SOLITUDE--	HOW THE OLD MOUNTAINS	291	20
UNTO LIKE STORY--TROUBLE HAS ENTICED ME--	UNTO LIKE STORY--TROUBLE	295	1
UNTO GUESSED CRESTS, MY MOANING FANCY, LEADS [LURES] ME,	UNTO LIKE STORY--TROUBLE	295	9
UNTO THE EAST AGAIN--	IT SIFTS FROM LEADEN	311	8
NOT UNTO [UPON] IT'S SUMMER--MORNING	HER--"LAST POEMS"--	312	7
UNTO MISERY--	SMILING BACK FROM	385	12
UNTO THE LADY'S FACE--	I HAD NOT MINDED--WALLS	398	14
UNTO [OVER] THE EAST, AND VICTORY--	A WIFE--AT DAYBREAK I	461	6
UNTO ITSELF--AND SMILE--AND SHAKE--	WHY MAKE IT DOUBT--IT	462	6
UNTO THE DAISY LOW--	THE HIMMALEH WAS KNOWN	481	2
UNTO THE DEAD	WE PRAY--TO HEAVEN--	489	8
AS HEAVEN [EDEN]--UNTO ME!	I ENVY SEAS, WHEREON HE	498	8
UNTO SUPREMEST NAME [TERM]--	I'M CEDED--I'VE STOPPED	508	10
WITH HIM REMAIN--WHO UNTO ME--	HER SWEET WEIGHT ON MY	518	9
AS UNTO CROWD--	TO HEAR AN ORIOLE SING	526	6
I SHOUT UNTO MY FEET--	I CROSS TILL I AM WEARY	550	19
AND YET, UNTO THE SINGLE DOE	ONE ANGUISH--IN A CROWD	565	3
UNTO THE SOFA OPPOSITE--	THE NIGHT WAS WIDE, AND	589	19
GIVE SPICES--UNTO MEN--	WHAT CARE THE DEAD, FOR	592	24
AS IF UNTO A JUBILEE [SACRAMENT]	I THINK I WAS ENCHANTED	593	19
THEY--SOLD [THEN--SELL] IT UNTO ME	OF BRUSSELS--IT WAS NOT	602	4
UNTO MY BOOKS--SO GOOD TO TURN--	UNTO MY BOOKS--SO GOOD	604	1
UNTO GOD--	ONLY GOD--DETECT THE	626	4
UNTO A VELVET LIMB--	YOU'LL KNOW HER--BY HER	634	8
NOR IS IT CLASPED UNTO OF BAND--	YOU'LL KNOW HER--BY HER	634	19
UNTO ALL [TO FOREIGN] HEART--	ME FROM MYSELF--TO	642	4
THE ANSWER OF THE SEA UNTO	I COULD SUFFICE FOR HIM,	643	13
HERSELF ADJUST HER TIDES--UNTO--	I COULD SUFFICE FOR HIM,	643	15
APPEAR--UNTO THE SEA--	I THINK TO LIVE--MAY BE	646	8
NO ROMANCE SOLD UNTO	NO ROMANCE SOLD UNTO	669	1
UNTO THE SAINTS' SLOW DILIGENCE [INDUSTRY]--	EACH LIFE CONVERGES TO	680	15
FADE I UNTO DIVINITY--	'TWOULD EASE--A	682	11
THE SOUL UNTO ITSELF	THE SOUL UNTO ITSELF	683	1
UNTO VITALITY!	THE ZEROES--TAUGHT US--	689	8
UNTO MY SEEMING--MAKE?	THE SUN KEPT SETTING--	692	12
WHITE--UNTO THE WHITE CREATOR--	PUBLICATION--IS THE	709	7
HER EYE UNTO THE SUMMER DEW	THE MOON WAS BUT A CHIN	737	7
WHAT DEED IS THEIR'S [THEY BEAR] UNTO THE GENERAL NATURE--	FOUR TREES--UPON A	742	13
UNTO ITSELF--	RENUNCIATION--IS A	745	13
NEED YOU--UNTO HIM--	NEVER FOR SOCIETY	746	12
DEATH--UNTO ITSELF--EXCEPTION--	ALL BUT DEATH, CAN BE	749	7
UNTO HER SACRAMENT--	MY WORTHINESS IS ALL MY	751	16
THAT I UNTO HIMSELF ADJUST	YOU CONSTITUTED TIME--	765	7
UNTO A NAMELESS MAN--	TO OFFER BRAVE	767	6
UNTO THE EVERLASTING SPRING	NO NOTICE GAVE SHE, BUT	804	15
UNTO SUCH, WERE SUCH ASSEMBLY	ONE DAY IS THERE OF THE	814	15
GIVEN IN MARRIAGE UNTO THEE	GIVEN IN MARRIAGE UNTO	817	1
APPOINTED UNTO MEN--	THIS CONSCIOUSNESS THAT	822	8
HOW ADEQUATE UNTO ITSELF	THIS CONSCIOUSNESS THAT	822	9
ITSELF UNTO ITSELF AND NONE	THIS CONSCIOUSNESS THAT	822	11
ADVENTURE MOST UNTO ITSELF	THIS CONSCIOUSNESS THAT	822	13
AND SHUT THE DOOR UNTO MY HOUSE	I SING TO USE THE	850	3
UNTO THIS PRESENT, RUN,	HE OUTSTRIPPED TIME WITH	865	6
LIST EVEN UNTO ME.	BECAUSE THE BEE MAY	869	3
UNTO THE LIPS IT EDDIED THROUGH--	I'VE NONE TO TELL ME TO	881	12
ATTRACTED MORE UNTO--	WHO OCCUPIES THIS HOUSE?	892	24
UNTO THE SCENE THAT WE DO NOT--	FAITH--IS THE PIERLESS	915	3
UNTO HIS NEST AGAIN	IF I CAN STOP ONE HEART	919	6
TO THE [UNTO] SOULS THAT SNOW--	ABSENT PLACE--AN APRIL	927	4
UNTO THE THOUGHT BEFORE--	I FELT A CLEAVING IN MY	937	6
AS SOMEONE HELD A LIGHT UNTO [UPON]	WHAT I SEE NOT, I BETTER	939	7
THAT MAY FURNISH THE FUSE [IGNITION] UNTO A SPARK	A MAN MAY MAKE A REMARK	952	3
A FLINT UNTO THIS DAY--PERHAPS--	WE MET AS SPARKS--	958 V	7
"UNTO ME?" I DO NOT KNOW YOU--	"UNTO ME?" I DO NOT KNOW	964	1
OF ME--WHEN FIRST UNTO THE DOOR	FITTER TO SEE HIM, I MAY	968	17
UNTO US--THE SUNS EXTINGUISH--	UNFULFILLED TO	972	5
UNTO THE DISK BEFORE--	THE DUST BEHIND I STROVE	992	2
BUT DISCPLINE UNTO	I KNEW THAT I HAD GAINED	1022	4
UNTO A NEIGHBOR'S BIN.	THE PRODUCTS OF MY FARM	1025	4
"GIVE OF THINE AN ACRE UNTO ME."	SAID DEATH TO PASSION	1033	2
AND SPIRIT TURNED [THE SPIRIT SAID] UNTO THE DUST	I HEARD, AS IF I HAD NO	1039	13
AND MET [UNTO] ETERNITY	I HEARD, AS IF I HAD NO	1039	16
UNTO AN EQUAL BUD	THE OPENING AND THE	1047	6
OF DANES, UNTO THE REST.	REPORTLESS SUBJECTS, TO	1048	4
EACH ONE UNTO THE OTHER	PAIN HAS BUT ONE	1049	3
THE BOLT UNTO [UPON] THE DOOR--	THE SOUL SHOULD ALWAYS	1055	6
GRACIOUS UNTO NONE--	THREE WEEKS PASSED SINCE	1061	8
UNTO A SILENT SKY	AT HALF PAST THREE, A	1084	2
UNTO A MISER'S EAR--	BECAUSE 'TWAS RICHES I	1093	8

	FIRST LINE	POEM	LINE
UNTO (CONTINUED)			
ASK [TO] HIM UNTO THE GALLOWS LED [CALLED]--	OH SUMPTUOUS MOMENT	1125	8
NOT UNTO NOMINATION	SHALL I TAKE THEE, THE	1126	11
THEN GAVE [BENT / BOWED] THE EAST UNTO THE WEST	THE WIND TOOK UP THE	1134	3
THE WIND--UNTO HIS [IT'S] CHAMBERS WENT	THE WIND TOOK UP THE	1134	9
COME UNTO ME ENACTED [ACCOMPLISHED] HOW	CONTAINED IN THIS SHORT	1165	V
UNTO A JUGGLER TURNED--	NATURE AFFECTS TO BE	1170	8
SINGING UNTO THE STONE	NOT WITH A CLUB, THE	1304	11
UNTO THE WHOLE--HOW ADD?	UNTO THE WHOLE--HOW ADD?	1341	1
CONSIDER IT UNTO MYSELF	ESCAPE IS SUCH A	1347	3
UNTO ITSELF A DIRGE	HIS LITTLE HEARSE LIKE	1522	2
INTO [UNTO] THE BEAUTIFUL.	AS IMPERCEPTIBLY AS	1540	16
THE MAPLE LENT UNTO THE ROAD	AS IMPERCEPTIBLY AS	1540	V
"COME UNTO ME" THE MOIETY	NO LADDER NEEDS THE BIRD	1574	7
"COME UNTO ME" THE MOIETY	TO HER DERIDED HOME	1586	11
UNTO A PURPLE WOOD	A LANE OF YELLOW LED THE	1650	2
UNTO A BROKEN HEART	UNTO A BROKEN HEART	1704	1
UN TO			
THAT WOULD TO [UN TO] SENSE HAVE DAZZLED	CONTAINED IN THIS SHORT	1165	V
UNTOLD			
UNTOLD TALE--	LET US PLAY YESTERDAY--	728	4
THE BIBLE IS AN ANTIQUE [UNTOLD] VOLUME--	THE BIBLE IS AN ANTIQUE	1545	1
PORTENTOUSLY UNTOLD	THEY TALK AS SLOW AS	1697	8
UNTOUCHED			
UNTOUCHED BY MORNING	SAFE IN THEIR ALABASTER	216	2
AND UNTOUCHED BY NOON--	SAFE IN THEIR ALABASTER	216	3
UNTOWARD			
AND THIS UNTOWARD TRANSPORT	HIGH FROM THE EARTH I	1723	17
UNTRAVELLED			
FERN ODORS ON UNTRAVELLED ROADS--	AN ALTERED LOOK ABOUT	140	12
UNTRAVERSED			
TO AN UNTRAVERSED SPOT--	COULD LIVE--DID LIVE--	43	7
UNTUMBLED			
UNTUMBLED THIS ABODE	TO THEIR APARTMENT DEEP	1701	3
UNTWIST			
AND OAKS UNTWIST [UNKNOT / UNKNIT / UNCLINCH] THEIR FISTS--	THE TRUTH--IS STIRLESS--	780	5
UNUSED			
LIPS UNUSED TO THEE--	COME SLOWLY--EDEN!	211	2
UNVARYING			
THE FINE--UNVARYING AXIS	THE OUTER--FROM THE	451	5
THOSE SAME UNVARYING EYES	SWEET MOUNTAINS--YE TELL	722	3
UNVEIL			
IF IMMORTALITY UNVEIL [DISCLOSE]	MY LIFE CLOSED TWICE	1732	3
UNVISITED			
UNVISITED OF SHORES--	AS IF THE SEA SHOULD	695	6
UNWEARIED			
UNWEARIED, ALL THE SUMMER LONG,	IF I COULD BRIBE THEM BY	179	10
WHEN KATIE RUNS UNWEARIED THEY FOLLOW ON THE ROAD,	WHEN KATIE WALKS, THIS	222	2
UNWHOLE			
THOUGH THE RING IS UNWHOLE, AND THE COMPANY BROKE	OF THE HEART THAT GOES	1098	3
UNWILLING			
TO THE STANCH [UNWILLING] DUST	TO THE STANCH DUST	1402	1
UNWIND			
UNWIND THE SOLEMN TWINE, AND TIE MY VALENTINE!	AWAKE YE MUSES NINE,	1	2
UNWINDS			
HIS YARN [COIL] OF PEARL--UNWINDS [EXPENDS]--	THE SPIDER HOLDS A	605	4
THE NOON UNWINDS HER BLUE	THE SUNRISE RUNS FOR	710	4
UNWITNESSED			
UNMANIFEST TO [UNWITNESSED OF THE / AS DOTH THE TIRED] SENSE	CONTAINED IN THIS SHORT	1165	V
UNWORTHY			
UNWORTHY, THAT A THOUGHT SO MEAN	THE SOUL HAS BANDAGED	512	9
THE MOST UNWORTHY FLOWER--	NATURE--THE GENTLEST	790	16
UNWORTHY OF HER BREAST	UNWORTHY OF HER BREAST	1414	1
UP			
APPROACH THAT TREE WITH CAUTION, THEN UP IT BOLDLY CLIMB,	AWAKE YE MUSES NINE,	1	35
PETER, PUT UP THE SUNSHINE;	"SIC TRANSIT GLORIA	3	13
BUT UP AND DOWN THE HILLS	ONE SISTER HAVE I IN OUR	14	14
ONE LITTLE BOAT GAVE UP IT'S STRIFE	ADRIFT! A LITTLE BOAT	30	7
AND LIFT IT UP TO THEE.	NOBODY KNOWS THIS LITTLE	35	4
BE RECKONED UP?	IF PAIN FOR PEACE	63	6
TENDERLY TOOK IT UP FROM TOIL	A POOR--TORN HEART-- A	78	11
WENT UP A YEAR THIS EVENING!	WENT UP A YEAR THIS	93	1
RECKON THE MORNING'S FLAGON'S UP	BRING ME THE SUNSET IN A	128	2
TOOK UP HER SIMPLE WARDROBE	SHE DIED--THIS WAS THE	150	3
"BERNARDINE" ANGELS, UP THE HIGHT	SHE DIED--THIS WAS THE	150	V 5
AND RISEN UP--AND GONE AWAY,	I'VE HEARD AN ORGAN TALK	183	5
IF I COULD SHUT HIM UP	IS IT TRUE, DEAR SUE?	218	5
THE SOUND ONES, LIKE THE HILLS--SHALL STAND [STAND UP]--	WHEN WE STAND ON THE	242	7
PLUCK UP IT'S STAKES, AND DISAPPEAR--	I'VE KNOWN A HEAVEN,	243	3
THEN SWALLOWED UP, OF VIEW.	I'VE KNOWN A HEAVEN,	243	17
THE HEARING HIM PUT HIS PLAYTHINGS UP	IT IS EASY TO WORK WHEN	244	3
BREAKS UP MY FEET--	I CAN WADE GRIEF--	252	5
STRUCK UP MY CHILDISH	DELIGHT IS AS THE FLIGHT	257	13

	FIRST LINE	POEM	LINE
UP (CONTINUED)			
PUT UP MY LUTE!	PUT UP MY LUTE!	261	1
MY LIFETIME FOLDING UP--	HE PUT THE BELT AROUND	273	4
PUT GENTLY UP THE EVENING BARS--	I'LL TELL YOU HOW THE	318	15
AND BEES--PICK UP--	I TEND MY FLOWERS FOR	339	10
DEFORMING--DWINDLING--GULPHING UP--	I HAD THE GLORY--THAT	349	6
LOOP UP A COUNTESS--WITH YOU--	I'LL CLUTCH--AND CLUTCH	427	10
TAKING UP THE FAIR IDEAL,	TAKING UP THE FAIR IDEAL	428	1
AND COVERED UP--OUR NAMES--	I DIED FOR BEAUTY--BUT	449	12
DUCAL--AT LAST--STAND UP BY THEE--	LOVE--THOU ART HIGH--	453	6
ARE SO HIGH UP--YOU SEE--	I KNOW WHERE WELLS GROW	460	12
THE QUIET AGES PICKED IT UP--	I MEANT TO HAVE BUT	476	19
JUST LOCKING UP--TO DIE.	SHE DEALT HER PRETTY	479	12
AND GOLDEN HANG--WHILE FARTHER UP--	A SOLEMN THING WITHIN	483	3
SCOOPING UP THE DUST AND CHANTING "LIVE"!	WHILE IT IS ALIVE	491	10
CHILDREN--MATURED [GROWN UP]--ARE WISER--MOSTLY--	BETTER--THAN MUSIC! FOR	503	13
WHEN THE LAST SAINT--GOES UP THE AISLES--	BETTER--THAN MUSIC! FOR	503	18
EXISTENCE'S WHOLE ARC, [WHOLE EYE / WHOLE RIM / SURMISE] FILLED UP,	I'M CEDED--I'VE STOPPED	508	12
IT WAS NOT DEATH, FOR I STOOD UP,	IT WAS NOT DEATH, FOR I	510	1
SHE FEELS SOME GHASTLY FRIGHT COME UP	THE SOUL HAS BANDAGED	512	3
AND THEN--HE CLOSES UP--	HE PARTS HIMSELF--LIKE	517	2
AND MADE AS HE WOULD EAT ME UP--	I STARTED EARLY--TOOK MY	520	13
AND FAILED TO WAKE THEM UP--	I HAD NO CAUSE TO BE	542	4
BLOCK IT UP	TO FILL A GAP	546	3
PUT UP--TO HIDE [HOLD] HER PARTING GRACE	MY FIRST WELL DAY--SINCE	574	23
AND LICK THE VALLEYS UP--	I LIKE TO SEE IT LAP	585	2
NOVEMBER LEFT--THEN CLAMBERED UP	THE NIGHT WAS WIDE, AND	589	7
LIT UP THE LOW--INFERIOR GRASS--	I THINK I WAS ENCHANTED	593	V 11
WENT UP FROM THE POTOMAC--	WHEN I WAS SMALL, A	596	3
THREE TIMES--THE BILLOWS THREW [TOSSED] ME UP--	THREE TIMES--WE PARTED--	598	5
AND I STOOD UP--AND LIVED--	THREE TIMES--WE PARTED--	598	16
IT SWALLOWS SUBSTANCE [BEING] UP--	THERE IS A PAIN--SO	599	2
HE FOUND MY BEING--SET IT UP--	HE FOUND MY BEING--SET	603	1
THEY SHUT ME UP IN PROSE--	THEY SHUT ME UP IN PROSE	613	1
DONT PUT UP MY THREAD & NEEDLE--	DONT PUT UP MY THREAD &	617	1
TAKE UP MY LITTLE VIOLIN--	I THINK THE LONGEST HOUR	635	15
PUTTING UP	I CANNOT LIVE WITH YOU--	640	6
TOO STEEP FOR LOOKING UP--	A PRISON GETS TO BE A	652	28
NOR ONCE LOOK UP--FOR NOON?	A LONG--LONG SLEEP--A	654	8
A THOUGHT WENT UP MY MIND TODAY--	A THOUGHT WENT UP MY	701	1
THAT TRUSTS HER--BOLDLY UP--	THE TRUTH--IS STIRLESS--	780	12
WHEN DEATH LIT ALL THE SHORTNESS UP [LIMIT--UP / BREVITY]	HER FINAL SUMMER WAS IT	795	7
WHEN DEATH LIT ALL THE SHORTNESS UP [LIMIT--UP / BREVITY]	HER FINAL SUMMER WAS IT	795	7
THE BIRDS PUT UP THE BARS TO NESTS--	THE WIND BEGUN TO KNEAD	824	13
WHEN ONE HAS GIVEN UP ONE'S LIFE	WHEN ONE HAS GIVEN UP	853	1
I'M TEMPTED HALF TO STITCH IT UP	THIS CHASM, SWEET, UPON	858	13
RETREATING UP, A BILLOW'S HIGHT	ESCAPING BACKWARD TO	867	5
GO UP BY TWO AND TWO.	'TIS ANGUISH GRANDER	984	8
YOU WILL NOT WAKE THEM UP."	THE FINGERS OF THE LIGHT	1000	8
HELD UP HIS CUP FOR LIGHT.	THE FINGERS OF THE LIGHT	1000	16
UP LIFE'S HILL WITH MY LITTLE BUNDLE	UP LIFE'S HILL WITH MY	1010	1
GROPED UP, TO SEE IF GOD WERE [WAS] THERE--	HE SCANNED IT--STAGGERED	1062	6
THE SWEEPING UP THE HEART	THE BUSTLE IN A HOUSE	1078	5
THE SUN WENT UP--NO MAN LOOKED ON--	THE SUN WENT DOWN--NO	1079	5
THE MORN WAS UP--THE MEADOWS OUT	THE BIRD DID PRANCE--THE	1107	5
THE WIND TOOK UP THE NORTHERN THINGS	THE WIND TOOK UP THE	1134	1
INSTINCT PICKING UP THE KEY	AFTER A HUNDRED YEARS	1147	11
FLING UP THY BALLS OF GOLD	MY GOD--HE SEES THEE--	1178	3
THAT MAKES THE HEART PUT UP IT'S FUN--	SEPTEMBER'S	1271	7
PUT UP MY HEART THY HOARY WORK	THE NOTICE THAT IS	1310	3
OH MARCH, COME RIGHT UP STAIRS WITH ME--	DEAR MARCH--COME IN--	1320	9
WHO [THAT] MUST BE UP TO CALL THE WORLD	HOW GOOD HIS LAVA BED,	1447	3
THE WINDS CAME CLOSER UP--	AS IMPERCEPTIBLY AS	1540	V
AND THEN HE LIFTED UP HIS THROAT	UPON HIS SADDLE SPRUNG A	1600	5
A CHILL CAME UP AS FROM A SHAFT	A CAP OF LEAD ACROSS THE	1649	5
THE TREES HELD UP	THE WIND DREW OFF	1694	7
WALK BOLDLY UP AND KNOCK	T'WAS COMFORT IN HER	1703	4
THAT HOLDS MY CHANCES UP.	A PIT--BUT HEAVEN OVER	1712	8
COMES UP TO FACE THE SKIES,	DROWNING IS NOT SO	1718	4
UPBORNE			
MYSELF ENDUED [UPHELD / UPBORNE / SUSTAINED] BALLOON	I WOULD NOT PAINT--A	505	14
UPBRAIDS			
AND THEN UPBRAIDS A PERFECTNESS	PERCEPTION OF AN OBJECT	1071	7
UPHELD			
MYSELF ENDUED [UPHELD / UPBORNE / SUSTAINED] BALLOON	I WOULD NOT PAINT--A	505	14
UPHELD IN ROLLING AIR	I WATCHED THE MOON	629	18
WAS ALL THAT SAVED [ALONE SUSTAINED-- / ALONE UPHELD--] A BEE	A SINGLE CLOVER PLANK	1343	2
UPHOLSTERER			
UPHOLSTERER OF THE PINES [SEA / LAND / HILLS]--IS HE--	OF BRUSSELS--IT WAS NOT	602	15
UPHOLSTERER--OF THE POND--	OF BRUSSELS--IT WAS NOT	602	16

	FIRST LINE	POEM	LINE
UPLIFTS			
THE TUBE UPLIFTS A SIGNAL BUD	THE DANDELION'S PALLID	1519	5
UPPER			
FOR THE UPPER AIR!	TO VENERATE THE SIMPLE	57	11
AND FRIGATES--IN THE UPPER FLOOR	I STARTED EARLY--TOOK MY	520	5
AND THE UPPER SIDE--IS THE SUN--	BY MY WINDOW HAVE I FOR	797	10
THE UPPER SURFACES OF THINGS	THE SYMPTOM OF THE GALE	1327	7
SOME CONFLICT WITH THOSE UPPER FRIENDS . .	A WILD BLUE SKY ABREAST	1415	5
TO WESTWARD [UPPER] OF THE TOWN--	IT WAS A QUIET SEEMING	1419	6
TO SOMETHING UPPER WOOING US	THE FASCINATING CHILL	1480	7
UPRIGHT			
AND SETTING IT UPRIGHT	YOU CANNOT MAKE	1508	4
UPSET			
WHEN WINDS--UPSET THE BASIN--	THE NAME--OF IT--IS	656	7
URCHIN			
NEITHER PATRIARCH NOR PUSSY [ANCESTOR NOR URCHIN]	ONE DAY IS THERE OF THE	814	5
ISAAC WAS AN URCHIN--	ABRAHAM TO KILL HIM	1317	3
URCHIN'S			
AND EVERY SEPARATE URCHIN'S SUM--	'TIS ONE BY ONE--THE	545	15
URGE			
TILL THE CHILDREN URGE [ASK]--	GLEE--THE GREAT STORM IS	619	11
A FEAR WILL URGE IT WHERE	I LIVED ON DREAD--	770	7
LOCATION DOUBTLESS HE WOULD PLEAD [URGE] .	SO MUCH OF HEAVEN HAS	1228	7
URGED			
SO AGONIZED URGED?	JUST ONCE! OH LEAST	1076	V 5
"UNCHANGED" I URGED WITH A CANDOR	I SAW THAT THE FLAKE WAS	1267	3
URGENCY			
OF GREEDINESS [URGENCY / VEHEMENCE] TO DIE--	HE FOUGHT LIKE THOSE	759	12
URGENT			
ADULT AND URGENT GROWN--	THE WAY TO KNOW THE	1279	18
URGING			
URGING THE FEET--THAT WOULD--NOT--FLY-- . .	BETTER--THAN MUSIC! FOR	503	12
URN			
AND EVEN IN THE URN, ...	OF ALL THE SOUNDS	321	16
IN INFAMY OR URN--	ALL MEN FOR HONOR	1193	4
US			
BANDITTI OFTEN PASSED US	THROUGH LANE IT LAY--	9	3
FIERCE FROM THE CRAG ABOVE US	THROUGH LANE IT LAY--	9	11
AN AGED BEE ADDRESSED US--	THE GENTIAN WEAVES HER	18	11
LET US GO WITH THEE!	THE GENTIAN WEAVES HER	18	16
LET US CHANT IT SOFTLY--	ALL THESE MY BANNERS BE.	22	18
SUCH TRUST HAD ONE AMONG US, ...	COULD LIVE--DID LIVE--	43	10
AMONG US NOT TODAY--	COULD LIVE--DID LIVE--	43	11
TO GIRD US FOR THE SUN, ...	IF PAIN FOR PEACE	63	8
MODEST, LET US WALK AMONG IT	I CANT TELL YOU--BUT YOU	65	9
FORGIVE US, IF AS DAYS DECLINE--	THE DAISY FOLLOWS SOFT	106	8
COULD SCARE US ANY MORE!	WHERE BELLS NO MORE	112	12
HEAVEN TO US, IF TRUE.	AS WATCHERS HANG UPON	121	12
TO US--THE DULLER SCHOLARS [CORNETS] . . .	TO LEARN THE TRANSPORT	167	15
THAT QUICKENED US LIKE WINE!	IN EBON BOX, WHEN YEARS	169	8
TAKE US SIMULTANEOUS--LORD--	WE DONT CRY--TIM AND I,	196	27
WONT THEY SCOLD US--WHEN WE'RE HUNGRY [HOMESICK]--	WHAT IS--"PARADISE"--	215	9
THEN--MAYBE, IT WOULD PUZZLE US	I'VE NOTHING ELSE--TO	224	7
"FORBID US NOT"--	TEACH HIM--WHEN HE MAKES	227	8
'TIS'NT ALL HOCK--WITH US--	WE--BEE AND I--LIVE BY	230	2
THAT SPURNED US--YESTERDAY!	"HEAVEN"--IS WHAT I	239	12
JUST FINDING OUT--WHAT PUZZLED US--	FOREVER AT HIS SIDE TO	246	15
AND HELPS US TO FORGET--	TO DIE--TAKES JUST A	255	8
THAT BUT FOR LOVE OF US--	TO DIE--TAKES JUST A	255	10
HEAVENLY HURT, IT GIVES US--	THERE'S A CERTAIN SLANT	258	5
SENT US OF THE AIR--	THERE'S A CERTAIN SLANT	258	12
CHARGED US TO FORGET HIM--	DID WE DISOBEY HIM?	267	3
THEY CANNOT TAKE ME [US]--ANY MORE!	WHAT IF I SAY I SHALL	277	7
THAT AFTER HORROR--THAT 'TWAS US--	THAT AFTER HORROR--THAT	286	1
THEN THERE'S A PAIR OF US!	I'M NOBODY! WHO ARE YOU?	288	3
DONT TELL! THEY'D BANISH US [ADVERTISE]--YOU KNOW!	I'M NOBODY! WHO ARE YOU?	288	4
ELATE US--TILL WE ALMOST WEEP--	LIKE SOME OLD FASHIONED	302	11
INHERITANCE, IT IS, TO US--	OF ALL THE SOUNDS	321	9
'TIS NOT THAT DYING HURTS US SO--	'TIS NOT THAT DYING	335	1
'TIS LIVING--HURTS US MORE--	'TIS NOT THAT DYING	335	2
THEY LEAVE US WITH THE INFINITE.	THEY LEAVE US WITH THE	350	1
WOOS, AS HE STATES US--BY HIS SON--	GOD IS A DISTANT--	357	2
ENTREAT US TENDERLY	DEATH SETS A THING	360	4
REMIND US THAT WE DIED.	REHEARSAL TO OURSELVES	379	8
ON THE HEADS THAT STARTED WITH US--	SMILING BACK FROM	385	3
SO NOT TO SEE US--BUT THEY SAY	I NEVER FELT AT HOME--	413	11
PERENNIAL BEHOLDS US--	I NEVER FELT AT HOME--	413	13
BUT DO ONE FACE US SUDDENLY--	SUNSET AT NIGHT--IS	415	7
NOT AUDIBLE--AS OUR'S--TO US--	A MURMUR IN THE TREES--	416	7
MEET US--WITH A SMILE--	TAKING UP THE FAIR IDEAL	428	17
BUT PROVES US	UNDUE SIGNIFICANCE A	439	6
TO BEAR ON US UNSHADED--	I TIE MY HAT--I CREASE	443	23
AS LIFE--DISSOLVED BE--FOR US--	IT FEELS A SHAME TO BE	444	15
ENTITLES US--BY CONTRAST--	THIS WAS A POET--IT IS	448	11
THEY GIVE US PRESENTS MOST--YOU KNOW-- . .	IT WAS GIVEN TO ME BY	454	3
THEY PUT US FAR APART--	THEY PUT US FAR APART--	474	1
THEY THWARTED US WITH GUNS--	THEY PUT US FAR APART--	474	6

	FIRST LINE	POEM	LINE
US (CONTINUED)			
THEY SUMMONED US TO DIE--	THEY PUT US FAR APART--	474	13
ENOUGH FOR US	"WHY DO I LOVE" YOU, SIR	480	9
BUT THAT THYSELF FATIGUE OF US--	WE COVER THEE--SWEET	482	3
THOU NOTICE US--NO MORE--	WE COVER THEE--SWEET	482	6
SUFFICIENTLY DEVELOPED--HE'D HIRE US	MYSELF WAS FORMED--A	488	7
ANTICIPATING US	THOSE FAIR--FICTITIOUS	499	18
ESTEEMING US--AS EXILE--	THOSE FAIR--FICTITIOUS	499	21
AND HE AND I, PERPLEX US	WITHIN MY GARDEN, RIDES	500	13
'TWAS WARM--AT FIRST--LIKE US--	'TWAS WARM--AT FIRST--	519	1
SACRAMENT, SAINTS PARTOOK [INDORSED] BEFORE US--	TO PUT THIS WORLD DOWN,	527	12
IT [THEY] WOULD HURT US--WERE WE AWAKE--	WE DREAM--IT IS GOOD WE	531	2
BUT SINCE IT IS PLAYING--KILL US,	WE DREAM--IT IS GOOD WE	531	3
COOL US TO SHAFTS OF GRANITE--	WE DREAM--IT IS GOOD WE	531	13
PERHAPS 'TIS KINDLY--DONE US--	WE SEE--COMPARATIVELY--	534	9
THE THING BELONGED TO US--	WE SEE--COMPARATIVELY--	534	12
TO US--GIGANTIC SUM--	HE GAVE AWAY HIS LIFE--	567	2
ALL THESE--REMIND US OF THE PLACE	"HEAVEN" HAS DIFFERENT	575	15
AND SO AND SO--HAD BEEN TO US [ME],	I CRIED AT PITY--NOT AT	588	15
SALUTE US, WITH THEIR WINGS--	OF NEARNESS TO HER	607	16
WHO RECOLLECTED US	I ROSE--BECAUSE HE SANK	616	18
THEIR GRASPLESS MANNERS--MOCK US--	THE TINT I CANNOT TAKE--	627	21
AS HARASS US--LIKE LIFE--AND DEATH--	I WATCHED THE MOON	629	25
ALARMS US--THO' HIS YELLOW FEET	THE LIGHTNING PLAYETH--	630	7
THEY'D JUDGE US--HOW--	I CANNOT LIVE WITH YOU--	640	29
FITTER FEET--OF HER [FOR THE FEET] BEFORE US--	HER SWEET TURN TO LEAVE	649	13
IT DEAL US [FURNISH]--STATED AS OUR FOOD--	A PRISON GETS TO BE A	652	7
ARE PRESENT TO US--AS OUR OWN--	A PRISON GETS TO BE A	652	23
GOES WITH US--JUST A LITTLE WAY--	AGAIN--HIS VOICE IS AT	663	20
'TIS THIS ENAMORS [AFFLICTS US] IN THE EAST--	THE LOVE A LIFE CAN SHOW	673	10
THE ZEROES--TAUGHT US--PHOSPHORUS--	THE ZEROES--TAUGHT US--	689	1
HIS TABLE'S SPREAD TOO HIGH FOR US--	VICTORY COMES LATE--	690	8
OR RATHER--HE PASSED US--	BECAUSE I COULD NOT STOP	712	13
LET US PLAY YESTERDAY--	LET US PLAY YESTERDAY--	728	1
THAT ARISE AND SET ABOUT US--	DRAMA'S VITALLEST	741	2
WHY FLOODS BE SERVED TO US--IN BOWLS--	ONE BLESSING HAD I THAN	756	19
THESE--ADJUST--THAT RAN TO MEET US--	THESE--SAW VISIONS--	758	12
SUFFICE US--FOR A CROWD--	ON A COLUMNAR SELF--	789	9
OF SAVORS--MAKE US CONSCIOUS--	DESPAIR'S ADVANTAGE IS	799	9
AS SOME [US] SHE NEVER KNEW--	NO NOTICE GAVE SHE, BUT	804	20
A DOUBT IF IT BE US	A DOUBT IF IT BE US	859	1
THAT DISTANCE WAS BETWEEN US	THAT DISTANCE WAS	863	1
AND GRANT US ALL THEIR COUNTENANCE	THEY ASK BUT OUR DELIGHT	868	3
HIS MIGHTY PLEASURE SUITS US NOT	THE SUN IS GAY OR STARK	878	7
FROM US SHE WANDERED NOW A YEAR,	FROM US SHE WANDERED NOW	890	1
THE NEARER THEY DEPARTED US	SWEET, TO HAVE HAD THEM	901	3
THEN THOUGHT OF US, AND STAYED.	SWEET, TO HAVE HAD THEM	901	9
NO NEED--HADST THOU--OF US"?	HAD I NOT THIS, OR THIS,	904	8
BUT FLOWERS--NEGOTIATE BETWEEN US--	BETWEEN MY COUNTRY--AND	905	3
THAT LOOKS A HARDER SKILL TO US--	ONLY A SHRINE, BUT MINE	918	9
HOW HE STRETCHED HIS ANGUISH [SPIRIT] TO US	HOW THE WATERS CLOSED	923	3
AFFECT US, AND RETURN--	THERE IS A JUNE WHEN	930	8
DEATH LEAVES US HOMESICK, WHO BEHIND,	DEATH LEAVES US HOMESICK	935	1
THE WITNESSING, TO US--	ON THAT DEAR FRAME THE	940	4
WHAT BEES--FOR US--TO HUM--	I LEARNED--AT LEAST--	944	10
TILL SUNRISE TAKE [CALL] US BACK TO SCENE--	I LEARNED--AT LEAST--	944	25
LET US DIVIDE [DEPORT]--WITH SKILL--	A MAN MAY MAKE A REMARK	952	5
LET US DISCOURSE [DISCLOSE]--WITH CARE--	A MAN MAY MAKE A REMARK	952	6
UNTO US--THE SUNS EXTINGUISH--	UNFULFILLED TO	972	5
FRONTING US--WITH [TURNING US--THEIR] NIGHT.	UNFULFILLED TO	972	8
FRONTING US--WITH [TURNING US--THEIR] NIGHT.	UNFULFILLED TO	972	8
INCLUDE US [SCAN BETTER / CONVEY US]--AS THEY GO--	WE MISS HER, NOT BECAUSE	993	8
INCLUDE US [SCAN BETTER / CONVEY US]--AS THEY GO--	WE MISS HER, NOT BECAUSE	993	8
TO SIMULATE, TO US.	AURORA IS THE EFFORT	1002	4
IS OPTIONAL WITH US--	DID WE ABOLISH FROST	1014	4
WITH US, 'TIS HARVEST ALL THE YEAR	THE PRODUCTS OF MY FARM	1025	5
THAT SUCH HAVE DIED ENABLE US	THAT SUCH HAVE DIED	1030	1
NO SEASONS WERE TO US--	IT WAS A QUIET WAY--	1053	17
GOD SENDS [GIVES] US WOMEN--	TITLE DIVINE--IS MINE!	1072	7
NATURE, LIKE US IS SOMETIMES CAUGHT	THE SKY IS LOW--THE	1075	7
WAS RECENTLY AMONG US--	WE LEARN IN THE	1083	3
EXCEPT THE DYING--THIS TO US	THE LAST NIGHT THAT SHE	1100	3
MORE INTIMATE WITH US BECOME	THE MURMURING OF BEES,	1115	15
THAT LIFTS US FROM THE GROUND	EXHILIRATION IS THE	1118	2
AND LEAVES US IN ANOTHER PLACE	EXHILIRATION IS THE	1118	3
RETURNS US NOT, BUT AFTER TIME	EXHILIRATION IS THE	1118	5
WHOSE HAVING LIVED IS HELD BY US IN NOBLE HOLIDAY	LEST ANY DOUBT THAT WE	1156	2
A TRANSPORT MAY [MIGHT] RECEIPT US	THE PAST IS SUCH A	1203	3
LICENSE TO THINK OF [CHERISH] US--	WHATEVER IT IS--SHE HAS	1204	12
BUT WHEN IT LEAVES US FOR A TIME	IMMORTAL IS AN AMPLE	1205	3
THE EXCELLENCE [QUALITY] DEFIES US--	TO DISAPPEAR ENHANCES--	1209	15
OCCUPY TO US THOUGH PERHAPS TO THEM	SOME WE SEE NO MORE,	1221	2
LEAVE US TO PRESUME	SOME WE SEE NO MORE,	1221	5
OH GOD OF WIDTH, DO NOT FOR US	SOMEWHERE UPON THE	1231	11
BESIDE US LIKE A BLAND ABYSS	POWER IS A FAMILIAR	1238	3
AND WHAT HAD THEY TO DO WITH US [ME]	WHO WERE "THE FATHER AND	1258	3

	FIRST LINE	POEM	LINE
US (CONTINUED)			
HE TELLS US CERTAINLY	BECAUSE THAT YOU ARE	1260	36
HE WILL REFUND US FINALLY	BECAUSE THAT YOU ARE	1260	39
TO TAKE US [ONE] LANDS AWAY	THERE IS NO FRIGATE LIKE	1263	2
IT MADE US ALL ASHAMED [DEMEANED]	SO PROUD SHE WAS TO DIE	1272	2
WHERE NONE OF US SHOULD [WOULD] BE . . .	SO PROUD SHE WAS TO DIE	1272	6
CONFRONTING US AGAIN!	THE BONE THAT HAS NO	1274	12
LAIN IN NATURE--SO SUFFICE US	LAIN IN NATURE--SO	1288	1
WOULD STRIKE US INSTANT DEAD	I NEVER HEAR THAT ONE IS	1323	12
BECAUSE "GOD TOOK HIM" MENTION--[TELL US] .	"WAS NOT" WAS ALL THE	1342	7
ENJOINING US TO PART	AN ANTIQUATED GRACE	1345	4
THAT MAKE US RICH AN HOUR--	DREAMS ARE THE SUBTLE	1376	2
THEN FLING US POOR	DREAMS ARE THE SUBTLE	1376	3
A FEW OF US--BELIEVED--	SUMMER--WE ALL HAVE SEEN	1386	2
HER PANTING NOTE [JOYFUL CRY / CORDIAL NOTE] EXALTS US-- . . .	AFTER ALL BIRDS HAVE	1395	6
HER GALLANT NOTE ENDOWS US LIKE A FRIEND .	AFTER ALL BIRDS HAVE	1395 V	6
. . . US THERE [HERE]--	PERHAPS THEY DO NOT GO	1399	8
BETRAYS [REPORTS] US, AS HIS FIRST BETROTHAL	MARCH IS THE MONTH OF	1404	7
NOT ONLY MUST CONFIRM US	THE FACT THAT EARTH IS	1408	5
THAT IT IS NOT FOR US	THE FACT THAT EARTH IS	1408	6
BUT THAT IT WOULD AFFRONT US	THE FACT THAT EARTH IS	1408	7
RESERVED FOR US TO KNOW	HOW HUMAN NATURE DOTES	1417	6
SO LET US GATHER--EVERY DAY--	TO EARN IT BY DISDAINING	1427	5
WHO LED US WHILE HE STAYED.	NOT THAT HE GOES--WE	1435	2
THE CONSCIENCE OF US ALL	BELSHAZZAR HAD A LETTER	1459	6
THOUGH TO TRUST US--SEEM TO US	"HEAVENLY FATHER"--TAKE	1461	5
THOUGH TO TRUST US--SEEM TO US	"HEAVENLY FATHER"--TAKE	1461	5
WHO FAILED TO TOUCH US ALL	ONE OF THE ONES THAT	1466	2
THOUGH NEITHER OF US SPOKE--	WE TALKED WITH EACH	1473	2
ARKS OF REPRIEVE HE OFFERED [OPENED] TO US--	WE TALKED WITH EACH	1473	7
WHEN FATE INCORPORATED US--	ESTRANGED FROM BEAUTY--	1474 V	4
TO SOMETHING UPPER WOOING US	THE FASCINATING CHILL	1480	7
EACH ONE OF US SHALL BE--	'TIS WHITER THAN AN	1482	10
DESCENDING [CONSENTING / ESTABLISHED / IMPARTED] TO ENAMOR US	THE FACE IN EVANESCENCE	1490	7
BE ONCE DISCLOSED TO US	COULD THAT SWEET	1493	2
AND [BUT] THEN THEY SCARE US LIKE A SPECTRE	FACTS BY OUR SIDE ARE	1497	3
NOT ONE OF US WILL OWN	I SAW THE WIND WITHIN	1502 V	
"GO TRAVELING WITH US!"	"GO TRAVELING WITH US!"	1513	1
BUT THINK ENLARGED OF ALL THAT THEY WILL TELL US	THE THINGS THAT NEVER	1515	7
FATE--FOLLOWING--BEHIND US BOLTS IT-- . .	WE NEVER KNOW WE GO WHEN	1523	3
AND EACH OF US WERE SLAIN	'TIS SEASONS SINCE THE	1529	3
OR USHER US--A STRANGER--	ON THAT SPECIFIC PILLOW	1533	5
THAT WOULD EXPAND [BETRAY] US ALL--	THE LIFE THAT TIED TOO	1535 V	8
THE WELL IN WHICH THEY LAY US	OF DEATH I TRY TO THINK	1558	2
THAT MENACED NOT TO SLAY US, ...	OF DEATH I TRY TO THINK	1558	4
DECOYING BUT TO GREET US--	OF DEATH I TRY TO THINK	1558	8
WITHHELD US BY IT'S ROARING	OF DEATH I TRY TO THINK	1558	12
PURSUING [SUBDUING] WINDS THAT CENSURE [SUNDER] US	NO BRIGADIER THROUGHOUT	1561	5
WHEN HEAVEN LOOKED UPON US ALL	NO BRIGADIER THROUGHOUT	1561	11
PANGLESS EXCEPT FOR US--	PASS TO THY RENDEZVOUS	1564	2
AROUND US, EVERY DAY--	WITCHCRAFT WAS HUNG, IN	1583	4
AND SHOUTED [BUBBLED / GURGLED] LET US PRAY--	THE BOBOLINK IS GONE--	1591	7
HAVE NOT EACH ONE OF US THE RIGHT	FEW, YET ENOUGH,	1596	4
THE CRIME, FROM US, IS HIDDEN--	OF GOD WE ASK ONE FAVOR,	1601	4
EACH THAT WE LOSE TAKES PART OF US!	EACH THAT WE LOSE TAKES	1605	1
WHOSE BUGLES CALL THE LEAST OF US	TALK NOT TO ME OF SUMMER	1634	7
EACH ONE OF US HAS TASTED	A WORD MADE FLESH IS	1651	5
"MADE FLESH AND DWELT AMONG US	A WORD MADE FLESH IS	1651	13
REMAINED A FEW SLOW YEARS WITH US	I WATCHED HER FACE TO	1667	5
OR LONGING--AND IS THAT FOR US	THE LOOK OF THEE, WHAT	1689	7
NOTWITHSTANDING IT COST US EXISTENCE ONCE .	TO DO A MAGNANIMOUS	1699	7
'TWOULD START US WHERE WE SIT	A PIT--BUT HEAVEN OVER	1712	12
IT MAKES US THINK OF ALL THE DEAD	THE SADDEST NOISE, THE	1764	9
THAT SAUNTERED WITH US HERE, ...	THE SADDEST NOISE, THE	1764	10
IT MAKES US THINK OF WHAT WE HAD, ...	THE SADDEST NOISE, THE	1764	13
EXPERIMENT ESCORTS [ACCOSTS] US LAST-- . .	EXPERIMENT ESCORTS US	1770	1
INSTRUCTS US BY DEPARTING [DERISION] NOW [MORE]	THE SUMMER THAT WE DID	1773	3
USE			
HAD NOT A FURTHER USE--	HE FOUGHT LIKE THOSE	759	4
I SING TO USE THE WAITING	I SING TO USE THE	850	1
WE SHALL NOT WANT TO USE AGAIN	THE BUSTLE IN A HOUSE	1078	7
IT WAS NO USE TO WAIT--	THIS SLOW DAY MOVED	1120	6
WHAT USE HAS IT FOR ME--	HOW SOFT A CATERPILLAR	1448	8
USED			
WHERE IT USED TO BE--	FREQUENTLY THE WOODS ARE	6	8
AS NEW ENGLAND USED TO BE!	WHAT IS--"PARADISE"--	215	18
I'M USED TO THAT--	I CAN WADE GRIEF--	252	3
GOODBYE TO THE LIFE I USED TO LIVE--	TIE THE STRINGS TO MY	279	13
AND THE WORLD I USED TO KNOW--	TIE THE STRINGS TO MY	279	14
I USED TO--WHEN A BOY--	THERE'S BEEN A DEATH, IN	389	12
I AM NOT USED TO HOPE--	IT MIGHT BE LONELIER	405	9
THE FEET--I FORMER USED--	IT WOULD NEVER BE COMMON	430	14
THE FROCK I USED TO WEAR--	IT WOULD NEVER BE COMMON	430	31
GODS USED TO KNOW--	KNOWS HOW TO FORGET!	433	8
I WAS USED--TO THE BIRDS--BEFORE--	BETTER--THAN MUSIC! FOR	503	2

	FIRST LINE	POEM	LINE
USED (CONTINUED)			
THE VEINS THAT USED TO RUN	I'VE DROPPED MY BRAIN--	1046	2
MOSES WAS'NT FAIRLY USED--	SO I PULL MY STOCKINGS	1201	7
USELESS			
WERE USELESS AS NEXT MORNING'S SUN-- . . .	I SHOULD NOT DARE TO	205	15
'TWERE USELESS TELL.	THE MOST IMPORTANT	1746	6
USES			
NATURE RARER USES YELLOW	NATURE RARER USES YELLOW	1045	1
USHER			
AND USHER LIBERTY.	THE DUTIES OF THE WIND	1137	4
OR USHER US--A STRANGER--	ON THAT SPECIFIC PILLOW	1533	5
USHERED			
AND USHERED GRAND OLD MOSES	IT ALWAYS FELT TO ME--A	597	19
USHERS			
GREAT CLOUDS--LIKE USHERS--LEANING [PLACING]--	DEPARTED--TO THE	524	3
USING			
IS FINISHED USING, NOW, ...	I'M CEDED--I'VE STOPPED	508	4
IN USING, WEAR AWAY, ...	SHE ROSE TO HIS	732	8
TWO--BE FINISHED USING--	ONE AND ONE--ARE ONE--	769	2
USUAL			
AS IT HAS USUAL DONE--	IF I SHOULD DIE,	54	6
USUALLY			
USUALLY SO STILL--	I HAVE NEVER SEEN	175	4
WITH USUALLY [GENERALLY] A SOBER BIRD-- . .	A FIELD OF STUBBLE,	1407 V	5
USURPED			
SEE! I USURPED THY CRUCIFIX TO HONOR MINE! .	PROUD OF MY BROKEN HEART	1736	8
USURPS			
USURPS IT--OF ITSELF--	LOVE--IS THAT LATER	924	4
NOW DEATH USURPS MY PREMIUM	I DID NOT REACH THEE	1664	33
UTMOST			
IS THE UTMOST OF YOUR HAND--	TAKE YOUR HEAVEN FURTHER	388	7
BE WHOLLY [CHIEFEST / UTMOST] BEAUTIFUL-- .	I PLAY AT RICHES--TO	801	24
UTMOST, IS MUNIFICENCE--	ALL I MAY, IF SMALL,	819	7
A WORM, HIS UTMOST GOAL.	HIS BILL AN AUGUR IS	1034	4
INCREASED [ENLARGED] BEYOND MY UTMOST SCOPE	I HAD A DAILY BLISS	1057	7
THAT REACHES TO OUR UTMOST HAIR	WE LIKE A HAIRBREADTH	1175	7
THE TRYING ON THE [AN] UTMOST	WHILE WE WERE FEARING IT	1277	9
UTMOST IS RELATIVE--	UNTIL THE DESERT KNOWS	1291	7
OR UTMOST AN ULTERIOR?	UNTO THE WHOLE--HOW ADD?	1341	3
THE CRICKET IS HER UTMOST	THE EARTH HAS MANY KEYS.	1775	7
UTTER			
FOR UTTER JUBILEE--	THE MORNING AFTER WO--	364	4
THERE IS A PAIN--SO UTTER--	THERE IS A PAIN--SO	599	1
THEN HALF--THEN UTTER HID--	THE TREES LIKE TASSELS--	606	10
A UNIVERSE'S UTTER ART	UPON HIS SADDLE SPRUNG A	1600 V	7
GOOD-BYE--THE GOING UTTER ME--	SOME SAY GOODNIGHT--AT	1739	3
UTTERED			
UTTERED IN BETHLEEM!	"THEY HAVE NOT CHOSEN ME	85	4
ROBIN--UTTERED [PUBLISHED / LAVISHED] HALF THE TUNE--	HER--"LAST POEMS"--	312	8
WHICH UTTERED, WOULD DISCOURAGE NATURE . .	THERE IS NO SILENCE IN	1004	3
UTTEREST			
WHICH ANGUISH WAS THE UTTEREST--THEN-- . .	'TWAS LIKE A MAELSTROM,	414	24
UTTERLY			
DISSOLVED AS UTTERLY--	I'VE KNOWN A HEAVEN,	243	13
WHAT IS FORBIDDEN [DENIED] UTTERLY	I ENVY SEAS, WHEREON HE	498	7
REFUSED TOO UTTERLY--	THE BIRDS REPORTED FROM	743	12
SO UTTERLY UNMOVED--	HAD WE OUR SENSES	1284	8
SECRETED [RESERVED] UTTERLY	I SEND YOU A DECREPIT	1324 V	8
UTTERS			
THAT ORDINATION--UTTERS--	I GOT SO I COULD HEAR	293	20
VACANT			
STARE STOLID [VACANT / HORRID] INTO MINE .	I YEARS HAD BEEN FROM	609	5
TO STILL IT'S NOISY [HELP IT'S VACANT] HANDS--	AT LEISURE IS THE SOUL	618	8
VACATION			
NO MORE VACATION!	ALWAYS MINE!	839	2
THEY ARE THE SPIRITS STILL VACATION	THE LASSITUDES OF	1592	3
VACILLATING			
NO VACILLATING GOD	THOUGH THE GREAT WATERS	1599	4
VACUUM			
TO FILL THE AWFUL VACUUM [LONGITUDE] . . .	SEVERER SERVICE OF	786	3
VAGABOND			
A VAGABOND [SORCERER] FROM GENESIS	THE CLOCK STRIKES ONE	1569	3
VAGRANT			
BUT YESTERDAY A VAGRANT--	TO DISAPPEAR ENHANCES--	1209	5
VAGUE			
TOO VAGUE--THE FACE--	YOU SEE I CANNOT SEE--	253	8
VAGUE CALAMITY--	ROBBED BY DEATH--BUT	971	12
VAIL SEE VEIL			
MY CLASSICS VAIL THEIR FACES--	THE FEET OF PEOPLE	7	21
THEN VAIL MY TOO INSPECTING FACE	A SOMETHING IN A	122	10
UPON MY SIDE THE VAIL--	A SINGLE SCREW OF FLESH	263	4
IT DEALS CELESTIAL [FLINGS A CRYSTAL] VAIL .	IT SIFTS FROM LEADEN	311	12
A LIMIT LIKE THE VAIL	I HAD NOT MINDED--WALLS	398	13
THE LADY DARE NOT LIFT HER VAIL	A CHARM INVESTS A FACE	421	3
IT JOINS--BEHIND THE VAIL	FAITH--IS THE PIERLESS	915	8
TO WALK WITHIN THE VAIL.	THE LAST OF SUMMER IS	1353	8
LAUREL--VAIL YOUR [THY] DEATHLESS TREE-- .	LAY THIS LAUREL ON THE	1393	3
VAILED			
WITH OUR FACES VAILED--	I CANT TELL YOU--BUT YOU	65	10

	FIRST LINE	POEM	LINE
VAILED (CONTINUED)			
LOVE--THOU ART VAILED--	LOVE--THOU ART HIGH--	453	13
ALONE--IF THOSE "VAILED FACES"--BE--	AGAIN--HIS VOICE IS AT	663	24
VAILING			
VAILING THE PURPLE, AND THE PLUMES--	IN RAGS MYSTERIOUS AS	117	3
VAILING THE ERMINE SO.	IN RAGS MYSTERIOUS AS	117	4
VAIN			
AND EARTH IS QUITE COQUETTISH, AND BESEEMETH IN VAIN TO SUE.	AWAKE YE MUSES NINE,	1	24
THIS FAITH THAT WATCHED FOR STAR IN VAIN,	THIS HEART THAT BROKE SO	145	3
SURGEONS ASSUAGE IN VAIN,	AH, NECROMANCY SWEET!	177	5
THEY STRIVE TO CLIMB--IN VAIN--	THE LONESOME FOR THEY	262	6
UPON SO VAIN A HILL--	THEY CALLED ME TO THE	628	6
ITSELF IS NOT IN VAIN--	THE JUDGE IS LIKE THE	699	8
DID SUPPLICATE IN VAIN--	THE BEGGAR LAD--DIES	717	16
OR TAKE THE ROYAL NAMES IN VAIN--	SWEET MOUNTAINS--YE TELL	722	5
HE SHALL SEEK IN VAIN--	NEVER FOR SOCIETY	746	2
FIRST SUITOR NOT IN VAIN.	HOW FORTUNATE THE GRAVE	897	4
I SHALL NOT LIVE IN VAIN	IF I CAN STOP ONE HEART	919	2
I SHALL NOT LIVE IN VAIN.	IF I CAN STOP ONE HEART	919	7
HOW SWEET I SHALL NOT LACK IN VAIN--	FITTER TO SEE HIM, I MAY	968	25
ALIEN AND VAIN WHATEVER CLIME	FRIGID AND SWEET HER	1318	3
SO MODEST AND SO VAIN--	'TIS SEASONS SINCE THE	1529	6
IN VAIN TO PUNISH HONEY--	HER LOSSES MAKE OUR	1562	7
SOEVER MADE IN VAIN,	WE SEND THE WAVE TO FIND	1604	6
PERCEIVE THEIR PRAYER IS VAIN.	THERE COMES AN HOUR WHEN	1751	3
VAINER			
TILL I HAVE FINER [VAINER / FURTHER] TRIED--	SHALL I TAKE THEE, THE	1126	4
VALE			
SWEEP VALE--AND HILL--AND TREE!	A LADY RED--AMID THE	74	6
VALENTINE			
VALENTINE WEEK	AWAKE YE MUSES NINE,	1	T
UNWIND THE SOLEMN TWINE, AND TIE MY VALENTINE!	AWAKE YE MUSES NINE,	1	2
VALID			
IS VALID AS A STAR--	TO HER DERIDED HOME	1586	V
VALLEY			
THE VALLEY MURMURED "COME"--	THROUGH LANE IT LAY--	9	14
UPON THE VALLEY GLOW--	MY LIFE HAD STOOD--A	754	10
VALLEYS			
WHICH IN THE VALLEYS LIE?	WHOSE ARE THE LITTLE	142	2
AND LICK THE VALLEYS UP--	I LIKE TO SEE IT LAP	585	2
THE UNIVERSE--[THE VALLEYS--ARE] HER SHOE--	THE MOON WAS BUT A CHIN	737	18
FORCES THE BROODS IN LONELY VALLEYS	AS THE STARVED MAELSTROM	872	3
THE VALLEYS STOPPED BELOW	THE MOUNTAINS STOOD IN	1278	2
VALOR			
BUT "YOU"--SHE RETURNED WITH VALOR	I SAW THAT THE FLAKE WAS	1267	5
VALUE			
STILL, HAD IT SUCH A VALUE	I HAD A GUINEA GOLDEN--	23	5
AND COULD NOT VALUE--AIR?	ONE YEAR AGO--JOTS WHAT?	296	31
A VALUE--FOR THE GREATNESS' SAKE--	HAD I PRESUMED TO HOPE--	522	3
THE VALUE OF IT'S TEN--	'TIS ONE BY ONE--THE	545	4
FOR THIS NEW VALUE [FORTUNE / PORTION] IN THE SOUL--	ONE BLESSING HAD I THAN	756	11
A VALUE [NATURE] STRUGGLE--IT EXIST--	A PLATED LIFE--	806	5
THE VALUE COULD NOT BE--	THE SNOW THAT NEVER	1133	14
WITH SUPERSTITIOUS VALUE [MERIT / MOMENT]	TO DISAPPEAR ENHANCES--	1209	7
LEST LOVE SHOULD VALUE LESS	HAD THIS ONE DAY NOT	1253	5
WHAT LOSS WOULD VALUE MORE	HAD THIS ONE DAY NOT	1253	6
VALUED			
THAT WHAT WE CHERISHED, SO UNKNOWN [VALUED SO DEVOID / HOARDED . . .	SO PROUD SHE WAS TO DIE	1272	3
VALUES			
BETTER THAN LARGER VALUES--	THEIR HIGHT IN HEAVEN	696	13
OR VALUES MORE SEVERE--	THE LOOK OF THEE, WHAT	1689	8
VALVES			
SEALED ARE THE SPICY VALVES--	BESIDES THE AUTUMN POETS	131	10
THEN--CLOSE THE VALVES [LIDS] OF HER ATTENTION--	THE SOUL SELECTS HER OWN	303	11
VAN			
INTO VAN DIEMAN'S LAND.	IF YOU WERE COMING IN	511	12
AND SIGNED THE FETE [SHOW / VAN] AWAY--	A DROP FELL ON THE APPLE	794	16
. . . THRILLING / FLUTTERING / COWERING] VAN	TO FLEE FROM MEMORY	1242	6
VANDYKES			
VANDYKES DELINEATION	THE TREES LIKE TASSELS--	606	27
VANE			
THE VANE A LITTLE TO THE EAST--	A SHADY FRIEND--FOR	278	5
AND ASKS A VANE, THE WAY--	THIS WORLD IS NOT	501	16
'TIS FIRST [YOU SEE] HE STEPS UPON THE VANE--	MY FAITH IS LARGER THAN	766	5
VANE'S			
SOMETIMES--A VANE'S FOREFINGER--	THE ANGLE OF A LANDSCAPE	375	11
VANISH			
VANISH UNRECORDED	GLOWING IS HER BONNET,	72	7
DIP--AND VANISH LIKE ORIOLES!	THIS--IS THE LAND--THE	266	9
VANISHED			
SO HAS A DAISY VANISHED	SO HAS A DAISY VANISHED	28	1
SWEETER THAN A VANISHED FROLIC	I CANT TELL YOU--BUT YOU	65	5
FROM A VANISHED GREEN!	I CANT TELL YOU--BUT YOU	65	6
I PAUSE ABOVE THAT VANISHED HEAD	WHERE I HAVE LOST, I	104	3
OF VANISHED DAMES--AND MEN!	MUSICIANS WRESTLE	157	15
IN VANISHED FASHIONS SET!	IN EBON BOX, WHEN YEARS	169	16

	FIRST LINE	POEM	LINE
VANISHED (CONTINUED)			
DEMOSTHENES HAS VANISHED	HIS MANSION IN THE POOL	1379	15
AND HOUSES VANISHED WITH A ROAR	IT WAS A QUIET SEEMING	1419	8
VANISHES			
AND AS [WHEN] SHE VANISHES, REMORSE . . .	I CANNOT MEET THE SPRING	1051	7
VANITY			
WHO SHALL CHARGE THE VANITY	RIBBONS OF THE YEAR--	873	7
THE VANITY DIVULGE	HIS LITTLE HEARSE LIKE	1522	4
VANQUISH			
TO VANQUISH OTHER BLOOMS.	LIKE TRAINS OF CARS ON	1224	8
VANQUISHED			
THAT VANQUISHED HIM--	PUT UP MY LUTE!	261	8
HAS VANQUISHED [SATED] FLAME'S CONDITIONS, .	DARE YOU SEE A SOUL AT	365	5
BUT VANQUISHED HER [HIM] WITH MY DEFEAT . .	THE STARS ARE OLD, THAT	1249	7
THAT VANQUISHED HER--DEFEATED FEAT-- . . .	THE PRETTY RAIN FROM	1426	7
I WATCHED [BOUGHT] THE FLUTTERING [VANQUISHED] SPIRIT	I SAW THE WIND WITHIN	1502	V
VANQUISHED, MY SOUL WILL KNOW	I'VE GOT AN ARROW HERE.	1729	5
VANS			
AND VANS WITHOUT A NAME	HOW KNOW IT FROM A	1364	6
VARIED			
'TIS VARIED BY THE DREAM	DOOM IS THE HOUSE	475	5
HE VARIED BY A RIBBON'S WIDTH	HOW MANY SCHEMES MAY DIE	1150	7
VARIES			
IT VARIES--IN THE CHIN--	YOU KNOW THAT PORTRAIT	504	6
VARIETY			
THAT BREWS THAT RARE VARIETY!	THE NEAREST DREAM	319	13
VARIOUS			
'TIS VARIOUS--AS THE VARIOUS TASTE--	'TIS CUSTOMARY AS WE	440	5
'TIS VARIOUS--AS THE VARIOUS TASTE--	'TIS CUSTOMARY AS WE	440	5
THERE IS THE VARIOUS CAUSE--	I MEASURE EVERY GRIEF I	561	26
SENT VARIOUS--SCATTERED WAYS--	WE MET AS SPARKS--	958	2
VASCILLATING			
TO OUR FAR, VASCILLATING FEET	FAITH--IS THE PIERLESS	915	11
VASE			
MY EYE IS FULLER THAN MY VASE--	MY EYE IS FULLER THAN MY	202	1
THAT FADING FROM YOUR VASE, ...	I HIDE MYSELF WITHIN MY	903	2
VASSAL			
THE VASSAL OF THE SNOW--	THE FEET OF PEOPLE	7	4
VAST			
VAST--IN IT'S FADING RATIO	AS BY THE DEAD WE LOVE	88	7
AND VISIONS VAST AND SMALL--	ON SUCH A NIGHT, OR SUCH	146	22
ITSELF, TOO GREAT [VAST], FOR INTERRUPTING--MORE--	I GOT SO I COULD HEAR	293	27
'TIS VAST--AS OUR CAPACITY--	HEAVEN IS SO FAR OF THE	370	5
ENLARGE MY MESSAGE--IF TOO VAST	A TONGUE--TO TELL HIM I	400	16
VAST [WIDE] PRAIRIES OF AIR	MY PERIOD HAD COME FOR	564	12
ETERNITY'S VAST [WIDE] POCKET, PICKED-- . .	EMPTY MY HEART, OF THEE	587	14
A LONG--LONG [VAST--VAST / BRAVE--BRAVE] SLEEP--A FAMOUS--SLEEP--	A LONG--LONG SLEEP--A	654	1
A LONG--LONG [VAST--VAST / BRAVE--BRAVE] SLEEP--A FAMOUS--SLEEP--	A LONG--LONG SLEEP--A	654	1
VAST SOCIETY--	CONSCIOUS AM I IN MY	679	16
ON WHICH SO VAST DEPENDS--	MY FAITH IS LARGER THAN	766	14
MORE [TWO]--WOULD BE TOO VAST	ONE AND ONE--ARE ONE--	769	7
OF THAT VAST DARK--	GRIEF IS A MOUSE--	793	7
TIME FEELS SO VAST THAT WERE IT NOT . . .	TIME FEELS SO VAST THAT	802	1
HOW VAST AN ONE	WE LEARN IN THE	1083	2
NOT HOPING FOR HIS NOTICE VAST [FAR / FINE]	BECAUSE HE LOVES HER	1229	9
TO BREAK SO VAST A HEART	TO BREAK SO VAST A HEART	1312	1
REQUIRED A BLOW AS VAST--	TO BREAK SO VAST A HEART	1312	2
AND FELT [THOUGHT] "HOW VAST A DESTINY"-- .	A DEW SUFFICED ITSELF--	1437	3
VASTER			
TILL I TAKE VASTER ATTITUDES [MANNERS]-- .	OF BRONZE--AND BLAZE--	290	10
TODAY'S--HAVE VASTER CLAIMS [FORM]-- . . .	I COULD NOT PROVE THE	563	8
AND VASTER [THIS ONE / DIFFERENT]--OF THE WORLD'S.	THAT FIRST DAY, WHEN YOU	659	8
BUT DID BECAUSE [VASTER THAT] THEY DIED . .	I NOTICED PEOPLE	1149	7
BUT LABOR VASTER THAN MYSELF	THE FROST WAS NEVER SEEN	1202	19
THAN VASTER SUING--	COME SHOW THY DURHAM	1542	9
VASTEST			
BALKED IN THE VASTEST INSTANCE	COULD HOPE INSPECT HER	1283	5
THE VASTEST EARTHLY DAY	THE VASTEST EARTHLY DAY	1328	1
VASTLY			
A VISTA VASTLY WARMER--	THE ROBIN IS A GABRIEL	1483	8
VASTNESS			
A VASTNESS, AS A NEIGHBOR, CAME, ...	THE CRICKETS SANG	1104	9
VAT			
FIRST--AT THE VAT--AND LATEST AT THE VINE--	WE--BEE AND I--LIVE BY	230	14
VATICAN			
ITSELF--A GALLERY [VATICAN] TOO RARE-- . .	IT'S THOUGHTS--AND JUST	495	10
VATS			
NOT ALL THE FRANKFORT BERRIES [VATS UPON THE RHINE]	I TASTE A LIQUOR NEVER	214	3
VAULTED			
SHE VAULTED OUT OF GAZE--	I WATCHED THE MOON	629	32
VAUNT			
BUT FOR THE GREED [VAUNT / LIKE] OF HIM-- .	MY HEART RAN SO TO THEE	1237	13
WITHOUT A VAUNT OR SHEEN	THE GENTIAN HAS A	1424	5

	FIRST LINE	POEM	LINE
VEGETATION'S			
'TIS VEGETATION'S JUGGLER--	THE MUSHROOM IS THE ELF	1298	9
VEHEMENCE			
OF GREEDINESS [URGENCY / VEHEMENCE] TO DIE--	HE FOUGHT LIKE THOSE	759	12
VEHICLE			
ANOTHER SUCH A VEHICLE	I MET A KING THIS	166	19
I ONLY KNOW [SIGH]--NO CURRICLE [VEHICLE] THAT RUMBLE THERE	A LITTLE ROAD--NOT MADE	647	7
AS WAS HIS VEHICLE--	ELIJAH'S WAGON KNEW NO	1254	4
VEHICLES			
THE EPICURE OF FIRMAMENTS [VEHICLES / COURTESY / PURPOSES]	A SPARROW TOOK A SLICE	1211	V 7
VEIL SEE VAIL			
THE ELEMENTAL VEIL	SHAME IS THE SHAWL OF	1412	4
VEIN			
A VEIN--ALONG THE ROAD--	THE NAME--OF IT--IS	656	4
THE PURPLE--IN MY VEIN--	AGAIN--HIS VOICE I , AT	663	27
WITH ARTERY AND VEIN--	OH GIVE IT MOTION--DECK	1527	2
VEINS			
SHE BORE IT TILL THE SIMPLE VEINS	SHE BORE IT TILL THE	144	1
TEARS OPEN HER IMPERIAL VEINS--	YOU'VE SEEN BALLOONS SET	700	15
THE VEINS OF OTHER FLOWERS	THE VEINS OF OTHER	811	1
DAINTY ADORNED WITH VEINS AND TISSUES	AS THE STARVED MAELSTROM	872	7
THE VEINS THAT USED TO RUN	I'VE DROPPED MY BRAIN--	1046	2
VELLUM			
OLD VOLUMES SHAKE THEIR VELLUM HEADS	A PRECIOUS--MOULDERING	371	27
VELOCITY			
AS OF FRUGALITY [VELOCITY / AMENITY / PROPRIETY]--	A SPARROW TOOK A SLICE	1211	V 8
VELOCITY OR PAUSE	TWO LENGTHS HAS EVERY	1295	6
VELVET			
MY VELVET LIFE TO CLOSE--	IF SHE HAD BEEN THE	44	4
VELVET PEOPLE FROM VEVAY--	PIGMY SERAPHS--GONE	138	2
WIPING AWAY THE VELVET DUST	IN EBON BOX, WHEN YEARS	169	3
OF VELVET, IS HIS COUNTENANCE,	A FUZZY FELLOW, WITHOUT	173	3
HE STIRRED HIS VELVET HEAD	A BIRD CAME DOWN THE	328	12
UNTIL THE VELVET PRODUCT	THERE ARE TWO RIPENINGS	332	3
SYLLABLES OF VELVET--	ALL THE LETTERS I CAN	334	3
UNTO A VELVET LIMB--	YOU'LL KNOW HER--BY HER	634	8
I THOUGHT YOU'D CHOOSE A VELVET CHEEK	THEMSELF ARE ALL I HAVE	1094	3
THEIR VELVET MASONRY	LIKE TRAINS OF CARS ON	1224	4
FROM SUCH A VELVET WORLD IT COMES [CAME]	HOW SOFT A CATERPILLAR	1448	3
VENDED			
OF LIQUORS THAT ARE VENDED	THROUGH THOSE OLD	1753	5
VENERABLE			
HIS VENERABLE HAND TO TAKE--	A PRECIOUS--MOULDERING	371	5
TO VENERABLE BIRDS	AN ANTIQUATED TREE	1514	4
VENERATE			
TO VENERATE THE SIMPLE DAYS	TO VENERATE THE SIMPLE	57	1
VENETIAN			
LIKE A VENETIAN--WAITING--	THE ANGLE OF A LANDSCAPE	375	5
VENGEANCE			
NOR MISSILE [VENGEANCE] EVER COMES	THE CLOUDS THEIR BACKS	1172	8
VENI			
OH "VENI, VIDI, VICI!"	"SIC TRANSIT GLORIA	3	5
VENICE			
VENICE COULD NOT SHOW A CHEEK	PIGMY SERAPHS--GONE	138	7
VENOMS			
AND [THE] VENOMS HE MISTOOK FOR BALMS	ARROWS ENAMORED OF HIS	1629	3
VENTURE			
WE TALK IN CARELESS [VENTURE]--AND IN TOSS--	AGAIN--HIS VOICE IS AT	663	13
UNGAINED--IT MAY BE--BY [IN] A LIFE'S LOW VENTURE--	EACH LIFE CONVERGES TO	680	17
HOW IMMINENT THE VENTURE--	THE HEAVEN VESTS FOR	694	9
DARE NOT VENTURE--NOW--	LIFE--IS WHAT WE MAKE IT	698	16
FINITE--TO FAIL, BUT INFINITE TO VENTURE--	FINITE--TO FAIL, BUT	847	1
MAIMED--WAS I--YET NOT BY VENTURE--	STRUCK, WAS I, NOR YET	925	5
SUIT [PLEASE] ME AT A VENTURE	FORTITUDE INCARNATE	1217	11
FILLED WAS THE AIR WITH MERRY VENTURE	GLASS WAS THE STREET--IN	1498	3
VENTURED			
HAVE VENTURED ALL UPON A THROW!	'TIS SO MUCH JOY! 'TIS	172	4
AND NATURE VENTURED OUT--	THE WIND TOOK UP THE	1134	10
IF WE [I] HAD VENTURED LESS	WE LIKE A HAIRBREADTH	1175	5
VERA			
COLORS--FROM VERA CRUZ--	I COULD BRING YOU JEWELS	697	4
VERB			
AND LEFT THE VERB AND THE PRONOUN OUT--	GOING TO HIM! HAPPY	494	5
VERDICT			
VERDICT FOR BOOT!	IS BLISS THEN, SUCH	340	14
THIS MORNING'S FINER VERDICT--	WE SEE--COMPARATIVELY--	534	5
VERDURE			
TWICE HAD SUMMER HER FAIR VERDURE	TWICE HAD SUMMER HER	846	1
VERGE			
THEMSELVES THE VERGE OF SEAS TO BE--	AS IF THE SEA SHOULD	695	7
VERILY			
VERILY, A VICARIOUS COURTSHIP--	GOD IS A DISTANT--	357	3
VERMILLION			
A PRINT OF A VERMILLION FOOT--	AN ALTERED LOOK ABOUT	140	5
IT GATHERS RUDDY [STANDS IN--RUDDY / MAKES VERMILLION--] POOLS--	THE NAME--OF IT--IS	656	10

	FIRST LINE	POEM	LINE
VERMILLION (CONTINUED)			
UPON VERMILLION WHEELS--	THE NAME--OF IT--IS	656	12
IN THE VERMILLION THAT IT WORE	THERE IS A JUNE WHEN	930	7
SUFFER THE VERMILLION--	SANG FROM THE HEART,	1059	6
IDLE HIS VERMILLION	ON THE WORLD YOU COLORED	1171	3
TILL SAFFRON IN VERMILLION SLID	OF YELLOW WAS THE OUTER	1676	3
VERMIN'S			
'TIS THE VERMIN'S WILL.	DEATH IS LIKE THE INSECT	1716	12
VERRIERE			
LESS SKILLFUL THAN LE VERRIERE	SHE WENT AS QUIET AS THE	149	7
VERY			
HOW VERY BLITHE THE FINGERS [MAIDEN]	IF RECOLLECTING WERE	33	7
IT'S VERY MEAN OF SCIENCE	"ARCTURUS" IS HIS OTHER	70	3
WERE NOTHING VERY STRANGE!	A LADY RED--AMID THE	74	16
SURGEONS MUST BE VERY CAREFUL	SURGEONS MUST BE VERY	108	1
WHERE VERY NIMBLE GENTLEMEN	WHERE BELLS NO MORE	112	3
TO FIGHT ALOUD, IS VERY BRAVE--	TO FIGHT ALOUD, IS VERY	126	1
A VERY FEW--A BIRD OR TWO--	THESE ARE THE DAYS WHEN	130	2
IT SHONE SO VERY SMALL--	I CAME TO BUY A SMILE--	223	6
YOU ARE VERY FAR--	AH, MOON--AND STAR!	240	2
THOUGH YOU'RE VERY FAR--	AH, MOON--AND STAR!	240	14
THE VERY PROFILE OF THE THOUGHT	THAT AFTER HORROR--THAT	286	7
HE'S A TRANSITIVE FELLOW--VERY--	THE WIND DID'NT COME	316	5
HER VERY HAT--	'TWAS THE OLD--ROAD--	344	14
HE KEEPS HIS SECRETS SAFELY--VERY--	FUNNY--TO BE A CENTURY--	345	5
AS THE VERY LEAST	I TIE MY HAT--I CREASE	443	3
TO TELL THE VERY LAST THEY SAID	WHY MAKE IT DOUBT--IT	462	5
THE VERY BROW--THE STOOPING EYES--	YOU KNOW THAT PORTRAIT	504	3
THE VERY PATTERN OF THE CHEEK--	YOU KNOW THAT PORTRAIT	504	5
SIP, GOBLIN, FROM THE VERY LIPS	THE SOUL HAS BANDAGED	512	7
TO THE VERY SQUARE--HIS FOOT IS PASSING--	I COULD DIE--TO KNOW--	570	10
PIERCE--BY THE VERY PRESS	INCONCEIVABLY SOLEMN!	582	3
FOR VERY LUNACY OF LIGHT	I THINK I WAS ENCHANTED	593	7
THE VERY COLOR OF MY HAIR--	PRECIOUS TO ME--SHE	727	4
TO FORFEIT THEE? THE VERY NAME	IF BLAME BE MY SIDE--	775	3
SOME HOUSES VERY OLD,	WHO OCCUPIES THIS HOUSE?	892	10
THE LIFE WE HAVE IS VERY GREAT.	THE LIFE WE HAVE IS VERY	1162	1
AND THOUGHT IT VERY NICE	A SPARROW TOOK A SLICE	1211	2
'TIS VERY COMFORTABLE INDEED	TO MEND EACH TATTERED	1442	7
BOYS THAT "BELIEVE" ARE VERY LONESOME [BASTINADOED]--	THE BIBLE IS AN ANTIQUE	1545	11
THAT VERY INSTANT PASSED--	THERE CAME A WIND LIKE A	1593	8
WHEN AT MY VERY DOOR ARE THOSE POSSESSING MORE,	TAKE ALL AWAY FROM ME,	1640	4
THE VERY FOOD DEBATED	A WORD MADE FLESH IS	1651	7
WHO WOULD BE VERY GLAD	I KNOW OF PEOPLE IN THE	1665	2
THE VERY STRING WITH WHICH	IN WINTER IN MY ROOM	1670	18
THAT VERY PHYSIOGNOMY	NO MAN SAW AWE, NOR TO	1733	15
THE VERY NEAREST ROOM	ELYSIUM IS AS FAR AS TO	1760	2
VESPERS			
VESPERS--ARE SWEETER THAN MATINS--SIGNOR--	I SHALL KEEP SINGING!	250	9
VESSEL			
THE ONLY VESSEL THAT IS SHUNNED	IF WRECKED UPON THE	1469	3
VEST			
DELAYED TILL IN IT'S VEST OF SNOW	DELAYED TILL SHE HAD	58	2
IN A SATIN VEST!	PORTRAITS ARE TO DAILY	170	4
A VEST THAT LIKE HER BODDICE, DANCED--	THE ROSE DID CAPER ON	208	13
SWELLED--LIKE HORIZONS--IN MY BREAST [VEST]--	A SOLEMN THING--IT WAS--	271	15
IN SHAGGIER VEST--	ONE YEAR AGO--JOTS WHAT?	296	20
I HAD NOT DEEMED A VEST	THE MALAY--TOOK THE	452	12
LIKE CHARIOTS--IN THE VEST--	THE TINT I CANNOT TAKE--	627	16
YOU'LL KNOW HER--BY HER VEST--	YOU'LL KNOW HER--BY HER	634	9
VESTMENTS			
HER VESTMENTS AS THE SILVER FLEECE--	SHE DIED AT PLAY,	75	8
VESTS			
THE HEAVEN VESTS FOR EACH	THE HEAVEN VESTS FOR	694	1
VESUVIAN			
IT IS AS A VESUVIAN FACE	MY LIFE HAD STOOD--A	754	11
VESUVIUS			
VESUVIUS AT HOME	VOLCANOES BE IN SICILY	1705	8
VETO			
MINE--HERE--IN VISION--AND IN VETO!	MINE--BY THE RIGHT OF	528	5
VEVAY			
VELVET PEOPLE FROM VEVAY--	PIGMY SERAPHS--GONE	138	2
BUT TEACH THE FOOTMAN FROM VEVAY--	THE FLOWER MUST NOT	206	4
VEX			
THE DUST, WILL VEX YOUR FAME--	ALTHOUGH I PUT AWAY HIS	366	25
'TIS LATE YOUR SUNRISE VEX THEIR FACE--	WHAT CARE THE DEAD, FOR	592	3
FLAGS--VEX A DYING FACE--	THE WORLD--FEELS DUSTY	715	5
VEXT			
SOME DISEASE HAD VEXT	THREE WEEKS PASSED SINCE	1061	2
VIAND			
LET HIM BE QUICK--THE VIAND FLITS [BANQUET COOLS]--	MINE ENEMY IS GROWING	1509	5
VIANDS			
OF YOUR VIANDS, AND YOUR WINES!	TALK WITH PRUDENCE TO A	119	4
VIBRATING			
TO JUST VIBRATING BLOSSOMS!	WITHIN MY GARDEN, RIDES	500	19
VIBRATIONS			
SHOT THE LITHE SLEDS LIKE SHOD VIBRATIONS	GLASS WAS THE STREET--IN	1498	5

	FIRST LINE	POEM	LINE
VICARIOUS			
VERILY, A VICARIOUS COURTSHIP--	GOD IS A DISTANT--	357	3
VICARIOUSLY			
BUT [WHEN / IF] DEFACED VICARIOUSLY--	HE WHO IN HIMSELF	969	7
VICI			
OH "VENI, VIDI, VICI!"	"SIC TRANSIT GLORIA	3	5
VICINITY			
VICINITY TO LAWS	A NEARNESS TO	963	4
BUT IT'S VICINITY INFER,	OF PARADISE' EXISTENCE	1411	4
. . . POSSIBLE / VICINITY--]	WHO NEVER WANTED--	1430	7
VICIOUS			
HEAVES BALLS OF SPECKS, LIKE VICIOUS BOY	TO INTERRUPT HIS YELLOW	591	5
VICISSITUDE			
ABOVE OSTENSIBLE VICISSITUDE.	AFTER ALL BIRDS HAVE	1395	4
VICTIM			
HER VICTIM STARED UPON--	THE MORNING AFTER WO--	364	8
VICTOR			
SUCH A VICTOR COULD NOT [CANNOT] BE--	LAY THIS LAUREL ON THE	1393	V
VICTORIOUS			
ASCEND IN CEASELESS [BREAKS IN VICTORIOUS] CAROL--	TO LEARN THE TRANSPORT	167	13
WHILE HE, VICTORIOUS TILTS AWAY	LIKE TRAINS OF CARS ON	1224	7
VICTORS			
OF VICTORS, DESIGNATE--	OF TRIBULATION--THESE	325	4
VICTORY			
THERE IS IT'S VICTORY!	THERE IS A WORD	8	14
MIGHT DATE A VICTORY!	A DAY! HELP! HELP!	42	4
ANY FORGOT BY VICTORY	DELAYED TILL SHE HAD	58	14
SO CLEAR OF VICTORY	SUCCESS IS COUNTED	67	8
AND BELLS KEEP SAYING "VICTORY"	I HAVE A KING, WHO DOES	103	11
THIS SIDE THE VICTORY!	'TIS SO MUCH JOY! 'TIS	172	6
DEFEAT WHETS VICTORY--THEY SAY--	I SHOULD HAVE BEEN TOO	313	19
UNTO [OVER] THE EAST, AND VICTORY--	A WIFE--AT DAYBREAK I	461	6
REVERSED--IN VICTORY?	I CROSS TILL I AM WEARY	550	25
CONFIRM [WITHDRAW]--IN VICTORY--	AN IGNORANCE A SUNSET	552	10
WHEN THEY TOGETHER VICTORY MAKE--	"HEAVEN" HAS DIFFERENT	575	11
HIS FACE ALL VICTORY	WHEN I WAS SMALL, A	596	4
A PALER LUCK THAN VICTORY--	MY PORTION IS DEFEAT--	639	2
HOW DIFFERENT VICTORY	MY PORTION IS DEFEAT--	639	16
VICTORY COMES LATE--	VICTORY COMES LATE--	690	1
AND CREATURES CLAD IN MIRACLE [VICTORY]	'TIS ANGUISH GRANDER	984	7
TRI VICTORY--	TITLE DIVINE--IS MINE!	1072	V
AND THEN I DROPPED MY VICTORY	MY TRIUMPH LASTED TILL	1227	3
'TWAS VICTORY WAS SLAIN.	THE STARS ARE OLD, THAT	1249	8
VIDI			
OH "VENI, VIDI, VICI!"	"SIC TRANSIT GLORIA	3	5
VIEW			
I "VIEW THE LANDSCAPE O'ER;"	"SIC TRANSIT GLORIA	3	22
AND VIEW THE LANDSCAPE O'ER"	WHERE BELLS NO MORE	112	10
HID HEAVEN AND EARTH FROM VIEW.	AN AWFUL TEMPEST MASHED	198	4
THEN SWALLOWED UP, OF VIEW.	I'VE KNOWN A HEAVEN,	243	17
AND LEAN--AND VIEW IT SIDEWISE--	I AM ALIVE--I GUESS--	470	13
ETERNALLY FROM VIEW--	THE TREES LIKE TASSELS--	606	14
OH THE VIEW	WHAT TWIGS WE HELD BY--	1086	2
VIEWED			
WHEN VIEWED THROUGH PAIN--	DELIGHT--BECOMES	572	2
I HALF INDIFFERENT VIEWED	I HAD A DAILY BLISS	1057	2
WISDOM IS MORE BECOMING VIEWED	I WORKED FOR CHAFF AND	1269	7
VIEWS			
HAS VIEWS OF BRIDLES AND OF BARNS	THE LIFE THAT TIED TOO	1535	V 7
VIGILANCE			
OUR VIGILANCE AT WASTE	THE FROST WAS NEVER SEEN	1202	10
VIGOROUS			
HOW VIGOROUS A FORCE	THE TRUTH--IS STIRLESS--	780	9
VILIFY			
MIGHT VILIFY THE JOY--	THE TREASON OF AN ACCENT	1358	V 2
VILLAGE			
HOW FAR THE VILLAGE LIES--	THE FEET OF PEOPLE	7	18
WHICH WALK NO MORE THE VILLAGE STREET--	THERE IS A MORN BY MEN	24	8
I OFTEN PASSED THE VILLAGE	I OFTEN PASSED THE	51	1
SOFT SAUNTERED THRO' THE VILLAGE--	WITHIN MY REACH!	90	4
CHEERFUL--AS TO THE VILLAGE--	WENT UP A YEAR THIS	93	5
BELLS, ALSO, IN THE VILLAGE	ONE DIGNITY DELAYS FOR	98	7
BENEATH THE VILLAGE DOOR,	PERHAPS YOU'D LIKE TO	134	6
A TYRIAN LIGHT THE VILLAGE FILLS--	AN ALTERED LOOK ABOUT	140	2
UPON THE VILLAGE STREET--	SHE BORE IT TILL THE	144	12
HOW A SMALL DUSK CRAWLS ON THE VILLAGE	HOW THE OLD MOUNTAINS	291	13
THE VILLAGE LIES--TODAY--	IT WILL BE SUMMER--	342	8
LEAST VILLAGE HAS [BOASTS] IT'S BLACKSMITH	DARE YOU SEE A SOUL AT	365	9
UPON THE VILLAGE I PERCEIVED--	THE SUN KEPT SETTING--	692	3
THOUGH ALL THE VILLAGE LOOKED--	NO NOTICE GAVE SHE, BUT	804	10
'TWAS WITH TEXT AND VILLAGE [ANTIQUE] SINGING	THREE WEEKS PASSED SINCE	1061	3
VILLAGES			
TAKING VILLAGES FOR BREAKFAST,	I HAVE NEVER SEEN	175	7
THROUGH VILLAGES OF ETHER--	I WOULD NOT PAINT--A	505	13
MY [THE] VILLAGES BE SEEN--	HAVE ANY LIKE MYSELF	736	22
IN VILLAGES REMOTELY SET	THE FROST WAS NEVER SEEN	1202	7
VINDICATE			
I'LL VINDICATE THE LAW--	I HAD SOME THINGS THAT I	116	14

	FIRST LINE	POEM	LINE
VINE			
FIRST--AT THE VAT--AND LATEST AT THE VINE--	WE--BEE AND I--LIVE BY	230	14
VINEYARD			
AND THE PALPITATING VINEYARD	I HAVE NEVER SEEN	175	15
VIOLATE			
OR VIOLATE A STAR--	WHAT SOFT--CHERUBIC	401	4
VIOLET			
THE VIOLET--IS NOON--	THE RED--BLAZE--IS THE	469	2
AS STALACTITE [VIOLET]--	MUST BE A WO--	571	8
EXCELLING VIOLET--	I SEE THEE BETTER--IN	611	4
PERPLEXED! ESTATES OF VIOLET TROUBLE NE'ER LOOKED ON!	WOULD YOU LIKE SUMMER?	691	5
THEIR FAR--SLOW--VIOLET GAZE--	SWEET MOUNTAINS--YE TELL	722	6
ESPOUSED A VIOLET,	TO THIS WORLD SHE	830	5
VIOLETS			
THE VIOLETS LIE	ONE SISTER HAVE I IN OUR	14	21
AND VIOLETS ARE DONE--	WHEN ROSES CEASE TO	32	2
SO UNSUSPECTED VIOLETS	WITHIN MY REACH!	90	6
VIOLIN			
THE VIOLIN IN BAIZE REPLACED--	LIKE SOME OLD FASHIONED	302	15
TAKE UP MY LITTLE VIOLIN--	I THINK THE LONGEST HOUR	635	15
THE MUSIC IN THE VIOLIN	THE SPIRIT LASTS--BUT IN	1576	5
VIRTUE			
RENUNCIATION--IS A PIERCING VIRTUE--	RENUNCIATION--IS A	745	1
PERFIDY IS THE VIRTUE	THE DEVIL--HAD HE	1479	5
VISAGE			
THE VISAGE OF THE SOUL	THIS DIRTY--LITTLE--	1311	7
THE MAKER'S CORDIAL VISAGE,	DROWNING IS NOT SO	1718	9
VISIBLE			
STAMPED VISIBLE--IN STONE--	MY PORTION IS DEFEAT--	639	13
THE ROOF WAS SCARCELY VISIBLE--	BECAUSE I COULD NOT STOP	712	19
TO MAKE ME VISIBLE--	TO MY QUICK EAR THE	891	8
VISION SEE OUTVISION			
SOME VISION OF THE WORLD CASHMERE--	SOME RAINBOW--COMING	64	2
INTENT UPON THE [A] VISION	A POOR--TORN HEART-- A	78	7
ASCENDED FROM OUR VISION	WENT UP A YEAR THIS	93	21
THEN--FIT OUR VISION TO THE DARK--	WE GROW ACCUSTOMED TO	419	7
THE VISION FLUTTERS IN THE DOOR,	A WIFE--AT DAYBREAK I	461	V 12
OFFEND THE VISION--AND IT FLEE--	WHY MAKE IT DOUBT--IT	462	10
JUST TO BE POOR--FOR BAREFOOT VISION [PLEASURE]	SWEET--YOU FORGOT--BUT I	523	11
MINE--HERE--IN VISION--AND IN VETO!	MINE--BY THE RIGHT OF	528	5
THEN--THE LICENSE [VISION / PAGEANT] CLOSES--	SOME SUCH BUTTERFLY BE	541	4
A VISION ON THE RETINA	A DYING TIGER--MOANED	566	7
DEPRECIATE THE VISION--	I GAVE MYSELF TO HIM--	580	9
YOUR VISION--WAS IN JUNE--	OURSELVES WERE WED ONE	631	2
THE VISION--PONDERED LONG--	I THINK TO LIVE--MAY BE	646	21
PRESERVED THE CHARM [VISION SURE / VISION CLEAR] SECURE	HAVE ANY LIKE MYSELF	736	18
PRESERVED THE CHARM [VISION SURE / VISION CLEAR] SECURE	HAVE ANY LIKE MYSELF	736	18
SMALLER--THAT COVERED [FLOODED / SATED] VISION--HERE--	RENUNCIATION--IS A	745	16
FOR THE STUPENDOUS VISION [VOLUME]	TIME FEELS SO VAST THAT	802	7
'TIS COMPOUND VISION--	THE ADMIRATIONS--AND	906	9
THAT PORTION OF THE VISION	SHALL I TAKE THEE, THE	1126	9
A VISION TO PROVIDE	THAN HEAVEN MORE REMOTE,	1436	8
VISIONS			
AND VISIONS VAST AND SMALL--	ON SUCH A NIGHT, OR SUCH	146	22
THESE ARE THE VISIONS FLITTED [FASHIONS--BAFFLED--] GUIDO--	HOW THE OLD MOUNTAINS	291	21
THESE--SAW VISIONS--	THESE--SAW VISIONS--	758	1
VISIT			
THE [FOR] HOSTS--DO VISIT ME--	ALONE, I CANNOT BE--	298	2
IF GOD COULD MAKE A VISIT--	I NEVER FELT AT HOME--	413	9
AND VISIT ONLY WHERE I LIKED	COULD I BUT RIDE	661	3
AND NO ONE VISIT ME	COULD I BUT RIDE	661	4
NEITHER IF HE VISIT OTHER--	CONSCIOUS AM I IN MY	679	17
TO THOSE WHO VISIT HIM	'TIS MY FIRST NIGHT	1122	8
EMPLOYED A FACT TO VISIT ME	I BET WITH EVERY WIND	1215	3
THE ROSE RECEIVED HIS VISIT	A BEE HIS BURNISHED	1339	5
VISITED			
HE VISITED--STILL FLITTING--	THE WIND--TAPPED LIKE A	436	17
AND VISITED THE SEA--	I STARTED EARLY--TOOK MY	520	2
NOR VISITED IN HEAVEN--	I NEVER SAW A MOOR--	1052	6
SUPPOSED THEY VISITED REMOTE	I NOTICED PEOPLE	1149	3
NOW KNOW I--THEY BOTH VISITED	I NOTICED PEOPLE	1149	5
VISITER			
FOR VISITER--OR SACRAMENT--	EXHILIRATION--IS WITHIN	383	7
FOR VISITER--OR SUNDOWN--	I LIVE WITH HIM--I SEE	463	3
VISITERS			
OF VISITERS--THE FAIREST--	I DWELL IN POSSIBILITY--	657	9
VISITING			
UPON HIMSELF BE VISITING	THE SOUL THAT HATH A	674	7
VISITOR			
IT'S FREQUENT VISITOR--	A MIEN TO MOVE A QUEEN--	283	8
A VISITOR IN MARL--	A VISITOR IN MARL--	391	1
MY VISITOR IN PARADISE--	A DROP FELL ON THE APPLE	794	V
HER VISITOR, NO MORE--	THE SOUL SHOULD ALWAYS	1055	8
I FELT MYSELF A [THE] VISITOR	ALONE AND IN A	1167	7

	FIRST LINE	POEM	LINE
VISITOR (CONTINUED)			
MY GUEST "TODAY [VISITOR] IN PARADISE" . .	"REMEMBER ME" IMPLORED	1180	3
VISITORS			
SO VISITORS MAY COME--	I AM ALIVE--I GUESS--	470	12
SO VISITORS MAY KNOW	I AM ALIVE--I GUESS--	470	22
VISITS			
WHO VISITS IN THE NIGHT--	A VISITOR IN MARL--	391	5
VISTA			
A VISTA VASTLY WARMER--	THE ROBIN IS A GABRIEL	1483	8
WHOSE VISTA IS A HILL, ...	THE GOING FROM A WORLD	1603	4
VITAL			
SO--MANY--DROPS--OF VITAL SCARLET-- . . .	BOUND--A TROUBLE--	269	4
ASSERT HER VITAL PRIVILEGE--[HIS PRIMOGENITURE]	NO CROWD THAT HAS	515	7
A VITAL KINSMANSHIP IMPORT	BEREAVEMENT IN THEIR	645	3
WHO, VITAL ONLY TO OUR THOUGHT--	BEREAVEMENT IN THEIR	645	9
IF VITAL LIGHT	THE POETS LIGHT BUT	883	4
BUT WHEN THE VITAL AXLE TURNS	IDEALS ARE THE FAIRY OIL	983	3
UNTIL A VITAL WORD	I HEARD, AS IF I HAD NO	1039	2
VITALITY			
THE BEST VITALITY	I REASON, EARTH IS SHORT	301	6
THERE'S NO VITALITY	THERE IS A LANGUOR OF	396	16
UNTO VITALITY!	THE ZEROES--TAUGHT US--	689	8
VITALITY TO CLOG	SEVERER SERVICE OF	786	12
FOR LOVE REFORMS VITALITY [IS IMMORTALITY] .	UNABLE ARE THE LOVED TO	809	5
THEY DIED, VITALITY BEGUN.	A DEATH BLOW IS A LIFE	816	4
WITH VITALITY.	STRUCK, WAS I, NOR YET	925	4
PRESUMPTION IS VITALITY	AS FROST IS BEST	951	11
VITALITY IS CARVED AND COOL.	I'VE DROPPED MY BRAIN--	1046	5
THE ORDNANCE OF VITALITY	'TWAS FIGHTING FOR HIS	1188	3
THAN LEAST [BESIDE] VITALITY.	THE HARM OF YEARS IS ON	1280	8
DETAINED VITALITY.	NO MAN SAW AWE, NOR TO	1733	8
VITALIZE			
TO VITALIZE THE GRACE--	A TOOTH UPON OUR PEACE	459	4
VITALIZES			
'TIS THIRSTING [PARCHING]--VITALIZES WINE--	I SHOULD HAVE BEEN TOO	313	23
VITALLESS			
IS NUMB--AND VITALLESS--	I LIVED ON DREAD--	770	5
VITALLEST			
DRAMA'S VITALLEST EXPRESSION IS THE COMMON DAY	DRAMA'S VITALLEST	741	1
VITALLY			
DIE OFTENER--NOT SO VITALLY--	NATURE--SOMETIMES SEARS	314	8
VITALS			
A SMALL LEECH--ON THE VITALS--	ONE ANGUISH--IN A CROWD	565	9
VIVAMUS			
"DUM VIVIMUS VIVAMUS,"	"SIC TRANSIT GLORIA	3	3
VIVE			
MEEK [LOW] MY VIVE LE ROI, ...	MUTE THY CORONATION--	151	2
VIVID			
BUT WHEN THE VIVID [QUICKENED] ORE	DARE YOU SEE A SOUL AT	365	4
WHOSE PEAT LIFE--AMPLY VIVID--	MORE LIFE--WENT OUT--	422	17
VIVIDER			
TRANSMUTED--VIVIDER--	I LEARNED--AT LEAST--	944	26
VIVIMUS			
"DUM VIVIMUS VIVAMUS,"	"SIC TRANSIT GLORIA	3	3
VOCAL			
AND VOCAL--WHEN WE DIE--	A COUNTERFEIT--A PLATED	1453	7
VOICE			
THE CRIER'S VOICE W'D [WOULD] TELL ME-- . .	IF THOSE I LOVED WERE	29	2
A LITTLE TREMOR IN MY VOICE	WHERE I HAVE LOST, I	104	11
A VOICE THAT ALTERS--LOW	A MIEN TO MOVE A QUEEN--	283	16
I LIVE WITH HIM--I HEAR HIS VOICE-- . . .	I LIVE WITH HIM--I SEE	463	9
"POOR CHILD"--AND SOMETHING IN HER VOICE .	I CRIED AT PITY--NOT AT	588	3
YOU'LL KNOW HER--BY HER VOICE--	YOU'LL KNOW HER--BY HER	634	21
AGAIN--HIS VOICE IS AT THE DOOR--	AGAIN--HIS VOICE IS AT	663	1
OF INDIVIDUAL VOICE--	A SOUTH WIND--HAS A	719	2
HER VOICE AMONG THE AISLES	NATURE--THE GENTLEST	790	13
OF IT'S VOICE--TO AFFIRM--WHEN THE WIND IS WITHIN--	BY MY WINDOW HAVE I FOR	797	13
THE VOICE THAT STANDS FOR FLOODS TO ME . .	THE VOICE THAT STANDS	1189	1
THERE'S RANSOM IN A VOICE--	SILENCE IS ALL WE DREAD.	1251	2
HAS NOT A VOICE TO SPARE--	CONFIRMING ALL WHO	1268	4
HER CONSCIENTIOUS VOICE WILL SOAR UNMOVED .	AFTER ALL BIRDS HAVE	1395	3
WHY, KATIE, TREASON HAS A VOICE--	I SHALL NOT MURMUR IF AT	1410	7
HIS VOICE DECREPIT WAS WITH JOY--	HIS VOICE DECREPIT WAS	1476	1
NOT ANY VOICE IMPLY [DENOTE] IT HERE . . .	'TIS WHITER THAN AN	1482	5
THE TIPPET THAT IGNORES [RESISTS] HIS VOICE	THE JAY HIS CASTANET HAS	1635	3
VOICES			
WHOSE VOICES--TRAINED--[STANZA, HUSHED,] BELOW--	TO LEARN THE TRANSPORT	167	12
THEIR VOICES [NUMBERS] DID EXPEND	THE BIRDS BEGUN AT FOUR	783	6
VOLCANIC			
IF THE STILLNESS IS VOLCANIC	I HAVE NEVER SEEN	175	9
A STILL--VOLCANO [VOLCANIC]--LIFE--	A STILL--VOLCANO--LIFE--	601	1
VOLCANIC CLOUD	THE WIND DREW OFF	1694	5
VOLCANO			
A STILL--VOLCANO [VOLCANIC]--LIFE--	A STILL--VOLCANO--LIFE--	601	1
ON MY VOLCANO GROWS THE GRASS	ON MY VOLCANO GROWS THE	1677	1
THE RETICENT VOLCANO KEEPS	THE RETICENT VOLCANO	1748	1

	FIRST LINE	POEM	LINE
VOLCANOES			
I HAVE NEVER SEEN "VOLCANOES"--	I HAVE NEVER SEEN	175	1
VOLCANOES BE IN SICILY	VOLCANOES BE IN SICILY	1705	1
VOLCANOES NEARER HERE	VOLCANOES BE IN SICILY	1705	4
VOLUME			
FOR THE STUPENDOUS VISION [VOLUME]	TIME FEELS SO VAST THAT	802	7
THE BIBLE IS AN ANTIQUE [UNTOLD] VOLUME--	THE BIBLE IS AN ANTIQUE	1545	1
VOLUMES			
OLD VOLUMES SHAKE THEIR VELLUM HEADS	A PRECIOUS--MOULDERING	371	27
VOTE			
ELECTION--VOTE--	MY REWARD FOR BEING, WAS	343	10
I SHALL VOTE FOR LANDS WITH LOCKS	WHAT WE SEE WE KNOW	1195	5
VOTED			
THE JURY VOTED HIM--	I READ MY SENTENCE--	412	8
VOUCH			
I CANNOT VOUCH THE MERRY DUST	OF ALL THE SOUNDS	321	17
WITHOUT A BUTTON--I C'D VOUCH--	YOU'LL KNOW HER--BY HER	634	7
VOUCHES			
VOUCHES, WITH HYPERBOLIC ARCHNESS--	GOD IS A DISTANT--	357	7
VOW			
"I VOW TO PAY	WHAT WOULD I GIVE TO SEE	247	24
HER HEART MISGIVES HER, FOR HER VOW--	I KNOW A PLACE WHERE	337	7
PAST INTERVIEW, AND VOW--	IF ANYBODY'S FRIEND BE	509	22
GOD KEEP HIS OATH [VOW] TO SPARROWS--	VICTORY COMES LATE--	690	13
VOWS			
THEIR SPIRITS MEET TOGETHER, THEY MAKE THEM SOLEMN VOWS,	AWAKE YE MUSES NINE,	1	19
GOD'S OLD FASHIONED VOWS--	IT DID NOT SURPRISE ME--	39	8
VULGAR			
A VULGAR GRIMACE IN THE FLESH--	SHE DEALT HER PRETTY	479	7
VULTURE			
THE HUNGRY VULTURE SCREAMED--	THROUGH LANE IT LAY--	9	12
AS THE VULTURE TEAZED	AS THE STARVED MAELSTROM	872	2
WADE			
I CAN WADE GRIEF--	I CAN WADE GRIEF--	252	1
AND STEP [WADE] IN LIBERTY!	WHAT IF I SAY I SHALL	277	6
WADED			
I SHALL HAVE WADED DOWN ONE DAY".	IT DONT SOUND SO	426	9
THEN--HOW THEY WADED [STAMMERED]--SLOW--SLOW--	GOING TO HIM! HAPPY	494	7
ALL WADED--WE LOOK BACK FOR PLAY,	IF I MAY HAVE IT, WHEN	577	24
INVIGORATED, WADED [FULLY]	A SPARROW TOOK A SLICE	1211	5
WADES			
WADES--SO--THRO' POLAR AIR!	THROUGH THE STRAIT PASS	792	12
WADING			
WADING IN THE WATER	SO I PULL MY STOCKINGS	1201	2
WAFTS			
IT WAFTS THIS SORDID FLESH	WITH PINIONS OF DISDAIN	1431	5
THAT WAFTS THE CHERUBIM.	NO LADDER NEEDS THE BIRD	1574	8
THAT WAFTS THE SERAPHIM--	TO HER DERIDED HOME	1586	12
WAGGONS			
WAGGONS LIKE MESSENGERS HURRY ABOUT	AFTER THE SUN COMES OUT	1148	3
WAGON			
PINIONS--THE SERAPH'S WAGON	THE FEET OF PEOPLE	7	11
AND SUCH A WAGON! WHILE I LIVE	I MET A KING THIS	166	17
THAT WAGON NEVER REACHED--	A HOUSE UPON THE HIGHT--	399	2
ELIJAH'S WAGON KNEW [HAD] NO THILL	ELIJAH'S WAGON KNEW NO	1254	1
WAGONS			
THE WAGONS QUICKENED ON THE STREET [STREETS]--	THE WIND BEGUN TO KNEAD	824	9
WAGONS--HAVE YOU--TO CONVEY ME?	"UNTO ME?" I DO NOT KNOW	964	5
WAGS			
A LITTLE DOG THAT WAGS HIS TAIL	A LITTLE DOG THAT WAGS	1185	1
WAILING			
AND A DEAL OF SAD REFLECTION, AND WAILING INSTEAD OF SONG?	AWAKE YE MUSES NINE,	1	30
ESSENTIAL HOST, IN LIFE'S FAINT, WAILING INN,	AIR HAS NO RESIDENCE, NO	1060	6
WAINSCOT			
AND CHOOSES WAINSCOT IN THE BREAST	GRIEF IS A MOUSE--	793	2
WAIT			
I WAIT THY FAR, FANTASTIC BELLS--	THERE IS A MORN BY MEN	24	22
AND SEE IF DOLLIE'S COMING! WAIT!	DYING! DYING IN THE	158	10
ROUND WHICH THE FOOTMEN WAIT	I MET A KING THIS	166	26
WAIT TILL THE MAJESTY OF DEATH	WAIT TILL THE MAJESTY OF	171	1
WAIT TILL IN EVERLASTING ROBES	WAIT TILL THE MAJESTY OF	171	5
OBSEQUIOUS ANGELS WAIT!	WAIT TILL THE MAJESTY OF	171	10
THE CHARIOTS WAIT--	IF HE DISSOLVE--THEN--	236	11
WHAT IF I SAY I SHALL NOT WAIT!	WHAT IF I SAY I SHALL	277	1
WAIT! LOOK! HER LITTLE BOOK--	'TWAS THE OLD--ROAD--	344	12
HOW SICK--TO WAIT--IN ANY PLACE--BUT THINE--	HOW SICK--TO WAIT--IN	368	1
SHE DOTH NOT WAIT FOR JUNE--	THERE IS A FLOWER THAT	380	13
DIAMONDS--WAIT--	I'LL CLUTCH--AND CLUTCH	427	4
ARE WE THAT WAIT--SUFFICIENT WORTH--	IT FEELS A SHAME TO BE	444	13
WHILE I--DREAM [WAIT]--HERE--	I COULD DIE--TO KNOW--	570	12
FOR ONE MUST WAIT	I CANNOT LIVE WITH YOU--	640	14
TO WAIT AN HOUR--IS LONG--	TO WAIT AN HOUR--IS LONG	781	1
TO WAIT ETERNITY--IS SHORT--	TO WAIT AN HOUR--IS LONG	781	3
IN IT WAIT TILL JUDGMENT BREAK	AMPLE MAKE THIS BED--	829	3
WITH "I AM GREAT AND CANNOT WAIT	THE FINGERS OF THE LIGHT	1000	3
HE WILL NOT BE OBLIGED TO WAIT	THE SOUL SHOULD ALWAYS	1055	3
WHOSE PERFECT SEASONS WAIT--	THERE IS A ZONE WHOSE	1056	4
WAIT YOUR CHORALS--	SANG FROM THE HEART,	1059	14

	FIRST LINE	POEM	LINE
WAIT (CONTINUED)			
THE WIND COULD WAIT WITHOUT THE GATE	THE SPRY ARMS OF THE	1103	7
IT WAS NO USE TO WAIT--	THIS SLOW DAY MOVED	1120	6
IT WOULD NOT WAIT FOR ME	MY HEART RAN SO TO THEE	1237	2
TIME'S WILY CHARGERS WILL NOT WAIT	TIME'S WILY CHARGERS	1458	1
WHAT OMNIPRESENCE LIES IN WAIT	ALL THAT I DO	1496	10
WHY, RESURRECTION HAD TO WAIT	A PANG IS MORE	1530	7
ALAS--THAT FROWNS [DUSK] SHOULD LIE IN WAIT	FROM ALL THE JAILS THE	1532	7
WAITED			
BENT TO THE SCAFFOLD, OR IN DUNGEONS--CHANTED [WAITED]--	UNTO LIKE STORY--TROUBLE	295	5
I PUSHED MY DIMPLES BY, AND WAITED--	I FELT MY LIFE WITH BOTH	351	10
WE WAITED WHILE SHE PASSED--	THE LAST NIGHT THAT SHE	1100	17
AND WENT OR WAITED AS THEY LIKED	THE MOUNTAINS STOOD IN	1278	3
I TELL THE WHILE I WAITED [FAMISHED]--	ART THOU THE THING I	1282	5
WAITING			
TELL LUNA, TEA IS WAITING,	"SIC TRANSIT GLORIA	3	15
LIKE A VENETIAN--WAITING--	THE ANGLE OF A LANDSCAPE	375	5
AND WE ARE WAITING FOR THE COACH--	I THINK THE LONGEST HOUR	635	3
YOU TAUGHT ME WAITING WITH MYSELF--	YOU TAUGHT ME WAITING	740	1
I SING TO USE THE WAITING	I SING TO USE THE	850	1
NOT IF THEIR PARTY WERE WAITING,	WHAT DID THEY DO SINCE I	900	9
THE LILY--WAITING TO BE WED--	'TIS SUNRISE--LITTLE	908	7
IN THE NEAREST ORCHARD DWELLING [WAITING]	STRUCK, WAS I, NOR YET	925	15
THE WAITING--THEN--WILL SEEM SO WORTH	FITTER TO SEE HIM, I MAY	968	6
WAS WAITING [ASSEMBLED] TO BE POURED	HIS BILL IS CLASPED--HIS	1102	6
WAITS			
MY RIVER WAITS REPLY--	MY RIVER RUNS TO THEE--	162	3
NOT "REVELATION"--'TIS--THAT WAITS,	NOT "REVELATION"--'TIS--	685	1
IT WAITS UPON THE LAWN,	A LIGHT EXISTS IN SPRING	812	9
AND NATURE NOTHING WAITS TO DO	FURTHER IN SUMMER THAN	1068	V
WAITS ANY INDURATED MATE	THAT ODD OLD MAN IS DEAD	1130	7
WAKE			
THE TRUMPET, SIR, SHALL WAKE THEM,	"SIC TRANSIT GLORIA	3	49
AS CHILDREN CAPER WHEN THEY WAKE	AS CHILDREN BID THE	133	5
NEAREST THE DOOR--TO WAKE THE FIRST--	WHOSE ARE THE LITTLE	142	11
THE BUMBLE BEES WILL WAKE THEM	WHOSE ARE THE LITTLE	142	27
FOR CHANTICLEER TO WAKE IT--	ON SUCH A NIGHT, OR SUCH	146	13
I SHALL NOT CHEATED WAKE--	YOU LOVE ME--YOU ARE	156	3
IF IT BE, I WAKE A BOURBON,	I'M SAYING EVERY DAY	373	5
THAT EVERY TIME I WAKE--	THE ANGLE OF A LANDSCAPE	375	2
I WAKE--TO FIND NO--EMERALDS--	THE ANGLE OF A LANDSCAPE	375	15
IF ONE WAKE AT MORN--	DREAMS--ARE WELL--BUT	450	2
IF ONE WAKE AT MIDNIGHT--BETTER--	DREAMS--ARE WELL--BUT	450	3
AND FAILED TO WAKE THEM UP--	I HAD NO CAUSE TO BE	542	4
EXCEPT A WAKE OF MUSIC	OF BEING IS A BIRD	653	9
YOU WILL NOT WAKE THEM UP."	THE FINGERS OF THE LIGHT	1000	8
AND IF THOU LIVE BEFORE THOU WAKE--	NOW I LAY THEE DOWN TO	1539	3
WAKED			
TO FIND THAT WHAT ONE WAKED FOR,	A DARTING FEAR--A POMP--	87	3
CONJECTURED, AND WAKED SUDDEN IN--	'TIS SO MUCH JOY! 'TIS	172	17
I WAKED, TO FIND IT FIRST AWAKE--	BEREAVED OF ALL, I WENT	784	9
WAKELESSNESS			
TOO WISE HE SEEMS FOR WAKELESSNESS,	THE DUTIES OF THE WIND	1137	15
WAKENS			
HUSH! EPIGEA WAKENS!	WHOSE ARE THE LITTLE	142	21
WAKES			
I ENVY LIGHT--THAT WAKES HIM--	I ENVY SEAS, WHEREON HE	498	17
IT'S JOURNEY NEVER WAKES MY HAND	HOW SOFT A CATERPILLAR	1448	V
WAKING			
A WAKING ON A MORN	A DARTING FEAR--A POMP--	87	2
HE--WAKING--FINDS THE FLOWER THERE--	THE DAISY FOLLOWS SOFT	106	4
AND--WAKING--LONG BEFORE THE MORN--	MUSICIANS WRESTLE	157	4
THE WAKING IN A GNAT'S--EMBRACE--	WE SEE--COMPARATIVELY--	534	15
WAKING'S			
DREAMS--ARE WELL--BUT WAKING'S BETTER,	DREAMS--ARE WELL--BUT	450	1
WALK			
THE STORM DOTH WALK THE SEASHORE HUMMING A MOURNFUL TUNE,	AWAKE YE MUSES NINE,	1	17
WHICH WALK NO MORE THE VILLAGE STREET--	THERE IS A MORN BY MEN	24	8
ONE WILL WALK TODAY--	I HAV'NT TOLD MY GARDEN	50	16
MODEST, LET US WALK AMONG IT	I CANT TELL YOU--BUT YOU	65	9
AND WHEN HIS GOLDEN WALK IS DONE--	THE DAISY FOLLOWS SOFT	106	2
SMILING WHEN WE WALK BAREFOOT	IN RAGS MYSTERIOUS AS	117	7
I SHANT WALK THE "JASPER"--BAREFOOT--	WHAT IS--"PARADISE"--	215	15
WHERE OTHERS, DARE NOT GO [WALK] AT NOON,	WHEN WE STAND ON THE	242	11
FOREVER AT HIS SIDE TO WALK--	FOREVER AT HIS SIDE TO	246	1
I GOT SO I COULD WALK ACROSS	I GOT SO I COULD HEAR	293	5
A BIRD CAME DOWN THE WALK--	A BIRD CAME DOWN THE	328	1
AND WALK STEADY, AWAY,	TO PUT THIS WORLD DOWN,	527	2
WE WALK--I LEAVE MY DOG--AT HOME [BEHIND]--	AGAIN--HIS VOICE IS AT	663	18
LIKE MEN AND WOMEN SHADOWS WALK	LIKE MEN AND WOMEN	1105	1
TO WALK ON SEAS [TIDES] REQUIRES CEDAR FEET	THERE IS A STRENGTH IN	1113	6
THAT WALK THIS PLANK OF BALM--	THIS IS THE PLACE THEY	1264	6
TO WALK WITHIN THE VAIL.	THE LAST OF SUMMER IS	1353	8
MY RIGHT TO WALK UPON THE EARTH	I KNOW OF PEOPLE IN THE	1665	7
WALK BOLDLY UP AND KNOCK	T'WAS COMFORT IN HER	1703	4
WALKED			
WALKED SINGING ON THE SHORE.	THE FEET OF PEOPLE	7	8
I WALKED--AS WINGS--MY BODY BORE--	IT WOULD NEVER BE COMMON	430	13

	FIRST LINE	POEM	LINE
WALKED (CONTINUED)			
THE THINKING HOW THEY WALKED ALIVE--	IF ANYBODY'S FRIEND BE	509	3
THENCEFORWARD--WE--TOGETHER DWELT [WALKED]--	THE BIRDS REPORTED FROM	743	21
A MOURNER WALKED [LURKED] AMONG THE CHILDREN	A LOSS OF SOMETHING EVER	959	5
BUT SHE STRAIGHTER WALKED FOR FREIGHT . .	HAD WE KNOWN THE TON SHE	1124	3
IT WALKED AS WET AS ANY WAVE	LIKE RAIN IT SOUNDED	1235	3
YOU MUST HAVE WALKED--	DEAR MARCH--COME IN--	1320	5
WALKING			
THE FEET OF PEOPLE WALKING HOME	THE FEET OF PEOPLE	7	1
WHAT IS ONLY WALKING	BEFORE THE ICE IS IN THE	37	11
WALKS			
WHEN KATIE WALKS, THIS SIMPLE PAIR ACCOMPANY HER SIDE,	WHEN KATIE WALKS, THIS	222	1
THIS ME--THAT WALKS AND WORKS--MUST DIE, .	THIS ME--THAT WALKS AND	1588	1
WALL			
AND THEN HOPPED SIDEWISE TO THE WALL	A BIRD CAME DOWN THE	328	7
BETWEEN MY CURTAIN AND THE WALL	THE ANGLE OF A LANDSCAPE	375	3
WHO STAY [DWELL] UPON THE WALL	THOSE FAIR--FICTITIOUS	499	6
AS ON THE TIER [ROW] OF WALL	WHAT CARE THE DEAD, FOR	592	6
THEN--GLANCING NARROW, AT THE WALL-- . . .	THE WAY I READ A	636	9
THAT CALM IS BUT A WALL	THE HEART HAS NARROW	928	9
TO PUNCTUATE THE WALL, ...	THE DYING NEED BUT	1026	4
ON REVELATION'S WALL--	BELSHAZZAR HAD A LETTER	1459	8
EXISTENCE WITH A WALL	ADVANCE IS LIFE'S	1652	6
WALLS			
AND SO THE WALLS--DONT TELL--	I KNOW SOME LONELY	289	17
I HAD NOT MINDED--WALLS--	I HAD NOT MINDED--WALLS	398	1
AS ONE SHOULD PRY THE WALLS--	I TRIED TO THINK A	532	13
THE WALLS--BEGUN TO TELL--	TO MY QUICK EAR THE	891	6
ON ELIGIBLE WALLS--	THOSE CATTLE SMALLER	1388	8
ALARM IT'S WALLS AWAY--	GO NOT TOO NEAR A HOUSE	1434	4
WALTZED			
AND WALTZED UPON A FARM--	TWO BUTTERFLIES WENT OUT	533	2
WAMPUM			
WHO COUNTS THE WAMPUM OF THE NIGHT	BRING ME THE SUNSET IN A	128	17
WAN			
THE STOUTEST [FORTHWITH THE] MIND IS WAN . .	THE MIND LIVES ON THE	1355	V 6
MY LOW [ONE / MEEK / WAN] RENOWN	TO BE FORGOT BY THEE	1560	V 12
WANDER			
TO WANDER--NOW--IS MY REPOSE [ABODE]-- . .	I MEANT TO FIND HER WHEN	718	9
REMAIN, OR WANDER, ...	THE DUTIES OF THE WIND	1137	7
WANDERED			
IT WANDERED FROM THE SAME.	I HAD A GUINEA GOLDEN--	23	20
TO EDEN, WANDERED IN--	AS IF SOME LITTLE ARCTIC	180	10
MY FEET, TOO, THAT HAD WANDERED SO--	HE TOUCHED ME, SO I LIVE	506	10
MINE TO STAY--WHEN ALL HAVE WANDERED-- . .	PROMISE THIS--WHEN YOU	648	9
AND WANDERED IN MY FACE--	THE SUN KEPT SETTING--	692	8
FROM US SHE WANDERED NOW A YEAR, ...	FROM US SHE WANDERED NOW	890	1
AND WANDERED OUT OF LIFE.	HE SCANNED IT--STAGGERED	1062	9
WANDERING SEE WIDE-WANDERING			
LEAD THE WANDERING SAILS.	A POOR--TORN HEART-- A	78	16
WENT WANDERING DOWN THE LATITUDES	AS IF SOME LITTLE ARCTIC	180	3
FOR THY WANDERING BIRD?	TWICE HAD SUMMER HER	846	8
WHOSE WANDERING IS DONE--	LET DOWN THE BARS, OH	1065	4
A WANDERING "ALAS"--	A SINGLE CLOVER PLANK	1343	16
WHOSE TILLAGE [PASTURE] IS THE PASSING [WANDERING] CRUMB--	THOSE CATTLE SMALLER	1388	3
IS THERE NO WANDERING ROUTE OF GRACE	OH FUTURE! THOU SECRETED	1631	3
WANDERINGS			
GATHERED FROM MANY WANDERINGS--	ALL OVERGROWN BY CUNNING	148	V
WANE			
THAN WANE [LIVE] IS EASIER--	I'D RATHER RECOLLECT A	1349	8
THEN WANED [TO WANE] WITHOUT DISPARAGEMENT .	THESE HELD THEIR WICK	1390	5
WANED			
THEN WANED [TO WANE] WITHOUT DISPARAGEMENT .	THESE HELD THEIR WICK	1390	5
WANES			
AS ACCENT FADES [WANES] TO INTERVAL	THE MURMURING OF BEES,	1115	11
WANING			
IT MIGHT--HAVE BEEN THE WANING LAMP	GOOD NIGHT! WHICH PUT	259	10
WANT			
THE WANT OF DIADEMS!	THE SUN--JUST TOUCHED	232	12
TEAZING THE WANT--	YOU SEE I CANNOT SEE--	253	14
LEST INTERVIEW--ANNUL A WANT	A CHARM INVESTS A FACE	421	7
BUT MORN--DID'NT WANT ME--NOW--	GOOD MORNING--MIDNIGHT--	425	7
THERE'S GRIEF OF WANT--AND GRIEF OF COLD-- .	I MEASURE EVERY GRIEF I	561	29
WE WANT THE DEW--THEN--	THE WORLD--FEELS DUSTY	715	3
IT INTIMATES THE FINER WANT--	WE THIRST AT FIRST--'TIS	726	5
"I WANT"--IT PLEADED--ALL IT'S LIFE-- . . .	"I WANT"--IT PLEADED--	731	1
I WANT--WAS CHIEF IT SAID	"I WANT"--IT PLEADED--	731	2
I KNEW NO MORE OF WANT--OR COLD--	ONE BLESSING HAD I THAN	756	9
WANT--IS A MEAGRE ART	NONE CAN EXPERIENCE	771	5
WITH WANT, AND OPPORTUNITY--	I PLAY AT RICHES--TO	801	5
HOW ['TIS] FITTER THEY WILL [I SHALL] BE--FOR [BY] WANT--	I PLAY AT RICHES--TO	801	21
IF OTHERS WANT TO SEE	LIGHT IS SUFFICIENT TO	862	2
WANT--A QUIET COMISSARY	SATISFACTION--IS THE	1036	3
WE SHALL NOT WANT TO USE AGAIN	THE BUSTLE IN A HOUSE	1078	7
NOT WANT OF FRIEND OCCASIONS IT	THERE IS ANOTHER	1116	3
I WANT A BROOK--COME NOW"!	THE SEA SAID "COME" TO	1210	4
I CANNOT WANT IT MORE--	I CANNOT WANT IT MORE--	1301	1

	FIRST LINE	POEM	LINE
WARY			
OF THIS MAN--I AM WARY--	I FEAR A MAN OF FRUGAL	543	7
WASHED			
STAINS--ALL WASHED--	TAKING UP THE FAIR IDEAL	428	15
A SOFT SEA WASHED AROUND THE HOUSE	A SOFT SEA WASHED AROUND	1198	1
WASHES			
THIS--IS THE LAND--THE SUNSET WASHES--	THIS--IS THE LAND--THE	266	1
WASTE			
LET ME NOT SPILL [LOSE / WASTE]--IT'S SMALLEST CADENCE--	BETTER--THAN MUSIC! FOR	503	21
JUST TO BE RICH--TO WASTE MY GUINEAS [GUINEA]	SWEET--YOU FORGOT--BUT I	523	9
COULD WASTE [MELT] THE SNOW BEFORE THEIR GATE--	WHAT CARE THE DEAD, FOR	592	11
OUR VIGILANCE AT WASTE	THE FROST WAS NEVER SEEN	1202	10
TILL YOU WASTE [FURL / LAME] YOUR EYE--	FOLLOW WISE ORION	1538	2
WASTED			
IT WASTED FROM MY SIGHT	I HAD A DAILY BLISS	1057	6
WASTES			
LIKE EYES THAT LOOKED ON WASTES--	LIKE EYES THAT LOOKED ON	458	1
WASTES OF LIVES--RESOWN WITH COLORS	ALL BUT DEATH, CAN BE	749	5
WATCH			
A WATCH--SOME ANCIENT [ANTIQUE] BROOCH	I KNOW SOME LONELY	289	28
JEHOVAH'S WATCH--IS WRONG.	SUNSET AT NIGHT--IS	415	8
ALTHOUGH BY NATURE'S STERLING WATCH	THE SYMPTOM OF THE GALE	1327	11
WATCHED			
THIS FAITH THAT WATCHED FOR STAR IN VAIN,	THIS HEART THAT BROKE SO	145	3
SLOW--NIGHT--THAT MUST BE WATCHED AWAY--	A NIGHT--THERE LAY THE	471	5
I WATCHED THE MOON AROUND THE HOUSE	I WATCHED THE MOON	629	1
I WATCHED [BOUGHT] THE FLUTTERING [VANQUISHED] SPIRIT	I SAW THE WIND WITHIN	1502	V
I WATCHED THE PRECIOUS [SUBTLE] BEGGAR	I SAW THE WIND WITHIN	1502	V
I WATCHED HER FACE TO SEE WHICH WAY	I WATCHED HER FACE TO	1667	1
WATCHER			
AS THAT SAME WATCHER, WHEN THE EAST	AS WATCHERS HANG UPON	121	7
WATCHERS			
AS WATCHERS HANG UPON THE EAST,	AS WATCHERS HANG UPON	121	1
WATER			
HAS IT FEET LIKE WATER LILIES?	WILL THERE REALLY BE A	101	5
WATER, IS TAUGHT BY THIRST.	WATER, IS TAUGHT BY	135	1
TO TELL WHAT WATER IS	TO ONE DENIED TO DRINK	490	2
WITH WATER, IN THE COUNTRY CHURCH	I'M CEDED--I'VE STOPPED	508	3
OF WATER--AND OF ME--	A DYING TIGER--MOANED	566	8
THEY'RE WATER--EQUALLY--	'TIS GOOD--THE LOOKING	660	12
A LITTLE WATER SUPPLICATE--	WE THIRST AT FIRST--'TIS	726	3
IS THAT GREAT WATER IN THE WEST--	WE THIRST AT FIRST--'TIS	726	7
THOUGH COOLER THAN THE WATER WAS	I COULD NOT DRINK IT,	818	3
BENT TO THE WATER, STRUGGLED [SHIVERED] SCARCE--	THE LAST NIGHT THAT SHE	1100	23
WADING IN THE WATER	SO I PULL MY STOCKINGS	1201	2
AND MAKE THE WATER SLOW	A STAGNANT PLEASURE LIKE	1281	4
THAT WATER GROWS	UNTIL THE DESERT KNOWS	1291	2
I THINK THAT THE ROOT OF THE WIND IS WATER--	I THINK THAT THE ROOT OF	1302	1
THE WATER LIVES SO FAR--	WHAT MYSTERY PERVADES A	1400	2
BUT LEAVES THE WATER WHOLE--	THE INUNDATION OF THE	1425	4
WATER MAKES MANY BEDS	WATER MAKES MANY BEDS	1428	1
THAT MAKE THE WATER LIVE, ESTRANGED	THE SPIRIT LASTS--BUT IN	1576	11
WATER'S			
A GLASS OF WATER'S ALL,	THE DYING NEED BUT	1026	2
WATERS			
UPON THE WATERS BORNE--	TWO SWIMMERS WRESTLED ON	201	7
OF PEARLS IN EASTERN WATERS,	REMOVED FROM ACCIDENT OF	424	7
THOSE WATERS SOUND SO GRAND--	I KNOW WHERE WELLS GROW	460	18
TO PUT A CURRENT [THE WATERS] BACK--	THE BRAIN, WITHIN IT'S	556	5
THE WATERS--STROVE TO STAY.	THREE TIMES--WE PARTED--	598	4
THE WATERS WRECKED THE SKY--	THE WIND BEGUN TO KNEAD	824	18
HOW THE WATERS CLOSED ABOVE HIM	HOW THE WATERS CLOSED	923	1
WHOSE WATERS ARE THE BRAWLING [NAMELESS] BROOK	CONTAINED IN THIS SHORT	1165	V 7
YOU CHERISHED"--"LEARNED WATERS--	THE SEA SAID "COME" TO	1210	7
IN WATERS [FORUMS] GREEN--	HIS MANSION IN THE POOL	1379	16
THE TORRENTS [WATERS] OF ETERNITY	HOW MUCH THE PRESENT	1380	7
WHERE WATERS COOL AROUND THE MOSSES CRAWL--	THESE FEVERED DAYS--TO	1441	2
DECLAIMING WATERS NONE MAY DREAD--	DECLAIMING WATERS NONE	1595	1
BUT WATERS THAT ARE STILL	DECLAIMING WATERS NONE	1595	2
THOUGH THE GREAT WATERS SLEEP,	THOUGH THE GREAT WATERS	1599	1
THE WATERS MURMUR NEW	I DID NOT REACH THEE	1664	30
THE WATERS CHASED HIM AS HE FLED,	THE WATERS CHASED HIM AS	1749	1
WAVE			
THE WAVE WITH EYE SO PENSIVE, LOOKETH TO SEE THE MOON,	AWAKE YE MUSES NINE,	1	18
'TWAS SUCH A GREEDY, GREEDY WAVE	'TWAS SUCH A LITTLE--	107	5
A WAVE OF GOLD--	A SLASH OF BLUE--	204	7
IT WALKED AS WET AS ANY WAVE	LIKE RAIN IT SOUNDED	1235	3
WE SEND THE WAVE TO FIND THE WAVE--	WE SEND THE WAVE TO FIND	1604	1
WE SEND THE WAVE TO FIND THE WAVE--	WE SEND THE WAVE TO FIND	1604	1
WAVED			
TILL ALL THE GRIEF WITH SUMMER--WAVED [BLEW]	'TIS GOOD--THE LOOKING	660	7
WAVERING			
TO WHOM HE COULD ENTRUST HIS WAVERING GAZE--	TO KNOW JUST HOW HE	622	3
WAVES			
THE WAVES GREW SLEEPY--[THE	THREE TIMES--WE PARTED--	598	13

	FIRST LINE	POEM	LINE
WAVES (CONTINUED)			
OCEAN--TIRED-- / THE OCEAN-- . . .			
WAXING			
AND JACOB, WAXING STRONG,	A LITTLE EAST OF JORDAN,	59	6
WAY			
BY WAY OF A GYMNASTIC .	"SIC TRANSIT GLORIA	3	35
NOR HEEDLESS BY THE WAY	I HAV'NT TOLD MY GARDEN	50	14
THE ANGELS--HAPPENING THAT WAY .	A POOR--TORN HEART-- A	78	9
SAUNTERING THIS WAY	HEART, NOT SO HEAVY AS	83	10
UPON A [THE] DUSTY [TOILSOME] WAY--	HEART, NOT SO HEAVY AS	83	14
I MIGHT HAVE CHANCED THAT WAY!	WITHIN MY REACH!	90	3
DAISIES POINT THE WAY THERE--	SEXTON! MY MASTER'S	96	7
FOR MY WILL GOES THE OTHER WAY,	I HAVE A KING, WHO DOES	103	17
SOME LOSE THEIR WAY!	OUR SHARE OF NIGHT TO	113	6
COULD THE CHILDREN FIND THE WAY THERE--	"HOUSES"--SO THE WISE	127	7
SHE DIED--THIS WAS THE WAY SHE DIED.	SHE DIED--THIS WAS THE	150	1
SO I CAN SEE WHICH WAY TO GO	DYING! DYING IN THE	158	3
THIS WAY, JESUS, LET HIM PASS!	DYING! DYING IN THE	158	8
A BIRD--BY CHANCE--THAT GOES THAT WAY--	THE SKIES CANT KEEP	191	5
ALWAYS LOST THE WAY!	WE DONT CRY--TIM AND I,	196	20
SOME SCARLET PATCHES ON THE WAY,	A SLASH OF BLUE--	204	3
BEGUILES THE CENTURIES OF WAY!	THO' I GET HOME HOW LATE	207	13
TO FIND OUR WAY HOME--	I'VE NOTHING ELSE--TO	224	8
YOU'RE RIGHT--"THE WAY IS NARROW"--	YOU'RE RIGHT--"THE WAY	234	1
ON THEIR WAY TO YELLOWER CLIMES--	I SHALL KEEP SINGING!	250	3
THE RAINBOW'S WAY--	DELIGHT IS AS THE FLIGHT	257	4
TOOK RAINBOWS, AS THE COMMON WAY,	DELIGHT IS AS THE FLIGHT	257	16
PETITION'S WAY,	I GOT SO I COULD HEAR	293	18
IT CARE, IN SOME REMOTER WAY,	I GOT SO I COULD HEAR	293	24
SUBLIMER SORT [THING / WAY]--THAN SPEECH--	GIVE LITTLE ANGUISH--	310	8
HIS WAY--OF A JUNE DAY--	THE WIND DID'NT COME	316	16
A WAY HE HAS	THE WIND DID'NT COME	316	V 16
AND A HOARSE "GET OUT OF THE WAY, I SAY,"	THE WIND DID'NT COME	316	20
AND KNOW NO OTHER WAY--	BEFORE I GOT MY EYE PUT	327	4
BUT DYING--IS A DIFFERENT WAY--	'TIS NOT THAT DYING	335	3
A WOODEN WAY .	AFTER GREAT PAIN, A	341	7
'TIS FREQUENTLY THE WAY--	THE MORNING AFTER WO--	364	2
I'D DO THIS WAY--	I'M SAYING EVERY DAY	373	3
I SAW NO WAY--THE HEAVENS WERE STITCHED--	I SAW NO WAY--THE	378	1
THAT INTERDICTED WAY,	A TONGUE--TO TELL HIM I	400	6
SO GO YOUR WAY--AND I'LL GO MINE--	A MURMUR IN THE TREES--	416	19
THE HILLS--HAVE A WAY--THEN--	GOOD MORNING--MIDNIGHT--	425	11
SAY "WHEN TOMORROW COMES THIS WAY--	IT DONT SOUND SO	426	8
AND YET--EXISTENCE--SOME WAY BACK--	I TIE MY HAT--I CREASE	443	11
AND SO, I THOUGHT THE OTHER WAY,	'TWAS JUST THIS TIME,	445	22
INLAID WITH EMERALD--HALF WAY DOWN--	I KNOW WHERE WELLS GROW	460	7
TAUGHT ME--BY TIME--THE LOWER WAY--	I LIVE WITH HIM--I SEE	463	13
'TWAS MAJOR ANDRE'S WAY--	THE MANNER OF IT'S DEATH	468	4
LOCATION'S NARROW WAY IS FOR OURSELVES--	WE PRAY--TO HEAVEN--	489	7
YOU GUESSED--FROM THE WAY THE SENTENCE TOILED--	GOING TO HIM! HAPPY	494	11
THE WAY OURSELF, MUST COME--	THOSE FAIR--FICTITIOUS	499	24
AND ASKS A VANE, THE WAY--	THIS WORLD IS NOT	501	16
SO SHORT WAY OFF IT SEEMS--	IF ANYBODY'S FRIEND BE	509	11
'TIS THE SCARLET WAY	TO PUT THIS WORLD DOWN,	527	4
IT'S SUCH CONGENIAL TIMES [WAY]	I'M SORRY FOR THE DEAD--	529	2
DONT FEEL A LONESOME WAY--	I'M SORRY FOR THE DEAD--	529	18
BEST BEAUTY'S WAY--	MUST BE A WO--	571	4
A FOND--ILLUSIVE WAY--	MY FIRST WELL DAY--SINCE	574	12
THAT THIS WAY--THOU COULD'ST NOTICE [SPEAK TO] ME--	IF I MAY HAVE IT, WHEN	577	21
THE MORE CONVENIENT WAY--	THE BODY GROWS WITHOUT--	578	2
THAT HUNGER--WAS A WAY	I HAD BEEN HUNGRY, ALL	579	18
WAS RATIFIED, THIS WAY--	I GAVE MYSELF TO HIM--	580	4
IT SEEMED THE COMMON WAY,	I CRIED AT PITY--NOT AT	588	6
SO WHEN SHE COMES THIS WAY,	I CRIED AT PITY--NOT AT	588	18
WITHOUT A GLANCE MY WAY--	I ASKED NO OTHER THING--	621	6
AND DID THE SUNSHINE FACE HIS WAY--	TO KNOW JUST HOW HE	622	8
ANOTHER WAY--TO SEE--	THE TINT I CANNOT TAKE--	627	24
SHE'D PASS FOR BAREHEAD--SHORT WAY OFF--	YOU'LL KNOW HER--BY HER	634	15
THE WAY I READ A LETTER'S--THIS [SO]--	THE WAY I READ A	636	1
CAME THE DARKER WAY--	HER SWEET TURN TO LEAVE	649	2
I WISHED A WAY [SORT] MIGHT BE	WITHOUT THIS--THERE IS	655	9
GOES WITH US--JUST A LITTLE WAY--	AGAIN--HIS VOICE IS AT	663	20
BUT DID NOT FINISH--SOME WAY BACK--	A THOUGHT WENT UP MY	701	3
AND CAME MY WAY NO MORE--	A THOUGHT WENT UP MY	701	12
THAT TOOK IT'S CAMBRIC WAY--	THE BEGGAR LAD--DIES	717	6
FOR CERTAINTY SHE TAKE HER WAY	THE MOON WAS BUT A CHIN	737	15
MOST SHE WON ME BY THE WAY	MOST SHE TOUCHED ME BY	760	2
A THREADLESS WAY [COURSE]	FROM BLANK TO BLANK--	761	2
TO SHOW THE SUN THE WAY--	MY FAITH IS LARGER THAN	766	4
LEST IF HE FLINCH--THE EYE THAT WAY	GRIEF IS A MOUSE--	793	10
MAY BE EASIER REACHED [BETTER ATTAINED / EASIER GAINED]--THIS WAY--	BY MY WINDOW HAVE I FOR	797	8
I THAT WAY WORSHIP THEE.	BECAUSE THE BEE MAY	869	12
A SLOW AND CAUTIOUS WAY	I STEPPED FROM PLANK TO	875	2
LOSE MY WAY LIKE A LITTLE CHILD	HOW HAPPY I WAS IF I	898	7
TOO LITTLE WAY THE HOUSE MUST LIE	TOO LITTLE WAY THE HOUSE	911	1
DEATH IS THE OTHER [FURTHER] WAY--	THOSE WHO HAVE BEEN IN	922	4
AS FAR AS DEATH THIS WAY--	HOW FAR IS IT TO HEAVEN?	929	2

	FIRST LINE	POEM	LINE
WAY (CONTINUED)			
AS FAR AS DEATH THIS WAY--	HOW FAR IS IT TO HEAVEN?	929	6
THIS PATTERN--OF THE WAY--	I LEARNED--AT LEAST--	944	6
WOULD SEEM TO ME THE MORE THE WAY	OF TOLLING BELL I ASK	947	7
THIS WAY, I KEEP FROM MISSING	WE'LL PASS WITHOUT THE	996	7
CAME ALL THE WAY FROM LIFE TO ME	I HEARD, AS IF I HAD NO	1039	3
IT WAS A QUIET WAY--	IT WAS A QUIET WAY--	1053	1
IS THIS--THE WAY?	TITLE DIVINE--IS MINE!	1072	14
HE FORKED HIS WAY ALONG	THE FROST OF DEATH WAS	1136	13
RECOLLECT THE WAY--	AFTER A HUNDRED YEARS	1147	10
THE WAY IS CLOSED THEY CAME.	THIS IS THE PLACE THEY	1264	8
THE WAY TO KNOW THE BOBOLINK	THE WAY TO KNOW THE	1279	1
HE RESTITUTES IN SOME SWEET WAY	NOT ONE BY HEAVEN	1303	3
. . . MIGHTY / GALLANT / SYLVAN / AMPLE / PERFECT] WAY	SUMMER--WE ALL HAVE SEEN	1386	6
TO GO IT'S CONVALESCENT WAY	THE HEALED HEART SHOWS	1440	5
THE WAY HOPE BUILDS HIS HOUSE	THE WAY HOPE BUILDS HIS	1481	1
AND THAT'S THE WAY TO GRIEVE--	THE BUTTERFLY UPON THE	1521	8
AND WENT THE WAY OF DUSK	HE LIVED THE LIFE OF	1525	2
BUT ANGELS HAVE THAT MODEST WAY	FOREVER HONORED BE THE	1570	7
WHAT HEART WOULD RISK [COULD FIND] THE WAY--	WHERE ROSES WOULD NOT	1582	2
AND OF WHOEVER ASK THEIR WAY	COSMOPOLITES WITHOUT A	1589 V	3
WHEN OPENING THE SABBATH IN THEIR AFFLICTIVE WAY	THE BOBOLINK IS GONE--	1591	5
IN A PORTENTOUS WAY--	THE BOBOLINK IS GONE--	1591	11
AND WENT THE WAY OF DUSK,	WHO ABDICATED AMBUSH	1616	2
TO TRY TO SPEAK, AND MISS THE WAY	TO TRY TO SPEAK, AND	1617	1
TO THE SAME PAGEANT WENDS ITS WAY	NO LIFE CAN POMPLESS	1626	3
A "THIS WAY" BECKONS SPACIOUSLY--	NO LIFE CAN POMPLESS	1626	7
THE RIGHT OF WAY TO TRIPOLI	THE PEDIGREE OF HONEY	1627	7
AND WINDS DO GO THAT WAY AT NOON [TIMES]	TALK NOT TO ME OF SUMMER	1634	5
GO THY GREAT WAY!	GO THY GREAT WAY!	1638	1
WHEN EVERY WAY WE FLY	WHY SHOULD WE HURRY--WHY	1646	2
I WATCHED HER FACE TO SEE WHICH WAY	I WATCHED HER FACE TO	1667	1
BOTH EYES HIS WAY	IN WINTER IN MY ROOM	1670	33
MY WISDOM LOSES WAY	THE ONES THAT	1690	6
WAYLAID			
NOR WE WHO HAVING ONCE INHALED [WAYLAID] IT--	IN MANY AND REPORTLESS	1382	11
WAYLAYING			
DEATH'S WAYLAYING NOT THE SHARPEST	DEATH'S WAYLAYING NOT	1296	1
OF THAT WAYLAYING LIGHT--	THE FARTHEST THUNDER	1581	16
WAYS			
DID I NOT TAKE IT FROM THE WAYS	NOBODY KNOWS THIS LITTLE	35	3
AND WAYS I KNEW NOT THAT I KNEW--TILL THEN--	I ROSE--BECAUSE HE SANK	616	22
OF SHRINKING WAYS--SHE DID NOT [FOREBORE HER] FRIGHT	NO NOTICE GAVE SHE, BUT	804	9
OF PRETTY WAYS OF COVENANT--	I LEARNED--AT LEAST--	944	3
SENT VARIOUS--SCATTERED WAYS--	WE MET AS SPARKS--	958	2
THE WINDS WENT OUT THEIR MARTIAL WAYS	THE DAY GREW SMALL,	1140	5
WAYWARD			
THE WAYWARD NUN--BENEATH THE HILL--	SWEET MOUNTAINS--YE TELL	722	8
WAYWARDEST			
THE FEEBLEST [DULLEST]--OR THE WAYWARDEST--	NATURE--THE GENTLEST	790	3
WE			
PEDESTRIAN ONCE--AS WE--	THE FEET OF PEOPLE	7	12
WE MIGHT E'EN DIVIDE--	I NEVER TOLD THE BURIED	11	19
SHE DID NOT SING AS WE DID--	ONE SISTER HAVE I IN OUR	14	9
AND THEN WE KNELT IN PRAYER--	THE GENTIAN WEAVES HER	18	12
WE TRUST THAT SHE WAS WILLING--	THE GENTIAN WEAVES HER	18	13
WE ASK THAT WE MAY BE.	THE GENTIAN WEAVES HER	18	14
WE ASK THAT WE MAY BE.	THE GENTIAN WEAVES HER	18	14
WE LOSE--BECAUSE WE WIN--	WE LOSE--BECAUSE WE WIN	21	1
WE LOSE--BECAUSE WE WIN--	WE LOSE--BECAUSE WE WIN	21	1
MORNS LIKE THESE--WE PARTED--	MORNS LIKE THESE--WE	27	1
WHAT WE TOUCH THE HEMS OF	BEFORE THE ICE IS IN THE	37	9
WE WHO SAW THE LAUNCHING	COULD LIVE--DID LIVE--	43	12
WE--PRONE TO PERIPHRASIS,	THERE'S SOMETHING	45	15
HEART! WE WILL FORGET HIM!	HEART! WE WILL FORGET	47	1
WHEN WE WITH DAISIES LIE--	IF I SHOULD DIE,	54	12
"OH LORD--HOW FRAIL ARE WE"!	"ARCTURUS" IS HIS OTHER	70	8
BRED AS WE, AMONG THE MOUNTAINS,	EXULTATION IS THE GOING	76	5
FOR YOU KNOW WE DO NOT MIND OUR DRESS	GOING TO HEAVEN!	79	18
WHEN WE ARE GOING HOME--	GOING TO HEAVEN!	79	19
AND WE LOOK FARTHER ON!	OUR LIVES ARE SWISS--	80	5
WE SHOULD NOT MIND SO SMALL A FLOWER--	WE SHOULD NOT MIND SO	81	1
OUR LITTLE GARDEN THAT WE LOST	WE SHOULD NOT MIND SO	81	3
AS BY THE DEAD WE LOVE TO SIT,	AS BY THE DEAD WE LOVE	88	1
AS FOR THE LOST WE GRAPPLE	AS BY THE DEAD WE LOVE	88	3
WE ESTIMATE OUR PRIZE	AS BY THE DEAD WE LOVE	88	6
WE MIGHT LOOK FOR HIM!	WENT UP A YEAR THIS	93	12
AS WE RIDE GRAND ALONG!	ONE DIGNITY DELAYS FOR	98	8
WHAT SERVICE WHEN WE PAUSE!	ONE DIGNITY DELAYS FOR	98	10
WE ARE THE FLOWER--THOU THE SUN!	THE DAISY FOLLOWS SOFT	106	7
WE NEARER STEAL TO THEE!	THE DAISY FOLLOWS SOFT	106	9
"OH COULD WE CLIMB WHERE MOSES STOOD,	WHERE BELLS NO MORE	112	9
GOOD NIGHT, BECAUSE WE MUST,	GOOD NIGHT, BECAUSE WE	114	1
SMILING WHEN WE WALK BAREFOOT	IN RAGS MYSTERIOUS AS	117	7
WE MUST AN ANGUISH PAY	FOR EACH EXTATIC INSTANT	125	2
WE TRUST, IN PLUMED PROCESSION	TO FIGHT ALOUD, IS VERY	126	9
WHERE WE--WITH LATE--CELESTIAL FACE--	MUSICIANS WRESTLE	157	17

WE (CONTINUED)

	FIRST LINE	POEM	LINE
COULD WE STAND WITH THAT OLD "MOSES"--	IF THE FOOLISH, CALL	168	9
DOUBTLESS, WE SHOULD DEEM SUPERFLUOUS	IF THE FOOLISH, CALL	168	13
GRANT THAT WE MAY STAND,	IF THE FOOLISH, CALL	168	18
WE MEN AND WOMEN DIE!	IT'S SUCH A LITTLE THING	189	4
DAY KNOCKED--AND WE MUST PART--	HE WAS WEAK, AND I WAS	190	9
WE DID'NT DO IT--THO'!	HE WAS WEAK, AND I WAS	190	12
WE DONT CRY--TIM AND I,	WE DONT CRY--TIM AND I,	196	1
WE ARE FAR TOO GRAND--	WE DONT CRY--TIM AND I,	196	2
BUT WE BOLT THE DOOR TIGHT	WE DONT CRY--TIM AND I,	196	3
THEN WE HIDE OUR BRAVE FACE	WE DONT CRY--TIM AND I,	196	5
WE ARE FAR TOO GRAND--	WE DONT CRY--TIM AND I,	196	8
DO WE CONDESCEND--	WE DONT CRY--TIM AND I,	196	10
WE JUST SHUT OUR BROWN EYE	WE DONT CRY--TIM AND I,	196	11
THEN--WE SHAKE--TIM AND I--	WE DONT CRY--TIM AND I,	196	15
AND WE BOTH PRAY--	WE DONT CRY--TIM AND I,	196	18
WE MUST DIE--BY AND BY--	WE DONT CRY--TIM AND I,	196	21
HOW SHALL WE ARRANGE IT--	WE DONT CRY--TIM AND I,	196	25
OR TELL GOD--HOW CROSS WE ARE--	WHAT IS--"PARADISE"--	215	10
MAYBE, WE SHOULD'NT MIND THEM--	I'VE NOTHING ELSE--TO	224	5
WE--BEE AND I--LIVE BY THE QUAFFING--	WE--BEE AND I--LIVE BY	230	1
BUT IT'S DIM CHAT OF THINGS BURGUND, WE KNOW--	WE--BEE AND I--LIVE BY	230 V	4
WE CHANT--FOR CHEER--WHEN THE WINES--FAIL--	WE--BEE AND I--LIVE BY	230	5
DO WE "GET DRUNK"?	WE--BEE AND I--LIVE BY	230	6
DO WE "BEAT" OUR "WIFE"?	WE--BEE AND I--LIVE BY	230	8
WHEN WE STAND ON THE TOPS OF THINGS--	WHEN WE STAND ON THE	242	1
WHOM WE CAN NEVER LEARN--	FOREVER AT HIS SIDE TO	246	11
WE CAN FIND NO SCAR,	THERE'S A CERTAIN SLANT	258	6
TILL WE--ARE STOUTER--	READ--SWEET--HOW OTHERS	260	2
TILL WE--ARE LESS AFRAID--	READ--SWEET--HOW OTHERS	260	4
TILL WE--ARE HELPED--	READ--SWEET--HOW OTHERS	260	6
DID WE DISOBEY HIM?	DID WE DISOBEY HIM?	267	1
BUT WE COULD'NT LEARN!	DID WE DISOBEY HIM?	267	4
WHAT WOULD WE--DO?	DID WE DISOBEY HIM?	267	6
FOR WE MUST RIDE TO THE JUDGMENT--	TIE THE STRINGS TO MY	279	7
WE SHOW THEM--PRAYER--	'TIS SO APPALLING--IT	281	12
BUT WE, WHO KNOW,	'TIS SO APPALLING--IT	281	13
EXISTING, WHILE WE STARE,	HOW NOTELESS MEN, AND	282	6
WHY DID'NT WE DETAIN [RETAIN] THEM [IT]?	HOW NOTELESS MEN, AND	282	9
WE BREATHED--	ONE YEAR AGO--JOTS WHAT?	296	26
I REASON, WE COULD [SHOULD] DIE--	I REASON, EARTH IS SHORT	301	5
ELATE US--TILL WE ALMOST WEEP--	LIKE SOME OLD FASHIONED	302	11
NOUGHT--THAT [YET, IF] WE--NO POET'S KINSMAN--	HER--"LAST POEMS"--	312	16
WE--WHO HAVE THE SOULS--	NATURE--SOMETIMES SEARS	314	7
WE KNOW [SAY] HE HAS CLIMBED A FIR--	THE WIND DID'NT COME	316	8
THE HEAVEN WE CHASE,	THE NEAREST DREAM	319	2
WE PLAY AT PASTE--	WE PLAY AT PASTE--	320	1
LEST WE TOO AWKWARD SHOW	THERE CAME A DAY AT	322	15
WE GAVE NO OTHER BOND--	THERE CAME A DAY AT	322	24
SUFFICIENT TROTH, THAT WE SHALL [SHE WILL] RISE--	THERE CAME A DAY AT	322	25
BUT WE--STOOD--WHISPERING IN THE HOUSE--	OF TRIBULATION--THESE	325	15
AND ALL WE SAID--WAS	OF TRIBULATION--THESE	325	16
SO GLAD WE ARE--A STRANGER'D DEEM	SO GLAD WE ARE--A	329	1
'TWAS SORRY, THAT WE WERE--	SO GLAD WE ARE--A	329	2
WE--ARE THE BIRDS--THAT STAY.	'TIS NOT THAT DYING	335	8
WE STIPULATE--TILL PITYING SNOWS	'TIS NOT THAT DYING	335	11
THAT WE CAN TOUCH THE SPACES--	WHEN NIGHT IS ALMOST	347	3
AND WONDER WE COULD CARE	WHEN NIGHT IS ALMOST	347	6
BUT WE MIGHT LEARN TO LIKE THE HEAVEN,	I FELT MY LIFE WITH BOTH	351	15
WE WILL NOT DROP THE DIRK--	REHEARSAL TO OURSELVES	379	5
BECAUSE WE LOVE THE WOUND	REHEARSAL TO OURSELVES	379	6
REMIND US THAT WE DIED.	REHEARSAL TO OURSELVES	379	8
WE KNOW NOT--	FOR DEATH--OR RATHER	382	11
ONES WE FORMER KNEW--	SMILING BACK FROM	385	6
WE TWO--LOOKED SO ALIKE--	'TWAS LOVE--NOT ME--	394	10
AND WHAT IT WAS--WE NEVER LISPED--	A HOUSE UPON THE HIGHT--	399	11
IF WHAT WE COULD--WERE WHAT WE WOULD--	IF WHAT WE COULD--WERE	407	1
IF WHAT WE COULD--WERE WHAT WE WOULD--	IF WHAT WE COULD--WERE	407	1
WE GROW ACCUSTOMED TO THE DARK--	WE GROW ACCUSTOMED TO	419	1
A MOMENT--WE UNCERTAIN STEP	WE GROW ACCUSTOMED TO	419	5
WHEN A FRACTURE--WE DISCOVER--	TAKING UP THE FAIR IDEAL	428	3
WE BEHOLD HER--GLORIFIED--	TAKING UP THE FAIR IDEAL	428	11
WE ADORED--FOR WHOLE--	TAKING UP THE FAIR IDEAL	428	14
'TIS CUSTOMARY AS WE PART	'TIS CUSTOMARY AS WE	440	1
WE CANNOT PUT OURSELF AWAY	I TIE MY HAT--I CREASE	443	13
WE CAME TO FLESH--UPON--	I TIE MY HAT--I CREASE	443	16
TO COVER WHAT WE ARE	I TIE MY HAT--I CREASE	443	20
WE--COULD TREMBLE--	I TIE MY HAT--I CREASE	443	26
BUT SINCE WE GOT A BOMB--	I TIE MY HAT--I CREASE	443	27
THEREFORE--WE DO LIFE'S LABOR--	I TIE MY HAT--I CREASE	443	30
WHAT LITTLE OF HIM WE--POSSESSED	IT FEELS A SHAME TO BE	444	7
DO WE DESERVE--A THING--	IT FEELS A SHAME TO BE	444	10
BEFORE WE MAY OBTAIN?	IT FEELS A SHAME TO BE	444	12
ARE WE THAT WAIT--SUFFICIENT WORTH--	IT FEELS A SHAME TO BE	444	13
WE WONDER IT WAS NOT OURSELVES	THIS WAS A POET--IT IS	448	7
WE BRETHEREN, ARE", HE SAID--	I DIED FOR BEAUTY--BUT	449	8
WE TALKED BETWEEN THE ROOMS--	I DIED FOR BEAUTY--BUT	449	10
WHO KNOWS BUT WE--	LOVE--THOU ART HIGH--	453	4
WHEN WE ARE NEW--AND SMALL.	IT WAS GIVEN TO ME BY	454	4

		FIRST LINE	POEM	LINE
WE	(CONTINUED)			
	WE PERISH--THO' WE REIGN--	LIKE EYES THAT LOOKED ON	458	16
	WE PERISH--THO' WE REIGN--	LIKE EYES THAT LOOKED ON	458	16
	SHALL WE REMEMBER PARCHING--THEN?	I KNOW WHERE WELLS GROW	460	17
	WE DO NOT PLAY ON GRAVES--	WE DO NOT PLAY ON GRAVES	467	1
	AND SO WE MOVE AS FAR	WE DO NOT PLAY ON GRAVES	467	9
	WE SIGNIFIED "THESE SEE"--	THEY PUT US FAR APART--	474	4
	WE STOOD UPON OUR STAPLED FEET--	THEY PUT US FAR APART--	474	15
	WE TURNED OUR BACKS UPON THE SUN	THEY PUT US FAR APART--	474	19
	AND WE KNOW NOT--	"WHY DO I LOVE" YOU, SIR	480	8
	WE COVER THEE--SWEET FACE--	WE COVER THEE--SWEET	482	1
	NOT THAT WE TIRE OF THEE--	WE COVER THEE--SWEET	482	2
	WE FOLLOW THEE UNTIL	WE COVER THEE--SWEET	482	5
	WE WERE CONTENT TO SHOW--	WE COVER THEE--SWEET	482	10
	OF ONLY TASTE WE CARED TO PLEASE	TO MAKE ONE'S TOILETTE--	485	3
	HAD WE THE ART OF BOARDS	MYSELF WAS FORMED--A	488	6
	THE BENCH, WHERE WE HAD TOILED--	MYSELF WAS FORMED--A	488	10
	WE--TEMPLES BUILD--I SAID--	MYSELF WAS FORMED--A	488	12
	WE PRAY--TO HEAVEN--	WE PRAY--TO HEAVEN--	489	1
	WE PRATE--OF HEAVEN--	WE PRAY--TO HEAVEN--	489	2
	TELL HIM [HER]--NIGHT [DAY] FINISHED--BEFORE WE FINISHED--	GOING TO HIM! HAPPY	494	18
	WE WOULD NOT HAVE CORRECT--	IT'S THOUGHTS--AND JUST	495	26
	WE TRUST--IN PLACES PERFECTER--	THOSE FAIR--FICTITIOUS	499	9
	REMEMBERING OURSELVES, WE TRUST--	THOSE FAIR--FICTITIOUS	499	13
	YET BLESSEDER--THAN WE--	THOSE FAIR--FICTITIOUS	499	14
	THROUGH KNOWING--WHERE WE ONLY HOPE [GUESS]--	THOSE FAIR--FICTITIOUS	499	15
	RECEIVING [BEHOLDING]--WHERE WE--PRAY--	THOSE FAIR--FICTITIOUS	499	16
	IF POSITIVE, 'TWERE WE--	WITHIN MY GARDEN, RIDES	500	14
	BUT--ISHMAEL--SINCE WE MET--'TIS LONG--	YOU KNOW THAT PORTRAIT	504	7
	UNTIL WE MET THE SOLID TOWN--	I STARTED EARLY--TOOK MY	520	21
	WE DREAM [ARE DREAMING / SHOULD DREAM]--IT IS GOOD WE ARE DREAMING--	WE DREAM--IT IS GOOD WE	531	1
	WE DREAM [ARE DREAMING / SHOULD DREAM]--IT IS GOOD WE ARE DREAMING--	WE DREAM--IT IS GOOD WE	531	1
	IT [THEY] WOULD HURT US--WERE WE AWAKE--	WE DREAM--IT IS GOOD WE	531	2
	AND WE ARE PLAYING--SHRIEK--	WE DREAM--IT IS GOOD WE	531	4
	BUT WE--ARE DYING IN DRAMA--	WE DREAM--IT IS GOOD WE	531	7
	CAUTIOUS--WE JAR EACH OTHER--	WE DREAM--IT IS GOOD WE	531	9
	WE SEE--COMPARATIVELY--	WE SEE--COMPARATIVELY--	534	1
	WE COULD NOT GRASP IT'S SEGMENT [ANGLE]	WE SEE--COMPARATIVELY--	534	3
	THE INSTANT THAT WE MEET--	I CROSS TILL I AM WEARY	550	21
	THEY PERISH [STAGGER]--DO WE DIE--	I CROSS TILL I AM WEARY	550	23
	WE START--AS IF DETECTED	AN IGNORANCE A SUNSET	552	11
	WE--TELL A HURT--TO COOL IT--	THE BLACK BERRY--WEARS A	554	9
	AS WORTHILY [PRIVATELY] AS WE.	SHE HIDETH HER THE LAST	557	8
	AND QUICKENING [RIPENING]--AS WE SOWED--	HE GAVE AWAY HIS LIFE--	567	13
	AND WHEN WE TURNED TO NOTE THE GROWTH--	HE GAVE AWAY HIS LIFE--	567	15
	WE LEARNED THE WHOLE OF LOVE--	WE LEARNED THE WHOLE OF	568	1
	THE SUMMER DEEPENED, WHILE WE STROVE--	MY FIRST WELL DAY--SINCE	574	9
	ITSELF BE FAIRER--WE SUPPOSE--	"HEAVEN" HAS DIFFERENT	575	17
	ALL WADED--WE LOOK BACK FOR PLAY,	IF I MAY HAVE IT, WHEN	577	24
	WE TALKED AS GIRLS DO--	WE TALKED AS GIRLS DO--	586	1
	WE SPECULATED FAIR, ON EVERY SUBJECT, BUT THE GRAVE--	WE TALKED AS GIRLS DO--	586	3
	WE HANDLED DESTINIES, AS COOL--	WE TALKED AS GIRLS DO--	586	5
	AS WE--DISPOSERS--BE--	WE TALKED AS GIRLS DO--	586	6
	AS WE EVENTUAL--BE--	WE TALKED AS GIRLS DO--	586	10
	WE--OCCUPY--DEGREE [TOO--PARTAKE]--	WE TALKED AS GIRLS DO--	586	12
	WE PARTED WITH A CONTRACT	WE TALKED AS GIRLS DO--	586	13
	AND CARRIED, WE SUPPOSE--[I SUPPOSED] TO HEAVEN,	I CRIED AT PITY--NOT AT	588	11
	THREE TIMES--WE PARTED--BREATH--AND I--	THREE TIMES--WE PARTED--	598	1
	THE SHAPES WE BURIED, DWELL ABOUT,	OF NEARNESS TO HER	607	5
	SINCE WE--OLD MORNINGS, CHILDREN--PLAYED--	OF NEARNESS TO HER	607	11
	AS WE--IT WERE--THAT PERISHED--	OF NEARNESS TO HER	607	17
	THEMSELF--HAD JUST REMAINED TILL WE REJOIN THEM--	OF NEARNESS TO HER	607	18
	WE BOUGHT--TO EASE THEIR PLACE--	YOU'LL FIND--IT WHEN YOU	610	16
	IF WE WERE TRUE--	I ROSE--BECAUSE HE SANK	616	19
	THAT WE CAN SHOW--TODAY?"	I ASKED NO OTHER THING--	621	8
	AND WE APPROACH [ACCOST] HIM--STERN--	THE LIGHTNING PLAYETH--	630	4
	NOR WE SO MUCH AS CHECK OUR SPEECH--	THE LIGHTNING PLAYETH--	630	11
	AND YET, ONE SUMMER, WE WERE QUEENS [WED]--	OURSELVES WERE WED ONE	631	15
	AND WE ARE WAITING FOR THE COACH--	I THINK THE LONGEST HOUR	635	3
	SO WE MUST MEET APART--	I CANNOT LIVE WITH YOU--	640	45
	WHOM WE HAVE NEVER SEEN--	BEREAVEMENT IN THEIR	645	2
	WE COME TO LOOK WITH GRATITUDE [FONDNESS / PLEASURE]	A PRISON GETS TO BE A	652	5
	WE LEARN TO KNOW THE PLANKS--	A PRISON GETS TO BE A	652	9
	THE LIBERTY WE KNEW	A PRISON GETS TO BE A	652	29
	WE THOUGHT THE MIGHTY [MONSTROUS] FUNERAL--	'TIS GOOD--THE LOOKING	660	3
	WE TALK IN CARELESS [VENTURE]--AND IN TOSS--	AGAIN--HIS VOICE IS AT	663	13
	WE WALK--I LEAVE MY DOG--AT HOME [BEHIND]--	AGAIN--HIS VOICE IS AT	663	18
	AND--THEN--WE ARE ALONE--	AGAIN--HIS VOICE IS AT	663	21
	WE CANNOT COUNT--ON HIGH!	AGAIN--HIS VOICE IS AT	663	25
	"NATURE" IS WHAT WE SEE--	"NATURE" IS WHAT WE SEE	668	1
	NATURE IS WHAT WE HEAR--	"NATURE" IS WHAT WE SEE	668	5
	NATURE IS WHAT WE KNOW--	"NATURE" IS WHAT WE SEE	668	9
	WE LEARNED TO LIKE THE FIRE	THE ZEROES--TAUGHT US--	689	2

WE (CONTINUED)

	FIRST LINE	POEM	LINE
UNLESS [EXCEPT] WE DINE ON TIPTOE--	VICTORY COMES LATE--	690	9
ILL! WE HAVE BERRIES, FOR THE PARCHING!	WOULD YOU LIKE SUMMER?	691	3
CAPTIVE! WE BRING REPRIEVE OF ROSES!	WOULD YOU LIKE SUMMER?	691	6
WE ALMOST CEASE TO FEAR--	THE HEAVEN VESTS FOR	694	14
LIFE--IS WHAT WE MAKE IT--	LIFE--IS WHAT WE MAKE IT	698	1
DEATH--WE DO NOT KNOW--	LIFE--IS WHAT WE MAKE IT	698	2
POSSIBLY--BUT WE--WOULD RATHER	PUBLICATION--IS THE	709	5
WE SLOWLY DROVE--HE KNEW NO HASTE	BECAUSE I COULD NOT STOP	712	5
WE PASSED THE SCHOOL, WHERE CHILDREN STROVE	BECAUSE I COULD NOT STOP	712	9
WE PASSED THE FIELDS OF GAZING GRAIN--	BECAUSE I COULD NOT STOP	712	11
WE PASSED THE SETTING SUN--	BECAUSE I COULD NOT STOP	712	12
WE PAUSED BEFORE A HOUSE THAT SEEMED	BECAUSE I COULD NOT STOP	712	17
WHEN WE STOP TO DIE--	THE WORLD--FEELS DUSTY	715	2
WE WANT THE DEW--THEN--	THE WORLD--FEELS DUSTY	715	3
JUST WE TWO--MEET--	WHERE THOU ART--THAT--IS	725	10
WE THIRST AT FIRST--'TIS NATURE'S ACT--	WE THIRST AT FIRST--'TIS	726	1
AND LATER--WHEN WE DIE--	WE THIRST AT FIRST--'TIS	726	2
WE ACTUALLY HEAR	THE SPIRIT IS THE	733	2
WHEN WE INSPECT--THAT'S AUDIBLE--	THE SPIRIT IS THE	733	3
THAT WERE NOT, WE ARE SURE--	HAVE ANY LIKE MYSELF	736	5
AND ARE TODAY--IF WE EXIST--	HAVE ANY LIKE MYSELF	736	7
THENCEFORWARD--WE--TOGETHER DWELT [WALKED]--	THE BIRDS REPORTED FROM	743	21
AND NOW WE ROAM IN [THE] SOVREIGN WOODS--	MY LIFE HAD STOOD--A	754	5
AND NOW WE HUNT THE DOE--	MY LIFE HAD STOOD--A	754	6
THIS--WE STROKED--	THESE--SAW VISIONS--	758	7
THESE--WE HELD AMONG [FONDLED IN] OUR OWN--	THESE--SAW VISIONS--	758	9
AND YET WE GUESSED IT NOT--	HER FINAL SUMMER WAS IT	795	2
YET WE SUSPECTED NOT	HER FINAL SUMMER WAS IT	795	V 2
PERVADED HER, WE THOUGHT	HER FINAL SUMMER WAS IT	795	4
WE WONDERED AT OUR BLINDNESS	HER FINAL SUMMER WAS IT	795	9
SO LEISURELY--WERE WE--	HER FINAL SUMMER WAS IT	795	16
WE QUESTION IF THE MAN--	I PLAY AT RICHES--TO	801	14
AS WE--WHO NEVER CAN--	I PLAY AT RICHES--TO	801	16
AND WE--IMPLORING DREW--	NO NOTICE GAVE SHE, BUT	804	18
WE PASS, AND SHE ABIDES.	THE VEINS OF OTHER	811	5
WE CONJUGATE HER SKILL	THE VEINS OF OTHER	811	6
IT PASSES AND WE STAY--	A LIGHT EXISTS IN SPRING	812	16
WE--DIFFICULT--ACQUIRE	AWAY FROM HOME ARE SOME	821	6
NOT WHAT WE DID, SHALL BE THE TEST	NOT WHAT WE DID, SHALL	823	1
BUT WHAT OUR LORD INFERS [INFERRED] WE WOULD	NOT WHAT WE DID, SHALL	823	3
HAD WE DIVINER BEEN--	NOT WHAT WE DID, SHALL	823	4
BEFORE HE COMES WE WEIGH THE TIME!	BEFORE HE COMES WE WEIGH	834	1
WE JOURNEY TO THE DAY	I SING TO USE THE	850	6
AND TELL EACH OTHER HOW WE SUNG	I SING TO USE THE	850	7
PRECISER WHAT WE ARE	THERE IS A FINISHED	856	6
IF WE DEMUR, IT'S GAPING SIDES	THIS CHASM, SWEET, UPON	858	5
TENDERNESS DECREASES AS WE PROVE--	ABSENCE DISEMBODIES--SO	860	4
WE OUTGROW LOVE, LIKE OTHER THINGS	WE OUTGROW LOVE, LIKE	887	1
IS THE MOST WE CAN	CRISIS IS A HAIR	889	6
WE IGNORANT MUST BE--	FROM US SHE WANDERED NOW	890	6
WE ONLY KNOW WHAT TIME OF YEAR	FROM US SHE WANDERED NOW	890	7
WE TOOK THE MYSTERY.	FROM US SHE WANDERED NOW	890	8
AND WHAT WE SAW NOT	THE ADMIRATIONS--AND	906	5
WE DISTINGUISH CLEAR--	THE ADMIRATIONS--AND	906	6
WHAT WE SAW BEFORE--	THE ADMIRATIONS--AND	906	8
BUT SINCE WE HOLD A MUTUAL DISC--	I MAKE HIS CRESCENT FILL	909	9
SUPPORTING WHAT WE SEE	FAITH--IS THE PIERLESS	915	2
UNTO THE SCENE THAT WE DO NOT--	FAITH--IS THE PIERLESS	915	3
TO WHAT, COULD WE PRESUME	FAITH--IS THE PIERLESS	915	9
WE CAN BUT FOLLOW TO THE SUN--	WE CAN BUT FOLLOW TO THE	920	1
WE GO NO FURTHER WITH THE DUST	WE CAN BUT FOLLOW TO THE	920	5
AND WE BEHOLD--NO MORE	WE CAN BUT FOLLOW TO THE	920	8
WE SHALL NEVER KNOW--	HOW THE WATERS CLOSED	923	2
THAT WE BUT RECOLLECT THE ONE	THERE IS A JUNE WHEN	930	15
THAT IS SOLEMN [TENDER / SACRED] WE HAVE ENDED	THAT IS SOLEMN WE HAVE	934	1
WE HAVE UNDERSTOOD FOR BETTER	THAT IS SOLEMN WE HAVE	934	7
THROUGH ALL THEIR [IT'S] FORMER PLACES, WE	DEATH LEAVES US HOMESICK	935	5
IN WHICH WE FIRST EXPERIENCED LIGHT	ON THAT DEAR FRAME THE	940	3
WE SO NEW BESTOW	SNOW BENEATH WHOSE	942	6
WE MET AS SPARKS--DIVERGING FLINTS	WE MET AS SPARKS--	958	1
WE PARTED AS THE CENTRAL FLINT	WE MET AS SPARKS--	958	3
SUBSISTING ON THE LIGHT WE BORE	WE MET AS SPARKS--	958	5
BEFORE WE FELT THE DARK--	WE MET AS SPARKS--	958	6
WE KNEW BY CHANGE BETWEEN ITSELF	WE MET AS SPARKS--	958	7
WE KNOW	BESIDES THIS MAY	977	2
SOME KNOW HIM [IT] WHOM WE KNEW--	BESIDES THIS MAY	977	6
A PARTY THAT [WHOM] WE KNEW--	AS SLEIGH BELLS SEEM IN	981	6
WITH WHICH WE HELP THE WHEEL	IDEALS ARE THE FAIRY OIL	983	2
WE QUESTIONED TO, AGAIN.	'TIS ANGUISH GRANDER	984	4
WE MISS HER, NOT BECAUSE WE SEE--	WE MISS HER, NOT BECAUSE	993	1
WE MISS HER, NOT BECAUSE WE SEE--	WE MISS HER, NOT BECAUSE	993	1
WE KNOW THAT THEIR SUPERIOR EYES	WE MISS HER, NOT BECAUSE	993	7
THE FIRST WE KNEW OF HIM WAS DEATH--	THE FIRST WE KNEW OF HIM	1006	1
DID WE ABOLISH FROST	DID WE ABOLISH FROST	1014	1
WE CHIEFLY WONDER THEN	SO LARGE MY WILL	1024	14
WE JUST REVERSE THE ZODIAC	THE PRODUCTS OF MY FARM	1025	7
WE ACHIEVE THE JOY--	SATISFACTION--IS THE	1036	6
A SINGLE BLOOM WE CONSTITUTE	HERE, WHERE THE DAISIES	1037	11
A FALLACY, A FIGMENT, WE KNEW--	NOT SO THE INFINITE	1040	4

WE (CONTINUED)	FIRST LINE	POEM	LINE
WE SHALL NOT WANT TO USE AGAIN	THE BUSTLE IN A HOUSE	1078	7
WE LEARN IN THE RETREATING	WE LEARN IN THE	1083	1
WHAT TWIGS WE HELD BY--	WHAT TWIGS WE HELD BY--	1086	1
WE PAUSE BEFORE A FURTHER PLUNGE	WHAT TWIGS WE HELD BY--	1086	4
TO SINK, IF WE HAD LABORED, FOND	WHAT TWIGS WE HELD BY--	1086	12
WE MISS A KINSMAN MORE	WE MISS A KINSMAN MORE	1087	1
TILL WE, WHO SMILED AT PYRRHENEES--	WE MISS A KINSMAN MORE	1087	7
WE SPY THE FORESTS AND THE HILLS	DEW--IS THE FRESHET IN	1097	5
AND MENTION WHAT WE SAW.	DEW--IS THE FRESHET IN	1097	8
WE NOTICED SMALLEST THINGS--	THE LAST NIGHT THAT SHE	1100	5
AS WE WENT OUT AND IN	THE LAST NIGHT THAT SHE	1100	9
WE WAITED WHILE SHE PASSED--	THE LAST NIGHT THAT SHE	1100	17
AND WE--WE PLACED THE HAIR--	THE LAST NIGHT THAT SHE	1100	25
AND WE--WE PLACED THE HAIR--	THE LAST NIGHT THAT SHE	1100	25
AND BOROUGHS [LIMITS] WHERE WE LIVE--	LIKE MEN AND WOMEN	1105	8
WE DO NOT KNOW THE TIME WE LOSE--	WE DO NOT KNOW THE TIME	1106	1
WE DO NOT KNOW THE TIME WE LOSE--	WE DO NOT KNOW THE TIME	1106	1
AS EMIGRANTS WE COME	THE BIRD DID PRANCE--THE	1107	V 10
TILL WHAT WE SPECULATE, HAS BEEN	THE MURMURING OF BEES,	1115	13
TILL WHAT WE COULD NOT SEE [FACE / CHOOSE / PROVE] HAS COME . . .	THE MURMURING OF BEES,	1115	V 13
AND THOUGHTS WE WILL NOT SHOW	THE MURMURING OF BEES,	1115	14
THAN PERSONS, THAT WE KNOW.	THE MURMURING OF BEES,	1115	16
WE SOBERLY DESCEND	EXHILIRATION IS THE	1118	6
WE WENT AND PLAYED AND CAME AGAIN	THIS SLOW DAY MOVED	1120	7
HAD WE KNOWN THE TON [WEIGHT / LOAD] SHE BORE	HAD WE KNOWN THE TON SHE	1124	1
WE HAD HELPED THE TERROR	HAD WE KNOWN THE TON SHE	1124	2
WE MISS HIS STATED HAT.	THAT ODD OLD MAN IS DEAD	1130	2
WE STERN AND FORMER KNEW	THE SNOW THAT NEVER	1133	10
WE BUY WITH CONTRAST--PANG IS GOOD	THE SNOW THAT NEVER	1133	15
WE FOUGHT MORTALITY.	THE FROST OF DEATH WAS	1136	4
OUR PASSIVE FLOWER WE HELD TO SEA--	THE FROST OF DEATH WAS	1136	5
WE PRIED HIM BACK	THE FROST OF DEATH WAS	1136	9
OURSELVES WE WEDGED	THE FROST OF DEATH WAS	1136	10
WE HUNTED HIM TO HIS RAVINE	THE FROST OF DEATH WAS	1136	16
WE CHASED HIM TO HIS DEN--	THE FROST OF DEATH WAS	1136	17
WE HATED DEATH AND HATED LIFE	THE FROST OF DEATH WAS	1136	18
THE FACE WE CHOOSE TO MISS--	THE FACE WE CHOOSE TO	1141	1
OURSELVES WE DO INTER WITH SWEET DERISION.	OURSELVES WE DO INTER	1144	1
LEST ANY DOUBT THAT WE ARE GLAD THAT THEY WERE BORN TODAY	LEST ANY DOUBT THAT WE	1156	1
THE LIFE WE HAVE IS VERY GREAT.	THE LIFE WE HAVE IS VERY	1162	1
THE LIFE THAT WE SHALL SEE	THE LIFE WE HAVE IS VERY	1162	2
SURPASSES IT, WE KNOW, BECAUSE	THE LIFE WE HAVE IS VERY	1162	3
WHAT WE DID NOT SUSPECT WAS MARKED--	WERE IT TO BE THE LAST	1164	3
WE [I] LIKE A HAIRBREADTH 'SCAPE	WE LIKE A HAIRBREADTH	1175	1
IF WE [I] HAD VENTURED LESS	WE LIKE A HAIRBREADTH	1175	5
WE NEVER KNOW HOW HIGH WE ARE	WE NEVER KNOW HOW HIGH	1176	1
WE NEVER KNOW HOW HIGH WE ARE	WE NEVER KNOW HOW HIGH	1176	1
TILL WE ARE ASKED [CALLED] TO RISE	WE NEVER KNOW HOW HIGH	1176	2
AND THEN IF WE ARE TRUE TO PLAN [GROWTH]	WE NEVER KNOW HOW HIGH	1176	3
THE HEROISM WE RECITE	WE NEVER KNOW HOW HIGH	1176	5
WE ENTER BUT THE GAIN,	OF SO DIVINE A LOSS	1179	2
WITH WHICH WE CITE THIS MIGHTIEST CASE	"REMEMBER ME" IMPLORED	1180	7
OF ALL WE ARE ALLOWED TO HOPE	"REMEMBER ME" IMPLORED	1180	9
THAT THIS WAS DUE WHERE MOST [SOME] WE FEAR	"REMEMBER ME" IMPLORED	1180	11
THE DAYS THAT WE CAN SPARE	THE DAYS THAT WE CAN	1184	1
WE LET GO ALL OF TIME WITHOUT	THE DAYS THAT WE CAN	1184	7
AS POSITIVE ARE WE	THE PUNGENT ATOM IN THE	1191	6
WHAT WE SEE WE KNOW SOMEWHAT	WHAT WE SEE WE KNOW	1195	1
WHAT WE SEE WE KNOW SOMEWHAT	WHAT WE SEE WE KNOW	1195	1
WHAT WE DONT SURMISE WE DO	WHAT WE SEE WE KNOW	1195	3
WHAT WE DONT SURMISE WE DO	WHAT WE SEE WE KNOW	1195	3
WHEN WE HAVE PUT IT DOWN--	I SHOULD NOT DARE TO BE	1197	4
AND WE WHO NEVER SAW	I SHOULD NOT DARE TO BE	1197	6
UNPROVED IS MUCH WE KNOW--	THE FROST WAS NEVER SEEN	1202	13
UNKNOWN THE WORST WE FEAR--	THE FROST WAS NEVER SEEN	1202	14
WHEN WHAT WE NEED IS BY	IMMORTAL IS AN AMPLE	1205	2
WE FUNDAMENTAL KNOW	IMMORTAL IS AN AMPLE	1205	6
HE PREACHED UPON [ABOUT] "BREADTH" TILL IT ARGUED HIM [WE . . .	HE PREACHED UPON	1207	1
WE TAMPER WITH "AGAIN"	TO DISAPPEAR ENHANCES--	1209	8
WE HASTEN TO ADORN--	TO DISAPPEAR ENHANCES--	1209	12
THAT JUST AS WE DISCERN	TO DISAPPEAR ENHANCES--	1209	14
WE LIKE MARCH.	WE LIKE MARCH.	1213	1
WE INTRODUCE OURSELVES	WE INTRODUCE OURSELVES	1214	1
SOME WE SEE NO MORE, TENEMENTS OF WONDER	SOME WE SEE NO MORE,	1221	1
THAT OBLIQUE BELIEF WHICH WE CALL CONJECTURE	SOME WE SEE NO MORE,	1221	6
THE RIDDLE WE CAN [THAT WE] GUESS	THE RIDDLE WE CAN GUESS	1222	1
THE RIDDLE WE CAN [THAT WE] GUESS	THE RIDDLE WE CAN GUESS	1222	1
WE SPEEDILY DESPISE--	THE RIDDLE WE CAN GUESS	1222	2
WE WILL PRY AND SEE IF SHE IS FAIR	BECAUSE HE LOVES HER	1229	2
THAT WE SO FAR BEHIND--	BECAUSE HE LOVES HER	1229	6
AND THEN I [WE] KNEW 'TWAS WIND--	LIKE RAIN IT SOUNDED	1235	2
WE CLUTCH THE GRACE THE TIGHTER	LIKE TIME'S INSIDIOUS	1236	3
THOUGH [WHILE / BUT] WE RESENT THE CREASE	LIKE TIME'S INSIDIOUS	1236	4
HAD WE THE WINGS	TO FLEE FROM MEMORY	1242	2
WE BOTH AND NEITHER PROVE--	TO PILE LIKE THUNDER TO	1247	6
SILENCE IS ALL WE DREAD.	SILENCE IS ALL WE DREAD.	1251	1

		FIRST LINE	POEM	LINE
WE	(CONTINUED)			
	WE [I] PONDERED WHEN A CHILD,	WHO WERE "THE FATHER AND	1258	2
	WE [I] THOUGHT, AT LEAST THEY ARE NO WORSE	WHO WERE "THE FATHER AND	1258	7
	DID WE [I] DEMAND TODAY	WHO WERE "THE FATHER AND	1258	10
	WHEN WE [I] DESIRED TO KNOW,	WHO WERE "THE FATHER AND	1258	14
	WE BETTER FRIENDS HAD BEEN, PERHAPS,	WHO WERE "THE FATHER AND	1258	15
	WE START--TO LEARN THAT WE BELIEVE	WHO WERE "THE FATHER AND	1258	17
	WE START--TO LEARN THAT WE BELIEVE	WHO WERE "THE FATHER AND	1258	17
	WE BLUSH, THAT HEAVEN IF WE ACHIEVE [BEHOLD]--	WHO WERE "THE FATHER AND	1258	21
	WE BLUSH, THAT HEAVEN IF WE ACHIEVE [BEHOLD]--	WHO WERE "THE FATHER AND	1258	21
	WE SHALL HAVE SHUNNED UNTIL ASHAMED	WHO WERE "THE FATHER AND	1258	23
	WE THINK THAT HE MUST BE	BECAUSE THAT YOU ARE	1260	34
	WE MAY [AND WE] INHALE DESPAIR	A WORD DROPPED CARELESS	1261	6
	WE MAY [AND WE] INHALE DESPAIR	A WORD DROPPED CARELESS	1261	6
	THEY SPEAK OF WHAT WE OWE--	IS HEAVEN A PHYSICIAN?	1270	6
	THAT WHAT WE CHERISHED, SO UNKNOWN [VALUED SO DEVOID / HOARDED . . .	SO PROUD SHE WAS TO DIE	1272	3
	AND YET WE KNEW THAT GENTLE CLOCK	'TWAS LATER WHEN THE	1276	3
	WHILE WE WERE [I WAS] FEARING IT, IT CAME--	WHILE WE WERE FEARING IT	1277	1
	WE FELT HOW NEIGHBORLY A THING	THE MOUNTAINS STOOD IN	1278	11
	HAD WE OUR SENSES	HAD WE OUR SENSES	1284	1
	HAD WE THE EYES WITHIN OUR HEAD [HEADS]--	HAD WE OUR SENSES	1284	5
	HOW WELL THAT [PRUDENT] WE ARE BLIND--	HAD WE OUR SENSES	1284	6
	WE COULD NOT LOOK UPON THE EARTH [WORLD]--	HAD WE OUR SENSES	1284	7
	WHEN WE ADVERTISE EXISTENCE	LAIN IN NATURE--SO	1288	3
	WHILE WE SHREWDLY SPECULATE [SAGE INVESTIGATE / SHREWD INVESTIGATE]	YESTERDAY IS HISTORY,	1292	7
	THE THINGS WE THOUGHT THAT WE SHOULD DO	THE THINGS WE THOUGHT	1293	1
	THE THINGS WE THOUGHT THAT WE SHOULD DO	THE THINGS WE THOUGHT	1293	1
	WE OTHER THINGS HAVE DONE	THE THINGS WE THOUGHT	1293	2
	THE LANDS WE THOUGHT THAT WE SHOULD SEEK	THE THINGS WE THOUGHT	1293	5
	THE LANDS WE THOUGHT THAT WE SHOULD SEEK	THE THINGS WE THOUGHT	1293	5
	THE HEAVEN, IN WHICH WE HOPED TO PAUSE	THE THINGS WE THOUGHT	1293	9
	WE COMMEND OURSELVES TO THEE	RECOLLECT THE FACE OF ME	1305	7
	WE TRUST THAT SHE PARTOOK	ELIZABETH TOLD ESSEX	1321	6
	AND MIGHT WE NOT AS WELL--	OUR LITTLE SECRETS SLINK	1326	4
	"WE DREAMED IT"? SHE INTERROGATES--	THE SYMPTOM OF THE GALE	1327	15
	"GOOD MORNING"--WE PROPOUND?	THE SYMPTOM OF THE GALE	1327	16
	UNKNOWN--FOR ALL THE TIMES WE MET--	WITHOUT A SMILE--WITHOUT	1330	4
	NOT WHEN WE KNOW, THE POWER ACCOSTS--	LET ME NOT MAR THAT	1335	5
	WE AND OUR PLOTTING HEART [GAUDY HEART / SCHEMING TINSEL / . . .	AN ANTIQUATED GRACE	1345	5
	AND YET WE SOONER SAY	AS SUMMER INTO AUTUMN	1346	2
	WE TURN THE SUN [SPELL] AWAY,	AS SUMMER INTO AUTUMN	1346	4
	THE ONE THAT WE HAVE LOVED--	AS SUMMER INTO AUTUMN	1346	8
	SO WE EVADE THE CHARGE OF YEARS	AS SUMMER INTO AUTUMN	1346	9
	NOT ALONE WE FLY--	LIFT IT--WITH THE	1348	2
	WE SPURNED [DISOWNED]--	LUCK IS NOT CHANCE--	1350	7
	I [WE] KEEP ONE RAY	OF THEIR PECULIAR LIGHT	1362	2
	WE KNOW THAT WE ARE WISE--	HOW FITS HIS UMBER COAT	1371	9
	WE KNOW THAT WE ARE WISE--	HOW FITS HIS UMBER COAT	1371	9
	CONVICTED--COULD WE BE	A SAUCER HOLDS A CUP	1374	13
	IS HEARTIER THAN WE--	A SAUCER HOLDS A CUP	1374	16
	POSSESSED [ABHORRED / WE OWNED] BEFORE--	DREAMS ARE THE SUBTLE	1376	6
	WE FEEL A JOY--	IN MANY AND REPORTLESS	1382	2
	PROFANE IT BY A SEARCH [PURSUIT]--WE CANNOT	IN MANY AND REPORTLESS	1382	9
	NOR WE WHO HAVING ONCE INHALED [WAYLAID] IT--	IN MANY AND REPORTLESS	1382	11
	SUMMER--WE ALL HAVE SEEN--	SUMMER--WE ALL HAVE SEEN	1386	1
	TO NATURE WE REMAND THEM	THOSE CATTLE SMALLER	1388	15
	EMBELLISH ALL WE OWN--	HOPE IS A STRANGE	1392	8
	ECLIPSE--WAS ALL WE COULD SEE AT THE WINDOW	IT SOUNDED AS IF THE	1397	3
	AND AWE--WAS ALL WE COULD FEEL.	IT SOUNDED AS IF THE	1397	4
	AS WE [YOU] WHO STAY, SUPPOSE--	PERHAPS THEY DO NOT GO	1399	2
	HOW SHORT WE HAVE TO FEAR	PERHAPS THEY DO NOT GO	1399	6
	WE SAFE [SOFT] COMMIT THEE--	TO THE STANCH DUST	1402	2
	THE THINGS WE DO NOT KNOW--	MARCH IS THE MONTH OF	1404	2
	WE FEEL IT BY THE FLUCTUATION	MARCH IS THE MONTH OF	1404	V 3
	WE TRY TO SHOW BECOMING FIRMNESS [CALMNESS]--	MARCH IS THE MONTH OF	1404	5
	WE SHUN BECAUSE WE PRIZE HER FACE	I SHALL NOT MURMUR IF AT	1410	V
	ALL WE KNOW	OF PARADISE' EXISTENCE	1411	2
	IN WHICH WE WRAP THE SOUL	SHAME IS THE SHAWL OF	1412	2
	WE CHIEFLY HAVE!	UNWORTHY OF HER BREAST	1414	6
	THAT WE DEPLORE PECULIARLY	A WILD BLUE SKY ABREAST	1415	7
	WHERE GO WE--	HOW HUMAN NATURE DOTES	1417	11
	GO WE ANYWHERE	HOW HUMAN NATURE DOTES	1417	12
	WE COMPREHENDED [POSTULATED / RECOLLECTED] BY THE AWE	IT WAS A QUIET SEEMING	1419	10
	WE SHUN BECAUSE WE PRIZE HER FACE	WE SHUN BECAUSE WE PRIZE	1429	1
	WE SHUN BECAUSE WE PRIZE HER FACE	WE SHUN BECAUSE WE PRIZE	1429	1
	KNEW WE OF THEE--	SPURN THE TEMERITY--	1432	4
	NOT THAT HE GOES--WE LOVE HIM MORE	NOT THAT HE GOES--WE	1435	1
	AND VOCAL--WHEN WE DIE--	A COUNTERFEIT--A PLATED	1453	7
	IF THEN WE CANNOT OWN THEM BOTH--	OPINION IS A FLITTING	1455	3
	MORE RESPECTFUL--"WE ARE DUST"--	"HEAVENLY FATHER"--TAKE	1461	6
	WE APOLOGIZE TO THEE	"HEAVENLY FATHER"--TAKE	1461	7
	WE KNEW NOT THAT WE WERE TO LIVE--	WE KNEW NOT THAT WE WERE	1462	1
	WE KNEW NOT THAT WE WERE TO LIVE--	WE KNEW NOT THAT WE WERE	1462	1
	NOR WHEN--WE ARE TO DIE--	WE KNEW NOT THAT WE WERE	1462	2
	WE WEAR MORTALITY	WE KNEW NOT THAT WE WERE	1462	4
	ONE THING OF IT WE [THEE I] BORROW	ONE THING OF IT WE	1464	1

WE (CONTINUED)

	FIRST LINE	POEM	LINE
ONE THING OF IT WE [THEE I] COVET--	ONE THING OF IT WE	1464	5
SO DAZZLING WE MISTAKE HIM	ONE OF THE ONES THAT	1466	7
WE TALKED WITH EACH OTHER ABOUT EACH OTHER	WE TALKED WITH EACH	1473	1
WE WERE LISTENING TO [TOO ENGROSSED WITH] THE SECONDS	WE TALKED WITH EACH	1473	3
ARARATS--WE TOOK--	WE TALKED WITH EACH	1473	8
BUT WE DEMAND [BINDLESS IS] THE FLAME	FAME IS THE ONE THAT	1475	8
WE SHALL FIND THE CUBE OF THE RAINBOW.	WE SHALL FIND THE CUBE	1484	1
BUT WE PRESUME	THE ROAD TO PARADISE IS	1491	4
WE NEVER KNOW--	FACTS BY OUR SIDE ARE	1497	6
SEE HOW WELL WE SPURN HIM--	SUMMER IS SHORTER THAN	1506	6
WE DO NOT MOURN FOR TRAVELER, OR SAILOR,	THE THINGS THAT NEVER	1515	5
NOT SEEING, STILL WE KNOW--	NOT SEEING, STILL WE	1518	1
WE NEVER KNOW WE GO WHEN WE ARE GOING--	WE NEVER KNOW WE GO WHEN	1523	1
WE NEVER KNOW WE GO WHEN WE ARE GOING--	WE NEVER KNOW WE GO WHEN	1523	1
WE NEVER KNOW WE GO WHEN WE ARE GOING--	WE NEVER KNOW WE GO WHEN	1523	1
WE JEST AND SHUT THE DOOR--	WE NEVER KNOW WE GO WHEN	1523	2
AND WE ACCOST NO MORE--[WE KNOW]	WE NEVER KNOW WE GO WHEN	1523	4
AND WE ACCOST NO MORE--[WE KNOW]	WE NEVER KNOW WE GO WHEN	1523	4
AS CONFIDENT OF HIM AS WE--	HE LIVED THE LIFE OF	1525	5
IMPREGNABLE WE ARE--	HE LIVED THE LIFE OF	1525	6
TO THAT PINK STRANGER WE CALL DUST--	OH GIVE IT MOTION--DECK	1527	5
IN WHICH WE EACH WERE CONQUEROR	'TIS SEASONS SINCE THE	1529	2
WITHOUT A FORMULA WE FOUGHT	'TIS SEASONS SINCE THE	1529	7
WHEREVER WE REMOVE--	WHO HAS NOT FOUND THE	1544	4
WE HOVERED BY DESIGN--	MEETING BY ACCIDENT,	1548	2
REBUKE IT IF WE CAN	BLISS IS THE PLAYTHING	1553	4
BUT SIMPLY--WE--OBEYED--	"GO TELL IT"--WHAT A	1554	4
WE WEAR OUR SOBER DRESSES WHEN WE DIE,	WE WEAR OUR SOBER	1572	1
WE WEAR OUR SOBER DRESSES WHEN WE DIE,	WE WEAR OUR SOBER	1572	1
WE DEEM WE DREAM--	TO THE BRIGHT EAST SHE	1573	9
WE DEEM WE DREAM--	TO THE BRIGHT EAST SHE	1573	9
WE SHUN IT ERE IT COMES,	WE SHUN IT ERE IT COMES,	1580	1
FIND ALL THE WITCHCRAFT THAT WE NEED	WITCHCRAFT WAS HUNG, IN	1583	3
WE ALL HAVE FOLLOWED THEE--	EXPANSE CANNOT BE LOST--	1584	12
WE BARRED THE WINDOWS AND THE DOORS	THERE CAME A WIND LIKE A	1593	5
'TIS NOT THE SWAYING FRAME WE MISS,	'TIS NOT THE SWAYING	1597	1
WE CANNOT DOUBT--	THOUGH THE GREAT WATERS	1599	3
OF GOD WE ASK ONE FAVOR,	OF GOD WE ASK ONE FAVOR,	1601	1
THAT WE MAY BE FORGIVEN--	OF GOD WE ASK ONE FAVOR,	1601	2
WE REPRIMAND THE HAPPINESS	OF GOD WE ASK ONE FAVOR,	1601	7
THE GOING FROM A WORLD WE KNOW	THE GOING FROM A WORLD	1603	1
WE SEND THE WAVE TO FIND THE WAVE--	WE SEND THE WAVE TO FIND	1604	1
WE MAKE THE WISE DISTINCTION [SAGE DECISION] STILL,	WE SEND THE WAVE TO FIND	1604	5
EACH THAT WE LOSE TAKES PART OF US;	EACH THAT WE LOSE TAKES	1605	1
ENHANCING WHAT WE SEE	SUNSET THAT SCREENS,	1609	2
THAT WE HAVE NEVER MET,	PARTING WITH THEE	1614	2
AS CONFIDENT OF HIM AS WE--	WHO ABDICATED AMBUSH	1616	5
IMPREGNABLE WE ARE--	WHO ABDICATED AMBUSH	1616	6
WE THIS MOMENT KNEW--	IS IT TOO LATE TO TOUCH	1637	2
THAT WE ARE OF THE SKY	EXTOL THEE--COULD I--	1643	6
WHY SHOULD WE [I] HURRY--WHY INDEED	WHY SHOULD WE HURRY--WHY	1646	1
WHEN EVERY WAY WE FLY	WHY SHOULD WE HURRY--WHY	1646	2
WE ARE MOLESTED EQUALLY	WHY SHOULD WE HURRY--WHY	1646	3
WE BORROWED AT HER GRAVE--	THE IMMORTALITY SHE GAVE	1648	2
WE COULD NOT FIND THE MIGHTY FACE	A CAP OF LEAD ACROSS THE	1649	3
IS BETTER WE CONSIDER	ADVANCE IS LIFE'S	1652	7
AS WE PASS HOUSES MUSING SLOW	AS WE PASS HOUSES MUSING	1653	1
WE ARE ENFORCED TO SAIL	DOWN TIME'S QUAINT	1656	3
WE DWELL IN EVERY DAY	EDEN IS THAT	1657	2
UNTIL WE DRIVE AWAY	EDEN IS THAT	1657	4
WE SAUNTERED FROM THE DOOR	EDEN IS THAT	1657	6
SO SHORT WE HAVE TO GO	I DID NOT REACH THEE	1664	15
TO PLAY TOGETHER WE ARE PRONE	I DID NOT REACH THEE	1664	16
BUT WE MUST LABOR NOW	I DID NOT REACH THEE	1664	17
THAT WE HAVE HAD TO DRAW	I DID NOT REACH THEE	1664	19
WE MUST HAVE PASSED THE MIDDLE SEA	I DID NOT REACH THEE	1664	23
ALMOST WE WISH THE END	I DID NOT REACH THEE	1664	24
WE STEP LIKE PLUSH	I DID NOT REACH THEE	1664	28
WE STAND LIKE SNOW	I DID NOT REACH THEE	1664	29
HOW DEAD WE ARE--	NOT ANY SUNNY TONE	1674	9
WE SAY AS OF A STATION	THE BLUNDER IS IN	1684	3
WHEN WE HAVE CEASED TO CARE	WHEN WE HAVE CEASED TO	1706	1
FOR WHICH WE GAVE THE EARTH	WHEN WE HAVE CEASED TO	1706	3
'TWOULD START US WHERE WE SIT	A PIT--BUT HEAVEN OVER	1712	12
WE SEE ACUTER [DISTINCTER / SINCERER], QUITE,	BY A DEPARTING LIGHT	1714	2
IS SHUNNED, WE MUST ADMIT IT,	DROWNING IS NOT SO	1718	11
THAT WE HAD RATHER NOT WITH HIM	GOD IS INDEED A JEALOUS	1719	3
THAT WE DESIRE WITH OURSELVES	GOD IS INDEED A JEALOUS	1719	V 3
HOW DIFFERENT WE ARE!	HIGH FROM THE EARTH I	1723	20
PARTING IS ALL WE KNOW OF HEAVEN,	MY LIFE CLOSED TWICE	1732	7
AND ALL WE NEED OF HELL.	MY LIFE CLOSED TWICE	1732	8
WE ENVY THE DESPAIR	SOFTENED BY TIME'S	1738	6
UNTIL WE MEET A SNAKE;	SWEET IS THE SWAMP WITH	1740	2
'TIS THEN WE SIGH FOR HOUSES,	SWEET IS THE SWAMP WITH	1740	3
BELIEVING WHAT WE DON'T BELIEVE	THAT IT WILL NEVER COME	1741	3
AND THEN, THAT WE HAVE FOLLOWED THEM,	THE DISTANCE THAT THE	1742	5
WE MORE THAN HALF SUSPECT,	THE DISTANCE THAT THE	1742	6

	FIRST LINE	POEM	LINE
WE (CONTINUED)			
SO INTIMATE HAVE WE BECOME	THE DISTANCE THAT THE	1742	7
NOR SEED THAT WE CAN SOW, ...	THE JOY THAT HAS NO STEM	1744	2
WHILE WE WHO DARE TO LIVE	THIS DOCILE ONE INTER	1752	2
IT MAKES US THINK OF WHAT WE HAD, ...	THE SADDEST NOISE, THE	1764	13
AND WHAT WE NOW DEPLORE.	THE SADDEST NOISE, THE	1764	14
WE ALMOST WISH THOSE SIREN THROATS . . .	THE SADDEST NOISE, THE	1764	15
WE WISH THE EAR HAD NOT A HEART	THE SADDEST NOISE, THE	1764	19
IS ALL WE KNOW OF LOVE;	THAT LOVE IS ALL THERE	1765	2
WE ARE NOT SCOURGED TO SERVE--	HOW FLEET--HOW	1771	4
THE SUMMER THAT WE DID NOT PRIZE, ...	THE SUMMER THAT WE DID	1773	1
WEAK			
HE WAS WEAK, AND I WAS STRONG--THEN-- . .	HE WAS WEAK, AND I WAS	190	1
I WAS WEAK, AND HE WAS STRONG THEN-- . . .	HE WAS WEAK, AND I WAS	190	3
AND TURNS SO WEAK AWAY--	I KNOW SUSPENSE--IT	1285	2
WEAKNESS			
HOW WEAKNESS PASSED--OR FORCE--AROSE-- . .	IF ANY SINK, ASSURE THAT	358	4
NOT TO DISCOVER WEAKNESS IS	NOT TO DISCOVER WEAKNESS	1054	1
WEALTH			
BUT THIS, MUST BE A DIFFERENT WEALTH-- . .	YOUR RICHES--TAUGHT ME--	299	15
LEST SKIES IMPEACH A WEALTH SO WONDERFUL-- .	I'LL CLUTCH--AND CLUTCH	427	23
'TIS BLISS [WEALTH / RIGHT] I CANNOT WEIGH--	IF I MAY HAVE IT, WHEN	577	6
I LOOKED IN WINDOWS, FOR THE WEALTH [THINGS]	I HAD BEEN HUNGRY, ALL	579	7
THE WEALTH MIGHT DISAPPOINT--	I GAVE MYSELF TO HIM--	580	5
THE WEALTH I HAD--CONTENTED ME--	THEIR HIGHT IN HEAVEN	696	9
THE POVERTY THAT WAS NOT WEALTH--	NONE CAN EXPERIENCE	771	7
IT IS THAT POVERTY WAS WEALTH	NONE CAN EXPERIENCE	771	V 7
AND WEALTH--AND COMPANY.	A DOOR JUST OPENED ON A	953	4
GRACE OF WEALTH, AND GRACE OF STATION . .	ALL FORGOT FOR	966	5
DEATH IS THE WEALTH	SANG FROM THE HEART,	1059	7
DEMEANING BY EXCLUSIVE WEALTH	A MINE THERE IS NO MAN	1117	3
WEALTHIER			
BLANKET WEALTHIER THE NEIGHBOR	SNOW BENEATH WHOSE	942	5
WEALTHILY			
ILL IT BECOMETH [IS IT BECOMING] ME TO DWELL SO WEALTHILY	TAKE ALL AWAY FROM ME,	1640	3
WEALTHS			
IN LITTLE WEALTHS, AS GIRLS COULD [CAN] BOAST	YOUR RICHES--TAUGHT ME--	299	3
WEALTHY			
THE WEALTHY [HAPPY] FLY, UPON HIS PANE-- .	I ENVY SEAS, WHEREON HE	498	11
WAS DIM AS TO THE WEALTHY	IT STOLE ALONG SO	1457	3
WEAR			
ANSWER ME TO WEAR?	BEFORE THE ICE IS IN THE	37	16
I HAD RATHER WEAR HER GRACE	PIGMY SERAPHS--GONE	138	12
THO' SHE WEAR A SILVER APRON--	THO' MY DESTINY BE	163	3
NEVER A THIMBLE--MORE--SHALL WEAR-- . . .	HOW MANY TIMES THESE LOW	187	8
DO THEY WEAR "NEW SHOES"--IN "EDEN"-- . .	WHAT IS--"PARADISE"--	215	7
AND WEAR--IF GOD SHOULD COUNT ME FIT-- . .	A SOLEMN THING--IT WAS--	271	3
I JUST WEAR MY WINGS--	SOME KEEP THE SABBATH	324	6
WEAR NOTHING COMMONER THAN SNOW--	OF TRIBULATION--THESE	325	7
FOR FOREHEAD LOW AS MINE, TO WEAR, . . .	ALTHOUGH I PUT AWAY HIS	366	3
RUSTICS--WEAR--	I'M SAYING EVERY DAY	373	31
MURDER--WEAR!	IT DONT SOUND SO	426	17
WEAR YOU ON HEM--	I'LL CLUTCH--AND CLUTCH	427	9
THE FROCK I USED TO WEAR--	IT WOULD NEVER BE COMMON	430	31
FOR ME--MY SOUL--TO WEAR--	I AM ASHAMED--I HIDE--	473	12
TO WEAR THAT PERFECT--PEARL--	THE WORLD--STANDS--	493	6
THE FASHION OF THE GOWN I WEAR--	PRECIOUS TO ME--SHE	727	3
IN USING, WEAR AWAY, ...	SHE ROSE TO HIS	732	8
YOU, UNSUSPECTING, FEEL FOR ME [WEAR ME TOO]--	I HIDE MYSELF WITHIN MY	903	3
A SUMMER FURTHER I MUST WEAR, ...	HER LITTLE PARASOL TO	1038	5
DEMEANS [DEGRADES] THE DRESS I WEAR-- . .	MY COCOON TIGHTENS--	1099	4
FROM FEATURES OTHERS WEAR.	BECAUSE HE LOVES HER	1229	4
IT'S FOND SUBJECTION WEAR--	WARM IN HER HAND THESE	1313	4
THOSE IT FITS, TOO FAIR TO WEAR IT--	"FAITHFUL TO THE END"	1357	V
AND THOUGH IT DO NOT WEAR	TO MEND EACH TATTERED	1442	5
WE WEAR MORTALITY	WE KNEW NOT THAT WE WERE	1462	4
WE WEAR OUR SOBER DRESSES WHEN WE DIE, . .	WE WEAR OUR SOBER	1572	1
FOR I WEAR THE "THORNS" TILL SUNSET-- . .	REARRANGE A "WIFE'S"	1737	15
WEARIED			
. . . WEARIED--] BREATH--DID NOT--	THREE TIMES--WE PARTED--	598	13
I WEARIED--TOO--OF MINE--	OURSELVES WERE WED ONE	631	4
WEARIEST			
HIS WEARIEST COMMANDMENT--	ALTHOUGH I PUT AWAY HIS	366	17
WEARINESS			
WITHOUT THE WEARINESS--	TO DIE--TAKES JUST A	255	12
WEARINESS OF HIM, WERE QUAINTER	CONSCIOUS AM I IN MY	679	13
WEARING			
WEARING THE SOD GOWN--	DROPPED INTO THE ETHER	665	2
THAT WEARING ON YOUR BREAST--	I HIDE MYSELF WITHIN MY	903	V 2
IS TERRIBLER THAN WEARING IT	WHILE WE WERE FEARING IT	1277	11
YET NEVER WEARING OUT--	HOPE IS A STRANGE	1392	4
WEARS			
THE MAPLE WEARS A GAYER SCARF--	THE MORNS ARE MEEKER	12	5
IT WEARS A SPRIG UPON IT'S BREAST--	THERE'S SOMETHING	45	3
BUT THIS ONE, WEARS IT'S MERRIMENT . . .	A HAPPY LIP--BREAKS	353	5
THE BLACK BERRY--WEARS A THORN IN HIS SIDE--	THE BLACK BERRY--WEARS A	554	1
THE TATTERS THAT HE WEARS--	TO TRY TO SPEAK, AND	1617	4
AND WEARS A PROPER COAT	THE BUTTERFLY OBTAINS	1685	6

	FIRST LINE	POEM	LINE
WEARY			
OUR FATHERS BEING WEARY,	"SIC TRANSIT GLORIA	3	45
WEARY FOR MY----	DISTRUSTFUL OF THE	20	5
WHO NEVER CLIMBED THE WEARY LEAGUE--	WHO NEVER LOST, ARE	73	5
PERHAPS, WEARY [TIRED] AND SORE--	HEART, NOT SO HEAVY AS	83	18
NEW WEARY SLEEP BELOW--	NEW FEET WITHIN MY	99	6
THAT, WEARY OF THIS BEGGAR'S FACE--	IF I COULD BRIBE THEM BY	179	17
HE--DOES'NT WEARY--	JUST SO--JESUS--RAPS--	317	2
CHILLED--OR WEARY--	JUST SO--JESUS--RAPS--	317	8
SLOW--SLOW--AS FEET DID WEARY--GROW--	'TWAS THE OLD--ROAD--	344	10
YOUR SERVANT, SIR, WILL WEARY--	ALTHOUGH I PUT AWAY HIS	366	22
WHO WEARY OF THE DAY--	THE MONTHS HAVE ENDS--	423	10
I CROSS TILL I AM WEARY	I CROSS TILL I AM WEARY	550	1
WEARY! FURLOUGHS OF DOWN!	WOULD YOU LIKE SUMMER?	691	4
WISER MEN [ONE / EAR] MAY WEARY--	NEVER FOR SOCIETY	746	5
I STROVE TO WEARY BRAIN AND BONE--	SEVERER SERVICE OF	786	9
AS WILLING LID O'ER WEARY EYE	AS WILLING LID O'ER	1050	1
TILL THE DAY ITS WEARY KEEPER	REARRANGE A "WIFE'S"	1737	19
WEATHER			
THE WEATHER--HOW THE RAINS	MYSELF CAN READ THE	1089	5
A LITTLE WEATHER WORN	BEFORE YOU THOUGHT OF	1465	6
WEAVER			
TELL ME WHAT TIME THE WEAVER SLEEPS	BRING ME THE SUNSET IN A	128	5
WHO IS TO BLAME? THE WEAVER?	A SHADY FRIEND--FOR	278	9
WEAVES			
THE GENTIAN WEAVES HER FRINGES--	THE GENTIAN WEAVES HER	18	1
WEB			
THE WEB OF LIFE WOVEN--	BY SUCH AND SUCH AN	38	3
WE'D			
WHO KNOWS--BUT WE'D REACH THE SUN?	LOVE--THOU ART HIGH--	453	12
WED			
I--NEVER WED--	WE--BEE AND I--LIVE BY	230	9
SINCE I WAS WED--TO HIM--	THE WORLD--STANDS--	493	2
OURSELVES WERE WED ONE SUMMER--DEAR--	OURSELVES WERE WED ONE	631	1
AND YET, ONE SUMMER, WE WERE QUEENS [WED]--	OURSELVES WERE WED ONE	631	15
THE LILY--WAITING TO BE WED--	'TIS SUNRISE--LITTLE	908	7
WEDDING			
AND THEY MAKE MERRY WEDDING, WHOSE GUESTS ARE HUNDRED LEAVES;	AWAKE YE MUSES NINE,	1	14
WEDGE			
AND WEDGE CANNOT DIVIDE	ON A COLUMNAR SELF--	789	6
WEDGED			
I THOUGHT JUST HOW RED--APPLES WEDGED	'TWAS JUST THIS TIME,	445	9
OURSELVES WE WEDGED	THE FROST OF DEATH WAS	1136	10
WEDLOCK			
NO WEDLOCK--GRANTED ME--	I LIVE WITH HIM--I SEE	463	8
WEDLOCK OF WILL, DECAY--	GIVEN IN MARRIAGE UNTO	817	6
WEDNESDAY			
BRIGHT WEDNESDAY AFTERNOONS--	I NEVER FELT AT HOME--	413	8
SOME WEDNESDAY AFTERNOON.	DEW--IS THE FRESHET IN	1097	12
WEED			
ALL INTERSPERSED WITH WEED,	ALL OVERGROWN BY CUNNING	148	2
DEVELOPE PEARL, AND WEED,	SHE ROSE TO HIS	732	10
A WEED OF SUMMER CAME--	TO HER DERIDED HOME	1586	2
WEEDS			
WEEDS TRIUMPHANT RANGED	AFTER A HUNDRED YEARS	1147	5
WEEK			
VALENTINE WEEK	AWAKE YE MUSES NINE,	1	T
THE FROGS GOT HOME LAST WEEK--	BEE! I'M EXPECTING YOU!	1035	5
WEEKS			
THREE WEEKS PASSED SINCE I HAD SEEN HER--	THREE WEEKS PASSED SINCE	1061	1
WEEP			
I WOULD NOT WEEP IF I WERE THEY--	THERE'S SOMETHING	45	9
IT'S SUCH A LITTLE THING TO WEEP--	IT'S SUCH A LITTLE THING	189	1
TILL I STIR [GROPE / START], AND WEEP--	MANY A PHRASE HAS THE	276	12
ELATE US--TILL WE ALMOST WEEP--	LIKE SOME OLD FASHIONED	302	11
SHE'S TEARFUL--IF SHE WEEP AT ALL--	SHE'S HAPPY, WITH A NEW	535	5
'TIS OURS--TO WINCE--AND WEEP--	HE GAVE AWAY HIS LIFE--	567	9
I COULD'NT WEEP--FOR SO MANY SMILING	TRUDGING TO EDEN,	1020	7
WEEPING			
TO WIPE MY WEEPING E'E.	"SIC TRANSIT GLORIA	3	60
WEIGH			
I THINK JUST HOW MY LIPS WILL WEIGH--	I THINK JUST HOW MY	237	5
WEIGH, HELPLESS, IN HIS PAWS--	'TWAS LIKE A MAELSTROM,	414	13
THAT ANCHORED THERE--I WEIGH	I TIE MY HAT--I CREASE	443	8
'TIS BLISS [WEALTH / RIGHT] I CANNOT WEIGH--	IF I MAY HAVE IT, WHEN	577	6
BEFORE HE COMES WE WEIGH THE TIME!	BEFORE HE COMES WE WEIGH	834	1
WEIGHED			
THE THIMBLE WEIGHED TOO HEAVY--	DEATH SETS A THING	360	9
THE HEAVENS WEIGHED THE MOST--BY FAR [WERE THE WEIGHTIEST--FAR]--	IT TROUBLED ME AS ONCE I	600	5
THEY WEIGHED ME, DUST BY DUST--	I TOOK ONE DRAUGHT OF	1725	5
WEIGHETH			
BUT HE WHO WEIGHETH--WHILE THE REST--	I FEAR A MAN OF FRUGAL	543	5
WEIGHS			
I WONDER IF IT WEIGHS LIKE MINE--	I MEASURE EVERY GRIEF I	561	3
WEIGHT			
A WEIGHT WITH NEEDLES ON THE POUNDS--	A WEIGHT WITH NEEDLES ON	264	1
HER SWEET WEIGHT ON MY HEART A NIGHT	HER SWEET WEIGHT ON MY	518	1
'TWAS LOWERED, LIKE A WEIGHT [FREIGHT]--	'TWAS WARM--AT FIRST--	519	14

	FIRST LINE	POEM	LINE
WEIGHT (CONTINUED)			
THE BRAIN IS JUST THE WEIGHT OF GOD--	THE BRAIN--IS WIDER THAN	632	9
A HONEY'S WEIGHT [WORTH]	LEAST BEE THAT BREW--	676	2
HAD WE KNOWN THE TON [WEIGHT / LOAD] SHE BORE	HAD WE KNOWN THE TON SHE	1124	1
'TWOULD CRUMBLE WITH THE WEIGHT.	COULD MORTAL LIP DIVINE	1409	4
OR TOO MUCH WEIGHT TO FLY--	TOO HAPPY TIME DISSOLVES	1774	4
WEIGHTIEST			
THE HEAVENS WEIGHED THE MOST--BY FAR [WERE THE WEIGHTIEST--FAR]--	IT TROUBLED ME AS ONCE I	600	5
WEIGHTS			
TILL WEIGHTS--WILL HANG--	I CAN WADE GRIEF--	252	12
WITH HUNDRED WEIGHTS--TO SPARE--	RISK IS THE HAIR THAT	1239	4
WELCOME			
BLUE SEA! WILT WELCOME ME?	MY RIVER RUNS TO THEE--	162	2
WHO DRILLS [NAILS] HIS WELCOME IN--	THAT AFTER HORROR--THAT	286	16
THE SOUNDS OF WELCOME--THERE!	ME--COME! MY DAZZLED	431	4
BUT WELCOME WHEN HE GOES.	WINTER IS GOOD--HIS HOAR	1316	8
FOR SERVICE [HONOR / WELCOME] OR FOR GLEE--	A CHILLY PEACE INFESTS	1443	6
WELCOMES			
THE HORROR WELCOMES HER, AGAIN,	THE SOUL HAS BANDAGED	512	23
WELD			
IF I WELD THE RIVET FASTER--	BY A FLOWER--BY A LETTER	109	3
WE'LL			
AFTER A LIFE--A DEATH--WE'LL SAY--	IF I MAY HAVE IT, WHEN	577	11
WE'LL PASS WITHOUT THE PARTING	WE'LL PASS WITHOUT THE	996	1
WELL			
I RECOLLECT IT WELL!	WENT UP A YEAR THIS	93	2
FLOWERS--WELL--IF ANYBODY	FLOWERS--WELL--IF	137	1
A FURTIVE LOOK YOU KNOW AS WELL--	AN ALTERED LOOK ABOUT	140	14
IT IS JUST AS WELL!	IF THE FOOLISH, CALL	168	4
WILL SUIT ME JUST AS WELL--	I CAME TO BUY A SMILE--	223	4
SOBBING--WILL SUIT--AS WELL AS PSALM!	PUT UP MY LUTE!	261	5
INTO THE MYSTIC [PURPLE] WELL--	A SOLEMN THING--IT WAS--	271	6
I SIMULATE THE BREATH, SO WELL--	I BREATHED ENOUGH TO	272	3
I LIKED AS WELL TO SEE--	BEFORE I GOT MY EYE PUT	327	2
AS WELL AS OUR OLD HOME!"	I FELT MY LIFE WITH BOTH	351	16
AS WELL THE SKY	I GAINED IT SO--	359	6
DREAMS--ARE WELL--BUT WAKING'S BETTER,	DREAMS--ARE WELL--BUT	450	1
SO WELL THAT I CAN LIVE WITHOUT--	SO WELL THAT I CAN LIVE	456	1
I LOVE THEE--THEN HOW WELL IS THAT?	SO WELL THAT I CAN LIVE	456	2
AS WELL AS JESUS?	SO WELL THAT I CAN LIVE	456	3
I THINK A LITTLE WELL--LIKE MINE--	I KNOW WHERE WELLS GROW	460	19
OUR SOULS SAW--JUST AS WELL--	THEY PUT US FAR APART--	474	12
TO LEAD HIM TO THE WELL	TO ONE DENIED TO DRINK	490	5
MY FIRST WELL DAY--SINCE MANY ILL--	MY FIRST WELL DAY--SINCE	574	1
ILL FLUTTERED OUT--IN EVERLASTING WELL--	TO KNOW JUST HOW HE	622	17
'TIS GOOD [WELL]--THE LOOKING BACK ON GRIEF--	'TIS GOOD--THE LOOKING	660	1
HOW WELL I KNEW THE LIGHT BEFORE--	THE SUN KEPT SETTING--	692	13
I SHUT MY EYES--AND GROPED AS WELL	FROM BLANK TO BLANK--	761	9
WELL ENOUGH FOR SCHOOLS--	ONE AND ONE--ARE ONE--	769	3
ENLIGHTENING SO WELL--	I PLAY AT RICHES--TO	801	22
YET BOTH SO WELL KNEW ME	NATURE AND GOD--I	835	2
HOW WELL I KNEW HER NOT	HOW WELL I KNEW HER NOT	837	1
SUPERSTITION HELPS, AS WELL AS LOVE--	ABSENCE DISEMBODIES--SO	860	3
'TIS WELL THE NAME AND AGE	WHO OCCUPIES THIS HOUSE?	892	4
I RECOLLECT IT--AS WELL--	THE FIRST DAY THAT I WAS	902	4
WHAT DEATH--KNOWS SO WELL--	COLOR--CASTE--	970	14
THE WELL UPON THE BROOK	THE WELL UPON THE BROOK	1091	1
THE SMALL MUST [DO] DIE, THE SAME [AS WELL] AS HE--	THAT THIS SHOULD FEEL	1112	6
NATURE KNOWS AS WELL	HER SOVREIGN PEOPLE	1139	2
THAT SORT ACCOMPLISH WELL--	'TWAS FIGHTING FOR HIS	1188	2
'TIS WELL TO HOARD ANEW--	OUR OWN POSSESSIONS--	1208	2
AND WILL AT HOME AND WELL	A DEED KNOCKS FIRST AT	1216	4
BELIEF, IT DOES NOT FIT SO WELL	WHO WERE "THE FATHER AND	1258	19
BUT A CONFIDING GUEST CONSULT AS WELL,	I CANNOT SEE MY SOUL BUT	1262	4
BUT [THO'] PERHAPS 'TIS WELL THEY'RE NOT AT HOME	HAD WE OUR SENSES	1284	2
HOW WELL THAT [PRUDENT] WE ARE BLIND--	HAD WE OUR SENSES	1284	6
DID YOU LEAVE NATURE WELL--	DEAR MARCH--COME IN--	1320	8
DOES NOT LOOK AS WELL--	FLOSS WONT SAVE YOU FROM	1322	V 4
AND EVERY STOP A WELL--	FLOSS WONT SAVE YOU FROM	1322	6
AND MIGHT WE NOT AS WELL--	OUR LITTLE SECRETS SLINK	1326	4
AS WELL AS [BETTER THAN] PRIME	AN ANTIQUATED GRACE	1345	3
WHAT MYSTERY PERVADES A WELL!	WHAT MYSTERY PERVADES A	1400	1
SEE HOW WELL WE SPURN HIM--	SUMMER IS SHORTER THAN	1506	6
WHOSE CORPORATION [UNSUSPECTING / WELL INTENTIONED] COAT	AN ANTIQUATED TREE	1514	5
THE WELL IN WHICH THEY LAY US	OF DEATH I TRY TO THINK	1558	2
OUR NOON BECAME A WELL	A CAP OF LEAD ACROSS THE	1649	6
HE RECOLLECTS IT WELL.	ONE CROWN THAT NO ONE	1735	8
WELLS			
AND LILY TUBES--LIKE WELLS--	WHAT WOULD I GIVE TO SEE	247	10
I KNOW WHERE WELLS GROW--DROUGHTLESS WELLS--	I KNOW WHERE WELLS GROW	460	1
I KNOW WHERE WELLS GROW--DROUGHTLESS WELLS--	I KNOW WHERE WELLS GROW	460	1
THE WELLS HAVE BUCKETS TO THEM THERE--	I KNOW WHERE WELLS GROW	460	15
BUT WELLS--OF FAILLESS GROUND!	THE WELL UPON THE BROOK	1091	4
IT FILLED THE WELLS, IT PLEASED THE POOLS	LIKE RAIN IT SOUNDED	1235	9
WENDING			
WENDING LATE HOME--	HEART, NOT SO HEAVY AS	83	2

	FIRST LINE	POEM	LINE
WENDS			
TO THE SAME PAGEANT WENDS ITS WAY	NO LIFE CAN POMPLESS	1626	3
WENT			
WHETHER MY BARK WENT DOWN AT SEA-- . . .	WHETHER MY BARK WENT	52	1
WENT UP A YEAR THIS EVENING!	WENT UP A YEAR THIS	93	1
WENT HOME A CENTURY AGO	WHERE I HAVE LOST, I	104	15
BLESS GOD, HE WENT AS SOLDIERS, ...	BLESS GOD, HE WENT AS	147	1
SHE WENT AS QUIET AS THE DEW	SHE WENT AS QUIET AS THE	149	1
I WENT ONE WINTER MORNING	I CAUTIOUS, SCANNED MY	178	7
WENT WANDERING DOWN THE LATITUDES	AS IF SOME LITTLE ARCTIC	180	3
'TWAS'NT DARK--FOR HE WENT--TOO--	HE WAS WEAK, AND I WAS	190	6
IT LISTENING--LISTENING--WENT TO SLEEP-- .	I SHOULD NOT DARE TO	205	11
YET--STRANGEST--HEAVIER SINCE IT WENT-- . .	SAVIOR! I'VE NO ONE ELSE	217	11
WHO WENT TOO NEAR	A BURDOCK--CLAWED MY	229	4
AND WENT TO SLEEP--	I HELD A JEWEL IN MY	245	2
AND SHAME [SCORN] WENT STILL [DUMB]-- . .	UNTO LIKE STORY--TROUBLE	295	8
WHEN SPEECH WENT NUMB--	UNTO LIKE STORY--TROUBLE	295	20
THE SUN, AS COMMON, WENT ABROAD, ...	THERE CAME A DAY AT	322	5
I WENT TO THANK HER--	I WENT TO THANK HER--	363	1
WHO WENT TO THANK HER--	I WENT TO THANK HER--	363	6
I WENT TO HEAVEN--	I WENT TO HEAVEN--	374	1
WENT OUT UPON CIRCUMFERENCE--	I SAW NO WAY--THE	378	7
MORE LIFE--WENT OUT--WHEN HE WENT	MORE LIFE--WENT OUT--	422	1
MORE LIFE--WENT OUT--WHEN HE WENT	MORE LIFE--WENT OUT--	422	1
I WENT TO SCHOOL	KNOWS HOW TO FORGET!	433	V
WHILE OTHER--WENT THE SEA TO FILL-- . . .	FORGET! THE LADY WITH	438	14
AND OTHER--WENT TO TURN THE MILL-- . . .	FORGET! THE LADY WITH	438	15
WHEN RICHARD WENT TO MILL--	'TWAS JUST THIS TIME,	445	6
AND CARTS WENT STOOPING ROUND THE FIELDS .	'TWAS JUST THIS TIME,	445	11
WENT PAST MY SIMPLE SHOE--	I STARTED EARLY--TOOK MY	520	10
TWO BUTTERFLIES WENT OUT AT NOON-- . . .	TWO BUTTERFLIES WENT OUT	533	1
AND WENT AGAINST THE WORLD--	I TOOK MY POWER IN MY	540	2
A'BLOSSOM JUST WHEN I WENT IN	MY FIRST WELL DAY--SINCE	574	5
EVER WENT BY ONE--	INCONCEIVABLY SOLEMN!	582	10
NO SQUIRREL WENT ABROAD--	THE NIGHT WAS WIDE, AND	589	9
WENT UP FROM THE POTOMAC--	WHEN I WAS SMALL, A	596	3
AND HE PASSED [WENT] QUICKLY [SOFTLY] ROUND--	WHEN I WAS SMALL, A	596	8
FOR RECOLLECTING SUCH AS WENT--	YOU'LL FIND--IT WHEN YOU	610	3
A THOUGHT WENT UP MY MIND TODAY--	A THOUGHT WENT UP MY	701	1
NOR WHERE IT WENT--NOR WHY IT CAME . . .	A THOUGHT WENT UP MY	701	5
AND SO AROUND THE WORDS I WENT--	IF HE WERE LIVING--DARE	734	3
BIRD WENT PRAISING EVERYWHERE--	WHEN I HOPED, I	768	15
BEREAVED OF ALL, I WENT ABROAD--	BEREAVED OF ALL, I WENT	784	1
A FEW WENT OUT TO HELP THE BROOK	A DROP FELL ON THE APPLE	794	5
THAT [WHO] WENT TO HELP THE SEA--	A DROP FELL ON THE APPLE	794	6
TO SHUT THE DOOR AND IT WENT OUT	I CANNOT BUY IT--'TIS	840	5
THE TALELESS DAYS WENT ON	TWO TRAVELLERS PERISHING	933	12
I NOTWITHSTANDING WENT [STOLE] ABOUT . . .	A LOSS OF SOMETHING EVER	959	6
PASSED [WENT] INFINITE BY ME--	IT BLOOMED AND DROPT, A	978	20
AND TIME WENT OUT TO TELL THE NEWS . . .	I HEARD, AS IF I HAD NO	1039	15
THE SUN WENT DOWN--NO MAN LOOKED ON-- . .	THE SUN WENT DOWN--NO	1079	1
HE TRIUMPHED, AND WENT ON--	THE SUN WENT DOWN--NO	1079	4
THE SUN WENT UP--NO MAN LOOKED ON-- . . .	THE SUN WENT DOWN--NO	1079	5
AS WE WENT OUT AND IN	THE LAST NIGHT THAT SHE	1100	9
WE WENT AND PLAYED AND CAME AGAIN	THIS SLOW DAY MOVED	1120	7
HIS FADED LAMP WENT OUT.	THAT ODD OLD MAN IS DEAD	1130	4
THE WIND--UNTO HIS [IT'S] CHAMBERS WENT . .	THE WIND TOOK UP THE	1134	9
HOW WENT THE AGILE KERNEL OUT	TOO COLD IS THIS	1135	6
THE WINDS WENT OUT THEIR MARTIAL WAYS . .	THE DAY GREW SMALL,	1140	5
THE WORK OF HER THAT WENT, ...	THE WORK OF HER THAT	1143	1
BUT WHEN THEY WENT TO TAKE THEM OUT . . .	OF PAUL AND SILAS IT IS	1166	3
WENT TO HEAVEN PERHAPS AT DEATH	SO I PULL MY STOCKINGS	1201	5
BOTH WENT TO SEE--	THE SHOW IS NOT THE SHOW	1206	6
'TWAS LATER WHEN THE SUMMER WENT	'TWAS LATER WHEN THE	1276	1
'TWAS SOONER WHEN THE CRICKET WENT . . .	'TWAS LATER WHEN THE	1276	5
AND WENT OR WAITED AS THEY LIKED	THE MOUNTAINS STOOD IN	1278	3
WHICH NEVER WENT AWAY?	THE INFINITE A SUDDEN	1309	4
THE SUN WENT OUT TO WORK--	A DEW SUFFICED ITSELF--	1437	5
THE DAY WENT OUT TO PLAY	A DEW SUFFICED ITSELF--	1437	6
AND WENT THE WAY OF DUSK	HE LIVED THE LIFE OF	1525	2
AS IF A DRUM [THE DRUMS] WENT ON AND ON . .	A PANG IS MORE	1530	V
KNEW WHERE THEY WENT--	THOSE--DYING THEN,	1551	2
THEY WENT TO GOD'S RIGHT HAND--	THOSE--DYING THEN,	1551	3
AND WENT THE WAY OF DUSK, ...	WHO ABDICATED AMBUSH	1616	2
HE WENT BY SLEEP THAT DROWSY ROUTE . . .	HE WENT BY SLEEP THAT	1662	1
AND WENT ALONG.	IN WINTER IN MY ROOM	1670	9
WHO SINCE THEY WENT TO THEIR ACCOUNT . . .	HOW DARE THE ROBINS SING	1724	3
OR THAT THAT WENT TO SLEEP	WHICH MISSES MOST,	1759	8
A TRAIN WENT THROUGH A BURIAL GATE, ...	A TRAIN WENT THROUGH A	1761	1
WEPT			
WILL THE FROCK I WEPT IN	BEFORE THE ICE IS IN THE	37	15
WE'RE			
OF WHOM WE'RE WHISPERING HERE?	SHE BORE IT TILL THE	144	16
WONT THEY SCOLD US--WHEN WE'RE HUNGRY [HOMESICK]--	WHAT IS--"PARADISE"--	215	9
BECAUSE, WE'RE ORCHARD SPRUNG--	THE ROBIN'S MY CRITERION	285	7
WE'RE FEARING THAT THEIR HEARTS WILL DROP--	WE DO NOT PLAY ON GRAVES	467	7
AND SINCE WE'RE MUTUAL MONARCH	ME FROM MYSELF--TO	642	9
I'M KNEELING--[WE'RE PLEADING] STILL-- . .	AH, TENERIFFE!	666	10

	FIRST LINE	POEM	LINE
WEST			
IN THE PEACEFUL [SILENT] WEST	ON THIS WONDROUS SEA	4	7
FLOWED SILVER TO THE WEST--	A POOR--TORN HEART-- A	78	4
ENAMORED OF THE PARTING WEST--	THE DAISY FOLLOWS SOFT	106	10
AS AN EVENING WEST,	PORTRAITS ARE TO DAILY	170	2
OH HOUSEWIFE IN THE EVENING WEST--	SHE SWEEPS WITH	219	3
TO TAKE MY RANK--BY--IN THE WEST--	THE FACE I CARRY WITH ME	336	3
IT HINDER FROM THE WEST	I CROSS TILL I AM WEARY	550	11
RETURNING TO THE WEST--	"HEAVEN" HAS DIFFERENT	575	14
DID PLACE ABOUT THE WEST--TONIGHT--	WHOLE GULFS--OF RED, AND	658	3
FAR AS SOUTH AND WEST--EXPANDING [DISCLOSING]--	BLOOM UPON THE MOUNTAIN	667	15
AND TINTS THE TRANSIT IN THE WEST	THE LOVE A LIFE CAN SHOW	673	11
BEFORE THE WEST BEGIN--	BEHIND ME--DIPS ETERNITY	721	6
IS THAT GREAT WATER IN THE WEST--	WE THIRST AT FIRST--'TIS	726	7
AT A WINDOW [IN A CHAMBER] FACING WEST--	WHEN I HOPED, I	768	3
ENTIRELY THE WEST	WHEN ONE HAS GIVEN UP	853	4
HIS EYE, IT IS THE EAST AND WEST--	THE SUN AND MOON MUST	871	5
RALLIES HER GLOW [THE WEST], LIKE A DYING FRIEND--	FAIRER THROUGH FADING--	938	5
WHO IS THE WEST?	WHO IS THE EAST?	1032	5
RESITUATED IN THE WEST	SAID DEATH TO PASSION	1033	8
THEN GAVE [BENT / BOWED] THE EAST UNTO THE WEST	THE WIND TOOK UP THE	1134	3
OF ONE COROLLA IS THE WEST--	THE LILAC IS AN ANCIENT	1241	9
THE WEST A LITTLE WORN--	THE STARS ARE OLD, THAT	1249	2
THESE HELD THEIR WICK ABOVE THE WEST--	THESE HELD THEIR WICK	1390	1
IN HUMAN NATURE'S WEST--	LOOK BACK ON TIME, WITH	1478	4
THE SUN IN REINING TO THE WEST	THE SUN IN REINING TO	1636	1
I HAVE A NAVY IN THE WEST	"RED SEA," INDEED! TALK	1642	3
IN THAT LOW SUMMER OF THE WEST	A LANE OF YELLOW LED THE	1650	7
WESTERLY			
GONE WESTERLY, TODAY--	THE SUNSET STOPPED ON	950	4
WESTERN			
THESE--ARE THE WESTERN MYSTERY!	THIS--IS THE LAND--THE	266	4
WEST-INDIAN			
AS WEST-INDIAN--	EXCEPT THE SMALLER SIZE	1067	V
WESTMINSTER			
AND LOWER LAY IN LOW WESTMINSTER	SHE ROSE AS HIGH AS HIS	1011	3
WESTS			
WITHDREW THE SUN--TO OTHER WESTS--	I COULD SUFFICE FOR HIM,	643	9
WESTWARD			
TO WESTWARD [UPPER] OF THE TOWN--	IT WAS A QUIET SEEMING	1419	6
WET			
IT WALKED AS WET AS ANY WAVE	LIKE RAIN IT SOUNDED	1235	3
WE'VE			
THAT WE'VE IMMORTAL PLACE	IT IS AN HONORABLE	946	5
WHARF			
AND THEN--THE WHARF IS STILL!	WHERE SHIPS OF PURPLE--	265	4
IF WRECKED UPON THE SHOAL [WHARF / CAPE / DOCK / BAY] OF THOUGHT	IF WRECKED UPON THE	1469	1
WHATEVER			
WHATEVER PRANK BETIDES!	"ARCTURUS" IS HIS OTHER	70	25
ME PROVE IT NOW--WHOEVER [WHATEVER] DOUBT	ME PROVE IT NOW--WHOEVER	537	1
THAN WHATEVER BROW	HER SWEET TURN TO LEAVE	649	14
WHATEVER IT IS [BE]--SHE HAS TRIED IT--	WHATEVER IT IS--SHE HAS	1204	1
ALIEN AND VAIN WHATEVER CLIME	FRIGID AND SWEET HER	1318	3
ACRID WHATEVER FATE.	FRIGID AND SWEET HER	1318	4
WHATEVER REALM I FORFEIT, LORD,	TO OWN A SUSAN OF MY OWN	1401	3
WHATEVER STRATA OF INIQUITY	A COUNTERFEIT--A PLATED	1453	3
WHATEVER FLOWER FAIL TO COME	NATURE CAN DO NO MORE	1673	3
WHATSOEVER			
AND WHATSOEVER INSECT PASS--	THERE IS A FLOWER THAT	380	5
AND WHATSOEVER MOUTH HE KISSED--	A VISITOR IN MARL--	391	11
THAT "WHATSOEVER YE SHALL ASK--	I MEANT TO HAVE BUT	476	23
IN WHATSOEVER PRESENCE MAKES	THE LUXURY TO APPREHEND	815	5
FROM WHATSOEVER SEA--	A CHILLY PEACE INFESTS	1443	8
HIMSELF--AT WHATSOEVER FATHOM	THE THINGS THAT NEVER	1515	12
IN WHATSOEVER REALM--	OBTAINING BUT OUR OWN	1543	2
AND WHATSOEVER IS CONSUMED	HOPE IS A SUBTLE GLUTTON	1547	7
IN WHATSOEVER HELL	ONE CROWN THAT NO ONE	1735	6
WHEAT			
I WORKED FOR CHAFF AND EARNING WHEAT	I WORKED FOR CHAFF AND	1269	1
I TASTED WHEAT AND HATED CHAFF	I WORKED FOR CHAFF AND	1269	5
WHEEL			
MY WHEEL IS IN THE DARK!	MY WHEEL IS IN THE DARK!	10	1
WHEEL SOLEMNLY [POMPOUSLY] AWAY!	PAPA ABOVE!	61	9
AND THE CYCLES WHEEL!	JUST LOST, WHEN I WAS	160	19
KEPT NARROWING IT'S BOILING WHEEL	'TWAS LIKE A MAELSTROM,	414	3
THAT REGULATES THE WHEEL--	THE OUTER--FROM THE	451	6
UPON A SINGLE WHEEL--	WITHIN MY GARDEN, RIDES	500	2
MY FAITH MUST TAKE THE PURPLE WHEEL	MY FAITH IS LARGER THAN	766	3
WITH WHICH WE HELP THE WHEEL	IDEALS ARE THE FAIRY OIL	983	2
UPON A WHEEL OF CLOUD.	LIKE RAIN IT SOUNDED	1235	16
WAS INNOCENT [IGNORANT / NOT ENFORCED / UNENFORCED] OF WHEEL	ELIJAH'S WAGON KNEW NO	1254	2
. . . RENEWING] WHEEL--	A ROUTE OF EVANESCENCE	1463	2
WHEELING			
MEANWHILE--HER WHEELING KING--	THE SUN--JUST TOUCHED	232	8

	FIRST LINE	POEM	LINE
WHILE (CONTINUED)			
BUT [WHILE] THIS--IN LADY'S DRAWER	ESSENTIAL OILS--ARE	675	6
WHILE NATURE	RESTS AT NIGHT	714	5
WHILE SHE CREATES AND FEDERATES	THE VEINS OF OTHER	811	7
WHILE CUBES IN A DROP	BANISH AIR FROM AIR--	854	4
WHILE IT SUSPENDS THE LIVES.	A DOUBT IF IT BE US	859	8
WHILE I REPEAT [RECITE] YOUR	SANG FROM THE HEART,	1059	15
WHILE SHE MUST FINISH QUITE	THE LAST NIGHT THAT SHE	1100	14
WE WAITED WHILE SHE PASSED--	THE LAST NIGHT THAT SHE	1100	17
WHILE EVERYTHING TO CORNERS SLUNK	THE WIND TOOK UP THE	1134	7
THOUGH [WHILE] A STATLIER TALE	TELL AS A MARKSMAN--WERE	1152	6
WHILE I DELAY [DELAYED] TO GUESS [DRESS]	OH SHADOW ON THE GRASS,	1187	6
WHILE HE, VICTORIOUS TILTS AWAY	LIKE TRAINS OF CARS ON	1224	7
THOUGH [WHILE / BUT] WE RESENT THE CREASE	LIKE TIME'S INSIDIOUS	1236	4
WHILE THAT DELUSIVE [OBLIGING / ENCHANTING] HAIR	RISK IS THE HAIR THAT	1239	10
WHILE EVERYTHING CREATED HID	TO PILE LIKE THUNDER TO	1247	3
WHILE WE WERE [I WAS] FEARING IT, IT CAME--	WHILE WE WERE FEARING IT	1277	1
I TELL THE WHILE I WAITED [FAMISHED]--	ART THOU THE THING I	1282	5
WHILE WE SHREWDLY SPECULATE [SAGE INVESTIGATE / SHREWD INVESTIGATE]	YESTERDAY IS HISTORY,	1292	7
WHILE FAITHFUL AND AFAR	WARM IN HER HAND THESE	1313	2
WHILE THEIR COMMUTED FEET	HOW MUCH THE PRESENT	1380	6
WHO LED US WHILE HE STAYED.	NOT THAT HE GOES--WE	1435	2
WHICH WHILE YOU TASTE SO NATIVE [ADJACENT] SEEMS	YOUR THOUGHTS DONT HAVE	1452	5
WHILE RAPTURE CHANGED IT'S DRESS	THE THRILL CAME SLOWLY	1495	6
AND WHILE BY STEPPING [STANDING] ON MY HEART	THE PILE OF YEARS IS NOT	1507	5
WHILE PONTIUS PILATE LIVES	ONE CROWN THAT NO ONE	1735	5
WHILE HER FATHER ABUTS THE TEMPEST	THE PARASOL IS THE	1747	3
WHILE WE WHO DARE TO LIVE	THIS DOCILE ONE INTER	1752	2
WHIM			
THE BUTTERCUP'S, MY WHIM FOR BLOOM--	THE ROBIN'S MY CRITERION	285	6
EXCEPT IT WERE A WHIM OF HIS	THE TREES LIKE TASSELS--	606	15
I'M SURE, AT MANY A WHIM	IF NATURE SMILES--THE	1085	2
OUR AFFLUENCE A WHIM	THE DAYS THAT WE CAN	1184 V	6
WHIMPERED			
SO WHIMPERED FOR THE SPRING--	I THOUGHT THE TRAIN	1449	4
WHIMPERING			
CROWNED--CROWING [WHIMPERING / DANGLING]--ON MY FATHER'S BREAST--	I'M CEDED--I'VE STOPPED	508	15
WHIMPERS			
WHAT SHALL I DO--IT WHIMPERS SO--	WHAT SHALL I DO--IT	186	1
WHINING			
WOULD IT STOP WHINING--IF TO THEE--	WHAT SHALL I DO--IT	186	6
WHIP			
JOURNEY OF DOWN--AND WHIP OF DIAMOND--	DROPPED INTO THE ETHER	665	7
HAVE PASSED, I THOUGHT, A WHIP LASH	A NARROW FELLOW IN THE	986	13
THE SUN TOOK DOWN HIS YELLOW WHIP	THE SUN AND FOG	1190	3
A WHIP SO SMALL YOU COULD NOT SEE IT	NOT WITH A CLUB, THE	1304	3
WHIPPOWIL			
THY MUSIC STILL, WHEN WHIPPOWIL	SUMMER FOR THEE, GRANT I	31	3
A FEATHER FROM THE WHIPPOWIL	A FEATHER FROM THE	161	1
LIKE A WHIPPOWIL--	MANY A PHRASE HAS THE	276	8
PLEAD--LIKE A WHIPPOWIL--	I AM ASHAMED--I HIDE--	473	17
WHIP'S			
YET THAT WHIP'S NAME	NOT WITH A CLUB, THE	1304	7
WHIRLS			
IT SOARS--AND SHIFTS--AND WHIRLS--	OF BEING IS A BIRD	653	5
WHIRR			
LETHARGIC POOLS RESUME THE WHIRR	SOME RAINBOW--COMING	64	8
WHISPER			
TO SUCH, IF THEY SH'D WHISPER	MY NOSEGAYS ARE FOR	95	5
AS THE LAUGHTER--AND THE WHISPER--	SWEET--SAFE--HOUSES--	457	8
WHISPERED			
A BILLOW WHISPERED IN HIS EAR,	THE WATERS CHASED HIM AS	1749	3
WHISPERING			
FOR SIGHING, AND GENTLE WHISPERING, AND UNITY MADE OF TWAIN.	AWAKE YE MUSES NINE,	1	4
OF WHOM WE'RE WHISPERING HERE?	SHE BORE IT TILL THE	144	16
BUT WE--STOOD--WHISPERING IN THE HOUSE--	OF TRIBULATION--THESE	325	15
WHIST			
HIST! WHIST! I'D COME!	IS IT TRUE, DEAR SUE?	218	11
WHISTLE			
WHEN THE BIRDS BEGIN TO WHISTLE--	DONT PUT UP MY THREAD &	617	3
HOW SLOW THE WHISTLE SANG--	I THOUGHT THE TRAIN	1449	2
WHISTLED			
WHISTLED ITSELF A TUNE--	HEART, NOT SO HEAVY AS	83	4
AND WHISTLED IN THE AIR--	AN AWFUL TEMPEST MASHED	198	6
THE BOYS THAT WHISTLED ARE EXTINCT--	A FADED BOY--IN SALLOW	1524	5
WHISTLING			
WHISTLING UNDER MY WINDOW	HEART, NOT SO HEAVY AS	83	T
WHITE			
A LADY WHITE, WITHIN THE FIELD	A LADY RED--AMID THE	74	3
IN EPAULETTED WHITE--	BLESS GOD, HE WENT AS	147	6
THERE'S THAT LONG [THEN THERE'S THAT] TOWN OF WHITE--TO CROSS--	IT CANT BE "SUMMER"!	221	4
THE DEAD SHALL GO IN WHITE--	IT CANT BE "SUMMER"!	221	8
IN THE "WHITE ROBE"--	WHY--DO THEY SHUT ME OUT	248	10
A WOMAN--WHITE--TO BE--	A SOLEMN THING--IT WAS--	271	2

	FIRST LINE	POEM	LINE
WHITE (CONTINUED)			
DENOTED BY THE WHITE.	OF TRIBULATION--THESE	325	2
DARE YOU SEE A SOUL AT THE WHITE HEAT?	DARE YOU SEE A SOUL AT	365	1
SEE--IN WHITE!	TAKE YOUR HEAVEN FURTHER	388	12
FEELS HER WHITE FOOT--NO TREPIDATION--	THROUGH THE DARK SOD--AS	392	3
THE COLOR OF THE GRAVE IS WHITE--	THE COLOR OF THE GRAVE	411	9
NOT ALL THE SNOWS C'D MAKE IT WHITE--	THE COLOR OF THE GRAVE	411	19
FASHION MY SPIRIT QUAINT--WHITE--	I AM ASHAMED--I HIDE--	473	20
MINE--BY THE RIGHT OF THE WHITE ELECTION!	MINE--BY THE RIGHT OF	528	1
ETERNITY'S WHITE [COOL] FLAG--BEFORE [IN FRONT]--	OUR JOURNEY HAD ADVANCED	615	11
AND THAT WHITE SUSTENANCE--[EXERCISE / PRIVILEGE]	I CANNOT LIVE WITH YOU--	640	49
IF WHITE--A RED--MUST BE!	THE ZEROES--TAUGHT US--	689	6
WHITE--UNTO THE WHITE CREATOR--	PUBLICATION--IS THE	709	7
WHITE--UNTO THE WHITE CREATOR--	PUBLICATION--IS THE	709	7
IT'S WHITE FOOT TRIPPED--	IT TOSSED--AND TOSSED--	723	7
A WHITE INHABITANT--	TOO LITTLE WAY THE HOUSE	911	4
IT--IS THE WHITE EXPLOIT--	THOSE WHO HAVE BEEN IN	922	6
THIS WAS IN THE WHITE OF THE YEAR--	THIS WAS IN THE WHITE OF	995	1
UPON AN ARC OF WHITE.	A SPIDER SEWED AT NIGHT	1138	3
WHITE AS AN INDIAN PIPE	WHITE AS AN INDIAN PIPE	1250	1
AT HIS NEW WHITE HOUSE THE EARTH	I SUPPOSE THE TIME WILL	1381	11
HOW COUNTERFEIT THE WHITE	UNWORTHY OF HER BREAST	1414	5
WHITER			
A WHITER GIFT--WITHIN--	THE WORLD--STANDS--	493	10
THAT COOLER [WHITER] HOST.	ONE NEED NOT BE A	670	8
'TIS WHITER THAN AN INDIAN PIPE--	'TIS WHITER THAN AN	1482	1
HER HAND WAS WHITER THAN THE SPERM	HER FACE WAS IN A BED OF	1722	3
WHITES			
AS FLOODS--ON WHITES OF WHEELS--	JOY TO HAVE MERITED THE	788	20
WHITHER			
WHERE IT ROSE--OR WHITHER IT RUSHES--	THIS--IS THE LAND--THE	266	3
WHITTLES			
AND WHITTLES AT THE TWIG	AS ONE DOES SICKNESS	957	6
WHIZZING			
DREAD, BUT THE WHIZZING, BEFORE THE BALL--	IF ANY SINK, ASSURE THAT	358	6
WHOLE			
COULD SMILE UPON THE WHOLE	COULD LIVE--DID LIVE--	43	3
SOFT OVERHEARS THE WHOLE--	THE SKIES CANT KEEP	191	6
WHOLE POOLS OF IT--	I CAN WADE GRIEF--	252	2
THE WHOLE OF ME--FOREVER--	DOUBT ME! MY DIM	275	5
TILL GOD'S FULL TIME [WHOLE--WILL]--	UNTO LIKE STORY--TROUBLE	295	6
HID GOLDEN, FOR THE WHOLE OF DAYS,	OF ALL THE SOUNDS	321	15
WE ADORED--FOR WHOLE--	TAKING UP THE FAIR IDEAL	428	14
THE STAR'S WHOLE SECRET--IN THE LAKE--	THE OUTER--FROM THE	451	15
EXISTENCE'S WHOLE ARC, [WHOLE EYE / WHOLE RIM / SURMISE] FILLED UP,	I'M CEDED--I'VE STOPPED	508	12
EXISTENCE'S WHOLE ARC, [WHOLE EYE / WHOLE RIM / SURMISE] FILLED UP,	I'M CEDED--I'VE STOPPED	508	12
EXISTENCE'S WHOLE ARC, [WHOLE EYE / WHOLE RIM / SURMISE] FILLED UP,	I'M CEDED--I'VE STOPPED	508	12
I OFFER THEM THE WHOLE [HALF] OF HEAVEN	I CROSS TILL I AM WEARY	550	20
WE LEARNED THE WHOLE OF LOVE--	WE LEARNED THE WHOLE OF	568	1
TO COMPREHEND THE WHOLE--	I RECKON--WHEN I COUNT	569	6
THE SUN SHONE WHOLE AT INTERVALS--	THE TREES LIKE TASSELS--	606	9
WHOLE--LIKE HIS PRINCIPLE--	THE CHILD'S FAITH IS NEW	637	2
"WOULD I BE WHOLE" HE SUDDEN BROACHED--	I COULD SUFFICE FOR HIM,	643	5
POURED LIKE THIS--MY WHOLE [BEST] LIBATION--	PROMISE THIS--WHEN YOU	648	13
A LESSER THAN THE WHOLE--	WITHOUT THIS--THERE IS	655	6
WHOLE GULFS--OF RED, AND FLEETS--OF RED--	WHOLE GULFS--OF RED, AND	658	1
I KNOW THE WHOLE--OBSCURES THE PART--	PRECIOUS TO ME--SHE	727	9
WERE A CRUMB MY WHOLE POSSESSION--	MOST SHE TOUCHED ME BY	760	5
THE WHOLE OF IT CAME NOT AT ONCE--	THE WHOLE OF IT CAME NOT	762	1
WHOLE CHAOSES [OBLIVIONS] ON HIM--	A PLATED LIFE--	806	8
ODORS RETURN WHOLE	BANISH AIR FROM AIR--	854	8
WHOLE STATURED--BY THE SIDE	NOT ALL DIE EARLY, DYING	990	6
FOR WHOM THE WHOLE WERE SMALL	SO LARGE MY WILL	1024	6
HER WHOLE RESPONSIBILITY--	HER LITTLE PARASOL TO	1038	3
A WHOLE EXISTENCE THROUGH.	WHILE WE WERE FEARING IT	1277	12
AND YET IT'S WHOLE CAREER [ALIEN PLACE / COVERT PLACE]	THE MUSHROOM IS THE ELF	1298	6
THIS WHOLE [SUDDEN / FAIR / GAY / BRIGHT / FLEET / SWEET / . . .	A LITTLE MADNESS IN THE	1333	5
UNTO THE WHOLE--HOW ADD?	UNTO THE WHOLE--HOW ADD?	1341	1
BUT LEAVES THE WATER WHOLE--	THE INUNDATION OF THE	1425	4
IS GUILTY OF THE WHOLE.	WHOEVER DISENCHANTS	1451	4
THE WHOLE OF IMMORTALITY INTRENCHED [SECRETED / DEPUTED]	HE LIVED THE LIFE OF	1525	7
PRECEPTOR OF THE WHOLE--	IMAGE OF LIGHT, ADIEU--	1556	4
IMMURED THE WHOLE OF LIFE	OF GOD WE ASK ONE FAVOR,	1601	5
THE WHOLE OF IMMORTALITY	WHO ABDICATED AMBUSH	1616	7
SUPERFLUOUS MY WHOLE CAREER	CONFERRING WITH MYSELF	1655	7
SO NEAR THE WHOLE TO STAND	I DID NOT REACH THEE	1664	27
WHOLESOME			
IS WHOLESOME EVEN FOR THE KING,	A LITTLE MADNESS IN THE	1333	2
WHOLLY			
AS WHOLLY AS A DEW	I STARTED EARLY--TOOK MY	520	14
BE WHOLLY [CHIEFEST / UTMOST] BEAUTIFUL--	I PLAY AT RICHES--TO	801	24

	FIRST LINE	POEM	LINE
WILDERNESS (CONTINUED)			
IT MAY BE WILDERNESS--WITHOUT--	UNTO MY BOOKS--SO GOOD	604	9
NO BANKRUPTCY [SEPULCHRE / WILDERNESS]--NO DOOM--	I THINK TO LIVE--MAY BE	646	16
THROUGH DESERT OR THE WILDERNESS	STRONG DRAUGHTS OF THEIR	711	3
A WILDERNESS OF SIZE.	THERE IS A FINISHED	856	4
IF WILDERNESS PREVENT HER FEET	FROM US SHE WANDERED NOW	890	3
BUT LIGHT A NEWER WILDERNESS	HAD I NOT SEEN THE SUN	1233	3
MY WILDERNESS HAS MADE--	HAD I NOT SEEN THE SUN	1233	4
HE ONLY SELLS THE WILDERNESS,	THE AUCTIONEER OF	1612	5
NO WILDERNESS REMAIN [RETAIN]	THIS DOCILE ONE INTER	1752	6
WILE			
OR WILE OF BUTTERFLY	FORGET! THE LADY WITH	438	7
WILL			
"FATHER, THY WILL BE DONE" TODAY	I HAVE A KING, WHO DOES	103	16
FOR MY WILL GOES THE OTHER WAY,	I HAVE A KING, WHO DOES	103	17
THY WINDY WILL TO BEAR!	BESIDES THE AUTUMN POETS	131	16
TAKETH AWAY MY WILL--	THE MURMUR OF A BEE	155	7
AND THEIR YOUNG WILL	UNTO LIKE STORY--TROUBLE	295	4
TILL GOD'S FULL TIME [WHOLE--WILL]--	UNTO LIKE STORY--TROUBLE	295	6
I'LL DO THY WILL--	FORGET! THE LADY WITH	438	16
BUT SOMETHING HELD MY WILL.	'TWAS JUST THIS TIME,	445	8
WITH WILL [POWER] TO CHOOSE, OR TO REJECT,	I'M CEDED--I'VE STOPPED	508	18
THE WILL OF IT'S INQUISITOR	THE HEART ASKS PLEASURE	536	7
HIMSELF HAS BUT TO WILL	THEY SHUT ME UP IN PROSE	613	9
TO BE ALIVE--AND WILL!	TO BE ALIVE--IS POWER--	677	5
WERE SUCH HER SILVER WILL--	THE MOON WAS BUT A CHIN	737	12
TO DO HIS GOLDEN WILL--	MY FAITH IS LARGER THAN	766	8
WEDLOCK OF WILL, DECAY--	GIVEN IN MARRIAGE UNTO	817	6
THE LEISURE OF HIS WILL--	ALL CIRCUMSTANCES ARE	820	6
WHEN ACT AND WILL ARE DONE	NOT WHAT WE DID, SHALL	823	2
THE GOOD WILL OF A FLOWER	THE GOOD WILL OF A	849	1
THE WILL IT IS THAT SITUATES--	THAT DISTANCE WAS	863	3
STILL--JUST AS EASY, IF IT BE THY WILL	ONLY A SHRINE, BUT MINE	918	10
THAT WOULD NOT LET THE WILL--	'TWAS CRISIS--ALL THE	948	10
WHOSE WILL--A NUMB SIGNIFICANCE--[BLANK INTELLIGENCE]	DENIAL--IS THE ONLY FACT	965	3
SO LARGE MY WILL	SO LARGE MY WILL	1024	1
WHEN THE WINDS OF WILL ARE STIRRED	REVOLUTION IS THE POD	1082	3
AND THEN--IT KNOCKS AT WILL--	A DEED KNOCKS FIRST AT	1216	2
AND WILL AT HOME AND WELL	A DEED KNOCKS FIRST AT	1216	4
SECRETED IN HIS WILL--	NOT ONE BY HEAVEN	1303	4
MY WILL ENDEAVORS FOR IT'S WORD	TO TELL THE BEAUTY WOULD	1700	5
'TIS THE VERMIN'S WILL.	DEATH IS LIKE THE INSECT	1716	12
WILLED			
I WILLED MY KEEPSAKES--SIGNED AWAY	I HEARD A FLY BUZZ--WHEN	465	9
HAD GOD WILLED DIFFERENTLY.	I CRIED AT PITY--NOT AT	588	16
WILLIAM			
BY THIS--WAS WILLIAM KIDD	TRUST IN THE UNEXPECTED	555	2
WILLING			
WE TRUST THAT SHE WAS WILLING--	THE GENTIAN WEAVES HER	18	13
WHEN YOU WERE WILLING--	WHAT SHALL I DO--IT	186	12
AS WILLING LID O'ER WEARY EYE	AS WILLING LID O'ER	1050	1
TOO WILLING, TO BE CALLED	LET DOWN THE BARS, OH	1065	V 8
WILLS			
WILLS SILENCE--EVERYWHERE--	NATURE--THE GENTLEST	790	24
WILT			
AND THEY'LL WILT, LIKE MEN--	I CAN WADE GRIEF--	252	14
WILTED			
THE WILTED [BLACKENED] COUNTENANCE	AS FROST IS BEST	951	8
HIS FEATHERS WILTED LOW--	HIS BILL IS CLASPED--HIS	1102	2
WILY			
THAT WILY--SUBTERRANEAN [UNSUBSTANTIAL] INN	NO PASSENGER WAS KNOWN	1406	3
TIME'S WILY CHARGERS WILL NOT WAIT	TIME'S WILY CHARGERS	1458	1
WIN			
WE LOSE--BECAUSE WE WIN--	WE LOSE--BECAUSE WE WIN	21	1
WHO WIN, AND NATIONS DO NOT SEE--	TO FIGHT ALOUD, IS VERY	126	5
TO WIN, BECOME THEIR [MY] TURN--	I PLAY AT RICHES--TO	801	20
WINCE			
'TIS OURS--TO WINCE--AND WEEP--	HE GAVE AWAY HIS LIFE--	567	9
WINCED			
AND [BUT] NEVER WINCED [SHOOK / QUAKED] BEFORE.	I YEARS HAD BEEN FROM	609	16
WINCES			
WINCES [ACHES] WITH DELIGHT	INCONCEIVABLY SOLEMN!	582	14
WINCING			
. . . WINCING NATURES--]	WE SEE--COMPARATIVELY--	534	13
UPON MY WINCING HEAD--	WHO IS IT SEEKS MY	1598	6
WIND			
THE WIND DOTH WOO THE BRANCHES, THE BRANCHES THEY ARE WON,	AWAKE YE MUSES NINE,	1	15
IN CASE THE WIND SHOULD BLOW!	"SIC TRANSIT GLORIA	3	28
WHETHER IT WAS THE WIND--	I CAUTIOUS, SCANNED MY	178	14
WIND AND SUN--WILT THEE ARRAY!	POOR LITTLE HEART!	192	12
THE WIND--IS PRINCE OF THOSE--	THE DAY CAME SLOW--TILL	304	12
THE WIND DID'NT COME FROM THE ORCHARD--TODAY--	THE WIND DID'NT COME	316	1
THE WIND DOES--WORKING LIKE A HAND,	OF ALL THE SOUNDS	321	5
WHOSE FORCES SPHERIC WIND [ROUND]	THERE ARE TWO RIPENINGS	332	2
BUT WHEN THE SOUTH WIND STIRS THE POOLS	I KNOW A PLACE WHERE	337	5
AGAINST THE WIND--BE SEEN--	THERE IS A FLOWER THAT	380	16

	FIRST LINE	POEM	LINE
WIND (CONTINUED)			
A WIND WITH FINGERS--GOES--	THEY DROPPED LIKE FLAKES	409	5
NOT LOUD ENOUGH--FOR WIND--	A MURMUR IN THE TREES--	416	2
YOU, OR THE WIND?	IT IS DEAD--FIND IT--	417	4
THE WIND--TAPPED LIKE A TIRED MAN--	THE WIND--TAPPED LIKE A	436	1
THE WIND DOES NOT REQUIRE THE GRASS	"WHY DO I LOVE" YOU, SIR	480	3
TURNED BY THE WIND--	IT'S THOUGHTS--AND JUST	495	21
I'D WIND THE MONTHS IN BALLS--	IF YOU WERE COMING IN	511	6
IN THE MEADOW--WHEN THE WIND	BEAUTY--BE NOT CAUSED--	516	5
THE WIND PURSUED THE LITTLE BUSH--	THE NIGHT WAS WIDE, AND	589	5
THE WIND--UNROLLED IT FAST--	OF BRUSSELS--IT WAS NOT	602	13
THE SLEET--THE BITTER WIND--	THE BEGGAR LAD--DIES	717	12
A SOUTH WIND--HAS A PATHOS	A SOUTH WIND--HAS A	719	1
THE WIND--	FOUR TREES--UPON A	742	6
AFAR [REMOTE / ASTRAY] UPON THE WIND	IT IS A LONESOME GLEE--	774	4
OF IT'S VOICE--TO AFFIRM--WHEN THE WIND IS WITHIN--	BY MY WINDOW HAVE I FOR	797	13
THE WIND BEGUN TO KNEAD [ROCK] THE GRASS--	THE WIND BEGUN TO KNEAD	824	1
FOR LANGUAGE, AND THE WIND	TWO TRAVELLERS PERISHING	933	8
SHY AS THE WIND OF HIS CHAMBERS [LODGINGS]	THIS IS A BLOSSOM OF THE	945	5
OFFENDED [INSULTED / ASSAULTED] BY THE WIND--	SHE SPED AS PETALS OF A	991	2
THE CAPSULE OF THE WIND	BEST THINGS DWELL OUT OF	998	5
ADJUST THE HEAT--ELUDE THE WIND--	BLOOM--IS RESULT--TO	1058	11
A NARROW WIND COMPLAINS ALL DAY	THE SKY IS LOW--THE	1075	5
THE SPRY [LONG] ARMS OF THE WIND	THE SPRY ARMS OF THE	1103	1
THE WIND COULD WAIT WITHOUT THE GATE	THE SPRY ARMS OF THE	1103	7
AND TAKES THE WIND AT PRIME--	'TIS MY FIRST NIGHT	1122	6
THE WIND TOOK UP THE NORTHERN THINGS	THE WIND TOOK UP THE	1134	1
THE WIND--UNTO HIS [IT'S] CHAMBERS WENT	THE WIND TOOK UP THE	1134	9
THE DUTIES OF THE WIND ARE FEW,	THE DUTIES OF THE WIND	1137	1
THE PLEASURES OF THE WIND ARE BROAD,	THE DUTIES OF THE WIND	1137	5
THE KINSMEN OF THE WIND ARE PEAKS	THE DUTIES OF THE WIND	1137	9
THE LIMITATIONS OF THE WIND	THE DUTIES OF THE WIND	1137	13
LIKE PARAGRAPHS [ARTICLES] OF WIND	WE LIKE A HAIRBREADTH	1175	4
I BET WITH EVERY WIND THAT BLEW	I BET WITH EVERY WIND	1215	1
AS FORESTS [BRANCHES] TOUCH THE WIND	BECAUSE HE LOVES HER	1229	8
AND THEN I [WE] KNEW 'TWAS WIND--	LIKE RAIN IT SOUNDED	1235	2
THE SNOW AND WIND	LIKE BROOMS OF STEEL	1252	2
A WIND THAT ROSE	A WIND THAT ROSE	1259	1
A WIND THAT WOKE A LONE DELIGHT	A WIND THAT ROSE	1259	6
I THINK THAT THE ROOT OF THE WIND IS WATER--	I THINK THAT THE ROOT OF	1302	1
A SUDDEN FREIGHT OF WIND ASSUMED [TOOK ON--]	A SINGLE CLOVER PLANK	1343	11
THE FLAKE THE WIND EXASPERATE	THE FLAKE THE WIND	1361	1
FIRST AT THE MARCH--COMPETING WITH THE WIND--	AFTER ALL BIRDS HAVE	1395	5
HOW LONESOME THE WIND MUST FEEL NIGHTS--	HOW LONESOME THE WIND	1418	1
HOW POMPOUS THE WIND MUST FEEL NOONS	HOW LONESOME THE WIND	1418	5
HOW MIGHTY THE WIND MUST FEEL MORNS	HOW LONESOME THE WIND	1418	9
TO QUALIFY THE WIND--	HOW RUTHLESS ARE THE	1439	4
I SAW THE WIND WITHIN HER	I SAW THE WIND WITHIN	1502	1
HOW SLOW THE WIND--	HOW SLOW THE WIND--	1571	1
THERE CAME A WIND LIKE A BUGLE--	THERE CAME A WIND LIKE A	1593	1
WITHOUT A SURETY FROM THE WIND	DOWN TIME'S QUAINT	1656	9
THE WIND DREW OFF	THE WIND DREW OFF	1694	1
TOO STOLID FOR THE WIND--	THEY TALK AS SLOW AS	1697	4
A SHORT RELIEF TO HAVE THE WIND	T'WAS COMFORT IN HER	1703	3
UPON A PILE OF WIND	HIGH FROM THE EARTH I	1723	6
WINDING			
JUST WINDING ROUND A STONE--	THE TREES LIKE TASSELS--	606	20
WINDOW			
WHISTLING UNDER MY WINDOW	HEART, NOT SO HEAVY AS	83	T
AS IT PASSED MY WINDOW	HEART, NOT SO HEAVY AS	83	3
AH [OH] BUGLE! BY MY [THE] WINDOW	HEART, NOT SO HEAVY AS	83	19
UPON THE WINDOW PANE--	THE SUN KEPT STOOPING--	152	6
BUZZ THE DULL FLIES--ON THE CHAMBER WINDOW--	HOW MANY TIMES THESE LOW	187	9
HOAR--IS THE WINDOW--AND NUMB--THE DOOR--	SAFE IN THEIR ALABASTER	216	V
. . . ORIEL] WINDOW	BLAZING IN GOLD AND	228	5
UPON THE WINDOW PANE--	BEFORE I GOT MY EYE PUT	327	19
A WINDOW OPENS LIKE A POD--	THERE'S BEEN A DEATH, IN	389	7
THAT JUST ABROAD HIS WINDOW	I ENVY SEAS, WHEREON HE	498	13
MORNING'S BOLD FACE--STARES IN THE WINDOW--	I COULD DIE--TO KNOW--	570	5
UPON THE WINDOW PANE	IT WOULD HAVE STARVED A	612	14
THEY CALLED ME TO THE WINDOW, FOR	THEY CALLED ME TO THE	628	1
AND DOME [SPIRE / CHURCH]--AND WINDOW PANE--	THE DAY UNDRESSED--	716	16
AT WINDOW--AND AT DOOR--	REMORSE--IS MEMORY--	744	4
AT A WINDOW [IN A CHAMBER] FACING WEST--	WHEN I HOPED, I	768	3
BY MY WINDOW HAVE I FOR SCENERY	BY MY WINDOW HAVE I FOR	797	1
WAS THE PINE AT MY WINDOW A "FELLOW	BY MY WINDOW HAVE I FOR	797	22
IT CAN BE HAD ON WINDOW PANES	LIGHT IS SUFFICIENT TO	862	3
IS ALWAYS AT THE WINDOW	I KNOW SUSPENSE--IT	1285	5
ECLIPSE--WAS ALL WE COULD SEE AT THE WINDOW	IT SOUNDED AS IF THE	1397	3
WINDOWS			
AND SHUT THE WINDOWS DOWN SO CLOSE	BRING ME THE SUNSET IN A	128	20
TO FIND THE WINDOWS DARK--	YOU LOVE ME--YOU ARE	156	11
AND SAINTS--TO WINDOWS RUN--	I TASTE A LIQUOR NEVER	214	14
AND WINDOWS HANGING LOW,	I KNOW SOME LONELY	289	4
WHOSE WINDOWS--NIGHT AND MORN--	A HOUSE UPON THE HIGHT--	399	6
AND THEN THE WINDOWS FAILED--AND THEN	I HEARD A FLY BUZZ--WHEN	465	15
I LOOKED IN WINDOWS, FOR THE WEALTH [THINGS]	I HAD BEEN HUNGRY, ALL	579	7
OF PERSONS [CREATURES] OUTSIDE WINDOWS--	I HAD BEEN HUNGRY, ALL	579	19
I SCANNED THE WINDOWS O'ER--	I YEARS HAD BEEN FROM	609	V 10

	FIRST LINE	POEM	LINE
WINS			
THAT WINS AT LAST--	DEATH IS THE SUPPLE	1445	2
WINTER			
IF SPRINGS FROM WINTER RISE,	IF PAIN FOR PEACE	63	4
SOME, TOO FRAGILE FOR WINTER WINDS	SOME, TOO FRAGILE FOR	141	1
I WENT ONE WINTER MORNING	I CAUTIOUS, SCANNED MY	178	7
WHEN WINTER SHOOK THE BOUGHS!	IF I COULD BRIBE THEM BY	179	12
WINTER AFTERNOONS--	THERE'S A CERTAIN SLANT	258	2
WINTER, WERE LIE--TO ME--	THE ROBIN'S MY CRITERION	285	14
BECAUSE THERE WAS A WINTER--ONCE--	THE WINTERS ARE SO SHORT	403	11
IN WINTER--TILL THE SUN--	THE COLOR OF THE GRAVE	411	12
THOUGH WINTER FIRE--SING CLEAR AS PLOVER--	IT'S THOUGHTS--AND JUST	495	15
ADDS [GIVES] POIGNANCY TO WINTER--	CONJECTURING A CLIMATE	562	3
WHAT [NOR] CARE THE DEAD FOR WINTER?	WHAT CARE THE DEAD, FOR	592	17
WHEN WINTER SHAKE THE DOOR--	GLEE--THE GREAT STORM IS	619	10
THE BELLS A WINTER NIGHT	PEACE IS A FICTION OF	912	2
MAKE THEIR FIRST REPOSE THIS WINTER	SNOW BENEATH WHOSE	942	3
LIKE WINTER AS A FACE	THE SNOW THAT NEVER	1133	9
HAD SWEPT THE WINTER STREET--	LIKE BROOMS OF STEEL	1252	3
THAN WHEN THE WINTER CAME	'TWAS LATER WHEN THE	1276	6
WINTER IS GOOD--HIS HOAR DELIGHTS	WINTER IS GOOD--HIS HOAR	1316	1
OF BARNS FOR WINTER--BLAMELESS [IGNORANT]--	THOSE CATTLE SMALLER	1388	5
AND WINTER INSTANTLY BECOMES	THE DANDELION'S PALLID	1519	3
PUT ON YOUR MUFF [BELLS] FOR WINTER	THE JAY HIS CASTANET HAS	1635	2
OF WINTER AND OF HELL	A CAP OF LEAD ACROSS THE	1649	8
IN WINTER IN MY ROOM	IN WINTER IN MY ROOM	1670	1
WINTER UNDER CULTIVATION	WINTER UNDER CULTIVATION	1707	1
TO WINTER TO REMOVE	'TWAS HERE MY SUMMER	1756	5
WITH WINTER TO ABIDE	'TWAS HERE MY SUMMER	1756	6
WINTER'S			
UPON A WINTER'S DAY,	A SCIENCE--SO THE SAVANS	100	9
TWICE A WINTER'S SILVER FRACTURE	TWICE HAD SUMMER HER	846	3
WINTERS			
THE WINTERS ARE SO SHORT--	THE WINTERS ARE SO SHORT	403	1
WITH SUMMERS, AND WITH WINTERS, GROW,	FITTER TO SEE HIM, I MAY	968	3
WINTERWORN			
WHOSE APPLE WINTERWORN	FOREVER HONORED BE THE	1570	2
WIPE			
TO WIPE MY WEEPING E'E.	"SIC TRANSIT GLORIA	3	60
WIPING			
WIPING AWAY THE VELVET DUST	IN EBON BOX, WHEN YEARS	169	3
WISDOM			
THE WISDOM IT BE SO--	"WHY DO I LOVE" YOU, SIR	480	10
THE POWER [WISDOM] TO PRESUME--	HER SWEET WEIGHT ON MY	518	8
ALAS, THAT WISDOM IS SO LARGE--	WE LEARNED THE WHOLE OF	568	11
SO IMPOTENT OUR WISDOM IS [BE]	"NATURE" IS WHAT WE SEE	668	11
WHAT COMFORT WAS IT WISDOM--WAS--	DENIAL--IS THE ONLY FACT	965	7
A WISDOM, WITHOUT FACE, OR NAME,	THE CRICKETS SANG	1104	10
WISDOM IS STALE--TO ME"	THE SEA SAID "COME" TO	1210	8
WISDOM IS MORE BECOMING VIEWED	I WORKED FOR CHAFF AND	1269	7
MY WISDOM LOSES WAY	THE ONES THAT	1690	6
WISDOMS			
NOR ACTION [WISDOMS] NEW--	I HAVE NO LIFE BUT THIS	1398	6
WISE			
OH SOME WISE MAN FROM THE SKIES!	WILL THERE REALLY BE A	101	10
"HOUSES"--SO THE WISE MEN TELL ME--	"HOUSES"--SO THE WISE	127	1
THAN THAT--BE SWEETER WISE--	NOT IN THIS WORLD TO SEE	418	9
RABBI OF THE WISE BOOK	KNOWS HOW TO FORGET!	433	V
AND SO--UPON THIS WISE--I PRAYED--	I MEANT TO HAVE BUT	476	9
THEY MIGHT AS WISE HAVE LODGED A BIRD	THEY SHUT ME UP IN PROSE	613	7
THE WISE CONVEY IT HOME	THIS IS A BLOSSOM OF THE	945	10
TOO WISE HE SEEMS FOR WAKELESSNESS,	THE DUTIES OF THE WIND	1137	15
THE WISE DECEIVES	"TOMORROW"--WHOSE	1367	2
WE KNOW THAT WE ARE WISE--	HOW FITS HIS UMBER COAT	1371	9
THE SAGE [WISE] CANNOT CONJECTURE	FACTS BY OUR SIDE ARE	1497	10
FOLLOW WISE [FINE] ORION	FOLLOW WISE ORION	1538	1
WE MAKE THE WISE DISTINCTION [SAGE DECISION] STILL,	WE SEND THE WAVE TO FIND	1604	5
THEY LAUGH AS WISE AS PLOTS OF WIT	THEY TALK AS SLOW AS	1697	5
WISENESS			
AND FAINTER, TOO, AS WISENESS IS--	A LOSS OF SOMETHING EVER	959	10
WISER			
THEN WISER THAN A "SURROGATE",	COCOON ABOVE! COCOON	129	11
NEED THE WISER, TELL?	IF THE FOOLISH, CALL	168	2
"HAPPY"? WHICH IS WISER--	IT IS DEAD--FIND IT--	417	3
BUT WAS NOT WISER	KNOWS HOW TO FORGET!	433	V
CHILDREN--MATURED [GROWN UP]--ARE WISER--MOSTLY--	BETTER--THAN MUSIC! FOR	503	13
A WISER [WORDLESS / SILENT / SPEECHLESS] SYMPATHY	THE BIRDS REPORTED FROM	743	24
WISER MEN [ONE / EAR] MAY WEARY--	NEVER FOR SOCIETY	746	5
ELDER, TODAY, A SESSION WISER	A LOSS OF SOMETHING EVER	959	9
TO WISER BE [GROW] TOO SOON--	I THOUGHT THE TRAIN	1449	10
WISH			
MY HEART WOULD WISH IT BROKE BEFORE--	I SHOULD NOT DARE TO	205	13
I WISH I WERE A HAY--	THE GRASS SO LITTLE HAS	333	20
BUT NOT TO TOUCH, OR WISH FOR,	I CRIED AT PITY--NOT AT	588	13
I WISH I KNEW THAT WOMAN'S NAME--	I CRIED AT PITY--NOT AT	588	17
WONT YOU WISH YOU'D SPOKEN	NO MATTER--NOW--SWEET--	704	3
BUT WONT YOU WISH YOU'D SPARED ONE	NO MATTER--NOW--SWEET--	704	7

	FIRST LINE	POEM	LINE
WISH (CONTINUED)			
WONT YOU WISH YOU'D SMILED--JUST-- . . .	NO MATTER--NOW--SWEET--	704	15
I WISH I HAD NOT BROKEN IT--	THE MOST PATHETIC THING	1290	7
ALMOST WE WISH THE END	I DID NOT REACH THEE	1664	24
WE ALMOST WISH THOSE SIREN THROATS . . .	THE SADDEST NOISE, THE	1764	15
WE WISH THE EAR HAD NOT A HEART	THE SADDEST NOISE, THE	1764	19
WISHED			
I WISHED THE GRASS WOULD HURRY--	I DREADED THAT FIRST	348	13
I WISHED THEY'D STAY AWAY	I DREADED THAT FIRST	348	18
AND THEN YOU WISHED YOU HAD EYES IN YOUR PAGES--	GOING TO HIM! HAPPY	494	8
I WISHED A WAY [SORT] MIGHT BE	WITHOUT THIS--THERE IS	655	9
AND WISHED MYSELF WERE THEY.	MY TRIUMPH LASTED TILL	1227	8
WISHES			
AND WISHES--AND DENIES--	A CHARM INVESTS A FACE	421	6
AND WISHES--HAD HE ANY--	TO KNOW JUST HOW HE	622	13
WISHFULNESS			
AND WISHFULNESS IN ME AROSE--	I HAD NO CAUSE TO BE	542	11
A WISHFULNESS THEIR FAR CONDITION	A SICKNESS OF THIS WORLD	1044	3
WISHING			
WISHING YOU GOOD DAY--	NOT AT HOME TO CALLERS	1590	4
WIT			
BAPTIZED [TO WIT] AMERICA--	TRUST IN THE UNEXPECTED	555	12
EMACIATE THE WIT--	THE MIND LIVES ON THE	1355	6
BALKING OUR WIT	THE RAT IS THE CONCISEST	1356	5
THEY LAUGH AS WISE AS PLOTS OF WIT . . .	THEY TALK AS SLOW AS	1697	5
WITCH			
THE [DIM / FAR] ABSENCE OF THE WITCH DOES NOT [CANNOT]	LONG YEARS APART--CAN	1383	3
WHO SAYS THE ABSENCE OF A WITCH	LONG YEARS APART--CAN	1383 V	4
WITCHCRAFT			
A WITCHCRAFT--YIELDETH ME--	THE MURMUR OF A BEE	155	2
TO TOMES OF SOLID WITCHCRAFT--	I THINK I WAS ENCHANTED	593	29
'TIS [THAT'S] THIS--AND WITCHCRAFT--NATURE KEEPS [KNOWS / HAS]	THE COLOR OF A QUEEN, IS	776	7
WERE IT A WITCHCRAFT--WERE IT DEATH-- . .	I'VE DROPPED MY BRAIN--	1046	15
BEST WITCHCRAFT IS GEOMETRY	BEST WITCHCRAFT IS	1158	1
WITCHCRAFT WAS HUNG, IN HISTORY, ...	WITCHCRAFT WAS HUNG, IN	1583	1
FIND ALL THE WITCHCRAFT THAT WE NEED . . .	WITCHCRAFT WAS HUNG, IN	1583	3
WITCHCRAFT HAS NOT A PEDIGREE	WITCHCRAFT HAS NOT A	1708	1
WITHDRAW			
TWO [THE] WORLDS--LIKE AUDIENCES--DISPERSE [DISSOLVE / WITHDRAW / RETIRE]	DEPARTED--TO THE	524	7
CONFIRM [WITHDRAW]--IN VICTORY--	AN IGNORANCE A SUNSET	552	10
AND THEN THE PROPS WITHDRAW	THE PROPS ASSIST THE	1142	3
THE MARTIAL TREES WITHDRAW	THEIR BARRICADE AGAINST	1471	2
WITHDRAWN			
HAVE INFINITE WITHDRAWN--	THE SOUL'S SUPERIOR	306	4
OF A WITHDRAWN DELIGHT--	REHEARSAL TO OURSELVES	379	2
SUN--WITHDRAWN TO RECOGNITION--	STRUCK, WAS I, NOR YET	925	11
A LITTLE FROM REMARK WITHDRAWN--	THE MOUNTAINS STOOD IN	1278	7
HER SORCERER WITHDRAWN!	THE WAY TO KNOW THE	1279	24
THE FIGURE WAS WITHDRAWN--	A CAP OF LEAD ACROSS THE	1649	4
WITHDRAWS			
WITHDRAWS--AND LEAVES THE DAZZLED SOUL . .	DID OUR BEST MOMENT LAST	393	11
THE SUPERHUMAN THEN WITHDRAWS	I SHOULD NOT DARE TO BE	1197	5
WITHDRAWS THE WORTHLESS THING [ONE]	TO DISAPPEAR ENHANCES--	1209	10
BUT THE HEART WITHDRAWS--	"FAITHFUL TO THE END"	1357 V	
WITHDREW			
THE LARGER, AS HER [MY] FACE WITHDREW-- . .	I SHOWED HER HIGHTS SHE	446	11
THE CHERUBIM--WITHDREW--	I MEANT TO HAVE BUT	476	14
AT ME--THE SEA WITHDREW--	I STARTED EARLY--TOOK MY	520	24
WHEN [TILL] GENOA--WITHDREW	TRUST IN THE UNEXPECTED	555	10
WITHDREW THE SUN--TO OTHER WESTS--	I COULD SUFFICE FOR HIM,	643	9
WITHDREW THE FURTHEST STAR	I COULD SUFFICE FOR HIM,	643	10
THE ABSOLUTE--REMOVED [WITHDREW]	YOU CONSTITUTED TIME--	765	5
A CLOUD WITHDREW FROM THE SKY	A CLOUD WITHDREW FROM	895	1
AND HURRIEDLY [HASTILY] WITHDREW	ALONE AND IN A	1167	8
WITHELD			
THAN WHEN WITHELD OF OCEANS	WE MISS A KINSMAN MORE	1087	3
A FACT WITHELD THE LITTLE CHILD--	I NOTICED PEOPLE	1149	8
WITHELD INVINCIBLY--	I SEND YOU A DECREPIT	1324	8
WITHELD TO THE ARRIVED [DEBARRED / DENIED]--	CRISIS IS SWEET AND YET	1416 V	4
WITHERED			
THE WORDS ARE WITHERED [SPEECH IS STOLEN] AWAY	WHATEVER IT IS--SHE HAS	1204 V	8
WITHES			
BY WITHES OF SUPPLE BLUE?	BRING ME THE SUNSET IN A	128	15
WITHHELD			
DISPELLED [ABASED / WITHHELD / DEPRIVED] FROM THERE--	I HAVE NO LIFE BUT THIS	1398	4
WITHHELD US BY IT'S ROARING	OF DEATH I TRY TO THINK	1558	12
AUSPICIOUSLY WITHHELD--	THE BAT IS DUN, WITH	1575	12
FROM SUCH A GIANT [BEGGAR] WERE WITHHELD .	LOVE CAN DO ALL BUT	1731	3
BUT OTHERWISE WITHHELD.	THROUGH THOSE OLD	1753	16
WITHIN			
ONE WITHIN MY BOSOM	IT DID NOT SURPRISE ME--	39	11
WITHIN THIS INNER ROOM!	THERE'S SOMETHING	45	2
HINT THAT WITHIN THE RIDDLE	I HAV'NT TOLD MY GARDEN	50	15
RESERVE WITHIN THY KINGDOM	PAPA ABOVE!	61	4
A LADY WHITE, WITHIN THE FIELD	A LADY RED--AMID THE	74	3

	FIRST LINE	POEM	LINE
WITHIN (CONTINUED)			
WITHIN MY REACH!	WITHIN MY REACH!	90	1
WITHIN THE MEADOWS GO--	WITHIN MY REACH!	90	7
NEW FEET WITHIN MY GARDEN GO--	NEW FEET WITHIN MY	99	1
WITHIN THE ORCHARD, IS NOT HEARD,	I HAVE A KING, WHO DOES	103	14
AND STILL WITHIN A SUMMER'S NIGHT	A SOMETHING IN A	122	7
THE PURPLE BROOK WITHIN THE BREAST	A SOMETHING IN A	122	14
WHO CHARGE WITHIN THE BOSOM	TO FIGHT ALOUD, IS VERY	126	3
WITHIN THAT JACKET'S POCKET TOO!	I MET A KING THIS	166	8
BEAR WITHIN--APPALLING ORDNANCE,	I HAVE NEVER SEEN	175	5
ART THOU WITHIN THE LITTLE BARN	I CAUTIOUS, SCANNED MY	178	19
THIS LITTLE HOUND WITHIN THE HEART	WHAT SHALL I DO--IT	186	2
THE LAMP BURNS SURE--WITHIN--	THE LAMP BURNS SURE--	233	1
BY COURIERS WITHIN--	ALONE, I CANNOT BE--	298	10
THEN CROUCH WITHIN THE DOOR--	DARE YOU SEE A SOUL AT	365	2
THAT SOUNDLESS TUGS--WITHIN--	DARE YOU SEE A SOUL AT	365	12
EXHILIRATION--IS WITHIN--	EXHILIRATION--IS WITHIN	383	1
WITHIN HIS CLOSET--BEST YOU CAN	EXHILIRATION--IS WITHIN	383	11
AND SOMETHING'S ODD--WITHIN--	THE FIRST DAY'S NIGHT	410	17
THE COLOR OF THE GRAVE WITHIN--	THE COLOR OF THE GRAVE	411	17
OR STAR--COME OUT--WITHIN--	WE GROW ACCUSTOMED TO	419	12
THE ETHIOP WITHIN.	MORE LIFE--WENT OUT--	422	12
MY RESIDENCE WITHIN	THE WIND--TAPPED LIKE A	436	4
WITHIN MY INCOME--THESE COULD LIE	I MEANT TO HAVE BUT	476	3
A SOLEMN THING WITHIN THE SOUL	A SOLEMN THING WITHIN	483	1
A WHITER GIFT--WITHIN--	THE WORLD--STANDS--	493	10
WITHIN MY GARDEN, RIDES A BIRD	WITHIN MY GARDEN, RIDES	500	1
IS OF WITHIN.	TO HEAR AN ORIOLE SING	526	12
WITHIN THE CLUTCH OF THOUGHT--	I TRIED TO THINK A	532	9
WITHIN OPPOSING CELLS--	I TRIED TO THINK A	532	15
THE BRAIN, WITHIN IT'S GROOVE	THE BRAIN, WITHIN IT'S	556	1
AS ONE WITHIN A SWOON--	THERE IS A PAIN--SO	599	6
IT WAS WITHIN THE FRUGAL PURSE	OF BRUSSELS--IT WAS NOT	602	7
AND IT IS BELLS--WITHIN--	UNTO MY BOOKS--SO GOOD	604	12
THE LUNGS--WITHIN--	IN FALLING TIMBERS	614	4
AND SINEW FROM WITHIN--	I ROSE--BECAUSE HE SANK	616	21
UPON A BANK [WITHIN A HUT] OF STONE	A LONG--LONG SLEEP--A	654	6
DIVINER CROWD AT HOME [WITHIN]--	THE SOUL THAT HATH A	674	3
BUT THE MAN WITHIN	NEVER FOR SOCIETY	746	6
GRAVITATES WITHIN--	GROWTH OF MAN--LIKE	750	2
DEVELOPED FROM WITHIN--	HER FINAL SUMMER WAS IT	795	6
OF IT'S VOICE--TO AFFIRM--WHEN THE WIND IS WITHIN--	BY MY WINDOW HAVE I FOR	797	13
WHO COURT OBTAIN WITHIN HIMSELF	WHO COURT OBTAIN WITHIN	803	1
TO OWN THE ART WITHIN THE SOUL	TO OWN THE ART WITHIN	855	1
TO FAIL WITHIN A CHANCE--	EACH SECOND IS THE LAST	879	5
I HIDE MYSELF WITHIN MY FLOWER,	I HIDE MYSELF WITHIN MY	903	1
PATIENCE--LOOK WITHIN--	PATIENCE--HAS A QUIET	926	2
DRIFT MAY BLOCK WITHIN IT	ABSENT PLACE--AN APRIL	927	5
SHOULD SOFTLY PLACE WITHIN OUR OWN	ON THAT DEAR FRAME THE	940	7
AGES COIL [LURK] WITHIN	PAIN--EXPANDS THE TIME--	967	2
BUT ONCE WITHIN THE TOWN	THE FINGERS OF THE LIGHT	1000	10
STRIKES TRUE WITHIN--	BIND ME--I STILL CAN	1005	3
THE "BIRD WITHIN THE HAND"	WHICH IS BEST? HEAVEN--	1012	5
MY BODY BUT WITHIN	I HEARD, AS IF I HAD NO	1039	10
BUT MEAT WITHIN, IS REQUISITE	EXPERIMENT TO ME	1073	7
AND IF THE SOUL'S WITHIN	THE SPRY ARMS OF THE	1103	V 10
WITHIN A SELLER'S SHRINE	A DIAMOND ON THE HAND	1108	5
THE RUIN [HAVOC / DAMAGE] WAS WITHIN	A GREAT HOPE FELL	1123	3
BUT IS WITHIN OR NEGATIVE	THE MERCHANT OF THE	1131	3
OH CHEEK [HEART] WITHIN THE COAL	THE SMOULDERING EMBERS	1132	2
TILL IT IS LAID WITHIN.	WHO GOES TO DINE MUST	1223	4
WITHIN A CAPSULE GAY,	THIS IS THE PLACE THEY	1264	4
HAD WE THE EYES WITHIN OUR HEAD [HEADS]--	HAD WE OUR SENSES	1284	5
WITHIN OUR POWER	IN THIS SHORT LIFE	1287	4
TO WALK WITHIN THE VAIL.	THE LAST OF SUMMER IS	1353	8
WITHIN [BETWEEN] HIS RUSSET LIPS--	A SAUCER HOLDS A CUP	1374	10
HOW LUSCIOUS LIES WITHIN THE POD	FORBIDDEN FRUIT A FLAVOR	1377	3
WITHIN IT'S REACH [HOPE], THOUGH YET [AND JUST] UNGRASPED	WHO NEVER WANTED--	1430	5
I SAW THE WIND WITHIN HER	I SAW THE WIND WITHIN	1502	1
WITHIN [IN / TO] A STAR--	HE LIVED THE LIFE OF	1525	8
AT LEAST WITHIN MY TREE	COME SHOW THY DURHAM	1542	5
WITHIN THY GRAVE!	WITHIN THY GRAVE!	1552	1
THOUGH I WITHIN SUPPOSE	I GROPED FOR HIM BEFORE	1555	6
THE SPIRIT LURKS WITHIN THE FLESH	THE SPIRIT LASTS--BUT IN	1576	9
LIKE TIDES WITHIN THE SEA	THE SPIRIT LASTS--BUT IN	1576	10
FROM THESE [THOSE] WITHIN MY HAND	COSMOPOLITES WITHOUT A	1589	4
THE BELL WITHIN THE STEEPLE WILD	THERE CAME A WIND LIKE A	1593	13
WITHIN A MAGIC PRISON	OF GOD WE ASK ONE FAVOR,	1601	6
WITHIN THAT LITTLE HIVE	WITHIN THAT LITTLE HIVE	1607	1
IS HAD WITHIN--	SPEECH IS ONE SYMPTOM OF	1681	6
THE MOB WITHIN THE HEART	THE MOB WITHIN THE HEART	1745	1
WITHIN ITS PRECINCTS HOPES HAVE PLAYED,--	SWEET HOURS HAVE	1767	3
WITHOLD			
AND WITHOLD A STAR--	ALL I MAY, IF SMALL,	819	6
IF A DISCOURAGEMENT WITHOLD ME--	UP LIFE'S HILL WITH MY	1010	3
WHO WAS SHE TO WITHOLD FROM ME	FRIGID AND SWEET HER	1318	7
WITHOLDEN			
DISCERNED--STILL WITHOLDEN	TRUST IN THE UNEXPECTED	555	7

	FIRST LINE	POEM	LINE
WITHOLDING			
WITHOLDING NOT A CRESCENT	A BEE HIS BURNISHED	1339	7
WITHOUT			
WITHOUT COMMANDER! COUNTLESS! STILL!	SOME RAINBOW--COMING	64	19
WITHOUT A QUICKER BLOOD,	I NEVER HEAR THE WORD	77	2
WITHOUT THE KNOWING WHY!	HEART, NOT SO HEAVY AS	83	16
A FUZZY FELLOW, WITHOUT FEET,	A FUZZY FELLOW, WITHOUT	173	1
WITHOUT THE SOUND OF BOARDS	I'VE KNOWN A HEAVEN,	243	4
WITHOUT THE LEXICON!	FOREVER AT HIS SIDE TO	246	16
AND SINGS THE TUNE WITHOUT THE WORDS--	"HOPE" IS THE THING WITH	254	3
WITHOUT THE WEARINESS--	TO DIE--TAKES JUST A	255	12
POURED THEE, WITHOUT A STINT--	DOUBT ME! MY DIM	275	4
WITHOUT A [BUT DEIGN NO] SYLLABLE--	HOW NOTELESS MEN, AND	282	12
WITHOUT THE SNOW'S TABLEAU	THE ROBIN'S MY CRITERION	285	13
WITHOUT A MOMENT'S BELL--	THAT AFTER HORROR--THAT	286	10
WITHOUT--TREMENDOUS GAIN--	I GOT SO I COULD HEAR	293	2
WITHOUT THAT FORCING, IN MY BREATH--	I GOT SO I COULD HEAR	293	11
WITHOUT A STINT--WITHOUT A BLAME,	YOUR RICHES--TAUGHT ME--	299	19
WITHOUT A STINT--WITHOUT A BLAME,	YOUR RICHES--TAUGHT ME--	299	19
WITHOUT THE FEAR--TO JUSTIFY--	I SHOULD HAVE BEEN TOO	313	16
THE PALM--WITHOUT THE CALVARY--	I SHOULD HAVE BEEN TOO	313	17
WITHOUT EXTERNAL SOUND	THERE CAME A DAY AT	322	22
WITHOUT DESIGN--THAT I COULD TRACE	FROM COCOON FORTH A	354	5
WITHOUT A COLOR, BUT THE LIGHT	DARE YOU SEE A SOUL AT	365	7
WITHOUT A MISERY--	I KNOW LIVES, I COULD	372	2
WITHOUT THE PRIVILEGE TO KNOW	HOW MANY FLOWERS FAIL IN	404	3
WITHOUT THE LONELINESS--	IT MIGHT BE LONELIER	405	2
SALUTE, AND PASS, WITHOUT A HINT--	I READ MY SENTENCE--	412	13
THE BRUSH WITHOUT THE HAND--	THE OUTER--FROM THE	451	10
BLISS--WERE AN ODDITY--WITHOUT THEE--	LOVE--THOU ART HIGH--	453	16
SO WELL THAT I CAN LIVE WITHOUT--	SO WELL THAT I CAN LIVE	456	1
WITHOUT THE OTHER--THEREFORE--	LIKE EYES THAT LOOKED ON	458	15
DOOM IS THE HOUSE WITHOUT THE DOOR--	DOOM IS THE HOUSE	475	1
PARTAKES WITHOUT ALIGHTING	WITHIN MY GARDEN, RIDES	500	7
SHE RUNS WITHOUT THE LOOK OF FEET--	SHE SIGHTS A BIRD--SHE	507	3
BAPTIZED, BEFORE, WITHOUT THE CHOICE,	I'M CEDED--I'VE STOPPED	508	8
AND COULD NOT BREATHE WITHOUT A KEY,	IT WAS NOT DEATH, FOR I	510	15
WITHOUT A CHANCE, OR SPAR--	IT WAS NOT DEATH, FOR I	510	22
CAN GO, ITSELF, WITHOUT A FAN--	YOU CANNOT PUT A FIRE	530	3
WITHOUT DISCLOSING WHAT IT BE	I'VE SEEN A DYING EYE	547	7
THE BODY GROWS WITHOUT [OUTSIDE]--	THE BODY GROWS WITHOUT--	578	1
WITHOUT THE ENTERING--	IT ALWAYS FELT TO ME--A	597	4
WITHOUT A BOLT--THAT I COULD PROVE--	IT TROUBLED ME AS ONCE I	600	7
WITHOUT ERASING [ENDANGERING] SIGHT--	A STILL--VOLCANO--LIFE--	601	4
IT MAY BE WILDERNESS--WITHOUT--	UNTO MY BOOKS--SO GOOD	604	9
OUTSIDE [WITHOUT]--THE SPADES--WERE PLYING--	IN FALLING TIMBERS	614	3
WITHOUT A THING TO DO--	AT LEISURE IS THE SOUL	618	4
WITHOUT A GLANCE MY WAY--	I ASKED NO OTHER THING--	621	6
WITHOUT DEBATE [CERTIFICATE]--OR PAUSE--	FOREVER--IS COMPOSED OF	624	9
WITHOUT A BUTTON--I C'D VOUCH--	YOU'LL KNOW HER--BY HER	634	7
'TWAS NOON--WITHOUT THE NEWS [REPORT] OF NIGHT--	TO MY SMALL HEARTH HIS	638	7
WITHOUT MY RIGHT OF FROST--	I CANNOT LIVE WITH YOU--	640	19
WITHOUT THIS--THERE IS NOUGHT--	WITHOUT THIS--THERE IS	655	1
WITHOUT A FURTHER FUNCTION--	TO BE ALIVE--IS POWER--	677	3
WITHOUT AN INSTANT'S RESPITE--	I SOMETIMES DROP IT, FOR	708	7
RETIRED [LAID DOWN] WITHOUT A CARE--	THE DAY UNDRESSED--	716	12
WITHOUT DESIGN	FOUR TREES--UPON A	742	2
ENTERTAIN--WITHOUT ADDRESSING	SO THE EYES ACCOST--AND	752	5
WITHOUT--THE POWER TO DIE--	MY LIFE HAD STOOD--A	754	24
WITHOUT ATTEMPT--EXHAUSTION--	THE MOUNTAINS--GROW	757	3
TO GO WITHOUT THE SPECTRE'S AID [HELP]	I LIVED ON DREAD--	770	8
DELIGHT WITHOUT A CAUSE--	IT IS A LONESOME GLEE--	774	6
THE SERVICE WITHOUT HOPE--	THE SERVICE WITHOUT HOPE	779	1
STANDS WITHOUT A BONE--	THE TRUTH--IS STIRLESS--	780	8
THAT HOLDS WITHOUT A PROP--	THE TRUTH--IS STIRLESS--	780	10
GOOD, WITHOUT ALARM	EXPECTATION--IS	807	6
WITHOUT A SYLLABLE.	THE VEINS OF OTHER	811	8
WITHOUT THE FORMULA OF SOUND	A LIGHT EXISTS IN SPRING	812	15
WITHOUT A CORDIAL INTERVIEW	SPRING IS THE PERIOD	844	7
HERSELF, WITHOUT A PARLIAMENT	APOLOGY FOR HER	852	3
WITHOUT THE INCIDENT OF FAME	WHEN I HAVE SEEN THE SUN	888	5
DEEPER THAN WITHOUT--	ABSENT PLACE--AN APRIL	927	6
CIRCUMFERENCE WITHOUT RELIEF--	A COFFIN--IS A SMALL	943	11
WITHOUT DELIGHT, OR BEAM--	DENIAL--IS THE ONLY FACT	965	6
WITHOUT A TIGHTER BREATHING	A NARROW FELLOW IN THE	986	23
WE'LL PASS WITHOUT THE PARTING	WE'LL PASS WITHOUT THE	996	1
THE DYING MULTIFOLD--WITHOUT	TOO SCANTY 'TWAS TO DIE	1013	7
TO DIE--WITHOUT THE DYING	TO DIE--WITHOUT THE	1017	1
AND LIVE--WITHOUT THE LIFE	TO DIE--WITHOUT THE	1017	2
A GRACE WITHOUT A FRIEND.	MY SEASON'S FURTHEST	1019	4
BORNE WITHOUT DISSENT OF EITHER [ANY]	THREE WEEKS PASSED SINCE	1061	9
THE WIFE--WITHOUT THE SIGN!	TITLE DIVINE--IS MINE!	1072	2
BETROTHED--WITHOUT THE SWOON	TITLE DIVINE--IS MINE!	1072	6
WITHOUT HER DIADEM.	THE SKY IS LOW--THE	1075	8
THE WIND COULD WAIT WITHOUT THE GATE	THE SPRY ARMS OF THE	1103	7
A WISDOM, WITHOUT FACE, OR NAME,	THE CRICKETS SANG	1104	10
DISCOVERED IS WITHOUT SURPRISE	THE LARGEST FIRE EVER	1114	3
PROCEEDS WITHOUT CONCERN--	THE LARGEST FIRE EVER	1114	4
CONSUMES AND NO [WITHOUT] REPORT TO MEN	THE LARGEST FIRE EVER	1114	5

	FIRST LINE	POEM	LINE
WITHOUT (CONTINUED)			
REBUILT ANOTHER MORNING [IN TIME NEXT MORNING / WITHOUT . . .	THE LARGEST FIRE EVER	1114	7
THAT MANY DIE WITHOUT--	THERE IS ANOTHER	1116	2
WITHOUT DISCREET ALARM--	THESE ARE THE NIGHTS	1128	14
WITHOUT A LIGHT	A SPIDER SEWED AT NIGHT	1138	2
TO BREATHE MY BLANK WITHOUT THEE	THROUGH WHAT TRANSPORTS	1153	3
WITHOUT THE DATE, LIKE CONSCIOUSNESS OR IMMORTALITY--	LEST ANY DOUBT THAT WE	1156	3
GOD MADE NO ACT WITHOUT A CAUSE, ...	GOD MADE NO ACT WITHOUT	1163	1
NOR HEART WITHOUT AN AIM, ...	GOD MADE NO ACT WITHOUT	1163	2
WE LET GO ALL OF TIME WITHOUT	THE DAYS THAT WE CAN	1184	7
WITHOUT AN EARTHLY CAUSE	A LITTLE DOG THAT WAGS	1185	6
WITHOUT THE FORMULA.	SOMEHOW MYSELF SURVIVED	1194	4
THAT SAILED WITHOUT A CARE--	A SOFT SEA WASHED AROUND	1198	4
THE TABLE IS NOT LAID WITHOUT	WHO GOES TO DINE MUST	1223	3
WITHOUT OFFENCE [OPPRESS] OF TOLL-- . . .	THERE IS NO FRIGATE LIKE	1263	6
THAT HINTS WITHOUT ASSUMING--	SEPTEMBER'S	1271	5
AND DINE [GROW] WITHOUT LIKE GOD-- . . .	ART THOU THE THING I	1282	8
GIVEN TO ME WITHOUT THE SUIT	FRIGID AND SWEET HER	1318	5
WITHOUT THE CHANCE OF LIFE	I NEVER HEAR THAT ONE IS	1323	2
WITHOUT A SMILE--WITHOUT A THROE	WITHOUT A SMILE--WITHOUT	1330	1
WITHOUT A SMILE--WITHOUT A THROE	WITHOUT A SMILE--WITHOUT	1330	1
WITHOUT A RHYTHMIC RUMOR	WHAT TENEMENTS OF CLOVER	1338	7
WITHOUT CELESTIAL MAIL--	THE LAST OF SUMMER IS	1353	6
AUDACIOUS AS WITHOUT A KNOCK	THE LAST OF SUMMER IS	1353	7
AND VANS WITHOUT A NAME	HOW KNOW IT FROM A	1364	6
COMBINED WITHOUT A SEAM	HOW FITS HIS UMBER COAT	1371	3
IT COMES, WITHOUT A CONSTERNATION-- . . .	IN MANY AND REPORTLESS	1382	5
WITHOUT A NAME--	IN MANY AND REPORTLESS	1382	8
THEN WANED [TO WANE] WITHOUT DISPARAGEMENT .	THESE HELD THEIR WICK	1390	5
WITHOUT, PERHAPS, THE RIOT	SUMMER HAS TWO	1422	5
WITHOUT A VAUNT OR SHEEN	THE GENTIAN HAS A	1424	5
CAN READ WITHOUT IT'S GLASSES	BELSHAZZAR HAD A LETTER	1459	7
WITHOUT A SINGLE LEAF	BEFORE YOU THOUGHT OF	1465	14
THE DEVIL--WITHOUT QUESTION [SO AMENDED--] .	THE DEVIL--HAD HE	1479	7
WITHOUT DAY.	LOVE IS DONE WHEN LOVE'S	1485	5
WITHOUT A FORMULA WE FOUGHT	'TIS SEASONS SINCE THE	1529	7
INTRO WITHOUT MY TRANS--	A PANG IS MORE	1530	V
AND THUS, WITHOUT A WING	AS IMPERCEPTIBLY AS	1540	13
WITHOUT A CHANGE OF WINGS, ...	TO THE BRIGHT EAST SHE	1573	4
A CRASH WITHOUT A SOUND, ...	THE FARTHEST THUNDER	1581	18
COSMOPOLITES WITHOUT A PLEA	COSMOPOLITES WITHOUT A	1589	1
BEFORE A FENCE WITHOUT A FARE	UPON HIS SADDLE SPRUNG A	1600	3
WITHOUT DIMINUET PROCEED!	OH WHAT A GRACE IS THIS,	1615	5
WITHOUT A REVERY--	A DRUNKARD CANNOT MEET A	1628	2
TO WHICH WITHOUT A TICKET GO	SOME ONE PREPARED THIS	1644	2
WITHOUT AN OAR	DOWN TIME'S QUAINT	1656	2
WITHOUT A SURETY FROM THE WIND	DOWN TIME'S QUAINT	1656	9
WITHOUT SUSPECTING OUR ABODE	EDEN IS THAT	1657	3
WITHOUT THE HIGH PREROGATIVE	UNTO A BROKEN HEART	1704	3
WITHOUT APPARENT BURDEN	HIGH FROM THE EARTH I	1723	13
WITHOUT A HINT FROM ME, ...	IF EVER THE LID GETS OFF	1727	4
THOU CAN'ST NOT BOAST, LIKE JESUS, DRUNKEN WITHOUT COMPANION	PROUD OF MY BROKEN HEART	1736	5
WITHOUT A LISTENER?	THE RETICENT VOLCANO	1748	8
WITHOUT THE STERILE PERQUISITE, ...	TO LOSE THEE--SWEETER	1754	7
WITHOUT THE STRENGTH TO SHAPE?	WHICH MISSES MOST,	1759	10
WITHSTAND			
COULD I SUCH A PLEA [FACE] WITHSTAND-- . . .	MOST SHE TOUCHED ME BY	760	8
WITHSTANDS			
WITHSTANDS UNTIL THE SWEET ASSAULT . . .	LIKE TRAINS OF CARS ON	1224	5
WITNESS			
THE HOSTS OF WITNESS STAND!	SLEEP IS SUPPOSED TO BE	13	6
TILL RANKS OF SEEDS THEIR WITNESS BEAR-- .	THESE ARE THE DAYS WHEN	130	10
HOW MANY TIMES THEY--BORE THE FAITHFUL WITNESS--	READ--SWEET--HOW OTHERS	260	5
THEY DOUBT TO WITNESS IT--	THE DOOMED--REGARD THE	294	4
HANDS--NOT SO STOUT--HOISTED THEM--IN WITNESS--	UNTO LIKE STORY--TROUBLE	295	19
THAT WAS THE WITNESS FOR THE GRACE--	THE DAY THAT I WAS	356	15
TO WITNESS HER GOODBYE--	WE GROW ACCUSTOMED TO	419	4
AND FILL MY LUNGS, FOR WITNESS--	DO PEOPLE MOULDER	432	7
TO WITNESS TO THE CERTAINTY	I LIVE WITH HIM--I SEE	463	11
LET NOT MY WITNESS HINDER THEM [THEM IMPAIR--]	'TIS TRUE--THEY SHUT ME	538	5
OUR LORD--INDEED--MADE [BORE] COMPOUND WITNESS--	ONE CRUCIFIXION IS	553	13
WITNESS, IS NOT HERE--	BLOOM UPON THE MOUNTAIN	667	12
MY WITNESS--WAS THE CRAPE [BLACK] I BORE-- .	THE BIRDS REPORTED FROM	743	19
HER--WITNESS--WAS HER DEAD--	THE BIRDS REPORTED FROM	743	20
CONVEX--AND CONCAVE WITNESS--	THE ADMIRATIONS--AND	906	13
WERE WITNESS FOR THE CROWN--	THE SUN WENT DOWN--NO	1079	8
AND LET NO WITNESS IN	A GREAT HOPE FELL	1123	5
THAT ALL MAY THEM--IT--EXAMINE [WITNESS IT AND MORE]	SOME ONE PREPARED THIS	1644	5
BUT WITNESS FOR HER LAND, ...	THE EARTH HAS MANY KEYS.	1775	5
AND WITNESS FOR HER SEA, ...	THE EARTH HAS MANY KEYS.	1775	6
WITNESSED			
ONCE WITNESSED OF THE GAUZE--	A SINGLE SCREW OF FLESH	263	5
BE WITNESSED--IN THE ROOM--	I HEARD A FLY BUZZ--WHEN	465	8

	FIRST LINE	POEM	LINE
WON (CONTINUED)			
THE BRANCHES THEY ARE WON, BUT TENS HAVE WON AN ALL--	SOUL, WILT THOU TOSS	139	4
MOST SHE WON ME BY THE WAY	MOST SHE TOUCHED ME BY	760	2
I WON AS NEAR AS THIS	THROUGH WHAT TRANSPORTS	1153	6
I WON IT WITH A BUN--	THIS DIRTY--LITTLE--	1311	3
DISSENTING [DEFYING] TO BE WON	THE FACE IN EVANESCENCE	1490	6
WONDER			
ONLY A BIRD WILL WONDER--	NOBODY KNOWS THIS LITTLE	35	9
WONDER UPON WONDER	BEFORE THE ICE IS IN THE	37	7
WONDER UPON WONDER	BEFORE THE ICE IS IN THE	37	7
BEGUILING THUS THE WONDER	WENT UP A YEAR THIS	93	17
CONCLUDE THE WONDER GAY--	A SOMETHING IN A	122	20
AND I HAVE CEASED TO WONDER WHY--	I SHALL KNOW WHY--WHEN	193	2
AND I--FOR WONDER AT HIS WOE--	I SHALL KNOW WHY--WHEN	193	6
TO WONDER WHAT MYSELF WILL SAY,	THO' I GET HOME HOW LATE	207	11
AND WONDER WE COULD CARE	WHEN NIGHT IS ALMOST	347	6
THEY WONDER IF IT DIED--ON THAT--	THERE'S BEEN A DEATH, IN	389	11
WE WONDER IT WAS NOT OURSELVES	THIS WAS A POET--IT IS	448	7
LEST THEY--WONDER WHY--	SWEET--SAFE--HOUSES--	457	15
AND WONDER HOW THE FINGERS FEEL	I WOULD NOT PAINT--A	505	5
A WONDER IF THE SEPULCHRE	I'M SORRY FOR THE DEAD--	529	17
I WONDER IF IT WEIGHS LIKE MINE--	I MEASURE EVERY GRIEF I	561	3
I WONDER IF THEY BORE IT LONG--	I MEASURE EVERY GRIEF I	561	5
I WONDER IF IT HURTS TO LIVE--	I MEASURE EVERY GRIEF I	561	9
I WONDER IF WHEN YEARS HAVE PILED--	I MEASURE EVERY GRIEF I	561	17
AND WONDER--AND DECAY	HE GAVE AWAY HIS LIFE--	567	10
I WONDER HOW THE RICH--MAY FEEL--	GOD GAVE A LOAF TO EVERY	791	13
SWEET WONDER--	BESIDES THIS MAY	977	7
WE CHIEFLY WONDER THEN	SO LARGE MY WILL	1024	14
SOME WE SEE NO MORE, TENEMENTS OF WONDER	SOME WE SEE NO MORE,	1221	1
WONDER--IS NOT PRECISELY KNOWING	WONDER--IS NOT PRECISELY	1331	1
I OFTEN WONDER HE	WHAT MYSTERY PERVADES A	1400	10
TO ONE A WONDER STILL	THE GOING FROM A WORLD	1603	2
WONDERED			
AND WONDERED WHAT THEY DID THERE--	I OFTEN PASSED THE	51	3
I WONDERED WHICH WOULD MISS ME, LEAST,	'TWAS JUST THIS TIME,	445	13
WE WONDERED AT OUR BLINDNESS	HER FINAL SUMMER WAS IT	795	9
WONDERFUL			
WONDERFUL ROTATION!	FREQUENTLY THE WOODS ARE	6	11
LEST SKIES IMPEACH A WEALTH SO WONDERFUL--	I'LL CLUTCH--AND CLUTCH	427	23
A WONDERFUL--TO FEEL THE SUN	A SOLEMN THING WITHIN	483	7
ARE MAGICAL [WERE WONDERFUL / ARE TERRIBLE / ARE MIRACULOUS / . . .	CONTAINED IN THIS SHORT	1165	2
WONDERING			
SO--WONDERING--THRO' THE HOURS MEEK	I HAVE A KING, WHO DOES	103	2
AND IN MY WONDERING HAND	AS IF I ASKED A COMMON	323	2
WONDROUS			
ON THIS WONDROUS SEA	ON THIS WONDROUS SEA	4	1
THAT WAS A WONDROUS BOOTY--	I NEVER TOLD THE BURIED	11	10
NE'ER SAW I SUCH A WONDROUS SCENE--	THERE IS A MORN BY MEN	24	13
BECOME SO WONDROUS DEAR--	AS BY THE DEAD WE LOVE	88	2
THE WONDROUS NEARER DREW--	WENT UP A YEAR THIS	93	18
WONT			
I WAS WONT TO SEE--	FREQUENTLY THE WOODS ARE	6	6
'TWAS NOT THY WONT, TO HINDER SO--	'TIS SUNRISE--LITTLE	908	3
WOO			
THE WIND DOTH WOO THE BRANCHES, THE BRANCHES THEY ARE WON,	AWAKE YE MUSES NINE,	1	15
THE WORM DOTH WOO THE MORTAL, DEATH CLAIMS A LIVING BRIDE,	AWAKE YE MUSES NINE,	1	21
NOR PROVE, NOR WOO,	THAN HEAVEN MORE REMOTE,	1436	13
WOOD			
THROUGH CLEARING AND THRO' WOOD--	THROUGH LANE IT LAY--	9	2
NOR BY THE WOOD ARE FOUND--	THERE IS A MORN BY MEN	24	9
BACK TO HER NATIVE WOOD!	THERE'S SOMETHING	45	12
THE REGIMENTS OF WOOD AND HILL	SOME RAINBOW--COMING	64	20
WITH THEE IN THE TAMARIND WOOD--	WITH THEE, IN THE DESERT	209	3
AND WHERE WAS THE WOOD--	HOW THE OLD MOUNTAINS	291	18
IT POWDERS ALL THE WOOD [FIELD].	IT SIFTS FROM LEADEN	311	2
HOW MANY FLOWERS FAIL IN WOOD--	HOW MANY FLOWERS FAIL IN	404	1
IMPORTED TO THE WOOD--	LIKE FLOWERS, THAT HEARD	513	9
UNTO A PURPLE WOOD	A LANE OF YELLOW LED THE	1650	2
WOODEN			
WOODEN BARRED,	I KNOW SOME LONELY	289	3
A WOODEN WAY	AFTER GREAT PAIN, A	341	7
I LAUGHED A CRUMBLING [WOODEN] LAUGH	I YEARS HAD BEEN FROM	609	13
WOODS			
FREQUENTLY THE WOODS ARE PINK--	FREQUENTLY THE WOODS ARE	6	1
SHE BECKONS, AND THE WOODS START--	BAFFLED FOR JUST A DAY	17	5
BUT WHEN THE WOODS WERE PAINTED,	I HAD A GUINEA GOLDEN--	23	11
I [WHO] ROBBED THE WOODS--	I ROBBED THE WOODS--	41	1
THE TRUSTING WOODS.	I ROBBED THE WOODS--	41	2
I PULL A FLOWER FROM THE WOODS--	"ARCTURUS" IS HIS OTHER	70	9
THE WOODS EXCHANGE A SMILE!	A LADY RED--AMID THE	74	10
I FOUND HER--"PLEIAD"--IN THE WOODS	WHOSE CHEEK IS THIS?	82	4
THE PRETTY PEOPLE IN THE WOODS	THE BEE IS NOT AFRAID OF	111	3
AN AXE SHRILL SINGING IN THE WOODS--	AN ALTERED LOOK ABOUT	140	11
SHE'S DREAMING OF THE WOODS!	WHOSE ARE THE LITTLE	142	24
WHEN APRIL WOODS ARE RED.	WHOSE ARE THE LITTLE	142	28

	FIRST LINE	POEM	LINE
WOODS (CONTINUED)			
AMONG THE APRIL WOODS!	IF I COULD BRIBE THEM BY	179	9
IT'S LIKE THE WOODS--	IT'S LIKE THE LIGHT--	297	5
NOT ALL PIANOS IN THE WOODS	I DREADED THAT FIRST	348	7
THE WINDS DID BUY IT OF THE WOODS--	OF BRUSSELS--IT WAS NOT	602	3
WILD FLOWERS--KINDLE IN THE WOODS--	IT MAKES NO DIFFERENCE	620	5
AND NOW WE ROAM IN [THE] SOVREIGN WOODS--	MY LIFE HAD STOOD--A	754	5
WOOED			
I--WOOED IT--TOO--	THE MALAY--TOOK THE	452	15
WOOING			
BOASTING [WOOING] MY PREMIUM--	MY HEART RAN SO TO THEE	1237	14
IT IS A STEALTHY WOOING	DEATH IS THE SUPPLE	1445	3
TO SOMETHING UPPER WOOING US	THE FASCINATING CHILL	1480	7
WOOL			
IT FILLS WITH ALABASTER WOOL	IT SIFTS FROM LEADEN	311	3
IN CRAYON, OR IN WOOL,	DEATH SETS A THING	360	6
SO FINER 'TIS THAN WOOL--	YOU'LL KNOW HER--BY HER	634	17
WOOS			
WOOS, AS HE STATES US--BY HIS SON--	GOD IS A DISTANT--	357	2
WORD			
THERE IS A WORD	THERE IS A WORD	8	1
I NEVER HEAR THE WORD "ESCAPE"	I NEVER HEAR THE WORD	77	1
FROM ACCENT HARSH, OR RUTHLESS WORD--	WHERE I HAVE LOST, I	104	6
AND UNDERSTOOD NO WORD IT SAID--	I'VE HEARD AN ORGAN TALK	183	3
THO' IGNORANT OF A WORD	I GOT SO I COULD HEAR	293	19
GOD--SPELL THE WORD! I--CANT--	ONE YEAR AGO--JOTS WHAT?	296	2
THE SYMBOL [FALLING / FIGURE] OF A WORD	THERE CAME A DAY AT	322	10
A SMILE TOO FEW--A WORD TOO MUCH	NOT PROBABLE--THE BAREST	346	2
WHAT WORD HAD THEY, FOR ME?	I DREADED THAT FIRST	348	20
PRONOUNCING EVERY WORD	THE MORNING AFTER WO--	364	10
PUT FROM MY SIMPLE SPEECH ALL PLAIN WORD--	I'M SAYING EVERY DAY	373	20
HOW COULD I BREAK MY WORD?	A MURMUR IN THE TREES--	416	18
I DEALT A WORD OF GOLD	IT WOULD NEVER BE COMMON	430	18
NOR CONFIRM--BY WORD--	CONSCIOUS AM I IN MY	679	4
TRIVIAL A WORD--JUST--	NO MATTER--NOW--SWEET--	704	5
I OFFERED HER NO WORD--	THE BIRDS REPORTED FROM	743	18
IF IT HAD NO WORD,	IF IT HAD NO PENCIL	921	5
WITH WHOM I SPOKE NO WORD--	MY BEST ACQUAINTANCES	932	2
UNTIL A VITAL WORD	I HEARD, AS IF I HAD NO	1039	2
TO THE PROPOUNDED WORD?	SHALL I TAKE THEE, THE	1126	2
THE WORD APPLIED TO FILL	SHALL I TAKE THEE, THE	1126	10
IMMORTAL IS AN AMPLE WORD	IMMORTAL IS AN AMPLE	1205	1
A WORD IS DEAD	A WORD IS DEAD	1212	1
A WORD DROPPED CARELESS ON A PAGE	A WORD DROPPED CARELESS	1261	1
HE KEPT HIS WORD A TRILLION YEARS	OUR LITTLE SECRETS SLINK	1326	3
ESCAPE IS SUCH A THANKFUL WORD	ESCAPE IS SUCH A	1347	1
UPON THIS TRUSTY WORD--	ESCAPE IS SUCH A	1347	12
"SECRETS" IS A DAILY WORD	"SECRETS" IS A DAILY	1385	1
WORD TO A FRIEND	I HAVE NO LIFE BUT THIS	1398	T
A LITTLE OVERFLOWING WORD	A LITTLE OVERFLOWING	1467	1
A WORD MADE FLESH IS SELDOM	A WORD MADE FLESH IS	1651	1
A WORD THAT BREATHES DISTINCTLY	A WORD MADE FLESH IS	1651	9
NOR MOULD IT INTO WORD	IF I COULD TELL HOW GLAD	1668	4
MY WILL ENDEAVORS FOR IT'S WORD	TO TELL THE BEAUTY WOULD	1700	5
WORDLESS			
A WISER [WORDLESS / SILENT / SPEECHLESS] SYMPATHY	THE BIRDS REPORTED FROM	743	24
WORDS			
AND SINGS THE TUNE WITHOUT THE WORDS--	"HOPE" IS THE THING WITH	254	3
I HEARD SUCH WORDS AS "RICH"--	IT WAS GIVEN TO ME BY	454	9
SHE DEALT HER PRETTY WORDS LIKE BLADES--	SHE DEALT HER PRETTY	479	1
THE ALPHABET--THE WORDS--	WE LEARNED THE WHOLE OF	568	2
I FOUND THE WORDS [PHRASE] TO EVERY THOUGHT	I FOUND THE WORDS TO	581	1
AND SO AROUND THE WORDS I WENT--	IF HE WERE LIVING--DARE	734	3
EACH OTHER WITH THE WORDS [NEWS]	TWO TRAVELLERS PERISHING	933	4
LIKE A LOVER'S WORDS.	NATURE RARER USES YELLOW	1045	8
WORDS ARE HANDED [LANGUAGE IS DRIVEN] AWAY--	WHATEVER IT IS--SHE HAS	1204	8
THE WORDS ARE WITHERED [SPEECH IS STOLEN] AWAY	WHATEVER IT IS--SHE HAS	1204	V 8
YOUR THOUGHTS DONT HAVE WORDS EVERY DAY	YOUR THOUGHTS DONT HAVE	1452	1
HER WORDS DID TOTTER SO	HIS VOICE DECREPIT WAS	1476	2
UPON IT'S FASTENED LIPS LAY WORDS--	OH GIVE IT MOTION--DECK	1527	3
BY HOMELY GIFT AND HINDERED WORDS	BY HOMELY GIFT AND	1563	1
HE ATE AND DRANK THE PRECIOUS WORDS--	HE ATE AND DRANK THE	1587	1
THE WORDS THE HAPPY SAY	THE WORDS THE HAPPY SAY	1750	1
WORE			
AND WORE MY LAST YEAR'S GOWN--	ONE SISTER HAVE I IN OUR	14	6
WHO ONCE THE COCKADE WORE--	THE SUN KEPT STOOPING--	152	12
BUT SURE I AM HE ERMINE WORE	I MET A KING THIS	166	5
HE HAD [WORE] NO SANDAL ON HIS FOOT--	THE ONLY GHOST I EVER	274	3
I WORE--AN HOUR AGO--	I GAINED IT SO--	359	15
IN JUST THE DRESS HIS CENTURY WORE--	A PRECIOUS--MOULDERING	371	3
AND BEATRICE WORE	A PRECIOUS--MOULDERING	371	18
FORGOT SHE WORE IT AT HER HEART	FORGET! THE LADY WITH	438	2
OVAL--AS FEUDAL LADIES WORE--	I AM ASHAMED--I HIDE--	473	14
IN JUST THE JACKET THAT HE WORE--	OF NEARNESS TO HER	607	9
SHE WORE WHEN SHE WAS BORN--	YOU'LL KNOW HER--BY HER	634	12
I THINK THE HEART I FORMER WORE	I THINK TO LIVE--MAY BE	646	5
LIKE COSTUMES GRANDSIRES WORE.	WE OUTGROW LOVE, LIKE	887	4
IN THE VERMILLION THAT IT WORE	THERE IS A JUNE WHEN	930	7
WAS ALL OUR TIMID MOTHER WORE	LET ME NOT MAR THAT	1335	7

	FIRST LINE	POEM	LINE
WORE (CONTINUED)			
THEY WORE [KNEW] NO LEXICONS--	"WAS NOT" WAS ALL THE	1342	4
WORK			
HER FINGERS FUMBLED AT HER WORK--	THE ROSE DID CAPER ON	208	5
IT IS EASY TO WORK WHEN THE SOUL IS AT PLAY--	IT IS EASY TO WORK WHEN	244	1
MAKES WORK DIFFICULT--THEN--	IT IS EASY TO WORK WHEN	244	4
SOME--WORK FOR IMMORTALITY--	SOME--WORK FOR	406	1
AND SO TO MEND HER--GAVE ME WORK	THE FIRST DAY'S NIGHT	410	7
TO SIMULATE--IS STINGING WORK--	I TIE MY HAT--I CREASE	443	19
COOL OF EYE, AND CRITICAL OF WORK--	A SOLEMN THING WITHIN	483	10
BEQUEATHING--RATHER--TO THEIR WORK--	THE MARTYR POETS--DID	544	6
SHE DOTH HER PURPLE WORK--	SHE HIDETH HER THE LAST	557	5
IT BEGS YOU GIVE IT WORK--	AT LEISURE IS THE SOUL	618	5
TO TAKE THE HONORABLE WORK	SHE ROSE TO HIS	732	3
BY STINT [END]--REWARDED WORK--	THE SERVICE WITHOUT HOPE	779	4
WHEN SHE HAD PUT AWAY HER WORK	SEVERER SERVICE OF	786	7
COULD LIFT MY FOREHEAD FROM MY WORK	THE MISSING ALL,	985	7
RUIN IS FORMAL--DEVILS WORK	CRUMBLING IS NOT AN	997	9
ARE SETTLED, AND AT WORK--	BEE! I'M EXPECTING YOU!	1035	6
TO JOINT THIS AGATE WERE A WORK [FEAT]--	TOO COLD IS THIS	1135	4
THE WORK OF HER THAT WENT,	THE WORK OF HER THAT	1143	1
PUT THEIR WORK AWAY	THERE'S THE BATTLE OF	1174	4
ALL MEN FOR HONOR HARDEST WORK	ALL MEN FOR HONOR	1193	1
PAID AFTER THEY HAVE CEASED TO WORK	ALL MEN FOR HONOR	1193	3
PUT UP MY HEART THY HOARY WORK	THE NOTICE THAT IS	1310	3
HOW LITTLE WORK [WHAT LITTLE ACT] IT BE--	WITH PINIONS OF DISDAIN	1431	10
THE SUN WENT OUT TO WORK--	A DEW SUFFICED ITSELF--	1437	5
BUT WORK MIGHT BE ELECTRIC REST	THE BIRD HER PUNCTUAL	1585	7
FOR BREATHING IS THE ONLY WORK	NO MAN SAW AWE, NOR TO	1733	11
WORKED			
AND NOTWITHSTANDING BEE--THAT WORKED--	FROM COCOON FORTH A	354	18
YOU ALMOST PITIED IT--YOU--IT WORKED SO--	GOING TO HIM! HAPPY	494	14
I WORKED FOR CHAFF AND EARNING WHEAT	I WORKED FOR CHAFF AND	1269	1
WORKING			
THE WIND DOES--WORKING LIKE A HAND,	OF ALL THE SOUNDS	321	5
WHO QUIT THEIR SHINING WORKING	TRUSTY AS THE STARS	1369	2
OF TRANSPORT'S WORKING CLASSES--	THE ROBIN IS A GABRIEL	1483	4
WORKMAN			
SING--AT IT'S PAIN--AS ANY WORKMAN--	BOUND--A TROUBLE--	269	9
WORKMANSHIPS			
TO PONDER LITTLE WORKMANSHIPS	DEATH SETS A THING	360	5
WORKMEN			
AND WORKMEN FINISHED ONE BY ONE	THE CRICKETS SANG	1104	3
WORKS			
THIS ME--THAT WALKS AND WORKS--MUST DIE,	THIS ME--THAT WALKS AND	1588	1
WORLD			
GOD HATH MADE NOTHING SINGLE BUT THEE IN HIS WORLD SO FAIR!	AWAKE YE MUSES NINE,	1	6
AND BID THE WORLD GOODMORROW, AND GO TO GLORY HOME!	AWAKE YE MUSES NINE,	1	40
AND THE EARTH [WORLD]--THEY TELL ME--	FREQUENTLY THE WOODS ARE	6	9
SOME VISION OF THE WORLD CASHMERE--	SOME RAINBOW--COMING	64	2
WHAT ALL THE WORLD SUSPECT?	COCOON ABOVE! COCOON	129	3
JUST FELT [HEARD] THE WORLD GO BY!	JUST LOST, WHEN I WAS	160	2
I LOST A WORLD--THE OTHER DAY!	I LOST A WORLD--THE	181	1
IN YOUR NEW-FASHIONED WORLD!	THE SKIES CANT KEEP	191	16
UPON A SPOTTED WORLD--	WHEN WE STAND ON THE	242	14
WHOSE INVITATION, KNOW YOU NOT [FOR THIS WORLD--]	HE PUT THE BELT AROUND	273	15
AND THE WORLD I USED TO KNOW--	TIE THE STRINGS TO MY	279	14
AND HIT A WORLD, AT EVERY PLUNGE [CRASH],	I FELT A FUNERAL, IN MY	280	19
CAME ONCE A WORLD--DID YOU?	ONE YEAR AGO--JOTS WHAT?	296	14
THE WORLD, WILL HAVE IT'S OWN--TO DO--	ALTHOUGH I PUT AWAY HIS	366	24
BEFORE THE WORLD BE GREEN--	THERE IS A FLOWER THAT	380	14
AND SWEPT THE WORLD AWAY--	THE WINTERS ARE SO SHORT	403	14
NOT IN THIS WORLD TO SEE HIS FACE--	NOT IN THIS WORLD TO SEE	418	1
AND DOWERED--ALL THE WORLD--	IT WOULD NEVER BE COMMON	430	20
THIS IS MY LETTER TO THE WORLD	THIS IS MY LETTER TO THE	441	1
THE WORLD--STANDS--SOLEMNER--TO ME--	THE WORLD--STANDS--	493	1
THIS WORLD IS NOT CONCLUSION.	THIS WORLD IS NOT	501	1
THE FROST--POSSESS [OBTAIN] THE WORLD--	HE PARTS HIMSELF--LIKE	517	17
TO PUT THIS WORLD DOWN, LIKE A BUNDLE--	TO PUT THIS WORLD DOWN,	527	1
AND WENT AGAINST THE WORLD--	I TOOK MY POWER IN MY	540	2
OR WORLD--	IT KNEW NO LAPSE, NOR	560	8
A MIGHTY LOOK RUNS ROUND THE WORLD	"HEAVEN" HAS DIFFERENT	575	5
HOW ALL THE CLOCKS STOPPED IN THE WORLD--	IF I MAY HAVE IT, WHEN	577	16
DIVIDED--BY A WORLD--	OF NEARNESS TO HER	607	12
AND WHEN THIS WORLD--SETS FURTHER BACK--	YOU'LL FIND--IT WHEN YOU	610	9
I TOLD HIM WORLDS [A WORLD] I KNEW	I ROSE--BECAUSE HE SANK	616	16
CREDITS THE WORLD--	THE CHILD'S FAITH IS NEW	637	9
IN DYING--'TIS AS IF OUR SOULS [WORLD / SELVES / SUN]	BEREAVEMENT IN THEIR	645	11
I LOOK ON ALL THIS WORLD CONTAINS--	AGAIN--HIS VOICE IS AT	663	11
BLUE IS BLUE--THE WORLD THROUGH--	OUT OF SIGHT? WHAT OF	703	8
THE WORLD--FEELS DUSTY	THE WORLD--FEELS DUSTY	715	1
EXACTLY [PRECISELY]--AS THE WORLD--	THE DAY UNDRESSED--	716	5
AND HAPLY, IN THE WORLD--	THE BEGGAR LAD--DIES	717	4
THE CRUEL--SMILING--BOWING WORLD--	THE BEGGAR LAD--DIES	717	5
UPON THE WORLD BELOW--	THE MOON WAS BUT A CHIN	737	4
ALL ELSE [THE WORLD] ACCUSED ME--AND	MY SOUL--ACCUSED ME--AND	753	3

	FIRST LINE	POEM		LINE
WORLD (CONTINUED)				
I SMILED--				
AND THEN ABROAD THE WORLD HE GO	MY FAITH IS LARGER THAN	766		7
THE DAY CONTROLLED [RESUMED] THE WORLD--	THE BIRDS BEGUN AT FOUR	783		22
TO BESTOW A WORLD	ALL I MAY, IF SMALL,	819		5
TO THIS WORLD SHE RETURNED.	TO THIS WORLD SHE	830		1
THERE IS NO OTHER IN THE WORLD--	I CANNOT BUY IT--'TIS	840		2
TILL ALL THE WORLD IS AJAR--	NOON--IS THE HINGE OF	931		4
PARTING WITH A WORLD	THAT IS SOLEMN WE HAVE	934		6
THIS WORLD, AND IT'S SPECIES [NATIONS / FASHIONS / SYMBOLS / . . .	THIS DUST, AND IT'S	936		9
AND HAUNT THE WORLD.	THERE IS NO SILENCE IN	1004		4
SPRING COMES ON THE WORLD--	SPRING COMES ON THE	1042		1
A SICKNESS OF THIS WORLD IT MOST OCCASIONS	A SICKNESS OF THIS WORLD	1044		1
A WORLD MUST BE	A SICKNESS OF THIS WORLD	1044		6
THIS [THE] WORLD DID DROP AWAY	IT WAS A QUIET WAY--	1053		9
THESE STRANGERS, IN A FOREIGN WORLD,	THESE STRANGERS, IN A	1096		1
HOW IT ALTERS THE WORLD--	AFTER THE SUN COMES OUT	1148		2
ON THE WORLD YOU COLORED	ON THE WORLD YOU COLORED	1171		1
AND SANG FOR NOTHING SCRUTABLE [IN THE WORLD]	THE MOST TRIUMPHANT BIRD	1265		5
WE COULD NOT LOOK UPON THE EARTH [WORLD]--	HAD WE OUR SENSES	1284		7
WITH SUMMER, OR THE WORLD--	WINTER IS GOOD--HIS HOAR	1316		4
THAT EVERY MAN [ALL THE WORLD] BEHOLD	YOU CANNOT TAKE ITSELF	1351		6
NOR PLEA FOR WORLD [WORLDS] TO COME	I HAVE NO LIFE BUT THIS	1398	V	5
A NEIGHBOR FROM ANOTHER WORLD	WHAT MYSTERY PERVADES A	1400		3
A FENCE [WORLD] OR TWO FROM THEE--	MY MAKER--LET ME BE	1403	V	2
WHO [THAT] MUST BE UP TO CALL THE WORLD	HOW GOOD HIS LAVA BED,	1447		3
FROM SUCH A VELVET WORLD IT COMES [CAME]	HOW SOFT A CATERPILLAR	1448		3
LIVES HE IN ANY OTHER WORLD	LIVES HE IN ANY OTHER	1557		1
THAT RENOVATES THE WORLD--	BY HOMELY GIFT AND	1563		5
THE WORLD THAT THOU HAST OPENED	EXPANSE CANNOT BE LOST--	1584		9
AND YET ABIDE [REMAIN] THE WORLD!	THERE CAME A WIND LIKE A	1593		17
THE GOING FROM A WORLD WE KNOW	THE GOING FROM A WORLD	1603		1
A WORLD MADE PENNINILESS BY THAT [HIS] DEPARTURE	A WORLD MADE PENNINILESS	1623		1
THERE IS A WORLD [TOMB / CHAIR / SEAT] FOR ALL	NO LIFE CAN POMPLESS	1626	V	8
AND THE WORLD--IF THE WORLD BE LOOKING ON--	IF EVER THE LID GETS OFF	1727		5
AND THE WORLD--IF THE WORLD BE LOOKING ON--	IF EVER THE LID GETS OFF	1727		5
WORLD'S				
AND VASTER [THIS ONE / DIFFERENT]--OF THE WORLD'S.	THAT FIRST DAY, WHEN YOU	659		8
IF NOTHING LARGER THAN A WORLD'S	THE MISSING ALL,	985		3
MAKES A WORLD'S SUSPENSE	TRUSTY AS THE STARS	1369		7
WORLDS				
WORLDS SCOOP THEIR ARCS--	SAFE IN THEIR ALABASTER	216	V	
WORLDS [THE MILLER]--A FLOOD--	"MORNING"--MEANS	300		8
TWO [THE] WORLDS--LIKE AUDIENCES--DISPERSE [DISSOLVE / WITHDRAW / RETIRE]	DEPARTED--TO THE	524		7
I TOLD HIM WORLDS [A WORLD] I KNEW	I ROSE--BECAUSE HE SANK	616		16
WORLDS WERE LYING OUT TO [SWIMMING IN THE / LYING IN THE] SUN--	WHEN I HOPED, I	768		11
HIS AUDITORS TWO WORLDS	HIS MANSION IN THE POOL	1379		5
NOR PLEA FOR WORLD [WORLDS] TO COME	I HAVE NO LIFE BUT THIS	1398	V	5
WORM				
THE WORM DOTH WOO THE MORTAL, DEATH CLAIMS A LIVING BRIDE,	AWAKE YE MUSES NINE,	1		21
MANY A WORM	SO FROM THE MOULD	66		7
I SLEW A WORM THE OTHER DAY--	"ARCTURUS" IS HIS OTHER	70		5
AND LEFT THE LITTLE ANGLE WORM	OUR LITTLE KINSMEN--	885		11
OR DOME OF WORM--	DRAB HABITATION OF WHOM?	893		3
NEVER A WORM SO CONFIDENT	AND THIS OF ALL MY HOPES	913		7
A WORM, HIS UTMOST GOAL.	HIS BILL AN AUGUR IS	1034		4
TO PACK THE BUD--OPPOSE THE WORM--	BLOOM--IS RESULT--TO	1058		9
I CAME UPON A WORM	IN WINTER IN MY ROOM	1670		2
BUT AS HE WAS A WORM	IN WINTER IN MY ROOM	1670		4
IN FEATURE AS THE WORM BEFORE	IN WINTER IN MY ROOM	1670		16
WORMS				
LIKE GLOW WORMS, FLEE AWAY--	THE SUN AND MOON MUST	871		8
LIKE WORMS BENEATH [BEFORE] THE POWER--	THE WIND TOOK UP THE	1134	V	8
AND WORMS PRESUME	IN WINTER IN MY ROOM	1670		5
WORN				
WORN FAIR	UNTO LIKE STORY--TROUBLE	295		10
AND THIS WORN SHOE JUST FITS THE TRACK--	'TWAS THE OLD--ROAD--	344		15
OR RHODODENDRON--WORN--	THERE IS A FLOWER THAT	380		12
WHEN CRESCENT--THOU ART WORN--I NOTE [MIND]--	YOU KNOW THAT PORTRAIT	504		11
AND HOW THEY'RE MOSTLY WORN--	I MEASURE EVERY GRIEF I	561		38
FOR I HAD WORN IT, EVERY DAY,	IT CEASED TO HURT ME,	584		6
AS TRINKET--WORN BY FADED CHILD--	I'LL SEND THE FEATHER	687		4
WORN TO NATURE'S PARTY ONCE	RIBBONS OF THE YEAR--	873		3
IN HIS LONG ABSENCE WORN	EACH SCAR I'LL KEEP FOR	877		3
WORN--NOW--AND DULL--SWEET,	IF IT HAD NO PENCIL	921		3
ON THAT DEAR FRAME THE YEARS HAD WORN	ON THAT DEAR FRAME THE	940		1
THE WEST A LITTLE WORN--	THE STARS ARE OLD, THAT	1249		2
FOR A SPAN SO WORN--	NOT ANY MORE TO BE	1344		4
A LITTLE WEATHER WORN	BEFORE YOU THOUGHT OF	1465		6
AS SUDDENLY BE WORN	AS IMPERCEPTIBLY AS	1540	V	
WORRIED				
I HUNTED [WORRIED] ALL THE SAND--	A DYING TIGER--MOANED	566		2
I WORRIED NATURE WITH MY WHEELS	SEVERER SERVICE OF	786		5

	FIRST LINE	POEM	LINE
WORSE			
WE [I] THOUGHT, AT LEAST THEY ARE NO WORSE .	WHO WERE "THE FATHER AND	1258	7
WORSHIP			
FOR [TO] THOSE WHO WORSHIP [TRUST IN / ASK OF] THEM--	I RECKON--WHEN I COUNT	569	14
IT CRAVED THE GRACE TO WORSHIP	THE HEAVEN VESTS FOR	694	3
HER LATEST WORSHIP--WHEN THE DAY	SWEET MOUNTAINS--YE TELL	722	10
I THAT WAY WORSHIP THEE.	BECAUSE THE BEE MAY	869	12
WORSHIPPED			
I WORSHIPPED--DID NOT "PRAY"--	MY PERIOD HAD COME FOR	564	20
WORSHIPPING			
TO LIVES THAT THOUGHT THE WORSHIPPING . .	LIKE FLOWERS, THAT HEARD	513	14
WORST			
I HOPE I'M READY FOR "THE WORST"-- . . .	"ARCTURUS" IS HIS OTHER	70	24
AT LEAST, TO KNOW THE WORST, IS SWEET! . .	'TIS SO MUCH JOY! 'TIS	172	10
TO KNOW THE WORST, LEAVES NO DREAD MORE-- .	'TIS SO APPALLING--IT	281	4
TELL THAT THE WORST, IS EASY IN A MOMENT-- .	IF ANY SINK, ASSURE THAT	358	5
THE LONELINESS WHOSE WORST ALARM	THE LONELINESS ONE DARE	777	5
THIS MERIT HATH THE WORST--	THIS MERIT HATH THE	979	1
BUT WHEN HER WORST WAS DONE	FATE SLEW HIM, BUT HE	1031	6
UNKNOWN THE WORST WE FEAR--	THE FROST WAS NEVER SEEN	1202	14
WORSTED			
FOUND HE HAD WORSTED GOD!	A LITTLE EAST OF JORDAN,	59	16
WORTH			
MY KINGDOM'S WORTH OF BLISS!	WHAT WOULD I GIVE TO SEE	247	29
ARE WE THAT WAIT--SUFFICIENT WORTH-- . . .	IT FEELS A SHAME TO BE	444	13
MAKES SCARCELY WORTH THE TOIL--	WE SEE--COMPARATIVELY--	534	6
A HONEY'S WEIGHT [WORTH]	LEAST BEE THAT BREW--	676	2
THE WAITING--THEN--WILL SEEM SO WORTH . .	FITTER TO SEE HIM, I MAY	968	6
IS WORTH ITSELF OR DISTANCE	I CANNOT WANT IT MORE--	1301	7
THE ONLY THING WORTH LARCENY	TAKE ALL AWAY--	1365	2
THAT ONE SHOULD COMPREHEND THE WORTH . . .	HIS MIND LIKE FABRICS OF	1446	7
YOU CANNOT COMPREHEND ITS PRICE [WORTH] . .	YOUR THOUGHTS DONT HAVE	1452	7
TO WHICH HE [SHE] GAVE THE WORTH, ...	CLIMBING TO REACH THE	1566	2
BUT SO DECLINED IN WORTH	WHEN WE HAVE CEASED TO	1706	5
THEN HANDED ME MY BEING'S WORTH--	I TOOK ONE DRAUGHT OF	1725	7
WORTHIER			
EXHIBIT WORTHIER.	WHO GOES TO DINE MUST	1223	8
WORTHIEST			
WORTHIEST--TO HAVE GAINED--	PROMISE THIS--WHEN YOU	648	V 33
WORTHILY			
AS WORTHILY [PRIVATELY] AS WE.	SHE HIDETH HER THE LAST	557	8
WORTHINESS			
MY WORTHINESS IS ALL MY DOUBT--	MY WORTHINESS IS ALL MY	751	1
THE WORTHINESS [EXCELLENCE / QUALITY] OF SUFFERING LIKE	DESPAIR'S ADVANTAGE IS	799	5
THE WORTHINESS OF DEATH	DESPAIR'S ADVANTAGE IS	799	6
WORTHLESS			
IS WORTHLESS--TO THE BEE--	THERE IS AN ARID	782	8
WITHDRAWS THE WORTHLESS THING [ONE] . . .	TO DISAPPEAR ENHANCES--	1209	10
WORTHLESSNESS			
THE WORTHLESSNESS [EMPTINESS] OF EARTHLY THINGS	THE WORTHLESSNESS OF	1373	1
WORTHY			
WORTHY--THE DESTINY--	THE MALAY--TOOK THE	452	6
WORTHY TO BE FORGOT	TO BE FORGOT BY THEE	1560	11
THAT I WAS WORTHY TO FORGET	THAT SHE FORGOT ME WAS	1683	3
WOUND			
BECAUSE WE LOVE THE WOUND	REHEARSAL TO OURSELVES	379	6
A NOT ADMITTING OF THE WOUND	A GREAT HOPE FELL	1123	10
TO OWN OF IT IS WOUND--	BEHOLD THIS LITTLE BANE	1438	6
THE WOUND THAT WAS NOT WOUND NOR SCAR-- . .	THEIR BARRICADE AGAINST	1471	11
THE WOUND THAT WAS NOT WOUND NOR SCAR-- . .	THEIR BARRICADE AGAINST	1471	11
WOUNDED			
A WOUNDED DEER--LEAPS HIGHEST--	A WOUNDED DEER--LEAPS	165	1
WOVE			
WITH CUNNING CARE SHE WOVE--	MAMA NEVER FORGETS HER	164	6
A COBWEB--WOVE IN ADAMANT--	I HAD NOT MINDED--WALLS	398	11
WOVEN			
THE WEB OF LIFE WOVEN--	BY SUCH AND SUCH AN	38	3
WRAP			
TO WRAP IT'S SHINING YARDS--	I'VE KNOWN A HEAVEN,	243	2
IN WHICH WE WRAP THE SOUL	SHAME IS THE SHAWL OF	1412	2
WRAPS			
IT WRAPS IT RAIL BY RAIL	IT SIFTS FROM LEADEN	311	10
THAT WRAPS THE EVERLASTING HILL	SUMMER BEGINS TO HAVE	1682	8
WRATH			
AND THEN OUR WRATH BEGUN [BEGAN]--	THE FROST OF DEATH WAS	1136	15
WRECK			
BETWEEN THE INSTANT OF A WRECK--	THE DIFFERENCE BETWEEN	305	3
AND WHEN THE WRECK HAS BEEN--	THE DIFFERENCE BETWEEN	305	4
OH CUNNING WRECK THAT TOLD NO TALE	A GREAT HOPE FELL	1123	4
WRECKED			
WRECKED, SOLITARY, HERE--	I FELT A FUNERAL, IN MY	280	16
AND BOTH WERE WRECKED [DROWNED / QUENCHED / WHELMED] IN NOON--	TWO BUTTERFLIES WENT OUT	533	V
AS WRECKED MEN--DEEM THEY SIGHT THE LAND-- .	I MANY TIMES THOUGHT	739	3
THE WATERS WRECKED THE SKY--	THE WIND BEGUN TO KNEAD	824	18
THE MAN THAT WAS NOT LOST [WRECKED / ROBBED / KILLED]	HOW MANY SCHEMES MAY DIE	1150	5

	FIRST LINE	POEM	LINE
WRECKED (CONTINUED)			
IF WRECKED UPON THE SHOAL [WHARF / CAPE / DOCK / BAY] OF THOUGHT	IF WRECKED UPON THE	1469	1
HAS WRECKED THE PENDULUM--	THE CLOCK STRIKES ONE	1569	4
WRECKETH			
WHAT WRECKETH THEE?	SWEET PIRATE OF THE	1546	3
WRECKS			
AND WRECKS IN PEACE A PURPLE TAR, ...	A SLOOP OF AMBER SLIPS	1622	3
WREN			
SOME LITTLE WREN GOES SEEKING ROUND-- . .	FOR EVERY BIRD A NEST--	143	3
THE LITTLE WREN DESIRES--	FOR EVERY BIRD A NEST--	143	9
OR LOWER--LIKE THE WREN--	YOU SAID THAT I "WAS	738	6
WRENCH			
SOME--RESCINDED THE WRENCH--	NOT ANY MORE TO BE	1344	13
WRENCHED			
WHEN EYES THAT FONDLED IT ARE WRENCHED . .	TO MAKE ONE'S TOILETTE--	485	7
WRENCHING			
THE WRENCHING--FOR HIS FIRMAMENT	WE SEE--COMPARATIVELY--	534	11
WREN'S			
AND YET A WREN'S PERUKE	A MIEN TO MOVE A QUEEN--	283	10
WREST			
WHAT ANSWER [TIDINGS] WREST FROM THEE . .	STILL OWN THEE--STILL	1633	6
WRESTLE			
DID WRESTLE LONG AND HARD--	A LITTLE EAST OF JORDAN,	59	4
MUSICIANS WRESTLE [WRESTLING] EVERYWHERE-- .	MUSICIANS WRESTLE	157	1
OTHERS, CAN WRESTLE--	'TIS SO APPALLING--IT	281	19
THE WRESTLE IN HER SIMPLE THROAT	THE PRETTY RAIN FROM	1426	5
WRESTLED			
ARTISTS WRESTLED HERE!	ARTISTS WRESTLED HERE!	110	1
TWO SWIMMERS WRESTLED ON THE SPAR-- . . .	TWO SWIMMERS WRESTLED ON	201	1
AND WRESTLED WITH A SMILE.	IT WAS GIVEN TO ME BY	454	12
WRESTLER			
A GYMNAST AND AN ANGEL [A WRESTLER]	A LITTLE EAST OF JORDAN,	59	3
AND THE BEWILDERED GYMNAST [ASTONISHED WRESTLER]	A LITTLE EAST OF JORDAN,	59	15
WRESTLERS			
AND DNIEPER WRESTLERS, RUN.	I THINK THE HEMLOCK	525	16
WRESTLES			
THE DROP, THAT WRESTLES IN THE SEA--	THE DROP, THAT WRESTLES	284	1
THAT WRESTLES IN THE GROUND, ...	LONGING IS LIKE THE SEED	1255	2
WHOSE GARDEN WRESTLES WITH THE DEW, . . .	HOW DARE THE ROBINS SING	1724	15
WRESTLING			
MUSICIANS WRESTLE [WRESTLING] EVERYWHERE-- .	MUSICIANS WRESTLE	157	1
WRETCH			
DELIRIUM--DIVERTS THE WRETCH	I SOMETIMES DROP IT, FOR	708	9
UPON THE GALLOWS HUNG A WRETCH, ...	UPON THE GALLOWS HUNG A	1757	1
WRETCHED			
SOME WRETCHED CREATURE, SAVIOR TAKE . . .	SOME WRETCHED CREATURE,	1111	1
WRING			
WHAT MISERS WRING THEIR HANDS TONIGHT . .	A MINE THERE IS NO MAN	1117	7
DID NOT SO MUCH AS WRING FROM HIM	A SINGLE CLOVER PLANK	1343	15
WRING THE TREE AND LEAVE IT, ...	DEATH IS LIKE THE INSECT	1716	11
WRINKLE			
NOR RIP, NOR WRINKLE INDICATE	TOO COLD IS THIS	1135	8
. . . FORECLOSING / REPEALING] WRINKLE . .	LIKE TIME'S INSIDIOUS	1236	1
WRINKLED			
BE WRINKLED--MUCH AS HER--	THE DAY UNDRESSED--	716	8
WRINKLED ANY SEA, ...	ONE DAY IS THERE OF THE	814	14
OR A WRINKLED PEARL--	RIBBONS OF THE YEAR--	873	6
IT WRINKLED, AND WAS GONE--	A NARROW FELLOW IN THE	986	16
HIS WRINKLED COMING HOME?	THAT ODD OLD MAN IS DEAD	1130	8
TILL YOUR WRINKLED FINGER	ON THE WORLD YOU COLORED	1171	9
HOARY [EVIL / RIGID / WRINKLED / ARID / SHRUNKEN] THE FRUITION	FORTITUDE INCARNATE	1217	7
THE WRINKLED MAKER [AUTHOR] LIE	A WORD DROPPED CARELESS	1261	4
THE BAT IS DUN, WITH WRINKLED WINGS-- . .	THE BAT IS DUN, WITH	1575	1
WRINKLES			
THE WRINKLES OF THE ROAD--	IT SIFTS FROM LEADEN	311	4
WRISTS			
IT RUFFLES WRISTS OF POSTS	IT SIFTS FROM LEADEN	311	17
WRIT			
ARE WRIT UPON THE DOOR	WHO OCCUPIES THIS HOUSE?	892	5
WRITE			
ANGELS! WRITE [MARK] "PROMOTED"	WHO NEVER LOST, ARE	73	15
WRITE ME HOW MANY NOTES THERE BE	BRING ME THE SUNSET IN A	128	7
ALL THE LETTERS I CAN [COULD] WRITE	ALL THE LETTERS I CAN	334	1
YOU WRITE HIM--EVERY DAY--	YOU LOVE THE LORD--YOU	487	2
TELL HIM [HER] THE PAGE I DID'NT WRITE--[NEVER WROTE!]	GOING TO HIM! HAPPY	494	3
SO I WRITE--POETS--ALL--	I RECKON--WHEN I COUNT	569	8
TO CHERISH, AND [RECOLLECT] TO WRITE	WE TALKED AS GIRLS DO--	586	14
I DARE NOT WRITE UNTIL I HEAR--	A PANG IS MORE	1530	V
WRITER			
TELL HIM [HER]--IT WAS'NT A PRACTISED WRITER--	GOING TO HIM! HAPPY	494	10
WRITING			
WRITING MUCH TO THEE.	IF IT HAD NO PENCIL	921	4
WRITTEN			
WRITTEN BY FADED [UNKNOWN] MEN	THE BIBLE IS AN ANTIQUE	1545	2
WRONG			
JEHOVAH'S WATCH--IS WRONG.	SUNSET AT NIGHT--IS	415	8

	FIRST LINE	POEM	LINE
WRONG (CONTINUED)			
'THO' FOR WHAT WRONG	HE STRAINED MY FAITH--	497	11
IT ALWAYS FELT TO ME--A WRONG	IT ALWAYS FELT TO ME--A	597	1
BUT WRONG THE MORE	T'WAS COMFORT IN HER	1703	7
HOW ALWAYS WRONG IS LOVE--	HOW FLEET--HOW	1771	2
WROTE			
THAT NEVER WROTE TO ME--	THIS IS MY LETTER TO THE	441	2
TELL HIM [HER] THE PAGE I DID'NT WRITE--[NEVER WROTE!]	GOING TO HIM! HAPPY	494	3
THEN CARVED [HE WROTE] HIS NAME--UPON IT--	HE FOUND MY BEING--SET	603	3
HAD NOT SHAKESPEARE WROTE--	DRAMA'S VITALLEST	741	9
"AM NOT CONSUMED," OLD MOSES WROTE,	NO MAN SAW AWE, NOR TO	1733	13
WROUGHT			
MY PLANE--AND I, TOGETHER WROUGHT	MYSELF WAS FORMED--A	488	3
BUT WROUGHT THEIR PANG IN SYLLABLE--	THE MARTYR POETS--DID	544	2
WHO WROUGHT CARRARA IN ME	I'VE DROPPED MY BRAIN--	1046	13
WRUNG			
THE EYES AROUND--HAD WRUNG THEM DRY--	I HEARD A FLY BUZZ--WHEN	465	5
WRUNG ME--WITH ANGUISH--	HE STRAINED MY FAITH--	497	9
ESSENTIAL OILS--ARE WRUNG--	ESSENTIAL OILS--ARE	675	1
YACHT			
ROWER, AND YACHT--SOME SOVREIGN SUMMER--	LOVE--THOU ART HIGH--	453	11
YARDS			
TO WRAP IT'S SHINING YARDS--	I'VE KNOWN A HEAVEN,	243	2
OF SMALL AND SPICY YARDS [BREADTHS]--	OF BRUSSELS--IT WAS NOT	602	9
YARN			
HIS YARN [COIL] OF PEARL--UNWINDS [EXPENDS]--	THE SPIDER HOLDS A	605	4
YAWN			
WITH OTHER--AND 'TWILL YAWN THE MORE--	TO FILL A GAP	546	4
YAWNING			
THE YAWNING CONSCIOUSNESS,	I NEVER HEAR THAT ONE IS	1323	8
YCLEPT			
BY MEN, YCLEPT CATERPILLAR!	A FUZZY FELLOW, WITHOUT	173	17
YE			
AWAKE YE MUSES NINE, SING ME A STRAIN DIVINE,	AWAKE YE MUSES NINE,	1	1
ARE YE THEN WITH GOD?	SO HAS A DAISY VANISHED	28	8
THAT "WHATSOEVER YE SHALL ASK--	I MEANT TO HAVE BUT	476	23
ONE MORE--"YE BLESSED"--TO BE TOLD--	THERE IS A SHAME OF	551	7
SWEET MOUNTAINS--YE TELL ME NO LIE--	SWEET MOUNTAINS--YE TELL	722	1
NO CLUSTER--YE [YOU] SHALL FIND--	EXCEPT THE SMALLER SIZE	1067	V
YEAR			
I DID NOT KNOW THE YEAR THEN--	I OFTEN PASSED THE	51	5
WENT UP A YEAR THIS EVENING!	WENT UP A YEAR THIS	93	1
STUDENT OF THE YEAR!	ARTISTS WRESTLED HERE!	110	4
ONE YEAR AGO--JOTS WHAT?	ONE YEAR AGO--JOTS WHAT?	296	1
SHE--EACH YEAR--LEADS HER DAISIES BACK--	I KNOW A PLACE WHERE	337	3
THE LILACS--BENDING MANY A YEAR--	IT WILL BE SUMMER--	342	9
HERE--SAID THE YEAR--	ANSWER JULY--	386	18
PUT THE THOUGHT IN ADVANCE--A YEAR--	IT DONT SOUND SO	426	15
TO LOVE THEE YEAR BY YEAR--	TO LOVE THEE YEAR BY	434	1
TO LOVE THEE YEAR BY YEAR--	TO LOVE THEE YEAR BY	434	1
'TWAS JUST THIS TIME, LAST YEAR, I DIED.	'TWAS JUST THIS TIME,	445	1
HOW JUST THIS TIME, SOME PERFECT YEAR--	'TWAS JUST THIS TIME,	445	23
IF I COULD SEE YOU IN A YEAR,	IF YOU WERE COMING IN	511	5
IT'S TIME O' YEAR FOR HAY.	I'M SORRY FOR THE DEAD--	529	4
THEIR SUMMER--LASTS A SOLID YEAR--	I RECKON--WHEN I COUNT	569	9
I COULD NOT FIX THE YEAR--	A THOUGHT WENT UP MY	701	4
ALL SEASONS OF THE YEAR,	HAVE ANY LIKE MYSELF	736	20
NOT PRESENT ON THE YEAR	A LIGHT EXISTS IN SPRING	812	2
RIBBONS OF THE YEAR--	RIBBONS OF THE YEAR--	873	1
FROM US SHE WANDERED NOW A YEAR,	FROM US SHE WANDERED NOW	890	1
WE ONLY KNOW WHAT TIME OF YEAR	FROM US SHE WANDERED NOW	890	7
WERE THE DAY YEAR LONG,	UNDER THE LIGHT, YET	949	8
SOME PASSING YEAR--A TRAIT [CHARM] BESTOW	FITTER TO SEE HIM, I MAY	968	4
THIS SEASON OF THE YEAR,	PURPLE--IS FASHIONABLE	980	2
THIS WAS IN THE WHITE OF THE YEAR--	THIS WAS IN THE WHITE OF	995	1
WITH US, 'TIS HARVEST ALL THE YEAR	THE PRODUCTS OF MY FARM	1025	5
LAST YEAR,	WHEN THEY COME BACK--IF	1080	8
THE LOWER METRES OF THE YEAR	THE MURMURING OF BEES,	1115	5
THAT ODD OLD MAN IS DEAD A YEAR--	THAT ODD OLD MAN IS DEAD	1130	1
THAT COMES A SINGLE TIME A YEAR	THE SNOW THAT NEVER	1133	3
HE STAYED AWAY A YEAR TO CALL	DEAR MARCH--COME IN--	1320	21
AND AID AN AGED YEAR	THE GENTIAN HAS A	1424	12
NO BRIGADIER THROUGHOUT THE YEAR	NO BRIGADIER THROUGHOUT	1561	1
TWO DESERTS BUT THE YEAR IS COLD	I DID NOT REACH THEE	1664	7
AND FINLAND OF THE YEAR	THESE ARE THE DAYS THAT	1696	4
HAVE SETTLED WITH THE YEAR!--	HOW DARE THE ROBINS SING	1724	4
FOR MANY AN ARDENT [A FRUITLESS] YEAR.	THE DISTANCE THAT THE	1742	4
THAT FIRST ABANDONED [ABSCONDED] YEAR.	THE DISTANCE THAT THE	1742	V 4
FOR EVERY PALATE IN THE YEAR,"--	THE WATERS CHASED HIM AS	1749	7
YEARNS			
... YEARNS NO MORE]	THE INUNDATION OF THE	1425	7
YEAR'S			
AND WORE MY LAST YEAR'S GOWN--	ONE SISTER HAVE I IN OUR	14	6
WHEN LAST YEAR'S DISTAFF IDLE HUNG	THERE IS A MORN BY MEN	24	11
OF LAST YEAR'S SUNDERED TUNE!	SOME RAINBOW--COMING	64	9
YEARS			
LONG YEARS OF PRACTISE BORE	THE FEET OF PEOPLE	7	6
THE YEARS AMONG,	ONE SISTER HAVE I IN OUR	14	18
LO, WHAT [THE] "AUGUSTAN" YEARS	IF PAIN FOR PEACE	63	2

	FIRST LINE	POEM	LINE
YEARS (CONTINUED)			
SHARP PITTANCES OF YEARS--	FOR EACH EXTATIC INSTANT	125	6
IN EBON BOX, WHEN YEARS HAVE FLOWN	IN EBON BOX, WHEN YEARS	169	1
GRAND GO THE YEARS--IN THE CRESCENT--ABOVE THEM--	SAFE IN THEIR ALABASTER	216	V
AND THO' 'TIS YEARS AGO--THAT DAY--	THE FIRST DAY'S NIGHT	410	15
THE MONTHS HAVE ENDS--THE YEARS--A KNOT--	THE MONTHS HAVE ENDS--	423	1
SUCH BLISS--HAD I--FOR ALL THE YEARS--	IT WOULD NEVER BE COMMON	430	7
I WONDER IF WHEN YEARS HAVE PILED--	I MEASURE EVERY GRIEF I	561	17
I COULD NOT PROVE THE YEARS HAD FEET--	I COULD NOT PROVE THE	563	1
I HAD BEEN HUNGRY, ALL THE YEARS--	I HAD BEEN HUNGRY, ALL	579	1
THE YEARS, OUR PILFERED THINGS--	OF NEARNESS TO HER	607	14
I YEARS HAD BEEN FROM HOME	I YEARS HAD BEEN FROM	609	1
I SEE THEE BETTER FOR THE YEARS	I SEE THEE BETTER--IN	611	5
AND YEARS--EXHALE IN YEARS--	FOREVER--IS COMPOSED OF	624	8
AND YEARS--EXHALE IN YEARS--	FOREVER--IS COMPOSED OF	624	8
NO DIFFERENT [AS INFINITE] OUR YEARS WOULD BE	FOREVER--IS COMPOSED OF	624	11
THE SURFACES OF YEARS--	IF HE WERE LIVING--DARE	734	6
THE CICATRICE OF YEARS--	HE TOLD A HOMELY TALE	763	4
ON THAT DEAR FRAME THE YEARS HAD WORN	ON THAT DEAR FRAME THE	940	1
THERE IS A ZONE WHOSE EVEN YEARS	THERE IS A ZONE WHOSE	1056	1
HAST THOU SURVIVED SO MANY NIGHTS [YEARS]?	THE SMOULDERING EMBERS	1132	3
AS ABSENT AS A HUNDRED YEARS,	THE FACE WE CHOOSE TO	1141	3
AFTER A HUNDRED YEARS	AFTER A HUNDRED YEARS	1147	1
SOME EIGHTEEN THOUSAND YEARS--	AS OLD AS WOE--	1168	3
THEY ARE OF EQUAL YEARS	AS OLD AS WOE--	1168	6
SO MANY YEARS AGAIN--	I SHOULD NOT DARE TO BE	1197	2
THE HARM OF YEARS IS ON HIM--	THE HARM OF YEARS IS ON	1280	1
RANSOMED FROM YEARS--	LEFT IN IMMORTAL YOUTH	1289	5
HE KEPT HIS WORD A TRILLION YEARS	OUR LITTLE SECRETS SLINK	1326	3
SO WE EVADE THE CHARGE OF YEARS	AS SUMMER INTO AUTUMN	1346	9
LONG YEARS APART--CAN MAKE NO	LONG YEARS APART--CAN	1383	1
THE EMBERS OF A THOUSAND YEARS	LONG YEARS APART--CAN	1383	5
SEVENTY YEARS IS SPENT AS QUICK	SUMMER IS SHORTER THAN	1506	3
THE PILE OF YEARS IS NOT SO HIGH	THE PILE OF YEARS IS NOT	1507	1
THAT HAD IT BEAT A THOUSAND YEARS,	'TIS NOT THE SWAYING	1597	3
REMAINED A FEW SLOW YEARS WITH US	I WATCHED HER FACE TO	1667	5
SEVEN YEARS OF TROTH HAVE TAUGHT THEE	REARRANGE A "WIFE'S"	1737	7
AND UNDERMINED THE YEARS.	SOFTENED BY TIME'S	1738	4
YELLOW			
UNTIES HER YELLOW BONNET	PERHAPS YOU'D LIKE TO	134	5
THESE--ARE THE BANKS OF THE YELLOW SEA--	THIS--IS THE LAND--THE	266	2
THAT [WHICH] LITTLE YELLOW BOYS AND GIRLS	I'LL TELL YOU HOW THE	318	11
FOR FEAR THEIR YELLOW GOWN	I DREADED THAT FIRST	348	10
A LONG--LONG YELLOW--ON THE LAWN--	A MURMUR IN THE TREES--	416	5
I THOUGHT HOW YELLOW IT WOULD LOOK--	'TWAS JUST THIS TIME,	445	5
THE YELLOW--DAY--IS FALLING--	THE RED--BLAZE--IS THE	469	3
OR SUNSET'S YELLOW PLAY	AS FAR FROM PITY, AS	496	8
BETWEEN WHOSE YELLOW EYE--	DID YOU EVER STAND IN A	590	10
TO INTERRUPT HIS YELLOW PLAN	TO INTERRUPT HIS YELLOW	591	1
ALARMS US--THO' HIS YELLOW FEET	THE LIGHTNING PLAYETH--	630	7
ON WHOM I LAY A YELLOW EYE--	MY LIFE HAD STOOD--A	754	19
AND IF HIS YELLOW FEET SHOULD MISS--	MY FAITH IS LARGER THAN	766	9
THE LIGHTNING SHOWED A YELLOW HEAD [BEAK]--	THE WIND BEGUN TO KNEAD	824	11
LET NO SUNRISE' YELLOW NOISE	AMPLE MAKE THIS BED--	829	7
AND FAINTING, ON HER YELLOW KNEE	THE LADY FEEDS HER	941	7
THE YELLOW MAN	WHO IS THE EAST?	1032	2
WHO MAY BE YELLOW IF HE CAN	WHO IS THE EAST?	1032	7
NATURE RARER USES YELLOW	NATURE RARER USES YELLOW	1045	1
YELLOW SHE AFFORDS	NATURE RARER USES YELLOW	1045	6
IT'S YELLOW SHORTNESS DROPT--	THE DAY GREW SMALL,	1140	4
THE LIGHTNING IS A YELLOW FORK	THE LIGHTNING IS A	1173	1
THE SUN TOOK DOWN HIS YELLOW WHIP	THE SUN AND FOG	1190	3
AND CROUCHED BEHIND HIS YELLOW DOOR	A WILD BLUE SKY ABREAST	1415	3
A LANE OF YELLOW LED THE EYE	A LANE OF YELLOW LED THE	1650	1
LIGHTLY STEPPED A YELLOW STAR	LIGHTLY STEPPED A YELLOW	1672	1
OF YELLOW WAS THE OUTER SKY	OF YELLOW WAS THE OUTER	1676	1
IN YELLOWER YELLOW HEWN	OF YELLOW WAS THE OUTER	1676	2
THE YELLOW LIGHTNING SHONE--	THE WIND DREW OFF	1694	6
YELLOWER			
ON THEIR WAY TO YELLOWER CLIMES--	I SHALL KEEP SINGING!	250	3
IN YELLOWER YELLOW HEWN	OF YELLOW WAS THE OUTER	1676	2
YES			
HAVE GAINED! YES! HESITATED SO--	'TIS SO MUCH JOY! 'TIS	172	5
THEY MAY NOT FINALLY SAY, YES--	IF I COULD BRIBE THEM BY	179	18
SHE [I] COULD NOT FIND HER [MY] YES--	I SHOWED HER HIGHTS SHE	446	8
IF 'TIS NAY--OR YES--	HER SWEET TURN TO LEAVE	649	22
YESTERDAY			
SO SAILORS SAY--ON YESTERDAY--	ADRIFT! A LITTLE BOAT	30	5
SO ANGELS SAY--ON YESTERDAY--	ADRIFT! A LITTLE BOAT	30	9
OH LAGGING YESTERDAY!	DELAYED TILL SHE HAD	58	6
AS FLAKES OF SNOW STOOD [DID] YESTERDAY--	SOME RAINBOW--COMING	64	14
YESTERDAY, UNDISTINGUISHED!	AMBITION CANNOT FIND HIM	68	5
YESTERDAY, AND TODAY,	SHE DIED AT PLAY,	75	7
THAT SPURNED US--YESTERDAY!	"HEAVEN"--IS WHAT I	239	12
THAT DAZZLED, YESTERDAY,	I'VE KNOWN A HEAVEN,	243	10
HAD PRINTED YESTERDAY,	A SINGLE SCREW OF FLESH	263	8
OR WHO DIED--YESTERDAY!	WHAT IF I SAY I SHALL	277	12
I KNEW SO PERFECT--YESTERDAY--	I SHOULD HAVE BEEN TOO	313	10
AND YESTERDAY, OR CENTURIES BEFORE?	AFTER GREAT PAIN, A	341	4

	FIRST LINE	POEM	LINE
YESTERDAY (CONTINUED)			
YESTERDAY."	I'M SAYING EVERY DAY	373	9
UNAIDED--YESTERDAY--	WE SEE--COMPARATIVELY--	534	4
THAT FELT SO AMPLE--YESTERDAY--	I COULD NOT PROVE THE	563	7
THE MASON BUILDED, YESTERDAY,	WHAT CARE THE DEAD, FOR	592	7
LET US PLAY YESTERDAY--	LET US PLAY YESTERDAY--	728	1
THAN YESTERDAY?	LET US PLAY YESTERDAY--	728	28
HAD I BUT LINGERED YESTERDAY--	IT BLOOMED AND DROPT, A	978	11
WAS SAYING YESTERDAY	BEE! I'M EXPECTING YOU!	1035	2
YESTERDAY--ENDOWED WITH PARADISE.	I'VE DROPPED MY BRAIN--	1046	8
YESTERDAY [LIVERPOOL] IS OLD--	AFTER THE SUN COMES OUT	1148	4
BUT YESTERDAY A VAGRANT--	TO DISAPPEAR ENHANCES--	1209	5
YESTERDAY IS HISTORY,	YESTERDAY IS HISTORY,	1292	1
YESTERDAY IS POETRY--	YESTERDAY IS HISTORY,	1292	3
YESTERDAY IS MYSTERY--	YESTERDAY IS HISTORY,	1292	5
YESTERDAY'S			
AS YESTERDAY'S SURPRISE--	THE RIDDLE WE CAN GUESS	1222	4
YESTERDAYS			
AS YESTERDAYS IN PAIRS,	THE FIRST DAY'S NIGHT	410	10
YESTERMORN			
TWO GABRIELS YESTERMORN.	FOREVER HONORED BE THE	1570	4
YET			
THINE EYES ARE SADLY BLINDED, BUT YET THOU MAYEST SEE	AWAKE YE MUSES NINE,	1	33
YET THEY ARE SLEEPING STILL,--	"SIC TRANSIT GLORIA	3	48
YET DO I NOT REPINE	I HAVE A BIRD IN SPRING	5	7
YET KNOW IT'S DRIPPING FEET	MY WHEEL IS IN THE DARK!	10	3
YET HAVE ALL ROADS	MY WHEEL IS IN THE DARK!	10	7
THERE MAY YET BE LAND!	ONCE MORE, MY NOW	48	8
I HAV'NT TOLD MY GARDEN YET--	I HAV'NT TOLD MY GARDEN	50	1
YET SHE CANNOT SPEAK.	GLOWING IS HER BONNET,	72	4
THE NEIGHBORS DO NOT YET SUSPECT!	A LADY RED--AMID THE	74	9
AND YET, HOW STILL THE LANDSCAPE STANDS!	A LADY RED--AMID THE	74	13
AND YET IT WILL BE DONE	GOING TO HEAVEN!	79	8
YET TO MY IRRITATED EAR	HEART, NOT SO HEAVY AS	83	7
YET IS SHE MORE CONVINCING	THE RAINBOW NEVER TELLS	97	3
YET ELOQUENT DECLARE	THE RAINBOW NEVER TELLS	97	6
AND YET YOUR LITTLE DRAUGHT OF LIFE	HAVE YOU GOT A BROOK IN	136	7
YET WHO OF ALL THE THRONG	FOR EVERY BIRD A NEST--	143	16
YET NOT IN ALL THE NESTS I MEET--	ALL OVERGROWN BY CUNNING	148	11
YET TAKE HER FROM THE LAWN	EXCEPT TO HEAVEN, SHE IS	154	10
AND YET, AS POOR AS I,	'TIS SO MUCH JOY! 'TIS	172	3
YET DOTH EXCEEDING RUN!	A FUZZY FELLOW, WITHOUT	173	2
YET--TO MY FRUGAL EYE,	I LOST A WORLD--THE	181	6
YET HELD MY BREATH, THE WHILE--	I'VE HEARD AN ORGAN TALK	183	4
YET--KNOW NOT WHAT WAS DONE TO ME	I'VE HEARD AN ORGAN TALK	183	7
MAY YET, A TRANSPORT BE--	A TRANSPORT ONE CANNOT	184	2
AND YET, IT WILL NOT GO--	WHAT SHALL I DO--IT	186	4
AND YET--BY TRADES--THE SIZE OF THESE	IT'S SUCH A LITTLE THING	189	3
YET--STRANGEST--HEAVIER SINCE IT WENT--	SAVIOR! I'VE NO ONE ELSE	217	11
IT'S EARLY--YET--FOR "SPRING"!	IT CANT BE "SUMMER"!	221	3
YET, NEVER, IN EXTREMITY,	"HOPE" IS THE THING WITH	254	11
YET I--FOR IT--WOULD PAY--	ONE LIFE OF SO MUCH	270	2
YET--NOT SO DENSE A CROWD--	ONE LIFE OF SO MUCH	270	14
YET NOT TOO FAR [NEAR ENOUGH--] TO COME AT CALL--	HE PUT THE BELT AROUND	273	9
AND YET A WREN'S PERUKE	A MIEN TO MOVE A QUEEN--	283	10
YET SMALL--SHE SIGHS--IF ALL--IS ALL--	THE DROP, THAT WRESTLES	284	5
PHRASELESS--YET IT STIRS	IT'S LIKE THE LIGHT--	297	7
WHILE JUST [YET] A GIRL AT SCHOOL.	YOUR RICHES--TAUGHT ME--	299	32
AND YET THE LARGEST WOMAN'S HEART	FOR LARGEST WOMAN'S	309	3
IT TRAVERSES--YET HALTS--	IT SIFTS FROM LEADEN	311	V
NOUGHT--THAT [YET, IF] WE--NO POET'S KINSMAN--	HER--"LAST POEMS"--	312	16
YET--THOU--NOT THERE--	I TEND MY FLOWERS FOR	339	18
FOR YET TO BUY ANOTHER PAIR	IS BLISS THEN, SUCH	340	6
ARE ONE--AND YET THE FORMER	THE DAY THAT I WAS	356	7
CLASPED YET--TO HIM--AND ME--	NOT IN THIS WORLD TO SEE	418	6
AND YET--MY PRIMER SUITS ME SO	NOT IN THIS WORLD TO SEE	418	7
(AND YET, WITH AMBER HANDS--	THE MOON IS DISTANT FROM	429	2
AND YET--EXISTENCE--SOME WAY BACK--	I TIE MY HAT--I CREASE	443	11
AT MIDNIGHT, I AM BUT [YET] A MAID,	A WIFE--AT DAYBREAK I	461	3
THERE YET REMAINS A LOVE	THE MANNER OF IT'S DEATH	468	6
NEVER YET--CONSUMED--	THE RED--BLAZE--IS THE	469	8
YET INTERDICT--MY BLOSSOM--	I ENVY SEAS, WHEREON HE	498	21
YET BLESSEDER--THAN WE--	THOSE FAIR--FICTITIOUS	499	14
AND YET, IT TASTED, LIKE THEM ALL,	IT WAS NOT DEATH, FOR I	510	9
THOUGH NEVER YET, IN ANY PORT--	TWO BUTTERFLIES WENT OUT	533	7
AS YET--MY HEART BE DRY--	ME PROVE IT NOW--WHOEVER	537	6
THEY STRIVE--AND YET DELAY--	I CROSS TILL I AM WEARY	550	22
AND YET--	ONE CRUCIFIXION IS	553	14
CORRECTLY--YET TO ME	I MEASURE EVERY GRIEF I	561	34
YET CONFIDENT THEY RUN	I COULD NOT PROVE THE	563	2
AND YET, UNTO THE SINGLE DOE	ONE ANGUISH--IN A CROWD	565	3
YET [BUT] MIGHTY--BY RELATION	ONE ANGUISH--IN A CROWD	565	13
NOT YET, OUR EYES CAN SEE--	"HEAVEN" HAS DIFFERENT	575	20
YET ANY PASSING BY	TO INTERRUPT HIS YELLOW	591	12
AND YET THE HEAVENS--HELD--	IT TROUBLED ME AS ONCE I	600	4
YET BLUE--AND SOLID [EASY]--STOOD--	IT TROUBLED ME AS ONCE I	600	6
THEY NEVER YET DID SATISFY--	THE TREES LIKE TASSELS--	606	7
AND YET I WAS A LIVING CHILD--	IT WOULD HAVE STARVED A	612	3

YET (CONTINUED)

	FIRST LINE	POEM	LINE
BUT EARLY, YET, FOR GOD--	IT WAS TOO LATE FOR MAN	623	2
AND YET, ONE SUMMER, WE WERE QUEENS [WED]--	OURSELVES WERE WED ONE	631	15
YET SWAYING ALL--	THE CHILD'S FAITH IS NEW	637	16
YET HESITATING FRACTIONS--BOTH	I COULD SUFFICE FOR HIM,	643	3
YET [BUT] HAVE NO ART TO SAY--	"NATURE" IS WHAT WE SEE	668	10
YET PERSEVERED TOWARD--SURER [STRICTER]--FOR THE DISTANCE--	EACH LIFE CONVERGES TO	680	13
YET WHY SO LITTLE SOUND--MYSELF	THE SUN KEPT SETTING--	692	11
AND YET THE CROWD APPLAUD, BELOW--	YOU'VE SEEN BALLOONS SET	700	11
SINCE THEN--'TIS CENTURIES--AND YET . . .	BECAUSE I COULD NOT STOP	712	21
AND YET THE NEWEST STAR--	THE DAY UNDRESSED--	716	6
YET--THERE IS A SCIENCE MORE--	YOU TAUGHT ME WAITING	740	8
OWNER CANNOT [NEVER YET WAS] SHUT-- . . .	DRAMA'S VITALLEST	741	15
YET BLAMED THE FATE THAT FRACTURED--[FLUNG IT] LESS	IT DROPPED SO LOW--IN MY	747	5
YET HOW NATURE FROZE--	WHEN I HOPED, I	768	12
YET SANCTIFIES THE MIND--	IT IS A LONESOME GLEE--	774	2
YET ONE--REJOICES FLOWERS--	THERE IS AN ARID	782	5
AND YET [YET ALL] THE BAND WAS GONE-- . .	THE BIRDS BEGUN AT FOUR	783	20
AND YET [YET ALL] THE BAND WAS GONE-- . .	THE BIRDS BEGUN AT FOUR	783	20
AND YET WE GUESSED IT NOT--	HER FINAL SUMMER WAS IT	795	2
YET WE SUSPECTED NOT	HER FINAL SUMMER WAS IT	795	V 2
YET BOTH SO WELL KNEW ME	NATURE AND GOD--I	835	2
YET NEITHER TOLD--THAT I COULD LEARN-- . .	NATURE AND GOD--I	835	5
YET UPON HIS PURPLE PROGRAMME	ALWAYS MINE!	839	8
AND YET SO BOLDER EVERY DAY	THIS CHASM, SWEET, UPON	858	11
IT WAS A GRAVE, YET BORE NO STONE	IT WAS A GRAVE, YET BORE	876	1
"AND YET THOU ART INDUSTRIOUS--	HAD I NOT THIS, OR THIS,	904	7
ALAS--AND ART THOU SLEEPING YET?	'TIS SUNRISE--LITTLE	908	6
STRUCK, WAS I, NOR YET BY LIGHTNING-- . .	STRUCK, WAS I, NOR YET	925	1
MAIMED--WAS I--YET NOT BY VENTURE-- . . .	STRUCK, WAS I, NOR YET	925	5
ROBBED--WAS I--INTACT TO [YET MET NO] BANDIT--	STRUCK, WAS I, NOR YET	925	9
YET WAS NOT THE FOE--OF ANY--	STRUCK, WAS I, NOR YET	925	13
STILL [YET] TO BE EXPLAINED.	THAT IS SOLEMN WE HAVE	934	8
YET PRECIOUS AS THE HOUSE	ON THAT DEAR FRAME THE	940	2
YET ABLE TO CONTAIN	A COFFIN--IS A SMALL	943	2
YET AMPLER THAN THE SUN--	A COFFIN--IS A SMALL	943	6
UNDER THE LIGHT, YET UNDER, ...	UNDER THE LIGHT, YET	949	1
OVER THE LIGHT, YET OVER, ...	UNDER THE LIGHT, YET	949	9
NOT YET SUSPECTED--[STILL UNSUSPECTED] BUT FOR FLASH [FORK]--	THE SOUL'S DISTINCT	974	7
YET [BUT] WHEN A BOY, AND BAREFOOT-- . . .	A NARROW FELLOW IN THE	986	11
AND YET I KNEW NOT HOW	I KNEW THAT I HAD GAINED	1022	2
YET KNOW I HOW THE HEATHER LOOKS	I NEVER SAW A MOOR--	1052	3
YET CERTAIN AM I OF THE SPOT	I NEVER SAW A MOOR--	1052	7
REMIT AS YET NO GRACE	FURTHER IN SUMMER THAN	1068	13
YET [BUT] A DRUIDIC DIFFERENCE	FURTHER IN SUMMER THAN	1068	15
YET [BUT] EVEN ON HIS SCARLET SHELF . . .	THE FROST OF DEATH WAS	1136	7
YET [BUT] EASY AS THE [A] NARROW SNAKE . .	THE FROST OF DEATH WAS	1136	12
MIGHT YET [STILL] REPLY [DESTROY]. . . .	THE PAST IS SUCH A	1203	8
YET NEWER GLOWS THE ONLY GOLD	THE STARS ARE OLD, THAT	1249	3
AND YET WE KNEW THAT GENTLE CLOCK	'TWAS LATER WHEN THE	1276	3
YET THAT PATHETIC PENDULUM	'TWAS LATER WHEN THE	1276	7
YET EVEN THIS SHALL ROUSE [STIR] ITSELF . .	A STAGNANT PLEASURE LIKE	1281	7
AND YET IT'S WHOLE CAREER [ALIEN PLACE / COVERT PLACE]	THE MUSHROOM IS THE ELF	1298	6
AND YET IT NOTHING IS	I CANNOT WANT IT MORE--	1301	5
YET THAT WHIP'S NAME	NOT WITH A CLUB, THE	1304	7
AND YET WE SOONER SAY	AS SUMMER INTO AUTUMN	1346	2
I SUED THE NEWS--YET FEARED--THE NEWS . .	I SUED THE NEWS--YET	1360	1
YET BIRDS EXAMINE IT AND FLEE--	HOW KNOW IT FROM A	1364	5
YET BY THIS COUNTRYMAN--	HOW FITS HIS UMBER COAT	1371	11
YET DOES NOT EXIST--	"SECRETS" IS A DAILY	1385	2
BUT [YET] PRONE TO SHUT IT'S [HIS] SPOTTED [SUBTLE] FAN	THE BUTTERFLY'S NUMIDIAN	1387	4
THEY MIGHT NOT NEED ME--YET THEY MIGHT-- .	THEY MIGHT NOT NEED ME--	1391	1
YET NEVER WEARING OUT--	HOPE IS A STRANGE	1392	4
BUT [YET] IT'S UNIQUE MOMENTUM	HOPE IS A STRANGE	1392	7
BUT NATURE [SUSAN] IS A STRANGER YET; . .	WHAT MYSTERY PERVADES A	1400	17
CRISIS IS SWEET AND YET THE HEART	CRISIS IS SWEET AND YET	1416	1
WITHIN IT'S REACH [HOPE], THOUGH YET [AND JUST] UNGRASPED	WHO NEVER WANTED--	1430	5
YET [AND] NONE HATH SUCH A CROWD.	HOW BRITTLE ARE THE	1433	4
THOSE NOT LIVE YET	THOSE NOT LIVE YET	1454	1
THE [A] CRASH OF NOTHING, YET [AND] OF ALL--	MORE THAN THE GRAVE IS	1503	5
A [THE] COURTEOUS, YET [BUT] HARROWING GRACE,	AS IMPERCEPTIBLY AS	1540	11
AND YET--INSPECTED CLOSELY	HOPE IS A SUBTLE GLUTTON	1547	3
BUT ARM IN ARM WITH TOUCH, YET TOUCH . . .	THE SPIRIT LASTS--BUT IN	1576	7
AND YET ABIDE [REMAIN] THE WORLD!	THERE CAME A WIND LIKE A	1593	17
FEW, YET ENOUGH, ...	FEW, YET ENOUGH,	1596	1
IS STRICKEN BY IT YET--	UPON HIS SADDLE SPRUNG A	1600	8
AND YET IF YOU COMPARE THE LASTS, ...	A FLOWER WILL NOT	1621	2
GUILELESS, YET OF SUCH GLORY FINE	"RED SEA," INDEED! TALK	1642	5
YET HAD NOT SEEN!	SPEECH IS ONE SYMPTOM OF	1681	8
YET HE DID NOT GUESS	THE EVENT WAS DIRECTLY	1686	2
YET MAN HAS NOT OF ALL THE THRONG	THE HILLS ERECT THEIR	1688	3
AND YET A PIT--	A PIT--BUT HEAVEN OVER	1712	3
YET BUT A NAME.	AS SUBTLE AS TOMORROW	1713	4
IT YET REMAINS TO SEE	MY LIFE CLOSED TWICE	1732	2

	FIRST LINE	POEM	LINE
YET (CONTINUED)			
"YET SAW HIM FACE TO FACE"--	NO MAN SAW AWE, NOR TO	1733	14
AND YET [ALTHOUGH] THE HIGHEST HEAD	ONE CROWN THAT NO ONE	1735	2
YIELD			
YIELD HER MOAT OF PEARL--	DID THE HAREBELL LOOSE	213	6
YIELD SUCH AN ALCOHOL!	I TASTE A LIQUOR NEVER	214	4
DID IT THEN--YIELD?	HE STRAINED MY FAITH--	497	4
THE "BUSH" MAY YIELD ME	WHICH IS BEST? HEAVEN--	1012	7
YIELD GROUPS OF ONES--	EXCEPT THE SMALLER SIZE	1067	V
OF HEAVEN AND HELL I ALSO YIELD	BECAUSE THAT YOU ARE	1260	29
ITALIC FLAVOR YIELD--	WINTER IS GOOD--HIS HOAR	1316	2
YIELDED			
YIELDED GRAPE--AND MAISE--	SOIL OF FLINT, IF STEADY	681	V
YIELDETH			
A WITCHCRAFT--YIELDETH ME--	THE MURMUR OF A BEE	155	2
YIELDING			
I SHOULD NOT MISS IN YIELDING, THOUGH	THIS CHASM, SWEET, UPON	858	15
YIELDS			
THE GRAVE YIELDS BACK HER ROBBERIES--	OF NEARNESS TO HER	607	13
YONDER			
I'D TOSS IT YONDER, LIKE A RIND,	IF YOU WERE COMING IN	511	15
IN YONDER [SCARLET] MARYLAND--	WHEN I WAS SMALL, A	596	20
YORKSHIRE			
SINCE YORKSHIRE HILLS ARE GREEN--	ALL OVERGROWN BY CUNNING	148	10
YOU			
AT YOU AND I!	MY WHEEL IS IN THE DARK!	10	15
AS STOOD YOU HERE--	I NEVER TOLD THE BURIED	11	6
YOU AND I THE SECRET	ALL THESE MY BANNERS BE.	22	16
BE SURE YOU COUNT--SH'D I FORGET	IT'S ALL I HAVE TO BRING	26	5
AND SEND THE ROSE TO YOU.	IF SHE HAD BEEN THE	44	8
YOU AND I--TONIGHT!	HEART! WE WILL FORGET	47	2
YOU MAY FORGET THE WARMTH HE GAVE--	HEART! WE WILL FORGET	47	3
WHEN YOU HAVE DONE, PRAY TELL ME	HEART! WE WILL FORGET	47	5
SO WHEN YOU ARE TIRED--	I OFTEN PASSED THE	51	13
AND YOU SHOULD LIVE--	IF I SHOULD DIE,	54	2
THAT FROM YOU OR I,	TO VENERATE THE SIMPLE	57	4
I CANT TELL YOU--BUT YOU FEEL IT--	I CANT TELL YOU--BUT YOU	65	1
I CANT TELL YOU--BUT YOU FEEL IT--	I CANT TELL YOU--BUT YOU	65	1
NOR CAN YOU TELL ME--	I CANT TELL YOU--BUT YOU	65	2
NOT FOR YOU--TO SAY	I CANT TELL YOU--BUT YOU	65	14
TO THINK OF ANSWERING YOU!	GOING TO HEAVEN!	79	5
IF YOU SH'D GET THERE FIRST	GOING TO HEAVEN!	79	13
FOR YOU KNOW WE DO NOT MIND OUR DRESS	GOING TO HEAVEN!	79	18
I PRAY YOU PASS [STROLL] ONCE MORE.	HEART, NOT SO HEAVY AS	83	20
WHEN SIMPLE YOU, AND I,	ONE DIGNITY DELAYS FOR	98	14
YOU--TOO--TAKE COBWEB ATTITUDES	TO HANG OUR HEAD--	105	7
WONT YOU TELL THEM TO?	GOOD NIGHT, BECAUSE WE	114	8
YOU HAVE PASSED ENFRANCHIZED FEET!	TALK WITH PRUDENCE TO A	119	6
WHICH, SIR, ARE YOU AND WHICH AM I	IN LANDS I NEVER SAW--	124	7
STEALTHY COCOON, WHY HIDE YOU SO	COCOON ABOVE! COCOON	129	2
IF YOU WOULD LIKE TO BORROW,	PERHAPS YOU'D LIKE TO	134	3
HAVE YOU GOT A BROOK IN YOUR LITTLE HEART,	HAVE YOU GOT A BROOK IN	136	1
A FURTIVE LOOK YOU KNOW AS WELL--	AN ALTERED LOOK ABOUT	140	14
YOU CANNOT FIND OUT ALL ABOUT	DUST IS THE ONLY SECRET	153	3
YOU LOVE ME--YOU ARE SURE--	YOU LOVE ME--YOU ARE	156	1
YOU LOVE ME--YOU ARE SURE--	YOU LOVE ME--YOU ARE	156	1
BE SURE YOU'RE SURE--YOU KNOW--	YOU LOVE ME--YOU ARE	156	14
YOU STING--AGAIN!	YOU LOVE ME--YOU ARE	156	19
YOU AND I, AND DR HOLLAND,	THO' MY DESTINY BE	163	11
IF I MUST TELL YOU, OF A HORSE	I MET A KING THIS	166	13
IF I COULD'NT THANK YOU,	IF I SHOULD'NT BE ALIVE	182	5
YOU WILL KNOW I'M TRYING	IF I SHOULD'NT BE ALIVE	182	7
WOULD YOU UNTIE IT, WERE YOU ME--	WHAT SHALL I DO--IT	186	5
WOULD YOU UNTIE IT, WERE YOU ME--	WHAT SHALL I DO--IT	186	5
IT SHOULD NOT TEASE YOU--	WHAT SHALL I DO--IT	186	8
WHEN YOU WERE WILLING--	WHAT SHALL I DO--IT	186	12
TRY--CAN YOU STIR THE AWFUL RIVET--	HOW MANY TIMES THESE LOW	187	3
TRY--CAN YOU LIFT THE HASPS OF STEEL!	HOW MANY TIMES THESE LOW	187	4
LIFT--IF YOU CARE--THE LISTLESS HAIR--	HOW MANY TIMES THESE LOW	187	6
EAST INDIA--FOR YOU!	MY EYE IS FULLER THAN MY	202	4
YOU ARE SURE THERE'S SUCH A PERSON	WHAT IS--"PARADISE"--	215	11
IS IT TOO LARGE FOR YOU?	SAVIOR! I'VE NO ONE ELSE	217	12
YOU DROPPED A PURPLE RAVELLING IN--	SHE SWEEPS WITH	219	5
YOU DROPPED AN AMBER THREAD--	SHE SWEEPS WITH	219	6
COULD YOU AFFORD TO SELL--	I CAME TO BUY A SMILE--	223	8
YOU KNOW WHAT DIAMONDS ARE?	I CAME TO BUY A SMILE--	223	10
I'VE NOTHING ELSE--TO BRING, YOU KNOW--	I'VE NOTHING ELSE--TO	224	1
SHOULD YOU BUT FAIL AT--SEA--	SHOULD YOU BUT FAIL AT--	226	1
UNTIL HE LET YOU IN!	SHOULD YOU BUT FAIL AT--	226	7
THAT YOU--SO LATE--"CONSIDER" ME--	I THINK JUST HOW MY	237	7
KILL YOUR BALM--AND IT'S ODORS BLESS YOU--	KILL YOUR BALM--AND IT'S	238	1
OH, COULD YOU CATCH HER LAST REFRAIN--	KILL YOUR BALM--AND IT'S	238	6
YOU ARE VERY FAR--	AH, MOON--AND STAR!	240	2
FARTHER THAN YOU--	AH, MOON--AND STAR!	240	4
DO YOU THINK I'D STOP	AH, MOON--AND STAR!	240	5
AND BE WITH [LEAP TO] YOU--TONIGHT!	AH, MOON--AND STAR!	240	12
THERE IS ONE--FARTHER THAN YOU--	AH, MOON--AND STAR!	240	15
YOU KNOW WHO "JUNE" IS--	WHAT WOULD I GIVE TO SEE	247	7
YOU SEE I CANNOT SEE--YOUR LIFETIME--	YOU SEE I CANNOT SEE--	253	1
I'M BANISHED--NOW--YOU KNOW IT--	IF I'M LOST--NOW--	256	10

YOU (CONTINUED)	FIRST LINE	POEM	LINE
TURNS SO--AWAY FROM YOU--	IF I'M LOST--NOW--	256	13
AH, FRIEND, YOU LITTLE KNEW	GOOD NIGHT! WHICH PUT	259	3
EXTINGUISHED--NOW--FOR YOU!	GOOD NIGHT! WHICH PUT	259	6
OH, WOULDN'T YOU?	DID WE DISOBEY HIM?	267	8
WHOSE INVITATION, KNOW YOU NOT [FOR THIS WORLD--]	HE PUT THE BELT AROUND	273	15
OH, CAVILER, FOR YOU!	DOUBT ME! MY DIM	275	25
I'M NOBODY! WHO ARE YOU?	I'M NOBODY! WHO ARE YOU?	288	1
ARE YOU--NOBODY--TOO?	I'M NOBODY! WHO ARE YOU?	288	2
DONT TELL! THEY'D BANISH US [ADVERTISE]--YOU KNOW!	I'M NOBODY! WHO ARE YOU?	288	4
IF YOUR NERVE, DENY YOU--	IF YOUR NERVE, DENY YOU	292	1
WAS'T GLORY? THAT--WILL DO ['TWAS JUST YOU]--	ONE YEAR AGO--JOTS WHAT?	296	4
CAME ONCE A WORLD--DID YOU?	ONE YEAR AGO--JOTS WHAT?	296	14
OH, HAD YOU TOLD ME SO--	ONE YEAR AGO--JOTS WHAT?	296	15
YOU SAID IT HURT YOU--MOST--	ONE YEAR AGO--JOTS WHAT?	296	17
YOU SAID IT HURT YOU--MOST--	ONE YEAR AGO--JOTS WHAT?	296	17
BUT, HAD YOU LOOKED IN--	ONE YEAR AGO--JOTS WHAT?	296	22
A GIANT--EYE TO EYE WITH YOU, HAD BEEN--	ONE YEAR AGO--JOTS WHAT?	296	23
BECAUSE IT WAS A CHILD, YOU KNOW--	ONE YEAR AGO--JOTS WHAT?	296	30
YOU DRIFTED YOUR DOMINIONS--	YOUR RICHES--TAUGHT ME--	299	5
FOR LIFE'S ESTATE WITH YOU--	YOUR RICHES--TAUGHT ME--	299	8
TO THOSE WHO LOOK ON YOU--	YOUR RICHES--TAUGHT ME--	299	18
HE STUNS YOU BY DEGREES--	HE FUMBLES AT YOUR SOUL	315	4
WERE YOU EVER THERE?	THE WIND DID'NT COME	316	10
WOULD YOU--SAY--	THE WIND DID'NT COME	316	22
WOULD YOU BE THE FOOL TO STAY?	THE WIND DID'NT COME	316	23
I'LL TELL YOU HOW THE SUN ROSE--	I'LL TELL YOU HOW THE	318	1
FOR MINE--I TELL YOU THAT MY HEART	BEFORE I GOT MY EYE PUT	327	7
IN KINGDOMS--YOU HAVE HEARD THE RAISED--	THE FACE I CARRY WITH ME	336	7
YOU MARVEL HOW THEY HELD--	I TEND MY FLOWERS FOR	339	15
YOU FOR YOU, AND I, FOR YOU AND ME	THEY LEAVE US WITH THE	350	10
YOU FOR YOU, AND I, FOR YOU AND ME	THEY LEAVE US WITH THE	350	10
YOU FOR YOU, AND I, FOR YOU AND ME	THEY LEAVE US WITH THE	350	10
IT DOES'NT STATE YOU HOW	A HAPPY LIP--BREAKS	353	2
DARE YOU SEE A SOUL AT THE WHITE HEAT?	DARE YOU SEE A SOUL AT	365	1
YOU, SIR, TAUGHT FIRST--TO ME.	ALTHOUGH I PUT AWAY HIS	366	33
FOR FUN--AT YOU--	SHE LAY AS IF AT PLAY	369	12
AND TELL YOU ALL YOUR DREAMS--WERE TRUE--	A PRECIOUS--MOULDERING	371	23
YOU BEG HIM NOT TO GO--	A PRECIOUS--MOULDERING	371	26
AND WHOM YOU TOLD IT TO--BESIDE--	A SECRET TOLD--	381	7
WITHIN HIS CLOSET--BEST YOU CAN	EXHILIRATION--IS WITHIN	383	11
YOU CANNOT PRICK WITH SAW--	NO RACK CAN TORTURE ME--	384	5
HAD YOU EARLIER BLUNDERED IN	TAKE YOUR HEAVEN FURTHER	388	3
POSSIBLY, E'EN YOU HAD SEEN	TAKE YOUR HEAVEN FURTHER	388	4
DRESSED TO MEET YOU--	TAKE YOUR HEAVEN FURTHER	388	11
ENTERS--WITH A "YOU KNOW ME--SIR"?	IT'S COMING--THE	390	4
AND HE WILL TELL YOU--SKILL IS LATE--	THERE IS A LANGUOR OF	396	13
THEN--LOOK FOR ME. BE SURE YOU SAY--	A TONGUE--TO TELL HIM I	400	28
YOU DID NOT STATE--YOUR PRICE--	I PAY--IN SATIN CASH--	402	2
YOU WOULD NOT KNOW IT FROM THE FIELD--	THE COLOR OF THE GRAVE	411	3
YOU WOULD NOT KNOW IT FROM THE DRIFTS--	THE COLOR OF THE GRAVE	411	11
WHEN THAT YOU MET IT WITH BEFORE--	THE COLOR OF THE GRAVE	411	23
AND YOU DROPT, LOST,	'TWAS LIKE A MAELSTROM,	414	7
AND LET YOU FROM A DREAM--	'TWAS LIKE A MAELSTROM,	414	9
UNTIL YOU FELT YOUR SECOND	'TWAS LIKE A MAELSTROM,	414	12
AND YOU WERE FROZEN LED	'TWAS LIKE A MAELSTROM,	414	19
YOU, OR THE WIND?	IT IS DEAD--FIND IT--	417	4
"CONSCIOUS"? WONT YOU ASK THAT--	IT IS DEAD--FIND IT--	417	5
YOU'LL KNOW IT--AS YOU KNOW 'TIS NOON--	YOU'LL KNOW IT--AS YOU	420	1
AS YOU DO THE SUN--	YOU'LL KNOW IT--AS YOU	420	3
AS YOU WILL IN HEAVEN--	YOU'LL KNOW IT--AS YOU	420	5
"HOW SHALL YOU KNOW"?	YOU'LL KNOW IT--AS YOU	420	14
YOU--ARE NOT SO FAIR--MIDNIGHT--	GOOD MORNING--MIDNIGHT--	425	13
I'LL STRING YOU--IN FINE NECKLACE--	I'LL CLUTCH--AND CLUTCH	427	7
WEAR YOU ON HEM--	I'LL CLUTCH--AND CLUTCH	427	9
LOOP UP A COUNTESS--WITH YOU--	I'LL CLUTCH--AND CLUTCH	427	10
AND DOUBT THAT YOU ARE MINE--	I'LL CLUTCH--AND CLUTCH	427	13
I'LL SHOW YOU AT THE COURT--	I'LL CLUTCH--AND CLUTCH	427	15
BEAR YOU--FOR ORNAMENT	I'LL CLUTCH--AND CLUTCH	427	16
THAT EVERY SIGH--MAY LIFT YOU	I'LL CLUTCH--AND CLUTCH	427	18
IN MEEK ARRAY--DISPLAY YOU--	I'LL CLUTCH--AND CLUTCH	427	21
I SAY TO YOU, SAID JESUS--	DO PEOPLE MOULDER	432	9
I WOULD GIVE YOU--	KNOWS HOW TO FORGET!	433	13
DONT YOU KNOW?	KNOWS HOW TO FORGET!	433	V
ASSENT--AND YOU ARE SANE--	MUCH MADNESS IS DIVINEST	435	6
THEY GIVE US PRESENTS MOST--YOU KNOW--	IT WAS GIVEN TO ME BY	454	3
ARE SO HIGH UP--YOU SEE--	I KNOW WHERE WELLS GROW	460	12
THE POWER TO BE TRUE TO YOU,	THE POWER TO BE TRUE TO	464	1
ITSELF BE GIVEN YOU"--	I MEANT TO HAVE BUT	476	24
"WHY DO I LOVE" YOU, SIR?	"WHY DO I LOVE" YOU, SIR	480	1
DO NOT YOU--	"WHY DO I LOVE" YOU, SIR	480	7
YOU HEAR A BEING--DROP--	A SOLEMN THING WITHIN	483	6
YOU THOUGHT WAS FINISHED--	A SOLEMN THING WITHIN	483	9
YOU LOVE THE LORD--YOU CANNOT SEE--	YOU LOVE THE LORD--YOU	487	1
YOU LOVE THE LORD--YOU CANNOT SEE--	YOU LOVE THE LORD--YOU	487	1
YOU WRITE HIM--EVERY DAY--	YOU LOVE THE LORD--YOU	487	2
A LITTLE NOTE--WHEN YOU AWAKE--	YOU LOVE THE LORD--YOU	487	3
AN AMPLE LETTER--HOW YOU MISS--	YOU LOVE THE LORD--YOU	487	5

YOU (CONTINUED)

	FIRST LINE	POEM	LINE
AND MINE'S--IN HEAVEN--YOU SEE.	YOU LOVE THE LORD--YOU	487	8
AND THEN YOU WISHED YOU HAD EYES IN YOUR PAGES--	GOING TO HIM! HAPPY	494	8
AND THEN YOU WISHED YOU HAD EYES IN YOUR PAGES--	GOING TO HIM! HAPPY	494	8
SO YOU COULD SEE WHAT MOVED THEM SO--	GOING TO HIM! HAPPY	494	9
YOU GUESSED--FROM THE WAY THE SENTENCE TOILED--	GOING TO HIM! HAPPY	494	11
YOU COULD HEAR THE BODDICE TUG, BEHIND YOU--	GOING TO HIM! HAPPY	494	12
YOU COULD HEAR THE BODDICE TUG, BEHIND YOU--	GOING TO HIM! HAPPY	494	12
YOU ALMOST PITIED IT--YOU--IT WORKED SO--	GOING TO HIM! HAPPY	494	14
YOU ALMOST PITIED IT--YOU--IT WORKED SO--	GOING TO HIM! HAPPY	494	14
TELL HIM [HER]--NO--YOU MAY QUIBBLE THERE--	GOING TO HIM! HAPPY	494	15
AND THEN YOU AND I, WERE SILENTER.	GOING TO HIM! HAPPY	494	17
AND YOU--GOT SLEEPY--AND BEGGED TO BE ENDED--	GOING TO HIM! HAPPY	494	20
TELL HIM [HER]--JUST HOW SHE SEALED YOU--CAUTIOUS!	GOING TO HIM! HAPPY	494	22
BUT--IF HE [SHE] ASK WHERE YOU ARE HID	GOING TO HIM! HAPPY	494	23
DONT YOU KNOW--ME?	HE STRAINED MY FAITH--	497	16
WHERE ARE THEY--CAN YOU TELL--	THOSE FAIR--FICTITIOUS	499	V 8
YOU KNOW THAT PORTRAIT IN THE MOON--	YOU KNOW THAT PORTRAIT	504	1
YOU ALMOST BATHED YOUR TONGUE--	SHE SIGHTS A BIRD--SHE	507	10
YOU ALMOST FEEL THE DATE--	IF ANYBODY'S FRIEND BE	509	10
HOW PLEASED THEY WERE [LOOKED], AT WHAT YOU SAID--	IF ANYBODY'S FRIEND BE	509	13
YOU TRY TO TOUCH [REACH] THE SMILE	IF ANYBODY'S FRIEND BE	509	14
WHEN WAS IT--CAN YOU TELL--	IF ANYBODY'S FRIEND BE	509	16
YOU ASKED THE COMPANY TO TEA--	IF ANYBODY'S FRIEND BE	509	17
THAT DONT REMEMBER YOU--	IF ANYBODY'S FRIEND BE	509	20
IF YOU WERE COMING IN THE FALL,	IF YOU WERE COMING IN	511	1
IF I COULD SEE YOU IN A YEAR,	IF YOU WERE COMING IN	511	5
AND STILL IT HURT YOU, AS SOME BIRD	HER SMILE WAS SHAPED	514	3
THAT YOU NEVER DO IT--	BEAUTY--BE NOT CAUSED--	516	8
YOU SQUANDER ON [SPEND UPON] THE DEAD,	ENDOW THE LIVING--WITH	521	2
SWEET--YOU FORGOT--BUT I REMEMBERED	SWEET--YOU FORGOT--BUT I	523	1
THROUGH DECAY [FATIGUE / THE LAPSE] OF YOU--	SWEET--YOU FORGOT--BUT I	523	4
HAPPY IT BE FOR YOU--A BEGGAR'S--	SWEET--YOU FORGOT--BUT I	523	7
YOU--SWEET [SIR]--SHUT ME OUT--	SWEET--YOU FORGOT--BUT I	523	12
YOU CANNOT [NO MAN--] PUT A FIRE OUT--	YOU CANNOT PUT A FIRE	530	1
YOU CANNOT FOLD A FLOOD--	YOU CANNOT PUT A FIRE	530	5
AS THE STARS--YOU KNEW LAST NIGHT--	SOME SUCH BUTTERFLY BE	541	7
FOREIGNERS [KNOW NOT YOU]--THIS MORNING--	SOME SUCH BUTTERFLY BE	541	8
YOU CANNOT SOLDER AN ABYSS [PLUG A SEPULCHRE]	TO FILL A GAP	546	5
'TWERE EASIER FOR YOU--	THE BRAIN, WITHIN IT'S	556	4
CREATOR--WAS IT YOU?	MY PERIOD HAD COME FOR	564	4
I'LL TELL YOU HOW I TRIED TO KEEP	IF I MAY HAVE IT, WHEN	577	22
A SMILE, TO SHOW YOU, WHEN THIS DEEP	IF I MAY HAVE IT, WHEN	577	23
DID YOU EVER STAND IN A CAVERN'S MOUTH--	DID YOU EVER STAND IN A	590	1
AND FLY, AS 'TWERE PURSUING YOU?	DID YOU EVER STAND IN A	590	7
DID YOU EVER LOOK IN A CANNON'S FACE--	DID YOU EVER STAND IN A	590	9
IF YOU REMEMBER, AND WERE SAVED--	DID YOU EVER STAND IN A	590	15
YOU'LL FIND--IT WHEN YOU TRY TO DIE--	YOU'LL FIND--IT WHEN YOU	610	1
YOU COULD NOT SPARE--YOU KNOW.	YOU'LL FIND--IT WHEN YOU	610	4
YOU COULD NOT SPARE--YOU KNOW.	YOU'LL FIND--IT WHEN YOU	610	4
YOU CHOSE THE NEWER NAMES [TIMES]--	YOU'LL FIND--IT WHEN YOU	610	8
IT BEGS YOU GIVE IT WORK--	AT LEISURE IS THE SOUL	618	5
WHERE YOU HAD PUT ME DOWN--	OURSELVES WERE WED ONE	631	6
BUT YOU--WERE CROWNED [YOUR'S WAS FIRST--] IN JUNE--	OURSELVES WERE WED ONE	631	16
WITH EASE--AND YOU--BESIDE--	THE BRAIN--IS WIDER THAN	632	4
YOU CANNOT FEEL THE SEAM--	YOU'LL KNOW HER--BY HER	634	18
YOU BEG THE ROBIN IN YOUR BRAIN	YOU'LL KNOW HER--BY HER	634	27
TO NO ONE THAT YOU--KNOW--	THE WAY I READ A	636	14
I CANNOT LIVE WITH YOU--	I CANNOT LIVE WITH YOU--	640	1
I COULD NOT DIE--WITH YOU--	I CANNOT LIVE WITH YOU--	640	13
YOU--COULD NOT--	I CANNOT LIVE WITH YOU--	640	16
AND SEE YOU--FREEZE--	I CANNOT LIVE WITH YOU--	640	18
NOR COULD I RISE--WITH YOU--	I CANNOT LIVE WITH YOU--	640	21
EXCEPT THAT YOU THAN HE	I CANNOT LIVE WITH YOU--	640	27
FOR YOU--SERVED HEAVEN--YOU KNOW,	I CANNOT LIVE WITH YOU--	640	30
FOR YOU--SERVED HEAVEN--YOU KNOW,	I CANNOT LIVE WITH YOU--	640	30
BECAUSE YOU SATURATED SIGHT--	I CANNOT LIVE WITH YOU--	640	33
AND WERE YOU LOST, I WOULD BE--	I CANNOT LIVE WITH YOU--	640	37
AND WERE YOU--SAVED--	I CANNOT LIVE WITH YOU--	640	41
WHERE YOU WERE NOT--	I CANNOT LIVE WITH YOU--	640	43
YOU THERE--I--HERE--	I CANNOT LIVE WITH YOU--	640	46
YOU LEFT ME--SIRE [SWEET]--TWO LEGACIES--	YOU LEFT ME--SIRE--TWO	644	1
YOU LEFT ME BOUNDARIES OF PAIN--	YOU LEFT ME--SIRE--TWO	644	5
PROMISE THIS--WHEN YOU BE DYING--	PROMISE THIS--WHEN YOU	648	1
JUST THAT YOU SHOULD SEE	PROMISE THIS--WHEN YOU	648	14
IMITATING [MORE RESEMBLING] YOU--	PROMISE THIS--WHEN YOU	648	16
THAT FIRST DAY, WHEN YOU PRAISED ME, SWEET,	THAT FIRST DAY, WHEN YOU	659	1
AND THOUGH THE WO YOU HAVE TODAY	'TIS GOOD--THE LOOKING	660	9
PURPLES OF AGES--PAUSE [HALT] FOR YOU--	AH, TENERIFFE!	666	3
DAY--DROPS YOU HER [HIS] RED ADIEU!	AH, TENERIFFE!	666	5
WOULD YOU LIKE SUMMER? TASTE OF OURS.	WOULD YOU LIKE SUMMER?	691	1
I COULD BRING YOU JEWELS--HAD I A MIND TO--	I COULD BRING YOU JEWELS	697	1
BUT YOU HAVE ENOUGH--OF THOSE--	I COULD BRING YOU JEWELS	697	2
I COULD BRING YOU ODORS FROM ST DOMINGO--	I COULD BRING YOU JEWELS	697	3

	FIRST LINE	POEM	LINE
YOU (CONTINUED)			
AND IF IT SERVE YOU FOR A HOUSE--	THE JUDGE IS LIKE THE	699	7
YOU'VE SEEN BALLOONS SET--HAV'NT YOU?	YOU'VE SEEN BALLOONS SET	700	1
IT IS AS SWANS--DISCARDED YOU,	YOU'VE SEEN BALLOONS SET	700	3
WONT YOU WISH YOU'D SPOKEN	NO MATTER--NOW--SWEET--	704	3
BUT WONT YOU WISH YOU'D SPARED ONE	NO MATTER--NOW--SWEET--	704	7
WONT YOU WISH YOU'D SMILED--JUST--	NO MATTER--NOW--SWEET--	704	15
WHOSE SERVICE--IS TO YOU--	SWEET MOUNTAINS--YE TELL	722	9
TO LIFT HER BROWS ON YOU--	SWEET MOUNTAINS--YE TELL	722	12
TO CREW AND YOU--	IT TOSSED--AND TOSSED--	723	10
TO BREAK FOR YOU--	IT TOSSED--AND TOSSED--	723	12
YOU--AND ETERNITY--THE	LET US PLAY YESTERDAY--	728	3
WHEN YOU TROUBLED THE ELLIPSE--	LET US PLAY YESTERDAY--	728	15
I WILL--OF YOU--	ALTER! WHEN THE HILLS DO	729	8
YOU SAID THAT I "WAS GREAT"--ONE DAY--	YOU SAID THAT I "WAS	738	1
YOU TAUGHT ME WAITING WITH MYSELF--	YOU TAUGHT ME WAITING	740	1
YOU TAUGHT ME FORTITUDE OF FATE--	YOU TAUGHT ME WAITING	740	3
THE HEAVEN YOU KNOW--TO UNDERSTAND	YOU TAUGHT ME WAITING	740	9
THAT YOU BE NOT ASHAMED	YOU TAUGHT ME WAITING	740	10
BUT YOU MUST GO AWAY	THE BIRDS REPORTED FROM	743 V	4
NEED YOU--UNTO HIM--	NEVER FOR SOCIETY	746	12
YOU CONSTITUTED TIME--	YOU CONSTITUTED TIME--	765	1
'TIS FIRST [YOU SEE] HE STEPS UPON THE VANE--	MY FAITH IS LARGER THAN	766	5
WHEN ONE [YOU] HAS FAILED TO STOP THEM--	TO OFFER BRAVE	767	3
UPON THE FURTHEST SLOPE YOU KNOW	A LIGHT EXISTS IN SPRING	812	11
IT ALMOST SPEAKS TO YOU.	A LIGHT EXISTS IN SPRING	812	12
TILL YOU HAD TASTED FIRST,	I COULD NOT DRINK IT,	818	2
I'LL TELL IT YOU [SIGNIFY / TESTIFY]--	THE ONLY NEWS I KNOW	827	12
PERHAPS YOU THINK ME STOOPING	PERHAPS YOU THINK ME	833	1
DIVIDE LIGHT IF YOU DARE--	BANISH AIR FROM AIR--	854	2
I MENTION IT TO YOU,	THIS CHASM, SWEET, UPON	858	2
LOOSE THE FLOOD--YOU SHALL FIND IT PATENT--	SPLIT THE LARK--AND	861	5
GUSH AFTER GUSH, RESERVED FOR YOU--	SPLIT THE LARK--AND	861	6
NOW, DO YOU DOUBT THAT YOUR BIRD WAS TRUE?	SPLIT THE LARK--AND	861	8
PRECISELY, AS TO YOU [ME].	LIGHT IS SUFFICIENT TO	862	8
YOU, UNSUSPECTING, FEEL FOR ME [WEAR ME TOO]--	I HIDE MYSELF WITHIN MY	903	3
WILL HOLD YOU TILL YOUR PRIVILEGE	TILL DEATH--IS NARROW	907	3
BUT HE WHOSE LOSS PROCURES YOU	TILL DEATH--IS NARROW	907	5
THE LOVE YOU OFFER--	I CANNOT BE ASHAMED	914	3
AND THEN AWAY TO YOU TO PASS--	I LEARNED--AT LEAST--	944	23
"UNTO ME?" I DO NOT KNOW YOU--	"UNTO ME?" I DO NOT KNOW	964	1
WAGONS--HAVE YOU--TO CONVEY ME?	"UNTO ME?" I DO NOT KNOW	964	5
YOU MAY HAVE MET HIM--DID YOU NOT	A NARROW FELLOW IN THE	986	3
YOU MAY HAVE MET HIM--DID YOU NOT	A NARROW FELLOW IN THE	986	3
AND WHOSE "I'LL MEET YOU" HESITATES	SUPERFLUOUS WERE THE SUN	999	7
BUT SWEAR, AND I WILL LET YOU BY	THE FINGERS OF THE LIGHT	1000	7
YOU WILL NOT WAKE THEM UP."	THE FINGERS OF THE LIGHT	1000	8
TOO SCANTY 'TWAS TO DIE FOR YOU,	TOO SCANTY 'TWAS TO DIE	1013	1
PERCEIVE, WHEN YOU ARE GONE.	THE DYING NEED BUT	1026	8
BEE! I'M EXPECTING YOU!	BEE! I'M EXPECTING YOU!	1035	1
TO SOMEBODY YOU KNOW	BEE! I'M EXPECTING YOU!	1035	3
THAT YOU WERE DUE--	BEE! I'M EXPECTING YOU!	1035	4
NO CLUSTER--YE [YOU] SHALL FIND--	EXCEPT THE SMALLER SIZE	1067 V	
WHEN YOU--HOLD--GARNET TO GARNET--	TITLE DIVINE--IS MINE!	1072	8
HERE'S--WHAT I HAD TO "TELL YOU"--	TITLE DIVINE--IS MINE!	1072 V	
YOU WILL TELL NO OTHER?	TITLE DIVINE--IS MINE!	1072 V	
WOULD YOU--INSTEAD OF ME?	THEMSELF ARE ALL I HAVE	1094	5
ON ANGELS--SQUANDERING FOR YOU	HIS BILL IS CLASPED--HIS	1102	11
WOULD YOU SERVE [SEEK] IT SO?	NONE WHO SAW IT EVER	1110	8
YOU HEARD NO NOISE [CRASH]	A GREAT HOPE FELL	1123	2
PHANTOMS ENTERED "AND NOT YOU."	TRUST ADJUSTS HER	1161	2
ON THE WORLD YOU COLORED	ON THE WORLD YOU COLORED	1171	1
COULD YOU COMPREHEND IT	THERE'S THE BATTLE OF	1174	7
YOU WOULD CHASTENED STARE--	THERE'S THE BATTLE OF	1174	8
THE SEA SAID "THEN YOU WILL BE A SEA--	THE SEA SAID "COME" TO	1210	3
YOU CHERISHED"--"LEARNED WATERS--	THE SEA SAID "COME" TO	1210	7
UNLESS YOU LEAVE HIM--THEN RETURN	SO MUCH OF HEAVEN HAS	1228	11
DISPROVE [DISPEL] THAT AND YOU MAY--	POWER IS A FAMILIAR	1238	8
SUPPLANTING ME AND YOU	DOMINION LASTS UNTIL	1257	8
BECAUSE THAT YOU ARE GOING	BECAUSE THAT YOU ARE	1260	1
THAT YOU, WHO WERE EXISTENCE	BECAUSE THAT YOU ARE	1260	15
UNTIL THE REALM OF YOU--	BECAUSE THAT YOU ARE	1260	20
BUT "YOU"--SHE RETURNED WITH VALOR	I SAW THAT THE FLAKE WAS	1267	5
THAT SACRED CLOSET WHEN YOU SWEEP--	THAT SACRED CLOSET WHEN	1273	1
YOU CANNOT SUPERSEDE ITSELF	THAT SACRED CLOSET WHEN	1273	11
BUT IT CAN SILENCE YOU--	THAT SACRED CLOSET WHEN	1273	12
AND YOU WILL [SHALL] LODGE A GIANT	I THOUGHT THAT NATURE	1286	11
IS PLAY I HEAR FROM YOU--	THE MOST PATHETIC THING	1290	2
YOU KNEW IT [THAT] WAS NOT TRUE	THE MOST PATHETIC THING	1290	6
GOLIAH--SO WOULD YOU--	THE MOST PATHETIC THING	1290	8
A WHIP SO SMALL YOU COULD NOT SEE IT	NOT WITH A CLUB, THE	1304	3
YOU EFFACE THE SHEEN.	WHICH IS THE BEST--THE	1315	4
I HOPED [LOOKED] FOR YOU BEFORE--	DEAR MARCH--COME IN--	1320	3
YOU MUST HAVE WALKED--	DEAR MARCH--COME IN--	1320	5
HOW OUT OF BREATH YOU ARE--	DEAR MARCH--COME IN--	1320	6
DEAR MARCH, HOW ARE YOU, AND THE REST--	DEAR MARCH--COME IN--	1320	7
DID YOU LEAVE NATURE WELL--	DEAR MARCH--COME IN--	1320	8
THE MAPLES NEVER KNEW THAT YOU WERE COMING--TILL I CALLED	DEAR MARCH--COME IN--	1320	12
ALL THOSE HILLS YOU LEFT FOR ME TO HUE--	DEAR MARCH--COME IN--	1320	15

	FIRST LINE	POEM		LINE
YOU (CONTINUED)				
YOU TOOK IT ALL WITH YOU--	DEAR MARCH--COME IN--	1320		17
YOU TOOK IT ALL WITH YOU--	DEAR MARCH--COME IN--	1320		17
AS SOON AS [THE INSTANT THAT] YOU HAVE COME	DEAR MARCH--COME IN--	1320		24
FLOSS WONT SAVE YOU FROM AN ABYSS	FLOSS WONT SAVE YOU FROM	1322		1
BUT I TELL YOU EVERY STEP IS A TROUGH [SLUICE]--	FLOSS WONT SAVE YOU FROM	1322		5
NOW WILL YOU HAVE THE ROPE OR THE FLOSS?	FLOSS WONT SAVE YOU FROM	1322		7
I SEND YOU A DECREPIT FLOWER	I SEND YOU A DECREPIT	1324		1
FLEE AS IF YOU TROD UNTHINKING	KNOCK WITH TREMOR--	1325		4
SHOULD THEY REND YOU WITH "HOW ARE YOU"	KNOCK WITH TREMOR--	1325		8
SHOULD THEY REND YOU WITH "HOW ARE YOU"	KNOCK WITH TREMOR--	1325		8
WHAT HAVE YOU TO SHOW?	KNOCK WITH TREMOR--	1325		9
YOU CANNOT TAKE ITSELF	YOU CANNOT TAKE ITSELF	1351		1
EMPTY THE HEARTS THAT PURCHASED YOU--	BROTHER OF INGOTS--AH	1366		2
SUBTLE THE SUM THAT PURCHASE YOU--	BROTHER OF INGOTS--AH	1366	V	2
HONOR, THE SHORTEST ROUTE TO YOU.	BROTHER OF INGOTS--AH	1366	V	2
HIM YOU CHASTEN, [THOU CHASTENEST-- / YOU CHASTENED] THAT IS [WAS] HE!	LAY THIS LAUREL ON THE	1393		4
HIM YOU CHASTEN, [THOU CHASTENEST-- / YOU CHASTENED] THAT IS [WAS] HE!	LAY THIS LAUREL ON THE	1393		4
THE REALM OF [LOVING] YOU--	I HAVE NO LIFE BUT THIS	1398		8
AS WE [YOU] WHO STAY, SUPPOSE--	PERHAPS THEY DO NOT GO	1399		2
LIKE LOOKING EVERY TIME YOU PLEASE	WHAT MYSTERY PERVADES A	1400		7
AND SHE WOULD TELL YOU [ANSWER] SIGHING--	CRISIS IS SWEET AND YET	1416		7
AND SHE WILL POINT UNDOUBTEDLY [YOU FONDLY-- / YOU LONGINGLY]	CRISIS IS SWEET AND YET	1416	V	7
AND SHE WILL POINT UNDOUBTEDLY [YOU FONDLY-- / YOU LONGINGLY]	CRISIS IS SWEET AND YET	1416	V	7
HIS OUTLETS--WOULD YOU SEE [KNOW]	SUCH ARE THE INLETS OF	1421		2
PROVOKING LOVER, WHEN YOU CAME	I THOUGHT THE TRAIN	1449		7
WHICH WHILE YOU TASTE SO NATIVE [ADJACENT] SEEMS	YOUR THOUGHTS DONT HAVE	1452		5
YOU CANNOT COMPREHEND ITS PRICE [WORTH]	YOUR THOUGHTS DONT HAVE	1452		7
BEFORE YOU THOUGHT OF SPRING	BEFORE YOU THOUGHT OF	1465		1
YOU SEE--GOD BLESS HIS SUDDENNESS--	BEFORE YOU THOUGHT OF	1465		3
AS IF FOR YOU TO CHOOSE--	BEFORE YOU THOUGHT OF	1465		10
WHEN YOU APPROACH THE PLACE--	'TIS WHITER THAN AN	1482		4
NOT ME--NOR YOU--	THE ROAD TO PARADISE IS	1491		8
AS YOU OR I [COWARDS DO]--	FACTS BY OUR SIDE ARE	1497		13
AS WHEN YOU CAME BEFORE	THE PILE OF YEARS IS NOT	1507		2
YOU CANNOT MAKE REMEMBRANCE GROW	YOU CANNOT MAKE	1508		1
NOR CAN YOU CUT REMEMBRANCE DOWN	YOU CANNOT MAKE	1508		9
"IF YOU DARE"?	NOT SEEING, STILL WE	1518		8
IS JUST AS HIGH AS YOU AND I,	THE BUTTERFLY UPON THE	1521		5
I WANT TO SEND IT TO YOU	HE LIVED THE LIFE OF	1525	V	
TILL YOU WASTE [FURL / LAME] YOUR EYE--	FOLLOW WISE ORION	1538		2
WITH A SNEER AT YOU--	FOLLOW WISE ORION	1538	V	
WISHING YOU GOOD DAY--	NOT AT HOME TO CALLERS	1590		4
"DID YOU" OR "DID YOU NOT," TO ASK--	WHO IS IT SEEKS MY	1598		3
"DID YOU" OR "DID YOU NOT," TO ASK--	WHO IS IT SEEKS MY	1598		3
PURSUING YOU IN YOUR TRANSITIONS,	PURSUING YOU IN YOUR	1602		1
AND YET IF YOU COMPARE THE LASTS,	A FLOWER WILL NOT	1621		2
IS IT TOO LATE TO TOUCH YOU, DEAR?	IS IT TOO LATE TO TOUCH	1637		1
I SHRANK--"HOW FAIR YOU ARE"!	IN WINTER IN MY ROOM	1670		22
YOU ARE PUNCTUAL--	LIGHTLY STEPPED A YELLOW	1672		8
YOU CANNOT EVEN DIE	THE RIGHT TO PERISH	1692		6
TO PAY YOU SCRUTINY--	THE RIGHT TO PERISH	1692		8
BAFFLE, IF IT COST YOU	DEATH IS LIKE THE INSECT	1716		7
EVERYTHING YOU ARE.	DEATH IS LIKE THE INSECT	1716		8
I'LL TELL YOU WHAT I PAID--	I TOOK ONE DRAUGHT OF	1725		2
THEIR NAMES, UNLESS YOU KNOW THEM,	THE MOST IMPORTANT	1746		5
YOU'D				
PERHAPS YOU'D LIKE TO BUY A FLOWER,	PERHAPS YOU'D LIKE TO	134		1
YOU'D SCARCE RECOGNIZE HIM!	A FUZZY FELLOW, WITHOUT	173		16
WONT YOU WISH YOU'D SPOKEN	NO MATTER--NOW--SWEET--	704		3
BUT WONT YOU WISH YOU'D SPARED ONE	NO MATTER--NOW--SWEET--	704		7
WONT YOU WISH YOU'D SMILED--JUST--	NO MATTER--NOW--SWEET--	704		15
I THOUGHT YOU'D CHOOSE A VELVET CHEEK	THEMSELF ARE ALL I HAVE	1094		3
YOU'D THINK [SWEAR] HE TOOK A DEED	HOW DESTITUTE IS HE	1477	V	7
SO STRAIGHT YOU'D SCARCE SUSPECT	A PIT--BUT HEAVEN OVER	1712		13
YOU'LL				
WHEN I HAVE LOST, YOU'LL KNOW BY THIS--	WHERE I HAVE LOST, I	104		9
IF YOU'LL JUST TELL ME SO--	YOU LOVE ME--YOU ARE	156		16
YOU'LL KNOW IT BY THE ROW OF STARS	I LOST A WORLD--THE	181		3
YOU'LL KNOW--SIR--WHEN THE SAVIOR'S FACE	IF I'M LOST--NOW--	256		12
NO FEAR YOU'LL MISS THE ROAD.	A MURMUR IN THE TREES--	416		20
YOU'LL KNOW IT--AS YOU KNOW 'TIS NOON--	YOU'LL KNOW IT--AS YOU	420		1
YOU'LL FIND--IT WHEN YOU TRY TO DIE--	YOU'LL FIND--IT WHEN YOU	610		1
YOU'LL KNOW HER--BY HER FOOT--	YOU'LL KNOW HER--BY HER	634		1
YOU'LL KNOW HER--BY HER VEST--	YOU'LL KNOW HER--BY HER	634		9
YOU'LL KNOW HER--BY HER VOICE--	YOU'LL KNOW HER--BY HER	634		21
SPLIT THE LARK--AND YOU'LL FIND THE MUSIC--	SPLIT THE LARK--AND	861		1
YOU'LL GET MY LETTER BY	BEE! I'M EXPECTING YOU!	1035		9
YOUNG				
AND THEIR YOUNG WILL	UNTO LIKE STORY--TROUBLE	295		4
TO TIMES WHEN HE--WAS YOUNG--	A PRECIOUS--MOULDERING	371		8
TOO YOUNG THAT ANY SHOULD SUSPECT	A LOSS OF SOMETHING EVER	959		4
NOT ALL DIE EARLY, DYING YOUNG--	NOT ALL DIE EARLY, DYING	990		1

YOUR	FIRST LINE	POEM	LINE
AND CALL YOUR BROTHER MARS!	"SIC TRANSIT GLORIA	3	16
YOUR PRAYERS, OH PASSER BY!	A DAY! HELP! HELP!	42	2
HOW GAY UPON YOUR TABLE	IF SHE HAD BEEN THE	44	3
WITH YOUR MAJESTIC LEAVE!	GREAT CAESAR! CONDESCEND	102	4
JOVE! CHOOSE YOUR COUNSEL--	I HAD SOME THINGS THAT I	116	15
OF YOUR VIANDS, AND YOUR WINES!	TALK WITH PRUDENCE TO A	119	4
OF YOUR VIANDS, AND YOUR WINES!	TALK WITH PRUDENCE TO A	119	4
YOUR SECRET, PERCHED IN EXTASY	COCOON ABOVE! COCOON	129	5
HAVE YOU GOT A BROOK IN YOUR LITTLE HEART,	HAVE YOU GOT A BROOK IN	136	1
AND YET YOUR LITTLE DRAUGHT OF LIFE	HAVE YOU GOT A BROOK IN	136	7
AT LAST, THE LAMPS UPON THY [YOUR] SIDE	AT LAST, TO BE	174	2
ONLY, YOUR INFERENCE THEREFROM!	AS IF SOME LITTLE ARCTIC	180	12
BY YOUR CHAIR--OR, ON THE MAT--	WHAT SHALL I DO--IT	186	9
OR IF IT DARE--TO CLIMB YOUR DIZZY KNEE--	WHAT SHALL I DO--IT	186	10
OR--SOMETIMES AT YOUR SIDE TO RUN--	WHAT SHALL I DO--IT	186	11
SO KEEP YOUR SECRET--FATHER!	THE SKIES CANT KEEP	191	13
IN YOUR NEW-FASHIONED WORLD!	THE SKIES CANT KEEP	191	16
THE SMALLEST ONE UPON YOUR FACE [CHEEK]	I CAME TO BUY A SMILE--	223	3
THE "SPARROW" OF YOUR CARE--	I THINK JUST HOW MY	237	8
KILL YOUR BALM--AND IT'S ODORS BLESS YOU--	KILL YOUR BALM--AND IT'S	238	1
BARE YOUR JESSAMINE--TO THE STORM--	KILL YOUR BALM--AND IT'S	238	2
HAPLY--YOUR SUMMER NIGHT TO CHARM--	KILL YOUR BALM--AND IT'S	238	4
STAB THE BIRD--THAT BUILT IN YOUR BOSOM--	KILL YOUR BALM--AND IT'S	238	5
YOU SEE I CANNOT SEE--YOUR LIFETIME--	YOU SEE I CANNOT SEE--	253	1
STRAIN TILL YOUR [HER] LAST SURMISE--	DOUBT ME! MY DIM	275	19
AND NOT THE PILLOW AT YOUR CHEEK	'TIS SO APPALLING--IT	281	17
TO TELL YOUR [ONE'S] NAME--THE LIVELONG JUNE--	I'M NOBODY! WHO ARE YOU?	288	7
IF YOUR NERVE, DENY YOU--	IF YOUR NERVE, DENY YOU	292	1
GO ABOVE YOUR NERVE--	IF YOUR NERVE, DENY YOU	292	2
IF YOUR SOUL SEESAW [STAGGER]--	IF YOUR NERVE, DENY YOU	292	9
YOUR RICHES--TAUGHT ME--POVERTY.	YOUR RICHES--TAUGHT ME--	299	1
YOU DRIFTED YOUR DOMINIONS--	YOUR RICHES--TAUGHT ME--	299	5
HE FUMBLES AT YOUR SOUL	HE FUMBLES AT YOUR SOUL	315	1
PREPARES YOUR BRITTLE NATURE [SUBSTANCE]	HE FUMBLES AT YOUR SOUL	315	5
YOUR BREATH HAS TIME [CHANCE] TO STRAIGHTEN--	HE FUMBLES AT YOUR SOUL	315	9
YOUR BRAIN--TO BUBBLE COOL--	HE FUMBLES AT YOUR SOUL	315	10
THAT SCALPS [PEELS] YOUR NAKED SOUL--	HE FUMBLES AT YOUR SOUL	315	12
YOUR SERVANT, SIR, WILL WEARY--	ALTHOUGH I PUT AWAY HIS	366	22
THE DUST, WILL VEX YOUR FAME--	ALTHOUGH I PUT AWAY HIS	366	25
THE COLD WILL FORCE YOUR TIGHTEST DOOR	ALTHOUGH I PUT AWAY HIS	366	26
TO MAKE YOUR COTTAGE GAY--	ALTHOUGH I PUT AWAY HIS	366	29
AND TELL YOU ALL YOUR DREAMS--WERE TRUE--	A PRECIOUS--MOULDERING	371	23
TAKE YOUR HEAVEN FURTHER ON--	TAKE YOUR HEAVEN FURTHER	388	1
IS THE UTMOST OF YOUR HAND--	TAKE YOUR HEAVEN FURTHER	388	7
NEARER TO YOUR COURTESIES	TAKE YOUR HEAVEN FURTHER	388	9
YOU DID NOT STATE--YOUR PRICE--	I PAY--IN SATIN CASH--	402	2
OF YOUR DELIRIOUS HEM--	'TWAS LIKE A MAELSTROM,	414	6
UNTIL YOU FELT YOUR SECOND	'TWAS LIKE A MAELSTROM,	414	12
AS IF YOUR SENTENCE STOOD--PRONOUNCED--	'TWAS LIKE A MAELSTROM,	414	18
AND WHEN THE FILM HAD STITCHED YOUR EYES	'TWAS LIKE A MAELSTROM,	414	22
SO GO YOUR WAY--AND I'LL GO MINE--	A MURMUR IN THE TREES--	416	19
CONSULT YOUR EYE!	YOU'LL KNOW IT--AS YOU	420	15
PRESUMPTUOUS OF YOUR PLACE--	THE POWER TO BE TRUE TO	464	4
TO GIVE YOUR CORE--A LOOK--	A SOLEMN THING WITHIN	483	12
YOUR CHANCE IN HARVEST MOVES	A SOLEMN THING WITHIN	483	14
AND THEN YOU WISHED YOU HAD EYES IN YOUR PAGES--	GOING TO HIM! HAPPY	494	8
GESTURE COQUETTE--AND SHAKE YOUR HEAD!	GOING TO HIM! HAPPY	494	25
JESUS--IT'S YOUR LITTLE "JOHN"!	HE STRAINED MY FAITH--	497	15
YOU ALMOST BATHED YOUR TONGUE--	SHE SIGHTS A BIRD--SHE	507	10
AND DIP [MIX] YOUR FINGERS IN THE FROST--	IF ANYBODY'S FRIEND BE	509	15
AROUND YOUR FIRESIDE--	ENDOW THE LIVING--WITH	521	4
AND TELL YOUR CEDAR FLOOR--	YOU CANNOT PUT A FIRE	530	8
SUBJECT [PRESENT] TO YOUR PLUCKING--	SOME SUCH BUTTERFLY BE	541	6
HOW WOULD YOUR OWN--BEGIN?	I FOUND THE WORDS TO	581	6
AND LOOK--AND SHUDDER, AND BLOCK YOUR BREATH--	DID YOU EVER STAND IN A	590	3
EXTEMPORIZING IN YOUR EAR	DID YOU EVER STAND IN A	590	13
'TIS LATE YOUR SUNRISE VEX THEIR FACE--	WHAT CARE THE DEAD, FOR	592	3
YOUR VISION--WAS IN JUNE--	OURSELVES WERE WED ONE	631	2
AND WHEN YOUR LITTLE LIFETIME FAILED,	OURSELVES WERE WED ONE	631	3
YOUR COTTAGE--FACED THE SUN--	OURSELVES WERE WED ONE	631	10
'TIS TRUE, YOUR GARDEN LED THE BLOOM,	OURSELVES WERE WED ONE	631	13
SHE SQUANDERS ON YOUR HEAD [EAR]	YOU'LL KNOW HER--BY HER	634	25
YOU BEG THE ROBIN IN YOUR BRAIN	YOU'LL KNOW HER--BY HER	634	27
BECAUSE YOUR FACE	I CANNOT LIVE WITH YOU--	640	22
YOUR CONSCIOUSNESS--AND ME--	YOU LEFT ME--SIRE--TWO	644	8
MINE BELONG YOUR LATEST SIGHING--	PROMISE THIS--WHEN YOU	648	3
MINE--TO BELT YOUR EYE--	PROMISE THIS--WHEN YOU	648	4
YOUR LOW [MEEK] EYES--DEMAND--	PROMISE THIS--WHEN YOU	648	8
MINE--TO GUARD YOUR NARROW PRECINCT--	PROMISE THIS--WHEN YOU	648	17
LONGEST [LATEST] ON YOUR SOUTH, TO LINGER,	PROMISE THIS--WHEN YOU	648	19
TO DEMAND, IN YOUR LOW FAVOR	PROMISE THIS--WHEN YOU	648	21
JUST [STILL] TO FOLLOW YOUR DEAR FEATURE--	PROMISE THIS--WHEN YOU	648	29
STILL--CLAD IN YOUR MAIL OF ICES--	AH, TENERIFFE!	666	6
BESIDE YOUR PALACE [TWINKLING / GLIMMERING] DOOR--	THE MOON WAS BUT A CHIN	737	16
YOUR LIFE HAD LEFT BEHIND--	SEVERER SERVICE OF	786	4
OVER YOUR IMPOTENCE	BANISH AIR FROM AIR--	854	11
SAVED FOR YOUR EAR WHEN LUTES BE OLD.	SPLIT THE LARK--AND	861	4

	FIRST LINE	POEM	LINE
YOUR (CONTINUED)			
NOW, DO YOU DOUBT THAT YOUR BIRD WAS TRUE?	SPLIT THE LARK--AND	861	8
THAT FADING FROM YOUR VASE,	I HIDE MYSELF WITHIN MY	903	2
THAT WEARING ON YOUR BREAST--	I HIDE MYSELF WITHIN MY	903	V 2
WILL HOLD YOU TILL YOUR PRIVILEGE	TILL DEATH--IS NARROW	907	3
YOUR LIFE TOO ABJECT FOR ITSELF	TILL DEATH--IS NARROW	907	7
YOUR PROBLEM [LABOR]--OF THE BRAIN--	I LEARNED--AT LEAST--	944	15
WHERE MAY BE YOUR HOUSE?	"UNTO ME?" I DO NOT KNOW	964	2
AND THEN IT CLOSES AT YOUR FEET	A NARROW FELLOW IN THE	986	7
PAUSE IN YOUR LITURGIES--	SANG FROM THE HEART,	1059	13
WAIT YOUR CHORALS--	SANG FROM THE HEART,	1059	14
WHILE I REPEAT [RECITE] YOUR	SANG FROM THE HEART,	1059	15
"SECURE [PROTECT] YOUR FLOWER" SAID HE.	THE FROST OF DEATH WAS	1136	2
TILL YOUR WRINKLED FINGER	ON THE WORLD YOU COLORED	1171	9
MAY OVERLOOK [MISINFER / MISCONCEIVE] YOUR TRACK--	BECAUSE THAT YOU ARE	1260	4
I RECOGNIZE YOUR OWN--	BECAUSE THAT YOU ARE	1260	24
CURTAILED BY YOUR OBSCURING [REMOVING] FACE	BECAUSE THAT YOU ARE	1260	27
A GIANT IS YOUR TENANT	I THOUGHT THAT NATURE	1286	V 11
PUT DOWN YOUR HAT--	DEAR MARCH--COME IN--	1320	4
I GOT YOUR LETTER, AND THE BIRDS--	DEAR MARCH--COME IN--	1320	11
THESE SECEDED FROM YOUR SUMMONS [SUMMITS / SUBJECTS / SUBSTANCE]	KNOCK WITH TREMOR--	1325	6
SPARE YOUR "CROWN OF LIFE"--	"FAITHFUL TO THE END"	1357	V
TO YOUR CHAGRIN	HIS MANSION IN THE POOL	1379	14
LAUREL--VAIL YOUR [THY] DEATHLESS TREE--	LAY THIS LAUREL ON THE	1393	3
LAUREL--FELL YOUR [THY] FUTILE TREE--	LAY THIS LAUREL ON THE	1393	V
YOUR THOUGHTS DONT HAVE WORDS EVERY DAY	YOUR THOUGHTS DONT HAVE	1452	1
TRUTH ADJOURN YOUR BOON	LOVE IS DONE WHEN LOVE'S	1485	4
. . . MOUNTAIN] WITH YOUR FACE	THE PILE OF YEARS IS NOT	1507	7
TILL YOU WASTE [FURL / LAME] YOUR EYE--	FOLLOW WISE ORION	1538	2
WERE SHINING IN YOUR [ONE'S] HAND.	TO SEE HER IS A PICTURE	1568	8
PURSUING YOU IN YOUR TRANSITIONS,	PURSUING YOU IN YOUR	1602	1
YOUR REQUISITION BE.	PURSUING YOU IN YOUR	1602	4
YOUR CONNOISSEUR IN LIQUORS	A DRUNKARD CANNOT MEET A	1628	11
PUT ON YOUR MUFF [BELLS] FOR WINTER	THE JAY HIS CASTANET HAS	1635	2
CUP, IT WAS YOUR FAULT,	HAD I KNOWN THAT THE	1720	5
GO MANACLE YOUR ICICLE	'TWAS HERE MY SUMMER	1756	7
AGAINST YOUR TROPIC BRIDE	'TWAS HERE MY SUMMER	1756	8
YOU'RE			
HASTE! LEST WHILE YOU'RE LAGGING	HEART! WE WILL FORGET	47	7
PERHAPS YOU'RE GOING TOO!	GOING TO HEAVEN!	79	11
I NEED NOT START--YOU'RE SURE--	YOU LOVE ME--YOU ARE	156	8
BE SURE YOU'RE SURE--YOU KNOW--	YOU LOVE ME--YOU ARE	156	14
AND "YOU'RE HURT" EXCLAIM!	A WOUNDED DEER--LEAPS	165	12
YOU'RE RIGHT--"THE WAY IS NARROW"--	YOU'RE RIGHT--"THE WAY	234	1
THOUGH YOU'RE VERY FAR--	AH, MOON--AND STAR!	240	14
DEMUR--YOU'RE STRAIGHTWAY DANGEROUS--	MUCH MADNESS IS DIVINEST	435	7
AND YOU'RE AN INFIDEL--	YOU'LL KNOW HER--BY HER	634	V 28
"YOU'RE SOON," THE TOWN REPLIED,	THE FINGERS OF THE LIGHT	1000	5
YOUR'S			
YOUR'S, IS DONE--	'TIS SO APPALLING--IT	281	20
WHOSE INVITATION--YOUR'S REDUCED	THE POWER TO BE TRUE TO	464	7
A HEAVEN NOT SO LARGE AS YOUR'S,	I MEANT TO HAVE BUT	476	11
THAT YOUR'S AND MINE, SHOULD BE--	IF YOU WERE COMING IN	511	14
AND YOUR'S--THE JUDGMENT INTERVENED--	DID YOU EVER STAND IN A	590	11
BUT YOU--WERE CROWNED [YOUR'S WAS FIRST--] IN JUNE--	OURSELVES WERE WED ONE	631	16
HAD IT BEEN YOUR'S, TO READ!	ENDED, ERE IT BEGUN--	1088	6
THE UNIVERSE IS YOUR'S.	NOT WITH A CLUB, THE	1304	16
YOURS			
YOURS, FLY.	BEE! I'M EXPECTING YOU!	1035	12
NO MORE FROM YOURS AT PRESENT	THE JAY HIS CASTANET HAS	1635	8
NO, LIP IT WAS YOURS,	HAD I KNOWN THAT THE	1720	7
YOURSELF			
I HAD NOT HAD--BUT FOR YOURSELF--	OF COURSE--I PRAYED--	376	7
AS NEAR YOURSELF--TODAY--	AS FAR FROM PITY, AS	496	6
A REVELATION OF YOURSELF--	YOU CONSTITUTED TIME--	765	3
YOURSELF, FOR HIS PURSUIT	TILL DEATH--IS NARROW	907	10
BEFRIEND THEM, LEST YOURSELF IN HEAVEN	THESE STRANGERS, IN A	1096	3
YOURSELF FORGOT TO LIVE--	BECAUSE THAT YOU ARE	1260	16
SEEK--IT IS YOURSELF.	THE HEART IS THE CAPITAL	1354	8
TRY IT ON YOURSELF--	"FAITHFUL TO THE END"	1357	V
. . . IT / SANCTION IT / FASTEN IT] YOURSELF.	SUMMER LAID HER SIMPLE	1363	4
YOUTH			
UPON AN EXCELLENTER YOUTH--	FITTER TO SEE HIM, I MAY	968	24
LEFT IN IMMORTAL YOUTH	LEFT IN IMMORTAL YOUTH	1289	1
YOU'VE			
AND NOW YOU'VE LITTERED ALL THE EAST	SHE SWEEPS WITH	219	7
YOU'VE SEEN THE COLOR--MAYBE--	THE COLOR OF THE GRAVE	411	21
YOU'VE SEEN IT ON A CAST'S FACE [CHEEK]--	IT KNEW NO MEDICINE--	559	11
YOU'VE SEEN BALLOONS SET--HAV'NT YOU?	YOU'VE SEEN BALLOONS SET	700	1
ZEALOUS			
AND FLOWER--THAT ZEALOUS BLEW--	FROM COCOON FORTH A	354	19
HER ZEALOUS NOTE DELIGHTS IT TO ASCEND.	AFTER ALL BIRDS HAVE	1395	V 6
ZENITH			
IS "ZENITH" NOW--	"ARCTURUS" IS HIS OTHER	70	18
ZENZIBAR			
ROSES A DAY FROM ZENZIBAR--	WHAT WOULD I GIVE TO SEE	247	9

	FIRST LINE	POEM	LINE
ZEPHYR			
A JEALOUS ZEPHYR--NOT A DOUBT--	GOOD NIGHT! WHICH PUT	259	2
UNTIL A ZEPHYR PUSHED [CHASED / FLUNG / SPURNED / SCOURGED] THEM	TWO BUTTERFLIES WENT OUT	533	V
NO ZEPHYR FELLED THIS CEDAR STRAIGHT-- . .	TO BREAK SO VAST A HEART	1312	3
ZERO			
FOR SOME--AN AMPLER ZERO--	MORE LIFE--WENT OUT--	422	9
AND ZERO AT THE BONE--	A NARROW FELLOW IN THE	986	24
ZEROES			
THE ZEROES--TAUGHT US--PHOSPHORUS-- . . .	THE ZEROES--TAUGHT US--	689	1
ZEST			
INVEST THIS ALABASTER ZEST	PRAISE IT--'TIS DEAD--	1384	6
WHICH IS THE ZEST OF SWEETNESS	OF DEATH I TRY TO THINK	1558	6
ZIGZAG			
I CAN MAKE THE ZIGZAG STITCHES	DONT PUT UP MY THREAD &	617	15
ZION			
TILL SYNODS ARE [ZION IS] INORDINATE-- . .	THE WORTHLESSNESS OF	1373	4
ZODIAC			
WE JUST REVERSE THE ZODIAC	THE PRODUCTS OF MY FARM	1025	7
ZONE			
OR THAT ETHERIAL ZONE	FROM US SHE WANDERED NOW	890	4
BY ALTERNATING ZONE--	'TWAS AWKWARD, BUT IT	973	8
THERE IS A ZONE WHOSE EVEN YEARS	THERE IS A ZONE WHOSE	1056	1
TO AN ADJOINING ZONE--	THE SPRY ARMS OF THE	1103	4
THE HOUR, AND THE CLIME [ZONE]--	LONGING IS LIKE THE SEED	1255	5
FROM ANY FERVENT ZONE	NOT ANY SUNNY TONE	1674	2
ZONES			
FROSTS UNHOOK--IN THE NORTHERN ZONES-- . .	SAFE IN THEIR ALABASTER	216	V
FOR IN THE ZONES OF PARADISE	THE SUN AND MOON MUST	871	3
MUCH FLOWERS OF THIS AND FURTHER ZONES . .	IT BLOOMED AND DROPT, A	978	13
THE PREY OF [IN SPANS IN] UNKNOWN ZONES-- .	COULD MORTAL LIP DIVINE	1409	V

APPENDIX

Index Words in Order of Frequency

1682
I

980
AS

755
MY

719
BE

616
ME

579
HER

563
WE

521
HIS

462
HE

378
YOU

354
ALL

352
ONE

349
LIKE

252
HIM

248
OUR

244
JUST

232
DAY

230
KNOW

226
LITTLE

223
THEE

218
SHE

216
AWAY

202
US

191
NEVER

189
MORE

178
SOME

174
TILL

170
SUN

156
LIFE

152
GO

151
YET

146
SEE

143
HEAVEN

141
DEATH
FACE
SUCH

140
WITHOUT

135
TELL

130
GOD
TIME

128
BEFORE

127
COME

125
SOUL

124
HEART

123
YOUR

122
SEA

121
NIGHT

119
ONLY

117
STILL
THOU

115
WAY

114
OUT

112
EVERY
FAR
SUMMER

110
NATURE

107
ANY
MINE

106
FIRST
LOVE
UNTO

102
BIRD

100
SAY

96
SWEET

94
DIE

93
MAN

92
EYE

90
MEN

89
MAKE

88
EYES

87
PUT
TAKE
UP

86
BEE
HOME
LOOK
THY
WITHIN

85
DOWN

83
FEET

82
LIGHT
OH

81
LAST

80
KNEW
MYSELF
OLD

79
BECAUSE
HAND
LET
MIND
OWN

78
UNTIL

77
SKY

76
DOOR
NOON
PLACE
WENT

75
NEW

74
HOUSE
WORLD

72
FLOWER
LONG
WHILE

69
ROSE
THOUGHT

68
BEEN
MORNING
SAID

67
FAIR
THING

66
ONCE
TWO

65
SMALL

64
BETWEEN
MANY
WIND

63
AIR
GRACE

61
AGAIN
FIND

60
DONE
GRAVE
SHOW

59
BIRDS
I'M

58
DEAD
FRIEND
NAME

57
BEST
EARTH
PAIN
PARADISE

56
LIVE

55
CAME
MOST

54
FURTHER

53
BEHIND
FEAR
PLAY
PURPLE
SNOW
TODAY

52
NONE
WELL

51
GONE
LOST
SINCE
SLOW

50
BACK
ETERNITY
EVEN
HEARD
LEST
MADE
MUCH

49
EAR
SINGLE

48
DYING
LOW
SIGHT

47
DELIGHT

46
DUST
SEEN
THINGS

45
EXCEPT
FAITH
HIMSELF
MAKES
TOLD
TREE

44
FINGERS
GOOD
HUMAN
IMMORTALITY
KEEP
ROUND
SIDE

43
ALONE
BETTER
JOY
LEFT
THINK

42
DAYS
EASY
HELD
HILL
MEET

41
BLISS
EVER
HEAR
LIE
MORN
POWER
REST

40
BEYOND
PASSED
PERHAPS
TOOK
WHOLE
YEARS

39
BEAR
ENOUGH
FEEL
NEAR
STAND
YEAR

38
DROP
FULL
HEAD
NEWS
NOTHING
PASS
SAME
SLEEP
SOFTLY
SPIRIT

37
AFTER
CARE
FLOWERS
GOLD
GRASS
HOUR
LEAST
NATURE'S
NEED
SAW

36
CHILDREN
COMES
GIVE
HOLD
PROVE
STAR
SURE
TUNE
VERY

35
BLUE
BORE
BRIGHT
FELT
FLY
GOING
HALF
PAST
ROAD
SOUND
TRUE

34
ABOVE
ALMOST
AMONG
DEW
HILLS
I'LL
MET
SMILE
UNKNOWN
WORD

33
BEGUN
DIVINE
EAST
FOUND
GREAT
HANDS
MIGHTY
SIMPLE

32
ABROAD
ANGUISH
ASK
BOY
BREATH
DARE
KNOWN
RED
SUNRISE

31
AH
BELOW
FATHER
FOOT
FORGOT
FROST
GAY
I'D
KNOWS
ROOM
TOUCH
TURN

30
BELLS
DAWN
DIED
DREAM
FEW
GAIN
HIGH
LAND
LOOKED
OURSELVES
RIGHT
RUN
SIR
STONE
STOP
TOWN

29
ABOUT
DARK
DESPAIR
INFINITE
LATE
OFF
SET
SKIES
STARS
STAY
UNIVERSE
WAIT
WILL (noun)
YELLOW

28
BEES
DIFFERENT
FIT
GLORY
HOPE
LEAVE
MOMENT
OVER
SECOND
STIR

27
AROUND
BOLD
BUTTERFLY
CLOSE
DOUBT
FORGET
GOES
GROUND
HAPPY
HERSELF
I'VE
LESS
LIPS
PEACE
SHUT
SILVER
SUDDEN
WEAR
WEST
WHITE

26
ANGELS

26 (cont.)
BRAIN
CALL
COLD
COMMON
DROPPED
EVERLASTING
FAME
GUESS
HAIR
PEOPLE
PLAIN
SECRET
SOLEMN
SOMETHING
SUNSET
THINE
WINTER
WONDER
WORK
YESTERDAY

25
BEING
BREAST
CHILD
COOL
DWELL
FIRE
GOWN
INDEED
LEAVES
LORD
MOON
NEXT
PRIVILEGE
RECOLLECT
SPRING
SUMMER'S
TRUTH

24
ART (noun)
BLAME
BRAVE
CHEEK
COMING
CONSCIOUSNESS
EVENING
FINE
GREW
INSTANT
LIFE'S
LIFT
LIVES
MEMORY
MISS
NARROW
OFTEN
PERISH
QUIET
ROBIN
STANDS
STOOD
TRUST

23
ALIVE
ALONG
AMBER
AMPLE
BLOOM
BRING
CHANCE
DEAR
DISTANCE
DISTANT
FACES
GROW
LADY
LAY
MEAN
MIDNIGHT
PEARL
RETURN
SEEK
WINDS

22
AFRAID
AFTERNOON
BEHOLD
CENTURIES
DEITY
FATE
MUSIC
NOUGHT
PART
PRESENT
SOFT
SOMETIMES
TRANSPORT
TURNED

21
AGAINST
AWE
AWFUL
CHOOSE
CROWN
FOREHEAD
GUEST
HAT
HELP
JESUS
JUNE
KEPT
LAID
REMAIN
SCENE
SHORT
SIGH
SILENCE
SIZE
TOMB
TRY
WANT
WARM
WINDOW

20
BROOK
CONTENT
COUNTENANCE
DEEP
DOOM
GAVE
GOT
HIDE
MARCH
NOTICE
PERFECT
PRAY
PRAYER
QUICK
RATHER
REACH
SEEMS
TIMES
TIMID
TREES
VISION
WITNESS

19
ALWAYS
BUTTERFLIES
CREATURE
DEEM
EARLY
EASIER
FAIL
FOREIGN
GARDEN
GOLDEN
GRIEF
MORTAL
NEARER
NEST
NUMB
PRICE
SEEMED
SOON
STEP
STRAIGHT
SUM
SUPERIOR
SURPRISE
TONGUE
VAST
VICTORY
WALK

18
BENEATH
BONE
CALLED
CEASE
COMPANY
CRUMB
EDEN
FINISHED
FIRMAMENT
FORCE
GIVEN
GREEN
HOLIDAY
LARGE
LARGER
LIBERTY
LIES
LOOKING
MELODY
NEIGHBOR
PARTING
PAUSE
REMEMBER
ROYAL
SIGN
SING
SON
SPEECH
STOPPED
TOUCHED
VAIN
VOICE
WATER
WOODS

17
ASKED
BEAUTY
BEGGAR
BEGIN
BELIEVE
BOOK
BORNE
BOYS
BREAK
BUY
CIRCUMFERENCE
CLOUD
COLOR
CREATURES
DEPARTED
DREW
FELL
FLESH
GET
GROWN
HEAVENLY
HOUSES
LIVED
LIVING
LOSS
NAY
ONES
OUR'S
PASSING
PLEASE
RISE
SAKE
SCARLET
SEASONS
SETTING
STRANGER
SUFFICIENT
WATERS
WEARY
WINGS

16
BORN
BREEZE
CROWD
DAISY
DIM
ELSE
END
ESTIMATE
EXISTENCE
FAILED
FEELS
FELLOW
FIGURE
GATE
GIRL
HOLDS
HONOR
INSTEAD
LIGHTNING
LIP
PERISHED
PRESENCE
PRETTY
QUEEN
QUITE
READ
REALM
REPLY
SAVED
SEED
SHAME
SKILL
SOUTH
SOVREIGN
STATE
STORM
SYLLABLE
WO
WORDS
WORE

15
ANSWER
BALM
BED
BELIEF
BELOVED
BESIDE
BRIEF
CEASED
COUNT
CROSS
DEGREE
DENIED
DUMB
EXIST
FACT
FALL
FIRM
GRAND
GROWS
HIGHT
HURT
JOURNEY
KEEPS
LIMIT
LOOKS
MYSTERY
O'ER
OBTAIN
PLEASURE
PRECISELY
SAND
SCARCELY
SHY
SOMEWHAT
STEADY
STREET

15 (cont.)
STRONG
SUFFICE
TRIED
TWICE
VILLAGE
WAKE
WORN

14
ACT
BEAUTIFUL
BECOME
BLOSSOM
BRIDE
BROKE
CHANGE
CONSCIOUS
COUNTRY
DEATH'S
DIFFERENCE
DUE
DULL
ESTATE
EXTASY
FAINT
FAMILIAR
FINER
FLOOR
FOREVER
FORMER
GLASS
GLOW
GRANT
HEAVENS
HID
HOURS
LOSE
MISERY
MOUNTAIN
NORTH
NOTE
OURSELF
PINK
POOR
POSSIBLY
PUSH
RENOWN
ROBINS
SACRAMENT
STROVE
SUBTLE
THREE
TOWARD
TROUBLE
UNDER
WILD
WILDERNESS
WINE
WISE
WOMEN

13
ABODE
ACRE
AGO
APRIL
BONNET
BROAD
BUSY
CONTENTED
DECAY
DOUBTLESS
EARN
ECSTASY
EMPTY
FASHIONED
FINAL
FLED
FURTHEST
GIANT
GLEE
IMMORTAL
INTIMATE
KNOWING
LEAD
LEARNED
LED
LONESOME
LOVED
LUXURY
MAID
MAJESTY
MINOR
MISTAKE
MOUNTAINS
NAMES
NOBODY
POVERTY
RAPTURE
RING
SAINTS
SCARCE
SCHOOL
SENSATION
SEPULCHRE
SERVICE
SHORE
SILENT
SMALLER
STATELY
SUIT
SUNS
SUNSHINE
SUSPECT
TALK
TASTE
TAUGHT
TINT
TIRED
TOGETHER
TOMORROW
TRIUMPH
USED
WOMAN

12
ABSOLUTE
ACROSS
ADEQUATE
ALSO
ASHAMED
BALL
BLOOD
BLOSSOMS
CELESTIAL
CERTAIN
CLIMB
CLOVER
CUP
CURIOUS
DAILY
DIFFICULT
DOWER
EQUAL
EQUALLY
ESCAPE
ESTEEM
FADED
FIELDS
FILL
FLEE
FORESTS
FREIGHT
GAINED
GATHERED
GAZE
GENTLE
GLAD
HEADS
HUE
HUNDRED
JUDGMENT
KING
LETTER
LOVER
MAGIC
MEADOW
MEEK
MIGHT (noun)
MINUTE
MIRACLE
NERVE
ODD
OPPOSITE
PAY
PERIOD
RANK
REPOSE
RUNS
SCANT
SHOWS
SMALLEST
SMILING
SOLID
SPARE
SPEAK
START
STEM
SURMISE
TABLE
TIME'S
TURNS
UNCONSCIOUS
UNDERSTAND
VITALITY
WEALTH
WHEREFORE
WINDOWS
WORTH
YOU'LL

11
AGES
AUTUMN
BALLS
BESIDES
BLANK
BOBOLINK
BOSOM
CALVARY
CAUSE
CLOUDS
CONVICTION
CRESCENT
CRICKET
DAISIES
DATE
DEPARTING
DISCLOSE
DRESS
DRINK
DROPT
DRUMS
EARL
EASE
EMERALD
ENEMY
EXPERIENCE
FAST
FLEET
FRIENDS
FROSTS
GENERAL
HANG
HARM
HELL
IGNORANT
IMPERIAL
INFINITY
LAIN
LANDSCAPE
LATER
LAUGH
LEARN
LONELINESS
NATIVE
NIGHTS
OPEN
ORCHARD
PATIENT
PERCEIVE
PRAISE
PROSPECTIVE
QUAINT
QUESTION
RARE
REMEMBERED
REMOTE
SATIN
SEAS
SHONE
SIGNAL
SORT
SPOKE
SPOT
SPURN
STOOPING
SUDDENLY
SUPPOSED
TEACH
TEARS
THUNDER
TIGHT
VELVET
WHEEL
WIDE
WISH
WORM

10
ADAMANT
AFFAIR
ALARM
ARM
ARRAY
ATTEMPT
AWKWARD
BAREFOOT
BELL
BENT
BERRY
BLIND
BLOW
BODY
BROOKS
BUILD
BUMBLE
BURN
CAUGHT
CAUTIOUS
CERTAINTY
CHAMBER
CHURCH
CIRCUMSTANCE
CLOCK
CREATION
DANGER
DEFEAT
DESERT
DIADEM
DREAMS
DUSK
EVERYWHERE
EXISTS
EXPERIMENT
EXPRESS
FAITHFUL
FAN
FASHION
FEATURES
FICTITIOUS
FLIGHT
FOLLOW
FOOD
FUTURE
HEARTS
HOMELY
HOST
HUNGRY
INTERRUPT
INTERVIEW
JUSTIFY
KIND
LINE
LIT
MEANS
MEASURE
MENTION
MERRY

10 (cont.)
MILES
MORNING'S
MOVED
MUTUAL
NE'ER
NOISE
OFFER
ORCHARDS
PANE
PILLOW
PLAN
PLUSH
POSSIBLE
PRESUME
PUSHED
RAIN
RAN
REAL
REPORT
REVERSE
RICH
RICHES
RIDE
ROOMS
ROUTE
SAFE
SEAM
SELDOM
SEND
SHINING
SHOOK
SLOWLY
SOMEWHERE
SOULS
SPOTTED
STARE
SUPERFLUOUS
SUPPOSE
SWEETER
TAKES
TALE
THIRST
THYME
TONIGHT
TREASON
UNCERTAIN
UTMOST
VALUE
WAITING
WOOD
YOU'RE

9
ABIDE
ACCUSTOMED
ACTION
AFFLICTION
AFFRONT
AGONY
ALAS
ANYBODY
APPLE
ASLEEP
AWAKE
BEAM
BEHELD
BLAZE
BLOCK
BLUSH
BOLDLY
BOON
BROKEN
BROWN
BUBBLE
BUD
BYE
CHARGE
CHILDISH
CHILL
CHOSE
CIRCUIT
CLEAR
CONTAIN
CORN
CRY
DEWS
DIVINER
DIVINITY
DOCILE
DOG
DOMINION
DRY
ENAMORED
ENTERTAIN
ETHERIAL
EVERYTHING
EXPECTATION
FASHIONS
FEATHERS
FITTED
FLING
FOND
FORCES
FORFEIT
FORGIVE
FRESH
FRUGAL
GHOST
GIRLS
GODS
GRATITUDE
HAPLY
HAY
HOMESICK
HYMN
ILL
IMPOTENT
JUSTIFIED
LEISURE
LENGTH
LID
LIGHTLY
LOT
LOVING
MARTIAL
MAY (noun)
MEADOWS
MERIT
MINDS
MOSTLY
MOUSE
MOUTH
MOVE
NEIGHBORS
ONE'S
OVERTAKE
PENCIL
PERPETUAL
PITY
POD
POSSESSION
POSSIBILITY
PRECIOUS
PREFERRED
PROUD
PUNCTUAL
PUTS
REMAINED
RESURRECTION
RIVER
ROW
SCIENCE
SECRETS
SECURE
SEEM
SENT
SHOE
SHOT
SINGING
SOCIETY
SOD
SOWN
SPICES
SQUIRREL
STEEL
STIMULATE
STOLE
STORY
SUPREME
SUSPENSE
TEAR
TENDER
TERM
TEST
TIE
TIM
TUNES
TWILIGHT
UNLESS
VAIL
WALL
WHATEVER
WHATSOEVER
WISDOM
WISER
WITHDREW
WOE
WRINKLED
YOURSELF

8
ACCIDENT
ACCOST
ACHIEVE
ADVANCE
AFTERWARD
AJAR
APPALLING
ARMS
BARS
BASHFUL
BECAME
BELONG
BELT
BESTOW
BIG
BLACK
BLEW
BOUGH
BREAKING
BROW
BUSINESS
CARED
CARRIED
CAST
CHAIR
CHERISHED
CHRIST
COMFORT
CONFIDENT
CONJECTURE
CONSTANCY
CONSUMMATE
CONTRAST
COURTESY
DAFFODIL
DARKNESS
DEMAND
DEPART
DIAMONDS
DISTINCT
DRAMA
DREAD
DRUNKEN
DWELT
ENABLE
ERECT
ESTEEMED
FEATHER
FEELING
FENCE
FILM
FLAKE
FOE
FRAME
FREE
GAINS
GRACIOUS
HINDER
HINDERED
HINT
HISTORY
HONEY
HORROR
HUM
HUMMING
HUNG
HURRY
IDENTITY
IGNORANCE
IMPREGNABLE
INDUSTRY
KEY
KINSMEN
KNOCK
LABOR
LAMP
LANDS
LEADS
LEAN
LEAP
LESSER
LIKED
LONGING
MARBLE
MISSED
MODEST
MORTALITY
MOSES
MOTION
MURMUR
NESCESSITY
NEWER
NOTICED
OBTAINED
ODORS
OFT
OPPORTUNITY
PACE
PATIENCE
PEBBLE
PLANK
PLAYED
PORT
PRESUMPTION
QUALITY
RACE
RAISED
REMEMBERING
RESIDENCE
RESULT
REWARD
RIDDLE
RISK
ROOT
ROSES
SALUTE
SANG
SATISFIED
SAVE
SAVIOR
SEALED
SETTLED
SHAPE
SHOWED
SLIPPED
SOLITUDE
SOUNDS
SPACE
SPECIES
SPLIT
STAIN
STEAL
STEPPED
STEPS
STIRRED
STOLID
STRAIN
STRANGE
STRENGTH
STRUCK
SUMMERS
SURRENDERED
SWEPT
TASTED
TENDERER
TIDE
TOIL
TWIG

8 (cont.)
UNMOVED
UNSUSPECTING
VANISHED
VENTURE
VEST
VISIT
WALKED
WEIGHT
WIDTH
WITCHCRAFT
WORST
WRITE
YOU'D
YOUR'S

7
ABSENCE
ABYSS
ACRES
ADJUST
ADVERSITY
AFFORD
ALIKE
ALTERED
APPEAR
ARC
ARISE
ARROW
AUGUST
BARN
BASE
BEARS
BEGINS
BERRIES
BIND
BLONDE
BOW
BREAD
BREATHE
BREATHED
BRITTLE
BUILT
CAREER
CHARM
CHASTENED
CHIEF
CHIMNEY
CITIZEN
CLOSED
CLOSER
CLUTCH
COAT
COCOON
CONFERRED
CONFIRM
CONTINUAL
CONTRACT
CROWDED
CUNNING
CURIOSITY
DAY'S
DEED
DEPARTURE
DESIRE
DIES
DISCLOSED
DRAW
DRUM
DUN
EARTHLY
ECLIPSE
ELATE
ENTERED
ENTIRELY
ENVY
ERE
ERMINE
ETHER
EVENT
EVIDENCE
EXCHANGE
FADING
FARTHER
FATHOMS
FEATURE
FETCH
FIELD
FIGURES
FINGER
FIRMAMENTS
FLAG
FLOODS
FLUNG
FORBID
FOREST
FRAUD
FRECKLED
FUNCTION
GALE
GALLANT
GIANTS
GOD'S
GRANITE
GROPED
GUESSED
HALLOWED
HEAVY
HIGHER
HOPED
HOPELESS
HORIZON
HORIZONS
HURRIED
INFER
INFERENCE
INN
INSTANT'S
INVISIBLE
INVITED
JAY
LAPSE
LARGEST
LATEST
LAW
LEAF
LEAVING
LONGER
LOUD
LOVE'S
LOWER
MADNESS
MANKIND
MANNER
MANSION
MEANT
MEETING
MOMENTS
MOTHER
NAMELESS
NATIONS
NEAREST
NEEDLE
NOONS
NOTWITHSTAND-
ING
NOWHERE
OUGHT
OUTER
OUTSIDE
OWNED
PARTED
PARTIES
PARTY
PATTERN
PAUSED
PEARLS
PENINSULA
PERSON
PETER
PICTURE
PIERCE
PILE
POINT
POLAR
POOLS
PRINCE
PRISON
PROCESS
PURSUED
PUZZLED
RAPID
REACHED
REACHES
READY
REALMS
REMAINING
REMEMBRANCE
RETURNING
REVELATION
RIVERS
ROCK
SAILOR
SAT
SCAN
SCANNED
SCANTY
SENTENCE
SEPARATE
SERVE
SHORTER
SHUN
SIGHING
SIGNIFICANCE
SINGS
SNAKE
SONG
SOUGHT
SOW
SPECIFIC
SPELL
SPICE
SPICY
SPIDER
SPRINGS
STATION
STEADFAST
STINT
STIRS
STRIKE
SUBJECTS
SUFFERING
SUMPTUOUS
SUPPLE
SURPASSES
SWEEP
SWEETEST
SWIFT
TENDERLY
TERROR
THANK
THIEF
THOUSAND
THROWN
TRADITION
TRAGEDY
TRINKET
TURNING
UNROLLED
UPPER
VERMILLION
VIEW
VITAL
WANDERED
WANDERING
WEEP
WHEELS
WORLDS
WRECKED
YIELD

6
ABSENT
ACCOMPLISHED
ACQUAINTANCE
ADAM
ADJUSTED
AMETHYST
ANEW
ANGEL
ANGLE
ANTIQUE
APPROACH
APRON
ASCEND
ASCERTAIN
ATOM
ATTENTION
AWARE
BANISH
BEING'S
BEND
BLEAK
BOAT
BOLDER
BOOT
BOUGHS
BOUND
BOUNTY
BREAKFAST
BREATHLESS
BROTHER
BROUGHT
BURIAL
BURIED
BURST
BUSH
CAPACITY
CARELESS
CASHMERE
CASPIAN
CATTLE
CHASE
CHEER
CHIEFEST
CHILDHOOD
CLAW
CLAY
CLOSING
COACH
COMPANION
COMPETENT
COMPREHEND
CONCERN
CONDITION
CONFER
CONFRONTING
CONSEQUENCE
CONVENIENT
CORDIAL
COURSE
COURT
COVERT
CRAWL
CREASE
CRIMSON
DAPPLED
DAZZLED
DEEMED
DEEPER
DELAY
DELAYED
DENY
DESCEND
DESERTS
DESIGN
DESTINY
DIAMOND
DIMPLES
DISHONOR
DISSOLVE
DISSOLVED
DISTINGUISHED
DIVIDE
DOORS
DOUBTFUL
DRAWER
DROPS
DUKE
DUNGEONS
DUPLICATE
EAGER
ELECTRIC
EMPEROR
ENACTED
ENDED
ENDURE
ENTER
ERRAND
EXTREMITY

6 (cont.)
FADE
FAMINE
FILLED
FINEST
FINITE
FLAGS
FLAKES
FLIES
FLOOD
FOG
FOLD
FORGETTING
FORGOTTEN
FREQUENTLY
FRONT
FUNDAMENTAL
GEM
GENTLY
GETS
GNAT
GOAL
GOBLIN
GRAY
GUARD
GUESTS
HABIT
HASTE
HATED
HAZE
HE'LL
HONEST
HURRYING
HURTS
IMPOSSIBLE
INDIFFERENT
INFERIOR
INFERRED
INNER
JUDGE
KILL
KISS
KNEE
LACK
LADY'S
LASTS
LATITUDES
LAUGHTER
LAWN
LEAPED
LETS
LIFETIME
LIFTED
LILY
LO
LOAD
LOCK
LONE
LONGEST
MADDEST
MAKER
MANSIONS
MILL
MINUTEST
MISSING
MORNINGS
MURMURING
MUTE
OCCUPIED
OCEAN
OFFERED
OVERCOME
OWNER
PANG
PARTAKE
PARTOOK
PASSIVE
PECULIAR
PERFIDY
PERMITTED
PHANTOM
PLATED
PLEA
PLEADING
PLEASED
PLUCKING
POETS
PORTION
POSITIVE
POSSESS
PREFER
PRESENTS
PRESUMED
PREVAIL
PRIZE
PROFOUND
PROOF
RAISE
RAVISHED
REASON
RECOGNITION
RECOLLECTING
RECORD
REMOTEST
REMOVED
RETROSPECT
REVEAL
REVERSED
ROBBED
ROOF
SACRED
SAFER
SAYING
SCRUTINY
SEAL
SEAMS
SECRETED
SEEKING
SELF
SHADOWS
SHAKE
SHEEN
SHELF
SHIPS
SICKNESS
SIMPLICITY
SMILED
SMILES
SNOWS
SOIL
SOMEBODY
SOUL'S
SPACIOUS
SPECTRE
STARTED
STATED
STIMULUS
STOPS
STREETS
STRING
SUE
SUFFERED
SURRENDER
TERRITORY
THICK
THINKING
THREAD
THRONG
TITLE
TONE
TOSS
TRADE
TRANQUIL
TRAVELLER
TROPIC
TROTH
VANQUISHED
VASTER
VIOLET
VISITOR
WALLS
WATCHED
WAVE
WAYS
WEARS
WELLS
WE'RE
WICK
WIFE
WITHDRAWN
WON
YE
ZONE

5
ACCENT
ACHE
ACHIEVED
ADIEU
ADMITTED
ADORE
ADORED
AFTERNOONS
AGE
ALWAY
AMPLER
ANTIQUATED
APART
APPEARS
APPOINTED
ASSAULT
AUDIENCE
AXIS
AZURE
BACKWARD
BAFFLED
BALLOON
BALMS
BAND
BANKS
BANQUET
BAR
BARE
BATTLE
BECOMES
BEE'S
BEG
BEGAN
BELIEVED
BELIEVES
BENDING
BERYL
BETRAY
BEWILDERED
BILLOWS
BLAND
BOAST
BODDICE
BOG
BOLT
BOMB
BOND
BOUGHT
BOWING
BRAVEST
BREEZES
BRIGADIER
BROOMS
BUBBLED
BURNED
BUZZ
CALM
CANDLE
CAPER
CARPENTER
CATCH
CEDAR
CENTRE
CENTURY
CERTIFICATE
CHAMBERS
CHANT
CHARACTER
CHARIOTS
CHARITY
CHASED
CHILDHOOD'S
CHIVALRY
CHOSEN
CITADEL
CLAIM
CLOSES
CLOSET
CLOVERS
COCHINEAL
COLORS
COMPARE
COMPREHENSION
CONCLUSION
CONDEMNED
CONSUMMATED
CONTINENT
CONVEY
COOLER
CORPOREAL
COST
COVER
CRASH
CREATOR
CRUCIFIX
CRUCIFIXION
CUSTOM
DAFFODILS
DAINTY
DARED
DEAL
DECIDE
DEEMING
DEFINITION
DELICIOUS
DELIGHTS
DELIRIOUS
DESCRIED
DETECT
DILIGENCE
DINE
DISAPPEARED
DISC
DISDAIN
DISMAY
DISPLAYED
DISSOLVES
DOME
DREAMING
DRESSED
DROVE
DURING
DWELLING
EAT
EFFACE
EFFORT
ELEMENT
ELEMENTAL
EMERGE
ENDS
ENDURED
ENTIRE
ESTRANGED
ETERNAL
ETERNALLY
EXCELLENT
EXHIBIT
EXTENT
FAINTER
FAINTING
FAIRER
FAIREST
FAIRY
FARMER
FATHER'S
FEARED
FEARING
FELICITY
FELLOWS
FICKLE
FIGHT
FIRMER
FITTER
FITTING
FLEW
FLIT
FLOWN
FORGETS
FORMULA
FORTITUDE
FORTUNE
FOUR
GABRIEL
GALES
GATHER

5 (cont.)
GAUZE
GENTLEMEN
GIFT
GILDED
GIVES
GLANCE
GLOWS
GROWTH
GUINEA
HALL
HANDED
HARASS
HEEDLESS
HELPED
HELPLESS
HEM
HENCEFORTH
HESITATE
HOMES
HONORED
HORSES
HOUND
HOUSEWIFE
HUMBLE
HUMILITY
HUNGER
HUNTED
IMITATE
IMMEDIATELY
INCLUDE
INDIA
INDUSTRIOUS
INFAMY
INNOCENT
INSPECT
INTERVAL
INVITATION
INVITES
JEALOUS
JEWEL
KATIE
KINGDOM
LANGUAGE
LATITUDE
LAWFUL
LEANED
LIBYAN
LIQUOR
LIST
LOADED
LONELY
LYING
MAKING
MAR
MATCH
MAYBE
MEASURING
MEAT
MERELY
MESSAGE
MILE
MINES
MONTHS
MORNS
MOULD
MURMURED
MYSTIC
NAIL
NAKED
NEEDLESS
NEWEST
NORTHERN
OCCASION
OCEANS
OIL
OMNIPOTENCE
OPAL
OPENED
OPPOSING
ORDERLY
OVERLOOKED
PAGEANT
PAID
PAIR
PALATE
PANTING
PARADE
PARCHING
PASSES
PATENT
PENURY
PERENNIAL
PERJURY
PERMISSION
PERSONS
PETALS
PHILOSOPHER
PICK
PILED
PILGRIM
PINE
PLACES
PLAYING
PLAYMATES
PLENTY
PLUCKED
POET
POLITE
POMP
PORTENTOUS
POSSESSED
POSTURE
POUND
PRIDE
PROMISE
PROSPERITY
PROVED
PRUDENT
PUNGENT
RAIMENT
RAINBOW
RECOGNIZE
REDEMPTION
REDUCE
REGARD
REJOICE
RELUCTANT
REMOVE
REPORTLESS
RESUME
RETAIN
RETIRE
RETREATING
RETURNED
REVERE
REVERY
REVOLUTION
RHINE
RIPE
ROBIN'S
RODE
ROLLED
RUDDY
SAIL
SAILS
SANDS
SATIETY
SAYS
SCAR
SCATTERED
SCHOLARS
SEARCH
SEAT
SEEDS
SEES
SELL
SERAPHIC
SERE
SERENE
SEVERAL
SEVERE
SHAWL
SHE'S
SHIFT
SINEW
SIRE
SITE
SLAY
SLEEPING
SLEET
SLID
SLOWER
SOAR
SORROW
SORRY
SPARK
SPIED
SPURNED
SPY
SQUIRRELS
STANDING
STAYED
STAYS
STEEPLE
STEEPLES
STIFF
STING
STOOP
STRAINS
STRANGERS
STRETCH
SUBJECT
SUBLIME
SUBSTANCE
SUITS
SURPASSING
SWERVE
SYLLABLES
SYMBOL
TEAZE
TEMERITY
TEN
TENANT
TENT
TESTIFY
THEME
THOUGHTS
THREW
THROAT
THROE
TIDES
TIED
TOOTH
TRACK
TRAIN
TRAIT
TRANSITIVE
TRANSPORT'S
TRAVELLING
TREMENDOUS
TRIFLE
TROUBADOR
TROUBLED
TRUDGING
ULTIMATE
UNDERSTOOD
UNDONE
UNEXPECTED
UNOBTRUSIVE
USE
UTTER
UTTERLY
VALLEYS
VEINS
VISITED
WAITED
WAITS
WARRANT
WASTE
WED
WEIGH
WELCOME
WING
WISHED
WITHHELD
WOMAN'S
WONDROUS
WOUND
WRONG
WROTE

4
ABILITY
ABLE
ACCENTS
ACCEPT
ACCOMPANY
ACCORDING
ADD
ADDED
ADDRESSED
ADJOINING
ADJUSTS
ADORNED
ADVANCING
AFAR
AFFECTION
AFFIDAVIT
AFFORDS
AFFRONTED
AGED
ALIGHTING
ALLOW
ALMS
ALPS
AMID
ANALYSIS
ANCIENT
ANSWERED
ANYWHERE
APARTMENT
APPARITION
ARCTIC
AROSE
ARTERY
ASSASSIN
ASSEMBLY
ASSISTED
ASTERISK
ATOMS
AURORA
BALD
BANDS
BAPTIZED
BARK
BARNS
BAY
BEDS
BEGGARS
BEGGED
BEGGING
BEGINNING
BESTOWED
BETHLEHEM
BEWARE
BILLOW
BLAMELESS
BLESS
BLESSED
BLISSFUL
BLOWN
BOLDEST
BOLTS
BORROW
BOX
BRAKE
BRANCHES
BRAND
BREAKS
BREATHING
BRIDGE
BURNS
BUSTLE
BUTTERCUP
CAMPAIGN
CANDIDATE
CAPSULE
CARGO
CARRIAGE
CARRIES
CARRY
CARTS
CAT
CAUTION
CEASELESS
CENTRAL
CERTAINLY
CHANTICLEER
CHARTER

4 (cont.)
CHEAT
CHERISH
CHERISHING
CHERUBIM
CHRIST'S
CLASP
CLIMBING
CLOCKS
COAST
COBWEB
COLORED
COMPASS
COMPETITION
COMPOSED
COMPOUND
CON
CONCEALED
CONCLUDE
CONCLUDED
CONFIDING
CONTAINED
CONTEMPLATION
CONTENTMENT
CONTINENTS
CONVICTED
CORDIALITY
CORE
CORONATION
COTTAGE
COUNTERFEIT
COVENANT
CRACK
CRAG
CRAWLED
CREATED
CREST
CREW
CRISIS
CROUCH
CROWNED
CURTAINS
CUT
DANCE
DANDELION'S
DAZZLING
DEALT
DEBATE
DECADE
DECEIVES
DECKS
DECLARE
DECREE
DEFIES
DEFINE
DEFRAUDED
DEMUR
DENYING
DEPRIVED
DEPTH
DEPUTED
DERISION
DESPISE
DIADEMS
DIP
DIRECTLY
DISCOVER
DISCOVERY
DISGRACE
DISK
DISPLAY
DISSEMBLING
DISTANCES
DOMINGO
DOT
DRIFTS
DUCAL
DULLER
DUSTY
DUTIES
EARNED
EARS
EAVES
EDIFICE
E'EN
ELEGY
ELUDE
EMBERS
ENABLED
ENACT
ENAMOR
ENCHANTED
ENDEAR
ENDEAVOR
ENDOW
ENGLAND
ENGROSSED
ENLARGED
ENTERS
ENTITLED
ESTABLISHED
ESTIMATES
ETERNITY'S
EXCELLENCE
EXCLUSIVE
EXPERIENCED
EXPIRE
EXQUISITE
EXTATIC
EXTINCT
FABRICS
FANCY
FARM
FASTENED
FATAL
FATIGUE
FAVOR
FEARS
FEAT
FED
FEED
FENCES
FIDELITY
FILLS
FINISH
FISTS
FITS
FLAME
FLEECE
FLINGS
FLINT
FLITS
FLOSS
FLUENT
FLUTTERED
FLUTTERING
FLYING
FOLLOWED
FONDNESS
FOOL
FORGE
FORM
FORSOOK
FORTH
FOUGHT
FRACTION
FREEZING
FREQUENT
FRIGHT
FRONTIER
FUNERAL
FURNITURE
FUSE
FUTILE
FUZZ
GAILY
GAIT
GALLOP
GENESIS
GENTIAN
GETHSEMANE
GLITTERING
GLOWING
GNAT'S
GOODNIGHT
GRAVES
GRAVITY
GROWING
GUN
HALT
HANGS
HAUNT
HAVING
HEAL
HEAT
HERB'S
HE'S
HIMMALEH
HIT
HOAR
HOARY
HOISTED
HOLY
HOMESTEAD
HORRID
IDLE
IDLENESS
IMMENSITY
IMMINENT
INDICATE
INDIVIDUAL
INIQUITY
INLAID
INQUIRE
INSCRUTABLE
INSTINCT
INSUFFICIENT
INTACT
INTEGRITY
INTERIOR
IODINE
ITALIC
JACKET
JAR
JEHOVAH'S
JOYFUL
JUGGLER
JUSTICE
KEEPER
KERNEL
KINDLY
KINGDOMS
KINSMAN
KISSED
KNOCKS
KNOWEST
LAD
LADIES
LANE
LAP
LARK
LATTER
LAUREL
LAWS
LEAGUE
LEAGUES
LEASE
LEGACY
LIDS
LILAC
LINGER
LISTENING
LIVID
LOVERS
MAELSTROM
MAGNITUDE
MAIL
MAJESTIC
MANNERS
MASTER
MAT
MATTER
MEND
MENTIONED
MERCHANT
MERCY
MIGHTIEST
MISTS
MONOTONY
MOOR
MOSS
MOULDERING
MOURN
MULTITUDES
NATURES
NEEDS
NEIGHBORING
NESTS
NIGHT'S
NIMBLE
NODS
NOTES
NOVEL
NOVEMBER
NUMEROUS
NUT
OBJECT
OBLITERATE
OBLIVION
OBSCURED
OBSERVATION
OCCASIONAL
OCCASIONALLY
OCCIDENT
OCCUPY
O'CLOCK
OFTENER
OPENING
OPENS
OPTIONAL
ORDAINED
ORDER
ORIOLE
ORNAMENT
OTHERWISE
PACK
PAGE
PALLID
PALM
PALTRY
PARDON
PARLOR
PASSER
PASSION
PATHETIC
PAUSING
PEASANTS
PENDULUM
PENSIVE
PENURIOUS
PERCEIVED
PERDITION
PERFECTNESS
PERIODS
PERISHING
PERMIT
PERSUADED
PETAL
PHEBE
PHILOSOPHY
PHYSIOGNOMY
PIT
PITIFUL
POETRY
POMPOUS
POND
PONDER
PONDERED
POOREST
PRACTISE
PRANK
PRESS
PRESUMING
PRISM
PROBLEM
PROCEED
PRONOUNCED
PROVES
PUBLIC
PURSUING
QUALIFIED
QUESTIONED
QUICKENED
QUIVERING
RAINBOW'S
RANSOMED
RAPT
RAT
RATIFIED
RECEDING

4 (cont.)
RECEIVE
REGRET
REMAINS
REMIND
REMOTER
REPEAT
REPRIEVE
REQUEST
RESIST
RESPITE
RETIRED
RETURNS
REVELATIONS
REVIEW
RIDES
RIND
RISES
ROADS
ROBES
ROLL
ROPE
RUBIES
RUSSET
SABBATH
SAD
SAGACIOUS
SAGE
SANCTITY
SAPPHIRE
SAUNTERED
SCAFFOLD
SCORN
SCRUTINIZE
SECONDS
SEEKS
SEIZE
SERMON
SETS
SHADOW
SHAFT
SHAM
SHARE
SHARPER
SHOUTS
SHOWN
SHRINE
SHUNNED
SHUTS
SIGNOR
SIGNS
SILL
SIMPLY
SIMULATE
SISTER
SIT
SKIP
SLAIN
SLEEPY
SLEPT
SLEW
SLIM
SLIP
SLIPS
SLIT
SMOOTH
SMOULDERING
SNEER
SOBER
SOFTER
SOLD
SOLITARY
SOMEHOW
SORER
SOUNDLESS
SPAR
SPARROWS
SPECULATE
SPEECHLESS
SPENT
SPHERE
SPILL
SPIRITS
SPUN
STAKED
STANZA
STARES
STARTLED
STARVE
STARVED
STATEMENT
STEAD
STEEP
STILLER
STILLNESS
STOOPED
STORE
STRICKEN
STROKE
STRUGGLE
STUPENDOUS
SUBSEQUENT
SUBSIST
SUFFER
SUMMON
SUMMONED
SUMS
SUNDER
SUNDOWN
SURVIVE
SUSPENDED
SWEAR
SWEETNESS
SWING
SWUNG
SYMPATHY
SYMPTOM
SYSTEMS
TAKING
TALKED
TALL
TEA
TEETH
TELLS
TERMED
TERMS
TERRIBLE
THRILLING
THRONE
THROW
THRUST
TINY
TOES
TORRID
TOSSED
TRAVELLERS
TRAVELS
TREASURES
TRICK
TRIUMPHANT
TRIVIAL
TRYING
TUN
TWIGS
TWINE
TYRANNY
UNFURNISHED
UNNOTICED
UNSUSPECTED
VARIOUS
VILLAGES
VOW
WADED
WAGON
WAKING
WANTED
WAR
WEARING
WHIM
WHIP
WHIPPOWIL
WHITER
WHO'S
WHOSO
WILLING
WIT
WITHDRAW
WITHDRAWS
WITHELD
WITNESSED
WONDERFUL
WORSHIP
WRESTLE
YES
YOUNG
YOU'VE
ZONES

3
ABIDES
ABJECT
ABLATIVE
ABRAHAM
ABSCONDED
ABSTINENCE
ABUNDANT
ACCEPTED
ACCLIMATED
ACCOMPANYING
ACCOSTS
ACCOUNTED
ACCUSED
ACQUAINTANCES
ADDRESS
ADJACENT
ADORN
ADVANCED
AFFLICTS
AFFLUENCE
AFFORDED
AID
AIMS
AISLE
AISLES
ALABASTER
ALIBI
ALIEN
ALLOWED
ALOUD
ALTER
ALTERS
AMBUSH
AMERICA
ANCESTOR
ANNUL
ANODYNE
ANTICIPATE
APOLOGIZE
APOLOGY
APPARATUS
APPEASED
APPENINE
APPLAUD
APPLAUSE
APPROACHED
AREA
ARID
ARMIES
ARRANGE
ARROGANCE
ASHES
ASIDE
ASKS
ASSISTANCE
ASSISTS
ASSUMED
ASSURE
ASSURED
ASTER
ASTIR
ASTONISHED
ASTRAY
ASTUTE
ATMOSPHERE
ATTAIN
ATTAR
ATTITUDE
AUDIBLE
AUSTERE
AUTHORITY
AUTHORIZED
AVARICE
AVOID
BABBLE
BABBLER
BAFFLE
BALLAD
BANDAGED
BANK
BARD
BASIS
BASKET
BEADS
BEAT
BEATING
BECKONS
BECOMING
BEFALL
BEGGAR'S
BELLES
BEREAVED
BESTOWS
BETRAYS
BILL
BINDS
BIRD'S
BIRTHDAY
BIT
BLAZING
BLINDNESS
BONNETS
BONNIE
BOOKS
BOOTY
BOQUET
BORDER
BOUNDLESS
BOWED
BOWS
BREADTH
BREADTHS
BREATHES
BREWED
BRIAR
BRIBE
BRIDEGROOM
BRIG
BRINGING
BRINGS
BRITISH
BROOCH
BROOM
BROWS
BRUSH
BUCKLE
BUDS
BUILDED
BULB
BUR
BURDEN
BUTTERCUP'S
BUTTERCUPS
CADENCE
CALLS
CALYX
CANVAS
CAP
CAPTIVE
CARAVAN
CARESS
CARMINE
CAROL
CART
CARVED
CASE
CASTLE
CEASES
CEDED
CELLAR
CERTIFIED
CHAFF
CHAGRIN
CHANCES
CHARGED
CHECK
CHIEFLY
CHOICE
CHOOSING
CHRISTMAS
CHRYSALIS

3 (cont.)
CIRCUMSTANCES
CLAIMS
CLASPED
CLAUSE
CLIMBED
CLIME
CLIMES
CLOTHES
CLOVER'S
CLUSTER
CLUTCHED
COEVAL
COLUMNS
COMBINED
COMMAND
COMMEMORATE
COMMERCE
COMPACT
COMPARISON
COMPASSION
COMPETING
COMPETITIONS
COMPUTED
CONCEIVE
CONFIDE
CONFIDENCE
CONFIRM
CONJECTURED
CONQUER
CONSECRATED
CONSIDER
CONSTANT
CONSTERNATION
CONSUMED
CONTEMPLATE
CONTROL
CONVERSATION
COOLED
COOLLY
CORDILLERA
CORNER
CORNERS
CORNETS
CORRECT
COSTLY
COTTAGES
COUNTED
COUNTS
COURTIERS
COVERED
COVET
COWARD
COY
CRAFT
CRAPE
CREDIT
CREEP
CREPT
CRITERION
CROCUS
CROOKED
CROW
CRUMBLING
CRYSTAL
CUPS
CURL
CURLS
CUSTOMS
DAMASK
DAMSEL
DANCED
DANCING
DANGEROUS
DARKER
DART
DATELESS
DATES
DAYBREAK
DEBATED
DECADES
DECISION
DECK
DECLINE
DECLINED
DEEPEST
DEFEATED
DEGREES
DELUSIVE
DEMOCRAT
DEN
DENOTE
DENSE
DENT
DEPRIVE
DESCENDING
DETAINED
DEVELOPED
DICE
DIFFER
DIMLY
DINNER
DIPS
DISAPPEAR
DISAPPOINT
DISCERN
DISCIPLINE
DISCOURSE
DISCREET
DISPARAGEMENT
DISPLAYS
DISSENT
DISSOLUTION
DISTINCTION
DISTINCTLY
DITTY
DIVERSIFIED
DIVIDED
DIVINEST
DIZZY
DOLLIE
DOMINIONS
DOOMED
DOOM'S
DOUBLE
DOUBTS
DRANK
DRIP
DRIPPING
DRIVES
DROPPING
DRUNK
DUSKY
DWELLS
EARLIER
EARTH'S
EASED
EASILY
EASTERN
ECONOMY
ELDER
ELIJAH'S
ELOQUENT
EMBELLISH
EMBRYO
ENABLES
ENABLING
ENCHANTING
ENFORCED
ENTERTAINS
ENTICED
ENTOMOLOGY
EPICURE
EQUITY
ESCAPING
ESOTERIC
ESPIED
ESSENTIAL
ESTATES
EVE
EXCEL
EXCUSE
EXILE
EXPANSE
EXPLANATION
EXPLORE
EXTANT
EXTINGUISH
EXTRAVAGANT
EXULTATION
FAILING
FAILS
FAILURE
FALLING
FAMILY
FANTASTIC
FARMERS
FARTHEST
FARTHINGS
FAT
FATHOM
FEARLESS
FEAST
FEATS
FEBUARY
FEEDS
FELLED
FICTION
FILAMENT
FINALLY
FINDING
FIR
FIRES
FIRMAMENTAL
FLAGONS
FLASH
FLAVORS
FLEECES
FLICKERING
FLITTED
FLOWER'S
FLUTTER
FOLIAGE
FONDLED
FOOLISH
FORBIDDEN
FOREIGNER
FORGIVEN
FORK
FORWARD
FRACTURE
FRAIL
FREELY
FRIGHTENED
FRIGID
FRILL
FROCK
FROG
FROWN
FUCHSIA'S
FULFILLED
FUN
FURNISHED
FURROW
GALLOPED
GAMBOLS
GARMENT
GARNET
GARRET
GAUDY
GAYER
GAZING
GENERATIONS
GENTLEMAN
GERM
GETTING
GHOSTS
GIDDY
GILT
GLEAM
GLIMMERING
GLOBE
GLOVE
GRANTED
GRASP
GREATER
GREEDY
GREET
GROOVE
GUARANTY
GUSH
HAPPENING
HAPPINESS
HARD
HARDLY
HARROWING
HATE
HATS
HAUNTED
HAUNTING
HAUNTS
HEALTH
HEARING
HEART'S
HEARTY
HE'D
HEFT
HEIGHT
HELPS
HEMISPHERES
HEMS
HENCE
HERD
HEROIC
HIDDEN
HIGHEST
HINTS
HO
HOARSE
HOCK
HOLINESS
HOPES
HOPING
HORSE
HOSPITABLE
HOSPITALITY
HOSTS
HOT
HOVERED
HUGE
HUNT
HURLED
HURRICANE
HUT
IDEAL
IGNORES
IMPATIENT
IMPETUS
IMPLAUSIBLE
IMPLEMENTS
IMPOTENCE
IMPUDENT
INCOME
INCREASE
INDEPENDANT
INDEPENDENT
INDIAN
INDIVIDUALS
INDORSED
INEBRIATE
INFIDEL
INSECURE
INSURES
INTENT
INTERCEDE
INTERVENE
INTRINSIC
INTRODUCE
INTRUDE
INTUITION
INVENTION
INVEST
INVINCIBLE
INVIOLATE
INVITE
ISLES
JANUARY
JASON
JEALOUSY
JEST
JEW
JOHN
JOIN
JOYS
JUDGED
JUNIOR
KEEN
KEEPSAKE
KNEES
KNOCKING

3 (cont.)
KNOLL
LACES
LAMPS
LARCENY
LATCH
LATELY
LAUGHS
LAYING
LEANING
LEAPS
LEECH
LEGEND
LEGIONS
LENT
LEOPARD
LETTING
LIFELESS
LIFTS
LINGERED
LISP
LOAF
LOCALITY
LOCATION
LOCKS
LODGED
LOFTY
LOOP
LOOSE
LOVES
LOWLY
LUNGS
MADDER
MADONNA
MAGICAL
MAGNANIMOUS
MAIDEN
MAINTAIN
MAJORITY
MAKER'S
MANIFOLD
MAPLE
MARKED
MASSACRE
MASTER'S
MATHEMATICS
MATTERS
MEANWHILE
MEASURES
MECHLIN
MEDICINE
MELLOW
MEMORIAL
MENACE
MERIDIAN
MERRIMENT
MIDNIGHT'S
MIEN
MINGLED
MINISTRY
MINUTER
MISTOOK
MOB
MOLD
MONSTER
MONSTROUS
MORTISED
MOSSES
MOURNER
MOURNERS
MOURNFUL
MR
MULTIPLY
MURDER
MUSHROOM
MUSKET
MYSTERIOUS
NATION
NAVIES
NEARNESS
NEEDLES
NEGATIVE
NEIGHBORLY
NERVES
NUMBERS
NUTS
OATH
OBLIGATION
OBLIGED
OBSCURE
OBSERVED
OBTAINS
OCCURRED
OCTOBER
ODDITY
OER
OFFERING
OMNIPOTENT
ONSET
OPERA
OPINION
OPTION
ORDINARY
ORIENT
ORIENTAL
OURS
OUTGROWN
OVERFLOW
OWL
OXYGEN
PALACE
PALACES
PALL
PARASOL
PARTAKES
PARTS
PASSENGER
PATHOS
PAUL
PAWN
PEDIGREE
PEEP
PEER
PERADVENTURE
PERCEIVELESS
PERCEIVES
PERCEPTION
PERCHANCE
PERU
PERUSAL
PHILOLOGY
PHRASE
PICTURES
PIER
PIERCING
PIERS
PILLAGE
PILOT
PINIONS
PINS
PIOUS
PIPE
PLANE
PLATE
PLAYS
PLEASANT
PLEIAD
PLY
POCKET
POMPOSITY
PONDEROUS
POOL
POPULATION
POSSESSING
POURED
PRATE
PRAYED
PRECARIOUS
PRECISE
PREMIUM
PREPARE
PREPARED
PRESUMPTUOUS
PREVIOUS
PREY
PRIME
PRIMER
PRINT
PRIVACY
PROCESSION
PROCLAIM
PROFILE
PROGNOSTIC'S
PROGRESS
PRONE
PROPERTY
PROPITIATE
PROPORTIONED
PROPOUNDED
PROPS
PROSPECT
PROVIDED
PRY
PUNISH
PURER
PURPLES
PURSUE
PURSUES
PURSUIT
PUTTING
QUAINTEST
QUALIFY
QUANTITY
QUIETLY
QUIVERED
RACES
RACK
RAGGED
RAIL
RATIO
RAW
REALITY
REASONS
RECEIPTED
RECEIVED
RECEIVES
RECESS
RECOLLECTED
RECOLLECTION
RECOMPENSE
RECORDED
REELING
REFUSE
REIGN
REJOIN
RELEASE
REMARK
REMINDED
REMIT
REMORSE
RENEW
RENOWNED
RENT
RENUNCIATION
REPEAL
REQUIRES
RESERVE
RESERVED
RESIGNED
RESISTS
RESPECTFUL
RESUMED
RESUMING
RETRIEVELESS
RETROGRADE
RETROSPECTION
REVEALED
REVEL
REVELRY
REVERENTIAL
REVISITING
RICHER
RIDING
RIOT
RIP
RISING
RIVET
ROBE
ROCKED
ROMANCE
ROUTES
ROYALTY
RUBY
RULE
RUMOR
RUMOR'S
RUTHLESS
SACRIFICE
SAFELY
SAGES
SAILED
SAILORS
SANDALS
SANK
SAUNTERING
SCARE
SCENERY
SEARCHING
SECOND'S
SEEING
SENDS
SERVICES
SEXTON
SHADE
SHAPES
SHARED
SHARP
SHARPEST
SHIFTED
SHINE
SHIP
SHOD
SHOES
SHORES
SHORTEST
SHREWD
SHRINKING
SHUTTING
SIDES
SIDEWISE
SIGNED
SILENTLY
SIMILAR
SIMULTANEOUS
SINK
SIP
SIREN
SITS
SITUATES
SIX
SLAKE
SLANT
SLEEPS
SLIGHT
SLINK
SLIPPING
SMITTEN
SMOKE
SMUGGLED
SNATCH
SNUG
SOFTNESS
SOLDERED
SOLE
SOLSTICE
SOMETIME
SOONER
SOONEST
SORCERY
SORDID
SOUVENIR
SOWED
SPADE
SPAN
SPANGLED
SPARED
SPARROW
SPEAKS
SPECIFY
SPECTRES
SPECULATION
SPED
SPEND
SPOKES
SPRANG
SPREAD
SPREADS
ST
STAB
STAGGER

3 (cont.)
STAGGERED
STAIR
STAKE
STALE
STAMPED
STAPLES
STARVING
STATURE
STEALTH
STEALTHY
STIPULATE
STIRRUP
STITCHES
STRATEGY
STRIKES
STRINGS
STRUGGLED
SUBLIMER
SUBTERRANEAN
SUCCESS
SUDDENNESS
SUFFOCATE
SUING
SUITOR
SUNG
SUNNY
SUPERCILIOUS
SUPPLICATE
SUPPLIED
SUPPLY
SUPREMACY
SUPREMER
SURFACES
SURGEONS
SURVEYED
SUSAN
SUSPECTED
SUSPICION
SUSTAIN
SWANS
SWAYING
SWEEPING
SWEEPS
SWELLING
SWIM
SWINGING
SWORD
SYLVAN
TABERNACLES
TAKEN
TAMPER
TAPPED
TARE
TARRY
TASK
TASSELS
TEAZING
TELLING
TEMPEST
TEMPLE
TENDERNESS
TENEMENTS
TENERIFFE
TERMINATE
TERRIBLER
THANKSGIVING
THEREON
THICKER
THIMBLE
THIRD
THIRSTY
THORN
THREATENED
THRILL
TIGHTER
TINSEL
TIP
TOILETTE
TOILS
TOLL
TOMBS
TOPAZ
TORMENT
TORN
TOUCHING
TRACE
TRADES
TRAINS
TRANCE
TRANSIT
TRANSPORTING
TRAVERSE
TRAVERSED
TREAD
TREMBLING
TREMOR
TRINKETS
TRIPOLI
TRIPS
TROD
TRUMPET
TUMBLE
TURRET
TYPIC
TYRIAN
UNANNOINTED
UNFOLD
UNFREQUENTED
UNHEARD
UNIQUE
UNPERCEIVED
UNSUBSTANTIAL
UNTOLD
UNWORTHY
UPHELD
URGE
USING
UTTERED
VAILED
VAN
VANE
VEHICLE
VEIN
VENTURED
VEX
VICINITY
VIEWED
VIOLETS
VIOLIN
VISIBLE
VISIONS
VOLCANIC
VOLCANO
VOLCANOES
WAFTS
WAKED
WARDROBE
WARMTH
WATCH
WEAK
WEED
WEIGHED
WHISPERING
WHISTLED
WHOSOEVER
WIN
WINES
WITHOLD
WITNESSES
WIZARD
WONDERED
WOO
WOODEN
WOOING
WOOL
WORKED
WORKING
WORLD'S
WORMS
WORTHINESS
WORTHY
WRECK
WREN
WRESTLED
WRESTLES
WRING
WROUGHT
WRUNG
YEAR'S
YOURS
ZEPHYR

2
ABBEY
ABDICATION
ABHOR
ABHORRED
ABOLISH
ABSORB
ABSORBED
ACCIDENTAL
ACCURATE
ACHIEVEMENT
ACHIEVES
ACHIEVING
ACHING
ACKNOWLEDGED
ACORN
ACQUAINTED
ACQUIRE
ACRID
ACTS
ACTUAL
ACUTE
ACUTER
ADJOURN
ADMIRING
ADMIT
ADMITS
ADMONITION
ADORING
ADOWN
ADRIFT
ADROITLY
ADULT
ADVANTAGE
ADVENTURE
ADVERTISE
ADVOCATE
AFFLICTED
AFFLICTIVE
AFFLUENT
AFFRONTS
AFRESH
AGGRANDIZE-
MENT
AGGREGATE
AGLOW
AGONIZED
AGONIZING
AGROUND
AIDED
AIM
AIRS
ALARMS
ALGEBRA
ALIGHT
ALIMENT
ALL'S
ALLURED
ALMIGHTY
ALPHABET
ALTITUDE
AMAZING
AMENDED
AMHERST
AMISS
AMPLEST
AMPLITUDE
AMPLY
AMULET
ANALYZE
ANCHOR
ANCLE
ANEMONE
ANNIHILATE
ANNIHILATION
ANNUAL
ANNULS
ANONYMOUS
ANTELOPE
ANTERIOR
ANTICS
ANYONE
ANYTHING
APARTMENTS
APOCALYPSE
APOSTLE
APPALLS
APPARELED
APPARENT
APPEARANCE
APPLES
APPRECIATION
APPREHENSION
APTITUDE
ARCHITECT
ARDENT
ARDUOUS
ARGUE
ARGUES
ARISTOCRACY
ARMED
ARRANGED
ARREST
ARRESTED
ARROGANT
ARROWS
ARTICLES
ARTIFICE
ARTIST
ASCENDED
ASIATIC
ASKETH
ASPIRE
ASSAULTED
ASSERT
ASSOCIATES
ASSUAGE
ASSUREDLY
ASTRAL
ASTRONOMY
ATE
ATTAINED
ATTEMPTED
ATTENDANCE
ATTENDED
ATTEST
ATTIRED
ATTITUDES
AUBURN
AUDIBLER
AUDIENCES
AUGHT
AUGUR
AURORAL
AUTUMN'S
AVERSE
AWAIT
AWAITED
AWAKEN
AXE
AXIOM
AXLE
BABY
BACKS
BADINAGE
BAFFLES
BALANCE
BALLADS
BALTIC
BANE
BANNERS
BARRED
BASELESS
BASKS
BASS
BATHED
BATTLEMENT
BATTLES
BEAK
BEARER
BEAST
BECKONED
BECOMETH
BEETLE
BEETLES
BEGETS
BEGS

2 (cont.)
BEGUILE
BEGUILES
BEHOLDS
BELIEVING
BELONGED
BENEDICTION
BENEFIT
BERNARDINE
BESEECHING
BESTIR
BESTIRS
BETHLEEM
BETRAYED
BETROTHED
BIBLE
BID
BIN
BIOGRAPHY
BISECT
BISECTED
BITTER
BLAMED
BLANCH
BLANKET
BLAST
BLEAKER
BLEEDING
BLESSEDER
BLESSING
BLEST
BLINDED
BLOCKED
BLUNDER
BLUR
BLUSHING
BOARDS
BOBOLINKS
BODILESS
BOILING
BONDAGE
BONDS
BOOTS
BORROWED
BOSOMS
BOTTOM
BOUNDARIES
BOUNTEOUS
BOUNTIFUL
BOUT
BOWER
BRASS
BRAVERIES
BRAVOES
BRAZIL
BRAZILIAN
BREATHS
BRETHEREN
BREVITY
BREW
BRIDES
BRIDGES
BRIEFLY
BRIMMING
BRITAIN
BROACHED
BROADEST
BROCADE
BRONZE
BROOD
BROTHERS
BUCKET
BUCKETS
BUCKLED
BUGLE
BUGLES
BUILDS
BULLETS
BUMBLEBEE
BUMBLEBEES
BUN
BUNDLE
BURDOCK'S
BURGLAR
BURNING
BURNISHED
BURY
BUSHES
BUTTERFLY'S
BUTTON
CABINETS
CAESAR
CALAMITY
CANAAN
CANCELLED
CANDID
CANDLES
CANDOR
CANNON
CAPITAL
CAPSULES
CAPTIVES
CAPTIVITY
CARBON
CARDINAL
CAREFUL
CAREFULLY
CARES
CARNATIONS
CAROLLED
CARRARA
CARS
CASES
CASUAL
CATACOMB
CATERPILLAR
CATHEDRAL
CAUSED
CAUTIOUSLY
CAVERNS
CAVILER
CEDARS
CEILING
CELEBRATE
CELEBRATED
CELLS
CENTRES
CERTAINTIES
CERTIFYING
CHANCEL
CHANCE'S
CHANGED
CHANTING
CHAPEL
CHART
CHASM
CHAT
CHEATED
CHECKS
CHEEKS
CHEMIST
CHERUBIC
CHESTNUT
CHID
CHIEFER
CHILD'S
CHILLY
CHIN
CHINTZ
CHOOSES
CHRYSOLITE
CIRCASSIAN
CIRCUMSPECT
CITE
CITIES
CLAD
CLAMOR
CLARIFIED
CLASS
CLEARING
CLEMENCY
CLICK
CLIMATE
CLOG
COACHES
COAL
COAX
COFFIN
COGS
COIL
COLUMBUS
COMB
COMELY
COMEST
COMFORTS
COMMEND
COMMONER
COMMONWEALTH
COMMUNE
COMMUNION
COMMUTED
COMPARATIVE
COMPARED
COMPELLING
COMPENSATE
COMPENSATION
COMPLAIN
COMPLEXION
COMPLIED
COMPLIMENTS
COMPREHENDED
COMPRISE
COMPRISED
COMPRISING
COMPROMISE
COMPROMISED
CONCEAL
CONCEDES
CONCEIT
CONCEIVED
CONCENTRATE
CONDESCEND
CONDITIONS
CONDUCT
CONFERRING
CONGENIAL
CONQUERS
CONSCIENCE
CONSCIENTIOUS
CONSECRATE
CONSIDERED
CONSOLATION
CONSPICUOUS
CONSTITUTE
CONSULT
CONSUMES
CONTAINS
CONTEMN
CONTENTEDER
CONTENTS
CONTESTED
CONTINUALLY
CONTINUE
CONTRACTING
CONTRASTING
CONTROLLED
CONVALESCENT
CONVINCED
CONVULSION
CONVULSIVE
COOLS
CORKLESS
COROLLA
CORRIDORS
COSTLIER
COUNTENANCES
COUNTER
COUNTERACT
COUNTIES
COUNTLESS
COUNTRIES
COURAGE
COURTEOUS
COURTESIES
COURTIER
COVERS
COVETING
COW
CRAWLS
CREASES
CREATURE'S
CREDIBILITY
CREDITS
CRESTS
CRICKETS
CRIED
CROSSED
CROWDS
CROWNS
CROWS
CRUCIFIXAL
CRUEL
CRUISING
CRUMBLE
CRUMBLESS
CRUMBS
CUBIT
CUBITS
CURRENCY
CURRENT
CURTAIL
CURTAIN
CURVE
CUSHIONS
CUTLERY
CYCLES
CZAR
DAINTIER
DAMS
DANGLE
DARING
DARLING
DAUGHTER
DAUNTLESS
DAVID
DAWNS
DEADLY
DEAF
DEALS
DEARER
DEATHLESS
DEBAR
DEBAUCHEE
DEBONNAIRE
DECALOGUE
DECAMPING
DECAYS
DECLINES
DECORATE
DECOYS
DECREPIT
DEER
DEFACE
DEFERENCE
DEFIANT
DEFINED
DEFYING
DEGRADES
DEIFIED
DEIGN
DEJECTED
DELAYS
DELIBERATELY
DELIGHTED
DELIRIUM
DELIVERED
DELL
DELLS
DEMURRED
DENIES
DENIZEN
DENOMINATED
DENOTES
DEPARTMENT
DEPARTS
DEPLORE
DEPOSE
DESERVE
DESIGNATE
DESIRED
DESPATCH
DESPOT
DESTITUTE
DESTITUTION
DETECTED
DEVELOPES
DEVIL
DEVILS
DEVOID
DIAL

2 (cont.)
DILIGENT
DIMINUTION
DIMITIES
DIMMER
DIMNESS
DIMPLE
DIMPLED
DINING
DIRECT
DIRK
DISAPPEARS
DISAPPOINTED
DISCARDED
DISCERNING
DISCERNS
DISCLOSING
DISCOVERED
DISDAINED
DISDAINING
DISEASE
DISPARAGE
DISPELLED
DISPERSE
DISPUTE
DISSOLVING
DISTINCTER
DITCH
DIVERGING
DIVESTED
DIVIDEND
DIVIDES
DIVISION
DIVORCE
DIVULGE
DOE
DOLLARS
DOLLIE'S
DOLLS
DOMAIN
DON
DOUBLY
DOUBTING
DOVE
DOWERED
DOWERLESS
DRAGON
DRAM
DRAMS
DRAPED
DRAUGHT
DRAWERS
DREADED
DREAMED
DREARY
DRESSES
DREST
DRIFT
DRIFTED
DRILL
DRINKER
DRIVE
DRIVEN
DROSS
DROWSING
DRUNKARD
DUCHESS
DUNCE
DUNGEONED
DUTY
DWELLETH
DWINDLED
DYES
DYNASTY
EAGERNESS
EARTHQUAKE
EARTHS
EASIEST
EASING
EBON
ECCENTRIC
ECHOES
ECLIPSES
ECONOMICAL
ECSTASY'S
EDDIES
EDIBLE
EDUCATION
E'ER
EFFACES
EFFACING
EFFECT
EGG
EIDER
ELECTION
ELEMENTS
ELIGIBLE
ELIJAH
ELOQUENCE
ELSEWHERE
ELUDES
EMBARRASSMENT
EMBRACE
EMERGENCY
EMIGRANT
EMINENCE
EMINENT
EMOLUMENT
EMPIRE
EMPLOY
EMPLOYED
EMPTINESS
ENCHANTMENT
ENCHANTMENT'S
ENCHANTS
ENCLOSE
ENCLOSES
ENCORE
ENCOUNTER
ENDEAVORING
ENDOWED
ENDOWS
ENFOLD
ENFORCES
ENGLISH
ENHANCES
ENJOINING
ENLIGHTENED
ENLIGHTENING
ENORMOUS
ENSUING
ENTERING
ENTERPRISE
ENTHRALL
ENTICE
ENTOMBED
ENTRANCE
EPAULETTED
EQUIPAGE
ERROR
ERUDITE
ESCAPED
ESCAPELESS
ESCAPES
ESCUTSCHEON
ESSEX
ETHIOP
ETRUSCAN
EVADE
EVADES
EVANESCENCE
EVENING'S
EVENINGS
EXACTING
EXAMINE
EXCLUDES
EXETER
EXHALE
EXHIBITED
EXHIBITION
EXHILIRATE
EXHILIRATES
EXHILIRATION
EXIGENCIES
EXPANDS
EXPECTED
EXPECTING
EXPEND
EXPENDED
EXPENDS
EXPENSIVE
EXPLAINED
EXPOUND
EXPRESSED
EXTENDED
EXTERNAL
EXTINGUISHED
EXTOL
FABULOUS
FACED
FACTS
FADES
FAILLESS
FAINTEST
FAINTS
FALLACY
FALLS
FAME'S
FAMISH
FAMISHING
FAMOUS
FANTASY
FAREWELL
FARMS
FASHIONABLE
FASTEN
FASTER
FAULT
FAVORITE
FEE
FEIGN
FERVENT
FEVER
FIGHTING
FIGMENT
FILAMENTS
FILE
FILMS
FINDS
FIRE'S
FIRESIDE
FIRMEST
FIXED
FLAMINGO
FLANKED
FLASK
FLASKS
FLAVOR
FLAW
FLESHLESS
FLITTING
FLOATING
FLOCK
FLOCKS
FLOW
FLUTES
FOCUS
FOLDING
FOLK
FOLKS
FOLLOWING
FOLLOWS
FOOTING
FOOTMAN
FOOTMEN
FORBIDS
FORCED
FOREHEADS
FORESTALLING
FOREVERMORE
FORFEITED
FORMAL
FORMERLY
FORMS
FORSAKE
FORSAKES
FORTRESS
FORTY
FORUMS
FOUNDED
FOUNDERING
FOX
FRACTURED
FRAGRANT
FRANKFORT
FRANTIC
FREEZE
FRIENDLY
FRIEND'S
FRIGATE
FRINGES
FRO
FROCKS
FROZE
FROZEN
FRUCTIFIED
FRUIT
FRUITION
FRUITLESS
FULLER
FULLEST
FULLY
FUMBLE
FUMBLED
FURLONG
FURNISH
FURTIVE
GABLES
GALLERIES
GALLOWS
GAMBOL
GASPED
GENERALLY
GENTIANS
GEOGRAPHY
GESTURE
GHASTLY
GIFTS
GIRT
GLAZE
GLEAMED
GLOAT
GNOME
GOLIAH
GOODBYE
GOODS
GOSSAMER
GRADUAL
GRAINS
GRAPHIC
GRASPED
GRATE
GRATEFUL
GRAVE'S
GRAVITATION
GREEK
GRIEFS
GRIEVED
GROPE
GROPES
GROUPS
GUAGE
GUESSING
GUIDE
GUIDES
GUILE
GUILELESS
GUILT
GUILTY
GUINEAS
GULF
GUNS
GURGLED
GYMNAST
HALCYON
HALLOW
HALLOWING
HALTS
HALVES
HAMLET
HAMMER
HAMMERS
HANDLE
HANDLED
HANGING
HARBOR
HARDER
HARDEST
HAREBELL
HARVEST

2 (cont.)
HASTEN
HASTENED
HAUGHTY
HAZARD
HAZEL
HEARTH
HEAVEN'S
HEAVES
HEAVIER
HEAVIEST
HEDGE
HEMISPHERE
HEMLOCK
HEMLOCKS
HERESIES
HERMETIC
HEROES
HEROISM
HESITATED
HESITATES
HESITATING
HEWN
HIDING
HIGHTS
HILLSIDE
HINGE
HITHERTO
HOARD
HOARDED
HOIST
HOLIDAYS
HOMELESS
HOMELIER
HONESTY
HONORABLE
HONORS
HOOFS
HOPPED
HORROR'S
HOUSEHOLD
HOUSEWIFE'S
HOUSEWIVES
HOVERING
HUES
HUGEST
HUMBLEST
HUMS
HUNCH
HURRAH
HURRIES
HUSH
HYACINTH
ICE
ICICLE
ICICLES
IDENTIFIED
IDOLATRY
IGNOBLE
IGNOMINY
IGNOMINY'S
ILLUMINATE
ILLUSIVE
ILLUSTRIOUS
IMAGE
IMITATING
IMMURED
IMPAIR
IMPALPABLE
IMPASSIVE
IMPEACH
IMPEL
IMPERCEPTIBLE
IMPERFECT
IMPLORE
IMPLY
IMPORT
IMPORTUNED
IMPORTUNITY
IMPOSING
IMPOSSIBILITY
IMPRISONMENT
INCENSE
INCESSANTLY
INCH
INCOMPLETE
INCREASED
INCREDULOUS
INDEFINITE
INDEMNITY
INDIFFERENCE
INDUSTRIES
INEFFABLE
INFERS
INFINITER
INFINITES
INFORM
INGOTS
INHABITANTS
INHERITED
INNOCENCE
INNS
INNUENDO
INORDINATE
INQUEST
INSCRIBES
INSECT
INSOLVENT
INSPECTING
INSPIRITING
INSTANTS
INSTRUCTED
INSTRUCTS
INSULTED
INTEMPERANCE
INTER
INTERCOURSE
INTERDICT
INTERDICTED
INTERNAL
INTERRUPTING
INTERVALS
INTOXICATION
INTRENCHED
INUNDATION
INVALIDATES
INVESTED
INVESTIGATE
INVESTS
INVITING
INVOLVES
IRIS
IRON
ISAAC
ISCARIOT
ITALY
IVORY
JACKET'S
JACOB
JAIL
JASPER
JEHOVAH
JOGGLE
JOINS
JOINTS
JOLLY
JUBILEE
JUDEA
JUG
JUGGLER'S
JUGULAR
JULY
JUSTEST
KEYS
KIDD
KINDRED
KINGDOM'S
KINSMANSHIP
KNEELING
KNELL
KNIGHT
KNIT
KNITS
KNOCKED
KNOT
KNOWLEDGE
LABORED
LADEN
LAGGING
LAMB
LANDLORD
LANES
LAPS
LARDER
LASH
LATIN
LAUGHED
LAVA
LAYS
LE
LEANS
LEGACIES
LEND
LETTERS
LEXICON
LIAR
LIGHTED
LIGHTER
LIGHTNING'S
LIGHTS
LIKES
LIKEST
LILIES
LIMB
LINES
LINGERING
LIQUORS
LISPED
LISTENER
LISTLESS
LISTS
LOCATION'S
LOCKING
LODGE
LODGINGS
LOG
LOGARITHM
LONELIER
LONGED
LOOM
LOOSENED
LORE
LOSES
LOUDEST
LOVER'S
LOYAL
LUCK
LULLABY
LULLS
LUSCIOUS
LUTE
LUTES
MAD
MAGICIAN'S
MAGISTRATE
MAGNANIMITY
MAGNIFY
MAIDS
MAILED
MAIN
MAJESTIES
MAJOR
MALADY
MALAY
MALIGNITY
MANACLE
MANGLE
MAN'S
MARINE
MARK
MARKET
MARKSMAN
MARRIAGE
MARROW
MARS
MARSHALLED
MARTYR
MARTYRS
MARVEL
MASON
MASONRY
MASTS
MATCHED
MATE
MATURITY
MAYEST
MEAGRE
MEANINGS
MECHANIC
MEDDLE
MEDITERRANEAN
MELT
MEMBERS
MEMORIES
MENAGERIE
MENDED
MERCIFUL
MESH
MESSENGER
METALLIC
METEOR
METRE
METRES
METROPOLIS
MICE
MIDAS
MIDDLE
MIDSUMMER
MIGHTIER
MILD
MILLINERY
MINDED
MINISTER
MINTED
MISERIES
MISSES
MIST
MISTAKEN
MISTLETOE
MISTRESS
MIX
MIXED
MIXING
MOAN
MOAT
MOCKERY
MODESTY
MODIFY
MOIETY
MOMENTOUS
MOMENT'S
MOMENTUM
MONARCH
MONARCHS
MONARCHY
MONITION
MONTH
MOONS
MOORING
MORAL
MORTALITY'S
MOTH
MOURNED
MOVES
MUFFLED
MULTITUDE
MUNIFICENCE
MUSCLE
NAILS
NAPLES
NAVIGATION
NAVY
NECROMANCY
NECTAR
NECTARS
NEIGHBORHOODS
NEIGHBOR'S
NEWLY
NICE
NICODEMUS'
NIGGARDLY
NIGHTFALL
NIGHTGOWNS
NOBLE
NODDING
NOISY
NOOKS
NOSEGAYS
NOTCHED
NOTELESS

2 (cont.)
NOTORIETY
NUN
NURSE
NUTRIMENT
NUTRITION
OAKS
OAR
OARS
OBEDIENT
OBEISANCE
OBEY
OBEYED
OBLIGING
OBLIQUE
OBLIQUITY
OBLIVION'S
OBSCURING
OBSERVE
OBSTACLE
OBVIATED
OCCASIONS
OCCUPANT
OFFENCE
OFFEND
OFFENDED
OLDEST
OLD-FASHIONED
OMEN
OMIT
OMITTED
OMNIPRESENCE
ONESELF
OPHIR
OPULENCE
ORCHESTRA
ORCHIS
ORDINATION
ORDNANCE
ORE
ORTHOGRAPHY
OSTENSIBLY
OUTCAST
OUTGROW
OUTSTRIPPED
OVERFLOWING
OVERHEAD
OVERLOOK
OVERTAKELESS-
NESS
OWE
PAGEANTRY
PAGES
PAINTED
PALE
PALLIATE
PALSIED
PANELS
PARALLEL
PARALYSIS
PARCEL
PARCHED
PARE
PARISH
PARLEY
PARLIAMENT
PARLORS
PARTITION
PASSAGE
PASTE
PASTURE
PASTURES
PATENTED
PATH
PATTERNS
PAWS
PEAKS
PEEVISH
PENCE
PENINSULAS
PERCEIVING
PERCEPTIBLE
PERFECTED
PERFECTER
PERFUME
PERIL
PERPLEXED
PERSUADE
PETITE
PHANTASM
PHILIP
PHOSPHORUS
PHRASELESS
PICKED
PICTURESQUE
PILATE
PINES
PIONEER
PIRATE
PITIED
PLACED
PLACID
PLACING
PLAINER
PLANKS
PLANT
PLAUDIT
PLAUSIBILITY
PLAUSIBLE
PLAYTHING
PLAYTHINGS
PLEAD
PLEDGES
PLIES
PLIGHT
PLODDING
PLOT
PLUCK
PLUMB
PLUMED
PLUMES
PLUNDER
PLUNGE
POEMS
POINTERS
POISE
POISED
POLICE
PONIARDS
POORER
POPULATE
PORCELAIN
PORCH
PORTER
PORTRAIT
POSTERIOR
POSTHUMOUS
POSTS
POTENTIAL
POTOSI
POUNDS
POURS
POUTING
POWERLESS
PRACTISED
PRANCE
PRECEDED
PRECEDING
PRECINCT
PRECIPICE
PREDESTINED
PREPARES
PRESIDE
PRESSED
PREVENT
PRICELESS
PRICES
PRINCIPALLY
PRINCIPLE
PRISCILLA
PRITHEE
PRIVATE
PRIZES
PROBED
PROBITY
PROCEEDS
PROCESSES
PROCLAIMED
PROCURES
PRODIGAL
PRODUCT
PRODUCTS
PROFANED
PROFANES
PROHIBIT
PROJECTS
PROMISED
PROMPT
PROMPTER
PROMPTLY
PRONOUNCING
PROP
PROPOSED
PROPOUND
PROSE
PROTRACTED
PROUDEST
PROVINCE
PROVISO
PRUDENTER
PRUDENTIAL
PSALM
PUBLICITY
PUBLISHES
PULL
PULPIT
PUMPKINS
PUNCTURE
PURCHASER
PURE
PURPOSES
PUSHING
PUSSY
QUAINTER
QUAINTLY
QUALITIES
QUARRY
QUARTZ
QUEENS
QUEST
QUESTIONS
QUICKLY
RAFTER
RAINBOWS
RAINS
RALLIES
RANG
RANGED
RANKLE
RAPTURE'S
RARER
RATTLE
RAVELLED
REACHING
REALLY
REAR
RECALLS
RECEIPT
RECENTLY
RECITATION
RECITE
RECKON
RECOGNIZED
RECORDLESS
RECTITUDE
RECURRENT
REDBREAST
REDDER
REDEEM
REDOUBT
REFRAIN
REFRESHING
REFUND
REFUSED
REGARDED
REGARDS
REGIMENTS
REGIONS
REHEARSAL
REIN
REJECTED
RELATE
RELATED
RELATIVE
RELAY
RELIEF
RELIGION
RELUCTANTLY
RELY
REMANDED
REMEDY
REMEMBERS
REMOVING
REND
RENDERED
RENOUNCED
REPAIR
REPAIRED
REPAST
REPAY
REPEALLESS
REPEATED
REPINE
REPLACED
REPLIED
REPORTED
REPORTS
REPUDIATE
REPUDIATES
REQUISITE
RESCINDED
RESEMBLANCE
RESEMBLE
RESEMBLING
RESERVING
RESIDUE
RESIGN
RESONANCE
RESPONDED
RESPONSIBILITY
RESTED
RESTORE
RESTORED
RESTRICTED
RESUMPTION
RETAKEN
RETICENCE
RETICENT
RETINUE
RETREAT
REVEALS
REVELATION'S
REVERENTLY
REVERING
REVERSES
REVILED
REVOLVING
RIBALDRY
RIBBON
RIBBONS
RIDGE
RILL
RIM
RIME
RIPENING
ROAM
ROAR
ROB
ROBBER
ROLLING
ROPES
ROSY
ROTATION
ROWING
ROWS
RUDDIER
RUDE
RUDIMENT
RUIN
RUNNING
RUSH
RUSHES
SADDLE
SAGACITY
SAHARA
SAINT
SALARY
SANE
SANITY
SATED

2 (cont.)
SATISFIES
SATISFY
SAUCER
SAUCY
SAVANS
SAVES
SAVORY
SCAFFOLDS
SCALDS
SCALPS
SCANTEST
SCANTILY
SCARES
SCARF
SCATTERS
SCHEDULE
SCHEMES
SCHOOLBOY
SCHOOLS
SCIENCES
SCOLD
SCOOP
SCOOPED
SCORE
SCOURGED
SCRAPS
SCRUPLE
SCRUPULOUS
SEAMLESS
SEASON
SEATS
SECRECY
SECURED
SECURES
SECUREST
SECURITY
SEDATE
SEEKETH
SEEMING
SELECT
SENSES
SENTENCED
SENTIMENTS
SEPARATION'S
SEPULCHRAL
SEQUENCE
SEQUESTERED
SERAPH
SERAPHIM
SERAPHS
SERENER
SERIES
SERVANT
SERVED
SESSION
SETTLER
SEVEN
SEVERER
SHAKES
SHALLOW
SHAMED
SHAPELESS
SHATTER
SHEET
SHELL
SHELTER
SHIFTS
SHILY
SHIMMERING
SHIVER
SHORTNESS
SHOULDER
SHOUT
SHOWING
SHRANK
SHREDS
SHREWDER
SHRIEK
SHRILL
SHRIVELLED
SHRIVEN
SHROUD
SHRUNKEN
SHUDDER
SICILY
SICK
SICKENED
SIGHS
SIGNALIZE
SIGNIFIED
SIGNIFY
SILK
SIMPLER
SIN
SINCERE
SINCERITY
SINEWS
SINGETH
SINKING
SITTING
SKEIN
SLATE
SLAVE
SLENDER
SLOPE
SLOWEST
SMART
SMILE'S
SMOTE
SNAP
SNEERED
SOARING
SOFA
SOLDIER'S
SOLDIERS
SOLEMNEST
SOLVE
SOMBRE
SOMEONE
SOPHISTRIES
SORCERER
SORE
SOUNDED
SOURCES
SOWING
SPADES
SPARKLED
SPARKS
SPECIAL
SPECIFIED
SPECK
SPECTACLE
SPECTRE'S
SPECULATIONS
SPENDING
SPHERES
SPIN
SPIRE
SPIRES
SPLITS
SPOKEN
SPOOLS
SPRUNG
SPURNS
SQUARE
STAGGERING
STAID
STAINS
STAKES
STALACTITE
STALK
STANDARDS
STAPLED
STARING
STAR'S
STATELIER
STATES
STATIONED
STAYING
STEADILY
STEALS
STEALTHILY
STEMS
STEPPING
STEPT
STERILE
STERN
STIFFENS
STILE
STIRLESS
STIRRING
STITCH
STITCHED
STOCKING
STOCKS
STONES
STOPLESS
STOUTEST
STRAIGHTEN
STRAIGHTENED
STRAIGHTER
STRAIGHTWAY
STRANDED
STRANGER'S
STRANGEST
STRANGLES
STRAY
STRAYED
STRICT
STRICTLY
STRIDING
STRIFE
STRIVE
STRIVES
STROLL
STROLLED
STRONGEST
STRUGGLES
STRUGGLING
STRUT
STRUTS
STUBBLE
STUDENT
STUMBLING
STUN
STUNS
STUPENDOUSNESS
STUPOR
STURDY
STYLE
SUBSISTING
SUCCEED
SUCCESSFUL
SUCCOR
SUED
SUGGESTION
SUGGESTS
SUMMONS
SUNDAY
SUNDERED
SUN'S
SUNSETS
SUPERSEDE
SUPERSEDING
SUPPER
SUPPLANTS
SUPPORTS
SUPPOSITION
SUPREMEST
SURELY
SURER
SURGEON
SURGERY
SURLY
SURMISING
SURPASS
SURPLICE
SURPRISED
SURREPTITIOUS
SURVIVED
SUSPECTING
SUSTAINED
SUSTENANCE
SWAGGERS
SWAM
SWARTHY
SWEETS
SWELL
SWELLED
SWELLS
SWIFTER
SWIMMING
SWINGS
SWOON
SYCAMORE
SYMBOLS
TABERNACLE
TABLES
TAKETH
TAMARIND
TAMBORIN
TANKARDS
TANKS
TAPESTRIES
TARDY
TARGET
TASTES
TATTERED
TAWNY
TAX
TEARFUL
TEAZED
TECHNICALITY
TEMPERATURE
TEMPTATION
TENDEREST
TENTS
TEPID
TERRENE
TERRESTRIAL
TERSE
TESTIFIED
TESTING
THANKED
THEMES
THENCE
THENCEFORWARD
THILL
THOMAS
THOROUGH
THOROUGHLY
THOUGHTFUL
THRIFT
THRONES
THRONGS
THROUGHOUT
TICK
TICKED
TICKETS
TIDINGS
TIGER
TIGHTEST
TILLING
TIMIDLY
TINDER
TINGLES
TIPPET
TIPTOE
TITANTIC
TITLED
TO-DAY
TOILED
TOKEN
TOLLING
TON
TONGUES
TO-NIGHT
TOOLS
TOP
TOPS
TORE
TOTAL
TOTTER
TOUCHES
TOWNS
TOY
TRACED
TRACKS
TRACT
TRAILED
TRAITOR
TRAMP
TRANSACTION
TRANSFIGURED
TRANSIENT
TRANSPORTED
TRANSPORTS
TRAP
TRAVEL

2 (cont.)
TRAVELLED
TRAVERSES
TREADING
TREASURE
TREMBLE
TRESS
TRIBES
TRIES
TRIFLES
TRIFLING
TRIPLE
TRITEST
TRIUMPHED
TRODDEN
TRUDGE
TRUMPETS
TRUNK
TRUSTY
TUBE
TUG
TULLE
TUMULT
TUMULTUOUS
TUNNEL
TWAIN
TWELVE
TWIN
TWINKLED
TWINKLING
TWIXT
UMBER
UNABLE
UNARMED
UNBROKEN
UNCONSCIOUS-
NESS
UNDERNEATH
UNDEVELOPED
UNDISCOVERED
UNDISPUTED
UNDIVINE
UNFITTED
UNIT
UNIVERSE'S
UNNUMBERED
UNQUALIFIED
UNREMITTING
UNSEEN
UNSUSTAINED
UNTHINKING
UNTIE
UNTOUCHED
UNVARYING
UNWEARIED
UNWINDS
UPHOLSTERER
URCHIN
URGED
URN
USELESS
USHER
USUALLY
USURPS
VACANT
VACATION
VAGUE
VAILING
VALENTINE
VALLEY
VALUES
VALVES
VANISH
VANITY
VARIED
VASE
VASTEST
VAUNT
VELOCITY
VENERABLE
VERDICT
VEVAY
VICTORIOUS
VIRTUE
VISAGE
VISITER
VISITORS
VISTA
VIVID
VOICES
VOLUME
VOTE
VOUCH
VOWS
VULTURE
WADE
WAGONS
WAILING
WAKES
WALKING
WALKS
WAN
WANDER
WANE
WANTS
WARMING
WARNING
WASHED
WASTES
WAYLAYING
WEAKNESS
WEALTHY
WEARIED
WEARINESS
WEATHER
WEAVER
WEDGED
WEDLOCK
WEDNESDAY
WEEK
WEIGHTS
WE'LL
WHARF
WHEAT
WHEREAS
WHISPER
WHISTLE
WHOLLY
WICKS
WIDER
WIDTHS
WILLED
WILTED
WILY
WINCING
WINGED
WINNING
WINTER'S
WINTERS
WISHES
WISHFULNESS
WITCH
WOKE
WOLFE
WONDERING
WONT (noun)
WORRIED
WORTHLESS
WOVE
WRAP
WRAPS
WRESTLER
WRETCH
WRINKLE
YARDS
YELLOWER
YONDER
YOUTH
ZEALOUS
ZERO
ZEST

1
ABASED
ABASH
ABASHETH
ABASHING
ABASHLESS
ABATED
ABATES
ABBEYS
ABBREVIATE
A—B—C
ABDICATE
ABDICATED
ABDUCTED
ABETS
ABHORRENCE
ABHORRENT
ABHORS
ABILITIES
ABJURED
ABLENESS
A'BLOSSOM
A-BLOW
ABODES
ABOLISHED
ABOLITION
ABREAST
ABRIDGE
ABRIDGES
ABROGATE
ABRUPT
ABSCONDING
ABSCONDS
ABSENTEE
ABSENTLY
ABSOLVED
ABSTEMIOUS
ABSTEMIOUSLY
ABSTEMIOUSNESS
ABSURD
ABSURDITY
ABUNDANCE
ABUTS
ABYSS'S
ACCEDED
ACCENTED
ACCEPTS
ACCESSIBLE
ACCOMMODATE
ACCOMPANIED
ACCOMPANIES
ACCOMPLISH
ACCORDINGLY
ACCOSTAL
ACCOSTED
ACCOUNT
ACCOUTRED
ACCREDITED
ACCRUE
ACCUSE
A'CHASE
ACHES
A'CHIRRUP
ACKNOWLEDGE-
MENT
ACORN'S
A COURTING
ACQUIESCENCE
ACQUIRED
ACQUISITION
ACQUITTED
ACTUALIZE
ACTUALLY
ADAMANTINE
ADDER
ADDERS
ADDETH
ADDICTED
ADDINGS
ADDRESSING
ADDS
ADEQUATELY
ADHERE
ADHERES
ADHESION'S
ADJECTIVE
ADJOURNING
ADJOURNS
ADJUNCT
ADJURE
ADMINISTER
ADMIRABLER
ADMIRALTY
ADMIRATIONS
ADMIRED
ADMISSION
ADMITTING
ADMONISH
ADMONISHED
ADORATION
ADORES
ADORNING
A-DREAMING
ADROIT
ADROITER
ADVENTURES
ADVENTUROUS
ADVISE
ADZ
ADZE
AERIAL
AESTHETICS
AFFABLE
AFFAIRS
AFFECT
AFFECTING
AFFECTINGLY
AFFECTS
AFFIANCE
AFFIRM
AFFIRMED
AFFIRMING
AFFIXED
AFFLICT
AFFRIGHT
AFLOAT
A-FOG
AFORETIME
AFRICAN
AFTERWARDS
AGATE
AGENT
AGGRANDIZED
AGGRAVATE
AGILE
AILED
AIMED
AIMLESS
A JAR
ALACRITY
ALARMED
ALARMING
ALBAN
ALBUMS
ALCOHOL
ALDEN
ALE
ALLEYS
ALLIED
ALLIES
ALLOTTED
ALLOYS
ALLUDED
ALLURE
ALLURES
ALMANAC'S
ALMANACS
ALOFT
ALOOF
ALPINE
ALTERNATING
ALTERNATIVE
A LULL
A MARCHING
AMAZED
AMAZES
AMBITION
AMBLING
AMBUSCADE
AMEN
AMENABLE
AMEND
AMENITY
AMITIES
AMMUNITION
AMOUNT
AMPHITRITE
AMPUTATE

1 (cont.)
AMPUTATED
AMULETS
ANALYTIC
ANANIAS
ANATOMY
ANCESTORS
ANCHORED
ANCHORS
ANCIENTER
ANDRE'S
ANECDOTES
ANEMONES
ANGELS'
ANGER
ANGLED
ANGLEWORM
ANGLO-FLORENTINE
ANIMALS
ANKLES
ANNEALED
ANNIHILATING
ANNIVERSARY
ANNO
ANNOUNCED
ANNOUNCING
ANNULLED
ANODYNES
ANOMALY
ANSWERING
ANTEDATE
ANTEDATES
ANTHRACITE
ANTI
ANTICIPATING
ANTICIPATION
ANTIDOTE
ANTIQUARY
ANTIQUER
ANTIQUEST
ANTIQUITY
ANTLERS
ANVIL
ANVIL'S
ANXIOUS
ANYBODY'S
APE
APOCALYPTIC
APOSTACY
APOSTASY
APOSTATE
APPAL
APPALLED
APPALS
APPARENTLY
APPARITIONS
APPARRELED
APPEALED
APPEALING
APPEASE
APPETITE
APPLICATION
APPLIED
APPOINTMENT
APPOINTS
APPREHEND
APPREHENSION'S
APPREHENSIONS
APPRENTICED
APPROACHING
APPROPRIATE
APPROVING
APRICOT
APRILS
APRONS
AQUATIC
ARABLE
ARAGON
ARARATS
ARBITRATE
ARCH
ARCHANGEL'S
ARCHANGELS
ARCHER'S
ARCHLY
ARCHNESS
ARCS
ARCTURUS
ARDOR
ARGENT
ARGUED
ARGUMENT
ARGUMENTS
ARISTOCRAT
ARITHMETIC
ARKS
AROMA
AROMATIC
ARRAGON
ARRAIGN
ARRAIGNS
ARRAYED
ARRAYS
ARRESTLESS
ARRIVE
ARRIVED
ARROGANTLY
ARTERIAL
ARTICLE
ARTIFICIAL
ARTILLERY
ARTISAN
ARTISANS
ARTISTS
ARTLESS
ARTS
A SAILING
ASCENDING
ASCENSION
ASCERTAINED
ASCETIC
ASCRIBE
A'SELF
ASHINE
ASHORE
ASIA
ASKEW
ASKING
ASLANT
ASPECTS
ASPERITY
ASPHODEL
ASPIRES
ASPIRING
ASSAULTING
ASSEMBLE
ASSEMBLED
ASSEMBLIES
ASSEMBLING
ASSENT
ASSERTING
ASSIDUOUSLY
ASSIGNABLE
ASSIGNS
ASSIST
ASSISTING
ASSOCIATION
ASSUAGES
ASSUMES
ASSUMING
ASSUMPTION
ASTERISKS
ASTEROID
ASTERS
ASTONISHES
ASTONISHMENT
ASTROLOGY
ASTRONOMER
ATHEIST
ATHENS
ATMOSPHERES
ATOM'S
ATONE
ATROPOS
ATTACHES
ATTACKS
ATTAINMENTS
ATTAR'S
ATTARS
ATTEMPTING
ATTEND
ATTENDANTS
ATTENDETH
ATTENTION'S
ATTESTED
ATTESTS
ATTIRETH
ATTRACTED
ATTRACTS
AUCTION
AUCTIONEER
AUDACIOUS
AUDACITY
AUDITORS
AUGMENTED
AUGUSTAN
AURORAN
AUSPICIOUSLY
AUSTERER
AUSTERITY
AUSTIN
AUSTRIAN
AUTHENTIC
AUTHOR
AUTOCRATIC
AUTO DA FE
AUTUMNS
AUXILIARIES
AUXILIARY
AVAIL
AVAILED
AVALANCHES
AVENGE
AVENGING
AVERRING
AVOCATION
AVOIDED
AVOWING
AWAITING
AWAKENED
AWARD
AWARDED
AWARDS
AWED
AWES
AWHILE
AXLES
AYRE
AZOF
BABBLERS
BABBLES
BABBLING
BACCALAUREATE
BAD
BADE
BAFFLING
BAGATELLES
BAGGAGE
BAGS
BAHAMAS
BAILIFF
BAILIFF'S
BAIT
BAIZE
BAKES
BALANCED
BALANCING
BALCONY
BALES
BALK
BALKED
BALKING
BALLAD'S
BALLET
BALLOONS
BALLOT
BALLOTS
BALSAM
BAN
BANDIT
BANDITTI
BANISHED
BANISHMENT
BANJO
BANKER
BANKRUPT
BANKRUPTCY
BANNED
BANNER
BANQUET'S
BANQUETS
BANQUETTINGS
BAPTIZES
BARABBAS'
BARBED
BARBS
BARDS
BAREHEAD
BARELY
BAREST
BARGAIN
BARGEMEN
BAROMETER
BARONIAL
BARRICADE
BARTSIA
BASEMENT
BASES
BASIN
BASK
BASKING
BASTINADOED
BAT
BATES
BATIZE
BATON
BATTERED
BATTERIES
BATTLEMENTS
BATTLE'S
BAUBLE
BAYONET
BAYONET'S
BAYS
BAZAAR
BEACH
BEAD
BEARD
BEARDED
BEARD'S
BEAREST
BEARING
BEATIFIED
BEATRICE
BEAUTY'S
BECK
BECKONING
BECLOUDED
BEDECKED
BEDTIME
BEETLE'S
BEFALLEN
BEFALLING
BEFEL
BEFITS
BEFRIEND
BEGET
BEGGARED
BEGGARY
BEGINNINGS
BEGONE
BEGUILED
BEGUILING
BEHAVIOR
BEHEADS
BEHOLDING
BEHOOVETH
BELATED
BELIEF'S
BELIEFS
BELLOWS
BELSHAZZAR
BELSHAZZAR'S
BELTED
BEMOANING
BEMUMBED
BENCH
BENDED
BENDS

1 (cont.)
BENEFACTOR
BENEFICENT
BENIGN
BENUMBED
BENUMBING
BEQUEATHES
BEQUEATHING
BEQUEATHS
BEQUEST
BEREAVEMENT
BEREAVES
BEREFT
BERRY'S
BESEECH
BESEEMETH
BESETS
BESTOWAL
BESTOWING
BET
BETAKES
BETHLEHEM'S
BETHOUGHT
BETIDES
BETIMES
BETOKEN
BETROTHAL
BEWILDERING
BIDS
BIER
BIGGEST
BILLION
BILLOW'S
BINDLESS
BIOGRAPHER
BIRDLING
BIRMINGHAM
BIRTH
BISCAYAN
BISECTING
BITE
BITTERER
BITTEREST
BITTERNESS
BLACKBIRDS
BLACKENED
BLACKSMITH
BLADE
BLADES
BLANDLY
BLANKETLESS
BLARE
BLASPHEME
BLAZED
BLEAKNESS
BLEATING
BLEATS
BLEEDS
BLEMÍSHLESS
BLEND
BLENT
BLESSES
BLINDING
BLINDS
BLISS'
BLISTER
BLISTERED
BLISTERS
BLITHE
BLOCKS
BLOOMED
BLOOMING
BLOOMS
BLOT
BLOTTED
BLOWS
BLUE-BIRD
BLUEST
BLUNDERED
BLURS
BLUSHES
BOANERGES
BOARD
BOASTING
BOASTS
BOBADILO
BODE
BODIES
BOGGY
BOGS
BOHEA
BOLIVIAN
BOOMING
BORED
BORER
BOROUGHS
BORROWS
BOSPORUS
BOUNDARY
BOUNDLESSNESS
BOUQUET
BOURBON
BOURNE
BOWL
BOWLS
BOXES
BOYISH
BRACED
BRAG
BRAID
BRAMBLE
BRANCH
BRAVER
BRAVO
BRAWLING
BRAYED
BREACH
BREAKERS
BREAKFASTED
BREASTS
BRED
BREEDS
BREWS
BRICK
BRIDAL
BRIDALLED
BRIDGET
BRIDLES
BRIEFER
BRIGAND
BRIGHTER
BRIGHTEST
BRIM
BRIMS
BRINDLED
BRISKLY
BROADCLOTH
BROADER
BROKER
BROKER'S
BROKERS
BRONTE
BROOCHES
BROODS
BRUISE
BRUISES
BRUSHED
BRUSSELS
BRYANT'S
BUBBLES
BUCANEERS
BUCCANEER
BUCCANEERING
BUCKLES
BUENOS
BUILDER
BUILDING
BULK
BULLETINS
BULLION
BULWARK
BUMBLE-BEES
BUNDLES
BUNG
BUNKER
BUOYANT
BURDOCK
BURGOYNE
BURGUND
BURGUNDY
BURMAH
BURNISH
BURR
BURROWED
BURS
BURSTING
BUSIER
BUST
BUSTLED
BUSTLES
BUSTLING
BUSTS
BUTTONED
BUTTONHOLE
BYSTANDERS
BY-THYME
CACTUS
CADENCES
CAESARS
CAGE
CAGES
CAJOLES
CAJOLING
CAKES
CALCULATIONS
CALLERS
CALLETH
CALLING
CALMNESS
CALUMNIES
CALVARIES
CAMBRIC
CAMEL'S
CAMEST
CAMP
CANCELED
CANDIDATES
CANES
CANNON'S
CANTICLE
CANTONS
CAPABILITIES
CAPACIOUS
CAP-A-PIE
CAPE
CAPERED
CAPITOL
CAPRICES
CAPRICORN
CAPTAIN
CAPTION
CAPTIVATE
CAPTIVATED
CAPTIVATES
CAPUCHIN
CAPUT
CARBONATES
CARD
CAREERS
CARELESSLY
CARESSED
CARESSES
CARGOES
CARLO
CARNIVAL
CARNIVALS
CARP
CARPENTERS
CARRIAGES
CARRYING
CASEMENT
CASH
CASK
CASKETS
CASQUE
CASTANET
CASTE
CAST'S
CASUALLY
CATARACT
CATCHING
CATO
CATO'S
CAUCUS
CAUSES
CAUTERIZE
CAVALIER
CAVALRY
CAVE
CAVERN'S
CAVIL
CAW
CEILINGS
CELEBRATES
CELERITY
CELL
CELLARS
CENOTAPH
CENSURE
CENTIPEDE
CENTS
CEREMENTS
CEREMONIOUS
CHAFE
CHAFES
CHAFING
CHAIN
CHALK
CHALLENGED
CHALLENGING
CHAMOIS'
CHANCED
CHANGES
CHANNEL
CHANTED
CHANTS
CHAOS
CHAOSES
CHAPEAU
CHAPEAUX
CHAPTER
CHARCOAL
CHARGERS
CHARIOT
CHARMED
CHARMING
CHARMS
CHARTED
CHASTEN
CHASTENEST
CHASTENS
CHASTISE
CHASTISING
CHATTED
CHATTER
CHEATS
CHEEKED
CHEERED
CHEERFUL
CHEERS
CHEMICAL
CHEMISTRY
CHERISHES
CHERRIES
CHILDREN'S
CHILLED
CHILLEST
CHIMBORAZO
CHIME
CHINK
CHIPS
CHIRPING
CHIVALRIES
CHOIRS
CHORALS
CHORISTER
CHRISTIAN
CHRONICLE
CHRYSOPHRAS
CHRYSOPRASE
CHUBBY
CHUCKLED
CHUCKLES
CHUMS
CHURCHES
CHURCHYARD
CICATRICE
CIGAR
CIMITAR
CINDER

1 (cont.)
CINDERELLA'S
CINNAMON
CIPHER
CIPHERS
CIRCLE
CIRCUMSCRIBES
CIRCUMSCRIPTION
CIRCUMVENT
CIRCUMVENTION
CITADELS
CITES
CITY
CIVIC
CIVILITY
CIVILIZATION
CLAIMED
CLAMBERED
CLAMORING
CLAMORS
CLANS
CLAP
CLAPS
CLARIFIES
CLARIFY
CLARIFYING
CLASPS
CLASSES
CLASSICS
CLASSIFY
CLASSIFYING
CLAUS
CLAWED
CLAWS
CLEAN
CLEARED
CLEARER
CLEAVE
CLEAVES
CLEAVING
CLEF
CLEMATIS
CLEOPATRA'S
CLERGYMAN
CLERGYMEN
CLERKS
CLIMBS
CLING
CLIPT
CLOAK
CLOSELY
CLOTH
CLOUDIER
CLOUDING
CLOVE
CLOVEN
CLOWN
CLOY
CLUB
CLUE
CLUMSY
CLUNG
CLUSTERS
COALS
COCKADE
COCKS
COCOA
CODES
CODICIL
CO-ETERNITY
COFFEE
COFFERS
COHERE
COHESIVE
COIN
COINS
COLONNADE
COLOR'S
COLOSSAL
COLUMBA
COLUMBINE
COLUMNAR
COMBINATION
COMBINE
COMBINEDLY
COMBINES
COMELIER
COMET'S
COMFORTABLE
COMFORTED
COMFORTING
COMISSARY
COMMANDER
COMMANDMENT
COMMENCES
COMMENSURATE
COMMENTATORS
COMMIT
COMMITTED
COMMONEST
COMMONLY
COMMUNICATE
COMMUNICATION
COMMUTE
COMPANIES
COMPARATIVELY
COMPASSED
COMPELLED
COMPELLETH
COMPENSATED
COMPENSATES
COMPETE
COMPETELESS
COMPETENCE
COMPETES
COMPETITOR
COMPLACENCE
COMPLAINED
COMPLAINING
COMPLAINS
COMPLAINT
COMPLEMENT
COMPLETED
COMPLICATE
COMPOSE
COMPOSER
COMPREHENDETH
COMPREHENSIVE
COMPUTES
COMRADE
COMRADES
CONCAVE
CONCEDE
CONCEIVELESS
CONCEPTION
CONCERNING
CONCERNLESS
CONCIEVE
CONCISEST
CONCLUDES
CONCLUDING
CONCLUSIVE
CONCOMITANT
CONDEMN
CONDENSED
CONDENSES
CONDESCENDED
CONDESCENDING
CONDESCENSION
CONDUCTED
CONFEDERATE
CONFEDERATES
CONFESS
CONFIDED
CONFIDENTIAL
CONFIDENTLY
CONFIDES
CONFIRMING
CONFIRMS
CONFISCATED
CONFISCATES
CONFLICT
CONFORM
CONFRONT
CONFRONTS
CONFUSED
CONFUSION
CONGEALED
CONJECTURE'S
CONJECTURING
CONJUGATE
CONJUROR
CONNECT
CONNECTION
CONNOISSEUR
CONQUERED
CONQUEROR
CONSCIOUSER
CONSCIOUSLY
CONSCIOUSNESS'
CONSECUTIVE
CONSENT
CONSENTED
CONSENTING
CONSIDERS
CONSIGNED
CONSOLED
CONSOLELESSLY
CONSOLES
CONSOLIDATE
CONSOLIDATES
CONSORT
CONSPIRE
CONSTANCY'S
CONSTELLATION
CONSTERNA-
TION'S
CONSTITUTED
CONSTRAINED
CONSTRUCTED
CONSTRUCTS
CONSULATE
CONSULTING
CONSULTS
CONSUME
CONTEMPLATED
CONTEMPLATING
CONTEMPT
CONTEMPTS
CONTENDED
CONTENDING
CONTENTETH
CONTENTMENT'S
CONTINGENT
CONTRA
CONTRABAND
CONTRACTS
CONTRADICT
CONTRASTED
CONTRITION
CONTRIVES
CONTROVERTIBLE
CONTUSION
CONVERGES
CONVERSION
CONVERT
CONVEX
CONVEYING
CONVICTIONS
CONVICTS
CONVINCE
CONVINCING
COOLING
COPIED
COPY
COQUETTE
COQUETTISH
CORAL
CORALS
CORDAGE
CORDIALLY
CORDS
CORINTHIANS
CORK
CORNICE
CORONAL
CORONER
CORONET
CORPORAL
CORPORATION
CORRECTING
CORRECTLY
CORRESPONDENT
CORROBORATION
CORRODE
CORRODELESS
CORRUPTION
COSMOPOLITES
COSTS
COSTUME
COSTUMELESS
COSTUMES
COTEMPORANE-
OUS
COTERIE
COUCH
COUNSEL
COUNTERFEITS
COUNTERPASS
COUNTESS
COUNTING
COUNTRYMAN
COUNTRYMEN
COUNTRY'S
COUPLE
COURIERS
COURSERS
COVETED
COVETS
COWARDS
COWERING
COWS
COWSLIP
CRACKLING
CRADLE
CRADLES
CRAM
CRANNY
CRASHED
CRASHE'S
CRASHING
CRATER
CRAVAT
CRAVE
CRAVED
CRAYON
CRAYONS
CREAK
CREASED
CREATE
CREATES
CREATOR'S
CREDIBILITY'S
CREDULOUS
CREEPING
CREEPS
CRESTED
CREVICES
CREWS
CRIB
CRIBS
CRIER
CRIER'S
CRIME
CRITICAL
CRITICIZE
CRITICS
CROONED
CROSS'
CROUCHED
CROWING
CRUCIFY
CRUELLY
CRUISE
CRUMBLED
CRUMPLED
CRUNCHES
CRUSADE'S
CRUSH
CRUST
CRUZ
CRYPTS
CUBE
CUBES
CUBIT'S
CUCKOO
CUFFS
CUIRASS
CULMINATE
CULPABLER

1 (cont.)
CULPRIT
CULTIVATE
CULTIVATION
CULTURE
CUNNINGLY
CUPBOARDS
CUPIDITY
CUPID'S
CURDLED
CURELESS
CURLED
CURLING
CURRENT'S
CURRER
CURRICLE
CURTAILED
CURTNESS
CURVED
CUSTOMARY
CUTICLE
CYCLE
CYNIC
CYPHER
CYPHERER
CYPHERLESS
CZARS
DAINTILY
DAM
DAMAGE
DAME
DAMES
DAMSONS
DANCER
DANCES
DANDELION
DANDELIONS
DANES
DANGEROUSLY
DANGLED
DANGLES
DANGLING
DANIEL
DANTE
DAPPERER
DARES
DARKNESSES
DARLINGS
DARTING
DATED
DATING
DAYLIGHT
DAZZINGLY
DAZZLE
DAZZLES
DEADEN
DEARTH
DEATHLESSNESS
DEBARRED
DEBASE
DEBASES
DEBATES
DEBT
DECALOGUES
DECAMP
DECAYED
DECIDING
DECIDUOUS
DECIMALS
DECLAIM
DECLAIMING
DECLIVITY
DECOMPOSITION
DECOY
DECOYED
DECOYING
DECREASE
DECREASES
DEDICATED
DEDUCTING
DEEDS
DEEMS
DEEPENED
DEEPENS
DEFACED
DEFACES
DEFAULT
DEFAULTER
DEFAULTING
DEFENCES
DEFENDING
DEFER
DEFERRED
DEFIED
DEFILES
DEFINITELY
DEFORMED
DEFORMING
DEFRAYS
DEFT
DEFY
DEGREELESS
DEIGNED
DEITY'S
DELAPIDATION'S
DELAYING
DELIBERATE
DELICATE
DELIGHT'S
DELINEATION
DELINQUENT
DELIVER
DELUGE
DEMANDED
DEMANDETH
DEMANDS
DEMEAN
DEMEANED
DEMEANING
DEMEANS
DEMIJOHN
DEMOCRATIC
DEMOLISHES
DEMOSTHENES
DEMURER
DEMURRAL
DENIAL
DENOMINATION
DENOTED
DENOUNCED
DENUDED
DEPEND
DEPENDENT
DEPENDS
DEPLOYS
DEPORT
DEPORTMENTS
DEPOSED
DEPOSES
DEPOSIT
DEPOSITING
DEPOSITS
DEPRECIATE
DEPREDATION
DEPTHS
DEPUTIES
DEPUTY
DERIDED
DERIDING
DERIVE
DERIVES
DESCRIBED
DESCRIBING
DESCRY
DESERVED
DESERVING
DESIGNATED
DESIGNED
DESIRELESS
DESIRE'S
DESIRES
DESIST
DESOLATION
DESPAIRED
DESPAIR'S
DESPATCHED
DESPOILED
DESTINIES
DESTROY
DETACHMENT
DETACHMENTS
DETAIN
DETECTING
DETECTION
DETECTS
DETENTION
DETERMINATELY
DETERMINE
DETERRED
DETRIMENT
DEVASTATED
DEVASTATES
DEVELOPE
DEVISE
DEVISED
DEVISING
DEVOTEE
DEVOUR
DEVOURED
DIAGNOSIS
DIAGRAM
DIALECT
DIALOGUE
DIAMETERS
DIEMAN'S
DIFFERED
DIFFERENTLY
DIFFIDENT
DIFFUSES
DIGGERS
DIGNIFIED
DIGNITY
DIKES
DILAPIDATIONS
DILUTE
DIMENSIONS
DIMINISHED
DIMINUET
DIMITY
DIN
DINES
DINGLE
DINGY
DIPPED
DIPPING
DIRECTION
DIRGE
DIRKS
DIRT
DIRTY
DISAPPOINTING
DISAPPOINTMENT
DISAPPROVES
DISARMS
DISASTER
DISAVOWS
DISBAND
DISBURSE
DISCARD
DISCERNED
DISCERNIBLE
DISCIPLE
DISCLOSER
DISCLOSES
DISCLOSURE
DISCOMFIT
DISCONTENT
DISCORD
DISCOUNT
DISCOURAGE
DISCOURAGED
DISCOURAGEMENT
DISCPLINE
DISCREETLY
DISCRETION
DISCS
DISDAINFUL
DISEMBODIES
DISENCHANTS
DISENTHRALL
DISHEVELED
DISHEVELS
DISHONORED
DISINTEGRATES
DISLOCATE
DISMISS
DISOBEDIENCE'
DISOBEY
DISOWNED
DISPARITY
DISPEL
DISPELS
DISPERSES
DISPOSED
DISPOSERS
DISPROVE
DISPUTING
DISRESPECT
DISRESPECTFUL
DISSECT
DISSEMBLER
DISSEMINATED
DISSEMINATING
DISSENTING
DISSIPATE
DISSOLUTE
DISSUADE
DISTAFF
DISTIL
DISTILLED
DISTILLS
DISTILS
DISTINCTNESS
DISTINGUISH
DISTRACTS
DISTRUSTFUL
DISTURBED
DITCHES
DITTIES
DIVE
DIVER
DIVER'S
DIVERSE
DIVERSIFY
DIVERSION
DIVERTS
DIVEST
DIVINELY
DIVING
DIVISIONS
DIVORCED
DIVULGELESS
DIVULGING
DNIEPER
DOCK
DOCTOR
DOCTOR'S
DOCTRINES
DODGES
DOGMAS
DOG'S
DOGS
DOING
DOLL
DOLLAR
DOMAINS
DOMENICHINO
DOMINIE
DOMINIES
DOOMS
DOON
DORMANT
DOTE
DOTES
DOTS
DOTTED
DOUBLET
DOUBLOONS
DOUBTED
DOUGH
DOWER'S
DOWERS
DOWNIEST
DOWRIES
DOZEN
DR
DRAB
DRAG
DRAGONS
DRAMA'S

1 (cont.)
DRAUGHTS
DRAWN
DREAMY
DREAR
DREARIER
DREGS
DRESSING
DRIED
DRIFTING
DRILLED
DRILLS
DRINKING
DRIVING
DROUGHT
DROUGHTLESS
DROWN
DROWNED
DROWNING
DROWNS
DROWSE
DROWSIEST
DROWSINESS
DROWSY
DRUG
DRUID
DRUIDIC
DRUMMER
DUCATS
DUG
DUKES
DULLEST
DULLNESS
DUM
DUMBER
DUMBLY
DUNGEON
DUNGEON'S
DUPLICITY
DURABLE
DURABLER
DURABLY
DURHAM
DUSKER
DUSTIEST
DWARF
DWELLINGS
DWINDLING
DYER
DYNASTIES
EAGLE
EAGLE'S
EAGLES
EARLDOM
EARL'S
EARNEST
EARNING
EARNS
EARRING
EARRINGS
EARTHEN
EASEL
EASES
EASTER
EATS
EBBED
EBBING
EBBS
ECCENTRICITIES
ECCENTRICITY
ECHO
ECHOED
ECLAT
ECSTASIES
ECSTATIC
ECSTATICALLY
EDDIED
EDEN'LL
EDEN'S
EDIFICES
EDITION
E'E
EFFACED
EFFACELESS
EFFERVESCE
EFFERVESCED
EFFLORESCENCE
EFFULGENCIES
EGG-LIFE
EGGS
EGYPTIAN
EIDER-DUCK'S
EIGHTEEN
EJECTED
ELASTIC
ELDERLY
ELECT
ELECTED
ELECTRICAL
ELECTRICITY
ELEGANT
ELEPHANT'S
ELEPHANTS
ELF
ELF'S
ELICIT
ELIGIBLY
ELIZA
ELIZABETH
ELLIPSE
ELM
ELOQUENTLY
ELVES
ELYSIUM
EMACIATE
EMBARK
EMBARKED
EMBARRASSED
EMBARRASSES
EMBARRASSMENTS
EMBLEM
EMBLEMS
EMBODIED
EMBOLDEN
EMELINE
EMERALDS
EMERGED
EMERGES
EMIGRANT'S
EMIGRANTS
EMIGRATE
EMILY
EMINENTLY
EMIT
EMITS
EMPEROR'S
EMPERORS
EMPERY
EMPHASIZE
EMPHASIZED
EMPHATIC
EMPOWERED
EMPRESS
EMPTIED
ENACTING
ENACTS
ENAMEL
ENAMELED
ENAMELLED
ENAMORING
ENAMORS
ENCAMPING
ENCHANT
ENCHANTLESS
ENCLOSED
ENCOMIUM
ENCORES
ENCOUNTERED
ENCOUNTERING
ENCOURAGE
ENCOURAGEMENT
ENCOURAGES
ENCROACHED
ENDANGER
ENDANGERING
ENDEARMENT
ENDEARS
ENDEAVORS
ENDLESS
ENDORSE
ENDORSEMENT
ENDOWAL
ENDOWING
ENDUED
ENDURES
ENEMIES
ENEMY'S
ENERGY
ENFEEBLES
ENFOLDING
ENFOLDS
ENFORCE
ENFRANCHIZED
ENGAGE
ENGINERY
ENGLANDLY
ENGROSS
ENGULPH
ENHANCING
ENLARGE
ENLARGES
ENLARGING
ENLIST
ENMITY
ENO'
ENROLLED
ENSNARES
ENSUE
ENTAILED
ENTERTAINED
ENTERTAINING
ENTHRALLING
ENTITLES
ENTOMBER
ENTRANCING
ENTREAT
ENTREATED
ENTREATY
ENTRENCHED
ENTRUST
ENTRUSTED
ENVELOPES
ENVIES
ENVOY
EPICURES
EPIGEA
EPITAPH
EPOCH
EQUATION
EQUATOR
EQUILIBRIUM
EQUINOX
EQUIP
EQUIVALENT
ERASE
ERASING
ERECTS
ERRAND'S
ERRED
ERRORS
ESCAPADE
ESCORT
ESCORTED
ESCORTS
ESPIES
ESPOUSE
ESPOUSED
ESPOUSING
ESPY
ESSAY
ESTABLISH
ESTABLISHES
ESTEEMING
ESTIMABLE
ESTIMATING
ESTRANGING
ETCHINGS
ETERNITIES
ETHEREAL
ETHICS
ETHIOPIAN
ETIQUETTE
ETIQUETTES
ETNA
ETNA'S
EULOGY
EVANESCE
EVANGELISTS
EVENLY
EVENTIDE
EVENTS
EVENTUAL
EVENTUALLY
EVERGREENS
EVERYDAY
EVERYONE
EVE'S
EVES
EVIL
EVOKES
EVOLVED
EXACTLY
EXACTNESS
EXALT
EXALTED
EXALTS
EXAMPLE
EXASPERATE
EXCEEDING
EXCEEDS
EXCELLENTER
EXCELLING
EXCEPTING
EXCEPTION
EXCESSES
EXCHEQUER
EXCLAIM
EXCLUDE
EXCLUSION
EXCLUSIVELY
EXCURSION
EXECUTE
EXECUTIVE
EXECUTORS
EXEGESIS
EXEMPT
EXERCISE
EXERCISING
EXERT
EXERTION
EXHALED
EXHALES
EXHAUSTION
EXHIBITING
EXHIBITS
EXHILARATE
EXILES
EXISTENCE'S
EXISTENCES
EXISTING
EXODY
EXORBITANT
EXORCISED
EXPAND
EXPANDING
EXPECTANT
EXPEDITION
EXPENSE
EXPIATION
EXPIRES
EXPIRING
EXPLAIN
EXPLOIT
EXPLORING
EXPONENT
EXPORT
EXPOSED
EXPOSES
EXPOSITION
EXPOSITOR
EXPRESSION
EXTACIES
EXTEMPORANEOUS
EXTEMPORIZING
EXTEND
EXTENTS
EXTERIOR
EXTERMINATE
EXTERNALLY
EXTINCTION

1 (cont.)
EXTINCTION'S
EXTORTED
EXTRAVAGANCE
EXTREMELY
EXTREMER
EXTREMEST
EXTRINSIC
EXUBERANCE
EXUDE
EXULT
EXULTANT
EYELIDS
FABLE
FABLES
FACILITATE
FACING
FACTORIES
FADELESS
FAGOT
FAILEST
FAIN
FAINTED
FAINT-GOING
FAINTLY
FAIRLY
FAIRNESS
FALLEN
FALLIBLE
FALLOW
FALSEHOOD
FALTER
FALTERING
FAMELESS
FAMES
FAMILIARITIES
FAMISHED
FANCIED
FARE
FARED
FARMER'S
FARMING
FARNESS
FASCINATED
FASCINATES
FASCINATING
FASHIONING
FASHIONLESS
FASTENINGS
FASTIDIOUS
FASTNESS
FASTS
FATALLER
FATE'S
FATHER'D
FATHERS
FATHOMED
FATHOMING
FATIGUED
FATUITY
FATUUS
FAVORABLY
FAVORITES
FEALTY
FEBUARY'S
FEDERATES
FEEBLE
FEEBLEST
FEEBLY
FEEDING
FELLOWMEN
FELLOWSHIP
FELON
FERN
FEROCIOUS
FERRET
FERVENTLY
FERVOR
FERVOR'S
FERVORS
FESTAL
FESTIVAL
FETCHED
FETCHES
FETCHING
FETE
FEUDAL
FEVERED
FEWER
FICTION'S
FIEND
FIERCE
FIERCER
FIERCEST
FIFE
FIFE'S
FIFTEEN
FIFTH
FILES
FILLING
FINALLEST
FINANCIERS
FINGER'S
FINISHING
FINITENESS
FINITUDE
FINITY
FINLAND
FIRING
FIRMAMENT'S
FIRMNESS
FISH
FISHERMAN
FISHERMAN'S
FISSURE
FISSURES
FIST
FITNESS
FITTEST
FIVE
FIX
FLAGGED
FLAGON'S
FLAIL
FLAMBEAU
FLAMBEAUX
FLAME'S
FLAP
FLARE
FLASHING
FLATTENS
FLATTERED
FLAUNTED
FLAVORLESS
FLEEING
FLEES
FLEETER
FLEETING
FLEETS
FLESHLY
FLICKERED
FLICKERS
FLIGHTS
FLINCH
FLINGING
FLINTS
FLIPPANT
FLIRT
FLOODED
FLOODING
FLOORLESS
FLOORS
FLORA
FLOURISHING
FLOWED
FLOWING
FLOWS
FLUCTUATES
FLUCTUATION
FLUENTLY
FLURRIEDLY
FLUTE
FLUTTERS
FOLDED
FOLDS
FONDER
FONDEST
FONDLY
FOOD'S
FOOLISHER
FOOTLESS
FOP
FORCING
FORD
FOREBORE
FORECLOSED
FORECLOSING
FOREFATHERS
FOREFINGER
FOREIGNERS
FOREIGNHOOD
FORESHADOWED
FORESTALL
FORETOLD
FORGIVENESS
FORKED
FORMED
FORSWEARS
FORTHWITH
FORTIFIED
FORTUNATE
FORTUNE'S
FOUL
FOUNDER
FOUNDERED
FOUNDETH
FOUNDS
FOUNTAIN
FOURSCORE
FOURTH
FOXGLOVE'S
FRACTIONS
FRAGILE
FRAMES
FRANK
FREEDOM
FRENZIED
FRENZIES
FRENZY
FRESHER
FRESHEST
FRESHET
FRESHET'S
FRESHETS
FRET
FRETTED
FRIENDSHIP
FRIGATES
FRILLED
FRINGE
FRINGED
FRISK
FRITTERS
FROGS
FROLIC
FRONTING
FROWNS
FRUGALITY
FRUITLESSER
FULFILLING
FUMBLES
FUND
FUNNELED
FUNNY
FURL
FURLOUGHS
FURNISHES
FURROWED
FURZE
FUSCHZIA'S
FUSTIAN
FUTURES
FUZZY
GABRIEL'S
GABRIELS
GAD
GAG
GAIETY
GAINING
GALA
GALAXIES
GALLANTER
GALLANTLY
GALLERY
GAMBLERS
GAMBOGE
GAMBOLLED
GAMBRELS
GAME
GAMMUTS
GAP
GAPING
GARLAND
GARLANDS
GARMENTS
GARNER
GARRISONED
GARTER
GASH
GASPING
GATES
GATHERING
GATHERS
GAZED
GAZES
GEMS
GEM-TACTICS
GENERATE
GENERIC
GENESIS'
GENEVA'S
GENIAL
GENIUS
GENOA
GENTILE
GENTILITY
GENTLEFOLK
GENTLEST
GENTLEWOMEN
GENUINE
GEOMETRIC
GEOMETRY
GERANIUM
GERANIUMS
GERMINATION
GERM'S
GESSLER
GHENT
GIANTURE
GIBBETS
GIBRALTAR
GIBRALTAR'S
GIFTED
GIG
GIGANTIC
GIGGLE
GIGGLING
GIMBLETS
GIPSEY
GIPSY
GIRD
GIRDLE
GIRLHOOD'S
GIRL'S
GIRTH
GIVING
GLACIERS
GLADDENED
GLANCED
GLANCES
GLANCING
GLARE
GLASSES
GLAZES
GLEE'S
GLID
GLIMMER
GLIMMERS
GLISTENING
GLOBULES
GLOOM
GLORIA
GLORIES
GLORIFIED
GLORY'S
GLOSS
GLOVES
GLOWED
GLUTTON
GNASH

1 (cont.)
GNASHED
GNOMES
GOAD
GOADS
GOALLESS
GOALS
GOER
GOLCONDA
GOLDS
GOOD-BY
GOOD-BYE
GOODMORROW
GORED
GORSE
GOSSIPED
GOSSIPPED
GOTTEN
GOURMAND
GOVERNMENT
GOWNS
GRACIOUSLY
GRADUALLY
GRAIN
GRANDAME'S
GRANDER
GRANDFATHER
GRANDMAMA
GRANDSIRES
GRANITIC
GRAPE
GRAPHICER
GRAPPLE
GRAPPLED
GRAPPLES
GRAPPLING
GRASPLESS
GRATITUDE'S
GRAVITATES
GRAVITATIONS
GRAYEST
GRAZE
GREATNESS
GREATNESS'
GREED
GREEDINESS
GREENER
GREENWOOD
GRIEVE
GRIM
GRIMACE
GRIMED
GRIN
GRINNING
GRISLY
GROOM
GROPING
GROSS
GROUNDS
GRUMBLED
GUAGES
GUAGING
GUIDO
GUILLOTINE
GUILTLESS
GUITAR
GULFS
GULPHING
GURGLE
GUSHED
GUSHES
GUST
GUSTS
GYMNASIUM
GYMNASTIC
HABILIMENT
HABILIMENTS
HABITATION
HAGGARD
HAIRBREADTH
HAIR'S
HALLELUJAH
HALLELUJAHS
HALLUCINATION
HALVED
HAME
HAMMOCK'S
HANDSOME
HANGED
HAPPEN
HAPPENED
HAPPENS
HAPPILY
HARANGUER
HARDENED
HARE
HARK
HARKS
HARMLESS
HARMONY
HARMS
HARRIET
HARSH
HARVESTS
HASPS
HASTENING
HASTILY
HATEFUL
HAULED
HAVENS
HAVOC
HAWORTH
HAZARDOUS
HEADLANDS
HEALED
HEALTHY
HEAPED
HEARKENED
HEARS
HEARSE
HEARTED
HEARTIER
HEATHER
HECTIC
HEED
HEEDING
HEEL
HELMET
HELMSMAN
HEMLOCK'S
HEMPEN
HENCEFORWARD
HERB
HEREIN
HERES
HERESY
HERO
HEROINE
HERSCHEL'S
HESITATION
HESPERIAN
HESPERIDES
HIDETH
HIE
HIGHLAND
HILLOCKS
HILLSIDES
HINDERING
HINDERS
HINDRANCE
HINTED
HIP
HIRE
HISSED
HISSING
HIST
HISTORIES
HITHER
HIVE
HOE
HOISTS
HOLDING
HOLLAND
HOLLOW
HOLLOWS
HOMELESSNESS
HOMELIEST
HOMESICKNESS
HOMOGENEOUS
HONESTLY
HONEY'S
HONEYS
HONORLESS
HOOD
HOODED
HOODS
HOOKED
HOOTING
HOPELESSLY
HOPE'S
HOPPER
HORIZONTAL
HORNS
HORSEMAN
HORSEMEN
HOSTILER
HOST'S
HOTTEST
HOUNDS
HOUSEHOLDS
HOVER
HOVERS
HUBBUB
HUELESS
HUG
HUMBLED
HUMBLER
HUMBLES
HUMMED
HUMMING-BIRD
HUMORS
HUNCHED
HUNDREDS
HUNGERED
HUNGERS
HUNTER
HURLS
HURRIEDLY
HUSBAND
HUSHED
HUSK
HYBLA
HYPERBOLE
HYPERBOLIC
HYPHEN
HYPOTHESIS
ICES
IDEA
IDEALS
IDENTIFY
IDLY
IDOL'S
I. E.
IGNIS
IGNITE
IGNITED
IGNITION
ILLEGIBLE
ILLEGITIMATE
ILLNESS
ILLOCALITY
ILLUME
ILLUMINATION
ILLUMINE
ILLUMINES
ILLUSTRATION
IMAGERY
IMAGINATION
IMITATION
IMMATERIAL
IMMENSE
IMPALED
IMPANELLED
IMPART
IMPARTED
IMPARTS
IMPASSABLE
IMPEDE
IMPEDIMENT
IMPEDING
IMPELLED
IMPENDING
IMPERATIVE
IMPERATOR
IMPERCEPTIBLY
IMPERFECTLY
IMPERTINENCE
IMPERTINENTLY
IMPERVIOUS
IMPETUOUS
IMPLIES
IMPLORED
IMPLORING
IMPORTANT
IMPORTED
IMPORTUNATE
IMPORTUNES
IMPOSE
IMPOVERISH
IMPREGNABILITY
IMPRINTED
IMPROVING
IMPS
IMPUTE
INACTIVE
INADEQUATE
INADVERTENT
INANITION
INAUDIBLE
INCARCERATED
INCARCERATION
INCARNATE
INCAUTIOUS
INCIDENT
INCIDENTS
INCISIONS
INCISIVE
INCITE
INCIVILITY
INCLEMENT
INCLINE
INCLINED
INCLUDED
INCLUDING
INCOGNITO
INCONCEIVABLY
INCORPORATED
INCORPOREAL
INCREDIBLE
INCUR
INCURRED
INDEBTEDNESS
INDELIBLE
INDESTRUCTIBLE
INDIAMAN
INDICATES
INDICATING
INDICATIVE
INDIES
INDIGENCE
INDIGNANT
INDIGNATION
INDIGO
INDISCREET
INDOLENT
INDORSEMENT
INDUCED
INDUCES
INDURATED
INDUSTRIOUSNESS
INERTIA
INFANT
INFECTION
INFECTS
INFESTING
INFESTS
INFINITENESS
INFINITUDE
INFIRM
INFLATE
INFLATES
INFLECTION
INFLICTS
INFLUENCE
INFLUENCES
INFLUENTIAL
INFORMED
INFORMING
INFREQUENCY
INGREDIENT

1 (cont.)
INHABIT
INHABITANT
INHALE
INHALED
INHALES
INHERE
INHERED
INHERENTLY
INHERES
INHERITANCE
INHERITING
INHERITORS
INITIAL
INJURY
INLAND
INLANDS
INLETS
INMATES
INMOST
INNOMINATE
INNUENDOES
INNUTRITIOUS
INQUIRES
INQUIRY
INQUISITOR
INSANITY
INSCRIPTION
INSCRUTABLY
INSECT'S
INSECURITY
INSERT
INSERTING
INSIDE
INSIDIOUS
INSIGHT
INSINUATES
INSOLVENCY
INSPECTED
INSPECTION
INSPECTION'S
INSTABILITY
INSTANCE
INSTANCES
INSTANTLY
INSTIGATES
INSTIL
INSTINCTS
INSTITUTE
INSTITUTION
INSTRUCT
INSTRUCTING
INSULATORS
INSULTING
INSURANCE
INSURING
INTEGRAL
INTELLECTS
INTELLIGENCE
INTENDING
INTENSIFY
INTENTION
INTENTIONED
INTERCEDING
INTERCEPTING
INTERCEPTIVE
INTERCHANGE
INTEREST
INTERESTED
INTERESTS
INTERFERE
INTERLOCUTORS
INTERMIT
INTERMITTENT
INTERPOSED
INTERROGATE
INTERROGATES
INTERRUPTED
INTERRUPTION
INTERRUPTIONS
INTERSECT
INTERSPERSED
INTERSPERSION
INTERVENED
INTIMATES
INTONATIONS
INTOXICATE
INTOXICATED
INTRENCHMENT
INTRENCHMENTS
INTRICATE
INTRICATELY
INTRO
INTRODUCED
INTRODUCTION
INTRODUCTIONS
INTROSPECTIVE
INTRUSION
INTUITIONS
INUNDATE
INURED
INVADES
INVADING
INVALIDATE
INVENT
INVENTED
INVESTIGATED
INVESTIGATING
INVESTMENT'S
INVIGORATED
INVINCIBLY
INVIOLABLE
INVITATIONS
INVOKE
INVOLVED
INVOLVING
IRONIC
IRONS
IRONY
IRRESOLUTE
IRREVERENCE
IRREVERENCED
IRRITATED
ISHMAEL
ISLAND
ISOLATE
ISOLATION
ISRAEL'S
ISSUES
ITALICIZE
ITALICIZED
JADED
JAGGED
JAILS
JAMAICAS
JAMES
JARRED
JAWS
JAYS
JEALOUSIES
JEHOVAHS
JEOPARDIZE
JEOPARDY
JERUSALEM
JESSAMINE
JESSAMINES
JESUIT
JESUS'
JEWELS
JIB
JIG
JOCOSER
JOCUND
JOGGLING
JOINT
JOINTED
JOKE
JOLT
JORDAN
JOSTLE
JOSTLED
JOTS
JOURNEYING
JOURNEYS
JOVE
JOYOUS
JOY'S
JUDAS
JUGS
JUICES
JUICY
JULEP
JULEPS
JULIET
JUMBLED
JUMP
JUNCTION
JUPITER
JURY
JUSTIFYING
KEEL
KEENEST
KEEPING
KEEPSAKES
KENNEL
KEYLESS
KID
KIDDERMINSTER
KILLED
KILLS
KINDER
KINDLE
KINDS
KINGS
KINSMANLESS
KIRTLE
KISSING
KITCHEN
KITCHEN'D
KNEAD
KNEELED
KNEELS
KNELT
KNEWEST
KNIFE
KNITTING
KNOCKER
KNOTS
KNOW'ST
LABORETH
LABORING
LABORIOUS
LABORS
LACE
LACERATING
LACKED
LACONIC
LADDER
LADDER'S
LADDERS
LADS
LAKE
LAMBS
LAME
LANDING
LANDINGS
LANDLORDS
LANDSCAPES
LANGUID
LANGUOR
LANK
LAPLAND'S
LAPSED
LAPWING'S
LARK'S
LARKS
LASSITUDES
LASTED
LATHED
LATITUDELESS
LAUNCH
LAUNCHING
LAUREATE
LAUREATES
LAURELS
LAVISHED
LAWNS
LAZY
LEA
LEADEN
LEADER
LEADER'S
LEADING
LEAFLETS
LEAGUELESS
LEAK
LEAKAGE
LEAKED
LEAKING
LEANETH
LEANT
LEAPING
LEARNETH
LEARNS
LEARNT
LEASED
LEASES
LEDGE
LEDGES
LEGENDS
LEGIBLE
LEGISLATURE
LEGITIMATE
LEISURELY
LENGTHS
LENS
LENSES
LEONTODON
LEONTODON'S
LEOPARD'S
LEOPARDS
LETHARGIC
LETHE
LET'S
LETTER'S
LETTRES
LEVEL
LEVELED
LEVELLED
LEVER
LEXICONS
LEXINGTON
LIABLE
LIBATION
LIBERTY'S
LIBRARY
LICENSED
LICK
LICKED
LIEF
LIGHTEST
LIKENESS
LIKER
LIKING
LILACS
LIMBS
LIMITATIONS
LIMITED
LIMITLESS
LIMITS
LINCOLN
LINEAGE
LINGERS
LINNET
LIQUID
LISPING
LISPS
LISTENS
LITANIES
LITERATURE
LITHE
LITHEST
LITIGANTS
LITTERED
LITURGIES
LIVELONG
LIVERPOOL
LOAVES
LOCATIONS
LOCKED
LODGING
LOGIC
LOGICIAN
LOINS
LONG-CHEATED
LONGINGLY
LONGITUDE
LOOKETH
LOOSED
LORD'S

1 (cont.)
LORDS
LOSSES
LOSSES'
LOTH
LOTUS
LOUDER
LOVELINESS
LOVELY
LOVEST
LOWERED
LOWLIER
LOWLIEST
LOYALLY
LUCRATIVE
LULL
LULLED
LUNA
LUNACY
LUNG
LURE
LURES
LURK
LURKED
LURKS
LUSTRAL
LUSTRE
LUSTROUS
LUXURIES
LUXURIOUS
LYBIAN
MACHINERY
MADAM
MADONNAS
MAGICIANS
MAGNETIZE
MAGNIFIED
MAGNIFIES
MAIDENS
MAINTAINING
MAISE
MAIZE
MAKETH
MAK'ST
MALARIA
MAMA
MANACLES
MANCHESTER
MANDOLIN
MANGLED
MANGLES
MANIFEST
MANOR
MANSE
MANTEL'S
MANUFACTORING
MANY-COLORED
MANY'S
MANZANILLA
MAPLE'S
MAPLES
MAPPED
MARAUDER
MARAUDING
MARAUDS
MARBLES
MARCHED
MARITIME
MARKETS
MARL
MARQUIS
MARRIED
MARROWLESS
MARROWS
MARRY
MARSHALLING
MARSHALLINGS
MARYLAND
MASHED
MASHES
MASQUERADE
MASS
MASSACRES
MAST
MASTERED
MASTIFF
MATERIAL
MATES
MATINS
MATTRASS
MATTRESS
MATURED
MATURER
MATURING
MAUSOLEUM
MAYS
MAZARIN
MEAD
MEAGRES
MEAL
MEALS
MEANER
MEANEST
MEANING
MEASURELESS
MECHANICAL
MECHANICALLY
MEDDLED
MEDITATE
MEDITATION
MEDITATIVE
MEED
MEEKER
MEEKEST
MEEKLY
MEETS
MEETST
MEMBER
MEMENTO
MEMNON
MEM'RY
MENACED
MENACES
MENACING
MERCHANTMAN
MERCHANTMEN
MERCURY
MERCURY'S
MERCY'S
MERE
MEREST
MERINO
MERITED
MERMAIDS
MERRIER
MESMERIC
MESSENGERS
METAL
METTLE
MEXICO
MICROSCOPES
MICROSCOPIC
MIDGE
MIDNIGHTS
MIDST
MIGHTINESS
MILITANT
MILKING
MILLER
MILLINER
MILLINER'S
MILLIONAIRE
MILLS
MINER'S
MINE'S
MINGLE
MINIATURE
MINISTERED
MINNOWS
MINT
MINTS
MINUETS
MINUTES
MINUTIAE
MIRACLES
MIRACULOUS
MIRACULOUSLY
MIRAGE
MIRROR
MIRRORRS
MIRTH
MIS
MISCELLANEOUS
MISCONCEIVE
MISERABLE
MISER'S
MISERS
MISFORTUNE
MISGIVES
MISGIVING
MISINFER
MISSILE
MISSILES
MISSION
MISSIONARY
MISTAKING
MIST'S
MITRED
MITTENS
MOANED
MOANING
MOATS
MOCCASIN
MOCHAS
MOCK
MOCKING
MOCKS
MODE
MODERATE
MODERATELY
MODERN
MODESTIES
MODESTLY
MOLD-LIFE
MOLE
MOLESTED
MOLTEN
MOMENTLY
MONAD
MONEY
'MONG
MONSTER'S
MONTCALM
MOOD
MOONLESS
MOON'S
MOORINGS
MORALS
MORI
MORROW
MORSEL
MORTALS
MORTGAGED
MOSAIC
MOTE
MOTES
MOTIONED
MOTIONLESS
MOTIONS
MOTIVE
MOTTLES
MOULDER
MOULDERED
MOUND
MOUNT
MOUNTS
MOUTH'S
MOUTHS
MOVING
MOWER
MOWER'S
MOWERS
MOZART
MUD
MUFF
MUFFLE
MULTIFOLD
MULTIPLIED
MUMBLED
MUNDI
MUSCLES
MUSED
MUSES
MUSICIANS
MUSIC'S
MUSING
MUSLIN
MUTENESS
MUTINEER
MUTINY
MYRIAD
MYRIADS
MYRMIDONS
MYRRHS
MYSTERIES
MYTHS
NAMED
NAP
NAPOLEON
NARCOTIC
NARCOTICS
NARRATES
NARROWING
NARROWLY
NATURAL
NAUGHTY
NAZARENE
NAZARETH
NEARING
NEARLY
NEARS
NEBO
NECESSARY
NECKLACE
NECKLACES
NECROLOGY
NECROMANCER
NEEDING
NEEDY
NEGLECT
NEGLECTED
NEGLECTING
NEGOTIATE
NEGOTIATION
NEGRO
NEIGH
NEIGHBORHOOD
NEIGHING
NEIGHS
NERVOUS
NESCESSARY
NESTLED
NEUTRALIZED
NEVERMORE
NEW-FASHIONED
NEW-MAILED
NEWNESS
NEWS-BOYS
NIBBLE
NIBBLES
NICELY
NICKNAMED
NIGGARD
NIGHTINGALE
NINE
NOAH
NOBLENESS
NOD
NOISELESS
NOMINATED
NOMINATION
NONCHALANCE
NONCHALANT
NORMAL
NORSEMAN'S
NORWEGIAN
NOTABILITY
NOTCH
NOTCHING
NOTED
NOTELESSLY
NOTICES
NOTICING
NOTIFIED
NOWS
NULL
NULLIFIED
NULLIFY
NULLS
NUMBER

1 (cont.)
NUMBERED
NUMBER'S
NUMERAL
NUMERALS
NUMIDIAN
NUPTIAL
NURTURED
O'
OAK
OBDURATE
OBELISK
OBJECTION
OBJECTIVE
OBJECT'S
OBLIGATIONS
OBLIVIONS
OBLOQUIES
OBLOQUY
OBSCURES
OBSEQUIOUS
OBSERVING
OBSOLETE
OBSTRUCTS
OBTAINING
OBTRUDE
OBTUSER
OBVIATE
OCCIDENTAL
OCCUPANTS
OCCUPATION
OCCUPIES
OCCUPYING
OCCUR
OCCURS
OCEAN'S
OCTAVE'S
ODDEST
ODE
ODIOUSER
ODOR
ODORLESS
O'ERLOOKING
O'ERPOWERED
O'ERSPENT
O'ERTAKELESS
O'ERTOOK
OFFENSE
OFFERS
OFFICE
OFFICERS
OFTENTIMES
OGLE
OILS
OLDER
OMINOUS
OMNIFOLD
OMNIPOTENCE'
ONYX
OOZE
OOZED
OPAQUE
OPAQUEST
OPINIONS
OPPOSE
OPPOSITELY
OPPOSITES
OPPRESS
OPPRESSED
OPPRESSES
OPPROBRIUM
OPTIZAN
OPULENT
ORANGE
ORATOR
ORATORIO
ORBIT
ORCHIS'
ORDAIN
ORDINANCE
ORES
ORGAN
ORGANDY
ORGANIZED
ORIEL
ORIENT'S
ORIOLES
ORION
ORLEANS
ORNITHOLOGY
ORPHEUS'
OR'TER
OSTENSIBLE
OSTENTATION
OTTER'S
OUTCAST'S
OUTGLOW
OUTLASTS
OUTLETS
OUTLIVED
OUTRAGED
OUTSHOW
OUTSTARING
OUTVIE
OUTVISIONS
OUTWEIGHS
OVAL
OVENS
OVERBOLD
OVERCAME
OVERCOAT
OVERGROWN
OVERHEAR
OVERHEARD
OVERHEARS
OVERSETS
OVERSLEEP
OVERTAKEN
OVERTAKING
OVERTHROWN
OVERTOOK
OVERTURNED
OVERTURNS
OVERWHELMED
OWLS
OWNER'S
OWNEST
OWNS
PACES
PACKED
PAEANS
PAGEANTS
PAID'ST
PAIN'S
PAINT
PAINTERS
PAINTS
PAIRS
PALATES
PALER
PALLS
PALMLEAF
PALMS
PALPITATING
PAMPAS
PANES
PANGLESS
PANTHER
PANTOMIME
PANTRY
PAPA
PARADES
PARADISE'
PARADOX
PARAGON
PARAGRAPH
PARAGRAPHS
PARALLAX
PARALYZE
PARALYZED
PARALYZING
PARASITE
PARASOLS
PARD
PARDONED
PARIAN
PARIS
PARISHES
PARTAKEN
PARTAKING
PARTICLE
PARTICLES
PARTITIONS
PARTLY
PARTRIDGE
PASSENGERS
PASSIVER
PASTED
PAST'S
PATCHES
PATCHWORK
PATER
PATERNAL
PATIENCE'
PATIENTEST
PATRIARCH
PATRIARCH'S
PATRIOT
PATRIOTIC
PATRONS
PATTIE
PAUPER
PAUSELESS
PAUSES
PAYING
PAYS
PEA
PEACEFUL
PEACOCK
PEACOCK'S
PEAK
PEAL
PEARLY
PEASANTRY
PEAT
PECULIARLY
PEDANTIC
PEDDLER
PEDDLER'S
PEDESTRIAN
PEELS
PEEPED
PEERED
PEERING
PEERLESS
PEERS
PEG
PELF
PELLET
PELLETS
PELTETH
PENALTY
PENETRATE
PENIEL
PENINSULAR
PENNILESS
PENNINILESS
PENTATEUCHAL
PEOPLES
PER
PERCH
PERCHED
PERCHES
PERFECTEST
PERFIDIOUS
PERFORMED
PERIHELION
PERIL'S
PERIPHERY
PERIPHRASIS
PERISHES
PERMANENCE
PERMITS
PERMITTING
PERNICIOUS
PERPENDICULAR
PERPENDICULARS
PERPLEX
PERPLEXEDLY
PERPLEXITY
PERQUISITE
PERSERVERED
PERSIAN
PERSISTS
PERSONAL
PERSONALLY
PERSPICACITY
PERSUADING
PERSUASIVE
PERTURBATION
PERTURBED
PERTURBLESS
PERUKE
PERUSE
PERUSER
PERVADE
PERVADED
PERVADES
PERVERSE
PERVERSITY
PETITION
PETITION'S
PETTICOAT
PETTY
PHAETON
PHANTASMS
PHANTOMS
PHARAOH
PHARMACY
PHEBES
PHIALS
PHLEGMATIC
PHOSPHORIC
PHYSICIAN
PHYSICIAN'S
PIANOS
PICKING
PICTORIAL
PIECE
PIECED
PIECES
PIERCES
PIERLESS
PIGMY
PILES
PILFERED
PIN
PINCHED
PINCHING
PINKS
PINNACE
PINNACLE
PINNED
PIPPIN
PIROUETTE
PITTANCE
PITTANCES
PITYING
PIZARRO
PIZARRO'S
PLACARD
PLANET
PLANETARY
PLANET'S
PLANETS
PLANNED
PLANTED
PLANTS
PLASH
PLASHING
PLASHLESS
PLATES
PLATO
PLATOON
PLAUSIBLY
PLAYERS
PLAYETH
PLAYFELLOW
PLAYFUL
PLAYMATE
PLEADED
PLEADER
PLEADS
PLEASANTER
PLEASES
PLEASING
PLEASURES
PLEDGE

1 (cont.)
PLEIAD'S
PLEIADS
PLIANT
PLIED
PLOTS
PLOTTED
PLOTTING
PLOVER
PLUCKS
PLUG
PLUMBED
PLUMBING
PLUMMET
PLUMMETLESS
PLUMP
PLUMPER
PLUPOTENTIAL
PLUSHES
PLYING
POCKETS
PODS
POESY
POET'S
POIGNANCY
POIGNANT
POINARDS
POINTED
POISING
POLES
POLITENESS
POLLUTES
POLTROON
POMPADOUR
POMPEII
POMPLESS
POMPOUSLY
POMPS
PONDERING
PONDERS
PONTOON
POPE
POPOCATAPEL
POPPY
POPULAR
POPULATES
POPULOUS
PORE
PORED
PORTABLE
PORTENTOUSLY
PORTICO
PORTLY
PORTRAITS
PORTRAY
PORTS
POSITIVELY
POSSESSETH
POSSESSIONS
POSSIBLER
POSSIBLE'S
POST
POSTPONELESS
POSTULATE
POSTULATED
POTOMAC
POUNCE
POUR
POWDER
POWDERED
POWDERS
POWERFUL
PRACTICES
PRACTICING
PRACTISING
PRAIRIE
PRAIRIES
PRAISED
PRAISES
PRAISING
PRANCING
PRANKS
PRATER
PRATTLE
PRAYERS
PRAYING
PREACHED
PREACHES
PREAPPOINTED
PRECEDES
PRECEPT
PRECEPTOR
PRECINCTS
PRECISER
PRECONCERTED
PREDICTED
PREFACE
PREFACES
PREFERMENT
PRELIMINARY
PREMATURE
PREMISES
PREPARATION
PREROGATIVE
PRESBYTERIAN
PRESENTED
PRESENTIMENT
PRESENTING
PRESERVED
PREST
PRESUMES
PRETENSE
PREVAILING
PREVAILS
PREVALENT
PREVENTED
PREVISION
PRICK
PRICKLED
PRICKLIER
PRICKLY
PRICKS
PRIED
PRIESTS
PRIG
PRIMA
PRIMEVAL
PRIMOGENITURE
PRIMROSE
PRINCES
PRINTED
PRISONER
PRISONS
PRIVATELY
PROBABILITY
PROBABLE
PROBABLY
PROBING
PROBLEMS
PROCESSIONS
PROCLAIMING
PROCLAMATION
PROCURE
PROCURED
PROCURING
PRODIGIOUS
PRODUCE
PROFANE
PROFFERED
PROFOUNDER
PROGENITOR
PROGNOSTICA-
TION
PROGRAMME
PROGRESS'
PROGRESSIVE
PROJECTED
PROMETHEUS
PROMOTE
PROMOTED
PROMPTED
PROMPTNESS
PRONOUN
PRONOUNCE
PROOF'S
PROPAGATES
PROPENSITY
PROPER
PROPERTIES
PROPHETIC
PROPITIATION'S
PROPITIOUS
PROPORTION
PROPOSITION
PROPOUNDETH
PROPRIETY
PROSAIC
PROSPECT'S
PROSY
PROTECT
PROTECTED
PROTECTION
PROTECTS
PROTRUDING
PROUDER
PROVIDE
PROVIDENCE
PROVINCIAL
PROVINCIALLY
PROVING
PROVOKES
PROVOKING
PROWESS
PROWLING
PRUDENCE
PRUDENTLY
PSALTERIES
PUBLICATION
PUBLISH
PUBLISHED
PUCK'S
PULLED
PULPY
PULSE
PUNCTUALITY
PUNCTUATE
PUNCTUATION
PUNISHMENT
PUPPET
PURCHASE
PURCHASED
PURCHASING
PUREST
PURLED
PURPOSELESS
PURRS
PURSE
PUTTETH
PUZZLE
PUZZLES
PUZZLEST
PYRAMIDAL
PYRAMIDS
PYRITES
PYRRHENEES
QUAFFING
QUAILED
QUAKE
QUAKED
QUARTER
QUARTERING
QUEEN'S
QUENCH
QUENCHED
QUENCHING
QUESTIONING
QUIBBLE
QUIBBLED
QUICKENING
QUICKER
QUICKEST
QUIETER
QUIETNESS
QUIT
QUIVER
QUIVERS
QUOTH
RABBI
RACKED
RACKET
RAFFLE
RAFT
RAFTERS
RAGS
RALLYING
RAMBLE
RAMBLED
RAMBLES
RAMPANT
RANGE
RANGES
RANKS
RANSACK
RANSOM
RAP
RAPIDS
RAPS
RASCALITY
RASHNESS
RATES
RATTLES
RAVAGE
RAVELLING
RAVES
RAVINE
RAY
RAYS
READINESS
READING
READS
REAPERS
REAP'ST
REARED
REARRANGE
REARS
REASONABLE
REBECCA
REBELLED
REBELS
REBUILT
REBUKE
REBUKED
RECALL
RECALLLESS
RECANT
RECEDE
RECEDED
RECEDES
RECEIVING
RECEPTACLE
RECEPTION
RECIEVED
RECITED
RECKONED
RECKONS
RECOGNIZING
RECOLLECTION'S
RECOLLECTS
RECORDING
RECORDS
RECOUNTING
RECOVER
RECOVERED
RECOVERER
RECTIFIED
RECUSANCE
REDDEN
REDDEST
REDECKED
REDEEMED
REDEEMER'S
REDIGNIFIED
REDOUBLED
REDOUBTABLEST
REDRESS
REDS
REDUCED
REDUCELESS
REDUCES
REED
REEF
REEFS
REEL
REELS
RE-ENDURE
REFER
REFERS
REFINED
REFINING
REFLECTION

1 (cont.)
REFLEX
REFORMED
REFORMS
REFRACTED
REFRAINS
REFRESH
REFUGEE
REFUTES
REGALE
REGALING
REGARDLESS
REGIMENT
REGISTER
REGISTERED
REGULATE
REGULATES
REIMBURSE
REIMBURSED
REINDEER
REINFORCED
REINING
REJECT
REJECTS
REJOICES
REKINDLED
REKNOWN
RELATION
RELATIONS
RELEGATES
RELENT
RELIEVES
RELIGIOUS
RELINQUISHED
RELISHED
RELISHES
REMAINETH
REMAND
REMEDILESSLY
REMINDS
REMISS
REMITS
REMITTED
REMNANT
REMOTELY
REMOTENESS
REMOVES
RENDEZVOUS
RENEGADE
RENEWING
RENOUNCE
RENOUNCHED
RENOVATES
RENTS
REORGANIZES
REPAIRING
REPAIRS
REPEALED
REPEALING
REPELS
REPENTANCE
REPITITION
REPLACING
REPLENISH
REPLENISHED
REPLEVYS
REPLIES
REPLYING
REPORTER
REPOSED
REPREHEND
REPREIVE
REPRESENTATIVE
REPRESSED
REPRIEVES
REPRIEVING
REPRIMAND
REPRODUCE
REPRODUCED
REPUBLIC
REPUGNANT
REPUGNANTLY
REPULSE
REQUIRE
REQUIRED
REQUIREMENT
REQUIREMENTS
REQUIRING
REQUISITION
RE-ROYALIZED
RESCUED
RESEARCH
RESEMBLES
RESENT
RESENTS
RESERVATION
RESERVOIR
RESIDE
RESIDENCES
RESIDING
RESISTLESS
RESITUATED
RESOLUTE
RESOLUTER
RESOURCE
RESOWN
RESPECT
RESPITES
RESPLENDENT
RESPONSIBLE
RESPONSIVE
RESTING
RESTITUTES
RESTITUTION
RESTRAINING
RESTS
RESUMES
RESURGAM
RESURRECTIONS
RETARD
RETARDED
RETARDS
RETINA
RETIRES
RETRACT
RETRIEVE
RETRIEVER
RETRIEVES
RETRIMMED
RETROSPECTS
REVEILLE
REVENGE
REVENUES
REVERBERATION
REVERED
REVERENT
REVERTED
REVIEWED
REVIEWING
REVIEWS
REVIVE
REVOLTING
REVOLVER
REWALKS
REWARDED
RHINOCEROS
RHODODENDRON
RHODORA'S
RHYME
RHYMES
RHYTHM
RHYTHMIC
RIBBON'S
RIBIN
RIBS
RICHARD
RID
RIGHTEOUS
RIGHTEOUSNESS
RIGID
RIGOR
RINGED
RINGING
RINGLET
RINGS
RIPEN
RIPENESS
RIPENINGS
RIPEST
RIPPLE
RIPPLES
RISEN
RISKS
RITARDANDO
RITE
RITES
RITUAL
RIVAL
RIVETS
ROAMING
ROAMS
ROARING
ROASTED
ROBBER'D
ROBBERIES
ROBBING
ROBS
ROBUST
ROCKING
ROCKS
ROD
ROE
ROGUES
ROI
ROMEO
ROOFS
ROSEMARY
ROSIER
ROUGE
ROUGHEST
ROUNDER
ROUSE
ROUTINE
ROWDY
ROWED
ROWER
RUB
RUBBED
RUBBERS
RUBY'S
RUDIMENTS
RUFF
RUFFLE
RUFFLED
RUFFLES
RUGGED
RULER
RULES
RUM
RUMBLE
RUMBLES
RUMORED
RUNE
RUPTURE
RURAL
RUSSETLY
RUSSIAN
RUST
RUSTICS
RUSTLE
RUSTLING
RUSTY
RUT
SABACTHINI
SABLE
SABRE
SABRES
SACKCLOTH
SACRAMENTAL
SACRIFICIAL
SADDENED
SADDEST
SADLY
SADNESS
SAFEST
SAFETY
SAFFRON
SAGEST
SAILING
SAILOR'S
SAINTED
SAINTS'
SAITH
SALE
SALES
SALLOW
SALUBRIOUS
SALUTES
SALUTING
SALVATION
SANCTIFIES
SANCTIFYING
SANCTION
SANDAL
SANTA
SAP
SAPLING
SAPPED
SAPPHO
SARAH
SATAN
SATIRIST
SATISFACTION
SATURATED
SATURN'S
SATYR'S
SATYRS
SAVAN
SAVING
SAVIOR'S
SAVIORS
SAVORS
SAWING
SAXON
SCALDING
SCALED
SCANNING
SCANS
SCANTLY
'SCAPE
'SCAPING
SCARCER
SCARCITY
SCARLETS
SCATHING
SCENES
SCENTS
SCEPTIC
SCEPTRE
SCHEME
SCHEMING
SCHISM
SCHOLAR
SCHOLASTIC
SCHOOLMATES
SCHOOLROOM
SCIENTIST
SCIMITAR
SCION
SCOOPING
SCOPE
SCORNING
SCOURGE
SCOUTS
SCOWLED
SCRABBLE
SCREAMED
SCREAMS
SCREEN
SCREENS
SCREW
SCREWS
SCRUTABLE
SCUTCHEON
SCUTTLE
SCYTHE
SEALS
SEAR
SEARCHED
SEARCHES
SEARS
SEASHORE
SEASON'S
SEATED
SECEDED
SECESSION
SECONDARY
SECRETING
SECTION
SECURELY

1 (cont.)
SECURER
SEDGE
SEDITIOUS
SEDUCE
SEDUCTIVE
SEDULOUS
SEESAW
SEESAWING
SEGMENT
SELDOMLY
SELECTLY
SELECTS
SELLER'S
SELLS
SELVES
SENDING
SENTENCES
SENTIMENT
SENTINELS
SEPAL
SEPARATED
SEPARATING
SEPARATION
SEPTEMBER'S
SEPULTURE
SEQUEL
SERAPH'S
SERFS
SERPENT
SERPENT'S
SERVILE
SESSIONS
SETTEST
SETTLE
SETTLEMENT
SETTLERS
SETTLES
SEVENTEENTH
SEVENTY
SEVERALLY
SEVERELY
SEVEREST
SEVERITY
SEVRES
SEWED
SEWING
SHACKLES
SHADY
SHAFTS
SHAGGIER
SHAKESPEARE
SHAMELESS
SHAMES
SHANTIES
SHAPED
SHARES
SHATTERED
SHAVEN
SHAW
SHEAVES
SHE'D
SHEETS
SHELLS
SHELVES
SHEPHERD'S
SHERRY
SHEWN
SHIELD
SHIFTING
SHINES
SHIVERED
SHIVERERS
SHIVERING
SHOAL
SHOALS
SHOCK
SHOOT
SHOPMAN
SHOPS
SHORED
SHORTENED
SHOULDERS
SHOUTED
SHOUTING
SHOVED
SHOWER
SHOWETH
SHOWMAN
SHOW'S
SHREWDLY
SHROUDED
SHRUB
SHUNNING
SHUNS
SHUTTER
SHYLOCK
SICKER
SIEVES
SIFT
SIFTS
SIGHTED
SIGHTLESS
SIGHT'S
SIGHTS
SIGNALS
SIGNIFICANT
SIGNIFYING
SILAS
SILENCED
SILENTER
SILKEN
SILLS
SILLY
SIMILITUDE
SIMPLE-HEARTED
SIMPLEST
SIMPLIFIED
SIMULTANEOUSLY
SINCERER
SINISTER
SINKS
SINS
SIPPED
SIPS
SIROCCOS
SISTERS
SITELESS
SITES
SITUATE
SITUATED
SITUATIONS
SIXPENCE
SKATER'S
SKATERS
SKEPTIC
SKEPTICISM
SKILFUL
SKILLFUL
SKIM
SKIPPED
SKIPPER
SKIRMISH
SKIRTED
SKIRTING
SKIRTS
SLACKED
SLACKENS
SLACKER
SLAM
SLANTED
SLANTING
SLANTS
SLASH
SLASHING
SLEDS
SLEEK
SLEEVE
SLEIGH
SLICE
SLIDE
SLIDES
SLIGHTEST
SLIGHTLY
SLILY
SLIPPER
SLIPPERS
SLIPT
SLIVER
SLOOP
SLOWNESS
SLUICE
SLUMBER
SLUMBERETH
SLUMBERING
SLUNK
SLY
SMARTNESS
SMIT
SMITES
SMOKED
SMOOTHED
SNAKE'S
SNAPT
SNARE
SNATCHES
SNOW'S
SNOWY
SNUGLY
SOARED
SOARS
SOB
SOBBED
SOBBING
SOBERER
SOBERLY
SOBRIETY
SOCIALLY
SOCKET
SOCKETS
SOE'ER
SOEVER
SOFTENED
SOLACED
SOLACES
SOLDER
SOLDIER
SOLELY
SOLEMNER
SOLEMNITY
SOLEMNIZES
SOLEMNLY
SOLIDITIES
SOLO
SOMEBODY'S
SOMETHING'S
SOOTHED
SOOTY
SOPHOCLES
SOREST
SORROWFUL
SOTO
SOUNDEST
SOUNDING
SOURCE
SOUTHERN
SOVREIGN'S
SOVREIGNS
SOVREIGNTIES
SOWER
SPACE'S
SPACES
SPACIOUSLY
SPANGLES
SPANIEL
SPANS
SPARKLES
SPARKLING
SPARROW'S
SPARTAN
SPEAR
SPECIFICAL
SPECIMENS
SPECIOUS
SPECKS
SPECTACLES
SPECTRAL
SPECULATED
SPECULATION'S
SPEEDILY
SPELLED
SPENDS
SPERM
SPHERIC
SPICELESS
SPICE'S
SPICIEST
SPIES
SPIGOT
SPIKENARDS
SPILLED
SPILLS
SPILT
SPINNING
SPINS
SPIRIT'S
SPIRITUAL
SPLASHING
SPLENDOR
SPLENDORS
SPLINTER
SPLINTERED
SPOIL
SPOILER
SPONGES
SPONTANEITY
SPOON
SPORT
SPORTSMAN
SPORTSMAN'S
SPOTLESS
SPOTS
SPRAY
SPREADING
SPRIG
SPRIGHTLY
SPRINKLED
SPRINKLES
SPRITE
SPROUT
SPRY
SPUR
SPURNING
SQUANDER
SQUANDERED
SQUANDERING
SQUANDERS
SQUARELY
SQUIRREL'S
STABBED
STABILITY
STABLE
STACK
STAG
STAGINGS
STAGNANT
STAINED
STAIRS
STAKING
STALLS
STAMENS
STAMMERED
STAMP
STANCH
STANCHED
STANDARD
STANZAS
STAPLE
STARED
STARK
STARKEST
STARLESS
STARTLE
STATEMENTS
STATESMAN'S
STATLIER
STATURED
STATURES
STATUS
STATUTE
STATUTES
STAUNCH
STEADFASTNESS
STEALING
STEALTH'S

1 (cont.)
STEAM
STEED
STEEL'S
STEEPEST
STEEPLE'S
STEERSMAN
STEMLESS
STEPHEN
STERILITY
STERLING
STERNEST
STERNLY
STICKS
STIFFEN
STIFFLY
STIFFNESS
STIFLED
STIGMA
STILLEST
STILLS
STIMULANTS
STIMULATED
STINGING
STINGS
STINTLESS
STIPULUS
STIRREST
STIRRINGS
STOCKINGS
STOCK'S
STOLEN
STOOPS
STOP-SENSATION
STORES
STORMY
STOUT
STOUTER
STOW
STRAGGLED
STRAINED
STRAIT
STRAITS
STRANDS
STRANGER'D
STRAPPED
STRATA
STRATEGEM
STRATEGIST
STRAW
STRAWBERRIES
STRAYING
STRAYS
STREAKS
STREAM
STREAMS
STRENGTHENING
STRENGTHENS
STRESS
STRETCHED
STREWS
STRICTER
STRICTEST
STRIPE
STRIPPED
STRIVEN
STRIVING
STROKED
STROKES
STROKING
STROLLING
STRONGER
STRUNG
STUBBLE'S
STUBBORN
STUFF
STUMP
STUNG
STUPIDITY
STYLES
SUBDIVIDE
SUBDUE
SUBDUED
SUBDUING
SUBJECTED
SUBJECTION
SUBJUGATE
SUBJUGATED
SUBJUGATING
SUBJUNCTIVE
SUBLIMELY
SUBLIMEST
SUBMERGED
SUBMERGES
SUBMIT
SUBMITTING
SUBORDINATE
SUBSCRIBE
SUBSEQUENTLY
SUBSIDES
SUBSIDING
SUBSIDY
SUBSTANCES
SUBSTANTIATE
SUBSTANTIATES
SUBSTITUTE
SUBTERFUGE
SUBTRACT
SUBTRACTING
SUBTRACTION
SUBURB
SUBURBS
SUCCEEDING
SUCCESSOR
SUFFERER
SUFFICED
SUFFICES
SUFFICETH
SUFFICIENCY
SUFFICIENTLY
SUFFICING
SUFFUSE
SUFFUSED
SUFFUSES
SUGGEST
SUITABLE
SULKED
SULLEN
SULLIED
SULPHURETS
SUMMERTIME
SUMMIT
SUMMITS
SUMPTUOUSNESS
SUNBURNED
SUNBURNT
SUNRISE'
SUNSET'S
SUPERB
SUPERFICIES
SUPERFINE
SUPERHUMAN
SUPERIORITY
SUPERLATIVE
SUPERSEDES
SUPERSTITION
SUPERSTITIOUS
SUPPLANTED
SUPPLANTING
SUPPLEMENTS
SUPPLEST
SUPPLICATING
SUPPLIES
SUPPORT
SUPPORTING
SUPPRESS
SUPPRESSED
SURCINGLES
SURETIES
SURETY
SURFEIT
SURGE
SURMISED
SURPASSED
SURRENDERING
SURREPTITIOUSLY
SURROGATE
SURROUNDED
SURVEY
SURVEYING
SURVIVING
SUSCEPTIVE
SUSPEND
SUSPENDS
SUSPENSE'S
SUSPICIOUS
SUSTAINS
SWAGGER
SWAIN
SWALLOWED
SWALLOWS
SWAMP
SWAMPS
SWANG
SWARM
SWAY
SWAYS
SWERVED
SWERVELESS
SWERVES
SWIFTLY
SWIFTNESS
SWIMMERS
SWINDLED
SWINDLERS
SWISS
SWOLLEN
SYLLABLE-LESS
SYMPTOMS
SYNDICATE
SYNODS
SYNONYME
SYNTAX
SYNTHESIS
SYSTEM
TABLEAU
TABLE'S
TACTICS
TAIL
TAILOR
TAINTS
TALELESS
TALISMANIC
TALKS
TALLEST
TANGIBLE
TANKARD
TANTALIZE
TANTALIZING
TANTAMOUNT
TAPER
TAPESTRY
TAR
TARNISHED
TARRIED
TARRYING
TASTELESS
TASTING
TATTERS
TAUNTED
TAUNTING
TAUNTS
TAWDRY
TEAM
TEASE
TEAZES
TELEGRAM
TELEGRAMS
TELEGRAPHIC
TELESCOPE
TELESCOPES
TELESCOPIC
TELLER
TELLER'S
TEMPER
TEMPESTS
TEMPLES
TEMPTATION'S
TEMPTED
TENANTLESS
TEND
TENDENCY
TENDS
TENEMENT
TENERIFFE'S
TENETS
TENS
TENTACLES
TENURE
TERMINABLE
TERMINATES
TERMINUS
TERRESTIAL
TERRITORIES
TERROR'S
TESTAMENT
TESTED
TETHERED
TEXT
THANKFUL
THANKS
THEATRE
THEATRICALS
THEFTS
THEOLOGY
THEORIES
THEREAFTER
THEREAT
THEREFROM
THEREIN
THERMOPYLAE
THESES
THESSALY
THEW
THEWS
THICKEST
THIGH
THIN
THIRSTED
THIRSTING
THITHER
THOMSON'S
THORNS
THO'T
THOUGHTFULNESS
THOU'RT
THOUSANDS
THREADED
THREADING
THREADLESS
THREADS
THREATEN
THREATENING
THREESCORE
THRENODIES
THRESHOLD
THRICE
THRIFTY
THRILLED
THRILLS
THRIVES
THRIVING
THROATS
THRONGING
THRUM
THUMB
THUNDERBOLT
THUNDERING
THUNDER'S
THUNDERS
THWARTED
TIARAS
TICKET
TICKING
TIDE'S
TIDY
TIER
TIGHTENING
TIGHTENS
TILLAGE
TILLED
TILTS
TIMBERS
TIMBRELS
TIMBUCTOO
TIMIDITY
TIMIDNESS
TINCTURE

1 (cont.)
TINCTURED
TINGE
TINTING
TINTS
TIPPED
TIPPLER
TIPS
TIPTOED
TIRE
TISSUE
TISSUES
TITIAN
TOAD
TOADS
TOBY'S
TODAY'S
TODDLED
TOE
TOILING
TOILSOME
TOLERATES
TOMES
TO-MORROW
TONGUELESS
TONIC
TOPOGRAPHY
TORRENTS
TORTOISE
TORTURE
TOSSES
TOSSING
TOTALLER
TOTALNESS
TOTTERED
TOTTERS
TOURIST
TOWERING
TOYED
TOYS
TRACING
TRACKLESS
TRACTS
TRADITION'S
TRADITIONS
TRAFFIC
TRAFFICKING
TRAGIC
TRAILING
TRAINED
TRAITS
TRAMPLED
TRANQUILITY
TRANQUILLER
TRANQUILLY
TRANS
TRANSATLANTIC
TRANSCENDENTAL
TRANSCENDING
TRANSFER
TRANSFUSE
TRANSGRESSION
TRANSITIONS
TRANSLATED
TRANSLATION
TRANSMIGRATION
TRANSMUTED
TRANSPIRING
TRANSPLANTED
TRAVELER
TRAVELING
TRAVELLER'S
TRAVERSING
TREATED
TREATISE
TREBLE
TREMBLINGLY
TREMENDOUSNESS
TREMULOUS
TRENCH
TREPIDATION
TRI
TRIBULATION
TRIBUNAL
TRIGGER
TRILLED
TRILLION
TRIP
TRIPLETS
TRIPPED
TRIPPING
TRIUMPHS
TROOPS
TROTWOOD
TROUBLES
TROUBLING
TROUGH
TROUGHS
TROUPE
TROWSERS
TRUER
TRUEST
TRUFFLED
TRULY
TRUNDLE
TRUSTED
TRUSTING
TRUSTS
TRUTH'S
TUBES
TUCKING
TUCKS
TUFTS
TUGGING
TUGS
TUMBLED
TUMBLES
TUNING
TUNIS
TURBANED
TURBID
TURBULENT
TURK
TURNPIKE
TURTLE
TUSCARORA
TWIRLED
TWISTS
TWITCHED
TWITCHING
TWITTER
TWO-FOLD
TYPIFY
TYRANNIES
ULTERIOR
ULTIMATES
UMBRELLA
UMBRELLA'S
UMPIRE
UNABATED
UNACCUSTOMED
UNACKNOWL-
EDGED
UNADORNED
UNAFRAID
UNAIDED
UNALTERED
UNANSWERING
UNAPPROACHED
UNATTEMPTED
UNAVAILABLE
UNAVAILING
UNAVOIDABLE
UNBARED
UNBEREFT
UNBLUSHINGLY
UNBORN
UNBRAIDING
UNCERTAINTY
UNCERTIFIED
UNCHALLENGED
UNCHANGED
UNCLAIMED
UNCLINCH
UNCOMELY
UNCOMMON
UNCONCERN
UNCONJECTURED
UNCONSPICUOUS
UNCOVERED
UNDECAYING
UNDEFEATED
UNDEPICTED
UNDERLIE
UNDERMINE
UNDERMINED
UNDERMINING
UNDERSTANDING
UNDERTAKE
UNDERTAKING
UNDESERVED
UNDISTINGUISHED
UNDIVERTED
UNDOUBTEDLY
UNDRAINED
UNDRESS
UNDRESSED
UNDUE
UNDULATING
UNELECTED
UNENFORCED
UNERUDITE
UNEVEN
UNEXPECTEDLY
UNFADING
UNFAIR
UNFORESEEN
UNFULFILLED
UNGAINED
UNGRACIOUS
UNGRASPED
UNHELPED
UNHOOK
UNHOOKED
UNIFORMS
UNIMPEACHABLE
UNINTENDING
UNITE
UNITS
UNITY
UNJADED
UNKNIT
UNKNOT
UNKNOWING
UNKNOWNS
UNLADEN
UNLIKE
UNMANIFEST
UNMEANING
UNMENTIONED
UNNESCESSARY
UNOBSERVED
UNOBTAINED
UNOPENED
UNPAID
UNPERVERTED
UNPLAUSIBLE
UNPREPARED
UNPRETENDING
UNPRETENSION
UNPROVED
UNPUZZLED
UNQUESTIONABLY
UNREALITY
UNREALIZED
UNRECORDED
UNRELIEVED
UNRELUCTANTLY
UNREMEMBERED
UNREPORTED
UNREVEALED
UNROLL
UNROLLS
UNSANCTIFIED
UNSCRUTINIZED
UNSHADED
UNSHARED
UNSHRIVEN
UNSOWN
UNSPEAKABLE
UNSPOKEN
UNSTEADY
UNSULLIED
UNSUMMONED
UNSURMISED
UNSUSPENDED
UNSUSPICIOUS
UNTARNISHED
UNTENABLE
UNTIED
UNTIES
UN TO
UNTOWARD
UNTRAVELLED
UNTRAVERSED
UNTUMBLED
UNTWIST
UNUSED
UNVEIL
UNVISITED
UNWHOLE
UNWILLING
UNWIND
UNWITNESSED
UPBORNE
UPBRAIDS
UPLIFTS
UPRIGHT
UPSET
URCHIN'S
URGENCY
URGENT
URGING
USES
USHERED
USHERS
USUAL
USURPED
UTTEREST
UTTERS
VACILLATING
VACUUM
VAGABOND
VAGRANT
VAINER
VALE
VALID
VALOR
VALUED
VANDYKES
VANE'S
VANISHES
VANQUISH
VANS
VARIES
VARIETY
VASCILLATING
VASSAL
VASTLY
VASTNESS
VAT
VATICAN
VATS
VAULTED
VEGETATION'S
VEHEMENCE
VEHICLES
VEIL
VELLUM
VENDED
VENERATE
VENETIAN
VENGEANCE
VENI
VENICE
VENOMS
VERA
VERB
VERDURE
VERGE
VERILY
VERMIN'S
VERRIERE
VESPERS
VESSEL
VESTMENTS
VESTS
VESUVIAN
VESUVIUS
VETO

1 (cont.)
VEXT
VIAND
VIANDS
VIBRATING
VIBRATIONS
VICARIOUS
VICARIOUSLY
VICI
VICIOUS
VICISSITUDE
VICTIM
VICTOR
VICTORS
VIDI
VIEWS
VIGILANCE
VIGOROUS
VILIFY
VINDICATE
VINE
VINEYARD
VIOLATE
VISITERS
VISITING
VISITS
VITALIZE
VITALIZES
VITALLESS
VITALLEST
VITALLY
VITALS
VIVAMUS
VIVE
VIVIDER
VIVIMUS
VOCAL
VOLUMES
VOTED
VOUCHES
VULGAR
WADES
WADING
WAGGONS
WAGS
WAINSCOT
WAKELESSNESS
WAKENS
WAKING'S
WALTZED
WAMPUM
WANDERINGS
WANED
WANES
WANING
WANTING
WANTON
WANTONED
WARBLED
WARBLING
WARES
WARMED
WARMER
WARMS
WARP
WARRANTED
WARRANTS
WARRIOR
WARS
WARY
WASHES
WASTED
WATCHER
WATCHERS
WATER'S
WAVED
WAVERING
WAVES
WAXING
WAYLAID
WAYWARD
WAYWARDEST
WEALTHIER
WEALTHILY
WEALTHS
WEARIEST
WEAVES
WEB
WE'D
WEDDING
WEDGE
WEEDS
WEEKS
WEEPING
WEIGHETH
WEIGHS
WEIGHTIEST
WELCOMES
WELD
WENDING
WENDS
WEPT
WESTERLY
WESTERN
WEST-INDIAN
WESTMINSTER
WESTS
WESTWARD
WET
WE'VE
WHEELING
WHELMED
WHENCE
WHEREIN
WHEREON
WHERESOE'ER
WHETS
WHETTING
WHIFFLETREE
WHIMPERED
WHIMPERING
WHIMPERS
WHINING
WHIP'S
WHIRLS
WHIRR
WHISPERED
WHIST
WHISTLING
WHITES
WHITHER
WHITTLES
WHIZZING
WHOLESOME
WIDEN
WIDE-WANDERING
WIFEHOOD
WIFE'S
WILDER
WILE
WILLIAM
WILLS
WILT
WINCE
WINCED
WINCES
WINDING
WIND'S
WINDY
WINK
WINKED
WINNOW
WINNOWED
WINS
WINTERWORN
WIPE
WIPING
WISDOMS
WISENESS
WISHING
WITHERED
WITHES
WITHOLDEN
WITHOLDING
WITHSTAND
WITHSTANDS
WITNESSING
WIVES
WOE'S
WOLF
WOOED
WOOS
WORDLESS
WORKMAN
WORKMANSHIPS
WORKMEN
WORKS
WORSE
WORSHIPPED
WORSHIPPING
WORSTED
WORTHIER
WORTHIEST
WORTHILY
WORTHLESSNESS
WOUNDED
WOVEN
WRATH
WRECKETH
WRECKS
WRENCH
WRENCHED
WRENCHING
WREN'S
WREST
WRESTLERS
WRESTLING
WRETCHED
WRINKLES
WRISTS
WRIT
WRITER
WRITING
WRITTEN
YACHT
YARN
YAWN
YAWNING
YCLEPT
YEARNS
YESTERDAY'S
YESTERDAYS
YESTERMORN
YIELDED
YIELDETH
YIELDING
YIELDS
YORKSHIRE
ZENITH
ZENZIBAR
ZEROES
ZIGZAG
ZION
ZODIAC